NEW YORK CONSOLIDATED LAWS SERVICE

GILBERT'S CRIMINAL PRACTICE ANNUAL

2006

Case Annotations • Legislative History

Criminal Procedure Law

Penal Law

Correction Law

Related Statutes and Court Rules

QUESTIONS ABOUT THIS PUBLICATION?

For questions about the **Editorial Content** appearing in these volumes or reprint permission, please call:

Jeanine M. Schupbach, J.D., at	1-800-252-9257 (ext. 2539)
E-mail Address	jeanine.schupbach@lexisnexis.com
Kathryn Calista, J.D., at	1-800-424-4200 (ext. 3465)
E-mail Address	kathryn.calista@lexisnexis.com

For assistance with replacement pages, shipments, billing or other customer service matters, please call:

Customer Services Department at	(800) 833-9844
Outside the United States and Canada, please call	(518) 487-3000
Fax number	(518) 487-3584
Customer Service Website	http://www.lexisnexis.com/custserv/

For information on other Matthew Bender Publications, please call

Your account manager or	(800) 223-1940
Outside the United States and Canada, please call	(518) 487-3000

This publication is designed to provide accurate and authoritative information in regard to the subject matter covered. It is sold with the understanding that the publisher is not engaged in rendering legal, accounting, or other professional services. If legal advice or other expert assistance is required, the services of a competent professional should be sought.

LexisNexis, the knowledge burst logo, and Michie are trademarks of Reed Elsevier Properties Inc, used under license. Matthew Bender is a registered trademark of Matthew Bender Properties Inc.

ISBN 0-8205-6263-7

Editorial Offices
744 Broad Street, Newark, NJ 07102 (973) 820-2000
201 Mission St., San Francisco, CA 94105-1831 (415) 908-3200
www.lexis.com

MATTHEW◆BENDER

FEATURES OF THIS PRODUCT

The **NY CLS Desk Edition Gilbert's Criminal Practice Annual** compiles in one portable reference the **statutes and court rules** frequently consulted by criminal law practitioners. A **Table of Amendments** as well as **concise legislative history** for each statutory section highlight revisions and additions to the statutory language. **Selected case annotations** examine how the courts have interpreted and applied the statute.

EXPAND YOUR RESEARCH ON LEXIS.COM

The **New York Consolidated Laws Service** on *www.lexis.com* provides **comprehensive case annotations**, an enhanced Table of Contents, easy access to **Shepard's**, and, through the **Practitioner's Toolbox for Statutes**, immediate access to Practice Insights, Case Notes, Legislative History, Legislative Alerts, Treatises and Practice Guides, Practice Forms, Checklists, and Related Statutes and Rules.

To locate a NY code section using its citation

- Click on **Get a Document** from the navigation bar at the top of the screen.
- Enter the appropriate statute and section number and click **Get**. For example, "NY CPLR 205" for NY Civil Practice Law and Rules 205.

To search NY CLS by subject matter

- Click the **Find a Source** tab.
- Type "new york consolidated" and click **Find**.
- Click on **NY-New York Consolidated Laws**.
- Browse the Table of Contents
  or
- Enter your search query using terms and connectors or natural language.

<u>Terms and Connectors:</u> Search using words and connectors to create phrases and concepts based on specific rules of search logic. Statutes containing the specific combinations of words in your search request will be retrieved. Use connectors OR, AND, W/# (where # is the number of words between terms linked by this connector) to define the relationships between your search words. Use the exclamation mark "!" to replace an infinite number of letters following the word root (litigat! finds variations of the litigate litigator, litigated, litigation, litigating).

To find statutes discussing a prosecutor's duty to disclose, you may use this search:

duty W/5 prosecutor W/5 disclos!

The search finds documents where "duty," "prosecutor" and word root beginning with "disclos" (disclosed, disclosing, etc.) are all within five words of each other.

<u>Natural Language:</u> Search using plain English, without the need for any special terms and connectors. To develop a natural language search, simply select **Natural Language** and use words that you might use when describing your research topic to another person.

Prosecutor's duty to disclose

FIND YOUR SOURCE THROUGH THE PRACTITIONER'S TOOLBOX

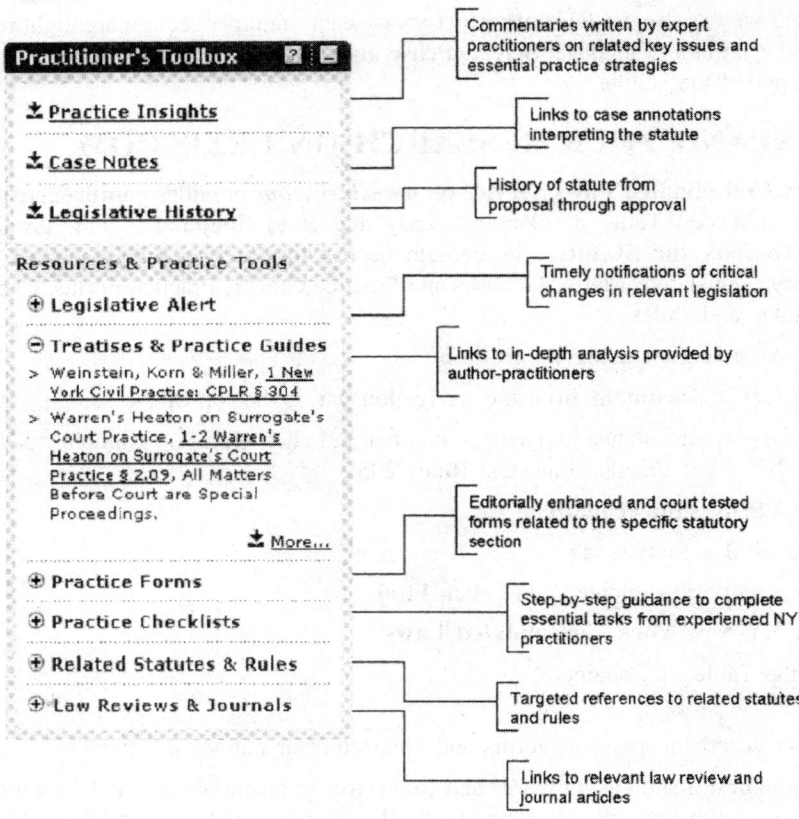

Commentaries written by expert practitioners on related key issues and essential practice strategies

Links to case annotations interpreting the statute

History of statute from proposal through approval

Timely notifications of critical changes in relevant legislation

Links to in-depth analysis provided by author-practitioners

Editorially enhanced and court tested forms related to the specific statutory section

Step-by-step guidance to complete essential tasks from experienced NY practitioners

Targeted references to related statutes and rules

Links to relevant law review and journal articles

For more help with legal research on lexis.com, consult the help buttons throughout lexis.com or call **800-543-6862** or select **Take a Tour** at the login page.

Publication *Table of Contents*

FAMILY COURT ACT

JUDICIARY LAW

PUBLIC HEALTH LAW

PART 3: MISCELLANEOUS COURT RULES

RULES OF THE CHIEF JUDGE

RULES OF THE CHIEF ADMINISTRATOR OF THE COURTS

UNIFORM RULES FOR THE NEW YORK STATE TRIAL COURTS

RULES OF THE COURT OF APPEALS OF THE STATE OF NEW YORK

RULES OF THE FIRST JUDICIAL DEPARTMENT APPELLATE DIVISION

RULES OF THE FIRST JUDICIAL DEPARTMENT APPELLATE TERM

RULES OF THE SECOND JUDICIAL DEPARTMENT APPELLATE DIVISION

RULES OF THE SECOND JUDICIAL DEPARTMENT APPELLATE TERM

RULES OF THE THIRD JUDICIAL DEPARTMENT APPELLATE DIVISION

PART 4: SENTENCING GUIDES

PART 5: NEW YORK COURT STRUCTURE CHART AND DIRECTORY

PART 6: INDEX   I–1

TABLE OF 2005 AMENDMENTS
Current through Laws of 2005, Chapters 1 through 653, except 243, 356, 434, 438, 446, 499, 544, 553, 574, 584, 604, 609, 645, 647, 648, 649, 650, 651, 652

CRIMINAL PROCEDURE LAW

PENAL LAW

1021	amended	3 (Part A)
1022(a)	amended	3 (Part A)
1022(b)	amended	3 (Part A)
1026(c)	amended	3 (Part A)
1027	amended	3 (Part A)
1035(a)	amended	3 (Part A)
1035(c)	amended	3 (Part A)
1042	amended	3 (Part B)
1051(f)(i)	amended	3 (Part A)
1055	amended	3 (Part A)
1055-a	repealed and replaced	3 (Part A)
1058	amended	3 (Part A)

JUDICIARY LAW

Section	Effect	Chapter
751	expiration note amended	31
849-g	amended	524

VEHICLE AND TRAFFIC LAW

Section	Effect	Chapter
510	expiration notes amended	56 (Part D); 60 (Parts D & E)
510(2)(b)(xiii)	added	223
510(6)(b)	amended	60 (Part E)
510(6)(c)	amended	60 (Part E)
510(6)(d)(i)	amended	60 (Part E)
510-a(1)	amended	60 (Part E)
510-a(2)	amended	60 (Part E)
510-a(4)	amended	60 (Part E)
510-a(4-a)	added	60 (Part E)
516-b	expiration note amended	60 (Part D)
600	amended	49
1193	expiration note amended	60 (Part D)
1193(2)(b)(5)	amended	60 (Part E)
1193(2)(e)(3)(b)	amended	60 (Part E)
1194(2)d)(1)(c)	amended	60 (Part E)
1196	expiration note amended	60 (Part D)
1196(7)(g)	amended	60 (Part E)
1198	expiration note amended	56 (Part D)
1809	expiration note amended	56 (Part D)
1809(8)	amended	56 (Part D)
1809-a	expiration note amended	56 (Part D)
1809-d	added	223

PART 1
CRIMINAL JUSTICE STATUTES

STATE OF NEW YORK

CRIMINAL PROCEDURE LAW

AN ACT

To establish a criminal procedure law, constituting chapter eleven-A of the consolidated laws, and to repeal the code of criminal procedure

The People of the State of New York, represented in Senate and Assembly, do enact as follows:

CHAPTER 11-A OF THE CONSOLIDATED LAWS

CRIMINAL PROCEDURE LAW
SYNOPSIS OF ARTICLES

PART ONE—GENERAL PROVISIONS

TITLE A—SHORT TITLE, APPLICABILITY AND DEFINITIONS

ARTICLE 1—SHORT TITLE, APPLICABILITY AND DEFINITIONS

Section

§ 1.00. Short title.

This chapter shall be known as the criminal procedure law, and may be cited as "CPL."

§ 1.10. Applicability of chapter to actions and matter occurring before and after effective date.

1. The provisions of this chapter apply exclusively to:

(a) All criminal actions and proceedings commenced upon or after the effective date thereof and all appeals and other post-judgment proceedings relating or attaching thereto; and

(b) All matters of criminal procedure prescribed in this chapter which do not constitute a part of any particular action or case, occurring upon or after such effective date.

2. The provisions of this chapter apply to (a) all criminal actions and proceedings commenced prior to the effective date thereof but still pending on such date, and (b) all appeals and other post-judgment proceedings commenced upon or after such effective date which relate or attach to criminal actions and proceedings commenced or concluded prior to such effective date; provided that, if application of such provisions in any particular case would not be feasible or would work injustice, the provisions of the code of criminal procedure * apply thereto.

3. The provisions of this chapter do not impair or render ineffectual any proceedings or procedural matters which occurred prior to the effective date thereof.

* Repealed.

§ 1.20. Definitions of terms of general use in this chapter.

Except where different meanings are expressly specified in subsequent provisions of this chapter, the term definitions contained in section 10.00 of the penal law are applicable to this chapter, and, in addition, the following terms have the following meanings:

1. "Accusatory instrument" means an indictment, an indictment ordered reduced pursuant to subdivision one-a of section 210.20 of this chapter, an information, a simplified information, a prosecutor's information, a superior court information, a misdemeanor complaint or a felony complaint. Every accusatory instrument, regardless of the person designated therein as accuser, constitutes an accusation on behalf of the state as plaintiff and must be entitled "the people of the state of New York" against a designated person, known as the defendant.

2. "Local criminal court accusatory instrument" means any accusatory instrument other than an indictment or a superior court information.

3. "Indictment" means a written accusation by a grand jury, more fully defined and described in article two hundred, filed with a superior court, which charges one or more defendants with the commission of one or more offenses, at least one of which is a crime, and which serves as a basis for prosecution thereof.

3-a. "Superior court information" means a written accusation by a district attorney more fully defined and described in articles one hundred ninety-five and two hundred, filed with a superior court pursuant to article one hundred ninety-five, which charges one or more defendants with the commission of one or more offenses, at least one of which is a crime, and which serves as a basis for prosecution thereof.

4. "Information" means a verified written accusation by a person, more fully defined and described in article one hundred, filed with a local criminal court, which charges one or more defendants with the commission of one or more offenses, none of which is a felony, and which may serve both to commence a criminal action and as a basis for prosecution thereof.

5. [See also subd. 5 below] "Simplified traffic information" means a written accusation by a police officer or other public servant authorized by law to issue same, more fully defined and described in article one hundred, filed with a local

criminal court, which, being in a brief or simplified form prescribed by the commissioner of motor vehicles, charges a person with one or more traffic infractions or misdemeanors relating to traffic, and which may serve both to commence a criminal action for such offense and as a basis for prosecution thereof.

5. [*See also* subd. 5 *above*] (a) "Simplified information" means a simplified traffic information, a simplified parks information, or a simplified environmental conservation information.

(b) "Simplified traffic information" means a written accusation by a police officer, or other public servant authorized by law to issue same, more fully defined and described in article one hundred, filed with a local criminal court, which, being in a brief or simplified form prescribed by the commissioner of motor vehicles, charges a person with one or more traffic infractions or misdemeanors relating to traffic, and which may serve both to commence a criminal action for such offense and as a basis for prosecution thereof.

(c) "Simplified parks information" means a written accusation by a police officer, or other public servant authorized by law to issue same, filed with a local criminal court, which, being in a brief or simplified form prescribed by the commissioner of parks and recreation, charges a person with one or more offenses, other than a felony, for which a uniform simplified parks information may be issued pursuant to the parks and recreation law and the navigation law, and which may serve both to commence a criminal action for such offense and a basis for prosecution thereof.

(d) "Simplified environmental conservation information" means a written accusation by a police officer, or other public servant authorized by law to issue same, filed with a local criminal court, which being in a brief or simplified form prescribed by the commissioner of environmental conservation, charges a person with one or more offenses, other than a felony, for which a uniform simplified environmental conservation simplified* information may be issued pursuant to the environmental conservation law, and which may serve both to commence a criminal action for such offense and as a basis for prosecution thereof.

6. "Prosecutor's information" means a written accusation by a district attorney, more fully defined and described in article one hundred, filed with a local criminal court, which charges one or more defendants with the commission of one or more offenses, none of which is a felony, and which serves as a basis for prosecution thereof.

7. "Misdemeanor complaint" means a verified written accusation by a person, more fully defined and described in article one hundred, filed with a local criminal court, which charges one or more defendants with the commission of one or more offenses, at least one of which is a misdemeanor

and none of which is a felony, and which serves to commence a criminal action but which may not, except upon the defendant's consent, serve as a basis for prosecution of the offenses charged therein.

8. "Felony complaint" means a verified written accusation by a person, more fully defined and described in article one hundred, filed with a local criminal court, which charges one or more defendants with the commission of one or more felonies and which serves to commence a criminal action but not as a basis for prosecution thereof.

9. "Arraignment" means the occasion upon which a defendant against whom an accusatory instrument has been filed appears before the court in which the criminal action is pending for the purpose of having such court acquire and exercise control over his person with respect to such accusatory instrument and of setting the course of further proceedings in the action.

10. "Plea," in addition to its ordinary meaning as prescribed in sections 220.10 and 340.20, means, where appropriate, the occasion upon which a defendant enters such a plea to an accusatory instrument.

11. "Trial." A jury trial commences with the selection of the jury and includes all further proceedings through the rendition of a verdict. A non-jury trial commences with the first opening address, if there be any, and, if not, when the first witness is sworn, and includes all further proceedings through the rendition of a verdict.

12. "Verdict" means the announcement by a jury in the case of a jury trial, or by the court in the case of a non-jury trial, of its decision upon the defendant's guilt or innocence of the charges submitted to or considered by it.

13. "Conviction" means the entry of a plea of guilty to, or a verdict of guilty upon, an accusatory instrument other than a felony complaint, or to one or more counts of such instrument.

14. "Sentence" means the imposition and entry of sentence upon a conviction.

15. "Judgment." A judgment is comprised of a conviction and the sentence imposed thereon and is completed by imposition and entry of the sentence.

16. "Criminal action." A criminal action (a) commences with the filing of an accusatory instrument against a defendant in a criminal court, as specified in subdivision seventeen; (b) includes the filing of all further accusatory instruments directly derived from the initial one, and all proceedings, orders and motions conducted or made by a criminal court in the course of disposing of any such accusatory instrument, or which, regardless of the court in which they occurred or were made, could properly be considered as a part of the record of the case by an appellate court upon an appeal from a judgment of conviction;

and (c) terminates with the imposition of sentence or some other final disposition in a criminal court of the last accusatory instrument filed in the case.

17. "Commencement of criminal action." A criminal action is commenced by the filing of an accusatory instrument against a defendant in a criminal court, and, if more than one accusatory instrument is filed in the course of the action, it commences when the first of such instruments is filed.

18. "Criminal proceeding" means any proceeding which (a) constitutes a part of a criminal action or (b) occurs in a criminal court and is related to a prospective, pending or completed criminal action, either of this state or of any other jurisdiction, or involves a criminal investigation.

19. "Criminal court" means any court defined as such by section 10.10.

20. "Superior court" means any court defined as such by subdivision two of section 10.10.

21. "Local criminal court" means any court defined as such by subdivision three of section 10.10.

22. "Intermediate appellate court" means any court possessing appellate jurisdiction, other than the court of appeals.

23. "Judge" means any judicial officer who is a member of or constitutes a court, whether referred to in another provision of law as a justice or by any other title.

24. "Trial jurisdiction." A criminal court has "trial jurisdiction" of an offense when an indictment or an information charging such offense may properly be filed with such court, and when such court has authority to accept a plea to, try or otherwise finally dispose of such accusatory instrument.

25. "Preliminary jurisdiction." A criminal court has "preliminary jurisdiction" of an offense when, regardless of whether it has trial jurisdiction thereof, a criminal action for such offense may be commenced therein, and when such court may conduct proceedings with respect thereto which lead or may lead to prosecution and final disposition of the action in a court having trial jurisdiction thereof.

26. "Appearance ticket" means a written notice issued by a public servant, more fully defined in section 150.10, requiring a person to appear before a local criminal court in connection with an accusatory instrument to be filed against him therein.

27. "Summons" means a process of a local criminal court or superior court, more fully defined in section 130.10, requiring a defendant to appear before such court for the purpose of arraignment upon an accusatory instrument filed therewith by which a criminal action against him has been commenced.

28. "Warrant of arrest" means a process of a local criminal court, more fully defined in section 120.10, directing a police officer to arrest a defendant and to bring him before such court for the purpose of arraignment upon an accusatory instrument filed therewith by which a criminal action against him has been commenced.

29. "Superior court warrant of arrest" means a process of a superior court directing a police officer to arrest a defendant and to bring him before such court for the purpose of arraignment upon an indictment filed therewith by which a criminal action against him has been commenced.

30. "Bench warrant" means a process of a criminal court in which a criminal action is pending, directing a police officer, or a uniformed court officer, pursuant to paragraph b of subdivision two of section 530.70 of this chapter to take into custody a defendant in such action who has previously been arraigned upon the accusatory instrument by which the action was commenced, and to bring him before such court. The function of a bench warrant is to achieve the court appearance of a defendant in a pending criminal action for some purpose other than his initial arraignment in the action.

31. "Prosecutor" means a district attorney or any other public servant who represents the people in a criminal action.

32. "District attorney" means a district attorney, an assistant district attorney or a special district attorney, and, where appropriate, the attorney general, an assistant attorney general, a deputy attorney general or a special deputy attorney general.

33. "Peace officer" means a person listed in section 2.10 of this chapter.

34. "Police officer." The following persons are police officers:

(a) A sworn member of the division of state police;

(b) Sheriffs, under-sheriffs and deputy sheriffs of counties outside of New York City;

(c) A sworn officer of an authorized county or county parkway police department;

(d) A sworn officer of an authorized police department or force of a city, town, village or police district;

(e) A sworn officer of an authorized police department of an authority or a sworn officer of the state regional park police in the office of parks and recreation;

(f) A sworn officer of the capital police force of the office of general services;

(g) An investigator employed in the office of a district attorney;

(h) An investigator employed by a commission created by an interstate compact who is, to a substantial extent, engaged in the enforcement of the criminal laws of this state;

(i) The chief and deputy fire marshals, the supervising fire marshals and the fire marshals of the bureau of fire investigation of the New York City fire department;

(j) A sworn officer of the division of law enforcement in the department of environmental conservation;

(k) A sworn officer of a police force of a public authority created by an interstate compact;

(l) Long Island railroad police.

(m) A special investigator employed in the statewide organized crime task force, while performing his assigned duties pursuant to section seventy-a of the executive law.

(n) A sworn officer of the Westchester county department of public safety services who, on or prior to June thirtieth, nineteen hundred seventy-nine was appointed as a sworn officer of the division of Westchester county parkway police or who was appointed on or after July first, nineteen hundred seventy-nine to the title of police officer, sergeant, lieutenant, captain or inspector or who, on or prior to January thirty-first, nineteen hundred eighty-three, was appointed as a Westchester county deputy sheriff.

(o) A sworn officer of the water-supply police employed by the city of New York, appointed to protect the sources, works, and transmission of water supplied to the city of New York, and to protect persons on or in the vicinity of such water sources, works, and transmissions.

(p) Persons appointed as railroad policemen pursuant to section eighty-eight of the railroad law.

(q) [*Effective until Oct. 31, 2007.*] An employee of the department of taxation and finance (i) assigned to enforcement of the taxes imposed under or pursuant to the authority of article twelve-A of the tax law and administered by the commissioner of taxation and finance, taxes imposed under or pursuant to the authority of article eighteen of the tax law and administered by the commissioner, taxes imposed under article twenty of the tax law, or sales or compensating use taxes relating to automotive fuel or cigarettes imposed under article twenty-eight or pursuant to the authority of article twenty-nine of the tax law and administered by the commissioner or (ii) designated as a revenue crimes specialist and assigned to the enforcement of the taxes described in paragraph (c) of subdivision four of section 2.10 of this title, for the purpose of applying for and executing search warrants under article six hundred ninety of this chapter, for the purpose of acting as a claiming agent under article thirteen-A of the civil practice law and rules in connection with the enforcement of the taxes referred to above and for the purpose of executing warrants

of arrest relating to the respective crimes specified in subdivision four of section 2.10 of this title.

(q) [*Effective Oct. 31, 2007.*] An employee of the department of taxation and finance (i) assigned to enforcement of the taxes imposed under or pursuant to the authority of article twelve-A of the tax law and administered by the commissioner of taxation and finance, taxes imposed under article twenty of the tax law, or sales or compensating use taxes relating to automotive fuel or cigarettes imposed under article twenty-eight or pursuant to the authority of article twenty-nine of the tax law and administered by the commissioner of taxation and finance or (ii) designated as a revenue crimes specialist and assigned to the enforcement of the taxes described in paragraph (c) of subdivision four of section 2.10 of this title, for the purpose of applying for and executing search warrants under article six hundred ninety of this chapter, for the purpose of acting as a claiming agent under article thirteen-A of the civil practice law and rules in connection with the enforcement of the taxes referred to above and for the purpose of executing warrants of arrest relating to the respective crimes specified in subdivision four of section 2.10 of this title.

(r) Any employee of the Suffolk county department of parks who is appointed as a Suffolk county park police officer.

(s) A university police officer appointed by the state university pursuant to paragraph 1 of subdivision two of section three hundred fifty-five of the education law.

(t) A sworn officer of the department of public safety of the Buffalo municipal housing authority who has achieved or been granted the status of sworn police officer and has been certified by the division of criminal justice services as successfully completing an approved basic course for police officers.

(u) Persons appointed as Indian police officers pursuant to section one hundred fourteen of the Indian law.

34-a. "Geographical area of employment." The "geographical area of employment" of certain police officers is as follows:

(a) [*Expires and repealed Sept. 1, 2007.*] Except as provided in paragraph (d) of this subdivision, New York state constitutes the "geographical area of employment" of any police officer employed as such by an agency of the state or by an authority which functions throughout the state, or a police officer designated by the superintendent of state police pursuant to section two hundred twenty-three of the executive law;

(a) [*Effective Sept. 1, 2007.*] Except as provided in paragraph (d), New York state constitutes the "geographical area of employment" of any police officer employed as such by an agency of the state or by an authority which functions throughout the state;

(b) A county, city, town or village, as the case may be, constitutes the "geographical area of employment" of any police officer employed as such by an agency of such political subdivision or by an authority which functions only in such political subdivision; and

(c) Where an authority functions in more than one county, the "geographical area of employment" of a police officer employed thereby extends through all of such counties.

(d) The geographical area of employment of a police officer appointed by the state university is the campuses and other property of the state university, including any portion of a public highway which crosses or abuts such property.

35. "Commitment to the custody of the sheriff," when referring to an order of a court located in a county or city which has established a department of correction, means commitment to the commissioner of correction of such county or city.

36. "County" ordinarily means (a) any county outside of New York City or (b) New York City in its entirety. Unless the context requires a different construction, New York City, despite its five counties, is deemed a single county within the meaning of the provisions of this chapter in which that term appears.

37. "Lesser included offense." When it is impossible to commit a particular crime without concomitantly committing, by the same conduct, another offense of lesser grade or degree, the latter is, with respect to the former, a "lesser included offense." In any case in which it is legally possible to attempt to commit a crime, an attempt to commit such crime constitutes a lesser included offense with respect thereto.

38. "Oath" includes an affirmation and every other mode authorized by law of attesting to the truth of that which is stated.

39. "Petty offense" means a violation or a traffic infraction.

40. "Evidence in chief" means evidence, received at a trial or other criminal proceeding in which a defendant's guilt or innocence of an offense is in issue, which may be considered as a part of the quantum of substantive proof establishing or tending to establish the commission of such offense or an element thereof or the defendant's connection therewith.

41. "Armed felony" means any violent felony offense defined in section 70.02 of the penal law that includes as an element either:

(a) possession, being armed with or causing serious physical injury by means of a deadly weapon, if the weapon is a loaded weapon from which a shot, readily capable of producing death

or other serious physical injury may be discharged; or

(b) display of what appears to be a pistol, revolver, rifle, shotgun, machine gun or other firearm.

42. "Juvenile offender" means (1) a person, thirteen years old who is criminally responsible for acts constituting murder in the second degree as defined in subdivisions one and two of section 125.25 of the penal law and (2) a person fourteen or fifteen years old who is criminally responsible for acts constituting the crimes defined in subdivisions one and two of section 125.25 (murder in the second degree) and in subdivision three of such section provided that the underlying crime for the murder charge is one for which such person is criminally responsible; section 135.25 (kidnapping in the first degree); 150.20 (arson in the first degree); subdivisions one and two of section 120.10 (assault in the first degree); 125.20 (manslaughter in the first degree); subdivisions one and two of section 130.35 (rape in the first degree); subdivisions one and two of section 130.50 (criminal sexual act in the first degree); 130.70 (aggravated sexual abuse in the first degree); 140.30 (burglary in the first degree); subdivision one of section 140.25 (burglary in the second degree); 150.15 (arson in the second degree); 160.15 (robbery in the first degree); subdivision two of section 160.10 (robbery in the second degree) of the penal law; subdivision four of section 265.02 of the penal law, where such firearm is possessed on school grounds, as that phrase is defined in subdivision fourteen of section 220.00 of the penal law; or section 265.03 of the penal law, where such machine gun or such firearm is possessed on school grounds, as that phrase is defined in subdivision fourteen of section 220.00 of the penal law; or defined in the penal law as an attempt to commit murder in the second degree or kidnapping in the first degree.

43. "Judicial hearing officer" means a person so designated pursuant to provisions of article twenty-two of the judiciary law.

* As originally enacted.

Amended by L. 1973, Chs. 461, 780, 781, 782, 948; L. 1974, Chs. 22, 250, 281, 282, 467, 707, 877; L. 1975, Chs. 509, 667; L. 1976, Chs. 265, 590; L. 1977, Ch. 487; L. 1978, Chs. 205, 481, 655, 756; L. 1979, Chs. 330, 411, 533; L. 1980, Ch. 285, Ch. 843; L. 1981, Ch. 335; L. 1982, Ch. 658, L. 1983, Ch. 969; Ch. 840, eff. Apr. 1, 1983; L. 1985, Ch. 65; L. 1986, Ch. 318; L. 1988, Ch. 521; L. 1990, Ch. 209; L. 1991, Ch.166; L. 1991, Ch. 542, eff. July 23, 1991, added subd. 34(r), which shall apply to all employees appointed after the effective date of this act, and notwithstanding any inconsistent provision of law to those employees appointed prior to such date provided they have satisfactorily completed an approved municipal police basic training program pursuant to section 209-q of the general municipal law; L. 1993, Ch. 446; L. 1993, Ch. 508, amending subd. 34(q), eff. until Oct. 31, 1997; L. 1995, Ch. 2, § 68, amending subd. 34(q), eff. Sept. 1. 1995, repealed Oct. 31, 1997; L. 1995, Ch. 2, § 69, amending subd. 34(q), eff. Oct. 31, 1997; L. 1997, Ch. 389 Part A, § 103, extending expiration date of subd. 34(q) to Oct. 31, 2002, eff. Aug. 7, 1997; L. 1998, Ch. 424, §§ 1 and 2, eff. Jan. 1, 1999, and Ch. 435, § 1, eff. Nov. 1, 1998; L. 2000, Ch. 599, amending subd. 34(o), eff. Dec. 20, 2000; L. 2001, Ch. 95, § 2, eff. July 13, 2001, extending exp.

date of amendment to subd. 34-a(a) to Nov. 1, 2003, and Ch. 504, § 5, eff. Nov. 21, 2001, amending subd. 34(r); L. 2002, Ch. 318, §§ 1 and 2, amending subd. 34(q), eff. Aug. 6, 2002, and Ch. 85, Part F § 2, extending exp. date of amendment to subd. 34(q) to Oct. 1, 2007; L. 2003, Ch. 16, § 2, extending expiration date of subd. 34-a(a) to Sept. 1, 2005, eff. Mar. 31, 2003; Ch. 121, § 1, adding subd. 34(t), eff. July 1, 2003; L. 2003, Ch. 264, § 35, eff. Nov. 1, 2003, amending subd. 42; L. 2005, Ch. 558, § 2, adding subd. 34(u), eff. Aug. 23, 2005; L. 2005, Ch. 56, Part D, § 2, extending exp. date of amendment to subd. 34-a(a) to Nov. 1, 2007.

ANNOTATIONS

Accusatory instrument.—Defendant's inculpatory statement cannot be suppressed where the defendant waived his rights after pre-interrogation warnings and agreed to answer questions; no accusatory instrument had been prepared or signed and therefore no criminal action had been commenced and defendant's argument that because he was physically in police custody awaiting arraignment his right to counsel had attached was without merit. People v. Wilson, 56 N.Y.2d 692, 451 N.Y.S.2d 719, 436 N.E.2d 1321 (1982).

Arrest; seizure.—The mere service of a summons does not constitute an arrest. The simultaneous service of a subpoena duces tecum, to compel production of an allegedly obscene film on the return date, did not constitute a seizure. Under this circumstance, a prior judicial scrutiny of the film was not necessary. People v. P.A.J. Theater Corp., 72 Misc. 2d 354, 339 N.Y.S.2d 152 (Crim. Ct. N.Y. Co. 1972).

Definition of county; search warrant; issuance and execution.—The constitutional definition of a county must prevail where it conflicts with statutory language; therefore a Town Justice in Westchester County was without authority to issue search warrant to be executed in Queens County, since Queens and Westchester are not contiguous; nor could Peace Officer of such Town execute the warrant. People v. Donlin, 71 Misc. 2d 1035, 337 N.Y.S.2d 768 (Nassau Co. Ct. 1972).

Misdemeanor case; jurisdiction acquired.—In a misdemeanor case, a local criminal court acquires jurisdiction over a defendant upon his or her arraignment on a misdemeanor complaint. People v. Santos, 165 Misc. 2d 950, 630 N.Y.S.2d 908 (Crim. Ct. Bronx Co. 1995).

Subd. 9

Arraignment; absence of.—Absent arraignment, County Court never acquired the requisite control of defendant's person with respect to the accusatory instrument, and was therefore precluded from setting the course of further proceedings into action. People v. Mitchell, 235 A.D.2d 834, 652 N.Y.S.2d 827 (3d Dept. 1997).

Subd. 17

Commencement of criminal action.—A criminal action is commenced by the filing of the first accusatory instrument in a criminal court. People v. Raglin, 175 Misc. 2d 1003, 673 N.Y.S.2d 285 (Crim. Ct. Queens Co. 1998).

Extension of statute of limitations; ex post facto.—The Legislature's act of extending the statute of limitations did not make criminal an act which was innocent when done, did not aggravate an offense or change the punishment to make it greater than when the act was committed, and did not alter the rules of evidence to require less or different evidence than the law required at the time of commission of the offense. Periods of limitation are subject to the will of the Legislature, and may be changed or repealed altogether in any case where a right to acquittal has not been absolutely acquired by completion of the limitation period. People v. Pfitzmayer, 72 Misc. 2d 739, 340 N.Y.S.2d 85 (Sup. Ct. Nassau Co. 1972).

Subd. 32

District Attorney; exclusive jurisdiction to prosecute.—A party charged with committing a traffic offense and properly served with a traffic information and summons may not then act privately as a prosecutor of a different but related traffic offense against the police officer who issued the traffic information. People ex rel. Luceno v. Cuozzo, 97 Misc. 2d 871, 412 N.Y.S.2d 748 (City Ct. Westchester Co. 1978).

Jurisdiction; prosecution of indictment by District

Attorney instead of Special Prosecutor.—Supreme Court has jurisdiction to try attorney for attempt to bribe police officer to give false testimony in civil action but indictment must be prosecuted by District Attorney and not Special Prosecutor since attorney's alleged crime was not an act relating to the criminal justice system. Dondi v. Jones, 40 N.Y.2d 8, 386 N.Y.S.2d 4, 351 N.E.2d 650 (1976).

Village attorney.—The Village of Waterloo may by resolution authorize the village attorney or another attorney to prosecute violations of village ordinances providing such attorney is designated as an Assistant District Attorney as required by law. People v. Waterloo Stock Car Corp., 89 Misc. 2d 922, 392 N.Y.S.2d 839 (Seneca Co. Ct. 1977).

Subds. 33, 34

City marshals are not "peace officers" within the definition of CPL § 1.20(33).—Aponte v. The Dept. of Investigation of the City of New York, 51 A.D.2d 905, 381 N.Y.S.2d 57 (1st Dept. 1976).

Cooks and bakers.—Cooks and bakers in the Nassau Co. Correctional Center are not "peace officers" within the meaning of CPL § 1.20(33)(h). Ravalli v. County of Nassau, 67 A.D.2d 979, 413 N.Y.S.2d 443 (2d Dept. 1979).

Fire marshals.—Although Fire Marshals are police officers, New York City fire marshals are limited in their powers to arrest whatever else they may do as police officers by the Administrative Code (§ 487-a-15.0); this section restricts their power to make arrests to cases arising under laws relating to fires and extinguishment thereof, and to fire perils. People v. Lanzot, 67 A.D.2d 864, 413 N.Y.S.2d 399 (1st Dept. 1979).

Out-of-state officers.—New Jersey officers were not authorized by any New York statute to execute federal warrant in New York; CPL § 120.60 provides that warrants can be executed only by a police or peace officer, and the New Jersey officers did not so qualify under CPL §§ 1.20(33), (34), 2.10, or 120.60. People v. LaFontaine, 92 N.Y.2d 470, 682 N.Y.S.2d 671, 705 N.E.2d 663 (1998).

Part time deputy sheriff.—A part time deputy sheriff is not a peace officer and is not exempt from prosecution under PL § 265.20. People v. Smith, 105 Misc. 2d 586, 432 N.Y.S.2d 612 (Sup. Ct. N.Y. Co. 1980).

Special agents of the ASPCA.—Special agents of the ASPCA are included under the designation of "peace officer" as set forth in CPL § 1.20(33)(m) and are properly authorized to issue universal summonses. People v. Esteves, 95 Misc. 2d 70, 406 N.Y.S.2d 674 (Crim. Ct. N.Y.C. 1978).

Special Patrolmen.—Special Patrolmen licensed through the Administrative Code § 434a–7.0 may, in a proper case, be treated like peace officers and must give *Miranda* warnings and can arrest and search only upon probable cause. People v. Laurence, 100 Misc. 2d 612, 420 N.Y.S.2d 65 (N.Y.C. Crim. Ct. 1979).

Campus security officer.—Officers appointed pursuant to Education Law § 355(2) (m) are peace officers although not included as such in CPL § 1.20(33). People v. Wesley, 80 Misc. 2d 1002, 365 N.Y.S.2d 593 (City Ct. of Buffalo 1975).

Peace officers; license to carry firearms.—Special Officers of the Department of Social Services appointed pursuant to the Administrative Code of New York City, § 434a-7.0(e), are not peace officers exempt from the requirement of obtaining a license to carry firearms. Velez v. Sugarman, 75 Misc. 2d 746, 349 N.Y.S.2d 53 (Sup. Ct. N.Y. Co. 1973).

Subd. 37

Lesser included offense.—Harassment in the second degree is not a lesser included offense of menacing in the second degree; distinct from harassment, menacing does not require any form of "physical contact," but rather simply requires an intent to place another person in "reasonable fear of physical injury" by "displaying" a weapon or dangerous instrument. Thus, it is possible to commit menacing without harassment. People v. Bartkow, 96 N.Y.2d 770, 725 N.Y.S.2d 589, 749 N.E.2d 158 (2001).

—Driving while one's ability is impaired is a lesser included offense of driving while intoxicated but is not a lesser included offense of the blood alcohol level crime. People v. Brown, 53 N.Y.2d 979, 441 N.Y.S.2d 662, 424 N.E.2d 549 (1981).

—Lesser included offenses are not to be submitted for

consideration by the jury in reaching its verdict in every case; there must exist "a reasonable view of the evidence" upon which might be predicated a conclusion that the defendant did in fact commit a lesser, but not the greater offense; if there is no such reasonable view, a submission of lesser offenses is improper. People v. Scarborough, 49 N.Y.2d 364, 426 N.Y.S.2d 224, 402 N.E.2d 1127 (1980).

Interpretation.—"Impossible" in CPL § 1.20(37), does not mean impossible under any circumstances, but impossible under the particular facts of the case on trial. People v. Cioneck, 43 A.D.2d 256, 351 N.Y.S.2d 177 (3d Dept. 1974), aff'd, 35 N.Y.2d 924, 365 N.Y.S.2d 161, 324 N.E.2d 544 (1974).

Subd. 41

Armed felony.—Manslaughter in the first degree is not an armed violent felony offense. People v. Roye, 255 A.D.2d 464, 682 N.Y.S.2d 217 (2d Dept. 1998); People v. Marty, 150 A.D.2d 171, 171, 540 N.Y.S.2d 783, 784 (1st Dept. 1989).

—Attempted murder in the second degree does not meet the definition of an armed violent felony. People v. Staton, 242 A.D.2d 747, 663 N.Y.S.2d 57 (2d Dept. 1997); People v. Kuey, 155 A.D.2d 481, 481, 547 N.Y.S.2d 141, 142 (2d Dept. 1989); People v. Bartlett, 146 A.D.2d 705, 706, 537 N.Y.S.2d 58, 59 (2d Dept. 1989).

—Neither rape in the first degree nor sodomy in the first degree is an armed felony offense. People v. Samuels, 133 A.D.2d 785, 786, 520 N.Y.S.2d 172, 173 (2d Dept. 1987).

Attempted murder not armed felony.—Attempted murder in the second degree is not an armed violent felony for sentencing purposes because its elements do not include either possession of a deadly weapon or display of a firearm. People v. Lawrence, 97 A.D.2d 718, 469 N.Y.S.2d 1 (1st Dept. 1983), aff'd, 64 N.Y.2d 200, 485 N.Y.S.2d 233, 474 N.E.2d 593 (1984).

Robbery and burglary not armed felony.—Counts of robbery in the first degree and burglary in the first degree involving the use of a knife do not fall within the category of "armed felony" as defined in CPL § 1.20(41). People v. Griffin, 114 A.D.2d 756, 494 N.Y.S.2d 862 (1st Dept. 1985).

Robbery not armed felony.—Defendant could not be sentenced as an armed felony offender where each of defendants' robbery convictions involved the use of a knife. People v. Scarpetta, 114 A.D.2d 766, 494 N.Y.S.2d 867 (1st Dept. 1985).

Subd. 42

Juvenile offender.—The legislature added CPL § 1.20(42), defining a juvenile offender as including a person 14 to 15 years old who is criminally responsible for acts constituting the crimes defined in stated sections of the Penal Law; Penal Law § 30.00 was amended to make the juvenile offender criminally responsible for the acts specified in the new subdivision of CPL § 1.20. In re Nick C., 172 Misc. 2d 739, 659 N.Y.S.2d 969 (Fam. Ct. Bronx Co. 1997).

ARTICLE 2—PEACE OFFICERS

§ 2.10. Persons designated as peace officers.

Notwithstanding the provisions of any general, special or local law or charter to the contrary, only the following persons shall have the powers of, and shall be peace officers:

1. Constables or police constables of a town or village, provided such designation is not inconsistent with local law.

2. The sheriff, undersheriff and deputy sheriffs of New York city and sworn officers of the Westchester county department of public safety services appointed after January thirty-first, nineteen hundred eighty-three to the title of public safety officer and who perform the functions previously performed by a Westchester county deputy sheriff on or prior to such date.

3. Investigators of the office of the state commission of investigation.

4. Employees of the department of taxation and finance designated by the commissioner of taxation and finance as peace officers and assigned by the commissioner of taxation and finance

(a) to the enforcement of any of the criminal or seizure and forfeiture provisions of the tax law relating to (i) taxes imposed under or pursuant to the authority of article twelve-A of the tax law and administered by the commissioner of taxation and finance, (ii) taxes imposed under article twenty of the tax law, or (iii) sales or compensating use taxes relating to automotive fuel or cigarettes imposed under article twenty-eight or pursuant to the authority of article twenty-nine of the tax law and administered by the commissioner of taxation and finance or

(b) to the enforcement of any provision of the penal law relating to any of the taxes described in paragraph (a) of this subdivision and relating to crimes effected through the use of a statement or document filed with the department in connection with the administration of such taxes or

(c) as revenue crimes specialist and assigned to the enforcement of any of the criminal provisions of the tax law relating to taxes administered by the commissioner of taxation and finance other than those taxes set forth in paragraph (a) of this subdivision or any provision of the penal law relating to such taxes, and those provisions of the penal law (i) relating to any of the foregoing taxes and (ii) relating to crimes effected through the use of a statement or document filed with the department in connection with the administration of such foregoing taxes or

(d) to the enforcement of any provision of law which is subject to enforcement by criminal penalties and which relates to the performance by persons employed by the department of taxation and finance of the duties of their employment.

Provided, however, that nothing in this subdivision shall be deemed to authorize any such employee designated as a peace officer after November first, nineteen hundred eighty-five to carry, possess, repair or dispose of a firearm unless the appropriate license therefor has been issued pursuant to section 400.00 of the penal law, and further provided that, prior to such designation by the commissioner each such employee shall have successfully completed the training requirements specified in section 2.30 of this article. Provided, further, that any license issued to such employee pursuant to such peace officer designation by the commissioner shall relate only to the firearm issued to such employee by the department of taxation and finance and such permit shall not cover any other firearms. The foregoing sentence shall not be deemed to prohibit such peace officer from applying for a separate permit relating to non-departmental firearms.

5. Employees of the New York city department of finance assigned to enforcement of the tax on cigarettes imposed by title D of chapter forty-six of the administrative code of the city of New York by the commissioner of finance.

6. Confidential investigators and inspectors, as designated by the commissioner, of the department of agriculture and markets, pursuant to rules of the department.

7. Officers or agents of a duly incorporated society for the prevention of cruelty to animals.

7-a. Officers or agents of a duly incorporated society for the prevention of cruelty to children; provided, however, that nothing in this subdivision shall be deemed to authorize such officer or agent to carry, possess, repair, or dispose of a firearm unless the appropriate license therefor has been issued pursuant to section 400.00 of the penal law; and provided further that such officer or agent shall exercise the powers of a peace officer only when he is acting pursuant to his special duties.

8. Inspectors and officers of the New York city department of health when acting pursuant to their special duties as set forth in section 564-11.0 of the administrative code of the city of New York; provided, however, that nothing in this subdivision shall be deemed to authorize such officer to carry, possess, repair or dispose of a firearm unless the appropriate license therefor has been issued pursuant to section 400.00 of the penal law.

9. Park rangers in Suffolk county, who shall be authorized to issue appearance tickets, simplified traffic informations, simplified parks informations and simplified environmental conservation informations.

10. Broome county park rangers who shall be authorized to issue appearance tickets, simplified traffic informations, simplified parks informations, and simplified environmental conservation informations; provided, however, that nothing in this subdivision shall be deemed to authorize such officer to carry, possess, repair or dispose of a firearm unless the appropriate license therefor has been issued pursuant to section 400.00 of the penal law.

11. Park rangers in Onondaga and Cayuga counties, who shall be authorized to issue appearance tickets, simplified traffic informations, simplified parks informations and simplified environmental conservation informations, within the respective counties of Onondaga and Cayuga.

12. Special policemen designated by the commissioner and the directors of in-patient facilities in the office of mental health pursuant to section 7.25 of the mental hygiene law, and special policemen designated by the commissioner and the directors of facilities under his jurisdiction in the office of mental retardation and developmental disabilities pursuant to section 13.25 of the mental hygiene law; provided, however, that nothing in this subdivision shall be deemed to authorize such officers to carry, possess, repair or dispose of a firearm unless the appropriate license therefor has been issued pursuant to section 400.00 of the penal law.

13. Persons designated as special policemen by the director of a hospital in the department of health pursuant to section four hundred fifty-five of the public health law; provided, however, that nothing in this subdivision shall be deemed to authorize such officer to carry, possess, repair or dispose of a firearm unless the appropriate license therefor has been issued pursuant to section 400.00 of the penal law.

14. [*Repealed Jan. 1, 1999.*]

15. Uniformed enforcement forces of the New York state thruway authority, when acting pursuant to subdivision two of section three hundred sixty-one of the public authorities law; provided, however, that nothing in this subdivision shall be deemed to authorize such officer to carry, possess, repair or dispose of a firearm unless the appropriate license therefor has been issued pursuant to section 400.00 of the penal law.

16. Employees of the department of health designated pursuant to section thirty-three hundred eighty-five of the public health law; provided, however, that nothing in this subdivision shall be deemed to authorize such officer to carry, possess, repair or dispose of a firearm unless the appropriate license therefor has been issued pursuant to section 400.00 of the penal law.

17. Uniformed housing guards of the Buffalo municipal housing authority.

18. Bay constable of the city of Rye, the villages of Mamaroneck, South Nyack and bay constables of the towns of East Hampton, Hempstead, Oyster Bay, Riverhead, Southampton, Southold, Islip, Shelter Island, Brookhaven, Babylon, Smithtown, Huntington and North Hempstead; provided, however, that nothing in this subdivision shall be deemed to authorize the bay constables in the city of Rye, the village of South Nyack or the towns of Brookhaven, Babylon, Southold, East Hampton, Riverhead, Islip, other than a bay constable of the town of Islip who prior to April third, nineteen hundred ninety-eight served as harbormaster for such town and whose position was reclassified as bay constable for such town prior to such date, Smithtown, Huntington and Shelter Island to carry, possess, repair or dispose of a firearm unless the appropriate license therefor has been issued pursuant to section 400.00 of the penal law.

19. Harbor masters appointed by a county, city, town or village.

20. Bridge and tunnel officers, sergeants and lieutenants of the Triborough bridge and tunnel authority.

21.   a. Uniformed court officers of the unified court system.

b. Court clerks of the unified court system in the first and second departments.

c. Marshall, deputy marshall, clerk or uniformed court officer of a district court.

(d) * Marshalls or deputy marshalls of a city court, provided, however, that nothing in this subdivision shall be deemed to authorize such officer to carry, possess, repair or dispose of a firearm unless the appropriate license therefor has been issued pursuant to section 400.00 of the penal law.

e. Uniformed court officers of the city of Mount Vernon.

f. Uniformed court officers of the city of Jamestown.

22. Patrolmen appointed by the Lake George park commission; provided however that nothing

in this subdivision shall be deemed to authorize such officer to carry, possess, repair or dispose of a firearm unless the appropriate license therefor has been issued pursuant to section 400.00 of the penal law.

23. Parole officers or warrant officers in the division of parole.

23-a. Parole revocation specialists in the division of parole; provided, however, that nothing in this subdivision shall be deemed to authorize such employee to carry, possess, repair or dispose of a firearm unless the appropriate license therefor has been issued pursuant to section 400.00 of the penal law.

24. Probation officers.

25. Officials, as designated by the commissioner of the department of correctional services pursuant to rules of the department, and correction officers of any state correctional facility or of any penal correctional institution.

26. Peace officers designated pursuant to the provisions of the New York state defense emergency act, as set forth in chapter seven hundred eighty-four of the laws of nineteen hundred fifty-one, as amended, when acting pursuant to their special duties during a period of attack or imminent attack by enemy forces, or during official drills called to combat natural or man-made disasters, or during official drills in preparation for an attack by enemy forces or in preparation for a natural or man-made disaster; provided, however, that nothing in this subdivision shall be deemed to authorize such officer to carry, possess, repair or dispose of a firearm unless the appropriate license therefor has been issued pursuant to section 400.00 of the penal law; and provided further, that such officer shall have the powers set forth in section 2.20 of this article only during a period of imminent or actual attack by enemy forces and during drills authorized under section twenty-nine-b of article two-B of the executive law, providing for the use of civil defense forces in disasters. Notwithstanding any other provision of law, such officers shall have the power to direct and control traffic during official drills in preparation for an attack by enemy forces or in preparation for combating natural or man-made disasters; however, this grant does not include any of the other powers set forth in section 2.20 of this article.

27. New York city special patrolmen appointed by the police commissioner pursuant to subdivision c or e of section 434a-7.0 or subdivision c or e of section 14-106 of the administrative code of the city of New York; provided, however, that nothing in this subdivision shall be deemed to authorize such officer to carry, possess, repair or dispose of a firearm unless the appropriate license therefore has been issued pursuant to section 400.00 of the penal law and the employer has authorized such officer to possess a firearm

during any phase of the officers on-duty employment. Special patrolmen shall have the powers set forth in section 2.20 of this article only when they are acting pursuant to their special duties; provided, however, that the following categories of New York city special patrolmen shall have such powers whether or not they are acting pursuant to their special duties: school safety officers employed by the board of education of the city of New York; parking control specialists, taxi and limousine inspectors, urban park rangers and evidence and property control specialists employed by the city of New York; and further provided that, with respect to the aforementioned categories of New York city special patrolmen, where such a special patrolman has been appointed by the police commissioner and, upon the expiration of such appointment the police commissioner has neither renewed such appointment nor explicitly determined that such appointment shall not be renewed, such appointment shall remain in full force and effect indefinitely, until such time as the police commissioner expressly determines to either renew or terminate such appointment.

28. All officers and members of the uniformed force of the New York city fire department as set forth and subject to the limitations contained in section 487a-15.0 of the administrative code of the city of New York; provided, however, that nothing in this subdivision shall be deemed to authorize such officer to carry, possess, repair or dispose of a firearm unless the appropriate license therefor has been issued pursuant to section 400.00 of the penal law.

29. Special policemen for horse racing, appointed pursuant to the provisions of the pari-mutuel revenue law as set forth in chapter two hundred fifty-four of the laws of nineteen hundred forty, as amended; provided, however, that nothing in this subdivision shall be deemed to authorize such officer to carry, possess, repair or dispose of a firearm unless the appropriate license therefor has been issued pursuant to section 400.00 of the penal law.

30. Supervising fire inspectors, fire inspectors, the fire marshal and assistant fire marshals, all of whom are full-time employees of the county of Nassau fire marshal's office.

31. Supervisor of forest ranger services; assistant supervisor of forest ranger services; forest ranger 3; forest ranger 2; forest ranger 1 employed by the state department of environmental conservation.

32. Investigators of the department of motor vehicles, pursuant to section three hundred ninety-two-b of the vehicle and traffic law; provided, however, that nothing in this subdivision shall be deemed to authorize such officer to carry, possess, repair or dispose of a firearm unless the appropriate license therefor has been issued pursuant to section 400.00 of the penal law.

33. A city marshall of the city of New York who has received training in firearms handling from the federal bureau of investigation or in the New York city police academy, or in the absence of the available training programs from the federal bureau of investigation and the New York city police academy, from another law enforcement agency located in the state of New York, and who has received a firearms permit from the license division of the New York city police department.

34. Waterfront and airport investigators, pursuant to subdivision four of section ninety-nine hundred six of the unconsolidated laws; provided, however, that nothing in this subdivision shall be deemed to authorize such officer to carry, possess, repair or dispose of a firearm unless the appropriate license therefor has been issued pursuant to section 400.00 of the penal law.

35. Special investigators appointed by the state board of elections, pursuant to section 3-107 of the election law.

36. Investigators appointed by the state liquor authority, pursuant to section fifteen of the alcoholic beverage control law; provided, however, that nothing in this subdivision shall be deemed to authorize such officer to carry, possess, repair or dispose of a firearm unless the appropriate license therefor has been issued pursuant to section 400.00 of the penal law.

37. Special patrolmen of a political subdivision, appointed pursuant to section two hundred nine-v of the general municipal law; provided, however, that nothing in this subdivision shall be deemed to authorize such officer to carry, possess, repair or dispose of a firearm unless the appropriate license therefor has been issued pursuant to section 400.00 of the penal law.

38. A special investigator of the New York city department of investigation who has received training in firearms handling in the New York police academy and has received a firearms permit from the license division of the New York city police department.

39. Broome county special patrolman, appointed by the Broome county attorney; provided, however, that nothing in this subdivision shall be deemed to authorize such officer to carry, possess, repair or dispose of a firearm unless the appropriate license therefor has been issued pursuant to section 400.00 of the penal law.

40. Special officers employed by the city of New York or by the New York city health and hospitals corporation; provided, however, that nothing in this subdivision shall be deemed to authorize such officer to carry, possess, repair or dispose of a firearm unless the appropriate license therefor has been issued pursuant to section 400.00 of the penal law. The New York city health and hospitals corporation shall employ peace officers appointed pursuant to this subdivision to perform the patrol, investigation, and maintenance of the peace duties of special officer, senior special officer and hospital security officer, provided however that nothing in this subdivision shall prohibit managerial, supervisory, or state licensed or certified professional employees of the corporation from performing such duties where they are incidental to their usual duties, or shall prohibit police officers employed by the city of New York from performing these duties.

41. Fire police squads organized pursuant to section two hundred nine-c of the general municipal law, at such times as the fire department, fire company or an emergency rescue and first aid squad of the fire department or fire company are on duty, or when, on orders of the chief of the fire department or fire company of which they are members, they are separately engaged in response to a call for assistance pursuant to the provisions of section two hundred nine of the general municipal law; provided, however, that nothing in this subdivision shall be deemed to authorize such officer to carry, possess, repair or dispose of a firearm unless the appropriate license therefor has been issued pursuant to section 400.00 of the penal law.

42. Special deputy sheriffs appointed by the sheriff of a county within which any part of the grounds of Cornell university or the grounds of any state institution constituting a part of the educational and research plants owned or under the supervision, administration or control of said university are located pursuant to section fifty-seven hundred nine of the education law; provided, however, that nothing in this subdivision shall be deemed to authorize such officer to carry, possess, repair or dispose of a firearm unless the appropriate license therefor has been issued pursuant to section 400.00 of the penal law.

43. Housing patrolmen of the Mount Vernon housing authority, acting pursuant to rules of the Mount Vernon housing authority; provided, however, that nothing in this subdivision shall be deemed to authorize such officer to carry, possess, repair or dispose of a firearm unless the appropriate license therefor has been issued pursuant to section 400.00 of the penal law.

44. The officers, employees and members of the New York city division of fire prevention, in the bureau of fire, as set forth and subject to the limitations contained in subdivision one of section 487a-1.0 of the administrative code of the city of New York; provided, however, that nothing in this subdivision shall be deemed to authorize such officer to carry, possess, repair or dispose of a firearm unless the appropriate license therefor has been issued pursuant to section 400.00 of the penal law.

45. Persons appointed and designated as peace officers by the Niagara frontier transportation authority, pursuant to subdivision thirteen of

section twelve hundred ninety-nine-e of the public authorities law.

46. Persons appointed as peace officers by the Sea Gate Association pursuant to the provisions of chapter three hundred ninety-one of the laws of nineteen hundred forty, provided, however, that nothing in this subdivision shall be deemed to authorize such officer to carry, possess, repair or dispose of a firearm unless the appropriate license therefor has been issued pursuant to section 400.00 of the penal law.

47. Employees of the insurance frauds bureau of the state department of insurance when designated as peace officers by the superintendent of insurance and acting pursuant to their special duties; provided, however, that nothing in this subdivision shall be deemed to authorize such officer to carry, possess, repair or dispose of a firearm unless the appropriate license therefor has been issued pursuant to section 400.00 of the penal law.

48. New York state air base security guards when they are designated as peace officers under military regulations promulgated by the chief of staff to the governor and when performing their duties as air base security guards pursuant to orders issued by appropriate military authority; provided, however, that nothing in this subdivision shall be deemed to authorize such guards to carry, possess, repair or dispose of a firearm unless the appropriate license therefor has been issued pursuant to section 400.00 of the penal law.

49. Members of the army national guard military police and air national guard security personnel belonging to the organized militia of the state of New York when they are designated as peace officers under military regulations promulgated by the adjutant general and when performing their duties as military policemen or air security personnel pursuant to orders issued by appropriate military authority; provided, however, that nothing in this subdivision shall be deemed to authorize such military police or air security personnel to carry, possess, repair or dispose of a firearm unless the appropriate license therefor has been issued pursuant to section 400.00 of the penal law.

50. Transportation supervisors in the city of White Plains appointed by the commissioner of public safety in the city of White Plains; provided, however, that nothing in this subdivision shall be deemed to authorize such officer to carry, possess, repair or dispose of a firearm unless the appropriate license therefor has been issued pursuant to section 400.00 of the penal law.

51. Officers and members of the fire investigation division of the fire department of the city of Rochester, the city of Binghamton and the city of Utica, when acting pursuant to their special duties in matters arising under the laws relating to fires, the extinguishment thereof and fire perils; provided, however, that nothing in this subdivision shall be deemed to authorize such officer to carry, possess, repair or dispose of a firearm unless the appropriate license therefor has been issued pursuant to section 400.00 of the penal law.

52. Security hospital treatment assistants, as so designated by the commissioner of the office of mental health while transporting persons convicted of a crime to court, to other facilities within the jurisdiction of the office of mental health, or to any state or local correctional facility; provided, however, that nothing in this subdivision shall be deemed to authorize such employee to carry, possess, repair or dispose of a firearm unless the appropriate license therefor has been issued pursuant to section 400.00 of penal law.

53. Authorized agents of the municipal directors of weights and measures in the counties of Suffolk, Nassau and Westchester when acting pursuant to their special duties as set forth in section one hundred eighty-one of the agriculture and markets law; provided, however, that nothing in this subdivision shall be deemed to authorize such officer to carry, possess, repair or dispose of a firearm unless the appropriate license therefor has been issued pursuant to section 400.00 of the penal law.

54. Special policemen appointed pursuant to section one hundred fifty-eight of the town law; provided, however, that nothing in this subdivision shall be deemed to authorize such officer to carry, possess, repair or dispose of a firearm unless the appropriate license therefor has been issued pursuant to section 400.00 of the penal law.

55. [*Expired.*]

56. Dog control officers of the town of Brookhaven, who at the discretion of the town board may be designated as constables for the purpose of enforcing article twenty-six of the agriculture and markets law and for the purpose of issuing appearance tickets permitted under article seven of such law; provided, however, that nothing in this subdivision shall be deemed to authorize such officer to carry, possess, repair or dispose of a firearm unless the appropriate license therefor has been issued pursuant to section 400.00 of the penal law.

57. Harbor Park rangers employed by the Snug Harbor cultural center in Richmond county and appointed as New York city special patrolmen by the police commissioner pursuant to subdivision c of section 14-106 of the administrative code of the city of New York. Notwithstanding any provision of law, rule or regulation, such officers shall be authorized to issue appearance tickets pursuant to section 150.20 of this chapter, and shall have such other powers as are specified in section 2.20 of this article only when acting pursuant to their special duties. Nothing in this subdivision shall be deemed to authorize such officers to carry, possess, repair or dispose of a firearm unless the appropriate license therefore has been issued pursuant to section 400.00 of the penal law and

the employer has authorized such officer to possess a firearm during any phase of the officer's on-duty employment.

57-a. [*See also* subd. 57-a *below*] Seasonal park rangers of the Westchester county department of public safety while employed as authorized by the commissioner of public safety/sheriff of the county of Westchester; provided, however, that nothing in this subdivision shall be deemed to authorize such officer to carry, possess, repair or dispose of a firearm unless the appropriate license therefor has been issued pursuant to section 400.00 of the penal law.

57-a. [*See also* subd. 57-a *above*] Officers of the Westchester county public safety emergency force, when activated by the commissioner of public safety/sheriff of the county of Westchester; provided, however that nothing in this subdivision shall be deemed to authorize such officer to carry, possess, repair or dispose of a firearm unless the appropriate license therefor has been issued pursuant to section 400.00.

58. Uniformed members of the security force of the Troy housing authority provided, however, that nothing in this subdivision shall be deemed to authorize such officer to carry, possess, repair or dispose of a firearm unless the appropriate license therefor has been issued pursuant to section 400.00 of the penal law.

59. Officers and members of the sanitation police of the department of sanitation of the city of New York, duly appointed and designated as peace officers by such department; provided, however, that nothing in this subdivision shall be deemed to authorize such officer to carry, possess, repair or dispose of a firearm unless the appropriate license therefor has been issued pursuant to section 400.00 of the penal law. Provided, further, that nothing in this subdivision shall be deemed to apply to officers and members of the sanitation police regularly and exclusively assigned to enforcement of such city's residential recycling laws.

60. [*Expired.*]

[*In 1992 the Legislature added the following two subdivisions, which vary in content but are both numbered 61. It is assumed that the Legislature intended to number these consecutively, rather than identically.*]

61. Chief fire marshall, assistant chief fire marshall, fire marshall and fire marshall, all of whom are full-time employees of the Suffolk county department of fire, rescue and emergency services, when acting pursuant to their special duties in matters arising under the laws relating to fires, the extinguishment thereof and fire perils; provided, however, that nothing in this subdivision shall be deemed to authorize such officer to carry, possess, repair or dispose of a firearm unless the appropriate license therefor has been issued pursuant to section 400.00 of the penal law. [*Added by L. 1992, Ch. 257. See also subd. 61 below.*]

61. Investigators employed by the criminal investigations bureau when assigned to such bureau by the superintendent of banks and acting pursuant to their special duties as set forth in article two-B of the banking law; provided, however, that nothing in this subdivision shall be deemed to authorize such officer to carry, possess, repair or dispose of a firearm unless the appropriate license therefor has been issued pursuant to section 400.00 of the penal law. [*Added by L. 1992, Ch. 321. See also subd. 61 above.*]

[*In 1993 the Legislature added the following two subdivisions, which vary in content but are both numbered 62. It is assumed that the Legislature intended to number these consecutively, rather than identically.*]

62. Chief fire marshall, assistant chief fire marshall, fire marshall ii and fire marshall i, all of whom are full-time employees of the town of Babylon, when acting pursuant to their special duties in matters arising under the laws relating to fires, the extinguishment thereof and fire perils; provided, however, that nothing in this subdivision shall be deemed to authorize such officer to carry, possess, repair or dispose of a firearm unless the appropriate license therefor has been issued pursuant to section 400.00 of the penal law. [*Added by L. 1993, Ch. 204, effective July 6, 1993. See also subd. 62 below.*]

62. Employees of the division for youth assigned to transport and warrants units who are specifically designated by the director in accordance with section five hundred four-b of the executive law, provided, however, that nothing in this subdivision shall be deemed to authorize such employees to carry, possess, repair or dispose of a firearm unless the appropriate license therefor has been issued pursuant to section 400.00 of the penal law. [*Added by L. 1993, Ch. 687, effective 120 days after August 4, 1993. See also subd. 62 above.*]

[*In 1994 the Legislature added the following two subdivisions, which vary in content but are both numbered 63. It is assumed that the Legislature intended to number these consecutively, rather than identically.*]

63. Uniformed members of the fire marshal's office in the town of Southampton and the town of Riverhead, when acting pursuant to their special duties in matters arising under the laws relating to fires, the extinguishment thereof and fire perils; provided, however that nothing in this subdivision shall be deemed to authorize such officer to carry, possess, repair or dispose of a firearm unless the appropriate license therefor has been issued pursuant to section 400.00 of the penal law. [*Added by L. 1994, Ch. 519, as amended. See also subd. 63 below.*]

63. Employees of the town court of the town of Greenburgh serving as a security officer; provided, however, that nothing in this subdivision will be deemed to authorize such officer to carry, possess, repair or dispose of a firearm unless the appropriate license therefor has been issued pursuant to section 400.00 of the penal law

or to authorize such officer to carry or possess a firearm except while on duty. [*Added by L. 1994, Ch. 620. See also subd. 63 above.*]

64. Cell block attendants employed by the city of Buffalo police department; provided, however, that nothing in this subdivision shall be deemed to authorize such officer to carry, possess, repair or dispose of a firearm unless the appropriate license therefor has been issued pursuant to section 400.00 of the penal law.

65. Chief fire marshall, assistant chief fire marshall, fire marshall II and fire marshall I, all of whom are full-time employees of the town of Brookhaven, when acting pursuant to their special duties in matters arising under the laws relating to fires, the extinguishment thereof and fire perils; provided, however, that nothing in this subdivision shall be deemed to authorize such officer to carry, possess, repair or dispose of a firearm unless the appropriate license thereof has been issued pursuant to section 400.00 of the penal law.

66. Employees of the village court of the village of Spring Valley serving as security officers at such village court; provided, however, that nothing in this subdivision shall be deemed to authorize such officer to carry, possess, repair or dispose of a firearm unless the appropriate license therefor has been issued pursuant to section 400.00 of the penal law.

67. Employees of the town court of the town of Putnam Valley serving as a security officer; provided, however, that nothing in this subdivision will be deemed to authorize such officer to carry, possess, repair or dispose of a firearm unless the appropriate license therefor has been issued pursuant to section 400.00 of the penal law or to authorize such officer to carry or possess a firearm except while on duty.

[*In 2000 the Legislature renumbered subdivision 65 subdivision 68 and added four subdivisions which vary in content but are all numbered 68. It is assumed that the Legislature intended to number these consecutively, rather than identically.*]

68. Employees of the town court of the town of Southampton serving as uniformed court officers at such town court; provided, however, that nothing in this subdivision shall be deemed to authorize such officer to carry, possess, repair or dispose of a firearm unless the appropriate license therefor has been issued pursuant to section 400.00 of the penal law. [*Renumbered by L. 2000, Ch. 385, § 1, eff. Aug. 30, 2000. See also subds. 68 below.*]

68. The state inspector general and investigators designated by the state inspector general; provided, however, that nothing in this subdivision shall be deemed to authorize the state inspector general or such investigators to carry, possess, repair or dispose of a firearm unless the appropriate license therefor has been issued pursuant to section 400.00 of the penal law. [*Added by L. 2000, Ch. 168, § 1, eff. July 18, 2000. See also subd. 68 above, and subds. 68 below.*]

68. Dog control officers of the town of Arcadia, who at the discretion of the town board may be designated as constables for the purpose of enforcing article twenty-six of the agriculture and markets law and for the purpose of issuing appearance tickets permitted under article seven of such law; provided, however, that nothing in this subdivision shall be deemed to authorize such officer to carry, possess, repair or dispose of a firearm unless the appropriate license therefor has been issued pursuant to section 400.00 of the penal law. [*Added by L. 2000, Ch. 227, § 1, eff. Aug. 16, 2000. See also subds. 68 above and subds. 68 below.*]

68. Employees appointed by the sheriff of Livingston county, when acting pursuant to their special duties serving as uniformed marine patrol officers; provided, however, that nothing in this subdivision shall be deemed to authorize such officer to carry, possess, repair or dispose of a firearm unless the appropriate license has been issued pursuant to section 400.00 of the penal law or to authorize such officer to carry or possess a firearm except while on duty. [*Added by L. 2000, Ch. 381, § 1, eff. Aug. 30, 2000. See also subds. 68 above and subd. 68 below.*]

68. Persons employed by the Chautauqua county sheriff's office serving as court security officers; provided, however, that nothing in this subdivision shall be deemed to authorize such officer to carry, possess, repair or dispose of a firearm unless the appropriate license therefor has been issued pursuant to section 400.00 of the penal law. [*Added by L. 2000, Ch. 393, § 1, eff. Aug. 30, 2000. See also subds. 68 above.*]

69. Employees of the village court of the village of Amityville serving as uniformed court officers at such village court; provided, however, that nothing in this subdivision shall be deemed to authorize such officer to carry, possess, repair or dispose of a firearm unless the appropriate license therefor has been issued pursuant to section 400.00 of the penal law.

70. Employees appointed by the sheriff of Yates county, pursuant to their special duties serving as uniformed marine patrol officers; provided, however, that nothing in this subdivision shall be deemed to authorize such officer to carry, possess, repair or dispose of a firearm unless the appropriate license has been issued pursuant to section 400.00 of the penal law or to authorize such officer to carry or possess a firearm except while on duty.

71. Town of Smithtown fire marshalls when acting pursuant to their special duties in matters arising under the laws relating to fires, the extinguishment thereof and fire perils; provided, however, that nothing in this subdivision shall be deemed to authorize such officers to carry, possess, repair or dispose of a firearm unless the appropriate license therefor has been issued pursuant to section 400.00 of the penal law.

72. Persons employed by Canisius college as members of the security force of such college; provided, however, that nothing in this subdivision shall be deemed to authorize such officer to carry, possess, repair or dispose of a firearm unless the appropriate license therefor has been issued pursuant to section 400.00 of the penal law.

73. Employees of the town court of the town of Newburgh serving as uniformed court officers at such town court; provided, however, that nothing in this subdivision shall be deemed to authorize such officer to carry, possess, repair or dispose of a firearm unless the appropriate license therefor has been issued pursuant to section 400.00 of the penal law.

[There are four subd. 74. See below.]

74. *[Added by L. 2002, Ch. 260, § 1, eff. July 30, 2002.]* Employees of the village court of the village of Quogue, town of Southampton serving as uniformed court officers at such village court; provided, however, that nothing in this subdivision shall be deemed to authorize such officer to carry, possess, repair or dispose of a firearm unless the appropriate license therefor has been issued pursuant to section 400.00 of the penal law.

74. *[Added by L. 2002, Ch. 261, § 1, eff. July 30, 2002.]* Employees of the town court of the town of East Hampton serving as uniformed court officers at such town court; provided, however, that nothing in this subdivision shall be deemed to authorize such officer to carry, possess, repair or dispose of a firearm unless the appropriate license therefor has been issued pursuant to section 400.00 of the penal law.

74. *[Added by L. 2001, Ch. 120.]*

a. Special deputy sheriffs appointed by the sheriff of Tompkins county pursuant to paragraphs b and c of this subdivision; provided, however, that nothing in this subdivision shall be deemed to authorize such officer to carry, possess, repair or dispose of a firearm unless the appropriate license therefor has been issued pursuant to section 400.00 of the penal law.

b. For the protection of the grounds, buildings and property of Ithaca college the prevention of crime and the enforcement of law and order, and for the enforcement of such rules and regulations as the board of trustees of Ithaca college shall from time to time make, the sheriff of Tompkins county may appoint and remove following consultation with Ithaca college such number of special deputy sheriffs as is determined by the sheriff to be necessary for the maintenance of public order at Ithaca college, such appointments to be made from persons nominated by the president of Ithaca college. Such special deputy sheriffs shall comply with requirements as established by the sheriff and shall act only within Tompkins county. Such special deputy sheriffs so appointed shall be employees of the college and subject to its supervision and control as outlined in the terms and conditions to be mutually agreed upon between the sheriff and Ithaca college. Such special deputy sheriffs shall have the powers of peace officers and shall act solely within the said grounds or premises owned or administered by Ithaca college, except in those rare and special situations when requested by the sheriff to provide assistance on any public highway which crosses or adjoins such property. Ithaca college will provide legal defense and indemnification, and hold harmless the county of Tompkins, its officers and employees and the Tompkins county sheriff, its officers and employees, from all claims arising out of conduct by or injury to, such personnel while carrying out their law enforcement functions except in those situations when they are acting under the direct supervision and control of the county or sheriff's department.

c. Every special deputy sheriff so appointed shall, before entering upon the duties of his or her office, take and subscribe the oath of office prescribed by article thirteen of the constitution of the state of New York which oath shall be filed in the office of the county clerk of Tompkins county. Every special deputy sheriff appointed under this subdivision when on regular duty shall wear conspicuously a metallic shield with a designating number and the words "Special Deputy Sheriff Ithaca College" thereon.

74. *[Added by L. 2001, Ch. 548.]* Parks and recreation forest rangers employed by the office of parks, recreation and historic preservation; provided, however, that nothing in this subdivision shall be deemed to authorize such individuals to carry, possess, repair or dispose of a firearm unless the appropriate license therefor has been issued pursuant to section 400.00 of the penal law.

[There are three subd. 75. See below.]

75. *[Added by L. 2002, Ch. 320, § 1, eff. Aug. 6, 2002.]* Dog control officers of the town of Clarence, who at the discretion of the town board may be designated as constables for the purpose of enforcing article twenty-six of the agriculture and markets law and for the purpose of issuing appearance tickets permitted under article seven of the agriculture and markets law; provided, however, that nothing in this subdivision shall be deemed to authorize such officers to carry, possess, repair or dispose of a firearm unless the appropriate license therefor has been issued pursuant to section 400.00 of the penal law.

75. *[Added by L. 2002, Ch. 321, § 1, eff. Aug. 6, 2002.]* Airport security guards, senior airport security guards, airport security supervisors, retired police officers, and supervisors of same, who are designated by resolution of the town board of the town of Islip to provide security at Long Island MacArthur Airport when acting pursuant to their duties as such, and such authority being specifically limited to the grounds of the said airport. However, nothing in this subdivision shall be deemed to authorize such officer to carry,

possess, repair or dispose of a firearm unless the appropriate license therefor has been issued pursuant to section 400.00 of the penal law.

75. [*Added by L. 2002, Ch. 623, § 1, eff. Oct. 2, 2002. See also subd. 76 below.*] Officers and members of the fire investigation unit of the fire department of the city of Buffalo when acting pursuant to their special duties in matters arising under the laws relating to fires, the extinguishment thereof and fire perils; provided, however, that nothing in this subdivision shall be deemed to authorize such officer to carry, possess, repair or dispose of a firearm unless the appropriate license therefor has been issued pursuant to section 400.00 of the penal law.

[*There are two subd. 76. See below.*]

76. [*Added by L. 2003, Ch. 626, § 1, eff. Sept. 30, 2003. See also subd. 76 below.*] Employees of the village court of the village of Southampton, town of Southampton serving as uniformed court officers at such village court; provided, however, that nothing in this subdivision shall be deemed to authorize such officer to carry, possess, repair or dispose of a firearm unless the appropriate license therefor has been issued pursuant to section 400.00 of the penal law.

76. [*Added by L. 2003, Ch. 665, § 1, eff. Oct. 15, 2003. See also subd. 76 above.*] Animal control officers employed by the city of Peekskill; provided, however, that nothing in this subdivision shall be deemed to authorize such individuals to carry, possess, repair or dispose of a firearm unless the appropriate license therefor has been issued pursuant to section 400.00 of the penal law.

[*There are two subd. 77. See below.*]

77. [*Added by L. 2003, Ch. 654, § 1, eff. Oct. 7, 2003; Amended by L. 2004, Ch. 17, § 1, eff. Mar. 23, 2004. See also subd. 77 below.*]

(a) Syracuse University peace officers appointed by the chief law enforcement officer of the city of Syracuse pursuant to paragraphs (b), (c) and (d) of this subdivision, who shall be authorized to issue appearance tickets and simplified traffic informations; provided, however, that nothing in this subdivision shall be deemed to authorize any such officer to carry, possess, repair or dispose of a firearm unless the appropriate license therefor has been issued pursuant to section 400.00 of the penal law.

(b) For the protection of the grounds, buildings and property of Syracuse University, the prevention of crime and the enforcement of law and order, and for the enforcement of such rules and regulations as Syracuse University shall from time to time establish, the chief law enforcement officer of the city of Syracuse may appoint and remove, following consultations with Syracuse University; such number of Syracuse University peace officers as is determined by the chief law enforcement officer of the city of Syracuse to be necessary for the maintenance of public order at

such university, such appointments to be made from persons nominated by the chancellor of Syracuse University. Such peace officers shall comply with such requirements as shall be established by the chief law enforcement officer of the city of Syracuse. Such Syracuse University peace officers so appointed shall be employees of such university, and subject to its supervision and control and the terms and conditions to be mutually agreed upon between the chief law enforcement officer of the city of Syracuse and Syracuse University. Nothing in this paragraph shall limit the authority of Syracuse University to remove such peace officers. Such Syracuse University peace officers shall have the powers of peace officers within the geographical area of employment of the grounds or premises owned, controlled or administrated by Syracuse University within the county of Onondaga, except in those situations when requested by the chief law enforcement officer of the city of Syracuse or his or her designee, including by means of written protocols agreed to by the chief law enforcement officer of the city of Syracuse and Syracuse University, to provide assistance on any public highway which crosses or adjoins such grounds or premises. Syracuse University shall provide legal defense and indemnification, and hold harmless the city of Syracuse, and its officers and employees from all claims arising out of conduct by or injury to, such peace officers while carrying out their law enforcement functions, except in those situations when they are acting under the direct supervision and control of the chief law enforcement officer of the city of Syracuse, or his or her designee.

(c) Every Syracuse University peace officer so appointed shall, before entering upon the duties of his or her office, take and subscribe the oath of office prescribed by article thirteen of the state constitution, which oath shall be filed in the office of the county clerk of the county of Onondaga. Every such peace officer appointed pursuant to this subdivision when on regular duty shall conspicuously wear a metallic shield with a designating number and the words "Syracuse University Peace Officer" engraved thereon.

(d) To become eligible for appointment as a Syracuse University peace officer a candidate shall, in addition to the training requirements as set forth in section 2.30 of this article, complete the course of instruction in public and private law enforcement established pursuant to paragraph (c) of subdivision five of section sixty-four hundred fifty of the education law.

77. [*Added by L. 2004, Ch. 367, § 1, eff. Aug. 17, 2004. See also subd. 77 above.*] Chief fire marshal, assistant chief fire marshal, and fire marshals, all of whom are full-time employees of the town of East Hampton, when acting pursuant to their special duties in matters arising under the laws relating to fires, the extinguishment thereof and fire perils; provided, however, that nothing

in this subdivision shall be deemed to authorize such officer to carry, possess, repair or dispose of a firearm unless the appropriate license therefor has been issued pursuant to section 400.00 of the penal law.

78. [*Added by L. 2003, Ch. 689, § 3, eff. Oct. 21, 2003; Renumbered by L. 2004, Ch. 24 § 3, eff. Apr. 6, 2004.*] A security officer employed by a community college who is specifically designated as a peace officer by the board of trustees of a community college pursuant to subdivision five-a of section sixty-three hundred six of the education law, or by a community college regional board of trustees pursuant to subdivision four-a of section sixty-three hundred ten of the education law; provided, however, that nothing in this subdivision shall be deemed to authorize such officer to carry, possess, repair or dispose of a firearm unless the appropriate license therefor has been issued pursuant to section 400.00 of the penal law.

79. [*Added by L. 2004, Ch. 235, § 1, eff. July 27, 2004.*] Court security officers employed by the Wayne county sheriff's office; provided however, that nothing in this subdivision shall be deemed to authorize such officer to carry, possess, repair or dispose of a firearm unless the appropriate license therefor has been issued pursu ant to section 400.00 of the penal law.

79. [*Added by L. 2004, Ch. 241, § 1, eff. July 27, 2004.*] Supervisors and members of the arson investigation bureau and fire inspection bureau of the department of state's office of fire prevention and control when acting pursuant to their special duties in matters arising under the laws relating to fires, their prevention, extinguishment, investigation thereof, and fire perils; provided, however, that nothing in this subdivision shall be deemed to authorize such employees to carry, possess, repair, or dispose of a firearm unless the appropriate license therefor has been issued pursuant to section 400.00 of the penal law.

79. [*Added by L. 2004, Ch. 664, § 2, eff. Oct. 26, 2004.*] Peace officers appointed by the city university of New York pursuant to subdivision sixteen of section sixty-two hundred six of the education law, who shall have the powers set forth in section 2.20 of this article whether or not they are acting pursuant to their special duties; provided, however, that nothing in this subdivision shall be deemed to authorize such officer to carry, possess, repair or dispose of a firearm unless the appropriate license therefore has been issued pursuant to section 400.00 of the penal law.

79. [*Added by L. 2004, Ch. 752, § 1, eff. Jan. 28, 2005.*] Animal control officers of the city of Elmira, who at the discretion of the city council of the city of Elmira may be designated as constables for the purpose of enforcing article twenty-six of the agriculture and markets law, and for the purpose of issuing appearance tickets

permitted under article seven of such law; provided, however, that nothing in this subdivision shall be deemed to authorize such officer to carry, possess, repair or dispose of a firearm unless the appropriate license therefor has been issued pursuant to section 400.00 of the penal law.

80. Employees of the Onondaga county sheriff's department serving as uniformed court security officers at Onondaga county court facilities; provided, however, that nothing in this subdivision shall be deemed to authorize such officers to carry, possess, repair or dispose of a firearm unless the appropriate license therefor has been issued pursuant to section 400.00 of the penal law.

Amended by L. 1981, Ch. 175, Ch. 462, Ch. 523, Ch. 720; L. 1982, Ch. 658; L. 1983, Ch. 399; Ch. 969; L. 1984, Ch. 740; L. 1985, Ch. 65; L. 1985, Ch. 266; L. 1986, Ch. 318; Ch. 364; L. 1987, Chs. 24, 355; L. 1991, Ch. 371; L. 1987, Ch. 617; L. 1987, Ch. 734; L. 1988, Ch. 274; L. 1988, Ch. 141; L. 1988, Ch. 438; L. 1988, Ch. 694; L. 1988, Ch. 695; L. 1989, Ch. 189; L. 1990, Ch. 931; L. 1991, Ch. 166; L. 1992, Ch. 93; L. 1992, Ch. 294; L. 1992, Ch. 257; L. 1992, Ch. 321; L. 1992, Ch. 487; L. 1992, Ch. 858; L. 1993, Ch. 157; L. 1993, Ch. 204; L. 1993, Ch. 508, eff. until October 31, 1997, amending subds. 4(a) and 4(c); L. 1993, Ch. 687, eff. 120 days after Aug. 4, 1993, adding subds. 62; L. 1994, Ch. 466, § 1, eff. July 20, 1994, and expiring and deemed repealed Jan. 31, 1995, adding subd. 21(f); L. 1994, Ch. 519, § 1, eff. July 26, 1994, adding first subd. 63; L. 1994, Ch. 620, § 1, eff. July 26, 1994, adding second subd. 63; L. 1994, Ch. 665, § 1, eff. Aug. 2, 1994, amending subd. 30; L. 1994, Ch. 668, § 1, eff. Aug. 2, 1994, amending subd. 27; L. 1995, Ch. 2, § 70, amending subd. 4(a), eff. Sept. 1, 1995, repealed Oct. 31, 1997; L. 1995, Ch. 2, § 71, eff. Oct. 31, 1997; L. 1995, Ch. 658, § 1, adding subd. (f), eff. Aug. 8, 1995; L. 1995, Ch. 457, § 1, amending subd. 27, eff. Aug. 2, 1995; L. 1995, Ch. 206, Ch. 462, and Ch. 521, all § 1, adding subd. 64, eff. Sept. 24, 1995, Aug. 2, 1995, and Aug. 2, 1995, respectively; L. 1996, Ch. 314, § 1, adding subd. 64, eff. July 17, 1996; L. 1996, Ch. 379, § 1, adding subd. 65, eff. July 30, 1996; L. 1997, Ch. 389 Part A, § 103, extending expiration date of 4(a) and (c) to Oct. 31, 2002, eff. Aug. 7, 1997, and adding subd. 66, eff. Aug. 5, 1997, Ch. 555, § 1, eff. Sept. 10, 1997, adding a second subd. 66, and Ch. 562, § 1, eff. Sept. 10, 1997, adding a third subd. 66; L. 1998, Ch. 424, § 3 eff. Jan. 1, 1999 and Ch. 224, § 1, eff. July 7, 1998; L. 1999, Ch. 212, § 2, eff. July 6, 1999, amending subd. 31, and Ch. 584, § 1, adding subd. 67; L. 2000, Ch. 168, § 1, eff. July 18, 2000, adding subd. 68, Ch. 227, § 1, eff. Aug. 16, 2000, adding subd. 68, Ch. 381, § 1, eff. Aug. 30, 2000, adding subd. 68, Ch. 385, § 1, eff. Aug. 30, 2000, renumbering subds. 64–67 to subds. 65–72 and adding subd. 73, Ch. 393, § 1, eff. Aug. 30, 2000, adding subd. 68, Ch. 404, § 1, eff. Aug. 30, 2000, adding subd. 23-a; L. 2001, Ch. 120, § 1, eff. Aug. 6, 2001, adding subd. 74; Ch. 481, eff. Nov. 21, 2001, amending subd. 30, and Ch. 548, eff. Dec. 12, 2001, adding second subd. 74; L. 2002, Ch. 318, §§ 3 and 4, amending subd. 4, Ch. 85, Part F § 2, extending exp. dates in subd. 4 to Oct. 31, 2007, Ch. 260, § 1, adding third subd. 74, eff. July 30, 2002, Ch. 261, § 1, adding fourth subd. 74, eff. July 30, 2002, Ch. 320, § 1, adding subd. 75, eff. Aug. 6, 2002, Ch. 321, § 1, adding second subd. 75, eff. Aug. 6, 2002, Ch. 623, § 1, adding third subd. 75, eff. Oct. 2, 2002; L. 2003, Ch. 16, § 14, extending expiration date to Sept. 1, 2005; L. 2003, Ch. 626, § 1, eff. Sept. 30, 2003, adding first version of subd. 76; L. 2003, Ch. 638, § 1, eff. Oct. 7, 2003, amending the first version of subd. 63; L. 2003, Ch. 654, § 1, eff. Oct. 7, 2003, adding second version of subd. 76; L. 2003, Ch. 671, § 1, eff. Oct. 15, 2003, amending subd. 40; L. 2003, Ch. 665, § 1, eff. Oct. 15, 2003, adding subd. 76; L. 2003, Ch. 689, § 3, adding subd. 76, eff. Oct. 21, 2003; L. 2004, Ch. 17, § 1, renumbering and amending subd. 76 as subd. 77, eff. Mar. 23, 2004; L. 2004, Ch. 24, § 3, renumbering subd. 76 as subd. 78, eff. Apr. 6, 2004; L. 2004, Ch. 367, § 1, adding subd. 77, eff. Aug. 17, 2004; L. 2004, Ch. 235, § 1, adding subd. 79, eff. July 27, 2004; L. 2004, Ch. 241, § 1, adding subd. 79, eff. July 27, 2004; L. 2004, Ch. 664, § 3, eff. Oct. 26, 2004, amending subd. 27 and adding third version of subd. 79; L. 2004, Ch. 752, eff. Jan. 28, 2005, adding fourth version of subd. 79; L. 2005, Ch. 557, § 1, adding subd. 80, eff. Aug 23, 2005.

§ 2.15. Federal law enforcement officers; powers.

The following federal law enforcement officers shall have the powers set forth in paragraphs (a) (with the exception of the powers provided by paragraph (b) of subdivision one and paragraph (b) of subdivision three of section 140.25 of this chapter), (b), (c) and (h) of subdivision one of section 2.20 of this article:

1. Federal Bureau of Investigation special agents.

2. United States Secret Service special agents.

3. Immigration and Naturalization Service immigration inspectors, special agents, patrol officers and deportation officers.

4. United States Marshals and Marshals Service deputies.

5. Drug Enforcement Administration special agents.

6. Federal Protective Officers.

7. United States Customs Service special agents, inspectors and patrol officers.

8. United States Postal Service police officers and inspectors.

9. United States park police; provided, however that, notwithstanding any provision of this section to the contrary, such park police shall also have the powers set forth in paragraph (b) of subdivision one of section 140.25 of this chapter and the powers set forth in paragraphs (d), (e) and (g) of subdivision one of section 2.20 of this article.

10. United States probation officers.

11. United States General Services Administration special agents.

12. United States Department of Agriculture special agents.

13. Bureau of Alcohol, Tobacco and Firearms special agents.

14. Internal Revenue Service special agents and inspectors.

15. Officers of the United States bureau of prisons.

16. United States Fish and Wildlife special agents.

17. United States Naval Investigative Service special agents.

18. United States Department of State special agents.

19. Special agents of the defense criminal investigative service of the United States department of defense.

20. United States Department of Commerce, Office of Export Enforcement, special agents.

21. United States Department of Veterans Administration Police officers employed at the Veterans Administration Medical Center in Batavia.

22. Federal Reserve law enforcement officers.

23. Federal air marshal program special agents.

24. [*Added by L. 2004, Ch. 110.*] United States department of transportation federal police officers and police supervisors assigned to the United States Merchant Marine Academy in Kings Point, New York; provided, however that, notwithstanding any provision of this section to the contrary, such police shall also have the powers set forth in paragraph (b) of subdivision one of section 140.25 of this chapter and the powers set forth in paragraphs (d), (e) and (g) of subdivision one of section 2.20 of this article when acting pursuant to their special duties within the geographical area of their employment or within one hundred yards of such geographical area.

24. [*Added by L. 2004, Ch. 720.*] United States Coast Guard Investigative Service special agents.

Amended by L. 1982, Ch. 474; L. 1983, Ch. 683; L. 1985, Ch. 205; L. 1985, Ch. 392; L. 1986, Ch. 420; L. 1987, Ch. 644; L. 1988, Ch. 177; L. 1995, Ch. 177, § 1, amending subd. 9, eff. July 19, 1995; L. 1995, Ch. 522, § 1, amending subd. 3, eff. Aug. 2, 1995; L. 1997, Ch. 549, § 1, eff. Sept. 10, 1997, adding subd. 21; L. 2002, Ch. 92, § 1, eff. June 24, 2002, adding subd. 22; L. 2003, Ch. 299, § 1, eff. Aug. 5, 2003, adding subd. 23; L. 2004, Ch. 110, § 1, eff. June 15, 2004, adding subd. 24; L. 2004, Ch. 178, § 1, eff. July 20, 2004, amending subd. 24; L. 2004, Ch. 720, § 1, eff. Nov. 24, 2004, adding second version of subd. 24; L. 2005, Ch. 43, § 1, amending subd. 10, eff. May 24, 2005.

§ 2.16. Watershed protection and enforcement officers; powers, duties, jurisdiction for arrests.

1. Watershed protection and enforcement officers appointed by the city of Peekskill shall have the powers set forth in paragraphs (a), (b), (c), (f), (g), and (h) of subdivision one of section 2.20 of this article; provided, however, that nothing in this section shall be deemed to authorize such officer to carry, possess, repair, or dispose of a firearm unless the appropriate license therefor has been issued pursuant to section 400.00 of the penal law. Watershed protection and enforcement officers shall complete the training requirements set forth in section 2.30 of this article.

2. The city of Peekskill may appoint the following persons as watershed protection and enforcement officers:

(a) the water superintendent;

(b) the deputy assistant to the water superintendent; and

(c) the watershed inspector or inspectors.

3. The duties of the watershed protection and

enforcement officers shall be to enforce those provisions of the environmental conservation law and the penal law which relate to the contamination of water in those areas of the Hollow Brook watershed located within the city of Peekskill, including its reservoirs, shoreline, and tributaries, and those areas of the Hollow Brook watershed and Wiccopee reservoir located outside of the city of Peekskill in the counties of Putnam and Westchester, including its reservoirs, shoreline, and tributaries.

4. Notwithstanding paragraph (b) of subdivision thirty-four-a of section 1.20 of this title and paragraph (b) of subdivision five of section 140.25 of this chapter, watershed protection and enforcement officers are authorized to make arrests and issue appearance tickets in those areas of the Hollow Brook watershed and Wiccopee reservoir located outside of the city of Peekskill in the counties of Putnam and Westchester, including along its reservoirs, shoreline, and tributaries.

Added by L. 2004, Ch. 347, § 1, eff. Aug. 10, 2004.

§ 2.20. Powers of peace officers.

1. The persons designated in section 2.10 of this article shall have the following powers:

(a) The power to make warrantless arrests pursuant to section 140.25 of this chapter.

(b) The power to use physical force and deadly physical force in making an arrest or preventing an escape pursuant to section 35.30 of the penal law.

(c) The power to carry out warrantless searches whenever such searches are constitutionally permissible and acting pursuant to their special duties.

(d) The power to issue appearance tickets pursuant to subdivision three of section 150.20 of this chapter, when acting pursuant to their special duties. New York city special patrolmen shall have the power to issue an appearance ticket only when it is pursuant to rules and regulations of the police commissioner of the city of New York.

(e) The power to issue uniform appearance tickets pursuant to article twenty-seven of the parks, recreation and historic preservation law and to issue simplified traffic informations pursuant to section 100.25 of this chapter and section two hundred seven of the vehicle and traffic law whenever acting pursuant to their special duties.

(f) The power to issue a uniform navigation summons and/or complaint pursuant to section nineteen of the navigation law whenever acting pursuant to their special duties.

(g) The power to issue uniform appearance tickets pursuant to article seventy-one of the environmental conservation law, whenever acting pursuant to their special duties.

(h) The power to possess and take custody of firearms not owned by the peace officer, for the purpose of disposing, guarding, or any other lawful purpose, consistent with his duties as a peace officer.

(i) Any other power which a particular peace officer is otherwise authorized to exercise by any general, special or local law or charter whenever acting pursuant to his special duties, provided such power is not inconsistent with the provisions of the penal law or this chapter.

2. For the purposes of this section a peace officer acts pursuant to his special duties when he performs the duties of his office, pursuant to the specialized nature of his particular employment, whereby he is required or authorized to enforce any general, special or local law or charter, rule, regulation, judgment or order.

3. A peace officer, whether or not acting pursuant to his special duties, who lawfully exercises any of the powers conferred upon him pursuant to this section, shall be deemed to be acting within the scope of his public employment for purposes of defense and indemnification rights and benefits that he may be otherwise entitled to under the provisions of section fifty-k of the general municipal law, section seventeen or eighteen of the public officers law, or any other applicable section of law.

Amended by L. 1985, Ch. 722.

§ 2.30. Training requirements for peace officers.

1. Every peace officer in the state of New York, appointed after the effective date of this article, who works a full complement of hours which constitutes full-time employment for the officer's employer, must successfully complete a training program, a portion of which shall be prescribed by the municipal police training council and by his employer, the state or local agency, unit of local government, state or local commission, or public authority or private organization that employs him. The portion prescribed by the municipal police training council shall be comprised of subjects, and the hours each is to be taught, that shall be required of all types or classes of peace officers. The hours of instruction required by the municipal police training council shall not exceed thirty-five, unless a greater amount is either required by law or regulation, or is requested by the employer.

The segment prescribed by the employer for his employees shall be comprised of subjects, and the hours each is to be taught, relating to the special nature of the duties of the peace officers employed by him. Each state or local agency, unit of local government, state or local commission, or public authority, or public or private organization which employs peace officers shall provide the training mandated by this section, and transmit to the municipal police training council within six months after the effective date of this article the proposed training program for peace officers, comprised of subjects required by the employer, the cost of which will be borne by the employer. The program shall:

(a) List the subjects comprising the proposed curriculum and the number of hours each is to be taught;

(b) List the proposed instructors for each subject with their qualifications; and

(c) Indicate the proposed location of the school.

In the reviewing of the employer's submission, the instructors must be found qualified by background and experience and if so found, the course shall be certified by the municipal police training council. When the subjects prescribed by the employer are identical to the subjects in the training program required by the municipal police training council, the officer shall not be required to take duplicate training for those subjects. It is the responsibility of every employer to provide the training program certified by the municipal police training council. Each peace officer satisfactorily completing the course shall be awarded a certificate by the division of criminal justice services attesting to that effect, and no person appointed as a peace officer after the effective date of this article shall exercise the powers of a peace officer, unless he has received such certification within twelve months of appointment. Where an employer has authorized a peace officer to carry or use a weapon during any phase of the officer's official duties, which constitutes on-duty employment, the program shall include the same number of hours of instruction in deadly physical force and the use of firearms and other weapons as is required in the basic training program for police officers by the municipal police training council. The program shall include the information set forth in subdivision seven of section 265.10 of the penal law. No employer shall allow any peace officer, notwithstanding when the officer was appointed, to carry or use a weapon during any phase of the officer's official duties, which constitutes on-duty employment, unless the officer has satisfactorily completed a course of training approved by the municipal police training council in the use of deadly physical force and firearms and other weapons, and annually receives instruction in deadly physical force and the use of firearms and other weapons as approved by the municipal police training council. The course of training in the use of deadly physical force and firearms and other weapons shall be provided by the officer's employer, not later than six months from the date on which the officer was appointed where the officer is authorized to carry a weapon pursuant to law.

2. Upon the failure or refusal to comply with the requirements of subdivision one of this section, the commissioner of the division of criminal justice services shall apply to the supreme court for an order directed to the person responsible requiring compliance. Upon such application, the court may issue such order as may be just, and a failure to comply with the order of the court shall be a contempt of court and punishable as such.

3. Any individual who is a peace officer or a New York city special patrolman on the effective date of this article and has previously taken a formalized course of training while a peace officer or a New York city special patrolman, may apply, in writing, to the municipal police training council for certification. The application shall be granted or denied for reasons specifically and concisely stated in writing, and if granted, the exact extent of any waiver of the training then presently required for new appointees shall be set forth. The certification shall be granted only if the municipal police training council determines that the course of training previously taken by the applicant is in substantial compliance with the training then presently required for new appointees.

When an application is denied, it is the responsibility of the officer to obtain the training that is required in order to obtain certification. When a peace officer meets the training requirements specified herein, the division of criminal justice services shall issue that person a certificate attesting to the fact that he has satisfactorily completed the required training.

4. Any peace officer appointed after the effective date of this article who normally works on a part-time basis for less than the full complement of hours which would constitute full-time employment for their position as determined by their employer, shall receive training which may, in whole or in part, be in-service training. The portion of the training program required by the municipal police training council shall not exceed ten hours of instruction. The segment of the training program prescribed by the employer shall be comprised of subjects, and the hours each is to be taught, relating to the special nature of the duties of the peace officers employed by him. Every employer who employs part-time peace officers shall transmit to the municipal police training council within six months after the effective date of this article the proposed training program for its officers, in accordance with the procedure and requirements set forth in subdivision one of this section. Each peace officer satisfactorily completing the training requirements shall be issued a certificate by the division of criminal justice services attesting to that effect.

5. Every employer of peace officers shall annually report to the municipal police training council, in such form and at such time as the council may by regulation require, the names and

addresses of all peace officers who have, during the course of the year, satisfactorily completed any of the training requirements prescribed by this section.

6. A certificate attesting to satisfactory completion of the training requirements imposed under this section awarded to any peace officer by the executive director of the municipal police training council pursuant to this section shall remain valid:

(a) during the holder's continuous service as a peace officer; and

(b) for two years after the date of the commencement of an interruption in such service where the holder had, immediately prior to such interruption, served as a peace officer for less than two consecutive years; or

(c) for four years after the date of the commencement of an interruption in such service where the holder had, immediately prior to such interruption, served as a peace officer for two consecutive years or longer.

As used in this subdivision, the term "interruption" shall mean a period of separation from employment as a peace officer by reason of such officer's leave of absence, resignation or removal, other than removal for cause.

Amended by L. 1987, Ch. 543; L. 1988, Ch. 735; L. 1989, Ch. 766; L. 1991, Ch. 219; L. 1991, Ch. 474.

TITLE B—THE CRIMINAL COURTS

ARTICLE 10—THE CRIMINAL COURTS

Section

LexisNexis Cross References

Criminal Defense Techniques, Vol. 3A, Ch. 75, Criminal Court Management: Implications for the Defense; *New York Criminal Practice (2d ed.),* Vol. 1, Ch. 3, Local Criminal Courts.

§ 10.10. The criminal courts; enumeration and definitions.

1. The "criminal courts" of this state are comprised of the superior courts and the local criminal courts.

2. "Superior court" means:

(a) The supreme court; or

(b) A county court.

3. "Local criminal court" means:

(a) A district court; or

(b) The New York City criminal court; or

(c) A city court; or

(d) A town court; or

(e) A village court; or

(f) A supreme court justice sitting as a local criminal court; or

(g) A county judge sitting as a local criminal court.

4. "City court" means any court for a city, other than New York City, having trial jurisdiction of offenses of less than felony grade only committed within such city, whether such court is entitled a city court, a municipal court, a police court, a recorder's court or is known by any other name or title.

5. "Town court." A "town court" is comprised of all the town justices of a town.

6. "Village court." A "village court" is comprised of the justice of a village, or all the justices thereof if there be more than one, or, at a time when he or they are absent, an acting justice of a village who is authorized to perform the functions of a village justice during his absence.

7. Notwithstanding any other provision of this section, a court specified herein which possesses civil as well as criminal jurisdiction does not act as a criminal court when acting solely in the exercise of its civil jurisdiction, and an order or determination made by such a court in its civil capacity is not an order or determination of a criminal court even though it may terminate or otherwise control or affect a criminal action or proceeding.

ANNOTATIONS

General.—An appearance ticket is not an accusatory instrument and its filing does not give a criminal court jurisdiction over the defendant. People v. Weinberg, 146 Misc. 2d 441, 558 N.Y.S.2d 439 (App. Term, 9th and 11th Jud. Dists. 1990).

Jurisdiction; local criminal court; jury trial.—One charged with violation of zoning ordinance is not entitled to jury trial since it is less serious than a misdemeanor and it is the length of possible incarceration that is determinative. Absent a showing of indigency, it could not be assumed that defendant faced imprisonment because he might be unable to pay any fine imposed. Friscia v. Crowe, 71 Misc. 2d 79, 335 N.Y.S.2d 453 (Sup. Ct. Suffolk Co. 1972).

Jurisdiction of criminal court.— The jurisdiction of the Criminal Court is restricted to hearing, trying and determining criminal charges, specifically misdemeanors and petty offenses. People v. Marchetta, 177 Misc. 2d 701, 676 N.Y.S.2d 791 (Crim. Ct. Queens Co. 1998).

Juvenile delinquency proceedings; application of CPL.— Though juvenile delinquency proceedings are quasi-criminal in nature, they do not require full application of CPL, only the affording of constitutional protection of due process; failure to verify petition or supporting statement of complainant was not a denial of due process. *In re* White, 70 Misc. 2d 541, 334 N.Y.S.2d 476 (Fam. Ct. Nassau Co. 1972).

Local criminal courts; use of school building denial of open trial.—Arraignment held in parochial school classroom deprived the defendant of his right to a public trial since a school is not open to the public. People v. Rose, 82 Misc. 2d 429, 368 N.Y.S.2d 387 (Rockland Co. Ct. 1975).

Town and Village Justices.—Under the State Constitution the current practice of lay Town and Village Justices is authorized. People v. Skrynski, 42 N.Y.2d 218, 397 N.Y.S.2d 707, 366 N.E.2d 797 (1977).

§ 10.20. Superior courts; jurisdiction.

1. Superior courts have trial jurisdiction of all offenses. They have:

(a) Exclusive trial jurisdiction of felonies; and

(b) Trial jurisdiction of misdemeanors concurrent with that of the local criminal courts; and

(c) Trial jurisdiction of petty offenses, but only when such an offense is charged in an indictment which also charges a crime.

2. Superior courts have preliminary jurisdic-

tion of all offenses, but they exercise such jurisdiction only by reason of and through the agency of their grand juries.

3. Superior court judges may, in their discretion, sit as local criminal courts for the following purposes:

(a) conducting arraignments, as provided in subdivision two of section 170.15 and subdivision two of section 180.20 of this chapter;

(b) issuing warrants of arrests, as provided in subdivision one of section 120.70 of this chapter; and

(c) issuing search warrants, as provided in article six hundred ninety of this chapter.

Amended by L. 1992, Ch. 815, eff. Nov. 1, 1992, adding subd. 3 and L. 1992, Ch. 816, eff. Nov. 1, 1992, amending subd. 3.

ANNOTATIONS

County Court.—County Court has trial jurisdiction of petty offenses only when such offenses are charged in an indictment which also charges a crime. People v. Judges of the County Court of the County of Oswego, 56 A.D.2d 728, 392 N.Y.S.2d 760 (4th Dept. 1977).

Filing of accusatory instrument.—Jurisdiction is established in a court following the filing of a sufficient accusatory instrument. People v. Perez, 189 Misc. 2d 516, 734 N.Y.S.2d 398 (Co. Ct. Nassau Co. 2001) (citing People v. Casey, 95 N.Y.2d 354, 717 N.Y.S.2d 88, 740 N.E.2d 233).

Grand jury and felony cases.—A court's jurisdiction over a defendant in felony cases is based on the decision of a Grand Jury as expressed in an indictment. People v. Jackson, 153 Misc. 2d 270, 271, 582 N.Y.S.2d 336, 337 (Sup. Ct. Bronx Co. 1991).

Jurisdiction; incest.—Family Court Act did not confer exclusive jurisdiction over incest to Family Court and defendant's conviction in County Court was proper. People v. Lewis, 29 N.Y.2d 923, 329 N.Y.S.2d 100 (1972).

Jurisdiction; sodomy.—Defendant charged with sodomy involving 4-year-old son of his mistress with whom he lived could not transfer proceedings to Family Court where he was not legally adopting father and because Family Court jurisdiction was limited to physical abuse of a non-sexual nature. People v. Monsanto, 70 Misc. 2d 996, 335 N.Y.S.2d 451 (Sup. Ct. Bronx Co. 1972).

§ 10.30. Local criminal courts; jurisdiction.

1. Local criminal courts have trial jurisdiction of all offenses other than felonies. They have:

(a) Exclusive trial jurisdiction of petty offenses except for the superior court jurisdiction thereof prescribed in paragraph (c) of subdivision one of section 10.20; and

(b) Trial jurisdiction of misdemeanors concurrent with that of the superior courts but subject to divestiture thereof by the latter in any particular case.

2. Local criminal courts have preliminary jurisdiction of all offenses subject to divestiture thereof in any particular case by the superior courts and their grand juries.

3. Notwithstanding the provisions of subdivision one, a superior court judge sitting as a local criminal court does not have trial jurisdiction of any offense, but has preliminary jurisdiction only, as provided in subdivision two.

ANNOTATIONS

Jurisdiction of criminal court.—A criminal court is divested of jurisdiction over a felony complaint when an indictment is filed with a superior court. People v. Gervais, 195 Misc. 2d 129, 756 N.Y.S.2d 390 (N.Y.C. Crim. Ct. 2003).

—The jurisdiction of the Criminal Court is restricted to hearing, trying, and determining criminal charges, specifically misdemeanors and petty offenses. People v. Marchetta, 177 Misc. 2d 701, 676 N.Y.S.2d 791 (Crim. Ct. Queens Co. 1998).

Preliminary jurisdiction.—A city court's preliminary jurisdiction over felonies is limited to those for which a criminal action may be commenced in that court; city court does not have geographic jurisdiction over locations to be searched in towns outside its territorial borders. People v. Chrysler, 287 A.D.2d 7, 733 N.Y.S.2d 452 (2d Dept. 2001).

Return of property; local criminal court.—A local criminal court may order the release of the property when a defendant is found innocent of the charges and his ownership of the property is undisputed and there is no claim by the People that the property is further needed in the prosecution of the case or a claim by the Police Department that the property is contraband; in a case where ownership is disputed or proper objections to the release of property are raised by either the District Attorney or the Police Department, then the claimant's remedy is to be found in civil court rather than the criminal court. People v. Braunhut, 101 Misc. 2d 975, 422 N.Y.S.2d 602 (Crim. Ct. N.Y.C. 1979).

§ 10.40. Chief administrator to prescribe forms.

The chief administrator of the courts shall have the power to adopt, amend and rescind forms for the efficient and just administration of this chapter. A failure by any party to submit papers in compliance with forms authorized by this section shall not be grounds for that reason alone for denial or granting of any motion.

Added by L. 1984, Ch. 47.

TITLE C—GENERAL PRINCIPLES RELATING TO REQUIREMENTS FOR AND EXEMPTIONS FROM CRIMINAL PROSECUTION

ARTICLE 20—GEOGRAPHICAL JURISDICTION OF OFFENSES

Section

LexisNexis Cross Reference

New York Criminal Practice (2d ed.), Vol. 1, Ch. 2, Jurisdiction of Criminal Courts.

§ 20.10. Geographical jurisdiction of offenses; definitions of terms.

The following definitions are applicable to this article:

1. "This state" means New York State as its boundaries are prescribed in the state law, and the space over it.

2. "County" means any of the sixty-two counties of this state as its boundaries are prescribed by law, and the space over it.

3. "Result of an offense." When a specific consequence, such as the death of the victim in a homicide case, is an element of an offense, the occurrence of such consequence constitutes the "result" of such offense. An offense of which a result is an element is a "result offense."

4. "Particular effect of an offense." When conduct constituting an offense produces consequences which, though not necessarily amounting to a result or element of such offense, have a materially harmful impact upon the governmental processes or community welfare of a particular jurisdiction, or result in the defrauding of persons in such jurisdiction, such conduct and offense have a "particular effect" upon such jurisdiction.

ANNOTATIONS

Civil family offenses.—Civil family offense proceedings in family court are not subject to limits on geographical jurisdiction of criminal offenses, though family offenses were defined as acts that would also constitute offenses under Penal Law. Eileen W. v. Mario A., 169 Misc. 2d 484, 644 N.Y.S.2d 452 (Fam. Ct. N.Y. Co. 1996).

Assault aboard common carrier.—New York City court had jurisdiction over defendant who assaulted victim in New York aboard a PATH train en route to Hoboken, New Jersey, at which point defendant was removed by Port Authority Policeman and then returned to New York City. People v.

Bacon, 84 Misc. 2d 679, 376 N.Y.S.2d 839 (Crim. Ct. N.Y.C. 1975).

Burden of proof.—The question of whether the court has geographical jurisdiction over an offense is one of fact and need only be proven by a preponderance of the evidence. People v. Lovacco, 147 A.D.2d 592, 537 N.Y.S.2d 886 (2d Dept. 1989).

Objection to jurisdiction not waived by plea.—Defendant did not waive his objection to the geographical jurisdiction of the court by pleading guilty after his motion to dismiss the indictment for conspiracy was denied. People v. Kellerman, 102 A.D.2d 629, 479 N.Y.S.2d 815 (3d Dept. 1984).

Type of conduct.—CPL §§ 20.40(2) and 20.10(4) require that the conduct committed must cause a harmful impact, not on any individual or individuals, but on a whole community and the harm must be to "governmental processes" or to the welfare of an entire community. Steingut v. Gold, 54 A.D.2d 481, 388 N.Y.S.2d 622 (2d Dept. 1976), *aff'd,* 42 N.Y.2d 311, 397 N.Y.S.2d 765, 366 N.E.2d 854 (1977).

§ 20.20. Geographical jurisdiction of offenses; jurisdiction of state.

Except as otherwise provided in this section and section 20.30, a person may be convicted in the criminal courts of this state of an offense defined by the laws of this state, committed either by his own conduct or by the conduct of another for which he is legally accountable pursuant to section 20.00 of the penal law, when:

1. Conduct occurred within this state sufficient to establish:

(a) An element of such offense; or

(b) An attempt to commit such offense; or

(c) A conspiracy or criminal solicitation to commit such offense, or otherwise to establish complicity of at least one of the persons liable therefor; provided that the jurisdiction accorded by this paragraph extends only to conviction of those persons whose conspiratorial or other conduct of complicity occurred within this state; or

2. Even though none of the conduct constitut-

ing such offense may have occurred within this state:

(a) The offense committed was a result offense and the result occurred within this state. If the offense was one of homicide, it is presumed that the result, namely the death of the victim, occurred within this state if the victim's body or part thereof was found herein; or

(b) The statute defining the offense is designed to prevent the occurrence of a particular effect in this state and the conduct constituting the offense committed was performed with intent that it would have such effect herein; or

(c) The offense committed was an attempt to commit a crime within this state; or

(d) The offense committed was conspiracy to commit a crime within this state and an overt act in furtherance of such conspiracy occurred within this state; or

3. The offense committed was one of omission to perform within this state a duty imposed by the laws of this state. In such case, it is immaterial whether such person was within or outside this state at the time of the omission.

ANNOTATIONS

Burden of proof.—When jurisdiction under CPL § 20.20 is put in issue, the People must prove it beyond a reasonable doubt. People v. McLaughlin, 80 N.Y.2d 466, 591 N.Y.S.2d 966, 606 N.E.2d 1357 (1992).

Cause of illegal act occurred in New York; New York has jurisdiction.—Although the criminal act of illegally reproducing phonograph records occurred in New Jersey, it was caused by the defendant in New York when he ordered and prepaid for the records, and this was an element of the offense giving New York jurisdiction. People v. Winley, 105 Misc. 2d 474, 432 N.Y.S.2d 429 (Sup. Ct. N.Y. Co. 1980).

Federal prison.—Court rejected defendant's contention that the homicide was committed within the confines of a Federal prison, and thus the state of New York had no jurisdiction to indict him, because defendant failed to meet his burden of showing that the Federal Government clearly intended to exercise sole jurisdiction over crimes committed within Federal prisons. People v. Tate, 128 A.D.2d 652, 513 N.Y.S.2d 38, 39 (2d Dept. 1987).

Interstate crime operation.—In large interstate drug operation involving the transport of cocaine from California to New York, defendant challenged New York's territorial jurisdiction because the drugs he was charged with possessing were found in California, as was the defendant; using concept of constructive possession, court found ample evidence that, regardless of where he was situated, defendant at all times exercised continued dominion and control over the drugs that were ultimately seized in New York. People v. Carvajal, 14 A.D.3d 165, 786 N.Y.S.2d 450 (1st Dept. 2004), appeal granted, 4 N.Y.3d 762, 792 N.Y.S.2d 6, 825 N.E.2d 138 (2005).

Limited jurisdiction of out of state offenses.—Jurisdiction under CPL § 20.20(2)(b) is limited to those out of state offenses which, by their nature, produce palpably harmful consequences which are of necessity local and peculiarly injurious to the rights of this state or its citizens; excluded from this jurisdiction, where the charged crime was committed entirely outside the state, are those offenses pertaining to the general community welfare, e.g., offenses under PL § 220 and criminal facilitation thereof. People v. Puig, 85 Misc. 2d 228, 378 N.Y.S.2d 925 (Sup. Ct. N.Y. Co. 1976), aff'd, 42 N.Y.2d 311, 397 N.Y.S.2d 765, 366 N.E.2d 854 (1977).

Significant conduct in New York.—Defendant was properly prosecuted in New York for first degree attempted possession of a controlled substance based on the significant conduct that occurred in this state for an attempt offense effectuated when

he and his accomplices were offered heroin and tested samples of the narcotic in a neighboring state. Some of the significant conduct included forming the plan in New York, where the defendants resided and intended to return for the purposes of selling heroin. People v. Kassebaum, 95 N.Y.2d 611, 721 N.Y.S.2d 866, 744 N.E.2d 694, cert. denied, 532 U.S. 1069 (2001).

§ 20.30. Geographical jurisdiction of offenses; effect of laws of other jurisdictions upon this state's jurisdiction.

1. Notwithstanding the provisions of section 20.20, the courts of this state do not have jurisdiction to convict a person of an alleged offense partly committed within this state but consummated in another jurisdiction, or an offense of criminal solicitation, conspiracy or attempt in this state to commit a crime in another jurisdiction, or an offense of criminal facilitation in this state of a felony committed in another jurisdiction, unless the conduct constituting the consummated offense or, as the case may be, the conduct constituting the crime solicited, conspiratorially contemplated or facilitated, constitutes an offense under the laws of such other jurisdiction as well as under the laws of this state.

2. The courts of this state are not deprived of the jurisdiction accorded them by section 20.20 to convict a person of an offense defined by the laws of this state, partly committed in another jurisdiction but consummated in this state, or an offense of attempt or conspiracy in another jurisdiction to commit in this state a crime defined by the laws of this state, by the circumstance that the conduct constituting the consummated offense or, as the case may be, the crime attempted or conspiratorially contemplated, does not constitute an offense under the laws of such other jurisdiction.

§ 20.40. Geographical jurisdiction of offenses; jurisdiction of counties.

A person may be convicted in an appropriate criminal court of a particular county, of an offense of which the criminal courts of this state have jurisdiction pursuant to section 20.20, committed either by his own conduct or by the conduct of another for which he is legally accountable pursuant to section 20.00 of the penal law, when:

1. Conduct occurred within such county sufficient to establish:

(a) An element of such offense; or

(b) An attempt or a conspiracy to commit such offense; or

2. Even though none of the conduct constituting such offense may have occurred within such county:

(a) The offense committed was a result offense and the result occurred in such county; or

CPL

(b) The offense committed was one of homicide and the victim's body or a part thereof was found in such county; or

(c) Such conduct had, or was likely to have, a particular effect upon such county or a political subdivision or part thereof, and was performed with intent that it would, or with knowledge that it was likely to, have such particular effect therein; or

(d) The offense committed was attempt, conspiracy or criminal solicitation to commit a crime in such county; or

(e) The offense committed was criminal facilitation of a felony committed in such county; or

3. The offense committed was one of omission to perform a duty imposed by law, which duty either was required to be or could properly have been performed in such county. In such case, it is immaterial whether such person was within or outside such county at the time of the omission; or

4. Jurisdiction of such offense is accorded to the courts of such county pursuant to any of the following rules:

(a) An offense of abandonment of a child or non-support of a child may be prosecuted in (i) any county in which such child resided during the period of abandonment or non-support, or (ii) any county in which such person resided during such period, or (iii) any county in which such person was present during such period, provided that he was arrested for such offense in such county or the criminal action therefor was commenced while he was present therein.

(b) An offense of bigamy may be prosecuted either in the county in which such offense was committed or in (i) any county in which bigamous cohabitation subsequently occurred, or (ii) any county in which such person was present after the commission of the offense, provided that he was arrested for such offense in such county or the criminal action therefor was commenced while he was present therein.

(c) An offense committed within five hundred yards of the boundary of a particular county, and in an adjoining county of this state, may be prosecuted in either such county.

(d) An offense committed anywhere on the Hudson river southward of the northern boundary of New York City, or anywhere on New York bay between Staten Island and Long Island, may be prosecuted in any of the five counties of New York City.

(e) An offense committed upon any bridge or in any tunnel having terminals in different counties may be prosecuted in any terminal county.

(f) An offense committed on board a railroad train, aircraft or omnibus operating as a common carrier may be prosecuted in any county through or over which such common carrier passed during the particular trip, or in any county in which such trip terminated or was scheduled to terminate.

(g) An offense committed in a private vehicle during a trip thereof extending through more than one county may be prosecuted in any county through which such vehicle passed in the course of such trip.

(h) An offense committed on board a vessel navigating or lying in any river, canal or lake flowing through or situated within this state, may be prosecuted in any county bordering upon such body of water, or in which it is located, or through which it passes; and if such offense was committed upon a vessel operating as a common carrier, it may be prosecuted in any county bordering upon any body of water upon which such vessel navigated or passed during the particular trip.

(i) An offense committed in the Atlantic Ocean within two nautical miles from the shore at high water mark may be prosecuted in an appropriate court of the county the shore line of which is closest to the point where the offense was committed. A crime committed more than two nautical miles from the shore but within the boundary of this state may be prosecuted in the supreme court of the county the shore line of which is closest to the point where the crime was committed.

(j) An offense of forgery may be prosecuted in any county in which the defendant, or another for whose conduct the defendant is legally accountable pursuant to section 20.00 of the penal law, possessed the instrument.

(k) An offense of offering of a false instrument for filing, or of larceny by means of a false pretense therein, may be prosecuted (i) in any county in which such instrument was executed, in whole or in part, or (ii) in any county in which any of the goods or services for which payment or reimbursement is sought by means of such instrument were purported to have been provided.

(l) An offense of identity theft or unlawful possession of personal identification information may be prosecuted (i) in any county in which part of the offense took place regardless of whether the defendant was actually present in such county, or (ii) in the county in which the person who suffers financial loss resided at the time of the commission of the offense, or (iii) in the county where the person whose personal identification information was used in the commission of the offense resided at the time of the commission of the offense.

Amended by L. 1985, Ch. 575; L. 2002, Ch. 619, § 5, adding subd. 4(l), eff. Nov. 1, 2002.

ANNOTATIONS

Grand jury; determination of jurisdiction.—Indictment dismissed for lack of geographical jurisdiction where grand jury was not presented with any information that there was even an issue as to geographical jurisdiction and was not charged that it had to make a factual determination that the alleged crimes occurred in Franklin County within five hundred yards of the boundary of Essex County. People v. Bickford, 173 Misc. 2d 770, 662 N.Y.S.2d 386 (Co. Ct. Essex Co. 1997).

Standard of proof.—Geographical jurisdiction is a question of fact which must be proven by a preponderance of the evidence; testimony by the victim and his brother was sufficient to enable the jury to reasonably conclude that the incident occurred in St. Lawrence County. People v. Dendler, 244 A.D.2d 778, 666 N.Y.S.2d 276 (3d Dept. 1997).

Subd. 1(a)

Venue.—Advancing or profiting from unlawful gambling activity is a separate element of promoting gambling in the first degree and, if established by the evidence, could support jurisdiction in Nassau County. People v. Giordano, 87 N.Y.2d 441, 640 N.Y.S.2d 432, 663 N.E.2d 588 (1995).

—Prosecution for offering false instrument for filing was properly venued in county where defendant prepared victim's tax returns with intention of evading consequences in connection with his own tax returns. People v. Camiola, 225 A.D.2d 380, 639 N.Y.S.2d 35 (1st Dept. 1996).

—For purposes of venue in county in prosecution for forgery in second degree as accessory, People had to prove by preponderance of the evidence that defendant engaged in conduct in county sufficient to establish any one of elements of forgery in second degree or, in the alternative, that defendant possessed instrument in that county, and governing statute did not require that defendant possess "completed" instrument. People v. Selim, 227 A.D.2d 917, 644 N.Y.S.2d 448 (4th Dept. 1996).

Attempt to hire.—Where the only act perpetrated in Rensselaer County was the defendant's attempt to recruit an individual to carry out the scheme to murder his wife it was not sufficient to confer jurisdiction upon the court of Rensselaer County since there was no showing where the defendant's intent was formulated. People v. Hanley, 92 Misc. 2d 465, 400 N.Y.S.2d 319 (Rensselaer Co. Ct. 1977).

Bribe-receiving.—The Supreme Court of New York County lacked geographic jurisdiction over the offense of bribe receiving where the only conduct which occurred in New York County was the receipt and deposit of a contribution check by an innocent third party who was the designee of the defendant. People v. Hopkins, 95 Misc. 2d 716, 408 N.Y.S.2d 597 (Sup. Ct. N.Y. Co. 1978).

Criminal possession of controlled substance.—CPL § 20.40(1)(a) cannot supply a jurisdictional predicate for the crime of criminal possession of a controlled substance on the theory the knowledge occurred in one county and possession in another. People v. Cullen, 50 N.Y.2d 168, 428 N.Y.S.2d 456, 405 N.E.2d 1021 (1980).

Forgery.—Since there was no indication of where the forgery occurred, the jury could not have found by a preponderance of the evidence that venue was properly laid in Nassau County. People v. Schlatter, 55 A.D.2d 922, 390 N.Y.S.2d 441 (2d Dept. 1977).

Formation of intent.—Where proof showed that defendant, while in Nassau County, had formed an intent to commit rape which was actually committed in Suffolk County, Nassau County had jurisdiction to indict and try the defendant on rape charges. People v. Burgess, 107 A.D.2d 703, 484 N.Y.S.2d 58 (2d Dept. 1985).

Jurisdiction; indictment; larceny.—Where defendant represented Suffolk County resident in sale of Suffolk County property and closing was held in New York City with funds misappropriated there, indictment must be dismissed as no conduct occurred within Suffolk County sufficient to establish an element of such offense. People v. Brown, 69 Misc. 2d 412, 330 N.Y.S.2d 215 (Suffolk Co. Ct. 1972).

Multi-county crimes.—Albany County had geographical jurisdiction to prosecute defendant for promoting prostitution where the evidence revealed that Albany County was the place where defendant engaged in some management activities of his prostitutes. People v. Johnson, 128 A.D.2d 915, 917, 512 N.Y.S.2d 724, 726 (3d Dept. 1987).

—A felony murder indictment in which the underlying felony was committed in one county and the murder in another county may be tried in either county since conduct occurred in each county sufficient to constitute an element of such offenses (CPL

§ 20.40[1][a]), and since the felony murder may be tried in either county, so may the underlying felonies, and the failure to join in one county all the offenses based upon the same criminal transaction bars further prosecution of the unjoined crimes (CPL §§ 200.20, 40.40). People v. Ruzas, 54 A.D.2d 1083, 389 N.Y.S.2d 205 (4th Dept. 1976).

—If the evidence adduced before the Grand Jury permits a fair and reasonable inference that sufficient conduct occurred within that county to establish an element of the offense charged, jurisdiction will lie in that county. People v. Seifert, 113 A.D.2d 80, 495 N.Y.S.2d 543 (4th Dept. 1985).

—If a crime is continuous, then the alleged perpetrator may be tried in any locale where any of the different acts were done. People v. Brown, 159 Misc. 2d 11, 15, 603 N.Y.S.2d 256, 260 (Sup. Ct. Kings Co. 1993).

Subd. 1

Burden of proof.—The burden is on the People to prove by a preponderance of the evidence that the county where the crime is prosecuted is the proper venue because either the crime was committed there or one of the statutory exceptions is applicable. People v. Ribowsky, 77 N.Y.2d 284, 291, 567 N.Y.S.2d 392, 397, 568 N.E.2d 1197, 1202 (1991).

—Prosecution presented sufficient evidence from which the jury could have determined that venue in Suffolk County was proper, because the defendant deposited two of the subject checks at a Suffolk County branch of his bank and later withdrew those funds by means of checks drawn on his Suffolk County account. People v. Dickman, 233 A.D.2d 524, 650 N.Y.S.2d 761 (2d Dept. 1996).

Narcotics.—Kings County lacked jurisdiction to prosecute the alleged sale of narcotics where the undercover officer approached one defendant at a Kings County methadone clinic and she then led him to second defendant in a bar in that county and together they took the undercover officer to a location in New York County where one defendant obtained the narcotics and then gave them to the undercover officer and he paid for them in New York County. People v. King, 61 A.D.2d 1035, 403 N.Y.S.2d 109 (2d Dept. 1978).

Nassau County lacked jurisdiction; crime took place in New York County.—Nassau County lacked jurisdiction to prosecute defendant where defendant, after agreeing in Nassau County to assist an informant in obtaining peyote, then drove with the informant and a Nassau County undercover officer to New York County and there obtained the peyote and handed it to the officer and the three then drove back to Nassau County where he was arrested. People v. Cullen, 65 A.D.2d 594, 409 N.Y.S.2d 263 (2d Dept. 1978).

Situs of crime; unlawful sale of controlled substance.—Nassau County was endowed with geographical jurisdiction to prosecute defendant for criminal sales of a controlled substance on the basis of two agreements to sell made by defendant within the county even though the transaction was actually completed in New York County; CPL § 20.40(1)(a) predicates jurisdiction to prosecute upon commission of one element of the crime within the county and PL § 220.00 defines sale as including the mere offer or agreement to sell. People v. Pilgrim, 67 A.D.2d 554, 415 N.Y.S.2d 876 (2d Dept. 1979), aff'd, 52 N.Y.2d 730, 436 N.Y.S.2d 265, 417 N.E.2d 559 (1980).

Telephonic communications.—An agreement to sell a narcotic via the telephone between defendant seller, in Schenectady County, and buyer, in Albany County, was deemed to have been made in both counties pursuant to CPL § 20.60, and the requirements of CPL § 20.40 needed to establish the geographical jurisdiction of Albany County were satisfied. People v. Larowe, 99 Misc. 2d 842, 417 N.Y.S.2d 438 (Albany Co. Ct. 1979).

Venue; jury question.—In prosecution for first degree rape, where complainant was uncertain as to the location where the rape took place, the question of venue must be submitted to the jury. People v. Cavallerio, 71 A.D.2d 338, 422 N.Y.S.2d 691 (1st Dept. 1979).

Venue; insurance fraud.—Where defendant fraudulently sought insurance recovery for the loss by fire of store located in Bronx County as well as its contents, including merchandise, merchandise constituted "goods . . . for which payment of reimbursement was sought" within the meaning of CPL § 20.40(4)(k)(ii). Venue was also proper under CPL § 20.40(1)(b), since defendant was engaged in conduct in Bronx County.

People v. LanFranco, 278 A.D.2d 8, 717 N.Y.S.2d 140 (1st Dept. 2000).

Waiver.—The defendant waived his claim that Nassau County lacked geographical jurisdiction to prosecute him, since the defendant never requested the trial court to charge the jury with respect to geographical jurisdiction. People v. Hernandez, 198 A.D.2d 375, 603 N.Y.S.2d 187 (3d Dept. 1993).

Geographic jurisdiction; inter-county telephone calls.—Nassau County had geographic jurisdiction to prosecute defendants on gambling related charges based upon inter-county telephone conversations between one defendant in a wireroom in Queens County and the other defendant in his home in Nassau County; under CPL § 20.60(1), telephonic communications made by a person in one jurisdiction to a person in another jurisdiction is deemed to be conduct occurring in each jurisdiction. People v. Botta, 100 A.D.2d 311, 474 N.Y.S.2d 72 (2d Dept. 1984).

State jurisdiction over federal customshouse area.—State court had jurisdiction to try the defendant for a crime committed within the state borders but in a federal customshouse area; absent a showing that the federal government intended to exercise sole jurisdiction over a particular land area within a state, a burden of proof resting with the defendant, mere purchase or acquisition of such land by the federal government does not per se oust the state of sovereignty over the land. People v. Fisher, 97 A.D.2d 651, 469 N.Y.S.2d 187 (3d Dept. 1983).

Subd. 2(a)

Jurisdiction to consolidate all "universal summonses" and "requests to appear."—The Criminal Court of the City of New York has jurisdiction to consolidate all "universal summonses" and "requests to appear" for offenses committed in all five counties at a single location where they are for minor offenses since the maximum punishment is less than six months and CPL § 20.40 does not apply, the defendant can be tried anywhere within the jurisdiction of the court. People v. Hexner, 104 Misc. 2d 671, 428 N.Y.S.2d 860 (Crim. Ct. N.Y. Co. 1980).

Obscenity.—Defendant could be prosecuted in Nassau County where the wholesale transactions were made in New York County to a Nassau County dealer for resale purposes in Nassau County. People v. Brill, 82 Misc. 2d 865, 370 N.Y.S.2d 820 (Nassau Co. Ct. 1975).

Subd. 2(b)

Offense committed aboard aircraft over mid-Atlantic; no geographic jurisdiction in New York.—State did not have geographical jurisdiction to prosecute defendant for any offense committed when the defendant, while aboard an aircraft flying to New York, but still only midway across the Atlantic Ocean, attempted to set fire to the aircraft; neither proof to statutory requirements of CPL § 20.20(2)(b) were satisfied in that defendant's acts evinced a desire for immediate results without regard to any New York consequence and the defendant's conduct did not affect the governmental process or the community as a whole in New York. People v. Costa, 121 Misc. 2d 864, 469 N.Y.S.2d 545 (Sup. Ct. Queens Co. 1983).

Subd. 2(c)

Jurisdiction; testimony in another county.—Extraordinary Special Grand Jury of Kings County did not exceed its jurisdiction with respect to courts alleging perjury in Westchester County. Di Lorenzo v. Murtagh, 43 A.D.2d 938, 351 N.Y.S.2d 725 (2d Dept. 1974), dism'd, 34 N.Y.2d 722, 356 N.Y.S.2d 864, 313 N.E.2d 343 (1974), dism'd, 34 N.Y.2d 755, 357 N.Y.S.2d 1028 (1975).

Injured forum; requirements.—CPL § 20.40(2)(c) did not apply and the indictment was properly dismissed where the alleged illegal acts occurred in New York County and the prosecutor failed to place before the Kings County Grand Jury any evidence either that there was a materially harmful impact upon the governmental processes of Kings County or that the allegedly criminal activity was performed with the intent or knowledge that such a particular effect would occur in that county. Steingut v. Gold, 42 N.Y.2d 311, 397 N.Y.S.2d 765, 366 N.E.2d 854 (1977).

—Defendant may be prosecuted in Bronx County where his original sex crime was committed and where he still lives, even though the Sex Offender Monitoring Unit where defendant failed to register was in New York County. Bronx County has jurisdiction over this case pursuant to the injured forum statute, CPL 20.40(2)(c), because defendant's failure to register affects the Bronx in that the police and the community in the Bronx will not receive appropriate SORA notifications about defendant. People v. Patterson, 185 Misc. 2d 519, 708 N.Y.S.2d 815 (N.Y.C. Crim. Ct. 2000).

Type of conduct.—Extraterritorial jurisdiction is to be applied only in those limited circumstances where out-of-jurisdiction conduct is violative of a statute intended to protect the integrity of the governmental processes or is harmful to the community as a whole. People v. Fea, 47 N.Y.2d 70, 416 N.Y.S.2d 778, 390 N.E.2d 286 (1979).

—An accusatory instrument may be filed in a city court, even though none of the alleged illegal conduct constituting the offense may have occurred in that city, if the conduct had or was likely to have a particular effect on such city. People v. Chrysler, 287 A.D.2d 7, 733 N.Y.S.2d 452 (2d Dept. 2001).

—CPL §§ 20.40(2) and 20.10(4) require that the conduct committed must cause a harmful impact, not on any individual or individuals, but on a whole community and the harm must be to "governmental processes" or to the welfare of an entire community. Steingut v. Gold, 54 A.D.2d 1, 388 N.Y.S.2d 622 (2d Dept. 1976), aff'd, 42 N.Y.2d 311, 397 N.Y.S.2d 765, 366 N.E.2d 854 (1977).

—The materially harmful impact to Bronx County caused by defendant's alleged failure to register with a Sex Offender Monitoring Unit in New York County furnished grounds, pursuant to CPL § 20.40(2)(c), for the court to properly exercise jurisdiction over the prosecution. People v. Olivera, 184 Misc. 2d 327, 708 N.Y.S.2d 586 (Crim. Ct. Bronx Co. 2000).

Subd. 2(d)

Conspiracy.—Because Kings County has geographic jurisdiction over the conspiracy count, it also has geographic jurisdiction over the substantive crimes which were the object of the conspiracy, regardless of whether the elements of those crimes were committed in Kings County. Faraci v. Firetog, 308 A.D.2d 423, 764 N.Y.S.2d 188 (2d Dept. 2003).

—Conspiracy is a statutory exception and it may be prosecuted in the county in which defendant entered into the conspiracy or any county in which an overt act in furtherance of the conspiracy was committed by defendant or one of the co-conspirators. People v. Ormsby, — A.D.3d —, 774 N.Y.S.2d 191 (3d Dept. 2004).

Subd. 4(c)

Jurisdiction could be inferred.—Jurisdiction in county could be fairly and reasonably inferred from all facts and circumstances introduced into evidence before grand jury, even without explicit mention of statute providing that offense committed within 500 yards of boundary of particular county may be prosecuted in either county, and even though location of alleged drug deal was in different county within 365 yards of county boundary, where undercover officers involved in case were all from county of venue, and address of premises was repeated several times. People v. Rodriguez, 168 Misc. 2d 423, 641 N.Y.S.2d 975 (Sup. Ct. Bronx Co. 1996).

Jurisdiction over misdemeanors allegedly committed in one county, near another county's border.—The City Court of Mount Vernon did not lack jurisdiction over misdemeanors allegedly committed in Bronx County, 18 feet from the Mount Vernon, Westchester County border; pursuant to CPL § 20.40(4)(c) the offenses may be prosecuted in the appropriate court in either Bronx County or Westchester County. People v. Griffin, 99 Misc. 2d 874, 420 N.Y.S.2d 824 (Sup. Ct. 9th & 10th Dist. 1979).

Location of crimes was question of fact.—Whether the crimes charged were committed, as contended, 500 yards outside of the Kings County border was a question of fact for the jury. People v. Moore, 60 A.D.2d 638, 400 N.Y.S.2d 187 (2d Dept. 1977), aff'd, 46 N.Y.2d 1, 412 N.Y.S.2d 795, 385 N.E.2d 535 (1978).

Subd. 4(d)

Search; arrest without a warrant; close pursuit.—Where defendants were arrested after pre-arranged narcotics transaction involving large quantity of narcotics and auto chase through Lincoln Tunnel, search of auto without warrant was not illegal and recovered evidence would not be suppressed, even though arresting officers in close pursuit brought defendants to New York for arraignment instead of to a New Jersey magistrate in accordance with New Jersey statute. People v. Junco, 70 Misc. 2d 73, 333 N.Y.S.2d 142 (Sup. Ct. N.Y. Co. 1972).

Subd. 4(f)

Commuter train.—An offense committed on board a common carrier may be prosecuted in any county through which the carrier passed during the trip, and since the commuter train on which defendant was a passenger traveled through New York City and the trip also terminated there, the plain language of CPL § 20.40(4)(f) allows trial in New York County. People v. Greenberg, 89 N.Y.2d 553, 656 N.Y.S.2d 192, 678 N.E.2d 878 (1997).

International flight.—Jurisdiction to prosecute misdemeanor assault occurring during flight from Santo Domingo, Dominican Republic to JFK Airport in Queens County lay in Queens County; the Federal Aviation Act was passed to promote the efficient and safe operation of aircraft and it does not exclude state law not inconsistent with its purpose. People v. Corsino, 91 Misc. 2d 46, 397 N.Y.S.2d 342 (Crim. Ct. N.Y.C. 1977).

Subd. 4(g)

Charge; CPL § 20.40(4)(g).—Before the People are entitled to the benefit of a charge that Nassau County would have jurisdiction of the crimes if the jury found that the offenses occurred in a private vehicle during a trip through more than one county, the prosecutor must in good faith elicit all the facts tending to show the exact location where the crime was committed and if, after such an effort, the jury cannot determine whether the crime of possession occurred in New York County or Nassau County, then the properly instructed jury may find that either county has jurisdiction of the offense. People v. Cullen, 50 N.Y.2d 168, 428 N.Y.S.2d 456, 405 N.E.2d 1021 (1980).

—The People were entitled to rely upon the "private vehicle exception" where exact location of crime was unknown. People v. Bailey, 133 A.D.2d 462, 519 N.Y.S.2d 676 (2d Dept. 1987).

—Jury correctly determined that Westchester County was the proper venue for bringing weapon possession charges against the defendant since the evidence revealed that the defendant had constructive possession of the weapon during the entire automobile trip from Bronx County to White Plains in Westchester County. People v. Zannone, 130 A.D.2d 699, 699, 515 N.Y.S.2d 624, 625 (2d Dept. 1987).

Complainant able to identify place where crime was committed.—Crime may not be prosecuted in adjacent county by relying on the private vehicle trip statute (CPL § 20.40[4][g]), where the complainant was able to identify the place where the crime was allegedly committed. People v. Moore, 46 N.Y.2d 1, 412 N.Y.S.2d 795, 385 N.E.2d 535 (1978).

§ 20.50. Geographical jurisdiction of offenses; jurisdiction of cities, towns and villages.

1. The principles prescribed in section 20.40, governing geographical jurisdiction over offenses as between counties of this state, are, where appropriate, applicable to the determination of geographical jurisdiction over offenses as between cities, towns and villages within a particular county unless a different determination is required by the provisions of some other express provision of statute.

2. Where an offense prosecutable in a local criminal court is committed in a city other than New York City, or in a town or village, but within one hundred yards of any other such political subdivision, it may be prosecuted in either such political subdivision.

ANNOTATIONS

CPL § 20.50; county jurisdiction.—CPL § 20.50 is only applicable to situations where there is no question as to a particular county's jurisdiction of an offense but there is a question as to which political subdivision (city, town or village) of such county has jurisdiction (CPL § 20.50[1]); offenses committed in New York City which are prosecutable in a local criminal court are specifically excluded from the operation of this statute. People v. Griffin, 99 Misc. 2d 874, 420 N.Y.S.2d 824 (Sup. Ct. 9th & 10th Dists. 1979).

City court; lack of jurisdiction.—The City Court of Mount Vernon lacked geographical jurisdiction over a misdemeanor committed in New York City even though the crime was allegedly committed well within 100 yards of the line separating the two cities. People v. Thomas, 93 Misc. 2d 961, 404 N.Y.S.2d 254 (1978).

Jurisdiction of Justice Court.—Since no part of the alleged offenses occurred in the Town of Monroe or had a result or an effect therein, the Town Justice lacked jurisdiction of the offenses and was powerless to issue a search warrant. People v. Epstein, 47 A.D.2d 661, 364 N.Y.S.2d 38 (2d Dept. 1975).

Village court; lack of jurisdiction.—Village court did not have authority to issue search warrant for offense committed solely within the City of Syracuse and not within 100 yards of the village. People v. Beard, 77 Misc. 2d 927, 353 N.Y.S.2d 999 (Onondaga Co. Ct. 1974).

§ 20.60. Geographical jurisdiction of offenses; communications and transportation of property between jurisdictions.

For purposes of this article:

1. An oral or written statement made by a person in one jurisdiction to a person in another jurisdiction by means of telecommunication, mail or any other method of communication is deemed to be made in each such jurisdiction.

2. A person who causes property to be transported from one jurisdiction to another by means of mail, common carrier or any other method is deemed to have personally transported it in each jurisdiction, and if delivery is made in the second jurisdiction he is deemed to have personally made such delivery therein.

3. A person who causes by any means the use of a computer or computer service in one jurisdiction from another jurisdiction is deemed to have personally used the computer or computer service in each jurisdiction.

Amended by L. 1986, Ch. 514.

ANNOTATIONS

Jurisdiction under CPL § 20.60(4)(c).—CPL § 20.60(4)(c) is not limited to instances in which the precise location of the criminal act cannot be determined, and is applicable as long as the alleged conduct occurred within 500 yards of the boundary. People v. Berg, 101 Misc. 2d 726, 421 N.Y.S.2d 968 (Nassau Co. 1979).

Telephonic communications.—Although defendant was in Florida, his statements made over the telephone to an investigator in New York County are deemed to have been made in each jurisdiction. People v. Taylor, 304 A.D.2d 434, 758 N.Y.S.2d 634 (1st Dept. 2003).

—An agreement to sell a narcotic via the telephone between defendant seller, in Schenectady County, and buyer, in Albany

County, was deemed to have been made in both counties pursuant to CPL § 20.60, and the requirements of CPL § 20.40 needed to establish the geographical jurisdiction of Albany County were satisfied. People v. Larowe, 99 Misc. 2d 842, 417 N.Y.S.2d 438 (Albany Co. Ct. 1979).

Mail communications.—Since defendant caused funds to be mailed to him from New York County, he is deemed to have personally transported them in New York. People v. Taylor, 304 A.D.2d 434, 758 N.Y.S.2d 634 (1st Dept. 2003).

Conspiracy case.—Because Kings County has geographic jurisdiction over the conspiracy count, it also has geographic jurisdiction over the substantive crimes which were the object of the conspiracy, regardless of whether the elements of those crimes were committed in Kings County. Faraci v. Firetog, 308 A.D.2d 423, 764 N.Y.S.2d 188 (2d Dept. 2003).

ARTICLE 30—TIMELINESS OF PROSECUTIONS AND SPEEDY TRIAL

LexisNexis Cross References

Criminal Law Advocacy, Vol. 1, Ch. 11B, Asserting Defendant's Right to a Speedy Trial; *Criminal Defense Techniques,* Vol. 1A, Ch. 19, Speedy Trial; Vol. 6, Ch. 114, Speedy Trial Motions; *New York Criminal Practice (2d ed.),* Vol. 3, Ch. 26, Speedy Trial.

§ 30.10. Timeliness of prosecutions; periods of limitation.

1. A criminal action must be commenced within the period of limitation prescribed in the ensuing subdivisions of this section.

2. Except as otherwise provided in subdivision three:

(a) A prosecution for a class A felony may be commenced at any time;

(b) A prosecution for any other felony must be commenced within five years after the commission thereof;

(c) A prosecution for a misdemeanor must be commenced within two years after the commission thereof;

(d) A prosecution for a petty offense must be commenced within one year after the commission thereof.

3. Notwithstanding the provisions of subdivision two, the periods of limitation for the commencement of criminal actions are extended as follows in the indicated circumstances:

(a) A prosecution for larceny committed by a person in violation of a fiduciary duty may be commenced within one year after the facts constituting such offense are discovered or, in the exercise of reasonable diligence, should have been discovered by the aggrieved party or by a person under a legal duty to represent him who is not himself implicated in the commission of the offense.

(b) A prosecution for any offense involving misconduct in public office by a public servant may be commenced at any time during the defendant's service in such office or within five years after the termination of such service; provided however, that in no event shall the period of limitation be extended by more than five years beyond the period otherwise applicable under subdivision two.

(c) A prosecution for any crime set forth in title twenty-seven or * article seventy-one of the environmental conservation law may be commenced within four years after the facts constituting such crime are discovered or, in the exercise of reasonable diligence, should have been discovered by a public servant who has the responsibility to enforce the provisions of said title and article.

(d) A prosecution for any misdemeanor set forth in the tax law or chapter forty-six of the administrative code of the city of New York must be commenced within three years after the commission thereof.

(e) A prosecution for course of sexual conduct in the first degree as defined in section 130.75 of the penal law and course of sexual conduct in the second degree as defined in section 130.80 of the penal law may be commenced within five years of the commission of the most recent act of sexual conduct.

(f) For purposes of a prosecution involving a sexual offense as defined in article one hundred thirty of the penal law committed against a child less than eighteen years of age, incest as defined in section 255.25 of the penal law committed against a child less than eighteen years of age, or use of a child in a sexual performance as defined in section 263.05 of the penal law, the period of limitation shall not begin to run until the child has reached the age of eighteen or the offense is reported to a law enforcement agency or statewide central register of child abuse and maltreatment, whichever occurs earlier.

(g) A prosecution for any felony defined in article four hundred ninety of the penal law must be commenced within eight years after the commission thereof provided, however, that in a prosecution for a felony defined in article four hundred ninety of the penal law, if the commission of such felony offense resulted in, or created a foreseeable risk of, death or serious physical injury to another person, the prosecution may be commenced at any time; provided, however, that nothing in this paragraph shall be deemed to shorten or otherwise lessen the period, defined in any other applicable law, in which a prosecution for a felony designated in this paragraph may be commenced.

4. In calculating the time limitation applicable to commencement of a criminal action, the following periods shall not be included:

(a) Any period following the commission of the offense during which (i) the defendant was continuously outside this state or (ii) the whereabouts of the defendant were continuously unknown and continuously unascertainable by the exercise of reasonable diligence. However, in no event shall the period of limitation be extended by more than five years beyond the period otherwise applicable under subdivision two.

(b) When a prosecution for an offense is lawfully commenced within the prescribed period of limitation therefor, and when an accusatory instrument upon which such prosecution is based is subsequently dismissed by an authorized court under directions or circumstances permitting the lodging of another charge for the same offense or an offense based on the same conduct, the period extending from the commencement of the thus defeated prosecution to the dismissal of the accusatory instrument does not constitute a part of the period of limitation applicable to commencement of prosecution by a new charge.

* As originally enacted. Should probably be "of."

Amended by L. 1981, Ch. 719; L. 1985, Ch. 65; L. 1985, Ch. 765; L. 1986, Ch. 671; L. 1996, Ch. 122, § 1, adding subds. (3)(e), (f), eff. Aug. 1, 1996, which apply only to offenses occurring on and after the effective date; L. 2004, Ch. 1, Part A, § 2, eff. July 23, 2004, adding subd. 3(g).

Editor's Note:

ANNOTATIONS

Delay in prosecution; denial of motion to dismiss.—Where defendant made only a "routine like" claim of prejudice without any substantiation, motion to dismiss on ground that the preindictment delay in prosecution violated defendant's right to due process was properly denied. People v. Hoskins, 95 A.D.2d 899, 464 N.Y.S.2d 55 (3d Dept. 1983).

Delay due to defendant's absence from state.—Indictment was filed more than five years following the commission of the crime, but was nonetheless proper because statute of limitations was tolled during all periods defendant was "continuously outside" the State; defendant's absence from the state need not be a single, uninterrupted period of time, and all periods of a day or more that a nonresident defendant is out-of-State should be totaled and toll the statute of limitations. People v. Knobel, 94 N.Y.2d 226, 701 N.Y.S.2d 695, 723 N.E.2d 550 (1999).

Motion to dismiss; after arraignment.—A motion to dismiss the indictment pursuant to CPL § 30.10 is properly made after arraignment, and once the defense has been asserted the People have the burden of proof beyond a reasonable doubt. People v. O'Neil, 107 Misc. 2d 340, 433 N.Y.S.2d 977 (Suffolk Co. Ct. 1980).

Preindictment delay.—Preindictment delay was reasonable as it was caused by the People's good faith efforts to investigate the murder and the fact that the original witness's recantation of his identification of defendant rendered the People's case legally insufficient until years later when another witness came forward. People v. Delgado, 292 A.D.2d 212, 741 N.Y.S.2d 2 (1st Dept. 2002).

—Preindictment delay of six months and 21 days did not deprive defendant of his due process rights because 1) it was relatively brief, 2) the underlying charge, involving the security of the correctional facility, is serious in nature, 3) defendant failed to show that the delay impaired his defense and 4) because defendant was already incarcerated for a prior conviction, he

endured no further imposition on his freedom as a result of the delay. People v. Staton, 297 A.D.2d 876, 747 N.Y.S.2d 603 (3d Dept. 2002).

—Indictment was well within statutory five-year period of limitations, and preindictment delay was reasonable, especially in light of complete turnover in D.A.'s staff after election and numerous prosecutions arising out of prison riot that involved more than 300 prisoners. People v. Torres, 257 A.D.2d 772, 684 N.Y.S.2d 17 (3d Dept. 1998).

Waiver of statute of limitations.—The statute of limitations defense is a jurisdictional right which is waivable by the defendant only at trial or upon a plea of guilty and is not automatically waived if not raised within the time limitations for pretrial motions provided by CPL § 255.20. People v. Perico, 143 Misc. 2d 961, 963, 542 N.Y.S.2d 911, 913 (Dist. Ct. Nassau Co. 1989).

§ 30.20. Speedy trial; in general.

1. After a criminal action is commenced, the defendant is entitled to a speedy trial.

2. Insofar as is practicable, the trial of a criminal action must be given preference over civil cases; and the trial of a criminal action where the defendant has been committed to the custody of the sheriff during the pendency of the criminal action must be given preference over other criminal actions.

Amended by L. 1972, Ch. 184.

ANNOTATIONS

Taranovich factors.—The factors to consider in determining whether there has been a denial of a speedy trial right are: (1) the extent of the delay; (2) the reason for the delay; (3) the nature of the underlying charge; (4) whether or not there has been an extended period of pretrial incarceration; and (5) whether or not there is any indication that the defense has been impaired by the delay. People v. Taranovich, 37 N.Y.2d 442, 373 N.Y.S.2d 79, 335 N.E.2d 303 (1975); *see also* People v. Ling, 221 A.D.2d 372, 633 N.Y.S.2d 348 (2d Dept. 1995).

—In deciding a motion to dismiss an indictment upon speedy trial grounds, no one factor or combination of factors is necessarily decisive or determinative of the speedy trial claim, and each case must be considered in light of all the factors as they apply to it. People v. Lowery, 107 A.D.2d 716, 484 N.Y.S.2d 71 (2d Dept. 1985).

Constitution; exact time.—There is no exact time that is determinative of what constitutes a "speedy trial" for constitutional purposes. People v. Sirosis, 92 A.D.2d 618, 459 N.Y.S.2d 813 (2d Dept. 1983).

Delay.—Defendant incarcerated 16 months before trial; criminal possession of a controlled substance charge dismissed on CPL § 30.20 grounds. People v. Nelson, 197 A.D.2d 744, 746, 603 N.Y.S.2d 57, 59 (3d Dept. 1993).

Justifiable delay.—There was no deprivation of the right to a speedy trial although the delay of 15 or 16 months was attributable to the People since the very serious nature of the charge (assault, first degree, and possession of a weapon, felony) necessitated a slow and careful preparation of the case and defendant had not demonstrated that the delay impaired his defense. People v. Perez, 42 N.Y.2d 971, 398 N.Y.S.2d 269, 367 N.E.2d 867 (1977).

—Although 18 months elapsed between the date of defendant's arrest and the scheduled trial date, the charges involved class A-1 felonies, 15 defendants, and a multi-county drug trafficking investigation. While defendant was incarcerated for the entire period, most of the delay was occasioned by motions and hearings concerning defendant and his 14 co-defendants, and defendant failed to show any prejudice as a result of the delay. People v. Morobel, 273 A.D.2d 871, 709 N.Y.S.2d 743 (4th Dept. 2000).

Delay due to defendant's action.—Defendant's speedy trial motion was properly denied without an evidentiary hearing because it was made under CPL § 30.20 rather than CPL § 30.30 and of the thirteen months between the filing of the information and the date of the motion at least nine were the result of the pretrial conference and motions made by the defendant, and the affidavit failed to allege any impairment of his defense as a result of the delay. People v. Coffaro, 52 N.Y.2d 932, 437 N.Y.S.2d 666, 419 N.E.2d 344 (1981).

—Delays of 22 and 29 months from arrest to trial on two separate indictments did not constitute a denial of the right to speedy trial where much of the delays were due to the defendant's actions in replacing his counsel. Delay alone does automatically breach the defendant's constitutional and statutory rights, but each case must be determined on the basis of the conduct of both the prosecution and the defendant. People v. Timothy, 34 N.Y.2d 867, 359 N.Y.S.2d 114, 316 N.E.2d 580 (1974).

—Sixteen months elapsed between defendant's arraignment and trial for criminal possession of a weapon, grand larceny and reckless endangerment. Defendant's attorney had requested three postponements of trial, twice because of prior engagements, and that because of defendant's dissatisfaction with his retained lawyers successive assignments of counsel had to be made by the court. Held, despite defendant's motions for dismissal for failure to prosecute on three occasions, the District Attorney's policy of prosecuting cases in order of sequence was not the sole cause of the delay, and therefore defendant's right to speedy trial had not been denied. People v. Purdy, 29 N.Y.2d 800, 327 N.Y.S.2d 362, 277 N.E.2d 410 (1971).

—Court rejected defendant's speedy trial claim despite argument that witness died during the delay where witness' illness was known only to the defense and where some of the delay was attributable to action of the defendant. People v. Mann, 200 A.D.2d 910, 607 N.Y.S.2d 158 (3d Dept. 1994).

Denial of due process.—A 31-month unexplained delay in return of indictment, following arrest for criminal possession of stolen property and reckless endangerment and dismissal of charges at the request of the prosecutor so that they could be presented to Grand Jury, constituted a denial of due process; failure of prompt prosecution may require dismissal even in the absence of prejudice to the defendant. People v. Staley, 41 N.Y.2d 789, 396 N.Y.S.2d 339, 364 N.E.2d 1111 (1977).

—Defendant should have been granted a hearing on his application to dismiss his conviction of second degree manslaughter based on an assertion that the inordinate delay of nearly eight years between the time of the commission of the crime and the indictment violated his right to due process; due process requirement of a prompt prosecution is broader than the right to a speedy trial guaranteed by statute and the sixth amendment, and if commencement of the action has been delayed for a lengthy period, without good cause, defendant may be entitled to dismissal although there may be no showing of special prejudice. People v. Bryant, 79 A.D.2d 867, 434 N.Y.S.2d 558 (4th Dept. 1980).

Burden on People to show good cause for delay.—Although the People had the burden of establishing good cause for the delay of over three years in prosecuting the defendant for murder, their failure to do so should not be conclusive and the prosecutor should be afforded an opportunity to produce such proof. People v. Singer, 44 N.Y.2d 241, 405 N.Y.S.2d 17, 376 N.E.2d 179 (1978).

Ongoing criminal investigation.—A seven month delay between the cocaine sale and defendant's indictment thereon did not deprive him of due process of law so as to warrant dismissal of the indictment where the undercover police officer and confidential informant who helped arrange the transaction were involved in an ongoing drug investigation centered in the locale where defendant lived, and where defendant failed to establish any significant degree of actual prejudice resulting from the delay. People v. Bryant, 65 A.D.2d 333, 411 N.Y.S.2d 932 (2d Dept. 1978).

—One year delay between defendant's sale of cocaine to an undercover officer and his arrest did not deprive defendant of due process where the undercover purchase was part of a larger investigation of continuing drug activity, and the investigation required secrecy during at least a portion of the delay. People v. Kirkley, 295 A.D.2d 759, 745 N.Y.S.2d 81 (3d Dept. 2002).

—Three-month period between the second heroin sale and the indictment did not violate defendant's right to a speedy trial as the delay was amply justified by the desire of the police to continue the ongoing drug investigation. People v. James, 90 A.D.2d 920, 457 N.Y.S.2d 936 (3d Dept. 1982).

No prejudice shown.—Where defendant was incarcerated

on other charges, and there has been no showing that his defense has been impaired by reason of the unexplained six-month delay, the delay in prosecution did not constitute a deprivation of due process. People v. Rivera, 298 A.D.2d 612, 747 N.Y.S.2d 854 (3d Dept. 2002).

—Twenty-month delay between commission of the crime and the indictment did not violate defendant's right to a speedy trial where the defendant failed to show any prejudice. People v. King, 114 A.D.2d 650, 494 N.Y.S.2d 484 (3d Dept. 1985).

Pre-arrest delay.—Thirteen months of pre-arrest delay did not warrant dismissal of the indictment. People v. Mitchell, 192 A.D.2d 495, 495, 597 N.Y.S.2d 297, 298 (1st Dept. 1993).

Delay between arrest and trial.—Dismissal was warranted where 43 months expired between defendant's arrest and his trial. People v. Charles, 180 A.D.2d 868, 870, 580 N.Y.S.2d 99, 101 (3d Dept. 1992).

Applicability of statute to traffic infractions.—Statute entitling defendant to speedy trial "after a criminal trial has commenced" did not apply to defendant charged with traffic infraction; while defendant charged with traffic infraction may not have statutory right to speedy trial, he or she does have constitutional right to speedy trial. People v. Fisher, 167 Misc. 2d 850, 635 N.Y.S.2d 1002 (Crim. Ct. Richmond Co. 1995).

—The speedy trial protections of CPL § 30.30 do not apply to traffic infractions. People v. Wise, 141 Misc. 2d 409, 410, 532 N.Y.S.2d 833, 834 (Nassau Co. Dist. Court 1988).

—The constitutional right to a speedy trial applies to all prosecutions, even those for traffic infractions. People v. Thorpe, 160 Misc. 2d 558, 613 N.Y.S.2d 795, 796 (App. Term 1994).

Generally.—There are no steadfast rules regarding the amount of delay that will automatically entitle a defendant to a dismissal on these grounds. People v. Jones, 188 A.D.2d 745, 746, 591 N.Y.S.2d 555, 556 (3d Dept. 1992).

Guilty plea not waiver of speedy trial.—While a constitutional speedy trial claim survives a guilty plea or appeal waiver, defendant's failure to make any kind of speedy trial motion foreclosed the claim. People v. Arac, 297 A.D.2d 560, 747 N.Y.S.2d 87 (1st Dept. 2002).

—Where defendant's written speedy trial motion became lost in the confusion when a suppression hearing was terminated after the prosecution moved to dismiss a higher count of the indictment subject to acceptance of a guilty plea and Criminal Term took the plea on the erroneous assumption that a waiver of the speedy trial challenge was encompassed in the plea bargain which included a waiver of determination of the suppression motion, the speedy trial motion improperly became an item of barter in the plea negotiation and a vacatur of the plea was therefore required. People v. Diaz, 70 A.D.2d 601, 416 N.Y.S.2d 83 (2d Dept. 1979).

—The defendant has a right to raise the issue of a denial of a speedy trial as a constitutional violation of his right to due process following a plea of guilty. People v. Rathbun, 48 A.D.2d 149, 368 N.Y.S.2d 317 (3d Dept. 1975).

Habeas corpus; trial begins.—Where the action is brought to trial, habeas corpus brought on the ground of denial of the right to a speedy trial generally should be denied, without necessarily reaching the merits, but such denial does not preclude raising the issue again, provided it has been preserved by proper objection, motion or otherwise. People ex rel. McDonald v. Warden, New York City House of Detention for Men, 34 N.Y.2d 554, 354 N.Y.S.2d 939, 310 N.E.2d 537 (1974).

Homicide; speedy trial denied.—The mandate of a speedy trial, provided for in CPL § 30.20 was inapplicable to a consolidated indictment charging murder and robbery, first degree (CPL § 30.30(3)(a)). People v. Smith, 53 A.D.2d 652, 384 N.Y.S.2d 488 (2d Dept. 1976).

Out of state incarceration.—Where New York knew of defendant's whereabouts in a New Jersey prison and his availability for over three years, and did not extradite him, his right to a speedy trial was violated. People v. McLaurin, 38 N.Y.2d 586, 381 N.Y.S.2d 835, 345 N.E.2d 306 (1976).

Excessive delay.—A delay of 51 months in bringing defendant to trial after filing of felony information in prosecution for robbery was a denial of defendant's right to a speedy trial. One's right to a speedy trial is violated if there is an excessive delay between institution of the prosecution whether by felony information, complaint, detainer warrant, or indictment, and trial. It is the filing of the felony complaint that commences the criminal action for purposes of determining whether a defendant has been denied his right to a speedy trial. People v. White 32 N.Y.2d 393, 345 N.Y.S.2d 513, 298 N.E.2d 659 (1973).

—Four-year delay between commencement of prosecution and defendant's entry of a plea of guilty denied defendant his right to a speedy trial. People v. Willis, 149 A.D.2d 953, 540 N.Y.S.2d 86 (4th Dept. 1989).

—Delay of over 16 months was unreasonable where defendant was incarcerated during entire period, co-defendants had been released on bail during that time, prosecution was not a complex one, the required evidence and witnesses had been available to the People after 6 weeks, the delay was not borne of defense actions, and the delay prejudiced the defendant in that the co-defendant who played a major role in the crime died during that time. People v. Brown, 117 A.D.2d 978, 499 N.Y.S.2d 529 (4th Dept. 1986).

No speedy trial violation.—Twenty-five-month delay did not violate defendant's speedy trial right. People v. Allen, 203 A.D.2d 97, 610 N.Y.S.2d 40 (1st Dept. 1994).

—In narcotics prosecution, delay of 33 months did not deprive defendant of his constitutional right to a speedy trial. People v. Garcia, 208 A.D.2d 425, 617 N.Y.S.2d 307 (1st Dept. 1994).

Shortage in prosecutor's office.—Eighteen-month delay between arrest and guilty plea to manslaughter, second degree, during which time defendant was incarcerated, required reversal and dismissal of the indictment where the delay was due to shortage of personnel in the prosecutor's office and defendant had repeatedly sought a speedy trial and the record indicated that the delay prejudiced his case. People v. Johnson, 38 N.Y.2d 271, 379 N.Y.S.2d 735, 342 N.E.2d 525 (1975).

Review by another judge; improper.—It was error for a justice of coordinate jurisdiction to reconsider the denial of a speedy trial motion by another judge where the motion was based upon the same adjournments. People v. Calderon, 91 A.D.2d 1054, 458 N.Y.S.2d 659 (2d Dept. 1983).

Speedy trial; involuntary waiver; dismissal of indictment.—Defendant's waiver of speedy trial claim was ineffectual where prosecutor conditioned offer to recommend reduced plea upon withdrawal of claim, as condition made waiver inherently coercive and thus 34 month delay between indictment and motion for adjournment, in absence of good cause, required dismissal of the indictment. People v. Blakeley, 34 N.Y.2d 311, 357 N.Y.S.2d 459, 313 N.E.2d 763 (1974).

Unavailability of alibi witness.—Dismissal was required when, as a result of nineteen month post indictment delay, defendant was unable to locate his alibi witness, who possessed necessary and material evidence. People v. McDonald, 49 A.D.2d 589, 370 N.Y.S.2d 547 (2d Dept. 1975).

Waiver; failure to raise at trial.—Court of Appeals could not consider defendants' contention that they had been denied their right to a speedy trial (U.S. Const., 6th, 14th Amends.; CPL § 30.20; Civil Rights Law § 12) where defendants failed to raise the issue at trial. People v. Whisby, 48 N.Y.2d 834, 424 N.Y.S.2d 344, 400 N.E.2d 286 (1979).

—Defendant's claim of denial of his right to a speedy trial as guaranteed by the Sixth Amendment will not be reviewed on appeal if not raised in the trial court. People v. Primmer, 46 N.Y.2d 1048, 416 N.Y.S.2d 548, 389 N.E.2d 1070 (1979).

—The right to a speedy trial may be waived but the waiver must be both knowingly and voluntarily made. People v. Adams, 38 N.Y.2d 605, 381 N.Y.S.2d 847, 345 N.E.2d 318 (1976).

—By failing to move for dismissal of indictment pursuant to CPL § 30.20, defendant did not preserve claim for appellate review. People v. Martinez, 126 A.D.2d 942, 942, 989, 511 N.Y.S.2d 988 (2d Dept. 1987).

§ 30.30. Speedy trial; time limitations.

1. Except as otherwise provided in subdivision three, a motion made pursuant to paragraph (e) of subdivision one of section 170.30 or paragraph (g) of subdivision one of section 210.20 must be granted where the people are not ready for trial within:

(a) six months of the commencement of a criminal action wherein a defendant is accused of one or more offenses, at least one of which is a felony;

(b) ninety days of the commencement of a criminal action wherein a defendant is accused of one or more offenses, at least one of which is a misdemeanor punishable by a sentence of imprisonment of more than three months and none of which is a felony;

(c) sixty days of the commencement of a criminal action wherein the defendant is accused of one or more offenses, at least one of which is a misdemeanor punishable by a sentence of imprisonment of not more than three months and none of which is a crime punishable by a sentence of imprisonment of more than three months;

(d) thirty days of the commencement of a criminal action wherein the defendant is accused of one or more offenses, at least one of which is a violation and none of which is a crime.

2. Except as provided in subdivision three, where a defendant has been committed to the custody of the sheriff in a criminal action he must be released on bail or on his own recognizance, upon such conditions as may be just and reasonable, if the people are not ready for trial in that criminal action within:

(a) ninety days from the commencement of his commitment to the custody of the sheriff in a criminal action wherein the defendant is accused of one or more offenses, at least one of which is a felony;

(b) thirty days from the commencement of his commitment to the custody of the sheriff in a criminal action wherein the defendant is accused of one or more offenses, at least one of which is a misdemeanor punishable by a sentence of imprisonment of more than three months and none of which is a felony;

(c) fifteen days from the commencement of his commitment to the custody of the sheriff in a criminal action wherein the defendant is accused of one or more offenses, at least one of which is a misdemeanor punishable by a sentence of imprisonment of not more than three months and none of which is a crime punishable by a sentence of imprisonment of more than three months;

(d) five days from the commencement of his commitment to the custody of the sheriff in a criminal action wherein the defendant is accused of one or more offenses, at least one of which is a violation and none of which is a crime.

3. (a) Subdivisions one and two do not apply to a criminal action wherein the defendant is accused of an offense defined in sections 125.10, 125.15, 125.20, 125.25 and 125.27 of the penal law.

(b) A motion made pursuant to subdivisions one or two upon expiration of the specified period may be denied where the people are not ready for trial if the people were ready for trial prior to the expiration of the specified period and their present unreadiness is due to some exceptional fact or circumstance, including, but not limited to, the sudden unavailability of evidence material to the people's case, when the district attorney has exercised due diligence to obtain such evidence and there are reasonable grounds to believe that such evidence will become available in a reasonable period.

(c) A motion made pursuant to subdivision two shall not:

(i) apply to any defendant who is serving a term of imprisonment for another offense;

(ii) require the release from custody of any defendant who is also being held in custody pending trial of another criminal charge as to which the applicable period has not yet elapsed;

(iii) prevent the redetention of or otherwise apply to any defendant who, after being released from custody pursuant to this section or otherwise, is charged with another crime or violates the conditions on which he has been released, by failing to appear at a judicial proceeding at which his presence is required or otherwise.

4. In computing the time within which the people must be ready for trial pursuant to subdivisions one and two, the following periods must be excluded:

(a) a reasonable period of delay resulting from other proceedings concerning the defendant, including but not limited to: proceedings for the determination of competency and the period during which defendant is incompetent to stand trial; demand to produce; request for a bill of particulars; pre-trial motions; appeals; trial of other charges; and the period during which such matters are under consideration by the court; or

(b) the period of delay resulting from a continuance granted by the court at the request of, or with the consent of, the defendant or his counsel. The court must grant such a continuance only if it is satisfied that postponement is in the interest of justice, taking into account the public interest in the prompt dispositions of criminal charges. A defendant without counsel must not be deemed to have consented to a continuance unless he has been advised by the court of his rights under these rules and the effect of his consent; or

(c) (i) the period of delay resulting from the absence or unavailability of the defendant. A defendant must be considered absent whenever his location is unknown and he is attempting to avoid apprehension or prosecution, or his location cannot be determined by due diligence. A defendant must be considered unavailable whenever his location is known but his presence for trial cannot be obtained by due diligence; or

(ii) where the defendant has either escaped from custody or has failed to appear when required after having previously been released on bail or on his own recognizance, and provided the defendant is not in custody on another matter, the period extending from the day the court issues a bench warrant pursuant to section 530.70 because of the defendant's failure to appear in court when required, to the day the defendant subsequently appears in the court pursuant to a bench warrant or voluntarily or otherwise; or

(d) a reasonable period of delay when the defendant is joined for trial with a co-defendant as to whom the time for trial pursuant to this section has not run and good cause is not shown for granting a severance; or

(e) the period of delay resulting from detention of the defendant in another jurisdiction provided the district attorney is aware of such detention and has been diligent and has made reasonable efforts to obtain the presence of the defendant for trial; or

(f) the period during which the defendant is without counsel through no fault of the court; except when the defendant is proceeding as his own attorney with the permission of the court; or

(g) other periods of delay occasioned by exceptional circumstances, including but not limited to, the period of delay resulting from a continuance granted at the request of a district attorney if (i) the continuance is granted because of the unavailability of evidence material to the people's case, when the district attorney has exercised due diligence to obtain such evidence and there are reasonable grounds to believe that such evidence will become available in a reasonable period; or (ii) the continuance is granted to allow the district attorney additional time to prepare the people's case and additional time is justified by the exceptional circumstances of the case.

(h) the period during which an action has been adjourned in contemplation of dismissal pursuant to sections 170.55, 170.56 and 215.10 of this chapter.

(i) the period prior to the defendant's actual appearance for arraignment in a situation in which the defendant has been directed to appear by the district attorney pursuant to subdivision three of section 120.20 or subdivision three of section 210.10.

(j) the period during which a family offense is before a family court until such time as an accusatory instrument or indictment is filed against the defendant alleging a crime constituting a family offense, as such term is defined in section 530.11 of this chapter.

5. For purposes of this section, (a) where the defendant is to be tried following the withdrawal of the plea of guilty or is to be retried following a mistrial, an order for a new trial or an appeal or collateral attack, the criminal action and the

commitment to the custody of the sheriff, if any, must be deemed to have commenced on the date the withdrawal of the plea of guilty or the date the order occasioning a retrial becomes final;

(b) where a defendant has been served with an appearance ticket, the criminal action must be deemed to have commenced on the date the defendant first appears in a local criminal court in response to the ticket;

(c) where a criminal action is commenced by the filing of a felony complaint, and thereafter, in the course of the same criminal action either the felony complaint is replaced with or converted to an information, prosecutor's information or misdemeanor complaint pursuant to article 180 or a prosecutor's information is filed pursuant to section 190.70, the period applicable for the purposes of subdivision one must be the period applicable to the charges in the new accusatory instrument, calculated from the date of the filing of such new accusatory instrument; provided, however, that when the aggregate of such period and the period of time, excluding the periods provided in subdivision four, already elapsed from the date of the filing of the felony complaint to the date of the filing of the new accusatory instrument exceeds six months, the period applicable to the charges in the felony complaint must remain applicable and continue as if the new accusatory instrument had not been filed;

(d) where a criminal action is commenced by the filing of a felony complaint, and thereafter, in the course of the same criminal action either the felony complaint is replaced with or converted to an information, prosecutor's information or misdemeanor complaint pursuant to article 180 or a prosecutor's information is filed pursuant to section 190.70, the period applicable for the purposes of subdivision two must be the period applicable to the charges in the new accusatory instrument, calculated from the date of the filing of such new accusatory instrument; provided, however, that when the aggregate of such period and the period of time, excluding the periods provided in subdivision four, already elapsed from the date of the filing of the felony complaint to the date of the filing of the new accusatory instrument exceeds ninety days, the period applicable to the charges in the felony complaint must remain applicable and continue as if the new accusatory instrument had not been filed.

(e) where a count of an indictment is reduced to charge only a misdemeanor or petty offense and a reduced indictment or a prosecutor's information is filed pursuant to subdivisions one-a and six of section 210.20, the period applicable for the purposes of subdivision one of this section must be the period applicable to the charges in the new accusatory instrument, calculated from the date of the filing of such new accusatory instrument; provided, however, that when the aggregate of such period and the period of time,

excluding the periods provided in subdivision four of this section, already elapsed from the date of the filing of the indictment to the date of the filing of the new accusatory instrument exceeds six months, the period applicable to the charges in the indictment must remain applicable and continue as if the new accusatory instrument had not been filed;

(f) where a count of an indictment is reduced to charge only a misdemeanor or petty offense and a reduced indictment or a prosecutor's information is filed pursuant to subdivisions one-a and six of section 210.20, the period applicable for the purposes of subdivision two of this section must be the period applicable to the charges in the new accusatory instrument, calculated from the date of the filing of such new accusatory instrument; provided, however, that when the aggregate of such period and the period of time, excluding the periods provided in subdivision four of this section, already elapsed from the date of the filing of the indictment to the date of the filing of the new accusatory instrument exceeds ninety days, the period applicable to the charges in the indictment must remain applicable and continue as if the new accusatory instrument had not been filed.

6. The procedural rules prescribed in subdivisions one through seven of section 210.45 with respect to a motion to dismiss an indictment are also applicable to a motion made pursuant to subdivision two.

Repealed former § 30.30 and **Added** new § 30.30 by L. 1972, Ch. 184; **Amended** by L. 1974, Ch. 367; L. 1979, Ch. 412; L. 1981, Ch. 109; L. 1984, Ch. 670; L. 1986, Ch. 837; L. 1990, Ch. 209; L. 1993, Ch. 446; L. 1994, Ch. 222, § 29, eff. Jan. 1, 1995, adding subd. 4(j); L. 1996, Ch. 631, amending subd. 4(c), effective October 4, 1996.

ANNOTATIONS

Taranovich factors—While the 17-year delay in prosecution was extensive, there was good cause in light of the severity of the crime—a double murder in which two bar owners were shot at point blank range after defendant's cohort became enraged over a spilled drink; there was virtually no pretrial incarceration; the defense had not been impaired by the delay; and if anything, the delay made the case against defendant even harder to prove. People v. Vernace, 96 N.Y.2d 886, 730 N.Y.S.2d 778, 756 N.E.2d 66 (2001).

—The factors to consider in determining whether there has been a denial of a speedy trial right are: (1) the extent of the delay; (2) the reason for the delay; (3) the nature of the underlying charge; (4) whether or not there has been an extended period of pretrial incarceration; and (5) whether or not there is any indication that the defense has been impaired by the delay. People v. Taranovich, 37 N.Y.2d 442, 373 N.Y.S.2d 79, 335 N.E.2d 303 (1975).

—A one-year delay between the crime and indictment for a class C felony does not violate the defendant's constitutional right to a speedy trial even when it results from prosecutorial inattention, where there is no lengthy pretrial incarceration or impairment of the defense caused by the delay. People v. Taranovich, 37 N.Y.2d 442, 373 N.Y.S.2d 79, 335 N.E.2d 303 (1975).

Announcing readiness.—Announcing readiness requires the People to communicate their readiness on the trial court's record, and also to make a statement of readiness when the People are, in fact, ready to proceed. People v. Kendzia, 64 N.Y.2d 331, 486 N.Y.S.2d 888, 476 N.E.2d 287 (1985).

Absent defendant.—Defendant's absence was the cause of

the delay in the prosecution: the fact that defendant wilfully failed to appear in court; fled the jurisdiction and began another crime spree; used varied names, dates of birth, and social security numbers when he was arrested on numerous occasions for crimes in other jurisdictions, were all evidence that defendant was attempting to avoid responsibility for his crimes. People v. Chisolm, 232 A.D.2d 264, 649 N.Y.S.2d 127 (1st Dept. 1996).

—The issuance of a bench warrant does not excuse the People's obligation to exercise due diligence in attempting to locate the defendant. People v. Barasso, 193 A.D.2d 448, 597 N.Y.S.2d 681 (1st Dept. 1993).

—The seven-day period between the time that defendant failed to appear in court and the time that police attempted to locate him at his place of employment and at his parents' house was properly excluded from the time chargeable to the People as reasonable administrative delay inherent in the processing of a warrant. People v. Klavoon, 207 A.D.2d 979, 617 N.Y.S.2d 252 (4th Dept. 1994).

—Time was excludable where defendant was absent and warrant was stayed for his benefit. People v. Bryant, 158 Misc. 2d 86, 600 N.Y.S.2d 929 (Crim. Ct. Kings Co. 1993).

Indefinite search for defendant not required.—For speedy trial purposes, the police are not obligated to search for a defendant indefinitely in order to satisfy due diligence standards. People v. Seto, 162 Misc. 2d 255, 616 N.Y.S.2d 890, 894 (Sup. Ct. N.Y. Co. 1994).

Securing defendant's attendance.—Time between the defendant's arrest in Nassau County and his ultimate return to court in New York City was chargeable to the People since they failed to utilize the statutory procedure set forth in CPL § 560.10(2) to secure the defendant's attendance. People v. Cropper, 202 A.D.2d 603, 609 N.Y.S.2d 288 (2d Dept. 1994).

Accusatory instrument.—The obligation to obtain a proper accusatory instrument is the prosecutor's alone, and absent some reasonable ground the time used to obtain the indictment is ordinarily chargeable to the People. People v. Waring, 206 A.D.2d 329, 615 N.Y.S.2d 21 (1st Dept. 1994).

Adjournments.—Court rejected People's contention that an adjournment that is extended because the defense rejects the original date suggested by the People should be excludable from the time chargeable to them. People v. Smith, 82 N.Y.2d 676, 601 N.Y.S.2d 466, 619 N.E.2d 403 (1993).

—Preindictment adjournments requested by defense counsel constitute excludable time under CPL § 30.30. People v. Meierdiercks, 68 N.Y.2d 613, 505 N.Y.S.2d 51, 496 N.E.2d 210 (1986).

—Where adjournments are allowed at defendant's request, those periods of delay are expressly waived in calculating the People's trial readiness, without the need for the People to trace their lack of readiness to defendant's actions. People v. Kopciowski, 68 N.Y.2d 615, 505 N.Y.S.2d 52, 496 N.E.2d 211 (1986).

—Delays occasioned by defense motions, or requests for or consents to adjournments, are not chargeable to the People even where they occur prior to the conversion of the misdemeanor complaint to an information. People v. Worley, 66 N.Y.2d 523, 498 N.Y.S.2d 116, 488 N.E.2d 1228 (1985).

—Absent something in the record to indicate that defense counsel either expressly requested or consented to adjournments, adjournments "incident to plea negotiations" were not excludable. People v. Brown, 206 A.D.2d 326, 615 N.Y.S.2d 16 (1st Dept. 1994).

Appeal.—Reasonable period of time granted to the People following a request for an extension of time to perfect an appeal was excludable under CPL § 30.30(4). People v. Grafton, 73 N.Y.2d 779, 536 N.Y.S.2d 738, 533 N.E.2d 668 (1988).

—The statutory speedy trial provision was not violated where an appeal was pending and, if decided in the defendant's favor, it could have warranted the dismissal of the remaining indictments against him, since the prosecutor was entitled to await the outcome of the appeal before subjecting the defendant and his office to the expense and travail of a trial which might well have proved to be futile. People v. Dean, 45 N.Y.2d 651, 412 N.Y.S.2d 353, 384 N.E.2d 1277 (1978).

—Trial court's incorrect statement to defendant that statutory speedy trial issue could be raised on appeal did not require reversal of plea, in light of determination that such misstatement had no effect on defendant's decision to plead guilty and that

no speedy trial violation actually occurred. People v. Rivers, 228 A.D.2d 291, 644 N.Y.S.2d 208 (1st Dept. 1996).

—The Supreme Court erred in holding that the People had no right to take more than four months in perfecting their prior successful appeal; on the contrary, the People had every right to take nine months and to assume that their compliance with the rules of the court would shield them from the charge of having unreasonably delayed the prosecution of the case. People v. Aaron, 201 A.D.2d 574, 607 N.Y.S.2d 950 (2d Dept. 1994).

—Even though time between filing of notice of appeal by People and order of appellate order reversing dismissal of the indictment was excludable, the prosecution was charged with delay borne of failure to exercise due diligence in obtaining copy of lower court's written order dismissing the indictment. People v. Holmes, 206 A.D.2d 542, 615 N.Y.S.2d 52 (2d Dept. 1994).

—A reasonable time period to file a timely appeal is excludable. People v. Roesch, 153 Misc. 2d 668, 670, 582 N.Y.S.2d 916, 918 (Sup. Ct. Kings Co. 1992).

Appeal; inapplicable.—Five-year delay between the conviction and the granting of a new trial on appeal did not violate the defendant's right to a speedy appeal or retrial as CPL § 30.30 does not apply to appeals. People v. Cousart, 58 N.Y.2d 62, 458 N.Y.S.2d 507, 444 N.E.2d 971 (1982).

—Prosecutor was entitled to await outcome of appeal of dismissed charge before subjecting defendant and People to expense of trial which may have proven futile; thus, time during pendency of appeal was excluded from time charged to People for speedy trial purposes as to the remaining count, as long as appeal was perfected during a reasonable time. People v. Scott, 172 Misc. 2d 594, 659 N.Y.S.2d 697 (N.Y.C. Crim. Ct. 1997).

Desk appearance ticket.—When a defendant who has received a Desk Appearance Ticket (DAT) fails to appear in court on the return date, the speedy trial clock does not begin to run until the defendant actually appears in court, regardless of the reason for the failure to appear. People v. Parris, 79 N.Y.2d 69, 71, 580 N.Y.S.2d 167, 168, 588 N.E.2d 65, 66 (1991); see also People v. Felder, 132 A.D.2d 79, 503 N.Y.S.2d 509 (3d Dept. 1986); People v. Velie, 193 A.D.2d 1107, 1108, 598 N.Y.S.2d 636, 637 (4th Dept. 1993); People v. Brisotti, 169 Misc. 2d 672, 652 N.Y.S.2d 206 (App. T., 1st Dept. 1996).

Arraignment.—Delays between indictment and the arraignment do not prevent the People from being ready for trial and therefore are not excludable. People v. Correa, 77 N.Y.2d 930, 569 N.Y.S.2d 601, 572 N.E.2d 42 (1991); see also People v. Afshar, 152 Misc. 2d 615, 617, 578 N.Y.S.2d 372, 374 (Sup. Ct. N.Y. Co. 1991).

—The time between indictment and arraignment is chargeable to the People even where the court fixes the arraignment date. People v. Marte, 177 A.D.2d 347, 348, 576 N.Y.S.2d 122, 123 (1st Dept. 1991).

—For purposes of speedy trial, the People are entitled to a reasonable period in which to arrange the defendant's arraignment on an indictment. People v. Lopez, 149 A.D.2d 735, 540 N.Y.S.2d 518 (2d Dept. 1989).

—Where setting of arraignment date was within the control of court clerk and not People delay between indictment and arraignment was excludable. People v. Walton, 136 Misc. 2d 539, 518 N.Y.S.2d 930 (Sup. Ct. Queens Co. 1987).

Bench warrant.—The issuance of a bench warrant does not excuse the People's obligation to exercise due diligence in attempting to locate an absent defendant. People v. Barasso, 193 A.D.2d 448, 597 N.Y.S.2d 681 (1st Dept. 1993).

Bill of particulars.—The People's failure to file a bill of particulars is irrelevant on a CPL § 30.30 motion as the failure to serve a bill of particulars is in no way inconsistent with the prosecution's continued readiness. People v. Cole, 90 A.D.2d 27, 457 N.Y.S.2d 589 (3d Dept. 1983).

Both sides engaged elsewhere.—For the purpose of determining whether there was a delay in bringing a defendant to trial, a twenty-one day period during which both the prosecution and the defense attorney were actually engaged in other cases could not be charged to the People. People v. Green, 90 A.D.2d 705, 455 N.Y.S.2d 368 (1st Dept. 1982).

People's failure to submit opposition papers.—Court should summarily have granted defendant's speedy trial motion where People failed to submit opposition papers. People v. Cole, 73 N.Y.2d 957, 540 N.Y.S.2d 984, 538 N.E.2d 336 (1989).

Calendar notations.—In deciding the includability or excludability of time periods, a court may rely on its own file notations; while such notations are unofficial records, they may serve in the absence of minutes of adjournments, to resolve any disputed periods of time. People v. Williams, 147 Misc. 2d 420, 556 N.Y.S.2d 191 (Sup. Ct. N.Y. Co. 1990).

—Calendar notations do not bind the court that determines a speedy trial motion. People v. Nevarez, 142 Misc. 2d 1064, 1065, 539 N.Y.S.2d 645, 647 (Crim. Ct. N.Y. Co. 1989).

Burden on People to establish periods of exclusion.—Since the main thrust of CPL § 30.30 is to require the prosecution to be prepared within six months in all but the unusual case, once the defendant has shown the existence of a delay greater than six months, the burden of proving that certain periods within that time should be excluded falls upon the People. People v. Berkowitz, 50 N.Y.2d 333, 428 N.Y.S.2d 927, 406 N.E.2d 783 (1980).

—On a speedy trial motion, if the papers contain sworn allegations of an unexcused delay exceeding the time limit imposed by CPL § 30.30, it is the prosecution's burden to demonstrate that a particular period of time should be excluded from the calculation of the statutory limit. People v. Boyd, 189 A.D.2d 433, 436, 596 N.Y.S.2d 760, 762 (1st Dept. 1993).

—Where the People failed to call any witness at the CPL § 30.30 hearing it was difficult to conclude that the People carried any burden of proof that they might have had. People v. Canale, 159 A.D.2d 817, 817, 553 N.Y.S.2d 61, 62 (3d Dept. 1990).

Co-defendant.—Even though severance was ultimately granted, People were entitled to benefit of co-defendant's requests for adjournments which transpired prior to severance. People v. Vidal, 180 A.D.2d 447, 449, 580 N.Y.S.2d 13, 15 (1st Dept. 1992).

—People are not chargeable for a reasonable period of delay when the defendant is joined for trial with a co-defendant as to whom the time for trial pursuant to CPL § 30.30 has not run and good cause is not shown for granting a severance. People v. Robles, 139 A.D.2d 781, 782, 527 N.Y.S.2d 527, 528 (2d Dept. 1988).

—Periods of delay attributable to one defendant are attributable to all defendants. People v. Day, 139 Misc. 2d 222, 526 N.Y.S.2d 736 (Sup. Ct. Kings Co. 1988); People v. Barnett, 135 Misc. 2d 1127, 517 N.Y.S.2d 849 (Crim. Ct. Kings Co. 1987).

Commencement date for speedy trial purposes.—No matter how many times indictment is superseded, commencement date for speedy trial purposes remains date on which initial accusatory instrument was filed. People v. Tran, 177 Misc. 2d 63, 678 N.Y.S.2d 234 (Sup. Ct. N.Y. Co. 1998).

Commencement of action; first and second set of indictments.—An indictment which replaces an earlier one in the same criminal action should be related back to the original accusatory instrument for the purpose of computing excludable time under CPL § 30.30(4). People v. Sinjistaj, 67 N.Y.2d 236, 501 N.Y.S.2d 793, 492 N.E.2d 1209 (1986).

—Where the felony complaint and the indictment alleged separate and distinct criminal transactions, for the purposes of assessing the People's compliance with their speedy trial obligations, the criminal action was commenced upon the filing of the indictment. People v. Schaffer, 200 A.D.2d 695, 608 N.Y.S.2d 8 (2d Dept. 1994).

—Time between dismissal of first set of indictments and filing of second set of indictments was properly chargeable to the People. People v. Bryant, 153 A.D.2d 636, 544 N.Y.S.2d 661 (2d Dept. 1989).

—In order for a criminal action to be commenced, the prosecution must file a signed accusatory instrument. People v. Sagardia, 158 Misc. 2d 216, 217, 600 N.Y.S.2d 1022, 1023 (Crim. Ct. Kings Co. 1993).

Commencement of time period following appeal.—Speedy trial time period on order for retrial began to run on date Court of Appeals affirmed such order; failure of People to prove that District Attorney exercised due diligence in the location of the complaining witness or in obtaining a transcript required the inclusion of such time in the speedy trial period and dismissal of the indictment was warranted. People v. Holmes, 105 A.D.2d 803, 481 N.Y.S.2d 741 (2d Dept. 1984).

Competency.—Delay caused by psychiatric evaluation pursuant to CPL Art. 730 is an inherent delay in criminal justice system and therefore excludable from speedy trial considerations, even where delay comes prior to conversion to a jurisdictionally sufficient accusatory instrument. People v. Schwartz, 130 Misc. 2d 593, 497 N.Y.S.2d 293 (Crim. Ct. N.Y. Co. 1985).

Consent.—A failure to object to an adjournment is not the same as consent to an adjournment for speedy trial purposes. People v. Liotta, 79 N.Y.2d 841, 842, 580 N.Y.S.2d 184, 185, 588 N.E.2d 82, 83 (1992).

—Period of delay which was not objected to by defense counsel was excludable. People v. Robinson, 171 A.D.2d 475, 567 N.Y.S.2d 401 (1st Dept. 1991).

Counsel.—The period of adjournment to permit the retention of private counsel was excludable. People v. Drake, 205 A.D.2d 996, 613 N.Y.S.2d 961 (3d Dept. 1994).

—Defendant was not without counsel through the fault of the court, but rather, he knowingly and voluntarily waived his right to counsel, and thus, the People should not be charged with all periods of pre-readiness delay. People v. Berger, 2 Misc. 3d 46, 774 N.Y.S.2d 247 (App. T. 2d & 11th Jud. Depts. 2003).

—Where a defendant is without counsel due to the fault of the court, the time is not excludable under CPL § 30.30(4)(f). People v. Viken, 161 Misc. 2d 217, 613 N.Y.S.2d 824 (Sup. Ct. Queens Co. 1994).

Court's scheduling.—Adjournment attributable to court scheduling—done in order to conform with court rules—was chargeable to the People. People v. Collins, 82 N.Y.2d 177, 604 N.Y.S.2d 11, 624 N.E.2d 139 (1993).

—People were not chargeable with time between filing of indictment and arraignment where the date was fixed by the court and not the prosecutor. People v. Rivera, 160 A.D.2d 234, 235, 553 N.Y.S.2d 682, 683 (1st Dept. 1990).

—The negligence of the trial court cannot be imputed to the People or prosecutor, and thus the court's negligence in scheduling a jury trial may not serve as a basis for a motion to dismiss for failure to grant defendant a speedy trial. People v. Conrad, 93 Misc. 2d 655, 405 N.Y.S.2d 559 (Monroe Co. Ct. 1978), aff'd, 44 N.Y.2d 863, 407 N.Y.S.2d 694, 379 N.E.2d 220 (1978).

Court has no authority to dismiss case for "calendar control."—Trial court judges did not have the authority, inherent, statutory or otherwise, to dismiss a pending criminal proceeding for "failure to prosecute" or "calendar control" where statutory and Constitutional speedy trial time limits had not run. People v. Douglass, 60 N.Y.2d 194, 469 N.Y.S.2d 56, 456 N.E.2d 1179 (1983).

—Criminal term does not possess the inherent authority to dismiss a criminal action due to a delay in prosecution. People v. Cileli, 137 A.D.2d 829, 830, 525 N.Y.S.2d 291, 292 (2d Dept. 1988).

Effect of indictment where criminal action was dismissed.—The return of an indictment does not commence a new criminal action when the felony complaint initiating the criminal action against the defendant was dismissed because of the prosecutor's inexcusable delay. People v. Osgood, 52 N.Y.2d 37, 436 N.Y.S.2d 213, 417 N.E.2d 507 (1980).

Cooperation with federal authorities.—Eight month delay by District Attorney in proceeding further after indictment, due to an agreement between County and Federal authorities to keep secret the ongoing criminal investigation and grand jury proceedings conducted by the Federal authorities, was excluded from the computation of the period wherein the People were required to be ready for trial. People v. Tolkow, 80 Misc. 2d 1051, 364 N.Y.S.2d 756 (Suffolk Co. Ct. 1975).

Court congestion.—The announcement by the prosecution of readiness for trial exhausts the operational effect of CPL § 30.30 and the subsequent delay of 15 months before trial due to court congestion was excludable time. People v. Campbell, 91 A.D.2d 1075, 458 N.Y.S.2d 322 (3d Dept. 1983).

Defendant returned from without jurisdiction under CPL § 580.20 Article IV; right to omnibus pretrial motion.—Defendant, who was returned to New York from California pursuant to CPL § 580.20 Art. IV, was entitled to bring on his omnibus pretrial motion and to have it decided before he went to trial, thus he was unable to stand trial pending a decision on the motion and the time period was tolled accordingly (CPL § 580.20 (Art. IV[e]). People v. Chiofalo, 73 A.D.2d 673, 423 N.Y.S.2d 210 (2d Dept. 1979).

Defendant returned to jurisdiction pursuant to CPL

§ 580.—Trial Court committed error where it failed to exclude the period that elapsed from the filing of the detainer to the return of the defendant. People v. Chan, 81 A.D.2d 765, 439 N.Y.S.2d 112 (1st Dept. 1981).

Defense motions.—Forty-seven-day adjournment was excludable under CPL § 30.30(4)(a) as a delay resulting from other proceedings concerning the defendant, including pretrial motions, because it is of no consequence that defendant never actually filed the contemplated motion for which the adjournment was granted. People v. Brown, 99 N.Y.2d 488, 758 N.Y.S.2d 602, 788 N.E.2d 1030 (2003).

—Court initially failed to conform to procedural requirements for reduction of felony to misdemeanor pursuant to CPL § 180.50 and People had stated their readiness for trial before court properly reduced the charge; six months could not be charged to People because of defendant's numerous pretrial motions and changes of attorney, and furthermore, People's statement of readiness included the misdemeanor charge, which was unaffected by the procedural requirements of section 180.50. People v. Dion, 93 N.Y.2d 893, 689 N.Y.S.2d 685, 711 N.E.2d 963 (1999).

—Delay resulting from People's negligence in responding to defendant's motion to inspect and dismiss was chargeable to the People. People v. Harris, 82 N.Y.2d 409, 604 N.Y.S.2d 918, 624 N.E.2d 1013 (1993).

—The court's delay in determining the defendant's omnibus motion cannot be charged to the People on the ground that the court considered the motion "pro forma," for the law is clear that the People cannot be charged with the time a court takes to decide a defense motion. People v. Douglas, 209 A.D.2d 161, 617 N.Y.S.2d 765 (1st Dept. 1994).

Delay; defendant in federal custody.—Diligent efforts to return defendant from federal custody permit exclusion of the period of time involved. People v. Cook, 71 A.D.2d 801, 419 N.Y.S.2d 350 (4th Dept. 1979).

Delay; defendant in state psychiatric hospital.—Court properly charged the People with a seven-week delay, as defendant was not unavailable pursuant to CPL § 30.30(4)(c) because the prosecutor had information that defendant was in a state psychiatric hospital; delay cannot be charged to defendant on ground that his involuntary commitment to the hospital constituted a detention for purposes of CPL § 30.30(4)(e) unless the People made diligent efforts to obtain his presence in court. People v. Babbs, 232 A.D.2d 496, 648 N.Y.S.2d 649 (2d Dept. 1996).

Delay; psychiatric evaluations.—Delay occasioned by need for psychiatric evaluations was excludable under CPL 30.30(4)(a) because the examination fell within the category of other proceedings contemplated by the statute. People v. Jackson, 267 A.D.2d 183, 700 N.Y.S.2d 453 (1st Dept. 1999).

Delay in converting misdemeanor complaint to misdemeanor information.—The failure of the People to convert the misdemeanor complaint to a misdemeanor information did not in any way contribute to the delay in trial since the requirement to convert is one which can be met at a point in time close to the trial; the statutory pattern contemplates that a misdemeanor action is to proceed in its pretrial stages in the same fashion regardless of whether the accusatory instrument is an information or a complaint. People v. Callender, 101 Misc. 2d 958, 422 N.Y.S.2d 611 (Crim. Ct. N.Y.C. 1979), aff'd, 112 Misc. 2d 28, 448 N.Y.S.2d 92 (Sup. Ct. App. Term 1981).

Delays involving Grand Jury minutes.—The District Attorney was under no obligation to produce the Grand Jury minutes until ordered to do so, and he was entitled to a reasonable time to get them once the court directed their production. People v. Hancock, 173 A.D.2d 377, 377, 570 N.Y.S.2d 10, 11 (1st Dept. 1991).

—Delay attributable to failure of People to provide defense with Grand Jury minutes was excludable where defendant had not made a motion pursuant to CPL § 210.30. People v. Allen, 172 A.D.2d 542, 544, 568 N.Y.S.2d 132, 135 (2d Dept. 1991).

—Delay in producing Grand Jury minutes is not to be counted against the People; the delay in producing these materials did not impede the People's or the defendant's ability to prepare for trial, since such testimony, like Brady or Rosario material, may be provided at any time prior to the time the trial commences. People v. Corporan, 122 A.D.2d 152, 504 N.Y.S.2d 531 (2d Dept. 1986).

—Defendant was denied his statutory right to a speedy trial as a result of the People's post-readiness delay in providing the court with Grand Jury minutes. People v. Lloyd, 202 A.D.2d 1035, 610 N.Y.S.2d 111 (3d Dept. 1994).

—During the time that the People failed to provide the court with a transcript of the Grand Jury minutes, they could not be considered ready for trial. People v. Felder, 182 A.D.2d 1065, 1065, 583 N.Y.S.2d 697, 698 (4th Dept. 1992).

Discovery delay.—A delay by the People, subsequent to their announcement of readiness for trial, in answering a defendant's requests for discovery, even where such delay is unreasonable, does not vitiate the statement of readiness and is not chargeable against the People for purposes of speedy trial time limits; dismissal of the indictment on CPL § 30.30 grounds is not the appropriate remedy for such delay. People v. Jones, 105 A.D.2d 179, 483 N.Y.S.2d 345 (1st Dept. 1984).

—People cannot be charged with postreadiness delay in producing a document requested by the defendant, since the People's continuing readiness for trial was not affected, and to the extent that the delay impeded the defendant's readiness for trial, an alternative remedy was available to him. People v. Tinsley, 145 A.D.2d 448, 535 N.Y.S.2d 415 (2d Dept. 1988).

Dismissal of indictment; lack of due diligence.—Dismissal of indictment was properly based upon a failure to accord defendant a speedy trial where defendant was not arrested on a warrant issued in May 1977, on a sealed indictment, until November 1983, and the People failed to establish due diligence in locating the defendant. People v. Ray, 102 A.D.2d 876, 477 N.Y.S.2d 29 (2d Dept. 1984).

Dismissal required; witness available.—Defendant's motion for dismissal on CPL § 30.30 grounds was granted where the People failed to demonstrate that the state trooper was unavailable because they acknowledged that he was available at selected times. People v. Zimny, 188 Misc. 2d 600, 729 N.Y.S.2d 297 (Sup. Ct. Monroe Co. 2001).

Exceptional circumstances.—Period between the filing of information and defendant's arraignment was excludable as an "exceptional circumstance" where police detective prepared information without knowledge or involvement of prosecutor, and police did not advise prosecutor of the pending charges until the arraignment date; because the People, through no fault of their own, were unaware of the charges prior to arraignment, it was impossible for the People to prepare for trial, much less to announce readiness, within 30 days after the accusatory instrument was filed. People v. Smietana, 98 N.Y.2d 336, 746 N.Y.S.2d 678, 774 N.E.2d 743 (2002).

—Lengthy postreadiness delays attributable to defendant do not constitute an "exceptional fact or circumstance" within the meaning of CPL § 30.30(3)(b) sufficient to excuse adjournments resulting from the trial assistant's planned European vacation, particularly where the record suggested that another prosecutor could have been substituted. People v. Jones, 68 N.Y.2d 717, 506 N.Y.S.2d 315, 497 N.E.2d 682 (1986).

—Delay of seven months between indictment and arrest required dismissal despite People's claim of "exceptional circumstances" (CPL § 30.30(4)(g)) since the statutory exception is limited to instances in which the prosecution's inability to proceed is justified by the purposes of the investigation and credible, vigorous activity in pursuing it. People v. Washington, 43 N.Y.2d 772, 401 N.Y.S.2d 1007, 372 N.E.2d 795 (1977).

—After a thorough hearing, court properly determined that the period of 155 days during which the purchasing undercover officer was unavailable due to a family crisis and its tragic conclusion was excludable as a delay occasioned by exceptional circumstances. People v. Lopez, 2 A.D.3d 234, 768 N.Y.S.2d 468 (1st Dept. 2003).

—Speedy trial was not denied where the delay in arrest and trial was caused by a series of "substantial and vigorously pursued investigations," commenced as a result of an unexpected occurrence which took place after defendants were indicted, and which investigations continued until the time of arrest; the "exceptional circumstances" provision of CPL § 30.30(4)(g) authorizes the exclusion of delay caused by an ongoing investigation provided that the prosecution's inability to proceed is justified by the purposes of the investigation and credible, vigorous activity in pursuing it. People v. Capparelli, 68 A.D.2d 212, 416 N.Y.S.2d 798 (1st Dept. 1979).

—People did not sustain their burden of establishing that the period of delay was excludable due to exceptional circumstances since there was no evidence of "credible vigorous activity," but only the prosecutor's subjective assessment that the witnesses were in fear and were therefore unwilling to testify. People v. Meyers, 114 A.D.2d 861, 494 N.Y.S.2d 897 (2d Dept. 1985).

—Defendant's motion to dismiss the indictment was granted where the entire period of five months was chargeable to the People and the evidence established that the complaining witnesses were not unavailable but simply were not contacted; work load and shortage of personnel do not constitute "exceptional circumstances." People v. Warren, 85 A.D.2d 747, 445 N.Y.S.2d 797 (2d Dept. 1981).

—The delay due to a plea bargaining agreement with defendant whereby the People were to recommend lifetime probation upon defendant's plea of guilty to a class A-III felony in return for defendant's cooperation with the State Police in its narcotics investigation of certain individuals constituted a delay due to "exceptional circumstances" within the meaning of CPL § 30.30(4)(g) and was excludable from the computation of the time within which the People must be ready for trial. People v. Friscia, 70 A.D.2d 709, 416 N.Y.S.2d 669 (3d Dept. 1979).

—Although the unavailability of defendant did prevent the People from being ready for trial, that lack of readiness cannot be charged to the People because it was due to the exceptional fact or circumstance of the Governor's having signed an extradition order. People v. Buckley, 188 A.D.2d 1064, 1065, 591 N.Y.S.2d 913, 914 (4th Dept. 1992).

—Executive orders by governor mandated that any delay related to World Trade Center tragedy of September 11, 2001, during specified time period, constituted exceptional circumstances relieving prosecution of usual burden of demonstrating exceptional circumstances under speedy trial statute, and thus, delay during specified time period due to unavailability of police officer witness because of World Trade Center tragedy was excluded from speedy trial calculation in a misdemeanor prosecution as per se exceptional circumstance. People v. Wright, 193 Misc. 2d 207, 748 N.Y.S.2d 199 (N.Y.C. Crim. Ct. 2002). *But see* People v. Quinones, 190 Misc. 2d 648, 739 N.Y.S.2d 889 (Crim. Ct. Kings Co. 2002).

—Unavailability of evidence material to the prosecution's case may constitute exceptional circumstances sufficient to warrant exclusion of delays. People v. Mitchell, 158 Misc. 2d 768, 772, 601 N.Y.S.2d 677, 680 (Sup. Ct. Kings Co. 1993).

Plea bargain.—Seven-month delay, during which time police unsuccessfully sought defendant's cooperation, was not so excessive as to constitute an unreasonable delay, pursuant to CPL § 30.30(1)(a), where defendant had agreed to cooperate in police investigation as part of a plea bargain. People v. Friscia, 73 A.D.2d 702, 422 N.Y.S.2d 538 (3d Dept. 1979), *aff'd,* 51 N.Y.2d 845, 433 N.Y.S.2d 754, 413 N.E.2d 1168 (1980).

Co-defendant's motion.—Defendant's speedy trial motion was properly denied; during one of the periods of delay, the co-defendant's motion for severance was under consideration by the court, and thus, all of that time was excludable. People v. Coulter, 240 A.D.2d 756, 660 N.Y.S.2d 43 (2d Dept. 1997).

—Defendant was not denied his statutory right to a speedy trial because the time in which a co-defendant's motion to dismiss the indictment is pending is excludable. People v. Dary, 115 A.D.2d 996, 497 N.Y.S.2d 560 (4th Dept. 1985).

Fugitives.—People were entitled to rely on their general policy not to indict fugitive defendants and the period of the fugitive defendant's absence was properly excluded from the six month period contained in CPL § 30.30. People v. McShaw, 124 A.D.2d 829, 508 N.Y.S.2d 548 (2d Dept. 1986).

Due diligence.—Due diligence standard was not met where prosecution merely mailed a second letter to the defendant's last known address after a first letter had been returned marked "Address Not Known." People v. Orse, 118 A.D.2d 816, 500 N.Y.S.2d 173 (2d Dept. 1986).

Exceptional circumstances; unavailable witness due to medical reason. The unrefuted represented of the People constitutes sufficient proof of medical unavailability of a prosecution witness. The People are not required to show that the witness is completely immobilized or totally incapacitated or that they made extraordinary efforts to secure his presence. People v. Alcequier, 15 A.D.3d 162, 788 N.Y.S.2d 389 (1st Dept. 2005).

—Delay caused by officer's injury was properly excluded as exceptional circumstances, because the People represented to the court that the officer had broken her ankle and could not walk even with crutches. Such a representation by the People

was sufficient to permit the court to find that the adjournment was warranted. People v. Hernandez, 268 A.D.2d 344, 702 N.Y.S.2d 247 (1st Dept. 2000).

—Defendant's speedy trial claim was properly denied; the defendant failed to preserve his claim that the People furnished insufficient medical proof that the complainant was unable to testify during a period in which the court excluded under the exceptional circumstances exception. People v. Pagano, 207 A.D.2d 685, 616 N.Y.S.2d 366 (1st Dept. 1994).

—The 78-day delay attributable to the two arresting officers' subsequent injuries, fully documented by medical records, was properly excludable since the injuries constituted exceptional circumstances. People v. Pharr, 204 A.D.2d 126, 612 N.Y.S.2d 115 (1st Dept. 1994).

—Where necessary witness had a broken leg and was unable to testify, time was excludable under exceptional circumstances exception. People v. Celestino, 201 A.D.2d 91, 615 N.Y.S.2d 346 (1st Dept. 1994).

—Sixteen days should have been excluded from speedy trial period where a necessary witness was on medical leave during that time and unavailable to testify pursuant to CPL § 30.30(4)(g). People v. Moore, 234 A.D.2d 567, 651 N.Y.S.2d 590 (2d Dept. 1996).

—Delay borne of the undisputed medical unavailability of the complaining witness was excludable. People v. Martin, 142 A.D.2d 737, 531 N.Y.S.2d 312 (2d Dept. 1988).

—There is no requirement, in the speedy trial statute, that the unavailable evidence be critical or essential to the People's case before excluding an adjournment caused by the unavailability. People v. Wu, 136 Misc. 2d 558, 519 N.Y.S.2d 95 (Crim. Ct. N.Y. Co. 1987).

People's readiness.—Prosecution's request for a short delay in the continuation of the suppression hearing to permit the victim to make arrangements for a babysitter did not demonstrate the People's lack of readiness. People v. Hughes, 136 A.D.2d 916, 917, 89, 525 N.Y.S.2d 88 (4th Dept. 1988).

Court's delay.—The unavailability of the court due to vacation or for its own convenience is not chargeable to the People. People v. Brown, 195 A.D.2d 310, 311, 600 N.Y.S.2d 53, 54 (1st Dept. 1993); People v. Correa, 161 A.D.2d 391, 392, 555 N.Y.S.2d 715, 716 (1st Dept. 1990) (same).

Plea offer.—The period of delay resulting from giving the defendant more time to consider the plea offer was properly excludable. People v. Ali, 195 A.D.2d 368, 369, 600 N.Y.S.2d 55, 57 (1st Dept. 1993).

Excludable time.—Time properly chargeable to a party does not become chargeable to the opposition merely because the court subsequently renders a determination favorable to the proponent. People v. Bissereth, 194 A.D.2d 317, 318, 598 N.Y.S.2d 781, 782 (1st Dept. 1993).

—Delay from the filing of the indictment and issuance of the arrest warrant until the warrant squad's receipt of the warrant and commencement of its investigation is excludable as reasonable administrative delay inherent in processing of the warrant rather than a lack of due diligence. People v. Marrin, 187 A.D.2d 284, 285, 589 N.Y.S.2d 874, 876 (1st Dept. 1992).

—Time was excludable where People met their burden of showing the unavailability of a material witness, due diligence to secure her presence, and grounds for believing in her imminent availability. People v. Kato, 178 A.D.2d 381, 382, 578 N.Y.S.2d 143, 144 (1st Dept. 1991).

—Period in which defendant was the subject of a stayed bench warrant was excludable. People v. Espinosa, 170 A.D.2d 309, 310, 566 N.Y.S.2d 594, 595 (1st Dept. 1991); People v. Toro, 151 A.D.2d 142, 546 N.Y.S.2d 842 (1st Dept. 1989) (same).

—Adjournments requested by the People for the purpose of determining whether the victim of the crime would be able to testify were properly excluded pursuant to CPL § 30.30(4)(g). People v. Hammpud, 161 A.D.2d 179, 554 N.Y.S.2d 567 (1st Dept. 1990).

—Where People had announced their readiness for trial, time between deposition of Article 78 proceeding by Appellate Division and trial court placing the matter back on its calendar was excludable; the mere fact that the case was not restored to the court's calendar had no bearing on the People's readiness to proceed. People v. Chang, 176 A.D.2d 951, 952, 575 N.Y.S.2d 559, 560 (2d Dept. 1991).

—Delay was properly excluded where the prosecutor was

properly disqualified because of his association with the attorney representing the defendant earlier in the case. People v. Crandall, 199 A.D.2d 867, 606 N.Y.S.2d 357 (3d Dept. 1993).

—Where a trial is postponed to accommodate the court's calendar, the delay does not affect prosecutorial readiness, and is not chargeable to the People. People v. Vargas, 152 Misc. 2d 377, 380, 576 N.Y.S.2d 989, 991 (Sup. Ct. Bronx Co. 1991).

—Period of time during which the People investigated complaint of police brutality made by the co-defendant was excludable for speedy trial purposes. People v. Goggans, 150 Misc. 2d 79, 80, 568 N.Y.S.2d 1008, 1009 (Sup. Ct. Kings Co. 1991).

—Where a defendant has been given prior notice to appear in court and has failed to respond, resulting in the issuance of a bench warrant pursuant to CPL § 530.70, the period extending from the issuance of the warrant to the day defendant finally appears is excluded. People v. Brooks, 149 Misc. 2d 407, 565 N.Y.S.2d 955 (Sup. Ct. Kings Co. 1990).

Interstate situations.—Dismissal of indictment on ground defendant was not afforded a speedy trial was reversed where there was continuing communication between the office of the New York County District Attorney and the Pennsylvania authorities during 3 year period but Pennsylvania authorities held defendant pending the pursuit of their own criminal prosecution. People v. White, 51 A.D.2d 221, 380 N.Y.S.2d 230 (1st Dept. 1976).

—A 16-year delay between defendant's indictment and his return to New York after he was paroled in another state does not warrant dismissal because, during that time, the People diligently sought defendant's extradition from Virginia, where he was incarcerated, until those efforts proved futile. People v. Turner, 286 A.D.2d 514, 729 N.Y.S.2d 524 (2d Dept. 2001).

—When the district attorney made diligent and reasonable efforts to obtain return of defendant under the Interstate Agreement on Detainers but New Jersey officials refused, defendant was not denied a speedy trial because People were not ready for trial within six months of the commencement of the criminal action. People v. Mainor, 77 Misc. 2d 946, 355 N.Y.S.2d 263 (Sup. Ct. N.Y Co. 1974).

Failure to produce prisoner.—The District Attorney and the Department of Correctional Services are both agents of the State and the failure of the Department of Correctional Services to produce the defendant from September 21, 1973 to March 28, 1974 was chargeable to the District Attorney and the defendant's motion to dismiss the indictment was granted. People v. Scott, 56 A.D.2d 667, 392 N.Y.S.2d 55 (2d Dept. 1977).

Felony complaint dismissed in criminal court.—The six month period within which the People are required to be ready for trial is measured from the date of the filing of the felony complaint and not the indictment even when the complaint has been dismissed. People v. Haynes, 80 A.D.2d 620, 436 N.Y.S.2d 61 (2d Dept. 1981).

Filing of detainer insufficient to toll speedy trial period.—The mere filing of a detainer with regard to a defendant who is confined in another county, without any evidence that the District Attorney utilized the statutory procedures for securing the attendance of such defendant, is not a sufficient basis to exclude the period of defendant's incarceration from speedy trial calculations. People v. Billups, 105 A.D.2d 795, 481 N.Y.S.2d 430 (2d Dept. 1984).

—Defendant's claim of a denial of a speedy trial under CPL § 30.30 was abandoned when defendant proceeded to trial. People v. Rodriguez, 187 A.D.2d 291, 292, 589 N.Y.S.2d 873, 874 (1st Dept. 1992).

—Where People indicated that they had an available substitute trial assistant for the next day, the court also properly charged the People for only one additional day of post-readiness delay caused by the unavailability of the trial assistant. People v. Lourens, 208 A.D.2d 768, 617 N.Y.S.2d 779 (2d Dept. 1994).

Filing of notice.—The filing of a notice of intent to introduce statements or identification evidence at trial does not toll the running of the speedy trial statute, but the litigation prompted by the notice tolls the statute. People v. Bolden, 1 Misc. 3d 663, 766 N.Y.S.2d 324 (Crim. Ct. of City of N.Y. 2003).

Guilty plea.—By pleading guilty, defendant waived his statutory right to assert that he was entitled to dismissal because the People were not ready for trial within the time specified by CPL § 30.30, and therefore could not test the validity of that claim on appeal. People v. Thill, 52 N.Y.2d 1020, 438

N.Y.S.2d 297, 420 N.E.2d 95 (1981); *see also* People v. Friscia, 51 N.Y.2d 845, 433 N.Y.S.2d 754, 412 N.E.2d 1168 (1980); People v. Howe, 56 N.Y.2d 602, 450 N.Y.S.2d 477, 435 N.E.2d 1092 (1982); People v. Clary, 52 N.Y.2d 1023, 438 N.Y.S.2d 298, 420 N.E.2d 96 (1981).

— Violations of a defendant's right to a speedy trial are waived by a plea of guilty and the People's statement of readiness was not illusory merely because it antedated the defendant's timely arraignment. People v. McClure, 236 A.D.2d 633, 653 N.Y.S.2d 957 (2d Dept. 1997).

No retroactive invalidation of previous statement of readiness.—A statement on January 30, 1995 that the People were not then ready did not retroactively invalidate an earlier and otherwise valid statement of readiness. People v. Santana, 233 A.D.2d 344, 649 N.Y.S.2d 470 (2d Dept. 1996).

Habeas corpus.—Writ of habeas corpus may be used to obtain defendant's release pending trial of a felony indictment, pursuant to CPL § 30.30 (subd. 2), where People are not ready for trial within period of 90 days, and trial court must grant the motion by either setting a bail which the defendant can post or by releasing the defendant on his recognizance. People *ex rel.* Chakwin v. Wordan, 63 N.Y.2d 120, 480 N.Y.S.2d 719, 470 N.E.2d 146 (1984).

Hearing.—Court was not required to conduct a hearing on the speedy trial motion since the minutes of the adjournments conclusively established the excludability of the disputed periods. People v. Gama, 178 A.D.2d 173, 577 N.Y.S.2d 34 (1st Dept. 1991).

—In view of the considerable length of the delay between the defendant's arrest on unrelated charges and the return of the instant indictment—some 20 months—a proper balancing of the relevant factors demands that a hearing be conducted to determine the reasons if any for the prosecutorial hiatus and the degree to which the defense may have been prejudiced by the delay. People v. Vasquez, 79 A.D.2d 621, 433 N.Y.S.2d 471 (2d Dept. 1980).

—It was error for the trial court to summarily grant the defendant's motion to dismiss the indictment for violation of speedy trial rights without a hearing where the sworn allegations of fact essential to support the motion were neither conceded or conclusively established by unquestionable documentary proof. People v. Smith, 81 A.D.2d 965, 439 N.Y.S.2d 749 (3d Dept. 1981).

Incarceration within New York under an alias.—People should not be charged with that period of time in which defendant was incarcerated under a different name in a different county within the state and defendant's conduct, including his failure to appear for scheduled court dates and his use of different names, birthdays, social security numbers, and addresses strongly suggest that he was attempting to avoid apprehension. People v. Delacruz, 271 A.D.2d 452, 705 N.Y.S.2d 637 (2d Dept. 2000).

—Court erred in denying defendant's speedy trial motion without a hearing where several factual issues were raised in the motion papers as to whether the People exercised due diligence and made reasonable efforts to secure defendant's presence in the jurisdiction for trial. People v. Grant, 127 A.D.2d 965, 966, 512 N.Y.S.2d 747, 748 (4th Dept. 1987).

Intimidated witnesses.—Delay of seventeen years between date of crime and indictment in double homicide did not violate defendant's right to speedy trial where delay was based on good faith determination that prosecution could not go forward because witnesses were afraid to testify. Defendant was not prejudiced despite loss of police reports and gun linked to killings; moreover, remedies other than dismissal are available. People v. Vernace, 274 A.D.2d 595, 711 N.Y.S.2d 492 (2d Dept. 2000), *aff'd*, 96 N.Y.2d 886, 730 N.Y.S.2d 778, 756 N.E.2d 66 (2001).

Misdemeanor converted to felony; six-month period governs.—Where prosecution was commenced by filing of a misdemeanor complaint, but was later converted to felony prosecution, the case was governed by the six-month speedy trial period for felonies rather than the 90-day period for misdemeanors. People v. Cooper, 90 N.Y.2d 292, 660 N.Y.S.2d 546, 683 N.E.2d 11 (1997).

Murder cases.—Court erred in concluding that the time limitation of CPL § 30.30 was inapplicable to the prosecution because one of the charges was attempted murder in the first degree. People v. Williams, 130 A.D.2d 697, 698, 515 N.Y.S.2d 622, 623 (2d Dept. 1987).

—Statutory speedy trial considerations are inapplicable in cases where the defendant has been charged with a homicide. People v. Sullivan, 121 A.D.2d 658, 504 N.Y.S.2d 49 (2d Dept. 1986).

—Because the indictment charged defendant with murder in the second degree, the statutory speedy trial requirements do not apply. People v. Watson, 299 A.D.2d 735, 753 N.Y.S.2d 530 (3d Dept. 2002).

Motions generally.—Defendant's speedy trial motion was untimely where it was made after both sides announced their readiness for trial and there was a panel of jurors waiting outside the courtroom door. People v. Harvall, 196 A.D.2d 553, 554, 601 N.Y.S.2d 146, 148 (2d Dept. 1993).

Sister-state incarceration.—A sister-state incarceration may provide the requisite "good cause" if the prosecutor was unaware that the defendant was in the custody of the authorities of such state and could not with due diligence discover the defendant's whereabouts and secure his presence for trial in New York. People v. McLaurin, 38 N.Y.2d 123, 378 N.Y.S.2d 692, 341 N.E.2d 250 (1975).

Motion to dismiss information.—Defendant's motion was granted where shortly after the commencement of this action, the defendant absconded to Florida where he committed an offense unrelated to the present prosecution which the prosecution knew about; the prosecutor's failure to extradite him was a denial of his statutory right to a speedy trial. People v. Jensen, 109 Misc. 2d 952, 441 N.Y.S.2d 333 (1st Dist. Ct. Suffolk Co. 1981).

People's motion.—Speedy trial motion properly denied where the period in question was excludable as a reasonable delay resulting from the People's consolidation motion. People v. Wilson, 2 A.D.3d 185, 768 N.Y.S.2d 464 (1st Dept. 2003).

Effect of commencement of trial.—Motion to dismiss, on the ground that defendant's speedy trial rights were violated, was denied as untimely because the trial had commenced. People v. Warren, 81 A.D.2d 872, 439 N.Y.S.2d 41 (2d Dept. 1981).

Ninety-day rule; statute not tolled by delay caused by filing of improper instrument.—In granting motion to dismiss information on the ground that the People were not ready for trial within 90 days, the court ruled that the prosecution's error in drawing up a felony complaint, where the charge should have been a misdemeanor, would not be considered an "exceptional fact or circumstance" so as to toll the 90-day rule. People v. Lupo, 74 Misc. 2d 679, 345 N.Y.S.2d 348 (Crim. Ct. N.Y. Co. 1973).

Notice of readiness tolls clock.—Where People were not ready for trial, and the record was silent as to the length of adjournment the People sought, a notice of readiness satisfied the People's duty to be ready for trial, and served to toll the speedy trial clock from running. People v. Stirrup, 91 N.Y.2d 434, 671 N.Y.S.2d 433, 694 N.E.2d 434 (1998) (*abrogating* People v. Anderson, 231 A.D.2d 459, 647 N.Y.S.2d 737).

Offer of reduced plea.—People's offer to take a reduced plea did not automatically stop the running of their six months time in which to bring defendant to trial. People v. Wittman, 73 A.D.2d 1053, 425 N.Y.S.2d 416 (4th Dept. 1980).

Other proceedings.—Court improperly charged to People period of time during which People moved for leave to resubmit pursuant to CPL § 190.75(3). People v. Fluellen, 160 A.D.2d 219, 222, 553 N.Y.S.2d 670, 673 (1st Dept. 1990).

Effect of statute once readiness has been announced.—CPL § 30.30 requires that People be ready for trial within six months of commencement of criminal action, not that they are to afford defendant a trial within the prescribed statutory period, and once readiness for trial has been announced, the operational effect of the statute is exhausted. People v. Dillard, 79 A.D.2d 844, 434 N.Y.S.2d 509 (4th Dept. 1980).

Defendant's use of alias.—Indictment was dismissed because people failed to show what was done to apprehend defendant during the six year period following his indictment; the fact that he used another name is scarcely sufficient. People v. Beltran, 88 A.D.2d 830, 451 N.Y.S.2d 136 (1st Dept. 1982).

Placement of "P.I." calendar.—The burden is on the prosecution to bring defendant to trial within the prescribed time period, and no demand is required by him to trigger that obligation and the failure of the defendant to object to being placed on the "P.I." (Pending Indictment calendar) is not necessarily to be considered on acquiescence. People v. Magree,

103 Misc. 2d 212, 425 N.Y.S.2d 511 (Suffolk Co. Dist. Ct. 1980).

Placement of case on calendar by court.—The placement of the case on the trial calendar by the court without objection by the district attorney communicated the People's readiness for trial. People v. Burnoy, 90 A.D.2d 959, 456 N.Y.S.2d 894 (4th Dept. 1982).

Plea; appeal.—Defendant cannot preserve his statutory speedy trial claim for appellate review by obtaining the consent of the prosecutor and approval of the court at the time the plea was entered. People v. Thomas, 92 A.D.2d 876, 459 N.Y.S.2d 821 (2d Dept. 1983).

Plea of guilty; waiver of right to speedy trial.—A plea of guilty operates as a waiver of the right to a speedy trial. People v. Friscia, 51 N.Y.2d 845, 433 N.Y.S.2d 754, 413 N.E.2d 1168 (1980).

—Defendant forfeited his claim to dismissal of the indictment pursuant to CPL § 30.30 by his plea of guilty. People v. Howe, 56 N.Y.2d 602, 450 N.Y.S.2d 477, 435 N.E.2d 1092 (1982).

Readiness of People; absence of minutes.—Delays in production of court minutes were not chargeable to the People because the court reporters are not within the People's control. People v. Williams, 278 A.D.2d 44, 717 N.Y.S.2d 170 (1st Dept. 2000).

—Court erroneously attributed delay to People's failure to order the relevant minutes immediately upon receipt of defendant's motion, when the People were under no obligation to order the court minutes. Furthermore, the delay was caused by court stenographers, who are individuals not within the People's control. People v. Lacey, 260 A.D.2d 309, 690 N.Y.S.2d 182 (1st Dept. 1999).

—While burden is on People to ensure that an adequate record is made for court deciding a section 30.30 motion, People do not have burden of obtaining minutes of every adjourned date, challenged or not, in order to succeed on such a motion. People v. Notholt, 242 A.D.2d 251, 662 N.Y.S.2d 297 (1st Dept. 1997).

—People met speedy trial standards under CPL § 30.30 where they announced their readiness for trial within the required time, notwithstanding that they did not have the minutes from the defendant's parole revocation hearing when they announced their readiness; defendant was obviously aware of the statements made at the hearing and could have obtained the minutes thereof. People v. Anderson, 105 A.D.2d 38, 482 N.Y.S.2d 745 (1st Dept. 1984), *aff'd*, 66 N.Y.2d 529, 498 N.Y.S.2d 119, 488 N.E.2d 1231 (1985).

Readiness.—A statement of readiness for a hearing is not a substitute for a statement of trial readiness. People v. Chavis, 91 N.Y.2d 500, 673 N.Y.S.2d 29, 695 N.E.2d 1110 (1998).

—People cannot answer ready when wholly as a result of their own conduct defendant could not be arraigned, and thus trial could not commence. People v. England, 84 N.Y.2d 1, 613 N.Y.S.2d 854, 636 N.E.2d 1387 (1994).

—The unavailability of a particular assistant district attorney does not render the People's announcement of readiness ineffective, because another prosecutor could have tried the case. People v. Anderson, 252 A.D.2d 399, 676 N.Y.S.2d 549 (1st Dept. 1998).

—The People were not required to contact their witnesses on each and every adjourned date, and neither statute nor case law requires that the People have the ability to produce their witnesses instantaneously in order for a statement of readiness to be valid. People v. Dushain, 239 A.D.2d 151, 657 N.Y.S.2d 44 (1st Dept. 1997), *adhered to in* 247 A.2d 234, 669 N.Y.S.2d 30 (1st Dept. 1998).

—The trial court properly found that there was no speedy trial violation and excluded the time during which the People were prepared to go forward on the indictment while defendant was trial on another indictment; nor does CPL 30.30 impose an obligation on the People to be in regular contact with each of their witnesses while a defendant's other cases wind their way through the criminal justice system. People v. Hardy, 199 A.D.2d 49, 605 N.Y.S.2d 23 (1st Dept. 1993).

—The fact that formal laboratory results were not obtained until after the expiration of the CPL 30.30 statutory period did not mandate a finding that the prosecution's statement of readiness was illusory. People v. McCombs, 18 A.D.3d 888, 795 N.Y.S.2d 108 (3d Dept. 2005).

—The People cannot announce ready for trial prior to indictment; a notice of readiness served prior to the time of indictment is a nullity. People v. Benson, 200 A.D.2d 861, 606 N.Y.S.2d 828 (3d Dept. 1994).

—Announcement of readiness prior to arraignment is ineffective because a defendant may not be tried before he is arraigned. People v. Middlemiss, 198 A.D.2d 755, 756, 604 N.Y.S.2d 308, 309 (3d Dept. 1993).

—The People's statement of readiness was not illusory, even though they sought and obtained an adjournment for DNA testing after stating their readiness for trial. The People could have proceeded to trial without the DNA evidence, presenting the testimony of the victim and other witnesses. People v. Watkins, 17 A.D.3d 1083, 793 N.Y.S.2d 657 (4th Dept. 2005).

Readiness; defendant's presence unnecessary for announcement.—There is no requirement that a defendant be present in order to establish readiness for trial. People v. Carter, 91 N.Y.2d 795, 676 N.Y.S.2d 523, 699 N.E.2d 35 (1998).

Chargeable to the People.—The delay of over seven months which preceded defendant's arraignment in County Court constituted a direct impediment to commencement of the trial within the statutory period and was therefore chargeable to the People in the absence of any excuse or explanation for the delay. People v. Leavy, 204 A.D.2d 898 (3d Dept. 1994).

Readiness to proceed must be stated on the record.—The People, in order to be ready for trial so as to stop the running of speedy trial time, must communicate their readiness on the trial court's record, and that statement of readiness must be made when the People are in fact ready to proceed. People v. Kendzia, 64 N.Y.2d 331, 486 N.Y.S.2d 888, 476 N.E.2d 287 (1985).

—When the district attorney has announced his readiness on the record he has satisfied his obligation under CPL § 30.30. People v. Giordano, 56 N.Y.2d 524, 449 N.Y.S.2d 955, 434 N.E.2d 1333 (1982).

—The court refused to sustain the People's assertion that they were ready to proceed at an earlier date where the People had not communicated readiness for trial to the court on the record; it is insufficient as a matter of law to inform the court of such a claim for the first time in an affidavit submitted in response to a motion to dismiss the indictment. People v. Hamilton, 46 N.Y.2d 932, 415 N.Y.S.2d 208, 388 N.E.2d 345 (1979).

—Indictment should not have been dismissed on speedy trial grounds where prosecution answered ready within the necessary time, notwithstanding that the prosecution subsequently was not ready to proceed due to the absence of essential minutes of an earlier parole proceeding; the fact that the prosecution learned of such proceeding only after the initial statement of readiness did not negate such statement, especially since the defendant was aware of the prior proceeding and could have obtained the necessary minutes. People v. Anderson, 105 A.D.2d 38, 482 N.Y.S.2d 745 (1st Dept.), aff'd, 66 N.Y.2d 529, 498 N.Y.S.2d 119, 488 N.E.2d 1231 (1985).

—Prosecutor's statement of readiness, sent to court chambers, rather than to clerk, was sufficient. People v. Sutton, 199 A.D.2d 878, 606 N.Y.S.2d 408 (3d Dept. 1993).

—Six month limitation was not exceeded where the prosecutor communicated his readiness for trial by requesting the Administrative Judge to assign a judge to hear the case when no County Court judge was available. People v. Suarez, 80 A.D.2d 658, 436 N.Y.S.2d 408 (3d Dept. 1981), aff'd, 55 N.Y.2d 940, 449 N.Y.S.2d 176, 434 N.E.2d 245 (1982).

—The fact that the prosecutor provided notice of readiness to the court and not the court clerk does not mandate reversal, where, as here, defendant has suffered no prejudice as a result of this minor technical discrepancy. People v. Egan, 6 A.D.3d 1203, 776 N.Y.S.2d 667, subsequent appeal, 6 A.D.3d 1206, 775 N.Y.S.2d 714 (4th Dept. 2004).

—The mere announcement of readiness for trial by a prosecutor does not satisfy the People's statutory obligation because the People must be able to substantiate that they are in fact ready to proceed. People v. Hargo, 144 A.D.2d 971, 972, 534 N.Y.S.2d 274, 275 (4th Dept. 1988).

—Mere filing of supporting deposition without a further showing is insufficient to satisfy the "present readiness" requirement. People v. Foster, 135 Misc. 73, 77, 514 N.Y.S.2d 612, 615 (Crim. Ct. Kings Co. 1987).

Readiness to proceed; post-readiness delay.—Mere occurrence of delay by the People following a declaration of readiness does not warrant dismissal of the criminal action; inquiry must be made to determine whether the delay is excusable and whether, taking into account the delay before and after the announcement of readiness, the People's time to be ready for trial has expired. People v. Anderson, 66 N.Y.2d 529, 498 N.Y.S.2d 119, 488 N.E.2d 1231 (1985).

—A period of post-readiness delay may be charged to the People if the reason for the delay constitutes a direct and virtually insurmountable impediment to the trial's very commencement or has a direct bearing on the People's ability to present their case. People v. Sydney, 195 A.D.2d 763, 764, 600 N.Y.S.2d 358, 359 (3d Dept. 1993).

—Post-announcement delay caused by victim's medical problems is excludable. People v. Walker, 136 A.D.2d 949, 524 N.Y.S.2d 953 (4th Dept. 1988).

—An initial declaration of readiness does not end the People's continuing obligation to be ready for a trial, nor permanently deprive a defendant of the right to move for speedy trial relief. People v. Apodoca, 156 Misc. 2d 133, 137, 591 N.Y.S.2d 726, 729 (Sup. Ct. N.Y. Co. 1992).

Right to speedy trial; order for retrial.—Where there is an order for retrial in a felony case, the action is deemed to have been commenced, pursuant to CPL § 30.30(5)(a), on the date the order occasioning a retrial became final. People v. Pasquino, 100 Misc. 2d 1034, 420 N.Y.S.2d 658 (Sup. Ct. Westchester Co. 1979).

Six-month delay in execution of bench warrant.—Period of more than six months between the filing of the indictments and the first attempt to execute a bench warrant was not excludable from the speedy trial period; additionally, the period of more than six months between the dismissal of the felony complaint and the filing of the indictment also provided a basis for dismissal of the indictment. People v. Fuggazzatto, 62 N.Y.2d 862, 477 N.Y.S.2d 619, 466 N.E.2d 159 (1984).

Speedy trial after withdrawal of guilty plea.—For purposes of determining whether there was a denial of a speedy trial, the criminal action was deemed to have commenced when the defendant was permitted to withdraw his guilty plea (CPL § 30.30[5][a]). People v. Williams, 72 A.D.2d 950, 422 N.Y.S.2d 237 (4th Dept. 1979).

Speedy trial; dismissal of indictment for failure to prosecute; adjournments.—It was an abuse of discretion for trial court to dismiss indictment of possession of forged instruments and devices for failure to prosecute where the only request for adjournment made by the prosecution was to await decision from a federal court on a related case and where all prior adjournments were at request of defense or on consent. People v. Cangiano, 40 A.D.2d 528, 334 N.Y.S.2d 510 (2d Dept. 1972).

Speedy trial issue improperly raised on appeal.—A defendant who desires to raise the issue whether there has been compliance with the speedy trial statute must do so formally rather than as an added argument in an appellate brief, so that the People will have sufficient opportunity to put their side of the question before the court. People v. Hardy, 47 N.Y.2d 500, 419 N.Y.S.2d 49, 392 N.E.2d 1233 (1979).

Speedy trial; waiver of rights.—Defendant waived speedy trial claim by failing to raise such issue before or at trial in the trial court, notwithstanding that defendant did raise the issue before the Appellate Division in a pretrial habeas corpus motion that was denied and later dismissed on appeal to the Court of Appeals. People v. Jordan, 62 N.Y.2d 825, 477 N.Y.S.2d 605, 466 N.E.2d 145 (1984).

Speedy trial claim waived by guilty plea.—Defendant's plea of guilty operated as a waiver of speedy trial claim, claim that indictment was defective in that venue was not properly established as to two of the charged offenses, offenses were improperly joined, and that the evidence presented to the grand jury was insufficient. People v. Spears, 106 A.D.2d 417, 482 N.Y.S.2d 340 (2d Dept. 1984).

—Defendant waived appellate review of his statutory right to a speedy trial under CPL § 30.30 by pleading guilty. People v. Smith, 272 A.D.2d 679, 708 N.Y.S.2d 485 (3d Dept. 2000).

Fleeing defendant.—Defendant's speedy trial motion was properly denied where the four-year delay was caused primarily by defendant's failure to return to court for scheduled court dates, his interstate flight, and his use of an alias in order to avoid prosecution. People v. Hawkins, 290 A.D.2d 320, 736 N.Y.S.2d 39 (1st Dept. 2002).

—Defendant's use of a different name and other information in subsequent arrest established his intent to evade apprehension and prosecution and thereby relieved People of using due diligence to locate him. People v. Motz, 256 A.D.2d 46, 682 N.Y.S.2d 30 (1st Dept. 1998).

—Delay caused by the defendant's nonappearance for arraignment, due to the fact that he was, unbeknownst to the People, in jail on an unrelated charge under a different name, was excludable. People v. Johnson, 191 A.D.2d 709, 710, 595 N.Y.S.2d 515, 516 (2d Dept. 1993).

Defendant contributes to delay.—Delays occasioned by defendant's inadvertent release from the county jail and those occasioned at the request of the defendant were properly excluded in determining whether he was timely brought to trial. People v. Patterson, 38 N.Y.2d 623, 381 N.Y.S.2d 858, 345 N.E.2d 330 (1976).

—Delays of 22 and 29 months from arrest to trial on two separate indictments did not constitute a denial of the right to speedy trial where much of the delays were due to the defendant's actions in replacing his counsel. Delay alone does automatically breach the defendant's constitutional and statutory rights, but each case must be determined on the basis of the conduct of both the prosecution and the defendant. People v. Timothy, 34 N.Y.2d 867, 359 N.Y.S.2d 114, 316 N.E.2d 580 (1974).

—Defendant waived his constitutional right to a speedy trial where he affirmatively chose to remain in Vermont for a period of nine months to contest his extradition. People v. Iversen, 82 A.D.2d 895, 440 N.Y.S.2d 286 (2d Dept. 1981).

—A delay of 39 months between defendant's arrest and his plea of guilty did not violate his right to a speedy trial where much of the delay was due to interlocutory appeals, the court's calendar, and defense counsel's actions, and during this time the defendant remained at liberty; further, the defendant did not demonstrate any actual impairment of his defense. People v. Cole, 112 A.D.2d 472, 490 N.Y.S.2d 885 (3d Dept. 1985).

Time taken by court to rule on defendant's motions not includable for speedy trial purposes.—The court should not charge against the People for speedy trial purposes time taken to rule on defendant's motions where the District Attorney stated his readiness to proceed on the particular dates in question. People v. Moorhead, 61 N.Y.2d 851, 473 N.Y.S.2d 967, 462 N.E.2d 144 (1984).

—Time between date defendant was arraigned upon the first indictment and moved to dismiss the same, and the date the motion was returnable, was excludable since the delay resulted from defendant's pretrial motion notwithstanding the People's subsequent consent to the relief requested. People v. Pappas, 128 A.D.2d 556, 558, 512 N.Y.S.2d 493, 495 (2d Dept. 1987).

—People's tardiness in responding to defense motions, following their previous readiness for trial on two occasions, did not undermine their ability to proceed to trial and dismissal on speedy trial grounds was not a proper remedy; remedy for such tardiness was for the defendant to move to preclude the prosecution from controverting the allegations of the defendant's motion and for a decision upon the facts as alleged by the defense. People v. Amendolara, 135 Misc. 170, 179, 514 N.Y.S.2d 598, 605 (Sup. Ct. Kings Co. 1987).

Job suspension of defendant combined with 32-month delay.—Motion to dismiss for failure to grant a speedy trial was granted where thirty-two months had elapsed from the date of the incident and the defendant was a police officer who was suspended from the force for this period without pay. People v. Faulkner, 81 Misc. 2d 764, 366 N.Y.S.2d 965 (Sup. Ct. Westchester Co. 1975), aff'd, 54 A.D.2d 1141, 389 N.Y.S.2d 212 (1976).

Defendant's absence when the indictment was returned.—Since the period between the commencement of the criminal action and the time when the People were ready for trial, after deducting periods properly excludable, exceeded six months, the defendant was entitled to dismissal of the indictment for failure to afford her a speedy trial; defendant's absence of one and a half months when the indictment was returned did not result in a delay, attributable to her, since the finding of the indictment was in no way impeded or prevented by her

absence. People v. Sturgis, 38 N.Y.2d 625, 381 N.Y.S.2d 860, 345 N.E.2d 331 (1976).

Summons; action commenced.—For the purposes of a speedy trial in a prosecution instituted by the issuance of a summons, the time begins to run as of the date of issuance of the summons. People v. Eckert, 117 Misc. 2d 504, 458 N.Y.S.2d 494 (City Ct. Syracuse 1983).

Trial; voluntary absence from courtroom by defendant after warning; waiver of rights.—Where defendant voluntarily refused to attend trial after court order him to, he waived his right to be present and conviction for sodomy and assault were affirmed. People v. Epps, 71 Misc. 2d 1075, 338 N.Y.S.2d 297 (Sup. Ct. Kings Co. 1972), aff'd, 46 A.D.2d 890, 361 N.Y.S.2d 689 (2d Dept. 1974), aff'd, 37 N.Y.2d 343, 372 N.Y.S.2d 606, 334 N.E.2d 566 (1975).

Traffic infraction; speedy trial.—The right to a speedy trial does not attach to traffic violations, except for those traffic offenses that are classified as misdemeanors. People v. Pilewski, 173 Misc. 2d 800, 660 N.Y.S.2d 525 (Nassau Co. Ct. 1997).

—The mandate of CPL § 30.30 does not apply to criminal actions in which the defendant had been accused only of a traffic infraction from the outset. People v. Matute, 141 Misc. 2d 988, 535 N.Y.S.2d 524 (Crim. Ct. Bronx Co. 1988).

Trial of other charges.—Merely awaiting trial does not, without more, constitute participation in "other proceedings" or the actual "trial of other charges" within the meaning of CPL § 30.30(4). People v. Boyd, 123 A.D.2d 638, 506 N.Y.S.2d 904 (2d Dept. 1986).

Violation of probation hearing; inapplicability of speedy trial statute—A hearing on a violation of probation was not a criminal action but a criminal proceeding brought after completion of the criminal action, with the purpose of determining if defendant's subsequent actions violated the terms and conditions of his original sentence; since the time limitations of CPL article 30 are applicable only to criminal actions, the speedy trial provisions of CPL 30.30 do not apply to matters relating to a violation of probation. People v. Wong, 180 Misc. 2d 749, 692 N.Y.S.2d 904 (Sup. Ct. Queens Co. 1999).

Waiver of right to speedy trial.—A speedy trial motion must be made in writing prior to the commencement of trial or entry of a guilty plea and upon reasonable notice to the people; a failure to follow this statutorily prescribed procedure results in a waiver of the claim. People v. Lawrence, 64 N.Y.2d 200, 485 N.Y.S.2d 233, 474 N.E.2d 593 (1984).

—Only an intentional relinquishment or abandonment will suffice to surrender the constitutional right to a speedy trial; a silent record will not overcome the presumption against waiver. People v. Rodriquez, 50 N.Y.2d 553, 429 N.Y.S.2d 631, 407 N.E.2d 475 (1980).

—Where defendant did not argue before the motion court that the People's failure to respond to his speedy trial motion required dismissal of the indictment, that question was not preserved for appellate review. People v. Lugo, 161 A.D.2d 122, 123, 554 N.Y.S.2d 849, 850 (1st Dept. 1990).

—By failing to move to dismiss the indictment before trial on statutory speedy trial grounds, defendant waived any argument that he was denied his right to a speedy trial. People v. Felder, 201 A.D.2d 884, 607 N.Y.S.2d 792 (4th Dept. 1994).

Subd. 5

Reduction of charges; effect on readiness time-frame.—If a reduction in charges from a felony complaint to an information occurs early enough in the prosecution, as here, the 30.30(1) time frame associated with the most serious offense will determine the readiness time frame. CPL § 30.30(5)(c) was implicated when the felony complaint was replaced by an information three weeks after the filing of the initial accusatory instrument. A second reduction from class A to class B misdemeanor charges occurred. The subsequent reduction was not among the exceptions enumerated in CPL § 30.30(5), and it had no effect on the readiness equation because the People only expended 73 days of chargeable time. Accordingly, the prosecution was timely. People v. Cooper, 98 N.Y.2d 541, 750 N.Y.S.2d 258, 779 N.E.2d 1006 (2002).

ARTICLE 40—EXEMPTION FROM PROSECUTION BY REASON OF PREVIOUS PROSECUTION

LexisNexis Cross References

Defense of Drunk Driving Cases, Vol. 1, Ch. 7, Double Jeopardy and Rules Prohibiting Multiple Punishments and Prosecutions for a Single Act; *New York Criminal Practice (2d ed.),* Vol. 5, Ch. 55, Double Jeopardy.

§ 40.10. Previous prosecution; definitions of terms.

The following definitions are applicable to this article:

1. "Offense." An "offense" is committed whenever any conduct is performed which violates a statutory provision defining an offense; and when the same conduct or criminal transaction violates two or more such statutory provisions each such violation constitutes a separate and distinct offense. The same conduct or criminal transaction also establishes separate and distinct offenses when, though violating only one statutory provision, it results in death, injury, loss or other consequences to two or more victims, and such result is an element of the offense as defined. In such case, as many offenses are committed as there are victims.

2. "Criminal transaction" means conduct which establishes at least one offense, and which is comprised of two or more or a group of acts either (a) so closely related and connected in point of time and circumstance of commission as to constitute a single criminal incident, or (b) so closely related in criminal purpose or objective as to constitute elements or integral parts of a single criminal venture.

ANNOTATIONS

Appeals.—A double jeopardy defense based on the State and Federal Constitutions poses a question of law reviewable in the Court of Appeals despite the failure to raise it at the trial level. People v. Michael, 48 N.Y.2d 1, 420 N.Y.S.2d 371, 394 N.E.2d 1134 (1979).

—Although a defendant's statutory previous prosecution claim is waived by a plea of guilty, the constitutional double jeopardy claim survives a plea and may be raised for the first time on appeal. People v. Prescott, 66 N.Y.2d 216, 495 N.Y.S.2d 955, 486 N.E.2d 813 (1985).

Criminal transaction; definition.—The phrase "criminal transaction" in subd. (1)(a)(viii) of the first-degree murder statute was properly construed as incorporating the technical statutory definition contained in CPL 40.10(2). People v. Duggins, 3 N.Y.3d 522, 788 N.Y.S.2d 638, 821 N.E.2d 942 (2004).

Defense of double jeopardy valid.—The People are barred from appealing a trial order dismissing certain counts of defendant's indictment because it constitutes double jeopardy. People v. Consolazio, 40 N.Y.2d 446, 387 N.Y.S.2d 62, 354 N.E.2d 801, *cert. denied,* 433 U.S. 914 (1976).

Defense of double jeopardy waived.—Voluntarily entering guilty plea is a waiver of defense of double jeopardy. People *ex rel.* Williams v. Follette, 30 A.D.2d 693, 292 N.Y.S.2d 190 (2d Dept. 1968), *aff'd,* 24 N.Y.2d 949, 302 N.Y.S.2d 584, 250 N.E.2d 71 (1969).

—Defendant's plea constituted a valid waiver of any double jeopardy claim. People v. Almonte, 288 A.D.2d 632, 732 N.Y.S.2d 705 (3d Dept. 2001).

—New York and federal courts have recognized habeas corpus as a proper remedy on a claim of double jeopardy. People *ex rel.* Pendleton v. Smith, 83 Misc. 2d 503, 371 N.Y.S.2d 316 (Wyoming County Ct. 1975), *aff'd,* 54 A.D.2d 195, 388 N.Y.S.2d 426 (4th Dept. 1976).

Prior charges dismissed.—For defendant to be deemed to have been previously prosecuted, his prior charges must have proceeded to trial or terminated in conviction upon a plea; because prior charges against defendant were dismissed in City Court, double jeopardy did not bar his subsequent conviction. People v. Ruise, 248 A.D.2d 749, 669 N.Y.S.2d 711 (3d Dept. 1998).

Same transaction.—Joint trial of co-defendant charged in separate indictment with the sale of heroin and defendant and co-defendant jointly charged in second indictment with drug possession was proper since all of the offenses charged in both indictments stemmed from the same criminal transaction where evidence of the sale of heroin and of the presence of weapons in the bedroom would have been proper before the jury as a natural part of the narrative of events regardless of whether the indictments were consolidated for trial. People v. Lopez, 59 A.D.2d 767, 398 N.Y.S.2d 718 (2d Dept. 1977).

Same victim, offenses at different times.—Two rapes were perpetrated against the same victim, but the rape charge in the information arose out of an incident that occurred July 5, 1991 in Wells, and the rape charges in the indictment are based on incidents that took place in Lake Pleasant, between July 11, 1991 and September 25, 1991. Because of the temporal and spatial differences between the acts, the prosecution of the indictment was not barred by double jeopardy. People v. Van Nostrand, 217 A.D.2d 800, 630 N.Y.S.2d 101 (3d Dept. 1995).

Waiver of defense; second guilty plea waives double jeopardy defense as to first.—Where defendant with counsel entered a second plea without protest of double jeopardy and received a greater penalty upon resentencing, he has waived double jeopardy defense. People v. Soules, 38 A.D.2d 637, 326 N.Y.S.2d 894 (3d Dept. 1971).

§ 40.20. Previous prosecution; when a bar to second prosecution.

1. A person may not be twice prosecuted for the same offense.

2. A person may not be separately prosecuted for two offenses based upon the same act or criminal transaction unless:

(a) The offenses as defined have substantially different elements and the acts establishing one offense are in the main clearly distinguishable from those establishing the other; or

(b) Each of the offenses as defined contains an element which is not an element of the other, and the statutory provisions defining such offenses are designed to prevent very different kinds of harm or evil; or

(c) One of such offenses consists of criminal possession of contraband matter and the other offense is one involving the use of such contraband matter, other than a sale thereof; or

(d) One of the offenses is assault or some other offense resulting in physical injury to a person, and the other offense is one of homicide based upon the death of such person from the same physical injury, and such death occurs after a prosecution for the assault or other non-homicide offense; or

(e) Each offense involves death, injury, loss or other consequence to a different victim; or

(f) One of the offenses consists of a violation of a statutory provision of another jurisdiction, which offense has been prosecuted in such other jurisdiction and has there been terminated by a court order expressly founded upon insufficiency of evidence to establish some element of such offense which is not an element of the other offense, defined by the laws of this state; or

(g) The present prosecution is for a consummated result offense, as defined in subdivision three of section 20.10, which occurred in this state and the offense was the result of a conspiracy, facilitation or solicitation prosecuted in another state.

(h) One of such offenses is enterprise corruption in violation of section 460.20 of the penal law, racketeering in violation of federal law or any comparable offense pursuant to the law of another state and a separate or subsequent prosecution is not barred by section 40.50 of this article.

Amended by L. 1984, Ch. 624; L. 1986, Ch. 516.

ANNOTATIONS

Acquittal of one defendant; subsequent trial of co-defendant.—An acquittal of one defendant on a prior trial does not operate to preclude a subsequent trial or conviction of a second defendant, although both were indicted in connection with the same transaction, or even where the second was charged with aiding and abetting the first. People v. Rasero, 62 A.D.2d 845, 406 N.Y.S.2d 458 (1st Dept. 1978).

Administrative penalty; no double jeopardy.—Double jeopardy was not violated by defendant's administrative penalty of confinement to a special housing unit as a disciplinary sanction for his prison escape and defendant's criminal penalty of 3½to 7-year prison term for the same escape. People v. Hart, 244 A.D.2d 715, 664 N.Y.S.2d 645 (3d Dept. 1997).

Collateral estoppel.—The doctrine of collateral estoppel did

not preclude the People from relitigating suppression issues previously resolved in Federal Court since at least two of the legal criteria for the doctrine, identity of the parties and identity of the issues, were not satisfied. People v. Nezaj, 154 A.D.2d 296, 297, 546 N.Y.S.2d 373, 374 (1st Dept. 1989).

—A Grand Jury's decision not to return an indictment on the ground of insufficient legal evidence does not contain the finality requisite to the application of the doctrine of collateral estoppel. People v. Estes, 202 A.D.2d 516, 609 N.Y.S.2d 62 (2d Dept. 1994).

—Collateral estoppel applies in criminal matters only when there has been a valid and final judgment in the prior proceeding. People v. Moore, 142 A.D.2d 895, 896, 531 N.Y.S.2d 397, 398 (3d Dept. 1988).

—Collateral estoppel will apply in a criminal case only if the parties are the same or are so closely related that they may be deemed as one for these purposes and the issues are identical. People v. De Simone, 138 Misc. 2d 722, 525 N.Y.S.2d 520 (Sup. Ct. Queens Co. 1988).

Conviction of lesser included offense.—The acquit-first instruction discussed in *People v. Boettcher,* 69 N.Y.2d 174, 513 N.Y.S.2d 83, 505 N.E.2d 594 (1987), which requires a unanimous verdict of not guilty of the greater offense before the jury may consider any lesser-included offense, is mandatory and, in this case, the effect of the trial court's improper instruction was that it operated under the Double Jeopardy Clause to bar retrial on unresolved murder and manslaughter charges because the jury convicted defendant of criminally negligent homicide as a lesser included offense of manslaughter. People v. Helliger, 96 N.Y.2d 462, 729 N.Y.S.2d 654, 754 N.E.2d 756 (2001). *See also* People v. Helliger, 189 Misc. 2d 227, 730 N.Y.S.2d 846 (Sup. Ct. N.Y. Co. 2001) (subsequent decision in which the trial judge who presided over the case explained that he would in the future give an acquittal-first instruction).

—Trial judge accepted a partial verdict in which the jury acquitted on both robbery counts, convicted on third degree assault, but deadlocked on second degree assault. After defendant was sentenced for third degree assault, he was retried and convicted of second degree assault, which was error. Defendant was deemed acquitted of second degree assault when the jury failed to reach a verdict on that count, but found him guilty of the lesser included third degree assault. Retrial was prohibited under double jeopardy. People v. Fuller, 96 N.Y.2d 881, 730 N.Y.S.2d 773, 756 N.E.2d 61 (2001).

Two distinct statutory provisions.—The test for determining whether two offenses are the same within the meaning of the double jeopardy clause is whether two distinct statutory provisions each require proof of a fact that the other does not. People v. Prescott, 66 N.Y.2d 216, 495 N.Y.S.2d 955, 486 N.E.2d 813 (1985).

—The defendant could only be convicted of one count where his burglary convictions were based on the same illegal entry. People v. Sillaway, 144 A.D.2d 959, 534 N.Y.S.2d 615 (4th Dept. 1988).

Defense of double jeopardy valid.—A person who has previously pleaded guilty to the misdemeanor of driving while intoxicated as well as to a related traffic infraction, may not be subsequently prosecuted on homicide, assault and other charges arising out of the same incident when the prosecution concedes its intention to use the facts underlying the former conviction to establish the elements of the latter crimes. Corbin v. Hillery, 74 N.Y.2d 71, 545 N.Y.S.2d 71, 543 N.E.2d 714 (1989).

—The indictment for murder in New York must be dismissed where the defendant had previously been acquitted in Maryland of the crime of conspiracy to commit the murder. Wiley v. Altman, 76 A.D.2d 701, 431 N.Y.S.2d 826 (1st Dept. 1980), *aff'd,* 52 N.Y.2d 410 438 N.Y.S.2d 490, 420 N.E.2d 371 (1981).

Demand-waiver rule.—The "demand-waiver" rule provides that when a demand for a mistrial is at the defendant's request it operates as a waiver of any double jeopardy claim that a defendant might have to the reprosecution of the case before the same or a different tribunal, since the defendant sought the relief of the new trial. People v. Cavallerio, 104 Misc. 2d 436, 428 N.Y.S.2d 585 (Sup. Ct. Bronx Co. 1980).

Dismissal for insufficient evidence; acquittal.—Supreme Court's withdrawal of intentional murder counts from jury's consideration on the ground that there was insufficient evidence to support those charges constituted an acquittal for purposes of double jeopardy, and the first-degree manslaughter was the same offense as intentional murder for constitutional double jeopardy purposes such that an acquittal of the greater offense precluded further prosecution for the lesser offense. People v. Biggs, 1 N.Y.3d 225, 771 N.Y.S.2d 49, 803 N.E.2d 370 (2003).

—A dismissal for insufficient evidence at the end of a prior trial is an acquittal for double jeopardy purposes. People v. Davis, 91 A.D.2d 948, 458 N.Y.S.2d 563 (1st Dept. 1983).

Dismissal for insufficient evidence; indictment on same facts in another county; no double jeopardy.—Where eavesdropping warrant and search warrant are controverted and the evidence suppressed and the indictment is dismissed for insufficient evidence, there was no prosecution and an indictment in another county on the same facts is not double jeopardy. McGrath v. Gold, 36 N.Y.2d 406, 369 N.Y.S.2d 62, 330 N.E.2d 35 (1975).

Dismissal for insufficient evidence; retrial.—Defendant motion's to dismiss the indictment which was made prior to start of second trial should have been granted, where the only count in the indictment had been dismissed during the first trial due to insufficiency of evidence and the court later declared a mistrial because the jury was unable to reach a verdict on the lesser counts submitted to them, since the sole count it contains is not prosecutable under settled double jeopardy principles; however, further prosecution was not foreclosed pursuant to a new indictment containing such criminal charges as are not barred by the double jeopardy rule. People v. Mayo, 48 N.Y.2d 245, 422 N.Y.S.2d 361, 397 N.E.2d 1166 (1979).

Different victims.—Regardless of whether the court found that the offenses charged under the indictments 534 and 535 were based upon the same act or transaction, there was no bar on the ground of double jeopardy under CPL § 40.20(2)(e) since the offenses under each indictment involved loss or other consequence to different victims. People v. Dean, 56 A.D.2d 242, 392 N.Y.S.2d 134 (4th Dept. 1977), aff'd, 45 N.Y.2d 651, 412 N.Y.S.2d 353, 384 N.E.2d 1277 (1978).

—Different victims exception set forth in CPL § 40.20 (2e) is available only where each of the offenses, in the separate prosecutions, involves one or more specific, individually identifiable victims. Kaplan v. Ritter, 71 N.Y.2d 222, 525 N.Y.S.2d 1, 519 N.E.2d 882 (1987).

Different offenses.—Defendant's alleged receipt of bribes from contractors was not same transaction as his offering of bribes to fellow public servant who assisted him in leaking information to the contractors, so that his acquittal on charges of accepting bribes did not preclude conviction for offering bribes. People v. Simpson, 214 A.D.2d 352, 625 N.Y.S.2d 488 (1st Dept. 1995).

—Perjury was not same offense as second-degree murder or manslaughter for purposes of constitutional and statutory protections against double jeopardy. People v. Esposito, 225 A.D.2d 928, 640 N.Y.S.2d 274 (3d Dept. 1996).

—Because right to indictment by grand jury is public fundamental right, which is basis of jurisdiction to try and punish individual, filing of indictment bars prosecution, by any other means in any state court, of any offense arising out of same criminal transaction, except to extent permitted by statute governing separate prosecution for two offenses based upon same act or criminal transaction. Cummings v. Koppell, 212 A.D.2d 11, 627 N.Y.S.2d 480 (3d Dept. 1995).

Double jeopardy not present.—Where the legislature intended to impose cumulative punishments for a single offense, no constitutional double jeopardy claim is implicated. People v. Gonzalez, 99 N.Y.2d 76, 751 N.Y.S.2d 830, 781 N.E.2d 894 (2002).

—The prohibition against double jeopardy is not implicated when a defendant receives cumulative or multiple punishments for the same offense in a single prosecution as opposed to successive prosecutions. People v. Leung, 272 A.D.2d 88, 712 N.Y.S.2d 88 (1st Dept. 2000).

—An order setting aside a verdict on the grounds of legal insufficiency immediately after a bench trial is not tantamount to an acquittal. People v. Fowler, 154 A.D.2d 272, 273, 546 N.Y.S.2d 97, 98-99 (1st Dept. 1989).

—Treble-damage remedy provided for in Social Services Law did not violate constitutional provision against double jeopardy although defendant had previously pleaded guilty to crimes involving the filing of the false Medicaid claim forms. S

Harvey-Cook v. Miroff, 130 A.D.2d 621, 515 N.Y.S.2d 551 (2d Dept. 1987).

—After defendants' convictions under the Federal Travel Act were overturned on appeal, the defendants were indicted for conspiracy, bribery, and other offenses based upon the same act or criminal transaction in the state court and claimed double jeopardy; however, since the federal offense was terminated because of insufficient evidence to show use of interstate facilities and this is not an essential element in the crimes prosecuted under the Penal Law, the subsequent state prosecution is permissible. Klein v. Murtagh, 44 A.D.2d 465, 355 N.Y.S.2d 622 (2d Dept. 1974), aff'd, 34 N.Y.2d 988, 360 N.Y.S.2d 416, 318 N.E.2d 606 (1974).

—The provisions against double jeopardy do not bar prosecution for larceny arising out of a fraudulent multi-county investment scheme in one county although defendant was convicted on similar charges in another county, where the larcenies charged in each count are separate and distinct from each other and from the larcenies charged in the other county, and the alleged takings were not from a common owner and did not take place at the same time or from the same place. People v. Luongo, 58 A.D.2d 896, 397 N.Y.S.2d 98 (2d Dept. 1977), aff'd, 47 N.Y.2d 418, 418 N.Y.S.2d 365, 391 N.E.2d 1341 (1979).

—Defendant's successful appeal from his conviction did not result in a double jeopardy bar to reprosecution. People v. Putnam, 150 A.D.2d 925, 926, 541 N.Y.S.2d 269, 270 (3d Dept. 1989).

—Prosecution for second degree murder in New York was not barred by reason of a previous Maryland prosecution for conspiracy since the Maryland conspiracy statute and the New York homicide statute (1) each contained an element which was not an element of the other and (2) the two statutes were designed to prevent very different kinds of harm or evil. People v. Wiley, 104 Misc. 2d 114, 429 N.Y.S.2d 519 (Sup. Ct. N.Y. Co. 1980).

Felony murder and burglary; no double jeopardy.—Defendant's previous burglary conviction did not preclude on statutory double jeopardy grounds the subsequent prosecution for felony murder based on burglary, and the subsequent prosecution was also not precluded on constitutional double jeopardy grounds. People v. Carr, 267 A.D.2d 1062, 703 N.Y.S.2d 846 (4th Dept. 1999).

Prohibition available for offenses based on same act.—Since criminal possession of a weapon is a continuing offense, defendant was protected by double jeopardy principle from being prosecuted in two separate counties for his possession of the same weapon at different times, and places during the six days he possessed it. Johnson v. Morgenthau, 69 N.Y.2d 148, 150, 512 N.Y.S.2d 797, 799-800, 505 N.E.2d 240, 241 (1987).

—Petitioners, who had previously been convicted of conspiracy in federal court, sought relief in nature of prohibition after being charged with narcotics offenses where one of the overt acts proved in federal conspiracy prosecution was possession of the same drugs which formed the basis of the State charges; court held that prohibition was available as to the offenses based on the same act but relief should not have been extended to barring prosecution on other charges. Abraham v. Justices of N.Y. Sup. Ct. Bronx Co., 37 N.Y.2d 560, 376 N.Y.S.2d 79, 338 N.E.2d 597 (1975).

Merger.—As a matter of definition, the Constitution precludes only "the prosecution of a defendant who has himself previously been acquitted of another crime based on the same transaction, where the prior acquittal necessarily involved a rejection by the jury of some factual element necessary to the new prosecution"; double jeopardy cannot therefore be implicated within the context of a single prosecution. People v. Burgos, 177 A.D.2d 314, 315, 576 N.Y.S.2d 101, 102 (1st Dept. 1991).

—Defendant failed to preserve for appellate review his claim that his conviction for kidnapping was barred by the judicially-created merger doctrine. People v. Salami, 159 A.D.2d 658, 552 N.Y.S.2d 964 (2d Dept. 1990).

—Where asportation of the victims was for the purpose of accomplishing the sexual assaults, the kidnapping were an inherent part of those crimes and the merger doctrine should be applied. People v. Williams, 141 A.D.2d 783, 784, 529 N.Y.S.2d 859, 861 (2d Dept. 1988).

Double jeopardy; plea to misdemeanor over prosecutor's

objection.—Double jeopardy principles will not apply where court unlawfully reduced pending felony complaint charges to a misdemeanor without the consent of the district attorney, allowed the defendant to plead guilty and sentenced defendant on the reduced charge in full satisfaction of the complaint, and defendant was thereafter indicted. People *ex rel.* Leventhal v. Warden, 102 A.D.2d 317, 477 N.Y.S.2d 332 (1st Dept. 1984).

Guilty plea.—A guilty plea will not constitute a waiver if there is or has been a vindictive or retaliatory escalation of crime charged or sentence imposed for a defendant who pursued his constitutional rights. A similar preclusion of waiver may arise if the plea proceedings are directly affected by antecedent unconstitutionality. People v. La Ruffa, 37 N.Y.2d 58, 371 N.Y.S.2d 434, 332 N.E.2d 312 (1975).

—While a constitutional claim of double jeopardy survives a guilty plea, a claim of statutory previous prosecution does not. People v. Ortiz, 127 A.D.2d 305, 308, 515 N.Y.S.2d 317, 319 (3d Dept. 1987).

Impanelling and swearing of jury.—Defendant's contention that he was prosecuted twice for the same offense was without merit since at the time the court declared a mistrial as to one of the counts of the indictment no juror had been impaneled and sworn. People v. Hushie, 145 A.D.2d 506, 535 N.Y.S.2d 445 (2d Dept. 1988).

—Defendant was not placed in jeopardy where mistrial was granted, after four jurors were selected and sworn, due to unavailability of indispensable witness since the statute provided that jeopardy attached only after first witness was sworn and federal standard, extended to states by Benton v. Maryland, was that jury must be impaneled and sworn before jeopardy attaches. People v. Scott, 40 A.D.2d 933, 337 N.Y.S.2d 640 (4th Dept. 1972).

Juvenile.—In juvenile cases, like adult proceedings, jeopardy does not attach until the first witness has been sworn. Kevin B. v. Timothy L., 128 A.D.2d 63, 514 N.Y.S.2d 971 (1st Dept. 1987), *aff'd,* 71 N.Y.2d 835, 527 N.Y.S.2d 734, 522 N.E.2d 1032 (1988).

Mistrial.—Where a court declares a mistrial without obtaining the defendant's consent—defendant acquitted of assault—our State constitution and the Federal Constitution prohibit a retrial for the same crime unless there is a manifest necessity for the mistrial, or the ends of public justice would otherwise be defeated. People v. Michael, 48 N.Y.2d 1, 420 N.Y.S.2d 371, 394 N.E.2d 1134 (1979).

—No double jeopardy bar to a retrial existed where the declaration of a mistrial during the original trial was based on unavailability of a critical witness and was clearly based on "manifest necessity." People v. Sorenson, 80 A.D.2d 878, 436 N.Y.S.2d 745 (2d Dept. 1981).

—Petitioner's constitutional right not to be placed in double jeopardy would be violated by re-prosecution where court declared a mistrial without first granting a brief adjournment in order to give petitioner an opportunity to be present at his trial. Torres v. Justices of the Supreme Court, 82 A.D.2d 892, 440 N.Y.S.2d 294 (2d Dept. 1981).

Manifest necessity for mistrial; no double jeopardy.—Where a mistrial is declared without the consent of defense counsel, state and federal law prohibit retrial for the same crime, unless there is a manifest necessity for the declaration of a mistrial or the ends of public justice would otherwise be defeated. Enright v. Siedlecki, 59 N.Y.2d 195, 464 N.Y.S.2d 418, 451 N.E.2d 176 (1983).

Mistrial; no double jeopardy.—Double jeopardy does not bar retrial of a defendant where the first trial was aborted, without the defendant's consent, when the jurors reached an impasse and were unable to arrive at a verdict. People v. Baptiste, 72 N.Y.2d 356, 533 N.Y.S.2d 853, 530 N.E.2d 377 (1988).

—Mistrial granted on application of the People, after the jury had been sworn but before any witnesses had been called, did not preclude a subsequent trial because of double jeopardy either within the New York rule or within the federal rule, where the missing witnesses had been threatened by the defendant. People v. Paquette, 31 N.Y.2d 379, 339 N.Y.S.2d 959, 292 N.E.2d 17 (1972).

—Contrary to defendant's contentions, CPL §§ 300.50(4) and 300.40(3) do not require that his petit larceny conviction at his first trial be deemed an acquittal of the robbery charge, upon which the first jury was unable to reach a unanimous verdict.

Accordingly, his retrial on the robbery count did not violate double jeopardy. People v. Williams, 298 A.D.2d 163, 751 N.Y.S.2d 170 (1st Dept. 2002).

—Where a juror was hospitalized after the jury had already begun deliberating and the alternate jurors had already been dismissed, it was proper for the court to declare a mistrial over defendant's objection, and double jeopardy did not bar retrial. People v. Ramchair, 308 A.D.2d 601, 764 N.Y.S.2d 725 (2d Dept. 2003).

—Where a mistrial was granted at the request of the defendant's trial counsel and there is no evidence of bad faith, or of an attempt by the prosecutor to provoke a mistrial motion, retrial is not barred by the double jeopardy protections. Jordan v. O'Dwyer, 152 A.D.2d 671, 543 N.Y.S.2d 737 (2d Dept. 1989).

—Absent a showing that the prosecutor deliberately provoked the mistrial, a defendant's motion for a mistrial bars a double jeopardy claim. People v. Holmes, 128 A.D.2d 727, 728, 513 N.Y.S.2d 221, 222 (2d Dept. 1987); People v. Ilker, 81 A.D.2d 645, 438 N.Y.S.2d 149 (2d Dept. 1981) (same).

—Reprosecution was not barred by defendant's double jeopardy right where court ordered a mistrial and discharged the jury when it could not reach a verdict. People v. Brown, 128 A.D.2d 886, 887, 513 N.Y.S.2d 810, 811 (2d Dept. 1987).

—Mistrial granted due to inadvertent testimony of prosecution witness did not give rise to double jeopardy bar to retrial where the error was not attributable to any bad faith or intentional act on the part of the prosecutor or his witness. People v. Gemmill, 146 A.D.2d 951, 537 N.Y.S.2d 80 (3d Dept. 1989).

—Where a mistrial is ordered on a defendant's motion, double jeopardy is not a bar to a retrial unless the error which prompted the defendant's motion was the result of deliberate prosecutorial conduct which was intended to provoke the defendant into moving for a mistrial. Owen v. Harrigan, 131 A.D.2d 20, 22, 520 N.Y.S.2d 271, 273 (3d Dept. 1987).

—Where mistrial was granted on the defendant's motion and there was no evidence that the prosecutor intentionally provoked it, the reprosecution was not barred by the double jeopardy clauses of either the Federal or State Constitutions. People v. Presley, 136 A.D.2d 949, 525 N.Y.S.2d 84 (4th Dept. 1988).

Offenses different in time.—The act of possession of obscene material on September 26, 1976 was sufficiently separate in point of time as to be clearly distinguishable from possession of obscene material on October 2, 1976, and defendant could properly be charged with promotion of obscene materials on both days. Braunstein v. Frawley, 64 A.D.2d 772, 407 N.Y.S.2d 250 (3d Dept. 1978).

Offenses different in time and substance.—Where defendant discharged loaded handgun, abandoned the weapon, and later retrieved it, court held that successive prosecutions for his separate possessions of the weapon did not violate the defendant's constitutional or statutory double jeopardy rights. Pemberton v. Turner, 124 A.D.2d 338, 508 N.Y.S.2d 294 (3d Dept. 1986).

Previous prosecution in federal court.—Each of federal crime committed by defendants contained element that is not element of any of state crime for which defendants were prosecuted; thus, sequential state prosecution was lawful. People v. Bryant, 92 N.Y.2d 216, 677 N.Y.S.2d 286, 699 N.E.2d 910 (1998).

—The statutory previous prosecution claim, pursuant to CPL § 40.20, was waived by the defendant's plea of guilty and was not preserved for appellate review. People v. Dodson, 48 N.Y.2d 36, 421 N.Y.S.2d 47, 396 N.E.2d 194 (1979).

—Defendant's conviction in Federal court for conspiracy to distribute cocaine precluded subsequent prosecution in this State for the sale which concededly was part of the conspiracy and whether the sale was alleged, proven or even known to the Federal authorities is of no consequence. People v. Vera, 47 N.Y.2d 825, 418 N.Y.S.2d 575, 392 N.E.2d 562 (1979).

—When the substantive drug offense was not, but could have been, alleged and proved in the prior Federal conspiracy prosecution, subsequent State prosecution offends the statutory mandate; whether charges are disposed of by plea or trial bears no functional or logical relationship to whether they arise out of the same "criminal transaction." People v. Abbamonte, 43 N.Y.2d 74, 400 N.Y.S.2d 766, 371 N.E.2d 485 (1977).

—State was not precluded from charging defendant with sale of cocaine where federal court could have alleged it in the conspiracy prosecution since the defendant's own testimony revealed that the drug sale was a separate transaction. People v. Lieberman, 79 A.D.2d 175, 436 N.Y.S.2d 12 (1st Dept. 1981).

Previous prosecution in a state court.—Later prosecution was barred where the prosecution for criminal sale of a controlled substance was based upon acts which were or could have been received as proof of the conspiracy for which defendant had been previously prosecuted. People v. Nunez, 74 A.D.2d 652, 425 N.Y.S.2d 37 (2d Dept. 1980).

—Motion to dismiss was granted where the defendant was convicted of larceny in Massachusetts and was subsequently indicted for criminal possession of the same stolen property in New York because the crimes were so closely related in criminal purpose and objective as to constitute elements of a single criminal venture. People v. Lennon, 80 A.D.2d 672, 436 N.Y.S.2d 385 (3d Dept. 1981).

—Where court improperly vacated defendant's plea without defendant's consent, and defendant was thereafter tried on the indictment charging him with the same acts charged in the felony complaint to which he had pleaded guilty, he was twice prosecuted for the same offense and his double jeopardy rights were violated. People v. Searcy, 2 A.D.3d 1395, 770 N.Y.S.2d 493 (4th Dept. 2003).

Prior proceedings nullified; no double jeopardy.—Where, as here, proceedings constituting a prior prosecution are subsequently nullified by a court order directing a new trial of the same accusatory instrument, the nullified proceedings do not bar further prosecution of the offense under the same accusatory instrument. Kelly v. Bruhn, 3 A.D.3d 783, 771 N.Y.S.2d 561 (3d Dept. 2004).

Prison disciplinary proceeding; no double jeopardy.—It is well settled that state and federal constitutional double jeopardy provisions do not protect defendant from being sentenced in criminal prosecution for conduct which had been subject of prison disciplinary sanctions. People v. Walnut, 253 A.D.2d 910, 679 N.Y.S.2d 159 (3d Dept. 1998).

—Being punished for the same offense as the result of a prior prison disciplinary matter does not bar a subsequent criminal conviction based on the same conduct. People v. Taylor, 235 A.D.2d 719, 653 N.Y.S.2d 385 (3d Dept. 1997); *see also* People v. Thomas, 236 A.D.2d 764, 655 N.Y.S.2d 107 (3d Dept. 1997).

—A prison disciplinary proceeding which results in the loss of an inmate's privileges, including one year of good time, but does not result in the imposition of an additional sentence, does not form the basis for a claim of double jeopardy as to criminal charges based on the same acts covered by the disciplinary hearing. People v. Briggs, 108 A.D.2d 1058, 485 N.Y.S.2d 861 (3d Dept. 1985).

Reconsideration of the verdict by the judge.—Reversal was warranted where judge, after rendering a verdict, allowed prosecutor to reopen his case thereby violating the defendant's protection against double jeopardy. People v. Warren, 80 A.D.2d 905, 437 N.Y.S.2d 19 (2d Dept. 1981).

Single indictment and plea; no double jeopardy.—Conviction of DWI (VTL § 1192(1)) and first degree aggravated unlicensed operation of motor vehicle (VTL § 511(3)) did not violate or implicate double jeopardy; although commission of DWI is an element of AUO in the first degree and does not require proof of an additional fact which AUO in the first degree does not, because both charges were contained in a single indictment and were disposed of by a single plea, and the sentences for both convictions must be concurrent. People v. Khan, 291 A.D.2d 898, 737 N.Y.S.2d 738 (4th Dept. 2002).

Sufficient evidence; no double jeopardy.—Because the evidence with respect to the burglary charge was legally sufficient at the first trial, the retrial on that charge did not violate the constitutional prohibition against double jeopardy. People v. Montgomery, 1 A.D.3d 984, 767 N.Y.S.2d 533 (4th Dept. 2003).

Trial order of dismissal; no double jeopardy.—A mistrial and the subsequent erroneous granting of a trial order of dismissal does not constitute a legal bar to a future trial, because the trial order of dismissal was made at a time when the indictment was in a pretrial stage, that is prior to a second trial and the order did not constitute a resolution of the facts during trial in favor of the defendant. People v. Gallo, 75 A.D.2d 148, 431 N.Y.S.2d 1009 (1st Dept. 1980).

VTL offenses.—VTL §§ 1192(3) and 1193(2)(e)(7) do not have the same statutory elements, and one is not the lesser included offense of the other, so they do not constitute the same offense for double jeopardy purposes. People v. Steele, 172 A.D.2d 860, 661 N.Y.S.2d 908 (2d Dept. 1997); *see also* People v. Busby, 175 Misc. 2d 509, 670 N.Y.S.2d 960 (2d Dept. App. Term 1997) (same).

—A pre-trial driver's license suspension pursuant to VTL 1193(2)(e)(7) and a post-conviction license suspension pursuant to VTL 1193(2)(b)(2) do not violate the double jeopardy clause since pre-trial license suspensions are judicially ordered civil sanctions. People v. DeRojas, 196 Misc. 2d 171, 763 N.Y.S.2d 386 (App. T. 2d Dept. 2003).

Waiver.—By making application for a change of venue defendant effectively waived his right to raise the defense of double jeopardy upon retrial. People v. Brensic, 136 A.D.2d 169, 526 N.Y.S.2d 968 (2d Dept. 1988).

Waiver by guilty plea.—Defendant's statutory protection under CPL § 40.20 was waived by his failure to raise it until after his plea of guilty; however defendant did not waive his constitutional protection against double jeopardy by his plea of guilty or his failure to raise the argument before he entered the plea. People v. Artis, 74 A.D.2d 644, 425 N.Y.S.2d 142 (2d Dept. 1980).

Writ of prohibition.—Writ was granted where defendants had been prosecuted in federal court for conspiracy to possess the identical drugs specified in the state court indictments. Abraham v. Justices of New York, Inc, 43 A.D.2d 414, 352 N.Y.S.2d 451 (1st Dept. 1974), *modified,* 37 N.Y.2d 560, 376 N.Y.S.2d 79, 338 N.E.2d 597 (1975).

Retrial; failure to object.—Where a defendant is retried, despite a constitutional double jeopardy defense, a failure to object is not fatal to his claim. People v. Gonzalez, 99 N.Y.2d 76, 751 N.Y.S.2d 830, 781 N.E.2d 894 (2002).

—The extraordinary writ of prohibition has traditionally been available to bar a retrial on double jeopardy grounds. Collins v. Quinones, 202 A.D.2d 569, 616 N.Y.S.2d 306 (2d Dept. 1994).

§ 40.30. Previous prosecution; what constitutes.

1. Except as otherwise provided in this section, a person "is prosecuted" for an offense, within the meaning of section 40.20, when he is charged therewith by an accusatory instrument filed in a court of this state or of any jurisdiction within the United States, and when the action either:

(a) Terminates in a conviction upon a plea of guilty; or

(b) Proceeds to the trial stage and a jury has been impaneled and sworn or, in the case of a trial by the court without a jury, a witness is sworn.

2. Despite the occurrence of proceedings specified in subdivision one, a person is not deemed to have been prosecuted for an offense, within the meaning of section 40.20, when:

(a) Such prosecution occurred in a court which lacked jurisdiction over the defendant or the offense; or

(b) Such prosecution was for a lesser offense than could have been charged under the facts of the case, and the prosecution was procured by the defendant, without the knowledge of the appropriate prosecutor, for the purpose of avoiding prosecution for a greater offense.

3. Despite the occurrence of proceedings specified in subdivision one, if such proceedings are

subsequently nullified by a court order which restores the action to its pre-pleading status or which directs a new trial of the same accusatory instrument, the nullified proceedings do not bar further prosecution of such offense under the same accusatory instrument.

4. Despite the occurrence of proceedings specified in subdivision one, if such proceedings are subsequently nullified by a court order which dismisses the accusatory instrument but authorizes the people to obtain a new accusatory instrument charging the same offense or an offense based upon the same conduct, the nullified proceedings do not bar further prosecution of such offense under any new accusatory instrument obtained pursuant to such court order or authorization.

Amended by L. 1974, Ch. 80.

ANNOTATIONS

No double jeopardy protection.—Prison disciplinary hearing on charges arising out of stabbing incident did not constitute a previous prosecution affording inmate the constitutional safeguards of double jeopardy clause. Cordero v. Lalor, 227 A.D.2d 848, 642 N.Y.S.2d 399 (3d Dept. 1996), aff'd, 89 N.Y.2d 521, 655 N.Y.S.2d 870, 678 N.E.2d 482, cert. denied, 522 U.S. 846 (1997).

Dual sovereign doctrine.—State prosecutions are more restricted under New York's expansive statutory double jeopardy protections than under "dual sovereign" doctrine, as statutory provisions offer more protection than "dual sovereign" doctrine would tolerate. Booth v. Clary, 83 N.Y.2d 675, 635 N.E.2d 279, 613 N.Y.S.2d 110 (1994).

Defective accusatory instrument.—If an accusatory instrument is so radically defective that it would not support a judgment of conviction, jeopardy never attaches and retrial upon correction of the defect is not barred. People v. Laspina, 135 Misc. 422, 427, 515 N.Y.S.2d 694, 697 (Crim. Ct. Bronx Co. 1987).

Dismissal for insufficiency; filing second accusatory instrument charging same offense.—The dismissal of an accusatory instrument before trial on the ground that it is insufficient on its face in no way bars the filing of a second accusatory instrument charging the same offense and a subsequent trial thereon. People v. Bock, 77 Misc. 2d 350, 353 N.Y.S.2d 647 (Broome Co. Ct. 1974).

Court martial.—Court martial constitutes a previous prosecution for double jeopardy purposes. Booth v. Clary, 83 N.Y.2d 675, 613 N.Y.S.2d 110, 635 N.E.2d 279 (1994).

Reindictment or retrial.—When an accused avails himself of a course of legal redress with regard to a particular criminal prosecution, such as a motion or appeal, which results in reindictment or retrial, such individual may not raise double jeopardy. People v. Gonzalez, 81 A.D.2d 838, 438 N.Y.S.2d 842 (2d Dept. 1981).

—Where defendant was acquitted on count one but convicted on count two, a retrial on count two was not barred by double jeopardy. People v. Moore, 274 A.D.2d 959, 710 N.Y.S.2d 231 (4th Dept. 2000).

—Double jeopardy does not prevent a retrial where the orders terminating the prior trial were at the defendant's request for reasons not related to the defendant's guilt or innocence. People v. Zagarino, 74 A.D.2d 115, 427 N.Y.S.2d 40 (2d Dept. 1980).

First conviction reversed; no double jeopardy.—Defendant's retrial was not barred on double jeopardy grounds where his first conviction was reversed on grounds of prosecutorial misconduct. People v. Hammock, 182 A.D.2d 1114, 681 N.Y.S.2d 184 (4th Dept. 1998).

Illness of co-defendant.—Jeopardy attached and retrial was prohibited where, after the selection and swearing of a jury and delivery of opening statements, a mistrial was declared for the reason that a co-defendant became ill and was unable to continue the trial; further, the court denied appellant's request to

sever her case so that she might proceed with trial immediately. People v. Morgenthau, 102 A.D.2d 168, 476 N.Y.S.2d 841 (1st Dept. 1984).

Stipulation concerning witnesses' testimony.—Trial court's dismissal of prosecutor's information prior to the swearing of first witness was not on the merits, since Jeopardy did not attach after parties' stipulation concerning the testimony of certain witnesses. People v. Gingello, 84 Misc. 2d 63, 374 N.Y.S.2d 276 (Monroe Co. Ct. 1975).

Family Court proceedings.—Defendant's ex-wife obtained two orders of protection, one through City Court and one through Family Court, and defendant was later was found guilty in Family Court of violating the order of protection. Thereafter, defendant was indicted for first degree criminal contempt, second degree aggravated harassment, and first degree harassment. Defendant's conviction of criminal contempt was reversed, and remaining counts were dismissed on double jeopardy grounds. People v. Wood, 95 N.Y.2d 509, 719 N.Y.S.2d 639, 742 N.E.2d 114 (2000).

—Family Court proceeding did not amount to a prosecution, where defendant was not convicted of any offense therein and the permanent order of protection issued by that court did not amount to punishment. Accordingly, double jeopardy had no application to his subsequent guilty plea in Justice Court. People v. Runyon, 195 Misc. 2d 185, 757 N.Y.S.2d 669 (App. T. 2d Dept. 2002).

—Family Court action which removed children from defendant's home did not bar a criminal prosecution for endangering the welfare of a child. People v. Pettiford, 135 Misc. 2d 602, 605, 516 N.Y.S.2d 586, 588 (Sup. Ct. Kings Co. 1987).

Unreported partial verdict.—Where an unreported partial verdict was held invalid for failure to conform to statutory requirements for the rendering of a verdict, and where the jury was subsequently discharged as deadlocked, no jeopardy attached and a retrial was permitted. Oliver v. Justices of New York Supreme Court, 44 A.D.2d 823, 356 N.Y.S.2d 52 (1st Dept. 1974), aff'd, 36 N.Y.2d 53, 364 N.Y.S.2d 874, 324 N.E.2d 348.

Impaneling of jurors.—Jeopardy did not attach since the entire jury had not been impaneled and sworn at the time of the declaration of the mistrial. People v. Jenkins, 135 A.D.2d 733, 522 N.Y.S.2d 636 (2d Dept. 1987).

—Even if state could maintain appeal from order precluding introduction of identification evidence, double jeopardy barred further prosecution inasmuch as dismissal of indictment due to evidentiary failure occurred after jury had been impaneled and sworn, at which time jeopardy attached. People v. Austin, 208 A.D.2d 990, 618 N.Y.S.2d 115 (3d Dept. 1994).

—Retrial was not barred by because jeopardy never attached at first trial; entire jury had not been impaneled and sworn at the time mistrial was declared. People v. Moyer, 292 A.D.2d 793, 738 N.Y.S.2d 810 (4th Dept. 2002).

Knowledge; prosecutor.—Defendant did not violate CPL § 40.30(2)(b) when he pleaded guilty to the reduced charge in the Federal Court without the consent of the Westchester County District Attorney; this subdivision is intended to apply to a situation where a defendant is permitted by a judge to plead guilty to a reduced charge without the knowledge of the appropriate prosecutor in whose jurisdiction the offense occurred. People v. Daby, 56 A.D.2d 873, 392 N.Y.S.2d 325 (2d Dept. 1977).

Different victims.—Defendant's conviction in Suffolk County of the crime of larceny by false pretenses did not preclude his trial in Nassau County in connection with charges arising out of the same plan which was the predicate for the Suffolk convictions since none of the victims in the Suffolk County indictment were subjects of the subsequent Nassau County prosecution; each larceny was an independent criminal transaction which could be prosecuted independently. People v. Luongo, 47 N.Y.2d 418, 418 N.Y.S.2d 365, 391 N.E.2d 1341 (1979).

Mistrial.—Where defendant moved for mistrial after testimony was taken because of prosecution's failure to make exculpatory statements of witnesses available, and after impasse was reached in getting prosecutor to provide the names of the witnesses, court ordered mistrial, upon which defendant declared his readiness to proceed; it was not double jeopardy if defendant was charged again. Napoli v. The Supreme Court, 40 A.D.2d 159, 338 N.Y.S.2d 721 (1st Dept. 1972), aff'd, 33

N.Y.2d 980, 353 N.Y.S.2d 740, 309 N.E.2d 137, *cert. denied*, 417 U.S. 947 (1974).

—Retrial was proper when the first trial judge, after jury had been selected but before any evidence was taken, upon being informed by co-defendant's attorney that he wished to withdraw because the co-defendant intended to perjure himself, declared a mistrial on the motion of the co-defendant and with the acquiescence of defendant's attorney. People v. Miller, 52 A.D.2d 425, 385 N.Y.S.2d 457 (1st Dept. 1976), *aff'd*, 43 N.Y.2d 789, 402 N.Y.S.2d 392, 373 N.E.2d 286 (1977).

—Double jeopardy generally will bar a retrial when a mistrial is granted over the defendant's objection, unless the mistrial is granted as the product of manifest necessity. People v. Ramchair, 308 A.D.2d 601, 764 N.Y.S.2d 725 (2d Dept. 2003).

—The principles of double jeopardy will not bar a retrial where the first jury was discharged on consent. Helbrans v. Owens, 205 A.D.2d 775, 613 N.Y.S.2d 924 (2d Dept. 1994).

—Court's ruling to vacate, granted on defendant's motion, was the functional equivalent of a mistrial, which does not bar a second trial. DeCanzio v. Kennedy, 67 A.D.2d 111, 415 N.Y.S.2d 513 (4th Dept. 1979).

Mistrial; nonjury trial.—Declaration of mistrial by judge hearing charges without jury because of improper contacts between defendant's relatives and judge's relatives although judge had no contact with defendant or his relatives. The acts which formed the basis of the mistrial were not so improper or prejudicial that verdict could not have been reached. Defendant cannot be retried without being subjected to double jeopardy. Ferlito v. Judges of County Court, Suffolk County, 39 A.D.2d 17, 331 N.Y.S.2d 229 (2d Dept.), *aff'd*, 31 N.Y.2d 416, 340 N.Y.S.2d 635, 292 N.E.2d 779 (1972).

Murder conviction modified to manslaughter on appeal.—Defendant could not be retried for murder second degree after his conviction of murder, second degree, was modified upon appeal to Appellate Division to manslaughter, first degree and overturned in Federal Court. Retrial of defendant on murder charge was error since the earlier appellate court decision modifying the conviction and denying leave to appeal to the Court of Appeals, had the same finality as that of a verdict of acquittal of the greater charge. People v. Graham, 43 A.D.2d 182, 350 N.Y.S.2d 458 (3d Dept. 1973), *aff'd*, 36 N.Y.2d 633, 370 N.Y.S.2d 888, 331 N.E.2d 673 (1975).

Parole revocation hearing.—Dismissal of charges lodged against the defendant at the conclusion of a final parole revocation hearing did not bar a later prosecution of criminal charges based on the same acts. People v. Fagan, 66 N.Y.2d 481, 498 N.Y.S.2d 335, 489 N.E.2d 222 (1985).

Previous federal prosecution; bar to second prosecution.—The prior prosecution of a defendant on a federal indictment charging him with an attempt to distribute heroin and conspiracy to possess heroin with intent to distribute bars the State from prosecuting that defendant on an indictment charging possession of heroin and possession of heroin with intent to sell. The definition of "sale" in the Penal Law must be read to include "distribution," and therefore the federal indictment charged a sale. Accordingly, defendant's application to prohibit a State prosecution against him for possession of heroin and possession of heroin with intent to sell was granted; however, the State could prosecute the defendant for possession of cocaine, since this charge was not made in the federal indictment. Cirillo v. Justices of the Supreme Court, 43 A.D.2d 4, 349 N.Y.S.2d 129 (2d Dept. 1973), *aff'd*, 34 N.Y.2d 990, 360 N.Y.S.2d 416, 318 N.E.2d 607 (1974).

Previous prosecution; restoration of misdemeanor to calendar.—A misdemeanor may be restored to the calendar for trial after having once been dismissed on motion of the District Attorney, and double jeopardy is not involved inasmuch as a trial was never commenced by the swearing of a witness. People v. Krum, 68 Misc. 2d 763, 328 N.Y.S.2d 167 (Crim. Ct. N.Y. Co. 1972).

Prison disciplinary proceeding; no double jeopardy.—A prison disciplinary proceeding does not form the predicate for a claim of double jeopardy upon the indictment and trial of the inmate for alleged crimes based on acts on which the disciplinary proceeding was also based, even if the defendant loses good time credit as a result of the disciplinary proceeding. People v. Rivera, 189 A.D.2d 920, 921, 592 N.Y.S.2d 482, 483 (2d Dept. 1993).

—A prison disciplinary proceeding does not trigger double

jeopardy protection so as to bar a criminal prosecution based on the same incident. People v. Lane, 132 A.D.2d 855, 856, 518 N.Y.S.2d 207, 208 (3d Dept. 1987).

—Prison disciplinary proceedings do not form the basis for a double jeopardy claim, since they represent a loss of privileges with respect to a sentence already being served by a defendant, not an imposition of an additional sentence. People v. Simms, 124 A.D.2d 349, 507 N.Y.S.2d 290 (3d Dept. 1986).

—A prison disciplinary proceeding which results in the loss of an inmate's privileges, including one year of good time, but does not result in the imposition of an additional sentence, does not form the basis for a claim of double jeopardy as to criminal charges based on the same acts covered by the disciplinary hearing. People v. Briggs, 108 A.D.2d 1058, 485 N.Y.S.2d 861 (3d Dept. 1985).

Probation proceedings.—Finding, in a prior probation revocation proceeding, that the Department of Probation failed to prove, by a preponderance of the evidence, that petitioner had violated his probation by committing the acts underlying the robbery and assault charges did not bar a criminal prosecution for robbery and assault. Maisonet v. Merola, 69 N.Y.2d 965, 516 N.Y.S.2d 646, 509 N.E.2d 341 (1987).

—The revocation of probation and imposition of a more severe sentence did not place defendant in double jeopardy. People v. Tucker, 272 A.D.2d 992, 709 N.Y.S.2d 721 (4th Dept. 2000).

Prosecutor's opening statement.—Retrial was permissible where the court granted defendant's motion to dismiss because the prosecutor's opening statement was inadequate as a matter of law; the order of dismissal was not a determination of defendant's guilt or innocence since the determination was not based on the merits of any evidence presented during the trial but simply decided that the People had erred procedurally in failing to comply with CPL § 260.30(3). People v. Kurtz, 101 Misc. 2d 964, 422 N.Y.S.2d 352 (Jefferson Co. Ct. 1979), *aff'd*, 51 N.Y.2d 380, 434 N.Y.S.2d 200, 414 N.E.2d 699 (1980), *cert. denied*, 451 U.S. 911 (1981).

Trial after vacatur of guilty plea not double jeopardy.— Where the court, upon discovering that its acceptance of defendant's plea to a class D felony in satisfaction of an indictment including an A-II felony count was erroneous as a matter of law under CPL § 220.10(6)(a), vacated the plea of guilty as to that count and reinstated pleas of not guilty as to all counts, subsequent trial of defendant on the indictment did not place defendant in double jeopardy as CPL § 40.30(3) is controlling and provides in substance that acceptance of a plea in satisfaction is not the equivalent of an acquittal of the satisfied counts. People v. Bartley, 47 N.Y.2d 965, 419 N.Y.S.2d 956, 393 N.E.2d 1029 (1979).

Reinstatement of indictment permissible where no double jeopardy violation—Court has power to reinstate an indictment upon reargument without the necessity of a new grand jury presentation; there is no constitutional impediment to a court's power to modify its decisions, provided those decisions do not subject defendant to double jeopardy. People v. Rosa, 265 A.D.2d 167, 696 N.Y.S.2d 138 (1st Dept. 1999).

Tribal court proceedings.—Courts of other states are included within courts of "any jurisdiction within the United States," and Indian nations are no different from other states because they are free to adopt laws and regulations independent of any outside influence. Accordingly, defendant's acquittal by the Oneida Nation Tribal court operated as a double jeopardy bar to prosecution by state court on a charge arising out of the same incident. Hill v. Eppolito, 196 Misc. 2d 616, 766 N.Y.S.2d 509 (Sup. Ct. Madison Co. 2003), *aff'd*, 5 A.D.3d 854, 772 N.Y.S.2d 634 (3d Dept. 2004).

Civil forfeiture action.—Double jeopardy was not implicated by orders of attachment against defendant under civil forfeiture, because the orders were not punitive in nature; civil forfeiture action does not constitute criminal punishment within the meaning of the double jeopardy clause. People v. Edmonson, 300 A.D.2d 317, 751 N.Y.S.2d 280 (2d Dept. 2002).

§ 40.40. Separate prosecution of jointly prosecutable offenses; when barred.

1. Where two or more offenses are joinable in a single accusatory instrument against a person

by reason of being based upon the same criminal transaction, pursuant to paragraph (a) of subdivision two of section 200.20, such person may not, under circumstances prescribed in this section, be separately prosecuted for such offenses even though such separate prosecutions are not otherwise barred by any other section of this article.

2. When (a) one of two or more joinable offenses of the kind specified in subdivision one is charged in an accusatory instrument, and (b) another is not charged therein, or in any other accusatory instrument filed in the same court, despite possession by the people of evidence legally sufficient to support a conviction of the defendant for such uncharged offense, and (c) either a trial of the existing accusatory instrument is commenced or the action thereon is disposed of by a plea of guilty, any subsequent prosecution for the uncharged offense is thereby barred.

3. When (a) two or more of such offenses are charged in separate accusatory instruments filed in the same court, and (b) an application by the defendant for consolidation thereof for trial purposes, pursuant to subdivision five of section 200.20 or section 100.45, is improperly denied, the commencement of a trial of one such accusatory instrument bars any subsequent prosecution upon any of the other accusatory instruments with respect to any such offense.

ANNOTATIONS

Separate prosecution impermissible.—Where husband and wife owners were present during robbery of their bar, and where original indictment filed by People pertained solely to wife, first count of new indictment pertaining to husband was properly dismissed upon remand after reversal of first-degree robbery conviction for insufficiency of the evidence, as People had sufficient evidence at time of original indictment with which to proceed on indictment against defendant with respect to robbery of husband. People v. Owens, 227 A.D.2d 256, 642 N.Y.S.2d 874 (1st Dept. 1996).

—As the crimes charged in the indictment are based on the same criminal transaction, they are joinable pursuant to CPL § 200.20(2)(a) and, therefore, defendant cannot be separately prosecuted for the crimes. Lewis v. Sheriff of Schenectady Co., 220 A.D.2d 190, 645 N.Y.S.2d 339 (3d Dept. 1996).

Different victim.—Second Department rejected defendant's contention that because the murder charge and a robbery charge were based on the same criminal transaction, the prosecution was barred pursuant to CPL § 40.40(2) from separately prosecuting these offenses, finding that CPL § 40.40(2) does not operate as a bar to such prosecution because the alleged robbery occurred after the shooting and at a separate location, involved a different victim, and was not part of the same criminal transaction. People v. Rossi, 222 A.D.2d 717, 636 N.Y.S.2d 84 (2d Dept. 1995).

ACD (adjourned in contemplation of dismissal), felony indictment; arising from single criminal transaction.—Defendant, arrested and charged with possession of a dangerous drug as a misdemeanor, was later indicted for the felonies of criminal sale and criminal possession of a dangerous drug arising from same transaction. The misdemeanor charge was ACD and defendant claimed double jeopardy. The ACD was not a disposition but a nullification of an arrest and criminal proceeding and did not bar prosecution on the felony indictments. People v. Kephart, 77 Misc. 2d 921, 353 N.Y.S.2d 652 (Nassau Co. Ct. 1974).

Consolidation; request for.—Since the prohibition against separate prosecution of jointly prosecutable offenses applies only if the defendant has requested consolidation thereof for trial purposes and the request is denied, defendant's failure to

move for consolidation was deemed a waiver. People v. Dean, 56 A.D.2d 242, 392 N.Y.S.2d 134 (4th Dept. 1977), aff'd, 45 N.Y.2d 651, 412 N.Y.S.2d 353, 384 N.E.2d 1277 (1978).

—Where offenses are based on same act or transaction, but are properly prosecuted separately, pursuant to the exceptions to CPL § 40.20(2), a defendant may still cause a single prosecution of such offenses by moving to consolidate said prosecutions pursuant to CPL § 200.20(5). People v. Green, 89 Misc. 2d 639, 392 N.Y.S.2d 804 (Dist. Ct. Nassau Co. 1977).

—CPL § 40.40 prohibits consecutive prosecutions founded on one criminal transaction, but does not prohibit two separate proceedings commenced simultaneously. People v. Chestnut, 89 Misc. 2d 894, 392 N.Y.S.2d 1010 (Sup. Ct. N.Y. Co. 1977).

Conviction on two counts arising from same act; no double jeopardy.—Where defendant was convicted of driving with more than .15% of blood-alcohol content, it was not double jeopardy to find him guilty also of driving while intoxicated, even though conviction on both counts arose from the same act. People v. Rudd, 41 A.D.2d 875, 343 N.Y.S.2d 17 (3d Dept. 1973).

Multi-county crimes.—A felony murder indictment in which the underlying felony was committed in one county and the murder in another county may be tried in either county since conduct occurred in each county sufficient to constitute an element of such offenses (CPL § 20.40[1][a]), and since the felony murder may be tried in either county so may the underlying felonies and the failure to join in one county all the offenses based upon the same criminal transaction bars further prosecution of the unjoined crimes (CPL § 200.20, 40.40). People v. Ruzas, 54 A.D.2d 1083, 389 N.Y.S.2d 205 (4th Dept. 1976).

Previous prosecution in a state court.—Defendant's motions to dismiss Nassau County indictment were granted, pursuant to CPL § 40.20 and 210.20(1)(e), where defendant has already been sentenced to prison after pleading guilty to criminal possession of stolen property in Queens County committed in the same criminal transaction since the interest of justice would not have been served by a separate prosecution; separate charges arising from the same criminal transaction were barred by CPL § 40.20 and because the offenses were joinable in one accusatory instrument (CPL § 40.40[2]). People v. Riley, 58 A.D.2d 816, 396 N.Y.S.2d 271 (2d Dept. 1977).

—Where a felony complaint and a simplified traffic information charging a joinable offense were filed on the same date, in the District Court, and the latter instrument was disposed of by a plea of guilty, the prosecution of the felony offense was not barred by the CPL § 40.40(2) and the subsequent Grand Jury indictment charging the same offenses as were charged in the felony complaint did not bar prosecution. People v. Easterling, 59 A.D.2d 537, 397 N.Y.S.2d 125 (2d Dept. 1977).

Separate offenses; circumstances of commission.—Since driving while intoxicated (VTL § 1192) and failing to stop for a red light (VTL § 1111) have different elements of proof they are triable separately (CPL § 40.20[2]) however, where they arise out of the same transaction they are joinable (CPL § 200.20[2][a]), and in order to prevent separate trials, the defendant must apply for consolidation and if the application is improperly denied, the commencement of trial of one accusatory instrument bars any subsequent prosecution (CPL § 40.40[3]). Serignese v. Henry, 101 Misc. 2d 982, 424 N.Y.S.2d 810 (Sup. Ct. Suffolk Co. 1978).

—The offenses of driving with a revoked license and assault, second degree, have substantially different elements and the statutory provisions defining such offenses are designed to prevent very different kinds of evil; thus even though both offenses were based upon the same criminal transaction, in the absence of circumstances as set forth in CPL § 40.40(2) or (3), the trial of the assault charges was not barred by defendant's previous guilty plea to the driving offense in the Suffolk County District Court. People v. Durant, 88 Misc. 2d 731, 389 N.Y.S.2d 533 (Suffolk Co. Ct. 1976).

Separate prosecution of jointly prosecutable offenses; barred.—The prosecutor could not prosecute the defendant in 1978 and 1980 by two separate indictments when the evidence he had in his possession at the time of the 1978 indictment was legally sufficient to support a conviction of the defendant for offenses charged in the 1980 indictment. Auer v. Smith, 77 A.D.2d 172, 432 N.Y.S.2d 926 (4th Dept. 1980).

Simplified traffic informations.—The filing of two separate "simplified traffic informations" in two separate and distinct forums, charging the defendant with two offenses which arose from the same criminal transaction, in fact constitutes separate prosecutions, and upon a plea of guilty to one, dismissal of the second is mandated, pursuant to CPL § 40.40. People v. Montone, 82 Misc. 2d 234, 368 N.Y.S.2d 410 (Dist. Ct. Nassau Co. 1975).

§ 40.50. Previous prosecution; enterprise corruption.

1. The following definitions are applicable to this section:

(a) A criminal act or offense is "specifically included" when a count of an accusatory instrument charging a person with enterprise corruption alleges a pattern of criminal activity and the act or offense is alleged to be a criminal act within such pattern.

(b) A criminal act is "a part of" a pattern of criminal activity alleged in a count of enterprise corruption when it is committed prior to commencement of the criminal action in which enterprise corruption is charged and was committed in furtherance of the same common scheme or plan or with intent to participate in or further the affairs of the same criminal enterprise to which the crimes specifically included in the pattern are connected.

(c) A person "is prosecuted" for an offense when he is prosecuted for it within the meaning of section 40.30 of this article or when an indictment or a count of an indictment charging that offense is dismissed pursuant to section 210.20 of this chapter without authorization to submit the charge to the same or another grand jury, or the indictment or the count of the indictment charging that offense is dismissed following the granting of a motion to suppress pursuant to article 710 of this chapter, unless an appeal from the order granting the motion to dismiss or suppress is pending.

(d) An offense was "not prosecutable" in an accusatory instrument in which a person was charged with enterprise corruption when there was no geographical jurisdiction of that offense in the county where the accusatory instrument was filed, or when the offense was prosecutable in the county and was not barred from prosecution by section 40.20 or 40.40 of this article or by any other provision of law but the prosecutor filing the accusatory instrument was not empowered by law to prosecute the offense.

2. A person who has been previously prosecuted for an offense may not be subsequently prosecuted for enterprise corruption based upon a pattern of criminal activity in which that prior offense, or another offense based upon the same act or criminal transaction, is specifically included unless:

(a) he was convicted of that prior offense; and

(b) the subsequent pattern of criminal activity in which he participated includes at least one criminal act for which he was not previously prosecuted, which was a felony, and which occurred after that prior conviction.

3. A person who has been previously prosecuted for enterprise corruption may not be subsequently prosecuted for an offense specifically included in the pattern of criminal activity upon which it was based, or another offense based upon the same act or criminal transaction, unless the offense is a class A felony and was not prosecutable in the accusatory instrument in which the person was charged with enterprise corruption.

4. A person may not be separately prosecuted for enterprise corruption and for an offense specifically included in the pattern of criminal activity upon which it is based or another offense based upon the same act or transaction, unless the offense is a class A felony and is not prosecutable in the accusatory instrument in which the person is charged with enterprise corruption.

5. A person who has been previously prosecuted for enterprise corruption may not be subsequently prosecuted for an offense which, while not specifically included in the pattern of criminal activity on which the prior charge of enterprise corruption was based, was nonetheless a part of that pattern, unless the offense was a class A or B felony and either the offense was not prosecutable in the accusatory instrument in which the person was charged with enterprise corruption or the people show, by clear and convincing evidence, that the prosecutor did not possess evidence legally sufficient to support a conviction of that offense at the time of the earlier prosecution and evidence of that offense was not presented as part of the case in chief in the earlier prosecution.

6. A person who has been previously prosecuted for enterprise corruption may not be subsequently prosecuted for enterprise corruption based upon a pattern of criminal activity that specifically includes a criminal act that was also specifically included in the pattern upon which the prior charge of enterprise corruption was based.

7. A person may not be separately prosecuted for enterprise corruption in two accusatory instruments based upon a pattern of criminal activity, alleged in either instrument, that specifically includes a criminal act that is also specifically included in the pattern upon which the other charge of enterprise corruption is based.

8. When a person is charged in an accusatory instrument with both one or more counts of enterprise corruption and with another offense or offenses specifically included in or otherwise a part of the pattern or patterns of criminal activity upon which the charge or charges of enterprise corruption is or are based, and the court orders that any of the counts be tried separately pursuant to subdivision one of section 200.40 of this chapter, this section shall not apply and

subsequent prosecution of the remaining counts or offenses shall not be barred.

9. A person who has been previously prosecuted for racketeering pursuant to federal law, or any comparable offense pursuant to the law of another state may not be subsequently prosecuted for enterprise corruption based upon a pattern of criminal activity that specifically includes a criminal act that was also specifically included in the pattern of racketeering activity upon which the prior charge of racketeering was based provided, however, that this section shall not be construed to prohibit the subsequent prosecution of any other offense specifically included in or otherwise a part of a pattern of racketeering activity alleged in any such prior prosecution for racketeering or other comparable offense.

Added by L. 1986, Ch. 516.

ANNOTATION

Enterprise corruption.—CPL § 40.50(2) allows prosecution for enterprise corruption where up to two of the three patterns acts with which a person is charged have already been prosecuted as substantive crimes, as long as earlier prosecutions resulted in conviction. People v. Ciauri, 166 Misc. 2d 615, 632 N.Y.S.2d 404 (Sup. Ct. N.Y. Co. 1995).

See also cases cited in this text under Penal Law Article 460—Enterprise Corruption.

ARTICLE 50—COMPULSION OF EVIDENCE BY OFFER OF IMMUNITY

Section

50.10   Compulsion of evidence by offer of immunity; definitions of terms.

50.20   Compulsion of evidence by offer of immunity.

50.30   Authority to confer immunity in criminal proceedings; court a competent authority.

LexisNexis Cross References

Criminal Defense Techniques, Vol. 4, Ch. 79, Cross-Examining the Witness Who Has Received Immunity or Leniency From the Government; *New York Criminal Practice (2d ed.),* Vol. 5, Ch. 50, Immunity from Prosecution and Statute of Limitations; *Criminal Practice Handbook (2d ed.),* Ch. 3, Grand Jury Representation.

§ 50.10. Compulsion of evidence by offer of immunity; definitions of terms.

The following definitions are applicable to this article:

1. "Immunity." A person who has been a witness in a legal proceeding, and who cannot, except as otherwise provided in this subdivision, be convicted of any offense or subjected to any penalty or forfeiture for or on account of any transaction, matter or thing concerning which he gave evidence therein, possesses "immunity" from any such conviction, penalty or forfeiture. A person who possesses such immunity may nevertheless be convicted of perjury as a result of having given false testimony in such legal proceeding, and may be convicted of or adjudged in contempt as a result of having contumaciously refused to give evidence therein.

2. "Legal proceeding" means a proceeding in or before any court or grand jury, or before any body, agency or person authorized by law to conduct the same and to administer the oath or to cause it to be administered.

3. "Give evidence" means to testify or produce physical evidence.

ANNOTATIONS

Attorney.—Incriminating testimony given by an attorney, following a grant of immunity, may be used as evidence against him in a disciplinary proceedings. Anonymous Attorneys v. Bar Ass'n of Erie Co., 41 N.Y.2d 506, 393 N.Y.S.2d 961, 362 N.E.2d 592 (1977).

Complete immunity.—Complete immunity from prosecution may be granted only by strict compliance with the procedural requirements of the immunity statutes; if a witness gives evidence without asserting his privilege against self-incrimination, he does not receive immunity. People v. Flihan, 131 A.D.2d 269, 270, 520 N.Y.S.2d 686, 687 (4th Dept. 1987), *aff'd,* 73 N.Y.2d 729, 535 N.Y.S.2d 590, 532 N.E.2d 96 (1988).

General.—An agreement of immunity from prosecution exacted by defendant in exchange for the return of children to their lawful custodians pursuant to a Family Court order is unenforceable. Schrotenboer v. Soloff, 74 N.Y.2d 597, 550 N.Y.S.2d 256, 549 N.E.2d 458 (1989).

Grand jury; immunity.—Absent a waiver, a witness before the Grand Jury responding directly to questioning legally addressed to him, cannot be convicted of an offense for any transaction concerning which he gave testimony. People v. Williams, 81 A.D.2d 418, 440 N.Y.S.2d 935 (2d Dept. 1981), *aff'd,* 56 N.Y.2d 916, 453 N.Y.S.2d 430, 438 N.E.2d 1146 (1982).

—Where defendant testified in a grand jury proceeding that he understood the concepts of immunity, perjury, and contempt, as well as the scope of the immunity, he was not permitted to avail himself (in a prosecution for criminal contempt) of the defense that the explanation of "transactional immunity" was inadequate, especially where defendant was represented and advised by counsel. People v. Breindel, 73 Misc. 2d 734, 342 N.Y.S.2d 428 (Sup. Ct. N.Y. Co. 1973).

Grand jury testimony; immunity against violation of probation.—Defendant was entitled to immunity against violation of probation when called upon to testify before the grand jury. People v. Moschelle, 96 Misc. 2d 1030, 410 N.Y.S.2d 764 (Sup. Ct. Suffolk Co. 1978).

Grand jury; scope of immunity; responsiveness of answers.—The limitation of the scope of the immunity that is afforded under CPL 190.40 with regard to answers that are "responsive" does not violate the Due Process Clause of the Fourteenth Amendment on the ground of vagueness. The statute is not a penal statute nor a trap for the unwary, but a legal barrier to witnesses who intentionally give information not sought in an effort to frustrate and prevent criminal prosecution. People v. Breindel, 73 Misc. 2d 734, 342 N.Y.S.2d 428 (Sup. Ct. N.Y. Co. 1973), *aff'd,* 45 A.D.2d 691, 356 N.Y.S.2d 626, *aff'd,* 35 N.Y.2d 928, 365 N.Y.S.2d 163, 324 N.E.2d 545 (1974).

Grand jury; perjury, contempt.—The statute expressly provides, and the witness should be informed, that he will not be immune from prosecution for perjury if he lies, or for contempt if he refuses to answer or gives evasive replies, however this should not require an extended explanation, nor should the prosecutor be required to repeat the admonition, nor have the court direct an answer, every time the witness' testimony becomes vague or evasive. People v. Rappaport, 47 N.Y.2d 308, 418 N.Y.S.2d 306, 391 N.E.2d 1284 (1979).

Grand jury; eavesdropping; motion to suppress.—Defendant, served subsequent to his grand jury appearance with notice that he had been subjected to prior electronic surveillance, was not entitled to a suppression hearing during pendency of the grand jury proceedings; and failure of the prosecutor, during proceedings prior to trial, to answer defendant's questions concerning the surveillance was no defense to his contempt charge for refusal to answer questions, since he had been given "transactional immunity." People v. Breindel, 73 Misc. 2d 734, 342 N.Y.S.2d 428 (Sup. Ct. N.Y. Co. 1973), *aff'd,* 45 A.D.2d 691, 356 N.Y.S.2d 626, *aff'd,* 35 N.Y.2d 928, 365 N.Y.S.2d 163, 324 N.E.2d 545 (1974).

Grand jury; evidence.—A grand jury witness who testified only that she had "sold drugs in the past" and "got busted" was not entitled to immunity as to such matters. The admission of having sold drugs did not specifically relate to crimes charged; further, since a grant of immunity is afforded against testimony that is self-incriminatory and the fact of an arrest is a matter of public record, the testimony that the witness "got busted" does not confer immunity as to the activity which prompted the arrest. People v. McFarlan, 52 A.D.2d 112, 383 N.Y.S.2d 4 (1st Dept. 1976).

Grant of statutory immunity; evasive answers equivalent to refusal to testify; contempt.—Police officers, subpoenaed to testify before the New York City Commission of Investigation, gave evasive answers (after having been advised that they would be subject to dismissal from the police force if they refused to answer questions but that if they did testify, neither their answers nor any evidence or information gained by reason of their answers could be used against them in a criminal proceeding). The court ruled that the officers' testimony was so evasive as to amount to a refusal to answer legal and pertinent questions, and it ruled that the exclusionary rule applicable to testimony of public employees under threat of job forfeiture for refusal to testify did not bar the use of compelled testimony in a contempt proceeding under CPLR § 2308(b). Ruskin v. Detken, 32 N.Y.2d 293, 344 N.Y.S.2d 933, 298 N.E.2d 101 (1973).

Grand jury; prosecution for contempt.—Where defendant moved to quash a grand jury indictment on ground that his appearance before the grand jury resulted from an unlawful search of his car and himself, he could not avail himself of this defense, since, while before the grand jury, he did not urge the illegality of the proceeding and search as a ground for refusing to testify, but only asserted the privilege against self-incrimination. Defendant waived any other ground he may have had for refusing to testify, and thus could be prosecuted for contempt. People v. de Salvo, 32 N.Y.2d 12, 343 N.Y.S.2d 65 (1973), *cert. denied,* 415 U.S. 919 (1974).

Handwriting exemplars.—The term "gives evidence" expressly encompasses both testimony and the production of physical evidence which includes handwriting exemplars. People v. Csabon, 79 A.D.2d 609, 433 N.Y.S.2d 487 (2d Dept. 1980).

—A court ordered handwriting exemplar will be authorized (1) when, in the interest of justice, or when in the interest of public or private safety, it is necessary to determine authorship, validity, or authenticity of a questioned handwritten instrument or document and (2) when it appears that an identifiable person, or persons, have exercised such control over and have had such access to the questioned instruments that there is probable cause to believe that such person, or persons, wrote or authored the questioned documents; however, the court is required to make a factual determination upon notice to all parties to determine the reasonableness and constitutional validity of the requested submission of an identifiable and known exemplar. Special Prosecutor (Onondaga Co.) v. G.W., 95 Misc. 2d 298, 407 N.Y.S.2d 112 (Sup. Ct. Onondaga Co. 1978).

Parole revocation.—Since parole revocation procedures are not criminal in nature, the immunity granted to a witness before a Grand Jury, pursuant to CPL § 190.40 as defined in CPL § 50.10(1), does not extend to proceedings to revoke parole. In re Dellacroce, 91 Misc. 2d 755, 398 N.Y.S.2d 811 (Sup. Ct. Suffolk Co. 1977).

Qualified privilege.—Oral statements made by complainant to the District Attorney concerning a possible criminal act by a candidate for judicial appointment and his statements to the New York City Department of Investigation concerning the same matter should be afforded a qualified privilege. Toker v. Pollak, 44 N.Y.2d 211, 405 N.Y.S.2d 1, 376 N.E.2d 163 (1978).

Prosecutor's conduct erroneous.—Where witness did not seek immunity for any false statements they might make at trial, but when confronted with the prosecutor's ominous injunction that they be consistent above all else, they sought assurance that any misstatements or inconsistencies they may have uttered during the course of their prior testimony would not suddenly become prosecutable after their appearance on defendant's behalf, the prosecutor's refusal to extend immunity could have served no purpose other than to irretrievably bind the witnesses to their previous sworn versions, accurate or not, and thus impermissibly affected their meaningful exercise of their Fifth Amendment rights. People v. Shapiro, 50 N.Y.2d 747, 431 N.Y.S.2d 422, 409 N.E.2d 897 (1980).

Transactional immunity.—Defendant testified before the Grand Jury investigating his charges of police brutality stemming from his arrest for being in an altercation with an off-duty police officer. Court found that there was nothing unimportant, imaginary, or speculative about defendant's admission that his testimony provided a link in the chain of facts, and that his testimony was responsive to the Special Prosecutor's inquiries. Accordingly, the court found that defendant's Grand Jury testimony conferred transactional immunity upon him. People v. Henderson, 257 A.D.2d 213, 694 N.Y.S.2d 191 (3d Dept. 1999).

—In determining whether sufficient nexus exists between prior testimony and subject crime, so that witness is conferred with transactional immunity, "it is 'the context of the circumstances which ultimately governs.'" People v. McKenna, 250 A.D.2d 240, 685 N.Y.S.2d 110 (3d Dept. 1998).

§ 50.20. Compulsion of evidence by offer of immunity.

1. Any witness in a legal proceeding, other than a grand jury proceeding, may refuse to give evidence requested of him on the ground that it may tend to incriminate him and he may not, except as provided in subdivision two, be compelled to give such evidence.

2. Such a witness may be compelled to give evidence in such a proceeding notwithstanding an assertion of his privilege against self-incrimination if:

(a) The proceeding is one in which, by express provision of statute, a person conducting or connected therewith is declared a competent authority to confer immunity upon witnesses therein; and

(b) Such competent authority

(i) orders such witness to give the requested evidence notwithstanding his assertion of his privilege against self-incrimination, and

(ii) advises him that upon so doing he will receive immunity.

3. A witness who is ordered to give evidence pursuant to subdivision two and who complies with such order receives immunity. Such witness is not deprived of such immunity because such competent authority did not comply with statutory provisions requiring notice to a specified public servant of intention to confer immunity.

4. A witness who, without asserting his privilege against self-incrimination, gives evidence in a legal proceeding other than a grand jury proceeding does not receive immunity.

5. The rules governing the circumstances in which witnesses may be compelled to give evidence and in which they receive immunity therefor in a grand jury proceeding are prescribed in section 190.40.

ANNOTATIONS

Criminal contempt conviction supported by defendant's answers in Grand Jury.—Conviction for criminal contempt was affirmed where defendant, who had been granted transactional immunity, had testified evasively before grand jury, stating with regard to cryptic entries in his black book that "he don't remember," "I don't recall," and "I don't know" and that the money involved went to no one specifically. People v. Gottfried, 61 N.Y.2d 617, 471 N.Y.S.2d 844, 459 N.E.2d 1281 (1983).

Denial of immunity to defendant's witness.—Defendant's conviction for robbery was affirmed where the prosecutor refused to grant immunity to one of the defendant's prospective witnesses, since to do so would have been an abuse of the immunity statute. People v. Adams, 53 N.Y.2d 241, 440 N.Y.S.2d 902, 423 N.E.2d 379 (1981).

—A prosecutor is free to withhold immunity from a potential defense witness absent abuse, as for example, when "the prosecutor builds his case with immunized witnesses but denies the defendant a similar opportunity." People v. Thomas, 169 A.D.2d 553, 564 N.Y.S.2d 406 (1st Dept. 1991).

District attorney's refusal to confer full transactional immunity; good faith.—District attorney's refusal to confer full transactional immunity to witness was appropriate where the witness was an extremely disreputable individual with a significant criminal history who might avoid liability for more serious crimes. People v. Osorio, 86 A.D.2d 233, 449 N.Y.S.2d 968 (1st Dept. 1982).

Effect of federal immunity on state indictments.—Where defendants were subpoenaed to appear before simultaneous but independent federal and state grand juries investigating identical activities, a grant of transactional immunity in the federal investigation given in order to compel the testimony of the defendant acted to bar state indictments in regard to such activities, even through the state indictments were the result of a totally independent investigation and were not the result of information given to the federal grand jury. People v. Stievater, 77 Misc. 2d 761, 356 N.Y.S.2d 915 (Erie Co. Ct. 1972).

Grand jury; prosecution for contempt.—Where defendant moved to quash a grand jury indictment on ground that his appearance before the grand jury resulted from an unlawful search of his car and himself, he could not avail himself of this defense, since, while before the grand jury, he did not urge the illegality of the proceeding and search as a ground for refusing to testify, but only asserted the privilege against self-incrimination. Defendant waived any other ground he may have had for refusing to testify, and thus could be prosecuted for contempt. People v. De Salvo, 32 N.Y.2d 12, 343 N.Y.S.2d 65 (1973), *cert. denied*, 415 U.S. 919 (1974).

Informal promise of nonprosecution.—An informal "promise" of non-prosecution, cannot confer immunity from prosecution. People v. Dunbar, 53 N.Y.2d 868, 440 N.Y.S.2d 613, 423 N.E.2d 36 (1981).

"Ordered."—The term "ordered," as used in CPL § 50.20(2), is not a term of art and need not be given its precise literal meaning, at least where the record leaves no doubt that the witness fully understood that he was under judicial compulsion to answer the prosecutor's questions and that he would be held in contempt if he refused. O'Neil v. Kasler, 53 A.D.2d 310, 385 N.Y.S.2d 684 (4th Dept. 1976).

Silence; no inference of guilt proper.—The defense did not object to the court's questioning a witness, in front of the jury, on the defendant's refusal to be interrogated in the absence of counsel. Furthermore, the court stated in its charge to the jury that no inference could or should be drawn from the defendant's silence. Defendant's confession, made after his refusal to answer questions, rendered harmless any prejudice resulting from the testimony that the defendant had wished to remain silent. People v. Wheeler, 40 A.D.2d 348, 340 N.Y.S.2d 196 (2d Dept. 1973), *cert. denied*, 412 U.S. 931 (1973).

Independent inference; effect on right to remain silent.—A defendant's right to remain silent is unimpaired by the fact that an independent inference may arise from his unexplained possession of the fruits of a crime. People v. Wheeler, 40 A.D.2d 348, 340 N.Y.S.2d 196 (2d Dept. 1973), *cert. denied*, 412 U.S. 931 (1973).

Prosecutor acted within discretion in refusing to immunize a defense witness.—Prosecutor did not abuse her discretion by refusing to immunize a witness who would have been called to testify by the defense as to witness's sexual relations with the rape victim on or shortly before the day of the crime, apparently to explain the presence of sperm on the victim's underwear. People v. Owens, 63 N.Y.2d 824, 482 N.Y.S.2d 250, 472 N.E.2d 26 (1984).

Statutory duty to report traffic accident; not inconsistent with fifth amendment guarantee against self-incrimination.—Vehicle & Traffic Law § 600 requiring an operator of a motor vehicle to remain at the scene of an accident, identify himself, and report the accident to the police is a valid exercise of the police powers of the State in furtherance of the regulation of public safety; it does not constitute a violation of the privilege against self-incrimination. People v. Samuels, 29 N.Y.2d 252, 327 N.Y.S.2d 321, 277 N.E.2d 381 (1971).

Transactional immunity.—Defendant did not receive transactional immunity during examination by Attorney General since no offer of transactional immunity was made and defendant did not respond to questioning under duress, but simply refused to answer certain questions, invoking his Fifth Amendment rights, and continued in his refusal to answer questions after being advised of possible criminal sanctions. People v. Linick, 79 A.D.2d 925, 434 N.Y.S.2d 423 (1st Dept. 1981).

Complete immunity.—Complete immunity from prosecution may be obtained only by strict compliance with the procedural requirements of the immunity statutes. People v. D'Amico, 138 A.D.2d 943, 526 N.Y.S.2d 280 (4th Dept. 1988).

—Narcotics defendant did not receive transactional immunity absent assertion of his privilege against self-incrimination and order by judge that he testify; prosecutor's promise, when defendant gave information, not to use testimony against him in court of law, and court's similar promise that he would not be prosecuted as result of testimony he gave, entitled defendant only to use immunity, in that he could have such testimony suppressed should prosecutor seek to use it against him. People v. Flihan, 131 A.D.2d 269, 520 N.Y.S.2d 686 (4th Dept. 1987).

—Transactional immunity gives protection from "any transaction, matter or thing concerning which the witness" might give evidence and granting immunity from specified crimes only was not complete and coextensive with the witness' constitutional protection against self-incrimination. Felder v. New York State Supreme Court, 44 A.D.2d 1, 352 N.Y.S.2d 706 (4th Dept. 1974).

Witnesses; waiver of privilege against self-incrimination.—When defendant took the stand in his own defense in a prosecution for assault in the second degree and reckless endangerment in the second degree, he waived his constitutional and statutory protection against self-incrimination. The waiver did not extend, however, to the rules governing the competence and admissibility of evidence, particularly those dealing with privileged communications between attorney and client. No implication of a waiver of the attorney-client privilege could be made by the fact that defendant took the stand in his own defense. People v. Moore, 42 A.D.2d 268, 346 N.Y.S.2d 363 (2d Dept. 1973).

§ 50.30. Authority to confer immunity in criminal proceedings; court a competent authority.

In any criminal proceeding, other than a grand jury proceeding, the court is a competent authority to confer immunity in accordance with the provisions of section 50.20, but only when expressly requested by the district attorney to do so.

ANNOTATIONS

Duty to grant immunity.—Absent knowledge of specific exculpatory material or a specific source of such material, the People have no duty to grant immunity based on speculation or conjecture as a pseudo-fulfillment of the rule prohibiting suppression of "evidence favorable to an accused." People v. Sapia, 48 A.D.2d 524, 370 N.Y.S.2d 604 (1st Dept. 1975), *aff'd*, 41 N.Y.2d 160, 391 N.Y.S.2d 93, 359 N.E.2d 688 (1976).

—Family Court is empowered to grant a witness immunity at a fact finding hearing in accordance with CPL § 50.30. *In re* Barry M., 93 Misc. 2d 882, 403 N.Y.S.2d 979 (Fam. Ct. Queens Co. 1978).

Prosecutor's refusal to grant immunity to defense witness.—Prosecutor acted within discretion in refusing to grant immunity. People v. Rodriguez, 197 A.D.2d 546, 602 N.Y.S.2d 210 (2d Dept. 1993).

—Prosecutor did not abuse its discretion in denying immunity to witness who recanted his testimony incriminating defendant, where there was no evidence of bad faith or misconduct on the part of the prosecution. People v. Donahue, 235 A.D.2d 954, 653 N.Y.S.2d 968 (3d Dept. 1997).

—District Attorney abused his discretion in a murder prosecution and violated defendant's due process right to a fair trial and vital exculpatory testimony when he refused to grant immunity to a witness who previously testified and wished to recant such earlier testimony but invoked his Fifth Amendment rights prior to testifying on the second occasion especially since the witness was only seeking protection from perjury charges and not for past crimes. People v. Priester, 98 A.D.2d 820, 470 N.Y.S.2d 478 (3d Dept. 1983).

TITLE D—RULES OF EVIDENCE, STANDARDS OF PROOF AND RELATED MATTERS

ARTICLE 60—RULES OF EVIDENCE AND RELATED MATTERS

LexisNexis Cross References

See generally Bender's New York Evidence—CPLR; *Criminal Defense Techniques,* Vol. 1, Ch. 4B, Suppression of Illegally Obtained Evidence: Visual Surveillance; Vol. 1, Ch. 4C, Inventory Searches; Vol. 2, Ch. 51, Defending Drunk Driving Cases: Evidence Problems; Vol. 3A, Ch. 68, Developing and Presenting Psychological Evidence in Criminal Defense Proceedings; Vol. 4, Ch. 80 Suppression of Illegally Obtained Evidence: Private Searches; Vol. 4, Ch. 83, Suppression of Illegally Obtained Evidence: Pretext Searches; *New York Civil Practice: CPLR (2d ed.),* Vol. 9, Article 45, Evidence; *see generally New York Suppression Manual*; *New York Criminal Practice (2d ed.),* Vol. 2, Ch. 18, Motion to Suppress Evidence; *Prosecution and Defense of Sex Crimes,* Ch. 15, DNA Evidence; *Sexual Assault Trials (2d ed.),* Vol. 1, Ch. 1, Pretrial Issues, Discovery, and Motions; Vol. 1, Ch. 5, Direct and Cross-Examination of Complaining Witness; *Criminal Evidentiary Foundations,* Ch. 5, Rule 403 and Legal Relevance Limitations on Credibility Evidence; Ch. 6, Legal Relevance Limitations on Evidence That Is Relevant to the Historical Merits of the Case.

§ 60.10. Rules of evidence; in general.

Unless otherwise provided by statute or by judicially established rules of evidence applicable to criminal cases, the rules of evidence applicable to civil cases are, where appropriate, also applicable to criminal proceedings.

ANNOTATIONS

Admissibility of victim's clothing.—Defendant's contention that the admission into evidence of the stabbing victim's shirt inflamed the passion of the jury is unpersuasive since, under the circumstances of the case, the victim's clothing was of probative value. People v. Sears, 58 A.D.2d 693, 395 N.Y.S.2d 756 (3d Dept. 1977).

Arresting officer's testimony.—It was proper to allow the arresting officer to testify that he arrested defendant "because there was a certain description" and defendant was wearing a jacket like "what the undercover described to us," because such testimony demonstrated the basis for the backup officer's appearance on the scene and arrest of the particular person described. People v. Batista, 233 A.D.2d 195, 650 N.Y.S.2d 103 (1st Dept. 1996).

Composite sketch.—People sought to admit composite sketch to prove defendant's guilt and urged the jury to infer guilt based on his resemblance to the sketch. The Court has long considered composite sketches to be hearsay, but as an exception to the hearsay rule, a composite sketch may be admissible as a prior consistent statement where the testimony of an identifying witness is assailed as a recent fabrication. The court erred in admitting the sketch on the People's second application. It was inadmissible to rehabilitate the victim's identification because nothing about the cross-examination of the detective had suggested that the victim had lied in identifying defendant as the non-shooter. The court's erroneous admission of the sketch was not harmless error. The Court declined to equate a challenged police investigation with an allegation of recent fabrication. People v. Maldonado, 97 N.Y.2d 522, 743 N.Y.S.2d 389, 769 N.E.2d 1281 (2002).

—A composite sketch may be introduced in suppression hearing where issue is probable cause for arrest or reasonable suspicion for a stop. It may also be introduced by defendant on cross-examination to show inconsistencies between courtroom identification and prior description as recorded in sketch. People v. Griffin, 29 N.Y.2d 91, 323 N.Y.S.2d 964, 272 N.E.2d 477 (1971).

—Any error in the admission into evidence of a police composite sketch was harmless, given the overwhelming evidence of guilt, including highly probative DNA evidence of defendant's reliable and voluntary confession. In light of the powerful evidence of guilt, the recently decided case of People v. Maldonado, 97 N.Y.2d 522, 743 N.Y.S.2d 389, 769 N.E.2d 1281, does not affect the outcome of this appeal. Maldonado was reversed because the "thinnest of threads" of proof connected the defendant to the crimes charged. People v. Jones, 295 A.D.2d 243, 745 N.Y.S.2d 15 (1st Dept. 2002).

—Court should have permitted one of the defense witnesses to state whether she thought the composite sketch of the murderer, prepared by an eyewitness, looked like someone other than the defendant. People v. Moore, 140 A.D.2d 600, 527 N.Y.S.2d 862 (2d Dept. 1988).

Background information.—Trial court did not abuse its discretion in admitting the police officer's testimony concerning an unidentified cab driver's report of a recent encounter with the armed defendant, because the testimony was admitted not for its truth, but to provide background information as to how and why the police pursued and confronted defendant. People v. Tosca, 98 N.Y.2d 660, 746 N.Y.S.2d 276, 773 N.E.2d 1014 (2002).

—Court properly exercised its discretion in admitting background testimony about street-level drug operations in order to explain the fact that no drugs or pre-recorded buy money were recovered from defendant or the codefendant. People v. Garcia, 309 A.D.2d 514, 764 N.Y.S.2d 696 (1st Dept. 2003).

—Defendant was not unfairly prejudiced by the admission of background evidence concerning the procedures used in street level purchases of narcotics, since the evidence helped to provide the jury with an understanding of the officers' behavior.

People v. Ramos, 192 A.D.2d 324, 595 N.Y.S.2d 477 (1st Dept. 1993).

—Testimony describing an accomplice as an "enforcer" for the numbers corporation and describing the corporation's reason for ordering the arsons was necessary background information. People v. Morgan, 172 A.D.2d 312, 568 N.Y.S.2d 613 (1st Dept. 1991).

—Testimony that a search warrant for the premises had been obtained was permissible to alert the jury to the proper reasons for the police attention to the location. People v. Roman, 171 A.D.2d 562, 567 N.Y.S.2d 445 (1st Dept. 1991).

—The general testimony of uncharged crimes by the undercover officer was admitted as background material to complete a coherent narrative of the entire incident. People v. Reyes, 171 A.D.2d 461, 462, 567 N.Y.S.2d 225, 226 (1st Dept. 1991).

Impeachment.—While the People may not use a plea or the contents of a plea allocution on either their direct case or for impeachment, they may use statements made before plea negotiations and testimony given afterward. People v. Curdgel, 191 A.D.2d 743, 594 N.Y.S.2d 410 (3d Dept. 1993), aff'd, 83 N.Y.2d 862, 611 N.Y.S.2d 827, 634 N.E.2d 199 (1994).

Joint statements.—Before a joint statement may be received in evidence, the People must establish that the statement was made by defendant and that it can be effectively redacted for the jury without prejudice to the defendant. People v. Charles, 78 N.Y.2d 1044, 1045, 576 N.Y.S.2d 81, 82, 581 N.E.2d 1336, 1337 (1991).

Behavior of an animal.—In a prosecution for the robbery of a gas station, it was proper for the trial court to allow testimony by the gas station attendant of the gas station dog's behavior with respect to the defendant, other employees and strangers before, during, and after the crime. People v. Clow, 62 A.D.2d 880, 406 N.Y.S.2d 598 (3d Dept. 1978).

—Court properly admitted evidence of the trailing of the victim by a bloodhound after the prosecution laid the proper foundation for that evidence and the court gave the required cautionary instruction. People v. Muggelberg, 132 A.D.2d 988, 518 N.Y.S.2d 285 (4th Dept. 1987).

Best evidence.—The introduction of a photocopy did not violate the best evidence rule since the People sufficiently explained the unavailability of the primary evidence and did not procure its loss or destruction in bad faith. People v. Hamilton, 3 A.D.3d 405, 771 N.Y.S.2d 104 (1st Dept. 2004).

—Facsimile copy of business record properly admitted under best evidence rule since a proper excuse was offered for the nonproduction of the original certificate. People v. Miller, 199 A.D.2d 692, 605 N.Y.S.2d 160 (3d Dept. 1994).

—Court erred in permitting a co-defendant to testify during the prosecutor's direct case regarding the contents of a letter that was not produced; admission of that testimony violated the best evidence rule, which requires that one who desires to prove the contents of a writing, do so by producing the writing itself unless sufficient reasons is shown for its absence. People v. Pennick, 204 A.D.2d 988, 612 N.Y.S.2d 723 (4th Dept. 1994).

—The best evidence rule requires production of an original writing where its contents are in dispute and sought to be proven. Under a long-recognized exception to the best evidence rule, secondary evidence of the contents of an unproduced original may be admitted upon threshold factual findings that the proponent of the substitute has sufficiently explained the unavailability of the primary evidence and that the derivative proof "is a reliable and accurate portrayal of the original." People v. Jiminez, 8 Misc. 3d 803, 796 N.Y.S.2d 232 (Sup. Ct. Bronx Co. 2005).

Bruton issue.—At joint trial of defendant and co-defendant, trial court committed reversible error in admitting confession of nontestifying co-defendant that implicated the defendant. People v. Evans, 99 A.D.2d 452, 471 N.Y.S.2d 279 (1st Dept. 1984).

Chain of custody.—When evidence is not patently identifiable or is capable of being replaced or altered, admissibility generally requires that all those who have handled the item identify it and testify as to its custody and unchanged condition. People v. Rutter, 202 A.D.2d 123, 616 N.Y.S.2d 598 (1st Dept. 1994).

—Court properly admitted into evidence deformed bullet found next to the victim's body, even though it could not be definitively linked to the weapon that fired several other bullets into the victim's body; the fact merely went to the weight, rather than the admissibility, of that evidence. People v. Jamison, 208 A.D.2d 360, 616 N.Y.S.2d 735 (1st Dept. 1994).

—Where there are reasonable assurances of the identity and unchanged condition of the evidence, deficiencies in the chain of custody go to the weight of the evidence and not to its admissibility. People v. Rivera, 184 A.D.2d 153, 592 N.Y.S.2d 697 (1st Dept. 1993).

—Reasonable assurances of the identity and unchanged condition of the drugs was present where the drugs remained in police custody the entire time and the chemists testified that the envelopes they received were sealed. People v. Smith, 189 A.D.2d 652, 592 N.Y.S.2d 355 (1st Dept. 1993).

—While the People's failure to call all subsequent police handlers of the buy money might affect the weight accorded to that evidence, it does not preclude its admissibility. People v. Jackson, 182 A.D.2d 455, 582 N.Y.S.2d 179 (1st Dept. 1992).

—In prosecution for criminal possession of a weapon in the third degree, court improperly admitted into evidence five shell casings recovered from the ground at the scene of the shooting, where police ballistics experts were unable to connect the shells to defendant's gun, abandoned near the scene; however, error was harmless since nearly all of the witnesses testified, without defense objection, that several shots had been fired and that there were shell casings on the sidewalk. People v. Sumpter, 286 A.D.2d 450, 729 N.Y.S.2d 506 (2d Dept. 2001).

—Any gap in custody between the officer's sealing of the vouchered narcotics envelope and the chemist's receipt did not operate to bar admission of the narcotics into evidence. People v. Brathwaite, 204 A.D.2d 733, 613 N.Y.S.2d 26 (2d Dept. 1994).

—The fact that the police chemist who initially analyzed the contents of the vials did not testify at trial was not fatal to establishing the requisite chain of custody. People v. Leach, 203 A.D.2d 484, 611 N.Y.S.2d 17 (2d Dept. 1994).

—A chain of custody should be tested not by the satisfaction of a technical series of steps but by whether the proof satisfies the rationale for requiring an evidentiary foundation; the gap in custody between the officer's sealing of the vouchered narcotics envelope and the chemist's receipt thereof does not operate to bar its admission into evidence. People v. Stephens, 189 A.D.2d 837, 592 N.Y.S.2d 470 (2d Dept. 1993).

—Where the prosecutor testified that the tape was a fair and accurate representation of the conversation in question, and that it had not been altered, proof of a chain of custody was not required for admission of the tape-recorded conversation. People v. Holland, 179 A.D.2d 822, 578 N.Y.S.2d 917 (2d Dept. 1992).

—Any claimed gaps in the chain of custody go to the weight of the evidence, not its admissibility. People v. Davis, 193 A.D.2d 885, 597 N.Y.S.2d 780 (3d Dept. 1993).

—There is no requirement that the People establish the "chain of custody" of an item before it comes under the control of the authorities. People v. Taylor, 206 A.D.2d 904, 616 N.Y.S.2d 116 (4th Dept. 1994).

—The court properly admitted the rifle and ammunition into evidence where there were reasonable assurances of the identity and unchanged condition of the evidence; any deficiencies in the chain of custody merely affected the weight of that evidence. People v. Roman, 201 A.D.2d 933, 607 N.Y.S.2d 762 (4th Dept. 1994).

Character evidence.—The jury may not ignore the People's evidence tending to establish guilt and, consider only the defendant's evidence of good character, and render an acquittal based solely thereon. People v. Aharonowicz, 71 N.Y.2d 678, 682, 529 N.Y.S.2d 736, 738, 525 N.E.2d 458, 460 (1988).

—Character evidence is only admissible in the form of a defendant's general reputation in the community. People v. Taylor, 162 A.D.2d 175, 556 N.Y.S.2d 307 (1st Dept. 1990).

—Court did not err in precluding defendant from introducing character evidence of his reputation for truth and veracity; because the evidence did not relate to a trait involved in the charge of sodomy, sexual abuse, or endangering the welfare of a child, the trial court acted properly. People v. Sulkey, 195 A.D.2d 1026, 600 N.Y.S.2d 858 (4th Dept. 1993).

—Court did not err in precluding the defendant from introducing character evidence as to his reputation for truth and veracity as such evidence did not relate to the traits involved in the

charges against him, which were assault and reckless endangerment. People v. Sullivan, 150 Misc. 2d 10, 567 N.Y.S.2d 599 (Sup. Ct. Albany Co. 1991).

Conduct at line-up.—Court properly received into evidence a copy of the lineup form to clarify confusing testimony as to whether the lineup witness had selected the third person from the left or the third person from the right. People v. Sanders, 173 A.D.2d 391, 570 N.Y.S.2d 23 (1st Dept. 1991).

—There was no merit to defendant's contention that the admission of evidence at the trial regarding his apparent exchange of name and clothing for purposes of the line-up violated his privilege against self-incrimination, since defendant voluntarily engaged in such conduct and this evidence was admissible to show consciousness of guilt. People v. Pilgrim, 67 A.D.2d 1011, 413 N.Y.S.2d 751 (2d Dept. 1979).

Consciousness of guilt.—Court properly admitted testimony that defendant made a threatening gesture to a prosecution witness during a break in that witness's testimony; the throat-slitting gesture was highly probative of defendant's consciousness of guilt and was admissible, regardless of the possibility of innocent explanations. People v. Herrera, 245 A.D.2d 12, 665 N.Y.S.2d 643 (1st Dept. 1997).

—Evidence of a telephone threat was properly admitted; although the witness was unfamiliar with the defendant's voice, the circumstances made it highly likely that the call was by the defendant, and not an imposter or similarly named person. People v. Joseph, 207 A.D.2d 750, 616 N.Y.S.2d 733 (1st Dept. 1994).

—There was no error in the prosecutor's questioning of defendant concerning whether he was aware that he was being sought by the authorities prior to his arrest. People v. Brown, 192 A.D.2d 356, 596 N.Y.S.2d 36 (1st Dept. 1993).

—Prosecutor properly commented upon flight evidence where police attempted to locate defendant for two weeks to no avail. People v. Rosa, 176 A.D.2d 187, 574 N.Y.S.2d 311 (1st Dept. 1991).

—Defendant's claim that the court erred in permitting into evidence that at a meeting, at which his attorney was present, he attempted to secure his release from jail in exchange for information regarding the source of the drugs he planned to sell, was not preserved for review by timely objection and was in any event without merit; the defendant could have sought as a condition for the negotiations an agreement from the prosecutor not to use his statements against him. People v. Melo, 160 A.D.2d 600, 554 N.Y.S.2d 530 (1st Dept. 1990).

—The People contended that defendant's alteration of a tattoo on his arm was admissible as evidence of consciousness of guilt. The People and defendant had stipulated that defendant at one time had a tattoo on his arm which said "Pike," the name by which defendant was known. At the time of trial, the word "Pike" had been covered with a picture of a panther, which was shown to the jury. The trial court properly allowed the alteration of defendant's tattoo to be considered as evidence of consciousness of guilt because there was sufficient evidence from which it could be inferred that the tattoo was altered after the shooting and the court gave a comprehensive instruction regarding evidence of consciousness of guilt. People v. Spruill, 299 A.D.2d 374, 750 N.Y.S.2d 312 (2d Dept. 2002).

—Co-defendant's testimony—that, while in a holding cell, the defendant had admitted possessing the gun that was the subject of the indictment, and said, "Yo, Steve, take the rap for the gun because I got a record. You know I got a record, and I can't afford it"—was properly admitted as evidence of consciousness of guilt. People v. Knight, 191 A.D.2d 713, 595 N.Y.S.2d 797 (2d Dept. 1993).

—False statements of a defendant can reasonably be interpreted as establishing consciousness of guilt. People v. Holmes, 170 A.D.2d 534, 566 N.Y.S.2d 93 (2d Dept. 1991).

—Flight and consciousness of guilt are factors which, although of slight probative value, are to be considered by the trier of fact, even where the People have not excluded every other possible motivation for the defendant's flight. People v. Guthrie, 157 A.D.2d 668, 549 N.Y.S.2d 770 (2d Dept. 1990).

—Evidence that a defendant threatened a witness to change his testimony is highly probative and properly admitted as indicative of consciousness of guilt. People v. Sherman, 156 A.D.2d 889, 550 N.Y.S.2d 109 (3d Dept. 1990).

—Court did not error in allowing the complainant's mother to testify that, about two months after the incident, defendant and his wife came to her place of work and that defendant told her that she had "better watch out" and that what her daughter said "wasn't true"; such testimony was probative on the issue of consciousness of guilt. People v. Croft, 176 A.D.2d 1225, 576 N.Y.S.2d 719 (4th Dept. 1991).

—The prosecutor should refrain from implying that defendant's visit to his attorney's office immediately after the stabbing indicated a consciousness of guilt. People v. Henderson, 162 A.D.2d 1038, 557 N.Y.S.2d 813 (4th Dept. 1990).

Defense; generally.—Where perpetrator held knife during the robbery in his left hand, reversal was required when the court precluded the defendant from introducing evidence that he was right handed. People v. Felder, 143 A.D.2d 839, 533 N.Y.S.2d 322 (2d Dept. 1988).

—Trial court properly precluded defendant from introducing evidence of three other uncharged sex crimes committed in the area on dates when the defendant could not have committed them. People v. Capozzi, 152 A.D.2d 985, 543 N.Y.S.2d 95 (4th Dept. 1989).

—The right to present a defense does not give criminal defendants carte blanche to circumvent the rules of evidence. People v. Cepeda, 208 A.D.2d 364, 616 N.Y.S.2d 737 (1st Dept. 1994).

—A defendant has a right to introduce secondary evidence when (1) the evidence bears sufficient indicia of reliability, and (2) the witness is not longer available. People v. Phan, 208 A.D.2d 659, 617 N.Y.S.2d 480 (2d Dept. 1994).

Demonstrations.—Given the variations in the conditions of a courtroom and a moving train, it was not an abuse of discretion for the court to prevent defendant and his attorney from demonstrating defendant's struggle with the decedent. People v. Esquilin, 207 A.D.2d 686, 616 N.Y.S.2d 364 (1st Dept. 1994).

—It was not error to admit, as a demonstrative aid, a knife similar to, but not the same as, that used in the robbery. People v. Felder, 182 A.D.2d 495, 582 N.Y.S.2d 20 (1st Dept. 1992).

—Court did not abuse its discretion in permitting the complainant to show the jury the scars on his chest, which were the result of the robbery charges for which the defendant was being tried, since the sole purpose of this display was to demonstrate the seriousness of the injuries and not to arouse the emotions of the jury and to prejudice the defendant. People v. Hunter, 131 A.D.2d 877, 517 N.Y.S.2d 234 (2d Dept. 1987).

—Court did not err in having the defendant stand before jury in order for it to determine whether or not he was cross-eyed since the complaining witness had previously testified that one of the perpetrators had possessed this characteristic. People v. Brown, 133 A.D.2d 464, 519 N.Y.S.2d 680 (2d Dept. 1987).

Dismissal of accomplice's case not admissible.— Court properly precluded elicitation of testimony that the case against the accomplice was dismissed, which supposedly suggested a motive for the police to falsify evidence against defendant because the testimony was "not probative of the proposition it was offered to support." People v. Tejada, 249 A.D.2d 208, 671 N.Y.S.2d 755 (1st Dept. 1998).

Dog-tracking evidence; no *Frye* hearing required.—*Frye* hearing was unnecessary to determine admissibility of dog-tracking evidence for human scent because use of canine was investigative rather than scientific procedure; all the People needed to do was lay a proper foundation for admission of dog-tracking evidence. People v. Roraback, 242 A.D.2d 400, 662 N.Y.S.2d 327 (3d Dept. 1997).

Evidence of threat to prosecution witness.—Trial court improperly admitted statements that victim made concerning violent and threatening behavior of defendant, and admission was an unwarranted expansion of *People v. Geraci*, 85 N.Y.2d 359, 625 N.Y.S.2d 469, 649 N.E.2d 817, because there was no evidence that defendant's acts against absent witness were motivated by a desire to prevent victim from testifying, but error was harmless. People v. Maher, 89 N.Y.2d 456, 654 N.Y.S.2d 1004, 677 N.E.2d 728 (1997).

—Court properly found that defendant had forfeited his right of confrontation with respect to eyewitness's grand jury testimony and properly allowed prosecution to introduce that testimony as part of its direct case, where evidence presented at *Sirois* hearings supported court's determination that the eyewitness had been threatened with death if she testified that defendant was responsible for or acquiesced in witness's intimidation, and the eyewitness subsequently testified at trial but claimed total ignorance of the crime. People v. Brown, 308 A.D.2d 379, 764 N.Y.S.2d 272 (1st Dept. 2003).

—Court properly admitted testimony that defendant made a threatening gesture to a prosecution witness during a break in that witness's testimony; the throat-slitting gesture was highly probative of defendant's consciousness of guilt and was admissible, regardless of the possibility of innocent explanations. People v. Herrera, 245 A.D.2d 12, 665 N.Y.S.2d 643 (1st Dept. 1997).

Habit evidence.—Court properly received evidence concerning victim's habit of carrying cash on his person, where the testimony evidenced a deliberate and repetitive practice sufficient to allow the inference of its persistence. People v. D'Arton, 289 A.D.2d 711, 734 N.Y.S.2d 309 (3d Dept. 2001).

—Court did not err in admitting evidence of victim's business habits; habit evidence is probative when it relates to one's routine business or professional undertakings; such evidence may also be adduced to establish one's personal habit or routine, including one's habit of carrying a particular item on one's person; the People were thus properly permitted to establish that it was the business and personal practice of the victim to carry large sums of money on his person; they presented adequate foundation for such evidence, including four witnesses who testified that the victim always carried large amounts of cash for specified purposes. People v. LoPiccolo, 288 A.D.2d 913, 733 N.Y.S.2d 560 (4th Dept. 2001).

Failure to preserve evidence; dismissal of indictment improper.—Trial court improperly dismissed two informations because the People failed to preserve evidence that was seized from the defendant since less drastic remedies, such as appropriate instructions to the jury, could have eliminated any prejudice to the defendant. People v. Kelly, 62 N.Y.2d 516, 478 N.Y.S.2d 834, 467 N.E.2d 498 (1984).

Flight.—Evidence of flight was competent where defendant tried to escape while officer was investigating area where drugs were thought to be concealed, since, unexplained, it tended to show consciousness of guilt. People v. Bryant, 60 A.D.2d 810, 401 N.Y.S.2d 76 (1st Dept. 1978).

—Evidence of flight is admissible as circumstantial evidence of consciousness of guilt. People v. Yaghnam, 135 A.D.2d 763, 522 N.Y.S.2d 668 (2d Dept. 1987).

—Evidence of flight of a co-defendant is admissible into evidence by the defendant to show the absconding co-defendant's guilty knowledge and defendant's lack of knowledge as to the presence of marijuana; and exclusion of this evidence by the court denied the defendant his right to establish his defense. People v. Ofunniyin, 114 A.D.2d 1045, 495 N.Y.S.2d 485 (2d Dept. 1985).

—Defendant's proffering of an innocent explanation for his flight, that he believed the police wanted him because he neglected to appear in court on a misdemeanor charge for which an arrest warrant was outstanding, did not serve as a bar to evidence of flight but rather presented the jury an alternative reason for his fleeing, which it was free to accept or reject. People v. Snyder, 124 A.D.2d 394, 507 N.Y.S.2d 493 (3d Dept. 1986).

Fingerprints.—Fingerprint evidence is deemed sufficient to establish guilt beyond a reasonable doubt. People v. Collins, 150 A.D.2d 476, 541 N.Y.S.2d 79 (2d Dept. 1989).

Miscellaneous.—Court properly allowed testimony as to why officers approached the suspects with their weapons drawn. People v. Brown, 160 A.D.2d 440, 554 N.Y.S.2d 492 (1st Dept. 1990), *aff'd*, 78 N.Y.2d 874, 573 N.Y.S.2d 67, 577 N.E.2d 58 (1991).

—It was not error to refuse defendant's offer of the UF-61 report into evidence where the report was a summary of what the police officer was told by the two eyewitnesses and, in the circumstances presented, the apparent composite description recorded in the report without attribution was not an inconsistent statement. People v. Fortunato, 191 A.D.2d 221, 594 N.Y.S.2d 245 (1st Dept. 1993).

—References to police surveillance of the apartment from which defendant was seen exiting were not unduly prejudicial to the defendant. People v. Baez, 208 A.D.2d 638, 617 N.Y.S.2d 203 (2d Dept. 1994). *See also* People v. McCallop, 159 A.D.2d 731, 553 N.Y.S.2d 212 (2d Dept. 1990).

—Although proof aimed at establishing a motive to fabricate is never collateral and may not be excluded on that ground, a trial court may, in the exercise of its discretion, properly exclude such proof where it is too remote or speculative. People v. Rodriguez, 191 A.D.2d 723, 595 N.Y.S.2d 799 (2d Dept. 1993).

—The trial court correctly ruled that extrinsic evidence of the weather on the day of the crime, directed solely to impeach the complainant's memory and powers of observation, was collateral and thus inadmissible. People v. Windley, 181 A.D.2d 703, 581 N.Y.S.2d 220 (2d Dept. 1992).

—The admission of testimony indicating that the defendant was of Colombian origin did not deprive him of a fair trial; the prosecutor sought to adduce testimony regarding the defendant's pedigree information as given to the police after the arrest in order to negate the defense that defendant's arrest was based on misidentification. People v. Vargas, 161 A.D.2d 822, 556 N.Y.S.2d 145 (2d Dept. 1990).

—Prior inconsistent statements used for the purposes of testimonial impeachment have no substantial or independent evidentiary value. People v. Hall, 208 A.D.2d 1044, 617 N.Y.S.2d 579 (3d Dept. 1994).

—Where an object possesses unique characteristics or markings and is not subject to material alteration that would not be readily apparent, a simple identification is sufficient to warrant admission into evidence; witness testified that the bat looked "exactly like the bat I turned over." People v. Weiler, 194 A.D.2d 894, 599 N.Y.S.2d 149 (3d Dept. 1993).

—It was manifest injustice to allow the People to put into evidence only those portions of defendant's statement which incriminated him, while deleting the exculpatory portion. People v. Lewis, 182 A.D.2d 1083, 583 N.Y.S.2d 81 (4th Dept. 1992).

—Victim's blood-stained pants were properly admitted into evidence as probative on the issue of whether any force was used in the sexual assault. People v. Hill, 163 A.D.2d 852, 558 N.Y.S.2d 380 (4th Dept. 1990).

Motive.—Evidence of defendant's lifestyle and precarious financial condition at the time of the killing were properly admitted on the issue of motive. People v. Glanda, 5 A.D.3d 945, 774 N.Y.S.2d 576 (3d Dept. 2004), cert. denied, — U.S. —, 125 S. Ct. 973 (2005).

Grand jury testimony.—Reversal was warranted where court permitted admission of recalcitrant witness's Grand Jury testimony. People v. Russ, 79 N.Y.S.2d 173, 581 N.Y.S.2d 152, 589 N.E.2d 375 (1992).

—The defendants forfeited their right to confrontation or to otherwise object to the admissibility of the Grand Jury testimony of an eyewitness where the People proved that the defendants or someone acting on their behalf caused the death of the eyewitness. People v. La Torres, 186 A.D.2d 479, 590 N.Y.S.2d 187 (1st Dept. 1992).

—Court erred in permitting the People to use Grand Jury testimony to rehabilitate a witness who had been impeached. People v. Thornton, 139 A.D.2d 787, 527 N.Y.S.2d 532 (2d Dept. 1988).

—Court erred in admitting grand jury testimony of store owner in place of her live testimony at trial because the People failed to establish that the witness's unavailability was procured by the defendant, and all of the threats warning the store owner not to testify were made by a suspected accomplice, not defendant; nonetheless, the error was harmless. People v. Perkins, 289 A.D.2d 940, 735 N.Y.S.2d 273 (4th Dept. 2001).

For more annotations related to grand jury testimony, see annotations under CPL § 670.10, Use in a criminal proceeding of testimony given in a previous proceeding; when authorized.

Grand jury testimony; recantation.—Once prosecution witnesses recanted their grand jury testimony regarding the defendant's alleged admission of participation in a murder, the use of the prior grand jury testimony constituted only impeachment evidence and not direct evidence of the substance thereof; the remaining evidence, being purely circumstantial in nature, was insufficient to sustain the conviction. People v. Rodriguez, 102 A.D.2d 874, 476 N.Y.S.2d 925 (2d Dept. 1984).

Witness died prior to trial.—Court did not err in allowing into evidence testimony taken at a pretrial hearing of a witness, who died prior to the trial, since the defendant was afforded ample opportunity to cross-examine the witness at the hearing with respect to the subject matter for which the testimony was used at trial. People v. Claudio, 130 A.D.2d 759, 515 N.Y.S.2d 845 (2d Dept. 1987).

—Where defense counsel at suppression hearing was not afforded right to cross-examine police officer on issue of voluntariness and accuracy of defendant's alleged statements, and officer died before trial, his testimony at the hearing on the issues of voluntariness and accuracy could not be admitted into evidence at the trial. To do so would violate defendant's right of cross-examination. People v. Mayo, 35 A.D.2d 469, 319 N.Y.S.2d 764 (4th Dept. 1971), dism'd, 31 N.Y.2d 707, 337 N.Y.S.2d 515, 289 N.E.2d 556 (1972).

Witness dies during cross-examination.—During cross-examination of Investigator Cotter the court adjourned for the weekend during which the witness died in an auto accident. Defendant moved for a mistrial. There was no prejudice in the denial of the motion since the cross-examination prior to the witness's death was extensive. People v. Loewinger, 37 A.D.2d 675, 323 N.Y.S.2d 98 (3d Dept. 1972), aff'd, 30 N.Y.2d 587, 330 N.Y.S.2d 801, 281 N.E.2d 847 (1974).

Handwriting exemplars.—A court ordered handwriting exemplar will be authorized (1) when, in the interest of justice, or when in the interest of public or private safety, it is necessary to determine authorship, validity, or authenticity of a questioned handwritten instrument or document and (2) when it appears that an identifiable person, or persons, have exercised such control over and have had such access to the questioned instruments that there is probable cause to believe that such person, or persons, wrote or authored the questioned documents; however, the court is required to make a factual determination upon notice to all parties to determine the reasonableness and constitutional validity of the requested submission of an identifiable and known exemplar. Special Prosecutor (Onondaga Co.) v. G.W., 95 Misc. 2d 298, 407 N.Y.S.2d 112 (Sup. Ct. Onondaga Co. 1978).

Handwriting comparison.—CPLR 4536 provides that comparison of a disputed writing with a satisfactory standard is permissible, and the jury in its deliberation may make such comparison whether or not an expert offers an opinion. People v. Hunter, 34 N.Y.2d 432, 358 N.Y.S.2d 360, 315 N.E.2d 436 (1974).

—It was not violative of the Fifth Amendment to compel defendants, who were indicted for grand larceny, to submit handwriting exemplars where the defendants had exercised sufficient control over and/or have had access to the instruments with which exemplars are sought for comparison. In re District Attorney of Bronx Co., 96 Misc. 2d 154, 408 N.Y.S.2d 924 (Sup. Ct. Bronx Co. 1978).

—Defendant's jury waiver, which was executed in the presence of the court immediately prior to trial, and was part of the record before the court, could be utilized by the trial judge in his capacity as the trier of facts as the basis for authenticating defendant's purported signature on the checks and corporate resolutions in evidence. People v. Reilly, 93 Misc. 2d 63, 403 N.Y.S.2d 400 (1978).

Intent to sell; evidence of.—Court did not improperly allow prosecutor to elicit testimony about defendant's possession of beeper and cell phone as well as the undercover detective's testimony that detective had previously used a beeper and cell phone to contact drug dealers because testimony was probative of defendant's intent to sell an illegal substance. People v. Cartagena, 9 A.D.3d 468, 780 N.Y.S.2d 288 (2d Dept. 2004).

HEARSAY

Res gestae.—Where statements of third party explained and characterized the drug sale between declarant and the undercover officer, they were admissible as part of the res gestae. People v. Woods, 202 A.D.2d 1043, 610 N.Y.S.2d 108 (4th Dept. 1994).

Admissions.—It was error to allow a purported confession into evidence where it is handwritten by a law enforcement official, never signed or orally acknowledged by the defendant nor read to or by him. People v. Lee, 159 A.D.2d 238, 552 N.Y.S.2d 218 (1st Dept. 1990).

—A confession is a voluntary express acknowledgment by the accused that he engaged in conduct which constitutes the crime charged, or an essential part of it. People v. Alexander, 153 A.D.2d 507, 544 N.Y.S.2d 595 (1st Dept. 1989), aff'd, 75 N.Y.2d 979, 556 N.Y.S.2d 508, 555 N.E.2d 905 (1990); People v. Edwards, 147 A.D.2d 586, 537 N.Y.S.2d 879 (2d Dept. 1989).

—Defendant's grand jury testimony was properly admitted as an admission. People v. Rodriguez, 191 A.D.2d 597, 595 N.Y.S.2d 73 (2d Dept. 1993).

—Defendant's silence in response to co-defendant's statement inculpating them constituted an admission by silence. People v. Benanti, 158 A.D.2d 698, 551 N.Y.S.2d 963 (2d Dept. 1990).

—Any act or declaration of the accused inconsistent with his innocence is admissible as an admission. People v. Harris, 148 A.D.2d 474, 538 N.Y.S.2d 621 (2d Dept. 1989).

—Defendant's statement was a tacit acknowledgment of guilt and was properly admitted as an admission. People v. Williams, 154 A.D.2d 724, 546 N.Y.S.2d 907 (2d Dept. 1989).

—Judicial admissions are only binding and conclusive in the proceeding in which they are made; in other, separate actions, they are converted to informal judicial admissions, receivable in evidence as an admission, but subject to being explained or contested. People v. Jacobs, 149 A.D.2d 112, 544 N.Y.S.2d 1011 (3d Dept. 1989).

—Where defendant stated to prosecutor before case went to trial that "he could not do the time," People sought to introduce the statement as an admission. Court excluded the statement as hearsay and as ambiguous, finding that an individual's plea that he cannot do the time could no more be attributed as an admission of guilt than to an innocent person wishing to forestall the potential jail sentence which could be imposed following an erroneous conviction. People v. Ballinger, 176 Misc. 2d 803, 675 N.Y.S.2d 494 (Sup. Ct. Kings Co. 1998).

Declaration against penal interest; admissibility.—The admission of a non-testifying codefendant's plea allocution was subject to the requirements of the Sixth Amendment's Confrontation Clause. Crawford v. Washington, 541 U.S. 36, 124 S. Ct. 1354, 158 L. Ed. 2d 177 (2004) (rejecting Ohio v. Roberts, 448 U.S. 56, 100 S. Ct. 2531, 65 L. Ed. 2d 597 (1980)).

—Court erred in allowing People's use of redacted version of codefendant's plea allocution at defendant's trial because it was a testimonial statement that was not subject to cross-examination, but the error was harmless. People v. Douglas, 4 N.Y.3d 777, 793 N.Y.S.2d 825, 826 N.E.2d 796 (2005).

—Trial court erred in admitting the plea allocution of a non-testifying codefendant, and the admission was not harmless error because the prosecution heavily relied on the allocution in presenting its case, and the jury heavily relied on it, in a case where the only evidence inculpating the defendant was the testimony of a witness who had a long criminal history and there were no identifying witnesses. People v. Hardy, 4 N.Y.3d 192, 791 N.Y.S.2d 513, 824 N.E.2d 953 (2005).

—When the People seek to introduce a declaration against penal interest of an unavailable third party to inculpate a defendant, through the testimony of an in-court witness, and the defendant claims that such evidence is unreliable, the trial court should conduct a hearing to determine whether the criteria for admissibility are actually satisfied. People v. Brensic, 70 N.Y.2d 9, 15, 517 N.Y.S.2d 120, 123, 509 N.E.2d 1226, 1228 (1987).

—Statements in plea allocutions are neither admissible nor inadmissible as declarations against penal interest. People v. Thomas, 68 N.Y.2d 294, 507 N.Y.S.2d 973, 500 N.E.2d 293 (1986).

—Letters from the defendant's father which were written a few days before the father's suicide and in which the father claimed responsibility for the decedent's death were not admissible as declarations against the father's penal interest due to the strong motivation of the father to exculpate his son as well as the father's inability to provide some possible explanation for the decedent's death; it should also benoted that the defendant had previously made inculpatory statements to the police fully describing his actions in killing the decedent. People v. Shortridge, 65 N.Y.2d 309, 491 N.Y.S.2d 298, 480 N.E.2d 1080 (1985).

—Only when there is other evidence tending to show that the declarant or someone he implicates as his accomplice actually committed a crime, may a declaration against penal interest be said to display the degree of reliability sufficient to overcome the dangers of admitting hearsay evidence. People v. Settles, 46 N.Y.2d 154, 412 N.Y.S.2d 874, 385 N.E.2d 612 (1978).

—Court properly admitted a non-testifying codefendant's plea allocution as a declaration against penal interest, since it possessed sufficient guarantees of trustworthiness and met all the constitutional requirements for admission of such a declaration. People v. Douglas, 309 A.D.2d 597, 765 N.Y.S.2d 349 (1st Dept. 2003), aff'd, 4 N.Y.3d 777, 793 N.Y.S.2d 825, 826 N.E.2d 796 (2005).

—A statement may qualify as a declaration against penal interest even when made to a friend, trusted by the declarant not to reveal it to police. People v. Thomas, 264 A.D.2d 691, 697 N.Y.S.2d 1 (1st Dept. 1999).

—The statement was admissible as a declaration against penal interest where (1) the declarant was unavailable at the time of the trial; (2) the declarant was aware that the statement was adverse to his penal interest; (3) the declarant had knowledge of the facts; (4) there was independent proof of the trust worthiness of the statement, and there was a satisfactory showing that resort to such proof was necessary to the discovery of the truth and that the evidence was reliable. People v. Green, 75 A.D.2d 502, 426 N.Y.S.2d 736 (1st Dept. 1980); see also People v. Scalise, 70 A.D.2d 346, 421 N.Y.S.2d 637 (3d Dept. 1979).

—Third party statements used against the accused may be admitted only when competent independent evidence is presented to establish that the declaration was spoken under circumstances which renders it highly probable that it is truthful; declarations which exculpate a defendant, however, are subject to a more lenient standard; supportive evidence is sufficient if it establishes a reasonable possibility that the statement might be true. People v. Fonfrias, 204 A.D.2d 736, 612 N.Y.S.2d 421 (2d Dept. 1994).

—Where prosecution seeks admission of hearsay declarations tending to inculpate defendant, it is subjected to more exacting scrutiny as compared to exculpatory statements of which defendant is the proponent, and a declaration against penal interest should be admitted only "to the extent the statement is disserving to declarant." People v. Campney, 252 A.D.2d 734, 677 N.Y.S.2d 393 (3d Dept. 1998).

Declaration of future intention.—Declarations of future intent are admissible to infer subsequent acts of the declarant when there is a basis in the record premised on evidence independent of the statement of future intent that supports the inference that the act was carried out; such a declaration is inadmissible where, as here, there is no evidence before the jury to give credence to the desired inference. People v. Rivers, 177 Misc. 2d 738, 677 N.Y.S.2d 427 (Sup. Ct. Bronx Co. 1998).

—Testimony did not constitute hearsay where it was evidence of the victim's intent to meet the defendant. People v. Smythe, 172 A.D.2d 1028, 569 N.Y.S.2d 287 (4th Dept. 1991).

Dying declarations.—In a manslaughter prosecution deceased's in-hospital statement identifying her assailant was not admissible as a dying declaration since it was not shown decedent knew she was dying without the slightest chance of recovery; however, considering the trustworthiness of the proffered evidence in light of all of the relevant circumstances, the statement was admissible as an excited utterance. People v. Nieves, 108 A.D.2d 165, 488 N.Y.S.2d 654 (1st Dept. 1985).

—The victim's statements were made under a sense of impending death and at a time when she had no hope of recovery, where she repeatedly told the neighbors attending her that she was dying and she expressed concern for her children's future and she was losing blood rapidly from multiple stab wounds although she erroneously believed herself to be shot and were dying declarations; other statements, however, were clearly opinions of what she thought happened and not what she knew happened, since dying declarations are admissible only to the extent that they state facts and not opinions or conclusions, it was error to receive the latter statements. People v. Liccione, 63 A.D.2d 305, 407 N.Y.S.2d 753 (4th Dept. 1978), aff'd, 50 N.Y.2d 850, 430 N.Y.S.2d 36, 407 N.E.2d 1333 (1980).

Excited utterances.—Where challenged declaration was made in narrative form and in response to prompting a full hour after the startling event, and the declarant had become more relaxed, court could not say that declarant's capacity for deliberation and reflection remained stilled, but admission was harmless because of eyewitness testimony. People v. Johnson, 1 N.Y.3d 302, 772 N.Y.S.2d 238, 804 N.E.2d 402 (2003) (case discusses the excited utterance exception).

—Statement of victim did not constitute an "excited utterance" where, from declarant's level of responsiveness, his activity and his condition, it could not reasonably be concluded that the remarks were not made under the impetus of studied reflection. People v. Norton, 79 N.Y.2d 808, 580 N.Y.S.2d 174, 588 N.E.2d 72 (1991).

—Unless the questioning causes some interruption of or moderation in declarant's continued stress and excitement from the shocking event, it does not, standing alone—any more than do other specific circumstances—defeat the admissibility of the responses as excited utterances. People v. Brown, 70 N.Y.2d 513, 522, 522 N.Y.S.2d 837, 842, 517 N.E.2d 515, 519 (1987).

—Court of Appeals refused to adopt a rule that fixed an arbitrary limitation on the permissible period between the event and the excited utterance. People v. Brooks, 71 N.Y.2d 753, 527 N.Y.S.2d 753, 522 N.E.2d 1051 (1988).

—Trial court properly admitted statements made by complainant to police as excited utterances, where she spoke while under the stress or influence of the excitement caused by the rape so that her reflective capacity was stilled. People v. Powell, 288 A.D.2d 5, 732 N.Y.S.2d 216 (1st Dept. 2001).

—A tape recording of the complainant's 911 call was properly admitted into evidence as an excited utterance. People v. Gonzalez, 193 A.D.2d 360, 597 N.Y.S.2d 44 (1st Dept. 1993).

—The statement constituted an excited utterance even though it came some 45 minutes after the startling event. People v. Garcia, 189 A.D.2d 587, 592 N.Y.S.2d 43 (1st Dept. 1993).

—Court improperly admitted statement as "excited utterance" where the witness was not in shock at the time of the statement, had never lost consciousness and at the time of his statement had the capacity to fabricate and in fact had provided his informed consent for surgery and where the defendant was a member of the declarant's archival gang. People v. Lee, 177 A.D.2d 288, 576 N.Y.S.2d 97 (1st Dept. 1991).

—Court properly admitted as an excited utterance the stabbing victim's out-of-court statement identifying the defendant as his assailant because the victim made the statement while under the influence of nervous excitement caused by his life-threatening injury and at a time when he was incapable of reasoned reflection and deliberation. People v. Corker, 309 A.D.2d 816, 765 N.Y.S.2d 660 (2d Dept. 2003).

—Trial court improperly overruled defense counsel's objection to testimony by the complainant's aunt that the complainant had told her that the defendant set fire to the apartment, finding that the testimony was admissible as an excited utterance. Since the complainant did not observe the defendant set the fire, her statement to her aunt did not qualify as an excited utterance, and the judgment was reversed. People v. Boston, 296 A.D.2d 576, 746 N.Y.S.2d 28 (2d Dept. 2002).

—Court properly admitted as an excited utterance a recording of the 911 emergency telephone call in which the caller identified defendant as the person who shot her husband. People v. Joseph, 287 A.D.2d 742, 732 N.Y.S.2d 248 (2d Dept. 2001).

—The evidence was legally sufficient to establish defendant's guilt of criminal mischief in the fourth degree, where defendant allegedly drove a school bus through a red light, hitting a car and causing injuries to the driver. However, the Second Department ordered a new trial, finding it was not harmless error where the trial court refused to admit as excited utterances the defendant's statements immediately after the accident to the only passenger on the bus. People v. Cannon, 228 A.D.2d 513, 644 N.Y.S.2d 311 (2d Dept. 1996).

—The fact that the victim's statements were made in response to questioning did not necessitate a finding that they were not excited utterances. People v. Colon, 187 A.D.2d 445, 589 N.Y.S.2d 537 (2d Dept. 1992).

—Statement by victim which was made to police 30 minutes after being shot in the stomach constituted an excited utterance. People v. Evans, 183 A.D.2d 780, 583 N.Y.S.2d 510 (2d Dept. 1992).

—The "excited utterance" exception to the hearsay rule is based on the assumption that a person under the influence of the excitement precipitated by an external startling event will lack the reflective capacity essential for fabrication, and accordingly any utterance he makes will be spontaneous and trustworthy. People v. McFarlane, 181 A.D.2d 798, 581 N.Y.S.2d 243 (2d Dept. 1992).

—Court properly admitted into evidence testimony by witness that a bystander had told him that the defendant had just robbed the complainant and asked for his assistance to chase the perpetrators; statement properly characterized as an excited utterance notwithstanding that it was not made in response to a question. People v. McNeil, 163 A.D.2d 329, 557 N.Y.S.2d 162 (2d Dept. 1990).

—The criteria for admissibility of a statement as a spontaneous declaration or excited utterance are (1) the existence of an exciting event, and 2) whether it was prompted thereby without time to reflect, that is whether it was dominated by the nervous

excitement of the event. People v. Sostre, 70 A.D.2d 40, 418 N.Y.S.2d 662 (2d Dept. 1979), aff'd, 51 N.Y.2d 958, 435 N.Y.S.2d 702, 416 N.E.2d 1038 (1980).

—The trial court properly permitted the victim to testify that, several minutes after he was shot, he told an ambulance attendant that defendant was the person who shot him; the record supported the determination that the victim's response to the attendant's questions about who shot him constituted excited utterance. People v. Huggins, 199 A.D.2d 1025, 606 N.Y.S.2d 496 (4th Dept. 1994).

—Statements and gestures made by the stabbing victim some 20-30 minutes after the event were properly admitted as excited utterances; neither the lapse of time between the event and the statements nor the manner of police questioning diminished the stressful impact of the event upon the victim. People v. Cartledge, 147 A.D.2d 906, 537 N.Y.S.2d 378 (4th Dept. 1989).

Past recollection recorded.—Court erred by admitting a printed description of the alleged perpetrator prepared by the victim as a past recollection recorded; since the witness had no difficulty in recollecting the perpetrator's features, there was no basis for admission of the document as a past recollection recorded. People v. Riggio, 144 A.D.2d 951, 534 N.Y.S.2d 262 (4th Dept. 1988).

Hearsay evidence.—Hearsay pleading defects in the factual portion of a local criminal court information must be preserved in order to be reviewable as a matter of law on appeal; because defendant failed to interpose a timely objection or motion before the trial court which addressed the hearsay defect in the misdemeanor information in this case, Court of Appeals was precluded from considering it. People v. Casey, 95 N.Y.2d 354, 717 N.Y.S.2d 88, 740 N.E.2d 233 (2000).

—Whenever People allege specific facts that demonstrate "distinct possibility" that criminal defendant has engaged in witness tampering, court must grant *Sirois* hearing to test validity of that claim; at *Sirois* hearing, People must demonstrate by clear and convincing evidence that defendant, by violence, threats, or chicanery, caused witness' unavailability. If People meet that burden, defendant is precluded from asserting either "the constitutional right of confrontation or the evidentiary rules against the admission of hearsay in order to prevent the admission of the witness's out-of-court declarations." In this case, the People satisfied their burden. People v. Cotto, 92 N.Y.2d 68, 677 N.Y.S.2d 35, 699 N.E.2d 394 (1998).

—Trial court properly excluded statement defendant allegedly made to his sister within two hours after the shooting that the defendant believed the victim had been armed; although defendant claimed that the evidence was offered solely to establish his state of mind, and thus was not hearsay, the statement was irrelevant unless offered to prove the matter asserted—that defendant believed the victim was armed—and for that purpose it was inadmissible hearsay. People v. Reynoso, 73 N.Y.2d 816, 537 N.Y.S.2d 113, 534 N.E.2d 30 (1988).

—Testimony from defendant's mother concerning what the victim's mother had told her about defendant not having been involved in the crime constituted inadmissible double hearsay with no purpose other than to prove the truth of the matter asserted. People v. Boatwright, 297 A.D.2d 603, 748 N.Y.S.2d 541 (1st Dept. 2002).

—The trial court properly denied admission of the police laboratory analysis report as a "certified medical report," as the certification failed to state that the report was made in the regular course of business, that it was the regular course of the business to make the report, and that the report was made contemporaneously with the event recorded. People v. Cirilo, 191 A.D.2d 342, 596 N.Y.S.2d 7 (1st Dept. 1993).

—Out-of-court statements that are offered for the truth of their content constitute hearsay, and may not be admitted unless they come within an exception to the hearsay rule. People v. Slaughter, 189 A.D.2d 157, 596 N.Y.S.2d 22 (1st Dept. 1993).

—Where the alleged hearsay evidence elicited was not offered for its truth but was brought out to explain matters first brought up on cross-examination, the evidence did not constitute inadmissible hearsay. People v. Diaz, 189 A.D.2d 574, 592 N.Y.S.2d 29 (1st Dept. 1992).

—The spontaneous declaration exception rule applies to statements made by bystanders as well as participants. People v. Alexander, 173 A.D.2d 296, 569 N.Y.S.2d 689 (1st Dept. 1991).

—Testimony of witness to the effect that defendant had agreed to co-defendant's plan to commit a robbery using a shotgun was hearsay but it was properly received into evidence as an admission. People v. Pelt, 161 A.D.2d 284, 555 N.Y.S.2d 57 (1st Dept. 1990).

—The law does not permit the defendant to avoid taking the witness stand and to avoid being cross-examined by allowing his story to be presented through the hearsay testimony of another witness. People v. Williams, 203 A.D.2d 498, 610 N.Y.S.2d 596 (2d Dept. 1994); see also People v. Dvorznak, 127 A.D.2d 785, 512 N.Y.S.2d 180 (2d Dept. 1987).

—The general rule is that a party's self-serving statement is inadmissible at trial when offered in his or her favor, and it may not be introduced through the testimony of the party or through the testimony of a third person. People v. Oliphant, 201 A.D.2d 590, 607 N.Y.S.2d 739 (2d Dept. 1994).

—Court was within its discretion when it refused to allow the defendant to testify as to his conversation with a drug dealer prior to a sale of cocaine since any testimony concerning the conversation between the two would have been offered for the truth of the matter asserted and thus would have constituted inadmissible hearsay. People v. Lisyansky, 177 A.D.2d 509, 575 N.Y.S.2d 910, 911 (2d Dept. 1991).

—It was error for trial court to permit arresting officers to testify that they heard unidentified members of a crowd of bystanders state that "he did it" and thereafter placed defendant under arrest; although the statements may have been admissible as spontaneous declarations, there was no proof of who the declarants were and whether they had an adequate opportunity to observe the event. People v. Matos, 107 A.D.2d 823, 484 N.Y.S.2d 844 (2d Dept. 1985).

Hearsay; agency exception.—The rationale of the agency exception to the hearsay rule is simply that if a party has made an interpreter an agent for the purpose of translating what he or she says, the interpreter's translations may be received as party admissions. People v. Romero, 78 N.Y.2d 355, 362, 575 N.Y.S.2d 802, 805, 581 N.E.2d 1048, 1051 (1991).

Hearsay; co-conspirator's exception.—A declaration by a co-conspirator during the course of and in furtherance of the conspiracy is admissible against another co-conspirator as an exception to the hearsay rule; however, this evidence may be admitted only upon a showing that a prima facie case of conspiracy has been established. People v. Bac Tran, 80 N.Y.2d 170, 589 N.Y.S.2d 845, 603 N.E.2d 950 (1992).

—Since the declarant died before trial, a surreptitiously taped conversation between him and an informant could be used against a co-conspirator where declarant had full knowledge of the criminal activity in question, and believed he was speaking to a cohort in the activity; death satisfied the "unavailability" prong of the Ohio v. Roberts, 448 U.S. 56, 100 S. Ct. 235, 65 L. Ed. 2d 597 (1980), test for allowing in hearsay, and the circumstances in which declarant was taped satisfied the second prong of the test by bearing "indicia of reliability" allowing a satisfactory basis for evaluating the truth of the prior statement. People v. Sanders, 56 N.Y.2d 51, 451 N.Y.S.2d 30, 436 N.E.2d 480 (1982).

—The redacted plea allocution of defendant's co-conspirator met all of the requirements for admissibility as a declaration against penal interest, and it was properly admitted for the limited purpose of establishing the existence of a conspiracy. People v. Coscia, 279 A.D.2d 352, 719 N.Y.S.2d 80 (1st Dept. 2001).

—Statements may be admitted under the co-conspirator exception to the hearsay rule even if they are made before the defendant joins the conspiracy. People v. Reynolds, 192 A.D.2d 320, 595 N.Y.S.2d 451 (1st Dept. 1993).

—The hearsay testimony of a co-conspirator can be admitted subject to the establishment by the prosecution of a prima facie case that a conspiracy existed. People v. Green, 188 A.D.2d 662, 592 N.Y.S.2d 53 (2d Dept. 1992).

—The trial court erred in admitting the statement of a co-conspirator because the People failed to establish either that he was unavailable at the time of trial or that the statement bore some indicia of reliability. People v. Porter, 179 A.D.2d 1018, 580 N.Y.S.2d 117 (4th Dept. 1992).

—The fact that defendant is not charged with conspiracy does not preclude application of the co-conspirator exception to the hearsay rule. People v. Comfort, 151 A.D.2d 1019, 542 N.Y.S.2d 84 (4th Dept. 1989).

Prompt outcry.—A complaint is timely for purposes of the prompt outcry exception if made at the first suitable opportunity.

People v. McDaniel, 81 N.Y.2d 10, 17, 595 N.Y.S.2d 364, 368, 611 N.E.2d 265, 265 (1993).

—Proof that the victim promptly complained of being raped is admissible to show the reliability of the complaint. People v. Williams, 75 N.Y.2d 858, 552 N.Y.S.2d 917, 918, 552 N.E.2d 165 (1990).

—Admission of complaining witness' account of a description of her assailant given to the police shortly after she was raped was properly admitted for a non-hearsay purpose. People v. Huertas, 75 N.Y.2d 487, 554 N.Y.S.2d 444, 553 N.E.2d 992 (1990).

—Testimony of the complainant and police officers concerning a description of the perpetrator given by the complainant to the police immediately after the rape did not fall within the prompt-outcry exception to the hearsay rule. However the error was harmless. People v. Rice, 75 N.Y.2d 929, 555 N.Y.S.2d 677, 554 N.E.2d 1265 (1990).

—Although witnesses who have heard a victim complain may testify to the complaint, the complaint must be promptly made for the testimony to be admissible. People v. Seiver, 187 A.D.2d 683, 590 N.Y.S.2d 248 (2d Dept. 1992).

—Although witnesses who have heard a victim's prompt complaint may testify to the complaint, the testimony should be limited to the fact of the complaint and should not include details of the incident as related by the victim. People v. Beaulieu, 184 A.D.2d 1061, 1062, 584 N.Y.S.2d 367, 368 (4th Dept. 1992).

—Hearsay testimony in the nature of a prompt complaint is admissible only to bolster the victim's credibility in the face of a claim of recent fabrication. People v. Knapp, 139 A.D.2d 931, 527 N.Y.S.2d 914 (4th Dept. 1988).

—Prompt outcry evidentiary exception is limited to sex offenses of which assault is not one. People v. Rizzo, 189 Misc. 2d. 649, 735 N.Y.S.2d 916 (Dist. Ct. Nassau Co. 2001).

Present sense impression.—911 tapes were erroneously admitted under the present sense impression exception to the hearsay rule, because the shooting occurred at 4:30 a.m. and the 911 phone call was made at about 7:00 a.m., which was an extended interval that fell far beyond any acceptable time frame for admissibility under the exception. People v. Kello, 96 N.Y.2d 740, 723 N.Y.S.2d 111, 746 N.E.2d 166 (2001).

—Two 911 tapes were properly admitted—one under the present sense impression exception because it contained the caller's statements concerning his observations of the defendant, made contemporaneously with those observations, and the second under the excited utterance exception because it contained the caller's statements made immediately after watching the defendant stab the victim. People v. Carr, 277 A.D.2d 246, 716 N.Y.S.2d 59 (2d Dept. 2000).

—Court admitted 911 tape under present sense impression exception to the hearsay rule where declarant testified at trial. People v. Buie, 201 A.D.2d 156, 615 N.Y.S.2d 794 (4th Dept. 1994).

Prior consistent statement not admissible.—Admission of 911 tape of complainant's prior consistent statement to police was reversible error since it was inadmissible hearsay. People v. Jiminez, 102 A.D.2d 439, 477 N.Y.S.2d 170 (1st Dept. 1984).

Spontaneous declaration by victim.—Where deceased victim was shot six times at close range, and was bleeding profusely, his statements, to his landlady while awaiting medical aid, made within ten minutes of the shooting were admissible as spontaneous declarations. People v. McCullough, 73 A.D.2d 310, 425 N.Y.S.2d 982 (1st Dept. 1980).

—The testimony of the complaining witness, that about three minutes after the assault, he told a friend that "Ziggy stabbed me" even though in response to a question, was admissible under the spontaneous declaration rule. People v. Wortherly, 68 A.D.2d 158, 416 N.Y.S.2d 594 (1st Dept. 1979).

Spontaneous declaration or excited utterance by defendant.—A statement made by a defendant to her attorney over the telephone that was inadvertently overheard by a police officer, is admissible as a spontaneous statement. People v. Harris, 57 N.Y.2d 335, 456 N.Y.S.2d 694 (1982), cert. denied, 460 U.S. 1047 (1983).

—The criteria for admissibility of a statement as a spontaneous declaration or excited utterance are (1) the existence of an exciting event, and (2) whether it was prompted thereby without time to reflect, that is whether it was dominated by the nervous excitement of the event. People v. Sostre, 70 A.D.2d 40, 418 N.Y.S.2d 662 (2d Dept. 1979), aff'd, 51 N.Y.2d 958, 435 N.Y.S.2d 702, 416 N.E.2d 1038 (1980).

Spontaneous declaration by witness.—Statement by a murder victim that "Mr. Edie (the defendant) is trying to kill me" was held admissible under the spontaneous declaration exception to the hearsay rule even though it was made in response to the question of a would be rescuer; to pivot the admissibility of a subsequent statement, however spontaneous, on the question of whether it was prompted by an equally spontaneous inquiry would serve no useful purpose—instead, this is merely one of the factors to be weighed in determining whether the surrounding circumstances demonstrate that the utterance was instinctive. People v. Edwards, 47 N.Y.2d 493, 419 N.Y.S.2d 45 (1979).

—A spontaneous exclamation made by a nonparticipant who has had adequate opportunity to observe the event is admissible since the unexpected exciting event may just as effectively produce a natural and spontaneous declaration by a bystander as by a participant. People v. Caviness, 38 N.Y.2d 227, 379 N.Y.S.2d 695, 342 N.E.2d 496 (1975).

—Court properly admitted testimony of witnesses concerning statements made by defendant's wife after she regained consciousness and escaped from the fire; given the sudden and dangerous nature of the event, the emotional trauma the victim likely suffered and the brief time between the incident and the statements, the court properly concluded that the statements were spontaneous declarations made while the victim was still under the influence of the excitement precipitated by the event. People v. Boerman, 162 A.D.2d 971, 557 N.Y.S.2d 197 (4th Dept. 1990).

State of mind.—Court erred in precluding defendant from testifying as to his state of mind when he purchased the cocaine. People v. McBee, 143 A.D.2d 773, 533 N.Y.S.2d 477 (2d Dept. 1988).

—An extra-judicial declaration as to a declarant's state of mind existing prior to or after an occurrence, is admissible in evidence provided it was made spontaneously and naturally and under circumstances which are free from suspicion. People v. Sostre, 70 A.D.2d 40, 418 N.Y.S.2d 662 (2d Dept. 1979), aff'd, 51 N.Y.2d 958, 435 N.Y.S.2d 102, 416 N.E.2d 1038 (1980).

—Evidence of a victim's prior threats against a defendant is admissible to show both the victim's and the defendant's state of mind in a case where justification is asserted as a defense. People v. Diallo, 297 A.D.2d 247, 746 N.Y.S.2d 479 (1st Dept. 2002).

Business records.—Three foundation requirements for introduction of business records are that record was made in regular course of business, reflecting routine, regularly conducted business activity, that it is regular course of business to make record, such that record was made pursuant to established procedures for routine, habitual, systematic making of such record, and that record must have been made at time of act, transaction, occurrence or event, or within reasonable time thereafter, assuring that recollection is fairly accurate and entries routinely made. People v. Cratsley, 86 N.Y.2d 81, 629 N.Y.S.2d 992, 653 N.E.2d 1162 (1995).

—"Linesheet" entries made in the course of police surveillance operation are admissible in evidence under the business exception to the hearsay rule. People v. Guidice, 83 N.Y.2d 630, 612 N.Y.S.2d 350, 634 N.E.2d 951 (1994).

—The trial court correctly admitted as business records, certificates that showed analysis of a breathalyzer ampule; they were prepared in the ordinary course of police laboratory business and listed the date of analysis, the individual who conducted the test, the material analyzed and the results. People v. Farrell, 58 N.Y.2d 637, 458 N.Y.S.2d 514, 444 N.E.2d 978 (1982).

—Employment application and W4 tax form completed by defendant's wife containing information connecting defendant to a drug location were properly admitted into evidence under the business records exception to the hearsay rule; although at the time of her application she was not yet an employee, she was in the process of becoming one, and she was under a business duty to provide accurate personal information upon which the hiring company would rely. Furthermore, maintaining accurate tax and personnel records is a necessary function of any business. People v. McKissick, 281 A.D.2d 212, 721 N.Y.S.2d 646 (1st Dept. 2001).

—Although defense counsel established through the sergeant who prepared it, that the police report was prepared in the normal course of business, the statement of the child's aunt contained in the report was not made pursuant to a duty to relay the information and thus the police report was not admissible as a business record. People v. Torres, 165 A.D.2d 801, 564 N.Y.S.2d 61 (1st Dept. 1990).

—New trial ordered where court refused to allow defense counsel to cross-examine police officer regarding a notation in his report which may have indicated an unsuccessful buy attempt; the document qualified as one kept in the regular course of business, was properly admitted into evidence, and defense counsel should have been permitted to cross-examine the witness with respect to the notations. People v. Hill, 271 A.D.2d 546, 706 N.Y.S.2d 702 (2d Dept. 2000).

—"Sprint" report improperly admitted into evidence as business record where source of the information was unknown. People v. Morrow, 204 A.D.2d 356, 612 N.Y.S.2d 604 (2d Dept. 1994).

—Trial court erred in ruling that memo book prepared by police officer in regular course of his business was not admissible as evidence, but error was harmless in light of overwhelming quality of evidence and defense counsel's reference to document during cross-examination of officer, by virtue of which counsel was able to convey to jury sense of what memo book contained, and what it did not contain. People v. Nunez, 194 A.D.2d 696, 599 N.Y.S.2d 119 (2d Dept. 1993).

—Court did not err in admitting, pursuant to the business records exception to the hearsay rule, the portion of the complainant's hospital records indicating that the complainant had "claimed he was hit with a fist, and there was a metal object in the fist"; the statement was relevant to the diagnosis and treatment of the complainant's injuries. People v. Goode, 179 A.D.2d 676, 578 N.Y.S.2d 611 (2d Dept. 1992).

Admissibility of hospital record.—Diagnosis in hospital record stating "gunshot wound of chest and upper arm," where no bullet was discovered, was held admissible under the business record exception to the hearsay rule because it constituted an entry relating to diagnosis or treatment. People v. Davis, 95 A.D.2d 837, 463 N.Y.S.2d 876 (2d Dept. 1983).

—Where the entries in the hospital records related to diagnosis and treatment, they were properly admitted. People v. Anderson, 184 A.D.2d 1005, 584 N.Y.S.2d 349 (4th Dept. 1992).

—**For more annotations about business records, see the annotations following CPLR § 4518 in this text.**

Hypnosis; safeguards.—It was harmless error to admit the rape victim's testimony as to her pre-hypnotic recall without considering expert testimony, or any other evidence, on the question of whether the hypnotic procedures that had been employed were so impermissibly suggestive as to have tainted the victim's prior recollections. People v. Hughes, 72 N.Y.2d 1035, 534 N.Y.S.2d 931, 531 N.E.2d 652 (1988).

—An expert may rely on hypnosis to gather information, and may therefore refer to such information at trial whether or not the statements themselves would be admissible as evidence of the truth of the matter asserted. People v. Santana, 159 Misc. 2d 301, 604 N.Y.S.2d 1016 (Sup. Ct. Queens Co. 1993).

—In determining the ability of testimony to be given by one who has been hypnotized, and in order to protect the due process rights of any defendant with regard to such evidence the following safeguards have developed with regard to hypnosis: (1) the person conducting the hypnotic session should be a qualified professional; (2) the qualified professional should be independent, not acting in concert with or responsible to the prosecutor, investigator or the defense; (3) the qualified professional should be given only such information as is essential for him to have, in order to conduct the hypnotic session; (4) all contact between the qualified professional and subject should be videotaped; (5) no representative of the police, prosecutor or subject should be present during the hypnotic session; (6) a lengthy pre-hypnotic interview should take place between the subject and the hypnotist; (7) the qualified professional should elicit from the subject, prior to hypnosis, a detailed description of the facts surrounding the subject matter of the hypnotic session, as the subject recalls them; (8) the qualified professional should make every effort to avoid adding any new elements to the subject's memory; (9) all facts given during the session should be independently corroborated. People v. McDowell, 103 Misc. 2d 831, 427 N.Y.S.2d 181 (Sup. Ct. Onondaga Co. 1980).

Identification by bite mark.—Identification of a perpetrator of a crime through a human bite mark, while the subject of some dispute in the scientific community, is permissible since the test is not whether a particular procedure in unanimously endorsed by the scientific community, but whether it is generally accepted as reliable. People v. Smith, 63 N.Y.2d 41, 479 N.Y.S.2d 706, 468 N.E.2d 879 (1984).

—Bite-mark evidence, the comparison of impressions made upon a person's body with the dentition of another, has gained general acceptance in the scientific community as a reliable means of identification, and such evidence is therefore admissible in a criminal case so long as the methods and techniques used are generally accepted in the scientific community. People v. Bethune, 105 A.D.2d 262, 484 N.Y.S.2d 577 (2d Dept. 1985).

Inadvertent destruction of evidence.—Inadvertent destruction of evidence permits the trial court to admit testimony regarding the previously existing item and does not mandate reversal. People v. Pasciuta, 104 A.D.2d 1010, 480 N.Y.S.2d 916 (2d Dept. 1984).

Interested observer doctrine.—Where a prime witness is so mentally or physically incapacitated that his ability to testify is impeded, a person who has demonstrated an interest in the health, education or general welfare of said witness and who has actually observed the witness for a reasonable period of time, may testify objectively—as an aid to jury understanding concerning the condition of the witness and the nature of his infirmity; such witness may be a psychologist, psychiatrist, physician, teacher, parent or any other lay or professional person who fits the prerequisites. People v. Acklin, 102 Misc. 2d 596, 424 N.Y.S.2d 633 (Sup. Ct. N.Y. Co. 1980).

Intoxication.—It was proper for the prosecutor to introduce evidence of defendant's refusal to take a chemical test and to comment upon such evidence in summation after the defendant had contended that he had requested to take a chemical test and that the police refused to administer one. People v. Torrey, 144 A.D.2d 865, 534 N.Y.S.2d 807 (3d Dept. 1988).

Membership in an organization.—There is no rule of evidence that permits a prosecutor to show that a defendant is a member of an organization and then impeach him with the alleged illegal, immoral or vicious acts of that organization. People v. Torres, 72 A.D.2d 754, 421 N.Y.S.2d 275 (2d Dept. 1979).

Third-party culpability evidence.—To determine whether a court should admit at trial third-party culpability evidence that would show that someone other than defendant committed the crime charged in the indictment, the court must allow the defense to make an offer of proof outside the jury's presence and must permit the prosecutor to make counter-arguments. The defendant must show proof of connection with it, such as a train of facts or circumstances that tend clearly to point to someone other than the defendant as the guilty party. The court should preclude the evidence, as in this case, if admitting it would cause undue delay, prejudice, and confusion. People v. Schulz, 4 N.Y.3d 521, 797 N.Y.S.2d 24, 829 N.E.2d 1192 (2005).

—Trial court improperly precluded ballistics report for gun that was used to shoot a victim in an unrelated crime by a third person who was also present at scene of shooting in instant case; report was admissible because it was relevant insofar as it linked a third person to gun, and its probative value outweighed the dangers of delay, prejudice, and confusion. People v. Primo, 96 N.Y.2d 351, 728 N.Y.S.2d 735, 753 N.E.2d 164 (2001).

—While a defendant has a right to introduce evidence that a third party committed the crime charged, the prospective evidence must do more than raise a mere suspicion that a third party committed the crime; there must be a clear connection between the specified third party and the crime. People v. Jiminez, 172 A.D.2d 367, 568 N.Y.S.2d 624 (1st Dept. 1991).

—While the defendant's right to present a defense includes the right to present evidence that someone else committed the crimes alleged, there must be more than a mere suspicion that it was a different person that committed the crime. People v. Pack, 189 A.D.2d 787, 592 N.Y.S.2d 393 (2d Dept. 1993).

—Court did not err in precluding defendant from introducing evidence that another person was the true perpetrator of the crime where there was no clear link between the third party and the crime in question. People v. Brown, 187 A.D.2d 662, 590 N.Y.S.2d 896 (2d Dept. 1992).

Misidentification evidence.—There was no merit to defendant's claim that court erred in refusing to allow proof that he was misidentified in unrelated robbery nine months after the instant crime; the misidentification was irrelevant to the instant crime. People v. Drake, 247 A.D.2d 855, 668 N.Y.S.2d 809 (4th Dept. 1998).

Models.—Court properly exercised its discretion in admitting a model "stun gun" into evidence since the device was a unique one which the jury would otherwise have had difficulty in visualizing and the complainant testified that the device was similar to the one he claimed was used upon him by the defendant. People v. Pike, 131 A.D.2d 890, 517 N.Y.S.2d 246 (2d Dept. 1987).

Mold or cast of teeth.—It was not an unreasonable intrusion for the Court to direct that a mold or cast of defendant's teeth be taken where deceased had bite marks on his body, the defendant was shown to have been present at or about the time of the crime, and the D.A. had been informed by a dentist that if he could examine the defendant's mouth and make molds of his teeth, he could determine whether the defendant had caused the bite marks. People v. Middleton, 76 A.D.2d 762, 428 N.Y.S.2d 688 (1st Dept. 1980), aff'd, 54 N.Y.2d 42, 444 N.Y.S.2d 581, 429 N.E.2d 100 (1981).

Nickname.—Witness's reference to defendant by nickname "Murder Mike" was prejudicial and witness could have just as easily referred to defendant as "Mike," but overwhelming evidence rendered the error harmless. People v. Santiago, 255 A.D.2d 63, 691 N.Y.S.2d 22 (1st Dept. 1999).

—Evidence that certain witnesses knew defendant's nickname, Bloody Bad Ass, was properly admitted as highly probative with respect to the question of their ability to identify him as the perpetrator. People v. Caver, 302 A.D.2d 604, 758 N.Y.S.2d 335 (2d Dept. 2003).

—Defendant claimed it was improper for the prosecutor to repeatedly refer to defendant's nickname, "Killer", but the reference was relevant to his identity as one of the shooters because defendant was generally known by his nickname and an eyewitness and one of the victims identified him by his nickname. People v. Crowder, 2 A.D.3d 454, 767 N.Y.S.2d 805 (2d Dept. 2003).

Offer of proof.—Court properly refused to permit defendant to elicit prior violent acts allegedly committed by the victim where she failed to clearly and unambiguously make known her offer of proof to demonstrate the relevance of the evidence; moreover, there was no proof adduced that defendant was aware of specific violent acts previously committed by the victim which were reasonably related to the crime charged. People v. Cotto, 159 A.D.2d 385, 552 N.Y.S.2d 639 (1st Dept. 1990).

—A defendant is required to clearly and unambiguously make his or her offer of proof to demonstrate the relevance of the evidence. People v. Cotto, 159 A.D.2d 385, 552 N.Y.S.2d 639 (1st Dept. 1990).

—Where a court seeks to limit cross-examination, on demand for an offer of proof, counsel is required to provide some good faith basis for the proposed questions. People v. Ashner, 190 A.D.2d 238, 597 N.Y.S.2d 975 (2d Dept. 1993).

—Where there is a *bona fide* objection to the offer of certain evidence, the proponent of such evidence must take advantage of the opportunity to make an offer of proof in order to demonstrate the relevance of the disputed evidence. People v. Billups, 132 A.D.2d 612, 518 N.Y.S.2d 9 (2d Dept. 1987).

—Since defense counsel failed to make a specific offer of proof as to the admissibility of certain testimony after the People's objection thereto had been sustained by the trial court, and since the admissibility of the testimony could have been resolved by a proper offer of proof at trial, the issue cannot be raised for the first time on appeal. People v. Zambrabo, 114 A.D.2d 872, 494 N.Y.S.2d 904 (2d Dept. 1985).

Opening the door.—A trial court should decide whether a defendant has opened the door to the admission of otherwise inadmissible evidence by considering whether, and to what extent, the evidence or argument said to open the door is incomplete or misleading and what, if any, otherwise inadmissible evidence is reasonably necessary to correct the misleading impression. People v. Massie, 2 N.Y.3d 179, 777 N.Y.S.2d 794, 809 N.E.2d 1102 (2004).

—Defendant's simple denial of involvement in the crime charged was insufficient to open the door to the introduction of prior crimes for impeachment purposes, and court erred in modifying the *Sandoval* ruling to permit the People to cross-examine defendant regarding the details of similar, uncharged crimes. People v. Moore, 238 A.D.2d 228, 656 N.Y.S.2d 749 (1st Dept.), aff'd, 92 N.Y.2d 823, 677 N.Y.S.2d 56, 699 N.E.2d 415 (1998).

—Defendant opened the door for limited inquiry into her prior out-of-state conviction when she testified on cross-examination about her conversations with the arresting officers, in which she tried to portray herself as an innocent person who was in the wrong place at the wrong time, and was being victimized by the police; defendant's denial that there was anything more to one conversation with a detective opened the door to further cross-examination about one conversation in which she had raised her New Jersey conviction and claimed that she had taken the blame for someone else's conduct; testimony was clearly relevant to her credibility about the current claims. People v. Ali, 286 A.D.2d 272, 729 N.Y.S.2d 136 (1st Dept. 2001).

—The court did not abuse its discretion in modifying its Sandoval ruling to allow the prosecutor to inquire into the facts underlying defendant's prior convictions, the court having specifically cautioned trial counsel that the ruling was subject to change depending upon defendant's testimony; the defendant opened the door to such inquiry in the explanations given in his direct testimony. People v. Rich, 207 A.D.2d 299, 615 N.Y.S.2d 676 (1st Dept. 1994).

—When defendant elicited the fact of a photo identification, the People were properly permitted to elicit the photo identification procedures to correct the jury's potential misimpression that the police had unfairly shown the victim a single photo. People v. Nieves, 199 A.D.2d 97, 605 N.Y.S.2d 60 (1st Dept. 1993).

—When the defendant used one police document on cross-examination to suggest that an attempted robbery had not been contemporaneously reported, the trial court properly received, on redirect, an additional report referring to the robbery attempt; where a defendant opens the door by using only part of certain material, the unused portion may be used to refute the inference raised by the defendant's partial use. People v. King, 197 A.D.2d 440, 603 N.Y.S.2d 36 (1st Dept. 1993).

—Defendant's testimony, on direct examination, that he did not engage in any sale of drugs permitted cross-examination, for impeachment purposes, as to whether he had sold drugs to the man and woman who had approached him on the street prior to the sale which served as the basis for the indictment charges. People v. Terry, 179 A.D.2d 351, 577 N.Y.S.2d 623 (1st Dept. 1992).

—Where defense counsel, in his opening statement, alleged that the drugs recovered from defendant could have been prescription drugs for personal use, the prosecutor was properly permitted to ask the arresting officer whether the defendant had explained why he possessed Valium. People v. Spigner, 176 A.D.2d 457, 574 N.Y.S.2d 359 (1st Dept. 1991).

—When defense counsel, on cross-examination, elicited that the victim saw defendant on a later occasion but did not call the police, the People were properly allowed to establish on redirect that the victim had seen defendant being arrested on an unrelated crime, thus obviating any imminent need to call police. People v. Richardson, 172 A.D.2d 438, 568 N.Y.S.2d 944 (1st Dept. 1991).

—The People's reference on their redirect case to defendant's post-arrest silence did not violate defendant's right to remain silent or his right against self-incrimination where defense counsel opened the door to such testimony. People v. Desterdick, 173 A.D.2d 312, 570 N.Y.S.2d 2 (1st Dept. 1991).

—Murder defendant opened the door to questioning about his marital difficulties when he testified that his marriage was "wonderful." People v. Peradze, 15 A.D.3d 678, 791 N.Y.S.2d 586 (2d Dept. 2005).

—Although court had originally precluded evidence that the defendant had previously beaten the victim, once the defendant testified on his direct examination that he "would never do anything to hurt that woman," he put his character into issue and the People were entitled to rebut that evidence by asking the defendant about his previous acts against the complainant. People v. Qynn, 208 A.D.2d 576, 617 N.Y.S.2d 62 (2d Dept. 1994).

—Where in his opening argument defense counsel set forth his trial strategy of convincing the jury that the investigatory techniques employed by the police had been improper, the trial court did not improvidently exercise its broad discretion by permitting the arresting officer to testify concerning his training over a defense objection as to relevancy. People v. Walls, 199 A.D.2d 292, 604 N.Y.S.2d 594 (2d Dept. 1993).

—By his cross-examination suggesting that the police had deliberately used an unfair photographic array the defense attorney opened the door to the admission of the arrest photographs. People v. Rosado, 172 A.D.2d 700, 568 N.Y.S.2d 647 (2d Dept. 1991).

Real evidence; admissibility; chain of possession.—Real evidence is admissible when it is sufficiently connected with the defendants to be relevant to an issue in the case. A failure to completely trace the chain of possession of the evidence once it was seized did not render it inadmissible in grand jury proceedings when there was no indication of any improper access or tampering with the evidence. People v. Connelly, 35 N.Y.2d 171, 359 N.Y.S.2d 266, 316 N.E.2d 706 (1974).

—The deficiencies in the chain of custody went to the weight and not the admissibility of the cocaine. People v. Springer, 153 A.D.2d 959, 545 N.Y.S.2d 766 (2d Dept. 1989). See also People v. Consiglio, 145 A.D.2d 431, 535 N.Y.S.2d 410 (2d Dept. 1988) (audiotapes); People v. Smith, 130 A.D.2d 783, 516 N.Y.S.2d 72 (2d Dept. 1987) (photo pack); People v. Strouder, 124 A.D.2d 841, 508 N.Y.S.2d 559 (2d Dept. 1986) (packet of cocaine).

—When real evidence is purported to be the actual object associated with a crime, the party offering it must show that the evidence is identical and that it has not been tampered with. People v. Mathis, 145 A.D.2d 965, 536 N.Y.S.2d 336 (3d Dept. 1989).

—Fact that seal on the "rape kit" was inexplicably broken did not warrant concern about evidence tampering since the breaking occurred after the pertinent analysis had been completed. People v. Catron, 143 A.D.2d 468, 532 N.Y.S.2d 589 (3d Dept. 1988).

Circumstantial evidence; test required.—The traditional test required of circumstantial evidence is "that the proof point logically to guilt and exclude to a moral certainly every other reasonable hypothesis." People v. Buford, 37 A.D.2d 38, 324 N.Y.S.2d 100 (2d Dept.), aff'd, 37 A.D.2d 699, 324 N.Y.S.2d 105 (2d Dept. 1971).

—A conviction based on circumstantial evidence must be reversed where the facts from which the inference of guilt was drawn are not inconsistent with his innocence and do not exclude to a moral certainty every other reasonable hypothesis except guilty. People v. Burdick, 66 A.D.2d 459, 414 N.Y.S.2d 410 (4th Dept. 1979).

Physical condition inadmissible where defendant unable to notice.—It is the defendant's state of mind and mental culpability at the time the fatal shot was fired with respect to the defense of justification that matters, therefore physical limitations and body markings which were wholly unknown to the defendant, and of which he could in no way be charged with notice were irrelevant and should have been excluded. People v. Monaco, 57 N.Y.2d 645, 454 N.Y.S.2d 64 (1982).

Polygraphs.—Since the reliability of the polygraph test has not been demonstrated with sufficient certainty to be admissible in this State, it was not error for the trial court to preclude a defense psychiatrist from stating that his conclusions were based in whole or in part on such a test. People v. Angelo, 208 A.D.2d 939, 618 N.Y.S.2d 77 (2d Dept. 1994), aff'd, 88 N.Y.2d 217, 644 N.Y.S.2d 460, 666 N.E.2d 1333 (1996).

—Evidence of the results of a polygraph examination is inadmissible in New York. People v. Smith, 61 A.D.2d 91, 401 N.Y.S.2d 353 (4th Dept. 1978).

—Reliability of polygraph evidence was not established to give it evidentiary standing where 4-pen machine was used to record respiration rate, blood pressure, pulse rate, galvanic skin responses, as well as muscular activity, and it was administered by "control-question" method. People v. Vinson, 104 Misc. 2d 664, 428 N.Y.S.2d 832 (Sup. Ct. Westchester Co. 1980).

—Defendant's motion to suppress statements made by him during the pre-test interview and the polygraph examination itself were denied, where defendant was not in custody at the time he was interviewed by the polygraph operator and had been fully advised of his rights and had made a knowing and intelligent waiver. People v. Rhodes, 102 Misc. 2d 377, 423 N.Y.S.2d 437 (Sup. Ct. Monroe Co. 1979).

—Defendant's polygraph examination was admissible at trial where the case hinged on a single eyewitness identification, and the reliability of the instrument and the qualifications of the examiner were properly exhibited. People v. Donials, 102 Misc. 2d 540, 422 N.Y.S.2d 832 (Sup. Ct. Westchester Co. 1979).

—Results of defendant's polygraph examinations were admissible at *Clayton* hearing (People v. Clayton, 41 A.D.2d 204, 342 N.Y.S.2d 106) where the probative evidence of guilt was essentially circumstantial and the defendant's intoxication at the time of the crime left him without means to contravene it; the People were accorded the right to cross-examine the polygraphers and to produce their own experts. People v. Vernon, 89 Misc. 2d 472, 391 N.Y.S.2d 959 (Sup. Ct. N.Y. Co. 1977).

Rebuttal evidence.—Because the proposed rebuttal was both cumulative to, and duplicative of, evidence already presented on defendant's direct case, with only the same relevancy, it was within the trial court's discretion to disallow the presentation of that evidence on rebuttal. People v. Harris, 98 N.Y.2d 452, 749 N.Y.S.2d 766, 779 N.E.2d 705 (2002).

—The relevant principles concerning rebuttal evidence dictate that evidence concerning a defendant's consciousness of guilt should be presented in the prosecution's case-in-chief. People v. McCann, 90 A.D.2d 554, 455 N.Y.S.2d 134 (2d Dept. 1982).

Smile evidence.—Court cautioned against admission of evidence of a smile as circumstantial evidence of consciousness of guilt; Court said that this type of evidence is of questionable and limited probative value but admission was not reversible error here. People v. Harris, 98 N.Y.2d 452, 749 N.Y.S.2d 766, 779 N.E.2d 705 (2002).

—A post-arrest smile is generally inadmissible to establish consciousness of guilt because it can convey many different states of mind and is therefore often ambiguous and minimally probative. However, where, as here, the defendant made his state of mind a crucial issue, the People were entitled to prove that defendant's demeanor was inconsistent with that state of mind. People v. Graziosa, 194 Misc. 2d 799, 756 N.Y.S.2d 825 (N.Y.C. Crim. Ct. 2003).

Failure to fingerprint; evidence explaining.—Court properly admitted evidence that defendant had no pads on his fingertips, which was relevant to explain why the police officer failed to fingerprint the toolbox found in defendant's possession, and the evidence did not without more evoke bad character or a propensity to commit crimes. People v. Anderson, 304 A.D.2d 450, 758 N.Y.S.2d 625 (1st Dept. 2003).

Recantation.—Defendant was denied due process and a fair trial where prosecution waited until after defendant introduced into evidence a written confession of the crime by a third party, as a statement against penal interest before disclosing to defendant's attorney that the third party was then in custody and had recanted the confession. People v. Jimenez, 79 A.D.2d 442, 437 N.Y.S.2d 95 (1st Dept. 1981).

Relevance.—Evidence is relevant if it has any tendency in reason to prove a material fact; unless its admission violates some exclusionary rule, all relevant evidence is admissible. People v. Till, 201 A.D.2d 43, 614 N.Y.S.2d 727 (1st Dept. 1994).

—Court properly precluded defendant's admission of medical records concerning his hernia operation, because that evidence was completely irrelevant to the defendant's ability to commit the robbery 16 days after his discharge, and would have invited the jury to engage in speculation. People v. Young, 295 A.D.2d 631, 745 N.Y.S.2d 177 (2d Dept. 2002).

—Admission of testimony that defendant was in custody in Pennsylvania on unrelated charges at the time he made statements to the police about the instant case was irrelevant under the facts of the case and should not be admitted on his new trial if defendant, as he did in the first trial, admits the voluntariness of his statements. People v. Morgan, 290 A.D.2d 566, 737 N.Y.S.2d 108 (2d Dept. 2002).

—Court erred in admitting into evidence the untested tinfoil packages that were found scattered elsewhere throughout the basement, but not in room in which defendant was found; the prejudicial effect of such evidence, particularly since they were never tested for cocaine, outweighed any probative value they might have had. People v. Scott, 206 A.D.2d 392, 614 N.Y.S.2d 739 (2d Dept. 1994).

—Relevant evidence means evidence having any tendency to make the existence of any fact that is of consequence to the determination of the action more probable or less probable than it would be without the evidence; the fact that this evidence is equivocal or consistent with suppositions other than guilt does not render it inadmissible for such arguments go to the weight rather than the admissibility of the evidence. People v. Shegog, 155 A.D.2d 891, 547 N.Y.S.2d 725 (4th Dept. 1989). *Accord*

People v. Kyser, 183 A.D.2d 238, 591 N.Y.S.2d 276 (4th Dept. 1992).

Scientific proof not required.—Because drug test (EMIT) employed by the probation officer has been generally recognized as scientifically reliable and is accepted by the courts of this state, no scientific proof as to the reliability of such test is necessary. People v. Whalen, 1 A.D.3d 633, 766 N.Y.S.2d 458 (3d Dept. 2003).

Self-incrimination.—Trial ruling requiring the defendant to display his tattooed arms for the witness did not violate his privilege against self-incrimination, since it merely compelled the defendant to exhibit physical characteristics. People v. Shannon, 137 A.D.2d 850, 525 N.Y.S.2d 315 (2d Dept. 1988).

—Since a photograph is not testimonial in nature, admission of defendant's arrest photograph did not violate his Fifth Amendment right against self-incrimination. People v. Peters, 135 A.D.2d 841, 522 N.Y.S.2d 944 (2d Dept. 1987).

Shoe print comparison; no *Frye* hearing required.—Court properly denied defendant's application for a *Frye* hearing in connection with proposed testimony about shoe print comparison because the procedure involved mere physical comparison rather than a novel scientific technique. People v. Abdul, 244 A.D.2d 237, 665 N.Y.S.2d 406 (1st Dept. 1997), *cert. denied*, 525 U.S. 880 (1998).

Silence; upon arrest.—The fact that a defendant is silent at the time of arrest may not be used to impeach him at trial. People v. Arce, 42 N.Y.2d 179, 397 N.Y.S.2d 619, 366 N.E.2d 279 (1977).

—The prosecution's use of defendant police officer's silence immediately after his arrest properly admitted to impeach his exculpatory story. People v. Bowen, 65 A.D.2d 364, 411 N.Y.S.2d 573 (1st Dept. 1978), *aff'd*, 50 N.Y.2d 915, 431 N.Y.S.2d 449, 409 N.E.2d 924 (1980).

—Admission of evidence of defendant's pre-arrest silence was proper. People v. DeGeorge, 142 A.D.2d 589, 530 N.Y.S.2d 245 (2d Dept. 1988).

—It was fundamentally unfair and a denial of the right to due process for the prosecution to cross-examine the defendant about his post-arrest and pretrial silence concerning his alibi defense and to comment upon such silence in summation; similarly, such silence by an alibi witness may not be used as a means of discrediting the witness, either upon cross-examination or during summation. People v. Smoot, 59 A.D.2d 898, 399 N.Y.S.2d 133 (2d Dept. 1977). *See also* People v. Wilson, 60 A.D.2d 920, 401 N.Y.S.2d 576 (2d Dept. 1978).

Tape recording.—In the absence of any indication that the tape had been altered, the uncontradicted testimony of the victim, who identified the recording as a fair and accurate reproduction of the conversation, was sufficient to support the decision of the trial court to admit the recording into evidence. People v. Arena, 48 N.Y.2d 944, 425 N.Y.S.2d 60, 401 N.E.2d 183 (1979).

—Even though one tape contained static and the other was inaudible in parts, the transactions between the undercover officer, the defendant or his co-conspirator were audible and, as a result, the infirmities went to the weight of the evidence and not to its admissibility. People v. Wilson, 207 A.D.2d 463, 615 N.Y.S.2d 769 (2d Dept. 1994).

—Trial court did not err in refusing to exclude from evidence a redacted videotape of the defendant's attack on the police officers where a proper foundation was laid for the admission of the tape, the prejudicial portions of the tape were redacted, and the jury was instructed not to speculate as to the inaudible portions of the tape. People v. Kent, 143 A.D.2d 278, 532 N.Y.S.2d 152 (2d Dept. 1988).

—Foundation for introduction of tape recording was properly provided by the accomplice. People v. Fischman, 191 A.D.2d 841, 594 N.Y.S.2d 865 (3d Dept. 1993).

—Court properly allowed into evidence the audible tapes and the transcripts of the tapes after the officers, who prepared the transcripts, testified to their accuracy, and the transcripts were admitted for the limited purpose of assisting the jury in understanding the tapes. People v. Godley, 130 A.D.2d 791, 515 N.Y.S.2d 122 (3d Dept. 1987).

—For a tape-recorded conversation to be admissible, clear and convincing proof is required establishing that the offered evidence is genuine and that there has been no tampering with it. People v. Encarnaction, 187 A.D.2d 1007, 591 N.Y.S.2d 127 (4th Dept. 1992).

—The witness' unequivocal and positive testimony that the tape of his conversation with defendant fully and accurately reflected the entire contents of that conversation established a sufficient foundation for the admission of the tape into evidence. People v. Arena, 65 A.D.2d 182, 411 N.Y.S.2d 466 (4th Dept. 1978), aff'd, 48 N.Y.2d 944, 425 N.Y.S.2d 60, 401 N.E.2d 183 (1979).

Court's refusal to play tape at trial.—It was prejudicial error to deprive defendant of the opportunity of having the jury hear the words spoken and evaluating the inflection and tone of voice from the tapes. People v. Harding, 44 A.D.2d 800, 355 N.Y.S.2d 394 (1st Dept. 1974).

Tape recording; uncharged crimes; failure to redact.—Admission into evidence of unredacted recording of defendant's conversation in which defendant admitted to the crime charged, but which also contained detailed plans for an unrelated and uncharged robbery was error. People v. Ward, 62 N.Y.2d 816, 477 N.Y.S.2d 602, 466 N.E.2d 142 (1984).

Transcripts.—Court did not abuse its discretion in providing the jury with transcripts as an aid to understanding the tapes. People v. Weaver, 200 A.D.2d 696, 607 N.Y.S.2d 58 (2d Dept. 1994). See also People v. Owens, 202 A.D.2d 449, 608 N.Y.S.2d 501 (2d Dept. 1994) (court instructed jury that transcripts could not be used as evidence); People v. Wade, 173 A.D.2d 662, 570 N.Y.S.2d 236 (2d Dept. 1991) (admissible even though portions of transcript inaudible).

—It is within the court's discretion to allow the use of transcripts as an assistance once the audibility of tapes is established. People v. Watson, 172 A.D.2d 882, 568 N.Y.S.2d 182 (3d Dept. 1991).

—Court properly permitted jury to use transcripts as an aid to understanding tapes. People v. Soto, 163 A.D.2d 889, 559 N.Y.S.2d 73 (4th Dept. 1990).

Trial; cross-examination; selling narcotics.—Defense was entitled to complete inquiry into circumstances of prosecution witness's conditional discharge where defendant's conviction was based solely on witness's observations of LSD sale transaction. People v. Roth, 30 N.Y.2d 99, 330 N.Y.S.2d 375, 281 N.E.2d 174 (1972).

Utterances.—The use of utterances as verbal acts has four limitations. (1) the conduct to be characterized by the words must be material to the issue; (2) the conduct must be equivocal in its nature; (3) the words must aid in giving legal significance to the conduct; and (4) the words must accompany the conduct. People v. Sostre, 70 A.D.2d 40, 418 N.Y.S.2d 662 (2d Dept. 1979), aff'd, 51 N.Y.2d 958, 435 N.Y.S.2d 702, 416 N.E.2d 1038 (1980).

Videotape recording.—Unless specifically interdicted by the Legislature, videotape evidence is not to be excluded by the court. People v. Teicher, 73 A.D.2d 136, 425 N.Y.S.2d 315 (1st Dept. 1980), aff'd, 52 N.Y.2d 638, 439 N.Y.S.2d 846, 422 N.E.2d 506 (1981).

—The trial court properly admitted into evidence the videotaped recording of the victim's body to prove some of the wounds inflicted upon the victim and to corroborate the defendant's admission to the police. People v. Fardan, 188 A.D.2d 1012, 592 N.Y.S.2d 162 (4th Dept. 1992).

Voice identification.—A defendant does not have an absolute right to admission of voice exemplar evidence; whether such evidence should be admitted as real or demonstrative evidence is not whether the proposed exemplar would be communicative, but whether it is relevant and reliable. People v. Scarola, 71 N.Y.2d 769, 530 N.Y.S.2d 83, 525 N.E.2d 728 (1988).

—Trial court did not err in denying defendant's motion without holding a Wade hearing pursuant to CPL § 710.60 to determine whether a voice identification made at the station house was unduly suggestive since there was no factual support in the record for the contention that the identification procedure was suggestive. People v. Allweiss, 48 N.Y.2d 40, 421 N.Y.S.2d 341, 396 N.E.2d 735 (1979).

—Inasmuch as the complainant did not rely on voice identification and that the defendant's brother-in-law was not an expert in linguistics, the court committed no error in precluding the defendant's brother-in-law from testifying that the defendant did not speak with a Jamaican accent. People v. King, 183 A.D.2d 918, 584 N.Y.S.2d 153 (2d Dept. 1992).

—Claim that all voice identification testimony should be excluded as unreliable was rejected as contrary to long-established law. People v. Carroll, 182 A.D.2d 693, 582 N.Y.S.2d 281 (2d Dept. 1992).

—Court erred in refusing to hold a hearing regarding the admissibility of certain spectographic voice evidence, but error did not require reversal. People v. Jeter, 163 A.D.2d 421, 558 N.Y.S.2d 138 (2d Dept. 1990), aff'd, 80 N.Y.2d 818, 587 N.Y.S.2d 583, 600 N.E.2d 214 (1992).

—The trial court did not improvidently exercise its discretion by precluding the defendant from providing a voice exemplar to establish that he had a southern drawl rather than a Jamaican accent. People v. Veal, 158 A.D.2d 633, 551 N.Y.S.2d 602 (2d Dept. 1990).

—Voice exemplar evidence is not admissible as of right but lies within the sound discretion of the trial court which is in the best position to weigh its relevance, reliability and whether "its probative value is substantially outweighed by the danger it will unfairly prejudice the other side or mislead the jury." People v. Williams, 160 A.D.2d 754, 554 N.Y.S.2d 58 (2d Dept. 1990).

—Contempt conviction for failing to provide voice exemplars could not stand because the mandate requiring the exemplars ignored due process requirements, where the defendant was orally ordered by the court during trial to submit to the test, since no prior notice of the prosecutions intention to apply for that relief was given to the defendant, the necessity for the relief was not established on any papers served on the defendant, and defendant was not afforded the opportunity to controvert the grounds for the application. People v. Giglio, 74 A.D.2d 348, 428 N.Y.S.2d 27 (2d Dept. 1980).

Voice stress evaluation test.—Evidence obtained through a voice stress evaluation test, like that obtained from polygraph tests, is generally inadmissible because the reliability of the test has not yet been sufficiently established. People v. Tarsia, 67 A.D.2d 210, 415 N.Y.S.2d 120 (3d Dept. 1979), aff'd, 50 N.Y.2d 1, 427 N.Y.S.2d 944, 405 N.E.2d 188 (1982).

Spectrographic analysis.—Since the effects of many variables on the process of spectrographic analysis or voice identification have not been determined and since the results of the process are often arrived at in a manner purely subjective, spectrographic analysis does not presently meet the standards of reasonable accuracy and general scientific acceptance necessary for admission into evidence. People v. Collins, 94 Misc. 2d 704, 405 N.Y.S.2d 365 (Sup. Ct. Kings Co. 1978).

PHOTOGRAPHS

Driver's license photograph of defendant.—A driver's license bearing defendant's photograph but a different name was properly admitted to establish defendant's change in appearance. People v. Solano, 182 A.D.2d 591, 583 N.Y.S.2d 366 (1st Dept. 1992).

Arrest photographs.—A photograph of defendant was properly admitted into evidence after the witness's in-court identification to demonstrate that defendant had changed his appearance since the time of his arrest, a fact that could otherwise have affected the jury's ability to consider whether the complaining witness's description had been accurate. People v. Nogueras, 196 A.D.2d 448, 601 N.Y.S.2d 289 (1st Dept. 1993).

—Court properly permitted arrest photograph into evidence to establish defendant's appearance on the date of the crime. People v. Santana, 162 A.D.2d 191, 556 N.Y.S.2d 316 (1st Dept. 1990).

—The court erred in permitting the People to introduce the defendant's arrest photograph into evidence for the purpose of corroborating the complainant's testimony that she did not immediately report the crime because she was afraid of the defendant; the People never established that the complainant's fear was due to the defendant's appearance or that the photograph, taken 19 days later, depicted the defendant's appearance at the time of the crime. People v. Rivera, 193 A.D.2d 995, 596 N.Y.S.2d 108 (2d Dept. 1993).

—A defendant's arrest photograph was admissible where his appearance had changed since the time of his arrest on the day after the crime was committed. People v. Milbank, 187 A.D.2d 459, 589 N.Y.S.2d 901 (2d Dept. 1992).

—Defendant's arrest photo was properly admitted into evidence on redirect examination where the defendant's appearance had changed in the 6 years since the incident. People v. Esdaille, 160 A.D.2d 811, 554 N.Y.S.2d 258, 259 (2d Dept. 1990).

—While arrest photos may not be admitted if irrelevant to the issues at trial, the photo here was relevant to the jury's determination whether defendant, who had changed his appearance since his arrest, matched the description given. Any error in admission of the photo was harmless. People v. Lee, 6 A.D.3d 751, 774 N.Y.S.2d 601 (3d Dept. 2004).

Sealed photographs.—Sealed photograph of defendant taken in connection with unrelated arrest was properly received in evidence where the photo was redacted to conceal its origin from the jury and it was relevant to an issue that arose during trial concerning defendant's appearance. People v. Torres, 291 A.D.2d 273, 738 N.Y.S.2d 312 (1st Dept. 2002).

Miscellaneous photographs.—Court properly admitted photographs replicating the magnification provided by binoculars used by the observing officer, as relevant and admissible to demonstrate to the jury the power of the binoculars and how close they made objects appear. People v. Mathison, 287 A.D.2d 384, 732 N.Y.S.2d 2 (1st Dept. 2001).

—Court did not err in precluding the introduction of a photograph of defendant's family members; under the circumstances, the similarity or lack thereof between defendant and another family member was a collateral issue. People v. Duke, 181 A.D.2d 442, 580 N.Y.S.2d 353 (1st Dept. 1992).

—Court properly admitted certain photographs of the room where the victims were shot since they showed the layout of the room and corroborated and illustrated trial testimony. People v. Pride, 173 A.D.2d 645, 570 N.Y.S.2d 226 (2d Dept. 1991).

—Where defendant failed to establish that photographs taken of the crime scene after the assault were a fair and accurate representation of the scene at the time of the crime, the court properly denied admission of them. People v. Wrigglesworth, 204 A.D.2d 758, 611 N.Y.S.2d 678 (3d Dept. 1994).

—Reversal was required where the court admitted photographs of the suppressed evidence. People v. Simmons, 75 N.Y.2d 738, 551 N.Y.S.2d 196, 550 N.E.2d 449 (1990).

Photographs of murder victim.—Admission of 44 photographs and slides of homicide victim and crime scene did not constitute an abuse of discretion by the trial court. People v. Wood, 79 N.Y.2d 958, 582 N.Y.S.2d 992, 591 N.E.2d 1178 (1992).

—Four colored photographs of deceased's body were properly admitted as bearing on material issue whether defendant shot his wife or whether wife was shot by burglar in appeal for conviction of murder. The general rule regarding photographs of deceased is that they are admissible if they tend to prove or disprove a disputed or material issue, to illustrate or elucidate other relevant evidence, or to corroborate or disprove some other evidence offered or to be offered, and admission of the photographs is generally within the trial court's discretion. Photographic evidence should be excluded only if its sole purpose is to arouse the jury's emotions and prejudice the defendant. People v. Pobliner, 32 N.Y.2d 356, 345 N.Y.S.2d 482, 298 N.E.2d 637 (1973), cert. denied, 416 U.S. 905 (1974). See also People v. Arca, 72 A.D.2d 205, 424 N.Y.S.2d 569 (4th Dept. 1980).

—Court erred in permitting into evidence 22 color photographs of the murder scene, including several gruesome, close-up pictures of the decedent's mutilated body since the photographs were lacking any probative value. People v. Blake, 139 A.D.2d 110, 530 N.Y.S.2d 578 (1st Dept. 1988).

—Court improperly admitted 17 post-mortem photographs of the victim into evidence because the photographs did not tend to prove or disprove a disputed or material issue and they did not illustrate, elucidate, or corroborate other evidence, but because there was overwhelming evidence of defendant's guilt, the admission of the photographs was harmless error. People v. Chambers, 18 A.D.3d 571, 795 N.Y.S.2d 307 (2d Dept. 2005).

—Prosecution properly introduced into evidence five photographs of the deceased to illustrate the medical examiner's testimony concerning the fatal injuries sustained by him. People v. Washington, 182 A.D.2d 791, 582 N.Y.S.2d 740 (2d Dept. 1992).

—Photographs of the decedent were admitted to show the body as well as to corroborate the testimony of the medical examiner. People v. Moore, 161 A.D.2d 733, 555 N.Y.S.2d 868 (2d Dept. 1990).

—The trial court did not abuse its discretion in allowing the prosecution to introduce into evidence a photograph of the victim, taken shortly after the discovery of the body, since the photograph tended to corroborate the medical examiner's testimony that the victim died as a result of asphyxiation. People v. Long, 155 A.D.2d 558, 547 N.Y.S.2d 413 (2d Dept. 1989). See also People v. Harris, 141 A.D.2d 457, 528 N.Y.S.2d 156 (2d Dept. 1988); People v. Carini, 139 A.D.2d 753, 527 N.Y.S.2d 502 (2d Dept. 1988); People v. Flayhart, 136 A.D.2d 767, 523 N.Y.S.2d 225 (3d Dept.), aff'd, 72 N.Y.2d 737, 536 N.Y.S.2d 727, 533 N.E.2d 657 (1988); People v. Scott, 203 A.D.2d 911, 611 N.Y.S.2d 725 (4th Dept. 1994); People v. Snyder, 161 A.D.2d 1205, 555 N.Y.S.2d 994 (4th Dept. 1990); People v. Ford, 158 A.D.2d 914, 550 N.Y.S.2d 958 (4th Dept. 1990).

—Admission into evidence of photograph depicting the murder victim, a frail, elderly man tied to the post of his bed, was proper to corroborate testimony of People's witness concerning manner in which crime was committed. People v. Harris, 149 A.D.2d 433, 539 N.Y.S.2d 778 (2d Dept. 1989).

—Photographs of murder victim were properly admitted to illustrate the testimony of the medical examiner and to help prove the defendant's intent to kill and to dispute his claim of self-defense. People v. Shade, 127 A.D.2d 862, 512 N.Y.S.2d 241 (2d Dept. 1987).

—The admissibility of photographic evidence which is relevant to prove or disprove a material issue is within the discretion of the trial court and such evidence should be excluded only if its sole purpose is to arouse the emotions of the jury. People v. Garraway, 187 A.D.2d 761, 589 N.Y.S.2d 942 (3d Dept. 1992).

—Generally, photographs of a deceased victim are admissible when they illustrate or elucidate other relevant evidence which has been introduced at trial. People v. Longo, 182 A.D.2d 1019, 582 N.Y.S.2d 832 (3d Dept. 1992).

—Photographs of murder victim were properly admitted into evidence where they corroborated medical evidence offered by the prosecution and were pertinent to certain issues in dispute. People v. Paige, 120 A.D.2d 808, 502 N.Y.S.2d 532 (3d Dept. 1986).

—Court properly permitted introduction of photographs showing the victim's skull at the time of the autopsy. People v. Secore, 187 A.D.2d 1008, 591 N.Y.S.2d 126 (4th Dept. 1992).

—Photographs of the deceased are admissible in a homicide case if they tend to prove a disputed or material issue or corroborate some other evidence. People v. Murray, 140 A.D.2d 949, 529 N.Y.S.2d 628 (4th Dept. 1988).

Photographs of children.—Photographs of the dead child were properly admitted into evidence, since the People introduced the photographs to demonstrate that the defendant acted with a depraved indifference to human life, an element of the crime with which he was charged. People v. Quinones, 155 A.D.2d 244, 546 N.Y.S.2d 854 (1st Dept. 1989).

—Photographs depicting the deceased infant were properly admitted to illustrate the medical examiner's testimony and to corroborate the testimony of the other prosecution witnesses. People v. Ellwood, 205 A.D.2d 553, 613 N.Y.S.2d 197 (2d Dept. 1994).

—Admission of photograph which depicted the body of the deceased child was proper. People v. Mercado, 154 A.D.2d 556, 546 N.Y.S.2d 396 (2d Dept. 1989).

—Photographs of charred remains of the child were properly admitted as they tended to disprove the defendant's claim that he had mistaken a pillow for the child in a rescue attempt and also corroborated the expert testimony that the child was not in the normal fetal position usually seen after death in a fire. People v. Medina, 120 A.D.2d 749, 502 N.Y.S.2d 792 (2d Dept. 1986).

—Court did not err in admitting photographs of the deceased child in murder prosecution. People v. Sika, 142 A.D.2d 999, 530 N.Y.S.2d 719 (4th Dept. 1988).

Photographs of victim; relevance.—Admission into evidence of photographs of a victim being treated in the hospital was not an abuse of discretion as a matter of law where such photographs were not gory, although they were startling in that they showed a knife embedded in the victim's back, and they were relevant to defendant's complicity. People v. Bell, 63 N.Y.2d 769, 481 N.Y.S.2d 324, 471 N.E.2d 137 (1984).

—The court erred in admitting into evidence a photograph of the victim while she was alive, where the photograph was not relevant to any issue at trial and undoubtedly evoked sympathy from the jury. People v. Daughtry, 202 A.D.2d 686, 610 N.Y.S.2d 54 (2d Dept. 1994).

—Court properly admitted photograph of the victim's head wounds, since it showed the nature of the injury and therefore tended to prove that the defendant intended to cause physical injury to the victim, which was an element of the crime charged. People v. Duprey, 192 A.D.2d 716, 597 N.Y.S.2d 147 (2d Dept. 1993).

—Photographs of the victim's body were properly admitted into evidence since they corroborated testimony regarding the injuries to the victim and tended to prove that the defendant or his accomplice acted with the intent to kill. People v. Kaiser, 204 A.D.2d 572, 612 N.Y.S.2d 67 (2d Dept. 1994).

—Court properly admitted into evidence photographs of the crime scene and the complainant's injuries; although some of the photographs were graphic, they served to illustrate the testimony of the People's witnesses and tended to prove the People's theory that the defendant, not a fall, was the cause of the complainant's injuries. People v. Snyder, 189 A.D.2d 836, 592 N.Y.S.2d 469 (2d Dept. 1992).

—Court did not err in admitting into evidence two photographs of the complaining witness taken the day after the assault since the photographs tended to prove the physical injury suffered by the complainant in the attempted robbery and assault. People v. Burris, 160 A.D.2d 809, 553 N.Y.S.2d 846 (2d Dept. 1990).

—Photograph of one of the victims taken at the hospital was properly received into evidence where it served to corroborate the testimony of an oral surgeon who described the appearance and fracture of the victim's jaw. People v. Baez, 131 A.D.2d 687, 516 N.Y.S.2d 764 (2d Dept. 1987).

—In homicide case, it was error to admit a photograph of the victim when he was healthy, because it was irrelevant to the crimes charged, but the error was harmless based upon all of the evidence of guilt. People v. Dove, 233 A.D.2d 751, 650 N.Y.S.2d 444 (3d Dept. 1996).

Photographs of defendant; tattoos.—In case involving an attack on two Mexican day laborers, court did not violate defendant's privilege against self-incrimination by allowing the People to introduce photographs, taken over defendant's objection, of defendant's tattoos which contained images involving racial and ethnic stereotypes, as evidence of defendant's motive for committing a hate crime. People v. Slavin, 1 N.Y.3d 392, 775 N.Y.S.2d 210, 807 N.E.2d 259 (2004), cert. denied, — U.S. —, 125 S. Ct. 64 (2004).

EXPERT OPINION

Expert opinion.—Expert testimony is not a prerequisite to the admissibility of radar evidence. People v. Knight, 72 N.Y.2d 481, 482, 534 N.Y.S.2d 353, 354, 530 N.E.2d 1273, 1274 (1988).

—Opinion evidence must be based upon facts in the record or personally known to the witness; an expert cannot reach his conclusion by assuming material facts not supported by the evidence. People v. Bethea, 261 A.D.2d 629, 691 N.Y.S.2d 79 (2d Dept. 1999).

—Although the right to present witnesses of one's own choosing is fundamental, the admissibility and extent of expert testimony is addressed to the discretion of the trial court. People v. Roth, 139 A.D.2d 605, 527 N.Y.S.2d 97 (2d Dept. 1988).

—Detective did not have to be an expert to testify regarding his observations of footprints in the snow, discovered at the crime scene, and his observations of the defendant's boot prints. People v. Rosa, 138 A.D.2d 756, 526 N.Y.S.2d 569 (2d Dept. 1988).

—Although the court's twin rulings that the People's medical witness was not qualified as an expert in semen and spermatozoa testing and characteristics but could nevertheless render expert opinions on those subjects were inconsistent, the admission of his testimony was not improper since the witness had sufficient knowledge, training, and experience in the subject to render reliable testimony, and should have been qualified as an expert. People v. Robinson, 123 A.D.2d 455, 506 N.Y.S.2d 876 (2d Dept. 1986).

—Expert testimony concerning the nature of defendant's personality, in general, is not sufficiently relevant to outweigh the confusion that would be created by interjecting a collateral issue. People v. Lea, 144 A.D.2d 863, 864, 534 N.Y.S.2d 588, 590 (3d Dept. 1988).

—Expert testimony was improperly admitted where the opinion of the People's expert was not based on professional or medical knowledge but rather was based on inferences and conclusions drawn from various statements presented to her by police. Moreover, the expert's statement that infant died from "homicidal" suffocation improperly states a conclusion about defendant's intent. People v. Eberle, 265 A.D.2d 881, 697 N.Y.S.2d 218 (4th Dept. 1999).

—Court erred in ruling that defendant would be permitted to introduce his expert testimony only if he waived his right to challenge certain evidence that was inadmissible. People v. Stokes, 170 A.D.2d 946, 566 N.Y.S.2d 119 (4th Dept. 1991).

—Court erred when it allowed the medical examiner to testify that in his opinion the victim's death was a homicide. People v. Emmick, 136 A.D.2d 892, 525 N.Y.S.2d 77 (4th Dept. 1988).

—Medical examiner's testimony that the cause of death was "probable drowning" should have been excluded; however, the error in admitting it was harmless. People v. Violante, 144 A.D.2d 995, 534 N.Y.S.2d 281 (4th Dept. 1988).

Expert opinion; narcotics.—Trial court did not abuse its discretion in allowing arresting officer to testify, as a narcotics expert, that the packaging of the drugs recovered from the defendant was inconsistent with personal use and consistent with the packaging the officer had encountered in previous drug sale arrests. The average juror may not be aware of the quantity and packaging of heroin carried by someone who sells drugs, as opposed to someone who merely uses them. People v. Hicks, 2 N.Y.3d 750, 778 N.Y.S.2d 745, 811 N.E.2d 7 (2004).

—Court abused its discretion in allowing expert testimony as to the money handling aspects of street-level, multi-member narcotics operations, where the evidence presented was of a single transaction involving only the defendant and an undercover officer, but the error was harmless. People v. Smith, 2 N.Y.3d 8, 776 N.Y.S.2d 209, 808 N.E.2d 344 (2004).

—Trial court properly allowed the introduction of expert testimony by a police officer regarding the general operating methods and terminology used in street-level narcotics transactions, where defendant's primary defense was misidentification, and the testimony enabled the prosecution to offer one plausible explanation as to why a person might not possess money or drugs shortly after selling narcotics to an undercover officer. People v. Brown, 97 N.Y.2d 500, 743 N.Y.S.2d 374, 769 N.E.2d 1266 (2002).

—The trial court properly permitted admission of the undercover officer's testimony explaining the use and meaning of code words contained in two tape-recorded telephone negotiations regarding one of the drug sales involved in the case; such testimony need not have been admitted as qualified expert testimony, but was properly admissible for the purpose of allowing the undercover officer, as a party to the conversation, to explain his understanding of the code words. People v. Lozado, 180 A.D.2d 410, 579 N.Y.S.2d 82 (1st Dept. 1992).

—It was not error to allow a detective to be qualified as an expert for the purpose of explaining the methodology of street drug sales, with particular reference to the use of beepers and the reason for the means of record-keeping by street dealers. People v. Diaz, 181 A.D.2d 595, 581 N.Y.S.2d 329 (1st Dept. 1992).

—Court did not err in denying defendant's application to present the expert testimony of an "addictionologist," who would have explained that the ingestion of crack cocaine vastly diminishes the outward signs of intoxication cause by alcohol and also produces the possibility of hallucinations; defendant wished to use such testimony to impeach statements of the rape victim. People v. Benson, 206 A.D.2d 674, 614 N.Y.S.2d 808 (3d Dept. 1994).

Expert testimony.—Defendant moved to introduce testimony of "psychological expert" for purpose of explaining to the jury the factors that may influence the perception and memory of a witness and affect the reliability of identification testimony. Initially the trial court summarily rejected defendant's motion on the ground that such testimony was per se inadmissible, but the court subsequently entertained defendant's renewed request for an introduction of the testimony at which time the court was aware of corroborating evidence in addition to the identification testimony. Under these circumstances, the Court of Appeals declined to find that the trial court had abused its discretion in denying defendant's motion to introduce the expert testimony. People v. Lee, 96 N.Y.2d 157, 726 N.Y.S.2d 361, 750 N.E.2d 63 (2001).

—Authorized use of facts from outside the evidentiary record does not alter the basic principle that an expert's opinion not based on facts is worthless. People v. Jones, 73 N.Y.2d 427, 428, 541 N.Y.S.2d 340, 341, 539 N.E.2d 96, 97 (1989).

—Expert testimony is admissible if the analysis involved is beyond the ken of the typical juror and the results would be relevant to an issue in the case; conclusive results are not required, it is sufficient if the expert can state his opinion with a reasonable degree of certainty; a higher standard is applicable only when the expert is called to assess credibility. People v. Allweiss, 48 N.Y.2d 40, 421 N.Y.S.2d 341, 396 N.E.2d 735 (1979).

—Where the sole reason for questioning the "expert" witness is to bolster the testimony of another witness by explaining that his version of the events is more believable than the defendant's, the "expert's" testimony is equivalent to an opinion that the defendant is guilty, and the receipt of such testimony may not be condoned. People v. Ciaccio, 47 N.Y.2d 431, 418 N.Y.S.2d 371, 391 N.E.2d 1347 (1979).

—Court properly allowed an expert prosecution witness to provide background information about the illegal firearms trade, where the jury was faced with a large-scale gun trafficking case involving issues that called for technical knowledge beyond the knowledge of the typical juror. People v. Brown, 287 A.D.2d 404, 731 N.Y.S.2d 704 (1st Dept. 2001), aff'd, 99 N.Y.2d 488, 758 N.Y.S.2d 602, 788 N.E.2d 1030 (2003).

—Court properly admitted testimony of blood spatter analysis expert whose testimony included professional or technical knowledge beyond the ken of an average juror. People v. Whitaker, 289 A.D.2d 84, 734 N.Y.S.2d 149 (1st Dept. 2001).

—There is no requirement that a trial court formally "certify" a witness as an expert. People v. Gordon, 202 A.D.2d 166, 608 N.Y.S.2d 192 (1st Dept. 1994).

—Expert opinion is admissible in the discretion of the trial court if it would be beneficial to the jury. People v. Miranda, 179 A.D.2d 391, 578 N.Y.S.2d 160 (1st Dept. 1992); People v. Kroger, 200 A.D.2d 637, 606 N.Y.S.2d 746 (2d Dept. 1994) (same).

—Court properly precluded expert testimony about steroid rage, a behavioral state of hostility and anger resulting from prolonged use of steroids, because there was no evidence that the decedent, against whom defendant was allegedly defending himself and his friend, was under the influence of steroids at the time of the incident, and therefore, there was no foundation upon which the expert could base his opinion. People v. Kruglik, 256 A.D.2d 592, 682 N.Y.S.2d 440 (2d Dept. 1998).

—The fact that the defendant's expert offered an opinion contrary to the People's experts on the issue of sanity merely presented a factual issue for the jury. People v. Rahman, 202 A.D.2d 696, 609 N.Y.S.2d 290 (2d Dept. 1994).

—A complainant who is not qualified to testify as an expert is nevertheless competent to supply evidence of original cost. People v. Jackson, 194 A.D.2d 691, 599 N.Y.S.2d 114 (2d Dept. 1993).

—While it was improper for a doctor to testify that the victim had been "raped," as this constituted the ultimate question for the jury, given the overwhelming evidence of the defendant's guilt, the error was harmless. People v. Perry, 180 A.D.2d 766, 580 N.Y.S.2d 79 (2d Dept. 1992).

—Expert testimony is admissible if the analysis involved is beyond the ken of the typical juror and the results would be relevant to an issue in the case. People v. Crawford, 183 A.D.2d 775, 583 N.Y.S.2d 506 (2d Dept. 1992).

—The trial court did not err in precluding expert testimony on the issue of the reliability of eyewitness identification testimony. People v. Gibbs, 157 A.D.2d 799, 550 N.Y.S.2d 400 (2d Dept. 1990).

—Practical experience may properly substitute for academic training in determining whether an individual has acquired the training necessary to be qualified as an expert witness. People v. Donaldson, 107 A.D.2d 758, 484 N.Y.S.2d 123 (2d Dept. 1985).

—Blood stain pattern analysis is a proper subject of expert testimony, and court properly admitted it. People v. Delosh, 2 A.D.3d 1047, 770 N.Y.S.2d 141 (3d Dept. 2003).

—Fourier Transform Infrared Spectroscopy is generally accepted in the scientific community, and therefore, Supreme Court had a proper basis upon which to admit the testimony of a State Police Forensic Scientist who concluded that cement dust samples from various locations at the crime scene were consistent with safe lining cement which could have come from the victims' safe. People v. Roraback, 247 A.D.2d 647, 668 N.Y.S.2d 781 (3d Dept. 1998).

—Court did not abuse its discretion in admitting testimony of accident reconstruction expert as to where the point of impact occurred, as the expert demonstrated a degree of confidence in his conclusions sufficient to satisfy accepted standards of reliability. People v. Spurling, 199 A.D.2d 624, 604 N.Y.S.2d 997 (3d Dept. 1993).

—Court properly permitted testimony of accident reconstruction expert regarding the estimated pre-impact and post-impact speeds of the two vehicles. People v. Moore, 155 A.D.2d 725, 547 N.Y.S.2d 685 (3d Dept. 1989).

—Court properly allowed emergency room physician to testify concerning the type of force necessary to cause the victim's injuries because it involved a matter not within the ken of the average juror. People v. Mason, 281 A.D.2d 893, 722 N.Y.S.2d 840 (4th Dept. 2001).

—The court erred in admitting opinion testimony of People's handwriting expert that spray paint writing on the victim's vehicles corresponded to defendant's handwriting where the People failed to make the threshold showing that comparing handwriting to spray paint writing is scientifically reliable. People v. Michallow, 201 A.D.2d 915, 607 N.Y.S.2d 781 (4th Dept. 1994).

—In murder prosecution, People's expert was properly permitted to conclude that the circumstances of the case indicated a pathological condition called "piquerism," which is the realization of sexual satisfaction from penetrating a victim by sniper activity or by stab and bite wounds and the fact that such testimony tended to prove intent did not render it inadmissible. People v. Drake, 129 A.D.2d 963, 514 N.Y.S.2d 280 (4th Dept. 1987).

Battered child syndrome.—Defendant killed his stepfather, asserting a justification defense; defendant, his mother, and his stepbrother had all been physically abused by the deceased for years and the family had been in counseling with a social worker; the social worker and defendant's expert, a psychologist, testified at trial. Defendant was permitted to adduce some testimony about battered child/posttraumatic stress syndrome, but was precluded from introducing the social worker's records into evidence. This was error under the circumstances of the case. People v. Lovelace, 287 A.D.2d 652, 731 N.Y.S.2d 745 (2d Dept. 2001).

Battered woman syndrome.—Expert testimony on battered woman syndrome should be admissible only to address an issue that is inherently confusing to the jury and when there is no other evidence to address it. The admission of this testimony is not necessary to aid the trier of fact in this case to assess the circumstances surrounding the minimal delay in the complainant's reporting of the alleged offense, and the probative value is outweighed by the prejudicial impact. People v. White, 4 Misc. 3d 797, 780 N.Y.S.2d 727 (Dist. Ct. Nassau Co. 2004).

Child sexual abuse syndrome.—The People properly offered the doctor's testimony about child sexual abuse accommodation syndrome for the purpose of instructing the jury about reasons why a child might not report incidents of sexual abuse immediately. People v. Carroll, 95 N.Y.2d 375, 718 N.Y.S.2d 10, 740 N.E.2d 1084 (2000).

—Court properly admitted expert testimony about Child Sexual Abuse Accommodation Syndrome, which tended to explain matters beyond the ken of the typical juror, including a general explanation of such victim's untimely disclosures. People v. Gilley, 4 A.D.3d 127, 770 N.Y.S.2d 868 (1st Dept. 2004). Accord People v. Gillard, 7 A.D.3d 540, 776 N.Y.S.2d 95 (2d Dept. 2004).

—Expert testimony concerning child sexual abuse syndrome was relevant and helpful to the jury's understanding of child abuse victims, a subject not within the ken of the average juror. People v. Sanchez, 200 A.D.2d 363, 606 N.Y.S.2d 185 (1st Dept. 1994).

—Expert testimony was properly admitted to establish how a child could be raped without suffering physical injury. People v. Smith, 202 A.D.2d 366, 610 N.Y.S.2d 190 (1st Dept. 1994).

—The expert testimony on child sex abuse syndrome was properly limited to a general explanation of victim's untimely disclosures. People v. Guzman, 202 A.D.2d 272, 608 N.Y.S.2d 654 (1st Dept. 1994).

—The court properly admitted the expert testimony about child abuse accommodation syndrome. People v. Lopez, 187 A.D.2d 533, 589 N.Y.S.2d 920 (2d Dept. 1992).

—Court did not improvidently exercise its discretion in admitting expert testimony as to the psychological and behavioral characteristics and reaction typically shared by children who are victims of sexual abuse in a familiar setting. People v. Webb, 177 A.D.2d 524, 575 N.Y.S.2d 913 (2d Dept. 1991).

—Court did not err in admitting expert testimony about child sexual abuse accommodation syndrome (CSAAS). It was properly admitted after the victim testified to offer explanations to the jury as to why the victim delayed reporting the abuse, i.e., to rebut the defense's extended attempts on cross-examination to impair the victim's credibility by evidence that she had not promptly complained, that she had continued to maintain a close relationship with the defendant and that she initially denied the abuse. The expert's testimony was general and theoretical in nature and not directly linked to the specific facts or testimony. The expert did not attempt to bolster the victim's testimony. People v. Carroll, 300 A.D.2d 911, 753 N.Y.S.2d 148 (3d Dept. 2002). [Note: The Third Department's decision in *Carroll* was a subsequent appeal from People v. Carroll, 95 N.Y.2d 375, 718 N.Y.S.2d 10, 740 N.E.2d 1084 (2000).]

—Judgment reversed where court permitted expert testimony of child sexual abuse accommodation syndrome for the purpose of proving that the child was sexually abused. People v. Duell, 163 A.D.2d 866, 558 N.Y.S.2d 395 (4th Dept. 1990).

Cross-racial identification.—Despite a growing body of scientific research suggesting that witnesses may experience bias toward their own race that impairs the accuracy of cross-racial identification, the court would not permit expert testimony regarding the quality of cross-racial witness identification on the grounds that it falls within the ambit of jurors' general knowledge and life experience. People v. Carrieri, 4 Misc. 3d 307, 777 N.Y.S.2d 627 (Sup. Ct. Queens Co. 2004).

DNA testimony.—DNA profiling evidence has been accepted and found reliable by the relevant scientific community and is admissible. People v. Wesley, 83 N.Y.2d 417, 611 N.Y.S.2d 97, 633 N.E.2d 451 (1994).

Shaken baby syndrome.—Since shaken baby syndrome is no longer a novel scientific theory, no *Frye* hearing was required, and the court did not err in permitting the physician to present a computer-generated video demonstrating the mechanics of shaken baby syndrome. People v. Yates, 290 A.D.2d 888, 736 N.Y.S.2d 798 (3d Dept. 2002).

—The court properly permitted expert medical testimony that the victim dies from injuries consistent with shaken-baby syndrome and that his injuries were intentionally inflicted; the expert did not address defendant's awareness of the risk of death, the ultimate issue for the jury. People v. Benjamin, 204 A.D.2d 996, 612 N.Y.S.2d 517 (4th Dept. 1994).

Expert opinion; identification of marijuana.—Defendant cannot be convicted of sale of marijuana solely on purchaser's testimony that the substance bought was marijuana. Conviction must be based upon expert identification of the substance as marijuana. People v. Kenny, 30 N.Y.2d 154, 331 N.Y.S.2d 392, 282 N.E.2d 295 (1972).

—Habitual users of marihuana and phencyclidine can testify as expert witnesses on the question of whether or not, in their opinion, certain substances sold by the defendant to them were marihuana and phencyclidine based upon their prior consumption of the substances. People v. Lynch, 85 A.D.2d 126, 447 N.Y.S.2d 549 (4th Dept. 1982).

Expert opinion; parental alienation syndrome.—Defendant sought to introduce testimony about "parental alienation syndrome," a psychological syndrome in which one parent programs a child into a campaign of denigration directed at the other parent, and the child then contributes to the efforts of the programming parent. Based on the hearing testimony, the court did not allow the testimony at trial because defendant failed to establish general acceptance in the scientific community of parental alienation syndrome. People v. Fortin, 184 Misc. 2d 10, 706 N.Y.S.2d 611 (Co. Ct. Nassau Co. 2000).

Rape trauma syndrome.—In order for an expert on rape trauma syndrome to testify concerning victim's behavior during the crime, as opposed to following it, the trial court must make two determinations: whether the evidence has the requisite scientific basis, and whether its potential value outweighs the possibility of undue prejudice to defendant or interference with the jury's province of determining credibility. People v. Bennett, 79 N.Y.2d 464, 473, 583 N.Y.S.2d 825, 831, 593 N.E.2d 275, 285 (1992).

—Expert testimony that a complaining witness has exhibited behavior consistent with "rape trauma syndrome" is admissible. People v. Taylor, 75 N.Y.2d 277, 552 N.Y.S.2d 883, 552 N.E.2d 131 (1990).

Sexual assault; physical trauma.—The court properly exercised its discretion in permitting a nurse practitioner, who was also a sexual assault forensics examiner, to give expert opinion testimony on circumstances under which a sexual assault would not be likely to cause physical trauma, since the witness's extensive training and experience rendered her qualified to provide such an opinion. People v. Lewis, 16 A.D.3d 173, 790 N.Y.S.2d 132 (1st Dept. 2005).

UNCHARGED CRIMES EVIDENCE; *MOLINEUX* DOCTRINE

Uncharged crimes evidence improper.—In some instances, evidence of uncharged crimes may be allowable as background or narrative because juries might "wander helpless" trying to sort out ambiguous, but material, facts. Here, there was no ambiguity that could not easily have been dealt with by far less prejudicial means than introducing testimony about an uncharged car theft. People v. Resek, 3 N.Y.3d 385, 787 N.Y.S.2d 683, 821 N.E.2d 108 (2004).

—Trial court should have excluded uncharged crime evidence, because it was neither relevant to any material issue in the case nor necessary to "complete the narrative" or otherwise aid the jury in determining defendant's guilt or innocence, and because it was unduly prejudicial to the defendant. People v. Foster, 295 A.D.2d 110, 743 N.Y.S.2d 429 (1st Dept. 2002).

—Absent a unique modus operandi, it was an abuse of discretion for the trial court to admit evidence of prior robbery attempts for the purpose of establishing defendant's identity. People v. Bines, 137 A.D.2d 431, 432, 524 N.Y.S.2d 212, 213 (1st Dept. 1988).

—Court properly allowed the People to offer evidence of the defendant's prior participation in a robbery with the codefendant to prove the defendant's intent, and refute his claim that he had been carjacked and forced to participate in the robbery. People v. Maxwell, 299 A.D.2d 370, 750 N.Y.S.2d 97 (2d Dept. 2002).

—In an attempted murder case where defendant was charged with throwing paint remover and lighting matches at his girlfriend in their apartment, the trial court erred in permitting the People to introduce evidence that one year after the incident, the defendant set fire to the house of another girlfriend when she was not home; evidence of the subsequent arson was improperly admitted for the purpose of establishing defendant's identity, since he did not raise mistaken identity as a defense; the trial court's instruction permitted the jurors to draw the inference that the defendant had the propensity to commit the charged crime, and accordingly, the error could not be deemed harmless; new trial granted. People v. Negron, 280 A.D.2d 557, 721 N.Y.S.2d 75 (2d Dept. 2001).

—It was error to allow defendant's ex-wife to testify as to his violations of prior orders of protection, since there was nothing sufficiently unique about the defendant's prior acts to allow such testimony as evidence of modus operandi. People v. Harris, 191 A.D.2d 643, 595 N.Y.S.2d 217 (2d Dept. 1993).

—In defendant's trial for sexual abuse, where defendant had entered a locked home through a window, the admission of defendant's subsequent "peeping Tom" incident was not admissible under the intent exception of *Molineux*; the peeping incident was relevant only for the improper purposes of lending credibility to the victim's version and indicating a propensity for the defendant to engage in voyeurism and sexual misconduct. People v. Reilly, 19 A.D.3d 736, 796 N.Y.S.2d 726 (3d Dept. 2005).

—Conviction reversed where uncharged crime evidence was improperly admitted; the prejudicial effect outweighed the probative value, and the court's limiting instructions did not overcome the natural tendency to find guilt based on defendant's apparent propensity to commit similar crimes. People v. Chaney, 298 A.D.2d 617, 748 N.Y.S.2d 182 (3d Dept. 2002).

Uncharged crimes evidence proper.—When appropriate, as

here, in light of the relationship between defendant and complainant as paramours, evidence of a defendant's prior abusive behavior toward a complainant may be admissible to prove the element of forcible compulsion in a rape case. People v. Cook, 93 N.Y.2d 840, 688 N.Y.S.2d 89, 710 N.E.2d 654 (1999).

—Evidence that, at the time of defendant's arrest, a credit card belonging to one of the robbery victims was recovered from a sales clerk following defendant's attempt to use it, was probative and admissible to connect the card to defendant; although the use of the card in an attempt to purchase merchandise fraudulently constituted an uncharged crime, this circumstance was necessary to explain the chain of events and link defendant to the card, since it was recovered from the sales clerk and not defendant. People v. Kemp, 291 A.D.2d 236, 738 N.Y.S.2d 25 (1st Dept. 2002).

—Court properly admitted uncharged crimes evidence, which provided necessary background as to how the victim first spoke to defendant about the abuse and as to how an acrimonious relationship developed between the two men; evidence also explained defendant's statements to the victim at the time of the assault. People v. Rochez, 289 A.D.2d 63, 734 N.Y.S.2d 136 (1st Dept. 2001).

—Trial court properly permitted prosecution to inquire into defendant's court appearances on prior unrelated cases to rebut the defendant's assertion, in defense to charge of bail jumping, that he was generally unfamiliar with court procedure. People v. Martin, 285 A.D.2d 614, 729 N.Y.S.2d 491 (2d Dept. 2001).

—Evidence that on one prior occasion the defendant threatened his wife and mother-in-law with a gun was properly admitted for the limited purpose of refuting the defendant's claim that he did not own or use a gun during the attack in question. People v. Woodford, 259 A.D.2d 717, 688 N.Y.S.2d 167 (2d Dept. 1999).

—In prosecution for criminal sale of a controlled substance, evidence regarding the uncharged drug sale was admissible to demonstrate that the defendant, as charged in the indictment, was acting in concert with the other individuals who were also arrested. People v. Guzman, 146 A.D.2d 799, 537 N.Y.S.2d 277 (2d Dept. 1989).

—Defendant's possession of a .25 caliber pistol and his discharge of it at person's home shortly before his arrest nearby for possessing the .38 caliber pistol was probative of his intent to use the latter weapon against another. People v. Richardson, 148 A.D.2d 476, 538 N.Y.S.2d 625 (2d Dept. 1989).

—In determining when proof of an uncharged crime may be admitted, the trial court must confirm that the evidence is probative of either an element of a charged crime or an issue material to the prosecution's case. People v. Tucker, 291 A.D.2d 663, 738 N.Y.S.2d 710 (3d Dept. 2002).

—In cases involving charges of child abuse, evidence of a defendant's prior conduct is relevant to establish that the injuries were not accidental or were not caused by another individual. People v. Engler, 150 A.D.2d 827, 540 N.Y.S.2d 591 (3d Dept. 1989), *accord* People v. Neer, 129 A.D.2d 829, 513 N.Y.S.2d 566 (3d Dept. 1987).

—In a prosecution for murder of defendant's infant child, trial court correctly held that evidence of the circumstances surrounding the deaths of two of defendant's other children was probative on the issues of intent and absence of mistake or accident. People v. Tinning, 142 A.D.2d 402, 536 N.Y.S.2d 193 (3d Dept. 1988).

—Where defendant was charged with promoting prostitution and coercion, it was proper for the witness to testify to uncharged crimes demonstrating a history of force used by defendant to force complainant into prostitution in order to show intent, motive and a common plan, scheme or design to commit the crimes charged. People v. Grant, 104 A.D.2d 674, 479 N.Y.S.2d 914 (3d Dept. 1984).

—Evidence of uncharged incidents of sexual relations between defendant and his daughters, who were under 14 years of age, were properly admissible at his trial on charges of rape, incest and sexual abuse involving his daughters; evidence of such other crimes were directly probative of the crimes charged in that they indicated an ongoing continuing relationship showing the defendant's "amorous design." People v. James, 98 A.D.2d 863, 471 N.Y.S.2d 158 (3d Dept. 1983).

—The testimony of a threatening telephone call by defendant and co-defendant to a prosecution witness was properly admitted on the issue of consciousness of guilt, although it was

evidence of prior bad acts, because the probative value exceeded its potential for prejudice. People v. Pugh, 236 A.D.2d 810, 653 N.Y.S.2d 994 (4th Dept. 1997).

Evidence of other crimes.—In prosecution for grand larceny, court found defendant's claim that the trial court constructively amended the indictment by permitting the jury to consider the evidence of 146 uncharged forged checks as direct evidence to be without merit. People v. Bayne, 82 N.Y.2d 673, 601 N.Y.S.2d 464, 619 N.E.2d 401 (1993).

—While evidence of other crimes cannot be proffered solely for the purpose of showing that a defendant is of a such criminal bent that he is likely to have committed the crime charged, it is within the discretion of the trial judge to decide whether the probative worth of evidence of other crimes on the issue of defendant's credibility outweighs the risk of unfair prejudice. People v. Pavao, 59 N.Y.2d 282, 464 N.Y.S.2d 458, 451 N.E.2d 216 (1983).

—The court did not abuse its discretion in refusing to preclude the People from seeking a ruling on the admissibility of any bad acts committed by defendant of which the People had not yet learned by the time of the *Sandoval* hearing. People v. Brown, 202 A.D.2d 266, 609 N.Y.S.2d 2 (1st Dept. 1994).

—While evidence of two instances of defendant's prior physical abuse toward his mother were improperly admitted, error was harmless in light of overwhelming evidence of defendant's guilt, including strong corroborating testimony of two neighbors who overheard altercation and observed defendant holding his mother in headlock. People v. Davis, 259 A.D.2d 706, 687 N.Y.S.2d 653 (2d Dept. 1999).

—When fraudulent intent is in issue, evidence of other similar acts are admissible to negate the existence of an innocent state of mind. People v. Lowenstein, 203 A.D.2d 304, 610 N.Y.S.2d 61 (2d Dept. 1994).

—When the People are forced to refute a claim of entrapment, evidence of similar uncharged crimes become relevant to prove that the defendant was, in fact, predisposed to commit the crime charged. People v. Harrison, 208 A.D.2d 648, 617 N.Y.S.2d 349 (2d Dept. 1994).

—Court did not err in permitting the People to introduce evidence that the defendant sold crack cocaine to an undercover officer before the heroin sale for which she was charged; such testimony was admissible to rebut the defendant's agency defense. People v. Rodriguez, 193 A.D.2d 705, 598 N.Y.S.2d 48 (2d Dept. 1993).

—In robbery prosecution, complainant's testimony that when the defendant first approached him he asked where he could purchase crack, was properly admissible to complete the narrative of events. People v. Martin, 154 A.D.2d 554, 546 N.Y.S.2d 394 (2d Dept. 1989).

— Witness' testimony that defendant was "high" and had offered to sell her pills when she conversed with him earlier on the evening of the crime was relevant to complete her narrative of the episode and to establish her ability to identify the defendants. People v. Bradley, 150 A.D.2d 592, 541 N.Y.S.2d 460 (2d Dept. 1989).

—The fact that prior adjudications involved conduct similar to the crimes charged did not automatically bar their use for impeachment purposes. People v. Doane, 208 A.D.2d 971, 617 N.Y.S.2d 232 (3d Dept. 1994).

—Court erred in failing to conduct *Ventimiglia* hearing prior to receipt of evidence of subsequent bad acts; conviction reversed due to erroneous admission of such evidence. People v. Pena-Martinez, 206 A.D.2d 858, 614 N.Y.S.2d 850 (4th Dept. 1994).

—People are required to obtain an advance ruling where they intend to introduce evidence of other crimes by the defendant. People v. Powell, 152 A.D.2d 918, 543 N.Y.S.2d 818 (4th Dept. 1989).

—The *Molineux* doctrine is applicable to bad acts allegedly committed by defendant after the crime for which he is tried. People v. Noriega, 160 Misc. 2d 632, 610 N.Y.S.2d 739 (Sup. Ct. Bronx Co. 1994).

Molineux; **evidence of other uncharged crimes.**—Evidence of other uncharged crimes committed by a defendant is admissible where that evidence tends to show (1) motive; (2) intent; (3) the absence of mistake or accident; (4) a common scheme or plan embracing the commission of two or more crimes so related to each other that proof of one tends to establish the others; (5) the identity of the person charged with the commission of the crime on trial. People v. Molineux, 168 N.Y. 264, 61 N.E. 286 (1901).

—For a discussion of the Molineux doctrine, see People v. Vega, 3 A.D.3d 239, 771 N.Y.S.2d 30 (1st Dept. 2004).

Admissibility of evidence of unconnected, uncharged criminal conduct.—It is immaterial that the People can establish a prima facie case without evidence of uncharged crimes; the People are not bound to stop after presenting minimum evidence but can go on and present all the admissible evidence available to them. People v. Alvino, 71 N.Y.2d 233, 244, 525 N.Y.S.2d 7, 13, 519 N.E.2d 808, 814 (1987).

—Evidence of uncharged crimes is not admissible if the sole purpose is to show that the defendant was predisposed to commit the crime charged, unless the defendant places this in issue by claiming that he was estopped or coerced into committing a crime to which he was not otherwise disposed. Evidence of other crimes may be admitted to show inter alia, motive, intent, the absence of mistake or accident, a common plan or scheme or the identity of the guilty party. People v. Allweiss, 48 N.Y.2d 40, 421 N.Y.S.2d 341, 396 N.E.2d 735 (1979).

—Evidence of uncharged crimes may be introduced only when the testimony is relevant and necessary to the prosecution's case; in determining the admissibility of such evidence, a balance must be struck between the probative value of the testimony in connection with the crimes charged and the danger of undue prejudice to the defendant. People v. Cook, 42 N.Y.2d 204, 397 N.Y.S.2d 697, 366 N.E.2d 788 (1977).

—Evidence of unconnected, uncharged criminal conduct is inadmissible if its purpose is to establish a predisposition to commit a crime; however, such evidence may be admissible for a relevant purpose, such as the showing of a common scheme or plan. People v. Fiore, 34 N.Y.2d 81, 356 N.Y.S.2d 38, 312 N.E.2d 174 (1974).

—The court reversed a conviction on the ground that testimony relating to an earlier, unproved complaint concerning the defendant's apartment was irrelevant and might have prejudiced the defendant. People v. Green, 35 N.Y.2d 437, 363 N.Y.S.2d 910, 323 N.E.2d 160 (1974).

—The trial court did not err in granting the People's application to present evidence of a prior sale of cocaine by defendant from the same apartment at which the search warrant was executed. People v. Contreras, 191 A.D.2d 235, 594 N.Y.S.2d 254 (1st Dept. 1993).

—The testimony concerning the defendant's and his mother's involvement with the male victim's drug business was admissible for the purpose of completing the narrative and of demonstrating the defendant's motive for committing the crime. People v. Garcia, 173 A.D.2d 399, 570 N.Y.S.2d 30 (1st Dept. 1991).

—The arresting officer's remark that defendant "struggled" with the officers upon being arrested did not constitute improper evidence of an uncharged crime. People v. Almonte, 177 A.D.2d 403, 576 N.Y.S.2d 247 (1st Dept. 1991).

—Evidence of defendant's prior thefts from his mother was properly admitted for the limited purpose of establishing the intent element of the burglary charge. People v. Scott, 176 A.D.2d 184, 185, 574 N.Y.S.2d 308, 309 (1st Dept. 1991).

—The detective's testimony concerning the "Ghost Shadows" gang to which defendant belonged was properly admitted. People v. Chang, 160 A.D.2d 469, 470, 554 N.Y.S.2d 141, 142 (1st Dept. 1990).

—The admission of testimony concerning an assault committed earlier in the day by defendant against the victim of the assault charged in the indictment did not require reversal. People v. Cheeseboro, 162 A.D.2d 286, 287, 556 N.Y.S.2d 637, 638 (1st Dept. 1990).

—The testimony outlining the stormy relationship between the defendant and a woman, and the subsequent animosity between the defendant and the woman's brother, was central to establishing the defendant's motive for setting fire to the building where the woman's brother lived. People v. Aviles, 234 A.D.2d 466, 652 N.Y.S.2d 48 (2d Dept. 1996), citing People v. Chase, 85 N.Y.2d 493, 626 N.Y.S.2d 721, 650 N.E.2d 379 (1995).

—In order for a pattern to establish a modus operandi, it is not necessary that the pattern be ritualistic to be considered distinctive; it is sufficient that it is a pattern that is distinctive. People v. Jason, 190 A.D.2d 689, 594 N.Y.S.2d 41 (2d Dept. 1993).

—Testimony about the defendant's involvement with drug dealers was admissible because it was relevant to motive and was necessary to complete the narrative of events. People v. McDowell, 191 A.D.2d 515, 594 N.Y.S.2d 347 (2d Dept. 1993).

—The court properly admitted evidence concerning the defendant's prior physical abuse of the complainant—as relevant on the issue of the defendant's intent with respect to the crimes charged—especially in view of the defendant's position that he had struck the complainant by accident. People v. Robinson, 191 A.D.2d 595, 594 N.Y.S.2d 801 (2d Dept. 1993).

—While the prosecutor should have obtained a ruling from a trial court regarding the admissibility of the uncharged drug transaction before the evidence was introduced into the case, the error was harmless as the evidence was admissible in any event. People v. Williams, 197 A.D.2d 722, 602 N.Y.S.2d 910 (2d Dept. 1993).

—Limited reference to a "drug related" shooting merely served to complete the narrative of the events leading up to the defendant's commission of the charged offense and was admissible. People v. Pope, 177 A.D.2d 658, 576 N.Y.S.2d 360 (2d Dept. 1991).

—Conversations between the undercover police officer and the defendant, regarding a $600 debt and the method of payment, which only tended to indicate prior dealings, were admissible because they were so inextricably intertwined with the transactions at bar that it would have been impossible to delete them, without impairing the jury's ability to follow the entire transaction. People v. Vails, 56 A.D.2d 939, 393 N.Y.S.2d 55 (2d Dept.), aff'd, 43 N.Y.2d 364, 401 N.Y.S.2d 479, 372 N.E.2d 320 (1977).

—In homicide prosecution, court did not err in admitting evidence of defendant's prior bad acts consisting of his prior abusive behavior toward the victim. People v. Jordan, 193 A.D.2d 890, 597 N.Y.S.2d 807 (3d Dept. 1993).

—Court's refusal to dismiss, for lack of corroborative evidence, three counts in the indictment until the close of the proof was not tantamount to the impermissible introduction of evidence of uncharged transactions; court was unpersuaded by the argument that the Molineux prohibition should be extended to include crimes charged in the indictment. People v. Rosica, 171 A.D.2d 931, 567 N.Y.S.2d 324 (3d Dept. 1991).

PRIVILEGES

Privileged communications.—Fee information sought by the prosecution is neither privileged nor directly incriminatory of the lawyer's clients who were already indicted. In re Stewart, 156 A.D.2d 294, 548 N.Y.S.2d 679 (1st Dept. 1989).

—Defendant's communications to rabbi for the secular purpose of seeking assistance in the retention of counsel, and in negotiating with the prosecutor's office and securing other assistance in connection with the preparation of his defense, were not made in confidence to the rabbi in his professional character as a spiritual adviser and were thus not privileged. People v. Drelich, 123 A.D.2d 441, 506 N.Y.S.2d 746 (2d Dept. 1986).

Parent-child privilege.—Court properly permitted two police officers to testify to an inculpatory statement which they overheard the defendant make to his mother at the police precinct; such testimony did not violate the parent-child privilege. People v. Robertson, 149 A.D.2d 442, 539 N.Y.S.2d 785 (2d Dept. 1989).

—Mother had conversations with defendant, her son, following an alleged homicide, but she refused to answer questions before the grand jury, claiming that such conversations were protected by a child-parent privilege; however, parent-child privilege did not apply to 28-year-old, financially independent defendant who had lived away from home for at least seven years. People v. Hilligas, 175 Misc. 2d 842, 670 N.Y.S.2d 744 (Sup. Ct. Erie Co. 1998).

Attorney-client privilege.—Attorney-client communications translated by an official court interpreter acting at the court's direction carry a reasonable expectation of confidentiality and thus are privileged. People v. Sin, 278 A.D.2d 181, 718 N.Y.S.2d 333 (1st Dept. 2000).

—Defendant waived the attorney-client privilege with regard to counsel's disclosure of defendant's admission that he acted as a lookout during the robbery, in light of the fact that, during the plea proceeding, defendant admitted that he and two others forcibly stole the complainant's wallet and since defendant challenged counsel's representation. People v. Dixon, 204 A.D.2d 234, 612 N.Y.S.2d 145 (1st Dept. 1994).

—Statements made by defendant to two former employees, who were associated with the law firm which once represented the defendant in an unrelated matter, were not shielded by the attorney-client privilege where there was no evidence presented from which to conclude that the phone calls were made for the purpose of obtaining legal advice. People v. Wiesner, 129 A.D.2d 753, 514 N.Y.S.2d 514 (2d Dept. 1987).

—The attorney-client privilege protects from disclosure the substance of communications between the parties, not the demeanor and mental capacity of the client during that communication. People v. Kinder, 126 A.D.2d 60, 512 N.Y.S.2d 597 (4th Dept. 1987).

Marital privilege.—Presumption that communications between spouses are conducted "under the mantle of confidentiality" is not rebutted by the fact that the parties are not living together at the time of the communications, or that their marriage had deteriorated, for even in a stormy relationship disclosures to a spouse may be induced by absolute confidence in the marital relationship. People v. Fediuk, 66 N.Y.2d 881, 498 N.Y.S.2d 763, 489 N.E.2d 732 (1985).

—Confidential marital communication privilege did not preclude wife from testifying, in husband's arson trial, that husband admitted to setting fire, since evidence indicated that crime was directed at wife; husband and wife were estranged and wife was living with her mother, wife testified that husband told her that he had started fire because he thought she would be forced to return to him in aftermath, and, in telephone conversation shortly before fire, husband threatened his mother-in-law by warning that she better take wife far away. People v. Capobianco, 218 A.D.2d 707, 630 N.Y.S.2d 386 (2d Dept. 1995).

—While communication by husband to his wife that he has committed crime is privileged as communication which would not have been made except in reliance upon free and unrestrained privacy of marital relationship, privilege is inapplicable where crime was directed against other spouse. People v. Capobianco, 218 A.D.2d 707, 630 N.Y.S.2d 386 (2d Dept. 1995).

—Acts as well as words may be the subject of a confidential communication between spouses. People v. Yakoumakis, 156 A.D.2d 499, 548 N.Y.S.2d 576 (2d Dept. 1989).

—Court properly ruled admissible those portions of a conversation between the defendant and his wife, which were made in the presence of two police officers, and were therefore not made in reliance upon the marital relationship. People v. Gorman, 150 A.D.2d 797, 542 N.Y.S.2d 225 (2d Dept. 1989).

—Court erred in allowing defendant's wife to testify that defendant had showed her the weapon on a prior occasion because acts as well as words may be the subject of communications. The People did not rebut the presumption that the act of defendant in showing the weapon to his wife was confidential and protected by the marital privilege. However, the error was harmless because of the overwhelming evidence. People v. Marinaccio, 15 A.D.3d 932, 788 N.Y.S.2d 784 (4th Dept. 2005).

—The spousal privilege falls when the substance of the communication is revealed to third parties. Because the substance of the communication between murder defendant and his wife was revealed to his wife's sister by both defendant and his wife, he could not assert the privilege. People v. Weeks, 15 A.D.3d 845, 789 N.Y.S.2d 373 (4th Dept. 2005).

Physician-patient privilege.—Defendant would waive physician-patient privilege if he affirmatively placed his medical condition in issue. People v. O'Connor, 290 A.D.2d 519, 738 N.Y.S.2d 55 (2d Dept. 2002).

—Physician's observation in emergency room that defendant was extremely intoxicated could have been made by a lay person and did not depend upon any confidential communication by a defendant, thereby placing the physician's testimony regarding intoxication outside the physician-patient privilege. People v. Hedges, 98 A.D.2d 950, 470 N.Y.S.2d 61 (4th Dept. 1983).

—CPLR 4504 does not include Emergency Medical Technicians (EMT) or paramedics within its list of health care professionals who are expressly covered by the privilege, but where an EMT speaks to a patient and obtains medical information and then reports that to the hospital's medical staff, the privilege applies. People v. Mirque, 195 Misc. 2d 375, 758 N.Y.S.2d 471 (Crim. Ct. Bronx Co. 2003).

—There is no public interest exception to the physician-patient privilege. People v. Saaruto, 143 Misc. 2d 1075, 541 N.Y.S.2d 889 (Sup. Ct. Bronx Co. 1989).

Insanity defense; waiver of doctor-patient relationship.—When insanity is asserted as a defense and the defendant offers evidence tending to show his insanity in support of this plea, a complete waiver is affected, and the prosecution is then permitted to call psychiatric experts to testify regarding his sanity even though they may have treated the defendant during period he was unfit to stand trial. People v. Abjul Karim Al Kanani, 33 N.Y.2d 260, 351 N.Y.S.2d 969, 307 N.E.2d 43 (1973), cert. denied, 417 U.S. 916 (1974).

§ 60.15. Rules of evidence; what witnesses may be called.

1. Unless otherwise expressly provided, in any criminal proceeding involving a defendant in which evidence is or may be received, both the people and the defendant may as a matter of right call and examine witnesses, and each party may cross-examine every witness called by the other party.

2. A defendant may testify in his own behalf, but his failure to do so is not a factor from which any inference unfavorable to him may be drawn.

ANNOTATIONS

Alibi witness's delay in informing police.—The District Attorney may lay a proper foundation for the cross-examination of a defense witness concerning his failure to come forward at an earlier date by just demonstrating that the witness was aware of the nature of the charges pending against the defendant, had reason to recognize that he possessed exculpatory information, had a reasonable motive for acting to exonerate the defendant, and finally, was familiar with the means to make such information available to law enforcement authorities. People v. Dawson, 50 N.Y.2d 311, 428 N.Y.S.2d 914, 406 N.E.2d 771 (1980).

Amnesia; proof of.—Reversal was required when the court refused to permit a defense psychiatrist to testify that the defendant was "suffering from amnesia, a true lack of memory of the entire incident" because the defendant did not take the stand and lay a proper foundation; defendant was not required to waive his constitutional privilege against self incrimination in order to place a fact relevant to the case before the jury. People v. Reed, 40 N.Y.2d 204, 386 N.Y.S.2d 371, 352 N.E.2d 558 (1976).

Co-defendant as witness; privilege against self incrimination.—When the trial court recognized the claim of privilege asserted by defendant's witness, who had been a participant in the crime and had earlier pleaded guilty, the error, if any, was not preserved for appellate review since the defendant failed to object or otherwise raise any question as to the witness' right to assert the privilege. People v. Tyler, 40 N.Y.2d 1065, 392 N.Y.S.2d 250, 360 N.E.2d 928 (1976).

—It was error to refuse defense demand for co-defendant to take witness stand where there was not shown a clear right of co-defendant not to testify because of privilege against self incrimination, he having been convicted for a crime arising out of the same transaction and not having appealed. People v. Ciraulo, 40 A.D.2d 834, 337 N.Y.S.2d 389 (2d Dept. 1972).

—Reversal was required when the prosecutor improperly called an indicted co-defendant and accomplice to testify knowing that he would assert his Fifth Amendment privilege in response to questions concerning defendants' direct involvement in the crime charged. People v. Paulino, 60 A.D.2d 769, 400 N.Y.S.2d 421 (4th Dept. 1977).

Cross-examination.—During the cross-examination of defendant's witness—his Legal Aid attorney who represented him at arraignment—it was appropriate for the prosecutor to inquire into the witness's ability to observe and recall defendant's physical appearance, as well as the witness's methods of recording such, and to elicit the fact that the witness had no way of knowing whether the defendant had worn a particular item of clothing when he was arrested 48 hours before the arraignment. People v. Montero, 192 A.D.2d 420, 596 N.Y.S.2d 396 (1st Dept. 1993).

—Defendant's claim that it was impermissibly prejudicial for the prosecutor to ask, during cross-examination, whether the defendant had heard the testimony of the People's witnesses was found to be without merit. People v. Forbes, 190 A.D.2d 816, 594 N.Y.S.2d 46 (2d Dept. 1993).

—Prosecutor's unsuccessful attempt to refresh the defendant's recollection with respect to a prior vicious act by offering him a document to review did not exceed the bounds of propriety where the document was not identified or described in the presence of the jury or admitted into evidence. People v. Sellan, 143 A.D.2d 690, 533 N.Y.S.2d 109 (2d Dept. 1988).

—Where defendant did not suffer any "specific demonstrable prejudice" as a result of alleged prosecutorially-impaired access to witnesses, he was not entitled to reversal. People v. Barcena, 131 A.D.2d 688, 689, 516 N.Y.S.2d 765, 767 (2d Dept. 1987).

—Since subject witness was never hypnotized, any error which may have been committed by the trial court in restricting defense counsel's attempts to cross-examine the witness on the subject of hypnosis must be considered harmless beyond a reasonable doubt. People v. York, 133 A.D.2d 130, 518 N.Y.S.2d 665 (2d Dept. 1987).

—It was improper for the prosecutrix to force the defendant to characterize the testimony of prosecution witnesses, including a policeman and an assistant principal as either lies or at least mistakes. People v. Lazarus, 78 A.D.2d 862, 432 N.Y.S.2d 629 (2d Dept. 1980).

—It was unfair for the prosecutor, on cross-examination of defense witness and over defense objection, to ask several questions which required the witness to say whether a particular witness for the People had been lying or telling the truth. People v. McDowell, 59 A.D.2d 948, 399 N.Y.S.2d 475 (2d Dept. 1977), aff'd, 47 N.Y.2d 858, 419 N.Y.S.2d 62, 392 N.E.2d 1245 (1979).

—Defendant's attempt to impeach the missing witness/informant by cross-examining police witnesses about his extensive police record was correctly disallowed since there is no right of confrontation where a witness provides no evidence at trial. People v. Pollak, 130 A.D.2d 911, 516 N.Y.S.2d 511 (3d Dept. 1987).

—A witness has the right to invoke his constitutional protection against self-incrimination and curtailment of cross-examination by this invocation does not offend the confrontation clause if the unanswered questions are completely collateral to the direct evidence, such as his prior criminal acts or criminal record. People v. Farruggia, 77 A.D.2d 447, 433 N.Y.S.2d 950 (4th Dept. 1980).

Cross-examination; holding of in-court line-up not allowed.—It was not error for the trial court to refuse to allow defense to cross-examine a prosecution witness by holding a line-up in court with the defendant's brother participating. People v. Pearce, 48 N.Y.2d 897, 424 N.Y.S.2d 887, 400 N.E.2d 1339 (1979).

Curative instructions.—Prosecutor's reference to defendant's failure to testify or to present witnesses on his behalf, while improper, did not entitle defendant to new trial, as trial court's curative instructions were sufficient to eliminate any prejudice and proof of defendant's guilt was overwhelming. People v. DeFigueroa, 182 A.D.2d 772, 582 N.Y.S.2d 496 (2d Dept. 1992).

Emergency room doctor's testimony.—The testimony of the emergency room doctor that the complainant's behavior after the attack was common among victims of a sexual assault was properly admitted into evidence, despite the fact that the doctor was never qualified as an expert because there is no requirement that a trial court formally certify a witness as an expert, and here, defense counsel did not object to the court's failure to qualify the doctor. People v. Abrams, 232 A.D.2d 240, 649 N.Y.S.2d 5 (1st Dept. 1996).

Reopening defense.—County court abused its discretion in denying defendant's motion, after defense rested and during charge conference, to reopen defense to permit him to testify. People v. Burke, 176 A.D.2d 1000, 574 N.Y.S.2d 859 (3d Dept. 1991).

Cross-examination; limitation by court.—It is settled that an accused's right to cross-examine witnesses and present a defense is not absolute. People v. Williams, 81 N.Y.2d 303, 313, 598 N.Y.S.2d 167, 171, 614 N.E.2d 730, 734 (1993).

—Trial courts retain wide discretion to limit cross-examination in order to address concerns about, among other things, harassment, prejudice, confusion of the issues, the witness's safety, or interrogation that is repetitive or only marginally relevant. People v. Ashner, 190 A.D.2d 238, 597 N.Y.S.2d 975 (2d Dept. 1993); see also People v. Abney, 193 A.D.2d 608, 597 N.Y.S.2d 431 (2d Dept. 1993).

—Not every error that curtails the right of the accused to cross-examine a prosecution witness is per se reversible error. People v. Jones, 193 A.D.2d 696, 598 N.Y.S.2d 40 (2d Dept. 1993).

—It is axiomatic that the nature and extent of cross-examination is a matter within the sound discretion of the trial court. People v. Jay, 187 A.D.2d 454, 589 N.Y.S.2d 529 (2d Dept. 1992).

—Trial court properly precluded further inquiry by defense counsel as to whether a third party was the perpetrator of the crime where the only other evidence linking such party to the crime was that he matched the description given by the complainant, although the complainant also stated, upon being shown a photograph of the third party, that such person did not look familiar; such evidence was not sufficient to allow extended inquiry into irrelevant, speculative and potentially confusing areas. People v. Austin, 112 A.D.2d 242, 491 N.Y.S.2d 458 (2d Dept. 1985).

—After an in camera examination of the file, the trial court properly refused to permit the defendant to cross-examine the key prosecution witness about her psychiatric history and to examine her file at the Albany County Mental Health Department since there was no evidence that she had ever been psychotic; however, the court did admit into evidence three psychiatric reports, none of which indicated either distress or any psychosis, and then permitted inquiry into the witness's past drug use and juvenile record. People v. Ely, 115 A.D.2d 171, 495 N.Y.S.2d 240 (3d Dept. 1985).

Cross-examination; prosecution witness.—Reversal was required where complainant lied about criminal background which deprived defendant of adequate opportunity to cross-examine that witness, and where court relying on the complainant's false testimony incorrectly charged that she had been convicted of a seemingly innocuous misdemeanor when it was actually a felony. People v. Santiago, 138 A.D.2d 327, 526 N.Y.S.2d 456 (1st Dept. 1988).

—Court erred in not permitting defense counsel to fully cross-examine one of the People's witnesses about his personal interest in the outcome in the case. People v. Kress, 192 A.D.2d 722, 597 N.Y.S.2d 124 (2d Dept. 1993).

—Although complainant was, in part, unresponsive during cross-examination, the defendant was not deprived of his right to confrontation since he, nonetheless, subjected the witness to extensive cross-examination. People v. Burke, 127 A.D.2d 842, 511 N.Y.S.2d 946 (2d Dept. 1987).

—Defendant was entitled to attempt to show through cross-examination that the informant's motive to lie was increased because of the sentence she faced before she agreed to become an informant and to plead guilty and receive a sentence of probation. People v. Bryant, 77 A.D.2d 603, 430 N.Y.S.2d 101 (2d Dept. 1980).

Cross-examination; prosecution witness; grant of immunity.—It was not error for the trial court to prevent defense counsel from cross-examining the witness concerning the possibility of her receiving a life sentence, a risk to which defendant was also exposed, in order to explain to the jury the extent of the arrangement the witness had made with the prosecutor for a grant of immunity. People v. DeVito, 56 N.Y.2d 846, 453 N.Y.S.2d 168, 438 N.E.2d 874 (1982).

Cross-examination; selling narcotics.—Defense was entitled to complete inquiry into circumstances of prosecution witness's conditional discharge where defendant's conviction was based solely on witness's observations of LSD sale transaction. People v. Roth, 30 N.Y.2d 99, 330 N.Y.S.2d 375, 281 N.E.2d 174 (1972).

Cross-examination; witness's failure to volunteer evidence.—Trial court properly precluded further inquiry by defense counsel as to whether a third party was the perpetrator of the crime where the only other evidence linking such party to the crime was that he matched the description given by the complainant, although the complainant also stated, upon being shown a photograph of the third party, that such person did not look familiar; such evidence was not sufficient to allow extended inquiry into irrelevant, speculative and potentially confusing areas. People v. Austin, 112 A.D.2d 242, 491 N.Y.S.2d 458 (2d Dept. 1985).

—It was improper for the court to allow the prosecutor to

cross-examine two defense witnesses as to their failure to come forward to the police or the grand jury with evidence which would have exonerated defendant, without first determining the good faith basis for such questioning or holding a bench conference to determine the reason for the witness' silence. People v. Muniz, 89 A.D.2d 611, 452 N.Y.S.2d 450 (2d Dept. 1982).

Fifth Amendment; invocation by non-party witness.— Court committed reversible error in permitting prosecutor to repeatedly question accomplice about the identity of his helper where the accomplice refused to answer; the accomplice's silence served to identify the defendant but denied him his right of confrontation on that issue. People v. Roberts, 70 N.Y.2d 682, 518 N.Y.S.2d 790, 512 N.E.2d 311 (1987).

—Where areas sought to be probed had already been sufficiently probed, witness' invocation of Fifth Amendment privilege did not deprive defendants of constitutional right to confront witnesses. People v. Chin, 67 N.Y.2d 22, 499 N.Y.S.2d 638, 490 N.E.2d 505 (1986).

—The witness did not waive her Fifth Amendment privilege by testifying for the People and being fully cross-examined by the defense as a non-party witness concerning facts that were not self-incriminating because they did not directly inculpate the witness on the charges at issue; upon being recalled by the defendant the witness could invoke the Fifth Amendment to avoid threatened perjury charges to which the witness had not subjected herself during her initial testimony. People v. Bagby, 65 N.Y.2d 410, 492 N.Y.S.2d 562, 482 N.E.2d 41 (1985).

Forensic chemist.—The court should not have permitted the prosecuting attorney to elicit on re-direct examination of the police chemist that the defendant had made no request to have the substance tested by a chemist on her behalf; unfavorable inferences may not be drawn from the failure of the defendant to call witnesses. People v. Strong, 60 A.D.2d 792, 400 N.Y.S.2d 661 (4th Dept. 1977).

Collateral matter.—The collateral issue rule bars the cross-examiner from offering evidence contradicting the cross-examined party on a collateral issue; it does not or should not bar the cross-examined party from explaining his admissions or offering, within reason, proof from others to explain his partial admissions. People v. Catalanotte, 36 N.Y.2d 192, 366 N.Y.S.2d 403, 325 N.E.2d 866 (1975).

—A cross-examiner is bound by the answers of a witness to questions concerning collateral matters. People v. Inniss, 192 A.D.2d 553, 596 N.Y.S.2d 98 (2d Dept. 1993).

—It is well established that the party who is cross-examining a witness may not introduce extrinsic documentary evidence or call other witnesses to contradict a witness's answers concerning collateral matters, solely for the purpose of impeaching that witness's credibility. People v. Griffin, 194 A.D.2d 738, 599 N.Y.S.2d 825 (2d Dept. 1993).

—Reversal was required where the prosecutor, called an investigator from the District Attorney's office, to rebut defendant's alibi witness' denial on cross examination of making a certain statement in a prior interview with the prosecutor since the alibi witness's answer was binding upon the People. People v. Napoletano, 58 A.D.2d 83, 395 N.Y.S.2d 469 (2d Dept. 1977).

Of defendant.—Proof of subsequent bad acts by a defendant may be admissible if offered for a purpose other than to raise an inference that a defendant has a criminal propensity. People v. Ingram, 71 N.Y.2d 474, 527 N.Y.S.2d 363, 522 N.E.2d 439 (1988).

—Reversible error was committed in sodomy prosecution by admitting evidence that the defendant was a member of an organization advocating sexual activity between adults and boys, that he had been previously known to the police as a pedophile and that he had raised a constitutional challenge in federal court to the statute under which he was being prosecuted. People v. Bagarozy, 132 A.D.2d 225, 522 N.Y.S.2d 848 (1st Dept. 1987).

—Evidence of uncharged robbery did not deprive defendant of fair trial where the record reflected that the defendant did not participate in and was not present during that crime and the trial court issued prompt curative instructions adequate to dispel any possible prejudicial effect attributable to such evidence. People v. Cottle, 123 A.D.2d 326, 506 N.Y.S.2d 218 (2d Dept. 1986).

—People were properly permitted to introduce into evidence defendant's post-arrest threat to kill the complainant. People v. Jones, 124 A.D.2d 749, 508 N.Y.S.2d 250 (2d Dept. 1986).

—It is reversible error for the prosecutor to repeatedly try to have the defendant state that the police officer was a liar and for the prosecutor to vouch for the police officer's testimony. People v. Santiago, 78 A.D.2d 666, 432 N.Y.S.2d 216 (2d Dept. 1980).

—Insinuations, during cross-examination by the prosecutor, that defendant had obtained the money as a bribe to remain silent created an atmosphere of prejudice, notwithstanding that the innuendo lacked foundation in fact, and was improper. People v. Colgan, 50 A.D.2d 932, 377 N.Y.S.2d 602 (2d Dept. 1975).

—Proof of defendant's heavy gambling debts was admissible to establish defendant's motive to commit the crime of forgery. People v. Lawson, 124 A.D.2d 853, 508 N.Y.S.2d 623 (3d Dept. 1986).

Previous crimes.—Defendant's prior conviction was properly admitted into evidence where the complainant in the instant case had been instrumental in persuading the victim of the prior crime to testify against the defendant, as it was probative of motive. People v. McKinley, 123 A.D.2d 362, 506 N.Y.S.2d 374 (2d Dept. 1986).

—Defendant cannot be cross-examined about a criminal charge on which he has been acquitted, or as to whether he stands indicted of other crimes; likewise, he cannot be questioned concerning immoral, vicious and criminal acts if the intent of such questions is to show from character or experience a propensity on the part of the defendant to commit the crime for which he is on trial. People v. Reingold, 44 A.D.2d 191, 353 N.Y.S.2d 978 (4th Dept. 1974).

Military violations.—It was error to permit the prosecutor to cross-examine defendant concerning his A.W.O.L. and use of disrespectful language to a superior while in the service, with the error compounded by allowing prosecutor to confront defendant with his prior statement refuting the denials, for such offenses were not "immoral, vicious or criminal acts" bearing on his credibility. People v. Perez, 44 A.D.2d 614, 353 N.Y.S.2d 818 (3d Dept. 1974).

Witness' residence.—It is permissible to cross-examine a witness as to his residence under the 6th and 14th amendments and it was error to deny defendant the right to cross-examine witness as to his present incarceration at Riker's Island but not reversible where jury could draw inference from other testimony or statements made in court. People v. Stridiron, 33 N.Y.2d 287, 352 N.Y.S.2d 179, 307 N.E.2d 242 (1973).

Police officer.—It was improper for the trial court to wholly exclude the evidence relating to the defendant's civilian complaint against a fellow police officer of the arresting officers; such evidence should have been allowed in attempted impeachment of the policemen's testimony. People v. Thomas, 92 A.D.2d 992, 402 N.Y.S.2d 273 (1st Dept. 1977).

—On cross-examination officer testified that the woman in the room where drugs were found stated that she and defendant were living there as man and wife, and that he had previously gone to the city to obtain heroin; the evidence was hearsay, but it was not accomplice testimony and did not require corroboration. People v. Parker, 46 A.D.2d 699, 360 N.Y.S.2d 99 (3d Dept. 1974).

Defendant; right to testify.—When defendant's request to take the stand took place after attorneys' closing arguments, it was not untimely and refusal of the request constituted reversible error. People v. Washington, 130 A.D.2d 605, 515 N.Y.S.2d 533 (2d Dept. 1987).

Defendant's failure to testify or call witnesses; prosecution's comments.—Where defendant failed to testify and prosecutor stated in summation that the undercover police officer's testimony was uncontroverted, this statement alluded to defendant's failure to take stand and thus constituted reversible error. People v. Brown, 91 A.D.2d 615, 456 N.Y.S.2d 405 (2d Dept. 1982).

—Defendant is under no obligation to take stand and testify or to call witnesses and D.A.'s comments on these omissions are prejudicial and combined with the prosecutor's references to unproved prior possession of drugs by the defendant, result in prejudicial error warranting reversal and new trial. People v. Conklin, 39 A.D.2d 160, 332 N.Y.S.2d 826 (3d Dept. 1972); see also People v. Rencher, 49 A.D.2d 609, 370 N.Y.S.2d 199 (2d Dept. 1975).

Failure of prosecution to call witness.—Defendant is entitled to charge that failure to produce police officer as witness entitled jury to infer testimony would be adverse to prosecution.

People v. Miles, 48 A.D.2d 706, 368 N.Y.S.2d 255 (2d Dept. 1975).

Defendant's failure to call witnesses under his control.— The fact finder may infer from defendant's failure to call a witness that if the witness had been called he would not have supported the defense testimony on the issue of which he possessed knowledge. People v. Paylor, 70 N.Y.2d 146, 518 N.Y.S.2d 102, 51 N.E.2d 370 (1987).

—The failure of a defendant, who has testified, to call a co-defendant who was an accomplice but who was not presently on trial or already adjudged guilty of perpetrating the same act or offense as that for which the defendant was being prosecuted and who was present and under the defendant's control and had information material to the case, could not be brought to the jurors' attention. People v. DeJesus, 42 N.Y.2d 519, 399 N.Y.S.2d 196, 369 N.E.2d 752 (1977).

—Ordinarily a court may not comment on a defendant's failure to testify or otherwise come forward with evidence, but once a defendant does so, his failure to call an available witness who is under defendant's control and has information material to the case that is not privileged, or confidential, may be brought to the attention of the jury for their consideration. People v. Rodriguez, 38 N.Y.2d 95, 378 N.Y.S.2d 665, 341 N.E.2d 231 (1975).

Direct examination; prosecution witness.—Since the defendant's attorney raised the defense of entrapment and duress during jury selection, during his opening statement and in cross-examination, the trial court did not err when it permitted evidence relating to the defendant's criminal predisposition to be introduced on the People's direct. People v. Grama, 124 A.D.2d 746, 508 N.Y.S.2d 247 (2d Dept. 1986).

—In a prosecution for second degree murder and criminal possession of a weapon in the second degree, it was wholly improper for the district attorney to bring out on the direct examination of a police officer that defendant was in custody on another charge at the time of his arrest and a new trial was ordered. People v. Lyles, 63 A.D.2d 740, 405 N.Y.S.2d 293 (2d Dept. 1978).

Exculpatory witness's silence.—Error was not preserved for review by the Court of Appeals where, after prosecutor had asked 19 questions of defense witness concerning witness' failure to come forward with exculpatory information, defense registered an unembellished "objection" since the protest was neither timely nor effective. People v. Maschi, 49 N.Y.2d 784, 426 N.Y.S.2d 727, 403 N.E.2d 449 (1980).

—Prosecutor's cross-examination of defendant about his silence at time of arrest was not prejudicial where defense had brought out same information in his cross-examination of police officer. People v. Simon, 75 A.D.2d 516, 426 N.Y.S.2d 753 (1st Dept. 1980).

—No stigma is ascribed to an exculpatory witness because he cooperated with the defense and did not divulge beforehand to law enforcement authorities the information he possessed. People v. Dale, 65 A.D.2d 625, 409 N.Y.S.2d 525 (2d Dept. 1978).

Failure of prosecutor to call witnesses.—Defendant was not deprived of due process because the prosecutor did not call certain witnesses, where the names and addresses of these persons and their statements were furnished defense counsel at the close of the People's case. People v. Stridiron, 33 N.Y.2d 287, 352 N.Y.S.2d 179, 307 N.E.2d 242 (1973).

Failure to produce unavailable informant.—It could not be said as a matter of law that the People failed to exercise due diligence in their search for the informant where the police acted promptly when the court concluded that the evidence at trial indicated that defendant should be permitted to call the informant to testify and when the People had not been directed earlier to produce or retain the informer. People v. Budd, 46 N.Y.2d 930, 415 N.Y.S.2d 207 (1979).

—The conviction was upheld where the identity of the informer, who was not an eyewitness to the criminal transactions, was disclosed to defense counsel and his disappearance, six months before trial, was not procured by the People and the trial court found the efforts made by the People to comply with defendant's mid-trial request that he be located were acceptable. People v. Santiago, 44 N.Y.2d 924, 408 N.Y.S.2d 7, 379 N.E.2d 1138 (1978).

—An absolute duty of production, or, alternatively, dismissal of the prosecution's case is required only where the People have intentionally procured the disappearance of the informant when they knew or should have known that the testimony would be material and relevant to the defense, or have exerted inadequate efforts to locate the informant, to avoid his or her presence at trial. People v. Jenkins, 41 N.Y.2d 307, 392 N.Y.S.2d 587, 360 N.E.2d 1288 (1977).

Heroin.—Generally, evidence of narcotic addiction is admissible to impeach a witness' credibility if tending to show that the witness was under the influence of drugs while testifying, or at the time of the events to which the testimony relates, or that the witness' power of perception or recollection, were actually impaired by the habit. People v. Friedand, 36 N.Y.2d 518, 369 N.Y.S.2d 649, 330 N.E.2d 611 (1975).

—It was error for the court to restrict the defendant's cross-examination concerning the witness' use of heroin or other drugs on the morning of the victim's death as well as the days on which she testified at trial since the witness' drug use at the specific times at which her ability to perceive and recollect were most in question was a relevant issue which the defense should have been allowed to fully explore. People v. Knatz, 76 A.D.2d 891, 428 N.Y.S.2d 709 (2d Dept. 1980).

Hypnotized witness; pretrial hearing necessary.—Where a victim is hypnotized during a criminal investigation, the trial court must hold a pretrial hearing to determine whether there has been a substantial impairment of the defendant's ability to meaningfully cross-examine the victim as a result of hypnotic suggestion and the burden is upon the prosecution to demonstrate no substantial impairment of defendant's right to cross-examine by clear and convincing proof. People v. Tunstall, 63 N.Y.2d 1, 479 N.Y.S.2d 192, 468 N.E.2d 30 (1984).

Illegal wiretap; bug.—Even if the taps and bug were illegal, the intercepted conversations could still be used to impeach the defendants' credibility on cross-examination. People v. Brooks, 56 A.D.2d 634, 391 N.Y.S.2d 886 (2d Dept. 1977).

In camera **testimony; failure to release.**—Failure of trial judge to release a portion of the *ex parte in camera* testimony of a prosecution witness was improper since the witness's answer could have been useful to the defense in cross-examination as it may have shown that the witness lied to the jury. People v. Unroch, 64 N.Y.2d 905, 488 N.Y.S.2d 374, 477 N.E.2d 615 (1985).

Mental condition of witness.—The following conditions must exist for admissibility of the testimony of a specialist or interested observer: (1) the complainant or a crucial witness has an infirmity or impairment which may affect his capacity to testify; (2) the infirm or handicapped witness must be found legally competent to testify; (3) the infirm or impaired witness must actually testify; (4) the testimony of such witness must be crucial to the case; (5) the ability of the infirm or impaired witness to testify must actually be in issue; (6) the testimony of the impaired witness must be otherwise admissible under recognized rules of evidence; and (7) the testimony of the specialist or interested observer must not be used merely to bolster the testimony of the impaired or infirm witness. People v. Freshley, 87 A.D.2d 104, 451 N.Y.S.2d 73 (1st Dept. 1982).

—It was reversible error to permit a psychologist to testify as "an interested observer" on the competency of a mentally retarded witness without making available all of the data he examined or relied upon in coming to his conclusion, including intelligence tests administered or examined by the psychologist as a basis for his testimony. People v. Freshley, 87 A.D.2d 104, 451 N.Y.S.2d 73 (1st Dept. 1982).

—Since the details of the prosecution's principal witness's confinement and illness in Gowanda State Hospital were already before the jury, the court properly denied defense offer of psychiatric testimony to establish the nature of the witness's mental condition upon his credibility and the further defense offer for an opportunity to present psychiatric evidence solely as to the nature of the defendant's illness. People v. Spano, 57 A.D.2d 715, 395 N.Y.S.2d 548 (4th Dept. 1977).

—The jury is entitled to be made aware that there is "something mentally wrong" with a witness and that a witness may not be "normal." People v. Kampshoff, 53 A.D.2d 325, 385 N.Y.S.2d 672 (4th Dept. 1976), *cert denied*, 433 U.S. 911.

Motive to fabricate.—If a witness is assailed for having a motive to fabricate, it is competent to put in evidence statements made by him consistent with what he says on the stand, made before the motive arose. People v. White, 57 A.D.2d 669, 393 N.Y.S.2d 615 (3d Dept. 1977).

Part of statement used on direct examination; cross examination.—Where only a part of a statement is drawn out on cross-examination, the other parts may be produced on redirect examination for the purpose of explaining or clarifying that statement. People v. Torres, 42 N.Y.2d 1036, 399 N.Y.S.2d 203, 369 N.E.2d 761 (1977).

Preclusion of testimony; lack of trustworthiness. —Court properly excluded from evidence an allegedly exculpatory statement by a person who was with the defendant during the drug sale where, although such person was unavailable for trial, his statement lacked sufficient indicia of trustworthiness since the portion of the statement which exculpated the defendant was not against the declarant's penal interest. People v. Nicholson, 108 A.D.2d 929, 485 N.Y.S.2d 821 (2d Dept. 1985).

Preclusion of witnesses.—Though court's ruling improperly impeded defendant's ability to present his own witnesses to establish a defense, where evidence of guilt was overwhelming and where the testimony excluded would have been cumulative to that adduced through other witnesses, the error was harmless; there was no significant probability that the jury would have acquitted the defendant but for the error. People v. Gilmore, 66 N.Y.2d 863, 498 N.Y.S.2d 752, 489 N.E.2d 721 (1985).

Prior immoral or criminal acts; cross-examination.— Reversal was required despite failure of defense counsel to object where prosecutrix questioned defendant concerning details of a prior rape case that had been dismissed against him and focused on this case in her summation; the entire line of questioning was improper for it served no purpose but to show defendant's propensity to commit the crime of rape. People v. Walker, 59 A.D.2d 666, 398 N.Y.S.2d 285 (1st Dept. 1977).

—Where the prosecutor, during cross-examination of the defendant, inquired about a rape indictment pending in another county, without mentioning the words "rape" and "indictment," and defendant denied it, it was error for the prosecutor to read an excerpt from the court proceedings involving the other indictment which clearly showed that the defendant was lying. People v. Worrell, 54 A.D.2d 768, 387 N.Y.S.2d 694 (2d Dept. 1976).

—When a defendant chooses to testify he may be cross-examined concerning his immoral, vicious or prior criminal acts which have a bearing on his credibility as a witness, provided the prosecutor acts in good faith and upon a reasonable basis of fact; however, cross-examination as to such prior acts will not be permitted when the obvious intent is to show a propensity to commit the same crime for which defendant is on trial. People v. Brown, 70 A.D.2d 1043, 417 N.Y.S.2d 560 (4th Dept. 1979).

Prior statements of witness.—Although as a general rule, the credibility of any witness can be attacked by showing an inconsistency between his testimony at trial and what he has said on previous occasions, as this testimony is often collateral to the ultimate issue before the jury and bears only upon the credibility of the witness, its admissibility is entrusted to the discretion of the trial judge and if admitted a proper foundation must be laid as to the time, place and substance of the prior statement. People v. Duncan, 46 N.Y.2d 74, 412 N.Y.S.2d 833, 385 N.E.2d 572 (1978).

—Reversal was required where the court prevented defense counsel from placing in evidence a prior statement of the chief prosecution witness which was inconsistent with his trial testimony; the inconsistency itself was a jury question to be decided by the triers of fact like any other credibility factor such as interest, bias, ability to observe, and prejudice. People v. Stauris, 75 A.D.2d 507, 426 N.Y.S.2d 741 (1st Dept. 1980).

Promise of leniency by District Attorney.—Refusal to permit defense, during cross-examination, to ask witness whether he was testifying as a result of a deal or other arrangement for lenient treatment, deprived defendant of substantial right and constituted prejudicial error even though the trial court ruled as a matter of law that there was no such deal. People v. Leonard, 58 A.D.2d 1018, 396 N.Y.S.2d 956 (4th Dept. 1977).

Rebuttal testimony.—Since a cross-examiner is bound by the witness' answers on collateral matters, it was improper for the prosecutor to elicit on its rebuttal case evidence that defendant had engaged in prior drug transactions where the defendant had denied that any sales had occurred in his cross-examination. People v. Crandall, 67 N.Y.2d 111, 118, 500 N.Y.S.2d 635, 639, 491 N.E.2d 1092, 1096 (1986).

—In prosecution for fourth-degree criminal possession of a controlled substance, beeper and currency properly admitted to rebut the claim raised in the opening statement by defense counsel that the defendant was unaware of the presence of drugs in the glove compartment of the car. People v. Davis, 196 A.D.2d 880, 602 N.Y.S.2d 169 (2d Dept. 1993).

—On People's rebuttal case, the officer should not have been permitted to testify as to a prior inconsistent statement of a defense witness because the statement was relevant only to the issue of the credibility of the witness. People v. Torres, 199 A.D.2d 442, 605 N.Y.S.2d 380 (2d Dept. 1993).

Striking of testimony.—Trial court did not err in striking the defendant's testimony on direct examination and continuing the trial in his absence when he failed to appear after a recess for his own cross-examination. People v. Falchetti, 119 A.D.2d 690, 500 N.Y.S.2d 812 (2d Dept. 1986).

Prosecutor's remark.—Prosecutor's comments regarding the defendant's failure to admit his presence in the restaurant, in which robbery took place, were not improper since the prosecutor merely sought to point out inconsistencies between the defendant's testimony and the testimony of the complaining witness. People v. Rochester, 131 A.D.2d 791, 517 N.Y.S.2d 79 (2d Dept. 1987).

Trial minutes; availability to defense counsel.—Where minutes of prior trial were in court room, were requested by defense counsel as aid to cross-examination, and refused by District Attorney and Trial Judge declined to direct that they be made available, there was no error since there was no showing of defendant's indigency or inability to obtain copy. However, ordinary professional courtesy suggests that minutes be made available in such a case. People v. Zanotti, 30 N.Y.2d 926, 335 N.Y.S.2d 682 (1972).

Uncharged crimes.—The evidence of defendant's involvement in the drug trade was not admitted solely to establish a criminal propensity on the part of the defendant; rather, the evidence was properly admitted to show motive. People v. Cascoigne, 189 A.D.2d 714, 592 N.Y.S.2d 722 (1st Dept. 1993).

—There was no error in the admission of the background testimony regarding a "stabbing" with which defendant was never charged, nor of the fact that the defendant was in possession of $1600 when he was arrested. People v. Scianameo, 189 A.D.2d 691, 592 N.Y.S.2d 383 (1st Dept. 1993).

—To the extent that the defendant preserved his claim relating to the admissibility of background evidence concerning police procedures, the evidence in question was properly admitted to aid the jury in understanding the officer's conduct and was probative of their credibility. People v. Hamilton, 189 A.D.2d 620, 592 N.Y.S.2d 320 (1st Dept. 1993).

—Evidence of uncharged crimes was admissible to complete the narrative and was pertinent to defendant's motive. People v. Cintron, 181 A.D.2d 552, 581 N.Y.S.2d 190 (1st Dept. 1992).

—Uncharged crimes evidence properly admitted to complete a coherent narrative of the incident and to avoid speculation as to the subsequent actions of the police leading to defendant's arrest. People v. Grant, 181 A.D.2d 579, 581 N.Y.S.2d 323 (1st Dept. 1992).

—Court properly denied defendant's motion for a mistrial, since defendant was not prejudiced by prosecution's failure to advise defense counsel of the existence of evidence of uncharged drug sales until after voir dire and the swearing of the jury, but prior to counsel's opening statement. People v. Hicks, 189 A.D.2d 782, 592 N.Y.S.2d 398 (2d Dept. 1993).

—Questioning concerning other crimes is not automatically precluded simply because those crimes are similar to the crimes charged. People v. Dillon, 189 A.D.2d 775, 592 N.Y.S.2d 403 (2d Dept. 1993).

—Evidence of uncharged drug sales is admissible on the issue of the defendant's intent. People v. DeJesus, 189 A.D.2d 774, 592 N.Y.S.2d 62 (2d Dept. 1993).

—It was error to admit detective's testimony concerning the Drug Enforcement Administration's activities and surveillance photographs. People v. Martin, 182 A.D.2d 834, 582 N.Y.S.2d 793 (2d Dept. 1992).

—Trial court did not err in admitting the testimony regarding the defendant's previous threats and assaults against the victim; the testimony was relevant to the defendant's motive and intent. People v. Carver, 183 A.D.2d 907, 584 N.Y.S.2d 142 (2d Dept. 1992).

—Evidence of a prior drug sale is admissible to rebut an agency defense. People v. Alers, 182 A.D.2d 822, 582 N.Y.S.2d 789 (2d Dept. 1992).

—Evidence of uncharged crimes is not admissible when it is offered solely to raise an inference that a defendant has a criminal propensity. People v. Rios, 183 A.D.2d 734, 583 N.Y.S.2d 306 (2d Dept. 1992).

—Particularly in cases involving child abuse, evidence of prior bad acts is highly relevant to establish a lack of mistake or accident. People v. Basir, 179 A.D.2d 662, 578 N.Y.S.2d 604 (2d Dept. 1992).

—Court erred in permitting defendant's written and videotaped confessions, which contained references to prior uncharged crimes, to be submitted unredacted for the jury's consideration. People v. Jones, 182 A.D.2d 708, 582 N.Y.S.2d 476 (2d Dept. 1992).

—Evidence of prior uncharged crimes may not be introduced simply to demonstrate a defendant's propensity to commit the crime at issue. People v. Intelisano, 188 A.D.2d 881, 591 N.Y.S.2d 883 (3d Dept. 1992).

—Testimony that defendant had been under investigation by the police as a suspected drug dealer constituted improper use of character evidence. People v. Roberts, 188 A.D.2d 735, 591 N.Y.S.2d 559 (3d Dept. 1992).

Post-arrest reports.—Post-arrest report, UF61, prepared by undercover officer, which tended to confirm his testimonial version of events leading to the arrests, should not have been received into evidence after the defense cross-examined the officer with regard to a motive to fabricate the entire case from its inception; such report was irrelevant under the circumstances since it could not have been made prior to the time when the charged motive to falsify arose. People v. Davis, 44 N.Y.2d 269, 405 N.Y.S.2d 428, 376 N.E.2d 901 (1978).

—The DD-5 (an official police department Supplementary Complaint Report) can be used for impeachment purposes but cannot be admitted as evidence. People v. Massey, 44 A.D.2d 785, 355 N.Y.S.2d 120 (1st Dept. 1974), aff'd, 355 N.Y.S.2d 1006 (1974).

Witnesses.—It is not incumbent upon the prosecution to call at trial every witness to a crime or to make a complete and detailed accounting to the defense of all law enforcement investigatory work. People v. Buckler, 39 N.Y.2d 895, 386 N.Y.S.2d 396, 352 N.E.2d 583 (1976).

—The prosecutor's refusal to grant immunity to a defense witness who would not testify based on the assertion of fifth amendment privilege did not deprive defendant of due process or a fair trial when the witness was not a law enforcement agent or in any way a part of the prosecutorial apparatus. People v. Arroyo, 46 N.Y.2d 928, 415 N.Y.S.2d 205, 388 N.E.2d 342 (1979).

Witness in hiding; use of preliminary hearing testimony permitted.—Preliminary hearing testimony was properly admissible where the complaining witness in a robbery prosecution failed to appear and it was established that he was deliberately hiding, apparently because the defendant had paid him not to testify and where cross-examination of the complaining witness had not been restricted in any way at a preliminary hearing. People v. Corley, 77 A.D.2d 835, 431 N.Y.S.2d 21 (1st Dept. 1980).

Youthful offender.—Defendant's conviction was reversed since it was improper to bring out on defendant's cross-examination that defendant, previously adjudicated a youthful offender for resisting arrest, was in possession of a stolen car and had been charged or processed for car theft, although not convicted of this offense; furthermore, defendant did not open door to disclosure of facts concerning his previously being processed as a juvenile where he only acknowledged his prior juvenile status in response to those questions posed by the prosecution. People v. Cook, 37 N.Y.2d 591, 376 N.Y.S.2d 110, 338 N.E.2d 619 (1975).

—In robbery and grand larceny prosecution, court properly allowed the prosecutor to cross-examine the defendant, for impeachment purposes, concerning the illegal larcenous acts underlying his prior youthful offender adjudication. People v. Horne, 139 A.D.2d 765, 527 N.Y.S.2d 512 (2d Dept. 1988).

§ 60.20. Rules of evidence; testimonial capacity; evidence given by children.

1. Any person may be a witness in a criminal proceeding unless the court finds that, by reason of infancy or mental disease or defect, he does not possess sufficient intelligence or capacity to justify the reception of his evidence.

2. Every witness more than nine years old may testify only under oath unless the court is satisfied that such witness cannot, as a result of mental disease or defect, understand the nature of an oath. A witness less than nine years old may not testify under oath unless the court is satisfied that he or she understands the nature of an oath. If under either of the above provisions, a witness is deemed to be ineligible to testify under oath, the witness may nevertheless be permitted to give unshorn evidence if the court is satisfied that the witness possesses sufficient intelligence and capacity to justify the reception thereof. A witness understands the nature of an oath if he or she appreciates the difference between truth and falsehood, the necessity for telling the truth, and the fact that a witness who testifies falsely may be punished.

3. A defendant may not be convicted of an offense solely upon unsworn evidence given pursuant to subdivision two.

Amended by L. 1975, Ch. 133; L. 2000, Ch. 1, amending subd. 2, eff. Feb. 1, 2001; L. 2003, Ch. 264, § 36, eff. Nov. 1, 2003, amending subd. 2.

ANNOTATIONS

Child testimony; preliminary examination.—Trial court erroneously permitted testimony by an 8-year-old child where the preliminary examination of such child did not clearly establish that such witness understood and appreciated the nature of an oath. People v. Smith, 104 A.D.2d 160, 481 N.Y.S.2d 879 (2d Dept. 1984).

Confidentiality.—In prosecution involving sex crime of child under the age of 16, testimony by social worker concerning communications by victim to him did not serve to breach confidentiality of records of such communications as provided for by statute. People v. Tissois, 131 A.D.2d 612, 516 N.Y.S.2d 314 (2d Dept. 1987), aff'd, 72 N.Y.2d 75, 531 N.Y.S.2d 228, 526 N.E.2d 1086 (1988).

Corroboration requirement.—Pursuant to CPL § 60.20(3) corroborative evidence may not rely to any extent on the complaining witness's testimony for to do so would be bootstrapping. People v. Badia, 163 A.D.2d 4, 558 N.Y.S.2d 500 (1st Dept. 1990).

—Corroboration is not required for rape in the third degree, where a victim's incapacity to consent is a product of her age; neither physical injury nor screaming is required for a conviction of first degree rape. People v. Alford, 287 A.D.2d 884, 731 N.Y.S.2d 563 (3d Dept. 2001).

—While corroboration of a minor's testimony may be necessary if the child is unable to understand the nature of an oath, the County Court, after an extensive voir dire, properly determined that the victim understood the nature of the oath and that she was competent to give sworn testimony. People v. Rogowski, 228 A.D.2d 728, 644 N.Y.S.2d 334 (3d Dept. 1996).

—In a prosecution for forcible rape, first degree, (PL § 130.35[1]), the conviction was affirmed where the nine-year-old complainant's testimony was corroborated by circumstantial evidence consisting of the police officer's testimony of defendant's admission that he was "in the bedroom with the little girl" and "in the bed" and defendant's mother's testimony that she saw defendant in bed with the complainant although the testimony of the examining doctor was inconclusive; however this evidence was not sufficient to establish a statutory rape. People v. Fuller, 67 A.D.2d 890, 412 N.Y.S.2d 703 (3d Dept. 1979), *aff'd,* 50 N.Y.2d 628, 431 N.Y.S.2d 357, 409 N.E.2d 834 (1980).

—Unsworn testimony of nine-year-old complainant in sodomy trial was sufficiently corroborated by evidence tending to establish crime and connecting defendant with its commission and was corroborated by defendant's statement that itself required corroboration; cross-corroboration is permitted in cases when corroboration requirements of each statement are set forth in different statutes for different reasons. People v. Bitting, 224 A.D.2d 1012, 637 N.Y.S.2d 820 (4th Dept. 1996).

—Where the complaining witness is alleged to suffer from any mental disease or defect that may otherwise affect his capacity to understand the nature of an oath, the defendant is to be afforded the protection of an examination of the person's capacity to corroborate the charges in a supporting deposition similar to the requirement of CPL § 60.20 that is applicable to trial testimony. People v. McDermott, 158 Misc. 2d 823, 601 N.Y.S.2d 1017 (Crim. Ct. Kings Co. 1993).

General reasons for corroboration requirement.—The rules of evidence which require corroboration of other testimony are embodied in both the Penal Law and CPL. The corroboration requirements under both these statutes demand the same standard of sufficiency—it must tend to show the probable truth of the initial testimony and establish all the elements of the crime. Corroboration is required in the Penal Law due to the nature of the crime while it is required in the Criminal Procedure Law due to the nature of the witness. The indictment or conviction will stand or fall upon such other sworn evidence. People v. Curtis, 76 Misc. 2d 128, 350 N.Y.S.2d 315 (Sup. Ct. N.Y. Co. 1973).

Corroboration of unsworn testimony.—There was independent evidence to corroborate unsworn complainant's testimony where complainant's mother and brothers testified that complainant's behavior changed noticeably immediately after incident. In absence of any other explanation for sudden rift between complainant and his uncle, the latter's changed behavior constitutes corroborative evidence. People v. Cordero, 257 A.D.2d 372, 684 N.Y.S.2d 192 (1st Dept. 1999).

—A person cannot be convicted solely on the testimony of an unsworn witness. People v. Maldonado, 199 A.D.2d 563, 606 N.Y.S.2d 258 (2d Dept. 1993).

—Unsworn testimony of a witness must be corroborated before it can serve to convict a defendant; the proof presented must tend to connect the defendant with the commission of the crime so that the trier of fact is reasonably satisfied that the unsworn witness is telling the truth. People v. Tomczak, 189 A.D.2d 926, 592 N.Y.S.2d 486 (3d Dept. 1993).

—The sworn testimony of a ten-year-old witness was sufficient to corroborate the unsworn testimony of his seven-year-old brother, in a prosecution for sodomy. People v. Kalicki, 49 A.D.2d 1032, 374 N.Y.S.2d 501 (4th Dept. 1975).

—Infant's unsworn testimony was adequately corroborated by defendant's written confession, testimony of other witnesses and the infant's palm print on the trunk of defendant's car. People v. Zimmerman, 46 A.D.2d 725, 360 N.Y.S.2d 127 (4th Dept. 1974).

Cross-corroboration.—Complainant's six-year-old son's unsworn trial testimony was sufficient to corroborate complainant's trial testimony of sodomy under former PL § 130.15 which required corroboration of the victim's testimony; cross corroboration is permitted when the witnesses are required to be corroborated under different statutes and for different reasons. People v. Coleman, 42 N.Y.2d 500, 399 N.Y.S.2d 185, 369 N.E.2d 742 (1977).

—Child's testimony could corroborate defendant's statement and vice versa since cross-corroboration is permitted where the corroboration requirements of each statement are set forth in different statutes for different reasons. People v. Knights, 131 A.D.2d 924, 516 N.Y.S.2d 969 (3d Dept. 1987).

—The corroborating evidence need not be positive and direct, it may be circumstantial only but must extend to proof of circumstances legitimately tending to show the existence of the material facts of the crime. People v. St. John, 74 A.D.2d 85, 426 N.Y.S.2d 863 (3d Dept. 1980).

—Corroboration of the unsworn testimony of the defendant's six year-old niece as to sexual abuse was not established by the mere presence of the defendant in the same home of the victim when the premises were also occupied at that time by several other individuals. People v. Doellner, 87 A.D.2d 987, 450 N.Y.S.2d 114 (4th Dept. 1982).

Grand jury; unsworn testimony of one witness is insufficient to corroborate the unsworn testimony of another.—Complainant's testimony without oath is sufficient where the corroboration evidence is sworn. Unsworn corroborative testimony would be sufficient where the evidence in chief (i.e. complainant's testimony) is sworn. However, under statutory and case law, an indictment may not be based solely upon unsworn testimony and the unsworn testimony of one witness is insufficient to corroborate the unsworn testimony of another. People v. Curtis, 76 Misc. 2d 128, 350 N.Y.S.2d 315 (Sup. Ct. N.Y. Co. 1973).

Recorded statement inadmissible.—The 7-year-old child's recorded statement was inadmissible as a past recorded recollection since the test for such admissibility, that he believed the statement was correct at the time made was not met, i.e., the infant challenged the accuracy of the statement. People v. Bici, 87 A.D.2d 844, 449 N.Y.S.2d 250 (2d Dept. 1982).

Right of defense counsel to cross-examine witness in voir dire.—It is accepted practice here and elsewhere for the court to examine an 11-year-old complaining witness' testimonial capacity without the intervention of counsel. Although there is nothing to preclude the court from permitting defense counsel to participate in the examination by submitting questions or, cross-examining, the conduct of the voir dire by counsel for defendant is not a constitutional right. People v. Byrnes, 33 N.Y.2d 343, 352 N.Y.S.2d 913, 308 N.E.2d 435 (1974).

Sworn testimony; child less than 12 years.—Although it was obvious that the eight-year-old child did not understand the nature of an oath, the voir dire of this witness demonstrated that she undoubtedly possessed the requisite capacity and intelligence to justify the reception of her unsworn testimony. People v. Nisoff, 36 N.Y.2d 560, 369 N.Y.S.2d 686, 330 N.E.2d 638 (1975).

—Ten-year-old boy was properly sworn as witness; trial court was in best position to determine child's capabilities as witness and determined that child was sufficiently aware of nature and obligations of telling the truth and of recalling and relating prior events; that ten-year-old witness did not know meaning of word "oath" and that court did not inform him that he could face criminal sanctions for lying did not mean that he should not have been sworn as witness. People v. Young, 225 A.D.2d 339, 638 N.Y.S.2d 630 (1st Dept. 1996).

—Court properly allowed five-year-old complainant to testify under oath because she adequately demonstrated that she appreciated the difference between truth and falsehood, the necessity for telling the truth, and the fact that a witness may be punished for telling a lie in court. People v. McIver, 15 A.D.3d 677, 791 N.Y.S.2d 587 (2d Dept. 2005).

—Trial court properly allowed seven-year-old victim to give sworn testimony at criminal trial, despite court's purported failure to explain to victim the meaning of an oath where voir dire examination revealed that child could understand the difference between telling a lie and the truth, the meaning of a promise to tell the truth, that she would be punished if she did not keep a promise to God, and that she would have to tell the truth in court. People v. Dorsey, 265 A.D.2d 567, 697 N.Y.S.2d 305 (2d Dept. 1999).

—Court did not err in allowing seven-year-old complainant to testify under oath, where her responses to the court's preliminary questioning indicated that she had some conception of the obligations of an oath and the consequences of false testimony, including the fact that she could be punished by God. People v. Robrigado, 254 A.D.2d 438, 680 N.Y.S.2d 109 (2d Dept. 1998).

—Trial court improperly permitted unsworn testimony of five-year-old complainant, in sex crimes prosecution, without first conducting preliminary examination to determine whether she understood nature of oath and could, therefore, offer sworn testimony or whether she possessed sufficient intelligence and capacity to justify reception of unsworn testimony. People v. Rose, 223 A.D.2d 607, 637 N.Y.S.2d 172 (2d Dept. 1996).

—Where witness was a bright six-year-old child who understood that she was obligated to tell the truth, the trial court's decision to put her under oath was not an abuse of discretion. People v. Fernandez, 138 A.D.2d 733, 526 N.Y.S.2d 547 (2d Dept. 1988).

—Defendant failed to preserve for review his contention that court's *voir dire* of 10-year-old sodomy victim was inadequate and that court's finding of competency was erroneous since he expressed no dissatisfaction with the *voir dire* at the trial and he failed to object to court's competency determination. People v. Danza, 127 A.D.2d 781, 512 N.Y.S.2d 175 (2d Dept. 1987).

—Nine-year-old victim was competent to give sworn testimony because voir dire by court indicated that witness understood concept and obligations of oath, difference between truth and falsity, and consequences of giving false testimony. People v. Christie, 241 A.D.2d 699, 659 N.Y.S.2d 958 (3d Dept. 1997).

—Corroboration was not required in conviction for course of sexual conduct against a child in the first degree where the 11-year-old victim gave sworn testimony and she was not incapable of consent because of mental defect or incapacity. People v. McLoud, 291 A.D.2d 867, 737 N.Y.S.2d 216 (4th Dept. 2002).

—Because the eight-year-old victim did not testify under oath, the trial court did not need to determine whether the victim was competent to give sworn testimony. Furthermore, the victim's responses to questioning demonstrated that she possessed sufficient intelligence and capacity to justify the admission of her unsworn testimony. People v. Wacht, 261 A.D.2d 932, 689 N.Y.S.2d 795 (4th Dept. 1999).

Sworn testimony; mentally ill person.—The mere fact that the complainant is mentally ill does not *per se* render his testimony incompetent or incredible. People v. Green, 75 A.D.2d 502, 426 N.Y.S.2d 736 (1st Dept. 1980).

Testimony of others.—It was not error to permit the complainant's teacher to testify, to the jury, with respect to the mental condition of the complainant; however, the teacher could not express a view as to the credibility or believability of the complainant. People v. Parks, 41 N.Y.2d 36, 390 N.Y.S.2d 848, 359 N.E.2d 358 (1976).

—The trial court properly exercised its discretion in allowing the complainant's mother to make a limited statement as to her daughter's mental infirmity. People v. Riss, 58 A.D.2d 697, 396 N.Y.S.2d 89 (3d Dept. 1977).

§ 60.22. Rules of evidence; corroboration of accomplice testimony.

1. A defendant may not be convicted of any offense upon the testimony of an accomplice unsupported by corroborative evidence tending to connect the defendant with the commission of such offense.

2. An "accomplice" means a witness in a criminal action who, according to evidence adduced in such action, may reasonably be considered to have participated in:

(a) The offense charged; or

(b) An offense based upon the same or some of the same facts or conduct which constitute the offense charged.

3. A witness who is an accomplice as defined in subdivision two is no less such because a prosecution or conviction of himself would be barred or precluded by some defense or exemption, such as infancy, immunity or previous prosecution, amounting to a collateral impediment to such a prosecution or conviction, not affecting the conclusion that such witness engaged in the conduct constituting the offense with the mental state required for the commission thereof.

ANNOTATIONS

Accomplice; charge to the jury.—Where defendant was convicted of felony murder, the predicate felony being robbery, and evidence at trial showed that witness was present in victim's apartment during both the conversation concerning the possible robbery and the commission of the crime but the record was devoid of any direct proof that witness aided in the preparation or execution of the crimes of which the defendant was charged, trial judge properly submitted to the trier of facts the question of whether or not the witness was an accomplice. People v. Dorta, 46 N.Y.2d 818, 414 N.Y.S.2d 114, 386 N.E.2d 1081 (1978).

Accomplice; definition.—A witness may be stamped an accomplice only if there is a showing that he took part in the preparation or perpetration of the crime with the intent to assist therein or that he counseled, induced or encouraged the crime. The generally accepted test is whether he himself could have been convicted either as a principal or accessory. People v. Wheatman, 31 N.Y.2d 12, 334 N.Y.S.2d 842, 286 N.E.2d 234 (1972), *cert. denied*, 409 U.S. 1027 (1972), *reh'g denied*, 409 U.S. 1119 (1973); *see also* People v. Basck, 36 N.Y.2d 154, 365 N.Y.S.2d 836, 325 N.E.2d 156 (1975).

—A witness who is merely an accessory after the fact is not an accomplice for the purpose of the corroboration requirements of CPL § 60.22. People v. Brooks, 170 A.D.2d 182, 565 N.Y.S.2d 491 (1st Dept. 1991).

—Whether or not a witness was an accomplice as a matter of fact is properly submitted to the jury where different inferences can reasonably be drawn from the proof. People v. Rachles, 177 A.D.2d 357, 576 N.Y.S.2d 230 (1st Dept. 1991).

—A person who receives stolen property is not to be considered an accomplice of the thief unless it is demonstrated that the receiver aided the thief in the commission of the crime. People v. Lynch, 158 A.D.2d 472, 550 N.Y.S.2d 923 (2d Dept. 1990).

—Purchaser of drugs was an accomplice as a matter of law whose testimony had to be corroborated in order to convict the defendant. People v. Arnott, 143 A.D.2d 761, 533 N.Y.S.2d 470 (2d Dept. 1988).

—Test to decide witness's status as an accomplice is whether the witness theoretically could have been convicted of any crime based on at least some of the same facts that must be proven in order to convict the defendant. People v. Teitelbaum, 138 A.D.2d 647, 526 N.Y.S.2d 230 (2d Dept. 1988).

—Court properly left for the jury the question of the construction supervisor's status as an accomplice where his statement that he had feared losing his job if he did not give the defendant a bribe for each field inspection created a situation whereby different inferences could reasonably have been drawn as to whether he had the necessary intent to participate in the crime charged. People v. Romeo, 130 A.D.2d 523, 515 N.Y.S.2d 102 (2d Dept. 1987).

—Whether the testimony of a witness should be considered as that of an accomplice depends upon whether his participation in the offense, or conspiracy from which the offense directly emanated, was criminally corrupt. People v. Cona, 60 A.D.2d 318, 401 N.Y.S.2d 239 (2d Dept. 1978), *modified on other grounds*, 49 N.Y.2d 26, 424 N.Y.S.2d 146, 399 N.E.2d 1167 (1979).

—Wife, who failed to report the commission of the homicide by her husband and prevented the attendance of witnesses to the disposal of the body, was not an accomplice to his criminal actions. People v. LeGrand, 61 A.D.2d 815, 402 N.Y.S.2d 209 (2d Dept.), *cert. denied*, 439 U.S. 835 (1978).

—When the witness testified, under a grant of immunity, that he had driven the three defendants to the general area of the crime and that he had expected to share in the proceeds of the burglary, he was an accomplice as a matter of law, and the jury should have been so charged. People v. Schlictcroll, 59 A.D.2d 545, 396 N.Y.S.2d 898 (2d Dept. 1977).

—A witness is an accomplice as a matter of law if the jury could reach no conclusion other than that he or she participated in the offense charged or another offense based on the same facts which constitute that offense; court improperly failed to charge the jury that the wife of one of the men who pleaded guilty to burglarizing a store was an accomplice, where she had testified that she believed that by babysitting for the children of the defendant, she was providing him with the opportunity to commit the burglary. People v. Adams, 307 A.D.2d 475, 763 N.Y.S.2d 347 (3d Dept. 2003).

—Witnesses who did not know about or participate in, the commission of the crimes committed by defendant could not be considered accomplices, therefore, no corroboration of their testimony was required. People v. Aleshus, 81 A.D.2d 696, 438 N.Y.S.2d 650 (3d Dept.), aff'd, 55 N.Y.2d 775, 447 N.Y.S.2d 243, 431 N.E.2d 968 (1981).

—Where an informant acts as an agent of police without the intent to commit a crime, the informant is not an accomplice whose testimony must be corroborated. People v. Cleveland, 273 A.D.2d 787, 709 N.Y.S.2d 751 (4th Dept. 2000).

—Defendant claimed that People failed to corroborate testimony of two witnesses who were accomplices. However, one witness took no part in crimes charged in indictment and was involved only as accomplice after the fact. Thus, corroboration requirement of CPL § 60.22(1) did not apply to that witness because he learned of defendant's acts only after they had been committed, and his only involvement was in disposing of the evidence or fruits of the previous crimes. People v. Pepe, 259 A.D.2d 949, 689 N.Y.S.2d 310 (4th Dept. 1999).

—Although conduct establishes that the witness may have been an accessory after the fact it does not establish that he is an accomplice for the purpose of the corroboration requirement. People v. Brazeau, 162 A.D.2d 979, 557 N.Y.S.2d 205 (4th Dept. 1990).

Accomplice testimony; lack of corroboration.—Robbery conviction was reversed where there was no evidence to corroborate accomplice's testimony that defendant participated in the crime for which defendant was tried; defendant's admission that he participated in several robberies did not link him to the particular robbery in issue. People v. Thomas, 103 A.D.2d 854, 478 N.Y.S.2d 369 (2d Dept. 1984).

—Despite defendant's contention that the testimony of the accomplice was not corroborated, the court found that considering the "minimal requirements" of the corroboration statute, the evidence in the record was sufficient; it connected defendant with the commission of the crime so as to reasonably satisfy the jury that the accomplice was telling the truth. People v. Gonsa, 220 A.D.2d 27, 644 N.Y.S.2d 346 (3d Dept. 1996).

Accomplice's testimony sufficiently corroborated.—Accomplice's testimony was sufficiently corroborated by fact that defendant was apprehended inside a courtyard that was accessible only from inside the school defendant allegedly burglarized. People v. Lewis, 105 A.D.2d 758, 481 N.Y.S.2d 409 (2d Dept. 1984).

Accomplice's testimony sufficiently corroborated by police observations.—Accomplice's testimony inculpating the defendant as the "wheelman" was sufficiently corroborated by police observations of the defendant acting suspiciously in the manner of a lookout combined with the defendant's admission that he drove the accomplice to the area. People v. Cuevas, 99 A.D.2d 553, 471 N.Y.S.2d 640 (2d Dept. 1984).

Charge.—When it is apparent that the case against the defendant rests substantially on the testimony of an accomplice, it is the better practice for the Trial Judge to charge the jury, even without a request from the defendant, that the accomplice's testimony must be corroborated in accordance with CPL § 60.22. People v. Ramos, 68 A.D.2d 748, 418 N.Y.S.2d 103 (2d Dept. 1979).

Conflicting exculpatory statements.—Defendant's false alibi and a later admission of his presence at the scene of the crime constituted conflicting exculpatory statements which satisfied the statutory requirement of other evidence tending to connect the defendant with the commission of the offense. People v. Lewis, 90 A.D.2d 844, 455 N.Y.S.2d 662 (2d Dept. 1982).

Conspiracy.—The acts and declarations of one coconspirator which occur while the conspiracy is in progress and which are in furtherance of the common scheme are admissible and provable as to all other co-conspirators as part of the res gestae and as a recognized exception to the hearsay rule. People v. Rastelli, 37 N.Y.2d 240, 371 N.Y.S.2d 911, 333 N.E.2d 182, cert. denied, 423 U.S. 995 (1975).

—Given the similarity of the crimes, the close time frame in which they were committed, and the proximate locations of the establishments burglarized, there was ample evidence that the crimes were committed as part of a common plan or scheme. People v. Spencer, 272 A.D.2d 682, 708 N.Y.S.2d 488 (3d Dept. 2000).

Corroborating evidence; nature of testimony.—Evidence is sufficient under CPL § 60.22 if the unsworn victim's testimony is corroborated by evidence tending to establish the crime

and connecting defendant with its commission. People v. Groff, 71 N.Y.2d 13, 524 N.Y.S.2d 13, 518 N.E.2d 908 (1987).

—Independent proof of defendant's participation in the crime was effectively provided where witness heard a shot, and saw three men near murder victim's body who walked away and then returned for a moment to the crime scene and defendant was identified as one of the three. People v. Smith, 55 N.Y.2d 945, 449 N.Y.S.2d 177, 434 N.E.2d 246 (1982).

—Testimony corroborating that of an accomplice need not exclude to a moral certainty every hypothesis but that of wrongdoing. It is sufficient that it have a tendency to furnish the necessary connection between defendant and the crime. People v. Kohut, 30 N.Y.2d 183, 331 N.Y.S.2d 416, 282 N.E.2d 312 (1972).

—Independent evidence supporting defendant's conviction for murder in second degree was sufficient to satisfy accomplice corroboration requirement; defendant's own admissions on tape recordings made by accomplice turned police informant and those made to jailhouse informant reflected familiarity with parties involved in murder conspiracy and certain details of crime that tended to connect him to commission of crime, and defendant's admission on tape that no one else knew that he and accomplice had orchestrated killing stood on its own footing without reference to accomplice's testimony. People v. Stern, 226 A.D.2d 238, 641 N.Y.S.2d 248 (1st Dept. 1996).

—Corroboration required of accomplice testimony must be independent of and not draw its weight or probative value from accomplice's testimony. People v. Stern, 226 A.D.2d 238, 641 N.Y.S.2d 248 (1st Dept. 1996).

—Testimony of each of several accomplices is not corroborative of the other, nor is testimony tending merely to establish the credibility of an accomplice sufficient. People v. Ohlstein, 54 A.D.2d 109, 387 N.Y.S.2d 860 (1st Dept. 1976), aff'd, 44 N.Y.2d 896, 407 N.Y.S.2d 696, 379 N.E.2d 222 (1978).

—The corroboration required by CPL § 60.22(1) must be independent of, and may not draw its weight and probative value from, the accomplice's testimony. People v. Argueta, 192 A.D.2d 538, 595 N.Y.S.2d 821 (2d Dept. 1993).

—The role of independent proof to meet the requirements for corroboration under CPL § 60.22(1) is to connect the defendant with the commission of the crime, not to prove he committed it. People v. Jackson, 178 A.D.2d 438, 577 N.Y.S.2d 299 (2d Dept. 1991).

—Pursuant to CPL § 60.22, the requisite independent proof need only connect the defendant to the commission of the crime charged; it need not prove that he committed it. People v. Sanchez, 153 A.D.2d 646, 544 N.Y.S.2d 666 (2d Dept. 1989).

—Testimony of admitted accomplice to murder and conspiracy which implicated defendant was adequately corroborated by evidence that person matching defendant's description was seen at crime scene, that package bearing defendant's palm print was found at victim's house, and that defendant told friend not to say anything about murder or they would all be dead and, thus, accomplice's testimony was admissible. People v. Sledge, 223 A.D.2d 922, 636 N.Y.S.2d 930 (3d Dept. 1996).

—Corroborative evidence under CPL § 60.22 need not prove guilt or actually connect the defendant with the commission of the crime. People v. Mahan, 195 A.D.2d 881, 601 N.Y.S.2d 638 (3d Dept. 1993).

—Evidence corroborating an accomplice's testimony need only connect the defendant to the crime so as reasonably to satisfy the jury that the accomplice is telling the truth. People v. Williams, 195 A.D.2d 889, 600 N.Y.S.2d 836 (3d Dept. 1993).

—Where the chief evidence against the defendant was the testimony of an accomplice to whom the defendant was accused of having sold hallucinogenic substances, the accomplice's testimony was sufficiently corroborated by evidence that the accomplice did in fact wire money to the defendant for the purchase of drugs. People v. Cunningham, 64 A.D.2d 722, 406 N.Y.S.2d 899 (3d Dept. 1978), aff'd, 48 N.Y.2d 938, 425 N.Y.S.2d 59, 401 N.E.2d 182 (1979).

—Evidence sufficiently connected defendant to crimes to satisfy the corroboration requirement, where four people who accepted forged checks positively identified defendant as the individual who cashed the checks, and the People introduced evidence that defendant was employed at the company that owned the blank payroll checks. People v. Giguere, 265 A.D.2d 941, 690 N.Y.S.2d 354 (4th Dept. 1999).

—The testimony of one accomplice cannot be used to corroborate the testimony of another accomplice. People v. Pynes, 170 A.D.2d 981, 566 N.Y.S.2d 143 (4th Dept. 1991).

—The evidence necessary to corroborate an accomplice may be supplied by the defendant himself. People v. Goldfeld, 60 A.D.2d 1, 400 N.Y.S.2d 229 (4th Dept. 1977).

Corroboration of accomplice; false alibi insufficient.—False alibi of defendant did not constitute evidence of a material fact that tended to implicate the defendant in the crime and was insufficient corroboration for the incriminating testimony of an accomplice. People v. Moses, 63 N.Y.2d 299, 482 N.Y.S.2d 228, 472 N.E.2d 4 (1984).

Corroboration of accomplice testimony.—Evidence that sheriff's assistant had tracked the defendant from the scene of the crime with a bloodhound and that defendant was found with co-defendant in a nearby field with the same amount of money that was taken in the crime was sufficient to corroborate the testimony of an accomplice who implicated the defendant. People v. Tillotson, 63 N.Y.2d 731, 480 N.Y.S.2d 199, 469 N.E.2d 520 (1984).

—In satisfaction of CPL 60.22, accomplice testimony was corroborated by, among other things, testimony of a witness who saw defendant outside the restaurant shortly before the robbery occurred, and witness described what defendant was wearing and stated that second robber to enter restaurant was wearing such clothing. People v. Medina, 265 A.D.2d 429, 697 N.Y.S.2d 86 (2d Dept. 1999).

—Defendant's mere presence at scene and his own testimony was sufficient to corroborate testimony of accomplice. People v. Kelley, 142 A.D.2d 690, 531 N.Y.S.2d 32 (2d Dept. 1988).

—There was sufficient evidence to corroborate defendant's participation in assault, where requisite corroboration was provided by defendant's sister, who confirmed defendant's presence at the scene, repeated commands to attack the victim, and his active efforts to block assistance to the victim. People v. McLean, 307 A.D.2d 586, 762 N.Y.S.2d 700 (3d Dept. 2003).

Sufficiency of tapes.—Where portions of tapes were sufficiently audible to corroborate accomplice's evidence and there was other overwhelming proof of guilt, fact that tapes were in the main unintelligible would not warrant reversal. People v. Kee, 45 A.D.2d 704, 357 N.Y.S.2d 81 (1st Dept. 1974).

—The requisite independent proof necessary to corroborate accomplice testimony need only connect the defendant to the commission of the crime; it need not prove that he committed it, nor need it establish the elements of the crime. People v. Johnson, 188 A.D.2d 552, 591 N.Y.S.2d 453 (2d Dept. 1992).

—The fact that witness, who had been a co-conspirator but who was presently an informer for the prosecutor, was no longer a co-conspirator at the time he taped recorded incriminatory conversations with the other co-conspirators did not negate the requirement of independent corroboration with respect to his testimony about such conversations. People v. Cona, 60 A.D.2d 318, 401 N.Y.S.2d 239 (2d Dept. 1978), *modified on other grounds*, 49 N.Y.2d 26, 424 N.Y.S.2d 146, 399 N.E.2d 1167 (1979).

Corroboration; prostitution; testimony of patron.—Patron was an accomplice of prostitute and promoter as one criminally implicated in offense, and corroboration of his testimony was necessary to convict defendants which could not be supplied by policemen whose evidence was supplied entirely by patron's admissions, but there was reasonable cause to hold defendants for trial even though it might be an exercise in futility. People v. Jackson, 69 Misc. 2d 793, 331 N.Y.S.2d 216 (Crim. Ct. N.Y. Co. 1972).

Corroboration; testimony of prostitute.—Prostitutes are the accomplices of the promoter and their testimony must be corroborated and one prostitute cannot corroborate the testimony of another. People v. Griffin, 83 A.D.2d 180, 443 N.Y.S.2d 935 (4th Dept. 1981).

Corroboration of accomplice insufficient.—Testimony of one co-defendant, who had earlier pleaded guilty, that he was with defendant on the day of the crime was insufficient to corroborate testimony of third accomplice who also testified against the defendant. People v. Tillotson, 63 N.Y.2d 731, 480 N.Y.S.2d 199, 469 N.E.2d 520 (1984).

—Corroboration was insufficient where the evidence to corroborate the testimony of defendant's accomplice fails to establish anything more than defendant's mere presence at the crime scene. People v. Johnson, 1 A.D.3d 891, 767 N.Y.S.2d 548 (4th Dept. 2003).

—Conviction reversed and indictment dismissed where there was no evidence other than testimony of the accomplice that tended to connect defendant to the crime. People v. McGrath, 262 A.D.2d 1043, 693 N.Y.S.2d 358 (4th Dept. 1999).

Corroboration of accomplice testimony sufficient.—Accomplice testimony was sufficiently corroborated to prove defendant guilty beyond reasonable doubt in homicide prosecution; testimony of defendant and other witnesses placed defendant at scene of crime during and immediately after shooting, and defendant's presence, furtive behavior and false statement to police were sufficient independent evidence tending to connect him to crimes. People v. Blaho, 221 A.D.2d 650, 634 N.Y.S.2d 193 (2d Dept. 1995).

—Accomplice's testimony that defendant intended to act as lookout and share in the proceeds of a burglary was sufficiently corroborated by independent evidence placing the defendant in the accomplice's car shortly before and after the burglary combined with other evidence of a circumstantial nature. People v. Roselle, 97 A.D.2d 656, 469 N.Y.S.2d 183 (3d Dept. 1983).

Enterprise corruption.—In enterprise corruption case, the jury was properly charged that the testimony of accomplices need not be corroborated for each pattern act but was sufficiently corroborated if the jury determined that some independent evidence tended to connect defendants to the offense of enterprise corruption. People v. Besser, 96 N.Y.2d 136, 726 N.Y.S.2d 48, 749 N.E.2d 727 (2001).

—Accomplice corroboration was required for the offense of enterprise corruption but not for each of the underlying pattern acts. People v. Ciauri, 266 A.D.2d 164, 699 N.Y.S.2d 341 (1st Dept. 1999), *aff'd*, 96 N.Y.2d 136, 726 N.Y.S.2d 48, 749 N.E.2d 727 (2001).

Family Court.—Family Court adjudication of delinquency may not be sustained without independent corroboration of testimony of two accomplices. *In re* S, 44 A.D.2d 826, 355 N.Y.S.2d 158 (2d Dept. 1974).

Requirements generally.—The corroboration requirement is satisfied if the nonaccomplice evidence "tends to connect a defendant to the crime in a manner sufficient to satisfy the jury that an accomplice is telling the truth." People v. Bates, 299 A.D.2d 727, 751 N.Y.S.2d 73 (3d Dept. 2002).

—Requirement of CPL § 60.22(1) is satisfied by production of evidence from independent source, which need not establish commission of crime but rather need only "connect the defendant with the crime in such a way that the jury may be reasonably satisfied that the accomplice is telling the truth." People v. Bass, 255 A.D.2d 689, 681 N.Y.S.2d 101 (3d Dept. 1998).

—Court properly denied defendant's request to submit to the jury the issue whether the only eyewitness to the crime was an accomplice; there was no evidence presented from which the jury could reasonably infer that the witness participated in the offenses and thus no basis for an accomplice-in-fact instruction. Furthermore, the mere presence of the witness in the rear seat of the car, without more, did not constitute a reasonable basis for the jury to conclude that he was an accomplice within the meaning of CPL § 60.22. People v. Young, 277 A.D.2d 910, 716 N.Y.S.2d 267 (4th Dept. 2000).

—Whether identification evidence sufficiently corroborates the testimony of an accomplice does not require a positive identification; rather, it is sufficient that the victim believes the defendant is the culprit and offers some examples of physical similarity between the defendant and the participant in the crime. People v. Jones, 202 A.D.2d 979, 609 N.Y.S.2d 995 (4th Dept. 1994).

—The accomplice corroboration requirement is satisfied by independent evidence tending to connect the defendant with the commission of the crime; the corroborative evidence need not independently establish elements of the offense. People v. Harrison, 251 A.D.2d 893, 677 N.Y.S.2d 637 (3d Dept. 1998); People v. Lewis, 204 A.D.2d 1025, 613 N.Y.S.2d 306 (4th Dept. 1994), *aff'd*, 85 N.Y.2d 823, 623 N.Y.S.2d 836, 647 N.E.2d 1344 (1995).

—The rules of evidence which require corroboration of other testimony are embodied in both the Penal Law and CPL. The corroboration requirements under both these statutes demand the same standard of sufficiency—it must tend to show the probable truth of the initial testimony and establish all the elements of the crime. Corroboration is required in the Penal Law due to the nature of the crime while it is required in the Criminal Procedure Law due to the nature of the witness. The indictment or conviction will stand or fall upon such other sworn evidence. People v. Curtis, 76 Misc. 2d 128, 350 N.Y.S.2d 315 (Sup. Ct. N.Y. Co. 1973).

Corroboration; solicitation of perjury.—Although the crime of solicitation, in general, requires no corroboration of testimony, where the crime solicited is perjury and the sole testimony against the defendant is that of the solicitee/perjurer, corroboration is require. People v. Berger, 70 A.D.2d 622, 416 N.Y.S.2d 312 (2d Dept. 1979), aff'd, 52 N.Y.2d 214, 437 N.Y.S.2d 272, 418 N.E.2d 1291 (1981).

Discrepancy in testimony of nonaccomplice witness.—Discrepancies in testimony of nonaccomplice witness who overheard defendant in conversation with accomplices, merely raised questions of credibility for the jury and did not render the corroborative evidence insufficient as a matter of law. People v. Neal, 95 A.D.2d 872, 463 N.Y.S.2d 890 (3d Dept. 1983).

Failure to charge co-defendants were accomplices.—Failure to charge the jury that co-defendants were accomplices as a matter of law and that therefore the defendant could not be convicted on their testimony without corroborating evidence is necessarily harmful error. People v. Jenner, 29 N.Y.2d 695, 325 N.Y.S.2d 652, 275 N.E.2d 23 (1971).

—Defendant's conviction was reversed on the law and a new trial ordered where the trial court had allowed the jury to decide whether prosecution witness was an accomplice after such witness had been indicted for the same crimes as the defendant and had been named as a co-conspirator in the indictment against defendant since such witness was an accomplice as a matter of law and his testimony had to be corroborated. People v. Cohen, 73 A.D.2d 603, 422 N.Y.S.2d 117 (2d Dept. 1979).

Failure to object to jury charge.—At trial, defendant did not make any request concerning the court's charge pertaining to accomplices, nor did he except to the charge as given, thus the issue was not preserved for review. People v. Henn, 70 A.D.2d 622, 434 N.Y.S.2d 496 (4th Dept. 1980).

—Though it was error for the judge to fail to submit to the jury the question of whether defendant's girlfriend was an accomplice in her mother's murder, whose testimony needed corroboration, the error was rendered harmless since the defense strategy at trial was to portray the girlfriend as the actual sole perpetrator of the murder, and the defendant did not request an accomplice corroboration charge at trial nor except to the court's failure to charge. People v. Walker, 87 A.D.2d 725, 449 N.Y.S.2d 330 (3d Dept. 1982).

—Defendant failed to preserve issues for appeal where he neither requested a charge that a witness was an accomplice whose testimony needed to be corroborated nor excepted to the failure to so charge. People v. Graham, 111 A.D.2d 831, 490 N.Y.S.2d 253 (2d Dept. 1985).

Grand jury; corroboration.—Corroboration requirement set forth in CPL § 60.22 relates only to evidence necessary to obtain or sustain a conviction and corroboration of accomplice testimony is not required to sustain an indictment by a grand jury. People v. Glowa, 87 Misc. 2d 471, 384 N.Y.S.2d 673 (Sup. Ct. Kings Co. 1976); People v. King, 48 A.D.2d 457, 370 N.Y.S.2d 52 (1st Dept. 1975); People v. Clarkson, 50 A.D. 903, 377 N.Y.S.2d 555 (2d Dept. 1975). However, earlier cases expressly required corroboration; see People v. Eason, 45 A.D.2d 863, 358 N.Y.S.2d 546 (2d Dept. 1974), and People v. Dunleavy, 41 A.D.2d 717, 341 N.Y.S.2d 500 (1st Dept. 1973), aff'd, 33 N.Y.2d 573, 347 N.Y.S.2d 448, 301 N.E.2d 432 (1973).

—The indictment was sustained where the corroborating testimony of the undercover agent before the Grand Jury, given after investigation and surveillance, established that defendant was in the company of persons possessing and preparing large quantities of the drugs for sale, and harmonized with the accomplice's narrative so as to have a tendency to furnish the necessary connection between the defendant and the crime. People v. Laws, 54 A.D.2d 518, 386 N.Y.S.2d 251 (3d Dept. 1976).

—The corroboration of an accomplice is required before a Grand Jury just as it is required to obtain a conviction. People v. Murray, 88 Misc. 2d 668, 388 N.Y.S.2d 848 (Suffolk Co. Ct. 1976).

—While CPL § 60.22(1) precludes conviction without the necessary corroboration of accomplice testimony, that is not a necessary prerequisite for indictment where the evidence otherwise meets the standard set forth in CPL § 190.65(1). People v. Clarkson, 50 A.D.2d 903, 377 N.Y.S.2d 555 (2d Dept. 1975).

—Gamblers who testified that they had given bribes to various policemen in order to "protect" their gambling operations were not accomplices of such policemen where the bribes were made out of fear of reprisals by the police, thus, the testimony of such gamblers did not require corroboration in order to obtain an indictment against the police officer involved. People v. Court, 52 A.D.2d 891, 383 N.Y.S.2d 66 (2d Dept. 1976), aff'd, 43 N.Y.2d 817, 402 N.Y.S.2d 569, 373 N.E.2d 368 (1977).

Informants, not acting as agents, were accomplices as a matter of law.—Testimony of informants who were not acting as agents of the police at the time of the drug transaction charged in the indictment required the trial court to charge the jury that they were accomplices as a matter of law and that their testimony as to defendant's cocaine sale to them must be corroborated by other evidence. People v. Tune, 103 A.D.2d 990, 479 N.Y.S.2d 832 (3d Dept. 1984).

Instruction.—Any error in omitting the accomplice instruction was harmless since the record contained ample corroborating evidence connecting the defendant to the crime so as to reasonably satisfy the jury that the accomplice was telling the truth. People v. Woodham, 158 A.D.2d 494, 550 N.Y.S.2d 941 (2d Dept. 1990).

—It was proper for the court to instruct the jury that if they found that the witness was not an accomplice, then they could rely on his testimony as corroborating the testimony of the actual accomplices in the case. People v. Tuck, 155 A.D.2d 491, 547 N.Y.S.2d 154 (2d Dept. 1989).

Jury charge on accomplice testimony.—The question of whether or not defendant was an accomplice is a question of fact for the jury and a charge to the jury which in effect instructed the jury that even if it believed defendant's testimony that he was an innocent bystander who acted out of fear for his life, he was the co-defendant's accomplice was error. People v. Calhoun, 87 A.D.2d 825, 448 N.Y.S.2d 759 (2d Dept. 1982).

—It was reversible error for the court to recharge the jury on the subject of accomplice testimony as follows: ". . . to find that one is an accomplice, you must come to the conclusion that the evidence establishes that he or she criminally participated with the defendants in the commission of the crime charged. This participation must appear to you to have been in all of the elements of the crime . . . and that such accomplice acted with the intent required to charge him with the crime. There must be evidence tending to show that the purported accomplice took part in the preparation or perpetration of the crime with the intent to assist." This instruction is contrary to the clear language of CPL 60.22(2)(b). People v. Craft, 67 A.D.2d 1097, 415 N.Y.S.2d 150 (4th Dept. 1979).

Jury charge on corroborative evidence.—The trial court's charge that corroborative evidence must tend to connect defendant with the commission of the crime so as to reasonably satisfy the jury that the accomplice was telling the truth was proper. People v. Clickner, 95 A.D.2d 925, 463 N.Y.S.2d 943 (3d Dept. 1983).

Nature of corroborating evidence.—Although corroborative evidence must be truly independent, and may not draw its probative value from the accomplice testimony, it need not itself prove commission of the crime; it is sufficient if the corroborative evidence tends to connect the defendant to the crime so as to reasonably satisfy the jury that the accomplice is telling the truth. People v. Glasper, 52 N.Y.2d 970, 438 N.Y.S.2d 282, 420 N.E.2d 80 (1981).

—Independent corroborating evidence must be material evidence other than that of the accomplice which fairly and reasonably tends to connect defendant with the commission of the crime, not necessarily proving that defendant did in fact commit the crime, and may not depend for its probative weight upon the testimony of accomplices. People v. Hudson, 50 N.Y.2d 233, 433 N.Y.S.2d 1004, 414 N.E.2d 385 (1980).

—Accomplice's testimony was amply corroborated by the defendant's statements to the police that he was in company of other participants in the crime when they were "getting ready" to commit the crime and that he thereafter was also present at the scene when the crime occurred. People v. Burgin, 40 N.Y.2d 953, 390 N.Y.S.2d 410, 358 N.E.2d 1035 (1976).

—In drug possession prosecution, police testimony that there was drugs and paraphernalia on kitchen table when they entered defendant's apartment was sufficient corroboration of accomplice's testimony, especially since the presence of contraband and co-defendants in the apartment was a sufficient basis on which the jury could conclude that the accomplice was telling the truth when he testified that each of the defendants was involved in the drug business with him. People v. Daniels, 37 N.Y.2d 624, 376 N.Y.S.2d 436, 339 N.E.2d 139 (1975).

—Independent evidence is sufficient if it tends to connect the defendant with the commission of the crime in such a way as may reasonably satisfy the jury that the accomplice is telling the truth. People v. Wheatman, 31 N.Y.2d 12, 334 N.Y.S.2d 842, 286 N.E.2d 234 (1972), cert. denied, 409 U.S. 1027, reh'g denied, 409 U.S. 1119 (1973). See also People v. Devaul, 54 A.D.2d 1038, 388 N.Y.S.2d 382 (3d Dept. 1976); People v. Arce, 42 N.Y.2d 179, 397 N.Y.S.2d 619, 366 N.E.2d 279 (1977).

—Evidence which does no more than tend to establish the credibility of the accomplice is insufficient as a matter of law to satisfy the corroboration requirement. People v. Velasquez, 151 A.D.2d 159, 547 N.Y.S.2d 6 (1st Dept. 1989), aff'd, 76 N.Y.2d 905, 561 N.Y.S.2d 911, 563 N.E.2d 282 (1990).

—There was ample independent proof, including telephone records, eyewitness testimony and other evidence gathered, by the police, in their investigation, tending to connect the defendant with his accomplice and the commission of the crime, sufficient to meet the requirements for accomplice testimony of CPL § 60.22(1). People v. Garcia, 232 A.D.2d 578, 648 N.Y.S.2d 959 (2d Dept. 1996).

—The requisite independent proof (for accomplice corroboration) need not prove that the defendant committed the crime, or establish the elements of the crime. People v. Reyes, 204 A.D.2d 361, 611 N.Y.S.2d 563 (2d Dept. 1994).

—The evidence necessary to corroborate an accomplice's testimony need only connect the defendant to the crime so as to reasonably satisfy the jury that the accomplice was truthful. People v. Mariani, 203 A.D.2d 717, 610 N.Y.S.2d 967 (3d Dept. 1994).

—Defendant's post-arrest statement to accomplice, "Looks like they got us" provided sufficient corroboration of accomplice's testimony. People v. Springer, 127 A.D.2d 250, 514 N.Y.S.2d 555 (3d Dept. 1987), aff'd, 71 N.Y.2d 997, 529 N.Y.S.2d 275, 524 N.E.2d 876 (1988).

—Accomplice corroboration must consist of evidence from an independent source of some material fact tending to show that defendant was implicated in the crime. People v. Gonzalez, 201 A.D.2d 906, 607 N.Y.S.2d 805 (4th Dept. 1994).

Perjury.—Persons who testified at defendant's trial for perjury with respect to his and their own activities in connection with bribery payments to him were not accomplices. While each may have participated in bribery, such activity constituted no part of the crime of perjury and they were not "in some way implicated" in the perjury charge. People v. McAuliffe, 36 N.Y.2d 820, 370 N.Y.S.2d 900, 331 N.E.2d 681 (1975).

—Where the issue was whether the defendant had lied to the Grand Jury, testimony given at trial by two witnesses that they had bribed the defendant did not warrant a charge as to corroboration of accomplice's testimony since the witnesses were not accomplices to the perjury; by giving such a charge, the trial judge committed only harmless error. People v. Reardon, 58 A.D.2d 749, 396 N.Y.S.2d 222 (1st Dept. 1977).

Presence at crime scene.—Presence at crime scene may provide the necessary corroboration where there was no plausible hypothesis other than that the defendant was a likely participant in the crime or even if there were an innocent explanation, if the circumstances of the crime itself were otherwise corroborating. People v. Johnson, 1 A.D.3d 891, 767 N.Y.S.2d 548 (4th Dept. 2003).

Preservation.—Defendant argued that the trial court erred in failing to submit as a factual question for the jury to resolve the witness's alleged status as an accomplice; claim was unpreserved and, in any event, court properly denied the request, where the evidence was insufficient to establish that the witness participated in the offense. People v. Young, 235 A.D.2d 441, 653 N.Y.S.2d 124 (2d Dept. 1997).

Previously dismissed co-defendants not accomplices.— Prosecution witnesses were not accomplices of defendant as a matter of law where, in a previous trial, a trial order of dismissal was issued as to such former co-defendants as to both the murder charge and all lesser including charges. People v. Pagan, 105 A.D.2d 810, 481 N.Y.S.2d 441 (2d Dept. 1984).

Question of whether witnesses were accomplices.—In light of the requirement of CPL 60.22 that a defendant may not be convicted of any offense upon the testimony of an accomplice unsupported by corroborative evidence tending to connect the defendant with the crime and the lack of such corroborative evidence, it was reversible error for the trial court to submit to the jury the question of whether the witnesses were accomplices. People v. Ramirez, 94 A.D.2d 965, 463 N.Y.S.2d 966 (4th Dept. 1983).

Receiver of stolen property.—Receiver of stolen property is not accomplice of the thief when there is no proof of a prior agreement between them, and thus all requirements of corroboration of the testimony of either is eliminated. People v. Brooks, 34 N.Y.2d 475, 358 N.Y.S.2d 395, 315 N.E.2d 460 (1974).

Reversal of convictions stemming from impropriety of reduced sentence "deal."—Defendants' convictions for robbery, grand larceny and possession of a weapon were vacated on grounds that they were denied a fair trial, where the pretrial judge extracted a promise from the attorney for defendant-accomplice that the attorney would not reveal to the accomplice a "deal" made for a reduced plea and sentence, provided the accomplice would testify against his co-defendants, and where the prosecutor's office denied any knowledge of the plea bargain. People v. Graziano, 38 A.D.2d 127, 327 N.Y.S.2d 942 (2d Dept. 1972).

Sufficiency of corroborative testimony.—Testimony of nonaccomplice that he observed sale and overheard incriminatory statement of accomplice was sufficient to corroborate testimony of accomplice. People v. Swanchak, 95 A.D.2d 957, 464 N.Y.S.2d 60 (3d Dept. 1983), aff'd, 61 N.Y.2d 830, 473 N.Y.S.2d 973, 462 N.E.2d 150 (1984).

Sodomy.—Court sustained the sodomy conviction of defendant based solely upon the testimony of seven of his child victims, aged 13 and 14 years, since the child victims were not accomplices of defendant as a matter of law and were all victims of defendant on different occasions and in different combinations. People v. Fielding, 39 N.Y.2d 607, 385 N.Y.S.2d 17, 350 N.E.2d 393 (1976).

Solicitation of police decoy.—Defendant solicited a police-woman, decoyed as a prostitute, to perform a sex act. Since officer acted solely with the purpose of obtaining evidence for prosecution she was not an accomplice at law. People v. Bronski, 76 Misc. 2d 341, 351 N.Y.S.2d 73 (Crim. Ct. N.Y.C. 1973).

Testimony of others.—Where the 15-year-old complainant had an extensive history of mental illness which necessitated lengthy periods of hospitalization, the trial court committed reversible error in refusing to grant the defendants access to the mental health and hospital records of the complainant; without such records the defendants were in no position to evaluate the veracity of the psychologist's professional conclusions by resort to her own records and were severely handicapped in their cross-examination. People v. Baier, 73 A.D.2d 649, 422 N.Y.S.2d 734 (2d Dept. 1979).

Testimony of accomplice to one crime as corroboration of testimony of accomplice to second crime.—Where multiple crimes are charged and the record shows that the crimes involved a common plan or scheme, evidence corroborating the accomplice on one crime is sufficient to provide the required corroboration on the others. People v. Spencer, 272 A.D.2d 679, 708 N.Y.S.2d 485 (3d Dept. 2000).

—Where indictment charges commission of same crime on two different occasions, the testimony of an accomplice to one of the crimes may be used to corroborate the testimony of an accomplice provided the accomplices were not conspiring together in the commission of both crimes. This is a question of fact to be determined by the jury. People v. Chamberlain, 38 A.D.2d 306, 329 N.Y.S.2d 61 (4th Dept. 1972).

Undercover police agent.—The defendant could not be convicted on the basis of the undercover officer's uncorroborated testimony where the undercover officer, originally assigned to investigate police corruption, subsequently joined the police officers he was investigating in accepting funds to protect gamblers. People v. Cona, 49 N.Y.2d 26, 424 N.Y.S.2d 146, 399 N.E.2d 1167 (1979).

§ 60.25. Rules of evidence; identification by means of previous recognition in absence of present identification.

1. In any criminal proceeding in which the defendant's commission of an offense is in issue, testimony as provided in subdivision two may be given by a witness when:

(a) Such witness testifies that:

(i) He observed the person claimed by the people to be the defendant either at the time and place of the commission of the offense or upon some other occasion relevant to the case; and

(ii) On a subsequent occasion he observed, under circumstances consistent with such rights as an accused person may derive under the constitution of this state or of the United States, a person whom he recognized as the same person whom he had observed on the first or incriminating occasion; and

(iii) He is unable at the proceeding to state, on the basis of present recollection, whether or not the defendant is the person in question; and

(b) It is established that the defendant is in fact the person whom the witness observed and recognized on the second occasion. Such fact may be established by testimony of another person or persons to whom the witness promptly declared his recognition on such occasion.

2. Under circumstances prescribed in subdivision one, such witness may testify at the criminal proceeding that the person whom he observed and recognized on the second occasion is the same person whom he observed on the first or incriminating occasion. Such testimony, together with the evidence that the defendant is in fact the person whom the witness observed and recognized on the second occasion, constitutes evidence in chief.

Amended by L. 1977, Ch. 479.

ANNOTATIONS

Admissibility.—Victim, by indicating that he could no longer identify defendant as perpetrator of robbery, laid proper foundation for testimony about his prior out-of-court identification. People v. Davis, 205 A.D.2d 403, 613 N.Y.S.2d 610 (1st Dept. 1994).

Accidental or unarranged "show-ups."—Accidental or unarranged "show-ups" are not unnecessarily or impermissibly suggestive since unavoidable and not due to the fault of the police or prosecutor. People v. Gonzalez, 61 A.D.2d 666, 403 N.Y.S.2d 514 (1st Dept. 1978), aff'd, 46 N.Y.2d 1011, 416 N.Y.S.2d 239, 389 N.E.2d 834 (1979).

Confession of co-defendant; prejudice.—Motion was made to vacate judgment, since co-defendant's confession had been introduced into evidence and had been redacted only to the extent of replacing defendant's name with the letter "X." Although the trial court instructed the jury not to speculate as to the identity of X, references made to the confession during the trial, the prosecutor's summation, and the charge left no doubt as to who "X" was. The error could not be considered harmless error, since, aside from the co-defendant's confession, the People's case against the defendant rested entirely on a questionable identification made of him by the victim. People

v. Tinsley, 31 N.Y.2d 905, 340 N.Y.S.2d 640, 292 N.E.2d 783 (1972).

Corroboration of identification by police officer.—Trial court improperly admitted police officer's testimony about now-deceased robbery victim's lineup identification of defendant. The testimony of a third party non-identifying witness is allowed as evidence-in-chief under CPL § 60.25 only when coupled with the real identifying witness's testimony as to the prior identification, and the testimony of the third party, who witnessed the identification but not the crime, standing alone, cannot provide the indispensable safeguards of affording the defendant the benefit of cross-examination. Here, since the officer's testimony fell short of the CPL § 60.25 requirements, and identification was crucial, it was reversible error. People v. Patterson, 93 N.Y.2d 80, 688 N.Y.S.2d 101, 710 N.E.2d 665 (1999).

—Police officer's testimony of prior identification of defendant by complainant in court house on an unrelated charge was inadmissible to bolster complainant's identification. People v. Sarmiento, 40 A.D.2d 562, 334 N.Y.S.2d 210 (2d Dept. 1972).

Failure to previously note unique characteristic.—Reversal and new trial resulted where arresting officer's detailed identification report made no note of tattoos or scars on upper body then visible to officer, but at trial defendant removed shirt to display an upper body virtually covered with tattoos, together with several prominent scars. People v. Diaz, 53 A.D.2d 587, 384 N.Y.S.2d 844 (1st Dept. 1976).

General.—Court erred by permitting a witness to testify as to his prior identification of the defendant where the witness stated that the defendant was not the perpetrator; CPL § 60.25 was inapplicable since there was no failure to make an identification. People v. Cover, 198 A.D.2d 514, 604 N.Y.S.2d 192 (2d Dept. 1993).

Identification from photograph inadmissible.—It is improper to admit testimony from complaining witness that she identified defendant through a "mug-shot" at the police station. People v. Sarmiento, 40 A.D.2d 562, 334 N.Y.S.2d 210 (2d Dept. 1972).

—No error was committed, where photograph of defendant, taken upon his arrest the day after the crime, was introduced into evidence after complainant testified it was a fair and accurate representation of defendant as he appeared at time of crime. People v. Greenidge, 46 A.D.2d 947, 362 N.Y.S.2d 212 (3d Dept. 1974).

Identification; show-up; presence of counsel.—In a situation where the defendant was observed face to face by the victim of the robbery for 2 to 3 minutes under street lamp lighting and victim's description led to defendant's arrest 35 minutes later, showing the defendant to the victim after arrest was not suggestive of mistaken identification because there was minimal risk of mistake under the circumstances. Wade-Gilbert-Stovall rules did not require presence of counsel at show-up. People v. Martin, 39 A.D.2d 558, 331 N.Y.S.2d 952 (2d Dept. 1972).

Identification; spontaneous declaration; juvenile delinquency proceeding.—Testimony by arresting officer at Family Court fact finding hearing that victim cried "That's him" upon seeing defendant, who was brought back to the scene of the robbery by the officer, was properly admissible as a spontaneous declaration; CPL § 60.25 does not alter the rule recognizing the admissibility of such evidence in criminal prosecutions or similar proceedings as an exception to the hearsay rule. In re Danny R., 50 N.Y.2d 1026, 431 N.Y.S.2d 687, 409 N.E.2d 1361 (1980).

Identification; testimony of previous identification.—Based on changes in defendant's appearance that were critical to her identification, the People's witness was properly permitted to refer to her earlier identification and the People had the right to introduce evidence that witness had previously identified defendant as shooter based on his clothing and body build, not based on recollection of his face. People v. Vasquez, 216 A.D.2d 176, 629 N.Y.S.2d 213 (1st Dept. 1995), aff'd, 88 N.Y.2d 561, 647 N.Y.S.2d 697, 670 N.E.2d 1328 (1996).

—Although Court instructed jury that testimony of witness that complainant told him on 2 separate occasions that defendant committed hold up was only to prove conversation happened, it was error to close question of fact because it served to bolster complainant's identification testimony in violation of Trowbridge rule. People v. Rosati, 39 A.D.2d 592, 331 N.Y.S.2d 771 (2d Dept. 1972); see also People v. Otero, 45 A.D.2d 952, 359 N.Y.S.2d 318 (1st Dept. 1974).

—It was error to permit witness, who had since recanted his identification, to testify at the trial, that he was sure at the time line-up was conducted that defendant was one of the perpetrators. People v. Brown, 60 A.D.2d 890, 401 N.Y.S.2d 290 (2d Dept. 1978).

—It was error to permit arresting officer on direct examination to corroborate complainant's testimony that after crime complainant located defendant and pointed him out to the police. People v. Burton, 46 A.D.2d 774, 360 N.Y.S.2d 463 (2d Dept. 1974).

In-court photographic identification improper.—Where defendant had substantially altered his appearance subsequent to arrest and prior to trial, identification witness, who was unable to make an in-court identification, was improperly permitted to view a single photo of defendant taken on the day of his arrest for in-court identification purposes rather than properly placing defendant's photo in an array of look-alike photos. People v. Powell, 105 A.D.2d 712, 481 N.Y.S.2d 157 (2d Dept. 1984).

Photographic identification; suggestibility.—Where eyewitnesses to supermarket robbery identified photographs of defendants and then were shown second set of photographs of subsequent robbery, known to them, which were marked by police who apprehended defendants, it was not impermissible to admit identifications, but where a photograph supplied by the police was identified by witness as one defendant and it was photograph of another, a new hearing was required. People v. Hinds, 40 A.D.2d 786, 337 N.Y.S.2d 594 (1st Dept. 1972).

—Photographic display procedure used by the police was unduly suggestive, however, where the witness had an independent basis for identifying the defendant, suppression of the identification was not warranted. People v. Hall, 81 A.D.2d 644, 438 N.Y.S.2d 148 (2d Dept. 1981).

—Where the victims of a robbery examined over 600 mug shots together and simultaneously identified that of defendant as the perpetrator, it was held on appeal that having the victims look at the photographs together introduced the danger that identification by one viewer could likely influence or cause an identification by other viewers. People v. Leite, 52 A.D.2d 895, 383 N.Y.S.2d 71 (2d Dept. 1976).

—Although it was "impermissively suggestive" to show a rape victim 10 pictures including one of the defendant with his name on the back after the victim had already indicated the first name of an assailant, it was proper for the court to permit the victim to identify the defendant as the perpetrator at the trial since she had adequate opportunity to observe her assailant during the commission of the crime and she testified that the defendant had been known to her before the crime had been committed. People v. Simms, 58 A.D.2d 720, 396 N.Y.S.2d 278 (3d Dept. 1977).

Presence of counsel at line-up not required if conducted before filing of accusatory instrument.—Although defendant is entitled to the presence of counsel at a post-indictment line-up, this right does not extend to a line-up conducted prior to the filing of any accusatory instrument. People v. Parish, 70 Misc. 2d 577, 343 N.Y.S.2d 631 (Nassau Co. Ct. 1972).

Pretrial identification improper; error for court not to have made finding as to whether subsequent in-court identification was tainted.—Since the trial court, after a *Wade* hearing, ruled that a photo identification by a transit patrolman was improper and thus inadmissible in evidence at the trial, it was reversible error for the court to refuse to make a finding as to whether such identification tainted the subsequent in-court identification of defendant and to allow the jury to pass on the issue of that pretrial identification. People v. Ghee, 42 A.D.2d 860, 346 N.Y.S.2d 852 (2d Dept. 1973).

Pretrial suppression hearing; tainted pre-trial identification.—Defendant was entitled to *Wade* hearing on issue of tainted pretrial identification and court is required to make findings on the question of its admissibility. People v. Hicks, 40 A.D.2d 836, 337 N.Y.S.2d 346 (2d Dept. 1972).

Prior identification; unable to identify in court.—In order to lay a proper foundation under CPL § 60.25 there must be testimony from the witness that establishes a lack of present recollection of the defendant as the perpetrator; the testimony may occur at the trial or it may occur at a hearing to suppress identification testimony and be the basis of a conclusion by the court not to permit the witness to identify the defendant at trial; where the testimony of the witness concerning his lack of

present recollection is ambiguous, the rule will not apply. People v. Quevas, 81 N.Y.2d 41, 595 N.Y.S.2d 721, 611 N.E.2d 760 (1993).

—Since the complainant's failure to identify the defendant in court was not due to deficient recollection, but rather to fear, his out-of-court identification should not have been admitted. People v. Johnson, 75 N.Y.2d 856, 857, 552 N.Y.S.2d 916, 917, 552 N.E.2d 164, 165 (1990).

—Where victim of hold up testified that she identified the perpetrator to the police shortly after the crime but was unable to identify him at trial, it was proper for the police officer, who was present at the previous identification to testify that the defendant was the person whom the witness previously identified and the testimony of both is "evidence in chief." People v. Nival, 33 N.Y.2d 391, 353 N.Y.S.2d 409, 308 N.E.2d 883 (1974), *dism'd,* 417 U.S. 903 (1974).

—Court properly admitted testimony of officer concerning the circumstances of victim's identification of defendant; the officer merely described his own observations prior to the arrest, and, the victim, by indicating that he could no longer identify the defendant, laid a proper foundation for testifying about his prior identification. People v. Davis, 205 A.D.2d 403, 613 N.Y.S.2d 610 (1st Dept. 1994).

—When the victim was unable to identify the defendant with certainty, the court did not err when it permitted a police detective to testify, pursuant to CPL § 60.25, concerning a prior positive lineup identification of defendant by one victim who was unable to identify defendant at trial. People v. Gonzalez, 188 A.D.2d 364, 591 N.Y.S.2d 173 (1st Dept. 1992).

—Once the witness stated that he had identified the defendant at the constitutionally permissible lineup but could not identify him at trial, testimony establishing that the defendant was the individual identified was properly admitted. People v. Whyte, 299 A.D.2d 378, 749 N.Y.S.2d 90 (2d Dept. 2002).

—CPL § 60.25 overrules the effect of People v. Trowbridge (305 N.Y. 471, 113 N.E.2d 841) by permitting the fact of the prior identification to be established by the testimony of another person when the identifying witness is unable to make an identification at the trial. Accordingly, when the witness was unable to identify the defendant at the trial, the police officer, who was present when the witness identified defendant as the man with whom the deceased argued earlier in the evening, could testify concerning the earlier identification. People v. Lagana, 36 N.Y.2d 71, 365 N.Y.S.2d 147, 324 N.E.2d 534 (1975), *rev'g* 43 A.D.2d 834, 350 N.Y.S.2d 747 (2d Dept. 1974), *cert denied,* 424 U.S. 942 (1976).

—Testimony of prosecutor that robbery victim had previously identified the defendant at a lineup was properly received since the victim was unable to identify the defendant at trial. People v. Rawlings, 144 A.D.2d 500, 533 N.Y.S.2d 1001 (2d Dept. 1988).

—Where a complainant stated that he had identified the defendant at proper showup but could not identify him at trial, testimony that the defendant was the individual identified was properly admitted. People v. Rocafuerte, 144 A.D.2d 395, 533 N.Y.S.2d 788 (2d Dept. 1988).

—CPL § 60.25(1)(b) allows third party testimony only to supply the necessary logical link between the defendant and the person identified out of court, that they are one and the same person; thus the testimony of a police officer that the victim had at the police station shortly after the robbery identified the respondent *with certainty* was held inadmissible hearsay. *In re* Pablo F., 98 Misc. 2d 919, 415 N.Y.S.2d 741 (Fam. Ct. N.Y.C. 1979).

—Motion to suppress identification testimony was denied where the identification was made on the basis of a combination of features other than facial: unusual height, hair color, weight, and distinctive apparel twenty-five minutes after the crime. People v. Armioia, 109 Misc. 2d 1038, 441 N.Y.S.2d 361 (Suffolk Co. Ct. 1981).

Previous identification by third party.—Reversible error occurred where the trial court elicited testimony from one of the arresting officers that the victim of the crime had identified the defendant. In the absence of other strong proof of identification or an allegation of recent fabrication by an eyewitness, it is error to admit testimony by a third person that an eyewitness identified the defendant. People v. Taylor, 45 A.D.2d 953, 359 N.Y.S.2d 313 (1st Dept. 1974).

Request for line-up denied.—Trial court did not abuse its discretion when it denied defendant's request for line-up made five months after the initial identification when defendant presented a somewhat altered appearance. People v. Ruiz, 52 N.Y.2d 929, 437 N.Y.S.2d 665, 419 N.E.2d 343 (1981).

"Resemblance" and "identification" testimony distinguished.—Distinguishing between "resemblance" and "identification" testimony, the court held that a witness whose in-court identification of the defendant was suppressed due to suggestive police procedures and the absence of an independent source could nevertheless testify as to a detailed description of a man he saw at the scene of the crime, which description closely fit the appearance of the defendant shortly thereafter. People v. Sanders, 108 A.D.2d 316, 489 N.Y.S.2d 348 (2d Dept. 1985).

Right to counsel.—Court-ordered line-up violated defendant's right to counsel because each line-up was conducted in the absence of counsel without a valid waiver. People v. Banks, 53 N.Y.2d 819, 439 N.Y.S.2d 916, 422 N.E.2d 576 (1981).

Statute inapplicable where in-court identification is based on present recollection.—CPL § 60.25 was inapplicable because that statute governs the admissibility of a witness's previous identification by means of third-party testimony where the witness is unable to make an in-court identification. Here, the witness' in-court identification was based on his present recollection. People v. Green, 270 A.D.2d 566, 705 N.Y.S.2d 93 (3d Dept. 2000).

Suggestive identification, not excluded *per se*.—Suppression was not required where the identification at the preliminary hearing was suggestive but the witness had the opportunity to observe the defendant for 15 minutes prior to the assault and again a half hour later, while the actual assault was taking place. People v. Moger, 85 A.D.2d 610, 444 N.Y.S.2d 676 (2d Dept. 1981).

—Reliability is the linchpin of admissibility in cases involving CPL § 60.25 and § 60.30; the court rejected the argument that a suggestive identification must *per se* be excluded even if the totality of circumstances surrounding it indicates that it is reliable. People v. Graham, 67 A.D.2d 172, 415 N.Y.S.2d 714 (4th Dept. 1979).

Viewing by witnesses to other crimes prohibited.—A defendant may not be viewed by witnesses to other crimes in the absence of a showing of probable cause to arrest him for each separate crime. Santucci v. Andrews, 117 Misc. 2d 616, 458 N.Y.S.2d 1007 (Sup. Ct. Queens Co. 1983).

Waiver of presence of counsel at line-up.—Defendant's right to counsel at a post-arraignment line-up conducted in the absence of counsel was waived where defendant's counsel, having arranged with the prosecutor the physical details of the line-up and the questions to be asked and having discussed with defendant his reasons for not remaining for the actual line-up and obtaining defendant's consent, advised the prosecutor that the line-up should proceed in his absence, even though defendant did not himself communicate the waiver to the prosecutor and counsel was not in defendant's presence when he did. People v. Yut Wai Tom, 53 N.Y.2d 44, 439 N.Y.S.2d 896, 422 N.E.2d 556 (1981).

Witness's refusal to make in-court identification. —While third-party testimony recounting a witness's pretrial identification of the defendant is admissible at trial in situations where the witness cannot on the basis of present recollection identify the defendant, it is not admissible where the witness refuses to make an identification at trial because of fear. People v. Bayron, 66 N.Y.S.2d 77, 495 N.Y.S.2d 24, 485 N.E.2d 231 (1985).

—CPL § 60.25 did not apply where the complainant did not state he was "unable" to identify defendant but rather, affirmatively testified defendant was not the robber since the witness was able to state "whether or not the defendant is the person in question" on the basis of his present recollection. People v. Rodriquez, 169 A.D.2d 618, 564 N.Y.S.2d 757 (1st Dept. 1991).

§ 60.30. Rules of evidence; identification by means of previous recognition, in addition to present identification.

In any criminal proceeding in which the defendant's commission of an offense is in issue, a witness who testifies that (a) he observed the person claimed by the people to be the defendant either at the time and place of the commission of the offense or upon some other occasion relevant to the case, and (b) on the basis of present recollection, the defendant is the person in question and (c) on a subsequent occasion he observed the defendant, under circumstances consistent with such rights as an accused person may derive under the constitution of this state or of the United States, and then also recognized him as the same person whom he had observed on the first or incriminating occasion, may, in addition to making an identification of the defendant at the criminal proceeding on the basis of present recollection as the person whom he observed on the first or incriminating occasion, also describe his previous recognition of the defendant and testify that the person whom he observed on such second occasion is the same person whom he had observed on the first or incriminating occasion. Such testimony constitutes evidence in chief.

Amended by L. 1977, Ch. 479.

ANNOTATIONS

Limits of CPL § 60.30.—*See* People v. Mato, 83 N.Y.2d 406, 633 N.E.2d 446, 611 N.Y.S.2d 92 (1994).

Appeal.—*Trowbridge*-type bolstering claim unpreserved where both arresting officers testified that they arrested the defendant in the garage in the presence of the owner. People v. Buie, 86 N.Y.2d 501, 634 N.Y.S.2d 415, 658 N.E.2d 192 (1995).

Testimony as to extrajudicial identification of defendant's photograph.—After the defendant introduced testimony showing that one identification witness incorrectly identified a photograph as a picture of the defendant, it might have been proper under these unusual circumstances to permit that identification witness, on rebuttal, to testify that he had previously assisted in making a composite sketch and had picked the defendant out of a photographic line-up shortly after the incident defendant was being prosecuted for; however, it was reversible error to permit another identification witness, whose credibility had not been attacked, to testify in a like manner. People v. Lindsay, 42 N.Y.2d 9, 396 N.Y.S.2d 610, 364 N.E.2d 1302 (1977).

—A witness may not testify as to an extrajudicial identification of a photograph of the defendant. People v. Griffin, 29 N.Y.2d 91, 323 N.Y.S.2d 964, 27 N.E.2d 477 (1971).

—The identification testimony as to the previous extrajudicial identification of defendant's photograph was harmless where the trial counsel's strategic decision made earlier in the trial was to elicit the prior identification on cross-examination and there was overwhelming evidence of defendant's guilt. People v. Hand, 85 A.D.2d 642, 445 N.Y.S.2d 11 (2d Dept. 1981).

Use of composite sketch; when allowed.—Conviction of attempted rape in the first degree (PL § 130.35) was reversed and a new trial ordered where, after the testimony showed that complainant had selected a photograph of someone other than the defendant as resembling her assailant, the prosecution was permitted on cross-examination to introduce a composite sketch which had been prepared with the complainant's help prior to her selection of the photograph introduced by the defense. People v. Falterman, 74 A.D.2d 585, 424 N.Y.S.2d 481 (2d Dept. 1980).

In-court identification valid despite hospital confrontation.—Where a chauffeur had ample opportunity to observe the defendant for a considerable length of time and under favorable conditions during the commission of the crime and his course of flight from the scene, it is clear that his courtroom identification was not based on or tainted by the potentially misleading circumstances attending his earlier identification at the hospital or police station. People v. Pharo, 37 A.D.2d 865, 325 N.Y.S.2d 5 (1971).

Belief based on "instinct" and "woman's intuition."—Reversible error was committed when, in a prosecution for burglary, rape and sodomy, the victim was permitted to testify that based upon her "instinct" she believed the defendant was the perpetrator and although she could not identify her assailant, she testified that it "might possibly" be the defendant, based only upon her "woman's intuition." People v. Reick, 70 A.D.2d 724, 416 N.Y.S.2d 866 (3d Dept. 1979).

Bolstering testimony.—The arresting officer's testimony regarding the undercover officer's drive by confirmatory identification procedure did not constitute impermissible bolstering. People v. Chapman, 202 A.D.2d 297, 609 N.Y.S.2d 177 (1st Dept. 1994).

—Reference to the complainant's lineup identifications of other perpetrators who were not tried with the defendant did not constitute improper bolstering. People v. McClain, 193 A.D.2d 515, 597 N.Y.S.2d 409 (1st Dept. 1993).

—No bolstering error was committed where officer testified that the defendant's arrest was based solely on the radio description transmitted and not on his personal observation of the incident. People v. Acevedo, 181 A.D.2d 596, 581 N.Y.S.2d 334 (1st Dept. 1992).

—Credibility of the complainant was not improperly bolstered through prompting by the court or the prosecutor; the court was not encouraging the complainant to change his testimony when it directed that he write down, rather than utter, the offensive language he claimed defendant had used during the failed robbery, but was instead facilitating the receipt of relevant evidence. People v. Gordon, 182 A.D.2d 422, 582 N.Y.S.2d 156 (1st Dept. 1992).

—Court rejected claim that defendant's identification was improperly bolstered by the testimony of the arresting officer that he arrested the defendant after the sergeant, his supervisor, gave him a "nod." People v. Walker, 182 A.D.2d 528, 582 N.Y.S.2d 700 (1st Dept. 1992).

—Testimony of the back-up officer that he received a radioed description of the individual who had just sold crack cocaine to the undercover officer does not constitute improper bolstering as it provides a necessary explanation of the events leading up to the defendant's arrest. People v. Cardona, 173 A.D.2d 364, 569 N.Y.S.2d 733 (1st Dept. 1991).

—*Trowbridge* claim rejected where there was no contested issue of identification. People v. Figueroa, 172 A.D.2d 387, 568 N.Y.S.2d 767 (1st Dept. 1991).

—There was no violation of *People v. Trowbridge* simply because the officer testified that he chased after defendant upon statements from non-witnesses to "get him"; these statements attributed to the non-witnesses served only as a predicate for subsequent police activity and were not used to bolster the identification testimony of the shooting victims, who knew the defendant from prior occasions. People v. Bailey, 155 A.D.2d 262, 547 N.Y.S.2d 28 (1st Dept. 1989).

—There was no bolstering violation where the investigating officer testified as to the procedures employed during the lineup, and the questions he asked of the complainant, but never testified as to what the complainant said or that the complainant had identified the defendant. People v. McIlwain, 205 A.D.2d 710, 613 N.Y.S.2d 674 (2d Dept. 1994).

—The detective's testimony at trial that, during the lineup, the defendant was the "suspect" and the other participants at trial were "fillers" did not constitute *Trowbridge* error. People v. Williams, 193 A.D.2d 826, 598 N.Y.S.2d 299 (2d Dept. 1993).

—Although the police officer did not state that the defendant matched the description given by the radio transmission, the jury could have reasonably so inferred; therefore the officer's testimony implicitly bolstered the identification testimony. People v. Larsen, 157 A.D.2d 672, 549 N.Y.S.2d 772 (2d Dept. 1990).

—The prosecutor did not bolster his case by repetitively eliciting the same testimony from the police witnesses. People v. Vega, 159 A.D.2d 218, 552 N.Y.S.2d 23 (2d Dept. 1990).

—Complainant's identification of the defendant was not bolstered by the fact that he testified that he had identified his assailant in two lineups. People v. Carlton, 146 A.D.2d 641, 537 N.Y.S.2d 38 (2d Dept. 1989).

—Defendant failed to object to the testimony of the victim's fiance with respect to the lineup on the ground that it constituted impermissible bolstering and thus has failed to preserve the claim that the court erred in admitting the testimony on that ground. In any event, the People were properly allowed to present the testimony as evidence in chief. People v. Davis, 294 A.D.2d 936, 742 N.Y.S.2d 758 (4th Dept. 2002).

Charge.—The charge properly apprised the jury that the reasonable doubt standard attached to the element of identification where it instructed the jury that "before you can convict a defendant you must be convinced of his guilt beyond a reasonable doubt." People v. Newton, 46 N.Y.2d 877, 414 N.Y.S.2d 680, 387 N.E.2d 612 (1979).

—The trial court should have instructed the jury to consider and balance, *inter alia,* such factors as the complaining witness' opportunity for observation, the duration and distance of the viewing, the lighting and weather conditions, the witness' ability to describe the assailant's physical features and apparel, and any other relevant factors. People v. Gardner, 59 A.D.2d 913, 399 N.Y.S.2d 146 (2d Dept. 1977).

Corroboration of witness's photo identification.—It was harmless error to admit, without objection, prosecutor's elicitation from witness of an earlier pretrial station house photo identification and corroboration of this by the police witness, where there was substantial ground to show that witness had known defendant before crime and courtroom identification was based on independent source. People v. Bryant, 39 A.D.2d 80, 332 N.Y.S.2d 143 (1st Dept. 1972), *aff'd,* 31 N.Y.2d 747, 338 N.Y.S.2d 115, 290 N.E.2d 152 (1972).

Credibility of identifying witnesses.—Since identification of defendant was primary issue before jury it was improper and highly prejudicial for prosecutor, in his summation, to tell jury that a vote of not guilty was the equivalent of saying that the two identifying witnesses had lied. People v. Ball, 77 A.D.2d 625, 430 N.Y.S.2d 122 (2d Dept. 1980).

Defendant in custody; line-up on unrelated charge.—It was proper to place defendant, who was in custody on an unrelated charge and represented by counsel, in a line-up after a detective, who was investigating a robbery, saw him by chance at the police precinct since it presented a much lesser intrusion on his legal rights than an arrest or a detention for the limited purpose of investigation. People v. Pickett, 71 A.D.2d 575, 418 N.Y.S.2d 619 (1st Dept. 1979), *aff'd,* 52 N.Y.2d 892, 437 N.Y.S.2d 301, 418 N.E.2d 1319 (1981).

Evidence; corroboration of identification by police officer.—It was error to admit the police mug shots notwithstanding that some effort had been made by paste overs to modify their appearance after defense counsel had offered to stipulate that the photographs identified by the victim before trial had been photographs of defendant. People v. Robbins, 38 N.Y.2d 913, 382 N.Y.S.2d 977, 346 N.E.2d 815 (1976).

—Where defendant was not apprehended until sometime after the alleged crime, it was error to permit a police officer to testify at the trial as to the events when the defendant was brought into the only eyewitness's presence in handcuffs and then identified, and to permit another officer to testify to the description, which fit the defendant, given to him on the day of the crime by its victim. People v. Michael J., 54 A.D.2d 655, 387 N.Y.S.2d 875 (1st Dept. 1976).

—It was error for police officers to testify over objections that the complaining witness identified the defendant as one of the culprits; this could be considered improper bolstering, and, the evidence of guilt not being overwhelming, the error could not be disregarded as harmless. People v. Reeves, 50 A.D.2d 746, 376 N.Y.S.2d 143 (1st Dept. 1975).

—It was reversible error for court to refuse to strike the testimony of the arresting officer as to the complainant's prior out-of-court identification of defendant where the verdict was entirely dependent upon complainant's testimony and identification of defendant as perpetrator; officer's testimony served no purpose other than to bolster the complainant's identification. People v. Jones, 75 A.D.2d 607, 426 N.Y.S.2d 809 (2d Dept. 1980).

—Introduction into evidence of uncharged crimes on the issue of defendant's identity as perpetrator of the alleged crimes and testimony of a policeman regarding another witness's earlier identification was admissible, since the eyewitness identification was subject to attack as to the witness's credibility and the uncharged crimes were admissible under the rule stated in People v. Condon, 26 N.Y.2d 139, 309 N.Y.S.2d 152, 257 N.E.2d 615 (1970). People v. Beam, 83 A.D.2d 82 444 N.Y.S.2d 300 (3d Dept. 1981), *aff'd,* 57 N.Y.2d 241, 455 N.Y.S.2d 575, 441 N.E.2d 1093 (1982).

Failure to previously note unique characteristic.— Reversal and new trial resulted where arresting officer's detailed identification report made no note of tattoos or scars on upper body then visible to officer, but at trial defendant removed shirt to display an upper body virtually covered with tattoos, together with several prominent scars. People v. Diaz, 53 A.D.2d 587, 384 N.Y.S.2d 844 (1st Dept. 1976).

Failure to identify a person other than defendant.—The People cannot introduce evidence of a complainant's failure to identify a person other than the defendant as the perpetrator of a crime. People v. Moss, 103 Misc. 2d 245, 425 N.Y.S.2d 521 (Sup. Ct. N.Y. Co. 1980).

Photographic identification permissible.—Where a police officer saw the defendant's face under excellent viewing conditions at the time of the crime, the fact that the officer's photographic identification took place 10 months later did not render such identification invalid where the officer chose the defendant's photograph from a group of 11 similar photographs of other men of the same general color, build, and stature as defendant. People v. Joyiens, 39 N.Y.2d 197, 383 N.Y.S.2d 259, 347 N.E.2d 621 (1976).

—The procedures did not give rise to a substantial likelihood of irreparable misidentification where the witness was shown seven photographs of black individuals with mustaches and hair styles similar to those of defendant; where each picture was a full view of the face and shoulders; and where there was no testimony that such witness was told anything about the progress of the investigation or that anyone else had identified the defendant. People v. Fox, 65 A.D.2d 880, 410 N.Y.S.2d 180 (3d Dept. 1978).

—Photograph taken of the defendant when he was legally arrested on a charge of driving without a license, can be used for identification by the arresting officer where he suspects that the defendant is the unidentified perpetrator of a robbery because the defendant's car was similar to the car described by the robbery victim, even though there could easily have been a line-up. People v. Dibble 46 A.D.2d 829, 361 N.Y.S.2d 77 (3d Dept. 1974).

—A witness is not precluded by CPL § 60.30 from testifying at trial about her identification of the defendant as he appeared in a videotape of a street scene. People v. Edmonson, 137 Misc. 408, 520 N.Y.S.2d 707 (Sup. Ct. N.Y. Co. 1987), aff'd, 150 A.D.2d 990, 543 N.Y.S.2d 600 (1st Dept. 1989).

Waiver.—Defendant's counsel opened the door to redirect testimony by one of the victims concerning her identification of the defendant from photographs where cross-examining her on that subject. People v. Jenkins, 133 A.D.2d 279, 519 N.Y.S.2d 68, 69 (2d Dept. 1987).

Hearing; pretrial photo identification.—Error to deny defendant's motion for a pretrial hearing concerning his photographic identification by the People's identification witness. People v. Poerschke, 44 A.D.2d 844, 355 N.Y.S.2d 640 (2d Dept. 1974).

In-court identification; physical characteristics.—Court order, at pretrial hearing, directing defendant to remove his eyeglasses for observation of his person without glasses by a witness was lawful and defendant's refusal to obey the lawful order constituted criminal contempt. People v. Sanders, 58 A.D.2d 525, 395 N.Y.S.2d 190 (1st Dept. 1977).

Improper bolstering.—The trial court committed error in admitting over objection the testimony of three police officers that the victim pointed to defendants when he confronted them shortly after the robbery; unquestionably the testimony improperly bolstered the victim's testimony; the error was harmless where the evidence of identity was so strong that there was no substantial issue on the point. People v. Mobley, 56 N.Y.2d 584, 450 N.Y.S.2d 302, 435 N.E.2d 672 (1982).

—Inferential reference to prior out-of-court identification of defendant constituted improper bolstering and required reversal in light of the close identification issue. People v. Hines, 112 A.D.2d 316, 491 N.Y.S.2d 764 (2d Dept. 1985).

—Testimony by a police officer to the effect that he arrested the defendant pursuant to a conversation that he had with the complaining witness, constituted improper bolstering especially where the evidence of identification was not "clear and strong." People v. Brown, 91 A.D.2d 639, 456 N.Y.S.2d 821 (2d Dept. 1982).

—It was not bolstering for the undercover officer, who went to Puerto Rico to bring the defendant back, to testify at the trial as to the circumstances of the meeting, as this was not an identification procedure and the testimony was merely cumulative on the question of identity. People v. Velasquez, 78 A.D.2d 905, 433 N.Y.S.2d 204 (2d Dept. 1980).

—A new trial was mandated where testimony at trial revealed that the sole identification of defendant at the time of sale was made by the undercover officer and the court permitted testimony from the officer in charge of the back-up team that the undercover officer had pointed defendant out to him on other occasions in the neighborhood as the seller; such testimony constituted improper bolstering. People v. Mack, 72 A.D.2d 753, 421 N.Y.S.2d 271 (2d Dept. 1979).

—Where proof of defendant's guilt was based almost solely on the complainant's identification of defendant eleven months after the crime was committed, it was error to admit companion's testimony that complainant told him "that's him, that's the fellow that raped me," approximately eleven months after the rape. People v. Best, 73 A.D.2d 651, 422 N.Y.S.2d 478 (2d Dept. 1979).

—Defendant failed to object to the testimony of the victim's fiance with respect to the lineup on the ground that it constituted impermissible bolstering and thus has failed to preserve the claim that the court erred in admitting the testimony on that ground. In any event, the People were properly allowed to present the testimony as evidence in chief. People v. Davis, 294 A.D.2d 936, 742 N.Y.S.2d 758 (4th Dept. 2002).

Identification from photo of lineup inadmissible.— Witness' identification of defendant was photographic, and therefore not admissible on People's direct case, where witness was unable to make a positive identification at the lineup, but four days later used a photo of the lineup to make a positive identification. People v. Pruitt, 112 Misc. 2d 914, 447 N.Y.S.2d 824 (Sup. Ct. Bronx Co. 1982).

Independent identification.—There was no reasonable nexus between the unlawful conduct of Suffolk authorities, who had illegally arrested the defendant and then notified the New York Police and the proposed identification testimony of the victim of a prior robbery in New York and who had an independent recollection, since the New York authorities had earlier obtained a description of an armed robbery suspect totally independent of the subsequent conduct of Suffolk authorities. People v. Pleasant, 76 A.D.2d 244, 430 N.Y.S.2d 592 (1st Dept. 1980), aff'd, 54 N.Y.2d 972, 446 N.Y.S.2d 29, 430 N.E.2d 905 (1981).

Independent basis for in-court identification.—The indictment against the defendant for burglary was reinstated where the police brought the eyewitness-victim to police headquarters and permitted defendant and victim to be in each others company for two hours; any taint that resulted from the confrontation was removed when the victim testified that he was a corrections officer and is required to identify people even though he had previously identified a photograph of the defendant's twin brother. People v. Hill, 83 A.D.2d 671, 442 N.Y.S.2d 228 (3d Dept. 1981).

Lack of sufficient independent basis.—Where there was no sufficient independent basis to allow in-court identification testimony by the victim, the motion to suppress should have been granted regarding such testimony; furthermore, since it could not be determined whether defendant's guilty plea was influenced by this error, the court vacated the plea. People v. Burrows, 46 N.Y.2d 957, 415 N.Y.S.2d 410, 388 N.E.2d 733 (1979).

Lineup; absence of counsel; adjournments.—When defendant waived his right to counsel and voluntarily appeared in line-up, and 3 witnesses with ample opportunity to observe perpetrator of crime identified him and where defendant's attorney had two weeks notice of the suppression hearing, there was no error in attempted robbery conviction. People v. Foster, 38 A.D.2d 721, 329 N.Y.S.2d 435 (3d Dept. 1972).

—Although the defendant's right to counsel attached prior to the court ordered line-up, the facts do not warrant suppression of testimony concerning the identification made at the line-up where Legal Aid supervisors were adequately notified that the line-up would take place, but failed to appoint substitute counsel after it became apparent that the particular attorney assigned to the defendant's case could not be present at the line-up. People v. Styles, 90 Misc. 2d 861, 395 N.Y.S.2d 1007 (Sup. Ct. N.Y. Co. 1977).

Line-up identification.—It was not error to permit in-court identification to be made where the evidence of the line-up was suppressed because of suggestive procedures employed. People v. Burnett, 81 A.D.2d 869, 438 N.Y.S.2d 882 (2d Dept. 1981), *aff'd*, 56 N.Y.2d 269, 451 N.Y.S.2d 705, 436 N.E.2d 1307 (1982).

—It was error to admit witness's in-court identification of defendant where it was established that the witness had been present at a line-up where other witnesses identified defendant and then pointed defendant out to this witness in the line-up. People v. Torres, 72 A.D.2d 754, 421 N.Y.S.2d 275 (2d Dept. 1979).

—The trial court did not err in refusing to suppress identification evidence, since petitioner was represented by counsel at all times, and had requested the line-up and chosen seven other black inmates to stand with him. People *ex rel.* Hall v. Casscles, 51 A.D.2d 623, 378 N.Y.S.2d 813 (3d Dept. 1976).

—Line-up identification of defendant was not unduly suggestive where the participants of the line-up were of different height since there were three suspects in the crime who were of different height, and the witnesses did not know which of the three suspects would be in the line-up, though they knew a suspect would be shown. People v. Woods, 84 A.D.2d 937, 446 N.Y.S.2d 687 (4th Dept. 1981).

Lineup; court ordered.—Motion to suppress line-up identification was granted and a new trial was ordered where defendant was arrested in Manhattan on an unrelated charge and was not given counsel after he had been ordered by the Supreme Court, Bronx County, to appear in a line-up in the Bronx; the order for production of the defendant in Bronx County to appear in the line-up commenced an adversary judicial proceeding against him and activated his right to counsel. People v. Banks, 73 A.D.2d 907, 424 N.Y.S.2d 439 (1st Dept. 1980), *aff'd*, 53 N.Y.2d 819, 439 N.Y.S.2d 916, 422 N.E.2d 576 (1981).

—Trial court's order that owner of car, seen leaving scene of shooting, be detained at line-up and be viewed by witnesses reversed where owner had not been arrested or charged with the commission of a crime and district attorney conceded that there was no probable cause to believe that the owner had committed a crime; such court-ordered detention amounted to a "seizure" sans adequate basis and would not be permitted. Alphonso C. v. Morgenthau, 50 A.D.2d 97, 376 N.Y.S.2d 126 (1st Dept. 1975).

Opportunity to observe defendant.—Identification testimony of resident of burglarized dwelling was admissible where he had an opportunity to observe the burglar for about 10 minutes at close range, under excellent lighting conditions. Accordingly, there was an adequate basis for his identification of the defendant and his testimony was not tainted in any way by his prior identification at the scene of the crime when the police presented defendant as a suspect approximately 30 minutes after the incident. People v. Bonds, 93 A.D.2d 951, 463 N.Y.S.2d 62 (3d Dept. 1983).

Post-indictment; pre-arraignment line-up.—A defendant in a post-indictment, prearraignment custodial setting, even though not then represented by an attorney, may not in the absence of counsel waive his right to have counsel appear at a corporeal identification, and any actions taken by the police with respect to an indicted but unarraigned defendant which impinge upon his right to counsel may not be used against him at trial. People v. Settles, 46 N.Y.2d 154, 412 N.Y.S.2d 874, 385 N.E.2d 612 (1978).

Prejudicial error; defense strategy.—It was prejudicial for the trial judge to preclude the defendant's unorthodox but rational trial strategy of admitting that two prior identification had been suppressed and this error was compounded by the judge's refusal to instruct the jury on the issue of identification. People v. Foti, 83 A.D.2d 641, 441 N.Y.S.2d 521 (2d Dept. 1981).

Presence of counsel at line-up not required if conducted before filing of accusatory instrument.—Despite the fact that the police were aware he was represented by counsel in another action, the identification made at a line-up conducted prior to the filing of another accusatory instrument and in the absence of counsel should not be suppressed since the defendant was arrested for a crime committed while awaiting sentence in the previous action. People v. Seymour, 104 Misc. 2d 482, 428 N.Y.S.2d 796 (Suffolk Co. Ct. 1980).

Pre-arraignment line-up.—Since counsel had not been previously retained, the defendant's request that an attorney be

obtained for the prearraignment line-up was not significant and it could not create a right to counsel where none existed. People v. Perez, 42 N.Y.2d 971, 398 N.Y.S.2d 269, 367 N.E.2d 867 (1977).

Pretrial show-up.—Although pretrial show-up identification of defendant alone at police station is impermissible, it does not render in-court identification illegal where it has an independent source. People v. Carter, 30 N.Y.2d 279, 332 N.Y.S.2d 865, 283 N.E.2d 746 (1972).

—Where the crime was committed in broad daylight, took several minutes to complete, and witness was only several feet away from the defendant, the showup of defendant at police station 45 minutes later was proper. People v. Smith, 46 A.D.2d 639, 360 N.Y.S.2d 256 (1st Dept. 1974), *aff'd*, 38 N.Y.2d 882, 382 N.Y.S.2d 745, 346 N.E.2d 546 (1976).

—Suppression of the identification evidence was granted because it was inherently suggestive for three witnesses to view the defendant simultaneously when a line-up could easily have been arranged. People v. Jackson, 80 A.D.2d 904, 437 N.Y.S.2d 20 (2d Dept. 1981).

—There was ample basis for finding that identification of defendant possessed an independent source and was not tainted by suggestive police procedures where there was a "show-up" of defendant through a one-way mirror after victim of a robbery who obtained a close view of defendant first gave police a detailed and accurate description of defendant and the clothes he was wearing, then positively identified defendant in a book of mug shots at the police headquarters, and permitted defendant and victim to be in each others station shortly after the crime, and again selected defendant from a photographic lineup which included defendant and nine others of similar features and appearance. People v. Van Buren, 87 A.D.2d 900, 449 N.Y.S.2d 366 (3d Dept. 1982).

Photographic array.—It was error for the trial court to permit the complaining witness to testify that she had been shown approximately 30 photographs by a police officer and that she had not selected any from the group since the testimony was hearsay and improperly bolstered her in-court identification of the defendant by implying that she had not picked out a photograph of someone other than the defendant from the photographs. People v. Rothaar, 75 A.D.2d 652, 427 N.Y.S.2d 272 (2d Dept. 1980).

Undercover officer.—Undercover police officer, while observed by backup officers, purchased drugs from defendant. Later that day, defendant was arrested by the backup officers and afterwards viewed through a two way mirror at the police station by the undercover officer, without a line-up. It was error to permit the undercover officer at the trial to testify to the station house identification because it was calculated to bolster the testimony of the backup officers identifying the defendant with the sale based on their observation a half block distant. People v. Momales, 43 A.D.2d 917, 352 N.Y.S.2d 938 (1st Dept. 1974), *aff'd*, 37 N.Y.2d 262, 372 N.Y.S.2d 25, 333 N.E.2d 339 (1975).

Pretrial show-up; due process.—Although pretrial show-up identification may be impermissibly suggestive or conducted out of presence of counsel, it was for defendant to show that it tainted the in-court identification and that existing procedure denied defendant an opportunity to assert claim of fundamental unfairness in violation of due process, in order for coram nobis relief to be warranted. People v. Bennett, 30 N.Y.2d 283, 332 N.Y.S.2d 867, 283 N.E.2d 747 (1972).

—Show-up at the scene of the crime was valid where the police had probable cause to arrest the defendant for burglary and it occurred ten minutes after the burglary and the complainant identified his clothing and body characteristics. People v. Wilmer, 90 A.D.2d 918, 457 N.Y.S.2d 934 (3d Dept. 1982).

—The trial court erred in failing to suppress the in-court identification of the defendant where the show-up identification of the defendant at the police station violated due process even though the prior photograph selection process was proper where another witness had identified the defendant as the perpetrator and no exigent circumstances appeared in the record to justify a show-up. People v. Rogers, 81 A.D.2d 980, 439 N.Y.S.2d 764 (3d Dept. 1981).

Pretrial show-up; suggestive misidentification.—Showup held two hours after the crime at which complainant, who had only two brief opportunities to view the attacker in indirect light, and who knew that the defendant was perceived by police and her sister as the principal suspect, and who was still emotionally distraught at the time of the showup, identified the defendant as the guilty party was so unnecessarily suggestive and conducive to mistaken identification that defendant was denied due process of law. People v. Dolphin, 77 A.D.2d 571, 429 N.Y.S.2d 732 (2d Dept. 1980).

—Victim of robbery saw defendant during 5 or 10 minutes of crime, policeman saw defendant and chased them always seeing or hearing them and victim re-identified defendant when policeman arrested them, thereby satisfying requirement that there was no unnecessarily suggestive identification so as to cause mistake. People v. Colon, 39 A.D.2d 556, 331 N.Y.S.2d 863 (2d Dept. 1972).

Pretrial viewing; presence of counsel.—Where hearing disclosed that victim had ample opportunity to observe defendant at close quarters during crime and had accurately described defendant, his gun and clothing, absence of counsel at pretrial viewing was at most harmless error. People v. Hill, 38 A.D.2d 919, 329 N.Y.S.2d 847 (1st Dept. 1972), aff'd, 33 N.Y.2d 889, 352 N.Y.S.2d 446, 307 N.E.2d 562 (1973).

Prior view may not taint in-court identification.—If no independent origin for an in-court identification by the victim was established, the jury should not have been permitted to consider any such testimony. People v. Robles, 46 A.D.2d 748, 360 N.Y.S.2d 665 (1st Dept. 1974).

—Defendant, positively identified by eyewitnesses at scene of crime, was not prejudiced by admission of further identification, without objection, regardless of its hearsay character. People v. Grier, 45 A.D.2d 688, 357 N.Y.S.2d 4 (1st Dept. 1974).

—Victim's in-court identification of defendant is admissible even though victim had observed defendant being interrogated by police prior to trial. Court denied that prior view of defendant tainted victim's identification—where prior view was not police arranged but happenstance. People v. Martin, 38 A.D.2d 536, 327 N.Y.S.2d 53 (1st Dept. 1971), aff'd, 32 N.Y.2d 771, 344 N.Y.S.2d 957, 298 N.E.2d 119 (1973).

Prosecutor's use of previously suppressed evidence.—Prosecutor's questioning of complaining witness at trial regarding an out-of-court identification of defendant, in direct contravention of a prior court order which, following a hearing, suppressed evidence of such identification, was per se reversible error. People v. Fraser, 79 A.D.2d 686, 434 N.Y.S.2d 37 (2d Dept. 1980).

"Regiscope"; pretrial identification.—In prosecution for possession of a forged instrument, the witness' observation of her "regiscope" photograph during the pretrial identification procedures used by the police did not taint the identification process. People v. Raco, 72 A.D.2d 857, 421 N.Y.S.2d 732 (3d Dept. 1979).

Showup; exigent circumstances.—Where police officers responding to a radio bulletin that the perpetrator of a liquor store robbery and his alleged accomplice were observed leaving the scene in a U-haul van bearing out of state license plates, approached defendant's van which bore California plates with gun drawn, ordered defendant and his companion out of the vehicle, frisked them for weapons, asked what they were doing, informed the two that they were suspects in the robbery case, handcuffed them, and drove them back a half mile to the liquor store where the owner positively identified defendant as the robber, the court upheld the show-up identification on the ground that the more formal Wade-Gilbert rules were outweighed by the station shortly after the crime, and again exigencies of the case. People v. Brnja, 70 A.D.2d 17, 419 N.Y.S.2d 591 (2d Dept. 1979), aff'd, 50 N.Y.2d 366, 429 N.Y.S.2d 173, 406 N.E.2d 1066 (1980).

Suggestive identification, not excluded per se.—Reliability is the linchpin of admissibility in cases involving CPL § 60.25 and § 60.30; the court rejected the argument that a suggestive identification must per se be excluded even if the totality of circumstances surrounding it indicates that it is reliable. People v. Graph, 67 A.D.2d 172, 415 N.Y.S.2d 714 (4th Dept. 1979).

Testimony as to extra-judicial identification.—It is reversible error to allow the complainant to testify she had previously been shown an array of photographs and failed to identify any of them and to allow a witness to testify about a prior identification by the complainant in a dry cleaning store some months after the crime because it bolsters the in-court identification. People v. Zanfordino, 78 A.D.2d 558, 432 N.Y.S.2d 15 (2d Dept. 1980).

—It was harmless error where the prosecution's prime witness revealed to the jury on cross-examination that he had viewed photographs and subsequently identified the defendant. People v. Whipset, 80 A.D.2d 986, 437 N.Y.S.2d 470 (4th Dept. 1981).

Prosecution; disclosure obligation.—The prosecution must disclose any possible discrepancy in a witness's identification of a defendant. People v. Turner, 48 A.D.2d 674, 367 N.Y.S.2d 562 (2d Dept. 1975).

Untainted in-court identification.—Failure of proof with respect to identification of the defendant as the perpetrator of the crime cannot be cured or waived by the defendant's willful absenting of himself from the trial. People v. Singleton, 62 A.D.2d 1042, 404 N.Y.S.2d 47 (2d Dept. 1978).

Use of photograph to refresh memory combined with suggestive pretrial showup.—Where the witness was unable to identify defendant at the trial, the prosecution's use of a single photograph, taken at the time of the arrest to refresh his recollection coupled with a suggestive pretrial showup, created a substantial likelihood that the complainant's in-court identification of defendant was not reliable, and consequently, the court should have conducted an inquiry to ascertain the reliability of the complainant's corporeal identification. People v. Rivera, 74 A.D.2d 857, 425 N.Y.S.2d 373 (2d Dept. 1980).

Wade hearing; order directing defendant to shave.—The prosecutor was not entitled to an order directing the defendant to shave off his beard and mustache since the purpose of a Wade hearing is to have the court determine the issue of taint in certain identification procedures and to elicit evidence as to whether there was an independent source for the identification, and defendant's present facial condition is not relevant. People v. Bowen, 99 Misc. 2d 1034, 417 N.Y.S.2d 852 (Sup. Ct. Kings Co. 1979).

§ 60.35. Rules of evidence; impeachment of own witness by proof of prior contradictory statement.

1. When, upon examination by the party who called him, a witness in a criminal proceeding gives testimony upon a material issue of the case which tends to disprove the position of such party, such party may introduce evidence that such witness has previously made either a written statement signed by him or an oral statement under oath contradictory to such testimony.

2. Evidence concerning a prior contradictory statement introduced pursuant to subdivision one may be received only for the purpose of impeaching the credibility of the witness with respect to his testimony upon the subject, and does not constitute evidence in chief. Upon receiving such evidence at a jury trial, the court must so instruct the jury.

3. When a witness has made a prior signed or sworn statement contradictory to his testimony in a criminal proceeding upon a material issue of the case, but his testimony does not tend to disprove the position of the party who called him and elicited such testimony, evidence that the witness made such prior statement is not admissible, and such party may not use such prior statement for the purpose of refreshing the recollection of the witness in a manner that discloses its contents to the trier of the facts.

ANNOTATIONS

Admissibility.—It was gross error to permit the prosecutor on redirect examination, over objection, to read into the record excerpts from a prior out-of-court conversation between the witness and another which was not signed by the witness or given under oath. People v. Wright, 41 N.Y.2d 118, 390 N.Y.S.2d 909, 359 N.E.2d 417 (1976).

—Where the only aspect of the witness's prospective trial testimony that would have been impeachable by his pretrial testimony concerned the location where the witness was situated during the stabbing, the lower court's prohibition of impeachment on this minor issue did not result in prejudice to defendant, especially since, as defense counsel recognized, the witness would still have identified defendant as the assailant. People v. Reid, 228 A.D.2d 362, 644 N.Y.S.2d 717 (1st Dept. 1996).

—Proffered audiotape was admissible because contrary to defendant's contention, it did not constitute a prior inconsistent statement of participants in the drug transaction, and it was not offered for impeachment purposes but rather as evidence-in-chief to establish the events that transpired in the informant's car. People v. Waxter, 268 A.D.2d 899, 702 N.Y.S.2d 434 (3d Dept. 2000).

—Defendant on trial for criminal possession of controlled substance could not question his co-defendant, who testified for defense, about his motive in pleading guilty, absent prior inconsistent statement by co-defendant. People v. Clark, 225 A.D.2d 559, 638 N.Y.S.2d 765 (2d Dept. 1996).

—Prosecutor did not improperly impeach witness on redirect examination by use of prior statement where prosecutor neither disclosed contents of prior testimony of witness nor repeatedly questioned him regarding specific instances of inconsistency, but made good faith effort to assist witness in refreshing his recollection. People v. Sullivan, 227 A.D.2d 895, 643 N.Y.S.2d 799 (4th Dept. 1996).

—If trial testimony of witness contradicts prior sworn statement but does not affirmatively damage case of party calling him, recollection of witness may be refreshed with the prior inconsistent statement, but only in such manner that does not disclose contents of statement to the jury. People v. Lawrence, 227 A.D.2d 893, 643 N.Y.S.2d 273 (4th Dept. 1996).

Appeal.—Defendant failed to preserve for appellate review his contention that he was deprived of a fair trial by the prosecutor's impeachment of his own witness with prior inconsistent statements and by the court's failure to provide a limiting instruction, in violation of CPL § 60.35. People v. Boyd, 222 A.D.2d 314, 635 N.Y.S.2d 586 (1st Dept. 1995).

Charge.—Since the witnesses' trial testimony adopted and went beyond their Grand Jury testimony, there was no inconsistency which required the giving of a cautionary instruction pursuant to CPL § 60.35. People v. Ramirez, 66 A.D.2d 902, 411 N.Y.S.2d 693 (2d Dept. 1978).

—The failure of the trial court to make any reference to a prior statement used by the prosecution to impeach the defendant's witness did not, in the context of the entire charge, the overwhelming evidence of defendant's guilt, and the absence of a request for such an instruction, constitute reversible error. People v. Williamson, 51 A.D.2d 843, 380 N.Y.S.2d 778 (3d Dept. 1976).

Confession of co-defendant; prejudice.—Motion was made to vacate judgment, since co-defendant's confession had been introduced into evidence and had been redacted only to the extent of replacing defendant's name with the letter "X." Although the trial court instructed the jury not to speculate as to the identity of X, references made to the confession during the trial, the prosecutor's summation, and the charge left no doubt as to who X was. The error could not be considered harmless error, since, aside from the co-defendant's confession, the People's case against the defendant rested entirely on a questionable identification made of him exigencies by the victim. People v. Tinsley, 31 N.Y.2d 905, 340 N.Y.S.2d 640, 292 N.E.2d 783 (1972).

Disappointing or unhelpful testimony.—Prior inconsistent statement may be used for the purpose of refreshing recollection where the witness' trial testimony, though disappointing or unhelpful, falls short of "disproving" the party's position, so long as its contents are not disclosed to the trier of the facts (CPL § 60.35(3)). People v. Reed, 40 N.Y.2d 204, 386 N.Y.S.2d 371, 352 N.E.2d 558 (1976).

Grand jury testimony.—Court properly permitted prosecution to use grand jury testimony to impeach two of its witnesses, since their trial testimony affirmatively damaged the People's case. People v. Agosto, 248 A.D.2d 301, 670 N.Y.S.2d 463 (1st Dept. 1998).

Impeachment of credibility of defendant as a witness.—When the credibility of defendant as a witness is assailed by compelling him upon cross-examination to give testimony which, although competent for purposes of impeachment, is collateral to the main issue, the prosecution at whose instance the collateral evidence is elicited, is bound thereby and cannot introduce evidence to contradict it. People v. Mapp, 39 A.D.2d 968, 333 N.Y.S.2d 539 (2d Dept. 1972).

Impeachment allowed.—People were properly permitted to impeach prosecution witness through the use of her prior statement where a sincere attempt was made to refresh her recollection "in a discreet [and] non-publicizing manner," and because a good faith effort was made, no error can be discerned. People v. Layman, 284 A.D.2d 558, 725 N.Y.S.2d 744 (3d Dept. 2001).

—People were properly permitted to impeach one of their witnesses pursuant to CPL § 60.35 after he gave testimony which varied with his prior sworn statement to a police investigator. People v. McNeil, 273 A.D.2d 608, 711 N.Y.S.2d 518 (3d Dept. 2000).

—Court properly permitted People to impeach their own witness with a prior inconsistent statement where the testimony of that witness was on a material issue and affirmatively damaged the People's case. People v. Murray, 17 A.D.3d 1042, 794 N.Y.S.2d 199 (4th Dept. 2005).

Impeachment not available when discrepancies only found upon cross-examination.—CPL § 60.35(1) only contemplates the introduction into evidence of prior inconsistent statements when the witness gives evidence tending to disprove a material issue upon direct examination of the party calling the witness; it was prejudicial error to allow the prosecution to introduce prior inconsistent statements made by one of its witnesses when the discrepancy arose only upon cross-examination. People v. Kearney, 89 A.D.2d 860, 453 N.Y.S.2d 39 (2d Dept. 1982).

—Court improperly allowed People to impeach their own witness where the testimony that the People sought to be impeached was elicited on cross-examination by defense counsel and thus impeachment by the prosecutor on redirect was improper. People v. Sanders, 2 A.D.3d 1420, 768 N.Y.S.2d 900 (4th Dept. 2003).

No impeachment when procedural requirements not met.—Court properly denied defendant's permission to impeach his own witness, where none of the CPL § 60.35 criteria were met, and where the information that defendant sought to elicit by impeaching his own witness was not critical to his defense, particularly since he elicited similar information from other witnesses. People v. Stewart, 295 A.D.2d 249, 745 N.Y.S.2d 151 (1st Dept. 2002), cert. denied, 538 U.S. 1003 (2003).

—Court properly exercised its discretion in precluding defendant from attempting to impeach his own witness, since he failed to satisfy the requirements of CPL § 60.35. People v. Hall, 266 A.D.2d 160, 700 N.Y.S.2d 105 (1st Dept. 1999).

—Defendant's generalized objections, followed later in trial by untimely mistrial motion, failed to preserve his challenge to prosecutor's attempt to impeach her own witness without satisfying the requirements of CPL § 60.35(1). People v. Kello, 267 A.D.2d 123, 700 N.Y.S.2d 150 (1st Dept. 1999), aff'd, 96 N.Y.2d 740, 723 N.Y.S.2d 111, 746 N.E.2d 166 (2001) (mem.).

—Court properly disallowed the defendant's attempt to impeach the testimony of his own witness using a police report which the witness neither signed nor made under oath. People v. Whittington, 267 A.D.2d 486, 699 N.Y.S.2d 733 (2d Dept. 1999).

Improper use of prior inconsistent statement.—Prosecutor's use of prior unsworn statements of a prosecution witness to impeach that witness violated CPL § 60.35(1), but error was harmless where unsworn statements were no different from the witness's sworn statements which were also used to impeach him, and the court repeatedly instructed the jury to disregard the evidence of the unsworn statements. People v. Shuler, 238 A.D.2d 528, 656 N.Y.S.2d 665 (2d Dept. 1997).

—Conviction reversed where prosecutor repeatedly impeached his own witnesses with prior inconsistent statements and compounded the error when, on summation, he denigrated their credibility and called attention to the fact that he had impeached their testimony with prior statements. People v. Dowdall, 236 A.D.2d 836, 654 N.Y.S.2d 72 (4th Dept. 1997).

Past recollection recorded; evidence.—A written

memorandum given by a witness who at trial, after reading it remains unable or unwilling to testify as to its contents is admissible at trial as substantive evidence of the truth of its contents provided that otherwise competent testimony establishes that (1) the witness once had knowledge of the contents of the memorandum; (2) the memorandum was prepared by the witness or at his direction; (3) the memorandum was prepared when the knowledge of the contents was fresh in the mind of the witness; and (4) the witness intended, when the memorandum was made that it be accurate. People v. Raja, 77 A.D.2d 322, 433 N.Y.S.2d 200 (2d Dept. 1980).

Preliminary hearing; ground for reversal.—Failure to provide pretrial minutes on timely demand is a ground for reversal without a showing of prejudice, and presumably may not be treated as harmless error. In this case, the guilt of the defendant had been established in part by identification by the victim; however, the victim's description at trial of defendant's facial hair differed from his earlier description at the hearing. People v. Peacock, 31 N.Y.2d 907, 340 N.Y.S.2d 642, 292 N.E.2d 785 (1972).

Prior inconsistent statement inadmissible where it does not tend to disprove position of party calling witness.— Prosecution was forewarned that witness would state at trial that he did not recollect matters to which he testified before grand jury; his grand jury testimony accordingly, was inadmissible as prior inconsistent statements, since noncommittal testimony of a failure to recollect is not testimony tending to disprove position of party calling witness, who was forewarned. People v. Fitzpatrick, 40 N.Y.2d 44, 386 N.Y.S.2d 28, 351 N.E.2d 675 (1976).

—Testimony by People's witness that she did not recall whether the defendant had admitted stabbing the decedent did not "tend to disprove" the People's case, but merely failed to corroborate or bolster it and was an insufficient basis to allow impeachment by introducing a prior written statement to police that defendant had told her that he had stabbed the decedent. People v. Knatz, 76 A.D.2d 889, 428 N.Y.S.2d 709 (2d Dept. 1980).

—Court erred in permitting the People to impeach a witness, Thomas, an inmate whom defendant attacked at Coxsackie Facility, with his grand jury testimony, because Thomas's testimony did not tend to disprove the People's possession or affirmatively damage the People's case, as required for impeachment by CPL § 60.35; however, in view of the overwhelming evidence, error was harmless. People v. Andujar, 290 A.D.2d 654, 736 N.Y.S.2d 159 (3d Dept. 2002).

Referral to written statement.—Prosecutor did not impeach his own witness in violation of CPL § 60.35 when he referred a witness with faulty recollection to a written statement without revealing its contents. People v. Edwards, 232 A.D.2d 342, 649 N.Y.S.2d 408 (1st Dept. 1996), *cert. denied,* 522 U.S. 1121 (1998).

View at scene, unable to identify suspect one hour later.— The complainant had an opportunity to view defendant at crime scene, was unable to identify him one hour later at the station house but identified him in court. When there is reason to believe that the witness' observations were not recorded or have since been forgotten, his opportunity to observe may be entitled to little or no significance and the People bear a heavier burden to show by other circumstances that the witness formed a firm image of the offender and that it persists. People v. McCullers. 33 N.Y.2d 806, 350 N.Y.S.2d 904, 305 N.E.2d 914 (1973).

Written statement of complainant.—Written statement of complaining witness not admissible to impeach third party who signed statement as a witness. People v. Dackowski, 50 N.Y.2d 962, 431 N.Y.S.2d 463, 409 N.E.2d 937 (1980).

§ 60.40. Rules of evidence; proof of previous conviction; when allowed.

1. If in the course of a criminal proceeding, any witness, including a defendant, is properly asked whether he was previously convicted of a specified offense and answers in the negative or in an equivocal manner, the party adverse to the one who called him may independently prove such conviction. If in response to proper inquiry whether he has ever been convicted of any offense the witness answers in the negative or in an equivocal manner, the adverse party may independently prove any previous conviction of the witness.

2. If a defendant in a criminal proceeding, through the testimony of a witness called by him, offers evidence of his good character, the people may independently prove any previous conviction of the defendant for an offense the commission of which would tend to negate any character trait or quality attributed to the defendant in such witness' testimony.

3. Subject to the limitations prescribed in section 200.60, the people may prove that a defendant has been previously convicted of an offense when the fact of such previous conviction constitutes an element of the offense charged, or proof thereof is otherwise essential to the establishment of a legally sufficient case.

ANNOTATIONS

Admissibility of uncharged crimes.—In sexual assault prosecution, the evidence regarding the defendant's repeated failure to pay child support and his demand for sex was properly admitted as supplying necessary background information. People v. Martinez, 202 A.D.2d 182, 608 N.Y.S.2d 206 (1st Dept. 1994).

—The trial court properly admitted evidence that the defendant and an unidentified perpetrator committed another robbery minutes after the charged crimes as being relevant to the issue of identity. People v. Archie, 200 A.D.2d 676, 607 N.Y.S.2d 55 (2d Dept. 1994).

—Evidence that the defendant menaced his acquaintance with a gun, and that he was on parole at the time, was properly admitted, because the defendant's motive for shooting the police officer arose from the fact that the officer had observed him with a loaded firearm in his hand, a violation of his parole. People v. Robinson, 200 A.D.2d 693, 606 N.Y.S.2d 908 (2d Dept. 1994).

—During the course of direct and cross-examination, the defendant placed his character and past conduct toward women in issue by testifying, in substance, that his personal attitudes and standards regarding the treatment of women precluded him from engaging in the type of conduct alleged during the trial. Therefore, the trial court did not err in ruling that the defendant had "opened the door" to limited questioning about the sexual misconduct case. People v. Mays, 187 A.D.2d 535, 589 N.Y.S.2d 922 (2d Dept. 1992).

—Certificate of conviction and Department of Motor Vehicles abstract were properly before grand jury which was considering charges of felony DWI and aggravated unlicensed operation of motor vehicle. People v. Keller, 214 A.D.2d 825, 625 N.Y.S.2d 325 (3d Dept. 1995).

—The trial court was correct in admitting evidence of prior uncharged crimes where the victim of a robbery was unable to identify her assailant and defendant had previously been involved in crimes involving the cutting of girls' hair, a pattern similar to the present case. People v. Rossman, 95 A.D.2d 873, 463 N.Y.S.2d 891 (3d Dept. 1983).

Age.—The fact that the court permitted limited inquiry into a conviction more than ten years old did not deprive the defendant of a fair trial. People v. Walker, 189 A.D.2d 620, 621, 592 N.Y.S.2d 321, 322 (1st Dept. 1993), *aff'd,* 83 N.Y.2d 455, 611 N.Y.S.2d 118, 633 N.E.2d 472 (1994).

—The mere staleness of a witness's prior conviction is not, alone, reason to preclude impeachment. People v. Clancy, 191 A.D.2d 346, 347, 596 N.Y.S.2d 3, 4 (1st Dept. 1993).

—The age of a conviction in and of itself does not preclude the prosecutor from using it to cross-examine the defendant, particularly where the court utilizes a *Sandoval* compromise. People v. Zillinger, 179 A.D.2d 382, 578 N.Y.S.2d 153 (1st Dept. 1992); People v. Teen, 200 A.D.2d 785, 606 N.Y.S.2d 922 (3d Dept. 1994).

Aliases.—Defendant was not deprived of a fair trial by virtue of testimony concerning his use of an alias when initially questioned by the police. People v. Dobbs, 148 A.D.2d 627, 539 N.Y.S.2d 90 (2d Dept. 1989).

Character evidence.—Court's pronouncement in criminal prosecution that provable reputation would be limited to that current in one's "residential neighborhood" was too restrictive; a reputation may grow wherever an individual's associations are of such quantity and quality as to permit him to be personally observed by a sufficient number of individuals to give reasonable assurance of reliability. People v. Bouton, 50 N.Y.2d 130, 428 N.Y.S.2d 218, 50 N.E.2d 130 (1980).

—Although it was error to permit cross-examination of defendant's wife regarding defendant's prior criminal record where the wife, on direct examination, had not testified as a character witness, in view of the court's curative instructions and the overwhelming evidence against defendant and the lack of significant probability of acquittal absent such testimony, this cross-examination constituted harmless error. People v. Cruz, 47 N.Y.2d 838, 418 N.Y.S.2d 578, 392 N.E.2d 565 (1979).

—The district attorney should not have asked defendant's character witness whether he would change his opinion of defendant's character if he had heard that defendant had committed a cold-blooded murder since the question improperly assumed that the defendant was guilty of the crime with which he was charged, the very issue toward the determination of which the character evidence was offered. People v. Lopez, 67 A.D.2d 624, 411 N.Y.S.2d 627 (1st Dept. 1979). *See also* People v. Pryor, 70 A.D.2d 805, 417 N.Y.S.2d 490 (1st Dept. 1979) (robbery).

—When defendant put his character into issue, the trial court properly permitted the People to cross-examine the defendant as to his illegal entries into the United States. People v. Bravo, 154 A.D.2d 690, 691, 546 N.Y.S.2d 892, 893 (2d Dept. 1989).

—It was error for the prosecutor to have referred to a character witness who could have been called by the defendant as it is clear that the defendant does not have a duty to call any witness. People v. Thompson, 75 A.D.2d 830, 427 N.Y.S.2d 464 (2d Dept. 1980).

Conviction of other crimes; admission into evidence not cured by subsequent striking and instructions to jury.— Reversal was required where evidence of the defendant's prior criminal record was placed before the jury since he had not testified and his character had not been placed in issue. People v. Mullin, 41 N.Y.2d 475, 393 N.Y.S.2d 938, 362 N.E.2d 571 (1977).

—Court's striking testimony that was inadmissible and admonishing jury not to consider it, done at conclusion of trial, could not cure error of allowing inadmissible testimony of other convictions into evidence in the first place. People v. Johnson, 38 A.D.2d 744, 329 N.Y.S.2d 914 (2d Dept. 1972).

Credibility.—Trial court did not abuse discretion by permitting the People to inquire into the underlying facts of defendant's numerous convictions merely because they were similar to the instant charge where such ruling was for the assessment of credibility and not to demonstrate defendant's propensity to commit such crimes. People v. Sito, 114 A.D.2d 1049, 495 N.Y.S.2d 487 (2d Dept. 1985).

Criminal bent.—While evidence of other crimes cannot be proffered solely for the purpose of showing that a defendant is of a such criminal bent that he is likely to have committed the crime charged, it is within the discretion of the trial judge to decide whether the probative worth of evidence of other crimes on the issue of defendant's credibility outweighs the risk of unfair prejudice. People v. Pavao, 59 N.Y.2d 282, 464 N.Y.S.2d 458, 451 N.E.2d 216 (1983).

Criminal record of witness.—Where the parties, long after the prosecution witness was excused and just before the case was submitted to the jury, learned of the witness's criminal record and stipulated to call it to the jury's attention, it was a practical solution designed to avoid delay in continuing the trial and met the desire of the defense to have the witness's criminal record before the jury. People v. Brown, 62 A.D.2d 715, 405 N.Y.S.2d 691 (1st Dept. 1978), *aff'd,* 48 N.Y.2d 921, 425 N.Y.S.2d 54, 401 N.E.2d 177 (1979).

—Prosecutor could be permitted to recall alibi witness in order to rebut witness' prior testimony as to record of convictions. People v. Musmacher, 181 A.D.2d 920, 581 N.Y.S.2d 440 (2d Dept. 1992).

Cross-examination; previous conviction; modus operandi.—Cross-examination as to the underlying facts of a similar crime, for which the defendant had been convicted, to show modus operandi was improper. People v. Vickerstaff, 68 A.D.2d 918, 414 N.Y.S.2d 192 (2d Dept. 1979).

Cross-examination; impeachment; prior convictions.— The age of the conviction, in and of itself, does not preclude the prosecutor from using it to cross-examine the defendant particularly where the court utilizes a *Sandoval* compromise. People v. Zillinger, 179 A.D.2d 382, 578 N.Y.S.2d 153 (1st Dept. 1992).

—The fact that the defendant was the only material source of testimony in support of his defense, while relevant, is but one factor to consider in determining whether inquiry should be permitted into a prior conviction. People v. Grice, 177 A.D.2d 271, 272, 576 N.Y.S.2d 13, 14 (1st Dept. 1991).

—In a prosecution involving the theft of an automobile, the People should not have been permitted to cross-examine the defendant, had he elected to testify, regarding two previous convictions for possession of stolen property, both of which involved the theft of an automobile; the crime of possession of stolen property is not one such as is inherently relevant to the question of defendant's credibility. People v. Johnson, 64 A.D.2d 907, 408 N.Y.S.2d 519 (2d Dept. 1978), *aff'd,* 48 N.Y.2d 674, 421 N.Y.S.2d 881, 397 N.E.2d 392 (1979).

—Questioning concerning other crimes is not automatically precluded simply because the crimes to be inquired about are similar to the crime charged. People v. Estrada, 171 A.D.2d 948, 567 N.Y.S.2d 893 (3d Dept. 1991).

Sandoval standing; federal rule distinguished from state rule.—Upon a retrial of an armed robbery case following a hung jury, the law of the case doctrine did not require the successor trial judge to adhere to the *Sandoval* ruling made at the first trial, and the judge was free to exercise his discretion in deciding whether to revisit the issue or to defer to the earlier discretionary ruling of the judge at the prior trial. People v. Evans, 94 N.Y.2d 499, 706 N.Y.S.2d 678, 727 N.E.2d 1232 (2000).

—In contrast to federal law, *Sandoval* does not require a defendant to take the stand in order to contest a trial court's ruling as to the scope of cross-examination permitted concerning prior convictions. People v. Contreras, 108 A.D.2d 627, 485 N.Y.S.2d 261 (1st Dept. 1985).

—Statute gives adverse party the discretion to cross-examine defendant for impeachment on basis of his answers concerning a prior criminal record as distinguished from Federal rule which gives discretion to Court. People v. Pritchett, 69 Misc. 2d 67, 329 N.Y.S.2d 147 (Sup. Ct. Queens Co. 1972).

Cross-examinations; offenses committed subsequent to crime charged.—Trial court abused discretion in denying motion to preclude cross-examination for purposes of impeachment regarding sexual offenses committed subsequent to one for which defendant was standing trial; such cross-examination prevented defendant from testifying without running risk of prejudicing himself before the jury. People v. Smith, 60 A.D.2d 963, 401 N.Y.S.2d 606 (4th Dept. 1978).

Cross-examination; prior conviction.—Cross-examination of defendant did not have to be limited to the mere existence of prior convictions, as the Appellate Division erroneously required, but it properly included the nature of the crimes, even where the prior crimes are similar to the pending charges. People v. Hayes, 97 N.Y.2d 203, 738 N.Y.S.2d 663, 764 N.E.2d 963 (2002).

—It was not error for the prosecutor to question defendant on the allegations that defendant misappropriated funds, as treasurer, from a corporation, since this is also relevant to defendant's credibility and a proper subject for cross-examination. People v. Antilla, 156 A.D.2d 189, 548 N.Y.S.2d 445 (1st Dept. 1989), *aff'd,* 77 N.Y.2d 853, 568 N.Y.S.2d 9, 569 N.E.2d 868 (1991).

—A court may permit questioning on a prior conviction pending on appeal, as long as the inquiry is limited to the fact of the conviction, and not the underlying facts. People v. Galvin, 253 A.D.2d 437, 676 N.Y.S.2d 626 (2d Dept. 1998).

—Court properly permitted prosecutor to make inquiry regarding the defendant's prior conviction for attempted possession of a forged instrument since that conviction involved an act of individual dishonesty ahead of the interest of society and was directly relevant to the issue of credibility. People v. Jones, 145 A.D.2d 509, 535 N.Y.S.2d 109 (2d Dept. 1988).

—A dismissal in satisfaction of a plea is not an acquittal which would preclude a prosecutor in the future from inquiring as to the underlying acts of the crime since it is not a dismissal on the merits. People v. Alberti, 77 A.D.2d 602, 430 N.Y.S.2d 6 (2d Dept.), *cert. denied,* 449 U.S. 1018 (1980).

—Cross-examination relative to defendant's prior murder conviction was proper despite the fact that an appeal was pending on the conviction. People v. Lee, 55 A.D.2d 658, 390 N.Y.S.2d 134 (2d Dept. 1976).

—Defendant was deprived of his right to a fair trial when the prosecutor persisted, on cross-examination, in delving at length and in detail into the underlying facts of defendant's prior conviction after the defendant had admitted the conviction on direct examination and the District Attorney again alluded to the former conviction as part of his assessment of defendant's character and reputation in his summation. People v. Burgess, 50 A.D.2d 1036, 377 N.Y.S.2d 724 (3d Dept. 1975).

—The court did not err in permitting the prosecutor to question the defendant about his alleged acts of sexual abuse against the daughter of a prosecution witness; such evidence was independently admissible to explain why the witness, previously friendly to and under the control of the defendant recanted her prior statement which exculpated the defendant. People v. Jones, 156 A.D.2d 934, 548 N.Y.S.2d 824 (4th Dept. 1989).

—Questioning concerning other crimes is not automatically precluded simply because the crimes to be inquired about are similar to the crimes charged. People v. Lotz, 145 A.D.2d 900, 536 N.Y.S.2d 281 (4th Dept. 1988).

Proof of previous convictions.—The exclusion of prior convictions is largely, if not completely, a matter of discretion which rests with the trial courts and fact-reviewing intermediate courts. People v. Shields, 46 N.Y.2d 764, 413 N.Y.S.2d 649, 386 N.E.2d 257 (1978).

—The methods provided by CPL § 60.30 of proving a prior conviction are not exclusive and the judgment of conviction could be proved by other competent proof, including the original court records. People v. Wenstley, 152 A.D.2d 1000, 1002, 544 N.Y.S.2d 96, 97 (4th Dept. 1989).

—It was error to rule admissible for impeachment purposes certain prior bail forfeitures and convictions relating to public intoxication which occurred eleven and twelve years earlier because of their remoteness in time coupled with the limited probative value of the type of offense involved under the *Sandoval* rule; the error was harmless where more recent convictions were ruled admissible, including one for assault second degree, and therefore there was little likelihood that the error prompted defendant not to testify or otherwise caused prejudice. People v. Williams, 84 A.D.2d 966, 446 N.Y.S.2d 716 (4th Dept. 1981).

Crime for which defendants had not been arrested.—Reference to defendant's possession of bullets did not constitute evidence of an uncharged crime. People v. Perez, 191 A.D.2d 285, 595 N.Y.S.2d 33 (1st Dept. 1993), *modified,* 83 N.Y.2d 269, 609 N.Y.S.2d 564, 631 N.E.2d 570 (1994).

—Although it was error for the trial court to permit cross-examination of the defendant charged with first degree manslaughter, regarding a prior assault that he had committed against the victim in the instant case, without giving a limiting instruction to the jury on the use of such testimony, where the totality of the proof against the defendant overwhelmingly established his guilt and there was no significant probability that the jury would have acquitted the defendant had the error not occurred the error must be considered harmless. People v. Brown, 78 A.D.2d 903, 433 N.Y.S.2d 208 (2d Dept. 1980).

—It was error to allow the prosecutor to portray defendant and co-defendant who had earlier pleaded guilty, as large-scale drug dealers and, thus, introduce evidence of uncharged crimes for the impermissible purpose of implying that the defendant was guilty of the crimes charged. People v. Bryant, 77 A.D.2d 603, 430 N.Y.S.2d 101 (2d Dept. 1980).

—In prosecution for arson and attempted grand larceny arising from the burning of defendant's insured residence, it was prejudicial error to receive, over objection, evidence relating to the burning of the defendant's residence four years earlier. People v. Vincek, 75 A.D.2d 412, 429 N.Y.S.2d 928 (4th Dept. 1980).

Defendant's witness; opening the door.—Where defendant's prior criminal record and the nature of the crime were disclosed by his witnesses, the door had been opened and cross-examination directed toward those matters was proper and the scope thereof rested solely in the sound discretion of the trial court. People v. Lewis, 43 A.D.2d 989, 352 N.Y.S.2d 248 (3d Dept. 1974).

Erroneous *Sandoval* ruling.—Despite sufficient evidence underlying charge of incest, conviction was reversed due to wrongful admission of prior uncharged incestuous acts the defendant allegedly committed with the victim. People v. Lewis, 69 N.Y.2d 321, 514 N.Y.S.2d 205, 506 N.E.2d 915 (1987).

—Admission into evidence of multitude of past similar crimes made it likely that the jury would have been improperly influenced by considerations of the defendant's propensity to commit the crime with which he was charged. People v. Coe, 95 A.D.2d 685, 463 N.Y.S.2d 795 (1st Dept. 1983).

—In manslaughter prosecution, court erred in allowing the defendant to be cross-examined about verbal threats he made to teachers while he was in high school. People v. Resnick, 133 A.D.2d 237, 519 N.Y.S.2d 37 (2d Dept. 1987).

Evidence; prior unindicted assault.—In rape and attempted sodomy prosecution, it was reversible error for the court to allow the introduction of evidence concerning a prior unindicted assault by defendant, to prove the complainant's fear of him, where the trial evidence disclosed that the victim had an opportunity to leave the defendant's hotel room but remained until he returned. People v. Gay, 63 A.D.2d 590, 404 N.Y.S.2d 856 (1st Dept. 1978).

Evidence of past crime.—A suspect whose right to counsel has attached with respect to a past crime may be subjected to questioning outside the presence of counsel by police who are investigating a new crime and evidence obtained thereby, if not otherwise violative of the suspect's rights, may be presented to prove the suspect's guilt of the past crime. People v. Mealer, 57 N.Y.2d 214, 455 N.Y.S.2d 562 (1982), *cert. denied,* 460 U.S. 1024 (1983).

Evidence of prior rape conviction improperly admitted.—Where primary issue in sodomy case was whether forcible compulsion was involved, trial court erred in *Sandoval* ruling permitting the cross-examination of the defendant concerning a 1978 rape conviction. People v. Cooke, 101 A.D.2d 983, 477 N.Y.S.2d 730 (3d Dept. 1984).

Evidence of uncharged illegal or immoral acts improperly admitted.—Although evidence that defendant was a member of a group antagonistic to the group of which the victim was a member was properly admitted as relevant to motive and intent, it was improper to admit extensive additional evidence as to alleged illegal, immoral or vicious acts of the defendant's group that were unrelated to the charge on trial. People v. Connally, 105 A.D.2d 797, 481 N.Y.S.2d 432 (2d Dept. 1984).

Generally.—A *Sandoval* ruling does not allow a defendant to deceive the jury and be free from confrontation; a defendant who takes the stand is obliged to speak truthfully and accurately. People v. Green, 207 A.D.2d 318, 615 N.Y.S.2d 685 (1st Dept. 1994).

—While it would have been better had the court not made the scope of its *Sandoval* ruling dependent on the nature of the defense presented at trial, defendant did not object to the court's ruling and did not demonstrate that he was prejudiced thereby. People v. Ryer, 181 A.D.2d 426, 580 N.Y.S.2d 752 (1st Dept. 1992).

—Court's *Sandoval* ruling should not be disturbed merely because the court did not provide a more detailed recitation of its underlying reasoning. People v. Ramirez, 206 A.D.2d 491, 614 N.Y.S.2d 746 (2d Dept. 1994).

Guilty plea; *Sandoval* ruling; plea; appeal.—Any objection to a *Sandoval* ruling is waived by the plea of guilty. People v. Gilliam, 65 A.D.2d 533, 409 N.Y.S.2d 401 (1st Dept. 1978).

—Defendant forfeited his right to challenge the court's adverse *Sandoval* ruling by his plea of guilty. People v. Thompson, 117 A.D.2d 637, 498 N.Y.S.2d 86 (2d Dept. 1986).

Improper change in *Sandoval* ruling.—Where court changed its *Sandoval* ruling after defendant took the stand, defendant was denied a fair trial because he had relied on court's previous *Sandoval* ruling in deciding to take the stand. People v. Grant, 234 A.D.2d 475, 651 N.Y.S.2d 564 (2d Dept. 1996).

***Sandoval*; scope of cross-examination.**—Where defendant, who had prior convictions for knife-point robberies in Central Park, made equivocal statements on cross-examination about whether Central Park was a dangerous place, the trial court erred in permitting the prosecutor to cross-examine defendant about his two prior crimes which the court's *Sandoval* ruling had previously disallowed; defendant's remarks on cross-examination were ambiguous and could not be construed, as the People urged, as assertions that he had not previously committed robberies in Central Park, which would thereby open the door to this questioning. People v. Moore, 92 N.Y.2d 823, 677 N.Y.S.2d 56, 699 N.E.2d 415 (1998).

—The considerations for determining when cross-examination should be allowed, enunciated in *Sandoval* are also applicable to alleged immoral, vicious or criminal acts, regardless of whether those acts resulted in convictions. People v. Kennedy, 47 N.Y.2d 196, 417 N.Y.S.2d 452, 391 N.E.2d 288 (1979).

—In prosecution for criminal sale of a controlled substance, third degree, the trial court committed reversible error in permitting extensive cross-examination of the defendant on prior drug possession charges since, under the circumstances, there was too great a danger that the evidence would demonstrate a propensity to commit the crime charged rather than impeach his credibility. People v. Carmack, 44 N.Y.2d 706, 405 N.Y.S.2d 446, 376 N.E.2d 919 (1978).

—Cross-examination with respect to crimes or conduct similar to that of which the defendant is presently charged may be highly prejudicial, in view of the risk, despite the most clear and forceful limiting instructions to the contrary, that the evidence will be taken as some proof of the commission of the crime charged rather than be reserved solely to the issue of credibility. People v. Dickman, 42 N.Y.2d 294, 397 N.Y.S.2d 754, 366 N.E.2d 843 (1977).

—The extent to which disparaging questions, not relevant to the issues, but bearing on the credibility of a witness, may be put upon cross-examination is discretionary with the trial court and it s rulings are not subject to review, unless it clearly appears that the discretion has been abused. People v. Duffy, 36 N.Y.2d 258, 367 N.Y.S.2d 236, 326 N.E.2d 84, *modified on other grounds*, 36 N.Y.2d 857, 370 N.Y.S.2d 919, 331 N.E.2d 695 (1975), *cert. denied*, 423 U.S. 861 (1975); *but see* People v. Santiago, 47 A.D.2d 476, 367 N.Y.S.2d 280 (1st Dept. 1975).

—Where defense counsel sought prospective ruling as to permissible scope of cross-examination regarding prior criminal acts, on basis of which defendant decided whether to take stand in own defense, it was not error to permit cross-examination to include evidence of prior criminal acts, bearing logically and reasonably on issue of credibility, but such evidence would be inadmissible when it has no purpose other than to show that defendant is of criminal character. People v. Sandoval, 34 N.Y.2d 371, 357 N.Y.S.2d 849, 314 N.E.2d 413 (1974).

—The similarity between the crimes charged and defendant's past convictions posed a special problem for the court but the mere fact that defendant's prior convictions were in the main sex crimes did not insulate him from cross-examination regarding them. People v. Harris, 162 A.D.2d 195, 196, 556 N.Y.S.2d 320, 321 (1st Dept. 1990).

—The fact that defendant chose to specialize in one type of criminal activity did not shield him from impeachment by use of prior convictions. People v. Mack, 6 A.D.3d 551, 775 N.Y.S.2d 345 (2d Dept. 2004).

—In prosecution for criminal possession of a controlled substance, the fact that the *Sandoval* ruling permitted inquiry into the fact of prior misdemeanor convictions for the sale of marijuana, conduct which bore directly on the defendant's credibility, did not warrant a conclusion that defendant was unduly prejudiced. People v. Brown, 195 A.D.2d 419, 601 N.Y.S.2d 701 (2d Dept. 1993).

—Questions concerning other crimes are not automatically precluded simply because the crimes to be inquired about are similar to the crimes charged. People v. Miller, 199 A.D.2d 422, 423, 605 N.Y.S.2d 342, 343 (2d Dept. 1993); People v. Guzman, 197 A.D.2d 705, 603 N.Y.S.2d 52 (2d Dept. 1993).

—The prosecution may inquire as to the facts underlying a youthful offender adjudication to impeach the defendant's credibility as long as no mention is made as to the ultimate disposition. People v. Kyser, 147 A.D.2d 590, 591, 537 N.Y.S.2d 884, 885 (2d Dept. 1989).

—Court did not commit reversible error in admitting into evidence testimony concerning the defendant's uncharged crimes since this evidence was probative as to the circumstances leading up to the crime charged in the indictment. People v. Gonzalez, 131 A.D.2d 778, 517 N.Y.S.2d 83 (2d Dept. 1987).

—In view of the asserted defense of lack of knowledge and intent, the admission of evidence regarding the defendant's prior criminal possession of a forged instrument constituted a proper exercise of the trial court's discretion in prosecution for criminal possession of a forged instrument. People v. Lopez, 120 A.D.2d 679, 502 N.Y.S.2d 275 (2d Dept. 1986).

—The repeated questioning of defendant on cross-examination about a purported bad act constituted error, where the prosecution had not disclosed any uncharged crimes or bad acts at the *Sandoval* hearing, and no limiting instruction was given to the jury. People v. Marrow, 301 A.D.2d 673, 753 N.Y.S.2d 205 (3d Dept. 2003).

—In prosecution involving charge of promoting prison contraband, trial court properly found inquiry into defendant's prior conviction for possession of a weapon probative. People v. Miller, 132 A.D.2d 848, 518 N.Y.S.2d 59 (3d Dept. 1987).

—Defendant's argument that 18 alleged "bad acts" relating to theft in 1963, and a 1967 conviction for third degree burglary should not be available for cross-examination since they were remote and not the product of "calculated violence" was unpersuasive, where, upon trial for first degree sexual abuse, the *Sandoval* Court precluded inquiry into the underlying basis of defendant's 1980 conviction for first degree rape. People v. Patterson, 88 A.D.2d 694, 451 N.Y.S.2d 321 (3d Dept. 1982), *aff'd*, 59 N.Y.2d 794, 464 N.Y.S.2d 751, 451 N.E.2d 498 (1983).

—Trial court did not abuse its discretion by ruling if defendant takes the stand he could be cross-examined regarding facts underlying a pending indictment charging him with another robbery. People v. Edwards, 80 A.D.2d 993, 437 N.Y.S.2d 479 (4th Dept. 1981).

Opening the door.—Trial court properly modified its *Sandoval* ruling where defendant's direct testimony at trial that he was just a drug user was misleading and conveyed the impression that he was not a seller, thereby opening the door to inquiry into his prior conviction for an attempted sale. People v. Jones, 238 A.D.2d 251, 656 N.Y.S.2d 611 (1st Dept. 1997).

Prior convictions; impeachment of defendant.— Defendant, by not testifying at trial, waived appellate review of his motion *in limine* under Rule 609(a), Fed. Rules of Evidence, to preclude the prosecution from using a prior conviction to impeach his testimony should he take the stand at trial; an appellate court is unable to weight the probative value of the conviction against its prejudicial impact without knowing the precise nature of defendant's testimony. Luce v. United States, 469 U.S. 38, 105 S. Ct. 460, 83 L. Ed. 2d 443 (1984).

—Court's *Sandoval* ruling was proper, particularly where it denied inquiry into over 15 other convictions or alleged bad acts, and simply allowed inquiry into 6 convictions and 2 bad acts. People v. Winney, 180 A.D.2d 913, 914, 580 N.Y.S.2d 801, 802 (3d Dept. 1992).

Prior criminal conduct admissible.—After a thorough *Ventimiglia* hearing, court properly admitted evidence of defendant's 1992 robbery conviction for the purpose of establishing his identification as the perpetrator of the crimes charged. Defendant's current and prior crimes shared a sufficiently distinctive modus operandi whereby defendant and his accomplices robbed persons in Manhattan's jewelry district, during the evening rush hour, as they carried packages of jewelry for delivery. The slight differences between the charged and prior crimes did not render the prior crime inadmissible. People v. Daily, 297 A.D.2d 562, 747 N.Y.S.2d 85 (1st Dept. 2002).

—In a prosecution based upon cashing bad checks, evidence of the defendant's prior criminal conduct involving the issuing of five bad checks was admissible to negate the possibility of mistake and to establish that the defendant acted with the requisite intent. People v. Renzulli, 100 A.D.2d 945, 474 N.Y.S.2d 834 (2d Dept. 1984).

Witness; *Sandoval* rule not applicable.—The *Sandoval* procedure is inapplicable to witnesses who are not defendants, however a trial court is not precluded from entertaining an application for a ruling *in limine* on the permissible scope of cross-examination concerning a nonparty's prior misdeeds, or, if it believes it best, from refusing to do so in advance of the time when the question presents itself in regular course; the point is that, as to a nondefendant, a court is under no compunction whatsoever to deal procedurally with cross-examination on prior criminal, vicious or immoral acts in any way that departs from that employed in the regulation of cross-examination generally. People v. Ocasio, 47 N.Y.2d 55, 416 N.Y.S.2d 581, 389 N.E.2d 1101 (1979).

—Judgment of conviction for assault, second degree, reversed and new trial ordered where the trial judge in considering defendant's *Sandoval* motion only took into account "the defendant's prior propensities for committing violent acts." People v. Mayrant, 43 N.Y.2d 165, 401 N.Y.S.2d 165, 372 N.E.2d 1 (1977).

—When the witness is not the defendant, there is no danger that the jury will apply the evidence of prior acts of misconduct to anything but the witness's credibility; therefore there is no proper basis for applying the *Sandoval* rule to cross examination of a nondefendant witness regarding prior immoral, vicious or criminal acts. People v. Allen, 67 A.D.2d 558, 416 N.Y.S.2d 49 (2d Dept. 1979), *aff'd,* 50 N.Y.2d 898, 430 N.Y.S.2d 588, 408 N.E.2d 917 (1980).

—The prosecution was under no duty to open its file to the defendant in the absence of any particularization in defendant's oral motion for information concerning prior "bad acts." People v. Travison, 59 A.D.2d 404, 400 N.Y.S.2d 188 (3d Dept. 1977), *aff'd,* 46 N.Y.2d 758, 413 N.Y.S.2d 648, 386 N.E.2d 256, *cert. denied,* 441 U.S. 949.

Sandoval **motion.**—The decision in People v. Dokes, 79 N.Y.2d 656, 584 N.Y.S.2d 761, 595 N.E.2d 836 (1992), is to apply retroactively. People v. Favor, 82 N.Y.2d 254, 604 N.Y.S.2d 494, 624 N.E.2d 633 (1993).

—A defendant has the right to be present during *Sandoval* hearing, except when his or her presence would be superfluous. People v. Dokes, 79 N.Y.2d 656, 584 N.Y.S.2d 761, 595 N.E.2d 836 (1992).

—There was no error in the court's *Sandoval* procedures, presuming that the court, sitting in its other capacity as fact finder, exercised objectivity in its consideration of defendant's criminal record. People v. Herrington, 194 A.D.2d 379, 598 N.Y.S.2d 501 (1st Dept. 1993).

—Defendant's claim that he was absent from the *Sandoval* hearing was rejected where he failed to overcome the presumption of regularity attached to the proceeding, as the record strongly suggested that he was in fact present. People v. Michalek, 194 A.D.2d 568, 569, 598 N.Y.S.2d 565, 567 (2d Dept. 1993), *modified.* 82 N.Y.2d 906, 609 N.Y.S.2d 172, 631 N.E.2d 114 (1994).

—Where a defendant fails to make a sufficiently broad *Sandoval* application, he will be deprived only of the benefit of an advance ruling regarding any prior convictions or misconduct not specified in the motion; he retains the right to object at trial to prejudicial cross-examination, and when his objection challenges inquiry into his prior misconduct, he is entitled to a ruling based upon the same criteria as would have been applied had the issue been raised before trial. People v. Ortero, 75 A.D.2d 168, 428 N.Y.S.2d 765 (2d Dept. 1980).

—It is defendant who has the burden of bringing to the court's attention the particular convictions for which he wants an advance ruling as to admissibility. People v. Munck, 190 A.D.2d 963, 964, 594 N.Y.S.2d 77, 79 (3d Dept. 1993).

—Reversal of the conviction was required because defendant's absence from the *Sandoval* hearing held in chambers deprived him of his constitutional right to be present during all material stages of the trial. People v. Brown, 195 A.D.2d 1055, 601 N.Y.S.2d 727 (4th Dept. 1993).

Sandoval; **necessity for hearing.**—Trial court must make a determination that the probative value of evidence of uncharged crimes outweighs its potential prejudice to the defendant before permitting such evidence before the jury, preferably at a hearing where the court can assess how the evidence came into the case, its relevance and probative value as against its prejudicial value and either admit or exclude it in whole or in part. People v. Sudler, 100 A.D.2d 915, 474 N.Y.S.2d 575 (2d Dept. 1984).

—If a *Sandoval* hearing is to be effective there must be at least an informal hearing at which a record is made so that the details of the prior crime or bad act may be elaborated for review and so that the defendant may be given an opportunity to demonstrate the prejudice accruing to him if the jury is permitted to hear the evidence. People v. Anderson, 75 A.D.2d 988, 429 N.Y.S.2d 117 (4th Dept. 1980).

Sandoval **hearing; waiver.**—Defendant waived right to a ruling on his *Sandoval* motion when he testified on his own

behalf at trial without first requesting a ruling on that portion of his pretrial motions upon which the court had previously reserved its decision. People v. Innis, 98 A.D.2d 808, 470 N.Y.S.2d 26 (2d Dept. 1983).

Sandoval; **court must exercise its discretion.**—Since the record of the *Sandoval* hearing gave no indication that the court engaged in any exercise of its discretionary power to weigh the various relevant factors and the only factor it appeared to consider was whether the prior convictions indicated defendant's willingness to place his own interests above those of society, the conviction was reversed and the case remitted for a new trial; willingness to place his own interests above those of society is only one of the factors to be considered and should not be definitive since nearly every crime indicates such a willingness. People v. Williams, 56 N.Y.2d 236, 451 N.Y.S.2d 690, 436 N.E.2d 1292 (1982).

—The general and preferable procedure is for a trial court to rule on the *Sandoval* issues before trial. People v. Atkinson, 171 A.D.2d 430, 431, 567 N.Y.S.2d 12, 13 (1st Dept. 1991).

—Court's abuse of discretion in deciding *Sandoval* motion did not warrant reversal in view of strong proof of guilt. People v. Holman, 172 A.D.2d 245, 246, 568 N.Y.S.2d 371, 372 (1st Dept. 1991).

—While the trial court should have made a complete record of its *Sandoval* ruling, remittitur is not warranted where the court's ruling clearly occurred after a review of the defendant's criminal history. People v. Coe, 133 A.D.2d 165, 166, 518 N.Y.S.2d 683, 684 (2d Dept. 1983).

Sandoval **rule; questions regarding aliases.**—It was improper for the prosecutor to question the defendant about aliases used in connection with arrests made where those arrests were not subject to cross-examination under a *Sandoval* ruling because this questioning elicited information which alerted the jury to criminal involvement by the defendant which was excluded under the ruling. People v. Evans, 88 A.D.2d 604, 449 N.Y.S.2d 762 (2d Dept. 1982).

Sandoval **timing of motions.**—*Sandoval* ruling permits motions both before and during trial when circumstances warrant. People v. Mackey, 49 N.Y.2d 274, 425 N.Y.S.2d 288, 401 N.E.2d 398 (1980).

Sandoval; **non-jury trials.**—*Sandoval* rule does not apply to non-jury trials. People v. Rosa, 96 Misc. 2d 491, 409 N.Y.S.2d 117 (Crim. Ct. N.Y.C. 1978).

Sandoval; **subsequent reversal of prior conviction about which defendant is cross-examined.**—Where defendant's *Sandoval* motion to prevent cross-examination regarding a prior conviction was denied, reversal of defendant's conviction was required and a new trial ordered when the prior conviction was subsequently reversed on appeal. People v. Pasquino, 65 A.D.2d 629, 409 N.Y.S.2d 518 (2d Dept. 1978).

Sandoval **compromise.**—The *Sandoval* compromise permits the prosecutor to ask the defendant one question: Has he even been convicted of a felony or a misdemeanor?; the prosecutor cannot go into the underlying facts of the convictions. People v. Bermudez, 98 Misc. 2d 704, 414 N.Y.S.2d 645 (Sup. Ct. N.Y. Co. 1979).

Sandoval **stipulation.**—It was error for the District Attorney, when questioning the defendant concerning a previous robbery conviction, to elicit that the victim had been stabbed in the back, after counsel had entered into a *Sandoval* stipulation to the effect that the defendant might be questioned about the prior robbery conviction but was not to be questioned with regard to an accompanying homicide for which the defendant was not convicted. People v. Moven, 70 A.D.2d 846, 418 N.Y.S.2d 9 (1st Dept. 1979).

Sandoval **ruling; balance required.**—*Sandoval* ruling which permitted examination of the defendant's criminal background without limitation was error since it did not strike a balance between the prosecutor's right to impeach defendant's credibility and the danger of establishing in the minds of the jury a propensity of defendant to the commit crimes charged; defendant did not testify and there was a close identification question and a strong alibi. People v. Perez, 102 A.D.2d 797, 477 N.Y.S.2d 338 (1st Dept. 1984).

Evidence; defendant asked about prior arrest.—In a prosecution for attempted rape, the Assistant District Attorney's question which tended to emphasize the similarity between the assault being tried and a prior one approached the outer limits of discretionary admissibility of prior immoral acts bearing on a defendant's credibility, but did not constitute reversible error since the defendant categorically denied the previous attack, and ADA did not dwell on these questions. People v. Bowen, 65 A.D.2d 364, 411 N.Y.S.2d 573 (1st Dept. 1978), aff'd, 50 N.Y.2d 915, 431 N.Y.S.2d 449, 409 N.E.2d 924 (1980).

—In prosecution for burglary in the second degree and other charges, the prosecutor's conduct in asking the defendant whether he recalled being arrested on a particular date while it did not require reversal of conviction, was improper. Asking a person charged with a crime whether he has previously been arrested is incompetent and irrelevant and tends to be prejudicial. People v. Woolson, 42 A.D.2d 824, 345 N.Y.S.2d 799 (4th Dept. 1973).

Evidence; identification from photographs inadmissible.—A new trial was required where police mug shots of the defendant, which predated the present trial offense, were admitted as evidence of his prior appearance since the prison numerals across defendant's chest in the photographs were taped over and could have had the effect of emphasizing their nature rather than ameliorating the problem. People v. Carroll, 61 A.D.2d 760, 402 N.Y.S.2d 8 (1st Dept. 1978).

Immoral acts.—In a case of robbery, burglary and assault, it was within the court's discretion to permit the prosecutor to impeach the defendant's credibility by questioning him about a prior conviction involving sodomy of an eight-year-old girl since defendant's conviction was not irrelevant to the question of his veracity. People v. Bennatte, 56 N.Y.2d 142, 451 N.Y.S.2d 647, 436 N.E.2d 1249 (1982).

—In a prosecution for murder of two members of a religious sect in the sect's church it was not reversible error to allow testimony as to the lifestyle, religious beliefs and moral values of members that lived in the church introduced as background to establish or explain a material fact, where the evidence tended to show acts of an unusual and perhaps immoral nature but were not such as to demonstrate a propensity to commit the murders charged. People v. LeGrand, 76 A.D.2d 706, 431 N.Y.S.2d 850 (2d Dept. 1980).

Impeachment; character evidence.—It was not error for the trial court to allow the prosecutor to impeach defendant's credibility as a witness by use of pamphlets the publication of which was attributable to defendant and which advocated the evasion of all sales taxes and the cheating of the telephone company. People v. Coleman, 56 N.Y.2d 269, 451 N.Y.S.2d 705, 436 N.E.2d 1307 (1982).

Improper expansion on witness' prostitution conviction.—The prosecutor improperly expanded upon the defense witness' prior conviction on a guilty plea to prostitution to suggest a homosexual relationship between the witness and the defendant. People v. DeJesus, 88 A.D.2d 554, 450 N.Y.S.2d 488 (1st Dept. 1982).

Improper cross-examination of defendant; prior drug conviction and other drug-related incidents.—Prosecutor, upon cross-examination of defendant charged with criminal sale of a dangerous drug, should not be permitted to extensively inquire into defendant's prior history of drug addiction because there is too great a danger that the evidence would tend to demonstrate a propensity to commit the very crime for which the defendant was on trial, rather than impeach his credibility. People v. Figueroa, 62 A.D.2d 971, 404 N.Y.S.2d 348 (1st Dept. 1978).

—Ruling by trial court that if defendant testified, the prosecution could question him as to prior drug conviction and other activities created serious risk to defendant not only because of similarity of past offense to present one, but because of the widespread acceptance of the notion that the drug users are habitual offenders and necessarily violate the law to supply their habits. People v. Carmack, 52 A.D.2d 264, 383 N.Y.S.2d 738 (4th Dept. 1976), aff'd, 44 N.Y.2d 706, 405 N.Y.S.2d 446, 376 N.E.2d 919 (1978).

Military discharge.—Cross-examination concerning defendant's 1960 undesirable discharge from the military on the ground of a single homosexual act exceeded the bounds of legitimate testing of his credibility. People v. Crosby, 51 A.D.2d 902, 380 N.Y.S.2d 670 (1st Dept. 1976).

Motive.—Testimony of the prosecution witness that the defendant and his associates planned and carried out the shooting of two policemen because they had a vicious ideological hatred for the police was properly admitted to show the motive for the shooting even though it reflected on the defendant's

character and the character of his associates which was not otherwise in issue and it was for the jury to determine whether it was entitled to any weight. People v. Moore, 42 N.Y.2d 421, 397 N.Y.S.2d 975, 366 N.E.2d 1330, cert. denied, 434 U.S. 987 (1977).

Number of convictions.—The trial court erred in failing to consider the possibility that the number of convictions permitted to be disclosed might be more damaging to the defendant than was appropriate or necessary to the jury's evaluation of his credibility; but where evidence of defendant's guilt was overwhelming, there was no reason to reverse the conviction. People v. Hicks, 88 A.D.2d 519, 450 N.Y.S.2d 15 (1st Dept. 1982).

Preclusion order; cross-examination of a witness.—Preclusion order, although related expressly to use of the material on examination of defendant, foreclosed inquiry with respect to August 8, 1974 transaction on interrogation of a witness as well. People v. Williams, 46 N.Y.2d 799, 413 N.Y.S.2d 915, 386 N.E.2d 826 (1978).

Prior arrest; co-defendant.—Defendant was denied a fair trial by detective's trial testimony as to co-defendant's previous arrest, since it was reasonable to conclude that when jury discovered co-defendant had an arrest record that this fact tainted its view of the defendant. People v. Watson, 55 A.D.2d 873, 390 N.Y.S.2d 116 (1st Dept. 1977).

Questioning defense witness about defendant's previous criminal acts.—A defense witness who has not testified as a character witness on direct examination may not be cross-examined about the defendant's criminal record. However, once the defendant has introduced character evidence, the People may question the defense witness about whether he or she has heard of the defendant's previous criminal acts and the prosecutor may rebut defendant's character evidence by calling witnesses to testify that defendant's reputation is other than what the defendant claims. People v. Jones, 278 A.D.2d 246, 717 N.Y.S.2d 270 (2d Dept. 2000).

Traffic violations.—Questions as to traffic violations should rarely, if ever, be permitted. People v. Oliver, 80 Misc. 2d 905, 365 N.Y.S.2d 422 (Sup. Ct. Queens Co. 1975).

Statements to private persons.—Judgment reversed where the trial court admitted the defendant's signed confession and signed photographs since the evidence was obtained by department store security personnel without advising defendant of his *Miranda* rights, and the participation of police officers in the arrest was of a significant enough level to have required that defendant be advised of his rights. People v. Jones, 61 A.D.2d 264, 402 N.Y.S.2d 28 (2d Dept. 1978), aff'd, 47 N.Y.2d 528, 419 N.Y.S.2d 447, 393 N.E.2d 443 (1979).

Reference in charge to 20-year-old minor convictions; reversible error.—It was error for court to refer, in its instruction to jury on how to evaluate the credibility of defendant, to three 20-year-old minor convictions for breaking a window and possession of policy slips, which had little or no effect on credibility. People v. Velazquez, 77 A.D.2d 845, 431 N.Y.S.2d 31 (1st Dept. 1980).

Review by Court of Appeals not warranted.—Since exclusion of prior convictions is a discretionary determination for the trial courts and fact-reviewing appellate courts, no further review by the Court of Appeals is warranted. People v. Brown, 48 N.Y.2d 921, 425 N.Y.S.2d 54, 401 N.E.2d 177 (1979).

Similar uncharged crime; inadmissibility.—It was reversible error to allow into evidence testimony of defendant's behavior in throwing away a bag which contained a watch when told to halt by police where that watch was not the one recently robbed from victim, since the watch was in no way connected to the robbery of victim, and only showed defendant was of a criminal disposition. People v. Rivera, 88 A.D.2d 892, 453 N.Y.S.2d 7 (1st Dept. 1982).

Trial judge may decide defendant's *Sandoval* motion and continue to preside.—A trial judge may properly decide a defendant's pretrial *Sandoval* motion and continue to preside at trial; absent a showing of prejudice, the judge, by virtue of his learning and experience is presumed to have considered only the competent evidence adduced at trial in reaching the verdict. People v. Lombardi, 76 A.D.2d 891, 482 N.Y.S.2d 709 (2d Dept. 1980).

Youthful offender.—Although it is impermissible to use a youthful offender or juvenile delinquency adjudication to impeach, the illegal or immoral acts underlying such adjudications can be employed for such a purpose. People v. Greer, 42 N.Y.2d 170, 397 N.Y.S.2d 613, 366 N.E.2d 273 (1977).

—Court's *Sandoval* ruling permitting the prosecutor to cross-examine the defendant about the underlying facts of a youthful offender adjudication did not constitute an improvident exercise of discretion. People v. Randolph, 181 A.D.2d 801, 581 N.Y.S.2d 242 (2d Dept. 1992).

—A youthful offender adjudication is not a judgment of conviction for a crime or any other offense. People v. Ramos, 153 Misc. 2d 277, 581 N.Y.S.2d 559 (Sup. Ct. Bronx Co. 1992).

§ 60.42. Rules of evidence; admissibility of evidence of victim's sexual conduct in sex offense cases.

Evidence of a victim's sexual conduct shall not be admissible in a prosecution for an offense or an attempt to commit an offense defined in article one hundred thirty of the penal law unless such evidence:

1. proves or tends to prove specific instances of the victim's prior sexual conduct with the accused; or

2. proves or tends to prove that the victim has been convicted of an offense under section 230.00 of the penal law within three years prior to the sex offense which is the subject of the prosecution; or

3. rebuts evidence introduced by the people of the victim's failure to engage in sexual intercourse, oral sexual conduct, anal sexual conduct or sexual contact during a given period of time; or

4. rebuts evidence introduced by the people which proves or tends to prove that the accused is the cause of pregnancy or disease of the victim, or the source of semen found in the victim; or

5. is determined by the court after an offer of proof by the accused outside the hearing of the jury, or such hearing as the court may require, and a statement by the court of its findings of fact essential to its determination, to be relevant and admissible in the interests of justice.

Added by L. 1975, Ch. 230; L. 2003, Ch. 264, § 37, eff. Nov. 1, 2003, amending subd. 3.

ANNOTATIONS

Constitutionality.—CPL § 60.42 is constitutional. People v. Smith, 56 A.D.2d 686, 391 N.Y.S.2d 734 (3d Dept. 1977).

Cross-examination.—Court properly precluded cross-examination of victim regarding incident of sexual abuse by her biological father six years earlier, in prosecution of victim's uncle for rape, despite uncle's contention that victim was confused between prior abuse and charged incident, where her testimony revealed that she specifically described separate incidents to both medical doctor and her counselor. People v. Rogowski, 228 A.D.2d 728, 644 N.Y.S.2d 334 (3d Dept. 1996).

Cross-examinations; offenses committed subsequent to crime charged.—Trial court abused discretion in denying motion to preclude cross-examination for purposes of impeachment regarding sexual offenses committed subsequent to one for which defendant was standing trial; such cross-examination prevented defendant from testifying without running risk of prejudicing himself before the jury. People v. Smith, 60 A.D.2d 963, 401 N.Y.S.2d 606 (4th Dept. 1978).

Cross-examination of victim.—Although the rape shield law has severely restricted impeachment of the victim by use of prior sexual history, court unreasonably curtailed cross-examination of complainant about alleged perjury regarding her landlord-tenant case at an administrative hearing, prior frivolous lawsuits by her, and her financial circumstances, because rape shield law does not protect alleged sex-crime victims against all other standard forms of impeachment. People v. Griffin, 242 A.D.2d 70, 671 N.Y.S.2d 34 (1st Dept.), *appeal dismissed*, 93 N.Y.2d 955 (1999).

—Reversal was required due to the spareness of the 12-year-old rape victim's testimony and the barring of proof offered by defendant concerning victim's previous sex experiences with a 14-year-old boy and the 14-year-old boy's sexual relations with the victim's mother. People v. Ruiz, 71 A.D.2d 569, 418 N.Y.S.2d 402 (1st Dept. 1979).

—County court erred in precluding sexual abuse defendant from examining and cross-examining 11-year-old complainant's mother and psychologist with respect to a previous allegedly false allegation of sexual abuse where the complainant's motive for making the instant allegations was strikingly similar to her motive for making the prior allegation. The psychologist-patient statutory privilege must yield to the defendant's constitutional right of confrontation. People v. Bridgeland, 19 A.D.3d 1122, 796 N.Y.S.2d 768 (4th Dept. 2005).

—Preclusion of questions about a victim's prior complaint of a sex crime does not constitute an abuse of discretion where, as here, defendant made no showing that the prior allegation was false. People v. Smith, 281 A.D.2d 957, 722 N.Y.S.2d 850 (4th Dept. 2001).

—Court did not abuse its discretion in limiting the cross-examination of the victim with respect to abuse committed by codefendants because it is within the court's discretion to limit questioning "not relevant to the issues, but bearing on the credibility of a witness." People v. Stroman, 286 A.D.2d 974, 730 N.Y.S.2d 612 (4th Dept. 2001).

—Court erred in concluding that complainant's allegedly false claims of rape could not be probed due to the language of CPL § 60.42. People v. Harris, 151 A.D.2d 982, 983, 542 N.Y.S.2d 71, 72 (4th Dept. 1989).

E-mail messages not subject to Rape Shield Law.— Redacted e-mail messages were not subject to the Rape Shield Law because they did not constitute evidence of the sexual conduct of the complainant, and they were merely evidence of statements made by the complainant about herself. Furthermore, the e-mails fell within a number of exceptions set forth within the statute. People v. Jovanovic, 263 A.D.2d 182, 700 N.Y.S.2d 156 (1st Dept. 1999), *appeal dismissed*, 95 N.Y.2d 846 (2000).

Evidence about victim.—Evidence to show victim's reluctance to permit her prior sexual partners to touch her breasts was not admissible. People v. Mandel, 48 N.Y.2d 952, 425 N.Y.S.2d 63, 401 N.E.2d 185 (1979).

—Trial court improperly determined that evidence of a victim's prior complaints of sexual assaults is barred by the Rape Shield Law, but the error was harmless. People v. Byrd, 309 A.D.2d 593, 765 N.Y.S.2d 354 (1st Dept. 2003).

—The People can introduce sexual history evidence and a defendant can make limited inquiry into complainant's sexual history to rebut such evidence offered by the People; here, the sexual history evidence was admissible as relevant to the issue of why complainant failed to immediately inform her husband of the rape, as well as defendant's contention that the sexual encounter was consensual in exchange for employment. People v. Wigfall, 253 A.D.2d 80, 690 N.Y.S.2d 2 (1st Dept. 1999).

—Pursuant to CPL § 60.42, the rape shield law, the court properly excluded evidence of a second semen stain, not belonging to the defendant, which was found on the same piece of clothing as defendant's semen. Without more, the defendant's speculation as to that second semen stain was deposited was not sufficient to overcome its exclusion pursuant to the rape shield law. People v. Rendon, 301 A.D.2d 665, 756 N.Y.S.2d 229 (2d Dept. 2003).

—DNA evidence of semen on victim's underwear other than defendant's was inadmissible; defendant argued that the presence of another man's semen established that someone else assaulted her. However, defendant's sperm was also found on victim's underwear and in her vagina; thus, the presence of foreign sperm on her underwear was properly determined to be irrelevant. People v. Mount, 285 A.D.2d 899, 727 N.Y.S.2d 819 (3d Dept. 2001).

—Prejudicial effect of disclosure of victim's sexual activities outweighed the probative value of the evidence, and admission of this evidence would circumvent the rape shield law inasmuch as it would have a tendency to suggest that the victim was unable to identify the father of her child because she had multiple sexual partners. People v. Thompson, 267 A.D.2d 602, 699 N.Y.S.2d 770 (3d Dept. 1999).

Generally.—Pursuant to CPL § 60.42, evidence of the complainant's sexual history is irrelevant and has no bearing on the issue of guilt or innocence. People v. Swain, 171 A.D.2d 765, 766, 567 N.Y.S.2d 318, 319 (2d Dept. 1991).

—The trial court properly excluded defendant's testimony that on the night of the crime the rape victim told defendant that "she was not whoring around" since evidence of a victim's sexual conduct is inadmissible unless, *inter alia,* it relates to specific instances of prior sexual contact with the accused. People v. Hauver, 129 A.D.2d 889, 890, 514 N.Y.S.2d 814, 815 (2d Dept. 1987).

—Evidence regarding sexual activity between complainant, age ten, and individuals other than defendant was irrelevant to issue whether defendant had sexual intercourse with complainant and was not otherwise admissible. People v. Mathews, 227 A.D.2d 954, 643 N.Y.S.2d 851 (4th Dept. 1996).

Offer of proof.—Under CPL § 60.42, the trial court did not err in precluding cross-examination regarding the victim's arrests for prostitution that did not lead to convictions. People v. Dixon, 199 A.D.2d 332, 333, 604 N.Y.S.2d 604, 605 (2d Dept. 1993).

—Where the defendant did not make an offer of proof concerning the complainant's past sexual conduct as required by CPL § 60.42(5), the contention that he was deprived of the opportunity to confront the complainant with evidence of such conduct at the trial was rejected. People v. Monko, 162 A.D.2d 553, 556 N.Y.S.2d 745 (2d Dept. 1990).

—Where defendant did not raise consent as a defense, no substantial right or defense was denied him by the retroactive application of CPL § 60.42 and there was no violation either of the ex post facto or the confrontation clauses of the Constitution. People v. Conyers, 86 Misc. 2d 754, 382 N.Y.S.2d 437 (Sup. Ct. N.Y. Co. 1976), *aff'd,* 63 A.D.2d 634, 405 N.Y.S.2d 409 (1978).

Retroactivity of statute.—Statute was properly applied where trial was commenced on October 21, 1975, after effective date of the section, although the criminal transaction on which the indictment was based occurred on April 4, 1975, prior to the effective date, and so applied statute was constitutional. People v. Mandel, 48 N.Y.2d 952, 425 N.Y.S.2d 63, 401 N.E.2d 185 (1979).

—Where the indictment was handed down before September 1, 1975, the effective date of CPL § 60.42, but the trial was begun after that date it was proper to apply the provisions of CPL § 60.42. People v. Patno, 50 A.D.2d 965, 390 N.Y.S.2d 468 (3d Dept. 1977).

§ 60.43. Rules of evidence; admissibility of evidence of victim's sexual conduct in non-sex offense cases.

Evidence of the victim's conduct, including the past sexual conduct of a deceased victim, may not be admitted in a prosecution for any offense, attempt to commit an offense or conspiracy to commit an offense defined in the penal law unless such evidence is determined by the court to be relevant and admissible in the interests of justice, after an offer of proof by the proponent of such evidence outside the hearing of the jury, or such hearing as the court may require, and a statement by the court of its findings of fact essential to its determination.

Added by L. 1990, Ch. 832.

ANNOTATIONS

Offer of proof rejected.—Trial court properly rejected defendant's offer of proof of evidence that deceased victim was homosexual and had engaged in sexual relations with other young boys in the past to establish the defenses of justification and extreme emotional disturbance; CPL § 60.43 specifically provides that the past sexual conduct of a deceased victim may not be admitted in the prosecution of any offense unless such evidence is determined to be relevant and admissible. People v. Tenace, 232 A.D.2d 896, 649 N.Y.S.2d 218 (3d Dept. 1996).

—Because the victim's past sexual conduct has absolutely no bearing on defendant's guilt of the charged crimes, county court's actions in precluding cross-examination of her on this subject and in prohibiting the introduction of provocative photographs was in all respects proper. People v. McGrath, 195 A.D.2d 831, 601 N.Y.S.2d 200 (3d Dept. 1993).

Hearing.—Court committed reversible error in failing to conduct a statutory hearing on the admissibility of evidence of victim's sexual conduct and in failing to issue the appropriate limiting instructions to the jury. People v. Setless, 213 A.D.2d 900, 625 N.Y.S.2d 304 (3d Dept. 1995).

Victim's sexual history admissible.—Evidence of deceased victim's homosexual affairs was relevant and admissible because it tended to explain why the defendant and victim were together in the motel room, tended to corroborate the defendant's statement that the victim grabbed his genitalia, and demonstrated the victim's state of mind in escorting the defendant to the hotel. People v. Childs, 161 Misc. 2d 749, 615 N.Y.S.2d 232 (Sup. Ct. Bronx Co. 1994).

§ 60.44. Use of anatomically correct dolls.

Any person who is less than sixteen years old may in the discretion of the court and where helpful and appropriate, use an anatomically correct doll in testifying in a criminal proceeding based upon conduct prohibited by article one hundred thirty, article two hundred sixty or section 255.25 of the penal law.

Added by L. 1986, Ch. 358.

Proper use of dolls.—There was no error in permitting child witness in sexual abuse case to testify with the use of anatomically correct dolls. People v. Guce, 164 A.D.2d 946, 560 N.Y.S.2d 53 (2d Dept. 1990).

—In the circumstances of the bench trial, considering the tender age of the youthful victim and his difficulty in expressing himself verbally, court did not abuse its discretion in seeking to clarify his testimony by use of anatomically correct dolls. People v. McGuire, 152 A.D.2d 945, 543 N.Y.S.2d 822 (4th Dept. 1989).

—The use of anatomically dolls that reflected the races of the defendant and the rape victim before the grand jury was not prejudicial, and the age of the witness does not prohibit the use of anatomically correct dolls. People v. Rich, 137 Misc. 2d 474, 520 N.Y.S.2d 911 (Sup. Ct. Monroe Co. 1987).

—There was no prejudice in using anatomically correct dolls, where witness, who was over 16, had a limited vocabulary, and even with the aid of leading questions, he could only give a limited narration of the events. People v. Herring, 135 Misc. 2d 487, 515 N.Y.S.2d 954 (Sup. Ct. Queens Co. 1987).

§ 60.45. Rules of evidence; admissibility of statements of defendants.

1. Evidence of a written or oral confession, admission, or other statement made by a defendant with respect to his participation or lack of participation in the offense charged, may not be received in evidence against him in a criminal proceeding if such statement was involuntarily made.

2. A confession, admission or other statement

is "involuntarily made" by a defendant when it is obtained from him:

(a) By any person by the use or threatened use of physical force upon the defendant or another person, or by means of any other improper conduct or undue pressure which impaired the defendant's physical or mental condition to the extent of undermining his ability to make a choice whether or not to make a statement; or

(b) By a public servant engaged in law enforcement activity or by a person then acting under his direction or in cooperation with him:

(i) by means of any promise or statement of fact, which promise or statement creates a substantial risk that the defendant might falsely incriminate himself; or

(ii) in violation of such rights as the defendant may derive from the constitution of this state or of the United States.

ANNOTATIONS

"Act" considered equivalent to "verbal statement."—An act performed solely for the purpose of communicating, such as pointing or nodding, is equivalent to a verbal statement for purposes of the statute. People v. Lanquetot, 104 Misc. 2d 179, 427 N.Y.S.2d 679 (Sup. Ct. N.Y. Co. 1980).

Admissibility of confession.—Despite the fact that no statement to that effect was made, defendants were deemed to be under arrest when they were handcuffed and placed in the police vehicle for transportation back to the robbery scene and since the arrest was illegal the confession must be suppressed. People v. Gordon, 87 A.D.2d 636, 448 N.Y.S.2d 217 (2d Dept. 1982).

—Reversible error was committed where statement of the defendant was taken subsequent to the execution of the arrest warrant in the absence of counsel. People v. Gooljar, 80 A.D.2d 860, 436 N.Y.S.2d 754 (2d Dept. 1981)

Spontaneous statements.—Defendant's statements to transporting police officer who was unfamiliar with murder investigation were admissible at trial as spontaneous statements. People v. Damiano, 87 N.Y.2d 477, 640 N.Y.S.2d 451, 663 N.E.2d 607 (1996).

—Defendant's inculpatory statement to interpreter at his arraignment was spontaneously volunteered and therefore not subject to suppression. People v. Gonzales, 75 N.Y.2d 938, 555 N.Y.S.2d 681, 682, 554 N.E.2d 1269, cert. denied, 498 U.S. 33 (1990).

—Where police officer, who was accompanying defendant during arraignment on an unrelated charge, and who had learned of the rape charge only during the arraignment, stated in response to defendant's query as to what the rape warrant was about, that "You should know, they are looking for you," such a statement was not conduct reasonably anticipated to evoke an incriminating statement from the defendant, and the defendant's admission was spontaneous. People v. Lynes, 49 N.Y.2d 286, 425 N.Y.S.2d 295, 401 N.E.2d 405 (1980).

—Statements elicited from the defendant while confined at the Suffolk County Jail awaiting trial did not qualify as spontaneous and voluntary utterance where they were in response to a correction officer's question as to how the defendant had made out in court; the query should never have been made because it played upon the natural penchant to volunteer that even a cautious witness will often exhibit and thereby violated stringent safeguards that surround the right to counsel. People v. Garofolo, 46 N.Y.2d 592, 415 N.Y.S.2d 810, 389 N.E.2d 123 (1979).

—For a statement to qualify as a spontaneously volunteered statement, the spontaneity has to be genuine and not the result of inducement, provocation, encouragement or acquiescence, no matter how subtly employed. People v. Rogers, 48 N.Y.2d 167, 422 N.Y.S.2d 18, 397 N.E.2d 709 (1979).

—"When, during processing at the police station, one officer asked another, within earshot of defendant, what type of weapon

was recovered, this did not constitute the functional equivalent of interrogation and defendant's unsolicited spontaneous responses were not subject to suppression." People v. Atkins, 273 A.D.2d 12, 708 N.Y.S.2d 109 (1st Dept. 2000).

—Court properly admitted statements defendant made to an unknown party in the course of a telephone conversation at police headquarters since the statements were spontaneous. People v. Elliott, 138 A.D.2d 396, 525 N.Y.S.2d 680 (2d Dept. 1988).

—Defendant's statement that "no one got shot" which came in the wake of the police officer's response to the defendant's inquiry about the charges he was facing was spontaneous and not the product of police interrogation. People v. Hampton, 129 A.D.2d 736, 514 N.Y.S.2d 496 (2d Dept. 1987).

—Defendant's statement was admissible where after hearing one police officer comment to another "Do you believe that a guy this size would have to stab an old man," the defendant responded "Well, the old man slapped me, that's why I stabbed him;" the mere fact that the officer's comment was in a sense answered by defendant's statement does not bar a finding of spontaneity where the remark was an isolated one and not a part of any course of conduct from which defendant might have inferred that the police officer had any interest in eliciting a statement from him. People v. Bryant, 87 A.D.2d 873, 449 N.Y.S.2d 314 (2d Dept. 1982), aff'd, 59 N.Y.2d 786, 464 N.Y.S.2d 729, 451 N.E.2d 476 (1983).

—A statement by the defendant "you got me" when he saw the undercover officer to whom he had sold narcotics while his pedigree was being taken at the station house prior to the Miranda warning was admissible as a spontaneous outburst. People v. Baez, 79 A.D.2d 608, 433 N.Y.S.2d 489 (2d Dept. 1980).

—Defendant's disclosures to police were spontaneous and not the result of police questioning or conduct. The police are not required to silence a chatterbox. People v. Taylor, 1 A.D.3d 623, 766 N.Y.S.2d 266 (3d Dept. 2003).

—Defendant's statement to police was genuinely spontaneous though made in presence of armed officers. People v. Hoyer, 141 A.D.2d 973, 530 N.Y.S.2d 637 (3d Dept. 1988).

—Where defendant initiated the conversation without any prompting from the guard defendant's statements to the jail guard were properly admitted into evidence. People v. Cardew, 132 A.D.2d 721, 723, 516 N.Y.S.2d 986, 988 (3d Dept. 1987).

—A statement by the defendant after he was arrested and given his Miranda rights in response to an answer given him by the police officer as to why he was being arrested, that "the checks were not his, he had not made them out or signed them and did not know they were forgeries until a couple of them were passed" was a spontaneous statement and admissible. People v. Rivers, 83 A.D.2d 978, 443 N.Y.S.2d 35 (3d Dept. 1981), aff'd, 56 N.Y.2d 476, 453 N.Y.S.2d 156, 438 N.E.2d 862 (1982).

—The defendant's statements were spontaneous outburst where the genesis of the statements came from within him and were not the result of any illegal police questioning and the defendant initiated the conversations concerning his involvement in the homicide. People v. Lipsky, 102 Misc. 2d 19, 423 N.Y.S.2d 599 (Monroe Co. Ct. 1979).

Admissions.—It was not improper for the prosecutor to use for impeachment purposes a statement made by defendant's attorney at a bail application which was made in defendant's presence and with his active participation. People v. Mahone, 206 A.D.2d 263, 614 N.Y.S.2d 409 (1st Dept. 1994).

—Defendant's statement that he "stole" the taxicab did not constitute an admission of stealing or larceny as defined in the Penal Law. People v. Pauli, 130 A.D.2d 389, 392, 515 N.Y.S.2d 251, 254 (1st Dept. 1987).

—Defendant was not in custody when he met with a caseworker in the office of a public school, the caseworker was not a law enforcement official or an agent of such a person, and there was no indication that the statement was not voluntary. People v. Davila, 223 A.D.2d 722, 637 N.Y.S.2d 200 (2d Dept. 1996).

—Trial court was not required to submit to jury the issue of voluntariness of rape the defendant's statements to his mother and her friend, on asserted basis that mother's promise to prevent prosecution and to obtain counseling for defendant created risk that he would falsely incriminate himself, where there was no evidence that the alleged promise impaired defendant's physical condition in any way and defendant thus failed to raise a factual dispute over whether statement was involuntarily made. People v. Price, 224 A.D.2d 1014, 637 N.Y.S.2d 536 (4th Dept. 1996).

—The police did not misrepresent the nature of the proof against defendant; their promises not to prosecute defendant for making a false statement if he gave them a "straight story" did not create "a substantial risk that the defendant might falsely incriminate himself" and did not create a risk that defendant's will was overborne. People v. Guthrie, 222 A.D.2d 1084, 636 N.Y.S.2d 239 (4th Dept. 1995).

Admissions; impeachment of prior inconsistent statement; immunity.—It was reversible error to permit defendant's friend to testify at the trial to admissions made by the defendant during a meeting with the friend requested by the prosecutor after the plea negotiations had been concluded since it was justifiable for defense counsel, in permitting the interview, to assume that the prosecutor, by his request, impliedly revived the plea negotiations and his attendant promise not to use anything the defendant said. People v. Jackson, 36 N.Y.2d 922, 373 N.Y.S.2d 536, 335 N.E.2d 845 (1975).

Admissibility of statements to witness.—At trial for murder, testimony concerning statements made to witness by defendant and accomplice was admissible since it was necessary to the prosecution, statements met several tests as exceptions to the hearsay rule, to wit, declarations against penal interest, spontaneous declarations and silence as tacit admission of truth, and were reliable because they were unsolicited, inculpatory remarks made immediately after the killing when the defendants had no reason to lie; truth of statements was well-supported by corroborating evidence, and the jury's consideration of them did not deprive defendant of due process or right to fair trial. People v. Egan, 78 A.D.2d 34, 434 N.Y.S.2d 55 (4th Dept. 1980).

Admissibility of admission; waiver of right to counsel at questioning.—Where detective knew at the time of interrogation that the defendant was represented by counsel on a prior charge, statement made by the defendant was required to be suppressed, notwithstanding fact that the interrogation took place after defendant waived his *Miranda* rights. People v. Bacote, 76 A.D.2d 866, 428 N.Y.S.2d 700 (2d Dept. 1980).

—People v. Samuels, 49 N.Y.2d 218, 424 N.Y.S.2d 892, 400 N.E.2d 1344 (1980), was not violated and his statement was admissible where there had been no significant judicial activity and the defendant had been given his *Miranda* rights, voluntarily submitted to questioning and there was no evidence that the police intentionally delayed filing an accusatory instrument so that they could interrogate him. People v. Yanus, 92 A.D.2d 674, 460 N.Y.S.2d 180 (3d Dept. 1983).

By-passing attorney.—Police did not violate defendant's right to counsel when they obtained oral statements from defendant, where public defender's telephone appearance on defendant's behalf occurred after completion of oral interview and before completion of written statement. People v. Linderberry, 222 A.D.2d 731, 634 N.Y.S.2d 571 (3d Dept. 1995).

—Where defendant, while in prison and represented by attorney, insisted on by-passing his counsel and confessing his guilt after receiving the appropriate warnings, the statement was admissible. People v. Carbone, 80 Misc. 2d 150, 362 N.Y.S.2d 677 (Sup. Ct. N.Y. Co. 1974).

Admissibility of admissions without *Miranda* warnings.—The fact that there may have been police questioning is not controlling; custodial admissions are not suppressible unless produced by a process of interrogation designed to elicit statements from the defendants. People v. Huffman, 41 N.Y.2d 29, 390 N.Y.S.2d 843, 359 N.E.2d 353 (1976).

—Custodial statements are admissible without *Miranda* warnings where they are not "produced by a process of interrogation designed to elicit statements from the defendant," but rather to protect police officer's safety and to establish ownership of property not plainly contraband; police, upon entering defendant's room asked him what he was doing there, whether a shoulder bag was his, and whether $64,000 found in a mattress was his; police had a reasonable suspicion that the bag contained a pistol, and wanted to establish the ownership of the money. People v. Johnson, 86 A.D.2d 165, 449 N.Y.S.2d 41 (1st Dept. 1982), aff'd, 59 N.Y.2d 1014, 466 N.Y.S.2d 957, 453 N.E.2d 1246 (1983).

Admissibility of admissions without *Miranda* warnings; lack of restraint.—Although it is settled that unauthorized

search or seizure by private individuals, including store detectives, does not render the evidence inadmissible at subsequent criminal proceedings, this does not mean that the government may avoid constitutional restrictions by using a private individual as its agent, nor can it claim that only a private act is involved when government officers subject to constitutional limitations have participated in the act. People v. Jones, 47 N.Y.2d 528, 419 N.Y.S.2d 447, 393 N.E.2d 443 (1979).

—Brief street investigatory inquiry in defendant's neighborhood was not custodial and therefore no preinterrogation warnings were necessary where police, in search of juvenile for whom warrant had been issued, stopped group of boys and viewed photograph in possession of one showing defendant, who was present in group, holding weapons; this gave reasonable suspicion to believe crime may have been committed and imposed upon police duty to inquire of photographed boy the whereabouts of weapons. Kwok T. v. Mauriello, 43 N.Y.2d 213, 401 N.Y.S.2d 52, 371 N.E.2d 814 (1977).

—Pedigree questions need not be preceded by *Miranda* warnings. People v. Nelson, 147 A.D.2d 774, 775, 537 N.Y.S.2d 995. 997 (3d Dept. 1989). *See also* People v. Jones, 84 Misc. 2d 737, 376 N.Y.S.2d 885 (Sup. Ct. Bronx Co. 1975) (*Miranda* was never intended to apply to biographical data necessary to enable the police properly to charge a defendant).

—A Labor Department investigator was not required to give *Miranda* warnings before interviewing the defendant for unlawfully receiving unemployment insurance benefits during a time when he was gainfully employed, even though the department's investigation had been completed and the clear purpose of its interrogation was to obtain an admission of guilt because the defendant was not in custody and his freedom of action was not curtailed. People v. Matkowski, 67 A.D.2d 1087, 415 N.Y.S.2d 168 (4th Dept. 1979).

Admissibility of confession at joint trial.—The fact that a co-defendant did not testify does not bar the admission of his or her confession at a joint trial where the defendant also made a full and voluntary confession virtually identical to the co-defendant's confession. People v. Close, 90 A.D.2d 562, 456 N.Y.S.2d 152 (3d Dept. 1982).

Admissibility of statements to parole officer while in custody for new crime.—The status of the defendant as a parolee and of his interrogator as a parole officer does not diminish his constitutional rights in a new prosecution; thus, statements take in the absence of previously assigned counsel and without "Miranda" warnings were suppressed. People v. Ferguson, 90 Misc. 2d 467, 395 N.Y.S.2d 330 (Sup. Ct. N.Y. Co. 1977).

Admissibility of statements to parole officer.—In a proceeding for revocation of probation or parole based on statements made to a parole officer, it need not be shown that *Miranda* was followed, however, in a prosecution for a separate offense it must be shown either that the interrogation was not in a custodial setting or the accused knew the rights he was waiving. People v. Parker, 100 Misc. 2d 800, 421 N.Y.S.2d 561 (Kings Co. 1979).

ADA who took videotape confession; summation.—The trial court granted defendant's motion to disqualify the A.D.A. who tried the case from making the summation to the jury where the A.D.A. had taken defendant's pretrial videotaped confession which had been admitted at the trial; the court further recommended that the A.D.A. who is to conduct the trial not be the same A.D.A. who took the initial videotape statement and/or confession. People v. Bonilla 101 Misc. 2d 146, 420 N.Y.S.2d 665 (Sup. Ct. Bronx Co. 1979).

Appeal to Court of Appeals; question of law only.—The Court of Appeals can overturn the finding of the Appellate Division that there was no custodial interrogation only if the court concludes, as a matter of law, that the proof was insufficient to establish that the investigation was noncustodial. People v. Centano, 76 N.Y.2d 837, 560 N.Y.S.2d 121, 559 N.E.2d 1280 (1990).

—A determination by the trial court and the appellate division as a factual issue that there was no custodial interrogation because the police came to appellant's home at her invitation cannot be overturned by the court of appeals in the absence of a showing as a matter of law that the proof was insufficient to establish that the interrogation was noncustodial. People v. Williamson, 51 N.Y.2d 801, 433 N.Y.S.2d 93, 412 N.E.2d 1319 (1980).

Attachment of right to counsel, filing of federal

complaint. —Filing of complaint in federal court, along with the issuance of a federal arrest warrant, does not constitute either a "critical stage" of proceedings or "significant judicial activity" with regard to New York State criminal charges relating to the same incident; the right to counsel had therefore not attached when defendant waived her *Miranda* rights and made statements to state authorities. People v. Ridgeway, 101 A.D.2d 555, 476 N.Y.S.2d 940 (4th Dept. 1984), *aff'd,* 64 N.Y.2d 952, 488 N.Y.S.2d 641, 477 N.E.2d 1095 (1985).

Charge; voluntariness. —Reversible error was committed where the court refused to charge on the issue of voluntariness of statements made that the testimony of two witnesses who stated that defendant had asked for counsel could be considered by the jury in determining the voluntariness of defendant's subsequent confession. People v. Griswold, 58 N.Y.2d 633, 458 N.Y.S.2d 513, 444 N.E.2d 977 (1982).

Civilian Complaint Review Board. —The Civilian Complaint Review Board of the Police Department, aware that the defendant had been arraigned, indicted and assigned counsel, was free to interview the defendant and to make use of the interview in connection with its inquiry into defendant's allegations of police misconduct, but the People were prohibited from using the inculpatory statements of the defendant in the prosecution of the criminal charges. People v. Townes, 41 N.Y.2d 97, 390 N.Y.S.2d 893, 359 N.E.2d 402 (1976). *See also* People v. Roberson, 41 N.Y.2d 106, 390 N.Y.S.2d 900, 359 N.E.2d 408 (1976).

Co-defendant's confession. —It was proper to admit the co-defendant's statements, although he did not testify where defendant's and co-defendant's confession were overlapping as to the willing participation in the robbery, the division of its proceeds, and the joint striking of the victim in some form, and the only unilateral claim was that of co-defendant that defendant had used a knife on the victim, and the import of this statement was reduced by the uncontradicted medical testimony that the death had been produced by the violent conduct in its totality, with the lacerations least likely to have been fatal. People v. Berzups, 49 N.Y.2d 417, 426 N.Y.S.2d 253, 402 N.E.2d 1155 (1980).

—With limited exceptions, a confession may be considered only against its maker; in some cases, the court may avoid the necessity of a severance, by forcefully cautioning the trier of fact that admissions may not be considered against another. *In re* Quinton A., 49 N.Y.2d 328, 425 N.Y.S.2d 788, 402 N.E.2d 126 (1980).

—It was not error to admit the co-defendant's written confession where the defendant's oral confession interlocked in all material respects with the written confession and when read to the defendant he stated "yes, that is what happened" since the written confession would have been admissible at a separate trial. People v. Woodward, 50 N.Y.2d 922, 431 N.Y.S.2d 452, 409 N.E.2d 926 (1980).

—Failure to grant a severance was not error where each defendant's confession contained the same material facts and the confessions were admitted at trial with repeated and explicit instructions that each defendant's confession was to be considered against the confessing defendant only, and not against the co-defendant. People v. Safian, 46 N.Y.2d 181, 413 N.Y.S.2d 118, 385 N.E.2d 1046 (1978).

Confession admissible. —Defendant was not deprived of any constitutional right by virtue of trial court's instruction on the voluntariness of defendant's confession where the charge was in accordance with New York law, trial court made pretrial finding that the confession was not involuntary, defendant did not challenge that ruling, and defendant had no constitutional right to have jury again pass upon the issue. People v. Alvares, 219 A.D.2d 520, 631 N.Y.S.2d 668 (1st Dept. 1995).

—Police officer's statement to defendant that defendant could be charged with a crime for making a false statement if his signed, written denial of criminal activity proved false did not rise to a level creating a substantial risk that the defendant would falsely incriminate himself and did not render defendant's confession inadmissible. People v. Lum, 102 A.D.2d 992, 477 N.Y.S.2d 860 (3d Dept. 1984).

Confession; issue of voluntariness; delay in arraignment. —Even if a delay in arraignment was improper and thus illegal, such delay is merely one factor to be considered on the issue of the voluntariness of defendant's confession. People v. Cunningham, 97 Misc. 2d 618, 411 N.Y.S.2d 963 (Allegany Co. Ct. 1978).

Confession; *Miranda* **warnings not necessary.** —Defendant's

statements in response to questioning about a chain snatching were not entitled to be suppressed where defendant was questioned in the unfamiliar surroundings of the precinct but his presence there was voluntary; and his mother was present during the questioning; the mode of questioning was uncoercive, short and, at the end, defendant was free to leave. People v. Krystof, 84 A.D.2d 566, 443 N.Y.S.2d 258 (2d Dept. 1981).

Confession; suppression as involuntary. —Confession was involuntary when it was made as a result of questioning by police in relays for several hours with repeated exhortations to confess, appeals to religious principles, superstitious fears, ethnic pride, worth as a man and the showing of gruesome photographs of the deceased. People v. Sunset Bay, 76 A.D.2d 592, 430 N.Y.S.2d 601 (1st Dept. 1980).

—The police officers' warrantless and nonconsensual entry into defendant's bedroom violated (*Payton v. New York,* 445 U.S. 573, 100 S. Ct. 1371, 63 L. Ed. 2d 639), and therefore the confession must be suppressed. People v. King, 92 A.D.2d 922, 460 N.Y.S.2d 140 (2d Dept. 1983), *aff'd,* 61 N.Y.2d 969, 475 N.Y.S.2d 275, 463 N.E.2d 616 (1984).

Confession; voluntary; suppression denied. —Two police officers charged with burglary could not have their statements suppressed since they were never ordered to talk or directed to waive their rights nor were either of them warned or in any way reminded of possible job-related repercussions a refusal to talk could have. People v. Lannon, 107 Misc. 2d 996, 436 N.Y.S.2d 177 (Sup. Ct. Westchester Co. 1981).

Custody; test. —*Miranda* warnings need not be given prior to questioning when a seizure of a person remains at the stop and frisk inquiry level and does not constitute a restraint on his or her freedom of movement of the degree associated with a formal arrest. People v. Brunet, 70 N.Y.2d 891, 524 N.Y.S.2d 378, 380, 519 N.E.2d 289 (1987).

—In the absence of a finding by the court that the defendant was in custody *Miranda* warnings are not mandated. People v. Waymorex, 53 N.Y.2d 1053, 442 N.Y.S.2d 490, 425 N.E.2d 878 (1981).

—Defendant voluntarily accompanied detectives to the police station, and the record supported that she was not in custody when she made the confession, especially where there was evidence of defendant's understanding that she was not being arrested and that she would be returning to her hotel room after speaking with the detectives. People v. Leung, 15 A.D.3d 272, 791 N.Y.S.2d 519 (1st Dept. 2005).

—Mere fact defendant was subject to frisk and asked a couple of non-coercive questions did not establish that he was in custody. People v. Morales, 129 A.D.2d 440, 442, 514 N.Y.S.2d 13, 15 (1st Dept. 1987).

—The fact that defendant was subjected to two polygraph examinations did not mean that defendant was in custody. People v. Bailey, 141 A.D.2d 331, 527 N.Y.S.2d 845 (2d Dept. 1988).

—Fact that defendant was advised of his constitutional rights at one point during his conversation with the detectives does not necessarily lead to the conclusion that he was in custody. People v. Eke-Spiff, 128 A.D.2d 889, 890, 513 N.Y.S.2d 814, 815 (2d Dept. 1987).

—Fact that officer had his gun drawn did not convert lawful detention into an arrest. People v. Perry, 133 A.D.2d 380, 519 N.Y.S.2d 377 (2d Dept. 1987), *aff'd,* 71 N.Y.2d 871, 527 N.Y.S.2d 760, 522 N.E.2d 1058 (1988).

—Giving the defendant *Miranda* warnings when the encounter began did not indicate that she was then in custody. People v. Kircher, 134 A.D.2d 285, 520 N.Y.S.2d 611 (2d Dept. 1987).

—Defendant was not in custody when he made statements to police officer, where defendant was questioned for about an hour by a plain-clothes police officer with no visible weapon, sitting at defendant's kitchen table, he was not informed of any accusatory statements, and defendant was able to get a beverage during the conversation. People v. Petrie, 3 A.D.3d 665, 771 N.Y.S.2d 242 (3d Dept. 2004).

—In determining whether a defendant was in custody when he made a statement, the court should consider: (1) the amount of time the defendant spent with the police; (2) whether his freedom was restricted in any significant manner; (3) the location and atmosphere in which the defendant was questioned; (4) the degree of cooperation exhibited by the defendant; (5) whether he was apprised of his constitutional rights; and (6) whether the questioning was investigatory or accusatory in nature. People v. Lunderman, 19 A.D.3d 1067, 796 N.Y.S.2d 481 (4th Dept. 2005).

—Questioning an individual in his own home, without more, is not sufficient to conclude that the interrogation was custodial. People v. Benz, 136 A.D.2d 958, 524 N.Y.S.2d 942 (4th Dept. 1988).

—The mere fact that a guilty person may feel threatened or restrained in the presence of police, not because of objective police conduct, but because of secret guilty knowledge does not render the situation custodial. People v. Johnson, 91 A.D.2d 327, 458 N.Y.S.2d 775 (4th Dept. 1983), aff'd, 61 N.Y.2d 932, 474 N.Y.S.2d 967, 463 N.E.2d 368 (1984).

—In deciding whether a defendant is in custody the test is not what the defendant thought, but rather what a reasonable man, innocent of any crime, would have thought in the defendant's position. People v. Byers, 71 A.D.2d 77, 421 N.Y.S.2d 462 (4th Dept. 1979).

—Mere presence in a police station does not necessitate a finding of custody. People v. Dross, 146 A.D.2d 783, 789, 551 N.Y.S.2d 1016, 1021 (Sup. Ct. Bronx Co. 1989).

Custodial interrogation; *Miranda* warnings required.— The appeal was held in abeyance and the case remitted to the trial court where defendant raised the issue of being questioned prior to being given his *Miranda* warnings; had this issue been raised at the suppression hearing the people might have offered proof to show that defendant had been advised of his rights when first taken into custody or that there was a definite break in the interrogation. People v. McGregor, 84 A.D.2d 610, 444 N.Y.S.2d 231 (3d Dept. 1981).

Declaration against penal interest.—A confession by the co-defendant implicating the defendant is not admissible as a declaration against penal interest where the co-defendant had a motive to falsify, namely powerful incentives to minimize his own role and to place primary blame on others. People v. Geoghegan, 51 N.Y.2d 45, 431 N.Y.S.2d 502, 409 N.E.2d 975 (1980).

—It was an abuse of discretion to admit the hearsay statements of deceased daughter as testified to by her mother and a detective where they contained no declarations against penal interest; the daughter made no admission of participating in the crime for which defendant stands accused and the deceased daughter may have had motives to fabricate that far outweighed the paltry proof offered to establish their reliability. People v. Maerling, 46 N.Y.2d 289, 413 N.Y.S.2d 316, 385 N.E.2d 1245 (1978).

Defendant not represented by counsel on pending charge.—Defendant's inculpatory statements to detective, made after waiver of right to counsel and after dismissal of earlier case in which defendant was represented by counsel, were properly admitted into evidence; since earlier case had been dismissed, defendant was not represented by counsel on any "pending" charge. People v. Mann, 60 N.Y.2d 792, 469 N.Y.S.2d 681, 457 N.E.2d 681 (1983).

Defendant's statement not made as a result of police "questioning."—Defendant's confession was not suppressible even though made while in police custody, without *Miranda* warnings, and was prompted by a police officer's assertion that the defendant had been picked in a photo identification and that the defendant was "a liar" when he denied knowledge of a burglary and sexual assault; the officer's statement constitutes a declaration rather than express questioning. People v. Huffman, 61 N.Y.2d 795, 473 N.Y.S.2d 945, 462 N.E.2d 122 (1984).

—Police officer's question, "Where's all this blood coming from?" was not interrogation, but was intended to clarify the situation, including defendant's physical condition where his clothes were bloody and he stated that he had been shot, and court properly denied defendant's motion to suppress his statements. People v. Valderas, — A.D.2d —, 776 N.Y.S.2d 41 (1st Dept. 2004).

—Where police asked defendant questions (about the contents of a shopping bag) that were directed at clarifying the situation and not as interrogation, the questions did not require *Miranda* warnings. People v. Williams, 271 A.D.2d 335, 708 N.Y.S.2d 56 (1st Dept. 2000).

Defendant's request to remain silent; further questioning.—Detective's failure to readvise defendant of his *Miranda* rights upon interrogating defendant 17 hours after he had invoked his right to remain silent required suppression of his statements. People v. Dow, 129 A.D.2d 535, 514 N.Y.S.2d 735 (1st Dept. 1987).

—The fact that the defendant initially chose to remain silent did not preclude the police from asking him questions upon reiteration of his *Miranda* rights. People v. Norman, 127 A.D.2d 799, 512 N.Y.S.2d 196, 198 (2d Dept. 1987).

Delay in arraignment.—The federal rule requiring the *per se* exclusion of a confession procured during a delay in arraignment is not a limitation imposed on the states by the due process clause; therefore a delay in arraignment is only one factor to be considered in assessing the voluntariness of a confession. People v. Crosby, 91 A.D.2d 20, 457 N.Y.S.2d 831 (2d Dept. 1983).

District Attorney's promise of leniency.—A promise of a substantially more lenient sentence if there was cooperation which was repeated to the defendant in a variety of forms by the Assistant District Attorney rendered defendant's confession involuntary. People v. DeJesus, 63 A.D.2d 148, 407 N.Y.S.2d 5 (1st Dept. 1978).

—District Attorney's promise that he would not ask the court to sentence defendant as a persistent felony offender did not create "a substantial risk that the defendant might falsely incriminate himself." People v. Johnson, 242 A.D.2d 855, 662 N.Y.S.2d 955 (4th Dept. 1997).

Erroneous admission into evidence; not harmless error.—It was not harmless error to allow into evidence defendant's admissions while in police custody without *Miranda* warnings, where the admission may have provided corroboration of an accomplice's incrimination of defendant. People v. Goodman, 54 N.Y.2d 451, 446 N.Y.S.2d 202, 430 N.E.2d 1255 (1981).

Failure to inform defendant.—It was reversible error for a trial court to allow the prosecutor to elicit testimony regarding defendant's statements where the prosecution failed to inform the defendant of the existence of those statements. People v. Hoover, 57 N.Y.2d 908, 456 N.Y.S.2d 756, 442 N.E.2d 1267 (1982).

Failure to inform of victim's death.—Confession was admissible where voluntarily made after *Miranda* warnings although defendant was not advised of victim's death. People v. Lewis, 43 A.D.2d 989, 352 N.Y.S.2d 248 (3d Dept. 1974).

Following polygraph test.—Defendant, not a prime suspect, consented to take a polygraph test after twice receiving *Miranda* warnings and being warned not to take test if he intended to lie, and when confronted with the results indicative of deception he confessed. Such confession was admissible since defendant knowingly and intelligently waived his rights and chose to speak. People v. Wilson, 78 Misc. 2d 468, 354 N.Y.S.2d 296 (Nassau Co. Ct. 1974).

Juvenile.—There is no requirement that police officers permit the family members of a competent 19-year-old adult, in custody, to communicate with him. People v. Huber, 144 A.D.2d 583, 534 N.Y.S.2d 225 (2d Dept. 1988).

—The confession was suppressed where the police had knowledge that the 16-year-old defendant wished the presence of his mother, who had sought to be present with him during his interrogation, and that the family attorney had directed that no questioning of defendant proceed in the absence of an attorney. People v. Kocik, 63 A.D.2d 230, 407 N.Y.S.2d 929 (4th Dept. 1978).

—Fifteen-year-old, prior to receipt of *Miranda* warnings, confessed to homicide and four hours later, after receipt of appropriate warnings, in his mother's presence, signed another confession. Second confession was voluntary; juvenile did not testify at suppression hearing that first confession influenced his later statement and evidence failed to show circumstances probative of such influence. In re O., 76 Misc. 2d 1016, 351 N.Y.S.2d 853 (Fam. Ct. N.Y. Co. 1974).

Juvenile delinquency proceeding; voluntariness of confession; parental influence.—If it be established that parental guidance or influence is not exercised by the parent independently but at the behest or on behalf of the prosecutor, such where several days after his circumstance should weigh heavily to indicate the involuntariness of a child's confession. In re Raymond W., 44 N.Y.2d 438, 406 N.Y.S.2d 27, 377 N.E.2d 471 (1978).

Juvenile; admissibility of confession; waiver of appointment of law guardian.—A juvenile subject to custodial interrogation is "a subject" of a juvenile delinquency proceeding for the purposes of FCA § 249-a, and thus the presumption that he lacks the requisite knowledge and maturity to waive the appointment of a law guardian cannot be addressed until the law guardian is appointed. *In re* Schaefer, 97 Misc. 2d 487, 411 N.Y.S.2d 977 (Fam. Ct. Onondaga Co. 1978).

Illegally obtained statements may be used to impeach testifying defendant.—Defendant's statements, even though secured in disregard of constitutional safeguards, could be used to impeach the defendant's credibility where the defendant takes the stand to testify in contradiction of the contents of the statements. People v. Ortega, 101 A.D.2d 661, 475 N.Y.S.2d 587 (3d Dept. 1984).

Confession illegally obtained; use of deception and trickery.—In a murder case, it was reversible error for the prosecution to use confession of 17-year-old defendant, where, in the course of obtaining the confession, the police, using trickery and deception, sealed off the most likely avenue by which the assistance of counsel could reach the defendant, and where the confession followed three inadmissible statements and was the product of a continuous interrogation. However, the People were entitled to use as evidence incriminating statements made by defendant to a friend. People v. Townsend, 33 N.Y.2d 37, 347 N.Y.S.2d 187, 300 N.E.2d 722 (1973).

Intoxicated driving; evidence of refusal to take test.—VTL § 1194(4) which provides that evidence of a defendant's refusal to submit to a chemical test to determine the alcoholic content of his blood is admissible in any trial based on a violation of VTL § 1192, provided he was given sufficient warning in clear and unequivocal language is constitutional; the introduction of such evidence in accordance with this statute does not violate the defendant's privilege against self-incrimination under either the Federal or State Constitution. People v. Thomas, 46 N.Y.2d 100, 412 N.Y.S.2d 845, 385 N.E.2d 584 (1978).

—Reversal was required where police failed to warn defendant, arrested for drunk driving, that his refusal to submit to a chemical test could be introduced into evidence at his subsequent trial, and such refusal was not only admitted into evidence but also covered in the court's charge; VTL § 1194 (4) authorizes the admission of such evidence only where a defendant is warned in clear and unequivocal language of the effect of his refusal. People v. Boone, 71 A.D.2d 859, 419 N.Y.S.2d 187 (2d Dept. 1979).

Intoxicating driving; evidence of refusal to take test is inadmissible without counsel's presence.—Where an attorney seeks to confer with his client, who is then in custody, and such conference will not improperly delay the timely administering of the chemical examination, that right must be granted, or else a refusal to take such examination may not be utilized against the alleged drunken driver, either in a criminal proceeding, or in a quasi-criminal proceeding to revoke the driver's license. Leopold v. Toffany, 68 Misc. 2d 3, 325 N.Y.S.2d 24, *aff'd*, 38 A.D.2d 550, 327 N.Y.S.2d 999 (1st Dept. 1971).

Miranda; **exact language unnecessary.**—The exact language set forth in *Miranda v. Arizona* need not be utilized by the police as long as the substance of what is said adequately informs the defendant of his constitutional rights. People v. Evans, 162 A.D.2d 702, 557 N.Y.S.2d 120 (2d Dept. 1990).

Preservation.—*Miranda* violations did not require reversal where defendant did not move to suppress post-arrest statements in the trial court and where the People did not offer any such statements against him during trial. People v. Dunn, 163 A.D.2d 260, 558 N.Y.S.2d 542 (1st Dept. 1990).

Miranda **rights; waiver; defendant of subnormal intelligence.**—An effective waiver of *Miranda* rights may be made by an individual of subnormal intelligence, in this case a 20-year-old functionally illiterate, borderline retarded man who also suffered from organic brain damage, so long as it is established that the individual understood the immediate meaning of the warnings; the inability to understand the larger context or legal import underlying these rights is not necessary. People v. Williams, 62 N.Y.2d 285, 476 N.Y.S.2d 788, 465 N.E.2d 327 (1984).

—A knowing waiver of *Miranda* rights may be made by a person of subnormal intelligence. People v. Turley, 162 A.D.2d 564, 556 N.Y.S.2d 750 (2d Dept. 1990).

—The mere fact that the defendant was dirty, disheveled and appeared to be a derelict did not, in and of itself, establish that the defendant lacked the mental capacity to understand the

nature and consequences of his *Miranda* waiver. People v. Womble, 161 A.D.2d 667, 555 N.Y.S.2d 452, 453 (2d Dept. 1990).

—An effective waiver of *Miranda* rights may be made by an accused of subnormal intelligence so long as it is established that he understood the immediate meaning of the warnings. People v. Zulvaga, 148 A.D.2d 480, 538 N.Y.S.2d 628 (2d Dept. 1989).

—A defendant's impaired intelligence is but one factor to be considered in deciding whether the accused understood the *Miranda* waiver. The inquiry focuses on defendant's ability to grasp the basic concepts that he or she could refuse to talk to an investigator or could ask to speak to a lawyer. People v. Comfort, 6 A.D.3d 871, 775 N.Y.S.2d 127 (3d Dept. 2004).

Miranda **warnings; failure to request counsel.**—Defendant's statements in answer to *Miranda* warnings that he did not want counsel is a functional equivalent to a denial that he had a lawyer and his subsequent confessions would not be suppressed; although the police had information that the defendant had two prior arrests, they did not know whether charges had been filed or were pending. People v. Bertolo, 102 A.D.2d 193, 478 N.Y.S.2d 19 (2d Dept. 1984), *aff'd*, 65 N.Y.2d 111, 490 N.Y.S.2d 75, 480 N.E.2d 61 (1985).

Nonverbal "interrogation" by police.—Where the defendant, after being given the *Miranda* rights, first declined to answer questions and then indicated he wanted to talk to a district attorney, the actions of the police in placing decedent's furs in front of defendant without any words being spoken, and without the *Miranda* warnings being repeated, constituted an "interrogation" that required the suppression of statements the defendant made thereafter. People v. Ferro, 63 N.Y.2d 316, 482 N.Y.S.2d 237, 472 N.E.2d 13 (1984).

Missing persons investigation.—Statements were suppressed since the "missing persons investigation" exception to the entry of counsel principle did not apply as the body had been discovered the previous day. People v. Weinman, 90 A.D.2d 220, 458 N.Y.S.2d 265 (3d Dept. 1982).

Questioned for unreasonable period.—Confession was suppressed where defendant was detained for more than 19 hours beginning at 1:00 A.M. in a single room and questioned persistently by the police; was deprived of food and sleep during almost the entire interrogation period; was deprived of the company of a family member and was not advised of his right to counsel and his right against self-incrimination for 13 hours. People v. Anderson, 42 N.Y.2d 35, 396 N.Y.S.2d 625, 364 N.E.2d 1318 (1977).

—The fact that the police called the defendant, drove him to the polygraph test and told him after the test that he failed does not by itself make the inculpatory statements made, the result of coercion and suppressible. People v. Knighton, 91 A.D.2d 1077, 458 N.Y.S.2d 320 (3d Dept. 1983). *See also* People v. Anderson, 46 A.D.2d 150, 361 N.Y.S.2d 454 (4th Dept. 1974) (more than 13 hours); People v. Bowers, 45 A.D.2d 241, 357 N.Y.S.2d 563 (4th Dept. 1974) (after two days of confinement).

Defendant proceeding pro se; failure of court to assist in production of witness to whom defendant confessed.—Failure of trial court to assist defendant who was defending pro se, in producing at the trial the person to whom defendant initially confessed was reversible error. People v. Reade, 29 N.Y.2d 493, 323 N.Y.S.2d 969, 272 N.E.2d 481 (1971).

Readministering *Miranda* warnings.—Police were not required to readminster *Miranda* warnings and waivers after a five hour break in questioning, because defendant had knowingly and intelligently waived those rights five hours earlier and had remained in continuous custody in a non-coercive environment during that period. People v. Shomo, 235 A.D.2d 208, 653 N.Y.S.2d 292 (1st Dept. 1997).

—Readministration of *Miranda* warnings was not required because the statements were made within a reasonable time after the defendant's waiver. People v. Myers, 17 A.D.3d 699, 793 N.Y.S.2d 537 (2d Dept. 2005).

Premeditation.—Defendant's statement that "they have a place for disposing of the body where we put people . . . and they haven't been found for months" was admissible for its probative value as to premeditation or murder and the plan of conspiracy. People v. Ventimiglia, 52 N.Y.2d 350, 438 N.Y.S.2d 261, 420 N.E.2d 59 (1981).

Statement to private person.—Where the police officers acted reasonably and lawfully in allowing the wife to speak to her husband, the defendant, the Federal Constitution did not forbid the use of the defendant's subsequent statements to her at his criminal trial. Arizona v. Mauro, 481 U.S. 520, 107 S. Ct. 1931, 95 L. Ed. 2d 458 (1987).

—A statement made by a defendant to her attorney over the telephone that was inadvertently overheard by a police officer is admissible as a spontaneous statement. People v. Harris, 57 N.Y.2d 335, 456 N.Y.S.2d 694 (1982), cert. denied, 460 U.S. 1047 (1983).

—Where an informer works independently of the prosecution, provides information on his own initiative, and the government role is limited to the passive receipt of such information, the informer is not, as a matter of law, an agent of the government. People v. Cardona, 41 N.Y.2d 333, 392 N.Y.S.2d 606, 360 N.E.2d 1306 (1977).

—Court rejected defendant's contention that the inculpatory statement he made to the victim's mother should have been suppressed on the ground that she was acting as an agent of the police in violation of his Miranda rights, where her action was neither instigated nor supervised by the police. People v. Lewis, 273 A.D.2d 254, 709 N.Y.S.2d 572 (2d Dept. 2000).

—Court did not err in admitting into evidence an inculpatory statement he allegedly made to the complainant while he was in custody since there was no proof adduced that the complainant was an agent of the police or was acting either at the direction of or in cooperation with the police at the time the statement was purportedly made. People v. Haile M., 160 A.D.2d 1027, 554 N.Y.S.2d 737 (2d Dept. 1990).

—Court rejected claim that defendant's statement, made to a group of private citizens, should have been suppressed as the product of coercion. People v. Singletary, 135 A.D.2d 757, 522 N.Y.S.2d 872 (2d Dept. 1987).

—Defendant's brother could not be considered an agent of the police where the police gave the brother no instructions, offered no assistance in obtaining the inculpatory statements, and the brief mention of the fund for confidential information was, at most, "generalized encouragement." People v. Johnson, 303 A.D.2d 830, 758 N.Y.S.2d 687 (3d Dept. 2003).

—Since volunteer fire investigation as to the cause and the origin of the fire did accommodate police objectives, volunteer fire investigator was required to apply Miranda standards to arson investigation. People v. Todd, 134 Misc. 2d 988, 513 N.Y.S.2d 941 (St. Lawrence Co. Ct. 1987), aff'd, 149 A.D.2d 826, 540 N.Y.S.2d 349 (1989).

—The threatened loss of one's business (livelihood) is sufficient to cause one to make involuntary statements to a private person. People v. Weiss, 102 Misc. 2d 830, 424 N.Y.S.2d 844 (Sup. Ct. N.Y. Co. 1980).

—A statement made to AMEX officials was not "involuntarily made," for case law clearly indicates that it prohibits the state, not private entities, from offering a citizen the Hobson's choice between self-incrimination or loss of employment. People v. Barysh, 95 Misc. 2d 616, 408 N.Y.S.2d 190 (Sup. Ct. N.Y.C. 1978).

Statements to store security guards.—Although store detectives are private persons and need not give Miranda warnings a special patrolman when acting as such must do so. People v. Glenn, 106 Misc. 2d 806, 435 N.Y.S.2d 516 (Crim. Ct. Queens Co. 1981).

—The mere fact that the store security guards were given forms by the police and instructed to fingerprint suspects detained was not such involvement by police as to make the security guards either "agents of" or working "in cooperation with" the police pursuant to CPL § 60.45 and hence the security guards were not required to advise defendant of his constitutional rights. People v. Johnson, 101 Misc. 2d 833, 422 N.Y.S.2d 296 (Dist. Ct. Nassau Co. 1979).

Statements made to undercover officer.—Motion to suppress statements made by defendant to an undercover correction officer was granted where the court found that defendant's statements peripherally referred to the charges for which he was then under indictment and represented by counsel. People v. Boyd, 94 Misc. 2d 1074, 406 N.Y.S.2d 963 (Sup. Ct. Kings Co. 1978).

Statement to relative who was police officer.—Where defendant's brother-in-law, a police officer spoke with defendant at the police station after his arrest, brother-in-law was not acting as a public servant engaged in law enforcement activity but was acting as a concerned brother-in-law attempting to help

his wife's brother by giving him, in his opinion, the best advice he could offer and the subsequent statement by defendant was admissible. People v. Bracy, 98 Misc. 2d 346, 413 N.Y.S.2d 969 (Sup. Ct. Bronx Co. 1979).

—Defendant's statement, after his Miranda warnings, during a telephone conversation with his brother over the precinct telephone were suppressed where he was not advised nor was he aware that his words in that phone call would damn him. People v. Smith, 100 Misc. 2d 823, 420 N.Y.S.2d 132 (Sup. Ct. Bronx Co. 1979).

Statement to police officer; "make a deal."—Where defendant had just been released from jail and was on parole and did not have permission to be in Albany County, his attempt to "make a deal" with police officer could not be construed as an express acknowledgment of guilt of the crime he was charged with committing. People v. Greenwaldt, 72 A.D.2d 836, 421 N.Y.S.2d 679 (3d Dept. 1979).

Suppression of statements made to police agent.—Suppression was required of statements made by defendant to his employer who was acting as an informer and therefore as an agent of the police after defendant's attorney had advised the police that the defendant was not to be questioned further in relation to the crime. People v. Knapp, 57 N.Y.2d 161, 455 N.Y.S.2d 539, 441 N.E.2d 1057 (1982), cert. denied, 462 U.S. 1106 (1983).

Testimony of police brutality.—It was proper at the pretrial suppression hearing to exclude defendant's tender of evidence of the alleged beatings by the police of two other participants in the gang rape since there was no suggestion that the defendant had witnessed or was otherwise informed of the alleged brutality to his confederates nor was there any offer to demonstrate a closer nexus than that the other alleged beatings were administered by unidentified members of the police force during the course of the interrogation of two other members of the same group of young men on the same evening that defendant was questioned. People v. LaMar McC., 47 N.Y.2d 731, 417 N.Y.S.2d 248, 390 N.E.2d 1172 (1979).

—Reversible error was committed when the court denied defendant's request for a Huntley hearing to suppress his confession in view of the defendant's allegation of police brutality and the submission of medical records in support of his claim. He "was entitled to full inquiry into the voluntary nature of his purported confession even though he denied having made any confession." People v. Armioia, 92 A.D.2d 549, 459 N.Y.S.2d 118, aff'd, 96 A.D.2d 514, 464 N.Y.S.2d 993 (2d Dept. 1983).

—Where evidence indicates that a defendant has somehow sustained physical injury while in the custody of public officials, the prosecution bears the burden of accounting for the defendant's condition, and in the absence of a satisfactory accounting, admissions made during such custodial period cannot be found voluntary beyond a reasonable doubt. People v. Yarter, 51 A.D.2d 835, 380 N.Y.S.2d 96 (3d Dept. 1976), aff'd, 41 N.Y.2d 830, 393 N.Y.S.2d 393, 361 N.E.2d 1041 (1977).

—Despite defendant's denial that he made any statement to the police, he was entitled to full inquiry into the voluntary nature of his purported confession in view of his testimony as to brutality. People v. Brown, 44 A.D.2d 769, 354 N.Y.S.2d 263 (4th Dept. 1974).

Defendant; retained or assigned counsel.—An individual who has requested counsel in a noncustodial setting can subsequently waive or withdraw that request. People v. Davis, 75 N.Y.2d 517, 521, 554 N.Y.S.2d 460, 463-64, 553 N.E.2d 1008, 1011 (1990).

—Reversal was required where the one statement taken in defiance of the fact that the right to counsel had attached was by far the longest and the most detailed statement and the jury could have inferred its narrative carried the authoritative ring of more precise and unharried deliberation; hence it cannot be said beyond a reasonable doubt that the erroneously admitted statement did not contribute to the defendant's conviction. People v. Schaeffer, 56 N.Y.2d 448, 452 N.Y.S.2d 561, 438 N.E.2d 94 (1982).

—Motion to suppress was granted where defendant's statement was made after his request for counsel and it was not spontaneous. People v. Carmine, 53 N.Y.2d 816, 439 N.Y.S.2d 915, 422 N.E.2d 575 (1981).

—A defendant who requests counsel after his arrest but then without provocation seeks to buy his way out by offering a bribe to the arresting officer may be questioned by the officer as to anything legitimately related to the bribe offer that would be asked by an officer intending to accept such an offer. People v. Middleton, 54 N.Y.2d 474, 446 N.Y.S.2d 211, 430 N.E.2d 1264 (1981).

—Decision in *People v. Rogers*, 48 N.Y.2d 167, 422 N.Y.S.2d 18, 397 N.E.2d 709 (1979), which restricted questioning of a defendant, in custody, once an attorney had entered the proceeding, should be given retroactive effect. People v. Albro, 52 N.Y.2d 619, 439 N.Y.S.2d 836, 422 N.E.2d 496 (1981).

—Statements made by defendant during a telephone call to his father were suppressed because they were obtained by an officer after defendant had been assigned counsel. People v. Grimaldi, 52 N.Y.2d 611, 439 N.Y.S.2d 833, 422 N.E.2d 493 (1981).

—Reversible error was committed where defendant's uncounseled, inculpatory statement made during extradition from Florida to New York was admitted into evidence after he had requested counsel. People v. Lucas, 53 N.Y.2d 678, 439 N.Y.S.2d 99, 421 N.E.2d 494 (1981).

—Statements elicited from defendant in the absence of counsel immediately prior to the anticipated administration of a polygraph examination should have been suppressed where it could not be concluded that a valid waiver, which contemplated questioning in the absence of counsel, took place when defendant and his attorney consented to the polygraph examination. People v. Tillman, 52 N.Y.2d 1019, 438 N.Y.S.2d 296, 420 N.E.2d 94 (1981).

—Defendant's motion to suppress was granted where the officer who questioned defendant knew that he had been arrested eight months earlier on a sodomy charge by the same police department, therefore the officer was under an obligation to inquire into whether defendant was represented by an attorney on the earlier charge. People v. Smith, 54 N.Y.2d 954, 445 N.Y.S.2d 145, 429 N.E.2d 823 (1981).

—The right to counsel did not apply where the defendant had retained counsel in connection with a grand jury probe into Medicare fraud and he thereafter offered a kickback to a customer and the conversation was taped as the tape did not pertain to the defendant's prior offense but only to the commission of the new offense. People v. Ferrara, 54 N.Y.2d 498, 446 N.Y.S.2d 222, 430 N.E.2d 1275 (1981).

—Statements by the defendant after his arrest must be suppressed where the defendant hired a lawyer to arrange for his surrender and he surrendered in the lawyer's office even though he had retained the lawyer solely to arrange his surrender, which fact the police did not know, as the surrender with counsel present showed that the defendant was not competent to deal with the authorities without legal advice. People v. Marrero, 51 N.Y.2d 56, 431 N.Y.S.2d 508, 409 N.E.2d 980 (1980).

—Statements elicited prior to telephone request by defense counsel to cease questioning are admissible when not directly dependent upon subsequent statements. People v. Byrne, 47 N.Y.2d 117, 417 N.Y.S.2d 42, 390 N.E.2d 760 (1979).

—Reversal was required where defendant, who had already confessed orally after being given his rights at the fourth squad room, signed a second written confession at a point in time after a lawyer contacted by defendant's father made several phone calls to the police trying to find out where defendant was being held and an officer at headquarters informed the lawyer that no one was under arrest at the fourth squad across the street; nor was the error rendered harmless by the fact that the untainted oral confession, which led to the discovery of physical evidence, was identical in all material respects with the written one since the conclusion is unavoidable that the jury gave the written one more weight. People v. Garofolo, 46 N.Y.2d 592, 415 N.Y.S.2d 810, 389 N.E.2d 123 (1979).

—Once a defendant is represented by an attorney, the police may not elicit from him any statements, except those necessary for processing or physical needs, nor may they seek waiver of this right except in the presence of counsel. People v. Rogers, 48 N.Y.2d 167, 422 N.Y.S.2d 18, 397 N.E.2d 709 (1979).

—Where following his arraignment, and prior to his being questioned at the county jail, defendant's assigned counsel sent a letter to the sheriff notifying him of the assignment and directing that no one, other than a relative be permitted to question or confer with the defendant, the police thereafter should not have questioned the defendant about a related burglary in the absence of counsel. People v. Carl, 46 N.Y.2d 806, 413 N.Y.S.2d 916, 386 N.E.2d 828 (1978).

—When a suspect makes known his desire for an attorney at the time of his arrest, the police upon reaching the station house may not immediately and actively seek a waiver of his right and then proceed to interrogate him in the absence of counsel. People v. Buxton, 44 N.Y.2d 33, 403 N.Y.S.2d 487, 374 N.E.2d 384 (1978).

—Suppression of the homicide statement was required when the prosecutor interrogated the defendant in the absence of counsel after his privately retained counsel at his arraignment on an unrelated drug charge proclaimed in the presence of the court and the police officer taking defendant into custody in connection with a homicide that "I have advised Mr. Santiago not to make any statements to these police officers who are taking him into custody." People v. Ramos, 40 N.Y.2d 610, 389 N.Y.S.2d 299, 357 N.E.2d 955 (1976).

—Statements made must be suppressed where the police officer knew the defendant had been arrested six weeks previously and in view of the uniform practice of assigning attorneys to defendants at or shortly after their arraignment for a felony, the officer was charged with the duty to inquire whether defendant was represented by counsel in that case which he failed to do. People v. Bernal, 92 A.D.2d 489, 459 N.Y.S.2d 83 (1st Dept. 1983).

—Any statement by a defendant, who had been arrested and retained counsel, given to an informer acting as an agent of the police must be suppressed as it violated People v. Hobson, 39 N.Y.2d 479, 384 N.Y.S.2d 419, 348 N.E.2d 894 (1976). People v. Brooks, 83 A.D.2d 349, 444 N.Y.S.2d 615 (1st Dept. 1981).

—Knowledge by the police officer that the defendant was represented by counsel who had instructed the police not to question the defendant in relation to the crime did not invalidate the admissions made by defendant during a noncustodial investigation when he bragged in an attempt to convince the officer that he was experienced in these matters as the statements were not solicited but were "elicited in the course of a good faith police investigation." People v. Schwimmer, 85 A.D.2d 549, 445 N.Y.S.2d 8 (1st Dept. 1981).

—Once a suspect has retained counsel, statements made by him where counsel was present are admissible even though counsel's representation was clearly inadequate. People v. Claudio, 85 A.D.2d 245, 447 N.Y.S.2d 972 (2d Dept. 1982).

—Defendant's conviction for murder was affirmed where he sought to have the holding in *People v. Rogers*, 48 N.Y.2d 167, 422 N.Y.S.2d 18, 397 N.E.2d 709, applied retroactively to his case which had completed the appellate process prior to the *Rogers'* decision. People v. Harris, 84 A.D.2d 769, 443 N.Y.S.2d 784 (2d Dept. 1981); People v. Townsend, 81 A.D.2d 899, 439 N.Y.S.2d 174 (2d Dept. 1981) (*Rogers* applied to cases that were pending on appeal at the time of the decision).

—Court's error in allowing into evidence defendant's statement to police admitting the murder after defendant had retained counsel on an unrelated charge was not rendered harmless by the introduction of a videotape conversation defendant gave to a television reporter in which defendant also admitted the murder, where the videotape presented the shooting in a light substantially more favorable to defendant. People v. Coulter, 84 A.D.2d 669, 446 N.Y.S.2d 618 (4th Dept. 1981).

—Defendant does not have the right to counsel at presentence probation department interview. People v. Palazo, 147 Misc. 2d 829, 831, 556 N.Y.S.2d 432, 435 (Sup. Ct. Kings Co. 1990).

Defendant; retained or assigned counsel; non-custodial questioning.—A defendant who had counsel on a prior unrelated matter does not have a right to counsel that can only be waived in the presence of an attorney. People v. Bing, 76 N.Y.2d 331, 559 N.Y.S.2d 474, 558 N.E.2d 1011 (1990), specifically overruling People v. Bartolomeo, 53 N.Y.2d 225, 440 N.Y.S.2d 894, 423 N.E.2d 371 (1981).

—It was reversible error not to suppress statements obtained where the interrogating officer knew that the accused had been arrested by the same law enforcement agency nine days ago on an unrelated charge when in fact the suspect was represented by an attorney on the unrelated charge even though this fact was not known by the officer, who should have inquired, in such circumstances defendant cannot effectively waive his right to counsel. People v. Bartolomeo, 53 N.Y.2d 225, 440 N.Y.S.2d 894, 423 N.E.2d 371 (1981), specifically overruled by People v. Bing, 76 N.Y.2d 331, 559 N.Y.S.2d 474, 558 N.E.2d 1011 (1990).

—Defendant's telephoning the precinct and informing them that he would voluntarily appear with his attorney affirmatively interposed an attorney between himself and the police and his right to counsel could not be waived in the absence of counsel. People v. Ellis, 58 N.Y.2d 748, 459 N.Y.S.2d 25, 445 N.E.2d 201 (1982).

—Statements obtained by the police in a non-custodial setting when they knew that the defendant was already represented by an attorney are inadmissible. People v. Skinner, 52 N.Y.2d 24, 436 N.Y.S.2d 207, 417 N.E.2d 501 (1980).

Defendant's testimony; earlier trial.—The prohibition against custodial interrogation after a lawyer has entered the proceedings, absent the presence of counsel or a waiver, is aimed at protecting a defendant from deliberate efforts by law enforcement officials to elicit incriminating statements in disregard of constitutional protections; however, where the police are engaged in no such deliberate attempt but are instead pursuing a good faith investigation, neither the need nor the purpose for the rule is furthered by its application. People v. Clark, 41 N.Y.2d 612, 394 N.Y.S.2d 593, 363 N.E.2d 319, cert. denied, 434 U.S. 864 (1977).

—Police officer should not have questioned either defendant where he did not know whether the attorney represented both or only one of the defendants, and if so which one. People v. Coleman, 42 N.Y.2d 500, 399 N.Y.S.2d 185, 369 N.E.2d 742 (1977).

—Defendant's subsequent confession to felony murder was suppressed due to the absence of assigned counsel where the record revealed that the detectives after questioning defendant about an assault and a felony murder simultaneously and securing confessions to both utilized defendant's arraignment on the assault charge, at which time he was assigned counsel, to detain him in custody during which time they further interrogated him, in the absence of counsel, about the felony murder and referred to defendant's confession to the assault in a subtle attempt to secure a confession to the more serious crime of felony murder. People v. Ermo, 61 A.D.2d 177, 401 N.Y.S.2d 831 (2d Dept. 1978), aff'd, 37 N.Y.2d 863, 419 N.Y.S.2d 65, 392 N.E.2d 1248 (1979).

—The *Hobson* rule may not be invoked where the defendant is represented by counsel in a proceeding unrelated to charges under investigation. People v. Dibble, 59 A.D.2d 796, 398 N.Y.S.2d 755 (3d Dept. 1977).

Defendant; retained or assigned counsel; retroactivity.—The rule established in *People v. Cunningham*, 49 N.Y.2d 203, 424 N.Y.S.2d 421, 400 N.E.2d 360 (1980), that once a suspect requests counsel the questioning must cease is not to be applied retroactively. People v. Gonzalez, 81 A.D.2d 892, 439, 439 N.Y.S.2d 38 (2d Dept. 1981); People v. Jones, 108 Misc. 2d 845, 439 N.Y.S.2d 80 (Sup. Ct. N.Y. Co. 1981).

Defendant's right to counsel; felony complaint filed.—An accused may not waive his right to presence of counsel, absent counsel, after a felony complaint has been filed. People v. Walls, 74 A.D.2d 833, 425 N.Y.S.2d 170 (2d Dept. 1980).

—The court held that questioning of a defendant who testified to an exculpatory version of events, and claims to have told the police the same version upon arrest is permissible, citing Doyle v. Ohio, 426 U.S. 610, 96 S. Ct. 2240, 49 L. Ed. 2d 91. People v. Savage, 67 A.D.2d 562, 415 N.Y.S.2d 845 (1st Dept. 1979).

—Defendant's statement to police "ain't nothing I got to tell you," when viewed in context, did not rise to the level of an invocation of his right to remain silent or notify the police to cease the interview. People v. Allen, 147 A.D.2d 968, 537 N.Y.S.2d 415 (4th Dept. 1989).

Defendant's right to silence; court instructions.—There is no affirmative duty on the part of an alibi witness to inform authorities before trial of details surrounding an alibi defense, likewise, defendant, after his arrest, has no obligation to tell prosecution or police that he has an alibi. People v. Nolasco, 70 A.D.2d 549, 416 N.Y.S.2d 610 (1st Dept. 1979).

—Failure of the court to instruct jury that prosecutor improperly questioned defendant repeatedly and made issue of her refusal to make statement after her arrest, was prejudicial error since defendant had no obligation to speak when in police custody and no damaging inferences were to be drawn. People v. Finney, 39 A.D.2d 749, 332 N.Y.S.2d 83 (2d Dept. 1972), aff'd, 33 N.Y.2d 536, 347 N.Y.S.2d 435, 301 N.E.2d 422 (1973).

—Although the erroneous cross-examination of defendant's post-arrest silence placed a piece of improper evidence before the jury, reversal was not required since the proof of guilt in

the case was strong. People v. Musolino, 54 A.D.2d 22, 386 N.Y.S.2d 710 (3d Dept. 1976), cert. denied, 430 U.S. 935 (1977).

Defendant's silence after warnings held not a waiver.—A defendant's silence in response to a police officer's inquiry after *Miranda* rights are read as to whether defendant wishes to answer questions without an attorney present cannot be deemed to constitute a valid waiver of his right to remain silent or a consent to be questioned. People v. Schroder, 71 A.D.2d 907, 419 N.Y.S.2d 611 (2d Dept. 1979).

Dunaway rule: lack of probable cause to arrest not overcome by inculpatory statements made after Miranda warnings.—Where defendant was locked in the back set of a police car, taken to the station house and questioned about her husband's escape from a state correctional facility for twenty minutes before *Miranda* warnings were administered, subsequent inculpatory statements were held inadmissible under the rule in *Dunaway v. New York*, 442 U.S. 200, 99 S. Ct. 2248, 60 L. Ed. 2d 824 (1979), namely that the taint of illegality stemming from an arrest for less than probable cause is not removed from a subsequent inculpatory statement made as a direct result of the seizure and in close temporal proximity thereto without any intervening circumstances because a defendant is advised of *Miranda* rights. People v. Gonzalez, 71 A.D.2d 775, 419 N.Y.S.2d 322 (3d Dept. 1979).

Dunaway rule; suppression hearing; probable cause.—It was error requiring a vacatur of defendant's guilty plea for the court at the suppression hearing held to determine the admissibility of inculpatory admissions and a signed statement made by defendant after *Miranda* warnings were administered to refuse to permit defendant's attorney to cross-examine the arresting police officers on the issue of probable cause to arrest; statements obtained by exploitation of unlawful police conduct or detention must be suppressed as violative of the Fourth Amendment and therefore a defendant must be accorded an opportunity to delve fully into the circumstances attendant upon his arrest or detention. People v. Misuis, 47 N.Y.2d 979, 419 N.Y.S.2d 961, 393 N.E.2d 1034 (1979).

—Confession was not suppressed where, although the initial police detention of defendant lacked probable cause and was therefore illegal, his confession was not gained through the exploitation of this illegality and was made only after police, by virtue of their having obtained a statement from a co-defendant which clearly implicated the defendant in these crimes, had obtained the probable cause necessary for a legal arrest. People v. Johnson, 75 A.D.2d 715, 427 N.Y.S.2d 120 (4th Dept. 1980).

Felony complaint filed; subsequent statements by defendant in the absence of counsel; inadmissible.—A confession obtained in the absence of counsel after a felony complaint had been filed in court was suppressed since the defendant's right to counsel attached when the felony complaint was filed and he could not thereafter waive his right without the assistance of counsel. People v. Samuels, 49 N.Y.2d 218, 424 N.Y.S.2d 892, 400 N.E.2d 1344 (1979).

—The filing of the felony complaint and the issuance of the warrant based thereon formally commenced the criminal proceeding against the defendant and placed him "in no position to safeguard his rights" and entitled him as of right to the assistance of counsel which could only be waived in the physical presence of counsel; *People v. Samuels*, 49 N.Y.2d 218, 428 N.Y.S.2d 892, 400 N.E.2d 1344, is to be applied retroactively. People v. Pepper, 76 A.D.2d 1006, 429 N.Y.S.2d 490 (3d Dept. 1980), aff'd, 53 N.Y.2d 213, 440 N.Y.S.2d 889, 423 N.E.2d 366 (1981). *See also* People v. Parker, 78 A.D.2d 580, 432 N.Y.S.2d 564 (4th Dept. 1980).

Grand jury proceeding; defendant's right to silence.—A defendant in a criminal proceeding may testify in his own behalf but failure to testify is not a factor from which any inference unfavorable to him may be drawn and no allusion may be made thereto, CPL § 60.15(2); this rule of evidence is also applicable to grand jury proceedings, CPL § 190.30(1). People v Scott, 70 A.D.2d 601, 416 N.Y.S.2d 83 (2d Dept. 1979).

Harmless error.—Although a criminal suspect had not been given his *Miranda* rights during the course of a custodial interrogation, the admission of his statement at trial constituted harmless error where other evidence of guilt was overwhelming. People v. Rivera, 57 N.Y.2d 453, 457 N.Y.S.2d 191, 443 N.E.2d 439 (1982).

Huntley hearing; right to produce witnesses who would

testify about police coercion.—Defendant was entitled at hearing to produce three witnesses who would testify about prearrest statements by police concerning what they might do to the defendant if he refused to testify. People v. Murray, 79 A.D.2d 993, 434 N.Y.S.2d 720 (2d Dept. 1981).

Hypnosis.—The reliability of defendant's statements while under hypnosis was not established where there was no video-tape of the interview session, a tape recording was made of part of the session only, there was no evidence of what transpired between the hypnotist and the defendant prior to the time hypnosis was induced, defendant's attorney was present at the hypnotic session, and there was testimony from the hypnotist indicating that a subject could lie under hypnosis as readily as if he were not hypnotized. People v. Lewis, 103 Misc. 2d 881, 427 N.Y.S.2d 177 (Sup. Ct. N.Y. Co. 1980).

Illegal arrest; attenuation of the taint.—Absent a showing of attenuation, a statement obtained by a suspect following a *Payton* violation must be suppressed. People v. Harris, 77 N.Y.2d 434, 568 N.Y.S.2d 702, 570 N.E.2d 1051 (1991).

—Even assuming *Payton* violation, statements by defendant were admissible where nearly 7 hours passed between the illegal arrest and the issuance of the statements, and defendant was not handcuffed and had the opportunity to speak to his girlfriend during that time. People v. Leandry, 130 A.D.2d 351, 515 N.Y.S.2d 11 (1st Dept. 1987).

—Since police had no probable cause to arrest defendants on charges of murder, their successful attempt to get the three to travel with them in separate police cars from Yonkers to Hauppague, Suffolk County, 58 miles away, on a windy snowy, bitterly cold night, backed up by a threat to call the Yonkers police on them for marihuana dealing if they did not comply rendered the defendant's subsequent confessions suppressible, as being fruit of the original illegal detention. People v. Biggs, 88 A.D.2d 960, 451 N.Y.S.2d 196 (2d Dept. 1982).

—The intervening circumstance attenuated the taint of the initial illegal detention and rendered the defendant's confession admissible where the defendant was involuntarily brought to the precinct in handcuffs, without probable cause, and during the illegal detention, but prior to questioning, a period of two hours, the police independently obtained probable cause to arrest him. People v. Calhoun, 78 A.D.2d 658, 432 N.Y.S.2d 226 (2d Dept. 1980).

—A statement made by defendant which is voluntary under Fifth Amendment standards will nevertheless be suppressed if it has been obtained through the exploitation of an illegal arrest unless there was sufficient attenuation to sustain the admissibility of the statements. People v. Calhoun, 73 A.D.2d 972, 424 N.Y.S.2d 247 (2d Dept. 1980).

Inadequate *Miranda* warning.—A conviction for criminal possession of a controlled substance must be reversed and a new trial ordered where the *Miranda* warning advised her that if she did not have an attorney one would be appointed for her but failed to advise her that she had a right to an attorney present before she answered any questions. People v. Graham, 78 A.D.2d 831, 433 N.Y.S.2d 148 (1st Dept. 1980).

—*Miranda* warnings administered to the defendant were deficient because the defendant was not advised that he had the right to consult with an attorney prior to and during the course of any police questioning. People v. DiLucca, 133 A.D.2d 779, 520 N.Y.S.2d 171 (2d Dept. 1987).

Inculpatory statements made after advise as to right to counsel but before counsel retained.—Motion to suppress was denied where defendant was questioned on an unrelated larceny charge before the criminal action had commenced and she was not represented by counsel on the charges she was arrested for. People v. Angus, 81 A.D.2d 971, 439 N.Y.S.2d 747 (3d Dept. 1981), *aff'd*, 56 N.Y.2d 549, 449 N.Y.S.2d 966, 434 N.E.2d 1344 (1982).

Inculpatory statement made after *Miranda* admissible.—Defendant's statement was admitted into evidence where he was given *Miranda* warnings, then indicated he did not want to say anything; thereafter during arraignment he made an inculpatory statement. People v. North, 81 A.D.2d 944, 439 N.Y.S.2d 698 (3d Dept. 1981).

Informers.—The mere fact that an informant, who was clearly acting on his own initiative, had provided information in the past in other cases did not render him an agent of the police for all purposes. People v. Belgrave, 172 A.D.2d 335, 568 N.Y.S.2d 404 (1st Dept. 1991).

Interrogation; unrelated crime.—A pending unrelated criminal case upon which an arrest warrant has issued does not bar the police from questioning a suspect when the suspect does not in fact have counsel on the unrelated charge. People v. Kazmarick, 52 N.Y.2d 322, 438 N.Y.S.2d 247, 420 N.E.2d 45 (1981).

—A lawful arrest upon a bench warrant, followed by lawful questioning about an arson, did not constitute illegality because the police intended prior to the arrest upon the warrant to interrogate defendant about the arson which had been committed after the bench warrant was issued. People v. Cypriano, 73 A.D.2d 902, 424 N.Y.S.2d 214 (1st Dept. 1980).

—The limited inquiry by police regarding defendant's pending weapon charge in New York City went no further than to elicit the fact that it existed, which the Schenectady police already knew, and the police elicited the most damaging information without any reference to the New York City charge. Court held under the circumstances that the questioning was not in violation of the principles of *People v. Cohen*, 90 N.Y.2d 632, 665 N.Y.S.2d 30, 687 N.E.2d 1313 (1997). People v. Grant, 260 A.D.2d 860, 690 N.Y.S.2d 139 (3d Dept. 1999).

—Although officer was aware of pending unrelated burglary charge against the defendant and failed to inquire of the defendant whether he was actually represented by counsel on that charge, there was no right to counsel violation where the defendant was not actually represented on that charge. People v. Brennan, 129 A.D.2d 892, 514 N.Y.S.2d 528 (3d Dept. 1987).

Interrogation.—Defendant's statement that a nearby garbage bag belonged to him was properly not suppressed because the officer's inquiry was not "interrogation" but solely to "clarify" the nature of the situation. People v. Suardy, 163 A.D.2d 85, 558 N.Y.S.2d 26 (1st Dept. 1990).

—Before questioning, the police were under no obligation to inform the defendant of the specific crime they were investigating. People v. Myers, 17 A.D.3d 699, 793 N.Y.S.2d 537 (2d Dept. 2005).

—A defendant's single, unwarned statement was not the result of relentless custodial interrogation, and it did not taint the defendant's post-*Miranda* statements which would require them to be suppressed under the continuous chain of events theory. Furthermore, the statement was not so incriminating that it committed defendant to confessing to the crime. People v. Jamison, 307 A.D.2d 368, 762 N.Y.S.2d 640 (2d Dept. 2003).

—Since the officer's single question as to the reason for the defendant's presence in house, which had been burglarized, had an investigatory purpose it did not require the giving of the *Miranda* warnings. People v. Harris, 142 A.D.2d 596, 530 N.Y.S.2d 276 (2d Dept. 1988).

—Officer's terse and pointed response to the defendant's questions concerning basis for arrest did not constitute the functional equivalent of interrogation. People v. Coleman, 142 A.D.2d 586, 530 N.Y.S.2d 242 (2d Dept. 1988).

—The detective was entitled to ask the defendant his identity without the necessity of formal warnings. People v. Vasquez, 141 A.D.2d 880, 530 N.Y.S.2d 159 (2d Dept. 1988).

—Defendant's statement to police after his arrest were not suppressible as part of a custodial interrogation where defendant's response to the arresting officer's questions of whether he had been previously arrested for driving while intoxicated and whether he would take a breathalyzer test was that "he had only three or four drinks because his wife has had a baby"; the notification of arrest and the officer's questions were proper, and not "interrogation." People v. Tarsczowicz, 88 A.D.2d 772, 451 N.Y.S.2d 507 (4th Dept. 1982).

—The Supreme Court of the United States has held that the term "interrogation" under *Miranda* refers not only to express questioning, but also to any words or actions on the part of the police (other than those normally attendant to arrest and custody) that the police should know are reasonably likely to elicit an incriminating response from the suspect (Rhode Island v. Innis, 446 U.S. 291, 100 S. Ct. 1682, 64 L. Ed. 2d 297); since the police cannot be held accountable for the unforeseeable results of their words or actions, the definition of interrogation can extend only to words or actions on the part of police officers that they should have known were reasonably likely to elicit an incriminating response. People v. Bodner, 75 A.D.2d 440, 430 N.Y.S.2d 433 (4th Dept. 1980).

Intoxication.—Statements to law enforcement officials will only be rendered involuntary as a result of intoxication if the defendant can demonstrate that he or she was intoxicated to a degree of mania or of being unable to understand the meaning of the statements. People v. Benjamin, 17 A.D.3d 688, 793 N.Y.S.2d 547 (2d Dept. 2005).

—Self-induced intoxication alone will not render a confession inadmissible unless it can be shown that the accused was intoxicated to the degree of mania, or of being unable to understand the meaning of his statements, or to the point where he had lost contact with reality. People v. Cureton, 139 A.D.2d 756, 527 N.Y.S.2d 505 (2d Dept. 1988).

—Self-induced intoxication alone will not render a confession inadmissible. Only where it is shown that the accused was intoxicated to the degree of mania, or of being unable to understand the meaning of his statements will reception of a confession be barred. People v. Durante, 48 A.D.2d 962, 369 N.Y.S.2d 560 (3d Dept. 1975).

Involuntary waiver of Miranda rights; use of polygraph test to coerce confession.—Combined effects of the taking of the polygraph test and the person administering the test informing defendant that she was lying added to the psychological coercion inducing the confession. People v. Zimmer, 68 Misc. 2d 1067, 329 N.Y.S.2d 17 (Wayne Co. Ct. 1972), aff'd, 40 A.D.2d 944, 339 N.Y.S.2d 671 (4th Dept. 1972).

Juvenile confession suppressed; refusal to permit parent visit.—A confession obtained after a refusal to allow the 16- and 17-year-old defendants to speak with their mother who was present and with whom they resided was suppressed. People v. Rivera, 78 A.D.2d 556, 431 N.Y.S.2d 1015 (2d Dept. 1980).

Lineup.—Where lineup was conducted pursuant to removal order and where defendant failed to waive his attorney's presence, testimony with respect to the lineup should have been suppressed. People v. Williams, 156 A.D.2d 497, 548 N.Y.S.2d 773 (2d Dept. 1990).

Lineups before formal prosecutorial proceedings; no right to counsel.—The Sixth and Fourteenth Amendments only require right to counsel after the initiation of formal prosecutorial proceedings, and Miranda warnings apply only to custodial interrogations; lineups do not initiate Miranda right to counsel because they are not interrogations; the limited benefits provided by counsel at investigatory lineups are far outweighed by the policy considerations against it, and there is no basis in the state constitution for requiring counsel at investigatory lineups; however if a suspect has already retained counsel, his attorney may not be actively excluded from the lineup. People v. Hawkins, 55 N.Y.2d 474, 450 N.Y.S.2d 159, 435 N.E.2d 376, cert. denied, 459 U.S. 846 (1982).

—If a defendant has actually engaged counsel prior to an investigatory lineup that attorney may not be deliberately excluded. People v. LaClere, 157 A.D.2d 473, 549 N.Y.S.2d 397 (1st Dept. 1990).

—There is no right to counsel at a pre-arraignment lineup. People v. Lewis, 161 A.D.2d 117, 554 N.Y.S.2d 548 (1st Dept. 1990).

—Contrary to the defendant's specific contention he was not entitled to counsel, although requested, at the investigatory lineup. People v. Wilson, 156 A.D.2d 743, 549 N.Y.S.2d 494 (2d Dept. 1990); see also People v. Quick, 158 A.D.2d 625, 551 N.Y.S.2d 594 (2d Dept. 1990) (investigatory corporeal identification proceedings).

—Although the State has no obligation to supply counsel at investigatory lineups, if a suspect already has counsel, his attorney may not be excluded from the lineup proceedings. People v. Riley, 158 A.D.2d 559, 551 N.Y.S.2d 537 (2d Dept. 1990).

Miranda; generally.—In issuing Miranda warnings, it is not necessary that the police mouth a ritualistic formula so long as the words used convey the requisite information. People v. Thomches, 172 A.D.2d 786, 569 N.Y.S.2d 158 (2d Dept. 1991).

—Threshold crime inquiries do not require Miranda warnings. People v. Karim, 172 A.D.2d 625, 568 N.Y.S.2d 429 (2d Dept. 1991).

Miranda warnings; defendant's refusal to answer questions ignored.—Confession was suppressed where defendant, upon his arrest and after being advised of his rights, told police officers that he would not answer any questions without an attorney present, but the officers, after bringing defendant to station and completing the paperwork on the arrest, proceeded to interrogate defendant without readvising him of his rights.

People v. Clark, 45 N.Y.2d 432, 408 N.Y.S.2d 463, 380 N.E.2d 290 (1978).

Miranda; waiver of rights.—The defendant implicitly waived his Miranda rights where the detective, at the defendant's request, obtained a card with the Miranda warnings written in Spanish and instructed the defendant to read it, record "yes" or "no" after each statement and, if he did not understand to so indicate, and defendant wrote "yes" next to each statement, did not ask any questions, and immediately proceeded to give a statement to the detective. People v. Sirno, 76 N.Y.2d 967, 563 N.Y.S.2d 730, 556 N.E.2d 479 (1990).

—The fact that the defendant was a patient in a psychiatric center at the time of the waiver does not invalidate the waiver. People v. Love, 57 N.Y.2d 998, 457 N.Y.S.2d 238, 443 N.E.2d 486 (1982).

—After receiving his Miranda rights, defendant waived them by nodding his head affirmatively, thus subsequent statements made were admissible into evidence where he had at least one previous felonious brush with the law. People v. Rooney, 82 A.D.2d 840, 439 N.Y.S.2d 659 (2d Dept. 1981).

Non-custodial interrogation; statements admissible.—The statement of a defendant, who voluntarily accompanied the police to the precinct after the Miranda warning, is admissible as the defendant was not in custody; in deciding whether a defendant is in custody, the test is not what the defendant or the police thought but, rather, what a reasonable person, innocent of any crime in the defendant's position would have thought. People v. McNeely, 77 A.D.2d 205, 433 N.Y.S.2d 293 (4th Dept. 1980).

Plea bargaining session; admissions not admissible.—Defendant's inculpatory statements must be suppressed, notwithstanding his knowing waiver of Miranda rights, where such statements were obtained from defendant during the course of a plea bargaining conference with the Assistant District Attorney pursuant to PL § 65.00(1)(b). People v. Smith, 94 Misc. 2d 384, 404 N.Y.S.2d 947 (Sup. Ct. New York Co. 1978).

Police have no obligation to inquire whether defendant is represented by counsel.—Court held in two unrelated cases that once a suspect denies that he is represented by counsel on a pending unrelated charge, the police are under no obligation to make further inquiry, so long as it is reasonable to believe the defendant's disclaimer of representation, as where the pending case is of a nonserious nature. People v. Lucarano, People v. Walker, 61 N.Y.2d 138, 472 N.Y.S.2d 894, 460 N.E.2d 1328 (1984).

—Admissions elicited from defendant less than two hours after his 5:00 PM arraignment and the following morning must be suppressed where defendant, at the time of his arraignment, requested assignment of counsel but such request was denied on the ground that he could not afford his own counsel; the police were not at liberty to elicit statements from defendant before he had the opportunity to obtain counsel. People v. Dunbar, 62 A.D.2d 1132, 404 N.Y.S.2d 464 (4th Dept. 1978).

Request to call family.—Defendant's oral confession must be suppressed, despite the fact that he was properly notified of his constitutional preinterrogation rights and did not request to see a lawyer, where defendant, an 18-year-old charged with murder, was taken to a different police station than the other perpetrators and was twice ignored by police when he asked to telephone his mother, and where, after the oral confession had been obtained, defendant's lawyer arrived and was not immediately allowed to see his client People v. Bevilaqua, 45 N.Y.2d 508, 410 N.Y.S.2d 549, 382 N.E.2d 1326 (1978).

—Court, in finding defendant's statement voluntary, rejected contention that will of recidivist defendant could have been easily overborne by the denial of a telephone call to his grandmother. People v. Ebron, 123 A.D.2d 783, 507 N.Y.S.2d 258 (2d Dept. 1986).

—Denying the request of a suspect undergoing custodial interrogation to phone his family makes inadmissible a subsequent confession. People v. Talamo, 55 A.D.2d 506, 391 N.Y.S.2d 474 (3d Dept. 1977).

Post-arraignment admissions; right to counsel.—Defendant's motion to suppress was granted where the statements were obtained from him following his uncounseled waiver of his right to remain silent after the filing, in court, of an accusatory instrument charging him with a crime. People v. Fauntleroy, 74 A.D.2d 612, 424 N.Y.S.2d 736 (2d Dept. 1980).

CPL

Post-indictment statements.—All post-indictment custodial interrogations in absence of counsel are bared, irrespective of whether counsel has actually entered the case at time of the interrogation. People v. Jamison, 73 A.D.2d 853, 423 N.Y.S.2d 184 (1st Dept. 1980).

—Defendant's post indictment statements made to police without the aid of counsel, after expressing an interest in cooperating as an informant, were deemed inadmissible as they violated his sixth amendment right to counsel. People v. Welch, 82 A.D.2d 899, 440 N.Y.S.2d 283 (2d Dept. 1981).

—Defendant's statement should have been suppressed where he was interrogated in Virginia with respect to robbery charges after he had been indicted in such charges in New York and counsel had appeared in the case on his behalf. People v. Couch, 74 A.D.2d 582, 424 N.Y.S.2d 304 (2d Dept. 1980).

Prior statements; used to impeach defendant.—A prior statement of a witness is admissible for impeachment purposes even though it does not directly contradict the witness's testimony; a more rigorous rule requiring direct contradiction would be at odds with the purpose underlying use of prior inconsistents, since such statements are admitted principally to assist the jury in its fact-finding role. People v. Wise, 46 N.Y.2d 321, 413 N.Y.S.2d 334, 385 N.E.2d 1262 (1978).

Redaction unnecessary.—County Court properly rejected defense counsel's request to redact the portion of defendant's statement that read, "I didn't want to go back to jail because I had just got out," because statement was admissible to show defendant's motive and intent, and its probable value outweighed its prejudicial. People v. Brumfield, 236 A.D.2d 839, 654 N.Y.S.2d 74 (4th Dept. 1997).

Refusal to take breathalyzer test; *Miranda* warning necessary.—Performance tests administered to a defendant arrested for drunk driving need not be preceded by *Miranda* warnings. People v. Jacquin, 71 N.Y.2d 825, 527 N.Y.S.2d 728, 729, 522 N.E.2d 1026 (1988).

—The refusal of defendant to submit to a breathalyzer test after being advised of his *Miranda* rights is admissible as evidence against the defendant. People v. Haitz, 65 A.D.2d 172, 411 N.Y.S.2d 57 (4th Dept. 1978).

"Res gestae" statement.—If it is determined that the statement in question is part of the *res gestae* then no notice pursuant to CPL § 710.30 is required; however, if the defendant raises the question of voluntariness of the statement, then a hearing is required under CPL § 60.45. People v. Bostic, 97 Misc. 2d 1039, 412 N.Y.S.2d 948 (Dist. Ct. Nassau Co. 1978).

Request for counsel.—Defendant's suggestions that he or the police might want to consult with his attorney with respect to certain matters did not constitute an unequivocal assertion of the right to counsel. People v. Freidman, 71 N.Y.2d 845, 527 N.Y.S.2d 737, 738, 522 N.E.2d 1035 (1988).

—Defendant's inquiry re police "Should I speak to a lawyer" did not unequivocally inform the police of his intention to retain counsel. People v. Hicks, 69 N.Y.2d 969, 516 N.Y.S.2d 648, 509 N.E.2d 343 (1987).

—Once a suspect in custody requests the assistance of counsel he may not be questioned further in the absence of an attorney; an uncounseled waiver of a constitutional right will not be deemed voluntary if it is made after the right to counsel has been invoked. People v. Cunningham, 49 N.Y.2d 203, 424 N.Y.S.2d 421, 400 N.E.2d 360 (1980).

—Defendant never made an unequivocal assertion of her right to remain silent where, at the end of *Miranda* warnings, when the detective asked her if she wanted to speak to the police, defendant answered in the negative, but immediately asked what the question meant, to which the officer replied with an explanation reiterating that the defendant was not obligated to speak to the police, and the defendant then agreed to answer questions. People v. Ingram, 19 A.D.3d 101, 795 N.Y.S.2d 592 (1st Dept. 2005).

—Defendant did not invoke his right to counsel by his question as to whether he would be furnished an attorney with whom he could consult as to the advisability of speaking to police. People v. Santiago, 133 A.D.2d 429, 519 N.Y.S.2d 413 (2d Dept. 1987), *aff'd*, 72 N.Y.2d 836, 530 N.Y.S.2d 546, 526 N.E.2d 36 (1988).

—Fact that the defendant asked the Assistant District attorney whether or not he should speak to an attorney did not serve to invoke his right to counsel. People v. Banks, 135 A.D.2d 643, 522 N.Y.S.2d 574 (2d Dept. 1987).

—Defendant's motion to suppress was granted where he responded to the inquiry of whether he wished to speak without the presence of an attorney by "Naa, I don't want to talk to you. I don't want to say anything." This effectively invoked his right to counsel and he could not thereafter waive that right in the absence of counsel; thus, the police violated his rights when they resumed questioning him concerning the ownership of the car, which was not a question of pedigree since it went to the essence of the crime. People v. Antonio, 86 A.D.2d 614, 446 N.Y.S.2d 96 (2d Dept. 1982).

—A defendant's invocation of his right against self-incrimination or to counsel in response to police questioning cannot be used against him during the People's direct case. This rule applies equally to situations in which a defendant responds to questioning, but declines to answer certain questions, or desires to halt questioning. People v. Hunt, 18 A.D.3d 891, 794 N.Y.S.2d 490 (3d Dept. 2005).

—An inquiry about whether or not one should contact an attorney does not, without more, constitute an unequivocal invocation of the right to counsel. People v. Hurd, 279 A.D.2d 892, 719 N.Y.S.2d 752 (3d Dept. 2001).

Request for counsel; failure to honor.—All statements made by defendant after he requested "either to have an attorney or a priest to talk to, to have present" were properly suppressed. People v. Stroh, 48 N.Y.2d 1000, 425 N.Y.S.2d 548, 401 N.E.2d 906 (1980).

—It could not be said that defendant's request for counsel was scrupulously honored and defendant's statements were ordered suppressed where defendant stated while in police custody that he wished to speak with an attorney and the police, rather than taking steps to assist defendant in obtaining counsel, merely returned him to a holding pen and a few hours later, after defendant had cooperated in certain respects, affirmatively sought and obtained a waiver of defendant's rights. People v. Dean, 47 N.Y.S.2d 967, 419 N.Y.S.2d 957, 393 N.E.2d 1030 (1979).

—A *Wade/Huntley* motion must be granted where a defendant who was a suspect in a robbery in Suffolk County when visiting his parole officer in New York City was asked to remain to speak to detectives from Suffolk County; requested an attorney which request was denied and subsequently made incriminating statements to the detective and was then placed in a line-up and identified; statements were inadmissible because the request for counsel to the parole officer, a law enforcement agent, must be deemed to have been made to the detectives. People v. Moore, 79 A.D.2d 619, 433 N.Y.S.2d 473 (2d Dept. 1980).

—The defendant's statements must be suppressed where when advised of his rights he refused to answer questions without an attorney yet the police officer continued to question him eliciting statements and the taint of such illegal questioning carried over to subsequent questioning by the district attorney two hours later as the offending officer at the first interrogation was present at and assisted in the second questioning. People v. Johnson, 79 A.D.2d 617, 433 N.Y.S.2d 477 (2d Dept. 1980).

—The statements made to the assistant district attorney should have been suppressed where, after the defendant had expressed his desire to consult with an attorney and to remain silent, the authorities failed to act on these requests and in fact tried to dissuade defendant from exercising these rights. People v. Laricos, 73 A.D.2d 652, 422 N.Y.S.2d 731 (2d Dept. 1979).

Right to counsel.—Defendant's right to counsel did not attach when his father informed a detective that an attorney was en route to the police station. While it is conceivable that a third party could reliably impart knowledge of counsel's involvement to the police, it would be unreasonable to require the police to cease a criminal investigation and begin a separate inquiry to verify whether defendant is actually represented by counsel. People v. Grice, 100 N.Y.2d 318, 763 N.Y.S.2d 227, 794 N.E.2d 9 (2003).

—Denial of defendant's right to counsel was not subject to harmless error analysis. People v. Hilliard, 73 N.Y.2d 584, 585, 542 N.Y.S.2d 507, 508, 540 N.E.2d 702, 703 (1989).

—Neither the federal nor the state constitutional guarantee of the right to counsel includes the right to have counsel present when a criminal enterprise is being planned or executed. People v. Bell, 73 N.Y.2d 153, 156, 538 N.Y.S.2d 754, 758, 535 N.E.2d 1294, 1297 (1989).

—When a defendant, who had been arrested for driving while intoxicated but not yet formally charged in court, did not request the assistance of counsel and made an uncounseled waiver of the statutory right to refuse a sobriety test, there was no basis for suppressing the sobriety test results. People v. Shaw, 72 N.Y.2d 1032, 1033, 534 N.Y.S.2d 929, 930, 531 N.E.2d 650, 651 (1988).

—The officer's inquiry, "Do you have an attorney?" and the defendant's answer "No," was sufficient to satisfy the People's obligation where the interrogating officer had knowledge that defendant had been arrested and processed in the officer's own precinct 6-1/2 months earlier on felony charges and thus was obligated to make further inquiry. People v. Shaves, 69 N.Y.2d 766, 513 N.Y.S.2d 105, 505 N.E.2d 614 (1986).

—Even though the right-to-counsel claim was never raised at trial level, the claim is so fundamental that it may be raised for the first time on appeal. People v. Sanders, 50 N.Y.2d 51, 451 N.Y.S.2d 30, 436 N.E.2d 480 (1982).

—It was within the power of the court to grant permission to the defendant to waive the presence of already retained counsel where the crime he is charged with is punishable only by a fine; however the trial judge must make a sufficiently searching inquiry into the waiver of counsel to be reasonably assured that the defendant appreciates the "dangers and disadvantages" of the waiver; the trial judge's inquiry was inadequate where he merely informed defendant of his right to counsel and asked whether defendant's waiver was "freely and voluntarily" made. People v. White, 56 N.Y.2d 110, 451 N.Y.S.2d 57, 436 N.E.2d 507 (1982).

—It was proper for the prosecutor to dismiss defendant's shoplifting case for the sole purpose of allowing detectives to question defendant without the presence of his attorney. People v. Murray, 129 A.D.2d 319, 517 N.Y.S.2d 515 (1st Dept. 1987).

—Defendant's question to detective concerning whether he should call his lawyer, after he showed the detective his lawyer's business card, did not constitute an unequivocal invocation of the right to counsel which would prevent further police interrogation. People v. Thompson, 271 A.D.2d 555, 706 N.Y.S.2d 136 (2d Dept. 2000).

—Reversal was required where during the cross-examination of the defendant, the trial court directed an overnight recess, and directed defense counsel, over his objection, not to discuss the defendant's testimony with the defendant "at all." People v. Blount, 159 A.D.2d 579, 552 N.Y.S.2d 441 (2d Dept. 1990).

—Right to counsel based on an individual's representation in a pending proceeding does not extend to unrelated proceedings of wholly civil nature, such as bankruptcy proceedings. People v. Patterson, 137 A.D.2d 729, 524 N.Y.S.2d 814 (2d Dept. 1988).

—Suppression of the statement was required where the detective had actual knowledge that the defendant had been arraigned earlier that day on another charge and he failed to inquire if he was represented by counsel on that charge as he had a duty to make such inquiry. People v. Levy, 86 A.D.2d 878, 447 N.Y.S.2d 290 (2d Dept. 1982).

—Defendant's response to question of whether he wanted counsel by asking whether he needed counsel after his warrantless arrest on probable cause does not constitute the kind of unequivocal invocation of right to counsel under People v. Cunningham which prevents further interrogation; subsequent admissions were admissible. People v. Walker, 87 A.D.2d 725, 449 N.Y.S.2d 330 (3d Dept. 1982).

—Defendant invoked his right to counsel when upon voluntarily accompanying police to headquarters he refused to discuss the crime and said that "he was somewhat confused and that he might possibly want a lawyer"; admissions to police three hours later, after three unsuccessful attempts to contact a lawyer must be suppressed. People v. Zamiela, 84 A.D.2d 942, 446 N.Y.S.2d 643 (4th Dept. 1981).

Right to counsel; exigent circumstances.—Police may question a suspect even after a request for legal counsel is made when the object of the questioning is to locate a victim in danger; however, once victim is found, alive or dead, questioning should cease since its only object at that time would be to produce evidence for use at trial. People v. Krom, 61 N.Y.2d 187, 473 N.Y.S.2d 139, 461 N.E.2d 276 (1984).

Right to counsel; Family Court proceedings. —Child abuse or neglect proceedings in Family Court are civil in nature, notwithstanding the requirement that the respondent in such proceedings has a right to counsel; the commencement of such proceedings does not trigger the respondent's right to counsel

with respect to criminal charges arising out of the same acts and such person may, in response to *Miranda* warnings, waive the rights to counsel without counsel being present. People v. Smith, 62 N.Y.2d 306, 476 N.Y.S.2d 797, 465 N.E.2d 336 (1984).

Right to counsel; police unaware of representation in unrelated proceeding.—Right to counsel was not violated when police questioned the defendant without knowledge that he was represented by counsel in an unrelated proceeding. People v. Johnson, 61 N.Y.2d 932, 474 N.Y.S.2d 967, 463 N.E.2d 368 (1984).

—The knowledge of one prosecutor of a suspect's pending cases cannot be automatically imputed to every other member of the large legal staff of the prosecutor's office. People v. Sanders, 128 A.D.2d 480, 513 N.Y.S.2d 413 (1st Dept. 1987).

—Where defendant's earlier charges are remote in time, it cannot be presumed that the police officers, who were aware of the earlier arrest, will know whether the charges are still pending. People v. Cortijo, 141 A.D.2d 830, 529 N.Y.S.2d 887 (2d Dept. 1988).

—Defendant's representation to police that he had pleaded guilty to an unrelated charge and was no longer represented by counsel on that matter foreclosed the need for any further inquiry by police on that subject. People v. Morales, 133 A.D.2d 281, 519 N.Y.S.2d 71 (2d Dept. 1987).

—Where there is no evidence of a joint investigation by two police agencies, knowledge on the part of one agency cannot be imputed to the other. People v. Ippoliti, 127 A.D.2d 897, 512 N.Y.S.2d 258 (3d Dept. 1987).

Right to counsel; time of attachment.—Defendant's appearance before a New Jersey magistrate for extradition did not constitute such significant judicial activity with regard to a New York prosecution that defendant's right to counsel indelibly attached; therefore defendant's statements made prior to his New York arraignment were admissible in view of the fact that *Miranda* rights were properly given. People v. Morton, 104 A.D.2d 569, 479 N.Y.S.2d 275 (2d Dept. 1984).

Right to counsel during interrogation; lack of knowledge of representation.—Fact that defendant had counsel in a pending case did not require suppression of statement based upon violation of the right to counsel, who was not present when *Miranda* rights were waived, since interrogating officer had no actual knowledge of pending case. People v. Beverly, 104 A.D.2d 996, 480 N.Y.S.2d 908 (2d Dept. 1984).

Right to counsel violated by delay in arraignment.—Defendant's conviction was reversed on the ground that a delay of approximately 24 hours between defendant's arrest and the filing of a felony complaint and arraignment, during which time the police and an assistant district attorney conducted negotiations and interrogation of the defendant, was deemed calculated to deprive the defendant of his right to counsel at a critical stage of the proceedings. People v. Cooper, 101 A.D.2d 1, 475 N.Y.S.2d 660 (4th Dept. 1984).

Suppression hearing; challenge to *Miranda* warnings.—Defendant who contended at the suppression hearing that he had been given none of the constitutionally mandated admonitions before interrogation could not on appeal claim that the portion of the admonition covering the right to counsel was deficient in its extent and explicitness since the People were afforded no opportunity to meet the theory first put forward on appeal. People v. Tutt, 38 N.Y.2d 1011, 384 N.Y.S.2d 444, 348 N.E.2d 920 (1976).

Social workers and case workers.—Motion to suppress was granted where defendant was in police custody for an extended period of time, and he had at several times requested an attorney. People v. Stoesser, 53 N.Y.2d 648, 438 N.Y.S.2d 990, 421 N.E.2d 110 (1981).

—The filing of a child abuse petition does not trigger the right to counsel, and thus a caseworker was not required to advise defendant of his *Miranda* rights before speaking with him. People v. Jackson, 4 A.D.3d 848, 772 N.Y.S.2d 149 (4th Dept. 2004).

—*Miranda* warnings were not required where husband, suspected of beating his three-month-old son, voluntarily sought out the social worker assigned to the investigation and was not in custody at the time of the interview. People v. Easter, 90 Misc. 2d 713, 395 N.Y.S.2d 926 (Albany Co. Ct. 1977).

Spontaneous statement suppressed; result of interrogation environment.—To entitle a spontaneous statement to be received in evidence it must be shown that it was in no way the product of an "interrogation environment"; the test is whether defendant spoke with genuine spontaneity "and not the result of inducement, provocation, encouragement or acquiescence, no matter how subtly employed." People v. Lanahan, 55 N.Y.2d 711, 447 N.Y.S.2d 139, 431 N.E.2d 624 (1981).

Statement made to parole officer.—A statement made to a parole officer by a parolee cannot be used against the parolee to establish his guilt with respect to a crime for which the parolee is indicted where he was not given his *Miranda* warnings and was represented by counsel on the indictment. People v. Parker, 82 A.D.2d 661, 442 N.Y.S.2d 803 (2d Dept. 1981), *aff'd,* 57 N.Y.2d 813, 455 N.Y.S.2d 600, 441 N.E.2d 1118 (1982).

Statement obtained through promise.—A statement "obtained by any direct or implied promises, however slight" is inadmissible. People v. Vail, 90 A.D.2d 917, 457 N.Y.S.2d 933 (3d Dept. 1982).

Statement to police officer.—Single question asked by an officer "who are you" did not constitute an interrogation to which *Miranda* warnings were applicable. People v. McMillen, 80 A.D.2d 966, 438 N.Y.S.2d 627 (3d Dept. 1981).

Statements at co-defendant's trial; admissible.—A defendant who, with the advice and in the presence of counsel, entered into a plea bargain and voluntarily testified at the trial of a co-defendant cannot suppress statements made by him to the district attorney in preparation for his testifying nor can he suppress his testimony at the trial when he subsequently goes to trial. People v. Evans, 58 N.Y.2d 14, 457 N.Y.S.2d 757, 444 N.E.2d 7 (1982).

Suppressed statements; impeachment use.—Before suppressed evidence can be used to impeach a defendant's credibility he must affirmatively open the door on his direct testimony by uttering facts in contradiction to the suppressed evidence; this rule did not permit the introduction on rebuttal of the blood stained mattress cover previously suppressed by the court as this was not an "admission." People v. Robbins, 78 A.D.2d 750, 432 N.Y.S.2d 737 (3d Dept. 1980).

—A statement by the defendant which had been previously suppressed could be used to impeach defendant's testimony that he had made no statement. People v. Adams, 101 A.D.2d 701, 475 N.Y.S.2d 685 (4th Dept. 1984).

Statements made without *Miranda* warnings; use for impeachment purposes.—Statements made by a defendant, who had not been given *Miranda* warnings at the time of arrest, may be used by the prosecution for impeachment purposes where the defendant takes the stand on his own behalf. People v. Conyers, 49 N.Y.2d 174, 424 N.Y.S.2d 402, 400 N.E.2d 342 (1980).

Suppression of statements; continuous interrogation.—Appellate Division reversed the conviction and suppressed all statements made by defendant, including those made at the scene, prior to *Miranda* warnings, and those made after *Miranda* warnings, during the trip to the police station and while at the police station; based upon a practical "assessment of external events," the Court concluded that the defendant was subjected to such a continuous interrogation that the subsequently administered *Miranda* warnings were insufficient to protect his rights. People v. Mayorga, 100 A.D.2d 853, 474 N.Y.S.2d 99 (1984).

Statements made to police in absence of appellate counsel admissible.—Defendant's statements to police should not have been suppressed, notwithstanding that they were made without the presence of the attorney representing him in the appeal of a prior criminal conviction; an appeal and the attorney prosecuting it are not part of a pending criminal action or charge. People v. Colwell, 103 A.D.2d 169, 479 N.Y.S.2d 904 (3d Dept. 1984), *aff'd,* 65 N.Y.2d 883, 493 N.Y.S.2d 298, 482 N.E.2d 1214 (1985).

Statements not suppressed; no knowledge of defendant's representation.—Defendant was not entitled to suppression of inculpatory statements made to police on the ground that his waiver of counsel was ineffective because he was represented by counsel on a pending unrelated charge where there was no evidence that the police or assistant district attorney handling the new complaint were aware of the pending charge; there was no basis for imputing knowledge of the defendant's representation from the district attorney's office to the police officers. People v. Cunningham, 60 N.Y.2d 930, 471 N.Y.S.2d 42, 459 N.E.2d 151 (1983).

Suppression of statements; potential for falsity.—Defendant's suppressed inculpatory statement, induced by a police officer's false promises, could not be used to impeach the defendant on cross-examination; the defendant's statements had such substantial potential for falsity that the prosecution should not be allowed to use it. People v. Cole, 100 A.D.2d 442, 474 N.Y.S.2d 149 (4th Dept. 1984).

Violation of right to counsel; harmless error.—Erroneous admission into evidence of defendant's written and oral statements, concededly taken in violation of the defendant's right to counsel, was "harmless beyond a reasonable doubt" where evidence was overwhelming that defendant's killing of his brother-in-law was intentional and not in self-defense. People v. Flecha, 60 N.Y.2d 766, 469 N.Y.S.2d 671, 457 N.E.2d 777 (1983).

Voluntariness of confession; waiver of rights by defendant with dull-normal intelligence.—Although defendant's score of 77 on an I.Q. test and an 83 on a Wechsler test may have indicated that he fell into the dull-normal or borderline range of intelligence, where defendant completed eighth grade, had served honorably in the armed forces, and was gainfully employed as a janitor, the People had sustained its burden of proving that defendant had knowingly and intelligently waived his rights and that his confession was voluntarily made. People v. Lux, 29 N.Y.2d 848, 328 N.Y.S.2d 2 (1971); *see also* People v. Tigner, 48 A.D.2d 762, 368 N.Y.S.2d 92 (4th Dept. 1975).

—Defendant was not necessarily precluded from voluntarily, knowingly and intelligently waiving her constitutional rights where she had been under psychiatric observation since childhood, had an I.Q. of 67 and had been described as mentally retarded and schizophrenic. People v. Morales, 62 A.D.2d 946, 404 N.Y.S.2d 345 (1st Dept. 1978).

—Defendant's inability to read or write and the fact that his intelligence quotient was only a 68 was not a bar to his making an effective waiver of *Miranda* rights as the record reflects that he understood the immediate meaning of the warnings. People v. Gerald, 128 A.D.2d 635, 512 N.Y.S.2d 883 (2d Dept. 1987).

—Defendant voluntarily, knowingly and intelligently waived his *Miranda* rights despite the fact that his I.Q. was in the range of 59 to 74 where police informed defendant of his rights three times and explained them to him in language which defendant indicated he understood; the defendant could read and write English on at least a third grade level and had a working vocabulary sufficient to enable him to carry on conversations; and, expert testimony indicated that defendant was intelligent enough to understand the *Miranda* warnings if they were explained to him and not merely read. People v. Miles, 115 A.D.2d 962, 497 N.Y.S.2d 532 (4th Dept. 1985).

Voluntariness; confessions.—Coercive police activity is a necessary predicate to the finding that a confession is not "voluntary" within the meaning of the Due Process Clause of the Fourteenth Amendment; the defendant's mental condition cannot, standing alone, support a finding of involuntariness. Colorado v. Connelly, 479 U.S. 157, 107 S. Ct. 515, 93 L. Ed. 2d 473 (1986).

—Statements voluntarily made by the defendant after *Miranda* warnings were admissible where the arrest was made with a fair basis for the judgment that probable cause existed, notwithstanding the questionable validity of the initial contact between the police and the defendant, and the interrogation at the precinct was undertaken by detectives who were not involved in the initial stop and who had previously uncovered leads linking defendant to a specific murder. People v. Martinez, 37 N.Y.2d 662, 376 N.Y.S.2d 469, 339 N.E.2d 162 (1975).

—Since the arresting officers assured the defendant that he would be let go if he showed them where the other drugs were, the statements rendered as well as the contraband seized were inadmissible in the absence of a *Miranda* warning. People v. Urowsky, 89 A.D.2d 520, 452 N.Y.S.2d 208 (1st Dept. 1982).

—"Defendant's claim that his statements were physically coerced is belied by his appearance in his arrest photo and his appearance and demeanor during his videotaped statement." People v. Chapman, 277 A.D.2d 392, 717 N.Y.S.2d 211 (2d Dept. 2000).

—The standard for voluntariness is whether the statement was precipitated by a coercive environment or police misconduct that could induce a false confession or that was in any other respect so fundamentally unfair as to deny due process. People v. Deskovic, 201 A.D.2d 579, 607 N.Y.S.2d 957 (2d Dept. 1994).

—Confronting the defendant with the evidence of his guilt did not render his statements involuntary. People v. Ross, 158 A.D.2d 561, 551 N.Y.S.2d 329 (2d Dept. 1990).

—Defendant's statement was voluntarily issued where he waived his *Miranda* rights, was not questioned continuously, was permitted to sleep for 4 hours during his 12 hour detention, and where he was given water upon request. People v. Padilla, 133 A.D.2d 353, 519 N.Y.S.2d 254 (2d Dept. 1987).

—Juvenile's plea was vacated and confession suppressed where he was summoned to the principal's office during school hours and questioned by a detective concerning burglary of the school and damage to school property as the principals participation in the questioning conflicted with his duty regarding the school and its property and his ability to act in *loco parentis.* People v. Benedict V., 85 A.D.2d 747, 445 N.Y.S.2d 798 (2d Dept. 1981).

—Although defendant was at the police station for 14 hours before he gave his confession, the confession was knowing, intelligent, and voluntary beyond a reasonable doubt. People v. Towndrow, 236 A.D.2d 821, 654 N.Y.S.2d 69 (4th Dept. 1997).

—Fact that police misrepresented to defendant that coperpetrator had admitted the murder did not render defendant's statement involuntary since that misrepresentation did not create a substantial risk that the defendant might falsely incriminate himself. People v. Green, 147 A.D.2d 955, 537 N.Y.S.2d 702 (4th Dept. 1989).

—Confronting the defendant with the unfavorable result of a polygraph test did not result in involuntariness. People v. Melendez, 149 A.D.2d 919, 540 N.Y.S.2d 51 (4th Dept. 1989).

—Defendant's limited mental capacity is but one factor in determining the voluntariness of a statement. People v. Matthews, 148 A.D.2d 272, 544 N.Y.S.2d 398 (4th Dept. 1989).

—Injuries defendant received in accident did not prevent him from knowingly and voluntarily waiving his rights. People v. Fuhrer, 154 A.D.2d 942, 545 N.Y.S.2d 884 (4th Dept. 1989).

Voluntary confrontation with police; no suppression of defendant's confession.—While evidence was insufficient to establish that police had probable cause to arrest defendant, confession given by defendant some fifteen minutes after voluntarily arriving at police station was admissible since confessions were not the product of an illegal detention. People v. Morales, 52 A.D.2d 818, 383 N.Y.S.2d 608 (1st Dept. 1976), *aff'd,* 42 N.Y.2d 129, 397 N.Y.S.2d 587, 366 N.E.2d 248 (1977).

Illegal arrest and detention; effect.—When defendant had voluntarily come to the police to report a very serious crime but was reluctant to get involved, statements made by him after an illegal arrest were not excludable where the statements were made sixteen hours after the illegal detention and during that time defendant was in a motel with his wife, and the police immediately stopped all questioning when the defendant requested an attorney. People v. Patterson, 73 A.D.2d 922, 423 N.Y.S.2d 499 (2d Dept. 1980), *aff'd,* 53 N.Y.2d 829, 440 N.Y.S.2d 172, 422 N.E.2d 817 (1981).

—Defendant, arrested on loitering charge, was not arraigned but was questioned concerning a burglary in which he was suspect and confessed to the crime. His illegal arrest and detention were merely circumstances to be considered in determining the voluntariness of his confession. People v. Robinson, 45 A.D.2d 909, 358 N.Y.S.2d 230 (3d Dept. 1974).

—Reversal of conviction was required where defendant was arrested on sham charge (PL § 240.35(6)–loitering) which had been declared unconstitutional three years ago and then questioned on his involvement in another crime; his confession to the latter crime, despite the fact that *Miranda* warnings were given, was tainted evidence obtained through an unlawful arrest. People v. Burley, 60 A.D.2d 973, 401 N.Y.S.2d 631 (4th Dept. 1978).

Seventeen-year-old defendant.—Defendant's statements were admissible into evidence where they were obtained, subsequent to an illegal arrest, as a result of confronting him with the physical evidence and his conversation with his brother, which evidence was unconnected with the illegal detention the original taint, was removed. People v. Rogers, 52 N.Y.2d 527, 439 N.Y.S.2d 96, 421 N.E.2d 491 (1981).

—Although the defendant was 17 years of age at the time she committed the crime of which she was convicted, spoke little English and might have had limited intellectual abilities, these factors did not constitute circumstances so unusual as to warrant

suppression of her spontaneous admission at the arraignment. People v. Paul, 116 A.D.2d 746, 498 N.Y.S.2d 40 (2d Dept. 1986).

—Statements of defendant, seventeen years old, a slow learner, unable to read or write, who was accompanied to Police Headquarters by parents and sister, were admissible where record demonstrated he was of sufficient intelligence and possessed of enough experience to comprehend the questions police asked and to respond to them. People v. Brundige, 43 A.D.2d 1009, 352 N.Y.S.2d 309 (4th Dept. 1974).

—Defendant, a youthful offender, after being advised of his *Miranda* rights, but not yet formally arrested, admitted to committing several burglaries; such statements could not be suppressed even if the detention was illegal because there was sufficient evidence that the required nexus between the detention and statements was absent. People v. John B.B., 81 A.D.2d 188, 440 N.Y.S.2d 387 (3d Dept. 1981), *aff'd,* 56 N.Y.2d 482, 453 N.Y.S.2d 158, 438 N.E.2d 864 (1982).

—Statements made by 17-year-old defendant in the police van were suppressed where he had requested the police to call his mother but police did not make a diligent effort to call the mother until other suspects involved in the crime had been arrested. People v. Coker, 103 Misc. 2d 703, 427 N.Y.S.2d 141 (Sup. Ct. Bronx Co. 1980).

Testimony concerning identification by other party.—It was permissible for a third party to testify concerning a prior identification made by a witness where the witness is unable to make an in-court identification. People v. Ponton, 90 A.D.2d 799, 455 N.Y.S.2d 409 (2d Dept. 1982).

Voluntariness of statement.—Reversible error was committed when the trial court denied defendant's request that the issue of the voluntariness of the statements be submitted to the jury as the involuntariness of a confession is an issue for the jury to decide even though the court at the pretrial *Huntley* hearing found the statements to have been made voluntarily. People v. Graham, 55 N.Y.2d 144, 447 N.Y.S.2d 918, 432 N.E.2d 790 (1982).

—To hold voluntary a statement obtained only after the defendant has been subjected to a prolonged and almost unbroken series of events which brought to bear enormous psychological pressure to confess, flies in the face of established constitutional principles. People v. Jackson, 41 N.Y.2d 146, 391 N.Y.S.2d 82, 359 N.E.2d 677 (1976).

—The failure of the police to advise the defendant of his right as Mexican national to consular notification of his arrest did not affect the voluntariness of his statement, and there is no reason for a jury to consider evidence of this violation. People v. Ortiz, 17 A.D.3d 190, 795 N.Y.S.2d 182 (1st Dept. 2005).

—Despite injuries that defendant sustained in a car crash, he was alert and coherent during the interview, he never asked for medication, a doctor, an interpreter, or for the interview to end; court properly concluded that his physical injuries did not interfere with his making a voluntary statement. People v. Walker, 235 A.D.2d 262, 652 N.Y.S.2d 274 (1st Dept. 1997).

—Fact that approximately 14 hours had elapsed from the time of the defendant's arrest until his final statements did not require a finding that his statements were coerced where he was not subject to continuous interrogation and was permitted to eat and sleep when he was not being questioned. People v. Benitez, 128 A.D.2d 628, 513 N.Y.S.2d 26 (2d Dept. 1987).

—That defendant was in custody for close to 12 hours before giving his inculpatory statement did not render the defendant's confession involuntary where the defendant was twice given his *Miranda* warnings, was not subjected to continuous interrogation, was fed, and was not threatened or abused in any way. People v. Croney, 121 A.D.2d 558, 503 N.Y.S.2d 608 (2d Dept. 1986).

—Interrogating officer's promise that the District Attorney would be made aware of defendant's cooperation, and the fact that the police officers suggested to the defendant that he tell them what happened and get it off his chest did not render defendant's statement involuntary. People v. Weisbrot, 124 A.D.2d 762, 508 N.Y.S.2d 481 (2d Dept. 1986).

—It is proper for police to capitalize on a defendant's sense of shame or reluctance to involve his family in a pending investigation. People v. Johnson, 177 A.D.2d 791, 576 N.Y.S.2d 407 (3d Dept. 1991).

—Mere use of stratagems by police does not require a finding that a confession was given involuntarily. People v. Hoyer, 140 A.D.2d 853, 528 N.Y.S.2d 440, 441 (3d Dept. 1988).

—Reasonable use of force in the execution of an arrest does not invalidate *Miranda* warnings or make statements made thereafter invalid. People v. White, 138 A.D.2d 863, 526 N.Y.S.2d 247 (3d Dept. 1988).

—The People failed to establish beyond a reasonable doubt the voluntariness of the defendants confession where the defendant was a patient in a psychiatric center, had been diagnosed as a chronic undifferentiated schizophrenic and his confession was disjointed, disorganized and made no mention of his accomplice. People v. White, 85 A.D.2d 787, 445 N.Y.S.2d 327 (3d Dept. 1981).

—Defendant's statements were suppressed when it was shown that the statements were given after the defendant was informed that if he would not talk, the officers would search the apartment he shared with the woman who owned it and if stolen property were found the woman would be arrested. People v. Helstrom, 50 A.D.2d 685, 375 N.Y.S.2d 189 (3d Dept. 1975), aff'd, 40 N.Y.2d 914, 389 N.Y.S.2d 366, 357 N.E.2d 1021 (1976).

—While unnecessary delay in arraigning the defendant is a relevant factor in asserting the voluntariness of any statement given, it is not dispositive of the issue. People v. Johnson, 49 A.D.2d 663, 390 N.Y.S.2d 462 (3d Dept. 1975), aff'd, 40 N.Y.2d 882, 389 N.Y.S.2d 347, 357 N.E.2d 1002 (1976).

—Defendant claims that the promises of leniency made by the police during the interrogation rendered his statement involuntary, but "the statement of the police officer that he would inform the district attorney of defendant's cooperation did not create a substantial risk that defendant might falsely incriminate himself." People v. Richards, 275 A.D.2d 886, 713 N.Y.S.2d 604 (4th Dept. 2000).

—Investigator's statements relative to obtaining psychiatric help for defendant did not constitute a promise which rendered defendant's statement involuntary under CPL § 60.45. People v. Fox, 120 A.D.2d 949, 502 N.Y.S.2d 848 (4th Dept. 1986).

Non-English speaking defendant; monosyllabic responses.—Where defendant, an uneducated non-English speaking woman, was arrested in one county and brought to the Special Prosecutor's office in another county, she did not waive her rights when she gave monosyllabic responses and nodded her head in response to *Miranda* warnings. People v. Andino, 80 Misc. 2d 155, 362 N.Y.S.2d 766 (Sup. Ct. N.Y. Co. 1974).

Voluntary confession; *Miranda* warnings.—A police officer need not mouth a ritualistic formula so long as the words used convey the substance of the *Miranda* rights with all the requisite information. People v. Anderson, 143 A.D.2d 638, 536 N.Y.S.2d 543 (2d Dept. 1989).

—Although defendant suffered an injury to his eye during the course of his arrest, the force used by the police in effectuating that arrest preceded his first inculpatory statement by about 3 hours and his videotaped statement by 5-1/2 hours, thus the use of such force was sufficiently attenuated from the defendant's later statements as to remove any taint which might have otherwise arisen therefrom. People v. Crews, 128 A.D.2d 799, 513 N.Y.S.2d 499 (2d Dept. 1987).

—Fact that the defendant appeared tired during the videotaped statement did not negate the validity of his waiver of his *Miranda* rights. People v. Utley, 130 A.D.2d 693, 515 N.Y.S.2d 616 (2d Dept. 1987).

—Defendant did not lack capacity to waive *Miranda* rights and to issue a voluntary statement despite the fact he was bleeding and seriously injured at the time he issued the statement. People v. Montero, 118 A.D.2d 811, 500 N.Y.S.2d 169 (2d Dept. 1986).

—A statement is not rendered inadmissible because the police did not elicit an express waiver of his constitutional rights where the totality of the circumstances including the defendant's extensive prior contacts with the police, his express indication that he understood his constitutional rights and his unhesitant replies to questioning which occurred over a relatively brief period of time, established beyond a reasonable doubt that the defendant knowingly and voluntarily waived his rights. People v. Harris, 79 A.D.2d 615, 433 N.Y.S.2d 480 (2d Dept. 1980).

—Detective's full recitation of investigation results immediately prior to reading the *Miranda* warnings did not unduly interfere with defendant's ability to make an unpressured decision whether to waive his rights. People v. Gross, 127 A.D.2d 892, 512 N.Y.S.2d 254 (3d Dept. 1987).

—Police interrogators must faithfully carry out the *Miranda* mandate at the threshold, but then they may proceed, without further specific warnings. People v. Johnson, 49 A.D.2d 663, 390 N.Y.S.2d 462 (3d Dept. 1975), aff'd, 40 N.Y.2d 882, 389 N.Y.S.2d 347, 357 N.E.2d 1002 (1976).

—Where a defendant attested for murder was twice given the *Miranda* warnings and confessed to police officers and to the District Attorney, his confession was properly admitted, even though he once expressed reservations about confessing if the victim were dead and one of the police officers present knew the victim was dead and did not so inform the defendant People v. Solari, 43 A.D.2d 610, 349 N.Y.S.2d 31 (3d Dept. 1973), aff'd, 35 N.Y.2d 876, 363 N.Y.S.2d 953, 323 N.E.2d 191 (1974).

Miscellaneous.—Defendant, a man of 27 years, was not denied his right to counsel merely because his mother's attempts to locate him were unsuccessful, and these efforts were aggravated in part by an apparently accidental dissemination of information by the police where the record indicated that he consciously chose to confront his interrogators, alone, and after being informed of his constitutional rights, did not ever ask to speak to either counsel or any member of his family. People v. Cassasa, 49 N.Y.2d 688, 427 N.Y.S.2d 769, 403 N.E.2d 1310 (1980), cert. denied, 449 U.S. 842 (1981).

—The constitutional right to counsel does not include a right to consult clergyman, physicians, or others whose capabilities in such situations vary materially from those of members of the bar. People v. Byrne, 47 N.Y.2d 117, 417 N.Y.S.2d 42, 390 N.E.2d 760 (1979).

—What was implied in *Pinzon* is now the explicit law: that good faith efforts are made to locate a defendant who is taken into custody does not absolve the police of their responsibility in cases where interference with a person's liberty becomes necessary, to keep track of those against whom the restraining hand and accusing finger of the state have come to rest but undue delay prevent anyone so circumstanced from securing the protections, including the right to counsel, to which he or she is entitled. People v. Garofolo, 46 N.Y.2d 592, 415 N.Y.S.2d 810, 389 N.E.2d 123 (1979).

—In view of the fact that the People knew that the defendant had been previously represented by counsel in connection with this case, and that the retainer had never been terminated to their knowledge, the conclusion that the defendant voluntarily waived his right to counsel could not be sustained since the defendant's attorney was not present at the time of the waiver and defendant's oral statements and written confession obtained in the absence of counsel were suppressed. People v. Singer, 44 N.Y.2d 241, 405 N.Y.S.2d 17, 376 N.E.2d 179 (1978).

—Once a person has been taken into custody, the burden is on the police to keep track of him and to establish and maintain procedures which will insure that an attorney representing him may communicate with him and with the officials responsible for the investigation without unreasonable delay. People v. Pinzon, 44 N.Y.2d 458, 406 N.Y.S.2d 268, 377 N.E.2d 721 (1978).

—The confession was suppressed where, defendant, a few minutes after receiving telephone call from his attorney and informing the police that his attorney had told him not to talk to the police, stated that he was going to talk anyway. People v. Tompkins, 45 N.Y.2d 748, 408 N.Y.S.2d 485, 380 N.E.2d 311 (1978).

—Admissibility of confessions is a matter of state procedure; when New York police officers obtained a statement in Texas from defendant for use in a New York proceeding emanating from a violent crime in New York, Texas law, such as the requirement that all statements be electronically recorded and that defendant must be informed of his right to have interrogation terminated, need not be considered, but only New York law consistent with *Miranda*. People v. Benson, 88 A.D.2d 229, 454 N.Y.S.2d 155 (3d Dept. 1982).

—A mildly mentally retarded defendant knowingly, intelligently, and voluntarily waived her *Miranda* rights before she confessed to killing two of her children 30 years earlier, where the police investigator read the *Miranda* rights slowly and paused after each right to ask whether she understood it; she was reread her rights before signing the confession; the People's expert witness, a psychiatrist, testified that defendant controlled the interview for the first two hours, communicated well, and had no difficulty stating her address, knew her rent, and that she had had one breech birth. People v. King, 234 A.D.2d 923, 653 N.Y.S.2d 464 (4th Dept. 1996).

—Police warnings that defendant "could refuse to answer any questions" and that he could "stop answering at any time," and that defendant "could call a lawyer if he wanted to; and we would wait for the lawyer to come before any questioning and defendant said he never had a lawyer and never wanted one" sufficiently complied with *Miranda*. People v. Handley, 85 A.D.2d 910, 446 N.Y.S.2d 790 (4th Dept. 1981).

Totality of the circumstances.—The inculpatory statement was suppressed where the totality of the circumstances indicated that the defendant, suffering from borderline mental retardation, was denied contact with his sister, was questioned for five hours, and the statements made to him by the police during the detention may have induced his admission. People v. Brown, 63 A.D.2d 584, 404 N.Y.S.2d 617 (1st Dept. 1978).

—Defendant was not shown to have waived his rights beyond a reasonable doubt even though he had been fully informed of his rights and acknowledged that he understood them and inculpatory statements were suppressed where the totality of the circumstances indicated that the police officer told defendant that if the gun was his, he should admit it before fingerprints were taken. People v. Campbell, 81 A.D.2d 300, 440 N.Y.S.2d 336 (2d Dept. 1981).

—Defendant was not subjected to a prolonged interrogation and no force or deception was used. No promises or threats were made and no evidence was introduced that defendant was incapable of functioning normally or of understanding and intelligently waiving his rights. Under all the circumstances, the People sustained their burden of proving the confession admissible. People v. Armlin, 43 A.D.2d 782, 350 N.Y.S.2d 795 (3d Dept. 1973), *rev'd on other grounds,* 37 N.Y.2d 167, 371 N.Y.S.2d 691, 332 N.E.2d 870 (1975). *Cf.* People v. Woodson 87 Misc. 2d 575, 385 N.Y.S.2d 998 (Sup. Ct. Bronx Co. 1976); People v. DeJesus, 63 A.D.2d 148, 407 N.Y.S.2d 5 (1st Dept. 1978).

Tainted questioning.—The *Huntley* hearing was ordered reopened where the defendant made an exculpatory statement and two inculpatory statements and the trial court held that the exculpatory statement was inadmissible but that the inculpatory statements were admissible, to determine whether the two inculpatory statements were a continuation of tainted questioning. People v. Pettiford, 78 A.D.2d 823, 433 N.Y.S.2d 143 (1st Dept. 1980).

Telephone statement to employer.—Defendant's recorded statements to his employer were admissible where defendant, during conversation with his former employer, had admitted that he had murdered the victim and the former employer thereafter notified police of the confession and agreed to place a recording device on his phone and not to ask any leading questions since the employer was not an agent of the police. People v. Dabney, 75 A.D.2d 822, 427 N.Y.S.2d 489 (2d Dept. 1980).

Trickery; deception.—The defendant's statements was admissible where he asserted his right to silence after being advised of his right to an attorney although the warning did not include an admonition that he had a right to have the attorney present at the interrogation he subsequently made a statement to the police after conferring with a friend. People v. Mandrachio, 79 A.D.2d 278, 436 N.Y.S.2d 642 (1st Dept. 1981), *aff'd,* 55 N.Y.2d 906, 449 N.Y.S.2d 24, 433 N.E.2d 1272 (1982).

—Although there was some measure of guile employed by the police, particularly the confrontation of the defendant with the polygraph test results and informing him that they showed that he was lying, such conduct did not render the defendant's statement involuntary. People v. Henry, 132 A.D.2d 673, 518 N.Y.S.2d 44 (2d Dept. 1987).

—Trickery or deception without more does not make a confession inadmissible, the deception must be accompanied by a threat or promise before a confession becomes involuntary. People v. McGuffin, 55 A.D.2d 772, 389 N.Y.S.2d 478 (3d Dept. 1976).

—Deceptive practices by the police are permissible as long as they are not fundamentally unfair or likely to produce a false confession. People v. Finkle, 192 A.D.2d 783, 596 N.Y.S.2d 549 (3d Dept. 1993).

—Court rejected defendant's contention that police officers violated his right to due process in falsely informing him that the victim had accused him of forcibly raping her, causing

defendant to assert that the intercourse was consensual; although the police employed some guile, it cannot be said that the deception induced the defendant to make a false confession. People v. Burke, 20 A.D.3d 932, 798 N.Y.S.2d 291 (4th Dept. 2005).

Voluntariness; voice stress evaluation test.—Generally, the use of a voice stress evaluation test (stress test) will not in and of itself render a confession inadmissible as the product of coercion, but its use or misuse is a factor to be considered in determining whether there was impermissible coercion based upon an examination of the totality of the circumstances surrounding the confession. People v. Tarsia, 67 A.D.2d 210, 415 N.Y.S.2d 120 (3d Dept. 1979), *aff'd,* 50 N.Y.2d 1, 427 N.Y.S.2d 944, 405 N.E.2d 188 (1980).

Waiver.—Failure of law enforcement officials to inform suspect of the intended subject matter of the interrogation does not bear upon the suspect's decision to waive his Fifth Amendment privilege in a constitutionally significant manner. Colorado v. Spring, 479 U.S. 564, 107 S. Ct. 851, 93 L. Ed. 2d 954 (1987).

—Defendant made a knowing and intelligent waiver of his *Miranda* rights where he responded to the officer's questions in an intelligent and direct manner indicating he understood the language and its import and he never took the stand or offered any evidence at the hearing to refute his demonstrated intelligent waiver. People v. Love, 85 A.D.2d 799, 445 N.Y.S.2d 607 (3d Dept. 1981), *aff'd,* 57 N.Y.2d 998, 457 N.Y.S.2d 238, 443 N.E.2d 486 (1982).

—Defendant's non-verbal nods constituted an effective waiver of his *Miranda* rights. People v. Walsh, 134 Misc. 2d 1071, 1073, 514 N.Y.S.2d 174, 176 (Sup Ct. Queens Co. 1987).

—*Miranda* rights belong to the individual; they are his constitutional safeguard, and cannot be waived by the mother of a juvenile. *In re* Hector G., 89 Misc. 2d 1081, 393 N.Y.S.2d 519 (Fam. Ct. N.Y. Co. 1977).

Waiver of *Miranda* rights; break in interrogation.—Notwithstanding that police violated defendant's rights by continuing to question him after he refused to speak after being Mirandized, later statements are admissible since defendant changed his mind voluntarily after a pronounced break in interrogation, made an unprompted decision to make a statement, and was given his *Miranda* warnings a second time prior to making any statement. People v. Kinnard, 62 N.Y.2d 910, 479 N.Y.S.2d 2, 467 N.E.2d 886 (1984).

Youthful age; voluntariness of waiver of counsel.—Sixteen year-old youth with a previous criminal background was found to have made a voluntary waiver of counsel where he repeated several times that he understood his pre-interrogation rights. People v. Boykins, 81 A.D.2d 922, 439 N.Y.S.2d 181 (2d Dept. 1981).

Youth's admission to parent; should be suppressed.—While in custody, defendant, a youthful suspect, admitted that he stabbed someone to his mother and the statement was introduced in evidence through the testimony of a detective who overheard it as he stood near defendant's cell; the court held that a privilege did arise with respect to the communication as a parent is a youth's primary source of assistance while in custody and while the statements should have been suppressed a reversal was not warranted as defendant's guilt was established by overwhelming evidence. People v. Harrell, 87 A.D.2d 21, 450 N.Y.S.2d 501 (2d Dept. 1982), *aff'd,* 59 N.Y.2d 620, 463 N.Y.S.2d 185, 449 N.E.2d 1263 (1983).

§ 60.46. Rules of evidence, family offense proceedings in family court.

Evidence of a written or oral admission or any testimony given by either party, or evidence derived therefrom, in a proceeding under article eight of the family court act without the benefit of counsel in such proceeding may not be received into evidence in a criminal proceeding except for the purposes of impeachment unless such party waives the right to counsel on the record. Nothing herein shall be deemed to prohibit any testimony or exhibits received into evidence in a criminal proceeding, or any orders, decisions or judgments arising from such proceeding from being received into evidence in any proceeding under article eight of the family court act.

Added by L. 1994, Ch. 222, § 30, eff. Jan. 1, 1995.

§ 60.48. Rules of evidence; admissibility of evidence of victim's manner of dress in sex offense cases.

Evidence of the manner in which the victim was dressed at the time of the commission of an offense may not be admitted in a prosecution for any offense, or an attempt to commit an offense, defined in article one hundred thirty of the penal law, unless such evidence is determined by the court to be relevant and admissible in the interests of justice, after an offer of proof by the proponent of such evidence outside the hearing of the jury, or such hearing as the court may require, and a statement by the court of its findings of fact essential to its determination.

Added L. 1994, Ch. 482, § 1, eff. Nov. 1, 1994.

ANNOTATION

Mistrial required.—Defense counsel's improper inquiries about what the victim was wearing injected evidence into the trial that the legislature has specified should be excluded as prejudicial; record supported court's determination that there was manifest necessity for a mistrial, and defendant's retrial was not barred by double jeopardy. Maynard v. Wait, 246 A.D.2d 853, 668 N.Y.S.2d 263 (3d Dept. 1998).

§ 60.50. Rules of evidence; statements of defendants; corroboration.

A person may not be convicted of any offense solely upon evidence of a confession or admission made by him without additional proof that the offense charged has been committed.

ANNOTATIONS

Charge.—By failing to request a charge pursuant to CPL § 60.50, defendant failed to preserve for court's review his present argument that the court should have charged the jury pursuant to that section. People v. Schleyer, 236 A.D.2d 835, 654 N.Y.S.2d 70 (4th Dept. 1997).

Confession; corroboration.—The proscription of CPL § 60.50 against conviction solely upon evidence of a confession or admission without proof that the offense charged has been committed does not require direct proof, other than the confession or admission, of death or criminal agency, although the body of the victim is never found and there is no direct evidence, other than the confession, that the defendant caused the victim's death. A jury question is presented by circumstantial evidence calculated to suggest that the victim is dead and implicating the defendant as the criminal agency, the key to which is furnished by the confession or admission. People v. Lipsky, 57 N.Y.2d 560, 457 N.Y.S.2d 451, 443 N.E.2d 925 (1982).

—A confession may provide all the necessary proof of defendant's culpability and CPL § 60.50 only requires that the confessed crime be proved to have occurred by independent evidence without any other connection with the defendant or his confession. People v. Safian, 46 N.Y.2d 181, 413 N.Y.S.2d 118, 385 N.E.2d 1046 (1978).

—Presence at the scene, proof of motive, evidence of flight and other conduct indicating a consciousness of guilt may be held to constitute the essential additional proof. People v. Murray, 40 N.Y.2d 327, 386 N.Y.S.2d 691, 353 N.E.2d 605 (1976), cert. denied, 430 U.S. 948 (1977).

—In a rape prosecution, the hospital records, indicating that complainant had an abortion, was evidence of a crime (sexual intercourse with an underage female) and was sufficient to corroborate the defendant's admissions. People v. Parks, 41 N.Y.2d 36, 390 N.Y.S.2d 848, 359 N.E.2d 358 (1976).

—Regardless of defendant's statements and conduct before the fire, touching on his motive and intent, there was competent evidence from the People's arson investigator, from which the jury could have concluded that the fire was of incendiary origin thus satisfying the requirement of corroboration of his confession. People v. Simms, 37 N.Y.2d 906, 378 N.Y.S.2d 381, 340 N.E.2d 743 (1975).

—Contrary to defendant's contention, complainant's testimony, that she witnessed defendant on her property holding a screwdriver, that defendant provided an implausible excuse for his presence, and that he fled, sufficiently corroborated defendant's confession that he entered complainant's property with intent to commit a crime. People v. Boatwright, 253 A.D.2d 887, 680 N.Y.S.2d 254 (2d Dept. 1998).

—Defendant's confession was sufficiently corroborated by proof that the defendant was present at the scene of the fire only 12 to 15 minutes prior to its discovery; that he had a motive for setting the fire, as 1 week prior to the incident he had been fired by the firm which occupied the building in question; and, that the fire was a product of human agency. People v. Noren, 123 A.D.2d 453, 506 N.Y.S.2d 756 (2d Dept. 1986).

—There must be proof that the crime charged was actually committed by someone. Where the cause of death is unexplained, doubt arises as to whether any criminal agency is involved. However, once a crime has been established, a confession alone is enough to implicate a defendant; the independent evidence need not connect, or even tend to connect, a defendant with the crime. The death of the victim by a criminal agency was sufficiently established here by the circumstantial evidence presented at trial. People v. Jennings, 40 A.D.2d 357, 340 N.Y.S.2d 25 (2d Dept.), aff'd, 33 N.Y.2d 880, 352 N.Y.S.2d 444, 307 N.E.2d 561 (1973).

—Statute providing that person may not be convicted solely upon confession or admission without additional proof that offense charged has been committed does not require corroboration of every detail of confession or admission, but only some proof, of whatever weight, that offense charged has, in fact, been committed by someone. People v. McAuliffe, 220 A.D.2d 859, 632 N.Y.S.2d 253 (3d Dept. 1995).

—Where case against defendant is based largely upon testimony of third party concerning admission made to that third party by defendant, and third party is not accomplice, evidence in addition to confession is sufficient to support conviction even though it fails to exclude every reasonable hypothesis save that of guilt. People v. Wright, 214 A.D.2d 759, 624 N.Y.S.2d 650 (3d Dept. 1995).

—Sufficient corroboration of defendant's statements in burglary prosecution came in the form of several witnesses, each of whom testified that their residences and in one instance an office building, had been unlawfully broken into, ransacked and property stolen, and where necessary the value of that property was proven. People v. Lacy, 127 A.D.2d 933, 512 N.Y.S.2d 517 (3d Dept. 1987).

—In arson prosecution, the corroboration requirement of CPL § 60.50 was satisfied by the fire chief's testimony that the fire in question was not caused by electricity, natural gas or spontaneous combustion and that heavy charring in a closet indicated that the fire was started in the closet itself; such testimony constituted competent evidence from which the jury could have concluded that the fire was of an incendiary nature. People v. Pettis, 62 A.D.2d 1110, 404 N.Y.S.2d 428 (3d Dept. 1978).

—Physician who examined the victim, defendant's two-and-one-half-year-old daughter, testified that she found conditions unusual in a child of that age and consistent with penile penetration; that proof sufficiently corroborated the admission of defendant that he engaged in sexual intercourse with his daughter. People v. Angel E., 233 A.D.2d 938, 649 N.Y.S.2d 878 (4th Dept. 1996).

—Unsworn testimony of victim provided sufficient corroboration of defendant's admissions to support conviction for sexual abuse in the first degree. People v. Hamelinck, 222 A.D.2d 1024, 635 N.Y.S.2d 916 (4th Dept. 1995).

—Circumstantial evidence that a crime was committed satisfies the corroboration requirement of CPL § 60.50. People v. Van Der Sluys, 151 A.D.2d 983, 542 N.Y.S.2d 73 (4th Dept. 1989).

—There must be proof of the corpus delicti, in a prosecution for murder second degree; the proof additional to the confession that the fire started in the stairway without proof of its incendiary origin by any person failed to meet the requirements of corroboration of the confession. People v. Kazmarick, 99 Misc. 2d 1012, 417 N.Y.S.2d 671 (Sullivan Co. Ct. 1979), aff'd, 52 N.Y.2d 322, 438 N.Y.S.2d 247, 420 N.E.2d 45 (1981).

Felony murder; corroboration of underlying felony.—In a prosecution for felony murder, CPL § 60.50 does not require corroboration of defendant's confession to the underlying predicate felony. People v. Davis, 46 N.Y.2d 780, 413 N.Y.S.2d 911, 386 N.E.2d 823 (1978).

—Corroboration of defendant's confession in felony murder prosecution was adduced when the People produced a corpus delicti, i.e., that the deceased was a victim of homicide resulting from someone's criminality. People v. Velez, 122 A.D.2d 178, 504 N.Y.S.2d 715 (2d Dept. 1986).

—Defendant's statement, which was used to prove his guilt of felony murder, was sufficiently corroborated by ample evidence that homicide did occur; corroboration of the underlying felony is not necessary. People v. Agard, 111 A.D.2d 821, 490 N.Y.S.2d 249 (2d Dept. 1985).

General requirement.—The requirements of CPL § 60.50 are not rigorous and sufficient corroboration exists when the confession is supported by independent evidence of the corpus delicti, such as the presence of defendant at the scene of the crime, his guilty appearance afterward, or other circumstances supporting an inference of guilt. People v. Booden, 69 N.Y.2d 185, 513 N.Y.S.2d 87, 89 505 N.E.2d 598 (1987).

—CPL § 60.50 does not require corroboration of the defendant's admission to the underlying predicate felony of a felony-murder prosecution. People v. Vargas, 181 A.D.2d 806, 581 N.Y.S.2d 239 (2d Dept. 1992).

—The purpose of the corroboration statute is to obviate the danger that there may be a conviction for a crime when in fact no such crime has been committed by anyone; it has been construed only as requiring proof by independent evidence that the confessed crime occurred. People v. Hamilton, 121 A.D.2d 395, 503 N.Y.S.2d 106 (2d Dept. 1986).

—The additional proof necessary to satisfy the statutory requirement of corroboration of a confession need only be of circumstances calculated to suggest the commission of the crime, and for the explanation of which the confession furnishes the key. People v. Fiacco, 132 A.D.2d 887, 518 N.Y.S.2d 231 (3d Dept. 1987).

Grounds for exercise of discretion; right to review.—Implicit in the four criteria set forth in PL § 65.00(1)(b) for thereafter the discretionary grant of a sentence of probation are the following two propositions: (1) that the Legislature did not intend to vest and unfettered exercise of discretion in the administrative judge in connection with so vital a matter but rather that any determination be made in accordance with these guidelines; and (2) that the Legislature did not intend to deprive the appellate division of its inherent right to review the discretion exercised in denying the application for concurrence in the imposition of a sentence of probation. People v. Nudelman, 70 A.D.2d 13, 419 N.Y.S.2d 674 (2d Dept. 1979).

Hindering prosecution; confession.—When defendant confesses to hindering prosecution, there must be confession corroboration of the existence of an underlying felony, because without the existence of an underlying felony committed by someone, there would be no crime, of any degree, irrespective of defendant's belief that he is aiding the perpetrator. People v. Chico, 90 N.Y.2d 585, 665 N.Y.S.2d 5, 687 N.E.2d 1288 (1997).

Homicide prosecution; evidence in addition to confession, necessary.—Defendant's admissions to the police and the examining pediatrician that he practiced karate on the deceased child was amply corroborated by the expert testimony on the part of three physicians that the child was the victim of the "battered child syndrome." People v. Eisenman, 39 N.Y.2d 810, 385 N.Y.S.2d 763, 351 N.E.2d 430 (1976).

—White a person may not be convicted of any offense solely on evidence of a confession or admission, without additional proof of the commission of the offense, in homicide prosecution where evidence, including evidence of defendant's wife's cremation in barbeque pit and evidence of defendant's conduct when wife was found missing was sufficient to establish that killing occurred through criminal agency and with defendant's

confession it was sufficient for jury on issue of guilt in murder prosecution. People v. Pendleton, 42 A.D.2d 144, 345 N.Y.S.2d 773 (4th Dept. 1973), dismissed, 35 N.Y.2d 690, 361 N.Y.S.2d 160, 319 N.E.2d 422 (1974).

Illegally obtained statement of defendant may be used for impeachment.—Statements taken from defendant pursuant to an allegedly illegal, warrantless arrest in his home, after being given Miranda warnings, could be used to impeach the defendant during cross-examination. People v. Ferguson, 105 A.D.2d 802, 481 N.Y.S.2d 434 (2d Dept. 1984).

Preservation of objection to lack of corroboration.—Defendant claimed that he received ineffective assistance of counsel because his attorney failed to preserve an objection as to the lack of evidence corroborating his confession as required by CPL 60.50. Court found claim without merit, holding that defense counsel's general motion to dismiss the counts charged at the close of evidence, coupled with the trial judge's specific findings as to corroboration, meant that the question on appeal was expressly decided by the court. People v. Prado, 4 N.Y.3d 725, 790 N.Y.S.2d 418, 823 N.E.2d 824 (2004) (two justices dissented), reargument denied, 4 N.Y.3d 795, 795 N.Y.S.2d 170, 828 N.E.2d 86 (2005).

§ 60.55. Rules of evidence; psychiatric testimony in certain cases.

1. When, in connection with the affirmative defense of lack of criminal responsibility by reason of mental disease or defect, a psychiatrist or licensed psychologist testifies at a trial concerning the defendant's mental condition at the time of the conduct charged to constitute a crime, he must be permitted to make a statement as to the nature of any examination of the defendant, the diagnosis of the mental condition of the defendant and his opinion as to the extent, if any, to which the capacity of the defendant to know or appreciate the nature and consequence of such conduct, or its wrongfulness, was impaired as a result of mental disease or defect at that time.

The psychiatrist or licensed psychologist must be permitted to make any explanation reasonably serving to clarify his diagnosis and opinion, and may be cross-examined as to any matter bearing on his competency or credibility or the validity of his diagnosis or opinion.

2. Any statement made by the defendant to a psychiatrist or licensed psychologist during his examination of the defendant shall be inadmissible in evidence on any issue other than that of the affirmative defense of lack of criminal responsibility, by reason of mental disease or defect. The statement shall, however, be admissible upon the issue of the affirmative defense of lack of criminal responsibility by reason of mental disease or defect, whether or not it would otherwise be deemed a privileged communication. Upon receiving the statement in evidence, the court must instruct the jury that the statement is to be considered only on the issue of such affirmative defense and may not be considered by it in its determination of whether the defendant committed the act constituting the crime charged.

Amended by L. 1980, Ch. 548; L. 1984, Ch. 668.

ANNOTATIONS

Scope.—Statute, by its terms, does not apply to this case where defendant did not assert the insanity defense, but sought instead to use psychiatric testimony to negate a necessary element of the offenses charged. People v. Angelo, 88 N.Y.2d 217, 644 N.Y.S.2d 460, 666 N.E.2d 1333 (1996).

Instructions.—Absent any request, or any issue other than lack of criminal responsibility by reason of mental disease or defect, trial court's failure to instruct jury pursuant to statute governing consideration of psychiatric testimony did not constitute reversible error in murder prosecution. People v. Smith, 209 A.D.2d 267, 618 N.Y.S.2d 347 (1st Dept. 1994).

—Limiting instruction was sufficient to protect defendant after psychiatrist testified about his opinion of defendant's credibility at psychiatric interview; jury was told that psychiatrist's testimony related solely to insanity defense and that jury was sole arbiter of credibility of all witnesses, including defendant. People v. Doczy, 210 A.D.2d 425, 620 N.Y.S.2d 408 (2d Dept. 1994).

Basis of testimony.—Court properly admitted the testimony of a forensic psychiatrist, who recounted certain out-of-court statements made to him by the defendant's cousin, inasmuch as the cousin's statements formed a basis of the expert's professional opinion. People v. Gordon, 237 A.D.2d 376, 655 N.Y.S.2d 61 (2d Dept. 1997).

—The doctor's testimony concerning a diagnosis of the defendant's mental condition was properly excluded where it was based wholly on a review of information which had been obtained and recorded by medical students and residents since there was no showing that it was the regular course of the hospital's business to make such records (CPLR 4518[a]) or that the records bore a certification or authentication by the head of the hospital (CPLR 4518[c]). People v. McKinley, 72 A.D.2d 470, 424 N.Y.S.2d 941 (4th Dept. 1980).

Insanity defense; testimony of psychiatrist.—CPL § 60.55 allows the psychiatrist's expert opinion to be admitted where the opinion is substantially, though not exclusively, based upon observation and examination of the defendant and the facts in evidence. People v. Stone, 35 N.Y.2d 69, 358 N.Y.S.2d 737, 315 N.E.2d 787 (1974).

—A prosecution psychiatric expert may base his opinion on the out-of-court written statement of a witness who testifies at the trial. People v. Sugden, 35 N.Y.2d 453, 363 N.Y.S.2d 923, 323 N.E.2d 169 (1974).

—Where defendant raised the defense of insanity on trial, it was incumbent upon the trial court to give cautionary instructions as to the use of the psychiatrist's testimony; his testimony could be considered on the issue of sanity but not that of guilt. People v. Finn, 64 A.D.2d 526, 406 N.Y.S.2d 800 (1st Dept. 1978).

—Reversal was required where prosecutor, in summation, attacked defendant's psychiatric witness for failing to examine the Grand Jury minutes, which had been examined by the prosecutor's psychiatrist, implying that the People permit a defendant's witness to examine Grand Jury minutes as a matter of course, since the prosecutor made himself an unsworn witness, and left the jury with the impression that the approach taken by defendant's psychiatrist was deficient. People v. Wise, 74 A.D.2d 929, 426 N.Y.S.2d 96 (2d Dept. 1980).

—The Trial Judge's determination of the qualifications of an expert whose testimony is offered on behalf of a litigant is not open to review by the Appellate Divisions, so long as there are facts to support the trial court's ruling. People v. Diaz, 70 A.D.2d 885, 417 N.Y.S.2d 101 (2d Dept. 1979), aff'd, 51 N.Y.2d 841, 433 N.Y.S.2d 751, 413 N.E.2d 1166 (1980).

—It was proper for the People's expert witness to testify as to defendant's sanity even though witness did not indicate that he was aware of the events that occurred or the acts performed by defendant on the day of the crime; under the CPL it is no longer necessary that an expert witness set forth the basis for his opinion. People v. Whitted, 67 A.D.2d 736, 412 N.Y.S.2d 674 (2d Dept. 1979).

—In a prosecution for sodomy and related crimes, failure of the People to offer expert testimony regarding defendant's defense of insanity was not fatal to the convictions, where defendant refused to cooperate with the psychiatrist retained by the People to examine him as to his mental state at the time of commission of the acts charged. People v. Davis, 38 A.D.2d 579, 328 N.Y.S.2d 332 (2d Dept. 1971).

Neonaticide syndrome.—Court did not err in narrowly precluding expert testimony on neonaticide syndrome, because

the reliability of the evidence had not been established. People v. Wernick, 89 N.Y.2d 111, 651 N.Y.S.2d 392, 674 N.E.2d 322 (1996).

Prosecution representation cannot be present at exam.—The People do not have the right to have a representative of the prosecution present at the psychiatric examination of a defendant by a defense psychiatrist. People v. Kindt, 182 Misc. 2d 659, 700 N.Y.S.2d 371 (Co. Ct. Cattaraugus Co. 1999).

Psychiatrist's ignorance of New York standard of responsibility.—It was proper for the court to strike the psychiatrist's testimony after it became apparent that the psychiatrist, who testified on behalf of the defendant, did not know the New York standard for criminal responsibility at the time he examined the defendant and at the trial and had examined the defendant and formed an opinion under another standard. People v. McKinley, 72 A.D.2d 470, 424 N.Y.S.2d 941 (4th Dept. 1980).

Psychiatric testimony; credibility.—It was reversible error for the prosecutor, in his direct case, to adduce testimony of the psychiatrist to attest to complaining witness' capacity to relate facts since such testimony amounted to opinion concerning credibility. People v. Garcia, 75 A.D.2d 836, 426 N.Y.S.2d 836 (2d Dept. 1980).

Waiver of doctor-patient relationship.—When insanity is asserted as a defense and the defendant offers evidence tending to show his insanity in support of this plea, a complete waiver is affected, and the prosecution is then permitted to call psychiatric experts to testify regarding his sanity even though they may have treated the defendant during period he was unfit to stand trial. People v. Abjul Karim Al Kanani, 33 N.Y.2d 260, 351 N.Y.S.2d 969, 307 N.E.2d 43 (1973), cert. denied, 417 U.S. 916 (1974).

Opinion evidence; limitation.—It was highly prejudicial for the People on redirect examination to elicit from their psychiatrist that he found defendant's version incredible together with an explanation of his reasons. This was equivalent to allowing the expert to testify that the defendant was guilty. People v. Graydon, 43 A.D.2d 842, 351 N.Y.S.2d 172 (2d Dept. 1974).

Privilege against self-incrimination at pretrial psychiatric examination.—Examination and admissibility of psychiatric testimony resulting therefrom are not barred by six-year hiatus since commission of crime; such testimonial relevancy, if any, is merely a factor for jury to consider. Lee v. County Ct. of Erie Co., 27 N.Y.2d 432, 318 N.Y.S.2d 705, 267 N.E.2d 452, cert. denied, 404 U.S. 823 (1971).

Responsibilities of court.—Where examination reports submitted to the court showed that each of the two designated psychiatrists was of the opinion that the defendant was not an incapacitated person, but the testimony given by the experts at the hearing actually showed a conflict, the court has the discretionary power to arrive at a conclusion based upon the psychiatrists' reports, their testimony, and other available evidence. People v. Claron, 103 Misc. 2d 841, 427 N.Y.S.2d 146 (Sup. Ct. N.Y. Co. 1980).

Therapist testimony.—Therapist, a psychiatric social worker, who was not qualified as an expert witness at trial, could testify as to her observations of defendant at the holding center but she could not testify as to her conclusions and opinions from these observations. People v. McKinley, 72 A.D.2d 470, 424 N.Y.S.2d 941 (4th Dept. 1980).

Waiver of attorney-client privilege.—A criminal defendant who puts his sanity in issue cannot thwart the introduction of testimony from a psychiatrist who is called at trial by invoking the attorney-client privilege anymore than he can do so by invoking the physician patient privilege. People v. Edney, 39 N.Y.2d 620, 385 N.Y.S.2d 23, 350 N.E.2d 400 (1976).

§ 60.60. Rules of evidence; certificates concerning judgments of conviction and fingerprints.

1. A certificate issued by a criminal court, or the clerk thereof, certifying that a judgment of conviction against a designated defendant has been entered in such court, constitutes presumptive evidence of the facts stated in such certificate.

2. A report of a public servant charged with the custody of official fingerprint records which contains a certification that the fingerprints of a designated person who has previously been convicted of an offense are identical with those of a defendant in a criminal action, constitutes presumptive evidence of the fact that such defendant has previously been convicted of such offense.

ANNOTATIONS

No certificates of conviction; questioning by prosecutor about convictions not prejudicial.—It was improper for the prosecutor to cross-examine defendant as to three out-of-state convictions with respect to which the prosecutor later stipulated that he had no certificates of conviction; this impropriety, however, was not prejudicial in this instance, especially since this was a nonjury case. People v. D'Abate, 37 N.Y.2d 922, 378 N.Y.S.2d 390, 340 N.E.2d 750 (1975).

Presumptive evidence of convictions.—Certificate of conviction produced by People was sufficient to establish that defendant was a second felony offender; in this case, the evidence offered by the People identified the defendant by name and by date of birth. People v. Melvin, 279 A.D.2d 481, 718 N.Y.S.2d 409 (2d Dept. 2001).

—The certificates of disposition attested to by the Clerk of Bronx County stating that defendant was previously convicted of criminal sale of a controlled substance in the third degree and manslaughter in the first degree constitute presumptive evidence of those convictions. People v. Compton, 277 A.D.2d 913, 716 N.Y.S.2d 263 (4th Dept. 2000).

§ 60.70. Rules of evidence; dangerous drugs destroyed pursuant to court order.

The destruction of dangerous drugs pursuant to the provisions of article seven hundred fifteen hereof shall not preclude the admission on trial or in a proceeding in connection therewith of testimony or evidence where such testimony or evidence would otherwise have been admissible if such drugs had not been destroyed.

Added by L. 1973, Ch. 750.

§ 60.75. Rules of evidence; chemical test evidence.

In any prosecution where two or more offenses against the same defendant are properly joined in one indictment or charged in two accusatory instruments properly consolidated for trial purposes and where one such offense charges a violation of any subdivision of section eleven hundred ninety-two of the vehicle and traffic law, chemical test evidence properly admissible as evidence of intoxication under subdivision one of section eleven hundred ninety-five of such law shall also, if relevant, be received in evidence with regard to the remaining charges in the indictments.

Added by L. 1984, Ch. 954.

ANNOTATION

Use of blood test results.—CPL § 60.75 does not limit the use of blood test results to prosecutions under the Vehicle and Traffic Law or to prosecutions linking Vehicle and Traffic Law and Penal Law offenses; the evidence, if legally obtained and relevant, should be admissible in Penal Law prosecutions, notwithstanding the absence of any charge under the Vehicle and Traffic Law. People v. Ladd, 89 N.Y.2d 893, 653 N.Y.S.2d 259, 675 N.E.2d 1211 (1996).

§ 60.76. Rules of evidence; rape crisis counselor evidence in certain cases.

Where disclosure of a communication which would have been privileged pursuant to section forty-five hundred ten of the civil practice law and rules is sought on the grounds that the privilege has been waived or that disclosure is required pursuant to the constitution of this state or the united states, the party seeking disclosure must file a written motion supported by an affidavit containing specific factual allegations providing grounds that disclosure is required. Upon the filing of such motion and affidavit, the court shall conduct an in camera review of the communication outside the presence of the jury and of counsel for all parties in order to determine whether disclosure of any portion of the communication is required.

Added by L. 1993, Ch. 432, eff. 180 days after July 26, 1993.

ARTICLE 65—USE OF CLOSED-CIRCUIT TELEVISION FOR CERTAIN CHILD WITNESSES

Section

* As originally enacted. Differs from section catchline, which refers to "procedures."

LexisNexis Cross References

Prosecution and Defense of Sex Crimes, Ch. 9, The Prosecution and Defense of Child Sexual Assault; *Sexual Assault Trials (2d ed.),* Vol. 1, Ch. 5, Direct and Cross-Examination of Complaining Witness.

§ 65.00. Definitions. [*Expires and repealed September 1, 2007.*]

As used in this article:

1. "Child witness" means a person fourteen years old or less who is or will be called to testify in a criminal proceeding, other than a grand jury proceeding, concerning an offense defined in article one hundred thirty of the penal law or section 255.25 of such law which is the subject of such criminal proceeding.

2. "Vulnerable child witness" means a child witness whom a court has declared to be vulnerable.

3. "Testimonial room" means any room, separate and apart from the courtroom, which is furnished comfortably and less formally than a courtroom and from which the testimony of a vulnerable child witness can be transmitted to the courtroom by means of live, two-way closed-circuit television.

4. "Live, two-way closed-circuit television" means a simultaneous transmission, by closed-circuit television, or other electronic means, between the courtroom and the testimonial room, in accordance with the provisions of section 65.30.

5. "Operator" means the individual authorized by the court to operate the closed-circuit television equipment used in accordance with the provisions of this article.

6. A person occupies "a position of authority with respect to a child" when he or she is a parent, guardian or other person responsible for the custody or care of the child at the relevant time or is any other person who maintains an ongoing personal relationship with such parent, guardian or other person responsible for custody or care, which relationship involves his or her living, or his or her frequent and repeated presence, in the same household or premises as the child.

Added by L. 1985, Ch. 505; **Amended** by L. 1988, Ch. 516; L. 1991, Ch. 455; L. 1996, Ch. 359, § 1, extending exp. date to Nov. 1, 2000; L. 2000, Ch. 449, § 1, extending exp. date to Sept. 1, 2001; L. 2001, Ch. 273, § 1, extending exp. date to Sept. 1, 2002; L. 2002, Ch. 163, § 1, extending exp. date to Sept. 1, 2003; L. 2003, Ch. 388, § 1, eff. Aug. 19, 2003, extending exp. date to Sept. 1, 2005; L. 2004, Ch. 362, § 2, amending subd. 1, eff. Nov. 1, 2004, and such amendment shall not affect the repeal of such section and shall be deemed repealed therewith; L. 2005, Ch. 577, § 1, eff. Aug. 23, 2005, extending exp. date to Sept. 1, 2007.

§ 65.10. Closed-circuit television; general rule; declaration of vulnerability. [*Expires and repealed September 1, 2007.*]

1. A child witness shall be declared vulnerable when the court, in accordance with the provisions of section 65.20, determines by clear and convincing evidence that it is likely, as a result of extraordinary circumstances, that such child witness will suffer severe mental or emotional harm if required to testify at a criminal proceeding without the use of live, two-way closed-circuit television and that the use of such live, two-way closed-circuit television will help prevent, or diminish the likelihood or extent of, such harm.

2. When the court declares a child witness to be vulnerable, it shall, except as provided in subdivision four of section 65.30, authorize the taking of the testimony of the vulnerable child witness from the testimonial room by means of live, two-way closed-circuit television. Under no circumstances shall the provisions of this article be construed to authorize a closed-circuit television system by which events in the courtroom are not transmitted to the testimonial room during the testimony of the vulnerable child witness.

3. Nothing herein shall be contrued* to preclude the court from exercising its power to close the courtroom or from exercising any authority it otherwise may have to protect the well-being of a witness and the rights of the defendant.

* As originally enacted.

Added by L. 1985, Ch. 505; **Amended** by L. 1988, Ch. 516; L. 1991, Ch. 455; L. 1996, Ch. 359, § 1, extending exp. date to Nov. 1, 2000; L. 2000, Ch. 449, § 1, extending exp. date to Sept. 1, 2001; L. 2001, Ch. 273, § 1, extending exp. date to Sept. 1, 2002; L. 2002, Ch. 163, § 1, extending exp. date to Sept. 1, 2003; L. 2003, Ch. 388, § 1, eff. Aug. 19, 2003, extending exp. date to Sept. 1, 2005; L. 2005, Ch. 577, § 1, eff. Aug. 23, 2005, extending exp. date to Sept. 1, 2007.

ANNOTATION

Constitutionality.—Article 65 of the CPL, which authorizes the examination of emotionally traumatized child victims by closed-circuit television, does not violate the defendant's constitutional rights of confrontation, effective assistance of counsel and due process. People v. Henderson, 132 Misc. 2d 51, 503 N.Y.S.2d 238 (Sup. Ct. Queens Co. 1986).

§ 65.20. Closed-circuit television; procedure for application and grounds for determination.

[Expires and repealed September 1, 2007.]

1. Prior to the commencement of a criminal proceeding; other than a grand jury proceeding, either party may apply to the court for an order declaring that a child witness is vulnerable.

2. A motion pursuant to subdivision one of this section must be made in writing at least eight days before the commencement of trial or other criminal proceeding upon reasonable notice to the other party and with an opportunity to be heard.

3. The motion papers must state the basis for the motion and must contain sworn allegations of fact which, if true, would support a determination by the court that the child witness is vulnerable. Such allegations may be based upon the personal knowledge of the deponent or upon information and belief, provided that, in the latter event, the sources of such information and the grounds for such belief are stated.

4. The answering papers may admit or deny any of the alleged facts and may, in addition, contain sworn allegations of fact relevant to the motion, including the rights of the defendant, the need to protect the child witness and the integrity of the truth-finding function of the trier of fact.

5. Unless all material facts alleged in support of the motion made pursuant to subdivision one of this section are conceded, the court shall, in addition to examining the papers and hearing oral argument, conduct an appropriate hearing for the purpose of making findings of fact essential to the determination of the motion. Except as provided in subdivision six of this section, it may subpoena or call and examine witnesses, who must either testify under oath or be permitted to give unsworn testimony pursuant to subdivision two of section 60.20 and must authorize the attorneys for the parties to do the same.

6. Notwithstanding any other provision of law, the child witness who is alleged to be vulnerable may not be compelled to testify at such hearing or to submit to any psychological or psychiatric examination. The failure of the child witness to testify at such hearing shall not be a ground for denying a motion made pursuant to subdivision one of this section. Prior statements made by the child witness relating to any allegations of conduct constituting an offense defined in article one hundred thirty of the penal law or incest as defined in section 255.25 of such law or to any allegation of words or conduct constituting an attempt to prevent, impede or deter the child witness from cooperating in the investigation or prosecution of the offense shall be admissible at such hearing, provided, however, that a declaration that a child witness is vulnerable may not be based solely upon such prior statements.

7. (a) Notwithstanding any of the provisions of article forty-five of the civil practice law and rules, any physician, psychologist, nurse or social worker who has treated a child witness may testify at a hearing conducted pursuant to subdivision five of this section concerning the treatment of such child witness as such treatment relates to the issue presented at the hearing, provided that any otherwise applicable statutory privileges concerning communications between the child witness and such physician, psychologist, nurse or social worker in connection with such treatment shall not be deemed waived by such testimony alone, except to the limited extent of permitting the court alone to examine in camera reports, records or documents, if any, prepared by such physician, psychologist, nurse or social worker. If upon such examination the court determines that such reports, records or documents, or any one or portion thereof, contain information material and relevant to the issue of whether the child witness is a vulnerable child witness, the court shall disclose such information to both the attorney for the defendant and the district attorney.

(b) At any time after a motion has been made pursuant to subdivision one of this section, upon the demand of the other party the moving party must furnish the demanding party with a copy of any and all of such records, reports or other documents in the possession of such other party and must, in addition, supply the court with a copy of all such reports, records or other documents which are the subject of the demand. At any time after a demand has been made pursuant to this paragraph, the moving party may demand that property of the same kind or character in possession of the party that originally made such demand be furnished to the moving party and, if so furnished, be supplied, in addition, to the court.

8. (a) Prior to the commencement of the hearing conducted pursuant to subdivision five of this section, the district attorney shall, subject to a protective order, comply with the provisions of subdivision one of section 240.45 of this chapter as they concern any witness whom the district attorney intends to call at the hearing and the child witness.

(b) Before a defendant calls a witness at such

hearing, he or she must, subject to a protective order, comply with the provisions of subdivision two of section 240.45 of this chapter as they concern all the witnesses the defendant intends to call at such hearing.

9. The court may consider, in determining whether there are such extraordinary circumstances as would cause the child witness to suffer severe mental or emotional harm, a finding that any one or more of the following factors have been established by clear and convincing evidence:

(a) The manner of the commission of the offense of which the defendant is accused was particularly heinous or was characterized by aggravating circumstances.

(b) The child witness is particularly young or otherwise particularly subject to psychological harm on account of a physical or mental condition which existed before the alleged commission of the offense.

(c) At the time of the alleged offense, the defendant occupied a position of authority with respect to the child witness.

(d) The offense or offenses charged were part of an ongoing course of conduct committed by the defendant against the child witness over an extended period of time.

(e) A deadly weapon or dangerous instrument was allegedly used during the commission of the crime.

(f) The defendant has inflicted serious physical injury upon the child witness.

(g) A threat, express or implied, of physical violence to the child witness or a third person if the child witness were to report the incident to any person or communicate information to or cooperate with a court, grand jury, prosecutor, police officer or peace officer concerning the incident has been made by or on behalf of the defendant.

(h) A threat, express or implied, of the incarceration of a parent or guardian of the child witness, the removal of the child witness from the family or the dissolution of the family of the child witness if the child witness were to report the incident to any person or communicate information to or cooperate with a court, grand jury, prosecutor, police officer or peace officer concerning the incident has been made by or on behalf of the defendant.

(i) A witness other than the child witness has received a threat of physical violence directed at such witness or to a third person by or on behalf of the defendant.

(j) The defendant, at the time of the inquiry, (i) is living in the same household with the child witness, (ii) has ready access to the child witness or (iii) is providing substantial financial support for the child witness.

(k) The child witness has previously been the victim of an offense defined in article one hundred thirty of the penal law or incest as defined in section 255.25 of such law.

(l) According to expert testimony, the child witness would be particularly suceptible[*] to psychological harm if required to testify in open court or in the physical presence of the defendant.

10. Irrespective of whether a motion was made pursuant to subdivision one of this section, the court, at the request of either party or on its own motion, may decide that a child witness may be vulnerable based on its own observations that a child witness who has been called to testify at a criminal proceeding is suffering severe mental or emotional harm and therefore is physically or mentally unable to testify or to continue to testify in open court or in the physical presence of the defendant and that the use of live, two-way closed-circuit television is necessary to enable the child witness to testify. If the court so decides, it must conduct the same hearing that subdivision five of this section requires when a motion is made pursuant to subdivision one of this section, and it must make findings of fact pursuant to subdivisions nine and eleven of this section, before determining that the child witness is vulnerable.

11. In deciding whether a child witness is vulnerable, the court shall make findings of fact which reflect the causal relationship between the existence of any one or more of the factors set forth in subdivision nine of this section or other relevant factors which the court finds are established and the determination that the child witness is vulnerable. If the court is satisfied that the child witness is vulnerable and that, under the facts and circumstances of the particular case, the defendant's constitutional rights to an impartial jury or of confrontation will not be impaired, it may enter an order granting the application for the use of live, two-way closed-circuit television.

12. When the court has determined that a child witness is a vulnerable child witness, it shall make a specific finding as to whether placing the defendant and the child witness in the same room during the testimony of the child witness will contribute to the likelihood that the child witness will suffer severe mental or emotional harm. If the court finds that placing the defendant and the child witness in the same room during the testimony of the child witness will contribute to the likelihood that the child witness will suffer severe mental or emotional harm, the order entered pursuant to subdivision eleven of this section shall direct that the defendant remain in the courtroom during the testimony of the vulnerable child witness.

[*] As originally enacted.

Added by L. 1985, Ch. 505; **Amended** by L. 1988, Ch. 516; L. 1991, Ch. 455, eff. July 19, 1991, amending subds. (10) & (11); L. 1996, Ch. 359, § 1, extending exp. date to Nov. 1, 2000; L. 2000, Ch. 449, § 1, extending exp. date to Sept. 1, 2001;

L. 2001, Ch. 273, § 1, extending exp. date to Sept. 1, 2002; L. 2002, Ch. 163, § 1, extending exp. date to Sept. 1, 2003; L. 2003, Ch. 388, § 1, eff. Aug. 19, 2003, extending exp. date to Sept.1, 2005; L. 2005, Ch. 577, § 1, eff. Aug. 23, 2005, extending exp. date to Sept. 1, 2007.

ANNOTATIONS

Vulnerable child witness.—Court properly permitted six-year-old complainant to testify via closed circuit television, where court relied on a combination of its own observations and the testimony of two witnesses, and the record supports its determination that the child witness would suffer severe mental and emotional harm if required to testify in defendant's presence. People v. Paramore, 288 A.D.2d 53, 732 N.Y.S.2d 410 (1st Dept. 2001).

—Complainant was a "vulnerable child witness" within the meaning of CPL article 65, because the testimony revealed that the complainant was particularly young and was threatened with physical violence if the incident were reported to any person, that she exhibited a great deal of fear whenever she encountered defendant in the street, and that in the opinion of each witness, personally familiar with the circumstances, the complainant would be particularly susceptible to psychological harm if required to testify in defendant's physical presence. People v. Biavaschi, 265 A.D.2d 268, 697 N.Y.S.2d 53 (1st Dept. 1999).

§ 65.30. Closed-circuit television; special testimonial procedures. [*Expires and repealed September 1, 2007.*]

1. When the court has entered an order pursuant to section 65.20, the testimony of the vulnerable child witness shall be taken in the testimonial room and the image and voice of the vulnerable child witness, as well as the image of all other persons other than the operator present in the testimonial room, shall be transmitted live by means of closed-circuit television to the courtroom. The courtroom shall be equipped with monitors sufficient to permit the judge, jury, defendant and attorneys to observe the demeanor of the vulnerable child witness during his or her testimony. Unless the courtroom has been closed pursuant to court order, the public shall also be permitted to hear the testimony and view the image of the vulnerable child witness.

2. In all instances, the image of the jury shall be simultaneously transmitted to the vulnerable child witness in the testimonial room. If the court order issued pursuant to section 65.20 specifies that the vulnerable child witness shall testify outside the physical presence of the defendant, the image of the defendant and the image and voice of the person examining the vulnerable child witness shall also be simultaneously transmitted to the vulnerable child witness in the testimonial room.

3. The operator shall place herself or himself and the closed-circuit television equipment in a position that permits the entire testimony of the vulnerable child witness to be transmitted to the courtroom but limits the ability of the vulnerable child witness to see or hear the operator or the equipment.

4. Notwithstanding any provision of this article, if the court in a particular case involving a vulnerable child witness determines that there is no live, two-way closed-circuit television equipment available in the court or another court in the county or which can be transported to the court from another county or that such equipment, if available, is technologically inadequate to protect the constitutional rights of the defendant, it shall not permit the use of the closed-circuit television procedures authorized by this article.

5. If the order of the court entered pursuant to section 65.20 requires that the defendant remain in the courtroom, the attorney for the defendant and the district attorney shall also remain in the courtroom unless the court is satisfied that their presence in the testimonial room will not impede full and private communication between the defendant and his or her attorney and will not encourage the jury to draw an inference adverse to the interest of the defendant.

6. Upon request of the defendant, the court shall instruct the jury that they are to draw no inference from the use of live, two-way closed-circuit television in the examination of the vulnerable child witness.

7. The vulnerable child witness shall testify under oath except as specified in subdivision two of section 60.20. The examination and cross-examination of the vulnerable child witness shall, in all other respects, be conducted in the same manner as if the vulnerable child witness had testified in the courtroom.

8. When the testimony of the vulnerable child witness is transmitted from the testimonial room into the courtroom, the court stenographer shall record the textimony* in the same manner as if the vulnerable child witness had testified in the courtroom.

* As originally enacted.

Added by L. 1985, Ch. 505; **Amended** by L. 1988, Ch. 516; L. 1991, Ch. 455; L. 1996, Ch. 359, § 1, extending exp. date to Nov. 1, 2000; L. 2000, Ch. 449, § 1, extending exp. date to Sept. 1, 2001; L. 2001, Ch. 273, § 1, extending exp. date to Sept. 1, 2002; L. 2002, Ch. 163, § 1, extending exp. date to Sept. 1, 2003; L. 2003, Ch. 388, § 1, eff. Aug. 19, 2003, extending exp. date to Sept. 1, 2005; L. 2005, Ch. 577, § 1, eff. Aug. 23, 2005, extending exp. date to Sept. 1, 2007.

ANNOTATION

Preservation.—Defendant's claim that the court failed to comply with CPL § 65.30(2) required preservation, and if the court were to review unpreserved claim, it would find that the record provided no support for defendant's purely speculative contention that the images of the jury and of defendant were not transmitted to the complainant as she testified via closed circuit television from the testimonial room. People v. Alicea, 255 A.D.2d 240, 682 N.Y.S.2d 12 (1st Dept. 1998).

ARTICLE 70—STANDARDS OF PROOF

Section

70.10 Standards of proof; definitions of terms.
70.20 Standards of proof for conviction.

LexisNexis Cross References

Bender's New York Evidence—CPLR, Vol. 2, Ch. 5, Circumstantial Evidence; Vol. 3, Ch. 6A, Proof of Value; Vol. 4, Ch. 10, Burden of Proof; *Courtroom Criminal Evidence (3d ed.)*, Vol. 2, Ch. 29, Burdens of Production and Proof.

§ 70.10. Standards of proof; definitions of terms.

The following definitions are applicable to this chapter:

1. "Legally sufficient evidence" means competent evidence which, if accepted as true, would establish every element of an offense charged and the defendant's commission thereof; except that such evidence is not legally sufficient when corroboration required by law is absent.

2. "Reasonable cause to believe that a person has committed an offense" exists when evidence or information which appears reliable discloses facts or circumstances which are collectively of such weight and persuasiveness as to convince a person of ordinary intelligence, judgment and experience that it is reasonably likely that such offense was committed and that such person committed it. Except as otherwise provided in this chapter, such apparently reliable evidence may include or consist of hearsay.

ANNOTATIONS

Grand Jury.—In the context of Grand Jury procedure, legally sufficient evidence means proof of a prima facie case, not proof beyond a reasonable doubt. People v. Gordon, 88 N.Y.2d 92, 643 N.Y.S.2d 498, 666 N.E.2d 203 (1996).

—Indictment is authorized when grand jury receives competent evidence sufficient to establish each element of offense and to provide probable cause to believe defendant committed offense. People v. Frazier, 224 A.D.2d 358, 638 N.Y.S.2d 88 (1st Dept. 1996).

Dismissal.—In evaluating motion for trial order of dismissal, evidence must be viewed in light most favorable to People with review limited solely to legal sufficiency of evidence. People v. Beecher, 225 A.D.2d 943, 639 N.Y.S.2d 863 (3d Dept. 1996).

Accusatory instrument; information; sufficiency thereof.—In a prosecution for refusal to comply with orders of the fire commissioner, the use of the fire department code incorporated by reference, does not violate the requirement that an information contain nonhearsay allegations and its use is not improper provided it is authenticated or certified. People v. Penn Central Railroad Co., 95 Misc. 2d 748, 417 N.Y.S.2d 822 (N.Y.C. Crim. Ct. 1979).

Arson; proof.—To constitute arson, there must be proof beyond a reasonable doubt that the fire was directly caused by a human being. People v. Trippoda, 40 A.D.2d 388, 341 N.Y.S.2d 66 (3d Dept. 1973).

Circumstantial evidence.—Defendant was arrested near the scene of a burglary in possession of currency which matched the description of the bills given by the victim. A rifle, also stolen, was found near where the defendant had been. The court held that the inferences that defendant entered the house, stole the money and rifle flow naturally from and are consistent with the circumstantial evidence and the cumulative effect was legally sufficient to establish a prima facie case. People v. Dudwoire, 95 A.D.2d 878, 463 N.Y.S.2d 894 (3d Dept. 1983).

Circumstantial evidence; sufficiency.—Even where the evidence against defendant is circumstantial, the standard for reviewing the sufficiency of the evidence is whether any rational trier of fact could have found the essential elements of the crime beyond a reasonable doubt. People v. Ficarrota, 91 N.Y.2d 244, 668 N.Y.S.2d 993, 691 N.E.2d 1017 (1997).

—To sustain a conviction based exclusively on circumstantial evidence the facts from which the inference of the defendant's guilt is drawn must be established with certainty, must be inconsistent with his innocence and must exclude to a moral certainty every other reasonable hypothesis. People v. Williams, 35 N.Y.2d 783, 362 N.Y.S.2d 152, 320 N.E.2d 867 (1974); People v. Sibbles, 63 A.D.2d 934, 406 N.Y.S.2d 84 (1st Dept. 1978).

—When a defendant's conviction is based entirely upon circumstantial evidence of his guilt, it is subject to strict judicial scrutiny, not because of any inherent weakness in the form of evidence, but to ensure that the jury has not relied upon equivocal evidence to draw unwarranted inferences or to make unsupported assumptions. The standard of proof in such cases is that the facts from which the inference of guilt is drawn must be "inconsistent with his innocence and must exclude to a moral certainty every other reasonable hypothesis." People v. Way, 59 N.Y.2d 361, 465 N.Y.S.2d 853, 452 N.E.2d 1181 (1983).

—In murder prosecution, where defendant, accompanied by several other men, was seen holding a gun while leading the victim toward the scene of the crime and a few minutes later a shot was heard and the group fled, the evidence against defendant was legally insufficient as it did not exclude to a moral certainty every other hypothesis but that defendant committed the crime, since a juvenile subsequently admitted to shooting the victim and pleaded guilty to a manslaughter charge in Family Court. People v. Kennedy, 63 A.D.2d 738, 405 N.Y.S.2d 485 (2d Dept. 1978).

Felony hearing; reasonable cause; oral statements of defendant.—At a preliminary hearing before a local criminal court, the same degree or proof or quality of evidence as is necessary for an indictment is not required; only that there be reasonable cause to believe that the defendant committed any felony that the evidence indicates. Oral statements allegedly made by defendant to police officer were admissible at preliminary felony hearing to aid Town Justice to pass upon sufficiency of evidence to hold defendant charged with felony murder and sodomy. Mattioli v. Brown. 71 Misc. 2d 99, 335 N.Y.S.2d 613 (Sup. Ct. Fulton Co. 1972).

Hearsay sufficient.—A probable cause assessment need not rise to the level of evidence sufficient to support a conviction or prove a prima facie case. Furthermore, it is well settled that probable cause may be provided through hearsay information where the individuals providing the information are reliable and have a basis for their knowledge. People v. Letendre, 264 A.D.2d 943, 696 N.Y.S.2d 538 (3d Dept. 1999), *aff'd,* 94 N.Y.2d 939, 709 N.Y.S.2d 497, 731 N.E.2d 153 (2000).

Indictment; evidence.—There is no constitutional requirement that grand jury indictments be founded upon sufficient legal proof. Miranda v. Isseks, 41 A.D.2d 176, 341 N.Y.S.2d 541 (2d Dept. 1973).

Indictment; sufficiency.—Indictment improperly dismissed in solicitation case where the Grand Jury could rationally infer from defendant's conversations with the officer that he intended the officer to commit the underlying crimes; in making a determination as to the legal sufficiency of an indictment, the inquiry is "whether the evidence viewed in the light most favorable to the People, if unexplained and uncontradicted, would warrant conviction by a petit jury." People v. Cheatham, 239 A.D.2d 595, 658 N.Y.S.2d 84 (2d Dept. 1997).

Legal sufficiency in Grand Jury.—"Legally sufficient" is defined in CPL § 70.10(1) as "competent evidence which, if accepted as true, would establish every element of an offense charged." In Grand Jury proceeding, legal sufficiency means prima facie proof of the crimes charged, not proof beyond a reasonable doubt. People v. Bello, 92 N.Y.2d 523, 683 N.Y.S.2d 168, 705 N.E.2d 1209 (1998).

Possession of dangerous weapon; taxicab is "place of business."—Although the evidence warranted holding the matter for trial, charge of possession of firearm found in defendant's cab could be reduced to a misdemeanor, since the cab constituted a "place of business" and was therefore an exception to the statute concerning possession of weapons. People v. Anderson, 74 Misc. 2d 415, 344 N.Y.S.2d 15 (Crim. Ct. Bronx Co. 1973).

Reasonable cause; generally.—Probable cause to arrest the defendant did not exist where the record disclosed that at most the defendant may have been placed in the near vicinity of the crimes around the time that they may have occurred. People v. Barber, 60 A.D.2d 747, 400 N.Y.S.2d 941 (4th Dept. 1977).

—The standard of "reasonable cause" as defined in CPL section 70.10(2) does away with the requirement of prima facie case. People ex rel. Fox v. Sherwood, 73 Misc. 2d 101, 341 N.Y.S.2d 161 (Sup. Ct. Orange Co. 1973).

—Mere suspicion is not probable cause. What in the common judgment of reasonable men would be regarded as good, sound cause that is probable cause. When a police officer views a hardcore pornographic film, that is offered for public viewing, he has probable cause to believe an offense is being committed in his presence. People v. Morgan, 68 Misc. 2d 667, 326 N.Y.S.2d 976 (N.Y.C. Crim. Ct. 1971).

Reasonable cause; 72-hour period for production of proof.—The People should be able to produce proof within 72 hours of those elements which were regarded as reasonable justification for the arrest of the defendant. People ex rel. Fox v. Sherwood, 73 Misc. 2d 101, 341 N.Y.S.2d 161 (Sup. Ct. Orange Co. 1973).

§ 70.20. Standards of proof for conviction.

No conviction of an offense by verdict is valid unless based upon trial evidence which is legally sufficient and which establishes beyond a reasonable doubt every element of such offense and the defendant's commission thereof.

ANNOTATIONS

Alibi defense.—It was reversible error for the judge to refuse to instruct the jury on alibi defenses where defendant presented one; defendant was entitled to have alibi testimony considered in rebuttal as prosecution evidence to create a reasonable doubt as to his guilt; jury also should have been instructed that the people still must prove every element of their case when defendant brings an alibi defense, and that the jury could disbelieve the alibi and still acquit. People v. Bacon, 84 A.D.2d 680, 446 N.Y.S.2d 634 (4th Dept. 1981).

Burden of proof; alibi.—A defendant need not prove the truth of his alibi in any way and the court's statement that the alibi testimony should be carefully scrutinized warranted reversal. People v. Orse, 91 A.D.2d 1003, 457 N.Y.S.2d 581 (2d Dept. 1983).

Guilt based on circumstantial evidence; jury charge.—Where the defendant's guilt was based entirely upon circumstantial evidence, the trial court erred in not charging the jury that, where circumstantial evidence is relied upon to establish guilt, the evidence must point logically to the defendant's guilt so as to exclude to a moral certainty any other reasonable hypothesis. People v. Morris, 42 A.D.2d 968, 347 N.Y.S.2d 975 (2d Dept. 1973), aff'd, 36 N.Y.2d 877, 372 N.Y.S.2d 210, 334 N.E.2d 10 (1975).

Necessary elements; homicide.—Where defendant shot the victim five times some two to five minutes after the victim had been fatally wounded by another, the evidence was legally insufficient to support a homicide conviction since it was impossible for the jury to conclude beyond a reasonable doubt that the victim was alive when the defendant shot him, but the evidence was sufficient for the jury to conclude that the defendant thought that the victim was alive and such conclusion established the attempt since factual or legal impossibility is no defense if the result intended by the actor is a crime. People v. Dlugash, 41 N.Y.2d 725, 395 N.Y.S.2d 419, 363 N.E.2d 1155 (1977).

No necessity of proving each allegation of indictment.—While the indictment included an allegation that the defendant was intoxicated, the defendant could be found guilty of criminally negligent homicide for driving his vehicle on the wrong side of the road while speeding even though he may not have been intoxicated at the time. It is not necessary in every case that the People prove all acts alleged in the indictment where the remaining acts alleged are sufficient to sustain a conviction. People v. Rooney, 57 N.Y.2d 822, 455 N.Y.S.2d 595, 441 N.E.2d 1113 (1982).

PART TWO—THE PRINCIPAL PROCEEDINGS

TITLE H—PRELIMINARY PROCEEDINGS IN LOCAL CRIMINAL COURT

ARTICLE 100—COMMENCEMENT OF ACTION IN LOCAL CRIMINAL COURT—LOCAL CRIMINAL COURT ACCUSATORY INSTRUMENTS

LexisNexis Cross Reference

New York Criminal Practice (2d ed.), Vol. 1, Ch. 4, Local Criminal Court Accusatory Instruments.

§ 100.05. Commencement of action; in general.

A criminal action is commenced by the filing of an accusatory instrument with a criminal court, and if more than one such instrument is filed in the course of the same criminal action, such action commences when the first of such instruments is filed. The only way in which a criminal action can be commenced in a superior court is by the filing therewith by a grand jury of an indictment against a defendant who has never been held by a local criminal court for the action of such grand jury with respect to any charge contained in such indictment. Otherwise, a criminal action can be commenced only in a local criminal court, by the filing therewith of a local criminal court accusatory instrument, namely:

1. An information; or

2. A simplified information; or

3. A prosecutor's information; or

4. A misdemeanor complaint; or

5. A felony complaint.

Amended by L. 1972, Ch. 661.

ANNOTATIONS

Parking ticket.—Parking summons was akin to an appearance ticket rather than an accusatory instrument. People v. Gilberg, 166 Misc. 2d 772, 637 N.Y.S.2d 917 (App. Term, 2d Dept. 1995).

Dismissal of misdemeanor complaint; later filing of prosecutor's information at Grand Jury's direction.—In order to be part of a single criminal action CPL § 1.20(16)(b) requires that the second accusatory instrument must void and supersede the initial accusatory instrument by virtue of superior power provided for in law; thus, where the court dismissed the misdemeanor complaint "in the exercise of the calendar control function" and the Grand Jury later directed a prosecutor's information on the same charge, it did not violate CPL § 100.05, since no earlier accusatory instrument was extant and the prosecutor's information was not, in law, a superseding one. People v. Nizza, 95 Misc. 2d 74, 407 N.Y.S.2d 388 (Crim. Ct. N.Y.C. 1978).

Jurisdiction; dismissal by Grand Jury.—Where Grand Jury heard evidence concerning assault, presented by District Attorney, and dismissed proceedings, criminal court was precluded from taking jurisdiction as only the Supreme Court could direct resubmission. Manford v. McCormack, 72 Misc. 2d 53, 337 N.Y.S.2d 914 (Crim. Ct. N.Y.C. 1972).

Juvenile delinquency proceedings; applicability of CPL provisions.—Court interpreted CPL §§ 1.20 and 100.05 to mean that there can only be one criminal action for each set of criminal charges brought against a particular defendant, notwithstanding that the original accusatory instrument may be replaced or superseded during the course of the action; this is true even where the original accusatory instrument is dismissed outright and the defendant brought into court on an entirely new indictment. People v. Lomax, 50 N.Y.2d 937, 428 N.Y.S.2d 937, 406 N.E.2d 793 (1980).

—If more than one accusatory instrument is filed in the same criminal action, the action is commenced upon the filing of the first accusatory instrument. People v. Easterling, 59 A.D.2d 537, 397 N.Y.S.2d 125 (2d Dept. 1977).

—Although there was a typographical error with respect to the time of day in the accusatory instrument attached to the information for delinquency, defendant's statutory and due process rights were met because he had adequate notice of the charges against him and an opportunity to be heard and to confront the People's witnesses. People v. Mallory, 191 A.D.2d 970, 595 N.Y.S.2d 266 (4th Dept. 1993).

§ 100.07. Commencement of action; effect of family court proceeding.

A criminal court shall have concurrent jurisdiction over cognizable family offenses, as defined in subdivision one of section 530.11 of this chapter and in subdivision one of section eight hundred twelve of the family court act, notwithstanding the fact that a family court has or may be exercising jurisdiction over a petition under article eight of the family court act containing substantially the same allegations as are set forth in the accusatory instrument or indictment.

Added by L. 1977, Ch. 449; **Amended** by L. 1978, Chs. 628 and 629; L. 1990, Ch. 577; L. 1994, Ch. 222, § 31, eff. Jan. 1, 1995.

ANNOTATIONS

Commencement in Family Court and then local criminal court.—The same person may commence a proceeding by filing a petition in Family Court and then filing a complaint and proceeding in the local criminal court instead. People v. Fisher, 153 Misc. 2d 86, 580 N.Y.S.2d 625 (Justice Ct. Westchester Co. 1991).

Parallel to Family Court Act.—CPL § 100.07 parallels section 812 of the Family Court Act and prohibits the commencement of a criminal action charging a family offense if a Family Court petition involving the same criminal transaction remained pending in Family Court for more than 72 hours. People v. Williams, 146 Misc. 2d 447, 551 N.Y.S.2d 442 (Crim. Ct. Queens Co. 1990).

Jurisdiction; Family Court.—A defendant can be subject to both a Family Court proceeding involving the charge of disorderly conduct and a criminal proceeding involving the charge of criminal mischief in the fourth degree, which is not within the Family Court's jurisdiction, and the exclusion provision of CPL § 100.07 does not apply. People v. Bulin, 142 Misc. 2d 776, 538 N.Y.S.2d 436 (Dist. Ct. Nassau Co. 1989).

§ 100.10. Local criminal court accusatory instruments; definitions thereof.

1. An "information" is a verified written accusation by a person, filed with a local criminal court, charging one or more other persons with the commission of one or more offenses, none of which is a felony. It may serve as a basis both for the commencement of a criminal action and for the prosecution thereof in a local criminal court.

2. (a) A "simplified traffic information" is a written accusation by a police officer or other public servant authorized by law to issue same, filed with a local criminal court, which charges a person with the commission of one or more traffic infractions and/or misdemeanors relating to traffic, and which, being in a brief or simplified form prescribed by the commissioner of motor vehicles, designates the offense or offenses charged but contains no factual allegations of an evidentiary nature supporting such charge or charges. It serves as a basis for commencement of a criminal action for such traffic offenses, alternative to the charging thereof by a regular information, and, under circumstances prescribed in section 100.25, it may serve, either in whole or in part, as a basis for prosecution of such charges.

(b) A "simplified parks information" is a written accusation by a police officer or other public servant authorized by law to issue same, filed with a local criminal court, which charges a person with the commission of one or more offenses, other than a felony, for which a uniform simplified parks information may be issued pursuant to the parks and recreation law and navigation law, and which being in a brief or simplified form prescribed by the commissioner of parks and recreation, designates the offense or offenses charged but contains no factual allegations of an evidentiary nature supporting such charge or charges. It serves as a basis for commencement of a criminal action for such offenses, alternative to the charging thereof by a regular information, and, under circumstances parescribed[*] in section 100.25, it may serve, either in whole or in part, as a basis for prosecution of such charges.

(c) A "simplified environmental conservation information" is a written accusation by a police officer or other public servant authorized by law to issue same, filed with a local criminal court, which charges a person with the commission of one or more offenses, other than a felony, for which a uniform simplified environmental conservation information may be issued pursuant to the environmental conservation law, and which being in a brief or simplified form prescribed by the commissioner of environmental conservation, designates the offense or offenses charged but contains no factual allegations of an evidentiary nature supporting such charge or charges. It serves as a basis for commencement of a criminal action for such offenses, alternative to the charging thereof by a regular information, and, under circumstances prescribed in section 100.25, it may serve, either in whole or in part, as a basis for prosecution of such charges.

3. A "prosecutor's information" is a written accusation by a district attorney, filed with a local criminal court, either (a) at the direction of a grand jury pursuant to section 190.70, or (b) at the direction of a local criminal court pursuant to section 180.50 or 180.70, or (c) at the district attorney's own instance pursuant to subdivision

two of section 100.50, or (d) at the direction of a superior court pursuant to subdivision one-a of section 210.20, charging one or more persons with the commission of one or more offenses, none of which is a felony. It serves as a basis for the prosecution of a criminal action, but it commences a criminal action only where it results from a grand jury direction issued in a case not previously commenced in a local criminal court.

4. A "misdemeanor complaint" is a verified written accusation by a person, filed with a local criminal court, charging one or more other persons with the commission of one or more offenses, at least one of which is a misdemeanor and none of which is a felony. It serves as a basis for the commencement of a criminal action, but it may serve as a basis for prosecution thereof only where a defendant has waived prosecution by information pursuant to subdivision three of section 170.65.

5. A "felony complaint" is a verified written accusation by a person, filed with a local criminal court, charging one or more other persons with the commission of one or more felonies. It serves as a basis for the commencement of a criminal action, but not as a basis for prosecution thereof.

* As originally enacted.

Amended by L. 1972, Chs. 315, 383, 661 and 729; L. 1974, Ch. 707; L. 1990, Ch. 209.

ANNOTATIONS

Traffic information.—Where motorist was charged by simplified information with vehicle and traffic law misdemeanor of aggravated unlicensed operation in third degree, standard of review for facial sufficiency was whether simplified information and supplementing supporting deposition provided reasonable cause to believe that motorist committed the offense. People v. Quarles, 168 Misc. 2d 638, 639 N.Y.S.2d 661 (Rochester City Ct. 1996).

Mandamus; filing of accusatory instrument.—Mandamus was granted compelling justice of police court and clerk thereof to accept for filing an accusatory instrument charging police officers with assault upon the petitioner. Artis v. Keegan, 77 Misc. 2d 638, 354 N.Y.S.2d 504 (Albany Co. Sup. Ct. 1974).

No prosecution on misdemeanor complaint in absence of waiver.—In the absence of a valid waiver of prosecution by information, a defendant need not even plead to a misdemeanor complaint. People v. Ryff, 100 Misc. 2d 505, 419 N.Y.S.2d 845 (Crim. Ct. Bronx Co. 1979).

Simplified traffic information.—A simplified traffic information is not required to have factual allegations of an evidentiary nature, whether hearsay or nonhearsay. The required provision of "reasonable cause to believe that the defendant committed the charged offense" may be supplied by facts that permit an inference that a required element, such as operation of a motor vehicle, was present, with no requirement or more direct proof. People v. Rose, 8 Misc. 3d 184, 794 N.Y.S.2d 630 (Dist. Ct. Nassau Co. 2005).

—Simplified traffic information charging defendant with having no highway use tax permit while operating a truck on a public highway, in violation of section 512, subd. 1(a) of the Tax Law, is not jurisdictionally defective and may serve as the basis for prosecution, since the use of the traffic summons is permitted to accommodate offenses found in statutes other than the Vehicle and Traffic Law that relate to traffic. People v. Ferri, 106 Misc. 2d 311, 431 N.Y.S.2d 765 (Dix Town Ct., Schuyler Co. 1980).

Universal summons.—The rules applicable to the simplified traffic information (CPL § 100.10) are also applicable to the Universal summons since the two are so similar in form and content; Universal summons need not contain factual allegations. People v. Oasis Cabana Spa, Inc., 95 Misc. 2d 59, 406 N.Y.S.2d 964 (N.Y.C. Crim. Ct. 1978).

Waiver of prosecution by information must be conscious and knowing.—People v. Gittens, 103 Misc. 2d 309, 425 N.Y.S.2d 771 (Crim. Ct. Bronx Co. 1980).

§ 100.15. Information, misdemeanor complaint and felony complaint; form and content.

1. An information, a misdemeanor complaint and a felony complaint must each specify the name of the court with which it is filed and the title of the action, and must be subscribed and verified by a person known as the "complainant." The complainant may be any person having knowledge, whether personal or upon information and belief, of the commission of the offense or offenses charged. Each instrument must contain an accusatory part and a factual part. The complainant's verification of the instrument is deemed to apply only to the factual part thereof and not to the accusatory part.

2. The accusatory part of each such instrument must designate the offense or offenses charged. As in the case of an indictment, and subject to the rules of joinder applicable to indictments, two or more offenses may be charged in separate counts. Also as in the case of an indictment, such instrument may charge two or more defendants provided that all such defendants are jointly charged with every offense alleged therein.

3. The factual part of such instrument must contain a statement of the complainant alleging facts of an evidentiary character supporting or tending to support the charges. Where more than one offense is charged, the factual part should consist of a single factual account applicable to all the counts of the accusatory part. The factual allegations may be based either upon personal knowledge of the complainant or upon information and belief. Nothing contained in this section, however, limits or affects the requirement, prescribed in subdivision one of section 100.40, that in order for an information or a count thereof to be sufficient on its face, every element of the offense charged and the defendant's commission thereof must be supported by non-hearsay allegations of such information and/or any supporting depositions.

4. Where a felony complaint charges a violent felony offense defined in section 70.02 of the penal law and such offense is an armed felony as defined in subdivision forty-one of section 1.20,

(a) the accusatory part of the instrument must designate the offense as an armed felony, and

(b) the factual part of the instrument must allege facts of an evidentiary character supporting or tending to support such designation.

Amended by L. 1978, Ch. 481.

ANNOTATIONS

Family offense.—Because family offense proceeding before family court is civil proceeding, rules governing sufficiency and contents of criminal accusatory instruments are not applicable, and petitioner need only file petition which contains allegation that respondent has committed one or more family offenses. Eileen W. v. Mario A., 169 Misc. 2d 484, 644 N.Y.S.2d 452 (Family Ct. N.Y. Co. 1996).

Accusatory instrument; verification misdemeanor complaint; reasonable cause; sufficiency.—Necessary elements for information to be sufficient on its face include: substantial conformity to statutory requirements for information, in form and content; allegations in factual part of information or any supporting depositions that establish reasonable cause to believe defendant committed offense charged; and nonhearsay allegations in information or any supporting depositions that would establish, if true, every element of offense charged, or in other words, establish prima facie case. People v. Henry, 167 Misc. 2d 1027, 641 N.Y.S.2d 1003 (Dist. Ct. Nassau Co. 1996).

—Since the CPL provision regarding verifications was remedial, verification before notary supported by complainants reference to deposition in accusatory instrument, and deponents statement, was not violative of statute and instrument, was not violative of statute and instrument would be treated as misdemeanor complaint sufficiently stating facts that person of ordinary intelligence, etc., would reasonably believe constituted bookmaking violation, but complaint had to be superseded by information, unless waived, so that every element of the crime charged is established. People v. Minuto, 71 Misc. 2d 800, 337 N.Y.S.2d 88 (Batavia City Ct. 1972).

Accusatory instrument; information; sufficiency thereof.—As long as the factual allegations of an information give an accused sufficient notice to prepare a defense and are adequately detailed to prevent a defendant from being tried twice for the same offense, they should be given a fair and not overly restrictive or technical reading. People v. Konieczny, 2 N.Y.3d 569, 780 N.Y.S.2d 546, 813 N.E.2d 626 (2004) (citing People v. Casey, 95 N.Y.2d 354, 717 N.Y.S.2d 88, 740 N.E.2d 233 (2000)).

—It is a fundamental and non-waivable jurisdictional prerequisite that an information state the crime with which the defendant is charged and the particular facts constituting that crime; every element of the crime charged and the defendant's commission thereof must be alleged. People v. Hall, 48 N.Y.2d 927, 425 N.Y.S.2d 56, 401 N.E.2d 179 (1979).

—A valid and sufficient accusatory instrument is a non-waivable jurisdictional prerequisite to a criminal prosecution, and an objection to the substantive sufficiency of the information, such as one that it does not state a crime, as distinguished from an objection to the form of the instrument, is not waived by a plea of guilty. People v. Case, 42 N.Y.2d 98, 396 N.Y.S.2d 841, 365 N.E.2d 872 (1977).

—An information does not need to contain the most precise words or phrases which most clearly express the thought, but only needs to allege the crime and set forth the specifics so that a defendant can prepare for trial and so that a defendant will not be tried again for the same offense. People v. Hall, 4 Misc. 3d 60, 781 N.Y.S.2d 395 (App. T. 9th & 10th Jud. Dists. 2004).

—There is no authority for defendant's contention that the People must assert the operability of a gravity knife in a complaint or an information and defendant's motion to dismiss the accusatory instrument is denied. People v. William, 188 Misc. 2d 869, 729 N.Y.S.2d 826 (Crim. Ct. Kings. Co. 2001), aff'd, 191 Misc. 2d 293, 742 N.Y.S.2d 772 (App. T. 2d Dept. 2002).

—It is a fundamental principle that an information must allege each and every element of the offense charged. People v. Butt, 153 Misc. 2d 751, 583 N.Y.S.2d 732 (Crim. Ct. Kings Co. 1992).

—An accusatory instrument will be dismissed as facially insufficient if it fails to allege non-hearsay facts of an evidentiary nature that support or tend to support each and every element of the offense charged and the defendant's commission thereof. However, an accusatory instrument is facially sufficient when it establishes a "prima facie" case; it need not establish defendant's guilt beyond a reasonable doubt. People v. Ensley, 183 Misc. 2d 141, 702 N.Y.S.2d 752 (Crim. Ct. N.Y. Co. 1999).

—In order to constitute a legally sufficient information, an accusatory instrument must consist of verified, non-hearsay allegations which would establish, if true, the defendant's commission of every element of each offense charged. People v. Phillips, 142 Misc. 2d 574, 538 N.Y.S.2d 400 (Crim. Ct. Kings Co. 1989).

—When an accusatory instrument cites the specific statutes under which the defendant is charged, this may satisfy the "accusatory part" requirements, but it does not satisfy the factual part requirements. People v. Frazier, — Misc. 2d —, 759 N.Y.S.2d 631 (City Ct. Monroe Co. 2003).

—The failure of an information to allege an element of the offense charged is a nonwaivable jurisdictional defect, and the People have until the statutory period of CPL § 30.30 to correct the defect. People v. Volkes, 1 Misc. 3d 829, 771 N.Y.S.2d 797 (Richmond Co. 2003).

Obscenity; motion to suppress arrest warrant; sufficiency of information.—It was unnecessary to have a prior adversary hearing or judicial scrutiny before issuance of arrest warrant of defendant to police officer who purchased two books and one film in bookstore managed by defendant and statute was not unconstitutional solely because it permitted exception in cases of scientific, educational or governmental purchases. People v. Kokich, 72 Misc. 2d 124, 338 N.Y.S.2d 463 (Dist. Ct. Suffolk Co. 1972).

Title of action required.—The information should recite the title of the action as "the People of the State of New York against . . . [the named defendant]." People v. Brickel, 67 Misc. 2d 848, 325 N.Y.S.2d 28 (Justice Ct. 1971).

Evidentiary facts not conclusions are required.—For a misdemeanor information to be facially sufficient, the factual portion must allege facts of an be evidentiary nature supportinor tending to support the charges; nonhearsay allegations must establish, if true, every element of each offense charged as well as defendant's commission thereof. People v. Howell, 158 Misc. 2d 653, 601 N.Y.S.2d 778 (Crim. Ct. Kings Co. 1993).

Felony complaint; factual allegations.—It is not necessary in a felony complaint to specifically state the basis of the allegations, since the defendant will learn this at the felony hearing. People v. Ferro, 77 Misc. 2d 226, 353 N.Y.S.2d 854 (Nassau Co. District Ct. 1974).

Misdemeanor complaint; factual allegations.—The factual part of a misdemeanor complaint must allege "facts of an evidentiary character" demonstrating "reasonable cause" to believe the defendant committed the crime charged. People v. Dumas, 68 N.Y.2d 729, 506 N.Y.S.2d 319, 497 N.E.2d 686 (1986).

Ministerial mislabeling of information.—Where clerk mislabeled instrument containing only non-hearsay allegations as misdemeanor complaint instead of information, error was ministerial and not decisive of the nature of the instrument. People v. Vlasto, 78 Misc. 2d 419, 355 N.Y.S.2d 983 (Crim. Ct. N.Y. Co. 1974).

Information need not be phrased in the most precise words; sufficient if crime alleged and specifics set forth.—A complaint must contain a statement of facts of an evidentiary nature supporting or tending to support the charges. People v. Diouf, 153 Misc. 2d 887, 583 N.Y.S.2d 746 (Crim. Ct. N.Y. Co. 1992).

—The law does not require that the most precise words or the phrase which most clearly expresses the thought be required in an information; it only requires that the crime be alleged and the specifics set forth so that a defendant can prepare himself for trial, and so that he will not be tried again for the same offense. Under these tests, the information in instant case was sufficient and, accordingly, defendants' motion to dismiss was denied. People v. Shea, 68 Misc. 2d 271, 326 N.Y.S.2d 70 (N.Y. Ct. Special Sessions 1971).

Insufficiency of charge; felony complaint.—Where the felony complaint, charging criminal possession of stolen property failed to state the value of the property or that the defendants were pawnbrokers or were dealers in property, the evidentiary portion of the affidavit only spelled out a misdemeanor. People v. Scerbo, 91 Misc. 2d 97, 397 N.Y.S.2d 351 (Crim. Ct. N.Y.C. 1977).

Insufficiency of charge; information.—The factual part of an information charging custodial interference must set forth in evidentiary form the manner of "enticement," together with some evidentiary statement manifesting the intent of the defendant to hold the child either permanently or at least for some protracted period. People v. Page, 77 Misc. 2d 277, 353 N.Y.S.2d 358 (Amherst Town Ct. 1974).

Insufficiency of charge; plea of guilty.—Any claim of insufficiency in the factual allegations of the information is waived upon defendant's entry of a guilty plea. People v. LaGrave, 122 A.D.2d 294, 503 N.Y.S.2d 914 (3d Dept. 1986).

Juvenile delinquency proceedings; applicability of CPL provisions.—Except as to constitutional due process provisions, the procedures of the Family Court, as they affect juvenile delinquency proceedings, are not criminal in nature and the CPL does not apply. In re Parks, 78 Misc. 2d 281, 356 N.Y.S.2d 440 (Family Ct. Dutchess Co. 1974).

Right to counsel.—The filing of an accusatory instrument initiates the criminal proceedings, thus, a defendant can not waive his right to counsel without counsel being present. People v. Rainey, 83 A.D.2d 525, 441 N.Y.S.2d 457 (1st Dept. 1981).

Sufficiency; animal cruelty prosecution.—Motion to dismiss for facial insufficiency denied in animal cruelty prosecution, where acts of cutting off the heads of three conscious iguanas are acts which certainly injure, maim, mutilate, and kill. People v. Voelker, 172 Misc. 2d 564, 658 N.Y.S.2d 180 (Crim. Ct. Kings Co. 1997).

Unlicensed general vending; insufficiency of accusatory instrument.—Bare allegation that defendant displayed clothing and offered it for sale does not convey sufficient evidentiary definiteness to satisfy pleading requirements, because allegation is too conclusory by itself; accusatory instrument lacks enough additional specific evidence to support a conclusion that defendant was in fact offering goods for sale and engaging in prohibited activity of unlicensed general vending. People v. Montanez, 177 Misc. 2d 506, 676 N.Y.S.2d 785 (Crim. Ct. N.Y. Co. 1998).

§ 100.20. Supporting deposition; definition, form and content.

A supporting deposition is a written instrument accompanying or filed in connection with an information, a simplified information, a misdemeanor complaint or a felony complaint, subscribed and verified by a person other than the complainant of such accusatory instrument, and containing factual allegations of an evidentiary character, based either upon personal knowledge or upon information and belief, which supplement those of the accusatory instrument and support or tend to support the charge or charges contained therein.

Amended by L. 1972, Ch. 661.

ANNOTATION

Accusatory instrument; verification; misdemeanor complaint; reasonable cause; sufficiency.—Since the CPL provision regarding verifications was remedial, verification before notary supported by complainant's reference to deposition in accusatory instrument, and deponent's statement, was not violative of statute and instrument would be treated as misdemeanor complaint sufficiently stating facts that person of ordinary intelligence, etc. would reasonably believe constituted bookmaking violation, but complaint had to be superseded by information, unless waived, so that every element of the crime charged is established. People v. Minuto, 71 Misc. 2d 800, 337 N.Y.S.2d 88 (Batavia City Ct. 1972).

§ 100.25. Simplified information; form and content; defendant's right to supporting deposition; notice requirement.

1. A simplified information must be substantially in the form prescribed by the commissioner of motor vehicles, the commissioner of parks and recreation, or the commissioner of environmental conservation, as the case may be.

2. A defendant charged by a simplified information is, upon a timely request, entitled as a matter of right to have filed with the court and served upon him, or if he is represented by an attorney, upon his attorney, a supporting deposition of the complainant police officer or public servant, containing allegations of fact, based either upon personal knowledge or upon information and belief, providing reasonable cause to believe that the defendant committed the offense or offenses charged. To be timely, a request must, except as otherwise provided herein and in subdivision three of this section, be made before entry of a plea of guilty to the charge specified and before commencement of a trial thereon, but not later than thirty days after the date the defendant is directed to appear in court as such date appears upon the simplified information and upon the appearance ticket issued pursuant thereto. If the defendant's request is mailed to the court, the request must be mailed within such thirty day period. Upon such a request, the court must order the complainant police officer or public servant to serve a copy of such supporting deposition upon the defendant or his attorney, within thirty days of the date such request is received by the court, or at least five days before trial, whichever is earlier, and to file such supporting deposition with the court together with proof of service thereof. Notwithstanding any provision to the contrary, where a defendant is issued an appearance ticket in conjunction with the offense charged in the simplified information and the appearance ticket fails to conform with the requirements of subdivision two of section 150.10, a request is timely when made not later than thirty days after (a) entry of the defendant's plea of not guilty when he or she has been arraigned in person, or (b) written notice to the defendant of his or her right to receive a supporting deposition when a plea of not guilty has been submitted by mail.

3. When at least one of the offenses charged in a simplified information is a misdemeanor, the court may, upon motion of the defendant, for good cause shown and consistent with the interest of justice, permit the defendant to request a supporting deposition beyond the thirty day request period set forth in subdivision two of this section provided, however, that no motion may be brought under this subdivision after ninety days has elapsed from the date the defendant is directed to appear in court as such date appears upon the simplified information and upon the appearance ticket issued pursuant thereto.

4. Notwithstanding any provision of law to the contrary, where a person is charged by a simplified information and is served with an appearance ticket as defined in section 150.10, such appearance ticket shall contain the following language:

"NOTICE: YOU ARE ENTITLED TO RE-
CEIVE A SUPPORTING DEPOSITION FUR-
THER EXPLAINING THE CHARGES PRO-
VIDED YOU REQUEST SUCH SUPPORTING
DEPOSITION WITHIN THIRTY DAYS FROM
THE DATE YOU ARE DIRECTED TO AP-
PEAR IN COURT AS SET FORTH ON THIS
APPEARANCE TICKET. DO YOU REQUEST
A SUPPORTING DEPOSITION? [ ]YES [ ]NO"

Amended by L. 1973, Ch. 614; L. 1974, Ch. 707; L. 1985,
Ch. 225; L. 1986, Ch. 431; L. 1996, Ch. 67, § 1, amending
heading; L. 1996, Ch. 67, § 2, amending subd. 2, and § 3,
adding subds. 3 and 4, eff. Oct. 27, 1996.

ANNOTATIONS

Appearance by counsel.—Defense counsel's appearance
letter neither constituted nor dispensed with the need for an
arraignment, and therefore the People were under no statutory
obligation to furnish a supporting deposition. People v. Perry,
87 N.Y.2d 353, 639 N.Y.S.2d 307, 662 N.E.2d 787 (1996).

—Once defendant is represented by counsel, it is defendant's
attorney, and not defendant, who should be served with supporting deposition. People v. Suarez, 167 Misc. 2d 189, 638
N.Y.S.2d 1020 (Justice Ct. Nassau Co. 1996).

**Driving while intoxicated; supporting deposition must
contain sufficient allegations of fact.**—In a prosecution for
operating a motor vehicle while intoxicated, a requested supporting deposition must contain "allegations of fact providing
reasonable cause to believe that the defendant committed the
offense." Recitations in the supporting deposition filed by the
police officer in this traffic case: that the officer saw defendant
driving the vehicle; that defendant swerved and struck a parked
car; and that the officer felt from his observations that defendant
was intoxicated did not constitute the "allegations of fact"
necessary under the law (CPL 100.25[2]). People v. Hust, 74
Misc. 2d 887, 346 N.Y.S.2d 303 (Broome Co. Ct. 1973).

Simplified information; sufficiency on face.—The fact that
the date had been changed prior to issuance of the ticket, and
that the officer used two different signatures—one on the ticket
and one to verify the information—and that he failed to indicate
whether defendant was charged with a traffic infraction or
misdemeanor, was not sufficiently fatal to divest this court of
jurisdiction over the charge. People v. Perlman, 89 Misc. 2d
973, 392 N.Y.S.2d 985 (Dist. Ct. Suffolk Co. 1977).

Simplified traffic information.—The court dismissed the
simplified traffic information where the signature of the issuing
officer did not appear beneath the words "Affirmed under
penalty of perjury" and the inapplicable portions of the printed
form were not struck out. People v. Lennox, 94 Misc. 2d 730,
405 N.Y.S.2d 581 (Justice Ct. Westchester Co. 1978).

—Because defendant was charged by way of four simplified
traffic informations, alleged defects complained of do not render
instruments jurisdictionally defective; simplified traffic informations need only be in substantial compliance with the form
prescribed by the commissioner of motor vehicles. People v.
Weinert, 178 A.D.2d 675, 683 N.Y.S.2d 690 (2d Dept. 1998).

—As long as the act of filing occurs within a reasonable time,
service of supporting depositions within the 30-day period
specified in CPL § 100.25(2) is sufficient to sustain continued
prosecution by simplified traffic information. People v. Brady,
196 Misc. 2d 993, 768 N.Y.S.2d 157 (Dist. Ct. Nassau Co.
2003).

**Simplified traffic information inconsistent with deposi-
tion.**—Defendant, who was originally charged in a simplified
traffic information and requested a supporting deposition, was
granted a dismissal where the supporting deposition was inconsistent with the simplified traffic information in that it alleged
that the offense charged occurred on different dates and at
different times and the People sought to supersede the simplified
traffic information instead of curing the defects by amendment.
People v. Baron, 107 Misc. 2d 59, 438 N.Y.S.2d 425 (App.
Term 9-10 Jud. Dist. 1980).

Supporting deposition.—CPL § 100.25(2) does not force
a defendant to wait until arraignment to request a supporting
deposition; while a defendant cannot ask for a supporting
deposition later than 30 days after the return date on the

appearance ticket, nothing in CPL § 100.25 or elsewhere
precludes a request prior to the return date, as long as the
defendant has not pleaded guilty and the trial has not started.
People v. Tyler, 1 N.Y.3d 493, 776 N.Y.S.2d 199, 808 N.E.2d
334 (2004).

—The CPL does not provide for the service of supporting
depositions for crimes to be prosecuted in the superior courts,
and defendant waived any claim about service of supporting
depositions when he consented to prosecution by superior court
information. People v. Condon, 10 A.D.3d 811, 782 N.Y.S.2d
163 (3d Dept. 2004).

—If a supporting deposition is requested for a simplified traffic
information, it can be based on hearsay or nonhearsay as long
as it provides reasonable cause to believe that defendant committed the charged offenses. People v. Rose, 8 Misc. 3d 184,
794 N.Y.S.2d 630 (Dist. Ct. Nassau Co. 2005).

—The new language of CPL § 100.25 explicitly contemplates
that a defendant's request for a supporting deposition runs from
the time the appearance ticket is issued and expires 30 days
from the return date indicated on the appearance ticket, irrespective of whether the defendant has been arraigned. People v.
Guerrerio, 181 Misc. 2d 517, 694 N.Y.S.2d 619 (Justice Ct.
Nassau Co. 1999).

—Under the amendment to section 100.25, the time frame
within which a defendant may request a supporting deposition
is severely circumscribed, and if the request is made before 30
days after the return date shown on the ticket, it is timely even
if made by mail and without reference to whether defendant
has been validly arraigned. People v. Guerrerio, 181 Misc. 2d
517, 694 N.Y.S.2d 619 (Justice Ct. Nassau Co. 1999).

—Plain language of CPL § 100.25 requires that complainant
officer serve defendant with a supporting deposition, but officer
failed to do so; because a valid and sufficient accusatory
instrument is a jurisdictional prerequisite to criminal prosecution, local court lacked jurisdiction to hear this case. People v.
Noblett, 172 Misc. 2d 826, 660 N.Y.S.2d 517 (Monroe Co. Ct.
1997).

—There is no conflict between CPL § 100.20, which requires
that the supporting deposition be subscribed and verified by a
person other than the complainant, and CPL § 100.25 which
provides that a defendant is entitled as a matter of right to
receive a supporting deposition from the complainant police
officer, as each section refers to a different deposition; to hold
otherwise would require two police officers in every patrol car
or a civilian witness at the scene of every vehicular arrest,
willing and available to subscribe and verify a petition. People
v. Quinn, 100 Misc. 2d 582, 419 N.Y.S.2d 811 (Cohoes City
Police Ct. 1979).

—A defendant charged with an offense contained in a simplified
information, has the right, following the entry of a not guilty
plea by mail pursuant to VTL § 1806, to a supporting deposition and his time to apply for the deposition does not commence
running until he has been duly informed of that right pursuant
to CPL §§ 170.10(4)(c) and 170.10(5). People v. DiGioia, 98
Misc. 2d 359, 413 N.Y.S.2d 825 (Sup. Ct. App. Term 1978).

**Traffic infractions; failure to serve supporting deposi-
tions; dismissal.**—Where a defendant charged with traffic
offenses made a demand for a supporting deposition within 30
days after entry of a plea of not guilty, but did not receive it
prior to the trial date, the court dismissed the informations on
the ground that defendant was entitled to the supporting deposition as a matter of right under CPL § 100.25(2). People v.
Mercurio, 93 Misc. 2d 1126, 404 N.Y.S.2d 252 (1978).

Traffic infraction; supporting deposition.—The procedural requirements with respect to supporting depositions as
provided by CPL § 100.25(2) are not applicable to summonses
issued for traffic infractions under Article 2-A of the Vehicle
and Traffic Law. Steiger v. Wozniak,72 A.D.2d 944, 422
N.Y.S.2d 228 (4th Dept. 1979).

—Since the supporting deposition and the simplified traffic
information failed to set forth facts which provided reasonable
cause to believe that defendant committed every necessary
element of the offense charged a dismissal would have been
proper had the motion to dismiss been in writing and upon
notice to the People, however, where the motion was made
orally and without notice, at trial, it should have been denied.
People v. Key, 87 Misc. 2d 262, 391 N.Y.S.2d 781 (App. Term
9-10 Jud. Dist. 1976), aff'd, 45 N.Y. 111, 408 N.Y.S.2d 16,
379 N.E.2d 1147 (1978).

—A supporting deposition in a traffic case initiated by a simplified traffic information must set forth facts in a plain and concise manner which provide a reasonable cause to believe that the defendant committed every necessary element of the offense charged. People v. Key, No. 251, November 1975 Term, 87 Misc. 2d 262, 383 N.Y.S.2d 953 (9-10 Jud. Dists. 1976).

—Defendant, who requests supporting deposition, has an absolute right under the statute thereto before the commencement of trial and failure to comply warrants dismissal. People v. DeFeo, 77 Misc. 2d 523, 355 N.Y.S.2d 905 (App. Term 2d Dept. 1974).

—A defendant accused under a simplified information is, upon proper request, entitled unconditionally to a supporting deposition setting forth in some detail the acts which allegedly make up the offense charged. Such a guarantee is necessary in traffic infraction cases. People v. Zagorsky, 73 Misc. 2d 420, 341 N.Y.S.2d 791 (Broome Co. Ct. 1973).

§ 100.30. Information, misdemeanor complaint, felony complaint, supporting deposition and proof of service of supporting deposition; verification.

1. An information, a misdemeanor complaint, a felony complaint, a supporting deposition, and proof of service of a supporting desposition may be verified in any of the following manners:

(a) Such instrument may be sworn to before the court with which it is filed.

(b) Such instrument may be sworn to before a desk officer in charge at a police station or police headquarters or any of his superior officers.

(c) Where such instrument is filed by any public servant following the issuance and service of an appearance ticket, and where by express provision of law another designated public servant is authorized to administer the oath with respect to such instrument, it may be sworn to before such public servant.

(d) Such instrument may bear a form notice that false statements made therein are punishable as a class A misdemeanor pursuant to section 210.45 of the penal law, and such form notice together with the subscription of the deponent constitute a verification of the instrument.

(e) Such instrument may be sworn to before a notary public.

2. An instrument specified in subdivision one may be verified in any manner prescribed therein unless in a particular case the court expressly directs verification in a particular manner prescribed in said subdivision one.

Amended by L. 1984, Ch. 201, eff. June 12, 1984; L. 1986, Ch. 71.

ANNOTATIONS

Accusatory instrument; verification; misdemeanor complaint; reasonable cause; sufficiency.—Since the CPL provision regarding verifications was remedial, verification before notary supported by complainant's reference to deposition in accusatory instrument, and deponent's statement, was not violative of statute and instrument would be treated as misdemeanor complaint sufficiently stating facts that person of ordinary intelligence, etc., would reasonably believe constituted book-making violation, but complaint had to be superseded by

information, unless waived, so that every element of the crime charged is established. People v. Minuto, 71 Misc. 2d 800, 337 N.Y.S.2d 88 (Batavia City Ct. 1972).

Probable cause for arrest.—The court refused to declare defendant's arrest null and void despite the failure of complainant to appear and sign complaint and the resultant dismissal, where the supporting deposition of the complainant supplied probable cause for the arrest. People v. Revine, 80 Misc. 2d 292, 362 N.Y.S.2d 989 (Dist. Co. Nassau Co. 1975).

Proper verification required.—Complainant police officer must read and sign the accusatory instrument in front of the desk officer in charge; an information that is not properly verified must be dismissed. People v. Ryan, 185 Misc. 2d 477, 713 N.Y.S.2d 447 (Dist. Ct. Suffolk Co. 2000).

Reading and signing oath is sufficient.—There is no requirement that a complainant raise his hand and orally recite an oath; it was sufficient for him to read and sign the oath in front of the officer. People v. Pagan, 93 N.Y.2d 891, 689 N.Y.S.2d 686, 711 N.E.2d 964 (1999).

Signature; information.—The failure to place the form notice advising deponent of criminal liability, pursuant to Penal Law § 210.45, above deponent's signature did not render the verification of the information defective. People v. Coldiron, 79 Misc. 2d 731, 360 N.Y.S.2d 788 (Sup. Ct. App. Term 1974).

§ 100.35. Prosecutor's information; form and content.

A prosecutor's information must contain the name of the local criminal court with which it is filed and the title of the action, and must be subscribed by the district attorney by whom it is filed. Otherwise it should be in the form prescribed for an indictment, pursuant to section 200.50, and must, in one or more counts, allege the offense or offenses charged and a plain and concise statement of the conduct constituting each such offense. The rules prescribed in sections 200.20 and 200.40 governing joinder of different offenses and defendants in a single indictment are also applicable to a prosecutor's information.

§ 100.40. Local criminal court accusatory instruments; sufficiency on face.

1. An information, or a count thereof, is sufficient on its face when:

(a) It substantially conforms to the requirements prescribed in section 100.15; and

(b) The allegations of the factual part of the information, together with those of any supporting depositions which may accompany it, provide reasonable cause to believe that the defendant committed the offense charged in the accusatory part of the information; and

(c) Non-hearsay allegations of the factual part of the information and/or of any supporting depositions establish, if true, every element of the offense charged and the defendant's commission thereof.

2. A simplified information is sufficient on its face when, as provided by subdivision one of section 100.25, it substantially conforms to the requirements therefor prescribed by or pursuant to law; provided that when the filing of a supporting deposition is ordered by the court pursuant

to subdivision two of said section 100.25, a failure of the complainant police officer or public servant to comply with such order within the time provided by subdivision two of said section 100.25 renders the simplified information insufficient on its face.

3. A prosecutor's information, or a count thereof, is sufficient on its face when it substantially conforms to the requirements prescribed in section 100.35.

4. A misdemeanor complaint or a felony complaint, or a count thereof, is sufficient on its face when:

(a) It substantially conforms to the requirements prescribed in section 100.15; and

(b) The allegations of the factual part of such accusatory instrument and/or any supporting depositions which may accompany it, provide reasonable cause to believe that the defendant committed the offense charged in the accusatory part of such instrument.

Amended by L. 1972, Ch. 661; L. 1985, Ch. 225.

ANNOTATIONS

Sufficiency.—Fact that documents supporting accusatory instrument were not supporting depositions, but rather, were public records of court proceedings involving defendant supporting allegations of complainant as stated in instrument, did not preclude court from examining documents and incorporating them into instrument for purpose of determining facial sufficiency of information. People v. Henry, 167 Misc. 2d 1027, 641 N.Y.S.2d 1003 (Dist. Ct. Nassau Co. 1996).

Accusatory instrument; verification; misdemeanor complaint; reasonable cause; sufficiency.—Since the CPL provision regarding verifications was remedial, verification before notary supported by complainant's reference to deposition in accusatory instrument, and deponent's statement, was not violative of statute and instrument would be treated as misdemeanor complaint sufficiently stating facts that person of ordinary intelligence, etc., would reasonably believe constituted book-making violation, but complaint had to be superseded by information, unless waived, so that every element of the crime charged is established. People v. Minuto, 71 Misc. 2d 800, 337 N.Y.S.2d 88 (Batavia City Ct. 1972).

Animal cruelty; motion to dismiss.—Motion to dismiss for facial insufficiency denied in animal cruelty prosecution, since acts of cutting off the heads of three conscious iguanas are acts which certainly injure, maim, mutilate, and kill. People v. Voelker, 172 Misc. 2d 564, 658 N.Y.S.2d 180 (Crim. Ct. Kings Co. 1997).

Applicability of subd. 1(b).—CPL § 100.40(1)(b) governs the sufficiency of "informations" and has no applicability to Prosecutor's Informations. Rather, CPL § 100.40(3) governs the form and content of Prosecutor's Informations. People v. DeShazo, 183 Misc. 2d 719, 703 N.Y.S.2d 907 (Dist. Ct. Nassau Co. 2000).

Certified copy of teletype message; competent proof in information.—Where a certified copy of a police teletype message was used to arrest defendants for unauthorized use of a vehicle, such business entry was held to be competent proof in an information charge, since it passed the test of civil rule relating to the admissibility of business records. People v. Fields, 74 Misc. 2d 109, 344 N.Y.S.2d 413 (Dist. Ct. Nassau Co. 1973).

Complaining witness' deposition; necessity of filing.—The mandate that supporting depositions be filed where charges are on information and belief is built into CPL 100.40. At this post-*Gault* date, it should be unnecessary to repeat that, insofar as the fact-finding stages of juvenile procedure are concerned, and particularly as regards constitutionally-acceptable notice of pending charges, these rights are specifically guaranteed. Even

McKewer, which seemed to limit the *Kent-Gault-Winship* trend, emphasized that sufficient notice in fact-finding proceedings is a basic constitutional requirement. *In re* Anthony S., 73 Misc. 2d 187, 341 N.Y.S.2d 11 (Fam. Ct. Richmond Co. 1973).

Dismissal for insufficiency; filling second accusatory instrument charging same offense.—The dismissal of an accusatory instrument before trial on the ground that it is insufficient on its face in no way bars the filing of a second accusatory instrument charging the same offense and a subsequent trial thereon. People v. Bock, 77 Misc. 2d 350, 353 N.Y.S.2d 647 (Broome Co. Ct. 1974).

Information; non-hearsay allegation.—To be sufficient, an information must not only substantially conform to the requirements set forth in CPL § 100.15(1) but must also contain non-hearsay allegations. People v. Gibble, 2 Misc. 3d 510, 773 N.Y.S.2d 499 (N.Y.C. Crim. Ct. 2003).

—Where defendant "waived all defects" at the time the felony complaint was reduced, amended and deemed a misdemeanor information and pled not guilty, the requirement that the offense charged be supported by nonhearsay allegations was effectively waived by him and no jurisdictional impediment exists to his prosecution. People v. Poll, 94 Misc. 2d 905, 405 N.Y.S.2d 943 (Dist. Ct. Suffolk Co. 1978).

—This section now requires that an information be supported by non-hearsay allegations that would establish the defendant's commission of the crime charged. People v. Conoscenti, 83 Misc. 2d 842, 373 N.Y.S.2d 443 (Dist. Ct. Suffolk Co. 1975).

Jurisdictionally defective.—Prosecutor's information is jurisdictionally defective if the original information it supersedes and any supporting depositions do not contain adequate factual allegations that establish, if true, every element of the crime charged and the defendant's commission of each. People v. Inserra, 4 N.Y.3d 30, 790 N.Y.S.2d 72, 823 N.E.2d 437 (2004).

Ministerial mislabeling of information.—Where clerk mislabeled instrument containing only non-hearsay allegations as misdemeanor complaint instead of information, error was ministerial and not decisive of the nature of the instrument. People v. Vlasto, 78 Misc. 2d 419, 355 N.Y.S.2d 983 (Crim. Ct. N.Y. Co. 1974).

Misdemeanor complaint; factual sufficiency.—The factual part of a misdemeanor complaint must allege "facts of an evidentiary character" demonstrating "reasonable cause" to believe the defendant committed the crime charged. People v. Dumas, 68 N.Y.2d 729, 506 N.Y.S.2d 319, 497 N.E.2d 686 (1986).

Motion to dismiss information; certified copy of police teletype message held to be non-hearsay.—A certified copy of a police teletype message from city police to county police, identifying defendant's car as one reported stolen, was found to be "non-hearsay," and therefore was sufficient, if true, to establish the charge of unauthorized use of a vehicle, where the statute required that nonhearsay allegations of factual part of information, if true, establish every element of the offense charged. People v. Fields, 74 Misc. 2d 109, 344 N.Y.S.2d 413 (Dist. Ct. Nassau Co. 1973).

Obscenity; motion to suppress arrest warrant; sufficiency of information.—It was unnecessary to have a prior adversary hearing or judicial scrutiny before issuance of arrest warrant of defendant to police officer who purchased two books and one film in bookstore managed by defendant and statute was not unconstitutional solely because it permitted exception in cases of scientific, educational or governmental purchases. People v. Kokich, 72 Misc. 2d 124, 338 N.Y.S.2d 463 (District Ct. Suffolk Co. 1972).

Reading and signing oath is sufficient.— There is no requirement that a complainant raise his hand and orally recite an oath; it was sufficient for him to read and sign the oath in front of the officer. People v. Pagan, 93 N.Y.2d 891, 689 N.Y.S.2d 686, 711 N.E.2d 964 (1999).

Simplified information; supporting deposition.—Where a defendant fails to make a timely written motion to dismiss a simplified information and is thereafter tried and found guilty upon proof which establishes all the elements of the crime, he may not raise the defect on appeal from the judgment of conviction, however, a different result occurs where the defendant pleads guilty since the plea only admits those facts contained in the factual part of the information and thus, the judgment of conviction may be attacked on the ground that defendant has not been convicted of a crime even though no motion was made to dismiss the information. People v. Fattizzi, 98 Misc. 2d 288, 413 N.Y.S.2d 804 (Sup. Ct. App. Term 1978).

Sufficiency of information.—An accusatory instrument is defective on its face when it does not conform to the requirements of CPL § 100.40, however, the instrument may not be dismissed as defective, but must be amended when the defect or irregularity is of a kind that may be cured by amendment, and the People move to so amend (CPL § 100.35[1][a]). People v. Pacifico, 105 Misc. 2d 396, 432 N.Y.S.2d 588 (Crim. Ct. Queens Co. 1980).

—An information must be sufficient alone, without resort to testimony or record of evidence, in order to withstand a motion to dismiss for insufficiency; it is required to show a legally sufficient case, as well as "reasonable cause"; where the information is insufficient in law, no jurisdiction is conferred upon the court. People v. Crisofulli, 91 Misc. 2d 424, 398 N.Y.S.2d 120 (Crim. Ct. N.Y.C. 1977).

Traffic infraction; supporting deposition.—A defendant accused under a simplified information is, upon proper request, entitled unconditionally to a supporting deposition setting forth in some detail the acts which allegedly make up the offense charged. Such a guarantee is necessary in traffic infraction cases. People v. Zagorsky, 73 Misc. 2d 420, 341 N.Y.S.2d 791 (Broome Co. Ct. 1973).

Unlicensed general vending; insufficiency of accusatory instrument.—Bare allegation that defendant displayed clothing and offered it for sale does not convey sufficient evidentiary definiteness to satisfy pleading requirements, because allegation is too conclusory by itself; accusatory instrument lacks enough additional specific evidence to support conclusion that defendant was in fact offering goods for sale and engaging in prohibited activity of unlicensed general vending. People v. Montanez, 177 Misc. 2d 506, 676 N.Y.S.2d 785 (Crim. Ct. N.Y. Co. 1998).

§ 100.45. Information, prosecutor's information, misdemeanor complaint; severance, consolidation, amendment, bill of particulars.

1. Where appropriate, the provisions of sections 200.20 and 200.40, governing severance of counts of an indictment and severance of defendants for trial purposes, and governing consolidation of indictments for trial purposes, apply to informations, to prosecutor's informations and to misdemeanor complaints.

2. The provisions of section 200.70 governing amendment of indictments apply to prosecutor's informations.

3. At any time before the entry of a plea of guilty to or the commencement of a trial of an information, the court may, upon application of the people and with notice to the defendant and opportunity to be heard, order the amendment of the accusatory part of such information by addition of a count charging an offense supported by the allegations of the factual part of such information and/or any supporting depositions which may accompany it. In such case, the defendant must be accorded any reasonable adjournment necessitated by the amendment.

4. The provisions of section 200.95, governing bills of particulars with respect to indictments, apply to informations, to misdemeanor complaints and to prosecutor's informations.

Amended by L. 1982, Ch. 558.

ANNOTATIONS

Amendment of information; lewdness to obscenity.—Failure of prosecutor to move to amend the information changing the charge from lewdness to obscenity, the latter section specifically dealing with the "erotic dance" performance involved, and in the absence of proof sufficient to meet the standards for a conclusion of nonprotected obscenity or lewdness, warrants acquittal of the defendant. People v. Conrad, 70 Misc. 2d 408, 334 N.Y.S.2d 180 (Buffalo City Ct. 1972).

Amending an information.—Despite stipulation entered into the record by defense counsel consenting thereto, the information was dismissed where two supplemental menacing counts were added to the information after the commencement of the trial. People v. Harper, 37 N.Y.2d 96, 371 N.Y.S.2d 467, 332 N.E.2d 336 (1975).

—Prosecutor's amendment of the information as to the date of the crime was of no import since defendant did not object to the amendment and no prejudice accrued to him as a result thereof. People v. Hairston, 122 A.D.2d 340, 504 N.Y.S.2d 310 (3d Dept. 1986).

—The People's motion to amend the information so as to change the date, time, and basis of knowledge to "on information and belief," rather than on the police officer's personal knowledge, was granted. The amendment did not change the theory of the prosecution or prejudice the defendant. People v. Diggs, 72 Misc. 2d 898, 339 N.Y.S.2d 712 (Dist. Ct. Nassau Co. 1973).

Amendment of accusatory instrument not permitted after both People and defendant had rested.—Statute allowing the accusatory instrument to be amended at any time before commencement of trial must be strictly construed, thus, accusatory instrument concerning alleged violation of VTL section for altering an operator's license could not be amended after both the People and the defendant had rested, but before closing arguments, to correct errors in the accusatory part of the information to conform to the factual part of the instrument which designated the offense as "unlicensed driver," even though the defendant was well aware that he was charged with the former violation. People v. Law, 106 Misc. 2d 351, 431 N.Y.S.2d 648 (Crim. Ct. N.Y. Co. 1980).

Juvenile delinquency petition.—A juvenile delinquency petition is not akin to a prosecutor's information (or indictment) but is tantamount to an indictment. In re Parsons, 108 Misc. 2d 738, 438 N.Y.S.2d 933 (Fam. Ct. Queens Co. 1981).

Lesser included count.—Harassment, although supported by the factual allegations of the information is not a lesser included offense of disorderly conduct or resisting arrest, and could only be added upon application of the People with notice to the defendant prior to the commencement of trial. People v. Davis, 82 Misc. 2d 41, 370 N.Y.S.2d 328 (App. Term 2d-3d Jud. Dist. 1975).

Multiple counts; charging intoxication while driving.—In order to find a person guilty of violating both subd. 2 and 3 of VTL § 1192 the court suggested that, in driving while intoxicated cases, the People should (1) immediately file an information charging VTL § 1192(3) and when the additional factual allegations become available to support VTL § 1192(2) a second information charging that offense be filed and a consolidation application be filed pursuant to CPL §§ 200.20(4) and 100.45, or (2) immediately filing a misdemeanor complaint charging violation of both subdivisions and then subsequently filing a supporting deposition supplying the necessary factual allegations to support the VTL § 1192(2) charge. People v. Meikrantz, 77 Misc. 2d 892, 351 N.Y.S.2d 549 (Broome Co. Ct. 1974).

Replacement.—The prosecution may file a replacement information which includes new factual material and additional charges. People v. Henry, 166 Misc. 2d 824, 634 N.Y.S.2d 983 (Crim. Ct. Kings Co. 1995).

Separate trials; good cause not shown.—A defendant's assertion that a co-defendant may offer a defense antagonistic to him does not, in and of itself, constitute good cause to grant a severance. People v. Lerner, 122 A.D.2d 813, 505 N.Y.S.2d 195 (2d Dept. 1986).

—Court properly denied defendant's motion for a severance since his own extrajudicial admissions were sufficiently interlocking with the confessions made by his co-defendants to render negligible any resulting prejudice from improper consideration of their confessions. People v. Johnson, 122 A.D.2d 649, 504 N.Y.S.2d 486 (2d Dept. 1986).

Superseding information.—The People cannot amend a misdemeanor complaint, but CPL § 100.50 provides that a superseding information may be filed at any time prior to entry of the guilty plea or the commencement of trial, and it is proper to file a superseding information in response to a defense motion to dismiss the original instrument for insufficiency. People v. McDonald, 179 Misc. 2d 479, 689 N.Y.S.2d 600 (Crim. Ct. N.Y. Co. 1999).

§ 100.50. Superseding informations and prosecutor's informations.

1. If at any time before entry of a plea of guilty to or commencement of a trial of an information or a prosecutor's information, another information or, as the case may be, another prosecutor's information is filed with the same local criminal court charging the defendant with an offense charged in the first instrument, the first such instrument is, with respect to such offense, superseded by the second and, upon the defendant's arraignment upon the latter, the count of the first instrument charging such offense must be dismissed by the court. The first instrument is not, however, superseded with respect to any count contained therein which charges an offense not charged in the second instrument.

2. At any time before entry of a plea of guilty to or commencement of a trial of an information, the district attorney may file with the local criminal court a prosecutor's information charging any offenses supported, pursuant to the standards prescribed in subdivision one of section 100.40, by the allegations of the factual part of the original information and/or any supporting depositions which may accompany it. In such case, the original information is superseded by the prosecutor's information and, upon the defendant's arraignment upon the latter, is deemed dismissed.

3. A misdemeanor complaint must or may be replaced and superseded by an information pursuant to the provisions of section 170.65.

Amended by L. 1972, Ch. 610.

ANNOTATIONS

Simplified information.—Simplified information cannot be superseded by information inasmuch as superseding information may only be substituted for information, prosecutor's information, or misdemeanor complaint. People v. Kaid, 165 Misc. 2d 489, 629 N.Y.S.2d 617 (Crim. Ct. Kings Co. 1995).

—Though law permits filing of prosecutor's information at any time prior to commencement of trial, information cannot contain new factual allegations not part of original information. People v. Pratt, 164 Misc. 2d 498, 625 N.Y.S.2d 869 (Crim. Ct. N.Y. Co. 1995).

Motion to dismiss prosecutor's information; failure to comply with statute.—Motion to dismiss was granted where district attorney without any direction from the court, superseded a felony complaint with a prosecutor's information. People v. Thomas, 107 Misc. 2d 947, 436 N.Y.S.2d 153 (Dist. Ct. Suffolk Co. 1981).

Superseding information.—The People may file a new information that alleges additional facts or charges offenses that were not included in a previously filed information, but stem from the same criminal transaction. People v. Thomas, 4 N.Y.3d 143, 791 N.Y.S.2d 68, 824 N.E.2d 499 (2005).

—Prosecutor's information is jurisdictionally defective if the original information it supersedes and any supporting depositions do not contain adequate factual allegations that establish, if true, every element of the crime charged and the defendant's commission of each. People v. Inserra, 4 N.Y.3d 30, 790 N.Y.S.2d 72, 823 N.E.2d 437 (2004).

—The People cannot amend a misdemeanor complaint (CPL § 100.45[3]), but CPL § 100.50 provides that a superseding information may be filed at any time prior to entry of the guilty plea or the commencement of trial, and it is proper to file a superseding information in response to a defense motion to dismiss the original instrument for insufficiency. People v. McDonald, 179 Misc. 2d 479, 689 N.Y.S.2d 600 (Crim. Ct. N.Y. Co. 1999).

Superseding information cannot be used to consolidate criminal cases.—Defendant's motion to dismiss the district attorney's superseding information on the grounds that using the superseding information to consolidate the criminal cases was improper, was granted to allow the People to consolidate criminal cases by means of a superseding information gives them a superior position to defendant because he has no comparable right. There is no absolute right to consolidation of criminal cases. Only the court can, pursuant to statute, in its discretion direct such consolidation and then only on a showing of good cause. People v. Cunningham, 74 Misc. 2d 631, 345 N.Y.S.2d 903 (Crim. Ct. N.Y. Co. 1973).

§ 100.55. Local criminal court accusatory instruments; in what courts filed.

1. Any local criminal court accusatory instrument may be filed with a district court of a particular county when an offense charged therein was allegedly committed in such county or that part thereof over which such court has jurisdiction.

2. Any local criminal court accusatory instrument may be filed with the New York City criminal court when an offense charged therein was allegedly committed in New York City.

3. Any local criminal court accusatory instrument may be filed with a city court of a particular city when an offense charged therein was allegedly committed in such city.

4. An information, a simplified information, a prosecutor's information or a misdemeanor complaint may be filed with a town court of a particular town when an offense charged therein was allegedly committed anywhere in such town other than in a village thereof having a village court.

5. An information, a simplified information, a prosecutor's information or a misdemeanor complaint may be filed with a village court of a particular village when an offense charged therein was allegedly committed in such village.

6. A felony complaint may be filed with any town court or village court of a particular county when a felony charged therein was allegedly committed in some town of such county. Such court need not be that of the town or village in which such felony was allegedly committed.

7. An information, a simplified information, a misdemeanor complaint or a felony complaint may be filed with a judge of a superior court

CPL

sitting as a local criminal court when an offense charged therein was allegedly committed in a county in which such judge is then present and in which he either resides or is currently holding, or has been assigned to hold, a term of a superior court.

8. Where it is otherwise expressly provided by law that a particular kind of accusatory instrument may under given circumstances be filed with a local criminal court other than one authorized by this section, nothing contained in this section precludes the filing of such accusatory instrument accordingly.

9. In any case where each of two or more local criminal courts is authorized as a proper court with which to file an accusatory instrument, such an instrument may, in the absence of an express provision of law to the contrary, be filed with any one of such courts but not with more than one.

10. For purposes of this section, an offense is "committed in" a particular county, city, town, village or other specified political subdivision or area, not only when it is in fact committed therein but also when it is, for other reasons specified in sections 20.40 and 20.50, prosecutable in the criminal courts having geographical jurisdiction over such political subdivision or area.

Amended by L. 1972, Ch. 661.

ANNOTATIONS

Accusatory instrument.—Formal criminal proceedings are commenced by the filing of an accusatory instrument. People v. Fredenburg, 289 A.D.2d 868, 735 N.Y.S.2d 239 (3d Dept. 2001).

Delay.—Delay in arrestee's arraignment could not serve as basis for civil rights claim against arresting officer where delay was direct result of distance between county in which arrest took place and county in which vehicle was stolen and legal requirement that defendant be arraigned in county in which criminal conduct occurred. Wade v. Fisk, 176 A.D.2d 1087, 575 N.Y.S.2d 394 (3d Dept. 1991).

Jurisdiction; city court transfer to town court.—Although the statute provides for transfers from Village Justice Courts to Town Courts, there is no valid reason to exclude transfer from City to Town Court even in absence of statutory authority, when disqualification of City Court judge would render case in limbo without transfer. In re Jones, 69 Misc. 2d 640, 330 N.Y.S.2d 424 (Cortland Co. Ct. 1972).

Jurisdiction; transfers; disqualification of judge.—Where a City Court judge was disqualified from considering criminal case, court would transfer matter to Town or Village Court even in the absence of specific statutory authority, to conform to statutory objectives. In re Jones, 69 Misc. 2d 640, 330 N.Y.S.2d 424 (Cortland Co. Ct. 1972).

ARTICLE 110—REQUIRING DEFENDANT'S APPEARANCE IN LOCAL CRIMINAL COURT FOR ARRAIGNMENT

LexisNexis Cross Reference

New York Criminal Practice (2d ed.), Vol. 1, Ch. 4, Local Criminal Court Accusatory Instruments.

§ 110.10. Methods of requiring defendant's appearance in local criminal court for arraignment; in general.

1. After a criminal action has been commenced in a local criminal court by the filing of an accusatory instrument therewith, a defendant who has not been arraigned in the action and has not come under the control of the court may under certain circumstances be compelled or required to appear for arraignment upon such accusatory instrument by:

(a) The issuance and execution of a warrant of arrest, as provided in article one hundred twenty; or

(b) The issuance and service upon him of a summons, as provided in article one hundred thirty; or

(c) Procedures provided in articles five hundred sixty, five hundred seventy, five hundred eighty, five hundred ninety and six hundred for securing attendance of defendants in criminal actions who are not at liberty within the state.

2. Although no criminal action against a person has been commenced in any court, he may under certain circumstances be compelled or required to appear in a local criminal court for arraignment upon an accusatory instrument to be filed therewith at or before the time of his appearance by:

(a) An arrest made without a warrant, as provided in article one hundred forty; or

(b) The issuance and service upon him of an appearance ticket, as provided in article one hundred fifty.

ANNOTATION

Accusatory instrument.—Until an accusatory instrument is filed, a court cannot issue a summons or warrant of arrest to compel a defendant's appearance. People v. Brisotti, 167 Misc. 2d 688, 635 N.Y.S.2d 442 (Crim. Ct. Bronx Co. 1995).

§ 110.20. Local criminal court accusatory instruments; notice thereof to district attorney.

When a criminal action in which a crime is charged is commenced in a local criminal court, other than the criminal court of the city of New York, a copy of the accusatory instrument shall be promptly transmitted to the appropriate district attorney upon or prior to the arraignment of the defendant on the accusatory instrument. If a police officer or a peace officer is the complainant or the filer of a simplified information, or has arrested the defendant or brought him before the local criminal court on behalf of an arresting person pursuant to subdivision one of section 140.20, such officer or his agency shall transmit the copy of the accusatory instrument to the appropriate district attorney. In all other cases, the clerk of the court in which the defendant is arraigned shall so transmit it.

Added by L. 1977, Ch. 353; **Amended** by L. 1980, Ch. 843.

CPL

ARTICLE 120—WARRANT OF ARREST

LexisNexis Cross References

New York Criminal Practice (2d ed.), Vol. 1, Ch. 6, Warrants of Arrest and Summonses; Local Criminal Courts and Superior Courts; *New York Suppression Manual*, Ch. 8, Arrest Warrants; Ch. 10, Procedures After Arrest.

§ 120.10. Warrant of arrest; definition, function, form and content.

1. A warrant of arrest is a process issued by a local criminal court directing a police officer to arrest a defendant designated in an accusatory instrument filed with such court and to bring him before such court in connection with such instrument. The sole function of a warrant of arrest is to achieve a defendant's court appearance in a criminal action for the purpose of arraignment upon the accusatory instrument by which such action was commenced.

2. A warrant of arrest must be subscribed by the issuing judge and must state or contain (a) the name of the issuing court, and (b) the date of issuance of the warrant, and (c) the name or title of an offense charged in the underlying accusatory instrument, and (d) the name of the defendant to be arrested or, if such be unknown, any name or description by which he can be identified with reasonable certainty, and (e) the police officer or officers to whom the warrant is addressed, and (f) a direction that such officer arrest the defendant and bring him before the issuing court.

3. A warrant of arrest may be addressed to a classification of police officers, or to two or more classifications thereof, as well as to a designated individual police officer or officers. Multiple copies of such a warrant may be issued.

Amended by L. 1980, Ch. 843; L. 1998, Ch. 424, § 4, eff. Jan. 1, 1999.

ANNOTATIONS

Arresting officer's unsubstantiated procurement of warrant.—An arresting officer in the ordinary course of events may rely upon the fact that he possesses a judicially issued arrest warrant and thus be insulated from a claim of false imprisonment; however, he may not so insulate himself from such a claim where he has personally procured the issuance of the warrant based upon his own false and unsubstantiated statements. Ross v. Village of Wappingers Falls, 62 A.D.2d 892, 406 N.Y.S.2d 506 (2d Dept. 1978).

Content of application.—Where warrant application contained the unsworn statement of defendant's landlord that he had entered defendant's mobile home and observed marihuana apparatus and plants, reliability of the statement was presumed because defendant's landlord was an identified citizen-informant. People v. Montague, 273 A.D.2d 840, 710 N.Y.S.2d 219 (4th Dept. 2000).

Police conduct after warrant arrest; reasonable anticipation of statement from defendant.—Defendant's right to counsel attached indelibly upon the filing of the accusatory instrument which provided the basis for the issuance of the arrest warrant. People v. Rivers, 56 N.Y.2d 476, 453 N.Y.S.2d 156, 438 N.E.2d 862 (1982).

Second complaint; warrant of arrest.—A second complaint which does not commence an action does not provide the basis for issuance of an arrest warrant. People v. Jones, 108 Misc. 2d 137, 436 N.Y.S.2d 970 (City Ct. Erie Co. 1981).

Warrant invalid.—Although the warrant was signed by a County Court judge who is authorized to sit as a local criminal court, (CPL § 10.10[3][g]), it bore no indication of which local criminal court was the issuing court. Since there must be strict compliance with the requirements for the issuance of a warrant of arrest, this warrant is invalid on its face. People v. Johnson, 165 Misc. 2d 227, 629 N.Y.S.2d 371 (Rochester City Court 1995).

Warrant; misdemeanor traffic violation.—When police officer arrested defendant, pursuant to arrest warrant, on misdemeanor charge of driving while his license was suspended or revoked, he could lawfully frisk or search defendant. People v. Troiano, 35 N.Y.2d 476, 363 N.Y.S.2d 943, 323 N.E.2d 183 (1974).

§ 120.20. Warrant of arrest; when issuable.

1. When a criminal action has been commenced in a local criminal court by the filing therewith of an accusatory instrument, other than

a simplified traffic information, against a defendant who has not been arraigned upon such accusatory instrument and has not come under the control of the court with respect thereto:

(a) such court may, if such accusatory instrument is sufficient on its face, issue a warrant for such defendant's arrest; or

(b) if such accusatory instrument is not sufficient on its face as prescribed in section 100.40, and if the court is satisfied that on the basis of the available facts or evidence it would be impossible to draw and file an accusatory instrument that is sufficient on its face, the court must dismiss the accusatory instrument.

2. Even though such accusatory instrument is sufficient on its face, the court may refuse to issue a warrant of arrest based thereon until it has further satisfied itself, by inquiry or examination of witnesses, that there is reasonable cause to believe that the defendant committed an offense charged. Upon such inquiry or examination, the court may examine, under oath or otherwise, any available person whom it believes may possess knowledge concerning the subject matter of the charge.

3. Notwithstanding the provisions of subdivision one, if a summons may be issued in lieu of a warrant of arrest pursuant to section 130.20, and if the court is satisfied that the defendant will respond thereto, it may not issue a warrant of arrest. Upon the request of the district attorney, in lieu of a warrant of arrest or summons, the court may instead authorize the district attorney to direct the defendant to appear for arraignment on a designated date if it is satisfied that the defendant will so appear.

Amended by L. 1993, Ch. 446; L. 2000, Ch. 506, amending subd. 1, eff. Nov. 1, 2000.

ANNOTATIONS

Arrest warrant.—The court acted properly in issuing an arrest warrant where the defendant had not yet been arraigned on the felony charges but had been arraigned on misdemeanor charges arising out of the same criminal transaction. People v. Gaston, 83 A.D.2d 761, 443 N.Y.S.2d 491 (4th Dept. 1981).
—The filing of an accusatory instrument is a precondition to issuing an arrest warrant; leaving an accusatory instrument with a judge at her home or in chambers does not constitute a "filing." People v. Shipp, 137 Misc. 2d 495, 521 N.Y.S.2d 366 (City Ct. Monroe Co. 1987).
—The language in CPL § 120.20(3) is not a mandatory direction to use a summons as the first resource, it is merely permissive; the use of the arrest warrant remains a permissible instrument by which a defendant may be subjected to the jurisdiction of the Court. People v. McNeil, 90 Misc. 2d 180, 393 N.Y.S.2d 662 (Sup. Ct. Suffolk Co. 1977).
Warrant of arrest; felony complaint; standard of proof.—The language of CPL § 180.70(1) is similar to that of § 120.20(2), which provides that the court may refuse to issue a warrant of arrest based on an accusatory instrument until it has further satisfied itself, by inquiry or by examination of witnesses, that there is a reasonable cause to believe that the defendant committed the offense charged. People ex rel. Fox v. Sherwood, 73 Misc. 2d 101, 341 N.Y.S.2d 161 (Sup. Ct. Orange Co. 1973).
Misdemeanor complaint as basis for arrest warrant.—If found to be sufficient on its face, the misdemeanor complaint

alone may serve as the basis for issuing an arrest warrant. People v. Dumas, 68 N.Y.2d 729, 506 N.Y.S.2d 319, 497 N.E.2d 686 (1986).
Right to counsel.—The right to counsel attaches contemporaneously with the issuance of an arrest warrant. People v. Harris, 19 A.D.3d 871, 797 N.Y.S.2d 614 (3d Dept. 2005).

§ 120.30. Warrant of arrest; by what courts issuable and in what courts returnable.

1. A warrant of arrest may be issued only by the local criminal court with which the underlying accusatory instrument has been filed, and it may be made returnable in such issuing court only.

2. The particular local criminal court or courts with which any particular local criminal court accusatory instrument may be filed for the purpose of obtaining a warrant of arrest are determined, generally, by the provisions of section 100.55. If, however, a particular accusatory instrument may pursuant to said section 100.55 be filed with a particular town court and such town court is not available at the time such instrument is sought to be filed and a warrant obtained, such accusatory instrument may be filed with the town court of any adjoining town of the same county. If such instrument may be filed pursuant to said section 100.55 with a particular village court and such village court is not available at the time, it may be filed with the town court of the town embracing such village, or if such town court is not available either, with the town court of any adjoining town of the same county.

ANNOTATIONS

Jurisdiction; city court transfer to town court.—Although the statute provides for transfers from Village Justice Courts to Town Courts, there is no valid reason to exclude transfer from City to Town Court even in absence of statutory authority when disqualification of City Court judge would render case in limbo without transfer. In re Jones, 69 Misc. 2d 640, 330 N.Y.S.2d 424 (Cortland Co. Ct. 1972).
Jurisdiction; transfers; disqualification of judge.—Where a City Court Judge was disqualified from considering criminal case, court would transfer matter to Town or Village Court even in the absence of specific statutory authority, to conform to statutory objectives. In re Jones, 69 Misc. 2d 640, 330 N.Y.S.2d 424 (Cortland Co. Ct. 1972).

§ 120.40. Warrant of arrest; attaching accusatory instrument to warrant of town court, village court or city court.

A town court, village court or city court which issues a warrant of arrest may attach thereto a duplicate copy of the underlying accusatory instrument. If one or more duplicate copies of the warrant are issued, such court may attach as many copies of such accusatory instrument to copies of such warrant as it chooses. In any case where, pursuant to subdivision five of section 120.90, a defendant arrested upon such a warrant of arrest is brought before a local criminal court other than the town court, village court or city court in which the warrant is returnable, a copy of the accusatory instrument constitutes a valid basis for arraignment, as provided in subdivision one of section 170.15.

Amended by L. 1973, Ch. 61; L. 1988, Ch. 324.

§ 120.50. Warrant of arrest; to what police officers addressed.

A warrant of arrest may be addressed to any police officer or classification of police officers whose geographical area of employment embraces either the place where the offense charged was allegedly committed or the locality of the court by which the warrant is issued.

Amended by L. 1980, Ch. 843; L. 1998, Ch. 424, § 5, eff. Jan. 1, 1999.

§ 120.55. Warant* of arrest; defendent* under parole or probation supervision.

If the defendant named within a warrant of arrest issued by a local criminal court pursuant to the provisions of this article, or by a superior court issued pursuant to subdivision three of section 210.10 of such chapter, is under the supervision of the state division of parole or a local or state probation department, then a warrant for his arrest may be executed by a parole officer or probation officer, when authorized by his probation director, within his geographical area of employment. The execution of the warrant by a parole officer or probation officer shall be upon the same conditions and conducted in the same manner as provided for execution of a warrant by a police officer.

* As originally enacted.

Added by L. 1979, Ch. 492; Amended by L. 1981, Ch. 456.

§ 120.60. Warrant of arrest; what police officers may execute.

1. A warrant of arrest may be executed by (a) any police officer to whom it is addressed, or (b) any other police officer delegated to execute it under circumstances prescribed in subdivisions two and three.

2. A police officer to whom a warrant of arrest is addressed may delegate another officer to whom it is not addressed to execute such warrant as his agent when:

(a) He has reasonable cause to believe that the defendant is in a particular county other than the one in which the warrant is returnable; and

(b) The warrant is, pursuant to section 120.70, executable in such other county without endorsement by a local criminal court thereof; and

(c) The geographical area of employment of the delegated police officer embraces the locality where the arrest is to be made.

3. Under circumstances specified in subdivision two, the police officer to whom the warrant is addressed may inform the delegated officer, by telecommunication, mail or any other means, of the issuance of the warrant, of the offense charged in the underlying accusatory instrument and of all other pertinent details, and may request him to act as his agent in arresting the defendant pursuant to such warrant. Upon such request, the delegated police officer is to the same extent as the delegating officer, authorized to make such arrest pursuant to the warrant within the geographical area of such delegated officer's employment. Upon so arresting the defendant, he must proceed as provided in subdivisions two and four of section 120.90.

Amended by L. 1980, Ch. 843; L. 1998, Ch. 424, § 6, eff. Jan. 1, 1999.

ANNOTATIONS

Out-of-state officers.—New Jersey officers were not authorized by any New York statute to execute federal warrant in New York; CPL § 120.60 provides that warrants can be executed only by a police or peace officer, and the New Jersey officers did not so qualify under CPL §§ 1.20(33), (34), 2.10, or 120.60. People v. LaFontaine, 92 N.Y.2d 470, 682 N.Y.S.2d 671, 705 N.E.2d 663 (1998).

Wiretap order; jurisdiction to execute.—The Nassau County Police had jurisdiction to execute a wiretap order on telephones located in Queens and Brooklyn which were used by defendants who were engaging in criminal activities (illegal bookmaking) in Nassau County, since warrants addressed to a law enforcement agency whose jurisdiction encompasses the entire county in which the issuing court is located are generally executable anywhere in the state. People v. Fusco, 75 Misc. 2d 981, 348 N.Y.S.2d 858 (Nassau Co. Ct. 1973).

§ 120.70. Warrant of arrest; where executable.

1. A warrant of arrest issued by a district court, by the New York city criminal court or by a superior court judge sitting as a local criminal court may be executed anywhere in the state.

2. A warrant of arrest issued by a city court, a town court or a village court may be executed:

(a) In the county of issuance or in any adjoining county; or

(b) Anywhere else in the state upon the written endorsement thereon of a local criminal court of the county in which the arrest is to be made. When so endorsed, the warrant is deemed the process of the endorsing court as well as that of the issuing court.

ANNOTATIONS

Arrest pursuant to canceled arrest warrant; seized evidence suppressed.—Defendant's arrest for robbery, pursuant to an arrest warrant which, unknown to the police, had been canceled, was invalid despite the good faith of the police, and a watch seized from the defendant and a statement made by him on the day of such arrest were suppressed as "poisoned fruits of that unlawful arrest." People v. Watson, 100 A.D.2d 452, 474 N.Y.S.2d 978 (2d Dept. 1984).

Arrest warrant; attachment of right to counsel.—Where defendant was arrested pursuant to an arrest warrant, which must be preceded by the filing of an accusatory instrument, criminal proceedings had commenced and defendant could not waive the right to counsel without counsel being present. People v. Howard, 106 A.D.2d 663, 482 N.Y.S.2d 917 (2d Dept. 1984).

§ 120.80. Warrant of arrest; when and how executed.

1. A warrant of arrest may be executed on any day of the week and at any hour of the day or night.

2. Unless encountering physical resistance, flight or other factors rendering normal procedure impractical, the arresting police officer must inform the defendant that a warrant for his arrest for the offense designated therein has been issued. Upon request of the defendant, the officer must show him the warrant if he has it in his possession. The officer need not have the warrant in his possession, and, if he has not, he must show it to the defendant upon request as soon after the arrest as possible.

3. In order to effect the arrest, the police officer may use such physical force as is justifiable pursuant to section 35.30 of the penal law.

4. In order to effect the arrest, the police officer may, under circumstances and in the manner prescribed in this subdivision, enter any premises in which he reasonably believes the defendant to be present; provided, however, that where the premises in which the officer reasonably believes the defendant to be present is the dwelling of a third party who is not the subject of the arrest warrant, the officer shall proceed in the manner specified in article 690 of this chapter. Before such entry, he must give, or make reasonable effort to give, notice of his authority and purpose to an occupant thereof, unless there is reasonable cause to believe that the giving of such notice will:

(a) Result in the defendant escaping or attempting to escape; or

(b) Endanger the life or safety of the officer or another person; or

(c) Result in the destruction, damaging or secretion of material evidence.

5. If the officer is authorized to enter premises without giving notice of his authority and purpose, or if after giving such notice he is not admitted, he may enter such premises, and by a breaking if necessary.

Amended by L. 1980, Ch. 843, eff. Sept. 1, 1980; L. 1991, Ch. 504, eff. Nov. 1, 1991, amending subd. (4); L. 1998, Ch. 424, § 7, eff. Jan. 1, 1999.

ANNOTATIONS

Notice.—Failure by officers executing arrest warrant to make reasonable effort to give notice of their authority and purpose to occupant before entering premises listed in the warrant until they were well inside apartment made entry and seizure unlawful, thus requiring suppression of evidence seized from defendant's apartment absent any indication of exigent circumstances justifying noncompliance with statutory requirements. People v. Cabral, 147 Misc. 2d 1000, 560 N.Y.S.2d 71 (Sup. Ct. Kings Co. 1990).

Arrest on warrant; right to counsel.—A defendant cannot waive his right to counsel in the absence of counsel after being arrested pursuant to an arrest warrant; an infringement of his right to counsel can be raised for the first time on appeal. People v. Cullen, 50 N.Y.2d 168, 428 N.Y.S.2d 456, 405 N.E.2d 1021 (1980).

—Defendant was in custody at moment the arresting officer informed defendant that he had a warrant for defendant's arrest, and any admissions obtained thereafter without *Miranda* warnings should have been suppressed. People v. Duncan, 241 A.D.2d 566, 660 N.Y.S.2d 81 (3d Dept. 1997).

Arrest without warrant; probable cause; search without warrant.—Where, after 3-4 week surveillance police obtained warrant to search premises for heroin traffic and premises appeared hastily vacated, the search of another premises designated by informants as new operation quarters of defendants was justified and seizure of heroin and paraphernalia in plain view did not violate constitutional limitations. People v. Cage, 40 A.D.2d 234, 339 N.Y.S.2d 6 (3d Dept. 1972).

Search of apartment; arrest warrant only.—Where police officer reasonably believed the defendant to be present and he made a reasonable effort to give notice of authority and purpose, he has complied with the statute and has the right to enter and seize evidence in clear view. People v. Narayan, 83 Misc. 2d 215, 372 N.Y.S.2d 849 (Sup. Ct. Queens Co. 1975).

§ 120.90. Warrant of arrest; procedure after arrest.

1. Upon arresting a defendant for any offense pursuant to a warrant of arrest in the county in which the warrant is returnable or in any adjoining county, or upon so arresting him for a felony in any other county, a police officer, if he be one to whom the warrant is addressed, must without unnecessary delay bring the defendant before the local criminal court in which such warrant is returnable.

2. Upon arresting a defendant for any offense pursuant to a warrant of arrest in a county adjoining the county in which the warrant is returnable, or upon so arresting him for a felony in any other county, a police officer, if he be one delegated to execute the warrant pursuant to section 120.60, must without unnecessary delay deliver the defendant or cause him to be delivered to the custody of the officer by whom he was so delegated, and the latter must then proceed as provided in subdivision one.

3. Upon arresting a defendant for an offense other than a felony pursuant to a warrant of arrest in a county other than the one in which the warrant is returnable or one adjoining it, a police officer, if he be one to whom the warrant is addressed, must inform the defendant that he has a right to appear before a local criminal court of the county of arrest for the purpose of being released on his own recognizance or having bail fixed. If the defendant does not desire to avail himself of such right, the officer must request him to endorse such fact upon the warrant, and upon such endorsement the officer must without unnecessary delay bring him before the court in which the warrant is returnable. If the defendant does desire to avail himself of such right, or if he refuses to make the aforementioned endorsement, the officer must without unnecessary delay bring him before a local criminal court of the county of arrest. Such court must release the defendant on his own recognizance or fix bail for his appearance on a specified date in the court in

which the warrant is returnable. If the defendant is in default of bail, the officer must without unnecessary delay bring him before the court in which the warrant is returnable.

4. Upon arresting a defendant for an offense other than a felony pursuant to a warrant of arrest in a county other than the one in which the warrant is returnable or one adjoining it, a police officer, if he be one delegated to execute the warrant pursuant to section 120.60, may hold the defendant in custody in the county of arrest for a period not exceeding two hours for the purpose of delivering him to the custody of the officer by whom he was delegated to execute such warrant. If the delegating officer receives custody of the defendant during such period, he must proceed as provided in subdivision three. Otherwise, the delegated officer must inform the defendant that he has a right to appear before a local criminal court for the purpose of being released on his own recognizance or having bail fixed. If the defendant does not desire to avail himself of such right, the officer must request him to make, sign and deliver to him a written statement of such fact, and if the defendant does so, the officer must retain custody of him but must without unnecessary delay deliver him or cause him to be delivered to the custody of the delegating police officer. If the defendant does desire to avail himself of such right, or if he refuses to make and deliver the aforementioned statement, the delegated or arresting officer must without unnecessary delay bring him before a local criminal court of the county of arrest and must submit to such court a written statement reciting the material facts concerning the issuance of the warrant, the offense involved, and all other essential matters relating thereto. Upon the submission of such statement, such court must release the defendant on his own recognizance or fix bail for his appearance on a specified date in the court in which the warrant is returnable. If the defendant is in default of bail, the officer must retain custody of him but must without unnecessary delay deliver him or cause him to be delivered to the custody of the delegating officer. Upon receiving such custody, the latter must without unnecessary delay bring the defendant before the court in which the warrant is returnable.

5. Whenever a police officer is required pursuant to this section to bring an arrested defendant before a town court in which a warrant of arrest is returnable, and if such town court is not available at the time, such officer must, if a copy of the underlying accusatory instrument has been attached to the warrant pursuant to section 120.40, instead bring such defendant before any village court embraced, in whole or in part, by such town, or any local criminal court of an adjoining town or city of the same county or any village court embraced, in whole or in part, by such adjoining town. When the court in which the warrant is returnable is a village court which is not available at the time, the officer must in such circumstances bring the defendant before the town court of the town embracing such village or any other village court within such town or, if such town court or village court is not available either, before the local criminal court of any town or city of the same county which adjoins such embracing town or, before the local criminal court of any village embraced in whole or in part by such adjoining town. When the court in which the warrant is returnable is a city court which is not available at the time, the officer must in such circumstances bring the defendant before the local criminal court of any adjoining town or village embraced in whole or in part by such adjoining town of the same county.

6. Before bringing a defendant arrested pursuant to a warrant before the local criminal court in which such warrant is returnable, a police officer must without unnecessary delay perform all fingerprinting and other preliminary police duties required in the particular case. In any case in which the defendant is not brought by a police officer before such court but, following his arrest in another county for an offense specified in subdivision one of section 160.10, is released by a local criminal court of such other county on his own recognizance or on bail for his appearance on a specified date before the local criminal court before which the warrant is returnable, the latter court must, upon arraignment of the defendant before it, direct that he be fingerprinted by the appropriate officer or agency, and that he appear at an appropriate designated time and place for such purpose.

7. Upon arresting a juvenile offender, the police officer shall immediately notify the parent or other person legally responsible for his care or the person with whom he is domiciled, that the juvenile offender has been arrested, and the location of the facility where he is being detained.

Amended by L. 1971, Ch. 762; L. 1979, Ch. 411; L. 1980, Ch. 893; L. 1984, Ch. 695; L. 1986, Ch. 5; L. 1987, Ch. 382; L. 1988, Ch. 324; L. 1998, Ch. 424, § 8, eff. Jan. 1, 1999.

ARTICLE 130—THE SUMMONS

Section

LexisNexis Cross Reference

New York Criminal Practice (2d ed.), Vol. 1, Ch. 6, Warrants of Arrest and Summonses; Local Criminal Courts and Superior Courts.

§ 130.10. Summons; definition, function, form and content.

1. A summons is a process issued by a local criminal court directing a defendant designated in an information, a prosecutor's information, a felony complaint or a misdemeanor complaint filed with such court, or by a superior court directing a defendant designated in an indictment filed with such court, to appear before it at a designated future time in connection with such accusatory instrument. The sole function of a summons is to achieve a defendant's court appearance in a criminal action for the purpose of arraignment upon the accusatory instrument by which such action was commenced.

2. A summons must be subscribed by the issuing judge and must state or contain (a) the name of the issuing court, and (b) the name of the defendant to whom it is addressed, and (c) the name or title of an offense charged in the underlying accusatory instrument, and (d) the date of issuance of the summons, and (e) the date and time when it is returnable, and (f) a direction that the defendant appear before the issuing court at such time.

Amended by L. 1993, Ch. 446.

ANNOTATION

Service of summons not an arrest; seizure.—The mere service of a summons does not constitute an arrest. The simultaneous service of a subpoena duces tecum, to compel production of an allegedly obscene film on the return date, did not constitute a seizure. Under this circumstance, a prior judicial scrutiny of the film was not necessary. People v. P.A.J. Theater Corp., 72 Misc. 2d 354, 339 N.Y.S.2d 152 (Crim. Ct. N.Y. Co. 1972).

§ 130.20. Summons; by what courts issuable and in what courts returnable.

A summons may be issued only by the local criminal court or superior court with which the accusatory instrument underlying it has been filed, and it may be made returnable in such issuing court only.

Amended by L. 1993, Ch. 446.

§ 130.30. Summons; when issuable.

A local criminal court may issue a summons in any case in which, pursuant to section 120.20, it is authorized to issue a warrant of arrest based upon an information, a prosecutor's information, a felony complaint or a misdemeanor complaint. If such information, prosecutor's information, felony complaint or misdemeanor complaint is not sufficient on its face as prescribed in section 100.40, and if the court is satisfied that on the basis of the available facts or evidence it would be impossible to draw and file an authorized accusatory instrument that is sufficient on its face, the court must dismiss the accusatory instrument. A superior court may issue a summons in any case in which, pursuant to section 210.10, it is authorized to issue a warrant of arrest based upon an indictment.

Amended by L. 1993, Ch. 446; L. 2000, Ch. 506, eff. Nov. 1, 2000.

ANNOTATION

Accusatory instrument.—Until an accusatory instrument is filed, a Court cannot issue a summons or warrant of arrest to compel a defendant's appearance. People v. Brisotti, 167 Misc. 2d 688, 635 N.Y.S.2d 442 (Crim. Ct. Bronx Co. 1995).

§ 130.40. Summons; service.

1. A summons may be served by a police officer, or by a complainant at least eighteen years old or by any other person at least eighteen years old designated by the court.

2. A summons may be served anywhere in the county of issuance or anywhere in an adjoining county.

ANNOTATIONS

Personal delivery.—Where the defendant is not present at the time of issuance of a ticket, the policy considerations favoring personal delivery are especially strong. People v. DiLorenzo, 149 Misc. 2d 791, 566 N.Y.S.2d 458 (Crim. Ct. Bronx Co. 1990).

Federal rules; distinction.—The distinction between CPL 130.40 and Federal Rules of Criminal Procedure Rule 4 is that the NY legislature saw fit to omit the "suitable age and discretion" from the statute, whereas Congress included it in the federal statute; service in criminal actions is limited to personal delivery upon a natural person. People v. Turkel, 130 Misc. 2d 47, 494 N.Y.S.2d 984 (Crim. Ct. N.Y. Co. 1985).

§ 130.50. Summons; defendant's failure to appear.

If after the service of a summons the defendant does not appear in the designated local criminal or superior court at the time such summons is returnable, the court may issue a warrant of arrest.

Amended by L. 1993, Ch. 446.

§ 130.60. Summons; fingerprinting of defendant.

1. Upon the arraignment of a defendant whose court attendance has been secured by the issuance and service of a summons, based upon an indictment, a prosecutor's information or upon an information, felony complaint or misdemeanor complaint filed by a complainant who is a police officer, the court must, if the offense charged in the accusatory instrument is one specified in subdivision one of section 160.10, direct that the defendant be fingerprinted by the appropriate police officer or agency, and that he or she appear at an appropriate designated time and place for such purpose.

2. Upon the arraignment of a defendant whose court attendance has been secured by the issuance and service of a summons based upon an information or misdemeanor complaint filed by a complainant who is not a police officer, and who has not previously been fingerprinted, the court may, if it finds reasonable cause to believe that the defendant has committed an offense specified in subdivision one of section 160.10, direct that the defendant be fingerprinted by the appropriate police officer or agency, and that he appear at an appropriate designated time and place for such purpose. A defendant whose court appearance has been secured by the issuance and service of a criminal summons based upon a misdemeanor complaint or information filed by a complainant who is not a police officer, must be directed by the court, upon conviction of the defendant, to be fingerprinted by the appropriate police officer or agency and the court must also direct that the defendant appear at an appropriate designated time and place for such purpose, if the defendant is convicted of any offense specified in subdivision one of section 160.10.

Amended by L. 1971, Ch. 762; L. 1986, Ch. 396; L. 1991, Ch. 95; L. 1993, Ch. 446.

ANNOTATION

Return of fingerprints; sentence for failure to post bond.—One sentenced for 30 days to correctional institution for failure to post bond in alimony default was not convicted of crime and must be released and have his fingerprints, etc. returned on demand. Hofman v. Malcolm, 71 Misc. 2d 251, 335 N.Y.S.2d 938 (Sup. Ct. N.Y. Co. 1972).

ARTICLE 140—ARREST WITHOUT A WARRANT

LexisNexis Cross References

Defense of Speeding, Reckless Driving & Vehicular Homicide, Vol. 3, Ch. 35, Arrest Without a Warrant; *Apprehending and Prosecuting the Drunk Driver,* Ch. 5, Arrest and Booking Procedures; *Criminal Defense Techniques,* Vol. 4, Ch. 82, Warrantless Home Arrests; *Defense of Narcotics Cases,* Vol. 1, Ch. 3C, Warrantless Searches; *New York Criminal Practice (2d ed.),* Vol. 2, Ch.19, Warrantless Arrests; *New York Suppression Manual,* Ch. 7, Warrantless Arrests; Ch. 12, Exigent Circumstances and the Emergency Doctrine; Ch. 13, Search Incident to Arrest; Ch. 14, Automobile Searches; Ch. 15, Plain View; Ch. 18, Consent Searches.

§ 140.05. Arrest without a warrant; in general.

A person who has committed or is believed to have committed an offense and who is at liberty within the state may, under circumstances prescribed in this article, be arrested for such offense although no warrant of arrest therefor has been issued and although no criminal action therefor has yet been commenced in any criminal court.

ANNOTATIONS

Probable cause.—A police officer may arrest for an offense without a warrant if he has reasonable cause to believe that a person has committed that offense in his presence. People v. Maldonado, 86 N.Y.2d 631, 635 N.Y.S.2d 155, 658 N.E.2d 1028 (1995).

—There is no requirement that probable cause derive from a suspect's actions at the time of his arrest, and defendant's argument to this effect is entirely contrary to law. People v. Vasquez, 215 A.D.2d 118, 626 N.Y.S.2d 111 (1st Dept. 1995).

—Suspicion of criminality was supported by probable cause to believe defendant was committing the crime of trespass. People v. Velasquez, 217 A.D.2d 510, 630 N.Y.S.2d 303 (1st Dept. 1995).

—Where probable cause to arrest is predicated in whole or part on hearsay statement of informant, it must be demonstrated that information is reliable and informant had sufficient basis for his or her knowledge, but citizen informant's reliability is assumed. People v. Dollison, 221 A.D.2d 654, 634 N.Y.S.2d 194 (2d Dept 1995).

—Police officer had reasonable cause for warrantless arrest of defendant after assault victim, defendant's former girlfriend, identified him; police officer observed victim to be very upset and observed bruises on legs and scratches, blood, and contusions on her right arm, and there was knowledge of defendant's violent tendencies. People v. Alpern, 217 A.D.2d 853, 630 N.Y.S.2d 106 (3d Dept. 1995).

—Superseding information alleging that defendant, a candidate for judge, was told to stop distributing literature at church feast in church parking lot by authorized representative of church and by police officers and, upon failing to stop was told to leave, but did not, was sufficient to charge offense of trespass, despite defendant's contention that information lacked requisite element of knowledge. People v. Raab, 163 Misc. 2d 382, 621 N.Y.S.2d 440 (Nassau Co. Ct. 1994).

—Police officer had probable cause to make warrantless arrest of defendant based on information received from informant; informant stated that defendant was wanted for homicide and identified defendant from lineup, and officer then determined that informant had provided reliable information in the past and that defendant was wanted in connection with murder committed five years earlier. People v. Jacobo, 154 Misc. 2d 540, 585 N.Y.S.2d 665 (Sup. Ct. N.Y. Co. 1992).

Arrest; dismissal of accusatory instrument.—The making of an "on the scene" arrest for driving while intoxicated and the subsequent filing of simplified informations pertaining thereto were two separate and distinct legal matters. While the later dismissal of the simplified informations halted the criminal action it had no effect upon the defendant's prior arrest since he was not discharged and the court retained jurisdiction over him pending the filing of the long form informations. People v. Bock, 77 Misc. 2d 350, 353 N.Y.S.2d 647 (Broome Co. Ct. 1974).

Arrest; public place.—When an arrest occurs in a public place, no requirement exists that a warrant be obtained simply because there is time to do so. People v. Reynolds, 132 A.D.2d 632, 517 N.Y.S.2d 785 (2d Dept. 1987).

Arrest; without jurisdiction; outside state.—Defendant, accused of murder in the second degree, went to South Carolina where he subsequently voluntarily surrendered to a New York police officer and was brought back to New York; although a general statute authorizing arrests for crime applies only to crimes committed within the state, where a party has unlawfully been arrested by an officer without his jurisdiction, he waives his objection to the illegality of the arrest by failing to object and voluntarily accompanying the officer, or by giving bail. People v. Gilmore, 76 A.D.2d 548, 430 N.Y.S.2d 854 (2d Dept. 1980).

§ 140.10. Arrest without a warrant; by police officer; when and where authorized.

1. Subject to the provisions of subdivision two, a police officer may arrest a person for:

(a) Any offense when he has reasonable cause to believe that such person has committed such offense in his presence; and

(b) A crime when he has reasonable cause to believe that such person has committed such crime, whether in his presence or otherwise.

2. A police officer may arrest a person for a petty offense, pursuant to subdivision one, only when:

(a) Such offense was committed or believed by him or her to have been committed within the geographical area of such police officer's employment or within one hundred yards of such geographical area; and

(b) Such arrest is made in the county in which such offense was committed or believed to have been committed or in an adjoining county; except that the police officer may follow such person in continuous close pursuit, commencing either in the county in which the offense was or is believed to have been committed or in an adjoining county, in and through any county of the state, and may arrest him in any county in which he apprehends him.

3. A police officer may arrest a person for a crime, pursuant to subdivision one, whether or not such crime was committed within the geographical area of such police officer's employment, and he may make such arrest within the state, regardless of the situs of the commission of the crime. In addition, he may, if necessary, pursue such person outside the state and may arrest him in any state the laws of which contain provisions equivalent to those of section 140.55.

4. [*Expires and repealed September 1, 2007.*] Notwithstanding any other provisions of this section, a police officer shall arrest a person, and shall not attempt to reconcile the parties or mediate, where such officer has reasonable cause to believe that:

(a) a felony, other than subdivision three, four, nine or ten of section 155.30 of the penal law, has been committed by such person against a member of the same family or household, as member of the same family or household is defined in subdivision one of section 530.11 of this chapter; or

(b) a duly served order of protection or special order of conditions issued pursuant to subparagraph (i) or (ii) of paragraph (o) of subdivision one of section 330.20 of this chapter is in effect, or an order of which the respondent or defendant has actual knowledge because he or she was present in court when such order was issued, where the order appears to have been issued by a court of competent jurisdiction of this or another state, territorial or tribal jurisdiction; and

(i) Such order directs that the respondent or defendant stay away from persons on whose behalf the order of protection or special order of conditions has been issued and the respondent or defendant committed an act or acts in violation of such "stay away" provision of such order; or

(ii) The respondent or defendant commits a family offense as defined in subdivision one of section eight hundred twelve of the family court act or subdivision one of section 530.11 of this chapter in violation of such order of protection or special order of conditions.

The provisions of this subdivision shall apply only to orders of protection issued pursuant to sections two hundred forty and two hundred fifty-two of the domestic relations law, articles four, five, six and eight of the family court act and section 530.12 of this chapter, special orders of conditions issued pursuant to subparagraph (i) or (ii) of paragraph (o) of subdivision one of section 330.20 of this chapter insofar as they involve a victim or victims of domestic violence as defined by subdivision one of section four hundred fifty-nine-a of the social services law or a designated witness or witnesses to such domestic violence, and to orders of protection issued by courts of competent jurisdiction in another state, territorial or tribal jurisdiction. In determining whether reasonable cause exists to make an arrest for a violation of an order issued by a court of another state, territorial or tribal jurisdiction, the officer shall consider, among other factors, whether the order, if available, appears to be valid on its face or whether a record of the order exists on the statewide registry of orders of protection and warrants established pursuant to section two hundred twenty-one-a of the executive law or the protection order file maintained by the national crime information center; provided, however, that entry of the order of protection or special order of conditions into the statewide registry or the national protection order file shall not be required for enforcement of the order. When a special order of conditions is in effect and a defendant or respondent has been taken into custody pursuant to this paragraph, nothing contained in this paragraph shall restrict or impair a police officer from acting pursuant to section 9.41 of the mental hygiene law; or

(c) a misdemeanor constituting a family offense, as described in subdivision one of section 530.11 of this chapter and section eight hundred twelve of the family court act, has been committed by such person against such family or household member, unless the victim requests otherwise. The officer shall neither inquire as to whether the victim seeks an arrest of such person nor threaten the arrest of any person for the purpose of discouraging requests for police intervention. Notwithstanding the foregoing, when an officer has reasonable cause to believe that more than one family or household member has committed such a misdemeanor, the officer is not required to arrest each such person. In such circumstances, the officer shall attempt to identify and arrest the primary physical aggressor after considering: (i) the comparative extent of any injuries inflicted by and between the parties; (ii) whether any such person is threatening or has threatened future harm against another party or another family or household member; (iii) whether any such person has a prior history of domestic violence that the officer can reasonably ascertain; and (iv) whether any such person acted defensively to protect himself or herself from injury. The officer shall evaluate each complaint separately to determine who is the primary physical aggressor and shall not base the decision to arrest or not to arrest on the willingness of a person to testify or otherwise participate in a judicial proceeding.

Nothing contained in this subdivision shall be deemed to (a) require the arrest of any person when the officer reasonably believes the person's conduct is justifiable under article thirty-five of title C of the penal law; or (b) restrict or impair the authority of any municipality, political subdivision, or the division of state police from promulgating rules, regulations and policies requiring the arrest of persons in additional circumstances where domestic violence has allegedly occurred.

No cause of action for damages shall arise in favor of any person by reason of any arrest made by a police officer pursuant to this subdivision, except as provided in sections seventeen and eighteen of the public officers law and sections fifty-k, fifty-l, fifty-m and fifty-n of the general municipal law, as appropriate.

5. Upon investigating a report of a crime or offense between members of the same family or household as such terms are defined in section 530.11 of this chapter and section eight hundred twelve of the family court act, a law enforcement officer shall prepare and file a written report of the incident, on a form promulgated pursuant to section eight hundred thirty-seven of the executive law, including statements made by the victim and by any witnesses, and make any additional reports required by local law enforcement policy or regulations. Such report shall be prepared and filed, whether or not an arrest is made as a result of the officers' investigation, and shall be retained by the law enforcement agency for a period of not less than four years. Where the reported incident involved an offense committed against a person who is sixty-five years of age or older a copy of the report required by this subdivision shall be sent to the New York state committee for the coordination of police services to elderly persons established pursuant to section eight hundred forty-four-b of the executive law.

Amended by L. 1994, Ch. 222, § 32, and L. 1994, Ch. 224, §§ 5-a and 16, eff. July 1, 1995, and expiring and deemed repealed on July 1, 1999, adding subd. 4; L. 1994, Ch. 222, § 32, and L. 1994, Ch. 224, § 6, eff. Jan. 1, 1995, adding subd. 5; L. 1995, Ch. 17, § 1 amending effective date of subd. 4, as commencing January 1, 1996, and expiring January 1, 2000; L. 1995, Ch. 349, § 4, amending subd. 4(b)(ii), and amendment repealed July 1, 1999; L. 1996, Ch. 511, § 1, amending subd. 4(a), eff. Nov. 6, 1996; L. 1996, Ch. 533, § 2, extending expiration date of subd. 4 to July 1, 2001; L. 1997, Ch. 4, eff. Jan. 12, 1998, amending second undesignated paragraph of subd. 4 and subd. 4(c), and Ch. 626, eff. Sept. 17, 1997, amending subd. 5; L. 1998, Ch. 597, § 10, eff. Dec. 22, 1998; L. 2001, Chs. 63, 105, and 118, extending expiration date of subd. 4 to Sept. 1, 2003; L. 2003, Ch. 300, § 1, eff. Nov. 1, 2003, amending subd. 2(a); L. 2003, Ch. 303, § 1, Aug. 5, 2003, extending expiration date of subd. 4 to Sept. 1, 2005; L. 2004, Ch. 107, § 5, eff. June 8, 2004, amending subd. 4(b); L. 2004, Ch. 642, § 4, eff. Oct. 26, 2004, amending subd. 5, such amendment repealed by L. 2005, Ch. 87, § 3, deemed eff. Oct. 26, 2004; L. 2005, Ch. 56, Part D, § 19, eff. Apr. 1, 2005, extending expiration date of subd. 4 to Sept. 1, 2007.

ANNOTATIONS

Anonymous "tip"; no probable cause.— Judgment reversed and motion to suppress physical evidence granted; "anonymous tip stating that person of certain description was walking on particular street carrying a black plastic bag containing a gun did not create reasonable suspicion to stop and frisk individual matching that description; tip consisted essentially of description of person's visible attributes and came from an unaccountable informant." People v. Ballard, 279 A.D.2d 529, 719 N.Y.S.2d 267 (2d Dept. 2001).

—Police lacked probable cause to arrest defendant where basis of arrest was information supplied by anonymous caller and scant account by one of the victims of her observations of a purported robber in a gray car; because lineup identification was the fruit of an illegal arrest, it should have been suppressed. Defendant entitled to new trial and hearing to determine whether independent source existed for the victims' ability to identify defendant. People v. Brown, 256 A.D.2d 414, 682 N.Y.S.2d 229 (2d Dept. 1998).

—Defendant's arrest was improper where it was based on a telephone call by an individual who identified himself as an agent of the DEA to an airline service manager and who stated, without giving the basis for it, that a particular package contained material of a "suspicious nature"; such statement did not provide probable cause to believe that the package contained contraband and the suppression of evidence seized pursuant to the arrest was required. People v. Miranda, 106 A.D.2d. 407, 482 N.Y.S.2d 328 (2d Dept. 1984).

Arrest; identification by victim of crime.—Probable cause to arrest was demonstrated where a named citizen informed the police that he had just witnessed the defendant assault the complainant with a knife. People v. Burgos, 129 A.D.2d 804, 514 N.Y.S.2d 796 (2d Dept. 1987).

Apartment search; arrest in hallway.—Warrantless search of the apartment for a gun was not incident to arrest nor conducted under exigent circumstances, and was *per se* unreasonable where police had traced defendant, suspected of attempted murder to his apartment and subdued him in the hallway of the building after he attacked them with a machete. People v. Maldonado, 75 A.D.2d 558, 427 N.Y.S.2d 414 (1st Dept. 1980).

Inadequate description; effect.—The officer did not have reasonable ground to believe the defendant committed the felony and was liable for false arrest where defendant was arrested thirteen days after the crime, and the description given at crime scene by complainant when compared to defendant involved a five-inch discrepancy in height, an 8 to 18 year discrepancy in age, and discrepancies as to build and use of eyeglasses. Smith v. County of Nassau, 34 N.Y.2d 18, 355 N.Y.S.2d 349, 311 N.E.2d 489 (1974).

—Police lacked reasonable suspicion to forcibly detain defendant in connection with armed robbery where the vague and general description of a black male wearing black clothing was insufficient to provide reasonable suspicion that he was the perpetrator. After the robbery, defendant was apprehended several blocks from the crime scene while standing in line to purchase a sweater at a store, and he was wearing dark blue clothing. There was no evidence that he was out of breath, engaged in any suspicious behavior, or made any attempt to flee. People v. Thomas, 300 A.D.2d 416, 752 N.Y.S.2d 70 (2d Dept. 2002).

Observation based on informant's report.—After informant was arrested on drug charges he telephoned his supplier with police overhearing conversation and arranged drug buy; later the location was changed in telephone call received by informer and relayed to police. Probable cause to arrest defendant existed when police observed informant meet with defendant at location mentioned in second telephone conversation. People v. Adragna, 44 A.D.2d 505, 355 N.Y.S.2d 662 (4th Dept. 1974), aff'd, 40 N.Y.2d 609, 394 N.Y.S.2d 591, 363 N.E.2d 316 (1974).

Arrest without warrant; probable cause; search without warrant.—The arrest was supported by probable cause to believe that a crime was being committed, and the drugs seized during the search incident to that arrest were properly admitted into evidence where a taxicab proceeding toward a marked police car at 3:15 a.m. flashed its high beam lights and blew its horn, and the use of the high beam signal appeared to be a sign of trouble pursuant to the police department's temporary operating procedure and when approached by the officers on foot, the cab driver indicated that he was in the process of being robbed. People v. Blakely, 46 N.Y.2d 1026, 416 N.Y.S.2d 538, 389 N.E.2d 1060 (1979).

—Since at the time of the arrest, the police could have conducted a full-blown search of defendant and the unlocked suitcase within his immediate control in the baggage claim area, the fact that this did not occur and that the search took place as soon as defendant was in a place where the search could be performed without endangering innocent bystanders and without public embarrassment to the defendant was reasonable under the circumstances. People v. DeSantis, 46 N.Y.2d 82, 412 N.Y.S.2d 838, 385 N.E.2d 577 (1978).

Arrest; identification by citizen.—Since the police had probable cause to arrest defendant with respect to forged prescriptions presented to a pharmacy and in the course of questioning immediately following the arrest defendant admitted that his car was parked alongside the pharmacy and contained additional forged prescriptions as well as illegally obtained drugs, a search of the vehicle by the police without a warrant was permissible. People v. Orlando, 56 N.Y.2d 441, 452 N.Y.S.2d 559, 438 N.E.2d 92 (1982).

—Probable cause existed since the identified off-duty officer, who gave the arresting officer the details of the crime and identified defendant, was an eyewitness to the attempted burglary and thus had the requisite reliable basis of knowledge. People v. Pope, 208 A.D.2d 356, 616 N.Y.S.2d 742 (1st Dept. 1994).

—There was probable cause to arrest defendant based on the statements of his mother's common-law husband, a citizen-informer who went voluntarily to the police and revealed that defendant had confessed his involvement in the crime to him. People v. Diaz, 206 A.D.2d 314, 615 N.Y.S.2d 6 (1st Dept. 1994).

—Information provided to the police by an identified citizen is presumed to be reliable. People v. Allen, 209 A.D.2d 425, 618 N.Y.S.2d 104 (2d Dept. 1994).

—Unlike a paid or anonymous informant, an eyewitness-victim of a crime can provide probable cause for the arrest of his assailant despite the fact that his reliability has not been previously established or his information corroborated; an accusation against a specific individual from an identified citizen is presumed reliable. People v. Gonzalez, 138 A.D.2d 622, 526 N.Y.S.2d 208 (2d Dept. 1988).

—A citizen that provides sufficient information to believe a defendant has committed a crime does not have to testify at a pretrial suppression hearing; his reliability is assumed since he can be prosecuted if his report were a fabrication. People v. Inman, 80 A.D.2d 622, 436 N.Y.S.2d 63 (2d Dept. 1981).

Arrest without warrant; probable cause; search incident to arrest.—Police were justified in searching defendant's briefcase after his arrest for failing to pay his subway fare, where, at the time of initial detention defendant admitted not having a pass and police noted he was wearing a bulletproof vest; police may contemporaneously search the inside of a briefcase, package, or the like, carried by the arrested person or effectively in his possession, after the object has been removed so that the arrested person no longer has ready access to it. People v. Smith, 89 A.D.2d 549, 452 N.Y.S.2d 886 (1st Dept. 1982), aff'd, 59 N.Y.2d 454, 465 N.Y.S.2d 896, 452 N.E.2d 1224 (1983).

Arrest; stop of vehicle.—A police officer has probable cause to arrest and search the occupants of a van where he had received a report of a robbery and a description of the van with out-of-state license plates, driven by a white male with dark hair and the motor of the van was hot and it was less than a mile from the scene of the robbery which occurred fifteen minutes previously. People v. Brnja, 50 N.Y.2d 366, 429 N.Y.S.2d 173, 406 N.E.2d 1016 (1980).

Authority of police officer.—Since a police officer may make an arrest on a 24-hour basis for any offense which he has reasonable cause to believe a person has committed in his presence, it was irrelevant that the officer at the time was engaged in outside employment as a village constable. People v. Neuschatz, 88 Misc. 2d 433, 389 N.Y.S.2d 507 (App. Term 9-10th Dist. 1975), aff'd, 40 N.Y.2d 935, 390 N.Y.S.2d 61, 358 N.E.2d 885 (1976).

Border search.—The "border search" exception to the requirement of probable cause accorded to Customs officials by statute (U.S.C. Title 19, §§ 482, 1496, 1582) is a limited power. It permits such officials to search for contraband coming into the country but it does not extend to searches of baggage going out of the country upon which no duty is payable and on which no prohibitions are placed. People v. Esposito, 37 N.Y.2d 156, 371 N.Y.S.2d 681, 332 N.E.2d 863 (1975).

—Hashish was properly seized from defendant's luggage by a customs inspector at Kennedy Airport since the facts established a "border search" because no probable cause or warrant was required. People v. Mitchell, 72 A.D.2d 589, 421 N.Y.S.2d 13 (2d Dept. 1979).

—It is well-settled that the border patrol may stop a vehicle at a fixed checkpoint for brief questioning of its occupants "even though there is no reason to believe that the particular vehicle contains illegal aliens." People v. Sinzheimer, 15 A.D.2d 732, 790 N.Y.S.2d 554 (3d Dept. 2005).

—The passage of the Scott Bader across a functional border into the jurisdictional waters of the United States created a reasonable basis for a customs search by the Coast Guard. People v. Nissen, 97 Misc. 2d 1000, 412 N.Y.S.2d 999 (Sup. Ct. Suffolk Co. 1979).

—Enforcement of its laws concerning the sale or possession of a controlled substance by the State of New York is entirely compatible with the federal laws regulating customs procedures unless the state had ceded the land where the offense occurred and jurisdiction over it to the United States government; thus, New York may properly charge and try defendant for possession of 22 pounds of marijuana found in his suitcase during a border search at Kennedy Airport after a trans-Atlantic flight. People v. Mitchell, 90 Misc. 2d 463, 395 N.Y.S.2d 340 (Sup. Ct. Queens Co. 1977).

Consent, valid substitute for probable cause.—Where defendant voluntarily consented to accompany the police to the police station to assist in the investigation of a homicide and two knives were discovered in his jacket as he was preparing to leave his room, his consent was a valid substitute for probable cause. People v. Hodge, 44 N.Y.2d 553, 406 N.Y.S.2d 736, 378 N.E.2d 99 (1978).

—Where defendant voluntarily consented to accompany the officers to the station house, and such consent was free, voluntary and intelligently given, it did not constitute a submission to superior official presence even though the officers did not advise suspect that she had a right to refuse their request. People v. Joynes, 72 A.D.2d 799, 421 N.Y.S.2d 629 (2d Dept. 1979).

—A prosecutor seeking to rely upon consent to justify the lawfulness of a search has the burden of proving by clear and convincing evidence that the consent was unequivocally, voluntary and freely given. People v. Tinneny, 99 Misc. 2d 962, 417 N.Y.S.2d 840 (Sup. Ct. Kings Co. 1979).

DeBour.—Where police officers boarded a bus that had arrived from New York City, announced that they were conducting a drug interdiction, and asked everyone on board to produce bus tickets and identification, the request to produce documentation did not meet the *DeBour* standard and was conducted without an objective, credible reason. The ensuing search of defendant's bag and jacket was unlawful even though investigator obtained consent to search defendant's bag. People v. McIntosh, 96 N.Y.2d 521, 730 N.Y.S.2d 265, 755 N.E.2d 329 (2001).

Description by undercover officer.—Probable cause to arrest defendant was established by the fact that the undercover officer gave "buy money" to one Henley who went into an alley, conversed for 10 seconds with a man in a black tee shirt whose face the undercover could not see, and returned to give drugs to the undercover who then gave the description of the defendant as wearing a black tee shirt to backup team which promptly arrested the defendant at that location. People v. Witherspoon, 115 A.D.2d 572, 496 N.Y.S.2d 235 (2d Dept. 1985).

Disclosure of informant's identity; reliability of informant; reliability of information.—Where evidence of the reliability of the informant and reliability of the information exist, it is unnecessary to demonstrate further the informer's existence by disclosing his name. Reliability may be demonstrated by evidence of the informant's past performance; reliability of the information may be determined on the basis of the specificity and immediacy of the informer's accurate report, corroborated by the officer's own observation. People v. Castro, 29 N.Y.2d 324, 327 N.Y.S.2d 632, 277 N.E.2d 654 (1971).

Emergency doctrine.—Warrantless entry into defendant's apartment was justified under the emergency doctrine based on information officers had about defendant's violent conduct, threats, and disturbed mental condition, which information came from an identified victim, from persons the officers encountered on the street, and from the officers' own observations. People v. Salazar, 290 A.D.2d 256, 736 N.Y.S.2d 20 (1st Dept. 2002).

—Emergency doctrine did not justify a search of defendant's apartment by detective who accompanied father of apparent narcotic overdose victim, where victim was already being treated, and their action would have no bearing on the victim's condition. People v. Matta, 76 A.D.2d 844, 428 N.Y.S.2d 491 (2d Dept. 1980).

—Police officer's seizure of crack cocaine from a pantry shelf in plain view in defendant's apartment was proper pursuant to emergency exception, where the People established at the suppression hearing that when no one responded to their knocking, firefighters forcibly entered defendant's apartment to determine whether a fire in the apartment below had spread to defendant's apartment. A police officer proceeded to defendant's apartment after being advised that firefighters had forcibly entered the apartment. People v. Crawford, 298 A.D.2d 850, 747 N.Y.S.2d 618 (4th Dept. 2002).

—Warrantless entry into defendant's apartment by police was justified under the emergency exception to the search warrant requirement, in response to a foul odor emanating from the apartment, reported in a 911 call from a tenant; the odor was so foul it necessitated the use of charcoal masks, and the source of the odor was a decomposing body found in a closet. People v. Molnar, 288 A.D.2d 911, 732 N.Y.S.2d 788 (4th Dept. 2001), aff'd, 98 N.Y.2d 328, 746 N.Y.S.2d 673, 774 N.E.2d 738 (2002).

Exclusionary rule; independent act involving calculated risk.—Although the initial seizure of the defendant was unlawful since the police lacked evidence of probable cause, his subsequent action while in the police car of throwing a loaded revolver out the window of the car was not a spontaneous act but an independent act involving a calculated risk and the purpose of the exclusionary rule would not be served granting the motion to suppress. People v. Boodle, 47 N.Y.2d 398, 418 N.Y.S.2d 352, 391 N.E.2d 1321 (1979).

Exigent circumstances.—The contents of a radio run, report of shots fired from occupants of the building, and the screams and sounds emanating from the apartment provided a sufficient predicate for the warrantless entry into the apartment. People v. Rivera, 171 A.D.2d 560, 567 N.Y.S.2d 266 (1st Dept. 1991).

—Police were justified in entering defendant's apartment without a valid search warrant in light of exigent circumstances, where the record indicated that police received reliable information that defendant had killed two men and was in the process of destroying evidence by painting over blood-stained walls and disposing of the bodies. People v. Saunders, 290 A.D.2d 461, 736 N.Y.S.2d 90 (2d Dept. 2002).

—Police entry into apartment where defendant's arrest took place and the subsequent pat-down and warrantless arrest were proper and justified by a report of a violent fight involving a gun inside the apartment, clearly constituting exigent circumstances, statements by a person in the apartment that defendant had a gun and the finding of a gun on the defendant's person. People v. Lewis, 108 A.D.2d 833, 485 N.Y.S.2d 367 (2d Dept. 1985).

—No amount of probable cause can justify a warrantless seizure absent exigent circumstances; exigent circumstances exist where the police will be unable to make a seizure for which probable cause exists unless they act quickly. People v. Clark, 103 Misc. 2d 498, 426 N.Y.S.2d 692 (Sup. Ct. N.Y. Co. 1980).

Flashlight; vehicle.—Where there was no basis for suspicion other than defendant's prior presence in a rented car and his walking about the block, the police use of a flashlight to illuminate the interior of the car was an unwarranted intrusion into the interior of the vehicle and the firearm and the drugs discovered were suppressed. People v. Smith, 42 N.Y.2d 961, 398 N.Y.S.2d 142, 367 N.E.2d 648 (1977).

—Arrest was proper, where officer stopped vehicle for nonoperative tail lights, and later shone his flashlight into glove compartment while passenger was obtaining vehicle insurance card and observed a holstered gun. People v. Hale, 75 A.D.2d 606, 426 N.Y.S.2d 827 (2d Dept. 1980).

—Where the initial police approach to the defendant's vehicle was proper, the officer's use of his flashlight to illuminate the contents of a car, which but for the dark, would have been in plain view was fully justified and the resulting seizure of the gun was proper. People v. Duncan, 75 A.D.2d 823, 427 N.Y.S.2d 472 (2d Dept. 1980).

—The shining of a flashlight into the vehicle where the officer saw a gun was lawful. The action of a police officer in shining his flashlight to illuminate the interior of a car without probable cause to search the car violated no right secured by the fourth amendment. People v. Blankymsee, 196 Misc. 2d 240, 764 N.Y.S.2d 331 (Sup. Ct. Queens Co. 2003).

Flight.—Flight, combined with other specific circumstances indicating that the suspected may be engaged in criminal activity, could provide the predicate necessary to justify pursuit. People v. Holmes, 81 N.Y.2d 1056, 601 N.Y.S.2d 459, 619 N.E.2d 396 (1993).

—Flight alone is generally an insufficient basis for either seizure or the limited detention involved in pursuit. People v. Manning, 199 A.D.2d 621, 604 N.Y.S.2d 993 (3d Dept. 1993).

—Although flight is a factor to consider on the issue of probable cause, other facts must exist to show that a crime was committed and that the defendant committed it. People v. Woldeguiorguis, 195 A.D.2d 1004, 600 N.Y.S.2d 568 (4th Dept. 1993).

—Flight alone, or even in conjunction with equivocal circumstances that might justify a police request for information, is insufficient to justify pursuit because an individual has a right to be let alone and refuse to respond to police inquiry. People v. Smith, 161 Misc. 2d 832, 615 N.Y.S.2d 243 (Sup. Ct. N.Y. Co. 1994).

Jurisdiction.—As to petty offenses (violations and traffic infractions), arrests by a police officer may be made only in the county of commission of the offense or an adjoining county and only if the offense was committed in the arresting officer's officer jurisdiction (bailiwick). Here, the arresting officer lacked jurisdiction to arrest defendant for the petty offenses, and accordingly, the indictment was dismissed. People v. Graham, 192 Misc. 2d 528, 748 N.Y.S.2d 203 (Sup. Ct. Erie Co. 2002), aff'd, 1 A.D.3d 1066, 767 N.Y.S.2d 383 (4th Dept. 2003).

Lawful stop; acquiring probable cause.—Here, one of the officers had previously arrested defendant and recalled that defendant's license had been revoked. The officers saw defendant sitting in the driver's seat of the parked but running vehicle and thus had an objective, credible reason for approaching defendants to request information. Only seconds into the encounter, the officers acquired probable cause to arrest defendants based on one officer's observation of bags of cocaine in plain view on the floor of the vehicle. People v. Grady, 272 A.D.2d 952, 708 N.Y.S.2d 765 (4th Dept. 2000).

Line-up identification of non-suspect.—Defendant's Fourth Amendment rights were not violated by police who required him to stand in at a line-up involving a crime for which he was not a suspect and in which he was then identified as the perpetrator of a murder. People v. Whitaker, 64 N.Y.2d 347, 486 N.Y.S.2d 895, 476 N.E.2d 294 (1985).

Location.—Location alone does not justify police intrusion against citizens who happen to live, work, or travel in such "high crime areas." People v. Hampton, 200 A.D.2d 466, 606 N.Y.S.2d 628 (1st Dept. 1994).

Mere suspicion insufficient for arrest.—Detective's "belief" that watches and jewelry in a yellow nylon bag were stolen, even when combined with statements of defendant's companions that they saw him with the bag and saw him asking if anyone wanted to buy a watch, amounted to nothing more than mere suspicion and did not give probable cause for the defendant's arrest; statements made by the defendant following his improper arrest should have been suppressed. People v. Robinson, 100 A.D.2d 945, 474 N.Y.S.2d 836 (2d Dept. 1984).

Observation based on informant's report.—When the basis of the informant's knowledge is not given, personal police observation corroborative of data received from the informant should be regarded as sufficient only when the police observe facts suggestive of criminal activity. People v. Ilwell, 50 N.Y.2d 231, 428 N.Y.S.2d 655, 406 N.E.2d 471 (1980).

Payton.—The doorway to a private house is a public place for purposes of fourth amendment analysis, since a defendant has no legitimate expectation of privacy while standing there, exposed to public view. Since the defendant was arrested at the threshold of his residence, the defendant's arrest did not implicate *Payton* rights. People v. Reynoso, 309 A.D.2d 769, 765 N.Y.S.2d 54 (2d Dept. 2003), *aff'd,* 2 N.Y.3d 820, 781 N.Y.S.2d 284, 814 N.E.2d 456 (2004).

Plain view doctrine.—The Court of Appeals was without power of review where the trial court explicitly found on the basis of legally sufficient evidence that the items in question had been lying "in plain view" and had been found by the police purely by chance and that this factual determination was affirmed by the Appellate Division. People v. Martin, 50 N.Y.2d 1029, 431 N.Y.S.2d 689, 409 N.E.2d 1363 (1980).

—Observation by police officers, after they were admitted by defendant to his premises, of a revolver in plain view on his bed constituted probable cause to arrest defendant. People v. Phiefer, 43 N.Y.2d 719, 401 N.Y.S.2d 483, 372 N.E.2d 323 (1977).

—The officers were justified in seizing the coat and the other items revealed during the course of the seizure when they were lawfully in the hallway outside the defendant's room and observed through the open doorway of the room an item of clothing matching that described by the victim of the crime. People v. Jackson, 41 N.Y.2d 146, 391 N.Y.S.2d 82, 359 N.E.2d 677 (1976).

Probable cause to arrest.—The arrest and search was invalid where the officer arrested the defendant based on a teletype communication that there was an outstanding parole violation against the defendant when in fact there was none. People v. Jennings, 54 N.Y.2d 518, 446 N.Y.S.2d 229, 430 N.E.2d 1282 (1981).

—A probable cause determination involving mixed questions of law and fact is beyond the review powers of the Court of Appeals in those instances when conflicting inferences may be drawn from the record; whenever reasonable minds may differ as to the inferences which ultimately determine whether the arrest was justified, the Court of Appeals may not interfere with the affirmed findings of that court possessing authority to resolve the issues of fact. People v. Wharton, 46 N.Y.2d 924, 415 N.Y.S.2d 204, 338 N.E.2d 341 (1979).

—The question of "probable cause" is a mixed question of law and fact; determination of the facts and circumstances bearing on the issue, which hinges primarily on questions of witness credibility, is a question of fact; however, it is a question of law whether the facts found to exist are sufficient to constitute probable cause and where more than one inference may be drawn from the facts, the question of probable cause is primarily one of fact over which the Court of Appeals has limited powers of review. People v. Morales, 42 N.Y.2d 129, 397 N.Y.S.2d 587, 366 N.E.2d 248 (1977).

—There was unquestionable probable cause to arrest defendant where plainclothed police officers, unknown to defendant, observed him run back into a building and while following him up the stairs observed the barrel of a shotgun beneath his coat and then observed him throw the shotgun through a window onto a roof. People v. Simmons, 43 N.Y.2d 806, 402 N.Y.S.2d 391, 373 N.E.2d 285 (1977).

—Officer did not have probable cause to arrest defendants where, while observing one defendant open a small purse in his possession and take matches therefrom, the officer also saw either a glassine envelope or a Hershey bar in the purse since defendant's actions were susceptible of an innocent explanation. People v. Davis, 36 N.Y.2d 280, 367 N.Y.S.2d 256, 326 N.E.2d 818, *cert. denied,* 423 U.S. 376 (1975).

—The officer had probable cause to arrest defendant who had been accurately described and specifically located by an undisclosed informant of past reliability. After every other detail of informant's information had been verified the officer was warranted in believing that the remaining detail that defendant was in present possession of a drug, was also correct. Officer was warranted in thereupon finding probable cause in defendant's dropping to the ground a cigarette package—a known drug cover—when the arresting officer and two fellow officers stopped their car, jumped from it and started in defendant's direction. People v. Castro, 29 N.Y.2d 324, 327 N.Y.S.2d 632, 277 N.E.2d 654 (1971).

—Probable cause does not require proof beyond a reasonable doubt of the elements of the crime suspected by the police. People v. Marte, 295 A.D.2d 102, 747 N.Y.S.2d 74 (1st Dept. 2002).

—Officer had reasonable suspicion to stop and detain defendant for investigative purposes, after observing defendant exit and walk away from a car with an alarm that had just been activated, behavior that is contrary to the conduct of a person lawfully occupying or using the car. People v. Jones, 287 A.D.2d 300, 731 N.Y.S.2d 429 (1st Dept. 2001).

—The exchange of money is a much more important factor in establishing probable cause for arrest that evidence of a drug prone location and the officer's experience, which would become relevant in the absence of an exchange for money. People v. Carmona, 208 A.D.2d 369, 617 N.Y.S.2d 20 (1st Dept. 1994).

—Complainant's gesturing together with defendant's and co-defendant's flight led the arresting officer to believe that a crime had been committed, notwithstanding his inability to comprehend Spanish. People v. Casanas, 170 A.D.2d 257, 566 N.Y.S.2d 7 (1st Dept. 1991).

—De facto arrest of defendant occurred where defendant was stopped on a street by a detective who suspected him of having committed the crime at issue six days earlier, defendant was taken in a police car to the station, his wallet was thoroughly searched for identification, and he was not informed that he would be released if he were not arrested, he was also placed in a locked cell upon proclaiming his innocence. Since the arrest was not supported by probable cause, the subsequent showup identification by the complainant should have been suppressed and the complainant's in-court identification of defendant should not have been admitted since there was no pretrial independent source hearing. The error was not harmless, and the conviction was reversed. People v. Jackson, 286 A.D.2d 688, 729 N.Y.S.2d 783 (2d Dept. 2001).

—Officers had reasonable suspicion to stop a livery cab when they noticed the unusual, violent hand and upper body movements of its occupants, and had probable cause to arrest the defendant when they saw what appeared to be cocaine on the floor of the cab. People v. Brantley, 235 A.D.2d 546, 653 N.Y.S.2d 31 (2d Dept. 1997).

—Probable cause existed where defendant was observed by a department store security guard placing 15 boxes of flatware into a shopping bag and then exiting the store without paying for the merchandise. People v. Vega, 197 A.D.2d 552, 602 N.Y.S.2d 207 (2d Dept. 1993).

—The police had probable cause to arrest the defendant when they acted upon the sworn statement of an identified individual setting forth facts based on the affiant's personal observations, coupled with information from other individuals in the community which verified the reliability of the sworn statement. People v. Masi, 171 A.D.2d 760, 567 N.Y.S.2d 315 (2d Dept. 1991).

—Based upon the identification by the victim of the robbery, the police obtained probable cause to arrest. People v. Castillo, 158 A.D.2d 533, 551 N.Y.S.2d 300 (2d Dept. 1990).

—Unlike a paid or anonymous informant, an eyewitness-victim of a crime can provide probable cause for the arrest of his assailant despite the fact that his reliability has not been previously established or his information corroborated, the victim's reliability is assured because he can be prosecuted if his report is a fabrication. People v. Crespo, 70 A.D.2d 661, 417 N.Y.S.2d 19 (2d Dept. 1979).

—When the required probable cause is based on hearsay information from an informant, probable cause exists if it is determined that the informant has an adequate basis for the knowledge transmitted to the police and that such information is reliable. People v. Muir, 3 A.D.3d 597, 771 N.Y.S.2d 220 (3d Dept. 2004).

—Observation of baggies with white powder and glassine envelopes gave rise to probable cause. People v. Wolf, 160 A.D.2d 1076, 553 N.Y.S.2d 560 (3d Dept. 1990).

—Probable cause does not require proof beyond a reasonable doubt sufficient to warrant a conviction but merely information sufficient to support a reasonable belief that an offense has been or is being committed, or that evidence of a crime may be found in a certain place. People v. Flanders, 192 A.D.2d 1072, 596 N.Y.S.2d 227 (4th Dept. 1993); People v. Brockington, 166 A.D.2d 881, 560 N.Y.S.2d 540 (4th Dept. 1990).

—In the context of a "buy and bust" operation, an officer has probable cause to arrest a defendant where he relies "on information from another officer on the narcotics team who had personally witnessed the defendant commit the crime prior to the radio transmission." People v. Crespo, 189 A.D.2d 700, 592 N.Y.S.2d 717 (1st Dept. 1993).

—Since defendant failed to raise the issue of the warrantless arrest in her home in the lower court, the issue would not be reviewed on appeal for the first time. People v. Pettiway, 176 A.D.2d 1069, 575 N.Y.S.2d 380 (3d Dept. 1991).

Probable cause; search without arrest.—Existence of probable cause to arrest did not justify a full search of defendant when the arrest was not made until one month after the search. People v. Evans, 43 N.Y.2d 160, 400 N.Y.S.2d 810, 371 N.E.2d 528 (1977).

—An officer may only seize and take into custody an individual when the officer has probable cause to believe that the person has committed a crime. People v. Rosario, 202 A.D.2d 699, 609 N.Y.S.2d 316 (2d Dept. 1994).

—Victim's delay of 8 months before claiming she was raped by the defendant did not prevent finding of probable cause to arrest. Minott v. City of New York, 203 A.D.2d 265, 609 N.Y.S.2d 334 (2d Dept. 1994).

—Probable cause requires the existence of facts and circumstances which, when viewed together, would lead a reasonable person possessing the same expertise as the arresting officer to conclude that an offense has been or is being committed and that the person to be arrested is the perpetrator of the crime. People v. Pegram, 203 A.D.2d 391, 610 N.Y.S.2d 291 (2d Dept. 1994).

Probable cause; based on co-defendant's statements.— Probable cause for defendant's arrest was furnished by co-defendant's implication of defendant, co-defendant's ability to lead the police to the defendant and co-defendant's accurate description of defendant. People v. Berzups, 49 N.Y.2d 417, 426 N.Y.S.2d 253, 402 N.E.2d 1155 (1980).

—Sufficiently detailed statements regarding a homicide committed by the defendant given by an informant who incriminated himself in the same crime established the probable cause needed to justify the defendant's arrest. People v. Smith, 107 A.D.2d 633, 484 N.Y.S.2d 17 (1st Dept. 1985).

—Co-defendant's statements to the police and the prosecutor specifically implicated the defendant in the crime and provided probable cause for the defendant's arrest. People v. Rivera, 124 A.D.2d 611, 507 N.Y.S.2d 755 (2d Dept. 1986).

Probable cause for arrest; informant's tip.—Probable cause for the defendant's arrest was sufficient where an identified informant with no apparent motive to lie told the investigating officer that the crimes in question had been committed by the defendant and a named other person and that each other person had so informed the informant. People v. Murphy, 97 A.D.2d 873, 469 N.Y.S.2d 238 (3d Dept. 1983).

Glassine envelope.—Uniformed police officer, experienced in narcotics investigations, had probable cause to arrest defendant after he observed him holding a quantity of glassine envelopes in his hand and as he approached, defendant dropped or threw them away. People v. Alexander, 37 N.Y.2d 202, 371 N.Y.S.2d 876, 333 N.E.2d 157 (1975).

—No probable cause existed to arrest defendants when the arresting officer saw only containers appropriate to hold narcotics—of two types, glassine envelopes seen to be empty, and a folded bill not seen to contain anything. People v. Bryant, 37 N.Y.2d 208, 371 N.Y.S.2d 881, 333 N.E.2d 161 (1975).

Official police communication.—In making an arrest a police officer may rely upon information communicated to him by another police officer that an individual is the subject named in a warrant and should be taken into custody in the execution of the warrant. People v. Allen, 146 Misc. 2d 701, 550 N.Y.S.2d 997, 1003 (Seneca Co. Ct. 1990).

—Out-of-state official police communication, unsupported by background information, did not constitute probable cause unless there was additional verification of some form which tended to corroborate the initial facts. People v. Blackman, 81 Misc. 2d 12, 364 N.Y.S.2d 704 (Sup. Ct. Queens Co. 1975).

Not incident to arrest nor in plain view.—Suppression of the contraband seized in the apartment following defendant's arrest in the hallway outside the apartment was required since there was no evidence to suggest the presence of any other persons in the apartment to justify the search nor was the "plain view" exception applicable when the narcotics were found in the kitchen. People v. Fields, 45 N.Y.2d 986, 413 N.Y.S.2d 113, 385 N.E.2d 1041 (1978).

Probable cause for arrest and seizure not tainted by illegal search by police in another state where independent cause exists for such arrest.—In suppression proceedings, the N.Y. police's inspection, surveillance and arrest were not necessarily predicated wholly or in part on the results of the L.A. police's illegal search and seizure, but was preempted by the initial discovery made by airline employee, and the L.A. police had acted merely as a conduit through which to transmit his findings to the N.Y. police. People v. Reisman, 29 N.Y.2d 278, 327 N.Y.S.2d 342 (1971), cert. denied, 405 U.S. 1041 (1972).

Probable cause; information from another officer.— Police officer acts pursuant to probable cause if he arrests an individual on the direction of a fellow officer who has probable cause or he effects an arrest, without such direction, based on information received from a fellow officer and such information itself or together with that known to arresting police officer establishes probable cause. People v. Brnja, 50 N.Y.2d 366, 429 N.Y.S.2d 173, 406 N.E.2d 1066 (1980).

—It was not necessary for the arresting officer himself to have information sufficient for probable cause, when he arrested the defendant at the direction of another officer who had sufficient information to establish probable cause. People v. Loewel, 50 A.D.2d 483, 378 N.Y.S.2d 521 (4th Dept. 1976), aff'd, 41 N.Y.2d 609, 394 N.Y.S.2d 591, 363 N.E.2d 316 (1977).

Probable cause; information from another police department.—Probable cause for the warrantless arrest of the defendant for unlawful possession of marijuana existed where the Syracuse police received and verified information from the San Diego police that an experienced member of the San Diego department had observed brick shaped objects on the X-ray examination of the luggage and detected the odor of talcum powder coming from the bags. People v. Fritschler, 81 Misc. 2d 106, 364 N.Y.S.2d 801 (Sup. Ct. Onondaga Co. 1975).

Radio call sufficiently verified by personal observations of police.—Probable cause was furnished when the officer observed the defendant running with a gun in his hand from the gas station which had been robbed. People v. Gee, 143 A.D.2d 1039, 533 N.Y.S.2d 768 (2d Dept. 1988).

—Probable cause to arrest the defendant was established where the defendant matched the description relayed over the police radio and was observed standing in a bush counting money near the scene of the crime within 5 to 10 minutes after the occurrence. People v. Ridley, 124 A.D.2d 610, 507 N.Y.S.2d 753 (2d Dept. 1986).

—Police officers were justified in detaining the defendant on the basis of a radio call based upon an anonymous tip and describing two black males with guns, one wearing a blue jacket and the other a black jacket, which description was verified by the officers' personal observations within minutes of the call. People v. Belk, 100 A.D.2d 908, 474 N.Y.S.2d 564 (2d Dept. 1984).

Search; arrest without a warrant; close pursuit; out-of-state.—Where defendants were arrested after pre-arranged narcotic transaction involving large quantity of narcotics and auto chase through Lincoln Tunnel, search of auto without warrant was not illegal and recovered evidence would not be suppressed, even though arresting officers in close pursuit brought defendants to New York for arraignment instead of to a New Jersey magistrate in accordance with New Jersey statute. People v. Junco, 70 Misc. 2d 73, 333 N.Y.S.2d 142 (Sup. Ct. N.Y. Co. 1972).

Search and seizure; probable cause.—The arrest and subsequent search of defendant was lawful and the weapon was not produced as a result of unlawful police action, where the defendant shortly after entering the police vehicle at the request of the detectives, who were investigating a homicide, reached down about his waist and threw a gun through the car window while the vehicle was moving. People v. Boodle, 62 A.D.2d 966, 404 N.Y.S.2d 598 (1st Dept. 1978), aff'd, 47 N.Y.2d 398, 418 N.Y.S.2d 352, 391 N.E.2d 1329, cert. denied, 444 U.S. 969 (1979).

—Where defendant was arrested and searched on insufficient probable cause, the fact that the search was successful in producing contraband did not vitiate the unlawfulness of the arrest. People v. Martin, 32 N.Y.2d 123, 343 N.Y.S.2d 343 (1973); People v. Bruno, 45 A.D.2d 1025, 358 N.Y.S.2d 183 (2d Dept. 1974).

Search and seizure; probable cause; motion to suppress.—Where the police observed the defendant in the company of two other persons at the time of an apparent narcotics transaction between said persons, but defendant himself was engaged in no overt criminal activity, this did not give sufficient probable cause to arrest the defendant, and subsequent search of defendant which produced dangerous drugs was therefore unjustified and should have been suppressed. People v. Martin, 32 N.Y.2d 123, 343 N.Y.S.2d 343, 296 N.E.2d 245 (1973).

—Minimal intrusion of calling defendant over to police car without reasonable suspicion, did not taint the retrieval of a jacket which the defendant afterwards abandoned. People v. Hogya, 80 A.D.2d 621, 436 N.Y.S.2d 62 (2d Dept. 1981).

Search and seizure; warrantless search not incident to arrest.—The seized imitation pistol was suppressed where, after defendant was arrested and handcuffed in the hallway adjoining the door of his apartment or immediately inside the door in the foyer, the police, without a warrant, proceeded to search defendant's living room and bedroom seeking a stolen television set and found the imitation pistol similar to that used in the robbery lying in "plain view" in a partially open dresser drawer. People v. Bryant, 37 N.Y.2d 206, 371 N.Y.S.2d 880, 333 N.E.2d 160 (1975).

—Where police made warrantless search of car and discovered container of marijuana subsequent to chase and capture of defendant for possession of lone marijuana cigarette, denial of motion to suppress marijuana was error since police controlled trunk and handcuffed arrestees, and there was ample chance to secure warrant and no basis for believing that anything connected with arrests or of any violation was in trunk. People v. Kreichman, 45 A.D.2d 697, 357 N.Y.S.2d 82 (1st Dept. 1974).

Search incident to arrest.—Search of knapsack as search incident to arrest was improper, since defendant was subdued and knapsack was no longer in his control. People v. Chisolm, 7 A.D.3d 728, 777 N.Y.S.2d 502 (2d Dept. 2004).

Search without warrant; fire marshals.—The evidence gathered by the fire marshals was properly admitted where the fire marshals were summoned to fire scene by the firefighters combating the blaze but did not arrive until four hours later when the fire had been extinguished. People v. Calhoun, 49 N.Y.2d 398, 426 N.Y.S.2d 243, 402 N.E.2d 1145 (1980).

Automobile search.—The search of defendant's person and his automobile was not justified when the officers stopped his vehicle in order to give him a warning after they had observed him driving through a red light. People v. Erwin, 42 N.Y.2d 1064, 399 N.Y.S.2d 637, 369 N.E.2d 1170 (1977).

—The physical evidence seized was suppressed since the record disclosed no more than "mere whim, caprice, or idle curiosity" for the stop of defendant's automobile. People v. Simone, 39 N.Y.2d 818, 385 N.Y.S.2d 765, 351 N.E.2d 432 (1976).

—Police observation of a passenger, in possession of what they reasonably believed to be a marijuana cigarette, in an automobile driven by defendant, coupled with defendant's refusal to stop and high speed flight through the city streets; the subsequent flight by the passenger from the stopped automobile; and later finding of hand rolled cigarette in his possession; warranted a reasonable belief that the automobile contained additional contraband of some kind and constituted probable cause to search the vehicle. People v. Kreichman, 37 N.Y.2d 693, 376 N.Y.S.2d 497, 339 N.E.2d 182 (1975).

—While an interstate police bulletin alone can furnish probable cause for a warrantless motor vehicle search, the presumption of probable cause that originally cloaked the action disappears where a motion to suppress is made and the People must demonstrate that the sender or sending agency itself possessed the requisite probable cause to act. People v. Lypka, 36 N.Y.2d 210, 366 N.Y.S.2d 622, 326 N.E.2d 294 (1975).

—Warrantless search was proper where automobile registered in name of wife of person whom police had been informed was engaged in a series of burglaries of elderly persons' homes was found near scene of similar burglary and burglary tools were in plain view through windows of auto. Accordingly, prompt search was necessary to establish or confirm identity of burglars in order to aid in their apprehension before they escaped area. People v. Singletary, 30 N.Y.2d 528, 364 N.Y.S.2d 435, 324 N.E.2d 103 (1974).

—Because of the innocuous nature of the pestle, a club-like cooking utensil, which was under the driver's seat of defendant's car, the police did not have the requisite probable cause to arrest and search defendant, and the drugs should have been suppressed. People v. Buhagiar, 185 Misc. 2d 203, 713 N.Y.S.2d 114 (App. Term, 2d Dept. 2000).

—Search of an automobile and its driver was proper where officers, with extensive experience and training in marijuana detection, stopped vehicle for traffic violation and then noted odor of the drug emanating from the car. People v. Chestnut, 43 A.D.2d 260, 351 N.Y.S.2d 26 (3d Dept. 1974), aff'd, 36 N.Y.2d 971, 373 N.Y.S.2d 564, 335 N.E.2d 865 (1975).

—Where the defendant was arrested for a traffic violation and gave an unsatisfactory explanation for the possession of a rented vehicle, and ammunition and burglar tools were found during a lawful search after arrest, a further search of the entire vehicle was justified. People v. McLaughlin, 48 A.D.2d 722, 367 N.Y.S.2d 362 (3d Dept. 1975).

—If exigent circumstances exist when a vehicle is first seized, a later search, not too removed in time from the seizure, is proper even though no exigent circumstances might exist thereafter. People v. Hartford, 50 A.D.2d 1054, 377 N.Y.S.2d 712 (3d Dept. 1975).

Inventory of vehicle contents following arrest.—The People failed to show that the search of the glove compartment box was a proper inventory search. An inventory search should be conducted pursuant to an established procedure clearly limiting the conduct of individual officers that assures that the searches are carried out consistently and reasonably. People v. Johnson, 1 N.Y.3d 252, 771 N.Y.S.2d 64, 803 N.E.2d 385 (2003).

—The warrantless search of defendant's automobile was proper where defendant was apprehended in the act of burglarizing a store in a shopping center after midnight and had in his possession the keys to the automobile in question, which was the only car parked in the lot not belonging to one of the stores and was hidden behind a truck; having established a nexus between the crime and the car itself, it was obvious that the vehicle could very well have concealed stolen property, burglar tools or criminal instrumentalities. People v. Clark, 45 N.Y.2d 432, 408 N.Y.S.2d 463, 380 N.E.2d 290 (1978).

—The vehicle search was valid when conducted after lawful arrest of defendant and pursuant standard police procedure to inventory the contents of auto, and the items discovered were properly admissible as evidence. People v. Butter, 44 A.D.2d 423, 355 N.Y.S.2d 172 (2d Dept. 1974), aff'd, 36 N.Y.2d 990, 374 N.Y.S.2d 604, 337 N.E.2d 120 (1975).

—Even where impoundment of an automobile is lawful, the evidence seized during an inventory search is admissible at trial only if the inventory search was conducted according to standardized criteria or established routine procedures. People v. Miles, 3 Misc. 3d 566, 774 N.Y.S.2d 647 (City Ct. City of Rochester 2003).

Search and seizure where routine inspection of car finds marijuana in plain view.—Initial decision to impound vehicle was proper because the defendant, the driver and sole occupant of the vehicle, did not have a valid license, and when the officer leaned into the car to begin an inventory search, he detected the odor of marihuana, which gave the officer probable cause to believe the vehicle might contain drugs, justifying a search of the vehicle and its contents. People v. Figueroa, 6 A.D.3d 720, 776 N.Y.S.2d 574 (2d Dept. 2004).

—Police officers have a right to rely upon information furnished by private citizens who report crimes that they have witnesses or were perpetrated against them. People v. Cunningham, 135 A.D.2d 725, 522 N.Y.S.2d 626 (2d Dept. 1987).

—The contents of the carton were suppressed where the police, acting on information, stopped a vehicle, and after arresting the driver obtained the keys to the trunk and upon observing a sealed carton proceeded to open it and found marijuana since there could have been no reasonable belief that the carton would be removed or destroyed by the driver or anyone else, or that the contents presented any danger to the arresting officer. People v. Spencer, 74 A.D.2d 77, 426 N.Y.S.2d 605 (4th Dept. 1980).

Sufficiency of teletype communication to support arrest.—Probable cause for arrest was not shown where police made an arrest pursuant to a teletype communication, but no evidence was presented as to any physical description of a suspect contained in such communication; although the information contained in the teletype may be assumed by the arresting officer to be reliable, there is no presumption as to its sufficiency. People v. Dodt, 61 N.Y.2d 408, 474 N.Y.S.2d 441, 462 N.E.2d 1159 (1984).

Traffic infraction.—After traffic violation, police were justified in stopping minivan in which defendant was a passenger; police were justified in chasing defendant, who exited quickly after the lawful stop, and began grasping his waist area; police were justified in pursuing defendant and recovery of weapons was lawful. People v. Rivera, 286 A.D.2d 235, 729 N.Y.S.2d 481 (1st Dept. 2001).

—Court could discern no reason why the police, out of safety concerns, should be prevented from requiring the driver and/or passengers to remain in the car until a valid traffic stop is over. People v. Yates, 307 A.D.2d 593, 762 N.Y.S.2d 452 (3d Dept. 2003), aff'd, 3 N.Y.3d 625, 782 N.Y.S.2d 395, 816 N.E.2d 184 (2004).

—Under CPL § 140.10(1)(a) and VTL § 155, a police officer may arrest a person for a traffic infraction if it is committed in his presence. People v. Vierno, 159 Misc. 2d 770, 606 N.Y.S.2d 557 (Crim. Ct. Richmond Co. 1993).

Wanted poster; defendant's resemblance.—Based on defendant's resemblance to an individual in a wanted poster, the police had the right to approach him to request information. Defendant's subsequent flight when officers asked if they could speak to him provided reasonable suspicion to pursue and stop him, and his abandonment of a weapon during the chase provided probable cause to arrest. People v. Wilson, 5 A.D.3d 408, 773 N.Y.S.2d 95 (2d Dept. 2004).

Warrantless arrest; waiver.—The issue was waived when defendant failed to raise before the suppression court the claim that physical evidence should have been suppressed because his warrantless arrest was effectuated in his home in the absence of exigent circumstances. People v. Roache, 105 A.D.2d 811, 481 N.Y.S.2d 442 (2d Dept. 1984).

Warrantless arrest in defendant's home required suppression of evidence seized.—Defendant's arrest within his home, without an arrest or search warrant and in the absence of exigent circumstances, was violative of the Fourth Amendment and required that evidence seized pursuant to such arrest be suppressed. People v. Burden, 99 A.D.2d 552, 471 N.Y.S.2d 638 (2d Dept. 1984).

Warrantless search and arrest; lack of probable cause.—Incidence of high crime in neighborhood is relevant circumstance in determining probable cause but passing of glassine envelope observed by police at a distance in high-crime neighborhood is insufficient to establish probable cause. People v. Oden, 36 N.Y.2d 382, 368 N.Y.S.2d 508, 329 N.E.2d 188 (1975).

—Having no basis to credit the informant's tip, either by the informant's statement as to how he obtained his information or by their own independent observations, the police lacked probable cause to arrest defendant and the conviction was reversed. People v. West, 44 N.Y.2d 656, 405 N.Y.S.2d 29, 376 N.E.2d 190 (1978).

White envelope.—There was probable cause to arrest the defendant when experienced police officers saw the passing to the defendant of two white envelopes and also observed three other suspicious transactions in which there was an exchange of currency at a location known for drug trafficking. People v. Brown, 124 A.D.2d 592, 507 N.Y.S.2d 736 (2d Dept. 1986).

§ 140.15. Arrest without a warrant; when and how made by police officer.

1. A police officer may arrest a person for an offense, pursuant to section 140.10, at any hour of any day or night.

2. The arresting police officer must inform such person of his authority and purpose and of the reason for such arrest unless he encounters physical resistance, flight or other factors rendering such procedure impractical.

3. In order to effect such an arrest, such police officer may use such physical force as is justifiable pursuant to section 35.30 of the penal law.

4. In order to effect such an arrest, a police officer may enter premises in which he reasonably believes such person to be present, under the same circumstances and in the same manner as would be authorized, by the provisions of subdivisions four and five of section 120.80, if he were attempting to make such arrest pursuant to a warrant of arrest.

ANNOTATIONS

Pre-*Miranda* statements.—Defendant's statements before receiving *Miranda* warnings were spontaneous, not subject to suppression as product of police interrogation or its functional equivalent, where there was no evidence that arresting officer's statement to defendant advising him of reason for his arrest was reasonably likely to evoke incriminating response. People v. Hylton, 198 A.D.2d 301, 603 N.Y.S.2d 560 (2d Dept. 1993).

Falsehood by police.—Falsehood by police violated the statutory requirements of CPL § 140.15(2). But a statutory, as opposed to a constitutional, violation, does not itself trigger suppression. People v. Henry, 185 A.D.2d 1, 591 N.Y.S.2d 1018 (1st Dept. 1992).

Use of handcuffs.—Officer was justified in using handcuffs to protect safety of others and bystanders, and this does not necessarily constitute arrest. People v. Foster, 85 N.Y.2d 1012, 630 N.Y.S.2d 968, 654 N.E.2d 1216 (1995).

Arrest without warrant; probable cause; search without warrant.—On the basis of disclosures by defendant's wife, and a house search, the police had probable cause to arrest defendant resting on a reasonable belief that he had committed a misdemeanor, namely, possession of a contraband sawed-off shotgun. People v. Scull, 37 N.Y.2d 838, 378 N.Y.S.2d 30, 340 N.E.2d 466 (1975).

—Where after 3-4 week surveillance police obtained warrant to search premises for heroin traffic and premises appeared hastily vacated, the search of another premises designated by informants as new operation quarters of defendants was justified and seizure of heroin and paraphernalia in plain view did not violate Constitutional Limitations. People v. Cage, 40, A.D.2d 234, 339 N.Y.S.2d 6 (3d Dept. 1972).

Police officer's use of binoculars.—There was probable cause to arrest defendant and seize 29 glassine envelopes with heroin by the back-up team when they were advised by fellow officers to make the arrest after a fellow officer on a rooftop, who had narcotics experience, used binoculars to watch defendant in the street and saw him pass glassine envelopes to three different people and receive U.S. currency in exchange within a half-hour period. People v. Maxwell, 51 A.D.2d 922, 381 N.Y.S.2d 86 (1st Dept. 1976).

Of apartment following gun battle.—Where a gun battle with police had gone on for twenty minutes prior to their entry of apartment and upon entering police observed eight people and various types of armaments and ammunition as well as three pounds of narcotics, it was proper for the police to search the entire apartment and to open and inspect a suitcase found under a bed. People v. Sturgis, 76 Misc. 2d 1053, 352 N.Y.S.2d 942 (Sup. Ct. N.Y. Co. 1973).

Detentive stop of auto.—Officers had reasonable suspicion to make a detentive stop and question defendants when in a neighborhood where daytime burglaries were frequent they observed defendants walking in a furtive manner carrying a plastic bag to a rented auto where they opened the bag and removed identification papers, credit cards, a jewelry box, calculator, and an electric razor; there was probable cause to arrest defendants when defendants gave evasive, inconsistent, and incorrect answers to their questions. People v. Thurman, 81 A.D.2d 548, 438 N.Y.S.2d 312 (1st Dept. 1981).

What constitutes.—Mere fact that a suspect is handcuffed does not mean that he has been arrested. People v. Allen, 73 N.Y.2d 378, 540 N.Y.S.2d 971, 972, 538 N.E.2d 323 (1988).

—Detention of defendant constituted a lawful investigatory stop, rather than an arrest, where the defendant, without objection, was merely transported by police to the crime scene for purposes of a showup and he was not handcuffed at the time and there was no evidence that the police had their guns drawn at any point. People v. Hicks, 68 N.Y.2d 234, 508 N.Y.S.2d 163, 500 N.E.2d 163 (1986).

—Where defendant was handcuffed and placed in a patrol car, despite his prior indication that he would voluntarily accompany the detectives to the precinct, he was seized within the meaning of the Fourth Amendment. People v. Marrero, 152 A.D.2d 746, 544 N.Y.S.2d 198 (2d Dept. 1989).

—The exhibition of a police officer's badge and his identification of himself as a police officer does not constitute an arrest. In re B., 45 A.D.2d 724, 356 N.Y.S.2d 344 (2d Dept. 1974).

Indictment dismissed; police gained entry by ruse.—Conviction for illegal possession of dangerous drugs was reversed and indictment dismissed because the search and arrest violated defendant's constitutional rights in that police obtained entry into apartment by false representation that they were police officers investigating a gas leak. People v. Jefferson, 43 A.D.2d 112, 350 N.Y.S.2d 3 (1st Dept. 1973).

Payton.—No *Payton* issue is presented where the defendant is arrested outside of the home. People v. Roe, 73 N.Y.2d 1004, 541 N.Y.S.2d 759, 760, 539 N.E.2d 587 (1989).

—There is no authority that requires an arrest warrant where a person is arrested in his place of business. People v. Linden, 142 Misc. 2d 964, 539 N.Y.S.2d 279 (Sup. Ct. N.Y. Co. 1989).

Retroactivity of *Payton v. New York.*—The rule enunciated by the Supreme Court in *Payton v. New York,* 445 U.S. 73, 100 S. Ct. 1371, 63 L. Ed. 2d 639, is not to be applied retroactively. People v. Delgaizo, 81 A.D.2d 548, 444 N.Y.S.2d 368 (3d Dept. 1981).

Search and seizure; motion to suppress.—Defendant's failure to raise the issue within the context of his initial motion to suppress that a weapon found in his home should have been suppressed because his arrest was effectuated without a warrant and in the absence of exigent circumstances resulted in a failure to preserve the issue for appellate review. People v. Gonzales, 55 N.Y.2d 887, 449 N.Y.S.2d 18, 433 N.E.2d 1266 (1982).

—Motion to suppress was granted where the police knew only that a person entered the apartment with marked money and departed without it, but they did not know whether he had obtained the drugs found on him at the time of his arrest from the apartment or whether he had the drugs before entering; they did not know whether the defendant was in the apartment or actually lived there; or whether the defendant had engaged in the sale of narcotics at all. People v. Laskaris, 82 A.D.2d 34, 441 N.Y.S.2d 110 (2d Dept. 1981).

§ 140.20. Arrest without a warrant; procedure after arrest by police officer.

1. Upon arresting a person without a warrant, a police officer, after performing without unnecessary delay all recording, fingerprinting and other preliminary police duties required in the particular case, must except as otherwise provided in this section, without unnecessary delay bring the arrested person or cause him to be brought before a local criminal court and file therewith an appropriate accusatory instrument charging him with the offense or offenses in question. The arrested person must be brought to the particular local criminal court, or to one of them if there be more than one, designated in section 100.55 as an appropriate court for commencement of the particular action; except that:

(a) If the arrest is for an offense other than a class A, B, C or D felony or a violation of section 130.25, 130.40, 205.10, 205.17, 205.19 or 215.56 of the penal law committed in a town, but not in a village thereof having a village court, and the town court of such town is not available at the time, the arrested person may be brought before the local criminal court of any village within such town or, any adjoining town, village embraced in whole or in part by such adjoining town, or city of the same county; and

(b) If the arrest is for an offense other than a class A, B, C or D felony or a violation of section 130.25, 130.40, 205.10, 205.17, 205.19 or 215.56 of the penal law committed in a village having a village court and such court is not available at the time, the arrested person may be brought before the town court of the town embracing such village or any other village court within such town, or, if such town or village court is not available either, before the local criminal court of any adjoining town, village embraced in whole or in part by such adjoining town, or city of the same county; and

(c) If the arrest is for an offense committed in a city, and the city court thereof is not available at the time, the arrested person may be brought before the local criminal court of any adjoining town or village, or village court embraced by an adjoining town, within the same county as such city; and

(d) If the arrest is for a traffic infraction or for a misdemeanor relating to traffic, the police officer may, instead of bringing the arrested person before the local criminal court of the political subdivision or locality in which the offense was allegedly committed, bring him before the local criminal court of the same county nearest available by highway travel to the point of arrest.

2. If the arrest is for an offense other than a class A, B, C or D felony or a violation of section 130.25, 130.40, 205.10, 205.17, 205.19 or 215.56 of the penal law, the arrested person need not be brought before a local criminal court as provided in subdivision one, and the procedure may instead be as follows:

(a) A police officer may issue and serve an appearance ticket upon the arrested person and release him from custody, as prescribed in subdivision two of section 150.20; or

(b) The desk officer in charge at a police station, county jail or police headquarters, or any of his superior officers, may, in such place fix pre-arraignment bail and, upon deposit thereof, issue and serve an appearance ticket upon the arrested person and release him from custody, as prescribed in section 150.30.

3. If (a) the arrest is for an offense other than a class A, B, C or D felony or a violation of section 130.25, 130.40, 205.10, 205.17, 205.19 or 215.56 of the penal law, and (b) owing to unavailability of a local criminal court the arresting police officer is unable to bring the arrested person before such a court with reasonable promptness, either an appearance ticket must be served unconditionally upon the arrested person or pre-arraignment bail must be fixed, as prescribed in subdivision two. If pre-arraignment bail is fixed but not posted, such arrested person may be temporarily held in custody but must be brought before a local criminal court without unnecessary delay. Nothing contained in this subdivision requires a police officer to serve an appearance ticket upon an arrested person or release him from custody at a time when such person appears to be under the influence of alcohol, narcotics or other drug to the degree that he may endanger himself or other persons.

4. If after arresting a person, for any offense, a police officer upon further investigation or inquiry determines or is satisfied that there is not reasonable cause to believe that the arrested person committed such offense or any other offense based upon the conduct in question, he need not follow any of the procedures prescribed in subdivisions one, two and three, but must immediately release such person from custody.

5. Before service of an appearance ticket upon an arrested person pursuant to subdivision two or three, the issuing police officer must, if the offense designated in such appearance ticket is one of those specified in subdivision one of section 160.10, cause such person to be fingerprinted in the same manner as would be required were no appearance ticket to be issued or served.

6. Upon arresting a juvenile offender without a warrant, the police officer shall immediately notify the parent or other person legally responsible for his care or the person with whom he is domiciled, that the juvenile offender has been arrested, and the location of the facility where he is being detained.

Amended by L. 1971, Ch. 762; L. 1979, Ch. 411; L. 1984, Ch. 695; L. 1986, Ch. 5; L. 1987, Ch. 382; L. 1987, Chs. 549, 550; L. 1988, Ch. 324.

ANNOTATIONS

Arrest; dismissal of accusatory instrument.—The making of an "on the scene" arrest for driving while intoxicated and the subsequent filing of simplified informations pertaining thereto were two separate and distinct legal matters. While the later dismissal of the simplified informations halted the criminal action it had no effect upon the defendant's prior arrest since he was not discharged and the court retained jurisdiction over him pending the filing of the long form informations. People v. Bock, 77 Misc. 2d 350, 353 N.Y.S.2d 647 (Broome Co. Ct. 1974).

Body cavity search incident to arrest.—A warrantless body cavity search made incident to arrest is valid only if the People satisfy the requirements of Schmerber v. California, 384 U.S. 757, 86 S. Ct. 1826, 16 L. Ed. 2d 908 (1966). People v. Barnville, 7 Misc. 3d 688, 794 N.Y.S.2d 847 (Sup. Ct. Bronx Co. 2005).

Defendant over 16 years old.—Inasmuch as defendant was over 16 years old, the police had no duty to contact his legal guardian. People v. Morales, 228 A.D.2d 525, 644 N.Y.2d 303 (2d Dept. 1996).

Juvenile defendant misrepresents identity or age.— Hearing court properly declined to suppress defendant's confession under CPL § 140.20(6), where defendant's own deception that he was 17 years old, rather than his true age of 15, supplied police with lawful basis to question him without parental or guardian notification as long as adult protections of *Miranda* warnings were provided. People v. Wilson, 254 A.D.2d 316, 680 N.Y.S.2d 255 (2d Dept. 1998).

—CPL § 140.20(6) requires that when a juvenile offender is arrested without a warrant, the parent or guardian of the juvenile must be notified of the arrest; however, when the defendant misrepresents his identity and address, as in this case, the police cannot be found in dereliction of their duty under the statute. People v. Abiodun "L," 241 A.D.2d 774, 660 N.Y.S.2d 761 (3d Dept. 1997).

No suppression of defendant's statements.—Interrogating officers' statement at *Huntley* hearing that reason defendant was not taken for arraignment at 9:30 a.m. following his arrest in connection with stabbing death of former girlfriend was that police "wanted to talk to him" did not establish that arraignment was postponed for sole purpose of depriving defendant of right to counsel and that "unnecessary delay" required suppression of defendant's incriminating statements. People v. Ortlieb, 84 N.Y.2d 989, 622 N.Y.S.2d 501, 646 N.E.2d 803 (1994).

Prearraignment delay; waiver of claim.—While an unwarranted period of prearraignment delay can be a factor in assessing whether a confession was voluntary, a claimed violation of CPL § 140.20(1) must be raised at the trial level in order to afford the People an opportunity to put forth other reasons for the alleged delay in arraignment. People v. Seeber, 4 A.D.3d 620, 772 N.Y.S.2d 122 (3d Dept. 2004).

Prompt arraignment statute.—A delay in arraignment for the purpose of further police questioning does not establish a deprivation of the state constitutional right to counsel—the delay in arraignment claim must instead be advanced under CPL § 140.20(1). Defendant has not stated a valid right to counsel claim but rather asserts a violation of the prompt arraignment statute (CPL § 140.20), which must be preserved for appellate review. Defendant's failure to do so renders his claim unreviewable. People v. Ramos, 99 N.Y.2d 27, 750 N.Y.S.2d 821, 780 N.E.2d 506 (2002).

§ 140.25. Arrest without a warrant; by peace officer.

1. A peace officer, acting pursuant to his special duties, may arrest a person for:

(a) Any offense when he has reasonable cause to believe that such person has committed such offense in his presence; and

(b) A crime when he has reasonable cause to believe that such person has committed such crime, whether in his presence or otherwise.

2. A peace officer acts "pursuant to his special duties" in making an arrest only when the arrest is for:

(a) An offense defined by a statute which such

peace officer, by reason of the specialized nature of his particular employment or by express provision of law, is required or authorized to enforce; or

(b) An offense committed or reasonably believed by him to have been committed in such manner or place as to render arrest of the offender by such peace officer under the particular circumstances an integral part of his specialized duties.

3. A peace officer, whether or not he is acting pursuant to his special duties, may arrest a person for an offense committed or believed by him to have been committed within the geographical area of such peace officer's employment, as follows:

(a) He may arrest such person for any offense when such person has in fact committed such offense in his presence; and

(b) He may arrest such person for a felony when he has reasonable cause to believe that such person has committed such felony, whether in his presence or otherwise.

4. A peace officer, when outside the geographical area of his employment, may, anywhere in the state, arrest a person for a felony when he has reasonable cause to believe that such person has there committed such felony in his presence, provided that such arrest is made during or immediately after the allegedly criminal conduct or during the alleged perpetrator's immediate flight therefrom.

5. For the purposes of this section, the "geographical area of employment" of a peace officer is as follows:

(a) The "geographical area of employment" of any peace officer employed as such by any agency of the state consists of the entire state;

(b) The "geographical area of employment" of any peace officer employed as such by an agency of a county, city, town or village consists of (i) such county, city, town or village, as the case may be, and (ii) any other place where he is, at a particular time, acting in the course of his particular duties or employment;

(c) The "geographical area of employment" of any peace officer employed as such by any private organization consists of any place in the state where he is, at a particular time, acting in the course of his particular duties or employment.

Amended by L. 1980, Ch. 843.

ANNOTATIONS

Peace officers.—Because the alleged traffic infractions and the seizure of the defendant occurred outside the geographical jurisdiction of the housing authority peace officers, there was no authority for the peace officers to apprehend defendant, and the Court rejected the People's assertion that the stop was a valid citizen's arrest. People v. Williams, 4 N.Y.3d 535, 797 N.Y.S.2d 35, 829 N.E.2d 1203 (2005).

—Parole officer is a peace officer. People v. Dyla, 142 A.D.2d 423, 536 N.Y.S.2d 799 (2d Dept. 1988).

—Officer may make arrest outside his presence for a

misdemeanor. Brown v. Roland, 215 A.D.2d 1000, 627 N.Y.S.2d 791 (3d Dept. 1995).

—Auxiliary police have no arrest powers beyond that of private citizens, but a detainment by such an officer will constitute an arrest. People v. Rotger, 162 Misc. 2d 459, 617 N.Y.S.2d 425 (Bronx Co. Crim. Ct. 1994).

—Federal officer is a peace officer. People v. Nezaj, 139 Misc. 2d 366, 528 N.Y.2d 491 (Sup. Ct. Bronx Co. 1988).

Customs agent.—Although search of flight bag and interior of the car by custom officers at Kennedy Airport was proper, a gun found in the trunk of the auto was suppressed, since officers did not have reasonable suspicion that the trunk contained any dutiable merchandise. People v. Briedenback, 90 Misc. 2d 213 393 N.Y.S.2d 855 (Sup. Ct. Queens Co. 1977).

—If there is no proximity to the border, absent other factors, a Customs Agent stands on equal footing with any other law enforcement agent and needs probable cause to conduct a search. People v. Scoffa, 81 Misc. 2d 17, 365 N.Y.S.2d 475 (Crim. Ct. Queens Co. 1975).

Search; arrest without a warrant; close pursuit.—Where defendants were arrested after pre-arranged narcotic transaction involving large quantity of narcotics and auto chase through Lincoln Tunnel, search of auto without warrant was not illegal and recovered evidence would not be suppressed, even though arresting officers in close pursuit brought defendants to New York for arraignment instead of to a New Jersey magistrate in accordance with Jersey statute. People v. Junco, 70 Misc. 2d 73, 333 N.Y.S.2d 142 (Sup Ct. N.Y. Co. 1972).

Search and seizure; probable cause; warrantless arrest.—Defendant's conviction was affirmed where knowledge on the part of police officer that an armed robbery had recently taken place in the vicinity during which the perpetrators exchanged gunfire with the police, coupled with his confrontation within a few minutes with the defendant in a crouching position and hiding in the corner of a dark room in a nearby abandoned building, after following fresh footprints leading from the scene of the robbery, and the discovery of the weapon on the defendant, was sufficient probable cause to believe that a crime had been committed and defendant was one of the perpetrators. People v. Egrant, 83 A.D.2d 277, 443 N.Y.S.2d 878 (2d Dept. 1981).

Search and seizure; motion to suppress.—It was reversible error for the trial court to deny defendant's motion to suppress where after he had been handcuffed and placed in the police car, police searched his vehicle and found contraband. People v. Williamson, 81 A.D.2d 962, 439 N.Y.S.2d 752 (3d Dept. 1981).

Offense; crime; inquiry.—Harassment, one of the lesser offenses designated a "violation," falls within the generic term "offense," and conviction for harassment was therefore a proper subject of inquiry during trial. If the legislature had intended a different result, it merely had to use the word "crime." People v. Gray, 41 A.D.2d 125, 341 N.Y.S.2d 485 (3d Dept. 1973), aff'd, 34 N.Y.2d 903, 359 N.Y.S.2d 286, 316 N.E.2d 719, cert. denied, 419 U.S. 1055 (1974).

Border search.—Search conducted by a Customs Patrol Officer at Brooklyn pier was a "border search." People v. Mason, 50 A.D.2d 804, 375 N.Y.S.2d 405 (2d Dept. 1975).

Special state investigators; untaxed cigarettes.—Case remanded and testimony of investigator for the State Special Investigation Bureau held incredible where he claimed that probable cause for the arrest arose when, as he passed defendant on the street, he observed through a tear in a carton in an open bag defendant was carrying that the cigarettes therein did not contain tax stamps. People v. Garafolo, 44 A.D.2d 86, 353 N.Y.S.2d 500 (2d Dept. 1974).

—Visual surveillance of customers, who were in a closed fitting room by a "Special Patrolman," licensed by the Police Commissioner, for Gimbel's Department Store, constituted an unreasonable search within the meaning of the Fourth Amendment. People v. Diaz, 85 Misc. 2d 41, 376 N.Y.S.2d 849 (Crim. Ct. N.Y.C. 1975).

—Special Investigator for the State of New York did not have probable cause to arrest for possession of untaxed cigarettes where arrest was made on private property and he did not look into any of the packages or question defendant concerning the contents prior to the arrest. People v. Dwyer, 76 Misc. 2d 401, 351 N.Y.S.2d 297 (Sup Ct. Kings Co. 1973), aff'd, 48 A.D.2d 664, 371 N.Y.S.2d 375 (1975).

§ 140.27. Arrest without a warrant; when and how made; procedure after arrest by peace officer.

1. The rules governing the manner in which a peace officer may make an arrest, pursuant to section 140.25, are the same as those governing arrests by police officers, as prescribed in section 140.15.

2. Upon arresting a person without a warrant, a peace officer, except as otherwise provided in subdivision three, must without unnecessary delay bring him or cause him to be brought before a local criminal court, as provided in section 100.55 and subdivision one of section 140.20, and must without unnecessary delay file or cause to be filed therewith an appropriate accusatory instrument. If the offense which is the subject of the arrest is one of those specified in subdivision one of section 160.10, the arrested person must be fingerprinted and photographed as therein provided. In order to execute the required post-arrest functions, such arresting peace officer may perform such functions himself or he may enlist the aid of a police officer for the performance thereof in the manner provided in subdivision one of section 140.20.

3. If (a) the arrest is for an offense other than a class A, B, C or D felony or a violation of section 130.25, 130.40, 205.10, 205.17, 205.19 or 215.56 of the penal law and (b) owing to unavailability of a local criminal court such peace officer is unable to bring or cause the arrested person to be brought before such a court with reasonable promptness, the arrested person must be brought to an appropriate police station, county jail or police headquarters where he must be dealt with in the manner prescribed in subdivision three of section 140.20, as if he had been arrested by a police officer.

4. If the arrest is for an offense other than a class A, B, C or D felony or a violation of section 130.25, 130.40, 205.10, 205.17, 205.19 or 215.56 of the penal law, the arrested person need not be brought before a local criminal court as provided in subdivision two, and the procedure may instead be as follows:

(a) The arresting peace officer, where he is specially authorized by law to issue and serve an appearance ticket, may issue and serve an appearance ticket upon the arrested person and release him from custody; or

(b) The arresting peace officer, where he is not specially authorized by law to issue and serve an appearance ticket, may enlist the aid of a police officer and request that such officer issue and serve an appearance ticket upon the arrested person, and upon such issuance and service the latter must be released from custody.

5. Upon arresting a juvenile offender without a warrant, the peace officer shall immediately notify the parent or other person legally responsible for his care or the person with whom he is domiciled, that the juvenile offender has been arrested, and the location of the facility where he is being detained.

Amended by L. 1975, Ch. 78; L. 1979, Ch. 411; L. 1980, Ch. 843, eff. Sept. 1, 1980; L. 1987, Chs. 549, 550.

ANNOTATIONS

Notification provision.—This section's notification provision is similar to the FCA § 724. People v. Ward, 95 A.D.2d 351, 466 N.Y.S.2d 686 (2d Dept. 1983).

Non-felony arrest.—If arrest without a warrant is not for a felony, officer may issue DAT and suspect may be released. People v. Ashkinadze, 167 Misc. 2d 80, 636 N.Y.S.2d 554 (Sup. Ct. Kings Co. 1995).

§ 140.30. Arrest without a warrant; by any person; when and where authorized.

1. Subject to the provisions of subdivision two, any person may arrest another person (a) for a felony when the latter has in fact committed such felony, and (b) for any offense when the latter has in fact committed such offense in his presence.

2. Such an arrest, if for a felony, may be made anywhere in the state. If the arrest is for an offense other than a felony, it may be made only in the county in which such offense was committed.

ANNOTATIONS

Auxiliary police.—Auxiliary police have no arrest powers beyond that of private citizens, but a detainment by such an officer will constitute an arrest. People v. Rotger, 162 Misc. 2d 459, 617 N.Y.S.2d 425 (Bronx Co. Crim. Ct. 1994).

Peace officers.—An individual employed as a peace officer who acts under the color of law and with all of the accoutrements of an official cannot effect a citizen's arrest. People v. Williams, 4 N.Y.3d 535, 797 N.Y.S.2d 35, 829 N.E.2d 1203 (2005).

Store detective.—Observations of the store detective were those of a private individual employed by store and having no connection with a governmental agency, either directly or by agency, and were in pursuance of his responsibility to provide security for his employer; fourth amendment protection has not been applied to searches and seizures by persons other than government officers and agents. People v. LaFauci, 91 Misc. 2d 980, 398 N.Y.S.2d 981 (Dist. Ct. Nassau Co. 1977).

§ 140.35. Arrest without a warrant; by person acting other than as a police officer or a peace officer; when and how made.

1. A person may arrest another person for an offense pursuant to section 140.30 at any hour of any day or night.

2. Such person must inform the person whom he is arresting of the reason for such arrest unless he encounters physical resistance, flight or other factors rendering such procedure impractical.

3. In order to effect such an arrest, such person may use such physical force as is justifiable pursuant to subdivision four of section 35.30 of the penal law.

Amended by L. 1980, Ch. 843.

ANNOTATIONS

Not citizen's arrest.—Complainant's defensive action in encountering defendant and grabbing him did not constitute citizen's arrest, and, thus, did not terminate attempted burglary, where there was no evidence that complainant either intended to effect such arrest or followed statutory procedure of informing defendant of reason for such arrest, and defendant had directed complainant to immediately release his hold on defendant under penalty of death by use of displayed knife. People v. Mitchell, 214 A.D.2d 364, 625 N.Y.S.2d 157 (1st Dept. 1995).

Unconscious prisoner.—Verbal instructions as to the fact and cause of arrest for driving while intoxicated were not necessary where the prisoner was unconscious at the time of the arrest. People v. McGroder, 81 Misc. 2d 1081, 367 N.Y.S.2d 714 (Webster Town Ct., Monroe Co. 1975).

§ 140.40. Arrest without a warrant; by person acting other than as a police officer or a peace officer; procedure after arrest.

1. A person making an arrest pursuant to section 140.30 must without unnecessary delay deliver or attempt to deliver the person arrested to the custody of an appropriate police officer, as defined in subdivision five. * For such purpose, he may solicit the aid of any police officer and the latter, if he is not himself an appropriate police officer, must assist in delivering the arrested person to an appropriate officer. If the arrest is for a felony, the appropriate police officer must, upon receiving custody of the arrested person, perform all recording, fingerprinting and other preliminary police duties required in the particular case. In any case, the appropriate police officer, upon receiving custody of the arrested person, except as otherwise provided in subdivisions two and three, must bring him, on behalf of the arresting person, before an appropriate local criminal court, as defined in subdivision five * and the arresting person must without unnecessary delay file an appropriate accusatory instrument with such court.

2. If (a) the arrest is for an offense other than a class A, B, C or D felony or a violation of section 130.25, 130.40, 205.10, 205.17, 205.19 or 215.56 of the penal law and (b) owing to unavailability of a local criminal court the appropriate police officer having custody of the arrested person is unable to bring him before such a court with reasonable promptness, the arrested person must be dealt with in the manner prescribed in subdivision three of section 140.20, as if he had been arrested by a police officer.

3. If the arrest is for an offense other than a class A, B, C or D felony or a violation of section 130.25, 130.40, 205.10, 205.17, 205.19 or 215.56 of the penal law, the arrested person need not be brought before a local criminal court, as provided in subdivision one, and the procedure may instead be as follows:

(a) An appropriate police officer may issue and serve an appearance ticket upon the arrested person and release him from custody, as prescribed in subdivision two of section 150.20; or

(b) The desk officer in charge at the appropriate police officer's station, county jail or police headquarters, or any of his superior officers, may, in such place, fix pre-arraignment bail and, upon deposit thereof, issue and serve an appearance ticket upon the arrested person and release him from custody, as prescribed in section 150.30.

4. Notwithstanding any other provision of this section, a police officer is not required to take an arrested person into custody or to take any other action prescribed in this section on behalf of the arresting person if he has reasonable cause to believe that the arrested person did not commit the alleged offense or that the arrest was otherwise unauthorized.

5. If a police officer takes an arrested juvenile offender into custody, the police officer shall immediately notify the parent or other person legally responsible for his care or the person with whom he is domiciled, that the juvenile offender has been arrested, and the location of the facility where he is being detained.

6. As used in this section:

(a) An "appropriate police officer" means one who would himself be authorized to make the arrest in question as a police officer pursuant to section 140.10;

(b) An "appropriate local criminal court" means one with which an accusatory instrument charging the offense in question may properly be filed pursuant to the provisions of section 100.55.

* Renumbered subd. 6 by L. 1979, Ch. 411, § 4.

Amended by L. 1970, Ch. 997; L. 1971, Ch. 762; L. 1975, Ch. 78; L. 1979, Ch. 411; L. 1980, Ch. 843; L. 1987, Chs. 549, 550.

ANNOTATION

No right to frisk.—Police officer, who did not testify that he saw defendant in possession of the dice, could not have reasonably suspected defendant was promoting gambling in the second degree or that defendant was in possession of gambling device and therefore officer did not have a right to frisk defendant or to issue him an appearance ticket for those misdemeanors. People v. King, 102 A.D.2d 710, 476 N.Y.S.2d 847 (1st Dept. 1984).

§ 140.45. Arrest without a warrant; dismissal of insufficient local criminal court accusatory instrument.

If a local criminal court accusatory instrument filed with a local criminal court pursuant to section 140.20, 140.25 or 140.40 is not sufficient on its face, as prescribed in section 100.40, and if the court is satisfied that on the basis of the available facts or evidence it would be impossible to draw and file an accusatory instrument which is sufficient on its face, it must dismiss such accusatory instrument and discharge the defendant.

Amended by L. 1987, Chs. 549, 550.

ANNOTATIONS

Insufficient accusatory instrument.—Misdemeanor complaint was improperly dismissed at arraignment for facial insufficiency, and defendant's oral dismissal motion should not have been entertained because an application to dismiss an accusatory instrument filed in a local criminal court can only be heard after arraignment via a formal motion made in writing upon reasonable notice to the People; even if the misdemeanor complaint were facially insufficient, amendment rather than dismissal would be the remedy. People v. Gonzalez, 184 Misc. 2d 262, 708 N.Y.S.2d 564 (App. Term, 1st Dept. 2000).

—Instrument charging defendant with attempted illegal possession of vehicle identification number (VIN) failed to meet standards of information or complaint; accusatory instrument provided no facts from which inference of knowledge by defendant might be drawn, there were no facts to explain in what manner VIN plate was improperly affixed or expertise of deponent to determine that plate was not installed by manufacturer, and defendant produced documentation indicating that vehicle was registered to and insured by member of his immediate family. People v. McCabe, 157 Misc. 2d 373, 596 N.Y.S.2d 1021 (Kings Co. Crim. Ct. 1993).

—A local criminal court may dismiss a facially insufficient felony complaint at arraignment. People v. Marcus, 151 Misc. 2d 190, 573 N.Y.S.2d 110 (Bronx Co. Crim. Ct. 1991).

§ 140.50. Temporary questioning of persons in public places; search for weapons.

1. In addition to the authority provided by this article for making an arrest without a warrant, a police officer may stop a person in a public place located within the geographical area of such officer's employment when he reasonably suspects that such person is committing, has committed or is about to commit either (a) a felony or (b) a misdemeanor defined in the penal law, and may demand of him his name, address and an explanation of his conduct.

2. Any person who is a peace officer and who provides security services for any court of the unified court system may stop a person in or about the courthouse to which he is assigned when he reasonably suspects that such person is committing, has committed or is about to commit either (a) a felony or (b) a misdemeanor defined in the penal law, and may demand of him his name, address and an explanation of his conduct.

3. When upon stopping a person under circumstances prescribed in subdivisions one and two a police officer or court officer, as the case may be, reasonably suspects that he is in danger of physical injury, he may search such person for a deadly weapon or any instrument, article or substance readily capable of causing serious physical injury and of a sort not ordinarily carried in public places by law-abiding persons. If he finds such a weapon or instrument, or any other property possession of which he reasonably believes may constitute the commission of a crime, he may take it and keep it until the completion of the questioning, at which time he shall either return it, if lawfully possessed, or arrest such person.

Amended by L. 1972, Ch. 911; L. 1973, Chs. 159, 714; L. 1985, Ch. 237.

ANNOTATIONS

Reasonable suspicion to stop.—The authority to frisk is incidental to the right conferred by CPL § 140.50 to forcibly stop and temporarily detain for questioning a person reasonably suspected of committing a crime, and it requires that the officer entertain a reasonable suspicion that his physical safety is in danger. People v. Turriago, 219 A.D.2d 383, 644 N.Y.S.2d 178 (1st Dept. 1996), *modified on other grounds,* 90 N.Y.2d 77, 659 N.Y.S.2d 183, 681 N.E.2d 350 (1997).

—The observation of a gun in the waistband of one of defendant's companions justified the officers' suspicion that their physical safety was endangered so as to implicate the corollary statutory right to frisk the suspects for weapons. People v. Pagan, 203 A.D.2d 158, 610 N.Y.S.2d 787 (1st Dept. 1994).

—Police officers had reasonable suspicion to stop automobile since vehicle and its occupants closely matched descriptions set forth in radio transmission regarding suspects in a multiple shooting and officers observed the vehicle in fairly close physical and temporal proximity to the crime. People v. Bond, 227 A.D.2d 412, 642 N.Y.S.2d 320 (2d Dept. 1996), *aff'd,* 90 N.Y.2d 877 (1997).

—Arresting officer's observation of defendant and his companion, who were in close proximity to location given in radio call reporting attempted vehicle break-in and were only individuals present that closely matched descriptions received, properly assumed reliability of radio report and was justified in taking precaution of keeping his weapon at the ready but pointed toward the ground when approaching defendant, and protective frisk of defendant was warranted. People v. Perez, 224 A.D.2d 313, 638 N.Y.S.2d 441 (2d Dept.), *aff'd,* 88 N.Y.2d 1059 (1996).

—An anonymous tip will not of itself constitute reasonable suspicion thereby warranting a stop and frisk of anyone who happens to fit that description People v. Andrades, 219 A.D.2d 656, 631 N.Y.S.2d 712 (2d Dept. 1995).

—Police had reasonable suspicion to stop suspected stolen vehicle which defendant was driving, where police initially approached vehicle to issue citation for double-parking, observed that steering column was cracked and wires were hanging loose, canvassed area to look for suspects, and returned two minutes later to see same vehicle being driven away followed by another vehicle without a rear license plate. People v. Fox, 215 A.D.2d 583, 626 N.Y.S.2d 840 (2d Dept. 1995).

—Detention of defendant for several minutes for showup identification was reasonable where police officers had reasonable suspicion that defendant had committed felony or misdemeanor. People v. Miranda, 213 A.D.2d 560, 624 N.Y.S.2d 436 (2d Dept. 1995).

Airlines weapon search; drugs lawfully seized.—There was a legitimate basis for the patdown search of defendant, who was selected by an airport Customs Inspector for a routine luggage inspection. As he was approached, defendant walked very gingerly and during questioning, appeared nervous, was sweating, and was evasive. During the patdown, bags of cocaine were found hidden in the defendant's shoes. People v. Johnson, 300 A.D.2d 678, 752 N.Y.S.2d 700 (2d Dept. 2002).

—Search of airline passenger by airport official in conjunction with federal anti-hijacking program was not unreasonable, and narcotics found in the possession of defendant were therefore lawfully seized. A law enforcement officer is not required to close his eyes to one type of contraband simply because he is searching for another. People v. Lopez, 73 Misc. 2d 537, 342 N.Y.S.2d 420 (Sup. Ct. N.Y. Co. 1973).

—Search of defendant by custom's agent at airport was found to be reasonable, where defendant fitted behavioral profile of a potentially suspicious person, and his clothing tripped a metal-detecting device. Narcotics accidentally found were held to be legally seized, because of the reasonableness of the search. People v. Boyles, 73 Misc. 2d 576, 341 N.Y.S.2d 967 (Sup. Ct. Queens Co. 1973).

Anonymous tip.—Where an anonymous phone tip giving a general description and location of a "man with a gun" is the sole predicate, it will generate only a belief that criminal activity is afoot and by itself does not constitute reasonable suspicion to warrant a stop and frisk of anyone fitting that description; the police may only inquire until additional information can be acquired. People v. Stewart, 41 N.Y.2d 65, 390 N.Y.S.2d 870, 359 N.E.2d 379 (1976).

—Where police operator at 911 received an anonymous telephone tip that a light-haired white man wearing a silver jacket was standing on a specified corner and that he had a gun and was "out to kill people," the responding officers, who observed defendant at the location and he was the only one fitting the description, did not violate defendant's constitutional rights when they approached him with guns drawn and badges displayed and proceeded with a pat-down search which produced a gun. People v. Sustr, 73 A.D.2d 582, 423 N.Y.S.2d 166 (1st Dept. 1979).

—Police officers had cause to approach defendants, based on the radio report of "men with guns" and their own confirmation of the location of the car, its color, license plate number and the presence of men in the car, and when they discovered a gun on one defendant, who was in close proximity to the car and had been apparently in conversation with its occupants, the officers had authority to frisk the car occupants so as to ensure that the result of their inquiry would not be a hail of bullets. People v. Sterling, 63 A.D.2d 210, 406 N.Y.S.2d 478 (1st Dept. 1978).

—Police possession of information prior to defendant's arrest, that two to four blacks were seen in the vicinity of the crime was insufficient to establish the defendant's presence at scene of the crime. People v. Butler, 80 A.D.2d 644, 436 N.Y.S.2d 76 (2d Dept. 1981).

Arrest; lack of probable cause.—Searching, handcuffing, and transporting to police headquarters constituted an intrusion upon liberty amounting to an arrest and therefore, probable cause was required. People v. Foster, 91 A.D.2d 1046, 458 N.Y.S.2d 645 (2d Dept. 1983), dism'd, 61 N.Y.2d 640, 471 N.Y.S.2d 851, 459 N.E.2d 1288 (1983).

—A confession must be suppressed when it was obtained while the defendant was in custody and there was no probable cause to arrest the defendant. People v. Grant, 80 A.D.2d 862, 436 N.Y.S.2d 847 (2d Dept. 1981).

Anonymous tip insufficient to support frisk.—The frisk was illegal when conducted by police after receiving an anonymous 911 report describing location and female defendant, the automobile defendant was in, and stating that defendant passed a handgun to a man in the car, without further observation of police, such as, an evasive answer by defendant, a suspicious bulge, or furtive or concealed movement. People v. Pruss, 61 N.Y.2d 693, 472 N.Y.S.2d 601, 460 N.E.2d 1086 (1984).

—Sole predicate for stop of defendant was anonymous tip, which was insufficient here to justify police conduct. There was no verification of the information received over the radio, and on cross-examination the arresting officer testified that defendant's behavior was neither suspicious nor furtive and he did not appear nervous, and there were no exigent circumstances which would have precluded the police from making a common-law right of inquiry. People v. Oliver, 262 A.D.2d 335, 692 N.Y.S.2d 405 (2d Dept. 1999).

Anonymous tip sufficiently detailed to justify stop of defendant.—The intrusion by police officers in stopping the defendant and examining his suitcases, with his consent, was justified by an anonymous phone tip giving extremely specific information identifying the defendant, the time and place and what he would be carrying. People v. Roth, 99 A.D.2d 626, 472 N.Y.S.2d 164 (3d Dept. 1984).

Arrest; search; policeman's right to make non-incriminating inquiries.—Officer was justified in stopping defendant and asking for identification after he saw him leaving a house that had been receiving special attention as the site of prior burglaries; knew that the man did live in the house and observed that the occupants of the house had not seen this stranger at the door; and a second man appeared to be waiting for the suspect out of the immediate range of vision of the front of the house. People v. Murriel, 75 A.D.2d 628, 426 N.Y.S.2d 831 (2d Dept. 1980).

—When defendant was seen by police officer entering and leaving building where policeman had made a number of narcotic arrests and was approached for inquiry, but ran, officer had right to pursue him and when assaulted, to arrest and make

search incident to arrest. People v. Archiopoli, 39 A.D.2d 748, 332 N.Y.S.2d 166 (2d Dept. 1972).

Arrest; stop and frisk.—Defendant was unlawfully stopped where police based their actions on the fact that the defendant had a prior record, was walking in a residential area in which there had been burglaries and was looking at houses; there was no basis to believe that defendant was engaged in or was about to engage in criminal conduct. People v. Johnson, 64 N.Y.2d 617, 485 N.Y.S.2d 33 (1984).

—A suspect may not be frisked by a police officer investigating a recent robbery and shooting who personally had no grounds for believing that the suspect was armed and dangerous and did so solely on the basis of information received from a patron of a bar that there were two men in the bar who looked suspicious. People v. Carney, 58 N.Y.2d 51, 457 N.Y.S.2d 776, 474 N.E.2d 241 (1982).

—The officers were justified in stopping defendant after they received a radio report of an armed robbery and then observed him walking on a deserted street in the vicinity of the crime and he met the description of the robber, and the limited "pat down" was proper after defendant refused to furnish his name or address and repeatedly removed his hands from the radio car and shuffled them around since it was quite reasonable for the officer to investigate the suspicious bulges in his jacket pocket. People v. Spivey, 46 N.Y.2d 1014, 416 N.Y.S.2d 534, 389 N.E.2d 1056 (1979).

—The initial seizure of the defendant was unlawful and the fruit of the seizure, the pistol, was suppressed where the police, after observing defendant in an apartment apparently smoking marijuana, tailed him home and surrounded him as he exited from his vehicle and discovered a pistol in the ensuing search. People v. Cantor, 36 N.Y.2d 106, 365 N.Y.S.2d 509, 324 N.E.2d 872 (1975); cf. People v. Dread, 49 A.D.2d 401, 375 N.Y.S.2d 993 (1st Dept. 1975), aff'd, 41 N.Y.2d 871, 393 N.Y.S.2d 993, 362 N.E.2d 623; People v. Jose F., 60 A.D.2d 918, 401 N.Y.S.2d 573 (2d Dept. 1978).

—There was no justification for the officer to conduct a searching examination of the inside of defendant's jacket pocket after the frisk disclosed a small soft object but no weapon. People v. Gonzalez, 115 A.D.2d 73, 499 N.Y.S.2d 400 (1st Dept. 1986).

—Reasonable suspicion of police officer that defendant possessed narcotics, combined with the defendant's patently false answers to the officer's initial inquiries, justified a further search which resulted in the finding of stolen baseball tickets. People v. McNatt, 107 A.D.2d 1, 485 N.Y.S.2d 253 (1985).

—The mere purchase of a holster from a forty-second street novelty shop without the presence of additional objective criteria indicating that "criminal activity is afoot" does not permit a further intrusion upon the purchaser, other than the mere inquiry by the police and the threshold of impermissible conduct was crossed when the officer ordered the defendant to open his coat. People v. Johnson, 79 A.D.2d 936, 434 N.Y.S.2d 996 (1st Dept. 1980), aff'd, 54 N.Y.2d 958, 445 N.Y.S.2d 146, 429 N.E.2d 824 (1981).

—CPL § 140.50 did provide the police with the authority to perform a frisk at another time and another place after they had arrested suspects without probable cause. People v. Batista, 68 A.D.2d 515, 417 N.Y.S.2d 724 (1st Dept. 1979), aff'd, 51 N.Y.2d 996, 435 N.Y.S.2d 980, 417 N.E.2d 92 (1980).

—Merely walking in front of a building in which police officers believed a crime was taking place did not constitute sufficient cause to detain and frisk defendant and evidence found in defendant's possession was suppressed. People v. Monsanto, 73 A.D.2d 576, 423 N.Y.S.2d 476 (1st Dept. 1979), aff'd, 52 N.Y.2d 931, 437 N.E.2d 669, 419 N.E.2d 347 (1981).

—The police may not forcibly detain civilians in order to question them without a reasonable suspicion of criminal activity. People v. Voliton, 190 A.D.2d 764, 593 N.Y.S.2d 822 (2d Dept. 1993), aff'd, 83 N.Y.2d 192, 608 N.Y.S.2d 945, 630 N.E.2d 641 (1994).

—Brief detention of defendant and forcing him to remove his hands from his jacket pockets were justified, in part, by fact that defendant and companion fit description of alleged drug sellers and were in a "drug-prone" location late at night. People v. Kimble, 153 A.D.2d 591, 544 N.Y.S.2d 383 (2d Dept. 1989).

Automobile stop.—As established in People v. Robinson, 97 N.Y.2d 341, 741 N.Y.S.2d 147, 767 N.E.2d 638, provided a traffic stop is supported by probable cause, "neither the primary motivation of the officer nor a determination of what a reasonable traffic officer would have done under the circumstances is relevant"; because there is evidence to support the undisturbed finding of the suppression court that the trooper had probable cause to believe defendant committed a muffler violation of the VTL, the stop was lawful. People v. Wright, 98 N.Y.2d 657, 746 N.Y.S.2d 273, 773 N.E.2d 1011 (2002).

—Cops made lawful stop of a vehicle but when the officers approached, the car pulled away, and the cops chased the car with the sirens activated. This stop and pursuit cycle repeated itself and the vehicle nearly struck a pedestrian. The officers noticed defendant turn in the backseat and make a motion as if hiding something. Under these circumstances, the limited police intrusion in that area of the car where the furtive movements had been seen was justified. People v. Mundo, 99 N.Y.2d 55, 750 N.Y.S.2d 837, 780 N.E.2d 522 (2002).

—Confining the occupants to the car, even temporarily, is at least equivalent to a stop constituting a limited seizure of the person which at least requires reasonable suspicion. People v. Harrison, 57 N.Y.2d 470, 457 N.Y.S.2d 199, 443 N.E.2d 447 (1982).

—Reasonableness is the touchstone by which police-citizen encounters are measured. Police officers may direct a driver to exit his vehicle out of concern for their safety, even though they lack any particularized reason for believing the driver possesses a weapon. People v. Alvarez, 2003 N.Y. App. Div. LEXIS 9160, 764 N.Y.S.2d 42 (1st Dept. 2003).

—Stop of vehicle, in which the defendant was riding, was reasonable since it was based upon the fact that it had only one operating headlight, a violation of the Vehicle and Traffic Law. People v. Williams, 137 A.D.2d 569, 524 N.Y.S.2d 309 (2d Dept. 1988).

—Police initial stop of defendants vehicle, before they received the results of a stolen vehicle check, was permissible where the officers were able to determine that the vehicle, which had extensive damage, was a rented car, and the officers, in their many years on the police force, had never seen a rented vehicle on the road in such poor condition. People v. Roman, 74 A.D.2d 589, 424 N.Y.S.2d 489 (2d Dept. 1980).

—Although the fact that the vehicle was stopped at bus stop may have constituted an "articulable basis" under People v. Ingle, 36 N.Y.2d 413, 369 N.Y.S.2d 67, 330 N.E.2d 39 (1975), for approaching defendant and asking to see his license and registration, there was no justification for reaching into the vehicle and conducting a visual search of its interior; the act of opening the car door and leaning inside was clearly a search and since there was no evidence that the detective believed or had reason to believe he was in physical danger, which may have justified such an intrusion, the contraband seized was suppressed and the charge dismissed. People v. Vidal, 71 A.D.2d 962, 420 N.Y.S.2d 19 (2d Dept. 1979).

—Court adopted and followed federal view that the subjective reason of the police for stopping an automobile is irrelevant in ascertaining probable cause as long as the stop is reasonable. People v. Robinson, 271 A.D.2d 17, 711 N.Y.S.2d 384 (1st Dept. 2000), aff'd, 97 N.Y.2d 341, 741 N.Y.S.2d 147, 767 N.E.2d 638 (2001).

—Stop of car was justified where police officer credibly testified that rear license plate on defendant's automobile lacked illumination, in violation of VTL § 375(2)(a)(4). People v. Sanchez, 178 Misc. 2d 695, 681 N.Y.S.2d 428 (Crim. Ct. N.Y. Co. 1998).

Border checkpoint.—It is well-settled that the border patrol may stop a vehicle at a fixed checkpoint for brief questioning of its occupants "even though there is no reason to believe that the particular vehicle contains illegal aliens." People v. Sinzheimer, 15 A.D.2d 732, 790 N.Y.S.2d 554 (3d Dept. 2005).

—The temporary checkpoint by Border Patrol agents was authorized and properly conducted. Questions do not need to be limited to the topic of citizenship, but may include a traveler's alienage and travel plans. However, the agents did not have a founded suspicion of criminality to justify the nearly one-hour detention for eventual dog sniff of the defendant's vehicle. People v. White, 8 Misc. 3d 935, 796 N.Y.S.2d 902 (Co. Ct. St. Lawrence Co. 2005).

Consent; burden of proof.—Upon searching the vehicle with the driver's consent the trooper was authorized to direct the defendant/passenger out of the car as a precautionary measure. People v. Setzer, 199 A.D.2d 548, 608 N.Y.S.2d 6 (2d Dept. 1994).

—The People have the burden of proving the voluntariness of a defendant's consent to a search and the prosecution must "demonstrate that the consent was in fact voluntarily given and not the result of duress or coercion, express or implied." People v. Springer, 92 A.D.2d 209, 460 N.Y.S.2d 86 (2d Dept. 1983).

Detentive stop; minimum requirements met.—A request to search a suspect's bag is not permitted under the right to inquire. People v. Hallman, 79 N.Y.2d 181, 581 N.Y.S.2d 619, 590 N.E.2d 204 (1992).

—Reasonable grounds upon which to stop cab and remove defendant and his companion at gunpoint were presented where although description of perpetrators of robbery did not precisely match those of the defendant and his companion, they generally conformed to the description, and they were the only people on the street in the vicinity within minutes after the robbery; the police were justified in taking precautionary measures to insure their own safety. People v. Boyd, 78 A.D.2d 225, 434 N.Y.S.2d 221 (1st Dept. 1980).

—The minimum requirements for a lawful detentive stop were met where police officers, patrolling in a high-crime area during the early afternoon, observed one defendant, wearing a "dirty" coat and who didn't look like the sort of fellow that would be taking a cab, "throw a blue bag and pillowcase into a double-parked taxi" and saw the co-defendant, who hesitated when he saw the police car, leave the building with a television set in his hands. People v. Skinner, 65 A.D.2d 704, 410 N.Y.S.2d 84 (1st Dept. 1978), aff'd, 48 N.Y.2d 889, 424 N.Y.S.2d 884, 400 N.E.2d 1336 (1979).

—The minimum requirements for a lawful detentive stop were met where police officers were called to investigate a report of men with guns on the eighth or ninth floor of a building where recent arrests for gun possession had been made and where such officers, upon ascending the second flight of stairs, encountered a woman who called to those behind her "Police are here, police are coming," and upon proceeding to the second floor, they observed the defendant about to enter an apartment. People v. Hill, 65 A.D.2d 706, 410 N.Y.S.2d 89 (1st Dept. 1978).

—Police officers are authorized to stop a motor vehicle when a traffic offense has been committed in their presence. People v. Perrin, 201 A.D.2d 853, 608 N.Y.S.2d 332 (3d Dept. 1994).

Detentive stop; subsequent confession.—A new suppression hearing was required since no determination had been made as to whether the police officers had probable cause to take defendant into custody or if they did not have probable cause and his detention was thus illegal whether there were such attenuating circumstances as to establish that his subsequent confession was neither the product of his illegal arrest nor obtained in consequence of its exploitation. People v. Coleman, 56 N.Y.2d 669, 451 N.Y.S.2d 712, 436 N.E.2d 1314 (1982).

Frisk; unidentified informer.—Policeman, having been told by an unidentified citizen on the street, in a high-crime area, that defendant was carrying a concealed weapon, acted reasonably in conducting a limited search. People v. Bronk, 31 N.Y.2d 995, 341 N.Y.S.2d 450, 293 N.E.2d 826 (1973).

—There was no basis for the stop of the defendant when the police acted solely on the basis of a tip from an anonymous informer who reported no criminal act having been committed by the defendant, other than the alleged possession of a gun, and the officers observed no suspicious conduct on the defendant's part. People v. La Pene, 49 A.D.2d 604, 370 N.Y.S.2d 192 (2d Dept. 1975), aff'd, 40 N.Y.2d 210, 386 N.Y.S.2d 375, 352 N.E.2d 562 (1976).

Probation Officer.—Although "stop and frisk" power is restricted to police officers, the vital ability to conduct a search for weapons upon the reasonable belief that one's life or limb may be in danger is in no way meant to be arbitrarily limited; thus, a probation officer in an appropriate situation can conduct a limited search for weapons. People v. Thompson, 77 Misc. 2d 700, 353 N.Y.S.2d 698 (Sup. Ct. N.Y. Co. 1974).

Frisk; non-public places.—The frisk of the defendants was illegal where the police stopped the vehicle in which they were riding based upon information received from a radio call, and upon making initial inquiries for a driver's license and automobile registration which the defendants could not produce, the officer neither arrested nor searched the defendants, but merely detained them for 10–15 minutes until the state police arrived; and when the state police arrived, they frisked the defendants and found jewelry in a sock in the defendant's jacket as the defendants exhibited no violent tendencies, and there was no showing that the state trooper could have reasonably inferred that the defendants were dangerous. People v. Randall, 85 A.D.2d 754, 445 N.Y.S.2d 251 (3d Dept. 1981).

—Although our "stop and frisk" statute applies to activity "abroad in a public place" (CPL 140.50, subd. 1), CPL § 690.15, subd. 2 appears to authorize a similar frisk in a non-public place (such as an apartment) upon a legal entry. People v. Finn, 73 Misc. 2d 266, 340 N.Y.S.2d 807 (Crim. Ct. Bronx Co. 1973).

Frisk on less than probable cause.—Officer could make a limited frisk in order to pursue his investigation after he responded at night to call, in high crime area, of "man armed with a gun" and defendant, who matched description given by the caller, gave unintelligible, unresponsive reply to his inquiry. People v. Stroller, 42 N.Y.2d 1052, 399 N.Y.S.2d 207, 369 N.E.2d 763 (1977).

—Motion to suppress was granted where police, who had reason to believe owner of premises was engaging in an illegal activity made a blanket seizure of all individuals in the bar and found narcotics upon the defendant's patron. People v. James, 81 A.D.2d 795, 439 N.Y.S.2d 125 (1st Dept. 1981).

—Defendant's conviction for possession of a weapon was reversed where a police department policy requiring that as a safety precaution all suspects about to enter a police vehicle must be subjected to a pat-down search; since this policy may not be employed as justification to search a person impermissibly seized without probable cause for the purpose of transporting him to police headquarters for further interrogation. People v. Howington, 83 A.D.2d 756, 443 N.Y.S.2d 519 (4th Dept. 1981).

—Motion to suppress was granted where defendant's conduct, appearance, and demeanor was neither suspicious nor furtive and bespoke no harm to either officer. People v. Hauser, 80 A.D.2d 460, 439 N.Y.S.2d 562 (4th Dept. 1981).

Suppression of evidence obtained during unjustified frisk.—Conduct by defendant of looking into store windows and twice reaching under his jacket toward his stomach could not justify police frisk and the gun found on the defendant must be suppressed. People v. Roberts, 94 A.D.2d 237, 464 N.Y.S.2d 111 (1st Dept. 1983).

Frisk on less than probable cause; informant's tip.—Warrantless search of defendant will not be sustained where informant, who did not indicate the basis of his knowledge, claimed defendant was in possession of heroin and police officers did not themselves observe conduct indicating that defendant was involved in the criminal activity alleged by informant; weapon discovered in defendant's possession pursuant to search should be suppressed and indictment dismissed. People v. Eaddy, 78 A.D.2d 761, 433 N.Y.S.2d 635 (4th Dept. 1980).

Frisk; position of suspect.—The nature of a frisk, as opposed to a search, is that it is essentially a pat down; the position of the suspect during the pat down does not convert the frisk into a search. People v. Chestnut, 69 A.D.2d 41, 418 N.Y.S.2d 390 (1st Dept. 1979).

—Defendants had privacy interests in opaque garbage bags they were carrying, and thus, search of the bags was unjustified where police, upon the tip of a school custodian, were informed that two "suspicious" men had asked for the bags and placed a television set, stereo, and other property in the bags, and upon finding two men fitting the description, the police asked what was in the bags, and opened one of them before getting a response when there was no indication that the police were in danger entitling them to search "defendants for their protection." People v. McNally, 89 A.D.2d 971, 454 N.Y.S.2d 122 (2d Dept. 1982), dism'd, 58 N.Y.2d 1029, 462 N.Y.S.2d 440, 448 N.E.2d 1351 (1983).

Frisk, following commission of violation.—Where defendant was approached by police for having committed a violation and then ran into a nearby store and closed the door forcing the officer to pry it open, the officer had the right to frisk the defendant because of his suspicious conduct, notwithstanding that being stopped for a violation ordinarily does not justify a frisk. People v. King, 65 N.Y.2d 702, 492 N.Y.S.2d 1, 481 N.E.2d 541 (1985).

Police stop; "wanted flyer" as basis.—Police may stop and investigate an individual where they reasonably suspect that such person was involved in or is wanted in connection with a completed felony; police had a reasonable basis to stop and investigate the defendant based upon a "wanted flyer" issued by a neighboring police department for the defendant with regard to a robbery specified in the flyer. United States v. Hensley, 469 U.S. 221, 105 S. Ct. 675, 83 L. Ed. 2d 604 (1985).

—Based on defendant's resemblance to an individual in a wanted poster, the police had the right to approach him to request information. Defendant's subsequent flight when officers asked if they could speak to him provided reasonable suspicion to pursue and stop him, and his abandonment of a weapon during the chase provided probable cause to arrest. People v. Wilson, 5 A.D.3d 408, 773 N.Y.S.2d 95 (2d Dept. 2004).

Reasonable cause; sufficiency of description.—Police had reasonable suspicion to stop and frisk defendant because he matched a radioed description of the assailant, which included the fact that he was wearing a black knit skull cap, along with a jacket of a particular color and bore a specific brand name on the back and the gunman's sex, race, and height. Furthermore, defendant was found, in the early morning hours, in the suspect's general direction of flight. "The specificity of the description outweighed the fact that approximately two hours had transpired since the shooting." People v. Applewhite, 298 A.D.2d 136, 748 N.Y.S.2d 4 (1st Dept. 2002).

—Bare description that "four male Hispanics with guns," one wearing a red and white shirt and one wearing a blue shirt with jeans, would not constitute constitutionally adequate reasonable grounds for stop and frisk of defendant. People v. Bezares, 103 A.D.2d 717, 478 N.Y.S.2d 16 (1st Dept. 1984).

Reasonable cause to stop automobile.—Court held that officers possessed the requisite reasonable suspicion to stop defendant's automobile and search it where one passenger was identified as having recently been arrested for robbery, where car's occupants fit physical and clothing description of persons wanted for robberies in neighborhood, and where subsequent to the stop all occupants attempted to flee without producing requested license and registration. People v. Diaz, 103 A.D.2d 82, 478 N.Y.S.2d 629 (1st Dept. 1984).

Reasonable suspicion; particular crime.—Although the defendant was in a high crime area, carrying a woman's vanity case, and made "furtive" movements (repeated glances, change of direction, quickened pace) policemen patrolling the area were only permitted to keep the defendant under further observation or make an investigative stop; they could not pursue or seize the defendant. People v. Howard, 50 N.Y.2d 583, 430 N.Y.S.2d 578, 408 N.E.2d 908, cert. denied, 449 U.S. 1023 (1980).

—When the police lack a reasonable suspicion that a particular person has committed, is committing, or is about to commit a felony or misdemeanor, which is necessary to justify a forcible stop, they cannot stop an individual who exercises his right to be let alone and refuse to respond to police inquiry by slowly driving away as the police approach his or her vehicle to make a common-law inquiry. People v. Adams, 194 A.D.2d 102, 605 N.Y.S.2d 120, 122 (3d Dept. 1993).

Reasonable suspicion; failure to return property upon completion of questioning.—Where there was reasonable suspicion that a suspect was involved in the commission of a misdemeanor or felony, police officers were acting under the authority of the statute and the Constitution when, for their own protection, they took possession of two sticks carried by suspect, which could have posed a danger to them had suspect become violent; while the suspect was entitled to return of the sticks upon completion of the officers' questioning of him, the failure of the officers to return them was a violation of statute, not of a constitutional right, and, thus, the exclusionary rule was not implicated and suppression of the sticks at trial was not warranted. People v. Harris, 48 N.Y.2d 208, 422 N.Y.S.2d 43, 397 N.E.2d 733 (1979).

Reasonable suspicion of involvement in unlawful activity; relevant factors to determine.—The size of the area to be investigated, the number of persons expected to be there, and the time elapsed between notification and arrival of police are all relevant to the issue of reasonable suspicion, since they determine the likelihood of the presence of innocent persons whose privacy could be unreasonably invaded. People v. Taylor, 76 A.D.2d 892, 428 N.Y.S.2d 705 (2d Dept. 1980).

Right to inquire.—Although defendant and his companion did not perfectly match the radio description, there were enough similarities to provide the police with, at a minimum, the right to make a common law inquiry, especially where the men were found in close temporal and spatial proximity to a reported robbery. People v. Cintron, 304 A.D.2d 254, 758 N.Y.S.2d 636 (1st Dept. 2003).

—The common law right of inquiry is triggered by a reasonable suspicion that criminal activity is afoot and mere inquiry constitutes only a minor inconvenience to an individual. People v. Gray, 90 A.D.2d 405, 457 N.Y.S.2d 125 (2d Dept. 1982).

—Defendant's mere proximity to another person whom the police had probable cause to arrest for possession of drugs justified only a stop and request for an explanation of conduct as to that defendant and not a frisk since the officer did not reasonably suspect himself to be in danger of harm. People v. Ballejo, 114 A.D.2d 902, 495 N.Y.S.2d 75 (2d Dept. 1985).

—Where circumstances are suspicious but equivocal, the common-law right to inquire permits an intrusion upon one's liberty only to the extent necessary to gain explanatory information, but short of a forcible seizure. People v. Bramble, 158 Misc. 2d 411, 600 N.Y.S.2d 1005 (Sup. Ct. Kings Co. 1993), aff'd, 207 A.D.2d 407, 615 N.Y.S.2d 896 (2d Dept. 1994).

Roadblocks.—The suspicionless roadblock stop of defendant's vehicle contravened the fourth amendment because the hearing testimony of the officers who set up and operated the roadblock pointed to a series of unprioritized purposes, i.e., to reduce crime, educate cab drivers, prevent cab robberies and carjackings, and interdict drugs and guns. Many of these objectives were related only to general crime control and the evidence seized was properly suppressed. People v. Jackson, 99 N.Y.2d 125, 752 N.Y.S.2d 271, 782 N.E.2d 67 (2002).

—Stop in question was flawed where officer, who was not part of a sobriety checkpoint, stopped a car simply because he thought the driver was trying to evade the checkpoint. People v. Bigger, 2 Misc. 2d 937, 771 N.Y.S.2d 826 (Just. Ct. Monroe Co. 2004).

Informant's tips; lower standard of probable cause required.—Where police receive an informant's tip, the standard of reasonable suspicion for stopping a person is lower than the standard of probable cause for a arrest, if it has bee determined that the informant's tip has sufficient indicia of reliability to justify stopping and searching the person. People v. Moore, 32 N.Y.S.2d 67, 343 N.Y.S.2d 107, 295 N.E.2d 780 (1973), cert. denied, 414 U.S. 1011 (1973).

—Police had probable cause to stop and conduct a warrantless search of defendant's vehicle based upon information provided by a confidential informant who had purchased drugs from defendant for the police a few days earlier and who gave a number of details concerning the defendant's trip to his supplier which were confirmed by police observations. People v. Picone, 108 A.D.2d 932, 485 N.Y.S.2d 824 (2d Dept. 1985).

Investigation warranted, but probable cause to searching lacking.—An officer, before searching a suspect, must first stop and question him regarding his conduct; the officer can then search defendant if he can then reasonably suspects that he is in danger of physical harm. People v. Sanchez 38 N.Y.2d 72, 378 N.Y.S.2d 346 340 N.E.2d 718 (1975).

—Though police were justified in investigating the defendant, seen carrying a crowbar and an automobile battery with torn cables, search of the defendant was without probable cause, where defendant did not attempt to escape, was not evasive, was afforded scant opportunity to explain his possession of the items, and where there had been no report of a car break-in. Thus, drugs found during search of defendant were suppressed from being introduced. People v. Brown, 32 N.Y.2d 172, 344 N.Y.S.2d 356 (1973).

During traffic check.—Once a car has been lawfully stopped for a traffic infraction, the police may order the driver out even if he has indulged in no suspicious behavior but passengers may not be ordered out absent some suspicion directed at them. People v. Marin, 80 A.D.2d 541, 436 N.Y.S.2d 292 (1st Dept. 1981).

—The officers had an articulable basis to justify their request for defendant's license and registration after they observed the defendant behind the steering wheel of a double-parked car. People v. Duncan, 75 A.D.2d 823, 427 N.Y.S.2d 472 (2d Dept. 1980).

Mere observance of bulge.—Mere observance of a bulge in a person's pocket cannot provide the basis for a frisk. People v. Marquez, 80 A.D.2d 837, 436 N.Y.S.2d 333 (2d Dept. 1981). See also People v. Blackman, 61 A.D.2d 916, 403 N.Y.S.2d 3 (1st Dept. 1978).

Minimal intrusion.—A police officer had been given information to be on the lookout for two males, one tall and one short, who had committed a series of robberies at particular subway stations. At the scene of one of the stations, the officer observed two men fitting the description approaching an elderly man. When the two suspects noticed the officer they began walking in the opposite direction. He stopped them, requested identification and observed a bulge in one of the defendant's pockets. The officer felt the bulge from the outside detecting that it was a gun. The court held that the search was legal. The touching of the outside of the pocket was a minimal intrusion, reasonable under the circumstances. People v. Clee, 89 A.D.2d 188, 455 N.Y.S.2d 8 (1st Dept. 1982), dism'd, 61 N.Y.2d 899, 474 N.Y.S.2d 482, 462 N.E.2d 1200 (1984).

—While officer was not authorized to conduct patdown of pouch being held by passenger of vehicle, he was authorized to hold the pouch during the ensuing trip to the precinct in order to ensure his own safety; thus officer's attempt to take the pouch from the passenger, who resisted that effort, was proper. People v. Brewer, 200 A.D.2d 579, 606 N.Y.S.2d 292 (2d Dept. 1994).

Nature of police conduct; forcible seizure.—Police conduct could not be considered a mere stop and frisk under CPL § 140.50 where three officers emerged from their car with guns drawn and said to defendant, "Police, don't move"; such aggressive conduct constituted no minimal intrusion into defendant's life, but rather, bespoke a violent and forcible seizure and gun subsequently found was suppressed. People v. Figueroa, 58 A.D.2d 655, 396 N.Y.S.2d 63 (2d Dept. 1977).

—After police officer responded to a call of "suspicious conduct," and asked to see motorist's license and registration in a non-detentive setting, there was no unlawful search and seizure when he asked whose woman's pocketbook was in the front seat of the car, and where she lived; the motorist's response was incomplete as to both counts, and the officer's action of asking to look in the pocketbook, to which defendant did not object, and pulling it out of the car, was neither unjustified nor without consent. People v. Lanahan, 89 A.D.2d 629, 452 N.Y.S.2d 918 (3d Dept. 1982).

Probable cause; analysis.—When analyzing probable cause, the emphasis should not be narrowly focused on a recognizable drug package or any other single factor, but on an evaluation of the totality of circumstances which takes into account the "realities of everyday life unfolding before a trained officer who has to confront, on a daily basis, similar incidents." People v. Watts, 309 A.D.2d 1256, 764 N.Y.S.2d 737 (4th Dept. 2003).

School official.—A school official has the right to "frisk" a child based on a reasonable suspicion that he has a gun since the mere fact that a child may have a loaded gun in a school creates exigencies affecting the security of all of the children in the school. In re Ronald B., 61 A.D.2d 204, 401 N.Y.S.2d 544 (2d Dept. 1978).

Search and seizure; probable cause.—Where defendant was arrested and searched on insufficient probable cause, the fact that the search was successful in producing contraband did not vitiate the unlawfulness of the arrest. People v. Martin, 32 N.Y.2d 123, 343 N.Y.S.2d 343, 296 N.E.2d 245 (1973).

Search and seizure; probable cause; motion to suppress.—Where the police observed the defendant in the company of two other persons at the time of an apparent narcotics transaction between said persons, but defendant himself was engaged in no overt criminal activity, this did not give sufficient probable cause to arrest the defendant, and subsequent search of defendant which produced dangerous drugs was therefore unjustified and should have been suppressed. People v. Martin, 32 N.Y.2d 123, 343 N.Y.S.2d 343, 296 N.E.2d 245 (1973).

—Upon reaching the area where an alarm was ringing, the police officer observed only two pedestrians near the site. He approached them thinking they might have seen someone or something. As the officer approached, they avoided him and upon his request for identification, they were evasive. The stop was held proper and statements made were admissible. People v. Scruggs, 90 A.D.2d 520, 455 N.Y.S.2d 22 (2d Dept. 1982).

—Motion to suppress was denied where police stopped defendant after observing him going in the wrong direction on a one way street; upon his exit from the automobile; a bulge in defendant's pocket similar to a gun, was discovered and the police could have reasonably inferred he was a threat to their safety and could make a weapons search. People v. Behlin, 83 A.D.2d 557, 440 N.Y.S.2d 948 (2d Dept. 1981).

Search and seizure; suppression; abandonment of contraband.—Seizure of LSD was proper notwithstanding police officer's invalid arrest for trespass, since the prior illegal conduct of police did not precipitate the abandonment of the wallet which contained the unlawful drug. People v. James S. Branson, 81 A.D.2d 1031, 440 N.Y.S.2d 427 (4th Dept. 1981).

Stop and frisk; probable cause.—Gunpoint stop and frisk of defendant was justified by information given to a police officer that the informant had been threatened with a gun by her husband, a description of the husband and the location where he might be found, together with the confirming observations of the police officer. People v. Mumit, 106 A.D.2d 411, 482 N.Y.S.2d 333 (2d Dept. 1984).

"Stop and frisk"; probable cause present.—Court denied motion to suppress a gun where police had been directed to defendant, a man walking on the street with a shopping bag in his hand, by a civilian witness who stated "Defendant had a gun," and where police "frisked" the shopping bag and located a gun therein. People v. Tratch, 104 A.D.2d 501, 479 N.Y.S.2d 249 (2d Dept. 1984).

Stop and frisk; reasonable cause; motion to suppress.—Simply because the defendant was standing alongside a man who was alleged to possess a gun did not provide a reasonable basis to suspect that he committed or was about to commit a crime and subsequent frisk of defendant was unlawful. People v. Trapier, 47 A.D.2d 481, 367 N.Y.S.2d 276 (1st Dept. 1975).

—Motion to suppress was granted where subsequent to a stop of a car for investigation purposes, police officer without justification or provocation opened door to passenger side, revealing a weapon upon the defendant. People v. David L., 81 A.D.2d 893, 439 N.Y.S.2d 152 (2d Dept.), aff'd, 54 N.Y.2d 900, 444 N.Y.S.2d 919, 429 N.E.2d 426 (1981).

—Reasonable cause to frisk was lacking where police observed defendant and another man exiting a bar in a noisy and boisterous manner and defendant shattering a bottle to the ground; at most defendant's conduct prior to the search constituted disorderly conduct. People v. St. Clair, 80 A.D.2d 692, 436 N.Y.S.2d 449 (3d Dept. 1981).

Stop and frisk: reasonable cause; dangerous weapon.—Police officers who had received a report that a person fitting the defendant's description was seen waving a gun in the street and who thereafter conducted a valid stop and frisk could also examine personal items capable of concealing a weapon within the suspect's grabbable reach upon the grounds of safety and precaution. People v. Brooks, 65 N.Y.2d 1021, 494 N.Y.S.2d 103, 484 N.E.2d 132 (1985).

—Existence of "reasonable suspicion" is a mixed question of law and fact and, in light of the evidence in the record that supported the finding of the trial court that the officer had grounds to stop and frisk, it was beyond the power of review of the Court of Appeals. People v. Van Luven, 64 N.Y.2d 625, 485 N.Y.S.2d 39, 474 N.E.2d 247 (1984).

—Defendant's purchase of a pistol holster and his failure to respond to detective's inquiry, coupled with the potentially menacing action of placing his hand in his coat pocket and refusing to remove it, provided sufficient basis for the detective's grabbing the hand through the coat, for he had reason to believe defendant was armed and dangerous, and the weapon discovered in defendant's pocket should not be suppressed. People v. Samuels, 50 N.Y.2d 1035, 431 N.Y.S.2d 694, 409 N.E.2d 1368, cert. denied, 449 U.S. 984 (1980).

—At least three aspects of each handgun seizure by the police should be considered in determining the propriety of the seizure (1) was there proof of a describable object or of describable conduct that provides a reasonable basis for the police officer's belief that the defendant had a gun in his possession; (2) was the manner of the officer's approach to the defendant and the seizure of the gun from him reasonable in the circumstance; (3) was there evidence of probative worth that there had been a pretext stop and frisk or that the police were otherwise motivated by an improper or irrelevant purpose. People v. Prochilo, 41 N.Y.2d 759, 395 N.Y.S.2d 634, 363 N.E.2d 1379 (1977).

—The warrantless search of the defendant's handbag at the police station and the subsequent seizure of a loaded, .22 caliber revolver were upheld where, following the husband's arrest for menacing the defendant, his wife, and while en route to the station house, the husband informed the officers that the defendant had a gun in her possession. People v. Moore, 32 N.Y.2d 67, 343 N.Y.S.2d 107, 295 N.E.2d 780, cert. denied, 414 U.S. 1011 (1973).

—Police officer had reasonable cause to frisk defendant when defendant, who had been apparently loitering in a high volume drug trafficking area, responded to a demand to produce identification by reaching into a front jacket pocket, which triggered policeman's fear that defendant might be reaching for a weapon. People v. Stone, 86 A.D.2d 347, 449 N.Y.S.2d 972 (1st Dept. 1982).

—Anonymous telephone call to police that a "little dude" named Donald, wearing a black overcoat and a black hat, standing in front of a named bar on 125th Street had a gun, provided sufficient basis for the police who responded to the call to stop and frisk defendant when they observed him standing on the sidewalk at the location wearing a black coat and hat and the resulting "feel" of a gun justified the search and removal of the gun from defendant's person. People v. Williams, 52 A.D.2d 520, 381 N.Y.S.2d 874 (1st Dept.), aff'd, 41 N.Y.2d 65, 390 N.Y.S.2d 870, 359 N.E.2d 379 (1976).

Stop and frisk; reasonable suspicion.—When police reasonably suspected that defendant was about to commit a crime involving a forged instrument, they could demand of defendant his name, address and an explanation of his conduct. People v. Richardson, 41 N.Y.2d 886, 393 N.Y.S.2d 983, 362 N.E.2d 613 (1977).

—Neither the stop nor the frisk were justified by reasonable suspicions of police where they responded to radio alarm that unidentified caller reported two suspicious male Negroes at a gas station and found defendant and another at a second gas station, the defendant possessing narcotic paraphernalia. Absent an articulable foundation, the suspicions remain "hunches" and are not "reasonable" within meaning of statute. People v. Johnson, 30 N.Y.2d 929, 335 N.Y.S.2d 684, 287 N.E.2d 378 (1972).

—It was a permissible intrusion for the officer to have called out for the defendant to stop, based upon reasonable suspicion provided by his flight from the bank with money in his hand, his continued glances over his shoulder, his entry into a vestibule to remove sunglasses and a hat, and his placing money in his knapsack. People v. Cummings, 207 A.D.2d 657, 616 N.Y.S.2d 43 (1st Dept. 1994).

—Frisk of defendant was justified because arresting officer reasonably suspected that he was in danger of physical injury. People v. Douglas, 254 A.D.2d 367, 679 N.Y.S.2d 147 (2d Dept. 1998).

—The arresting officer's testimony that he observed the defendant violate several provisions of the Vehicle and Traffic Law provided a sufficient basis to justify a stop of the vehicle. People v. Close, 207 A.D.2d 905, 616 N.Y.S.2d 669 (2d Dept. 1994).

—A police officer may stop a motor vehicle on a public highway when the stop is premised upon a reasonable suspicion that the vehicle's occupant's had been, are then, or are about to engage in conduct in violation of the law. People v. Riggio, 202 A.D.2d 609, 609 N.Y.S.2d 257 (2d Dept. 1994).

—Where police observed the outline of a gun in the defendant's jacket pocket, they were justified in conducting frisk of defendant. People v. Trulio, 135 A.D.2d 758, 522 N.Y.S.2d 663, 664 (2d Dept. 1987).

—Defendant's suspicious response to improper questioning by police officer could not serve as the lawful predicate for the officer's subsequent detention of the defendant and the order to him to get into his vehicle and produce his driver's license. People v. Cirrincione, 206 A.D.2d 833, 615 N.Y.S.2d 197 (4th Dept. 1994).

Suspicionless stops.—Where defendant was stopped pursuant to the Police Department's Taxi/Livery Robbery Inspection Program (TRIP), the TRIP stop at issue passed constitutional muster. Suspicionless stops may be upheld where reasonable. Under TRIP, the officer's discretion in the field is significantly constrained by the limitation of the program to participating vehicles—ones that have elected to participate. The owner of the car can also opt out of the program. People v. Abad, 98 N.Y.2d 12, 744 N.Y.S.2d 353, 771 N.E.2d 235 (2002).

Stop and frisk; reasonable cause; radio bulletin.—Police officers, responding to a radio call advising that there were men with guns at a specific street location, had sufficient reasonable suspicion to justify a limited patdown search when the defendant, who was standing on the sidewalk as the officers approached, stepped backwards and reached beneath his jacket to the rear of his waistband. People v. Benjamin, 51 N.Y.2d 267, 434 N.Y.S.2d 144, 414 N.E.2d 645 (1981).

Warrantless search of auto; probable cause.—The use of coat hanger to open defendant's car and search it when it was a few feet from the police station and a woman in the station had accused the defendant of menacing her with a gun and had seen it and defendant stated he had thrown away the keys to his expensive car was valid as probable cause existed. People v. Cabral, 91 A.D.2d 944, 458 N.Y.S.2d 559 (1st Dept.), *dism'd,* 59 N.Y.2d 704, 463 N.Y.S.2d 439, 450 N.E.2d 245 (1983).

§ 140.55. Arrest without a warrant; by peace officers of other states for offense committed outside state; uniform close pursuit act.

1. As used in this section, the word "state" shall include the District of Columbia.

2. Any peace officer of another state of the United States, who enters this state in close pursuit and continues within this state in such close pursuit of a person in order to arrest him, shall have the same authority to arrest and hold in custody such person on the ground that he has committed a crime in another state which is a crime under the laws of the state of New York, as police officers of this state have to arrest and hold in custody a person on the ground that he has committed a crime in this state.

3. If an arrest is made in this state by an officer of another state in accordance with the provisions of subdivision two, he shall without unnecessary delay take the person arrested before a local criminal court which shall conduct a hearing for the sole purpose of determining if the arrest was in accordance with the provisions of subdivision two, and not of determining the guilt or innocence of the arrested person. If such court determines that the arrest was in accordance with such subdivision, it shall commit the person arrested to the custody of the officer making the arrest, who shall without unnecessary delay take him to the state from which he fled. If such court determines that the arrest was unlawful, it shall discharge the person arrested.

4. This section shall not be construed so as to make unlawful any arrest in this state which would otherwise be lawful.

5. Upon the taking effect of this section it shall be the duty of the secretary of state to certify a copy of this section to the executive department of each of the states of the United States.

6. This section shall apply only to peace officers of a state which by its laws has made similar provision for the arrest and custody of persons closely pursued within the territory thereof.

7. If any part of this section is for any reason declared void, it is declared to be the intent of this section that such invalidity shall not affect the validity of the remaining portions of this section.

8. This section may be cited as the uniform act on close pursuit.

ANNOTATION

Out-of-state officers in New York.—Only an officer specially authorized to make arrests in New York can execute a federal warrant in New York for New York prosecution purposes; out-of-state police officers may be authorized to make arrests in New York, but generally only when they are in hot pursuit, which did not occur in the instant case. People v. LaFontaine, 92 N.Y.2d 470, 682 N.Y.S.2d 671, 705 N.E.2d 663 (1998).

ARTICLE 150—THE APPEARANCE TICKET

Section

150.10   **Appearance ticket; definition, form and content.**

150.20   **Appearance ticket; when and by whom issuable.**

150.30   **Appearance ticket; issuance and service thereof after arrest upon posting of pre-arraignment bail.**

150.40   **Appearance ticket; where returnable; how and where served.**

150.50   **Appearance ticket; filing a local criminal court accusatory instrument; dismissal of insufficient instrument.**

150.60   **Appearance ticket; defendant's failure to appear.**

150.70   **Appearance ticket; fingerprinting of defendant.**

150.75   **Appearance ticket; certain cases.**

§ 150.10. Appearance ticket; definition, form and content.

1. An appearance ticket is a written notice issued and subscribed by a police officer or other public servant authorized by state law or local law enacted pursuant to the provisions of the municipal home rule law to issue the same, directing a designated person to appear in a designated local criminal court at a designated future time in connection with his alleged commission of a designated offense. A notice conforming to such definition constitutes an appearance ticket regardless of whether it is referred to in some other provision of law as a summons or by any other name or title.

2. When an appearance ticket as defined in subdivision one of this section is issued to a person in conjunction with an offense charged in a simplified information, said appearance ticket shall contain the language, set forth in subdivision four of section 100.25, notifying the defendant of his right to receive a supporting deposition.

Amended by L. 1978, Ch. 495; L. 1996, Ch. 67, § 4, adding subd. 2, eff. 180 days after Oct. 27, 1996.

ANNOTATIONS

Accusatory instrument.—Issuance of desk appearance ticket (DAT) does not obviate need for filing of accusatory instrument. People v. Brisotti, 167 Misc. 2d 688, 635 N.Y.S.2d 442 (Bronx Co. Crim. Ct. 1995), aff'd, 169 Misc. 2d 672, 652 N.Y.S.2d 206 (App. Term, 1st Dept. 1996).

Jurisdiction.—An appearance ticket is not an accusatory instrument and does not give a court jurisdiction over a defendant; thus, the failure to file with the court a proper accusatory instrument mandates reversal and dismissal of the appearance ticket. People v. Lowry, 184 Misc. 2d 306, 708 N.Y.S.2d 811 (App. Term, 2d Dept. 2000).

—Parking violation summonses are the functional equivalent of appearance tickets; an appearance ticket is not an accusatory instrument, and its filing does not confer jurisdiction over defendant. People v. Gabbay, 175 Misc. 2d 421, 670 N.Y.S.2d 962 (2d Dept. App. Term 1997).

—"Appearance ticket" is written notice to appear in local criminal court on designated future time in connection with alleged commission of designated offense, and does not confer upon court jurisdiction over defendant or subject matter; rather, to do so, police officer who has issued and served such ticket must, at or before return date, file with local criminal court a misdemeanor complaint, simplified information, or information charging person named in ticket with offense specified therein. People v. Ashkinadze, 167 Misc. 2d 80, 636 N.Y.S.2d 554 (Kings Co. Crim. Ct. 1995).

Form and content.—A notice conforming to statutory definition of an appearance ticket qualifies as one regardless of whether it is called a summons or any other name or title, and statement signed by defendant when he was released on bail after arrest for driving while intoxicated contained all facts required by statute for appearance ticket. People v. Scott, 71 Misc. 2d 266, 335 N.Y.S.2d 659 (Port Jervis City Ct. 1972). Cf. People v. Cleland, 88 Misc. 2d, 704, 388 N.Y.S.2d 856 (Just. Ct. Town of Canton, St. Lawrence Co. 1976).

§ 150.20. Appearance ticket; when and by whom issuable.

1. Whenever a police officer is authorized pursuant to section 140.10 to arrest a person without a warrant for an offense other than a class A, B, C or D felony or a violation of section 130.25, 130.40, 205.10, 205.17, 205.19 or 215.56 of the penal law, he may, subject to the provisions of subdivisions three and four of section 150.40, instead issue to and serve upon such person an appearance ticket.

2. (a) Whenever a police officer has arrested a person without a warrant for an offense other than a class A, B, C or D felony or a violation of section 130.25, 130.40, 205.10, 205.17, 205.19 or 215.56 of the penal law pursuant to section 140.10, or

(b) whenever a peace officer, who is not authorized by law to issue an appearance ticket, has arrested a person for an offense other than a class A, B, C or D felony or a violation of section 130.25, 130.40, 205.10, 205.17, 205.19 or 215.56 of the penal law pursuant to section 140.25, and has requested a police officer to issue and serve upon such arrested person an appearance ticket pursuant to subdivision four of section 140.27, or

(c) whenever a person has been arrested for an offense other than a class A, B, C or D felony or a violation of section 130.25, 130.40, 205.10, 205.17, 205.19 or 215.56 of the penal law and has been delivered to the custody of an appropriate police officer pursuant to section 140.40, such police officer may, instead of bringing such person before a local criminal court and promptly filing or causing the arresting peace officer or arresting person to file a local criminal court accusatory instrument therewith, issue to and serve upon such person an appearance ticket. The issuance and service of an appearance ticket under such circumstances may be conditioned upon a deposit of pre-arraignment bail, as provided in section 150.30.

3. A public servant other than a police officer, who is specially authorized by state law or local law enacted pursuant to the provisions of the municipal home rule law to issue and serve appearance tickets with respect to designated offenses other than class A, B, C or D felonies or violations of section 130.25, 130.40, 205.10, 205.17, 205.19 or 215.56 of the penal law, may in such cases issue and serve upon a person an appearance ticket when he has reasonable cause to believe that such person has committed a crime, or has committed a petty offense in his presence.

Amended by L. 1972, Ch. 661; L. 1975, Ch. 78; L. 1978, Ch. 495; L. 1987, Chs. 549, 550.

ANNOTATIONS

Jurisdiction.—Parking violation summonses are the functional equivalent of appearance tickets; an appearance ticket is not an accusatory instrument, and its filing does not confer jurisdiction over defendant. People v. Gabbay, 175 Misc. 2d 421, 670 N.Y.S.2d 962 (2d Dept. App. Term 1997).

—Appearance ticket is not accusatory instrument, and its filing does not give criminal court jurisdiction over defendant. People v. Weinberg, 146 Misc. 2d 441, 558 N.Y.S.2d 439 (App. Term 1990).

Advise by judge.—A judge in the Summons Part need not advise a respondent-appearing for the purpose of determining if he should be charged with a crime of a right to counsel and the free assistance of counsel. People v. Doherty, 98 Misc. 2d 878, 414 N.Y.S.2d 844 (Crim. Ct. N.Y.C. 1979).

Frisk; stop for erratic driving was improper.—The fruits of the search were suppressed as the arrest was not necessary because use of appearance ticket was available where the police proceeded to frisk defendant merely because they observed what they thought to be erratic driving. People v. Howell, 49 N.Y.2d 778, 426 N.Y.S.2d 477, 403 N.E.2d 182 (1980).

§ 150.30. Appearance ticket; issuance and service thereof after arrest upon posting of pre-arraignment bail.

1. Issuance and service of an appearance ticket by a police officer following an arrest without a warrant, as prescribed in subdivision two of section 150.20, may be made conditional upon the posting of a sum of money, known as pre-arraignment bail. In such case, the bail becomes forfeit upon failure of such person to comply with the directions of the appearance ticket. The person posting such bail must complete and sign a form which states (a) the name, residential address and occupation of each person posting cash bail; and (b) the title of the criminal action or proceeding involved; and (c) the offense or offenses which are the subjects of the action or proceeding involved, and the status of such action or proceeding; and (d) the name of the principal and the nature of his involvement in or connection with such action or proceeding; and (e) the date of the principal's next appearance in court; and (f) an

acknowledgment that the cash bail will be forfeited if the principal does not comply with the directions of the appearance ticket; and (g) the amount of money posted as cash bail. Such pre-arraignment bail may be posted as provided in subdivision two or three.

2. A desk officer in charge at a police station, county jail, or police headquarters, or any of his superior officers, may in such place, fix pre-arraignment bail, in an amount prescribed in this subdivision, and upon the posting thereof must issue and serve an appearance ticket upon the arrested person, give a receipt for the bail, and release such person from custody. Such pre-arraignment bail may be fixed in the following amounts:

(a) If the arrest was for a class E felony, any amount not exceeding seven hundred fifty dollars.

(b) If the arrest was for a class A misdemeanor, any amount not exceeding five hundred dollars.

(c) If the arrest was for a class B misdemeanor or an unclassified misdemeanor, any amount not exceeding two hundred fifty dollars.

(d) If the arrest was for a petty offense, any amount not exceeding one hundred dollars.

3. A police officer, who has arrested a person without a warrant pursuant to subdivision two of section 150.20 of this chapter for a traffic infraction, may, where he reasonably believes that such arrested person is not licensed to operate a motor vehicle by this state or any state covered by a reciprocal compact guaranteeing appearance as is provided in section five hundred seventeen of the vehicle and traffic law, fix pre-arraignment bail in the amount of fifty dollars; provided, however, such bail shall be posted by means of a credit card or similar device. Upon the posting thereof, said officer must issue and serve an appearance ticket upon the arrested person, give a receipt for the bail, and release such person from custody.

4. The chief administrator of the courts shall establish a system for the posting of pre-arraignment bail by means of credit card or similar device, as is provided by section two hundred twelve of the judiciary law. The head of each police department or police force and of any state department, agency, board, commission or public authority having police officers who fix pre-arraignment bail as provided herein may elect to use the system established by the chief administrator or may establish such other system for the posting of pre-arraignment bail by means of credit card or similar device as he or she may deem appropriate.

Amended by L. 1986, Ch. 708; L. 1987, Ch. 111; L. 1987, Ch. 549; L. 1987, Ch. 805.

ANNOTATIONS

Defendant's behavior before completion of bail process.— Since the bail process had not been completed, the desk officer

CPL

properly exercised his discretion in not releasing defendant based upon defendant's belligerent and insolent behavior. People v. Johnson, 148 A.D.2d 940, 539 N.Y.S.2d 178 (4th Dept.), aff'd, 74 N.Y.2d 906, 549 N.Y.S.2d 957, 549 N.E.2d 148 (1989).

Appearance ticket; form and content.—A notice conforming to statutory definition of an appearance ticket qualifies as one regardless of whether it is called a summons or any other name or title, and statement signed by defendant when he was released on bail after arrest for driving while intoxicated contained all facts required by statute for appearance ticket. People v. Scott, 71 Misc. 2d 266, 335 N.Y.S.2d 659 (Port Jervis City Ct. 1972).

Pre-arraignment bail; excessiveness.—Though police officer placed defendant under arrest and fixed pre-arraignment bail at $300 instead of statutory maximum of $250 it was not excessive and did not warrant dismissal of charges. People v. Scott, 71 Misc. 2d 266, 335 N.Y.S.2d 659 (Port Jervis City Ct. 1972).

§ 150.40. Appearance ticket; where returnable; how and where served.

1. An appearance ticket must be made returnable in a local criminal court designated in section 100.55 as one with which an information for the offense in question may be filed.

2. An appearance ticket, other than one issued for a traffic infraction relating to parking, must be served personally, except that an appearance ticket issued for the violation of a local zoning ordinance or zoning law, or of a building or sanitation code may be served in any manner authorized for service under section three hundred eight of the civil practice law and rules.

3. An appearance ticket may be served anywhere in the county in which the designated offense was allegedly committed or in any adjoining county, and may be served elsewhere as prescribed in subdivision four.

4. A police officer may, for the purpose of serving an appearance ticket upon a person, follow him in continuous close pursuit, commencing either in the county in which the alleged offense was committed or in an adjoining county, in and through any county of the state, and may serve such appearance ticket upon him in any county in which he overtakes him.

Amended by L. 2004, Ch. 415, §1, eff. Aug. 17, 2004, amending subd. 2; L. 2005, Ch. 642, § 1, amending subd. 2, eff. Aug. 30, 2005.

ANNOTATIONS

Appearance ticket; where returnable.—CPL § 150.40(1) serves as a coordinating function tying the place where the DAT is returnable to the Court where the accusatory instrument is to be filed. Thus, a DAT issued in New York County cannot be made returnable to a criminal court in Bronx County. This section does not address where within the Courthouse edifice the DAT is returnable and, thus, where the defendant must appear. People v. Weaver, 166 Misc. 2d 488, 634 N.Y.S.2d 968 (Bronx Co. Crim. Ct. 1995).

Appearance ticket; service.—Service of desk appearance tickets by mail on director and clergyman associated with local religious centers for violating local law for failing to operate existing structures with proper exit lighting with regard to premises over which director and clergyman were allegedly in control and for which they were allegedly mailed prior notice

was invalid. People v. Neuberger, 149 Misc. 2d 1, 570 N.Y.S.2d 256 (N.Y. Crim. Ct. 1991).

§ 150.50. Appearance ticket; filing a local criminal court accusatory instrument; dismissal of insufficient instrument.

1. A police officer or other public servant who has issued and served an appearance ticket must, at or before the time such appearance ticket is returnable, file or cause to be filed with the local criminal court in which it is returnable a local criminal court accusatory instrument charging the person named in such appearance ticket with the offense specified therein. Nothing herein contained shall authorize the use of a simplified information when not authorized by law.

2. If such accusatory instrument is not sufficient on its face, as prescribed in section 100.40, and if the court is satisfied that on the basis of the available facts or evidence it would be impossible to draw and file an accusatory instrument which is sufficient on its face, it must dismiss such accusatory instrument.

Amended by L. 1972, Ch. 661; L. 1987, Ch. 549; L. 2004, Ch. 415, § 1, eff. Aug. 17, 2004, amending subd. 2.

ANNOTATIONS

Transmission of data.—The transmission of data to the computer of the court below did not in any event constitute the filing of an accusatory instrument, particularly in the absence of a verified, written accusation. The parking summons, moreover, was akin to an appearance ticket rather than an accusatory instrument and the filing of an accusatory instrument was necessary for the court below to acquire jurisdiction. People v. Gilberg, 166 Misc. 2d 772, 637 N.Y.S.2d 917 (Sup. Ct. App. Term 1995).

Late filing.—Although CPL § 150.50 explicitly requires the People to file an accusatory instrument on or before the return date of a DAT, the statute is silent as to the effect of late filing. People v. Brisotti, 167 Misc. 2d 688, 635 N.Y.S.2d 442 (Bronx Co. Crim. Ct. 1995), aff'd, 169 Misc. 2d 672, 652 N.Y.S.2d 206 (App. Term, 1st Dept. 1996).

Accusatory instrument; necessity.—If a defendant voluntarily appears in court in response to an appearance ticket, a judge cannot arraign him unless an accusatory instrument has been filed or unless the officer is present to charge him and an accusatory instrument is filed. People v. Rodriguez, 90 Misc. 2d 356, 394 N.Y.S.2d 542 (Village Ct. of Rockville Centre 1977).

§ 150.60. Appearance ticket; defendant's failure to appear.

If after the service of an appearance ticket and the filing of a local criminal court accusatory instrument charging the offense designated therein, the defendant does not appear in the designated local criminal court at the time such appearance ticket is returnable, the court may issue a summons or a warrant of arrest based upon the local criminal court accusatory instrument filed.

Amended by L. 1987, Ch. 549.

ANNOTATIONS

Accusatory instrument.—Until an accusatory instrument is filed, a court cannot issue a summons or warrant of arrest to compel a defendant's appearance. People v. Brisotti, 167 Misc. 2d 688, 635 N.Y.S.2d 442 (Bronx Co. Crim. Ct. 1995).

—Court may only issue summons or arrest warrant with respect to a desk appearance ticket (DAT) when the People have filed an accusatory instrument and the accused failed to appear in court on the return date specified in the DAT. People v. Fysekis, 164 Misc. 2d 627, 625 N.Y.S.2d 861 (Bronx Co. Crim. Ct. 1995).

§ 150.70. Appearance ticket; fingerprinting of defendant.

Upon the arraignment of a defendant who has not been arrested and whose court attendance has been secured by the issuance and service of an appearance ticket pursuant to subdivision one of section 150.20, the court must, if an offense charged in the accusatory instrument is one specified in subdivision one of section 160.10, direct that the defendant be fingerprinted by the appropriate police officer or agency, and that he appear at an appropriate designated time and place for such purpose.

Amended by L. 1971, Ch. 762.

ANNOTATION

Mandatory fingerprinting.—If offense charged in accusatory instrument is one for which fingerprinting is mandatory, court must direct that defendant be fingerprinted by appropriate police officer or agency. People v. Ashinadze, 167 Misc. 2d 80, 636 N.Y.S.2d 554 (Kings Co. Crim. Ct. 1995).

§ 150.75. Appearance ticket; certain cases.

1. The provisions of this section shall apply in any case wherein the defendant is alleged to have committed an offense defined in section 221.05 of the penal law, and no other offense is alleged, notwithstanding any provision of this chapter or any other law to the contrary.

2. Whenever the defendant is arrested without a warrant, an appearance ticket shall promptly be issued and served upon him, as provided in this article. The issuance and service of the appearance ticket may be made conditional upon the posting of pre-arraignment bail as provided in section 150.30 of this chapter but only if the appropriate police officer (a) is unable to ascertain the defendant's identity or residence address; or (b) reasonably suspects that the identification or residence address given by the defendant is not accurate; or (c) reasonably suspects that the defendant does not reside within the state. No warrant of arrest shall be issued unless the defendant has failed to appear in court as required by the terms of the appearance ticket or by the court.

Added by L. 1977, Ch. 360.

ANNOTATION

Arrest prior to issuance of appearance ticket.—Police were authorized to arrest defendant for possession of marijuana before issuance of appearance ticket. People v. Conte, 159 A.D.2d 993, 552 N.Y.S.2d 743 (4th Dept. 1990).

ARTICLE 160—FINGERPRINTING AND PHOTOGRAPHING OF DEFENDANT AFTER ARREST—CRIMINAL IDENTIFICATION RECORDS AND STATISTICS

LexisNexis Cross References

Criminal Defense Techniques, Vol. 3A, Ch. 66, The Polygraph; *Forensic Sciences,* Vol. 3, Ch. 34, The Polygraph: Basic Information and Admissibility of Evidence; *New York Criminal Practice (2d ed.),* Vol. 1, Ch. 9, Local Criminal Court Arraignment and Related Issues; *New York Suppression Manual* Ch. 10, Procedures After Arrest; Ch. 22, Interrogation and Confessions: Voluntariness; *see generally Police Investigation Handbook.*

§ 160.10. Fingerprinting; duties of police with respect thereto.

1. Following an arrest, or following the arraignment upon a local criminal court accusatory instrument of a defendant whose court attendance has been secured by a summons or an appearance ticket under circumstances described in sections 130.60 and 150.70, the arresting or other appropriate police officer or agency must take or cause to be taken fingerprints of the arrested person or defendant if an offense which is the subject of the arrest or which is charged in the accusatory instrument filed is:

(a) A felony; or

(b) A misdemeanor defined in the penal law; or

(c) A misdemeanor defined outside the penal law which would constitute a felony if such person had a previous judgment of conviction for a crime; or

(d) Loitering, as defined in subdivision three of section 240.35 of the penal law; or

(e) Loitering for the purpose of engaging in a prostitution offense as defined in subdivision two of section 240.37 of the penal law.

2. In addition, a police officer who makes an arrest for any offense, either with or without a warrant, may take or cause to be taken the fingerprints of the arrested person if such police officer:

(a) Is unable to ascertain such person's identity; or

(b) Reasonably suspects that the identification given by such person is not accurate; or

(c) Reasonably suspects that such person is being sought by law enforcement officials for the commission of some other offense.

3. Whenever fingerprints are required to be taken pursuant to subdivision one or permitted to be taken pursuant to subdivision two, the photograph and palmprints of the arrested person or defendant, as the case may be, may also be taken.

4. The taking of fingerprints as prescribed in this section and the submission of available information concerning the arrested person or the defendant and the facts and circumstances of the crime charged must be in accordance with the standards established by the commissioner of the division of criminal justice services.

Amended by L. 1971, Ch. 762; L. 1972, Ch. 399; L. 1976, Ch. 344.

ANNOTATIONS

Jurisdiction.—Failure of state police to fingerprint motorist when arrested on driving while intoxicated charge did not deprive court of jurisdiction. People v. Crandall, 228 A.D.2d 794, 644 N.Y.S.2d 817 (3d Dept. 1996).

Admission of fingerprint card tending to imply prior criminal activity of the accused.—It was reversible error to admit into evidence a fingerprint card containing caption "arrest record," prepared in connection with an unrelated crime since it failed to protect the defendant adequately against the prejudicial jury inference that he had a criminal history. People v. Balone, 52 A.D.2d 216, 383 N.Y.S.2d 726 (4th Dept. 1976).

Delay in arraignment.—The delay in an arraignment occasioned by fingerprinting and the shuttling of defendant from police officer to police officer was "required in the particular case" within the meaning of CPL § 140.20(1) and CPL § 160.10(2)(b) and (c) where the arresting officer reasonably suspected that the identification given by defendant was not accurate and that defendant was being sought for the commission of some other offense. People v. Cunningham, 97 Misc. 2d 618, 411 N.Y.S.2d 963 (Allegany Co. Ct. 1978).

Palm prints.—CPL § 160.10(2) provided the court with jurisdiction to compel the defendants arrested for one crime to submit to palm printing in connection with another crime since the section grants a police officer who makes an arrest for an offense the right to secure fingerprints and palm prints when he "reasonably suspects such person is being sought by law enforcement officials for the commission of some other offense." People v. Mineo, 85 Misc. 2d 919, 381 N.Y.S.2d 179 (Sup. Ct. Queens Co. 1976).

Return of fingerprints; sentence for failure to post bond.—One sentenced for 30 days to correctional institution for failure to post bond in alimony default was not convicted of crime and must be released and have his fingerprints returned on demand. Hofman v. Malcolm, 71 Misc. 2d 251, 335 N.Y.S.2d 938 (Sup. Ct. N.Y. Co. 1972).

Right to photograph.—CPL § 160.10(3) authorizes the taking of photograph of an arrestee, and thus, it was proper for the photograph to be taken of defendant's upper body tattoos depicting racial and ethnic stereotypes in case involving an attack of two Mexican day laborers. People v. Slavin, 1 N.Y.3d 392, 775 N.Y.S.2d 210, 807 N.E.2d 259 (2004), *cert. denied*, — U.S. —, 125 S. Ct. 64 (2004).

—When the police, without probable cause and not incidental to an arrest, detain and photograph an individual it is a deliberate violation of the Fourth Amendment, and is even more egregious when that photograph becomes a permanent mug shot. People v. Johnson, 88 Misc. 2d 749, 389 N.Y.S.2d 766 (Onondaga Co. Ct. 1976).

Fingerprinting not required.—Sentence for violation of the Agriculture and Markets Law is not an offense specified in CPL § 160.10 and does not require fingerprinting of the defendant before sentence may be executed. People v. O'Rourke, 83 Misc. 2d 51, 371 N.Y.S.2d 603 (Crim. Ct. N.Y.C. 1975).

§ 160.20. Fingerprinting; forwarding of fingerprints.

Upon the taking of fingerprints of an arrested person or defendant as prescribed in section 160.10, the appropriate police officer or agency must without unnecessary delay forward two copies of such fingerprints to the division of criminal justice services.

Amended by L. 1973, Ch. 108.

ANNOTATIONS

Procedure.—Police officers have a statutory obligation to take fingerprints and to submit them to the proper agency. People v. Johnson, 168 A.D.2d 700, 564 N.Y.S.2d 206 (3d Dept. 1990).

—After the fingerprints are obtained by the police, they are transmitted to the Division of Criminal Justice. The Division of Criminal Justice generates a "NYSID" sheet and promptly transmits it to the police. People v. Ashkinadze, 167 Misc. 2d 80, 636 N.Y.S.2d 554 (Kings Co. Crim. Ct. 1995).

§ 160.30. Fingerprinting; duties of division of criminal justice services.

1. Upon receiving fingerprints from a police officer or agency pursuant to section 160.20 of this chapter, the division of criminal justice services must, except as provided in subdivision two of this section, classify them and search its records for information concerning a previous record of the defendant, including any adjudication as a juvenile delinquent pursuant to article three of the family court act, or as a youthful

offender pursuant to article seven hundred twenty of this chapter, and promptly transmit to such forwarding police officer or agency a report containing all information on file with respect to such defendant's previous record, if any, or stating that the defendant has no previous record according to its files. Such a report, if certified, constitutes presumptive evidence of the facts so certified.

2. If the fingerprints so received are not sufficiently legible to permit accurate and complete classification, they must be returned to the forwarding police officer or agency with an explanation of the defects and a request that the defendant's fingerprints be retaken if possible.

Amended by L. 1971, Ch. 762; L. 1972, Ch. 399; L. 1977, Ch. 447; L. 1982, Ch. 920.

§ 160.40. Fingerprinting; transmission of report received by police.

1. Upon receipt of a report of the division of criminal justice services as provided in section 160.30, the recipient police officer or agency must promptly transmit such report or a copy thereof to the district attorney of the county and two copies thereof to the court in which the action is pending.

2. Upon receipt of such report the court shall furnish a copy thereof to counsel for the defendant or, if the defendant is not represented by counsel, to the defendant.

Amended by L. 1971, Ch. 762; L. 1972, Ch. 399; L. 1975, Ch. 531.

§ 160.45. Polygraph tests; prohibition against.

1. No district attorney, police officer or employee of any law enforcement agency shall request or require any victim of a sexual assault crime to submit to any polygraph test or psychological stress evaluator examination.

2. As used in this section, "victim of a sexual assault crime" means any person alleged to have sustained an offense under article one hundred thirty or section 255.25 of the penal law.

Added by L. 1987, Ch. 589; **Amended** by L. 1990, Ch. 78; L. 1996, Ch. 17, § 1, amending subd. 1, eff. Feb. 27, 1996.

§ 160.50. Order upon termination of criminal action in favor of the accused.

1. Upon the termination of a criminal action or proceeding against a person in favor of such person, as defined in subdivision three of this section, unless the district attorney upon motion with not less than five days notice to such person or his or her attorney demonstrates to the satisfaction of the court that the interests of justice require otherwise, or the court on its own motion with

not less than five days notice to such person or his or her attorney determines that the interests of justice require otherwise and states the reasons for such determination on the record, the record of such action or proceeding shall be sealed and the clerk of the court wherein such criminal action or proceeding was terminated shall immediately notify the commissioner of the division of criminal justice services and the heads of all appropriate police departments and other law enforcement agencies that the action has been terminated in favor of the accused, and unless the court has directed otherwise, that the record of such action or proceeding shall be sealed. Upon receipt of notification of such termination and sealing:

(a) every photograph of such person and photographic plate or proof, and all palmprints and fingerprints taken or made of such person pursuant to the provisions of this article in regard to the action or proceeding terminated, except a dismissal pursuant to section 170.56 or 210.46 of this chapter, and all duplicates and copies thereof, except a digital fingerprint image where authorized pursuant to paragraph (e) of this subdivision, shall forthwith be, at the discretion of the recipient agency, either destroyed or returned to such person, or to the attorney who represented such person at the time of the termination of the action or proceeding, at the address given by such person or attorney during the action or proceeding, by the division of criminal justice services and by any police department or law enforcement agency having any such photograph, photographic plate or proof, palmprint or fingerprints in its possession or under its control;

(b) any police department or law enforcement agency, including the division of criminal justice services, which transmitted or otherwise forwarded to any agency of the United States or of any other state or of any other jurisdiction outside the state of New York copies of any such photographs, photographic plates or proofs, palmprints and fingerprints, including those relating to actions or proceedings which were dismissed pursuant to section 170.56 or 210.46 of this chapter, shall forthwith formally request in writing that all such copies be destroyed or returned to the police department or law enforcement agency which transmitted or forwarded them, and, if returned, such department shall, at its discretion, either destroy or return them as provided herein, except that those relating to dismissals pursuant to section 170.56 or 210.46 of this chapter shall not be destroyed or returned by such department or agency;

(c) all official records and papers, including judgments and orders of a court but not including published court decisions or opinions or records and briefs on appeal, relating to the arrest or prosecution, including all duplicates and copies thereof, on file with the division of criminal justice services, any court, police agency, or prosecutor's office shall be sealed and not made available to any person or public or private agency;

(d) such records shall be made available to the person accused or to such person's designated agent, and shall be made available to (i) a prosecutor in any proceeding in which the accused has moved for an order pursuant to section 170.56 or 210.46 of this chapter, or (ii) a law enforcement agency upon ex parte motion in any superior court, if such agency demonstrates to the satisfaction of the court that justice requires that such records be made available to it, or (iii) any state or local officer or agency with responsibility for the issuance of licenses to possess guns, when the accused has made application for such a license, or (iv) the New York state division of parole when the accused is on parole supervision as a result of conditional release or a parole release granted by the New York state board of parole, and the arrest which is the subject of the inquiry is one which occurred while the accused was under such supervision or (v) any prospective employer of a police officer or peace officer as those terms are defined in subdivisions thirty-three and thirty-four of section 1.20 of this chapter, in relation to an application for employment as a police officer or peace officer; provided, however, that every person who is an applicant for the position of police officer or peace officer shall be furnished with a copy of all records obtained under this paragraph and afforded an opportunity to make an explanation thereto, or (vi) the probation department responsible for supervision of the accused when the arrest which is the subject of the inquiry is one which occurred while the accused was under such supervision; and

(e) where fingerprints subject to the provisions of this section have been received by the division of criminal justice services and have been filed by the division as digital images, such images may be retained, provided that a fingerprint card of the individual is on file with the division which was not sealed pursuant to this section or section 160.55 of this article.

2. A report of the termination of the action or proceeding in favor of the accused shall be sufficient notice of sealing to the commissioner of the division of criminal justice services unless the report also indicates that the court directed that the record not be sealed in the interests of justice. Where the court has determined pursuant to subdivision one of this section that sealing in not in the interest of justice, the clerk of the court shall include notification of that determination in any report to such division of the disposition of the action or proceeding.

3. For the purposes of subdivision one of this section, a criminal action or proceeding against a person shall be considered terminated in favor of such person where:

(a) an order dismissing the entire accusatory

instrument against such person pursuant to article four hundred seventy was entered; or

(b) an order to dismiss the entire accusatory instrument against such person pursuant to section 170.30, 170.50, 170.55, 170.56, 180.70, 210.20, 210.46 or 210.47 of this chapter was entered or deemed entered, or an order terminating the prosecution against such person was entered pursuant to section 180.85 of this chapter, and the people have not appealed from such order or the determination of an appeal or appeals by the people from such order has been against the people; or

(c) a verdict of complete acquittal was made pursuant to section 330.10 of this chapter; or

(d) a trial order of dismissal of the entire accusatory instrument against such person pursuant to section 290.10 or 360.40 of this chapter was entered and the people have not appealed from such order or the determination of an appeal or appeals by the people from such order has been against the people; or

(e) an order setting aside a verdict pursuant to section 330.30 or 370.10 of this chapter was entered and the people have not appealed from such order or the determination of an appeal or appeals by the people from such order has been against the people and no new trial has been ordered; or

(f) an order vacating a judgment pursuant to section 440.10 of this chapter was entered and the people have not appealed from such order or the determination of an appeal or appeals by the people from such order has been against the people, and no new trial has been ordered; or

(g) an order of discharge pursuant to article seventy of the civil practice law and rules was entered on a ground which invalidates the conviction and the people have not appealed from such order or the determination of an appeal or appeals by the people from such order has been against the people; or

(h) where all charges against such person are dismissed pursuant to section 190.75 of this chapter. In such event, the clerk of the court which empaneled the grand jury shall serve a certification of such disposition upon the division of criminal justice services and upon the appropriate police department or law enforcement agency which upon receipt thereof, shall comply with the provisions of paragraphs (a), (b), (c) and (d) of subdivision one of this section in the same manner as is required thereunder with respect to an order of a court entered pursuant to said subdivision one; or

(i) prior to the filing of an accusatory instrument in a local criminal court against such person, the prosecutor elects not to prosecute such person. In such event, the prosecutor shall serve a certification of such disposition upon the division of criminal justice services and upon the appropriate police department or law enforcement agency which, upon receipt thereof, shall comply with the provisions of paragraphs (a), (b), (c) and (d) of subdivision one of this section in the same manner as is required thereunder with respect to an order of a court entered pursuant to said subdivision one.

(j) following the arrest of such person, the arresting police agency, prior to the filing of an accusatory instrument in a local criminal court but subsequent to the forwarding of a copy of the fingerprints of such person to the division of criminal justice services, elects not to proceed further. In such event, the head of the arresting police agency shall serve a certification of such disposition upon the division of criminal justice services which, upon receipt thereof, shall comply with the provisions of paragraphs (a), (b), (c) and (d) of subdivision one of this section in the same manner as is required thereunder with respect to an order of a court entered pursuant to said subdivision one.

(k) (i) the accusatory instrument alleged a violation of article two hundred twenty or section 240.36 of the penal law, prior to the taking effect of article two hundred twenty-one of the penal law, or a violation of article two hundred twenty-one of the penal law;

(ii) the sole controlled substance involved is marijuana;

(iii) the conviction was only for a violation or violations; and

(iv) at least three years have passed since the offense occurred.

(l) An order dismissing an action pursuant to section 215.40 of this chapter was entered.

4. A person in whose favor a criminal action or proceeding was terminated, as defined in paragraph (a) through (h) of subdivision two of this section, prior to the effective date of this section, may upon motion apply to the court in which such termination occurred, upon not less than twenty days notice to the district attorney, for an order granting to such person the relief set forth in subdivision one of this section, and such order shall be granted unless the district attorney demonstrates to the satisfaction of the court that the interests of justice require otherwise. A person in whose favor a criminal action or proceeding was terminated, as defined in paragraph (i) or (j) of subdivision two of this section, prior to the effective date of this section, may apply to the appropriate prosecutor or police agency for a certification as described in said paragraph (i) or (j) granting to such person the relief set forth therein, and such certification shall be granted by such prosecutor or police agency.

Added by L. 1976, Ch. 877; **Amended** by L. 1977, Chs. 835, 905; L. 1980, Ch. 192; L. 1981, Ch. 122; L. 1985, Ch. 208; L. 1986, Ch. 294; Ch. 837; L. 1991, Ch. 142; L. 1994, Ch. 169; L. 1995, Ch. 3, § 54, extending expiration date of subd. 1 to Sept. 1; L. 1997, Ch. 435, § 63, eff. Aug. 20, 1997, deleting expiration date of subd. 1; L. 2001, Ch. 487, eff. Nov. 1, 2002, amending subd. 3(b); L. 2004, Ch. 518, § 1, eff. November 1, 2004.

ANNOTATIONS

Statutory purpose.—Purpose of statute providing for sealing of record when criminal proceeding terminates in favor of accused is to insure that one who is charged but not convicted of offense suffers no stigma as result of his having once been object of unsustained accusation. People v. White, 169 A.D.2d 89, 642 N.Y.S.2d 492 (Sup. Ct. Bronx Co. 1996).

Appealability of ruling.—A court's ruling on a CPL § 160.50 motion is a civil matter and is thus appealable by defendant, who is an aggrieved party. People v. Anonymous, 7 A.D.3d 309, 776 N.Y.S.2d 282 (1st Dept. 2004).

Application of statute.—Although the sealing provision is generally invoked by those seeking to protect their civilian reputation and employment prospects, nothing in the statute prevents its full and intended application to that part of petitioner's RAP sheet which reflects that he was arrested on resisting arrest and disorderly conduct and that the charges were ultimately dismissed. Burr v. Goord, 283 A.D.2d 891, 725 N.Y.S.2d 151 (3d Dept. 2001).

Arrest photographs.—Absence at trial of arrest photographs used in confirmatory identification procedure did not require suppression of identification, since absence was result of return of photographs, which were needed in unrelated prosecution, by court order. People v. Cuevas, 167 Misc. 2d 738, 634 N.Y.S.2d 992 (Kings Co. Sup. Ct. 1995).

Grand jury minutes.—CPL § 160.50(1)(c), which embraces "all official records and papers . . . relating to the arrest and prosecution," includes and it is applicable to grand jury minutes. In re Attorney General, 101 Misc. 2d 36, 420 N.Y.S.2d 685 (Sup. Ct. Suffolk Co. 1979).

Defendant convicted of violation and acquitted of misdemeanor.—Where defendant, charged with a misdemeanor and two violations was convicted of the violation of disorderly conduct and acquitted of the misdemeanor, he was entitled to have photographs and prints returned and the record sealed pursuant to CPL § 160.50 since he would not have been photographed and fingerprinted if the initial accusations had only been violations. People v. Burns, 104 Misc. 2d 415, 428 N.Y.S.2d 588 (City Ct. Westchester Co. 1980).

District Attorney; motion to restore cause to calendar.—On the District Attorney ex parte motion, the court directed the clerk to calendar the matter under a suitable fictitious pseudonym and to deliver the sealed docket directly to the court on the date set for hearing the District Attorney's motion, on notice to the defendant, to restore the cause to the calendar, for temporary unsealing during the argument and forthwith resealing thereafter, if appropriate. People v. Anonymous, 99 Misc. 2d 537, 416 N.Y.S.2d 994 (Crim. Ct. N.Y.C. 1979).

—Family Court can issue a sealing order when Juvenile Delinquency proceedings terminates in juvenile's favor within the meaning of CPL § 160.50. In re Tony W., 91 Misc. 2d 700, 398 N.Y.S.2d 528 (Fam. Ct. N.Y. Co. 1977).

DNA profile.—Where defendant was prosecuted for rape, the use of a DNA profile of him kept by the Office of Chief Medical Examiner from a previous case in 1997, in which he was acquitted, did not violate CPL 160.50, which requires a sealing of records in court files upon termination of a criminal action in favor of the defendant, insofar as DNA evidence is not specifically mentioned in the statute and the court declined to expand the statutory provisions to include DNA. People v. Midgley, 196 Misc. 2d 19, 763 N.Y.S.2d 419 (Sup. Ct. Kings Co.), related proceeding, Midgley v. Goldberg, 2 A.D.3d 735, 768 N.Y.S.2d 624 (2d Dept. 2003).

Guilty pleas.—By pleading guilty, defendant waived his claim that his arrest and lineup identification resulted from DNA evidence that had been obtained in violation of the sealing requirements of CPL § 160.50, and in any event, a violation of CPL § 160.50 would not entitle defendant to suppression of the lineup identification or dismissal of the indictment. People v. Mosquea, 18 A.D.3d 228, 794 N.Y.S.2d 51 (1st Dept. 2005).

—CPL § 160.50 requires records be sealed where the criminal action is terminated in favor of the accused, as set forth in that statute. In this case, the charges that defendant seeks to have sealed were "satisfied" by a guilty plea in another court because this disposition is not specifically enumerated in CPL § 160.50 as a disposition constituting a termination in favor of the accused, the defendant does not have a right to have the records sealed. People v. Schleyer, 192 Misc. 2d 113, 746 N.Y.S.2d 365 (City Ct. of Rochester 2002.)

—Where defendant pleaded to "cover" three offenses, there was no favorable termination as to any of three offenses as provided in CPL § 160.50(2). People v. Ebner, 95 Misc. 2d 781, 408 N.Y.S.2d 234 (Crim. Ct. N.Y.C. 1978).

Juvenile.—Juvenile delinquent whose case was ACD and later dismissed by Family Court was entitled to have his records sealed and his arrest made a nullity, pursuant to CPL § 160.50. In re Kenneth M., 92 Misc. 2d 351, 399 N.Y.S.2d 843 (Fam. Ct. N.Y. Co. 1977).

Family offense proceeding; motion for return of fingerprints and photos.—Arrestee's motion for an order directing the return to him of all photos, fingerprints and other identification material, as well as the sealing of all official records, should be granted notwithstanding the fact that the matter had been transferred to the Family Court pursuant to Art. 8 of the Family Court Act, and therein dismissed for failure of prosecution. Schwartz v. Schwartz, 94 Misc. 2d 1071, 406 N.Y.S.2d 253 (Fam. Ct. Suffolk Co. 1978).

Motion to unseal in the interest of justice; when authorized.—CPL § 160.50(1) does not authorize the unsealing of records where a defendant-attorney has been acquitted in a criminal case for purposes of assisting the bar association grievance committee in determining whether or not to institute disciplinary proceedings. Hynes v. Karassik, 47 N.Y.2d 659, 419 N.Y.S.2d 942, 393 N.E.2d 1015 (1979); see also In re "R" anonymous, 81 A.D.2d 901, 439 N.Y.S.2d 172 (2d Dept. 1981).

—Investigation and audit reports prepared by the Office of the Special Prosecutor during the investigation and previous prosecution of defendants, do not constitute "official records and papers" within the meaning of CPL § 160.50(1)(c). People v. Neuman, 104 Misc. 2d 324, 428 N.Y.S.2d 577 (Sup. Ct. Westchester Co. 1980).

Plea of guilty to a violation.—After the defendant pled guilty to a violation in satisfaction of a misdemeanor charge the court directed that the Commissioner of Criminal Justice Services and the heads of all police departments and other law enforcement agencies return copies of the fingerprints, palmprints and photographs to the defendant and that records of arrest at these agencies be amended to reflect the arrest and conviction for the violation and that the court records also be amended accordingly. People v. Robertson, 97 Misc. 2d 1026, 412 N.Y.S.2d 982 (Crim. Ct. N.Y. Co. 1979).

—A plea of guilty to a violation after being charged with a misdemeanor is not a "favorable termination" under CPL § 160.50 and a writ of prohibition was granted where Criminal Court Judge exceeds his powers in ordering the return of fingerprints, palmprints and photographs to defendant under these circumstances. Morgenthau v. Becker, 102 Misc. 2d 507, 423 N.Y.S.2d 977 (Sup. Ct. N.Y. Co. 1979).

Miscellaneous.—Even in a criminal proceeding, evidence obtained through violation of CPL § 160.50 order need not be suppressed if no constitutional right is implicated. Charles Q. v Constantine, 204 A.D.2d 904, 612 N.Y.S.2d 687 (3d Dept. 1994), aff'd, 85 N.Y.2d 571, 626 N.Y.S.2d 992, 650 N.E.2d 839 (1995).

—The mere retention and use of a photograph in violation of CPL § 160.50, for identification purposes in a homicide investigation, did not violate defendant's due process of law rights guaranteed under the Fifth and Fourteenth Amendments or abridge the defendant's Fourth Amendment rights against an unreasonable search and seizure. People v. Anderson, 97 Misc. 2d 408, 411 N.Y.S.2d 830 (Sup. Ct. Bronx Co. 1978).

—The dismissal of an information based upon the inherent power of a court to control its calendar does not constitute a termination of the action in favor of the defendant as contemplated by CPL § 160.50. People v. Bell, 95 Misc. 2d 360, 407 N.Y.S.2d 944 (Crim. Ct. Queens Co. 1978).

—CPL § 160.50 relief is not to be automatically denied to a petitioner who has a criminal record without the further showing that the interests of justice so require such denial. People ex rel. Phoenix v. District Attorney of Onondaga Co., 95 Misc. 2d 573, 407 N.Y.S.2d 790 (Onondaga Co. Ct. 1978).

Prosecutor's motion in opposition.—Prosecutor's motion in opposition to defendant's motion for return of any fingerprints or photographs was timely even though not made until four months after defendant's motion, as CPL § 160.50 does not require prosecutor to move within any particular time, but only requires that he give five days' notice to defendant that he opposes the application. People v. Neuman, 104 Misc. 2d 324, 428 N.Y.S.2d 577 (Sup. Ct. Westchester Co. 1980).

Return of fingerprints and photos.—Defendant who was arrested and charged with resisting arrest, a class A misdemeanor, and harassment, a violation, and a traffic infraction, was entitled to return of his fingerprints and photographs after he pleaded guilty to harassment and was fined $75. Dwyer v. Guido, 54 A.D.2d 956, 388 N.Y.S.2d 636 (2d Dept. 1976).

—CPL § 160.50, which governs the sealing of records, is mandatory. People v. Abedi, 159 Misc. 2d 1010, 607 N.Y.S.2d 862 (Sup. Ct. N.Y. Co. 1994).

—Defendant who waived his right to the return of his fingerprints, photographs, and the sealing of the file, was entitled to have the waiver vacated in the interest of justice after ACD became final. People v. Martin C., 107 Misc. 2d 1007, 436 N.Y.S.2d 524 (Justice Ct. Westchester Co. 1981).

—An adjournment in contemplation of dismissal under CPL § 170.55 is a favorable termination of the proceeding under CPL § 160.50(2)(b) and the file must be sealed and the fingerprints returned. People v. Joseph P., 106 Misc. 2d 1075, 433 N.Y.S.2d 335 (Justice Ct. Westchester Co. 1980).

—The termination in favor of a defendant cannot be merely a plea down from a misdemeanor to a violation and defendant who pleaded guilty to the violations of trespass (PL § 140.45) and disorderly conduct (PL § 240.20) after being arrested and charged with the crimes of petit larceny (PL § 155.25) and criminal possession of burglar's tools (PL § 140.35) was not entitled to return of his fingerprints and photographs and to the sealing of the official record and papers relating to his arrest or prosecution. People v. Casella, 90 Misc. 2d 442, 395 N.Y.S.2d 909 (Crim. Ct. N.Y.C. 1977).

—Defendant, originally charged with driving while intoxicated, a printable offense, was not entitled to return of her photographs and fingerprints and sealing of the record after she pleaded guilty to the lesser non-printable offense of Disorderly Conduct (PL § 240.20) contained in the same accusatory instrument, since the plea-down did not constitute a termination of the criminal action in favor of the defendant, as defined in CPL § 160.50(2). People v. Blackman, 90 Misc. 2d 977, 396 N.Y.S.2d 982 (Crim. Ct. Queens Co. 1977).

—Since CPL § 160.50(2) does not define an adjudication as a youthful offender as the termination of proceeding in favor of the accused, the relief provided in CPL §§ 160.50 and 160.60 was denied. People v. Dugan, 91 Misc. 2d 239, 397 N.Y.S.2d 878 (Dutchess Co. Ct. 1977).

Refusal to issue "seal order."—Court refused to issue "seal order" after defendant had been acquitted of violation of VTL § 1192(3), a misdemeanor. People v. Jarnet, 100 Misc. 2d 988, 420 N.Y.S.2d 481 (City Ct. of Buffalo, Erie Co. 1979).

Subsequent pistol license proceeding.—Even though criminal proceedings against pistol licensee arising from an incident involving two police officers terminated in licensee's favor, the reports or evidence from the prior proceedings are properly made available to the pistol permit department pursuant to the statutory exception in CPL § 160.50(1)(d). St. Oharra v. Colucci, 67 A.D.2d 1104, 415 N.Y.S.2d 142 (4th Dept. 1979).

Use of sealed criminal records in civil action arising from the same incident.—Plaintiff, who brought action for false imprisonment and malicious prosecution, could not continue to enforce his right to suppress the criminal record (CPL § 160.50) while simultaneously prosecuting the civil claim for damages arising out of the same incident and identical facts since commencement of the civil action negated the purpose of the statutory protection and placed the defendant in an impossible, intolerable, unjust and nondefensible litigation posture. Maxie v. Gimbel Bros., Inc., 102 Misc. 2d 296, 423 N.Y.S.2d 802 (Sup. Ct. N.Y. Co. 1979).

—In a civil suit for false arrest and malicious prosecution a motion by the state to unseal the criminal record pursuant to CPL § 160.50(1)(d) is denied but if the claimant within 30 days after service of the order does not deliver an appropriate consent and authorization to the defendant for the procurement of the sealed records of the criminal proceeding at issue, claimant will be precluded from introducing at trial any evidence relating to the claims of false arrest and malicious prosecution. Iazzetta v. State, 105 Misc. 2d 567, 432 N.Y.S.2d 991 (Ct. of Claims N.Y. 1980).

Use of sealed criminal records for investigative purposes.—Violation of CPL § 160.50 based on identification of defendant from a photograph used in a dismissed and sealed case did not require suppression of the identification testimony or dismissal of the indictment. People v. Williams, 271 A.D.2d 363, 708 N.Y.S.2d 57 (1st Dept. 2000).

—The use of defendant's photograph in violation of CPL § 160.50 did not require suppression of the victim's identification testimony. People v. Lau, 171 A.D.2d 581, 567 N.Y.S.2d 661 (1st Dept. 1991).

—Police are not proscribed from using for identification purposes a mugshot of a defendant taken as a result of a previous arrest for a crime for which the defendant was acquitted; even assuming that the police illegally retained defendant's photograph in violation of CPL § 160.50, a subsequent identification of defendant in a later offense would not be suppressed simply because the illegally retained photograph was used, for the statute was not designed to immunize a defendant from a law enforcement official's investigatory display of a photograph. People v. London, 124 A.D.2d 254, 508 N.Y.S.2d 262 (3d Dept. 1986).

Subd. 3

"Terminated favorably."—A person whose indictment has been dismissed pursuant to CPL § 730.50(3) and (4) is not a person whose criminal actions have been terminated favorably under CPL § 160.50(3), and thus, such person is not entitled to the sealing of a court file and record. People v. Willingham, 195 Misc. 2d 241, 758 N.Y.S.2d 780 (Sup. Ct. Kings Co. 2003).

§ 160.55. Order upon termination of criminal action by conviction for noncriminal offense; entry of waiver; administrative findings.

1. Upon the termination of a criminal action or proceeding against a person by the conviction of such person of a traffic infraction or a violation, other than a violation of loitering as described in paragraph (d) or (e) of subdivision one of section 160.10 of this chapter or the violation of operating a motor vehicle while ability impaired as described in subdivision one of section eleven hundred ninety-two of the vehicle and traffic law, unless the district attorney upon motion with not less than five days notice to such person or his or her attorney demonstrates to the satisfaction of the court that the interests of justice require otherwise, or the court on its own motion with not less than five days notice to such person or his or her attorney determines that the interests of justice require otherwise and states the reasons for such determination on the record, the clerk of the court wherein such criminal action or proceeding was terminated shall immediately notify the commissioner of the division of criminal justice services and the heads of all appropriate police departments and other law enforcement agencies that the action has been terminated by such conviction. Upon receipt of notification of such termination:

(a) every photograph of such person and photographic plate or proof, and all palmprints and fingerprints taken or made of such person pursuant to the provisions of this article in regard to the action or proceeding terminated, and all duplicates and copies thereof, except a digital fingerprint image where authorized pursuant to paragraph (e) of this subdivision, shall forthwith be, at the discretion of the recipient agency, either destroyed or returned to such person, or to the attorney who represented such person at the time of the termination of the action or proceeding, at the address given by such person or attorney during the action or proceeding, by the division of criminal justice services and by any police department or law enforcement agency having any such photograph, photographic plate or proof, palmprints or fingerprints in its possession or under its control;

(b) any police department or law enforcement agency, including the division of criminal justice services, which transmitted or otherwise forwarded to any agency of the united states or of any other state or of any other jurisdiction outside the state of New York copies of any such photographs, photographic plates or proofs, palmprints and fingerprints, shall forthwith formally request in writing that all such copies be destroyed or returned to the police department or law enforcement agency which transmitted or forwarded them, and upon such return such department or agency shall, at its discretion, either destroy or return them as provided herein;

(c) all official records and papers relating to the arrest or prosecution, including all duplicates and copies thereof, on file with the division of criminal justice services, police agency, or prosecutor's office shall be sealed and not made available to any person or public or private agency;

(d) the records referred to in paragraph (c) of this subdivision shall be made available to the person accused or to such person's designated agent, and shall be made available to (i) a prosecutor in any proceeding in which the accused has moved for an order pursuant to section 170.56 or 210.46 of this chapter, or (ii) a law enforcement agency upon ex parte motion in any superior court, if such agency demonstrates to the satisfaction of the court that justice requires that such records be made available to it, or (iii) any state or local officer or agency with responsibility for the issuance of licenses to possess guns, when the accused has made application for such a license, or (iv) the New York state division of parole when the accused is under parole supervision as a result of conditional release or parole release granted by the New York state board of parole and the arrest which is the subject of the inquiry is one which occurred while the accused was under such supervision, or (v) the probation department responsible for supervision of the accused when the arrest which is the subject of the inquiry is one which occurred while the accused was under such supervision; and

(e) where fingerprints subject to the provisions of this section have been received by the division of criminal justice services and have been filed by the division as digital images, such images may be retained, provided that a fingerprint card of the individual is on file with the division which was not sealed pursuant to this section or section 160.50 of this article.

2. A report of the termination of the action or proceeding by conviction of a traffic violation or a violation other than a violation of loitering as described in paragraph (d) or (e) of subdivision one of section 160.10 of this chapter or the violation of operating a motor vehicle while ability impaired as described in subdivision one of section eleven hundred ninety-two of the vehicle and traffic law, shall be sufficient notice of the sealing to the commissioner of the division of criminal justice services unless the report also indicates that the court directed that the record not be sealed in the interests of justice. Where the court has determined pursuant to subdivision one of this section that sealing is not in the interests of justice, the clerk of the court shall include notification of that determination in any report to such division of the disposition of the action or proceeding.

3. A person against whom a criminal action or proceeding was terminated by such person's conviction of a traffic infraction or violation other than a violation of loitering as described in paragraph (d) or (e) of subdivision one of section 160.10 of this chapter or the violation of operating a motor vehicle while ability impaired as described in subdivision one of section eleven hundred ninety-two of the vehicle and traffic law, prior to the effective date of this section, may upon motion apply to the court in which such termination occurred, upon not less than twenty days notice to the district attorney, for an order granting to such person the relief set forth in subdivision one of this section, and such order shall be granted unless the district attorney demonstrates to the satisfaction of the court that the interests of justice require otherwise.

4. This section shall not apply to an action terminated in a manner described in paragraph (k) of subdivision two of section 160.50 of this chapter.

5. (a) When a criminal action or proceeding is terminated against a person by the entry of a waiver of a hearing pursuant to paragraph (c) of subdivision ten of section eleven hundred ninety-two of the vehicle and traffic law or section forty-nine-b of the navigation law, the record of the criminal action shall be sealed in accordance with this subdivision. Upon the entry of such waiver, the court or the clerk of the court shall immediately notify the commissioner of the division of criminal justice services and the heads of all appropriate police departments and other law enforcement agencies that a waiver has been entered and that the record of the action shall be

sealed when the person reaches the age of twenty-one or three years from the date of commission of the offense, whichever is the greater period of time. At the expiration of such period, the commissioner of the division of criminal justice services and the heads of all appropriate police departments and other law enforcement agencies shall take the actions required by paragraphs (a), (b) and (c) of subdivision one of section 160.50 of this article.

(b) Where a person under the age of twenty-one is referred by the police to the department of motor vehicles for action pursuant to section eleven hundred ninety-two-a or eleven hundred ninety-four-a of the vehicle and traffic law, or section forty-nine-b of the navigation law and a finding in favor of the motorist or operator is rendered, the commissioner of the department of motor vehicles shall, as soon as practicable, but not later than three years from the date of commission of the offense or when such person reaches the age of twenty-one, whichever is the greater period of time, notify the commissioner of the division of criminal justice services and the heads of all appropriate police departments and other law enforcement agencies that such finding in favor of the motorist or operator was rendered. Upon receipt of such notification, the commissioner of the division of criminal justice services and the heads of such police departments and other law enforcement agencies shall take the actions required by paragraphs (a), (b) and (c) of subdivision one of section 160.50 of this article.

(c) Where a person under the age of twenty-one is referred by the police to the department of motor vehicles for action pursuant to section eleven hundred ninety-two-a or eleven hundred ninety-four-a of the vehicle and traffic law, or section forty-nine-b of the navigation law, and no notification is received by the commissioner of the division of criminal justice services and the heads of all appropriate police departments and other law enforcement agencies pursuant to paragraph (b) of this subdivision, such commissioner of the division of criminal justice services and such heads of police departments and other law enforcement agencies shall, after three years from the date of commission of the offense or when the person reaches the age of twenty-one, whichever is the greater period of time, take the actions required by paragraphs (a), (b) and (c) of subdivision one of section 160.50 of this article.

Added by L. 1980, Ch. 192; Amended by L. 1981, Ch. 249; L. 1982, Ch. 174,; L. 1986, Ch. 294; L. 1991, Ch. 142, eff.

Nov. 1, 1991, amended subd. (1), renumbered subds. (2), (3) to (3), (4) and added new subd. (2); L. 1992, Ch. 249, eff. June 30, 1992, amending subd. (1); L. 1994, Ch. 169; L. 1995, Ch. 3, § 54, extending expiration date of subd. 1 to Sept. 1, 1997; L. 1996, Ch. 196, § 22, amending heading; L. 1996, Ch. 196, § 24, adding subd. 5, eff. Nov. 1; L. 1997, Ch. 435, § 63, eff. Aug. 20, 1997, deleting expiration date of subd. 1; L. 1998, Ch. 391, § 6, eff. Apr. 1, 1999.

ANNOTATIONS

Prosecutor's failure to disclose.—Prosecutor's failure to disclose that one of state's witnesses previously had been convicted of disorderly conduct did not result in reversible error, in light of fact that conviction was sealed violation and, thus, prosecutor's inquiries addressed to criminal records centers would not have revealed conviction. People v. Clark, 228 A.D.2d 326, 644 N.Y.S.2d 236 (1st Dept. 1996).

Retroactive.—CPL § 160.55(2) is retroactive and applied to a motion pursuant to CPL § 160.50 despite the people's claim that if CPL § 160.55(2) were in effect at the time of the plea the people would have insisted on a waiver of the sealing rights prior to accepting a plea as is currently the policy. People v. Gartenberg, 105 Misc. 2d 657, 432 N.Y.S.2d 785 (Dist. Ct. Nassau Co. 1980).

§ 160.60. Effect of termination of criminal actions in favor of the accused.

Upon the termination of a criminal action or proceeding against a person in favor of such person, as defined in subdivision two of section 160.50 of this chapter, the arrest and prosecution shall be deemed a nullity and the accused shall be restored, in contemplation of law, to the status he occupied before the arrest and prosecution. The arrest or prosecution shall not operate as a disqualification of any person so accused to pursue or engage in any lawful activity, occupation, profession, or calling. Except where specifically required or permitted by statute or upon specific authorization of a superior court, no such person shall be required to divulge information pertaining to the arrest or prosecution.

Added by L. 1976, Ch. 877.

ANNOTATIONS

Prosecutor's failure to disclose.—It was not error for prosecutor to fail to disclose confidential information that complainant had two prior arrests which have been sealed by court order nor was it error for complainant to deny existence of prior arrests during direct examination given statute providing that sealed records pertaining to dismissal of charges are treated as a nullity. People v. Ellis, 184 A.D.2d 307, 584 N.Y.S.2d 569 (1st Dept. 1992).

Return of photographs.—A defendant has no inherent or constitutional right to the return of photographs, fingerprints or other indicia of arrest where charges are dismissed. People v. Patterson, 78 N.Y.2d 711, 579 N.Y.S.2d 617, 587 N.E.2d 255 (1991).

ARTICLE 170—PROCEEDINGS UPON INFORMATION, SIMPLIFIED TRAFFIC INFORMATION, PROSECUTOR'S INFORMATION AND MISDEMEANOR COMPLAINT FROM ARRAIGNMENT TO PLEA

LexisNexis Cross References

Criminal Defense Techniques, Vol. 5, Ch. 103, Arraignment; *New York Criminal Practice (2d ed.),* Vol. 1, Ch. 5, Indictments and Superior Court Informations; Vol. 1, Ch. 7, Securing Attendance of Defendants for Arraignment and Prosecution; Vol. 1, Ch. 9, Local Criminal Court Arraignment and Related Issues.

§ 170.10. Arraignment upon information, simplified traffic information, prosecutor's information or misdemeanor complaint; defendant's presence, defendant's rights, court's instructions and bail matters.

1. Following the filing with a local criminal court of an information, a simplified information, a prosecutor's information or a misdemeanor complaint, the defendant must be arraigned thereon. The defendant must appear personally at such arraignment except under the following circumstances:

(a) In any case where a simplified information is filed and a procedure is provided by law which is applicable to all offenses charged in such simplified information and, if followed, would dispense with an arraignment or personal appearance of the defendant, nothing contained in this section affects the validity of such procedure or requires such personal appearance;

(b) In any case in which the defendant's appearance is required by a summons or an appearance ticket, the court in its discretion may, for good cause shown, permit the defendant to appear by counsel instead of in person.

2. Upon any arraignment at which the defendant is personally present, the court must immediately inform him, or cause him to be informed in its presence, of the charge or charges against him and must furnish him with a copy of the accusatory instrument.

3. The defendant has the right to the aid of counsel at the arraignment and at every subsequent stage of the action. If he appears upon such arraignment without counsel, he has the following rights:

(a) To an adjournment for the purpose of obtaining counsel; and

(b) To communicate, free of charge, by letter or by telephone, for the purposes of obtaining counsel and informing a relative or friend that he has been charged with an offense; and

(c) To have counsel assigned by the court if he is financially unable to obtain the same; except that this paragraph does not apply where the accusatory instrument charges a traffic infraction or infractions only.

4. Except as provided in subdivision five, the court must inform the defendant:

(a) Of his rights as prescribed in subdivision three; and the court must not only accord him opportunity to exercise such rights but must itself take such affirmative action as is necessary to effectuate them; and

(b) Where a traffic infraction or a misdemeanor relating to traffic is charged, that a judgment of conviction for such offense would in addition to subjecting the defendant to the sentence provided therefor render his license to drive a motor vehicle and his certificate of registration subject to suspension and revocation as prescribed by law and that a plea of guilty to such offense constitutes a conviction thereof to the same extent as a verdict of guilty after trial; and

(c) Where the accusatory instrument is a simplified traffic information, that the defendant has a right to have a supporting deposition filed, as provided in section 100.25; and

(d) Where the accusatory instrument is a misdemeanor complaint, that the defendant may not be prosecuted thereon or required to enter a plea thereto unless he consents to the same, and that in the absence of such consent such misdemeanor complaint will for prosecution purposes have to be replaced and superseded by an information; and

5. In any case in which a defendant has appeared for arraignment in response to a summons or an appearance ticket, a printed statement upon such process of any court instruction required by the provisions of subdivision four, other than those specified in paragraphs (d) and (e)* thereof, constitutes compliance with such provisions with respect to the instruction so printed.

6. If a defendant charged with a traffic infraction or infractions only desires to proceed without the aid of counsel, the court must permit him to do so. In all other cases, the court must permit the defendant to proceed without the aid of counsel if it is satisfied that he made such decision with knowledge of the significance thereof, but if it is not so satisfied it may not proceed until the defendant is provided with counsel, either of his own choosing or by assignment. Regardless of the kind or nature of the charges, a defendant who proceeds at the arraignment without counsel

does not waive his right to counsel, and the court must inform him that he continues to have such right as well as all the rights specified in subdivision three which are necessary to effectuate it, and that he may exercise such rights at any stage of the action.

7. Upon the arraignment, the court, unless it intends to make a final disposition of the action immediately thereafter, must, as provided in subdivision one of section 530.20, issue a securing order either releasing the defendant on his own recognizance or fixing bail for his future appearance in the action; except that where a defendant appears by counsel pursuant to paragraph (b) of subdivision one of this section, the court must release the defendant on his own recognizance.

8. Notwithstanding any other provision of law to the contrary, a local criminal court may not, at arraignment or within thirty days of arraignment on a simplified traffic information charging a violation of subdivision two, three or four of section eleven hundred ninety-two of the vehicle and traffic law and upon which a notation has been made pursuant to subdivision twelve of section eleven hundred ninety-two of the vehicle and traffic law, accept a plea of guilty to a violation of any subdivision of section eleven hundred ninety-two of the vehicle and traffic law, nor to any other traffic infraction arising out of the same incident, nor to any other traffic infraction, violation or misdemeanor where the court is aware that such offense was charged pursuant to an accident involving death or serious physical injury, except upon written consent of the district attorney.

9. Nothing contained in this section applies to the arraignment of corporate defendants, which is governed generally by the provisions of article six hundred.

* Para. (e) was repealed by L. 1972, Ch. 697.

Amended by L. 1972, Chs. 243, 661, 697; L. 1992, Ch. 449, eff. Nov. 14, 1992, renumbering subd. (8) to (9) and adding a new subd. (8).

ANNOTATIONS

General rule.—The general rule is that a defendant must personally appear in court for arraignment; the Legislature has carved out two exceptions whereby a defendant charged in a simplified information may be arraigned without a court appearance. The first exception, set forth in CPL § 170.10(1)(a), applies when an alternative provision of law dispenses with the need for an arraignment or defendant's personal appearance. People v. Perry, 87 N.Y.2d 353, 639 N.Y.S.2d 307, 662 N.E.2d 787 (1996).

Right to counsel; traffic infractions.—There is no statutory right to the assignment of counsel in traffic infraction prosecutions or appeals therefrom. People v. Farinaro, 36 N.Y.2d 283, 367 N.Y.S.2d 258, 326 N.E.2d 818 (1975).

—There is a constitutional right to counsel at a criminal trial where conviction would lead to a sentence of imprisonment, but this is inapposite to an appeal of a conviction for a traffic infraction where defendant no longer faces the possibility of imprisonment. There is no statutory right to the assignment of counsel in traffic infraction prosecutions. People v. Russo, 149 A.D.2d 255, 545 N.Y.S.2d 211 (2d Dept. 1989).

—Defendants charged with traffic violations and subject to

possible imprisonment, must be advised of their right to counsel and to have counsel assigned where the defendant is financially unable to obtain same. People v. Weinstock, 80 Misc. 2d 510, 363 N.Y.S.2d 878 (App. Term 9-10th Jud. Dist. 1974).

Grand jury; jurisdiction; district attorney; divestiture and removal.—Indictment by Grand Jury after presentation of evidence by District Attorney with apparent personal interest in the prosecution, would be dismissed and case remanded and removed to another local criminal court with appointment of a special prosecutor. People v. Krstovich, 72 Misc. 2d 90, 338 N.Y.S.2d 132 (Greene Co. Ct. 1972).

Defendant; right to defend himself.—A defendant in a criminal case may invoke the right to defend himself provided: the request is unequivocal and timely asserted; there has been a knowing and intelligent waiver of the right to counsel; and the defendant has not engaged in conduct which would prevent the fair and orderly exposition of the issues. People v. McIntyre, 36 N.Y.2d 10, 364 N.Y.S.2d 837, 324 N.E.2d 322 (1974).

Subd. 3

Adequate aid of counsel; conflict of interest.—Defendant was deprived of effective representation by his attorney who represented him at trial as well as his co-defendant who pleaded guilty and testified against him. Attorney's representation did not terminate until after sentence and thus constituted a divergent interest between defendants. People v. Lamere, 39 A.D.2d 15, 331 N.Y.S.2d 178 (3d Dept. 1972).

Right to counsel; competency of counsel; insanity defense.—Where defendant charged with first degree robbery had history of mental instability and confinement, failure of his assigned counsel to investigate background as aid in defense of insanity demonstrated incompetency of counsel and deprived defendant of fundamental right to fair trail. People v. Bennett, 29 N.Y.2d 462, 329 N.Y.S.2d 801, 280 N.E.2d 637 (1972).

Right to effective aid of counsel; conflict of interest between defendants.—Defendant who was convicted of assault together with co-defendant, and both were acquitted of murder arising out of fight during a crap game, did not have conflict of interest with co-defendant, as both sought to discredit prosecution witnesses and establish self defense. Record shows that attorney who represented both pressed favorable arguments of defendant even though he also represented gun wielding co-defendant. People v. Gonzalez, 30 N.Y.2d 27, 330 N.Y.S.2d 54, cert. denied, 409 U.S. 859 (1972).

Right to change counsel.—Once a trial has begun, a defendant's right to change counsel is not absolute, but rests within the court's discretion. People v. Johnson, 57 A.D.2d 844, 394 N.Y.S.2d 39 (2d Dept. 1977).

Right to counsel; indigent.—An indigent defendant is entitled to competent counsel and not counsel of his own choosing. People v. Pettiford, 51 A.D.2d 927, 381 N.Y.S.2d 245 (1st Dept. 1976).

—Even in traffic infraction cases, if there is a possibility of a sentence of imprisonment which is not waived by the Justice, the defendant is entitled to assigned counsel, absent his waiver of counsel. Davis v. Shepard, 92 Misc. 2d 181, 399 N.Y.S.2d 836 (Sup. Ct. Steuben Co. 1977).

Trial; conflict of interest between defendants.—It was error to proceed with trial of defendant for possession of dangerous weapon and burglar tools where counsel asked to be relieved for either of two co-defendants because there was a conflict of interest between them. People v. Austin, 38 A.D.2d 594, 328 N.Y.S.2d 695 (2d Dept. 1971).

Subd. 4

Prosecution on misdemeanor complaint.—In the absence of an effective admonition of the right to be prosecuted by information, a waiver or consent to prosecution by misdemeanor complaint cannot be presumed. People v. Weinberg, 34 N.Y.2d 429, 358 N.Y.S.2d 357, 315 N.E.2d 434 (1974).

Supporting deposition.—A defendant charged with an offense contained in a simplified information, has the right, following the entry of a not guilty plea by mail pursuant to VTL § 1806, to a supporting deposition and his time to apply for the deposition does not commence running until he has been duly informed of that right pursuant to CPL §§ 170.10(4)(c) and 170.10(5). People v. DiGioia, 98 Misc. 2d 359, 413 N.Y.S.2d 825 (Sup. Ct. App. Term 1978).

Subd. 6

Right to defend oneself.—A defendant in a criminal case may invoke the right to defend pro se provided: (1) the request is unequivocal and timely asserted, (2) there is a knowing and intelligent waiver of the right to counsel, and (3) the defendant has not engaged in conduct which would prevent the fair and orderly exposition of the issues. People v. McIntyre, 36 N.Y.2d 10, 364 N.Y.S.2d 837, 324 N.E.2d 322 (1974).

—The waiver of the right to counsel must be knowing and intelligent; a new trial is warranted where the court failed to properly inform defendant of the risks of self-representation. People v. Merriwether, 87 A.D.2d 804, 448 N.Y.S.2d 787 (2d Dept. 1982).

§ 170.15. Removal of action from one local criminal court to another.

Under circumstances prescribed in this section, a criminal action based upon an information, a simplified information, a prosecutor's information or a misdemeanor complaint may be removed from one local criminal court to another:

1. When a defendant arrested by a police officer for an offense other than a felony, allegedly committed in a city or town, has, owing to special circumstances and pursuant to law, not been brought before the particular local criminal court which by reason of the situs of such offense has trial jurisdiction thereof, but, instead, before a local criminal court which does not have trial jurisdiction thereof, and therein stands charged with such offense by information, simplified information or misdemeanor complaint, such local criminal court must arraign him upon such accusatory instrument. If the defendant desires to enter a plea of guilty thereto immediately following such arraignment, such local criminal court must permit him to do so and must thereafter conduct the action to judgment. Otherwise, it must remit the action, together with all pertinent papers and documents, to the local criminal court which has trial jurisdiction of the action, and the latter court must then conduct such action to judgment or other final disposition.

2. When a defendant arrested by a police officer for an offense other than a felony has been brought before a superior court judge sitting as a local criminal court for arraignment upon an information, simplified information or misdemeanor complaint charging such offense, such judge must, as a local criminal court, arraign the defendant upon such accusatory instrument. Such judge must then remit the action, together with all pertinent papers and documents, to a local criminal court having trial jurisdiction thereof. The latter court must then conduct such action to judgment or other final disposition.

3. At any time within the period provided by section 255.20, where a defendant is arraigned upon an information, a simplified information, a prosecutor's information or a misdemeanor complaint pending in a city court, a town court or a village court having trial jurisdiction thereof, a judge of the county court of the county in which such city court, town court or village court is

located may, upon motion of the defendant or the people, order that the action be transferred for disposition from the court in which the matter is pending to another designated local criminal court of the county, upon the ground that disposition thereof within a reasonable time in the court from which removal is sought is unlikely owing to:

(a) Death, disability or other incapacity or disqualification of all the judges of such court; or

(b) Inability of such court to form a jury in a case, in which the defendant is entitled to and has requested a jury trial.

4. Notwithstanding any provision of this section to the contrary, in any county outside a city having a population of one million or more, upon or after arraignment of a defendant on an information, a simplified information, a prosecutor's information or a misdemeanor complaint pending in a local criminal court, such court may, upon motion of the defendant and with the consent of the district attorney, order that the action be removed from the court in which the matter is pending to another local criminal court in the same county which has been designated a drug court by the chief administrator of the courts, and such drug court may then conduct such action to judgement or other final disposition; provided, however, that an order of removal issued under this subdivision shall not take effect until five days after the date the order is issued unless, prior to such effective date, the drug court notifies the court that issued the order that:

(a) it will not accept the action, in which event the order shall not take effect, or

(b) it will accept the action on a date prior to such effective date, in which event the order shall take effect upon such prior date.

Upon providing notification pursuant to paragraph (a) or (b) of this subdivision, the drug court shall promptly give notice to the defendant, his or her counsel and the district attorney.

Amended by L. 1972, Ch. 661; L. 1974, Chs. 837, 763; L. 1984, Ch. 695; L. 1998, Ch. 77, § 1, eff. June 2, 1998; L. 1999, Ch. 565, § 1, eff. Nov. 1, 1999; L. 2000, Ch. 67, § 1, eff. Nov. 1, 2000, amending subd. 4.

ANNOTATIONS

Jurisdiction.—Village justice court located within territorial jurisdiction of district court did not have jurisdiction over simplified information charging misdemeanor aggravated unlicensed operator of vehicle in second degree, but court could transfer proceeding to another court, such as district court; defendant had tendered plea of not guilty, so statute, providing that local court must permit defendant to enter guilty plea immediately after arraignment when he so desires, did not apply. People v. Caltabiano, 154 Misc. 2d 860, 586 N.Y.S.2d 714 (Suffolk Co. Justice Ct. 1992).

Allegation that defendant cannot obtain a fair and impartial trial.—The County Court found sufficient and proper basis for removal of the misdemeanor trial to another Town Court, where defendant alleged that he could not obtain a fair and impartial jury trial in the Town Court of Dryden because the members of the jury panel would be prejudiced against him. People v. Roberts, 95 Misc. 2d 41, 406 N.Y.S.2d 432 (Tompkins Co. Ct. 1978).

Bias or prejudice not grounds for removal.—A motion to change venue is not the correct procedure for raising issues of bias or prejudice of a presiding judge, and where disqualification cannot be grounded on Jud. Law § 14, the subject judge is the sole arbiter of recusal. The issue can be raised on appeal. People v. Tiffany, 176 Misc. 2d 271, 672 N.Y.S.2d 973 (Co. Ct. Westchester Co. 1998).

—There is no statutory provision for removal from one local criminal court to another based on prejudice. Unlike CPL § 230.20(2) this section makes no provision for change of venue where it is claimed that an impartial trial cannot be had. Disqualification is discretionary with the judge. Jud. Law § 14. *In re* Capuano, 68 Misc. 2d 481, 327 N.Y.S.2d 17 (Monroe Co. Ct. 1971).

—County Court Judge cannot transfer a matter from one local criminal court to another because of local bias, even if such bias is established. People v. Smith, 93 Misc. 2d 326, 402 N.Y.S.2d 766 (Rensselaer Co. Ct. 1978).

—Disability of the defendant's attorney to practice in Town Justice Court; not adequate grounds to change venue and place of trial. People v. Berg, 76 Misc. 2d 430, 351 N.Y.S.2d 525 (Dutchess Co. Ct. 1974).

Jurisdiction; transfer to Town Court.—The town court of the town of Sharon could not remit the action to the town court of Experance pursuant to CPL § 170.15[1] because the defendant when arrested was not before the town court of Sharon "owing to special circumstances and pursuant to law." People v. Myles, 107 Misc. 2d 960, 436 N.Y.S.2d 134 (Schoharie Co. Ct. 1981).

—Although the statute provides for transfers from Village Justice Courts to Town Courts, there is no valid reason to exclude transfer from City to Town Court even in absence of statutory authority when disqualification of City Court judge would render case in limbo without transfer. *In re* Jones, 69 Misc. 2d 640, 330 N.Y.S.2d 424 (Cortland Co. 1972).

Justice of the peace also member of the town board.—The constitutional requirement of due process of law is violated when a justice of the peace, who is also a member of the town board, is called upon to decide the guilt or innocence of an accused charged with violating an ordinance of town. People v. Kessler, 77 Misc. 2d 640, 354 N.Y.S.2d 517 (Suffolk Co. Ct. 1974).

Supreme Court; jurisdiction.—The Supreme Court has the right to try criminal offenses of any nature or quality despite restrictions a passing legislative body seeks to place upon its powers. It also has the authority to accept a guilty plea to the crime charged or to a lesser one. People v. Darling, 81 Misc. 2d 487, 366 N.Y.S.2d 982 (Sup. Ct. Rensselaer Co. 1975), *modified*, 50 A.D.2d 1038, 377 N.Y.S.2d 718 (1975).

§ 170.20. Divestiture of jurisdiction by indictment; removal of case to superior court at district attorney's instance.

1. If at any time before entry of a plea of guilty to or commencement of a trial of a local criminal court accusatory instrument containing a charge of misdemeanor, an indictment charging the defendant with such misdemeanor is filed in a superior court, the local criminal court is thereby divested of jurisdiction of such misdemeanor charge and all proceedings therein with respect thereto are terminated.

2. At any time before entry of a plea of guilty to or commencement of a trial of an accusatory instrument specified in subdivision one, the district attorney may apply for an adjournment of the proceedings in the local criminal court upon the ground that he intends to present the misdemeanor charge in question to a grand jury with a view to prosecuting it by indictment in a

superior court. In such case, the local criminal court must adjourn the proceedings to a date which affords the district attorney reasonable opportunity to pursue such action, and may subsequently grant such further adjournments for that purpose as are reasonable under the circumstances. Following the granting of such adjournment or adjournments, the proceedings must be as follows:

(a) If such charge is presented to a grand jury within the designated period and either an indictment or a dismissal of such charge results, the local criminal court is thereby divested of jurisdiction of such charge, and all proceedings in the local criminal court with respect thereto are terminated.

(b) If the misdemeanor charge is not presented to a grand jury within the designated period, the proceedings in the local criminal court must continue.

ANNOTATIONS

Indictment.—Indictment of defendant for second-degree burglary "resulted" when grand jury voted for indictment, rather than when indictment was filed, and, thus, criminal court was divested of jurisdiction over trespass charges arising out of same facts and defendant's guilty plea in that court did not bar, on double jeopardy grounds, prosecution for burglary; grand jury voted to indict one day before defendant pled guilty to misdemeanor, but indictment was not filed until five days after plea. People v. Brancoccio, 83 N.Y.2d 638, 612 N.Y.S.2d 353, 634 N.E.2d 954 (1994).

Divestiture of jurisdiction upon People's motion; constitutionality of statute.—The court turned aside a challenge to the constitutionality of section 170.20(2), rejecting the defendant's contention that the statute can be manipulated by unscrupulous District Attorneys to deny defendants a speedy trial. People v. Butor, 75 Misc. 2d 558, 348 N.Y.S.2d 89 (Dutchess Co. Ct. 1973).

Grand jury.—Since the misdemeanor complaint was dismissed before the defendant was placed in jeopardy, the prosecutor had the right to present the case to the grand jury without the permission of the court, which approval perhaps would have been required if that complaint had still been extant at the time. People v. Nizza, 92 Misc. 2d 823, 402 N.Y.S.2d 95 (Crim. Ct. N.Y.C. 1977).

Grand Jury.—The local criminal court lost jurisdiction when the indictment was voted. People v. Brancoccio, 147 Misc. 2d 1030, 558 N.Y.S.2d 803, 804 (Sup. Ct. Kings Co. 1990), aff'd, 189 A.D.2d 525, 596 N.Y.S.2d 856 (2d Dept. 1993), aff'd, 83 N.Y.2d 638, 612 N.Y.S.2d 353, 634 N.E.2d 954 (1994).

Divestiture of jurisdiction; subsequent plea in local criminal court a nullity.—Defendant's plea of guilty in a local criminal court was a nullity and the promise of a sentence of conditional discharge was thus unenforceable where prior to such plea, but unbeknownst to defendant and Assistant District Attorney, an indictment had been filed by a Grand Jury and the Criminal Court was accordingly divested of jurisdiction. People v. Phillips, 66 A.D.2d 696, 411 N.Y.S.2d 259 (1st Dept. 1978).

Grand jury; jurisdiction; district attorney; divestiture and removal.—Indictment by Grand Jury after presentation of evidence by District Attorney with apparent personal interest in the prosecution would be dismissed and case remanded and removed to another local criminal court with appointment of a special prosecutor. Divestiture statute at option of District Attorney was repugnant in its operation to equal protection of the laws. People v. Krstovich, 72 Misc. 2d 90, 338 N.Y.S.2d 132 (Greene Co. Ct. 1972).

Right to plead guilty.—CPL § 220.10(2) does not require the trial court to accept the defendant's offer to plead guilty to a charge in a misdemeanor complaint, and does not relieve the court of its duty, pursuant to CPL § 170.20(2), to order an adjournment to allow the District Attorney to present evidence against the defendant to a Grand Jury. People v. Barkin, 49 N.Y.2d 901, 428 N.Y.S.2d 193, 405 N.E.2d 674 (1980).

—A defendant has no unconditional right to plead guilty, in a local criminal court, to misdemeanor charges against him or her where the prosecutor has concurrently requested an adjournment pursuant to CPL § 170.20(2) for the purpose of presenting the charges against the defendant to a Grand Jury. Johnson v. Andrews, 179 A.D.2d 417, 579 N.Y.S.2d 332 (1st Dept. 1992).

Speedy trial; divestiture of jurisdiction to proceed by indictment.—The grand jury was not divested of power to indict the defendant where the District Attorney requested and was granted permission to submit the charge to the Grand Jury and the District Court subsequently dismissed the misdemeanor charge, on defendant's oral motion, for failure to prosecute since the action of the District Court reflected an impatience with the People's failure to move promptly and was not intended as action on a speedy trial motion. People v. Morgan, 90 Misc. 2d 416, 395 N.Y.S.2d 363 (Sup. Ct. Suffolk Co. 1977).

—Where defendant urged that delay of more than five months between his arrest and his indictment was proof that he was denied his right to a speedy trial, the court determined that part of the delay was caused by an adjournment requested by the People but agreed to by the defendant, and that the other "delays" were statutorily mandated since the District Attorney had requested adjournments to present the case to the grand jury. The court therefore refused to dismiss the indictment. People v. Butor, 75 Misc. 2d 558, 348 N.Y.S.2d 89 (Dutchess Co. Ct. 1973).

§ 170.25. Divestiture of jurisdiction by indictment; removal of case to superior court at defendant's instance.

1. At any time before entry of a plea of guilty to or commencement of a trial of a local criminal court accusatory instrument containing a charge of misdemeanor, a superior court having jurisdiction to prosecute such misdemeanor charge by indictment may, upon motion of the defendant made upon notice to the district attorney, showing good cause to believe that the interests of justice so require, order that such charge be prosecuted by indictment and that the district attorney present it to the grand jury for such purpose.

2. Such order stays the proceedings in the local criminal court pending submission of the charge to the grand jury. Upon the subsequent filing of an indictment in the superior court, the proceedings in the local criminal court terminate and the defendant must be required to appear for arraignment upon the indictment in the manner prescribed in subdivisions one and two of section 210.10. Upon the subsequent filing of a grand jury dismissal of the charge, the proceedings in the local criminal court terminate and the superior court must, if the defendant is not at liberty on his own recognizance, discharge him from custody or exonerate his bail, as the case may be.

3. At any time before entry of a plea of guilty to or commencement of a trial of or within thirty days of arraignment on an accusatory instrument specified in subdivision one, whichever occurs first, the defendant may apply to the local criminal court for an adjournment of the proceedings therein upon the ground that he intends to make a motion in a superior court, pursuant to subdivision one, for an order that the misdemeanor

charge be prosecuted by indictment. In such case, the local criminal court must adjourn the proceedings to a date which affords the defendant reasonable opportunity to pursue such action, and may subsequently grant such further adjournments for that purpose as are reasonable under the circumstances. Following the granting of such adjournment or adjournments, the proceedings must be as follows:

(a) If a motion in a superior court is not made by the defendant within the designated period, the proceedings in the local criminal court must continue.

(b) If a motion in a superior court is made by the defendant within the designated period, such motion stays the proceedings in the local criminal court until the entry of an order determining such motion.

(c) If the superior court enters an order granting the motion, such order stays the proceedings in the local criminal court as provided in subdivision two; and upon a subsequent indictment or dismissal of such charge by the grand jury, the proceedings in the local criminal court terminate as provided in subdivision two.

(d) If the superior court enters an order denying the motion, the proceedings in the local criminal court must continue.

4. Upon application of a defendant who on the basis of an order issued by a superior court pursuant to subdivision one is awaiting grand jury action, and who, at the time of such order or subsequent thereto, has been committed to the custody of the sheriff pending grand jury action, and who has been confined in such custody for a period of more than forty-five days without the occurrence of any grand jury action or disposition, the superior court which issued such order must release him on his own recognizance unless:

(a) The lack of a grand jury disposition during such period of confinement was due to the defendant's request, action or condition, or occurred with his consent; or

(b) The people have shown good cause why such order of release should not be issued. Such good cause must consist of some compelling fact or circumstance which precluded grand jury action within the prescribed period or rendered the same against the interest of justice.

Amended by L. 1973, Ch. 592; L. 1974, Ch. 509.

ANNOTATIONS

Indictment not defective.—Indictment against defendant accused of criminal possession of forged instrument in second degree was not defective; indictment followed language of statute governing that offense and set forth time and place of alleged crime and particular instrument involved. People v. Showers, 200 A.D.2d 864, 606 N.Y.S.2d 816 (3d Dept. 1994).

Article 78; prohibition.—Since alternative relief of transference to a Superior Court pursuant to CPL § 170.25 is available, the extraordinary remedy of prohibition does not lie to prevent Town Justices from making or entering any order, or entertaining any further proceedings in the prosecution or trial of

petitioners, with regard to pending criminal charges against them. Carter v. Hults, 51 A.D.2d 547, 378 N.Y.S.2d 423 (2d Dept. 1976).

Grand jury; jurisdiction; district attorney; divestiture and removal.—Indictment by Grand Jury after presentation of evidence by District Attorney with apparent personal interest in the prosecution, would be dismissed and case remanded and removed to another local criminal court with appointment of a special prosecutor. Divestiture statute at option of District Attorney was repugnant in its operation to equal protection of the laws. People v. Krstovich, 72 Misc. 2d 90, 338 N.Y.S.2d 132 (Greene Co. Ct. 1972).

By agreement.—Agreement between prosecution and defense to present the misdemeanor charges to the grand jury is binding even though a formal motion was not filed, for the agreement has the effect of a motion to have the misdemeanor charges presented to the grand jury. Mooney v. Cahn, 79 Misc. 2d 703, 361 N.Y.S.2d 118 (Sup Ct. Nassau Co. 1974).

Indictment; counts same as misdemeanor information; consolidation.—District Attorney would be directed to present bad check misdemeanor informations against defendant to Grand Jury so that they could be consolidated with related counts of indictment to dispose of all issues at one trial. People v. Consolazio, 72 Misc. 2d 73, 338 N.Y.S.2d 217 (Nassau Co. Ct. 1972).

Removal.—Defendant's motion to remove charge of intoxicated driving (VTL § 1192) from the Town Court to a superior court because the Justice of the Town Court was not an attorney and because the charge could result in the revocation of his operator's license was denied. *In re* Hewitt, 81 Misc. 2d 202, 365 N.Y.S.2d 760 (Tompkins Co. Ct. 1975).

Removal; interests of justice.—Defendant, a 58-year-old man, was charged with Reckless Endangerment, second degree and Endangering the Welfare of a Child, both misdemeanors. The victim was 8 years old and the witnesses under twelve years of age. In removing the case from the Town Court to County Court, upon defendant's application, the court held that if the charges are presented by indictment, all sides of the controversy will benefit from the restraining influence of an impartial tribunal (grand jury) and the ends of justice achieved according to the form and spirit of the law. People v. Banaszak, 76 Misc. 2d 397, 351 N.Y.S.2d 104 (Monroe Co. Ct. 1973).

Town and village courts with lay justices.—There is no evident federal infirmity in the New York State system of town and village courts with lay Justices since CPL § 170.25 provides for a procedure to divest the town and village courts, of, and remove to a superior court, the power to try and determine a criminal case People v. Skrynski, 42 N.Y.2d 218, 397 N.Y.S.2d 707, 366 N.E.2d 797 (1977).

—When the misdemeanor charged was punishable by a sentence of confinement up to one year, and the lower court was presided over by a lay justice, the case was removable as of right on the motion of the defendant for prosecution by indictment in a superior court. People v. Dean, 96 Misc. 2d 781, 409 N.Y.S.2d 647 (Sup. Ct. Chemung Co. 1978).

§ 170.30. Motion to dismiss information, simplified information, prosecutor's information or misdemeanor complaint.

1. After arraignment upon an information, a simplified information, a prosecutor's information or a misdemeanor complaint, the local criminal court may, upon motion of the defendant, dismiss such instrument or any count thereof upon the ground that:

(a) It is defective, within the meaning of section 170.35; or

(b) The defendant has received immunity from prosecution for the offense charged, pursuant to sections 50.20 or 190.40; or

(c) The prosecution is barred by reason of a

previous prosecution, pursuant to section 40.20; or

(d) The prosecution is untimely, pursuant to section 30.10; or

(e) The defendant has been denied the right to a speedy trial; or

(f) There exists some other jurisdictional or legal impediment to conviction of the defendant for the offense charged; or

(g) Dismissal is required in furtherance of justice, within the meaning of section 170.40.

2. A motion pursuant to this section, except a motion pursuant to paragraph (e) of subdivision one, should be made within the period provided by section 255.20. A motion made pursuant to paragraph (e) of subdivision one should be made prior to the commencement of trial or entry of a plea of guilty.

3. Upon the motion, a defendant who is in a position adequately to raise more than one ground in support thereof should raise every such ground upon which he intends to challenge the accusatory instrument. A subsequent motion based upon such a ground not so raised may be summarily denied, although the court, in the interest of justice and for good cause shown, may in its discretion entertain and dispose of such a motion on the merits notwithstanding.

Amended by L. 1972, Chs. 184, 661; L. 1974, Ch. 763.

ANNOTATIONS

Dismissal of complaint.—Complaint may be dismissed by the court because it concluded that the facts alleged by the People were not legally sufficient to support the charge. Mac-Fawn v. Kresler, 88 N.Y.2d 859, 644 N.Y.S.2d 486, 666 N.E.2d 1359 (1996).

Amending an information.—The People's motion to amend the information so as to change the date, time, and basis of knowledge to "on information and belief," rather than on the police officer's personal knowledge, was granted. The amendment did not change the theory of the prosecution or prejudice the defendant. People v. Diggs, 72 Misc. 2d 898, 339 N.Y.S.2d 712 (Dist. Ct. Nassau Co. 1973).

Accusatory instrument; verification; misdemeanor complaint; reasonable cause; sufficiency.—Since the CPL provision regarding verifications is remedial, verification before notary supported by complainant's reference to deposition in accusatory instrument, and deponent's statement, was not violative of statute and instrument would be treated as misdemeanor complaint sufficiently stating facts that person of ordinary intelligence, etc. would reasonably believe constituted bookmaking violation, but complaint had to be superseded by information, unless waived, so that every element of the crime charged is established. People v. Minuto, 71 Misc. 2d 800, 337 N.Y.S.2d 88 (Batavia City Ct. 1972).

Constitutionality of an ordinance may be challenged by defendant, pursuant to CPL § 170.30, after trial.—People v. Dahlman, 82 Misc. 2d 927, 371 N.Y.S.2d 60 (Dist. Ct. Nassau Co. 1975), aff'd, 87 Misc. 2d 261, 383 N.Y.S.2d 946 (9-10 Jud. Dist. 1976).

Criminal court; lack of jurisdiction when case not legally withdrawn from Grand Jury.—Where judicial authorization was required for lower court to obtain jurisdiction over case, but no verification had been provided that prosecution sought permission from the impaneling court to legally withdraw case from Grand Jury and proceed as a misdemeanor information, criminal court did not have jurisdiction over case, and further prosecution of defendant by misdemeanor information was not

proper. People v. Page, 177 Misc. 2d 448, 677 N.Y.S.2d 689 (N.Y.C. Crim. Ct. 1998).

Speedy trial.—CPL § 170.30(1)(e) does not contemplate a "speedy trial" motion being initiated by anyone but the defendant. People v. Nizza, 92 Misc. 2d 823, 402 N.Y.S.2d 95 (Crim. Ct. N.Y.C. 1977).

Dismissal of a misdemeanor "for failure to prosecute" is a bar to further prosecution.—People v. Scerbo, 91 Misc. 2d 97, 397 N.Y.S.2d 351 (Crim. Ct. N.Y.C. 1977).

Double jeopardy.—Where the motion to dismiss the information because of a deficiency is discoverable and capable of being made prior to trial, the right to assert the defense of double jeopardy when the motion is made during trial should be deemed waived. People v. Key, 87 Misc. 2d 262, 391 N.Y.S.2d 781 (App. Term 9-10 Jud. Dist. 1976), aff'd, 45 N.Y.2d 111, 408 N.Y.S.2d 16, 379 N.E.2d 1147 (1978).

Failure to prosecute.—Dismissal of a felony complaint for failure to prosecute based upon the inherent power of a court to control its calendar, is not a bar to the renewed prosecution as a misdemeanor based on the same charge. People v. Chandler, 111 Misc. 2d 654, 444 N.Y.S.2d 814 (Crim. Ct. N.Y. Ct. 1981).

Felony complaint dismissed in criminal court; indictment subsequently filed in Supreme Court; speedy trial.—Where a felony complaint is dismissed in the Crim. Ct. and subsequently an indictment is filed in Supreme Court, the period of time as prescribed in the "speedy trial" rule commenced with the filing of the indictment. People v. Boykin, 102 Misc. 2d 381, 423 N.Y.S.2d 366 (Sup. Ct. N.Y. Co. 1979).

Improper dismissal.—Misdemeanor complaint was improperly dismissed at arraignment for facial insufficiency, and defendant's oral dismissal motion should not have been entertained because an application to dismiss an accusatory instrument filed in a local criminal court can only be heard after arraignment via a formal motion made in writing upon reasonable notice to the People; even if the misdemeanor complaint were facially insufficient, amendment rather than dismissal would be the remedy. People v. Gonzalez, 184 Misc. 2d 262, 708 N.Y.S.2d 564 (App. Term, 1st Dept. 2000).

Investigative services; indigent defendant.—The court is empowered to allow counsel for an indigent defendant to obtain investigative services for his client at county expense if the demanded services are necessary and defendant is financially unable to obtain them. People v. Pride, 79 Misc. 2d 581, 360 N.Y.S.2d 572 (Westchester Co. Sup. Ct. 1974).

Prostitution; no corroboration needed.—The crime of prostitution is by itself prohibited by law, and requires no reciprocity. Thus, police officer to whom offer was allegedly made could not be considered an accomplice of the prostitute, and his testimony required no corroboration. People v. Thomas, 74 Misc. 2d 6, 343 N.Y.S.2d 1010 (Rochester City Ct. 1973).

Traffic infraction; supporting deposition.—A defendant accused under a simplified information is, upon proper request, entitled unconditionally to a supporting deposition setting forth in some detail the acts which allegedly make up the offense charged. Such a guarantee is necessary in traffic infraction cases. People v. Zagorsky, 73 Misc. 2d 420, 341 N.Y.S.2d 791 (Broome Co. Ct. 1973).

Exposure of a female; statute constitutional.—There is the presumption that a statute is constitutional until proven otherwise beyond a reasonable doubt. Women, or particular classes of women, may be singled out for special treatment in the exercise of the State's protective power without violation of the Fourteenth Amendment, and classification may be based on difference either in their physical characteristics or in the social conditions which surround their employment. People v. Gilbert, 72 Misc. 2d 795, 339 N.Y.S.2d 743 (Crim. Ct. N.Y. Co. 1973).

Motion to dismiss.—Criminal court does not have jurisdiction to dismiss a felony complaint for violation of the defendant's speedy trial rights where that complaint was not reduced to a misdemeanor complaint. People v. Senise, 111 Misc. 2d 477, 444 N.Y.S.2d 535 (Crim. Ct. Queens Co. 1981).

—Motion by a defendant to dismiss an information upon the grounds of denial of a speedy trial and in the interest of justice (CPL § 170.30[1][e], [g]) must be made in writing and upon reasonable notice to the People. People v. De Rosa, 84 Misc. 2d 316, 375 N.Y.S.2d 777 (App. Term Sup. Ct. 9-10 Jud. Dist. 1975), aff'd, 42 N.Y.2d 872, 397 N.Y.S.2d 780, 366 N.E.2d 868 (1977).

Reversal of conviction; unconstitutionality of statute.— Defendant's conviction for loitering must be reversed as the statute that he violated is unconstitutional in that it prohibits loitering "under circumstances which justify suspicion" that the person loitering "may be engaged or about to engage in a crime" and where the person loitering "upon inquiry by a peace officer, refuses to identify himself or fails to give a reasonably credible account of his conduct and purposes." The statute fails to give adequate notice as to what constitutes criminal conduct, depriving defendants of notice of the conduct to be avoided, and giving police complete discretion without guidelines to determine what conduct violates the statute, resulting in arbitrary and discriminatory enforcement, and hence violates due process. The statute also violates the Fourth Amendment requirement that arrests be made only for "probable cause" by permitting arrests for "suspicion." People v. Berck, 32 N.Y.2d 567, 347 N.Y.S.2d 33, cert. denied, 414 U.S. 1093 (1973).

Pre-arraignment; absence of complainant and arresting officer from arraignment.—The pre-arraignment procedure which excused the complainant and the arresting officer from appearing at the arraignment violated the defendant's right to reasonable bail guaranteed by section 510.30 of the CPL, the Eighth Amendment, and the Fourteenth Amendment, since the absence of these parties prevented the court from ascertaining facts from them on which it needed to rely in fixing bail. However, since this defendant was paroled and therefore suffered no harm, his motion to dismiss the charges against him was denied. People v. Vasquez, 76 Misc. 2d 5, 348 N.Y.S.2d 1007 (Crim. Ct. Bronx Co. 1973).

Right to a speedy trial; motion to dismiss information.— Where the People were not ready to try the defendant for misdemeanors punishable by sentences of more than three months until more than ninety days had elapsed since the commencement of the criminal action, defendant's motion to dismiss the information on the ground that he had been denied his right to a speedy trial was granted. People v. Feliciano, 75 Misc. 2d 921, 348 N.Y.S.2d 945 (Crim. Ct. Kings Co. 1973).

Unavailability of preliminary hearing minutes.—A reconstruction preliminary hearing was ordered where the hearing minutes were lost through no lack of diligence on the part of the District Attorney and there was a likelihood that a fair reconstruction of the original testimony could be achieved. People v. Hicks, 85 Misc. 2d 649, 381 N.Y.S.2d 794 (Crim. Ct. N.Y.C. 1976).

§ 170.35. Motion to dismiss information, simplified information, prosecutor's information or misdemeanor complaint; as defective.

1. An information, a simplified information, a prosecutor's information or a misdemeanor complaint, or a count thereof, is defective within the meaning of paragraph (a) of subdivision one of section 170.30 when:

(a) It is not sufficient on its face pursuant to the requirements of section 100.40; provided that such an instrument or count may not be dismissed as defective, but must instead be amended, where the defect or irregularity is of a kind that may be cured by amendment and where the people move to so amend; or

(b) The allegations demonstrate that the court does not have jurisdiction of the offense charged; or

(c) The statute defining the offense charged is unconstitutional or otherwise invalid.

2. An information is also defective when it is filed in replacement of a misdemeanor complaint

pursuant to section 170.65 but without satisfying the requirements stated therein.

3. A prosecutor's information is also defective when:

(a) It is filed at the direction of a grand jury, pursuant to section 190.70, and the offense or offenses charged are not among those authorized by such grand jury direction; or

(b) It is filed by the district attorney at his own instance, pursuant to subdivision two of section 100.50, and the factual allegations of the original information underlying it and any supporting depositions are not legally sufficient to support the charge in the prosecutor's information.

Amended by L. 1972, Ch. 661.

ANNOTATIONS

Accusatory instrument; sufficiency.—A legally sufficient accusatory instrument is a fundamental and nonwaivable jurisdictional predicate to a valid criminal prosecution. People v. Pratt, 164 Misc. 2d 498, 625 N.Y.S.2d 869 (N.Y. Co. Crim. Ct. 1995).

—An information or a count thereof is facially sufficient if it contains allegations in the factual part of the accusatory instrument which, when read together with any supporting depositions which may accompany the instrument, (1) provide reasonable cause to believe that the defendant committed the offense charged and (2) establish, if true, by non-hearsay allegations, every element of the offense(s) charged and the defendant's commission thereof. People v. Figueroa, 164 Misc. 2d 814, 625 N.Y.S.2d 839 (Kings Co. Crim. Ct. 1995).

Defect in information.—Defect in simplified traffic information, in that there was typographical error in one digit of license number, was amendable irregularity. People v. Kreismann, 162 Misc. 2d 726, 619 N.Y.S.2d 253 (Nassau Co. Justice Ct. 1994).

Accusatory instrument; verification; misdemeanor complaint; reasonable cause; sufficiency.—Since the CPL provision regarding verifications is remedial, verification before notary supported by complainant's reference to deposition in accusatory instrument, and deponent's statement, was not violative of statute and instrument would be treated as misdemeanor complaint sufficiently stating facts that person of ordinary intelligence, etc., would reasonably believe constituted bookmaking violation, but complaint had to be superseded by information, unless waived, so that every element of the crime charged is established. People v. Minuto, 71 Misc. 2d 800, 337 N.Y.S.2d 88 (Batavia City Ct. 1972).

Defects; insufficiency of evidence.—Defects or insufficience of evidence in the grand jury proceeding are matters which occur in the superior court rather than a local criminal court and should be determined by the superior court, and defendant's attack upon the direction and order of a higher court or a motion to amend such, by the prosecution, should be brought before the superior court. People v. Cai Adjustors Inc., 84 Misc. 2d 221, 375 N.Y.S.2d 554 (Crim. Ct. N.Y.C. 1975).

Dismissal of information; unconstitutionality of statute.— Informations charging violation of a city ordinance proscribing disorderly conduct in private premises were dismissed under CPL § 170.35(1)(c) because PL § 240.20 which does not mention private premises preempts varying local laws under the "home rule" provision of the State Constitution, Article 9, Section 2(c)(ii)(c)(10), thereby rendering the ordinance unconstitutional. People v. O'Neal, 93 Misc. 2d 953, 404 N.Y.S.2d 250 (City Ct. of Rome 1978).

Impermissible amendments.—Like indictments and informations, prosecutor's informations can be amended with respect to time, place, and the names of persons, but unlike indictments, informations do not have the limitations imposed by CPL § 200.70(2)(a) and (b), i.e., that there can be no amendment to cure the failure to state an offense or legal insufficiency of the factual allegations. People v. Kurtz, 175 Misc. 2d 980, 670 N.Y.S.2d 1008 (Crim. Ct. Queens Co. 1998).

Motion to dismiss simplified information in traffic case;

no adequate supporting deposition.—Where complainant police officer has not provided defendant with an adequate supporting deposition (as required by court order pursuant to CPL 100.25(2)) within a reasonable time before trial, a motion made on that day to dismiss the simplified information as defective within the meaning of CPL § 170.35(1) should be granted. It would not be proper at that time to permit the prosecutor to serve defendant with an amended supporting deposition. People v. Hust, 74 Misc. 2d 887, 346 N.Y.S.2d 303 (Broome Co. Ct. 1973).

Reversal of conviction; unconstitutionality of statute.—Defendant's conviction for loitering must be reversed as the statute that he violated is unconstitutional in that it prohibits loitering "under circumstances which justify suspicion" in that the person loitering "may be engaged or about to engage in a crime" and where the person loitering "upon inquiry by a peace officer, refuses to identify himself or fails to give a reasonably credible account of his conduct and purposes." The statute fails to give adequate notice as to what constitutes criminal conduct, depriving defendants of notice of the conduct to be avoided, and giving police complete discretion without guidelines to determine what conduct violates the statute, resulting in arbitrary and discriminatory enforcement, and hence violates due process. The statute also violates the Fourth Amendment requirement that arrests be made only for "probable cause" by permitting arrests for "suspicion." People v. Berck, 32 N.Y.2d 567, 347 N.Y.S.2d 33, 300 N.E.2d 411, cert. denied, 414 U.S. 1093 (1973).

Sufficiency of information.—Misdemeanor information was not jurisdictionally defective where it charged defendant with issuing a bad check and alleged that defendant knew of his insufficient funds or that payment would be refused; such allegation sufficiently complied with the requirement that the information allege facts supporting the charges. People v. Miles, 64 N.Y.2d 731, 485 N.Y.S.2d 747, 475 N.E.2d 118 (1984).

—An information must be sufficient alone, without resort to testimony or record of evidence, in order to withstand a motion to dismiss for insufficiency; it is required to show a legally sufficient case, as well as "reasonable cause"; where the information is insufficient in law, no jurisdiction is conferred upon the court. People v. Crisofulli, 91 Misc. 2d 424, 398 N.Y.S.2d 120 (Crim. Ct. N.Y.C. 1977).

—An accusatory instrument is defective on its face when it does not conform to the requirements of CPL § 100.40, however, the instrument may not be dismissed as defective, but must be amended when the defect or irregularity is of a kind that may be cured by amendment, and the People move to so amend (CPL 100.35[1][a]). People v. Pacifico, 105 Misc. 2d 396, 432 N.Y.S.2d 588 (Crim. Ct. Queens Co. 1980).

Traffic infraction; supporting deposition.—A defendant accused under a simplified information is, upon proper request, entitled unconditionally to a supporting deposition setting forth in some detail the acts which allegedly make up the offense charged. Such a guarantee is necessary in traffic infraction cases. People v. Zagorsky, 73 Misc. 2d 420, 341 N.Y.S.2d 791 (Broome Co. Ct. 1973).

§ 170.40. Motion to dismiss information, simplified traffic information, prosecutor's information or misdemeanor complaint; in furtherance of justice.

1. An information, a simplified traffic information, a prosecutor's information or a misdemeanor complaint, or any count thereof, may be dismissed in the interest of justice, as provided in paragraph (g) of subdivision one of section 170.30 when, even though there may be no basis for dismissal as a matter of law upon any ground specified in paragraphs (a) through (f) of said subdivision one of section 170.30, such dismissal is required as a matter of judicial discretion by the existence of some compelling factor, consideration or circumstance clearly demonstrating that conviction or prosecution of the defendant upon such accusatory instrument or count would constitute or result in injustice. In determining whether such compelling factor, consideration, or circumstance exists, the court must, to the extent applicable, examine and consider, individually and collectively, the following:

(a) the seriousness and circumstances of the offense;

(b) the extent of harm caused by the offense;

(c) the evidence of guilt, whether admissible or inadmissible at trial;

(d) the history, character and condition of the defendant;

(e) any exceptionally serious misconduct of law enforcement personnel in the investigation, arrest and prosecution of the defendant;

(f) the purpose and effect of imposing upon the defendant a sentence authorized for the offense;

(g) the impact of a dismissal on the safety or welfare of the community;

(h) the impact of a dismissal upon the confidence of the public in the criminal justice system;

(i) where the court deems it appropriate, the attitude of the complainant or victim with respect to the motion;

(j) any other relevant fact indicating that a judgment of conviction would serve no useful purpose.

2. An order dismissing an accusatory instrument specified in subdivision one in the interest of justice may be issued upon motion of the people or of the court itself as well as upon that of the defendant. Upon issuing such an order, the court must set forth its reasons therefor upon the record.

Amended by L. 1979, Ch. 216.

ANNOTATIONS

Dismissal.—In order to allege that a criminal act occurred during a hockey game, factual portion of information must allege acts that show intent to inflict physical injury which was unrelated to the athletic event, and injuries must be so severe as to be unacceptable in normal competition; court dismissed charge in interest of justice, finding that Penal Law could not "be imposed on a hockey game without running afoul of the policy of encouraging athletic competition." People v. Schacker, 175 Misc. 2d 834, 670 N.Y.S.2d 308 (Dist. Ct. Suffolk Co. 1998).

—Motions for dismissal in interests of justice are addressed to sound discretion of court and must be evaluated in light of factors enumerated in statute. People v. Shaughnessy, 168 Misc. 2d 53, 642 N.Y.S.2d 487 (Suffolk Co. Dist. Ct. 1996).

—Charge of criminal mischief in fourth degree, based on allegation that defendant intentionally damaged complainant's door, would be dismissed in interest of justice, where defendant was merely complying with court order to nail order for contempt to complainant's door at time of incident; defendant had reasonable ground to believe she had right to do what was reasonably necessary to nail court order to complainant's door. People v. Cantalino, 166 Misc. 2d 624, 632 N.Y.S.2d 445 (N.Y.C. Crim. Ct. 1995).

—In determining whether to dismiss criminal case in interest of justice, court must make value judgment based upon "sensitive balancing" of individual and state interests in assessing its reason for this remedy. People v. Doe, 158 Misc. 2d 863, 602 N.Y.S.2d 507 (N.Y.C. Crim. Ct. 1993).

Dismissal of information; discretion of court.—A judge who grants a CPL § 170.40 motion need only state the reasons for this action in "written or orally delivered on the record" and is not required to state which of paragraphs (a) thru (j) he relies on. People v. Rickert, 58 N.Y.2d 122, 459 N.Y.S.2d 734, 446 N.E.2d 419 (1983).

—When deciding a motion to dismiss in the interest of justice, it is not necessary to engage in a point-by-point discussion of all 10 factors of CPL 170.40(1). Court must consider the factors individually and collectively. In dismissing case against 17-year-old high school student who participated in an anti-war demonstration and blocked the flow of pedestrian traffic, court considered the defendant's age, background, character, lack of criminal record, and extensive volunteer work, among other factors. People v. Gragert, 1 Misc. 3d 646, 765 N.Y.S.2d 471 (Crim. Ct. City of New York 2003).

—The court did not abuse its discretion when it dismissed the information in furtherance of justice after the Assistant District Attorney twice failed to appear in court on scheduled dates. People v. Fagg, 86 Misc. 2d 1046, 385 N.Y.S.2d 743 (Ontario Co. Ct. 1976).

Failure of the prosecutor and complainant to appear.—The prosecutor had requested an early call but, on the day set for trial, both he and the complainant failed to answer two trial calls. The informations were dismissed "in the interests of justice." People v. Wingard, 33 N.Y.2d 192, 351 N.Y.S.2d 385, 306 N.E.2d 402 (1973).

Family Court.—A Family Court Judge is authorized under the present law to dismiss a juvenile delinquency petition in the furtherance of justice and the same standards applicable under CPL §§ 210.40 and 170.40 should be followed. In re Stephens, 98 Misc. 2d 137, 413 N.Y.S.2d 591 (Fam. Ct. Oneida Co. 1979).

General.—A court need not pursue a ritual adherence to the criteria in CPL § 170.40; it may give any element of said criteria greater, even controlling, weight over any other element or factor. People v. Pius, 157 Misc. 2d 805, 598 N.Y.S.2d 693 (Dist. Ct. Suffolk Co. 1993).

Improper use of Grand Jury subpoena.—Motion by defense counsel to dismiss the charges against the defendants because the District Attorney had improperly used grand jury subpoenas to interrogate witnesses was denied. People v. Boulet, 88 Misc. 2d 353, 388 N.Y.S.2d 350 (City Court of Rochester 1976).

Loss of evidence.—Where the television set and tapes of conversations between defendant and law enforcement officers were lost while in the constructive possession of the prosecutor, the court dismissed the charges in the interest of justice because of the irreparable denial of the defendant's right to adequately prepare for and maintain his own defense. People v. Churba, 76 Misc. 2d 1028, 353 N.Y.S.2d 130 (Criminal Ct. N.Y.C. 1974).

Permit issued by mistake; dismissal in interest of justice.—Town clerk issued a permit to defendant to erect a radio tower in violation of recently enacted Zoning law and thereafter defendant was prosecuted for violation of the ordinance. The court dismissed the charge finding that the existence of a compelling factor, consideration or circumstance clearly demonstrated that conviction or prosecution of the defendant upon such accusatory instrument would constitute or result in injustice. People v. Hacker, 76 Misc. 2d 610, 350 N.Y.S.2d 67 (Dist. Ct. Suffolk Co. 1973).

Pre-arraignment; absence of complainant and arresting officer from arraignment.—The pre-arraignment procedure which excused the complainant and the arresting officer from appearing at the arraignment violated the defendant's right to reasonable bail guaranteed by section 510.30 of the CPL, the Eighth Amendment, and the Fourteenth Amendment, since the absence of these parties prevented the court from ascertaining facts from them on which it needed to reply in fixing bail. However, since this defendant was paroled and therefore suffered no harm, his motion to dismiss the charges against him was denied. People v. Vasquez, 76 Misc. 2d 5, 348 N.Y.S.2d 1007 (Crim. Ct. Bronx Co. 1973).

Prosecutorial misconduct; dismissal in interest of justice.—Dismissal was granted where prosecutor on at least two occasions conducted a dialogue with the defendant, who was without counsel, regarding a plea and restitution after the filing of an information. People v. Eubanks, 108 Misc. 2d 108, 436 N.Y.S.2d 953 (Crim. Ct. Richmond Co. 1981).

Purpose.—Where a bona fide defense or other evidence to weaken the People's case exists, this is a matter that requires resolution at a trial rather than by way of a pretrial motion to dismiss; a motion to dismiss in the interests of justice is not intended to be a substitute for a trial, but rather to be used solely when some compelling factor requires the prosecution to be discontinued. People v. Prunty, 101 Misc. 2d 163, 420 N.Y.S.2d 703 (Crim. Ct. N.Y.C. 1979).

Statutory factors.—When an action is dismissed in the interest of justice pursuant to CPL § 170.40, the judge must consider individually and collectively the specific factors listed and must state the reasons on the record. Where the record does not indicate that the Town Justice took into consideration the factors enumerated in CPL § 170.40, the court reversed and reinstated the simplified traffic information. People v. Berrus, 1 N.Y.3d 535, 770 N.Y.S.2d 691, 802 N.E.2d 1089 (2003).

§ 170.45. Motion to dismiss information, simplified traffic information, prosecutor's information or misdemeanor complaint; procedure.

The procedural rules prescribed in section 210.45 with respect to the making, consideration and disposition of a motion to dismiss an indictment are also applicable to a motion to dismiss an information, a simplified traffic information, a prosecutor's information or a misdemeanor complaint.

ANNOTATION

Accusatory instruments.—An accusatory instrument based upon sworn incorrect statements which the affiant says are not true under oath should not serve as the basis for a prosecution. People v. Pappas, 163 Misc. 2d 1029, 623 N.Y.S.2d 83 (Kings Co. Crim. Ct. 1994).

§ 170.50. Motion in superior court to dismiss prosecutor's information.

1. At any time after arraignment in a local criminal court upon a prosecutor's information filed at the direction of a grand jury and before entry of a plea of guilty thereto or commencement of a trial thereof, the local criminal court wherein the prosecutor's information is filed may, upon motion of the defendant, dismiss such prosecutor's information or a count thereof upon the ground that:

(a) The evidence before the grand jury was not legally sufficient to support the charge; or

(b) The grand jury proceeding resulting in the filing of such prosecutor's information was defective.

2. The criteria and procedures for consideration and disposition of such motion are the same as those prescribed in sections 210.30 and 210.35, governing consideration and disposition of a motion to dismiss an indictment on the ground of insufficiency of grand jury evidence or of a

defective grand jury proceeding; and, where appropriate, the general procedural rules prescribed in section 210.45 for consideration and disposition of a motion to dismiss an indictment are also applicable.

3. Upon dismissing a prosecutor's information or a count thereof pursuant to this section, the court may, upon application of the people, in its discretion authorize the people to resubmit the charge or charges to the same or another grand jury. In the absence of such authorization, such charge or charges may not be resubmitted to a grand jury. The rules prescribed in subdivisions eight and nine of section 210.45 concerning the discharge of a defendant from custody or exoneration of bail in the absence of an authorization to resubmit an indictment to grand jury, and concerning the issuance of a securing order and the effective period thereof where such an authorization is issued, apply equally where a prosecutor's information is dismissed pursuant to this section.

Amended by L. 1973, Ch. 530; L. 1981, Ch. 247.

ANNOTATIONS

Dismissal.—Prosecutor's information charging defendants with criminal possession of weapon in fourth degree and resisting arrest was subject to dismissal on ground that evidence before grand jury was legally insufficient, where there was no testimony that one defendant resisted arrest, and there was no ballistics evidence presented as to operability of loaded firearms. People v. Patterson, 148 Misc. 2d 528, 561 N.Y.S.2d 502 (Kings Co. Crim. Ct. 1990).

—Statute stating that when motion to dismiss prosecutor's information directed by grand jury for legally insufficient evidence is granted by local criminal court, such charges may not be resubmitted to grand jury in absence of such authorization to resubmit, does not preclude People from superseding prosecutor's information with an information. People v. Patterson, 148 Misc. 2d 528, 561 N.Y.S.2d 502 (Kings Co. Crim. Ct. 1990).

Preliminary hearing.—The preliminary hearing upon misdemeanor charges authorized by CPL § 170.75, after arraignment, upon a prosecutor's information, does not apply when the prosecutor's information was filed by direction of the grand jury. In this situation, the defendant is relegated to the remedy outlined in CPL § 170.50. People v. Harper, 86 Misc. 2d 789, 371 N.Y.S.2d 86 (Crim. Ct. N.Y.C. 1975).

§ 170.55. Adjournment in contemplation of dismissal.

1. Upon or after arraignment in a local criminal court upon an information, a simplified information, a prosecutor's information or a misdemeanor complaint, and before entry of a plea of guilty thereto or commencement of a trial thereof, the court may, upon motion of the people or the defendant and with the consent of the other party, or upon the court's own motion with the consent of both the people and the defendant, order that the action be "adjourned in contemplation of dismissal," as prescribed in subdivision two.

2. An adjournment in contemplation of dismissal is an adjournment of the action without date ordered with a view to ultimate dismissal of the accusatory instrument in furtherance of justice. Upon issuing such an order, the court must release the defendant on his own recognizance. Upon application of the people, made at any time not more than six months, or in the case of a family offense as defined in subdivision one of section 530.11 of this chapter, one year, after the issuance of such order, the court may restore the case to the calendar upon a determination that dismissal of the accusatory instrument would not be in furtherance of justice, and the action must thereupon proceed. If the case is not so restored within such six months or one year period, the accusatory instrument is, at the expiration of such period, deemed to have been dismissed by the court in furtherance of justice.

3. In conjunction with an adjournment in contemplation of dismissal the court may issue a temporary order of protection pursuant to section 530.12 or 530.13 of this chapter, requiring the defendant to observe certain specified conditions of conduct.

4. Where the local criminal court information, simplified information, prosecutor's information, or misdemeanor complaint charges a crime or violation between spouses or between parent and child, or between members of the same family or household, as the term "members of the same family or household" is defined in subdivision one of section 530.11 of this chapter, the court may as a condition of an adjournment in contemplation of dismissal order require that the defendant participate in an educational program addressing the issues of spousal abuse and family violence.

5. The court may grant an adjournment in contemplation of dismissal on condition that the defendant participate in dispute resolution and comply with any award or settlement resulting therefrom.

6. The court may as a condition of an adjournment in contemplation of dismissal order, require the defendant to perform services for a public or not-for-profit corporation, association, institution or agency. Such condition may only be imposed where the defendant has consented to the amount and conditions of such service. The court may not impose such conditions in excess of the length of the adjournment.

7. The court may, as a condition of an adjournment in contemplation of dismissal order, where a defendant is under twenty-one years of age and is charged with (a) a misdemeanor or misdemeanors other than section eleven hundred ninety-two of the vehicle and traffic law, in which the record indicates the consumption of alcohol by the defendant may have been a contributing factor, or (b) a violation of paragraph (a) of subdivision one of section sixty-five-b of the alcoholic beverage control law, require the defendant to attend an alcohol awareness program established pursuant to subdivision (a) of section 19.07 of the mental hygiene law.

8. The granting of an adjournment in

contemplation of dismissal shall not be deemed to be a conviction or an admission of guilt. No person shall suffer any disability or forfeiture as a result of such an order. Upon the dismissal of the accusatory instrument pursuant to this section, the arrest and prosecution shall be deemed a nullity and the defendant shall be restored, in contemplation of law, to the status he occupied before his arrest and prosecution.

Amended by L. 1972, Ch. 661; L. 1980, Chs. 24, 530; L. 1981, Ch. 847; L. 1982, Ch. 134; L. 1984, Ch. 156; L. 1985, Ch. 672; L.1988, Ch. 39; L. 1990, Ch. 683; L. 1994, Ch. 222, § 33, eff. Jan. 1, 1995, amending subd. 2; L. 1998, Ch. 383, § 8, eff. Jan. 1, 1999, amending subd. 7, and amendment to expire on Jan. 1, 2002; L. 2001, Ch. 549, § 2, eff. Dec. 12, 2001, deleting expiration note set forth in L. 1998, Ch. 383.

ANNOTATIONS

ACD.—An ACD may be granted only before the entry of a guilty plea or the commencement of trial. *In re* Edwin L., 88 N.Y.2d 593, 648 N.Y.S.2d 850, 671 N.E.2d 1247 (1996).

—When action is adjourned in contemplation of dismissal, state may move, within six months, to restore action to calendar, and court may deny application or grant it, if it determines in its discretion that dismissal would not be in furtherance of justice. People v. Meyerson, 165 Misc. 2d 476, 628 N.Y.S.2d 934 (Bronx Co. Crim. Ct. 1995).

Adjournment in contemplation of dismissal; People's consent necessary.—Despite District Attorney's opposition, the court granted defendant's motion to restore the case to the calendar for trial after it had been ACOD. People v. Paar, 89 Misc. 2d 11, 390 N.Y.S.2d 776 (Dist. Ct. Nassau Co. 1976).

—A defendant has no constitutional or statutory right to an adjournment in contemplation of dismissal and it cannot be granted without the consent of the people. People v. McDonnell, 83 Misc. 2d 907, 373 N.Y.S.2d 971 (Sup. Ct. Queens Co. 1975).

Adjournment in contemplation of dismissal; statutory right to recover fingerprints.—The sealing of all defendant's records relating to marihuana arrest and prosecution effectively forecloses defendant's right to recover his fingerprints as such action is not a determination in his favor but renders the arrest a nullity to enable defendant to avoid stigma of arrest in non-criminal matters. Kushner v. De La Rosa, 72 Misc. 2d 319, 338 N.Y.S.2d 645 (Queens Co. 1972).

A.C.O.D.; conditions.—Westchester County District Attorney requirement that defendant waive his rights to return of fingerprints (CPL § 160.50) as a condition for the People's acquiescence in adjournment in contemplation of dismissal should be enforced like any other contract. People v. Wei Chen, 104 Misc. 2d 1067, 430 N.Y.S.2d 469 (Westchester Co. 1980).

—Prosecutor may not condition A.C.D. on matters extraneous to the criminal process involving the defendant's exercise of certain constitutional or civil rights. People v. Wilmot, 104 Misc. 2d 412, 428 N.Y.S.2d 568 (Crim. Ct. Kings Co. 1980).

—The People having legitimately determined not to prosecute by consenting to an A.C.O.D. may not reverse this position solely because defendant refused to abide with District Attorney's condition that the defendant release his civil right to sue to the County of Nassau. People v. Siragrisa, 81 Misc. 2d 368, 366 N.Y.S.2d 336 (Dist. Ct. Nassau Co. 1975).

Court has no discretion in ruling on A.C.O.D. motion.—The court's authority for granting or denying an A.C.O.D. (Adjournment in Contemplation of Dismissal) is dependent upon the action of the prosecutor and is not a matter of the court's independent discretion; if the People move for an A.C.O.D. even without the consent of the defendant, the court must grant it. People v. Ruggieri, 100 Misc. 2d 585, 419 N.Y.S.2d 869 (City Ct. Poughkeepsie 1979).

Defined.—"ACOD" is not a disposition, judgment or decree in favor of a defendant in a criminal action, but is the nullification of an arrest and criminal proceedings by operation of law which does not constitute double jeopardy grounds in later prosecution. People v. Kephart, 77 Misc. 2d 921, 353 N.Y.S.2d 652 (Nassau Co. Ct. 1974).

Dismissal of charges; return of fingerprints.—An order

dismissing the accusatory instrument pursuant to CPL § 170.55 is a favorable termination of the proceeding and the file must be sealed and the fingerprints returned. People v. Joseph P., 106 Misc. 2d 1075, 433 N.Y.S.2d 335 (Justice Ct. Westchester Co. 1980).

—Petitioner was granted an adjournment in contemplation of dismissal, and the charge was subsequently deemed dismissed. Petitioner then requested the return or destruction of his fingerprints and photographs, pursuant to section 79-e of the Civil Rights Law. Unfortunately, the county court had no jurisdiction to entertain such a motion. *In re* Foster, 72 Misc. 2d 1029, 340 N.Y.S.2d 758 (Erie Co. Ct. 1973).

Pending civil litigation.—People improperly attempted to restore defendant's adjournment in contemplation of dismissal to trial calendar in order to affect pending civil litigation. People v. Clark, 123 Misc. 2d 674, 474 N.Y.S.2d 409 (Crim. Ct. N.Y.C. 1984).

Restoration.—Restoration of an ACD because the People have had a change of heart is not appropriate. People v. Verardi, 158 Misc. 2d 1039, 602 N.Y.S.2d 318, 321 (Crim. Ct. Kings Co. 1993).

—The court had the jurisdiction and power to restore a case in A.C.D. status to the calendar absent the application of the People. People v. Pomerantz, 76 Misc. 2d 766, 351 N.Y.S.2d 613 (Crim. Ct. N.Y. Co. 1974).

—On application of the People, the court is required to restore the case to the calendar. People v. Hurt, 78 Misc. 2d 43, 355 N.Y.S.2d 728 (Crim. Ct. Bronx Co. 1974).

—Where the district attorney makes a motion to restore a case to the calendar within six months after an ACOD was obtained, the court must grant the motion since it has no discretion under the statute to do otherwise; moreover, it is well established that defendant is not entitled to notice of such motion or to a hearing thereon. People v. Goldstein, 79 Misc. 2d 996, 361 N.Y.S.2d 994 (Crim. Ct. N.Y. Co. 1974).

Restoration of adjournment in contemplation of dismissal; interests of justice.—Renewal of criminal prosecution by restoration of adjournment in contemplation of dismissal because of defendant's failure to fulfill restitution agreement due to indigency in six-month period between disposition and final dismissal is impermissible and warrants dismissal in the interests of justice; review of ACD arrangements on a case-by-case basis is necessary to insure that defendant has not entered into an agreement that is unconstitutional or improper, or one that becomes so upon restoration. People v. Cunningham, 106 Misc. 2d 326, 431 N.Y.S.2d 785 (Crim. Ct. Kings Co. 1980).

Not available for indictment.—An adjournment in contemplation of dismissal is not available to dismiss charges contained in an indictment. Hennessey v. Gorman, 87 A.D.2d 29, 450 N.Y.S.2d 638 (4th Dept. 1982).

§ 170.56. Adjournment in contemplation of dismissal in cases involving marihuana.

1. Upon or after arraignment in a local criminal court upon an information, a prosecutor's information or a misdemeanor complaint, where the sole remaining count or counts charge a violation or violations of section 221.05, 221.10, 221.15, 221.35, or 221.40 of the penal law and before the entry of a plea of guilty thereto or commencement of a trial thereof, the court, upon motion of a defendant, may order that all proceedings be suspended and the action adjourned in contemplation of dismissal, or upon a finding that adjournment would not be necessary or appropriate and the setting forth in the record of the reasons for such findings, may dismiss in furtherance of justice the accusatory instrument; provided, however, that the court may not order such adjournment in contemplation of dismissal or dismiss the accusatory instrument if: (a) the

defendant has previously been granted such adjournment in contemplation of dismissal, or (b) the defendant has previously been granted a dismissal under this section, or (c) the defendant has previously been convicted of any offense involving controlled substances, or (d) the defendant has previously been convicted of a crime and the district attorney does not consent or (e) the defendant has previously been adjudicated a youthful offender on the basis of any act or acts involving controlled substances and the district attorney does not consent.

2. Upon ordering the action adjourned in contemplation of dismissal, the court must set and specify such conditions for the adjournment as may be appropriate, and such conditions may include placing the defendant under the supervision of any public or private agency. At any time prior to dismissal the court may modify the conditions or extend or reduce the term of the adjournment, except that the total period of adjournment shall not exceed twelve months. Upon violation of any condition fixed by the court, the court may revoke its order and restore the case to the calendar and the prosecution thereupon must proceed. If the case is not so restored to the calendar during the period fixed by the court, the accusatory instrument is, at the expiration of such period, deemed to have been dismissed in the furtherance of justice.

3. Upon or after dismissal of such charges against a defendant not previously convicted of a crime, the court shall order that all official records and papers, relating to the defendant's arrest and prosecution, whether on file with the court, a police agency, or the New York state division of criminal justice services, be sealed and, except as otherwise provided in paragraph (d) of subdivision one of section 160.50 of this chapter, not made available to any person or public or private agency; except, such records shall be made available under order of a court for the purpose of determining whether, in subsequent proceedings, such person qualifies under this section for a dismissal or adjournment in contemplation of dismissal of the accusatory instrument.

4. Upon the granting of an order pursuant to subdivision three, the arrest and prosecution shall be deemed a nullity and the defendant shall be restored, in contemplation of law, to the status he occupied before his arrest and prosecution.

Amended by L. 1973, Ch. 276; L. 1977, Chs. 360, 905.

ANNOTATIONS

Applicability.—Section applicable to Family Court juvenile delinquency proceeding. *See In re* G., 68 Misc. 2d 80, 326 N.Y.S.2d 483 (Fam. Ct. 1971).

Adjournment in contemplation of dismissal; statutory right to recover fingerprints.—The sealing of all defendant's records relating to marihuana arrest and prosecution effectively forecloses defendant's right to recover his fingerprints as such action is not a determination in his favor but renders the arrest a nullity to enable defendant to avoid stigma of arrest in non-criminal matters. Kushner v. De La Rosa, 72 Misc. 2d 319, 338 N.Y.S.2d 645 (Queens Co. 1972).

Adjournment of twelve months; commits another crime.—Defendant qualified for ACD treatment and at the conclusion of this period the judge ordered that all official records and papers be sealed. Thereafter, it was learned that defendant had been convicted of another offense during the twelve month period. The court refused to vacate the dismissal but ordered the records and papers unsealed. People v. Connor, 76 Misc. 2d 361, 351 N.Y.S.2d 67 (Dist. Ct. Nassau Co. 1973).

Adjournment granted without D.A.'s consent where defendant had been granted prior adjournment.—Defendant was granted an adjournment in contemplation of dismissal under CPL § 170.56, without the approval of the District Attorney, where he had previously been granted a prior adjournment under CPL § 170.55. People v. Ford, 104 Misc. 2d 458, 428 N.Y.S.2d 612 (Crim. Ct. Kings Co. 1980).

Cases involving marihuana; reliability of informant.—An informant's reliability is measured in part by the accuracy of information supplied in previous cases. Where an informant supplied information that resulted in the arrest of two persons on a marihuana charge, his credibility in the present action should not be challenged on the grounds that the previous action was adjourned in contemplation of dismissal, and as such, was not a "conviction." People v. Campo, 71 Misc. 2d 6, 335 N.Y.S.2d 199 (Mount Vernon City Ct. 1972).

False information; restored to calendar.—An adjournment in contemplation of dismissal based upon false information supplied by the defendant could be restored to the calendar by the court even though it was a year after the adjournment in Contemplation of dismissal was granted. People v. Mann, 83 Misc. 2d 412, 372 N.Y.S.2d 902 (Dist. Ct. Nassau Co. 1975).

Sealing of records; testimony still permitted.—There is no specific CPL provision prohibiting officers or other agencies from giving testimony after a criminal action has terminated in favor of the accused; therefore where marihuana charges against two West Point cadets were dismissed pursuant to CPL § 170.56, the court ruled that police or prosecution personnel could testify at disciplinary hearings at the academy, although they could not use official records or papers or copies thereof. People v. A., 99 Misc. 2d 295, 415 N.Y.S.2d 919 (Crim. Ct. Orange Co. 1979).

§ 170.60. Requirement of plea to information, simplified information or prosecutor's information.

Unless an information, a simplified information or a prosecutor's information is dismissed or the criminal action thereon terminated or abated pursuant to a provision of this article or some other provision of law, the defendant must be required to enter a plea thereto.

Amended by L. 1972, Ch. 661.

§ 170.65. Replacement of misdemeanor complaint by information and waiver thereof.

1. A defendant against whom a misdemeanor complaint is pending is not required to enter a plea thereto. For purposes of prosecution, such instrument must, except as provided in subdivision three, be replaced by an information, and the defendant must be arraigned thereon. If the misdemeanor complaint is supplemented by a supporting deposition and such instruments taken together satisfy the requirements for a valid information, such misdemeanor complaint is deemed to have been converted to and to constitute a replacing information.

2. An information which replaces a misdemeanor complaint need not charge the same offense or offenses, but at least one count thereof must charge the commission by the defendant of an offense based upon conduct which was the subject of the misdemeanor complaint. In addition, the information may, subject to the rules of joinder, charge any other offense which the factual allegations thereof or of any supporting depositions accompanying it are legally sufficient to support, even though such offense is not based upon conduct which was the subject of the misdemeanor complaint.

3. A defendant who has been arraigned upon a misdemeanor complaint may waive prosecution by information and consent to be prosecuted upon the misdemeanor complaint. In such case, the defendant must be required, either upon the date of the waiver or subsequent thereto, to enter a plea to the misdemeanor complaint.

ANNOTATIONS

Converting misdemeanor complaint to information.—Absent a waiver by defendant, a misdemeanor complaint must be converted to an information before defendant can be prosecuted. People v. Santos, 165 Misc. 2d 950, 630 N.Y.S.2d 908 (Crim. Ct. Bronx Co. 1995).

Delay in converting misdemeanor complaint to misdemeanor information.—The failure of the People to convert the misdemeanor complaint to a misdemeanor information did not in any way contribute to the delay in trial since the requirement to convert is one which can be met at a point in time close to the trial; the statutory pattern contemplates that a misdemeanor action is to proceed in its pretrial stages in the same fashion regardless of whether the accusatory instrument is an information or a complaint. People v. Callender, 101 Misc. 2d 958, 422 N.Y.S.2d 611 (Crim. Ct. N.Y.C. 1979), aff'd, 112 Misc. 2d 28, 448 N.Y.S.2d 92 (Sup. Ct. App. Term, 1st Dept. 1981).

Prosecution on misdemeanor complaint.—In the absence of an effective admonition of the right to be prosecuted by information, a waiver or consent to prosecution by misdemeanor complaint cannot be presumed. People v. Weinberg, 34 N.Y.2d 429, 358 N.Y.S.2d 357, 315 N.E.2d 434 (1974).

—The court held that the sworn testimony of the complaining witness given at the preliminary hearing on the felony complaint served as a "supporting deposition," within the meaning of CPL § 170.65(1), when the former charge was reduced to a misdemeanor at the completion of the hearing. People v. Rodriguez, 94 Misc. 2d 645, 405 N.Y.S.2d 218 (Crim. Ct. Bronx Co. 1978).

Replacing complaint with an information.—Where a defendant is charged with the possession or sale of cocaine or heroin, a laboratory report is an absolute necessity in order to convert the complaint to an information. People v. Burton, 133 Misc. 2d 701, 507 N.Y.S.2d 809 (Crim. Ct. N.Y. Co. 1986).

—CPL § 170.65(1) required the replacing of the felony complaint, which was reduced to a misdemeanor complaint, by an information within a reasonable time period after arraignment and the lapse of more than one year from the date of arraignment without replacing the misdemeanor complaint was far beyond a reasonable time considering that CPL § 30.30(1) requires the People to be ready for trial on a felony within six months.

People v. Smith, 103 Misc. 2d 640, 426 N.Y.S.2d 952 (Crim. Ct. Kings Co. 1980).

Right to prosecution by information; waiver.—Defendant charged with a misdemeanor, criminal sale of marijuana, based upon a misdemeanor complaint waived his absolute right to be prosecuted upon a non-hearsay information (CPL § 170.65, subds. 1, 3) by waiving a reading of his rights and charges at arraignment and by making no request for prosecution by information prior to his trial or the prosecution of his appeal. People v. Connor, 63 N.Y.2d 11, 479 N.Y.S.2d 197, 468 N.E.2d 35 (1984).

Use of AT&T interpreters; corroboration of complaint.—Where complainant had some ability to read and speak English, and an AT&T interpreter was merely used as a precaution for the interpretation of the complaint to the complainant over the telephone, the complaint was sufficiently corroborated and thereby converted into an information. People v. Honshj, 176 Misc. 2d 170, 671 N.Y.S.2d 934 (Crim. Ct. Kings Co. 1998).

§ 170.70. Release of defendant upon failure to replace misdemeanor complaint by information.

Upon application of a defendant against whom a misdemeanor complaint is pending in a local criminal court, and who, either at the time of his arraignment thereon or subsequent thereto, has been committed to the custody of the sheriff pending disposition of the action, and who has been confined in such custody for a period of more than five days, not including Sunday, without any information having been filed in replacement of such misdemeanor complaint, the criminal court must release the defendant on his own recognizance unless:

1. The defendant has waived prosecution by information and consented to be prosecuted upon the misdemeanor complaint, pursuant to subdivision three of section 170.65; or

2. The court is satisfied that there is good cause why such order of release should not be issued. Such good cause must consist of some compelling fact or circumstance which precluded replacement of the misdemeanor complaint by an information or a prosecutor's information within the prescribed period.

ANNOTATIONS

Calculation of five-day time period.—In calculating the five-day period, the first day of custody should be counted, unless it preceded the day of arraignment or was a Sunday. People ex rel. Neufeld v. McMickens, 70 N.Y.2d 763, 520 N.Y.S.2d 744, 514 N.E.2d 1368 (1987).

Statutory purpose.—Purpose of CPL § 170.70 is to protect defendant's right to prosecution by information only and, more specifically, to guarantee that defendant will not be deprived of his or her liberty beyond a reasonable, finite period if the prosecution has violated that right. People ex rel. Alvarez v. Warden, Bronx House of Detention, 178 Misc. 2d 254, 680 N.Y.S.2d 153 (Sup. Ct. Bronx Co. 1998).

ARTICLE 180—PROCEEDINGS UPON FELONY COMPLAINT FROM ARRAIGNMENT THEREON THROUGH DISPOSITION THEREOF

LexisNexis Cross References

Criminal Defense Techniques, Vol. 5, Ch. 103, Arraignment; *New York Criminal Practice (2d ed.),* Vol. 1, Ch. 5, Indictments and Superior Court Informations; Vol. 1, Ch. 7, Securing Attendance of Defendants for Arraignment and Prosecution; Vol. 1, Ch. 9, Local Criminal Court Arraignment and Related Issues; *Criminal Practice Handbook (2d ed.),* Ch. 2, Bail, Arraignment, and Lower Court Practice.

§ 180.10. Proceedings upon felony complaint; arraignment; defendant's rights, court's instructions and bail matters.

1. Upon the defendant's arraignment before a local criminal court upon a felony complaint, the court must immediately inform him, or cause him to be informed in its presence, of the charge or charges against him and that the primary purpose of the proceedings upon such felony complaint is to determine whether the defendant is to be held for the action of a grand jury with respect to the charges contained therein. The court must furnish the defendant with a copy of the felony complaint.

2. The defendant has a right to a prompt hearing upon the issue of whether there is sufficient evidence to warrant the court in holding him for the action of a grand jury, but he may waive such right.

3. The defendant has a right to the aid of counsel at the arraignment and at every subsequent stage of the action, and, if he appears upon such arraignment without counsel, has the following rights:

(a) To an adjournment for the purpose of obtaining counsel; and

(b) To communicate, free of charge, by letter or by telephone, for the purpose of obtaining counsel and informing a relative or friend that he has been charged with an offense; and

(c) To have counsel assigned by the court in any case where he is financially unable to obtain the same.

4. The court must inform the defendant of all rights specified in subdivisions two and three. The court must accord the defendant opportunity to exercise such rights and must itself take such affirmative action as is necessary to effectuate them.

5. If the defendant desires to proceed without the aid of counsel, the court must permit him to do so if it is satisfied that he made such decision with knowledge of the significance thereof, but if it is not so satisfied it may not proceed until the defendant is provided with counsel, either of his own choosing or by assignment. A defendant who proceeds at the arraignment without counsel does not waive his right to counsel, and the court must inform him that he continues to have such right as well as all the rights specified in subdivision three which are necessary to effectuate it, and that he may exercise such rights at any stage of the action.

6. Upon the arraignment, the court, unless it intends immediately thereafter to dismiss the felony complaint and terminate the action, must

issue a securing order which, as provided in subdivision two of section 530.20, either releases the defendant on his own recognizance or fixes bail or commits him to the custody of the sheriff for his future appearance in such action.

ANNOTATIONS

Mootness doctrine.—Court would not review denial of inmate's petition for prompt preliminary hearing on charge of murdering another inmate after issue was mooted by grand jury's issuance of indictment, under exception to mootness doctrine, since issue of whether inmate who was already incarcerated for previous conviction and therefore not eligible for statutory remedy was denied prompt preliminary hearing was not significant or important question. Angell on Behalf of Brown v. Ferris, 227 A.D. 2d 475, 643 N.Y.S.2d 124 (2d Dept. 1996).

Arraignment; counsel.—Once a criminal action has been commenced, the burden devolves upon the authorities to insure that the defendant's right to be represented by counsel is protected and it is their duty to ascertain whether defendant intends to obtain counsel or have one assigned. People v. Blasingame, 65 A.D.2d 455, 412 N.Y.S.2d 153 (2d Dept. 1978).

Arraignment.—Pursuant to the dictates of the CPL, a local criminal court must upon arraignment of an individual charged with a felony, either dismiss the action or issue a securing order which either releases the defendant on his own recognizance or fixes bail or commits him to the custody of the sheriff for his future appearance in such action. In re Delaney, 75 A.D.2d 642, 427 N.Y.S.2d 284 (2d Dept. 1980).

18-B Attorney, assignment nunc pro tunc.—Article 18-B of the County Law does not authorize the court to pay for legal services and disbursements of retained counsel. People v. Berkowitz, 97 Misc. 2d 277, 411 N.Y.S.2d 164 (Sup. Ct. Kings Co. 1978).

Article 78 in nature of mandamus; failure to afford defendant preliminary hearing.—Neither mandamus nor prohibition would lie to direct prosecution to hold preliminary hearing as to crimes charged or to stay prosecution from presenting evidence to grand jury until after preliminary hearing was held. Friess v. Morgenthau, 86 Misc. 2d 852, 383 N.Y.S.2d 784 (Sup. Ct. N.Y. Co. 1975).

No hearing required.—CPL § 180.10 does not require a preliminary hearing where the sole charge before the local criminal court is a misdemeanor. People v. Anderson, 45 A.D.2d 561, 360 N.Y.S.2d 712 (3d Dept. 1974).

Adequate aid of counsel; conflict of interest.—A new trial will be ordered when the defendants demonstrate that a conflict of interest or at least the significant possibility thereof exists and the trial court made no inquiry to ascertain whether the defendants perceived the potential risks inherent to joint representation. People v. Richard M., 75 A.D.2d 389, 430 N.Y.S.2d 695 (3d Dept. 1980).

Denial of request to call parent is not equivalent to a denial of attorney.—Waiver of the right to counsel was voluntary, competent and intelligent where defendant, a 19-year-old, had been arrested twice previously on similar charges and retained counsel; the denial of defendant's request to call his mother was not a denial of defendant's right to representation. People v. Fuschino, 87 A.D.2d 716, 448 N.Y.S.2d 904 (3d Dept. 1982).

Counsel's failure to make pretrial motions not ineffective representation.—Defendant was not deprived of his constitutional right to effective counsel by reason of counsel's failure to make pretrial motions for discovery or suppression; prior to trial the prosecutor's file was opened to defendant and discoverable items were made available and on the facts a motion to suppress would have been denied so counsel's failure to bring such motion was not so grave an error as to constitute ineffective assistance of counsel. People v. Mitchell, 87 A.D.2d 663, 448 N.Y.S.2d 848 (3d Dept. 1982).

Failure to afford hearing.—Failure to accord defendant a prompt hearing, while it might secure his release from confinement (CPL § 180.80), would certainly not affect the power of a grand jury to consider the evidence against him or the authority of the District Attorney to place the matter before that body. People v. Lohman, 49 A.D.2d 75, 371 N.Y.S.2d 170 (3d Dept. 1975).

Indigent.—An indigent defendant is entitled to competent counsel and not counsel of his own choosing. People v. Pettiford, 51 A.D.2d 927, 381 N.Y.S.2d 245 (1st Dept. 1976).

—Defendant's concession, that she was not indigent, precluded a determination that she was financially unable to obtain counsel. People v. Wheat, 80 Misc. 2d 844, 365 N.Y.S.2d 363 (Suffolk Co. Ct. 1975).

Legal Aid Society representing co-perpetrators.—As a matter of law when the Legal Aid Society represents alleged coperpetrators of the same criminal transaction, it does so with full knowledge that a prima facie conflict exists and that it must affirmatively rebut the presumption of conflict and that failing rebuttal thereof, it is incumbent upon it to show that both alleged coperpetrators were made fully aware of the conflict and exercised informed waivers thereof. In re Bruce W., 114 Misc. 2d 91, 450 N.Y.S.2d 734 (Family Ct. Queens Co. 1982).

Motion to dismiss indictment; waiver of motion time.—Where defendant has an agreement with the State to plead guilty to misdemeanor charges and grand jury later indicts defendant on felony charges without giving him notice so he can appear before the grand jury, in the interests of justice defendant's motion to dismiss will be granted (even though not timely made), on condition that within five days defendant execute necessary waiver of immunity and then appear and testify. If the defendant failed to execute such waiver, the motion to dismiss would be denied. People v. Carter, 73 Misc. 2d 1040, 343 N.Y.S.2d 431 (Sup. Ct. Special Narcotics Ct. 1973).

Motion to dismiss indictment; withdrawal of waiver allowed.—Where defendant made an agreement with the prosecution to plead guilty to a misdemeanor charge (reduced from a felony) and the grand jury later indicted defendant on felony charges, he was entitled to withdraw his waiver of a preliminary hearing. People v. Carter, 73 Misc. 2d 1040, 343 N.Y.S.2d 431 (Sup. Ct. Special Narcotics Ct. 1973).

No right to counsel at lineup before initiation of formal prosecutorial proceedings.—There is no automatic entitlement to counsel at pre-accusatory, investigatory lineups, including in the context of juvenile delinquency proceedings. People v. Mitchell, 2 N.Y.3d 272, 778 N.Y.S.2d 427, 810 N.E.2d 879 (2004).

—The Sixth and Fourteenth Amendments only require right to counsel after the initiation of formal prosecutorial proceedings, and Miranda warnings only apply to custodial interrogations; lineups do not initiate Miranda rights because they are not interrogations; the limited benefits provided by counsel at investigatory lineups are far outweighed by the policy considerations against it, and there is no basis in the state constitution for requiring counsel at investigatory lineups; however, if a suspect already has counsel, his attorney may not be actively excluded from the lineup. People v. Hawkins, 55 N.Y.2d 474, 450 N.Y.S.2d 159, 453 N.E.2d 376, cert. denied, 459 U.S. 846 (1982).

Plea; request to withdraw; lack of sympathy of assigned counsel.—Where the only reason for withdrawal of plea given by defendant was his possible imprisonment, the fact that assigned counsel was unsympathetic and advised against withdrawal did not warrant withdrawal and sentencing was proper. People v. Sutton, 39 A.D.2d 820, 332 N.Y.S.2d 983 (4th Dept. 1972).

Possession of dangerous weapon; taxicab is "place of business."—Although the evidence warranted holding the matter for trial, charge of possession of firearm found in defendant's cab could be reduced to a misdemeanor, since the cab constituted a "place of business" and was therefore an exception to the statute concerning possession of weapons. People v. Anderson, 74 Misc. 2d 415, 344 N.Y.S.2d 15 (Crim. Ct. Bronx Co. 1973).

Precinct identification prior to arraignment; effect of nonappearance of counsel.—Uncounseled prearraignment viewings before the filing of an accusatory instrument does not invariably require exclusion of the identification thus obtained; the limited benefits obtained by counsel's relatively passive presence at identification viewing must be balanced against countervailing policy considerations, and thus the importance of staging a prompt viewing is paramount to the desirability of counsel's presence at such identification. People v. Blake, 35 N.Y.2d 331, 361 N.Y.S.2d 881, 320 N.E.2d 625 (1974).

Preliminary hearing.—The defendant's right to a prompt preliminary hearing only applies when the defendant is in custody or has been released on bail and the court is being asked to "hold" the defendant for grand jury action. People v. Hogan, 5 Misc. 3d 151, 780 N.Y.S.2d 883 (City Ct. Monroe Co. 2004).

—The District Attorney may not deliberately avoid conducting a preliminary hearing since the defendant has a right to the hearing and it is the District Attorney's obligation to conduct the hearing and the court has an obligation to see that he does it. People v. Heredia, 81 Misc. 2d 777, 367 N.Y.S.2d 925 (Dist. Ct. Suffolk Co. 1975).

Preliminary hearing; denial of right to counsel.— Defendant's conviction of escape was reversed and a new trial ordered where a preindictment preliminary hearing on that charge was conducted in the absence of retained counsel; by no means did the grand jury proceeding compensate for the hearing without counsel. People v. Hodge, 53 N.Y.2d 313, 441 N.Y.S.2d 231, 423 N.E.2d 1060 (1981).

Preliminary hearing; reasonable cause; station house identification.—Due to limited scope of preliminary hearing, namely, to determine if it is reasonably likely that defendant committed a felony, it was not error to deny defense counsel the right to cross examine the complaining witness concerning identification and the arresting officer as a witness on station house identification, where broad outline of facts justified charging defendant. People ex rel. Pierce v. Thomas, 70 Misc. 2d 629, 334 N.Y.S.2d 666 (Sup. Ct. Bronx Co. 1972).

Preliminary hearing; waiver of counsel and hearing; habeas corpus relief.—Eighteen-year-old defendant charged with felony could not waive counsel or preliminary hearing unless he was fully apprised of primary purpose of proceeding, namely, to determine if he was to be held for grand jury action, and then knowingly, intelligently and understandingly gave it cognizant of the consequences. So long as petition for writ of habeas corpus was made on behalf of the detained person and stated the illegal nature of the detention, it could be entertained. State ex rel. Pulver v. Pavlak, 71 Misc. 2d 95, 335 N.Y.S.2d 721 (Greene Co. Ct. 1972).

Right to defend oneself.—A defendant in a criminal case may invoke the right to defend pro se provided: (1) the request is unequivocal and timely asserted, (2) there has been a knowing and intelligent waiver of the right to counsel, and (3) the defendant had not engaged in conduct which would prevent the fair and orderly exposition of the issues. People v. McIntyre, 36 N.Y.2d 10, 364 N.Y.S.2d 837, 324 N.E.2d 322 (1974).

Right to counsel.—A defendant has a fundamental right to be represented by counsel of his own choosing and, in the absence of a showing that substitution of counsel would have resulted in a further delay, the denial of the motion improperly deprived the defendant of his right to counsel. People v. Walker, 92 A.D.2d 905, 460 N.Y.S.2d 101 (2d Dept. 1983).

—The defendant's right to counsel was violated where, in view of the defendant's responses that he wanted an attorney but did not want the attorney assigned to represent him because of a possible conflict of interest, and that defendant was not competent to represent himself, the trial court granted the defense counsel's motion to be relieved of the case and noted for the record that defendant would proceed pro se. People v. Sawyer, 83 A.D.2d 205, 443 N.Y.S.2d 926 (4th Dept. 1981), aff'd, 57 N.Y.2d 462, 453 N.Y.S.2d 418, 438 N.E.2d 1133 (1982), cert. denied, 459 U.S. 1178 (1983).

Right to counsel; competency of counsel; insanity defense.—Where defendant charged with 1st degree robbery had history of mental instability and confinement, failure of his assigned counsel to investigate background as aid to defense of insanity demonstrated incompetency of counsel and deprived defendant of fundamental right to fair trial. People v. Bennett, 29 N.Y.2d 462, 329 N.Y.S.2d 801, 280 N.E.2d 637 (1972).

—Although it was error for the Justice Court to fail to appoint counsel for defendant upon his initial arraignment, such error was cured upon the return of the indictment; furthermore since there was no reasonable possibility that the error might have contributed to defendant's conviction, upon a guilty plea, it was harmless. People v. Winck, 50 A.D.2d 948, 376 N.Y.S.2d 21 (3d Dept. 1975).

Right to effective aid of counsel; conflict of interest between defendants.—Defendant who was convicted of assault together with co-defendant, and both were acquitted of murder arising out of fight following a crap game, did not have conflict of interest with co-defendants as both sought to discredit prosecution witnesses and establish self defense as a defense.

Record shows that attorney who represented both pressed favorable arguments of defendant even though that he also represented gun wielding co-defendant. People v. Gonzalez, 30 N.Y.2d 28, 330 N.Y.S.2d 54, 280 N.E.2d 882, cert. denied, 409 U.S. 859 (1972).

—The failure of the trial judge to inquire whether the defendants were aware of the risk involved in their joint representation by the same attorney required reversal of the convictions in view of the different roles allegedly played by the defendants in the burglary and the differing nature of their defenses. People v. Biondo, 67 A.D.2d 1004, 413 N.Y.S.2d 739 (2d Dept. 1979).

Right to counsel; right to appear before grand jury.— Defendant was denied his right to counsel due to the inaction of the legal aid society and their failure to assign new counsel prior to the grand jury presentation, thus, the defendant was precluded from exercising his right to appear and testify before the grand jury. People v. Lincoln, 80 A.D.2d 877, 436 N.Y.S.2d 782 (2d Dept. 1981).

Submission to blood test and hair examination; attorney to be present.—Where defendant was required to submit to blood test and examination of facial, pubic, and scalp hair, the motion directing defendant to submit to such procedures provided that defendant's attorney was to be permitted to be present throughout. People v. Longo, 74 Misc. 2d 905, 347 N.Y.S.2d 321 (Nassau Co. Ct. 1973).

Trial; conflict of interest between defendants.—It was error to proceed with trial of defendant for possession of dangerous weapon and burglar tools where counsel asked to be relieved for either of two co-defendants because there was a conflict of interest between them. People v. Austin, 38 A.D.2d 594, 328 N.Y.S.2d 695 (2d Dept. 1971).

Waiver of right to counsel. —Although the court has the authority to allow the defendant to forego the assistance of counsel, before doing so it must first undertake "a sufficiently searching inquiry for it to be reasonably assured that the defendant appreciated the "dangers and disadvantages' of giving up the fundamental right to counsel." People v. Barnhill, 92 A.D.2d 759, 460 N.Y.S.2d 288 (1st Dept. 1983).

Subd. 4

Felony complaint; factual allegations.—It is not necessary in a felony complaint to specifically state the basis of the allegations, since defendant will learn this at the felony hearing. People v. Ferro, 77 Misc. 2d 226, 353 N.Y.S.2d 854 (Nassau Co. District Ct. 1974).

Grand jury; jurisdiction; district attorney; divestiture and removal.—Indictment by Grand Jury, after presentation of evidence by District Attorney with apparent personal interest in the prosecution, would be dismissed and case remanded and removed to another local criminal court with appointment of a special prosecutor. Divestiture statute at option of District Attorney was repugnant in its operation to equal protection of the laws. People v. Krstovich, 72 Misc. 2d 90, 338 N.Y.S.2d 132 (Greene Co. Ct. 1972).

§ 180.20. Proceedings upon felony complaint; removal of action from one local criminal court to another.

Under circumstances prescribed in this section, a criminal action based upon a pending felony complaint may be removed from one local criminal court to another:

1. When a defendant arrested by a police officer for a felony allegedly committed in a town has not been brought before the town court of the town, or as the case may be before the village court of the village, in which the felony charged was allegedly committed, but, instead, to another local criminal court of the county and there stands charged with such offense by felony complaint, such latter court must arraign him upon such felony complaint. Such court must then either:

(a) Dispose of the felony complaint pursuant to this article. If such disposition results in a reduction of the felony charge and the filing of an information or prosecutor's information charging a misdemeanor or a petty offense pursuant to section 180.50 or subdivision two or three of section 180.70, such court must conduct the action to judgment or other final disposition; or

(b) Remit the action upon the felony complaint, together with all pertinent papers and documents, to the town court of the town, or as the case may be to the village court of the village, in which the felony charged was allegedly committed. In such case, the latter court must dispose of the felony complaint pursuant to this article.

1-a. When a defendant arrested by a police officer for a felony allegedly committed in a city has not been brought before the city court of such city but, instead, to the local criminal court of an adjoining town or village of the same county and there stands charged with such offense by felony complaint, such latter court must arraign him upon such felony complaint. Such court must then either:

(a) Dispose of the felony complaint pursuant to this article. If such disposition results in a reduction of the felony charge and the filing of an information or prosecutor's information charging a misdemeanor or a petty offense pursuant to section 180.50 or subdivision two or three of section 180.70 of this article, such court must conduct the action to judgment or other final disposition; or

(b) Remit the action upon the felony complaint, together with all pertinent papers and documents, to the city court of the city in which the felony charged was allegedly committed. In such case, the latter court must dispose of the felony complaint pursuant to this article.

2. When a defendant arrested by a police officer for a felony has been brought before a superior court judge sitting as a local criminal court for arraignment upon a felony complaint charging such felony, such judge must, as a local criminal court, arraign the defendant upon such felony complaint. Such court must then either:

(a) Dispose of the felony complaint pursuant to this article. If however, such disposition results in a reduction of the charge and the filing of an information or prosecutor's information charging a misdemeanor or a petty offense, such judge, after arraigning the defendant upon such accusatory instrument, must remit the action, together with all pertinent papers and documents, to a local criminal court having trial jurisdiction of the offense charged, and the latter court must then conduct the action to judgment or other final disposition; or

(b) Remit the action upon the felony complaint, together with all pertinent papers and

documents, to a local criminal court having geographical jurisdiction over the area in which the felony charged was allegedly committed. In such case, such latter court must dispose of the felony complaint pursuant to this article.

3. Notwithstanding any provision of this section to the contrary, in any county outside a city having a population of one million or more, upon or after arraignment of a defendant on a felony complaint pending in a local criminal court having preliminary jurisdiction thereof, such court may, upon motion of the defendant and with the consent of the district attorney, order that the action be removed from the court in which the matter is pending to another local criminal court in the same county which has been designated a drug court by the chief administrator of the courts, and such drug court may then dispose of such felony complaint pursuant to this article; provided, however, that an order of removal issued under this subdivision shall not take effect until five days after the date the order is issued unless, prior to such effective date, the drug court notifies the court that issued the order that:

(a) it will not accept the action, in which event the order shall not take effect, or

(b) it will accept the action on a date prior to such effective date, in which event the order shall take effect upon such prior date.

Upon providing notification pursuant to paragraph (a) or (b) of this subdivision, the drug court shall promptly give notice to the defendant, his or her counsel and the district attorney.

Amended by L. 1984, Ch. 695; L. 1986, Ch. 5; L. 1998, Ch. 77, § 2, eff. June 2, 1998; L. 1999, Ch. 565, § 2, eff. Nov. 1, 1999; L. 2000, Ch. 67, § 2, eff. Nov. 1, 2000, amending subd. 3.

§ 180.30. Proceedings upon felony complaint; waiver of hearing; action to be taken.

If the defendant waives a hearing upon the felony complaint, the court must either:

1. Order that the defendant be held for the action of a grand jury of the appropriate superior court with respect to the charge or charges contained in the felony complaint. In such case, the court must promptly transmit to such superior court the order, the felony complaint, the supporting depositions and all other pertinent documents. Until such papers are received by the superior court, the action is deemed to be still pending in the local criminal court; or

2. Make inquiry, pursuant to section 180.50, for the purpose of determining whether the felony complaint should be dismissed and an information, a prosecutor's information or a misdemeanor complaint filed with the court in lieu thereof.

ANNOTATIONS

Transfer.—The transfer of a matter to County Court

presumptively establishes that a defendant has been held for action of the Grand Jury in accordance with CPL § 180.30(1). People v. Windley, 228 A.D.2d 875, 645 N.Y.S.2d 103 (3d Dept. 1996).

Dismissal of indictment denied; no showing that defendant was not afforded an opportunity to appear and testify before grand jury.—Defendant's motion was timely made, that defendant waived his felony examination and thereby the felony complaint was disposed of prior to the commencement of the grand jury proceedings and no notice by the People was required. Furthermore, defendant failed to serve notice upon the District Attorney of an intent to testify as required by CPL § 190; the court, therefore, denied defendant's motion in all respects. People v. Napoli, 67 Misc. 2d 1010, 326 N.Y.S.2d 144 (1971).

Waiver; defendant's failure to object to procedure.—Although the defendant did not object to being held for grand jury action without a preliminary hearing, the court ruled that the failure to object did not constitute a waiver of the right to the hearing or an acquiescence to such action. People v. Lupo, 74 Misc. 2d 679, 345 N.Y.S.2d 348 (Crim. Ct. N.Y. Co. 1973).

Waiver to grand jury.—Defendant could not execute an informed waiver to the grand jury, after his request for assigned counsel but prior to the attorney's actual functioning on his behalf. People v. Simmons, 95 Misc. 2d 497, 408 N.Y.S.2d 204 (Crim. Ct. N.Y.C. 1978).

Grand Jury indictment.—It was no defense for defendant that the Town Justice failed to transmit order, felony complaint, and other pertinent documents to the Superior Court before the Grand Jury indicted him for burglary. People v. Talham, 41 A.D.2d 354, 342 N.Y.S.2d 921 (3d Dept. 1973).

§ 180.40. Proceedings upon felony complaint; application in superior court following hearing or waiver of hearing.

Where the local criminal court has held a defendant for the action of a grand jury, the district attorney may, at any time before such matter is submitted to the grand jury, apply, ex parte, to the appropriate superior court for an order directing that the felony complaint and other papers transmitted to such court pursuant to subdivision one of section 180.30 be returned to the local criminal court for reconsideration of the action to be taken. The superior court may issue such an order if it is satisfied that the felony complaint is defective or that such action is required in the interest of justice.

Amended by L. 1974, Ch. 83.

ANNOTATIONS

Constitutionality.—CPL § 180.40 is constitutional under the Federal and State Constitutions. Corr v. Clavin, 96 Misc. 2d 185, 409 N.Y.S.2d 334 (Sup. Ct. Nassau Co. 1978).

Mandatory youthful offender.—Where the Assistant District Attorney, pursuant to CPL § 180.40, prior to the grand jury presentation had the cases returned to the Crim. Ct. and the felony charges reduced to misdemeanors, the defendants, who were then eligible for mandatory youthful offender treatment were not entitled to a jury trial; the provisions of CPL § 340.40(2) and (7) are constitutional. People v. Gray, 97 Misc. 2d 285, 411 N.Y.S.2d 170 (Crim. Ct. N.Y. Co. 1978).

Reduction of felony to misdemeanor.—CPL § 180.40 does not provide that a motion to return a case to the Crim. Ct. has the effect of reducing felony charges to misdemeanors, it provides for the return of the case "to the local court for reconsideration of the action to be taken" and the prosecution remains a felony prosecution until the charges are actually reduced to misdemeanor charges. People v. Fulcher, 97 Misc. 2d 239, 411 N.Y.S.2d 167 (Crim. Ct. N.Y. Co. 1978).

§ 180.50. Proceedings upon felony complaint; reduction of charge.

1. Whether or not the defendant waives a hearing upon the felony complaint, the local criminal court may, upon consent of the district attorney, make inquiry for the purpose of determining whether (a) the available facts and evidence relating to the conduct underlying the felony complaint provide a basis for charging the defendant with an offense other than a felony, and (b) if so, whether the charge should, in the manner prescribed in subdivision three, be reduced from one for a felony to one for a non-felony offense. Upon such inquiry, the court may question any person who it believes may possess information relevant to the matter, including the defendant if he wishes to be questioned.

2. If after such inquiry the court is satisfied that there is reasonable cause to believe that the defendant committed an offense other than a felony, it may order the indicated reduction as follows:

(a) If there is not reasonable cause to believe that the defendant committed a felony in addition to the non-felony offense in question, the court may as a matter of right order a reduction of the charge to one for the non-felony offense;

(b) If there is reasonable cause to believe that the defendant committed a felony in addition to the non-felony offense, the court may order a reduction of the charge to one for the non-felony offense only if (i) it is satisfied that such reduction is in the interest of justice, and (ii) the district attorney consents thereto; provided, however, that the court may not order such reduction where there is reasonable cause to believe that the defendant committed a class A felony, other than those defined in article two hundred twenty of the penal law, or any armed felony as defined in subdivision forty-one of section 1.20.

3. A charge is "reduced" from a felony to a non-felony offense, within the meaning of this section, by replacing the felony complaint with, or converting it to, another local criminal court accusatory instrument, as follows:

(a) If the factual allegations of the felony complaint and/or any supporting depositions are legally sufficient to support the charge that the defendant committed the non-felony offense in question, the court may:

(i) Direct the district attorney to file with the court a prosecutor's information charging the defendant with such non-felony offense; or

(ii) Request the complainant of the felony complaint to file with the court an information charging the defendant with such non-felony offense. If such an information is filed, any supporting deposition supporting or accompanying the felony complaint is deemed also to support or accompanying the replacing information; or

(iii) Convert the felony complaint, or a copy thereof, into an information by notations upon or attached thereto which make the necessary and appropriate changes in the title of the instrument and in the names of the offense or offenses charged. In case of such conversion, any supporting deposition supporting or accompanying the felony complaint is deemed also to support or accompany the information to which it has been converted;

(b) If the non-felony offense in question is a misdemeanor, and if the factual allegations of the felony complaint together with those of any supporting depositions, though providing reasonable cause to believe that the defendant committed such misdemeanor are not legally sufficient to support such misdemeanor charge, the court may cause such felony complaint to be replaced by or converted to a misdemeanor complaint charging the misdemeanor in question, in the manner prescribed in subparagraphs two and three of paragraph (a) of this subdivision.

(c) An information, a prosecutor's information or a misdemeanor complaint filed pursuant to this section may, pursuant to the ordinary rules of joinder, charge two or more offenses, and it may jointly charge with each offense any two or more defendants originally so charged in the felony complaint;

(d) Upon the filing of an information, a prosecutor's information or a misdemeanor complaint pursuant to this section, the court must dismiss the felony complaint from which such accusatory instrument is derived. It must then arraign the defendant upon the new accusatory instrument and inform him of his rights in connection therewith in the manner provided in section 170.10.

4. Upon making any finding other than that specified in subdivision two, the court must conduct a hearing upon the felony complaint, unless the defendant has waived the same. In the case of such waiver the court must order that the defendant be held for the action of a grand jury.

* As originally enacted.

Amended by L. 1978, Ch. 481.

ANNOTATIONS

Speedy trial.—Since the felony charge was "reduced" within the meaning of CPL § 180.50 to a non-felony offense charging defendant with a class A misdemeanor, CPL § 30.30(5)(c) applies for the purpose of modifying the original speedy trial time period. People v. Sommersell, 166 Misc. 2d 774, 638 N.Y.S.2d 272 (2d Dept. 1995).

Double jeopardy; prosecutor's information.—Defendants were not subjected to double jeopardy or unconstitutional denial of equal protection, where grand jury ordered filing of a prosecutor's information covering a misdemeanor that was previously dismissed by the Criminal Court. People v. McClafferty, 73 Misc. 2d 666, 342 N.Y.S.2d 208 (Crim. Ct. Queens Co. 1973).

Failure to file prosecutor's information pursuant to court order upon reduction of felony charges.—The prosecutor's failure to file a prosecutor's information pursuant to a court order under CPL § 180.50(3)(a)(i) upon reduction of felony charges to misdemeanor level within six months of the filing of the original felony complaint as required by CPL

§ 30.30(5)(c) resulted in dismissal of all charges against defendant on speedy trial grounds. People v. Ryff, 100 Misc. 2d 505, 419 N.Y.S.2d 845 (Crim. Ct. Bronx Co. 1979).

Statute inapplicable for reduction to lower grade felony.—CPL § 180.50 applies to the reduction of a charge in a felony complaint to a "non-felony" offense, and has no application to the instant case, in which the crime charged in the felony complaint is reduced to a lower grade felony. People v. McLaurin, 260 A.D.2d 944, 690 N.Y.S.2d 289 (3d Dept. 1999).

Reduction to misdemeanor; need for hearing.—Once there has been a reduction pursuant to CPL § 180.50, the case is to be treated as a misdemeanor and there is no longer a right to a preliminary hearing. People v. Ortiz, 99 Misc. 2d 1069, 418 N.Y.S.2d 517 (Sup. Ct. Bronx Co. 1979).

Reduction to nonfelony.—If prosecutor consents to reducing charges in felony complaint to offenses other than felonies, local criminal court must first inquire into whether facts and evidence provide basis for charging nonfelony offense; if court is satisfied, after such an inquiry, that there is reasonable cause to believe that defendant committed a nonfelony offense, court may order the indicated reduction. People v. Yolles, 92 N.Y.2d 960, 683 N.Y.S.2d 160, 705 N.E.2d 1201 (1998).

—The District Attorney must present a pending felony to the grand jury unless the case is returned to the lower court for reconsideration and upon reconsideration the matter is prosecuted as a misdemeanor. People v. Massaro, 196 Misc. 2d 478, 764 N.Y.S.2d 791 (Monroe Co. 2003).

—A court can effectively reduce a felony to a misdemeanor without questioning any person who may possess relevant information, because the inquiry requirement of CPL § 180.50(1) can be satisfied by examining the sufficiency of the factual allegations and/or supporting depositions. People v. Liburb, 182 Misc. 2d 356, 697 N.Y.S.2d 919 (Crim. Ct. Bronx Co. 1999).

Reduction to nonexistent crime.—Pretrial dismissal of the accusatory instrument was not the appropriate remedy following the reduction from unlawful practice of the profession of massage in violation of Education Law, a class E felony, to the nonexistent crime of attempted unlawful practice of the profession of massage. Pursuant to CPL § 180.50(3)(d), once the felony complaint is converted to a misdemeanor accusatory instrument, the prevailing authority makes it clear that where the reduction was invalid at its inception, the purported reduction, conversion, and dismissal of the felony complaint are of no legal effect and the felony complaint remains pending. People v. Carrabotta, 2 Misc. 3d 685, 774 N.Y.S.2d 279 (NYC Crim. Ct. Queens Co. 2003).

Speedy trial rights.—Defendant was not denied his right to a speedy trial where the court attached a "blueback" to the felony complaint and its supporting deposition and wrote in the names of the new charges on his blueback; the information came into existence at that moment. People v. Franco, 109 Misc. 2d 695, 440 N.Y.S.2d 961 (Crim. Ct. Bronx Co. 1981).

§ 180.60. Proceedings upon felony complaint; the hearing; conduct thereof.

A hearing upon a felony complaint must be conducted as follows:

1. The district attorney must conduct such hearing on behalf of the people.

2. The defendant may as a matter of right be present at such hearing.

3. The court must read to the defendant the felony complaint and any supporting depositions unless the defendant waives such reading.

4. Each witness, whether called by the people or by the defendant, must, unless he would be authorized to give unsworn evidence at a trial, testify under oath. Each witness, including any defendant testifying in his own behalf, may be cross-examined.

5. The people must call and examine witnesses and offer evidence in support of the charge.

6. The defendant may, as a matter of right, testify in his own behalf.

7. Upon request of the defendant, the court may, as a matter of discretion, permit him to call and examine other witnesses or to produce other evidence in his behalf.

8. Upon such a hearing, only non-hearsay evidence is admissible to demonstrate reasonable cause to believe that the defendant committed a felony; except that reports of experts and technicians in professional and scientific fields and sworn statements of the kinds specified in subdivisions two and three of section 190.30 are admissible to the same extent as in a grand jury proceeding, unless the court determines, upon application of the defendant, that such hearsay evidence is, under the particular circumstances of the case, not sufficiently reliable, in which case the court shall require that the witness testify in person and be subject to cross-examination.

9. The court may, upon application of the defendant, exclude the public from the hearing and direct that no disclosure be made of the proceedings.

10. Such hearing should be completed at one session. In the interest of justice, however, it may be adjourned by the court but, in the absence of a showing of good cause therefor, no such adjournment may be for more than one day.

Amended by L. 1975, Ch. 307.

ANNOTATIONS

Prior proceedings.—"Prior proceedings," in which testimony of now unavailable witness may be offered in subsequent criminal proceedings, are previous trials, preliminary hearings, and conditional examinations. People v. Concepcion, 228 A.D. 204, 644 N.Y.S.2d 498 (1st Dept. 1996).

Appeal.—The finding of a preliminary hearing is intermediate in nature and not itself appealable; defendant's remedy would be by appeal from a judgment of conviction under CPL § 450.10. People v. Solomon, 91 Misc. 2d 760, 398 N.Y.S.2d 643 (Crim. Ct. N.Y.C. 1977).

Auto theft; reasonable cause; use of business records; presumption of unauthorized possession.—Absence of vehicle owner at preliminary hearing did not prevent testimony of police officer, as to observations concerning recklessly driven stolen car and capture of defendant corroborated by police stolen car records identifying owner report of theft, value of car and other factors, from establishing reasonable cause that crime was committed and to hold defendant for grand jury. People v. Giesa, 71 Misc. 2d 506, 337 N.Y.S.2d 233 (Crim. Ct. Queens Co. 1972).

Closure of hearing.—Closure of the preliminary hearing was a proper exercise of discretion, where the crime had become a sensationalized news event. Reilly v. McKnight, 80 A.D.2d 333, 439 N.Y.S.2d 727 (3d Dept. 1981).

Defendant's witnesses.—CPL § 180.60(7) only permits a defendant to testify in his own behalf; he cannot as a matter of right call witnesses as it is completely within the court's discretion to permit a defendant to call and examine witnesses; (suggests procedure for subpoena of defendant's witnesses). In re Davis, 88 Misc. 2d 938, 389 N.Y.S.2d 1015 (Crim. Ct. N.Y.C. 1976).

Exclusion of public from hearing is discretionary.—CPL § 180.60(9) allowing exclusion of public from a preliminary hearing is discretionary rather than mandatory. Gannett County,

Inc. v. Weidman, 102 Misc. 2d 888, 424 N.Y.S.2d 972 (Sup. Ct. Livingston Co. 1980).

Felony complaint; factual allegations.—It is not necessary in a felony complaint to specifically state the basis of the allegations, since the defendant will learn this at the felony hearing. People v. Ferro, 77 Misc. 2d 226, 353 N.Y.S.2d 854 (Nassau Co. District Ct. 1974).

Felony complaint; misdemeanor charge included.—Where the misdemeanor charged in the felony complaint was part of the same transaction in which the felony charge arose, the court was empowered, at the preliminary hearing, to decide whether there was reasonable cause to hold the defendant on either or both the felony or misdemeanor charges. People on Complaint of Astarita v. Barclift, 97 Misc. 2d 994, 412 N.Y.S.2d 991 (Crim. Ct. Queens Co. 1979).

Hearing; commencement; continuation.—The burden on the prosecution is to commence a hearing before the magistrate within the time limitation. A continuation may thereafter be obtained from the magistrate for good cause shown, and it is conceivable that a reasonable adjournment might be granted. Here time was needed to obtain further proof of the nature of the chemical substances involved. People ex rel. Fox v. Sherwood, 73 Misc. 2d 101, 341 N.Y.S.2d 161 (Sup. Ct. Orange Co. 1973).

Lost minutes.—Whether or not the loss of preliminary hearing minutes requires another preliminary hearing should be left to the sound discretion of the trial court which should consider such things as the availability of other discovery materials and the need to expedite the disposition of cases. People v. Aviles, 89 Misc. 2d 1, 391 N.Y.S.2d 303 (Sup. Ct. N.Y. Co. 1977).

Minutes; request for.—Since the failure of the defendant to make a timely request for the minutes had not been adequately explained on the record, standing alone, it was sufficient to warrant denial of the motion to dismiss the indictment upon the ground that the minutes of his preliminary hearing were unavailable, however, in the interests of simple justice, the court directed that attorneys for the respective parties should attempt a reconstruction of the criminal court proceedings and if this could not be accomplished the court further directed that Criminal Term should issue an appropriate order directing the prosecutor to turn over to the defense counsel, prior to trial, all Grand Jury testimony and all non-privileged police and prosecutor's records relating to statements of the witnesses in the case. People v. Pinion, 56 A.D.2d 664, 392 N.Y.S.2d 53 (2d Dept. 1977).

Minutes not furnished to defendant; dismissal of indictment not required.—Motion to dismiss an indictment for failure to furnish defendant with minutes of preliminary hearing was not granted since the court was able to reconstruct the proceedings at the preliminary hearing and, from such, determine that the People has established reasonable cause to believe that defendant had committed the felony charged. People v. Degout, 94 Misc. 2d 883, 406 N.Y.S.2d 218 (Sup. Ct. Bronx Co. 1974).

Preliminary hearing; reasonable cause; station house identification.—Due to limited scope of preliminary hearing, namely, to determine if it is reasonably likely that defendant committed a felony, it was not error to deny defense counsel the right to cross examine the complaining witness concerning identification and the arresting officer as a witness on station house identification, where broad outline of facts justified charging defendant, People ex rel. Pierce v. Thomas, 70 Misc. 2d 629, 334 N.Y.S.2d 666 (Sup. Ct. Bronx Co. 1972).

Preliminary hearing; no hearsay.—Although hearsay is generally admissible to establish probable cause it is inadmissible in a preliminary felony hearing. In re Renaldo Q., 83 Misc. 2d 945, 373 N.Y.S.2d 993 (Family Ct. Bronx Co. 1975).

Preliminary hearing; hearsay evidence; sworn statements.—At a preliminary hearing on a felony complaint the court may require the testimony and cross-examination of the complainant, notwithstanding the fact that such complainant had submitted sworn statements in accordance with the provisions of CPL § 190.30(3), where the complainant is actually present to give testimony in open court. People v. Staton, 94 Misc. 2d 1002, 406 N.Y.S.2d 242 (Crim. Ct. Bronx Co. 1978).

Preliminary hearing; use of affidavit.—CPL § 180.60(8), which allows use, at the preliminary hearing, of affidavits of certain witnesses under certain circumstances, does not deny defendant the right to confrontation of witnesses, but merely puts the right off until trial and is constitutional. People v. Campbell, 92 Misc. 2d 732, 401 N.Y.S.2d 152 (Crim. Ct. Kings Co. 1978).

Preliminary hearing; defendant's right to waive appearance.—Although the court committed in refusing defendant's request to waive his appearance at the preliminary hearing it was harmless. People v. Allman, 133 A.D.2d 638, 519 N.Y.S.2d 747 (2d Dept. 1987).

—A criminal defendant has the right to waive his personal appearance at a felony hearing, pursuant to CPL § 180.60(2) and Federal and State constitutional guarantees, as long as the hearing judge determines that such waiver was being exercised knowingly, voluntarily and intelligently, and any in-court identification evidence obtained in violation of defendant's right to waive his appearance at such hearing should be suppressed. People v. Chambliss, 106 Misc. 2d 342, 431 N.Y.S.2d 771 (Westchester Co. Ct. 1980).

Procedure.—The court's sole duty at the felony hearing is to determine whether the People have met the burden required of them by statute. The judge at the hearing need not decide the questions of law regarding the corroboration of a defendant's statements or whether a witness is considered an accomplice whose testimony must be corroborated. Nor must corroboration be offered at a felony hearing in order for the People to sustain their burden. People v. Martinez, 80 Misc. 2d 735, 364 N.Y.S.2d 338 (Crim. Ct. N.Y. Co. 1975).

Family Court.—Complete prohibition of cross-examination at hearing in Family Court was an improvident exercise of discretion and deprived juvenile of benefit of hearing. People ex rel. Lauring v. Mucci, 44 A.D.2d 479, 355 N.Y.S.2d 786 (1st Dept. 1974).

Proof; absence of rebuttal.—The charge that the defendant possessed burglar's tools with intent to use them to commit theft could be sustained despite the lack of direct proof as to the ownership of the vehicle from which the plates were being detached. In addition to the police report, there were circumstances strongly supporting the inferences which spelled out a prima facie case of possession of the tools for an unlawful purpose. The defendant did not elect to testify at the hearing, and did not offer to produce witnesses to provide an innocent explanation of his possession of the plates. People v. Meyers, 72 Misc. 2d 1003, 340 N.Y.S.2d 505 (Crim. Ct. N.Y. Co. 1973).

§ 180.70. Proceedings upon felony complaint; disposition of felony complaint after hearing.

At the conclusion of a hearing, the court must dispose of the felony complaint as follows:

1. If there is reasonable cause to believe that the defendant committed a felony, the court must, except as provided in subdivision three, order that the defendant be held for the action of a grand jury of the appropriate superior court, and it must promptly transmit to such superior court the order, the felony complaint, the supporting depositions and all other pertinent documents. Until such papers are received by the superior court, the action is deemed to be still pending in the local criminal court.

2. If there is not reasonable cause to believe that the defendant committed a felony but there is reasonable cause to believe that he committed an offense other than a felony, the court may, by means of procedures prescribed in subdivision three of section 180.50, reduce the charge to one for such non-felony offense.

3. If there is reasonable cause to believe that the defendant committed a felony in addition to a non-felony offense, the court may, instead of ordering the defendant held for the action of a grand jury as provided in subdivision one, reduce the charge to one for such non-felony offense as provided in subdivision two, if (a) it is satisfied that such reduction is in the interest of justice, and (b) the district attorney consents thereto; provided, however, that the court may not order such reduction where there is reasonable cause to believe the defendant committed a class A felony, other than those defined in article two hundred twenty of the penal law, or any armed felony as defined in subdivision forty-one of section 1.20.

4. If there is not reasonable cause to believe that the defendant committed any offense, the court must dismiss the felony complaint and discharge the defendant from custody if he is in custody, or, if he is at liberty on bail, it must exonerate the bail.

Amended by L. 1978, Ch. 481.

ANNOTATIONS

Subd. 1.—The felony complaint charging defendant with offenses that were the subject of the grand jury proceeding had been disposed of by a preliminary hearing pursuant to CPL § 180.70(1), and thus the People had no obligation to inform defendant of the grand jury proceeding. People v. Walker, 15 A.D.3d 902, 789 N.Y.S.2d 780 (4th Dept. 2005).

Grand Jury.—A defendant can only be ordered held for the action of a Grand Jury following waiver of a hearing on a felony complaint, or upon a finding made at the conclusion of a hearing on a felony complaint that there is reasonable cause to believe that the defendant committed a felony. People v. Chamberain, 221 A.D. 869, 634 N.Y.S.2d 249 (3d Dept. 1995).

Felony hearing; reasonable cause; oral statement of defendant.—At a preliminary hearing before a local criminal court, the same degree of proof or quality of evidence as is necessary for an indictment is not required; only that there be reasonable cause to believe that the defendant committed any felony that the evidence indicates. Oral statements allegedly made by defendant to police officer were admissible at preliminary felony hearing to aid Town Justice to pass upon sufficiency of evidence to hold defendant charged with felony murder and sodomy. Mattioli v. Brown, 71 Misc. 2d 99, 335 N.Y.S.2d 613 (Sup. Ct. Fulton Co. 1972).

Preliminary hearing; sexual abuse; corroboration.—Court need not dismiss information charging sexual abuse and assault arising out of alleged sexual attack by defendant upon female victim where corroboration is lacking since only requirement at preliminary hearing is to have reasonable cause or ground to believe defendant committed crime. People v. Scarpsoi, 69 Misc. 2d 264, 329 N.Y.S.2d 850 (Cr. Ct. N.Y. Co. 1972).

Standard of proof.—People are not required to present a prima facie case, and thus failure to establish one or more elements of an offense to the degree required at trial or in the grand jury does not require dismissal of the complaint. People v. Soto, 76 Misc. 2d 491, 352 N.Y.S.2d 144 (Crim. Ct. Bronx Co. 1974).

Double jeopardy; prosecutor's information.—Defendants were not subjected to double jeopardy or unconstitutional denial of equal protection, where grand jury ordered filing of a prosecutor's information covering a misdemeanor that was previously dismissed by the Criminal Court. People v. McCafferty, 73 Misc. 2d 666, 342 N.Y.S.2d 208 (Crim. Ct. Queens Co. 1973).

Auto theft; reasonable cause; use of business records; presumption of unauthorized possession.—Absence of vehicle owner at preliminary hearing did not prevent testimony of police officer as to observations concerning recklessly driven stolen car and capture of defendant corroborated by police stolen car records identifying owner, report of theft, value of car and other factors, from establishing reasonable cause that crime was committed and to hold defendant for grand jury. People v.

Giesa, 71 Misc. 2d 506, 337 N.Y.S.2d 233 (Crim. Ct. Queens Co. 1972).

Hearing; commencement; continuation.—The burden on the prosecution is to commence a hearing before the magistrate within the time limitation. A continuation may thereafter be obtained from the magistrate for good cause shown, and it is conceivable that a reasonable adjournment might be granted. Here time was needed to obtain further proof of the nature of the chemical substances involved. People ex rel. Fox v. Sherwood, 73 Misc. 2d 101, 341 N.Y.S.2d 161 (Sup. Ct. Orange Co. 1973).

Preliminary hearing: reasonable cause; station house identification.—Due to limited scope of preliminary hearing, namely to determine if it is reasonably likely that defendant committed a felony, it was not error to deny defense counsel the right to cross examine the complaining witness concerning identification and the arresting officer as a witness on station house identification, where broad outline of facts justified charging defendant. People ex rel. Pierce v. Thomas, 70 Misc. 2d 629, 34 N.Y.S.2d 666 (Sup. Ct. Bronx Co. 1972).

Reasonable cause; 72-hour period for production of proof.—The People should be able to produce proof within 72 hours of those elements which were regarded as reasonable justification for the arrest of the defendant. People ex rel. Fox v. Sherwood, 73 Misc. 2d 101, 341 N.Y.S.2d 161 (Sup. Ct. Orange Co. 1973).

Standard of proof; arrest.—The court must dispose of a felony complaint by ordering that the defendant be held for the action of a grand jury if there is reasonable cause to believe that the defendant committed a felony. People ex rel. Fox v. Sherwood, 73 Misc. 2d 101, 341 N.Y.S.2d 161 (Sup. Ct. Orange Co. 1973).

Standard of proof; felony complaint.—The standard of proof for a felony complaint is a less stringent requirement than the standard for an indictment by a grand jury, and less stringent than that required for conviction. People ex rel. Fox v. Sherwood, 73 Misc. 2d 101, 341 N.Y.S.2d 161 (Sup. Ct. Orange Co. 1973).

Subd. 4; dismissal.—District Attorney's office did not appear at preliminary hearing requested by defendant because of District Attorney's general practice not to appear at preliminary hearings of defendants who are not incarcerated; citing CPL § 180.70(4), which requires a local court to dismiss a felony complaint if there is not reasonable cause to believe that the defendant committed any offense, the court dismissed the felony complaint against the defendant because the prosecution had declined to participate and, thus, the court had received no evidence. People v. Cleghorn, 190 Misc. 2d 421, 739 N.Y.S.2d 879 (Justice Ct. Tompkins Co. 2001).

Warrant of arrest; felony complaint; standard of proof.—The language of CPL section 180.70(1) is similar to that of section 120.20(2), which provides that the court may refuse to issue a warrant of arrest on an accusatory instrument until it has further satisfied itself, by inquiry or by examination of witnesses, that there is reasonable cause to believe that the defendant committed the offense charged. People ex rel. Fox v. Sherwood, 73 Misc. 2d 101, 341 N.Y.S.2d 161 (Sup. Ct. Orange Co. 1973).

§ 180.75. Proceedings upon felony complaint; juvenile offender.

1. When a juvenile offender is arraigned before a local criminal court, the provisions of this section shall apply in lieu of the provisions of sections 180.30, 180.50 and 180.70 of this article.

2. If the defendant waives a hearing upon the felony complaint, the court must order that the defendant be held for the action of the grand jury of the appropriate superior court with respect to the charge or charges contained in the felony complaint. In such case the court must promptly transmit to such superior court the order, the felony complaint, the supporting depositions and all other pertinent documents. Until such papers are received by the superior court, the action is deemed to be still pending in the local criminal court.

3. If there be a hearing, then at the conclusion of the hearing, the court must dispose of the felony complaint as follows:

(a) If there is reasonable cause to believe that the defendant committed a crime for which a person under the age of sixteen is criminally responsible, the court must order that the defendant be held for the action of a grand jury of the appropriate superior court, and it must promptly transmit to such superior court the order, the felony complaint, the supporting depositions and all other pertinent documents. Until such papers are received by the superior court, the action is deemed to be still pending in the local criminal court; or

(b) If there is not reasonable cause to believe that the defendant committed a crime for which a person under the age of sixteen is criminally responsible but there is reasonable cause to believe that the defendant is a "juvenile delinquent" as defined in subdivision one of section 301.2 of the family court act, the court must specify the act or acts it found reasonable cause to believe the defendant did and direct that the action be removed to the family court in accordance with the provisions of article seven hundred twenty-five of this chapter; or

(c) If there is not reasonable cause to believe that the defendant committed any criminal act, the court must dismiss the felony complaint and discharge the defendant from custody if he is in custody, or if he is at liberty on bail, it must exonerate the bail.

4. Notwithstanding the provisions of subdivisions two and three of this section, a local criminal court shall, at the request of the district attorney, order removal of an action against a juvenile offender to the family court pursuant to the provisions of article seven hundred twenty-five of this chapter if, upon consideration of the criteria specified in subdivision two of section 210.43 of this chapter, it is determined that to do so would be in the interests of justice. Where, however, the felony complaint charges the juvenile offender with murder in the second degree as defined in section 125.25 of the penal law, rape in the first degree as defined in subdivision one of section 130.35 of the penal law, criminal sexual act in the first degree as defined in subdivision one of section 130.50 of the penal law, or an armed felony as defined in paragraph (a) of subdivision forty-one of section 1.20 of this chapter, a determination that such action be removed to the family court shall, in addition, be based upon a finding of one or more of the following factors: (i) mitigating circumstances that bear directly upon the manner in which the crime was committed; or (ii) where the defendant was not the sole participant in the crime, the

defendant's participation was relatively minor although not so minor as to constitute a defense to the prosecution; or (iii) possible deficiencies in proof of the crime.

5. Notwithstanding the provisions of subdivision two, three, or four, if a currently undetermined felony complaint against a juvenile offender is pending in a local criminal court, and the defendant has not waived a hearing pursuant to subdivision two and a hearing pursuant to subdivision three has not commenced, the defendant may move in the superior court which would exercise the trial jurisdiction of the offense or offenses charged were an indictment therefor to result, to remove the action to family court. The procedural rules of subdivision one and two of section 210.45 of this chapter are applicable to a motion pursuant to this subdivision. Upon such motion, the superior court shall be authorized to sit as a local criminal court to exercise the preliminary jurisdiction specified in subdivisions two and three of this section, and shall proceed and determine the motion as provided in section 210.43 of this chapter; provided, however that the exception provisions of paragraph (b) of subdivision one of such section 210.43 shall not apply when there is not reasonable cause to believe that the juvenile offender committed one or more of the crimes enumerated therein, and in such event the provisions of paragraph (a) thereof shall apply.

6. (a) If the court orders removal of the action to family court, it shall state on the record the factor or factors upon which its determination is based, and the court shall give its reasons for removal in detail and not in conclusory terms.

(b) The district attorney shall state upon the record the reasons for his consent to removal of the action to the family court where such consent is required. The reasons shall be stated in detail and not in conclusory terms.

(c) For the purpose of making a determination pursuant to subdivision four or five, the court may make such inquiry as it deems necessary. Any evidence which is not legally privileged may be introduced. If the defendant testifies, his testimony may not be introduced against him in any future proceeding; except to impeach his testimony at such future proceeding as inconsistent prior testimony.

(d) Where a motion for removal by the defendant pursuant to subdivision five has been denied, no further motion pursuant to this section or section 210.43 of this chapter may be made by the juvenile offender with respect to the same offense or offenses.

(e) Except as provided by paragraph (f), this section shall not be construed to limit the powers of the grand jury.

(f) Where a motion by the defendant pursuant to subdivision five has been granted, there shall be no further proceedings against the juvenile offender in any local or superior criminal court for the offense or offenses which were the subject of the removal order.

Added by L. 1978, Ch. 481; **Amended** by L. 1979, Ch. 411; L. 2003, Ch. 264, § 38, eff. Nov. 1, 2003, amending subd. 4.

ANNOTATIONS

Constitutionality.—CPL § 180.75(4)(b) is constitutional. People v. Lugo, 98 Misc. 2d 115, 414 N.Y.S.2d 243 (Crim. Ct. Kings Co. 1979).

—CPL § 180.75(4)(a) is constitutional. People v. Williams, 97 Misc. 2d 24, 410 N.Y.S.2d 978 (Dutchess Co. Ct. 1978).

Closure.—The legislature has not required that CPL § 180.75 proceedings be conducted in closed court and it appears to be a matter of discretion which should be exercised against closure. People v. Williams, 97 Misc. 2d 24, 410 N.Y.S.2d 978 (Dutchess Co. Ct. 1978).

Felony hearing.—Motion to transfer prosecution to family court was denied where there had been a finding in a felony hearing in criminal court of probable cause sufficient to hold defendant for Grand Jury; even in the absence of Grand Jury indictment, such hearing converted the complaint to an information and hence it cannot qualify as a "complaint" as used in FCA § 1014(b). People v. Edwards, 101 Misc. 2d 747, 422 N.Y.S.2d 324 (Crim. Ct. N.Y. Co. 1979).

Hearsay.—The prohibition of hearsay evidence found in CPL § 180.60(8) was inapplicable to a removal proceeding conducted pursuant to CPL § 180.75(5) and the sworn felony complaints were admissible into evidence in the inquiry into the factual events of the alleged crime. People v. Martinez, 97 Misc. 2d 598, 412 N.Y.S.2d 276 (Crim. Ct. N.Y.C. 1978).

Juvenile; murder, second degree; removal to Family Court.—The court may remove an action charging a juvenile with murder, second degree, to the Family Court provided the District Attorney consents on the record and provided that the court finds one or more of the factors enumerated in CPL § 180.75(4)(b)(i), (ii) and (iii). People v. Kimball, 100 Misc. 2d 323, 418 N.Y.S.2d 890 (Onondaga Co. Ct. 1979).

Records; Commissioner of Social Services.—Defense attorney, representing juveniles accused of robbery, second degree, could apply to Supreme Court for a subpoena duces tecum, pursuant to CPL § 610.20(3), directing the New York City Commissioner of Social Services to disclose to the Criminal Court, records relating to defendants' recent placement as Persons In Need of Supervision (PINS -FCA Art. 7) and the Crim. Ct. could inspect the documents in camera and redact all entries which were irrelevant or immaterial to the issues sub judice and then disclose the redacted records to both defense and prosecution so that the interests of both the juvenile and the State could be adequately represented. In re Roman, 97 Misc. 2d 782, 412 N.Y.S.2d 325 (Sup. Ct. N.Y. Co. 1979).

Removal to Family Court.—CPL § 180.75(5) does not permit the District Attorney, by motion, or the local criminal court, to divest a superior court's mandatory duty to determine a removal motion on its merits. People v. Gregory C., 158 Misc. 2d 872, 602 N.Y.S.2d 492 (Sup. Ct. Erie Co. 1993).

—A 15-year-old defendant, charged with burglary, second degree, an act for which a juvenile may be prosecuted as a degree as defined in subdivision one of § 130.50 of the penal juvenile offender (FCA § 725.00), cannot be transferred to Family Court; CPL § 180.75 only authorizes removal when the defendant is accused as a juvenile offender. People v. Mote, 106 Misc. 2d 1090, 432 N.Y.S.2d 1000 (Fam. Ct. Oneida Co. 1980).

—Juvenile defendant's robbery, first degree, charge was removed to Family Court where the evidence revealed that there was an absence of injuries to the complainant, the crime was not committed in a particularly heinous manner and the evidence strongly indicated that the incident was an isolated occurrence rather than representative of a pattern of criminal behavior. People v. Martinez, 97 Misc. 2d 598, 412 N.Y.S.2d 276 (Crim. Ct. N.Y. Co. 1978).

—Removal to the Family Court would not be in the interest of justice where the 15 year old defendant, accused of robbery, first degree, had a violent and disruptive personality, was mature, tough, and street-wise, and was protective toward those of her peers that she considered friends and intimidating and violent toward those who are not. People v. Martinez, 97 Misc. 2d 598, 412 N.Y.S.2d 276 (Crim. Ct. N.Y. Co. 1978).

Removal; requirement of prosecutor's consent.—The legislature, by requiring a prosecutor's preliminary consent to removal of a juvenile offender to Family Court, (CPL § 210.43 subd. b), has not invested him with a judicial function or with a vehicle for trespassing on judicial turf and hence the statute is not violative of the doctrine of separation of powers. People v. Putland, 102 Misc. 2d 517, 423 N.Y.S.2d 999 (Co. Ct. Dutchess Co. 1979).

Removal to Family Court; subsequent indictment.—Defendant's motion to dismiss an indictment filed against him in Supreme Court after his case had been removed to the Family Court pursuant to CPL § 180.74(4)(a) was denied because the powers of the grand jury cannot be curtailed or diminished except by constitutional amendment or statutory enactment and there is no express provision in either the Criminal Procedure Law or Family Court Act restraining the powers of the grand jury in this situation. People v. Rodriguez, 97 Misc. 2d 379, 411 N.Y.S.2d 526 (Sup. Ct. Kings Co. 1978).

Transfer to Grand Jury; subsequent Grand Jury action.—Neither the Prosecutor nor the Grand Jury may divest the local Criminal court of its legislatively-granted authority to determine whether the Family Court should have jurisdiction unless prior to such determination the Grand Jury has acted. Rodriguez v. Myerson, 69 A.D.2d 162, 418 N.Y.S.2d 936 (2d Dept. 1979).

§ 180.80. Proceedings upon felony complaint; release of defendant from custody upon failure of timely disposition.

Upon application of a defendant against whom a felony complaint has been filed with a local criminal court, and who, since the time of his arrest or subsequent thereto, has been held in custody pending disposition of such felony complaint, and who has been confined in such custody for a period of more than one hundred twenty hours or, in the event that a Saturday, Sunday or legal holiday occurs during such custody, one hundred forty-four hours, without either a disposition of the felony complaint or commencement of a hearing thereon, the local criminal court must release him on his own recognizance unless:

1. The failure to dispose of the felony complaint or to commence a hearing thereon during such period of confinement was due to the defendant's request, action or condition, or occurred with his consent; or

2. Prior to the application:

(a) The district attorney files with the court a written certification that an indictment has been voted; or

(b) An indictment or a direction to file a prosecutor's information charging an offense based upon conduct alleged in the felony complaint was filed by a grand jury; or

3. The court is satisfied that the people have shown good cause why such order of release should not be issued. Such good cause must consist of some compelling fact or circumstance which precluded disposition of the felony complaint within the prescribed period or rendered such action against the interest of justice.

Amended by L. 1982, Chs. 556, 557.

ANNOTATIONS

Grand Jury.—Grand jury certification was a nullity and was void of any legal consequence, and, therefore, defendant had to be released pursuant to statute requiring release of defendant against whom no grand jury action has been taken within specified time, where defendant had not been provided his absolute statutory right to testify before grand jury; acceptance of prosecution's argument that court was bound by certification would make it participant in flouting the law. People v. Griffin, 163 A.D.2d 43, 619 N.Y.S.2d 931 (Crim. Ct. Kings Co. 1995).

Calculation of 72-hour period.—Intervening Saturdays, Sundays and holidays are included in the calculation of the seventy two hour period. People v. Malcolm, 85 A.D.2d 313, 448 N.Y.S.2d 176 (1st Dept. 1982).

Defendant must be released on his own recognizance.—A delay in arraignment from arrest one Saturday night until Monday morning, where defendant could have been arraigned on a Sunday, renders the police guilty of unnecessary delay as a matter of law and the defendant must be released on his own recognizance even where he had been convicted of two prior felonies and the criminal court ordinarily would not have jurisdiction to fix bail under CPL § 530.20(2). People v. Davis, 118 Misc. 2d 122, 460 N.Y.S.2d 260 (Justice Ct. Westchester Co. 1983).

Failure to hold preliminary hearing; felony complaint not dismissed.—Reversal was required when the Co. Court dismissed the indictment on the ground that the Town Justice had failed to fully inform defendant of his rights, pursuant to CPL § 180.10, which included the right to a prompt hearing to determine if there was sufficient evidence to warrant the court in holding him for the action of the Grand Jury; CPL § 180.80 is notice to the District Attorney that he must act expeditiously or face the consequence of the local criminal court releasing the defendant on his own recognizance. People v. Aaron, 55 A.D.2d 653, 390 N.Y.S.2d 157 (2d Dept. 1976).

—While a failure to accord a defendant a prompt hearing might secure his release from confinement under CPL § 180.80, it does not affect the power of a grand jury to consider the evidence against him. People v. Phillips, 88 A.D.2d 672, 450 N.Y.S.2d 925 (3d Dept. 1982).

—If the People refuse or fail to proceed with a preliminary hearing contrary to the defendant's wishes, the sole remedy for that failure is to release the defendant on his own recognizance pursuant to CPL § 180.80. People v. Davis, 170 Misc. 2d 987, 653 N.Y.S.2d 789 (City Ct. Poughkeepsie 1996).

—A felony complaint will not be dismissed where the district attorney has indicated that he would not conduct a preliminary hearing but instead present the case to the grand jury without an order of the local criminal court. Under such circumstances the defendant may be released on his own recognizance but the local criminal court retains jurisdiction until the grand jury either finds an indictment or dismisses the charges. People v. Cummings, 70 Misc. 2d 1016, 333 N.Y.S.2d 625 (Batavia City Ct. 1972).

Hearing; commencement; continuation.—The burden on the prosecution is to commence a hearing before the magistrate within the time limitation. A continuation may thereafter be obtained from the magistrate for good cause shown, and it is conceivable that a reasonable adjournment might be granted. Here time was needed to obtain further proof of the nature of the chemical substances involved. People ex rel. Fox v. Sherwood, 73 Misc. 2d 101, 341 N.Y.S.2d 161 (Sup. Ct. Orange Co. 1973).

Preliminary hearing; reasonable cause; station house identification.—Due to limited scope of preliminary hearing, namely to determine if it is reasonably likely that defendant committed a felony, it was not error to deny defense counsel the right to cross examine the complaining witness concerning identification and the arresting officer as a witness on station house identification, where broad outline of facts justified charging defendant. People ex rel. Pierce v. Thomas, 70 Misc. 2d 629, 334 N.Y.S.2d 666 (Sup. Ct. Bronx Co. 1972).

Reasonable cause; 72-hour period for production of proof.—The court held that the statute does not equate "72 hours" with "three court days." People v. Lethenia, 87 Misc. 2d 713, 386 N.Y.S.2d 799 (Crim. Ct. N.Y.C. 1976).

—The People should be able to produce proof within 72 hours

of those elements which were regarded as reasonable justification for the arrest of the defendant. People *ex rel.* Fox v. Sherwood, 73 Misc. 2d 101, 341 N.Y.S.2d 161 (Sup. Ct. Orange Co. 1973).

Removal of defendant from arrest processing.—Arrestee's removal from Central Booking, however justified, is a break in the chain of arrest processing and most often, necessarily precludes an arraignment without unnecessary delay. The removal of a defendant from arrest processing for investigation on a new charge must be deemed the functional equivalent of an arrest for the purpose of vindicating a defendant's 180.80 rights on the new matter. People v. Mejia, 2 Misc. 3d 494, 773 N.Y.S.2d 514 (Crim. Ct. Kings Co. 2003).

Right to counsel; right to conduct own defense.—A defendant was not deprived of counsel where, despite the efforts of the court, he chose to conduct his own defense, as was his constitutional right. In the absence of evidence of lack of mental capacity of the defendant, the court was not warranted in interfering with defendant's conduct of his own defense. People v. Yates, 45 A.D.2d 778, 356 N.Y.S.2d 713 (3d Dept. 1974).

Sister-state arrest.—CPL § 180.80 is not dependent on sister-state arrest. People v. Smiley, 3 Misc. 2d 430, 776 N.Y.S.2d 710 (N.Y.C. Crim. Ct. Kings Co. 2004) (case analyzes CPL § 180.80).

§ 180.85. Termination of prosecution.

1. After arraignment of a defendant upon a felony complaint, other than a felony complaint charging an offense defined in section 125.10, 125.15, 125.20, 125.25 or 125.27 of the penal law, either party or the local criminal court or superior court before which the action is pending, on its own motion, may move in accordance with the provisions of this section for an order terminating prosecution of the charges contained in such felony complaint on consent of the parties.

2. A motion to terminate a prosecution pursuant to this section may only be made where the count or counts of the felony complaint have not been presented to a grand jury or otherwise disposed of in accordance with this chapter. Such motion shall be filed in writing with the local criminal court or superior court in which the felony complaint is pending not earlier than twelve months following the date of arraignment on such felony complaint. Upon the filing of such motion, the court shall fix a return date and provide the parties with at least thirty days' written notice of the motion and return date.

3. Where, upon motion to terminate a prosecution pursuant to this section, both parties consent to such termination, the court, on the return date of such motion, shall enter an order terminating such prosecution. For purposes of this subdivision, a party that is given written notice of a motion to terminate a prosecution shall be deemed to consent to such termination unless, prior to the return date of such motion, such party files a notice of opposition thereto with the court. Except as otherwise provided in subdivision four, where such a notice of opposition is filed, the court, on the return date of the motion, shall enter an order denying the motion to terminate the prosecution.

4. Notwithstanding any other provision of this section, where the people file a notice of opposition pursuant to subdivision three, the court, on the return date of the motion, may defer disposition of such motion for a period of forty-five days. In such event, if the count or counts of such felony complaint are presented to a grand jury or otherwise disposed of within such period, the court, upon the expiration thereof, shall enter an order denying the motion to terminate the prosecution. If such count or counts are not presented to a grand jury or otherwise disposed of within such period, the court, upon the expiration thereof, shall enter an order terminating the prosecution unless, within the forty-five day period, the people, on at least five days' written notice to the defendant, show good cause for their failure to present or otherwise dispose of such count or counts. If such good cause is shown, the court, upon expiration of the forty-five day period, shall enter an order denying the motion to terminate the prosecution.

5. Notwithstanding any other provision of law, the defendant's appearance in court on the return date of the motion or on any other date shall not be required as a prerequisite to entry of an order under this section.

6. The period from the filing of a motion pursuant to this section until entry of an order disposing of such motion shall not, by reason of such motion, be considered a period of delay for purposes of subdivision four of section 30.30, nor shall such period, by reason of such motion, be excluded in computing the time within which the people must be ready for trial pursuant to such section 30.30.

7. Where a prosecution is terminated pursuant to this section, nothing contained herein shall preclude the people from subsequently filing an indictment charging the same count or counts provided such filing is in accordance with the provisions of this section, article thirty and any other relevant provisions of this chapter. Where the people indicate their intention to seek an indictment following the entry of an order terminating a prosecution pursuant to this section, the court shall, notwithstanding any provision of section 160.50 to the contrary, stay sealing under that section for a reasonable period not to exceed thirty days to permit the people an opportunity to pursue such indictment.

8. Where an order denying a party's motion to terminate a prosecution is entered pursuant to this section, such party may not file a subsequent motion to terminate the prosecution pursuant to this section for at least six months from the date on which such order is entered.

9. Notwithstanding any other provision of this section, where a motion to terminate a prosecution is filed with a local criminal court pursuant to subdivision two, and, prior to the determination thereof, such court is divested of jurisdiction by the filing of an indictment charging the offense or offenses contained in the felony complaint,

such motion shall be deemed to have been denied as of the date of such divestiture.

10. The chief administrator of the courts, in consultation with the director of the division of criminal justice services and representatives of appropriate prosecutorial and criminal defense organizations in the state, shall adopt forms for the motion to terminate a prose-cution authorized by subdivision one and for the notice of opposition specified in subdivision three.

Added by L. 2004, Ch. 518, § 2, eff. Nov. 1, 2004.

Editor's Note: Section 4 of L. 2004, Ch. 518 provides: "This act shall take effect on the first of November next succeeding the date on which it shall have become a law, and shall apply to all criminal actions, whenever commenced, except that, with respect to actions commenced prior to such effective date, the written notice required by subdivision two of section 180.85 of the criminal procedure law, as added by section two of this act, may be given no earlier than twelve months from the date of arraignment on the felony complaint in such action or sixty days from such effective date, whichever is later."

ARTICLE 182—ALTERNATE METHOD OF COURT APPEARANCE

[Expired and repealed Dec. 31, 2006, pursuant to L. 1993, Ch. 689, § 2, as amended.]

Section

    182.10   **Definition of terms.**

    182.20   **Electronic appearance; general rule.**

    182.30   **Electronic appearance; conditions and limitations.**

    182.40   **Approval by the chief administrator of the courts.**

§ 182.10. Definition of terms. [*Expires and repealed Dec. 31, 2006, pursuant to L. 1993, Ch. 689, § 2, as amended.*]

As used in this article:

1. "Independent audio-visual system" means an electronic system for the transmission and receiving of audio and visual signals, encompassing encoded signals, frequency domain multiplexing or other suitable means to preclude the unauthorized reception and decoding of the signals by commercially available television receivers, channel converters, or other available receiving devices.

2. "Electronic appearance" means an appearance in which various participants, including the defendant, are not present in the court, but in which, by means of an independent audio-visual system, (a) all of the participants are simultaneously able to see and hear reproductions of the voices and images of the judge, counsel, defendant, police officer, and any other appropriate participant, and (b) counsel is present with the defendant, or if the defendant waives the presence of counsel on the record, the defendant and his or her counsel are able to see and hear each other and engage in private conversation.

Amended by L. 1998, Ch. 605, § 1, extending the repeal date to Dec. 31, 2001, eff. Sept. 30, 1998; L. 2001, Ch. 315, § 1, extending the repeal date to Dec. 31, 2004; L. 2004, Ch. 172, § 1, extending the repeal date to Dec. 31, 2006.

§ 182.20. Electronic appearance; general rule. [*Expires and repealed Dec. 31, 2006, pursuant to L. 1993, Ch. 689, § 2, as amended.*]

1. Notwithstanding any other provision of law and except as provided in section 182.30 of this article, the court, in its discretion, may dispense with the personal appearance of the defendant, except an appearance at a hearing or trial, and conduct an electronic appearance in connection with a criminal action pending in Albany, Bronx, Broome, Erie, Kings, New York, Niagara, Oneida, Onondaga, Ontario, Queens, Richmond, St. Lawrence, Tompkins, Chautauqua, Cattaraugus, Clinton, Montgomery, Rensselaer, Warren, Westchester or Franklin county, provided that

the chief administrator of the courts has authorized the use of electronic appearance and the defendant, after consultation with counsel, consents on the record. Such consent shall be required at the commencement of each electronic appearance to such electronic appearance.

2. If, for any reason, the court determines on its own motion or on the motion of any party that the conduct of an electronic appearance may impair the legal rights of the defendant, it shall not permit the electronic appearance to proceed. If, for any other articulated reason, either party requests at any time during the electronic appearance that such appearance be terminated, the court shall grant such request and adjourn the proceeding to a date certain. Upon the adjourned date the proceeding shall be recommenced from the point at which the request for termination of the electronic appearance had been granted.

3. The electronic appearance shall be conducted in accordance with rules issued by the chief administrator of the courts.

4. When the defendant makes an electronic appearance, the court stenographer shall record any statements in the same manner as if the defendant had made a personal appearance. No electronic recording of any electronic appearance may be made, viewed or inspected except as may be authorized by the rules issued by the chief administrator of the courts.

Amended by L. 1994, Ch. 521 and 522, § 1, eff. July 26, 1994, amending subd. 1, and not affecting expiration and repeal provided for in L. 1993, Ch. 689; L. 1995, Ch. 124, § 1, extending repeal date to Dec. 31, 1998, and § 2, amending subd. 1, eff. July 5, 1995; L. 1998, Ch. 177, § 1, eff. July 7, 1998, and Ch. 430, § 1, eff. July 22, 1998; L. 1998, Ch. 605, § 1, extending the repeal date to Dec. 31, 2001, eff. Sept. 30, 1998, and § 2, amending subd. 1, eff. Sept. 30, 1998; L. 1999, Chs. 426 and 430, § 1, amending subd. 1, eff. Aug. 31, 1999; L. 2000, Ch. 514, § 1, amending subd. 1, eff. Oct. 4, 2000; L. 2001, Ch. 315, § 1, extending the repeal date to Dec. 31, 2004, and § 2, amending subd. 1, eff. Sept. 19, 2001; L. 2002, Ch. 57, § 1, eff. May 7, 2002, and Ch. 62, § 1, eff. May 7, 2002, both amending subd. 1; L. 2004, Ch. 167, § 1, eff. July 20, 2004, amending subd. 1; Ch. 172, § 1, extending the repeal date to Dec. 31, 2006.

§ 182.30. Electronic appearance; conditions and limitations. [*Expires and repealed Dec. 31, 2006, pursuant to L. 1993, Ch. 689, § 2, as amended.*]

The following conditions and limitations apply to all electronic appearances:

1. The defendant may not enter a plea of guilty to, or be sentenced upon a conviction of, a felony.

2. The defendant may not enter a plea of not responsible by reason of mental disease or defect.

3. The defendant may not be committed to the state department of mental hygiene pursuant to article seven hundred thirty of this chapter.

4. The defendant may not enter a plea of guilty to a misdemeanor conditioned upon a promise of incarceration unless such incarceration will be imposed only in the event that the defendant fails to comply with a term or condition imposed under the original sentence.

5. A defendant who has been convicted of a misdemeanor may not be sentenced to a period of incarceration which exceeds the time the defendant has already served when sentence is imposed.

Amended by L. 1998, Ch. 605, § 1, extending the repeal date to Dec. 31, 2001, eff. Sept. 30, 1998; L. 2001, Ch. 315, § 1, extending the repeal date to Dec. 31, 2004; Ch. 172, § 1, extending the repeal date to Dec. 31, 2006.

§ 182.40. Approval by the chief administrator of the courts. [*Expires and repealed Dec. 31, 2006, pursuant to L. 1993, Ch. 689, § 2, as amended.*]

1. The appropriate administrative judge shall submit to the chief administrator of the courts a written proposal for the use of electronic appearance in his or her jurisdiction. If the chief administrator of the courts approves the proposal, installation of an independent audiovisual system may begin.

2. Upon completion of the installation of an independent audio-visual system, the commission on cable television shall inspect, test, and examine the independent audiovisual system and certify to the chief administrator of the courts whether the system complies with the definition of an independent audio-visual system and is technically suitable for the conducting of electronic appearances as intended.

3. The chief administrator of the courts shall issue rules governing the use of electronic appearances.

Amended by L. 1998, Ch. 605, § 1, extending the repeal date to Dec. 31, 2001, eff. Sept. 30, 1998; L. 2001, Ch. 315, § 1, extending the repeal date to Dec. 31, 2004; Ch. 172, § 1, extending the repeal date to Dec. 31, 2006.

TITLE I—PRELIMINARY PROCEEDINGS IN SUPERIOR COURT

ARTICLE 190—THE GRAND JURY AND ITS PROCEEDINGS

LexisNexis Cross References

Criminal Constitutional Law, Vol. 2, Ch. 6, Grand Jury Procedures; *Criminal Defense Techniques,* Vol. 1, Ch. 6, Representing a Witness Before a Grand Jury; Vol. 5, Ch. 105, Grand Jury Motions; *Business Crime,* Vol. 1, Ch. 1, Grand Jury Practice; *New York Criminal Practice (2d ed.),* Vol. 1, Ch. 11, Grand Jury; *Criminal Practice Handbook (2d ed.),* Ch. 3, Grand Jury Representation.

§ 190.05. Grand jury; definition and general functions.

A grand jury is a body consisting of not less than sixteen nor more than twenty-three persons, impaneled by a superior court and constituting a part of such court, the functions of which are to hear and examine evidence concerning offenses and concerning misconduct, nonfeasance and neglect in public office, whether criminal or otherwise, and to take action with respect to such evidence as provided in section 190.60.

ANNOTATIONS

Death penalty.—Legislature enacted many changes to the CPL to implement the death penalty, but left the discovery statute unaltered, which indicates "a clear indication that the existing rule is operative in capital cases"; the CPL does not authorize a defendant to present mitigating evidence to the grand jury, and the fact that defendant could face the death penalty does not change the grand jury's function. People v. Campos, 176 Misc. 2d 637, 672 N.Y.S.2d 1001 (Sup. Ct. Kings Co. 1998).

Statutory period.—Obtaining and keeping quorum of grand jurors to hear case to its conclusion was not good cause to extend statutory period during which grand jury action must be taken or defendant must be released from custody. People v. Griffin, 163 Misc. 2d 43, 619 N.Y.S.2d 931 (Crim. Ct. Kings Co. 1994).

Prosecutorial discretion.—Authority of court to assess fairness of grand jury presentation is particularly important since current grand jury system vests considerable discretion with prosecution and such discretion should not be permitted to go unchecked. People v. Dzeloski, 161 Misc. 2d 867, 615 N.Y.S.2d 624 (Sup. Ct. Bronx Co. 1994).

Due process.—Calling defendant to testify before grand jury did not violate due process. People v. Stepteau, 178 A.D.2d 376, 578 N.Y.S.2d 540 (1st Dept. 1991).

Function.—The Grand Jury is an investigatory body with

broad exploratory powers, the scope of which are not to be limited narrowly by questions of propriety or forecasts of the probable result of the investigation, or by doubts whether any particular individual will be found properly subject to an accusation of crime. Kuriansky v. Seewald, 148 A.D.2d 238, 544 N.Y.S.2d 336, 338 (1st Dept. 1989).

Indictment for offense which is violation.—Grand jury has no authority to indict defendant for commission of an offense which is only a violation. People v. Star Supermarkets, Inc., 67 Misc. 2d 483, 324 N.Y.S.2d 514 (Co. Ct. 1971).

Motion to dismiss indictment; procedure.—To sustain a dismissal of an indictment, something more is required than the bare allegation that grand jury proceedings were defective. To dismiss an indictment, a court must have before it a preponderance of facts which establish clear violations of Article 190 of the CPL, and which are sufficient to overcome the presumption of regularity which applies to all grand jury proceedings. Motion to dismiss based on facts outside the pleadings must be supported by sworn allegations of fact supporting the grounds asserted. People v. Pfitzmayer, 72 Misc. 2d 739, 340 N.Y.S.2d 85 (Sup. Ct. Nassau Co. 1972).

Witnesses' grand jury testimony; availability to defendant at trial.—Although *Rosario* rule allows defense to obtain pre-trial statements of prosecution witnesses given to grand jury concerning accusations against defendant, this right is limited to non-confidential statements relating to the subject matter of the testimony used for impeachment purposes only and does not cover undercover investigator's grand jury testimony of illegal acts of Nassau County jail employees as to those not yet tried or indicted. People v. Bartholomew, 71 Misc. 2d 876, 337 N.Y.S.2d 906 (Nassau Co. Ct. 1972).

§ 190.10. Grand jury; for what courts drawn.

The appellate division of each judicial department shall adopt rules governing the number and the terms for which grand juries shall be drawn and impaneled by the superior courts within its department; provided, however, that a grand jury may be drawn and impaneled for any extraordinary term of the supreme court upon the order of a justice assigned to hold such term.

ANNOTATIONS

Statutory purpose.—Purpose of CPL § 190.10 was to effect a more flexible administrative approach. People v. Leibowitz, 112 A.D.2d 383, 491 N.Y.S.2d 839 (2d Dept. 1985).

Duration; extraordinary Grand Jury.—Duration of an extraordinary grand jury impaneled under CPL § 190.10 is coextensive with that of the extraordinary term; failure to limit duration as required for grand juries impaneled under CPL § 190.15 was not fatal to jurisdiction. Tyler v. Polsky, 57 A.D.2d 422, 395 N.Y.S.2d 21 (1st Dept. 1977).

§ 190.15. Grand jury; duration of term and discharge.

1. A term of a superior court for which a grand jury has been impaneled remains in existence at least until and including the opening date of the next term of such court for which a grand jury has been designated. Upon such date, or within five days preceding it, the court may, upon declaration of both the grand jury and the district attorney that such grand jury has not yet completed or will be unable to complete certain business before it, extend the term of court and the existence of such grand jury to a specified future date, and may subsequently order further extensions for such purpose.

2. At any time when a grand jury is in recess

and no other appropriate grand jury is in existence in the county, the court may, upon application of the district attorney or of a defendant held by a local criminal court for the action of a grand jury, order such grand jury reconvened for the purpose of dealing with a matter requiring grand jury action.

ANNOTATIONS

Dismissal of indictment.—Even if indictment against defendant was filed by grand jury whose term had not been extended, defendant was not entitled to dismissal, where grand jury had been legally constituted, and there was no showing of prejudice or that fundamental integrity of grand jury process had been impaired. People v. Soto, 163 A.D.2d 889, 559 N.Y.S.2d 73 (4th Dept. 1990).

—By prosecutor's posing of question to grand jury to vote to extend its term to hear witness for defendant, in terms of choice of having to return or not, prosecutor impaired integrity of grand jury and prejudiced defendant, which warranted dismissal of indictment. People v. Tillery, 166 Misc. 2d 879, 636 N.Y.S.2d 583 (Sup. Ct. Kings Co. 1995).

Improperly constituted grand jury.—Grand jury which had prepared, signed and filed indictment, had completed its investigation without unfinished business, and whose term had expired, was neither legally constituted grand jury nor "de facto grand jury" authorized to sign so-called "corrected" indictment which prosecution prepared in lieu of superseding or re-presented indictment after discovering that original indictment mistakenly charged different offense than that which grand jury had voted. People v. Livoti, 166 Misc. 2d 925, 632 N.Y.S.2d 425 (Sup. Ct. Bronx Co. 1995).

Extension of grand jury term; technical violation.—Grand jury was functioning continuously since its inception and failure of court to extend it to "specified date" as required by statute, did not violate defendants constitutional rights, was highly technical and did not warrant dismissal of indictment based on evidence sufficient to convict, if unexplained and uncontradicted, and failure of grand jury to join in application for extension was insignificant in view of their continuing operation which is deemed an acquiescence. People v. Kovacs, 72 Misc. 2d 39, 338 N.Y.S.2d 155 (Dutchess Co. Ct. 1972).

Term of Grand Jury.—A Grand Jury whose term has been extended due to uncompleted business under CPL § 190.15(1) may not consider entirely new matters during its extended term. People v. Williams, 73 N.Y.2d 84, 538 N.Y.S.2d 222, 223, 535 N.E.2d 275 (1989).

—CPL § 190.15 relates to the extension of existing grand juries and neither limits the original impaneling of grand juries nor the power of the Administrative Judge to determine when or for how long a grand jury can be originally impaneled. Seidenberg v. County Ct. of Rockland County, 34 N.Y.2d 499, 358 N.Y.S.2d 416, 315 N.E.2d 475 (1974).

§ 190.20. Grand jury; formation, organization and other matters preliminary to assumption of duties.

1. The mode of selecting grand jurors and of drawing and impaneling grand juries is governed by the judiciary law.

2. Neither the grand jury panel nor any individual grand juror may be challenged, but the court may:

(a) At any time before a grand jury is sworn, discharge the panel and summon another panel if it finds that the original panel does not substantially conform to the requirements of the judiciary law; or

(b) At any time after a grand juror is drawn,

refuse to swear him, or discharge him after he has been sworn, upon a finding that he is disqualified from service pursuant to the judiciary law, or incapable of performing his duties because of bias or prejudice, or guilty of misconduct in the performance of his duties such as to impair the proper functioning of the grand jury.

3. After a grand jury has been impaneled, the court must appoint one of the grand jurors as foreman and another to act as foreman during any absence or disability of the foreman. At some time before commencement of their duties, the grand jurors must appoint one of their number as secretary to keep records material to the conduct of the grand jury's business.

4. The grand jurors must be sworn by the court. The oath may be in any form or language which requires the grand jurors to perform their duties faithfully.

5. After a grand jury has been sworn, the court must deliver or cause to be delivered to each grand juror a printed copy of all the provisions of this article, and the court may, in addition, give the grand jurors any oral and written instructions relating to the proper performance of their duties as it deems necessary or appropriate.

6. If two or more grand juries are impaneled at the same court term, the court may thereafter, for good cause, transfer grand jurors from one panel to another, and any grand juror so transferred is deemed to have been sworn as a member of the panel to which he has been transferred.

Amended by L. 2000, Ch. 497, § 1, amending subd. 5, eff. Nov. 1, 2000.

ANNOTATIONS

Prosecutorial authority.—Prosecutor has no obligation to advise grand jury of its authority to cause witnesses to be called, nor is there requirement that grand jury be so advised prior to submission of each and every case for consideration; rather, grand jury is informed of its powers through distribution of copies of applicable statute. People v. Smith, 182 A.D.2d 725, 582 N.Y.S.2d 454 (2d Dept. 1992).

—Prosecutor has authority to excuse grand juror from participating in particular case, and that power is granted to the impanelling court as well. People v. Cipolla, 163 Misc. 2d 144, 619 N.Y.S.2d 939 (Westchester Co. Ct. 1994).

—Exercise by court or prosecutor of power to excuse grand juror from participating in a particular case must find some support in the record, but failure to excuse grand juror in case about which he or she professes to have some knowledge must also be justified with at least a showing that grand juror is able to follow law and render impartial verdict despite the knowledge. People v. Cipolla, 163 Misc. 2d 144, 619 N.Y.S.2d 939 (Westchester Co. Ct. 1994).

Subd. 3

Correction officer holding the defendant in custody.—The conviction was affirmed where the correction officer who was assigned to guard the defendant during his grand jury testimony, subsequently appeared as a trial witness as his testimony was of a limited nature, relating solely to the County Sheriff's Department regulation as to who may possess handcuff keys and there was no showing that his presence created a possibility of prejudice or impaired the grand jury proceeding. People v. Hyde, 85 A.D.2d 745, 445 N.Y.S.2d 800 (2d Dept. 1981).

Grand jury; composition.—There was no implied bias inferred from fact that 13 of 21 grand jurors were employed by IBM or wives of IBM employees so as to render dismissal of indictment against defendant charging perjury and theft and possession involving IBM equipment. People v. Reilly, 71 Misc. 2d 227, 335 N.Y.S.2d 841 (Dutchess Co. Ct. 1972).

Instructions.—The Grand Jury was adequately informed of its duties where the impanelling Judge orally instructed the jurors as to their duties and distributed printed copies of CPL Article 190 amongst the members, and the District Attorney could later instruct with respect to significance, legal effect or evaluation of evidence presented in a particular matter. People v. Valenti, 91 Misc. 2d 669, 399 N.Y.S.2d 363 (Suffolk Co. Ct. 1977).

Cognizable class.—Neither the young nor the poor describe groups that are distinctive within the contemplation of the fair cross-section requirement, and defendant has failed to show that the grand jury selection violates either equal protection or due process right to grand jury drawn from a fair cross-section. People v. Taylor, 191 Misc. 2d 672, 743 N.Y.S.2d 253 (Sup. Ct. Queens Co. 2002).

—One who identified himself as an Orthodox Jew is not part of cognizable class. People v. Goodman, 92 Misc. 2d 927, 402 N.Y.S.2d 114 (Sup. Ct. Bronx Co. 1978).

Equal protection claim; systematic underrepresentation.—Defendant argued that poor people, persons aged 18 to 34, Hispanics, Blacks, and women were systematically underrepresented at every stage of the grand jury process. Defendant then changed his claim to just Hispanics, the young, and the poor. An equal protection claim demands a showing of purposeful discrimination against members of an underrepresented group. After a hearing in which the court called witnesses to explain the jury selection procedures in Queens County, the court found that the evidence established that the intention at all levels of the jury selection process is to be more inclusive, not to discriminate against any recognizable or distinct class of citizens. Because there was no showing of any discriminatory intent at any stage of the jury selection process, defendant's equal protection claim failed. People v. Taylor, 191 Misc. 2d 672, 743 N.Y.S.2d 253 (Sup. Ct. Queens Co. 2002).

§ 190.25. Grand jury; proceedings and operation in general.

1. Proceedings of a grand jury are not valid unless at least sixteen of its members are present. The finding of an indictment, a direction to file a prosecutor's information, a decision to submit a grand jury report and every other affirmative official action or decision requires the concurrence of at least twelve members thereof.

2. The foreman or any other grand juror may administer an oath to any witness appearing before the grand jury.

3. Except as provided in subdivision three-a of this section, during the deliberations and voting of a grand jury, only the grand jurors may be present in the grand jury room. During its other proceedings, the following persons, in addition to witnesses, may, as the occasion requires, also be present:

(a) The district attorney;

(b) A clerk or other public servant authorized to assist the grand jury in the administrative conduct of its proceedings;

(c) A stenographer authorized to record the proceedings of the grand jury;

(d) An interpreter. Upon request of the grand jury, the prosecutor must provide an interpreter to interpret the testimony of any witness who does not speak the English language well enough to be readily understood. Such interpreter must, if he has not previously taken the constitutional oath of office, first take an oath before the grand jury that he will faithfully interpret the testimony of the witness and that he will keep secret all matters before such grand jury within his knowledge;

(e) A public servant holding a witness in custody. When a person held in official custody is a witness before a grand jury, a public servant assigned to guard him during his grand jury appearance may accompany him in the grand jury room. Such public servant must, if he has not previously taken the constitutional oath of office, first take an oath before the grand jury that he will keep secret all matters before it within his knowledge.

(f) An attorney representing a witness pursuant to section 190.52 of this chapter while that witness is present.

(g) An operator, as that term is defined in section 190.32 of this chapter, while the videotaped examination of either a special witness or a child witness is being played.

(h) A social worker, rape crisis counselor, psychologist or other professional providing emotional support to a child witness twelve years old or younger who is called to give evidence in a grand jury proceeding concerning a crime defined in article one hundred thirty, article two hundred sixty, section 120.10, 125.10, 125.15, 125.20, 125.25, 125.27 or 255.25 of the penal law provided that the district attorney consents. Such support person shall not provide the witness with an answer to any question or otherwise participate in such proceeding and shall first take an oath before the grand jury that he or she will keep secret all matters before such grand jury within his or her knowledge.

3-a. Upon the request of a deaf or hearing-impaired grand juror, the prosecutor shall provide a sign language interpreter for such juror. Such interpreter shall be present during all proceedings of the grand jury which the deaf or hearing-impaired grand juror attends, including deliberation and voting. The interpreter shall, if he or she has not previously taken the constitutional oath of office, first take an oath before the grand jury that he or she will faithfully interpret the testimony of the witnesses and the statements of the prosecutor, judge and grand jurors; keep secret all matters before such grand jury within his or her knowledge; and not seek to influence the deliberations and voting of such grand jury.

4. (a) Grand jury proceedings are secret, and no grand juror or other person specified in subdivision three of this section or section 215.70 of the penal law, may, except in the lawful discharge of his duties or upon written order of the court, disclose the nature or substance of any grand jury testimony, evidence, or any decision, result or other matter attending a grand jury proceeding. For the purpose of assisting the grand jury in conducting its investigation, evidence obtained by a grand jury may be independently examined by the district attorney, members of his staff, police officers specifically assigned to the investigation, and such other persons as the court may specifically authorize. Such evidence may not be disclosed to other persons without a court order. Nothing contained herein shall prohibit a witness from disclosing his own testimony.

(b) When a district attorney obtains evidence during a grand jury proceeding which provides reasonable cause to suspect that a child has been abused or maltreated, as those terms are defined by section ten hundred twelve of the family court act, he must apply to the court supervising the grand jury for an order permitting disclosure of such evidence to the state central register of child abuse and maltreatment. A district attorney need not apply to the court for such order if he has previously made or caused a report to be made to the state central register of child abuse and maltreatment pursuant to section four hundred thirteen of the social services law and the evidence obtained during the grand jury proceeding, or substantially similar information, was included in such report. The district attorney's application to the court shall be made *ex parte* and in camera. The court must grant the application and permit the district attorney to disclose the evidence to the state central register of child abuse and maltreatment unless the court finds that such disclosure would jeopardize the life or safety of any person or interfere with a continuing grand jury proceeding.

5. The grand jury is the exclusive judge of the facts with respect to any matter before it.

6. The legal advisors of the grand jury are the court and the district attorney, and the grand jury may not seek or receive legal advice from any other source. Where necessary or appropriate, the court or the district attorney, or both, must instruct the grand jury concerning the law with respect to its duties or any matter before it, and such instructions must be recorded in the minutes.

Amended by L. 1977, Ch. 451; L. 1978, Chs. 415; L. 1984, Ch. 804; L. 1985, Ch. 677; L. 1985, Ch. 650; L. 1986, Ch. 63; L. 1987, Ch. 613; L. 1994, Ch. 198.

ANNOTATIONS

Role of prosecutor.—The Criminal Procedure Law designates both the District Attorney and the court as legal advisors to the Grand Jury. People v. Huston, 88 N.Y.2d 400, 646 N.Y.S.2d 69, 668 N.E.2d 1362 (1996).

—Because Grand Jury proceedings are conducted by the prosecutor alone, this function confers upon the prosecutor broad powers and duties, as well as wide discretion in presenting the People's case. The prosecutor's discretion during Grand Jury proceedings, however, is not absolute. As legal advisor to the Grand Jury, the prosecutor performs dual functions: that of public officer and that of advocate. The prosecutor is thus charged with the duty not only to secure indictments but also to see that justice is done. People v. Huston, 88 N.Y.2d 400, 646 N.Y.S.2d 69, 668 N.E.2d 1362 (1996).

—As legal advisor to grand jury, prosecutor must, where

necessary or appropriate, instruct jurors on exculpatory defenses such as justification. People v. Brunson, 226 A.D.2d 1093, 641 N.Y.S.2d 935 (4th Dept. 1996).

—Evidence presented to grand jury must support prima facie case, and district attorney must instruct grand jury on law with respect to matters before it. People v. Mount Hope Asphalt Corp., 163 Misc. 2d 778, 623 N.Y.S.2d 74 (Suffolk Co. Ct. 1994).

Disclosure of minutes.—In determining whether statutorily authorized disclosure of grand jury minutes is appropriate, trial court must evaluate whether party seeking disclosure has shown a compelling and particularized need for the grand jury testimony, and when that threshold is met, trial court must weigh factors to assess competing public policies of disclosure versus secrecy blanketing grand jury proceedings. Lungen v. Kane, 88 N.Y.2d 861, 644 N.Y.S.2d 487, 666 N.E.2d 1360 (1996).

Defective indictment; remedy.—When sought by defendant, dismissal is proper remedy for indictment that is defective due to concurrence of fewer than 12 grand jurors. People v. Livoti, 166 Misc. 2d 925, 632 N.Y.S.2d 425 (Sup. Ct. Bronx Co. 1995).

Video camera.—Statutes authorizing presence at grand jury proceedings of "operator" of video camera to record examination of child witness do not require showing that district attorney formally hired and agreed to pay person to operate video camera, but rather it is sufficient if individual in question is operating video camera at district attorney's specific request. People v. Sayavong, 83 N.Y.2d 702, 613 N.Y.S.2d 343, 635 N.E.2d 1213 (1994).

Criminal proceeding; prospective witness's right to transcript of his grand jury testimony rejected.—Whether to allow a prospective prosecution witness to review the transcript of his prior grand jury testimony lies wholly within the prosecutor's discretionary mode of preparing for trial; disclosure is not a right to be claimed by the witness. In re Kinsella, 95 Misc. 2d 915, 408 N.Y.S.2d 17 (Sup. Ct. Onondaga Co. 1978).

Furnishing grand jury minutes.—Printed record on appeal from trial court's dismissal of indictment was not defective on grounds that it omitted copy of grand jury minutes, as state properly supplied appellate court with confidential minutes under separate cover. People v. Jiminez, 223 A.D.2d 558, 636 N.Y.S.2d 110 (2d Dept. 1996).

Constitutionality.—Section upheld as constitutional. People v. Taylor, 68 Misc. 2d 93, 325 N.Y.S.2d 702 (Co. Ct. 1972).

Scope of witness' right to counsel.—A witness appearing before the grand jury has the right to consult with counsel and may solicit the aid of his counsel outside the grand jury room, but the lawyer for a witness is not entitled to be present in the grand jury room. People v. Taylor, 68 Misc. 2d 93, 325 N.Y.S.2d 702 (Co. Ct. 1972), citing leading case, People v. Ianniello, 21 N.Y.2d 418, 288 N.Y.S.2d 462, 235 N.E.2d 439, cert. denied, 393 U.S. 827 (1968).

—There is no right to consultation in the midst of grand jury testimony for strategic, as opposed to legal, advice. People v. Langella, 82 Misc. 2d 410, 370 N.Y.S.2d 381 (Sup. Ct. N.Y. Co. 1975).

Intoxication charge; death penalty case.—Where sufficient evidence supports a claim of intoxication in connection with a first degree murder charge, such an instruction to the grand jury is required; intoxication instruction was not required in the instant case because defendant's claim of intoxication, taken in the context of his version of the incident, bears no relationship to the first degree murder charge. People v. Harris, 174 Misc. 2d 654, 666 N.Y.S.2d 876 (Sup. Ct. Kings. Co. 1997).

Unsealing order denied.—Court denied application by various news media organizations for an order unsealing certain evidence presented to the grand jury that returned indictments charging a number of individuals with crimes relating to the handling of matrimonial cases, finding that before any substantive proceedings take place, and without a showing of a compelling and particularized need, it would be inappropriate for the court to release grand jury evidence consisting of the fruits of untested, electronic surveillance dealing with sensitive matrimonial matters. In re NYP Holdings, Inc., 196 Misc. 2d 708, 766 N.Y.S.2d 477 (Sup. Ct. Kings Co. 2003).

Subd. 1

Voting of indictment.—In order to dismiss a charge, there must be a formal vote of the grand jury, and 12 of its members must concur in that result. People v. Aarons, 2 N.Y.3d 547, 780 N.Y.S.2d 533, 813 N.E.2d 613 (2004).

—A valid indictment is one which is voted by a legally constituted Grand Jury, i.e., one in which at least 12 of the members of the Grand Jury concur; the twelve who have voted to indict must have heard all of the "essential and critical evidence" presented against all of the defendants. People v. Gelfand, 131 Misc. 268, 499 N.Y.S.2d 573 (Sup. Ct. Kings Co. 1986).

—Procedure was proper where, after presentation of the evidence to the grand jury, the prosecutor outlined the appropriate provisions of law, the grand jury voted an indictment and afterwards the indictment was typed and signed by the foreman and the prosecutor. People v. Roberts, 76 Misc. 2d 887, 352 N.Y.S.2d 791 (Dutchess Co. Ct. 1974).

Subd. 3

Assistant district attorney.—The fact that the Assistant District Attorney, who presented the evidence to the Grand Jury, was not admitted to the bar, did not negate his authority to be present in the Grand Jury room. People v. Carter, 77 N.Y.2d 95, 564 N.Y.S.2d 992, 566 N.E.2d 119 (1990).

Attorney General.—The Attorney General has latent power to appear before a term of the Supreme Court or its grand jury; however that power must be triggered by statutory authority. L & S Hosp. & Institutional Supplies v. Hynes, 84 Misc. 2d 431, 375 N.Y.S.2d 934 (Sup. Ct. N.Y. Co. 1975), aff'd, 51 A.D.2d 515, 378 N.Y.S.2d 78 (1st Dept 1976).

Authorized person.—The integrity of the grand jury was not impaired by the presence of a caseworker from the Department of Social Services who provided support for the child victim during her testimony, because the caseworker was an authorized person within the meaning of CPL 190.25(3)(h), and the court determined after a hearing that the caseworker did not provide the witness with answers or participate in the proceedings. People v. Litzenberger, 234 A.D.2d 947, 652 N.Y.S.2d 912 (4th Dept. 1996).

Grand Jury instructions.—While instructions to the Grand Jury need not be as precise as those given to a petit jury, they may not be so misleading or incomplete as to substantially undermine the integrity of the proceedings. People v. Caraciola, 78 N.Y.2d 1021, 576 N.Y.S.2d 74, 581 N.E.2d 1329 (1991).

—The instructions to Grand Jury were sufficient where the prosecutor read the complete statutory definition of justification. People v. Sierra, 143 A.D.2d 1065, 533 N.Y.S.2d 751 (2d Dept. 1988).

—The People did not improperly allow a witness to charge the jurors on the law when it allowed the witness to testify concerning the requirements of various Medicaid regulations, since that testimony did not concern the requirements of the Penal Law. People v. Perry, 199 A.D.2d 889, 605 N.Y.S.2d 790 (3d Dept. 1993).

—The prosecutor, in his capacity as legal advisor, must instruct the Grand Jury with respect to the matters before it; although the instructions need not be as precise as a court's instructions to a petit jury must be, the prosecutor's paramount obligation is to provide the Grand Jury with enough information to enable it intelligently to decide whether a crime has been committed. People v. Crump, 157 Misc. 2d 566, 597 N.Y.S.2d 1010, 1011 (Westchester Co. Ct. 1993).

—Although the prosecutor, in a Grand Jury presentation, may read the applicable statutes in instructing the Grand Jury, where he elaborates by giving erroneous, misleading, and sometimes incomprehensible explanations of the law, dismissal of the indictment is required. People v. Ehrlich, 136 Misc. 2d 514, 518 N.Y.S.2d 742, 746 (Sup. Ct. N.Y. Co. 1987).

Minutes.—Grand Jury minutes provided by the District Attorney's office for inspection are original documents and are not required to be certified by the specific reporter. People v. Velez, 144 Misc. 2d 18, 543 N.Y.S.2d 238 (Sup. Ct. Queens Co. 1989).

Grand jury; jurisdiction; district attorney; divestiture and removal.—Indictment by Grand Jury after presentation of evidence by District Attorney with apparent personal interest in the prosecution, would be dismissed and case remanded and removed to another local criminal court with appointment of a special prosecutor. Divestiture statute at option of District Attorney was repugnant in its operation to equal protection of the laws. People v. Krstovich, 72 Misc. 2d 90, 338 N.Y.S.2d 132 (Greene Co. Ct. 1972).

Improper person before Grand Jury; Special Prosecutor.—Indictment of person not listed in appointing order, was an *ultra vires* act which compelled dismissal of indictment since the judicial appointment of a Special District Attorney was limited to a "particular case." People v. Leahy, 72 N.Y.2d 510, 534 N.Y.S.2d 658, 531 N.E.2d 290 (1988).

—Where a Special Prosecutor lacks the requisite authority he is not a proper person before the Grand Jury and those proceedings conducted by him before the Grand Jury are defective. People v. DiFalco, 44 N.Y.2d 482, 406 N.Y.S.2d 279, 377 N.E.2d 732 (1978).

—Presentation to Grand Jury by an unauthorized prosecutor impairs the integrity of the grand jury and any resulting indictment must be dismissed. People v. Gallagher, 140 Misc. 2d 894, 531 N.Y.S.2d 970 (Sup. Ct. Suffolk Co. 1988).

Unqualified grand juror.—The discovery that one or more grand jurors who participated in the proceedings of the panel were technically unqualified to sit is, alone, insufficient for dismissal of an indictment. People v. Colebut, 86 Misc. 2d 729, 383 N.Y.S.2d 985 (Sup. Ct. N.Y. Co. 1976).

Subd. 4

Adoption records.—Order quashing the Grand Jury subpoenas *duces tecum* issued against the Clerk of the Family Court of Suffolk County and the Clerk of the Nassau County Surrogate's Court ordering them to appear before the Grand Jury of New York County and produce designated adoption records reversed on the grounds that the Grand Jury is not a "person" within the contemplation of DRL § 114 which forbids access to sealed adoption record and that Grand Jury proceedings are secret. *In re* Grand Jury Subpoenas Duces Tecum v. Weeks, 58 A.D.2d 1, 395 N.Y.S.2d 645 (1st Dept. 1977).

Private litigation.—Court denied claimant's request for examination of the grand jury minutes in aid of private litigation seeking money damages. Carey v. State of New York, 92 Misc. 2d 316, 402 N.Y.S.2d 100 (Sup. Ct. Wyoming Co. 1977), *aff'd,* 68 A.D.2d 220, 416 N.Y.S.2d 904 (4th Dept. 1979).

Court order to turn over grand jury minutes.—Family Court, as a court of limited jurisdiction, lacks the jurisdiction to compel production of Grand Jury minutes. *In re* Brittini "F", 193 A.D.2d 846, 597 N.Y.S.2d 528 (3d Dept. 1993).

—Although there is no specific statutory authority for the court to direct the district attorney to turn over a copy of the grand jury minutes to defense counsel, CPL § 190.25(4) clearly implies such authority in providing that such proceedings may not be disclosed except "upon written order of the court," nor "without a court order"; where there is a motion to dismiss an indictment for legal insufficiency of evidence presented to the grand jury, and complex issues of law have been raised, the court may properly order such a turnover so that the defendant may better prepare material for use by the court in deciding the pending motion. People v. Kazmarick, 96 Misc. 2d 1024, 410 N.Y.S.2d 187 (Sullivan Co. Ct. 1978).

Court's power to release minutes.—By statute the court has jurisdiction over Grand Jury minutes and has discretionary power to release them. (Judiciary Law § 325; CPL § 190.25[4]). *In re* Scott, 33 A.D.2d 282, 385 N.Y.S.2d 639 (4th Dept. 1976).

Inspection by municipal agency.—Release to the Corporation Counsel of the grand jury minutes relating to the testimony of a police officer indicted for perjury and criminal contempt was denied because of the potential prejudice to his right to a fair trial, which outweighed the public interest in presently disclosing the substance of the officer's testimony. *In re* Corporation Counsel of the City of Buffalo, 61 A.D.2d 32, 401 N.Y.S.2d 339 (4th Dept. 1978).

—Inspection of Grand Jury proceedings by Department of Investigation was allowed where the indictment had been dismissed and the action had terminated in all respects; the witnesses had filed written releases of testimony; and the District Attorney had consented. People v. Werfel, 82 Misc. 2d 1029, 372 N.Y.S.2d 510 (Sup. Ct. Queens Co. 1975).

General.—The name of a Grand Jury witness is among those matters attending a grand jury proceeding which is required by law to be kept secret. People v. Sanoguet, 157 Misc. 2d 771, 597 N.Y.S.2d 854 (Sup. Ct. Bronx Co. 1993).

***In camera* hearing on subpoena duces tecum.**—Since Grand Jury proceedings are secret, an *in camera* hearing was an acceptable means for the court to become apprised of the purposes of the subpoena duces tecum (to investigate criminal activities other than those alleged in the previous indictment), while preserving the secrecy of the Grand Jury proceedings. Hynes v. Lerner, 44 N.Y.2d 329, 405 N.Y.S.2d 649, 376 N.E.2d 1294 (1978).

—The court must balance the competing needs for grand jury secrecy and public access to information for a public purpose; the inviolability of grand jury proceedings will be presumed, and the burden is on the party seeking disclosure to rebut the presumption. *In re* District Attorney of Suffolk County, 86 A.D.2d 294, 449 N.Y.S.2d 1004 (2d Dept. 1982), *aff'd,* 58 N.Y.2d 436, 461 N.Y.S.2d 773, 448 N.E.2d 440 (1983).

Resubmission of charges.—A motion to resubmit may be made *ex parte,* however, if a defendant has testified before a previous grand jury he should, absent compelling circumstances, be given notice of resubmission so as to be given a chance to testify again, and the new additional evidence is not required to meet the standards which justify a new trial after conviction. People v. Ladsen, 111 Misc. 2d 374, 444 N.Y.S.2d 362 (Sup. Ct. N.Y. Co. 1981).

Taking of notes.—Article 6 of the United States Constitution does not extend to the right to take notes of each question presented to a Grand Jury witness nor does it extend to the right to take notes of the answers. People v. Doe, 95 Misc. 2d 175, 406 N.Y.S.2d 650 (Sup. Ct. Albany Co. 1978).

Releasing minutes; court authorized.—Only the court in charge of the Grand Jury is authorized to release the statements from the secrecy requirements of CPL § 190.25(4). New York v. Quigley, 59 A.D.2d 825, 399 N.Y.S.2d 734 (4th Dept. 1977).

Use of grand jury testimony; absence of specific testimony.—Although it was error to receive into evidence, during the People's case-in-chief, the portion of defendant's grand jury testimony in which he acknowledged a prior conviction, such portion of the transcript could have been redacted and the error avoided if defense counsel had brought this matter to the attention of the trial court by means of a specific objection. The absence of a specific objection to the introduction of the prior conviction prevented this court from reviewing the issue. People v. Rullo, 31 N.Y.2d 894, 340 N.Y.S.2d 405, 292 N.E.2d 674 (1972).

—Until such time as defendant serves a notice of alibi the People's motion to unseal the grand jury minutes containing defendant's testimony pertaining to an unrelated incident, which People intended to use in the event the defendant testified and interposed an alibi inconsistent with his prior grand jury testimony, was premature. People v. Lester, 135 Misc. 205, 514 N.Y.S.2d 861, 863 (Sup. Ct. Bronx Co. 1987).

Use of grand jury testimony in civil proceeding.—After weighing the public interest in disclosure against the public interest in Grand Jury secrecy, the court properly refused to permit the defendant in a civil suit to inspect Grand Jury minutes as a discovery device to enable him to prepare his defense. Zinna v. Rensselaer Co. Grand Jury, 63 A.D.2d 800, 404 N.Y.S.2d 1015 (3d Dept. 1978).

—One seeking disclosure must first demonstrate a compelling and particularized need for access. *In re* New York State Temporary Comm'n of Investigation, 155 Misc. 2d 822, 590 N.Y.S.2d 169, 172 (Westchester Co. Ct. 1992).

—Complainants by their demand for the Grand Jury minutes and their expected use of them in pending civil litigation waived the consideration of secrecy usually attached to such records for the benefit of the witnesses testifying before the Grand Jury, and disclosure was allowed to the defendant as well; here the District Attorney presented no facts which indicated that third persons or the public interest would be adversely affected by this disposition. People v. Schittone, 86 Misc. 2d 576, 385 N.Y.S.2d 703 (Sup. Ct. Schenectady Co. 1976).

—The court refused to permit discovery of defendant's testimony before Grand Jury in plaintiff's subsequent civil action for false arrest and malicious prosecution but permitted the trial judge to allow the use of the grand jury testimony for impeachment purposes should the defendant take the stand. Albert v. Zahner's Sales Company, Inc., 81 Misc. 2d 103, 364 N.Y.S.2d 410 (Sup. Ct. Queens Co. 1975), *aff'd,* 51 A.D.2d 541, 378 N.Y.S.2d 414 (1976).

—Where the Administratrix of estate of individual shot by a

policeman sought minutes and exhibits of grand jury proceedings for use in civil action, the court ordered that the grand jury minutes involved be turned over to the custody of the trial justice, who would make the pertinent portions available as witnesses were called to testify at the trial. Such testimony could be used for impeachment, to refresh recollection, or to lead a hostile witness. Herring v. City of Syracuse, 81 Misc. 2d 1060, 367 N.Y.S.2d 698 (Onondaga Co. Ct. 1975).

—Where defendant pleaded guilty to manslaughter, plaintiff in a subsequent wrongful death action by victim's estate was permitted to examine the grand jury minutes since it would result in no interference or prejudice to a pending criminal prosecution and the public policy sought to be protected by the privilege would not be violated. Hopson v. Pinckney, 77 Misc. 2d 391, 353 N.Y.S.2d 664 (Sup. Ct. Suffolk Co. 1974).

Subd. 5

Presumption of regularity.—Defendant challenging grand jury proceeding failed to overcome presumption of regularity; 17 of 18 grand jurors who heard all evidence in continued case were present at time indictment was voted, grand jury minutes had been reviewed by two different judges, and defendant failed to establish that grand jurors were not provided with general instructions advising which jurors were entitled to vote. People v. Grant, 215 A.D.2d 114, 626 N.Y.S.2d 87 (1st Dept. 1995).

The Grand Jury is the sole arbiter of the credibility of witnesses and the weight to be given to evidence. —People v. Gleichmann, 89 Misc. 2d 648, 392 N.Y.S.2d 227 (Nassau Co. Ct. 1977).

Subd. 6

Witness' legal advice to Grand Jury.—Witness' advice to grand jury concerning the law requires dismissal of indictment only if there is some possibility that prejudice to defendant could result. People v. Keller, 214 A.D.2d 825, 625 N.Y.S.2d 325 (3d Dept. 1995).

Failure to record grand jury instructions; dismissal of indictment.—The fact that instructions to the Grand Jury were not recorded will not compel dismissal of an indictment unless it resulted in an impairment of the Grand Jury's integrity and a possibility of prejudice to the defendant. People v. Meachem, 50 A.D.2d 953, 375 N.Y.S.2d 678 (3d Dept. 1975).

—Failure to record instructions given to Grand Jury vitiates the entire Grand Jury proceedings. People v. Percy, 74 Misc. 2d 522, 345 N.Y.S.2d 276 (Suffolk Co. Ct. 1973), *modified*, 45 A.D.2d 284, 358 N.Y.S.2d 434 (2d Dept. 1974), *aff'd*, 38 N.Y.2d 806, 382 N.Y.S.2d 39, 345 N.E.2d 582 (1975).

—CPL § 190.25(6) requires that instructions to the jury made by the court or the District Attorney be recorded. However, in order to constitute a defect under CPL §§ 210.20(1) and 210.35, it must be shown that the failure to conform was "to such degree that the integrity" of the indictment is thereby "impaired and prejudice to the defendant may result." People v. Rallo, 46 A.D.2d 518, 363 N.Y.S.2d 851 (4th Dept. 1975), *aff'd*, 39 N.Y.2d 217, 383 N.Y.S.2d 271 (1976).

Dismissal unnecessary in simple cases.—In uncomplicated cases, if the proof is clear and the charge established, no good purpose will be served in dismissing indictment and requiring resubmission for failure to record the prosecutor's instructions. However, in complex cases where the potential of prejudice is great this procedure is proper. People v. Percy, 45 A.D.2d 284, 358 N.Y.S.2d 434 (2d Dept. 1974), *aff'd*, 38 N.Y.2d 806, 382 N.Y.S.2d 39, 345 N.E.2d 582 (1975).

Grand jury; harmless error.—Any comment by the District Attorney relative to the blood test could be considered harmless in light of the overall facts presented to the grand jury. People v. Flynn, 73 Misc. 2d 178, 340 N.Y.S.2d 837 (Seneca Co. Ct. 1973).

Instructions.—Like a mitigating defense, intoxication only reduces the gravity of the offense by negating an element, and thus, the People were not required to instruct the grand jury on intoxication. People v. Harris, 98 N.Y.2d 452, 749 N.Y.S.2d 766, 779 N.E.2d 705 (2002), *habeas corpus denied*, Harris v. Goord, 2004 LEXIS U.S. Dist. 14017 (E.D.N.Y. July 23, 2004.

—Defendant's claim—that the Grand Jury proceeding was defective due to the prosecutor's reliance on legal instructions given earlier in the day to the same Grand Jury but respect to different cases—was not preserved for review, where the defendant's omnibus motion did not specify that ground for objection

but rather specified another ground. People v. Brown, 81 N.Y.2d 798, 595 N.Y.S.2d 370, 371, 611 N.E.2d 27 (1993).

—An exculpatory defense which would wholly vitiate criminal liability must be charged where the evidence would reasonably support it. People v. Ortiz, 188 A.D.2d 389, 591 N.Y.S.2d 385 (1st Dept. 1992).

—Failure to instruct the Grand Jury on the limited purpose of the evidence of the defendant's prior bad acts and convictions did not warrant dismissal of the indictment. People v. Hardison, 181 A.D.2d 506, 581 N.Y.S.2d 675 (1st Dept. 1992).

—Evidence before grand jury required the district attorney to give a charge on justification, and the failure to do so impaired the integrity of that body to such a degree that defendant may have been prejudiced by an unwarranted prosecution. People v. Samuels, 12 A.D.3d 695, 785 N.Y.S.2d 485 (2d Dept. 2004).

—Court rejected claim that indictment should be dismissed because prosecutor failed to deliver a circumstantial evidence charge; there is no legal requirement that the prosecutor deliver any particular charge to the Grand Jury. People v. McLaurin, 196 A.D.2d 511, 601 N.Y.S.2d 139 (2d Dept. 1993).

—Although it might have been preferable for the People to have instructed the grand jury as to the generally accepted definitions of the term lewd, the word is not so arcane as to escape the understanding of the average juror. People v. Pinkoski, 300 A.D.2d 834, 752 N.Y.S.2d 421 (3d Dept. 2002).

—The prosecutor's duty under CPL § 190.25(6) is satisfied where the Grand Jury has been provided with sufficient information to intelligently determine whether a crime has been committed and whether legally sufficient evidence establishes the material elements thereof; it is not error when the prosecutor fails to read statutory definitions of terms that have an obvious meaning, such as "attempt" and "intent." People v. Levens, 252 A.D.2d 665, 677 N.Y.S.2d 390 (3d Dept. 1998).

—The District Attorney's failure to instruct the Grand Jury about corroboration did not warrant dismissal of the indictment. People v. Vincente, 183 A.D.2d 940, 583 N.Y.S.2d 573 (3d Dept. 1992).

—Instructions to the Grand Jury need not be as precise as those given to a petit jury, but they may not be so misleading or incomplete as to substantially undermine the integrity of the Grand Jury proceedings. People v. Scott, 188 A.D.2d 932, 592 N.Y.S. 2d 94 (3d Dept. 1992).

—A prosecutor must instruct a Grand Jury as to exculpatory but not mitigating defenses. People v. Jones, 157 Misc. 2d 45, 595 N.Y.S.2d 869 (Sup. Ct. Queens Co. 1993).

—Prosecutor was not required to charge the defense of alibi in the Grand Jury. People v. Crump, 157 Misc. 2d 566, 597 N.Y.S.2d 1010 (Westchester Co. Ct. 1993).

—Article 190 of the Criminal Procedure Law contains no provision comparable to CPL § 300.50 specifically setting forth when a prosecutor may or must submit a lesser included offense to the Grand Jury; a Grand Jury need not consider a lesser included offense that a reasonable view of the evidence might support. People v. Crumbaugh, 156 Misc. 2d 782, 594 N.Y.S.2d 553 (Sup. Ct. Bronx Co. 1993).

—Grand Jury should have been instructed on the definition of the term "operates," in reference to a motor vehicle. People v. Dymond, 158 Misc. 2d 677, 601 N.Y.S.2d 1001, 1003 (Greene Co. Ct. 1993).

—It is improper to advise a Grand Jury that indictment of a specific individual is a "now or never" proposition. People v. Dukes, 156 Misc. 2d 386, 592 N.Y.S.2d 220 (Sup. Ct. Kings Co. 1992).

—Prosecutor's failure to instruct Grand Jury that car presumption was rebuttable was not rendered harmless by an instruction to that effect which was given at another juncture. People v. Bacote, 143 Misc. 2d 535, 541 N.Y.S.2d 305 (Sup. Ct. Kings Co. 1989).

Overzealous prosecutor.—There is a paramount judicial responsibility to prevent unfairness in Grand Jury proceedings since the Grand Jury is considered an arm of the court. People v. Lewis, 157 Misc. 2d 937, 599 N.Y.S.2d 777 (Sup. Ct. Kings Co. 1993).

—A Grand Jury has the duty to protect a witness from an overzealous prosecutor to prevent a manipulated perjury entrapment; at any time that the witness feels he is subject to such manipulation he may complain to the foreman, and his attorney and seek a court decision on the alleged infringement. People

v. Doe, 95 Misc. 2d 175, 406 N.Y.S.2d 650 (Sup. Ct. Albany Co. 1978).

Perjury.—Recantations of witnesses did not render the original Grand Jury testimony perjurious. People v. Martin, 195 A.D.2d 293, 600 N.Y.S.2d 220 (1st Dept. 1993).

—When a prosecutor learns of any perjury committed before the Grand Jury, the prosecutor is under a duty to immediately inform the court and defense counsel. People v. Johnson, 156 Misc. 2d 159, 591 N.Y.S.2d 325 (Sup. Ct. N.Y. Co. 1992).

Procedure.—A Grand Jury need not be instructed with the same degree of precision that is required when a petit jury is instructed on the law, it is sufficient if the prosecutor provides the Grand Jury with enough information to enable it intelligently to decide whether a crime has been committed and to determine whether there exists legally sufficient evidence to establish the material elements of the crime; failure to furnish complete instructions regarding the proper legal standard for assessing obscenity did not render the indictment legally defective. People v. Calbud, Inc., 49 N.Y.2d 389, 426 N.Y.S.2d 238, 402 N.E.2d 1140 (1980).

—Prosecutor's responses to jurors questions were proper where the questions concerned matters not in evidence and were not relevant to the inquiry. People v. Collins, 154 A.D.2d 901, 545 N.Y.S.2d 959 (4th Dept. 1989).

Recording Grand Jury proceedings.—Any unrecorded conversation between a prosecutor and a grand juror does not automatically impair the integrity of the grand jury process and create the possibility of prejudice to the defendant. People v. Erceg, 82 A.D.2d 947, 440 N.Y.S.2d 726 (3d Dept. 1981).

—In close case that included a justification charge, grand jury process was impaired because grand jury warden replied to and instructed the grand jury on its authority to reconsider its earlier action, an impairment that was exacerbated by the absence of a record of the colloquy, which is a further violation of CPL § 190.25(6). People v. Shammas, 5 Misc. 3d 702, 785 N.Y.S.2d 874 (Crim. Ct. Kings Co. 2004).

§ 190.30. Grand jury; rules of evidence.

1. Except as otherwise provided in this section, the provisions of article sixty, governing rules of evidence and related matters with respect to criminal proceedings in general, are, where appropriate, applicable to grand jury proceedings.

2. A report or a copy of a report made by a public servant or by a person employed by a public servant or agency who is a physicist, chemist, coroner or medical examiner, firearms identification expert, examiner of questioned documents, fingerprint technician, or an expert or technician in some comparable scientific or professional field, concerning the results of an examination, comparison or test performed by him in connection with a case which is the subject of a grand jury proceeding, may, when certified by such person as a report made by him or as a true copy thereof, be received in such grand jury proceeding as evidence of the facts stated therein.

2-a. When the electronic transmission of a certified report, or certified copy thereof, of the kind described in subdivision two or three-a of this section or a sworn statement or copy thereof, of the kind described in subdivision three of this section results in a written document, such written document may be received in such grand jury proceeding provided that: (a) a transmittal memorandum completed by the person sending the report contains a certification that the report has not been altered and a description of the report specifying the number of pages; and (b) the

person who receives the electronically transmitted document certifies that such document and transmittal memorandum were so received; and (c) a certified report or a certified copy or sworn statement or sworn copy thereof is filed with the court within twenty days following arraignment upon the indictment; and (d) where such written document is a sworn statement or sworn copy thereof of the kind described in subdivision three of this section, such sworn statement or sworn copy thereof is also provided to the defendant or his counsel within twenty days following arraignment upon the indictment.

3. A written or oral statement, under oath, by a person attesting to one or more of the following matters may be received in such grand jury proceeding as evidence of the facts stated therein:

(a) that person's ownership or lawful custody of, or license to occupy, premises, as defined in section 140.00 of the penal law, and of the defendant's lack of license or privilege to enter or remain thereupon;

(b) that person's ownership of, or possessory right in, property, the nature and monetary amount of any damage thereto and the defendant's lack of right to damage or tamper with the property;

(c) that person's ownership or lawful custody of, or license to possess property, as defined in section 155.00 of the penal law, including an automobile or other vehicle, its value and the defendant's lack of superior or equal right to possession thereof;

(d) that person's ownership of a vehicle and the absence of his consent to the defendant's taking, operating, exercising control over or using it;

(e) that person's qualifications as a dealer or other expert in appraising or evaluating a particular type of property, his expert opinion as to the value of a certain item or items of property of that type, and the basis for his opinion;

(f) that person's identity as an ostensible maker, drafter, drawer, endorser or other signator of a written instrument and its falsity within the meaning of section 170.00 of the penal law.

Provided, however, that no such statement shall be admitted when an adversarial examination of such person has been previously ordered pursuant to subdivision 8 of section 180.60, unless a transcript of such examination is admitted.

3-a. A sex offender registration form, sex offender registration continuation/supplemental form, sex offender registry address verification form, sex offender change of address form or a copy of such form maintained by the division of criminal justice services concerning an individual who is the subject of a grand jury proceeding, may, when certified by a person designated by the commissioner of the division of criminal justice services as the person to certify such records, as a true copy thereof, be received in such grand jury proceeding as evidence of the facts stated therein.

4. An examination of a child witness or a special witness by the district attorney videotaped pursuant to section 190.32 of this chapter may be received in evidence in such grand jury proceeding as the testimony of such witness.

5. Nothing in subdivisions two, three or four of this section shall be construed to limit the power of the grand jury to cause any person to be called as a witness pursuant to subdivision three of section 190.50.

6. Wherever it is provided in article sixty that the court in a criminal proceeding must rule upon the competency of a witness to testify or upon the admissibility of evidence, such ruling may, in an equivalent situation in a grand jury proceeding, be made by the district attorney.

7. Whenever it is provided in article sixty that a court presiding at a jury trial must instruct the jury with respect to the significance, legal effect or evaluation of evidence, the district attorney, in an equivalent situation in a grand jury proceeding, may so instruct the grand jury.

Amended by L. 1971, Ch. 797; L. 1975, Ch. 307; L. 1976, Ch. 586; L. 1984, Ch. 804; L. 1985, Ch. 188; L. 1987, Ch. 751; L. 1998, Ch. 360, § 1, eff. Nov. 1, 1998; L. 1999, Ch. 453, §§ 21 and 22, eff. Jan. 1, 2000, amending subds. 2-a and 3-a.

ANNOTATIONS

Instructions.—Given lesser standards for measuring sufficiency of grand jury instructions, instructions given to Grand Jury were adequate regarding investigation of defendants for criminal possession of controlled substance. People v. Dillon, 87 N.Y.2d 885, 639 N.Y.S.2d 1007, 663 N.E.2d 319 (1995).

Laboratory report rather than live testimony.—Statute authorizing submission of certified laboratory report to Grand Jury in place of live testimony of technician who performed tests on controlled substance is limited exception to general prohibition against hearsay in grand jury proceedings, but does not require state to present laboratory report to support indictment for drug offense. People v. Swamp, 84 N.Y.2d 725, 622 N.Y.S.2d 472, 646 N.E.2d 774 (1995).

—Even though chemist's report does not include the phrase "performed by me," it was enough for the chemist to sign the report, signify that he performed the test, and the omission did not render the indictment invalid. People v. Washington, 228 A.D.2d 23, 652 N.Y.S.2d 750 (2d Dept. 1997).

—A report properly certified to insure the "expert both performed the test and made the report" is admissible without technician's testimony, but People should not be allowed to use report to establish facts not related to scientific study performed. People v. Landon, 175 Misc. 2d 861, 670 N.Y.S.2d 968 (Seneca Co. Ct. 1998).

Defendant's prior convictions.—Statute governing defendant's testimony before grand jury envisions that district attorney will make ruling on admissibility of defendant's prior convictions for purpose of impeaching defendant's testimony and that defendant's sole remedy for any prejudicial cross-examination will be motion to dismiss the indictment on ground that integrity of grand jury proceeding was impaired. People v. Thomas, 213 A.D.2d 73, 628 N.Y.S.2d 707 (2d Dept. 1995), aff'd, 88 N.Y.2d 821, 646 N.Y.S.2d 518, 666 N.E.2d 1364 (1996).

Admissibility of evidence.—While general criminal trial evidentiary rules apply to grand jury proceeding, validity of indictment does not turn on mere flaw, error, or skewing of proceeding, and thus receipt of evidence which might not be admissible at trial does not necessarily impair integrity of grand jury proceeding. People v. Diaz, 209 A.D.2d 1, 624 N.Y.S.2d 113 (1st Dept. 1995).

Affidavits.—An affidavit submitted to a Grand Jury pursuant to CPL § 190.30(3), wherein the owner states in conclusory terms the worth of allegedly stolen property and the amount of physical damage to it, without indicating the basis for the valuation, cannot sustain an indictment where value is an element of the offense charged. People v. Lopez, 79 N.Y.2d 402, 583 N.Y.S.2d 356, 592 N.E.2d 1360 (1992).

Brady **material need not be presented.**—The prosecutor was not required to put before the Grand Jury evidence that would have been helpful in overcoming the presumption contained in Penal Law § 265.15(3). People v. Sergeant, 193 A.D.2d 417, 597 N.Y.S.2d 350 (1st Dept. 1993).

—A prosecutor has wide discretion in presenting evidence to the Grand Jury, which may include the decision not to present exculpatory material; of course, in exercising this discretion, the prosecutor must balance the right to present the evidence against the Grand Juror's right to hear the full story. People v. Kaba, 177 A.D.2d 506, 575 N.Y.S.2d 716 (2d Dept. 1991).

—Court correctly denied defendant's motion to dismiss the indictment on the ground that the People should have submitted to the Grand Jury the results of a polygraph examination the complainant allegedly failed since polygraphs are not considered competent evidence at trial. People v. Ricigliano, 138 A.D.2d 751, 526 N.Y.S.2d 565 (2d Dept. 1988).

—The People are not required to present to the Grand Jury all the evidence in their possession that is favorable to the accused. People v. Lloyd, 141 A.D.2d 669, 529 N.Y.S.2d 801 (2d Dept. 1988).

—People need not present all evidence that is favorable to the accused, nor uncover evidence which is helpful to him, nor explore every defense suggested by the evidence, but they must instruct on defenses which may eliminate criminal liability altogether. People v. Nezaj, 139 Misc. 2d 366, 528 N.Y.S.2d 491 (Sup. Ct. Bronx Co. 1988).

—So long as the defendant's counsel is made aware of the exculpatory type evidence and the defendant is afforded the opportunity to have it aired before and weighed by the petit jury, he has not been denied due process in not having this evidence presented to the Grand Jury. People v. Perez, 105 Misc. 2d 845, 433 N.Y.S.2d 541 (Sup. Ct. Bronx Co. 1980).

Competency.—Assistant district attorney is not among those authorized to administer an oath in the Grand Jury to an underage victim witness, and in the absence of an oath properly administered either by the foreman or any other grand juror, the indictment was properly dismissed. People v. Rivers, 145 A.D.2d 319, 534 N.Y.S.2d 986 (1st Dept. 1988).

—A court, as well as the District Attorney, is empowered to pass upon the testimonial capacity of a witness in the Grand Jury. People v. DiFabio, 170 A.D.2d 1028, 566 N.Y.S.2d 172 (4th Dept. 1991).

Death penalty case; no mitigating evidence.—Legislature enacted many changes to the CPL to implement the death penalty, but left the discovery statute unaltered, which indicates "a clear indication that the existing rule is operative in capital cases"; the CPL does not authorize a defendant to present mitigating evidence to the grand jury, and the fact that defendant could face the death penalty does not change the grand jury's function. People v. Campos, 176 Misc. 2d 637, 672 N.Y.S.2d 1001 (Sup. Ct. Kings Co. 1998).

Evidence.—Court erred in concluding that the People were required to present defendant's exculpatory statements to the Grand Jury; they constituted inadmissible hearsay, and evidence is admissible in the grand jury only if it would be admissible at trial. People v. Mitchell, 183 A.D.2d 503, 583 N.Y.S.2d 432 (1st Dept. 1992).

—A prosecutor has wide discretion in presenting evidence to the Grand Jury, which may include the decision not to present exculpatory evidence. People v. Perry, 187 A.D.2d 678, 590 N.Y.S.2d 251 (2d Dept. 1992).

—The People enjoy wide discretion in presenting their case to the Grand Jury; failure to present evidence merely bearing upon credibility of witnesses was not cause for dismissal. People v. Martucci, 153 A.D.2d 866, 545 N.Y.S.2d 385 (2d Dept. 1989).

—The test for determining in what situations the prosecutor is obligated to present exculpatory evidence to the Grand Jury is whether such evidence might materially influence the Grand Jury's investigation. People v. Johnson, 155 Misc. 2d 791, 590 N.Y.S.2d 153 (Sup. Ct. Monroe Co. 1992).

Sale of LSD; sufficiency of grand jury evidence.—Testimony of undercover agent, before Grand Jury, that defendant sold him a tablet containing LSD, together with his testimony about the actual sale, was sufficient circumstantial evidence of the corpus delicti, and it was not necessary to introduce the tablet into evidence. People v. Peluso, 29 N.Y.2d 605, 324 N.Y.S.2d 404, 273 N.E.2d 134 (1971).

Grand jury proceeding; defendant's right to silence.—A defendant in a criminal proceeding may testify in his own behalf but failure to testify is not a factor from which any inference unfavorable to him may be drawn and no allusion may be made thereto, CPL § 60.15(2); this rule of evidence is also applicable to grand jury proceedings, CPL § 190.30(1). People v. Scott, 70 A.D.2d 601, 416 N.Y.S.2d 83 (2d Dept. 1979).

Grand jury subpoena; confidential relationship.—Federal statute concerning the confidentiality of records and information of patients being treated in methadone programs prohibited the disclosure of the pictures of patients in the program to the police who were investigating a homicide allegedly committed by a patient in the program. People v. Newman, 32 N.Y.2d 379, 345 N.Y.S.2d 502 (1973), *cert. denied*, 414 U.S. 814 (1975).

Grand Jury; presumption of regularity.—In his motion to dismiss the indictment defendant cannot successfully urge surmise and supposition upon the court and ask it to conclude that the Grand Jury corruptly acted or corruptly failed to act when defendants refuse to submit whatever evidence they may have concerning official misconduct to the Grand Jury. The court can only presume that the Grand Jury, as long as it remains sitting, shall take and act upon evidence in conformity with its oath and obligation. People v. John, 76 Misc. 2d 582, 350 N.Y.S.2d 44 (Erie Co. Sup. Ct. 1973).

Instructions.—Given lesser standards for measuring sufficiency of grand jury instructions, instructions given to Grand Jury were adequate regarding investigation of defendants for criminal possession of controlled substance. People v. Dillon, 87 N.Y.2d 885, 639 N.Y.S.2d 1007, 663 N.E.2d 319 (1995).

—It is not permissible for a District Attorney to inform grand jurors, who by statute and the Constitution, have the unique responsibility to decide whether to vote an indictment, that as a matter of law the prosecutor has already determined that there is enough evidence to warrant that action. People v. Batashure, 75 N.Y.2d 306, 552 N.Y.S.2d 896, 552 N.E.2d 144 (1990).

—Prosecutor's failure to charge the Grand Jury with respect to the complete defense of agency necessitated dismissal of the indictment. People v. Jenkins, 157 A.D.2d 854, 550 N.Y.S.2d 736, 737 (2d Dept. 1990).

—Due to the simple nature of the facts, it was not prejudicial error for the prosecutor to instruct the Grand Jury merely by reading the statutes defining reckless endangerment, first degree, and the defense of justification. People v. Banner, 59 A.D.2d 621, 398 N.Y.S.2d 168 (2d Dept. 1977).

—Although it might have been preferable for the People to have instructed the grand jury as to the generally accepted definitions of the term lewd, the word is not so arcane as to escape the understanding of the average juror. People v. Pinkoski, 300 A.D.2d 834, 752 N.Y.S.2d 421 (3d Dept. 2002).

—Defendant waived his claim that the prosecutor erroneously failed to give limiting instructions to the Grand Jury concerning evidence of defendant's prior convictions by his failure to move to dismiss the indictment on that ground. People v. Brooks, 163 A.D.2d 864, 558 N.Y.S.2d 768 (4th Dept. 1990).

—Instruction on the rebuttable nature of the statutory presumption pertaining to the possession of a weapon in a vehicle was not required where the defendant did not testify in the Grand Jury. People v. Wilt, 155 A.D.2d 895, 547 N.Y.S.2d 490 (4th Dept. 1989).

Photographic identification.—Evidence before the Grand Jury was sufficient to sustain an indictment where the complaining witness stated that she had identified the defendant, notwithstanding that it was not revealed that such identification was made from photographs. People v. Brewster, 63 N.Y.2d 419, 482 N.Y.S.2d 724, 472 N.E.2d 686 (1984).

—Since photographic identification evidence may now be used in Grand Jury proceedings, witness's mention in Grand Jury that he had previously identified defendant by photograph did not violate the integrity of the proceedings. People v. Diaz, 107 A.D.2d 706, 484 N.Y.S.2d 60 (2d Dept. 1985).

Preliminary hearing; hearsay evidence; sworn statements.—At a preliminary hearing on a felony complaint the court may require the testimony and cross-examination of the complainant, notwithstanding the fact that such complainant had submitted sworn statements in accordance with the provisions of CPL § 190.30(3), where the complainant is actually present to give testimony in open court. People v. Staton, 94 Misc. 2d 1002, 406 N.Y.S.2d 242 (Crim. Ct. Bronx Co. 1978).

Reviewability on appeal.—Defendant's claim that the laboratory reports presented to the grand jury failed to meet the requirements of CPL § 190.30(2) and that the evidence was insufficient is not reviewable on appeal from a judgment of conviction. People v. Caldwell, 245 A.D.2d 89, 666 N.Y.S.2d 133 (1st Dept. 1997).

Subpoena.—A subpoena requiring an attorney to appear before a Grand Jury and produce records concerning the fee arrangements with a defendant should be enforced upon a showing by the People of the relevance of the material sought, no reasonable and legally sufficient alternative source, and good faith in issuing the subpoena. *In re* Grand Jury Subpoena of Stewart, 144 Misc. 2d 1012, 545 N.Y.S.2d 974, 976 (Sup. Ct. N.Y. Co. 1989).

—A grand jury subpoena is presumptively valid and can be quashed only when the recipient proves that the materials subpoenaed have no relation to the matter under investigation. People v. Patel, 144 Misc. 2d 59, 542 N.Y.S.2d 906 (Sup. Ct. Bronx Co. 1989).

—A Grand Jury subpoena is presumptively valid and even on a motion to quash, there is no burden on the Grand Jury to set forth reasons for its issuance. *In re* Grand Jury Applications, 142 Misc. 2d 241, 536 N.Y.S.2d 939 (Sup. Ct. N.Y. Co. 1988).

§ 190.32. Videotaped examination; definitions, application, order and procedure.

1. Definitions. As used in this section:

(a) "Child witness" means a person twelve years old or less whom the people intend to call as witness in a grand jury proceeding to give evidence concerning any crime defined in article one hundred thirty or two hundred sixty or section 255.25 of the penal law of which the person was a victim.

(b) "Special witness" means a person whom the people intend to call as a witness in a grand jury proceeding and who is either:

(i) Unable to attend and testify in person in the grand jury proceeding because the person is either physically ill or incapacitated; or

(ii) More than twelve years old and who is likely to suffer very severe emotional or mental stress if required to testify in person concerning any crime defined in article one hundred thirty or two hundred sixty or section 255.25 of the penal law to which the person was a witness or of which the person was a victim.

(c) "Operator" means a person employed by the district attorney who operates the video camera to record the examination of a child witness or a special witness.

2. In lieu of requiring a witness who is a child witness to appear in person and give evidence in a grand jury proceeding, the district attorney may cause the examination of such witness to be

videotaped in accordance with the provisions of subdivision five of this section.

3. Whenever the district attorney has reason to believe that a witness is a special witness, he may make an *ex parte* application to the court for an order authorizing the videotaping of an examination of such special witness and the subsequent introduction in evidence in a grand jury proceeding of that videotape in lieu of the live testimony of such special witness. The application must be in writing, must state the grounds of the application and must contain sworn allegations of fact, whether of the district attorney or another person or persons, supporting such grounds. Such allegations may be based upon personal knowledge of the deponent or upon information and belief, provided, that in the latter event, the sources of such information and the grounds for such belief are stated.

4. If the court is satisfied that a witness is a special witness, it shall issue an order authorizing the videotaping of such special witness in accordance with the provisions of subdivision five of this section. The court order and the application and all supporting papers shall not be disclosed to any person except upon further court order.

5. The videotaping of an examination either of a child witness or a special witness shall proceed as follows:

(a) An examination of a child witness or a special witness which is to be videotaped pursuant to this section may be conducted anywhere and at any time provided that the operator begins the videotape by recording a statement by the district attorney of the date, time and place of the examination. In addition, the district attorney shall identify himself, the operator and all other persons present.

(b) An accurate clock with a sweep second hand shall be placed next to or behind the witness in such position as to enable the operator to videotape the clock and the witness together during the entire examination. In the alternative, a date and time generator shall be used to superimpose the day, hour, minute and second over the video portion of the recording during the entire examination.

(c) A social worker, rape crisis counselor, psychologist or other professional providing emotional support to a child witness or to a special witness, as defined in subparagraph (ii) of paragraph (b) of subdivision one of this section, or any of those persons enumerated in paragraphs (a), (b), (c), (d), (e), (f) and (g) of subdivision three of section 190.25 may be present during the videotaping except that a doctor, nurse or other medical assistant also may be present if required by the attendant circumstances. Each person present, except the witness, must, if he has not previously taken a constitutional oath of office or an oath that he will keep secret all matters

before a grand jury, must take an oath on the record that he will keep secret the videotaped examination.

(d) The district attorney shall state for the record the name of the witness, and the caption and the grand jury number, if any, of the case. If the witness to be examined is a child witness, the date of the witness' birth must be recorded. If the witness to be examined is a special witness, the date of the order authorizing the videotaped examination and the name of the justice who issued the order shall be recorded.

(e) If the witness will give sworn testimony, the administration of the oath must be recorded. If the witness will give unsworn testimony, a statement that the testimony is not under oath must be recorded.

(f) If the examination requires the use of more than one tape, the operator shall record a statement of the district attorney at the end of each tape declaring that such tape has ended and referring to the succeeding tape. At the beginning of such succeeding tape, the operator shall record a statement of the district attorney identifying himself, the witness being examined and the number of tapes which have been used to record the examination of such witness. At the conclusion of the examination the operator shall record a statement of the district attorney certifying that the recording has been completed, the number of tapes on which the recording has been made and that such tapes constitute a complete and accurate record of the examination of the witness.

(g) A videotape of an examination conducted pursuant to this section shall not be edited unless upon further order of the court.

6. When the videotape is introduced in evidence and played in the grand jury, the grand jury stenographer shall record the examination in the same manner as if the witness had testified in person.

7. Custody of the videotape shall be maintained in the same manner as custody of the grand jury minutes.

Added L. 1984, Ch. 804; **Amended** by L. 1995, Ch. 91, § 1, eff. June 28,

ANNOTATIONS

Failure to comply with statute.—People's failure to comply with the technical requirements of CPL § 190.32—specifically, failing to record the date of the order authorizing the videotaping procedure and the name of the issuing judge—did not require dismissal of the indictment where, as here, defense counsel was provided with a copy of the order. People v. Smith, 289 A.D.2d 1056, 735 N.Y.S.2d 693 (4th Dept. 2001).

Secrecy principles.—Secrecy principles governing conduct of personal grand jury appearances and proceedings apply with equal force to videotaped examinations. People v. Sayavong, 83 N.Y.2d 702, 613 N.Y.S.2d 343, 635 N.E.2d 1213 (1994).

—Person whose presence at grand jury proceedings seriously threatens any goal of bedrock secrecy requirement governing such proceedings cannot be authorized to attend grand jury proceedings under aegis of statutory provision for which that person may technically qualify. People v. Sayavong, 83 N.Y.2d 702, 613 N.Y.S.2d 343, 635 N.E.2d 1213 (1994).

§ 190.35. Grand jury; definitions of terms.

The term definitions contained in section 50.10 are applicable to sections 190.40, 190.45 and 190.50.

§ 190.40. Grand jury; witnesses, compulsion of evidence and immunity.

1. Every witness in a grand jury proceeding must give any evidence legally requested of him regardless of any protest or belief on his part that it may tend to incriminate him.

2. A witness who gives evidence in a grand jury proceeding receives immunity unless:

(a) He has effectively waived such immunity pursuant to section 190.45; or

(b) Such evidence is not responsive to any inquiry and is gratuitously given or volunteered by the witness with knowledge that it is not responsive.

(c) The evidence given by the witness consists only of books, papers, records or other physical evidence of an enterprise, as defined in subdivision one of section 175.00 of the penal law, the production of which is required by a subpoena duces tecum, and the witness does not possess a privilege against self-incrimination with respect to the production of such evidence. Any further evidence given by the witness entitles the witness to immunity except as provided in subparagraphs (a) and (b) of this subdivision.

Amended by L. 1975, Ch. 454.

ANNOTATIONS

Fair trial; defendant not deprived.—Defendant was not deprived of fair trial by prosecution's refusal to grant immunity to defense witness even though another witness was granted immunity as a matter of law when he testified before grand jury. People v. Sipley, 209 A.D.2d 864, 619 N.Y.S.2d 216 (3d Dept. 1994).

—Defendant was not denied fair trial by prosecution's failure to disclose grant of immunity to its informant witness, where defendant was fully aware that informant had testified at first trial, on which occasion defendant had been furnished with copy of witness' grand jury testimony which demonstrated that witness did not execute waiver of immunity and answered responsively to all questions so received automatic immunity, and it was abundantly clear to jury that prosecution had agreed not to prosecute informant witness for prior criminal acts which were disclosed during extensive and searching cross-examination by defense counsel. People v. Barrett, 168 A.D.2d 800, 564 N.Y.S.2d 506 (3d Dept. 1990).

Disclosure.—Fact that witness had testified before Grand Jury which later indicted defendant, and that witness consequently received immunity from prosecution by operation of law, was not equivalent to prosecution making "secret deal" which was required to be revealed to defense. People v. Wooley, 200 A.D.2d 644, 606 N.Y.S.2d 738 (2d Dept. 1994).

Appellate review.—Defendant failed to preserve for appellate review issue that indictment against him should have been dismissed because he did not effectively waive immunity when he testified before Grand Jury where defendant never made motion to dismiss indictment on that ground either before or at trial. People v. Allen, 163 A.D.2d 396, 558 N.Y.S.2d 121 (2d Dept. 1990).

Appealability of order.—No appeal lay from the order of the Extraordinary Special and Trial Term of the Supreme Court denying petitioner's application to compel the Special State Prosecutor to inquire of Federal authorities as to whether they had conducted electronic surveillance of him and for the prosecutor to state whether the questions asked him before the Grand Jury were the product of any such surveillance. In the *In re* Santangello, 38 N.Y.2d 536, 381 N.Y.S.2d 472, 344 N.E.2d 404 (1976).

—A witness subject to a subpoena ad testificandum cannot raise an issue of privilege until he has actually appeared and been questioned. People v. Doe, 61 A.D.2d 426, 403 N.Y.S.2d 375 (4th Dept. 1978).

Child-parent communications.—Four fundamental conditions must be established in order for the child-parent communications privilege to arise (1) the communications must originate in confidence that they will not be disclosed; (2) this element of confidentiality must be essential to the full and satisfactory maintenance of the relation between the parties; (3) the relation must be one which, in the opinion of society, ought to be sedulously fostered; and (4) the injury that would inure to the relation by the disclosure of the communication must be greater than the benefit thereby gained for the correct disposal of litigation. People v. Doe, 61 A.D.2d 426, 403 N.Y.S.2d 375 (4th Dept. 1978).

Corporate officer or employee.—A corporate officer or employee is required to produce the corporate books or records pursuant to a subpoena duces tecum and is required to testify before the Grand Jury as to the identify of the books and records produced without gaining immunity from prosecution even if the documents would tend to incriminate him personally; however, if the corporate officer or employee, while testifying before the Grand Jury is compelled to answer questions, pursuant to CPL § 190.40, which would incriminate him as an individual then defendant's answers to these inquiries had afford him immunity from prosecution. People v. Lachlan, 58 A.D.2d 586, 395 N.Y.S.2d 106 (2d Dept. 1977).

Eavesdropping evidence.—Where the district attorney had already answered the crucial question as to electronic surveillance before the witness in open court prior to the appearance before the Grand Jury, and the court had not seen fit to make further inquiry, there was no purpose to be served by interrupting the proceedings for a further appearance before the judge. People v. Langella, 82 Misc. 2d 410, 370 N.Y.S.2d 381 (Sup. Ct. N.Y. Co. 1975).

Extent of immunity in other states.—Defendant, who testified before a New York State Grand Jury under a grant of immunity concerning possible criminal acts in New Jersey, received "transactional" immunity in New York State but only "use" immunity under the Fifth Amendment in New Jersey. People v. Lev, 91 Misc. 2d 241, 398 N.Y.S.2d 593 (Sup. Ct. Bronx Co. 1977).

Failure to give *Miranda* warnings to Grand Jury witness no bar to prosecution for perjury.—Defendant, as a witness before the Grand Jury was entitled to the protection of the Fifth Amendment, but the privilege against self-incrimination relates to past criminal acts and not to future acts such as perjury. People v. Robinson, 66 Misc. 2d 639, 323 N.Y.S.2d 573 (Sup. Ct. 1971).

Grand Jury; immunity.—Where defendant's refusal to answer Grand Jury questions after being granted immunity was based on his constitutional privilege against self-incrimination, he could not contend on appeal of his contempt conviction that the Grand Jury questions were based on information derived from unauthorized electronic eavesdropping. People v. Gentile, 39 N.Y.2d 779, 385 N.Y.S.2d 284, 350 N.E.2d 615 (1976).

—Police officers gained no immunity before the Grand Jury, when they stated before the Grand Jury, under no threat of forfeiture of their public office, that they knowingly and voluntarily waived immunity after receiving advice from counsel, and neither made any statement against self-incrimination, he could not contend on appeal of his contempt conviction that the Grand Jury questions were based on information derived from unauthorized electronic eavesdropping. People v. Gentile, 39 N.Y.2d 779, 385 N.Y.S.2d 284, 350 N.E.2d 615 (1976).

—Reversal was warranted when defendant was not granted immunity for his testimony before a grand jury that related to crimes for which he was subsequently convicted. People v. Pardo, 81 A.D.2d 530, 438 N.Y.S.2d 85 (1st Dept. 1981).

—Court properly concluded that defendant was under oath when he acknowledged that it was his signature that appeared on the written waiver introduced in evidence at the Grand Jury proceeding, and that the statutory requirement that a waiver of immunity must be sworn to before the Grand Jury was thus satisfied. People v. Cole, 196 A.D.2d 634, 601 N.Y.S.2d 352, 354 (2d Dept. 1993).

—Defendant did not receive immunity where the records which he provided, pursuant to subpoena duces tecum, were never presented to the Grand Jury. People v. Blum, 132 A.D.2d 933, 518 N.Y.S.2d 482 (4th Dept. 1987).

—A defendant may be granted partial immunity for testifying before the grand jury. People v. Davis, 173 Misc. 2d 358, 660 N.Y.S.2d 964 (Sup. Ct. Nassau Co. 1997).

—A dispositional order could not be entered where the juvenile, who had admitted committing an act of delinquency in an Article 7 delinquency proceeding, subsequently was compelled to testify before a Grand Jury concerning the same incident. In re Jaime T., 96 Misc. 2d 173, 408 N.Y.S.2d 901 (Fam. Ct. N.Y.C. 1978).

—The giving of defendant's address when he turned over the subpoenaed records to the Grand Jury did not constitute "further evidence"; the statute contemplates "further evidence" that is self-incriminatory. People v. Zelmanowicz, 93 Misc. 2d 491, 403 N.Y.S.2d 663 (Sup. Ct. Bronx Co. 1978).

—A defendant is entitled to a plenary determination of a timely pretrial motion to suppress made in the course of a proceeding in which he is charged with criminal contempt based upon his refusal to answer questions before the Grand Jury previously asserted by him to be derived from unlawful electronic surveillance (CPL § 210.20[1][h]); pretrial findings in the defendant's favor must abort the prosecution. People v. Lopez, 91 Misc. 2d 157, 397 N.Y.S.2d 1010 (Sup. Ct. N.Y. Co. 1977).

—Where defendant testified in a Grand Jury proceeding that he understood the concepts of immunity, perjury, and contempt, as well as the scope of the immunity, he was not permitted to avail himself (in a prosecution for criminal contempt) of the defense that the explanation of "transactional immunity" was inadequate, especially where defendant was represented and advised by counsel. People v. Breindel, 73 Misc. 2d 734, 342 N.Y.S.2d 428 (Sup. Ct. N.Y. Co. 1973), aff'd, 45 A.D.2d 691, 356 N.Y.S.2d 626, aff'd, 35 N.Y.2d 928, 356 N.Y.S.2d 163, 324 N.E.2d 545 (1974).

Grand Jury; obligation to appear.—The obligation to come forth with evidence before a Grand Jury is not dependent upon a prospective witness or his attorney being informed of the scope of the investigation; if public disclosure of the nature of an investigation by the Grand Jury or the identity of the persons under investigation were mandated, the very function of the Grand Jury would be undermined. Additional January 1979 Grand Jury of the Albany Supreme Court v. Doe, 50 N.Y.2d 14, 427 N.Y.S.2d 950, 405 N.E.2d 194 (1980).

Grand Jury; scope of immunity.—Witness before a Grand Jury was entitled to insist that he be brought before a judge to obtain an authoritative ruling as to whether the requested testimony would entitle him to immunity against violation of probation. People v. Moschelle, 96 Misc. 2d 1030, 410 N.Y.S.2d 764 (Sup. Ct. Suffolk Co. 1978).

Grand Jury; scope of immunity; responsiveness of answers.—Dismissal of the pending indictment charging defendant with selling drugs on June 4, 1974, was required where the defendant, while testifying under a grant of immunity on December 18, 1974, had been compelled to confess before the Grand Jury that her past means of support, until June 4, 1974, was the sale of drugs. People v. McFarlan, 89 Misc. 2d 905, 396 N.Y.S.2d 559 (Sup. Ct. N.Y. Co. 1975), aff'd, 42 N.Y.2d 896, 397 N.Y.S.2d 1003, 366 N.E.2d 1357.

—The limitation of the scope of the immunity that is afforded under CPL § 190.40 with regard to answers that are "responsive" does not violate the Due Process Clause of the Fourteenth Amendment on the ground of vagueness. The statute is not a penal statute nor a trap for the unwary, but a legal barrier to witnesses who intentionally give information not sought in an effort to frustrate and prevent criminal prosecution. People v. Breindel, 73 Misc. 2d 734, 342 N.Y.S.2d 428 (Sup. Ct. N.Y. Co. 1973).

Grand Jury; claim of justification; refusal to answer questions.—For a Grand Jury witness to claim the defense of justification the impending injury to the witness must clearly outweigh the injury sought to be prevented by the PL § 35.05

namely, the loss of Grand Jury testimony. Fuhrer v. Hynes, 72 A.D.2d 813, 421 N.Y.S.2d 906 (2d Dept. 1979).

Grand Jury; eavesdropping.—A request during the Grand Jury proceeding by the witness that he be brought before the court must be respected and once there the Presiding Justice may make appropriate inquiry whether the witness's objection is sound and the court may, in its discretion interrogate the prosecutor under oath, either in camera or in open court, whether or not the basis for the questioning of the witness was founded on illegally obtained wiretap evidence. People v. Einhorn, 35 N.Y.2d 948, 365 N.Y.S.2d 171, 324 N.E.2d 551 (1974).

Grand Jury proceedings.—Wife may not be compelled to testify before grand jury regarding conversations with or instructions given her by her husband in connection with his business and business records or regarding communications and records which were not received from or subsequently sent to third parties. In re Doe, 90 Misc. 2d 812, 396 N.Y.S.2d 145 (Oneida Co. Ct. 1977).

Grand Jury testimony; legality of eavesdropping; no bearing on matter.—Where a witness before the grand jury refused to answer questions until a hearing was granted on the issue of the legality of eavesdropping, no hearing was required where the electronic eavesdropping had been authorized by court order. In re George, 74 Misc. 2d 359, 343 N.Y.S.2d 471 (Sup. Ct. N.Y. Co. 1973).

Grand Jury; eavesdropping, motion to suppress.—Defendant, served subsequent to his grand jury appearance with notice that he had been subjected to prior electronic surveillance, was not entitled to a suppression hearing during pendency of the grand jury proceedings; and failure of the prosecutor, during proceedings prior to trial, to answer defendant's questions concerning the surveillance was no defense to his concept change for refusal to answer questions, since he had been granted "transactional immunity," People v. Breindel, 73 Misc. 2d 734, 342 N.Y.S.2d 428 (Sup. Ct. N.Y. Co. 1973), aff'd, 45 A.D.2d 691, 356 N.Y.S.2d 626, aff'd, 35 N.Y.2d 928, 365 N.Y.S.2d 163, 324 N.E.2d 545 (1974).

Grand Jury witness; right to waive immunity; presence of counsel.—Witness in a Grand Jury investigation of death has no absolute statutory right to waive immunity and thereby have counsel accompany witness before Grand Jury, but must accept automatic grant of transactional immunity, provided under CPL § 190.40, and answer questions without having attorney present; witness failing to do so adjudged in contempt of court. People v. Bowers, 78 A.D.2d 190, 434 N.Y.S.2d 68 (4th Dept. 1980).

Handwriting exemplars.—Involuntary production by the defendant of handwriting exemplars before the Grand Jury pursuant to a subpoena ad testificandum, was sufficient to inadvertently confer immunity pursuant to CPL § 190.40. People v. Perri, 72 A.D.2d 106, 423 N.Y.S.2d 674 (2d Dept. 1980).

—A court ordered handwriting exemplar will be authorized (1) when, in the interest of justice, or when in the interest of public or private safety, it is necessary to determine authorship, validity, or authenticity of a questioned handwritten instrument or document and (2) when it appears that an identifiable person, or persons, have exercised such control over and have had such access to the questioned instruments that there is probable cause to believe that such person, or persons, wrote or authored the questioned documents; however, the court is required to make a factual determination upon notice to all parties to determine the reasonableness and constitutional validity of the requested submission of an identifiable and known exemplar. In re Special Prosecutor (Onondaga Co.) v. G.W., 95 Misc. 2d 298, 407 N.Y.S.2d 112 (Sup. Ct. Onondaga Co. 1978).

Identification of defendant.—Prior photographic identification is admissible at the Grand Jury since any likelihood of irreparable misidentification in the photographic selection may be adequately addressed in pretrial and trial proceedings. People v. Ball, 89 A.D.2d 353, 455 N.Y.S.2d 444 (4th Dept. 1982).

Interruption; Grand Jury proceedings.—The interruption procedure announced by the Court of Appeals seems to specifically limit the judge to a ruling on three grounds: the pertinency of the questions; the extent of the witnesses' immunity from prosecution for a prior offense; and the merit of a claimed testimonial privilege. In re Di Cocco, 80 Misc. 2d 854, 364 N.Y.S.2d 990 (Sup. Ct. Schenectady Co. 1975).

Joint income tax returns sought by Grand Jury.—Grand

Jury witness was not justified in refusing to submit income tax returns on the ground that they were joint returns signed by the witness and his wife as the question of privilege is personal to each individual and may be raised only by the aggrieved party and since the witness' wife has not appeared any right that she may have in her own name will have no bearing on the validity of the subpoena affecting the respondent in the present action. Hynes v. Doe, 101 Misc. 2d 350, 420 N.Y.S.2d 978 (Queens Co. 1979).

Motion to quash.—Order quashing subpoena duces tecum was reversed since neither the disclosure law, the Fourth Amendment, nor the public interest privilege may be properly relied upon to shield production of financial disclosure statements, filed with the Suffolk County Board of Public Disclosure by a Suffolk County Public Official. People v. Doe, 84 A.D.2d 182, 445 N.Y.S.2d 768 (2d Dept. 1981).

—A subpoena *duces tecum* issued by the Grand Jury for medical and psychiatric records pursuant to a Medicare fraud investigation will not be quashed on Fifth Amendment grounds; however, extent of records released must be limited by *in camera* inspection in order to minimize the public exposure of otherwise privileged information between physician and patient. Y, M.D., P.C. v. Kuriansky, 113 A.D.2d 49, 495 N.Y.S.2d 365 (1st Dept. 1985).

—The application to quash a Grand Jury subpoena on the basis of a claimed parent-child privilege was premature; a witness cannot raise the issue of privilege until the witness actually appears and is questioned. *In re* Grand Jury Subpoena No. 2573/85, 111 A.D.2d 891, 491 N.Y.S.2d 29 (2d Dept. 1985).

Necessity to bring witness before the court.—Although in the summary proceedings a witness must be brought before the court and directed to answer before he is held in contempt, it is not a prerequisite to a charge of criminal contempt before the Grand Jury (PL § 215.51), however, the taking of the witness before the court may reduce stalling tactics and expedite the proceeding. People v. Rappaport, 47 N.Y.2d 308, 418 N.Y.S.2d 306, 391 N.E.2d 1284 (1979).

Order of witnesses.—The order in which witnesses appear before the grand jury is a matter of procedure and the court can require that the people's witnesses be presented to the grand jury before the person about to be charged appears pursuant to his own request. Morgenthau v. Altman, 58 N.Y.2d 1057, 462 N.Y.S.2d 629, 449 N.E.2d 409 (1983).

Parole revocation.—Since parole revocation procedures are not criminal in nature, the immunity granted to a witness before a Grand Jury, pursuant to CPL § 190.40 as defined in CPL § 50.10(1), does not extend to proceedings to revoke parole. *In re* Dellacroce, 91 Misc. 2d 755, 398 N.Y.S.2d 811 (Sup. Ct. Suffolk Co. 1977).

Records of school custodian.—School records maintained by school custodian were records of the Board of Education, the employing institution, and were not custodian's personal property subject to his personal privilege against self-incrimination; the custodian was required to maintain the records with respect to public moneys received and disbursed by him. Cappetta v. Santucci, 42 N.Y.2d 1066, 399 N.Y.S.2d 638, 369 N.E.2d 1172 (1977).

Refusal to produce subpoenaed records; witness statement.—Where a witness fails to comply with a subpoena duces tecum on advice of counsel and wishes to make a statement, substantial justice can be done by allowing the witness to simply state on the record that he has failed to produce the required documents on the grounds of legal privilege; at most, he can give a simple statement as to the nature of this privilege but he has no right to go into the factual basis and the matter can then be immediately brought "into open court for a ruling." Hynes v. Doe, 101 Misc. 2d 350, 420 N.Y.S.2d 978 (Queens Co. 1979).

Right to call witness; information available elsewhere.—It is for the Grand Jury to determine; the most efficacious procedure to carry out its investigation, and even assuming the Grand Jury could have obtained the answers to its stated questions from an alternate source, it was entitled to hear such answers from the witness and probe further into the facts so revealed if it deemed more extensive inquiry necessary to carry out its function. Keenan v. Gigante, 47 N.Y.2d 160, 417 N.Y.S.2d 226, 390 N.E.2d 1151 (1979).

Right to consult attorney.—In a proper case, the refusal to allow a defendant to see his lawyer outside the Grand Jury

room may result in dismissal; however the cases which sanction dismissal, all deal with contempt rather than perjury. People v. Lev, 91 Misc. 2d 241, 398 N.Y.S.2d 593 (Sup. Ct. Bronx Co. 1977).

Scope of immunity; conspiracy continuing before and after Grand Jury testimony.—Defendant was entitled to full immunity as to count in the indictment charging conspiracy, fourth degree, where such conspiracy was ongoing, with overt acts alleged both before and after his Grand Jury testimony; the people could not prove the conspiracy by presenting evidence dealing only with defendant's acts committed after his testimony since the elements of proof in the case were so intermingled that proof of past acts would invariably enter the picture and contaminate the present acts. People v. Lieberman, 93 Misc. 2d 655, 405 N.Y.S.2d 559 (Sup. Ct. Queens Co. 1978), *aff'd,* 44 N.Y.2d 863, 407 N.Y.S.2d 694, 379 N.E.2d 220 (1978).

Scope of immunity; criminal acts committed after Grand Jury testimony.—The immunity granted to a Grand Jury witness pursuant to CPL § 190.40 extends only to present criminality, and thus where an indictment charges the defendant with crimes committed after his testimony, he received no immunity from prosecution. People v. Lieberman, 93 Misc. 2d 655, 405 N.Y.S.2d 559 (Sup. Ct. Queens Co. 1978), *aff'd,* 44 N.Y.2d 863, 407 N.Y.S.2d 694, 379 N.E.2d 220 (1978).

Special witness.—Court properly found that the victim was a special witness, where the prosecutor identified the victim's psychiatrist as the source of his information concerning the victim's physical condition and informed the court of the psychiatrist's opinion with respect to the condition, and there is no evidence that there were unauthorized persons present during the videotaping of the victim's grand jury testimony. People v. Smith, 289 A.D.2d 1056, 735 N.Y.S.2d 693 (4th Dept. 2001).

Statute of limitations.—Statute of limitations does not bar a grand jury investigation nor furnish an excuse for a witness's refusal to give evidence before a grand jury. Johnson v. Keenan, 58 A.D.2d 756, 396 N.Y.S.2d 232 (1st Dept. 1977).

Transactional immunity.—In determining whether there is a sufficient nexus between the prior testimony and the subject crime, so that the witness is conferred with transactional immunity, "it is 'the context of the circumstances which ultimately governs.'" People v. McKenna, 250 A.D.2d 240, 685 N.Y.S.2d 110 (3d Dept. 1998).

Waiver of immunity.—The defendants did not effectively waive immunity before the Grand Jury where the waivers were executed by the defendants prior to their being placed under oath and the defendants were not questioned about their waivers after being sworn. People v. Goldson, 145 A.D.2d 982, 536 N.Y.S.2d 353 (4th Dept. 1988).

Witness; application to "cancel and vacate" subpoenas.—A witness may not delay the Grand Jury proceedings by an application to "cancel and vacate" a Grand Jury subpoena but must await the formal accusation of contempt and service of the required notice. Then he may appropriately inquire whether the questions asked by the Grand Jury were based upon an improperly issued electronic surveillance order and if they were, he can not be convicted for his refusal to answer. *In re* O'Brien, 76 Misc. 2d 303, 350 N.Y.S.2d 498 (Rockland Co. Ct. 1973).

§ 190.45. Grand jury; waiver of immunity.

1. A waiver of immunity is a written instrument subscribed by a person who is or is about to become a witness in a grand jury proceeding, stipulating that he waives his privilege against self-incrimination and any possible or prospective immunity to which he would otherwise become entitled, pursuant to section 190.40, as a result of giving evidence in such proceeding.

2. A waiver of immunity is not effective unless and until it is sworn to before the grand jury conducting the proceeding in which the subscriber has been called as a witness.

3. A person who is called by the people as a witness in a grand jury proceeding and requested by the district attorney to subscribe and swear to a waiver of immunity before giving evidence has a right to confer with counsel before deciding whether he will comply with such request, and, if he desires to avail himself of such right, he must be accorded a reasonable time in which to obtain and confer with counsel for such purpose. The district attorney must inform the witness of all such rights before obtaining his execution of such a waiver of immunity. Any waiver obtained, subscribed or sworn to in violation of the provisions of this subdivision is invalid and ineffective.

4. If a grand jury witness subscribes and swears to a waiver of immunity upon a written agreement with the district attorney that the interrogation will be limited to certain specified subjects, matters or areas of conduct, and if after the commencement of his testimony he is interrogated and testifies concerning another subject, matter or area of conduct not included in such written agreement, he receives immunity with respect to any further testimony which he may give concerning such other subject, matter or area of conduct and the waiver of immunity is to that extent ineffective.

Amended by L. 1974, Ch. 761.

ANNOTATIONS

Waiver.—By waiving the right to immunity, defendant who testifies before grand jury necessarily gives up Fifth Amendment privilege against self-incrimination. People v. Smith, 87 N.Y.2d 715, 642 N.Y.S.2d 568, 665 N.E.2d 138 (1996).

—Waiver of immunity was binding upon defendant charged with assault, criminal possession of weapon, riot and incitement to riot; defendant verified under oath before grand jury that signature on waiver of immunity form was his, and defendant also acknowledged that he was waiving immunity. People v. Hanley, 227 A.D.2d 144, 642 N.Y.S.2d 22 (1st Dept. 1996).

Forfeiture-of-office statute; effect of voluntary waiver of immunity.—Generally, as held in *Garrity v. New Jersey,* 385 U.S. 493, 87 S. Ct. 616, 17 L. Ed. 2d 562 (1967), the testimony of a public employee compelled under a forfeiture-of-office statute is inadmissible. However, this is not to be inexorably applied and where the defendant wishes to testify before the grand jury and voluntarily does so, the testimony is admissible at trial. People v. Glucksman, 35 N.Y.2d 341, 361 N.Y.S.2d 892, 320 N.E.2d 633 (1974), *modified,* 35 N.Y.2d 905, 364 N.Y.S.2d 896, 324 N.E.2d 364, *cert. denied,* 420 U.S. 981 (1975).

Forced to sign waiver.—A *Huntley* hearing must be held where it is alleged that the district attorney threatened the defendants with a murder indictment if they did not sign waivers of immunity and testify before the Grand Jury and failed to advise them of their right to counsel, since the issue is the voluntariness of a statement and no factual showing is needed. People v. Richard MM, 75 A.D.2d 389, 430 N.Y.S.2d 695 (3d Dept. 1980).

Handwriting exemplar; immunity.—Defendant "gave evidence," within the meaning of CPL § 50.10(3), and was thus entitled to immunity from prosecution where he was brought before the grand jury under *subpoena ad testificandam* and required to produce handwriting exemplars. People v. Perri, 95 Misc. 2d 767, 408 N.Y.S.2d 709 (Sup. Ct. Kings Co. 1978).

Public contractor; "target" of investigation.—The provision of the General Municipal Law § 103(b) which required the employing institution, and were not public contractor, under penalty of disqualification from future public contracts, to testify under a limited waiver of immunity and furnish incriminating evidence to a grand jury investigating his activities

violated the Constitution of the State, Art. 1 § 6. People v. Avant, 33 N.Y.2d 265, 352 N.Y.S.2d 161, 307 N.E.2d 230 (1973).

Scope of waiver.—CPL § 190.45(4) provides for a written agreement between the prosecutor and a grand jury witness that the interrogation will be limited to certain specific subjects, and the waiver of immunity will be restricted accordingly. People v. Davis, 173 Misc. 2d 358, 660 N.Y.S.2d 964 (Sup. Ct. Nassau Co. 1997).

Unsworn waiver.—Defendant's unsworn acknowledgment to the Grand Jury that he had executed the Waiver of Immunity, coupled with his later ratification of the waiver of immunity while under oath, satisfies the requirements of CPL § 190.45. People Ellwanger, 99 Misc. 2d 807, 417 N.Y.S.2d 402 (Suffolk Co. Ct. 1979).

Waiver of immunity; inference that prosecution witness' cooperation was bargained for.—That a prosecution witness' cooperation was bargained for, directly or indirectly, was not to be inferred simply from the fact that he did not waive the automatic immunity which is otherwise conferred by statute on all witnesses who testify before a Grand Jury. People v. Piazza, 48 N.Y.2d 151, 422 N.Y.S.2d 9, 397 N.E.2d 700 (1979).

Waiver to be sworn to before Grand Jury.—Subscribing and swearing to the waiver of immunity before the Grand Jury are distinct acts that must occur for there to be a valid waiver; here, the required undertaking of an oath as to the waiver was satisfied when defendant signed the waiver containing the oath in the presence of the Grand Jury. People v. Stewart, 92 N.Y.2d 965, 683 N.Y.S.2d 751, 706 N.E.2d 739 (1998).

—A waiver of immunity is not effective unless it is sworn to before the Grand Jury conducting the proceeding in which the subscriber is called as a witness, as the purpose of the statute is to provide the Grand Jury with the opportunity to discover whether the prospective witness knowingly and meaningfully renounces his right not to be a witness against himself. *In re* Saratoga City Grand Jury Reports, 77 A.D.2d 399, 434 N.Y.S.2d 768 (3d Dept. 1980).

Waiver of immunity; right to counsel.—Where a Grand Jury witness testifies under a constitutionally defective waiver of immunity the witness, whether voluntary or compelled, receives automatic transactional immunity. People v. Chapman, 69 N.Y.2d 497, 516 N.Y.S.2d 159, 508 N.E.2d 894 (1987).

—Where defendant's waiver of immunity before the Grand Jury was ineffective, he received immunity from prosecution for all acts or transactions that were the subject of his testimony. People v. Higley, 70 N.Y.2d 624, 518 N.Y.S.2d 778, 779, 512 N.E.2d 299 (1987).

—Absent an effective waiver of the right to counsel, the defendant's waiver of immunity before the grand jury was invalid and he acquired transactional immunity. People v. Valvano, 131 A.D.2d 615, 516 N.Y.S.2d 507, 508 (2d Dept. 1987).

—Defendant's Grand Jury testimony was tainted by his denial of his right to counsel, where the police, after the defendant's arrest and arraignment on a felony complaint for possession of a controlled substance, held conversations with him in the absence of his counsel and convinced him to waive immunity and appear before the Grand Jury. People v. Holcombe, 74 A.D.2d 700, 426 N.Y.S.2d 121 (3d Dept. 1980).

§ 190.50. Grand jury; who may call witnesses; defendant as witness.

1. Except as provided in this section, no person has a right to call a witness or appear as a witness in a grand jury proceeding.

2. The people may call as a witness in a grand jury proceeding any person believed by the district attorney to possess relevant information or knowledge.

3. The grand jury may cause to be called as a witness any person believed by it to possess relevant information or knowledge. If the grand jury desires to hear any such witness who was

not called by the people, it may direct the district attorney to issue and serve a subpoena upon such witness, and the district attorney must comply with such direction. At any time after such a direction, however, or at any time after the service of a subpoena pursuant to such a direction and before the return date thereof, the people may apply to the court which impaneled the grand jury for an order vacating or modifying such direction or subpoena on the ground that such is in the public interest. Upon such application, the court may in its discretion vacate the direction or subpoena, attach reasonable conditions thereto, or make other appropriate qualification thereof.

4. Notwithstanding the provisions of subdivision three, the district attorney may demand that any witness thus called at the instance of the grand jury sign a waiver of immunity pursuant to section 190.45 before being sworn, and upon such demand no oath may be administered to such witness unless and until he complies therewith.

5. Although not called as a witness by the people or at the instance of the grand jury, a person has a right to be a witness in a grand jury proceeding under circumstances prescribed in this subdivision:

(a) When a criminal charge against a person is being or is about to be or has been submitted to a grand jury, such person has a right to appear before such grand jury as a witness in his own behalf if, prior to the filing of any indictment or any direction to file a prosecutor's information in the matter, he serves upon the district attorney of the county a written notice making such request and stating an address to which communications may be sent. The district attorney is not obliged to inform such a person that such a grand jury proceeding against him is pending, in progress or about to occur unless such person is a defendant who has been arraigned in a local criminal court upon a currently undisposed of felony complaint charging an offense which is a subject of the prospective or pending grand jury proceeding. In such case, the district attorney must notify the defendant or his attorney of the prospective or pending grand jury proceeding and accord the defendant a reasonable time to exercise his right to appear as a witness therein;

(b) Upon service upon the district attorney of a notice requesting appearance before a grand jury pursuant to paragraph (a), the district attorney must notify the foreman of the grand jury of such request, and must subsequently serve upon the applicant, at the address specified by him, a notice that he will be heard by the grand jury at a given time and place. Upon appearing at such time and place, and upon signing and submitting to the grand jury a waiver of immunity pursuant to section 190.45, such person must be permitted to testify before the grand jury and to give any relevant and competent evidence concerning the case under consideration. Upon giving such evidence, he is subject to examination by the people.

(c) Any indictment or direction to file a prosecutor's information obtained or filed in violation of the provisions of paragraph (a) or (b) is invalid and, upon a motion made pursuant to section 170.50 or section 210.20, must be dismissed; provided that a motion based upon such ground must be made not more than five days after the defendant has been arraigned upon the indictment or, as the case may be, upon the prosecutor's information resulting from the grand jury's direction to file the same. If the contention is not so asserted in timely fashion, it is waived and the indictment or prosecutor's information may not thereafter be challenged on such ground.

6. A defendant or person against whom a criminal charge is being or is about to be brought in a grand jury proceeding may request the grand jury, either orally or in writing, to cause a person designated by him to be called as a witness in such proceeding. The grand jury may as a matter of discretion grant such request and cause such witness to be called pursuant to subdivision three.

7. Where a subpoena is made pursuant to this section, all papers and proceedings relating to the subpoena and any motion to quash, fix conditions, modify or compel compliance shall be kept secret and not disclosed to the public by any public officer or public employee or any other individual described in section 215.70 of the penal law. This subdivision shall not apply where the person subpoenaed and the prosecutor waive the provisions of this subdivision.

This subdivision shall not prevent the publication of decisions and orders made in connection with such proceedings or motions, provided the caption and content of the decision are written or altered by the court to reasonably preclude identification of the person subpoenaed.

Amended by L. 1978, Ch. 289.

ANNOTATIONS

Charges before Grand Jury and indictment not identical; waiver.—By failing to move to dismiss his indictment within five days of his arraignment, defendant waived his contention that the charges presented to the grand jury and subsequently enumerated in the indictment were not identical to those contained in the felony complaints. People v. Obee, 232 A.D.2d 430, 648 N.Y.S.2d 619 (2d Dept. 1996).

Circumstantial and direct evidence.—The court need not charge the grand jury as to circumstantial evidence where both circumstantial and direct evidence are presented. People v. Hill, 90 A.D.2d 835, 456 N.Y.S.2d 9 (2d Dept. 1982).

Failure to give *Miranda* warnings to Grand Jury witness no bar to prosecution for perjury.—Defendant, as a witness before the Grand Jury was entitled to the protection of the Fifth Amendment, but the privilege against self-incrimination relates to past criminal acts and not to future acts such as perjury. People v. Robinson, 66 Misc. 2d 639, 323 N.Y.S.2d 573 (Sup. Ct. 1971).

Dismissal of indictment denied; no showing that defendant was not afforded an opportunity to appear and testify before Grand Jury.—Defendant was denied her right to testify before the Grand Jury where the district attorney failed to advise her that the Grand Jury proceedings had been postponed and as to the future Grand Jury meeting. People v. Martinez, 111 Misc. 2d 67, 443 N.Y.S.2d 576 (Sup. Ct. Queens Co. 1981). People v. Jean-Charles, 122 A.D.2d 166, 504 N.Y.S.2d 544 (2d Dept. 1986).

Grand Jury subpoena.—A motion to quash a grand jury subpoena is limited in scope, challenging only the validity of the subpoena or the jurisdiction of the issuing authority and should be made prior to the return date. Santangello v. People, 38 N.Y.2d 536, 381 N.Y.S.2d 472, 344 N.E.2d 404 (1976).

—Petitioner's motion to quash the Grand Jury subpoena was untimely when it was made after he commenced testifying before the Grand Jury. Gammarano v. Gold, 51 A.D.2d 1012, 381 N.Y.S.2d 298 (2d Dept. 1976).

Grand Jury subpoena duces tecum.—Grand Jury subpoena duces tecum issued by the Special Prosecutor does not authorize the Special Prosecutor to seize or impound the records produced; if the circumstances warrant, the prosecutor may apply for an order of impoundment or inspection, which is within the inherent power of a court to grant. Heisler v. Hynes, 42 N.Y.2d 250, 397 N.Y.S.2d 727, 366 N.E.2d 817 (1977). See also People v. Fairview Nursing Home, 92 Misc. 2d 694, 401 N.Y.S.2d 390 (Sup. Ct. Queens Co. 1977).

Motion to dismiss; defendant's right to be witness.—Motion to dismiss was granted where the indictment against the defendant was founded upon a defective Grand Jury proceeding because the defendant after testifying for a short time was not allowed to complete his testimony. People v. Green, 80 A.D.2d 650, 436 N.Y.S.2d 420 (3d Dept. 1981).

—Where defendant was indicted for burglary, assault and sexual abuse and four days after arraignment moved to dismiss indictment as legally insufficient without making point that he was not advised of his right to appear and then one month later raised the latter point, he was deemed to have waived his right which must be asserted within five days of arraignment. In re DeContie, 40 A.D.2d 619, 336 N.Y.S.2d 328 (4th Dept. 1972).

—Defendant's motion to dismiss the indictment was granted where the police, arranged to have him photographed and fingerprinted and filed an "arrest report" but no felony complaint and police failed to give notice to the defendant of the proposed presentment of the case to the Grand Jury. People v. Smiley, 111 Misc. 2d 236, 443 N.Y.S.2d 798 (Greene Co. Ct. 1981), aff'd, 100 A.D.2d 294, 475 N.Y.S.2d 533 (3d Dept. 1984).

Motion to dismiss indictment; waiver of motion time.—Defendant's motion to dismiss indictment was untimely where it was made well after five-day limitation set forth in statute, and there was no showing of any other compelling factors or circumstances which could be the basis for dismissal in the interest of justice. People v. Barrett, 246 A.D.2d 848, 668 N.Y.S.2d 80 (3d Dept. 1998).

No obligation to produce defendant; People unaware of re-arrest.— Because District Attorney was unaware that defendant had been re-arrested and was incarcerated by the Division of Parole, an independent administrative agency, the District Attorney had no obligation to produce the defendant before the grand jury prior to obtaining a voted indictment. People v. Dabney, 172 Misc. 2d 458, 659 N.Y.S.2d 717 (Sup. Ct. Kings Co. 1997).

Notice of Grand Jury proceeding.—A defendant need not be advised of each and every potential charge relating to the alleged criminal transaction which is the subject of the complaint. People v. Diaz, 144 Misc. 2d 766, 545 N.Y.S.2d 516, 518 (Sup. Ct. Bronx Co. 1989).

—The defendant was not entitled to notice of specific time and place that his case would be presented to the Grand Jury where the defendant did not make a request to testify after he received initial notice that his case would be presented to the Grand Jury. People v. Lawrence, 106 Misc. 2d 482, 434 N.Y.S.2d 311 (Franklin Co. Ct. 1980).

No true bill; not a final determination.—The grand jury's refusal to indict is not a final determination that the acts alleged did not occur, and therefore, the People were not barred from questioning the defendant concerning the incident; defendant's contention that court erred in allowing prosecutor to cross-examine him regarding his presence in a vehicle where cocaine was found because a grand jury issued a "no bill" with respect to that incident rejected. People v. Stokes, 247 A.D.2d 919, 668 N.Y.S.2d 425 (4th Dept. 1998).

Off the record promise.—An off the record promise that defendant will not have to testify before subsequent grand juries is unenforceable as once the terms of a plea bargaining agreement are placed on the record, judicial recognition of additional promises or terms of the agreement will not be forthcoming except in a rare case. Benjamin S. v. Kuriansky, 55 N.Y.2d 116, 447 N.Y.S.2d 905, 432 N.E.2d 777 (1982).

Pending Grand Jury proceeding; clarification of "undisposed of" felony complaint.—Once the court concluded, after preliminary hearing, that the evidence warranted binding defendant over to the Grand Jury, and this had been done, the local criminal court's action thereby ended, and, under the statute providing that the prosecution does not have to inform a person that a Grand Jury proceeding against him is pending (if such person is a defendant who has been arraigned in a local court upon a currently undisposed of felony complaint), the complaint was no longer "undisposed of" within the meaning of the statute. People v. Monroe, 74 Misc. 2d 292, 344 N.Y.S.2d 752 (St. Lawrence Co. Ct. 1973).

Plea waived review of grand jury notice.—By pleading guilty, defendant waived appellate review of whether notice of grand jury proceeding was defective and thereby denied him of his right to appear and testify before grand jury. People v. Empey, 242 A.D.2d 839, 662 N.Y.S.2d 152 (3d Dept. 1997).

Records; high school custodian.—Grand Jury could lawfully subpoena the personnel records of the high school, the Workmen's Compensation reports, the monthly expenditure reports and the personal bank account records pertaining to the school since these documents deal with the expenditure of public funds received from the Board of Education for the maintenance and operation of a city high school. People ex rel Santucci, D.A. v. Cappetta, 89 Misc. 2d 937, 392 N.Y.S.2d 992 (Sup. Ct. Queens Co. 1977), aff'd, 42 N.Y.2d 1066, 399 N.Y.S.2d 638, 369 N.E.2d 1172 (1977).

Subpoena; income tax return.—The nondisclosure provision of Tax Law § 697(e) required the Department of Taxation and Finance to refuse to comply with a Grand Jury subpoena duces tecum for the production of an individual income tax return. New York State Dept of Tax v. New York State Dept. of Law, 44 N.Y.2d 575, 406 N.Y.S.2d 747, 378 N.E.2d 110 (1978).

Subd. 2

Evidence received by second Grand Jury.—Where minutes of first indictment were lost, and another indictment was filed by the Grand Jury, there was no restriction on the type of evidence that could be submitted to the second Grand Jury, nor was there any rule that the second Grand Jury only hear witnesses who were heard before the first. People v. Lunney, 84 Misc. 2d 1090, 378 N.Y.S 2d 559 (Sup. Ct. N.Y. Co. 1975).

Joint representation by counsel.—The court had the right to order each of ten Grand Jury witnesses to hire separate legal counsel and to deny the PBA retained counsel to practice law in the matter, where ten police officers, subpoenaed to appear before the Grand Jury in connection with a police incident were all represented by the same PBA retained counsel; a paramount right of the grand jury exists in this instance which takes precedence over the individual rights of the officer witnesses pursuant to the First and Sixth Amendment. In re Rodriguez, 102 Misc. 2d 153, 423 N.Y.S.2d 120 (Sup. Ct. Bronx Co. 1979).

Reporter.—No valid reason exists why reporters, if not otherwise privileged, any more than citizens, should be exempt from providing information that may help the Grand Jury in making its initial determination as to who shall be and who shall not be indicted. Andrews v. Andreoli, 92 Misc. 2d 410, 400 N.Y.S.2d 442 (Sup. Ct. Onondaga Co. 1977).

Subd. 3

Prosecutor's conduct.—Prosecutor's conduct did not impair integrity of Grand Jury; specifically, evidence failed to support contention that prosecutor improperly influenced Grand Jury to rescind its prior request for production of defense witness. People v. Chen, 217 A.D.2d 637, 629 N.Y.S.2d 771 (2d Dept. 1995).

—Assistant District Attorney's statement to grand jurors that "who comes in front of the grand jury and gives testimony is in the prosecutor's discretion" was erroneous in view of CPL § 190.50(3), which authorizes the grand jury to call witnesses who it believes possess relevant knowledge or information. People v. Stanton, 241 A.D.2d 687, 660 N.Y.S.2d 169 (3d Dept. 1997).

Order of impoundment.—An order of impoundment is necessary to retain records obtained by subpoena duces tecum but which were never actually introduced into evidence before the Grand Jury and the prosecutor must show "special circumstances" in order to prevail. People v. Fairview Nursing Home, 92 Misc. 2d 694, 401 N.Y.S.2d 390 (Sup. Ct. Queens Co. 1977).

Subpoena duces tecum records.—Once a Grand Jury returned an indictment, the right to retain subpoenaed material not presented directly to the Grand Jury ended unless there was an allegation that the books are needed as part of a continuing investigation. People v. Fairview Nursing Home, 96 Misc. 2d 694, 401 N.Y.S.2d 390 (Sup. Ct. Queens Co. 1977).

Subd. 5

E-mail notice insufficient.—An electronic mail message, commonly known as e-mail, sent to the prosecutor by defense counsel indicating the defendant's desire to testify before the grand jury did not constitute proper written notice to satisfy the requirements of the statute. People v. Welch, 190 Misc. 2d 195, 738 N.Y.S.2d 510 (Co. Ct. Monroe Co. 2002).

Notice to testify untimely.—Defendant's notice of intent to testify should be deemed timely served only if the People actually receive it before the filing of the indictment since the receipt of such notice triggers reciprocal obligations on the prosecutor's part that cannot be fulfilled without actual notice of such intent; here, defense counsel mailed the notice of intent six days before the case was presented to the grand jury, but the District Attorney received the notice five days after the presentation and four days after the filing of the indictment. Therefore, defendant's notice was untimely and the indictment should be reinstated. People v. Crisp, 246 A.D.2d 84, 677 N.Y.S.2d 356 (1st Dept. 1998), aff'd upon reargument, 268 A.D.2d 247, 700 N.Y.S.2d 693 (1st Dept. 2000).

Right to testify.—CPL § 190.50(5)(a) does not mandate a specific time period for notice, but "reasonable" time must be accorded to allow a defendant to consult with counsel and decide whether to testify before a grand jury. The concept of reasonableness is flexible and must be applied to the particular facts of a case as known at the time. Because this inquiry involves a mixed question of law and fact, where the determinations by courts with fact-finding authority are supported by the record, they are beyond the further review of the Court of Appeals. People v. Sawyer, 96 N.Y.2d 815, 727 N.Y.S.2d 381, 751 N.E.2d 460, reargument denied, 96 N.Y.2d 928, 733 N.Y.S.2d 363, 759 N.E.2d 361 (2001).

—Prospective defendant has no constitutional right to testify before Grand Jury; right is provided by statute, and upon serving proper notice, appearing at given time and place, and executing waiver of immunity, prospective defendant must be permitted to testify before Grand Jury and to give any relevant and competent evidence concerning case under consideration. People v. Smith, 87 N.Y.2d 715, 642 N.Y.S.2d 568, 665 N.E.2d 138 (1996).

—A prosecutor's examination of defendant before Grand Jury did not deprive defendant of fair opportunity to testify or warrant dismissal of charges; defendant was permitted to make full narrative statement before examination, and prosecutor properly clarified that defendant was not aware of any exculpatory fingerprint evidence and that defendant was not being forced to accept sole responsibility. People v. Germosen, 86 N.Y.2d 822, 633 N.Y.S.2d 472, 657 N.E.2d 493 (1995).

—Right of accused to appear and testify before Grand Jury may be lost when question arises as to defendant's competency. People v. Calvert, 167 Misc. 2d 823, 637 N.Y.S.2d 639 (Sup. Ct. Queens Co. 1996).

—Where a defendant serves timely CPL § 190.50 notice, he is entitled to testify prior to a vote by the Grand Jury. People v. Evans, 79 N.Y.2d 407, 583 N.Y.S.2d 358, 592 N.E.2d 1362 (1992).

—Counsel's oral notification of the defendant's wish to testify before the Grand Jury failed to comply with the requirements of CPL § 190.50. People v. Robinson, 187 A.D.2d 296, 589 N.Y.S.2d 453 (1st Dept. 1992).

Right to testify not violated.—The People did not violate defendants' rights in presenting case to grand jury immediately after arrests and prior to any arraignment, and there is no evidence that the prosecutor intentionally delayed arraignment in order to deprive defendants of notice of the grand jury proceeding and of a right to testify, especially in light of People's good faith reason for an immediate grand jury proceeding, which was that the victim, a foreign tourist, was about to leave the United States. People v. Brown, 14 A.D.2d 356, 789 N.Y.S.2d 106 (1st Dept. 2005).

—Defendant's right to testify was not violated where the failure to testify was attributable to defendant's failure to respond to defense counsel's mailgram telling him the date of the presentation. People v. Smith, 191 A.D.2d 598, 594 N.Y.S.2d 799 (2d Dept. 1993).

—Defense counsel's inability to contact defendant within five days does not render the People's notice to defendant unreasonable, and because the prosecution never received written notice of defendant's intention to testify, People properly presented the case and obtained an indictment without defendant's participation. People v. Ballard, 13 A.D.3d 670, 785 N.Y.S.2d 608 (3d Dept. 2004).

Right to testify; waiver of claim.—The issue of a violation of CPL § 190.50(5) notice was unpreserved as it was not raised before trial, during trial, or in defendant's motion to set aside the verdict; raising the issue for the first time in defendant's reply papers to the CPL § 330.30 motion, and then again in a CPL § 440.10 motion, could not cure the lack of preservation. People v. Pressley, 94 N.Y.2d 935, 708 N.Y.S.2d 32, 729 N.E.2d 689 (2000).

—Defendant's motion to dismiss the indictment pursuant to CPL § 190.50(5)(c) was properly denied since he failed to file any written notice of his intention to testify before the Grand Jury prior to the filing of the indictment, and this requirement is strictly enforced. People v. Madsen, 254 A.D.2d 152, 681 N.Y.S.2d 6 (1st Dept. 1998).

—Defendant waived any claim that he was denied his statutory right to testify before Grand Jury by failing to move to dismiss indictment and, instead, agreeing to testify before same Grand Jury that had already indicted him. People v. Ray, 224 A.D.2d 722, 638 N.Y.S.2d 706 (2d Dept. 1996).

—The defendant's right to notice of his right to testify before the Grand Jury is absolute and CPL § 190.50 contemplates "actual" rather than technical notice to the defendant, reasonably calculated to apprise the defendant of the Grand Jury proceeding so as to permit the defendant to exercise his or her right to testify. People v. Abdullah, 184 A.D.2d 195, 592 N.Y.S.2d 406 (2d Dept. 1993).

—Any alleged violation of a defendant's right to testify before the Grand Jury is waived by plea of guilty. People v. Ferrara, 99 A.D.2d 257, 472 N.Y.S.2d 407 (2d Dept. 1984).

—Objections to the prosecution's notice are waived if not raised by motion within five days after arraignment on the indictment. People v. Wright, 5 A.D.3d 873, 773 N.Y.S.2d 486 (3d Dept. 2004).

—Defendant waived claim that he was denied right to testify before grand jury, where he waited to make claim until 13 months after arraignment and after jury's verdict had been rendered. People v. Brown, 227 A.D.2d 691, 641 N.Y.S.2d 763 (3d Dept. 1996).

—Because defendant did not move to dismiss the indictment within five days of arraignment on the ground that he was denied the right to testify before the grand jury, he has waived his challenge to the grand jury proceedings. People v. Webb, 236 A.D.2d 872, 653 N.Y.S.2d 999 (4th Dept. 1997).

—Where defendant withdrew his request to testify before the Grand Jury, and reasserted that request after the Grand Jury had voted a true bill and ended its term, he waived his right to testify; the defendant did not seek to extend the term of the Grand Jury before it was disbanded. People v. Domalevski, 157 Misc. 2d 562, 598 N.Y.S.2d 143 (Sup. Ct. Queens Co. 1993).

Defendant's calling of witnesses.—A letter sent by the defense counsel to the Grand Jury Bureau Chief was insufficient to "designate" persons he wished to be called as Grand Jury witnesses, since the letter did not identify any particular individuals. People v. Puluso, 182 A.D.2d 783, 582 N.Y.S.2d 778 (2d Dept. 1992).

Denial of right to testify; assignment of counsel.—Defendant was deprived of her statutory rights to testify before the grand jury despite her failure to move to dismiss the indictment within five days after her arraignment thereon; defendant was represented by the public defender solely for purposes of arraignment and assigned counsel thereafter moved promptly within five days of his appointment for such dismissal. People v. Prest, 105 A.D.2d 1078, 482 N.Y.S.2d 172 (4th Dept. 1984).

Deprivation of right to testify before Grand Jury.—The defendant's contention that he was prejudiced by comments of prosecutor during the Grand Jury proceeding was forfeited by his failure to move to dismiss the indictment on this ground. People v. Silvestri, 201 A.D.2d 684, 607 N.Y.S.2d 964 (2d Dept. 1994).

—Defendant was deprived of his statutory right to testify before the Grand Jury where he was immediately examined by the prosecutor, thereby effectively preventing him of a reasonably fair and uninterrupted opportunity to first furnish the Grand Jury with his own version concerning matters being investigated. People v. Durante, 97 A.D.2d 851, 469 N.Y.S.2d 18 (2d Dept. 1983).

Expanded notice of Grand Jury proceedings.—Grand jury notice provisions of CPL § 190.50(5) do not impose an obligation upon prosecution to provide notice of separate charges presented to grand jury which are not included in pending felony complaint, especially where, as here, defendant was clearly aware that additional charges would be presented to grand jury. People v. Clark, 240 A.D.2d 325, 660 N.Y.S.2d 114 (1st Dept. 1997).

—People are not required to give Grand Jury notice regarding enhanced gun possession charge which is not contained in felony complaint but is subsequently voted by Grand Jury; there is no obligation on part of prosecution to give notice regarding expanded notice of Grand Jury proceedings inasmuch as People are not required to give notice with respect to separate charges which are not included in felony complaint. People v. Hernandez, 223 A.D.2d 351, 636 N.Y.S.2d 45 (1st Dept. 1996).

Change of counsel.—Even if defendant's change of counsel was a basis for extension of the statutory time period to make a CPL § 190.50 motion, the motion was still untimely. People v. Wilkins, 188 A.D.2d 320, 591 N.Y.S.2d 18 (1st Dept. 1992).

Cross-examination.—The cross-examination in the Grand Jury about the defendant's prior criminal history and drug selling was not to demonstrate that defendant had a propensity for selling drugs; rather, that cross-examination was directly relevant to defendant's specific testimony that he abhorred the drug trade and that he had been attacked because of his efforts to end the drug dealing in his apartment building and neighborhood. People v. Gonzalez, 201 A.D.2d 414, 607 N.Y.S.2d 670 (1st Dept. 1994).

Polygraph test.—Defendant has no right to present evidence concerning the administration and results of a polygraph test to the Grand Jury. People v. Frank, 101 Misc. 2d 736, 422 N.Y.S.2d 317 (Nassau Co. Ct. 1979).

Defendant's version heard first without interruption.—The prosecution had the right to cross-examine the defendant after the completion of his Grand Jury testimony, and the cross-examination properly included questions that bore on the defendant's credibility; the defendant's criminal record was thus a proper subject for cross-examination. People v. Burton, 191 A.D.2d 451, 594 N.Y.S.2d 300 (2d Dept. 1993).

—CPL § 190.50(5) confers on a putative criminal defendant the right to appear before the grand jury and offer his version of the facts under consideration first and without interruption before cross-examination by the district attorney; where the district attorney embarked on a lengthy examination of the prospective defendant who sought to testify before the grand jury pursuant to CPL § 190.50(5) and further objected to the witness's statement on the basis of relevancy before allowing the witness to relate his version, a subsequent indictment against the witness was ordered dismissed. People v. Dunbar, 100 Misc. 2d 389, 419 N.Y.S.2d 432 (Sup. Ct. Suffolk Co. 1979).

Dismissal of indictment; defendant not afforded opportunity to appear and testify before grand jury.—Defendant was improperly denied his right to appear before the Grand Jury and the indictment was dismissed where defense counsel waived a preliminary hearing and orally informed the prosecutor on September 12 that defendant wished to appear before the Grand Jury, and also promptly served a written notice of defendant's desire, and prosecutor presented the case and obtained an indictment on September 13 without giving defendant a chance to appear. People v. Gini, 72 A.D.2d 752, 421 N.Y.S.2d 269 (2d Dept. 1979).

—The mailing of an incorrectly addressed notice of Grand Jury proceeding to a defendant arraigned on an undisposed felony charge did not constitute sufficient notice and warranted dismissal of the indictment with authorization for the District Attorney to resubmit the charge. People v. Rakity, 77 Misc. 2d 324, 352 N.Y.S.2d 803 (Sup. Ct. Suffolk Co. 1974).

Effect of refusal to sign waiver on Grand Jury appearance.—Defendant was not denied opportunity to testify before

the Grand Jury where the deprivation was traceable to his refusal to sign a waiver of immunity. People v. Anderson, 127 A.D.2d 885, 512 N.Y.S.2d 646 (3d Dept. 1987).

—Where the defendant was accorded the opportunity of signing a waiver of immunity and testifying before the Grand Jury, and through confusion refused to do so, he effectively waived his right to re-present the case and the court is not authorized to order the district attorney to re-present the case so that defendant can testify. People v. Collice, 77 Misc. 2d 662, 354 N.Y.S.2d 830 (Nassau Co. Ct. 1974).

Ineffective assistance of counsel.—Defendant's allegations that trial counsel failed to effectuate his right to testify before the grand jury and failed to make a timely dismissal motion pursuant to CPL § 190.50(5)(c) would not constitute ineffective assistance of counsel, and defendant has not demonstrated that the result of the grand jury proceeding would have been any different had defendant testified. People v. Hook, 246 A.D.2d 470, 668 N.Y.S.2d 183 (1st Dept. 1998).

—Counsel's failure to comply with the defendant's desire to testify would not, standing alone, amount to a denial of effective assistance of counsel. People v. Hamlin, 153 A.D.2d 644, 544 N.Y.S.2d 859 (2d Dept. 1989).

—Defense counsel's purported failure to effectuate defendant's right to testify before the grand jury does not, per se, amount to ineffective assistance of counsel. People v. Mejias, 293 A.D.2d 819, 742 N.Y.S.2d 129 (3d Dept. 2002).

—Where defendant served a CPL § 190.50 notice of his desire to testify before the Grand Jury, he was denied effective assistance of counsel where he did not do so due to his former attorney's oversight of the People's reciprocal section 190.50 notice. People v. Jiminez, 180 A.D.2d 757, 580 N.Y.S.2d 393 (2d Dept. 1992).

Generally.—A criminal defendant may not be physically restrained in the presence of a jury unless there is a rational basis, articulated in the record, for the restraint; although it was error to require the defendant to appear before the Grand Jury in handcuffs, the error was harmless where the prosecutor gave cautionary instructions to the Grand Jury. People v. Felder, 201 A.D.2d 884, 607 N.Y.S.2d 793 (4th Dept. 1994).

—The prosecution has the authority to override a Grand Jury's decision to subpoena a witness by application to the court that empaneled the Grand Jury. People v. Latorre, 162 Misc. 2d 432, 617 N.Y.S.2d 282 (Crim. Ct. Kings Co. 1994).

—Every witness before the Grand Jury is subject to being recalled as a witness before the same Grand Jury. People v. Hughes, 159 Misc. 2d 663, 606 N.Y.S.2d 499 (Sup. Ct. Monroe Co. 1993).

Grand Jury indictment.—It was no defense for defendant that the Town Justice failed to transmit order, felony complaint, and other pertinent documents to the Superior Court before the Grand Jury indicted him for burglary. People v. Talham, 41 A.D.2d 354, 342 N.Y.S.2d 921 (3d Dept. 1973).

Incapacitated defendant's right to be a witness.—Where defendant, who had been arraigned in the criminal court on a felony complaint, was indicted more than 90 days after issuance of a temporary order of observation committing her to custody for no more than 90 days, the district attorney was not obliged to notify defendant of the pending Grand Jury proceeding and accord defendant time to exercise her right to appear as witness in grand jury because there was no longer a currently undisposed of felony complaint pending since it had been dismissed pursuant to CPL § 730.40(2). People v. Moss, 99 Misc. 2d 534, 416 N.Y.S.2d 741 (Sup. Ct. Queens Co. 1979).

—The People have the right to present the case to the Grand Jury while the defendant is committed pursuant to a temporary order of observation. Where the defendant has been returned as competent to stand trial within a month of his commitment and there is no doubt that if he were competent he would have exercised his right to be a witness and the People would not be prejudiced by a dismissal of the indictment and its resubmission to the grand jury, the indictment will be dismissed with leave to the People to resubmit on condition that the defendant appears and signs a waiver of immunity at the time and place specified by the grand jury. People v. Searles, 79 Misc. 2d 850, 361 N.Y.S.2d 568 (Sup. Ct. N.Y. Co. 1974).

Motion to dismiss.—Motion to dismiss on section 190.50 grounds properly denied where defendant merely submitted to the trial court an affirmation of retained counsel, who did not have personal knowledge as to whether defendant's prior counsel properly consulted with defendant; the affirmation was insufficient to meet the defendant's burden of establishing that his rights pursuant to section 190.50 were violated. People v. Fleming, 196 A.D.2d 551, 601 N.Y.S.2d 304 (2d Dept. 1993).

—Affidavit of substituted defense counsel in support of § 190.50 motion that did not state sources of information was deficient. People v. Richardson, 193 A.D.2d 969, 598 N.Y.S.2d 341 (3d Dept. 1993).

Notification.—People provided defendant's counsel with adequate notice of the date and time of the scheduled grand jury presentation; the People are not responsible for defendant's failure to remain in touch with his counsel. People v. Malik, 6 A.D.3d 313, 775 N.Y.S.2d 41 (1st Dept. 2004).

—Five days' notice of the impending Grand Jury presentation was a reasonable time for defendant to exercise his right to appear as a witness. People v. Pugh, 207 A.D.2d 503, 615 N.Y.S.2d 912 (2d Dept. 1994)

—Where the defendant had not yet been arraigned because he was in the hospital, the People were not obligated to serve 190.50 notice. People v. Munoz, 207 A.D.2d 418, 615 N.Y.S.2d 730 (2d Dept. 1994).

—Since the defendant had been held for the action of the Grand Jury and since he was, therefore, no longer the subject of an undisposed of felony complaint in a local criminal court, the District Attorney was under no affirmative obligation to notify the defendant of prospective or pending Grand Jury proceedings. People v. Conde, 131 A.D.2d 586, 516 N.Y.S.2d 295 (2d Dept. 1987).

—Because there was no pending felony complaint in a local criminal court upon which defendant had been arraigned, the District Attorney was under no obligation to notify defendant that a Grand Jury was going to convene. People v. Legree, 176 A.D.2d 983, 574 N.Y.S.2d 604 (3d Dept. 1991).

—The felony complaint charging defendant with offenses that were the subject of the grand jury proceeding had been disposed of by a preliminary hearing pursuant to CPL § 180.70(1), and thus the People had no obligation to inform defendant of the grand jury proceeding. People v. Walker, 15 A.D.3d 902, 789 N.Y.S.2d 780 (4th Dept. 2005).

—CPL § 190.50 notice need not inform the defendant of all of the possible charges that the Grand Jury is likely to consider; notice need only give defendant some idea of the "nature and scope of the Grand Jury's inquiry." People v. Simmons, 178 A.D.2d 972, 579 N.Y.S.2d 499 (4th Dept. 1992).

—Prosecutor had no duty to inform the defendant of his right to testify before the Grand Jury when he was arraigned in a local criminal court upon the complaint. People v. LaBounty, 127 A.D.2d 989, 512 N.Y.S.2d 950, 951 (4th Dept. 1987).

—Each method of service listed in CPLR 2103 is a proper method of serving the District Attorney with notice of a defendant's intention to testify before the Grand Jury. People v. Fulton, 162 Misc. 2d 360, 616 N.Y.S.2d 881 (Sup. Ct. Monroe Co. 1994).

Notification by District Attorney not required where defendant waived preliminary hearing.—Notice of Grand Jury proceeding to a defendant arraigned on undisposed of felony charge is not required where defendant has waived a preliminary hearing. People v. Otello, 48 A.D.2d 169, 368 N.Y.S.2d 592 (3d Dept. 1975).

Prior convictions.—Prior to appearance before the Grand Jury, a defendant is entitled to a ruling by the District Attorney on the admissibility of prior convictions to impeach his credibility. People v. Adams, 81 Misc. 2d 528, 366 N.Y.S.2d 311 (Sup. Ct. N.Y. Co. 1975).

Prosecutor's control of grand jury presentation.—Absent a breach of a statutory command or some indication of likely prejudice, there is no legal basis for interfering with the prosecutor's prerogatives in determining the manner in which a grand jury presentation is made. People v. Darrett, 2 A.D.3d 16, 769 N.Y.S.2d 14 (1st Dept. 2003).

Right to appear.—A defendant who gives proper notice of his or her intention to appear before the Grand Jury must be afforded the opportunity to testify in advance of the Grand Jury's vote whether to indict. People v. Hawkins, 193 A.D.2d 524, 598 N.Y.S.2d 455 (1st Dept. 1993).

—The failure of the Department of Corrections to produce a defendant did not excuse the prosecutor's failure to give effect to the defendant's right to testify before the Grand Jury voted. People v. Ward, 193 A.D.2d 433, 597 N.Y.S.2d 328 (1st Dept. 1993).

—Defendant's rejection of the People's offer to appear before a new Grand Jury for representment of the facts constituted waiver of his right to appear before that body even though defendant was originally deprived of proper notice of his right to appear before the Grand Jury. People v. Bethea, 159 A.D.2d 384, 553 N.Y.S.2d 10 (1st Dept. 1990).

—The People's failure to notify defendant of the Grand Jury proceeding against him did not violate defendant's due process rights for that proceeding was initiated by an indictment and not by a felony complaint. People v. Wong, 163 A.D.2d 738, 558 N.Y.S.2d 324 (4th Dept. 1990).

Corporation.—An inanimate corporation cannot testify although it may direct others to act for it and it is not embraced within the provisions of CPL § 190.50; its remedy is to request the foreman of the Grand Jury to call designated persons as witnesses, but the request need not be granted (CPL § 190.50[6]) and the failure to comply does not render the indictment invalid. People v. Sterling Chevrolet, Inc., 91 Misc. 2d 641, 398 N.Y.S.2d 496 (Sup. Ct. Suffolk Co. 1977).

Jurisdiction; district attorney; divestiture and removal.—Indictment by Grand Jury after presentation of evidence by District Attorney with apparent personal interest in the prosecution, would be dismissed and case remanded and removed to another local criminal court with appointment of a special prosecutor. Divestiture statute at option of District Attorney was repugnant in its operation to equal protection of the laws. People v. Krstovich, 72 Misc. 2d 90, 338 N.Y.S.2d 132 (Greene Co. Ct. 1972).

Oral notice.—Oral notice given by defense counsel of defendant's intention to testify before the Grand Jury was not sufficient to meet the requirements of CPL § 190.50(5)(a). People v. Harris, 150 A.D.2d 723, 541 N.Y.S.2d 593 (2d Dept. 1989).

—Defense counsel's oral notice that the defendant "may wish to testify" is insufficient notice under CPL § 190.50. People v. Green, 187 A.D.2d 528, 589 N.Y.S.2d 916 (2d Dept. 1992).

—Oral notice by the district attorney to defendant's attorney a week in advance of the scheduled date of presentment sufficiently complied with the People's obligation under CPL § 190.50(5). People v. Phillips, 88 A.D.2d 672, 450 N.Y.S.2d 925 (3d Dept. 1982).

Oral and written notification to attorney sufficient.—Oral and written notice to defendant's assigned counsel of appearance before the Grand Jury sufficiently complies with the states statutory obligation under CPL § 190.50(5). People v. Helm, 51 N.Y.2d 853, 433 N.Y.S.2d 757, 413 N.E.2d 1172 (1980).

Target.—Although the better practice is not to do so, it is settled law that no constitutional error is involved in requiring one who is a Grand Jury target to appear before that body and claim the privilege. People v. Davis, 49 N.Y.2d 910, 428 N.Y.S.2d 195, 405 N.E.2d 677 (1980).

Voice mail notice insufficient.—Prosecutor's attempt to serve notice on defendant by telephone, at the telephone number of defendant's then counsel, did not result in actual notice to defendant. The attempted voice mail communication did not actually reach defendant's former counsel, and the message did not provide a given time and place as required by 190.50(5)(b). Accordingly, defendant was denied actual notice that would have permitted him to assert his right to testify before the Grand Jury, and the motion to dismiss was granted with leave to represent. People v. Leggett, 196 Misc. 2d 727, 766 N.Y.S.2d 515 (Sup. Ct. Kings Co. 2003).

Written notification.—In order to be given effect, § 190.50 notice must be in writing. People v. Smith, 197 A.D.2d 411, 602 N.Y.S.2d 606 (1st Dept. 1993).

Subd. 6

Defendant's witness.—Grand Jury's failure to call the witnesses requested by defendant did not render its proceedings defective since the Grand Jury has complete discretion as to the witnesses it will call. People v. Moore, 132 A.D.2d 776, 517 N.Y.S.2d 584 (3d Dept. 1987).

Grand Jury; defendant's mental condition.—The fact that the ADA foreclosed exploration into the defendant's mental condition by the Grand Jury did not require that the indictment be dismissed. People v. Galuppo, 98 Misc. 2d 395, 413 N.Y.S.2d 880 (Sup. Ct. N.Y. Co. 1979).

§ 190.52. Grand jury; attorney for witness.

1. Any person who appears as a witness and has signed a waiver of immunity in a grand jury proceeding, has a right to an attorney as provided in this section. Such a witness may appear with a retained attorney, or if he is financially unable to obtain counsel, an attorney who shall be assigned by the superior court which impaneled the grand jury. Such assigned attorney shall be assigned pursuant to the same plan and in the same manner as counsel are provided to persons charged with crime pursuant to section seven hundred twenty-two of the county law.

2. The attorney for such witness may be present with the witness in the grand jury room. The attorney may advise the witness, but may not otherwise take any part in the proceeding.

3. The superior court which impaneled the grand jury shall have the same power to remove an attorney from the grand jury room as such court has with respect to an attorney in a courtroom.

Added by L. 1978, Ch. 447.

ANNOTATIONS

Right to counsel.—Defendant was not denied his right to counsel during Grand Jury proceeding, even if counsel sat 20 feet away from defendant; there was no indication in record either that prosecutor prevented defendant from conferring with counsel, or that defendant sought to confer with counsel and was unable to do so. People v. Diaz, 211 A.D.2d 402, 621 N.Y.S.2d 36 (1st Dept. 1995).

Advice by attorney.—The advice counsel gives the witness before the Grand Jury may not interfere improperly with the proceedings of the Grand Jury; unlike a trial, the defendant before a Grand Jury is not in a position to object, nor is his attorney, because it is the prosecutor who must initially determine the propriety of a particular line of questioning; nor is it appropriate for counsel to advise the witness in such a manner that the advice may be heard by the Grand Jurors and have a direct effect on their deliberations. People v. Smays, 156 Misc. 2d 621, 594 N.Y.S.2d 101 (Sup. Ct. N.Y. Co. 1993).

Attorney may take notes.—An attorney for a defendant who has waived immunity may take reasonable notes while the defendant is testifying before the Grand Jury. Matter Pending Before Grand Jury ex rel. Riley, 98 Misc. 2d 458, 414 N.Y.S.2d 441 (Sup. Ct. Queens Co. 1979).

Constitutionality.—CPL § 190.52 which permits a waiver witness the right to be represented by counsel in the Grand Jury room while denying that right to one testifying under a grant of immunity does not violate the equal protection clause of the Fourteenth Amendment. Lief v. Hynes, 98 Misc. 2d 817, 414 N.Y.S.2d 855 (Sup. Ct. Queens Co. 1979).

Grand Jury witness; right to waive immunity; presence of counsel.—Witness in a Grand Jury investigation of death has no absolute statutory right to waive immunity and thereby have counsel accompany witness before Grand Jury, but must accept automatic grant of transactional immunity, provided under CPL § 190.40, and answer questions without having attorney present; witness failing to do so adjudged in contempt of court. People v. Bowers, 78 A.D.2d 190, 434 N.Y.S.2d 68 (4th Dept. 1980).

§ 190.55. Grand jury; matters to be heard and examined; duties and authority of district attorney.

1. A grand jury may hear and examine evidence concerning the alleged commission of any offense prosecutable in the courts of the county, and concerning any misconduct, nonfeasance or neglect in public office by a public servant, whether criminal or otherwise.

2. District attorneys are required or authorized to submit evidence to grand juries under the following circumstances:

(a) A district attorney must submit to a grand jury evidence concerning a felony allegedly committed by a defendant who, on the basis of a felony complaint filed with a local criminal court of the county, has been held for the action of a grand jury of such county, except where indictment has been waived by the defendant pursuant to article one hundred ninety-five.

(b) A district attorney must submit to a grand jury evidence concerning a misdemeanor allegedly committed by a defendant who has been charged therewith by a local criminal court accusatory instrument, in any case where a superior court of the county has, pursuant to subdivision one of section 170.25, ordered that such misdemeanor charge be prosecuted by indictment in a superior court.

(c) A district attorney may submit to a grand jury any available evidence concerning an offense prosecutable in the courts of the county, or concerning misconduct, nonfeasance or neglect in public office by a public servant, whether criminal or otherwise.

Amended by L. 1974, Ch. 467.

ANNOTATIONS

Constitutionality.—CPL § 180.40 is constitutional under the Federal and State Constitutions. Corr. v. Clavin, 96 Misc. 2d 185, 409 N.Y.S.2d 334 (Sup. Ct. Nassau Co. 1978).

Complaint; jurisdiction; dismissal by Grand Jury.—Where Grand Jury heard evidence concerning assault, presented by District Attorney, and dismissed proceedings. Crim. Ct. was precluded from taking jurisdiction as only the Supreme Court could direct resubmission. Manford v. McCormack, 72 Misc. 2d 53, 337 N.Y.S.2d 914 (Cr. Ct. of N.Y.C. 1972).

Constructive possession; instructions.—Grand jury did not need to be instructed on constructive possession, where grand jury was informed that defendant was outside the premises with the key to the apartment on his person and utility and telephone bills in his name were found in the apartment; in any event, the People fulfilled the duty when another prosecutor gave this grand jury a thorough, detailed instruction as to constructive possession as part of another case earlier in the jury's term. People v. Hewitt, 233 A.D.2d 171, 649 N.Y.S.2d 663 (1st Dept. 1996).

Corroboration of a confession is not required for indictment.—People v. Kazmarick, 99 Misc. 2d 1012, 417 N.Y.S.2d 671 (Sullivan Co. Ct. 1979), aff'd, 52 N.Y.2d 322, 438 N.Y.S.2d 247, 420 N.E.2d 45 (1981).

Duty of prosecutor.—A prosecutor may not sit by silently while the prosecution witness testifies falsely that she did not receive any premise in return for the testimony. People v.

Novoa, 70 N.Y.2d 490, 522 N.Y.S.2d 504, 508, 517 N.E.2d 219 (1987).

—Where a prosecutor learns that an indictment is based upon evidence known to be false he is duty bound to obtain a superseding indictment on proper evidence or to disclose the facts and seek permission from the court to resubmit the case. People v. Alexander, 136 A.D.2d 332, 527 N.Y.S.2d 380 (1st Dept. 1988).

Exculpatory evidence; duty to present.—Prosecutor is not required to present at grand jury proceeding the exculpatory statements of a defendant as well as inculpatory statements where the exculpatory statements "were not part of a single statement in which inculpatory and exculpatory thoughts were expressed." People v. Jimenez, 175 Misc. 2d 714, 669 N.Y.S.2d 799 (Sup. Ct. Bronx Co. 1998), *citing* People v. Mitchell, 82 N.Y.2d 509, 605 N.Y.S.2d 655, 626 N.E.2d 630 (1993); *see also* People v. Brooks, 249 A.D.2d 572, 670 N.Y.S.2d 934 (3d Dept. 1998).

—Although there is no requirement that a prosecutor present exculpatory evidence to a Grand Jury, indictment was dismissed where prosecutor failed to inform defendant of an exculpatory witness known to the prosecutor prior to the Grand Jury presentation; such witness could have been called before the Grand Jury at defendant's request, had he been aware of such witness, notwithstanding that defendant himself did not testify before the Grand Jury. People v. Hunter, 126 A.D.2d 13, 480 N.Y.S.2d 1006 (Sup. Ct. N.Y. Co. 1984).

Grand Jury; gathering evidence after indictment.—After a defendant has been indicted, a prosecutor may not use a Grand Jury for the purpose of securing additional information or freezing testimony for the prospective trial, but a good faith inquiry into other charges within the scope of the prosecutor's authority is not prohibited even if it incidentally produces some additional evidence in the pending case. People v. Donaudy, 87 Misc. 2d 787, 386 N.Y.S.2d 326 (Sup. Ct. Suffolk Co. 1976).

Grand Jury; report on willful misconduct of public officers.—A Grand Jury report may not be filed as public record, but must be sealed, where it did not fall within statutory provisions specifying "misconduct, non-feasance or neglect in public office by a public servant." *In re* Report of January, 1972 Term, County Court Grand Jury, 40 A.D.2d 1003, 338 N.Y.S.2d 776 (2d Dept. 1972).

Grand Jury indictment.—It was no defense for defendant that the Town Justice failed to transmit order, felony complaint, and other pertinent documents to the Superior Court before the Grand Jury indicted him for burglary. People v. Talham, 41 A.D.2d 354, 342 N.Y.S.2d 921 (3d Dept. 1973).

Indictment for offense which is violation.—Grand Jury has no authority to indict defendant for commission of an offense which is only a violation. People v. Star Supermarkets, Inc., 67 Misc. 2d 483, 324 N.Y.S.2d 514 (Monroe Co. Ct. 1971).

Indictment for a violation dismissed; Grand Jury lacks authority to return same.—Dismissing indictment for the violation of criminal solicitation in the third degree, the court held that the Grand Jury has no authority to return an indictment for a violation as distinguished from a crime. People v. Claiborne, 36 A.D.2d 500, 323 N.Y.S.2d 527 (2d Dept.), *rev'd on other grounds,* 29 N.Y.2d 950, 329 N.Y.S.2d 580, 280 N.E.2d 366 (1972).

Mandamus.—The matter of presentation of evidence of an offense to a Grand Jury is a matter of prosecutorial discretion and the question of the existence of reasonable cause to hold defendants for Grand Jury action is a matter of judicial discretion; mandamus therefore will not issue to compel the performance of these discretionary acts. Coppola v. People, 87 Misc. 2d 801, 386 N.Y.S.2d 279 (Sup. Ct. Ulster Co. 1976).

§ 190.60.　Grand jury; action to be taken.

After hearing and examining evidence as prescribed in section 190.55, a grand jury may:

1. Indict a person for an offense, as provided in section 190.65;

2. Direct the district attorney to file a prosecutor's information with a local criminal court, as provided in section 190.70;

3. Direct the district attorney to file a request for removal to the family court, as provided in section 190.71 of this article;

4. Dismiss the charge before it, as provided in section 190.75;

5. Submit a grand jury report, as provided in section 190.85.

Amended by L. 1978, Ch. 481.

ANNOTATIONS

Aborting first presentation in the Grand Jury.—Where the People abort their first presentation to the Grand Jury and then commence a second one, a hearing should be held to determine whether the prosecutor's conduct was proper within the facts of the case or whether it was merely a pretext to circumvent the function of the Grand Jury. People v. Wilkins, 95 Misc. 2d 739, 408 N.Y.S.2d 291 (Sup. Ct. N.Y. Co. 1978).

Functional equivalent of dismissal.—Where the prosecution has withdrawn an essentially completed case from the grand jury prior to any action having been taken by that body, the result will be deemed the functional equivalent of a dismissal under CPL § 190.60(4), and the prosecutor cannot resubmit the matter to a second grand jury without leave of court under CPL § 190.75(3). People v. Hemstreet, 234 A.D.2d 609, 652 N.Y.S.2d 60 (2d Dept. 1996).

Grand Jury; effect of failure to act.—Where misdemeanor charges have been presented to the Grand Jury and the Grand Jury has not indicted, ordered the district attorney to file an information or filed a formal order of dismissal, the District Court has no authority to proceed with hearings in the case and if it attempts to do so the defendants proper remedy is a writ of prohibition. Mooney v. Cahn, 79 Misc. 2d 703, 361 N.Y.S.2d 118 (Sup. Ct. Nassau Co. 1974).

§ 190.65.　Grand jury; when indictment is authorized.

1. Subject to the rules prescribing the kinds of offenses which may be charged in an indictment, a grand jury may indict a person for an offense when (a) the evidence before it is legally sufficient to establish that such person committed such offense provided, however, such evidence is not legally sufficient when corroboration that would be required, as a matter of law, to sustain a conviction for such offense is absent, and (b) competent and admissible evidence before it provides reasonable cause to believe that such person committed such offense.

2. The offense or offenses for which a grand jury may indict a person in any particular case are not limited to that or those which may have been designated, at the commencement of the grand jury proceeding, to be the subject of the inquiry; and even in a case submitted to it upon a court order, pursuant to the provisions of section 170.25, directing that a misdemeanor charge pending in a local criminal court be prosecuted by indictment, the grand jury may indict the defendant for a felony if the evidence so warrants.

3. Upon voting to indict a person, a grand jury must, through its foreman or acting foreman, file an indictment with the court by which it was impaneled.

Amended by L. 1983, Ch. 28.

ANNOTATIONS

Indictment; arson.—The evidence before the Grand Jury was sufficient to establish arson where the expert testified that the fire was caused by a flammable accelerant; one of the fireman, who fought the blaze, had smelled gasoline inside the building; defendant had admitted the commission of the crime and a disinterested witness had placed defendant within a two-minute walk of the fire shortly after the blaze began. People v. Gulino, 73 A.D.2d 604, 422 N.Y.S.2d 115 (2d Dept. 1980).

Indictment; evidence; clear showing.—The evidence before the Grand Jury need not provide reasonable cause to believe the defendant committed the crime charged. People v. Mikuszewski, 73 N.Y.2d 407, 541 N.Y.S.2d 196, 197, 538 N.E.2d 1017 (1989).

—The test to be applied on a motion to dismiss an indictment for insufficiency of evidence is whether there has been a "clear showing" that the evidence before the grand jury, if unexplained and uncontradicted, would not warrant a conviction by a trial jury. The term "clear showing" has been construed to mean *prima facie* proof that the crime charged has been committed. People v. Dunleavy, 41 A.D.2d 717, 341 N.Y.S.2d 500 (1st Dept.), *aff'd,* 33 N.Y.2d 573, 347 N.Y.S.2d 448, 301 N.E.2d 432 (1973).

Indictment reinstated; sufficiency of evidence.—Order dismissing indictment was reversed, and the indictment reinstated, where evidence before the Grand Jury (including testimony that co-defendant disembarked from ship with ten pounds of marijuana and discarded the drugs after customs officials started in pursuit and that defendants in waiting car picked up the fleeing co-defendant) was found to be legally sufficient to hold defendants as accomplices and principals in commission of the offense of possession of a dangerous drug. People v. Feliciano, 32 N.Y.2d 140, 344 N.Y.S.2d 329, 297 N.E.2d 76 (1973).

Grand Jury; blood test.—A blood test and the results thereof can be introduced into evidence before a Grand Jury when no arrest has been made; any comment by the District Attorney relative to the blood test could be considered harmless in light of the overall facts presented to the grand jury. People v. Flynn, 73 Misc. 2d 178, 340 N.Y.S.2d 837 (Seneca Co. Ct. 1973).

Mitigation evidence; admissibility.—The prosecutor was not required to present mitigating defenses to a grand jury. People v. Harris, 98 N.Y.2d 452, 749 N.Y.S.2d 766, 779 N.E.2d 705 (2002), *habeas corpus denied,* Harris v. Goord, 2004 LEXIS U.S. Dist. 14017 (E.D.N.Y. July 23, 2004).

—Evidence submitted at grand jury must be competent, admissible, and legally sufficient to establish that crime was committed and that the accused committed it; mitigation evidence proffered by defendant in capital case is not admissible at grand jury because it has no bearing on defendant's guilt or innocence. People v. Harris, 173 Misc. 2d 248, 661 N.Y.S.2d 712 (Sup. Ct. Kings Co. 1997).

Sufficient evidence.—In order to return an indictment, the Grand Jury must have before it sufficient evidence, if unexplained or uncontradicted, to warrant a conviction. People v. Potwora, 44 A.D.2d 207, 354 N.Y.S.2d 492 (4th Dept. 1974).

Preliminary hearing; sexual abuse; corroboration.—Court need not dismiss information charging sexual abuse and assault arising out of alleged sexual attack by defendant upon female victim where corroboration is lacking since only requirement at preliminary hearing is to have reasonable cause or ground to believe defendant committed crime. People v. Scarposi, 69 Misc. 2d 264, 329 N.Y.S.2d 850 (Cr. Ct. N.Y. Co. 1972).

Reopening.—Following return of a true bill and prior to its filing the prosecutor may void the vote and reopen proceedings for the purpose of submitting additional evidence without judicial authorization. People v. Cade, 74 N.Y.2d 410, 548 N.Y.S.2d 137, 547 N.E.2d 339 (1989).

Circumstantial evidence.—In assessing when the evidence before the grand jury is wholly circumstantial, a reviewing court's inquiry is limited to "whether the facts, if proven, and the inferences that logically flow from those facts supply proof of every element of the charged crimes." People v. Hyde, 302 A.D.2d 101, 754 N.Y.S.2d 11 (1st Dept. 2003).

Subd. 1

Accomplice testimony.—Accomplice testimony must be corroborated in a grand jury proceeding. People v. Wallace, 101 Misc. 2d 127, 420 N.Y.S.2d 851 (Monroe Co. Ct. 1979).

Counts.—It is legally permissible for the Grand Jury on the same conduct to "no-bill" a charge of criminally negligent homicide and to find a true bill with respect to reckless driving, even though the mental state required for the lesser offense is higher than that required for the greater offense. People v. Ackroyd, 144 Misc. 2d 149, 543 N.Y.S.2d 848, 850 (Sup. Ct. Albany Co. 1989).

Indictment; dismissal.—The fact that each indictment contains only one count of perjury does not warrant dismissal, since at the time of trial, should the evidence warrant it, lesser included counts may also be considered. People v. Dunleavy, 41 A.D.2d 717, 341 N.Y.S.2d 500 (1st Dept.), *aff'd,* 33 N.Y.2d 573, 347 N.Y.S.2d 448, 301 N.E.2d 432 (1973).

—The testimony of the two witnesses, who were not present when the incident occurred, should not have been presented and was prejudicial rendering the Grand Jury proceedings defective. People v. Cornachio, 46 A.D.2d 690, 360 N.Y.S.2d 266 (2d Dept. 1974).

Indictment; evidence.—In the context of the Grand Jury procedure, legally sufficient means prima facie, not proof beyond a reasonable doubt; proof that seller handed proceeds of drug sale to the defendant immediately after the transaction was sufficient to support charge of criminal sale (acting in concert). People v. Matos, 195 A.D.2d 287, 599 N.Y.S.2d 598 (1st Dept. 1993).

—There is no constitutional requirement that Grand Jury indictments be founded upon sufficient legal proof. Miranda v. Isseks, 41 A.D.2d 176, 341 N.Y.S.2d 541 (2d Dept. 1973).

—In a case involving circumstantial evidence, it is irrelevant that other innocent inferences could possible be drawn from the facts as long as the Grand Jury could rationally have drawn the guilty inference. People v. Colon, 188 A.D.2d 708, 590 N.Y.S.2d 581 (3d Dept. 1992).

—A Grand Jury may indict a person when the evidence before it establishes all the elements of the crime and also establishes reasonable cause to believe that the accused committed the crime charged. People v. Van Buren, 187 A.D.2d 925, 590 N.Y.S.2d 362 (4th Dept. 1992).

Motion to dismiss indictment reversed; prima facie case.— Reasonable doubt is not the standard to apply to an indictment, only a prima facie case is required. People v. Steiner, 77 A.D.2d 13, 432 N.Y.S.2d 83 (1st Dept. 1980).

—The evidence presented to a Grand Jury must be the equivalent of prima facie proof that the crime charged has been committed. People v. Cahill, 54 A.D.2d 736, 387 N.Y.S.2d 666 (2d Dept. 1976).

—After the County Court dismissed a robbery indictment against the defendant, the People appealed and the order was reversed, since the testimony of the victim together with admissions of the defendant that he was involved in aspects of the robbery was sufficient to establish a prima facie case. People v. Karl, 41 A.D.2d 1001, 344 N.Y.S.2d 118 (3d Dept. 1973).

Parole revocation; preliminary hearing; application or incarcerated parolee.—Incarcerated parolee, charged with felony, and parole violations, could obtain preliminary hearing with notice of charges and right to counsel either in jail or elsewhere before posting bail on felony indictment. *In re* Way, 71 Misc. 2d 229, 335 N.Y.S.2d 812 (Sup. Ct. Nassau Co. 1972).

Sufficiency of indictment; appeal.—Since a defendant, by virtue of section 210.30(6), can no longer attack a conviction on the ground that the proof before the Grand Jury is legally insufficient to make out a crime, the court felt that judges at *nisi prius* should be most liberal in granting motions to inspect Grand Jury minutes, to the extent of examining them *in camera* for the purpose of determining their sufficiency. Miranda v. Isseks, 41 A.D.2d 176, 341 N.Y.S.2d 541 (2d Dept. 1973).

Trier of facts. The existence of amistake can only be determined by the trier of the facts, whether a petit juror or a trial justice presiding at a non-jury trial. People v. Dunleavy, 41 A.D.2d 717, 341 N.Y.S.2d 500 (1st Dept. 1973), *aff'd,* 33 N.Y.2d 573, 347 N.Y.S.2d 448, 301 N.E.2d 432 (1973).

Indictment; sufficiency of evidence.—In reviewing a grand jury's determination to indict, a court may not examine the quality or persuasiveness of the proof to establish reasonable cause, which is solely the responsibility of the factfinders on the grand jury panel. Judicial review is limited to whether the charge voted by the grand jury is supported by legally sufficient evidence. People v. Williams, 20 A.D.3d 72, 795 N.Y.S.2d 561 (1st Dept. 2005).

Photographic identification.—Indictment based upon testimony of complaining witnesses that they had identified the defendant was not defective for failure to inform the Grand Jury that the identification had been made from photographs; the identification testimony satisfied the requirements of a prima facie case. People v. Brewster, 63 N.Y.2d 419, 482 N.Y.S.2d 724, 472 N.E.2d 686 (1984).

Sufficiency of evidence before Grand Jury.—Absent exceptional circumstances not present here, determination by first judge, after reviewing Grand Jury minutes, that there was sufficient evidence presented to the Grand Jury to support the indictment was binding as the law of the case on second judge who improperly reexamined the Grand Jury minutes after conducting a Wade hearing and dismissed the indictment. People v. Finley, 104 A.D.2d 450, 479 N.Y.S.2d 63 (2d Dept. 1984), aff'd, 107 A.D.2d 709, 484 N.Y.S.2d 63 (2d Dept. 1985).

Subd. 2

Factual allegations of indictment; deviations permitted from those of local criminal court accusatory instrument.—There was no error when defendant was charged in Town Court with interfering with an arrest being made by one police officer and by indictment with interfering with an arrest being made by another police officer. Any proceeding in the Town Court was superseded by the subsequent indictment. People v. Fife, 39 A.D.2d 780, 331 N.Y.S.2d 545 (3d Dept. 1972).

Indictment for a higher crime than the one held for.—The Grand Jury has the right to indict a defendant for a crime higher than the one for which he is being held. People ex rel. Reynolds v. Vincent, 57 A.D.2d 851, 394 N.Y.S.2d 35 (2d Dept. 1977).

—The offenses for which the Grand Jury might indict a defendant are not limited to those designated in the felony complaint. People v. Simmons, 178 A.D.2d 972, 579 N.Y.S.2d 499 (4th Dept. 1991).

Motion to inspect Grand Jury Minutes; motion to dismiss indictment.—Where the indictment did not contain the factual allegations required by Section 210.30 of the Criminal Procedure Law, the court, in its discretion, read the transcript of the evidence presented to the Grand Jury, and determined that the evidence presented met the standard prescribed by Section 190.65 of the Criminal Procedure Law, in that legally sufficient evidence had been presented which provided reasonable cause for believing that the defendant committed the crime charged. People v. Kaufman & Broad Homes of Long Island, 84 Misc. 2d 811, 378 N.Y.S.2d 258 (Rockland Co. Ct. 1975), aff'd, 89 Misc. 2d 769, 393 N.Y.S.2d 144 (Sup. Ct. App. Term 1977).

§ 190.70. Grand jury; direction to file prosecutor's information and related matters.

1. Except in a case submitted to it pursuant to the provisions of section 170.25, a grand jury may direct the district attorney to file in a local criminal court a prosecutor's information charging a person with an offense other than a felony when (a) the evidence before it is legally sufficient to establish that such person committed such offense, and (b) competent and admissible evidence before it provides reasonable cause to believe that such person committed such offense. In such case, the grand jury must, through its foreman or acting foreman, file such direction with the court by which it was impaneled.

2. Such direction must be signed by the foreman or acting foreman. It must contain a plain and concise statement of the conduct constituting the offense to be charged, equivalent in content and precision to the factual statement required to

be contained in an indictment pursuant to subdivision seven of section 200.50. Subject to the rules prescribed in sections 200.20 and 200.40 governing joinder in a single indictment of multiple offenses and multiple defendants, such grand jury direction may, where appropriate, specify multiple offenses of less than felony grade and multiple defendants, and may direct that the prospective prosecutor's information charge a single defendant with multiple offenses, or multiple defendants jointly with either a single offense or multiple offenses.

3. Upon the filing of such grand jury direction, the court must, unless such direction is insufficient on its face, issue an order approving such direction and ordering the district attorney to file such a prosecutor's information in a designated local criminal court having trial jurisdiction of the offense or offenses in question.

ANNOTATIONS

Court discretion.—CPL § 190.70(3) does not give the court discretion to direct resubmission where the Grand Jury has ordered the matter back to the local criminal court for prosecution of a non-felony offense. Kerstanski v. Shapiro, 84 Misc. 2d 1049, 376 N.Y.S.2d 844 (Sup. Ct. Orange Co. 1975).

Double jeopardy; prosecutor's information.—Defendants were not subjected to double jeopardy or unconstitutional denial of equal protection, where Grand Jury ordered filing of a prosecutor's information covering a misdemeanor that was previously dismissed by the Criminal Court. People v. McClafferty, 73 Misc. 2d 666, 342 N.Y.S.2d 208 (Crim. Ct. Queens Co. 1973).

§ 190.71. Grand jury; direction to file request for removal to family court.

(a) Except as provided in subdivision six of section 200.20 of this chapter, a grand jury may not indict (i) a person thirteen years of age for any conduct or crime other than conduct constituting a crime defined in subdivisions one and two of section 125.25 (murder in the second degree); (ii) a person fourteen or fifteen years of age for any conduct or crime other than conduct constituting a crime defined in subdivisions one and two of section 125.25 (murder in the second degree) and in subdivision three of such section provided that the underlying crime for the murder charge is one for which such person is criminally responsible; 135.25 (kidnapping in the first degree); 150.20 (arson in the first degree); subdivisions one and two of section 120.10 (assault in the first degree); 125.20 (manslaughter in the first degree); subdivisions one and two of section 130.35 (rape in the first degree); subdivisions one and two of section 130.50 (criminal sexual act in the first degree); 130.70 (aggravated sexual abuse in the first degree); 140.30 (burglary in the first degree); subdivision one of section 140.25 (burglary in the second degree); 150.15 (arson in the second degree); 160.15 (robbery in the first degree); subdivision two of section 160.10 (robbery in the second degree) of the penal law; subdivision four of section 265.02 of the penal law, where such firearm is possessed on school grounds, as that phrase is defined in subdivision fourteen of section 220.00 of the penal law; or section 265.03 of the penal law, where such machine gun or such firearm is possessed on school grounds, as that phrase is defined in subdivision fourteen of section 220.00 of the penal law; or defined in the penal law as an attempt to commit murder in the second degree or kidnapping in the first degree.

(b) A grand jury may vote to file a request to remove a charge to the family court if it finds that a person thirteen, fourteen or fifteen years of age did an act which, if done by a person over the age of sixteen, would constitute a crime provided (1) such act is one for which it may not indict; (2) it does not indict such person for a crime; and (3) the evidence before it is legally sufficient to establish that such person did such act and competent and admissible evidence before it provides reasonable cause to believe that such person did such act.

(c) Upon voting to remove a charge to the family court pursuant to subdivision (b) of this section, the grand jury must, through its foreman or acting foreman, file a request to transfer such charge to the family court. Such request shall be filed with the court by which it was impaneled. It must (1) allege that a person named therein did any act which, if done by a person over the age of sixteen, would constitute a crime; (2) specify the act and the time and place of its commission; and (3) be signed by the foreman or the acting foreman.

(d) Upon the filing of such grand jury request, the court must, unless such request is improper or insufficient on its face, issue an order approving such request and direct that the charge be removed to the family court in accordance with the provisions of article seven hundred twenty-five of this chapter.

Added by L. 1978, Ch. 481; **Amended** by L. 1979, Ch. 411; L. 1980, Ch. 136; L. 1981; L. 1998, Ch. 435, § 2, Nov. 1, 1998; L. 2003, Ch. 264, § 39, eff. Nov. 1, 2003, amending subd. (a).

ANNOTATIONS

Removal; requirements.—CPL § 190.71(b) provides that the Grand Jury may vote to file a request to remove to the Family Court only where the three enumerated conditions are met. People v. Owens, 101 Misc. 2d 891, 422 N.Y.S.2d 343 (Sup. Ct. Queens Co. 1979).

Removal to Family Court.—The only authority for the Grand Jury to vote to file a request for removal is where a juvenile has committed an act for which they may not indict, and they do not indict such juvenile for any other crime, and the Grand Jury finds the evidence before it legally sufficient to establish that such person did such act and competent evidence before it provides reasonable cause to believe such person did such act. People v. Harris, 100 Misc. 2d 736, 420 N.Y.S.2d 102 (Sup. Ct. Kings Co. 1979).

Removal to Family Court; indictable offense.—The Grand Jury does not have the option to remove a robbery in the first degree, for which the juvenile can be indicted, to the Family Court. People v. Rios, 78 A.D.2d 642, 432 N.Y.S.2d 120 (2d Dept. 1980).

§ 190.75. Grand jury; dismissal of charge.

1. If upon a charge that a designated person committed a crime, either (a) the evidence before the grand jury is not legally sufficient to establish that such person committed such crime or any other offense, or (b) the grand jury is not satisfied that there is reasonable cause to believe that such person committed such crime or any other offense, it must dismiss the charge. In such case, the grand jury must, through its foreman or acting foreman, file its finding of dismissal with the court by which it was impaneled.

2. If the defendant was previously held for the action of the grand jury by a local criminal court, the superior court to which such dismissal is presented must order the defendant released from custody if he is in the custody of the sheriff, or, if he is at liberty on bail, it must exonerate the bail.

3. When a charge has been so dismissed, it may not again be submitted to a grand jury unless the court in its discretion authorizes or directs the people to resubmit such charge to the same or another grand jury. If in such case the charge is again dismissed, it may not again be submitted to a grand jury.

4. Whenever all charges against a designated person have been so dismissed, the district attorney must within ninety days of the filing of the finding of such dismissal, notify that person of the dismissal by regular mail to his last known address unless resubmission has been permitted pursuant to subdivision three of this section or an order of postponement of such service is obtained upon a showing of good cause and exigent circumstances.

Amended by L. 1977, Ch. 907.

ANNOTATIONS

Different charge; same complainant; not resubmission.—When an indictment was returned by the March Grand Jury against the defendant for burglary, grand larceny and assault, an indictment by the July Grand Jury for robbery with two witnesses before the March Grand Jury giving identical testimony is not a resubmission where the minutes of the first Grand Jury showed the charge of robbery was not considered. People v. Westbrook, 79 Misc. 2d 902, 361 N.Y.S.2d 584 (Nassau Co. Ct. 1974).

Double jeopardy; prosecutor's information.—Defendants were not subjected to double jeopardy or unconstitutional denial of equal protection, where Grand Jury ordered filing of a prosecutor's information covering a misdemeanor that was previously dismissed by the Criminal Court. People v. McClafferty, 73 Misc. 2d 666, 342 N.Y.S.2d 208 (Crim. Ct. Queens Co. 1973).

Grand Jury; failure to file dismissal; resubmission of charges.—A grand jury cannot be denied further deliberations once it has taken a single, inconclusive, preliminary vote. Where the grand jury never formally filed a "finding of dismissal," the grand jury was not barred from further consideration of the case without leave of court. People v. Aarons, 305 A.D.2d 45, 759 N.Y.S.2d 20 (1st Dept. 2003), aff'd, 2 N.Y.3d 547, 780 N.Y.S.2d 533, 813 N.E.2d 613 (2004).

—Where misdemeanor charges have been presented to the grand jury and the Grand Jury has not indicted, ordered the district attorney to file an information or filed a formal order of dismissal, the District Court has no authority to proceed with hearing in the case and if it attempts to do so the defendant's proper remedy is a writ of prohibition. Mooney v. Cahn, 79 Misc. 2d 703, 361 N.Y.S.2d 118 (Sup. Ct. Nassau Co. 1974).

—The court held that where the first session of the Grand Jury resulted in no indictment, the same charges could not be resubmitted to a second Grand Jury, absent a court order, even though the first Grand Jury failed to file a dismissal with the court by which it was impaneled. People v. DiLio, 75 Misc. 2d 711, 348 N.Y.S.2d 703 (Sup. Ct. Queens Co. 1973).

Complaint; jurisdiction; dismissal by Grand Jury.— Where Grand Jury heard evidence concerning assault presented by District Attorney, and dismissed proceedings, criminal court was precluded from taking jurisdiction as only the Supreme Court could direct resubmission. Manford v. McCormack, 72 Misc. 2d 53, 337 N.Y.S.2d 914 (Crim. Ct. of N.Y.C. 1972).

Functional equivalent of dismissal.—Where the prosecution has withdrawn an essentially completed case from the grand jury prior to any action having been taken by that body, the result will be deemed the functional equivalent of a dismissal under CPL § 190.60(4), and the prosecutor cannot resubmit the matter to a second grand jury without leave of court under CPL § 190.75(3). People v. Hemstreet, 234 A.D.2d 609, 652 N.Y.S.2d 60 (2d Dept. 1996).

Indictment after resubmission; motion to dismiss.—A judge, deliberating upon a motion to dismiss an indictment handed up by the second Grand Jury, should be permitted to determine whether the prosecutor has, in fact, presented the promised new evidence; if upon comparing the minutes of the evidence presented to the two grand juries the court determines that the People have failed to present the evidence proffered in the application to resubmit and that the second Grand Jury was presented with substantially the same evidence as that given to the first, it may dismiss the indictment in the furtherance of justice. CPL §§ 190.75, 210.40. People v. Martin, 71 A.D.2d 928, 419 N.Y.S.2d 724 (2d Dept. 1979).

Judicial scrutiny; application to resubmit.—Had the legislature deemed judicial scrutiny unnecessary it could have eliminated it entirely; the prosecutor is still required to make an application to the court shows that his dissatisfaction with the first grand jury's action is not itself sufficient reason to permit resubmission. People v. Martin, 71 A.D.2d 928, 419 N.Y.S.2d 724 (2d Dept. 1979).

Resubmission.—Because there was no concurrence by the grand jurors on any authorized action, it was not improper for prosecutor to ask grand juror to cease deliberations to hear additional evidence, and prosecutor was not required to seek leave of court before presenting the new evidence. People v. Aarons, 2 N.Y.3d 547, 780 N.Y.S.2d 533, 813 N.E.2d 613 (2004).

—A grand jury may not, without court permission pursuant to CPL § 190.75(3), reconsider its vote of a no true bill under circumstances which incontrovertibly indicate prosecutorial involvement in the grand jury's deliberative process. People v. Montanez, 90 N.Y.2d 690, 665 N.Y.S.2d 62, 687 N.E.2d 1345 (1997).

—Where co-defendant testified and implicated defendant after grand jury had voted no true bill for defendant, prosecutor received approval of supervising justice of the grand jury to resubmit the charge based on co-defendant's testimony, which constituted new evidence; however, prior to being informed of this order, grand jury reconsidered the dismissal *sua sponte* and voted to indict defendant. The decision to reconsider was independent and not the result of prosecutorial overreaching. People v. Green, 249 A.D.2d 157, 671 N.Y.S.2d 250 (1st Dept. 1998).

—An indictment must be dismissed when the identical charges are represented in a subsequent Grand Jury proceeding and rejected; the rejection of those charges by the second Grand Jury effectively nullifies the action of the first Grand Jury, rendering the original indictment invalid and thereby creating a legal impediment to the conviction of the defendant for the offenses charged. People v. Franco, 196 A.D.2d 357, 612 N.Y.S.2d 591 (2d Dept. 1994), *aff'd,* 86 N.Y.2d 493, 634 N.Y.S.2d 38, 657 N.E.2d 1321 (1995).

—Granting of leave to resubmit charges based upon the mere ground that it appeared from the assistant district attorney's affirmation that the dismissal was against the weight of evidence was without basis without any other indication of Grand Jury conflict, or irregularity in the proceedings; the court's power to grant resubmission should be exercised sparingly. People v. Dykes, 86 A.D.2d 191, 449 N.Y.S.2d 284 (2d Dept. 1982).

—Where withdrawal of a case takes place because of the possibility that the Grand Jury will vote against indictment, the Special Prosecutor must obtain court approval for resubmission to another Grand Jury. McGinley v. Hynes, 75 A.D.2d 897, 428 N.Y.S.2d 57 (2d Dept. 1980).

—The CPL clearly permits resubmission of charges to a Grand Jury with judicial permission when the first Grand Jury hearing the evidence has rejected it as insufficient. People v. Maye, 173 A.D.2d 891, 569 N.Y.S.2d 758, 759 (3d Dept. 1991).

—Prosecution's ex parte application to resubmit the charge of attempted murder to the grand jury was proper since there is no requirement that an application to resubmit be made on notice to defendant. People v. Taylor, 187 Misc. 2d 321, 723 N.Y.S.2d 345 (Sup. Ct. Kings. Co. 2001)

—The failure of the prosecutor to seek leave of the court pursuant to CPL § 190.75(3) to resubmit the charges originally not true billed, which were only reconsidered after prosecutorial overreaching, impaired the integrity of the proceedings and created the risk of prejudice to the defendants, which mandated the dismissal of the indictment. People v. Harris, 181 Misc. 2d 670, 695 N.Y.S.2d 215 (Sup. Ct. Bronx Co. 1999).

—Court granted People authority to resubmit chages due to factually inconsistent findings by Grand Jury. People v. Wesley, 161 Misc. 2d 786, 615 N.Y.S.2d 611, 616 (Sup. Ct. Kings Co. 1994).

—No court approval is required to resubmit for the purpose of obtaining a superseding indictment where there is no initial refusal of the Grand Jury to indict. People v. Boria, 144 Misc. 2d 600, 544 N.Y.S.2d 1018 (Orange Co. Ct. 1989).

§ 190.80. Grand jury; release of defendant upon failure of timely grand jury action.

Upon application of a defendant who on the basis of a felony complaint has been held by a local criminal court for the action of a grand jury, and who, at the time of such order or subsequent thereto, has been committed to the custody of the sheriff pending such grand jury action, and who has been confined in such custody for a period of more than forty-five days, or, in the case of a juvenile offender, thirty days, without the occurrence of any grand jury action or disposition pursuant to subdivision one, two or three of section 190.60, the superior court by which such grand jury was or is to be impaneled must release him on his own recognizance unless:

(a) The lack of a grand jury disposition during such period of confinement was due to the defendant's request, action or condition, or occurred with his consent; or

(b) The people have shown good cause why such order of release should not be issued. Such good cause must consist of some compelling fact or circumstance which precluded grand jury action within the prescribed period or rendered the same against the interest of justice.

Amended by L. 1979, Ch. 411.

ANNOTATIONS

Commencement of 45-day period.—The 45-day period of CPL § 190.80 commences with the local criminal court's order holding defendant for the grand jury or from defendant's commitment to custody, whichever is later. People v. Brecker, 191 Misc. 2d 203, 741 N.Y.S.2d 839 (Co. Ct. Greene Co. 2002).

Expiration of statutory period; effect of.—Statute that protects defendant from being held for more than 45 days while awaiting grand jury action does not prevent People from indicting defendant prior to expiration of statutory period but merely provides that, after the expiration of the statutory period, a defendant may apply for release upon his own recognizance. People v. Cooper, 283 A.D.2d 1022, 725 N.Y.S.2d 780 (4th Dept. 2001).

Indictment; power to dismiss.—The court has the inherent power to dismiss the prosecution if no indictment is found within six months from the date of arrest. People v. Farley, 72 Misc. 2d 1018, 341 N.Y.S.2d 187 (Sup. Ct. Queens Co. 1973).

Motion to dismiss prosecution.—The motion to dismiss the prosecution was not carried over from the CCP, nor is it included in section 210.20(1) of the CPL. It can only be assumed that this was a legislative oversight, or that it was contemplated that any failure to indict within a co-extensive time for trial could be rectified by the court on a case-to-case basis. People v. Farley, 72 Misc. 2d 1018, 341 N.Y.S.2d 187 (Sup. Ct. Queens Co. 1973); People v. Wright, 88 Misc. 2d 14, 387 N.Y.S.2d 49 (Sup. Ct. N.Y. Co. 1976).

§ 190.85. Grand jury; grand jury reports.

1. The grand jury may submit to the court by which it was impaneled, a report:

(a) Concerning misconduct, non-feasance or neglect in public office by a public servant as the basis for a recommendation of removal or disciplinary action; or

(b) Stating that after investigation of a public servant it finds no misconduct, non-feasance or neglect in office by him provided that such public servant has requested the submission of such report; or

(c) Proposing recommendations for legislative, executive or administrative action in the public interest based upon stated findings.

2. The court to which such report is submitted shall examine it and the minutes of the grand jury and, except as otherwise provided in subdivision four, shall make an order accepting and filing such report as a public record only if the court is satisfied that it complies with the provisions of subdivision one and that:

(a) The report is based upon facts revealed in the course of an investigation authorized by section 190.55 and is supported by the preponderance of the credible and legally admissible evidence; and

(b) When the report is submitted pursuant to paragraph (a) of subdivision one, that each person named therein was afforded an opportunity to testify before the grand jury prior to the filing of such report, and when the report is submitted pursuant to paragraph (b) or (c) of subdivision one, it is not critical of an identified or identifiable person.

3. The order accepting a report pursuant to paragraph (a) of subdivision one, and the report itself, must be sealed by the court and may not be filed as a public record, or be subject to subpoena or otherwise be made public until at least thirty-one days after a copy of the order and the report are served upon each public servant named therein, or if an appeal is taken pursuant to section 190.90, until the affirmance of the order

accepting the report, or until reversal of the order sealing the report, or until dismissal of the appeal of the named public servant by the appellate division, whichever occurs later. Such public servant may file with the clerk of the court an answer to such report, not later than twenty days after service of the order and report upon him. Such an answer shall plainly and concisely state the facts and law constituting the defense of the public servant to the charges in said report, and, except for those parts of the answer which the court may determine to be scandalously or prejudicially and unnecessarily inserted therein, shall become an appendix to the report. Upon the expiration of the time set forth in this subdivision, the district attorney shall deliver a true copy of such report, and the appendix if any, for appropriate action, to each public servant or body having removal or disciplinary authority over each public servant named therein.

4. Upon the submission of a report pursuant to subdivision one, if the court finds that the filing of such report as a public record, may prejudice fair consideration of a pending criminal matter, it must order such report sealed and such report may not be subject to subpoena or public inspection during the pendency of such criminal matter, except upon order of the court.

5. Whenever the court to which a report is submitted pursuant to paragraph (a) of subdivision one is not satisfied that the report complies with the provisions of subdivision two, it may direct that additional testimony be taken before the same grand jury, or it must make an order sealing such report, and the report may not be filed as a public record, or be subject to subpoena or otherwise be made public.

ANNOTATIONS

Answer to report.—The "answer" merely furnishes additional information not before the Grand Jury and attempts to refute the charges against those named in the reports; it does not precipitate an adversary proceeding but merely provides further assistance to the court in rendering its decision whether or not to accept the reports for filing. First Report of the October 1972 Grand Jury of the Supreme Court Albany County v. District Attorney of the County of Albany, 44 A.D.2d 855, 354 N.Y.S.2d 966 (3d Dept. 1974), dism'd, 34 N.Y.2d 915, 359 N.Y.S.2d 290, 316 N.E.2d 722 (1974).

Confidentiality of Grand Jury reports.—A target of a grand jury investigation threatened with stigmatization by unwarranted disclosure has standing, where disclosure will cause him injury, to seek to enforce the confidentiality of the Grand Jury report. In re District Attorney of Suffolk County, 58 N.Y.2d 436, 461 N.Y.S.2d 773, 448 N.E.2d 440 (1983).

Disclosure of report; consent of persons named.—The contents of a Grand Jury report that concerns misconduct and nonfeasance as well as recommendations for legislative and executive action can be made public where both of the aggrieved individuals mentioned in the report urge publication. In re report of March 1980 Grand Jury, 77 A.D.2d 58, 432 N.Y.S.2d 726 (3d Dept. 1980).

District Attorney; Attorney General.—When, in the judgment of the District Attorney, Attorney General, or Special Deputy Attorney General acting under appropriate authority, there is evidence which bears upon the propriety of the conduct of a public employee, which information may not otherwise come to the attention of the employer agency, it is only right and proper for him to act in the public interest and to ask the court to consider his request that the information in the Grand Jury minutes be transmitted to the agency concerned. Application of Scotti, 53 A.D.2d 282, 385 N.Y.S.2d 659 (4th Dept. 1976).

Grand Jury; report; neglect.—Critical report after Grand Jury investigation of South Mall project in Albany was sealed where charge of neglect was not supported by evidence that officials involved failed to perform obligatory duty since publication would damage public officials not afforded protections of an adversary proceeding. *In re* Investigation of South Mall Financing, 69 Misc. 2d 460, 330 N.Y.S.2d 170 (Albany Co. Ct. 1972).

Grand Jury reports.—The combining in the report of a recommendation for disciplinary action against an identified person (CPL § 190.85[1][a]) with a recommendation for legislative or administrative action (CPL § 190.85[1][c]) required that the report be forever sealed. *In re* Report of October 1975 Grand Jury, 55 A.D.2d 707, 388 N.Y.S.2d 949 (3d Dept. 1976).

—Court directed that the Grand Jury reports should remain sealed and not be published as a public record since the findings of wrongdoing were not supported by a preponderance of the credible and legally admissible evidence. *In re* Reports of Grand Jury No. 1 etc., 71 A.D.2d 1060, 420 N.Y.S.2d 946 (4th Dept. 1979).

—The inclusion in a report containing recommendations for legislative or administrative action, of material critical of an identified individual, requires that the report be forever sealed. *In re* Report of the September 1975 Grand Jury of the Supreme Court of St. Lawrence County, 55 A.D.2d 220, 390 N.Y.S.2d 251 (1976).

—Since the combination in one Grand Jury report of reports dealing with misconduct, nonfeasance or neglect in public office by a public servant and recommendation for legislative, executive, or administrative action is improper and requires the sealing of the report the court denied the New York State Select Committee on Crime's application for order authorizing the furnishing of a full copy of the Grand Jury minutes and exhibits concerning its investigation into the negotiation and execution of an amended lease for certain real property owned by the City of New York which resulted in a report making specific recommendations for legislative and administrative action. People v. Doe, 103 Misc. 2d 524, 426 N.Y.S.2d 426 (Sup. Ct. N.Y. Co. 1980).

—A Grand Jury report may be sealed upon some indication that fair consideration of a matter has been tainted by prejudice. *In re* of Nassau County Grand Jury, 87 Misc. 2d 453, 382 N.Y.S.2d 1013 (Sup. Ct. Nassau Co. 1976).

Grand Jury report; specific disciplinary recommendations.—A Grand Jury is not authorized by statute to recommend specific disciplinary measures; a court may accept only those recommendations in the report which basically track the statute in recommending "removal or disciplinary action." *In re* Report of August "A" 1977 Grand Jury of Westchester Co., 63 A.D.2d 984, 406 N.Y.S.2d 107 (2d Dept. 1978).

"Recommendation."—as used in the statutory provision constitutes the necessary predicate conclusion for the authority granted to file such a report and does not grant any authority to make a specific disciplinary recommendation. *In re* Richard Roe 46 A.D.2d 723, 360 N.Y.S.2d 123 (4th Dept. 1974).

—The Grand Jury exceeded its statutory authority in recommending a minimum disciplinary action and the recommendation was deleted and forever sealed. *In re* Report of March, 1975 Grand Jury v. Vogt, 53 A.D.2d 724, 383 N.Y.S.2d 927 (3d Dept. 1976).

Report must be sealed.—A Grand Jury report alleging misconduct, non-feasance or neglect in public office must be sealed when it is not supported by a preponderance of credible and legally admissible evidence. *In re* Report of Special Grand Jury, 77 A.D.2d 199, 433 N.Y.S.2d 300 (4th Dept. 1980).

§ 190.90. Grand jury; appeal from order concerning grand jury reports.

1. When a court makes an order accepting a report of a grand jury pursuant to paragraph (a) of subdivision one of section 190.85, any public

servant named therein may appeal the order; and when a court makes an order sealing a report of a grand jury pursuant to subdivision five of section 190.85, the district attorney or other attorney designated by the grand jury may appeal the order.

2. When a court makes an order sealing a report of a grand jury pursuant to subdivision five of section 190.85, the district attorney or other attorney designated by the grand jury may, within ten days after service of a copy of the order and report upon each public servant named in the report, appeal the order to the appellate division of the department in which the order was made, by filing in duplicate a notice of appeal from the order with the clerk of the court in which the order was made and by serving a copy of such notice of appeal upon each such public servant. Notwithstanding any contrary provision of section 190.85, a true copy of the report of the grand jury shall be served, together with such notice of appeal, upon each such public servant.

3. The mode of and time for perfecting an appeal pursuant to this section, and the mode of and procedure for the argument thereof, are determined by the rules of the appellate division of the department in which the appeal is brought. Such rules shall prescribe the matters referred to in subdivision one of section 460.70 and in section 460.80, except that such appeal is a preferred cause and the appellate division of each department shall promulgate rules to effectuate such preference.

4. The record and all other presentations on appeal shall remain sealed, except that upon reversal of the order sealing the report or dismissal of the appeal of the named public servant by the appellate division, the report of the grand jury, with the appendix, if any, shall be filed as a public record as provided in subdivision three of section 190.85.

5. The procedure provided for in this section shall be the exclusive manner of reviewing an order made pursuant to section 190.85 and the appellate division of the supreme court shall be the sole court having jurisdiction of such an appeal. The order of the appellate division finally determining such appeal shall not be subject to review in any other court or proceeding.

6. The grand jury in an appeal pursuant to this section shall be represented by the district attorney unless the report relates to him or his office, in which event the grand jury may designate another attorney.

Amended by L. 1985, Ch. 517.

ANNOTATION

Grand Jury; report; neglect.—Critical report after Grand Jury investigation of South Mall project in Albany was sealed where charge of neglect was not supported by evidence that officials involved failed to perform obligatory duty since publication would damage public officials not afforded protections

of an adversary proceeding. *In re* Investigation of South Mall
Fin., 69 Misc. 2d 460, 330 N.Y.S.2d 170 (Albany Co. Ct. 1972).

ARTICLE 195—WAIVER OF INDICTMENT

Section

195.10   Waiver of indictment; in general.

195.20   Waiver of indictment; written instrument.

195.30   Waiver of indictment; approval of waiver by the court.

195.40   Waiver of indictment; filing of superior court information.

LexisNexis Cross Reference

New York Criminal Practice (2d ed.), Vol. 1, Ch. 5, Indictments and Superior Court Informations.

§ 195.10. Waiver of indictment; in general.

1. A defendant may waive indictment and consent to be prosecuted by superior court information when:

(a) a local criminal court has held the defendant for the action of a grand jury; and

(b) the defendant is not charged with a class A felony; and

(c) the district attorney consents to the waiver.

2. A defendant may waive indictment pursuant to subdivision one in either:

(a) the local criminal court in which the order was issued holding the defendant for action of a grand jury, at the time such order is issued; or

(b) the appropriate superior court, at any time prior to the filing of an indictment by the grand jury.

Added by L. 1974, Ch. 467.

ANNOTATIONS

Waiver permissible.—The waiver procedure is available after indictment when the defendant is held for Grand Jury action on a new felony complaint. People v. D'Amico, 76 N.Y.2d 877, 561 N.Y.S.2d 411, 562 N.E.2d 488 (1990).

—The Legislature's use of the term "file" rather than "vote" when enacting the time limits set forth in CPL § 195.10(2)(b) for waiving an indictment in superior court demonstrates an intent to permit waiver after the Grand Jury votes a true bill but prior to the filing of the indictment with the court. People v. Mills, 154 A.D.2d 405, 545 N.Y.S.2d 792 (2d Dept. 1989).

Waiver impermissible.—When an accused is held for Grand Jury action upon a felony complaint that charges a class A felony, a waiver of indictment with respect to that felony complaint is unauthorized; where the murder count in the felony complaint was a Class A type, the People's proffered superior court information and defendant's waiver stretch beyond the drawn constitutional and statutory boundaries of case precedents. People v. Trueluck, 88 N.Y.2d 546, 647 N.Y.S.2d 476, 670 N.E.2d 977 (1996).

—Superior court information procedure was unavailable to defendant who was already subject to an extant, at least partially valid, indictment, even though Trial Judge discussed with the parties the possibility of Grand Jury representment. People v. Casdia, 78 N.Y.2d 1024, 576 N.Y.S.2d 75, 581 N.E.2d 1330 (1991).

—After indictment, a defendant's waiver of indictment and plea to a count interposed by Superior Court information rather than Grand Jury action, contravenes the unequivocal direction of CPL § 195.10(2)(b) and must, therefore, be nullified. People

v. Boston, 75 N.Y.2d 585, 555 N.Y.S.2d 27, 554 N.E.2d 64 (1990).

—Following indictment, defendant's waiver of indictment and plea to a count interposed by Superior Court information must be nullified. People v. Hughes, 215 A.D.2d 101, 625 N.Y.S.2d 909 (1st Dept. 1995).

—Defendant's waiver of indictment was ineffective because his waiver and consent to be prosecuted by Superior Court information occurred after an indictment covering the same criminal transactions; defendant's plea of guilty to the offenses in the Superior Court information was vacated and the parties were restored to the status quo by reinstatement of the indictment. People v. Libby, 246 A.D.2d 669, 668 N.Y.S.2d 397 (2d Dept. 1998).

—Defendant, charged with a class A felony, could not waive prosecution by indictment; thus, plea to the superior court information was a nullity and jeopardy did not attach. People v. Alfano, 75 A.D.2d 584, 426 N.Y.S.2d 572 (2d Dept. 1980).

—A defendant may not waive prosecution by indictment after an indictment has been filed by a Grand Jury. People v. Davis, 171 A.D.2d 957, 568 N.Y.S.2d 163 (3d Dept. 1991).

—A person charged with a class A felony cannot waive prosecution by indictment. People v. Woolson, 195 A.D.2d 949, 600 N.Y.S.2d 587 (4th Dept. 1993).

General.—A person charged by felony complaint with the commission of a class A felony and held for Grand Jury action on that complaint cannot waive his right to prosecution by Grand Jury indictment. People v. Woolson, 195 A.D.2d 949, 600 N.Y.S.2d 587 (4th Dept. 1993).

Information.—Defendant, charged with a class A felony, could not waive prosecution by indictment and the plea to the superior court information was therefore a nullity and jeopardy did not attach. People v. Alfano, 75 A.D.2d 584, 426 N.Y.S.2d 572 (2d Dept. 1980).

Prior to filing.—The Legislature's use of the term "file" rather than "vote" when enacting the time limitations set forth in CPL § 195.10(2)(b) for waiving an indictment in superior court, belies any intention to time-bar a waiver made after the Grand Jury votes a true bill but prior to the filing of the indictment with the court. People v. Mills, 154 A.D.2d 405, 545 N.Y.S.2d 792 (2d Dept. 1989).

—After indictment, a defendant's waiver of indictment and plea to a count interposed by Superior Court Information rather than the Grand Jury action, contravenes the unequivocal direction of CPL § 195.10 and must therefore be nullified. People v. Boston, 75 N.Y.2d 585, 555 N.Y.S.2d 27, 554 N.E.2d 64 (1990).

—A defendant may not waive prosecution by indictment after an indictment has been filed by a Grand Jury. People v. Davis, 171 A.D.2d 957, 568 N.Y.S.2d 163 (3d Dept. 1991).

New felony complaint.—The waiver procedure is available after indictment when the defendant is held for Grand Jury action on a new felony complaint. People v. D'Amico, 76 N.Y.2d 877, 561 N.Y.S.2d 411, 562 N.E.2d 488 (1990).

§ 195.20. Waiver of indictment; written instrument.

A waiver of indictment shall be evidenced by

a written instrument, which shall contain the name of the court in which it is executed, the title of the action, and the name, date and approximate time and place of each offense to be charged in the superior court information to be filed by the district attorney pursuant to section 195.40. The offenses named may include any offense for which the defendant was held for action of a grand jury and any offense or offenses properly joinable therewith pursuant to sections 200.20 and 200.40. The written waiver shall also contain a statement by the defendant that he is aware that:

(a) under the constitution of the state of New York he has the right to be prosecuted by indictment filed by a grand jury;

(b) he waives such right and consents to be prosecuted by superior court information to be filed by the district attorney;

(c) the superior court information to be filed by the district attorney will charge the offenses named in the written waiver; and

(d) the superior court information to be filed by the district attorney will have the same force and effect as an indictment filed by a grand jury.

The written waiver shall be signed by the defendant in open court in the presence of his attorney. The consent of the district attorney shall be endorsed thereon.

Added by L. 1974, Ch. 467.

ANNOTATIONS

Information; lesser included offense.—CPL § 195.20 plainly permits waiver upon an information charging only a lesser included offense of the offense charged in the felony complaint. People v. Menchetti, 76 N.Y.2d 473, 560 N.Y.S.2d 760, 561 N.E.2d 536 (1990).

Jurisdictional defect.—The instrument on which defendant was prosecuted was jurisdictionally defective because it charged defendant with an offense that was greater than the offenses charged in the felony complaint. People v. Colon, 16 A.D.3d 433, 792 N.Y.S.2d 100 (2d Dept. 2005).

—The accusatory instrument was jurisdictionally defective where defendant was held for action by the Grand Jury on a charge of rape in the first degree and the superior court information subsequently filed did not contain that charge; CPL § 195.20 must be strictly construed therefor a superior court information must include any offense for which the defendant was held for action of a Grand Jury. People v. Herne, 110 Misc. 2d 152, 441 N.Y.S.2d 936 (Franklin Co. Ct. 1981).

§ 195.30. Waiver of indictment; approval of waiver by the court.

The court shall determine whether the waiver of indictment complies with the provisions of sections 195.10 and 195.20. If satisfied that the waiver complies with such provisions, the court shall approve the waiver and execute a written order to that effect. When the waiver is approved by a local criminal court, the local criminal court shall promptly transmit to the appropriate superior court the written waiver and order approving the waiver, along with all other documents pertinent to the action. Until such papers are received by the superior court, the action is deemed to be pending in the local criminal court.

Added by L. 1974, Ch. 467.

ANNOTATION

Absence of indictment.—The prosecution of the defendant for a class A felony in the absence of an indictment was a nonwaivable jurisdictional defect which requires a reversal of the conviction, a vacatur of the superior court information, and reinstatement of the felony complaint with leave to the People to present the appropriate charges to a Grand Jury. People v. Murphy, 143 A.D.2d 715, 539 N.Y.S.2d 376 (2d Dept. 1989).

§ 195.40. Waiver of indictment; filing of superior court information.

When indictment is waived in a superior court the district attorney shall file a superior court information in such court at the time the waiver is executed. When indictment is waived in a local criminal court the district attorney shall file a superior court information in the appropriate superior court within ten days of the execution of the court order approving the waiver. Upon application of a defendant whose waiver of indictment has been approved by the court, and who, at the time of such approval or subsequent thereto, has been committed to the custody of the sheriff pending disposition of the action, and who has been confined in such custody for a period of more than ten days from the date of approval without the filing by the district attorney of a superior court information, the superior court must release him on his own recognizance unless:

(a) The failure of the district attorney to file a superior court information during such period of confinement was due to defendant's request, action or condition or occurred with his consent; or

(b) The people have shown good cause why such order of release should not be issued. Such good cause must consist of some compelling fact or circumstance which precluded the filing of the superior court information within the prescribed period.

Added by L. 1974, Ch. 467.

ARTICLE 200—INDICTMENT AND RELATED INSTRUMENTS

LexisNexis Cross References

Criminal Defense Techniques, Vol. 1, Ch. 6A, Sufficiency of Indictments; *New York Criminal Practice (2d ed.),* Vol. 1, Ch. 5, Indictments and Superior Court Informations; Vol. 2, Ch. 16, Motion to Dismiss Indictment; Vol. 2, Ch. 17, Discovery and Bills of Particular.

§ 200.10. Indictment; definition.

An indictment is a written accusation by a grand jury, filed with a superior court, charging a person, or two or more persons jointly, with the commission of a crime, or with the commission of two or more offenses at least one of which is a crime. Except as used in Article 190, the term indictment shall include a superior court information.

Amended by L. 1974, Ch. 467.

ANNOTATIONS

Defined.—True bill is the same as an indictment. People v. Marine, 142 Misc. 2d 449, 537 N.Y.S.2d 745 (Sup. Ct. Kings Co. 1989).

Delay.—In determining whether the defendant's due process rights have been violated depends on a balancing of: (1) the length of the delay; (2) the reason for the delay; (3) the degree of actual prejudice to the defendant and (4) the seriousness of the underlying offense. People v. Bonsauger, 91 A.D.2d 1001, 457 N.Y.S.2d 866 (2d Dept. 1983).

—Defendant's due process rights were not violated where the two year delay in obtaining the indictment was due to good cause and not any desire to obtain a tactical advantage. A premature indictment of any of the individuals would have compromised the ongoing investigation and the defendants only showing of prejudice was that he could not recall the events of the day in question. People v. Bonsauger, 91 A.D.2d 1001, 457 N.Y.S.2d 866 (2d Dept. 1983).

Purpose.—The purpose of an indictment is to provide defendant with notice of the accusations against him so he can prepare a defense, to insure that the defendant is tried on the same crime for which the Grand Jury indicted him, and to prevent later retrial for the same offense, in violation of the Double Jeopardy Clauses of the state and federal constitutions. People v. Grega, 72 N.Y.2d 489, 534 N.Y.S.2d 647, 531 N.E.2d 279 (1988).

—An indictment is intended to prevent the court or prosecution from usurping the powers of the Grand Jury by insuring that the crime for which the defendant is tried is the same one for which the Grand Jury indicted him. People v. Ralston, 112 A.D.2d 758, 492 N.Y.S.2d 259 (4th Dept. 1985).

§ 200.15. Superior court information; definition.

A superior court information is a written accusation by a district attorney filed in a superior court pursuant to article one hundred ninety-five, charging a person, or two or more persons jointly, with the commission of a crime, or with the commission of two or more offenses, at least one of which is a crime. A superior court information may include any offense for which the defendant was held for action of a grand jury and any offense or offenses properly joinable therewith pursuant to sections 200.20 and 200.40, but shall not include an offense not named in the written waiver of indictment executed pursuant to section 195.20. A superior court information has the same force and effect as an indictment and all procedures and provisions of law applicable to indictments are also applicable to superior court informations, except where otherwise expressly provided.

Added by L. 1974, Ch. 467.

ANNOTATIONS

Information; generally.—A superior court information is the same as an indictment. People v. Burke, 105 Misc. 2d 722, 432 N.Y.S.2d 832 (Crim. Ct. Queens Co. 1980).

Sufficiency.—Superior court information charging defendant with criminal possession of a weapon in the third degree was not defective for failure to allege that the firearm was operable. People v. Fields, 208 A.D.2d 1050, 617 N.Y.S.2d 583 (3d Dept. 1994).

—A superior court information is subject to the same rules as an indictment, and an indictment that states no more than the bare elements of the crime charged and parrots the Penal Law is legally sufficient. People v. Price, 234 A.D.2d 978, 652 N.Y.S.2d 453 (4th Dept. 1996).

§ 200.20. Indictment; what offenses may be charged; joinder of offenses and consolidation of indictments.

1. An indictment must charge at least one crime and may, in addition, charge in separate counts one or more other offenses, including petty offenses, provided that all such offenses are joinable pursuant to the principles prescribed in subdivision two.

2. Two offenses are "joinable" when:

(a) They are based upon the same act or upon the same criminal transaction, as that term is defined in subdivision two of section 40.10; or

(b) Even though based upon different criminal transactions, such offenses, or the criminal transactions underlying them, are of such nature that either proof of the first offense would be material and admissible as evidence in chief upon a trial of the second, or proof of the second would be material and admissible as evidence in chief upon a trial of the first; or

(c) Even though based upon different criminal transactions, and even though not joinable pursuant to paragraph (b), such offenses are defined by the same or similar statutory provisions and consequently are the same or similar in law; or

(d) Though not directly joinable with each other pursuant to paragraph (a), (b) or (c), each is so joinable with a third offense contained in the indictment. In such case, each of the three offenses may properly be joined not only with each of the other two but also with any further offense joinable with either of the other two, and the chain of joinder may be further extended accordingly.

3. In any case where two or more offenses or groups of offenses charged in an indictment are based upon different criminal transactions, and where their joinability rests solely upon the fact that such offenses, or as the case may be at least one offense of each group, are the same or similar in law, as prescribed in paragraph (c) of subdivision two, the court, in the interest of justice and for good cause shown, may, upon application of

either a defendant or the people, in its discretion order that any such offenses be tried separately from the other or others thereof. Good cause shall include but not be limited to situations where there is:

(a) Substantially more proof on one or more such joinable offenses than on others and there is a substantial likelihood that the jury would be unable to consider separately the proof as it relates to each offense.

(b) A convincing showing that a defendant has both important testimony to give concerning one count and a genuine need to refrain from testifying on the other, which satisfies the court that the risk of prejudice is substantial.

(i) Good cause, under this paragraph (b), may be established in writing or upon oral representation of counsel on the record. Any written or oral representation may be based upon information and belief, provided the sources of such information and the grounds of such belief are set forth.

(ii) Upon the request of counsel, any written or recorded showing concerning the defendant's genuine need to refrain from testifying shall be *ex parte* and in camera. The in camera showing shall be sealed but a court for good cause may order unsealing. Any statements made by counsel in the course of an application under this paragraph (b) may not be offered against the defendant in any criminal action for impeachment purposes or otherwise.

4. When two or more indictments against the same defendant or defendants charge different offenses of a kind that are joinable in a single indictment pursuant to subdivision two, the court may, upon application of either the people or a defendant, order that such indictments be consolidated and treated as a single indictment for trial purposes. If such indictments, in addition to charging offenses which are so joinable charge other offenses which are not so joinable, they may nevertheless be consolidated for the limited purpose of jointly trying the joinable offenses. In such case, such indictments remain in existence with respect to any nonjoinable offenses and may be prosecuted accordingly. Nothing herein precludes the consolidation of an indictment with a superior court information.

5. A court's determination of an application for consolidation pursuant to subdivision four is discretionary; except that where an application by the defendant seeks consolidation with respect to offenses which are, pursuant to paragraph (a) of subdivision two, of a kind that are joinable in a single indictment by reason of being based upon the same act or criminal transaction, the court must order such consolidation unless good cause to the contrary be shown.

6. Where an indictment charges at least one offense against a defendant who was under the age of sixteen at the time of the commission of

the crime and who did not lack criminal responsibility for such crime by reason of infancy, the indictment may, in addition, charge in separate counts one or more other offenses for which such person would not have been criminally responsible by reason of infancy, if:

(a) the offense for which the defendant is criminally responsible and the one or more other offenses for which he would not have been criminally responsible by reason of infancy are based upon the same act or upon the same criminal transaction, as that term is defined in subdivision two of section 40.10 of this chapter; or

(b) the offenses are of such nature that either proof of the first offense would be material and admissible as evidence in chief upon a trial of the second, or proof of the second would be material and admissible as evidence in chief upon a trial of the first.

Amended by L. 1974, Ch. 467; L. 1980, Ch. 136; L. 1984, Ch. 672.

ANNOTATIONS

Consolidation of charges.—In order to defeat a motion by the people to consolidate two indictments made on the ground that proof of one offense would be material and admissible upon a trial of the second offense, a defendant claiming that his wishes to testify as to the first allegedly criminal transaction but not as to the second must make a convincing showing that he has both important testimony to give concerning one offense and a strong need to refrain from testifying as to the other. People v. Lane, 56 N.Y.2d 1, 451 N.Y.S.2d 6, 436 N.E.2d 456 (1982).

Consolidation or joinder proper.—Charges were properly joined pursuant to CPL § 200.20(2)(b), since evidence of each of these highly similar robberies was admissible as to the others. Charges were also properly joined pursuant to CPL § 200.20(2)(c) as similar in law. People v. Rolling, 3 A.D.3d 436, 770 N.Y.S.2d 719 (1st Dept. 2004).

—Where defendant was charged in a single indictment with twelve counts of first degree robbery arising from eight distinctively similar robberies committed in a three-month period against various small commercial establishments in Manhattan, defendant claimed that the court should have severed the counts for trial; while defendant's claim was unpreserved, even if the court were to review the claim, it would have found that the robberies were characterized by a sufficiently unique modus operandi. The robberies were also properly joined as legally similar pursuant to CPL § 200.20(2)(c). People v. Marengo, 276 A.D.2d 358, 714 N.Y.S.2d 43 (1st Dept. 2000).

—Cases were joinable because, even though based on different criminal transactions, the offenses were of such nature that proof of any one would be material and admissible as evidence in chief upon a trial of the others. Once the court determined that the charges were properly joinable pursuant to CPL § 200.20(2)(b), "the court lacked statutory authority to sever" under CPL § 200.20(3), which applies where joinability rests solely on the fact that the charged offenses are the same or similar in law. People v. Zinaman, 259 A.D.2d 327, 687 N.Y.S.2d 316 (1st Dept. 1999).

—Homicide and drug charges were properly joined because proof of the homicide was admissible as evidence in chief on the drug charge, given that the drugs were found in open view near the victim's body. People v. Jiminez, 225 A.D.2d 413, 640 N.Y.S.2d 490 (1st Dept. 1996).

—Similarities in the series of robberies and robbery attempts carried out in the same manner and area gave rise to joinder. People v. Allah, 283 A.D.2d 436, 725 N.Y.S.2d 659 (2d Dept. 2001).

—The trial court properly joined for trial two indictments, each of which charged third degree burglary and criminal mischief where, in each case, the police responded to a burglar alarm at a store located in a one-story shopping center in the early morning hours, found that the roof had been broken through, and observed the defendant near the store carrying stolen merchandise, despite defendant's contention that there was substantially more proof of the liquor store burglary than of the variety store burglary. People v. Hall, 272 A.D.2d 412, 708 N.Y.S.2d 125 (2d Dept. 2000).

—Trial court properly joined two indictments for trial where one charged first degree robbery and the other charged attempted first degree robbery; in both cases, defendant grabbed the driver from behind and held a knife to his throat while demanding money, defendant was positively identified by each of the complainants shortly after the incidents, and proof of each crime was presented separately and clearly. People v. Jackson, 273 A.D.2d 253, 709 N.Y.S.2d 569 (2d Dept. 2000).

—Court acted within its discretion in consolidating the indictments, where the record does not show any prejudice suffered by defendant, evidence of defendant's guilt of the charges under each indictment was presented separately to the jury, the defendant had ample opportunity to defend against the charges, and the court instructed the jury to consider each charge on its own merit. People v. McQueen, 266 A.D.2d 240, 699 N.Y.S.2d 419 (2d Dept. 1999).

—Charges as to several different complainants were properly tried together because they were defined by the same or similar statutory provisions and consequently were the same or similar in law. People v. Berta, 213 A.D.2d 659, 624 N.Y.S.2d 211 (2d Dept. 1995).

—Defendant was properly tried jointly for two distinct incidents—an attempted robbery and a completed one—which were committed within a week of each other at separate locations. People v. Veeney, 215 A.D.2d 605, 626 N.Y.S.2d 844 (2d Dept. 1995).

—Although the offenses charged in the indictment arose out of two separate robberies, they were properly joined for trial pursuant to CPL § 200.20(2)(c) since the offenses were based on the same statutory provisions. People v. Bryan, 158 A.D.2d 530, 551 N.Y.S.2d 296 (2d Dept. 1990).

—Court did not err in consolidating two indictments because charges arising out of different transactions are joinable when the same or similar statutory provisions define the offenses, subject only to a motion for a discretionary severance "in the interest of justice and for good cause shown," which were lacking in this case. People v. Ferrer, 17 A.D.3d 777, 793 N.Y.S.2d 564 (3d Dept. 2005).

—Although the counts related to three different victims and different locations, the counts were statutorily joinable because they were "the same or similar in law," and proof of each charge was "separately presented, uncomplicated and easily distinguishable." People v. Nickel, 14 A.D.3d 869, 788 N.Y.S.2d 274 (3d Dept. 2005).

—Offenses were joinable under CPL § 200.20(2)(b) because evidence of the rape against one victim would be material and admissible as evidence-in-chief at the trial of the rape against the other victim, and once the offenses were properly joined, the court lacked statutory authority to sever; the offenses were also the same or similar in law and defendant failed to show good cause for severance. People v. Cornell, 17 A.D.3d 1010, 794 N.Y.S.2d 226 (4th Dept. 2005).

—Court properly denied the motions of defendant to sever the drug charge; possession of a controlled substance was so closely related in time, place, and date to the other charges to have been part of the same criminal transaction and was thus properly joined. People v. Boyd, 272 A.D.2d 898, 709 N.Y.S.2d 269 (4th Dept. 2000).

—Trial court properly denied motion for severance where defendant's robbery convictions arose out of four separate incidents charged in the indictment; the offenses were the same or similar in law and were thus properly joinable. People v. Daymon, 239 A.D.2d 907, 659 N.Y.S.2d 621 (4th Dept. 1997).

—Drug offenses arising from different transactions were properly joined despite defendant's argument that their joinder precluded his raising an entrapment defense. People v. McCune, 210 A.D.2d 978, 621 N.Y.S.2d 246 (4th Dept. 1994), *lv. denied,* 85 N.Y.2d 864 (1995).

Consolidation improperly granted.—The prosecutor's consolidation of the robbery and possession of a dangerous weapon indictments was improperly granted where defendant's possession of the weapon was not part of the same criminal transaction which resulted in the robbery; it was removed from the robbery both by time and place and had absolutely no connection therewith. People v. Connors, 83 A.D.2d 640, 441 N.Y.S.2d 523 (2d Dept. 1981).

Consolidation; no prejudice to defendant.—The denial of a motion to sever was not an abuse of discretion where the two robberies charged in the indictment were "the same or similar in law." People v. Jenkins, 50 N.Y.2d 981, 431 N.Y.S.2d 471, 409 N.E.2d 944 (1980).

—Defendant was not prejudiced by the trial court's denial of his motion to sever three consolidated indictments charging him with seven similar crimes. The court ruled that the jury's acquittal of the defendant on three counts proved that the defendant had not been prejudiced, and the court added that in the face of the overwhelming proof of defendant's guilt, it would be a waste of time to retry the case. People v. Peterson, 42 A.D.2d 937, 348 N.Y.S.2d 137 (1st Dept. 1973), aff'd, 35 N.Y.2d 659, 360 N.Y.S.2d 640, 318 N.E.2d 796 (1974).

—People's decision to present joinable offenses to the same Grand Jury did not deprive the defendant of his right to testify. People v. Hemmings, 264 A.D.2d 529, 694 N.Y.S.2d 469 (2d Dept. 1999).

Contents.—An indictment must charge all of the legally material elements of the crime charged and allege that the defendant committed the acts which comprise those elements. People v. Haff, 47 N.Y.2d 695, 420 N.Y.S.2d 209, 394 N.E.2d 278 (1979), aff'd, 53 N.Y.2d 997, 441 N.Y.S.2d 665, 424 N.E.2d 552 (1981).

Criminal transaction.—Although the possession of heroin and the burglary, third degree counts, constituted different criminal transactions, the two were properly joined in one trial since the proof necessary to convict under the second charge was material as evidence in chief upon the trial of the first charge. People v. Johnson, 64 A.D.2d 140, 408 N.Y.S.2d 972 (3d Dept. 1978), aff'd, 48 N.Y.2d 925, 425 N.Y.S.2d 55, 401 N.E.2d 178 (1979).

Consolidation improper.—Trial court abused its discretion in denying defendant's motion to sever indictment charging him with engaging in a course of homosexual sodomitic acts on various occasions over a 17-month period with eight different boys under the age of 17, from his trial on two other indictments charging him with the more serious crime of promoting such conduct, where no one who figured in the first indictment other than the defendant would have any reason to be called at trial on the other indictments, and defendant, who did not plan to take the stand on the first indictment, desired to do so at trial of the promotion charges. People v. Shapiro, 50 N.Y.2d 747, 431 N.Y.S.2d 422, 409 N.E.2d 897 (1980).

—Motion to sever should have been granted where both incidents involved drunken arguments and the use of a knife, since there was a strong possibility of a conviction based on the cumulative effect of evidence rather than its separate and distinct relevance to each incident. People v. Stanley, 81 A.D.2d 842, 438 N.Y.S.2d 848 (2d Dept. 1981).

—Trial court abused its discretion in permitting joinder for trial of indictments charging sodomy with infants, even though charges were similar in nature since the potential for prejudice was so great as to outweigh the convenience to the prosecution. People v. Jackson, 77 A.D.2d 630, 430 N.Y.S.2d 126 (2d Dept. 1980).

—Motion to sever trial of possession of stolen property and possession of a forged instrument was properly denied as severance is discretionary and will be granted only if a defendant can persuade the court that it should be granted "in the interests of justice for good cause shown" and the mere allegation that the defendant wishes to testify as to one charge and not the other is insufficient to require severance. People v. Lowe, 91 A.D.2d 1100, 458 N.Y.S.2d 357 (3d Dept. 1983).

Death penalty case; not duplicitous.—Defense counsel argued in capital case that certain counts were duplicitous due to People's failure to particularize and connect a particular entry of a three-story structure with a common front door to a particular charge involving burglary; court found that counts were not duplicitous, because each count alleged murder of different victim, at a different residence, and different acts formed the basis for the conduct. People v. Gordon, 175 Misc. 2d 67, 667 N.Y.S.2d 626 (Sup. Ct. Queens Co. 1997)

Joinder where evidence of separate crimes establishes identity and intent.—The charges were properly tried together for proof of the first crime was probative of the identity of the

perpetrator of the second where the murder and the assault both involved the brutal and repeated punching of the lone female victims in the face and eyes and took place within a city block and within 15 to 30 minutes of each other. People v. Ferringer, 120 A.D.2d 101, 507 N.Y.S.2d 938 (4th Dept. 1986).

Joinder of offenses; based upon different criminal transactions.—Joint trial of offenses of murder, second degree, and robbery, first degree, was authorized where after being charged with the robbery, defendant murdered his co-defendant, who had entered a plea of guilty and made statements in connection with the plea inculpating the defendant. People v. Green, 67 A.D.2d 893, 413 N.Y.S.2d 398 (1st Dept. 1979).

—Counts in the indictment which related to the shooting of two brothers were properly joinable under CPL § 200.20(2) with counts concerning the later attack on a police officer while he was attempting to arrest the defendant because of the similarity of statutory provisions (CPL § 200.20[2][c]). People v. Maldonado, 75 A.D.2d 558, 427 N.Y.S.2d 414 (1st Dept. 1980).

—CPL § 200.20 authorizes joinder in a single indictment of more than one offense, provided that all of the charged offenses are joinable and are defined by the same or similar statutory provisions. Gold v. Booth, 79 A.D.2d 1013, 435 N.Y.S.2d 325 (2d Dept. 1981).

Multi-county crimes.—Although two inconsistent charges in an indictment cannot both be proven beyond a reasonable doubt, they may be charged in the same indictment, provided the prosecutor proffers legally sufficient evidence to support both of the charges. People v. Jarrett, 118 A.D.2d 657, 500 N.Y.S.2d 263 (2d Dept. 1986).

Multiplicity.—While duplicitous counts are prohibited in criminal indictments, multiplicity of counts is not. Fletcher v. Coughlin, 161 A.D.2d 869, 556 N.Y.S.2d 411 (3d Dept. 1990).

—If a count charges more than one offense, it is void for duplicity; a count will not be found duplicitous, however, if the crime charged may by its nature, be committed either by one act or by multiple acts and readily permits characterization as a continuing offense over a period of time. People v. First Meridian Planning Corp., 201 A.D.2d 145, 614 N.Y.S.2d 811 (3d Dept. 1994), aff'd, 86 N.Y.2d 608, 635 N.Y.S.2d 144, 658 N.E.2d 1017 (1995).

No authority to sever.—Once the charges were properly consolidated, the motion court lacked statutory authority to sever. People v. Bridgewater, 242 A.D.2d 491, 662 N.Y.S.2d 120 (1st Dept. 1997).

§ 200.30. Indictment; duplicitous counts prohibited.

1. Each count of an indictment may charge one offense only.

2. For purpose of this section, a statutory provision which defines the offense named in the title thereof by providing, in different subdivisions or paragraphs, different ways in which such named offense may be committed, defines a separate offense in each such subdivision or paragraph, and a count of an indictment charging such named offense which, without specifying or clearly indicating the particular subdivision or paragraph of the statutory provision, alleges facts which would support a conviction under more than one such subdivision or paragraph, charges more than one offense.

ANNOTATIONS

Separate and distinct crimes.—The sequential killing of more than two persons, committed as part of the same criminal transaction in violation of PL § 125.27(1)(a)(viii) does not constitute a single continuing offense over time and, therefore, the acts do not need to be charged in a single count. People v. Taylor, 190 Misc. 2d 124, 738 N.Y.S.2d 497 (Sup. Ct. Queens Co. 2002).

—The two count indictment was proper, as the facts underlying the two counts were not identical, either as to the type of property or the identity of victims where first count of a robbery alleged that defendants did on a certain day forcibly steal automobile radios and audio equipment from two victims and the second count, which named the same defendants, same date, and the same county, and charged the forcible stealing of a credit card contained in a wallet. People v. Bianca, 103 Misc. 2d 358, 425 N.Y.S.2d 958 (Sup. Ct. Suffolk Co. 1980).

Charges duplicitous.—Although count charging sexual abuse in the first degree, on its face, was not duplicitous, the complainant's trial testimony indicating that the sexual abuse occurred on two occasions at different locations rendered the count duplicitous. People v. Davila, 198 A.D.2d 371, 603 N.Y.S.2d 185 (2d Dept. 1993).

—Where People offered evidence at trial that defendant entered the complainant's apartment twice, only minutes apart, and the court indicated that defendant could be convicted on the basis of either or both entries, it is impossible to determine whether the jury convicted the defendant on the basis of the first or second entry, or if they unanimously agreed on either. People v. Stanley, 173 A.D.2d 658, 571 N.Y.S.2d 28 (2d Dept. 1991).

—Reversal was not warranted on ground that indictment contained multiplicitous counts where defendant was sentenced to concurrent terms as to all counts of which he was convicted. People v. Cassidy, 133 A.D.2d 374, 519 N.Y.S.2d 275 (2d Dept. 1987).

Charges not duplicitous.—Indictment charging defendant with 10 criminal acts over a five-month period was not unreasonable; the complainant, who was eight years old at the time of the alleged abuse, could not further particularize the offenses, and under the circumstances, defendant was not likely to be able to raise an alibi offense. People v. Watt, 84 N.Y.2d 948, 620 N.Y.S.2d 817, 644 N.E.2d 1373 (1994).

—Perjury counts were not duplicitous; each count was predicated on defendant's conduct at a single proceeding and, although each encompassed multiple falsehoods, each falsehood related to the same subject matter and was intended to mislead the same party about the same events. People v. Ribowsky, 77 N.Y.2d 284, 567 N.Y.S.2d 392, 568 N.E.2d 1197 (1991).

—Indictment charging defendant with two counts of murder in the first degree was not multiplicitous because each count involved different victims. People v. Saunders, 290 A.D.2d 461, 736 N.Y.S.2d 90 (2d Dept. 2002).

—Defendant was properly charged with sexual acts occurring from November 1990 to February 1991, where each count of the indictment was premised upon a single sexual act. People v. Palaguachi, 210 A.D.2d 436, 620 N.Y.S.2d 429 (2d Dept. 1994).

—If multiple acts constitute one scheme to commit grand larceny against a single victim and each count alleges a separate scheme to commit grand larceny over a period of time, the count is not duplicitous. People v. Arnold, 15 A.D.3d 783, 790 N.Y.S.2d 291 (3d Dept. 2005).

Waiver.—Issue of whether count charging criminal use of a firearm is duplicitous as to counts charging robbery and burglary requiring the display of a firearm during the commission of the crime was not preserved for appellate review because counsel failed to challenge the indictment or object to the submission of the criminal use of a firearm charge to the jury. People v. Griffin, 114 A.D.2d 756, 494 N.Y.S.2d 862 (1st Dept. 1985).

§ 200.40. Indictment; joinder of defendants and consolidation of indictments against different defendants.

1. Two or more defendants may be jointly charged in a single indictment provided that:

(a) all such defendants are jointly charged with every offense alleged therein; or

(b) all the offenses charged are based upon a common scheme or plan; or

(c) all the offenses charged are based upon the same criminal transaction as that term is defined in subdivision two of section 40.10; or

(d) if the indictment includes a count charging enterprise corruption:

(i) all the defendants are jointly charged with every count of enterprise corruption alleged therein; and

(ii) every offense, other than a count alleging enterprise corruption, is a criminal act specifically included in the pattern of criminal activity on which the charge or charges of enterprise corruption is or are based; and

(iii) each such defendant could have been jointly charged with at least one of the other defendants, absent an enterprise corruption count, under the provisions of paragraph (a), (b) or (c) of this subdivision, in an accusatory instrument charging at least one such specifically included criminal act. For purposes of this subparagraph, joinder shall not be precluded on the ground that a specifically included criminal act which is necessary to permit joinder is not currently prosecutable, when standing alone, by reason of previous prosecution or lack of geographical jurisdiction.

Even in such case, the court, upon motion of a defendant or the people made within the period provided by section 255.20, may for good cause shown order in its discretion that any defendant be tried separately from the other or from one or more or all of the others. Good cause shall include, but not be limited to, a finding that a defendant or the people will be unduly prejudiced by a joint trial or, in the case of a prosecution involving a charge of enterprise corruption, a finding that proof of one or more criminal acts alleged to have been committed by one defendant but not one or more of the others creates a likelihood that the jury may not be able to consider separately the proof as it relates to each defendant, or in such a case, given the scope of the pattern of criminal activity charged against all the defendants, a particular defendant's comparatively minor role in it creates a likelihood of prejudice to him. Upon such a finding of prejudice, the court may order counts to be tried separately, grant a severance of defendants or provide whatever other relief justice requires.

2. When two or more defendants are charged in separate indictments with an offense or offenses but could have been so charged in a single indictment under subdivision one above, the court may, upon application of the people, order that such indictments be consolidated and the charges be heard in a single trial. If such indictments also charge offenses not properly the subject of a single indictment under subdivision one above, those offenses shall not be consolidated, but shall remain in existence and may be separately prosecuted. Nothing herein precludes the consolidation of an indictment with a superior court information.

Amended by L. 1984, Ch. 672; L. 1986, Ch. 516; L. 2000, Ch. 107 § 7, eff. Oct. 8, 2000.

ANNOTATIONS

Charge to jury; lack of exception precludes claim of error.—Court did not improvidently exercise its discretion in consolidating two indictments; the use of an extremely unusual sawed-off shotgun in both incidents as well as a common location was highly probative of identity and the defendant did not establish by clear and convincing evidence that he had reason to testify with respect to one indictment and not the other. People v. Cruz, 176 A.D.2d 953, 575 N.Y.S.2d 891 (2d Dept. 1991).

Counts of indictment not identical; verdict not repugnant.—Although a repugnant verdict cannot stand, a verdict finding a physician guilty on 23 out of 29 counts of an indictment charging unlawful prescription of drugs was not found to be repugnant, where the separate counts did not have identical elements and involved different drugs, dates, and parties. People v. Kass, 74 Misc. 2d 682, 346 N.Y.S.2d 641 (2d Dept.), aff'd, 32 N.Y.2d 855, 346 N.Y.S.2d 274, 299 N.E.2d 685 (1973).

Defendant at a joint trial retains his full panoply of rights.—The fact that defendant may be compelled to submit to a joint trial does not mean or imply that he thereby becomes guardian of the rights and interests of his co-defendant; to the contrary, a defendant at a joint trial retains his full panoply of rights, and may pursue his own interests, vigorously defending himself by all means lawfully at his command. People v. Carter, 86 A.D.2d 451, 450 N.Y.S.2d 203 (2d Dept. 1982).

Denial of motion for separate trial; co-defendants' statements substantially the same.—The court properly denied the motion for a severance where both defendant and co-defendant confessed to the crime, each implicated the other with strikingly similar confessions, and where defendant was afforded the opportunity to cross-examine co-defendant at the *Huntley* hearing; when a confessing co-defendant testifies at a *Huntley* hearing, although he does not take the stand at trial, Bruton v. United States, 391 U.S. 123, 88 S. Ct. 1620, 20 L. Ed. 2d 470 (1968), which allows severance where a co-defendant confesses but does not take the stand, does not apply. People v. Safian, 59 A.D.2d 20, 396 N.Y.S.2d 432 (2d Dept. 1977), aff'd, 46 N.Y.2d 181, 413 N.Y.S.2d 118, 385 N.E.2d 1046 (1978).

Denial of severance; no showing of prejudice.—The decision to grant or deny a separate trial is vested primarily in the sound judgment of the trial court, and the defendant's burden to demonstrate abuse of that discretion is a substantial one. People v. Mahboubian, 74 N.Y.2d 174, 544 N.Y.S.2d 769, 543 N.E.2d 34 (1989).

—The court properly denied defendants' motions for severance since most of the People's evidence was introduced to establish the joint enterprise, which evidence applied to all defendants. There was no irreconcilable conflict between the defenses presented nor was there a significant danger that any alleged conflict led the jury to infer any defendant's guilt. Severance was not required based on incidents during trial in which some defendants elicited evidence objectionable to other defendants, because no defendant took an aggressive adversarial stance against another and the evidence so elicited was cumulative or nonprejudicial. People v. De Los Angeles, 270 A.D.2d 196, 707 N.Y.S.2d 16 (1st Dept. 2000).

—Trial court did not abuse its discretion in denying motion to sever two counts of an indictment which dealt with different criminal transactions where there was no showing that the evidence of one offense tainted the jury with respect to the other and the evidence was solid as to each of the offenses; further, it appeared that the crimes were so interrelated that evidence of one would have been admissible in the other. People v. Napolitano, 106 A.D.2d 304, 482 N.Y.S.2d 753 (1st Dept. 1984).

—The Decision to grant or deny severance is within the sound discretion of the trial court. Where, as here, both defendants claimed that they had been misidentified and had not participated in the crime, their defenses were not in irreconcilable conflict with each other so as to compel severance. People v. Leon, 265 A.D.2d 344, 696 N.Y.S.2d 221 (2d Dept. 1999).

—Severance motions are addressed to the sound discretion of the trial court. People v. Apolinar, 208 A.D.2d 548, 617 N.Y.S.2d 32 (2d Dept. 1994).

—Where the proof against two or more defendants is supplied by the same evidence, only the most cogent reasons warrant separate trials. People v. Thomas, 197 A.D.2d 719, 602 N.Y.S.2d 913 (2d Dept. 1993).

—Severance is not required merely because of hostility between the defendants, differences in their trial strategies or inconsistencies in their defense. People v. Allaway, 172 A.D.2d 617, 568 N.Y.S.2d 154 (2d Dept. 1991).

—Court did not err in denying the defendant's motion for severance, where the defendant failed to make a proper showing that his co-defendants were willing to testify in his behalf if he were tried separately, or to show what the co-defendants testimony would be and that their testimony would tend to exculpate him. People v. Mouzon, 154 A.D.2d 626, 546 N.Y.S.2d 638 (2d Dept. 1989).

—Any objection raised by the defendant in regard to the admission of a statement made by his co-defendant which inculpated the defendant in the crime went on to testify. People v. Jackson, 149 A.D.2d 436, 539 N.Y.S.2d 780, 781 (2d Dept. 1989).

—Motion for severance need not be granted when the grounds for a severance are merely colorable or speculative. People v. Gonzalez, 137 A.D.2d 558, 524 N.Y.S.2d 297 (2d Dept. 1988).

—The trial court did not abuse its discretion in denying the defendant's motion for a severance although the alibi defense presented by the co-defendant was antagonistic to the defendant's defense, since it did not result in unfair prejudice to the defendant. People v. Teller, 130 A.D.2d 528, 515 N.Y.S.2d 108 (2d Dept. 1987).

—The trial court possesses broad discretion in deciding whether a severance is necessary to avoid undue prejudice and to assure a fair trial. People v. Goldsborough, 203 A.D.2d 719, 609 N.Y.S.2d 967 (3d Dept. 1994).

—The mere fact that only one defendant testified at the trial did not warrant reversal. People v. Everspaugh, 171 A.D.2d 950, 567 N.Y.S.2d 895 (3d Dept. 1991).

—An application for severance is addressed to the sound discretion of the trial court. People v. Bryant, 148 A.D.2d 953, 539 N.Y.S.2d 191 (4th Dept. 1989).

—Severance is not required solely because of hostility between the defendants, differences in their strategies, or inconsistencies in their defenses; it must appear that a joint trial necessarily will, or did, result in unfair prejudice to the moving party and substantially impair his defense. People v. Almond, 152 A.D.2d 974, 544 N.Y.S.2d 92 (4th Dept. 1989).

—The legal test for determining severance motions is whether a separate trial will assist or impede the administration of justice and secure to the accused the right to a fair trial. People v. Chastain, 137 Misc. 2d 950, 522 N.Y.S.2d 1022 (Dist. Ct. Nassau Co. 1987).

Improper denial of motion for severance.—Trial court committed reversible error in refusing to grant defendant's severance motion, where redaction of co-defendant's confession was effectively negated by the court's slip of the tongue in using the defendant's name in referring to the defendant's statement, and by evidence of the prosecutor which lent further inculpatory value to the co-defendant's statement. People v. Lopez, 68 N.Y.2d 683, 506 N.Y.S.2d 299, 497 N.E.2d 666 (1986).

Improper joinder.—Although it is generally within the sound judgment of the trial court to determine whether a severance is warranted, where a joint trial results in an impairment of the defendant's substantial rights, it amounts to an abuse of discretion to deny a motion to sever. Thus, if one defendant's ability to exculpate himself has a significant potential of being unfairly prejudicial to the co-defendant, a severance should be ordered. People v. Rodriguez, 91 A.D.2d 591, 457 N.Y.S.2d 268 (1st Dept. 1982).

—The court was without authority to order consolidation absent a request for consolidation by the People. Gold v. McShane, 74 A.D.2d 616, 425 N.Y.S.2d 341 (2d Dept. 1980).

Improper joinder; harmless error.—Although the consolidation for trial on charges of criminal possession of a controlled substance, of a defendant who was in the hallway with a co-defendant who was in the apartment was prejudicial to the defendant in the hallway, the consolidation as to the co-defendant was harmless error since the evidence showed that the apartment was a "drug factory" and that the co-defendant was engaged in the wholesale drug business. People v. Ortiz, 78 A.D.2d 786, 432 N.Y.S.2d 890 (1st Dept. 1980).

Joinder improper; codefendant faces unrelated charges.—A defendant may not be jointly tried with a codefendant when the codefendant is charged with additional unrelated sales of drugs. People v. Williams, 1 Misc. 3d 226, 768 N.Y.S.2d 146 (Sup. Ct. N.Y. Co. 2003).

Joint trial; right to severance; testimony of co-defendant.— There exists a strong public policy to join cases because it expedites the judicial process, reduces court congestion and avoids the necessity of recalling witnesses. People v. Perez, 161 A.D.2d 154, 554 N.Y.S.2d 866 (1st Dept. 1990).

—Defendant's motion to sever his trial from that of the co-defendant was properly denied, despite his contention that his co-defendant would give testimony exculpatory of him; the contention was made solely in a conclusory allegation of counsel in motion papers and was not enough of a showing to meet the heavy burden that falls on a movant seeking severance where the proof against the co-defendant is supplied by the same evidence. People v. Jaso, 158 A.D.2d 337, 551 N.Y.S.2d 25 (1st Dept. 1990).

—Severance is not necessarily required because differences arise between defendants as to trial strategies or inconsistencies in their defenses. People v. Mohammed, 156 A.D.2d 262, 549 N.Y.S.2d 3 (1st Dept. 1989).

—The court did not err in denying severance; the defendant was not unduly prejudiced by the admission of testimony regarding his co-defendant's threats to a witness, since the trial court instructed the jury that the evidence was only to be considered as evidence of the defendant's consciousness of guilt and was not to be used as direct evidence against the defendant. People v. Paulino, 187 A.D.2d 736, 590 N.Y.S.2d 532 (2d Dept. 1992).

—Where the proof against all of the defendants is supplied by the same evidence only the most cogent reasons warrant a severance. People v. Watts, 159 A.D.2d 740, 553 N.Y.S.2d 213 (2d Dept. 1990).

—The trial court did not improvidently exercise its discretion in denying the defendant's motion for separate trial where he failed to show that the co-defendant would testify if the trials were severed or that any testimony that the co-defendant would give would tend to exculpate him. People v. LeGrande, 162 A.D.2d 474, 556 N.Y.S.2d 168 (2d Dept. 1990).

—Where the proof against the defendants is supplied by the same evidence only the most cogent reasons warrant a severance. People v. Lopez, 162 A.D.2d 621, 557 N.Y.S.2d 93 (2d Dept. 1990).

—Court did not err in denying the defendant's motion for a severance since the proof against him and his co-defendant was supplied by the same evidence. People v. Key, 155 A.D.2d 481, 547 N.Y.S.2d 141 (2d Dept. 1989).

—In view of the fact that the judge granted leave to renew the application for severance at the close of the People's case and no such application was made, the trial judge did not abuse his discretion when he denied an oral motion for a severance, made over three months after indictment, even though two of the defendant's attorneys said that their clients would exonerate the third defendant if the latter was tried separately. People v. Codavid, 74 A.D.2d 578, 424 N.Y.S.2d 479 (2d Dept. 1980).

—Trial court did not abuse its discretion in denying severance of the trial where both defendants were within the warehouse at midnight, concededly unlawfully, with no attempt to offer an explanation for such presence; the co-defendant's statements were admissible because they were offered to prove the state of mind or intent of defendants. People v. Boyling, 84 A.D.2d 892, 444 N.Y.S.2d 760 (3d Dept. 1981).

Right to severance; testimony of co-defendant; prejudicial error.—Defendant's application to sever his trial from that of his co-defendant should have been granted where co-defendant's statement, even after reduction could only be read as implicating the defendant. People v. Wheeler, 62 N.Y.2d 867, 478 N.Y.S.2d 254, 466 N.E.2d 846 (1984).

—Where defendant's statement left doubt as to whether rape had been attempted, his rights were substantially prejudiced in felony murder trial when he was tried together with co-defendant who had admitted the underlying rape felony in his statement to police. People v. Payne, 35 N.Y.2d 22, 358 N.Y.S.2d 701, 315 N.E.2d 762 (1974).

—Failure to sever required reversal where the confessions of the defendants were not sufficiently redacted so that, when coupled with eyewitness testimony, the confessions inferentially incriminated the nonconfessing defendant. People v. Ruiz, 207 A.D.2d 917, 616 N.Y.S.2d 658 (2d Dept. 1994).

—Wrongful admission of pretrial statements of non-testifying co-defendant constituted harmless error. People v. Jefferson, 156 A.D.2d 716, 549 N.Y.S.2d 468 (2d Dept. 1990).

—Any error in admission of non-testifying co-defendant's confessions were rendered harmless by the identification evidence and the detailed nature of the defendant's confession. People v. Glover, 139 A.D.2d 530, 526 N.Y.S.2d 853 (2d Dept. 1988).

—Any error occasioned by the violation of the *Bruton* rule and the court's denial of the defendant's severance motion did not require reversal in light of overwhelming proof of guilt which included defendant's detailed confession, an in-court identification of the defendant by one complainant, evidence of flight, and the defendant's possession of stolen property. People v. Williams, 136 A.D.2d 581, 523 N.Y.S.2d 571 (2d Dept. 1988).

—Severance is compelled where the core of each defense is in irreconcilable conflict with the other and where there is a significant danger, as both defenses are portrayed to the court, that the conflict alone would lead the jury to infer the defendant's guilt. People v. McDermott, 201 A.D.2d 913, 607 N.Y.S.2d 784 (4th Dept. 1994).

—Court committed reversible error in denying defendant's motion for a separate trial and in admitting into evidence the confession of a non-testifying co-defendant. People v. Thompson, 156 A.D.2d 961, 550 N.Y.S.2d 757 (4th Dept. 1989).

Joinder of defendants, same evidence and crime.— Defendant was properly tried with his co-defendant for attempted murder, robbery criminal possession of a weapon and reckless endangerment, where they were charged with acting in concert, the same evidence would be used against both, and there was little chance of prejudice to defendant from a joint trial. People v. Miceli, 199 A.D.2d 542, 605 N.Y.S.2d 407 (2d Dept. 1993), *lv. denied,* 83 N.Y.2d 874 (1994).

—Court properly denied severance where defendant and co-defendant were charged with "acting in concert." For most of the offenses charged, the proof against the defendants was supplied by the same evidence and all of the offenses charged were based upon the same criminal transaction. People v. Philip, 205 A.D.2d 714, 613 N.Y.S.2d 649 (2d Dept.), *lv. denied,* 84 N.Y.2d 831 (1994).

—Defendant could be jointly tried with co-defendants, where they were all charged with acting in concert, the proof against all of then was supplied by the same evidence and the defendant failed to demonstrate that his defense and that of his co-defendants were in irreconcilable conflict. People v. Barbieri, 207 A.D.2d 554, 616 N.Y.S.2d 80 (2d Dept. 1994).

—The trial court erred in concluding that the charges against defendant were improperly joined with those against his two sons, since the crimes were so closely connected and related with regard to the time and circumstances of their commission as to constitute a single criminal transaction. People v. Ramjit, 203 A.D.2d 498, 612 N.Y.S.2d 600 (2d Dept.), *lv. denied,* 84 N.Y.2d 831 (1994).

—Defendants who were charged with possessing the same quantity of drugs at the same time and place were properly tried together. People v. Vogel, 216 A.D.2d 857, 629 N.Y.S.2d 157 (4th Dept. 1995).

Motion for severance, general.—An application for severance is addressed to the discretion of the trial judge, and the judge's ruling will ordinarily not be disturbed; however, the court's discretion is not absolute. People v. Cardwell, 78 N.Y.2d 996, 575 N.Y.S.2d 267, 580 N.E.2d 753 (1991).

—Defendant's trial motion for a severance, which was not made until the close of co-defendant's direct testimony, was untimely. People v. Ruiz, 176 A.D.2d 683, 575 N.Y.S.2d 828 (1st Dept. 1991), *lv. denied,* 79 N.Y.2d 952 (1992).

—While an application for a severance is addressed to a trial court's discretion and its ruling on that motion will normally not be disturbed, such discretion is not absolute. People v. Jones, 139 A.D.2d 272, 531 N.Y.S.2d 906, 908 (1st Dept. 1988).

—Unlike a motion for a separate trial which must be made within 45 days after arraignment, a motion to consolidate is not governed by any pretrial time strictures. People v. Pratt, 201 A.D.2d 745, 608 N.Y.S.2d 317 (2d Dept. 1994).

—It is well settled that severance motions are directed to the sound discretion of the trial court. People v. Correa, 188 A.D.2d

542, 591 N.Y.S.2d 447 (2d Dept. 1992), *lv. denied,* 81 N.Y.2d 883 (1993).

—The decision to grant or deny a separate trial is vested in the sound discretion of the trial judge. People v. Chaplin, 181 A.D.2d 828, 581 N.Y.S.2d 385 (2d Dept.), *lv. denied,* 79 N.Y.2d 1047 (1992).

—Motion for severance is addressed to the sound discretion of the trial court and its decision will not be overturned absent a showing of an abuse of discretion. People v. Larkin, 135 A.D.2d 834, 523 N.Y.S.2d 131 (2d Dept. 1987).

—The decision to sever a case for separate trial rests within the sound discretion of the trial court. People v. Shepherd, 176 A.D.2d 766, 574 N.Y.S.2d 979 (3d Dept. 1991), *lv. denied,* 79 N.Y.2d 832 (1992).

Severance motion, timeliness.—The defendant's motion for a separate trial was properly denied as untimely, since it was made in the midst of jury selection, rather than prior to trial. People v. Becker, 189 A.D.2d 881, 592 N.Y.S.2d 764 (2d Dept.), *lv. denied,* 81 N.Y.2d 837 (1993).

—A motion for a severance must be made prior to trial; defendant's application for a severance of his case from that of his co-defendant, made toward the end of his trial, was both untimely and improper. People v. James, 116 A.D.2d 663, 497 N.Y.S.2d 730 (2d Dept. 1986).

Irreconcilable defenses.—Court properly denied defendant's severance motion because the defenses of the defendant and his codefendants were not so irreconcilable as to require severance; on the contrary, although defendant and the codefendants were prosecuted under different theories, their defenses were compatible. People v. Carney, 18 A.D.3d 242, 795 N.Y.S.2d 10 (1st Dept. 2005).

—Defendant's trial claim that he was not a participant in the robbery with co-defendant was not irreconcilable with co-defendant's claim that the smashing of the jewelry case was accidental. People v. Harris, 193 A.D.2d 435, 597 N.Y.S.2d 331 (1st Dept. 1993).

—Reversal was required, where the court failed to sever defendant's case, although his defense was mutually exclusive and irreconcilable with that of his co-defendant. People v. Figueroa, 193 A.D.2d 452, 597 N.Y.S.2d 685 (1st Dept. 1993).

—Failure to sever required reversal where the confessions of the defendants were not sufficiently redacted so that, when coupled with eyewitness testimony, the confessions inferentially incriminated the nonconfessing defendant. People v. Ruiz, 207 A.D.2d 917, 616 N.Y.S.2d 658 (2d Dept. 1994).

—Defendant was not prejudiced by denial of his motion to sever since his own confession and trial testimony were substantially identical to the extra-judicial statements of his nontestifying co-defendants. People v. Campos, 108 A.D.2d 751, 484 N.Y.S.2d 907 (2d Dept. 1985).

—Severance is compelled where the core of each defense is in irreconcilable conflict with the other and where there is a significant danger, as both defenses are portrayed to the court, that the conflict alone would lead the jury to infer the defendant's guilt. People v. McDermott, 201 A.D.2d 913, 607 N.Y.S.2d 784 (4th Dept.), *lv. denied,* 83 N.Y.2d 855 (1994).

Co-defendant's testimony.—The court is not required to sever where the possibility of the co-defendant's testifying is merely colorable or speculative, or where there is no showing that defendant will be unduly prejudiced by a joint trial; defendant merely claimed that his co-defendant might give exculpatory testimony on his behalf. People v. Tolbert, 202 A.D.2d 171, 608 N.Y.S.2d 198 (1st Dept.), *lv. denied,* 84 N.Y.2d 833 (1994).

—Trial court did not abuse its discretion by denying defendant's motion for severance; the defendants had similar defenses, and, although the co-defendant testified that defendant directed him to the drugs, there was no significant danger that this testimony would prejudice defendant, since the undercover officer also testified that defendant acted as a "steerer." People v. Nesbitt, 198 A.D.2d 33, 603 N.Y.S.2d 121 (1st Dept.), *lv. denied,* 82 N.Y.2d 900 (1993).

Pretrial statements.—Wrongful admission of pretrial statements of non-testifying co-defendant constituted harmless error. People v. Jefferson, 156 A.D.2d 716, 549 N.Y.S.2d 468 (2d Dept.), *lv. denied,* 75 N.Y.2d 920 (1990).

—Any error occasioned by the violation of the Bruton rule and the court's denial of the defendant's severance motion did not require reversal in light of overwhelming proof of guilt, which included defendant's detailed confession, an in-court identification of the defendant by one complainant, evidence of flight, and the defendant's possession of stolen property. People v. Williams, 136 A.D.2d 581, 523 N.Y.S.2d 571 (2d Dept. 1988).

—Court committed reversible error in denying defendant's motion for a separate trial and in admitting into evidence the confession of a non-testifying co-defendant. People v. Thompson, 156 A.D.2d 961, 550 N.Y.S.2d 757 (4th Dept. 1989).

Severance; preservation for appellate review.—Defendant's motion to sever did not serve to preserve the issue concerning the admission of the co-defendant's redacted statements. People v. Russell, 71 N.Y.2d 1016, 530 N.Y.S.2d 101, 525 N.E.2d 747 (1988), motion for reargument denied, 79 N.Y.2d 975 (1992).

—Defendant's claim that the joint trial and timing of the acceptance of co-defendant's guilty plea deprived him of the opportunity to call co-defendant as a witness was rejected especially because the defendant never moved for severance. People v. Acosta, 157 A.D.2d 485, 549 N.Y.S.2d 672 (1st Dept.), *lv. denied,* 75 N.Y.2d 916 (1990).

—Defendant's claim of a Cruz violation was not preserved for appellate review. People v. Restrepo-Velez, 156 A.D.2d 488, 548 N.Y.S.2d 571 (2d Dept. 1989).

—Since the defendant explicitly declined to join in his co-defendant's motion for a severance of his and co-defendant's trial, he failed to preserve any issue of law with respect thereto for appellate review. People v. Eisenreich, 121 A.D.2d 561, 503 N.Y.S.2d 610 (2d Dept. 1986).

—Claim that court improperly admitted co-defendants' confessions was not preserved for appellate review by an objection to the admission of that evidence. People v. Jefferson, 139 A.D.2d 531, 527 N.Y.S.2d 243 (2d Dept. 1988).

—By his plea of guilty the defendant waived the issue concerning the propriety of the denial of his severance motion. People v. Bishop, 139 A.D.2d 817, 527 N.Y.S.2d 119 (3d Dept. 1988).

Separate trials; good cause not shown.—Court properly denied severance motion where defendant and co-defendant were charged with "acting in concert" most of the offenses charged, the proof against the defendants was supplied by the same evidence and all of the offenses charged were based upon the same criminal transaction. People v. Philip, 205 A.D.2d 714, 613 N.Y.S.2d 649 (2d Dept. 1994).

—The defendant's motion for a separate trial was properly denied since he and his co-defendants were charged with acting in concert, the proof against all of then was supplied by the same evidence and the defendant failed to demonstrate that his defense and that of his co-defendants were in irreconcilable conflict. People v. Barbieri, 207 A.D.2d 554, 616 N.Y.S.2d 80 (2d Dept. 1994).

—Defendant was not prejudiced by denial of his motion to sever since his own confession and trial testimony were substantially identical with the extra-judicial statements of his nontestifying co-defendants. People v. Campos, 108 A.D.2d 751, 484 N.Y.S.2d 907 (2d Dept. 1985).

Severance; generally.—An application for severance is addressed to the discretion of the trial judge, and the judge's ruling will ordinarily not be disturbed; however, the court's discretion is not absolute. People v. Cardwell, 78 N.Y.2d 996, 575 N.Y.S.2d 267, 580 N.E.2d 753 (1991).

—Defendant's trial motion for a severance, which was not made until the close of co-defendant's direct testimony, was untimely. People v. Ruiz, 176 A.D.2d 683, 575 N.Y.S.2d 828 (1st Dept. 1991).

—Unlike a motion for a separate trial which must be made within 45 days after arraignment, a motion to consolidate is not governed by any pretrial time strictures. People v. Pratt, 201 A.D.2d 745, 608 N.Y.S.2d 317 (2d Dept. 1994).

—The defendant's motion for a separate trial was properly denied as untimely, since it was made in the midst of jury selection, rather than prior to trial. People v. Becker, 189 A.D.2d 881, 592 N.Y.S.2d 764 (2d Dept. 1993).

—It is well settled that severance motions are directed to the sound discretion of the trial court. People v. Correa, 188 A.D.2d 542, 591 N.Y.S.2d 447 (2d Dept. 1992); People v. Chaplin, 181 A.D.2d 828, 581 N.Y.S.2d 385 (2d Dept. 1992); People v. Shepherd, 177 A.D.2d 766, 574 N.Y.S.2d 979 (3d Dept. 1991).

Severance; discretion of court; written and oral inculpatory statements.—Defendant's claim that the joint trial and timing of the acceptance of co-defendant's guilty plea deprived him of the opportunity to call co-defendant as a witness was rejected especially because the defendant never moved for severance. People v. Acosta, 157 A.D.2d 485, 549 N.Y.S.2d 672 (1st Dept. 1990).

—While an application for a severance is addressed to a trial court's discretion and its ruling on that motion will normally not be disturbed, such discretion is not absolute. People v. Jones, 139 A.D.2d 272, 531 N.Y.S.2d 906, 908 (1st Dept. 1988).

—Defendant's claim of a *Cruz* violation was not preserved for appellate review. People v. Restrepo-Velez, 156 A.D.2d 488, 548 N.Y.S.2d 571, 572 (2d Dept. 1989).

—Motion for severance is addressed to the sound discretion of the trial court and its decision will not be overturned absent a showing of an abuse of discretion. People v. Larkin, 135 A.D.2d 734, 523 N.Y.S.2d 131, 132 (2d Dept. 1987).

Severance motion; timeliness.—A motion for a severance must be made prior to trial; defendant's application for a severance of his case from that of his co-defendant, made toward the end of his trial, was both untimely and improper. People v. James, 116 A.D.2d 663, 497 N.Y.S.2d 730 (2d Dept. 1986).

§ 200.50. Indictment; form and content.

An indictment must contain:

1. The name of the superior court in which it is filed; and

2. The title of the action and, where the defendant is a juvenile offender, a statement in the title that the defendant is charged as a juvenile offender; and

3. A separate accusation or count addressed to each offense charged, if there be more than one; and

4. A statement in each count that the grand jury, or, where the accusatory instrument is a superior court information, the district attorney, accuses the defendant or defendants of a designated offense, provided that in any prosecution under article four hundred eighty-five of the penal law, the designated offense shall be the specified offense, as defined in subdivision three of section 485.05 of the penal law, followed by the phrase "as a hate crime", and provided further that in any prosecution under section 490.25 of the penal law, the designated offense shall be the specified offense, as defined in subdivision three of section 490.05 of the penal law, followed by the phrase "as a crime of terrorism"; and

5. A statement in each count that the offense charged therein was committed in a designated county; and

6. A statement in each count that the offense charged therein was committed on, or on or about, a designated date, or during a designated period of time; and

7. A plain and concise factual statement in each count which, without allegations of an evidentiary nature,

(a) asserts facts supporting every element of the offense charged and the defendant's or defendants' commission thereof with sufficient precision to clearly apprise the defendant or defendants

of the conduct which is the subject of the accusation; and

(b) in the case of any armed felony, as defined in subdivision forty-one of section 1.20, states that such offense is an armed felony and specifies the particular implement the defendant or defendants possessed, were armed with, used or displayed or, in the case of an implement displayed, specifies what the implement appeared to be; and

(c) in the case of any hate crime, as defined in section 485.05 of the penal law, specifies, as applicable, that the defendant or defendants intentionally selected the person against whom the offense was committed or intended to be committed; or intentionally committed the act or acts constituting the offense, in whole or in substantial part because of a belief or perception regarding the race, color, national origin, ancestry, gender, religion, religious practice, age, disability or sexual orientation of a person; and

(d) in the case of a crime of terrorism, as defined in section 490.25 of the penal law, specifies, as applicable, that the defendant or defendants acted with intent to intimidate or coerce a civilian population, influence the policy of a unit of government by intimidation or coercion, or affect the conduct of a unit of government by murder, assassination or kidnapping; and

8. The signature of the foreman or acting foreman of the grand jury, except where the indictment has been ordered reduced pursuant to subdivision one-a of section 210.20 of this chapter or the accusatory instrument is a superior court information; and

9. The signature of the district attorney.

Amended by L. 1974, Ch. 467; L. 1978, Ch. 481; L. 1990, Ch. 209; L. 2000, Ch. 107, § 7, eff. Oct. 8, 2000, amending subds. 4 and 7; L. 2001, Ch. 300, § 5, amending subds. 4 and 7, eff. Sept. 17, 2001.

ANNOTATIONS

Sufficiency of indictment; general.—A defendant should be clearly apprised of the conduct which is the subject of the accusation. People v. Rivera, 84 N.Y.2d 766, 622 N.Y.S.2d 671, 646 N.E.2d 1098 (1995).

—There is no legal requirement that each charge contained in an indictment be supported by its own probable cause to arrest. People v. Richardson, 202 A.D.2d 227, 608 N.Y.S.2d 627 (1st Dept. 1994).

—CPL § 200.50 requires only that the indictment allege where, when and what the defendant did, and it is usually sufficient to charge the language of the statute unless the language of the statute is too broad. People *ex rel.* Best v. Senkowski, 200 A.D.2d 808, 606 N.Y.S.2d 427 (3d Dept.), *lv. denied,* 83 N.Y.2d 951 (1994).

—Specific reference in an indictment to the statute claimed to have been violated by name and section operates without more to inform a defendant of the charge or charges against him so as to provide him with the opportunity to prepare his defense, the indictment need not allege every element of the crime where there is a specific reference to the statute. People v. Craft, 87 A.D.2d 662, 448 N.Y.S.2d 847 (3d Dept. 1982).

—The indictment satisfied the jurisdictional requirements for indictments where it made specific reference by name and section to the statute allegedly violated, and alleged the commission of each of the elements of the crime. People v. Botshon,

135 A.D.2d 1107, 523 N.Y.S.2d 293 (4th Dept. 1987), *aff'd*, 73 N.Y.2d 732 (1989).

Sufficiency of indictment; failure to plead specific facts.— Facts tolling statute of limitations need not be pleaded in the indictment; however, if the issue is raised by the defendant by motion or on trial the prosecution has the burden of persuasion beyond a reasonable doubt in establishing that the limitation has been tolled. People v. Kohut, 30 N.Y.2d 183, 331 N.Y.S.2d 416, 282 N.E.2d 312 (1972).

—The indictment was not required to allege the inapplicability of any exemptions from licensing requirements, and, in any event, the indictment alleged that defendant performed duties as a hospital resident "for which a license is required"; as for the claim that the defendant was exempt from the licensing requirement, that was waived by the guilty plea. People v. Bennett, 201 A.D.2d 440, 608 N.Y.S.2d 166 (1st Dept. 1994).

—The People are not required to specify any particular theory of larceny in the indictment. People v. Cannon, 194 A.D.2d 496, 599 N.Y.S.2d 809 (1st Dept. 1993), *lv. denied*, 82 N.Y.2d 715.

Sufficiency of indictment; elements of offense.—The method employed to bring about death is not an element of manslaughter, however, the People cannot omit all description of defendant's actions. People v. Grega, 72 N.Y.2d 489, 534 N.Y.S.2d 647, 531 N.E.2d 279 (1988).

—The indictments charging criminal usury fulfilled the statutory and constitutional mandates for a valid indictment where they charged each and every element of the crime of criminal usury and alleged that the defendant committed the acts which constituted that crime at a specified place during a specified time period. People v. Iannone, 45 N.Y.2d 589, 412 N.Y.S.2d 110, 384 N.E.2d 656 (1978).

—Felony murder count against juvenile, which set forth every element of felony murder, was not rendered jurisdictionally defective by its lack of specificity as to the degree of burglary alleged to be the underlying act; indictment provided defendant with ample notice. People v. Colon, 273 A.D.2d 100, 710 N.Y.S.2d 35 (1st Dept. 2000).

—Being "armed with a dangerous instrument" as charged in the indictment is an insufficient factual predicate for a charge or conviction of robbery in the first degree. People v. Sollars, 91 A.D.2d 909, 457 N.Y.S.2d 792 (1st Dept. 1983).

—Dismissal of an indictment was required where it failed to allege every material element of the subject crime. An indictment which omitted the allegation that defendant's possession of a weapon was outside of his home or business where he was accused of criminal possession of a weapon in the third degree, was jurisdictionally defective and could not be waived. People v. Newell, 95 A.D.2d 815, 463 N.Y.S.2d 538 (2d Dept. 1983).

—It is firmly established that an indictment must contain a factual allegation of every element of the crime charged, including an allegation that any exception set forth within the statute defining the offense is inapplicable. People v. Kirkham, 273 A.D.2d 509, 708 N.Y.S.2d 746 (3d Dept. 2000).

—Indictment charging crime of criminal possession of a weapon in the third degree which did not allege home or business exception was jurisdictionally defective. People v. Best, 132 A.D.2d 773, 517 N.Y.S.2d 582 (3d Dept. 1987).

—The indictment alleged that the defendant forcibly stole approximately $60 from the owner of the house, who was named in the indictment, and that the defendant used or threatened to use a dangerous instrument, namely, a hammer; however, the evidence established that the owner's son was the person threatened with a hammer. Because the People chose to specify a fact to support a material element of the crime, they were not at liberty to present evidence that affirmatively disproved it; the court therefore reversed defendant's first degree robbery conviction as legally insufficient. People v. Orso, 270 A.D.2d 947, 706 N.Y.S.2d 805 (4th Dept. 2000).

Sufficiency of indictment; principals and accomplices.— Where only a single pistol was used during robbery, and indictment indicated that defendant was charged not only for his own actions but also for those of another, jury could properly apply principle of accomplice liability in determining defendant's guilt. People v. McEachin, 188 A.D.2d 433, 591 N.Y.S.2d 1023 (1st Dept.), *lv. denied,* 81 N.Y.2d 889 (1992).

—As a general rule, a defendant may not legitimately claim to have been prejudiced when his guilt as a principal is proved, even though he was charged as an accessory, or where his guilt as an accomplice is proved, even though he is charged as a

principal. People v. Woods, 208 A.D.2d 874, 618 N.Y.S.2d 51 (2d Dept. 1994).

—There is no distinction between liability as a principal and criminal culpability as an accessory and the status for which the defendant is convicted has no bearing upon the theory of the prosecution. People v. Hilts, 191 A.D.2d 779, 594 N.Y.S.2d 408 (3d Dept.), *lv. denied,* 81 N.Y.2d 1074 (1993).

Designated time periods in which crime was committed.— Trial court properly charged jury that it could disregard a "minor" 15 minute variance between the time of the offense as charged in the indictment and the time of the offense as proven at trial, notwithstanding alibi defense; as the precise moment of a rape is not a material element of the crime of rape, reliance on the exact time contained in the indictment is not justified and any prejudice resulting from such reliance is not grounds for reversal. People v. Owens, 63 N.Y.2d 824, 482 N.Y.S.2d 250, 472 N.E.2d 26 (1984).

—Indictment that contains the correct time periods in which the crimes were committed but also includes time periods postdating the filing of the indictment, during which commission of offenses would have been impossible, is not jurisdictionally defective; an amendment to correct the form of the indictment was valid. People v. Parilla, 285 A.D.2d 157, 730 N.Y.S.2d 301 (1st Dept. 2001), *cert. denied,* 535 U.S. 1020 (2002).

—When time is not an essential element of an offense, the indictment need not set forth the actual date of the crime charged; it must, however, set forth a time interval that is not so vast as to deny the defendant his constitutional right to be informed of the nature and cause of the accusation. People v. Watt, 192 A.D.2d 65, 600 N.Y.S.2d 714 (2d Dept. 1993), *aff'd,* 84 N.Y.2d 948, 620 N.Y.S.2d 817, 644 N.E.2d 1373 (1994).

—Where indictment charged crime of receiving reward for official misconduct in that defendant, as employee for Department of Sanitation, permitted illegal dumping from September 1977 to March, indictment was sufficient to give reasonable and adequate notice, since witnesses were unable to provide precise dates and hours, which are not material elements of crimes charged. People v. Cassiliano, 103 A.D.2d 806, 477 N.Y.S.2d 435 (2d Dept. 1984), *cert. denied,* 469 U.S. 1210 (1985).

—An indictment is not jurisdictionally defective due to a technical mistake as to the date on which the crime occurred. People v. Kepple, 98 A.D.2d 783, 469 N.Y.S.2d 801 (2d Dept. 1983).

—As long as the time frame alleged in an indictment is not so large that it deprives defendant of the ability to prepare and present a defense, the indictment will survive a jurisdictional challenge. People v. Lanfair, 18 A.D.3d 1032, 795 N.Y.S.2d 390 (3d Dept. 2005).

—When it appeared that at least some of the elements of the crime occurred outside the time period indicated in the indictment and bill of particulars, reversal was not required where the defendant did not show that he was prejudiced by this technical defect. People v. Cunningham, 64 A.D.2d 722, 406 N.Y.S.2d 899 (3d Dept. 1978), *aff'd,* 48 N.Y.2d 938, 425 N.Y.S.2d 59, 401 N.E.2d 182 (1979).

—The crime of endangering the welfare of a child permits characterization as a continuing offense over time; here, the indictment was sufficient, insofar as it alleged that the crime of second degree sodomy occurred on March 29, 1998, without narrowing the time frame to a specific time of day. People v. Hutzler, 270 A.D.2d 934, 706 N.Y.S.2d 807 (4th Dept. 2000).

—When time is not an essential element of an offense, the indictment, as supplemented by a bill of particulars, may allege the time in approximate terms. People v. Risolo, 261 A.D.2d 921, 689 N.Y.S.2d 836 (4th Dept. 1999).

—Although the indictment did not contain the requisite specificity as to the dates of the crimes, the defendant was not prejudiced thereby where the court permitted the defendant to call an alibi witness without proper notice. People v. Kulzer, 155 A.D.2d 882, 547 N.Y.S.2d 716 (4th Dept. 1989).

—Indictment was dismissed as defective where it did not sufficiently designate the dates of the offenses for which defendant was being charged. People v. Pries, 81 A.D.2d 1039, 440 N.Y.S.2d 116 (4th Dept. 1981).

—Two-month period designated in each count of indictment was reasonably specific considering victim's age and physical handicap, the continuous and long term nature of the abuse inflicted upon her and the substantial lapse of time before she reported it to the prosecuting authorities. People v. Coveney, 134 Misc. 2d 894, 513 N.Y.S.2d 324 (Sup. Ct. Kings Co. 1987).

Designated time periods: sex crimes.—Time frames of up to 2 months alleged for sex offenses were not excessive. People v. Goulbourne, 199 A.D.2d 533, 606 N.Y.S.2d 50 (2d Dept. 1993), *lv. denied,* 83 N.Y.2d 853 (1994).

—Indictment alleging sex abuse incidents occurred during the spring, summer, and month of June, 1989, provided sufficient specificity as to time. People v. Bolden, 194 A.D.2d 834, 598 N.Y.S.2d 603 (3d Dept.), *lv. denied,* 82 N.Y.2d 714 (1993).

—Indictment which alleged that at unknown times between May, 1976 and December, 1977, defendant engaged in sexual intercourse with a female who was less than 11 years old, was patently defective. People v. MacAfee, 76 A.D.2d 157, 431 N.Y.S.2d 149 (3d Dept. 1980).

—Where People had not limited their allegations of child sex abuse to a single day, trial court was not required to give instruction requested by defense that offense occurred on or about Thanksgiving Day, during which defendant had an alibi. People v. Wosu, 213 A.D.2d 967, 624 N.Y.S.2d 479 (4th Dept. 1995), *aff'd,* 87 N.Y.2d 935, 640 N.Y.S.2d 870, 663 N.E.2d 911 (1996).

—Indictment was not defective for failure to specify dates of sex-related crimes involving a 14-year-old girl where it was alleged that several of the crimes occurred during a specific period in the home where both victim and defendant resided; the court noted that the basis of the trial defenses was not that the acts never occurred, but that there was no forcible compulsion. People v. Benjamin R., 103 A.D.2d 663, 481 N.Y.S.2d 827 (4th Dept. 1984).

—A charge in an accusatory instrument violates the constitutional guarantees of fair notice when the time interval during which the crime is alleged to have taken place is so unreasonably excessive that a defendant cannot possibly defend against the charges and prepare a defense. The time span is six months and eleven days, per se unreasonable in a sexual misconduct case, but court stayed the dismissal pending the filing by the district attorney within 21 days a prosecutor's information, superseding information, or bill of particulars alleging a shorter time period. People v. Evangelista, 1 Misc. 3d 873, 771 N.Y.S.2d 791 (Crim. Ct. Bronx Co. 2003).

Defective indictment.—Not all defects in the indictment mandate dismissal; the standard is one of reasonableness. People v. Riedd, 160 Misc. 2d 733, 609 N.Y.S.2d 997 (Sup. Ct. Bronx Co. 1994).

—Allowing defense to read and take notes from Grand Jury minutes did not remedy inadequacies in the indictment, since, *inter alia,* it did not meet double jeopardy concerns. People v. Sanchez, 84 N.Y.2d 440, 618 N.Y.S.2d 887, 643 N.E.2d 509 (1994).

Discretionary persistent offender charge.—Court rejected defendant's contention that the discretionary persistent felony offender sentence enhancement provisions violated his right to trial by jury and violated his right to a charge-specific indictment. A defendant has no constitutional right to a jury trial to establish the facts of his prior felony convictions; the indictment does not need to contain a discretionary persistent offender charge—the Supreme Court has held that "recidivism increasing the maximum penalty need not be charged." People v. Rosen, 96 N.Y.2d 329, 728 N.Y.S.2d 407, 752 N.E.2d 844, *cert. denied,* 534 U.S. 899, 122 S. Ct. 224 (2001).

Notice; bill of particulars and discovery.—Words "scheme or business of making or collecting usurious loans" are not impermissibly vague and do not therefore deny defendant his constitutional right to due process. People v. Lombardo, 61 N.Y.2d 97, 472 N.Y.S.2d 589, 460 N.E.2d 1074 (1984).

—Where the indictment itself provides a paucity of information, the court must be vigilant in safeguarding the defendant's rights to a bill of particulars and to effective discovery. People v. Iannone, 45 N.Y.2d 589, 412 N.Y.S.2d 110, 384 N.E.2d 656 (1978).

—An indictment charging the defendant with criminally negligent homicide in the language of the statute, coupled with a bill of particulars setting forth the specific acts of negligence underlying the charge satisfies the requirements of the long form indictment mandated under the CPL. People v. Fitzgerald, 45 N.Y.2d 574, 412 N.Y.S.2d 102, 384 N.E.2d 649 (1978).

—The purpose of an indictment is to provide the defendant with fair notice of the accusation against him and to allow him to prepare a defense, to insure that the crime for which the defendant is tried is the same as intended by the Grand Jury, and to protect the defendant against double jeopardy by specifying the specific crime for which he was tried. People v. Feliz, 136 Misc. 2d 701, 519 N.Y.S.2d 290 (Sup. Ct. Queens Co. 1987).

Waiver of objections.—A defendant's plea of guilty waives his right to dismiss a defective indictment. People v. Cohen, 52 N.Y.2d 584, 439 N.Y.S.2d 321, 421 N.E.2d 813 (1981).

—Defendant's challenge to the adequacy of the indictment pursuant to CPL § 200.50(7) is not preserved for appellate review where there is no timely objection raised. People v. Soto, 44 N.Y.2d 683, 405 N.Y.S.2d 434, 376 N.E.2d 907 (1978).

—Claim that counts did not adequately apprise defendant of the operative facts constituting the crimes charged was not preserved for appellate review where defendant did not raise it in his omnibus motion. People v. Waldron, 162 A.D.2d 485, 556 N.Y.S.2d 404 (2d Dept. 1990).

—A failure to include a challenge to the validity of an indictment as being too vague by means of a pretrial motion to dismiss acts as a waiver of such challenge. People v. DiNoia, 105 A.D.2d 799, 481 N.Y.S.2d 738 (2d Dept. 1984), *cert. denied,* 471 U.S. 1022

—Where defendant failed to raise issue of duplicity at trial, the issue was not preserved for appellate review. People v. Fiacco, 172 A.D.2d 994, 569 N.Y.S.2d 219 (3d Dept.), *lv. denied,* 78 N.Y.2d 965 (1991).

Subd. (8)

Foreperson's signature.—Although the foreperson's signature was absent from the actual indictment document, the record reveals that the indictment was handed up as a packet with various notices, which included a backer—signed by the foreperson—referring to the indictment by caption. The record also contains a sworn affidavit, signed by the foreperson, stating that the grand jury met and voted true bills, which is sufficient to establish that the indictment was properly authenticated. People v. Brown, 17 A.D.3d 869, 793 N.Y.S.2d 270 (3d Dept. 2005).

—Fact that grand jury foreperson did not sign the indictment as required by statute was a technical, nonjurisdictional defect which did not require dismissal, because the foreperson was present when the indictment was handed up and unsealed, and the foreperson swore under oath that the indictment had been voted on as a true bill by the required number of jurors. People v. Stauber, 307 A.D.2d 544, 763 N.Y.S.2d 854 (3d Dept. 2003).

§ 200.60. Indictment; allegations of previous convictions prohibited.

1. When the fact that the defendant has been previously convicted of an offense raises an offense of lower grade to one of higher grade and thereby becomes an element of the latter, an indictment for such higher offense may not allege such previous conviction. If a reference to previous conviction is contained in the statutory name or title of such an offense, such name or title may not be used in the indictment, but an improvised name or title must be used which, by means of the phrase "as a felony" or in some other manner, labels and distinguishes the offense without reference to a previous conviction. This subdivision does not apply to an indictment or a count thereof that charges escape in the second degree pursuant to subdivision two of section 205.10 of the penal law, or escape in the first degree pursuant to section 205.15 thereof.

2. An indictment for such an offense must be accompanied by a special information, filed by the district attorney with the court, charging that the defendant was previously convicted of a

specified offense. Except as provided in subdivision three, the people may not refer to such special information during the trial nor adduce any evidence concerning the previous conviction alleged therein.

3. After commencement of the trial and before the close of the people's case, the court, in the absence of the jury, must arraign the defendant upon such special information, and must advise him that he may admit the previous conviction alleged, deny it or remain mute. Depending upon the defendant's response, the trial of the indictment must then proceed as follows:

(a) If the defendant admits the previous conviction, that element of the offense charged in the indictment is deemed established, no evidence in support thereof may be adduced by the people, and the court must submit the case to the jury without reference thereto and as if the fact of such previous conviction were not an element of the offense. The court may not submit to the jury any lesser included offense which is distinguished from the offense charged solely by the fact that a previous conviction is not an element thereof.

(b) If the defendant denies the previous conviction or remains mute, the people may prove that element of the offense charged before the jury as a part of their case. In any prosecution under subparagraph (ix) of paragraph (a) of subdivision one of section 125.27 of the penal law, if the defendant denies the previous murder conviction or remains mute, the people may prove that element of the offense only after the jury has first found the defendant guilty of intentionally causing the death of a person as charged in the indictment, in which case the court shall then permit the people and the defendant to offer evidence and argument consistent with the relevant provisions of section 260.30 of this chapter with respect to the previous murder conviction.

4. Nothing contained in this section precludes the people from proving a prior conviction before a grand jury or relieves them from the obligation or necessity of so doing in order to submit a legally sufficient case.

Amended by L. 1995, Ch. 1, § 8, amending subd. 3(b), eff. Sept. 1, 1995.

ANNOTATIONS

Generally.—Under CPL § 200.60, when a defendant is charged with an offense which has as an element the fact that he has a prior conviction, the prosecution must follow certain statutory procedures. People v. Cooper, 78 N.Y.2d 476, 577 N.Y.S.2d 202, 583 N.E.2d 915 (1991).

—When defendant stood mute at his arraignment, the People had the burden of proving defendant's prior conviction as an element of the offense charged, and they could not simply rely on the certificate of conviction. People v. Vollick, 148 A.D.2d 950, 539 N.Y.S.2d 187 (4th Dept. 1989), *aff'd for the reasons stated below*, 75 N.Y.2d 877, 553 N.Y.S.2d 473, 553 N.E.2d 1021 (1990).

Guilty pleas.—CPL § 200.60(3) is by its terms inapplicable in the context of a guilty plea. People v. Dezimm, 193 A.D.2d 976, 598 N.Y.S.2d 124 (3d Dept. 1993).

—In guilty plea case, requirement that defendant be arraigned

on special information after commencement of trial and before completion of People's case was inapplicable. People v. Smart, 190 A.D.2d 942, 593 N.Y.S.2d 608 (3d Dept. 1993).

—Although prosecutor did not file a special information charging that defendant was previously convicted of specified offense, defendant admitted his prior conviction and agreed to plead to criminal possession of weapon in the third degree; prosecutor's failure to file special information was waived by defendant's voluntary guilty plea. People v. Mooney, 245 A.D.2d 1137, 666 N.Y.S.2d 532 (4th Dept. 1997).

—Where defendant pleaded guilty to the class B misdemeanor of engaging in a prostitution offense with a previous conviction for prostitution, and admitted to the prior conviction during the plea allocution, no special information was required. People v. Denise L., 159 Misc. 2d 1080, 608 N.Y.S.2d 40 (Crim. Ct., N.Y. Co. 1994).

Unpreserved claim.—Defendant did not preserve his claim pursuant to CPL § 200.60 that the court failed to follow the proper procedures for use of a prior conviction to elevate the level of a crime; because defense counsel stated on three occasions that defendant was not going to dispute a prior conviction elevating the weapon charge to a felony, and that the People were not obligated to prove the prior conviction, there was no need for the court again to offer defendant a chance to admit or deny the previous conviction. People v. Santiago, 244 A.D.2d 263, 664 N.Y.S.2d 771 (1st Dept. 1997).

Vehicular offenses.—CPL § 200.60 requires that the prescribed procedure for alleging and proving an earlier conviction must be followed in a prosecution for vehicular manslaughter in the first degree, which requires proof that defendant's license had been revoked following a prior conviction for a VTL offense. People v. Cooper, 78 N.Y.2d 476, 577 N.Y.S.2d 202, 583 N.E.2d 915 (1991).

—Where the predicate misdemeanor conviction was vacated, defendant's conviction for driving while intoxicated as a felony had to be reduced, since the aggravated charge was missing an essential element. People v. Frieary, 144 A.D.2d 382, 533 N.Y.S.2d 935 (2d Dept. 1988), *application for lv. dismissed*, 73 N.Y.2d 891 (1989).

§ 200.61. Indictment; special information for operators of for-hire vehicles.

1. The provisions of this section shall govern the procedures for determining whether a defendant is eligible to receive the sentence set forth in subdivision one of section 60.07 of the penal law upon conviction of a specified offense as defined in subdivision two of such section 60.07.

2. To receive the sentence set forth in subdivision one of section 60.07 of the penal law, an indictment for such specified offense must be accompanied by a special information, filed by the district attorney with the court, alleging that the victim of such offense was operating a for-hire vehicle in the course of providing for-hire vehicle services at the time of the commission of such offense.

3. Prior to the commencement of the trial, the court, in the absence of the jury, must arraign the defendant upon such special information, and must advise him that he may admit that the alleged victim of such offense was operating a for-hire vehicle in the course of providing for-hire vehicle services at the time of the alleged commission of such offense, deny such allegation or remain mute. Depending upon the defendant's response, the trial of the indictment must proceed as follows:

(a) If the defendant admits that the alleged victim of such specified offense charged was operating a for-hire vehicle in the course of providing for-hire vehicle services at the time of the commission of such alleged offense, such allegation, and only such allegation, shall be deemed established for purposes of eligibility, if the defendant is convicted of the underlying specified offense, for a sentence pursuant to subdivision one of section 60.07 of the penal law.

(b) If the defendant denies such allegation or remains mute, the people may, by proof beyond a reasonable doubt, prove as part of their case before the jury or, where the defendant has waived a jury trial, the court, that the alleged victim of such offense was operating a forhire vehicle in the course of providing for-hire vehicle services at the time of the commission of the offense.

4. Where a jury, pursuant to paragraph (b) of subdivision three of this section, is charged with determining whether the alleged victim of such specified offense was operating a for-hire vehicle in the course of providing for-hire vehicle services, such jury shall consider and render its verdict on such matter only if it convicts the defendant of such specified offense or specified offenses charged.

5. For purposes of this section, the terms "for-hire vehicle", "for-hire vehicle services" and "specified offense" shall have the meanings set forth in section 60.07 of the penal law.

Added by L. 2000, Ch. 148, § 5, eff. Nov. 1, 2000.

§ 200.62. Indictment; special information for child sexual assault offender.

1. Whenever a person is charged with the commission or attempted commission of an offense defined in article one hundred thirty of the penal law which constitutes a felony and it appears that the victim of such offense was less than fifteen years old, an indictment for such offense may be accompanied by a special information, filed by the district attorney with the court, alleging that the victim was less than fifteen years old at the time of the commission of the offense; provided, however, that such an information need not be filed when the age of the victim is an element of the offense.

2. Prior to trial, or after the commencement of the trial but before the close of the people's case, the court, in the absence of the jury, must arraign the defendant upon such information and advise him or her that he or she may admit such allegation, deny it or remain mute. Depending upon the defendant's response, the trial of the indictment must proceed as follows:

(a) If the defendant admits that the alleged victim was less than fifteen years old at the time of the commission or attempted commission of the offense, that allegation shall be deemed established for all subsequent purposes, including sentencing pursuant to section 70.07 of the penal law.

(b) If the defendant denies such allegation or remains mute, the people may, by proof beyond a reasonable doubt, prove before the jury or, where the defendant has waived a jury trial, the court, that the alleged victim was less than fifteen years old at the time of the commission or attempted commission of the offense.

(c) Nothing in this subdivision shall prevent the people, in a trial before the court or a jury, from making reference to and introducing evidence of the victim's age.

3. Where a jury, pursuant to paragraph (b) of subdivision two of this section, makes the determination of whether the alleged victim of the offense was less than fifteen years old, such jury shall consider and render its verdict on such issue only after rendering its verdict with regard to the offense.

4. A determination pursuant to this section that the victim was less than fifteen years old at the time of the commission of the offense shall be binding in any future proceeding in which the issue may arise unless the underlying conviction or determination is vacated or reversed.

Added by L. 2000, Ch. 1, eff. Feb. 1, 2001; L. 2003, Ch. 264, § 40, eff. Nov. 1, 2003, amending opening par. of subd. 2 and adding subd. 2(c).

§ 200.65. Indictment; special information for enterprise corruption and criminal possession or use of a biological weapon or chemical weapon.

When filing an indictment which charges enterprise corruption in violation of article four hundred sixty of the penal law, criminal possession of a chemical weapon or biological weapon in violation of section 490.37, 490.40, or 490.45 of the penal law, or criminal use of a chemical weapon or biological weapon in violation of section 490.47, 490.50, or 490.55 of the penal law, the district attorney must submit a statement to the court attesting that he or she has reviewed the substance of the evidence presented to the grand jury and concurs in the judgment that the charge is consistent with legislative findings in article four hundred sixty or four hundred ninety of the penal law, as applicable. For purposes of this section only, "district attorney" means the district attorney of the county, the attorney general, or the deputy attorney general in charge of the organized crime task force, or where such person is actually absent or disabled, the person authorized to act in his or her stead.

Added by L. 1986, Ch. 516; Amended by L. 2004, Ch. 1, §§ 1 and 10 (Part A), eff. July 23, 2004.

§ 200.70. Indictment; amendment of.

1. At any time before or during trial, the court may, upon application of the people and with notice to the defendant and opportunity to be heard, order the amendment of an indictment with respect to defects, errors or variances from the proof relating to matters of form, time, place, names of persons and the like, when such an amendment does not change the theory or theories of the prosecution as reflected in the evidence before the grand jury which filed such indictment, or otherwise tend to prejudice the defendant on the merits. Where the accusatory instrument is a superior court information, such an amendment may be made when it does not tend to prejudice the defendant on the merits. Upon permitting such an amendment, the court must, upon application of the defendant, order any adjournment of the proceedings which may, by reason of such amendment, be necessary to accord the defendant adequate opportunity to prepare his defense.

2. An indictment may not be amended in any respect which changes the theory or theories of the prosecution as reflected in the evidence before the grand jury which filed it; nor may an indictment or a superior court information be amended for the purpose of curing:

(a) A failure thereof to charge or state an offense; or

(b) Legal insufficiency of the factual allegations; or

(c) A misjoinder of offenses; or

(d) A misjoinder of defendants.

Amended by L. 1974, Ch. 467.

ANNOTATIONS

Amendments: accomplices and co-defendants.—There was no impermissible trial amendment of a conspiracy indictment which charged that defendant conspired with three co-conspirators while proof showed that he, in fact, conspired with only two of the three other co-conspirators named in the indictment. People v. Treuber, 64 N.Y.S.2d 817, 486 N.Y.S.2d 926, 476 N.E.2d 325 (1985).

—Trial court improperly charged the jury on the alternative theory of "acting in concert," even though there was no evidence linking defendant to an unlawful entry by others; this was a significant change in the theory of the prosecution at the close of trial, causing defendant serious prejudice. People v. Ortiz, 207 A.D.2d 279, 615 N.Y.S.2d 387 (1st Dept. 1994).

—The amendment of the indictment to reflect that the defendant and his co-defendant acted in concert with additional unnamed individuals did not change the theory of the case or unduly prejudice the defendant; the amendment was consistent with the initial theory, of which the defendant had notice, that he acted with another to commit a robbery. People v. Budhai, 182 A.D.2d 693, 582 N.Y.S.2d 730 (2d Dept.), lv. denied, 80 N.Y.2d 901 (1992).

—The court properly amended the indictment to read that the defendant acted in concert "with another" instead of with the co-defendant. People v. Roseboro, 182 A.D.2d 784, 582 N.Y.S.2d 780 (2d Dept. 1992).

—It was proper for the trial court to amend the indictment, prior to trial, to delete the name of the co-defendant, who had previously been acquitted of the instant charges, since this amendment did not prejudice the defendant in his defense on the merits or alter the theory of the People's case. People v. Reddy, 73 A.D.2d 977, 424 N.Y.S.2d 238 (2d Dept. 1980).

Amendments: dates.—Court's amendment of indictment, which moderately enlarged the time frame of defendant's drug possession, did not change the theory of the prosecution or prejudice the defendant, but merely modified the time frame in a manner that fit the complex and unusual fact pattern established in the grand jury and at trial. People v. Straniero, 17 A.D.3d 161, 792 N.Y.S.2d 466 (1st Dept. 2005).

—Where time was not a material element of offense, amendment of indictment, during trial, to reflect evidence presented during trial regarding time span of alleged scheme to defraud, was a minor amendment and did not constitute a material variance from theory of indictment. People v. O'Connor, 240 A.D.2d 764, 660 N.Y.S.2d 140 (2d Dept. 1997).

—Where the People err in alleging the date or time of an offense, the appropriate remedy is to permit amendment of the indictment and to provide the accused with a reasonable adjournment to prepare a defense. People v. Rogers, 141 A.D.2d 870, 530 N.Y.S.2d 834 (2d. Dept. 1988).

—Amendment of an indictment on the eve of trial, changing the date of the alleged crime by one day, was not prejudicial, even where defendant intended to interpose an alibi defense, since the trial was adjourned for one month immediately after the amendment. People v. Page, 89 A.D.2d 878, 453 N.Y.S.2d 222 (2d Dept. 1982).

—Reversal was required where the People amended the indictment by changing the date of the crime after a bill of particulars and notice of alibi had been served and a jury had been selected. People v. Covington, 86 A.D.2d 877, 447 N.Y.S.2d 292 (2d Dept. 1982).

—Court did not err in allowing the People to amend the indictment to change the date of the crime, where the amendment merely corrected an error of form, was not prejudicial on the merits, and did not alter the theory of the prosecution's case. People v. Bell, 206 A.D.2d 686, 614 N.Y.S.2d 790 (3d Dept. 1994).

—Court properly permitted the prosecution to amend four counts of the indictment to allege that the acts in question occurred in April 1994, rather than in April 1993, where the amendment did not change the theory of the prosecution, and defendant, who did not raise an alibi defense, was not otherwise prejudiced on the merits. People v. Pike, 254 A.D.2d 727, 681 N.Y.S.2d 706 (4th Dept. 1998).

Amendments: weapons, injuries.—Court properly permitted People, prior to summations, to amend the indictment to read, injuries were caused "by means of a deadly weapon" to replace the words, "by means of a dangerous instrument, namely, a handgun." People v. Sage, 204 A.D.2d 746, 612 N.Y.S.2d 648 (2d Dept.), lv. denied, 84 N.Y.2d 832 (1994).

—Amendment of indictment by changing the description of the weapon from "handgun" to "shotgun" was permissible. People v. Hood, 194 A.D.2d 556, 598 N.Y.S.2d 569 (2d Dept.), lv. denied, 82 N.Y.2d 720 (1993).

—Amendment of indictment in order to include "asphyxiation" in the description of lethal injuries inflicted upon the victim was proper. People v. Rodriguez, 181 A.D.2d 840, 581 N.Y.S.2d 395 (2d Dept.), lv. denied, 80 N.Y.2d 837 (1992).

Amending to correct clerical errors or make other nonmaterial changes.—It was permissible for the trial court to instruct the jury that it could find defendant guilty of robbery if they found that he had stolen illegal drugs from complainant rather than "jewelry or money" stated in the complaint, since the nature of the property stolen is not an essential element of the crime of robbery and the underlying facts of victim, time, place, and date were the same. People v. Spann, 56 N.Y.2d 469, 452 N.Y.S.2d 869, 438 N.E.2d 402 (1982).

—The trial court properly permitted the People to amend the indictment to refer to "heroin" rather than "cocaine." People v. Acevedo, 215 A.D.2d 115, 626 N.Y.S.2d 89 (1st Dept. 1995).

—Constructive amendment of the indictment, which took place off-the-record, deleting fact that the buyer of narcotics was a police officer, was a permissible amendment of a nonessential fact. People v. Brown, 196 A.D.2d 428, 601 N.Y.S.2d 282 (1st Dept.), lv. denied, 82 N.Y.2d 804 (1993).

—Changing the description of the property that defendant was accused of taking was a permissible amendment, since it did not involve a material element of the crime. People v. Goodman, 156 A.D.2d 713, 549 N.Y.S.2d 465 (2d Dept. 1989), lv. denied, 75 N.Y.2d 919 (1990).

—Defendant was not prejudiced by the fact that the People were permitted to slightly amend the last count of the indictment so as to more closely conform the indictment to the proof. People v. Nardo, 153 A.D.2d 972, 545 N.Y.S.2d 411 (3d Dept. 1989).

—Deletion from the indictment of the statement defendant "was being prepared for a shower" where he was charged with assaulting a correction officer did not alter the theory of the indictment as what he was doing at the time of the assault did not constitute an element of the crime charged. People v. LaBoy, 91 A.D.2d 1102, 458 N.Y.S.2d 361 (3d Dept. 1983).

—Court properly amended the indictment to reflect the possible dates on which the crime occurred; amendment did not change the theory of the prosecution or otherwise prejudice defendant, and defendant's motion for a mistrial based on the amendment was properly denied. People v. Hale, 236 A.D.2d 807, 654 N.Y.S.2d 60 (4th Dept. 1997).

—The fact that subsequent to an indictment it is discovered that the defendant's true name is other than the name that was presented to the Grand Jury does not alter the Grand Jury's intention to indict the person and, therefore, the trial court should permit the State to amend the indictment to substitute the defendant's true name for the name in the indictment. People v. Ganett, 68 A.D.2d 81, 416 N.Y.S.2d 914 (4th Dept. 1979), aff'd, 51 N.Y.2d 991, 435 N.Y.S.2d 976, 417 N.E.2d 88 (1980).

Impermissible amendments.—The trial court cannot amend the indictment to add a new count, even one that was voted by the Grand Jury and omitted from the indictment because of a clerical error. People v. Perez, 83 N.Y.2d 269, 609 N.Y.S.2d 564, 631 N.E.2d 570 (1994).

—Because court lacked authority to amend instant indictment to add an offense with which defendant had not been charged, conviction must be reversed and indictment dismissed. People v. Jones, 267 A.D.2d 89, 700 N.Y.S.2d 141 (1st Dept. 1999).

—When an indictment specifies that an accused committed sodomy through the use of actual force, it is error for the court to instruct the jury, over objection, that the crime may also be committed by the use of the threat of force. People v. Udzinski, 146 A.D.2d 245, 541 N.Y.S.2d 9 (2d Dept. 1989).

—A charge which constructively amends an indictment in such a way as to allow a variation in the theory of the prosecution is impermissible. People v. Spratley, 144 A.D.2d 769, 534 N.Y.S.2d 754 (3d Dept. 1988).

—Like indictments and informations, prosecutor's informations can be amended with respect to time, place, and the names of persons, but unlike indictments, informations do not have the limitations imposed by CPL § 200.70(2)(a) and (b), i.e., that there can be no amendment to cure the failure to state an offense or legal insufficiency of the factual allegations. People v. Kurtz, 175 Misc. 2d 980, 670 N.Y.S.2d 1008 (Crim. Ct. Queens Co. 1998).

Waiver of objections.—The defendant by pleading guilty waived any challenge to the amendment of the indictment. People v. Harris, 117 A.D.2d 752, 498 N.Y.S.2d 475 (2d Dept. 1986).

§ 200.80. Indictment; superseding indictments.

If at any time before entry of a plea of guilty to an indictment or commencement of a trial thereof another indictment is filed in the same court charging the defendant with an offense charged in the first indictment, the first indictment is, with respect to such offense, superseded by the second and, upon the defendant's arraignment upon the second indictment, the count of the first indictment charging such offense must be dismissed by the court. The first indictment is not, however, superseded with respect to any count contained therein which charges an offense not charged in the second indictment. Nothing herein precludes the filing of a superseding indictment when the first accusatory instrument is a superior court information.

Amended by L. 1974, Ch. 467.

ANNOTATIONS

Authorization for superseding indictment not required where dismissal was nullity.—A court is without authority to dismiss an indictment based upon the People's inability to proceed at trial, and because such dismissal in this case was a nullity, the first indictment remained effective, and authorization to seek a superseding indictment was not required. People v. Dexter, 259 A.D.2d 952, 688 N.Y.S.2d 289 (4th Dept.), aff'd, 94 N.Y.2d 847 (1999).

Effect of superseding indictment.—Any offense contained in the prior indictment which was also contained in the superseding indictment had to be dismissed by the court. Gold v. McShane, 74 A.D.2d 616, 425 N.Y.S.2d 341 (2d Dept. 1980), lv. denied, 52 N.Y.2d 704 (1981).

New evidence.—CPL § 200.80 allows a prosecutor to obtain a superseding indictment based upon new or additional evidence not previously submitted to the Grand Jury. People v. Cade, 74 N.Y.2d 410, 548 N.Y.S.2d 137, 547 N.E.2d 339 (1989).

§ 200.90. [*Repealed by L. 1982, Ch. 558, eff. Oct. 20, 1982.*]

§ 200.95. Indictment; bill of particulars.

1. Definitions. (a) "Bill of particulars" is a written statement by the prosecutor specifying, as required by this section, items of factual information which are not recited in the indictment and which pertain to the offense charged and including the substance of each defendant's conduct encompassed by the charge which the people intend to prove at trial on their direct case, and whether the people intend to prove that the defendant acted as principal or accomplice or both, and the items of factual information which are not recited in a special forfeiture information or prosecutor's forfeiture information containing one or more forfeiture counts and which pertain to the substance of each defendant's conduct giving rise to the forfeiture claim, the approximate value of the property for which forfeiture is sought, the nature and extent of the defendant's interest in such property, and the extent of the defendant's gain, if any, from the offense charged. However, the prosecutor shall not be required to include in the bill of particulars matters of evidence relating to how the people intend to prove the elements of the offense charged or how the people intend to prove any item of factual information included in the bill of particulars.

(b) "Request for a bill of particulars" is a written request served by defendant upon the people, without leave of the court, requesting a bill of particulars, specifying the items of factual information desired, and alleging that defendant cannot adequately prepare or conduct his defense without the information requested.

2. Bill of particulars upon request. Upon a timely request for a bill of particulars by a defendant against whom an indictment is pending, the prosecutor shall within fifteen days of the service of the request or as soon thereafter as is practicable, serve upon the defendant or his attorney, and file with the court, the bill of

particulars, except to the extent the prosecutor shall have refused to comply with the request pursuant to subdivision four of this section.

3. Timeliness of request. A request for a bill of particulars shall be timely if made within thirty days after arraignment and before the commencement of trial. If the defendant is not represented by counsel, and has requested an adjournment to obtain counsel or to have counsel assigned, the thirty day period shall commence, for the purposes of a request for a bill of particulars by the defendant, on the date counsel initially appears on his behalf. However, the court may direct compliance with a request for a bill of particulars that, for good cause shown, could not have been made within the time specified.

4. Request refused. The prosecutor may refuse to comply with the request for a bill of particulars or any portion of the request for a bill of particulars to the extent he reasonably believes that the item of factual information requested is not authorized to be included in a bill of particulars, or that such information is not necessary to enable the defendant adequately to prepare or conduct his defense, or that a protective order would be warranted or that the demand is untimely. Such refusal shall be made in a writing, which shall set forth the grounds of such belief as fully as possible, consistent with the reason for the refusal. Within fifteen days of the request or as soon thereafter as practicable, the refusal shall be served upon the defendant and a copy shall be filed with the court.

5. Court ordered bill of particulars. Where a prosecutor has timely served a written refusal pursuant to subdivision four of this section and upon motion, made in writing, of a defendant, who has made a request for a bill of particulars and whose request has not been complied with in whole or in part, the court must, to the extent a protective order is not warranted, order the prosecutor to comply with the request if it is satisfied that the items of factual information requested are authorized to be included in a bill of particulars, and that such information is necessary to enable the defendant adequately to prepare or conduct his defense and, if the request was untimely, a finding of good cause for the delay. Where a prosecutor has not timely served a written refusal pursuant to subdivision four of this section the court must, unless it is satisfied that the people have shown good cause why such an order should not be issued, issue an order requiring the prosecutor to comply or providing for any other order authorized by subdivision one of section 240.70.

6. Motion procedure. A motion for a bill of particulars shall be made as prescribed in section 255.20. Upon an order granting a motion pursuant to this section, the prosecutor must file with the court a bill of particulars, reciting every item of information designated in the order, and serve a copy thereof upon the defendant. Pending such filing and service, the proceedings are stayed.

7. Protective order. (a) The court in which the criminal action is pending may, upon motion of the prosecutor, or of any affected person, or upon determination of a motion of defendant for a court ordered bill of particulars, or upon its own initiative, issue a protective order denying, limiting, conditioning, delaying or regulating the bill of particulars for good cause, including constitutional limitations, danger to the integrity of physical evidence or a substantial risk of physical harm, intimidation, economic reprisal, bribery or unjustified annoyance or embarrassment to any person or an adverse effect upon the legitimate needs of law enforcement, including the protection of the confidentiality of informants, or any other factor or set of factors which outweighs the need for the bill of particulars.

(b) An order limiting, conditioning, delaying or regulating the bill of particulars may, among other things, require that any material copied or derived therefrom be maintained in the exclusive possession of the attorney for the defendant and be used for the exclusive purpose of preparing for the defense of the criminal action.

8. Amendment. At any time before commencement of trial, the prosecutor may, without leave of the court, serve upon defendant and file with the court an amended bill of particulars. At any time during trial, upon application of the prosecutor and with notice to the defendant and an opportunity for him to be heard, the court must, upon finding that no undue prejudice will accrue to defendant and that the prosecutor has acted in good faith, permit the prosecutor to amend the bill of particulars. Upon any amendment of the bill of particulars, the court must, upon application of defendant, order an adjournment of the proceedings or any other action it deems appropriate which may, by reason of the amendment, be necessary to accord the defendant an adequate opportunity to defend.

Added by L. 1982, Ch. 558; **Amended** by L. 1990, Ch. 655.

ANNOTATIONS

Purpose.—A bill of particulars is intended to clarify the indictment, not to be a discovery device. People v. Davis, 41 N.Y.2d 678, 394 N.Y.S.2d 865, 363 N.E.2d 572 (1977).

—Sole function of a bill of particulars is to clarify a pleading. Where, as here, the indictment adequately apprised defendant of the charges against him with sufficient specificity to enable him to prepare and conduct a defense, no bill of particulars was required. People v. Elliot, 299 A.D.2d 731, 751 N.Y.S.2d 331 (2002), aff'd after remand, 305 A.D.2d 704, 757 N.Y.S.2d 807 (3d Dept. 2003).

—Bill of particulars cannot be used to amend an indictment or cure a defective pleading. People v. MacAfee, 76 A.D.2d 157, 431 N.Y.S.2d 149 (3d Dept. 1980).

Amendment of bill of particulars.—The prosecution could amend its bill of particulars, where the amendment did not change its theory of the case, but merely corrected the location of the crime. People v. Jarvis, 215 A.D.2d 588, 626 N.Y.S.2d 832 (2d Dept. 1995).

—Amendment of the bill of particulars by the People nearly

four months before trial was statutorily permissible. People v. Hampton, 148 A.D.2d 633, 539 N.Y.S.2d 93 (2d Dept. 1989).

—Court properly allowed prosecution's amendment to bill of particulars because it did not expand or alter the People's theory of the case, prompt a request for an adjournment by defense counsel, prejudice defendant in any way, or stem from bad faith on the part of the People. People v. Wright, 13 A.D.3d 803, 785 N.Y.S.2d 809 (3d Dept. 2004).

—Court properly allowed pretrial amendments of the bill of particulars, because the amendments did not change the theory of the People's case, and defendant neither requested an adjournment nor demonstrated any undue prejudice or prosecutorial bad faith. Furthermore, count one of the indictment sufficiently apprised defendant of the offense charged, and the amendments did not constitute a constructive amendment of the indictment. People v. West, 271 A.D.2d 806, 708 N.Y.S.2d 478 (3d Dept. 2000).

Contents.—Names and addresses of witnesses are evidentiary material and therefore not properly included in a demand for a bill of particulars. People v. Contento, 146 A.D.2d 959, 537 N.Y.S.2d 88 (3d Dept. 1989).

—Bill of particulars need not include evidentiary material such as conversations between police officer and defendant. People v. Bignall, 195 A.D.2d 997, 600 N.Y.S.2d 560 (4th Dept.), *lv. denied,* 82 N.Y.2d 891 (1993).

—The People's responses to defendant's motions for a bill of particulars and discovery are presumed adequate absent an application by counsel made prior to the date set for trial after conferences between the attorney. People v. Niang, 160 Misc. 2d 500, 609 N.Y.S.2d 1017 (Crim. Ct. N.Y. Co. 1994).

—Defendant was given fair notice of the charges and the People's theory in the indictment and bill of particulars; the fact that his testimony also satisfied every requisite element of the charged crime under a different theory permitted supplemental jury instructions that the defendant could be found guilty on either the People's theory or the alternative theory arising from the defendant's own testimony. People v. Harvey, 202 A.D.2d 208, 608 N.Y.S.2d 220 (1st Dept. 1994).

Timeliness of request.—Defendants argued that reversal was warranted because of alleged inadequacies in the People's response to defendants' demand for a bill of particulars. However, this argument was unpersuasive given that defendants' demand was untimely, having been made more than 30 days after their arraignment and no excuse for their delay was proffered. People v. Duell, 266 A.D.2d 649, 698 N.Y.S.2d 87 (3d Dept. 1999).

Waiver of objections.—By failing to request a bill of particulars, the defendant waives claim that the indictment lacked information significant to the preparation of the defense. People v. McKenzie, 67 N.Y.2d 695, 499 N.Y.S.2d 923, 490 N.E.2d 842 (1986).

ARTICLE 210—PROCEEDINGS IN SUPERIOR COURT FROM FILING OF INDICTMENT TO PLEA

LexisNexis Cross References

Prosecution and Defense of Forfeiture Cases, Vol. 2, Ch. 14, Procedure in Criminal Forfeiture Cases; *Criminal Law Advocacy,* Vol. 1, Ch. 1, Steps in the Criminal Process; *Criminal Defense Techniques,* Vol. 5, Ch. 103, Arraignment; *New York Criminal Practice (2d ed.),* Vol. 1, Ch. 5, Indictments and Superior Court Informations; Vol. 1, Ch. 9, Local Criminal Court Arraignment and Related Issues; Vol. 2, Ch. 16, Motion to Dismiss Indictment; *New York Suppression Manual,* Ch. 10, Procedures After Arrest.

§ 210.05. Indictment and superior court information exclusive methods of prosecution.

The only methods of prosecuting an offense in a superior court are by an indictment filed therewith by a grand jury or by a superior court information filed therewith by a district attorney.

Amended by L. 1974, Ch. 467.

ANNOTATIONS

In general.—A court's jurisdiction over a defendant in felony case must be based on the decision of a grand jury as expressed in an indictment. People v. Livoti, 166 Misc. 2d 925, 632 N.Y.S.2d 425 (Sup. Ct. Bronx Co. 1995).

—An indictment can be filed only in a superior court. People v. Santos, 165 Misc. 2d 950, 630 N.Y.S.2d 908 (Crim. Ct. Bronx Co. 1995).

—"No person shall be held to answer for a capital or otherwise infamous . . . crime unless on indictment of a grand jury." People v. Rivera, 84 N.Y.2d 766, 622 N.Y.S.2d 671, 646 N.E.2d 1098 (1995) (citing N.Y. Const. art. I, § 6).

§ 210.10. Requirement of, and methods of securing defendant's appearance for arraignment upon indictment.

After an indictment has been filed with a superior court, the defendant must be arraigned thereon. He must appear personally at such arraignment, and his appearance may be secured as follows:

1. If the defendant was previously held by a local criminal court for the action of the grand jury, and if he is confined in the custody of the sheriff pursuant to a previous court order issued in the same criminal action, the superior court must direct the sheriff to produce the defendant for arraignment on a specified date and the sheriff must comply with such direction. The court must give at least two days notice of the time and place of the arraignment to an attorney, if any, who has previously filed a notice of appearance on behalf of the defendant with such superior court, or if no such notice of appearance has been filed, to an attorney, if any, who filed a notice of appearance in behalf of the defendant with the local criminal court.

2. If a felony complaint against the defendant was pending in a local criminal court or if the defendant was previously held by a local criminal court for the action of the grand jury, and if the defendant is at liberty on his or her own recognizance or on bail pursuant to a previous court order issued in the same criminal action, the superior

court must, upon at least two days notice to the defendant and his or her surety, to any person other than the defendant who posted cash bail and to any attorney who would be entitled to notice under circumstances prescribed in subdivision one, direct the defendant to appear before the superior court for arraignment on a specified date. If the defendant fails to appear on such date, the court may issue a bench warrant and, in addition, may forfeit the bail, if any. Upon taking the defendant into custody pursuant to such bench warrant, the executing police officer must without unnecessary delay bring the defendant before such superior court for arraignment. If such superior court is not available, the executing police officer may bring the defendant to the local correctional facility of the county in which such superior court sits, to be detained there until not later than the commencement of the next session of such court occurring on the next business day.

3. If the defendant has not previously been held by a local criminal court for the action of the grand jury and the filing of the indictment constituted the commencement of the criminal action, the superior court must order the indictment to be filed as a sealed instrument until the defendant is produced or appears for arraignment, and must issue a superior court warrant of arrest. Upon the request of the district attorney, in lieu of a superior court warrant of arrest, the court may issue a summons if it is satisfied that the defendant will respond thereto. Upon the request of the district attorney, in lieu of a warrant or summons, the court may instead authorize the district attorney to direct the defendant to appear for arraignment on a designated date if it is satisfied that the defendant will so appear. A superior court warrant of arrest is executable anywhere in the state. Such warrant may be addressed to any police officer whose geographical area of employment embraces either the place where the offense charged was allegedly committed or the locality of the court by which the warrant is issued. It must be executed in the same manner as an ordinary warrant of arrest, as provided in section 120.80, and following the arrest the executing police officer must without unnecessary delay perform all recording, fingerprinting, photographing and other preliminary police duties required in the particular case, and bring the defendant before the superior court. If such superior court is not available, the executing police officer may bring the defendant to the local correctional facility of the county in which such superior court sits, to be detained there until not later than the commencement of the next session of such court occurring on the next business day.

4. A superior court warrant of arrest may be executed by (a) any police officer to whom it is addressed or (b) any other police officer delegated to execute it under circumstances prescribed in subdivisions five and six.

5. The issuing court may authorize the delegation of such warrant. Where the issuing court has so authorized, a police officer to whom a superior court warrant of arrest is addressed may delegate another police officer to whom it is not addressed to execute such warrant as his agent when:

(a) He has reasonable cause to believe that the defendant is in a particular county other than the one in which the warrant is returnable; and

(b) The geographical area of employment of the delegated police officer embraces the locality where the arrest is to be made.

6. Under circumstances specified in subdivision five, the police officer to whom the warrant is addressed may inform the delegated officer, by telecommunication, mail or any other means, of the issuance of the warrant, of the offense charged in the underlying accusatory instrument and of all other pertinent details, and may request such officer to act as his or her agent in arresting the defendant pursuant to such warrant. Upon such request, the delegated police officer is to the same extent as the delegating officer, authorized to make such arrest pursuant to the warrant within the geographical area of such delegated officer's employment. Upon so arresting the defendant, he or she must without unnecessary delay deliver the defendant or cause the defendant to be delivered to the custody of the police officer by whom he or she was so delegated, and the latter must then without unnecessary delay bring the defendant before a court in which such warrant is returnable. If such court is not available, the delegating officer may bring the defendant to the local correctional facility of the county in which such court sits, to be detained there until not later than the commencement of the next session of such court occurring on the next business day.

Amended by L. 1974, Ch. 467; L. 1976, Ch. 696; L. 1984, Ch. 384; L. 1988, Ch. 565; L. 1990, Ch. 681; L. 1993, Ch. 446.

ANNOTATION

Judicial function.—Arraigning a defendant upon indictment is exclusively a court function; it is the court that must notify the defendant of the arraignment date and secure his appearance. People v. Goss, 87 N.Y.2d 792, 642 N.Y.S.2d 607, 665 N.E.2d 177 (1996).

§ 210.15. Arraignment upon indictment; defendant's rights, court's instructions and bail matters.

1. Upon the defendant's arraignment before a superior court upon an indictment, the court must immediately inform him, or cause him to be informed in its presence, of the charge or charges against him, and the district attorney must cause him to be furnished with a copy of the indictment.

2. The defendant has a right to the aid of counsel at the arraignment and at every subsequent stage of the action, and, if he appears upon such arraignment without counsel, has the following rights:

(a) To an adjournment for the purpose of obtaining counsel; and

(b) To communicate, free of charge, by letter or by telephone, for the purposes of obtaining counsel and informing a relative or friend that he has been charged with an offense; and

(c) To have counsel assigned by the court in any case where he is financially unable to obtain the same.

3. The court must inform the defendant of all rights specified in subdivision two. The court must accord the defendant opportunity to exercise such rights and must itself take such affirmative action as is necessary to effectuate them.

4. [*Repealed.*]

5. If the defendant desires to proceed without the aid of counsel, the court must permit him to do so if it is satisfied that he made such decision with knowledge of the significance thereof, but if it is not so satisfied it may not proceed until the defendant is provided with counsel, either of his own choosing or by assignment. A defendant who proceeds at the arraignment without counsel does not waive his right to counsel, and the court must inform him that he continues to have such right as well as all the rights specified in subdivision two which are necessary to effectuate it, and that he may exercise such rights at any stage of the action.

6. Upon the arraignment, the court, unless it intends to make a final disposition of the action immediately thereafter, must, as provided in section 530.40, issue a securing order, releasing the defendant on his own recognizance or fixing bail or committing him to the custody of the sheriff for his future appearance in such action.

Amended by L. 1972, Ch. 697; L. 1973, Ch. 472.

ANNOTATIONS

Right to counsel: counsel of choice.—The right of an indigent criminal defendant to the services of a court-appointed lawyer does not encompass a right to appointment of successive lawyers at defendant's option. People v. Sides, 75 N.Y.2d 822, 552 N.Y.S.2d 555, 551 N.E.2d 1233 (1990).

—Court correctly denied defendant's request to be assigned a different attorney at the close of opening statements, since defendant did not make a showing of "good cause" for the requested assignment. People v. Nesby, 161 A.D.2d 246, 554 N.Y.S.2d 894 (1st Dept. 1990).

—The ultimate test in determining whether the court properly denied defendant's request for new counsel is whether counsel has secured a beneficial sentence for his client and from the client's perspective at least, beneficial means lenient. People v. Thompson, 162 A.D.2d 153, 556 N.Y.S.2d 296 (1st Dept.), *lv. denied,* 76 N.Y.2d 945 (1990).

—Although the right to be represented by counsel of one's own choosing is a valued one, an indigent defendant does not have the right to the appointment of successive lawyers absent a showing of good cause for the substitution. People v. Maldonado, 178 A.D.2d 554, 577 N.Y.S.2d 645 (2d Dept. 1991).

—Defendant's generalized assertion that assigned counsel was not "properly taking care of" him did not constitute good cause for assignment of new counsel. People v. Harris, 173 A.D.2d 486, 570 N.Y.S.2d 106 (2d Dept.), *lv. denied,* 78 N.Y.2d 955 (1991).

—Court properly refused to substitute new counsel in place of assigned counsel on the eve of trial since defendant's dissatisfaction with his assigned counsel was merely based upon his perception that counsel had no confidence in his case and conclusory allegations that counsel had not attempted to assist him until the eve of trial. People v. Taitt, 146 A.D.2d 658, 536 N.Y.S.2d 856 (2d Dept. 1989).

—Court-appointed counsel will not be removed except when good cause is shown. People v. Williams, 143 A.D.2d 959, 533 N.Y.S.2d 742 (2d Dept. 1988).

—Court properly denied assigned counsel's request to be relieved because he and the defendant had an argument, since there was no indication in the record that the defendant was dissatisfied with his counsel. People v. Folk, 145 A.D.2d 505, 535 N.Y.S.2d 444 (2d Dept. 1988).

—Court rejected the contention that the lower court should have granted the defendant's application for substitute counsel which was made only one month before trial; a change of counsel at this stage would have had the inevitable effect of delaying the trial. People v. Jiminez, 179 A.D.2d 840, 579 N.Y.S.2d 173 (3d Dept.), *lv. denied,* 79 N.Y.2d 949 (1992).

—The court did not abuse its discretion by refusing defendant's request for a different assigned attorney because defendant failed to establish good cause for the substitution. People v. Taylor, 176 A.D.2d 1225, 576 N.Y.S.2d 718 (4th Dept. 1991).

—An indigent's request for the court to assign new counsel should not be granted casually but rather only upon a showing of good cause. People v. Simmons, 156 A.D.2d 1012, 549 N.Y.S.2d 294 (4th Dept. 1989).

Right to counsel: conflict of interest.—Failure of defense counsel and prosecution to bring fact of defense counsel's representation of the prosecution's chief witness to the court's attention was cause for reversal on conflict of interest grounds. People v. Wandell, 75 N.Y.2d 951, 555 N.Y.S.2d 686, 554 N.E.2d 1274 (1990).

—Although the defendant was represented by a Legal Aid Society attorney at trial, the court rejected claim that he was deprived of a fair trial because another Legal Aid Society attorney had previously represented the complainant in an unrelated trial; that fact alone was not sufficient to establish a conflict of interest. People v. Villanueva, 181 A.D.2d 702, 580 N.Y.S.2d 472 (2d Dept.), *lv. denied,* 79 N.Y.2d 1055 (1992).

—Court rejected claim that defendant was prejudiced by an alleged conflict of interest stemming from the fact that her trial attorney had in the past represented one of the prosecution witnesses in unrelated civil matters. People v. Corona, 173 A.D.2d 484, 570 N.Y.S.2d 105 (2d Dept.), *lv. denied,* 78 N.Y.2d 954 (1991).

—Dual representation of the complainant and the defendant by two Legal Aid attorneys who were unaware of the fact does not *per se* create a conflict of interest. People v. Liberty, 147 A.D.2d 502, 537 N.Y.S.2d 596 (2d Dept. 1989).

—Conflict of interest claim was rejected where the conduct of the defense was not affected by a conflict of interest created by defense counsel's concurrent representation of a prosecution witness on an unrelated civil matter. People v. Miller, 187 A.D.2d 930, 591 N.Y.S.2d 115 (4th Dept. 1992).

—A conflict of interest exists when a defendant's attorney represents a prosecution witness, even if the representation is on an unrelated charge. People v. Green, 145 A.D.2d 929, 536 N.Y.S.2d 611 (4th Dept. 1988).

Right to change counsel.—Defendant was entitled to evidentiary hearing on the issue of whether the Department of Correction obstructed defendant's efforts to secure counsel of his own choosing by delaying delivery to defendant of a letter from an attorney who had expressed a willingness to represent him. People v. Arroyare, 49 N.Y.2d 264, 425 N.Y.S.2d 282, 401 N.E.2d 393 (1980).

—Although an indigent defendant has a right to a court-appointed attorney, he does not have the right to his choice of assigned counsel. People v. Rua, 198 A.D.2d 311, 603 N.Y.S.2d 552 (2d Dept. 1993).

—Court-appointed counsel will not be removed except for good cause shown; defendant's bald statement that defense counsel had failed to take the steps necessary to comply with his desire to testify before the Grand Jury was insufficient to meet his burden of establishing that his rights pursuant to CPL § 190.50 were violated. People v. Sturgis, 199 A.D.2d 549, 606 N.Y.S.2d 241 (2d Dept. 1993).

Gomberg **inquiry; right to counsel: conflict of interest from joint representation.**—Defense counsel concurrently represented the defendant and the father of one of the victims, which was an inextricable conflict and prejudicial to the interests of the defendant-appellant. The trial court's failure to conduct a *Gomberg* inquiry (People v. Gomberg, 38 N.Y.2d 307, 379 N.Y.S.2d 769, 342 N.E.2d 550 [1975]) in the face of this conflict warranted the reversal and order of a new trial. People v. Krausz, 84 N.Y.2d 953, 620 N.Y.S.2d 821, 644 N.E.2d 1377 (1994).

—When the same attorney represents two or more defendants, the trial court must ascertain on the record whether each defendant is aware of the potential risks involved in the joint representation, and has knowingly chosen it. People v. Gomberg, 38 N.Y.2d 307, 379 N.Y.S.2d 769, 342 N.E.2d 550 (1975).

—Before accepting a guilty plea from a jointly represented defendant the court must ascertain, on the record, whether the defendant's decision to proceed with the attorney is an informed one. People v. Recupero, 73 N.Y.2d 877, 538 N.Y.S.2d 234, 535 N.E.2d 287 (1988).

—Prior to accepting a guilty plea from a jointly represented defendant, the court must ascertain, on the record, whether the "defendant's decision to proceed with his attorney is an informed decision" and a reversal will be warranted only when there is a "significant possibility" that a conflict of interest existed. People v. Monroe, 54 N.Y.2d 35, 444 N.Y.S.2d 578, 429 N.E.2d 97 (1981).

—Although the court confronted with two or more defendants represented by one attorney must personally address the defendants to ascertain whether each has an awareness of the potential risks involved in that course and has knowingly chosen it, there is no prescribed format or catechism that the court must follow. People v. Lloyd, 51 N.Y.2d 107, 432 N.Y.S.2d 685, 412 N.E.2d 371 (1980).

—A new trial was ordered where the trial court failed to ascertain on the record whether each defendant had an awareness of the potential risks of joint representation and defendants demonstrated the existence of a conflict of interest. People v. Macerola, 47 N.Y.2d 257, 417 N.Y.S.2d 908, 391 N.E.2d 990 (1979).

—Defendant, who was convicted of assault together with co-defendant, and both were acquitted of murder arising out of fight following a crap game, did not have conflict of interest with co-defendant as both sought to discredit prosecution witnesses and establish self-defense. Record shows that attorney who represented both pressed favorable arguments of defendant even though he also represented gun wielding co-defendant. People v. Gonzalez, 30 N.Y.2d 28, 330 N.Y.S.2d 54, 280 N.E.2d 882 (1972), *cert. denied,* 409 U.S. 859 (1972).

—The joint representations of multiple defendants is not *per se* violative of one's constitutional right to counsel; when defendants consented to joint representation they waived any claim of prejudice resulting from it. People v. Peters, 83 A.D.2d 842, 441 N.Y.S.2d 572 (2d Dept. 1981).

Right to counsel: access to counsel.—A defendant's right to the assistance of counsel was not violated by a trial court's order banning consultation between him and his attorney during a luncheon recess called during the course of cross-examination. People v. Enrique, 165 A.D.2d 13, 566 N.Y.S.2d 201 (1st Dept. 1991), *aff'd,* 80 N.Y.2d 869, 587 N.Y.S.2d 598, 600 N.E.2d 229 (1992).

—It is well-settled that joint representation constitutes reversible error only where the defendant has demonstrated that "a significant possibility of a conflict of interest existed bearing a substantial relationship to the conduct of the defense." People v. Valdez, 190 A.D.2d 834, 593 N.Y.S.2d 825 (2d Dept. 1993).

—A trial court may not bar consultation between a defendant and his attorney during an overnight recess, since such a consultation would likely include a variety of trial-related matters. People v. Schiliro, 179 A.D.2d 693, 578 N.Y.S.2d 259 (2d Dept.), *lv. denied,* 80 N.Y.2d 827 (1992).

—Not every restriction upon a defendant's access to his attorney constitutes reversible error *per se.* People v. Morgan, 176 A.D.2d 359, 574 N.Y.S.2d 592 (2d Dept. 1991), *lv. denied,* 79 N.Y.2d 861 (1992).

—A defendant's right to the assistance of counsel is not absolute but is, rather, subject to the right of the court to impose reasonable rules to control the conduct of the proceedings.

People v. Rosaldo, 178 A.D.2d 443, 577 N.Y.S.2d 303 (2d Dept. 1991), *lv. denied,* 79 N.Y.2d 923 (1992).

Right to counsel; competency of counsel.—Attorney's temporary ineligibility to practice law in New York due to failure to remit fees to Client's Security Fund did not diminish his competency as an attorney, and had no bearing on his ability to represent the defendant. People v. Kieser, 172 A.D.2d 626, 568 N.Y.S.2d 159 (2d Dept. 1991), *aff'd,* 79 N.Y.2d 936, 582 N.Y.S.2d 988, 591 N.E.2d 1174 (1992).

—Where defendant charged with 1st degree robbery had history of mental instability and confinement, failure of his assigned counsel to investigate background as aid to defense of insanity demonstrated incompetency of counsel and deprived defendant of fundamental right to fair trial. People v. Bennett, 29 N.Y.2d 462, 329 N.Y.S.2d 801, 280 N.E.2d 637 (1972).

Right to proceed *pro se.*—When a criminal defendant waives the right to counsel in favor of self-representation, the searching inquiry is aimed at ensuring that the defendant is aware of the dangers and disadvantages of proceeding without counsel. People v. Providence, 2 N.Y.3d 579, 780 N.Y.S.2d 552, 813 N.E.2d 632 (2004) (citing People v. McIntyre, 36 N.Y.2d 10, 364 N.Y.S.2d 837, 324 N.E.2d 322 (1974)).

—A defendant in a criminal case may invoke the right to defend *pro se* provided: (1) the request is unequivocal and timely asserted, (2) there has been a knowing and intelligent waiver of the right to counsel, and (3) the defendant had not engaged in conduct which would prevent the fair and orderly exposition of the issues. People v. McIntyre, 36 N.Y.2d 10, 364 N.Y.S.2d 837, 324 N.E.2d 322 (1974).

—Upon denying the defendant's specific request for new counsel, the trial court was not required to *sua sponte* inform him of his right to proceed *pro se.* People v. Allen, 161 A.D.2d 653, 555 N.Y.S.2d 430 (2d Dept. 1990).

—A defendant is not entitled to proceed *pro se* if his request is made after the trial has commenced unless there are compelling reasons for the late request. People v. Branch, 155 A.D.2d 473, 547 N.Y.S.2d 135 (2d Dept. 1989), *lv. denied,* 75 N.Y.2d 811 (1990).

—A defendant has the right to waive counsel and appear *pro se* so long as it is done knowingly and voluntarily. People v. Simmons, 182 A.D.2d 1018, 583 N.Y.S.2d 46 (3d Dept. 1992).

—The fact that defendant asserted an insanity defense did not, by itself, preclude him from being entitled to represent himself. People v. Meurer, 184 A.D.2d 1067, 584 N.Y.S.2d 370 (4th Dept.), *application for lv. to appeal dismissed,* 80 N.Y.2d 835 (1992).

Right to appear *pro se:* standby counsel.—Defendant has no right to hybrid representation or stand-by counsel. People v. Royster, 176 A.D.2d 587, 575 N.Y.S.2d 476 (1st Dept. 1991), *lv. denied,* 81 N.Y.2d 976 (1993).

—Although a trial court may appoint counsel to assist a *pro se* defendant, a defendant has no constitutional right to a hybrid form of representation. People v. Ford, 143 A.D.2d 841, 533 N.Y.S.2d 325 (2d Dept. 1988).

Right to expert services.—Court rejected claim that defendant was deprived of a fair trial because as an indigent he was unable to prepay the chemist approved by the County Court, pursuant to County Law § 722-c, to analyze the substance seized from defendant; subsequent reimbursement rather than prepayment is the method implicitly prescribed by County Law § 722-c. People v. Butchino, 152 A.D.2d 854, 544 N.Y.S.2d 64 (3d Dept. 1989).

Self-representation; court's duty to advise.—Before proceeding pro se a defendant must make a knowing, voluntary, and intelligent waiver of the right to counsel. Court should undertake a searching inquiry. Here, the trial court failed to secure an effective waiver of counsel necessary to allow defendant to represent himself. People v. Arroyo, 98 N.Y.2d 101, 745 N.Y.S.2d 796, 772 N.E.2d 1154 (2002).

—Court failed to make sufficient inquiry as to defendant's waiver of right to counsel where there was no inquiry of defendants on the record as to whether he appreciated the value of being represented by counsel and the difficulties and pitfalls of proceeding without counsel. People v. Mitchell, 61 N.Y.2d 580, 475 N.Y.S.2d 355, 463 N.E.2d 1207 (1984).

—Where a defendant chooses knowingly and voluntarily to waive his right to counsel and represent himself, the court's only further obligation is to insure that he is aware of the dangers and disadvantages of self-representation before allowing him to proceed, notwithstanding his lack of expertise or rashness of choice. People v. Vivenzio, 62 N.Y.2d 775, 477 N.Y.S.2d 318, 465 N.E.2d 1254 (1984).

—Defendant's waiver of counsel was insufficient and required reversal where court informed defendant that he was entitled to a lawyer, was facing serious charges and could receive a year's imprisonment, but did not adequately warn the defendant of the risks inherent in representing himself or appraise him of the value of counsel. People v. Kaltenbach, 60 N.Y.2d 797, 469 N.Y.S.2d 685, 457 N.E.2d 791 (1983).

—Trial court's failure to fully explain to the defendant the risks of self-representation was reversible error and such failure is not subject to harmless error analysis. People v. Bonds, 99 A.D.2d 759, 471 N.Y.S.2d 677 (2d Dept. 1984).

Self-representation; not an unlimited right.—Although a defendant has a constitutional right to represent himself at trial, he forfeits this right where he has "engaged in conduct which would prevent the fair and orderly exposition of the issues." During the proceedings defendant impugned the integrity of the transcript that would be made, accused the court of being very prejudiced and claimed that he was being railroaded. People v. Glover, 90 A.D.2d 776, 455 N.Y.S.2d 285 (2d Dept. 1982).

Waiver of counsel.—To establish a valid assertion of the right to represent oneself, the trial court must satisfy itself that the accompanying waiver of the right to counsel was competent, intelligent and voluntary. People v. Allen, 39 N.Y.2d 916, 386 N.Y.S.2d 404; 352 N.E.2d 951 (1976).

—Fact that defendant lacked the technical legal knowledge for effective examination of witnesses was not a basis for terminating his *pro se* defense. People v. Nelson, 72 A.D.2d 64, 424 N.Y.S.2d 543 (4th Dept. 1980).

When right to counsel attaches.—Defendant was not denied his right to counsel by the absence of counsel at the execution of sentence; the execution of sentence, as opposed to the imposition of sentence, is not a critical stage of the proceedings. People v. Blas, 192 A.D.2d 540, 596 N.Y.S.2d 438 (2d Dept.), *lv. denied,* 82 N.Y.2d 751 (1993).

—A suspect's right to counsel does not attach where he or she seeks only information and not representation from an attorney. People v. Beickert, 191 A.D.2d 499, 595 N.Y.S.2d 53 (2d Dept.), *lv. denied,* 81 N.Y.2d 967 (1993).

—There is no *per se* rule requiring reversal of a conviction and a new trial in every case for failure to provide counsel to a defendant at a preliminary hearing. People v. Wicks, 145 A.D.2d 828, 535 N.Y.S.2d 814 (3d Dept. 1988), *aff'd,* 76 N.Y.2d 128, 556 N.Y.S.2d 970.

§ 210.20. Motion to dismiss or reduce indictment.

1. After arraignment upon an indictment, the superior court may, upon motion of the defendant, dismiss such indictment or any count thereof upon the ground that:

(a) Such indictment or count is defective, within the meaning of section 210.25; or

(b) The evidence before the grand jury was not legally sufficient to establish the offense charged or any lesser included offense; or

(c) The grand jury proceeding was defective, within the meaning of section 210.35; or

(d) The defendant has immunity with respect to the offense charged, pursuant to section 50.20 or 190.40; or

(e) The prosecution is barred by reason of a previous prosecution, pursuant to section 40.20; or

(f) The prosecution is untimely, pursuant to section 30.10; or

(g) The defendant has been denied the right to a speedy trial; or

(h) There exists some other jurisdictional or legal impediment to conviction of the defendant for the offense charged; or

(i) Dismissal is required in the interest of justice, pursuant to section 210.40.

1-a. After arraignment upon an indictment, if the superior court, upon motion of the defendant pursuant to this subdivision or paragraph b of subdivision one of this section challenging the legal sufficiency of the evidence before the grand jury, finds that the evidence before the grand jury was not legally sufficient to establish the commission by the defendant of the offense charged in any count contained within the indictment, but was legally sufficient to establish the commission of a lesser included offense, it shall order the count or counts of the indictment with respect to which the finding is made reduced to allege the most serious lesser included offense with respect to which the evidence before the grand jury was sufficient, except that where the most serious lesser included offense thus found is a petty offense, and the court does not find evidence of the commission of any crime in any other count of the indictment, it shall order the indictment dismissed and a prosecutor's information charging the petty offense filed in the appropriate local criminal court. The motion to dismiss or reduce any count of an indictment based on legal insufficiency to establish the offense charged shall be made in accordance with the procedure set forth in subdivisions one through seven of section 210.45, provided however, the court shall state on the record the basis for its determination. Upon entering an order pursuant to this subdivision, the court shall consider the appropriateness of any securing order issued pursuant to article 510 of this chapter.

2. A motion pursuant to this section, except a motion pursuant to paragraph (g) of subdivision one, should be made within the period provided in section 255.20. A motion made pursuant to paragraph (g) of subdivision one must be made prior to the commencement of trial or entry of a plea of guilty.

3. Upon the motion, a defendant who is in a position adequately to raise more than one ground in support thereof should raise every such ground upon which he intends to challenge the indictment. A subsequent motion based upon any such ground not so raised may be summarily denied, although the court, in the interest of justice and for good cause shown, may in its discretion entertain and dispose of such a motion on the merits notwithstanding.

4. Upon dismissing an indictment or a count thereof upon any of the grounds specified in paragraphs (a), (b), (c) and (i) of subdivision one, or, upon dismissing a superior court information

or a count thereof upon any of the grounds specified in paragraphs (a) or (i) of subdivision one, the court may, upon application of the people, in its discretion authorize the people to submit the charge or charges to the same or another grand jury. When the dismissal is based upon some other ground, such authorization may not be granted. In the absence of authorization to submit or resubmit, the order of dismissal constitutes a bar to any further prosecution of such charge or charges, by indictment or otherwise, in any criminal court within the county.

5. If the court dismisses one or more counts of an indictment, against a defendant who was under the age of sixteen at the time of the commission of the crime and who did not lack criminal responsibility for such crime by reason of infancy, and one or more other counts of the indictment having been joined in the indictment solely with the dismissed count pursuant to subdivision six of section 200.20 is not dismissed, the court must direct that such count be removed to the family court in accordance with article seven hundred twenty-five of this chapter.

6. The effectiveness of an order reducing a count or counts of an indictment or dismissing an indictment and directing the filing of a prosecutor's information or dismissing a count or counts of an indictment charging murder in the first degree shall be stayed for thirty days following the entry of such order unless such stay is otherwise waived by the people. On or before the conclusion of such thirty-day period, the people shall exercise one of the following options:

(a) Accept the court's order by filing a reduced indictment, by dismissing the indictment and filing a prosecutor's information, or by filing an indictment containing any count or counts remaining after dismissal of the count or counts charging murder in the first degree, as appropriate;

(b) Resubmit the subject count or counts to the same or a different grand jury within thirty days of the entry of the order or such additional time as the court may permit upon a showing of good cause; provided, however, that if in such case an order is again entered with respect to such count or counts pursuant to subdivision one-a of this section, such count or counts may not again be submitted to a grand jury. Where the people exercise this option, the effectiveness of the order further shall be stayed pending a determination by the grand jury and the filing of a new indictment, if voted, charging the resubmitted count or counts;

(c) Appeal the order pursuant to subdivision one or one-a of section 450.20. Where the people exercise this option, the effectiveness of the order further shall be stayed in accordance with the provisions of subdivision two of section 460.40.

If the people fail to exercise one of the foregoing options, the court's order shall take effect and

the people shall comply with paragraph (a) of this subdivision.

Amended by L. 1972, Ch. 184; L. 1974, Chs. 467, 763; L. 1980, Ch. 136; L. 1990, Ch. 209; L. 1995, Ch. 1, § 9, amending subd. 6, eff. Sept. 1, 1995; L. 1999, Ch. 563, § 1, adding closing para. of subd. 6, eff. Nov. 2, 1999.

ANNOTATIONS

Dismissal for failure to prosecute, calendar control.—In the absence of speedy trial considerations, the court was without authority to dismiss the indictment because of a delay in prosecution, or for reasons of calendar control. People v. Merlo, 183 A.D.2d 730, 583 N.Y.S.2d 305 (2d Dept. 1992); People v. Moore, 158 A.D.2d 721, 552 N.Y.S.2d 169 (2d Dept. 1990); People v. Booker, 140 A.D.2d 616, 528 N.Y.S.2d 658 (2d Dept. 1988); People v. Sullivan, 142 A.D.2d 695, 531 N.Y.S.2d 295 (2d Dept. 1988).

—Failure to prosecute or calendar control do not, in and of themselves, constitute permissible grounds for dismissal. People v. Duke, 158 Misc. 2d 647, 606 N.Y.S.2d 516 (2d Dept., App. Term 1993).

Dismissal for speedy trial violations.—A defendant may waive his right to a speedy trial, but such waiver must be made knowingly and voluntarily, and during such time as a defendant is without counsel he does not have the burden of seeing to it that he is speedily brought to trial. People v. White, 32 N.Y.2d 393, 345 N.Y.S.2d 513, 298 N.E.2d 659 (1973).

—Except in certain circumstances, a motion to dismiss pursuant to CPL § 210.20 must be granted where the People are not ready for trial within six months of the commencement of a criminal action and one offense charged is a felony. People v. Daniel P., 94 A.D.2d 83, 463 N.Y.S.2d 838 (2d Dept. 1983).

—A plea of guilty is a waiver of the statutory right to dismissal of the indictment on the grounds that the People were not ready for trial within the prescribed period of CPL § 30.30. People v. Galente, 91 A.D.2d 690, 457 N.Y.S.2d 136 (2d Dept. 1982).

Delay in prosecution; dismissal of indictment.—Defendant's motion to dismiss the indictment was reversed where the prosecutor claimed that for most of the preindictment period the defendant could not be located despite diligent efforts by the police, and this claim, if substantiated, would constitute good cause for the prosecution's delay in obtaining an indictment. People v. Mitchell, 84 A.D.2d 822, 444 N.Y.S.2d 118 (2d Dept. 1981).

—It is not enough for People to allege calendar congestion as a cause for delay; it must be established on the record. Absent this, the indictment must be dismissed. People v. Clyde, 73 A.D.2d 1047, 425 N.Y.S.2d 425 (4th Dept. 1980).

Dismissal for insufficient evidence.—The relevant inquiry on a motion to dismiss for insufficient evidence is whether the evidence before the Grand Jury, viewed most favorably to the People, would support a determination of guilt. People v. Gordon, 88 N.Y.2d 92, 643 N.Y.S.2d 498, 666 N.E.2d 203 (1996). See also People v. Galatro, 84 N.Y.2d 160, 615 N.Y.S.2d 650, 639 N.E.2d 7 (1994).

—The court must confine its inquiry to legal sufficiency of the evidence; it may not weigh the proof or examine its adequacy; when the defendant moves to dismiss for insufficient evidence, the People must make a prima facie showing establishing all the elements of the crime. People v. Galatro, 84 N.Y.2d 160, 615 N.Y.S.2d 650, 639 N.E.2d 7 (1994).

—Order dismissing indictment was reversed, and the indictment reinstated, where evidence before the Grand Jury (including testimony that co-defendant disembarked from ship with ten pounds of marijuana and discarded the drugs after customs officials started in pursuit, and that defendants in waiting car picked up the fleeing co-defendant) was found to be legally sufficient to hold defendants as accomplices and principals in commission of the offense of possession of a dangerous drug. People v. Feliciano, 32 N.Y.2d 140, 344 N.Y.S.2d 329, 297 N.E.2d 76 (1973).

—The test to be applied on a motion to dismiss an indictment for insufficiency of evidence is whether there has been a "clear showing" that the evidence before the Grand Jury, if unexplained and uncontradicted, would not warrant a conviction by a trial jury. The term "clear showing" has been construed to mean prima facie proof that the crime charged has been committed. People v. Dunleavy, 41 A.D.2d 717, 341 N.Y.S.2d 500 (1st

Dept.), *aff'd*, 33 N.Y.2d 573, 347 N.Y.S.2d 448, 301 N.E.2d 432 (1973).

—By pleading guilty, defendant waived her claim that the evidence submitted to the grand jury was insufficient to support the indictment. People v. Jang, 17 A.D.3d 693, 793 N.Y.S.2d 540 (2d Dept. 2005).

—Court was without authority to sua sponte dismiss the indictment during the course of preliminary proceedings on the ground that the trial evidence would be insufficient. People v. Smedman, 184 A.D.2d 600, 584 N.Y.S.2d 627 (2d Dept. 1992).

—The court must determine if the grand jury could rationally have drawn the guilty inference from the facts, if proven. People v. Pease, 8 A.D.3d 692, 777 N.Y.S.2d 570 (3d Dept. 2004) (citing People v. Bello, 92 N.Y.2d 523, 683 N.Y.S.2d 168, 705 N.E.2d 1209 (1998)).

—On a motion to dismiss an indictment under CPL § 210.20(1)(b), the evidence before the grand jury is examined for legal sufficiency, to determine whether there is "competent evidence which, if accepted as true, would establish every element of an offense charged and the defendant's commission" of it. People v. Stanley, 19 A.D.3d 1152, 796 N.Y.S.2d 767 (4th Dept. 2005).

—The sufficiency of the evidence before the Grand Jury is no longer critical following a conviction. People v. McAvoy, 160 A.D.2d 1180, 555 N.Y.S.2d 190 (3d Dept. 1990).

—On a motion to dismiss the indictment under 210.20(1)(b), the evidence before the grand jury is examined for legal sufficiency, which is properly determined by inquiring whether the evidence viewed in the light most favorably to the People, if unexplained and uncontradicted, would warrant conviction by a petit case. People v. Woodruff, 4 A.D.3d 770, 771 N.Y.S.2d 620 (4th Dept. 2004).

—The sufficiency of an indictment is not reviewable on appeal from an ensuing judgment of conviction which is supported by legally sufficient trial evidence. People v. Haqq, 159 A.D.2d 983, 552 N.Y.S.2d 757 (4th Dept.), *lv. denied*, 76 N.Y.2d 736 (1990).

—CPL § 210.20(1)(b) permits a dismissal of an indictment on grounds of insufficiency of evidence only where evidence is insufficient to establish the offense charged or any lesser included offense. People v. Buthy, 85 A.D.2d 890, 446 N.Y.S.2d 756 (4th Dept. 1981), *lv. denied*, 56 N.Y.2d 650 (1982).

—A waiver of indictment and consent to proceed by superior court information does not constitute an admission that there is sufficient evidence to sustain the information and a motion to dismiss the information may be made and a hearing *in camera* should be held, in the absence of defendant and defense attorney to determine if the evidence is sufficient. People v. Burke, 105 Misc. 2d 722, 432 N.Y.S.2d 832 (Crim. Ct. Queens Co. 1980).

Dismissal for failure to disclose or produce witnesses or evidence; prosecutorial misconduct.—Court rejected notion that indictment had to be dismissed because two prosecutors had differing recollections of the complainant's description of the crime and did not inform defense counsel of the same. People v. Frazier, 200 A.D.2d 510, 606 N.Y.S.2d 682 (1st Dept.), *lv. denied*, 83 N.Y.2d 852 (1994).

—Dismissal of indictment was required as the only appropriate sanction for State's failure to preserve tape recordings between officer and defendant especially where the tapes might have constituted *Brady* material and could have made a difference in the outcome of the case with respect to entrapment. People v. Pantino, 106 A.D.2d 412, 482 N.Y.S.2d 334 (2d Dept. 1984).

—A defendant's right to obtain disclosure of the identity of a police informant turns on "the relevance of the informer's testimony to the guilt or innocence of the accused and it is not an abuse of discretion to deny disclosure because the informant's role in the actual sales was minimal and the evidence of defendant's guilt was overwhelming." People v. Martinez, 79 A.D.2d 661, 433 N.Y.S.2d 841 (2d Dept. 1980).

—While condemning the actions of the Special Prosecutor in obtaining the arrest, jailing and indictment of defendants for staged crime, the court held that the taint did not extend to indictments for perjury by the Special Extraordinary Grand Jury investigating corruption, which was fully informed of the facts. Nigrone v. Murtagh, 46 A.D.2d 343, 362 N.Y.S.2d 513 (2d Dept. 1974), *aff'd*, 36 N.Y.2d 421, 369 N.Y.S.2d 75, 330 N.E.2d 45 (1973).

Dismissal for defects in Grand Jury procedures.—Where police officer who investigated case and testified before Grand Jury also operated a video camera in the Grand Jury during the testimony of child witnesses, defendant was entitled to dismissal of the indictment. People v. Sayavong, 83 N.Y.2d 702, 613 N.Y.S.2d 343, 635 N.E.2d 1213 (1994).

—An audiotape recording played to the grand jury constituted inadmissible hearsay not subject to any exception. The presentation of that recording impaired the integrity of the grand jury proceedings, resulting in prejudice to the defendants and requiring dismissal of the indictment. People v. Barabash, 18 A.D.3d 474, 795 N.Y.S.2d 257 (2d Dept. 2005).

Failure to record Grand Jury instructions; dismissal of indictment.—In cases, if the proof is clear and the charge established, no good purpose will be served in dismissing indictment and requiring resubmission for failure to record the prosecutor's instructions. However, in complex cases where the potential of prejudice is great this procedure is proper. People v. Percy, 45 A.D.2d 284, 358 N.Y.S.2d 434 (2d Dept. 1974), *aff'd*, 38 N.Y.2d 806, 382 N.Y.S.2d 39, 345 N.E.2d 582 (1975).

—Defendant's motion to dismiss the indictment because the People did not afford him an opportunity to testify before the Grand Jury pursuant to his prior written notice was properly denied since the motion was not timely made and the circumstances were not sufficient to cause the court to extend that time in the interest of justice. People v. Darcy, 114 A.D.2d 968, 495 N.Y.S.2d 232 (2d Dept. 1985).

—Defendant's indictment was dismissed where the stenographer, rather than record and transcribe the instructions of the district attorney verbatim, merely noted the specific statutory section and later copied the text of the particular statute. People v. Boots, 83 A.D.2d 705, 442 N.Y.S.2d 286 (3d Dept. 1981).

Dismissal for selective prosecution.—In order to make out a claim of selective prosecution, the defendant must show that he was prosecuted while others in similar circumstances were not and that he was targeted for prosecution for an impermissible reason. People v. England, 191 A.D.2d 706, 595 N.Y.S.2d 793 (2d Dept. 1993).

—In order for a court to even consider whether a defendant has been selectively prosecuted, the defendant must overcome the presumption that the decision was made in good faith and without discrimination. People v. Bergen Beach Yacht Club, 160 Misc. 2d 939, 612 N.Y.S.2d 545 (Crim. Ct. Kings Co. 1994).

Dismissal on double jeopardy grounds.—Defendant's punishment for contempt of court pursuant to the Judiciary Law was for "criminal" contempt. Defendant's subsequent indictment for the same offense under § 600 of the former Penal Law was barred by the double jeopardy clause of the Federal Constitution. People v. Colombo, 31 N.Y.2d 947, 341 N.Y.S.2d 97, 293 N.E.2d 247 (1972).

Dismissal because of a jurisdictional or legal impediment.—When the People represent charges to a second Grand Jury which are already contained in an indictment voted by a prior Grand Jury, and the second Grand Jury refuses to indict, the second Grand Jury's determination creates a legal impediment to conviction, requiring dismissal of the indictment. People v. Franco, 86 N.Y.2d 493, 634 N.Y.S.2d 38, 657 N.E.2d 1321 (1995).

—Where a subsequent, formal laboratory test yields a negative result for the presence of cocaine in contradiction to the positive result from a field test, absent any other evidence of possession, there is a legal impediment to conviction, and the defendant is entitled to a dismissal. People v. Swamp, 84 N.Y.2d 725, 622 N.Y.S.2d 472, 646 N.E.2d 774 (1995).

—Due process requires a court to divest itself of jurisdiction over the person of a defendant where it has been acquired as a result of the government's deliberate, unnecessary and unreasonable invasion of the accused's constitutional rights. People v. Rao, 73 A.D.2d 88, 425 N.Y.S.2d 122 (2d Dept. 1980).

—The Federal Drug Enforcement Agency has concurrent jurisdiction with the state and where the same act may constitute a federal and state crime the offender may be prosecuted by both sovereigns. People v. Sheppard, 105 Misc. 2d 495, 432 N.Y.S.2d 467 (Sup. Ct. Queens Co. 1980).

Dismissal, general.—Defendant's sole basis for his motion to dismiss the indictment was that upon suppression of his statement, there was no probable cause to support his arrest; this is not a proper basis for dismissal under CPL § 210.20.

People v. Winn, 232 A.D.2d 438, 648 N.Y.S.2d 451 (2d Dept. 1996).

—A trial court order, pursuant to CPL § 210.20(1)(h) and (i), which dismissed the indictment for the failure of the People to state a prima facie case in their opening address to the jury, should have been reviewed by the intermediate appellate court notwithstanding the fact that the trial court's reliance on the statute may have been misplaced; any inquiry into the court's reliance on CPL § 210.20 should have been considered on the merits. People v. Coppa, 45 N.Y.2d 244, 408 N.Y.S.2d 365, 380 N.E.2d 195 (1978).

—Where the Special Narcotics part of the Supreme Court dismissed the indictments, no further prosecution of the charges could occur in Kings County unless authorization was obtained from the Special Narcotics Part to resubmit the charges to the same or another Grand Jury; the fact that the dismissals did not grant such authorization did not bar the People from seeking it. People v. Shukla, 58 A.D.2d 879, 396 N.Y.S.2d 700 (2d Dept. 1977), aff'd, 44 N.Y.2d 756, 405 N.Y.S.2d 686, 376 N.E.2d 1331.

—Showing that attorney-client conversations were intercepted is not sufficient to justify dismissal of the indictment; it must be shown that the interception undermined the right to counsel, that the interference could not be cured by holding a new trial; and it must appear that the prosecution could or would use the illegal evidence directly or indirectly. People v. Pobliner, 32 N.Y.2d 356, 345 N.Y.S.2d 482 (1973), cert. denied, 416 U.S. 905 (1974).

—The fact that each indictment contains only one count of perjury does not warrant dismissal, since at the time of trial, should the evidence warrant it, lesser included counts may also be considered. People v. Dunleavy, 41 A.D.2d 717, 341 N.Y.S.2d 500 (1st Dept.), aff'd, 33 N.Y.2d 573, 347 N.Y.S.2d 448, 301 N.E.2d 432 (1973).

—Trial term erred in dismissing a count of the indictment in order to avoid the requirements of sentencing for persistent violent felony offenders, especially where defendant was a habitual criminal. People v. Cruz, 114 A.D.2d 769, 495 N.Y.S.2d 162 (1st Dept. 1985).

—Court refused to grant either writ of mandamus or prohibition where petitioner sought dismissal of indictment on grounds of prosecution's refusal to grant potentially favorable defense witness immunity; prohibition may never lie as a means of seeking collateral review of an error of law; and mandamus, while available to compel a subordinate judicial tribunal to act, may not be used to direct such a tribunal to decide an application in a particular manner. In re Kramer v. Rosenberger, 107 A.D.2d 748, 484 N.Y.S.2d 111 (3d Dept. 1985).

—Criminal Term did not abuse its discretion in denying the People authorization to resubmit the counts to another Grand Jury in light of the fact that the application was based solely on unspecified representations by the prosecutor, who had no personal knowledge of the facts of the case concerning the additional evidence that the People would submit to the Grand Jury; however, under the circumstances of this case, the People should be afforded an opportunity to renew their application on proper papers for authorization to resubmit. People v. Scott, 75 A.D.2d 858, 427 N.Y.S.2d 840 (2d Dept. 1980).

—Trial court erred in dismissing certain counts of defendant's indictment since the court improperly took upon itself the factual determination of whether certain items of payment constituted salary payments and were therefore beyond the scope of the particular statute in question, rather than relying upon the factual determination of the Grand Jury. People v. Rider, 115 A.D.2d 123, 494 N.Y.S.2d 925 (3d Dept. 1985).

Dual slip presentment.—Where issue was whether it is inherently prejudicial to obtain an indictment against a civilian defendant from a grand jury that has also been asked to consider a police misconduct charge arising out of the same incident, court found no concrete prejudice from the "dual slip" presentment, and upheld the indictment. People v. Adessa, 89 N.Y.2d 677, 657 N.Y.S.2d 863, 680 N.E.2d 134 (1997).

Reduction of charges.—If the People fail to act within 30 days after a trial court reduces an indictment to a lesser count, they may still proceed on the reduced count. However, if they intend to resubmit the higher count, they must either do so within 30 days or seek leave for an extension of time. People v. Jackson, 87 N.Y.2d 782, 642 N.Y.S.2d 602, 665 N.E.2d 172 (1996).

Motion to dismiss; timeliness.—Where the motion to dismiss the defective indictment was not "made prior to . . . commencement of trial," the lower courts acted within their jurisdiction in refusing to consider it. People v. Quigley, 37 N.Y.2d 913, 378 N.Y.S.2d 386, 340 N.E.2d 747 (1975).

—Preindictment delay was reasonable, since it was caused by the People's good faith efforts to investigate the murder and the fact that the original witness's recantation of his identification of defendant rendered the People's case legally insufficient until years later when another witness came forward. People v. Delgado, 292 A.D.2d 212, 741 N.Y.S.2d 2 (1st Dept. 2002).

—Motion to dismiss due to pre-indictment delay was untimely when made after close of prosecution's case-in-chief. People v. Ramirez, 243 A.D.2d 734, 663 N.Y.S.2d 855 (2d Dept. 1997).

—Defendant's motion to dismiss the indictment on jurisdictional grounds, made after the jury had been selected, and after opening statements were given, was untimely. People v. Reynolds, 133 A.D.2d 499, 519 N.Y.S.2d 425 (3d Dept. 1987).

—Where failure to record grand jury instructions was a violation of CPL § 190.25(6), the court determined that it could entertain the motion to dismiss the indictment, notwithstanding the 30-day time limitation for the making of the motion, and it held that, in the interests of justice, the indictment should be dismissed. People v. Percy, 74 Misc. 2d 522, 345 N.Y.S.2d 276 (Suffolk Co. Ct. 1973), modified, 45 A.D.2d 284, 358 N.Y.S.2d 434 (2d Dept. 1974), aff'd, 38 N.Y.2d 806, 382 N.Y.S.2d 39, 345 N.E.2d 582 (1975).

Motion to dismiss; hearing.—A hearing should be held by the court before it dismisses an indictment on the grounds that two alibi witnesses were available at the first trial but were not allowed to testify and now cannot be found, to afford the People the opportunity to reconstruct their potential testimony or stipulate to it. People v. Cuevas, 91 A.D.2d 598, 457 N.Y.S.2d 493 (1st Dept. 1982).

—The denial of the defendant's motion without a hearing was not an abuse of discretion where the defendant's contentions were fully set forth in his motion papers, he did not dispute his complicity in the crimes and the record provided an unequivocal basis for the rejection of his claims. People v. Kaye, 91 A.D.2d 680, 457 N.Y.S.2d 137 (2d Dept. 1982).

Motion to dismiss; waiver of objections.—A defendant who pleads guilty after a denial of the motion to dismiss the indictment on grounds of special prosecution is foreclosed from pursuing his claim of special prosecution on appeal because a guilty plea waives all non-jurisdictional defects such as selective prosecution. People v. Rodriguez, 79 A.D.2d 539, 433 N.Y.S.2d 584 (1st Dept. 1980), aff'd, 55 N.Y.2d 776, 447 N.Y.S.2d 246, 431 N.E.2d 972 (1981).

Motion to dismiss; right to appeal.—Where defendant withdrew all pending motions and pleaded guilty, he could not appeal the denial of his motion to dismiss the indictment because of the denial of his right to testify before the Grand Jury. People v. Addison, 196 A.D.2d 875, 602 N.Y.S.2d 61 (2d Dept. 1993).

—The issue was not preserved for appellate review where defendant failed to challenge the adequacy of the indictment by a pretrial motion to dismiss. People v. Wong, 133 A.D.2d 84, 519 N.Y.S.2d 10 (2d Dept. 1987).

—Defendant's claim of violation of his constitutional right to a speedy trial is unpreserved because defendant failed to move to dismiss the superior court information as required by CPL § 210.20(1)(g) or (h). People v. Kwiatkowski, 263 A.D.2d 552, 694 N.Y.S.2d 779 (3d Dept. 1999).

Sufficiency of evidence.—Evidence that is legally sufficient to establish a prima facie case in the Grand Jury may nevertheless be inadequate to prove guilt beyond a reasonable doubt at trial. People v. Sylvester, 254 A.D.2d 711, 677 N.Y.S.2d 865 (4th Dept. 1998).

§ 210.25. Motion to dismiss indictment; as defective.

An indictment or a count thereof is defective within the meaning of paragraph (a) of subdivision one of section 210.20 when:

1. It does not substantially conform to the

requirements stated in article two hundred; provided that an indictment may not be dismissed as defective, but must instead be amended, where the defect or irregularity is of a kind that may be cured by amendment, pursuant to section 200.70, and where the people move to so amend; or

2. The allegations demonstrate that the court does not have jurisdiction of the offense charged; or

3. The statute defining the offense charged is unconstitutional or otherwise invalid.

ANNOTATIONS

Defect not fatal.—Five-month period given in indictment for 10 criminal sexual acts did not require dismissal, where 8-year-old complainant could not further particularize offenses. People v. Watt, 84 N.Y.2d 948, 620 N.Y.S.2d 817, 644 N.E.2d 1373 (1994).

—When prosecutor, after diligent investigation, was unable to state either in the indictment or bill of particulars the exact date and time of crime of sodomy involving a 5-year-old complainant other than the month and year, indictment will not be dismissed on the ground that lack of exactitude will make use of an alibi defense more difficult. People v. Morris, 61 N.Y.2d 290, 473 N.Y.S.2d 769, 461 N.E.2d 1256 (1984).

Waiver of defects.—Even though the robbery indictment may have been duplicitous, the judgment of conviction was affirmed since defendant did not raise the objection during trial. People v. Branch, 73 A.D.2d 230, 426 N.Y.S.2d 291 (2d Dept. 1980).

§ 210.30. Motion to dismiss or reduce indictment on ground of insufficiency of grand jury evidence; motion to inspect grand jury minutes.

1. A motion to dismiss an indictment or a count thereof, pursuant to paragraph (b) of subdivision one of section 210.20 or a motion to reduce a count or counts of an indictment pursuant to subdivision one-a of section 210.20 must be preceded or accompanied by a motion to inspect the grand jury minutes, as prescribed in subdivision two of this section.

2. A motion to inspect grand jury minutes is a motion by a defendant requesting an examination by the court and the defendant of the stenographic minutes of a grand jury proceeding resulting in an indictment for the purpose of determining whether the evidence before the grand jury was legally sufficient to support the charges or a charge contained in such indictment.

3. Unless good cause exists to deny the motion to inspect the grand jury minutes, the court must grant the motion. It must then proceed to examine the minutes and to determine the motion to dismiss or reduce the indictment. If the court, after examining the minutes, finds that release of the minutes, or certain portions thereof, to the parties is necessary to assist the court in making its determination on the motion, it may release the minutes or such portions thereof to the parties. Provided, however, such release shall be limited to that grand jury testimony which is relevant to

a determination of whether the evidence before the grand jury was legally sufficient to support a charge or charges contained in such indictment. Prior to such release the district attorney shall be given an opportunity to present argument to the court that the release of the minutes, or any portion thereof, would not be in the public interest.

4. If the court determines that there is not reasonable cause to believe that the evidence before the grand jury may have been legally insufficient, it may in its discretion either (a) deny both the motion to inspect and the motion to dismiss or reduce, or (b) grant the motion to inspect notwithstanding and proceed to examine the minutes and to determine the motion to dismiss or reduce.

5. In any case, the court must place on the record its ruling upon the motion to inspect.

6. The validity of an order denying any motion made pursuant to this section is not reviewable upon an appeal from an ensuing judgment of conviction based upon legally sufficient trial evidence.

7. Notwithstanding any other provision of law, where the indictment is filed against a juvenile offender, the court shall dismiss the indictment or count thereof where the evidence before the grand jury was not legally sufficient to establish the offense charged or any lesser included offense for which the defendant is criminally responsible. Upon such dismissal, unless the court shall authorize the people to resubmit the charge to a subsequent grand jury, and upon a finding that there was sufficient evidence to believe defendant is a juvenile delinquent as defined in subdivision (a) of section seven hundred twelve of the family court act and upon specifying the act or acts it found sufficient evidence to believe defendant committed, the court may direct that such matter be removed to family court in accordance with the provisions of article seven hundred twenty-five of this chapter.

Amended by L. 1980, Chs. 136, 841, 842; L. 1990, Ch. 209.

ANNOTATIONS

Sufficiency of evidence.—An off-the-record, preliminary assessment by the trial justice that sufficient evidence existed to support the indictments did not preclude a subsequent disclosure direction as authorized by CPL § 210.30. Attorney General of New York v. Firetog, 94 N.Y.2d 477, 706 N.Y.S.2d 666, 727 N.E.2d 1220 (2000).

—Since proper standard for reviewing the sufficiency of the evidence to support an indictment is "legal sufficiency," not "proof beyond a reasonable doubt," court below erroneously relied upon circumstantial evidence standard that every hypothesis but guilt be excluded to a "moral certainty." People v. Deegan, 69 N.Y.2d 976, 516 N.Y.S.2d 651, 509 N.E.2d 345 (1987).

—Where defendant has been indicted under a fictitious name because his true name was unknown or where some person other than the intended defendant is accused in the indictment, the instrument may be amended upon discovery of the true name of the person the Grand Jury intended to indict. People v. Ganett, 68 A.D.2d 81, 416 N.Y.S.2d 914 (4th Dept. 1979), *aff'd*, 51 N.Y.2d 991, 435 N.Y.S.2d 976, 417 N.E.2d 88 (1980).

—Criminal Term's review of a motion to dismiss an indictment for insufficiency of Grand Jury evidence is limited to a determination of whether the evidence makes out a prima facie case, not whether there is proof beyond a reasonable doubt. People v. Guzman, 180 A.D.2d 469, 579 N.Y.S.2d 386 (1st Dept. 1992).

—In a motion to dismiss the indictment, the defendant must clearly establish the insufficiency of the evidence. People v. Yip, 118 A.D.2d 472, 499 N.Y.S.2d 752 (1st Dept. 1986).

—A court may only grant a motion to dismiss the indictment where the evidence before the grand jury was not legally sufficient to establish the offense charged or any lesser included offense; the burden is on the defendant to make a clear showing of legal sufficiency. People v. Diaz, 201 A.D.2d 580, 607 N.Y.S.2d 959 (2d Dept.), lv. denied, 83 N.Y.2d 1007 (1994).

—On a motion to dismiss the indictment, all questions as to the quality or weight of the proof should be deferred, as this is a matter for the petit jury. People v. Scott, 131 A.D.2d 893, 517 N.Y.S.2d 248 (2d Dept. 1987).

—In review of sufficiency of Grand Jury testimony, all questions as to the quality of proof should be deferred, as this is a matter for the petit jury, and not the Grand Jury. People v. Glessing, 206 A.D.2d 786, 615 N.Y.S.2d 115 (3d Dept. 1994).

—On a motion to dismiss the indictment, the inquiry of the reviewing court is limited to the legal sufficiency of the evidence; the court may not examine the adequacy of the proof to establish reasonable cause, since that inquiry is exclusively within the province of the Grand Jury. People v. Hughes, 159 Misc. 2d 663, 606 N.Y.S.2d 499 (Sup. Ct. Monroe Co. 1993).

—A trial court is not empowered to dismiss any count of an indictment no matter how deficient the evidence presented to the grand jury, if any lesser included offense has been made out. People v. Enfeld, 136 Misc. 2d 252, 518 N.Y.S.2d 536 (Sup. Ct. N.Y. Co. 1987).

Illegal or improper evidence.—Where defendant was indicted by the Grand Jury upon testimony of a police officer that defendant had confessed to the crimes charged, the subsequent motion to dismiss the indictment should not have been granted although the trial court following a *Huntley* hearing had suppressed the confession. People v. Mauceri, 74 A.D.2d 833, 425 N.Y.S.2d 346 (2d Dept. 1980).

Waiver of issue by plea.—A plea of guilty vitiates any question as to the sufficiency of the Grand Jury minutes. People v. Topping, 74 A.D.2d 703, 426 N.Y.S.2d 116 (3d Dept. 1980).

—The issue of sufficiency of the proof to support the indictment may not be raised on appeal after a guilty plea. People v. Buthy, 85 A.D.2d 890, 446 N.Y.S.2d 756 (4th Dept. 1981).

Inspection of Grand Jury minutes.—Pursuant to CPL § 210.30, a trial court is without power to order disclosure of the Grand Jury proceedings to a defendant or his counsel on a motion seeking inspection and dismissal of the indictment; a writ of prohibition is an appropriate remedy to prevent such disclosure. Jaffe v. Scheinman, 47 N.Y.2d 188, 417 N.Y.S.2d 241, 390 N.E.2d 1165 (1979).

—Grand jury minutes can only be inspected in advance of trial ancillary to attack on indictment, not to assist defendant at trial by means of pretrial discovery; unrestricted inspection of minutes ordered by court would justify use of prohibition as remedy to prevent court from taking further proceedings beyond its jurisdictional authority. Proskin v. County Court of Albany County, 30 N.Y.2d 15, 330 N.Y.S.2d 44, 280 N.E.2d 875 (1972).

—It was an abuse of discretion for court to allow inspection of grand jury minutes where affidavit in support of motion to inspect presented no sufficient basis for the inspection. The court granted a writ of prohibition to prevent inspection for general discovery purposes. Proskin v. County Court, 37 A.D.2d 279, 324 N.Y.S.2d 426 (3d Dept. 1971), aff'd, 30 N.Y.2d 15, 330 N.Y.S.2d 44, 280 N.E.2d 875 (1972).

—After finding sufficient evidence in the Grand Jury to support an indictment, the court could not direct the People to provide defendant with the Grand Jury minutes. Brown v. Rotker, 215 A.D.2d 378, 625 N.Y.S.2d 643 (2d Dept. 1995).

Inspection of Grand Jury minutes, time to produce.—Any delay beyond a reasonable period—in this case, 36 days—in responding to defendant's motion to inspect Grand Jury minutes is chargeable to the People for speedy trial purposes. People v. Harris, 82 N.Y.2d 409, 604 N.Y.S.2d 918, 624 N.E.2d 1013 (1993).

—The People are entitled to a reasonable period within which to respond to defendant's motion to inspect and dismiss, and such a period—here, 14 days—is not chargeable for speedy trial purposes. People v. Harry, 213 A.D.2d 424, 623 N.Y.S.2d 607 (2d Dept. 1995).

—Where the People make no objection to a CPL § 210.30 motion seeking inspection of Grand Jury minutes, the People's obligation to produce the minutes within a reasonable time begins to run from the date the defendant's CPL § 210.30 motion is made. People v. Edwards, 215 A.D.2d 498, 626 N.Y.S.2d 825 (2d Dept. 1995).

—Where the People waited eight months after defendant moved to inspect to file Grand Jury minutes, his indictment would be dismissed on speedy trial grounds. People v. Schmadebeck, 214 A.D.2d 1016, 627 N.Y.S.2d 494 (4th Dept. 1995).

Review.—The validity of a supreme court's order denying a defendant's motion to inspect and dismiss the indictment on the ground that the grand jury evidence was legally insufficient to establish the offense charged was not reviewable on defendant's appeal from the ensuing judgment of conviction based on legally sufficient trial evidence. People v. Smith, 4 N.Y.3d 806, 796 N.Y.S.2d 1, 828 N.E.2d 958 (2005).

—When a judgment of conviction has been rendered based on legally sufficient trial evidence, appellate review of a claim alleging sufficiency of grand jury evidence is barred. People v. Wiggins, 89 N.Y.2d 872, 653 N.Y.S.2d 91, 675 N.E.2d 845 (1996).

—An order denying the motion to dismiss the indictment is not reviewable upon appeal where the judgment of conviction is based upon legally sufficient trial evidence. People v. Graham, 43 A.D.2d 182, 350 N.Y.S.2d 458 (3d Dept. 1973), aff'd, 36 N.Y.2d 633, 370 N.Y.S.2d 888, 331 N.E.2d 673 (1975); People v. Robinson, 133 A.D.2d 473, 519 N.Y.S.2d 571 (2d Dept. 1987).

—Defendant's challenge to the certification of the ballistics report presented to the grand jury is, in essence, a challenge to the sufficiency of the grand jury evidence and, as such, is not reviewable on appeal. People v. Cerda, 236 A.D.2d 292, 654 N.Y.S.2d 348 (1st Dept. 1997).

—Where petitioner's claim of a defective indictment was based on the legal sufficiency of the evidence presented to the grand jury, and petitioner already challenged the sufficiency of the evidence before the grand jury prior to his first trial, judicial review of this claim was barred under CPL § 210.30(6) by virtue of the fact that the court previously determined that the evidence adduced at petitioner's first trial under the instant indictment was legally sufficient. Rose v. Golia, 232 A.D.2d 567, 648 N.Y.S.2d 683 (2d Dept. 1996).

—Implicit under CPL § 210.30(6) is the premise that a conviction after trial upon legally sufficient evidence will not be set aside where, prior thereto, a prosecutor, although acting in good faith, inadvertently failed to make out a prima facie case before the Grand Jury based on competent and admissible evidence. People v. Rao, 73 A.D.2d 88, 425 N.Y.S.2d 122 (2d Dept. 1980).

—Pursuant to CPL § 210.30(6), the defendant could not challenge the sufficiency of the Grand Jury evidence on appeal from conviction. People v. Thomas, 148 A.D.2d 883, 539 N.Y.S.2d 693 (3d Dept. 1989).

—The defendant's contention on appeal that the legal proof before the Grand Jury was insufficient to find an indictment against him provided no basis for relief in view of the trial evidence presented against the defendant. People v. Canale, 76 A.D.2d 1032, 429 N.Y.S.2d 495 (3d Dept. 1980).

—By failing to move to dismiss the indictment, defendant failed to preserve his contention that the evidence before the Grand Jury was legally sufficient; in any event, sufficiency of the evidence before the Grand Jury is not reviewable on appeal from a conviction based on legally sufficient trial evidence. People v. Krouth, 201 A.D.2d 912, 608 N.Y.S.2d 590 (4th Dept. 1994).

§ 210.35. Motion to dismiss indictment; defective grand jury proceeding.

A grand jury proceeding is defective within the

meaning of paragraph (c) of subdivision one of section 210.20 when:

1. The grand jury was illegally constituted; or

2. The proceeding is conducted before fewer than sixteen grand jurors; or

3. Fewer than twelve grand jurors concur in the finding of the indictment; or

4. The defendant is not accorded an opportunity to appear and testify before the grand jury in accordance with the provisions of section 190.50; or

5. The proceeding otherwise fails to conform to the requirements of article one hundred ninety to such degree that the integrity thereof is impaired and prejudice to the defendant may result.

ANNOTATIONS

Subd. 1

Composition and selection of Grand Jurors.—Systematic and intentional exclusion of blacks from grand juries required that defendant's murder conviction be reversed; the fact that defendant was convicted after a fair trial did not render such discrimination harmless error. Vasquez v. Hillery, 474 U.S. 254, 106 S. Ct. 617, 88 L. Ed. 2d 598 (1986).

—Objection that grand jury was improperly selected because it systematically excluded students and women may be raised by a motion to dismiss the indictment but it may not be raised in a CPLR Art. 78 proceeding. Paciona v. Marshall, 35 N.Y.2d 289, 360 N.Y.S.2d 882, 319 N.E.2d 199 (1974).

—Absent a showing of prejudice or fraud, indictment would not be dismissed solely because one juror was not a county resident and was thus not qualified to serve. People v. Baker, 75 A.D.2d 966, 428 N.Y.S.2d 353 (3d Dept. 1980).

Subd. 3

Concurrence of 12 members required.—The grand jury must have the concurrence of at least twelve members during a vote to determine whether they wish to continue deliberations on any particular case or charge. People v. Harris, 181 Misc. 2d 670, 695 N.Y.S.2d 215 (Sup. Ct. Bronx Co. 1999).

Subd. 4

Denial of right to testify before grand jury.—Court did not err in refusing to dismiss the indictment on the basis of a denial of defendant's right to testify before the grand jury. When the defendant presented the issue to the court, he claimed that he had sent written notification of his request to both the District Attorney and the court, but the District Attorney denied receipt, and the court's search of its own records failed to verify defendant's claim. People v. Roman, 19 A.D.3d 739, 796 N.Y.S.2d 430 (3d Dept. 2005).

Subd. 5

Acting in concert.—Where defendant was charged with acting in concert with a co-defendant in connection with sale and possession of a controlled substance, evidence of a separate and similar drug sale by a co-defendant was clearly improper and prejudicial; motion to dismiss two counts was granted with leave for People to re-present those counts. People v. Dixon, 172 Misc. 2d 292, 659 N.Y.S.2d 386 (Dutchess Co. Ct. 1997).

Cross-complaints against police officers.—It is not inherently prejudicial to obtain an indictment against a civilian defendant from a grand jury that also has been asked to consider a police misconduct charge arising out of the same incident; court stressed that its holding was not a blanket approval of the practice of submitting criminal charges against citizens and cross-complaints against police officers to the same grand juries. People v. Adessa, 89 N.Y.2d 677, 657 N.Y.S.2d 863, 680 N.E.2d 134 (1997).

Dismissal; drastic remedy.—Dismissal is a drastic remedy and is limited to "those instances where prosecutorial wrongdoing, fraudulent conduct or errors potentially prejudice the ultimate decision" that the grand jury reached. People v. Serkiz, 17 A.D.3d 28, 790 N.Y.S.2d 296 (3d Dept. 2005).

Dismissal not warranted.—Under § CPL 210.35(5), dismissal of an indictment must meet a high test and is limited to instances of prosecutorial misconduct, fraudulent conduct, or errors which potentially prejudice the ultimate decision reached by the grand jury; dismissal not warranted in instant case, because indictment was not based on hearsay affidavit, but on sufficient sworn testimony from other witnesses. People v. Carey, 241 A.D.2d 748, 660 N.Y.S.2d 886 (3d Dept. 1997).

Grand Jury instructions.—A Grand Jury need not be instructed with the same degree of precision that is required when a petit jury is instructed on the law; it is sufficient if the prosecutor provides the Grand Jury with enough information to enable it intelligently to decide whether a crime has been committed and to determine whether there exists legally sufficient evidence to establish the material elements of the crime. Failure to furnish complete instructions regarding the proper legal standard for assessing obscenity did not render the indictment legally defective. People v. Calbud, Inc., 49 N.Y.2d 389, 426 N.Y.S.2d 238, 402 N.E.2d 1140 (1980).

—Prosecutor's failure to define "operable" in grand jury presentation of prosecution for weapons possession did not render the grand jury instruction so incomplete and misleading as to impair the integrity of the grand jury. People v. Hilaire, 270 A.D.2d 359, 705 N.Y.S.2d 382 (2d Dept. 2000).

—In uncomplicated cases, if the proof is clear and the charge established, no good purpose will be served in dismissing indictment and requiring resubmission for failure to record the prosecutor's instructions. However, in complex cases where the potential of prejudice is great this procedure is proper. People v. Percy, 45 A.D.2d 284, 358 N.Y.S.2d 434 (2d Dept. 1974), aff'd, 38 N.Y.2d 806, 382 N.Y.S.2d 39, 345 N.E.2d 582 (1975).

Integrity of the proceedings.—The statutory test is very precise and very high for impairment of the integrity of the Grand Jury process, and dismissal under this section is an "exceptional" remedy. People v. Darby, 75 N.Y.2d 449, 554 N.Y.S.2d 426, 553 N.E.2d 974 (1990).

—Court properly denied a motion to dismiss, where the defendant had claimed that the integrity of the Grand Jury proceedings was impaired by the introduction of a forged document, because the prosecutor had no reason to believe that the notarized document was a forgery, and the document played only a minor role in the Grand Jury presentation. People v. Ponnapula, 266 A.D.2d 32, 698 N.Y.S.2d 219 (1st Dept. 1999).

—An audiotape recording played to the grand jury constituted inadmissible hearsay not subject to any exception. The presentation of that recording impaired the integrity of the grand jury proceedings, resulting in prejudice to the defendants and requiring dismissal of the indictment. People v. Barabash, 18 A.D.3d 474, 795 N.Y.S.2d 257 (2d Dept. 2005).

—The introduction of evidence that the defendant previously committed an unrelated homicide did not impair the integrity of the proceedings or prejudice him in light of the overwhelming evidence before the grand jury that he committed the crimes charged, i.e., two eyewitnesses identified the defendant as the person who shot and killed the victim. People v. Ramirez, 298 A.D.2d 413, 751 N.Y.S.2d 248 (2d Dept. 2002).

—Court did not err in denying defendant's pretrial motion to dismiss indictment on the ground that the use of hearsay testimony impaired the integrity of the grand jury proceeding because not every improper comment, elicitation of inadmissible testimony, impermissible question, or mere mistake renders an indictment defective. People v. Butcher, 11 A.D.3d 956, 782 N.Y.S.2d 339 (4th Dept. 2004) (citing People v. Huston, 88 N.Y.2d 400, 646 N.Y.S.2d 69, 668 N.Y.S.2d 1362 (1996)).

—Assistant district attorney's unsolicited marshaling of the evidence constitutes an independent basis for the court to conclude that the integrity of the grand jury was impaired. People v. Shammas, 5 Misc. 3d 702, 785 N.Y.S.2d 874 (Crim. Ct. Kings Co. 2004).

—Where the prosecutor unintentionally adopted a witness's erroneous testimony that owners of land acquired for public use had bought the land for $350,000 on a no-money-down basis and realized a $610,000 profit, the error was held to be inflammatory and prejudicial to the defendants, and, coupled with other errors, formed a sufficient basis for the dismissal of the indictments in the interests of justice. People v. Percy, 74 Misc. 2d 522, 345 N.Y.S.2d 276 (Suffolk Co. Ct. 1973), *modified on other grounds,* 45 A.D.2d 284, 358 N.Y.S.2d 434 (2d Dept. 1974), *aff'd,* 38 N.Y.2d 806, 382 N.Y.S.2d 39, 345 N.E.2d 582 (1975).

—Where the Grand Jury testimony of the complainant alone was sufficient to support the indictment, the allegedly perjured testimony of his companion did not constitute an "impairment of integrity" of the Grand Jury process. People v. Avilla, 212 A.D.2d 800, 623 N.Y.S.2d 280 (2d Dept. 1995).

—Defendant sought dismissal of the indictment alleging that the prosecutor should have disclosed his accomplice's coopera-tion agreement to the grand jury, but court held that the evidence withheld pertained to credibility, a collateral issue, and was not essential to the grand jury's responsibility to determine whether a prima facie case existed. Defendant also sought dismissal of the indictment, claiming that perjured testimony given by his accomplice impaired the integrity of the grand jury; court found that the allegation of perjury was based on hearsay, and court noted the absence of any proof that the prosecutor knowingly used perjured testimony. People v. Hansen, 290 A.D.2d 47, 736 N.Y.S.2d 743 (3d Dept. 2002), *aff'd,* 99 N.Y.2d 339, 756 N.Y.S.2d 122, 786 N.E.2d 21 (2003).

—When five-year-old victim's mother accompanied him and remained in Grand Jury room while he testified, it did not warrant dismissal of the indictment since the presence of the mother in no way prejudiced the defendant or affected the truthfulness and reliability of the testimony of the witness. People v. Wilson, 77 A.D.2d 713, 430 N.Y.S.2d 715 (3d Dept. 1980).

—Defendant bears the burden of demonstrating the existence of defects impairing the integrity of a grand jury proceeding and giving rise to a possibility of prejudice. People v. Wood, 291 A.D.2d 824, 737 N.Y.S.2d 760 (4th Dept. 2002).

—While the People conceded that the prosecutor erred in showing the mug shot of defendant taken at a prior arrest to the grand jury, this isolated instance of misconduct did not "potentially prejudice the ultimate decision reached by the grand jury." People v. Workman, 277 A.D.2d 1029, 716 N.Y.S.2d 198 (4th Dept. 2000).

—A presumption of regularity places the burden on the defen-dant to make a specific showing of prejudice from publicity on the state of mind of the grand jurors. People v. Hussein, 150 Misc. 2d 119, 568 N.Y.S.2d 296 (Sup. Ct. N.Y. Co. 1991).

Grand jury; use of unconstitutional confession.—The indictment was dismissed where confession obtained from the defendant in violation of his constitutional right to counsel and subsequently suppressed after the indictment had been presented to the Grand Jury in violation of CPL Article 190 and was so highly prejudicial that the integrity of the Grand Jury proceeding was impaired. People v. Seaman, 104 Misc. 2d 10, 427 N.Y.S.2d 567 (Sullivan Co. Ct. 1980).

Review.—Defendant's claim that the laboratory reports pres-ented to the grand jury failed to meet the requirements of CPL § 190.30(2) and that the evidence was insufficient is not reviewable on appeal from a judgment of conviction. People v. Caldwell, 245 A.D.2d 89, 666 N.Y.S.2d 133 (1st Dept. 1997).

§ 210.40. Motion to dismiss indictment; in furtherance of justice.

1. An indictment or any count thereof may be dismissed in furtherance of justice, as provided in paragraph (i) of subdivision one of section 210.20, when, even though there may be no basis for dismissal as a matter of law upon any ground specified in paragraphs (a) through (h) of said subdivision one of section 210.20, such dismissal is required as a matter of judicial discretion by the existence of some compelling factor, consider-ation or circumstance clearly demonstrating that conviction or prosecution of the defendant upon such indictment or count would constitute or result in injustice. In determining whether such compelling factor, consideration, or circumstance

exists, the court must, to the extent applicable, examine and consider, individually and collec-tively, the following:

(a) the seriousness and circumstances of the offense;

(b) the extent of harm caused by the offense;

(c) the evidence of guilt, whether admissible or inadmissible at trial;

(d) the history, character and condition of the defendant;

(e) any exceptionally serious misconduct of law enforcement personnel in the investigation, arrest and prosecution of the defendant;

(f) the purpose and effect of imposing upon the defendant a sentence authorized for the offense;

(g) the impact of a dismissal upon the confi-dence of the public in the criminal justice system;

(h) the impact of a dismissal on the safety or welfare of the community;

(i) where the court deems it appropriate, the attitude of the complainant or victim with respect to the motion;

(j) any other relevant fact indicating that a judgment of conviction would serve no useful purpose.

2. In addition to the grounds specified in subdivision one of this section, a count alleging enterprise corruption in violation of article four hundred sixty of the penal law may be dismissed in the interest of justice where prosecution of that count is inconsistent with the stated legislative findings in said article. Upon a motion pursuant to this section, the court must inspect the evidence before the grand jury and such other evidence or information as it may deem proper.

3. An order dismissing an indictment in the interest of justice may be issued upon motion of the people or of the court itself as well as upon that of the defendant. Upon issuing such an order, the court must set forth its reasons therefor upon the record.

Amended by L. 1979, Ch. 216; L. 1986, Ch. 516.

ANNOTATIONS

Court's role.—Court may not dismiss indictment in the interest of justice merely because it deems plea offer unsatisfac-tory. People v. Molfino, 178 A.D.2d 238, 577 N.Y.S.2d 787 (1st Dept. 1991), *lv. denied,* 79 N.Y.2d 951 (1992).

—An indictment may be dismissed in furtherance of justice only when there exists some compelling factor, consideration or circumstance clearly demonstrating that conviction or prosecu-tion of the defendant would constitute or result in injustice. People v. Reyes, 174 A.D.2d 87, 579 N.Y.S.2d 34 (1st Dept. 1991).

—Trial court must articulate on the record its reason for granting a dismissal in the interest of justice, making reference to the statutory factors. People v. Pugh, 207 A.D.2d 503, 615 N.Y.S.2d 912 (2d Dept. 1994).

—The court's discretionary power to dismiss an indictment in the interest of justice is to be exercised sparingly. People v.

Serrano, 163 A.D.2d 497, 558 N.Y.S.2d 593 (2d Dept. 1990). *See also* People v. McGraw, 158 A.D.2d 719, 552 N.Y.S.2d 166 (2d Dept.), *lv. denied,* 76 N.Y.2d 739 (1990); People v. Ortiz, 152 A.D.2d 755, 544 N.Y.S.2d 204 (2d Dept. 1989); People v. Naik, 139 A.D.2d 535, 526 N.Y.S.2d 856 (2d Dept. 1988).

—A trial court's discretion to dismiss an indictment in furtherance of justice is not absolute. People v. Brown, 194 A.D.2d 548, 598 N.Y.S.2d 88 (2d Dept. 1993).

—The purpose of a motion to dismiss in the interest of justice is to allow justice to prevail over the strict letter of the law so as to prevent a miscarriage of justice. People v. Morrisey, 161 Misc. 2d 295, 614 N.Y.S.2d 686 (Crim. Ct. N.Y. Co. 1994).

—Dismissal in the interest of justice lies within the discretion of the trial judge, but such discretion is neither absolute nor uncontrolled. People v. A.T., 155 Misc. 2d 637, 589 N.Y.S.2d 980 (Crim. Ct. N.Y. Co. 1992).

Notice and hearing.—A motion to dismiss an indictment in the interest of justice may be decided without a hearing unless the papers raise a factual dispute on a material point which must be resolved before the court can decide the legal issue. People v. Schlessel, 104 A.D.2d 501, 479 N.Y.S.2d 249 (2d Dept. 1984).

—Statutory scheme of dismissals in the interests of justice contemplates a measured and deliberate procedure, calling for notice, hearing and the consideration of the pertinent factors which manifestly form the embodiment of the interests of justice; it is not adapted to the ebb and flow of a trial where determinations must be made speedily; thus, if circumstances arise during a trial which prejudice the defendant, the remedy lies in the direction of a mistrial, not the dismissal of indictment. People v. Zagarino, 74 A.D.2d 115, 427 N.Y.S.2d 40 (2d Dept. 1980).

—Before a court can dismiss an indictment in the interests of justice, either on its own motion or on the defendant's motion, it must give notice to all interested parties and provide a hearing where evidence and arguments may be raised to shed light on the issues. People v. Clayton, 41 A.D.2d 204, 342 N.Y.S.2d 106 (2d Dept. 1973).

—If a court considers sua sponte a dismissal in furtherance of justice, it should not do so until fair notice of its intention has been given to the parties and a hearing has been held. People v. Russ, 19 A.D.3d 746, 796 N.Y.S.2d 444 (3d Dept. 2005).

—A defendant must be arraigned before a *Clayton* hearing will be held on anyone's motion to dismiss in the interests of justice. People v. Thompson, 107 Misc. 2d 258, 433 N.Y.S.2d 961 (Co. Ct. Franklin Co. 1980).

Circumstances justifying dismissal.—It was not improper for lower court to consider defendant's mental retardation a factor among others supporting dismissal. People v. Colon, 86 N.Y.2d 861, 635 N.Y.S.2d 165, 658 N.E.2d 1038 (1995).

—Dismissal of the indictment by the Court was appropriate where a promise of leniency was made to the defendant to obtain his cooperation in a pending unrelated criminal investigation and the defendant performed valuable services placing himself in great danger even though he did not completely perform the agreed on services. People v. Delaney, 80 A.D.2d 835, 436 N.Y.S.2d 336 (2d Dept. 1981).

—Court abused its discretion in sua sponte dismissing an indictment against defendant in furtherance of justice pursuant to CPL § 210.40(1) where it concluded that prosecution would serve no useful purpose because defendant had been recently convicted of robbery in the first degree and sentenced to a lengthy term of incarceration arising out of a prior offense; case did not present one of those rare instances in which dismissal in the furtherance of justice is warranted. People v. Wright, 278 A.D.2d 820, 719 N.Y.S.2d 411 (4th Dept. 2000).

—Reversible error was committed where the trial court denied the defendant's motion to dismiss the indictment in the interests of justice, which the prosecution joined. Defendant's role in the drug sale consisted largely of introducing a supplier to a seller, his role was initiated by the seller, a friend who overcame defendant's resistance to involvement in the sale; the sale was to an undercover officer who immediately arrested defendant and seller, seized the drugs and recovered the buy money; upon release on bail he voluntarily assisted both state and federal authorities; it was his first involvement with drugs, he had no prior arrests and while on bail moved to another state where he completed college with honors, had been in no further trouble

and was employed as a newspaper reporter. People v. Hirsch, 85 A.D.2d 902, 447 N.Y.S.2d 80 (4th Dept. 1981).

—The indictment for reckless endangerment and reckless assault was dismissed in the interests of justice when the court found that the defendant, a 64-year-old attorney, was the victim of a robbery and pursued the robber and fired at him with a licensed gun, and a bullet hit a pedestrian in the leg inflicting a minor wound and the defendant, with no prior record, had liability insurance. People v. Jacobs, 105 Misc. 2d 616, 432 N.Y.S.2d 614 (Sup. Ct. N.Y. Co. 1980).

Circumstances not justifying dismissal.—The offense with which defendant was charged is a serious and harmful one, and the criteria prescribed in CPL § 210.40(1) indicate that dismissal in furtherance of justice is inappropriate. People v. Stewart, 230 A.D.2d 116, 656 N.Y.S.2d 210 (1st Dept. 1997), *app. dismissed,* 668 N.Y.2d 1000.

—Defendant's *Clayton* motion was properly denied since the prosecutor's improper inclusion of sealed records on the motion was not the type of misconduct that warrants dismissal in the furtherance of justice. People v. Bazemore, 203 A.D.2d 25, 610 N.Y.S.2d 19 (1st Dept.), *lv. denied,* 84 N.Y.2d 866 (1994).

—Fact that defendant had an exemplary background and no prior criminal record did not constitute compelling factors justifying the dismissal in the interests of justice of charges involving the sale of cocaine. People v. Varela, 106 A.D.2d 339, 483 N.Y.S.2d 13 (1st Dept. 1984).

—Court improperly dismissed indictment in the interest of justice on the ground that prior to the robbery, the defendant had been accepted in the United States Marine Corps, and he had no criminal record; the power to dismiss an indictment should be dismissed sparingly, and the defendant's lack of a criminal history and the prospect of mandatory incarceration are insufficient to warrant dismissal. People v. Crespo, 244 A.D.2d 563, 665 N.Y.S.2d 676 (2d Dept. 1997).

—Defendant's rehabilitation through participation in the Fortune Society's program did not warrant a dismissal in the interest in justice, since defendant was arrested and found engaging in the same pattern of criminal behavior shortly before finishing the program. People v. Smith, 217 A.D.2d 671, 630 N.Y.S.2d 84 (2d Dept. 1995).

—Police misconduct did not justify dismissal in the interest of justice, where it was not so egregious as to manifest disregard for cherished principles of law and order. People v. Ranta, 203 A.D.2d 307, 610 N.Y.S.2d 283 (2d Dept.), *lv. denied,* 83 N.Y.2d 970 (1994).

—Court rejected notion that indictment was properly dismissed in the interest of justice simply because the defendant was mentally retarded and adjudicated an incapacitated person. People v. Saunders, 161 A.D.2d 611, 554 N.Y.S.2d 952 (2d Dept.), *lv. denied,* 76 N.Y.2d 896 (1990).

—The fact that the defendant had no prior record by itself did not constitute compelling circumstances to justify the dismissal of a count of the indictment in the furtherance of justice. CPL § 210.40(1). People v. Andrew, 78 A.D.2d 683, 432 N.Y.S.2d 252 (2d Dept. 1980).

—While defendant's ill health is among the factors to be considered in a court's decision on whether to dismiss criminal charges, this factor alone is not sufficiently compelling here to warrant a dismissal; considering the nature of defendant's present crimes, his history of violence and theft-related activity, and the continuation of his conduct after learning about his terminal illness, court was not persuaded that the type of extraordinary circumstances contemplated by the statute exist in the instant case. People v. Kennard, 266 A.D.2d 718, 699 N.Y.S.2d 497 (3d Dept. 1999).

—The absence of a criminal record and an exemplary character standing alone are not sufficient to compel a dismissal in the interest of justice. People v. Doe, 159 Misc. 2d 799, 606 N.Y.S.2d 862 (Sup. Ct. N.Y. Co. 1994).

—Interest of justice motion denied as frivolous in driving while intoxicated prosecution; neither the fact that the defendant entered an alcohol treatment program after he was arrested nor the fact that this offense was "almost" a misdemeanor presented a compelling injustice which only dismissal could cure. People v. McGorman, 159 Misc. 2d 736, 606 N.Y.S.2d 566 (Sup. Ct. N.Y. Co. 1994).

—Neither the lack of a criminal record nor an exemplary background are sufficient to require a dismissal in furtherance of justice. People v. Berrios, 160 Misc. 2d 612, 610 N.Y.S.2d 748 (Crim. Ct. N.Y. Co. 1994).

AIDS.—It was not an abuse of discretion as a matter of law for the lower court to grant defendant's motion to dismiss in the interest of judgment based, inter alia, on the court's own observation of defendant's deterioration from his HIV infection, even in the absence of expert medical evidence or documentation. People v. Herman L., 83 N.Y.2d 958, 615 N.Y.S.2d 865, 639 N.E.2d 404 (1994).

—It was not an abuse of discretion as a matter of law for the lower court to grant defendant's motion to dismiss in the interest of judgment where, inter alia, defendant was homeless and was HIV infected with a deteriorating physical condition. People v. Lawson, 198 A.D.2d 71, 603 N.Y.S.2d 311 (1st Dept. 1993), aff'd, 83 N.Y.2d 958 (1994).

—Fact that defendant was HIV positive did not warrant dismissal in the furtherance of justice. People v. Sierra, 149 A.D.2d 588, 566 N.Y.S.2d 818 (Sup. Ct. Kings Co. 1990).

—Court granted motion to dismiss the indictment in the interest of justice where defendant, who was suffering from AIDS, was expected to live only five or six months. People v. Camargo, 135 Misc. 2d 987, 516 N.Y.S.2d 1004 (Sup. Ct. Bronx Co. 1987).

Appellate review.—Court of Appeals' review of a dismissal in the interest of justice is limited to the question whether the dismissal was an abuse of discretion as a matter of law. People v. Colon, 86 N.Y.2d 861, 635 N.Y.S.2d 165, 658 N.E.2d 1038 (1995). See also People v. Rickert, 58 N.Y.2d 122, 459 N.Y.S.2d 734, 446 N.E.2d 419 (1983).

—Where the Trial Term dismissed the indictment in the interest of justice, and the Appellate Division affirmed, the order before the Court of Appeals was nonreviewable absent an abuse of discretion. People v. Tyler, 46 N.Y.2d 264, 413 N.Y.S.2d 302, 385 N.E.2d 1231 (1978).

—Order dismissing the indictment "in the interest of justice," which was affirmed by the Appellate Division, was outside the scope of review by the Court of Appeals, unless it could be said that there was an abuse of discretion as a matter of law. People v. Belge, 41 N.Y.2d 60, 390 N.Y.S.2d 867, 359 N.E.2d 377 (1976).

§ 210.43. Motion to remove juvenile offender to family court.

1. After a motion by a juvenile offender, pursuant to subdivision five of section 180.75 of this chapter, or after arraignment of a juvenile offender upon an indictment, the superior court may, on motion of any party or on its own motion:

(a) except as otherwise provided by paragraph (b), order removal of the action to the family court pursuant to the provisions of article seven hundred twenty-five of this chapter, if, after consideration of the factors set forth in subdivision two of this section, the court determines that to do so would be in the interests of justice; or

(b) with the consent of the district attorney, order removal of an action involving an indictment charging a juvenile offender with murder in the second degree as defined in section 125.25 of the penal law; rape in the first degree, as defined in subdivision one of section 130.35 of the penal law; criminal sexual act in the first degree, as defined in subdivision one of section 130.50 of the penal law; or an armed felony as defined in paragraph (a) of subdivision forty-one of section 1.20, to the family court pursuant to the provisions of article seven hundred twenty-five of this chapter if the court finds one or more of the following factors: (i) mitigating circumstances that bear directly upon the manner in which the crime was committed; (ii) where the defendant was not the sole participant in the crime, the defendant's participation was relatively minor although not so minor as to constitute a defense to the prosecution; or (iii) possible deficiencies in the proof of the crime, and, after consideration of the factors set forth in subdivision two of this section, the court determined that removal of the action to the family court would be in the interests of justice.

2. In making its determination pursuant to subdivision one of this section the court shall, to the extent applicable, examine individually and collectively, the following:

(a) the seriousness and circumstances of the offense;

(b) the extent of harm caused by the offense;

(c) evidence of guilt, whether admissible or inadmissible at trial;

(d) the history, character and condition of the defendant;

(e) the purpose and effect of imposing upon the defendant a sentence authorized for the offense;

(f) the impact of a removal of the case to the family court on the safety or welfare of the community;

(g) the impact of a removal of the case to the family court upon the confidence of the public in the criminal justice system;

(h) where the court deems it appropriate, the attitude of the complainant or victim with respect to the motion; and

(i) any other relevant fact indicating that a judgment of conviction in the criminal court would serve no useful purpose.

3. The procedure for bringing on a motion pursuant to subdivision one of this section, shall accord with the procedure prescribed in subdivisions one and two of section 210.45 of this article. After all papers of both parties have been filed and after all documentary evidence, if any, has been submitted, the court must consider the same for the purpose of determining whether the motion is determinable on the motion papers submitted and, if not, may make such inquiry as it deems necessary for the purpose of making a determination.

4. For the purpose of making a determination pursuant to this section, any evidence which is not legally privileged may be introduced. If the defendant testifies, his testimony may not be introduced against him in any future proceeding, except to impeach his testimony at such future proceeding as inconsistent prior testimony.

5. a. If the court orders removal of the action to family court, it shall state on the record the factor or factors upon which its determination is

based, and, the court shall give its reasons for removal in detail and not in conclusory terms.

b. The district attorney shall state upon the record the reasons for his consent to removal of the action to the family court. The reasons shall be stated in detail and not in conclusory terms.

Added by L. 1979, Ch. 411; L. 2003, Ch. 264, § 41, eff. Nov. 1, 2003, amending subd. 1(b).

ANNOTATIONS

Basis for removal.—Where the evidence indicated that defendant would likely be convicted of the lesser-included offense of second-degree assault rather than first-degree assault, removal was justified. People v. Gregory C., 158 Misc. 2d 872, 602 N.Y.S.2d 492 (Sup. Ct. N.Y. Co. 1993).

Denial of motion for removal.—The statute does not create a right to have a particular case removed to Family Court, but only protects a defendant from arbitrarily being denied removal. People v. Murphy, 128 A.D.2d 177, 515 N.Y.S.2d 895 (3d Dept. 1987), *aff'd for the reasons stated below,* 70 N.Y.2d 969 (1988).

Grand Jury minutes.—Defendant in a juvenile delinquency proceeding originated by removal to Family Court is not automatically entitled to inspect or receive a copy of the minutes of any grand jury proceeding which must be transferred to Family Court; notice can be met by service of a copy of the order of removal and of other documents in the petition file without recourse to grand jury minutes. Larry W. v. Corp. Counsel, 55 N.Y.2d 244, 448 N.Y.S.2d 452, 433 N.E.2d 517 (1982).

§ 210.45. Motion to dismiss indictment; procedure.

1. A motion to dismiss an indictment pursuant to section 210.20 must be made in writing and upon reasonable notice to the people. If the motion is based upon the existence or occurrence of facts, the motion papers must contain sworn allegations thereof, whether by the defendant or by another person or persons. Such sworn allegations may be based upon personal knowledge of the affiant or upon information and belief, provided that in the latter event the affiant must state the sources of such information and the grounds of such belief. The defendant may further submit documentary evidence supporting or tending to support the allegations of the moving papers.

2. The people may file with the court, and in such case must serve a copy thereof upon the defendant or his counsel, an answer denying or admitting any or all of the allegations of the moving papers, and may further submit documentary evidence refuting or tending to refute such allegations.

3. After all papers of both parties have been filed, and after all documentary evidence, if any, has been submitted, the court must consider the same for the purpose of determining whether the motion is determinable without a hearing to resolve questions of fact.

4. The court must grant the motion without conducting a hearing if:

(a) The moving papers allege a ground constituting legal basis for the motion pursuant to subdivision one of section 210.20; and

(b) Such ground, if based upon the existence or occurrence of facts, is supported by sworn allegations of all facts essential to support the motion; and

(c) The sworn allegations of fact essential to support the motion are either conceded by the people to be true or are conclusively substantiated by unquestionable documentary proof.

5. The court may deny the motion without conducting a hearing if:

(a) The moving papers do not allege any ground constituting legal basis for the motion pursuant to subdivision one of section 210.20; or

(b) The motion is based upon the existence or occurrence of facts, and the moving papers do not contain sworn allegations supporting all the essential facts; or

(c) An allegation of fact essential to support the motion is conclusively refuted by unquestionable documentary proof.

6. If the court does not determine the motion pursuant to subdivision four or five, it must conduct a hearing and make findings of fact essential to the determination thereof. The defendant has a right to be present in person at such hearing but may waive such right.

7. Upon such a hearing, the defendant has the burden of proving by a preponderance of the evidence every fact essential to support the motion.

8. When the court dismisses the entire indictment without authorizing resubmission of the charge or charges to a grand jury, it must order that the defendant be discharged from custody if he is in the custody of the sheriff, or if he is at liberty on bail it must exonerate the bail.

9. When the court dismisses the entire indictment but authorizes resubmission of the charge or charges to a grand jury, such authorization is, for purposes of this subdivision, deemed to constitute an order holding the defendant for the action of a grand jury with respect to such charge or charges. Such order must be accompanied by a securing order either releasing the defendant on his own recognizance or fixing bail or committing him to the custody of the sheriff pending resubmission of the case to the grand jury and the grand jury's disposition thereof. Such securing order remains in effect until the first to occur of any of the following:

(a) A statement to the court by the people that they do not intend to resubmit the case to a grand jury;

(b) Arraignment of the defendant upon an indictment or prosecutor's information filed as a result of resubmission of the case to a grand jury. Upon such arraignment, the arraigning court must issue a new securing order;

(c) The filing with the court of a grand jury

dismissal of the case following resubmission thereof;

(d) The expiration of a period of forty-five days from the date of issuance of the order; provided that such period may, for good cause shown, be extended by the court to a designated subsequent date if such be necessary to accord the people reasonable opportunity to resubmit the case to a grand jury.

Upon the termination of the effectiveness of the securing order pursuant to paragraph (a), (c) or (d), the court must immediately order that the defendant be discharged from custody if he is in the custody of the sheriff, or if he is at liberty on bail it must exonerate the bail. Although expiration of the period of time specified in paragraph (d) without any resubmission or grand jury disposition of the case terminates the effectiveness of the securing order, it does not terminate the effectiveness of the order authorizing resubmission.

ANNOTATIONS

Defendant's burden to demonstrate defects.—It is defendant's burden to demonstrate, on written notice to the People, the existence of defects impairing the integrity of the Grand Jury proceeding and giving rise to a possibility of prejudice, and orderly procedures require that the People be given the opportunity to address any alleged defects prior to dismissal of an indictment. People v. Santmyer, 255 A.D.2d 871, 680 N.Y.S.2d 367 (4th Dept. 1998).

Motion to dismiss.—Criminal term erred in dismissing the indictment on ground other than that set forth by defendants in their motion to dismiss. People v. Novack, 74 A.D.2d 652, 425 N.Y.S.2d 133 (2d Dept. 1980).

Motion practice.—Although defendant's affidavit in support of his speedy trial motion omitted the date the People's time began to run, that alleged insufficiency was cured where the prosecutor furnished that date in his own affidavit. People v. Santos, 68 N.Y.2d 859, 508 N.Y.S.2d 411, 501 N.E.2d 19 (1986).

—The dismissal of an indictment upon the court's own motion requires observance of the procedure set forth in CPL § 210.45. People v. Alston, 191 A.D.2d 176, 594 N.Y.S.2d 37 (1st Dept. 1993).

—Defense counsel sufficiently complied with the requirements of CPL § 210.20 (1)(g) and 210.45(10) by orally joining in with the written request of counsel for co-defendant. People v. Haynes, 143 A.D.2d 571, 533 N.Y.S.2d 61 (1st Dept. 1988).

—CPL 210.45(1) requires that a motion to dismiss an indictment for failure to prosecute must be in writing. People v. Kitt, 93 A.D.2d 77, 460 N.Y.S.2d 799 (1st Dept.), *lv. denied,* 57 N.Y.2d 672 (1983). *See also* People v. Johnson, 134 A.D.2d 284, 520 N.Y.S.2d 455 (2d Dept. 1987); People v. Fanelli, 92 A.D.2d 573, 459 N.Y.S.2d 329 (2d Dept. 1983) (cannot be made orally on the day of the trial).

—Court properly denied defendant's oral motion to dismiss the indictment pursuant to CPL 30.30, where that provision was not referred to in defendant's papers, which predicated the motion to dismiss the indictment upon CPL 30.30. People v. Hardy, 119 A.D.2d 832, 501 N.Y.S.2d 459 (2d Dept. 1986); People v. Marrero, 85 A.D.2d 610, 444 N.Y.S.2d 679 (2d Dept. 1981); People v. Hansel, 208 A.D.2d 1112, 617 N.Y.S.2d 542 (3d Dept. 1994).

—The 45-day period for a defense motion challenging eavesdropping evidence commences not from the end of the 15 days after arraignment within which the copy of the warrant and application must be furnished, but within 45 days after the date of service of the eavesdropping documentation. People v. Mullen, 152 A.D.2d 260, 549 N.Y.S.2d 520 (3d Dept. 1990).

—An oral motion to dismiss charges on statutory double jeopardy grounds is not adequate. People v. Cruz, 161 A.D.2d 1182, 555 N.Y.S.2d 523 (4th Dept. 1990).

Notice and hearing.—Trial court committed no procedural error when it granted defendant's oral motion to dismiss the indictment after the conclusion of the undercover officers' testimony and following a colloquy between the Trial Judge and both counsel with reference to the disclosure procedure; the record revealed extensive argumentation and consideration of the right of defendant to disclosure; the prosecutor declined to comply with the court's disclosure order; no contention was then made by the prosecutor that the motion was not in writing, or that he had not been given reasonable notice or an opportunity to be heard, nor did he request the formality of any further hearing. People v. Singleton, 42 N.Y.2d 466, 398 N.Y.S.2d 871, 368 N.E.2d 1237 (1977).

—The court may summarily grant a motion to dismiss unless the papers submitted by the prosecutor show that there is a factual dispute which must be resolved at a hearing; however, where the information alleged may be solely within the knowledge or possession of the defendant or based upon information and belief, the prosecutor can ask the court to put the defendant to his proof. People v. Gruden, 42 N.Y.2d 214, 397 N.Y.S.2d 704, 366 N.E.2d 794 (1977).

Clayton.—Before a court can dismiss an indictment in the interests of justice, either on its own motion or on the defendant's motion, it must give notice to all interested parties and provide a hearing where evidence and arguments may be raised to shed light on the issues. People v. Clayton 41 A.D.2d 204, 342 N.Y.S.2d 106 (2d Dept. 1973).

Basis for dismissal.—The test to be applied on a motion to dismiss an indictment for insufficiency of evidence is whether there has been a "clear showing" that the evidence before the Grand Jury, if unexplained and uncontradicted, would not warrant a conviction by a trial jury. The term "clear showing" has been constituted to mean *prima facie* proof that the crime charged has been committed. The fact that each indictment contains only one court of perjury does not warrant dismissal, since at the time of trial, should the evidence warrant it, lesser included counts may also be considered. People v. Dunleavy, 41 A.D.2d 717, 341 N.Y.S.2d 500 (1st Dept.), *aff'd,* 33 N.Y.2d 573, 347 N.Y.S.2d 448, 301 N.E.2d 432 (1973).

—Defendant's statements and physical evidence were prima facie competent to support the indictment and subsequent suppression does not render the evidence insufficient. People v. Vega, 80 A.D.2d 867, 436 N.Y.S.2d 748 (2d Dept. 1981).

People's failure to answer; not grounds for dismissal.— Court erroneously deemed People's failure to submit answer to defendant's motion to dismiss as a default and granted the motion without considering the merits; order reversed because CPL § 210.45 does not provide that the failure to submit answering papers is a ground for dismissal of an accusatory instrument. People v. Suriel, 173 Misc. 2d 674, 663 N.Y.S.2d 464 (2d Dept. App. Term 1997).

Review.—No appeal lies from an intermediate order denying dismissal of an indictment. People v. Young, 149 A.D.2d 916, 540 N.Y.S.2d 392 (4th Dept. 1989).

—Court declined to review, on a motion to dismiss the indictment, the merits of a ruling of another judge of the same court, made during the Grand Jury proceedings relating to the presentation of evidence to the Grand Jury. People v. Davis, 162 Misc. 2d 662, 618 N.Y.S.2d 194 (Sup. Ct. Kings Co. 1994).

Securing order.—When dismissal of the indictment was without prejudice to the People representing the charges to another Grand Jury, defendant was subject to a securing order either releasing him on his own recognizance, fixing bail, or committing his to the sheriff's custody. People v. Kress, 192 A.D.2d 722, 597 N.Y.S.2d 124 (2d Dept. 1993).

—CPL § 210.45(9) requires that the court issue a securing order when the entire indictment filed against the defendant is dismissed; the securing order functions as a hold on the defendant while the People decide how to proceed. People v. Richardson, 146 Misc. 2d 179, 549 N.Y.S.2d 572 (Sup. Ct. Bronx Co. 1989).

§ 210.46. Adjournment in contemplation of dismissal in marihuana cases in a superior court.

Upon or after arraignment in a superior court upon an indictment where the sole remaining count or counts charge a violation or violations of section 221.05, 221.10, 221.15, 221.35 or 221.40 of the penal law and before the entry of a plea of guilty thereto or commencement of a trial thereof, the court, upon motion of a defendant, may order that all proceedings be suspended and the action adjourned in contemplation of dismissal or may dismiss the indictment in furtherance of justice, in accordance with the provisions of section 170.56 of this chapter.

Added by L. 1973, Ch. 901; Amended by L. 1977, Ch.

§ 210.47. Adjournment in contemplation of dismissal in misdemeanor cases in superior court.

Upon or after the arraignment in a superior court upon an indictment where the sole remaining count or counts charge a misdemeanor offense, and before the entry of a plea of guilty thereto or commencement of a trial thereof, the court, upon motion of the people or the defendant and with the consent of the other party, or upon the court's own motion with the consent of both the people and the defendant, may order that all proceedings be suspended and the action adjourned in contemplation of dismissal, in accordance with the provisions of section 170.55 of this chapter.

Added by L. 2001, Ch. 487, eff. Nov. 1, 2002.

§ 210.50. Requirement of plea.

Unless an indictment is dismissed or the criminal action thereon terminated or abated pursuant to the provisions of this article or some other provision of law, the defendant must be required to enter a plea thereto.

ANNOTATIONS

Nature of plea.—That a plea is merely a device, rather than a factual assertion of innocence, is emphasized by the legislative mandate requiring a defendant against whom an indictment is pending to enter a plea at arraignment, and if a plea were testimonial or evidentiary, the court would have no power to demand it. People v. Garcia, 169 A.D.2d 358, 573 N.Y.S.2d 257 (1st Dept. 1991).

Time to enter plea.—There is no statutory requirement that a defendant enter a plea at the time of arraignment; CPL § 210.50 does not specify when the plea must be entered. People v. Updike, 125 A.D.2d 735, 509 N.Y.S.2d 158 (3d Dept. 1986).

ARTICLE 215—ADJOURNMENT IN CONTEMPLATION OF DISMISSAL FOR PURPOSES OF REFERRING SELECTED FELONIES TO DISPUTE RESOLUTION

§ 215.10. Referral of selected felonies to dispute resolution.

Upon or after arraignment in a local criminal court upon a felony complaint, or upon or after arraignment in a superior court upon an indictment or superior court information, and before final disposition thereof, the court, with the consent of the people and of the defendant, and with reasonable notice to the victim and an opportunity for the victim to be heard, may order that the action be adjourned in contemplation of dismissal, for the purpose of referring the action to a community dispute center established pursuant to article twenty-one-A of the judiciary law. Provided, however, that the court may not order any action adjourned in contemplation of dismissal if the defendant is charged therein with: (i) a class A felony, or (ii) a violent felony offense as defined in section 70.02 of the penal law, or (iii) any drug offense as defined in article two hundred twenty of the penal law, or (iv) a felony upon the conviction of which defendant must be sentenced as a second felony offender, a second violent felony offender, or a persistent violent felony offender pursuant to sections 70.06, 70.04 and 70.08 of the penal law, or a felony upon the conviction of which defendant may be sentenced as a persistent felony offender pursuant to section 70.10 of such law.

§ 215.20. Victim; definition.

For purposes of section 215.10 of this article, "victim" means any person alleged to have sustained physical or financial injury to person or property as a direct result of the crime or crimes charged in a felony complaint, superior court information, or indictment.

§ 215.30. Adjournment in contemplation of dismissal; restoration to calendar; dismissal of action.

Upon issuing an order adjourning an action in contemplation of dismissal pursuant to section 215.10 of this article, the court must release the defendant on his own recognizance and refer the action to a dispute resolution center established pursuant to article twenty-one-A of the judiciary law. No later than forty-five days after an action has been referred to a dispute resolution center, such center must advise the district attorney as to whether the charges against defendant have been resolved. Thereafter, if defendant has agreed to pay a fine, restitution or reparation, the district attorney must be advised every thirty days as to the status of such fine, restitution or reparation. Upon application of the people, made at any time not more than six months after the issuance of an order adjourning an action in contemplation of dismissal, the court may restore the action to the calendar upon a determination that dismissal of the accusatory instrument would not be in furtherance of justice, and the action must thereupon proceed. Notwithstanding the foregoing, where defendant has agreed to pay a fine, restitution, or reparation, but has not paid such fine, restitution or reparation, upon application of the people, made at any time not more than one year after the issuance of an order adjourning an action in contemplation of dismissal, the court may restore the action to the calendar upon a determination that defendant has failed to pay such fine, restitution, or reparation, and the action must thereupon proceed.

§ 215.40. Dismissal of action; effect thereof; records.

If an action has not been restored to the calendar within six months, or where the defendant has agreed to pay a fine, restitution or reparation but has not paid such fine, restitution or reparation, within one year, of the issuance of an order adjourning the action in contemplation of dismissal, the accusatory instrument shall be deemed to have been dismissed by the court in furtherance of justice at the expiration of such six month or one year period, as the case may be. Upon dismissal of an action, the arrest and prosecution shall be deemed a nullity, and defendant shall be restored to the status he or she occupied before his or her arrest and prosecution. All papers and records relating to an action that has been dismissed pursuant to this section shall be subject to the sealing provisions of section 160.50 of this chapter.

TITLE J—PROSECUTION OF INDICTMENTS IN SUPERIOR COURTS—PLEA TO SENTENCE

ARTICLE 220—THE PLEA

LexisNexis Cross References

Criminal Constitutional Law, Vol. 3, Ch. 12, Pleas and Plea Bargaining; *see generally Criminal Law Advocacy,* Vol. 2, Guilty Pleas; *Criminal Defense Techniques,* Vol. 1A, Ch. 13, Negotiating a Plea; *New York Criminal Practice (2d ed.),* Vol. 1, Ch. 9, Local Criminal Court Arraignment and Related Issues; Vol. 1, Ch. 12, Superior Court Arraignment; *Criminal Practice Handbook (2d ed.),* Ch. 10, Disposition Alternatives Including Sentencing Issues; *Plea Bargaining.*

§ 220.10. Plea; kinds of pleas.

The only kinds of pleas which may be entered to an indictment are those specified in this section:

1. The defendant may as a matter of right enter a plea of "not guilty" to the indictment.

2. Except as provided in subdivision five, the defendant may as a matter of right enter a plea of "guilty" to the entire indictment.

3. Except as provided in subdivision five, where the indictment charges but one crime, the defendant may, with both the permission of the court and the consent of the people, enter a plea of guilty of a lesser included offense.

4. Except as provided in subdivision five, where the indictment charges two or more offenses in separate counts, the defendant may, with both the permission of the court and the consent of the people, enter a plea of:

(a) Guilty of one or more but not all of the offenses charged; or

(b) Guilty of a lesser included offense with respect to any or all of the offenses charged; or

(c) Guilty of any combination of offenses charged and lesser offenses included within other offenses charged.

5. (a) (i)　Where the indictment charges one of the class A felonies defined in article two hundred twenty of the penal law or the attempt to commit any such class A felony, then any plea of guilty entered pursuant to subdivision three or four of this section must be or must include at least a plea of guilty of a class B felony.

(ii) *[Repealed.]*

(iii) Where the indictment charges one of the class B felonies defined in article two hundred twenty of the penal law then any plea of guilty entered pursuant to subdivision three or four must be or must include at least a plea of guilty of a class D felony.

(b) Where the indictment charges any class B felony, other than a class B felony defined in article two hundred twenty of the penal law or a class B violent felony offense as defined in subdivision one of section 70.02 of the penal law, then any plea of guilty entered pursuant to subdivision three or four must be or must include at least a plea of guilty of a felony.

(c) Where the indictment charges a felony, other than a class A felony or class B felony defined in article two hundred twenty of the penal law or class B or class C violent felony offense as defined in subdivision one of section 70.02 of the penal law, and it appears that the defendant has previously been subjected to a predicate felony conviction as defined in penal law section 70.06 then any plea of guilty entered pursuant to subdivision three or four must be or must include at least a plea of guilty of a felony.

(d) Where the indictment charges a class A

felony, other than those defined in article two hundred twenty of the penal law, or charges a class B or class C violent felony offense as defined in subdivision one of section 70.02 of the penal law, then a plea of guilty entered pursuant to subdivision three or four must be as follows:

(i) Where the indictment charges a class A felony offense or a class B violent felony offense which is also an armed felony offense then a plea of guilty must include at least a plea of guilty to a class C violent felony offense;

(ii) Except as provided in subparagraph (i) of this paragraph, where the indictment charges a class B violent felony offense or a class C violent felony offense, then a plea of guilty must include at least a plea of guilty to a class D violent felony offense;

(iii) Where the indictment charges the class D violent felony offense of criminal possession of a weapon in the third degree as defined in subdivision four of section 265.02 of the penal law, and the defendant has not been previously convicted of a class A misdemeanor defined in the penal law in the five years preceding the commission of the offense, then a plea of guilty must be either to the class E violent felony offense of attempted criminal possession of a weapon in the third degree or to the class A misdemeanor of criminal possession of a weapon in the fourth degree as defined in subdivision one of section 265.01 of the penal law;

(iv) Where the indictment charges the class D violent felony offenses of criminal possession of a weapon in the third degree as defined in subdivision four of section 265.02 of the penal law and the provisions of subparagraph (iii) of this paragraph do not apply, or subdivision five, seven or eight of section 265.02 of the penal law, then a plea of guilty must include at least a plea of guilty to a class E violent felony offense.

(e) A defendant may not enter a plea of guilty to the crime of murder in the first degree as defined in section 125.27 of the penal law; provided, however, that a defendant may enter such a plea with both the permission of the court and the consent of the people when the agreed upon sentence is either life imprisonment without parole or a term of imprisonment for the class A-I felony of murder in the first degree other than a sentence of life imprisonment without parole.

(f) The provisions of this subdivision shall apply irrespective of whether the defendant is thereby precluded from entering a plea of guilty of any lesser included offense.

(g) Where the defendant is a juvenile offender, the provisions of paragraphs (a), (b), (c) and (d) of this subdivision shall not apply and any plea entered pursuant to subdivision three or four of this section, must be as follows:

(i) If the indictment charges a person fourteen or fifteen years old with the crime of murder in the second degree any plea of guilty entered pursuant to subdivision three or four must be a plea of guilty of a crime for which the defendant is criminally responsible;

(ii) If the indictment does not charge a crime specified in subparagraph (i) of this paragraph, then any plea of guilty entered pursuant to subdivision three or four of this section must be a plea of guilty of a crime for which the defendant is criminally responsible unless a plea of guilty is accepted pursuant to subparagraph (iii) of this paragraph;

(iii) Where the indictment does not charge a crime specified in subparagraph (i) of this paragraph, the district attorney may recommend removal of the action to the family court. Upon making such recommendation the district attorney shall submit a subscribed memorandum setting forth: (1) a recommendation that the interests of justice would best be served by removal of the action to the family court; and (2) if the indictment charges a thirteen year old with the crime of murder in the second degree, or a fourteen or fifteen year old with the crimes of rape in the first degree as defined in subdivision one of section 130.35 of the penal law, or criminal sexual act in the first degree as defined in subdivision one of section 130.50 of the penal law, or an armed felony as defined in paragraph (a) of subdivision forty-one of section 1.20 of this chapter specific factors, one or more of which reasonably supports the recommendation, showing, (i) mitigating circumstances that bear directly upon the manner in which the crime was committed, or (ii) where the defendant was not the sole participant in the crime, that the defendant's participation was relatively minor although not so minor as to constitute a defense to the prosecution, or (iii) possible deficiencies in proof of the crime, or (iv) where the juvenile offender has no previous adjudication's of having committed a designated felony act, as defined in subdivision eight of section 301.2 of the family court act, regardless of the age of the offender at the time of commission of the act, that the criminal act was not part of a pattern of criminal behavior and, in view of the history of the offender, is not likely to be repeated.

If the court is of the opinion based on specific factors set forth in the district attorney's memorandum that the interests of justice would best be served by removal of the action to the family court, a plea of guilty of a crime or act for which the defendant is not criminally responsible may be entered pursuant to subdivision three or four of this section, except that a thirteen year old charged with the crime of murder in the second degree may only plead to a designated felony act, as defined in subdivision eight of section 301.2 of the family court act.

Upon accepting any such plea, the court must specify upon the record the portion or portions of the district attorney's statement the court is relying upon as the basis of its opinion and that it believes the interests of justice would best be served by removal of the proceeding to the family court. Such plea shall then be deemed to be a juvenile delinquency fact determination and the court upon entry thereof must direct that the action be removed to the family court in accordance with the provisions of article seven hundred twenty-five of this chapter.

(h) where the indictment charges the class E felony offense of aggravated harassment of an employee by an inmate as defined in section 240.32 of the penal law, then a plea of guilty must include at least a plea of guilty to a class E felony.

6. The defendant may, with both the permission of the court and the consent of the people, enter a plea of not responsible by reason of mental disease or defect to the indictment in the manner prescribed in section 220.15 of this chapter.

Amended by L. 1973, Chs. 276, 277, 1051; L. 1974, Ch. 367; L. 1976, Ch. 480; L. 1978, Ch. 481; L. 1979, Chs. 410, 411; L. 1980, Chs. 233, 234, 548; L. 1982, Ch. 920; L. 1991, Ch. 496; L. 1995, Ch. 1, § 10, amending subd. 5(e); L. 1996, Ch. 92, § 3, adding subd. 5(h), eff. June 5, 1996; L. 1999, Ch. 33, § 5, eff. Nov. 1, 1999, amending subd. 5(d)(iv); L. 2000, Ch. 227, § 1, eff. Nov. 1, 2000, amending subd. 5(d)(iv); L. 2003, Ch. 264, § 42, eff. Nov. 1, 2003, amending subd. 5(g)(iii); L. 2004, Ch. 738, § 16, eff. Dec. 14, 2004, amending subd. 5(a)(i) and repealing subd. 5(a)(ii).

ANNOTATIONS

Alford plea.—A conviction premised on an *Alford* plea may generally be used for the same purposes as any other conviction, and a defendant may be properly cross-examined for impeachment purposes about a previous conviction even if it arose from an *Alford* plea. People v. Miller, 91 N.Y.2d 372, 670 N.Y.S.2d 978, 694 N.E.2d 61 (1998).

—A court is not obligated to accept an *Alford* plea, which is a plea of guilty to less than the entire indictment without admitting guilt. People v. Moret, 290 A.D.2d 250, 735 N.Y.S.2d 535 (1st Dept. 2002).

—In an unusual *Alford* plea agreement, defendant agreed that prior to sentencing, he would undergo a polygraph exam to be performed by the District Attorney's office, and that the charges would be dismissed if the exam revealed that defendant's denial of involvement in the charged robbery was truthful, and plea would stand if defendant's denials were found to be false. Defendant failed the polygraph, and court was not obligated to consider the results of a second test that the defendant independently underwent, because that test was not contemplated under the terms of the plea agreement. People v. Martin, 235 A.D.2d 551, 653 N.Y.S.2d 863 (2d Dept. 1997).

—Court did not improperly accept defendant's *Alford* plea. The defendant is not required to make a factual recitation confirming guilt. The court may accept the plea if satisfied that there is a sufficient factual basis for the plea based on its review of the information before it, and protestations of innocence do not preclude acceptance of an *Alford* plea. People v. Stewart, 307 A.D.2d 533, 763 N.Y.S.2d 688 (3d Dept. 2003).

—In New York, *Alford* plea is allowed only if it is the product of a voluntary and rational choice and the record before the court contains strong evidence of actual guilt. People v. Oberdorf, 5 A.D.3d 1000, 773 N.Y.S.2d 334 (4th Dept. 2004).

Constitutionality; subd. 5(e).—The provisions of the New York death penalty statute, specifically, CPL §§ 220.10(5)(e) and 220.30(3)(b)(vii), are unconstitutional for the same reason as the Federal Kidnaping Act—because by statutory mandate, the death penalty hangs over only those who exercise their constitutional rights to maintain innocence and demand a jury trial; accordingly, the court was compelled by *United States v. Jackson,* 390 U.S. 570, to invalidate those provisions. However, CPL § 220.60(2)(a) was not limited to first degree murder cases, and it does not, in the absence of CPL § 220.10(5)(e),

violate *Jackson.* Thus, CPL § 220.60(2)(a) does not need to be stricken. Hynes v. Tomei, 92 N.Y.2d 613, 684 N.Y.S.2d 177, 706 N.E.2d 1201 (1998), *cert. denied,* 527 U.S. 1015 (1999).

—CPL §§ 220.10(5)(e), 220.30(3)(b)(vii), and 220.60 are not unconstitutional to the extent that they provide that a sentence of death for first degree murder could only be imposed upon a conviction after trial and could not be imposed after a guilty plea, which can be entered only with People's consent and court's approval. People v. McIntosh, 173 Misc. 2d 727, 662 N.Y.S.2d 214 (Dutchess Co. Ct. 1997).

Guilty plea; general.—CPL § 300.40(3)(b) deals only with trials, and has no application to convictions obtained on plea of guilty; CPL § 220.10 permits the court to accept a plea of guilty to the entire indictment, even when a series of inclusory counts is involved. People v. Walton, 41 N.Y.2d 880, 393 N.Y.S.2d 979, 362 N.E.2d 610 (1977).

Guilty plea; without court's consent.—A defendant has the statutory right to plead guilty to the entire indictment without the permission of the court or the consent of the People. People v. White, 7 A.D.3d 471, 777 N.Y.S.2d 544 (3d Dept. 2004).

Effect of guilty plea.—A defendant who pleads guilty and thereafter, prior to sentencing, testifies in the Grand Jury concerning the same offense does not acquire statutory immunity from prosecution or punishment for the offense to which he has pleaded guilty. People v. Sobotker, 61 N.Y.2d 44, 471 N.Y.S.2d 78, 459 N.E.2d 187 (1984).

—A plea of guilty "is more than a confession which admits that the accused did various acts, it is itself a conviction [and] nothing [else] remains but to give judgment and determine punishment." People v. Lynn, 28 N.Y.2d 196, 321 N.Y.S.2d 74, 269 N.E.2d 794 (1971), *citing Boykin v. Alabama,* 395 U.S. 238, 242, 89 S. Ct. 1709, 1711, 23 L. Ed. 2d 274 (1969).

—Having pleaded guilty, defendant's conviction rested upon the sufficiency of his plea and not the legal or constitutional sufficiency of any proceedings which might have led to his conviction after trial. People v. Garcia, 172 A.D.2d 330, 568 N.Y.S.2d 402 (1st Dept. 1991).

Effect of guilty plea; waiver of issues.—A defendant forfeits a hearsay defect in an accusatory instrument by pleading guilty, even though an information should be based on non-hearsay allegations, because a purported hearsay defect in an accusatory instrument is nonjurisdictional. People v. Konieczny, 2 N.Y.3d 569, 780 N.Y.S.2d 546, 813 N.E.2d 626 (2004) (citing People v. Keizer, 100 N.Y.2d 114, 760 N.Y.S.2d 720, 790 N.E.2d 1149 (2003)).

—By his guilty plea, the defendant waived the issue of whether the People had established a proper foundation on the accuracy of the DuPont Automatic Clinical Analyzer used for blood alcohol tests. People v. Campbell, 73 N.Y.2d 481, 541 N.Y.S.2d 756, 539 N.E.2d 584 (1989).

—Defendant by his plea of guilty forfeited any claim of transactional immunity. People v. Flihan, 73 N.Y.2d 729, 535 N.Y.S.2d 590, 532 N.E.2d 96 (1988).

—By pleading guilty, defendant waived his claim that his arrest and lineup identification resulted from DNA evidence that had been obtained in violation of the sealing requirements of CPL § 160.50, and in any event, a violation of CPL § 160.50 would not entitle defendant to suppression of the lineup identification or dismissal of the indictment. People v. Mosquea, 18 A.D.3d 228, 794 N.Y.S.2d 51 (1st Dept. 2005).

—A statutory speedy trial violation is waived by defendant's guilty plea. People v. Jackson, 178 A.D.2d 305, 577 N.Y.S.2d 609 (1st Dept. 1991); People v. Mobley, 206 A.D.2d 681, 614 N.Y.S.2d 795 (3d Dept. 1994); People v. Campbell, 188 A.D.2d 754, 591 N.Y.S.2d 557 (3d Dept. 1992).

—A defendant cannot preserve a legal issue otherwise forfeited by a guilty plea merely by securing the acquiescence of the court and the prosecutor. People v. Nelson, 173 A.D.2d 205, 569 N.Y.S.2d 86 (1st Dept.), *lv. denied,* 78 N.Y.2d 956 (1991).

—By his plea of guilty, the defendant waived his claim that he was deprived of his right to testify before the Grand Jury. People v. Roberts, 163 A.D.2d 68, 557 N.Y.S.2d 85 (1st Dept. 1990); People v. Wallace, 188 A.D.2d 499, 591 N.Y.S.2d 60 (2d Dept. 1992); People v. Bernard, 207 A.D.2d 927, 616 N.Y.S.2d 415 (3d Dept. 1994); People v. Torra, 191 A.D.2d 738, 594 N.Y.S.2d 419 (3d Dept.), *lv. denied,* 81 N.Y.2d 1021 (1993); People v. Wheeler, 176 A.D.2d 1133, 575 N.Y.S.2d 951 (3d Dept. 1991), *lv. denied,* 79 N.Y.2d 924 (1992).

—By his guilty plea the defendant waived the claim that the court unduly restricted his cross-examination of witness during trial which terminated upon the plea of guilty. People v. Robles, 160 A.D.2d 252, 553 N.Y.S.2d 360 (1st Dept.), *lv. denied,* 75 N.Y.2d 923 (1990).

—By pleading guilty defendant has forfeited his right to challenge the geographic jurisdiction of New York County. People v. Rivera, 156 A.D.2d 177, 548 N.Y.S.2d 439 (1st Dept. 1989).

—Defendant's plea of guilty constituted a waiver of his claim that the statute in question was unconstitutional as applied to the defendant because of the Federal Supremacy Clause of the U.S. Constitution. People v. Greenfield, 100 A.D.2d 752, 474 N.Y.S.2d 19 (1st Dept. 1984).

—By pleading guilty, the defendant effectively waived appellate review of any alleged *Rosario* violation. People v. Agyman, 204 A.D.2d 731, 613 N.Y.S.2d 27 (2d Dept. 1994).

—By pleading guilty, the defendant forfeited her right to challenge the denial of her motion to dismiss the indictment in the interest of justice. People v. Travis, 205 A.D.2d 648, 613 N.Y.S.2d 252 (2d Dept. 1994); People v. Guerra, 123 A.D.2d 882, 507 N.Y.S.2d 660 (2d Dept. 1986) (pleading guilty to selling more than two ounces of cocaine).

—The defendant's claims regarding the adequacy of the indictment and the court's failure to hold a requested pretrial hearing did not relate to jurisdictional defects or fundamental matters and thus were waived by reason of the defendant's guilty plea. People v. Meslin, 201 A.D.2d 744, 608 N.Y.S.2d 484 (2d Dept.), *lv. denied,* 83 N.Y.2d 813 (1994).

—Since the defendant pleaded guilty, he waived any claim regarding the sufficiency of the evidence before the Grand Jury. People v. Phillips, 201 A.D.2d 255, 607 N.Y.S.2d 266 (1st Dept. 1994); People v. Jang, 17 A.D.3d 693, 793 N.Y.S.2d 540 (2d Dept. 2005); People v. Contestabile, 202 A.D.2d 442, 608 N.Y.S.2d 512 (2d Dept. 1994); People v. Pucak, 187 A.D.2d 934, 591 N.Y.S.2d 114 (4th Dept. 1992), *lv. denied,* 81 N.Y.2d 793 (1993).

—The defendant, by pleading guilty, forfeited his right to challenge the denial of his *Clayton* motion. People v. Merlo, 195 A.D.2d 576, 600 N.Y.S.2d 494 (2d Dept. 1993).

—A defendant may not seek to review issues of factual guilt following an admission of factual guilt. People v. Torres, 171 A.D.2d 825, 567 N.Y.S.2d 527 (2d Dept.), *lv. denied,* 78 N.Y.2d 927 (1991); People v. Freeman, 198 A.D.2d 725, 604 N.Y.S.2d 629 (3d Dept. 1993), *lv. denied,* 83 N.Y.2d 804 (1994); People v. Duboy, 150 A.D.2d 882, 540 N.Y.S.2d 905 (3d Dept. 1989).

—By pleading guilty the defendant waived his right to challenge the court's adverse *Sandoval* ruling. People v. Henderson, 170 A.D.2d 532, 566 N.Y.S.2d 92 (2d Dept. 1991); People v. Coon, 161 A.D.2d 657, 555 N.Y.S.2d 434 (2d Dept. 1990); People v. Johnson, 141 A.D.2d 848, 530 N.Y.S.2d 189 (2d Dept. 1988); People v. Emerson, 141 A.D.2d 924, 530 N.Y.S.2d 283 (3d Dept. 1988).

—The defendant's guilty plea forfeited his claim that his rights under CPL § 30.30 were violated. People v. Landy, 177 A.D.2d 653, 576 N.Y.S.2d 355 (2d Dept. 1991), *lv. denied,* 80 N.Y.2d 931 (1992); People v. Sharcoff, 137 A.D.2d 567, 524 N.Y.S.2d 306 (2d Dept. 1988); People v. Hedayat, 151 A.D.2d 1043, 542 N.Y.S.2d 98 (4th Dept. 1989).

—By his plea of guilty the defendant waived his claim that he was denied *Brady* material. People v. Williams, 156 A.D.2d 497, 548 N.Y.S.2d 772 (2d Dept. 1989); People v. Day, 150 A.D.2d 595, 541 N.Y.S.2d 463 (2d Dept. 1989).

—By pleading guilty the defendant forfeited his right to appellate review of the denial of his motion to sever the counts of the indictment. People v. Reyes, 156 A.D.2d 397, 548 N.Y.S.2d 347 (2d Dept. 1989).

—Where defendant pleaded guilty before his suppression motion was decided, appellate review of the issue was precluded. People v. Williams, 146 A.D.2d 724, 537 N.Y.S.2d 545 (2d Dept. 1989); People v. Mattison, 182 A.D.2d 917, 582 N.Y.S.2d 823 (3d Dept.), *lv. denied,* 80 N.Y.2d 896 (1992).

—By pleading guilty, the defendant waived his right to appeal the denial of his motion to dismiss the charge against him. People v. DeLise, 149 A.D.2d 724, 540 N.Y.S.2d 330 (2d Dept. 1989).

—Defendant's claim that the hearing court improperly denied his motion for a separate trial was waived by his entry of his guilty plea. People v. Ondrizek, 141 A.D.2d 770, 529 N.Y.S.2d 596 (2d Dept. 1988).

—By pleading guilty, defendant forfeited review of his claim that the prosecutor's conduct before the Grand Jury impaired its integrity. People v. Bowen, 122 A.D.2d 64, 504 N.Y.S.2d 480 (2d Dept. 1986).

—Defendant's contention addressing the arresting officer's lack of geographic jurisdiction was waived by his guilty plea. People v. Alfone, 206 A.D.2d 775, 615 N.Y.S.2d 110 (3d Dept. 1994).

—The right to have counsel present at a psychiatric examination does not survive a guilty plea. People v. Reiblein, 200 A.D.2d 281, 613 N.Y.S.2d 789 (3d Dept.), *lv. denied,* 84 N.Y.2d 831 (1994).

—By pleading guilty defendant waived any error made by court in allowing amendment of the indictment. People v. Hunt, 148 A.D.2d 836, 539 N.Y.S.2d 109 (3d Dept. 1989).

—Defendant's plea of guilty constituted a waiver of his right to challenge the propriety of his arrest on appeal. People v. Homer, 87 A.D.2d 687, 448 N.Y.S.2d 878 (3d Dept. 1982).

—By pleading guilty, defendant forfeited his right to raise the issue of whether he was entitled to notice of the Grand Jury proceedings. People v. Roberson, 149 A.D.2d 926, 540 N.Y.S.2d 60 (4th Dept. 1989).

—Defendant's *Batson* claim is subsumed within the waiver of his right to a jury trial and does not survive a guilty plea. People v. Green, 75 N.Y.2d 902, 554 N.Y.S.2d 821, 553 N.E.2d 1331 (1990), *cert. denied,* 498 U.S. 860 (1991).

—A constitutional speedy trial claim survives a guilty plea or appeal waiver, but is foreclosed by failure to make a speedy trial motion. People v. Arac, 297 A.D.2d 560, 747 N.Y.S.2d 87 (1st Dept. 2002).

—By pleading guilty, defendant forfeited his right to challenge the propriety of the grand jury proceedings. People v. Batista, 299 A.D.2d 270, 753 N.Y.S.2d 47 (1st Dept. 2002).

—By pleading guilty, defendant forfeited review of the court's *Molineux* ruling. People v. Brown, 305 A.D.2d 1068, 759 N.Y.S.2d 830 (4th Dept. 2003).

Guilty plea; no waiver of issues.—By his plea of guilty the defendant waived his speedy trial claim pursuant to CPL § 30.30; however, defendant's claim pursuant to CPL § 30.20 and the Federal Constitution survived the guilty plea. People v. Rozell, 162 A.D.2d 732, 557 N.Y.S.2d 129 (2d Dept. 1990), *lv. denied,* 77 N.Y.2d 843 (1991).

—Defendant's challenge to the legality of her sentence cannot be waived by her guilty plea. People v. Nephew, 200 A.D.2d 799, 606 N.Y.S.2d 452 (3d Dept. 1994).

—Court rejected the People's contention that defendant waived his right to appeal his sentencing as a predicate felon without a hearing when he accepted the plea agreement; the right to challenge the legality of a sentence is not subject to waiver. People v. Kilgore, 199 A.D.2d 1008, 608 N.Y.S.2d 12 (4th Dept. 1994).

Guilty plea; factual basis.—Where during the plea colloquy the defendant said that he fired three shots at the victim in his car, one could readily infer an intent to commit murder and the court was not required to inquire further before accepting the guilty plea. People v. Pascale, 66 A.D.2d 653, 410 N.Y.S.2d 818 (1st Dept. 1978), *aff'd,* 48 N.Y.2d 997, 425 N.Y.S.2d 547, 401 N.E.2d 904 (1980).

—A plea of guilty will be sustained in the absence of a factual recitation of the underlying circumstances of the crime if "there is no suggestion in the record or dehors the record that the guilty plea was improvident or baseless" especially when the defendant was represented by counsel and made no effort to withdraw the plea. People v. Moore, 91 A.D.2d 1050, 458 N.Y.S.2d 649 (2d Dept. 1983).

—A challenge to a plea of guilty based on an insufficient factual recitation after verdict is not preserved for appellate review, unlike a challenge based upon constitutional grounds, if there is no suggestion in the record or dehors the record that the guilty plea was improvident or baseless. People v. Perkins, 89 A.D.2d 956, 454 N.Y.S.2d 100 (2d Dept. 1982).

—Where the defendant's plea was knowing, voluntary and the result of a bargained agreement with the District Attorney, a factual basis for the particular crime confessed was not necessary. People v. Fehr, 170 A.D.2d 890, 566 N.Y.S.2d 721 (3d Dept. 1991).

—Despite a failure to make a postallocution motion, a defendant may challenge the sufficiency of the allocution if, as here, the trial court accepted the guilty plea after defendant's factual recitation negated an essential element of the crime, thereby casting significant doubt on defendant's guilt. People v. Pangburn, 298 A.D.2d 989, 747 N.Y.S.2d 672, *plea vacated*, 298 A.D.2d 990, 748 N.Y.S.2d 303 (4th Dept. 2002).

—Where the defendant's recitation of the facts of the underlying crime which he pleads to clearly cast doubt upon the defendant's guilt or otherwise calls into question the voluntariness of the plea, the trial court has a duty to inquire further whether the plea is knowing and voluntary. People v. Davis, 176 A.D.2d 1236, 576 N.Y.S.2d 731 (4th Dept. 1991).

—Defendant's plea should not have been accepted without further inquiry by the court because defendant's statement that he displayed only a "fake" gun should have alerted the court to the fact that defendant might have a valid defense to first degree robbery. People v. Moye, 171 A.D.2d 1036, 569 N.Y.S.2d 38 (4th Dept. 1991).

—It was error for court to accept defendant's plea to robbery in the first degree where defendant stated during the allocution that the gun used was not loaded, thereby alerting the court to facts supporting the affirmative defense established by statute. People v. Sobczak, 105 A.D.2d 1053, 482 N.Y.S.2d 171 (4th Dept. 1984).

Guilty plea; factual basis, lesser included offense.—Since the defendant bargained for a guilty plea to a lesser crime than charged, and was aware of the circumstances of the crime with which he was charged, the trial court was not required to elicit a factual basis for the crime to which the defendant pleaded guilty. People v. Jones, 166 A.D.2d 218, 564 N.Y.S.2d 93 (1st Dept.), *lv. denied,* 76 N.Y.2d 987 (1990).

—Since defendant pleaded guilty to a lesser crime than that with which he was charged he could not challenge the factual basis for the plea. People v. Risalek, 172 A.D.2d 870, 568 N.Y.S.2d 172 (3d Dept.), *lv. denied,* 78 N.Y.2d 1080 (1991).

Guilty plea; factual basis, preservation.—Defendant's contention that the allocution upon his plea of guilty was insufficient to establish all of the elements of the crime was not preserved for appeal due to failure of defendant to move to withdraw such plea at the time of sentence. People v. Harris, 100 A.D.2d 852, 474 N.Y.S.2d 99 (2d Dept. 1984).

—By failing to make a motion to withdraw his plea, defendant failed to preserve for appellate review the issue of the sufficiency of the allocution. People v. Lawrence, 100 A.D.2d 944, 474 N.Y.S.2d 848 (2d Dept. 1984).

Guilty plea; allocution.—Where defendant's attorney, prior to a guilty plea, informed defendant that the attorney planned to join the staff of the prosecution after the plea, and the plea bargain was reasonable from defendant's point of view at the time made, there is no "significant possibility" of an actual conflict and the Trial Judge need not probe as deeply as would be required in a case of joint representation to assure that defendant's decision is an informed one. People v. Jackson, 60 N.Y.2d 848, 470 N.Y.S.2d 136, 458 N.E.2d 377 (1983).

—There is no uniform catechism of pleading defendants. People v. Lau, 171 A.D.2d 580, 567 N.Y.S.2d 449 (1st Dept. 1991), *lv. denied,* 78 N.Y.2d 969 (1992).

—Defense counsel does not have the duty to warn a defendant of all collateral consequences of a plea such as deportation. People v. Avila, 177 A.D.2d 426, 576 N.Y.S.2d 534 (1st Dept. 1991), *lv. denied,* 79 N.Y.2d 918 (1992).

—Deportation is a collateral consequence of a criminal conviction, and a court is not required to inform the defendant as to this consequence before accepting a guilty plea. People v. Williams, 189 A.D.2d 910, 592 N.Y.S.2d 471 (2d Dept. 1993).

—There is no general requirement that during a guilty plea allocution a court must inquire into a defendant's possible affirmative defenses unless something on the record specifically suggests an affirmative defense may exist. People v. McAllister, 114 A.D.2d 910, 495 N.Y.S.2d 81 (2d Dept. 1985).

—The privilege against self-incrimination, the right to a jury trial, and the right of confrontation are all involved in the waiver that occurs when a plea of guilty is entered, and such a waiver cannot be presumed from a "silent" record. However, from all of the circumstances of this plea, it was readily apparent that the record was not silent, but rather one which clearly showed that defendant's plea was intelligently and voluntarily entered. People *ex rel.* Woodruff v. Mancusi, 41 A.D.2d 12, 341 N.Y.S.2d 663 (4th Dept. 1973), *dism'd,* 34 N.Y.2d 951, 359 N.Y.S.2d 566, 316 N.E.2d 879 (1974).

Guilty plea; voluntariness.—The failure to advise a defendant of post-release supervision mandates reversal. People v. Feehan, 18 A.D.3d 279, 796 N.Y.S.2d 42 (1st Dept. 2005).

—While it is the preferred practice that a defendant be advised of the post-release supervision aspect of his sentence prior to entering a plea, any failure of defense counsel to advise defendant of this was harmless because knowledge of the PRS component would not have affected defendant's decision to plead guilty. People v. Ammarito, 306 A.D.2d 99, 763 N.Y.S.2d 244 (1st Dept. 2003).

—Court properly declined to accept defendant's offer to plead guilty during trial after defendant had wavered back and forth between accepting and rejecting the plea offer; court found that the defendant's extreme vacillation undermined the voluntariness of the plea. People v. Hankins, 286 A.D.2d 639, 730 N.Y.S.2d 322 (1st Dept. 2001).

—Record did not support defendant's claim that AIDS-related mental problems rendered his plea involuntary. People v. Hernandez, 207 A.D.2d 659, 616 N.Y.S.2d 41 (1st Dept. 1994).

—Defendant's comments at sentencing that he was ill and did not know what was going on provided no reason to believe that he was incapacitated or otherwise unable to understand his circumstances at the time of the plea. People v. Sarelakos, 197 A.D.2d 460, 603 N.Y.S.2d 6 (1st Dept. 1993).

—It is not coercive for a court to inform a defendant as to the possible sentence available under the indictment. People v. Stephens, 188 A.D.2d 345, 591 N.Y.S.2d 25 (1st Dept. 1992).

—Court rejected claim that plea was involuntary because of the court's failure to advise him that he could be deported as a result of pleading guilty. People v. Ford, 205 A.D.2d 798, 613 N.Y.S.2d 688 (2d Dept. 1994), *aff'd,* 86 N.Y.2d 397 (1995).

—The record as a whole indicated that defendant voluntarily, knowingly and intelligently pleaded guilty although it indicated that the defendant complained of dizziness at the time of the plea, claiming he had been hit on the head in the holding cell, since the court thoroughly questioned defendant as to whether the incident had any effect on his plea and the defendant unequivocally responded that it did not. People v. Sileo, 117 A.D.2d 690, 498 N.Y.S.2d 430 (2d Dept. 1986).

—Defendant's plea was vacated where there was a possibility that he was confused when entering his guilty plea and that he lacked the requisite knowledge of the robbery at the time he drove the "getaway" car. People v. McKay, 85 A.D.2d 746, 445 N.Y.S.2d 799 (2d Dept. 1981).

—As a general rule, a court should always advise a defendant who is pleading guilty of the post-release supervision component of the sentence. People v. Van Deusen, 19 A.D.3d 747, 796 N.Y.S.2d 721 (3d Dept. 2005).

—The fact that defendant was required to accept the plea offer within a short period of time did not render the plea coercive; the prosecutor is free to dictate the terms under which a plea will be accepted. People v. Eaddy, 200 A.D.2d 896, 606 N.Y.S.2d 928 (3d Dept. 1994).

—Defendant's plea was valid despite the fact that he was using Dilantin. People v. Marziale, 182 A.D.2d 1035, 583 N.Y.S.2d 36 (3d Dept. 1992).

Brady.—A defendant was not entitled to withdraw his guilty plea upon showing that the State failed to disclose that the complaining witness had died four days before entry of the plea. Citing the Supreme Court's decision in Brady v. United States, 397 U.S. 742, 90 S. Ct. 1463, 25 L. Ed. 2d 747 (1970), the Court stated that "[a] defendant is not entitled to withdraw his plea merely because he discovers . . . that his calculus misapprehended the quality of the State's case." The Court noted in the instant case that the silence of the prosecutor, where there was no affirmative duty to speak, could not be equated with cases of positive misstatement which result in a right to withdraw a guilty plea. People v. Jones, 44 N.Y.2d 76, 404 N.Y.S.2d 85, 375 N.E.2d 41, *cert. denied,* 439 U.S. 846 (1978).

First-degree murder cases.—A defendant arraigned upon an indictment charging, inter alia, first-degree murder, may not plead to the entire indictment and avoid the possibility of the death penalty verdict until the District Attorney has either declined to file his CPL § 250.40 notice on the record, consents to such plea, or the 120-day period with any court-ordered extensions has expired. People v. Schroedel, 182 Misc. 2d 154, 697 N.Y.S.2d 904 (Co. Ct. Sullivan Co. 1999), *cert. denied,* 531 U.S. 860 (2000).

Guilty plea; excessive sentence.—It was not error for the court to sentence defendant to imprisonment upon plea of guilty to a misdemeanor in full satisfaction of 19 felony indictments where the court made clear at the time of the plea that it was not bound by the prosecutor's recommendation that the defendant be placed on probation. People v. Maney, 45 A.D.2d 765, 356 N.Y.S.2d 892 (2d Dept. 1974), *aff'd*, 37 N.Y.2d 229, 371 N.Y.S.2d 901, 333 N.E.2d 174 (1975).

—Having received the benefits of the plea bargain and a sentence in accordance with his plea bargain and within statutory guidelines, defendant should be bound by its terms and cannot be heard to complain that the sentence imposed was unduly harsh or severe. People v. Zuluaga, 158 A.D.2d 439, 552 N.Y.S.2d 12 (1st Dept.), *lv. denied*, 76 N.Y.2d 745 (1990).

—Where defendant entered his plea of guilty with a full understanding that he would receive the sentence which was thereafter imposed, he had no basis to challenge the sentence as excessive. People v. Pavesi, 144 A.D.2d 392, 533 N.Y.S.2d 784 (2d Dept. 1988).

—Sentence of 3 to 9 years imprisonment upon the defendant's conviction of a class B violent felony offense was a proper exercise of the trial court's discretion where the sentence was the result of a negotiated plea agreement which substantially reduced the defendant's sentencing exposure. People v. Perkins, 130 A.D.2d 521, 515 N.Y.S.2d 100 (2d Dept. 1987).

—Where the defendant received the sentence promised by the plea court, he had no basis to complain that his sentence is excessive. People v. Allrod, 122 A.D.2d 271, 505 N.Y.S.2d 182 (2d Dept. 1986).

—A defendant who has been permitted to plead guilty to a lesser charge in satisfaction of all the crimes charged, cannot claim that the imposition of the maximum sentence for the crime to which he pled guilty was unjust. People v. Colon, 91 A.D.2d 641, 456 N.Y.S.2d 824 (2d Dept. 1982).

Improper plea.—Criminal sale of a controlled substance in the third degree is not a lesser included offense of criminal possession under the general definition, and it is omitted from the classes of crimes deemed to be lesser included offenses of criminal possession for plea purposes; thus, defendant's plea to criminal sale of a controlled substance in the third degree conflicted with the express plea constraints set forth in CPL § 220.10. People v. Johnson, 89 N.Y.2d 905, 653 N.Y.S.2d 265, 675 N.E.2d 1217 (1996).

Plea bargain; general.—In essence, a defendant forfeits the benefit of the deal by electing to go to trial. People v. Simon, 180 A.D.2d 866, 580 N.Y.S.2d 493 (3d Dept. 1992).

—Restitution may be an element of a plea bargain package. People v. Connell, 188 A.D.2d 825, 591 N.Y.S.2d 563 (3d Dept. 1992), *lv. denied*, 81 N.Y.2d 883 (1993).

Plea bargain; breach of promise.—Statement by prosecutor at sentence implying that defendant deserved a substantial prison term, violated his plea bargaining agreement not to take a position at sentence; sentence imposed was vacated and case remitted for sentencing before a different judge. People v. Tindle, 61 N.Y.2d 752, 472 N.Y.S.2d 919, 460 N.E.2d 1354 (1984).

—Defendant is entitled to specific performance of a plea bargain agreement requiring defendant to testify on behalf of the prosecution at the trial of an accomplice, which defendant did, notwithstanding the fact that the prosecutor had transmitted incorrect information to the court as to sentence recommendations for two other accomplices, that counsel was informed of Court's intentions not to abide by the agreement prior to testimony of defendant at accomplice's trial, and that defendant had been arrested and/or convicted in subsequent non-serious criminal cases. People v. Danny G., 61 N.Y.2d 169, 473 N.Y.S.2d 131, 461 N.E.2d 268 (1984).

—If a special prosecutor makes a representation within the scope of his power, and defendant acts in reliance upon the representation, defendant may be entitled to have the representation enforced, at least where merely vacating the plea would result in significant prejudice to defendant. Chaipis v. State Liquor Authority, 44 N.Y.2d 57, 404 N.Y.S.2d 76, 375 N.E.2d 32 (1978).

—Where a court finds that it cannot honor its sentence promise, it must give the pleading defendant the option of either accepting an enhanced sentence on the plea or withdrawing the plea and going to trial. People v. Easterling, 191 A.D.2d 579, 594 N.Y.S.2d 805 (2d Dept. 1993).

—Where court failed to keep original sentence promise, proper remedy was merely to vacate sentence rather than permit withdrawal of the plea; since the indictments under which the prosecution arose were more than four years old, it would prejudice the People to allow the defendant to withdraw his plea and go to trial. People v. White, 144 A.D.2d 711, 535 N.Y.S.2d 72 (2d Dept. 1988).

—Where defendant rejected the earlier plea offer, he was not entitled to specific performance as to that offer. People v. Hamilton, 192 A.D.2d 738, 596 N.Y.S.2d 175 (3d Dept. 1993).

—Where the defendant did not perform any services for the prosecutor under the terms of the original plea agreement and the defendant did not suffer any detriment in reliance upon the agreements, he was not entitled to specific performance. People v. German, 153 A.D.2d 588, 544 N.Y.S.2d 223 (2d Dept. 1989).

Plea bargain; off-the-record promises.—Defendant was not entitled to enforcement of an off-the-record agreement between him and the prosecutor which was never approved by the court. People v. Huertas, 85 N.Y.2d 898, 626 N.Y.S.2d 750, 650 N.E.2d 408 (1995).

—Defendants were not entitled to specific performance of an off-the-record plea bargain agreement which was withdrawn by the prosecution prior to the entry of the agreement on the record. People v. Hood, 62 N.Y.2d 863, 477 N.Y.S.2d 621, 466 N.E.2d 161 (1984).

—In order to avoid disputes as to what promises were in fact made when a guilty plea was entered, the terms of the plea agreement should be stated explicitly and unambiguously on the record. People v. Rosenberg, 148 A.D.2d 346, 538 N.Y.S.2d 558 (1st Dept. 1989).

—Promises concerning a plea agreement which are not placed on the record are not enforceable. District Attorney of Kings County v. Roman, 141 A.D.2d 601, 529 N.Y.S.2d 522 (2d Dept. 1988).

Plea bargain; breach of condition.—Where defendant publicly repudiated his Grand Jury testimony that was provided pursuant to plea agreement, he was not entitled to specific performance of that agreement; moreover, the People were properly permitted to use the defendant's Grand Jury testimony against him. People v. Curdgel, 83 N.Y.2d 862, 611 N.Y.S.2d 827, 634 N.E.2d 199 (1994).

—A sentence can be enhanced if defendant violates explicit conditions of plea negotiation. People v. Decoste, 203 A.D.2d 726, 611 N.Y.S.2d 40 (3d Dept. 1994).

Plea bargain; People's consent.—When the People do not consent thereto, a court is without power or jurisdiction to accept a defendant's plea to less than the full indictment. Morgenthau v. Gold, 189 A.D.2d 617, 592 N.Y.S.2d 696 (1st Dept. 1993).

—The People have the power to specify terms and conditions under which they will consent to a guilty plea to a lesser included count. People v. Perez, 156 A.D.2d 7, 553 N.Y.S.2d 659 (1st Dept. 1990).

—"Since the record does not support the defendant's claim that he was willing to enter a plea to the entire indictment, the trial court properly declined to permit the plea in the absence of the prosecutor's consent." People v. Machare, 264 A.D.2d 487, 695 N.Y.S.2d 112 (2d Dept. 1999).

—A prosecutor may not be held to any aspect of a plea bargain to which he or she has not, in fact, consented. People v. Burton, 191 A.D.2d 703, 595 N.Y.S.2d 512 (2d Dept.), *lv. denied*, 81 N.Y.2d 1011 (1993).

—Court erred in concluding that it was without discretion to consider a sentence below that negotiated through plea discussion; however, if court chooses to impose a more lenient sentence it may entertain an application by the People to withdraw consent to the plea agreement. People v. Montoya, 138 A.D.2d 528, 526 N.Y.S.2d 35 (2d Dept. 1988).

—Defendant is not entitled as a matter of right to plead guilty to a lesser included offense of the crime charged (CPL § 220.10[3]). Turdo v. Rubin, 77 A.D.2d 608, 430 N.Y.S.2d 360 (2d Dept. 1980).

—Where defendant pleaded to the entire indictment, the consent of the People to the plea was not required. Carney v. Feldstein, 193 A.D.2d 1016, 597 N.Y.S.2d 982 (3d Dept. 1993).

—Court refused to endorse a court's general policy of not permitting plea bargains on the eve of trial. People v. Compton,

157 A.D.2d 903, 550 N.Y.S.2d 148 (3d Dept.), *lv. denied*, 75 N.Y.2d 918 (1990).

—It is well settled that a defendant has no absolute right to have his plea accepted by the court and that the decision whether to accept a reduced plea is a matter within the court's discretion. People v. Williams, 158 A.D.2d 930, 551 N.Y.S.2d 94 (4th Dept.), *lv. denied*, 75 N.Y.2d 971 (1990).

—Defendant's constitutional rights were not violated by the People's withdrawal of their prior plea offer; a prosecutor has broad discretion whether to grant permission to enter a lesser plea and may withdraw a prior plea offer. People v. Brown, 144 A.D.2d 975, 534 N.Y.S.2d 278 (4th Dept. 1988).

—There is no constitutional right to a plea bargain. People v. Barnwell, 143 Misc. 2d 922, 541 N.Y.S.2d 664 (Crim. Ct. N.Y. Co. 1989).

Plea bargain; restrictions.—Acceptance by court of guilty plea to class D Felony was a nullity where trial court has no authority to accept guilty plea to less than class A Felony by virtue of CPL § 20.10(5)(a) and as the order setting aside the defective plea was not an acquittal, the defendant was not subjected to double jeopardy. People v. Bartley, 60 A.D.2d 283, 401 N.Y.S.2d 71 (1st Dept. 1977), *aff'd*, 47 N.Y.2d 965, 419 N.Y.S.2d 956, 393 N.E.2d 1029 (1979).

—CPL § 220.10(5)(e) is constitutional as there is a rational basis in requiring a dependent charged by indictment with a class B or class C violent felony offense, and who wished to plead guilty, to plead guilty to at least a violent felony offense, while no such restrictions are placed on an individual charged with the same offense by felony complaint. People v. Elliby, 80 A.D.2d 875, 436 N.Y.S.2d 784 (2d Dept. 1981).

—The plea-bargaining restrictions contained in CPL § 220.10 are not triggered by the filing of a felony complaint. People v. McLaurin, 260 A.D.2d 944, 690 N.Y.S.2d 289 (3d Dept. 1999).

—Defendant's negotiated plea of guilty to robbery third degree, in full satisfaction of the indictment was illegal and must be vacated since robbery first degree and burglary first degree are class B violent felonies and under CPL § 220.10(5)(d) defendant was required to plead to a violent felony offense and robbery in the third degree is not such an offense. People v. Hicks, 79 A.D.2d 887, 434 N.Y.S.2d 530 (4th Dept. 1980).

Plea bargain; waiver of right to appeal.—Waiver of right to appeal will not be valid unless there is a basis in the record for concluding that it was voluntary, knowing and intelligent. Court should ascertain on the record that defendant in fact signed waiver and was aware of its contents. People v. Callahan, 80 N.Y.2d 273, 590 N.Y.S.2d 46, 604 N.E.2d 108 (1992). *See also* People v. Rozo, 196 A.D.2d 514, 600 N.Y.S.2d 752 (2d Dept.), *lv. denied*, 82 N.Y.2d 853 (1993).

—Defendant validly waived her right to raise excessiveness of sentence on appeal; the record demonstrated a voluntary and intelligent waiver of her negotiated sentence, even though court stated at sentencing that she was waiving her right to appeal "anything that has happened up to this point." The court intended that statement to mean that the waiver was all encompassing. People v. Allen, 82 N.Y.2d 761, 603 N.Y.S.2d 820, 623 N.E.2d 1170 (1993).

—The right to appeal may be waived as a condition of a sentence or plea bargain. People v. Seaberg, 74 N.Y.2d 1, 543 N.Y.S.2d 968, 541 N.E.2d 1022 (1989).

—Requirement that defendant withdraw his motion to suppress evidence was a reasonable condition for acceptance of a plea of guilty to a class B felony rather than a class A felony. People v. Esajerre, 35 N.Y.2d 463, 363 N.Y.S.2d 931, 323 N.E.2d 175 (1974).

—The legality of a sentence may not be waived as part of a plea bargain. People v. Cordoba, 208 A.D.2d 420, 617 N.Y.S.2d 305 (1st Dept. 1994).

—A waiver of the right to appeal a criminal conviction entered by a defendant as a condition to a negotiated plea does not bar the appellate court from reviewing the defendant's sentence as a matter of discretion in the interest of justice. People v. Bourne, 139 A.D.2d 210, 531 N.Y.S.2d 899 (1st Dept. 1988).

—Where the court specifically asked the defendant before he waived his right to appeal, if he had discussed that right with his attorney and the defendant answered "Yes, your Honor," the court enforced the waiver. People v. Khan, 201 A.D.2d 586, 607 N.Y.S.2d 737 (2d Dept. 1994).

—Where prior to the acceptance of his plea of guilty the defendant withdrew all of his pretrial motions, decided and undecided, he was precluded from raising on appeal the issues raised in those motions. People v. Rodriguez, 193 A.D.2d 821, 598 N.Y.S.2d 293 (2d Dept. 1993).

—At the time of the guilty plea, the defendant's attorney expressly withdrew all undecided motions, including his pending motion to dismiss the indictment on constitutional speedy trial grounds; it was not necessary for the defendant to repeat the words of his attorney in order for those words to be given effect. People v. Nilson, 182 A.D.2d 715, 582 N.Y.S.2d 482 (2d Dept.), *lv. denied*, 80 N.Y.2d 932 (1992).

—Although it may be preferable for the record to clearly state that waiver applies to plea and sentence, a lack of those specific words will not automatically render the waiver invalid, if the record otherwise demonstrates that it was knowing and voluntary. People v. Burk, 181 A.D.2d 74, 586 N.Y.S.2d 140 (2d Dept.), *lv. denied*, 80 N.Y.2d 927 (1992).

—Waiver of a statutory right to appeal the denial of a suppression motion is an acceptable condition of a plea bargain. People v. Roberts, 152 A.D.2d 678, 544 N.Y.S.2d 157 (2d Dept. 1989).

—Where, pursuant to plea bargain, the defendant waived his right to raise on appeal any question with respect to the admissibility of his confession and certain physical evidence, he was precluded from raising those issues on appeal. People v. Cerce, 137 A.D.2d 542, 524 N.Y.S.2d 283 (2d Dept. 1988).

—Appeal would be dismissed where defendant waived his right to appeal as a condition of the plea. People v. Ocana, 135 A.D.2d 743, 522 N.Y.S.2d 646 (2d Dept. 1988).

—Where defendant waived his right to appeal propriety of suppression ruling as a condition of the plea, he could not contest admissibility of his confession on appeal. People v. McGinley, 135 A.D.2d 740, 522 N.Y.S.2d 642 (2d Dept. 1987).

—The appeal was not precluded by defendant's waiver of his right to appeal because a defendant cannot waive the right to challenge the legality of a sentence. People v. Defino, 200 A.D.2d 907, 607 N.Y.S.2d 170 (3d Dept. 1994).

—A waiver of appeal will not foreclose a defendant's right to challenge the competency of the legal representation relied upon in accepting the plea bargain and entering the guilty plea. People v. Rosado, 199 A.D.2d 833, 606 N.Y.S.2d 368 (3d Dept. 1993).

—A bargained-for waiver of the right to appeal is ineffective to the extent that it impairs the defendant's ability to obtain appellate review of a constitutional speedy trial claim. People v. Ferguson, 192 A.D.2d 800, 596 N.Y.S.2d 533 (3d Dept. 1993).

—A defendant ordinarily may waive his or her right to appeal as part of a negotiated plea as long as the waiver is knowingly and voluntarily made. People v. Korona, 197 A.D.2d 788, 603 N.Y.S.2d 88 (3d Dept.), *lv. denied*, 82 N.Y.2d 926 (1993).

—A general waiver of the right to appeal can be accomplished without specific enumeration of the scope of the waiver. People v. Crouch, 161 A.D.2d 834, 555 N.Y.S.2d 883 (3d Dept. 1990).

—The People need not particularize some legitimate State interest to justify conditioning a plea bargain on defendant's waiver of the right to appeal. People v. Moissett, 154 A.D.2d 786, 546 N.Y.S.2d 463 (3d Dept.), *lv. denied*, 76 N.Y.2d 909 (1989).

—Waiver of the right to appeal is valid where the sentence was lawful and the waiver was knowing, voluntary and intelligent. People v. Maye, 143 A.D.2d 483, 532 N.Y.S.2d 609 (3d Dept. 1988).

—Court rejected the defendant's argument that the prosecution's policy of requiring waiver of appeal as a condition of offering a plea to a lesser charge is illegal and unconstitutional. People v. Walker, 201 A.D.2d 896, 607 N.Y.S.2d 815 (4th Dept. 1994).

—Waiver of right to appeal was invalid to the extent that it foreclosed review of defendant's claim that he was illegally sentenced as a second felony offender. People v. Stephens, 193 A.D.2d 1087, 598 N.Y.S.2d 410 (4th Dept.), *lv. denied*, 82 N.Y.2d 727 (1993).

—Where, as part of the plea bargain, the defendant waived his right to appeal the denial of his suppression motion, he could not raise the suppression issue on appeal. People v. Correa, 149 A.D.2d 909, 540 N.Y.S.2d 45 (4th Dept. 1989).

Plea conditions; enforceability of.—Conditions agreed upon as part of a plea bargain are generally enforceable, unless violative of statute or public policy. People v. Hicks, 98 N.Y.2d 185, 746 N.Y.S.2d 441, 774 N.E.2d 205 (2002).

§ 220.15. Plea; plea of not responsible by reason of mental disease or defect.

1. The defendant may, with both the permission of the court and the consent of the people, enter a plea of not responsible by reason of mental disease or defect to the entire indictment. The district attorney must state to the court either orally on the record or in a writing filed with the court that the people consent to the entry of such plea and that the people are satisfied that the affirmative defense of lack of criminal responsibility by reason of mental disease or defect would be proven by the defendant at a trial by a preponderance of the evidence. The district attorney must further state to the court in detail the evidence available to the people with respect to the offense or offenses charged in the indictment, including all psychiatric evidence available or known to the people. If necessary the court may conduct a hearing before accepting such plea. The district attorney must further state to the court the reasons for recommending such plea. The reasons shall be stated in detail and not in conclusory terms.

2. Counsel for the defendant must state that in his opinion defendant has the capacity to understand the proceedings and to assist in his own defense and that the defendant understands the consequences of a plea of not responsible by reason of mental disease or defect. Counsel for the defendant must further state whether in his opinion defendant has any viable defense to the offense or offenses charged in the indictment other than the affirmative defense of lack of criminal responsibility by reason of mental disease or defect. Counsel for the defendant must further state in detail the psychiatric evidence available to the defendant with respect to such latter affirmative defense.

3. Before accepting a plea of not responsible by reason of mental disease or defect, the court must address the defendant in open court and determine that he understands each of the following:

(a) The nature of the charge to which the plea is offered, and the consequences of such plea;

(b) That he has the right to plead not guilty or to persist in that plea if it has already been entered;

(c) That he has the right to be tried by a jury, the right to the assistance of counsel, the right to confront and cross-examine witnesses against him, and the right not to be compelled to incriminate himself;

(d) That if he pleads not responsible by reason of mental disease or defect there will be no trial with respect to the charges contained in the indictment, so that by offering such plea he waives the right to such trial;

(e) That if he pleads not responsible by reason of mental disease or defect the court will ask him questions about the offense or offenses charged in the indictment and that he will thereby waive his right not to be compelled to incriminate himself; and

(f) That the acceptance of a plea of not responsible by reason of mental disease or defect is the equivalent of a verdict of not responsible by reason of mental disease or defect after trial.

4. The court shall not accept a plea of not responsible by reason of mental disease or defect without first determining that there is a factual basis for such plea. The court must address the defendant personally in open court and determine that the plea is voluntary, knowingly made, and not the result of force, threats, or promises. The court must inquire whether the defendant's willingness to plead results from prior discussions between the district attorney and counsel for the defendant. The court must be satisfied that the defendant understands the proceedings against him, has sufficient capacity to assist in his own defense and understands the consequences of a plea of not responsible by reason of mental disease or defect. The court may make such inquiry as it deems necessary or appropriate for the purpose of making the determinations required by this section.

5. Before accepting a plea of not responsible by reason of mental disease or defect, the court must find and state each of the following on the record in detail and not in conclusory terms:

(a) That it is satisfied that each element of the offense or offenses charge* in the indictment would be established beyond a reasonable doubt at a trial;

(b) That the affirmative defense of lack of criminal responsibility by reason of mental disease or defect would be proven by the defendant at a trial by a preponderance of the evidence;

(c) That the defendant has the capacity to understand the proceedings against him and to assist in his own defense;

(d) That such plea by the defendant is knowingly and voluntarily made and that there is a factual basis for the plea;

(e) That the acceptance of such plea is required in the interest of the public in the effective administration of justice.

6. When a plea of not responsible by reason of mental disease or defect is accepted by the court and recorded upon the minutes, the provisions of section 330.20 of this chapter shall govern all subsequent proceedings against the defendant.

* As originally enacted.

Added by L. 1980, Ch. 548; Amended by L. 1984, Ch.

§ 220.20. Plea; meaning of lesser included offense for plea purposes.

1. A "lesser included offense," within the meaning of subdivisions four and five of section 220.10 relating to the entry of a plea of guilty to an offense of lesser grade than one charged in a count of an indictment, means not only a "lesser included offense" as that term is defined in subdivision thirty-seven of section 1.20, but also one which is deemed to be such pursuant to the following rules:

(a) Where the only culpable mental state required for the crime charged is that the proscribed conduct be performed intentionally, any lesser offense consisting of reckless or criminally negligent, instead of intentional, performance of the same conduct is deemed to constitute a lesser included offense;

(b) Where the only culpable mental state required for the crime charged is that the proscribed conduct be performed recklessly, any lesser offense consisting of criminally negligent, instead of reckless, performance of the same conduct is deemed to constitute a lesser included offense;

(c) Where according to the allegations of a count a defendant's participation in the crime charged consisted in whole or in part of solicitation of another person to engage in the proscribed conduct, the offense of criminal solicitation, in any appropriate degree, is, with respect to such defendant, deemed to constitute a lesser included offense;

(d) Where according to the allegations of a count a defendant's participation in the crime charged consisted in whole or in part of conspiratorial agreement or conduct with another person to engage in the proscribed conduct, the crime of conspiracy, in any appropriate degree, is, with respect to such defendant, deemed to constitute a lesser included offense;

(e) Where according to the allegations of a count charging a felony a defendant's participation in such felony consisted in whole or in part of providing another person with means or opportunity for engaging in the proscribed conduct, the crime of criminal facilitation, in any appropriate degree, is, with respect to such defendant, deemed to constitute a lesser included offense;

(f) Where the crime charged is assault or attempted assault, in any degree, allegedly committed by intentionally causing or attempting to cause physical injury to a person by the immediate use of physical force against him, or where the crime charged is menacing, as defined in section 120.15 of the penal law, the offense of harassment, as defined in subdivision one of section 240.25 of the penal law, is deemed to constitute a lesser included offense;

(g) Where the crime charged is murder in the second degree as defined in subdivision three of section 125.25 of the penal law, allegedly committed in the course of the commission or attempted commission of a designated one of the underlying felonies enumerated in said subdivision, or during immediate flight therefrom, such designated underlying felony or attempted felony is deemed to constitute a lesser included offense. If such designated underlying felony is alleged to be robbery, burglary, kidnapping, or arson, without specification of the degree thereof, or an attempt to commit the same, a plea of guilty may be entered to the lowest degree thereof only, or as the case may be to attempted commission of such felony in its lowest degree, unless the allegations of the count clearly indicate the existence of all the elements of a higher degree;

(h) Where the crime charged is criminal sale of a controlled substance, any offense of criminal sale or possession of a controlled substance, in any degree, is deemed to constitute a lesser included offense.

(i) where the crime charged is criminal possession of a controlled substance, any offense of criminal possession of a controlled substance, in any degree, is deemed to constitute a lesser included offense.

(j) Where the offense charged is unlawful disposal of hazardous wastes in violation of section 27-0914 of the environmental conservation law, any offense of unlawful disposal or possession of hazardous wastes as set forth in sections 71-2707, 71-2709, 71-2711 and 71-2713 of such law, in any degree, is deemed to constitute a lesser included offense;

(k) Where the offense charged is unlawful possession of hazardous wastes in violation of section 27-0914 of the environmental conservation law, any offense of unlawful possession of hazardous wastes as set forth in sections 71-2707 and 71-2709 of such law, in any degree, is deemed to constitute a lesser included offense.

2. An offense is deemed to be a lesser included offense with respect to a crime charged in an indictment, pursuant to the provisions of subdivision one, only for purposes of conviction upon a plea of guilty and not for purposes of conviction by verdict. For the latter purpose, an offense constitutes a lesser included one only when it conforms to the definition of that term contained in subdivision thirty-seven of section 1.20.

Amended by L. 1973, Chs. 276, 1051; L. 1974, Ch. 367; L. 1976, Ch. 480; L. 1979, Ch. 410; L. 1981, Ch. 719.

ANNOTATIONS

Factual basis for guilty plea to a lesser offense.—A factual basis for a guilty plea is unnecessary when the defendant pleads to a lesser crime than the one charged in the indictment. People v. Hall, 71 N.Y.2d 1002, 530 N.Y.S.2d 94, 525 N.E.2d 460 (1988). *See also* People v. Cantu, 202 A.D.2d 1033, 610 N.Y.S.2d 113 (4th Dept. 1994); People v. Birks, 144 A.D.2d 566, 534 N.Y.S.2d 223 (2d Dept. 1988); People v. Rivera, 143 A.D.2d 783, 533 N.Y.S.2d 483 (2d Dept. 1988); People v. Filomeno, 138 A.D.2d 734, 526 N.Y.S.2d 548 (2d Dept. 1988).

—A bargained guilty plea to a lesser crime makes it unnecessary to establish a factual basis for the particular crime confessed. People v. Clairborne, 29 N.Y.2d 950, 329 N.Y.S.2d 580, 280 N.E.2d 366 (1972). *See also* People v. Johnson, 118 A.D.2d 1005, 500 N.Y.S.2d 374 (3d Dept. 1986).

—Although defendant pled down to first-degree manslaughter, court set aside plea because the accused had denied intending to kill or cause serious injury and claimed self-defense. People v. Thomas, 159 A.D.2d 529, 552 N.Y.S.2d 394 (2d Dept. 1990).

Not lesser offenses.—Because possession of explosives can, under no circumstances, be regarded as a lesser included offense of robbery in any degree, the defendant could not plead guilty to first degree criminal possession of a dangerous weapon in satisfaction of an indictment charging defendant with first and second degree robbery; defendant can only plead to offenses actually charged in the indictment or to lesser included offenses. People v. Crute, 236 A.D.2d 208, 653 N.Y.S.2d 549 (1st Dept. 1997).

§ 220.30. Plea; plea of guilty to part of indictment; plea covering other indictments.

1. A plea of guilty not embracing the entire indictment, entered pursuant to the provisions of subdivision four or five of section 220.10, is a "plea of guilty to part of the indictment."

2. The entry and acceptance of a plea of guilty to part of the indictment constitutes a disposition of the entire indictment.

3. (a) (i) Except as provided in paragraph (b), or in paragraph (c) dealing with juvenile offenders, a plea of guilty, whether to the entire indictment or to part of the indictment, may, with both the permission of the court and the consent of the people, be entered and accepted upon the condition that it constitutes a complete disposition of one or more other indictments against the defendant then pending.

(ii) If the other indictment or indictments are pending in a different court or courts, they shall not be disposed of under this subdivision unless the other courts and the appropriate prosecutors also transmit their written permission and consent as provided in subdivision four of section 220.50 of this article; in such a case the court in which the plea is entered shall so notify the other courts which, upon such notice, shall dismiss the appropriate indictments pending therein.

(b) (i) A plea of guilty, whether to the entire indictment or to part of the indictment for any crime other than a class A felony, may not be accepted on the condition that it constitutes a complete disposition of one or more other indictments against the defendant wherein is charged

a class A-I felony as defined in article two hundred twenty of the penal law or the attempt to commit any such class A-I felony, except that an eligible youth, as defined in subdivision two of section 720.10, may plea to a class B felony, upon consent of the district attorney, for purposes of adjudication as a youthful offender.

(ii) Where it appears that the defendant has previously been subjected to a predicate felony conviction as defined in paragraph (b) of subdivision (1) of section 70.06 of the penal law, a plea of guilty, whether to the entire indictment or to part of the indictment, of any offense other than a felony may not be accepted on the condition that it constitutes a complete disposition of one or more other indictments against the defendant wherein is charged a felony, other than a class A felony or a class B or class C violent felony offense as defined in subdivision one of section 70.02 of the penal law.

(iii) A plea of guilty, whether to the entire indictment or part of the indictment for any crime other than a class A felony or a class B or class C violent felony offense as defined in subdivision one of section 70.02 of the penal law, may not be accepted on the condition that it constitutes a complete disposition of one or more other indictments against the defendant wherein is charged a class A felony, other than those defined in article two hundred twenty of the penal law, or a class B violent felony offense which is also an armed felony offense.

(iv) Except as provided in subparagraph (iii) of this paragraph, a plea of guilty, whether to the entire indictment or part of the indictment, for any crime other than a class A felony or a class B, C, or D violent felony offense as defined in subdivision one of section 70.02 of the penal law, may not be accepted on the condition that it constitutes a complete disposition of one or more other indictments against the defendant wherein is charged a class B or class C violent felony offense as defined in subdivision one of section 70.02 of the penal law.

(v) A plea of guilty, whether to the entire indictment or part of the indictment, for any crime other than a violent felony offense as defined in section 70.02 of the penal law, may not be accepted on the condition that it constitutes a complete disposition of one or more other indictments against the defendant wherein is charged the class D violent felony offenses of criminal possession of a weapon in the third degree as defined in subdivision four, five, seven or eight of section 265.02 of the penal law; provided, however, a plea of guilty, whether to the entire indictment or part of the indictment, for the class A misdemeanor of criminal possession of a weapon in the fourth degree as defined in subdivision one of section 265.01 of the penal law may be accepted on the condition that it constitutes a complete disposition of one or more other indictments against the defendant wherein is charged the class D violent felony offense of criminal possession of a weapon in the third degree as defined in subdivision four of section 265.02 of the penal law when the defendant has not been previously convicted of a class A misdemeanor defined in the penal law in the five years preceding the commission of the offense.

(vi) A plea of guilty, whether to the entire indictment or to part of the indictment for any crime other than a felony, may not be accepted on the condition that it constitutes a complete disposition of one or more other indictments against the defendant wherein is charged a class B felony other than a class B violent felony offense as defined in subdivision one of section 70.02 of the penal law.

(vii) A defendant may not enter a plea of guilty to the crime of murder in the first degree as defined in section 125.27 of the penal law; provided, however, that a defendant may enter such a plea with both the permission of the court and the consent of the people when the agreed upon sentence is either life imprisonment without parole or a term of imprisonment for the class A-I felony of murder in the first degree other than a sentence of life imprisonment without parole.

(viii) A plea of guilty, whether to the entire indictment or to part of the indictment for any crime other than a class A or a class B felony may not be accepted on condition that it constitutes a complete disposition of one or more other indictments against the defendant wherein is charged a class A-II felony defined in article two hundred twenty of the penal law or the attempt to commit any such felony.

(ix) A plea of guilty, whether to the entire indictment or to part of the indictment for any crime other than a class B, a class C, or a class D felony, may not be accepted on condition that it constitutes a complete disposition of one or more other indictments against the defendant wherein is charged a class B felony defined in article two hundred twenty of the penal law.

(c) Where the defendant is a juvenile offender, a plea of guilty, whether to the entire indictment or to part of the indictment, of any offense other than one for which the defendant is criminally responsible may not be accepted on the condition that it constitutes a complete disposition of one or more other indictments against the defendant.

Amended by L. 1973, Chs. 276, 277, 1051; L. 1974, Ch. 367; L. 1976, Chs. 187, 480; L. 1978, Ch. 481; L. 1979, Ch. 410; L. 1980, Chs. 233, 234, 548; L. 1995, Ch. 1, § 11, eff. Sept. 1, 1995, amending subd. 3(b)(vii); L. 1999, Ch. 33, § 6, eff. Nov. 1, 1999, amending subd. 3(b)(v); L. 2000, Ch. 189, § 2, eff. Nov. 1, 2000, amending subd. 3(b)(v).

ANNOTATIONS

Constitutionality; subd. 3(b)(vii).—After defendant pleaded guilty to first degree murder pursuant to an agreement in which prosecutors agreed to the withdraw notice of intent to seek the death penalty, defendant claimed that his plea was invalid on the basis that his Fifth and Sixth Amendment rights were impermissibly burdened, pointing to the fact that after entry of his plea but before sentencing, the Court of Appeals decided *Hynes v. Tomei,* 92 N.Y.2d 613, 684 N.Y.S.2d 177, 706 N.E.2d 1201 (1998), *cert. denied,* 527 U.S. 1015 (1999), which found plea provisions of the death penalty statute unconstitutional. The fact that defendant could not anticipate this subsequent decision did not impugn the truth or reliability of the plea, which was otherwise valid. People v. Edwards, 96 N.Y.2d 445, 729 N.Y.S.2d 410, 754 N.E.2d 169 (2001).

—The provisions of the New York death penalty statute, specifically, CPL §§ 220.10(5)(e) and 220.30(3)(b)(vii), are unconstitutional for the same reason as the Federal Kidnapping Act, because by statutory mandate, the death penalty hangs over only those who exercise their constitutional rights to maintain innocence and demand a jury trial. Accordingly, the Court was compelled by *United States v. Jackson,* 390 U.S. 570, to invalidate those provisions. However, CPL § 220.60(2)(a) was not limited to first degree murder cases, and it does not, in the absence of CPL § 220.10(5)(e), violate *Jackson.* Therefore, CPL § 220.60(2)(a) does not need to be stricken. Hynes v. Tomei, 92 N.Y.2d 613, 684 N.Y.S.2d 177, 706 N.E.2d 1201 (1998), *cert. denied,* 527 U.S. 1015 (1999).

—Court upheld the constitutionality of CPL §§ 220.10(5)(e), 220.30(3)(b)(vii), and 220.60, which defendant challenged to the extent that they provide that a sentence of death for first degree murder could only be imposed upon a conviction after trial and could not be imposed after a guilty plea, a plea that can be entered only with People's consent and court's approval. People v. McIntosh, 173 Misc. 2d 727, 662 N.Y.S.2d 214 (Dutchess Co. Ct. 1997).

Voluntariness of plea.—Defendant's plea of guilty in 1957, after an earlier conviction of guilty was overturned on appeal, constituted a voluntary and intelligent waiver of the right against double jeopardy under the existing constitutional law. People v. La Ruffa, 34 N.Y.2d 242, 356 N.Y.S.2d 849, *cert. denied,* 419 U.S. 959, *remanded,* 37 N.Y.2d 58, 371 N.Y.S.2d 434, 332 N.E.2d 312 (1974).

Judicial role.—The CPL prohibits acceptance of a plea to a crime less than a felony where the defendant is a prior felony offender and is indicted for a felony. A court may not circumvent this statutory prohibition by dismissing the indictment in the interests of justice and accepting a plea to a class A misdemeanor. People v. Cook, 93 A.D.2d 942, 463 N.Y.S.2d 59 (3d Dept. 1983).

Prosecutor's role.—The sentence was vacated, and the matter remitted for resentencing before a different judge so that promise might be fulfilled where as part of plea bargain, the prosecutor had agreed not to make any sentence recommendation, but at sentencing, he asked the court to give the defendant the maximum permissible sentence. People v. Bushey, 75 A.D.2d 910, 427 N.Y.S.2d 326 (3d Dept. 1980).

Plea bargain; breach of condition.—When the promised sentence is conditioned upon the defendant's appearance on the sentencing date, a harsher sentence may be imposed if the condition is not fulfilled. People v. Webster, 202 A.D.2d 710, 608 N.Y.S.2d 552 (3d Dept. 1994).

§ 220.35. Hearing on predicate felony conviction.

In any case where the defendant offers to enter a plea of guilty of a misdemeanor to constitute a disposition of the entire indictment or to constitute a complete disposition of one or more other indictments, or both, and the permission of the court and the consent of the people must be withheld solely upon the ground that it appears the defendant has previously been subjected to a predicate felony conviction as defined in paragraph (b) of subdivision one of section 70.06 of the penal law the court, if the defendant does not admit such predicate felony conviction, may conduct the hearing required by section 400.21 for the purpose of determining whether the plea may be entered or must be rejected. The finding upon any such hearing shall also be binding upon the defendant for the purpose of sentence.

Added by L. 1973, Ch. 277.

ANNOTATION

Failure to advise defendant of second felony status.— While the court should have advised defendant at the time of his plea and agreement that he would be sentenced as a second felony offender, and that he had the right to contest the prior conviction on a constitutional basis, the failure to do so was not significant, since defendant's status as a second felony offender at the time of sentence was freely admitted and not contested. People v. Demand, 115 A.D.2d 139, 495 N.Y.S.2d 523 (3d Dept. 1985).

§ 220.40. Plea; plea of not guilty; meaning.

A plea of not guilty constitutes a denial of every allegation of the indictment.

ANNOTATION

Generally.—A plea of not guilty is not the equivalent of a factual assertion of innocence, but is merely the device by which a person accused of a crime informs the prosecutor and the court that he or she intends to put the government to its proof and preserves the right to defense; the plea of not guilty automatically constitutes a denial of every allegation in the indictment and imposes on the People the burden of proving every fact and element of the crime charged beyond a reasonable doubt. People v. Garcia, 169 A.D.2d 358, 573 N.Y.S.2d 257 (1st Dept. 1991).

§ 220.50. Plea; entry of plea.

1. A plea to an indictment, other than one against a corporation, must be entered orally by the defendant in person; except that a plea to an indictment which does not charge a felony may, with the permission of the court, be entered by counsel upon submission by him of written authorization of the defendant.

2. A plea to an indictment against a corporation must be entered by counsel.

3. If a defendant who is required to enter a plea to an indictment refuses to do so or remains mute, the court must enter a plea of not guilty to the indictment in his behalf.

4. Where the permission of the court and the consent of the people are a prerequisite to the entry of a plea of guilty, the court and the prosecutor must either orally on the record or in a writing filed with the indictment state their reason for granting permission or consenting, as the case may be, to entry of the plea of guilty.

5. When a sentence is agreed upon by the prosecutor and a defendant as a predicate to entry of a plea of guilty, the court or the prosecutor must orally on the record, or in writing filed with the court, state the sentence agreed upon as a condition of such plea.

6. Where the defendant consents to a plea of guilty to the indictment, or part of the indictment, or consents to be prosecuted by superior court information as set forth in section 195.20 of this chapter, and if the defendant and prosecutor agree that as a condition of the plea or the superior court information certain property shall be forfeited by the defendant, the description and present estimated monetary value of the property shall be stated in court by the prosecutor at the time of plea. Within thirty days of the acceptance of the plea or superior court information by the court, the prosecutor shall send to the commissioner of the division of criminal justice services a document containing the name of the defendant, the description and present estimated monetary value of the property, and the date the plea or superior court information was accepted. Any property forfeited by the defendant as a condition to a plea of guilty to an indictment, or a part thereof, or to a superior court information, shall be disposed of in accordance with the provisions of section thirteen hundred forty-nine of the civil practice law and rules.

7. [*Repealed Sept. 1, 2009.*] Prior to accepting a defendant's plea of guilty to a count or counts of an indictment or a superior court information charging a felony offense, the court must advise the defendant on the record, that if the defendant is not a citizen of the United States, the defendant's plea of guilty and the court's acceptance thereof may result in the defendant's deportation, exclusion from admission to the United States or denial of naturalization pursuant to the laws of the United States. Where the plea of guilty is to a count or counts of an indictment charging a felony offense other than a violent felony offense as defined in section 70.02 of the penal law or an A-I felony offense other than an A-I felony as defined in article two hundred twenty of the penal law, the court must also, prior to accepting such plea, advise the defendant that, if the defendant is not a citizen of the United States and is or becomes the subject of a final order of deportation issued by the United States Immigration and Naturalization Service, the defendant may be paroled to the custody of the Immigration and Naturalization Service for deportation purposes at any time subsequent to the commencement of any indeterminate or determinate prison sentence imposed as a result of the defendant's plea. The failure to advise the defendant pursuant to this subdivision shall not be deemed to affect the voluntariness of a plea of guilty or the validity of a conviction, nor shall it afford a defendant any rights in a subsequent proceeding relating to such defendant's deportation, exclusion or denial of naturalization.

Amended by L. 1973, Chs. 276, 277; L. 1984, Ch. 671, eff. Aug. 31, 1984; L. 1990, Ch. 655; L. 1995, Ch. 3, § 30, adding subd. 7, eff. June 15, 1995, pursuant to L. 1995, Ch. 3, § 74, para. (b), and repealed Sept. 30, 2005, pursuant to L. 1995, Ch. 3, § 74, para. (d); L. 2004, Ch. 738, § 17, eff. Dec. 14, 2004, amending subd. 7, and such amendments shall not affect the expiration and repeal of such subdivision and shall expire and be deemed repealed therewith; L. 2005, Ch. 56, Part D, § 20, eff. Apr. 1, 2005, extending repeal date of subd. 7 to Sept. 1, 2009.

ANNOTATIONS

Voluntariness; knowing waiver of constitutional rights.— Where there exists evidence demonstrating a motivation to plead guilty on the defendant's part independent of an erroneous suppression ruling, then vacatur of the plea is not warranted. People v. Lloyd, 66 N.Y.2d 964, 498 N.Y.S.2d 785, 489 N.E.2d 754 (1985).

—Convictions based upon pleas of guilty were not invalid where record indicated that defendants knowingly, voluntarily and intelligently relinquished their rights upon their guilty pleas; it is not necessary that the trial judge enumerate all of the "Boykin" rights to which a defendant is entitled and elicit from a defendant a list of detailed waivers before accepting a guilty plea; rather, the questioning of the defendant is within the trial court's discretion, considering such facts as the seriousness of the crime, the competency, experience and participation of counsel, the rationality of the "plea bargain" and the pace of the proceedings. People v. Harris, 61 N.Y.2d 9, 471 N.Y.S.2d 61, 459 N.E.2d 170 (1983).

—Where the trial court in the colloquy with the defendant in taking the guilty plea was explicit that it was trying to put the matter in layman's language so the defendant would understand what it was saying, the effort should not be subjected to legalistic hypertechnical examination. People v. Castro, 37 N.Y.2d 818, 376 N.Y.S.2d 922, 339 N.E.2d 620 (1975).

—There is no uniform mandatory catechism of pleading defendants, only that it be demonstrable that the plea was voluntary, knowing and intelligent. People v. Reyes, 202 A.D.2d 190, 608 N.Y.S.2d 426 (1st Dept. 1994).

—Plea was voluntarily and knowingly made notwithstanding defendant's unfamiliarity with the English language, absent evidence that he could not understand the interpreter who was present and assisted defendant throughout the entire proceeding, and in light of the great pains taken by the trial court to ensure that defendant and the interpreter understood each other. People v. Mohammed, 208 A.D.2d 1118, 617 N.Y.S.2d 955 (3d Dept. 1994), *lv. denied*, 85 N.Y.2d 941 (1995).

—It is not necessary that a defendant admit his guilt to enter a plea, provided the plea is informed and intelligent. People v. Bruington, 186 A.D.2d 504, 589 N.Y.S.2d 419 (1st Dept. 1992).

—It is well established that there is no uniform catechism which the court must elicit to render a defendant's plea appropriate. People v. Ramirez, 159 A.D.2d 392, 553 N.Y.S.2d 94 (1st Dept. 1990).

—A guilty plea will not be found invalid because the judge failed to enumerate all the rights to which the defendant was entitled. People v. Jones, 183 A.D.2d 918, 584 N.Y.S.2d 151 (2d Dept. 1992).

—Reversible error was committed where the court failed to insure that the defendant had an adequate understanding of the consequences of the plea and also failed to negate or establish the defense of justification or to indicate a knowing waiver thereof by defendant. People v. Riley, 91 A.D.2d 671, 457 N.Y.S.2d 122 (2d Dept. 1982).

—Defendant's previous plea of guilty was not constitutionally infirm merely because the court failed to specifically enumerate those rights waived by the plea and obtain waivers with respect to each of those rights. People v. Pacheco, 114 A.D.2d 913, 495 N.Y.S.2d 83 (2d Dept. 1985).

—The fact that the court failed to enumerate specifically and obtain waivers of all rights to which a defendant is entitled at trial and which he waives by pleading guilty does not render the plea invalid where the allocution established the requisite elements of the crime pleaded to and the plea was knowingly and intelligently made. People v. Nicastro, 114 A.D.2d 979, 495 N.Y.S.2d 423 (2d Dept. 1985).

—A guilty plea will be upheld if it was entered knowingly, voluntarily and with an understanding of the consequences, and will not be vacated merely because the defendant was unwilling or unable to describe or admit to the underlying facts of the crime charged, especially where defendant made a rational choice to limit the possible penalty to which he would be exposed had he gone to trial. People v. Brown, 114 A.D.2d 1036, 495 N.Y.S.2d 475 (2d Dept. 1985).

—The fact that the court failed to enumerate and obtain waivers of all rights to which the defendant is entitled at trial, and which he waives by pleading guilty, does not render the plea invalid where defendant's allocution established the requisite elements of the crime to which he is pleading guilty, and the defendant knowingly and intelligently pleaded guilty thereto. People v. Kennedy, 114 A.D.2d 1042, 495 N.Y.S.2d 482 (2d Dept. 1985).

—Plea was voluntarily and knowingly made notwithstanding defendant's unfamiliarity with the English language where an interpreter was present and assisted defendant throughout the entire proceeding. People v. Martes, 154 A.D.2d 946, 545 N.Y.S.2d 885 (4th Dept. 1989).

Voluntariness; defendant's competence to plead.—Having made the threshold determination that psychiatric inquiry was indicated, the trial court's failure to secure the second psychiatric report, as required by CPL § 730.20, was not an insubstantial error in light of the defendant's prior history of mental illness and the case was remitted to the trial court, but before another judge, for proper determination of defendant's mental capacity. People v. Armlin, 37 N.Y.2d 167, 371 N.Y.S.2d 691, 332 N.E.2d 870 (1975).

—If the record indicates a reason to doubt the accused's competency to plead guilty, the court has a *sua sponte* obligation to order a psychiatric examination. People v. Gensler, 72 N.Y.2d 239, 532 N.Y.S.2d 72, 527 N.E.2d 120 (1988).

—Trial court did not err in accepting defendant's plea without sua sponte ordering a competency examination, where defendant exhibited no delusional behavior at plea or at sentencing, and defense counsel did not raise the issue of defendant's fitness to proceed or request an examination pursuant to CPL § 730.30(2). People v. Carbonel, 296 A.D.2d 858, 745 N.Y.S.2d 367 (4th Dept. 2002).

—Defendant was competent to enter guilty plea, despite having been diagnosed with an antisocial personality disorder and a drug dependency. People v. Jones, 247 A.D.2d 883, 668 N.Y.S.2d 801 (4th Dept. 1998).

Adequate factual allocution.—A defendant does not have to be warned that one of the consequences of his plea will be an enhanced sentence in the event he should be subsequently convicted of another crime. People v. Silvers, 163 A.D.2d 71, 558 N.Y.S.2d 25 (1st Dept. 1990).

—A predicate conviction arising out of a guilty plea is not defective merely because a judge failed to enumerate all the rights to which a defendant is entitled. People v. Barry, 159 A.D.2d 353, 553 N.Y.S.2d 1 (1st Dept. 1990).

—It does not matter that it was the attorney who made the explicit statements showing why the defendant was taking the plea rather than going to trial as there is no requirement that the defendant shall himself admit to the underlying facts making out the crime. People v. Colon, 77 A.D.2d 370, 433 N.Y.S.2d 766 (1st Dept. 1980).

—The court did not err in accepting the defendant's guilty plea without inquiring as to whether he was knowingly and voluntarily waiving certain defenses, where a review of the plea minutes failed to indicate that the defendant's factual recitation negated an essential element of the crime or raised any defenses. People v. Sarlo, 188 A.D.2d 624, 591 N.Y.S.2d 847 (2d Dept. 1992).

—There is no general requirement that a court inquire into a defendant's possible affirmative defense unless something on the record specifically indicates that an affirmative defense may exist. People v. Martinez, 127 A.D.2d 855, 512 N.Y.S.2d 10 (2d Dept. 1987).

—The plea was factually sufficient although there was some discussion on the record as to whether the gun was unloaded and/or inoperable, where the defendant was well aware that he was pleading guilty to robbery in the first degree and was clearly informed of the necessary elements of that offense. People v. Glenn, 127 A.D.2d 787, 512 N.Y.S.2d 181 (2d Dept. 1987).

—Defendant failed to raise his objections to the adequacy of his plea allocutions in the court of first instance and accordingly has not preserved his claims for appellate review. People v. Frascella, 116 A.D.2d 587, 497 N.Y.S.2d 445 (2d Dept. 1986).

—A guilty plea can be accepted in the absence of a defendant's personal recitation of all the elements of the crime charged when there is no suggestion in the record that the plea is improvident or baseless. People v. Langhorn, 119 A.D.2d 844, 501 N.Y.S.2d 470 (2d Dept. 1986).

—Plea allocution is sufficient if defendant's affirmative responses to court's questions establish the elements of the crimes charged and there is no indication in the record that the voluntary plea was baseless or improvident. People v. Coles, 13 A.D.3d 665, 786 N.Y.S.2d 595 (3d Dept. 2004).

—All of the circumstances surrounding the plea must be considered in determining its sufficiency and the absence of an admission to an element of the crime standing alone is not dispositive. People v. Oliver, 191 A.D.2d 815, 594 N.Y.S.2d 839 (3d Dept. 1993).

—Defendant's professed inability to recall the events forming the basis for the subject prosecution did not preclude a valid plea of guilty. People v. DiPaola, 143 A.D.2d 487, 532 N.Y.S.2d 606 (3d Dept. 1988).

—Defendant's statement during plea allocution that he intended to "sell" or "distribute" cocaine was sufficient to establish the intent element of the crime notwithstanding the failure to prove the person or persons to whom the sale or distribution was to made or the amount of the cocaine to be sold or distributed. People v. Jerome, 142 A.D.2d 889, 531 N.Y.S.2d 390 (3d Dept. 1988).

—Judgment reversed where court failed to conduct any inquiry into the facts underlying defendant's pleas, but deferred to defense counsel's assertion that defendant would prefer not to discuss the matter in open court. People v. Fedora, 154 A.D.2d 918, 546 N.Y.S.2d 66 (4th Dept. 1989).

—Mere mouthing of the word "guilty" was insufficient to indicate that the plea was being entered knowingly and intelligently. People v. Bougas, 129 A.D.2d 967, 514 N.Y.S.2d 576 (4th Dept. 1987).

Adequate factual allocution; defenses.—Where there was no proof in the record that the defendant was legally insane at the time of the crime, the court was under no obligation to inquire whether defendant was aware of the possible defense of mental disease. People v. Hicks, 201 A.D.2d 831, 608 N.Y.S.2d 543 (3d Dept. 1994).

—Defendant's statement to the court, that he was so "loaded" at the time the offense was committed that he had no recollection of the events, required further inquiry by the court to ensure that the defendant was knowingly waiving defense of intoxication, and failure to conduct inquiry warranted vacatur of plea. People v. Braman, 136 A.D.2d 382, 527 N.Y.S.2d 104 (3d Dept. 1988).

Adequate factual allocution not required.—There is no requirement for a uniform, mandatory catechism of pleading; for plea to be effective, defendant does not have to acknowledge committing every element of the pleaded-to offense or provide a factual exposition for each element. People v. Seeber, 4 N.Y.3d 780, 793 N.Y.S.2d 826, 826 N.E.2d 797 (2005).

—Having accepted the bargained-for plea, the defendant forfeited the right to challenge the factual basis for that plea. People v. Jackson, 180 A.D.2d 755, 580 N.Y.S.2d 390 (2d Dept. 1992).

—It is well settled that a bargained-for guilty plea to a lesser crime makes unnecessary a factual basis for the crime charged. People v. Perrotti, 153 A.D.2d 992, 545 N.Y.S.2d 436 (2d Dept. 1989).

—Court did not err in accepting defendant's pleas of guilty to 166 felony counts, as set forth in three indictments, without requiring the defendant to give a factual allocution with respect to each count. People v. Samuel, 141 A.D.2d 778, 529 N.Y.S.2d 599 (2d Dept. 1988).

—A guilty plea can be accepted in the absence of a defendant's personal recitation of all the elements of the charged crime when there is no suggestion on the record that the plea was improvident or baseless. People v. Phelps, 140 A.D.2d 637, 528 N.Y.S.2d 673 (2d Dept. 1988).

—Defendant's failure to admit sufficient facts to establish each and every element of the charged offense at his allocution did not, as a matter of law, preclude a valid plea of guilty. People v. Smith, 146 A.D.2d 828, 536 N.Y.S.2d 233 (3d Dept. 1989).

—A guilty plea may be accepted in the absence of a defendant's actual recitation of all the elements of the crime where there is no indication the plea is improvident or baseless. People v. Everett, 146 A.D.2d 950, 536 N.Y.S.2d 911 (3d Dept. 1989).

—There is no requirement that defendant recite the underlying facts during the plea colloquy. People v. Baxtron, 8 A.D.3d 1010, 778 N.Y.S.2d 350 (4th Dept. 2004).

—Where defendant admitted his guilt, the fact that he did not set forth a factual basis for his guilty plea did not render the plea invalid. People v. Lowe, 149 A.D.2d 939, 540 N.Y.S.2d 73 (4th Dept. 1989).

Adequate factual allocution not required; lesser included offenses.—Defendant's plea to a lesser included offense of one

of the charges contained in the indictment served to forfeit his right to challenge the factual basis of the plea. People v. Hereida, 187 A.D.2d 272, 589 N.Y.S.2d 431 (1st Dept. 1992). *See also* People v. Lancaster, 163 A.D.2d 614, 559 N.Y.S.2d 42 (2d Dept. 1990); People v. Tillman, 147 A.D.2d 599, 537 N.Y.S.2d 894 (2d Dept. 1989); People v. McVay, 148 A.D.2d 474, 538 N.Y.S.2d 622 (2d Dept. 1989); People v. Filomeno, 138 A.D.2d 734, 526 N.Y.S.2d 548 (2d Dept. 1988); People v. Rivera, 143 A.D.2d 783, 533 N.Y.S.2d 483 (2d Dept. 1988); People v. Provosty, 141 A.D.2d 867, 529 N.Y.S.2d 894 (2d Dept. 1988); People v. Hadden, 158 A.D.2d 856, 552 N.Y.S.2d 53 (3d Dept. 1990); People v. DuBray, 76 A.D.2d 976, 429 N.Y.S.2d 76 (3d Dept. 1980); People v. Meyers, 151 A.D.2d 1002, 542 N.Y.S.2d 441 (4th Dept. 1989); People v. Middleton, 158 Misc. 2d 157, 599 N.Y.S.2d 460 (Sup. Ct. N.Y. Co. 1993).

—Court did not exceed its discretion in accepting defendant's plea because pleaded-to crime was a lesser offense than the crime charged and each crime involved the same victim and essentially the same factual circumstances. People v. Hahn, 10 A.D.3d 809, 782 N.Y.S.2d 161 (3d Dept. 2004).

Erroneous information; effect on plea.—Defendant's plea was properly vacated after trial court erroneously told him that deliberating jury was leaning 10 to 2 for conviction. Randall v. Rothwax, 78 N.Y.2d 494, 577 N.Y.S.2d 211, 583 N.E.2d 924 (1991).

—Where a plea of guilty is bargained for, mistake of counsel with respect to the minimum sentence does not rise to the level of ineffective assistance of counsel, the test being reasonable competence, not perfect representation. People v. Modica, 64 N.Y.2d 828, 486 N.Y.S.2d 931, 476 N.E.2d 330 (1985).

—The voluntariness of the defendant's plea was not materially affected by the court's erroneous statement concerning the maximum legal sentence, because defendant had acknowledged, after consultation with his attorney and mother, that the plea offer was favorable. People v. Wright, 196 A.D.2d 700, 601 N.Y.S.2d 618 (1st Dept. 1993).

—Plea vacated where it was based on the People's misrepresentation that a ballistics report linked him to a homicide. People v. Pilotti, 127 A.D.2d 23, 511 N.Y.S.2d 248 (1st Dept. 1987).

—Defendant who, prior to his guilty plea, received erroneous advice from counsel as to his possible maximum prison exposure nevertheless received meaningful representation and was not deprived of effective assistance of counsel since his plea bargain resulted in significantly less prison time than his true maximum exposure. People v. Marcano, 114 A.D.2d 976, 495 N.Y.S.2d 419 (2d Dept. 1985).

—Guilty plea and sentence upheld despite the fact the judge, at time of pleading, erroneously informed defendant that sentencing alternative, included probation, conditional or unconditional discharge whereas court could only sentence him to prison, or a rehabilitation program. People v. Caputo, 44 A.D.2d 572, 353 N.Y.S.2d 35 (2d Dept. 1974), aff'd, 36 N.Y.2d 653, 371 N.Y.S.2d 847, 325 N.E.2d 164 (1975).

—Prosecutor's erroneous representation that defendant was exposed to consecutive sentences did not warrant vacatur of the plea. People v. Wilkinson, 151 A.D.2d 801, 542 N.Y.S.2d 50 (3d Dept. 1989).

Prosecutor's role.—So long as the plea agreement is voluntarily, knowingly, and intelligently made, the fact that it is linked to the prosecutor's acceptance of a plea bargain favorable to a third person does not, by itself, make defendant's plea illegal. People v. Fiumefreddo, 82 N.Y.2d 536, 605 N.Y.S.2d 671, 626 N.E.2d 646 (1993).

—It is entirely proper for the court to conduct the plea allocution with the participation of the prosecuting attorney. People v. Anthony, 188 A.D.2d 477, 591 N.Y.S.2d 181 (2d Dept. 1992).

—Plea allocution was upheld notwithstanding the court's practice of delegating the plea allocution to the prosecutor. People v. Bonneau, 142 A.D.2d 890, 531 N.Y.S.2d 391 (3d Dept. 1988).

—Where the practice of allowing a prosecutor to conduct the plea allocution is not approved, the fact that the prosecuting attorney participates in the plea allocution does not necessarily constitute reversible error. People v. Empey, 141 A.D.2d 987, 531 N.Y.S.2d 37 (3d Dept. 1988).

Plea bargains; conditions.—A plea bargain may require that the defendant avoid being arrested before sentence. However, where the defendant claims a new arrest was baseless, he must be given an opportunity to challenge the validity of the new case. People v. Outley, 80 N.Y.2d 702, 594 N.Y.S.2d 683, 610 N.E.2d 356 (1993).

—A plea bargain may require that all defendants plead guilty. People v. Hunt, 176 A.D.2d 528, 574 N.Y.S.2d 718 (1st Dept. 1991).

—A plea is not coerced even though co-defendant would only be allowed to plead if appellant also pled guilty. People v. Bermudez, 157 A.D.2d 533, 549 N.Y.S.2d 1022 (1st Dept. 1990).

—Where defendant breached the plea agreement, the court was free, pursuant to the plea agreement, to impose a greater sentence. People v. Julio S., 181 A.D.2d 424, 580 N.Y.S.2d 749 (1st Dept. 1992).

—A plea bargain may be conditioned on the defendant's testifying against a co-defendant at trial. People v. Cuadrado, 161 A.D.2d 232, 554 N.Y.S.2d 618 (1st Dept. 1990).

—The trial court did not have the authority to enhance defendant's conviction from manslaughter in the first degree to murder in the second degree because of his failure to abide by the conditions of his plea agreement. Instead, the court should have vacated his plea of guilty and given him the opportunity to either plea guilty to murder or proceed to trial. People v. Aponte, 213 A.D.2d 415, 623 N.Y.S.2d 333 (2d Dept. 1995).

—Where a condition for the promise of concurrent terms of imprisonment had not been met, the court was not obligated to allow the defendant to withdraw his guilty plea. People v. Boyd, 179 A.D.2d 815, 579 N.Y.S.2d 696 (2d Dept. 1992).

—Where defendant failed to appear on the scheduled sentencing date, as required by the plea arrangement, the court was free to impose a higher sentence. People v. Malatesta, 172 A.D.2d 692, 568 N.Y.S.2d 836 (2d Dept. 1991).

—Where the defendant fails to comply with a condition of the guilty plea, the court is not bound by its original sentencing promise. People v. Moore, 176 A.D.2d 968, 575 N.Y.S.2d 687 (2d Dept. 1991).

—A plea bargain may be conditioned on the defendant's testifying against a co-defendant at trial. People v. Grant, 99 A.D.2d 536 (2d Dept. 1984).

—The court's allowance of the defendant to plead guilty to two counts of robbery in the first degree in full satisfaction of indictments pending against him and a promise to impose specific concurrent sentences only on the condition that defendant withdraw motion to dismiss and plead guilty immediately, such conditions may be attached so long as they are reasonable and do not amount to overreaching or denial of defendant's right to fundamental fairness. People v. Miller, 79 A.D.2d 687, 434 N.Y.S.2d 36 (2d Dept. 1980).

—Where defendant did not challenge the validity of his post-plea arrest and had been told when he agreed to plead guilty that he would face a higher sentence if he was arrested prior to sentence, court could impose a sentence greater than promised without conducting an inquiry into the foundation for the arrest. People v. McKinnie, 216 A.D.2d 868, 629 N.Y.S.2d 155 (4th Dept. 1995).

—A court may properly condition its sentence promise on defendant not being arrested between the date of the plea and the day of sentencing. People v. Ayers, 192 A.D.2d 1134, 596 N.Y.S.2d 630 (4th Dept. 1993).

Plea bargain; promises.—Defendant was entitled to withdraw his guilty plea where the court promised him a sentence that it could not legally impose. People v. Rogers, 81 A.D.2d 564, 438 N.Y.S.2d 338 (1st Dept. 1981).

—The Supreme Court's review of the victim impact statements contained in the presentence report provided a sufficient basis for the court's departure from the original sentencing promise; since defendant did not claim that he detrimentally relied on the original sentencing agreement, and he was given an opportunity to withdraw his pleas, he was not entitled to specific performance of the original sentencing agreement. People v. Jones, 287 A.D.2d 741, 732 N.Y.S.2d 246 (2d Dept. 2001).

—In order to give effect to a plea commitment, where a manslaughter conviction is reversed, the court must also reverse a defendant's robbery conviction where defendant pleaded guilty to both the robbery and the manslaughter charge on the understanding that he would receive a 5 to 10 year sentence for each to run concurrently. People v. Moore, 87 A.D.2d 639, 448 N.Y.S.2d 213 (2d Dept. 1982).

—A guilty plea induced by an unfulfilled sentence promise must either be vacated or the promise honored. People v. Urquidez, 84 A.D.2d 795, 444 N.Y.S.2d 16 (2d Dept. 1981).

Sentence.—A sentencing court retains discretion in fixing an appropriate sentence up until the time of the sentencing. People v. Schultz, 73 N.Y.2d 75, 536 N.Y.S.2d 46, 532 N.E.2d 1274 (1988).

—Prosecutor is entitled to withdraw his consent to plea where the sentence to be imposed is less than originally negotiated by the parties. People v. Farrar, 52 N.Y.2d 302, 437 N.Y.S.2d 961, 419 N.E.2d 864 (1981).

—Where the sentences imposed were those promised to the defendant at the time of the pleas, the defendant had no basis to complain that the sentences were excessive. People v. Brown, 153 A.D.2d 754, 544 N.Y.S.2d 887 (2d Dept. 1989).

—Court must exercise its discretion at sentencing notwithstanding that a sentence was negotiated at the time of the plea and must be free to impose a lesser penalty if warranted; defendant is entitled to be resentenced in accordance with People v. Farrar, 52 N.Y.2d 302, 437 N.Y.S.2d 961, 419 N.E.2d 864 (1981), and the People have the right to withdraw their consent to the plea in the event the sentence to be imposed is less than that originally negotiated. People v. Biagini, 87 A.D.2d 634, 448 N.Y.S.2d 222 (2d Dept. 1982).

—It is fundamental that a court retains discretion to impose an appropriate sentence notwithstanding the terms of the plea agreement and must exercise that authority. People v. Terry, 152 A.D.2d 822, 543 N.Y.S.2d 766 (3d Dept. 1989).

Preservation; general.—Defendant's claim that the plea should be vacated because of a defective allocution was not preserved by a timely motion to withdraw her plea pursuant to CPL § 220.60(3) or a motion to vacate the judgment of conviction pursuant to CPL § 440.10. People v. Johnson, 82 N.Y.2d 683, 601 N.Y.S.2d 468, 619 N.E.2d 405 (1993). See also People v. Galvan, 197 A.D.2d 394, 602 N.Y.S.2d 380 (1st Dept. 1993).

—Where defendant did not move to withdraw his plea before the imposition of sentence, he did not preserve for appellate review his challenge to the sufficiency of the plea. People v. Ramirez, 159 A.D.2d 392, 553 N.Y.S.2d 94 (1st Dept. 1990).

—Where the defendant failed to move to vacate his plea on the ground that he was unable to hear and understand the proceedings because of a hearing infirmity, the issue was not preserved for appellate review as a matter of law. People v. Robinson, 156 A.D.2d 598, 549 N.Y.S.2d 106 (2d Dept. 1989).

—By failing to make a motion in the trial court to withdraw his plea, the defendant has failed to preserve for appellate review the issue of the sufficiency of the plea allocution. People v. Thompson, 143 A.D.2d 858, 533 N.Y.S.2d 339 (2d Dept. 1988).

—Defendant did not preserve his claim regarding defects in the guilty pleas because he did not move, pursuant to CPL § 440.10, to vacate the judgment. People v. Smith, 145 A.D.2d 517, 535 N.Y.S.2d 110 (2d Dept. 1988).

—Defendant did not preserve for appellate review his claim that his plea of guilty was not voluntarily given since he failed to move on that ground either to withdraw his plea prior to the imposition of sentence or to vacate the judgment of conviction. People v. Walker, 114 A.D.2d 917, 495 N.Y.S.2d 86 (2d Dept. 1985).

—Defendant who failed to raise his objections to the adequacy of his plea allocution to the court's taking the plea did not preserve that issue for appellate review, and in any event, a guilty plea will be sustained unless there is a suggestion either within or dehors the record that the plea was improvident or baseless. People v. Richardson, 114 A.D.2d 980, 495 N.Y.S.2d 235 (2d Dept. 1985).

—By failing to move to withdraw his guilty plea or to vacate the judgment of conviction, defendant failed to preserve for appellate review his claim that the plea allocution was insufficient. People v. Tranka, 191 A.D.2d 903, 595 N.Y.S.2d 250 (3d Dept. 1993). See also People v. Pryslopski, 180 A.D.2d 839, 579 N.Y.S.2d 764 (3d Dept. 1992).

—Issue of conformity of the sentence to defendant's plea agreement was reviewable on appeal despite the absence of a formal CPL § 440.10 or 440.20 motion where the issue was put forth and ruled upon immediately following sentencing. People v. Auslander, 146 A.D.2d 936, 536 N.Y.S.2d 914 (3d Dept. 1989).

Waiver of issues by plea.—Guilty plea will not be vacated merely because defendant stated that he was intoxicated at the time of the commission of the crime and that, therefore, a defense of intoxication may have been available to him; by failing to move to either withdraw the plea or to vacate the judgment, the defendant did not preserve for appellate review the issue of the plea allocution's sufficiency. People v. Bryant, 107 A.D.2d 817, 484 N.Y.S.2d 654 (2d Dept. 1985).

—A defendant does not waive the right to a competency hearing by pleading guilty and may raise for the first time on appeal the issue of capacity to stand trial. People v. Frazier, 114 A.D.2d 1038, 495 N.Y.S.2d 478 (2d Dept. 1985).

—Defendant's plea of guilty waived her claim of error of the trial court's refusal to grant her motion for severance. People v. Cleveland, 81 A.D.2d 944, 439 N.Y.S.2d 697 (3d Dept. 1981).

Waiver of right to appeal.—The defendant's waiver of his right to appeal was conditioned on the premise that the sentence which would ultimately be imposed was the promised sentence; because the court ultimately imposed a harsher sentence than that promised, the waiver should not be enforced. People v. Poole, 202 A.D.2d 450, 608 N.Y.S.2d 502 (2d Dept. 1994).

—The waiver was effective where defendant entered his pleas of guilty and waived his right to appeal the denial of the motion to suppress voluntarily, with full knowledge of the consequences, and on advice of counsel. People v. Andrus, 81 A.D.2d 676, 437 N.Y.S.2d 800 (3d Dept. 1981).

—Defendant's plea which was conditioned on his waiver of his right to appeal the denial of a suppression motion was valid because it was knowingly and voluntarily entered into. People v. Jasper, 107 Misc. 2d 992, 436 N.Y.S.2d 185 (Sup. Ct. N.Y. Co. 1981).

§ 220.60. Plea; change of plea.

1. A defendant who has entered a plea of not guilty to an indictment may as a matter of right withdraw such plea at any time before rendition of a verdict and enter a plea of guilty to the entire indictment pursuant to subdivision two, but subject to the limitation in subdivision five of section 220.10.

2. A defendant who has entered a plea of not guilty to an indictment may, with both the permission of the court and the consent of the people, withdraw such plea at any time before the rendition of a verdict and enter: (a) a plea of guilty to part of the indictment pursuant to subdivision three or four but subject to the limitation in subdivision five of section 220.10, or (b) a plea of not responsible by reason of mental disease or defect to the indictment pursuant to section 220.15 of this chapter.

3. At any time before the imposition of sentence, the court in its discretion may permit a defendant who has entered a plea of guilty to the entire indictment or to part of the indictment, or a plea of not responsible by reason of mental disease or defect, to withdraw such plea, and in such event the entire indictment, as it existed at the time of such plea, is restored.

4. When a special information has been filed pursuant to section 200.61 or 200.62 of this chapter, a defendant may enter a plea of guilty to the count or counts of the indictment to which the special information applies without admitting the allegations of the special information. Whenever a defendant enters a plea of guilty to the count or counts of the indictment to which the

special information applies without admitting the allegations of the special information, the court must, unless the people consent otherwise, conduct a hearing in accordance with paragraph (b) of subdivision two of section 200.62 or paragraph (b) of subdivision three of section 200.61 of this chapter, whichever is applicable.

Amended by L. 1973, Chs. 276, 277, 278; L. 1974, Ch. 367; L. 1980, Ch. 548; L. 1995, Ch. 1, § 12, eff. Sept. 1, 1995, amending subd. 2; L. 2000, Ch. 1, eff. Feb. 1, 2001.

ANNOTATIONS

Plea withdrawal; generally.—In a trilogy of cases concerning defendants' right to withdraw guilty plea, the court, inter alia, held generally that (1) where defendant denies guilt, or court believes him innocent and guilty plea is not otherwise justified as intelligently made, the guilty plea should be rejected, (2) the failure or inability to fulfill a promise requires either that the plea of guilty be vacated or the promise kept and the sentencing court has the discretion to choose; (3) where the court cannot or will not impose the sentence previously promised it should specify, on the record, the reason for its changed view. The court also held that when at the time of the guilty plea, the court promised no imprisonment and relied on the minimal involvement of the defendant, it could later, if it discovered that he was a major piece rather than a pawn in the fraudulent scheme, refuse to impose promised sentence and allow him to withdraw the plea. The court further held that a promise made by the prosecutor to defendant without the knowledge of the court could not, as a matter of law, be relied on by defendant. People v. Selikoff, 35 N.Y.2d 227, 360 N.Y.S.2d 623, 318 N.E.2d 784, *cert. denied,* 419 U.S. 1122 (1974).

—Guilty plea withdrawal is in the court's discretion. A guilty plea may not be withdrawn absent some evidence or claim of innocence, fraud, or mistake in its inducement. People v. Griffin, 4 A.D.3d 674, 772 N.Y.S.2d 747 (3d Dept. 2004).

—Where the negotiated terms of sentence were statutorily unauthorized, the underlying plea agreement was invalid from its inception. People v. Curkendall, 141 A.D.2d 891, 529 N.Y.S.2d 402 (3d Dept. 1988).

Constitutionality; subd. 2(a).—The provisions of the New York death penalty statute, specifically, CPL §§ 220.10(5)(e) and 220.30(3)(b)(vii), are unconstitutional for the same reason as the Federal Kidnapping Act, because by statutory mandate, the death penalty hangs over only those who exercise their constitutional rights to maintain innocence and demand a jury trial. Accordingly, the court was compelled by *United States v. Jackson,* 390 U.S. 570, to invalidate those provisions. However, CPL § 220.60(2)(a) was not limited to first degree murder cases, and it does not, in the absence of CPL § 220.10(5)(e), violate *Jackson.* Therefore, CPL § 220.60(2)(a) does not need to be stricken. Hynes v. Tomei, 92 N.Y.2d 613, 684 N.Y.S.2d 177, 706 N.E.2d 1201 (1998), *cert. denied,* 527 U.S. 1015 (1999).

—Court upheld the constitutionality of CPL §§ 220.10(5)(e), 220.30(3)(b)(vii), and 220.60, which defendant challenged to the extent that they provide that a sentence of death for first degree murder could only be imposed upon a conviction after trial and could not be imposed after a guilty plea, a plea that can be entered only with People's consent and court's approval. People v. McIntosh, 173 Misc. 2d 727, 662 N.Y.S.2d 214 (Dutchess Co. Ct. 1997).

Court's role on motion to withdraw plea.—There is no absolute right to withdraw a guilty plea and a motion for such relief is within the trial court's discretion. People v. Arias, 161 A.D.2d 176, 554 N.Y.S.2d 560 (1st Dept. 1990).

—The determination as to whether to allow a defendant to withdraw a previously entered plea of guilty rests within the sound discretion of the sentencing court. People v. Alexander, 97 N.Y.2d 482, 743 N.Y.S.2d 45, 769 N.E.2d 802 (2002); People v. White, 226 A.D.2d 750, 641 N.Y.S.2d 856 (2d Dept. 1996); *see also* People v. DeJesus, 199 A.D.2d 529, 606 N.Y.S.2d 255 (2d Dept. 1993); People v. Ladelokun, 192 A.D.2d 723, 597 N.Y.S.2d 123 (2d Dept. 1993); People v. Fulmore, 189 A.D.2d 823, 592 N.Y.S.2d 449 (2d Dept. 1993); People v. Saunders, 188 A.D.2d 624, 591 N.Y.S.2d 473 (2d

Dept. 1992); People v. Gordon, 183 A.D.2d 915, 584 N.Y.S.2d 318 (2d Dept. 1992); People v. Lewis, 170 A.D.2d 538, 566 N.Y.S.2d 95 (2d Dept.), *lv. denied,* 77 N.Y.2d 997 (1991); People v. O'Callaghan, 171 A.D.2d 706, 567 N.Y.S.2d 167 (2d Dept. 1991); People v. Walters, 176 A.D.2d 277, 574 N.Y.S.2d 384 (2d Dept. 1991); People v. Dickerson, 163 A.D.2d 610, 559 N.Y.S.2d 40 (2d Dept. 1990); People v. Cance, 155 A.D.2d 764, 547 N.Y.S.2d 702 (3d Dept. 1990); People v. Murray, 207 A.D.2d 999, 617 N.Y.S.2d 253 (4th Dept. 1994).

—A motion to withdraw a plea of guilty is addressed to the sound discretion of the court and only in the rare instance will a defendant be entitled to an evidentiary hearing. People v. Rodriguez, 150 A.D.2d 812, 542 N.Y.S.2d 234 (2d Dept.), *lv. denied,* 74 N.Y.2d 818 (1989).

—Application to withdraw a guilty plea is addressed to the sound discretion of the trial court and, absent a showing of abuse, the court's determination should not be disturbed. People v. Franco, 145 A.D.2d 837, 535 N.Y.S.2d 823 (3d Dept. 1988).

—It is the acceptance by the Court, and not the proffer by defendant, that makes a guilty plea cognizable, because in New York, a guilty plea carrying a promised sentence cannot be entered without the permission of the court. People v. Smelefsky, 182 Misc. 2d 11, 695 N.Y.S.2d 689 (Sup. Ct. Queens Co. 1999).

Court's role on motion to withdraw plea: power to vacate.—A trial court lacks inherent power to vacate an illegally imposed plea and sentence once the criminal proceeding has terminated by entry of judgment. Kisloff v. Covington, 73 N.Y.2d 445, 541 N.Y.S.2d 737, 539 N.E.2d 565 (1989).

—The court had the inherent power to vacate a "not responsible" plea where the prosecutor showed that such plea was obtained by defendant's fraud in that he misrepresented himself to be a Vietnam veteran. Lockett v. Juviler, 65 N.Y.2d 182, 490 N.Y.S.2d 764, 480 N.E.2d 378 (1985).

—Guilty plea by defendant of low level education and tubercular, who, with district attorney, Judge and defense counsel, was under mistaken belief that he was not a fourth felony offender could be withdrawn sentence of 15 years vacated. People v. Nettles, 30 N.Y.2d 841, 335 N.Y.S.2d 83, 286 N.E.2d 467 (1972).

—After its acceptance and full agreement on sentence reached, in the absence of fraud the court has no inherent power to set aside the plea without defendant's consent; where a court sets aside a plea under those circumstances, the order may be the subject of an Article 78 proceeding. Crooms v. Corriero, 206 A.D.2d 275, 614 N.Y.S.2d 511 (1st Dept.), *lv. denied,* 84 N.Y.2d 809 (1994).

—In the absence of fraud, once a court accepts a guilty plea it has no inherent power to set aside the plea without the defendant's consent; however, a court may vacate a plea on application of the prosecutor where it was obtained by fraud or misrepresentation, provided there is no constitutional impediment. People v. Franco, 158 A.D.2d 33, 557 N.Y.S.2d 7 (1st Dept. 1990).

—The court could not sua sponte vacate defendant's guilty plea because defendant's probation report stated that defendant denied involvement in the crime charged; in the absence of fraud, once a court accepts a plea, it has no inherent power to set the plea aside without defendant's consent. People v. Prato, 89 A.D.2d 852, 453 N.Y.S.2d 41 (2d Dept. 1982).

—The sentencing court generally must adhere to the terms of the plea in the absence of relevant new information becoming available between the time of the taking of the plea and the date of sentencing. People v. Carner, 142 A.D.2d 789, 531 N.Y.S.2d 50 (3d Dept. 1988).

—If a court exceeds its judicial authority by vacating a plea without a defendant's consent, a writ of prohibition pursuant to CPLR Article 78 is a proper remedy. Moran v. Daley, 12 A.D.3d 1074, 785 N.Y.S.2d 264 (2004), *petition granted,* 16 A.D.3d 1045, 792 N.Y.S.2d 884 (4th Dept. 2005) (order prohibiting judge from reinstating indictment because court vacated plea in absence of defendant's consent).

—Court lacked authority to vacate the plea without defendant's consent where, as here, there was no new evidence, fraud, or clerical error to justify vacatur. People v. Searcy, 2 A.D.3d 1395, 770 N.Y.S.2d 493 (4th Dept. 2003).

First-degree murder cases.—A defendant arraigned upon an indictment charging, inter alia, first-degree murder, may not plead to the entire indictment and avoid the possibility of the death penalty verdict until the District Attorney has either declined to file his CPL § 250.40 notice on the record, consents to such plea, or the 120-day period with any court ordered extensions has expired. People v. Schroedel, 182 Misc. 2d 154, 697 N.Y.S.2d 904 (Co. Ct. Sullivan Co. 1999), *cert. denied,* 531 U.S. 860 (2000).

Right to a hearing on motion to withdraw plea.—Where defendant orally moves at sentencing to withdraw a guilty plea, the court may, in the exercise of sound discretion, hold an evidentiary hearing. People v. Miller, 42 N.Y.2d 946, 398 N.Y.S.2d 133, 367 N.E.2d 640 (1977).

—Withdrawal of guilty plea, tendered at completion of People's case-in-chief during which strong evidence of defendant's guilt was presented, was properly denied without an additional hearing where, even though defendant did not admit allegations, there was no evidence that defendant misunderstood or misapprehended the charges. People v. Friedman, 39 N.Y.2d 463, 384 N.Y.S.2d 408, 348 N.E.2d 883 (1976).

—Denial of defendant's motion, at time of sentencing, to withdraw his plea of guilty was not an abuse of discretion where the court reviewed the events taking place before entry of the plea and read into the record the minutes of the proceedings at the time of entry of the plea which included an admission of defendant's identity as the person who committed the crime, a waiver of his rights, an acknowledgment of a discussion of the plea and its effect with his attorney and of his understanding of the proceedings and a disclaimer of any coercion or promise as a motivation of the plea. People v. Garret, 43 A.D.2d 503, 352 N.Y.S.2d 713 (4th Dept. 1974), *aff'd,* 36 N.Y.2d 727, 367 N.Y.S.2d 975, 328 N.E.2d 487 (1975).

—The nature and extent of the fact-finding procedures prerequisite to the disposition of a motion to withdraw a plea of guilty rest largely in the discretion of the judge to whom the motion is made. Only in the rare instance will a defendant be entitled to an evidentiary hearing; often a limited interrogation by the court will suffice. People v. Tinsley, 35 N.Y.2d 926, 365 N.Y.S.2d 161, 324 N.E.2d 544 (1974).

—Court was not required either to grant defendant's pro se motion to withdraw his guilty plea or hold an immediate hearing on the voluntariness of the plea, since the court was sufficiently familiar with the defendant and the facts of the case to summarily dispose of defendant's last-ditch effort to avoid detention. People v. Guerrone, 208 A.D.2d 383, 617 N.Y.S.2d 16 (1st Dept. 1994).

—Whether an evidentiary hearing is necessary to determine a motion to withdraw a plea is a matter left to the discretion of the judge hearing the motion, and only in rare instances will a defendant be entitled to such a hearing. People v. Martinez, 204 A.D.2d 230, 612 N.Y.S.2d 40 (1st Dept.), *lv. denied,* 84 N.Y.2d 908 (1994).

—The court properly denied, without a hearing, the defendant's motion to withdraw his plea, where he failed to substantiate his allegations of innocence, coercion and ignorance as to the ramifications of the plea. People v. Baez, 188 A.D.2d 365, 591 N.Y.S.2d 40 (1st Dept. 1992).

—A statutorily-mandated post-release supervision is a direct consequence of a plea, but case was remitted under the circumstances for a hearing to determine if defendant would not have pleaded guilty had he been so informed. People v. Melio, 304 A.D.2d 247, 760 N.Y.S.2d 216 (2d Dept. 2003), *aff'd on appeal after remand,* — A.D.2d —, 775 N.Y.S.2d 346 (3d Dept. 2004).

—Only in rare instances will an evidentiary hearing be required on a defendant's application to withdraw his guilty plea. People v. Sendel, 158 A.D.2d 726, 552 N.Y.S.2d 173 (2d Dept. 1990).

—A hearing was required when defendant sought to withdraw his guilty plea and alleged that counsel misrepresented the nature of his experience in criminal law and the defendant relied on that misrepresentation in pleading guilty, which could affect whether the plea was rational or knowing. People v. Parizo, 78 A.D.2d 863, 432 N.Y.S.2d 627 (2d Dept. 1980).

—Court properly refused to conduct a full evidentiary hearing on defendant's application to withdraw his guilty plea where the court had afforded the defendant a full and complete opportunity to propound and substantiate his claim. People v. Zuk, 130 A.D.2d 886, 515 N.Y.S.2d 657 (3d Dept.), *lv. denied,* 70 N.Y.2d 659 (1987).

—A plea of guilty may be withdrawn when there is some evidence or claim of innocence, fraud or mistake in inducing the plea. People v. Bryan D.D., 77 A.D.2d 963, 429 N.Y.S.2d 77 (3d Dept. 1980).

Inadequate reason to withdraw plea.—Court denied defendant's motion to withdraw his plea "for reasons of his own"; defendant was given an ample opportunity to state the basis for his application to withdraw his plea, and the basis given by him was facially without merit. People v. Hyman, 247 A.D.2d 553, 668 N.Y.S.2d 484 (2d Dept. 1998).

Right to a hearing on motion to withdraw plea; claims of innocence.—"A defendant is not entitled to withdraw of his guilty plea based on a subsequent unsupported claim of innocence, where the guilty plea was voluntarily made with the advice of counsel following an appraisal of all the relevant factors including defendant's numerous prior convictions, the likelihood of eyewitness testimony confronting him at a trial and the hope of a reduced charge and sentence." People v. Dixon, 29 N.Y.2d 55, 323 N.Y.S.2d 825, 272 N.E.2d 329 (1971).

—The sentencing court did not abuse its discretion in refusing to allow defendant to withdraw his guilty plea based on his bare assertion of innocence and his fear that his criminal history would necessarily lead to a conviction. People v. Carreras, 200 A.D.2d 534, 607 N.Y.S.2d 16 (1st Dept. 1994).

—Where the totality of the circumstances demonstrate that a plea was knowingly and voluntarily entered, its validity is not undermined by subsequent protestations of innocence. People v. Graham, 191 A.D.2d 353, 595 N.Y.S.2d 759 (1st Dept. 1993).

—The determination as to whether to allow a defendant to withdraw a previously entered plea of guilty rests within the sound discretion of the sentencing court. Only in rare instances will a defendant be entitled to an evidentiary hearing upon a motion to withdraw a plea. People v. Sain, 261 A.D.2d 488, 691 N.Y.S.2d 64 (2d Dept. 1999).

—The sentencing court properly denied defendant's request to withdraw his plea and imposed sentence without further inquiry because the defendant's assertion of innocence was conclusory in nature. People v. Billings, 208 A.D.2d 941, 617 N.Y.S.2d 864 (2d Dept. 1994).

—A defendant may not withdraw a guilty plea by an unsupported assertion of innocence where the plea was voluntarily made with the advice of competent counsel following an appraisal of all relevant facts. People v. Youmans, 177 A.D.2d 679, 576 N.Y.S.2d 373 (2d Dept. 1991).

—In the absence of anything in the record to suggest that the defendant's plea was either improvident or baseless, the sentencing court did not abuse its discretion in denying the defendant's application to withdraw his plea, predicated upon a bare assertion of innocence and having been under personal pressure at the time the plea was entered. People v. Suba, 129 A.D.2d 611, 515 N.Y.S.2d 106 (2d Dept. 1987).

—Court properly denied, without a hearing, the defendant's motion to withdraw his plea of guilty where he failed to substantiate his bald allegations of innocence, coercion, and ignorance as to the ramifications of the plea, which arguments were rendered particularly unpersuasive in light of his prior experience with the law. People v. Kafka, 128 A.D.2d 895, 513 N.Y.S.2d 820 (2d Dept. 1987).

—A defendant may not withdraw his guilty plea by proffering an unsupported claim of innocence where the plea was voluntarily made with the advice of competent counsel following an appraisal of all relevant factors. People v. Tannenbaum, 116 A.D.2d 677, 497 N.Y.S.2d 745 (2d Dept. 1986).

—A defendant who requests to withdraw his plea at the time of sentence must be given a reasonable opportunity to advance his claims; however, only in the rare instance will a defendant be entitled to an evidentiary hearing; often, a limited interrogation will suffice. People v. Colon, 114 A.D.2d 967, 495 N.Y.S.2d 414 (2d Dept. 1985).

—A court should not impose sentence over defendant protestations of innocence after his guilty plea without at the very least undertaking a "limited interrogation" of the defendant concerning his claim. People v. King, 88 A.D.2d 938 450 N.Y.S.2d 868 (2d Dept. 1982).

—Defendant's motion to withdraw guilty plea on a claim of innocence was properly denied without a hearing because defendant made no claims of innocence during the plea allocution. People v. Zakrzewski, 7 A.D.3d 881, 776 N.Y.S.2d 377 (3d Dept. 2004).

—Where the defendant never protested his innocence or complained of the adequacy of his counsel, or the excessiveness of his sentence, and had fully admitted his guilt of the crime to which he pleaded guilty, the court properly exercised its discretion in summarily denying defendant's motion to withdraw his plea. People v. Normandin, 122 A.D.2d 348, 504 N.Y.S.2d 316 (3d Dept. 1986).

—Defendant's generalized claim of innocence, which was not made during the plea allocution did not entitle him to withdraw his guilty plea. People v. O'Keefe, 170 A.D.2d 1020, 566 N.Y.S.2d 166 (4th Dept. 1991).

—On a motion to withdraw a guilty plea conclusory allegations of innocence and coercion are insufficient to warrant a hearing. People v. Price, 140 A.D.2d 927, 529 N.Y.S.2d 607 (4th Dept.), *appeal withdrawn,* 72 N.Y.2d 913 (1988).

Motion to withdraw plea; sufficiency of evidence.—Court properly rejected defendant's argument in support of motion to withdraw guilty plea on the ground that he did not admit intent element of assault in the first degree; although at one point in the plea colloquy defendant stated that the gun went off accidentally, defendant responded affirmatively to court's specific inquiry as to whether he admitted shooting one of the victim's with the intent to cause serious physical injury. People v. Jackson, 130 A.D.2d 810, 514 N.Y.S.2d 834 (2d Dept. 1987).

—Court did not abuse its discretion in denying defendant's motion to withdraw his guilty plea since the defendant, on at least three occasions during his plea allocution, admitted his guilt of the charged crime. People v. McDonald, 135 A.D.2d 837, 522 N.Y.S.2d 940 (2d Dept. 1987).

—Trial court properly denied defendant's motion to withdraw his guilty plea without a hearing where defendant's narrative of the events surrounding the commission of the crime established his guilt of all the elements of the crime involved. People v. Kepple, 98 A.D.2d 783, 469 N.Y.S.2d 801 (2d Dept. 1983).

—Where defense attorneys represented that based upon prior proceedings, their discussions with the D.A.'s office, their years of experience, and after full consultation with their clients, the defendants decided to plead guilty pursuant to North Carolina v. Alford, 400 U.S. 25, 91 S. Ct. 160, 27 L. Ed. 2d 162 (1970), and People v. Serrano, 15 N.Y.2d 304, 258 N.Y.S.2d 386, 206 N.E.2d 330 (1965), and the record was clear that all participants believed that the requirements of a knowing and voluntary plea were present, the essential elements of a valid guilty plea were present though no underlying factual basis was placed on the record. People v. Bruno, 74 A.D.2d 577, 424 N.Y.S.2d 299 (2d Dept. 1980).

—The Court properly denied defendant's motion to withdraw his plea of guilty where there was strong evidence of his actual guilt and it was clear that defendant's plea was made after careful consideration of all his options in consultation with his attorney. People v. Dubay, 95 A.D.2d 900, 463 N.Y.S.2d 918 (3d Dept. 1983).

—Trial court's refusal to permit withdrawal of defendant's guilty plea was not error where defendant made a written statement the day of the crime detailing his participation and his counsel's comment, made during sentencing, that defendant had the "weakest defense that I have run across in this case." People v. Magnini, 80 A.D.2d 940, 440 N.Y.S.2d 728 (3d Dept. 1981).

Motion to withdraw plea; voluntariness.—Trial court did not abuse its discretion in denying defendant's motion to withdraw plea, because court was able to firsthand assess whether defendant was alert and knowledgeable enough to plead guilty voluntarily, and court considered defendant's familiarity with the criminal justice system. People v. Alexander, 97 N.Y.2d 482, 743 N.Y.S.2d 45, 769 N.E.2d 802 (2002).

—In prosecution for disorderly conduct and resisting arrest, it was error for the court to deny defendant's motion to withdraw his guilty plea without a hearing where defendant claimed that such plea, entered without the advice of counsel, was made as a result of his conversation with a police officer who stated that defendant would be released on his own recognizance if he pleaded guilty, and where the People's only challenge to this claim consisted of the district attorney's vague affidavit, based on information and belief, which asserted that the conversation in question never took place. People v. Wheaton, 45 N.Y.2d 769, 408 N.Y.S.2d 498, 380 N.E.2d 324 (1978).

—Where court advised defendant of its personal policy of sentencing predicate felony offenders who are convicted after trial to the high end of the sentencing chart, specifically 12½ to 25 years, it was coercion that rendered involuntary defendant's guilty plea to another charge under the plea agreement, because the court's policy would have exposed defendant to almost four times the sentence under the plea offer; motion to withdraw plea should have been granted. People v. Wilson, 245 A.D.2d 161, 666 N.Y.S.2d 164 (1st Dept. 1997).

—A new fact-finding hearing was required where the judge erroneously failed to explain to the juvenile that he was waiving his constitutional rights to trial, confrontation, cross-examination, and did not explain the consequences flowing from such waiver. In re Daniel, B., etc., 82 A.D.2d 761, 440 N.Y.S.2d 207 (1st Dept. 1981).

—Defendant's plea of guilty was vacated where, after being convicted by a jury of one charge of robbery, first degree (PL § 160.15), but before sentence was imposed, he was induced to plead guilty to a second charge by the explicit threat of a heavier sentence should he choose to proceed to trial. People v. Hollis, 74 A.D.2d 585, 424 N.Y.S.2d 483 (2d Dept. 1980).

—Court found no merit to defendant's contention that his plea was not knowingly entered because of a lack of fluency in English, since defendant provided detailed information with no apparent language difficulty during plea colloquy. People v. Torres, 4 A.D.3d 624, 772 N.Y.S.2d 125 (3d Dept. 2004).

—Court did not abuse discretion in denying defendant's motion to withdraw his plea where record reflects that before accepting plea, the court ascertained that defendant understood the nature and consequences of his plea, including the rights being relinquished and that he was thinking clearly. People v. Kagonyera, 304 A.D.2d 984, 759 N.Y.S.2d 785 (3d Dept. 2003).

—Court properly denied defendant's motion to withdraw his guilty plea, rejecting defendant's claim that he entered the plea as a result of the stress of the situation and ineffective assistance of counsel; record revealed that plea was entered into knowingly and voluntarily, and defendant stated unequivocally that his plea was not induced by force or threat. People v. Merck, 242 A.D.2d 792, 661 N.Y.S.2d 881 (3d Dept. 1997).

—Trial court properly refused to grant defendant's motion to withdraw his guilty plea where he was advised that the plea was the same as a conviction following a jury trial, he freely admitted his guilt, discussed the guilty plea with his attorney and understood the plea bargain agreement. People v. Jones, 95 A.D.2d 869, 463 N.Y.S.2d 888 (3d Dept. 1983).

Motion to withdraw plea; voluntariness, coercion, and duress.—Coercion by defendant's family members was no reason to vacate a guilty plea. People v. Lewis, 46 N.Y.2d 825, 414 N.Y.S.2d 116, 386 N.E.2d 1084 (1978).

—The defendant's appeal from his conviction on the ground that his guilty plea was coerced was denied where the defendant had requested and received two adjournments for the purpose of deciding whether to plead guilty or to go to trial. People v. Esajerre, 43 A.D.2d 541, 349 N.Y.S.2d 108 (1st Dept. 1973), aff'd, 35 N.Y.2d 463, 363 N.Y.S.2d 931, 323 N.E.2d 175 (1974).

—A plea of guilty may be withdrawn when the plea was made to secure removal from local jail in which defendant was detained and in which he had been sexually abused and beaten by other inmates and was in potential danger of his life. The plea cannot stand even if it was motivated only in part by the duress visited upon defendant by anarchic and criminal conditions in the jail. It is immaterial that there were other motivations, as well, for the plea. People v. Flowers, 30 N.Y.2d 315, 333 N.Y.S.2d 393, 284 N.E.2d 454 (1972).

—The defendant's allegations of coercion and inadequate representation made in his motion two months after his plea, were belied by the record of both the plea and sentencing proceedings, in which the defendant expressed the fact that he understood the plea he was entering and that his motive in entering the plea was a promise of early parole. People v. Campbell, 200 A.D.2d 364, 606 N.Y.S.2d 186 (1st Dept.), lv. denied, 83 N.Y.2d 869 (1994).

—Defendant's bald assertions of coercion, allegedly due to the prosecutor's withholding of consent to accept the guilty pleas unless both defendants entered such pleas, were properly rejected. People v. Bermudez, 157 A.D.2d 533, 549 N.Y.S.2d 1022 (1st Dept.), lv. denied, 75 N.Y.2d 964 (1990).

—The defendant's protestations at sentencing that he was coerced into pleading guilty and that he was innocent were refuted by the record of the plea proceedings, in which he had stated under oath that he was not being coerced into pleading guilty, that he possessed cocaine with the intent to sell it, and that he was satisfied with the representation being given by his counsel. People v. Lisbon, 187 A.D.2d 457, 589 N.Y.S.2d 527 (2d Dept. 1992).

—Defendant's conclusory allegation at sentencing, that he had been coerced by his attorney into pleading guilty did not provide a basis for withdrawal of his guilty plea. People v. Scialphi, 178 A.D.2d 569, 577 N.Y.S.2d 655 (2d Dept. 1991).

—Defense counsel's vague and conclusory allegation of police coercion was belied by the defendant's own statements at the time of the pleas to the effect that he was freely and voluntarily admitting his guilt, and no evidentiary hearing on the issue was required inasmuch as the defendant was afforded an ample opportunity to state the basis for the withdrawal application. People v. Martin, 157 A.D.2d 674, 549 N.Y.S.2d 776 (2d Dept. 1990).

—The fact that counsel made defendant aware of his sentencing exposure cannot be a basis for finding coercion; while the pressures of considering a plea may be stressful, they do not constitute duress or coercion. People v. Kelly, 157 A.D.2d 227, 552 N.Y.S.2d 32 (2d Dept. 1990).

—Court properly denied the defendant's motion to withdraw his guilty plea where any reluctance on the part of defendant in entering his guilty plea was attributable not to threats or coercion but to defendant's unhappiness with the harsh realities of his situation. People v. Wilmer, 191 A.D.2d 850, 595 N.Y.S.2d 123 (3d Dept.), lv. denied, 81 N.Y.2d 1022 (1993).

—Defendant's conclusory statements of coercion and duress did not require a hearing on his motion to withdraw his guilty plea. People v. DeGaspard, 170 A.D.2d 835, 566 N.Y.S.2d 667, 670 (3d Dept.), lv. denied, 77 N.Y.2d 994 (1991).

—Defendant's factual admission of guilt was not coerced by County Court or by defense counsel's alleged misrepresentation concerning the potential incarceration, because by the time of his sentencing, defendant had twice been found competent, and there is nothing in the record to suggest that at the time of the plea, he was unable to understand the charges or assist in his defense. People v. Lioto, 261 A.D.2d 883, 691 N.Y.S.2d 225 (4th Dept. 1999).

Motion to withdraw plea; defendant's use of drugs or medication.—Court properly denied defendant's request to withdraw his plea based on on claim that he was under the influence of anxiety medication at plea entry which caused him to experience difficulty concentrating and to be emotionally ambivalent, where counsel testified that defendant appeared to understand the proceedings and did not exhibit a mental impairment. People v. Stone, 303 A.D.2d 782, 758 N.Y.S.2d 176 (3d Dept. 2003).

Counsel; during guilty plea proceedings.—When a defendant waives his right to counsel and pleads guilty, there should be a painstaking effort by the trial court to make sure that the accused understands the consequences of the waiver and plea and that defendant committed an act which constituted a crime and which would furnish a basis for the plea. People v. Gina M.M., 40 N.Y.2d 595, 388 N.Y.S.2d 899, 357 N.E.2d 370 (1976).

—The court properly denied, without a hearing, the defendant's pro se motion to withdraw his guilty plea; defendant's allegations of coercion and inadequate representation, made at sentencing, were belied by the record of the plea proceedings, in which he expressly stated, under oath, that he was pleading guilty of his own free will and that he had no complaints about the representation being provided to him. People v. Alicea, 191 A.D.2d 702, 595 N.Y.S.2d 528 (2d Dept.), lv. denied, 81 N.Y.2d 1069 (1993).

—The defendant's conclusory and unsubstantiated claim of ineffective assistance of counsel and his generalized assertion of innocence were patently inadequate to warrant withdrawal of the plea. People v. Carter, 191 A.D.2d 640, 595 N.Y.S.2d 219 (2d Dept. 1993).

—Sentencing court did not abuse its discretion in denying the defendant's motion to withdraw his guilty pleas since there was absolutely no support for the defendant's claim that his assigned counsel was, in effect, not affording him adequate representation. People v. Perez, 119 A.D.2d 838, 501 N.Y.S.2d 464 (2d Dept. 1986).

—Defendant's guilty plea was not a knowing one where his attorney failed to explain that a plea of guilty extinguishes the right to appeal denial of a motion pursuant to CPL § 30.30. People v. Schurman, 81 A.D.2d 898, 439 N.Y.S.2d 151 (2d Dept. 1981).

—Court properly denied without a hearing the defendant's motion to withdraw a guilty plea as being a product of duress; defendant's appellate claim that he entered his guilty plea solely to obtain his temporary release so that he could witness the birth of his son was raised, explored, and expressly refuted at the plea proceeding prior to acceptance of defendant's plea. People v. Dale, 235 A.D.2d 565, 652 N.Y.S.2d 335 (3d Dept. 1997).

—It is not enough for a defendant seeking to set aside a plea to aver that counsel incorrectly appraised the facts or failed to pursue certain factual inquiries which might have uncovered other defenses or possible constitutional infirmities. People v. Hibbard, 150 A.D.2d 929, 41 N.Y.S.2d 272 (3d Dept. 1989).

—Tactical decision to forego making pretrial motions when an advantageous plea bargain had been struck may not be attacked on appeal and labeled ineffective assistance of counsel where overwhelming evidence implicated defendant in the crime and the defendant faced a potentially life-long period of incarceration. People v. Lewis, 116 A.D.2d 778, 497 N.Y.S.2d 297 (3d Dept. 1986).

—Court rejected claim that lack of communication with defense counsel and fear that a life sentence would result if he went to trial caused defendant such duress as to render his plea involuntary; record furnished no support for the charge that communication with counsel was wanting, and the pressures which confronted defendant, no neophyte in the criminal justice system, were those commonly faced by a defendant evaluating a plea. People v. Yarber, 122 A.D.2d 433, 504 N.Y.S.2d 830 (3d Dept. 1986).

—Where defendant's guilty plea was made following extensive consultation with counsel and after thorough interrogation by court during which defendant made an intelligent waiver of his trial rights, admitted commission of the crime to which he was pleading, and stated that his plea was voluntary and made without any promise as to punishment, the court properly refused to permit defendant to withdraw his plea, on grounds of inadequacy of counsel, where defendant's claim lacked specificity and factual support in the record; refusal to permit withdrawal of prior guilty plea is not an abuse of discretion absent some evidence or claim of innocence, fraud or mistake in inducing the plea. People v. Randolph, 78 A.D.2d 566, 431 N.Y.S.2d 734 (3d Dept. 1980).

—By requiring defense counsel to give his opinion that defendant had voluntarily pleaded guilty and would lose if his case went to trial, the court denied defendant the effective assistance of counsel on his motion to withdraw his plea. People v. Welsh, 207 A.D.2d 1025, 617 N.Y.S.2d 107 (4th Dept. 1994).

Counsel; on motion to withdraw plea.—The fact that defense counsel allowed the defendant to proceed pro se on his application to withdraw his guilty plea did not constitute ineffective assistance of counsel. People v. Pernell, 189 A.D.2d 833, 592 N.Y.S.2d 466 (2d Dept. 1993).

—Trial court committed reversible error where it determined defendant's pro se motion to withdraw his negotiated plea, without first assigning the defendant different counsel. People v. Stanley, 81 A.D.2d 842, 438 N.Y.S.2d 848 (2d Dept. 1981).

—Defense counsel's failure to actively participate in the defendant's application to withdraw his plea did not constitute ineffective assistance of counsel because the defendant was provided adequate opportunity to present his contention and counsel's lack of participation worked no discernible prejudice. People v. Bell, 141 A.D.2d 749, 529 N.Y.S.2d 845 (2d Dept. 1988).

—As the defendant's counsel was able to negotiate a plea which satisfied the two-count A-1 felony indictment in addition to three other pending, unrelated felony charges, his performance cannot be deemed ineffective. People v. Michalgo, 120 A.D.2d 675, 502 N.Y.S.2d 270 (2d Dept. 1986).

—Once counsel has been compelled to become a witness with respect to the merits of defendant's claim of innocence at a hearing on a motion to withdraw his plea he can no longer represent the defendant and new counsel should be assigned. People v. Wilson, 91 A.D.2d 1052, 458 N.Y.S.2d 655 (2d Dept. 1983).

—Court rejected claim that it was error for counsel to fail to participate in the defendant's application to withdraw his plea where the record revealed that the defendant was hostile and uncooperative. People v. Lynch, 156 A.D.2d 884, 550 N.Y.S.2d 104 (3d Dept.), lv. denied, 75 N.Y.2d 921 (1990).

—Defense counsel's failure to actively participate in the defendant's application to withdraw his guilty plea did not constitute ineffective assistance of counsel, since the defendant was provided an adequate opportunity to present his contentions and counsel's lack of participation worked no discernible prejudice. People v. Rodriguez, 188 A.D.2d 623, 591 N.Y.S.2d 846 (2d Dept. 1992), lv. denied, 81 N.Y.2d 891 (1993).

Plea bargain; conditions.—Defendant's claim that he was not given his promised sentence is to be tested against an objective reading of the bargain and not against his subjective interpretations thereof. People v. Acosta, 187 A.D.2d 329, 590 N.Y.S.2d 77 (1st Dept. 1992).

—Whether or not a defendant has performed his end of a plea bargain is not tested by the defendant's subjective interpretation but rather by an objective interpretation of the agreement. People v. Cuadrado, 161 A.D.2d 232, 554 N.Y.S.2d 618 (1st Dept. 1990).

—The defendant's motion to withdraw his guilty plea should have been granted where the transcript of the plea proceeding did not indicate that the defendant was told nor could it be implied therefrom that he understood that if he failed to appear on the date scheduled for sentencing, the court could impose a harsher sentence than the one promised. People v. Cook, 130 A.D.2d 503, 515 N.Y.S.2d 84 (2d Dept. 1987).

—Defendant could not be heard to complain about a harsher sentence where he was specifically informed by the plea court that if it was discovered that he had been convicted of a predicate felony, he would be subject to different or additional punishment. People v. Atkinson, 127 A.D.2d 841, 512 N.Y.S.2d 232 (2d Dept. 1987).

—Court abused its discretion in increasing the defendant's negotiated sentence based upon his mere violation of a plea condition that the information he conveys during the probation department interview conform with the facts recited at the allocution. People v. Carr, 135 A.D.2d 722, 522 N.Y.S.2d 623 (2d Dept. 1987).

—A sentencing court need not permit a defendant to withdraw a plea where the defendant himself has failed to fulfill an explicit condition underlying the sentence agreement. People v. Patterson, 208 A.D.2d 987, 617 N.Y.S.2d 221 (3d Dept. 1994).

—Once the defendant was found to have breached one of the conditions of the plea agreement, the court was free to impose enhanced sentences without allowing withdrawal of the plea. People v. Smith, 201 A.D.2d 804, 607 N.Y.S.2d 752 (3d Dept. 1994).

—A plea bargain that attaches specific conditions and provides for an enhanced penalty in the event of their violation is enforceable. People v. Murphy, 142 A.D.2d 776, 530 N.Y.S.2d 673 (3d Dept. 1988).

—The court did not violate the plea bargain agreement which promised a sentence of one and one-half to three years conditioned on the defendant's appearance for sentencing immediately after his release from the hospital when the defendant failed to immediately appear. The court was justified in imposing a greater sentence. People v. Chevalier, 92 A.D.2d 944, 460 N.Y.S.2d 632 (3d Dept. 1983).

Plea bargain; promises.—Defendant was entitled to vacatur of a plea to a drug charge which was induced by the promise that his sentence would run concurrently with another sentence, on another conviction, which was later vacated and then defendant was acquitted. People v. Pichardo, 1 N.Y.3d 126, 769 N.Y.S.2d 791, 802 N.E.2d 141 (2003).

—Permitting defendant to withdraw his plea and proceed to trial is a satisfactory remedy, when by pleading guilty, the defendant has given up nothing but his right to trial; however, where the defendant not only waives his right to trial, but performs other services for the prosecutor as well, services that involve considerable risk or sacrifice, merely undoing the plea is small compensation, if any, and specific performance of the plea bargain should be allowed. People v. McConnell, 49 N.Y.2d 340, 425 N.Y.S.2d 794, 402 N.E.2d 133 (1980).

—Defendant's motion to withdraw his guilty plea on the basis of an alleged unkept promise made to defendant's attorney with regard to sentencing was properly denied and no evidentiary hearing was required where defendant had the opportunity to submit detailed affirmations in support of his motion, and where the court had access to the transcript of the plea hearing and such transcript revealed the painstaking efforts taken by the court to insure that the defendant was not prompted to plead guilty by reason of an undisclosed sentence promise. People v. Frederick, 45 N.Y.2d 520, 410 N.Y.S.2d 555, 382 N.E.2d 1332 (1978).

—Where the People were unable to fulfill their part of the plea agreement, the trial court properly vacated the guilty plea. People v. Cohen, 176 A.D.2d 596, 575 N.Y.S.2d 40 (1st Dept. 1991), lv. denied, 79 N.Y.2d 945 (1992).

—Where court accepted defendant's guilty plea after full agreement that sentence would be three to six years and court did not reserve right to withdraw the plea and probation report did not indicate circumstances warranting such withdrawal, court erred in subsequently offering defendant option of withdrawing guilty plea or accepting a sentence of four to eight years due to complaining witness' request that the court impose substantial punishment. People v. Pendleton, 73 A.D.2d 857, 423 N.Y.S.2d 181 (1st Dept. 1980).

—It is well settled that a plea induced by an unfulfilled promise must be vacated or the promise honored; here, the defendant did not receive the benefit of his plea agreement and thus the court should have allowed the defendant to withdraw his plea. People v. Jackson, 272 A.D.2d 342, 708 N.Y.S.2d 416 (2d Dept. 2000).

—Having failed to accept the court's offer to withdraw his plea when the court could not fulfill the plea promise, the defendant had no claim to specific performance of the original sentencing representations. People v. Richard, 158 A.D.2d 627, 551 N.Y.S.2d 597 (2d Dept. 1990).

—Despite court's failure to adhere to promise that it would grant defendant youthful offender status, plea would not be vacated where the defendant declined to withdraw plea prior to sentencing and chose instead to obtain the desired term of incarceration. People v. Cuozzo, 128 A.D.2d 888, 513 N.Y.S.2d 813 (2d Dept. 1987).

—A defendant must be given the opportunity to withdraw his guilty plea where such plea was induced by a promise that the sentence thereon would be concurrent with that to be imposed in another case upon defendant's conviction after trial and where the jury conviction was thereafter reversed on appeal. People v. Martin, 115 A.D.2d 565, 496 N.Y.S.2d 85 (2d Dept. 1985).

—When a prosecutor reneges on a promise which induces a plea of guilty, the defendant must be permitted to withdraw his plea unless the promise was one which could not have been legally performed. People v. Marrow, 95 A.D.2d 839, 464 N.Y.S.2d 25 (2d Dept. 1983).

—Where the court made a promise to defendant as to sentencing at time of guilty plea and the court was subsequently unable to fulfill that promise, it was not prejudicial to the defendant to offer him the opportunity to withdraw his plea and be restored to his position before the promise was made. People v. Selikoff, 41 A.D.2d 376, 343 N.Y.S.2d 387 (2d Dept. 1973), aff'd, 35 N.Y.2d 227, 360 N.Y.S.2d 623, 318 N.E.2d 784, cert. denied, 419 U.S. 1122 (1974).

—Although a sentencing court is not bound to impose a sentence in accordance with the People's recommendation, the plea must be vacated where defendant did not receive the sentence commitment upon which the plea was expressly premised. People v. Shahid, 262 A.D.2d 670, 691 N.Y.S.2d 591 (3d Dept. 1999).

—Sentence was vacated and defendant's application to withdraw his guilty plea was granted where defendant was promised a sentence of 2-6 years on a burglary conviction but was sentenced to a term of 3-6 years when the court apprised that he was a predicate felon; a defendant's right to performance of a plea bargain may not be altered in such a "roughshod fashion." People v. Traynor, 101 A.D.2d 898, 475 N.Y.S.2d 590 (3d Dept. 1984).

—Reversal was required where defendant's plea of guilty to violation of probation was part of a plea agreement covering other offenses, including a charge of forgery and the trial court's determination that it would not accept a plea to the forgery charge required defendant to have an opportunity to withdraw his plea. People v. Salem, 84 A.D.2d 769, 443 N.Y.S.2d 783 (2d Dept. 1981).

—Where a prosecutor promises, as a condition of a guilty plea, not to make a sentence recommendation, he or she must adhere

to that promise. People v. Stripling, 136 A.D.2d 772, 523 N.Y.S.2d 230 (3d Dept. 1988).

—A guilty plea induced by an unfulfilled promise must be vacated or the promise honored. People v. Carlton, 2 A.D.3d 1353, 770 N.Y.S.2d 502 (4th Dept. 2003).

—It is well established that either a defendant or a prosecutor who had detrimentally relied upon a plea agreement has the right to its specific performance. People v. D'Amico, 147 Misc. 2d 731, 556 N.Y.S.2d 456 (Sup. Ct. Suffolk Co. 1990), aff'd, 179 A.D.2d 671 (2d Dept.), lv. denied, 79 N.Y.2d 999 (1992).

Plea bargain; off-the-record promises.—Court was not required to conduct a hearing on motion to withdraw plea based upon defendant's claim that he was induced to plead guilty by certain off-the-record promises. People v. Sanchez, 184 A.D.2d 537, 584 N.Y.S.2d 164 (2d Dept. 1992).

—Defendant's assertion of an alleged off-the-record statement by his attorney that he would be sentenced to a lesser term than he actually received upon the People obtaining a conviction of his co-defendant was not binding upon the court. People v Duff, 158 A.D.2d 711, 552 N.Y.S.2d 160 (2d Dept. 1990).

—The defendant was not entitled to a sentence of lifetime probation in return for his cooperation with law enforcement officials in the absence of an on-the-record promise, made at the time of entry of his guilty plea, that he would receive that particular sentence. People v. Lance P., 163 A.D.2d 333, 557 N.Y.S.2d 165 (2d Dept. 1990).

—Although the prosecutor conceded at sentencing that there was some conversation between him and defense counsel during the trial concerning a sentence recommendation, where no actual promise of a recommendation was placed on the record, any such promise was not entitled to judicial recognition. People v. Rodriguez, 123 A.D.2d 404, 506 N.Y.S.2d 603 (2d Dept. 1986).

Sentence.—When defendant interposed a plea of guilty to two counts with the understanding that he would receive concurrent sentences of 4 to 12 years on each, and the plea to the second count was vacated for failure to suppress statements, the pleas should be vacated in their entirety since the pleas covered both counts and were expressly conditioned on the negotiated agreement that the defendant would receive concurrent sentences on the separate counts to which he pleaded. People v. Salja, 430 N.Y.S.2d 865 (2d Dept. 1980), aff'd, 54 N.Y.2d 616, 442 N.Y.S.2d 491, 425 N.E.2d 879 (1981).

—Where defendant was sentenced in accordance with his plea bargain and within statutory guidelines he should be bound by the terms of the agreement. People v. Toro, 171 A.D.2d 524, 567 N.Y.S.2d 428 (1st Dept. 1991).

—If the court intentionally imposed a more severe sentence than had been promised based on new information, then the defendant should have been given the opportunity to withdraw his plea or if the court mistakenly imposed a harsher sentence, then the mistake should be corrected. People v. Bonilla, 87 A.D.2d 746, 448 N.Y.S.2d 677 (1st Dept. 1982).

—The proper procedure when the court determines that it cannot sentence a defendant as indicated prior to the acceptance of the plea, is to permit the defendant the choice of either withdrawing his plea or accepting sentence. People v. Reid, 140 A.D.2d 641, 529 N.Y.S.2d 9 (2d Dept. 1988).

—Where the court intended to sentence the defendant to a greater sentence than that promised at the time of the plea, it was required to allow the defendant the opportunity to withdraw his plea. People v. Lopez, 135 A.D.2d 739, 522 N.Y.S.2d 641 (2d Dept. 1987).

—Sentence was vacated where defendant was not offered an opportunity to withdraw his plea when it was apparent that the sentence promise would not be fulfilled. People v. Declemente, 108 A.D.2d 868, 485 N.Y.S.2d 364 (2d Dept. 1985).

—Sentencing court was authorized to impose a sentence harsher than that recommended by the prosecutor where the defendant was apprised during plea allocution that prosecutor's promise as to sentence was not binding on the court. People v. Anonymous Appellant, 130 A.D.2d 497, 515 N.Y.S.2d 80 (2d Dept. 1980).

—The trial court did not err in refusing to execute the plea bargain agreement when, subsequent to the plea allocution and prior to sentencing, the court became aware of a prior felony conviction which might subject the defendant to persistent felony treatment and the trial court properly gave the defendant the opportunity to withdraw his plea since the "sentence" promise at the plea was conditional upon its being lawful and appropriate. People v. Daniels, 77 A.D.2d 745, 430 N.Y.S.2d 981 (3d Dept. 1980).

—A sentencing court is under no obligation to adhere to a sentencing promise after receiving information affecting the sentence, provided the court affords defendant the opportunity to withdraw his plea. People v. Wood, 207 A.D.2d 1001, 617 N.Y.S.2d 248 (4th Dept. 1994).

—Where the sentencing court determines that it cannot adhere to its sentencing promise indicated prior to the acceptance of the plea, the proper procedure is to afford defendant the option of either withdrawing his plea or accepting an appropriate sentence. People v. D'Avolia, 176 A.D.2d 1245, 576 N.Y.S.2d 739 (4th Dept. 1991).

Appeal.—Principle prohibiting vacatur of a plea upon application of the People after defendant has commenced serving his sentence is applicable when the guilty plea is entered after the dismissal of one count of multicount indictment and the dismissal ruling has subsequently been reversed on the People's appeal. People v. Moquin, 77 N.Y.2d 449, 568 N.Y.S.2d 710, 711, 570 N.E.2d 1059 (1991).

—The legal sufficiency of a conceded set of facts to support a judgment of conviction entered upon a guilty plea may not be saved for appellate review by conditioning the plea on defendant's right to appeal that issue, even though the prosecutor consents, and the trial judge approves. People v. Thomas, 53 N.Y.2d 338, 441 N.Y.S.2d 650, 424 N.E.2d 537 (1981).

—On an appeal from the denial of a motion to withdraw a plea of guilty, review is limited to whether there was an abuse of discretion. People v. Brown, 177 A.D.2d 460, 576 N.Y.S.2d 557 (1st Dept. 1991).

Appeal; preservation.—Since defendant failed to move in the trial court to withdraw his plea or to vacate the judgment of conviction, and his case did not fall within the "rare case" exception to the preservation doctrine, his conviction was affirmed. People v. Toxey, 86 N.Y.2d 725, 631 N.Y.S.2d 119, 655 N.E.2d 160 (1995).

—Where defendant failed to preserve his claim that his plea allocution was defective by a motion to withdraw the plea or vacate the judgment of conviction, the Court could not review his claim on appeal. People v. Johnson, 82 N.Y.2d 683, 601 N.Y.S.2d 468, 619 N.E.2d 405 (1993).

—Challenges to the validity of a guilty plea are subject to the contemporaneous objection requirement, except for those cases which fit the "rare case" exception, where "the defendant's recitation of the facts underlying the crime pleaded to clearly casts significant doubt upon the defendant's guilt or otherwise calls into question the voluntariness of the plea." People v. Lopez, 71 N.Y.2d 662, 529 N.Y.S.2d 465, 525 N.E.2d 5 (1988).

—By raising an objection prior to the prosecutor's comments at sentencing, defendant preserved for appellate review prosecutor's failure to abide by promise not to take position at sentencing. People v. Torres, 67 N.Y.2d 659, 499 N.Y.S.2d 668, 490 N.E.2d 535 (1986).

—To preserve a challenge to the facial insufficiency of a plea allocution, defendant must make a CPL § 220.60(3) motion to withdraw the plea or, where applicable, a CPL § 440.10 motion to vacate the conviction. People v. Wallace, 247 A.D.2d 257, 669 N.Y.S.2d 26 (1st Dept. 1998)

—Defendant's waiver of his right to appeal did not preclude review of his claim that his plea was not knowingly and voluntarily entered on the basis that he was not advised of the ramifications of the Sex Offender Registration Act, but this claim is unpreserved because he did not move to withdraw his plea or vacate the judgment of conviction on that ground. People v. Melio, 6 A.D.3d 552, 775 N.Y.S.2d 346 (2d Dept. 2004).

—Since the defendant's motion to withdraw his plea prior to sentencing was not specifically based upon the fact that his factual allocution at the time of the plea was insufficient, his objection to the sufficiency of his allocution was not preserved for appellate review as a matter of law. People v. Smith, 127 A.D.2d 864, 512 N.Y.S.2d 243 (2d Dept. 1987).

—Failure to object to the adequacy of the plea or to move to withdraw the plea bars the defendant from raising the issue on appeal as a matter of law. People v. Vicks, 91 A.D.2d 1052, 458 N.Y.S.2d 654 (2d Dept. 1983).

—Where defendant's recitation of the underlying facts clearly

negates an essential element of the crime to which he or she is pleading and the court fails to make further inquiry to ensure that the plea is intelligent and voluntary, the acceptance of such plea is an abuse of discretion, and the defendant may challenge the sufficiency of the plea allocution on direct appeal. Here, the record clearly indicated that defendant's recitation at the plea allocution not only failed to establish the elements of arson in the second degree, but also negated at least one of those elements. Thus, defendant's request for appellate review falls within an exception to the preservation rule. People v. Makas, 273 A.D.2d 510, 709 N.Y.S.2d 650 (3d Dept. 2000).

—Because defendant moved to withdraw his plea prior to sentencing, his contention concerning the adequacy of the plea allocution is preserved for appellate review. However, defendant pleaded guilty to a reduced charge and thus no factual colloquy was required. People v. Dillard, 262 A.D.2d 1044, 693 N.Y.S.2d 360 (4th Dept. 1999).

—Because defendant failed to move to withdraw his guilty plea or to vacate the judgment of conviction, defendant has failed to preserve for appellate review his challenge to the factual sufficiency of the plea allocution. People v. Harris, 233 A.D.2d 959, 649 N.Y.S.2d 584 (4th Dept. 1996).

Waiver of right to appeal.—While there is no requirement that the trial court engage in any particular litany in order to satisfy itself that the standards of a proper waiver of appeal are met, a knowing and voluntary waiver cannot be inferred from a silent record. People v. Callahan, 80 N.Y.2d 273, 590 N.Y.S.2d 46, 604 N.E.2d 108 (1992).

—Defendant waived his right to appeal from the denial of his suppression motion where his plea was voluntarily entered, with full comprehension on defendant's part of both the plea and the associated condition, waiver of his right to appeal on the suppression issue. People v. Huggins, 36 N.Y.2d 827, 370 N.Y.S.2d 904, 331 N.E.2d 684 (1975).

—Where, during entry of plea, defendants expressly agreed to limit their appeals with respect to their suppression motions to the issue of probable cause for the issuance of a wiretap warrant, they were precluded from raising the issue of the sufficiency of the affidavit submitted in support of the wiretap warrant with respect to the use of other investigative procedures, however, they did not waive their right to question the overbroadness of the eavesdropping warrant inasmuch as the scope of a warrant is inexorably intertwined with the existence of probable cause to support it. People v. Juliano, 74 A.D.2d 881, 426 N.Y.S.2d 23 (2d Dept. 1980).

—Defendant's waiver of his right to appeal does not preclude his challenge to the voluntariness of his plea; it is well-settled that the question of whether to permit a defendant to withdraw a guilty plea rests within the sound discretion of the trial court and "[w]here a defendant has been fully informed of the rights he is waiving by pleading guilty and proceeds to admit the acts constituting the crime, a subsequent protestation of innocence which is not substantiated by any evidence is generally insufficient to support a request for vacatur of the plea." People v. Gibson, 261 A.D.2d 710, 691 N.Y.S.2d 195 (3d Dept. 1999).

Plea based on misunderstanding or misinformation.—Where both the trial judge and defense counsel labor under a misapprehension as to the correct minimum sentence in a plea bargain, the plea of guilty will not be set aside on that ground; the defendant however, must be resentenced. People v. Modica, 64 N.Y.2d 828, 486 N.Y.S.2d 931, 476 N.E.2d 330 (1985).

—If sentencing court keeps the promises it made at time it accepted guilty plea, defendant should not be permitted to withdraw the plea on the sole ground that he misinterpreted the agreement; compliance with plea bargain must be tested against an objective reading of the bargain, not against defendant's subjective interpretation thereof, since otherwise any defendant could withdraw his plea solely because he was disappointed with the sentence even though the court kept its word in such respect. People v. Cataldo, 39 N.Y.2d 578, 384 N.Y.S.2d 763, 349 N.E.2d 863 (1976).

—Critical to defendant's rights to withdraw his plea of guilty is whether he was misled by the court's advice to him before his guilty plea was accepted. To establish reliance on the Court's representations he must show that he believed them and that he was not otherwise advised by his lawyer or anyone else before he pleaded guilty. People v. Caputo, 36 N.Y.2d 653, 365 N.Y.S.2d 847, 325 N.E.2d 164 (1975).

—The contention that defendant's attorney misled him as to

the sentence which might be imposed following his plea of guilty did not warrant reversal. People v. Johnson, 34 N.Y.2d 623, 355 N.Y.S.2d 367, 311 N.E.2d 502 (1974).

—Defendant's guilty plea was "fatally defective" because court, its clerk, and defense counsel made numerous uncorrected misstatements in naming the crime charged and the crime to which defendant was pleading guilty; the vagueness in the factual allocution compounded these misstatements. People v. Ford, 14 A.D.3d 347, 786 N.Y.S.2d 742 (1st Dept. 2005).

—A defendant is not entitled to withdraw his guilty plea merely because he discovers that he did not understand the quality of the State's case. People v. Lesesne, 173 A.D.2d 407, 570 N.Y.S.2d 40 (1st Dept. 1991).

—A defendant is not entitled to withdraw his guilty plea merely because he discovers that he misapprehended the quality of the prosecution case and his chance of prevailing on a suppression motion. People v. Greene, 208 A.D.2d 950, 618 N.Y.S.2d 412 (2d Dept. 1994); *accord* People v. Cantu, 202 A.D.2d 1033, 610 N.Y.S.2d 113 (4th Dept. 1994).

—Since an objective reading of the plea bargain agreement was susceptible to but one interpretation, the defendant's misunderstanding of, or disappointment with the agreement did not suffice as a reason for vacating the guilty plea. People v. Walker, 152 A.D.2d 644, 543 N.Y.S.2d 171 (2d Dept. 1989).

—The court properly denied defendant's motion to withdraw his plea in view of the complete allocution at the defendant's plea, his unequivocal admission of guilt and the fact that he made no showing in support of his claim that his plea was the product of a unilateral mistake concerning the potential sentence being considered by the court. People v. Williams, 120 A.D.2d 693, 502 N.Y.S.2d 279 (2d Dept. 1986).

—The fact that the defendant was unaware at the time of his guilty plea that it constituted a waiver of his right to raise on appeal that he was denied a speedy trial does not constitute sufficient grounds to withdraw the plea. People v. Williams, 91 A.D.2d 1028, 457 N.Y.S.2d 899 (2d Dept. 1983).

—Guilty plea was vacated in the interest of justice where the record showed that defendant entered the plea based on assurance by the trial court that he had not, by virtue of the plea, "waived" his right to contest the constitutionality of the statutory presumption in Penal Law § 165.15(6), since in the absence of a factual record which indicated to what extent, if any, the presumption was relied upon that there could be no viable constitutional challenge. People v. Neis, 73 A.D.2d 938, 423 N.Y.S.2d 942 (2d Dept. 1980).

—Where defendant's claim of misunderstanding of terms of plea agreement was belied by the record, the court properly denied the defendant's motion to withdraw his plea. People v. Garcia, 117 A.D.2d 928, 499 N.Y.S.2d 234 (3d Dept.), *lv. denied,* 67 N.Y.2d 943 (1986).

Subsequent use of plea.—The rule that a guilty plea once withdrawn is out of the case forever and for all purposes applies both to the fact of the plea and the contents of the plea; such material may not be used either on the People's direct case or for impeachment purposes should the defendant take the stand. People v. Moore, 66 N.Y.2d 1028, 499 N.Y.S.2d 393, 489 N.E.2d 1295 (1985).

—Reference to fact that defendant had withdrawn a plea of guilty (but not the contents of actual plea colloquy) was proper where defense counsel persisted in eliciting testimony establishing that a co-defendant had pleaded guilty; the reference was necessary to rebut suggestion that because the co-defendant had admitted his guilt and the defendant had not that the defendant must be innocent. People v. Perez, 118 A.D.2d 431, 499 N.Y.S.2d 716 (1st Dept. 1986).

ARTICLE 230—REMOVAL OF ACTION

Section

230.10   **Removal of action; from supreme court to county court and from county court to supreme court; at instance of court.**

230.20   **Removal of action; removal from county court to supreme court and change of venue; upon motion of party.**

230.30   **Removal of action; stay of trial pending motion therefor.**

230.40   **Removal of action; determinations and rulings before and after removal; by which courts made.**

LexisNexis Cross References

Criminal Defense Techniques, Vol. 5, Ch. 107, Venue; *Criminal Law Advocacy,* Vol. 1, Ch. 18, Pretrial Publicity; *New York Criminal Practice (2d ed.),* Vol. 3, Ch. 25, Removal and Change of Venue; *Sexual Assault Trials (2d ed.),* Vol. 1, Ch. 2, Fair Trial, Free Press, and Dealing With Publicity.

§ 230.10. Removal of action; from supreme court to county court and from county court to supreme court; at instance of court.

Upon order of an appropriate court or judge, made at its or his own instance pursuant to rules established by the appellate division of the appropriate department, (a) an indictment filed with the supreme court at a term held in a particular county outside of New York City may, prior to entry of a plea of guilty thereto or commencement of a trial thereof, be removed to the county court of such county, and (b) an indictment filed in a county court may similarly be removed to the supreme court at a term held or to be held in the same county. Each of the appellate divisions of the second, third and fourth departments may establish rules authorizing such removals with respect to the superior courts within its department, and prescribing the courts or judges who may order such removals and other procedural matters involved therein.

ANNOTATION

Fitness to proceed—Court properly exercised its discretion in denying defense counsel's application for a new competency examination pursuant to CPL art. 730, since the court's own observations and totality of the circumstances did not establish that defendant lacked the capacity to understand the proceedings and assist in his own defense. The record warrants the inference that defendant was feigning mental illness, where the most recent psychiatric examination was conducted three months earlier and found defendant fit to proceed. People v. Mendez, 306 A.D.2d 143, 762 N.Y.S.2d 592 (1st Dept. 2003).

Jurisdiction; transfer without order; presumption of regularity.—Defendant convicted of 1st degree robbery was tried in County Court, Albany County after transfer without order, but by standard practice, from Supreme Court, Albany County, and not having raised objection through trial and appeal, if not waiver, it is not a rebuttal of the presumption of regularity. People *ex rel.* Fairley v. Zelker, 38 A.D.2d 960, 331 N.Y.S.2d 889 (2d Dept. 1972), *aff'd,* 35 N.Y.2d 804, 362 N.Y.S.2d 460, 321 N.E.2d 551 (1974).

§ 230.20. Removal of action; removal from county court to supreme court and change of venue; upon motion of party.

1. At any time within the period provided by section 255.20, the appellate division of the department embracing the county, upon motion of either the defendant or the people, may, for good cause shown, order that the indictment and action be removed from the county court to the supreme court at a term held or to be held in the same county.

2. At any time within the period provided by section 255.20, the appellate division of the department embracing the county in which the superior court is located may, upon motion of either the defendant or the people demonstrating reasonable cause to believe that a fair and impartial trial cannot be had in such county, order either:

(a) that the indictment and action be removed from such superior court to a designated superior court of or located in another county; or

(b) that the commissioner of jurors of such county, in consultation with the appropriate administrative judge of the judicial district in which the county is located, expand the pool of jurors to encompass prospective jurors from the jury lists of counties that are within the judicial district in which, and that are geographically contiguous with the county in which, such superior court is located.

In making such determination the appellate division shall consider, among other factors, the hardship on potential jurors and the potential depletion of a county's qualified juror list that may result from an order expanding the jury pool. An order of removal under paragraph (a) herein must, if the defendant is in custody at the time, include a provision for transfer of custody by the sheriff or other appropriate public servant of the county of confinement to the sheriff or other appropriate public servant of the county to which the action has been removed. If the order is issued upon motion of the people, the appellate division may impose such conditions as it deems equitable and appropriate to insure that the removal does not subject the defendant to an unreasonable burden in making his defense. Any additional cost to the people incurred in complying with the order must be borne by the county from which the action originated.

3. Any motion made pursuant to this section must be based upon papers stating the grounds therefor, and must be made within the period provided by section 255.20 and upon five days notice thereof together with service of the moving papers upon, as the case may be, (a) the district attorney or (b) either the defendant or his counsel. In any case, the motion must be made returnable either during the appellate division term during which such moving papers are served or during the next term thereof.

4. If the appellate division grants the motion and orders a removal of the action, a certified copy of such order must be filed with the clerk of the superior court in which the indictment is pending. Such clerk must thereupon transmit such instrument, together with the pertinent papers and proceedings of the action, including all undertakings for appearances of the defendant and of the witnesses, or a certified copy or copies of the same, to the term of the superior court to which the action has been removed. Such latter court must then proceed to conduct the action to judgment or other final disposition.

Amended by L. 1974, Ch. 763; L. 1985, Ch. 257.

ANNOTATIONS

Constitutionality.—CPL § 230.20(2) does not violate Art. 1 § 2 of the New York Constitution or the Sixth Amendment of the Constitution of the United States. People v. Goldswer, 39 N.Y.2d 656, 385 N.Y.S.2d 274, 350 N.E.2d 604 (1976), *stay denied,* 428 U.S. 908.

Change of venue; grounds for motion.—There is no bright-line test whereby a fixed percentage of veniremen expressing a preconceived opinion, standing alone, requires a change of venue; pretrial publicity, even if pervasive, does not necessarily lead to an unfair trial. People v. McClary, 150 A.D.2d 631, 541 N.Y.S.2d 503 (2d Dept. 1989).

—In determining a change of venue motion, court must examine the totality of the circumstances to determine whether the pretrial publicity has so permeated the community as to render it impossible to obtain a fair and impartial trial. People v. Ryan, 151 A.D.2d 528, 542 N.Y.S.2d 665 (2d Dept. 1989).

Change of venue; pretrial publicity.—This death penalty case did not warrant a pre-voir dire change of venue where the county was not deluged by a tidal wave of prejudicial publicity to such an extent that even an attempt to select an unbiased jury would be fruitless. People v. Cahill, 2 N.Y.3d 14, 777 N.Y.S.2d 332, 809 N.E.2d 561 (2003).

—A very localized and prejudicial publicity surrounding a case can be fairly easily avoided by transferring the case to a nearby venue in the first instance. People v. Culhane, 33 N.Y.2d 90, 350 N.Y.S.2d 381, 305 N.E.2d 469 (1973).

—Defendants were entitled to change in venue where co-defendants had recently been tried in the same county, there was extensive pretrial publicity and a significant percentage of the veniremen had expressed an opinion which they could not set aside. People v. Boudin, 97 A.D.2d 84, 469 N.Y.S.2d 89 (2d Dept. 1983).

—A pre voir dire change of venue was not warranted as publicity surrounding a Brinks robbery and murders was not so localized and incessant, nor the atmosphere in Rockland County so emotionally charged as to preclude the selection of a fair and impartial jury; notwithstanding the submission of two conflicting surveys, which were inconclusive. People v. Boudin, 87 A.D.2d 133, 451 N.Y.S.2d 153 (2d Dept. 1982).

—Court rejected defendant's claim that she did not receive a fair trial because of pretrial publicity, where she sought neither a change of venue nor an adjournment because of pretrial publicity, and the court conducted an adequate inquiry of the prospective jurors concerning the effect, if any, that pretrial publicity would have on their ability to judge the evidence; moreover, the defendant willingly participated in pretrial publicity by giving a statement to the media. People v. Ruger, 288 A.D.2d 686, 732 N.Y.S.2d 727 (3d Dept. 2001).

—Where case went to trial one and a half years after publicity about defendant prisoner's assault of a guard, and there was an exhaustive voir dire focused on the effect of pretrial publicity, a change of venue was not required. People v. Bosket, 216 A.D.2d 791, 629 N.Y.S.2d 296 (3d Dept. 1995).

Change of venue; timeliness of motion.—Change of venue motion premature; if it develops during voir dire that a fair and impartial jury cannot be drawn, then an appropriate application may be made. People v. Mateo, 239 A.D.2d 965, 662 N.Y.S.2d 279 (4th Dept. 1997); *see also* People v. Green, 122 A.D.2d 622, 504 N.Y.S.2d 917 (4th Dept. 1986); *see also* People v. Green, 122 A.D.2d 622, 504 N.Y.S.2d 917 (4th Dept. 1986).

§ 230.30. Removal of action; stay of trial pending motion therefor.

1. At any time when a timely motion for removal of an action from the county court to the supreme court or for a change of venue may be made pursuant to section 230.20, a justice holding a term of the supreme court in the district in which the indictment is pending, or a justice of the appellate division of the department in which the indictment is pending, upon application of either the defendant or the people, may, in his discretion and for good cause shown, order that the trial of such indictment be stayed for a designated period, not to exceed thirty days from the issuance of such order, to allow the applicant party to make a motion in the appropriate court for removal of the action from a county court to the supreme court or for a change of venue.

2. Such an order may be issued only upon an application made in writing and after reasonable notice and opportunity to be heard has been accorded the other party.

3. Upon issuing the order, the supreme court justice or appellate division justice must cause the order to be filed with the clerk of the court in which the indictment is pending. Thereafter, no further proceedings may be had in such court until a motion for removal or change of venue, as the case may be, if made within the designated period, has been determined, or until such designated period has expired without any such motion having been made.

4. When such an application for a stay has been made to and denied by a justice of the supreme court or a justice of the appellate

division, a second such application may not be made to any other such justice.

§ 230.40. Removal of action; determinations and rulings before and after removal; by which courts made.

Upon any removal of an indictment and action from one superior court to another pursuant to the provisions of this article, determinations and rulings with respect to the action made before such removal are not thereby rendered invalid. All subsequent determinations and rulings must be made by the court to which the action is removed; and such latter court is deemed to have control of the grand jury minutes underlying the indictment for the purpose of determining post-removal motions addressed to the legal sufficiency of the grand jury evidence or the validity of the grand jury proceeding.

ARTICLE 240—DISCOVERY

LexisNexis Cross References

Criminal Constitutional Law, Vol. 2, Ch. 10, Disclosure and Discovery; *Defense of Speeding, Reckless Driving and Vehicular Homicide,* Vol. 2, Ch. 22, Discovery; *Bender's New York Evidence—CPLR,* Vol. 5, Discovery; *Criminal Law Advocacy,* Vol. 1, Ch. 9, Discovery; *Criminal Defense Techniques,* Vol. 1A, Pretrial Discovery of Prosecution Witnesses in State Courts; Vol. 1A, Ch. 15, The Evolution of Discovery in Criminal Cases; *Defense of Drunk Driving Cases,* Vol. 4, Ch. 43, Pretrial Discovery; *New York Criminal Practice (2d ed.),* Vol. 2, Ch. 17, Discovery and Bills of Particular; *Sexual Assault Trials (2d ed.),* Vol. 1, Ch. 1, Pretrial Issues, Discovery, and Motions; *see generally Mastering Written Discovery: Procedures and Tactics.*

§ 240.10. Discovery; definition of terms.

The following definitions are applicable to this article:

1. "Demand to produce" means a written notice served by and on a party to a criminal action, without leave of the court, demanding to inspect property pursuant to this article and giving reasonable notice of the time at which the demanding party wishes to inspect the property designated.

2. "Attorneys' work product" means property to the extent that it contains the opinions, theories or conclusions of the prosecutor, defense counsel or members of their legal staffs.

3. "Property" means any existing tangible personal or real property, including but not limited to, books, records, reports, memoranda, papers, photographs, tapes or other electronic recordings, articles of clothing, fingerprints, blood samples, fingernail scrapings or handwriting specimens, but excluding attorneys' work product.

4. "At the trial" means as part of the people's or the defendant's direct case.

ANNOTATIONS

Capital cases.—Discovery that is unavailable pursuant to statute may not be ordered in either capital or noncapital cases. Sacket v. Bartlett, 241 A.D.2d 97, 671 N.Y.S.2d 156 (3d Dept. 1998).

Reciprocal discovery.—Prosecutor's request for discovery of "other documents" was denied where there was no showing of need or justification and the property had not been specifically designated. People v. Miller, 108 Misc. 2d 528, 437 N.Y.S.2d 543 (Co. Ct. Nassau Co. 1981).

—The 38-page handwritten statement made by the defendant at the request of his attorney, and supplied to defense psychiatrist, was ordered to be inspected in camera and all portions of the statement deemed relevant to the specific issue of the defense of insanity will be material discoverable by the prosecution. People v. Hairston, 111 Misc. 2d 691, 444 N.Y.S.2d 853 (Sup. Ct. Bronx Co. 1981).

Pretrial statements of witnesses.—The prosecutor's worksheets containing capsulized witnesses responses to questions relating directly to material issues raised on defendant's trial come within the *Rosario* rule and should be given to the defendant. People v. Consolazio, 40 N.Y.2d 446, 387 N.Y.S.2d 62, 354 N.E.2d 801 (1976), *cert. denied,* 433 U.S. 914 (1977).

Exempt property.—Prior to ordering defense counsel to furnish interview notes of a defense witness to the prosecutor, the court should have conducted an in-court inspection of the notes to determine the legitimacy of the claim that the notes constituted "work product"; error deemed harmless as notes were indeed discoverable. People v. Nielson, 115 A.D.2d 972, 497 N.Y.S.2d 537 (4th Dept. 1985).

Informants.—Where the disclosure of the identity of an informant is pertinent to establishing probable cause for arrest and search, an ex parte in camera hearing with respect to the existence of the informant and the alleged communication from that person strikes a proper balance between the defendant's rights and the competing interests of the State. People v. Liberatore, 79 N.Y.2d 208, 581 N.Y.S.2d 634, 590 N.E.2d 219 (1992).

—A *Darden* hearing is an extension of the suppression hearing because it validates the existence of the informant and his communications with the police. People v. Hepburn, 189 A.D.2d 914, 593 N.Y.S.2d 85 (3d Dept. 1993).

Handwritten notes.—Notes made by the arresting officer at the scene of the arrest do not constitute "exempt property." People v. Paranzino, 40 N.Y.2d 1005, 391 N.Y.S.2d 391, 359 N.E.2d 981 (1976).

Police reports and records.—Although certain documents demanded by the defendant were not produced, the representation of the prosecutor that the documents did not exist sufficed to establish their nonexistence. People v. Ciola, 134 A.D.2d 1, 523 N.Y.S.2d 553 (2d Dept. 1988).

Subpoenas.—A subpoena duces tecum, unlike a search warrant, does not have to be supported by probable cause. *In re* Grand Jury Subpoenas, 72 N.Y.2d 307, 532 N.Y.S.2d 722, 727, 528 N.E.2d 1195 (1988).

§ 240.20. Discovery; upon demand of defendant.

1. Except to the extent protected by court order, upon a demand to produce by a defendant against whom an indictment, superior court information, prosecutor's information, information, or simplified information charging a misdemeanor is pending, the prosecutor shall disclose to the defendant and make available for inspection, photographing, copying or testing, the following property:

(a) Any written, recorded or oral statement of the defendant, and of a co-defendant to be tried jointly, made, other than in the course of the criminal transaction, to a public servant engaged in law enforcement activity or to a person then acting under his direction or in cooperation with him;

(b) Any transcript of testimony relating to the criminal action or proceeding pending against the defendant, given by the defendant, or by a co-defendant to be tried jointly, before any grand jury;

(c) Any written report or document, or portion thereof, concerning a physical or mental examination, or scientific test or experiment, relating to the criminal action or proceeding which was made by, or at the request or direction of a public servant engaged in law enforcement activity, or which was made by a person whom the prosecutor intends to call as a witness at trial, or which the people intend to introduce at trial;

(d) Any photograph or drawing relating to the criminal action or proceeding which was made or completed by a public servant engaged in law enforcement activity, or which was made by a person whom the prosecutor intends to call as a witness at trial, or which the people intend to introduce at trial;

(e) Any photograph, photocopy or other reproduction made by or at the direction of a police officer, peace officer or prosecutor of any property prior to its release pursuant to the provisions of section 450.10 of the penal law, irrespective of whether the people intend to introduce at trial the property or the photograph, photocopy or other reproduction.

(f) Any other property obtained from the defendant, or a co-defendant to be tried jointly;

(g) Any tapes or other electronic recordings which the prosecutor intends to introduce at trial, irrespective of whether such recording was made during the course of the criminal transaction;

(h) Anything required to be disclosed, prior to trial, to the defendant by the prosecutor, pursuant to the constitution of this state or of the United States.

(i) The approximate date, time and place of the offense charged and of defendant's arrest.

(j) In any prosecution under penal law section 156.05 or 156.10, the time, place and manner of notice given pursuant to subdivision six of section 156.00 of such law.

(k) In any prosecution commenced in a manner set forth in this subdivision alleging a violation of the vehicle and traffic law, in addition to any material required to be disclosed pursuant to this article, any other provision of law, or the constitution of this state or of the United States, any written report or document, or portion thereof, concerning a physical examination, a scientific test or experiment, including the most recent record of inspection, or calibration or repair of machines or instruments utilized to perform such scientific tests or experiments and the certification certificate, if any, held by the operator of the machine or instrument, which tests or examinations were made by or at the request or direction of a public servant engaged in law enforcement activity or which was made by a person whom the prosecutor intends to call as a witness at trial, or which the people intend to introduce at trial.

2. The prosecutor shall make a diligent, good faith effort to ascertain the existence of demanded property and to cause such property to be made available for discovery where it exists but is not within the prosecutor's possession, custody or control; provided, that the prosecutor shall not be required to obtain by subpoena duces tecum demanded material which the defendant may thereby obtain.

Amended by L. 1982, Ch. 558; L. 1983, Ch. 317; L. 1984, Ch. 795; L. 1986, Ch. 514; L. 1989, Ch. 536.

ANNOTATIONS

Pretrial statements of witnesses.—The prosecutor's worksheets containing capsulized witnesses responses to questions relating directly to material issues raised on defendant's trial come within the *Rosario* rule and should be given to the defendant. People v. Consolazio, 40 N.Y.2d 446, 387 N.Y.S.2d 62, 354 N.E.2d 801 (1976), *cert. denied,* 433 U.S. 914 (1977).

Exempt property.—Prior to ordering defense counsel to furnish interview notes of a defense witness to the prosecutor, the court should have conducted an in-court inspection of the notes to determine the legitimacy of the claim that the notes constituted "work product"; error deemed harmless as notes were indeed discoverable. People v. Nielson, 115 A.D.2d 972, 497 N.Y.S.2d 537 (4th Dept. 1985).

Informants.—Where the disclosure of the identity of an informant is pertinent to establishing probable cause for arrest and search, an ex parte in camera hearing with respect to the existence of the informant and the alleged communication from that person strikes a proper balance between the defendant's rights and the competing interests of the State. People v. Liberatore, 79 N.Y.2d 208, 581 N.Y.S.2d 634, 590 N.E.2d 219 (1992).

—A *Darden* hearing is an extension of the suppression hearing because it validates the existence of the informant and his communications with the police. People v. Hepburn, 189 A.D.2d 914, 593 N.Y.S.2d 85 (3d Dept. 1993).

Handwritten notes.—Notes made by the arresting officer at the scene of the arrest do not constitute "exempt property." People v. Paranzino, 40 N.Y.2d 1005, 391 N.Y.S.2d 391, 359 N.E.2d 981 (1976).

Police files.—The police "nickname" file sought by defendant did not constitute *Rosario* material because it was not a written statement, report, or document, made by a prospective prosecution witness; nor was it *Brady* material because there was not evidence to support defendant's assertion that the nickname file contained the names of other individuals who were known by the nickname "Ski." People v. Turner, 233 A.D.2d 932, 649 N.Y.S.2d 571 (4th Dept. 1996).

—While a witness's feelings are understandable, the allegation that a witness is generally apprehensive about disclosure of his name and address or would simply prefer that such information not be disclosed, should not serve as a bar to disclosure to the defendant. People v. Leon, 134 Misc. 2d 757, 512 N.Y.S.2d 991 (Westchester Co. Ct. 1987).

Police reports and records.—Although certain documents demanded by the defendant were not produced, the representation of the prosecutor that the documents did not exist sufficed to establish their nonexistence. People v. Ciola, 134 A.D.2d 1, 523 N.Y.S.2d 553 (2d Dept. 1988).

Duty to preserve evidence.—The responsibility to safeguard and preserve evidence gathered against an accused lies with the prosecution, and the People must meet a heavy burden in establishing that a failure to preserve the evidence was not intentional, deliberate or in bad faith. People v. Davis, 109 Misc. 2d 230, 439 N.Y.S.2d 798 (Onondaga Co. Ct. 1981).

Subpoenas.—A subpoena duces tecum, unlike a search warrant, does not have to be supported by probable cause. *In re* Grand Jury Subpoenas, 72 N.Y.2d 307, 532 N.Y.S.2d 722, 727, 528 N.E.2d 1195 (1988).

Pretrial discovery; general.—Promises made to a defendant by one prosecutor are generally binding on others in the criminal law enforcement system and certainly promises made by a superior are binding on subordinates in the same office. People v. Steadman, 82 N.Y.2d 1, 603 N.Y.S.2d 382, 623 N.E.2d 509 (1993).

—Defense efforts, or lack thereof, are irrelevant on the issue of the prosecutor's affirmative obligation to disclose *Brady* or *Rosario* material. People v. Ramos, 201 A.D.2d 78, 614 N.Y.S.2d 977 (1st Dept. 1994).

—The mere fact that defense counsel did not engage in some pretrial procedures available to defendant, in itself, does not indicate ineffectiveness of counsel. People v. Peters, 90 A.D.2d 618, 456 N.Y.S.2d 234 (3d Dept. 1982).

Pretrial discovery; exculpatory evidence.—Defendant cannot use an exculpatory statement signed by a prosecution witness unless the statement is produced for inspection and examination by the district attorney, if the document is not a forgery, it is nontestimonial and thus discoverable. People v. Garay, 105 Misc. 2d 1, 420 N.Y.S.2d 867 (Albany Co. Ct. 1980).

Pretrial discovery; defendant's statements.—Because a defendant's own statements to police are highly material and relevant to a criminal prosecution, these statements are always discoverable, even if the People do not intend to offer them at trial. Thus, when documentary television crew made videotapes of the early stages of questioning of the defendant by homicide detectives, the Court found that—notwithstanding trial court's denial of defendant's motion to suppress his later statement—defendant was entitled to present evidence to the jury that he had been coerced into making the statement through techniques employed during the earlier interrogation that the television crew recorded; defendant met his burden under the "Shield Law" for production of the television crew's videotape. People v. Combest, 4 N.Y.3d 341, 795 N.Y.S.2d 481, 828 N.E.2d 583 (2005).

—Defendant's statements to civilian witnesses were not discoverable. People v. Rivera, 210 A.D.2d 178, 620 N.Y.S.2d 365 (1st Dept. 1994).

—Defendant's pedigree statements were not discoverable. People v. Fortunato, 161 A.D.2d 455, 555 N.Y.S.2d 366 (1st Dept. 1990).

—Court rejected defendant's position that she was improperly denied request for disclosure of a letter that she wrote from jail to her neighbor, which was later used by the People during its cross-examination of defendant; defendant was not entitled to disclosure because an accused's statements to civilian witnesses are not discoverable. People v. Mitchell, 289 A.D.2d 776, 734 N.Y.S.2d 353 (3d Dept. 2001).

—Statements made to civilian witnesses are not discoverable; court properly admitted a letter written by defendant to his former girlfriend while he was in jail, where the ex-girlfriend testified that she was familiar with defendant's handwriting and the letter was in his writing. The prosecutor was not required to disclose the letter, which was not made to someone in any law enforcement capacity, and it was sufficiently inculpatory to warrant its admission. People v. Swart, 273 A.D.2d 503, 709 N.Y.S.2d 653 (3d Dept. 2000).

—There was no prosecutorial error in failing to provide defendant with the contents of any contemporaneous or additional oral statements he may have made which were not recorded; the notice that the oral admission existed, and the further advice that it was, in "sum and substance," the same pursuant to the constitution of this state or as the written confession, plainly fulfilled the obligation imposed by CPL § 710.30. People v. Bennett, 80 A.D.2d 68, 438 N.Y.S.2d 389 (3d Dept. 1981).

—Defendant's oral statements to the police should have been disclosed to the defense before the eve of trial; however, the People's failure to timely disclose them did not require reversal. People v. Watson, 213 A.D.2d 996, 624 N.Y.S.2d 710 (4th Dept. 1995).

—Prosecution's use of oral statements made by the defendant to the District Attorney, which were not previously disclosed to defense counsel, was proper since disclosure of the statements were neither required by statute nor specifically provided for in the parties agreed reciprocal discovery. People v. Berger, 129 A.D.2d 971, 514 N.Y.S.2d 284 (4th Dept. 1987).

—Conversations taking place during a controlled substance sale between defendant, a police officer and any other person are specifically excluded by the new discovery statute as statements, written, recorded, or orally made by defendant "in the course of a criminal transaction." (CPL § 240.20[1][a]). People v. Finkle, 103 Misc. 2d 985, 427 N.Y.S.2d 374 (Sullivan Co. Ct. 1980).

Pretrial discovery; material evidence favorable to defendant.—Whether other, sufficient evidence of guilt was produced in response to defendant's discovery demand was irrelevant if the prosecutor, in violation of his statutory duty to facilitate the discovery of exculpatory evidence, prejudiced defendant's ability to obtain the evidence before trial by misrepresenting that it had been preserved and would be available to him. People v. Bryce, 88 N.Y.2d 124, 643 N.Y.S.2d 516, 666 N.E.2d 221 (1996).

—It was error to deny defendant pretrial disclosure of statement by defense witness that contained exculpatory evidence. People v. Stanley, 81 A.D.2d 842, 438 N.Y.S.2d 848 (2d Dept. 1981).

Pretrial discovery; when authorized.—Law enforcement authorities are not ordinarily required to notify counsel of an impending investigatory lineup absent a specific request to do so. People v. Mitchell, 2 N.Y.3d 272, 778 N.Y.S.2d 427, 810 N.E.2d 879 (2004).

—Drug detecting dog need not be produced pursuant to CPL § 240.20 where defendant has failed to present any evidence rebutting People's documentary proof of dog's ability to detect. People v. Price, 54 N.Y.2d 557, 446 N.Y.S.2d 906, 431 N.E.2d 267 (1981).

—CPL makes no provision for preindictment disclosure, even on a defendant's specific request. People v. Gudz, 18 A.D.3d 11, 793 N.Y.S.2d 556 (3d Dept. 2005).

—Defendant had no right to discovery prior to indictment. People v. Walker, 15 A.D.3d 902, 789 N.Y.S.2d 780 (4th Dept. 2005).

—Items that are not enumerated in CPL 240.20 are not discoverable as a matter of right unless constitutionally or otherwise specifically mandated. People v. Blankymsee, 196 Misc. 2d 240, 764 N.Y.S.2d 331 (Sup. Ct. Queens Co. 2003).

—Article 240 of the CPL provides no authority for a court to order discovery where the accusatory instrument is a simplified information charging a traffic infraction. People v. McGettrick, 139 Misc. 2d 403, 528 N.Y.S.2d 758 (City Ct. Columbia Co. 1988).

—There can be no discovery on a felony complaint; discovery may be obtained when the felony complaint is reduced to an information (CPL § 240.20[1]); the appropriate method resulting in the least confusion to all parties is to serve a demand upon the People at the time an information is first filed, and to run the time for compliance from that date. People v. Webb, 105 Misc. 2d 660, 432 N.Y.S.2d 826 (Crim. Ct. Queens Co. 1980).

—Defendants may not obtain pretrial discovery of evidentiary matter with respect to tainted identification and electronic eavesdropping. Defendants may obtain such material in the course of a suppression hearing if defendants show that such material was unlawfully acquired. People v. Bennett, 75 Misc. 2d 1040, 349 N.Y.S.2d 506 (Sup. Ct. Erie Co. 1973).

Pretrial discovery; physical examination of victim.—Court did not abuse its discretion in denying defendant's motion, made only two weeks before trial and one year after the incident, for an independent physical examination of the victim, because such discovery is not provided by CPL § 240.20 and when measured against the traumatic effect the examination would have on the victim, there was nothing in the record justifying the exam in the interest of justice. People v. James, 233 A.D.2d 903, 649 N.Y.S.2d 550 (4th Dept. 1996).

Pretrial discovery; names of witnesses.—Names of prospective witnesses should be obtained from the attorneys outside the presence of the jury and presented to prospective jurors during voir dire without attribution to either party. People v. Boyd, 53 N.Y.2d 912, 440 N.Y.S.2d 631, 423 N.E.2d 54 (1981).

—Defendant's right to discover a potentially material witness must be balanced against a founded fear that such discovery might lead to intimidation of the witness or the influencing of his testimony; it should be disclosed, with the proper safeguards, if the evidence is of material importance to the defense on the question of guilt or innocence. People v. Andre W., 44 N.Y.2d 179, 404 N.Y.S.2d 578, 375 N.E.2d 758 (1978).

—Absent compelling circumstances, such as the danger of intimidation, there should be disclosure of the names of the prosecution witnesses, particularly where the evidence to be given by the witness is material to the defendant's guilt or innocence. People v. Rivera, 119 A.D.2d 517, 501 N.Y.S.2d 38 (1st Dept. 1986).

—Where there has been a showing that divulging a witness' name raises justifiable fear for his or her own safety, the burden of establishing the materiality of the pretrial revelation of the witness' name shifts to the defendant. People v. Robinson, 207 A.D.2d 363, 615 N.Y.S.2d 451 (2d Dept. 1994).

—Names, addresses, and statements of confidential witnesses compiled during a criminal investigation are exempt from disclosure under the Freedom of Information Law. Allen v. Strojnowski, 129 A.D.2d 700, 514 N.Y.S.2d 463 (2d Dept. 1987).

—Defendant does not have a constitutional or statutory right to pretrial disclosure of the identity of the prosecution witnesses. People v. Coleman, 178 A.D.2d 842, 577 N.Y.S.2d 900 (3d Dept. 1991).

—It is within a trial judge's discretion to order the pretrial disclosure of the names and addresses of witnesses. People v. Arrellano, 150 Misc. 2d 574, 569 N.Y.S.2d 574 (Crim. Ct. Kings Co. 1991).

Pretrial discovery; witness' pretrial statements.—Prosecutor's failure to give defendant, prior to trial, the memorandum of a statement previously made by a prosecution witness did not warrant reversal where the defendant had obtained duplicative material and used it. People v. Payne, 52 N.Y.2d 743, 436 N.Y.S.2d 271, 417 N.E.2d 564 (1980).

Pretrial discovery; police reports and records—Court

allowed discovery of any internal police memoranda that the prosecutor intended to use at trial. People v. Bissonette, 107 Misc. 2d 1049, 436 N.Y.S.2d 607 (City Ct. Saratoga Co. 1981).

—Defense counsel is entitled to have produced at trial or at a hearing, for possible impeachment purposes, any police reports, records or memoranda, prepared by testifying police officers, and such reports, unless falling within the category of exempt or work papers are discoverable. People v. McLoughlin, 104 Misc. 2d 730, 429 N.Y.S.2d 149 (Dist. Ct. Nassau Co. 1980).

—Statistical data relating to the arrest and prosecution of persons for prostitution-related offenses is not discoverable under CPL §§ 240.20 and 240.40 and is not discoverable on the authority of *Brady* because it does not address the guilt or innocence of the defendant; a claim of discriminatory enforcement should not be treated as a defense to a criminal charge but as an application to the court for a dismissal or quashing of the prosecution upon constitutional grounds. People v. Nelson, 103 Misc. 2d 847, 427 N.Y.S.2d 194 (City Ct. of Syracuse 1980).

Pretrial discovery; *Rosario* material.—New trial ordered where People failed to turn over copy of transcript of mentally disabled complainant at her first swearability hearing, which indicated that she did not know her attacker's full name; *Rosario* violation was reversible error because attacker's identity was central issue at trial. People v. LaSalle, 243 A.D.2d 490, 663 N.Y.S.2d 79 (2d Dept. 1997).

No pretrial discovery; capital case.—Discovery that is unavailable pursuant to statute may not be ordered in either capital or noncapital cases. Sacket v. Bartlett, 241 A.D.2d 97, 671 N.Y.S.2d 156 (3d Dept. 1998).

—There is no common law right to discovery prior to indictment, and there is no statutory right to discovery based upon the filing of a felony case; "unless the defendant in a potential capital case can cite specific statutory authority for the grant of procedural rights other and different than those enjoyed by all other criminal defendants in New York State, any imagined so called 'heightened due process rights' simply do not exist." People v. Leftenant, 175 Misc. 2d 605, 671 N.Y.S.2d 917 (Suffolk Co. Ct. 1998); *see also* Brown v. Appelman, 241 A.D.2d 279, 672 N.Y.S.2d 373 (2d Dept. 1998) ("[t]here simply is no heightened right to preindictment discovery in capital cases").

—The Criminal Procedure Law does not contain any provision entitling an individual who is facing capital charges to earlier or expanded discovery. People v. Davis, 184 Misc. 2d 680, 709 N.Y.S.2d 345 (Sup. Ct. Kings Co. 2000).

Pretrial notice of use; defendant's statements.—Suppression was denied even though notice of the People's intent to introduce at trial the defendant's statement was not made within 15 days of his arraignment, as required by CPL § 710.30(2) since the defendant nonetheless received ample pretrial notice. People v. Brown, 92 A.D.2d 939, 460 N.Y.S.2d 365 (2d Dept. 1983).

Pretrial notice; not required.—Contrary to defendant's contentions, CPL § 240.20 contains no mandate that the People use the discovery process or otherwise give pretrial notice of their intention to compel defendant to display his tattoo of the name "Polo" for the jury, which defendant was directed to do at trial after two witnesses testified to knowing defendant by that name. People v. Holmes, 304 A.D.2d 1043, 758 N.Y.S.2d 212 (3d Dept. 2003).

Duty to preserve evidence.—The loss or destruction of evidence prior to trial does not necessarily require dismissal of the charge since dismissal is considered a drastic remedy and is rarely invoked as an appropriate sanction for the People's failure to preserve evidence. People v. Haupt, 71 N.Y.2d 929, 528 N.Y.S.2d 808, 524 N.E.2d 129 (1988).

—Inadvertent destruction of "rape kit" did not provide basis for reversal where defendant was aware of its existence some eight months before it was destroyed but never sought its production or expressed an interest in performing independent tests until its destruction was disclosed in the middle of trial. People v. Allgood, 70 N.Y.2d 812, 523 N.Y.S.2d 431, 517 N.E.2d 1316 (1987).

—FBI's destruction of the pubic hair found near the victim's body which had been found to be microscopically indistinguishable from samples taken from the defendant did not deprive the defendant of a fair trial since the hair had been available for examination prior to the defendant's initial guilty plea and was destroyed by the F.B.I. some time thereafter in the good-faith belief that it was no longer necessary to preserve it as evidence. People v. Sunset Bay, 67 N.Y.2d 787, 501 N.Y.S.2d 19, 492 N.E.2d 127 (1986).

—With respect to the blanket in which the deceased's body was found wrapped, it was undisputed that the failure to preserve the evidence was attributable to the Medical Examiner's Office, not law enforcement personnel. People v. Santiago, 200 A.D.2d 370, 606 N.Y.S.2d 200 (1st Dept. 1994).

—Destruction of 911 tapes, in the course of routine police procedure, does not have *Rosario* consequences when it does not prejudice the defendant. People v. Segui, 208 A.D.2d 447, 617 N.Y.S.2d 718 (1st Dept.), *lv. denied*, 84 N.Y.2d 1038 (1994).

—The police do not have the duty to preserve all material which might be of conceivable evidentiary significance. People v. Bradshaw, 172 A.D.2d 328, 568 N.Y.S.2d 401 (1st Dept. 1991).

—In the absence of bad faith, the failure of the People to preserve evidentiary material—a rape kit—of which no more can be said than that it could have been tested and that the result may have helped the defendant does not violate the *Brady* rule. People v. Callendar, 207 A.D.2d 900, 616 N.Y.S.2d 667 (2d Dept.), *lv. denied*, 84 N.Y.2d 1029 (1994).

—Testimony regarding the narcotics which were seized from the female purchaser was properly admitted into evidence despite the pretrial destruction of the narcotics since the destruction was inadvertent and because defendant never sought production of the evidence prior to trial. People v. Hernandez, 138 A.D.2d 627, 526 N.Y.S.2d 211 (2d Dept. 1988).

—The defendant could not be heard to complain about its destruction where knife recovered from crime scene was destroyed pursuant to an internal departmental policy to destroy investigatory evidence that was being held by the property clerk's office for a period in excess of one year, and the knife was deemed investigatory evidence because the defendant was still at large trying to avoid apprehension. People v. Taylor, 127 A.D.2d 714, 511 N.Y.S.2d 908 (2d Dept. 1987).

—Failure of law enforcement authorities to retain evidence did not warrant reversal where the loss was traceable to the 16-year period of time between arrest and trial occasioned by the defendant's incompetency rather than to bad faith. People v. Haupt, 128 A.D.2d 172, 515 N.Y.S.2d 537 (2d Dept. 1987).

—By his guilty plea, the defendant waived the issue concerning the People's alleged failure to properly preserve for purposes of discovery a second vial of blood taken from the defendant. People v. Mills, 124 A.D.2d 600, 507 N.Y.S.2d 743 (2d Dept. 1986).

—The conviction was reversed and the indictment dismissed where police deliberately destroyed bank surveillance photographs taken during the robbery. People v. Springer, 122 A.D.2d 87, 504 N.Y.S.2d 232 (2d Dept. 1986).

—The conviction for criminal sale of a controlled substance was reversed where law enforcement officials deliberately for reasons of economy, erased a series of tape recordings of conversations between a law enforcement official and the defendant. People v. Saddy, 84 A.D.2d 175, 445 N.Y.S.2d 601 (2d Dept. 1981).

—Inadvertent loss of a tape recording of a telephone conversation had with defendant and the deliberate erasure of a tape of a conversation had with defendant when the equipment malfunctioned shortly after the tape started did not require reversal where police officers testified that the second tape lacked any evidentiary value whatsoever, and there was no demonstration that either tape contained any exculpatory material. People v. Frye, 129 A.D.2d 985, 514 N.Y.S.2d 295 (4th Dept. 1987).

—The loss or destruction of evidence in necessary testing by the prosecution does not violate a defendant's due process rights when authorities are acting in good faith and in accordance with their normal practice, the destroyed evidence is not likely to have been exculpatory, and the defendant has alternative means of demonstrating his innocence. People v. Monagas, 161 Misc. 2d 898, 615 N.Y.S.2d 633 (Sup. Ct. N.Y. Co. 1994).

—The responsibility to safeguard and preserve evidence gathered against an accused lies with the prosecution and the People must meet a heavy burden in establishing that a failure to preserve the evidence was not intentional, deliberate or in bad faith. People v. Davis, 109 Misc. 2d 230, 439 N.Y.S.2d 798 (Onondaga Co. Ct. 1981).

Reciprocal discovery.—The prosecution's right to discovery is not an independent right, but is triggered only by a defense request for discretionary discovery and is restricted to like property. Moreover, production of an accused's purely private papers may not be compelled, for there the State extracts testimonial disclosure, invading the "private inner sanctum of individual feeling and thought" that the Fifth Amendment was designed to protect. People v. Copicotto, 50 N.Y.2d 222, 428 N.Y.S.2d 649, 406 N.E.2d 465 (1980).

Exempt material; work product rule.—Prior to ordering defense counsel to furnish interview notes of a defense witness to the prosecutor, the court should have conducted an in-court inspection of the notes to determine the legitimacy of the claim that the notes constituted "work product"; error deemed harmless as notes were indeed discoverable. People v. Nielson, 115 A.D.2d 972, 497 N.Y.S.2d 537 (4th Dept. 1985).

Brady **material; scope of discovery.**—The police do not have an affirmative duty to gather evidence for the accused. People v. Kirkland, 157 Misc. 2d 38, 595 N.Y.S.2d 905 (Yates Co. Ct. 1993).

Brady **material; defendant's burden to present clear factual record.**—Where People, in compliance with *Brady*, claimed a statement was turned over to the defense, but the defense did not recall receiving it, court declined to decide whether the statement constituted *Brady* material, as it could not determine from the record whether the material was withheld from the defense, and it was the defense's burden to present a clear factual record for the court's review. People v. Licitra, 236 A.D.2d 559, 654 N.Y.S.2d 631 (2d Dept. 1997).

—Defendant failed to establish that, had the prosecutor disclosed the material, the result of the trial would have been different. People v. Mellerson, 15 A.D.3d 964, 788 N.Y.S.2d 746 (4th Dept. 2005).

Brady **material; time of disclosure.**—People's failure to disclose *Brady* material to defendant until the defense case did not require reversal, since trial court gave the defense the opportunity to recall witnesses, introduce the evidence, and refer to the material during summation. People v. Jagopat, 216 A.D.2d 583, 628 N.Y.S.2d 763 (2d Dept. 1995).

—It is well settled that defendant's constitutional right to a fair trial is not violated where he was given a meaningful opportunity to use the allegedly exculpatory material to cross-examine the People's witnesses or as evidence during his case. People v. Barnes, 200 A.D.2d 751, 607 N.Y.S.2d 92 (2d Dept.), *lv. denied*, 83 N.Y.2d 849 (1994); *accord* People v. Warren, 304 A.D.2d 594, 758 N.Y.S.2d 127 (2d Dept. 2003).

—The rule of *Brady* does not require that disclosure be made at any particular point of the proceedings, but only that it be made in time for the defense to use it effectively. People v. White, 178 A.D.2d 674, 578 N.Y.S.2d 227 (2d Dept. 1991); People v. Bolling, 157 A.D.2d 733, 550 N.Y.S.2d 27 (2d Dept. 1990).

—Prosecution did not commit *Brady* violation by failing to disclose victim's misidentification of defendant until the eve of trial because this exculpatory evidence had been disclosed directly to defendant's counsel by the investigating detective well before trial commenced, giving defendant a meaningful opportunity to use the information. People v. Cyrus, 18 A.D.3d 1020, 794 N.Y.S.2d 755 (3d Dept. 2005).

—No *Brady* violation occurred where the evidence was presented to the defendant well in advance of the trial and in sufficient time for its effective use. People v. Zambito, 153 A.D.2d 975, 545 N.Y.S.2d 414 (3d Dept. 1989).

—Over three-month period before trial, the People disclosed that three items had been removed from the victim's car—a gun, a bolt action for the gun, and two shells. Although the production of the *Brady* material was delayed, defendant was given a meaningful opportunity to use the allegedly exculpatory material to cross-examine the People's witnesses or as evidence during his case; thus, the court affirmed the conviction. People v. Duncan, 277 A.D.2d 997, 716 N.Y.S.2d 516 (4th Dept. 2000).

Brady **material; exculpatory evidence.**—Evidence that witness misidentification of one of the perpetrators—proof that such person was in the hospital at the time of the crime—constituted *Brady* material that should have been disclosed to the defense; reversal required. People v. Davis, 81 N.Y.2d 281, 598 N.Y.S.2d 156, 614 N.E.2d 719 (1993).

—Contested evidence was not *Brady* material, but was nothing more than an innocuous statement that a police officer over-heard, devoid of context, and even if it was exculpatory mate-rial, the defendant was given a meaningful opportunity to use the material to cross-examine the People's witnesses or as evidence in his own case. People v. Brims, 19 A.D.3d 433, 796 N.Y.S.2d 696 (2d Dept. 2005).

—Reversal was required where prosecutor withheld from defen-dant information concerning a possible conspiracy against the defendant predating the crime for which he was arrested and tried, and which involved a police officer and two persons with suspected ties to organized crime. People v. Smith, 127 A.D.2d 864, 512 N.Y.S.2d 244 (2d Dept. 1987).

—There was no merit to claim that failure of one of the victims to identify defendant's photograph during the Grand Jury pro-ceedings constituted *Brady* material that should have been disclosed to him; the Grand Jury minutes were provided to defendant at trial and he had the opportunity to cross-examine that witness. People v. McGee, 171 A.D.2d 1081, 569 N.Y.S.2d 527 (4th Dept.), *lv. denied*, 78 N.Y.2d 924 (1991).

—Court rejected claim that 911 tape constituted *Brady* material where the claim merely rested in speculation that the tape may have contained potentially exculpatory material. People v. Cachoian, 135 Misc. 2d 1116, 517 N.Y.S.2d 362, 364 (Crim. Ct. Bronx Co. 1987).

***Brady* material; relating to a victim.**—Court properly de-nied defendant access to the sodomy victim's school, counseling and medical records and the medical records pertaining to the suicide of the victim's father; inasmuch as the defendant sought the records merely in the hope of discovering material to impeach the victim's credibility, the court acted properly. People v. Gutkaiss, 206 A.D.2d 628, 614 N.Y.S.2d 599 (3d Dept.), *lv. denied*, 84 N.Y.2d 936 (1994).

—Court did not abuse its discretion in denying defendant's request for an independent psychiatric examination of the victim since the CPL does not authorize such a procedure; moreover, when measured against the traumatic effect that type of exami-nation would have on the victim, there was nothing in the record justifying such an examination in the interest of justice. People v. Gutkaiss, 206 A.D.2d 628, 614 N.Y.S.2d 599 (3d Dept.), *lv. denied*, 84 N.Y.2d 936 (1994).

—Court rejected argument that victim's post-indictment psychi-atric medical records constituted *Brady* material. People v. Cesar G., 154 Misc. 2d 17, 584 N.Y.S.2d 383 (Crim. Ct. N.Y. Co. 1991).

***Brady* material; relating to a witness.**—People's failure to disclose murder witness's initial statement to the police in which she denied witnessing the shooting was *Brady* material that had been specifically requested; reversal was required because her testimony was crucial to the People's theory that it was defen-dant alone who shot and killed the victim, despite other evidence that someone else was also at the scene and discharged his gun. People v. Bond, 95 N.Y.2d 840, 713 N.Y.S.2d 514, 735 N.E.2d 1279 (2000).

—In manslaughter prosecution where witness suffered from schizophrenia, paranoid type, methadone dependence, and anti-social personality and the court denied the defense request for the psychiatric records of the witness, reversal was required. People v. Rivera, 138 A.D.2d 169, 530 N.Y.S.2d 802 (1st Dept. 1988).

—Because defendant learned of relevant informationâthat a witness who provided the description for a composite sketch was later unable to identify defendant in a photo array at a suppression hearing more than one week before the trial, in time to allow defendant to make meaningful use of the evidence, and neither the prosecution nor defense called the witness at the trial, the prosecution's failure to turn over the information earlier did not deprive defendant of a fair trial. People v. Clarke, 5 A.D.3d 807, 772 N.Y.S.2d 630 (3d Dept. 2004).

—The People have a duty to disclose any material exculpatory information in their possession, and evidence affecting the credibility of witnesses falls within the general rule. People v. Haley, 199 A.D.2d 863, 606 N.Y.S.2d 359 (3d Dept. 1993).

—A witness' criminal background is evidence which must be disclosed under *Brady* principles. People v. Ramos, 146 Misc. 2d 168, 550 N.Y.S.2d 784 (Sup. Ct. Bronx Co. 1990).

—Prosecution was not required under *Brady* to disclose ticket-ing officer's retirement, where the officer was still available as a witness. People v. Perez, 193 Misc. 2d 169, 749 N.Y.S.2d 850 (Justice Ct. Nassau Co. 2002).

***Brady* material; information within defendant's knowl-edge.**—Evidence is not deemed to be *Brady* material when the defendant has knowledge of it. People v. LaRocca, 172 A.D.2d 628, 568 N.Y.S.2d 431 (2d Dept. 1991).

—Where the defendant knows the witness testifying on his behalf and the nature of her testimony, there can be no violation of the *Brady* rule; thus court rejected claim that he was improp-erly denied disclosure of Grand Jury minutes containing the testimony of his girlfriend. People v. Johnson, 157 A.D.2d 855, 550 N.Y.S.2d 430 (2d Dept. 1990).

—Evidence is not deemed *Brady* material where the defendant has knowledge of it. People v. Lacen, 151 A.D.2d 783, 543 N.Y.S.2d 111 (2d Dept. 1989).

—Defendant could not claim surprise due to People's failure to disclose existence of tire iron until during trial, where the tire iron had been obtained from him by one of the eyewitnesses to the burglary. People v. Rosario, 124 A.D.2d 683, 508 N.Y.S.2d 58 (2d Dept. 1986).

—Where defendant had knowledge of fingernail scrapings and oral swabs taken from the victim, they were not *Brady* material. People v. Buxton, 189 A.D.2d 996, 593 N.Y.S.2d 87 (3d Dept. 1993).

—Evidence is not deemed to be *Brady* material when the defendant has knowledge of it. People v. Cornell, 17 A.D.3d 1010, 794 N.Y.S.2d 226 (4th Dept. 2005).

***Brady* material; arrest photo.**—Court erred in failing to sanction the People for their failure to provide defendant with his arrest photo, and the failure to provide the photo prejudiced the defendant, warranting reversal. People v. Dudley, 268 A.D.2d 442, 703 N.Y.S.2d 489 (2d Dept. 2000).

***Brady* material; speculative claim.**—Prosecutor's failure to disclose the addresses and telephone numbers of potential prosecution witnesses did not violate *Brady*, where defendant's claim—that the addresses and telephone numbers may have led to potentially exculpatory material—was speculative. There is no statutory basis to compel such disclosure, and defense counsel had ample opportunity to subpoena the witnesses but failed to do so. People v. Estrada, 1 A.D.3d 928, 767 N.Y.S.2d 552 (4th Dept. 2003).

Documents from Chief Medical Examiner; not *Brady* material.—Ballistics and serology documents concerning tests conducted on a certain vehicle found two days after the murder of the victim were not *Brady* material because they were not in the People's possession, but rather were in the possession of the Office of the Chief Medical Examiner, which is not a law enforcement agency. People v. Stern, 270 A.D.2d 118, 704 N.Y.S.2d 569 (1st Dept. 2000).

Alcohol; blood, DNA tests.—Vehicle and Traffic Law § 1194 (7)(a) does not require a physician to be actually present, observing the procedure, when a laboratory technician draws a blood sample from a suspect for the purposes of conducting a test to determine its alcoholic or drug content. People v. Moser, 70 N.Y.2d 476, 522 N.Y.S.2d 497, 517 N.E.2d 212 (1987).

—People's failure to supply the defendant, until the first day of trial, with documents relating to the testing and calibration of the breathalyzer instrument used to test defendant's blood alcohol level required reversal where the documents bore upon the admissibility of the breathalyzer test results themselves, and the court refused to grant defendant a continuance in order to permit defense counsel an opportunity to adequately examine the documents. People v. Corley, 124 A.D.2d 390, 507 N.Y.S.2d 491 (3d Dept. 1986).

—Trial court committed reversible error by refusing defense counsel's request for the calibration records of a breathalyzer machine where defendant was charged with the crime of operat-ing a motor vehicle under the influence of alcohol. People v. English, 103 A.D.2d 979, 480 N.Y.S.2d 56 (3d Dept. 1984).

—Defendant's nine month delay in requesting the sample, during which time the sample became unusable for retesting does not bar the prosecution from using the results of its tests at trial where the district attorney not only did not question defendant's right to discover and inspect a blood sample, but additionally apprised him of the procedure to be observed in securing the sample. People v. Swanda, 87 A.D.2d 940, 451 N.Y.S.2d 240 (3d Dept. 1982).

—Court rejected argument that defendant's blood samples constituted *Brady* material. People v. Harris, 178 A.D.2d 919, 579 N.Y.S.2d 263, 265 (4th Dept. 1991).

—Prosecutor was not precluded from offering evidence of the blood specimen test where the blood sample was inadvertently lost and the parties stipulated to that fact. People v. Briggs, 81 A.D.2d 1017, 440 N.Y.S.2d 143 (4th Dept. 1981).

—There is no duty to capture and preserve the defendant's breath sample for preservation of a sample, because later testing is not mandated by statute and because the scientific reliability of the result of a test performed on a breath sample preserved for that purpose has not been established. People v. DiLorenzo, 134 Misc. 2d 1000, 513 N.Y.S.2d 938 (Nassau Co. Ct. 1987).

—Breathalyzer test results are neither testimony nor evidence relating to some communicative act by defendant, and therefore the test result is not inadmissible on privilege grounds. People v. Harrington, 111 Misc. 2d 648, 444 N.Y.S.2d 849 (Monroe Co. Ct. 1981).

—In prosecution for driving while intoxicated, defendant was entitled to discovery of all documentary evidence that the People intended to introduce as a foundation for the breathalyzer test results, but he was not entitled to discovery of the original ampule, its chemical contents, or the reference ampule used during test. People v. Amidon, 104 Misc. 2d 850, 427 N.Y.S.2d 727 (City Ct. Ontario Co. 1980).

—It was proper to deny motion to suppress evidence of breathalyzer test due to the fact that the test ampule used was not preserved because the preservation of the test ampule is neither feasible, practical nor relevant since subsequent testing will not give any scientifically reliable results due to the uncontrollable and unpredictable changes that occur in the Breathalyzer test ampule. People v. LePree, 105 Misc. 2d 1066, 430 N.Y.S.2d 778 (City Ct. Monroe Co. 1980).

Bank surveillance tape and photos.—Lost or destroyed bank surveillance videotape and photographs did not constitute *Brady* material because there was no showing that they were exculpatory and because they never came into possession of the prosecution or the police, and their non-production would not warrant dismissal of the indictment, where there was no showing of bad faith or that the videotape or still photographs would have been beneficial to defendant. People v. Brock, 246 A.D.2d 406, 667 N.Y.S.2d 730 (1st Dept. 1998).

Scientific tests.—Analysis notes made in the FBI laboratory during DNA testing should have been furnished to defendant without a prior court determination as to whether they constituted exculpatory *Brady* material. People v. Dagata, 86 N.Y.2d 40, 629 N.Y.S.2d 186, 652 N.E.2d 932 (1995).

—Defendant is entitled to an order of discovery permitting him to conduct his own scientific tests, under court supervision, with respect to the alleged dangerous drug on which his indictment is based; if there is a justifiable apprehension of danger of alteration as to size, shape, weight or composition by pretrial testing the defendant should be afforded this opportunity after the drug has been introduced on trial. People v. White, 40 N.Y.2d 797, 390 N.Y.S.2d 405, 358 N.E.2d 1031 (1976).

—*Brady* claim rejected; defendant's claim that DNA testing, if performed, would have proved to be exculpatory in nature is purely speculative and inasmuch as no testing was conducted, defendant could not reasonably argue that he was denied exculpatory material. People v. Smith, 204 A.D.2d 140, 612 N.Y.S.2d 113 (1st Dept. 1994).

—The trial court erred in denying defendant's discovery request to conduct independent testing of the drugs which were the subject of his conviction. People v. Metivier, 210 A.D.2d 260, 619 N.Y.S.2d 731 (2d Dept. 1994).

—Court did not err in denying defendant's motion to prohibit the introduction of any evidence related to the victim's body, wounds, or cause of death, on the ground that the body had been cremated before the defense could conduct its own examination; the body of the victim in a homicide case is not listed among the discoverable items the prosecution must produce upon demand by a defendant and the defendant failed to explain why disclosure of that evidence was necessary. People v. Rose, 122 A.D.2d 484, 505 N.Y.S.2d 244 (3d Dept. 1986).

Cooperation agreements.—Once witness testified he had no cooperation agreement, People were obligated to reveal their agreement with witness' attorney that he would have to go to prison if he testified against defendants, even if witness and trial assistant were purposely shielded from that information. People v. Steadman, 82 N.Y.2d 1, 603 N.Y.S.2d 382, 623 N.E.2d 509 (1993).

—A prosecutor is under a duty to disclose to defense counsel correspondence between the District Attorney's office and the Parole board advising of the cooperation of a principal prosecution witness in the trial of the witness' accomplices and expressing the hope that such cooperation will be taken into account when the witness is considered for parole. People v. Cwikla, 46 N.Y.2d 434, 414 N.Y.S.2d 102, 386 N.E.2d 1070 (1979).

—It is questionable whether witness's prior cooperation with the Homicide Investigation Unit on unrelated matters was *Brady* material; *People v. Wright,* 86 N.Y.2d 591, 635 N.Y.S.2d 136, 658 N.E.2d 1009, which held that a prosecution witness's prior activity as a police informant constituted *Brady* material under the circumstances of that case, did not establish a blanket rule. People v. Sibadan, 240 A.D.2d 30, 671 N.Y.S.2d 1 (1st Dept. 1998).

—A defendant must be made aware of the existence of immunity agreements between the prosecutor and a witness in order to comply with the principles of *Brady.* People v. Rathbun, 191 A.D.2d 720, 595 N.Y.S.2d 522 (2d Dept.), *lv. denied,* 81 N.Y.2d 1078 (1993).

—Once any understanding has been reached between the prosecutor and a witness, it is for the jury to determine how much value to assign it in terms of assessing the witness' credibility. People v. LaDolce, 196 A.D.2d 49, 607 N.Y.S.2d 523 (4th Dept. 1994).

Identity of confidential informant.—Whether an informant's identity should be disclosed following a *Darden* hearing is a matter entrusted to the sound discretion of the trial court. People v. Adrion, 82 N.Y.S.2d 628, 606 N.Y.S.2d 893, 627 N.E.2d 973 (1993).

—The People may not refuse to comply with a trial court's order to produce a confidential informant for a *Darden* inquiry on the ground that agency obtained enough confirmatory information through his own observations to justify a finding of probable cause; notwithstanding the arresting authorities' own observations of criminality, the People are obliged to either produce the informant or forfeit the resulting evidence. People v. Adrion, 82 N.Y.2d 628, 606 N.Y.S.2d 893, 617 N.E.2d 973 (1993).

—In order to establish the required materiality of the testimony of a missing informant, the defendant must demonstrate a reasonable probability that the outcome of the trial would have been different had the informant testified. People v. Lesiuk, 81 N.Y.2d 485, 600 N.Y.S.2d 931, 617 N.E.2d 1047 (1993).

—Where the defendant at the close of the People's case moves for the production of the informant, the court after an in camera examination of the informant can deny the motion where it finds that the disclosure would not advance the defendant's case either on the question of credibility or on any issue or substantive issue. People v. Lee, 39 N.Y.2d 388, 384 N.Y.S.2d 123, 348 N.E.2d 579 (1976).

—Defendant's request for access to sealed warrant, affidavit and minutes was properly denied, because the sealing of these materials in the interest of maintaining the informant's safety did not impair defendant's ability to litigate the suppression issue. People v. Castillo, 309 A.D.2d 533, 765 N.Y.S.2d 322 (1st Dept. 2003).

—Defendant was not entitled to a *Darden* hearing where there were no allegations that the police informant was imaginary or the communications fabricated. People v. Marin, 161 A.D.2d 393, 555 N.Y.S.2d 128 (2d Dept. 1990).

—Court rejects defendant's contention that prosecution was required to call as a witness the confidential informant, who had played a minor role in the narcotics sale which resulted in the defendant's arrest, where the informant could not be located by police and was in fact known and produced in court by the defendant. People v. Murray, 119 A.D.2d 702, 501 N.Y.S.2d 118 (2d Dept. 1986).

—Court properly refused to order the People to reveal the identity of a confidential informant, where his role in the narcotics sales was not significant and defendant was identified by several witnesses as the seller. People v. Sturgis, 202 A.D.2d 808, 609 N.Y.S.2d 393 (3d Dept.), *lv. denied,* 84 N.Y.2d 833 (1994).

—Since the issue of identification was not closely contested, the trial court did not abuse discretion by denying defendant's motion to order the prosecution to disclose the identity of the confidential informant who accompanied the undercover policewoman at the time she purchased drugs from the defendant.

People v. Yattaw, 106 A.D.2d 679, 484 N.Y.S.2d 140 (3d Dept. 1984).

—There was no error in the court's consideration of the information provided by the sworn informant to the issuing magistrate and the court's refusal to disclose that information to defendant. People v. Knighton, 202 A.D.2d 1022, 610 N.Y.S.2d 116 (4th Dept. 1994).

Subpoena.—Generally, a subpoena duces tecum may not be used for the purpose of discovery or to ascertain the existence of evidence. *In re* Terry D., 81 N.Y.2d 1042, 601 N.Y.S.2d 452, 619 N.E.2d 389 (1993).

—Subpoena for items in possession of social services department should have been quashed, since they were confidential, were not demonstrably relevant, and were not within the control of the district attorney. Sabol v. People, 203 A.D.2d 369, 610 N.Y.S.2d 93 (2d Dept. 1994).

—The law does not confer upon a prosecutor the power to employ a subpoena solely to conduct an investigation or to subpoena witnesses to attend his office or any other place where a grand jury or court is not convened. People v. Neptune, 161 Misc. 2d 781, 615 N.Y.S.2d 265 (Sup. Ct. Kings Co. 1994).

—A court cannot issue a subpoena where there is no proceeding or action before it. People v. Jones, 160 Misc. 2d 246, 608 N.Y.S.2d 795 (Crim. Ct. Kings Co. 1994).

—Although the district attorney was a party to the proceeding, he did not have standing to quash a subpoena addressed to the department of social services. People v. Grosunor, 108 Misc. 2d 932, 439 N.Y.S.2d 243 (Crim. Ct. Bronx Co. 1981).

§ 240.30. Discovery; upon demand of prosecutor.

1. Except to the extent protected by court order, upon a demand to produce by the prosecutor, a defendant against whom an indictment, superior court information, prosecutor's information, information, or simplified information charging a misdemeanor is pending shall disclose and make available for inspection, photographing, copying or testing, subject to constitutional limitations:

(a) any written report or document, or portion thereof, concerning a physical or mental examination, or scientific test, experiment, or comparisons, made by or at the request or direction of, the defendant, if the defendant intends to introduce such report or document at trial, or if the defendant has filed a notice of intent to proffer psychiatric evidence and such report or document relates thereto, or if such report or document was made by a person, other than defendant, whom defendant intends to call as a witness at trial; and

(b) any photograph, drawing, tape or other electronic recording which the defendant intends to introduce at trial.

2. The defense shall make a diligent good faith effort to make such property available for discovery where it exists but the property is not within its possession, custody or control, provided, that the defendant shall not be required to obtain by subpoena duces tecum demanded material that the prosecutor may thereby obtain.

Amended by L. 1980, Ch. 220; L. 1982, Ch. 558; L. 1983, Ch. 317.

ANNOTATIONS

Voice exemplars.—Compelling a defendant to speak solely for the purpose of physical identification does not violate the privilege against self-incrimination where the defendant had been arrested, indicted and present in court. People v. Smith, 86 A.D.2d 251, 450 N.Y.S.2d 57 (3d Dept. 1982).

Mental health records; examinations.—The defense psychiatrist's progress notes relating to his examination of defendant were discoverable under CPL § 240.30(1)(a). People v. Likovic, 215 A.D.2d 406, 626 N.Y.S.2d 244 (2d Dept. 1995).

—Discovery provisions only require the disclosure of written psychological reports where they exist, and the defense cannot be compelled to obtain written reports. Mulvaney v. Dubin, 80 A.D.2d 566, 435 N.Y.S.2d 761 (2d Dept.), *rev'd on other grounds,* 55 N.Y.2d 668 (1981).

Privileged communications.—Defendant's conviction reversed because his attorney turned over to the prosecution a lengthy, confidential letter defendant had written to defense counsel; disclosure of the confidential communication was protected by the attorney-client privilege, which was not overcome by the reciprocal discovery rules of CPL § 240.30. People v. Cosme, 169 A.D.2d 467, 564 N.Y.S.2d 345 (1st Dept. 1991), *aff'd,* 80 N.Y.2d 790 (1992).

Subd. 2; applicability.—CPL § 240.30(2) is expressly limited to any "written report" that "exists"; accordingly, trial court could not compel defendant's psychiatric expert to prepare a written report, but court could order defense expert to turn over any written or tape recordings that have already been made regarding this defendant. People v. Purdon, 175 Misc. 2d 775, 669 N.Y.S.2d 777 (Sullivan Co. Ct. 1997).

§ 240.35. Discovery; refusal of demand.

Notwithstanding the provisions of sections 240.20 and 240.30, the prosecutor or the defendant, as the case may be, may refuse to disclose any information which he reasonably believes is not discoverable by a demand to produce, pursuant to section 240.20 or section 240.30 as the case may be, or for which he reasonably believes a protective order would be warranted. Such refusal shall be made in a writing, which shall set forth the grounds of such belief as fully as possible, consistent with the objective of the refusal. The writing shall be served upon the demanding party and a copy shall be filed with the court.

ANNOTATION

Suggestive identification; disclosure of informant required.—Disclosure of the identity of the informant who arranged and was present at drug sale was required where suggestive post-arrest identification procedure raised a serious question as to the accuracy of the identification by the undercover detective. People v. Baez, 103 A.D.2d 746, 477 N.Y.S.2d 651 (2d Dept. 1984).

§ 240.40. Discovery; upon court order.

1. Upon motion of a defendant against whom an indictment, superior court information, prosecutor's information, information, or simplified information charging a misdemeanor is pending, the court in which such accusatory instrument is pending:

(a) must order discovery as to any material not disclosed upon a demand pursuant to section 240.20, if it finds that the prosecutor's refusal to disclose such material is not justified;

(b) must, unless it is satisfied that the people have shown good cause why such an order should not be issued, order discovery or any other order authorized by subdivision one of section 240.70 as to any material not disclosed upon demand pursuant to section 240.20 where the prosecutor has failed to serve a timely written refusal pursuant to section 240.35; and

(c) may order discovery with respect to any other property, which the people intend to introduce at the trial, upon a showing by the defendant that discovery with respect to such property is material to the preparation of his defense, and that the request is reasonable. Upon granting the motion pursuant to paragraph (c) hereof, the court shall, upon motion of the people showing such to be material to the preparation of their case and that the request is reasonable, condition its order of discovery by further directing discovery by the people of property, of the same kind or character as that authorized to be inspected by the defendant, which he intends to introduce at the trial.

2. Upon motion of the prosecutor, and subject to constitutional limitation, the court in which an indictment, superior court information, prosecutor's information, information, or simplified information charging a misdemeanor is pending:

(a) must order discovery as to any property not disclosed upon a demand pursuant to section 240.30, if it finds that the defendant's refusal to disclose such material is not justified; and

(b) may order the defendant to provide nontestimonial evidence. Such order may, among other things, require the defendant to:

(i) Appear in a line-up;

(ii) Speak for identification by witness or potential witness;

(iii) Be fingerprinted;

(iv) Pose for photographs not involving reenactment of an event;

(v) Permit the taking of samples of blood, hair or other materials from his body in a manner not involving an unreasonable intrusion thereof or a risk of serious physical injury thereto;

(vi) Provide specimens of his handwriting;

(vii) Submit to a reasonable physical or medical inspection of his body.

This subdivision shall not be construed to limit, expand, or otherwise affect the issuance of a similar court order, as may be authorized by law, before the filing of an accusatory instrument consistent with such rights as the defendant may derive from the constitution of this state or of the United States. This section shall not be construed to limit or otherwise affect the administration of a chemical test where otherwise authorized pursuant to section one thousand one hundred ninety-four-a of the vehicle and traffic law.

3. An order pursuant to this section may be denied, limited or conditioned as provided in section 240.50.

Amended by L. 1982, Ch. 558; L. 1983, Chs. 317, 481.

ANNOTATIONS

General.—While the CPL does not expressly compel pretrial discovery of evidentiary material which the prosecution intends to introduce at trial, the trial court, in its discretion, may order its early prosecutorial disclosure under certain defined circumstances defined in CPL § 240.40(1)(c). People v. Colavito, 87 N.Y.2d 423, 639 N.Y.S.2d 996, 663 N.E.2d 308 (1996).

—Where confidential information is sought in a criminal action, the applicant must demonstrate in good faith some factual predicate which would make it reasonably likely that the information sought would establish unreliability of the complaining witness. People v. Davis, 203 A.D.2d 300, 610 N.Y.S.2d 63 (2d Dept. 1994).

—CPL § 240.40 does not apply to defendants charged by a simplified information with a traffic infraction; the statute requires that a simplified information charging a misdemeanor be pending. People v. Cohen, 131 Misc. 2d 898, 502 N.Y.S.2d 123 (City Ct. Westchester Co. 1986).

DNA evidence.—The legislature must decide whether to authorize the DNA testing of arrestees or indicted individuals. People sought DNA testing of defendant, arguing that even though they have no information that the defendant committed any other crime, if defendant's DNA is compared to DNA profiles in the linkage database of the Office of the Chief Medical Examiner, defendant's commission of an uncharged crime may be uncovered. Court held that this type of fishing expedition was prohibited under CPL Article 240 and was irrelevant to the instant criminal proceeding in which defendant was charged with various sex crimes. People v. Rodriguez, 196 Misc. 2d 217, 764 N.Y.S.2d 305 (Sup. Ct. Kings Co. 2003).

Nontestimonial evidence.—CPL § 240.40(2) empowers the courts to order physical evidence to be taken from a defendant's person. Here, where the victim suffered a bite mark, and the People demonstrated that no less intrusive methods existed to obtain the evidence, a court-ordered dental examination was proper. People v. Randt, 142 A.D.2d 611, 530 N.Y.S.2d 266 (2d Dept. 1988).

—Authority exists for the issuance of an order to compel a mere suspect to supply non-testimonial evidence. In re Abitabile, 143 Misc. 2d 113, 539 N.Y.S.2d 1009 (City Ct. Columbia Co. 1989).

—Where probable cause was established for arrest, there was no constitutional violation for compelled submission to dental impressions prior to the defendant's indictment. People v. Smith, 110 Misc. 2d 118, 443 N.Y.S.2d 551 (Dutchess Co. Ct. 1981).

—"Handwriting" is a generic term, and it is undoubtedly intended to cover handprinted as well as handscripted writing and the court may direct the acquisition of a sufficient specimen to enable an expert to express an opinion as to the similarity of a specimen with the handwriting under examination. People v. Gabron, 103 Misc. 2d 783, 426 N.Y.S.2d 964 (Co. Ct. Dutchess Co. 1980).

Nontestimonial evidence; blood, hair or other samples.—In a situation where a suspect was a prime suspect in a homicide, but not arrested for the crime, though probable cause did exist, criminal term could order that the suspect submit to a blood test to see if his blood type matched that found in the deceased apartment, since the blood type was rare, and would have probative value in determining whether the suspect was involved in the fatal altercation, especially since he received injuries at about the time of the death, consistent to the type of struggle resulting in the victim's death, and his explanation was unsatisfactory. In re Abe A., 56 N.Y.2d 288, 452 N.Y.S.2d 6, 437 N.E.2d 265 (1982).

—Court properly granted People's application to take a blood sample from the defendant for scientific analysis because substantial probative evidence before the court on this application indicated that the blood sample would supply relevant, material evidence. People v. Pryor, 14 A.D.3d 723, 787 N.Y.S.2d 503 (3d Dept. 2004).

—A court order is necessary to obtain pubic hair in rape case prior to commencement of formal proceedings as no exigent circumstances exist. People v. Mott, 118 Misc. 2d 90, 460 N.Y.S.2d 259 (Sup. Ct. Monroe Co. 1983).

—In order to obtain an order pursuant to CPL § 240.40(2)(b) for blood samples, pubic hair samples and saliva samples the People must show a special need or justification. People v. Handley, 105 Misc. 2d 215, 431 N.Y.S.2d 982 (Sup. Ct. Monroe Co. 1980).

Nontestimonial evidence; lineups.—Prohibition did not lie to prohibit enforcement of court order compelling defendant to stand in lineup and to shave any facial hair so that he could appear in reasonably the same condition as was the perpetrator at the time of the crime; court rejected claim that forcible shaving or shaving would violate defendant's constitutional rights because his religious beliefs prevented him from shaving. Ford v. Kreindler, 206 A.D.2d 425, 614 N.Y.S.2d 439 (2d Dept. 1994).

—Defendant was required to appear and participate in a lineup at the district attorney's office where they alleged that they were in need of a lineup because certain eye witnesses were unable to make any positive identification through a photographic array. People v. West, 111 Misc. 2d 658, 444 N.Y.S.2d 805 (Co. Ct., Rockland, Co. 1981).

—The court could not order defendant to appear in a lineup after the filing of a felony complaint but had to wait for an indictment since CPL § 240.40(2)(i) permits only the court in which an indictment, superior court information, prosecutor's information or information is pending to issue such an order. People v. Steiner, 103 Misc. 2d 844, 427 N.Y.S.2d 176 (Nassau Co. Ct. 1980).

Nontestimonial evidence; photographs of defendant.—In case involving attack of two Mexican day laborers, trial court determined that defendant's tattoos depicting racial and ethnic stereotypes were relevant to defendant's motive for committing the hate crime of second-degree aggravated harassment, and thus, court properly granted People's motion to take a second set of photographs pursuant to CPL § 240.40. None of the testimony about the tattoos, presented through an expert witness on hate crime, implicated defendant's privilege against self-incrimination. People v. Slavin, 1 N.Y.3d 392, 775 N.Y.S.2d 210, 807 N.E.2d 259, cert. denied, — U.S. —, 125 S. Ct. 64 (2004).

Pendency of felony.—The pendency of a felony complaint does not entitle a defendant to discovery under CPL § 240.40. People v. Morgan, 178 Misc. 2d 615, 682 N.Y.S.2d 512 (Fulton Co. Ct. 1998).

Failure to comply with order; prosecution.—Defendant's right to a fair trial was denied because the prosecution did not produce, pursuant to pretrial order, a photograph of defendant in its possession and then at trial used the photograph to rebut testimony of defense witnesses that defendant had no facial hair at the time of the drug transaction in question. People v. Halikias, 106 A.D.2d 811, 484 N.Y.S.2d 182 (3d Dept. 1984).

Informant's identity.—Defendant was not entitled to disclosure of informant's identity absent an extremely strong showing of relevance where the information provided was of "marginal nature" in that she observed the defendant walking with the kidnap victim and gave the police the defendant's name and address. People v. Rios, 60 N.Y.2d 764, 469 N.Y.S.2d 670, 457 N.E.2d 776 (1983).

Duty to preserve evidence.—Failure of the prosecution to deliver test results on deceased's coat as soon as they were available was prejudicial to defendant's case and warranted reversal of conviction for manslaughter where defendant had moved for copies of all scientific or laboratory tests done for the purpose of the case; the coat had been misplaced, and found on the next to last day of trial testimony, and test results were available to the prosecution twenty minutes prior to the time the jury was to be charged; since this evidence helped to show how the shooting occurred, and tended to create doubts about some of the prosecution's testimony, a new trial was necessary. People v. Kitt, 86 A.D.2d 465, 450 N.Y.S.2d 319 (1st Dept. 1982).

—The court may order the discovery of police reports if the prosecutor intends to introduce them at the trial. People v. Finkle, 103 Misc. 2d 985, 427 N.Y.S.2d 374 (Sullivan Co. Ct. 1980).

Statutory purpose.—The purpose of CPL 240.40(2)(b)(v) is to provide discovery for the pending criminal action and not to permit the People to investigate unsolved crimes for which they have no reason to suspect a defendant. People v. Rodriguez, 196 Misc. 2d 217, 764 N.Y.S.2d 305 (Sup. Ct. Kings Co. 2003).

§ 240.43. Discovery; disclosure of prior uncharged criminal, vicious or immoral acts.

Upon a request by a defendant, the prosecutor

shall notify the defendant of all specific instances of a defendant's prior uncharged criminal, vicious or immoral conduct of which the prosecutor has knowledge and which the prosecutor intends to use at trial for purposes of impeaching the credibility of the defendant. Such notification by the prosecutor shall be made immediately prior to the commencement of jury selection, except that the court may, in its discretion, order such notification and make its determination as to the admissibility for impeachment purposes of such conduct within a period of three days, excluding Saturdays, Sundays and holidays, prior to the commencement of jury selection.

Added by L. 1987, Ch. 222, eff. Nov. 1, 1987.

ANNOTATION

Duty to disclose.—The statute did not prevent the People from seeking a ruling on bad acts committed by defendant which the People did not learn of until after the Sandoval hearing. People v. Brown, 202 A.D.2d 266, 609 N.Y.S.2d 2 (1st Dept.), lv. denied, 83 N.Y.2d 964 (1994).

§ 240.44. Discovery; upon pre-trial hearing.

Subject to a protective order, at a pre-trial hearing held in a criminal court at which a witness is called to testify, each party, at the conclusion of the direct examination of each of its witnesses, shall, upon request of the other party, make available to that party to the extent not previously disclosed:

1. Any written or recorded statement, including any testimony before a grand jury, made by such witness other than the defendant which relates to the subject matter of the witness's testimony.

2. A record of a judgment of conviction of such witness other than the defendant if the record of conviction is known by the prosecutor or defendant, as the case may be, to exist.

3. The existence of any pending criminal action against such witness other than the defendant if the pending criminal action is known by the prosecutor or defendant, as the case may be, to exist.

Added by L. 1982, Ch. 558.

ANNOTATIONS

Duty to disclose.—The People were under no obligation to turn over their Rosario material prior to the pretrial hearing; the material must be turned over to the defense only upon defense request at the conclusion of the People's direct examination at the pretrial hearing. People v. Zephir, 226 A.D.2d 408, 640 N.Y.S.2d 584 (2d Dept. 1996).

—Court should have ordered the production of notes prepared by a detective who testified at the Wade-Dunaway hearing. People v. Figueroa, 213 A.D.2d 669, 625 N.Y.S.2d 49 (2d Dept.), lv. denied, 85 N.Y.2d 972 (1995).

—The People are obligated to turn over Rosario material at hearings to determine a defendant's competency. People v. McPhee, 161 Misc. 2d 660, 614 N.Y.S.2d 884 (Sup. Ct. Queens Co. 1994).

Reversal required.—People bear the burden of demonstrating that the undisclosed notes used to refresh the officer's recollection at a Wade hearing are duplicative materials previously turned over to the defense. People did not sustain their burden and this is a per se error requiring reversal. People v. Dennis, 265 A.D.2d 271, 697 N.Y.S.2d 599 (1st Dept. 1999).

§ 240.45. Discovery; upon trial, of prior statements and criminal history of witnesses.

1. After the jury has been sworn and before the prosecutor's opening address, or in the case of a single judge trial after commencement and before submission of evidence, the prosecutor shall, subject to a protective order, make available to the defendant:

(a) Any written or recorded statement, including any testimony before a grand jury and an examination videotaped pursuant to section 190.32 of this chapter, made by a person whom the prosecutor intends to call as a witness at trial, and which relates to the subject matter of the witness's testimony;

(b) A record of judgment of conviction of a witness the people intend to call at trial if the record of conviction is known by the prosecutor to exist;

(c) The existence of any pending criminal action against a witness the people intend to call at trial, if the pending criminal action is known by the prosecutor to exist.

The provisions of paragraphs (b) and (c) of this subdivision shall not be construed to require the prosecutor to fingerprint a witness or otherwise cause the division of criminal justice services or other law enforcement agency or court to issue a report concerning a witness.

2. After presentation of the people's direct case and before the presentation of the defendant's direct case, the defendant shall, subject to a protective order, make available to the prosecutor:

(a) any written or recorded statement made by a person other than the defendant whom the defendant intends to call as a witness at the trial, and which relates to the subject matter of the witness's testimony;

(b) a record of judgment of conviction of a witness, other than the defendant, the defendant intends to call at trial if the record of conviction is known by the defendant to exist;

(c) the existence of any pending criminal action against a witness, other than the defendant, the defendant intends to call at trial, if the pending criminal action is known by the defendant to exist.

Amended by L. 1982, Ch. 558; L. 1984, Ch. 804.

ANNOTATIONS

CPL 660 examinations.—Since Art. 660 provides that the conditional examination may be utilized in place of and instead of an actual appearance of the victim at trial with prescribed safeguards, it follows that the timing of the disclosure requirements contained in 240.45 of the CPL are triggered by the

granting of the 660.10 examination. The material must be disclosed in toto at the outset of the prosecution's case, and not in piecemeal fashion immediately prior to the particular witness testifying. People v. Coyne, 192 Misc. 2d 507, 748 N.Y.S.2d 206 (County Ct. Onondaga Co. 2002).

General.—Since *Rosario* material relates solely to a witness's direct testimony, and the fact that the subject chemist had performed a mass spectrometry test was educed in the course of defendant's cross-examination, the lab book was not *Rosario* material. People v. Brown, 234 A.D.2d 15, 650 N.Y.S.2d 643 (1st Dept. 1996).

—The representation of a prosecutor that no prior statements of a witness exist is generally sufficient to obviate the need for further inquiry; but where the defendant can articulate a factual basis for the assertion that the prosecutor is improperly denying the existence of prior statements, it becomes incumbent upon the trial court to inspect the disputed document or the People's entire file, if necessary, to determine if the statements in question exist. People v. Farrell, 207 A.D.2d 560, 616 N.Y.S.2d 77 (2d Dept. 1994).

—Trial court lacks the authority to direct disclosure of *Rosario* material before the time period specified by statute, or to order the prosecutor to create *Rosario* material. Catterson v. Rohl, 202 A.D.2d 420, 608 N.Y.S.2d 696 (2d Dept.), *lv. denied*, 83 N.Y.2d 755 (1994).

—The People are obligated to turn over *Rosario* material at hearings to determine a defendant's competency. People v. McPhee, 161 Misc. 2d 660, 614 N.Y.S.2d 884 (Sup. Ct. Queens Co. 1994).

Timing of disclosure.—Where disclosure of police memo book entry occurs before both sides have rested, the material has been disclosed when it is still useful to the defense. People v. Jacob, 287 A.D.2d 740, 732 N.Y.S.2d 245 (2d Dept. 2001).

Criminal records; prosecution witnesses.—Although People failed to turn over a judgment of conviction of a prosecution witness, and People conceded that the witness testified untruthfully about his criminal record during direct examination, the evidence overwhelmingly demonstrated defendant's guilt, and there is no reasonable possibility that either error contributed to the jury's verdict. People v. Pressley, 91 N.Y.2d 825, 666 N.Y.S.2d 555, 689 N.E.2d 525 (1997).

—During cross-examination of People's witness, it was discovered that the witness had been previously convicted of disorderly conduct, of which the trial prosecutor was unaware; defendant was not entitled to a new trial because he was given a meaningful opportunity to use the allegedly exculpatory material to cross-examine the People's witness. People v. Osborne, 91 N.Y.2d 827, 666 N.Y.S.2d 556, 689 N.E.2d 526 (1997).

—Although the prosecutor's failure to turn over a witness' criminal record until mid-trial created the possibility of prejudice to defendant, this delay did not justify dismissal of the indictment but did justify a mistrial. People v. Torres, 201 A.D.2d 294, 607 N.Y.S.2d 303 (1st Dept. 1994).

—Where defendant had been fully informed of witnesses' prior criminal histories, the prosecution's failure to produce the actual certificates of convictions prior to trial did not require reversal of defendant's conviction. People v. Clark, 194 A.D.2d 868, 598 N.Y.S.2d 847 (3d Dept.), *lv. denied*, 82 N.Y.2d 752 (1993).

—Prosecutor had no obligation pursuant to CPL § 240.45 to disclose the juvenile delinquency adjudication of another witness because that adjudication is not a criminal conviction. People v. Bennett, 273 A.D.2d 914, 709 N.Y.S.2d 773 (4th Dept. 2000).

—The failure of the prosecutor to inform defense counsel of the criminal record of a prosecution witness did not warrant reversal because the error was harmless. People v. Welch, 154 A.D.2d 946, 545 N.Y.S.2d 884 (4th Dept. 1989).

—The People did not violate the letter of CPL § 240.45 in failing to disclose CCRB determination regarding detective who took allegedly coerced statement from defendant, because this was not a criminal conviction and it did not give rise to a criminal action in the instant case, but the spirit of CPL § 240.45 was apparently violated; however, after an in camera review of CCRB reports, court determined that the reports did not need to be disclosed because they were irrelevant. People v. Oglesby, 177 Misc. 2d 580, 676 N.Y.S.2d 430 (Sup. Ct. Kings Co. 1998).

—In the context of discovery, a matter which has been adjourned in contemplation of dismissal constitutes a "pending criminal action" and must be disclosed to the defendant. People v. Benjamin, 147 Misc. 2d 617, 558 N.Y.S.2d 825, 827 (Crim. Ct. N.Y. Co. 1990).

—People have an obligation to furnish defense with a current NYSIS of a prosecution witness upon trial notwithstanding a lack of knowledge on the prosecution's part of any pending charges against the witness. People v. Buckley, 131 Misc. 744, 501 N.Y.S.2d 554 (Sup. Ct. Monroe Co. 1986).

Duty to preserve Rosario material.—Not only do the People have a duty to produce Rosario material, they have a corresponding obligation to preserve such evidence until a request for disclosure is made. People v. Morton, 189 A.D.2d 488, 596 N.Y.S.2d 783 (1st Dept. 1993).

—When Rosario material exists, the People have the duty to preserve it; however, the People have no affirmative duty to create such material. People v. Littles, 192 A.D.2d 314, 595 N.Y.S.2d 463 (1st Dept.), lv. denied, 81 N.Y.2d 1016 (1993).

Medicaid payments.—Where the existence of the Medicaid payment records was necessarily known to defendant by virtue of his having billed Medicaid and received payment, the People had no Brady obligation to disclose the documents which defendant knew about and could have procured himself by maintaining orderly business records. People v. Doshi, 93 N.Y.2d 499, 693 N.Y.S.2d 87, 715 N.E.2d 113 (1999).

Rosario material; witness' prior statements, generally.— Defendant was not entitled to the personal version of the attack written by the attempted rape victim, a free-lance writer, two days after the attack since defendant conceded that the personal account constituted neither Rosario nor Brady material. People v. Reedy, 70 N.Y.2d 826, 523 N.Y.S.2d 438, 517 N.E.2d 1324 (1987).

—Statements that must be disclosed include notes or writings created either by the witness or by those who interviewed or spoke to the witness. "The character of a statement is not to be determined by the manner in which it is recorded," thus the absence of a signature is irrelevant. People v. Consolazio, 40 N.Y.2d 446, 387 N.Y.S.2d 62, 354 N.E.2d 801 (1976), cert. denied, 433 U.S. 914.

—The Rosario rule does not encompass hearsay, rumor or gossip attributable to a witness. In re Andrew T., 182 A.D.2d 630, 581 N.Y.S.2d 864 (2d Dept.), lv. denied, 80 N.Y.2d 757 (1992).

—People were required to make the videotape of a child sexual abuse victim available to the defense; Rosario violation required reversal even where defense counsel was provided with a copy of the minutes of the videotaped examination. People v. Gaskins, 171 A.D.2d 272, 575 N.Y.S.2d 564 (2d Dept. 1991).

—Synopses of statements by a witness may constitute Rosario material. People v. Machado, 159 Misc. 2d 94, 603 N.Y.S.2d 273 (Sup. Ct. Kings Co. 1993).

Rosario material; witness' prior statements, redaction.— There was no merit to defendant's claim that the complainant's address and phone number redacted from the sex crimes screening sheet was Rosario material to which he was improperly denied access, no showing having been made that defendant required that information, which could have been used to intimidate the complainant. People v. Garcia, 207 A.D.2d 718, 616 N.Y.S.2d 501 (1st Dept.), lv. denied, 84 N.Y.2d 1011 (1994).

—Limited redaction of residential information regarding prospective witnesses did not in any manner prejudice defendant's right to obtain prior recorded statements of the People's prospective witnesses. People v. Guzman, 176 A.D.2d 561, 575 N.Y.S.2d 26 (1st Dept. 1991).

Rosario material; prior testimony, transcripts.— Untranscribed plea minutes of a potential prosecution witness which have been ordered but not yet received by the prosecution do not constitute Rosario material. People v. Fishman, 72 N.Y.2d 884, 532 N.Y.S.2d 739, 528 N.E.2d 1212 (1988).

—New trial ordered where People failed to turn over copy of transcript of mentally disabled complainant at her first swearability hearing, which indicated that she did not know her attacker's full name; Rosario violation was reversible error because attacker's identity was central issue at trial. People v. LaSalle, 243 A.D.2d 490, 663 N.Y.S.2d 79 (2d Dept. 1997).

—Where defendant's sister was not called by the People to testify at trial, her Grand Jury testimony did not constitute Rosario material. People v. Gardner, 162 A.D.2d 466, 556 N.Y.S.2d 163 (2d Dept. 1990).

—Although Grand Jury transcribed minutes of witnesses are Rosario material, the stenographer's notes which are used to type the minutes are not. People v. Solomon, 160 Misc. 2d 945, 612 N.Y.S.2d 779 (Sup. Ct. Kings Co. 1994).

—Transcripts of testimony given in the presence of both the defendant and his counsel are not required to be produced by the Rosario rule or by the codifying statutes; the prosecutor is not required to provide the transcripts. People v. Yanowitch, 140 Misc. 2d 575, 530 N.Y.S.2d 975 (Nassau Co. Ct. 1988).

—In a nonjury trial the prosecutor shall make available to the defendant prior to offering of evidence, any written or recorded statement made by any person who the prosecutor intends to call as witness at trial, including minutes of preliminary hearing involving person minor was charged with acting in concert with, and corporation counsel is under affirmative obligation to produce same, prior to offering of evidence. In re John M., 104 Misc. 2d 725, 430 N.Y.S.2d 198 (Fam. Ct. 1980).

Rosario material; grand jury testimony.—Prosecutor's failure to disclose a witness' grand jury testimony after the trial jury was sworn and before his opening statement violated the clear directives of CPL § 240.25(1)(a) where the prosecutor expressed his intention to call the witness both before and after his opening statement; the fact that the witness ultimately did not testify did not retroactively excuse the prosecution from complying with the statute; this was especially true when the prosecution's remaining witness might have been defendant's accomplice, according to the grand jury testimony of the witness who did not testify at trial. People v. Hopper, 87 A.D.2d 193, 450 N.Y.S.2d 798 (1st Dept. 1982).

—Prosecutor's refusal to provide defendant with the Grand Jury testimony of a witness was reversible error where the minutes contained potentially exculpatory material regarding defendant's insanity defense, and the People provided the material to the their expert and not to the defense expert. People v. Gonzalez, 120 A.D.2d 464, 502 N.Y.S.2d 468 (1st Dept. 1986).

—Proper procedure in case where defense counsel requested Grand Jury testimony of People's witness would have been for trial court to inspect, in camera, the entire testimony before the Grand Jury of the witness to determine whether or not any relevant statements of the witness were present as opposed to merely accepting the representations of the prosecutor that although other Grand Jury statements existed, they were irrelevant to the testimony of the witness. People v. Baker, 75 A.D.2d 966, 428 N.Y.S.2d 353 (2d Dept. 1980).

Rosario material; grand jury synopsis sheet, data analysis sheet.—Data analysis of prosecutor may or may not constitute Rosario material depending upon whether or not it constitutes work product of the District Attorney's office. People v. Adgers, 75 N.Y.2d 723, 551 N.Y.S.2d 190, 550 N.E.2d 443 (1990).

—A curative instruction was a proper sanction for the prosecution's failure to preserve the data analysis form. People v. Marks, 208 A.D.2d 865, 618 N.Y.S.2d 380 (2d Dept.), lv. denied, 84 N.Y.2d 1013 (1994).

—Defendant's conviction was reversed, where the prosecutor failed to provide him with the early case assessment data sheet, which contained prosecutor's notes of interviews with prosecution witnesses. People v. Cecora, 186 A.D.2d 215, 587 N.Y.S.2d 748 (2d Dept. 1992), lv. denied, 81 N.Y.2d 786 (1993).

—Reversal was required where the People were not compelled to disclose the Data Analysis Form prepared by the assistant district attorney on duty the night of the defendant's arrest. People v. Munoz, 161 A.D.2d 807, 556 N.Y.S.2d 136 (2d Dept. 1990), lv. denied, 77 N.Y.2d 845 (1991).

—Grand Jury synopsis sheet did not constitute Rosario material since it was not an abbreviated summary of an interview with any of the People's witnesses. People v. Liles, 145 A.D.2d 509, 535 N.Y.S.2d 448 (2d Dept. 1988).

—Grand jury synopsis sheet did not constitute Rosario material since it was not an abbreviated summary of an interview with any of the People's witnesses. People v. Williams, 128 A.D.2d 912, 513 N.Y.S.2d 840 (2d Dept.), lv. denied, 69 N.Y.2d 1011 (1987).

Rosario material; 911 tapes.—Where 911 tape was destroyed as a matter of routine police procedure, no sanction was required, unless defendant demonstrated prejudice. People v. Segui, 208 A.D.2d 447, 617 N.Y.S.2d 718 (1st Dept.), lv. denied, 84 N.Y.2d 1038 (1994).

—911 tape constituted Rosario material under facts of case.

People v. Parker, 157 A.D.2d 519, 549 N.Y.S.2d 710 (1st Dept.), *lv. denied*, 76 N.Y.2d 793 (1990).

—The report of the arresting officer's taped telephone call to the emergency 911 number did not constitute *Rosario* material in the context of this case because the substance of the report did not relate to the subject matter of the witness's trial testimony. People v. Barrios, 163 A.D.2d 579, 559 N.Y.S.2d 31 (2d Dept. 1990), *lv. denied*, 77 N.Y.2d 875 (1991).

Rosario material; police reports.—To the extent that some information on Narcotics Investigative Tracking Recidivist Offender (NITRO) form may be construed to constitute *Rosario* material, defendant was not prejudiced by its destruction and not entitled to an adverse inference instruction, because the subject matter and approximate contents may be ascertained despite its destruction. Furthermore, besides being given a computer printout of the information contained on the destroyed NITRO, defendant rigorously cross-examined the police witnesses and utilized the failure to preserve the document in summation. People v. Grant, 259 A.D.2d 451, 688 N.Y.S.2d 130 (1st Dept. 1999).

—Conviction reversed and new trial ordered where original Request for Laboratory Analysis form was never disclosed to defendant, and photocopy of form that was provided to defense did not include certain alterations testified to by police witness and could not be considered duplicative equivalent; defense counsel's election not to cross-examine the witness further without the original does not excuse this violation, and no lesser sanction was available because the prosecution did not even attempt to establish that the original document was lost or destroyed. People v. Johnson, 245 A.D.2d 134, 666 N.Y.S.2d 160 (1st Dept. 1997).

—Prosecutor failed to provide defense with Daily Activity Report of sergeant who testified at trial regarding his role in arresting the defendants; absent a factual showing by prosecution that the report was lost or destroyed, the failure to turn it over requires reversal, regardless of prejudice. People v. Jennings, 248 A.D.2d 265, 670 N.Y.S.2d 438 (1st Dept. 1998).

—A "request for laboratory analysis" form, whose "details of offense" section contains a brief synopsis of the crimes, constitutes *Rosario* material. People v. Palma, 224 A.D.2d 363, 638 N.Y.S.2d 79 (2d Dept. 1996).

—Once the prosecution elicited testimony from the police officer detailing specifics concerning other arrests made at the same time he arrested the defendant, defense counsel was entitled to receive, as *Rosario* material, the reports prepared by the witness relevant to those arrests. People v. Ramos, 206 A.D.2d 260, 613 N.Y.S.2d 870 (1st Dept. 1994).

—Prosecutor's failure to disclose the memo books of the two police witnesses was a per se error requiring that the conviction be reversed and a new trial ordered. People v. Mayo, 207 A.D.2d 673, 616 N.Y.S.2d 28 (1st Dept. 1994).

—A questioned computer generated police form did not constitute *Rosario* material, as it contained no actual pretrial statements of witnesses but only a digest of certain portions of preexisting recorded witness statements that had been turned over to the defense at trial. People v. Moolenaar, 207 A.D.2d 711, 616 N.Y.S.2d 590 (1st Dept. 1994), *lv. denied*, 85 N.Y.2d 864 (1995).

—The defendant was clearly entitled to police DD-5 follow-up reports as *Rosario* material. People v. White, 200 A.D.2d 351, 606 N.Y.S.2d 172 (1st Dept. 1994).

—Police report prepared by the police officer based upon complainant's statement is a prior statement of a witness to which defendants were entitled. People v. Cadby, 75 A.D.2d 713, 427 N.Y.S.2d 121 (4th Dept. 1980).

Rosario material; police officer's notes.—A police officer's "scratch notes" made prior to completion of official police reports are *Rosario* material and must be disclosed. People v. Wallace, 76 N.Y.2d 953, 563 N.Y.S.2d 722, 565 N.E.2d 471 (1990).

—A police officer's notes and summaries made in the course of the officer's investigation are *Rosario* material and must be disclosed. People v. Martinez, 71 N.Y.2d 937, 528 N.Y.S.2d 813, 524 N.E.2d 134 (1988).

—A police officer's memo book constitutes *Rosario* material. People v. Rodney B., 69 N.Y.2d 687, 512 N.Y.S.2d 17, 504 N.E.2d 384 (1986).

—The court's adverse inference charge was an appropriate sanction for the People's failure to turn over the notes of a duty captain who interviewed complainant at the hospital; defendant waived his appellate argument that the sanction was inadequate because the People failed to carry their burden or establishing that the unproduced material did not exist or was not subject to disclosure by acquiescing in the court's proposed sanction, namely, an adverse inference charge. People v. Deas, 208 A.D.2d 467, 617 N.Y.S.2d 328 (1st Dept. 1994).

—Where defendant's ability to conduct cross-examination was impeded by the destruction of the scratch notes, some discovery sanction was required. People v. Dunn, 185 A.D.2d 54, 592 N.Y.S.2d 299 (1st Dept.), *lv. denied*, 81 N.Y.2d 970 (1993).

—Trial court abused its discretion in failing to grant the defendant's request for the imposition of sanctions for the officer's failure to preserve his notes, which constituted *Rosario* material. People v. Gamble, 172 A.D.2d 687, 568 N.Y.S.2d 644 (2d Dept. 1991).

Police files.—The police "nickname" file sought by defendant did not constitute *Rosario* material because it was not a written statement, report, or document, made by a prospective prosecution witness; nor was it *Brady* material because there was not evidence to support defendant's assertion that the nickname file contained the names of other individuals who were known by the nickname "Ski." People v. Turner, 233 A.D.2d 932, 649 N.Y.S.2d 571 (4th Dept. 1996).

Police blotter.—Where nondisclosed police blotter entry related to the subject matter of the arresting officer's testimony, the fact that the police withheld the evidence was immaterial, and the good faith of the prosecutor was also immaterial. People v. Jackson, 237 A.D.2d 179, 655 N.Y.S.2d 17 (1st Dept. 1997).

Rosario material; prosecutor's notes.—A prosecutor's summary of a witness' answers to questions is *Rosario* material. People v. Consolazio, 40 N.Y.2d 446, 387 N.Y.S.2d 62, 354 N.E.2d 801 (1976), *cert. denied*, 433 U.S. 914.

—Questions prepared by the prosecutor in preparation of his witness's testimony did not constitute *Rosario* material. People v. Gallardo, 196 A.D.2d 551, 601 N.Y.S.2d 150 (2d Dept. 1993).

—Notes of prosecutor consisting of catch words designed to jog the prosecutor's memory, and drafts of the questions the prosecutor intended to ask the witness did not constitute *Rosario* material. People v. Roberts, 178 A.D.2d 622, 577 N.Y.S.2d 672 (2d Dept. 1991).

Rosario material; not in prosecutor's possession.—Interview notes and reports of the State Division of Parole are not *Rosario* material, since they are not generally in the possession or control of prosecutors. People v. Kelly, 88 N.Y.2d 248, 644 N.Y.S.2d 475, 666 N.E.2d 1348 (1996).

—An audiotape of an autopsy performed by the Office of the Chief Medical Examiner does not constitute *Rosario* material where it is not in the actual possession of the prosecution. People v. Washington, 87 N.Y.2d 945, 641 N.Y.S.2d 223, 663 N.E.2d 1253 (1995).

—Material in the possession of a state administrative agency, such as the Department of Motor Vehicles, is not within the control of a local prosecutor and thus does not constitute *Rosario* material. People v. Flynn, 79 N.Y.2d 879, 581 N.Y.S.2d 160, 589 N.E.2d 383 (1992).

—Reports prepared by the Probation Department in connection with the testifying co-indictee were not *Rosario* material because they were confidential documents not within the possession or control of the People. People v. Figueroa, 258 A.D.2d 280, 685 N.Y.S.2d 53 (1st Dept. 1999).

—Defendant alleged *Rosario* violations because the Kings County District Attorney's Office had failed to turn over certain documents possessed by the Queens District Attorney's Office in connection with a separate prosecution of complainant's father; however, most of the Queens documents were not *Rosario* because they were not statements of the complainant which related to her testimony at defendant's trial, and defendant failed to show that the Kings County prosecutors had actual or constructive possession of any of the items. People v. Rajigah, 265 A.D.2d 580, 697 N.Y.S.2d 646 (2d Dept. 1999).

—Statements in possession of county attorney do not constitute *Rosario* material since the county attorney is a separate agency from the prosecutor's office. County of Nassau v. Sullivan, 194 A.D.2d 236, 606 N.Y.S.2d 249 (2d Dept. 1993).

—Memo books of private security guards did not constitute

Rosario material since they were not made at the direction of the police department and were never in the possession and control of the People. People v. Johnson, 131 A.D.2d 782, 599 N.Y.S.2d 861 (2d Dept. 1993).

—There is no merit to defendant's contention concerning an alleged *Rosario* violation with respect to a prior statement of a witness, because there was no evidence that the trial prosecutor ever had possession or control of the witness's prior statement, which had been given to a private investigator and an attorney for a third party. People v. Nance, 2 A.D.3d 1473, 770 N.Y.S.2d 524 (4th Dept. 2003).

—People did not violate CPL § 240.45(1)(a) by failing to turn over a teletype sent by and FBI agent to FBI headquarters in Washington, D.C., relating to a statement of a prosecution witness concerning the murder of which defendants were subsequently convicted, because the teletype was an internal FBI document that was never in the possession or control of the People or any State law enforcement agency, and thus, there was no *Rosario* violation. People v. Marvin, 258 A.D.2d 964, 685 N.Y.S.2d 499 (4th Dept. 1999).

—The nature of the entity or individual retaining the evidentiary material is determinative of *Rosario* issues. People v. Farrell, 159 Misc. 2d 992, 607 N.Y.S.2d 557 (Sup. Ct. Richmond Co. 1994).

—Files exclusively in the possession of the County Attorney are not within the control of the District Attorney; however, files in the possession of the police are clearly under the control of the District Attorney. People v. McIntosh, 157 Misc. 2d 551, 598 N.Y.S.2d 136 (Nassau Co. Ct. 1993).

—Motion to quash subpoena duces tecum served on the Assistant United States Attorney was granted where subpoena required the production of statement given to federal authorities not in the possession of the District Attorney, including testimony before a federal Grand Jury, by a witness the People intended to call and relating to the subject matter of the witness' testimony. People v. Carbonaro, 104 Misc. 2d 145, 427 N.Y.S.2d 701 (Sup. Ct. Kings Co. 1980).

Rosario **material; nontestifying witnesses, defense witnesses.**—Where letter was written by a person who was not a prosecution witness, it did not constitute *Rosario* material. People v. Copes, 200 A.D.2d 681, 606 N.Y.S.2d 752 (2d Dept. 1994).

—The failure of the prosecution to turn over a copy of the receipt the complainant signed before retrieving her property from the property clerk's office was not a *Rosario* violation since the information contained in the form was unrelated to the subject matter of the complainant's testimony. People v. Mobley, 190 A.D.2d 821, 593 N.Y.S.2d 839 (2d Dept.), *lv. denied,* 81 N.Y.2d 974 (1993).

—Need for adverse inference charge was rendered academic because witness who failed to preserve document in question was not called as a witness. People v. Hawkins, 193 A.D.2d 758, 598 N.Y.S.2d 72 (2d Dept. 1993).

—Since the detectives did not testify at the trial, their notes did not constitute *Rosario* material and defendant was not entitled to them. People v. Alejandro, 175 A.D.2d 873, 573 N.Y.S.2d 720 (2d Dept. 1991).

—Neither the holding of People v. Rosario nor the statutory codification of that rule requires that prior statements made by defense witnesses be produced by the People. People v. Medina, 208 A.D.2d 974, 617 N.Y.S.2d 230 (3d Dept. 1994).

—The People were not required to produce statements of individual who testified on behalf of the defendant and of a police witness who did not testify at the suppression hearing. People v. Love, 187 A.D.2d 1030, 591 N.Y.S.2d 111 (4th Dept. 1992).

Rosario **material; unconnected to subject matter of witness' testimony.**—Since the defense has failed to demonstrate that the material in question had any connection to the witness's testimony the *Rosario* rule was not violated. People v. Davis, 160 A.D.2d 718, 554 N.Y.S.2d 45 (2d Dept.), *lv. denied,* 76 N.Y.2d 786 (1990).

—Where notes of interview with witness did not contain any information concerning the subject matter of the witness's testimony, the notes did not constitute *Rosario* material. People v. Bianco, 183 A.D.2d 284, 591 N.Y.S.2d 287 (4th Dept. 1992), *lv. denied,* 81 N.Y.2d 785 (1993).

Rosario **material; unwritten, unrecorded, untranscri-**

bed.—Court rejected *Rosario* claim where the witness' statement to the prosecutor on the eve of trial was neither written nor recorded. People v. Minott, 208 A.D.2d 395, 617 N.Y.S.2d 160 (1st Dept.), *lv. denied,* 84 N.Y.2d 1013 (1994).

—A prosecutor's *Rosario* obligation does not extend to unrecorded oral statements. Catterson v. Rohl, 202 A.D.2d 420, 608 N.Y.S.2d 696 (2d Dept.), *lv. denied,* 83 N.Y.2d 755 (1994).

—Court rejected claim that there is an obligation on the part of police to prepare video or audio tapes of their questioning of a suspect. People v. Grimes, 191 A.D.2d 745, 594 N.Y.S.2d 392 (3d Dept. 1993).

—Where telephone conversation was never memorialized it did not constitute *Rosario* material. People v. Dudley, 156 A.D.2d 581, 549 N.Y.S.2d 89 (2d Dept. 1989).

Harmless error.—There is no due process violation where defendant made a general non-specific request for documentary evidence which was honored by the People notwithstanding the fact that a more specific exculpatory document existed but was not turned over; the evidence in question would not have created a reasonable doubt which would not have otherwise existed. People v. Smith, 63 N.Y.2d 41, 479 N.Y.S.2d 706, 468 N.E.2d 879 (1984), *cert. denied,* 469 U.S. 1227 (1985).

—Where prosecutor failed to turn over to defendant after jury selection the complainant's criminal record, it was error for court to deny defense motion for that record; however, the error was harmless since defendant's cross-examination of complainant elicited most, if not all, of the information concerning the witness' prior criminal record that would have been available if the record had been provided. People v. Torres, 103 A.D.2d 972, 480 N.Y.S.2d 60 (3d Dept. 1984).

Rosario; **per se error rule.**—Per se reversal rule does not require that all counts being tried jointly must be reversed, when undisclosed *Rosario* material related only to some of the counts. People v. Baghai-Kermani, 84 N.Y.2d 525, 620 N.Y.S.2d 313, 644 N.E.2d 1004 (1994).

—The per se reversal rule is designed to insure that defense counsel and not the court weighs and exercises defendant's fair trial advocacy interests by judging the potential for material from prosecution to be used for defenses purposes. People v. Flores, 84 N.Y.2d 184, 615 N.Y.S.2d 662, 639 N.E.2d 19 (1994).

—Violations of *Rosario* rule require reversal notwithstanding fact that non-disclosure may have been inadvertent or immaterial. People v. Jones, 70 N.Y.2d 547, 523 N.Y.S.2d 53, 57, 517 N.E.2d 865 (1987).

—The per se Rosario rule, limited to an appeal from a judgment of conviction, does not apply to an appeal from the denial of a CPL § 440.10 motion; on such motions a court must apply the statutory standard: that it is reasonably probable that disclosure of any of the documents would have led to a different verdict. People v. Howard, 127 A.D.2d 109, 513 N.Y.S.2d 973, 980 (1st Dept. 1987).

—Harmless error analysis is inappropriate with respect to *Rosario* material. People v. Jackson, 162 A.D.2d 470, 556 N.Y.S.2d 165 (2d Dept. 1990).

Rosario **material; duplicative.**—A document that has been destroyed can never be deemed the "duplicative equivalent" of one that exists and remains available for inspection. People v. Joseph, 84 N.Y.2d 995, 622 N.Y.S.2d 505, 646 N.E.2d 807 (1995).

—Two documents cannot be duplicative equivalents if there are variations or inconsistencies between them. People v. Young, 79 N.Y.2d 365, 582 N.Y.S.2d 977, 591 N.E.2d 1163 (1992).

—Even if statements are harmonious or consistent, it does not mean that they are duplicative equivalents. People v. Richardson, 203 A.D.2d 141, 610 N.Y.S.2d 509 (1st Dept.), *lv. denied,* 84 N.Y.2d 831 (1994).

—Where a document is unavailable for comparison, the trial court generally has no means of determining whether it constitutes a duplicative equivalent of another document. People v. Quiles, 198 A.D.2d 448, 604 N.Y.S.2d 154 (2d Dept. 1993), *lv. denied,* 83 N.Y.2d 857 (1994).

—There was no *Rosario* violation where the police report, which was not supplied to the defendant until after trial, duplicated other material which was furnished in a timely fashion. People v. Acevedo, 178 A.D.2d 536, 577 N.Y.S.2d 452 (2d Dept. 1991).

—When dealing with a failure to turn over *Rosario* material, the burden is on the People to establish that the omitted material was duplicative. People v. Rivera, 170 A.D.2d 544, 566 N.Y.S.2d 321 (2d Dept. 1991).

—Where officer's notes of interview with informant were duplicated in a deposition taken shortly thereafter, a copy of which was turned over to defense counsel, the failure to turn over the interview notes did not constitute error. People v. Atkinson, 122 A.D.2d 385, 505 N.Y.S.2d 203 (3d Dept. 1986).

Property release form; not *Rosario*.—The personal property release form prepared by a testifying police officer, which merely listed personal property returned to defendant, did not constitute a prior statement of the witness. People v. Polk, 247 A.D.2d 342, 669 N.Y.S.2d 217 (1st Dept. 1998).

Federal documents not *Rosario*.—People's failure to disclose FBI interview reports was neither a *Rosario* nor a *Brady* violation because the People did not possess the additional reports that defendant sought and the reports were in the hands of the FBI, an independent federal law enforcement agency not subject to State control. People v. Santorelli, 95 N.Y.2d 412, 718 N.Y.S.2d 696, 741 N.E.2d 493 (2000).

—No *Rosario* violation occurred with respect to federal documents because defendant received all of the *Rosario* made available by the federal agency, the People were not in control of the federal file, and there was no evidence of a joint investigation between the People and federal authorities. People v. Leo, 249 A.D.2d 251, 673 N.Y.S.2d 70 (1st Dept. 1998).

Witness list not *Rosario*.—CPL § 240.45 does not require that the People provide a witness list for the following day of trial to the defense. People v. Brown, 175 Misc. 2d 376, 668 N.Y.S.2d 877 (Suffolk Co. Ct. 1998).

Sanctions; delayed disclosure of *Rosario* material.—Although some *Rosario* violations may require a full hearing, the hearing court here was well within its discretion to reopen the hearing only to the extent necessary to cross-examine the People's witness as to the contents of the six *Rosario* documents. People v. Feerick, 93 N.Y.2d 433, 692 N.Y.S.2d 638, 714 N.E.2d 851 (1999).

—Reversal is required if delay in the disclosure of *Rosario* material substantially prejudices the defendant. People v. Martinez, 71 N.Y.2d 937, 528 N.Y.S.2d 813, 524 N.E.2d 134 (1988).

—People's belated disclosure of *Rosario* material did not warrant mistrial where there was no showing of bad faith, the defense was not prejudiced, and the *Rosario* violation resulted, at most, in some cross-examination of the complainant that was superfluous but not detrimental to the defense. People v. Martin, 249 A.D.2d 75, 671 N.Y.S.2d 73 (1st Dept. 1998).

—Unlike the situation of a failure to supply *Rosario* material, which constitutes per se reversible error, when the People delay in producing *Rosario* material, the reviewing court must ascertain whether the defense was substantially prejudiced by the delay. People v. Swindell, 157 A.D.2d 549, 549 N.Y.S.2d 733 (1st Dept. 1990).

—Defendant's receipt of *Rosario* material at the trial, while perhaps belated, did not require reversal. People v. Jiminez, 157 A.D.2d 575, 550 N.Y.S.2d 319 (1st Dept. 1990).

—Per se reversal is not required for belated disclosure of *Rosario* material as opposed to non-disclosure of *Rosario* material. People v. Tarantino, 156 A.D.2d 244, 548 N.Y.S.2d 504 (1st Dept. 1989).

—Defendant was substantially prejudiced by People's failure to provide a record book maintained by complainant, which was in People's control, until after she had been cross-examined; because prosecutor deliberately withheld the information which was likely to be elicited on cross-examination and would be damaging to defense, reversal was required. People v. Mackey, 249 A.D.2d 329, 670 N.Y.S.2d 879 (2d Dept. 1998).

—Prosecutor's delay in turning over to defendant the police report written by one of the prosecution witnesses was not grounds for reversal because the delay did not substantially prejudice the defense. People v. Jackson, 154 A.D.2d 930, 547 N.Y.S.2d 164 (4th Dept. 1989).

—Court dismissed indictment in forcible rape prosecution, due to People's delayed disclosure of *Rosario* and possible *Brady* materials that could have been used to cross-examine complainant. People v. Ariosa, 172 Misc. 2d 312, 660 N.Y.S.2d 255 (Monroe Co. Ct. 1997).

Speculative *Rosario* claims.—Defendant's showing of a mere possibility that the Office of the Corporation Counsel might have been in possession of interview notes that might have had some relevance to the instant case does not present a valid *Rosario* claim, and, in any event, such notes could not be *Rosario* material because the Office of the Corporation Counsel was acting in a civil capacity. People v. Cortijo, 254 A.D.2d 125, 680 N.Y.S.2d 208 (1st Dept. 1998).

Sanctions; loss, destruction of *Rosario* material.—A document that has been destroyed can never be deemed the "duplicative equivalent" of one that exists and remains available for inspection. People v. Joseph, 84 N.Y.2d 995, 622 N.Y.S.2d 505, 646 N.E.2d 807 (1995).

—Where the People fail to exercise due care in preserving *Rosario* material the trial court has discretion to determine the specific sanction to be imposed and it was an abuse of discretion to decline to impose any sanction where defendant was prejudiced by the discarding of *Rosario* material. People v. Wallace, 76 N.Y.2d 953, 563 N.Y.S.2d 722, 565 N.E.2d 471 (1990).

—The court's adverse inference charge was an appropriate sanction for the People's failure to turn over the notes of a duty captain who interviewed complainant at the hospital; defendant waived his appellate argument that the sanction was inadequate because the People failed to carry their burden of establishing that the unproduced material did not exist or was not subject to disclosure by acquiescing in the court's proposed sanction, namely, an adverse inference charge. People v. Deas, 208 A.D.2d 467, 617 N.Y.S.2d 328 (1st Dept. 1994).

—When a defendant is prejudiced by the People's failure to exercise due care in preserving *Rosario* material, the court is obliged to impose an appropriate sanction. People v. Watkins, 189 A.D.2d 623, 592 N.Y.S.2d 347 (1st Dept. 1993).

—Where defendant's ability to conduct cross-examination was impeded by the destruction of the scratch notes, some discovery sanction was required. People v. Dunn, 185 A.D.2d 54, 592 N.Y.S.2d 299 (1st Dept. 1993).

—Where the prosecution fails to exercise due care in preserving *Rosario* material and defendant is prejudiced thereby, the court must impose an appropriate sanction. People v. Nelson, 188 A.D.2d 67, 594 N.Y.S.2d 8 (1st Dept. 1993).

—Where police officer lost his memo book through lack of his due care, reversal was required under *Rosario* because there was a serious identification issue, the defendant was prejudiced by his inability to cross-examination using the missing memo book, and defense counsel requested the proper sanction of an adverse inference charge, but his application was denied. People v. White, 232 A.D.2d 436, 649 N.Y.S.2d 156 (2d Dept. 1996).

—Where *Rosario* material was not disclosed, court committed reversible error by refusing to allow defense to recall complainant for cross-examination and imposed no sanction. People v. Khadaidi, 201 A.D.2d 585, 608 N.Y.S.2d 471 (2d Dept. 1994).

—Where a document is unavailable for comparison, the trial court generally has no means of determining whether it constitutes a duplicative equivalent of another document. People v. Quiles, 198 A.D.2d 448, 604 N.Y.S.2d 154 (2d Dept. 1993).

—Where the People fail to exercise due care in preserving *Rosario* material, and the defendant is prejudiced thereby, the trial court must impose an appropriate sanction. People v. Smith, 182 A.D.2d 787, 582 N.Y.S.2d 499 (2d Dept. 1992).

—Trial court abused its discretion in failing to grant the defendant's request for the imposition of sanctions for the officer's failure to preserve his notes, which constituted *Rosario* material. People v. Gamble, 172 A.D.2d 687, 568 N.Y.S.2d 644 (2d Dept. 1991).

—Sanction to be imposed for a *Rosario* violation is dependent on the degree of prosecutorial fault and the resulting prejudice to the defendant. Adverse inference instruction was an adequate sanction for detective's loss of a witness's written statement because the court gave the instruction after the detective's testimony and again in the court's final charge. People v. Davis, 18 A.D.3d 1016, 795 N.Y.S.2d 785 (3d Dept. 2005).

—Where state police investigator typed defendant's statement on his laptop computer after defendant was advised of his *Miranda* rights and used the backspace key to make corrections as necessary, the prior drafts were lost or destroyed *Rosario* material, but there is no *Rosario* error because the investigator did not act in bad faith in failing to save the drafts and defendant was not prejudiced. Court did not err in refusing to apply the extreme sanction of preclusion. People v. Munroe, 307 A.D.2d 588, 763 N.Y.S.2d 691 (3d Dept. 2003).

—The nature and extent of a discovery sanction will depend on the degree of the prosecutor's bad faith, the importance of the evidence lost, and the evidence of guilt adduced at trial. People v. Torres, 190 A.D.2d 52, 597 N.Y.S.2d 492 (3d Dept. 1993).

—Pending charges against a prosecution witness do not constitute *Rosario* material. People v. Hendrix, 235 A.D.2d 575, 652 N.Y.S.2d 127 (3d Dept. 1997).

—When *Rosario* material is lost because the People did not use due care to protect it and defendant is prejudiced by the mistake, the court must impose an appropriate action. People v. Collins, 203 A.D.2d 888, 611 N.Y.S.2d 377, error coram nobis denied, 207 A.D.2d 1042 (4th Dept. 1994), *lv. denied*, 85 N.Y.2d 861 (1995).

—The drastic remedy of dismissal should not be invoked where less severe measures can rectify the harm done by the loss of evidence. People v. James, 178 A.D.2d 946, 578 N.Y.S.2d 741 (4th Dept. 1991), *appeal withdrawn*, 80 N.Y.2d 833 (1992).

Preservation; waiver.—Claimed *Rosario* and *Kastigar* violations were unpreserved for appellate review, where defendant failed to raise at trial the claims which were based on documents and facts that were unquestionably known to the defendants at trial. People v. Feerick, 93 N.Y.2d 433, 692 N.Y.S.2d 638, 714 N.E.2d 851 (1999).

—Once defense counsel becomes aware of a *Rosario* violation during trial, it behooves counsel to seek sanction for belated disclosure or nonproduction, or else the claim for violation is deemed abandoned. People v. Graves, 85 N.Y.2d 1024, 630 N.Y.S.2d 972, 654 N.E.2d 1220 (1995).

—Defendant's claim that court should have issued an adverse inference instruction for *Rosario* violation was waived where defendant failed to renew request for the charge after the court initially denied the request "subject to any further developments." People v. Cruz, 172 A.D.2d 365, 568 N.Y.S.2d 750 (1st Dept. 1991).

—Defendant's claim that *Rosario* violations occurred because he did not receive a laboratory report was not preserved since no protest was registered when the chemist testified. People v. Diaz, 170 A.D.2d 395, 566 N.Y.S.2d 283 (1st Dept. 1991).

—Defense counsel's request at suppression hearing for the striking of officer's testimony based upon *Rosario* violation did not preserve claim that identifying witness's showup identification should be excluded on ground that lost *Rosario* material contained that witness's description. People v. Rosado, 160 A.D.2d 505, 554 N.Y.S.2d 168 (1st Dept. 1990).

—Defendant failed to preserve for appellate review the claim that he was deprived of a fair trial because of the destruction of certain *Rosario* material. People v. Merchant, 171 A.D.2d 887, 567 N.Y.S.2d 812 (2d Dept. 1991).

—Where defense counsel made no claims of prejudice as a result of the belated disclosure of the police reports, *Rosario* claim was not preserved for appellate review. People v. Faison, 176 A.D.2d 752, 574 N.Y.S.2d 977 (2d Dept. 1991), *lv. denied*, 79 N.Y.2d 826 (1992).

—A defendant's actions or inaction may constitute a waiver of any *Rosario* claim. A defendant cannot, by withholding *Rosario* claims for a period of time, later advance them in order to gain an advantage. People v. Thompson, 177 Misc. 2d 803, 678 N.Y.S.2d 845 (Sup. Ct. Kings Co. 1998).

Post-appeal requirements.—A defendant who was deprived of *Rosario* material and who subsequently seeks to vacate a conviction under CPL § 440.10(1)(f) must demonstrate a reasonable possibility that the failure to disclose the *Rosario* material contributed to the verdict. People v. Jackson, 78 N.Y.2d 638, 578 N.Y.S.2d 483, 490, 585 N.E.2d 795 (1991).

—A defendant who has exhausted his direct appeal and raises a *Rosario* claim by a motion to vacate the judgment of conviction is required to make an actual showing of prejudice as a result of the People's failure to turn over the *Rosario* material. People v. Harden, 188 A.D.2d 426, 592 N.Y.S.2d 2 (1st Dept. 1992).

Crime Victim's Compensation Board application.—Where prosecution delayed turning over affidavit of rape victim seeking financial assistance from the Crime Victim's Compensation Board until prior to summations, defense counsel moved to recall the victim. Court took judicial notice of the victim's application for remuneration, but improperly denied defendant's request to recall victim and cross-examine her with respect to

the affidavit, which was *Rosario* material. Case remanded for a new trial. People v. King, 241 A.D.2d 329, 659 N.Y.S.2d 469 (1st Dept. 1997).

§ 240.50. Discovery; protective orders.

1. The court in which the criminal action is pending may, upon motion of either party, or of any affected person, or upon determination of a motion of either party for an order of discovery; or upon its own initiative, issue a protective order denying, limiting, conditioning, delaying or regulating discovery pursuant to this article for good cause, including constitutional limitations, danger to the integrity of physical evidence or a substantial risk of physical harm, intimidation, economic reprisal, bribery or unjustified annoyance or embarrassment to any person or an adverse effect upon the legitimate needs of law enforcement, including the protection of the confidentiality of informants, or any other factor or set of factors which outweighs the usefulness of the discovery.

2. An order limiting, conditioning, delaying or regulating discovery may, among other things, require that any material copied or derived therefrom be maintained in the exclusive possession of the attorney for the discovering party and be used for the exclusive purpose of preparing for the defense or prosecution of the criminal action.

3. A motion for a protective order shall suspend discovery of the particular matter in dispute.

4. Notwithstanding any other provision of this article, the personal residence address of a police officer or correction officer shall not be required to be disclosed except pursuant to an order issued by a court following a finding of good cause.

Amended by L. 1981, Ch. 195; L. 1985, Ch. 348.

ANNOTATIONS

Interview of complainant.—Defendant's attorney was entitled to review the portion of the report prepared by the Criminal Court assistant district attorney which contained a detailed, carefully prepared report of the district attorney's interview with the complaining witness after the preliminary hearing. People v. Gonzalez, 74 A.D.2d 763, 425 N.Y.S.2d 601 (1st Dept. 1980).

Identity of witnesses.—Where defendant had a history of threatening witnesses, and all *Rosario* material was turned over in time for defendant to use it effectively on cross-examination, defendant was not prejudiced by a protective order delaying disclosure of the identity of some of the People's witnesses until the day before trial. People v. Robinson, 200 A.D.2d 693, 606 N.Y.S.2d 908 (2d Dept.), *lv. denied*, 84 N.Y.2d 831 (1994).

§ 240.60. Discovery; continuing duty to disclose.

If, after complying with the provisions of this article or an order pursuant thereto, a party finds, either before or during trial, additional material subject to discovery or covered by such order, he shall promptly comply with the demand or order, refuse to comply with the demand where refusal is authorized, or apply for a protective order.

ANNOTATIONS

Generally.—People were not obligated to disclose report

prosecution witness had made to his employer where the People did not know of the statement's existence or contents, and that document was never in the People's possession or control. People v. Bailey, 73 N.Y.2d 812, 537 N.Y.S.2d 111, 534 N.E.2d 28 (1988).

—Defendant's conviction was affirmed although the prosecutor failed to inform the defense that a prosecution witness had been staying at a hotel at the State's expense during trial for security reasons. People v. Wolfe, 194 A.D.2d 399, 598 N.Y.S.2d 510 (1st Dept.), lv. denied, 82 N.Y.2d 729 (1993).

—Defendant's conviction was affirmed although the prosecutor failed to apprise the defense, one to two weeks before trial, that a witness had been located who saw some of the activity constituting the crimes charged; the error was harmless since another witness corroborated the testimony and there was full opportunity for cross-examination. People v. Delancey, 83 A.D.2d 616, 441 N.Y.S.2d 287 (2d Dept. 1981).

§ 240.70. Discovery; sanctions; fees.

1. If, during the course of discovery proceedings, the court finds that a party has failed to comply with any of the provisions of this article, the court may order such party to permit discovery of the property not previously disclosed, grant a continuance, issue a protective order, prohibit the introduction of certain evidence or the calling of certain witnesses or take any other appropriate action.

2. The failure of the prosecution to call as a witness a person specified in subdivision one of section 240.20 of this article or of any party to introduce disclosed material at the trial shall not, by itself, constitute grounds for any sanction or for adverse comment thereupon by any party in summation to the jury or at any other point.

3. A fee for copies of records required to be disclosed may be charged. Such fee shall not exceed twenty-five cents per photocopy not in excess of nine inches by fourteen inches, or the actual cost of reproducing any other record, except when a different fee is otherwise prescribed by law.

ANNOTATIONS

General.—Fashioning an appropriate remedy for the People's failure to timely comply with discovery demands is within the discretion of the trial court. People v. Cunningham, 189 A.D.2d 821, 592 N.Y.S.2d 447 (2d Dept.), lv. denied, 81 N.Y.2d 1071 (1993).

No sanction required.—Reversal was not required for the People's delayed disclosure of a police officer's memo book where there was no substantial prejudice to defendant. People v. Bowman, 211 A.D.2d 590, 622 N.Y.S.2d 22 (1st Dept. 1995).

—Court did not err in refusing to impose any sanction for the People's failure to preserve the 911 tapes; the People did not fail to exercise due diligence, since no specific request for the tapes was made until after they had been routinely destroyed. People v. Ortiz, 188 A.D.2d 292, 591 N.Y.S.2d 13 (1st Dept. 1992), lv. denied, 81 N.Y.2d 890 (1993).

—Loss of 911 tape did not require reversal where the loss of the tape was inadvertent, and the defendant was in possession of the Sprint report. People v. Figueroa, 156 A.D.2d 322, 549 N.Y.S.2d 381 (1st Dept. 1989).

—In prosecution for rape and incest, the failure of the People to preserve the semen stains on the victim's panties did not deny defendant a fair trial. People v. Ramos, 147 A.D.2d 718, 538 N.Y.S.2d 327 (2d Dept. 1989).

—Prosecutor's failure to furnish transcript of testimony given by one of the complaining witnesses at the Wade hearing of the defendant's accomplice did not require reversal where the prosecutor never possessed the transcript. People v. Jacome, 145 A.D.2d 570, 535 N.Y.S.2d 755 (2d Dept. 1988).

—Court did not err in failing to impose sua sponte a sanction for violation of the rule of People v. Rosario where defense counsel made no application for such relief. People v. Best, 145 A.D.2d 499, 535 N.Y.S.2d 108 (2d Dept. 1988), lv. denied, 73 N.Y.2d 1011 (1989).

—No sanction was required for the police officer's loss of his notes of his interview with the victim after he typed his notes into the computer; although People were negligent in failing to preserve the notes, where People did not introduce evidence of the interview, which was brought out by defendant, and defendant was not prejudiced. People v. Spinks, 205 A.D.2d 842, 613 N.Y.S.2d 288 (3d Dept.), lv. denied, 84 N.Y.2d 833 (1994).

—No sanction was required for the prosecution's failure to produce 18-year-old notes which had been destroyed in good faith as a matter of routine. People v. Pillbeam, 209 A.D.2d 934, 619 N.Y.S.2d 228 (4th Dept. 1994).

—The failure of the People to perform a secretor test or to keep the rape kit in cold storage did not deprive defendant of a fair trial. People v. Bridges, 184 A.D.2d 1042, 584 N.Y.S.2d 361 (4th Dept. 1992).

—Since the destruction of the dispatch tape by the police was inadvertent, the sanction of dismissal was not necessary to rectify whatever harm defendant may have suffered by the loss of this evidence; the court did not abuse its discretion in imposing an adverse inference charge as a lesser sanction for the failure to preserve the tape. People v. Perrin, 163 A.D.2d 809, 559 N.Y.S.2d 67 (4th Dept. 1990).

—Testimony of the prosecutor's expert witness concerning blood splatter was properly admitted even though defense counsel was not furnished with a written report of that testimony since the witness had not prepared any report. People v. Murray, 147 A.D.2d 925, 537 N.Y.S.2d 399 (4th Dept.), lv. denied, 73 N.Y.2d 1019 (1989).

—Untimely disclosure of chemist's notes to defense counsel did not warrant reversal where defense counsel obtained them in time for use during cross-examination. People v. Harris, 130 A.D.2d 939, 516 N.Y.S.2d 554 (4th Dept. 1987).

Sanctions; adverse inference instruction.—Where prosecution was unaware, until trial, that a police officer may have jotted down a description of the perpetrator, and the possibility of prejudice was remote, an adverse inference charge was an adequate sanction. People v. Martinez, 71 N.Y.2d 937, 528 N.Y.S.2d 813, 524 N.E.2d 134 (1988).

—Where evidence was "overwhelming," and there was no serious dispute about identification, adverse inference charge was an adequate remedy for a Rosario violation. People v. Morillo, 181 A.D.2d 532, 582 N.Y.S.2d 1 (1st Dept. 1992).

—Court's adverse instruction was appropriate remedy for People's failure to timely comply with defendant's discovery demand, and thus, court properly denied defendant's motion for a mistrial. People v. Hill, 265 A.D.2d 426, 697 N.Y.S.2d 627 (2d Dept. 1999).

—Adverse inference charge was an appropriate sanction where prosecution's failure to produce a police officer's handwritten notes prejudiced defendant. People v. Bell, 217 A.D.2d 585, 629 N.Y.S.2d 89 (2d Dept. 1995).

—Adverse inference instruction was an appropriate sanction for arresting officer's destruction of his "scratch notes." People v. Walker, 209 A.D.2d 460, 618 N.Y.S.2d 449 (2d Dept. 1994).

—Adverse inference charge was an adequate sanction for loss of handwritten notes, especially where typewritten report prepared from the missing notes was provided. People v. Liriano, 184 A.D.2d 788, 585 N.Y.S.2d 487 (2d Dept.), lv. denied, 80 N.Y.2d 931 (1992).

Sanctions; evidence preclusion.—Trial court did not abuse its discretion by denying defendant's motion for preclusion of evidence contained in a ballistics report that was allegedly first disclosed after defendant had begun to present his defense, where the purported untimely disclosure did not prevent defendant from contesting the People's theory that he was the lone shooter. People v. Jenkins, 98 N.Y.2d 280, 746 N.Y.S.2d 651, 774 N.E.2d 716 (2002).

—Court's preclusion of the People from calling witness due to their failure to timely disclose the statement of the witness was upheld since it eliminated any prejudice to the defendant.

People v. Vasquez, 143 A.D.2d 161, 532 N.Y.S.2d 8 (2d Dept. 1988).

—Though prosecutor did not make his report available to defense counsel upon demand, the drastic remedy of preclusion was not warranted since any potential prejudice arising from noncompliance could by cured by the granting of a continuance. People v. Eleby, 137 A.D.2d 708, 525 N.Y.S.2d 51 (2d Dept. 1988).

—Court did not err in refusing to preclude the People from admitting into evidence the hospital records of the complainant although they were not timely disclosed since there was a satisfactory explanation for the late disclosure and no prejudice accrued to the defendant as a result of the disclosure. People v. Johnstone, 131 A.D.2d 782, 517 N.Y.S.2d 69 (2d Dept.), *lv. denied*, 70 N.Y.2d 800 (1987).

—Contraband, alleged marihuana, was properly suppressed by Court where it was destroyed with the prosecution's knowledge prior to indictment and before the defense had the opportunity to analyze the vegetative matter in order to refute its character and weight. People v. Wagstaff, 107 A.D.2d 877, 484 N.Y.S.2d 264 (3d Dept. 1985).

—Where the People, in a gambling case, failed to comply with a demand for discovery and a court directing response to a demand for discovery, as well as a failure to respond to a motion for discovery, and for a request for a hearing on a motion to suppress, the Court, pursuant to CPL § 240.70 precluded the People from introducing any physical evidence seized from the defendants, or premises alleged to be under their control and from introducing any search warrant or supporting materials relevant to the proceedings. People v. Brown, 104 Misc. 2d 157, 427 N.Y.S.2d 722 (Crim. Ct. N.Y.C. 1980).

Sanctions; mistrial, reversal.—People's delay in furnishing defense counsel with daily activity report until after both sides had rested required reversal. People v. Goins, 73 N.Y.2d 989, 540 N.Y.S.2d 994, 995 N.E.2d 346 (1989).

—Granting of mistrial was sufficient remedy for *Brady* violation since it provided defendant with a sufficient opportunity to investigate the information belatedly disclosed. People v. Crespo, 188 A.D.2d 483, 591 N.Y.S.2d 57 (2d Dept. 1992).

Sanction; dismissal.—Dismissal is too harsh a sanction "where less severe measures can rectify the harm." People v. Kelly, 62 N.Y.2d 516, 478 N.Y.S.2d 834, 467 N.E.2d 498 (1984).

—Dismissal or preclusion of testimony is too harsh a sanction where less severe measures can rectify the harm done. People v. Beam, 161 A.D.2d 1153, 556 N.Y.S.2d 181 (4th Dept. 1990).

—The drastic remedy of dismissal should not be invoked where less severe measures can rectify the harm. People v. James, 178 A.D.2d 946, 578 N.Y.S.2d 741 (4th Dept. 1991), *app. withdrawn*, 80 N.Y.2d 833 (1992).

—Court dismissed indictment in forcible rape prosecution due to People's delayed disclosure of *Rosario* and possible *Brady* materials that could have been used to cross-examine complainant. People v. Ariosa, 172 Misc. 2d 312, 660 N.Y.S.2d 255 (Monroe Co. Ct. 1997).

§ 240.75. Discovery; certain violations.

The failure of the prosecutor or any agent of the prosecutor to disclose statements that are required to be disclosed under subdivision one of section 240.44 or paragraph (a) of subdivision one of section 240.45 of this article shall not constitute grounds for any court to order a new pre-trial hearing or set aside a conviction, or reverse, modify or vacate a judgment of conviction in the absence of a showing by the defendant that there is a reasonable possibility that the non-disclosure materially contributed to the result of the trial or other proceeding; provided, however, that nothing in this section shall affect or limit any right the defendant may have to a re-opened pre-trial hearing when such statements were disclosed before the close of evidence at trial.

Added by L. 2000, Ch. 1, eff. Feb. 1, 2001.

ANNOTATIONS

Failure to disclose; no prejudice.—The fact that the People did not disclose the Daily Activity Report at the suppression hearing, which defendant never sought to reopen, did not cause defendant any prejudice, because the report was disclosed by the time of trial, since defense counsel referred to it on cross-examination. People v. Malik, 6 A.D.3d 313, 775 N.Y.S.2d 41 (1st Dept. 2004).

Failure to disclose; prejudicial.—If an in camera review of the diary of the victim's mother contains a relevant portion regarding dates of alleged sexual abuse and the court determines that admission of that portion would lead to the conclusion "that there is a reasonable possibility that non-disclosure materially contributed to the result of the trial," then the relevant portions of the diary should be turned over and a new trial ordered. People v. Yavru-Sakuk, 4 N.Y.3d 814, 797 N.Y.S.2d 19, 829 N.E.2d 1187 (2005).

§ 240.80. Discovery; when demand, refusal and compliance made.

1. A demand to produce shall be made within thirty days after arraignment and before the commencement of trial. If the defendant is not represented by counsel, and has requested an adjournment to obtain counsel or to have counsel assigned, the thirty-day period shall commence, for purposes of a demand by the defendant, on the date counsel initially appears on his behalf. However, the court may direct compliance with a demand to produce that, for good cause shown, could not have been made within the time specified.

2. A refusal to comply with a demand to produce shall be made within fifteen days of the service of the demand to produce, but for good cause may be made thereafter.

3. Absent a refusal to comply with a demand to produce, compliance with such demand shall be made within fifteen days of the service of the demand or as soon thereafter as practicable.

Amended by L. 1982, Ch. 558.

ANNOTATION

Generally.—Defendant need not make his discovery demands until 30 days after his arraignment, and the People's response is not due until 15 days after service of defendant's demands. People v. Lopez, 84 N.Y.2d 425, 618 N.Y.S.2d 879, 643 N.E.2d 501 (1994).

§ 240.90. Discovery; motion procedure.

1. A motion by a prosecutor for discovery shall be made within forty-five days after arraignment, but for good cause shown may be made at any time before commencement of trial.

2. A motion by a defendant for discovery shall be made as prescribed in section 255.20 of this chapter.

3. Where the interests of justice so require, the court may permit a party to a motion for an order of discovery or a protective order, or other affected person, to submit papers or to testify *ex parte* or in camera. Any such papers and transcript

of such testimony shall be sealed, but shall constitute a part of the record on appeal.

ANNOTATIONS

Generally.—Violation of CPL § 240.90(1) does not require suppression or reversal unless constitutionally protected rights are implicated. People v. Finkle, 192 A.D.2d 783, 596 N.Y.S.2d 549 (3d Dept. 1993).

In camera **proceedings.**—Court did not abuse its discretion in conducting an *in camera* proceeding during the *Huntley* hearing to protect the identity of a witness who had expressed legitimate fears for his safety. People v. Rosa, 184 A.D.2d 323, 586 N.Y.S.2d 887 (1st Dept. 1992).

—It was proper for the court to base its protective order with respect to *Rosario* material on the prosecutor's *in camera* representations on the record that the defendant had a history of threatening witnesses. People v. Robinson, 200 A.D.2d 693, 606 N.Y.S.2d 908 (2d Dept. 1994).

ARTICLE 250—PRE-TRIAL NOTICES OF DEFENSES

LexisNexis Cross Reference

New York Criminal Practice (2d ed.), Vol. 1, Ch. 14, Mental Disease or Defect Precluding Fitness to Proceed; Vol. 3, Ch. 30, Trial Strategy; Vol. 5, Ch. 52, General Defenses; *Sexual Assault Trials (2d ed.),* Vol. 1, Ch. 1, Pretrial Issues, Discovery, and Motions.

§ 250.10. Notice of intent to proffer psychiatric evidence; examination of defendant upon application of prosecutor.

1. As used in this section, the term "psychiatric evidence" means:

(a) Evidence of mental disease or defect to be offered by the defendant in connection with the affirmative defense of lack of criminal responsibility by reason of mental disease or defect.

(b) Evidence of mental disease or defect to be offered by the defendant in connection with the affirmative defense of extreme emotional disturbance as defined in paragraph (a) of subdivision one of section 125.25 of the penal law and paragraph (a) of subdivision two of section 125.27 of the penal law.

(c) Evidence of mental disease or defect to be offered by the defendant in connection with any other defense not specified in the preceding paragraphs.

2. Psychiatric evidence is not admissible upon a trial unless the defendant serves upon the people and files with the court a written notice of his intention to present psychiatric evidence. Such notice must be served and filed before trial and not more than thirty days after entry of the plea of not guilty to the indictment. In the interest of justice and for good cause shown, however, the court may permit such service and filing to be made at any later time prior to the close of the evidence.

3. When a defendant, pursuant to subdivision two of this section, serves notice of intent to present psychiatric evidence, the district attorney may apply to the court, upon notice to the defendant, for an order directing that the defendant submit to an examination by a psychiatrist or licensed psychologist as defined in article one hundred fifty-three of the education law designated by the district attorney. If the application is granted, the psychiatrist or psychologist designated to conduct the examination must notify the district attorney and counsel for the defendant of the time and place of the examination. Defendant has a right to have his counsel present at such examination. The district attorney may also be present. The role of each counsel at such examination is that of an observer, and neither counsel shall be permitted to take an active role at the examination.

4. After the conclusion of the examination, the psychiatrist or psychologist must promptly prepare a written report of his findings and evaluation. A copy of such report must be made available to the district attorney and to the counsel for the defendant. No transcript or recording of the examination is required, but if one is made, it shall be made available to both parties prior to the trial.

5. If the court finds that the defendant has willfully refused to cooperate fully in the examination ordered pursuant to subdivision three of this section it may preclude introduction of testimony by a psychiatrist or psychologist concerning mental disease or defect of the defendant at trial. Where, however, the defendant has other proof of his affirmative defense, and the court has found that the defendant did not submit to or cooperate fully in the examination ordered by the court, this other evidence, if otherwise competent, shall be admissible. In such case, the court must instruct the jury that the defendant did not submit to or cooperate fully in the pre-trial psychiatric examination ordered by the court pursuant to subdivision three of this section and that such failure may be considered in determining the merits of the affirmative defense.

Amended by L. 1980, Ch. 548; L. 1982, Ch. 558, eff. Oct. 20, 1982, amending subd. 1 and adding paragraphs (b) and (c) thereto; L. 1984, Ch. 668, eff. Nov. 1, 1984, amending subds. (1)(a) and (5), however, the amendment does not apply to any criminal action or proceeding relating to an offense committed prior to the effective date hereof.

ANNOTATIONS

Psychiatric examination; counsel's presence.—Because a pretrial psychiatric examination constitutes a critical stage in the prosecution of one accused of a crime, a defendant is entitled to have counsel present to make more effective his basic right of cross-examination. Absent unique circumstances, a court does not need to mandate recording or audiotaping of a pretrial psychiatric examination. People v. Chung, 8 Misc. 3d 321, 793 N.Y.S.2d 323 (Sup. Ct. Westchester Co. 2005).

Scope and purpose of the statute.—CPL § 250.10 is designed to create a format by which psychiatric evidence may be prepared and presented manageably and efficiently, eliminating the element of surprise. Here, because defendant did not comply with the statute, the trial court acted within its discretion in precluding defendant from offering psychiatric testimony. People v. Almonor, 93 N.Y.2d 571, 693 N.Y.S.2d 861, 715 N.E.2d 1054 (1999).

—The statute requires that any evidence regarding a mental disease or defect offered in relation to the defense of extreme emotional disturbance or any other defense be preceded by timely notice to the People, including expert psychiatric testimony not derived from an examination of the defendant. People v. Berk, 88 N.Y.2d 257, 644 N.Y.S.2d 658, 667 N.E.2d 308, *cert. denied,* 519 U.S. 849 (1997).

—The 30-day notice provision enables the People to have defendant examined by their own experts within close temporal proximity to the offense and to any examination by defense experts, thus preventing any disadvantage to the prosecution, and avoiding delays during the trial. People v. Berk, 88 N.Y.2d 257, 644 N.Y.S.2d 658, 667 N.E.2d 308, *cert. denied,* 519 U.S. 849 (1997).

—The term "mental disease or defect" as used in CPL § 250.10 necessarily includes mental infirmities that would not sustain an insanity defense. People v. Berk, 88 N.Y.2d 257, 644 N.Y.S.2d 658, 667 N.E.2d 308, *cert. denied,* 519 U.S. 849 (1996).

—Prosecution is clearly entitled to have its psychiatrist review defendant's hospital records prior to its examination of defendant because the defendant served and filed the required section 250.10(2) notice. People v. Chavis, 181 Misc. 2d 540, 696 N.Y.S.2d 365 (Sup. Ct. Bronx Co. 1999).

—Where defendant intended to raise defense of battered wife syndrome, she was required to file notice pursuant to CPL § 250.10 and submit to a psychiatric/psychological examination by the People. People v. Rossakis, 159 Misc. 2d 611, 605 N.Y.S.2d 825 (Sup. Ct. Queens Co. 1993).

Trial court's discretion.—Trial court's refusal to allow late notice and introduction of mental health evidence regarding the psychological impairment that results from a traumatic experience was not an abuse of discretion. People v. Berk, 88 N.Y.2d 257, 644 N.Y.S.2d 658, 667 N.E.2d 308, *cert. denied,* 519 U.S. 859 (1997).

—Decision to allow a defendant to serve and file late notice of intent to introduce psychiatric evidence is in the court's discretion. Court improvidently exercised its discretion in excluding the psychiatric testimony, where the People failed to advance any claim of prejudice from the delay, contending solely that the CPL § 250.10 notice was beyond the requisite 30-day time period, and it was clear that defendant's sanity and his ability to form the requisite intent to commit rape would be a significant factor at trial. People v. Gracius, 6 A.D.3d 222, 774 N.Y.S.2d 534 (1st Dept. 2004).

—The trial court's denial of defendant's request to admit psychological evidence concerning his low I.Q. was proper in light of defendant's failure to comply with notice requirements, where the request was not made until after the testimony of the first witness, although the evidence was in defense possession two months before trial. People v. Mai, 175 A.D.2d 692, 573 N.Y.S.2d 90 (1st Dept.), *lv. denied,* 78 N.Y.2d 1081 (1991).

—Contrary to defendant's contention, the court properly ordered him to submit to a psychiatric examination upon his service of notice pursuant to CPL § 250.10 of his intention to use psychiatric evidence, where, in support of his justification defense, defendant sought to introduce expert testimony about how some people behave as if on "automatic pilot" under extremely stressful situations. People v. Kruglik, 256 A.D.2d 592, 682 N.Y.S.2d 440 (2d Dept. 1998).

—County court did not abuse its discretion in determining that no undue prejudice flowed from any delay on the part of the People's expert in preparing his report, where the only specific prejudice defense counsel articulated from the delay was the additional time that defendant would remain in jail awaiting trial, and defense counsel delayed for considerably more than

30 days before giving notice to the People that he would be presenting psychiatric evidence. People v. Berry, 235 A.D.2d 571, 652 N.Y.S.2d 785 (3d Dept. 1997).

—Court did not abuse its discretion in rejecting defendant's attempt to serve a late CPL § 250.10 notice during the retrial where defendant has never offered a reason for failing to serve such notice. People v. Brown, 4 A.D.3d 886, 772 N.Y.S.2d 143, *rearguement denied,* 6 A.D.3d 1250, 776 N.Y.S.2d 530 (4th Dept. 2004).

—People's failure to submit amended psychiatric report and the delay in disclosing their expert's opinion did not require reversal where defendant was not prejudiced by the delay in disclosure, the court offered defendant an adjournment before commencing the cross-examination, the People's psychiatrist testified that he considered no additional facts in changing his conclusion, and his defense counsel conducted a thorough and effective cross-examination of the psychiatrist regarding his amended conclusion. People v. McCaffrey, 270 A.D.2d 822, 706 N.Y.S.2d 793 (4th Dept. 2000).

—County Court did not abuse its discretion in precluding defendant from offering psychiatric evidence negating an intent to cause physical injury, where defendant failed to serve and file a timely and sufficient notice of intent to offer such evidence, defendant failed to offer an explanation for serving and filing a late and insufficient notice of intent, and defendant did not establish that he should be allowed to offer such evidence in the interest of justice. People v. Pitts, 254 A.D.2d 742, 679 N.Y.S.2d 229 (4th Dept. 1998), *aff'd,* 93 N.Y.2d 571, 693 N.Y.S.2d 861, 715 N.E.2d 1054 (1999); *accord* People v. Lewis, 302 A.D.2d 322, 758 N.Y.S.2d 1 (1st Dept. 2003).

—Trial court has the discretion to determine whether to permit a defendant to serve and file a late notice of intent to produce psychiatric evidence. People v. Holland, 173 Misc. 2d 286, 660 N.Y.S.2d 822 (Westchester Co. Ct. 1997); *see also* People v. DiDonato, 211 A.D.2d 842, 621 N.Y.S.2d 226 (3d Dept.), *aff'd,* 87 N.Y.2d 992, 642 N.Y.S.2d 616, 665 N.E.2d 186 (1996).

Waiver of physician-patient privilege.—Where defendant served CPL § 250.10(2) notice, he was precluded from asserting the physician-patient privilege to bar the release of his hospital psychiatric records for review by the prosecution's expert. People v. Chavis, 181 Misc. 2d 540, 696 N.Y.S.2d 365 (Sup. Ct. Bronx Co. 1999).

§ 250.20. Notice of alibi.

1. At any time, not more than twenty days after arraignment, the people may serve upon the defendant or his counsel, and file a copy thereof with the court, a demand that if the defendant intends to offer a trial defense that at the time of the commission of the crime charged he was at some place or places other than the scene of the crime, and to call witnesses in support of such defense, he must, within eight days of service of such demand, serve upon the people, and file a copy thereof with the court, a "notice of alibi," reciting (a) the place or places where the defendant claims to have been at the time in question, and (b) the names, the residential addresses, the places of employment and the addresses thereof of every such alibi witness upon whom he intends to rely. For good cause shown, the court may extend the period for service of the notice.

2. Within a reasonable time after receipt of the defendant's witness list but not later than ten days before trial, the people must serve upon the defendant or his counsel, and file a copy thereof with the court, a list of the witnesses the people propose to offer in rebuttal to discredit the defendant's alibi at the trial together with the residential addresses, the places of employment and the addresses thereof of any such rebuttal witnesses.

A witnesses who will testify that the defendant was at the scene of the crime is not such an alibi rebuttal witness. For good cause shown, the court may extend the period for service of the list of witnesses by the people.

3. If at the trial the defendant calls such an alibi witness without having served the demanded notice of alibi, or if having served such a notice he calls a witness not specified therein, the court may exclude any testimony of such witness relating to the alibi defense. The court may in its discretion receive such testimony, but before doing so, it must, upon application of the people, grant an adjournment not in excess of three days.

4. Similarly, if the people fail to serve and file a list of any rebuttal witnesses, the provisions of subdivision three, above, shall reciprocally apply.

5. Both the defendant and the people shall be under a continuing duty to promptly disclose the names and addresses of additional witnesses which come to the attention of either party subsequent to filing their witness lists as provided in this section.

Amended by L. 1971, Ch. 789; L. 1974, Ch. 420.

ANNOTATIONS

Cross-examination of alibi.—Proper foundation was laid pursuant to *People v. Dawson,* 50 N.Y.2d 311, 428 N.Y.S.2d 914, 406 N.E.2d 771, for the cross-examination of defendant's alibi witnesses concerning their third alleged opportunity to inform law enforcement officials of defendant's alibi. People v. Miller, 89 N.Y.2d 1077, 659 N.Y.S.2d 837, 681 N.E.2d 1283 (1997).

Preclusion of alibi witness as sanction for late or improper notice.—Court properly exercised its discretion in precluding alibi testimony on the ground of untimeliness of defendant's alibi notice, which was not offered without any showing of good cause, for the first time at the close of the People's case. People v. Walker, 294 A.D.2d 218, 743 N.Y.S.2d 403 (1st Dept. 2002).

—Trial court properly precluded defendant from calling a third alibi witness, since the defense concededly failed to give proper alibi notice pursuant to CPL § 250.20, and since the People were deprived of the opportunity to conduct a proper investigation regarding any of the alibi testimony. People v. Bohan, 257 A.D.2d 443, 684 N.Y.S.2d 514 (1st Dept. 1999).

—Trial court properly rejected defendant's late alibi notice, served approximately 27 months after the statutory deadline, since defendant failed to provide a sufficient explanation for the delay. People v. Bonner, 287 A.D.2d 728, 732 N.Y.S.2d 106 (2d Dept. 2001).

—Trial court did not improvidently exercise its discretion when it precluded the defendant from presenting an alibi witness for failure to provide adequate notice, since defendant did not proffer a sufficient reason for his failure to comply. People v. DeLaRosa, 215 A.D.2d 496, 626 N.Y.S.2d 827 (2d Dept. 1995).

—Trial court did not abuse its discretion by precluding defendant's alibi witnesses for failure to provide adequate notice, where defendant failed to give a reasonable excuse and his alibi contradicted what he himself told the complainant right before he shot her. People v. Bernard, 210 A.D.2d 419, 620 N.Y.S.2d 414 (2d Dept. 1994), *lv. denied,* 85 N.Y.2d 906 (1995).

—Court properly precluded defendant from calling an alibi witness because there was no good cause shown for the belated application to extend the period for service of notice of alibi and, under the facts presented, defendant would have had sufficient information about this witness to serve an alibi notice at the inception of the case. People v. Douglas, 243 A.D.2d 280, 662 N.Y.S.2d 315 (1st Dept. 1997).

—The trial court's refusal to allow the defendant to substitute an alibi witness on his list after the court had already allowed him to present three alibi witnesses for whom late notice was served was not an improvident exercise of discretion. People v. Grayson, 201 A.D.2d 667, 608 N.Y.S.2d 668 (2d Dept.), *lv. denied,* 83 N.Y.2d 1003 (1994).

—Trial court was justified in precluding defendant's three alibi witnesses from testifying for failure to give proper notice, where defendant did not proffer a reasonable explanation for the delay. People v. Toro, 198 A.D.2d 532, 604 N.Y.S.2d 189 (2d Dept. 1993).

—Where the court precluded an alibi witness from testifying when the defense failed to give the People notice until six months after demand, but two weeks prior to trial it was error for the court to preclude the witness since the People were not unduly prejudiced and CPL § 250.20 does not make a failure to make timely notice a fatal defect. People v. Peterson, 96 A.D.2d 871, 465 N.Y.S.2d 743 (2d Dept. 1983).

Use of notice of alibi to impeach.—The defense, after disavowing reliance on its alibi notice, but not withdrawing it, introduced two alibi witnesses who gave a new alibi relating to a different time frame. Court erred in allowing the prosecution to introduce the notice of alibi on its rebuttal case. The error was harmless because of overwhelming evidence of guilt. People v. Rodriguez, 3 N.Y.3d 462, 787 N.Y.S.2d 697, 821 N.E.2d 122 (2004).

—Trial court erred in permitting prosecutor to impeach defendant with statements made in the withdrawn alibi notice after he testified to a non-alibi defense, but the error was harmless because there is no significant probability that the jury would have acquitted absent the error. People v. Brown, 98 N.Y.2d 226, 746 N.Y.S.2d 422, 774 N.E.2d 186 (2002).

—Where defendant withdrew his alibi notice prior to trial and then presented an entirely different alibi defense, of which no prior notice had been given, court allowed prosecutor to introduce a redacted copy of the alibi notice for rebuttal to impeach the alibi witnesses. If there were an error in the admission of the alibi notice, it was harmless in light of the overwhelming evidence. People v. Rodriguez, 2 A.D.3d 296, 770 N.Y.S.2d 38 (1st Dept. 2003), *aff'd,* 3 N.Y.3d 462, 787 N.Y.S.2d 697, 821 N.E.2d 122 (2004).

—The prosecutor was properly allowed to impeach defendant with the notice of alibi, whether it is viewed as a prior inconsistent statement or an informal judicial admission. The notice was offered with defendant's active participation and it was a declaration made by defendant in the course of the proceedings inconsistent with the position at trial. People v. Shuff, 168 A.D.2d 348, 564 N.Y.S.2d 132 (1st Dept. 1990).

—People may not use the defendant's notice of alibi to impeach him or his alibi witness; it is not his statement but merely a document prepared by the defense attorney. People v. Nelu, 157 A.D.2d 864, 550 N.Y.S.2d 905 (2d Dept. 1990).

Notice; rebuttal witnesses.—Court properly denied defendant's application to preclude People from calling an alibi rebuttal witness, made on the ground that the People's alibi rebuttal notice was untimely. Defendant did not avail himself of his statutory right to an adjournment, and did not establish a claim of incurable prejudice. People v. Wiener, 271 A.D.2d 319, 707 N.Y.S.2d 150 (1st Dept. 2000).

—Trial court properly permitted the People to put on a rebuttal witness whose testimony went to the heart of defendant's alibi defense despite their failure to timely serve notice, where the witness' testimony was preceded by a three-day adjournment. People v. Cade, 138 A.D.2d 388, 525 N.Y.S.2d 672 (2d Dept. 1988), *aff'd,* 73 N.Y.2d 904 (1989).

—New York's alibi statute (CPL § 250.20) comports with the requirements of the U.S. Supreme Court decision in *Wardius v. Oregon,* 412 U.S. 470, 93 S. Ct. 2208, 37 L. Ed. 2d 82 (1973), in that it obliges the People to serve a list of proposed alibi rebuttal witnesses if the defendant has first served a notice of alibi disclosing his alibi witnesses. People v. Peterson, 96 A.D.2d 871, 465 N.Y.S.2d 743 (2d Dept. 1983).

§ 250.30. Notice of defenses in offenses involving computers.

1. In any prosecution in which the defendant seeks to invoke any of the defenses specified in section 156.50 of the penal law, the defendant must within forty-five days after arraignment and

not less than twenty days before the commencement of the trial serve upon the people and file with the court a written notice of his intention to present such defense. For good cause shown, the court may extend the period for service of the notice.

2. The notice served must specify the subdivision or subdivisions upon which the defendant relies and must also state the reasonable grounds that led the defendant to believe that he had the authorization required by the statute or the right required by the statute to engage in such conduct.

3. If at the trial the defendant seeks to invoke any of the defenses specified in section 156.50 of the penal law without having served the notice as required, or seeks to invoke a subdivision or a ground not specified in the notice, the court may exclude any testimony or evidence in regard to the defense, or any subdivision or ground, not noticed. The court may in its discretion, for good cause shown, receive such testimony or evidence, but before doing so, it may, upon application of the people, grant an adjournment.

Added by L. 1986, Ch. 514.

§ 250.40. Notice of intent to seek death penalty.

1. A sentence of death may not be imposed upon a defendant convicted of murder in the first degree unless, pursuant to subdivision two of this section, the people file with the court and serve upon the defendant a notice of intent to seek the death penalty.

2. In any prosecution in which the people seek a sentence of death, the people shall, within one hundred twenty days of the defendant's arraignment upon an indictment charging the defendant with murder in the first degree, serve upon the defendant and file with the court in which indictment is pending a written notice of intention to seek the death penalty. For good cause shown the court may extend the period for service and filing of the notice.

3. Notwithstanding any other provisions of law, where the people file a notice of intent to seek the death penalty pursuant to this section the defendant shall be entitled to an additional sixty days for the purpose of filing new motions or supplementing pending motions.

4. A notice of intent to seek the death penalty may be withdrawn at any time by a written notice of withdrawal filed with the court and served upon the defendant. Once withdrawn the notice of intent to seek the death penalty may not be refiled.

Added by L. 1995, Ch. 1, § 13, eff. Sept. 1, 1995.

ANNOTATIONS

Constitutionality.—New York's statutory scheme for selecting candidates for the death penalty does not violate due process or the constitutional prohibition against cruel and unusual punishment. People v. Harris, 176 Misc. 2d 967, 675 N.Y.S.2d 742 (Sup. Ct. Kings Co. 1998).

Extension of time.—A finding of good cause is a condition precedent to granting an extension of time to file a notice of intent to seek the death penalty. Good cause exists here. People v. Winebrenner, 2 Misc. 3d 440, 768 N.Y.S.2d 588 (Co. Ct. Monroe Co. 2003).

Meaning of "serve upon defendant."—Defendant moved to strike the death penalty on the grounds that he was not personally served with the Notice of Intent to seek the death penalty pursuant to CPL § 250.40. Court denied defendant's motion because the words "serve upon the defendant" include service upon defendant's attorney and the statutory notice requirement was satisfied by the timely service of defendant's attorney on his behalf. People v. Edwards, 178 Misc. 2d 649, 682 N.Y.S.2d 538 (Schoharie Co. Ct. 1998).

Pleas.—A defendant arraigned upon an indictment charging, inter alia, first-degree murder, may not plead to the entire indictment and avoid the possibility of the death penalty verdict until the District Attorney has either declined to file his CPL § 250.40 notice on the record, consents to such plea, or the 120 day period with any court ordered extensions has expired. People v. Schroedel, 182 Misc. 2d 154, 697 N.Y.S.2d 904 (Co. Ct. Sullivan Co. 1999), *cert. denied,* 531 U.S. 860 (2000).

Tolling of time.—Where court has dismissed all first-degree murder counts before the time for filing the notice of intention to seek the death penalty has expired, and the District Attorney appeals the dismissal, the time period to file the notice of intent to seek the death penalty is tolled until the murder in the first degree charges are reinstated. People v. Butts, 178 Misc. 2d 531, 679 N.Y.S.2d 560 (Sup. Ct. Kings Co. 1998).

CPL

ARTICLE 255—PRE-TRIAL MOTIONS

Section
255.10   Definitions.
255.20   Pre-trial motions; procedure.

LexisNexis Cross References

Criminal Constitutional Law, Vol. 2, Ch. 11, Pretrial Motions; *Criminal Law Advocacy,* Vol. 1, Ch. 11, Motions Challenging the Indictment; *Criminal Defense Techniques,* Vol. 1, Ch. 1C, Pretrial Preparation for a White-Collar Crime Case; Vol. 1, Ch. 1D, State Pretrial Motion Tactics; Vol. 1A, Ch. 11, Pretrial Discovery of Prosecution Witnesses in State Courts; Vol. 1A, Ch. 20, Pretrial Conference; Vol. 5, Ch. 101, Introduction to Motion Practice; Vol. 5, Ch. 110, Motions to Suppress Confessions and Identification Evidence; Vol. 5, Ch. 111, Motions to Suppress Evidence; Vol. 6, Ch. 117, Motions To Disqualify Judge or Counsel; Vol. 6, Ch. 123, Miscellaneous Motions; *Defense of Narcotics Cases,* Vol. 1, Ch. 2, Pretrial Proceedings; *Business Crime,* Vol. 1, Ch. 4, Pretrial Motions Directed at Indictment; *New York Criminal Practice (2d ed.),* Vol. 2, Ch. 16, Motions to Dismiss Indictment; *Sexual Assault Trials (2d ed.),* Vol. 1, Ch. 1, Pretrial Issues, Discovery, and Motions; *Criminal Practice Handbook (2d ed.),* Ch. 4, Sample Pretrial Motions; *Criminal Evidentiary Foundations,* Ch. 2, Related Procedures.

§ 255.10. Definitions.

1.* "Pretrial motion" as used in this article means any motion by a defendant which seeks an order of the court:

(a) dismissing or reducing an indictment pursuant to article 210 or removing an action to the family court pursuant to section 210.43; or

(b) dismissing an information, prosecutor's information, simplified information or misdemeanor complaint pursuant to article 170; or

(c) granting discovery pursuant to article 240; or

(d) granting a bill of particulars pursuant to sections 100.45 or 200.90; or

(e) removing the action pursuant to sections 170.15, 230.20 or 230.30; or

(f) suppressing the use at trial of any evidence pursuant to article 710; or

(g) granting separate trials pursuant to article 100 or 200.
* No other subdivisions have been enacted.

Added by L. 1974, Ch. 763; **Amended** by L. 1979, Ch. 411; L. 1990, Ch. 209.

ANNOTATIONS

Change of venue.—Application for change of venue, which was made prior to jury selection, was premature. People v. Oakes, 130 A.D.2d 980, 516 N.Y.S.2d 1000 (4th Dept. 1987).

Motion for severance; directed to discretion of court.—Where the proof against the defendants is supplied by the same evidence, only the most cogent reasons warrant a severance. A proper showing of need for a County defendant's testimony imports that the movant clearly show what the co-defendant would testify to and that such testimony would tend to exculpate the movant. Severance is not required where possibility of co-defendant's testifying is merely colorable or speculative. People v. Bornholdt, 33 N.Y.2d 75, 350 N.Y.S.2d 369, 305 N.E.2d 461 (1973), *cert. denied,* 416 U.S. 905 (1974).

—Defendant's severance motion was properly denied, because it was untimely and because the motion did not establish a sufficient basis for severance, since the evidence against both defendants was essentially identical, their defenses were fundamentally similar, and defendant was not prejudiced in any way by a joint trial. People v. Montalbo, 265 A.D.2d 183, 697 N.Y.S.2d 6 (1st Dept. 1999).

Removal; prosecutor.—To recuse a prosecutor from trying a case there should be more than the mere taking of a statement by a prosecutor at the time of arrest and more than the mere possibility that opposing counsel may call the prosecutor; there should be some likelihood (1) that the prosecutor will be called, and (2) that the testimony will be relevant, i.e., tending to establish the contention of the side for whom it is being offered and if these criteria are met, then the prosecutor should disqualify himself from the trial of the case. People v. Arabadjis, 93 Misc. 2d 826, 403 N.Y.S.2d 674 (Sup. Ct. N.Y. Co. 1978).

§ 255.20. Pre-trial motions; procedure.

1. Except as otherwise expressly provided by law, whether the defendant is represented by counsel or elects to proceed pro se, all pretrial motions shall be served or filed within forty-five days after arraignment and before commencement of trial, or within such additional time as the court may fix upon application of the defendant made prior to entry of judgment. In an action in which an eavesdropping warrant and application have been furnished pursuant to section 700.70 or a notice of intention to introduce evidence has been served pursuant to section 710.30, such period shall be extended until forty-five days after the last date of such service. If the defendant is not represented by counsel and has requested an adjournment to obtain counsel or to have counsel

assigned, such forty-five day period shall commence on the date counsel initially appears on defendant's behalf.

2. All pre-trial motions, with supporting affidavits, affirmations, exhibits and memoranda of law, whenever practicable, shall be included within the same set of motion papers, and shall be made returnable on the same date, unless the defendant shows that it would be prejudicial to the defense were a single judge to consider all the pre-trial motions. Where one motion seeks to provide the basis for making another motion, it shall be deemed impracticable to include both motions in the same set of motion papers pursuant to this subdivision.

3. Notwithstanding the provisions of subdivisions one and two hereof, the court must entertain and decide on its merits, at anytime before the end of the trial, any appropriate pre-trial motion based upon grounds of which the defendant could not, with due diligence, have been previously aware, or which, for other good cause, could not reasonably have been raised within the period specified in subdivision one of this section or included within the single set of motion papers as required by subdivision two. Any other pretrial motion made after the forty-five day period may be summarily denied, but the court, in the interest of justice, and for good cause shown, may, in its discretion, at any time before sentence, entertain and dispose of the motion on the merits.

4. Any pre-trial motion, whether made before or after expiration of the period specified in subdivision one of this section, may be referred by the court to a judicial hearing officer who shall entertain it in the same manner as a court. In the discharge of this responsibility, the judicial hearing officer shall have the same powers as a judge of the court making the assignment, except that the judicial hearing officer shall not determine the motion but shall file a report with the court setting forth findings of fact and conclusions of law. The rules of evidence shall be applicable at any hearing conducted hereunder by a judicial hearing officer. A transcript of any testimony taken, together with the exhibits or copies thereof, shall be filed with the report. The court shall determine the motion on the motion papers, affidavits and other documents submitted by the parties thereto, the record of the hearing before the judicial hearing officer, and the judicial hearing officer's report.

Added by L. 1974, Ch. 763; **Amended** by L. 1976, Ch. 194; L. 1982, Ch. 369; L. 1983, Ch. 840.

ANNOTATIONS

Timeliness of application.—Defendant's motion to dismiss the indictment was untimely where it was made over three months after his arraignment. People v. Dean, 74 N.Y.2d 643, 542 N.Y.S.2d 512, 540 N.E.2d 707 (1989).

—Request for a suppression hearing made mid-trial was properly denied, absent adequate explanation why it could not have been made earlier. People v. Gibbs, 210 A.D.2d 4, 618 N.Y.S.2d 813 (1st Dept. 1994).

—It was not an abuse of discretion to deny the defendant's motion to dismiss the indictment which was untimely because it was not made within 45 days after arraignment. People v. Figueroa, 203 A.D.2d 72, 610 N.Y.S.2d 25 (1st Dept. 1994).

—Court providently exercised its discretion in denying the defendant's request, made on the first day of jury selection, for an independent drug test because the motion was untimely and the defendant did not offer an adequate explanation for his failure to have the drugs tested, since they were available for inspection during pretrial discovery. People v. Delacruz, 271 A.D.2d 452, 705 N.Y.S.2d 637 (2d Dept. 2000).

—Motion to dismiss due to pre-indictment delay was untimely when made after close of prosecution's case-in-chief. People v. Ramirez, 243 A.D.2d 734, 663 N.Y.S.2d 855 (2d Dept. 1997).

—Motion to dismiss the indictment made well beyond 45 days after arraignment was untimely and court properly refused to consider it. Valle v. Moskowitz, 286 A.D.2d 572, 588 N.Y.S.2d 582 (2d Dept. 1992).

—Where defendant did not timely move to suppress his confession under CPL § 255.20 upon the ground that it was involuntarily made and proffered no excuse whatever for his failure, he waived his right to such hearing and the trial court was free to submit the issue to the jury without first conducting a separate hearing. People v. Selby, 53 A.D.2d 878, 385 N.Y.S.2d 335 (2d Dept. 1976), aff'd, 43 N.Y.2d 791, 402 N.Y.S.2d 392, 383 N.E.2d 286 (1977).

—The time restrictions of CPL § 255.20 are not casual, and contrary to defendant's contention, a stipulation in lieu of motion did not afford defendant additional time to file defendant's suppression motion. People v. Knowles, 12 A.D.3d 939, 785 N.Y.S.2d 561 (3d Dept. 2004).

—Motion to suppress breathalyzer test results, although not made until jury selection, could not be denied as untimely, since defendant did not obtain assigned counsel until a week before trial, and problems with the test were not generally recognized until more than a year after arraignment. People v. Colon, 180 A.D.2d 876, 580 N.Y.S.2d 95 (3d Dept. 1992).

—It was not an abuse of discretion to deny defendant leave to file a suppression motion 22 months after his arraignment and 4 months after engaging new counsel. People v. Petgen, 81 A.D.2d 951, 439 N.Y.S.2d 692 (3d Dept. 1981).

—County Court properly denied defendant's motion to suppress items of physical evidence without conducting a hearing, where the motion was made at the beginning of trial, was untimely, and was not made in writing or supported by sworn allegations of fact. People v. Adams, 252 A.D.2d 980, 676 N.Y.S.2d 361 (4th Dept. 1998).

—Court properly denied defendant's motion, made during jury selection, for production of the original audiotapes for scientific testing; defendant's motion was untimely, and defendant did not offer an adequate explanation for his failure to make the motion at an earlier time. People v. Molling, 238 A.D.2d 915, 661 N.Y.S.2d 129 (4th Dept. 1997).

—All pretrial motions, including a motion to suppress evidence, must be made within 45 days after arraignment unless defendant demonstrates good cause for delay in making the motion. People v. Broome, 187 A.D.2d 949, 590 N.Y.S.2d 349 (4th Dept. 1992).

—Application for change of venue, which was made prior to jury selection, was premature. People v. Oakes, 130 A.D.2d 980, 516 N.Y.S.2d 1000 (4th Dept. 1987).

—The trial court did not abuse its discretion in denying defendant's suppression motion, which was not made until six and one-half months after the prescribed 45 day period had expired, where defendant offered no excuse for the delay. People v. Stafford, 79 A.D.2d 435, 437 N.Y.S.2d 195 (4th Dept. 1981).

Waiver of statutory requirements.—Although pretrial motions to suppress evidence must be made in writing and upon reasonable notice to the People, the writing requirement may be waived by the People. People v. Mezon, 80 N.Y.2d 155, 589 N.Y.S.2d 839, 693 N.E.2d 943 (1992).

Suppression court's role.—CPL § 255.20(4) recognizes and preserves the trial court's nondelegable and exclusive authority to decide the suppression motion. People v. Scalza, 76 N.Y.2d 604, 562 N.Y.S.2d 14, 563 N.E.2d 705 (1990).

—CPL § 255.20 sets a maximum time in which a defendant must make his pretrial motions without application to the Court, no minimum time is set forth and the Trial Court may, in its discretion, require that pretrial motions be made at some point earlier than 45 days after arraignment. People v. Broome, 78 A.D.2d 718, 432 N.Y.S.2d 558 (3d Dept. 1980).

ARTICLE 260—JURY TRIAL—GENERALLY

Section
260.10 Jury trial; requirement thereof.
260.20 Jury trial; defendant's presence at trial.
260.30 Jury trial; in what order to proceed.

LexisNexis Cross References

See generally Criminal Law Advocacy, Vol. 6, Argument to the Jury; *Defense of Drunk Driving Cases,* Vol. 4, Ch. 47, Opening Statement; Ch. 50, Closing Argument; *Criminal Practice Handbook (2d ed.),* Ch. 6, Opening and Closing Statements.

§ 260.10. Jury trial; requirement thereof.

Except as otherwise provided in section 320.10, every trial of an indictment must be a jury trial.

ANNOTATIONS

Aggregate sentence.—Prosecution of consolidated petty offenses, with a potential aggregate sentence in excess of six months, does not add up to a constitutionally compelled right to a jury trial. People v. Foy, 88 N.Y.2d 742, 650 N.Y.S.2d 79, 673 N.E.2d 589 (1996).

Change of attorney.—Trial court did not abuse its discretion in granting counsel's motion to be relieved shortly before trial on the ground that a conflict of interest might arise from his representation of a confidential informant who would testify, and thereafter refusing to reinstate said defense counsel a few days later; it is not an abuse of discretion for a trial court, acting on the eve of trial, to consider the interests of judicial economy, the integrity of the judicial process, and the continuous vacillation of both defendant and counsel in denying the motion for reinstatement. People v. Tineo, 64 N.Y.2d 531, 490 N.Y.S.2d 159, 479 N.E.2d 795 (1985).

—Appellant was not denied effective assistance of counsel when the Trial Judge refused to replace his court-appointed lawyer since the court, in deciding whether "good cause" existed, took into account such circumstances as whether present counsel was reasonably likely to afford the defendant effective assistance and whether the defendant has unduly delayed in seeking new assignment. People v. Medina, 44 N.Y.2d 199, 404 N.Y.S.2d 588, 375 N.E.2d 768 (1978).

—A court should be hesitant to interfere in an established attorney-client relationship, even where the attorney joins in the application to be excused; the lawyer cannot terminate the relationship, ex parte, nor, on the other hand, may the client preclude termination. People v. Hall, 46 N.Y.2d 873, 414 N.Y.S.2d 678, 387 N.E.2d 610 (1978).

—The court properly exercised its discretion in denying defendant's request for the substitution of counsel following jury selection where defendant presented no exigent or compelling circumstances that justified the substitution nor did he demonstrate that the requested adjournment had been necessitated by forces beyond his control and was not simply a dilatory tactic. People v. Rivera, 201 A.D.2d 385, 607 N.Y.S.2d 932 (1st Dept. 1994).

—Although a defendant is constitutionally entitled to counsel of his own choosing, he may use that right to delay judicial proceedings. People v. Brown, 200 A.D.2d 435, 607 N.Y.S.2d 244 (1st Dept. 1994).

—The contentions that defense counsel called defendant names and failed to communicate adequately with him did not amount to a showing of good cause, or a conflict or irreconcilable conflict between defendant and counsel, justifying assignment of new counsel. People v. Benson, 203 A.D.2d 966, 611 N.Y.S.2d 407 (4th Dept. 1994).

Counsel.—In order to prevail on a conflict of interest claim, the defendant must establish that the conduct of his defense was in fact affected by the operation of the conflict of interest. People v. Jordan, 83 N.Y.2d 784, 610 N.Y.S.2d 952, 632 N.E.2d 1275 (1994).

—"Counsel," as the word is used in the Sixth Amendment, can mean nothing less than a licensed attorney at law; a lay person, regardless of his educational qualifications or experience, is not a constitutionally acceptable substitute for a member of the Bar; harmless error analysis is not applicable in these cases. People v. Felder, 47 N.Y.2d 287, 418 N.Y.S.2d 295, 391 N.E.2d 1274 (1979).

—The defendant was not denied his constitutional right of counsel by the court's order limiting his telephone privileges to calling his attorney only; there was no evidence that the granting of the order detrimentally affected the manner in which counsel represented defendant. People v. Boyd, 197 A.D.2d 365, 602 N.Y.S.2d 132 (1st Dept. 1993).

—Defendant's application for leave to appeal the denial of a motion to vacate judgment was dismissed without prejudice to a renewed application where it was submitted on the defendant's behalf by a fellow inmate; the inmate was not admitted to the practice of law in this State or of any other jurisdiction and, therefore, his attempted representation of the defendant was in violation of the proscription against the practice of law by non-lawyers. People v. Rodriguez, 129 A.D.2d 594, 514 N.Y.S.2d 90 (2d Dept. 1987).

—A defendant's right to be represented by counsel of his or her own choosing is qualified in the sense that he or she may not employ such right as a means to delay judicial proceedings. People v. Michalek, 195 A.D.2d 1007, 600 N.Y.S.2d 571 (4th Dept. 1993).

Judge substitution.—Judge may be substituted for another when original judge becomes incapacitated during jury trial, provided the substitute indicates on the record the requisite familiarity with the proceedings and there is no undue prejudice to defendant or People. People v. Thompson, 90 N.Y.2d 615, 665 N.Y.S.2d 21, 687 N.E.2d 1304 (1997).

Judge's ineffectiveness.—Where it was apparent from the outset that the presiding town justice was unfamiliar with the mechanics of a jury trial, to which defense counsel objected, and the judge had to be guided by the prosecutor through every aspect of jury selection, resulting in the judge's relinquishing control over the jury selection process, a new trial was ordered, because the judge's inexperience permeated the rest of the proceedings, and the prosecutor even instructed the jury following a readback request. People v. Stiggins, 1 N.Y.3d 529, 770 N.Y.S.2d 683, 802 N.E.2d 1081 (2003).

Withdrawal of counsel.—It was proper to permit the defendant to plead guilty *pro se* where he was repeatedly advised against doing so by both the court and the prosecutor, he had extensive prior exposure to the criminal justice system, and, he felt sufficiently comfortable with proceeding *pro se* as demonstrated by the numerous applications he made to the courts. People v. Knatz, 128 A.D.2d 896, 513 N.Y.S.2d 821 (2d Dept. 1987).

—Trial court erred in permitting counsel to withdraw on the eve of trial and compelling the defendant to proceed *pro se* where it failed to inquire into whether defendant understood the dangers of proceeding *pro se.* People v. Buckman, 127 A.D.2d 964, 512 N.Y.S.2d 748 (4th Dept. 1987).

Sidebar conferences; exclusion from.—A defendant in a criminal trial who has exercised the right to self-representation may not be arbitrarily and categorically excluded from sidebar conferences. People v. Rosen, 81 N.Y.2d 237, 597 N.Y.S.2d 914, 613 N.E.2d 946 (1993).

Associate counsel *pro se.*—The assignment of stand-by counsel is a matter of trial management, not a constitutional right. People v. Howell, 207 A.D.2d 412, 615 N.Y.S.2d 728 (2d Dept. 1994).

Disqualification of prosecutor.—Vacation of conviction was required because attorney who had initially represented the defendant and had participated activity in preparation of his defense was the chief assistant in the office of the prosecutor in the months preceding and during the defendant's trial, and thus gave both the defendant and the public the unmistakable appearance of impropriety. People v. Shinkle, 51 N.Y.2d 417, 434 N.Y.S.2d 918, 415 N.E.2d 909 (1980).

—The indictment should have been dismissed where the district attorney who presented the case to the grand jury failed to recuse himself when he was counsel to and a stockholder of the corporation against which the defendant was alleged to have committed the crimes with which he was charged since a conflict of interest existed. People v. Zimmer 51 N.Y.2d 390, 434 N.Y.S.2d 206, 414 N.E.2d 705 (1980).

—Court erred is disqualifying assistant district attorney in the absence of a significant showing that the prosecutor's prior investigative or prosecutorial conduct would be a material issue at the trial, or alternatively, any allegations that the prosecutor might seek to influence the jury by injecting his own credibility into the trial. Morgenthau v. Altman, 207 A.D.2d 685, 616 N.Y.S.2d 365 (1st Dept. 1994).

Excessive questioning by trial court.—A trial court may intervene in the proceedings in order to clarify the issues so long as it does so sparingly, and without partiality, bias or hostility. People v. Ayala, 120 A.D.2d 600, 502 N.Y.S.2d 75 (2d Dept. 1986).

—Inquiries by trial judge to two prosecution witnesses were not prejudicial but rather were part of an attempt to explain and clarify discrepancies that arose from the testimony as it was given and the persistent questioning of a defense witness was proper where that witness evaded and eluded responding to a question posed by the court. People v. Manor, 116 A.D.2d 921, 498 N.Y.S.2d 223 (3d Dept. 1986).

—The trial judge's two questions concerning the meaning of the words "cop" and "joint" while better left unasked, did not reveal the court's opinion of either the witness or the case or deprive the defendant of a fair trial. People v. Fantroy, 122 A.D.2d 291, 503 N.Y.S.2d 910 (3d Dept. 1986).

Fair trial.—When courtroom security measures are challenged as inherently prejudicial, the appropriate inquiry is whether the security measures presented a risk that the jury's deliberations were infected. People v. Terry, 188 A.D.2d 1020, 591 N.Y.S.2d 666 (4th Dept. 1992).

Gag order.—Imposition of a gag order upon the attorneys and other participants in the trial is constitutionally impermissible absent the requisite showing of necessity for prior restraints, i.e., threat to defendant's right to a fair trial. New York Times Company v. Rothwax, 143 A.D.2d 592, 533 N.Y.S.2d 73 (1st Dept. 1988).

—Reversal was required where the court's gag rule denied defendant the effective assistance of counsel by prohibiting the attorney from discussing the information divulged in court with anyone, including his client. People v. Chiarello, 82 A.D.2d 837, 439 N.Y.S.2d 664 (2d Dept. 1981).

Failure of judge to recuse himself after presiding over previous trial.—Reversal was required where the trial court failed to make a meaningful inquiry on the record to ascertain whether the defendant was cognizant of the potential risks inherent in his representation by the same counsel as his co-defendant, the significant possibility of a conflict of interest arising out of the differing types and quantum of evidence against each, including the disincentive to call the defendant to the stand despite his lack of a criminal record. People v. Fioretti, 49 N.Y.2d 976, 428 N.Y.S.2d 889, 406 N.E.2d 746 (1980).

—Trial judge was justified in believing he could preside impartially in a second trial on related charges, even though first trial resulted in a conviction and imposition of the mandatory sentence, and thus his refusal to recuse himself was not a basis for reversal, nonetheless, the court found it would have been wiser for trial judge to have recused himself. People v. Pellitteri, 76 A.D.2d 774, 429 N.Y.S.2d 6 (1st Dept. 1980).

—The affidavit of the co-defendant stating that he could exculpate the defendant was insufficient, by itself, to establish defendant's claim that the dual representation of himself and the co-defendant by the same counsel impaired his right to the effective assistance of counsel. People v. DeSuze, 77 A.D.2d 531, 429 N.Y.S.2d 464 (2d Dept. 1980).

Fair trial.—The defendant was not deprived of a fair trial simply because one juror inadvertently saw her in handcuffs. People v. Collazo 163 A.D.2d 581, 559 N.Y.S.2d 33 (2d Dept. 1990).

—The defendant was deprived of a fair trial by the fact that five inmate witnesses testifying on his behalf all appeared in court in shackles. People v. Bryant, 158 A.D.2d 808, 551 N.Y.S.2d 612 (3d Dept. 1990).

Interpreter.—County court's failure to appoint an interpreter to French-speaking defendant constituted harmless error, where defense counsel was fluent in French and was able to fully communicate with defendant and defendant offered no evidence of any instance when defendant's limited English-speaking abilities interfered with his understanding of what was said during any hearing. People v. Villeneuve, 232 A.D.2d 892, 649 N.Y.S.2d 80 (3d Dept. 1996).

Invocation of Fifth Amendment right by witness does not violate confrontation clause.—Invocation by a witness of the privilege against self incrimination during cross-examination with regard to the witness's own immoral or unlawful acts does not offend the confrontation clause where the unanswered question is completely collateral and relates solely to the credibility of the witness and not to the subject matter of direct examination. People v. Jones, 99 A.D.2d 471, 470 N.Y.S.2d 178 (2d Dept. 1984).

No right to trial before law-trained judge.—Defendant has no absolute due process right under New York or Federal law to trial before a law-trained judge, and to obtain removal for trial before lay justice in a town court must show a reason for possible prejudice or, on appeal, must show specific prejudice and trial error resulting from the conduct of the lay judge. People v. Charles F., 60 N.Y.2d 47, 470 N.Y.S.2d 342, 458 N.E.2d 801 (1983).

Prosecutor.—There was no impropriety in prosecutor instructing a witness that the witness did not have to speak to anyone if he did not want to; such an admonition was standard and did not constitute an attempt to persuade a witness to withhold or distort any information. People v. McCloe, 200 A.D.2d 787, 606 N.Y.S.2d 438 (3d Dept. 1994).

Prosecutorial misconduct; comment on defendant's post-arrest silence; waiver of error.—Prosecutor's comment on defendant's post-arrest silence is proper where the defendant testifies in contradiction to the arresting officer, that he said nothing at the time of arrest; however, where prosecutor's summation invited jury to infer guilt from silence, it was improper, except that defendant cannot now complain since trial counsel objected to prosecutor's suggestion of curative instruction. People v. Davis, 61 N.Y.2d 202, 473 N.Y.S.2d 146, 461 N.E.2d 283 (1984).

Prosecutorial misconduct in cross-examination.—Prosecutor committed reversible error when he repeatedly asked defendant on cross-examination whether the prosecution's witnesses, including the complainant and certain police detectives, lied during their testimony, because it was irrelevant whether the defendant believed that the other witnesses were lying. People v. Berrios, 298 A.D.2d 597, 750 N.Y.S.2d 302 (2d Dept. 2002).

—Reversal was mandated where prosecutor improperly cross-examined co-defendant, who had pleaded guilty one week prior to trial, concerning his failure to provide information exculpating the defendant during the many court appearances prior to his pleas. People v. Cruz, 98 A.D.2d 726, 469 N.Y.S.2d 138 (2d Dept. 1983).

—The repeated questioning of defendant on cross-examination about a purported bad act constituted error, where the prosecution had not disclosed any uncharged crimes or bad acts at the *Sandoval* hearing, and no limiting instruction was given to the jury. People v. Marrow, 301 A.D.2d 673, 753 N.Y.S.2d 205 (3d Dept. 2003).

Refusal to admit testimony by defendant's expert; abuse of discretion.—Trial Court erred in refusing to permit defendant's expert, a forensic psychiatrist skilled in drug and alcohol abuse, to testify as to the impact upon defendant of consumption of a case of beer, several marihuana cigarettes and 5 to 10 valium tablets with regard to defendant's ability to form the intent to commit the crime charged. People v. Cronim, 60 N.Y.2d 430, 470 N.Y.S.2d 110, 458 N.E.2d 351 (1983).

Removal of Legal Aid Society as counsel; request by People.—Where People intended to call as a witness a confidential informant who had been previously represented by the Legal Aid Society when he was a defendant, removal of the Legal Aid Society as counsel for defendant was not required, but counsel was directed not to attempt to ascertain confidential facts about the witness that might have been disclosed to the witness's previous Legal Aid attorney under the attorney-client relationship. People v. Spencer, 101 Misc. 2d 259, 420 N.Y.S.2d 868 (Sup. Ct. Kings Co. 1979).

Trial.—The Trial Judge is not without power, to be exercised with judicious restraint, to keep the proceedings within the reasonable confines of the issues and to encourage clarity rather than obscurity in the development of proof; thus, the court may put appropriate questions to witnesses and of course, make such rulings, evidentiary and otherwise, as the proper conduct of the case and the range of discretion entrusted to it for that purpose require. People v. Moulton, 43 N.Y.2d 944, 403 N.Y.S.2d 892, 374 N.E.2d 1243 (1978).

—The trial court was justified, indeed obligated, to assume aggressive control of the proceedings to ensure a fair trial when defense counsel persistently failed to obey proper evidentiary rulings and engaged in tactics designed to disrupt and infuriate throughout the trial and summation. People v. Gonzalez, 38 N.Y.2d 208, 379 N.Y.S.2d 397, 341 N.E.2d 822 (1975).

—An excessive display of security measures adversely affects the presumption of innocence and will not be tolerated absent a clear showing of necessity. People v. Lopez, 207 A.D.2d 658, 616 N.Y.S.2d 42 (1st Dept. 1994).

Termination of assignment of counsel.—Defendant was improperly tried and convicted in absentia of a misdemeanor without first having been given "*Parker*" warnings or informed that the trial would proceed in his absence. People v. Trendell, 61 N.Y.2d 728, 472 N.Y.S.2d 616, 460 N.E.2d 1101 (1984).

Violation of right to confrontation; self-representation at hearing.—Defendant's Sixth Amendment right of confrontation was violated when trial court admitted into evidence transcript of a preliminary hearing wherein defendant represented himself without the hearing court having made a sufficiently searching inquiry for it to be reasonably assured that defendant appreciated the dangers and disadvantages of giving up the fundamental right to counsel. People v. Jackson, 98 A.D.2d 458, 470 N.Y.S.2d 235 (4th Dept. 1983).

When jury trial is required.—The Sixth Amendment guarantee of trial by jury applies only to serious offenses and does not extend to petty crimes or offenses, such as criminal contempt offenses; defendant's contention that he was entitled to a jury trial because he faced a potential six-month aggregate sentence has already been rejected by the Court of Appeals in *People v. Foy*, 88 N.Y.2d 742, 650 N.Y.S.2d 79, 673 N.E.2d 589 (1996), and by the Supreme Court in *Lewis v. United States*, 518 U.S. 322, 116 S. Ct. 2163, 135 L. Ed. 2d 590 (1996). *In re* Hirshfeld, 184 Misc. 2d 119, 706 N.Y.S.2d 815 (Sup. Ct. N.Y. Co. 1999).

—A defendant does not have a right to trial by jury where he is charged with multiple offenses, each separately carrying a penalty of less than 6 months but potentially punishable in the aggregate to more than 6 months. However, if defendant has a non-jury trial, his maximum aggregate sentence should not exceed 6 months. People v. DiLorenzo, 153 Misc. 2d 1021, 585 N.Y.S.2d 670 (Crim. Ct. Bronx Co. 1992).

Six member jury.—Reversal was warranted because the conviction violated N.Y. Constitution § 18(a) of Article VI where defendant was indicted on two misdemeanor charges and over his objection, defendant was subsequently convicted on both counts before a six-person jury. People v. Dean, 80 A.D.2d 695, 436 N.Y.S.2d 455 (3d Dept. 1981).

Dual juries.—Dual juries are permissible if proper procedures are followed, even in the first jury's verdict is not sealed until the second verdict is returned, absent a showing a prejudice. People v. Irizarry, 83 N.Y.2d 557, 611 N.Y.S.2d 807, 634 N.E.2d 179 (1994).

—Nothing in the statute either authorizes or prohibits the use of multiple juries; where proof against co-defendants is primarily supplied by the same evidence, dual juries are appropriate,

but only after a full consideration of the impact the procedure will have on defendants' due process rights and after thorough precautions are taken to protect those rights. People v. Ricardo B., 73 N.Y.2d 228, 538 N.Y.S.2d 796, 535 N.E.2d 1336 (1989).

—The fact that defendant's jury trial was held jointly with a co-defendant's bench trial did not deprive him of a fair trial. People v. Cabrero, 213 A.D.2d 298, 624 N.Y.S.2d 152 (1st Dept.), *lv. denied,* 86 N.Y.2d 780 (1995).

—A joint trial with two juries was properly conducted where the defendant and his accomplice were tried on much the same evidence and each had made a confession implicating the other. People v. Lydon, 197 A.D.2d 640, 603 N.Y.S.2d 771 (2d Dept. 1993).

Absence of trial judge.—An integral component of the right to a trial by jury, is the supervision of a judge. Thus, the absence of the trial judge from the courtroom for a portion of the jury's deliberations, during which time they were supervised by his law secretary, constituted a denial of the right to jury trial. People v. Ahmed, 66 N.Y.2d 307, 496 N.Y.S.2d 984, 487 N.E.2d 894 (1985).

PUBLIC TRIAL/CLOSURE OF COURTROOM

Closure—The exclusion of a witness during summation did not deprive the defendant of the right to a public trial. People v. Walker, 156 A.D.2d 271, 548 N.Y.S.2d 661 (1st Dept. 1989).

Closure of courtroom proper.—People v. Ramos, 90 N.Y.2d 490, 662 N.Y.S.2d 739, 685 N.E.2d 492, *cert. denied,* 522 U.S. 1002 (1997), and companion case, People v. Ayala. In both cases, the records were sufficient to establish that any open-court testimony by the undercover officers would jeopardize their safety and effectiveness, the closure did not extend beyond the live testimony of the witnesses at risk, and neither defendant mentioned particular alternatives he was willing to adopt.

—Locking the courtroom doors during the charge to avoid disruption—allowing those already present to remain—did not seek to exclude the public or frustrate the salutary purposes of public scrutiny. People v. Colon, 71 N.Y.2d 410, 526 N.Y.S.2d 932, 521 N.E.2d 1075 (1988).

—Court did not deprive defendant of his right to a public trial when it ruled over defendant's objection that the wife of a juror would be excluded from the courtroom during the testimony of an undercover officer on the ground that the juror's wife was a member of the general public, to whom the courtroom was closed. People v. Ingram, 3 A.D.3d 437, 770 N.Y.S.2d 718 (1st Dept. 2004).

—Court properly closed the courtroom to public and defendant's family during testimony of undercover officer, because hearing testimony established that undercover officer was actively engaged in extensive, ongoing undercover operations in area where defendant was arrested and where defendant's family lived, that he had previously encountered threatening behavior by drug dealers, that he feared for his safety if courtroom remained open during his testimony, and that he found it necessary to protect his undercover status by entering courthouse through nonpublic doorway. People v. Powell, 246 A.D.2d 494, 667 N.Y.S.2d 988 (1st Dept. 1998).

—Representation by the district attorney that the witness is engaged as an undercover officer and reluctant to testify in public, is sufficient to support closure when the case is being tried in a narcotics part, and it is anticipated that drug dealers, some of whom may have come into contact with the undercover officer, might have occasion to enter the courtroom as defendants or for some other purpose. People v. Gross, 179 A.D.2d 138, 583 N.Y.S.2d 832 (1st Dept. 1992).

Closure of courtroom improper.—Closure order was broader than necessary to protect the People's interest, where the record was insufficient to establish a substantial probability that the officer's safety would be jeopardized by the presence of defendant's wife and children during his testimony. People v. Nieves, 90 N.Y.2d 426, 660 N.Y.S.2d 858, 683 N.E.2d 764 (1997).

—Defendant claimed that total closure of courtroom, which excluded his girlfriend and uncle, was overbroad. The court is obligated to ensure that closure was no broader than necessary to protect an officer's safety and must make adequate findings to support the closure. Those findings were not made here, and the absence of those findings was not cured in this case by any hearing evidence demonstrating that these individuals posed a risk. Thus, reversal was required. People v. Garcia, 271 A.D.2d 81, 710 N.Y.S.2d 345 (1st Dept.), *aff'd*, 95 N.Y.2d 946, 727 N.Y.S.2d 1, 750 N.E.2d 1049 (2000).

—Closure was broader than necessary, where nothing in the record demonstrated that defendant's friends resided or worked in the area where the undercover officer would be returning, and the People did not present sufficient evidence that the friends posed a threat to the officer. People v. Heslop, 307 A.D.2d 975, 763 N.Y.S.2d 327 (2d Dept. 2003).

—Defendant was deprived of his constitutional right to a public trial when the trial court closed the courtroom prior to charging the jury until after the announcement of the verdict, without either party requesting it and over defendant's objection. People v. Singh, 287 A.D.2d 748, 732 N.Y.S.2d 415 (2d Dept. 2001).

—Closure of courtroom during undercover's testimony was improper, because it did not appear that the officer would be returning to undercover work in the same area where defendant was arrested, and general testimony about the risks of undercover work and fear of open court, does not meet the standard for closure under *People v. Martinez*, 82 N.Y.2d 436, 604 N.Y.S.2d 932, 624 N.E.2d 1027 (1993). People v. Bobo, 236 A.D.2d 417, 653 N.Y.S.2d 617 (2d Dept. 1997).

—Court abused its discretion in closing the courtroom where the record neither reflected that the undercover offices were still operating in the locale of the defendant's arrest nor that they expected to return there and where the sole basis for closure proffered by the prosecution was that each undercover had "lost subjects" in the borough. People v. James, 202 A.D.2d 564, 616 N.Y.S.2d 75 (2d Dept. 1994).

—Court improperly closed courtroom as to supervisor of Legal Aid attorney where only basis was that it was court's practice to "exclude everybody." People v. Mercer, 204 A.D.2d 741, 612 N.Y.S.2d 650 (2d Dept. 1994).

—Court erred in closing courtroom during hearing on defendant's motion to suppress. Prosecutor's perfunctory assertions were insufficient to meet the standards for closure, and court did not make an adequate inquiry of the prosecutor, investigator, or spectators, nor did it hold a hearing to ascertain whether the investigator's public testimony would threaten her safety or the safety of others. Court also failed to articulate any findings of fact supporting closure. People v. Ward, 6 A.D.3d 741, 774 N.Y.S.2d 604 (3d Dept. 2004).

Closure of courtroom; screening procedures and alternatives to closure.—Court properly employed a screening procedure to control access to the courtroom during the undercover officer's testimony in light of the officer's *Hinton* hearing testimony that he continued to work in the area of defendant's arrest, had other cases pending in the same courthouse, had received threats in the past, feared for his safety, and always employed security precautions when appearing in court. People v. Medina, 288 A.D.2d 61, 732 N.Y.S.2d 411 (1st Dept. 2001).

—After *Hinton* hearing, court ruled that People had made a sufficient showing to warrant closure during undercover's testimony, but rather than actually closing the courtroom, the court decided, *sua sponte*, to post a court officer outside the courtroom with instructions to notify the court if anyone sought entry. Defendant made no objection to this alternative to closure, and so his current objection is unpreserved. In any event, the court's action was appropriate. This screening procedure was not a closure of the courtroom and would not have ripened into even a partial closure unless and until someone was denied entry. People v. Muniz, 273 A.D.2d 138, 710 N.Y.S.2d 896 (1st Dept. 2000).

—Closure of courtroom to the public during the undercover officer's testimony was proper, as was the narrowly-tailored alternative to closure with respect to defendant's family, allowing them to remain in the courtroom during the officer's testimony provided that a blackboard was placed to block their view of the undercover officer, where the officer testified that he had ongoing undercover operations and investigations within the area of the arrest, that he would be returning to the area, and that, if his identification was revealed, his safety and cases would be jeopardized. People v. Hargett, 293 A.D.2d 757, 742 N.Y.S.2d 638 (2d Dept. 2002).

Closure; waiver of claim.—By failing to oppose the People's request for closure of the courtroom during the testimony of the undercover officers, the defendant waived his claim that the closure resulted in the denial of his right to a public trial. People v. Riveria, 162 A.D.2d 728, 557 N.Y.S.2d 126 (2d Dept. 1990).

Exclusion of defendant's family members improper.—Court committed reversible error in exclusion of defendant's children from the courtroom, an act that also had the effect of excluding the defendant's wife. People v. Cole, 207 A.D.2d 273, 615 N.Y.S.2d 393 (1st Dept. 1994).

—Court improperly excluded defendant's aunt and her two sons from the courtroom during the undercover officer's testimony where the People failed to demonstrate that those relatives, who had no criminal history and lived outside the area where defendant was arrested, posed a threat to the officer's safety. People v. Brann, 290 A.D.2d 455, 736 N.Y.S.2d 107 (2d Dept. 2002).

—After *Hinton* hearing, trial court improperly excluded from the courtroom spectators that the defendant asserted were his common law wife and two children, where the People failed to demonstrate a substantial probability that the woman and children posed a threat to the undercover officer's safety. People v. Serrano, 274 A.D.2d 594, 711 N.Y.S.2d 485 (2d Dept. 2000).

—Defendant was entitled to a new trial, where trial court excluded defendant's sister from the courtroom during the testimony of the undercover officer, but nothing in the record demonstrates, and the trial court did not find, that defendant's sister posed a threat to the officer. People v. Perez, 252 A.D.2d 593, 676 N.Y.S.2d 215 (2d Dept. 1998).

Exclusion of defendant's family members proper.—Court properly closed the courtroom to the defendant's family during the brief testimony of one witness who had indicated at she had seen members of the defendant's family in the courtroom and that she had been threatened by at least one of them. People v. Woods, 156 A.D.2d 609, 549 N.Y.S.2d 116 (2d Dept. 1989).

—Court did not abuse its discretion in excluding defendant's six-year old child from a portion of the trial. People v. Covington, 154 A.D.2d 385, 545 N.Y.S.2d 774 (2d Dept. 1989).

—Defendant's right to public trial was not violated when his mother and aunt were excluded from the courtroom following their disruptive conduct in the jury's presence; court properly exercised its discretion to maintain order and decorum. People v. Cajigas, 288 A.D.2d 51, 733 N.Y.S.2d 8 (1st Dept. 2001).

Exclusion of press at pretrial hearing.—Press was properly excluded from a pretrial hearing on admissibility of evidence in a highly publicized murder case, where the victim was a female New York State Corrections Officer, in order to assure that certain inadmissible evidence would not become known by the jury, thereby denying defendant his right to a fair trial. Poughkeepsie Newspaper, Inc., v. Rosenblatt, as a Justice of the Supreme Court. 61 N.Y.2d 1005, 475 N.Y.S.2d 370, 463 N.E.2d 1005 (1984).

Exclusion of public from trial.—Defendant was denied his right to a public trial where trial court excluded defendant's girlfriend from the courtroom during the testimony of an undercover officer, and when defendant objected to her exclusion, the People offered no evidence that she would be a threat to the officer, nor did the court make findings that the girlfriend would pose a threat to the officer. People v. Gayle, 237 A.D.2d 532, 655 N.Y.S.2d 581 (2d Dept. 1997).

—Trial court's exclusion of defendant's family from the courtroom during the complainant's testimony in a rape trial did not constitute an abuse of discretion; further, the defendant did not request a hearing on the issue and made only a general objection to the court's ruling. People v. Salcedo, 98 A.D.2d 961, 470 N.Y.S.2d 58 (4th Dept. 1983), *cert. denied*, 467 U.S. 1229 (1984).

Pretrial suppression hearing; closure.—To avoid becoming a link in the chain of prejudicial disclosures, the trial court has the power to exclude the public from pretrial suppression hearings at the defendant's request; in so doing the courts should afford interested members of the news media an opportunity to be heard, not in the context of a full evidentiary hearing, but in a preliminary proceeding adequate to determine the magnitude of any genuine public interest; the public interest can be fully satisfied, consonant with constitutional free press guarantees, by affording the media access to transcripts redacted to exclude matters ruled inadmissible during the closed suppression hearing. Gannett Co., Inc. v. De Pasquale, 43 N.Y.2d 370, 401 N.Y.S.2d 756, 372 N.E.2d 544 (1977).

Public trial; exclusion of public during undercover agent's testimony.—A denial of the public trial right requires an affirmative act by the trial court excluding persons from the courtroom, which in effect explicitly overcomes the presumption of openness; the brief and inadvertent continuation of a proper courtroom closing, which was not noticed by any of the participants, did not violate the defendant's right to a public trial. People v. Peterson, 81 N.Y.2d 824, 595 N.Y.S.2d 383, 611 N.E.2d 824 (1993).

—A general objection by defendant's attorney to the People's request to close the courtroom during the testimony of the undercover detective and an informant, but made no request for a hearing, and failed to dispute the People's contention that the witnesses would be in danger if the general public was not excluded the Court did not err in granting closure. People v. Pollock, 50 N.Y.2d 547, 429 N.Y.S.2d 628, 407 N.E.2d 472 (1980).

—While there is no single rule to cover every case, no closing of the court to the public can be tolerated that is not preceded by an inquiry careful enough to assure the court that the defendant's right to a public trial is not being sacrificed for less than compelling reasons; where an appellate court finds that the exclusion was improperly granted a *per se* rule of reversal irrespective of prejudice is the only realistic means to implement this important constitutional guarantee. People v. Jones, 47 N.Y.2d 409, 418 N.Y.S.2d 359, 391 N.E.2d 1335 (1979). *See also* People v. Cuevas, 50 N.Y.2d 1022, 431 N.Y.S.2d 686, 409 N.E.2d 1360 (1980).

—Prosecution's main witness in a prosecution for selling and possessing a dangerous drug was an undercover agent who had purchased the drug from the defendant. During his testimony the public was excluded on grounds that (1) the agent was still operating in the community, (2) other narcotic investigations were pending, and (3) other targets of these investigations were present in the courtroom, thus jeopardizing the agent's life if his identity was exposed. A trial court has discretion to exclude the public when special circumstances are shown warranting the exclusion. The grounds in this case constituted such special circumstance. People v. Hinton, 31 N.Y.2d 71, 334 N.Y.S.2d 885 (1972), *cert. denied,* 410 U.S. 911 (1973).

Closure of courtroom in general.—A witness' anxiety or embarrassment might in appropriate circumstances warrant closure of the courtroom. People v. Mateo, 73 N.Y.2d 928, 539 N.Y.S.2d 727, 536 N.E.2d 1146 (1989).

—A defendant who asserts that his right to a fair trial may be compromised by an open proceeding bears the burden of supporting that contention; he must demonstrate a substantial probability that his right to fair trial will be prejudiced by publicity that closure would prevent and that reasonable alternatives to closure cannot adequately protect the defendant's rights. Associated Press v. Bell, 70 N.Y.2d 32, 517 N.Y.S.2d 444, 510 N.E.2d 313 (1987).

—At a *Hinton* hearing, an overriding law enforcement interest as well as the interests of personal safety may be established by the testimony of the officer that he still has ongoing operations or will be conducting operations in a limited area. People v. Badillo, 207 A.D.2d 742, 616 N.Y.S.2d 619 (1st Dept. 1994).

—Where the People move to deny the public access to the criminal proceedings in order to prevent the disclosure of sensitive information, they must demonstrate a compelling governmental interest necessitating closure. Associated Press v. Owens, 160 A.D.2d 902, 554 N.Y.S.2d 334 (2d Dept. 1990).

—Where the court erroneously closes the courtroom, no showing of prejudice need be demonstrated in order to justify reversal. People v. Thompson, 151 A.D.2d 626, 542 N.Y.S.2d 700 (2d Dept. 1989).

—Reversal was required where court failed to articulate an overriding interest or specific findings sufficient to warrant closing the courtroom; harmless error doctrine is not applicable to errors of that type. People v. Thomas, 130 A.D.2d 692, 515 N.Y.S.2d 615 (2d Dept. 1987).

Closure of courtroom during testimony of complainant in rape case.—Trial court's limited closure of the courtroom during the testimony of the complainant in a rape case did not constitute an abuse of discretion or a denial of defendant's right to a public trial where no spectator was to present at time of closure, none was seeking admittance, the defendant was told that anyone whom he desired to have present would be admitted and the court intended only to limit the "traffic" of courthouse employees who tended to enter the courtroom out of curiosity during such testimony. People v. Glover, 60 N.Y.2d 783, 469 N.Y.S.2d 677, 457 N.E.2d 783 (1983).

—Court properly closed the courtroom during a rape victim's testimony as permitted by the Judiciary Law since the charges involved sordid, demeaning acts and required embarrassing testimony. People v. Pasko, 115 A.D.2d 114, 495 N.Y.S.2d 100 (3d Dept. 1985).

INEFFECTIVE ASSISTANCE OF COUNSEL

Conflict of interest; attorney's acquaintance with prosecution witness.—Where defendant argued that trial court failed to conduct a sufficient inquiry into relationship of defendant's attorney and victim, who had been hired by a third party to perform security duties in connection with an unrelated trial involving defense counsel, defendant did not demonstrate that his attorney's representation was influenced or affected by any prior relationship with the victim and, accordingly, there is no basis to conclude that a conflict of interest "operated on" the defense. People v. Smart, 96 N.Y.2d 793, 726 N.Y.S.2d 343, 750 N.E.2d 45 (2001).

Conflict of interest; defense counsel is former prosecutor.—Defendant argues that the potential for divided loyalties resulting from his counsel's previous duties as a prosecutor impaired his defense. Here there is no evidence that the Public Defender obtained any information about defendant through her prior employment as an Assistant District Attorney that compromised her representation of him. No conflict operated on the conduct of defendant, where the attorney negotiated favorable plea agreements and defendant stated that he was satisfied with the lawyer. People v. Abar, 99 N.Y.2d 406, 757 N.Y.S.2d 219, 786 N.E.2d 1255 (2003), *aff'g,* 290 A.D.2d 592, 736 N.Y.S.2d 155 (3d Dept. 2002).

Conflict of interest; attorney's prior representation of prosecution witness.—Attorney's pretrial, unknowing, concurrent representation of a confidential informant—a key prosecution witness—on unrelated charges, was not a conflict of interest. Here, the representation was not affected by the potential conflict. The grand jury testimony had been given before the attorney began his representation of the informant, and during the attorney's brief pretrial representation of the defendant, he never learned the identity of the informant in defendant's case. People v. Harris, 99 N.Y.2d 202, 753 N.Y.S.2d 437, 783 N.E.2d 502 (2002).

—County Court did not err in failing to inform defendant of the possibility of a conflict of interest based on the fact that his trial counsel had previously represented a prosecution witness, and the court did not err in failing to conduct a *Gomberg* inquiry, where defense counsel's prior representation of the prosecution witness involved an entirely different matter, which ended years before defendant was charged with the crimes at issue. People v. Butts, 254 A.D.2d 823, 680 N.Y.S.2d 761 (4th Dept. 1998).

—Representation by the Legal Aid Society of both the defendant and a prosecution witness, either in the past or at the time of the defendant's trial, did not in itself deprive the defendant of effective representation. People v. Dakin, 199 A.D.2d 407, 605 N.Y.S.2d 108 (2d Dept. 1993).

Conflict of interest; attorney's representation of co-defendants.—Defendant's murder conviction was reversed due to his attorney's conflict of interest where the attorney also represented a co-defendant who had pleaded guilty and the court did not ask the defendant whether he was aware of the potential risk in such joint representation. People v. Ferrer, 99 A.D.2d 459, 471 N.Y.S.2d 290 (1st Dept. 1984).

—Court's failure to conduct *Gomberg* inquiry did not require reversal where defendant failed to demonstrate that defense counsel's alleged conflict of interest affected, operated on, or bore a substantial relation to the conduct of his defense. People v. Lashley, 193 A.D.2d 698, 598 N.Y.S.2d 42 (2d Dept. 1993).

—Joint representation is not per se forbidden, and a plea of guilty will be vacated only where the defendant demonstrates that a significant possibility of a conflict of interest existed bearing a substantial relationship to the conduct of the defense. People v. Fryar, 198 A.D.2d 298, 603 N.Y.S.2d 56 (2d Dept. 1993).

Conflict of interest; inquiries involved. A conflict-based ineffective assistance of counsel claim involves two inquiries: 1) the court must assess whether there were a potential conflict of interest in a defendant's representation; 2) a defendant must show that the conduct of his defense was in fact affected by the operation of the conflict of interest, or that the conflict operated on the representation. People v. Abar, 99 N.Y.2d 406, 757 N.Y.S.2d 219, 786 N.E.2d 1255 (2003), *aff'g,* 290 A.D.2d 592, 736 N.Y.S.2d 155 (3d Dept. 2002).

—In order to prevail on a conflict of interest claim, the defendant must establish that the conduct of his defense was in fact affected by the operation of the conflict of interest. People v. Jordan, 83 N.Y.2d 784, 610 N.Y.S.2d 952, 632 N.E.2d 1275 (1994).

Effective assistance of counsel.—A defense counsel's incorrect advice as to deportation consequences of a plea may constitute ineffective assistance of counsel, but defendant was not deprived of effective assistance where he failed to make the required showing of prejudice due to counsel's incorrect advice, specifically, that he would not have pleaded guilty but for counsel's error. People v. McDonald, 1 N.Y.3d 109, 769 N.Y.S.2d 781, 802 N.E.2d 131 (2003).

—All evidence should be weighed in context and as of the time of complete representation at the trial level for resolving ineffective assistance of counsel claims. People v. Flores, 84 N.Y.2d 184, 615 N.Y.S.2d 662, 639 N.E.2d 19 (1994).

—Except in most unusual circumstances, the State is not charged with the responsibility of guaranteeing effective legal representation upon the entry of counsel at the preaccusatory investigatory stage of a criminal matter, i.e., before the commencement of formal adversarial judicial criminal proceedings. People v. Claudio, 83 N.Y.2d 76, 607 N.Y.S.2d 912, 629 N.E.2d 384 (1994).

—Defense counsel's failure to make a suppression motion prior to negotiating a plea bargain for his client did not constitute ineffective assistance of counsel. People v. Strempack, 71 N.Y.2d 1015, 530 N.Y.S.2d 100, 101, 525 N.E.2d 746 (1988).

—Trial tactics which terminate unsuccessfully do not automatically indicate ineffectiveness of counsel. People v. Rivera, 71 N.Y.2d 705, 530 N.Y.S.2d 52, 525 N.E.2d 698 (1988).

—Where identification testimony was weak, attorney could not be deemed incompetent for failing to call a potential exculpatory witness; the strategy chosen by defense counsel to explore the deficiencies of the evidence of identification through cross-examination of the prosecutor's sole witness rather than to explore and present other evidence of misidentification, was reasonable. People v. Thompson, 69 N.Y.2d 661, 551 N.Y.S.2d 832, 503 N.E.2d 1369 (1987).

—Counsel was not incompetent for advising defendant to plead guilty where he thereby satisfied defendant's primary concern which was to avoid multiple criminal charges and a possible jail sentence. People v. Angelakos, 70 N.Y.2d 670, 518 N.Y.S.2d 784, 512 N.E.2d 305 (1987).

—Attorney's testimony at defendant's two trials was consistent with and strengthened his insanity defense and his unsuccessful trial tactics cannot be said to have provided defendant with ineffective assistance of counsel, as by testifying the attorney was able to introduce into evidence the fact that his client had committed a number of sexual assaults and murders and also that he could not recall making these admissions before a number of witnesses. People v. Baldi, 54 N.Y.2d 137, 444 N.Y.S.2d 893, 429 N.E.2d 400 (1981).

—While several of counsel's strategic decisions may not have proven successful, there was no reason to conclude that counsel's representation of defendant was ineffective. People v. Contreras, 192 A.D.2d 417, 596 N.Y.S.2d 393, 394 (1st Dept. 1993); People v. Gomez, 157 A.D.2d 480, 549 N.Y.S.2d 403 (1st Dept. 1990); People v. Mackey, 155 A.D.2d 297, 547 N.Y.S.2d 213 (1st Dept. 1989) (failure to request a *Sandoval* hearing was not in itself sufficient to warrant reversal).

—What constitutes effective assistance of counsel is not and cannot be fixed with yardstick precision, but varies according to the unique circumstances of each representation. People v. Brunskill, 200 A.D.2d 752, 607 N.Y.S.2d 94 (2d Dept. 1994).

—Merely because the defense counsel's tactics were not successful does not render his representation ineffective. People v. Joseph, 201 A.D.2d 506, 607 N.Y.S.2d 697 (2d Dept. 1994).

—Mere fact that attorney may have been under criminal indictment for a felony while representing the defendant did not lead to a per se conclusion that he was ineffective. People v. Thomas, 201 A.D.2d 687, 608 N.Y.S.2d 251 (2d Dept. 1994).

—Counsel was not ineffective for having failed to file notice of alibi where the record revealed that the defense counsel was not informed by his client of the purported evidence of an alibi witness until after the trial had started. People v. Bradford, 202 A.D.2d 441, 608 N.Y.S.2d 511 (2d Dept. 1994).

—Defense counsel's strategy in focusing on the defendant's claim that he fabricated the attempted robbery story in order to avoid being charged with murder, while ultimately unsuccessful, was diligently pursued and a claim of incompetent counsel was rejected. People v. Lewis, 203 A.D.2d 389, 610 N.Y.S.2d 288 (2d Dept. 1994).

—The imposition of discipline on an attorney previously qualified and in good standing will not and should not transform his services into ineffective assistance; thus, the disbarment of the defendant's trial counsel for misconduct in several unrelated matters three years after the defendant's conviction did not, by itself, constitute ineffective assistance of counsel. People v. Powell, 197 A.D.2d 544, 602 N.Y.S.2d 213 (2d Dept. 1993).

—The mere fact that different attorneys assisted the defendant's case at different times did not render their assistance ineffective. People v. Lopez, 197 A.D.2d 594, 602 N.Y.S.2d 872 (2d Dept. 1993).

—It is not the province of the appellate courts to second-guess whether a course chosen by defendant's counsel was the best trial strategy or even a good one, so long as defendant was afforded meaningful representation. People v. Hunt, 158 A.D.2d 543, 551 N.Y.S.2d 311 (2d Dept. 1990).

—In rejecting claim of ineffective counsel, court noted that since counsel was not the first attorney at the trial to conduct cross-examination or summation, there was little else which could have been adduced or added to the defense presented by the co-defendant's counsel. People v. Bossett, 157 A.D.2d 734, 550 N.Y.S.2d 29 (2d Dept. 1990).

—If there are matters outside the record which would support the defendant's claim of ineffective counsel the proper remedy is a proceeding pursuant to CPL § 440.10. People v. Reyes, 158 A.D.2d 626, 551 N.Y.S.2d 596 (2d Dept. 1990).

—Defendant failed to demonstrate any prejudice or error on part of his counsel based on their alleged hostile relationship, where defendant did not dispute that his attorney made appropriate pretrial motions and negotiated a favorable plea bargain on his behalf and defendant pointed to no specific errors on the part of his counsel. People v. Brooks, 273 A.D.2d 513, 708 N.Y.S.2d 197 (3d Dept. 2000).

—A necessary prerequisite to a finding of ineffectiveness is a showing of actual prejudice. People v. Frascatore, 200 A.D.2d 860, 607 N.Y.S.2d 144 (3d Dept. 1994).

—Notwithstanding counsel's failure to call witnesses to the results of an alleged beating by a police officer after defendant's arrest and before defendant gave a detailed statement to the police, defendant was not denied effective assistance of counsel where the issues concerning the alleged assault were fully explored at the suppression hearing. People v. Walker, 199 A.D.2d 689, 605 N.Y.S.2d 163 (3d Dept. 1993).

—Defense counsel's failure to inquire adequately into the defendant's prior psychiatric history warranted a hearing to determine validity of claim of incompetency of counsel. People v. Miller, 144 A.D.2d 867, 534 N.Y.S.2d 809 (3d Dept. 1988).

—Defendants are not entitled to error-free or perfect representation. People v. Standard, 273 A.D.2d 870, 709 N.Y.S.2d 294 (4th Dept. 2000).

—Although defense counsel's representation of defendant may not have been perfect, perfection is not required. People v. Kroemer, 204 A.D.2d 1017, 613 N.Y.S.2d 304 (4th Dept. 1994).

—The failure of counsel to make a pretrial motion, even one that might be successful, does not per se, constitute ineffective assistance of counsel; to prevail, defendant must demonstrate that there was no legitimate explanation for counsel's failure to make the motion. People v. Stauffer, 202 A.D.2d 1041, 609 N.Y.S.2d 467 (4th Dept. 1994).

—The failure of counsel to request a particular hearing without more does not constitute ineffective counsel. People v. Harris, 163 A.D.2d 898, 558 N.Y.S.2d 770 (4th Dept. 1990).

Effective assistance of counsel; appellate counsel.—The same standard—meaningful representation—that applies to claimed ineffective assistance of trial counsel, applies in assessing the effectiveness of appellate counsel. People v. Stultz, 2 N.Y.3d 277, 778 N.Y.S.2d 431, 810 N.E.2d 883, *reargument denied*, 3 N.Y.3d 702, 785 N.Y.S.2d 29, 818 N.E.2d 671 (2004).

Effective assistance of counsel; defendant voluntarily absent from trial.—A defendant who absents himself from trial may not succeed on appeal by raising counsel's purported ineffectiveness where counsel affirmatively, as a matter of trial strategy, sought to obstruct the trial of his client. People v.

Aiken, 45 N.Y.2d 394, 408 N.Y.S.2d 444, 380 N.E.2d 272 (1978).

Effective assistance of counsel; choice of trial tactics.— Defendant was not denied meaningful representation when his attorney called an alibi witness who failed to account for defendant's whereabouts on the night of the crime; counsel's failed attempt to establish an alibi was at most unsuccessful tactic that cannot be characterized as ineffective assistance. People v. Henry, 95 N.Y.2d 563, 721 N.Y.S.2d 577, 744 N.E.2d 112 (2000).

—Defendant was not deprived of effective assistance of counsel where defense counsel failed to request a lesser included offense as a result of an "all or nothing" tactic in pursuing intoxication defense to negate intent necessary to commit crime; nor was defendant denied effective assistance because counsel did not challenge the defendant's status as a second felony offender where a review of the defendant's challenges indicated that their assertion would have been futile. People v. Lane. 60 N.Y.2d 748, 469 N.Y.S.2d 663, 457 N.E.2d 769 (1983).

Effective assistance of counsel; denial of court interpreter.—Court denied defendant effective assistance of counsel and due process of law where it did not permit the defendant to have a court interpreter seated at counsel table to enable the defendant to converse with counsel and understand the court proceedings. People v. De Armas, 105 A.D.2d 928, 482 N.Y.S.2d 121 (2d Dept. 1984).

Effective assistance of counsel; waiver of.—In cases where defendants have refused self-representation and restricted the participation of counsel, it has been held that the defendants have voluntarily waived the right to the effective assistance of counsel. In this case, because the court directed defense counsel to remain available to assist defendant, defendant was aware at any time that he could change his mind and counsel would mount a defense, rather than refrain from participating in the trial, as defendant had requested. People v. Henriquez, 3 N.Y.3d 210, 785 N.Y.S.2d 384, 818 N.E.2d 1125 (2004).

Ineffective assistance of counsel.—Where defendant's attorney testified adversely to his client at the *Sirois* hearing, he transformed himself from defendant's advocate into his adversary, denying defendant of effective representation. People v. Lewis, 2 N.Y.3d 224, 777 N.Y.S.2d 798, 809 N.E.2d 1106 (2004).

—An attorney who presents a well-grounded but unsuccessful defense will not later be held to have provided ineffective assistance of counsel and thus a defendant will not be entitled to a vacatur on such basis. People v. Taylor, 1 N.Y.3d 174, 770 N.Y.S.2d 711, 802 N.E.2d 1109 (2003).

—Under the unique circumstances of this case, the defendant's right to effective assistance of counsel was compromised when defense counsel stipulated to facts directly contradicting defense witnesses' statements. The Court agreed with defendant's contention that the stipulation transformed his attorney into an adverse witness whose credibility was pitted against his other witnesses. People v. Berroa, 99 N.Y.2d 134, 753 N.Y.S.2d 12, 782 N.E.2d 1148 (2002).

—Among other errors, defendant was deprived of a fair trial by the prosecutor's 31 references to the defendant's highly prejudicial nickname, "Homicide" and was deprived of the effective assistance of counsel insofar as his attorney failed to object to any of these references. People v. Lauderdale, 295 A.D.2d 539, 746 N.Y.S.2d 163 (2d Dept. 2002).

—Defendant was denied effective representation where his attorney initially conceded that defendant shot victim but asserted the defense of justification and then chose in mid-stream to abandon the justification defense and to present an entirely inconsistent and contradictory defense of factual impossibility. People v. Lee, 129 A.D.2d 587, 514 N.Y.S.2d 84 (2d Dept. 1987).

—Defendant received ineffective assistance of counsel in rape case where defense counsel failed to object to the prosecutor's and victim's references to defendant's uncharged sexual assaults upon the victim, failed to request a limiting instruction regarding the jury's consideration of that evidence, and even elicited additional proof regarding those uncharged crimes during his cross-examination of the victim, with no tactical, strategic or other legitimate explanation. People v. Fleegle, 295 A.D.2d 760, 745 N.Y.S.2d 224 (3d Dept. 2002).

—Defendant received ineffective assistance of counsel where counsel's failure to challenge a prior conviction for a sex offense

resulted in defendant's improper sentencing as a second felony offender; this, combined with counsel's erroneous advice concerning the maximum sentence that defendant could receive if convicted of the crimes properly charged, demonstrates patent prejudice, because defendant was prevented from properly assessing the risks associated with proceeding to trial as opposed to concluding with a negotiated plea. People v. Perron, 287 A.D.2d 808, 731 N.Y.S.2d 512 (3d Dept. 2001).

—Defendant was denied meaningful representation, where defense counsel made it clear that defendant's cases were not a priority for him, he filed no motions on her behalf, and consistently requested adjournments, was ill-prepared for hearings and demonstrated an utter lack of proficiency in criminal matters. People v. Laraby, 305 A.D.2d 1121, 762 N.Y.S.2d 456, *subsequent appeal,* 305 A.D.2d 1123, 760 N.Y.S.2d 702 (4th Dept. 2003).

—Defendant was denied effective assistance of counsel on a retrial where defense counsel made no effort to impeach an important witness, never used the record of the prior trial in his cross-examination of any witness and demonstrated an obvious lack of pretrial preparation and a marked unfamiliarity with the earlier proceedings. People v. Riley, 101 A.D.2d 710, 475 N.Y.S.2d 691 (4th Dept. 1984).

Joint representation; conflict of interest.—It was error for trial court not to have inquired of defendant as to his awareness of risks involved in his representation by an attorney who had previously represented the People's chief witness against him; however, defendant is not entitled to a reversal of his conviction since vigorous representation of defendant by counsel failed to demonstrate a conflict of interest or even the significant possibility of a conflict, especially where counsel believed he was released from his obligation of confidentiality in consequence of witness' waiver of attorney-client privilege by his unrestricted cooperation with prosecution. People v. Lombardo, 61 N.Y.2d 97, 472 N.Y.S.2d 589, 460 N.E.2d 1074 (1984).

Joint representation; no conflict of interest.—"A defendant claiming ineffective assistance of counsel must do more than show that defense counsel had a potential conflict of interest. To prevail, defendant must demonstrate that 'the conduct of his defense was in fact affected by the operation of the conflict of interest,' or that the conflict 'operated on' counsel's representation." Defendant failed to make the showing in the instant case. People v. Longtin, 92 N.Y.2d 640, 684 N.Y.S.2d 463, 707 N.E.2d 418 (1998), *cert. denied,* 526 U.S. 1114 (1999).

—Defendant was not denied his constitutional right to effective assistance of counsel because his attorney previously also represented a co-defendant-giving rise to a potential conflict of interest where; following a post-trial hearing, the trial court determined that such prior representation had not affected the attorney's representation of the defendant; a defendant must demonstrate that the conduct of his defense was in fact affected by the operation of the conflict of interest. People v. Allicea, 61 N.Y.2d 23, 471 N.Y.S.2d 68, 459 N.E.2d 177 (1983).

—Defendant was not denied effective assistance of counsel because he and his co-defendant brother were represented by the same attorney at trial where neither an actual conflict of interest nor a significant possibility thereof was demonstrated. People v. Cruz, 101 A.D.2d 841, 475 N.Y.S.2d 502 (2d Dept.), *aff'd,* 63 N.Y.2d 848, 482 N.Y.S.2d 259, 472 N.E.2d 35 (1984).

§ 260.20. Jury trial; defendant's presence at trial.

A defendant must be personally present during the trial of an indictment; provided, however, that a defendant who conducts himself in so disorderly and disruptive a manner that his trial cannot be carried on with him in the courtroom may be removed from the courtroom if, after he has been warned by the court that he will be removed if he continues such conduct, he continues to engage in such conduct.

Amended by L. 1971, Ch. 789.

ANNOTATIONS

Trial in absentia.—Court improperly conducted summations and jury charge in defendant's absence where it failed to conduct an inquiry into the circumstances surrounding the defendant's failure to appear at those junctures. People v. Brooks, 75 N.Y.2d 898, 554 N.Y.S.2d 818, 553 N.E.2d 1328 (1990).

—Though defendant was advised by counsel that pretrial hearings were scheduled to commence on a certain date and the trial thereafter, since he was not informed that the trial and sentencing would proceed in his absence if he failed to appear, he was improperly tried in absentia. People v. Smith, 68 N.Y.2d 725, 506 N.Y.S.2d 318, 497 N.E.2d 685 (1986).

—Defendants who abscond knowing their trial is about to begin or after their trial has begun may be tried and sentenced *in absentia,* whether or not *Parker* warnings have been given, because they have unambiguously waived the right to be present. People v. Sanchez, 65 N.Y.2d 436, 492 N.Y.S.2d 577, 482 N.E.2d 56 (1985).

—Defendant forfeited his right to be present at trial where defendant was present at the time the judge instructed that should the parties run out of witnesses at the pretrial hearing, requiring that the hearing be adjourned, the trial was to begin at that point, or in any event, immediately following the conclusion of the hearing and defendant absconded after the third day of the hearing. People v. Smith, 66 N.Y.2d 755, 497 N.Y.S.2d 363, 488 N.E.2d 109 (1985).

—Defendant was improperly tried and convicted *in absentia* of a misdemeanor without first having been given *Parker* warnings or informed that the trial would proceed in his absence. People v. Trendell, 61 N.Y.2d 728, 472 N.Y.S.2d 616, 460 N.E.2d 1101 (1984).

—Defendant has a right to waive being present at his trial and voluntary participation in a prison boycott of court is a waiver. People v. Epps, 37 N.Y.2d 343, 372 N.Y.S.2d 606, 334 N.E.2d 566 (1975).

—Court properly proceeded in defendant's absence, where it made reasonable efforts to find out if his absence was deliberate, and police had attempted to locate him. People v. Herring, 204 A.D.2d 51, 611 N.Y.S.2d 517 (1st Dept.), *lv. denied,* 84 N.Y.2d 827 (1994).

—Defendant was improperly tried *in absentia* where he was never made aware that a trial could be held in his absence if he failed to appear, and where his conduct did not represent a clear desire not to be present at trial under any circumstances. People v. Martinez, 108 A.D.2d 618, 485 N.Y.S.2d 74 (1st Dept. 1985).

—Court did not abuse discretion by trying defendant *in absentia* and refusing an adjournment on medical grounds where defendant had been warned by the court on the record that if he did not appear for trial in the afternoon the trial would proceed without him and where defendant failed to submit a medical affidavit or other medical documentation justifying an adjournment. People v. Bermudez, 104 A.D.2d 314, 478 N.Y.S.2d 647 (1st Dept. 1984).

—Reversible error was committed where trial judge's highlighting of defendant's absence during the trial shifted the focus of the jury's attention from the issue of guilt or innocence to a question of whether defendant's absence is an indication of guilt. People v. Morales, 83 A.D.2d 804, 441 N.Y.S.2d 686 (1st Dept. 1981).

—Following a hearing relating to the People's efforts to locate the defendant, the trial properly proceeded in defendant's absence; court correctly determined that defendant had voluntarily absented himself from the trial after receiving *Parker* warnings and signing a statement embodying *Parker* warnings. People v. Cajigas, 240 A.D.2d 755, 660 N.Y.S.2d 28 (2d Dept. 1997).

—Defendant forfeited his right to be present at a pretrial *Rodriguez* independent source hearing, since, although he was present in the courtroom, he deliberately absented himself from the proceeding. People v. Griffin, 224 A.D.2d 957, 637 N.Y.S.2d 861 (2d Dept. 1996).

—Court properly took verdict in defendant's absence, where it was clear that he deliberately absconded from that proceeding. People v. Febo, 210 A.D.2d 251, 619 N.Y.S.2d 340 (2d Dept. 1994), *lv. denied,* 85 N.Y.2d 972 (1995).

—Court should not have tried defendant *in absentia,* where he had received *Parker* warnings a year earlier, had always appeared before, his parents believed he was on his way to court, and he actually appeared within 20 minutes of the trial's commencement, explaining he had transportation problems. People v. Smiley, 200 A.D.2d 777, 607 N.Y.S.2d 101 (2d Dept. 1994).

—Defendant was not denied his right to be present at trial because his request for a one-day adjournment for health reasons was denied; defendant's ailment did not prevent him from being present, but merely required him to avoid strenuous activity. People v. Medina-Hernandez, 205 A.D.2d 643, 613 N.Y.S.2d 228 (2d Dept.), *lv. denied,* 84 N.Y.2d 870 (1994).

—Court committed reversible error when it commenced trial in defendant's absence, despite being informed by counsel that the defendant would be late because he was waiting to be picked up by his witness. People v. Ramos, 207 A.D.2d 810, 616 N.Y.S.2d 400 (2d Dept. 1994).

—Where a defendant is absent during a material stage of his trial, the harmless error analysis is inapplicable. People v. Jones, 159 A.D.2d 644, 553 N.Y.S.2d 37 (2d Dept. 1990).

—Court properly tried defendant *in absentia,* where he had been given Parker warnings and after hearing was held which showed that reasonable efforts had been made to find defendant. People v. Bryan, 158 A.D.2d 530, 551 N.Y.S.2d 296 (2d Dept.), *lv. denied,* 76 N.Y.2d 731 (1990).

—Defendant was properly tried in absentia where nearly two months prior to the commencement of pretrial hearings, and over two months prior to the commencement of the trial, he was explicitly warned that the trial would proceed in his absence should he fail to appear. People v. Vasquez, 127 A.D.2d 716, 511 N.Y.S.2d 909 (2d Dept.), *lv. denied,* 69 N.Y.2d 956 (1987).

—Where a defendant informs the court that he will be temporarily absent for a particular aspect of the trial and has a justifiable excuse for such absence, the court is best advised to delay the proceeding until the defendant arrives in the courtroom. People v. Windley, 134 A.D.2d 386, 520 N.Y.S.2d 864 (2d Dept. 1987).

—Trial court quite reasonably continued trial in defendant's absence when defendant could not be located through a check of at least 18 hospitals and the police departments of Nassau and Suffolk Counties and New York City; court properly rejected defendant's claim that he had been hospitalized where a hospital record neither referred to defendant's name nor contained other descriptive matter relating to defendant and where the dates contained therein did not coincide with the trial dates. People v. Satchell, 116 A.D.2d 753, 497 N.Y.S.2d 941 (2d Dept.), *lv. denied,* 67 N.Y.2d 889 (1986).

—Defendant was properly tried *in absentia,* despite the failure to give *Parker* warnings, where he absconded prior to the commencement of pretrial proceedings in a multiple-defendant trial under circumstances where it was unlikely that he could have been located within a reasonable period of time and there would have been "enormous difficulties" in rescheduling the trial. People v. Smith, 106 A.D.2d 670, 483 N.Y.S.2d 437 (2d Dept. 1984).

—Where defendant was warned about the consequences of his failure to appear for trial and defense counsel was advised that defendant's trial could occur on 24 hours' notice, court found that defendant impliedly waived his right to be present during jury selection when he voluntarily decided to travel to Florida; however, the record does not demonstrate that the County Court considered any of the appropriate factors, such as the possibility that defendant could be located within a reasonable period of time, nor did it indicate the court's reason for proceeding with jury selection despite being informed that defendant was en route and would appear shortly; court's conduct was reversible error. People v. Lamb, 235 A.D.2d 829, 653 N.Y.S.2d 395 (3d Dept. 1997).

—Defendant willfully absented himself from court in an effort to delay his trial and by doing so forfeited his constitutional right to be present at trial. People v. Phoenix, 197 A.D.2d 755, 602 N.Y.S.2d 734 (3d Dept. 1993).

—Court did not err in conducting trial *in absentia* where the defendant was unequivocally instructed that the trial would proceed if he failed to appear; defendant's non-appearance on the day of trial constituted a waiver of the defendant's right to be present. People v. Daley, 207 A.D.2d 1000, 617 N.Y.S.2d 68 (4th Dept. 1994).

—Court rejected defendant's claim that his waiver of his right to be present was not voluntary because the court had denied his motion for an adjournment for 30 days to retain new counsel; defendant's remedy is to correct any perceived erroneous ruling by appealing and not by withdrawing from the trial. People v. Porter, 201 A.D.2d 881, 607 N.Y.S.2d 796 (4th Dept. 1994).

—A waiver of the right to be present at sentencing is effectuated where a defendant is advised that he will be sentenced in the event of his failure to appear and his failure to appear is deliberate. People v. Robinson, 181 A.D.2d 983, 582 N.Y.S.2d 305 (4th Dept. 1992).

—Where the defendant absconds before the trial date has been set after repeatedly being given the *Parker* warnings, the failure to actually notify the defendant of the date that her trial is to begin does not constitute a deprivation of the right to be present at trial. People v. Badia-Almonte, 188 A.D.2d 1001, 592 N.Y.S.2d 157 (4th Dept. 1992), *lv. denied,* 81 N.Y.2d 1069 (1993).

—Since the record failed to establish that defendant was advised of the date of trial, it was error to try the defendant *in absentia.* People v. Draper, 154 A.D.2d 882, 546 N.Y.S.2d 47 (4th Dept. 1989).

Right to be present; general.—A defendant in a criminal trial who has exercised the right to self-representation may not be arbitrarily and categorically excluded from sidebar conferences. People v. Rosen, 81 N.Y.2d 237, 597 N.Y.S.2d 914, 613 N.E.2d 946 (1993).

—A *de minimis* violation of the absolute right to be present at trial would not necessarily result in reversal. People v. Morales, 80 N.Y.2d 450, 591 N.Y.S.2d 825 (1992).

—A defendant has a fundamental constitutional right to be present at all material stages of a trial People v. Mehmedi, 69 N.Y.2d 759, 760, 513 N.Y.S.2d 100, 505 N.E.2d 610 (1987); People v. Lamour, 189 A.D.2d 825, 592 N.Y.S.2d 451 (2d Dept.), *lv. denied,* 81 N.Y.2d 973 (1993).

—A reconstruction hearing was warranted because the record did not reveal whether the defendant was absent or effectively denied the opportunity to provide input regarding his attorney's discretionary decision to excuse certain jurors; colloquy revealed an ambiguity as to the validity and scope of defendant's waiver of the right to be present at sidebar discussions. People v. Bennett, 238 A.D.2d 138, 655 N.Y.S.2d 509 (1st Dept. 1997).

Right to be present; waiver.—A defendant has a right to waive his or her right to be present at any material stage of the proceedings. People v. Epps, 37 N.Y.2d 343, 372 N.Y.S.2d 606, 334 N.E.2d 566 (1975), *cert. denied,* 423 U.S. 999.

—Court did not violate defendant Hoyt's right to the free exercise of his religion and did not force him to choose between that right and his right to be present at trial where the case was charged on a Thursday and the court properly refused to suspend deliberations until the following Monday so that defendant could attend religious services on Friday. Court had a compelling interest in completing trial without a three-day hiatus in deliberations, and court offered to make a reasonable effort to arrange for defendant to attend services near the court house if he came on Friday. Defendant chose not to come and court gave an appropriate instruction concerning his absence. People v. Hall, 2 A.D.3d 227, 769 N.Y.S.2d 28 (1st Dept. 2003).

—Defendant voluntarily waived right to be present at trial and to confront witness against him where, after being fully advised that the trial could proceed without him, he informed assigned counsel and court that he did not wish to remain, notwithstanding fact that appellant's claims were based on dissatisfaction with assigned counsel and that he was never advised that he could preserve this objection for review without absenting himself. People v. Johnson, 45 A.D.2d 1030, 357 N.Y.S.2d 892 (2d Dept. 1974), *aff'd,* 37 N.Y.2d 778, 375 N.Y.S.2d 97, 337 N.E.2d 605 (1975).

—Court did not deprive defendant of right to be present when it commenced a second felony offender hearing in his absence where defendant ratified the acts of his attorney performed during his absence and thereby waived his right to be present throughout the proceedings. People v. Lawson, 162 A.D.2d 962, 557 N.Y.S.2d 779 (4th Dept. 1990).

Right to be present; audibility hearing.—The trial judge did not exclude defendant from a material stage of the trial when he listened to a videotape, outside defendant's presence, to determine audibility, despite defendant's subsequent objection to audibility; because no arguments were heard at that juncture. Under the circumstances, defendant's presence would have been useless or the benefit but a shadow. People v. Rivera, 94 N.Y.2d 908, 707 N.Y.S.2d 620, 729 N.E.2d 339 (2000).

Right to be absent.—A defendant has the right to waive

his presence at a *Wade* hearing. People v. Foster, 205 A.D.2d 313, 612 N.Y.S.2d 414 (1st Dept. 1994).

—Defendant did not have the right to absent himself from the defense table during the complainant's testimony of his observations after the robbery, since he was not expected to identify defendant and, in any event, there was no real identification issue at trial. People v. Jackson, 190 A.D.2d 533, 593 N.Y.S.2d 216 (1st Dept.), *lv. denied,* 81 N.Y.2d 1015 (1993).

—Defendant was properly denied the right to absent himself from the defense table during the complainant's testimony, where his identification was never cast into doubt. People v. Hardy, 180 A.D.2d 447, 588 N.Y.S.2d 290 (1st Dept. 1992), *lv. denied,* 81 N.Y.2d 789 (1993).

—The suppression court acted improperly in denying the request by the defendant, as well as that of the co-defendant, to absent themselves from the courtroom during the witness's identification testimony. People v. Rayford, 158 A.D.2d 482, 551 N.Y.S.2d 257 (2d Dept. 1990).

—Although a defendant may waive his presence at trial, the People nevertheless have the right to require his presence for the purpose of identification by its witnesses. People v. Jackson, 135 A.D.2d 831, 522 N.Y.S.2d 675 (2d Dept. 1987).

Right to be present; pretrial hearings.—Defendant had the right to be present at a *Ventimiglia* hearing to determine whether the People could use his prior bad acts against him on their direct case; however, his attorney's request that defendant's presence be waived, made in defendant's presence, was sufficient to waive his right to be present. People v. Spotford, 85 N.Y.2d 593, 627 N.Y.S.2d 295, 650 N.E.2d 1296 (1995).

—An audibility hearing is an ancillary proceeding where the court is determining admissibility on a preliminary basis, and the nature of the determination usually involves no witness, and thus, it does not require the defendant's presence. People v. Rivera, 257 A.D.2d 172, 691 N.Y.S.2d 4 (1st Dept. 1999), *aff'd,* 94 N.Y.2d 908, 707 N.Y.S.2d 620, 729 N.E.2d 339 (2000).

—Defendant waived his right to be present at the suppression hearing; that the defendant expressed his choice through trial counsel did not render the waiver invalid. People v. Underwood, 201 A.D.2d 597, 607 N.Y.S.2d 955 (2d Dept.), *lv. denied,* 83 N.Y.2d 1008 (1994).

—Defendant did not have the right to attend a hearing concerning the identification of a co-defendant. People v. Keller, 215 A.D.2d 502, 626 N.Y.S.2d 822 (2d Dept. 1995).

—Defendant did not have the right to attend a *Wade* hearing which solely involved the co-defendant. People v. Morris, 187 A.D.2d 460, 590 N.Y.S.2d 104 (2d Dept. 1992).

—A defendant has a right to be present at all material stages of his trial including pretrial hearings. People v. Whitehead, 143 A.D.2d 1066, 533 N.Y.S.2d 753 (2d Dept. 1988), *lv. denied,* 75 N.Y.2d 777 (1990).

—Defendant did not have the right to attend a hearing on the prosecutor's motion to consolidate indictments. People v. Ortiz, 202 A.D.2d 860, 609 N.Y.S.2d 688 (3d Dept.), *lv. denied,* 83 N.Y.2d 970 (1994).

—Defendant's presence at the argument of the omnibus motion was not required because it involved only questions of law. People v. Shawcross, 192 A.D.2d 1128, 596 N.Y.S.2d 622 (4th Dept. 1993).

Right to be present; *Sandoval* hearings.—Defendant's right to be present was violated if he was absent from a "preliminary informal *Sandoval* hearing," at which a factual discussion of his prior arrests and convictions took place; the case was remanded for a hearing to determine whether or not he was present. People v. Monclavo, 87 N.Y.2d 1029, 643 N.Y.S.2d 470, 666 N.E.2d 175 (1996).

—Where the record was unclear as to whether defendant was present, either at a pretrial *in camera Sandoval* hearing at which a *Sandoval* compromise was reached with respect to one conviction, or at the reopened *Sandoval* hearing at trial, shortly before he was to testify, where the court decided to admit two other prior convictions, the case would be remanded for a reconstruction hearing. Since the outcome at neither stage was "wholly favorable" to defendant, he had a right to be present at both. People v. Michalek, 82 N.Y.2d 906, 609 N.Y.S.2d 172, 631 N.E.2d 114 (1994).

—Except in circumstances where the nature of the defendant's criminal history and the issues to be resolved at the *Sandoval* hearing render the defendant's presence superfluous, the hearing should not be conducted without the presence of the accused. People v. Odiat, 82 N.Y.2d 872, 609 N.Y.S.2d 166, 609 N.E.2d 166 (1993).

—A defendant has a right to be present during a *Sandoval* hearing, except where the outcome of the proceeding from which he was excluded was "wholly favorable" to him, and where the surrounding circumstances negate the possibility that he might have made a meaningful contribution to the colloquy. The remedy in cases involving a denial of the defendant's right to be present at a *Sandoval* hearing is a new trial rather than a new *Sandoval* hearing. A defendant's absence from the *Sandoval* hearing is not remedied by the trial court's reciting the gist of its *Sandoval* decision in defendant's presence. People v. Favor, 82 N.Y.2d 254, 604 N.Y.S.2d 494, 624 N.E.2d 631, *reargument denied,* 83 N.Y.2d 801 (1993).

—The ruling in *Dokes* requiring a defendant's presence at a *Sandoval* hearing is retroactive. People v. Favor, 82 N.Y.2d 254, 604 N.Y.S.2d 494, 624 N.E.2d 631, *reargument denied,* 83 N.Y.2d 801 (1993).

—Issue concerning defendant's absence from the *Sandoval* hearing was reviewable despite defendant's failure to object. People v. Gebrosky, 80 N.Y.2d 995, 592 N.Y.S.2d 650, 607 N.E.2d 797 (1992).

—Defendant's absence from the *Sandoval* hearing required reversal. People v. Beasley, 80 N.Y.2d 981, 592 N.Y.S.2d 644, 645, 607 N.E.2d 791 (1992), *reargument denied,* 81 N.Y.2d 759 (1993).

—A *Sandoval* hearing is a material stage of the trial at which the defendant's presence is required. People v. Dokes, 79 N.Y.2d 656, 584 N.Y.S.2d 761, 595 N.E.2d 836 (1992).

—Defendant was not prejudiced by his absence from a portion of a *Sandoval* proceeding, where the only issues resolved with finality were resolved in defendant's favor. People v. Ford, 205 A.D.2d 310, 612 N.Y.S.2d 575 (1st Dept. 1994).

—Defendant's presence was not required at the conference at which matters preparatory to the *Sandoval* hearing were discussed; the points discussed were repeated for the defendant upon her belated arrival in court, after which a de novo determination was made concerning the few prior bad acts into which inquiry had not been previously prohibited at the preparatory conference. People v. Allen-Collins, 207 A.D.2d 725, 616 N.Y.S.2d 597 (1st Dept.), *lv. denied,* 84 N.Y.2d 1008 (1994).

—Although the Spanish-speaking defendant attended his *Sandoval* hearing without the benefit of an interpreter, where the court ruled that no inquiry whatsoever would be allowed into the sole incident proffered by the People, the defendant's effective participation in the *Sandoval* hearing would have been superfluous. People v. Almanzar, 188 A.D.2d 654, 591 N.Y.S.2d 847 (2d Dept. 1992), *lv. denied,* 81 N.Y.2d 881 (1993).

—Where the court's in chambers *Sandoval* ruling was not entirely favorable, defendant's absence from that conference cannot be viewed as wholly superfluous. People v. Taylor, 201 A.D.2d 905, 607 N.Y.S.2d 806 (4th Dept. 1994).

—Reversal required due to defendant's absence from *Sandoval* hearing, where the court's ruling was not wholly favorable to the defendant. People v. Mitchell, 204 A.D.2d 1014, 613 N.Y.S.2d 83 (4th Dept. 1994).

Right to be present; proceedings on matters of law.—A defendant does not have a right to be present at a colloquy between the court and the attorneys regarding counsel's intent to present defendant's testimony in the narrative because this type of colloquy involves procedural matters, about which a defendant can offer no meaningful input. People v. Andrades, 4 N.Y.3d 355, 795 N.Y.S.2d 497, 828 N.E.2d 599 (2005).

—Defendant contends that by delivering an instruction through the verdict sheet, rather than recharging the jury in his presence, court violated defendant's right to be present during a material stage of the trial. Defendant's presence was not necessary because it involved purely legal argument to which defendant had nothing to contribute. People v. Collins, 99 N.Y.2d 14, 750 N.Y.S.2d 814, 780 N.E.2d 499 (2002)

—Defendant's presence was not required at a sidebar conference held outside his earshot to determine whether his direct testimony had "opened the door" to cross-examination about the underlying facts of a prior conviction which had been precluded under the court's *Sandoval* ruling. People v. Rodriguez, 85 N.Y.2d 586, 627 N.Y.S.2d 292, 650 N.E.2d 1293 (1995).

—Defendant's presence was not required at an appearance where defense counsel declined to controvert a finding that defendant was competent to stand trial. People v. Williams, 85 N.Y.2d 945, 626 N.Y.S.2d 1002, 650 N.E.2d 849 (1995).

—Defendant's absence and that of his attorney from a hearing conducted by the trial court, outside the presence of the jury, relating solely to the scope of defendant's telephone privileges did not violate defendant's right to be present. People v. Blair, 173 A.D.2d 172, 569 N.Y.S.2d 77 (1st Dept. 1991).

—Defendant was not prejudiced when the indictment was amended in his absence. People v. Martino, 161 A.D.2d 102, 554 N.Y.S.2d 838 (1st Dept. 1990).

—Defendant's absence from a conference involving the scope of cross-examination of one of the complainants did not constitute a denial of his right to be present at trial; a defendant has no right under CPL 260.20 or the federal due process clause to be present at sidebar conferences concerning only matters of law or procedure. People v. Page, 240 A.D.2d 765, 660 N.Y.S.2d 47 (2d Dept. 1997).

—New trial ordered where, outside of defendant's presence, the court, the prosecutor, and defense counsel discussed which portions of tape-recorded conversations between defendant and confidential informant would be redacted; the redaction did not involve purely legal issues. Since the defendant could have contributed to the proceeding and assisted in his own defense, he had a right to be present. People v. Tellier, 232 A.D.2d 509, 648 N.Y.S.2d 659 (2d Dept. 1996).

—Defendant did not have the right to attend a hearing on the prosecutor's motion to consolidate indictments. People v. Ortiz, 202 A.D.2d 860, 609 N.Y.S.2d 688 (3d Dept.), *lv. denied,* 83 N.Y.2d 970 (1994).

—Defendant's absence from conferences involving matters of law or procedure did not violate his right to be present. People v. Haley, 195 A.D.2d 873, 600 N.Y.S.2d 842 (3d Dept. 1993).

—Because only questions of law or procedure were involved during a particular hearing and defendant's absence did not in any way affect his ability to defend himself against the charges, he had no right to be physically present during that proceeding. People v. Deets, 188 A.D.2d 889, 591 N.Y.S.2d 879 (3d Dept. 1992).

—Defendant's presence at the argument of the omnibus motion was not required because argument involved only questions of law. People v. Shawcross, 192 A.D.2d 1128, 596 N.Y.S.2d 622 (4th Dept. 1993).

Right to be present; jury selection.—A CPL § 260.20 violation is not overcome merely because the venire person who was interviewed outside the defendant's presence was not seated on the jury. When a prospective juror is disqualified by the court for cause, defendant's absence from that hearing does not require reversal. When a prospective juror is peremptorily challenged by the People, defendant's absence from that hearing does not require reversal. Where the record does not negate the possibility that defendant could have provided input on his counsel's apparently discretionary choice to excuse venire persons, his exclusion from sidebar conferences with those jurors requires reversal. People v. Feliciano, 88 N.Y.2d 18, 643 N.Y.S.2d 10, 665 N.E.2d 1050 (1996).

—Defendant's right to be present is not violated by his absence from sidebar questioning of a prospective juror on ministerial matters, such as availability for jury service. The court's decision in People v. Sloan concerning the right to be present at voir dire sidebars did not apply retroactively. People v. Sprowal, 84 N.Y.2d 113, 615 N.Y.S.2d 328, 638 N.E.2d 973 (1994).

—Judgment reversed, where the County Court discharged a sworn juror in defendant's absence, because jury selection had not been completed, and the court's inquiry into the disqualification of the juror was still part of the formal impaneling of the jury. People v. Tucker, 256 A.D.2d 1019, 683 N.Y.S.2d 315 (3d Dept. 1998).

Antommarchi.—Court declined to speculate that the court reporter's failure to note defendant's presence at the challenged robing room conference, coupled with occasional references to his presence in other portions of the transcript, demonstrates that he must have been absent from the ancillary proceeding at issue. Defendant failed to meet his burden of rebutting the presumption of regularity. People v. Velasquez, 1 N.Y.3d 44, 769 N.Y.S.2d 156, 801 N.E.2d 376 (2003).

—At close of bench conference, counsel said "waived" to which the court immediately responded "Antommarchi." The better practice would have been to state the substance of the right being waived, but nothing in the record calls into question the effectiveness of defendant's waiver as announced by counsel, because the waiver occurred in open court in defendant's presence. People v. Velasquez, 1 N.Y.3d 44, 769 N.Y.S.2d 156, 801 N.E.2d 376 (2003).

—Record does not support defendant's contention that he was absent at the time counsel waived his *Antommarchi* rights, where the waiver occurred in open court after the trial judge had articulated the substance of the *Antommarchi* right, and neither defendant nor his counsel objected to his absence at sidebar colloquies during the three-day voir dire. Furthermore, defendant was not denied the right to be present at the ex parte conferences, which were held solely at the behest of the defense. Moreover, the People were excluded and not even furnished with a transcript, and the conferences involved procedural matters. People v. Keen, 94 N.Y.2d 533, 707 N.Y.S.2d 380, 728 N.E.2d 979 (2000).

—Defendants are entitled to hear questions intended to search out a prospective juror's bias, hostility or predisposition to believe or discredit the testimony of potential witnesses, and the venireperson's answers so that they have the opportunity to assess the juror's "facial expressions, demeanor and other subliminal responses." People v. Antommarchi, 80 N.Y.2d 247, 590 N.Y.S.2d 33, 604 N.E.2d 95 (1992).

—The rule of *People v. Antommarchi* should be applied prospectively only. People v. Mitchell, 80 N.Y.2d 519, 591 N.Y.S.2d 990, 606 N.E.2d 1301 (1992).

—A defendant has a right to hear and be present during a conference concerning issues such as jurors' knowledge of, and reaction to, pretrial publicity concerning the specific crime on trial and their attitude toward the prosecution's key witness. People v. Sloan, 79 N.Y.2d 386, 583 N.Y.S.2d 176, 592 N.E.2d 784 (1992).

—The record did not bear out defendant's claim that his right to be present at all material stages of his trial was infringed by the exercise of some challenges to jurors at a side-bar conference, there being no indication that defendant's position at the defense table prevented him from hearing the proceeding or conferring with his counsel throughout. People v. Walker, 202 A.D.2d 312, 609 N.Y.S.2d 201 (1st Dept. 1994).

—Because the two prospective jurors who were questioned in the defendant's absence were excused from the panel, no prejudice resulted from his absence. People v. Rodriguez, 203 A.D.2d 92, 610 N.Y.S.2d 217 (1st Dept. 1994).

—Since no jurors who were spoken with at sidebars that the defendant did not attend were selected to sit on the jury, there was no violation of the right to be present. People v. Shabani, 203 A.D.2d 142, 611 N.Y.S.2d 2 (1st Dept. 1994).

—The presence of neither defendant nor counsel was required at sidebar discussions where the trial court posed questions to unsworn prospective jurors relating solely to the qualification, in a general sense, of those individuals to sit as jurors, matters which are solely for the court. People v. Kirkland, 199 A.D.2d 54, 605 N.Y.S.2d 27 (1st Dept. 1993).

—Because record failed to disclose the subject matter of the sidebar conferences, meaningful appellate review of the issue was precluded. People v. Rodriguez, 240 A.D.2d 768, 660 N.Y.S.2d 30 (2d Dept. 1997).

—Where court, in at least one instance, dismissed a prospective juror after a private discussion without permitting any inquiry into the reasons for this action, the record supported defendant's contention that he was deprived of his statutory right to be present at sidebar discussions during jury selection. People v. Cherry, 237 A.D.2d 296, 654 N.Y.S.2d 800 (2d Dept. 1997).

—Defendant was not denied his right to be present when he was excluded when counsel exercised their challenges to the jury in chambers; while defendant was not present when the challenges were discussed, he was present during the entire voir dire and was present when the challenges were given effect, because the challenged jurors were excused and others were sworn in open court. People v. Evans, 207 A.D.2d 500, 615 N.Y.S.2d 914 (2d Dept.), *lv. denied,* 84 N.Y.2d 1031 (1994).

—The trial court's questioning, at a sidebar, of some prospective jurors concerning their ability to weigh evidence objectively and impartially, in the defendant's absence, did not require reversal since the conviction predated People v. Antommarchi. People v. McLamb, 196 A.D.2d 556, 600 N.Y.S.2d 766 (2d Dept. 1993), *lv. denied,* 85 N.Y.2d 911 (1994).

—Having failed to raise the claim that the court conducted a voir dire of potential jurors in his absence prior to his guilty plea, the defendant waived his right of review of that issue. People v. Bourdonnay, 160 A.D.2d 1014, 555 N.Y.S.2d 134 (2d Dept. 1990).

—Court rejected defendant's contention that his statutory right to be present at all material stages of his trial was violated by his absence from four sidebar conferences with individual prospective jurors; as set forth in *People v. Roman,* 88 N.Y.2d 18, 643 N.Y.S.2d 10, 665 N.E.2d 1050, a defendant's absence from a sidebar involving a prospective juror where the juror is ultimately peremptorily challenged by the People does not require reversal. People v. Thompson, 233 A.D.2d 755, 650 N.Y.S.2d 825 (3d Dept. 1996).

—Because the court's inquiry of jurors touched on matters of juror bias and prejudice, it was improper to conduct the discussions with neither defendant nor his attorney being present. People v. Wilson, 199 A.D.2d 631, 605 N.Y.S.2d 131 (3d Dept. 1993).

—Because prospective jurors were excused by the court for cause after a discussion in chambers, defendant was not denied the right to be present at a material stage of the trial. People v. McDermott, 244 A.D.2d 918, 665 N.Y.S.2d 187 (4th Dept. 1997).

—Court was not under an obligation, before accepting defendant's waiver of his right to be present at sidebars with prospective jurors, to recite the reasons for defendant's right to be present. People v. Howard, 206 A.D.2d 844, 616 N.Y.S.2d 122 (4th Dept. 1994).

—Where defendant did not object to court's conducting a portion of the voir dire at the bench in his absence, and where the defendant indicated that he waived his right to be present at the bench when questioned by the court, the error was not preserved for appellate review. People v. Dunlap, 161 A.D.2d 1114, 555 N.Y.S.2d 492 (4th Dept. 1990).

Right to be present; witness examination.—Defendant did not have the right to be present at a hearing to determine a child's competency to testify. People v. Morales, 80 N.Y.2d 450, 591 N.Y.S.2d 825, 606 N.E.2d 953 (1992).

—Reversal was required where court conducted inquiry with undercover officer concerning the latter's refusal to disclose the identify of the confidential informant, and such inquiry was conducted without the presence, knowledge or consent of either party or counsel. People v. Ortega, 78 N.Y.2d 1101, 578 N.Y.S.2d 123, 585 N.E.2d 372 (1991).

—Ex parte examination of prosecution identification witness to determine whether he had been tampered with was error, but harmless, where the witness did not identify defendant in court. People v. Mendez, 208 A.D.2d 358, 617 N.Y.S.2d 5 (1st Dept. 1994).

—Defendant was not deprived of his right to be present by his exclusion from a hearing to determine whether a prospective witness had been unduly influenced by what he had heard of another witness' testimony. People v. Yarborough, 184 A.D.2d 394, 585 N.Y.S.2d 372 (1st Dept.), *lv. denied,* 80 N.Y.2d 935 (1992).

Right to be present; questioning sworn jurors, juror removal.—Defendant was not deprived by his right to be present where trial court questioned juror in defendant's absence, juror said that defendant looked like someone she knew and might be related to that person, juror was dismissed with defense counsel's consent. People v. Torres, 80 N.Y.2d 944, 590 N.Y.S.2d 867, 605 N.E.2d 354 (1992), *reargument denied,* 81 N.Y.2d 784 (1993).

—The in-chambers questioning of a seated juror for possible disqualification to serve, which was conducted by the Trial Judge in the presence of the prosecutor and defense counsel but in the absence of the defendant, did not violate CPL § 260.20 or due process. People v. Mullen, 44 N.Y.2d 1, 403 N.Y.S.2d 470, 374 N.E.2d 369 (1978).

—Not every communication with a deliberating juror requires the participation of the court or the presence of the defendant. People v. Guadalupe, 202 A.D.2d 334, 610 N.Y.S.2d 1 (1st Dept. 1994).

—Defendant's absence during the trial court's questioning of a deliberating juror who sought to be excused because of illness did not deprive defendant of his right to be present, where defense counsel was present and there was no prejudice to defendant. People v. Johnson, 205 A.D.2d 375, 613 N.Y.S.2d 381 (1st Dept.), lv. denied, 84 N.Y.2d 868 (1994).

—Defendant's absence during the trial court's questioning of a deliberating juror to determine whether the juror was qualified to continue service, in the presence of defense counsel, who contributed his views and specifically stated his agreement with the court's determination that the juror was so qualified, did not deprive the defendant of his right to be present at a material stage of his trial. People v. Maldonado, 192 A.D.2d 381, 596 N.Y.S.2d 44 (1st Dept.), lv. denied, 81 N.Y.2d 1076 (1993).

—A defendant's presence is not required at hearings conducted in connection with juror misconduct, provided that defense counsel's presence ensures that defendant receives a fair and just hearing. People v. Hayes, 191 A.D.2d 368, 595 N.Y.S.2d 409 (1st Dept. 1993).

—The dismissal of two alternates jurors after the commencement of deliberations outside the presence of defendant and counsel did not require reversal, particularly since the regular jury was able to reach a verdict without recourse to the alternates. People v. Melendez, 173 A.D.2d 168, 569 N.Y.S.2d 23 (1st Dept. 1991).

—Defendant's absence from sidebar with juror did not require reversal where the juror was properly dismissed for cause. People v. Mills, 200 A.D.2d 771, 607 N.Y.S.2d 124 (2d Dept.), lv. denied, 83 N.Y.2d 855 (1994).

—Defendant's absence from in camera questioning of a juror who had just been mugged, resulting in her dismissal on consent did not deprive him of a fair trial. People v. Dewese, 198 A.D.2d 430, 604 N.Y.S.2d 575 (2d Dept. 1993), lv. denied, 83 N.Y.2d 804 (1994).

—The defendant's contention that his conviction should be reversed because a juror was questioned in his absence was not preserved for appellate review since no objection was made to the questioning of the juror in his absence. People v. Rodriguez, 180 A.D.2d 831, 580 N.Y.S.2d 448 (2d Dept. 1992).

—A sidebar conference with a juror is not a material stage of the trial at which a defendant has a right to be present. People v. Jack, 199 A.D.2d 980, 606 N.Y.S.2d 471 (4th Dept.), lv. denied, 83 N.Y.2d 854 (1994).

—Absence of defendant and counsel when court questioned four female jurors to ascertain the nature of a conversation that had occurred among those jurors and an alternate juror, who was later removed, did not require reversal. People v. Boatman, 147 A.D.2d 912, 537 N.Y.S.2d 693 (4th Dept. 1989), appeal withdrawn, 76 N.Y.2d 846 (1990).

Right to be present; charge conferences.—Defendant's absence from the pre-charge and post-charge conferences without objection was not error as it did not deprive defendant of his constitutional and statutory right to be present at all material stages of the criminal proceedings. People v. Torres, 171 A.D.2d 425, 567 N.Y.S.2d 5 (1st Dept. 1991).

—Defendant's absence from the charge conference was not a material stage of the trial at which defendant's absence without objection affected any substantial right of defendant, or bore any reasonable substantial relation to defendant's relation to defendant's opportunity to defend against the charges. People v. Davis, 172 A.D.2d 273, 568 N.Y.S.2d 95 (1st Dept. 1991).

—Defendant has no right to be present during either pre-charge conferences dealing with legal issues. People v. Peters, 175 A.D.2d 220, 572 N.Y.S.2d 81 (2d Dept.), lv. denied, 78 N.Y.2d 1014, 575 N.Y.S.2d 822, 581 N.E.2d 1068 (1991).

—Defendant's absence from a pre-charge conference did not deprive him of his right to be present. People v. GoPaul, 171 A.D.2d 754, 567 N.Y.S.2d 487 (2d Dept.), lv. denied, 78 N.Y.2d 966, 574 N.Y.S.2d 946, 580 N.E.2d 418 (1991).

Right to be present; ex parte communication.—Court rejected defendant's claim that his right to be present during a material stage of the trial was violated by his absence from the ex parte communication between the court and his attorney; the purpose of this proceeding was simply to place on the record matters which had already occurred regarding defendant's perjury and his attorney's response. Defendant's presence was not mandated because the proceeding had no bearing on his ability to defend against the charges or on the outcome of this jury trial. People v. DePallo, 96 N.Y.2d 437, 729 N.Y.S.2d 649, 754 N.E.2d 751 (2001).

Right to be present; jury instructions, deliberations.—Defendant's absence from courtroom when court responded to

jury note mandated reversal despite the presence of his attorney at that juncture and the absence of any timely protest. People v. Mehmedi, 69 N.Y.2d 759, 513 N.Y.S.2d 100, 505 N.E.2d 610 (1987).

—Despite clear evidence of defendant's guilt, court reversed conviction because defendant was absent from the read-back of instructions during jury deliberations, which is a material stage of the trial. People v. Mason, 308 A.D.2d 317, 764 N.Y.S.2d 80 (1st Dept. 2003).

—Defendant could not be produced because he had broken his jaw and was being treated in the hospital; his presence was not required when the trial court instructed the jury that there would be a delay in responding to its request for a readback of certain testimony. People v. Frye, 192 A.D.2d 412, 596 N.Y.S.2d 373 (1st Dept. 1993).

—Defendant's right to be present during supplemental instructions was not waived by defense counsel's consent to proceed in defendant's absence; counsel's waiver, purported exercised on behalf of his client, is thus a nullity. People v. Aguilar, 177 A.D.2d 197, 582 N.Y.S.2d 388 (1st Dept. 1992).

—Defendant's right to be present was not violated where court instructed a court officer to advise the jurors that certain requested reports were not in evidence, and this was done in the defendant's absence. People v. Roldan, 173 A.D.2d 233, 569 N.Y.S.2d 642 (1st Dept. 1991).

—Court rejected claim that defendant's right to be present was violated when the court dismissed the jury for the evening in his absence; the court's brief remarks that the jury should not deliberate was not a charge on fundamental legal principles. People v. Nixon, 172 A.D.2d 366, 569 N.Y.S.2d 2 (1st Dept. 1991).

—Action of court officer telling the jury that "we have some problems that we are going over to Monday morning at ten o'clock" did not deprive the defendant of his right to be present at all material stages of the proceeding, since that was a minor ministerial matter which did not occur at a critical state of the trial. People v. Suarez, 170 A.D.2d 264, 566 N.Y.S.2d 9 (1st Dept.), lv. denied, 77 N.Y.2d 967 (1991).

—Court rejected People's argument that, since the supplemental instruction given in defendant's absence related to only one of the charges, a reversal should be limited to that conviction; court held that the argument was "essentially an invitation to apply harmless error analysis" to the error. People v. Caballero, 221 A.D.2d 459, 634 N.Y.S.2d 392 (2d Dept. 1995).

—Defendant's presence was not required where court directed that the jurors should continue deliberating until about 6:00 p.m., and that they should not worry about meals and accommodations for the night. People v. Smith, 204 A.D.2d 748, 612 N.Y.S.2d 452 (2d Dept. 1994).

—The defendant's absence when the court turned over three previously admitted exhibits to the jury was not a violation of the defendant's right to be present during a critical stage of the trial. People v. Murphy, 176 A.D.2d 899, 575 N.Y.S.2d 363 (2d Dept. 1991), lv. denied, 79 N.Y.2d 861 (1992).

—The right of the defendant to be present during the instructions to the jury is absolute and unequivocal and cannot be waived by defense counsel. People v. Lopez, 156 A.D.2d 476, 548 N.Y.S.2d 762 (2d Dept. 1990).

—Court rejected defendant's unpreserved contention that he was deprived of his right to be present at a material stage of his trial in the use of the special verdict sheet. People v. Ribowsky, 156 A.D.2d 726, 549 N.Y.S.2d 480 (2d Dept. 1990), aff'd, 77 N.Y.2d 284, 567 N.Y.S.2d 392, 568 N.E.2d 1197 (1991).

—Reversal was not required despite the fact that during jury deliberations and in the absence of the defendant and counsel, the trial court visited the jury room and informed the jury, in response to their written request, that they were not permitted to read the trial transcript but could have it read back to them by the court reporter. People v. Aveille, 148 A.D.2d 461, 538 N.Y.S.2d 615 (2d Dept. 1989).

—There was no need to assemble the parties to rule on the jury's request for a document which had not been admitted into evidence. People v. Dittman, 127 A.D.2d 964, 513 N.Y.S.2d 62 (2d Dept. 1987).

Right to be present; material stage of defendant's trial.—Defendant was not entitled to be present when victim conferred with her attorney because victim's meeting with her attorney was not part of the defendant's trial. People v. Figueroa, 304 A.D.2d 475, 759 N.Y.S.2d 41 (1st Dept. 2003).

Right to be present; violation of.—Where an off-the-record conference dealt directly with matters that had potential for meaningful input from the defendant, his absence from that conference required reversal. People v. Casiano, 294 A.D.2d 277, 743 N.Y.S.2d 405 (1st Dept. 2002).

Defendant's outbursts.—Defendant's behavior in turning over a table and lying on the floor during the testimony of the identification witness, coupled with his clear and repeated requests to leave the courtroom and the Trial Judge's admonitions and explanation of the consequences were sufficient to constitute a waiver of his right to be present at trial. People v. Johnson, 37 N.Y.2d 778, 375 N.Y.S.2d 97, 337 N.E.2d 605 (1975).

—Where defendant was forcibly removed from the courtroom after his outburst during the reading of the verdict, he forfeited his right to be present when the jury was polled. People v. Myers, 215 A.D.2d 595, 626 N.Y.S.2d 852 (2d Dept.), lv. denied, 86 N.Y.2d 799 (1995).

—Trial court's comment, made in response to an outburst by the defendant, stating that he had an opportunity to make a statement under oath, if he so desired, tended to deprive the defendant of the full protection of his right not to have unfavorable inferences drawn from his failure to testify in his own behalf and required reversal. People v. Mercado, 120 A.D.2d 619, 502 N.Y.S.2d 87 (2d Dept. 1986).

—Defendant's actions in the courtroom, which included screaming, using profane language, and his explicit request to be removed from the courtroom, constituted a waiver of his right to be present at his trial and his subsequent removal during the testimony of the complaint was not improper. People v. Cornelius, 107 A.D.2d 757, 484 N.Y.S.2d 122 (2d Dept. 1985).

Prison garb; shackling, security measures.—When a defendant fails to request an instruction regarding his physical restraints, a court is under no obligation to instruct the jury to disregard them. People v. Rouse, 79 N.Y.2d 934, 582 N.Y.S.2d 986, 591 N.E.2d 1172 (1992).

—To forbid defendant to wear his own clothing and require him to appear in convict's attire denied him his right to appear in court with the dignity and the self-respect of a free and innocent man. People v. Roman, 35 N.Y.2d 978, 365 N.Y.S.2d 527, 324 N.E.2d 885 (1975).

—An excessive display of security measures adversely affects the presumption of innocence and will not be tolerated absent a clear showing of necessity. People v. Lopez, 207 A.D.2d 658, 616 N.Y.S.2d 42 (1st Dept. 1994).

—Defendant was not prejudiced by the fact that he was shackled during his trial, where the court placed a skirt around the defense table so that the jurors could not see the defendant's shackles, and when there were breaks in the proceedings, the court dismissed the jurors first so as to minimize any chance that they might see the shackles. People v. Bailey, 205 A.D.2d 789, 613 N.Y.S.2d 692 (2d Dept. 1994).

—The defendant was not deprived of a fair trial simply because one juror inadvertently saw her in handcuffs. People v. Collazo, 163 A.D.2d 581, 559 N.Y.S.2d 33 (2d Dept. 1990).

—Defendant was not unduly prejudiced due to his appearance before the jury in shackles, since the measure was justified by defendant's conduct. People v. Johnstone, 147 A.D.2d 589, 537 N.Y.S.2d 882 (2d Dept. 1989).

—Brief and inadvertent viewing of the defendant in handcuffs by jurors outside of the courtroom prior to the commencement of trial was not by itself sufficient to deny defendant a fair trial. People v. Walker, 139 A.D.2d 546, 526 N.Y.S.2d 856 (2d Dept. 1988).

—The defendant was deprived of a fair trial by the fact that five inmate witnesses testifying on his behalf all appeared in court in shackles. People v. Bryant, 158 A.D.2d 808, 551 N.Y.S.2d 612 (3d Dept. 1990).

—The inadvertent viewing of defendant in handcuffs did not deprive defendant of a fair trial. People v. Rescigno, 152 A.D.2d 853, 544 N.Y.S.2d 63 (3d Dept. 1989).

—Court erred in ruling that defendant would be handcuffed and shackled throughout the trial where the record contained no statement by the court giving any reasons for the order and the court failed to instruct the jury with regard to its consideration of the restraints. People v. Mixon, 120 A.D.2d 861, 502 N.Y.S.2d 299 (3d Dept. 1986).

—The shackling of a defendant in the presence of the jury is inherently prejudicial and constitutes reversible error unless a reasonable basis therefore is in the record or it is clear that the jury was not prejudiced thereby. People v. Vigliotti, 203 A.D.2d 898, 611 N.Y.S.2d 413 (4th Dept. 1994).

Defendant's exclusion because of misconduct.—It was proper to exclude defendant, charged with sex offenses against his 11-year-old daughter, from the courtroom during his daughter's testimony because of his deliberate and disruptive behavior calculated to intimidate the witness. People v. Byrnes, 33 N.Y.2d 343, 352 N.Y.S.2d 913, 308 N.E.2d 435 (1974).

—The loss of a defendant's right to be present at all proceedings of a case as a result of his repeated disruptive behavior is a forfeiture rather than a waiver. People v. Cumberbatch, 200 A.D.2d 376, 606 N.Y.S.2d 195 (1st Dept.), lv. denied, 83 N.Y.2d 803 (1994).

—Where at least two of the prosecution witnesses had been threatened and offered money not to testify, it was proper for the court to condition the defense counsel's attendance at an in camera hearing (regarding the prosecutor's request for an adjournment in order to locate two missing witnesses) upon counsel's agreement not to discuss the hearing with defendant. People v. Martinez, 204 A.D.2d 489, 612 N.Y.S.2d 59 (2d Dept. 1994).

—Trial of defendant in absentia, when he was removed for causing disruptions, did not require reversal since the defendant heard the proceedings in the room to which he was confined and was provided with direct telephone communication with his attorney, and the jury was repeatedly given curative instructions with respect to the defendant's absence. People v.Williams, 143 A.D.2d 859, 533 N.Y.S.2d 334 (2d Dept. 1988).

—Although a defendant has the right to be present and heard at sentencing, he forfeits that right by engaging in obstreperous conduct. People v. Fulton, 202 A.D.2d 1042, 610 N.Y.S.2d 109 (4th Dept. 1994).

§ 260.30. Jury trial; in what order to proceed.

The order of a jury trial, in general, is as follows:

1. The jury must be selected and sworn.

2. The court must deliver preliminary instructions to the jury.

3. The people must deliver an opening address to the jury.

4. The defendant may deliver an opening address to the jury.

5. The people must offer evidence in support of the indictment.

6. The defendant may offer evidence in his defense.

7. The people may offer evidence in rebuttal of the defense evidence, and the defendant may then offer evidence in rebuttal of the people's rebuttal evidence. The court may in its discretion permit the parties to offer further rebuttal or surrebuttal evidence in this pattern. In the interest of justice, the court may permit either party to offer evidence upon rebuttal which is not technically of a rebuttal nature but more properly a part of the offering party's original case.

8. At the conclusion of the evidence, the defendant may deliver a summation to the jury.

9. The people may then deliver a summation to the jury.

10. The court must then deliver a charge to the jury.

11. The jury must then retire to deliberate and, if possible, render a verdict.

ANNOTATIONS

Adjournments.—Decision to deny a defense adjournment request based on a purported need to call a police witness at the suppression hearing was within the court's discretion where the defense failed to proffer a bona fide factual predicate demonstrating that the witness possessed material noncumulative evidence. People v. Setteroth, 200 A.D.2d 533, 607 N.Y.S.2d 15 (1st Dept. 1994).

—Court properly denied request for an adjournment where the defendant waited until the eve of trial to make request in order to locate missing witnesses and also failed to show that their testimony would be material and that they could be located. People v. Sima-Rodriguez, 190 A.D.2d 596, 593 N.Y.S.2d 798 (1st Dept. 1993).

—Court did not abuse its discretion in granting a brief adjournment, as requested by defense counsel, in anticipation of a prospective defense witness, and in thereafter refusing to reopen the defense case for that witness' testimony when he appeared, for the first time, after the completion of the defense summation. People v. Rolon, 172 A.D.2d 252, 568 N.Y.S.2d 373 (1st Dept. 1991).

—Court did not err in denying defendant's request for a one day adjournment due to his medial condition, where that condition—fractured ribs and syncope—did not preclude him from participating fully in his defense. People v. Medina-Hernandez, 205 A.D.2d 643, 613 N.Y.S.2d 228 (2d Dept. 1994).

—An abuse or improvident exercise of discretion may occur where the refusal to grant an adjournment results in the deprivation of a defendant's fundamental right to confer with counsel. People v. Norris, 190 A.D.2d 871, 593 N.Y.S.2d 866 (2d Dept. 1993).

—Court improvidently exercised its discretion in denying the defendant's request for a one-day continuance where witnesses were identified to the court, appeared to have material testimony, were to be found within the jurisdiction, and were not located earlier because of the prosecution's failure to turn over *Brady* material to the defense, which revealed the existence of these witnesses. People v. Inswood, 180 A.D.2d 649, 580 N.Y.S.2d 39 (2d Dept. 1992).

—Court properly denied defendant's last minute request for an adjournment to permit him an opportunity to retain private counsel where he had not registered any complaint concerning his counsel's representation during the 17 months preceding the request. People v. Gibson, 137 A.D.2d 553, 524 N.Y.S.2d 294 (2d Dept. 1988).

—It was not an abuse of discretion for the trial court to deny the defendant's application, made on the eve of trial, for a two week adjournment so that he could call a particular psychiatrist as to his medical history, since the testimony sought from the psychiatrist would have been cumulative, and defense counsel had failed to exercise due diligence in attempting to procure him and had declined the trial court's offer of a short adjournment for that purpose. People v. Wood, 129 A.D.2d 598, 514 N.Y.S.2d 93 (2d Dept. 1987).

—Court did not err in denying defense request for an adjournment in order to produce a witness where the defendant failed to establish that he made a diligent effort to secure the witness, and the defendant's assertion that the witness' testimony would be favorable and material to the defense was supported by nothing more than the conclusory allegations of his attorney. People v. Vredenburg, 200 A.D.2d 797, 606 N.Y.S.2d 453 (3d Dept. 1994).

—Court did not abuse its discretion in denying defendant's request for an adjournment; decision to continue with the summations and jury charge while lying in a hospital bed did not constitute reversible error. People v. Torres, 173 A.D.2d 977, 569 N.Y.S.2d 485 (3d Dept. 1991).

—The court did not abuse its discretion in refusing to grant an adjournment to defendant's counsel when, shortly before trial, the prosecutor provided materials to counsel; the decision whether to grant an adjournment is within the sound discretion of the trial court. People v. Sargent, 195 A.D.2d 987, 601 N.Y.S.2d 736 (4th Dept. 1993).

—Where defendant's request for a transcript of the *Wade* hearing was not made prior to the conclusion of the hearing it was untimely, and court properly denied defense request for an adjournment of the trial until the *Wade* hearing transcript could be transcribed. People v. Green, 149 A.D.2d 919, 540 N.Y.S.2d 51 (4th Dept. 1989).

Adjournments; generally.—The granting of an adjournment is a matter of discretion for the court. People v. Singleton, 41 N.Y.S.2d 402, 393 N.Y.S.2d 353, 361 N.E.2d 1003 (1977).

—An abuse or improvident exercise of discretion may occur where the refusal to grant an adjournment results in the deprivation of a defendant's fundamental right to confer with counsel. People v. Norris, 190 A.D.2d 871, 593 N.Y.S.2d 866 (2d Dept. 1993).

—Requests for adjournments are addressed to the sound discretion of the trial court. People v. Rodriguez, 188 A.D.2d 494, 591 N.Y.S.2d 416 (2d Dept. 1992); People v. Brown, 177 A.D.2d 585, 576 N.Y.S.2d 300 (2d Dept. 1991); People v. Mingo, 155 A.D.2d 485, 547 N.Y.S.2d 146 (2d Dept. 1989), lv. denied, 75 N.Y.2d 773 (1990); People v. Moutinho, 146 A.D.2d 650, 536 N.Y.S.2d 549 (2d Dept. 1989); People v. Paul, 143 A.D.2d 107, 531 N.Y.S.2d 358 (2d Dept. 1988); People v. Wright, 192 A.D.2d 875, 596 N.Y.S.2d 896 (3d Dept. 1993); People v. Esquilan, 158 Misc. 2d 618, 601 N.Y.S.2d 673 (Sup. Ct. Bronx Co. 1993).

Adjournments to obtain witnesses; information.—After three times announcing their readiness for trial, the prosecutor sought an adjournment on the day the trial was to commence because he could not find the complaining witness. The trial court had the power to deny the People's request for an adjournment and proceed with jury selection. Hynes v. George, 76 N.Y.2d 500, 561 N.Y.S.2d 538, 562 N.E.2d 863 (1990).

—Decision to deny a defense adjournment request based on a purported need to call a police witness at the suppression hearing was within the court's discretion where the defense failed to proffer a bona fide factual predicate demonstrating that the witness possessed material noncumulative evidence. People v. Setteroth, 200 A.D.2d 533, 607 N.Y.S.2d 15 (1st Dept. 1994).

—Court properly denied request for an adjournment where the defendant waited until the eve of trial to make request in order to locate missing witnesses and also failed to show that their testimony would be material and that they could be located. People v. Sima-Rodriguez, 190 A.D.2d 596, 593 N.Y.S.2d 798 (1st Dept. 1993).

—Court did not abuse its discretion in granting a brief adjournment, as requested by defense counsel, in anticipation of a prospective defense witness, and in thereafter refusing to reopen the defense case for that witness' testimony when he appeared, for the first time, after the completion of the defense summation. People v. Rolon, 172 A.D.2d 252, 568 N.Y.S.2d 373, 374 (1st Dept.), lv. denied, 78 N.Y.2d 926 (1991).

—The party requesting the continuance bears the burden of showing that the witness is material. People v. Bell, 160 A.D.2d 477, 553 N.Y.S.2d 772 (1st Dept.), lv. denied, 76 N.Y.2d 784 (1990).

—Court improvidently exercised its discretion in denying the defendant's request for a one-day continuance where witnesses were identified to the court, appeared to have material testimony, were to be found within the jurisdiction, and were not located earlier because of the prosecution's failure to turn over *Brady* material, which revealed the existence of these witnesses. People v. Inswood, 180 A.D.2d 649, 580 N.Y.S.2d 39 (2d Dept. 1992).

—Trial court did not improvidently exercise its discretion when it refused to grant the defendant's application for a continuance to secure the presence of a witness since there was no showing that the potential testimony of the absent witness was material or relevant to any issue in the trial. People v. Whitehead 155 A.D.2d 567, 547 N.Y.S.2d 421 (2d Dept. 1989), lv. denied, 75 N.Y.2d 926 (1990).

—It was not an abuse of discretion for the trial court to deny the defendant's application, made on the eve of trial, for a two week adjournment so that he could call a particular psychiatrist as to his medical history, since the testimony sought from the psychiatrist would have been cumulative, and defense counsel had failed to exercise due diligence in attempting to procure him and had declined the trial court's offer of a short adjournment for that purpose. People v. Wood, 129 A.D.2d 598, 514 N.Y.S.2d 93 (2d Dept.), lv. denied, 70 N.Y.2d 719 (1987).

—Court did not abuse its discretion in denying defense request for adjournment so as to insure presence of witness at trail; there was no showing of a diligent and good faith attempt on the part of the defendant to insure officer's appearance in that defendant failed to avail himself of several week period of time in which to serve the officer with a subpoena. People v. Daniels, 128 A.D.2d 632, 512 N.Y.S.2d 881 (2d Dept. 1987).

—Court properly denied defense request for an adjournment to obtain the presence of alibi witnesses where there was no showing of a diligent and good faith attempt on the defendant's part to insure the witnesses' appearance at trial. People v. Green, 140 A.D.2d 370, 527 N.Y.S.2d 856 (2d Dept. 1983).

—Court did not err in denying defense request for an adjournment in order to produce a witness where the defendant failed to establish that he made a diligent effort to secure the witness, and the defendant's assertion that the witness' testimony would be favorable and material to the defense was supported by nothing more than the conclusory allegations of his attorney. People v. Vredenburg, 200 A.D.2d 797, 606 N.Y.S.2d 453 (3d Dept.), lv. denied, 83 N.Y.2d 859 (1994).

—The court did not abuse its discretion in refusing to grant an adjournment to defendant's counsel when, shortly before trial, the prosecutor provided materials to counsel; the decision whether to grant an adjournment is within the sound discretion of the trial court. People v. Sargent, 195 A.D.2d 987, 601 N.Y.S.2d 736 (4th Dept. 1993).

—Where defendant's request for a transcript of the *Wade* hearing was not made prior to the conclusion of the hearing it was untimely, and court properly denied defense request for a adjournment of the trial until the *Wade* hearing transcript could be transcribed. People v. Green, 149 A.D.2d 919, 540 N.Y.S.2d 51 (4th Dept. 1989).

Adjournments related to new counsel.—Where attorney assigned to represent defendant at the plea proceeding had been relieved, and the same day the trial court that new counsel was assigned, the court proceeded to sentencing over counsel's objection that he was unfamiliar with the case and had no opportunity to review defendant's probation report, court erred in refusing to adjourn sentencing until counsel had an opportunity to be sufficiently familiar with the case and defendant's background to make an effective presentation. People v. Stella, 188 A.D.2d 318, 590 N.Y.S.2d 478 (1st Dept. 1992).

—Court properly denied defendant's last minute request for an adjournment to permit him an opportunity to retain private counsel where he had not registered any complaint concerning his counsel's representation during the 17 months preceding the request. People v. Gibson, 137 A.D.2d 553, 524 N.Y.S.2d 294 (2d Dept. 1988).

—Court did not abuse its discretion in denying newly retained counsel's request for an adjournment where defendant was aware of the approximate trial date for almost two months prior thereto and no effort was made to replace his prior attorney until the eve of trial. People v. Gabler, 129 A.D.2d 733, 514 N.Y.S.2d 493 (2d Dept. 1987).

Adjournments related to illness.—Defendant was not denied his right to be present at trial because his request for a one-day adjournment for health reasons was denied; defendant's ailment did not prevent him from being present, but merely required him to avoid strenuous activity. People v. Medina-Hernandez, 205 A.D.2d 643, 613 N.Y.S.2d 228 (2d Dept.), lv. denied, 84 N.Y.2d 870 (1994).

—Court did not abuse its discretion in denying defendant's request for an adjournment; decision to continue with the summations and jury charge while lying in a hospital bed did not constitute reversible error. People v. Torres, 173 A.D.2d 977, 569 N.Y.S.2d 485 (3d Dept. 1991).

Leading questions.—Court properly allowed prosecutor to ask some leading questions of the complainant and also properly posed its own questions, in light of the language difficulty displayed by the complainant. People v. Williams, 242 A.D.2d 469, 662 N.Y.S.2d 118 (1st Dept. 1997).

Recesses.—Trial court acted within its discretion in permitting, during direct examination, the prosecutor to hold a brief private conference with a witness after that witness had given an unexpected and potentially damaging response. People v. Branch, 83 N.Y.2d 863, 612 N.Y.S.2d 365, 634 N.E.2d 966 (1994).

—Trial court abused its discretion in arbitrarily denying the defendant a brief delay in order to consult with counsel about taking the stand after the co-defendant testified and rested unexpectedly. People v. Spears, 64 N.Y.2d 698, 485 N.Y.S.2d 521, 474 N.E.2d 1189 (1984).

Order of trial; general.—It was not an abuse of discretion to permit an expert witness, who otherwise would have been unavailable, to testify out of turn. People v. Ramirez, 200 A.D.2d 377, 606 N.Y.S.2d 194 (1st Dept. 1994).

—The order of the presentation of the evidence at trial, including the decision to permit a party to recall a witness who has finished testifying, are matters generally resting within the sound discretion of the trial court. People v. Georgescu, 197 A.D.2d 352, 602 N.Y.S.2d 128 (1st Dept. 1993).

—Absent a compelling reason, the order of trial prescribed by CPL § 260.30 should be followed. People v. Fama, 212 A.D.2d 542, 622 N.Y.S.2d 732 (2d Dept. 1995).

—A one-week delay between summations and the jury charge was not improper. People v. Smith, 183 A.D.2d 794, 583 N.Y.S.2d 521 (2d Dept. 1992).

—Court committed reversible error in delivering a large portion of the charge to the jury prior to summations. People v. Fujah, 182 A.D.2d 774, 582 N.Y.S.2d 497 (2d Dept. 1992).

—In the absence of prejudice, a delay in swearing in the jury until the conclusion of the People's case did not warrant reversal of defendant's conviction. People v. Morales, 176 A.D.2d 825, 575 N.Y.S.2d 150 (2d Dept. 1991).

—While CPL § 260.30 spells out the order of a criminal jury trial in general, the trial court has discretion to alter the order of the proceedings up until the time the case is submitted to the jury. People v. Duplessis, 16 A.D.3d 846, 791 N.Y.S.2d 214 (3d Dept. 2005).

Opening statement; the People.—Prosecutor's opening statement was fatally deficient, where it failed to delineate particular offenses and demonstrate how they would be proven, and merely listed the names of prospective witnesses and briefly described the evidence. People v. Kurtz, 51 N.Y.2d 380, 434 N.Y.S.2d 200, 414 N.E.2d 699 (1980), cert. denied, 451 U.S. 911 (1981).

—People's opening statement, which included a reading of the indictment, delineated the particular offense with which defendant was charged, including the elements to be proven, and provided sufficient factual details so that the jury could intelligently understand the nature of the case. People v. Frazier, 291 A.D.2d 21, 738 N.Y.S.2d 16 (1st Dept. 2002).

—When the People fail to produce a witness referred to in opening statements, "the general rule is that, absent bad faith or undue prejudice, a trial will not be undone"; here, defendant conceded that the prosecutor did not act in bad faith, and there was overwhelming evidence against the defendant, thus, there is no significant probability that the jury would have acquitted him had it not heard the references to the witnesses. People v. Thompson, 276 A.D.2d 811, 716 N.Y.S.2d 397 (2d Dept. 2000).

—Prosecutor's opening failed to mention the depraved indifference count of the indictment, and the People declined to supplement their opening when the omission was pointed out; court properly denied defendant's motion to dismiss that count of indictment, because People stated sufficient allegations to support a finding that defendant acted with depraved indifference to human life. People v. Carter, 248 A.D.2d 722, 670 N.Y.S.2d 542 (2d Dept. 1998).

—People did not act in bad faith in failing to call witness mentioned in opening statement, where parties stipulated that witness was unavailable because of medical condition; any prejudice from witness's failure to testify was cured by court's prompt instructions prohibiting jury from speculating as to what her testimony would have been, along with court's preliminary instructions and jury charge, which instructed that statements of counsel were not evidence. People v. Seabrooks, 244 A.D.2d 514, 664 N.Y.S.2d 105 (2d Dept. 1997).

—Conviction reversed, where prosecutor represented in opening statement that he would present evidence that an additional victim was shot during the incident, and that the defendant was the shooter, but no such evidence was admitted at the trial, and prosecutor revealed at the conclusion of the trial that he had "no information" about that victim's whereabouts; prosecutor's reference to the victim was unduly prejudicial. People v. Bonnen, 236 A.D.2d 479, 653 N.Y.S.2d 648 (2d Dept. 1997).

—Absent bad faith or undue prejudice, the prosecutor's failure to prove every statement in his or her opening will not result in a jury's verdict being reversed. People v. Zienkowicz, 213 A.D.2d 435, 622 N.Y.S.2d 979 (2d Dept. 1995).

—Without imputing bad faith to the People, the court concluded that their opening was "unfulfilled and undoubtedly influenced the jury," constituting reversible error. People v. Camacho, 209 A.D.2d 534, 618 N.Y.S.2d 842 (2d Dept. 1994).

—The prejudice resulting from the prosecutor's unfulfilled opening was ineradicable and transcended the court's efforts, leading to reversal. People v. Gonzalez, 187 A.D.2d 630, 590 N.Y.S.2d 505 (2d Dept. 1992).

—Prosecutor's use in his opening of a nontestifying co-defendant's statement inculpating defendant by his nickname was error; however, since the error occurred only in the opening statement and was not repeated during the presentation of evidence, reversal was not warranted. People v. Sheppard, 168 A.D.2d 584, 562 N.Y.S.2d 801 (2d Dept. 1990).

—Prosecutor's opening should set forth the nature of the charges against the defendant and briefly state the facts the prosecution intends to prove and evidence which will be introduced in support thereof. People v. Brown, 158 A.D.2d 461, 550 N.Y.S.2d 913 (2d Dept. 1990), cert. denied, 498 U.S. 870.

—Prosecutor's act of banging a hammer on a table during his opening statement and later trying to introduce this hammer into evidence even though the prosecutor knew that the hammer was not the one used in the assault did not deprive the defendant of a fair trial. People v. Canada, 157 A.D.2d 793, 550 N.Y.S.2d 392 (2d Dept. 1990).

—Trial court's failure to dismiss the indictment upon the petitioner's motion and in the face of the prosecutor's deliberate refusal to deliver an opening statement constituted error. Mortillaro v. Posner, 147 A.D.2d 701, 538 N.Y.S.2d 311 (2d Dept. 1989).

—Absent bad faith or undue prejudice, a trial will not be undone for deficiencies in an opening statement. People v. Collins, 136 A.D.2d 720, 523 N.Y.S.2d 1018 (2d Dept. 1988); see also People v. Campos, 138 A.D.2d 500, 526 N.Y.S.2d 124 (2d Dept. 1988).

—Although prosecutor's opening statement may have failed sufficiently to relate the facts to the various crimes charged in the indictment, reversal was not required. People v. Edwards, 145 A.D.2d 503, 535 N.Y.S.2d 442 (2d Dept. 1988).

—People were entitled to read the indictment during their opening statement; moreover, the court properly instructed the jury that the indictment was merely an accusation and not evidence of guilt. People v. Davis, 208 A.D.2d 989, 617 N.Y.S.2d 220 (3d Dept. 1994).

—It was not error for trial court to deny defendant's motion to reserve opening statement until the close of People's case; the order of trial prescribed by statute should be followed unless there is a showing of a compelling reason for variation. People v. Theriault, 75 A.D.2d 971, 428 N.Y.S.2d 365 (3d Dept. 1980).

—The prosecutor's references in his opening statement to the victim's tortured childhood constituted an improper attempt to arouse the jury's sympathy. People v. Scott, 163 A.D.2d 855, 558 N.Y.S.2d 384 (4th Dept. 1990).

Opening statement; the defense.—Court imposed reasonable restriction on defense counsel's opening statement; court is entitled to control the content of a defense opening that goes beyond a brief outline of what would be supported by the evidence. People v. Frazier, 291 A.D.2d 211, 738 N.Y.S.2d 16 (1st Dept. 2002).

—Trial court properly curtailed counsel's opening statement, since it went beyond a brief outline of what the defense believed would be supported by the evidence. People v. Valentin, 211 A.D.2d 509, 621 N.Y.S.2d 67 (1st Dept.), lv. denied, 85 N.Y.2d 944 (1995).

—Trial court improperly gave the jury a message that there were things the defense had to prove by its comments during defense counsel's opening statement; curtailment of opening effectively denied defendant his statutory right to an opening. People v. Robinson, 202 A.D.2d 225, 608 N.Y.S.2d 456 (1st Dept.), lv. denied, 84 N.Y.2d 871 (1994).

Cross-examination.—A conviction premised on an Alford plea may generally be used for the same purposes as any other conviction, and a defendant may be properly cross-examined for impeachment purposes about a previous conviction even if it arose from an Alford plea. People v. Miller, 91 N.Y.2d 372, 670 N.Y.S.2d 978, 694 N.E.2d 61 (1998).

—Proper foundation was laid pursuant to People v. Dawson, 50 N.Y.2d 311, 428 N.Y.S.2d 914, 406 N.E.2d 771, for the cross-examination of defendant's alibi witnesses concerning their third alleged opportunity to inform law enforcement officials of defendant's alibi. People v. Miller, 89 N.Y.2d 1077, 659 N.Y.S.2d 837, 681 N.E.2d 1283 (1997).

—It is settled that an accused's right to cross-examine witnesses and present a defense is not absolute. People v. Williams, 81 N.Y.2d 303, 598 N.Y.S.2d 167, 614 N.E.2d 730 (1993).

—Court improperly precluded defendant's cross-examination of a police witness about a statement in a felony complain that had been prepared by the People and signed by the officer, since his in-court testimony flatly contradicted the description given in the complaint, but the error was harmless. People v. Castillo, 309 A.D.2d 533, 765 N.Y.S.2d 322 (1st Dept. 2003).

—Court properly exercised its discretion in limiting the scope of cross-examination of a People's witness concerning his immigration status. In any event, the issue of immigration status was only marginally relevant because the court, as the trier of fact in this case, was made aware of the issue and was free to credit the witness nonetheless. People v. Garcia, 237 A.D.2d 114, 654 N.Y.S.2d 740 (1st Dept. 1997).

—The scope of cross-examination rests in the sound discretion of the trial court and is reviewed on appeal only for plain abuse. People v. Smith, 205 A.D.2d 458, 613 N.Y.S.2d 885 (1st Dept. 1994).

—The rule limiting the scope of cross-examination to that of the direct examination may be relaxed by the trial court where the testimony would be material to major issues in the case. People v. Hadden, 95 A.D.2d 725, 464 N.Y.S.2d 134 (1st Dept. 1983).

—Prosecutor committed reversible error when he repeatedly asked defendant on cross-examination whether the prosecution's witnesses, including the complainant and certain police detectives, lied during their testimony, because it was irrelevant whether the defendant believed that the other witnesses were lying. People v. Berrios, 298 A.D.2d 597, 750 N.Y.S.2d 302 (2d Dept. 2002).

—New trial ordered where court refused to allow defense counsel to cross-examine police officer regarding a notation in his report which may have indicated an unsuccessful buy attempt; the document qualified as one kept in the regular course of business, was properly admitted into evidence, and defense counsel should have been permitted to cross-examine the witness with respect to the notations. People v. Hill, 271 A.D.2d 546, 706 N.Y.S.2d 702 (2d Dept. 2000).

—Reversal was required where the right to cross-examine had been significantly curtailed even without a showing of specific prejudice since counsel often cannot know in advance what pertinent facts may be elicited on cross-examination, it is sheer speculation to suggest that notwithstanding the improper restriction of the cross-examinations the defendants were later able to elicit all they might have had the warning never been given. People v. Carter, 86 A.D.2d 451, 450 N.Y.S.2d 203 (2d Dept. 1982).

—Prosecutor improperly asked questions on cross-examination that required defendant to characterize prosecution witnesses as liars, but error was harmless because of overwhelming proof of guilt. People v. Hubert, 237 A.D.2d 756, 655 N.Y.S.2d 140 (3d Dept. 1997).

—Scope of cross-examination is a matter addressed to the sound discretion of the trial court; such discretion includes limiting the scope of cross-examination concerning collateral issues designed solely to impeach the witness's credibility. People v. Perotti, 233 A.D.2d 936, 649 N.Y.S.2d 899 (4th Dept. 1996).

Redirect.—The trial court must limit the inquiry on redirect to the subject matter of the cross-examination which bears upon the question at issue and the "opening the door principle" merely allows a party to explain or clarify on redirect matters that have been put in issue for the first time on cross-examination and the trial court should normally "exclude all evidence which has not been made necessary by the opponents case in reply." People v. Melendez, 56 N.Y.2d 445, 449 N.Y.S.2d 946, 434 N.E.2d 1324 (1982).

—Any error in allowing the prosecutor, on redirect examination, to rehabilitate two witnesses was harmless in light of the overwhelming evidence of guilt. People v. Russell, 189 A.D.2d 901, 592 N.Y.S.2d 794 (2d Dept. 1993).

—The scope of redirect examination is left to the sound discretion of the trial court. People v. DeAndressi, 146 A.D.2d 642, 536 N.Y.S.2d 849 (2d Dept. 1989).

Rebuttal.—Because the proposed rebuttal was both cumulative to, and duplicative of, evidence already presented on defendant's direct case, with only the same relevancy, it was within the trial court's discretion to disallow the presentation of that evidence on rebuttal. People v. Harris, 98 N.Y.2d 452, 749 N.Y.S.2d 766, 779 N.E.2d 705 (2002).

—It was proper to elicit from undercover officer rebuttal that the street corner where the sale took place was not busy with people in order to establish that it was quiet enough for the undercover to have known whether or not defendant said that the cocaine was "beat"; to the extent that any of the testimony may not have been "technically of a rebuttal nature," it was properly admitted as a matter of discretion. People v. Payne, 235 A.D.2d 235, 652 N.Y.S.2d 273 (1st Dept. 1997).

—Once defendant used cross-examination to make broad assertions of innocence, the People were entitled to contradict his non-collateral testimony with rebuttal evidence. People v. Rojas, 200 A.D.2d 545, 606 N.Y.S.2d 698 (1st Dept.), lv. denied, 83 N.Y.2d 857 (1994).

—Although the court originally precluded the People from introducing into evidence the amount of money on the defendant's person at the time of his arrest, when the defendant and his girlfriend testified and made an issue of the amount of money on the defendant, the court properly permitted the People on their rebuttal case to introduce the evidence concerning the money. People v. Aarons, 183 A.D.2d 496, 583 N.Y.S.2d 438 (1st Dept. 1992).

—Trial court properly permitted People to present rebuttal testimony in response to evidence adduced by the defense; "[w]hile it was improper for the prosecutor to elicit testimony from the rebuttal witness concerning his involvement with a narcotics enforcement unit, any prejudice caused by this testimony was dissipated by the trial court's prompt curative instruction." People v. Biggs, 280 A.D.2d 484, 721 N.Y.S.2d 364 (2d Dept. 2001).

—Where matter of identification was crucial issue and the rebuttal case did not cause any undue prejudice to defendant, court properly allowed People to introduce rebuttal evidence concerning defendant's changed appearance at trial. People v. Harris, 232 A.D.2d 426, 648 N.Y.S.2d 620 (2d Dept. 1996).

—Court holds that alibi testimony may be rebutted by evidence of a witness's prior inconsistent statements, overruling prior cases. People v. Knight, 173 A.D.2d 646, 570 N.Y.S.2d 227 (2d Dept. 1991), lv. denied, 79 N.Y.2d 1046 (1992).

—Court properly permitted People, on rebuttal case, to introduce letters written by defendant to complainant which contained statements indicating consciousness of guilt to counter defendant's testimony regarding an accidental stabbing. People v. Oglesby, 153 A.D.2d 284, 519 N.Y.S.2d 153 (2d Dept. 1987).

—Court properly admitted as rebuttal testimony, testimony regarding the weather on the night of the drug sale since it was relevant to the issue of the ability of the police officers to observe the defendant from their surveillance posts on the street and where the defendant had attempted through his witnesses to prove that it was misty on the night in question. People v. Hewlett, 133 A.D.2d 418, 519 N.Y.S.2d 557 (2d Dept. 1987).

—The trial court did not err in permitting the prosecutor's rebuttal witness to testify even though she was present in the courtroom during the testimony presented by the defense; the violation of a stipulation between the parties that witnesses would be excluded from the courtroom did not render the witness incompetent to testify. People v. Cody, 182 A.D.2d 1089, 583 N.Y.S.2d 77 (4th Dept. 1992).

Recalling witnesses.—Although the complainant perjured himself with respect to background testimony, upon being advised by the complainant of this perjury, the prosecutor acted properly; the complainant was recalled after the close of the defendant's case to admit his perjury and to provide corrected testimony, and the jury was free to evaluate the complainant's testimony. People v. Franklin, 188 A.D.2d 366, 591 N.Y.S.2d 174 (1st Dept. 1992).

—Defendant's conviction was reversed and remanded for new trial because of the trial court's prejudicial error in denying defense counsel's application for permission to recall sole defense witness to rehabilitate him. People v. Johnson, 78 A.D.2d 298, 434 N.Y.S.2d 389 (1st Dept. 1981).

Reopening the case; the People.—Permitting People to reopen their case is permissible where the missing element is simple to prove and not seriously contested and where reopening the case does not unduly prejudice the defense. People v. Whipple, 97 N.Y.2d 1, 734 N.Y.S.2d 549, 760 N.E.2d 337 (2001).

—Reopening of case after jury began deliberations was reversible error where evidence did not supply an element in prosecution's case, which was overlooked, nor was it newly discovered evidence relating directly to issue of guilt but only served to give more credibility to a possible weakness in People's case. People v. Olsen, 34 N.Y.2d 349, 357 N.Y.S.2d 487, 313 N.E.2d 782 (1974).

—Trial court did not abuse its discretion in permitting the People to reopen their case so their witnesses could make an in-court identification of defendant, when the People's failure to do so on direct was the product of the trial assistant's inexperience and not an attempt to gain an unfair tactical advantage. People v. Murray, 165 A.D.2d 690, 564 N.Y.S.2d 15 (1st Dept. 1990), lv. denied, 77 N.Y.2d 880 (1991).

—Defendant failed to show how he was prejudiced by the mere reopening of the People's case well before jury deliberations to supply an easily provable element of their case. People v. Martin, 180 A.D.2d 602, 580 N.Y.S.2d 312 (1st Dept.), lv. denied, 80 N.Y.2d 906 (1992).

—The trial court acted properly in allowing the People to reopen their case to present the testimony of a police officer with regard to whom the defendant requested a missing witness charge. People v. Parilla, 158 A.D.2d 556, 551 N.Y.S.2d 326 (2d Dept. 1990).

—Court did not err in permitting the People to call a witness following the summations. People v. Hinkley, 178 A.D.2d 800, 581 N.Y.S.2d 253 (3d Dept.), lv. denied, 79 N.Y.2d 948 (1992).

Reopening the case; the defense.—Refusal of trial court to reopen trial to allow recantation testimony from a prosecution witness was not error; court did not abuse discretion particularly in light of evident pique of witness; additionally, it was open to counsel to make the appropriate post-conviction motion. People v. Escobar, 36 N.Y.2d 883, 372 N.Y.S.2d 213, 334 N.E.2d 12 (1975).

—Determination as to whether to reopen the case for further testimony and as to the qualifications of the witness to testify as an expert rested in the reasonable discretion of the trial Judge. People v. Ventura, 35 N.Y.2d 654, 360 N.Y.S.2d 419, 315 N.E.2d 609 (1974).

—The court did not abuse its discretion by refusing to reopen the defense case after jury deliberations had begun in order to allow the appearance of a witness who had been subpoenaed the day before, since the potential testimony was speculative, at best. People v. James, 200 A.D.2d 394, 608 N.Y.S.2d 800 (1st Dept. 1994).

—Court did not abuse its discretion in granting a brief adjournment, as requested by defense counsel, in anticipation of a prospective defense witness, and in thereafter refusing to reopen the defense case for that witness' testimony when he appeared, for the first time, after the completion of the defense summation. People v. Rolon, 172 A.D.2d 252, 568 N.Y.S.2d 373, 374 (1st Dept.), lv. denied, 78 N.Y.2d 926 (1991).

—The court abused its discretion in failing to reopen the case in order to afford defendant the opportunity to cross-examine the prosecution witness on a key fact that came to light while the jury was deliberating. People v. Parker, 125 A.D.2d 504, 509 N.Y.S.2d 586 (2d Dept. 1986).

Reopening the case; permitting the defendant to testify.—The court did not abuse its discretion as a matter of law when, accepting defense counsel's representation that it was his understanding that defendant had concluded he would not take the stand, he declined to reopen the case when, for the first time, defendant expressed a desire to testify after closing arguments. People v. Washington, 71 N.Y.2d 916, 528 N.Y.S.2d 531, 523 N.E.2d 818 (1988).

—Court properly denied defendant's request to testify, made for the first time after summations had been completed; the record sufficiently established that prior to summations defendant had accepted his counsel's recommendation against testifying, and there was no sound reason to permit defendant to change his mind and thereby disturb the normal order of trial. People v. Franco, 271 A.D.2d 383, 708 N.Y.S.2d 62 (1st Dept. 2000).

—The trial court abused its discretion by denying defendant's request to testify in his own behalf, notwithstanding that such request was made after the summation by defense counsel but prior to the prosecutor's summation. People v. Hendricks, 114 A.D.2d 510, 494 N.Y.S.2d 729 (2d Dept. 1985).

—Reversible error was committed when the trial court refused to allow the defendant to testify where the defense had rested but the jury had not been charged and there was no showing of prejudice to the People. People v. Harami, 93 A.D.2d 867, 461 N.Y.S.2d 376 (2d Dept. 1983).

Summations.—The trial court must be given great latitude in controlling the duration and limiting the scope of summations, and thus may limit counsel to a reasonable time and may terminate an argument when continuation would be repetitive and redundant. People v. Brown, 136 A.D.2d 1, 525 N.Y.S.2d 618 (2d Dept. 1988).

—Although summation is not an unbridled debate, defense counsel has the right to comment on every pertinent matter of fact bearing upon the questions which must be decided by the jury as long as it is limited to the four corners of the evidence. People v. Robinson, 137 A.D.2d 564, 524 N.Y.S.2d 304 (2d Dept. 1988).

—Court did not err in bifurcating the summations by directing both sides to sum up prior to the testimony of a witness, who had yet to be produced from an out-of-state correctional facility since the court permitted both sides to reopen their summations following that witness's testimony and instructed them to limit their summations to his testimony. People v. Hernandez, 137 A.D.2d 560, 524 N.Y.S.2d 300 (2d Dept. 1988).

Summations; propriety of prosecutor's remarks.—In response to defense counsel's argument on summation that the victim had been prompted by police to misidentify defendant, the prosecutor's response that the victim would have to have been "suicidal or foolish" to do so and repeated the remark twice more, exceeded the bounds of proper summation. The defendant was entitled to a curative instruction that the prosecutor's remarks were unfounded, improper and should be disregarded and the failure of the court to do so, over the request of defendant, constituted reversible error. People v. Trinidad, 59 N.Y.2d 820, 464 N.Y.S.2d 740, 451 N.E.2d 487 (1983).

—Though the prosecutor's summation comment suggesting that the defendant may have engaged in other criminal conduct was prejudicial in nature, the trial judge's curative instruction, following which neither any further objection nor any request for a mistrial was made, must be deemed to have corrected the error to defendant's satisfaction. People v. Williams, 46 N.Y.2d 1070, 416 N.Y.S.2d 792, 390 N.E.2d 299 (1979).

—A reversal of conviction on narcotics charges was warranted where the prosecutor, in his summation, conveyed the impression that the defendant had killed an informant, an accusation both unsupported by any evidence presented and irrelevant to the crime charged, thus depriving the defendant of a fair trial; counsel, in summing up, must stay within "the four corners of the evidence" and avoid comments unrelated to a legitimate issue in the case, especially as to matters which are inflammatory and tend to prejudice the jury. People v. Ashwal, 39 N.Y.2d 105, 383 N.Y.S.2d 204, 347 N.E.2d 564 (1976).

—Trial court unduly limited counsel's argument during summation regarding the defense's ricochet theory, which was reasonably based on the evidence adduced at trial. People v. Ventura, 233 A.D.2d 154, 650 N.Y.S.2d 2 (1st Dept. 1996).

—Where defendant necessarily pitted the credibility of People's witnesses, other than the victim, against the defendant, it was permissible for People in response to say that if there had been an agreement among these witnesses about what to say at trial, they "would have done a better job." People v. Silas, 233 A.D.2d 103, 649 N.Y.S.2d 428 (1st Dept. 1996).

—Although the prosecutor might have better utilized milder terms in summation than "a story" and "a frenzy of lies." his characterization of defendant's testimony as patently false was accurate. People v. Montez, 203 A.D.2d 616, 611 N.Y.S.2d 172 (1st Dept. 1994).

—Defendant's claim that he was deprived of a fair trial because the prosecutor impugned the integrity of his counsel by warning the jury not to let him "pull the wool over [their] eyes" and characterized the evidence elicited by the defense as a "red herring" rejected. People v. Richards, 207 A.D.2d 660, 616 N.Y.S.2d 40 (1st Dept. 1994).

—The prosecutor did not vouch for the truthfulness of an identification witness or mischaracterize the defense by remarking that the witness "would have not reason to come into this courtroom and lie." People v. Gibbs, 207 A.D.2d 739, 617 N.Y.S.2d 2 (1st Dept.), lv. denied, 84 N.Y.2d 935 (1994).

—A prosecutor's reminder to the jury that an asserted defense is not supported by any evidence does not shift the burden of proof. People v. Gathers, 207 A.D.2d 751, 616 N.Y.S.2d 732 (1st Dept. 1994).

—Summation comments of prosecutor constituted appropriate response to the defense summation which repeatedly argued that the police witness lied and deliberately arrested an innocent man to effect an unwritten "body quota." People v. Carraquillo, 202 A.D.2d 253, 608 N.Y.S.2d 461 (1st Dept. 1994).

—The purpose of summation is not to test a prosecutor's skills for purple rhetoric, nor a prosecutor's talents for hyperbole or metaphor. People v. Nevedo, 202 A.D.2d 183, 608 N.Y.S.2d 422 (1st Dept. 1994).

—Although not preserved for appellate review by appropriate objection, the court considered the question of the prosecutor's improper comments in summation in the interest of justice and reversed the conviction. People v. Bell, 191 A.D.2d 361, 595 N.Y.S.2d 191 (1st Dept. 1993).

—The characterization of the defense as a "smoke screen" was within the bounds of fair comment. People v. Flores, 191 A.D.2d 306, 595 N.Y.S.2d 173 (1st Dept. 1993).

—The prosecutor's use of rhetorical questions to note the absent central figure in the defense case did not ascribe an obligation to defendant to produce the witness. People v. Smith, 190 A.D.2d 522, 593 N.Y.S.2d 22 (1st Dept. 1993).

—The prosecutor's comments that defendant was the person "with the strongest motive to lie" and "the most interested witness" in the case were fair responses to defense counsel's attack on the credibility of the People's main witness. People v. Keough, 188 A.D.2d 312, 591 N.Y.S.2d 11 (1st Dept. 1992).

—A prosecutor has broad latitude in summation, particularly in responding to the defense counsel's summation. People v. D'Alessandro, 184 A.D.2d 114, 591 N.Y.S.2d 1001(1st Dept. 1992), lv. denied, 81 N.Y.2d 884 (1993).

—Prosecutor's comments, such as those concerning the absence of a potential witness, and his characterization of the defense as a "doozie," did not deprive the defendant of a fair trial. People v. Wilson, 181 A.D.2d 562, 582 N.Y.S.2d 87 (1st Dept. 1992).

—Prosecutor erred in summation by suggesting, without evidentiary support, that the defendant was a prostitute, and randomly commenting about people who sell sex for crack and the AIDS epidemic. People v. Fearnot, 200 A.D.2d 583, 606 N.Y.S.2d 288 (2d Dept. 1994).

—While it would have been better had the prosecutor not used the term "we" in his summation, he did not thereby inject the issue of his own credibility. People v. Alexander, 191 A.D.2d 498, 594 N.Y.S.2d 66 (2d Dept. 1993).

—Though the A.D.A. made numerous intemperate and improper remarks during the course of his summation, defendant never objected to the now complained-of statements, and the issue, therefore, has not been preserved for appellate review. People v. Mastropietro, 232 A.D.2d 725, 648 N.Y.S.2d 752 (3d Dept. 1996).

—Although there was no basis in the record for the prosecutor's comment that the police officers who testified at defendant's trial did not have criminal records, the prosecutor did not inject his own credibility into the case, and this minor departure from the evidence at trial did not prejudice defendant. People v. Artis, 232 A.D.2d 729, 648 N.Y.S.2d 722 (3d Dept. 1996).

—Rhetorical questions put to the jury do not constitute improper expressions of personal opinion by the prosecutor. People v. Smith, 192 A.D.2d 806, 596 N.Y.S.2d 539 (3d Dept. 1993).

—The prosecutor's comment to the jurors in summation—that they should "send a message to this community"—was improper. People v. Hanright, 187 A.D.2d 1021, 590 N.Y.S.2d 347 (4th Dept. 1992).

Jury charge; deliberations.—The trial court inadvertently began its charge to the jury before summations, and, upon realizing its mistake, decided to bifurcate its charge, with half of it given before, and half after, summations. Although no objection was made below, reversal required as a matter of law. People v. Fujah, 182 A.D.2d 774, 582 N.Y.S.2d 497 (2d Dept. 1992).

—Jury may change any decision it may have reached until

verdict is actually announced in court. People v. Faulkner, 77
A.D.2d 573, 429 N.Y.S.2d 735 (2d Dept. 1980).

ARTICLE 270—JURY TRIAL—FORMATION AND CONDUCT OF JURY

LexisNexis Cross References

See generally Criminal Law Advocacy, Vol. 2A, Jury Selection; *Criminal Defense Techniques,* Vol. 1A, Ch. 21, Voir Dire; Vol. 1A, Ch. 21A, Challenges to the Jury Pool; Vol. 6, Ch. 119, Jury Selection and Jurors; *Defense of Drunk Driving Cases,* Vol. 4, Ch. 46, Jury Selection; *New York Criminal Practice (2d ed.),* Vol. 3, Ch. 28, Jury and Non-Jury Trials; Vol. 3, Ch. 29, Formation and Conduct of Trial Jury; *Prosecution and Defense of Sex Crimes,* Ch. 16, Jury Selection in Sex Offenses Cases; *Criminal Practice Handbook (2d ed.),* Ch. 5, Jury Issues; *Sexual Assault Trials (2d ed.),* Vol. 1, Ch. 2, Fair Trial, Free Press, and Dealing With Publicity; Vol. 1, Ch. 3, Jury Selection.

§ 270.05. Trial jury; formation in general.

1. A trial jury consists of twelve jurors, but "alternate jurors" may be selected and sworn pursuant to section 270.30.

2. The panel from which the jury is drawn is formed and selected as prescribed in the judiciary law. The first twelve members of the panel returned for the term who appear as their names are drawn and called, and who are not excluded as prescribed by this article, must be sworn and thereupon constitute the trial jury.

ANNOTATIONS

General.—A defendant is entitled to insist that the jury be selected according to the methods established; the court cannot arbitrarily, and without cause, set aside a competent juror. Neither the court nor the parties can select the jury, except as authorized by the statute. People v. Thorpe, 223 A.D.2d 739, 637 N.Y.S.2d 212 (2d Dept. 1996).

Number of jurors.—Where one juror was left out of some parts of the deliberations, but all jurors confirmed the verdict as theirs during jury poll, defendant was not denied his right to a jury of 12. People v. Sampson, 201 A.D.2d 314, 607 N.Y.S.2d 290 (1st Dept.), *lv. denied,* 83 N.Y.2d 971 (1993).

—An indicted defendant cannot consent to a trial by fewer than 12 jurors. People v. Lester, 149 A.D.2d 975, 540 N.Y.S.2d 110 (4th Dept.), *lv. denied,* 74 N.Y.2d 742 (1989).

—When a deliberating juror became ill and had to be hospitalized for an extended period of time during a murder trial, the court determined that it was permissible for the defendant to waive the right to a jury trial by 12 and consent to deliberation

by 11. People v. Gajadahar, 194 Misc. 2d 142, 753 N.Y.S.2d 309 (Sup. Ct. N.Y. Co. 2002).

Multiple juries.—Dual juries are permissible if proper procedures are followed, even in the first jury's verdict is not sealed until the second verdict is returned, absent a showing a prejudice. People v. Irizarry, 83 N.Y.2d 557, 611 N.Y.S.2d 807, 634 N.E.2d 179 (1994).

—Nothing in the statute either authorizes or prohibits the use of multiple juries; where proof against co-defendants is primarily supplied by the same evidence, dual juries are appropriate, but only after a full consideration of the impact the procedure will have on defendants' due process rights and after thorough precautions are taken to protect those rights. People v. Ricardo B., 73 N.Y.2d 228, 538 N.Y.S.2d 796, 535 N.E.2d 1336 (1989).

—The fact that defendant's jury trial was held jointly with a co-defendant's bench trial did not deprive him of a fair trial. People v. Cabrero, 213 A.D.2d 298, 624 N.Y.S.2d 152 (1st Dept.), *lv. denied,* 86 N.Y.2d 780 (1995).

—A joint trial with two juries was properly conducted where the defendant and his accomplice were tried on much the same evidence and each had made a confession implicating the other. People v. Lydon, 197 A.D.2d 640, 603 N.Y.S.2d 771 (2d Dept. 1993).

§ 270.10. Trial jury; challenge to the panel.

1. A challenge to the panel is an objection made to the entire panel of prospective trial jurors returned for the term and may be taken to such panel or to any additional panel that may be ordered by the court. Such a challenge may be made only by the defendant and only on the ground that there has been such a departure from the requirements of the judiciary law in the

drawing or return of the panel as to result in substantial prejudice to the defendant.

2. A challenge to the panel must be made before the selection of the jury commences, and, if it is not, such challenge is deemed to have been waived. Such challenge must be made in writing setting forth the facts constituting the ground of challenge. If such facts are denied by the people, witnesses may be called and examined by either party. All issues of fact and law arising on the challenge must be tried and determined by the court. If a challenge to the panel is allowed, the court must discharge that panel and order another panel of prospective trial jurors returned for the term.

ANNOTATIONS

Claim of systematic discrimination.—By failing to comply with CPL § 270.10, defendant waived any objections he may have had to the composition of the jury panel, and his motion was deficient because it failed to allege facts demonstrating that the claimed underrepresentation of black persons was the result of systematic exclusion. People v. Faulk, 251 A.D.2d 345, 673 N.Y.S.2d 715 (2d Dept. 1998).

—Defendant showed neither that Hispanics were underrepresented in the jury pool or that they were excluded by the court's use of motor vehicle and income tax lists. People v. Rubeo, 158 A.D.2d 485, 550 N.Y.S.2d 936 (2d Dept.), *lv. denied*, 75 N.Y.2d 969 (1990).

—Court rejected defendant's claim that he was denied a representative venire from which to choose a jury because there was only one black person present and that person was not selected; defendant provided no facts tending to demonstrate the existence of a systematic exclusion of minorities or that black persons had been underrepresented on county juries for a significant period of time. People v. Woolfolk, 192 A.D.2d 883, 596 N.Y.S.2d 573 (3d Dept.), *lv. denied*, 82 N.Y.2d 729 (1993).

—Claim that college students were systematically excluded from the jury pool was rejected since college students do not fall into any distinctive group within the meaning of the fair cross-section of the community requirement for prospective jurors. People v. Robinson, 114 A.D.2d 120, 498 N.Y.S.2d 506 (3d Dept. 1986).

—Defendant waived the right to challenge the composition of the panel of prospective jurors because he failed to make a timely written motion; in any event, defendant's conclusory assertions were insufficient to demonstrate that the underrepresentation of African-Americans was the result of systematic exclusion. People v. Bradley, 247 A.D.2d 929, 668 N.Y.S.2d 788 (4th Dept. 1998).

Cognizable group.—Defendant failed to show that his right to equal protection was violated by underrepresentation of Hispanics in Grand Jury pool where it was shown that such underrepresentation was not the result intentional discrimination, but was due instead to a lower response rate to qualification summonses, a higher rate of disqualification for reasons of English literacy and women who were exempted at their own request because they had young children. People v. Guzman, 60 N.Y.2d 403, 469 N.Y.S.2d 916, 457 N.E.2d 1143 (1983), *cert. denied*, 466 U.S. 951 (1984).

—The standard by which a claim of an illegally constituted jury is to be measured is whether the complainant has submitted proof sufficient to establish the existence of intentional and systematic discrimination in the jury selection process. People v. Parks, 41 N.Y.2d 36, 390 N.Y.S.2d 848, 359 N.E.2d 358 (1976).

—Defendant's motion challenging the composition of the jury pool was rejected when he failed to support his contention that 18 to 24-year-olds constitute a recognizable group for the purpose of jury selection. People v. Abdullah, 134 A.D.2d 503, 521 N.Y.S.2d 286 (2d Dept. 1987), *lv. denied*, 71 N.Y.2d 965 (1988).

—Defendant's claim that black youths from ages 18 to 21 were systematically excluded from the jury pool was properly rejected, since there was an insufficient showing that said group

was a large and identifiable segment of the Suffolk County community. People v. Greene, 125 A.D.2d 697, 510 N.Y.S.2d 20 (2d Dept. 1986).

—Defendant failed to show that blacks between the ages of 18 and 21 years old constituted a recognizable group in the community, or that they were systematically excluded from the jury pool. People v. Waters, 125 A.D.2d 615, 510 N.Y.S.2d 8 (2d Dept. 1986), *lv. denied*, 69 N.Y.2d 956 (1987).

—There was no systematic exclusion of Jewish people from the jury pool, merely because the voir dire was conducted on a Jewish holiday. People v. Marrero, 110 A.D.2d 785, 487 N.Y.S.2d 853 (2d Dept. 1985).

—Whether a challenge to the jury selection process is based on the equal protection clause or the due process clause, it must be supported by a demonstration of the demographic breakdown of the jury panels selected in order to show some systematic discrimination. People v. Tucker, 115 A.D.2d 175, 495 N.Y.S.2d 244 (3d Dept. 1985), *lv. denied*, 69 N.Y.2d 956 (1986).

Procedural requirements for challenge.—An oral challenge to the panel does not comply with the requirements of this section and a denial is not appealable. People v. Consolazio, 40 N.Y.2d 446, 387 N.Y.S.2d 62, 354 N.E.2d 801 (1976), *cert. denied*, 433 U.S. 914 (1977).

—Challenge to the jury panel was not preserved for review since the motion was not in writing and no adequate specification of the objections was offered in advance of the selection of the jury to give either the Court or the People sufficient notice of the grounds to be relied upon. People v. Prim, 40 N.Y.2d 946, 390 N.Y.S.2d 407, 358 N.E.2d 1033 (1976).

—Where it appears that the parties did have advance notice and there is no claim of surprise or prejudice, the requirement of a written notice becomes a formality that may be waived by the court, in its discretion. People v. Parks, 41 N.Y.2d 36, 390 N.Y.S.2d 848, 359 N.E.2d 358 (1976).

Comments by excused panelist.—Comments by panelist, who was excused after she stated during voir dire that she recognized defendant, did not taint the remaining panelists so as to deprive defendant of a fair trial because the panelist did not reveal any negative information about defendant until she was at sidebar. People v. Diaz, 289 A.D.2d 184, 735 N.Y.S.2d 517 (1st Dept. 2001).

§ 270.15. Trial jury; examination of prospective jurors; challenges generally.

1.   (a) If no challenge to the panel is made as prescribed by section 270.10, or if such challenge is made and disallowed, the court shall direct that the names of not less than twelve members of the panel be drawn and called as prescribed by the judiciary law. Such persons shall take their places in the jury box and shall be immediately sworn to answer truthfully questions asked them relative to their qualifications to serve as jurors in the action. In its discretion, the court may require prospective jurors to complete a questionnaire concerning their ability to serve as fair and impartial jurors, including but not limited to place of birth, current address, education, occupation, prior jury service, knowledge of, relationship to, or contact with the court, any party, witness or attorney in the action and any other fact relevant to his or her service on the jury. An official form for such questionnaire shall be developed by the chief administrator of the courts in consultation with the administrative board of the courts. A copy of questionnaires completed by the members of the panel shall be given to the court and each attorney prior to examination of prospective jurors.

(b) The court shall initiate the examination of prospective jurors by identifying the parties and their respective counsel and briefly outlining the nature of case to all the prospective jurors. The court shall then put to the members of the panel who have been sworn pursuant to this subdivision and to any prospective jurors subsequently sworn, questions affecting their qualifications to serve as jurors in the action.

(c) The court shall permit both parties, commencing with the people, to examine the prospective jurors, individually or collectively, regarding their qualifications to serve as jurors. Each party shall be afforded a fair opportunity to question the prospective jurors as to any unexplored matter affecting their qualifications, but the court shall not permit questioning that is repetitious or irrelevant, or questions as to a juror's knowledge of rules of law. If necessary to prevent improper questioning as to any matter, the court shall personally examine the prospective jurors as to that matter. The scope of such examination shall be within the discretion of the court. After the parties have concluded their examinations of the prospective jurors, the court may ask such further questions as it deems proper regarding the qualifications of such prospective jurors.

1-a. The court may for good cause shown, upon motion of either party or any affected person or upon its own initiative, issue a protective order for a stated period regulating disclosure of the business or residential address of any prospective or sworn juror to any person or persons, other than to counsel for either party. Such good cause shall exist where the court determines that there is a likelihood of bribery, jury tampering or of physical injury or harassment of the juror.

2. Upon the completion of such examination by both parties, each, commencing with the people, may challenge a prospective juror for cause, as prescribed by section 270.20. If such challenge is allowed, the prospective juror must be excluded from service. After both parties have had an opportunity to challenge for cause, the court must permit them to peremptorily challenge any remaining prospective juror, as prescribed by section 270.25, and such juror must be excluded from service. The people must exercise their peremptory challenges first and may not, after the defendant has exercised his peremptory challenges, make such a challenge to any remaining prospective juror who is then in the jury box. If either party so requests, challenges for cause must be made and determined, and peremptory challenges must be made, within the courtroom but outside of the hearing of the prospective jurors in such manner as not to disclose which party made the challenge. The prospective jurors who are not excluded from service must retain their place in the jury box and must be immediately sworn as trial jurors. They must be sworn to try the action in a just and impartial manner, to the best of their judgment, and to render a verdict according to the law and the evidence.

3. The court may thereupon direct that the persons excluded be replaced in the jury box by an equal number from the panel or, in its discretion, direct that all sworn jurors be removed from the jury box and that the jury box be occupied by such additional number of persons from the panel as the court shall direct. In the court's discretion, sworn jurors who are removed from the jury box as provided herein may be seated elsewhere in the courtroom separate and apart from the unsworn members of the panel or may be removed to the jury room or be allowed to leave the courthouse. The process of jury selection as prescribed herein shall continue until twelve persons are selected and sworn as trial jurors. The juror whose name was first drawn and called must be designated by the court as the foreperson, and no special oath need be administered to him or her. If before twelve jurors are sworn, a juror already sworn becomes unable to serve by reason of illness or other incapacity, the court must discharge him or her and the selection of the trial jury must be completed in the manner prescribed in this section.

4. A challenge for cause of a prospective juror which is not made before he is sworn as a trial juror shall be deemed to have been waived, except that such a challenge based upon a ground not known to the challenging party at that time may be made at any time before a witness is sworn at the trial. If such challenge is allowed by the court, the juror shall be discharged and the selection of the trial jury shall be completed in the manner prescribed in this section, except that if alternate jurors have been sworn, the alternate juror whose name was first drawn and called shall take the place of the juror so discharged.

Amended by L. 1981, Chs. 301, 302; L. 1983, Ch. 684; L. 1985, Chs. 173, 467, 516; L. 1997, Ch. 634, eff. Sept. 24, 1997, amending subd. 3.

ANNOTATIONS

Anonymous jury; not allowed.—People sought to exclude from voir dire all inquiry into the names and exact addresses of the prospective jurors; CPL § 270.15 prohibits selection of an anonymous jury, but CPL § 270.45 gives the court discretion to sequester the jury for the entire trial. However, People did not establish basis for fully sequestered jury. People v. Watts, 173 Misc. 2d 373, 661 N.Y.S.2d 768 (Sup. Ct. Richmond Co. 1997).

Pretrial publicity.—Court's denial of motions for a continuance was upheld where the motions were based on publicity which occurred during the selection of the jury and concerned the defendant's involvement in the crime charged, reports of other crimes committed by the defendant and reports of similar crimes committed by individuals or groups associated with the defendant. People v. Moore, 42 N.Y.2d 421, 397 N.Y.S.2d 975, 366 N.E.2d 1330, cert. denied, 434 U.S. 987 (1977).

—The request for an adjournment to enable a county-wide opinion poll to be taken to assess the effects of allegedly prejudicial media coverage was properly denied as premature where the case had not yet progressed to the voir dire of potential jurors. People v. Begg, 86 A.D.2d 693, 446 N.Y.S.2d 514 (3d Dept. 1982).

Capital case.—In death penalty case, court granted defendant's motion, which was joined by the People, for an order prohibiting disclosure of names and addresses of prospective and sworn jurors to the media or public, in an effort to protect the anonymity of the jurors. People v. Owens, 186 Misc. 2d 923, 721 N.Y.S.2d 487 (Sup. Ct. Monroe Co. 2001).

Voir dire; generally.—It is vital that a defendant have the opportunity to personally view and scrutinize the panel of prospective jurors and to confer and participate with his counsel in the selection of the trial jury. People v. Ganett, 68 A.D.2d 81, 416 N.Y.S.2d 914 (4th Dept. 1979), aff'd, 51 N.Y.2d 991, 435 N.Y.S.2d 976, 417 N.E.2d 88 (1980).

—No matter how desirable it may be, it is unrealistic to expect and require jurors to be totally ignorant prior to trial of the facts and issues in certain cases. People v. Solomon, 172 A.D.2d 781, 569 N.Y.S.2d 101 (2d Dept. 1991).

—To safeguard the defendant's rights, the proper procedure requires that the Judge request the names of the prospective witnesses outside the presence of the jury and that he later present the names to the jury without attributing them to either party. People v. Boyd, 74 A.D.2d 647, 425 N.Y.S.2d 134 (2d Dept. 1980), aff'd, 53 N.Y.2d 912, 440 N.Y.S.2d 631, 423 N.E.2d 54 (1981).

—CPL § 270.15(1)(a) requires the court to swear the panel of prospective jurors prior to the voir dire; trial court's failure to do so was one of several errors that, in the aggregate, led to reversal. People v. Patterson, 203 A.D.2d 597, 611 N.Y.S.2d 597 (2d Dept. 1994).

—Being escorted in the courtroom did not prejudice the defendant, particularly where the viewing occurred during jury selection and it was unclear whether the two veniremen who saw him were ever chosen for the jury panel. People v. Lev, 128 A.D.2d 1000, 513 N.Y.S.2d 533 (3d Dept. 1987).

—While it is the better practice to record the voir dire, the failure of the court to do so did not warrant reversal where the defendant failed to demonstrate prejudice from the failure to do so. People v. Johnson, 140 A.D.2d 954, 529 N.Y.S.2d 631 (4th Dept.), lv. denied, 72 N.Y.2d 920 (1988).

Court's comments to venire persons.—The court's statement to the jurors during voir dire that if they were late, they would be fined, did not present a due process violation of defendant's right to a jury trial; defendant failed to submit any indication that any potential jurors were thereby kept off the jury. People v. Stansberry, 205 A.D.2d 317, 613 N.Y.S.2d 6 (1st Dept. 1994).

—The court did not err in failing to inquire of the eight jurors already sworn as to a statement by juror number one that he remembered the defendant from another case since no objection or motion with respect to these remarks was made until after trial nor did defense counsel request that the remarks be excluded or that the jury be directed to disregard them. People v. Mullen, 53 A.D.2d 933, 385 N.Y.S.2d 186 (3d Dept. 1976), aff'd, 44 N.Y.2d 1, 403 N.Y.S.2d 470, 374 N.E.2d 369 (1978).

Foreperson of jury.—Court's decision to designate second-drawn juror as foreperson, over defendant's objection, after first-drawn juror refused to serve in that capacity, does not warrant reversal; although CPL § 270.15(3) requires that the first-drawn juror perform that duty or be discharged, the designation of the second-drawn juror could not have caused any prejudice to defendant because the law recognizes no special function as the jury's spokesperson. People v. Burgess, 280 A.D.2d 264, 719 N.Y.S.2d 649 (1st Dept. 2001).

Restrictions on voir dire; generally.—Trial judge retains broad discretion in determining what inquiries may be made of prospective jurors, where such inquiries do not reach a constitutional dimension. People v. Stanard, 42 N.Y.2d 74, 396 N.Y.S.2d 825, 365 N.E.2d 857, cert. denied, 434 U.S. 986 (1977).

—A trial court possesses broad discretion to restrict the scope of voir dire by counsel and to preclude repetitive or irrelevant questioning. People v. Ellis, 202 A.D.2d 271, 608 N.Y.S.2d 652 (1st Dept. 1994).

—The trial court has broad discretion to control the scope of the voir dire. People v. Sorentino, 182 A.D.2d 418, 582 N.Y.S.2d 152 (1st Dept. 1992); People v. Mendoza, 191 A.D.2d 648, 595 N.Y.S.2d 113 (2d Dept. 1993); People v. Loliscio, 187 A.D.2d 172, 593 N.Y.S.2d 991 (2d Dept. 1993).

—Reversal was required because defense counsel was not permitted to ask potential jurors during the voir dire whether they would follow instructions from the court requiring them to disregard inculpatory statements made by the defendant

should the jury find them to have been involuntarily made. People v. DeFrancesco, 88 A.D.2d 920, 450 N.Y.S.2d 562 (2d Dept. 1982).

Restrictions on voir dire; time limits.—Time limits on each attorney's voir dire is permissible so long as defense counsel has a fair opportunity to question prospective jurors about relevant matters. People v. Jean, 75 N.Y.2d 744, 551 N.Y.S.2d 889, 551 N.E.2d 90 (1989).

—Questioning limited to 15 minutes in the first two rounds and 10 minutes in the third round was within the court's discretion. People v. Jean, 75 N.Y.2d 744, 551 N.Y.S.2d 889, 551 N.E.2d 90 (1989).

—Time limits of 10 minutes for first panel, 5 minutes for second panel, and only one question to the third panel, addressed to the panel as a whole; limits on third panel cannot be construed as a fair opportunity to question the panel members. People v. Rampersant, 182 A.D.2d 373, 581 N.Y.S.2d 784 (1st Dept. 1992).

—Limiting third round questions to 10 minutes is permissible. People v. Davis, 166 A.D.2d 453, 560 N.Y.S.2d 499 (2d Dept.), lv. denied, 76 N.Y.2d 985 (1990).

—Limiting questioning to 10 minutes in each of the first three rounds and 3 minutes in fourth round was within the court's discretion. People v. Garrow, 151 A.D.2d 877, 542 N.Y.S.2d 849 (3d Dept.), lv. denied, 74 N.Y.2d 948 (1989).

Restrictions on voir dire; scope of questioning.—It was improper for the court to preclude questions regarding whether the jurors would be able to fairly assess the testimony of a witness with a criminal record, and whether they would draw an adverse inference if he did not testify. People v. Porter, 220 A.D.2d 540, 632 N.Y.S.2d 205 (1st Dept.), lv. denied, 87 N.Y.2d 976 (1996).

—In reversing defendant's conviction, the court determined that the trial court's failure to permit defendant to examine prospective jurors concerning prejudice against persons of Italian origin was a reversible constitutional error. People v. Rubicco, 42 A.D.2d 719, 345 N.Y.S.2d 624 (2d Dept. 1973), aff'd, 34 N.Y.2d 841, 359 N.Y.S.2d 62, 316 N.E.2d 344 (1974).

—Prospective jurors may not be questioned as to their attitudes concerning matters of law since questions concerning prospective jurors' knowledge or attitudes relating to a particular law are irrelevant to their functions as triers of factual issues and, therefore, have no bearing on their qualifications as jurors. People v. Corbett, 68 A.D.2d 772, 418 N.Y.S.2d 699 (4th Dept. 1979), aff'd, 52 N.Y.2d 714, 436 N.Y.S.2d 273, 417 N.E.2d 567 (1980).

—Trial court properly precluded the defendant from questioning prospective jurors concerning the doctrine of self-defense, because it is not the province of counsel to question prospective jurors as to their attitudes or knowledge of matters of law. People v. Rodriguez, 240 A.D.2d 683, 659 N.Y.S.2d 495 (2d Dept. 1997).

Restrictions on voir dire; scope of questioning.—Court did not err in limiting defense counsel's questioning of prospective jurors concerning their possible bias toward police witnesses, because court has broad discretion to supervise the scope of voir dire to preclude repetitive, irrelevant, or otherwise improper questioning, including questioning of jurors with regard to their knowledge or attitude toward matters of law. People v. Bennett, 238 A.D.2d 898, 660 N.Y.S.2d 772 (4th Dept. 1997).

Requirement that court seat not less than 12 prospective jurors at same time.—The trial court called 18 prospective jurors for the initial round of jury selection, seven of whom were ultimately chosen to serve. The court then ordered one prospective juror at a time to be put into the jury box for questioning and challenges, over the objection of both sides. This procedure continued until the jury was selected. Defendant argued that this violated CPL § 270.15(3) and that at least five jurors should have been placed in the box. The trial court has the discretion to determine the number of prospective jurors to be placed in the jury box following completion of the first round of voir dire. Although the court's procedure was not unlawful, it should not be followed because it needlessly prolonged jury selection. People v. Williams, 2 N.Y.3d 725, 778 N.Y.S.2d 739, 811 N.E.2d 1 (2004).

—When the court swore in 52 prospective jurors, seated in the jury box and elsewhere in the courtroom for simultaneous voir dire by counsel, it did not violate CPL § 270.15 or defendant's constitutional right to select a jury; the procedure complied with the requirement that the court seat not less than 12 prospective jurors for examination at the same time. People v. Campbell, 259 A.D.2d 447, 687 N.Y.S.2d 343 (1st Dept. 1999).

Expanded jury box.—Court's use of an expanded jury box for voir dire did not violate CPL § 270.15(1)(a) or adversely affect defendant's ability to select a jury. People v. Serrano, 19 A.D.3d 303, 797 N.Y.S.2d 92 (1st Dept. 2005).

Jury challenges; general.—While the court erred in refusing to permit a challenge outside of the hearing of the prospective jurors in such manner as not to disclose which party made the challenge, a reversal of conviction was not warranted where the defendant failed to demonstrate any prejudice as a result of the error. People v. Pepper, 59 N.Y.2d 353, 465 N.Y.S.2d 850, 452 N.E.2d 1178 (1983).

Jury challenges; order.—The People must exercise their challenges first and may not exercise challenges after the defense has made their challenges; the statute is drafted to prevent the prosecutor from challenging a juror found acceptable to the defendant for that reason alone. People v. Roberts, 215 A.D.2d 148, 626 N.Y.S.2d 757 (1st Dept. 1995).

—Trial court committed error when, after defense counsel had made his peremptory challenges, it permitted the prosecutor to rectify an unintentional omission by belatedly exercising a peremptory challenge to a still unsworn, prospective juror, but defendant waived any objections to this irregularity in the jury selection process by failing to avail himself of the court's explicit invitation to place his objection on the record and by failing to request any curative relief at a time when the court could have corrected its error. People v. Lebron, 236 A.D.2d 423, 653 N.Y.S.2d 615 (2d Dept. 1997).

—Reversal, where the trial court improperly allowed the prosecutor to exercise a peremptory challenge after she had indicated she was finished and defense counsel had exercised his challenges. People v. McDermott, 199 A.D.2d 341, 606 N.Y.S.2d 986 (2d Dept. 1993).

—Trial court committed reversible error by permitting the prosecutor to exercise another peremptory challenge after he indicated to the court he had completed his challenges, and while defense counsel was exercising his challenges. People v. DeConto, 172 A.D.2d 684 (2d Dept. 1991), aff'd, 80 N.Y.2d 943 (1992).

—In no event may the People exercise a peremptory challenge after the defendant has exercised his or her peremptory challenges. Any action inconsistent with the statutorily delineated procedure warrants reversal. People v. Powell, 13 A.D.3d 975, 787 N.Y.S.2d 480 (3d Dept. 2004).

Jury challenges; for cause.—A hearing-impaired person is not, by reason of that impairment disqualified from service as a juror. People v. Guzman, 76 N.Y.2d 1, 556 N.Y.S.2d 7, 555 N.E.2d 259 (1990).

—In determining whether a juror must be disqualified, the trial court must question in camera each allegedly unqualified juror individually in the presence of the attorneys and the defendant. People v. Thomas, 196 A.D.2d 462, 601 N.Y.S.2d 608 (1st Dept.), lv. denied, 82 N.Y.2d 757 (1993).

—Court properly discharged a juror who was not a resident of the county. People v. Mikell, 183 A.D.2d 411, 583 N.Y.S.2d 266 (1st Dept. 1992).

—Court properly discharged juror where juror's home had been burned, and the juror expressed uncertainty as to when he could return. People v. Ray, 182 A.D.2d 387, 582 N.Y.S.2d 129 (1st Dept.), lv. denied, 79 N.Y.2d 1053 (1992).

—Challenge for cause was not justified although the juror apparently sought to be excused from duty, since he gave assurances that he would be fair and impartial. People v. Blyden, 225 A.D.2d 704, 640 N.Y.S.2d 131 (2d Dept. 1996).

—The defendant was not prejudiced by the trial court's failure to dismiss for cause a particular juror, since the prosecutor exercised a peremptory challenge and that juror was excused. People v. Dunkley, 189 A.D.2d 776, 592 N.Y.S.2d 401 (2d Dept.), lv. denied, 81 N.Y.2d 884 (1993).

—Reversal was required where court denied defense counsel's challenge to a juror who had served within the past two years. People v. Mandala, 195 A.D.2d 574, 600 N.Y.S.2d 492 (2d Dept. 1993).

—The fact that one of the jurors became aware that defendant had approached her son, a correction officer at the jail, and had a conversation with him did not require her disqualification.

People v. Peck, 192 A.D.2d 746, 596 N.Y.S.2d 209 (3d Dept. 1993).

Disqualified because of prior service.—A prospective juror was disqualified by reason of prior service when he appeared for jury service within the previous four years but never sat as a juror in a case; Judiciary Law § 524 is intended to include for disqualification individuals who fulfilled their jury service obligations by responding to a summons for jury duty through either actual physical attendance or telephone standby service. People v. Wynter, 95 N.Y.2d 504, 719 N.Y.S.2d 637, 742 N.E.2d 112 (2000)

Swearing in jurors.—Defendant's challenge to the court's failure to swear in the jurors immediately upon their selection, as mandated by CPL § 270.15(2), requires preservation, but this technical error was harmless because the court swore in the jurors before it delivered its preliminary instructions and proceeded with opening statements and testimony. People v. Quinones, 18 A.D.3d 330, 795 N.Y.S.2d 47 (1st Dept. 2005).

Requirement that sworn jurors remain in courtroom.—Defendant's claim that the court violated the jury selection procedures mandated by CPL § 270.15(3) in excusing sworn jurors from the courtroom without defendant's consent while the voir dire continued was unpreserved; moreover, the absence of the jurors caused defendant no real prejudice and therefore did not warrant a new trial. People v. Cruz, 204 A.D.2d 212, 612 N.Y.S.2d 35 (1st Dept. 1994).

—Violation of CPL § 270.15(3) does not constitute per se reversible error; rather, defendant must point to real prejudice resulting from absence of sworn jurors. People v. Cassado, 156 A.D.2d 183, 548 N.Y.S.2d 227 (1st Dept. 1989).

Juror properly discharged after being sworn.—Juror's statement that he would abandon his obligations in favor of personal concerns, which was brought to the court's attention after the juror had been sworn, justified juror's discharge. People v. Marquez, 264 A.D.2d 634, 696 N.Y.S.2d 422 (1st Dept. 1999).

§ 270.16. Capital cases; individual questioning for racial bias.

1. In any case in which the crime charged may be punishable by death, the court shall, upon motion of either party, permit the parties, commencing with the people, to examine the prospective jurors individually and outside the presence of the other prospective jurors regarding their qualifications to serve as jurors. Each party shall be afforded a fair opportunity to question a prospective juror as to any unexplored matter affecting his or her qualifications, including without limitation the possibility of racial bias on the part of the prospective juror, but the court shall not permit questioning that is repetitious or irrelevant, or questions as to a prospective juror's knowledge of rules of law. If necessary to prevent improper questioning as to any matter, the court shall personally examine the prospective jurors as to that matter. The scope of such examination shall be within the discretion of the court. After the parties have concluded their examinations of a prospective juror, the court may ask such further questions as it deems proper regarding the qualifications of the prospective juror.

2. The proceedings provided for in this section shall be conducted on the record; provided, however, that upon motion of either party, and for good cause shown, the court may direct that all or a portion of the record of such proceedings be sealed.

Added by L. 1995, Ch. 1, § 14, eff. Sept. 1, 1995, and

applying only to offenses committed on or after Sept. 1, 1995; offenses committed prior to such date shall be governed by the provisions of law in effect at the time the offense was committed.

ANNOTATIONS

Court's discretion.—Trial court has broad discretion to conduct voir dire in a capital case. People v. Santiago, 184 Misc. 2d 403, 708 N.Y.S.2d 269 (Co. Ct. Monroe Co. 2000).

Hybrid system of jury selection.—Court adopted a hybrid system of jury selection in capital case in order to minimize the risk of a conviction-prone jury. The court modified the "struck-jury system" to the extent that it would conduct an individualized voir dire until a sufficient pool was assembled and then it would allow both parties to question the jurors on issues unconnected to sentencing; once the sufficient pool was amassed, peremptory challenges would be exercised under the "jury box" method. People v. Webb, 187 Misc. 2d 451, 722 N.Y.S.2d 349 (Sup. Ct. Kings Co. 2001).

No superseding of CPL § 270.15.—"There is nothing to suggest that in adding CPL § 270.16, the Legislature intended to supersede CPL 270.15." People v. Harris, 98 N.Y.2d 452, 749 N.Y.S.2d 766, 779 N.E.2d 705 (2002), *habeas corpus denied,* Harris v. Goord, 2004 U.S. Dist. LEXIS 14017 (E.D.N.Y. July 23, 2004).

§ 270.20. Trial jury; challenge for cause of an individual juror.

1. A challenge for cause is an objection to a prospective juror and may be made only on the ground that:

(a) He does not have the qualifications required by the judiciary law; or

(b) He has a state of mind that is likely to preclude him from rendering an impartial verdict based upon the evidence adduced at the trial; or

(c) He is related within the sixth degree by consanguinity or affinity to the defendant, or to the person allegedly injured by the crime charged, or to a prospective witness at the trial, or to counsel for the people or for the defendant; or that he is or was a party adverse to any such person in a civil action; or that he has complained against or been accused by any such person in a criminal action; or that he bears some other relationship to any such person of such nature that it is likely to preclude him from rendering an impartial verdict; or

(d) He was a witness at the preliminary examination or before the grand jury or is to be a witness at the trial; or

(e) He served on the grand jury which found the indictment in issue or served on a trial jury in a prior civil or criminal action involving the same incident charged in such indictment; or

(f) The crime charged may be punishable by death and the prospective juror entertains such conscientious opinions either against or in favor of such punishment as to preclude such juror from rendering an impartial verdict or from properly exercising the discretion conferred upon such juror by law in the determination of a sentence pursuant to section 400.27.

2. All issues of fact or law arising on the challenge must be tried and determined by the court. If the challenge is allowed, the court must exclude the person challenged from service. An erroneous ruling by the court allowing a challenge for cause by the people does not constitute reversible error unless the people have exhausted their peremptory challenges at the time or exhaust them before the selection of the jury is complete. An erroneous ruling by the court denying a challenge for cause by the defendant does not constitute reversible error unless the defendant has exhausted his peremptory challenges at the time or, if he has not, he peremptorily challenges such prospective juror and his peremptory challenges are exhausted before the selection of the jury is complete.

Amended by L. 1974, Ch. 367; L. 1989, Ch. 68; L. 1995, Ch. 1, § 15, eff. Sept. 1, 1995, amending subd. 1(f).

ANNOTATIONS

Challenges for cause; general.—An erroneous ruling by the court, denying a challenge for cause, constitutes reversible error when the defendant peremptorily challenges the prospective juror and his peremptory challenges are exhausted before the jury selection process is complete. People v. Culhane, 33 N.Y.2d 90, 350 N.Y.S.2d 381, 305 N.E.2d 469 (1973).

—Despite legally sufficient evidence, new trial was ordered where defendant's challenge for cause should have been granted because juror's statement to defense counsel that "I think I could be impartial" fell short of the required unequivocal declaration of impartiality. People v. Sumpter, 237 A.D.2d 389, 654 N.Y.S.2d 817 (2d Dept. 1997).

—Where defendant has exhausted his peremptory challenges, an erroneous ruling by the court denying a challenge for cause is reversible error. People v. Branch, 59 A.D.2d 459, 399 N.Y.S.2d 930 (3d Dept. 1977), *aff'd,* 46 N.Y.2d 645, 415 N.Y.S.2d 985, 389 N.E.2d 467 (1979).

—To successfully object to a juror after a verdict, a party is required to demonstrate that the objectionable conduct was unknown to him beforehand and that it would not have been disclosed by proper inquiry before the jury was sworn. People v. Albright, 104 A.D.2d 508, 479 N.Y.S.2d 892 (3d Dept. 1984).

Challenges for cause; relationships with law enforcement.—Court properly denied defendant's challenge for cause to a police officer/panelist who became a sworn juror as a result of defendant's exhaustion of his peremptory challenges. The juror did not know any of the testifying officers and emphatically stated her ability to evaluate the credibility of police testimony fairly and to render an impartial verdict. Simply being a member of the same police force as the witnesses was not a disqualifying relationship under CPL § 270.20(1)(c). People v. Jones, 299 A.D.2d 283, 751 N.Y.S.2d 173 (1st Dept. 2002)

—It was error for the court to refuse a challenge for cause to a juror whose son was a police officer, where defendant was charged with shooting at police officers. People v. Johnson, 89 A.D.2d 506, 452 N.Y.S.2d 53 (1st Dept. 1982).

—Two prospective jurors, one who was a fiancee of a police officer and the other who was the spouse of a police officer, indicated that they could be fair and impartial; however, one of these prospective jurors said that she did have an affinity to police officers, and both stated that they did not believe police officers would lie. Two other prospective jurors indicated that their experiences as crime victims might affect their views of the case. The trial court erred in refusing to dismiss these prospective jurors, and because the defense counsel then exercised a peremptory challenge against each prospective juror, and eventually exhausted his allotment of peremptory challenges, defendant's conviction must be reversed. People v. Zachary, 260 A.D.2d 514, 689 N.Y.S.2d 156 (2d Dept. 1999).

—A juror's relationship with a police officer and even his position as a police officer are insufficient to constitute implied basis. People v. Butts, 140 A.D.2d 677, 527 N.Y.S.2d 880 (3d Dept. 1988).

Challenges for cause; relationships with defense or prosecution.—An expurgatory oath is not available to purge the taint of bias that is implied by the law from the existence of the relationships covered by the statute. People v. Provenzano, 50 N.Y.2d 420, 429 N.Y.S.2d 562, 407 N.E.2d 408 (1980).

—Court did not err in denying defendant's application to dismiss for cause a juror who claimed to be a passing acquaintance of the District Attorney; the relationship was not one proscribed by the CPL, and there was no substantial risk that the juror's pre-existing opinions would impede her ability to be a fair juror. People v. Rodriguez, 242 A.D.2d. 475, 662 N.Y.S.2d 478 (1st Dept. 1997).

—The respective relationships of two prospective jurors with people in the District Attorney's office and the trial prosecutor were so remote in all respects that it did not render them inherently biased, and the denial of defendant's challenges for cause as to these two prospective jurors was not error. People v. Rowe, 253 A.D.2d 831, 677 N.Y.S.2d 625 (2d Dept. 1998).

—The trial court properly rejected defendant's challenge for cause to a prospective juror whose cousin was an assistant district attorney, because the cousin was in no way involved in the prosecution of the case. People v. Horne, 203 A.D.2d 482, 610 N.Y.S.2d 867 (2d Dept. 1994).

—The trial court properly disqualified for cause a prospective juror whose brother was being prosecuted by the prosecutor's office in three state and at the same time as the defendant's trial. People v. Dockery, 204 A.D.2d 477, 612 N.Y.S.2d 608 (2d Dept.), lv. denied, 84 N.Y.2d 934 (1994).

—Implied bias existed where a juror had both a limited social acquaintance and a business relationship with the prosecution witness and no expurgatory oath could be given to overcome the possible bias as an expurgatory oath can only overcome actual bias. People v. Meyer, 78 A.D.2d 662, 432 N.Y.S.2d 219 (2d Dept. 1980).

—CPL § 270.20(1)(c) precludes taking into account any statements of impartiality made in an attempt to overcome a relationship that objectively is likely to preclude such impartiality. People v. Branch, 59 A.D.2d 459, 399 N.Y.S.2d 930 (3d Dept. 1977), aff'd, 46 N.Y.2d 645, 415 N.Y.S.2d 985, 389 N.E.2d 467 (1979).

Judge's absence.—Judge's absence from portions of the actual voir dire examination of jurors violated defendant's right to have a judge preside over and supervise the voir dire proceedings, because in the end, it is the judge who is the ultimate arbiter of a prospective juror's fitness to serve. People v. Toliver, 89 N.Y.2d 843, 652 N.Y.S.2d 728, 675 N.E.2d 463 (1996).

Challenges for cause; relationship to victim.—A panelist who was acquainted with the crime victims did not exhibit a state of mind that was likely to preclude her from rendering an impartial verdict based on the evidence at trial. People v. McDowell, 16 A.D.3d 102, 790 N.Y.S.2d 121 (1st Dept. 2005).

—Court properly dismissed juror as unqualified where she expressed uncertainty, because of her familial ties to the victim, about her capacity to render an objective verdict. People v. Benson, 123 A.D.2d 470, 506 N.Y.S.2d 480 (3d Dept. 1986).

Married jurors.—The prospective jurors' marriage was not a relationship that implicates CPL § 270.20(1)(c), and both jurors unequivocally stated that they could render an impartial verdict based solely on the evidence at trial. People v. Stamps, 254 A.D.2d 507, 681 N.Y.S.2d 31 (2d Dept. 1998).

Challenges for cause; defendant's decision not to testify.—Court did not err in denying cause challenges as to one juror who had two nephews in prison and another who stated that, should the defendant invoke his Fifth Amendment right not to testify at trial, he would wonder why the defendant did not testify; both prospective jurors, upon being questioned by the court, stated unequivocally that they would be able to decide the case solely on the evidence adduced at trial and that they would follow the instructions given to them by the court. People v. Perez, 204 A.D.2d 662, 612 N.Y.S.2d 620 (2d Dept. 1994).

—A prospective juror's statement that a defendant's decision not to testify "might" influence his or her ability to be impartial is sufficient to cast serious doubt on his or her ability to render a fair verdict, and the case must be reversed if the court denies a challenge for cause on this ground and the defendant subsequently exhausts his or her peremptory challenges. People v. Russell, 16 A.D.3d 776, 791 N.Y.S.2d 198 (3d Dept. 2005).

Challenges for cause: disabilities.—A visually impaired juror is not necessarily unable to properly evaluate the credibility of witnesses and thus it was not error to deny defendant's

challenge for cause. People v. Pagan, 191 A.D.2d 651, 595 N.Y.S.2d 486 (2d Dept.), lv. denied, 81 N.Y.2d 1017 (1993).

—A prospective juror may not be disqualified solely because he is deaf; a deaf person who communicates in signed English, as opposed to American Sign Language, and who otherwise meets the qualifications of a juror may communicate through a "signer," to be provided by the court. People v. Guzman, 125 Misc. 2d 457, 478 N.Y.S.2d 455 (Sup. Ct. N.Y. Co. 1984), aff'd, 148 A.D.2d 350, 538 N.Y.S.2d 986 (1989), aff'd, 76 N.Y.2d 1, 556 N.Y.S.2d 7, 555 N.E.2d 259 (1990).

Challenges for cause; juror's background.—Where prospective juror stated that she studied domestic violence extensively and that she had a "problem," those statements indicated that she herself questioned whether she could be impartial in any domestic violence case; court should have granted challenge for cause to this juror. People v. Arnold, 96 N.Y.2d 358, 729 N.Y.S.2d 51, 753 N.E.2d 846 (2001).

Challenges for cause; relationship or acquaintance with witness.—The fact that two prospective jurors were former police officers who had "nodding acquaintances" with several of the prospective witnesses did not render them so inherently biased to justify disqualification for cause. There was no allegation of misconduct by any police officer, the defense did not attack the credibility of an officer, and the charges did not pertain to the police. People v. Cassidy, 16 A.D.3d 1079, 791 N.Y.S.2d 259 (4th Dept. 2005).

—Court erred in denying defendant's challenge for cause to a prospective juror who informed the court during jury selection that he had attended school with a prosecution witness and who admitted that he would tend to believe that witness "more than somebody that [he] did not know." The juror further did not provide an unequivocal assurance that he could put his bias aside and render a fair and impartial verdict. Because defendant exhausted all of his peremptory challenges before the completion of jury selection, the court's erroneous ruling was reversible error. People v. McDonald, 291 A.D.2d 832, 737 N.Y.S.2d 446 (4th Dept. 2002).

Challenges for cause; prior jury service.—Reversal was warranted where the trial court denied defendant's challenge for cause of a juror who had been a juror within the last two years. People v. Mandala, 195 A.D.2d 574, 600 N.Y.S.2d 492 (2d Dept. 1993).

—Reversal was required pursuant to CPL § 270.20(1) where court improperly denied defendant's challenge for cause of a juror, who stated he had served on a Federal Grand Jury a year and a half prior to the trial, causing defendant to exercise one of his peremptory challenges and defendant exhausted all of his peremptories prior to the completion of jury selection. People v. O'Hare, 117 A.D.2d 757, 498 N.Y.S.2d 478 (2d Dept. 1986).

Challenges for cause; state of mind.—Juror's use of the phrase "I think so" did not negate the fact that, through the totality of her responses, she was able to provide an unequivocal assurance that she could be a fair juror. People v. Tyler, 17 A.D.3d 239, 793 N.Y.S.2d 44 (1st Dept. 2005); accord People v. Gonzalez, 16 A.D.3d 283, 792 N.Y.S.2d 407 (1st Dept. 2005) (court properly denied defendant's challenge for cause to prospective juror who initially expressed favorable inclination toward police testimony, but then gave unequivocal assurance of his impartiality to evaluate police testimony fairly; in context, juror's use of phrase "I think so" was not disqualifying); People v. McDowell, 16 A.D.3d 102, 790 N.Y.S.2d 121 (1st Dept. 2005) (panelist's use of word "think" was not disqualifying).

—Trial court properly granted People's request to excuse a juror for cause, where juror repeatedly expressed concern that she was uncomfortable with deciding innocence or guilt. People v. Johnson, 252 A.D.2d 532, 676 N.Y.S.2d 366 (4th Dept.), aff'd, 92 N.Y.2d 976, 683 N.Y.S.2d 754, 706 N.E.2d 742 (1998).

—Court properly refused to dismiss for cause a juror whose voir dire responses indicated that her scheduling conflict was manageable and that she did not have a state of mind likely to preclude her from rendering an impartial verdict.

Challenges for cause; expurgatory oath.—An expurgatory oath is not available to purge the taint of bias that is implied by the law from the existence of the relationships covered by the statute. People v. Provenzano, 50 N.Y.2d 420, 429 N.Y.S.2d 562, 407 N.E.2d 408 (1980).

—The expurgatory oath is unavailable where a juror is disqualified by virtue of CPL § 270.20(1)(c). People v. Branch, 46 N.Y.2d 645, 415 N.Y.S.2d 985, 389 N.E.2d 467 (1979).

—Judge's inquiry to jurors as a collective body whether they could remain impartial where certain jurors had been exposed to demonstrations against the judge's use of a racial reference in an unrelated case was inadequate to ensure impartiality of jurors. People v. Pascullo, 120 A.D.2d 687, 502 N.Y.S.2d 275 (2d Dept. 1986).

—Implied bias existed where a juror had both a limited social acquaintance and a business relationship with the prosecution witness and no expurgatory oath could be given to overcome the possible bias as an expurgatory oath can only overcome actual bias. People v. Meyer, 78 A.D.2d 662, 432 N.Y.S.2d 219 (2d Dept. 1980).

Inadequate assurance of impartiality.—Where one of the prospective jurors gave equivocal responses when questioned by defense counsel as to whether the victim's age (14 years old) would prevent her from being fair and impartial, since she had children of her own, and trial court failed to obtain a personal, unequivocal declaration or assurance of impartiality from that juror, it was reversible error because defendant had exhausted all of his peremptory challenges. People v. Henriques, 307 A.D.2d 937, 762 N.Y.S.2d 887 (2d Dept. 2003).

—Court erred in denying defendant's challenge for cause to a prospective juror who expressed doubt concerning his ability to be impartial based on what he had heard from bar patrons who were present on the night of the incident. Because the court failed to elicit or even seek an unequivocal assurance from the prospective juror that he would be able to render an impartial verdict based on the evidence, reversal was required. People v. Papineau, 19 A.D.3d 1149, 796 N.Y.S.2d 491 (4th Dept. 2005).

State of mind; defendant's prior convictions.—Where two prospective jurors indicated that defendant's prior conviction would lead them to believe that defendant was guilty of the present crime, the court was obligated, upon defendant's application, to discharge these jurors for cause unless a "personal, unequivocal assurance of impartiality" could be secured; because the court failed to do so and answers given by the entire panel failed to remedy this deficiency, court vacated defendant's conviction. People v. Thompkins, 287 A.D.2d 381, 731 N.Y.S.2d 457 (1st Dept. 2001).

—Where prospective juror gave equivocal responses when questioned by counsel as to whether the fact that defendant had a prior felony conviction would prevent her from being fair and impartial, failure to grant defendant's for cause challenge was reversible error. People v. Butler, 287 A.D.2d 647, 732 N.Y.S.2d 18 (2d Dept. 2001).

—Trial court erred in denying defendant's challenge for cause where prospective juror responded in the affirmative when asked if, upon learning that the defendant had prior felony convictions, she might believe "if he had done it before he might do it again"; such a response indicated that the juror had a state of mind likely to preclude her from rendering an impartial verdict based on the evidence. People v. Morton, 271 A.D.2d 702, 707 N.Y.S.2d 185 (2d Dept. 2000).

State of mind; defendant's drug use.—Trial court improperly denied defendant's challenge for cause to prospective juror, who had stated that he was "not sure" he could convict defendant on the basis of the evidence, and that he would "wonder why [the defendant] is still involved with drugs if he has a prior." These statements established that the prospective juror had a state of mind that was likely to preclude him from rendering an impartial verdict, and it was then incumbent on the trial court to seek clarification from the juror to ensure his ability to render an impartial verdict or, in the absence of such assurance, to dismiss the prospective juror for cause. Since the court did neither, and defendant exhausted his peremptory challenges before jury selection was complete, reversal is required. People v. Beldres, 262 A.D.2d 498, 692 N.Y.S.2d 114 (2d Dept. 1999).

—The trial court erred in refusing to dismiss a prospective juror for cause when the juror did not unequivocably state that he would not be influenced by his feelings with respect to the defendant's history of drug use. People v. Watts, 212 A.D.2d 650, 622 N.Y.S.2d 574 (2d Dept.), lv. denied, 85 N.Y.2d 981 (1995).

State of mind; attitudes toward law enforcement.—In murder trial, where the responses and affirmative nods of certain prospective jurors indicated their possible bias in favor of police testimony, the trial court should have obtained unequivocal assurances of impartiality from each of them, and its failure to

do so was reversible error because defendant eventually exhausted his peremptory challenges. People v. Nicholas, 98 N.Y.2d 749, 751 N.Y.S.2d 820, 781 N.E.2d 884 (2002).

—Defendant's challenge for cause should have been granted, where the prospective juror said he believed a police officer would not exaggerate and would tell the truth, and did not state in unequivocal terms that he could render an impartial verdict based on the evidence. People v. Punch, 215 A.D.2d 410, 626 N.Y.S.2d 246 (2d Dept. 1995).

State of mind; racial attitudes.—Trial court did not commit error by denying a challenge for cause to two jurors who had stated that although they did not associate with blacks and did not approve of interracial marriages, they could render a fair and impartial verdict notwithstanding evidence that the defendant, a black, had a white girlfriend with whom he had a child; there was no showing of a substantial risk that any juror's predisposition would affect the proper discharge of that juror's duties. People v. Williams, 63 N.Y.2d 882, 483 N.Y.S.2d 198, 472 N.E.2d 1026 (1984).

State of mind; juror or relative was crime victim.—Court correctly exercised its discretion in refusing to excuse for cause a prospective juror who indicated that a close friend had been shot to death, but that she would try not to let that affect her ability to be impartial in prosecution for criminal possession of a weapon and resisting arrest; prospective juror never expressed any actual bias, and therefore, she was not required to make an unequivocal declaration overcoming a bias that she never stated she possessed. People v. Washington, 254 A.D.2d 148, 679 N.Y.S.2d 31 (1st Dept. 1998).

—Court erred in denying defendant's challenge for cause of prospective juror who had been a crime victim and could only declare that she "hoped" her experience would not affect her. Where there remains any doubt in the wake of such statements, when considered in the context of the prospective juror's overall responses, the prospective juror should be discharged for cause. People v. Jackson, 265 A.D.2d 342, 697 N.Y.S.2d 288 (2d Dept. 1999).

—Court erred in denying defense counsel's for cause challenge to juror who indicated during voir dire that a relative had recently been assaulted, and she did not unequivocally state that she could render a fair and impartial verdict based on the evidence; reversal required because both defense counsel exhausted their peremptory challenges, including the one used to excuse this juror, and the court denied the request for additional peremptory challenges. People v. McFadden, 244 A.D.2d 887, 665 N.Y.S.2d 985 (4th Dept. 1997).

Subd. (1)(f); capital case.—Where court erroneously denied a for cause dismissal of a juror and erroneously granted another for cause dismissal, the errors did not warrant reversal because the errors related only to the jurors' ability to serve impartially during the penalty phase, and thus, were not of the type that would infect the guilt phase. People v. Cahill, 2 N.Y.3d 14, 777 N.Y.S.2d 332, 809 N.E.2d 561 (2003).

—"Where jurors express conscientious views concerning the death penalty yet still make clear that they are able to follow their oaths to act impartially, they cannot be excluded for cause from participating on the jury." Defendant failed to overcome the presumption of constitutionality of CPL § 270.20(1)(f). People v. Harris, 98 N.Y.2d 452, 749 N.Y.S.2d 766, 779 N.E.2d 705 (2002), habeas corpus denied, Harris v. Goord, 2004 U.S. Dist. LEXIS 14017 (E.D.N.Y. July 23, 2004).

—Defendant argued CPL § 270.20(1)(f) is unconstitutional because it permits a "death-qualified" jury to determine a capital defendant's guilt or innocence. The court rejected this argument and upheld the constitutionality of the statute. Defendant's prosecution was not affected by the constitutional infirmity of CPL §§ 220.10(5)(e) and 220.30(3)(b)(vii), which were determined to be unconstitutional in Hynes v. Tomei, a case decided after defendant was convicted and sentenced. People v. Parker, 304 A.D.2d 146, 755 N.Y.S.2d 521 (4th Dept. 2003).

—Where defendant claimed that the capital jury qualification process under New York law violated his rights to an impartial jury, due process, and a jury comprised of a fair cross-section of the community because it excluded individuals expressing qualms about capital punishment; the court found that "[a] shared attitude of conscientious objection to the death penalty is insufficient alone to create the kernel of a cognizable group." People v. Webb, 186 Misc. 2d 835, 721 N.Y.S.2d 475 (Sup. Ct. Kings Co. 2000).

—The legislature never intended or contemplated the creation of separate standards for asserting challenges for cause. People v. Webb, 186 Misc. 2d 835, 721 N.Y.S.2d 475 (Sup. Ct. Kings Co. 2000).

—There is no merit to defendants' contention that excluding jurors who have a conscientious objection to the death penalty necessarily results in a jury which is predisposed to imposing the death penalty and is also "pro-prosecution and predisposed to conviction"; CPL § 270.20(1)(f) is constitutional. People v. Arroyo, 178 Misc. 2d 362, 679 N.Y.S.2d 885 (Schoharie Co. Ct. 1998).

—CPL § 270.20(1)(f) provides that a prospective juror may be excused for cause in a capital case if he or she entertains such conscientious opinions either against or in favor of the death penalty "as to preclude such juror from rendering an impartial verdict or from properly exercising the discretion conferred upon such juror by law in the determination of a sentence. . .."; court determined that it would "grant valid defense challenges for cause when advanced against those prospective jurors whose views in favor of the death penalty would preclude or substantially impair their ability to perform as a juror in accordance with law." People v. McIntosh, 173 Misc. 2d 724, 662 N.Y.S.2d 212 (Dutchess Co. Ct. 1997).

Exhaustion of peremptories.—Where juror admitted that he would be swayed by evidence of defendant's prior convictions, juror should have been dismissed for cause and since defendant had to exercise a peremptory and it exhausted all of the peremptories, the court's denial of the for cause challenge was reversible error. People v. Webb, 5 A.D.3d 115, 772 N.Y.S.2d 333 (1st Dept. 2004).

—Because the People did not exhaust their peremptory challenges, the defendant's challenge to the removal of one of the prospective jurors for cause is not reviewable on appeal. People v. James, 259 A.D.2d 709, 688 N.Y.S.2d 163 (2d Dept. 1999).

—Trial court erred in refusing to dismiss a prospective juror for cause, where the juror indicated that he believed that an individual accused of a crime was probably guilty; because defense counsel then exercised a peremptory challenge against this prospective juror and eventually exhausted his peremptory challenges, the defendant's conviction must be reversed. People v. Molinari, 252 A.D.2d 532, 678 N.Y.S.2d 106 (2d Dept. 1998).

—Trial court's granting of prosecution's challenge for cause was not a basis for reversal, because the People had not exhausted all of their peremptory challenges before completion of jury selection. People v. Stone, 239 A.D.2d 872, 659 N.Y.S.2d 674 (4th Dept. 1997).

State of mind; trial in absentia.—Court did not commit reversible error when it denied defense counsel's challenge for cause to two jurors who said they were not sure when counsel asked the panel generally about their feelings regarding defendant's being tried in absentia. Jurors' response could not be said to reveal an inability to render an impartial verdict and counsel did not avail himself of the opportunity to pursue the issue any further. People v. Stroman, 6 A.D.3d 818, 775 N.Y.S.2d 117 (3d Dept. 2004).

§ 270.25. Trial jury; peremptory challenge of an individual juror.

1. A peremptory challenge is an objection to a prospective juror for which no reason need be assigned. Upon any peremptory challenge, the court must exclude the person challenged from service.

2. Each party must be allowed the following number of peremptory challenges:

(a) Twenty for the regular jurors if the highest crime charged is a class A felony, and two for each alternate juror to be selected.

(b) Fifteen for the regular jurors if the highest crime charged is a class B or class C felony, and two for each alternate juror to be selected.

(c) Ten for the regular jurors in all other cases, and two for each alternate juror to be selected.

3. When two or more defendants are tried jointly, the number of peremptory challenges prescribed in subdivision two is not multiplied by the number of defendants, but such defendants are to be treated as a single party. In any such case, a peremptory challenge by one or more defendants must be allowed if a majority of the defendants join in such challenge. Otherwise, it must be disallowed.

ANNOTATIONS

Peremptory challenges; general.—Peremptory strikes for which no reason need be assigned (CPL § 270.52[2]), constitute an important "part of the strategic arsenal of trial lawyers." People v. Allen, 86 N.Y.2d 101, 629 N.Y.S.2d 1003, 653 N.E.2d 1173 (1995).

Peremptory challenges; numbers.—"The clear statutory mandate of CPL § 270.25(2) bases the number of peremptory challenges allotted to each party on the degree of the highest crime charged." People v. McGee, 76 N.Y.2d 764, 559 N.Y.S.2d 953, 559 N.E.2d 647 (1990).

—Prohibition or mandamus under CPLR Article 78 was not available to the People for the purpose of reviewing the trial court's grant of 10 additional peremptory challenges to the defendants without a similar grant to the People. People v. King, 36 N.Y.2d 59, 364 N.Y.S.2d 879, 324 N.E.2d 351 (1975).

—When a defendant received 14 peremptory challenges instead of 15, following an inaccurate count by the court clerk, the defendant's deprivation of one of his allotted peremptory challenges did not irreparably taint the entire trial and did not require reversal. Furthermore, the defendant failed to preserve his claim that he was deprived of an allotted peremptory. People v. Mathis, 272 A.D.2d 250, 708 N.Y.S.2d 87 (1st Dept. 2000).

—Reversal was warranted where the trial court denied the defendant's request for an additional peremptory challenge after defendant utilized one to remove a juror that saw defendant being escorted in handcuffs. People v. Dixon, 81 A.D.2d 620, 438 N.Y.S.2d 6 (2d Dept. 1981).

Peremptory challenges; co-defendants.—The law provides that co-defendants be treated as a single defendant; there is no provision entitling a co-defendant who commits a more serious crime to additional peremptory challenges. People v. Hursey, 233 A.D.2d 464, 650 N.Y.S.2d 28 (2d Dept. 1996).

Improper dismissal.—Although court rejected as pretextual the prosecutor's explanation for the striking of a black prospective female juror, court erred procedurally by permitting the juror to be dismissed; new trial ordered. People v. Miller, 241 A.D.2d 465, 659 N.Y.S.2d 512 (2d Dept. 1997).

Recall of peremptorily challenged juror.—Trial court committed no error by accepting defense counsel's recall of a peremptorily challenged juror over defendant's preferred person; although defendant objected to the particular juror who was selected, defendant and counsel both consented to the procedure of withdrawing peremptory challenges, and defendant thus waived any argument to that procedure. People v. Colon, 90 N.Y.2d 824, 660 N.Y.S.2d 377, 682 N.E.2d 978 (1997).

Batson **challenges.**—In making a *Batson* challenge, the moving party has the initial burden of establishing that the other side is using peremptory strikes to remove a cognizable racial group and that other relevant circumstances support a finding that the use of these peremptory challenges excludes potential jurors because of their race. People v. James, 99 N.Y.2d 264, 755 N.Y.S.2d 43, 784 N.E.2d 1152 (2002).

—When one side makes a *Batson* challenge, the trial court must engage in a three-step process: (1) the party making the *Batson* claim must make a prima facie showing that the peremptory strikes were exercised because of race; (2) if that showing is made, the party seeking the excusals must come forward with a race-neutral reason for the strikes; (3) when the explanation is facially race-neutral, the trial court must determine whether the other side has proved purposeful racial discrimination, i.e., whether the "race-neutral" explanation is merely a pretext for racial discrimination. People v. Payne, 88 N.Y.2d 172, 643 N.Y.S.2d 949, 666 N.E.2d 542 (1996).

—Where prosecutor peremptorily challenged every black prospective juror, and the prosecutor's notes as to one of those prospective jurors were sketchy and prosecutor could not remember why he had challenged the juror, case was reversed and remanded for a new trial; court agreed with defendant's claim that prosecutor failed to provide a race-neutral reason for the peremptory challenge of this particular person. People v. Davis, 253 A.D.2d 634, 677 N.Y.S.2d 541 (1st Dept. 1998).

—Prosecutor improperly exercised his peremptory challenges where he used 12 of 17 of them to strike potential black jurors and failed to come forward with a neutral explanation for those challenged People v. Hockett, 128 A.D.2d 393, 512 N.Y.S.2d 679 (1st Dept. 1987).

—The *Batson* court specifically declined to express any view on what appropriate action a trial court should take in the event the prosecution failed to rebut a defendant's prima facie showing of racial discrimination in the use of peremptory challenges. People v. Frye, 191 A.D.2d 581, 595 N.Y.S.2d 84 (2d Dept.), *lv. denied*, 81 N.Y.2d 1014 (1993).

—Courts should refuse to reinstate peremptory challenges disallowed by a court pursuant to *Batson* for a later round of voir dire. In making the initial improper challenges, the party has violated the civil rights of the potential juror and in some circumstances, the defendant. To allow reinstatement of a challenge would be inconsistent with the court's objective of deterrence. People v. Johnson, 196 Misc. 2d 417, 765 N.Y.S.2d 199 (Sup. Ct. Kings Co. 2003).

Delayed *Batson* challenge.—When a defendant delays raising a *Batson* challenge until subsequent rounds of voir dire after the relevant jurors have been excused, the defendant limits the remedies available to the trial court. People v. Butler, 15 A.D.3d 415, 790 N.Y.S.2d 479 (2d Dept. 2005).

Reverse *Batson* challenges.—Although defense counsel proffered race neutral reasons, the record supports the court's conclusion that they were pretextual, i.e., defendant challenged one childless juror on the grounds that he would not be able to evaluate the teenage witness properly but failed to ask follow-up questions on this point, and similarly situated non-Caucasian jurors were not challenged. People v. Torres, 289 A.D.2d 136, 734 N.Y.S.2d 174 (1st Dept. 2001).

—The *Batson* ruling applies not only to the prosecution, but to the defense as well. People v. Kern, 149 A.D.2d 187, 545 N.Y.S.2d 4 (2d Dept. 1989), *aff'd*, 75 N.Y.2d 638, 555 N.Y.S.2d 647, 554 N.E.2d 1235 (1990), *cert. denied*, 498 U.S. 824.

—A proceeding pursuant to CPLR article 78, in the nature of prohibition, was not the proper procedural vehicle to challenge the trial court's requiring defense attorneys to respond to allegations that they are exercising peremptory challenges against black jurors on the ground of group bias alone, by articulating a neutral explanation for the use of such peremptory challenges. Ladone v. Demakos, 133 A.D.2d 435, 519 N.Y.S.2d 417 (2d Dept. 1987).

—The equal protection of the law clause of the Fourteenth Amendment is violated when a defendant exercises his peremptory challenges in a racially discriminatory manner. People v. Gary M., 138 Misc. 2d 1081, 526 N.Y.S.2d 986 (Sup. Ct. Kings Co. 1988).

Batson challenges; prima facie case.—"Since a party need give no reason at all for exercise of a peremptory challenge, the initial burden logically falls on the party opposing the strike to make out a prima facie case that a challenge has been [exercised] for an impermissible reason—step one of the *Batson* inquiry." People v. Allen, 86 N.Y.2d 101, 629 N.Y.S.2d 1003, 653 N.E.2d 1173 (1995).

—In order to give the trial court a proper foundation to evaluate that a *Batson* claim, as well as to ensure an adequate record for appellate review, a party asserting such a claim should articulate and develop all of the grounds supporting the claim, both factual and legal, during the colloquy in which the objection is raised and discussed; despite the absence of voir dire minutes, a trial or appellate court may determine, based on facts elicited during the *Batson* colloquy, whether a prima facie case of discriminatory use of peremptory challenges has been established. People v. Childress, 81 N.Y.2d 263, 598 N.Y.S.2d 146, 614 N.E.2d 709 (1993).

—A prima facie case may be made by making a record comparing the venirepersons of one race whom the opposing party accepted, with similarly situated venirepersons which the opposing party challenged, or by establishing objective facts indicating that the opposing party has challenged members of a particular racial group who might be expected to favor that side

because of their backgrounds. People v. Bolling, 79 N.Y.2d 317, 582 N.Y.S.2d 950, 591 N.E.2d 1136 (1992).

—A *Batson* violation is not avoided simply because notwithstanding the discriminatory use of peremptory strikes the prosecutor leaves some blacks on the jury panel and those left are enough to form a petit jury containing a percentage of blacks not significantly lower than the percentage of blacks in the local community. People v. Jenkins, 75 N.Y.2d 550, 555 N.Y.S.2d 10, 554 N.E.2d 47 (1990).

—While a pattern of strikes may suggest an improper use of challenges, a speculative numerical analysis does not satisfy the defense obligation to make a preliminary showing of impropriety. People v. Graham, 181 A.D.2d 504, 580 N.Y.S.2d 772 (1st Dept.), *lv. denied*, 80 N.Y.2d 831 (1992).

—Where a peremptory challenge is based on the prospective juror's employment, the concerns about the employment must be related to the factual circumstances of the case and the qualifications of the juror to serve on the case. People v. Campos, 290 A.D.2d 456, 736 N.Y.S.2d 108 (2d Dept. 2002).

—Prosecutor's explanation for striking a minority juror—that she only had a high school education—was pretextual under the circumstances of this case, and a new trial was ordered. People v. Davis, 272 A.D.2d 339, 708 N.Y.S.2d 119 (2d Dept. 2000).

—Defense counsel "wholly failed" to establish a prima facie case with the "bare fact" that prosecutor exercised five of his eight peremptory challenges against black venirepersons. People v. Vidal, 212 A.D.2d 553, 622 N.Y.S.2d 323 (2d Dept. 1995)

—Although the defendant, who is black, had standing to assert that Hispanics were improperly excluded, he could not successfully argue that regardless of race, minorities in general constitute a cognizable racial group. People v. Mathews, 201 A.D.2d 588, 607 N.Y.S.2d 738 (2d Dept. 1994).

—Since the purpose of the *Batson* rule is to eliminate discrimination and not to minimize it, the exclusion of any blacks solely because of their race is constitutionally forbidden. People v. Peart, 197 A.D.2d 599, 602 N.Y.S.2d 424 (2d Dept. 1993).

—Prosecution's exercise of a peremptory challenge to exclude the only black venire member was sufficient to raise an inference that the challenge was used for a discriminatory purpose. People v. Ware, 173 A.D.2d 903, 569 N.Y.S.2d 763 (2d Dept. 1991).

—Defendant failed to make out a prima facie case of discrimination, where his *Batson* claim was premised on the purported absence of any legitimate reason to challenge the juror, as opposed to actual facts or circumstances. People v. Beverly, 6 A.D.3d 874, 775 N.Y.S.2d 409 (3d Dept. 2004).

—The burden under *Batson* remains on the defendant to show that the challenged juror is a member of a cognizable racial group and that the prosecutor used the peremptory challenge on the basis of race. People v. Stubbs, 183 A.D.2d 178, 590 N.Y.S.2d 539 (3d Dept. 1992), *lv. denied*, 81 N.Y.2d 539 (1993).

Batson challenges; gender.—Because there was a substantially greater number of female venirepersons available, the fact that a disproportionate number of peremptory challenges was exercised against females did not reflect an impermissible discriminatory motive. People v. Rodriguez, 258 A.D.2d 270, 685 N.Y.S.2d 45 (1st Dept. 1999).

Batson challenges; race-neutral explanations.—All that is required of the challenged party is to come forward with an articulable neutral explanation for having excused particular jurors. The "explanation need not rise to the level for sustaining a challenge for cause." People v. Allen, 86 N.Y.2d 101, 629 N.Y.S.2d 1003, 653 N.E.2d 1173 (1995).

—Fact that prospective juror's son had been wrongly arrested and incarcerated for a crime he did not commit, and that other juror seemed to be hostile towards the prosecution and more receptive to the defense constituted sufficient race-neutral reasons. People v. Roberts, 208 A.D.2d 410, 617 N.Y.S.2d 174 (1st Dept. 1994).

—Discussion of race-neutral explanations in connection with defendant's peremptory challenges did not require defendant's presence. People v. Earl, 208 A.D.2d 430, 617 N.Y.S.2d 179 (1st Dept. 1994).

—Great deference is to be given the trial court in determining whether race-neutral reasons are pretextual. People v. Castro, 200 A.D.2d 359, 606 N.Y.S.2d 180 (1st Dept. 1994).

—A peremptory challenge based on a potential juror's status as a crime victim is not necessarily pretextual despite the high incidence of crime in the country. People v. Dixon, 202 A.D.2d 12, 615 N.Y.S.2d 904 (2d Dept. 1994).

—Although reason was facially race neutral—the prosecutor felt that the fact that juror wore a head scarf showed a certain disrespect for the proceedings—the court rejected it on credibility grounds due to inconsistent treatment in relation to nonblack prospective jurors. People v. Bennet, 206 A.D.2d 382, 614 N.Y.S.2d 430 (2d Dept. 1994).

—While a person's employment may, in an appropriate case, constitute a legitimate race-neutral reason for exclusion, the concerns must somehow be related to the factual circumstances of the case. People v. Payton, 204 A.D.2d 661, 613 N.Y.S.2d 25 (2d Dept.), *lv. denied*, 84 N.Y.2d 830 (1994).

—Although a proffered race-neutral reason need not rise to the level required for "cause," the burden cannot be met by merely claiming good faith and denying discrimination. People v. Rodney, 192 A.D.2d 626, 596 N.Y.S.2d 169 (2d Dept. 1993).

—It is for the trial court to determine if a race-neutral explanation for challenging a juror is a mere pretext, and the resolution of this issue by the trial court is entitled to great deference. People v. Mondello, 191 A.D.2d 462, 594 N.Y.S.2d 287 (2d Dept.), *lv. denied*, 81 N.Y.2d 1077 (1993).

—Although the prosecutor cited a race-neutral basis for his removal of two black potential jurors, this explanation was pretextual, since the prosecutor passed up the opportunity to use this basis to remove several non-black prospective jurors. People v. Manuel, 182 A.D.2d 711, 582 N.Y.S.2d 735 (2d Dept. 1992).

—A court's finding that the explanation offered for a peremptory challenge to a juror was or was not race neutral is entitled to great deference. People v. Green, 181 A.D.2d 693, 581 N.Y.S.2d 357 (2d Dept.), *lv. denied*, 79 N.Y.2d 1049 (1992).

—In the selection of jurors a general denial of racial basis is insufficient to rebut the defendant's prima facie showing of purposeful discrimination. People v. Mack, 143 A.D.2d 280, 532 N.Y.S.2d 161 (2d Dept. 1988).

—People proffered a race-neutral reason for their challenge, explaining that the juror stated that she would have difficulty in making a decision if the matter turned on the credibility of one witness over another. People v. Williams, 306 A.D.2d 691, 762 N.Y.S.2d 644 (3d Dept. 2003).

—A trial court's finding that an explanation is race-neutral and non-pretextual is a factual matter requiring an evaluation of the prosecutor's credibility, and is an assessment entitled to great deference. People v. Rios, 201 A.D.2d 762, 607 N.Y.S.2d 469 (3d Dept.), *lv. denied*, 83 N.Y.2d 875 (1994).

—Court properly denied defendant's *Batson* challenge to prosecutor's strike of an African-American prospective juror where the prosecutor explained that he exercised the strike because the prospective juror lived only four blocks away from the crime scene, might have shopped at the store where the incident began, and might know or encounter some of the witnesses and spectators at trial or others acquainted with defendant or the victim; thus, the reasons were race-neutral. People v. Gant, 291 A.D.2d 912, 736 N.Y.S.2d 820 (4th Dept. 2002).

—The prosecutor's reasons for the exercise of a peremptory challenge need not rise to the level justifying a challenge for cause. People v. Duncan, 177 A.D.2d 187, 582 N.Y.S.2d 847 (4th Dept.), *lv. denied*, 79 N.Y.2d 1048 (1992).

—Reversal was required when the prosecutor failed to provide a racially neutral explanation for his peremptory challenges excluding all blacks from the jury. People v. Stephens, 149 A.D.2d 949, 540 N.Y.S.2d 81 (4th Dept. 1989).

—Prosecutor's explanation—that he assumed that the defense would peremptorily challenge a particular white juror, thus leaving two other black prospective jurors to sit on the jury—was satisfactory. People v. Ortiz, 161 Misc. 2d 198, 612 N.Y.S.2d 764 (Sup. Ct. Queens Co. 1994).

Batson claim; relying on number of minority jurors challenged.—Although the prosecutor struck the only African-American on the first panel, three of the six potential African-American jurors in the second round, and two of at least four African-American jurors in the third round, leaving six African-Americans on the jury, these numbers were, without more, insufficient to create an inference establishing a prima facie case. People v. Jenkins, 84 N.Y.2d 1001, 622 N.Y.S.2d 509, 646 N.E.2d 811 (1994).

—In companion case to People v. Bolling, the Court found the prosecutor's exercise of three of her four challenges against African-Americans to be insufficient, standing alone, to establish a pattern of purposeful exclusion sufficient to raise an inference of discrimination. People v. Steele, 79 N.Y.2d 317, 582 N.Y.S.2d 950, 591 N.E.2d 1136 (1992).

—Prosecutor challenged four out of the six African-American venirepersons; prima facie case established. People v. Hawthorne, 80 N.Y.2d 873, 587 N.Y.S.2d 600, 600 N.E.2d 231 (1992).

—Defense counsel did not make a prima facie showing of discrimination in raising a *Batson* objection to the prosecutor's use of her three peremptory challenges. He relied solely on the number of black venirepersons challenged to support his request for race-neutral explanations and offered no showing of facts and circumstances sufficient to raise an inference of a pattern of discrimination. People v. Narvaez, 298 A.D.2d 603, 749 N.Y.S.2d 56 (2d Dept. 2002).

—Prosecutor challenged 89% of the prospective black jurors, prima facie case established. People v. McDougle, 203 A.D.2d 593, 611 N.Y.S.2d 23 (2d Dept. 1994).

—Prima facie case of discrimination made out where prosecutor challenged 80% of the potential black jurors. People v. Hameed, 183 A.D.2d 847, 584 N.Y.S.2d 94 (2d Dept. 1992)

Remedy for *Batson* violation.—Granting defendant one additional peremptory challenge was an adequate remedy for the *Batson* violation, where the subject juror had already been released from jury service. People v. Chin, 3 A.D.3d 574, 771 N.Y.S.2d 158 (2d Dept. 2004).

Preservation.—Notwithstanding the trial court's hasty and compressed *Batson* inquiry, defendant failed to meet his burden of establishing an equal protection violation, where the proffered reasons as to two of the jurors were clearly nonpretextual and the argument regarding a third juror was unpreserved. People v. Smocum, 99 N.Y.2d 418, 757 N.Y.S.2d 239, 786 N.E.2d 1275 (2003).

—If the court accepts the race neutral reasons given following a *Batson* challenge, the moving party must make a specific objection to the exclusion of any juror still claimed to have been the object of discrimination. Because defendant failed to preserve the *Batson* challenges for review on appeal, the Court of Appeals affirmed the orders upholding defendant's convictions. People v. James, 99 N.Y.2d 264, 755 N.Y.S.2d 43, 784 N.E.2d 1152 (2002).

—Where defense counsel did not indicate dissatisfaction with race neutral reasons proffered by the prosecutor, the issue was not preserved for appellate review. People v. Cruz, 200 A.D.2d 581, 606 N.Y.S.2d 291 (2d Dept.), *lv. denied*, 83 N.Y.2d 851 (1994).

—Where the defense argued to the trial court that the People failed to establish a prima facie case of discrimination, the issue is preserved for appellate review notwithstanding the fact that the defense offered a race-neutral explanation when required by the trial court to do so. People v. Stiff, 206 A.D.2d 235, 620 N.Y.S.2d 87 (2d Dept. 1994), *lv. denied*, 85 N.Y.2d 867 (1995).

—*Batson* issue was not preserved for appellate review where defense counsel neither controverted the prosecutor's explanations for the challenged strikes, requested a hearing or further ruling by the trial court, nor moved for a mistrial. People v. Campanella, 176 A.D.2d 813, 575 N.Y.S.2d 137 (2d Dept. 1991), *lv. denied*, 79 N.Y.2d 854 (1992).

—Because defense counsel failed to make a *Batson* challenge until after the jurors, including the alternates, were sworn, his objection was untimely and defendant's contention was not preserved for appellate review. People v. Williams, 206 A.D.2d 917, 614 N.Y.S.2d 842 (4th Dept. 1994).

Absence of stenographic record.—Absence of a stenographic record of some of the voir dire proceedings does not require reversal of defendant's conviction where defendant did not show that the failure to record the proceedings prejudiced him and never requested a reconstruction hearing. People v. Asencia, 280 A.D.2d 678, 721 N.Y.S.2d 105 (2d Dept. 2001).

—A large portion of the voir dire from trial transcript was missing, and at the reconstruction hearing, the trial judge, defense attorney, and prosecutor all indicated that they had no independent recollection of the voir dire. None could recall if any *Batson* or reverse-*Batson* challenges were made. Because court was unable to determine if proceeding was free of prejudice to defendant, reversal was required. People v. Smith, 248 A.D.2d 568, 670 N.Y.S.2d 46 (2d Dept. 1998).

Challenge based on prospective juror's employment.— Court properly rejected defendant's *Batson* claim regarding an African-American juror, where the court ruled that the reasons proffered by the prosecutor were based on employment and were race-neutral. People v. Stafford, 302 A.D.2d 325, 756 N.Y.S.2d 39 (1st Dept. 2003).

—Prosecutor challenged juror because, as a result of her job as a corporate trainer in the affirmative action program of her office, she might be sympathetic to defendant; court erroneously accepted this as a nonpretextual reason, where the prosecutor failed to relate concerns about the prospective juror's employment to the facts of the case, and a new trial was ordered. People v. Pierrot, 289 A.D.2d 511, 735 N.Y.S.2d 589 (2d Dept. 2001).

Hearing-impaired juror.—It was proper for prosecutor to use peremptory challenge with respect to prospective juror who was hearing-impaired where prosecutor was concerned that the hearing impairment of the prospective juror would affect her ability to assess the audiotape evidence because the inflections of defendant's voice on the audiotape were significant to the People's case. "Unlike race or gender, disability may legitimately affect a person's ability to serve as a juror." People v. Falkenstein, 288 A.D.2d 922, 732 N.Y.S.2d 817 (4th Dept. 2001).

§ 270.30. Trial jury; alternate jurors.

1. Immediately after the last trial juror is sworn, the court may in its discretion direct the selection of one or more, but not more than six additional jurors to be known as "alternate jurors," except that, in a prosecution under section 125.27 of the penal law, the court may, in its discretion, direct the selection of as many alternate jurors as the court determines to be appropriate. Alternate jurors must be drawn in the same manner, must have the same qualifications, must be subject to the same examination and challenges for cause and must take the same oath as the regular jurors. After the jury has retired to deliberate, the court must either (1) with the consent of the defendant and the people, discharge the alternate jurors or (2) direct the alternate jurors not to discuss the case and must further direct that they be kept separate and apart from the regular jurors.

2. In any prosecution in which the people seek a sentence of death, the court shall not discharge the alternate jurors when the jury retires to deliberate upon its verdict and the alternate jurors, in the discretion of the court, may be continuously kept together under the supervision of an appropriate public servant or servants until such time as the jury returns its verdict. If the jury returns a verdict of guilty to a charge for which the death penalty may be imposed, the alternate jurors shall not be discharged and shall remain available for service during any separate sentencing proceeding which may be conducted pursuant to section 400.27.

Amended by L. 1979, Ch. 267; L. 1992, Ch. 100; L. 1995, Ch. 1, § 16, eff. Sept. 1, 1995.

ANNOTATIONS

Use and selection of alternate jurors.—Trial court did not abuse its discretion by granting defendant's request that alternate jurors be selected before all sitting jurors were chosen, in order to expedite jury selection. People v. Blackmond, 212

A.D.2d 402, 622 N.Y.S.2d 45 (1st Dept.), *lv. denied*, 85 N.Y.2d 969 (1995).

—Trial court did not abuse its discretion by failing to impanel alternate jurors, when, because of mechanical difficulties, to do so might have caused a considerable delay in starting trial. People v. Ashley, 145 A.D.2d 782, 535 N.Y.S.2d 763 (3d Dept. 1988).

Preservation.—A violation of the statutory requirement that a deliberating jury be kept apart from the alternate jurors must be preserved by timely objection to raise a question of law. People v. Agramonte, 87 N.Y.2d 765, 642 N.Y.S.2d 594, 665 N.E.2d 164 (1996).

—Where defendant stated he had no objection to the court's method for selecting alternate jurors, he failed to preserve for appellate review his claim that the court erred by limiting the choice of alternatives to prior peremptorily challenged venirepersons. People v. Wade, 209 A.D.2d 733, 619 N.Y.S.2d 951 (2d Dept. 1994).

§ 270.35. Trial jury; discharge of juror; replacement by alternate juror.

1. If at any time after the trial jury has been sworn and before the rendition of its verdict, a juror is unable to continue serving by reason of illness or other incapacity, or for any other reason is unavailable for continued service, or the court finds, from facts unknown at the time of the selection of the jury, that a juror is grossly unqualified to serve in the case or has engaged in misconduct of a substantial nature, but not warranting the declaration of a mistrial, the court must discharge such juror. If an alternate juror or jurors are available for service, the court must order that the discharged juror be replaced by the alternate juror whose name was first drawn and called, provided, however, that if the trial jury has begun its deliberations, the defendant must consent to such replacement. Such consent must be in writing and must be signed by the defendant in person in open court in the presence of the court. If the discharged juror was the foreperson, the court shall designate as the new foreperson the juror whose name was second drawn and called. If no alternate juror is available, the court must declare a mistrial pursuant to subdivision three of section 280.10.

2. (a) In determining pursuant to this section whether a juror is unable to continue serving by reason of illness or other incapacity, or is for any other reason unavailable for continued service, the court shall make a reasonably thorough inquiry concerning such illness, incapacity or unavailability, and shall attempt to ascertain when such juror will be appearing in court. If such juror fails to appear, or if the court determines that there is no reasonable likelihood such juror will be appearing, in court within two hours of the time set by the court for the trial to resume, the court may presume such juror is unavailable for continued service and may discharge such juror. Nothing contained in this paragraph shall affect the court's discretion, under this or any other provision of law, to discharge a juror who repeatedly fails to appear in court in a timely fashion.

(b) The court shall afford the parties an opportunity to be heard before discharging a juror. If the court discharges a juror pursuant to this subdivision, it shall place on the record the facts and reasons for its determination that such juror is ill, incapacitated or unavailable for continued service.

(c) Nothing contained in this subdivision shall affect the requirements of subdivision one of this section pertaining to the discharge of a juror where the trial jury has begun its deliberations.

Amended by L. 1975, Ch. 77; L. 1996, Ch. 630, § 1, numbering the undesignated paragraph as 1, and adding subd. 2, effective Oct. 4, 1996; L. 1999, Ch. 594, § 1, amending subd. 1, eff. Nov. 1, 1999.

ANNOTATIONS

Discharge; grossly unqualified to serve.—Defendant's claim that the trial court should have used the "grossly unqualified" standard contained in CPL § 270.35 in determining whether the subject juror should be discharged is unpreserved for appellate review, because it was raised for the first time in support of defendant's motion to set aside the verdict. Furthermore, the court did not err as matter of law in discharging the subject juror by using the "for cause" standard of CPL § 270.20(1)(b), where defendant conceded in the pretrial colloquy that "for cause" was the applicable standard. People v. Johnson, 92 N.Y.2d 976, 683 N.Y.S.2d 754, 706 N.E.2d 742 (1998).

—A juror who stated after the first day of deliberations that she felt unable to continue was properly discharged as grossly unqualified to serve. But, since she stated she had felt capable of serving until then, the trial court properly accepted a partial verdict, since the jury had reached agreement on some of the counts after one day of deliberations. People v. Johnson, 88 N.Y.2d 880, 645 N.Y.S.2d 455, 668 N.E.2d 426 (1996).

—Sworn juror was "grossly unqualified" when, following opening statements, juror expressed repeated doubts that she could render a verdict based on the evidence as a result of her fear of retribution from defendant, a resident of her neighborhood, which was also the location of the arrest. People v. Carrasco, 262 A.D.2d 50, 691 N.Y.S.2d 465 (1st Dept. 1999).

—Court properly discharged a sworn juror, over defense objection, where the juror was found to have engaged in flirtatious conduct with a co-defendants's sister and then lied about it to the court, making the juror "grossly unqualified to serve," because she had "engaged in misconduct of a substantial nature. People v. De La Rosa, 233 A.D.2d 257, 650 N.Y.S.2d 641 (1st Dept. 1996).

—Court rejected defendant's double jeopardy argument; mistrial was properly declared where court questioned juror at length and elicited from juror his preoccupation with his ill wife, as well as his agitation with the fact that the jury had served beyond the court's anticipated schedule, and had distracted him to the point that he could no longer deliberate impartially. People v. Mason, 233 A.D.2d 271, 650 N.Y.S.2d 131 (1st Dept. 1996).

—A juror's bias against two of the People's witnesses—demonstrated by his statement that he was upset by his impression that they were not taking the case seriously—justified discharging the juror as grossly unqualified. People v. Aybinder, 215 A.D.2d 181, 626 N.Y.S.2d 150 (1st Dept. 1995).

—Trial court properly declared a mistrial after one of the jurors informed the court, for the first time during deliberations, that he suffered from panic attacks and claustrophobia. Court thoroughly questioned the juror, who revealed that the jury room was torture for him and that he could not think straight. Because no alternate juror was available, a mistrial was correctly declared. People v. Reed, 2 A.D.3d 463, 767 N.Y.S.2d 821 (2d Dept. 2003).

—Based upon a sworn juror's apprehension over the defendant's having a friend who was the juror's former student, and the juror's inability to state that he could continue to be fair and impartial because of his anxiety that his identity could become known, the trial court acted properly in discharging the juror as being "grossly unqualified" People v. White, 204 A.D.2d 750, 613 N.Y.S.2d 34 (2d Dept. 1994).

—Court properly discharged a juror, over defense counsel's objection where the juror, who knew a spectator in the courtroom, embraced that person during a recess and stated that she was unsure that she could remain fair and impartial as a result. People v. Lilly, 139 A.D.2d 671, 527 N.Y.S.2d 433 (2d Dept.), lv. denied, 72 N.Y.2d 862 (1988).

—Reversal was required where the court excused a sworn juror without conducting a probing inquiry but merely on the basis that the juror learned that defendant's sister was his coemployee. People v. Ballard, 149 A.D.2d 926, 540 N.Y.S.2d 59 (4th Dept. 1989).

—Court properly found that juror was grossly disqualified to serve where juror expressed familiarity with several material facts and was unsure whether he could determine the facts impartially. People v. Gozdalski, 239 A.D.2d 896, 659 N.Y.S.2d 677 (4th Dept. 1997).

Discharge; grossly unqualified, sleeping juror.—Court properly excused a juror as grossly unqualified after she acknowledged that she had been sleeping and had missed some testimony. People v. Smith, 18 A.D.3d 236, 794 N.Y.S.2d 50 (1st Dept. 2005).

—Where defendant failed to urge court to make an inquiry into whether a juror had been sleeping, and in fact, defendant took the position that the juror had not been sleeping, defendant waived his present claim that the court improperly permitted continued deliberations by a juror who had allegedly been asleep during portions of the trial. People v. Lin, 240 A.D.2d 319, 659 N.Y.S.2d 261 (1st Dept. 1997).

—Trial court properly dismissed a sworn juror for sleeping and bizarre behavior, where neither party objected to the dismissal. People v. La Torres, 186 A.D.2d 479, 590 N.Y.S.2d 187 (1st Dept. 1992), lv. denied, 81 N.Y.2d 842 (1993).

—Trial court could rely on its own observations and was not obligated to conduct an inquiry into whether a juror had been sleeping during jury instructions. People v. McIntyre, 193 A.D.2d 626, 597 N.Y.S.2d 442 (2d Dept.), lv. denied, 82 N.Y.2d 757 (1993).

—Juror who "drifted off" during testimony was properly discharged. People v. Williams, 202 A.D.2d 1004, 612 N.Y.S.2d 700 (4th Dept. 1994).

—Juror was disqualified who fell asleep on at least five occasions during the trial and when questioned about whether he had missed evidence, stated "I got most of it." People v. Dupont, 111 Misc.2d 328, 444 N.Y.S.2d 40 (Sup. Ct. N.Y. Co. 1981).

Discharge; substantial misconduct.—The court's decision to replace a juror, over defense objection, was based on ample proof, including the juror's own admissions and self-contradictory statements, taken together with other evidence, showing that the juror had engaged in substantial misconduct by attempting to discuss the credibility of a principal witness with a fellow juror during trial. People v. Vasquez, 208 A.D.2d 412, 617 N.Y.S.2d 299 (1st Dept. 1994).

—In light of juror's request prior to summations and charge, for information as to where grand larceny starts and petty larceny ends, trial court's denial of defendant's motion for mistrial without any inquiry into whether and to what extent jurors had violated their duty not to discuss case before it was submitted to them was error. People v. Gordon, 77 A.D.2d 663, 430 N.Y.S.2d 147 (2d Dept. 1980).

Discharge; unavailable for continued service—Court's discharge of two jurors on ground that they were not available was proper where the first juror discharged had informed a court officer that she was sick with the flu and that she would not be available for more than a couple of days, and the second juror discharged had indicated that her son was home sick with a fever and that she would not be available until after the illness was over since she had no one to look after him; there was no need for the court to personally speak to the jurors. People v. Harris, 204 A.D.2d 240, 612 N.Y.S.2d 157 (1st Dept. 1994).

—The trial court properly excused a sitting juror after ascertaining and placing on the record that the juror in question had experienced chest pains and was then in a hospital emergency room awaiting admission, with initial hospital tests indicating some damage to the heart that required admission. People v. Washington, 207 A.D.2d 759, 616 N.Y.S.2d 616 (1st Dept. 1994).

—Reversal required where court discharged juror who was "ill" without a reasonably thorough inquiry into the inability of the juror to appear. People v. Brown, 194 A.D.2d 443, 599 N.Y.S.2d 277 (1st Dept. 1993).

—The trial court properly replaced a sworn juror after personally speaking with him by telephone and learning that he would be disabled for at least two days and probably a week or two. People v. Morgan, 199 A.D.2d 143, 605 N.Y.S.2d 85 (1st Dept. 1993).

—Trial court properly dismissed a sworn juror, prior to the People's rebuttal case, after she called the court and stated that she had been "stricken seriously," was bedridden and too ill to attend the trial, since there was no indication that the juror would soon recover. People v. Gordon, 185 A.D.2d 199, 586 N.Y.S.2d 595 (1st Dept.), lv. denied, 80 N.Y.2d 904 (1992).

—It was proper not to discharge the juror where the juror had merely suffered a temporary fainting spell as a result of the heat in the courtroom and had recovered. People v. Torres, 183 A.D.2d 507, 583 N.Y.S.2d 447 (1st Dept. 1992).

—Reversal was required where the court excused the juror and the record does not reveal that any effort was made to determine the exact nature of the juror's illness and probable length of unavailability. People v. Dunn, 169 A.D.2d 394, 563 N.Y.S.2d 421 (1st Dept. 1991).

—Trial court properly discharged a sworn juror who had two asthmatic attacks during the second day of trial; court conducted a thorough inquiry of the juror, who could not give any assurance that her condition would not recur at any moment, and court placed its reasons for the discharge on the record. People v. Jackson, 240 A.D.2d 680, 659 N.Y.S.2d 479 (2d Dept. 1997).

—Claim that court erred in discharging an ill juror without conducting a reasonable inquiry is one that must be preserved for appellate review by way of an appropriate objection. People v. Correll, 207 A.D.2d 410, 615 N.Y.S.2d 86 (2d Dept. 1994).

—Discharge of sworn juror was proper where the juror informed the court, prior to conclusion of the defendant's evidence that his wife was to undergo surgery and that he would thus be unavailable for two days. People v. Riccardi, 199 A.D.2d 432, 605 N.Y.S.2d 112 (2d Dept. 1993), lv. denied, 83 N.Y.2d 809 (1994).

—The trial court properly exercised its discretion in discharging, prior to the commencement of trial, a sworn juror who had asked to be excused because his father, who was in the hospital and had just been diagnosed as having cancer and a broken hip, was to undergo surgery the following day and there was uncertainty as to whether he would survive the surgery; a more detailed inquiry by the court was not required. People v. Hill, 182 A.D.2d 640, 582 N.Y.S.2d 246 (2d Dept.), lv. denied, 80 N.Y.2d 832 (1992).

—Court properly discharged juror where juror made known his travel plan during voir dire and was assured that the trial would conclude before his scheduled departure date and thereafter was seated without objection. People v. Maxwell, 156 A.D.2d 476, 548 N.Y.S.2d 763 (2d Dept. 1990).

—Replacing a juror with an alternate so that the juror could go on vacation fell within trial judge's broad discretion. People v. Burns, 118 A.D.2d 864, 500 N.Y.S.2d 545 (2d Dept. 1986).

Discharge; timely objection.—Reversal required where court discharged juror who was "ill" without a reasonably thorough inquiry into the inability of the juror to appear. People v. Brown, 194 A.D.2d 443, 599 N.Y.S.2d 277 (1st Dept. 1993).

—Defendant's objection to the dismissal of a juror after the court learned that a friend of the defendant had made contact with the juror during a recess was untimely; notwithstanding the court's willingness to consider the defendant's objection on the merits, the objection was made after the juror was dismissed, when there was no way for the court to effectively change its ruling. People v. Simmons, 188 A.D.2d 668, 591 N.Y.S.2d 511 (2d Dept. 1992).

—Defendant's claim that he was denied his right to have a particular juror chosen was not preserved for appellate review because the defendant failed to object to the juror's dismissal at a time when the trial court could correct the claimed error. People v. Robinson, 180 A.D.2d 767, 580 N.Y.S.2d 80 (2d Dept. 1992).

Discharge; necessity and requisites of an inquiry.—Where a juror told a court officer during deliberations that she did not understand what was going on, and did not understand the lawyers or the judge, the court's inquiry of that juror was misdirected and incomplete, because the court only asked questions as to the juror's age, citizenship, criminal background, and ability to communicate in English, rather than resolving whether the juror should have been entrusted with the responsibilities of fact-finding. People v. Sanchez, 99 N.Y.2d 62, 760 N.Y.S.2d 391, 790 N.E.2d 766 (2003).

—In concluding that a sworn juror is grossly unqualified, a trial court may not speculate as to the likelihood of partiality, but rather, must be convinced, after a probing and tactful inquiry, that the sworn juror will be unable to deliberate fairly and render an impartial verdict. People v. Cargill, 70 N.Y.2d 687, 518 N.Y.S.2d 792, 512 N.E.2d 313 (1983).

—Case reversed because trial court failed, as required, to conduct an inquiry into whether some of the jurors were prematurely deliberating in violation of the court's instructions, which was alleged by an alternate juror who had participated in the premature discussions about the case. People v. Ordenana, 20 A.D.3d 39, 795 N.Y.S.2d 582 (1st Dept. 2005).

—Court properly discharged a sworn juror over defense objection following a "probing and tactful inquiry" where the juror informed the court that if he had to miss classes necessary for a job promotion, he could not give the case the attention it required and could not be a fair juror. People v. Sipas, 246 A.D.2d 408, 668 N.Y.S.2d 31 (1st Dept. 1998).

—Conviction reversed where, during deliberations, juror sent the court a note indicating that the jurors had agreed to reach a compromise not based on the evidence, but from a strong desire for deliberations to cease, and juror stated his clear intention to vote in a way that did not accord with his own findings about the evidence; court's failure to make an inquiry into this juror's position made it impossible for the Appellate Court to determine whether the juror did vote in a manner inconsistent with his views of the evidence. People v. Fermin, 235 A.D.2d 328, 653 N.Y.S.2d 316 (1st Dept. 1997).

—The trial court erred in failing to conduct an inquiry of a juror who, before jury deliberations commenced, wrote a note to her employer stating that she would be making it to work "beyond a reasonable doubt." People v. McClenton, 213 A.D.2d 1, 630 N.Y.S.2d 290 (1st Dept. 1995).

—The court violated the defendant's constitutional and statutory right to a trial by a jury of his choice when it discharged a sworn juror in the absence of the attorneys and the defendant. People v. Pegeise, 195 A.D.2d 337, N.Y.S.2d 26, 28 (1st Dept. 1993).

—There was no evidence that juror was unable to render an impartial verdict so as to be deemed grossly unqualified pursuant to CPL § 270.35, where juror had allegedly commented to another juror about the testimony of a witness, but both jurors were questioned by the court; the court properly refused to speculate about what the juror had said. People v. Rosario, 241 A.D.2d 502, 660 N.Y.S.2d 66 (2d Dept. 1997).

—A determination that a juror is grossly unqualified requires a probing and tactful inquiry into the unique facts of each case, and the trial court must carefully consider the juror's answers and demeanor to ascertain whether her state of mind will affect her deliberations; great deference is generally accorded to the trial court's findings. People v. Bamfield, 208 A.D.2d 853, 618 N.Y.S.2d 64 (2d Dept.), lv. denied, 84 N.Y.2d 1009 (1994).

—Unlike the situation where an inquiry is being made of a juror to determine if he or she should be dismissed as grossly unqualified, inquiries to determine the availability of a juror need not necessarily be in the presence of the defendant or his counsel. People v. Delgado, 187 A.D.2d 447, 589 N.Y.S.2d 536 (2d Dept. 1992).

—Court's discharge of juror, who failed to appear at appointed hour, without first causing an adequate inquiry to be made as to the juror's future availability constituted reversible error. People v. Hewlett, 133 A.D.2d 417, 519 N.Y.S.2d 555 (2d Dept. 1987).

—Where the trial judge has the benefit of his own observations and he states that he is satisfied that the juror did not display hostility towards or prejudice against the defense, there is no need to conduct an inquiry regarding the juror's alleged hostility towards the defense. People v. Garrow, 233 A.D.2d 856, 649 N.Y.S.2d 604 (4th Dept. 1996).

—Trial court committed reversible error by excusing a selected and sworn juror, prior to the entire jury being selected and sworn, outside of defendant's presence and without his consent, for reasons other than illness or other incapacity. People v. Wilson, 105 A.D.2d 311, 484 N.Y.S.2d 733 (4th Dept. 1985).

Discharge properly denied.—Juror's statement that he could not keep certain testimony that had been stricken out of his mind did not render him grossly unqualified, because the testimony did not pertain to material evidence in the case, and the juror never indicated that he could not view the evidence fairly and impartially. People v. Sweeney, 16 A.D.3d 602, 792 N.Y.S.2d 149 (2d Dept. 2005).

—Sworn juror was not grossly unqualified, even though she had informed the court on the first day of deliberations that she thought she recognized one of defendant's accomplices as "one of the persons who tried to rob her home," because she was not sure that she recognized the accomplice and she assured the trial court that she could remain fair and impartial. People v. Bunch, 278 A.D.2d 501, 717 N.Y.S.2d 385 (2d Dept. 2000).

—Court rejected defendant's contention that a juror should have been discharged as grossly unqualified because she had contact with a grand juror who was possibly familiar with defendant's case, because juror unequivocally stated that she did not accept the grand juror's statements as fact and that his statements did not affect her ability to be fair and impartial, and furthermore, the juror did not communicate the grand juror's statement to the other jurors and she did not have greater knowledge about the case than she had prior to her contact with the grand juror. People v. Harrison, 251 A.D.2d 681, 677 N.Y.S.2d 794 (2d Dept. 1998).

—Court did not err in refusing to discharge sworn juror who was disturbed by the presence of hypodermic needles at trial in view of the fact that juror's son had died from a drug overdose two months earlier; the juror repeatedly reassured the court that he would nonetheless be able to reach an impartial decision, and the juror agreed not to share his feelings with the other jurors. People v. Acevedo, 207 A.D.2d 842, 616 N.Y.S.2d 636 (2d Dept. 1994).

—Court properly denied a motion to dismiss a juror as grossly unqualified on grounds that juror revealed she was familiar with fast food restaurant where undercover purchases from defendant allegedly took place, where there was no real dispute at trial concerning the undercover's ability to observe the transaction and where the court questioned the juror and was convinced that she would refrain from using her knowledge of the scene during deliberations. People v. Johnson, 287 A.D.2d 792, 731 N.Y.S.2d 259 (3d Dept. 2001).

—Fact that juror observed defendant in a police van outside the courthouse banging on the window of the van in an attempt to attract her attention and that juror related that fact to other jurors, did not render jurors involved "grossly unqualified" where they all told the trial court that the incident would have no effect on their verdict. People v. Graham, 117 A.D.2d 832, 498 N.Y.S.2d 730 (3d Dept. 1986).

—Although the record made clear that there was a personality conflict involving the jurors, it is not obvious that juror possessed a state of mind which prevented her from rendering an impartial verdict, where she clearly articulated her concern that the defendant be treated fairly, and she was cooperative and agreeable when discussing the matter with the attorneys. People v. Bradford, 300 A.D.2d 685, 750 N.Y.S.2d 367 (3d Dept. 2002).

—The passing acquaintance of the juror with the witness together with his intermittent and brief face-to-face dealing with him at work while both were employed by a large corporation, did not constitute such a close relationship of a business or personal nature as to render the juror grossly unqualified to continue serving in the case, where the juror stated unequivocally that his acquaintance with and knowledge of the good reputation of the witness would not color his perception of the witness's testimony. People v. Telehany, 302 A.D.2d 927, 754 N.Y.S.2d 508 (4th Dept. 2003).

Substituting an alternate for a regular juror.— Substitution of an alternate juror for a regular juror, once the jury has begun deliberating, requires defendant's in-court, written consent. Where, as here, defendant gave his voluntary oral consent to the discharge of the juror prior to deliberations, no error lies. People v. Ortiz, 92 N.Y.2d 955, 683 N.Y.S.2d 158, 705 N.E.2d 1199 (1998).

—A defendant's oral consent to the substitution of an alternate for a regular juror is invalid once deliberations have begun. People v. Page, 88 N.Y.2d 1, 643 N.Y.S.2d 1, 665 N.E.2d 1041 (1996).

—By consenting to substitution of an alternate for a sick juror, defendant waived any argument that the substitution was improper, and the court did not impermissibly delegate its duty to make a reasonably thorough inquiry by relying, without objection, on information relayed by court employees about the juror's illness. People v. Smith, 304 A.D.2d 364, 758 N.Y.S.2d 33 (1st Dept. 2003).

—Defendant's conviction must be reversed and new trial ordered because the court replaced a juror after deliberations had commenced, with an alternate juror who had previously been discharged from jury service. People v. Gomez, 308 A.D.2d 460, 764 N.Y.S.2d 109 (2d Dept. 2003).

—A new trial was required because court did not obtain defendant's written and signed consent to replace a regular juror with an alternate juror after the jury began its deliberations. People v. Williams, 291 A.D.2d 466, 737 N.Y.S.2d 635 (2d Dept. 2002).

Two-hour rule.—CPL § 270.35(2) two-hour rule is not an arbitrary cut-off point; it strikes a constitutionally accepted balance between the need to avoid uncertainty and delay and the defendant's right to an orderly jury trial. People v. Jeanty, 94 N.Y.2d 507, 706 N.Y.S.2d 683, 727 N.E.2d 1237 (2000).

—Court properly discharged a juror who indicated that he had to attend his uncle's funeral and would not be at court in the morning; court was not required to wait two hours, since it complied with CPL § 270.35(2)(a) by determining that there was no reasonable likelihood that the juror would be appearing in court within two hours of the time set for the trial to resume. People v. Lopez, 18 A.D.3d 233, 795 N.Y.S.2d 6 (1st Dept. 2005).

—Court properly discharged a sworn juror who failed to appear in court within two hours of the time set by the court for the trial to resume. After conducting a thorough inquiry in which it spoke to the juror by telephone and also questioned the court officers, the court discredited the juror's claim that he had in fact appeared at the end of the luncheon recess and had been told that the trial had recessed for the day. People v. Jones, 305 A.D.2d 264, 759 N.Y.S.2d 467 (1st Dept. 2003).

§ 270.40. Trial jury; preliminary instructions by court.

After the jury has been sworn and before the people's opening address, the court must instruct the jury generally concerning its basic functions, duties and conduct. Such instructions must include, among other matters, admonitions that the jurors may not converse among themselves or with anyone else upon any subject connected with the trial; that they may not read or listen to any accounts or discussions of the case reported by newspapers or other news media; that they may not visit or view the premises or place where the offense or offenses charged were allegedly committed or any other premises or place involved in the case; that prior to discharge, they may not request, accept, agree to accept, or discuss with any person receiving or accepting, any payment or benefit in consideration for supplying any information concerning the trial; and that they must promptly report to the court any incident within their knowledge involving an attempt by any person improperly to influence any member of the jury.

Amended by L. 1990, Ch. 305.

ANNOTATIONS

Failure to give instructions as prescribed by statute.— Trial court committed reversible error by giving the jury written preliminary instructions, including elements of the crime. People v. Townsend, 67 N.Y.2d 815, 501 N.Y.S.2d 638, 492 N.E.2d 766 (1986).

—Trial court's failure to give the preliminary instructions as required by statute, one of the errors leading to reversal. People v. Wright, 215 A.D.2d 299, 627 N.Y.S.2d 13 (1st Dept. 1995).

—Appeals court "disapproves" of trial court's preliminary instructions which omitted the statutorily prescribed admonitions. People v. Nunez-Ramos, 160 A.D.2d 1029, 554 N.Y.S.2d 947 (2d Dept. 1990).

—The trial court is not mandated to give a "no adverse inference" charge regarding a defendant's failure to testify at trial, at the request of defendant, during the preliminary instructions. People v. Bell, 152 A.D.2d 700, 544 N.Y.S.2d 160 (2d Dept. 1989).

—Improper to omit preliminary instructions; case remand to determine whether preliminary instructions were given. People v. Benitez, 99 A.D.2d 841, 472 N.Y.S.2d 586 (2d Dept. 1984).

—Preliminary instructions which contained an outline of the elements of the crime charge against the defendant constituted reversible error. People v. Morris, 162 Misc. 2d 742, 621 N.Y.S.2d 434 (App. Term 1994).

Effect of preliminary instructions.—Preliminary charge on prosecution's burden of proof did not cure failure to so charge at end of trial. People v. Newman, 46 N.Y.2d 126, 412 N.Y.S.2d 860, 385 N.E.2d 598 (1978).

—Court's failure to include any reference to the presumption of innocence in its main charge was not cured by its having done so in its preliminary instructions. People v. Gayle, 76 A.D.2d 587, 431 N.Y.S.2d 18, *modified,* 78 A.D.2d 630 (1st Dept. 1980).

Preliminary instructions; purpose of.—CPL § 270.40 requires that, after the jury has been sworn and before the People's opening, the court must give the jury certain preliminary instructions, including an admonition not to converse among themselves or with anyone else about any subject connected with the trial; premature discussions can lead to a premature final decision. People v. Ordenana, 20 A.D.3d 39, 795 N.Y.S.2d 582 (1st Dept. 2005).

§ 270.45. Trial jury; when separation permitted.

During the period extending from the time the jurors are sworn to the time they retire to deliberate upon their verdict, the court may in its discretion either permit them to separate during recesses and adjournments or direct that they be continuously kept together during such periods under the supervision of an appropriate public servant or servants. In the latter case, such public servant or servants may not speak to or communicate with any juror concerning any subject connected with the trial nor permit any other person to do so, and must return the jury to the court room at the next designated trial session.

ANNOTATIONS

Generally.—CPL § 270.45 commits to the sound discretion of the trial judge the decision to permit separation of the jurors or their sequestration at any stage of the trial up until submission of the case to the jury. People v. D'Alvia, 171 A.D.2d 96, 575 N.Y.S.2d 495 (2d Dept. 1991).

—People sought to exclude from voir dire all inquiry into the names and exact addresses of the prospective jurors; CPL § 270.15 prohibits selection of an anonymous jury, but CPL § 270.45 gives the court discretion to sequester the jury for the entire trial. However, People did not establish basis for fully sequestered jury. People v. Watts, 173 Misc. 2d 373, 661 N.Y.S.2d 768 (Sup. Ct. Richmond Co. 1997).

§ 270.50. Trial jury; viewing of premises.

1. When the court is of the opinion that a viewing or observation by the jury of the premises or place where an offense on trial was allegedly committed, or of any other premises or place involved in the case, will be helpful to the jury in determining any material factual issue, it may in its discretion, at any time before the commencement of the summations, order that the jury be conducted to such premises or place for such purpose in accordance with the provisions of this section.

2. In such case, the jury must be kept together throughout under the supervision of an appropriate public servant or servants appointed by the court, and the court itself must be present throughout. The prosecutor, the defendant and counsel for the defendant may as a matter of right be present throughout, but such right may be waived.

3. The purpose of such an inspection is solely to permit visual observation by the jury of the premises or place in question, and neither the court, the parties, counsel nor the jurors may engage in discussion or argumentation concerning the significance or implications of anything under observation or concerning any issue in the case.

ANNOTATIONS

Trial court's discretion.—It is not error for the trial court to deny defense counsel's request that the jury view the scene even though the People raise no objection. People v. Jackson, 39 N.Y.2d 64, 382 N.Y.S.2d 736, 346 N.E.2d 537 (1976).

—Where there was nothing particularly uncommon or unique about the scene of the crime it was reasonable for the trial court to conclude that inspecting the location would be of questionable value in helping the jury decide any material issue of fact. People v. Kaufman, 156 A.D.2d 718, 549 N.Y.S.2d 471 (2d Dept. 1990).

—A trial court may permit a jury to view the place where the crime was allegedly committed if the court determines that such viewing would be helpful to the jury in resolving an issue of material fact, and the decision rests within the trial court's sound discretion. People v. Grenier, 250 A.D.2d 874, 672 N.Y.S.2d 499 (3d Dept. 1998).

Restrictions on jurors viewing the scene.—Action of two jurors at the scene, aimed at authenticating the eyewitness's version of the crime, exceeded the scope and manner of what counsel consented to, and converted a viewing of the scene to an impermissible experiment which essentially converted the two experimenting jurors into unsworn witnesses. Notwithstanding defendant's consent to the jury's view of the scene, reversal was mandated. People v. Stanley, 87 N.Y.2d 1000, 642 N.Y.S.2d 620, 665 N.E.2d 190 (1996).

—While it is within the court's discretion to permit the jury to view the crime scene, it is imperative that the potential of prejudice be avoided; since the hallway and vestibule were not substantially in the same condition as they were on the date of the incident, the walls were now a lighter color, there was a new door with a smaller window and the lighting was different and since visibility was an issue the visit by the jury created a strong possibility of prejudice requiring reversal. People v. McCurdy, 86 A.D.2d 493, 450 N.Y.S.2d 507 (2d Dept. 1982).

§ 270.55. Sentencing jury in capital cases.

During the period extending from when a jury returns a verdict of guilty upon a count of an indictment charging murder in the first degree as defined by section 125.27 of the penal law until a jury retires to deliberate on the sentence pursuant to section 400.27, the court may in its discretion either permit the jurors to separate during recesses and adjournments or direct that they be continuously kept together during such periods under the supervision of an appropriate public servant or servants. In the latter case, such public servant or servants may not speak to or communicate with any juror concerning any subject connected with the sentencing proceeding nor permit any other person to do so, and must return the jury to the court room at the next designated session. Unless otherwise provided for in section 400.27, the provisions of sections 270.35, 270.40 and 270.50 shall govern the sentencing proceeding provided for in section 400.27.

Added by L. 1995, Ch. 1, § 17, eff. Sept. 1, 1995.

ARTICLE 280—JURY TRIAL—MOTION FOR
A MISTRIAL

Section

280.10 Motion for mistrial.

280.20 Motion for mistrial; status of indictment upon new trial.

LexisNexis Cross References

Criminal Defense Techniques, Vol. 6, Ch. 120, Motions for Acquittal or New Trial; *New York Criminal Practice (2d ed.),* Vol. 3, Ch. 37, Mistrial and Trial Order of Dismissal.

§ 280.10. Motion for mistrial.

At any time during the trial, the court must declare a mistrial and order a new trial of the indictment under the following circumstances:

1. Upon motion of the defendant, when there occurs during the trial an error or legal defect in the proceedings, or conduct inside or outside the courtroom, which is prejudicial to the defendant and deprives him of a fair trial. When such an error, defect or conduct occurs during a joint trial of two or more defendants and a mistrial motion is made by one or more but not by all, the court must declare a mistrial only as to the defendant or defendants making or joining in the motion, and the trial of the other defendant or defendants must proceed;

2. Upon motion of the people, when there occurs during the trial, either inside or outside the courtroom, gross misconduct by the defendant or some person acting on his behalf, or by a juror, resulting in substantial and irreparable prejudice to the people's case. When such misconduct occurs during a joint trial of two or more defendants, and when the court is satisfied that it did not result in substantial prejudice to the people's case as against a particular defendant and that such defendant was in no way responsible for the misconduct, it may not declare a mistrial with respect to such defendant but must proceed with the trial as to him;

3. Upon motion of either party or upon the court's own motion, when it is physically impossible to proceed with the trial in conformity with law.

ANNOTATIONS

Mistrial; general.—When the jury told the court that it was deadlocked, the court declared a mistrial. Before the mistrial declaration had been communicated to the jury, it returned with a verdict. The court had the discretion to accept the verdict, since the trial is not terminated until the jury is discharged. People v. Dawkins, 82 N.Y.2d 226, 604 N.Y.S.2d 34, 624 N.E.2d 162 (1993).

—The defendant is free to withdraw a motion for a mistrial at any time before its grant and to continue before the already impaneled jury. People v. Catten, 69 N.Y.2d 547, 516 N.Y.S.2d 186, 508 N.E.2d 920 (1987).

—A reviewing court will be hesitant to interfere with the discretion given a trial judge to grant a mistrial out of deference to the judge who is in the best position to determine whether a mistrial is in fact necessary in a particular case. The granting of a mistrial based on the unavailability of a critical prosecution witness will be strictly scrutinized because the People are not entitled to a mistrial merely to gain a more favorable opportunity to convict. However, where a mistrial is based on the likelihood that the impartiality of the jurors is in question because of an improper comment, the trial judge's evaluation will be accorded the highest degree of respect. Enright v. Siedlecki, 59 N.Y.2d 195, 464 N.Y.S.2d 418, 451 N.E.2d 176 (1983).

—Decision to declare mistrial rests within sound discretion of trial court. People v. Knorr, 284 A.D.2d 411, 728 N.Y.S.2d 169 (2d Dept. 2001).

—The granting of a mistrial and the methods of dealing with disruptive behavior on the part of the defendant rests in the discretion of the trial court. People v. White, 199 A.D.2d 558, 606 N.Y.S.2d 49 (2d Dept. 1993), *lv. denied*, 83 N.Y.2d 859 (1994).

—The declaration of a mistrial after a verdict has been rendered is unauthorized. People v. Roberts, 91 A.D.2d 1099, 458 N.Y.S.2d 355 (3d Dept. 1983).

—Where multiple juries have been deadlocked, and the likelihood of a future jury reaching a verdict is slight, the court may dismiss an indictment. People v. Kirby, 112 Misc. 2d 906, 447 N.Y.S.2d 606 (Sup. Ct. N.Y. Co. 1982).

Mistrial; consent.—A defendant need not agree with counsel, or even be in the courtroom, when counsel moves for a mistrial. People v. Catten, 69 N.Y.2d 547, 516 N.Y.S.2d 186, 508 N.E.2d 920 (1987).

—Defendant's consent to a mistrial may be implied from a totality of the circumstances. People v. Barreto, 149 A.D.2d 428, 539 N.Y.S.2d 771 (2d Dept. 1989).

—A defendant's consent to a mistrial may be implied from the circumstances leading up to the dismissal of the jury. People v. Lilly, 187 A.D.2d 674, 590 N.Y.S.2d 253 (2d Dept. 1992).

Mistrial; double jeopardy.—Double jeopardy did not bar a retrial where defense counsel impliedly consented to court's declaration of a mistrial when he remained silent while the court addressed the jury concerning the need for a mistrial due to the hospitalization of a juror. People v. Ferguson, 67 N.Y.2d 383, 502 N.Y.S.2d 972, 494 N.E.2d 77 (1986).

—Where a mistrial is declared without the consent of defense counsel, state and federal law prohibit retrial for the same crime unless there is a manifest necessity for the declaration of a mistrial or the ends of public justice would otherwise be defeated. Enright v. Siedlecki, 59 N.Y.2d 195, 464 N.Y.S.2d 418, 451 N.E.2d 176 (1983).

—Where a court declares a mistrial without obtaining the defendant's consent, the double jeopardy provisions of both the State and Federal Constitutions prohibit a retrial for the same crime unless there is a manifest necessity for the mistrial, or the ends of public justice would otherwise be defeated. People v. Michael, 48 N.Y.2d 1, 420 N.Y.S.2d 371, 394 N.E.2d 1134 (1979).

—Mistrial granted on application of the People, after the jury had been sworn but before any witnesses had been called, did not preclude a subsequent trial because of double jeopardy either within the New York rule or within the federal rule, where the missing witnesses had been threatened by the defendant. People v. Paquette, 31 N.Y.2d 379, 339 N.Y.S.2d 959, 292 N.E.2d 17 (1972).

—The court's sua sponte grant of a mistrial occurred before an entire panel was selected and sworn; as such, jeopardy did not attach. People v. Singh, 190 A.D.2d 640, 594 N.Y.S.2d 165 (1st Dept.), *lv. denied*, 81 N.Y.2d 1020 (1993).

—Where defendant moved for mistrial after testimony was taken because of prosecution's failure to make exculpatory statements of witnesses available, and after impasse was reached in getting prosecutor to provide the names of the witnesses, court ordered mistrial, upon which defendant declared his readiness to proceed, it was not double jeopardy if defendant was charged again. Napoli v. The Supreme Court, 40 A.D.2d 159, 338 N.Y.S.2d 721 (1st Dept. 1972), *aff'd*, 33 N.Y.2d 980, 353 N.Y.S.2d 740, 309 N.E.2d 137, *cert. denied*, 417 U.S. 947 (1974).

—Based on juror's revealing, for the first time during deliberations, that he suffered from claustrophobia and the jury room was torture for him, court properly declared a mistrial because no alternate juror was available. Double jeopardy did not bar the retrial. People v. Reed, 2 A.D.3d 463, 767 N.Y.S.2d 821 (2d Dept. 2003).

Death penalty case.—In death penalty case where Capital Defender Office was substituted as lead defense counsel due to original cousel's illness, court found that the drastic remedy of declaring a mistrial was not necessitated, because all individual voir dire had been conducted on the record and in the presence of both defendant's associate counsel and jury consultant, and an attorney from the CDO was often present in the courtroom. Furthermore, the court would instruct the jurors about drawing negative inferences from the unforeseen delay, and defense counsel would have an opportunity to question the retained and as yet unquestioned jurors about the issue. People v. Owens, 186 Misc. 2d 767, 720 N.Y.S.2d 764 (Sup. Ct. Monroe Co. 2001).

Grounds for mistrial; alleged denial of right to confrontation.—Reversal was not required where court refused defendant's mistrial request after defendant learned that the statement given by his female friend to the police in which she denied being with defendant on the night of the crimes was inadvertently given to the jury during deliberations; although the statement was not in evidence and the female friend did not testify at trial, Court rejected defendant's claim that his right of confrontation was infringed. The evidence was overwhelming, and there was no reasonable possibility that the error might have contributed to the defendant's conviction. People v. Smith, 97 N.Y.2d 324, 740 N.Y.S.2d 279, 766 N.E.2d 941 (2002), *reversing*, 283 A.D.2d 908, 730 N.Y.S.2d 583 (4th Dept. 2001).

Grounds for mistrial; deadlocked jury.—Trial court did not abuse its discretion in declaring a mistrial when the jury announced itself deadlocked after only four and one-half hours of deliberation in a short, uncomplicated trial involving two witnesses for the prosecution and one for the defense and where the trial court adequately explored the genuineness of the deadlock; retrial of the defendant was therefore not barred by the guarantee against double jeopardy. Plummer v. Rothwax, 63 N.Y.2d 243, 481 N.Y.S.2d 657, 471 N.E.2d 429 (1984).

—While the jury first deliberated for only three hours before the trial court at defendant's first trial declared a mistrial, there is no minimum time a jury must deliberate before a mistrial is considered. People v. Campbell, 203 A.D.2d 127, 610 N.Y.S.2d 246 (1st Dept. 1994).

—The determination as to how long deliberating jurors will be kept together and required to continue their deliberations is a matter of sound judicial discretion which, if not improvidently exercised, will not be disturbed. People v. Bastien, 180 A.D.2d 691, 580 N.Y.S.2d 54 (2d Dept. 1992).

—Generally the declaration of a mistrial due to a deadlocked jury is a matter of discretion for the trial court and its decision should be given great deference. People v. Cheeseborough, 158 A.D.2d 542, 551 N.Y.S.2d 310 (2d Dept. 1990).

—Court properly denied defendant's motion for a mistrial based upon a deadlocked jury where it was made on only the second day of deliberations and much of jury's time had been consumed by the rereading of testimony. People v. Gonzalez, 140 A.D.2d 587, 527 N.Y.S.2d 855 (2d Dept. 1988).

—Defendant's motion for a mistrial, which was predicated upon the jury's inability to reach a verdict on only the second day of its deliberations, was properly denied where much of the jury's time was taken up by the rereading of testimony and the court's answering of certain questions. People v. Adorno, 124

A.D.2d 588, 507 N.Y.S.2d 733 (2d Dept. 1986), *lv. denied*, 69 N.Y.2d 708 (1987).

—Declaration of mistrial after the verdict is entered is unauthorized. People v. Collins, 72 A.D.2d 431, 424 N.Y.S.2d 954 (4th Dept. 1980).

—There existed manifest necessity to justify the declaration of a mistrial where jury was genuinely deadlocked after deliberating over a period of five days. People v. Leisner, 135 Misc. 2d 1081, 518 N.Y.S.2d 86 (Sup. Ct. N.Y. Co. 1987).

Grounds for mistrial; manifest necessity.—There was no deprivation of defendant's right to due process where the prosecutor placed himself in the position of becoming an unsworn witness when on voir dire he asked "will any of you have any problem with the fact that I took the statement?", referring to defendant's confession at the time of his arrest as the defense failed to show any substantial likelihood of prejudice flowing from the prosecutor's references to his pretrial involvement. People v. Ortiz, 54 N.Y.2d 288, 445 N.Y.S.2d 116, 429 N.E.2d 794 (1981).

—The decision to abort a criminal trial must rest, in the first instance, in the sound discretion of the trial court; when the Trial Judge had properly explored the appropriate alternatives, and there is a sufficient basis in the record for a mistrial, an appellate court will be hesitant to interfere with the exercise of this discretion, however, where the mistrial is premised upon a claimed unavailability of crucial prosecution evidence, the validity of that claim is subjected to the strictest scrutiny. Hall v. Potoker, 49 N.Y.2d 501, 427 N.Y.S.2d 211, 403 N.E.2d 1210 (1980).

—The mistrial procedure was not designed to provide an escape from the performance of an unpleasant duty. A mistrial in the public interest and against defendant's will must have some basis of demonstrable substance; according to the rule, the necessity must be "manifest." Ferlito v. Judges of the County Court, 31 N.Y.2d 416, 340 N.Y.S.2d 635, 292 N.E.2d 779 (1972).

—Court properly exercised its discretion in denying defendant's motion for a mistrial or for individual questioning of jurors concerning the effect of defendant's courtroom disruptions; court's questioning of the jurors concerning their ability to remain impartial, during which the court solicited a show of hands to specific questions, and its prompt curative instructions, were appropriate, and the court properly declined to reward defendant's violent and disruptive conduct with a mistrial. People v. Cosby, 271 A.D.2d 353, 708 N.Y.S.2d 58 (1st Dept. 2000).

—Mistrial properly declared where one juror claimed her diamond ring had disappeared, demanded that all the jurors be strip searched, and ultimately focused her accusation on a single juror, because it was impossible to proceed with the trial. People v. Green, 237 A.D.2d 218, 655 N.Y.S.2d 31 (1st Dept. 1997).

—Mistrial was not warranted merely because one of the jurors, sequestered for the night after the first day of deliberations, was observed attempting to leave the hotel on bed sheets via his second-story window. People v. Conyers, 189 A.D.2d 607, 592 N.Y.S.2d 694 (1st Dept.), *lv. denied*, 81 N.Y.2d 969 (1993).

—Court properly denied defendant's motion for a mistrial based upon delays during jury selection, because the court properly questioned the sworn jurors individually in chambers to ensure that they would not hold the delays against the People or the defendant. People v. Thom, 256 A.D.2d 481, 683 N.Y.S.2d 279 (2d Dept. 1998).

—Mistrial was not warranted by comment made by a prosecution witness during cross-examination which indicated that the defendant had previously been in prison. People v. Pought, 154 A.D.2d 628, 546 N.Y.S.2d 458 (2d Dept. 1989).

—Trial court did not abuse its discretion in denying defense counsel's application for a continuance based on his claim that he was too flustered by a violent outburst by the defendant, since the court took a 3 hour recess to allow defense counsel to regain his composure and where prosecution witnesses might have become unavailable had the case been adjourned. People v. Astacio, 130 A.D.2d 908, 516 N.Y.S.2d 508 (2d Dept. 1987).

—Trial court properly declared a mistrial on its own motion, after the court dismissed a sworn juror who possessed personal knowledge of the case, and after defense counsel advised the court of a possibility that the former juror would be called as a defense witness; the court correctly noted that it would be patently unfair for the jury to have to assess the credibility of a witness who had been a member of the jury panel. People v. Magee, 254 A.D.2d 825, 679 N.Y.S.2d 485 (4th Dept. 1998).

—Mistrial motion properly denied even though four jurors inadvertently saw a mug shot of the defendant which had not been introduced into evidence. People v. Martin, 179 A.D.2d 1044, 579 N.Y.S.2d 803, 804 (4th Dept. 1992).

—In the absence of a showing of prejudice the court did not err in refusing to order a mistrial when, during the trial, the co-defendant attempted to attack the defendant. People v. Campbell, 170 A.D.2d 982, 566 N.Y.S.2d 805 (4th Dept. 1991).

—Court did not err in refusing defendant's request for a mistrial where police officer referred to defendant's statement concerning a prior arrest; court struck the statement from the record and twice instructed the jury to disregard it. People v. Guise, 179 A.D.2d 1027, 579 N.Y.S.2d 515 (4th Dept. 1991).

—Declaration of a mistrial was warranted where trial court's failure to sign a material witness order resulted in the inability of the prosecution to call an essential witness. People v. Di-Marco, 134 Misc. 2d 863, 512 N.Y.S.2d 1004 (Sup. Ct. Bronx Co. 1987).

Intent to provoke a mistrial.—A defendant may specifically limit a motion to one for a mistrial "with prejudice" based on the ground that the prosecution engaged in misconduct intended to provoke a mistrial. If a defendant so delimits his motion, he must be given the opportunity to withdraw it if the total relief requested will not be granted. Davis v. Brown, 87 N.Y.2d 626, 641 N.Y.S.2d 819, 664 N.E.2d 884 (1996).

—Although in her opening statement the prosecutor improperly referred to the defendant as a "pimp," the record did not support the defendant's claim that she did so with the intent to provoke a mistrial; absent such bad-faith intent, the misconduct did not constitute the type of prosecutorial overreaching contemplated by the United States Supreme Court as requiring a barring of reprosecution on the grounds of double jeopardy. People v. Mitchell, 197 A.D.2d 709, 602 N.Y.S.2d 923 (2d Dept. 1993).

Curative instructions.—Trial court did not err in denying defendant's requests for a mistrial based on peripheral references to another criminal act allegedly performed by the defendant, in light of the availability of court instruction to alleviate whatever prejudice may have resulted. People v. Young, 48 N.Y.2d 995, 425 N.Y.S.2d 546, 401 N.E.2d 904 (1980).

—Defendant was not deprived of due process when the trial court denied his motion for a mistrial made upon the ground that he had been unduly prejudiced when two jurors inadvertently viewed him in handcuffs while returning from lunch recess, as such viewing was brief and inadvertent and, furthermore, defense counsel declined an express invitation by the trial judge to deliver a curative instruction and did not request the substitution of alternate jurors or an examination into the effect of the encounter. People v. Harper, 47 N.Y.2d 857, 419 N.Y.S.2d 61, 392 N.E.2d 1244 (1979).

—Defendant's mistrial motion was properly denied after jurors observed an elderly witness require medical assistance immediately following his testimony; the court made a thorough inquiry and each juror stated that he or she could be fair and that the events would have no impact on his or her verdict and that the court issued a curative instruction to the jurors instructing them to disregard what happened to the witness. People v. Martinez, 289 A.D.2d 62, 734 N.Y.S.2d 138 (1st Dept. 2001).

—Court properly exercised its discretion in denying defendant's motion for a mistrial or for individual questioning of jurors concerning the effect of defendant's courtroom disruptions. The court's questioning of the jurors concerning their ability to remain impartial, during which the court solicited a show of hands to specific questions, and its prompt curative instructions, were appropriate, and the court properly declined to reward defendant's violent and disruptive conduct with a mistrial. People v. Cosby, 271 A.D.2d 353, 708 N.Y.S.2d 58 (1st Dept. 2000).

—Where curative instructions are sufficient to alleviate prejudice, the court need not declare a mistrial. People v. Owens, 214 A.D.2d 480, 625 N.Y.S.2d 524 (1st Dept. 1995).

—The trial court appropriately exercised its discretion in denying defendant's motion for a mistrial on the ground of unsolicited testimony regarding an alleged exculpatory statement made by defendant to explain his presence near the scene of the crime, where prompt curative instructions were issued. People v. Zayas, 202 A.D.2d 324, 609 N.Y.S.2d 9 (1st Dept. 1994).

—Any prejudice caused by the prosecutor's comment during summation that the grand jury "saw enough evidence to indict the defendant for robbery in the first degree" was cured by the court's instruction that an indictment is not evidence. People v. James, 197 A.D.2d 429, 602 N.Y.S.2d 610 (1st Dept. 1993).

—Court properly denied appellant's motion for a mistrial based on a verbal confrontation between the counsel for codefendant and the prosecutor, which took place in front of the jury, because the prompt curative instructions were sufficient to cure any prejudicial effect of the confrontation, especially in light of the overwhelming evidence. People v. Seecharan, 267 A.D.2d 481, 700 N.Y.S.2d 479 (2d Dept. 1999).

—In sale prosecution, although it was improper for the prosecutor to elicit testimony concerning the large sum of money recovered from the defendant at the time of his arrest, the admission of the testimony did not warrant a mistrial where the court sustained defense counsel's objection and gave prompt curative instructions which were sufficient to dispel the prejudicial effect of the error. People v. Jones, 200 A.D.2d 764, 607 N.Y.S.2d 119 (2d Dept. 1994).

—Inadvertent observation by an alternate juror of the defendant being escorted by court officers did not create any prejudice in light of the court's inquiry of that individual and subsequent instructions to him. People v. Baron, 133 A.D.2d 833, 520 N.Y.S.2d 205 (2d Dept.), lv. denied, 70 N.Y.2d 929 (1987).

—Court's denial of defendant's motion for a mistrial after two brief incidents involving courtroom spectators was not improper, in view of court's observation that the first incident did not distract the jury from paying careful attention to the opening statements and the curative instructions given following the second incident. People v. Pantoliano, 127 A.D.2d 857, 512 N.Y.S.2d 235 (2d Dept.), lv. denied, 70 N.Y.2d 715 (1987).

—Use of curative instructions, rather than the granting of a mistrial, is a proper course where such instructions alleviate whatever prejudice may have resulted from the prejudicial testimony. People v. Nagi, 153 A.D.2d 964, 545 N.Y.S.2d 403 (3d Dept. 1989).

—While CPL § 280.10 provides that a court must grant a defendant's motion for mistrial when there occurs during the trial an error or legal defect in the proceedings which is prejudicial to the defendant and deprives him of a fair trial, where an unexpected prejudicial statement is given by the People's witness, not the product of any improper conduct by the prosecution, and the court immediately gave curative instructions in an attempt to remove the prejudice, it was not mandatory that the motion be granted where the error was not of such a magnitude that the defendant's right to a fair trial was violated. People v. Celeste, 95 A.D.2d 961, 464 N.Y.S.2d 295 (3d Dept. 1983).

Failure to move for mistrial; abandonment of motion.—Defendant did not object to the manner in which the trial court dealt with possible juror misconduct, and withdrew his motion for a mistrial, after which the court took other remedial measures on the assumption that defendant no longer wanted a mistrial. Although counsel subsequently changed his mind and attempted to renew his mistrial motion, the issue is unpreserved or waived for purposes of appeal. People v. Albert, 85 N.Y.2d 851, 623 N.Y.S.2d 848, 647 N.E.2d 1356 (1995).

—Defendant's failure to request mistrial at time of prosecutor's attempt to evoke before the jury the informant's answer regarding a completely unrelated heroin transaction barred later appeal on this issue, especially where defendant's counsel gambled on fact that the court, in striking the answer, gave an instruction to the jury on the point. People v. Miller, 50 A.D.2d 757, 376 N.Y.S.2d 168 (1st Dept. 1975), aff'd, 41 N.Y.2d 857, 393 N.Y.S.2d 705, 362 N.E.2d 256 (1977).

—Defendant abandoned his motion for a mistrial in pursuing his argument for a continuance. People v. Serrano, 203 A.D.2d 99, 610 N.Y.S.2d 38 (1st Dept. 1994).

—Statements made by defendant to probation officer for presentence report on previously withdrawn guilty plea were admissible, because counsel failed to move for a mistrial after his objection to the line of questioning was sustained. People v. Muzio, 91 A.D.2d 1050, 458 N.Y.S.2d 650 (2d Dept. 1983).

§ 280.20. Motion for mistrial; status of indictment upon new trial.

Upon a new trial resulting from an order

declaring a mistrial, the indictment is deemed to contain all the counts which it contained at the time the previous trial was commenced, regardless of whether any count was thereafter dismissed by the court prior to the mistrial order.

ANNOTATIONS

Retrial; counts not submitted to first jury.—If, at the first trial, counts were dismissed for insufficient evidence, they may not be submitted to a second jury on retrial. People v. Anderson, 111 A.D.2d 124, 489 N.Y.S.2d 721 (1st Dept. 1985).

—Where the court refused to submit certain counts to the first jury, the inference is warranted that the court dismissed them for insufficient evidence; thus the defendant may not be retried on those counts. People v. Sweeney, 122 A.D.2d 177, 504 N.Y.S.2d 714 (2d Dept. 1986).

—Where defendant's first trial ended in jury disagreement, but record contained a notation indicating that weapon possession count was not to be considered but did not indicate whether the court issued a trial order of dismissal as to a weapons possession count or simply failed to submit that charge to the jury, a hearing was required as to whether the double jeopardy clause barred a second trial on a weapon possession charge. People v. Coston, 77 A.D.2d 908, 431 N.Y.S.2d 81 (2d Dept. 1980).

ARTICLE 290—JURY TRIAL—TRIAL ORDER OF DISMISSAL

Section

290.10 Trial order of dismissal.

LexisNexis Cross Reference

New York Criminal Practice (2d ed.), Vol. 3, Ch. 37, Mistrial and Trial Order of Dismissal.

§ 290.10. Trial order of dismissal.

1. At the conclusion of the people's case or at the conclusion of all the evidence, the court may, except as provided in subdivision two, upon motion of the defendant, (a) issue a "trial order of dismissal," dismissing any count of an indictment upon the ground that the trial evidence is not legally sufficient to establish the offense charged therein or any lesser included offense, or (b) reserve decision on the motion until after the verdict has been rendered and accepted by the court. Where the court has reserved decision and the jury thereafter renders a verdict of guilty, the court shall proceed to determine the motion upon such evidence as it would have been authorized to consider upon the motion had the court not reserved decision. If the court determines that such motion should have been granted upon the ground specified in paragraph (a) herein, it shall enter an order both setting aside the verdict and dismissing any count of the indictment upon such ground. If the jury is discharged before rendition of a verdict the court shall proceed to determine the motion as set forth in this paragraph.

2. Despite the lack of legally sufficient trial evidence in support of a count of an indictment as described in subdivision one, issuance of a trial order of dismissal is not authorized and constitutes error when the trial evidence would have been legally sufficient had the court not erroneously excluded admissible evidence offered by the people.

3. When the court excludes trial evidence offered by the people under such circumstances that the substance or content thereof does not appear in the record, the people may, in anticipation of a possible subsequent trial order of dismissal emanating from the allegedly improper exclusion and erroneously issued in violation of subdivision two, and in anticipation of a possible appeal therefrom pursuant to subdivision two of section 450.20, place upon the record, out of the presence of the jury, an "offer of proof" summarizing the substance or content of such excluded evidence. Upon the subsequent issuance of a trial order of dismissal and an appeal therefrom, such offer of proof constitutes a part of the record on appeal and has the effect and significance prescribed in subdivision two of section 450.40. In the absence of such an order and an appeal therefrom, such offer of proof is not deemed a part of the record and does not constitute such for purposes of an ensuing appeal by the defendant from a judgment of conviction.

4. Upon issuing a trial order of dismissal which dismisses the entire indictment, the court must immediately discharge the defendant from custody if he is in custody of the sheriff, or, if he is at liberty on bail, it must exonerate the bail.

Amended by L. 1983, Ch. 170.

ANNOTATIONS

Dismissal warranted.—Trial court's dismissal of the indictment was proper after the prosecutor refused to produce the informer for an in camera examination where certain evidence elicited from the undercover police officers, at trial, had not been contained in either of the contemporaneous written police reports of the transaction and there was no other proof of any conversations or nonverbal acts which might be deemed to constitute an offer to sell emanating from defendant, nor was there any other evidence that defendant had provided the heroin, and the subject matter testimony which defendant sought to elicit from the informer could not be obtained from alternative sources. People v. Singleton, 42 N.Y.2d 466, 398 N.Y.S.2d 871, 368 N.E.2d 1237 (1977).

Trial court's authority.—Double jeopardy did not bar retrial where court reserved decision on motion for trial order of dismissal until after the jury had rendered a verdict. People v. Adames, 83 N.Y.2d 89, 607 N.Y.S.2d 919, 629 N.E.2d 391 (1994).

—A court lacks the authority to issue a non-appealable trial order of dismissal on the merits where no evidence has been presented. Holtzman v. Goldman, 71 N.Y.2d 564, 528 N.Y.S.2d 21, 523 N.E.2d 297 (1988).

—Trial court exceeded its authority by issuing a trial order of dismissal before commencement of the trial, as CPL 290.10 only grants the court the power to rule on insufficiency, not the power to terminate the proceedings by default. People v. Spellman, 233 A.D.2d 254, 650 N.Y.S.2d 132 (1st Dept. 1996).

—The trial court may reserve judgment on a motion to dismiss until after the jury returns its verdict, since granting the motion before the jury verdict would prevent the People from appealing the ruling. People v. Ali, 189 A.D.2d 770, 592 N.Y.S.2d 405 (2d Dept.), *lv. denied*, 81 N.Y.2d 881 (1993).

Trial court's authority; scope of its review.—In deciding a motion for a trial order of dismissal under CPL § 290.10(1), the trial court must limit its review solely to the legal sufficiency of the evidence as defined in CPL § 70.10(1); in this process the court must view the evidence in the light most favorable to the People. People v. Singh, 191 A.D.2d 731, 595 N.Y.S.2d 510 (2d Dept.), *lv. denied*, 81 N.Y.2d 1020 (1993).

—A trial order of dismissal may be granted only if the trial evidence, if accepted as true and without consideration as to its quality or weight, would not establish every element of the offense charged. People v. Davis, 208 A.D.2d 1062, 617 N.Y.S.2d 571 (3d Dept. 1994).

—A defense motion for a trial order of dismissal at the close of the People's proof should be granted where the evidence on the charge is wholly circumstantial and when viewed in the light most favorable to the People, it cannot be inferred that evidence of the defendant's criminal activity flowed naturally from the facts proved and excluded every reasonable hypothesis of innocence. People v. Halstead, 3 Misc. 3d 496, 776 N.Y.S.2d 754 (Crim. Ct. Kings Co. 2004).

Sufficiency of the evidence.—Reversing trial court's order of dismissal in perjury case, Court of Appeals found order dismissing the indictment appealable, and that circumstantial evidence produced at trial was legally sufficient. People v. Sabella, 35 N.Y.2d 158, 359 N.Y.S.2d 100, 316 N.E.2d 569 (1974).

People's right to appeal.—CPL § 450.20(2), providing that the People may appeal a trial order of dismissal entered pursuant to CPL § 290.10 is unconstitutional as violative of the right not to be placed twice in jeopardy for the same offense if "further proceedings of some sort, devoted to the resolution of factual issues going to the elements of the offense charged, would have been required upon reversal and remand." People v. Brown, 40 N.Y.2d, 381, 386 N.Y.S.2d 848, 353 N.E.2d 811 (1976), *cert. denied,* 433 U.S. 913 (1977).

—While the evidence was sufficient to establish accessorial liability under PL § 20.00, the trial court's dismissal of the count was non-appealable since an appellate reversal would result in a retrial of the defendant. People v Dlugash, 41 N.Y.2d 725, 395 N.Y.S.2d 419, 363 N.E.2d 1155 (1977).

ARTICLE 300—JURY TRIAL—COURT'S CHARGE AND INSTRUCTIONS TO JURY

Section

LexisNexis Cross References

Criminal Defense Techniques, Vol. 1B, Ch. 37, Jury Instructions in Criminal Cases; *Prosecution and Defense of Sex Crimes,* Ch. 4, Jury Instructions in Sex Offense Cases.

§ 300.10. Court's charge; in general.

1. At the conclusion of the summations, the court must deliver a charge to the jury.

2. In its charge, the court must state the fundamental legal principles applicable to criminal cases in general. Such principles include, but are not limited to, the presumption of the defendant's innocence, the requirement that guilt be proved beyond a reasonable doubt and that the jury may not, in determining the issue of guilt or innocence, consider or speculate concerning matters relating to sentence or punishment. Upon request of a defendant who did not testify in his own behalf, but not otherwise, the court must state that the fact that he did not testify is not a factor from which any inference unfavorable to the defendant may be drawn. The court must also state the material legal principles applicable to the particular case, and, so far as practicable, explain the application of the law to the facts, but it need not marshall or refer to the evidence to any greater extent than is necessary for such explanation.

3. Where a defendant has raised the affirmative defense of lack of criminal responsibility by reason of mental disease or defect, as defined in section 40.15 of the penal law, the court must, without elaboration, instruct the jury as follows: "A jury during its deliberations must never consider or speculate concerning matters relating to the consequences of its verdict. However, because of the lack of common knowledge regarding the consequences of a verdict of not responsible by reason of mental disease or defect, I charge you that if this verdict is rendered by you there will be hearings as to the defendant's present mental condition and, where appropriate, involuntary commitment proceedings."

4. The court must specifically designate and submit, in accordance with the provisions of sections 300.30 and 300.40, those counts and offenses contained and charged in the indictment which the jury are to consider. Such determination must be made, and the parties informed thereof, prior to the summations. In its charge, the court must define each offense so submitted and, except as otherwise expressly provided, it must instruct the jury to render a verdict separately and specifically upon each count submitted to it, and with respect to each defendant if there be more than one, and must require that the verdict upon each such count be one of the following:

(a) "Guilty" of the offense submitted, if there be but one; or

(b) Where appropriate, "guilty" of a specified one of two or more offenses submitted under the same count in the alternative pursuant to section 300.40; or

(c) "Not guilty"; or

(d) Where appropriate, "not responsible by reason of mental disease or defect."

5. Both before and after the court's charge, the parties may submit requests to charge, either orally or in writing, and the court must rule promptly upon each request. A failure to rule upon a request is deemed a denial thereof.

6. In a prosecution involving a charge of enterprise corruption, as defined in article four hundred sixty of the penal law, the court must specifically designate and separately submit for jury consideration those criminal acts which are contained and charged in the indictment and which are supported by legally sufficient trial evidence. Every criminal act which is not so supported shall be dismissed and stricken from the indictment. If legally sufficient trial evidence exists to support a lesser included offense which is also a criminal act within the meaning of subdivision one of section 460.10 of the penal law, such lesser offense shall be substituted. Such determination must be made and the parties informed thereof, prior to the summations. In its charge, the court must define each criminal act so submitted and, as when it may or must do so pursuant to sections 300.40 and 300.50 of this article, any lesser included offense that is also a criminal act within the meaning of subdivision one of section 460.10 of the penal law. It must instruct the jury to render a verdict separately and specifically upon each criminal act (and where

necessary, any submitted lesser included offense) submitted to it with respect to each defendant. It must further explain to the jury that they may not consider a charge of enterprise corruption against any defendant until they have separately and unanimously agreed that the defendant has committed each of at least three criminal acts alleged as part of the pattern of criminal activity, including any submitted lesser included offenses.

Amended by L. 1980, Ch. 548; L. 1984, Ch. 668; L. 1986, Ch. 516.

ANNOTATIONS

Law of the case.—If instructions are erroneous, and are not objected to at trial, they become the "law of the case," and the adequacy of the proof must be evaluated under the law as it was erroneously charged. People v. Malagon, 50 N.Y.2d 954, 431 N.Y.S.2d 460, 409 N.E.2d 9 (1980).

Limiting instructions.—It was reversible error for trial judge to fail to instruct jury that co-defendant's plea could not constitute or be considered as proof of defendant's guilt. People v. Barber, 81 A.D.2d 943, 439 N.Y.S.2d 699 (3d Dept. 1981).

—If evidence that a witness has received threats is introduced even though the threats cannot be connected to the defendant, the jury must be instructed that the sole value of such evidence is to explain the witness's fearful behavior, and the evidence may not be considered against the defendant. People v. Rivera, 160 A.D.2d 267, 553 N.Y.S.2d 707 (1st Dept. 1990).

—If a witness has been impeached with prior inconsistent statements, the trial judge should instruct the jury that such statements may be considered only on the issue of the witness's credibility, and not for their truth. People v. Martinez, 173 A.D.2d 310, 570 N.Y.S.2d 1 (1st Dept. 1991).

—The trial court committed reversible error when it failed to charge that the defendant's suppressed statement was admitted only for the purpose of impeaching his credibility and not for the truth of its content, even though the error was not preserved for appellate review. People v. Jackson, 90 A.D.2d 836, 456 N.Y.S.2d 7 (2d Dept. 1982).

Curative instructions.—Although the trial court sustained defendant's objection to the prosecution's improper summation argument, reversal was required because it improperly denied the defense request for an instruction directing the jury to disregard the argument. People v. Trinidad, 59 N.Y.2d 820, 464 N.Y.S.2d 740, 451 N.E.2d 487 (1983).

—Evidence of telephone conversations improperly admitted over the defendant's assertion of the marital privilege was so inherently prejudicial that curative instructions were not sufficient to dissipate the prejudice. People v. Knapper, 191 A.D.2d 207, 594 N.Y.S.2d 210 (1st Dept. 1993).

—Fact that trial court waited overnight before giving curative instruction deemed "particularly significant" in appeals court's decision to reverse. People v. Barranco, 174 A.D.2d 343, 570 N.Y.S.2d 555 (1st Dept. 1991).

—Any prejudice resulting from prosecution's misconduct in cross-examining defendant's psychiatrist on his reason for affirming rather than swearing prior to testifying and upon his religious beliefs was dissipated by the trial court's curative instruction on the right of a witness to either swear or affirm to tell the truth. People v. Wood, 107 A.D.2d 830, 484 N.Y.S.2d 671 (2d Dept. 1985).

General principles.—The test of a jury instruction is "whether the jury, hearing the whole charge, would gather from its language the correct rules which should be applied"; although the charge here was clear enough, in cases where the People allege an offer to sell drugs, the better practice is to indicate that this theory requires proof that the defendant had the intent and ability to make the sale. People v. Samuels, 99 N.Y.2d 20, 750 N.Y,.S.2d 828, 780 N.E.2d 513 (2002).

—On appeal, the court should read the charge as a whole against the background of the evidence produced at the trial. People v. Andujas, 79 N.Y.2d 113, 580 N.Y.S.2d 719, 588 N.E.2d 754 (1992).

—A reviewing court must presume that the jury appropriately applied the charged substantive and procedural rules of law to the determined events. People v. Acevedo, 69 N.Y.2d 478, 515 N.Y.S.2d 753, 760, 508 N.E.2d 665 (1987).

—If a judge gives both correct and incorrect instructions on a particular legal principle, however, it should not be assumed that the jury adopted the right one. People v. Lourido, 70 N.Y.2d 428, 522 N.Y.S.2d 98, 516 N.E.2d 1212 (1987).

—Even if instructions to the jury are erroneous, they provide the sole basis for determining whether a conviction must be reversed and dismissed as repugnant to an acquittal on another count. People v. Hampton, 61 N.Y.2d 963, 475 N.Y.S.2d 273, 463 N.E.2d 614 (1984).

—The trial court should not use the facts of reported cases as illustrations in his charge since a slight variance in the factual content of the cases might mislead the jury. People v. Hommel, 41 N.Y.2d 427, 393 N.Y.S.2d 371, 361 N.E.2d 1020 (1977).

—It is presumed that the jury adhered to the court's instructions. People v. Trevesu, 203 A.D.2d 202, 611 N.Y.S.2d 8 (1st Dept. 1994); People v. Russell, 179 A.D.2d 521, 579 N.Y.S.2d 18, 20 (1st Dept. 1992); People v. Carreras, 181 A.D.2d 613, 581 N.Y.S.2d 336 (1st Dept. 1992); People v. Barcliff, 178 A.D.2d 285, 577 N.Y.S.2d 371 (1st Dept. 1991); People v. Jackson, 126 A.D.2d 471, 574 N.Y.S.2d 661 (1st Dept. 1991); People v. Vigilante, 153 Misc. 2d 206, 581 N.Y.S.2d 261 (Sup. Ct. Kings Co. 1992).

—Since the legality of defendant's arrest was not a jury question, the court did not commit error in refusing to charge that the police were required to obtain an arrest warrant. People v. Diaz, 172 A.D.2d 417, 568 N.Y.S.2d 791 (1st Dept. 1991).

Fairness, neutrality of the charge.—The trial judge's frequent caustic remarks deprived defendant of the right to a fair trial before an unbiased court; counsel for defendant was forced to rebut not only the People's proof but also the implications imputed by the trial judge. People v. DeJesus, 42 N.Y.2d 519, 399 N.Y.S.2d 196, 369 N.E.2d 752 (1977).

—It was not error to advise the jury to "keep its eye on the ball" since it directed attention to the discrepancies in the evidence. People v. Garcia, 50 A.D.2d 544, 375 N.Y.S.2d 344 (1st Dept. 1975), aff'd, 40 N.Y.2d 1067, 392 N.Y.S.2d 251, 360 N.E.2d 929 (1976).

—A charge which ignores or unfairly discredits the contentions of either the People or the defense cannot be countenanced, particularly where there are closely contested factual issues; care must be taken to guard against "the possibility that the stated opinion of the trial court or even the suggestion of an opinion might be seized upon by the jury and eventually prove decisive." People v. Bell, 38 N.Y.2d 116, 378 N.Y.S.2d 686, 341 N.E.2d 246 (1975).

—A trial judge is not precluded from supplying hypothetical examples in its jury instructions as an aid to understanding the applicable law. People v. Wise, 204 A.D.2d 133, 612 N.Y.S.2d 117 (1st Dept. 1994).

—It is fundamental that the court's charge must avoid any encouragement to the jury that it should draw a certain inference from the facts. People v. Lee, 192 A.D.2d 308, 595 N.Y.S.2d 471 (1st Dept. 1993).

—The court's use of a hypothetical with facts "strikingly similar" to the facts in the present case may have been error, however, any prejudice was adequately dissipated by the subsequent curative instruction and alternative hypothetical. People v. Johnson, 171 A.D.2d 532, 567 N.Y.S.2d 430 (1st Dept. 1991).

—Reversal where certain rhetorical questions and descriptive comments posed by the trial judge during the charge communicated his disbelief of the defense arguments. People v. McLean, 172 A.D.2d 256, 568 N.Y.S.2d 376 (1st Dept. 1991).

—Court's reference to the race and background of the various parties in emphasizing the equal protection of the law to which both the complaining witness and the defendants were entitled, while inartistically phrased and essentially unnecessary, were not prejudicial to the defendant. People v. Hill, 158 A.D.2d 339, 551 N.Y.S.2d 27 (1st Dept. 1990).

—Court committed reversible error where it instructed the jury that fingerprints had not nothing to do with the case where key part of the defense strategy centered on absence of fingerprints on gun. People v. Rodriguez, 141 A.D.2d 382, 529 N.Y.S.2d 318 (1st. Dept. 1988).

—Reversal where, after juror stated during verdict poll that he had "a discrepancy," trial judge made a comment suggesting his opinion regarding a factual issue. People v. Bryant, 170 A.D.2d 520, 566 N.Y.S.2d 83 (2d Dept. 1991).

—Reversible error was committed when the court informed the jury that the defendant had been and remained incarcerated pending the completion of his trial and that the State had assigned an attorney to represent the defendant because of his indigence. People v. Connor, 137 A.D.2d 547, 524 N.Y.S.2d 287 (2d Dept. 1988).

—Defendant was denied a fair trial where the judge made improper statements to the jury that "a quorum of the 23 grand jurors handed down an indictment; the jury's failure to agree would result in an new trial with tremendous expense to the state; the question of punishment rests on the shoulders of this judge and you can be sure that my shoulders are big enough and broad enough to assume and carry that responsibility." People v. Brunch, 83 A.D.2d 855, 441 N.Y.S.2d 737 (2d Dept. 1981).

—Defendant, a podiatrist, was deprived of his due process right to a fair trial when trial court charged the jury on a different theory of Grand Larceny than the one posed in the indictment and the People's direct case. People v. Prubin, 101 A.D.2d 71, 474 N.Y.S.2d 348 (4th Dept. 1984).

—The court's charge was erroneous where the jury was informed that it could "draw the strongest inferences against the defendant that the opposing evidence permits" because the defendant failed to produce a witness, as it conflicted with the presumption of innocence, the People's burden of proof and created potential for speculation with regard to evidence not in the record. People v. Terry, 83 A.D.2d 491, 445 N.Y.S.2d 340 (4th Dept. 1981).

General principles; fairness, marshalling the evidence.— The court has an obligation to marshal or refer to the evidence only to the extent necessary to explain the application of the law to the facts. People v. Culhane, 45 N.Y.2d 757, 408 N.Y.S.2d 489, 380 N.E.2d 315 (1978).

—A new trial was required when the court pointed out the single inconsistency in the defendant's testimony but neglected to mention any of the numerous inconsistencies in the testimony of the witnesses for the prosecution. People v. Williamson, 40 N.Y.2d 1073, 392 N.Y.S.2d 255, 360 N.E.2d 933 (1976).

—The judge is under no obligation to marshal the evidence except as required to relate it to the applicable law. People v. Right, 180 A.D.2d 430, 579 N.Y.S.2d 661 (1st Dept.), lv. denied, 79 N.Y.2d 952 (1992).

—A trial court is not required to explain all of the contentions of both parties or outline all inconsistencies in the evidence; however, in its discretion, the court may summarize the facts for the jury. People v. Right, 180 A.D.2d 430, 579 N.Y.S.2d 661 (1st Dept. 1992).

—As the trial was not unduly long and did not involve complex legal and factual issues, the trial court did not err in failing to marshal the evidence. People v. Bowser, 287 A.D.2d 647, 732 N.Y.S.2d 28 (2d Dept. 2001).

—A court is required to summarize the evidence only to the extent necessary to explain the application of the law to the facts. People v. Filardi, 203 A.D.2d 301, 610 N.Y.S.2d 62 (2d Dept. 1994).

—When the trial court does refer to the evidence, it must do so fairly and in an even-handed manner, favoring neither the prosecution nor the defense. People v. James, 194 A.D.2d 558, 598 N.Y.S.2d 334 (2d Dept. 1993).

—Trial court's decision not to marshal the evidence would not be a basis for a reversal and a new trial, since the trial was relatively short and the jury was adequately apprised of the defendant's position. People v. Patterson, 121 A.D.2d 406, 502 N.Y.S.2d 806 (2d Dept. 1986).

—Court was not required to marshal the evidence where the trial was relatively short, the jury was adequately apprised of defendant's defense and the charge, taken in its entirety, was unquestionably fair to defendant. People v. Carter, 158 A.D.2d 851, 551 N.Y.S.2d 644 (3d Dept. 1990).

Invading the province of the jury.— In a Driving While Intoxicated trial it was error to charge the jurors, in substance, that they could ignore the failure of the police to administer the breathalyzer test in accordance with the rules and regulations of the Sheriff's Department. People v. Williams, 62 N.Y.2d 765, 477 N.Y.S.2d 315, 465 N.E.2d 1251 (1984).

—Reversal of defendant's conviction was required where the court's charge placed the defendant at the scene of the crime, one of the issues raised by the case and a fact contested by

counsel. People v. Martin, 115 A.D.2d 565, 496 N.Y.S.2d 85 (2d Dept. 1985).

—Court's charge to jury that it could either convict the defendant of murder or convict him of manslaughter usurped the jury function by directing a guilty verdict and constituted reversible error notwithstanding defense counsel's failure to object to the error. People v. Stahl, 138 A.D.2d 920, 526 N.Y.S.2d 868 (4th Dept. 1988).

Preservation; court's uninterrupted supervision.— Defendant did not preserve his argument that the trial court erred in directing assistance in the reading of its final charge to the jury; all instructions on the law were provided by the court, and the law secretary's reading of portions of the final charge necessitated by the judge's intermittent difficulties in reading due to recent eye surgery, was clearly at the direction and under the supervision of the court in compliance with CPL § 300.10, and protected defendant's right to trial by jury by the court's uninterrupted presence and active supervision. People v. Mays, 232 A.D.2d 332, 649 N.Y.S.2d 409 (1st Dept. 1996).

Subd. 2

Burden of proof.— Court of Appeals disapproves a charge which stated: "If the evidence in the case reasonably permits a conclusion of either guilt or innocence, you should adopt a conclusion of innocence;" however, although the phrase was "improper and should not have been used," the Court affirmed because the charge as a whole conveyed the correct standard. People v. Fields, 87 N.Y.2d 821, 637 N.Y.S.2d 355, 660 N.E.2d 1134 (1995).

—The trial court should not charge that the jurors must supply concrete reasons "based on the evidence" for their inclination to acquit; however, a trial judge does not err by charging the jury that "a reasonable doubt is a doubt based upon a reason. It is a doubt for which a juror could give a reason, if he or she were called upon to do so in the jury room." People v. Antonmarchi, 80 N.Y.2d 247, 590 N.Y.S.2d 33, 604 N.E.2d 95 (1992).

—Trial court did not err in instructing the jury that, if it found that the People had proved each of the elements of the crime beyond a reasonable doubt, it "must" find defendant guilty; while there is nothing to prevent the jury from acquitting although finding the prosecution has proved its case, this so-called "mercy-dispensing power" is not a legally sanctioned function of the jury and should not be encouraged by the court. People v. Goetz, 73 N.Y.2d 751, 536 N.Y.S.2d 45, 532 N.E.2d 1273 (1988), cert. denied, 489 U.S. 1053.

—The trial court must instruct the jury that the People are required to prove every element of the crime charged beyond a reasonable doubt, and the refusal to do so is per se error. People v. Sanders, 69 N.Y.2d 860, 514 N.Y.S.2d 711, 507 N.E.2d 304 (1987).

—Reversal required where court charged jurors that "if you had a reasonable doubt on any relative point... and one or more of your fellow jurors questioned you about it, [you] would be willing and able to give what you believe is a fair, calm explanation of your position based upon the evidence or lack of evidence." People v. Arce, 215 A.D.2d 277, 627 N.Y.S.2d 15 (1st Dept. 1995).

—It is undesirable for a court to use the phrase "the scales weigh even" in the reasonable doubt charge in a criminal case even if the charge is formally correct. People v. Ellis, 202 A.D.2d 301, 609 N.Y.S.2d 7 (1st Dept. 1994).

—Court did not err by charging the jury that a "reasonable doubt is a doubt based upon a reason. It is a doubt for which a juror could give a reason, if he or she were called upon to do so in the jury room." People v. Uraca, 195 A.D.2d 377, 600 N.Y.S.2d 458 (1st Dept. 1993).

—Defendant's argument that he was deprived of a fair trial by the court's instruction that the jury apply the reasonable doubt standard only after it first determined the credibility of the witnesses by means of a preponderance standard was unpreserved by objection. People v. Perez, 194 A.D.2d 455, 599 N.Y.S.2d 269 (1st Dept. 1993).

—Any error by the court in instructing the jury that it should decide "who's telling the truth?" was harmless when the court's charge was considered as a whole and in view of the overwhelming evidence of defendant's guilt. People v. Molina, 187 A.D.2d 356, 590 N.Y.S.2d 76 (1st Dept. 1992).

—Court properly instructed the jury that if it found that each element of the crime had been established beyond a reasonable doubt it "must" convict defendant. People v. Fields, 160 A.D.2d 166, 554 N.Y.S.2d 250 (1st Dept. 1990).

—Court erred in instructing the jury that it is possible to demand proof to a reasonable certainty and to that degree of proof the People must be held; such language subverts the standard of proof of guilt beyond a reasonable doubt. People v. Reyes, 151 A.D.2d 435, 542 N.Y.S.2d 637 (1st Dept. 1989).

—It was not error for the trial judge in his charge to equate the standard of proof of guilt beyond a reasonable doubt to proof "to a moral certainty." People v. Fox, 72 A.D.2d 146, 423 N.Y.S.2d 171 (1st Dept. 1980).

—A 3-judge majority upheld defendant's conviction, where court charged at length, and with examples, that reasonable doubt was a doubt for which a juror could give a reason if called upon to do so in the jury room; 2-judge dissent would reverse conviction, finding that the charge impermissibly shifted the burden of proof. People v. Robinson, 218 A.D.2d 673, 630 N.Y.S.2d 505 (2d Dept. 1995), aff'd, 88 N.Y.2d 1001, 648 N.Y.S.2d 869, 671 N.E.2d 1266 (1996).

—A court's failure to charge that a reasonable doubt can arise from a lack of evidence is not error. People v. Fenderson, 203 A.D.2d 585, 611 N.Y.S.2d 220 (2d Dept. 1994).

—The trial court's references to reasonable doubt as "something of consequence" and "something of substance," when viewed in the context of the entire charge, did not create a reasonable likelihood that the jury applied a standard of proof lower than due process requires. People v. Reyes, 207 A.D.2d 362, 615 N.Y.S.2d 450 (2d Dept.), lv. denied, 84 N.Y.2d 871 (1994).

—The trial court's statements at the end of its charge that "the essence of the jury system" and the "bottom line" and "you are looking for the truth, what actually happened," did not shift the burden of proof to the defendant; the court's charge, viewed in its entirety, explained the concepts of reasonable doubt and the People's burden of proof and made it clear that the defendant bore no burden of proof. People v. Griffith, 200 A.D.2d 760, 607 N.Y.S.2d 96 (2d Dept.), lv. denied, 83 N.Y.2d 853 (1994).

—Court's charge to the effect that the jury must acquit if the "scales are even" did not require reversal. People v. Jones, 156 A.D.2d 718, 549 N.Y.S.2d 470 (2d Dept. 1990).

—Court's apparently inadvertent use of the phrase "merely proof of guilty (sic) beyond a reasonable doubt" at the end of its otherwise proper charge on reasonable doubt was harmless beyond a reasonable doubt. People v. Allen, 127 A.D.2d 840, 512 N.Y.S.2d 231 (2d Dept. 1987).

—Although the trial court erred in employing the phrase "if your minds are wavering or if the scales are even" in charging the jury as to reasonable doubt, reversal was not required since the charge, when read in its entirety, conveyed to the jury the appropriate standard of proof. People v. Samuels, 121 A.D.2d 751, 504 N.Y.S.2d 166 (2d Dept. 1986).

—Court's charge was improper where, court said that presumption of fact of possession was something jury could accept or reject, and also said "the presumption is overcome only when the defendant produces substantial evidence to the contrary," as this improperly shifted burden of proof to defendant. People v. Sears, 86 A.D.2d 879, 447 N.Y.S.2d 289 (2d Dept. 1982).

—Court rejected challenge to charge which included language, "a doubt of the defendant's guilty to be a reasonable doubt must be a doubt for which some reason can be given"; standing alone, the words created no impression that a juror is obliged to articulate the reason, and the charge as delivered neither shifted the burden of proof to defendant nor suggested to the jury that they were required to give reasons for their doubts. People v. Martin, 206 A.D.2d 591, 614 N.Y.S.2d 467 (3d Dept. 1994).

—Court, in issuing reasonable doubt charge, is not required to add the proviso to the effect that jurors have no obligation to actually articulate the reason for their doubts. People v. Daniels, 204 A.D.2d 865, 612 N.Y.S.2d 463 (3d Dept. 1994).

—Court's failure to charge specifically the reasonable doubt standard with regard to identification of defendant and alibi defense did not warrant reversal where charge taken as a whole was adequate to convey proper standard. People v. House, 132 A.D.2d 807, 517 N.Y.S.2d 803 (3d Dept. 1987).

—The trial court erred in refusing to grant defense counsel's request to charge the jury that reasonable doubt could be found based on a lack of evidence. People v. Johnson, 189 A.D.2d 318, 596 N.Y.S.2d 255 (4th Dept. 1993).

—Court committed reversible error in charging the jury on reasonable doubt that "[i]t is a doubt which leaves your mind in such a state of suspense that you are unable to say that you are convinced, to a moral certainty, of defendant's guilt." People v. Melito, 195 A.D.2d 195, 601 N.Y.S.2d 745 (4th Dept. 1993).

—Court did not err in refusing to instruct the jury that reasonable doubt may be found in lack of evidence. People v. Rodriguez, 171 A.D.2d 1021, 569 N.Y.S.2d 31 (4th Dept. 1991).

—Defendant's request to charge that the People must prove each circumstantial fact upon which they rely beyond a reasonable doubt was properly denied; although the People must prove each element of the crime beyond a reasonable doubt, there is no requirement that they prove each fact beyond a reasonable doubt. People v. Man Lee Lo, 118 A.D.2d 225, 504 N.Y.S.2d 332 (4th Dept. 1986).

Failure of defendant to testify.—In the case of a charge error implicating defendant's right against self-incrimination, the exception to the preservation requirement may be invoked only where the language of the charge unambiguously or expressly conveys to the jury that the defendant should have testified. People v. Autry, 75 N.Y.2d 836, 552 N.Y.S.2d 908, 552 N.E.2d 156 (1990).

—Rule prohibiting a "no inference" charge absent the defendant's request applies to instructions given during the voir dire; should a venireman comment on the possible failure of the defendant to testify, the court need not only instruct that the juror is bound by the law, which the court will state at the appropriate time, inquire whether the juror can accept and apply the legal instructions as given, and excuse that juror for cause if he cannot follow the court's instructions; any further or more specific discussion of the "no inference" rule during voir dire is proper only if requested or consented to by defense counsel. People v. Koberstein, 66 N.Y.2d 1028, 499 N.Y.S.2d 379, 489 N.E.2d 1295 (1985).

—Where the court without request from the defendant, charged the jury that no adverse inference could be drawn from the defendant's failure to testify at the trial, the error committed in submitting the charge, if it was error at all, was harmless, since the proof of defendant's guilt was overwhelming. People v. Vereen, 45 N.Y..2d 856, 410 N.Y.S.2d 288, 382 N.E.2d 1151 (1978).

—It is reversible error where a trial judge fails to charge, when requested, that no inference unfavorable to the defendant may be drawn from his failure to testify during his trial. People v. Britt, 43 N.Y.2d 111, 400 N.Y.S.2d 785, 371 N.E.2d 504 (1977).

—Where defendant failed to object to the language used by the court in its instructions that no inference be drawn from the defendant's failure to testify, the issue was not preserved for appellate review. People v. Sachs, 162 A.D.2d 125, 556 N.Y.S.2d 72 (1st Dept. 1990), appeal dism'd, 77 N.Y.2d 881 (1991).

—Where the proof of guilt is overwhelming any error committed in submitting a no-adverse inference charge is deemed harmless. People v. Gonzalez, 157 A.D.2d 625, 550 N.Y.S.2d 643 (1st Dept. 1990).

—Where a defendant who has not testified makes no request for a no-adverse inference charge, the better practice is for a trial judge to ask defense counsel during the charge conference, out of the presence of the jury, if such a charge is desired. People v. Garcia, 160 A.D.2d 354, 553 N.Y.S.2d 416 (1st Dept. 1990).

—Trial court's expansive "no adverse inference" charge improperly implied that the defendant's exercise of his right not to testify was a tactical decision. People v. Rose, 223 A.D.2d 607, 637 N.Y.S.2d 172 (2d Dept. 1996).

—The jury is presumed to have followed the court's instructions not to draw any unfavorable inference from the fact that the defendant did not testify. People v. Brown, 196 A.D.2d 465, 601 N.Y.S.2d 296 (1st Dept. 1993).

—Reversal was not required where the trial court delivered an unrequested instruction on the defendant's failure to testify. People v. Gardner, 182 A.D.2d 638, 582 N.Y.S.2d 248, 249 (2d Dept.), lv. denied, 80 N.Y.2d 903 (1992).

—Court's deviation from statutory language of CPL § 300.10 with regard to the defendant's right not to testify constituted harmless error. People v. White, 154 A.D.2d 564, 546 N.Y.S.2d 168 (2d Dept. 1989).

—Court's failure to issue a charge that no unfavorable inference can be drawn from defendant's failure to take the stand after agreeing to issue one was not preserved for appellate review where the defendant failed to except to the court's omission. People v. Hall, 124 A.D.2d 246, 508 N.Y.S.2d 113 (3d Dept. 1986).

—Court did not err in failing to instruct the jury that defendant's failure to testify was not a factor from which an unfavorable inference may be drawn since the defendant never made a request for such a charge. People v. Ceppner, 122 A.D.2d 394, 505 N.Y.S.2d 208 (3d Dept. 1986).

—The court erred when it charged the jury in connection with defendant's failure to testify that "if there are witnesses that are in control of either party and are not produced by that party, you have the right to infer, if you so desire, that their testimony would be adverse to the party in whose control they are"; however, the error was not prejudicial or reversible since the erroneous charge was not accompanied by any improper remarks by the prosecutor in summation. People v. Renner, 80 A.D.2d 705, 437 N.Y.S.2d 749 (3d Dept. 1981).

Presumption of innocence.—Appellate Division erred in holding that failure to charge jury on the presumption of innocence required reversal as a matter of law even in the absence of timely objection at trial; however, case remitted to determine whether reversal should be granted as a matter of discretion. People v. Creech, 60 N.Y.2d 895, 470 N.Y.S.2d 572, 458 N.E.2d 1249 (1983).

—The trial judge may not downplay the importance of the presumption, by for example, calling it a "device" (one of the grounds for reversal). People v. McLean, 172 A.D.2d 256, 568 N.Y.S.2d 376 (1st Dept. 1991).

—While court did not approve of the trial court's introductory phrasing that "each defendant is presumed to be innocent in a sense it concluded that the remainder of the instruction properly set forth the principles intended to be conveyed and reinforced, rather than weakened the vitality of the presumption continuing until such time as the jury was convinced beyond a reasonable doubt of the defendant's guilt." People v. Jorge, 159 A.D.2d 237, 552 N.Y.S.2d 217 (1st Dept. 1990).

—Trial court's inadvertent failure to instruct the jury with regard to the presumption of innocence mandated reversal of conviction even though omission was not called to the court's attention and court had referred to the principal repeatedly during voir dire in his introductory remarks. People v. Gayle, 76 A.D.2d 587, 431 N.Y.S.2d 18 (1st Dept. 1980).

Acting in concert.—Where different inferences may reasonably be drawn from the proof adduced at trial as to witness' complicity in preparing for the murder, the accomplice role should have been given to the jury for its consideration. People v. Vataj, 69 N.Y.2d 985, 517 N.Y.S.2d 708, 510 N.E.2d 792, (1987).

—Failure to charge the jury that co-defendants were accomplices as a matter of law and that therefore the defendant could not be convicted on their testimony without corroborating evidence is necessarily harmful error. People v. Jenner, 29 N.Y.S.2d 695, 325 N.Y.S.2d 652 (1971).

—Court rejected defendant's contention that the court should recognize a purported "bodyguard exception" to accessorial liability, and declined to recognize the validity of any blanket exception. People v. Rosa, 176 A.D.2d 188, 574 N.Y.S.2d 312 (1st Dept. 1991).

—A jury is properly charged on accomplice liability when it is instructed to consider each defendant's guilt or innocence separately and that each defendant's conduct must be intentional and knowing. People v. Green, 161 A.D.2d 248, 554 N.Y.S.2d 896 (1st Dept. 1990).

—Charge that an individual is an accomplice as a matter of law "if you believe his testimony" was patently ambiguous, and rendered the charge defective. People v. Lanni, 73 A.D.2d 538, 422 N.Y.S.2d 700 (1st Dept. 1979).

—In this case involving the defendant and a co-defendant, the court erred in failing to instruct the jury to consider the evidence of guilt or innocence separately as to each individual, and the error was compounded by the failure of the trial court to properly charge accomplice liability. Accordingly, a new trial was ordered. People v. Robinson, 262 A.D.2d 505, 692 N.Y.S.2d 136 (2d Dept. 1999).

—Defendant who was charged on an "acting in concert" basis was not prejudiced by the court's instruction that jurors could find him guilty even if they did not believe that there was a

second perpetrator. People v. Richards, 207 A.D.2d 660, 616 N.Y.S.2d 40 (2d Dept.), lv. denied, 84 N.Y.2d 1037 (1995).

—The court erred during its acting in concert charge in instructing the jury that the defendant could be found liable even if he played no part at all in the criminal activity as long as he harbored a criminal intent. People v. King, 200 A.D.2d 765, 607 N.Y.S.2d 120 (2d Dept. 1994).

—Where the court gives an unwarranted instruction on acting in concert in a case where the prosecution proceeds on a single-perpetrator theory, it is not grounds for reversal. People v. Ranta, 203 A.D.2d 307, 610 N.Y.S.2d 283 (2d Dept. 1994).

—A witness may be an accomplice for purposes of the corroboration statute, if, according to the evidence presented, he or she may reasonably be considered to have participated in an offense based on the same or some of the same conduct which constituted the offense charged. People v. Walden, 181 A.D.2d 808, 581 N.Y.S.2d 236 (2d Dept. 1992).

—In order to be held accountable for the act as the principal actor, a defendant must be found to share a community of purpose with the principal. People v. Armistead, 178 A.D.2d 607, 577 N.Y.S.2d 667 (2d Dept. 1991).

—Where defendant did not request an accomplice charge, that omission constituted a waiver of his right to contest that issue on appeal. People v. Gerenstein, 179 A.D.2d 930, 580 N.Y.S.2d 489 (3d Dept. 1992).

—Where a conviction rests substantially on the testimony of an accomplice, failure to instruct the jury that an accomplice's testimony requires corroboration is error, even absent a request by defendant. People v. Murphy, 139 Misc. 2d 83, 526 N.Y.S.2d 905 (Sup. Ct. Kings Co. 1988).

Attempt.—A charge on attempt may be submitted to the jury when, although there is evidence of a consummation, the proof is also susceptible of a finding of an attempt. People v. Bouyea, 142 A.D.2d 757, 531 N.Y.S.2d 129 (3d Dept. 1988).

Circumstantial evidence.—Whenever a case relies wholly on circumstantial evidence to establish all elements of the charge, the jury should be instructed, in substance, that the evidence must establish guilt to a moral certainty; where a charge is supported with both circumstantial and direct evidence, the court need not so charge the jury. People v. Daddona, 81 N.Y.2d 990, 599 N.Y.S.2d 530, 615 N.E.2d 1014 (1993).

—Circumstantial evidence instruction containing erroneous language that some facts could be proved with less assurance than others was not cause for reversal where the charge as a whole adequately conveyed to the jury the appropriate standards. People v. Adams, 69 N.Y.2d 805, 513 N.Y.S.2d 381, 382 N.E.2d 946 (1987).

—Reversal was required where court failed to issue circumstantial evidence charge and case against defendant on the robbery was wholly circumstantial. People v. Silva, 69 N.Y.2d 858, 514 N.Y.S.2d 710, 507 N.E.2d 303 (1987).

—Reversible error was committed where the court erroneously failed to advise the jury as part of the circumstantial evidence charge that the facts proved must exclude every reasonable inference of innocence and where it incorrectly advised the jury that if it was satisfied beyond a reasonable doubt of the defendant's guilt it should convict even if some of the facts alleged have been proved with a lower degree of certainty. People v. Ford, 66 N.Y.2d 428, 497 N.Y.S.2d 637, 488 N.E.2d 458 (1985).

—In a circumstantial evidence charge it is not necessary that the words "moral certainty" be used, but the jury should be instructed in substance that it must appear that the inference of guilt is the only one that can fairly and reasonably be drawn from the facts, and that the evidence excludes beyond a reasonable doubt every reasonable hypothesis of innocence. People v. Sanchez, 61 N.Y.2d 1022, 475 N.Y.S.2d 376, 463 N.E.2d 1228 (1984).

—Trial court failed to charge that jury should have applied a circumstantial evidence standard to the prosecution's entire case where defendant's statements, in absence of other evidence, only placed him at the scene of the crime close in time to its commission, but the fact of his presence did not establish that he was the strangler. People v. Sanchez, 61 N.Y.2d 1022, 475 N.Y.S.2d 376, 463 N.E.2d 1228 (1984).

—Court erred in failing to give circumstantial evidence charge where evidence consisted of an admission by defendant not amounting to a confession, but from which the jury might or might not infer guilt. People v. Burke, 62 N.Y.2d 860, 477 N.Y.S.2d 618, 466 N.E.2d 158 (1984).

—Trial court's instruction was acceptable; although it would have been preferable for the instruction on circumstantial evidence to state that the hypothesis of guilt should flow naturally from the facts proved, and be consistent with them, and that the facts proved must exclude to a moral certainty every reasonable hypothesis of innocence. People v. Morris, 36 N.Y.2d 877, 372 N.Y.S.2d 210, 334 N.E.2d 10 (1975).

—The rule with respect to convictions based exclusively upon circumstantial evidence is that for guilt to be proven beyond a reasonable doubt the hypothesis of guilt should flow naturally from the facts proved, and be consistent with them; and the facts proved must exclude "to a moral certainty" every reasonable hypothesis of innocence. People v. Benzinger, 36 N.Y.2d 29, 364 N.Y.S.2d 855, 324 N.E.2d 334 (1974).

—Where a conviction is based upon circumstantial evidence, the facts from which the inference of guilty is drawn must be inconsistent with the defendant's innocence and must exclude to a moral certainty every other reasonable hypothesis. People v. Schepis, 206 A.D.2d 278, 614 N.Y.S.2d 719 (1st Dept. 1994).

—The circumstantial evidence standard does not apply to a situation where both direct and circumstantial evidence are employed to demonstrate a defendant's culpability. People v. Wright, 189 A.D.2d 612, 592 N.Y.S.2d 312 (1st Dept. 1993); see also People v. Monje, 179 A.D.2d 437, 578 N.Y.S.2d, 556 (1st Dept. 1992); People v. Garden, 176 A.D.2d 621, 575 N.Y.S.2d 63 (1st Dept. 1991); People v. Barnes, 176 A.D.2d 640, 575 N.Y.S.2d 292 (1st Dept. 1991); People v. Brossoit, 192 A.D.2d 900, 597 N.Y.S.2d 192 (3d Dept. 1993); People v. Holden, 187 A.D.2d 757, 590 N.Y.S.2d 939 (3d Dept. 1992); People v. Bowen, 172 A.D.2d 876, 568 N.Y.S.2d 179 (3d Dept. 1991).

—Court's circumstantial charge was proper; although the court chose not to employ either "moral certainty" language or the "exclusion concept," its instruction as a whole conveyed the substance of the appropriate standard for evaluating the evidence. People v. Walker, 194 A.D.2d 368, 598 N.Y.S.2d 495 (1st Dept. 1993).

—Defendant was properly denied an "inference of innocence" charge, which is "is only required where the People's case is based solely on circumstantial evidence . . . or where the People introduce evidence of the defendant's conduct from which they contend the jury may draw an inference that such conduct evidences guilt"; here, the prosecution relied on testimony of the undercover officer and his recorded conversations with defendant, and thus, its case was not based entirely on circumstantial evidence. People v. Delacruz, 289 A.D.2d 254, 733 N.Y.S.2d 699 (2d Dept. 2001).

—Where the case involved both direct and circumstantial evidence, the moral certainty standard did not apply. People v. Gonzalez, 199 A.D.2d 412, 605 N.Y.S.2d 110 (2d Dept. 1994); see also People v. Cassas, 194 A.D.2d 685, 599 N.Y.S.2d 107 (2d Dept. 1993); People v. Cave, 191 A.D.2d 704, 595 N.Y.S.2d 791 (2d Dept. 1993); People v. Burgos, 170 A.D.2d 689, 567 N.Y.S.2d 103 (2d Dept. 1991).

—Court properly denied request for circumstantial evidence charge; such a charge is proper only when the evidence of guilty is solely circumstantial, which was not the case. People v. Pilgrim, 208 A.D.2d 868, 617 N.Y.S.2d 847 (2d Dept. 1994), lv. denied, 84 N.Y.2d (1995).

—Where the evidence of guilt was not overwhelming, the court's failure to include in its circumstantial evidence charge language which clearly conveyed the concept that the evidence must exclude beyond a reasonable doubt every reasonable hypothesis but that of guilt required reversal. People v. Marsalis, 189 A.D.2d 89, 592 N.Y.S.2d 79 (2d Dept. 1993).

—Reversal was required where the circumstantial evidence charge given by the court failed to include language which clearly conveyed to the jury the concept that the evidence must exclude beyond a reasonable doubt every reasonable hypothesis of innocence. People v. Livingston, 157 A.D.2d 859, 550 N.Y.S.2d 739 (2d Dept. 1990).

—Defendant was not entitled to a circumstantial evidence charge where one witness testified that the defendant had admitted participation in the robbery and the shootout which resulted in the victim's death. People v. Jones, 153 A.D.2d 590, 544 N.Y.S.2d 382 (2d Dept. 1989).

—Defendant's admissible inculpatory statements constituted

direct evidence of his guilt and thus no circumstantial evidence charge was required. People v. Rivera, 154 A.D.2d 630, 546 N.Y.S.2d 641 (2d Dept. 1989).

—While the trial court's charge to the jury on circumstantial evidence was not a misstatement of law, it failed to adequately convey to the jury the reasoning process to be followed in assessing such proof, and in view of less than overwhelming proof of guilt reversal was required. People v. Perotta, 121 A.D.2d 659, 504 N.Y.S.2d 51 (2d Dept. 1986).

—Defendant was not entitled to circumstantial evidence charge because defendant's admission that he had consumed four beers, together with police testimony about defendant's condition and the eyewitness testimony about his erratic driving, constituted direct evidence of his impaired ability to operate his vehicle. People v. Crandall, 287 A.D.2d 881, 731 N.Y.S.2d 553 (3d Dept. 2001).

—Circumstantial evidence charge was not required where, as here, both direct and circumstantial evidence is presented to prove defendant's guilt, and any error was harmless because the circumstantial evidence adduced at trial overwhelmingly established defendant's guilt. People v. McHenry, 233 A.D.2d 866, 649 N.Y.S.2d 755 (4th Dept. 1996).

—Since there was direct evidence of a full confession made by the defendant to a fellow inmate, the circumstantial evidence charge need not have been given by the court. People v. Wallace, 159 A.D.2d 1022, 552 N.Y.S.2d 723 (4th Dept. 1990).

—Where defendant's statement could be interpreted by the trier of fact as a "relevant admission of guilt" the court properly declined to issue a circumstantial evidence charge. People v. Barnes, 162 A.D.2d 1039, 558 N.Y.S.2d 339 (4th Dept. 1990).

—"Moral certainty" standard has no application where circumstantial evidence relates to proof of only one element. People v. Tribunella, 149 A.D.2d 925, 540 N.Y.S.2d 58 (4th Dept. 1989).

—Court did not err in denying defendant's request for a "moral certainty" circumstantial evidence charge because the People also introduced direct evidence against the defendant. People v. Goss, 204 A.D.2d 984, 614 N.Y.S.2d 86 (4th Dept. 1994); see also People v. Glover, 206 A.D.2d 826, 616 N.Y.S.2d 128 (4th Dept. 1994); People v. Graham, 151 A.D.2d 979, 542 N.Y.S.2d 69 (4th Dept. 1989).

Consciousness of guilt.—The court properly charged the jury that the defendant's admitted use of an alias upon arrest could imply a consciousness of guilty but that such evidence must be weighed cautiously. People v. Severino, 200 A.D.2d 522, 607 N.Y.S.2d 9 (1st Dept. 1994).

—Court incorrectly charged that consciousness of guilt could be inferred from the failure of defendant or his family to preserve and to produce defendant's bloody clothing where there was not at least some evidence of defendant's knowledge, authorization on participation in the loss or destruction of the clothing. People v. Murphy, 128 A.D.2d 177, 515 N.Y.S.2d 895 (3d Dept. 1987).

Consciousness of guilt; flight.—Trial court's charge, suggesting that a strong inference could be drawn that defendant was fleeing from the robbery essentially equated defendant's flight with guilt as to the crimes charged and required reversal. People v. Williams, 66 N.Y.2d 789, 497 N.Y.S.2d 902, 488 N.E.2d 832 (1985).

—Where flight evidence has been admitted, the trial court should charge the jury that such proof of consciousness of guilt is only of slight value, and should explain why flight can also be consistent with innocence. People v. Moses, 63 N.Y.2d 299, 482 N.Y.S.2d 228, 472 N.E.2d 4 (1984).

—Although evidence of flight is admissible, the trial court is required to instruct the jury as to the limited probative value which may be attributed to such evidence. People v. Limage, 57 A.D.2d 906, 394 N.Y.S.2d 458 (2d Dept. 1977), aff'd, 45 N.Y.2d 845, 410 N.Y.S.2d 68, 382 N.E.2d 767 (1978).

—Flight charge was proper even though defendant merely walked, rather than ran, away from the police. People v. Exum, 208 A.D.2d 557, 616 N.Y.S.2d 670 (2d Dept. 1994), lv. denied, 85 N.Y.2d 908, 650 N.E.2d 1333 (1995).

—Court erred in giving instructions on flight where testimony established that defendant had been seen a couple of times shortly after the incident in the immediate neighborhood of the crime scene and did not go to Georgia until over a year after the crime. People v. Edmond, 118 A.D.2d 797, 500 N.Y.S.2d 165 (2d Dept. 1986).

—Where there was trial testimony concerning the defendant's flight, trial court erred in failing to charge the jury that if two inferences could be drawn from defendant's conduct, one consistent with consciousness of guilt and one consistent with an innocent purpose, the jury must draw that inference consistent with an innocent purpose, and this error was particularly prejudicial in light of improper prosecutorial comments during summation. People v. Jones, 104 A.D.2d 826, 480 N.Y.S.2d 49 (2d Dept. 1984).

—Evidence that defendant could not be found at home, or in the custody of the police, or in the custody of the Department of Correction, or in certain hospitals, or the city morgue, justified the court's issuance of a flight charge. People v. Anglin, 136 Misc. 2d 987, 519 N.Y.S.2d 586 (Sup. Ct. Kings Co. 1987).

Credibility, general.—Since proof that the victim promptly complained of being raped is admissible to show the reliability of that complaint, it is proper for the trial court to issue an instruction to that effect. People v. Williams, 75 N.Y.2d 858, 552 N.Y.S.2d 917, 918, 552 N.E.2d 16 (1990).

—Hypnotized witnesses require trial court to charge the jury, if requested by the defense, that a hypnotized witness usually acquires a measure of confidence in events recalled under hypnosis. People v. Smith, 63 N.Y.2d 41, 479 N.Y.S.2d 706, 463 N.E.2d 879 (1984), cert. denied, 469 U.S. 1227 (1985).

—Evidence of good character is not in and of itself insufficient to raise a reasonable doubt. Such evidence does not exist in a vacuum and its value, influence or the weight to be accorded it depends in great part upon the other evidence in the case, but if accepted and believed, it becomes a fact to be weighed with the other facts. People v. Miller, 35 N.Y.2d 65, 358 N.Y.S.2d 733, 45 N.E.2d 1043 (1974).

—Court's statement to the jury in relation to testimony of expert, "You don't have to automatically accept the opinion of an expert. You can reject it, if there's a reason in the record to do that," did not impermissibly shift the burden of proof, since the People's burden of proof and the evaluation of the credibility of all of the witnesses, including that of a person in an official position, were adequately explained in the court's charge viewed as a whole. People v. Caldwell, 196 A.D.2d 760, 602 N.Y.S.2d 14 (1st Dept.), lv. denied, 82 N.Y.2d 892 (1993).

—Although court should have charged the jury that it should consider any specific benefits conferred upon a witness for testifying, the failure to do so did not warrant reversal under the facts of the case. People v. Jamison, 188 A.D.2d 551, 591 N.Y.S.2d 450 (2d Dept. 1992).

—Portion of trial court's charge stating, "If the jury should say that every witness whose manners or morals they may not approve of must necessarily be perjuring herself or himself on the stand then a great many of the crimes that came before juries would go unpunished," is disapproved as to the last part of the quoted sentence; however, since no objection was taken, or request for curative instructions made, the error was not preserved for appellate review. People v. Robinson, 103 A.D.2d 852, 478 N.Y.S.2d 662 (2d Dept. 1984).

—In prosecution for rape and sodomy, the trial court erred in refusing to instruct the jury that it could consider the complainant's delay in reporting these crimes since prompt outcry, or lack thereof, on the part of the complainant may be relevant in determining the complainant's credibility. People v. Derrick, 96 A.D.2d 600, 465 N.Y.S.2d 292 (2d Dept. 1983).

Credibility; interested witnesses.—Defendant was an interested witness as a matter of law. People v. Agosto, 73 N.Y.2d 963, 540 N.Y.S.2d 988, 538 N.E.2d 740 (1989).

—Court's charge that as a matter of law a disinterested witness tells the truth was erroneous and warranted reversal. People v. Rawlins, 166 A.D.2d 64, 569 N.Y.S.2d 635 (1st Dept. 1991).

—Reversible error was committed when judge charged jury that testimony of an interested witness should be scrutinized more carefully than a disinterested witness. People v. Gadsden, 80A.D.2d 508, 435 N.Y.S.2d 601 (1st Dept. 1981).

—Defendant was deprived of his right to a public trial when the trial court closed the courtroom prior to charging the jury until after the announcement of the verdict, but without either party requesting it and over defendant's objection; court's interested witness charge was error, because it departed from the CJI and engrafted a concept that the defendant is "the most" interested witness. People v. Singh, 287 A.D.2d 748, 732 N.Y.S.2d 415 (2d Dept. 2001).

—Trial court properly denied the defendant's request to charge that complainants were interested witnesses as a matter of law; evidence of the complainants' civil lawsuits was before the jury, and the jury was charged to consider the interest or lack of interest of any witness in the outcome of the case, which might cause the witness who may benefit or lose, based on the outcome of the case, to intentionally or otherwise color his or her testimony. People v. Pereda, 200 A.D.2d 774, 607 N.Y.S.2d 98 (2d Dept.), lv. denied, 83 N.Y.2d 914 (1994).

—Reversal is required where trial court instructed the jury that the defendant had a "deep personal interest in his prosecution" of a character possessed by no other witness. People v. Isidron, 209 A.D.2d 718, 619 N.Y.S.2d 329 (2d Dept. 1994).

—Although the trial court should have charged the jury that it should consider any specific benefits conferred upon a witness for testifying, the failure to do so did not warrant reversal under the facts of the case. People v. Jamison, 188 A.D.2d 551, 591 N.Y.S.2d 450 (2d Dept. 1992).

—The trial court properly charged the jury that the defendant was an interested witness as a matter of law. People v. Herbert, 182 A.D.2d 639, 582 N.Y.S.2d 247 (2d Dept. 1992).

—Trial court erred in refusing to issue an interested witness charge to prosecution witness who was implicated in the murder by the defendant's testimony. People v. Dahan, 158 A.D.2d 708, 552 N.Y.S.2d 158 (2d Dept.), lv. denied, 76 N.Y.2d 733 (1990).

—The court properly charged that the defendant was an interested witness as a matter of law; however, there is no requirement that a trial court instruct that the People's witnesses are interested as a matter of law. People v. Wilson, 154 A.D.2d 566, 546 N.Y.S.2d 170 (2d Dept. 1989).

—Court's charge to the jury concerning interested witnesses was not improper as it only instructed that the jury could, if it so wished, find defendant's alibi witnesses to be interested witnesses. People v. Whitmore, 123 A.D.2d 336, 506 N.Y.S.2d 231 (2d Dept. 1986).

—In the absence of evidence that the victim had a direct penal or personal interest in the outcome of the case, the trial court did not have to issue an interested witness charge as to the victim. People v. Diaz, 150 A.D.2d 885, 540 N.Y.S.2d 907 (3d Dept. 1989).

—Court did not err in denying defendant's request to charge the jury that two witnesses were interested as a matter of law where those witnesses denied that promises of leniency had been made to them; furthermore, court properly instructed the jury that it could consider the interest of any witness in assessing credibility. People v. Gordon, 277 A.D.2d 1053, 716 N.Y.S.2d 839 (4th Dept. 2000).

Credibility, police officers.—Reversal required where, instead of giving the standard police witness charge, the trial court charged the jury that "you are to consider the fact that a person is a police officer in weighing that person's testimony." People v. Pegeise, 195 A.D.2d 337, 600 N.Y.S.2d 26 (1st Dept. 1993).

—While a police witness charge should usually be given, the failure to issue such a charge did not require reversal because the only witnesses were police witnesses and because the defendant did not testify, and thus his testimony was not singled out for special scrutiny. People v. Miller, 159 A.D.2d 224, 552 N.Y.S.2d 28 (1st Dept. 1990).

—Trial court improperly and inexplicable refused to give a police-witness charge; reversible error where the case turned critically on the credibility of the police and the proof of guilt was not overwhelming. People v. Lopez, 190 A.D.2d 866, 593 N.Y.S.2d 871 (2d Dept. 1993).

—The court's failure to charge that in evaluating the credibility of police officers, the jurors should accord their testimony no greater weight than that of any other witness, in part, warranted reversal. People v. McCain, 177 A.D.2d 513, 576 N.Y.S.2d 146 (2d Dept. 1991).

—As a matter of law police officers are not interested witnesses. People v. Melvin, 128 A.D.2d 647, 512 N.Y.S.2d 891 (2d Dept. 1987).

—The court did not err in refusing to charge that the police officers were interested witnesses as a matter of law; however, since the court charged that the defendant was an interested witness, it should have noted the potential interest of one of the police officers in the outcome of the case. People v. Gomez, 137 A.D.2d 556, 524 N.Y.S.2d 460 (2d Dept. 1988).

—Court properly refused to charge that police officers, who testified, were interested witnesses though one had previously been involved in an altercation with defendant and his brother; police officers are not, as a matter of law, interested witnesses. People v. Holmes, 117 A.D.2d 480, 504 N.Y.S.2d 245 (3d Dept. 1986).

Evidence.—Court's charge was proper in that it stated that the indictment is "nothing more than an accusation and has no evidentiary or probative value whatsoever, nor does it prove anything." People v. Lynch, 145 A.D.2d 440, 535 N.Y.S.2d 413 (2d Dept. 1988).

—Court's instructions concerning statement of co-defendant, given in a hospital just prior to his death, which closely followed the pattern jury instructions on declarations against penal interest were in accord with established principles of law. People v. Jacobsen, 135 A.D.2d 1118, 523 N.Y.S.2d 283 (4th Dept. 1987).

Jury charge on identification.—Although the better practice is to issue an expanded charge on identification, such a charge is not always required. People v. Perez, 77 N.Y.2d 928, 569 N.Y.S.2d 600, 572 N.E.2d 41 (1991).

—While failure to give a defendant's requested instruction regarding the unreliability of visual identification evidence is not required, it is better practice to give an expanded jury instruction especially where the mistaken identity defense is intertwined with an alibi defense. People v. Whalen, 59 N.Y.2d 273, 464 N.Y.S.2d 454, 451 N.E.2d 212 (1983).

—A charge stating that the defendant's identity "must be shown with sufficient certainty to preclude a reasonable probability of mistake" incorrectly implies that identification is governed by a lesser burden of proof than proof beyond a reasonable doubt. People v. Wright, 215 A.D.2d 299, 627 N.Y.S.2d 13 (1st Dept. 1995).

—Court's charge concerning identification was proper where is instructed the jury on evaluating the credibility of witnesses and that the People had to prove identification beyond a reasonable doubt. People v. Felix, 207 A.D.2d 729, 616 N.Y.S.2d 614 (1st Dept. 1994).

—The defendant is not entitled to an instruction on the lesser reliability of "cross-racial" identifications. People v. Jenkins, 167 A.D.2d 273, 561 N.Y.S.2d 774 (1st Dept. 1990).

—Court's erroneous substitution of the word "perpetrator" for the word "defendant" did not deprive the defendant of a fair trial. People v. West, 159 A.D.2d 378, 553 N.Y.S.2d 7 (1st Dept. 1990).

—Trial court did not abuse its discretion in refusing request for an expanded identification charge in a case with a close question of identity; failure to so charge is not reversible error per se. People v. Love, 244 A.D.2d 431, 664 N.Y.S.2d 91 (2d Dept. 1997).

—An identification charge is not warranted where, as here, the defendant's guilt turns largely on the credibility of the People's witnesses who knew the defendant prior to the commission of the crime, and not upon the nature and quality of their observations of the defendant during the commission of the crime, because there is not substantial issue of identification before the jury. People v. Quinones, 235 A.D.2d 437, 653 N.Y.S.2d 122 (2d Dept. 1997).

—The trial court need not given a fact specific charge as to identification but may give a general instruction on weighing credibility and state that the identification must be proven beyond a reasonable doubt by the People. People v. Smith, 201 A.D.2d 685, 607 N.Y.S.2d 978 (2d Dept. 1994).

—Where the only evidence against the defendant is an identification, an expanded charge on identification is desirable, but not required as a matter of law. People v. Boykin, 197 A.D.2d 585, 602 N.Y.S.2d 647 (2d Dept.), lv. denied, 82 N.Y.2d 891 (1993).

—Although desirable, a detailed charge on the issue of identification is not required as a matter of law. People v. James, 170 A.D.2d 694, 567 N.Y.S.2d 108 (2d Dept. 1991).

—Court did not err in failing to give an expanded charge on the issue of identification where it properly indicated to the jurors that the accuracy of the witness's identification of the defendant, as well as the question of his credibility, were to be considered by them in determining whether the defendant was in fact one of the robbers' because the identification testimony was neither conflicting nor confusing and the identification charge, as given, adequately informed the jury on the

issue. People v. Nalty, 160 A.D.2d 958, 554 N.Y.S.2d 935 (2d Dept. 1990).

—Since the question of the defendant's guilt turned largely on the credibility of the People's witnesses who knew the defendant, and not upon the nature and quality of their observations of the defendant during the commission of the crime, a Daniels-type charge was unwarranted. People v. Wade, 146 A.D.2d 589, 536 N.Y.S.2d 180 (2d Dept. 1989).

—Court did not err in refusing to issue a Daniels charge on identification where the issue of the defendant's guilt turned on the credibility of the witnesses and not upon the accuracy of their observations of the defendant during the commission of the crime. People v. Floyd, 150 A.D.2d 486, 541 N.Y.S.2d 225 (2d Dept. 1989).

—Court's use of the defendant's name instead of the term "the perpetrator" in its identification charge did not deprive the defendant of a fair trial. People v. Bennett, 144 A.D.2d 564, 534 N.Y.S.2d 422 (2d Dept. 1988).

—Court erred in its identification charge by substituting the word "defendant" for the word "perpetrator" on five occasions. People v. Willis, 140 A.D.2d 639, 527 N.Y.S.2d 870 (2d Dept. 1988).

—Court's refusal to issue a detailed identification charge was not error since court's charge properly conveyed to the jury the People's burden to prove identification beyond a reasonable doubt. People v. Robertson, 128 A.D.2d 815, 513 N.Y.S.2d 519 (2d Dept. 1987).

—Even if court's identification charge was insufficient, a new trial would not be warranted because the evidence offered at trial did not present a close identification question nor did the defendant raise an alibi defense. People v. Rodriguez, 130 A.D.2d 522, 515 N.Y.S.2d 101 (2d Dept. 1987).

—Where proof of guilt was not strong and defendant proffered a substantiated alibi the court's refusal to give the defendant's requested charge that the jury should consider the accuracy of a witness' prior description of the assailant in evaluating credibility constituted reversible error. People v. Knowell, 127 A.D.2d 794, 512 N.Y.S.2d 190 (2d Dept. 1987).

—Where the defendant's guilt hinged largely upon the credibility of the People's witnesses, and not upon the nature and quality of their observations of the defendant during the commission of the crime, the defendant was not entitled to a comprehensive identification instruction. People v. Blake, 124 A.D.2d 661, 507 N.Y.S.2d 912 (2d Dept. 1986).

—Refusal to issue identification charge amounted to harmless error where narcotics officers lost sight of defendant only momentarily after having observed him for approximately 3½ hours. People v. Johnson, 124 A.D.2d 677, 508 N.Y.S.2d 51 (2d Dept. 1986).

—Court's failure to give an appropriate charge which would have directed the jury to consider and balance such factors as the officers' opportunity for observation, the weather and lighting conditions and the duration and the distance of the viewing warranted reversal since identification was the primary issue. People v. Clark, 120 A.D.2d 542, 501 N.Y.S.2d 734 (2d Dept. 1986).

—Where identity of assailant was in controversy, the court committed reversible error by denying defense counsel's timely request for a detailed jury instruction on the issue of identification; court should have furnished an instruction directing the jury to focus on both the accuracy and veracity of identification testimony, and should have provided specific guidelines for the evaluation of such testimony. People v. Hambrick, 122 A.D.2d 163, 504 N.Y.S.2d 540 (2d Dept. 1986).

—Reversal of robbery conviction was required where trial court denied defense request for a specific identification charge in a case where the sole identification of the defendant was by one witness, the victim being unable to make a positive identification, and the defendant offered some evidence of an alibi. People v. Clarke, 108 A.D.2d 819, 485 N.Y.S.2d 295 (2d Dept. 1985).

—Failure to give identification charge did not require reversal of a rape conviction where complainant had an "extraordinary" opportunity to observe the defendant over a two-hour period, gave a detailed description to the police and identified the defendant in a line-up 18 days after the crime. People v. Scott, 108 A.D.2d 882, 485 N.Y.S.2d 379 (2d Dept. 1985).

—Court did not err in refusing to issue an identification charge where the primary issue in the case was one of credibility rather than identification. People v. Daniels, 161 A.D.2d 958, 557 N.Y.S.2d 531 (3d Dept. 1990).

—Although court refused to charge the jury that identification must be proven beyond a reasonable doubt, and although court's general charge on reasonable doubt was lacking, the error was harmless where in addition to the identification evidence the prosecution's case rested upon the defendant's confession and forensic evidence. People v. Ferkins, 112 A.D.2d 760, 497 N.Y.S.2d 159 (3d Dept. 1986).

—Since defendant's identification was not in issue—the crucial issue was one of the credibility of the eyewitnesses—there was no need for the court, even if it had been requested to do so, to give the jury special instruction for evaluating identification testimony. People v. Chrysler, 122 A.D.2d 460, 504 N.Y.S.2d 849 (3d Dept. 1986).

Missing witnesses, general.—A party requesting a missing witness charge with respect to a witness under the control of (and presumably favorable to) the opposite party "can hardly know what that witness knows or what the witness would say if called." Therefore, all the requesting party is required to show is that "from the witness' relationship to the issues or events in dispute that the witness was in a position to have knowledge of these issues or to have observed the events." People v. Kitching, 78 N.Y.2d 532, 577 N.Y.S.2d 231, 583 N.E.2d 944 (1991).

—Court's failure to issue missing witness charge where one was warranted required reversal. People v. Erts, 73 N.Y.2d 872, 537 N.Y.S.2d 796, 534 N.E.2d 833 (1988).

—While defendant failed to request a missing witness charge as to a police officer, trial court erred in charging, at the request of the prosecution, that the jury was forbidden to draw an negative inference from the prosecution's failure to call that officer. People v. Williams, 62 N.Y.2d 765, 477 N.Y.S.2d 315, 465 N.E.2d 1251 (1984).

—Where defendant testified at trial that he was at home with his wife at the time of the crime, trial court properly gave a missing witness charge when the wife was not called to testify in support of the alibi. People v. Wilson, 64 N.Y.2d 634, 485 N.Y.S.2d 40, 474 N.E.2d 248 (1984).

—Marital privilege was not violated where the court gave a missing witness charge with regard to the failure of defendant's wife to testify in support of his alibi; defendant's presence or absence from his apartment is not a communication which would not have been made but for the marital relationship. People v. Wilson, 64 N.Y.2d 634, 485 N.Y.S.2d 40, 474 N.E.2d 248 (1984).

—Court properly refused to deliver a missing witness charge against the People with regard to the complainant, who did not testify, because the People provided the court with information indicating that the complainant had resumed her relationship with defendant and that she would not cooperate with the prosecution. People v. Royster, 18 A.D.3d 375, 795 N.Y.S.2d 560 (1st Dept. 2005).

—The People were entitled to a missing witness charge even where defense counsel claimed that the witness would not testify and that defense counsel believed that the witness would assert his Fifth Amendment right against self-incrimination. People v. Macana, 193 A.D.2d 702, 598 N.Y.S.2d 46, 47 (2d Dept. 1993), aff'd, 84 N.Y.2d 173, 615 N.Y.S.2d 656, 639 N.E.2d 13 (1994).

—The party requesting a missing witness charge has the initial burden of demonstrating that the uncalled witness could be expected to have knowledge of a material issue and to testify favorably to the People. People v. Heredia, 196 A.D.2d 885, 602 N.Y.S.2d 164 (2d Dept. 1993).

—The People are not obligated to produce every witness to a crime so long as evidence potentially favorable to the defendant has not been suppressed. People v. Chisom, 170 A.D.2d 523, 566 N.Y.S.2d 86 (2d Dept. 1991).

—It is not incumbent upon the prosecution to call at trial every witness to a crime or to make a complete and detailed accounting to the defense of all law enforcement investigatory work. People v. Ramos, 159 A.D.2d 596, 552 N.Y.S.2d 454 (2d Dept. 1990).

—The court did not err in refusing to give a missing witness charge in view of defense counsel's refusal to consent to the reopening of the prosecution case to enable the prosecutor to present evidence to the jury as to why a certain witness had

not been called to testify. People v. Bartolomeo, 126 A.D.2d 375, 513 N.Y.S.2d 981 (2d Dept. 1987).

—Court properly refused to give missing witness charge as to a second arresting officer where defense counsel knew before-hand that due to illness the officer would not be called as a prosecution witness; it was suggested that if defendant wished to have the officer testify, he should serve a subpoena which he failed to do; and the officer's suppression hearing testimony demonstrated that his trial testimony could only have been cumulative. People v. Smith, 119 A.D.2d 776, 501 N.Y.S.2d 183 (2d Dept. 1986).

—In view of defendant's confession, court did not err in refusing to give missing witness charge as to sexual abuse victim's parents. People v. Jacobs, 148 A.D.2d 811, 538 N.Y.S.2d 647 (3d Dept. 1989).

—Defendants were not entitled to a missing witness charge because they failed to make the initial showing that the uncalled witness would naturally be expected to provide noncumulative testimony favorable to the prosecution. People v. Williams, 202 A.D.2d 1004, 612 N.Y.S.2d 700, 701 (4th Dept. 1994).

—Where a defendant comes forward with evidence, his failure to produce available evidence within his control creates an adverse inference which may be the subject of a charge to the jury. People v. Maddox, 159 A.D.2d 954, 552 N.Y.S.2d 786 (4th Dept. 1990).

—It is not incumbent upon the prosecution to call at trial every witness to a crime or to make a complete and detailed account-ing to the defense of all law enforcement investigatory work. People v. Fields, 152 A.D.2d 958, 543 N.Y.S.2d 1012 (4th Dept. 1989).

Missing witnesses, materiality and noncumulativeness.—Trial court properly denied request for missing witness charge where the designated arresting officer, who recorded undercover officer's radio description of defendant and was a few blocks away from location of drug sale, was not in position to have knowledge of material issues or to have observed anything that would make his testimony relevant to any material issue in the case. People v. Lyons, 81 N.Y.2d 753, 593 N.Y.S.2d 776, 609 N.E.2d 129 (1992).

—A missing witness charge should be given only where a witness is knowledgeable about a material issue in the case; a request to charge is properly denied where the prosecutor states that the witness in question will be produced if the defense wishes to call him. People v. Knowels, 187 A.D.2d 361, 590 N.Y.S.2d 95 (1st Dept. 1992), lv. denied, 81 N.Y.2d 842 (1993).

—Where the defendant failed to show that the probable testi-mony of the anonymous telephone caller was anything but cumulative, there was no merit in defendant's argument that a missing witness charge was necessary. People v. DeWitt, 155 A.D.2d 279, 547 N.Y.S.2d 43 (1st Dept. 1989).

—Trial court did not err in denying the request for a missing witness charge to the undercover officer's "ghost" since the sale took place inside a building and there was no evidence that the uncalled officer ever viewed the defendant or observed any part of the drug transaction. People v. Profit, 200 A.D.2d 639, 606 N.Y.S.2d 745 (2d Dept.), lv. denied, 83 N.Y.2d 875 (1994).

—Defendant's request for a missing witness charge was prop-erly denied where the People met their burden of establishing that the witness's testimony would have been cumulative. People v. Jones, 200 A.D.2d 763, 607 N.Y.S.2d 118 (2d Dept. 1994).

—No missing witness charge was required where the uncalled police officer's attention was focused on matters other than the commission of the crime at the time of its commission. People v. Knight, 187 A.D.2d 731, 590 N.Y.S.2d 529 (2d Dept. 1992), lv. denied, 81 N.Y.2d 888 (1993).

—Court properly refused to issue a missing witness charge where there was no indication that the officers in question would have provided material and noncumulative testimony. People v. Rushings, 159 A.D.2d 527, 552 N.Y.S.2d 653 (2d Dept. 1990).

—It was error to give a missing witness charge as to certain of the defendant's family members who resided in Puerto Rico where the testimony of the additional family members would have been cumulative. People v. Hernandez, 159 A.D.2d 722, 553 N.Y.S.2d 205 (2d Dept. 1990).

—Court properly refused to issue missing witness charge as to a second undercover officer where that officer merely drove the undercover officer who participated in the transaction to the site of the sale and there was no evidence that he actually witnessed the sale. People v. Torres, 146 A.D.2d 658, 536 N.Y.S.2d 857 (2d Dept. 1989).

—Court properly refused defense request for missing witness charge as to two other police officers who assisted in the defendant's apprehension, since the defendant failed to demonstrate that the two officers were knowledgeable about a pending material issue. People v. King, 128 A.D.2d 805, 513 N.Y.S.2d 507 (2d Dept. 1987).

—The court erroneously granted People's request for a missing witness charge with respect to the defendant's girlfriend, a nonmaterial witness who, at most, would have contradicted defendant's account of his activities before and after the crime, but not during its commission. People v. Williams, 112 A.D.2d 117, 490 N.Y.S.2d 856 (2d Dept. 1985).

—Court improperly denied defendant's request for a missing witness charge, and error was not harmless, where People did not demonstrate that troopers who were present during illegal drug sale were without material, relevant knowledge, and that their testimony would have been cumulative to that provided by the officer who did testify, or that they were unavailable. People v. Sergeant, 244 A.D.2d 702, 664 N.Y.S.2d 649 (3d Dept. 1997).

—The Court properly refused to issue a missing witness charge where the testimony of the police witness and the father of the victim would have been either cumulative or immaterial to the crime charged. People v. Hallaway, 132 A.D.2d 940, 518 N.Y.S.2d 487 (4th Dept. 1987).

Missing witnesses, control and availability.—In determining whether to issue a missing witness charge, control is a "relative concept" and the inquiry is directed to the relationship between the witness and the parties rather than physical availability. People v. Vasquez, 76 N.Y.2d 722, 557 N.Y.S.2d 873, 557 N.E.2d 109 (1990).

—When a party has it peculiarly within his power to produce witnesses whose testimony would elucidate the transaction, the fact that he does not do it creates the presumption that the testimony, if produced, would be unfavorable. People v. Dianda, 70 N.Y.2d 894, 524 N.Y.S.2d 381, 519 N.E.2d 289 (1987).

—Court properly granted People's request for a missing witness charge with respect to the friend whom defendant had alleged would corroborate his innocent bystander defense, who was present in court and spoke with defense counsel. The closeness of the friendship reflected in the record was sufficient under the circumstances to establish control. People v. Trent, 273 A.D.2d 50, 709 N.Y.S.2d 538 (1st Dept. 2000).

—The uncalled witnesses' casual friendship with the complaining witness did not place them within the People's control for purposes of a missing witness charge, nor were they in fact available for the People; accordingly, the request for a missing witness charge was properly denied. People v. Brunson, 270 A.D.2d 133, 707 N.Y.S.2d 1 (1st Dept. 2000).

—Court properly issued a missing witness charge as to the defendant's wife, even though he was separated from her and despite the fact that she was subpoenaed. People v. Ramirez, 208 A.D.2d 384, 617 N.Y.S.2d 17 (1st Dept. 1994).

—Defendant was not entitled to a missing witness charge as to a witness whose relationship to the complainant was not more than that of a friend. People v. Justice, 202 A.D.2d 362, 610 N.Y.S.2d 4 (1st Dept. 1994).

—For purposes of issuing a missing witness charge against a defendant, while a familial relationship may, under certain circumstances, be sufficient to establish the necessary element of control, there must be evidence that such a relationship exists. People v. Magett, 196 A.D.2d 62, 608 N.Y.S.2d 434 (1st Dept. 1994).

—The trial court properly declined to give a missing witness charge where the People demonstrated that the three witnesses were unavailable. People v. Thomas, 200 A.D.2d 419, 606 N.Y.S.2d 217 (1st Dept. 1994).

—Where the witness was equally available to the defendant, a missing witness charge is properly denied. People v. Costa, 183 A.D.2d 723, 583 N.Y.S.2d 301 (2d Dept. 1992).

—The defendant was not entitled to a missing witness charge in light of the unavailability of the uncalled witness. People v. Rafiqzada, 143 A.D.2d 688, 533 N.Y.S.2d 107 (2d Dept. 1988).

—Reversible error was committed when the court gave a

missing witness charge as the relationship between the defendant and the witness, the emancipated son of defendant's estranged wife, was not sufficient in itself to give rise to a presumption that one is under the other's control for the purpose of the missing witness rule. People v. Jasan, 92 A.D.2d 902, 459 N.Y.S.2d 897 (2d Dept. 1983).

—Defendant satisfied his initial burden of demonstrating that the uncalled witness, the robbery victim, was under the People's control and could be expected to give testimony favorable to the People on a material issue. Court erred in concluding that the request for the missing witness charge was untimely because the victim was on the People's witness list and the defendant timely made the request after the People rested without calling her, but the error was harmless in light of the overwhelming evidence of guilt. People v. Williams, 286 A.D.2d 918, 730 N.Y.S.2d 631 (4th Dept. 2001).

—Defendant was not entitled to a missing witness charge with respect to the accomplice where it was established that the accomplice was unavailable and diligent efforts to locate him were unsuccessful. People v. Sturgis, 154 A.D.2d 906, 546 N.Y.S.2d 58 (4th Dept. 1989).

Missing witness charge, timeliness of request.—Defendant's request for a missing witness charge, made after the parties had rested and after an unsuccessful motion to dismiss the indictment, was properly denied as untimely since it was not make as soon as practicable. People v. Alamo, 202 A.D.2d 349, 609 N.Y.S.2d 227 (1st Dept. 1994).

—The trial court did not err in denying the defendant's request, made only after both sides had rested, for a missing witness charge with respect to two men who were part of the crowd chasing defendant before his arrest. People v. Kaplan, 199 A.D.2d 82, 606 N.Y.S.2d 151 (1st Dept. 1993).

—Where defendant did not raise a claim at trial that he was deprived of a missing witness instruction, the matter may not be raised for the first time on appeal. People v. Ford, 176 A.D.2d 612, 575 N.Y.S.2d 52 (1st Dept. 1991).

—Where the defendant waited until both sides had rested at the close of the evidence to request a missing witness charge, the request was untimely and thus properly denied. People v. Simmons, 206 A.D.2d 396, 614 N.Y.S.2d 427 (2d Dept.), lv. denied, 84 N.Y.2d 939 (1994); see also People v. Sims, 201 A.D.2d 516, 607 N.Y.S.2d 693 (2d Dept. 1994); People v. Asphill, 208 A.D.2d 550, 617 N.Y.S.2d 31 (2d Dept. 1994); People v. Catoe, 181 A.D.2d 905, 582 N.Y.S.2d 29 (2d Dept. 1992); People v. Bradley, 160 A.D.2d 808, 554 N.Y.S.2d 72 (2d Dept. 1990).

—Defendant's request for a missing witness charge was untimely when it was not made until after both the trial and the charge had been completed. People v. Boyajian, 148 A.D.2d 740, 539 N.Y.S.2d 683 (2d Dept. 1989).

—Court properly denied defendant's request for a missing witness charge; although it was evident from the prosecutor's voir dire and opening statement that the victim would not testify, defendant would not request a missing witness charge until both sides had rested and therefore the request was untimely. People v. Castro-Garcia, 203 A.D.2d 899, 612 N.Y.S.2d 711 (4th Dept. 1994).

—Trial court did not err in denying defendant's request, made after summations of counsel, to consider a missing witness charge in the non-jury trial. People v. Martinez, 151 A.D.2d 965, 542 N.Y.S.2d 64 (4th Dept. 1989).

People's failure to preserve evidence.—Although the People were obligated to preserve the gun as evidence, the failure to do so does not mandate reversal where, as here, the court instructed the jury that it could infer that neither of defendant's fingerprints would have been found on the gun had it been tested for fingerprints; this charge adequately ameliorated any prejudice to defendants. People v. Dinsio, 286 A.D.2d 517, 729 N.Y.S.2d 208 (3d Dept. 2001), cert. denied, 536 U.S. 942 (2002).

Presumptions, general.—Trial court's omission of instruction that "indictment is not evidence of anything" did not warrant reversal, where, in the whole context, the court gave ample emphasis in the final charge that the jury's verdict must be based on an assessment only of the evidence and the defendant was always protected by the presumption of innocence. People v. Greaves, 94 N.Y.2d 775, 698 N.Y.S.2d 587, 720 N.E.2d 863 (1999).

—Jury's general verdict was deemed invalid since it could not have been known if the result was predicated on the erroneous "drug factory" presumption or on the lawful alternative theory of constructive possession without the aid of the presumption; harmless error analysis not applicable since there was some evidence supportive of the erroneous theory presented to the jury. People v. Martinez, 83 N.Y.2d 26, 607 N.Y.S.2d 610, 628 N.E.2d 1320 (1994).

—*Galbo* charge was proper in burglary prosecution, since jury was advised that the presumption could be used to find defendant guilty either of burglary or as possessor of stolen property. People v. Perry, 188 A.D.2d 392, 591 N.Y.S.2d 382 (1st Dept. 1992), *lv. denied*, 81 N.Y.2d 845 (1993).

—Court's charge "it is a fundamental rule of evidence that a person is presumed to intend the natural consequences of his acts" was not preserved for review where no objection was registered by defense counsel. People v. Colony, 54 N.Y.2d 913, 445 N.Y.S.2d 133, 429 N.E.2d 811 (1981).

—Although courts are better advised to avoid using a charge that a person is presumed to intend the natural consequences of his acts, there was no reversible error, as the court's further explanation made it clear that the jury had a choice and was to decide from all the circumstances whether the People had proved defendant's actual intent. People v. Green, 50 N.Y.2d 891, 43 N.Y.S.2d 267, 408 N.E.2d 675 (1980).

—Holding of Supreme Court in Sandstrom v. Montana, that where intent is an element of the crime charged, a charge that the law presumed that a person intends the ordinary consequences of his voluntary act, is violative of the Constitution is given retroactive effect. People v. Getch, 50 N.Y.2d 456, 429 N.Y.S.2d 579, 407 N.E.2d 425 (1980).

—Defendant's claim that he was denied a fair trial because the court failed to properly charge the presumption of innocence was not preserved for appellate review in the absence of an appropriate exception. People v. Torres, 173 A.D.2d 283, 569 N.Y.S.2d 676 (1st Dept. 1991).

—Trial court's inadvertent failure to instruct the jury with regard to the presumption of innocence mandated reversal of conviction even though omission was not called to the court's attention and court had referred to the principal repeatedly during voir dire in his introductory remarks. People v. Gayle, 76 A.D.2d 587, 431 N.Y.S.2d 18 (1st Dept. 1980).

—Court improperly charged the statutory gun presumption under PL § 265.15(3) since the evidence showed that the gun was at all times when it was seen in the exclusive possession of the co-defendant. People v. Williams, 146 A.D.2d 659, 537 N.Y.S.2d 39 (2d Dept. 1989).

—Defendant's false explanation that stolen items in car trunk were his together with his joint possession of the items in the trunk with those with whom he acted in concert, justified a charge on effect to be given recent and exclusive possession of the fruits of a crime. People v. Hawthorne, 145 A.D.2d 569, 536 N.Y.S.2d 122 (2d Dept. 1988).

—Trial court erred by repeatedly using the words "presumption of guilt" with regard to defendant's recent exclusive possession of stolen property. People v. Mitchell, 108 A.D.2d 759, 484 N.Y.S.2d 916 (2d Dept. 1985).

—Where defense case at trial, in which possession of controlled substance was charged, was that defendant had no knowledge of the existence of a controlled substance, and the proof of knowledge was a close question for the jury, trial court's failure to specifically inform the jury that knowledge from possession of the contraband was only a permissive inference was highly prejudicial and therefore error. People v. Ofunniyin, 114 A.D.2d 1045, 495 N.Y.S.2d 485 (2d Dept. 1985).

—Court's supplemental charges requiring defendant to rebut presumption of knowing possession of a weapon found in an automobile beyond a reasonable doubt improperly shifted the burden of proof to the defendant and reversal of conviction was required. People v. Velasquez, 114 A.D.2d 527, 494 N.Y.S.2d 427 (2d Dept. 1985).

—In prosecution for burglary in the third degree and criminal possession of stolen property in the third degree, it was error for the trial court during its charge on the "recent and exclusive possession" of the proceeds of a burglary not to charge that there were two permissible inferences of guilt which could be drawn from the facts of the case: (1) that defendant was involved in the burglary; or (2) that the defendant was merely the knowing possessor of the stolen ring; and since the court only charged the former, the error was highly prejudicial and warranted a

reversal in the interests of justice. People v. Seaman, 96 A.D.2d 603, 465 N.Y.S.2d 298 (2d Dept. 1983).

—Reversible error was committed when the court refused to charge that the presumption that a person who knowingly possesses stolen property is presumed to possess it with intent to benefit himself or a person other than the owner or to impede the recovery by the owner, was rebuttable where rebuttal evidence was presented. People v. Ornstein, 91 A.D.2d 788, 458 N.Y.S.2d 87 (3d Dept. 1982).

—Although the court erred in charging the jury as to the presumption of possession of weapon found in vehicle to all occupants, it was harmless error where the evidence of guilt was overwhelming. People v. Mace, 91 A.D.2d 864, 458 N.Y.S.2d 379 (4th Dept. 1982).

—Defendant's conviction of second degree murder (PL § 125.25) was reversed and a new trial ordered where the court, on the issue of intentional killing charged that "a person is presumed to intend the natural and probable consequences of his act and if the consequences are natural and probable, you will not be heard to say that he did not intend them"; such charge denied defendant his constitutional due process right to be free from conviction unless the People proved beyond a reasonable doubt every fact necessary to constitute the crime charged. People v. Egan, 72 A.D.2d 239, 424 N.Y.S.2d 546 (4th Dept. 1980).

—The court's charge, in homicide trial, that a man intends the ordinary and natural consequences of his act, that intent may be inferred from acts and the surrounding circumstances and that the jury must find that defendant formed in his mind a specific intent to kill before the act was committed did not create a presumption, but allowed an inference and did not shift the burden of proof to the defendant. People v. Barr, 75 A.D.2d 14, 428 N.Y.S.2d 116 (4th Dept. 1980).

Voluntariness of a confession.—The court, in submitting the voluntariness of the confession to the jury, did not err in refusing to charge that the police had an obligation to let family members or friends communicate with a competent adult in custody, especially where there was no evidence that these persons had retained counsel for the defendant, nor was there evidence that defendant sought the assistance of these individuals or that the police discouraged him from doing so. People v. Crimmins, 64 N.Y.2d 1072, 489 N.Y.S.2d 879, 479 N.E.2d 224 (1985).

—Reversible error was committed where the court refused to charge, on the issue of voluntariness of statements made, that the testimony of two witnesses who stated that defendant had asked for counsel could be considered by the jury in determining the voluntariness of defendant's subsequent confession. People v. Griswold, 58 N.Y.2d 633, 458 N.Y.S.2d 513, 444 N.E.2d 977 (1982).

—When a defendant raises a factual issue regarding the voluntariness of a confession, he is entitled to a voluntariness charge, despite an adverse ruling at a pretrial hearing regarding the admissibility of a defendant's statement. People v. Rose, 223 A.D.2d 607, 637 N.Y.S.2d 172 (2d Dept. 1996).

—Although it is error for the court to neglect to charge that the People have to prove that a defendant's statements were voluntary beyond a reasonable doubt, the error is harmless if the court has made it clear that the People were obliged to prove every material element of their case beyond a reasonable doubt. People v. Nelson, 171 A.D.2d 702, 566 N.Y.S.2d 943 (2d Dept.), *lv. denied*, 77 N.Y.2d 964 (1991).

—Voluntariness of defendant's admissions is not a proper subject for a charge to the jury where defendant fails to explore the issue at trial. People v. Stewart, 74 A.D.2d 516, 425 N.Y.S.2d 6 (1st Dept. 1980).

—When, as here, a defendant raises a factual issue regarding the voluntariness of a confession, he or she is entitled to a voluntariness charge. People v. Sanchez, 293 A.D.2d 499, 742 N.Y.S.2d 58 (2d Dept. 2002).

—It was not error for the court, in instructing the jury on the voluntariness of the defendant's confession, to fail to instruct the jury that the statements must be found to be truthful as well. People v. Bowen, 134 A.D.2d 356, 520 N.Y.S.2d 834 (2d Dept. 1987).

—The trial court should determine whether a defendant's statement is either a confession or an admission, but where the question is left to the jury, the trial court is obliged to instruct the jurors on the proper standard to be applied as a consequence of their determination that the statement is of one or the other type. People v. Sanchez, 92 A.D.2d 595, 459 N.Y.S.2d 488 (2d Dept. 1983), aff'd, 61 N.Y.2d 1022 (1984).

—A court's refusal to instruct the jury on the issue of voluntariness of defendant's statements, as mandated by CPL § 710.70(3) and against the request of defendant, may not be regarded as harmless error and requires a reversal on the law. People v. Iglesia, 96 A.D.2d 515, 464 N.Y.S.2d 557 (2d Dept. 1983).

Defenses; affirmative.—Trial court erred in submitted the affirmative defense of extreme emotional disturbance over defense objection. People v. Bradley, 88 N.Y.2d 901, 646 N.Y.S.2d 657, 669 N.E.2d 815 (1996).

—A defendant is entitled to submission of the affirmative defense to felony murder only if he demonstrates that there is a reasonable view of the evidence which would permit a jury to find that every one of the four elements of the defense was established by a preponderance of the evidence. People v. Diaz, 177 A.D.2d 500, 576 N.Y.S.2d 144 (2d Dept. 1991).

Defenses; agency.—It is error for the court to instruct the jury that it "must" charge the agency defense because the defendant raised the issue. People v. Schinas, 204 A.D.2d 362, 611 N.Y.S.2d 564 (2d Dept.), lv. denied, 83 N.Y.2d 971 (1994).

—Agency defense may not be raised for the first time on appeal, and there was no reason for the court to sua sponte issue an agency charge, especially where defendant testified and asserted a completely different defense. People v. Wright, 288 A.D.2d 28, 732 N.Y.S.2d 225 (1st Dept. 2001).

—In the absence of a reasonable view of the evidence indicating that the defendant acted merely as the agent of the buyer, the agency defense should not be submitted to the jury. People v. Davis, 189 A.D.2d 774, 592 N.Y.S.2d 404 (2d Dept.), lv. denied, 81 N.Y.2d 884 (1993).

—The agency defense was established where defendant exhibited no independent desire to promote the transaction; it was the undercover officer who suggested the purchase; the defendant's previous acquaintance, if any, with the actual seller was not established; the defendant exhibited no salesmanlike behavior; the defendant used the undercover officer's funds; and there was no evidence of a promised reward or any profit. People v. Matos, 123 A.D.2d 330, 506 N.Y.S.2d 225 (2d Dept. 1986).

—Where a defense of agency is asserted, it is preferable for the trial judge to provide the jury with detailed guidance concerning the application of the agency defense factors to the evidence adduced at trial, particularly the fact that receipt of some incidental financial benefit from the transaction, including a tip from the buyer, does not preclude the existence of an agency relationship. People v. Jones, 107 A.D.2d 714, 484 N.Y.S.2d 69 (2d Dept. 1985).

—Entitlement to an agency charge depends entirely on the relationship between the buyer and the defendant; unless some reasonable view of the evidence supports the theory that defendant was acting only on behalf of the buyer, the jury need not be instructed on the agency defense. People v. Hood, 288 A.D.2d 923, 732 N.Y.S.2d 522 (4th Dept. 2001).

Defenses; alibi.—A court's erroneous refusal to give an alibi charge does not require reversal if the charge as a whole conveys the necessary information regarding the prosecution's burden of proof. People v. Warren, 76 N.Y.2d 773, 559 N.Y.S.2d 954, 559 N.E.2d 648 (1990).

—Accused is not obligated to establish an ironclad alibi, i.e., that he was somewhere which made it impossible for him to commit the crime alleged, in order to be entitled to an alibi charge. People v. Jack, 74 N.Y.2d 708, 543 N.Y.S.2d 381, 541 N.E.2d 410 (1989).

—In light of court's instructions that defendant had no burden of proof with respect to his alibi and that the People must disprove the alibi beyond a reasonable doubt, the additional charge that the People need not prove that all the alibi evidence presented is false or mistaken merely clarified the weight of the People's burden and did not shift the burden of proof to the defendant. People v. Wintje, 68 N.Y.2d 637, 505 N.Y.S.2d 62, 496 N.E.2d 221 (1986).

—The trial court's denial, without explanation, of defendant's request for an alibi charge constituted reversible error where the defendant testified that, at the time the crime was committed, he was 11 blocks away from the crime scene. People v. Holt, 67 N.Y.2d 819, 501 N.Y.S.2d 641, 492 N.E.2d 769 (1986).

—Trial court is required to charge the jury that the People have the burden of disproving an alibi beyond a reasonable doubt and, without such language, any other charge may confuse the jury and erroneously lead it to believe that the defendant must prove the truth of the alibi. People v. Victor, 62 N.Y.2d 374, 477 N.Y.S.2d 97, 465 N.E.2d 817 (1984).

—A jury charge that a defendant is entitled to an acquittal when the proof as to his alibi raises a reasonable doubt was insufficient; an alibi charge must explicitly state that the People have the burden of disproving an alibi beyond a reasonable doubt. People v. Screven, 111 A.D.2d 208, 489 N.Y.S.2d 234 (1st Dept. 1985).

—The court's charge as to the alibi defense was valid where the court imposed no requirement that the jury must be satisfied as to the truth of the alibi but instead phrased it in terms of "if you, the jury, tend to believe the evidence" which is considerably less than a requirement that the jury be satisfied that the alibi is true. People v. Contes, 91 A.D.2d 562, 457 N.Y.S.2d 45 (1st Dept. 1982), aff'd, 60 N.Y.2d 620, 467 N.Y.S.2d 349, 454 N.E.2d 932 (1983).

—The court should instruct the jury that the prosecution must disprove the alibi defense beyond a reasonable doubt and that if the evidence as to alibi, in and of itself or when taken into consideration with all other evidence in the case, created a reasonable doubt as to the guilt of the defendant, the defendant was entitled to acquittal. People v. Jones, 74 A.D.2d 515, 425 N.Y.S.2d 5 (1st Dept. 1980).

—Testimony of defendant's mother that he was at her home having dinner minutes before his arrest was legally sufficient to raise the alibi defense; the mother had testified that although she was not wearing a watch or watching the clock, it was not more than 10 minutes after the defendant left her home when a neighbor came and told her that her son was being arrested outside. People v. McFarlane, 187 A.D.2d 734, 590 N.Y.S.2d 530 (2d Dept. 1992), lv. denied, 81 N.Y.2d 843 (1993).

—Court's failure to unequivocally state during its charge that the People bore the burden of disproving the defendant's alibi defense beyond a reasonable doubt did not require reversal where court's charge taken as a whole effectively conveyed the proper burden of proof with respect to the alibi defense. People v. Watford, 146 A.D.2d 590, 536 N.Y.S.2d 835 (2d Dept. 1989).

—Reversal was not required by court's failure to specifically state that the prosecution must disprove the defendant's alibi beyond a reasonable doubt where the court emphasized throughout the charge that the prosecution, not the defendant, bore the burden of proving beyond a reasonable doubt that it was the defendant who committed the crime. People v. Hydlebury, 127 A.D.2d 792, 512 N.Y.S.2d 188, 189 (2d Dept. 1987).

—Court's failure to give an alibi charge did not constitute reversible error since it is possible that due to the weakness of the defendant's alibi and the existence of the alternative defense of justification, that the failure to request an alibi charge was calculated trial strategy. People v. Ortiz, 120 A.D.2d 550, 501 N.Y.S.2d 739 (2d Dept. 1986).

—The court's charge to the jury that the alibi defense is a strong defense "if you believe it" required reversal as such instruction may have implied that the defendant had some burden of proving his alibi, especially in light of the court's failure to explicitly charge that the People have the burden of disproving an alibi despite defense counsel's request to so charge. People v. Jiminez, 111 A.D.2d 832, 490 N.Y.S.2d 256 (2d Dept. 1985).

—Trial court's instruction to jury that it must be satisfied as to the truth of the alibi and the failure to state that the People had the burden of disproving the alibi beyond a reasonable doubt impermissibly shifted the burden of proof to the defendant. People v. Torres, 111 A.D.2d 848, 490 N.Y.S.2d 783 (2d Dept. 1985).

—Trial court's charge to jury that it "carefully" examine defendant's alibi witness without a corresponding statement as to People's identification witnesses, while probably error, was cured by a proper and complete charge on the issue of identification. People v. Walkers, 104 A.D.2d 573, 479 N.Y.S.2d 363 (2d Dept. 1984).

—Any claim that trial court's alibi charge impermissibly shifted the burden of proof was waived by defense counsel's failure to object thereto. People v. Joiner, 105 A.D.2d 805, 481 N.Y.S.2d 437 (2d Dept. 1984).

—Conviction for robbery in the first degree was reversed where the trial court failed to instruct the jury that the prosecution had the burden of disproving the alibi defense beyond a reasonable doubt, notwithstanding that the jury was told that it could acquit the defendant if it found that the alibi raised a reasonable doubt. People v. Ciesluk, 106 A.D.2d 514, 483 N.Y.S.2d 49 (2d Dept. 1984).

—Refusal of trial judge to recharge jury on alibi and burden of proof in response to jury request which was clearly related to these issues was prejudicial error. People v. Mezzacap, 105 A.D.2d 808, 481 N.Y.S.2d 438 (2d Dept. 1984).

—The trial court's charge that the alibi defense should be "carefully scrutinized" was improper as it served to place the burden upon the defendant to prove the truth of his alibi. People v. Carreras, 83 A.D.2d 590, 441 N.Y.S.2d 118 (2d Dept. 1981).

—While the court's instructions to the jury as to the alibi defense were incorrect, the error did not constitute reversible error since it did not have the effect of shifting the burden of proof on the issue of alibi. People v. Peoples, 130 A.D.2d 694, 516 N.Y.S.2d 555 (4th Dept. 1987).

—It was reversible error for the court, in the absence of independent proof of fabrication to charge the jury that it could consider as some evidence of guilt a possible false alibi. People v. Wright, 86 A.D.2d 968, 448 N.Y.S.2d 293 (4th Dept. 1982).

Defenses; duress.—Defendant's testimony that he sold heroin to the undercover officer because he had been "threatened" did not form a sufficient factual predicate for a duress instruction. People v. Rodriguez, 145 A.D.2d 580, 535 N.Y.S.2d 761, 762 (2d Dept. 1988).

—Defendant's contention that trial court committed error by failing to point out to the jury that her defense of duress did not consist solely of the use or threatened use of physical force on third persons was waived since no objection was made to the omission. People v. Marshall, 124 A.D.2d 396, 507 N.Y.S.2d 495 (3d Dept. 1986).

Defenses; entrapment.—A defendant's testimony denying that he committed the proscribed conduct does not alone support or defeat a requested entrapment charge. People v. Brown, 82 N.Y.2d 869, 609 N.Y.S.2d 164, 631 N.E.2d 106 (1994).

—Inconsistency in claimed defenses or even between a defendant's testimony and a defense should not deprive defendant of the requested charge if the charge would otherwise be warranted by the evidence; defendant's denial that he made narcotics sales did not necessarily preclude issuance of entrapment charge. People v. Butts, 72 N.Y.2d 746, 536 N.Y.S.2d 731, 533 N.E.2d 660 (1988).

—Reversal was required where trial court instructed jury on the affirmative defense of entrapment over defendant's consistent protestations that he was not advancing an entrapment defense but was in fact putting forth a different defense. People v. DeGina, 72 N.Y.2d 768, 537 N.Y.S.2d 8, 533 N.E.2d 1037 (1988).

—Where defense to bribery charge was that the defendant intended only to catch and report to the authorities the public official he was accused of bribing, it was error for the court to charge as to the entrapment defense; the defense was not entrapment but, rather, lack of criminal intent and, by charging entrapment, the burden of proof was shifted to the defendant. People v. Albright, 65 N.Y.2d 666, 491 N.Y.S.2d 614, 481 N.E.2d 246 (1985).

—Although the court's entrapment charge differed from that which had been requested by defense counsel, it adequately apprised the jury of the law governing that defense; the statutory definition was fully narrated and the trial court took particular care to explain the operation of the burden of proof with regard to each count of the indictment. People v. Longwood, 116 A.D.2d 590, 497 N.Y.S.2d 450 (2d Dept. 1986).

—Trial court's charge that the jurors were to consider first whether defendants had by preponderance of the evidence proven their joint defense of entrapment, and, if jurors did not believe the defense, to then consider whether the State had proven defendant's guilty beyond a reasonable doubt, was erroneous and served to deprive defendants of fair trial. People v. Fusaro, 77 A.D.2d 627, 430 N.Y.S.2d 125 (2d Dept. 1980).

—County Court did not err in refusing to charge entrapment defense, because merely asking a defendant to commit a crime is not such inducement or encouragement as to constitute entrapment. People v. Delaney, 309 A.D.2d 968, 765 N.Y.S.2d 696 (3d Dept. 2003).

Defenses; insanity, extreme emotional disturbance.—

Proof was insufficient to support an extreme emotional disturbance defense where defendant had told the police he had not harmed his wife in any respect, never claimed that he suffered a loss of self-control or was under the influence of a mental disability. In addition, his actions prior to and immediately after the murder were inconsistent with the defense, because during this time he contrived a false explanation for the victim's wounds and he had the presence of mind to gather certain items from the apartment and remove them so that police would not discover them. Court reversed First Department, which had considered the proof that the defendant and his wife had a volatile relationship characterized by his wife's repeated yelling, berating, and making demands of defendant, including proof that on the day of the murder, she had made a number of demands which required defendant to walk up and down the stairs to their fifth-floor walk-up. People v. Roche, 98 N.Y.2d 70, 745 N.Y.S.2d 775, 772 N.E.2d 1133 (2002), reversing 286 A.D.2d 290, 729 N.Y.S.2d 722 (1st Dept. 2001).

—Extreme emotional disturbance mitigation is not limited to circumstances associated with traditional heat of passion doctrine but may be considered with respect to a broad range of situations where the trier of fact believes that such leniency should be afforded an emotionally disturbed defendant. People v. Harris, 95 N.Y.2d 316, 717 N.Y.S.2d 82, 740 N.E.2d 227 (2000).

—Extreme emotional disturbance is not a defense to a charge of depraved mind murder, and thus court properly refused to charge the jury on the affirmative defense. People v. Fardan, 82 N.Y.2d 638, 607 N.Y.S.2d 220, 628 N.E.2d 41 (1993).

—In order for the defendant to be entitled to an instruction on extreme emotional disturbance, the court must determine that sufficient credible evidence has been presented for the jury to find, by a preponderance of the evidence, that the defendant's conducted was influenced by an extreme emotional disturbance at the time of the alleged crime, and that there was a reasonable explanation or excuse for the emotional disturbance. People v. White, 79 N.Y.2d 900, 581 N.Y.S.2d 651, 590 N.E.2d 236 (1992).

—Trial court erroneously instructed jury that if they should find the defendant not guilty of murder by reason of insanity, they should acquit her of murder and then consider whether she was guilty of manslaughter; this charge created the impression that the insanity defense related only to the murder charge when such defense, if established, would relieve the defendant of responsibility for all her acts. People v. Young, 65 N.Y.2d 103, 490 N.Y.S.2d 179, 479 N.E.2d 815 (1985).

—Court committed reversible error in failing to charge the defense of extreme emotional disturbance where defendant's savage acts of mutilating and decapitating his victim, coupled with his statements to the police and prosecutor that "something snapped" inside him when she mocked and taunted him, that he went "bananas" and needed help, were evidence of a loss of self-control associated with that defense. People v. Moya, 66 N.Y.2d 887, 498 N.Y.S.2d 767, 489 N.E.2d 736 (1985).

—Defendant's conviction reversed, where trial court failed to charge that evidence of diminished capacity could be considered in determining whether defendant could form the requisite mens rea. People v. Wilcox, 194 A.D.2d 820, 599 N.Y.S.2d 131 (3d Dept. 1993).

—Where trial court responded with a simple "Yes" when the jury asked whether the defendant could be mentally ill and still be criminally responsible, and used one-sided examples in its main charge, reversal was required. People v. Justice, 173 A.D.2d 144, 579 N.Y.S.2d 502 (4th Dept. 1991).

Defenses; intoxication.—Evidence of intoxication requires more than a bare assertion by a defendant that he was intoxicated; a charge on intoxication should be given if there is sufficient evidence of intoxication in the record for a reasonable person to entertain a doubt as to the element of intent on that basis. People v. Gaines, 83 N.Y.2d 925, 615 N.Y.S.2d 309, 638 N.E.2d 964 (1994).

—A defendant is entitled to a charge on intoxication "if there is sufficient evidence of intoxication in the record for a reasonable person to entertain a doubt as to the element of intent on that basis." People v. Rodriguez, 76 N.Y.2d 918, 563 N.Y.S.2d 48, 564 N.E.2d 658 (1990).

—Where the issue on appeal is whether a particular theory of defense should have been charged to the jury, the evidence must be viewed in the light most favorable to the defendant, and here, based upon the appearance and conduct of defendant at time of arrest, the requested charge should have been given. People v. Farnsworth, 65 N.Y.2d 734, 492 N.Y.S.2d 12, 481 N.E.2d 552 (1985).

—Where defendant's testimony raised undisputed issue of his intoxication, the trial court improperly refused to charge intoxication; the intoxication charge should be given whenever there is "sufficient evidence of intoxication" . . . "for a reasonable person to entertain a doubt as to the element of intent on that basis." People v. Perry, 61 N.Y.2d 849, 473 N.Y.S.2d 966, 462 N.E.2d 143 (1984).

—Evidence of intoxication should be excluded whenever recklessness is an element of the offense; the trial court properly refused defendant's request that it charge jury as to intoxication with regard to a charge of "depraved indifference" murder as the mens rea for such crime is "recklessness." People v. Register, 60 N.Y.2d 270, 469 N.Y.S.2d 599, 457 N.E.2d 704 (1983).

—Trial judge did not err in charging that jury "may," instead of "must," consider evidence of intoxication in deciding defendant's guilt. Both statutory and case law use "may." People v. Jones, 27 N.Y.2d 222, 316 N.Y.S.2d 617, 265 N.E.2d 446 (1970).

—A person intoxicated by drugs, as well as alcohol, may be entitled to the charge. People v. Rodriguez, 190 A.D.2d 506, 593 N.Y.S.2d 37 (1st Dept. 1993) (crack cocaine).

—Trial court should have given intoxication charge, even if it was inconsistent with a proffered defense of justification. People v. Dawson, 173 A.D.2d 262, 569 N.Y.S.2d 659 (1st Dept.), lv. denied, 78 N.Y.2d 965 (1991).

—Jury rejected intoxication defense notwithstanding evidence that shortly before the crime was committed, a friend of the defendant slipped three mescaline tablets into the defendant's drink without the latter's knowledge. People v. Sanchez, 140 A.D.2d 725, 529 N.Y.S.2d 35 (2d Dept. 1988).

—Court was not required to instruct the jury that the People bore the burden of disproving intoxication beyond a reasonable doubt. People v. Gilbert, 136 A.D.2d 562, 523 N.Y.S.2d 557 (2d. Dept. 1988).

—There is no general requirement that the court specifically relate intoxication to the particular intent requirement of each of the crimes charged. People v. Morton, 117 A.D.2d 631, 498 N.Y.S.2d 81 (2d Dept. 1986).

—In a prosecution for murder in the second degree and manslaughter in the first degree, after intoxication had been raised by the defense, it was reversible error for the court in its charge to merely read PL § 15.25 to the jury with little elaboration. People v. Lawrence, 78 A.D.2d 702, 432 N.Y.S.2d 508 (2d Dept. 1980).

—Although intoxication does not automatically negate specific intent, it is a factor to be considered by the jury. People v. Sargent, 136 A.D.2d 869, 524 N.Y.S.2d 528 (3d Dept. 1988).

—Where defendant did not request a charge on the effect of intoxication, he failed to preserve the issue for appellate review. People v. Bargerstock, 192 A.D.2d 1058, 596 N.Y.S.2d 611 (4th Dept. 1993).

—While intoxication may negate the mens rea in a crime requiring specific intent, it may not negate the lower culpable mental state required in crimes of recklessness. People v. Tocco, 138 Misc. 2d 510, 525 N.Y.S.2d 137 (Sup. Ct. Bronx Co. 1988).

Defenses; justification.—Court did not err in declining to give a PL § 35.15(2)(a)(i) charge. Crediting defendant's testimony that he was attacked in the lobby, court concluded that defendant was not entitled to a "no duty to retreat" jury instruction, where the lobby and stairwell areas were not under defendant's exclusive possession and could not be characterized as defendant's living quarters. People v. Hernandez, 98 N.Y.2d 175, 746 N.Y.S.2d 434, 774 N.E.2d 198 (2002).

—Where a reasonable view of the evidence supported the defendant's claim that he chose to speed in order to avoid a perceived attack, the trial court was required to charge justification. People v. Maher, 79 N.Y.2d 978, 584 N.Y.S.2d 421, 594 N.E.2d 915 (1992).

—Where justification is in issue, a critical determination for the jury is whether the defendant "reasonably believed" that someone was about to use physical force or deadly physical force against him or a third person. This determination "requires an assessment of reasonableness which must be determined from the point of view of the particular defendant under the standard of a reasonable person in defendant's circumstances at the time of the incident." People v. Wesley, 76 N.Y.2d 555, 561 N.Y.S.2d 707, 563 N.E.2d 21 (1990).

—Justification is a defense to depraved indifference murder, and where evidence supporting the defense has been presented, refusal to instruct the jury that the People must disprove justification beyond a reasonable doubt is reversible error. People v. McManus, 67 N.Y.2d 541, 505 N.Y.S.2d 43, 496 N.E.2d 202 (1986).

—Justification is not a defense to criminal possession of a weapon, since weapons possession offenses do not require the use of force, but merely outlaw the unlawful possession of a weapon. People v. Pons, 68 N.Y.2d 264, 508 N.Y.S.2d 403, 501 N.E.2d 11 (1986).

—The failure to charge justification constitutes reversible error only when the defense is "supported by a reasonable view of the evidence—not by any view of the evidence, however artificial or irrational." People v. Rivers, 300 A.D.2d 63, 751 N.Y.S.2d 28 (1st Dept. 2002).

—Trial court erred in failing to instruct jury on justification arising from the threat of deadly physical force by a third man, where a reasonable view of the evidence would support a finding that the defendant responded to the use of deadly physical force from the third man, and that, in the struggle for the gun, it accidentally fired, killing the murder victim. People v. Morgan, 290 A.D.2d 566, 737 N.Y.S.2d 108 (2d Dept. 2002).

—Court properly denied defendant's request to charge the defense of justification where defendant's statement to police indicated that his wife threatened him with a knife but that he was able to wrest it from her. At that point, defendant's wife was no longer armed and, therefore, defendant was no longer facing the imminent use of deadly force against him. People v. Bennett, 279 A.D.2d 585, 719 N.Y.S.2d 281 (2d Dept. 2001).

—It is unnecessary for the defendant to admit inflicting the fatal wound to be entitled to a justification charge. People v. Badillo, 218 A.D.2d 811, 630 N.Y.S.2d 798 (2d Dept. 1995).

—It was an error to limit justification charge to those circumstances in which the use of deadly physical force would be justified. People v. Ogodor, 207 A.D.2d 461, 615 N.Y.S.2d 909 (2d Dept. 1994).

—County court properly denied defendant's request to charge justification through the use of ordinary physical force where defendant's use of a knife clearly constitutes use of a deadly force as a matter of law. People v. Mothon, 284 A.D.2d 568, 729 N.Y.S.2d 541 (3d Dept. 2001).

—Reversible error was committed when court, in issuing justification charge, failed to explain how the jury was to judge the reasonableness of the defendant's belief that the deceased was about to use deadly physical force, and failed to inform the jury of the need to take into account the accused's background or circumstances as they would have appeared to him. People v. Davis, 201 A.D.2d 827, 608 N.Y.S.2d 348 (3d Dept. 1994).

Matters of defense; generally.—It was reversible error for the trial court to persistently refuse, over defense counsel's timely objections, to charge the jury in any way as to the effect of any police custody or arrest of either participant as related to the felony murder count; the question whether the homicide occurred in the immediate flight from a felony is only rarely to be considered as one of law for the court. People v. Irby, 47 N.Y.2d 894, 419 N.Y.S.2d 477, 393 N.E.2d 472 (1979).

—Reversal was not warranted where the defendant, although possessing several vials of crack in a bag, and one vial in the mouth, received the proper jury charge clearly demonstrating that only one count of possession was charged, not two, and that to convict, defendant had to possess both items. People v. Bilbatua, 208 A.D.2d 404, 617 N.Y.S.2d 162 (1st Dept. 1994).

—The court had no obligation in a prosecution for reckless manslaughter to charge the jury with the definition of a "speed contest." People v. Killane, 203 A.D.2d 386, 610 N.Y.S.2d 547 (2d Dept. 1994).

—Court properly instructed the jury not to speculate as to fingerprints after defense counsel referred in summation to the lack of fingerprints, since there was no testimony adduced concerning fingerprints or the lack thereof. People v. Hernandez, 143 A.D.2d 842, 533 N.Y.S.2d 488 (2d Dept. 1988).

—The trial court properly refused defendant's request to charge the jury on the earnest resistance definition of forcible compulsion where the act of sodomy for which defendant was convicted did not occur prior to the July 1982 amendment of the statute defining forcible compulsion which abandoned the earnest resistance requirements. People v. Atkinson, 116 A.D.2d 584, 497 N.Y.S.2d 442 (2d Dept. 1986).

—Defendant does not have the right to have issues concerning the suppression of physical evidence submitted to the jury. People v. Moore, 156 Misc. 2d 583, 593 N.Y.S.2d 953, 955 (Sup. Ct. N.Y. Co. 1993).

Adverse inference charge.—The trial court properly gave an adverse inference charge instead of striking a police officer's testimony where the prosecution was unable to produce defendant's arrest pedigree report. People v. Brown, 276 A.D.2d 799, 715 N.Y.S.2d 251 (2d Dept. 2000).

Subd. 3

Instruction required.—Failure to give the required instruction regarding the affirmative defense of lack of criminal responsibility by reason of mental disease or defect when requested requires reversal, without regard to harmless error analysis. People v. Kinnitsky, 119 A.D.2d 159, 505 N.Y.S.2d 910 (2d Dept. 1987).

Subd. 4

Elements of the crime.—Upon request, the court must submit the issue of venue to the jury. People v. Sosnik, 77 N.Y.2d 858, 568 N.Y.S.2d 340, 569 N.E.2d 1019 (1991).

—Failure to submit the issue of venue to the jury was harmless where it necessarily found that venue was proper. People v. Ribowsky, 77 N.Y.2d 284, 567 N.Y.S.2d 392, 568 N.E.2d 1197 (1991).

—Reversal was required where court merely recited the statutory definitions of the crimes charged and failed to explain the essential elements of the crimes charged and failed to instruct the jury that the prosecution had the burden of proving beyond a reasonable doubt every element of the offenses charged. People v. Sanders, 69 N.Y.2d 860, 514 N.Y.S.2d 711 507 N.E.2d 304 (1987).

—Trial court erred by removing from its jury instructions all of the elements of the crimes charged for the jury's consideration except for identification, and the error was preserved for review by the timely objection of defense counsel. People v. Lewis, 64 N.Y.2d 57, 489 N.Y.S.2d 57, 478 N.E.2d 198 (1985).

—Failure of the trial judge to charge the jury as to the statutory definitions of "deprive" and "appropriate" was reversible error in an attempted larceny case where the defendant had requested such charge; the jury could have been misled into thinking that any withholding, either permanent or temporary, constituted larceny. People v. Blacknall, 63 N.Y.2d 912, 483 N.Y.S.2d 206, 472 N.E.2d 1034 (1984).

—Defendant robbed a drunken man and left him at the side of a highway, where he was killed when struck by a car. The court, in charging the jury, explained the applicable law of murder. Although the charge in regard to the issue of causation was not fully submitted to the jury, it was held that since the defendant's attorney took no exception and made no request as to causation, and failed to raise any question on appeal as to the sufficiency of the charge, a new trial would not be allowed. People v. Kibbe, 41 A.D.2d 228, 342 N.Y.S.2d 386 (4th Dept. 1973), aff'd, 35 N.Y.2d 407, 362 N.Y.S.2d 848, 321 N.E.2d 773 (1974).

—Trial judge's failure in assault prosecution, to reiterate, in supplementary charge, the requirements of the particular intent as to charge of assault in third degree, was not prejudicial where defendant was convicted of assault in the second degree. People v. Jones, 27 N.Y.2d 222, 316 N.Y.S.2d 617, 265 N.E.2d 446 (1970).

—Since the case involved "unlawful entry" and not "unlawful remaining" the court erred by denying defendant's request to eliminate the phrase "or remains" from its instructions on burglary. People v. Jackson, 202 A.D.2d 250, 608 N.Y.S.2d 631 (1st Dept. 1994).

—Defendant's conviction was reversed because the trial court omitted an element of bail jumping in supplemental charge, even though the element was included in the main charge. People v. Simpkins, 174 A.D.2d 341, 571 N.Y.S.2d 1 (1st Dept. 1991).

—Despite the fact that the defendant and his counsel suggested that the court omit the definitions of the elements of the crimes

charged in its instructions to the jury, the better practice would be for the court to define the elements of the crimes charged. People v. Carroll, 196 A.D.2d 546, 601 N.Y.S.2d 702 (2d Dept. 1993).

—Although the court's initial charge failed to distinguish robbery in the second degree from robbery in the first degree, upon the jury's request the court adequately explained the difference between the two crimes and thus cured its initial defective instructions. People v. Gildersleeve, 143 A.D.2d 361, 532 N.Y.S.2d 418 (2d Dept. 1988).

—Reversible error was committed when the court in the course of its charge on disorderly conduct injected the element of recklessness which expanded and changed the theory of the prosecution as reflected in the evidence before the grand jury. People v. Collesides, 79 A.D.2d 1063, 435 N.Y.S.2d 398 (3d Dept. 1981).

—Court's failure to instruct the jury on the operability requirement with respect to criminal trespass charge was harmless error, because the jury necessarily found that the weapon was operable when it found defendant guilty of criminal possession of a weapon in the third degree; furthermore, the evidence of operability was uncontroverted and there is no reasonable possibility that the jury would have acquitted defendant of the criminal trespass count if the court had instructed the jury on the operability requirement. People v. Cruz, 272 A.D.2d 922, 709 N.Y.S.2d 717 (4th Dept. 2000), aff'd on other grounds, 96 N.Y.2d 857, 730 N.Y.S.2d 29, 754 N.E.2d 1112 (2001).

Court's failure to inform the parties which counts would be submitted.—Trial court's error in failing to inform counsel of the lesser included charge prior to their summations was harmless since it could not be said that defense counsel's summation would have been affected by knowledge that the lesser charge would be submitted to the jury. People v. Miller, 70 N.Y.2d 903, 524 N.Y.S.2d 386, 519 N.E.2d 903 (1987).

—Although it is preferable for the parties to know all of the charges to be submitted to the jury before summations, CPL § 300.10(4) was not violated when the court interrupted defendant's summation to inform the parties that it had reversed its original ruling to deny the People's request for the lesser-included offense. Furthermore, since the charge was submitted after the court heard defense counsel's description of the trial evidence in his summation and defense counsel was permitted to alter his summation to address the submission of that count, there was no prejudice to defendant. People v. Young, 271 A.D.2d 263, 707 N.Y.S.2d 41 (1st Dept. 2000).

—A trial court's failure to provide notice of any lesser included offenses that will be submitted to the jury prior to summations deprives defense counsel of the opportunity to argue to the jury the evidence as it relates to the lesser crime, but reversal is not required where there is no prejudice to defendant; here, reversal was required because had defense counsel been informed that the lesser included offense of second-degree assault would be submitted to the jury, he would have argued that defendant lacked intent to cause any physical injury, and would not have argued, as he did, that defendant lacked the intent to cause serious physical injury. People v. Aruz, 253 A.D.2d 592, 677 N.Y.S.2d 322 (1st Dept. 1998).

—Defendant's request, made after the summations, for a lesser included offense, was untimely. People v. Stringfellow, 176 A.D.2d 447, 574 N.Y.S.2d 543 (1st Dept. 1991).

—Although the trial court did not state, prior to defense counsel's summation, the counts upon which it intended to render a verdict, the error was harmless in view of fact that defendant was convicted of the offenses specified in the indictment and not of any lesser included offenses. People v. Herman, 133 A.D.2d 377, 519 N.Y.S.2d 550 (2d Dept. 1987).

—Though court may have erred in failing to advise the parties prior to summation that it would charge the lesser included offense of manslaughter in the second degree, the error, which went unobjected to, was harmless in light of the fact that defendant was not convicted of the lesser offense but of the greater offense of murder in the second degree. People v. Bacote, 120 A.D.2d 539, 501 N.Y.S.2d 733 (2d Dept. 1986).

—Reversal not required due to court's error in failing to notify the parties prior to summation that it would consider a lesser included offense since the defense summation could not have been altered in any substantial way had he been properly informed of the offenses the court would consider. People v. Hampton, 124 A.D.2d 675, 507 N.Y.S.2d 916 (2d Dept. 1986).

—Court's failure to inform the parties prior to summation of its intent to charge lesser included offense violated (CPL §§ 300.10[3] and 300.30 and required reversal where defendant was convicted of the lesser included offense. People v. Garcia, 76 A.D.2d 867, 428 N.Y.S.2d 500 (2d Dept. 1980).

—Since the only issue in the case was one which was the same for all counts regardless of what crimes were actually submitted, i.e. identification, and because the defendants were convicted of the offenses charged in the indictment, it was harmless error to fail to inform defendants of counts and offenses which the court intended to submit to the jury before summation. People v. Coast, 77 A.D.2d 810, 430 N.Y.S.2d 762 (4th Dept. 1980).

Subd. 5

Requests to charge; exceptions.—A defendant cannot rely on the request of a co-defendant to preserve a charge error, since, for tactical reasons, co-defendants might take different positions on the desirability of various instructions. People v. Buckley, 75 N.Y.2d 843, 552 N.Y.S.2d 92 (1990).

—Where a trial judge agrees to give a particular charge but subsequently fails to do so, the requesting party must draw the error to the judge's attention or the error is waived. People v. Whalen, 59 N.Y.2d 273, 464 N.Y.S.2d 454, 451 N.E.2d 212 (1983).

—Defendant's request was properly denied as duplicative or cumulative where defendant requested a charge that he must be found not guilty of criminal possession of a weapon in the third degree (PL § 265.02) if the jury found "that defendant picked up the gun from the ground and then was arrested immediately" after the court had twice charged that "fleeting or momentary possession" was not sufficient to support a conviction on the possession counts. People v. Coonan, 48 N.Y.2d 772, 423 N.Y.S.2d 914, 399 N.E.2d 944 (1979).

—Issue concerning the court's failure to alert counsel as to the lesser included offenses which would be submitted to the jury was not preserved for appellate review. People v. Trial, 172 A.D.2d 320, 568 N.Y.S.2d 366 (1st Dept. 1991).

—While it was improper for the trial court to instruct the jury to disregard the personal opinions and theories of the attorneys as expressed during summations, the error was not preserved for appellate review. People v. Vasquez, 159 A.D.2d 262, 552 N.Y.S.2d 262 (1st Dept. 1990).

—A request to charge may properly be made after the completion of the charge to the jury and in response to a note by the jury; a protest need not be in the form of an exception and may be made at any subsequent time when the court has an opportunity of effectively charging the same. People v. Lewis, 116 A.D.2d 16, 499 N.Y.S.2d 709 (1st Dept. 1986).

—Although the court refused to charge certain language requested by the defendants, the charge contained the substance of the request and conveyed the appropriate rules of law. People v. Bryant, 122 A.D.2d 220, 504 N.Y.S.2d 753 (2d Dept. 1986).

—No error was committed by the court in not charging the jury that the witnesses had no obligation to come forward with exculpatory information since such a charge was never requested. People v. Carroll, 117 A.D.2d 815, 499 N.Y.S.2d 135 (2d Dept.), lv. denied, 67 N.Y.2d 940 (1986).

—Trial court was not required to instruct the jury with respect to the affirmative defense of duress where, prior to the charge, the defendant withdrew his request for such an instruction, and there was no evidence presented that any physical force or immediate threat of physical force was imposed upon defendant. People v. Wedgeworth, 121 A.D.2d 762, 504 N.Y.S.2d 169 (2d Dept.), lv. denied, 68 N.Y.2d 818 (1986).

—Defendant failed to preserve for review the issue of the propriety of the court's alibi charge, as there was no objection taken nor was there a refusal of a request for an additional charge. People v. Aponti, 122 A.D.2d 271, 505 N.Y.S.2d 182 (2d Dept. 1986).

—The defendant has failed to preserve for appellate review his claim that the trial court's instructions were insufficient since defense counsel neither objected to the proposed charges, nor excepted to the charges as a whole. People v. Moya, 115 A.D.2d 769, 497 N.Y.S.2d 147 (2d Dept. 1985).

—Where the charge taken in its entirety was adequate and trial counsel failed to make objections or take exceptions, alleged errors in the charge were not properly preserved for review. People v. Bowers, 107 A.D.2d 703, 484 N.Y.S.2d 57 (2d Dept. 1985).

Harmless error.—Although court failed to instruct that witness' prior inconsistent statements to the police could only be used for impeachment purposes and not as direct evidence, error was harmless in light of the overwhelming evidence of the defendant's guilt. People v. Hynes, 146 A.D.2d 587, 36 N.Y.S.2d 509 (2d Dept. 1989).

—While trial court improperly commented on the defendant's failure to testify, the error was harmless in light of the overwhelming proof of guilt and because the trial was conducted without a jury. People v. Jennings, 144 A.D.2d 696, 535 N.Y.S.2d 38 (2d Dept. 1988).

—Court's failure to instruct the jury on the operability requirement with respect to criminal trespass charge was harmless error, because the jury necessarily found that the weapon was operable when it found defendant guilty of criminal possession of a weapon in the third degree; furthermore, the evidence of operability was uncontroverted and there is no reasonable possibility that the jury would have acquitted defendant of the criminal trespass count if the court had instructed the jury on the operability requirement. People v. Cruz, 272 A.D.2d 922, 709 N.Y.S.2d 717 (4th Dept. 2000), aff'd on other grounds, 96 N.Y.2d 857, 730 N.Y.S.2d 29, 754 N.E.2d 1112 (2001).

Waiver of errors.—Where defense counsel supplies the court with the words of the charge in his written request, claim of error in charge is waived. People v. Candelario, 150 A.D.2d 791, 542 N.Y.S.2d 222 (2d Dept. 1989).

—Since defendant consented to the court's decision not to marshal the evidence, his contention on appeal concerning the court's failure to do so was not only not preserved for appellate review but was expressly waived by him. People v. Sanchez, 136 A.D.2d 751, 524 N.Y.S.2d 86 (2d Dept. 1988).

—Though court in its Sandoval ruling promised to issue limiting instructions concerning prior criminal acts, defendant waived issue of court's failure to issue such instructions where there was no request to charge on the issue or exception to the court's failure to so charge. People v. Moon, 121 A.D.2d 790, 504 N.Y.S.2d 239 (3d Dept. 1986).

—Defendant's contention that trial court committed error by failing to point out to the jury that her defense of duress did not consist solely of the use or threatened use of physical force on third persons was waived since no objection was made to the omission. People v. Marshall, 124 A.D.2d 396, 507 N.Y.S.2d 495 (3d Dept. 1986).

—Defendant waived trial court's error in not instructing the jury on necessity of corroboration for accomplice testimony by failing to either request such charge or except to its omission. People v. Smith, 103 A.D.2d 859, 477 N.Y.S.2d 917 (3d Dept. 1984).

§ 300.30. Court's charge; submission of indictment to jury; definitions of terms.

The following definitions are applicable to this article:

1. "Submission of a count" of an indictment means submission of the offense charged therein, or of a lesser included offense, or submission in the alternative of both the offense charged and a lesser included offense or offenses. When the court "submits a count," it must, at the least, submit the offense charged therein if such is supported by legally sufficient trial evidence, or if it is not, the greatest lesser included offense which is supported by legally sufficient trial evidence.

2. "Consecutive counts" means two or more counts of an indictment upon which consecutive sentences may be imposed in case of conviction thereon.

3. "Concurrent counts" means two or more counts of an indictment upon which concurrent

sentences only may be imposed in case of conviction thereon.

4. "Inclusory concurrent counts." Concurrent counts are "inclusory" when the offense charged in one is greater than any of those charged in the others and when the latter are all lesser offenses included within the greater. All other kinds of concurrent counts are "non-inclusory."

5. "Inconsistent counts." Two counts are "inconsistent" when guilt of the offense charged in one necessarily negates guilt of the offense charged in the other.

ANNOTATIONS

Inclusory concurrent counts.—Defendant could not be simultaneously convicted of assault in the first degree and the lesser concurrent count of assault in the second degree. People v. Allen, 147 A.D.2d 352, 537 N.Y.S.2d 174 (1st Dept.), *lv. denied,* 73 N.Y.2d 1010 (1989).

—Dismissal of the counts of robbery in the second degree and grand larceny in the third degree were warranted where the facts established they were inclusory concurrent counts of robbery in the first degree and the jury returned a guilty verdict on the latter charge. People v. Turner, 83 A.D.2d 844, 441 N.Y.S.2d 574 (2d Dept. 1981).

—Defendant's conviction of assault in the second degree had to be dismissed because it was a lesser-included offense of assault in the first degree, for which he was also convicted. People v. Walker, 275 A.D.2d 1009, 713 N.Y.S.2d 590 (4th Dept. 2000).

Non-inclusory counts.—Defendant's conviction for assault in the first degree was not an inclusory concurrent count of his conviction for robbery in the first degree; the assault charge required the infliction of serious physical injury in furtherance of the underlying felony—an element not required by the robbery charge. Thus, the assault was not a lesser included offense. People v. Abrew, 95 N.Y.2d 806, 710 N.Y.S.2d 833, 732 N.E.2d 940 (2000).

Order in which counts are considered.—Nothing contained in Article 300 directs the order in which the jury should consider the various offenses submitted to it, and the court may properly instruct the jury to consider counts and their lesser included offenses in alternating order. People v. Johnson, 88 N.Y.2d 880, 645 N.Y.S.2d 455, 668 N.E.2d 426 (1996).

§ 300.40. Court's charge; submission of indictment to jury; counts to be submitted.

The court may submit to the jury only those counts of an indictment remaining therein at the time of its charge which are supported by legally sufficient trial evidence, and every count not so supported should be dismissed by a trial order of dismissal. The court's determination as to which of the sufficient counts are to be submitted must be in accordance with the following rules:

1. If the indictment contains but one count, the court must submit such count.

2. If a multiple count indictment contains consecutive counts only, the court must submit every count thereof.

3. If a multiple count indictment contains concurrent counts of murder in the first degree, the court must submit every such count. In any other case, if a multiple count indictment contains concurrent counts only, the court must submit at least one such count, and may submit more than one as follows:

(a) With respect to non-inclusory concurrent counts, the court may in its discretion submit one or more or all thereof;

(b) With respect to inclusory concurrent counts, the court must submit the greatest or inclusive count and may or must, under circumstances prescribed in section 300.50, also submit, but in the alternative only, one or more of the lesser included counts. A verdict of guilty upon the greatest count submitted is deemed a dismissal of every lesser count submitted, but not an acquittal thereon. A verdict of guilty upon a lesser count is deemed an acquittal upon every greater count submitted.

4. If a multiple count indictment contains two or more groups of counts, with the counts within each group being concurrent as to each other but consecutive as to those of the other group or groups, the court must submit at least one count of each group, in the manner prescribed in subdivision three. If an indictment contains one or more of such groups of concurrent counts, and also one or more other counts each of which is consecutive as to every other count of the indictment, the court must submit each individual consecutive count and at least one count of each group of concurrent counts.

5. If an indictment contains two inconsistent counts, the court must submit at least one thereof. If a verdict of guilty upon either would be supported by legally sufficient trial evidence, the court may submit both counts in the alternative and authorize the jury to convict upon one or the other depending upon its findings of fact. In such case, the court must direct the jury that if it renders a verdict of guilty upon one such count it must render a verdict of not guilty upon the other. If the court is satisfied that a conviction upon one such count, though supported by legally sufficient trial evidence, would be against the weight of the evidence while a conviction upon the other would not, it may in its discretion submit the latter count only.

6. Notwithstanding any other provision of this section, the court is not required to submit any particular count to the jury when:

(a) The people consent that it not be submitted; except that nothing contained in this paragraph limits the right accorded a defendant by section 300.50 to the submission, in certain situations, of counts charging lesser included offenses; or

(b) The number of counts or the complexity of the indictment requires selectivity of counts by the court in order to avoid placing an unduly heavy burden upon the jury in its consideration of the case. In such case, the court may submit to the jury a portion of the counts which are representative of the people's case.

7. Every count not submitted to the jury is deemed to have been dismissed by the court. Where the court, over objection of the people, refuses to submit a count which is consecutive as to every count actually submitted, such count is deemed to have been dismissed by a trial order of dismissal even though no such order was expressly made by the court.

Amended by L. 1995, Ch. 1, § 18, amending subd. 3, eff. Sept. 1, 1995.

ANNOTATIONS

Non-inclusory concurrent counts.—Defendant's conviction for assault in the first degree was not an inclusory concurrent count of his conviction for robbery in the first degree; the assault charge required the infliction of serious physical injury in furtherance of the underlying felony—an element not required by the robbery charge. Thus, the assault was not a lesser included offense. People v. Abrew, 95 N.Y.2d 806, 710 N.Y.S.2d 833, 732 N.E.2d 940 (2000).

—Court properly determined not to submit to the jury the count of the indictment charging first-degree assault, a non-inclusory concurrent count, to avoid distracting the jury with the issue of the extent of the complainant's injury in a case turning on identity. Notably, defendant did not request submission of any lesser included offense and the absence of the assault count could not have caused any prejudice. People v. Smith, 260 A.D.2d 253, 690 N.Y.S.2d 6 (1st Dept. 1999).

—In first degree robbery case, court did not abuse its discretion by refusing to charge noninclusory concurrent count of unauthorized use of a vehicle in the third degree. People v. Pagano, 195 A.D.2d 487, 599 N.Y.S.2d 854 (2d Dept.), lv. denied, 82 N.Y.2d 757, 603 N.Y.S.2d 999, 624 N.E.2d 185 (1993).

—Defendant was properly convicted of burglary, criminal mischief and possession of stolen property, all committed during the same incident, because all three crimes contained unique elements and defendant could possibly have committed one without also committing the others. People v. Bolton, 103 A.D.2d 806, 477 N.Y.S.2d 685 (2d Dept. 1984).

—Assault in the first degree is not an inclusory concurrent count of attempted murder in the second degree. People v. Reed, 236 A.D.2d 866, 654 N.Y.S.2d 498 (4th Dept. 1997).

Inclusory concurrent counts.—Weapon possession count need not be dismissed upon conviction for robbery, first degree, since the former is not an inclusory concurrent count with respect to the latter, notwithstanding the fact that there was no evidence showing possession of the knife apart from the robbery. People v. Perez, 45 N.Y.2d 204, 408 N.Y.S.2d 343, 380 N.E.2d 174 (1978).

—CPL § 300.40(3)(b) deals only with trials, and has no application to convictions obtained on plea of guilty; CPL § 220.10 permits the court to accept a plea of guilty to the entire indictment, even when a series of inclusory counts is involved. People v. Walton, 41 N.Y.2d 880, 393 N.Y.S.2d 979, 362 N.E.2d 610 (1977).

—Since defendant could not have committed robbery without also committing grand larceny, the counts being conclusory and concurrent, the grand larceny conviction would not stand; where the verdict is comprised of inclusory concurrent counts, a verdict of guilty on the greatest count is deemed a dismissal of every lesser count. People v. Grier, 37 N.Y.2d 847, 378 N.Y.S.2d 37, 340 N.E.2d 471 (1975).

—Criminal possession of a controlled substance in the seventh degree is a lesser included offense of criminal possession of a controlled substance in the third degree, and therefore, defendant's conviction of the greater precluded his conviction of the lesser count. People v. Anderson, 253 A.D.2d 636, 678 N.Y.S.2d 315 (1st Dept. 1998).

—Count of criminal possession of a controlled substance in the seventh degree must be dismissed because it is an inclusory concurrent count of third-degree possession. People v. Santiago, 242 A.D.2d 462, 662 N.Y.S.2d 51 (1st Dept. 1997).

—Since defendant was convicted for robbery in the first degree under the first count of the indictment because of the serious physical injury he caused during the commission of the crime, a conviction under another count of the indictment for assault

in the first degree based upon the injury defendant gave complainant during the course of the same robbery must be reversed. People v. Preston, 88 A.D.2d 574, 451 N.Y.S.2d 396 (1st Dept. 1982).

—Defendant's conviction for sexual abuse was reversed where court found that the acts forming the basis of the sexual abuse charge were part and parcel of the continuous conduct culminating in the rape of the complainant for which the defendant was also convicted. People v. Grant, 108 A.D.2d 823, 485 N.Y.S.2d 299 (2d Dept. 1985).

—Under the facts of the case, criminal possession of a weapon in the fourth degree is an inclusory concurrent count of criminal possession of a weapon in the third degree and therefore, the criminal possession of a weapon in the fourth degree should have been dismissed when the jury returned a guilty verdict on the criminal possession in the third degree. People v. Cassesse, 80 A.D.2d 860, 436 N.Y.S.2d 758 (2d Dept.), cert. denied, 454 U.S. 822 (1981).

Inconsistent counts.—So long as the court instructs the jury that if it renders a verdict of guilty on one count, it must render a verdict of not guilty upon the other (inconsistent) count, it is not required to tell the jury why the counts are inconsistent, or even to explicitly instruct the jurors that the counts are inconsistent. People v. Harrison, 85 N.Y.2d 891, 626 N.Y.S.2d 747, 650 N.E.2d 405 (1995).

—Where a defendant is charged with a single homicide, in an indictment containing one count of intentional murder and one count of depraved mind murder, both counts may be submitted to the jury, but only in the alternative. People v. Gallagher, 69 N.Y.2d 525, 516 N.Y.S.2d 174, 508 N.E.2d 909 (1987).

—New trial ordered where inconsistent counts were improperly submitted in the conjunctive rather than in the alternative. People v. Trappier, 208 A.D.2d 351, 616 N.Y.S.2d 739 (1st Dept. 1994), modif'd, 87 N.Y.2d 55 (1995).

—Trial counsel waived claim that verdicts were repugnant by failing to request a charge that acquittal of robbery in the second degree would require an acquittal of lesser charge and by failing to move to set aside the verdict prior to discharge of the jury. People v. Lee, 102 A.D.2d 540, 477 N.Y.S.2d 655 (2d Dept. 1984).

—Trial court should not have denied defendant's motion to have second degree manslaughter and vehicular homicide in the second degree submitted to the jury in the alternative, since the counts required different mental states. People v. Spurling, 199 A.D.2d 624, 604 N.Y.S.2d 997 (3d Dept. 1993).

—Although intentional murder and depraved mind murder are inconsistent counts that must be charged in the alternative, defendant's conviction on both counts did not require reversal where defendant did not object when the court submitted both counts nor did he object to the jury verdict. People v. Jones, 163 A.D.2d 911, 558 N.Y.S.2d 774 (4th Dept. 1990).

—The court did not err in failing to submit the felony murder count in the alternative because felony murder does not depend upon a particular mental state. People v. Paxhia, 140 A.D.2d 962, 529 N.Y.S.2d 638 (4th Dept. 1988).

Dismissal of counts.—Since the definition of reckless endangerment in the first degree is virtually identical to that of assault in the first degree, except that it does not include the additional element of causing serious physical injury, a verdict of guilty of the greater count of first degree assault constitutes a dismissal of the endangerment count arising out of the same criminal transaction. People v. Cheung-Kok Lau, 88 A.D.2d 808, 451 N.Y.S.2d 95 (1st Dept. 1982).

—The fact that each indictment contains only one count of perjury does not warrant dismissal, since at the time of trial, should the evidence warrant it, lesser included counts may also be considered. People v. Dunleavy, 41 A.D.2d 717, 341 N.Y.S.2d 500 (1st Dept. 1973), aff'd, 33 N.Y.2d 573, 347 N.Y.S.2d 448, 301 N.E.2d 432 (1973).

—Trial court's refusal to present weapons possession charges to jury at first trial warrants inference that they were dismissed for insufficient evidence and therefore the defendant should not have been retried on those charges. People v. Kluck, 131 A.D.2d 590, 516 N.Y.S.2d 298 (2d Dept. 1987).

—Defendant's conviction for attempted murder in the second degree does not require the dismissal of his conviction for criminal possession of a weapon but it does require dismissal of his conviction for assault in the first degree. People v. Lewis, 81 A.D.2d 645, 438 N.Y.S.2d 150 (2d Dept. 1981).

§ 300.50. Court's charge; submission of lesser included offenses.

1. In submitting a count of an indictment to the jury, the court in its discretion may, in addition to submitting the greatest offense which it is required to submit, submit in the alternative any lesser included offense if there is a reasonable view of the evidence which would support a finding that the defendant committed such lesser offense but did not commit the greater. If there is no reasonable view of the evidence which would support such a finding, the court may not submit such lesser offense. Any error respecting such submission, however, is waived by the defendant unless he objects thereto before the jury retires to deliberate.

2. If the court is authorized by subdivision one to submit a lesser included offense and is requested by either party to do so, it must do so. In the absence of such a request, the court' s failure to submit such offense does not constitute error.

3. The principles prescribed in subdivisions one and two apply equally where the lesser included offense is specifically charged in another count of the indictment.

4. Whenever the court submits two or more offenses in the alternative pursuant to this section, it must instruct the jury that it may render a verdict of guilty with respect to any one of such offenses, depending upon its findings of fact, but that it may not render a verdict of guilty with respect to more than one. A verdict of guilty of any such offense is not deemed an acquittal of any lesser offense submitted, but is deemed an acquittal of every greater offense submitted.

5. Where the indictment charges a crime committed by the defendant while he was under the age of sixteen but a lesser included offense would be one for which the defendant is not criminally responsible by reason of infancy, such lesser included offense may nevertheless be submitted to the jury in the same manner as an offense for which the defendant would be criminally responsible notwithstanding the fact that a verdict of guilty would not result in a criminal conviction.

6. For purposes of this section, the offenses of rape in the third degree as defined in subdivision three of section 130.25 of the penal law and criminal sexual act in the third degree as defined in subdivision three of section 130.40 of the penal law, are not lesser included offenses of rape in the first degree, criminal sexual act in the first degree or any other offense. Notwithstanding the foregoing, either such offense may be submitted as a lesser included offense of the applicable first degree offense when (i) there is a reasonable view of the evidence which would support a finding that the defendant committed such lesser offense but did not commit the greater offense, and (ii) both parties consent to its submission.

Amended by L. 1978, Ch. 481; L. 2000, Ch. 1, eff. Feb. 1, 2001; L. 2003, Ch. 264, § 43, eff. Nov. 1, 2003, amending subd. 6.

ANNOTATIONS

Definitions.—A lesser offense is a lesser "included" offense only if it is "theoretically impossible to commit the greater crime without at the same time committing the lesser." People v. Glover, 57 N.Y.2d 61, 453 N.Y.S.2d 660, 439 N.E.2d 376 (1982).

—If the only difference between the lesser and the greater offense is the culpable mental state required, the lesser is an "included" offense, even if it would theoretically possible to commit the greater without committing the lesser. People v. Green, 56 N.Y.2d 427, 452 N.Y.S.2d 389, 437 N.E.2d 1146 (1982).

—Before a jury is charged concerning a lesser included offense two criteria must exist: (1) the offense being scrutinized for possible submission must meet the statutory definition of a "lesser included offense" (CPL § 1.20[37]); and (2) there must be a reasonable view of the evidence which would support a finding that the defendant committed the lesser offense but did not commit the greater (CPL § 300.50). People v. Johnson, 39 N.Y.2d 364, 384 N.Y.S.2d 108, 348 NE.2d 564 (1976).

Reasonable view of the evidence.—Request to charge a lesser included offense must be granted if there is a reasonable view of the evidence to support it. People v. Van Norstrand, 85 N.Y.2d 131, 623 N.Y.S.2d 767, 647 N.E.2d 1275 (1995).

—A lesser included offense must be charged only if, under any reasonable view of the evidence as seen in a light most favorable to defendant, the jury could find that defendant committed the lesser offense but not the greater. People v. Randolph, 81 N.Y.2d 868, 597 N.Y.S.2d 630, 613 N.E.2d 536 (1993).

—Lesser included offenses are not to be submitted for consideration by the jury in reaching its verdict in every case; there must exist "a reasonable view of the evidence" upon which might be predicated a conclusion that the defendant did in fact commit a lesser, but not the greater offense; if there is no such reasonable view, a submission of lesser offenses is improper. People v. Scarborough, 49 N.Y.2d 364, 426 N.Y.S.2d 224, 402 N.E.2d 1127 (1980).

—The test of whether a "lesser included offense" is to be submitted is whether on any reasonable view of the evidence it is possible for the trier of the facts to acquit the defendant on the higher count and still find him guilty on the lesser one. People v. Henderson, 41 N.Y.2d 233, 391 N.Y.S.2d 563, 359 N.E.2d 1357 (1976).

—The test for whether a lesser included offense should be charged is not whether there is any view of the evidence that defendant committed the lesser but not the greater offense, but whether there is a "reasonable view." People v. Scoggins, 167 A.D.2d 321, 562 N.Y.S.2d 70 (1st Dept. 1990).

—In prosecution for manslaughter in the first degree submission of lesser degree or included crime is justified only where there is basis in evidence for finding accused innocent of higher crime yet guilty of the lower one, but trial court may not permit jury to choose between crime charged and some lesser offense where evidence essential to support verdict of guilty of latter necessarily proves guilt of greater crime as well. People v. Ramirez, 76 A.D.2d 115, 430 N.Y.S.2d 83 (1st Dept. 1980).

Reasonable view of the evidence; specific cases.—The trial court erred in refusing defendant's request to charge as a lesser included offense robbery in the second degree; defendant's confession, admitted into evidence, stated that he used a toy gun. This provided a reasonable basis for jury to conclude that the firearm displayed by defendant "was not a loaded weapon . . . readily capable of producing death or serious physical injury." People v. Smith, 55 N.Y.2d 888, 449 N.Y.S.2d 19, 433 N.E.2d 1267 (1982).

—One who fails to perceive the possible danger inherent in holding a gun to another when he has no intention of using it is at least negligent, and he is reckless if he perceives the possibility that an outside blow might discharge the weapon; accordingly, such person is entitled to a charge on criminal negligent homicide in addition to one on second degree manslaughter. People v. Stanfield, 44 A.D.2d 780, 355 N.Y.S.2d 3 (1st Dept. 1974), aff'd, 36 N.Y.2d 467, 369 N.Y.S.2d 118, 330 N.E.2d 75 (1975).

—Evidence reasonably supported a finding that when defendant repeatedly shot his victim's chest and back, he acted with either intent to cause serious physical injury or with the intent to cause death, and because the jury could reasonably have found that defendant committed the lesser but not the greater crime, the submission of the lesser-included offense of first-degree manslaughter was proper. People v. Faison, 265 A.D.2d 422, 697 N.Y.S.2d 296 (2d Dept. 1999).

—Reasonable view of the evidence supported finding that defendant's shooting of victim during altercation was "reckless" and that defendant committed the lesser offense of second degree manslaughter but not greater offense second degree murder. People v. Alvarez, 201 A.D.2d 487, 607 N.Y.S.2d 137 (2d Dept.), *lv. denied*, 83 N.Y.2d 868 (1994).

—Where injury to complainant could have been caused by his falling on pavement and indictment charged assault in the first degree, it was error for the court to refuse defendant's request to charge assault in the third degree as a lesser included crime since a reasonable view of the evidence could support an acquittal as to the first degree charge and a conviction of the lesser charge by the jury. People v. Galvin, 104 A.D.2d 527, 479 N.Y.S.2d 896 (3d Dept. 1984).

—Reasonable view of the evidence supported conviction of the lesser offense of reckless assault in the third degree rather than the greater offense of second degree intentional assault, in light of evidence of intoxication at the time of the offense. People v. Williams, 212 A.D.2d 1065, 623 N.Y.S.2d 31 (4th Dept.), *lv. denied*, 85 N.Y.2d 916 (1995).

No reasonable view of the evidence; specific cases.—In case involving first degree criminal sale of a controlled substance, there was no reasonable view of the evidence which could support finding that weight of drugs was less than two ounces as required for the lesser offense of criminal sale in the third degree. People v. Flores, 84 N.Y.2d 957, 620 N.Y.S.2d 823, 644 N.E.2d 1379 (1994).

—Although criminal trespass in the third degree is a lesser included offense of burglary in the third degree, the trial court properly refused defense counsel's request to submit such lesser charge to the jury where there was no reasonable view of the evidence under which the jury could conclude that the defendant committed the trespass, but not the burglary. People v. Blim, 63 N.Y.2d 718, 480 N.Y.S.2d 192, 469 N.E.2d 513 (1984).

—Court properly refused to charge manslaughter (reckless homicide) where no reasonable view of the evidence would support defendant's claim that he only intended to have his wife physically assaulted (PL § 125.20[1]) and not killed (PL § 125.25[1]). People v. Safian, 59 A.D.2d 20, 396 N.Y.S.2d 432 (2d Dept. 1977), *aff'd*, 46 N.Y.2d 181, 413 N.Y.S.2d 118, 38 N.E.2d 1046 (1978).

—There was no reasonable view of the evidence to support a conviction on the lesser offense of seventh degree criminal possession of a controlled substance but not the greater offense of third degree criminal possession, where police officer's testimony established possession with intent to sell, defendant's testimony did not support his contention that he possessed drugs for personal use People v. Hernandez, 215 A.D.2d 179, 626 N.Y.S.2d 478 (1st Dept. 1995).

—Defendant was not entitled to charge of criminally negligent homicide as a lesser-included offense of manslaughter in the second degree where there was no reasonable view of the evidence that would support a finding that the defendant was unaware of the substantial and unjustifiable risk of death caused by his actions—defendant forcefully stabbed his wife three times in the front torso, puncturing her diaphragm, liver, and the final wound went through her heart with such force that the handle of the knife broke off when the blade struck bone and cartilage. People v. Anderson, 287 A.D.2d 574, 731 N.Y.S.2d 495 (2d Dept. 2001).

—In murder prosecution, court properly declined to issue manslaughter instruction where the defendant deliberately and repeatedly fired a gun into the victim's upper body from close range. People v. Ochoa, 142 A.D.2d 741, 531 N.Y.S.2d 124 (2d Dept. 1988).

—The court properly refused to charge manslaughter in the first degree as a lesser included offense in murder prosecution, in view of the execution-style murder and the evidence that the shotgun was held only 1 to 3 feet from the rear portion of the neck of the deceased when discharged. People v. Green, 134 A.D.2d 516, 521 N.Y.S.2d 291, 292 (2d Dept. 1987).

—Trial court properly refused to charge the jury as to the lesser included offense of criminal sale of a controlled substance in the third degree where the uncontroverted evidence of the People's expert established that the weight of heroin sold was in excess of one-half ounce; no reasonable view of the evidence would support such lesser count. People v. Carolina, 112 A.D.2d 244, 491 N.Y.S.2d 459 (2d Dept. 1985).

—Court properly denied defendant's request to charge on the lesser included offenses of manslaughter in the second degree and criminally negligent homicide, as there was no reasonable view of the evidence to support defendant's contention that he did not intend to cause the victim's death where defendant and others were hired to kill the victim, and victim was killed in an execution-style murder. People v. Williams, 283 A.D.2d 998, 725 N.Y.S.2d 775 (4th Dept. 2001).

—Where defendant stabbed the victim 13 times in the neck and chest, strangled her, left an ice pick in her neck and then sexually assaulted the victim's 11-year-old daughter, there was no reasonable view of the evidence justifying manslaughter second degree charge as lesser included offense of murder in the second degree. People v. West. 203 A.D.2d 947, 611 N.Y.S.2d 401 (4th Dept.), *lv. denied*, 84 N.Y.2d 834 (1994).

—Court did not err in refusing to charge manslaughter in the second degree as a lesser included offense of murder in the second degree where the evidence showed that defendant shot the decedent three time, twice as he was attempting to flee from the defendant. People v. Sapp, 163 A.D.2d 835, 558 N.Y.S.2d 764, 765 (4th Dept. 1990).

Notice of lesser offenses being submitted to jury.—After completion of summations, trial court, at the request of co-counsel and the prosecutor, improperly decided to submit to the jury certain lesser included offenses in violation of CPL § 300.10(4). People v. Reilly, 105 A.D.2d 716, 481 N.Y.S.2d 153 (2d Dept. 1984).

—The failure of the court to notify defendant, prior to summations, that it intended to submit to the jury the charge of manslaughter as a lesser included offense of murder was reversible error. People v. Bacalocostantis, 111 A.D.2d 991, 490 N.Y.S.2d 309 (3d Dept. 1985).

Requests to charge.—Where a single witness's testimony essential to support a verdict of guilt of the lesser offense was substantially identical to the testimony establishing guilt of the greater crime as well, officer's testimony was properly deemed integrated, and a charge-down to the lesser included offense was properly denied. People v. Negron, 91 N.Y.2d 788, 676 N.Y.S.2d 520, 699 N.E.2d 32 (1998).

—By affirmatively requesting that the trial court submit the lesser offense of escape in the second degree to the jury, defendant waived his right to challenge the submission of the lesser charge on appeal. People v. Richardson, 88 N.Y.2d 1049, 650 N.Y.S.2d 633, 673 N.E.2d 918 (1996).

—Court properly rejected defendant's request to charge that the jury could consider the lesser included offense where it was "unable to agree" on the greater offense; a jury may consider a lesser offense only upon reaching a unanimous verdict of not guilty on the greater offense. People v. Boettcher, 69 N.Y.2d 174, 513 N.Y.S.2d 83, 505 N.E.2d 594 (1987).

—By failing to make a request to submit the lesser included offense until after the jury had commenced its deliberations, defendant waived whatever right he may have had to have criminal facilitation submitted as a lesser included offense. People v. Duncan, 46 N.Y.2d 74, 412 N.Y.S.2d 833, 385 N.E.2d 572 (1978).

—Where defendant failed to request a lesser included offense, the court's failure to submit such offense, sua sponte, was not error. People v. Douglas, 194 A.D.2d 408, 599 N.Y.S.2d 230 (1st Dept.), *lv. denied*, 82 N.Y.2d 717 (1993).

—The defendant's request for a lesser included offense, which was made after the summations, was untimely. People v. Stringfellow, 176 A.D.2d 447, 574 N.Y.S.2d 543 (1st Dept. 1991), *lv. denied*, 79 N.Y.2d 864 (1992).

—Although a request for a charge on a lesser included offense should be made before summations, it cannot be rejected as untimely were, as here, it is made before the jury retires to deliberate. People v. McInnis, 179 A.D.2d 781, 579 N.Y.S.2d 144 (2d Dept.), *lv. denied*, 79 N.Y.2d 997 (1992).

Specific offenses.—Submission of nonexistent crime of attempted manslaughter in the first degree as a lesser included offense of attempted murder in the second degree was fundamental error. People v. Martinez, 81 N.Y.2d 810, 595 N.Y.S.2d 376, 611 N.E.2d 277 (1993).

—Criminal possession of a weapon in the fourth degree [involving any firearm] is a lesser included offense of third degree criminal possession of a weapon [loaded firearm other than in home or place of business]. People v. Menchetti, 76 N.Y.2d 473, 560 N.Y.S.2d 760, 561 N.E.2d 536 (1990).

—Defendant could not be simultaneously convicted of assault in the first degree and the lesser concurrent count of assault in the second degree. People v. Allen, 147 A.D.2d 352, 537 N.Y.S.2d 174 (1st Dept.), lv. denied, 73 N.Y.2d 1010 (1989).

—Robbery in the second degree, based upon the causing of physical injury, is a lesser included offense of robbery in the first degree based upon the causing of serious physical injury, since it is impossible to cause serious physical injury without at the same time causing physical injury to the victim. People v. Rivera, 123 A.D.2d 295, 506 N.Y.S.2d 569 (1st Dept. 1986).

—Criminally negligent homicide can be a lesser included offense under a charge of intentional murder, and where the defendant requests that the charge be submitted, to do so it must be viewed that the evidence will support such a finding. People v. Lewis, 53 A.D.2d 591, 444 N.Y.S.2d 450 (1st Dept. 1981).

—Assault, in the second degree, is not a lesser included offense of robbery in the first degree because intent to cause serious physical injury to another is an essential element of assault, in the second degree, and intent to cause serious physical injury need not be shown for a conviction of robbery in the first degree. People v. Strawder, 78 A.D.2d 810, 433 N.Y.S.2d 112 (1st Dept. 1980).

—Criminal possession of a controlled substance in the fourth degree [weight requirement] is not a lesser included offense of criminal possession in the third degree [intent to sell]. People v. Lee, 196 A.D.2d 509, 601 N.Y.S.2d 20 (2d Dept.), lv. denied, 82 N.Y.2d 851 (1993).

—Criminal facilitation is not a lesser included offense of criminal sale of a controlled substance. People v. Marrow, 183 A.D.2d 788, 583 N.Y.S.2d 514, 516 (2d Dept.), lv. denied, 82 N.Y.2d 906 (1992).

—Criminal possession of a weapon in the third degree is not a lesser included offense of criminal possession of a weapon in the second degree inasmuch as criminal possession of a weapon in the third degree includes the added element that it cannot occur in the defendant's home or place of business. People v. Ruiz, 144 A.D.2d 599, 534 N.Y.S.2d 1020 (2d Dept. 1988).

—Criminal facilitation in the fourth degree is not a lesser included offense of robbery in the first degree and assault in the first degree even where the defendant was charged with acting in concert with another since the phrase "acting in concert" is not an essential element of the crimes charged but rather concerned the theory of the case presented to the Grand Jury. People v. Hernandez, 135 A.D.2d 732, 522 N.Y.S.2d 634 (2d. Dept. 1987).

—Criminal possession of a weapon in the third degree is not a lesser included offense of criminal possession of a weapon in the second degree since the former crime, unlike the latter, contains the requirement that the possession not be in the defendant's home or place of business. People v. McGriff, 123 A.D.2d 646, 506 N.Y.S.2d 910 (2d Dept. 1986).

—Since it is theoretically possible for a defendant illegally to sell a drug without intending to aid anyone else in the commission of a felony, criminal facilitation in the fourth degree does not constitute a lesser included offense of the crime of criminal sale of a controlled substance. People v. Dunn, 122 A.D.2d 952, 506 N.Y.S.2d 98 (2d Dept. 1986).

—Robbery and burglary are not lesser included offenses of felony murder. People v. Zada, 82 A.D.2d 926, 440 N.Y.S.2d 672 (2d Dept. 1981).

—Possession of a weapon charge was not lesser included offense of burglary charge since one could threaten the immediate use of a dangerous instrument without actually possessing it; therefore, one could commit the burglary without also committing possession of a weapon. People v. Graham, 127 A.D.2d 443, 515 N.Y.S.2d 126 (3d Dept. 1987).

—Assault in the second degree is not a lesser included offense of attempted murder in the second degree. People v. Jansen, 118 A.D.2d 953, 499 N.Y.S.2d 984 (3d Dept. 1986); People v. Weibke, 119 A.D.2d 890, 501 N.Y.S.2d 189 (3d Dept. 1986).

—Because criminal facilitation requires some conduct which aids another in the commission of a crime, and such proof is unnecessary to establish criminal possession of stolen property in the second degree, there was no basis for request to have the former charged as a lesser included offense of the latter. People v. Calkins, 122 A.D.2d 452, 504 N.Y.S.2d 842 (3d Dept. 1986).

—Sexual abuse in any degree does not qualify as a lesser included offense of sodomy in the first degree since all degrees of sexual abuse require as an element that the sexual contact be for the purpose of gratifying the sexual desire of either party, whereas sodomy in the first degree does not. People v. Saddlemire, 121 A.D.2d 791, 504 N.Y.S.2d 240 (3d Dept. 1986).

Statutory purpose.—The purpose of the rule of 300.50(2) is not only to prevent the prosecution from failing where some element of the crime charged was not made out but also to empower the jury to extend mercy to an accused by finding a lesser degree of crime is established by the evidence. People v. Doyle, 3 A.D.3d 126, 770 N.Y.S.2d 318 (1st Dept. 2004).

Waiver.—A conviction for a lesser charge that is not a lesser included offense of one of the crimes charge is error, but is not jurisdictionally defective. If the defense has requested submission of the lesser charge, or has failed to object, the error is waived. People v. Ford, 62 N.Y.2d 275, 476 N.Y.S.2d 783, 465 N.E.2d 322 (1984).

—A court's erroneous submission of a lesser crime that arises out of the same transaction, but which does not qualify as a lesser included offense, is not a jurisdictional defect and is waived if timely objection is not made. People v. Hector, 295 A.D.2d 212, 744 N.Y.S.2d 370 (1st Dept. 2002).

—By specifically requesting that the court charge certain lesser included offenses, the defendant waived any alleged claim of error in connection with the submission of those offenses. People v. Green, 205 A.D.2d 637, 613 N.Y.S.2d 233 (2d. Dept. 1994).

—Defendant's argument that he was convicted of a lesser included offense which was not in fact a lesser included offense was not preserved for review since defendant failed to issue a trial protest and specifically requested that the court consider the charge in question. People v. Baldwin, 130 A.D.2d 666, 515 N.Y.S.2d 597 (2d Dept. 1987).

—Defense counsel waived trial court's error in submitting assault in the second degree as a lesser included offense of assault in the first degree by failing to object to the jury charge. People v. Haslip, 103 A.D.2d 807, 477 N.Y.S.2d 686 (2d Dept. 1984).

—Defendant waived any claim that court should have charged manslaughter in the first degree on the theory of extreme emotional disturbance where he neither requested such charge nor objected to the charge as given. People v. Mills, 105 A.D.2d 759, 481 N.Y.S.2d 411 (2d Dept. 1984).

—Pursuant to CPL § 300.50, it is well-settled that a defendant waives any error in submission of a lesser included offense unless an objection is made before the jury deliberations. People v. Heath, 269 A.D.2d 701, 705 N.Y.S.2d 85 (3d Dept. 2000).

—By failing to object to court's submission of charge of third-degree weapons possession as a lesser included offense, defendant waived any claim of error. People v. Dennis, 263 A.D.2d 618, 693 N.Y.S.2d 299 (3d Dept. 1999).

—Failure to object to the court's charge before the jury retires constitutes a waiver as to the charge on a lesser included offense. People v. Logolbo, 76 A.D.2d 990, 429 N.Y.S.2d 286 (3d Dept. 1980).

—Criminally negligent homicide is a lesser included offense of vehicular homicide. People v. White, 155 A.D.2d 953, 547 N.Y.S.2d 768 (4th Dept. 1990).

—Where the evidence is sufficient to support convictions for intentional murder and manslaughter in first degree, and defendant has requested a charge down to manslaughter in the second degree, he may not, on appeal, complain that the evidence will not sustain a conviction of the lesser charge. People v. Holliday, 74 A.D.2d 993, 427 N.Y.S.2d 105 (4th Dept. 1980).

Harmless error.—Defendant's challenge to the court's refusal to charge criminally negligent homicide was foreclosed by the jury's convicting him of manslaughter in the first degree, despite the availability of the lesser offense of manslaughter in the second degree. People v. Norman, 147 A.D.2d 717, 538 N.Y.S.2d 326 (2d Dept. 1989).

—Given the defendant's conviction on the top count of murder in the second degree despite the court's submission of the lesser-included count of manslaughter in the first degree, any error in failing to submit manslaughter in the second degree was harmless. People v. Hernandez, 148 A.D.2d 546, 538 N.Y.S.2d 874 (2d Dept. 1989).

—Court's error in informing jury that lesser included offense was being given at request of defense counsel was harmless. People v. McFayder, 127 A.D.2d 702, 511 N.Y.S.2d 904, 905 (2d Dept. 1987).

ARTICLE 310—JURY TRIAL—DELIBERATION AND VERDICT OF JURY

Section

LexisNexis Cross References

Criminal Law Advocacy, Vol. 2A, Ch. 5, Juror Misconduct; *Criminal Defense Techniques,* Vol. 1B, Ch. 38, Overturning Jury Verdicts; Vol. 1B, Ch. 38A, Impeachment of Partial Verdicts; *New York Criminal Practice (2d ed.),* Vol. 3, Ch. 39, Jury Deliberation and Verdict.

§ 310.10. Jury deliberation; requirement of; where conducted.

1. Following the court's charge, except as otherwise provided by subdivision two of this section, the jury must retire to deliberate upon its verdict in a place outside the courtroom. It must be provided with suitable accommodations therefor and must, except as otherwise provided in subdivision two of this section, be continuously kept together under the supervision of a court officer or court officers. In the event such court officer or court officers are not available, the jury shall be under the supervision of an appropriate public servant or public servants except when so authorized by the court or when performing administerial duties with respect to the jurors, such court officers or public servants, as the case may be, may not speak to or communicate with them or permit any other person to do so.

2. At any time after the jury has been charged or commenced its deliberations, and after notice to the parties and affording such parties an opportunity to be heard on the record outside of the presence of the jury, the court may declare the deliberations to be in recess and may thereupon direct the jury to suspend its deliberations and to separate for a reasonable period of time to be specified by the court, not to exceed twenty-four hours, except that in the case of a Saturday, Sunday or holiday, such separation may extend beyond such twenty-four hour period. Before each recess, the court must admonish the jury as provided in section 270.40 of this chapter and direct it not to resume its deliberations until all twelve jurors have reassembled in the designated place at the termination of the declared recess.

3. [*Repealed pursuant to L. 2001, Ch. 47, § 3, eff. May 30, 2001.*]

Amended by L. 2001, Ch. 47, amending subd. 2 and repealing subd. 3, eff. May 30, 2001.

ANNOTATIONS

Amendment; retroactive application of.—Amendment to CPL 310.10(2), which permits a court to declare jury deliberations to be in recess in any case without obtaining defendant's consent, is procedural and should be applied retroactively to defendant's case, in which trial court released deliberating jury for the weekend over defendant's objection and contrary to CPL 310.10 as it stood at that time. People v. Pena, 309 A.D.2d 687, 766 N.Y.S.2d 196 (1st Dept. 2003).

Judicial function; delegation, defendant's presence.—All communications with the jury, except those which are "ministerial" in nature, must be conveyed directly between the judge and the jury, in the presence of the defendant. People v. Torres, 72 N.Y.2d 1007, 534 N.Y.S.2d 914, 531 N.E.2d 635 (1988).

—The absence of the trial judge, and the delegation of some of his duties to his law secretary during part of the jury's deliberations, deprived the defendant of his right to a trial by jury, an integral component of which is the supervision of a judge, and the fact that defense counsel consented did not constitute a failure to preserve a question of law for our review or a waiver. People v. Ahmed, 66 N.Y.2d 307, 496 N.Y.S.2d 984, 487 N.E.2d 894 (1985).

—A trial court cannot delegate the judicial duty of communicating with the jury to a court officer unless the communication is deemed "ministerial" in nature. People v. Buxton, 192 A.D.2d 289, 601 N.Y.S.2d 132 (2d Dept.), *lv. denied,* 82 N.Y.2d 752 (1993).

—Only a "ministerial" communication can be had with the jury, by someone other than the trial judge and absent the presence of the defendant. People v. Lara, 199 A.D.2d 419, 605 N.Y.S.2d 339 (2d Dept. 1993).

Communications by court officers.—After jury had been instructed to cease deliberating, one or more of the jurors asked a court officer to inform the judge that a verdict had been reached. Court officer's supervisor told the jurors, without first contacting the court, that they would not be allowed to deliver the verdict until the next morning. The jury continued deliberating the next morning, and convicted the defendant of a count on which it had previously acquitted in the unreported verdict. Court found that the supervisor exceeded his ministerial duties and the scope of communications between court officers and jurors, resulting in the usurpation of the judicial function. Defendant was entitled to a new trial on the count for which he was convicted. People v. Khalek, 91 N.Y.2d 838, 666 N.Y.S.2d 1020, 689 N.E.2d 914 (1997).

—It is within the administerial duties of the court officer to tell jurors that they should stop deliberating and that they could start deliberating when they returned to court in the morning. People v. Nacey, 78 N.Y.2d 990, 575 N.Y.S.2d 265, 580 N.E.2d 751 (1991).

—Defendant was not entitled to reversal based on a communication between a court officer and the jury regarding procedures for disposal of the jury's confidential notes concerning their deliberations because the communication involved a purely administrative or ministerial matter that had nothing to do with any legal or factual issue or the mode of jury deliberations. People v. Bowen, 309 A.D.2d 600, 765 N.Y.S.2d 612 (1st Dept. 2003).

—Court officers were merely performing a ministerial act when they delivered copies of transcripts to the jury. People v. Espinal, 183 A.D.2d 407, 583 N.Y.S.2d 371 (1st Dept. 1992).

—Court's delegation to the court officer of the task of informing the jury that they shortly would be taken to dinner and sequestered concerned a ministerial matter and did not violate CPL § 310. People v. Ford, 161 A.D.2d 262, 554 N.Y.S.2d 905 (1st Dept. 1990).

—Court officer's unauthorized remark to a holdout juror that a jury could be sequestered for as long as five or six weeks before a mistrial would be declared constituted reversible error where the jury soon thereafter reached a verdict and the juror testified that, at the very least, she voted for conviction because of her concern about a lengthy sequestration even though she still believed the defendant to be not guilty. People v. Rukaj, 123 A.D.2d 277, 506 N.Y.S.2d 677 (1st Dept. 1986).

—Defendant was entitled to new trial where court officer usurped the court's function by permitting the jury to believe that it could allow one of their Spanish-speaking members to translate a letter written in Spanish into English; the juror's translation injected "nonrecord evidence into the calculus of judgment which a defendant cannot test or refute by cross-examination." People v. Flores, 282 A.D.2d 688, 725 N.Y.S.2d 655 (2d Dept. 2001).

—Court officer could properly perform the "ministerial" task of inquiring of the jurors, upon learning that they had reached a verdict, whether the verdict was unanimous. People v. Harrison, 192 A.D.2d 551, 596 N.Y.S.2d 97 (2d Dept.), lv. denied, 81 N.Y.2d 1073 (1993).

—Where the alleged communication between the court officer and the jury related to purely administrative matters—how late the jury would deliberate at the courthouse—the court was not required to conduct an inquiry into that communication. People v. Morales, 189 A.D.2d 785, 592 N.Y.S.2d 395 (2d Dept.), lv. denied, 81 N.Y.2d 1017 (1993).

—No error was committed where court officer, at the court's instruction, told the jurors to stop deliberating as they would be sequestered for the evening and that they should follow all of the court's prior instructions. People v. Smith, 181 A.D.2d 844, 581 N.Y.S.2d 398 (2d Dept. 1992).

—Court committed reversible error when it sent the clerk into the jury room with a message to "continue deliberating." People v. Jones, 159 A.D.2d 644, 553 N.Y.S.2d 37 (2d Dept. 1990).

—Defendant was not deprived of a fair trial by prison guard's entering jury room to obtain a cup of coffee since the guard did not speak to anyone. People v. Davilla, 120 A.D.2d 860, 502 N.Y.S.2d 535 (3d Dept. 1986).

—Court employee was merely performing a routinely undertaken and authorized administration duty when he inquired of the jury, while they were deliberating, whether they would need lodging accommodations for the evening or if they expected to reach a verdict, all made with the assurance that they were not being rushed; attendant was obviously prompted by a genuine concern for his ability of court personnel to ensure that motel rooms would be available for the jury panel should they be sequestered. People v. Demming, 116 A.D.2d 886, 498 N.Y.S.2d 203 (3d Dept.), lv. denied, 67 N.Y.2d 941 (1986).

Sequestration; keeping the jurors together.—Deviations from the statutory requirement that a deliberating jury be sequestered are unpreserved as a matter of law absent timely objection by defendants. People v. Agramonte, 87 N.Y.2d 765, 642 N.Y.S.2d 594, 665 N.E.2d 164 (1996).

—Court did not violate CPL § 310.10 by permitting one or more jurors to attend church services during the lunch recess after the trial had entered the deliberation phase. People v.

Fernandez, 81 N.Y.2d 1023, 599 N.Y.S.2d 911, 616 N.E.2d 497 (1993).

—Where defendant and his attorney have expressly agreed to the procedure, the court, in its discretion and with appropriate instructions, may permit deliberating jurors to return overnight to their homes separately and without supervision. People v. Webb, 78 N.Y.2d 335, 575 N.Y.S.2d 656, 581 N.E.2d 509 (1991).

—Trial court erred in allowing jurors during deliberations to go to their homes separately and unsupervised for dinner. People v. Coons, 75 N.Y.2d 796, 552 N.Y.S.2d 94, 551 N.E.2d 587 (1990).

—Court remanded for a hearing to determine whether or not a juror, who had been hospitalized after the commencement of deliberations, had been appropriately supervised and the nature and extent of conversations and outside contacts during the period of hospitalization. People v. Shanholtzer, 67 A.D.2d 860, 501 N.Y.S.2d 665 (1st Dept. 1986).

—Separation of jurors during deliberations for breaks to smoke cigarettes did not violate the sequestration requirement of CPL § 310.10, and the court officer's instruction to cease deliberations during the smoke breaks was ministerial in nature. People v. Manzo, 233 A.D.2d 529, 650 N.Y.S.2d 763 (2d Dept. 1996).

—It constitutes reversible error to permit alternate jurors to dine with regular jurors after deliberations have commenced. People v. Letizia, 155 A.D.2d 952, 547 N.Y.S.2d 767 (4th Dept. 1989).

—Reversible error was committed when, after the jurors had commenced deliberations, some of the jurors were transported to and from dinner unsupervised by court officers in direct contravention of the court's instructions. People v. Prosser, 130 A.D.2d 972, 516 N.Y.S.2d 559 (4th Dept. 1987).

—Reversible error was committed where one juror was allowed to go home while the remaining jurors were sequestered. People v. Thomas, 91 A.D.2d 857, 458 N.Y.S.2d 383 (4th Dept. 1982).

Sequestration; emergencies.—The trial court should determine in its discretion what course of action to follow when a juror becomes ill after deliberations commence; defense counsel, defendant and the public prosecutor should be informed as promptly as feasible, but treatment of an ill juror should not be required to await such notification, nor should the failure to notify counsel of such fact mandate reversal of the judgment, absent prejudice to the defendant; here the record established the fact that defendant suffered no prejudice by reason of the illness or the medical aid. People v. Prisco, 37 A.D.2d 369, 326 N.Y.S.2d 65 (1st Dept.), aff'd, 30 N.Y.2d 808, 334 N.Y.S.2d 905, 286 N.E.2d 279, cert. denied, 409 U.S. 1039 (1972).

—Where juror was complaining of symptoms related to an anxiety attack, trial judge properly sent the juror to the hospital accompanied by a court officer. People v. Colon, 211 A.D.2d 575, 621 N.Y.S.2d 606 (1st Dept.), lv. denied, 85 N.Y.2d 971 (1995).

—Trial court did not abuse its discretion when it released the jury over the weekend, after it had reached its verdict but before it could be announce, because a juror was rushed to the hospital; on Monday, the court recorded the verdict in the presence of the entire jury; by deliberately absenting himself from the courtroom on the day the verdict was announced, defendant forfeited his right to be present. People v. Webster, 205 A.D.2d 312, 613 N.Y.S.2d 12 (1st Dept. 1994).

—The need of a juror to respond to personal necessity does not constitute prohibited separation of the deliberating jury as contemplated by CPL § 310.10. People v. Russell, 179 A.D.2d 521, 579 N.Y.S.2d 18 (1st Dept. 1991).

—Court did not violate CPL § 310.10 by asking juror who claimed that he was nauseous to remain in the courtroom and be quickly examined by a medical technician while the other jurors were taken out of the courtroom. People v. Lee, 205 A.D.2d 558, 613 N.Y.S.2d 208 (2d Dept.), lv. denied, 84 N.Y.2d 828 (1994).

Sequestration; waiver.—Defendant does not have to personally consent to a waiver of sequestration pursuant to CPL § 310.10 People v. Bello, 82 N.Y.2d 862, 609 N.Y.S.2d 162, 631 N.E.2d 104 (1993).

—Defendant, by consenting to court's arrangements for accommodating jurors' religious observances, effectively waived his right to have the jury continuously sequestered. People v. Lilly, 187 A.D.2d 674, 590 N.Y.S.2d 253 (2d Dept. 1992), lv. denied, 81 N.Y.2d 973 (1993).

—Sequestration is not such an integral part of the right to a jury trial that it constitutes a fundamental or constitutional guaranteed right. People v. D'Alvia, 171 A.D.2d 96, 575 N.Y.S.2d 495 (2d Dept.), *lv. denied*, 78 N.Y.2d 1075 (1991).

—Defendant waived any claim that the court improperly failed to sequester the jury during deliberations, because the defendant, who was represented by counsel, agreed to allow the jury to go home. People v. Sealey, 239 A.D.2d 864, 659 N.Y.S.2d 639 (4th Dept. 1997).

—The trial court did not abuse its discretion by refusing to accept defendant's waiver of sequestration of the jury; the charges were serious and it was obvious from the responses of prospective jurors that the shootout and trial had received considerable attention in the media. People v. Alls, 195 A.D.2d 952, 601 N.Y.S.2d 749 (4th Dept.), *lv. denied*, 82 N.Y.2d 862 (1993).

§ 310.20. Jury deliberation; use of exhibits and other material.

Upon retiring to deliberate, the jurors may take with them:

1. Any exhibits received in evidence at the trial which the court, after according the parties an opportunity to be heard upon the matter, in its discretion permits them to take;

2. A written list prepared by the court containing the offenses submitted to the jury by the court in its charge and the possible verdicts thereon. Whenever the court submits two or more counts charging offenses set forth in the same article of the law, the court may set forth the dates, names of complainants or specific statutory language, without defining the terms, by which the counts may be distinguished; provided, however, that the court shall instruct the jury in its charge that the sole purpose of the notations is to distinguish between the counts; and

3. A written list prepared by the court containing the names of every witness whose testimony has been presented during the trial, if the jury requests such a list and the court, in its discretion, determines that such a list will assist the jury.

Amended by L. 1996, Ch. 630, § 2, amending subd. 2, effective October 4, 1996; L. 1999, Ch. 66, eff. June 8, 1999, amending subds. 1 and 2 and adding subd. 3; L. 2002, Ch. 588, eff. Sept. 24, 2002, amending subd. 2.

ANNOTATIONS

Note taking by jurors.—It is within the sound discretion of trial courts to allow note taking by jurors during a trial. Here, the trial court did not mandate that jurors take notes nor did it indicate that it was their duty to take notes, and it gave appropriate cautionary instructions at the beginning of the trial and prior to deliberations on the taking of notes and their use. People v. Hues, 92 N.Y.2d 413, 681 N.Y.S.2d 779, 704 N.E.2d 546 (1998).

—Mere fact that juror took notes of court's supplemental instruction, and took those notes into deliberation room, did not call for reversal. People v. Tucker, 77 N.Y.2d 861, 568 N.Y.S.2d 342, 569 N.E.2d 1021 (1991).

—The decision as to whether the jurors should be permitted to take notes is properly left to the discretion of the trial court; however, it is essential that preliminary cautionary instructions be given with respect to the taking and the use of such notes and these instructions should be repeated at the conclusion of the case as part of the court's charge prior to deliberations. People v. DiLuca, 85 A.D.2d 439, 448 N.Y.S.2d 730 (2d Dept. 1982).

Verdict sheet.—The submission of an annotated verdict sheet, not consented to by counsel, cannot be deemed harmless. People v. Damiano, 87 N.Y.2d 477, 640 N.Y.S.2d 451, 663 N.E.2d 607 (1996).

—The trial court did not err in including on the verdict sheet a direction regarding the order in which the submitted charges should be considered. People v. Cole, 85 N.Y.2d 990, 629 N.Y.S.2d 166, 652 N.E.2d 912 (1995).

—Unless the parties agree, it is reversible error for a trial court to give the jury a verdict sheet that, in addition to listing the counts, also lists some of the statutory elements of the counts. People v. Spivey, 81 N.Y.2d 356, 599 N.Y.S.2d 477, 615 N.E.2d 961 (1993).

—It was reversible error for the trial court to submit to the jury a verdict sheet which, in addition to enumerating the crimes charged and possible verdicts, instructed the jury on the order in which the charges should be considered and the effect of a determination that the prosecution failed to disprove justification. People v. Sotomayor, 79 N.Y.2d 1029, 584 N.Y.S.2d 431, 594 N.E.2d 925 (1992).

—It was error for the trial court to give the jury a verdict sheet, over defendant's objection, that, in addition to listing the charged crimes, also listed some of the robbery counts statutory elements. People v. Kelly, 76 N.Y.2d 1013, 565 N.Y.S.2d 754, 566 N.E.2d 1159 (1990).

—It is error to submit verdict sheets that, in addition to listing the charged crimes and the possible verdicts, also list some or all of the statutory elements, unless the parties consent. People v. Taylor, 76 N.Y.2d 873, 560 N.Y.S.2d 982, 561 N.E.2d 882 (1990).

—Reversal is required where the trial judge submits to the jury a verdict sheet listing the various counts and defining the elements of each count, in the absence of the consent of the parties. People v. Nimmons, 72 N.Y.2d 830, 530 N.Y.S.2d 543, 526 N.E.2d 33 (1988).

—Verdict sheet prepared by the court, pursuant to CPL § 310.20(2), which first enumerated the alternative of finding the defendant "not guilty of anything" and, thereafter, the fifteen possible permutations of charges under which the defendant could be found guilty of one or more, unduly emphasized the options of guilt and the better course would have been for the court simply to have instructed the jury that it could find the defendant guilty or not guilty on each of the four counts. People v. Piazza, 48 N.Y.2d 151, 422 N.Y.S.2d 9, 397 N.E.2d 700 (1979).

—A one-sentence procedural direction to the jury to consider the second count only in the alternative to the first, included by the trial court on the verdict sheet, was not improper. People v. Andujar, 202 A.D.2d 316, 609 N.Y.S.2d 205 (1st Dept. 1994).

—The annotations on co-defendant's verdict sheet were not inherently prejudicial to the defendant, and they provided the same information as did the court's instructions. People v. Bryant, 246 A.D.2d 662, 668 N.Y.S.2d 231 (2d Dept. 1998).

—Court did not violate CPL § 310.20(2) when it submitted a verdict sheet with notes instructing the jury on the order to consider the charges, because the notes were just directions regarding the order in which the submitted charges should be considered, and such directions are proper. People v. Amante, 242 A.D.2d 275, 660 N.Y.S.2d 589 (2d Dept. 1997).

—The court did not commit reversible error in directing a clerk to deliver a new verdict sheet with instructions to the members of the jury that they should use the new verdict sheet to record their verdict, where jurors had sent a note saying that they had made a written mistake on the original verdict sheet. People v. Jacob, 202 A.D.2d 444, 608 N.Y.S.2d 508 (2d Dept. 1994).

—A trial court may not given a jury a verdict sheet that, in addition to listing the counts, also lists some of the statutory elements of the counts. People v. Percinthe, 200 A.D.2d 773, 607 N.Y.S.2d 370 (2d Dept. 1994).

—The submission of a verdict sheet to the jury which specifies the elements of the count charged is not authorized by CPL § 310.20(2) and constitutes reversible error absent consent of the parties. People v. Rodriguez, 159 A.D.2d 736, 553 N.Y.S.2d 446 (2d Dept. 1990).

—Defendant's objection to the verdict sheet was untimely when it was made after the jury began deliberations. People v. McKenzie, 148 A.D.2d 472, 539 N.Y.S.2d 20 (2d Dept. 1989).

—It was improper for the court, after reciting its instructions orally, to submit to the jury a verdict sheet containing only certain portions of that charge for their use in deliberations. People v. Testaverde, 143 A.D.2d 208, 532 N.Y.S.2d 12 (2d Dept. 1988).

—Submission to the jury of a verdict sheet which defines the elements of each count contained therein is not authorized by CPL § 310.20(2) and absent the consent of the parties constitutes per se reversible error. People v. Valle, 143 A.D.2d 160, 531 N.Y.S.2d 929 (2d Dept. 1988).

—CPL § 310.20 has been amended to allow the submission of annotated verdict sheets but the amendment does not apply retroactively to defendant's trial. People v. Gerstner, 270 A.D.2d 837, 706 N.Y.S.2d 542 (4th Dept. 2000).

—Supreme Court was not required to obtain defendant's consent to include statutory language on the verdict sheet to assist the jury in distinguishing among three counts of second-degree murder. People v. Andrews, 267 A.D.2d 1071, 701 N.Y.S.2d 760 (4th Dept. 1999).

—Statutory amendments that allow annotated verdict sheets similar to the one employed by the court in this case do not apply retroactively; conviction reversed where court submitted annotated verdict sheet before the statute was amended. People v. Richardson, 234 A.D.2d 952, 652 N.Y.S.2d 173 (4th Dept. 1996).

Exhibits.—CPLR § 310.20(1) grants the trial court discretion to allow the jury to view any exhibit received in evidence at trial, but no provision authorizes submission of unadmitted exhibits; departure from this rule affects important rights since an unadmitted exhibit has not undergone the test of cross-examination and its consideration by the jury directly infringes on the defendant's right of confrontation. People v. Bouton, 50 N.Y.2d 130, 428 N.Y.S.2d 218, 405 N.E.2d 699 (1980).

—Court's refusal to allow the jury to experiment with a gun and shorts that had been introduced into evidence did not constitute reversible error. People v. Isaac, 214 A.D.2d 749, 625 N.Y.S.2d 635 (2d Dept. 1995).

—Court erred in granting jury's request to have an item not in evidence (an armless chair) sent into the jury room without first notifying counsel, however, error was harmless; claim that the jury used the chair in order to reenact the crime is sheer speculation. People v. Gallagher, 116 A.D.2d 299, 501 N.Y.S.2d 355 (2d Dept. 1986).

—The defendant was not prejudiced when an exhibit was inadvertently left out of the jury room during deliberations; the jury had full opportunity to hear testimony concerning this item and their understanding of this testimony would not have been heightened by the physical presence of this particular exhibit in the jury room. People v. Van Ostrand, 157 A.D.2d 875, 550 N.Y.S.2d 147 (3d Dept. 1990).

—The trial court should not have permitted the jury to bring a legal dictionary into the jury room, even though the defense consented. People v. Coleman, 210 A.D.2d 977, 621 N.Y.S.2d 244 (4th Dept. 1994).

Transcripts.—Court properly permitted jurors to use transcripts of tape recordings during deliberations, where their accuracy was sufficiently established, and the court delivered cautionary instructions. People v. Robinson, 158 A.D.2d 628, 551 N.Y.S.2d 599 (2d Dept. 1990).

—Court properly permitted the jury, during deliberations and at their request, to examine an English transcription of a tape recording in Spanish since there was sufficient proof as to the accuracy of the transcript and the admissibility of such a transcript is generally left to the sound discretion of the trial judge. People v. Tapia, 114 A.D.2d 983, 495 N.Y.S.2d 93 (2d Dept. 1985), lv. denied, 67 N.Y.2d 951 (1986).

—Court properly permitted jurors to use transcripts after giving appropriate cautionary instructions. People v. Charron, 198 A.D.2d 722, 604 N.Y.S.2d 311 (3d Dept. 1993), lv. denied, 83 N.Y.2d 803 (1994).

—Jurors' use of transcripts, which had been received in evidence, did not deprive defendant of a fair trial where the circumstances under which they were made and the persons responsible for them were subject to extensive cross-examination and the judge gave specific instructions both at the time the tapes were being played and in its charge. People v. Kuss, 81 A.D.2d 427, 42 N.Y.S.2d 313 (4th Dept. 1981).

Waiver of objections; verdict sheet.—Defendant failed to preserve challenge to the annotation of the verdict sheet; in any event, the annotations which merely indicated the date and

victim to which each of the virtually identical 42 counts applied, posed no risk of skewing the jury's deliberations. People v. McFarlane, 205 A.D.2d 447, 613 N.Y.S.2d 895 (1st Dept. 1994).

—Where defendant consented to the court's submission of a verdict sheet to the jury, the error, if any, was waived. People v. Sanders, 176 A.D.2d 309, 574 N.Y.S.2d 577 (1st Dept. 1991).

—In the absence of a protest the court declined to reach claim that trial court erred in submitting to the jury a verdict sheet containing the elements of the crimes charged. People v. Moore, 149 A.D.2d 739, 540 N.Y.S.2d 523 (2d Dept. 1989).

—Contention that submission of a verdict sheet to the jury deprived defendant of a fair trial was not preserved for appellate review. People v. Braithwaite, 154 A.D.2d 543, 546 N.Y.S.2d 164, 165 (2d Dept. 1989).

—Defendant's contention that the trial court committed reversible error when it sua sponte submitted a verdict sheet to the jury which contained selected portions of the court's oral charge was not preserved for appellate review since no objection was taken by the defense counsel. People v. Davis, 155 A.D.2d 609, 547 N.Y.S.2d 665 (2d Dept. 1989).

—A defendant may impliedly consent to submission of an annotated verdict sheet if the defendant is given an adequate opportunity to review the verdict sheet and objects only to a portion of it. The failure to object to the remainder of the verdict sheet constitutes implicit consent to the remaining annotations. People v. Washington, 9 A.D.3d 499, 779 N.Y.S.2d 303 (3d Dept. 2004).

Waiver of objections; general.—While appellate review of a trial court's improper use of a court clerk to instruct the jury foreperson concerning the verdict sheet would not be precluded by a defendant's failure to object thereto, review was precluded by the absence of any record of what the clerk said, if anything, to the foreperson; there is a presumption of regularity in the absence of substantial evidence to the contrary. People v. Pizarro, 190 A.D.2d 634, 594 N.Y.S.2d 159 (1st Dept. 1993).

—When an error in the charge comes at the request of the defendant, he may not be heard to complain on appeal. People v. Scarnati, 140 A.D.2d 469, 528 N.Y.S.2d 166 (2d Dept. 1988).

§ 310.30. Jury deliberation; request for information.

At any time during its deliberation, the jury may request the court for further instruction or information with respect to the law, with respect to the content or substance of any trial evidence, or with respect to any other matter pertinent to the jury's consideration of the case. Upon such a request, the court must direct that the jury be returned to the courtroom and, after notice to both the people and counsel for the defendant, and in the presence of the defendant, must give such requested information or instruction as the court deems proper. With the consent of the parties and upon the request of the jury for further instruction with respect to a statute, the court may also give to the jury copies of the text of any statute which, in its discretion, the court deems proper.

Amended by L. 1980, Ch. 208.

ANNOTATIONS

Jury questions, request for clarification.—Reversal was not required where the court's communication with the jury merely constituted a request for clarification as to what the jury wanted and conveyed no information pertaining to the law or facts of the case, and did not channel or limit the jury's question. People v. Lykes, 81 N.Y.2d 767, 593 N.Y.S.2d 779, 609 N.E.2d 132 (1993).

—Reversal required, where trial court improperly permitted the clerk, outside of its presence, to clarify its unlawful imprisonment charge to the jury, because this constituted an improper delegation of judicial authority, and it abridged defendant's right to be present at a critical stage of the trial; harmless error analysis was not applicable to this violation. People v. Galdamez, 234 A.D.2d 608, 652 N.Y.S.2d 65 (2d Dept. 1996).

Questions, requests by jurors: readback of testimony.— When a defendant objects to any technique that a trial court's proposes to use to provide testimony to a jury, which constitutes anything other than a readback—e.g., a transcript—the trial court must direct a readback in the courtroom, with defendant and counsel present. People v. Colon, 151 A.D.2d 146, 547 N.Y.S.2d 11 (1st Dept. 1989), *lv. denied*, 75 N.Y.2d 1052 (1990), *cert. denied*, 113 S. Ct. 2376.

—Court did not unduly restrict the jury's right to have testimony read back by suggesting that it would be "helpful" if the request for a read back of testimony was limited to relevant portions of the testimony which might aid the jury in its deliberations. People v. Charkow, 142 A.D.2d 734, 531 N.Y.S.2d 120, 121 (2d Dept. 1988).

—Court did not err in granting jury's request to have certain testimony read back during its deliberations on Sunday. People v. Kramer, 132 A.D.2d 708, 518 N.Y.S.2d 189 (2d Dept. 1987).

—The trial court improperly influenced the jury to rescind its request to hear certain testimony again where judge called a recess and insisted that the jury submit another written request if it wanted to hear certain testimony again. People v. Ravenell, 82 A.D.2d 868, 440 N.Y.S.2d (2d Dept. 1981).

—When court informed jury that there would be a delay in reading back requested testimony, and jury reached a verdict before hearing that testimony, reversal was not required since the court, prior to accepting the verdict, offered the testimony to the jury, and the jury declined the offer. People v. Sturgis, 124 A.D.2d 1045, 508 N.Y.S.2d 751 (4th Dept. 1986).

Response to jury questions, manner and timing.—The trial court's spontaneous response to an oral question posed by a deliberating juror while the court was in the midst of responding, after full consultation with counsel, to a written jury request for clarification on the charges, did not violate defendant's rights. People v. Maxwell, 235 A.D.2d 229, 652 N.Y.S.2d 271 (1st Dept. 1997).

—The court's failure to suspend jury deliberations until a response could be given to the jury's request in the defendant's presence warranted reversal. People v. Morse, 182 A.D.2d 781, 582 N.Y.S.2d 776 (2d Dept. 1992).

—Trial courts confronted with requests for supplemental instructions must perform the delicate operation of fashioning a response which meaningfully answers the jury's inquiry while at the same time working no prejudice to the defendant. People v. Williamson, 267 A.D.2d 487, 699 N.Y.S.2d 749 (3d Dept. 1999).

—Trial court erred by permitting a two-hour delay to take place between a jury question and court's response. People v. Hall, 101 A.D.2d 956, 477 N.Y.S.2d 439 (3d Dept. 1984).

Court's failure to disclose juror's note to defense counsel.—Where court responded to jury's note without first disclosing its contents to counsel outside the presence of the jury, court's conduct was inherently prejudicial and not subject to harmless error analysis. People v. Heath, 234 A.D.2d 388, 651 N.Y.S.2d 551 (2d Dept. 1996). *See also* People v. O'Rama, 78 N.Y.2d 270, 574 N.Y.S.2d 159, 579 N.E.2d 189 (1991); People v. Cook, 85 N.Y.2d 928, 626 N.Y.S.2d 1000, 650 N.E.2d 847 (1995).

—Where jury note to court stated, "[w]e feel we have quite a bit more time deliberating. How long will you want us to deliberate tonight? We will need to make calls if necessary," and record did not indicate that court disclosed contents of note to counsel, read it in open court, or responded to jury, court did not violate CPL § 310.30, because note was merely a response to a question posed by court in open court a few minutes earlier, the note did not request any substantive information or concern the crimes charged, the evidence, or any key issue. People v. Fontanez, 254 A.D.2d 762, 679 N.Y.S.2d 222 (4th Dept. 1998).

—Court erred by failing to read into the record a jury note requesting clarification of two counts of the indictment, and by failing to afford defense counsel an opportunity to be heard before responding; conviction under those counts was reversed. People v. Sanchez, 244 A.D.2d 922, 668 N.Y.S.2d 125 (4th Dept. 1997).

—Conviction of sexual abuse in first and second degree reversed, where trial court erred in failing to read into the record a jury note requesting further instruction on sexual abuse in the first and second degree, failing to make the note part of the record, and failing to give counsel notice of the actual specific content of the jurors' request. People v. Roberts, 236 A.D.2d 848, 653 N.Y.S.2d 1002 (4th Dept. 1997).

Refusal, failure to respond to jury questions, requests, and notes.—Court did not err in refusing the jury's request to "hear" the original police robbery report where the report in question was not in evidence. People v. Ramon, 182 A.D.2d 519, 582 N.Y.S.2d 196 (1st Dept. 1992).

—Not every failure to comply with a jury's request for information during deliberation is reversible error. People v. Hawkins, 173 A.D.2d 358, 569 N.Y.S.2d 728 (1st Dept. 1991).

—A court should have discretion to determine whether to permit jurors' questions. People v. Wilds, 141 A.D.2d 395, 529 N.Y.S.2d 325 (1st Dept. 1988).

—Since a summation is only one party's argument and does not constitute evidence, the trial court properly exercised its discretion in declining the jury's request to reread defense counsel's summation. People v. Santana, 121 A.D.2d 236, 502 N.Y.S.2d 751 (1st Dept. 1986).

—Court did not err in refusing jury's request to have defense counsel's summation reread since the content of counsel's summation was not evidence. People v. McClary, 197 A.D.2d 640, 602 N.Y.S.2d 680 (2d Dept. 1993); *see also* People v. Foster, 118 A.D.2d 654, 499 N.Y.S.2d 808 (2d Dept.), *lv. denied*, 67 N.Y.2d 1052 (1986).

—Where jury submitted a question to the court asking what the consequences of merely being present during a drug transaction were and whether presence was sufficient to establish guilt of a crime, court's refusal to respond directly to the inquiry did not constitute a meaningful response to the request, and the defendant was entitled to a new trial. People v. Henning, 271 A.D.2d 813, 706 N.Y.S.2d 748 (3d Dept. 2000).

Supplemental instructions, sufficiency.—The court did not err in denying a reinstruction on intoxication in the supplemental instruction inasmuch as the jury did not ask for reinstruction on that issue but only on the elements of the crime charged. People v. Allen, 69 N.Y.2d 915, 516 N.Y.S.2d 199, 200, 508 N.E.2d 934 (1987).

—Where jury requested guidance concerning a stain on the jeans of the rape victim, it was error for the court to fail to give, after a specific request, a cautionary instruction against the jury speculating on the meaning of any evidence before it. People v. Betts, 70 N.Y.2d 289, 520 N.Y.S.2d 370, 514 N.E.2d 865 (1987).

—While the trial court possesses some discretion in responding to inquiries from the jury during deliberations, it is well-settled that the court must respond meaningfully. People v. Faulkner, 195 A.D.2d 384, 600 N.Y.S.2d 231 (1st Dept. 1993).

—Court's mere rereading of elements of robbery in the third degree was in accordance with the jury's request notwithstanding the court's failure to reinstruct the jury on intent and force. People v. DeCosta, 149 A.D.2d 723, 540 N.Y.S.2d 513 (2d Dept. 1989).

—Court did not err in omitting from its supplemental charge a reinstruction on the intoxication issue inasmuch as the jury did not request instruction on that issue, but only on the law as it pertained to the mental operation of intent. People v. Wilkinson, 139 A.D.2d 682, 527 N.Y.S.2d 436 (2d Dept. 1988).

—Although the court accepted the jury's verdict prior to completion of the readback of the complainant's testimony, any error was harmless where the omitted portions pertained to charges of which the defendant was acquitted. People v. Louridio, 124 A.D.2d 598, 507 N.Y.S.2d 740 (2d Dept. 1986).

—Court erred by replying to such jury question as to whose responsibility it was to prove knowledge of the existence of a gun in a car as follows: "It doesn't really make any difference who proves what so long as when you look at that evidence, if you are satisfied beyond a reasonable doubt, you will find the defendant guilty," thereby failing to reply to the jury's question with a meaningful response. People v. Hall, 101 A.D.2d 956, 477 N.Y.S.2d 439 (3d Dept. 1984).

—While the manner in which a trial court responds to a jury request is largely discretionary, the response must be meaningful. People v. Berger, 188 A.D.2d 1073, 592 N.Y.S.2d 173 (4th Dept. 1992), *lv. denied*, 81 N.Y.2d 881 (1993).

Supplemental instructions; rereading original charge.— Where the jury requested clarification of the term "beyond a reasonable doubt," the court did not err in rereading its original charge, since the jury gave no indication after the repetition that their concerns about the definition were not satisfied. People v. Malloy, 55 N.Y.2d 296, 449 N.Y.S.2d 168, 434 N.E.2d 237 (1982), *cert. denied,* 459 U.S. 847 (1982).

—There is no prohibition against a rereading of an instruction when it is clear and unambiguous in the first instance. People v. Rodriguez, 153 A.D.2d 762, 545 N.Y.S.2d 44 (2d Dept. 1989), *lv. denied,* 75 N.Y.2d 775 (1990).

—In prosecution for drug possession the issue of whether the Trial Justice committed reversible error when he essentially reread his original charge defining "possession" "constructive possession" and "reasonable doubt" after the jury sought an explanation "in laymen's terms" of these concepts was not preserved for appeal since no objection was taken to the supplemental charge and in light of the overwhelming evidence of the defendant's guilt. People v. Gonzales, 77 A.D.2d 654, 430 N.Y.S.2d 655 (2d Dept. 1980).

—It was error for the court, on being requested six times for further instructions on the issue of justification, to reiterate original instructions; the court should have clarified initial charge and marshaled evidence to explain legal implications of possible findings of fact to law of justification. People v. Brabham, 77 A.D.2d 626, 430 N.Y.S.2d 123 (2d Dept. 1980).

—Court's response to jury note requesting reinstruction on the requirements for justification of reiterating its original instructions on justification was proper where the form of the jury's notes evinced no confusion or dissatisfaction with the court's charge and the jury asked no specific questions which the court failed to answer. People v. Davis, 118 A.D.2d 206, 504 N.Y.S.2d 885 (4th Dept.), *lv. denied,* 68 N.Y.2d 768 (1986).

Written instructions.—Defendant claims that the instruction to consider counts of second and third degree burglary in the alternative involved a substantive legal principle and the court was thus required to recall the jury and charge it orally to that effect. The court disagreed because CPL § 310.20(2) specifically authorized written communication. People v. Collins, 99 N.Y.2d 14, 750 N.Y.S.2d 814, 780 N.E.2d 499 (2002).

—The court erred in complying with a jury request for a written copy of the entire charge, including statutory textual material, over the defendant's objections. People v. Johnson, 81 N.Y.2d 980, 599 N.Y.S.2d 525, 615 N.E.2d 1009 (1993).

—Unlike the marshaling of evidence—which is statutorily authorized and constitutes error only when an imbalance results in prejudice to the defendant—the distribution of written instructions to the jury is not expressly authorized by law and error in such submissions cannot be deemed harmless. People v. Owens, 69 N.Y.2d 585, 516 N.Y.S.2d 619, 509 N.E.2d 314 (1987).

—An error in submitting written instructions to the jury may not be considered harmless. People v. Brooks, 70 N.Y.2d 896, 524 N.Y.S.2d 382, 519 N.E.2d 293 (1987).

—The consent of defense counsel is an "absolute precondition" to furnishing the jury with the text of a statute. People v. Sanders, 70 N.Y.2d 837, 523 N.Y.S.2d 444, 517 N.E.2d 1330 (1987).

—The decision of the trial court to give the jury a portion of the jury charge in writing, over defendant's objection, constituted reversible error. People v. Wilson, 149 A.D.2d 376, 540 N.Y.S.2d 242 (1st Dept. 1989).

—Submission of portions of the court's charge to the jury, over objection of the defendant, required reversal. People v. Westergren, 134 A.D.2d 185, 520 N.Y.S.2d 774 (1st Dept. 1987).

—Reversal was required where portions of the final charge submitted in writing, particularly that portion on identification, highlighted certain principles to the exclusion of others, without including the countervailing principles favorable to the defendant. People v. Rhyne, 121 A.D.2d 954, 504 N.Y.S.2d 665 (1st Dept. 1986).

—Error of court in providing the jury with final written instructions comprised solely of the elements of the crimes charged without any reference to countervailing principles favorable to the defendant was not subject to harmless error analysis. People v. Diaz, 145 A.D.2d 331, 534 N.Y.S.2d 992 (2d Dept. 1988).

Juror coercion; improper influence.—It is prejudicial error requiring reversal when a juror "tests" the veracity of a key witness' testimony be re-enacting the situation in which the witness stated he had observed the defendant and then relates the test results to other jurors People v. Brown, 48 N.Y.2d 388, 423 N.Y.S.2d 461, 399 N.E.2d 51 (1979).

—A charge that stresses the need for a verdict at expense of the individual juror's judgment mandates reversal. People v. Aponte, 306 A.D.2d 42, 759 N.Y.S.2d 486 (1st Dept. 2003), *aff'd,* 2 N.Y.3d 304, 778 N.Y.S.2d 447, 810 N.E.2d 899 (2004).

—Conviction should be reversed where a juror told the court during the course of deliberation about a genuine, perceived, physical coercion of herself by another juror and the court ignored it. People v. Lavender, 117 A.D.2d 253, 502 N.Y.S.2d 439 (1st Dept.), *appeal dism'd,* 68 N.Y.2d 195 (1986).

—Generally, post-verdict affidavits will only be considered for the purpose of impeaching a jury verdict when there is a showing of the injection of improper outside influences into the jurors' deliberations. People v. Hammond, 132 A.D.2d 849, 518 N.Y.S.2d 60 (3d Dept. 1987).

Jury coercion; *Allen* charge.—Court's supplemental instruction overemphasized the jury's obligation to return a verdict and failed to advise the jurors that they should not surrender a conscientiously held belief. Defendant was entitled to an uncoerced, unanimous jury verdict, not one tainted by the improper jury instructions the court gave. People v. Aponte, 2 N.Y.3d 304, 778 N.Y.S.2d 447, 810 N.E.2d 899 (2004).

—Court erred in its supplemental instruction to the deadlocked jury that it, the court, "could have decided this case in ten minutes, or less" and that the jurors should not "go in with a feeling that the person is guilty or not guilty." People v. Riley, 70 N.Y.2d 523, 522 N.Y.S.2d 842, 847, 517 N.E.2d 520 (1987).

—Allen charge was coercive and constituted reversible error where court repeatedly stressed the desirability of reaching a verdict by means of supplemental charges, singled out the dissenting juror by its comments, and suggested that the jury would continue deliberations until the court decided that said deliberations should be terminated. People v. Diaz, 66 N.Y.2d 744, 497 N.Y.S.2d 359, 488 N.E.2d 105 (1985).

—Judge's supplemental instructions to a deadlocked jury were proper where, in essence, he simply asked the jury to exert its best efforts and renew deliberations; no jurors were singled out for noncompliance with the majority or were there any threats or suggestions that the jury would be forced to continue deliberations indefinitely without outside communication should they fail to reach an agreement. People v. Pagan, 45 N.Y.2d 725, 408 N.Y.S.2d 473, 380 N.E.2d 299 (1978).

—The jury's verdict was proper where the jury, under the trial judge's instructions, was held until the verdict was rendered at 3:27 a.m., following an afternoon and evening of deliberation after a two-day, second trial since there was no evidence of fatigue or distress on the part of the jurors and the defense counsel had not requested that deliberations be recessed to the following day. People v. Crandall, 45 N.Y.2d 851, 410 N.Y.S.2d 66, 382 N.E.2d 766 (1978).

—The trial justice statement, absent improper conduct, remarks or innuendos, that if the jury were unable to reach a verdict within a period of approximately an hour and a quarter they would be sequestered at a hotel for the night was proper. People v. Sharff, 38 N.Y.2d 751, 381 N.Y.S.2d 48, 343 N.E.2d 765 (1975).

—A statement that the court or jury could have decided the case in a matter of minutes or less is as characterizing a case as simple or not difficult. People v. Grant, 163 A.D.2d 117, 558 N.Y.S.2d 927 (1st Dept. 1990).

—Characterizing a case as "a very simple case" can have the effect of embarrassing the jury for not having already reached a verdict and is an inappropriate statement for the court to make. People v. Stokes, 139 A.D.2d 428, 527 N.Y.S.2d 19 (1st Dept. 1988).

—Court's pride in its reputation for not having deadlocked juries is not an appropriate consideration to be presented to jurors in the discharge of their function. People v. King, 136 A.D.2d 475, 523 N.Y.S.2d 114 (1st Dept. 1988).

—It was reversible error for the trial judge to instruct the jury that the minority should reconcile their differences with the majority and that they have a responsibility to reach a verdict. People v. Robinson, 84 A.D.2d 732, 444 N.Y.S.2d 82 (1st Dept. 1981).

—The trial court did not coerce a verdict when it informed the jurors that the time required for dinner would preclude further deliberations that evening. People v. Ramos, 181 A.D.2d 837, 581 N.Y.S.2d 392 (2d Dept. 1992).

—Court's remark to jury at conclusion of its charge that "I think when you go in that jury room to deliberate that hopefully you might have a verdict this afternoon" did not prejudice the defendant where the jury continued its deliberations overnight. People v. Bilello, 124 A.D.2d 665, 507 N.Y.S.2d 910 (2d Dept. 1986).

—Court erred in directing its instructions with respect to the jurors' duty to reconcile their differing views only at the jurors who were in favor of acquittal, and in repeatedly urging the jurors to attempt to reach a verdict but only fleetingly alluding to the jurors' duty not to abandon their consciously-held beliefs. People v. Nieves, 124 A.D.2d 603, 507 N.Y.2d 747 (2d Dept. 1986).

—A new trial was granted where after a day of deliberation the trial judge instructed the jury that if they had not reached a verdict, they would be sequestered for the night, it is unclear whether the jury interpreted the remarks as coercive and prejudicial and, neither defendants nor their attorneys were present at the time. People v. Eadie, 83 A.D.2d 773, 443 N.Y.S.2d 477 (4th Dept. 1981).

Jury questions; translation of information.—Jurors were not entitled to hear an official translation of the Spanish-language *Miranda* form by a court interpreter during deliberations because permitting the official translation after the close of the evidence would have deprived the People of the right to cross-examine the court interpreter. People v. Arreaga, 17 A.D.3d 604, 793 N.Y.S.2d 179 (2d Dept. 2005).

Defendant's rights to notice and to be present.—Court violated defendant's right to be heard before court responded to a jury note, by refusing to permit defense counsel to suggest responses to the note. People v. Cook, 85 N.Y.2d 928, 626 N.Y.S.2d 1000, 650 N.E.2d 847 (1995).

—Defense counsel must have notice of jury requests, so counsel can be heard before the court's response is given. People v. DeRosario, 81 N.Y.2d 801, 595 N.Y.S.2d 372, 611 N.E.2d 273 (1993).

—Trial court committed reversible error when it failed to disclose contents of note from the jurors before responding with an *Allen* charge. People v. O'Rama, 78 N.Y.2d 270, 574 N.Y.S.2d 159, 579 N.E.2d 189 (1991).

—Defendant's right to be present was not violated by his absence from a colloquy between his attorney and the trial judge which took place outside the jury's presence, involving the sufficiency of the readback. People v. Rodriguez, 76 N.Y.2d 918, 563 N.Y.S.2d 48, 564 N.E.2d 658 (1990).

—The presence of the defendant and his counsel is constitutionally required whenever supplemental instructions are given, and failure to notify them is fundamental error. People v. Ciaccio, 47 N.Y.2d 431, 418 N.Y.S.2d 371, 391 N.E.2d 1347 (1979).

—The right to be present during supplemental instructions is absolute and unequivocal and cannot be waived by defense counsel. People v. Pegeise, 195 A.D.2d 337, 600 N.Y.S.2d 26 (1st Dept. 1993).

—The court committed reversible error when it gave supplemental instructions to the jury, in the absence of the defendant, without making inquiry and reciting on the record the facts and reasons it relied upon in determining that the defendant's absence was deliberate. People v. Aguilar, 177 A.D.2d 197, 582 N.Y.S.2d 383 (1st Dept. 1992).

—Not every communication with a deliberating jury requires the participation of the court or the presence of the accused. People v. Lanfronco, 176 A.D.2d 201, 574 N.Y.S.2d 323 (1st Dept. 1991), *lv. denied*, 79 N.Y.2d 828 (1992).

—Reversal was required where the court directed the court officer, outside the presence of the defendant and his attorney, to inform the jury that they were not to discuss the case among themselves until their return to court the following morning. People v. Hernandez, 157 A.D.2d 472, 549 N.Y.S.2d 396 (1st Dept. 1990).

—Court rejected defendant's contention that is was error for the trial court to respond orally, without prior notice to the attorneys, to certain questions by the jury during deliberations; while it would have been preferable for the court to observe the statutory requirement to give counsel meaningful prior notice of jury questions during deliberations, the court's failure to do so did not seriously prejudice the defendant under the facts of the case. People v. Austin, 199 A.D.2d 325, 605 N.Y.S.2d 103 (2d Dept. 1994).

—Reversal was required because of the court's supplemental instruction to the jury given in defendant's absence, given that there was no evidence of a forfeiture on the record. People v. Charles, 176 A.D.2d 891, 575 N.Y.S.2d 886 (2d Dept. 1991).

—Court's conversation with juror outside the presence of the attorneys for the parties, upon request of the juror, did not constitute reversible error where the court merely explained to the juror that juror secrecy precluded him from discussing any aspect of the deliberations with her and that she could, nonetheless, report to the court if any threats had been made against her. People v. Moran, 123 A.D.2d 646, 507 N.Y.S.2d 24 (2d Dept. 1986), *lv. denied*, 69 N.Y.2d 953 (1987).

—The provision of supplemental jury instructions is a material stage of the trial at which defendant's presence is required. People v. Vargas, 278 A.D.2d 807, 718 N.Y.S.2d 521 (4th Dept. 2000).

Trial judge's obligation to be present.—Judge's absence during readbacks did not require reversal, because the readbacks required no further rulings or instructions than those previously made by the court, and the record indicated clearly that all substantive rulings regarding the readbacks were made by the trial judge and no delegation of judicial authority occurred. People v. Hernandez, 94 N.Y.2d 552, 708 N.Y.S.2d 34, 729 N.E.2d 691 (2000).

—Reversible error was committed when court responded to written question posed by jury during deliberations outside the presence of defendant notwithstanding that defense counsel was present at the time and participated in forming the answer to the jury's inquiry and did not object to the defendant's absence. People v. Mehmedi, 69 N.Y.2d 759, 513 N.Y.S.2d 100, 505 N.E.2d 610, *rearg. denied*, 69 N.Y.2d 985 (1987).

—Reversal was not warranted because of a readback of testimony in the absence of the trial judge, as defendant consented to this procedure and the judge was available to maintain control over the readback, and did, in fact, appear to resolve a dispute as to the readback's scope. People v. Mai, 175 A.D.2d 692, 573 N.Y.S.2d 90 (1st Dept. 1991).

—Reversal was warranted when the trial judge improperly absented himself from the courtroom while the witness's testimony was being read back to the jury. People v. Rawlings, 178 A.D.2d 619, 577 N.Y.S.2d 493 (2d Dept. 1991).

—Court's direction to the court officer that "the jurors should be instructed not to deliberate anymore until I tell them to" was not an improper delegation of judicial authority. People v. Brickhouse, 178 A.D.2d 541, 577 N.Y.S.2d 453 (2d Dept. 1991).

Defendant forfeits right to be present.—Defendant forfeited his right to be present during the delivery of additional instructions to the jury by leaving the courthouse during deliberations despite instructions to remain in the building. People v. Watson, 121 A.D.2d 487, 503 N.Y.S.2d 584 (2d Dept.), *lv. denied*, 68 N.Y.2d 818 (1986).

Objections to supplemental charge; waiver.—Defense counsel failed to preserve for appeal asserted error of trial court in failing to question or further inquire of a juror who sent the court a note stating that he could not render a fair and just verdict; counsel did not join in the prosecutor's suggestion that the court conduct an inquiry, but instead moved only for mistrial, which was properly denied. People v. Lombardo, 61 N.Y.2d 97, 472 N.Y.S.2d 589, 460 N.E.2d 1074 (1984).

—Having failed to object to the supplemental instruction on identification, the defendant waived any appellate challenge to it as a matter of law. People v. Nieves, 157 A.D.2d 562, 550 N.Y.S.2d 305 (1st Dept. 1990).

§ 310.40. Verdict; rendition thereof.

1. The verdict must be rendered and announced by the foreperson of the jury in the courtroom in the presence of the court, a prosecutor, the defendant's counsel and the defendant; provided, however, that where the foreperson refuses or is unable to render and announce the verdict, the court may designate another member of the jury to do so.

2. Before rendering and announcing the verdict, the foreperson of the jury, or such other

member of the jury as may be designated by the court pursuant to subdivision one, must be asked whether the jury has agreed upon a verdict and must answer in the affirmative.

Amended by L. 1976, Ch. 181; L. 2001, Ch. 488, eff. Nov. 21, 2001, and shall apply to all trials commenced on or after such date.

ANNOTATIONS

Rendition of verdict.—Trial court should not have taken jury verdict in defendant's absence. People v. Williams, 186 A.D.2d 161, 587 N.Y.S.2d 704 (2d Dept. 1992), *lv. denied*, 81 N.Y.2d 767 (1993).

Partial verdict.—There was no verdict of acquittal where, after the jury was discharged as deadlocked, affidavits by nine jurors stated that they had reached a partial verdict of acquittal on one of the several counts charged. Such an unreported partial verdict does not conform to the statutory requirements for the rendering of a verdict. Oliver v. Justices of New York Supreme Court, 44 A.D.2d 823, 356 N.Y.S.2d 52 (1st Dept.), *aff'd*, 36 N.Y.2d 53, 364 N.Y.S.2d 874, 324 N.E.2d 34 (1974).

—The court is not obligated to inquire of the jury whether it reached a partial verdict after receiving a deadlock note, absent some indication that the jury wishes to return such a verdict. People v. Hymes, 208 A.D.2d 355, 616 N.Y.S.2d 742 (1st Dept. 1994).

§ 310.50. Verdict; form; reconsideration of defective verdict.

1. The form of the verdict must be in accordance with the court's instructions, as prescribed in article three hundred.

2. If the jury renders a verdict which in form is not in accordance with the court's instructions or which is otherwise legally defective, the court must explain the defect or error and must direct the jury to reconsider such verdict, to resume its deliberation for such purpose, and to render a proper verdict. If the jury persists in rendering a defective or improper verdict, the court may in its discretion either order that the verdict in its entirety as to any defendant be recorded as an acquittal, or discharge the jury and authorize the people to retry the indictment or a specified count or counts thereof as to such defendant; provided that if it is clear that the jury intended to find a defendant not guilty upon any particular count, the court must order that the verdict be recorded as an acquittal of such defendant upon such count.

3. If the court accepts a verdict which is defective or incomplete by reason of the jury's failure to render a verdict upon every count upon which it was instructed to do so, such verdict is deemed to constitute an acquittal upon every such count improperly ignored in the verdict.

4. In a prosecution involving a charge of enterprise corruption in violation of article four hundred sixty of the penal law, the jury must separately and specifically render a special verdict with regard to each criminal act and any lesser included offense submitted for its consideration as a part of a pattern of criminal activity in addition to its verdict on the charge of enterprise corruption. In the absence of a unanimous special verdict of guilty with regard to each of at least

three criminal acts and/or lesser included offenses submitted for its consideration and legally sufficient to constitute a person's participation in a pattern of criminal activity within the meaning of subdivision four of section 460.10 of the penal law, the court must order that the verdict on the count charging enterprise corruption be recorded as an acquittal.

Amended by L. 1986, Ch. 516.

ANNOTATIONS

Inconsistent; repugnant verdicts.—There is no per se rule requiring resubmission of inconsistent verdicts; rather, resubmission is required only where the verdict exhibits confusion on the part of the jury such that its intention with respect to the individual counts of the indictment is uncertain. People v. Loughlin, 76 N.Y.2d 804, 559 N.Y.S.2d 962, 559 N.E.2d 656 (1990).

—The Appellate Court erred in viewing the verdicts as repugnant by going beyond the elements of the crime, as charged and by making a factual analysis of the evidence. People v. Green, 71 N.Y.2d 1006, 530 N.Y.S.2d 97, 525 N.E.2d 742 (1988).

—Guilty verdict of robbery count and acquittal on weapon possession count was not repugnant since the jury may have found that the defendant may not have possessed a knife yet threatened to use one. People v. Johnson, 70 N.Y.2d 819, 523 N.Y.S.2d 434, 435, 517 N.E.2d 1320 (1987).

—Verdicts of not guilty on one count of rape and one count of sodomy were not legally inconsistent with the guilty verdict as to a remaining sodomy charge; although all of the charges arose from a single occurrence, the verdicts were not inherently inconsistent when viewed in light of the elements of each crime as charged to the jury. People v. Goodfriend, 64 N.Y.2d 695, 485 N.Y.S.2d 519, 474 N.E.2d 1187 (1984).

—A verdict of acquittal of the sale of narcotics as to one officer and the conviction of the sale of narcotics simultaneously to another officer is inconsistent but not repugnant as there were two independent fact findings required. People v. Satloff, 82 A.D.2d 896, 441 N.Y.S.2d 96 (2d Dept. 1981), *aff'd*, 56 N.Y.2d 745, 452 N.Y.S.2d 12, 437 N.E.2d 271 (1982).

—When two separate counts of different subdivisions of robbery in the second degree were charged by the trial court, consistency in the verdict between the two counts is not required, and an appellate court cannot look behind the jury's verdict to determine why it chose to acquit on one count and not another. People v. Gudson, 70 A.D.2d 740, 416 N.Y.S.2d 899 (3d Dept. 1979), *aff'd*, 51 N.Y.2d 233, 433 N.Y.S.2d 1004, 414 N.E.2d 385 (1980).

—Resubmission, where the jury has failed to comply with the court's instructions, is required only where the verdict exhibits confusion on the part of the jury such that its intention with respect to the individual counts of the indictment is uncertain. People v. Robinson, 45 N.Y.2d 448, 410 N.Y.S.2d 59, 382 N.E.2d 759 (1978).

—Defendant's acquittal of murder in the second degree and manslaughter in the first degree does not necessarily negate any of the elements of criminal possession of a weapon in the second degree. People v. Richardson, 235 A.D.2d 504, 652 N.Y.S.2d 989 (2d Dept. 1997).

—A compromise verdict is not to be condoned, but is not ground for reversal, provided that the verdict is not repugnant as a matter of law. People v. Martinez, 201 A.D.2d 671, 608 N.Y.S.2d 261 (2d Dept. 1994).

—The question of whether a verdict is inconsistent or repugnant is to be determined by reviewing the elements of the crimes charged by the trial court to determine whether the jury's findings in those counts can be reconciled. People v. Coleman, 199 A.D.2d 330, 605 N.Y.S.2d 105 (2d Dept. 1993), *lv. denied*, 83 N.Y.2d 850 (1994).

—Factual inconsistencies in a verdict do not constitute a ground for reversal provided that the verdict is not repugnant as a matter of law. People v. Fraser, 159 A.D.2d 587, 552 N.Y.S.2d 442 (2d Dept. 1990).

—Conviction for attempted murder of bystander was not repugnant to acquittal of intentional murder of the victim, since the elements of the two counts, as charged to the jury, were not the same. People v. Castro, 141 A.D.2d 658, 529 N.Y.S.2d 554 (2d Dept. 1988).

—Defendant's conviction for robbery on theory of being aided by another person present was not repugnant to co-defendant's acquittal on same charge; jury could have found that co-defendant aided the defendant in the commission of the robbery by providing the means or opportunity while at the same time finding that he did not participate in the robbery or possess the criminal intent necessary to commit the crime. People v. Greer, 126 A.D.2d 105, 512 N.Y.S.2d 714 (2d Dept. 1987).

—Defendant's contention that the jury verdict was internally inconsistent insofar as it found recklessness with respect to the depraved indifference murder conviction and intent to cause serious physical injury with respect to the first degree man-slaughter conviction was rejected by court; where two crimes require the same act and result and differ only as to the required mental state, it is impossible to commit the crime requiring the higher culpable mental state without concomitantly committing the lesser crime. People v. Brensic, 119 A.D.2d 281, 506 N.Y.S.2d 570 (2d Dept. 1986).

—Acquittal on arson charges was not repugnant to conviction of conspiracy to commit arson since conduct which will support a conviction for conspiracy does not perforce give rise to liability for the substantive crime as an accessory. People v. Torres, 118 A.D.2d 821, 500 N.Y.S.2d 178 (2d Dept. 1986).

—Verdicts convicting defendant of murder in the second degree and manslaughter in the first degree were not repugnant as defendant was convicted of two separate crimes which involved the killings of two victims occurring at two different locations under different circumstances. People v. Cornwall, 121 A.D.2d 735, 504 N.Y.S.2d 155 (2d Dept. 1986).

—Verdicts of guilty of robbery in the first degree and not guilty of criminal possession of a weapon in the second degree or of criminal use of a firearm in the first degree were not repugnant since the jury could have reasonably concluded that the defendant could be convicted of the crime of robbery on the basis that she intended to forcibly steal property from the victim, but that she did not knowingly and intentionally possess or use the loaded deadly weapon. People v. Ellis, 120 A.D.2d 743, 502 N.Y.S.2d 522 (2d Dept.), lv. denied, 68 N.Y.2d 811 (1986).

—Jury's finding of not guilty as to criminal sale of cocaine was not repugnant to its finding of guilt as to criminal sale of heroin since the elements of the crime, as charged to the jury, were not identical. People v. Baeza, 125 A.D.2d 318, 508 N.Y.S.2d 602 (2d Dept. 1986).

—A verdict will only be found repugnant if, in view of the actual charge given, it is inherently self-contradictory. People v. Cooper, 118 A.D.2d 721, 500 N.Y.S.2d 53 (2d Dept. 1986).

—A jury verdict is repugnant when a defendant is convicted of one crime and acquitted of another and the elements of each are identical; although repugnancy may be a ground for reversal, an inconsistent verdict is not such a ground if it is related to separate counts of the indictment. People v. James, 112 A.D.2d 380, 491 N.Y.S.2d 836 (2d Dept. 1985).

—Defendant's conviction of robbery in the second degree did not require dismissal of the charge of assault in the second degree, of which he was also convicted; since each crime has unique elements, there is no lesser included crime and the defendant could have committed assault in the second degree without also having committed robbery in the second degree. People v. Irazarry, 114 A.D.2d 1041, 495 N.Y.S.2d 481 (2d Dept. 1985).

—Defendant was properly convicted of burglary, criminal mischief and possession of stolen property, all committed during the same incident, because all three crimes contained unique elements and defendant could not possibly have committed one without also committing the others. People v. Bolton, 103 A.D.2d 806, 477 N.Y.S.2d 685 (2d Dept. 1984).

—Acquittal on charge of reckless endangerment was not repugnant to conviction on charge of discharging a firearm across a public highway. People v. Maille, 136 A.D.2d 829, 523 N.Y.S.2d 667 (3d Dept. 1988).

—Inconsistency in a verdict applies as to the various charges against each individual defendant and does not apply between co-defendants. People v. Layman, 112 A.D.2d 530, 491 N.Y.S.2d 468 (3d Dept. 1985).

Repugnant verdicts; waiver.—Defendant's claim that the verdict was repugnant was unpreserved for appellate review

since he failed to object to the verdict prior to the discharge of the jury. People v. Aponte, 194 A.D.2d 315, 598 N.Y.S.2d 237 (1st Dept. 1993).

—Where defendant failed to object to verdict prior to the discharge of the jury, the issue of repugnancy was not preserved for appellate review notwithstanding the trial court's decision to act sua sponte and reach the issue in a motion made pursuant to CPL Article 330.30 (1); the statute provides no express authority for such action unless an objection is taken to the verdict before the jury is discharged. People v. Hankinson, 119 A.D.2d 506, 501 N.Y.S.2d 36 (1st Dept. 1986).

—When there is a claim that repugnant jury verdicts have been rendered in response to a multiple-count indictment, a verdict as to a particular count shall be set aside only when it is inherently inconsistent when viewed in light of the elements of each crime as charged to the jury. People v. Feliciano, 187 A.D.2d 448, 589 N.Y.S.2d 534 (2d Dept. 1992), lv. denied, 84 N.Y.2d 825 (1994).

—Defendant's contention that the jury's verdict was repugnant was not preserved for appellate review where he failed to object to the verdict prior to the discharge of the jury. People v. White, 172 A.D.2d 790, 569 N.Y.S.2d 161 (2d Dept. 1991).

—The defendant's claim regarding the repugnancy of the verdict was not preserved for appellate review due to his failure to raise the issue prior to the discharge of the jury. People v. Zambrana, 158 A.D.2d 736, 552 N.Y.S.2d 181 (2d Dept. 1990).

—Defendant's claim of repugnancy was not preserved for appellate review where he failed to object to the verdict prior to the discharge of the jury. People v. Gomez, 149 A.D.2d 432, 539 N.Y.S.2d 776 (2d Dept.), lv. denied, 74 N.Y.2d 794 (1989).

—Issue of repugnancy was preserved for appellate review when defense counsel properly raised the issue prior to the discharge of the jury. People v. Hard, 139 A.D.2d 592, 527 N.Y.S.2d 86 (2d Dept. 1988).

—Defendant's claim of repugnancy in the verdict was waived for failure to object to the verdict prior to the discharge of the jury. People v. LaPella, 135 A.D.2d 735, 522 N.Y.S.2d 637 (2d Dept. 1987).

—Where there was a bench trial, defendant's failure to move to set aside the verdict or modify the verdict resulted in a waiver of the repugnancy issue. People v. DeMeo, 123 A.D.2d 879, 507 N.Y.S.2d 658 (2d Dept. 1986).

—Where defendant failed to raise repugnancy issue before the jury was discharged, he failed to preserve the issue for appellate review. People v. White, 121 A.D.2d 762, 504 N.Y.S.2d 170 (2d Dept. 1986).

—To preserve for appeal a claim of repugnancy of verdict, the defendant must raise that issue prior to the discharge of the jury. People v. Howard, 107 A.D.2d 712, 484 N.Y.S.2d 67 (2d Dept. 1985).

—Defense counsel waived any claim of repugnancy with regard to jury's verdict when he failed to complain prior to jury's discharge at which point it was impossible to remedy any possible defect by resubmission to the jury. People v. Suarez, 99 A.D.2d 473, 470 N.Y.S.2d 179 (2d Dept. 1984).

—Defense counsel waived claim that verdicts were repugnant by failing to request a charge that acquittal of robbery in the second degree would require an acquittal of lesser charge and by failing to move to set aside the verdict prior to discharge of the jury. People v. Lee, 102 A.D.2d 540, 477 N.Y.S.2d 655 (2d Dept. 1984).

—Defendant's failure to object to court's resubmission to jury after its initial rendering of an inconsistent verdict waived any argument regarding the resubmission. People v. Hope, 186 A.D.2d 872, 589 N.Y.S.2d 363 (3d Dept.), lv. denied, 80 N.Y.2d 1027 (1992).

—Claim of repugnancy was not preserved for appellate review where it was not raised until after the jury was discharged. People v. McCann, 149 A.D.2d 814, 540 N.Y.S.2d 341 (3d Dept. 1989).

—Where defendant did not object to the verdict or otherwise raise the repugnancy claim prior to the discharge of the jury, the issue was not preserved for review. People v. Brooks, 154 A.D.2d 940, 546 N.Y.S.2d 69 (4th Dept. 1989).

Polling the jury.—As defendant did not object to the continued polling of the jurors after juror number 9 had stated that she did not concur in the announced verdict, he did not preserve any claim of error for appellate review as a matter of law. People v. Pena, 188 A.D.2d 349, 591 N.Y.S.2d 166 (1st Dept. 1992).

—One reason to prohibit intrusion into the jury's deliberative process is that the jury, in reaching its verdict, may have exercised mercy. People v. Childs, 161 Misc. 2d 988, 615 N.Y.S.2d 972 (Sup. Ct. Bronx Co. 1994).

Defective verdicts.—The trial court properly dismissed the two counts of the indictment charging defendant with simple possession of a controlled substance after the jury, in apparent disregard of the court's instructions, had returned guilty verdicts on those counts as well as on the two counts charging possession of a controlled substance with intent to sell, and the jury, upon polling, confirmed their intent to convict defendant of both possession with intent to sell and simple possession. People v. Robinson, 45 N.Y.2d 448, 410 N.Y.S.2d 59, 382 N.E.2d 759 (1978).

—It was proper to resubmit the three counts in the indictment to the jury, after additional instructions, when the jury initially reported a verdict of guilty of the first two counts and not guilty on the third count after being instructed to find the defendant guilty of one of the counts, or not guilty of any of the three counts. People v. Salemmo, 38 N.Y.2d 357, 379 N.Y.S.2d 809, 342 N.E.2d 579 (1976).

—An inadvertent error on the verdict sheet—identifying the second count as burglary in the third degree rather than reversal in the second degree, did not render the verdict defective. Court rejects the Second Department cases, People v. Worthy,178 A.D.2d 454, and People v. Klos, 190 A.D.2d 754. People v. Justiniano, 203 A.D.2d 139, 610 N.Y.S.2d 238 (1st Dept.), *lv. denied*, 83 N.Y.2d 968 (1994).

—Even if the evidence is more supportive of a finding of reckless rather than intentional conduct, the verdict may not be set aside simply because one theory is more plausible than another. People v. Samuels, 203 A.D.2d 494, 610 N.Y.S.2d 593 (2d Dept. 1994).

—When the court clerk inadvertently asked for the jury's verdict on a count which the court had dismissed, instead of a count which had been submitted, and the jury foreman rendered a verdict, the verdict was defective and the court should have directed the jury to reconsider it. Under CPL § 310.50(3), both counts were dismissed. People v. Calderon, 113 A.D.2d 894, 493 N.Y.S.2d 611 (2d Dept. 1985), *lv. denied*, 67 N.Y.2d 881 (1986).

—The mere failure to follow instructions as to the order of deliberation does not require resubmission of the case to the jury in the absence of a verdict which is confusing as to the jury's intention or contains inconsistent or repugnant decisions. People v. Benedict, 202 A.D.2d 758, 609 N.Y.S.2d 100 (3d Dept. 1994).

§ 310.60. Discharge of jury before rendition of verdict and effect thereof.

1. A deliberating jury may be discharged by the court without having rendered a verdict only when:

(a) The jury has deliberated for an extensive period of time without agreeing upon a verdict with respect to any of the charges submitted and the court is satisfied that any such agreement is unlikely within a reasonable time; or

(b) The court, the defendant and the people all consent to such discharge; or

(c) A mistrial is declared pursuant to section 280.10.

2. When the jury is so discharged, the defendant or defendants may be retried upon the indictment. Upon such retrial, the indictment is deemed to contain all counts which it contained, except those which were dismissed or were

deemed to have resulted in an acquittal pursuant to subdivision one of section 290.10.

Amended by L. 1983, Ch. 170.

ANNOTATIONS

Deadlocked jury; instructions.—Trial court's direction to court officer to tell jury to continue deliberations where it had indicated it was deadlocked required reversal. People v. Torres, 72 N.Y.2d 1007, 534 N.Y.S.2d 914, 531 N.E.2d 635 (1988).

—Court erred in overemphasizing to one juror that if her request to be dismissed was granted a costly mistrial, unfair to defendant and others, would be required. People v. Rodriguez, 71 N.Y.2d 214, 524 N.Y.S.2d 422, 426, 519 N.E.2d 333 (1988).

—Court improperly singled out dissenting juror and suggested that deliberations would continue until court decided to terminate the discussion. People v. Diaz, 66 N.Y.2d 744, 497 N.Y.S.2d 359, 488 N.E.2d 105 (1985).

—Although the *Allen* charge properly stressed the importance of each juror's keeping an open mind to the arguments of other jurors, the court erred when it failed to balance that instruction by stressing that the verdict must be the verdict of each individual juror, and not a mere acquiescence in the conclusion of the others. People v. Ali, 65 A.D.2d 513, 409 N.Y.S.2d 12 (1st Dept. 1978), *aff'd*, 47 N.Y.2d 920, 419 N.Y.S.2d 487, 393 N.E.2d 481 (1979).

—Reversal was required when the trial judge leveled a pointed threat to the jury, and in particular to the lone dissenting juror, that they would be forced to continue their deliberations indefinitely and without outside communications. People v. Carter, 40 N.Y.2d 933, 389 N.Y.S.2d 835, 358 N.E.2d 517 (1976).

—Supplemental "Allen" charge (Allen v. United States, 164 U.S. 492, 17 S. Ct. 154, 41 L. Ed. 528 (1896)) to encourage jury to seek agreement after announcing deadlock was proper since not coercive. People v. Graham, 48 A.D.2d 646, 368 N.Y.S.2d 518 (1st Dept. 1975), *aff'd*, 39 N.Y.2d 775, 385 N.Y.S.2d 31, 350 N.E.2d 408 (1976).

—Unbalanced *Allen* charge which focused on difficulties and expense of a retrial without instructing jurors to impartially consider evidence and try to reach agreement without surrendering their individual views was improper. People v. Delaremore, 212 A.D.2d 804, 623 N.Y.S.2d 279 (2d Dept. 1995).

Deadlocked jury; partial verdict.—The court did not abuse its discretion and a retrial was proper when it indicated its intention to accept a partial verdict and discharge the jury and neither side objected after the jury reported a deadlock on the attempted murder count after deliberating for over five hours and the foreman informed the court that the situation would remain unchanged if deliberations were continued for another day. Wiley v. Couzens, 38 N.Y.2d 731, 381 N.Y.S.2d 39, 343 N.E.2d 757 (1975).

—The court is not obligated to inquire of the jury whether it reached a partial verdict after receiving a deadlock note, absent some indication that the jury wishes to return such a verdict. People v. Hymes, 208 A.D.2d 355, 616 N.Y.S.2d 742 (1st Dept. 1994).

Deadlocked jury; declaration of mistrial.—Defendant motion's to dismiss the indictment which was made prior to start of second trial should have been granted, where the only count in the indictment had been dismissed during the first trial due to insufficiency of evidence and the court later declared a mistrial because the jury was unable to reach a verdict on the lesser counts submitted to them; however further prosecution was not foreclosed pursuant to a new indictment containing those charges upon which the jury deadlocked. People v. Mayo, 48 N.Y.2d 245, 422 N.Y.S.2d 361, 397 N.E.2d 1166 (1979).

—Declaration of a mistrial without defendant's consent would have been a proper exercise of discretion because a unanimous verdict was unlikely and there would have been a substantial potential for coercion had the court required the jury to engage in further deliberations. People v. Peterson, 273 A.D.2d 88, 709 N.Y.S.2d 540 (1st Dept. 2000).

—Court did not abuse its discretion in declaring a mistrial after the jury deliberated three hours in a single issue case, where the defendant did not object until after the court had already declared the mistrial. People v. Campbell, 203 A.D.2d 127, 610 N.Y.S.2d 246 (1st Dept.), *lv. denied*, 84 N.Y.2d 823 (1994).

—The court's recalling of the jury after its discharge for the purpose of resuming deliberations was procedurally defective. People v. Bryant, 170 A.D.2d 520, 566 N.Y.S.2d 83, 85 (2d Dept. 1991).

Discharge of jury; effect of.—Discharge of jury terminated the trial, and the court thus lacked the power to reopen the trial and accept the jury's verdict after it had discharged the jury. Once the trial has been terminated, the judge's power to correct the record only extends to ministerial acts, and not to substantive reassessments of the jury's verdict. People v. Serrano, 182 Misc. 2d 498, 697 N.Y.S.2d 814 (Sup. Ct. Bronx Co. 1999).

§ 310.70.　Rendition of partial verdict and effect thereof.

1. If a deliberating jury declares that it has reached a verdict with respect to one or more but not all of the offenses submitted to it, or with respect to one or more but not all of the defendants, the court must proceed as follows:

(a) If the possibility of ultimate agreement with respect to the other submitted offenses or defendants is so small and the circumstances are such that if they were the only matters under consideration the court would be authorized to discharge the jury pursuant to paragraph (a) of subdivision one of section 310.60, the court must terminate the deliberation and order the jury to render a partial verdict with respect to those offenses and defendants upon which or with respect to whom it has reached a verdict;

(b) If the court is satisfied that there is a reasonable possibility of ultimate agreement upon any of the unresolved offenses with respect to any defendant, it may either:

(i) Order the jury to render its verdict with respect to those offenses and defendants upon which or with respect to whom it has reached agreement and resume its deliberation upon the remainder; or

(ii) Refuse to accept a partial verdict at the time and order the jury to resume its deliberation upon the entire case.

2. Following the rendition of a partial verdict pursuant to subdivision one, a defendant may be retried for any submitted offense upon which the jury was unable to agree unless:

(a) A verdict of conviction thereon would have been inconsistent with a verdict, of either conviction or acquittal, actually rendered with respect to some other offense, or

(b) The submitted offense which was the subject of the disagreement, and some other submitted offense of higher or equal grade which was the subject of a verdict of conviction, were so related that consecutive sentences thereon could not have been imposed upon a defendant convicted of both such offenses.

3. As used in this section, a "submitted offense" means any offense submitted by the court to the jury, whether it be one which was expressly charged in a count of the indictment or a lesser included offense thereof submitted pursuant to section 300.50.

Amended by L. 1974, Ch. 762.

ANNOTATIONS

Trial court's obligations when responding to a deadlocked jury.—Defendant's claim that trial court erred when, after rejecting a partial verdict, it told the jury to resume deliberations without explicitly stating that such should be "upon the entire case," is unpreserved for appellate review because defendant failed to object when the instruction was given and this error does not fall within the narrow class of error which need not be preserved by timely objection. People v. Freire, 232 A.D.2d 254, 649 N.Y.S.2d 407 (1st Dept. 1996).

—Trial court did not err in failing to poll jury as to seriousness of alleged deadlock prior to instructing jury to continue its deliberations, because the trial court properly found that there was a reasonable possibility of ultimate agreement on the unresolved offense. People v. Woods, 262 A.D.2d 668, 693 N.Y.S.2d 163 (2d Dept. 1999).

—Objections to the court's failure—after declining to accept a partial verdict—to instruct the jury to resume deliberations on the entire case must be preserved by timely objection. People v. Rios, 215 A.D.2d 509, 626 N.Y.S.2d 515 (2d Dept. 1995).

—Court was not required to inform jury that it could render a partial verdict; where, as here, the court is satisfied that there is a reasonable possibility of ultimate agreement, the court may refuse to accept a partial verdict and may order the jury to resume its deliberations on the entire case. People v. Le, 277 A.D.2d 1036, 716 N.Y.S.2d 189 (4th Dept. 2000).

Retrial.—The trial court's ruling that a verdict of acquittal of assault in the first degree warranted acquittal of defendant on the second count of assault in the second degree was error of a legal, not factual nature; since the merits of the second charge had not been reached, it was not double jeopardy for defendant to be retried on the lesser count where the prosecution was not given adequate opportunity to object to the Court's motion sua sponte. Pestrana v. Baker, 55 N.Y.2d 315, 449 N.Y.S.2d 461, 434 N.E.2d 697 (1982).

—Where all the counts of the indictment related to one inseparable event, the defendant's alleged attack upon the victim, upon rendition of a partial verdict of acquittal, since the unresolved counts were concurrent rather than consecutive, defendant could not be retried. People v. Walsh, 44 N.Y.2d 631, 407 N.Y.S.2d 472, 378 N.E.2d 1041 (1978).

—The several acts of perjury charged in the indictment were separate, and thus acquittal on some of the charges did not prevent retrial of the other perjury charges following a mistrial due to jury's inability to reach verdict on those charges. In re DiLorenzo, 36 N.Y.2d 306, 367 N.Y.S.2d 761, 327 N.E.2d 805 (1975).

—Defendant could not be retried for attempted murder after jury convicted him of reckless endangerment for same incident; jury could have concluded that defendant acted recklessly, and not with the intent to kill. People v. Albritton, 217 A.D.2d 553, 629 N.Y.S.2d 270 (2d Dept. 1995).

—Defendant's conviction of arson, fourth degree, after a retrial, was reversed and the indictment dismissed. Since defendant had been acquitted of the only count in the indictment, arson, third degree, and the jury at the first trial had been unable to agree on the lesser submitted count or arson, fourth degree, the original indictment could not serve as the basis for such further prosecution and a new indictment was required. People v. Fudger, 73 A.D.2d 1020, 424 N.Y.S.2d 759 (3d Dept. 1980).

§ 310.80.　Recording and checking of verdict and polling of jury.

After a verdict has been rendered, it must be recorded on the minutes and read to the jury, and the jurors must be collectively asked whether such is their verdict. Even though no juror makes any declaration in the negative, the jury must, if either party makes such an application, be polled and each juror separately asked whether the verdict announced by the foreman is in all respects his verdict. If upon either the collective or the separate inquiry any juror answers in the negative, the court must refuse to accept the verdict and must direct the jury to resume its deliberation. If no disagreement is expressed, the jury must be discharged from the case, except as otherwise provided in section 400.27.

Amended by L. 1995, Ch. 1, § 19, eff. Sept. 1, 1995.

ANNOTATIONS

Inquiry necessary.—Where a juror indicates that his verdict was the result of duress, the trial court must make an inquiry to determine whether it needs to take corrective action. People v. Pickett, 61 N.Y.2d 773, 473 N.Y.S.2d 157, 461 N.E.2d 294 (1984).

—The verdict was not defective although one juror answered "no" as to his verdict upon polling since the court subsequently asked him if he had misunderstood the question to which he replied, "yes" and the court again polled the members and all assented to the verdict. People v. Crandall, 53 A.D.2d 956, 386 N.Y.S.2d 108 (3d Dept. 1976), aff'd, 45 N.Y.2d 851, 410 N.Y.S.2d 66, 382 N.E.2d 766 (1978).

—A court is not obligated to inquire of the jury whether it reached a partial verdict in the absence of an indication that the jury wishes to reach such a verdict. People v. Hymes, 208 A.D.2d 355, 616 N.Y.S.2d 742 (1st Dept. 1994).

—Trial court properly sent the jury back to deliberate, rather than make an inquiry, after one polled juror said "no" when asked if his verdict was guilty. People v. Horn, 196 A.D.2d 886, 602 N.Y.S.2d 390 (2d Dept.), lv. denied, 82 N.Y.2d 850 (1993).

Polling jury.—Though juror was momentarily unable to articulate her verdict when the jury was polled, an inquiry would have served no statutory purpose because the record clearly reflects that the juror provided an unqualified affirmative response during polling; defendant was not deprived of right to unanimous verdict. People v. Mercado, 230 A.D.2d 488, 659 N.Y.S.2d 453 (1st Dept. 1997), aff'd, 91 N.Y.2d 960, 672 N.Y.S.2d 842, 695 N.E.2d 711 (1998) (where defendant claims that court failed to inquire further into an individual juror's vote on the verdict, claim was unpreserved because defendant failed to make this specific objection or request such procedures when the juror was being polled).

—Where defendant's outburst prevented the court from hearing counsel's request for individual polling of the jury, defendant cannot raise the court's failure to poll the jury on appeal. People v. Bembry, 209 A.D.2d 270, 618 N.Y.S.2d 344 (1st Dept. 1994), aff'd, 85 N.Y.2d 932, 628 N.Y.S.2d 45, 651 N.E.2d 913 (1995).

—It was not necessary for trial court to repoll a jury after the jury clearly manifested that the verdict was unanimous where it found the defendant guilty of minimal sale of a controlled substance and criminal possession of a controlled substance arising out of a single transaction and the jury was polled according to statute and each member indicated his assent, and thereafter the court dismissed the inclusory concurrent count. People v. Sea, 49 N.Y.2d 1032, 429 N.Y.S.2d 553, 407 N.E.2d 400 (1980).

—A defendant cannot claim on appeal that the court should have polled the jury, unless he objected at a time when the omission

could have been remedied. People v. Bembry, 209 A.D.2d 270, 618 N.Y.S.2d 344 (1st Dept. 1994).

—Trial court properly continued to individually poll the jurors after one responded "No," and then directed them to continue their deliberations. People v. Pena, 188 A.D.2d 349, 591 N.Y.S.2d 166 (1st Dept. 1992), lv. denied, 81 N.Y.2d 845 (1993).

Verdict improperly accepted.—Either party may request polling of the jury after a verdict has been rendered, and if "any juror answers in the negative, the court must refuse to accept the verdict and must direct the jury to resume its deliberations"; while the Supreme Court's inquiry to clarify the juror's ambiguous responses was proper, it did not resolve the uncertainty as to this juror's vote. The court should not have accepted the verdict and a new trial was ordered. People v. Francois, 297 A.D.2d 750, 748 N.Y.S.2d 384 (2d Dept. 2002).

§ 310.85. Verdict of guilty where defendant not criminally responsible.

1. Where a verdict of guilty is rendered with respect to a crime, but the defendant is not criminally responsible for such crime by reason of infancy, the court shall proceed as provided in this section.

2. If a verdict of guilty also is rendered with respect to a crime for which the defendant is criminally responsible, or if the defendant is awaiting sentence upon another criminal conviction or is under a sentence of imprisonment on another criminal conviction, the verdict rendered with respect to a crime for which he is not criminally responsible must be set aside and shall be deemed a nullity.

3. In any case where the verdict is not set aside pursuant to subdivision two or * this section, the court must order that the verdict be deemed vacated and replaced by a juvenile delinquency fact determination. Upon so ordering, the court must direct that the action be removed to the family court in accordance with the provisions of article seven hundred twenty-five of this chapter.

* As originally enacted.

Added by L. 1978, Ch. 481.

ARTICLE 320—WAIVER OF JURY TRIAL AND CONDUCT OF NON-JURY TRIAL

Section

320.10 Non-jury trial; when authorized.

320.20 Non-jury trial; nature and conduct thereof.

LexisNexis Cross Reference

New York Criminal Practice (2d ed.), Vol. 3, Ch. 28, Jury and Non-Jury Trials.

§ 320.10. Non-jury trial; when authorized.

1. Except where the indictment charges the crime of murder in the first degree, the defendant, subject to the provisions of subdivision two, may at any time before trial waive a jury trial and consent to a trial without a jury in the superior court in which the indictment is pending.

2. Such waiver must be in writing and must be signed by the defendant in person in open court in the presence of the court, and with the approval of the court. The court must approve the execution and submission of such waiver unless it determines that it is tendered as a stratagem to procure an otherwise impermissible procedural advantage or that the defendant is not fully aware of the consequences of the choice he is making. If the court disapproves the waiver, it must state upon the record its reasons for such disapproval.

Amended by L. 1974, Ch. 367.

ANNOTATIONS

Capital case.—Defendant in capital case was not entitled to bench trial, because CPL § 320.10 excludes capital cases from the provisions that govern jury trial waiver. People v. Cahill, 2 N.Y.3d 14, 777 N.Y.S.2d 332, 809 N.E.2d 561 (2003).

—Constitutionality of CPL § 320.10 upheld insofar as it prohibits a capital defendant from waiving a jury trial at either phase of trial; the prohibition against non-jury trials allows a jury to act as a safeguard between an individual and the tyranny of the state and reflects the legitimate reluctance to entrust plenary powers over life and liberty of the citizen to one judge. People v. Owens, 184 Misc. 2d 600, 710 N.Y.S.2d 790 (Sup. Ct. Monroe Co. 2000).

—Defendant moved for an order invalidating CPL § 320.10, which forbids waiver of jury trial in first degree murder cases; court upheld the statute, and found that a defendant has no recognized federal constitutional right to a bench trial in a capital case. People v. McIntosh, 173 Misc. 2d 727, 662 N.Y.S.2d 214 (Dutchess Co. Ct. 1997).

—Defendant who was charged with first-degree murder could waive his right to trial by jury, notwithstanding statute prohibiting waiver where indictment charges first degree murder; court allowed waiver in instant case because prosecution had elected not to seek the death penalty. People v. Elliott, 173 Misc. 2d 795, 662 N.Y.S.2d 701 (Sup. Ct. Kings Co. 1997).

Denial of application to waive jury trial.—The trial court did not err in refusing to permit defendant to waive a jury since the jury had already been impaneled and sworn. People v. Kitching, 78 N.Y.2d 532, 577 N.Y.S.2d 231, 583 N.E.2d 944 (1991).

—Defendant's conviction was vacated and the case was remitted for a new trial where the court denied defendant his constitutional rights to self-representation and to waiver of a trial by jury since defendant was intelligent, articulate and knowledgeable of the criminal justice system, had made a timely and unequivocal assertion of each right and had shown his lack of confidence in his three assigned counsels. People v. Davis, 49 N.Y.2d 114, 424 N.Y.S.2d 372, 400 N.E.2d 313 (1979).

—Trial court properly denied defendant's request for a bench trial, where it was an indirect attempt to obtain a severance which had previously been denied at his co-defendant's request. People v. Richiez, 173 A.D.2d 234, 569 N.Y.S.2d 442 (1st Dept. 1991).

—Trial court properly denied defendant's application to waive a jury trial where it determined that such waiver was a stratagem to obtain an impermissible procedural advantage—a severance from several co-defendants in a lengthy and complicated trial. People v. Firestone, 111 A.D.2d 696, 490 N.Y.S.2d 513 (1st Dept. 1985).

Waiver; procedural requirements.—Waiver was valid although defendant signed it before his colloquy with the court, where he discussed waiver on the record and understood the significance of the waiver. People v. Perez, 213 A.D.2d 351, 624 N.Y.S.2d 413 (1st Dept. 1995).

—Defendants have a right to waive trial by jury, and the court must accept the waiver if it is made knowingly and in accordance with statutory requirements. Defendant validly waived this right, in a written waiver, signed in open court after an extensive colloquy regarding defendant's condition and the benefits associated with a jury trial. People v. Saunders, 19 A.D.3d 744, 796 N.Y.S.2d 446 (3d Dept. 2005).

—Waiver of right to trial by jury was adequate, where defendant indicated at hearing that he was aware of his right to a jury trial and the consequences of his waiver of that right, that his decision was voluntary, that he had discussed the decision with his attorney and his daughter, that he was conscious of what he was doing, and that he had not had anything to eat or drink or taken any medication that would affect his ability to think. People v. Ahl, 243 A.D.2d 985, 663 N.Y.S.2d 907 (3d Dept. 1997).

—Conviction cannot be sustained in view of the fact that the defendant did not sign a written waiver of his right to a trial by jury. People v. Zawestowski, 168 A.D.2d 950, 564 N.Y.S.2d 902 (4th Dept. 1990).

—In order for a jury trial to be properly waived it must be in writing and signed by the defendant in person, in open court and with the approval of the court. People v. Minter, 157 Misc. 2d 54, 595 N.Y.S.2d 845 (Monroe Co. Ct. 1992).

Effect of waiver.—The court did not abuse its discretion in refusing the request for a jury trial where defendant knowingly and voluntarily waived his right to a jury trial and the case was adjourned until the next day; when the defense counsel advised the court that defendant had changed his mind and without any other reason requested that the waiver be vacated. People v. McQueen, 52 N.Y.2d 1025, 438 N.Y.S.2d 299, 420 N.E.2d 97 (1981).

—Trial court lacks the authority sua sponte to set aside its own verdict on ground defendant had not signed written waiver of his right to a jury trial. Zawistowski v. Arcara, 132 A.D.2d 1000, 518 N.Y.S.2d 474 (4th Dept. 1987).

§ 320.20. Non-jury trial; nature and conduct thereof.

1. A non-jury trial of an indictment must be

conducted by one judge of the superior court in which the indictment is pending.

2. The court, in addition to determining all questions of law, is the execlusive * trier of all issues of fact and must render a verdict.

3. The order of the trial must be as follows:

(a) The court must permit the parties to deliver opening addresses in the order provided for a trial by jury pursuant to section 260.30.

(b) The order in which evidence must or may be offered by the respective parties is the same as that applicable to a jury trial of an indictment as prescribed in subdivisions five, six and seven of section 260.30.

(c) The court must permit the parties to deliver summations in the order provided for a trial by jury pursuant to section 260.30.

(d) The court must then consider the case and render a verdict.

4. The provisions governing motion practice and general procedure with respect to a jury trial are, wherever appropriate, applicable to a non-jury trial.

5. Before considering a multiple count indictment for the purpose of rendering a verdict thereon, and before the summations if there be any, the court must designate and state upon the record the counts upon which it will render a verdict and the particular defendant or defendants, if there be more than one, with respect to whom it will render a verdict upon any particular count. In determining what counts, offenses and defendants must be considered by it and covered by its verdict, and the form of the verdict in general, the court must be governed, so far as appropriate and practicable, by the provisions of article three hundred governing the court's submission of counts and offenses to a jury upon a jury trial.

* As originally enacted.

Amended by L. 1976, Ch. 320; L. 1981, Ch. 333.

ANNOTATIONS

Declaration of mistrial.—Judge at bench trial should not have declared a mistrial because of improper contacts between defendant's relatives and judge's relatives. The judge had no contact with defendant or his relatives, and the acts which formed the basis of the mistrial were not so improper or prejudicial that verdict could not have been reached. Defendant cannot be retried without being subjected to double jeopardy. Ferlito v. Judges of County Court, Suffolk County, 39 A.D.2d 17, 331 N.Y.S.2d 229 (2d Dept.), *aff'd*, 31 N.Y.2d 416, 340 N.Y.S.2d 635, 292 N.E.2d 779 (1972).

Evidence considered.—Defendant was not deprived of fair trial when prosecutor briefly mentioned defendant's pretrial silence and asked questions about a prior bad act, because in a nonjury trial, fact finder is capable of distinguishing issues and making objective determination notwithstanding awareness of facts that cannot properly be relied on in decision. People v. Torres, 249 A.D.2d 229, 673 N.Y.S.2d 72 (1st Dept. 1998).

—A trial justice, sitting as the trier of fact, is presumed to have considered only the competent evidence adduced at the trial in reaching a verdict. People v. Dazi, 195 A.D.2d 571, 600 N.Y.S.2d 276 (2d Dept. 1993).

—Evidentiary error did not require reversal after nonjury trial where court indicated that it would not consider any improper

evidence. People v. McIlwain, 188 A.D.2d 666, 591 N.Y.S.2d 849 (2d Dept. 1992).

—The trial judge, sitting as the finder of fact, is presumed to have considered only the competent evidence adduced at the trial in reaching his verdict. People v. Livingston, 184 A.D.2d 529, 584 N.Y.S.2d 175, 176 (2d Dept. 1992).

—While the defendant was subjected to an improper line of questioning regarding prior traffic infractions, the error, arising in the context of a bench trial, was harmless. People v. Taylor, 135 A.D.2d 848, 523 N.Y.S.2d 136 (2d Dept. 1988).

—A trial judge is presumed to have considered only the legally competent evidence adduced at the trial and to have excluded inadmissible evidence from his deliberations and verdict. People v. Harris, 133 A.D.2d 649, 519 N.Y.S.2d 758 (2d Dept. 1987).

—In a nonjury trial the court is presumed, absent a showing of prejudice, to have considered only the competent evidence at the trial in reaching the verdict. People v. Sims, 127 A.D.2d 805, 511 N.Y.S.2d 935, 936 (2d Dept. 1987).

Court's fact-finding.—Following a non-jury trial, due deference is given to the trial court's factual conclusions and findings as to credibility. People v. Cambria, 204 A.D.2d 167, 612 N.Y.S.2d 22 (1st Dept. 1994).

—At a non-jury trial, issues of credibility are primarily for the trial court and its determination is entitled to great weight. People v. Balacky, 203 A.D.2d 471, 611 N.Y.S.2d 14 (2d Dept. 1994).

—Judge at a bench trial is presumed to consider only the competent evidence in reaching a determination. People v. Majeed, 204 A.D.2d 986, 613 N.Y.S.2d 69 (4th Dept. 1994).

—In a bench trial, no less than a jury trial, the resolution of credibility issues by the trier of fact and its determination of the weight to be given the evidence presented are entitled to great deference. People v. Van Akin, 197 A.D.2d 845, 602 N.Y.S.2d 450 (4th Dept. 1993).

Court's power to reassess its findings.—The Court of Appeals ordered a new trial on defendant's conviction for driving while intoxicated where, after a bench trial, the trial court applied a definition of intoxication which improperly lowered the prosecution's burden of proof, and upon defendant's motion to set aside the verdict, the judge reconsidered the evidence in light of the *Cruz* definition of intoxication and again found defendant guilty. The court's reconsideration of its verdict under a different standard that came too late and exceeded the scope of its authority. Allowing the second verdict to stand would permit the trial judge to engage in postverdict fact finding that would not be possible in a jury trial, thereby according less finality to the verdict of a trial judge when sitting as trier of fact than to a jury verdict. People v. Cunningham, 95 N.Y.2d 909, 717 N.Y.S.2d 68, 740 N.E.2d 213 (2000).

—A trial judge who has rendered a guilty verdict after a non-jury trial has neither inherent power nor statutory authority to reconsider his factual determination and change a guilty verdict to not guilty. People v. Carter, 63 N.Y.2d 530, 483 N.Y.S.2d 654, 473 N.E.2d 6 (1984).

—A trial judge, after a non-jury trial, has no authority to reassess the facts and change his verdict of guilty to not guilty. People v. Samuel, 135 Misc. 2d 60, 514 N.Y.S.2d 610 (Crim. Ct. Kings Co. 1987).

Recusal.—Defendant's recusal motion should have been granted where he sought a nonjury trial and the judge had previously accepted a guilty plea from the defendant's wife and imposed the maximum sentence after eliciting incriminating statements as to the defendant. People v. Zappacosta, 77 A.D.2d 928, 431 N.Y.S.2d 96 (2d Dept. 1980).

Delay in rendering a verdict.—The 82-day delay between the close of the trial and the rendering of the verdict was not unreasonable and did not violate defendant's right to a prompt verdict. People v. Francis, 189 A.D.2d 822, 592 N.Y.S.2d 448 (2d Dept.), *lv. denied*, 81 N.Y.2d 839, *on reconsideration, lv. denied*, 81 N.Y.2d 885 (1993).

—A justice sitting in a nonjury trial must render a verdict within a reasonable time after the close of trial. People v. Woodley, 141 A.D.2d 587, 529 N.Y.S.2d 193 (2d Dept. 1988).

—Eighteen-day delay between the close of proof and the rendering of a verdict did not deny the defendant his right to a prompt verdict. People v. Munn, 184 A.D.2d 1061, 584 N.Y.S.2d 366, 367 (4th Dept. 1992).

—Court's delay of 7 months in rendering its verdict was unreasonable as a matter of law. People v. Hyrn, 144 A.D.2d 961, 534 N.Y.S.2d 268 (4th Dept. 1988).

Right to summation.—Trial court's failure to inform defense counsel before summations that it would consider a lesser included offense was harmless error, since it could not be said that counsel's summation would have been affected by the knowledge. People v. Kloska, 191 A.D.2d 587, 595 N.Y.S.2d 78 (2d Dept. 1993).

—In a robbery and kidnapping prosecution it was merely harmless error and not reversible error for the trial court to fail to inform defendant prior to summation that it would consider the lesser included offenses of robbery in the first degree since defendant had based his defense on the theory of mental defect it cannot be argued he was denied his right to an effective summation. People v. Smith, 77 A.D.2d 712, 430 N.Y.S.2d 713 (3d Dept. 1980).

—Waiver of right to trial by jury was adequate, where defendant indicated at hearing that he was aware of his right to a jury trial and the consequences of his waiver of that right, that his decision was voluntary, that he had discussed the decision with his attorney and his daughter, that he was conscious of what he was doing, and that he had not had anything to eat or drink or taken any medication that would affect his ability to think.

People v. Ahl, 243 A.D.2d 985, 663 N.Y.S.2d 907 (3d Dept. 1997).

—While the trial court failed to inform defense counsel before summations that it would consider a lesser included offense, the error was harmless since the defense argument on summation applied to lesser offense as well. People v. Peterkin, 195 A.D.2d 1015, 600 N.Y.S.2d 579 (4th Dept.), *lv. denied*, 82 N.Y.2d 758 (1993).

Subd. 5

Specifying counts.—Court's failure to specify the counts which it would consider in rendering its verdict is harmless error because defendant was convicted only of offenses charged in the indictment. People v. Wright, 16 A.D.3d 982, 792 N.Y.S.2d 256 (3d Dept. 2005).

—Defendant failed to preserve for appellate review his claim that County Court erred by not advising counsel before summation of the offenses it would consider in rendering a verdict. In any event, the court's failure to comply with CPL § 320.20(5) was harmless error where defendant was convicted of offenses charged in the indictment, not lesser included offenses. People v. Mitchell, 254 A.D.2d 830, 679 N.Y.S.2d 761 (4th Dept. 1998).

ARTICLE 330—PROCEEDINGS FROM VERDICT
TO SENTENCE

LexisNexis Cross Reference

New York Criminal Practice (2d ed.), Vol. 4, Ch. 40, Proceedings from Verdict to Sentence.

§ 330.10. Disposition of defendant after verdict of acquittal.

1. Upon a verdict of complete acquittal, the court must immediately discharge the defendant if he is in the custody of the sheriff, or, if he is at liberty on bail, it must exonerate the bail.

2. Upon a verdict of not responsible by reason of mental disease or defect, the provisions of section 330.20 of this chapter shall govern all subsequent proceedings against the defendant.

Amended by L. 1980, Ch. 548.

§ 330.20. Procedure following verdict or plea of not responsible by reason of mental disease or defect.

1. Definition of terms. As used in this section, the following terms shall have the following meanings:

(a) "Commissioner" means the state commissioner of mental health or the state commissioner of mental retardation and developmental disability.

(b) "Secure facility" means a facility within the state office of mental health or the state office of mental retardation and developmental disabilities which is staffed with personnel adequately trained in security methods and is so equipped as to minimize the risk or danger of escapes, and which has been so specifically designated by the commissioner.

(c) "Dangerous mental disorder" means: (i) that a defendant currently suffers from a "mental illness" as that term is defined in subdivision twenty of section 1.03 of the mental hygiene law, and (ii) that because of such condition he currently constitutes a physical danger to himself or others.

(d) "Mentally ill" means that a defendant currently suffers from a mental illness for which care and treatment as a patient, in the in-patient services of a psychiatric center under the jurisdiction of the state office of mental health, is essential to such defendant's welfare and that his judgment is so impaired that he is unable to understand the need for such care and treatment; and, where a defendant is mentally retarded, the term "mentally ill" shall also mean, for purposes of this section, that the defendant is in need of care and treatment as a resident in the in-patient services of a developmental center or other residential facility for the mentally retarded and developmentally disabled under the jurisdiction of the state office of mental retardation and developmental disabilities.

(e) "Examination order" means an order directed to the commissioner requiring that a defendant submit to a psychiatric examination to determine whether the defendant has a dangerous mental disorder, or if he does not have dangerous mental disorder, whether he is mentally ill.

(f) "Commitment order" or "recommitment order" means an order committing a defendant to the custody of the commissioner for confinement in a secure facility for care and treatment for six months from the date of the order.

(g) "First retention order" means an order which is effective at the expiration of the period prescribed in a commitment order for * a recommitment order, authorizing continued custody of a defendant by the commissioner for a period not to exceed one year.

(h) "Second retention order" means an order which is effective at the expiration of the period prescribed in a first retention order, authorizing continued custody of a defendant by the commissioner for a period not to exceed two years.

(i) "Subsequent retention order" means an order which is effective at the expiration of the period prescribed in a second retention order or a prior subsequent retention order authorizing continued custody of a defendant by the commissioner for a period not to exceed two years.

(j) "Retention order" means a first retention order, a second retention order or a subsequent retention order.

(k) "Furlough order" means an order directing the commissioner to allow a defendant in confinement pursuant to a commitment order, recommitment order or retention order to temporarily leave the facility for a period not exceeding fourteen days, either with or without the constant supervision of one or more employees of the facility.

(l) "Transfer order" means an order directing the commissioner to transfer a defendant from a secure facility to a non-secure facility under the jurisdiction of the commissioner or to any non-secure facility designated by the commissioner.

(m) "Release order" means an order directing the commissioner to terminate a defendant's inpatient status without terminating the commissioner's responsibility for the defendant.

(n) "Discharge order" means an order terminating an order of conditions or unconditionally discharging a defendant from supervision under the provisions of this section.

(o) "Order of conditions" means an order directing a defendant to comply with this prescribed treatment plan, or any other condition which the court determines to be reasonably necessary or appropriate, and, in addition, where a defendant is in custody of the commissioner, not to leave the facility without authorization. In addition to such conditions, when determined to be reasonably necessary or appropriate, an order of conditions may be accompanied by a special order of conditions set forth in a separate document requiring that the defendant: (i) stay away from the home, school, business or place of employment of the victim or victims, or of any witness designated by the court, of such offense; or (ii) refrain from harassing, intimidating, threatening or otherwise interfering with the victim or victims of the offense and such members of the family or household of such victim or victims as shall be specifically named by the court in such special order. An order of conditions or special order of conditions shall be valid for five years from the date of its issuance, except that, for good cause shown, the court may extend the period for an additional five years.

(p) "District attorney" means the office which prosecuted the criminal action resulting in the verdict or plea of not responsible by reason of mental disease or defect.

(q) "Qualified psychiatrist" means a physician who (i) is a diplomate of the American board of psychiatry and neurology or is eligible to be certified by that board; or (ii) is certified by the American osteopathic board of neurology and psychiatry or is eligible to be certified by that board.

(r) "Licensed psychologist" means a person who is registered as a psychologist under article one hundred fifty-three of the education law.

(s) "Psychiatric examiner" means a qualified psychiatrist or a licensed psychologist who has been designated by the commissioner to examine a defendant pursuant to this section, and such designee need not be an employee of the department of mental hygiene.

2. Examination order; psychiatric examiners. Upon entry of a verdict of not responsible by reason of mental disease or defect, or upon the acceptance of a plea of not responsible by reason of mental disease or defect, the court must immediately issue an examination order. Upon receipt of such order, the commissioner must designate two qualified psychiatric examiners to conduct the examination to examine the defendant. In conducting their examination, the psychiatric examiners may employ any method which is accepted by the medical profession for the examination of persons alleged to be suffering from a dangerous mental disorder or to be mentally ill or retarded. The court may authorize a psychiatrist or psychologist retained by a defendant to be present at such examination. The clerk of the court must promptly forward a copy of the examination order to the mental hygiene legal service and such service may thereafter participate in all subsequent proceedings under this section.

In all subsequent proceedings under this section, prior to the issuance of a special order of conditions, the court shall consider whether any order of protection had been issued prior to a verdict of not responsible by reason of mental disease or defect in the case, or prior to the acceptance of a plea of not responsible by reason of mental disease or defect in the case.

3. Examination order; place of examination. Upon issuing an examination order, the court must, except as otherwise provided in this subdivision, direct that the defendant be committed to a secure facility designated by the commissioner as the place for such psychiatric examination. The sheriff must hold the defendant in custody pending such designation by the commissioner, and when notified of the designation, the sheriff must promptly deliver the defendant to such secure facility. When the defendant is not in custody at the time of such verdict or plea, because he was previously released on bail or on his own recognizance, the court, in its discretion, may direct that such examination be conducted on an out-patient basis, and at such time and place as the commissioner shall designate. If, however, the commissioner informs the court that confinement of the defendant is necessary for an effective examination, the court must direct that the defendant be confined in a facility designated by the commissioner until the examination is completed.

4. Examination order, duration. Confinement in a secure facility pursuant to an examination order shall be for a period not exceeding thirty

days, except that, upon application of the commissioner, the court may authorize confinement for an additional period not exceeding thirty days when a longer period is necessary to complete the examination. If the initial hearing required by subdivision six of this section has not commenced prior to the termination of such examination period, the commissioner shall retain custody of the defendant in such secure facility until custody is transferred to the sheriff in the manner prescribed in subdivision six of this section. During the period of such confinement, the physician in charge of the facility may administer or cause to be administered to the defendant such emergency psychiatric, medical or other therapeutic treatment as in his judgment should be administered. If the court has directed that the examination be conducted on an out-patient basis, the examination shall be completed within thirty days after the defendant has first reported to the place designated by the commissioner, except that, upon application of the commissioner, the court may extend such period for a reasonable time if a longer period is necessary to complete the examination.

5. Examination order; reports. After he has completed his examination of the defendant, each psychiatric examiner must promptly prepare a report of his findings and evaluation concerning the defendant's mental condition, and submit such report to the commissioner. If the psychiatric examiners differ in their opinion as to whether the defendant is mentally ill or is suffering from a dangerous mental disorder, the commissioner must designate another psychiatric examiner to examine the defendant. Upon receipt of the examination reports, the commissioner must submit them to the court that issued the examination order. If the court is not satisfied with the findings of these psychiatric examiners, the court may designate one or more additional psychiatric examiners pursuant to subdivision fifteen of this section. The court must furnish a copy of the reports to the district attorney, counsel for the defendant and the mental hygiene legal service.

6. Initial hearing; commitment order. After the examination reports are submitted, the court must, within ten days of the receipt of such reports, conduct an initial hearing to determine the defendant's present mental condition. If the defendant is in the custody of the commissioner pursuant to an examination order, the court must direct the sheriff to obtain custody of the defendant from the commissioner and to confine the defendant pending further order of the court, except that the court may direct the sheriff to confine the defendant in an institution located near the place where the court sits if that institution has been designated by the commissioner as suitable for the temporary and secure detention of mentally disabled persons. At such initial hearing, the district attorney must establish to the satisfaction of the court that the defendant has a dangerous mental

disorder or is mentally ill. If the court finds that the defendant has a dangerous mental disorder, it must issue a commitment order. If the court finds that the defendant does not have a dangerous mental disorder but is mentally ill, the provisions of subdivision seven of this section shall apply.

7. Initial hearing civil commitment and order of conditions. If, at the conclusion of the initial hearing conducted pursuant to subdivision six of this section, the court finds that the defendant is mentally ill but does not have a dangerous mental disorder, the provisions of articles nine or fifteen of the mental hygiene law shall apply at that stage of the proceedings and at all subsequent proceedings. Having found that the defendant is mentally ill, the court must issue an order of conditions and an order committing the defendant to the custody of the commissioner. The latter order shall be deemed an order made pursuant to the mental hygiene law and not pursuant to this section, and further retention, conditional release or discharge of such defendant shall be in accordance with the provisions of the mental hygiene law. If, at the conclusion of the initial hearing, the court finds that the defendant does not have a dangerous mental disorder and is not mentally ill, the court must discharge the defendant either unconditionally or subject to an order of conditions.

7-a. Whenever the court issues a special order of conditions pursuant to this section, the commissioner shall make reasonable efforts to notify the victim or victims or the designated witness or witnesses that a special order of conditions containing such provisions has been issued, unless such victim or witness has requested that such notice should not be provided.

8. First retention order. When a defendant is in the custody of the commissioner pursuant to a commitment order, the commissioner must, at least thirty days prior to the expiration of the period prescribed in the order, apply to the court that issued the order, or to a superior court in the county where the secure facility is located, for a first retention order or a release order. The commissioner must give written notice of the application to the district attorney, the defendant, counsel for the defendant, and the mental hygiene legal service. Upon receipt of such application, the court may, on its own motion, conduct a hearing to determine whether the defendant has a dangerous mental disorder, and it must conduct such hearing if a demand therefor is made by the district attorney, the defendant, counsel for the defendant, or the mental hygiene legal service within ten days from the date that notice of the application was given to them. If such a hearing is held on an application for retention, the commissioner must establish to the satisfaction of the court that the defendant has a dangerous mental disorder or is mentally ill. The district attorney shall be entitled to appear and present evidence at such hearing. If such a hearing is held on an

application for release, the district attorney must establish to the satisfaction of the court that the defendant has a dangerous mental disorder or is mentally ill. If the court finds that the defendant has a dangerous mental disorder it must issue a first retention order. If the court finds that the defendant is mentally ill but does not have a dangerous mental disorder, it must issue a first retention order and, pursuant to subdivision eleven of this section, a transfer order and an order of conditions. If the court finds that the defendant does not have a dangerous mental disorder and is not mentally ill, it must issue a release order and an order of conditions pursuant to subdivision twelve of this section.

9. Second and subsequent retention orders. When a defendant is in the custody of the commissioner pursuant to a first retention order, the commissioner must, at least thirty days prior to the expiration of the period prescribed in the order, apply to the court that issued the order, or to a superior court in the county where the facility is located, for a second retention order or a release order. The commissioner must give written notice of the application to the district attorney, the defendant, counsel for the defendant, and the mental hygiene legal service. Upon receipt of such application, the court may, on its own motion, conduct a hearing to determine whether the defendant has a dangerous mental disorder, and it must conduct such hearing if a demand therefor is made by the district attorney, the defendant, counsel for the defendant, or the mental hygiene legal service within ten days from the date that notice of the application was given to them. If such a hearing is held on an application for retention, the commissioner must establish to the satisfaction of the court that the defendant has a dangerous mental disorder or is mentally ill. The district attorney shall be entitled to appear and present evidence at such hearing. If such a hearing is held on an application for release, the district attorney must establish to the satisfaction of the court that the defendant has a dangerous mental disorder or is mentally ill. If the court finds that the defendant has a dangerous mental disorder it must issue a second retention order. If the court finds that the defendant is mentally ill but does not have a dangerous mental disorder, it must issue a second retention order and, pursuant to subdivision eleven of this section, a transfer order and an order of conditions. If the court finds that the defendant does not have a dangerous mental disorder and is not mentally ill, it must issue a release order and an order of conditions pursuant to subdivision twelve of this section. When a defendant is in the custody of the commissioner prior to the expiration of the period prescribed in a second retention order, the procedures set forth in this subdivision for the issuance of a second retention order shall govern the application for and the issuance of any subsequent retention order.

10. Furlough order. The commissioner may apply for a furlough order, pursuant to this subdivision, when a defendant is in his custody pursuant to a commitment order, recommitment order, or retention order and the commissioner is of the view that, consistent with the public safety and welfare of the community and the defendant, the clinical condition of the defendant warrants a granting of the privileges authorized by a furlough order. The application for a furlough order may be made to the court that issued the commitment order, or to a superior court in the county where the secure facility is located. The commissioner must give ten days written notice to the district attorney, the defendant, counsel for the defendant, and the mental hygiene legal service. Upon receipt of such application, the court may, on its own motion, conduct a hearing to determine whether the application should be granted, and must conduct such hearing if a demand therefor is made by the district attorney. If the court finds that the issuance of a furlough order is consistent with the public safety and welfare of the community and the defendant, and that the clinical condition of the defendant warrants a granting of the privileges authorized by a furlough order, the court must grant the application and issue a furlough order containing any terms and conditions that the court deems necessary or appropriate. If the defendant fails to return to the secure facility at the time specified in the furlough order, then, for purposes of subdivision nineteen of this section, he shall be deemed to have escaped.

11. Transfer order and order of conditions. The commissioner may apply for a transfer order, pursuant to this subdivision, when a defendant is in his custody pursuant to a retention order or a recommitment order, and the commissioner is of the view that the defendant does not have a dangerous mental disorder or that, consistent with the public safety and welfare of the community and the defendant, the clinical condition of the defendant warrants his transfer from a secure facility to a non-secure facility under the jurisdiction of the commissioner or to any non-secure facility designated by the commissioner. The application for a transfer order may be made to the court that issued the order under which the defendant is then in custody, or to a superior court in the county where the secure facility is located. The commissioner must give ten days written notice to the district attorney, the defendant, counsel for the defendant, and the mental hygiene legal service. Upon receipt of such application, the court may, on its own motion, conduct a hearing to determine whether the application should be granted, and must conduct such hearing if the demand therefor is made by the district attorney. At such hearing, the district attorney must establish to the satisfaction of the court that the defendant has a dangerous mental disorder or that the issuance of a transfer order is inconsistent with the public safety and welfare of the community. The court must grant the application and

issue a transfer order if the court finds that the defendant does not have a dangerous mental disorder, or if the court finds that the issuance of a transfer order is consistent with the public safety and welfare of the community and the defendant and that the clinical condition of the defendant warrants his transfer from a secure facility to a non-secure facility. A court must also issue a transfer order when, in connection with an application for a first retention order pursuant to subdivision eight of this section or a second or subsequent retention order pursuant to subdivision nine of this section, it finds that a defendant is mentally ill but does not have a dangerous mental disorder. Whenever a court issues a transfer order it must also issue an order of conditions.

12. Release order and order of conditions. The commissioner may apply for a release order, pursuant to this subdivision, when a defendant is in his custody pursuant to a retention order or recommitment order, and the commissioner is of the view that the defendant no longer has a dangerous mental disorder and is no longer mentally ill. The application for a release order may be made to the court that issued the order under which the defendant is then in custody, or to a superior court in the county where the facility is located. The application must contain a description of the defendant's current mental condition, the past course of treatment, a history of the defendant's conduct subsequent to his commitment, a written service plan for continued treatment which shall include the information specified in subdivision (g) of section 29.15 of the mental hygiene law, and a detailed statement of the extent to which supervision of the defendant after release is proposed. The commissioner must give ten days written notice to the district attorney, the defendant, counsel for the defendant, and the mental hygiene legal service. Upon receipt of such application, the court must promptly conduct a hearing to determine the defendant's present mental condition. At such hearing, the district attorney must establish to the satisfaction of the court that the defendant has a dangerous mental disorder or is mentally ill. If the court finds that the defendant has a dangerous mental disorder, it must deny the application for a release order. If the court finds that the defendant does not have a dangerous mental disorder but is mentally ill, it must issue a transfer order pursuant to subdivision eleven of this section if the defendant is then confined in a secure facility. If the court finds that the defendant does not have a dangerous mental disorder and is not mentally ill, it must grant the application and issue a release order. A court must also issue a release order when, in connection with an application for a first retention order pursuant to subdivision eight of this section or a second or subsequent retention order pursuant to subdivision nine of this section, it finds that the defendant does not have a dangerous mental disorder and is not mentally ill. Whenever a court issues a release order it must also issue an order

of conditions. If the court has previously issued a transfer order and an order of conditions, it must issue a new order of conditions upon issuing a release order. The order of conditions issued in conjunction with a release order shall incorporate a written service plan prepared by a psychiatrist familiar with the defendant's case history and approved by the court, and shall contain any conditions that the court determines to be reasonably necessary or appropriate. It shall be the responsibility of the commissioner to determine that such defendant is receiving the services specified in the written service plan and is complying with any conditions specified in such plan and the order of conditions.

13. Discharge order. The commissioner may apply for a discharge order, pursuant to this subdivision, when a defendant has been continuously on an out-patient status for three years or more pursuant to a release order, and the commissioner is of the view that the defendant no longer has a dangerous mental disorder and is no longer mentally ill and that the issuance of a discharge order is consistent with the public safety and welfare of the community and the defendant. The application for a discharge order may be made to the court that issued the release order, or to a superior court in the county where the defendant is then residing. The commissioner must give ten days written notice to the district attorney, the defendant, counsel for the defendant, and the mental hygiene legal service. Upon receipt of such application, the court may, on its own motion, conduct a hearing to determine whether the application should be granted, and must conduct such hearing if a demand therefor is made by the district attorney. The court must grant the application and issue a discharge order if the court finds that the defendant has been continuously on an out-patient status for three years or more, that he does not have a dangerous mental disorder and is not mentally ill, and that the issuance of the discharge order is consistent with the public safety and welfare of the community and the defendant.

14. Recommitment order. At any time during the period covered by an order of conditions an application may be made by the commissioner or the district attorney to the court that issued such order, or to a superior court in the county where the defendant is then residing, for a recommitment order when the applicant is of the view that the defendant has a dangerous mental disorder. The applicant must give written notice of the application to the defendant, counsel for the defendant, and the mental hygiene legal service, and if the applicant is the commissioner he must give such notice to the district attorney or if the applicant is the district attorney he must give such notice to the commissioner. Upon receipt of such application the court must order the defendant to appear before it for a hearing to determine if the defendant has a dangerous mental disorder. Such

order may be in the form of a written notice, specifying the time and place of appearance, served personally upon the defendant, or mailed to his last known address, as the court may direct. If the defendant fails to appear in court as directed, the court may issue a warrant to an appropriate peace officer directing him to take the defendant into custody and bring him before the court. In such circumstance, the court may direct that the defendant be confined in an appropriate institution located near the place where the court sits. The court must conduct a hearing to determine whether the defendant has a dangerous mental disorder. At such hearing, the applicant, whether he be the commissioner or the district attorney must establish to the satisfaction of the court that the defendant has a dangerous mental disorder. If the applicant is the commissioner, the district attorney shall be entitled to appear and present evidence at such hearing; if the applicant is the district attorney, the commissioner shall be entitled to appear and present evidence at such hearing. If the court finds that the defendant has a dangerous mental disorder, it must issue a recommitment order. When a defendant is in the custody of the commissioner pursuant to a recommitment order, the procedures set forth in subdivisions eight and nine of this section for the issuance of retention orders shall govern the application for and the issuance of a first retention order, a second retention order, and subsequent retention orders.

15. Designation of psychiatric examiners. If, at any hearing conducted under this section to determine the defendant's present mental condition, the court is not satisfied with the findings of the psychiatric examiners, the court may direct the commissioner to designate one or more additional psychiatric examiners to conduct an examination of the defendant and submit a report of their findings. In addition, the court may on its own motion, or upon request of a party, may designate one or more psychiatric examiners to examine the defendant and submit a report of their findings. The district attorney may apply to the court for an order directing that the defendant submit to an examination by a psychiatric examiner designated by the district attorney, and such psychiatric examiner may testify at the hearing.

16. Rehearing and review. Any defendant who is in the custody of the commissioner pursuant to a commitment order, a retention order, or a recommitment order, if dissatisfied with such order, may, within thirty days after the making of such order, obtain a rehearing and review of the proceedings and of such order in accordance with the provisions of section 9.35 or 15.35 of the mental hygiene law.

17. Rights of defendants. Subject to the limitations and provisions of this section, a defendant committed to the custody of the commissioner pursuant to this section shall have the rights granted to patients under the mental hygiene law.

18. Notwithstanding any other provision of law, no person confined by reason of a commitment order, recommitment order or retention order to a secure facility may be discharged or released unless the commissioner shall deliver written notice, at least four days excluding Saturdays, Sundays and holidays, in advance of such discharge or release to all of the following:

(a) the district attorney.

(b) the police department having jurisdiction of the area to which the defendant is to be discharged or released.

(c) any other person the court may designate.

The notices required by this subdivision shall be given by the facility staff physician who was treating the defendant or, if unavailable, by the defendant's treatment team leader, but if neither is immediately available, notice must be given by some other member of the clinical staff of the facility. Such notice must be given by any means reasonably calculated to give prompt actual notice.

19. Escape from custody; notice requirements. If a defendant is in the custody of the commissioner pursuant to an order issued under this section, and such defendant escapes from custody, immediate notice of such escape shall be given by the department facility staff to: (a) the district attorney, (b) the superintendent of state police, (c) the sheriff of the county where the escape occurred, (d) the police department having jurisdiction of the area where the escape occurred, (e) any person the facility staff believes to be in danger, and (f) any law enforcement agency and any person the facility staff believes would be able to apprise such endangered person that the defendant has escaped from the facility. Such notice shall be given as soon as the facility staff know that the defendant has escaped from the facility and shall include such information as will adequately identify the defendant and the person or persons believed to be in danger and the nature of the danger. The notices required by this subdivision shall be given by the facility staff physician who was treating the defendant or, if unavailable, by the defendant's treatment team leader, but if neither is immediately available, notice must be given by some other member of the clinical staff of the facility. Such notice must be given by any means reasonably calculated to give prompt actual notice. The defendant may be apprehended, restrained, transported to, and returned to the facility from which he escaped by any peace officer, and it shall be the duty of the officer to assist any representative of the commissioner to take the defendant into custody upon the request of such representative.

20. Required affidavit. No application may be made by the commissioner under this section without an accompanying affidavit from at least one psychiatric examiner supportive of relief

requested in the application, which affidavit shall be served on all parties entitled to receive the notice of application. Such affidavit shall set forth the defendant's clinical diagnosis, a detailed analysis of his or her mental condition which caused the psychiatric examiner to formulate an opinion, and the opinion of the psychiatric examiner with respect to the defendant. Any application submitted without the required affidavit shall be dismissed by the court.

21. Appeals. (a) A party to proceedings conducted in accordance with the provisions of this section may take an appeal to an intermediate appellate court by permission of the intermediate appellate court as follows:

(i) the commissioner may appeal from any release order, retention order, transfer order, discharge order, order of conditions, or recommitment order, for which he has not applied;

(ii) a defendant, or the mental hygiene legal service on his/or her behalf, may appeal from any commitment order, retention order, recommitment order, or, if the defendant has obtained a rehearing and review of any such order pursuant to subdivision sixteen of this section, from an order, not otherwise appealable as of right, issued in accordance with the provisions of section 9.35 or 15.35 of the mental hygiene law authorizing continued retention under the original order, provided, however, that a defendant who takes an appeal from a commitment order, retention order, or recommitment order may not subsequently obtain a rehearing and review of such order pursuant to subdivision sixteen of this section;

(iii) the district attorney may appeal from any release order, transfer order, discharge order, order of conditions, furlough order, or order denying an application for a recommitment order which he opposed.

(b) An aggrieved party may appeal from a final order of the intermediate appellate court to the court of appeals by permission of the intermediate appellate court granted before application to the court of appeals, or by permission of the court of appeals upon refusal by the intermediate appellate court or upon direct application.

(c) An appeal taken under this subdivision shall be deemed civil in nature, and shall be governed by the laws and rules applicable to civil appeals; provided, however, that a stay of the order appealed from must be obtained in accordance with the provisions of paragraph (d) hereof.

(d) The court from or to which an appeal is taken may stay all proceedings to enforce the order appealed from pending an appeal or determination on a motion for permission to appeal, or may grant a limited stay, except that only the court to which an appeal is taken may vacate, limit, or modify a stay previously granted. If the order appealed from is affirmed or modified, the stay shall continue for five days after service upon the appellant of the order of affirmance or modification with notice of its entry in the court to which the appeal was taken. If a motion is made for permission to appeal from such an order, before the expiration of the five days, the stay, or any other stay granted pending determination of the motion for permission to appeal, shall:

(i) if the motion is granted, continue until five days after the appeal is determined; or

(ii) if the motion is denied, continue until five days after the movant is served with the order of denial with notice of its entry.

22. Any special order of conditions issued pursuant to subparagraph (i) or (ii) of paragraph (o) of subdivision one of this section shall bear in a conspicuous manner the term "special order of conditions" and a copy shall be filed by the clerk of the court with the sheriff's office in the county in which anyone intended to be protected by such special order resides, or, if anyone intended to be protected by such special order resides within a city, with the police department of such city. The absence of language specifying that the order is a "special order of conditions" shall not affect the validity of such order. A copy of such special order of conditions may from time to time be filed by the clerk of the court with any other police department or sheriff's office having jurisdiction of the residence, work place, or school of anyone intended to be protected by such special order. A copy of such special order may also be filed by anyone intended to be protected by such provisions at the appropriate police department or sheriff's office having jurisdiction. Any subsequent amendment or revocation of such special order may be filed in the same manner as provided in this subdivision. Such special order of conditions shall plainly state the date that the order expires.

[*] As originally enacted. Should probably be "or."

Added by L. 1980, Ch. 548; **Amended** by L. 1982, Ch. 526; L. 1983, Ch. 976; L. 1985, Ch. 789; L. 1989, Ch. 693; L. 1993, Ch. 330, amending subd. 21; L. 2003, Ch. 525, §§ 1–4, eff. Sept. 17, 2003, amending subd. 1(o) and adding subds. 2 (second undesignated paragraph), 7-a, and 22; L. 2004, Ch. 107, §§ 1–4, eff. June 8, 2004, amending subds. 1(o), 2, 3, 7-a, and 22.

ANNOTATIONS

Commitment.—An acquittal by reason of mental disease or defect does not create a presumption that a person so acquitted currently suffers from mental disease or defect, but, rather, having raised this defense and having previously engaged in antisocial behavior, such a verdict creates sufficient grounds for further examination to determine his present need for treatment and confinement as opposed to immediate release; it is for this purpose only—a prompt examination and report as to sanity— that such a person may be automatically committed to the custody of the Commissioner of Mental Hygiene upon acquittal. *In re* Torsney, 47 N.Y.2d 667, 420 N.Y.S.2d 192, 394 N.E.2d 262 (1979).

—It was improper to direct that the petitioner, acquitted by reason of insanity in 1975 and not then hospitalized, be examined as to his present mental state on an outpatient basis; the examination required by CPL § 330.20(1) is to determine whether petitioner is dangerous and is best performed on an inpatient basis. People *ex rel.* Henig v. Commissioner of Mental Hygiene, 56 A.D.2d 398, 392 N.Y.S.2d 636 (1st Dept.), *aff'd*, 43 N.Y.2d 334, 401 N.Y.S.2d 462, 372 N.E.2d 304 (1977).

Escape risk; restrictions proper.—Court agreed with hospital's assessment that the defendant, an observer of Hasidic Judaism who had previously escaped, was still an escape risk, was diagnosed with a dangerous mental disorder, posed a danger to himself and others, and should be kept in the secure facility; accordingly, court found that restrictions on defendant's ability to practice his religion were not unconstitutional. People *ex rel.* Abraham J. v. Sarkis, 175 Misc. 2d 433, 668 N.Y.S.2d 435 (Sup. Ct. Kings Co. 1997).

Release.—CPL § 330.20 authorizes an order extending the conditions placed on an insanity acquittee's release from a psychiatric facility for a period greater than ten years. *In re* Oswald N., 87 N.Y.2d 98, 637 N.Y.S.2d 949, 661 N.E.2d 679 (1995).

—People's burden of proving defendant is "currently" suffering from a mental illness can be sustained by evidence regarding the likelihood of a relapse if defendant's level of confinement is lowered. People v. George L., 85 N.Y.2d 295, 624 N.Y.S.2d 99, 648 N.E.2d 475 (1995).

—Even when an insanity acquittee is not in the custody of the commissioner of the office of mental health, the court must retain supervisory authority over the acquittee. *In re* Jill ZZ, 83 N.Y.2d 133, 608 N.Y.S.2d 161, 629 N.E.2d 1040 (1994).

—A person who has been validly committed as a result of an acquittal by reason of mental defect or disease, and who at a later time seeks release on the claimed ground that he is no longer dangerous to either himself or others, is required to prove by a fair preponderance of the evidence that he may safely be released. Lublin v. Central Islip Psychiatric Center, 43 N.Y.2d 341, 401 N.Y.S.2d 466, 372 N.E.2d 307 (1977).

—Habeas corpus is a proper proceeding to test the right of the Commissioner of Mental Health to retain in custody a criminal offender who has been found not guilty by reason of mental disease or defect and committed to the Commissioner's custody when retention proceedings have not been had within the time schedule mandated by statute; however, in light of evidence of the present dangerous mental disorder, release would be ordered only if a retention hearing was not begun within ten days of the court's order. People *ex rel.* Thorpe v. Von Holden, 63 N.Y.2d 546, 483 N.Y.S.2d 662, 473 N.E.2d 14 (1984).

Recommitment.—A defendant absolved as not responsible for an otherwise criminal act by reason of mental disease or defect, who after an initial hearing is found not to be suffering from a dangerous mental disorder or a mental illness, may while subject to an order of conditions under the initial disposition nevertheless be recommitted to a secure psychiatric facility. People v. Stone, 73 N.Y.2d 296, 539 N.Y.S.2d 718, 536 N.E.2d 1137 (1989).

—If the applicant for recommitment establishes, by a preponderance of the evidence, that the defendant has a dangerous mental disorder, the court must issue a recommitment order, which means that all future proceedings regarding his retention and release will be governed by CPL § 330.20. *In re* Sheldon S., 9 A.D.3d 92, 778 N.Y.S.2d 180 (2d Dept. 2004).

Retention in secure facility.—To retain an insanity acquittee in a secure facility, the commissioner must show that the acquittee is mentally ill and that he poses a current threat to himself or others. Richard H. v. Consilvio, 6 A.D.3d 7, 773 N.Y.S.2d 356 (1st Dept. 2004) (explaining CPL 330.20).

—In determining whether an insanity acquittee constitutes a current physical danger to himself or others and is therefore in need of secure retention, the courts may consider the nature and recency of the defendant's criminal act; evidence of a history of relapses into violent behavior; substance abuse or dangerous activities upon release or termination of psychiatric treatment; or evidence establishing that continued medication is necessary to control defendant's violent tendencies and that the defendant is not likely to comply with prescribed medication. James M. v. Consilvio, 6 A.D.3d 153, 774 N.Y.S.2d 506 (1st Dept. 2004).

Review and reconsideration.—Although insanity acquittees who contest the terms of their physical confinement have rehearing and review rights comparable to civilly committed patients, acquittees are generally not entitled to all the same heightened procedural and substantive protections that apply to involuntarily committed civil patients. Acquittees are not entitled to the same form of reconsideration of their track status,

a determination that is unique to individuals who have committed criminal acts and inapplicable to involuntary civil patients. Reevaluation of the track determination must be limited to an appeal. *In re* Norman D., 3 N.Y.3d 150, 785 N.Y.S.2d 1, 818 N.E.2d 642 (2004).

§ 330.25. Removal after verdict.

1. Where a defendant is a juvenile offender who does not stand convicted of murder in the second degree, upon motion and with the consent of the district attorney, the action may be removed to the family court in the interests of justice pursuant to article seven hundred twenty-five of this chapter notwithstanding the verdict.

2. If the district attorney consents to the motion for removal pursuant to this section, he shall file a subscribed memorandum with the court setting forth (1) a recommendation that the interests of justice would best be served by removal of the action to the family court; and (2) if the conviction is of an offense set forth in paragraph (b) of subdivision one of section 210.43 of this chapter, specific factors, one or more of which reasonably support the recommendation, showing, (i) mitigating circumstances that bear directly upon the manner in which the crime was committed, or (ii) where the defendant was not the sole participant in the crime, that the defendant's participation was relatively minor although not so minor as to constitute a defense to prosecution, or (iii) where the juvenile offender has no previous adjudications of having committed a designated felony act, as defined in subdivision eight of section 301.2 of the family court act, regardless of the age of the offender at the time of commission of the act, that the criminal act was not part of a pattern of criminal behavior and, in view of the history of the offender, is not likely to be repeated.

3. If the court is of the opinion, based upon the specific factors set forth in the district attorney's memorandum, that the interests of justice would best be served by removal of the action to the family court, the verdict shall be set aside and a plea of guilty of a crime or act for which the defendant is not criminally responsible may be entered pursuant to subdivision three or four of section 220.10 of this chapter. Upon accepting any such plea, the court must specify upon the record the portion or portions of the district attorney's statement the court is relying upon as the basis of its opinion and that it believes the interests of justice would best be served by removal of the proceeding to the family court. Such plea shall then be deemed to be a juvenile delinquency fact determination and the court upon entry thereof must direct that the action be removed to the family court in accordance with the provisions of article seven hundred twenty-five of this chapter.

Added by L. 1978, Ch. 481; **Amended** by L. 1979, Ch. 411; L. 1982, Ch. 920.

ANNOTATION

Infancy issue.—The infancy issue can be raised at any time, and the CPL expressly provides the procedures for dealing with the issue at various stages of the criminal proceeding (*see* CPL §§ 180.75, 190.71, 210.43, 220[5][g], 310.85, 330.25). People v. Holmes, 220 A.D.2d 109, 645 N.Y.S.2d 115 (3d Dept.), *aff'd*, 89 N.Y.2d 838 (1996).

§ 330.30. Motion to set aside verdict; grounds for.

At any time after rendition of a verdict of guilty and before sentence, the court may, upon motion of the defendant, set aside or modify the verdict or any part thereof upon the following grounds:

1. Any ground appearing in the record which, if raised upon an appeal from a prospective judgment of conviction, would require a reversal or modification of the judgment as a matter of law by an appellate court.

2. That during the trial there occurred, out of the presence of the court, improper conduct by a juror, or improper conduct by another person in relation to a juror, which may have affected a substantial right of the defendant and which was not known to the defendant prior to the rendition of the verdict; or

3. That new evidence has been discovered since the trial which could not have been produced by the defendant at the trial even with due diligence on his part and which is of such character as to create a probability that had such evidence been received at the trial the verdict would have been more favorable to the defendant.

ANNOTATIONS

Generally.—In determining a motion to set aside the verdict, a court must draw every reasonable inference in the People's favor. People v. Floyd, 176 A.D.2d 554, 574 N.Y.S.2d 733 (1st Dept. 1991), *lv. denied*, 79 N.Y.2d 827 (1992).

—The grounds upon which a trial court may set aside a jury verdict before a sentence are limited to those set forth in CPL § 330.30. People v. Carthens, 171 A.D.2d 387, 577 N.Y.S.2d 249 (1st Dept. 1991).

—After granting a motion to set aside a verdict of guilty for criminal sale of a controlled substance when defendant contended there was a witness who would testify that defendant was not the seller, the court had power to vacate its order before final judgment after defendant's attorney informed the district attorney that the witness would not testify unless she was granted immunity from prosecution. People v. Phino, 80 A.D.2d 804, 437 N.Y.S.2d 104 (1st Dept. 1981).

—Only a claim of error that is properly preserved for appellate review may serve as the basis for a trial court to set aside a verdict. People v. Josey, 204 A.D.2d 571, 612 N.Y.S.2d 170 (2d Dept. 1994).

—Upon an application to set aside a verdict by the defendant, pursuant to CPL § 330.30(1), the court may set aside a verdict only when there appears in the record, a ground which, if raised upon an appeal from a prospective judgment of conviction, would require a reversal or modification of the judgment as a matter of law by an appellate court. People v. Collins, 72 A.D.2d 431, 424 N.Y.S.2d 954 (4th Dept. 1980).

—A CPL 330.30(1) motion is inappropriate if trial facts must be supplemented by an affidavit or if appellate discretion is involved. People v. Thompson, 177 Misc. 2d 803, 678 N.Y.S.2d 845 (Sup. Ct. Kings Co. 1998).

—CPL § 330.30(1) motion is inappropriate if trial facts must be supplemented by affidavit or if appellate discretion is involved. People v. Thompson, 177 Misc. 2d 803, 678 N.Y.S.2d 845 (Sup. Ct. Kings Co. 1998).

Juror misconduct.—While it would be improper for a juror

to engage in experimentation, investigation, and calculation that necessarily rely on facts outside the record and beyond the understanding of the average juror, jurors are not required to "check their life experiences at the door." Where juror, a patient care associate at a hospital, merely gave her lay opinions regarding the introduction of an I.V. line, drawing on both her life experiences and the trial evidence, it was proper and did not rise to the level of juror misconduct. People v. Santi, 3 N.Y.3d 234, 785 N.Y.S.2d 405, 818 N.E.2d 1146 (2004) (citing People v. Maragh, 94 N.Y.2d 569, 708 N.Y.S.2d 44, 729 N.E.2d 701 (2000)).

—A juror's concealment of any information during voir dire is not, by itself, a reason for automatic reversal. Court properly determined after a hearing that the juror's lack of disclosure of his acquaintance with a prosecutor did not cause any prejudice to defendant. People v. Rodriguez, 100 N.Y.2d 30, 760 N.Y.S.2d 74, 790 N.E.2d 247 (2003).

—Where nurse-jurors substituted their own professional opinions in place of expert proofs at trial and shared their opinions with the rest of the jury, a new trial was ordered. People v. Maragh, 94 N.Y.2d 569, 708 N.Y.S.2d 44, 729 N.E.2d 701 (2000), *limited by* People v. Arnold, 96 N.Y.2d 358, 729 N.Y.S.2d 51, 753 N.E.2d 846 (2001).

—A motion to set aside verdict is the appropriate vehicle for post-verdict allegations of improper influence of juror deliberation, and defendant is entitled to a hearing upon his assertion of facts indicating misconduct. People v. Irizarry, 83 N.Y.2d 557, 611 N.Y.S.2d 807, 634 N.E.2d 179 (1994).

—A motion to set aside a verdict may be granted when it is shown that improper conduct by a juror may have affected a substantial right of the defendant; however, not every misstep by a juror rises to the inherently prejudicial level at which reversal is required automatically. People v. Clark, 81 N.Y.2d 913, 597 N.Y.S.2d 646, 613 N.E.2d 552 (1993).

—There is no concrete test for the trial court to follow in assessing claims of improper jury influence; trial court did not abuse its discretion in denying defendant's challenge to the verdict where there was conflicting testimony at a post-verdict hearing as to the jurors' discussion during deliberations of a news report of a co-defendant's guilty plea and whether this had a substantial impact on the verdict. People v. Testa, 61 N.Y.2d 1008, 475 N.Y.S.2d 371, 463 N.E.2d 1223 (1984).

—Defendant was entitled to have verdict set aside based on juror misconduct because the evidence established that the jurors and alternate jurors discussed the trial testimony and credibility of witnesses and the defendant's guilt or innocence before deliberations commenced. Some of the jurors and alternate jurors read and discussed newspaper articles about the case, and there were improper communications between the jurors and the alternate jurors during deliberations. People v. Romano, 8 A.D.3d 503, 778 N.Y.S.2d 517 (2d Dept. 2004).

—Although deliberating juror stated that he voted guilty only because he capitulated to the pressure placed on him by the other jurors, a jury verdict may not be impeached by statements going to the tenor of the jury's deliberations. People v. Liguori, 149 A.D.2d 624, 540 N.Y.S.2d 291 (2d Dept. 1989).

—Jury's verdict will not be disturbed on basis of an affidavit by a juror in which she sought to impeach her verdict by reference to matters occurring during the deliberation process; defendant must establish outside influences on a jury which may have prejudiced the defendant or the discovery of a juror's lack of qualifications. People v. Maddox, 139 A.D.2d 597, 527 N.Y.S.2d 89 (2d Dept. 1988).

—The trial court properly denied the defendant's motion to set aside the verdict on the basis of the allegations of one juror concerning the behavior of another juror during deliberations where the defendant raised no issue of improper influence but rather sought to impeach the verdict by questioning the jury's deliberative processes. People v. Scales, 121 A.D.2d 578, 503 N.Y.S.2d 629 (2d Dept. 1986).

—Defendant's conviction was not tainted by the post-verdict statement of one of the jurors that she abandoned her position in favor of an acquittal and voted in favor of defendant's conviction only because she was ill and exhausted. People v. Rodriguez, 119 A.D.2d 599, 500 N.Y.S.2d 769 (2d Dept. 1986).

—Trial court did not abuse its discretion when it set aside the verdict where it appeared that the verdict of the jurors may have been the result of outside influences, to wit, the opinions of the alternate jurors, and extraneous material. People v. Marrero, 83 A.D.2d 565, 441 N.Y.S.2d 12 (2d Dept. 1981).

—Allegation by one juror that several jurors threatened others into a compromise verdict is insufficient for its impeachment where, as here, the proffer is solely proof of the tenor of its deliberations. People v. Browne, 307 A.D.2d 645, 763 N.Y.S.2d 695 (3d Dept. 2003).

—To the extent that one juror indicated a reliance on his nursing training, this required neither the granting of defendant's motion nor a hearing because the juror's use of personal professional expertise merely confirmed the medical proof adduced at trial; it was not communicated to the other jurors and did not violate defendant's right to have his case decided on the evidence adduced. People v. Camacho, 293 A.D.2d 876, 742 N.Y.S.2d 402 (3d Dept. 2002).

—Court properly denied defendant's motion to set aside verdict based on juror misconduct. Juror had installed appliances at the apartment complex where the crime occurred, and he shared his knowledge of the layout of the apartment with the other jurors. Juror testified that although he believed a diagram introduced into evidence was inaccurate, his knowledge of the layout of the apartment did not affect his verdict, and the other jurors testified that they were not influenced by the juror's comments. People v. Robinson, 1 A.D.3d 985, 768 N.Y.S.2d 50 (4th Dept. 2003).

—Defendant cannot impeach the jury's verdict by claiming that one of the jurors stated that the jury was confused about deliberations. People v. Paz, 159 A.D.2d 987, 552 N.Y.S.2d 753 (4th Dept.), *lv. denied,* 76 N.Y.2d 793 (1990), *on reconsideration, lv. denied,* 77 N.Y.2d 842 (1991).

—Juror's failure to reveal participation in court watcher's program did not provide sufficient ground to set aside the verdict. People v. Teitelbaum, 133 Misc. 2d 392, 506 N.Y.S.2d 936 (Sup. Ct. Queens Co. 1986), *aff'd,* 138 A.D.2d 647, 526 N.Y.S.2d 230 (2d Dept. 1988).

Improper juror experimentation.—Reversal was required where a juror conducted an experiment in the form of adjusting the lighting conditions and opening the curtains in her hotel room to simulate what she believed to be the conditions of the crime scene, based on the victim's testimony. People v. Legister, 75 N.Y.2d 832, 552 N.Y.S.2d 906, 552 N.E.2d 154 (1990).

—Prior familiarity with a neighborhood where a crime has occurred cannot be equated with a juror's impermissibly conscious, contrived experimentation. People v. Griffin, 173 A.D.2d 216, 569 N.Y.S.2d 97 (1st Dept.), *lv. denied,* 78 N.Y.2d 1076 (1991).

—Court did not err in granting the jury's request, during deliberations, for a magnifying glass, since use of it was for the purpose of enhancing the clarity of photographs admitted into evidence, similar to the use of reading glasses; it was not to be used for inadmissible purposes such as comparing fingerprints or determining whether a handwriting exhibit had been tampered with. People v. Moody, 195 A.D.2d 1016, 600 N.Y.S.2d 581 (4th Dept. 1993).

—Reversal was required where the jurors conducted an experiment in form of test-firing gun. People v. Andrew, 156 A.D.2d 978, 549 N.Y.S.2d 268 (4th Dept. 1989).

Ineffective assistance of counsel.—Trial court erred in granting motion to vacate judgment of conviction for murder based upon denial of effective assistance of counsel at trial, due to court's belief that the wrong trial strategy was chosen; defense counsel vigorously participated in the trial, and demonstrated reasonable competence which precluded a determination that the trial was a farce and a mockery of justice. People v. Natal, 102 A.D.2d 496, 478 N.Y.S.2d 889 (1st Dept. 1984), *aff'd,* 66 N.Y.2d 802 (1985).

—Defendant was deprived effective assistance of counsel, where the testimony at the CPL § 330.30 hearing revealed that defense counsel did not conduct an investigation into the defendant's alibi, and failed to obtain any report from the investigator he hired to interview the alibi witnesses. People v. Bussey, 6 A.D.3d 621, 775 N.Y.S.2d 364 (2d Dept. 2004).

—To the extent that defendant's motion pursuant to CPL § 330.30 to set aside the verdict was based on ground of ineffective assistance of counsel and relied on alleged deficiencies in his counsel's performance which were dehors the record, those claims were not properly before the Appellate Division on appeal from final judgment. People v. Wells, 265 A.D.2d 588, 696 N.Y.S.2d 893 (2d Dept. 1999).

Impeaching evidence.—Statements made in a civil proceeding by one of the victims that were allegedly inconsistent with the victim's testimony constituted impeaching evidence that would not justify reversal. People v. Casillas, 289 A.D.2d 1063, 736 N.Y.S.2d 207 (4th Dept. 2001).

Insufficient evidence.—A court adjudicating a CPL § 330.30 motion may consider only issues of law that would require a reversal or modification of the judgment as a matter of law by an appellate court; under this statutory standard, an insufficiency argument may not be addressed unless it has been properly preserved for review during the trial. People v. Hines, 97 N.Y.2d 56, 736 N.Y.S.2d 643, 762 N.E.2d 329 (2001), *reargument denied,* 97 N.Y.2d 678, 738 N.Y.S.2d 292, 764 N.E.2d 396 (2001).

—Jury's verdict of guilty was properly set aside where there was no evidence, direct or circumstantial, from which the inference of guilt must be drawn as inconsistent with innocence and the evidence failed to exclude to a moral certainty every other reasonable hypothesis except guilt. People v. Marin, 65 N.Y.2d 741, 492 N.Y.S.2d 16, 481 N.E.2d 556 (1985).

—Where the inferences that could be drawn from the evidence are consistent with innocence as well as with guilt, and there are logical gaps in the People's case that cannot be bridged by the drawing of reasonable, permissible inferences, the jury's verdict of guilty is not supported by sufficient evidence. People v. Giuliano, 65 N.Y.2d 766, 492 N.Y.S.2d 939, 482 N.E.2d 557 (1985).

—A jury's verdict of guilty and rejection of defendant's insanity defense will not be overturned because defendant's motivation for his criminal acts may have been bizarre and unlikely to succeed, especially where there was sufficient expert testimony to prove beyond a reasonable doubt that defendant had substantial capacity to know or appreciate the nature and consequences of his conduct and that the conduct was wrong. People v. Roldan, 64 N.Y.2d 821, 486 N.Y.S.2d 928, 476 N.E.2d 327 (1985).

—While the trial court can set aside a verdict for insufficient evidence, it cannot do so on the grounds that the verdict is against the weight of the evidence. People v. Carter, 63 N.Y.2d 530, 483 N.Y.S.2d 654, 473 N.E.2d 6 (1984).

—Court properly denied the motion of defendant to set aside the verdict on the ground that the People failed to disprove his alibi defense; pursuant to CPL § 330.30(1), a court may set aside a guilty verdict on any ground that, if raised on appeal, would require reversal or modification as a matter of law. Whether the People failed to disprove his alibi defense is a question of fact, not law; thus, court lacked authority to set aside the verdict on that ground. People v. South, 233 A.D.2d 910, 649 N.Y.S.2d 553 (4th Dept. 1996).

Newly discovered evidence.—Trial court properly denied motion for new trial on the ground of newly discovered evidence where defendant alleged that two police officers, who participated in drug raid on defendant's hotel room, had observed defendant in lobby rather than in room containing the contraband at time of arrest; testimony merely amounted to an inconsistent version of the circumstances surrounding the initial entry of the police into the hotel. People v. Slaughter, 37 N.Y.2d 596, 376 N.Y.S.2d 114, 338 N.E.2d 622 (1975).

—Trial court properly denied defendant's motion to set aside his conviction on the basis of newly discovered evidence where the claimed newly discovered evidence that defendant's friend had admitted to committing the crime was known to defendant and his attorney before trial and the withholding of such evidence was in furtherance of defendant's own deliberate tactic. People v. Messina, 73 A.D.2d 899, 424 N.Y.S.2d 219 (1st Dept. 1980).

—Defendant was not entitled to a new trial based on a recanting witness's affidavit, absent showing that a different result would probably have been reached had the affidavit been submitted earlier. People v. Lane, 212 A.D.2d 637, 622 N.Y.S.2d 590 (2d Dept. 1995).

—Recantation evidence is inherently unreliable and alone is not sufficient to require setting aside a conviction. People v. Legette, 153 A.D.2d 760, 545 N.Y.S.2d 296 (2d Dept. 1989).

—Since the testimony of the new witness was sufficiently impeached and the evidence of guilt was overwhelming, motion to set aside the verdict was denied because defendants failed to meet their burden of proof on the probable impact of the newly discovered evidence on the verdict. People v. Santiago, 88 A.D.2d 665, 450 N.Y.S.2d 514 (2d Dept. 1982).

—Where testimony of an undercover officer fully implicated

defendant and defendant's testimony was patently incredible, failure of the prosecutor to inform defendant that a co-defendant had threatened the life of the officer did not necessitate a new trial since the new evidence did not create a reasonable likelihood of a different result. People v. Cantone, 73 A.D.2d 936, 423 N.Y.S.2d 507 (2d Dept. 1980), *cert. denied,* 474 U.S. 835 (1985).

—Defendant failed to show that his brother's testimony constituted "newly discovered" evidence, considering that the brother had spoken with counsel the week before trial, other defense witnesses knew where he was living, no material witness order or subpoena was sought to secure his testimony, and the brother's testimony would not likely have changed the outcome because he planned to directly contradict his grand jury testimony, and every witness referred to the defendant's brother as always being drunk. People v. Ortiz, 16 A.D.3d 831, 791 N.Y.S.2d 709 (3d Dept. 2005).

—Where new evidence was, if believed, impeaching to a witness's testimony, court properly denied defendant's motion. People v. Bowers, 4 A.D.3d 558, 771 N.Y.S.2d 270 (3d Dept. 2004).

—Victim testified before the Grand Jury that the offense occurred "around" November 10, 1996, and defendant claimed after the trial that he was contacted by two alleged alibi witnesses regarding his whereabouts on that date; under those circumstances, the precise date of the offense could not be considered newly discovered evidence, because the alleged evidence could have been discovered before the trial through the exercise of due diligence. People v. Remillard, 267 A.D.2d 610, 699 N.Y.S.2d 558 (3d Dept. 1999).

—Court properly denied defendant's motion to set aside the verdict, where the minor errors made by the interpreter were known during trial and were thus not newly discovered evidence. People v. Casillas, 289 A.D.2d 1063, 736 N.Y.S.2d 207 (4th Dept. 2001).

—Court properly denied defendant's motion to set aside the verdict on the ground of newly discovered evidence because defendant's motion was made orally at the time of sentencing and thus failed to comply with the requirements of 330.40(2)(a). People v. Castleberry, 265 A.D.2d 921, 697 N.Y.S.2d 215 (4th Dept. 1999).

—A defendant who chooses to withhold evidence should not be given a new trial on the basis of the evidence withheld. People v. Moore, 147 A.D.2d 924, 537 N.Y.S.2d 691 (4th Dept. 1989).

Repugnant verdicts.—In nonjury cases the issue of a verdict's repugnancy may be raised in a motion to set aside the verdict pursuant to CPL § 330.30, since the court, as trier of the facts, is still available to correct repugnancies in the verdict if there be any. People v. Alfaro, 66 N.Y.2d 985, 499 N.Y.S.2d 378, 489 N.E.2d 1280 (1985).

—Defendant's CPL § 330.30 motion was actually a claim of repugnancy or inconsistency in the verdict; it was untimely, not having been made prior to discharge of the jury, and meritless because acquittal on the second degree grand larceny count did not negate any necessary element of the fourth degree grand larceny count as charged. People v. Echevarria, 233 A.D.2d 200, 650 N.Y.S.2d 98 (1st Dept. 1996).

—Verdict of guilty with respect to criminal possession of a controlled substance charge was not repugnant to acquittal on criminal possession of a weapon charge involving weapons found in the apartment. People v. Plower, 176 A.D.2d 214, 574 N.Y.S.2d 337 (1st Dept. 1991), *lv. denied,* 79 N.Y.2d 830 (1992).

—Defendant's acquittal of criminal sale charge was not repugnant to conviction of criminal possession charge. People v. Ortiz, 170 A.D.2d 396, 566 N.Y.S.2d 284 (1st Dept.), *lv. denied,* 78 N.Y.2d 1079 (1991).

—In assessing a repugnant verdict claim, review of the entire record in an attempt to divine the jury's collective mental process of weighing the evidence is inappropriate. People v. Loughlin, 154 A.D.2d 550, 546 N.Y.S.2d 390 (2d Dept.), *aff'd,* 74 N.Y.2d 804 (1989).

—Jury verdict acquitting defendant of charges in connection with alleged sale of cocaine to an undercover officer on one occasion and convicting him of similar charges arising out of the sale of cocaine two weeks later was not repugnant. People v. Cruz, 147 A.D.2d 584, 537 N.Y.S.2d 878 (2d Dept. 1989).

—Factual inconsistencies in a verdict, whether rendered by judge or jury, does not constitute a ground for reversal, provided, of course, that the verdict is not repugnant as a matter of law. People v. Montgomery, 116 A.D.2d 669, 497 N.Y.S.2d 737 (2d Dept. 1986).

—In determining whether a verdict is repugnant, the court must look only to the essential elements of the crime. People v. Sylvers, 149 A.D.2d 920, 540 N.Y.S.2d 52 (4th Dept. 1989).

—There is no inconsistency between a conviction for intentional murder and felony murder since no culpable mental state is essential to conviction for the latter; these are noninclusory concurrent counts which the court need not submit in the alternative. People v. Sampson, 145 A.D.2d 910, 536 N.Y.S.2d 291 (4th Dept. 1988).

—A court cannot set aside a verdict as repugnant or inconsistent merely because it considers the jury's decision to be irrational. People v. Gladney, 195 Misc. 2d 520, 760 N.Y.S.2d 309 (Nassau Co. Dist. Ct. 2003).

Appeal; preservation.—In order for an error to constitute an "error of law" as required for a new trial order under CPL § 330.30(2), there must be a timely protest. People v. Padro, 75 N.Y.2d 820, 552 N.Y.S.2d 555, 551 N.E.2d 1233 (1990).

—No separate appeal lies from an order denying a motion to set aside a verdict, although the determination of the motion is reviewed on appeal from the judgment. People v. Pollack, 67 A.D.2d 608, 412 N.Y.S.2d 12 (1st Dept. 1979), *aff'd,* 50 N.Y.2d 547, 429 N.Y.S.2d 628, 407 N.E.2d 472 (1980).

—No error was preserved for review where defendant claimed that his plea should be vacated because the elements of the crime were not clearly spelled out in his statements to the Court at the time he entered his plea since he did not raise the issue by motion to vacate or otherwise in the trial court. People v. Warren, 47 N.Y.2d 740, 417 N.Y.S.2d 251, 390 N.E.2d 1175 (1979).

—Trial court erred in granting defendant's motion made one month after verdict, to set aside verdict as repugnant because the defendant waived such claim by failing to register a protest to the verdict prior to the discharge of the jury, when any infirmity might have been remedied by resubmission to the jury for further consideration; further, the verdicts, acquitting the defendant of grand larceny in the third degree and convicting him of robbery in the second degree, were neither repugnant nor inconsistent since the grand larceny charge contained an element not found in the robbery charge, to wit, that property be taken from the person of another. People v. Barry, 100 A.D.2d 803, 474 N.Y.S.2d 731 (1st Dept. 1984).

—Defendant did not preserve his contention that the application of a statutory presumption was unconstitutional under the facts of his case by raising it in a motion to set aside the verdict pursuant to CPL § 330.30. People v. Grossfeld, 216 A.D.2d 319, 628 N.Y.S.2d 331 (2d Dept. 1995).

—Since the defendant's claim that the verdict was repugnant was not raised before the jury was discharged, it was waived. People v. Thompson, 145 A.D.2d 952, 536 N.Y.S.2d 322 (4th Dept. 1988).

Verdict improperly set aside.—Where the CPL § 330.30 order in this case essentially rested on trial court's factual review of the weight of the evidence, a power not statutorily extended to the trial court in a jury trial, reversal of the trial court's granting of the motion to set aside the verdict was ordered on procedural grounds. People v. Garcia, 272 A.D.2d 189, 707 N.Y.S.2d 441 (1st Dept. 2000).

—Trial court improperly set aside the verdict of guilt, because court's decision was based on the apparent discrepancy concerning the respective linguistic abilities of the perpetrator and of the defendant, which was a factual review involving the weighing of evidence; verdict reinstated. People v. Garcia, 237 A.D.2d 42, 668 N.Y.S.2d 5 (1st Dept. 1998), *rev'd on other grounds,* 93 N.Y.2d 42, 687 N.Y.S.2d 601, 710 N.E.2d 247 (1999).

§ 330.40. Motion to set aside verdict; procedure.

1. A motion to set aside a verdict based upon a ground specified in subdivision one of section 330.30 need not be in writing, but the people must be given reasonable notice thereof and an opportunity to appear in opposition thereto.

2. A motion to set aside a verdict based upon a ground specified in subdivisions two and three of section 330.30 must be made and determined as follows:

(a) The motion must be in writing and upon reasonable notice to the people. The moving papers must contain sworn allegations, whether by the defendant or by another person or persons, of the occurrence or existence of all facts essential to support the motion. Such sworn allegations may be based upon personal knowledge of the affiant or upon information and belief, provided that in the latter event the affiant must state the sources of such information and the grounds of such belief;

(b) The people may file with the court, and in such case must serve a copy thereof upon the defendant or his counsel, an answer denying or admitting any or all of the allegations of the moving papers;

(c) After all papers of both parties have been filed, the court must consider the same and, if the motion is determinable pursuant to paragraphs (d) or (e), must or may, as therein provided, determine the motion without holding a hearing to resolve questions of fact;

(d) The court must grant the motion if:

(i) The moving papers allege a ground constituting legal basis for the motion; and

(ii) Such papers contain sworn allegations of all facts essential to support such ground; and

(iii) All the essential facts are conceded by the people to be true.

(e) The court may deny the motion if:

(i) The moving papers do not allege any ground constituting legal basis for the motion; or

(ii) The moving papers do not contain sworn allegations of all facts essential to support the motion.

(f) If the court does not determine the motion pursuant to paragraphs (d) or (e), it must conduct a hearing and make findings of fact essential to the determination thereof;

(g) Upon such a hearing, the defendant has the burden of proving by a preponderance of the evidence every fact essential to support motion.

ANNOTATIONS

Procedure; motion papers.—Defendant's motion to set aside verdict was based on matters outside record, and thus motion should not have been entertained. People v. Leka, 209 A.D.2d 723, 619 N.Y.S.2d 144 (2d Dept. 1994), *lv. denied*, 85 N.Y.2d 911 (1995).

—Defendant's claim that he was entitled to a new trial based on newly-discovered evidence was not raised in the County Court by way of a motion, in writing, with reasonable notice to the People, and was thus not properly before the court. People v. Donovan, 141 A.D.2d 835, 530 N.Y.S.2d 174 (2d Dept. 1988).

—Court properly denied defense counsel's motion for an order

setting aside the verdict where it was made orally, and was unsupported by moving papers. People v. Williams, 134 A.D.2d 304, 520 N.Y.S.2d 631 (2d Dept. 1987), *lv. denied*, 71 N.Y.2d 904 (1988).

Hearing required.—Defendant's due process right to have his motion decided by an impartial tribunal based upon the evidence presented at the hearing was violated where a hearing was held following the verdict on the ground of juror misconduct; the trial court conducted its own investigation with participation by the District Attorney's office, and withheld the fruits of that inquiry from the defense counsel. People v. Lackomec, 86 A.D.2d 77, 449 N.Y.S.2d 71 (3d Dept. 1982).

—The court committed reversible error when it denied the motion without a hearing where the newly discovered evidence was not merely contradictory nor for the sole purpose of impeaching complainant's testimony and the statement by the witness was made for the first time after the trial. People v. Stokes, 83 A.D.2d 968, 443 N.Y.S.2d 12 (2d Dept. 1981).

Hearing not required.—Ordinarily, the court, when confronted with charges and allegations, that a court clerk had instructed the jury to continue deliberations, should hold a hearing to inquire into the truth of the factual averments, however, a hearing was not necessary where defense counsel, in his motion papers, alleged a legal basis for relief and submitted uncontroverted sworn affidavits of two jurors containing all facts essential to support the grounds for setting aside the verdicts and the People did not dispute any of these facts. People v. Ciaccio, 47 N.Y.2d 431, 418 N.Y.S.2d 371, 391 N.E.2d 1347 (1979).

—Defendant's CPL § 330.30 motion was properly denied without a hearing where defendant failed to establish that the evidence could not have been discovered before trial by the exercise of due diligence and that the evidence did not merely contradict former evidence introduced by the People. People v. Batista, 172 A.D.2d 386, 568 N.Y.S.2d 766 (1st Dept.), *lv. denied*, 78 N.Y.2d 961 (1991).

—Post-trial hearing was not required to inquire into whether a juror gave truthful answers on the voir dire, when the only evidence to justify such a hearing is the unsupported affidavit of a juror, who disputes what another juror allegedly said during deliberations, and where there is no claim that the juror who allegedly lied did anything to frustrate the fair and impartial consideration of the facts before the jury. People v. Morales, 121 A.D.2d 240, 503 N.Y.S.2d 374 (1st Dept. 1986).

—Trial court did not improvidently exercise its discretion in denying the defendant's motion to set aside the verdict based upon alleged juror misconduct without a hearing where it was based upon an affidavit containing hearsay allegations. People v. Bellamy, 158 A.D.2d 525, 551 N.Y.S.2d 291 (2d Dept.), *lv. denied*, 76 N.Y.2d 731 (1990).

—It was proper for the court to summarily deny the motion where newly discovered evidence, which served as basis for defendant's motion to set aside the verdict, consisted of hearsay. People v. Haddad, 133 A.D.2d 124, 518 N.Y.S.2d 656 (2d Dept. 1987).

§ 330.50. Motion to set aside verdict; order granting motion.

1. Upon setting aside or modifying a verdict or a part thereof upon a ground specified in subdivision one of section 330.30, the court must take the same action as the appropriate appellate court would be required to take upon reversing or modifying a judgment upon the particular ground in issue.

2. Upon setting aside a verdict upon a ground specified in subdivision two of section 330.30, the court must order a new trial.

3. Upon setting aside a verdict upon a ground specified in subdivision three of section 330.30, the court must, except as otherwise provided in this subdivision, order a new trial. If a verdict is set aside upon the ground that had the newly

discovered evidence in question been received at the trial the verdict probably would have been more favorable to the defendant in that the conviction probably would have been for a lesser offense than the one contained in the verdict, the court may either (a) set aside such verdict or (b) with the consent of the people modify such verdict by reducing it to one of conviction of such lesser offense.

4. Upon a new trial resulting from an order setting aside a verdict, the indictment is deemed to contain all the counts and to charge all the offenses which it contained and charged at the time the previous trial was commenced, regardless of whether any count was dismissed by the court in the course of such trial, except those upon or of which the defendant was acquitted or is deemed to have been acquitted.

ANNOTATION

New trial.—A new trial is the proper remedy where the evidence provided by the missing witness was "of such a character as to create a probability that had such evidence been received at the trial the verdict would have been more favorable to the defendant" and the trial evidence against the defendant was legally sufficient. People v. Barberas, 92 A.D.2d 871, 459 N.Y.S.2d 828 (2d Dept. 1983).

TITLE K—PROSECUTION OF INFORMATIONS IN LOCAL CRIMINAL COURTS—PLEA TO SENTENCE

ARTICLE 340—PRE-TRIAL PROCEEDINGS

LexisNexis Cross References

Criminal Law Advocacy, Vol. 1, Ch. 11A, Resisting Pretrial Disclosure on the Basis of the Fifth Amendment's Privilege Against Self-Incrimination; Vol. 1, Ch. 14, Miscellaneous Pretrial Motions; *see generally Criminal Law Advocacy,* Vol. 2, Guilty Pleas; *Criminal Defense Techniques,* Vol. 1, Ch. 1C, Pretrial Preparation for a White-Collar Crime Case; Vol. 1, Ch. 1D, State Pretrial Motion Tactics; Vol. 1A, Ch. 13, Negotiating a Plea; Vol. 1A, Ch. 15, The Evolution of Discovery in Criminal Cases; Vol. 1B, Ch. 29, Alibi Evidence; Vol. 1B, Ch. 30, Entrapment; Vol. 1B, Ch. 31, The Insanity Defense; Vol. 1B, Ch. 32, Diminished Capacity; *Defense of Narcotics Cases,* Vol. 1, Ch. 2, Pretrial Proceedings.

§ 340.10. Definitions of terms.

The following definitions are applicable to this title:

1. "Information," in addition to its meaning as defined in subdivision one of section 100.10, includes (a) a simplified information and (b) a prosecutor's information and (c) a misdemeanor complaint upon which the defendant, by a waiver executed pursuant to subdivision three of section 170.65, has consented to be prosecuted.

2. "Single judge trial" means a trial in a local criminal court conducted by one judge sitting without a jury.

3. "Jury trial" means a trial in a local criminal court conducted by one judge sitting with a jury.

Amended by L. 1971, Ch. 815; L. 1972, Ch. 661.

§ 340.20. The plea.

1. Except as provided in subdivisions two and three, the provisions of article two hundred twenty, governing the kinds of pleas to indictments which may be entered and related matters, are, to the extent that they can be so applied, applicable to pleas to informations, and changes of pleas thereto, in local criminal courts.

2. A plea to an information, other than one against a corporation, must be entered in the following manner:

(a) Subject to the provisions of paragraph (b), a plea to an information must be entered orally by the defendant in person unless the court permits entry thereof by counsel upon the filing by him of a written and subscribed statement by the defendant declaring that he waives his right to plead to the information in person and authorizing his attorney to enter a plea on his behalf as set forth in the authorization.

(b) If the only offense or offenses charged are traffic infractions, the procedure provided in sections eighteen hundred five, eighteen hundred six and eighteen hundred seven of the vehicle and traffic law, relating to pleas in such cases, is, when appropriate, applicable and controlling.

3. A plea to an information against a corporation must be entered by counsel.

4. When a sentence is agreed upon by the prosecutor and a defendant as a predicate to entry of a plea of guilty, the court or the prosecutor must orally on the record, or in writing filed with the court, state the sentence agreed upon as a condition of such plea.

Amended by L. 1973, Ch. 61; L. 1974, Ch. 430; L. 1984, Ch. 671.

ANNOTATION

Acceptance of plea.—In the absence of express consent by the district attorney to the acceptance of a reduced plea in a specific case, the court is without jurisdiction to accept it. Blumberg v. Lennon, 44 A.D.2d 769, 354 N.Y.S.2d 261 (4th Dept. 1974).

§ 340.30. Pre-trial discovery and notices of defenses.

The provisions of article two hundred forty,

concerning pre-trial discovery by a defendant under indictment in a superior court, and article two hundred fifty, concerning pre-trial notice to the people by a defendant under indictment in a superior court who intends to advance a trial defense of mental disease or defect or of alibi, apply to a prosecution of an information in a local criminal court.

§ 340.40. Modes of trial.

1. Except as otherwise provided in this section, a trial of an information in a local criminal court must be a single judge trial.

2. In any local criminal court a defendant who has entered a plea of not guilty to an information which charges a misdemeanor must be accorded a jury trial, conducted pursuant to article three hundred sixty, except that in the New York city criminal court, the trial of an information which charges a misdemeanor for which the authorized term of imprisonment is not more than six months must be a single judge trial. The defendant may at any time before trial waive a jury trial in the manner prescribed in subdivision two of section 320.10, and consent to a single judge trial.

3. A defendant entitled to a jury trial pursuant to subdivision two, shall be so entitled even though the information also charges an offense for which he is otherwise not entitled to a jury trial. In such case, the defendant is not entitled both to a jury trial and a separate single judge trial and the court may not order separate trials.

4. [Renumbered as subd. 3.]

5. [Omitted.]

6. [Omitted.]

7. Notwithstanding any other provision of law, in any local criminal court the trial of a person who is an eligible youth within the meaning of the youthful offender procedure set forth in article seven hundred twenty and who has not prior to commencement of the trial been convicted of a crime or adjudicated a youthful offender must be a single judge trial.

Amended by L. 1971, Chs. 815, 981; L. 1984, Ch. 673; L. 1987, Ch. 727; L. 1988, Ch. 190; L. 1989, Ch. 240.

ANNOTATION

Right to trial by jury.—A defendant does not have a right to trial by jury where he is charged with multiple offenses, each separately carrying a penalty of less than 6 months but potentially punishable in the aggregate to more than 6 months. However, if defendant has a non-jury trial, his maximum

aggregate sentence should not exceed 6 months. People v. DiLorenzo, 153 Misc. 2d 1021, 585 N.Y.S.2d 670 (Crim. Ct. Bronx Co. 1992).

§ 340.50. Defendant's presence at trial.

1. Except as provided in subdivision two or three, a defendant must be personally present during the trial.

2. On motion of a defendant represented by counsel, the court may, in the absence of an objection by the people, issue an order dispensing with the requirement that the defendant be personally present at trial. Such an order may be made only upon the filing of a written and subscribed statement by the defendant declaring that he waives his right to be personally present at the trial and authorizing his attorney to conduct his defense.

3. A defendant who conducts himself in so disorderly and disruptive a manner that his trial cannot be carried on with him in the courtroom may be removed from the courtroom if, after he has been warned by the court that he will be removed if he continues such conduct, he continues to engage in such conduct.

Amended by L. 1971, Ch. 789.

ANNOTATIONS

Psychiatric examination; fitness to proceed.—Although the accused was found to be a "paranoid personality" capable of standing trial, psychiatric examination had to be required to determine whether he had the capacity to represent himself, after accused exhibited erratic behavior, made outbursts in court, and insisted upon serving as his own counsel. People v. Jones, 74 Misc. 2d 767, 346 N.Y.S.2d 92 (Crim. Ct. Bronx Co. 1973).

Standard of fitness; capability of standing trial versus capacity to defend oneself.—The standard for capacity to defend oneself is markedly different from the standard required merely to assist counsel. Thus, although the accused was found to be a "paranoid personality" who was capable of standing trial, a hearing had to be required to determine his capacity to proceed pro se where defendant insisted upon conducting his own defense. People v. Jones, 74 Misc. 2d 767, 346 N.Y.S.2d 92 (Crim. Ct. Bronx Co. 1973).

Youthful offenders.—On its face CPL § 340.40(7) would appear to fit within the *Baldwin v. New York*, 399 U.S. 66, 90 S. Ct. 1886, 26 L. Ed. 2d 437 (1970), criterion, permitting denial of a jury trial, since Penal Law 60.02 limits the period of incarceration for mandatorily adjudicated youthful offenders pursuant to CPL § 340.40(7) to six months. People v. Denning, 98 Misc. 2d 369, 413 N.Y.S.2d 837 (Sup. Ct. App. Term. 1st Dept. 1979).

Mandatory youthful offenders.—Where the Assistant District Attorney, pursuant to CPL § 180.40, prior to the grand jury presentation had the cases returned to the Crim. Ct. and the felony charges reduced to misdemeanors, the defendants, who were then eligible for mandatory youthful offender treatment were not entitled to a jury trial; the provisions of CPL § 340.40(2) and (7) are constitutional. People v. Gray, 97 Misc. 2d 285, 411 N.Y.S.2d 170 (Crim. Ct. N.Y. Co. 1978).

ARTICLE 350—NON-JURY TRIALS

Section
350.10   Conduct of single judge trial.
350.20   Trial by judicial hearing officer.

LexisNexis Cross Reference

New York Criminal Practice (2d ed.), Vol. 3, Ch. 28, Jury and Non-Jury Trials.

§ 350.10. Conduct of single judge trial.

1. A single judge trial of an information in a local criminal court must be conducted pursuant to this section.

2. The court, in addition to determining all questions of law, is the exclusive trier of all issues of fact and must render a verdict.

3. The order of the trial must be as follows:

(a) The court may in its discretion permit the parties to deliver opening addresses. If the court grants such permission to one party, it must grant it to the other also. If both parties deliver opening addresses, the people's address must be delivered first.

(b) The order in which evidence must or may be offered by the respective parties is the same as that applicable to a jury trial of an indictment as prescribed in subdivisions five, six and seven of section 260.30.

(c) The court may in its discretion permit the parties to deliver summations. If the court grants such permission to one party, it must grant permission to the other also. If both parties deliver summations, the defendant's summation must be delivered first.

(d) The court must then consider the case and render a verdict.

4. The provisions governing motion practice and general procedure with respect to a jury trial of an indictment are, wherever appropriate, applicable to a non-jury trial of an information.

5. If the information contains more than one count, the court must render a verdict upon each count not previously dismissed or must otherwise state upon the record its disposition of each such count. A verdict which does not so dispose of each count constitutes a verdict of not guilty with respect to each undisposed of count.

6. In rendering a verdict of guilty upon a count charging a misdemeanor, the court may find the defendant guilty of such misdemeanor, if it is established by legally sufficient trial evidence, or guilty of any lesser included offense which is established by legally sufficient trial evidence.

ANNOTATIONS

Court's calling of witnesses.—Over defense objection, court erred in calling its own witness after both the People and the defendant rested at a bench trial, where the court gave no reason for calling the witness and did not articulate the consequences of doing so. The court assumed the parties' traditional role of deciding what evidence to present and introduced evidence that corroborated the prosecution's witnesses and discredited defendant on a key issue. People v. Arnold, 98 N.Y.2d 63, 745 N.Y.S.2d 782, 772 N.E.2d 1140 (2002).

Standard of proof.—Where court in bench trial stated that in its deliberations it would "consider the evidence in the light most favorable to the People," it applied a lesser standard of proof than the required standard of beyond a reasonable doubt; accordingly, a new trial was ordered. People v. Neff, 287 A.D.2d 809, 731 N.Y.S.2d 269 (3d Dept. 2001).

Verdict; timing.—In driving while impaired case, justice court's 76-day delay in rendering its verdict resulted in a loss of jurisdiction over the defendant, where the record is devoid of consent by the defendant to any delay exceeding two weeks, and the time of delay was unreasonable. People v. Plaza, 175 Misc. 2d 277, 670 N.Y.S.2d 299 (2d Dept. 1997).

—A justice sitting in a nonjury trial must render a verdict within a reasonable time after the close of trial. People v. Woodley, 141 A.D.2d 587, 529 N.Y.S.2d 193 (2d Dept. 1988).

§ 350.20. Trial by judicial hearing officer.

1. Notwithstanding any provision of section 350.10 of this article, in any case where a single judge trial of an information in a local criminal court is authorized or required, the court may, upon agreement of the parties, assign a judicial hearing officer to conduct the trial. Where such assignment is made, the judicial hearing officer shall entertain the case in the same manner as a court and shall:

(a) determine all questions of law;

(b) act as the exclusive trier of all issues of fact; and

(c) render a verdict.

2. In the discharge of this responsibility, the judicial hearing officer shall have the same powers as a judge of the court in which the proceeding is pending. The rules of evidence shall be applicable at a trial conducted by a judicial hearing officer.

3. Any action taken by a judicial hearing officer in the conduct of a trial shall be deemed the action of the court in which the proceeding is pending.

4. This section shall not apply where the single judge trial is of an information at least one count of which charges a class A misdemeanor.

5. Notwithstanding the provisions of subdivision one of this section, the administrative judge of Nassau county may, without the consent of the

parties, assign matters involving traffic and parking infractions except those described in paragraphs (a), (b), (c)(d),* (e) and (f) of subdivision two of section three hundred seventy-one of the general municipal law to a judicial hearing officer for all proceedings before the district court of Nassau county in accordance with the provisions of section sixteen hundred ninety of the vehicle and traffic law.

* As originally enacted.

Added by L. 1983, Ch. 840; **Amended** by L. 1990, Ch. 496.

ANNOTATION

Delay in rendering verdict.—Since the delay of 58 days from close of trial to rendition of verdict was unreasonable, the adjudication was vacated and the information dismissed. People v. South, 41 N.Y.2d 451, 393 N.Y.S.2d 695, 362 N.E.2d 246 (1977).

CPL

ARTICLE 360—JURY TRIAL

Section

LexisNexis Cross References

Defense of Narcotics Cases, Vol. 2, Ch. 5, The Trial; *see generally Criminal Law Advocacy,* Vol. 2A, Jury Selection; Vol. 6, Argument to the Jury; *Criminal Defense Techniques,* Vol. 6, Ch. 119, Jury Selection and Jurors; *New York Criminal Practice (2d ed.),* Vol. 3, Ch. 29, Formation and Conduct of Trial Jury; *Sexual Assault Trials (2d ed.),* Vol. 1, Ch. 3, Jury Selection; *Criminal Practice Handbook (2d ed.),* Ch. 5, Jury Issues.

§ 360.05. Jury trial; order of trial.

The provisions of section 260.30, governing the order of proceedings of a jury trial of an indictment in a superior court, are applicable to a jury trial of an information in a local criminal court.

§ 360.10. Trial jury; formation in general.

1. A trial jury consists of six jurors, but "alternate jurors" may be selected and sworn pursuant to section 360.35.

2. The panel from which the jury is drawn is formed and selected as prescribed in the uniform district court act, uniform city court act, and uniform justice court act. In the New York city criminal court the panel from which the jury is drawn is formed and selected in the same manner as is prescribed for the formation and selection of a panel in the supreme court in counties within cities having a population of one million or more.

Amended by L. 1971, Ch. 815.

§ 360.15. Trial jury; challenge to the panel.

1. A challenge to the panel is an objection made to the entire panel of prospective trial jurors returned for the trial of the action and may be taken to such panel or to any additional panel that may be ordered by the court. Such a challenge may be made only by the defendant and only on the ground that there has been such a departure from the requirements of the appropriate law in the drawing or return of the panel as to result in substantial prejudice to the defendant.

2. A challenge to the panel must be made before the selection of the jury commences, and, if it is not, such challenge is deemed to have been waived. Such challenge must be made in writing setting forth the facts constituting the ground of challenge. If such facts are denied by the people, witnesses may be called and examined by either party. All issues of fact and questions of law arising on the challenge must be tried and determined by the court. If a challenge to the panel is allowed, the court must discharge that panel and order the return of another panel of prospective trial jurors.

ANNOTATION

Jury pool.—After a hearing pursuant to CPL § 360.15, court found that there was no significant state interest advanced in using a centralized jury pool consisting of Monroe County residents for Rochester City Court trials, which was a process resulting in a disproportionate exclusion of distinct groups, and the court found that there were compelling reasons entitling defendants to a jury randomly selected from a fair cross-section of residents of the City of Rochester. People v. Miller, 170 Misc. 2d 367, 646 N.Y.S.2d 965 (City Ct. of Rochester, Monroe Co. 1996).

Review of challenges to panel.—While a local criminal court has no authority to supervise the administration or operation of the jury selection system, the court is vested with the power to review and determine a defendant's challenge to a jury panel that is returned for service in that court. The presiding judge has the sole jurisdiction to determine whether a prospective jury panel fairly represents a cross-section of the community. Oglesby v. McKinney, 6 Misc. 3d 905, 788 N.Y.S.2d 559 (Sup. Ct. Onondaga Co. 2004).

§ 360.20. Trial jury; examination of prospective jurors; challenges generally.

If no challenge to the panel is made as prescribed by section 360.15, or if such challenge is made and disallowed, the court must direct that the names of six members of the panel be drawn and called. Such persons must take their places in the jury box and must be immediately sworn to answer truthfully questions asked them relative to their qualifications to serve as jurors in the action. The procedural rules prescribed in section 270.15 with respect to the examination of the prospective jurors and to challenges are also applicable to the selection of a trial jury in a local criminal court.

ANNOTATION

Reversible error.—The trial court may not refuse to permit interrogation of prospective jurors on the voir dire as to possible prejudice against members of the defendant's race. People v. Williams, 41 A.D.2d 611, 340 N.Y.S.2d 504 (1st Dept. 1973).

§ 360.25. Trial jury; challenge for cause of an individual juror.

1. A challenge for cause is an objection to a prospective member of the jury and may be made only on the ground that:

(a) He does not have the qualifications required by the judiciary law; or

(b) He has a state of mind that is likely to preclude him from rendering an impartial verdict based upon the evidence adduced at the trial; or

(c) He is related within the sixth degree by consanguinity or affinity to the defendant, or to the person allegedly injured by the crime charged, or to a prospective witness at the trial, or to counsel for the people or for the defendant; or that he is or was a party adverse to any such person in a civil action; or that he has complained against or been accused by any such person in a criminal action; or that he bears some other relationship to any such person of such nature that it is likely to preclude him from rendering an impartial verdict; or

(d) He is to be a witness at the trial; or where a prosecutor's information was filed at the direction of a grand jury, he was a witness before the grand jury or at the preliminary hearing; or

(e) He served on a trial jury in a prior civil or criminal action involving the same conduct charged; or where a prosecutor's information was filed at the direction of a grand jury, he served on the grand jury which directed such filing.

2. All issues of fact or questions of law arising on the challenge must be tried and determined by the court. The provisions of subdivision two of section 270.20 with respect to challenges are also applicable to the selection of a trial jury in a local criminal court.

§ 360.30. Trial jury; peremptory challenge of an individaul* juror.

1. A peremptory challenge is an objection to a prospective juror for which no reason need be assigned. Upon any peremptory challenge, the court must exclude the person challenged from service.

2. Each party must be allowed three peremptory challenges. When two or more defendants are tried jointly, such challenges are not multiplied by the number of defendants, but such defendants are to be treated as a single party. In any such case, a peremptory challenge by one or more defendants must be allowed if a majority of the defendants join in such challenge. Otherwise, it must be disallowed.

* As originally enacted. Should be "individual."

§ 360.35. Trial jury; alternate juror.

1. Immediately after the last trial juror is sworn, the court may in its discretion direct the selection of either one or two additional jurors to be known as "alternate jurors." The alternate jurors must be drawn in the same manner, must have the same qualifications, must be subject to the same examination and challenges for cause and must take the same oath as the regular jurors. Whether or not a party has used its peremptory challenge in the selection of the trial jury, one peremptory challenge is authorized in the selection of the alternate jurors.

2. The provisions of section 270.35 with respect to alternate jurors are also applicable to a trial jury in a local criminal court.

§ 360.40. Trial jury; conduct of jury trial in general.

A jury trial of an information must be conducted generally in the same manner as a jury trial of an indictment, and the rules governing preliminary instructions by the court, supervision of the jury, motion practice and other procedural matters involved in the conduct of a jury trial of an indictment are, where appropriate, applicable to the conduct of a jury trial of an information.

ANNOTATION

Testimony; unrelated incident.—In a prosecution for criminal possession of a weapon, third degree, the defendant was deprived of a fair trial when testimony relating to a previous unrelated stabbing by the defendant was admitted. People v. Figueroa, 63 A.D.2d 954, 406 N.Y.S.2d 325 (1st Dept. 1978).

§ 360.45. Court's charge and instructions; in general.

The general principles, prescribed in section 300.10, governing the court's charge to the jury and requests to charge upon a trial of an indictment, are applicable to a jury trial of an information in a local criminal court.

§ 360.50. Court's submission of information to jury; counts and offenses to be submitted.

1. The term definitions contained in section 300.30 are applicable to this section, except that the word "information" is to be substituted for the word "indictment" wherever the latter appears in said section 300.30.

2. The court may submit to the jury only those counts of an information remaining therein at the time of its charge which are supported by legally sufficient trial evidence, and every count not so supported should be dismissed by a trial order of dismissal. If the trial evidence is not legally sufficient to establish a misdemeanor charged in a particular count which the court would otherwise be required to submit pursuant to this section, but is legally sufficient to establish a lesser included offense, the court may submit such lesser included offense and, upon the people's request, must do so. In submitting a count charging a misdemeanor established by legally sufficient trial evidence, the court in its discretion may, in addition to submitting such misdemeanor, submit in the alternative any lesser included offense if there is a reasonable view of the evidence which would support a finding that the defendant committed such lesser offense but did not commit the misdemeanor charged.

3. If the information contains but one count, the court must submit such count.

4. If a multiple count information contains consecutive counts only, the court must submit every count thereof.

5. In any case where the information may be more complex by reason of concurrent counts or inconsistent counts or other factors indicated in subdivisions three, four and five of section 300.40, relating to multiple count indictments, the court, in its submission of such information to the jury, should, so far as practicable, be guided by the provisions of the said subdivisions of said section 300.40.

6. Notwithstanding any other provision of this section, the court is not required to submit to the jury any particular count of a multiple count information if the people consent that it not be submitted.

7. Every count not submitted to the jury is deemed to have been dismissed by the court. Where the court, over objection of the people, refuses to submit a count which is consecutive as to every count actually submitted, such count is deemed to have been dismissed by a trial order of dismissal even though no such order was expressly made by the court.

§ 360.55. Deliberation and verdict of jury.

The provisions of article three hundred ten, governing the deliberation and verdict of a jury upon a jury trial of an indictment in a superior court, are applicable to a jury trial of an information in a local criminal court.

ARTICLE 370—PROCEEDINGS FROM VERDICT TO SENTENCE

Section
370.10   Proceedings from verdict to sentence.

LexisNexis Cross Reference

New York Criminal Practice (2d ed.), Vol. 4, Ch. 40, Proceedings from Verdict to Sentence.

§ 370.10. Proceedings from verdict to sentence.

The provisions of article three hundred thirty, governing the proceedings from verdict to sentence in an action prosecuted by indictment in a superior court, are applicable to a prosecution by information in a local criminal court; provided, however, where a judicial hearing officer has conducted the trial pursuant to section 350.20 of this chapter, all references to a court therein shall be deemed references to such judicial hearing officer.

Amended by L. 1983, Ch. 840.

TITLE L—SENTENCE

ARTICLE 380—SENTENCING IN GENERAL

LexisNexis Cross References

Criminal Defense Techniques, Vol. 1B, Ch. 40A, Sentencing Considerations in Computer Crime Cases; Vol. 1B, Ch. 41, Criteria for the Imposition of a Probationary Sentence; Vol. 6, Ch. 121, Sentencing; *New York Criminal Practice (2d ed.),* Vol. 4, Ch. 42, Classification of Offenses, Authorized Dispositions and Punishment; *Prosecution and Defense of Sex Crimes,* Ch. 13, Sentencing; *Criminal Practice Handbook (2d ed.),* Ch. 10, Disposition Alternatives Including Sentencing Issues.

§ 380.10. Applicability.

1. In general. The procedure prescribed by this title applies to sentencing for every offense, whether defined within or outside of the penal law; provided, however, where a judicial hearing officer has conducted the trial pursuant to section 350.20 of this chapter, all references to a court herein shall be deemed references to such judicial hearing officer.

2. Exception. Whenever a different or inconsistent procedure is provided by any other law in relation to sentencing for a non-criminal offense defined therein, such different or inconsistent procedure applies thereto.

Amended by L. 1983, Ch. 840.

ANNOTATION

Sentencing; unrehabilitated drug addict.—Defendant, an admitted drug addict, reverted back to drug use and committed two crimes after being discharged from a rehabilitation center. The trial justice did not abuse his discretion, therefore, in imposing sentence upon the defendant. People v. Failla, 41 A.D.2d 850, 343 N.Y.S.2d 64 (2d Dept. 1973).

§ 380.20. Sentence required.

The court must pronounce sentence in every case where a conviction is entered. If an accusatory instrument contains multiple counts and a conviction is entered on more than one count the court must pronounce sentence on each count.

ANNOTATIONS

Sentencing factors.—Under its discretionary sentencing power, a court may consider evidence of prior uncharged crimes, but trial court erred in considering a shooting incident when imposing sentence on defendant for other crimes, where the prosecutor's assertion that defendant was involved in shooting incident was based on pure speculation. People v. Naranjo, 89 N.Y.2d 1047, 659 N.Y.S.2d 826, 681 N.E.2d 1272 (1997).

—A court may not sentence a defendant based upon extraneous crimes unless there is evidence that defendant committed those crimes. People v. Thomas, 178 A.D.2d 162, 577 N.Y.S.2d 259 (1st Dept. 1991), *lv. denied,* 79 N.Y.2d 924 (1992).

—The fact that defendant may have tested positive for the HIV virus was not sufficient reason, standing alone, to conclude that the negotiated sentence was excessive. People v. Hafner, 199 A.D.2d 703, 605 N.Y.S.2d 487 (3d Dept. 1993), *lv. denied,* 83 N.Y.2d 805 (1994).

—There is no requirement that defendants in similar circumstances be sentenced equally. People v. Givens, 181 A.D.2d 1031, 582 N.Y.S.2d 577 (4th Dept.), *lv. denied,* 79 N.Y.2d 1049 (1992).

—Mere fact that other cases reveal a lesser sentence for the same crime does not mean that defendant's sentence was excessive. People v. Quezada, 145 A.D.2d 950, 536 N.Y.S.2d 617 (4th Dept. 1988).

Sentencing court's discretion.—The trial court was not bound to adopt the sentence recommendation of the Probation Department. People v. Hynes, 199 A.D.2d 667, 605 N.Y.S.2d 142 (3d Dept. 1994).

Enhanced sentence after trial.—Court rejected as meritless the defendant's contention that the sentence imposed impermissibly punished him for exercising his right to proceed to trial based on the disparity between the pretrial offer and the actual sentence imposed. People v. Kennedy, 199 A.D.2d 537, 606 N.Y.S.2d 254 (2d Dept.), *lv. denied,* 83 N.Y.2d 806 (1994).

—Sentences imposed after trial may be more severe than those proposed in connection with a plea. People v. Norfleet, 146 A.D.2d 812, 537 N.Y.S.2d 289 (2d Dept. 1989).

—The mere fact that a sentence imposed after trial is longer than one offered in exchange for a guilty plea does not constitute grounds for overturning the sentence in the absence of evidence that defendant was given the lengthier sentence solely as a punishment or exercising his right to a trial. People v. Morin, 192 A.D.2d 791, 596 N.Y.S.2d 508 (3d Dept.), *lv. denied,* 81 N.Y.2d 1077 (1993).

—Court may impose enhanced sentence based on defendant's perjury at trial. People v. Marchese, 160 Misc. 2d 212, 608 N.Y.S.2d 776 (Sup. Ct. Bronx Co. 1994).

Breach of plea agreement.—Defendant was required to be resentenced where he pled guilty based on the promise of the prosecutor that he would not take any position or make an statement on sentencing and subsequently, the prosecutor provided the news media with photographs and films of defendant perpetrating the crime, which were viewed by the trial judge who thereafter imposed the maximum sentence. People v. Tullio, 85 A.D.2d 783, 445 N.Y.S.2d 322 (3d Dept. 1981).

Procedural requirements.—Case remitted for resentencing where trial court failed to specifically pronounce sentence on each of the counts of which the defendant was convicted. People v. Frazier, 237 A.D.2d 618, 655 N.Y.S.2d 1007 (2d Dept. 1997).

—Sentencing court erred by pronouncing sentence only on the top count of the indictment and failing to pronounce a clear sentence on each of the remaining counts, so matter was remitted for resentencing on all counts. People v. Cuccuru, 236 A.D.2d 419, 653 N.Y.S.2d 370 (2d Dept. 1997).

—Sentencing court erred by imposing a single term of imprisonment for all four counts of the indictment to which defendant pled guilty. People v. McKinney, 215 A.D.2d 407, 625 N.Y.S.2d 667 (2d Dept. 1995).

—Defendant had to be resentenced where he was not sentenced on each count of the indictment to which he had pleaded guilty. People v. Charles, 98 A.D.2d 780, 469 N.Y.S.2d 797 (2d Dept. 1983).

—There is no statutory requirement that the prosecutor appear at sentencing. People v. Rieman, 153 A.D.2d 984, 545 N.Y.S.2d 426 (3d Dept. 1989).

—Even if the parties are able to waive their rights to proper sentencing, the court itself has a distinct responsibility to insure that its sentencing is done in accordance with the law. People v. Kade, 152 Misc. 2d 453, 577 N.Y.S.2d 555 (Sup. Ct. Kings Co. 1991).

§ 380.30. Time for pronouncing sentence.

1. In general. Sentence must be pronounced without unreasonable delay.

2. Court to fix time. Upon entering a conviction the court must:

(a) Fix a date for pronouncing sentence; or

(b) Fix a date for one of the pre-sentence proceedings specified in article four hundred; or

(c) Pronounce sentence on the date the conviction is entered in accordance with the provisions of subdivision three.

3. Sentence on date of conviction. The court may sentence the defendant at the time the conviction is entered if:

(a) A pre-sentence report or a fingerprint report is not required; or

(b) Where any such report is required, the report has been received.

Provided, however, that the court may not pronounce sentence at such time without inquiring as to whether an adjournment is desired by the defendant. Where an adjournment is requested, the defendant must state the purpose thereof and the court may, in its discretion, allow a reasonable time.

4. Time for pre-sentence proceedings. The court may conduct one or more of the pre-sentence proceedings specified in article four

hundred at any time before sentence is pronounced. Notice of any such proceeding issued after the date for pronouncing sentence has been fixed automatically adjourns the date for pronouncing sentence. In such case the court must fix a date for pronouncing sentence at the conclusion of such proceeding.

Amended by L. 1992, Ch. 55, and amendment expired Mar. 31, 1994.

ANNOTATIONS

Sentencing delay; unreasonable.—An unexcused delay of 39 months between guilty verdict and sentencing was unreasonable and resulted in a loss of jurisdiction by the court requiring a dismissal of the underlying indictment, notwithstanding that the trial court stated that such delay was due to extrajudicial pleas for leniency on behalf of the defendant by three different lawyers; the New York rule assumes the defendant to be prejudiced by unreasonable delay and defendant need not prove prejudice nor take affirmative action in demanding to be sentenced. People v. Drake, 61 N.Y.2d 359, 474 N.Y.S.2d 276, 462 N.E.2d 376 (1984).

—In absence of any explanation for a 26-month sentencing delay, the unexplained delay requires dismissal of charges of second-degree forgery. Prejudice is presumed when sentencing is unreasonably delayed. People v. Muro, 196 Misc. 2d 837, 763 N.Y.S.2d 457 (Sup. Ct. N.Y. Co. 2003).

—A deliberate refusal to set a date for sentencing or a permanent deferral of sentence is per se unreasonable and improper. People v. Harper, 137 Misc. 2d 357, 520 N.Y.S.2d 892, 894 (Crim. Ct. N.Y. Co. 1987).

Sentencing delay; not unreasonable.—Nineteen-year delay in sentencing defendant after his guilty plea was not unreasonable, where defendant absconded, used nearly two dozen aliases, and gave false pedigree information in connection with his numerous subsequent arrests and incarcerations in New York. People v. Allen, 309 A.D.2d 624, 766 N.Y.S.2d 24 (1st Dept. 2003).

—Defendant's right to be sentenced without unreasonable delay was not violated by the elapse of three years between the original sentencing and resentencing. The procedural error during the prompt initial sentencing did not render that sentence a nullity for purposes of speedy sentencing analysis and, in any event, the delay resulted from defendant's delay in seeking a remedy for the procedural defect in the original sentence. People v. Smith, 277 A.D.2d 178, 717 N.Y.S.2d 66 (1st Dept. 2000).

—Twelve-year delay between guilty plea and imposition of sentence did not deprive the sentencing court of jurisdiction. People v. Gee, 149 A.D.2d 728, 540 N.Y.S.2d 334 (2d Dept. 1989).

—Delay between defendant's initial guilty plea and his resentencing was not an unreasonable delay that would cause the court to lose jurisdiction and require dismissal where defendant knowingly waived his right to prompt sentencing during his plea allocution. People v. Slack, 288 A.D.2d 765, 733 N.Y.S.2d 746 (3d Dept. 2001).

—Although nine months elapsed between defendant's conviction and his sentencing, the delay was not unreasonable. People v. Coleman, 157 A.D.2d 935, 550 N.Y.S.2d 191 (3d Dept. 1990).

Delay; absconding defendant.—For purposes of sentencing, the People had no duty to make efforts to apprehend the absconding defendant so as to avoid a loss of jurisdiction. People v. Davidson, 158 A.D.2d 317, 551 N.Y.S.2d 4 (1st Dept.), lv. denied, 75 N.Y.2d 965 (1990).

—A lengthy delay brought about solely by a defendant's flight will not divest the court of jurisdiction to sentence the defendant, but it will have that effect if the People have failed to make a diligent effort to proceed against the absconder. People v. Miller, 130 A.D.2d 449, 515 N.Y.S.2d 782 (1st Dept. 1987).

—The People are under no obligation to make efforts to apprehend an absconding defendant in order to avoid a loss of jurisdiction to sentence the defendant. People v. Battles, 150 A.D.2d 785, 542 N.Y.S.2d 218 (2d Dept. 1989).

—Court lost jurisdiction to impose sentence based on seven-year delay between the entry of the plea and sentence. Although defendant absconded, the People had actual knowledge that defendant was incarcerated in Pennsylvania, and the record is devoid of any evidence that the People made any efforts to secure defendant's presence in New York. People v. Reyes, 15 A.D.3d 868, 789 N.Y.S.2d 588, *amended by* 16 A.D.3d 1179, 709 N.Y.S.2d 909 (4th Dept. 2005).

—Where delay in sentencing is caused by defendant's absconding, it is excusable. People v. Brazeau, 144 A.D.2d 977, 534 N.Y.S.2d 634 (4th Dept. 1988).

—While CPL § 380.30(1) mandates that a court may be divested of jurisdiction if there is an unreasonable delay in pronouncing sentence, a delay is excusable where it is caused by conduct of the defendant. Moreover, the People are not required to make efforts to apprehend an absconding defendant to avoid a loss of jurisdiction. People v. Matias, 182 Misc. 2d 599, 695 N.Y.S.2d 661 (Sup. Ct. N.Y. Co. 1999).

—Where there was a delay in trial court's pronouncement of sentence, court did not lose jurisdiction over defendant, who was incarcerated in a state correctional facility during the delay, because defendant used repeatedly false names and birth dates, and was "absconding" or hiding within the prison itself. People v. Alberto, 171 Misc. 2d 780, 655 N.Y.S.2d 812 (Sup. Ct. Kings Co. 1997).

—Eleven year delay in sentencing defendant did not strip sentencing court of jurisdiction where delay was caused by defendant's act of absconding. People v. Nasbit, 136 Misc. 2d 605, 519 N.Y.S.2d 84 (Crim. Ct. N.Y. Co. 1987).

Unreasonable delay claim survives waiver of appeal.—A claim of unreasonable delay in sentencing does not fall within the ambit of the waiver of the right to appeal, as it challenges the legality of the sentence. A CPL § 380.30(1) claim survives a general waiver of appeal and the fact-finding determination of the hearing court should be reviewed upon appeal. People v. Campbell, 97 N.Y.2d 532, 743 N.Y.S.2d 396, 769 N.E.2d 1288 (2002), *app. after remand*, 306 A.D.2d 495, 761 N.Y.S.2d 834 (2d Dept. 2003).

§ 380.40. Defendant's presence at sentencing.

1. **In general.** The defendant must be personally present at the time sentence is pronounced.

2. **Exception.** Where sentence is to be pronounced for a misdemeanor or for a petty offense, the court may, on motion of the defendant, dispense with the requirement that the defendant be personally present. Any such motion must be accompanied by a waiver, signed and acknowledged by the defendant, reciting the maximum sentence that may be imposed for the offense and stating that the defendant waives the right to be personally present at the time sentence is pronounced.

3. **Corporations.** Sentence may be pronounced against a corporation in the absence of counsel if counsel fails to appear on the date of sentence after reasonable notice thereof.

ANNOTATIONS

Resentencing.—A defendant has the right to be present at resentencing. People v. Lucks, 91 A.D.2d 896, 457 N.Y.S.2d 514 (1st Dept. 1983).

—Defendant's sentence was vacated where the trial court failed to have her produced at the resentencing; as she was denied her right to be present at sentencing and her right to speak on her own behalf. People v. Lee, 84 A.D.2d 699, 443 N.Y.S.2d 728 (1st Dept. 1981).

—Court's failure to have defendant produced at the proceeding at which it amended the sentence, after court determined that the original sentence was unlawful, violated the defendant's statutory right to be present at the time of sentence. People v. Garrison, 9 A.D.3d 436, 780 N.Y.S.2d 170 (2d Dept. 2004).

Forfeiture.—Prohibition is not available to defeat the court's power to impose sentence on an absconding petitioner at the appropriate and designated time. Whitley v. Cioffi, 74 A.D.2d 230, 427 N.Y.S.2d 23 (1st Dept.), *lv. denied*, 50 N.Y.2d 803 (1980).

—By absconding prior to sentencing, the defendant unambiguously indicated a defiance of the processes of law sufficient to effect a forfeiture of his right to be present at sentencing. People v. Hooper, 133 A.D.2d 347, 519 N.Y.S.2d 247 (2d Dept. 1987).

—Where defendant was disruptive at sentencing, he was properly removed from the courtroom and sentenced in absentia. People v. Fulton, 202 A.D.2d 1042, 610 N.Y.S.2d 109 (4th Dept.), *lv. denied*, 83 N.Y.2d 910 (1994).

Waiver.—Where the defendant was in a detention pen adjacent to the court and no effort was made to apprise him of his right to be present or to bring him into court for sentencing no waiver can be implied. People v. Stroman, 36 N.Y.2d 939, 373 N.Y.S.2d 548, 335 N.E.2d 853 (1975).

—The defendant's presence is required at sentencing absent an express waiver. People v. Brown, 155 A.D.2d 608, 547 N.Y.S.2d 664 (2d Dept. 1989).

—Defendant, who had pleaded guilty to a misdemeanor, waived her right to be present at sentencing, when, after being advised that she would be sentenced to a maximum sentence if she failed to appear, voluntarily absented herself from the court on the date set for sentencing. People v. Carson, 104 Misc. 2d 281, 428 N.Y.S.2d 123 (Crim. Ct. Bronx Co. 1979).

§ 380.50. Statements at time of sentence.

1. At the time of pronouncing sentence, the court must accord the prosecutor an opportunity to make a statement with respect to any matter relevant to the question of sentence. The court must then accord counsel for the defendant an opportunity to speak on behalf of the defendant. The defendant also has the right to make a statement personally in his or her own behalf, and before pronouncing sentence the court must ask defendant whether he or she wishes to make such a statement.

2. (a) For purposes of this section "victim" shall mean:

(1) the victim as indicated in the accusatory instrument; or

(2) if such victim is unable or unwilling to express himself or herself before the court or a person so mentally or physically disabled as to make it impracticable to appear in court in person or the victim is deceased, a member of the family of such victim, or the legal guardian or representative of the legal guardian of the victim where such guardian or representative has personal knowledge of and a relationship with the victim, unless the court finds that it would be inappropriate for such person to make a statement on behalf of the victim.

(b) If the defendant is being sentenced for a felony the court, if requested at least ten days prior to the sentencing date, shall accord the victim the right to make a statement with regard to any matter relevant to the question of sentence. The court shall notify the defendant no less than seven days prior to sentencing of the victim's intent to make a statement at sentencing. If the defendant does not receive timely notice pursuant to this subdivision, the defendant may request a reasonable adjournment.

(c) Any statement by the victim must precede any statement by counsel to the defendant or the defendant made pursuant to subdivision one of this section. The defendant shall have the right to rebut any statement made by the victim.

(d) Where the people and the defendant have agreed to a disposition which includes a sentence acceptable to the court, and the court intends to impose such sentence, any rebuttal by the defendant shall be limited to an oral presentation made at the time of sentencing.

(e) Where

(1) the defendant has been found guilty after trial or there is no agreement between the people and the defendant as to the proposed sentence or the court, after statement by the victim, chooses not to impose the proposed sentence agreed to by the parties;

(2) the statement by the victim includes allegations about the crime that were not fully explored during the proceedings or that materially vary from or contradict the evidence at the trial; and

(3) the court determines that the allegations are relevant to the issue of sentencing, then the court shall afford the defendant the following rights:

(a) a reasonable adjournment of the sentencing to allow the defendant to present information to rebut the allegations by the victim; and

(b) allow the defendant to present written questions to the court that the defendant desires the court to put to the victim. The court may, in its discretion, decline to put any or all of the questions to the victim. Where the court declines to put any or all of the questions to the victim it shall state its reasons therefor on the record.

(f) If the victim does not appear to make a statement at the time of sentencing, the right to make a statement is waived. The failure of the victim to make a statement shall not be cause for delaying the proceedings against the defendant nor shall it affect the validity of a conviction, judgment or order.

3. The court may, either before or after receiving such statements, summarize the factors it considers relevant for the purpose of sentence and afford an opportunity to the defendant or his or her counsel to comment thereon.

4. Regardless of whether the victim requests to make a statement with regard to the defendant's sentence, where the defendant is committed to the custody of the department of correctional services upon a sentence of imprisonment for conviction of a violent felony offense as defined in section 70.02 of the penal law or a felony defined in article one hundred twenty-five of such law, within sixty days of the imposition of sentence the prosecutor shall provide the victim with a form, prepared and distributed by the commissioner of the department of correctional services,

on which the victim may indicate a demand to be informed of the escape, absconding, discharge, parole, conditional release or release to post-release supervision of the person so imprisoned. If the victim submits a completed form to the prosecutor, it shall be the duty of the prosecutor to mail promptly such form to the department of correctional services.

5. Following the receipt of such form from the prosecutor, it shall be the duty of the department of correctional services, at the time such person is discharged, paroled, conditionally released or released to post-release supervision, to notify the victim of such occurrence by certified mail directed to the address provided by the victim. In the event such person escapes or absconds from a facility under the jurisdiction of the department of correctional services, it shall be the duty of such department to notify immediately the victim of such occurrence at the most current address or telephone number provided by the victim in the most reasonable and expedient possible manner. In the event such escapee or absconder is subsequently taken into custody by the department of correctional services, it shall be the duty of such department to notify the victim of such occurrence by certified mail directed to the address provided by the victim within forty-eight hours of regaining such custody. In no case shall the state be held liable for failure to provide any notice required by this subdivision.

6. Regardless of whether the victim requests to make a statement with regard to the defendant's sentence, where the defendant is sentenced for a violent felony offense as defined in section 70.02 of the penal law or a felony defined in article one hundred twenty-five of such law or any of the following provisions of such law sections 130.25, 130.30, 130.40, 130.45, 255.25, article 263, 135.10, 135.25, 230.05, 230.06, subdivision two of section 230.30 or 230.32, the prosecutor shall, within sixty days of the imposition of sentence, provide the victim with a form on which the victim may indicate a demand to be informed of any petition to change the name of such defendant. Such forms shall be maintained by such prosecutor. Upon receipt of a notice of a petition to change the name of any such defendant, pursuant to subdivision two of section sixty-two of the civil rights law, the prosecutor shall promptly notify the victim at the most current address or telephone number provided by such victim in the most reasonable and expedient possible manner of the time and place such petition will be presented to the court.

Amended by L. 1992, Ch. 307; L. 1993, Ch. 499; L. 1996, Ch. 173, § 1, eff. July 18, 1996; L. 1996, Ch. 198, § 1, amending subd. 2, eff. July 25, 1996; L. 1998, Ch. 1, § 41, eff. Aug 6, 1998; L. 2000, Ch. 549, § 5, adding subd. 6, eff. Jan. 24, 2001, as amended by L. 2005, Ch. 613, § 1, eff. Aug. 30, 2005, and shall apply to all convictions that are entered on, after or before such date for which a petition is filed on, after or before the effective date of this act [Jan. 24, 2001] and is pending before a court on or after the effective date of this act [Jan. 24, 2001].

ANNOTATIONS

Court's discretion in allowing statements.—Sentencing courts have discretion to allow more than one person to make a victim impact statement at sentencing, and court did not abuse its discretion in allowing five people to make statements at defendant's sentencing. People v. Hemmings, 2 N.Y.3d 1, 776 N.Y.S.2d 201, 808 N.E.2d 336 (2004).

—Court properly exercised its discretion in permitting family members of a police officer who died during this incident even though defendant was acquitted of all charges relating to the officer; even though those persons were not victims within the meaning of CPL § 380.50(2)(a), court read statute as granting victims the right to make statements at sentencing and not as limiting the court's discretion to permit additional persons to speak. People v. Rivers, 262 A.D.2d 108, 691 N.Y.S.2d 488 (1st Dept. 1999).

—In cases where defendant will be sentenced for a felony, court must permit the victim to make a statement relevant to the question of sentencing; there is no preclusion against statements offered by additional individuals. People v. Arroyo, 284 A.D.2d 735, 728 N.Y.S.2d 231 (3d Dept. 2001).

Defendant's right to make a statement.—Resentencing court's failure to ask defendant whether he wanted to make a statement on his own behalf was not an error of constitutional dimensions. People v. Green, 54 N.Y.2d 878, 444 N.Y.S.2d 908, 429 N.E.2d 415 (1981).

—Where the defendant was not afforded the opportunity, as required by CPL § 380.50, to make a statement on his behalf before the court pronounced sentence, case was remitted for resentencing to give the defendant an opportunity to make a statement on his own behalf, if he desired. People v. Crossland, 251 A.D.2d 509, 675 N.Y.S.2d 358 (2d Dept. 1998).

—Where defendant and his attorney had previously submitted presentence memorandum to the court, and the defendant was ably represented by attorney at time of sentencing, there was full compliance with the allocution statute, which gives the defense the right to make a statement prior to sentencing. Failure to make an actual oral statement where these particular facts are present will not be a valid reason for remitting case for resentencing. People v. McClain, 42 A.D.2d 868, 346 N.Y.S.2d 856 (2d Dept. 1973), aff'd, 35 N.Y.2d 483, 364 N.Y.S.2d 143, 323 N.E.2d 685 (1974), cert. denied, 423 U.S. 852 (1975).

—The defendant was effectively afforded the right to make a presentence statement in his own behalf, where the court twice asked whether he wished to make such a statement before pronouncing sentence. People v. Hayes, 43 A.D.2d 99, 349 N.Y.S.2d 869 (4th Dept. 1973), aff'd, 35 N.Y.2d 907, 364 N.Y.S.2d 897, 324 N.E.2d 365 (1974).

—While the sentencing minutes did not indicate a response by defendant to the court's invitation to make a presentencing statement, the more probable interpretation of the events is that defendant indicated her waiver of the opportunity to speak by way of a gesture. People v. Osorio, 161 A.D.2d 258, 555 N.Y.S.2d 51 (1st Dept.), lv. denied, 76 N.Y.2d 862 (1990).

—At resentencing both the defendant and his attorney have the right to be present and to be heard by the court. People v. Lucks, 91 A.D.2d 896, 457 N.Y.S.2d 514 (1st Dept. 1983).

—The failure to accord the defendant the opportunity to speak in his own behalf prior to the imposition of sentence was a violation of CPL § 380.50 and accordingly requires the vacation of the sentence imposed and remittance to the court for resentencing. People v. McCarroll, 95 A.D.2d 815, 463 N.Y.S.2d 538 (2d Dept. 1983).

Adequacy of allocution.—Although there was not conformity with the literal dictates of CPL § 380.50, governing the right of allocution, the allocution afforded the defendants substantially complied with the statutory requirement that each defendant be afforded an opportunity to make a statement personally in his own behalf of whatever character and thus did not require resentencing. People v. McClain, 35 N.Y.2d 483, 364 N.Y.S.2d 143, 323 N.E.2d 685, cert. denied, 423 U.S. 852 (1975); People v. DiLaura, 47 A.D.2d 806, 365 N.Y.S.2d 300 (4th Dept. 1975).

—The allocution requirements were not satisfied where the clerk prior to sentencing only asked whether he had "any legal cause to show why sentencing should not be pronounced." People v. Debnam, 92 A.D.2d 940, 460 N.Y.S.2d 367 (2d Dept. 1983).

Noncompliance with subd. 1.—Court's question at the beginning of the sentencing proceeding asking whether "anyone" wanted to be heard was not sufficient to be deemed substantial compliance with statutory mandate of CPL § 380.50(1). People v. Torres, 238 A.D.2d 933, 661 N.Y.S.2d 153 (4th Dept. 1997).

Representation by counsel.—Defendant was deprived of effective assistance of counsel at sentencing where the attorney representing the defendant at sentencing was not the attorney who represented him at trial and when asked by the court if he had anything to say stated that he had "nothing to add to the probation report" and when asked if he had seen the probation report stated "no, I have not." People v. Edmond, 84 A.D.2d 938, 447 N.Y.S.2d 60 (4th Dept. 1981).

Victim's statement.—CPL § 380.50(2)(b) is not unconstitutional; nothing in the State or Federal Constitution prohibits the court from considering the victim's own account of the defendant's crime in assessing the true dimensions of its psychological impact. People v. Oyola, 215 A.D.2d 597, 626 N.Y.S.2d 849 (2d Dept. 1995).

—Although the court was not authorized to permit the victim's attorney to speak at sentencing, the error was harmless. People v. Blaich, 201 A.D.2d 661, 608 N.Y.S.2d 265 (2d Dept. 1994).

—Error, if any, in permitting victim's mother and sister to testify at defendant's sentencing was harmless. People v. Knapp, 213 A.D.2d 740, 623 N.Y.S.2d 355 (3d Dept. 1995).

—Court did not err in asking questions of the victim to clarify her statement made pursuant to CPL § 380.50(2) because the court has broad powers to determine facts pertinent to sentencing. People v. Gilbert, 17 A.D.3d 1166, 793 N.Y.S.2d 846 (4th Dept. 2005).

Prosecutor's statement.—A presentence memorandum submitted to the court by the prosecution is acceptable where a lengthy oral statement by the people can be avoided or condensed; or where the nature of the case, the particular defendant involved, or the public interest in the subject matter justifies a more detailed and delineated recital of claimed aggravating or mitigating circumstances. People v. Gregorio, 110 Misc. 2d 1058, 443 N.Y.S.2d 589 (Sup. Ct. N.Y. Co. 1981).

Subd. 2; victim unable or unwilling to make statement.—The term victim encompasses the victim or a surrogate if the victim is deceased, unable or unwilling to appear at sentencing. People v. Hemmings, 2 N.Y.3d 1, 776 N.Y.S.2d 201, 808 N.E.2d 336 (2004).

§ 380.60. Authority for the execution of sentence.

Except where a sentence of death is pronounced, a certificate of conviction showing the sentence pronounced by the court, or a certified copy thereof, constitutes the authority for the execution of the sentence and serves as the order of commitment, and no other warrant, order of commitment or authority is necessary to justify or to require execution of the sentence.

§ 380.70. Minutes of sentence. [*Effective until Sept. 1, 2009.*]

In any case where a person receives an indeterminate or determinate sentence of imprisonment, a certified copy of the stenographic minutes of the sentencing proceeding and a certificate of conviction specifying the section and, to the extent applicable, the subdivision, paragraph and subparagraph of the penal law or other statute under which the defendant was convicted, must be delivered to the person in charge of the institution to which the defendant has been delivered within thirty days from the date such sentence was imposed; provided, however, that a sentence or commitment is not defective by reason of a failure to comply with the provisions of this section.

Amended by L. 1995, Ch. 3, § 31, eff. Oct. 1, 1995, pursuant to L. 1995, Ch. 3, § 74, paragraph (a), and repealed Sept. 30, 2005, pursuant to L. 1995, Ch. 3, § 74, paragraph (d); L. 2005, Ch. 56, Part D, § 20, eff. Apr. 1, 2005, extending repeal date to Sept. 1, 2009.

ANNOTATION

Missing transcript.—It was not sufficient to permit withdrawal of the guilty plea for defendant to show that the sentencing transcript was missing, but rather, the burden was on the defendant to demonstrate the existence of a specific appealable issue. People v. Sanchez, 75 A.D.2d 918, 427 N.Y.S.2d 538 (3d Dept. 1980).

§ 380.80. Reporting sentence to social services.

Whenever a person receives a sentence of imprisonment, the court that has sentenced such person shall deliver the certificate of conviction and provide notification of the sentence imposed to the commissioner of social services who, in turn, shall deliver the certificate of conviction and provide notification of the sentence imposed to the appropriate local commissioner of social services.

Added L. 1996, Ch. 700, § 2, eff. Jan. 7, 1997.

§ 380.90. Reporting sentences to schools.

1. "Designated educational official" shall mean (a) an employee or representative of a school district who is designated by the school district or (b) an employee or representative of a charter school or private elementary or secondary school who is designated by such school to receive records pursuant to this section and to coordinate the student's participation in programs which may exist in the school district or community, including: non-violent conflict resolution programs, peer mediation programs and youth courts, extended day programs and other school violence prevention and intervention programs.

2. Whenever a person under the age of nineteen who is enrolled as a student in a public or private elementary or secondary school is sentenced for a crime, the court that has sentenced such person shall provide notification of the conviction and sentence to the designated educational official of the school in which such person is enrolled as a student. Such notification shall be used by the designated educational official only for purposes related to the execution of the student's educational plan, where applicable, successful school adjustment and reentry into the community. Such notification shall be kept separate and apart from such student's school records and shall be accessible only by the designated educational official. Such notification shall not be part of such student's permanent school record and shall not be appended to or included in any documentation regarding such student and shall be destroyed at such time as such student is no longer enrolled in the school district. At no time shall such notification be used for any purpose other than those specified in this subdivision.

Added L. 2000, Ch. 181, § 14, eff. Nov. 1, 2000; **Amended** by L. 2001, Ch. 380, § 7, eff. Oct. 23, 2001, and deemed in full force and effect on and after Nov. 1, 2000, amending subd. 1.

ARTICLE 390—PRE-SENTENCE REPORTS

LexisNexis Cross References

New York Criminal Practice (2d ed.), Vol. 4, Ch. 41, Pre-Sentence Reports and Proceedings; *Sexual Assault Trials (2d ed.),* Vol. 1, Ch. 9, AIDS and Sexual Assault; *Criminal Practice Handbook (2d ed.),* Ch. 10, Disposition Alternatives Including Sentencing Issues.

§ 390.10. Requirement of fingerprint report.

In any case where the defendant is convicted of an offense specified in subdivision one of section 160.10, the court may not pronounce sentence until it has received a fingerprint report from the division of criminal justice services or a police department report with respect to the defendant's prior arrest record. For such purpose, the court may use the original fingerprint report obtained after the arrest or arraignment of the defendant, or it may direct that a new report be prepared and transmitted to it.

Amended by L. 1971, Ch. 762; L. 1972, Ch. 399.

§ 390.15. Requirement of HIV related testing in certain cases.

1.   (a) In any case where the defendant is convicted of a felony offense enumerated in any section of article one hundred thirty of the penal law, or any subdivision of section 130.20 of such law, where an act of "sexual intercourse," "oral sexual conduct" or "anal sexual conduct," as those terms are defined in section 130.00 of the penal law, is required as an essential element for the commission thereof, the court must, upon a request of the victim, order that the defendant submit to human immunodeficiency (HIV) related testing. The testing is to be conducted by a state, county, or local public health officer designated by the order. Test results, which shall not be disclosed to the court, shall be communicated to the defendant and the victim named in the order in accordance with the provisions of section twenty-seven hundred eighty-five-a of the public health law, but such results and disclosure need not be completed prior to the imposition of sentence.

(b) For the purposes of this section, the terms "defendant", "conviction" and "sentence" mean and include, respectively, an "eligible youth," a

"youthful offender finding" and a "youthful offender sentence" as those terms are defined in section 720.10 of this chapter. The term "victim" means the person with whom the defendant engaged in an act of "sexual intercourse", "oral sexual conduct" or "anal sexual conduct", as those terms are defined in section 130.00 of the penal law, where such conduct with such victim was the basis for the defendant's conviction of an offense specified in paragraph (a) of this subdivision.

2. Any request made by the victim pursuant to this section must be in writing, filed with the court and provided by the court to the defendant or his or her counsel. The request must be filed with the court prior to or within ten days after entry of the defendant's conviction; provided that, for good cause shown, the court may permit such request to be filed at any time before sentence is imposed.

3. Any requests, related papers and orders made or filed pursuant to this section, together with any papers or proceedings related thereto, shall be sealed by the court and not made available for any purpose, except as may be necessary for the conduct of judicial proceedings directly related to the provisions of this section. All proceedings on such requests shall be held in camera.

4. The application for an order to compel a convicted person to undergo an HIV related test may be made by the victim but, if the victim is an infant or incompetent person, the application may also be made by a representative as defined in section twelve hundred one of the civil practice law and rules. The application must state that (a) the applicant was the victim of the offense enumerated in paragraph (a) of subdivision one of this section of which the defendant stands convicted; and (b) the applicant has been offered counseling by a public health officer and been advised of (i) the limitations on the information

to be obtained through an HIV test on the proposed subject; (ii) current scientific assessments of the risk of transmission of HIV from the exposure he or she may have experienced, and (iii) the need for the applicant to undergo HIV related testing to definitively determine his or her HIV status.

5. The court shall conduct a hearing only if necessary to determine if the applicant is the victim of the offense of which the defendant was convicted. The court ordered test must be performed within fifteen days of the date on which the court ordered the test, provided, however, that whenever the defendant is not tested within the period prescribed by the court, the court must again order that the defendant undergo an HIV related test.

6. (a) Test results shall be disclosed subject to the following limitations, which shall be specified in any order issued pursuant to this section:

(i) disclosure of confidential HIV related information shall be limited to that information which is necessary to fulfill the purpose for which the order is granted;

(ii) disclosure of confidential HIV related information shall be limited to the person making the application; redisclosure shall be permitted only to the victim, the victim's immediate family, guardian, physicians, attorneys, medical or mental health providers and to his or her past and future contacts to whom there was or is a reasonable risk of HIV transmission and shall not be permitted to any other person or the court.

(b) Unless inconsistent with this section, the court's order shall direct compliance with and conform to the provisions of article twenty seven-f of the public health law. Such order shall include measures to protect against disclosure to others of the identity and HIV status of the applicant and of the person tested and may include such other measures as the court deems necessary to protect confidential information.

7. Any failure to comply with the provisions of this section or section twenty-seven hundred eighty-five-a of the public health law shall not impair or affect the validity of any sentence imposed by the court.

8. No information obtained as a result of a consent, hearing or court order for testing issued pursuant to this section nor any information derived therefrom may be used as evidence in any criminal or civil proceeding against the defendant which relates to events that were the basis for the defendant's conviction, provided however that nothing herein shall prevent prosecution of a witness testifying in any court hearing held pursuant to this section for perjury pursuant to article two hundred ten of the penal law.

Added by L. 1995, Ch. 76, § 1, eff. Aug. 1, 1995; L. 2003, Ch. 264, § 44, eff. Nov. 1, 2003, amending subd. 1(a), (b).

§ 390.20. Requirement of pre-sentence report.

1. Requirement for felonies. In any case where a person is convicted of a felony, the court must order a pre-sentence investigation of the defendant and it may not pronounce sentence until it has received a written report of such investigation.

2. Requirement for misdemeanors. Where a person is convicted of a misdemeanor a pre-sentence report is not required, but the court may not pronounce any of the following sentences unless it has ordered a pre-sentence investigation of the defendant and has received a written report thereof:

(a) A sentence of probation; except where the provisions of subparagraph (ii) of paragraph (a) of subdivision four of this section apply;

(b) A sentence of imprisonment for a term in excess of ninety days;

(c) Consecutive sentences of imprisonment with terms aggregating more than ninety days.

3. Permissible in any case. For purposes of sentence, the court may, in its discretion, order a pre-sentence investigation and report in any case, irrespective of whether such investigation and report is required by subdivision one or two.

4. Waiver. (a) Notwithstanding the provisions of subdivision one or two of this section, a pre-sentence investigation of the defendant and a written report thereon may be waived by the mutual consent of the parties and with consent of the judge, stated on the record or in writing, whenever:

(i) A sentence of imprisonment has been agreed upon by the parties and will be satisfied by the time served, or

(ii) A sentence of probation has been agreed upon by the parties and will be imposed, or

(iii) A report has been prepared in the preceding twelve months, or

(iv) A sentence of probation is revoked.

[*Effective until Sept. 1, 2009.*] Provided, however, a pre-sentence investigation of the defendant and a written report thereon shall not be waived if an indeterminate or determinate sentence of imprisonment is to be imposed.

[*Effective Sept. 1, 2009.*] Provided, however, a pre-sentence investigation of the defendant and a written report thereon shall not be waived if an indeterminate sentence of imprisonment is to be imposed.

(b) Whenever a pre-sentence investigation and report has been waived pursuant to subparagraph (i), (ii) or (iii) of paragraph (a) of this subdivision and the court determines that such information would be relevant to the court disposition, a victim impact statement shall be provided in accordance with this section.

Amended by L. 1974, Ch. 652; L. 1991, Ch. 413, eff. Oct. 17, 1991, amending subd. 2 and adding subd. 4; L. 1995, Ch. 3, § 32, amending subd. 4(a), eff. Oct. 1, 1995, and amendments repealed Sept. 1, 2009.

ANNOTATIONS

Confidentiality provisions.—Although defendant argued that his statements to the probation officer should have been suppressed as a result of the probation officer's alleged violation of the confidentiality provisions of CPL § 390.50 by reporting the statement to the District Attorney's office, the statute clearly provides that the prosecutor was entitled to see a copy of the presentence report; thus, there was no breach of confidentiality in the disclosure. People v. Cortijo, 291 A.D.2d 352, 739 N.Y.S.2d 19 (1st Dept. 2002).

Updated presentence report; not required.—In a case where the defendant had been continuously incarcerated in the time between the original sentence and resentence, the need for an updated report is a matter within the sentencing court's discretion. People v. Kuey, 83 N.Y.2d 278, 609 N.Y.S.2d 568, 681 N.E.2d 574 (1994).

—The resentencing court's failure to obtain an updated presentence report before imposing sentence did not require vacatur of the resentence as the resentence imposed was the minimum authorized sentence. People v. Jandelli, 158 A.D.2d 620, 551 N.Y.S.2d 590 (2d Dept. 1990).

—Where, as here, defendant has been continually incarcerated between the time of the initial sentencing and resentencing, there is no legal obligation to order an updated report. People v. James, 4 A.D.3d 774, 772 N.Y.S.2d 151 (4th Dept. 2004).

—"Although CPL § 390.20(1) requires a presentence investigation report when a sentence is imposed upon a felony conviction, where, as here, the court is fully familiar with any changes in defendant's status, conduct or condition since the original report was prepared, an updated report was not required." People v. Perry, 278 A.D.2d 933, 718 N.Y.S.2d 768 (4th Dept. 2000).

Updated presentence report; required.—It is well established that before sentencing a defendant convicted of a felony, the court must order, receive, and, of course, consider a current presentence report. People v. Gordon, 155 A.D.2d 225, 546 N.Y.S.2d 374 (1st Dept. 1989).

—Where defendant was resentenced without the benefit of an updated presentence report, the matter was remanded for resentencing. People v. Smith, 150 A.D.2d 313, 541 N.Y.S.2d 810 (1st Dept. 1989).

—A presentence report that was more than two years old was inadequate and sentence had to be vacated. People v. Laster, 140 A.D.2d 233, 528 N.Y.S.2d 831 (1st Dept. 1988).

—Absent the imposition of the minimum sentence or a bargained sentence and express waiver, a court imposing a sentence of imprisonment upon finding that the defendant violated the terms of probation must obtain and consider and updated presentence report. People v. Roman, 153 A.D.2d 594, 544 N.Y.S.2d 384 (2d Dept. 1989).

—Resentencing was required where sentencing court relied upon six-year-old presentence report. People v. Goolsby, 153 A.D.2d 759, 545 N.Y.S.2d 210 (2d Dept. 1989).

—Court's utilization of a presentence report which had been prepared 18 months earlier in connection with sentencing on an unrelated conviction required remittal for resentencing; the oral statements made by a probation officer at the time of sentencing did not constitute the functional equivalent of an updated report inasmuch as the probation officer did not provide the court with any updated information and did not participate in the proceedings until after the sentence was already imposed. People v. Martinez, 118 A.D.2d 661, 499 N.Y.S.2d 964 (2d Dept.), *lv. denied,* 67 N.Y.2d 1054 (1986).

—Vacatur of sentence and remittal for resentencing was mandated where court failed to obtain an updated presentence report despite the passage of 10 years between the original date set for sentencing and the date sentence was imposed. People v. Sierra, 99 A.D.2d 472, 470 N.Y.S.2d 51 (2d Dept. 1984).

—A period of more than one year between preparation of presentence report and resentencing of defendant required that

an updated report be submitted. People v. O'Dell, 105 A.D.2d 987, 482 N.Y.S.2d 134 (3d Dept. 1984).

Updated presentence report; probation violation.—Where a defendant is sentenced for a violation of probation, the presentence report upon which the probationary sentence was based must ordinarily be updated to reflect any changes in the defendant's new circumstances relevant to the new sentence; new matter asserted by defense counsel and accepted as true by the court is the "functional equivalent" of an updated presentence report. People v. Santiago, 187 A.D.2d 384, 590 N.Y.S.2d 200 (1st Dept. 1992).

—Where the time between imposition of the original sentence, and resentencing upon revocation of probation was brief, and defendant was incarcerated for much of that time, sentencing court did not abuse its discretion in failing to order an updated presentence report prior to imposing sentence. People v. Roberts, 214 A.D.2d 592, 625 N.Y.S.2d 569 (2d Dept.), *lv. denied,* 85 N.Y.2d 979 (1995).

—Where defendant's probation revocation sentencing took place only six months after his initial presentence report had been prepared, and he did not request that it be updated, an updated presentence report was not required. People v. Shattuck, 214 A.D.2d 1026, 626 N.Y.S.2d 602 (4th Dept. 1995).

Effect of sentencing without a complete presentence report.—Prior to the imposition of a one-year sentence upon defendant's conviction of endangering the welfare of a child, a pre-sentence investigation of defendant's mental condition and background should have been conducted. People v. Aiss, 29 N.Y.2d 403, 328 N.Y.S.2d 438, 278 N.E.2d 647 (1972).

—A defendant who has pleaded or been found guilty after trial of a felony should not be sentenced without a presentence report, notwithstanding that where a defendant pleads guilty conditioned upon a specified sentence, requests immediate sentencing, and knowingly waives a presentence report, he cannot thereafter assert that the sentence was improper. People v. Andujar, 110 A.D.2d 606, 488 N.Y.S.2d 653 (1st Dept. 1985).

—Where defendant was sentenced without preparation of presentence report and the prosecutor had specifically asked that defendant not be sentenced without a presentence report, the sentence imposed was invalid. People v. Thomas, 269 A.D.2d 411, 704 N.Y.S.2d 96 (2d Dept. 2000).

—Defendant cannot complain on appeal that his absence, by virtue of the fact that he had absconded, resulted in the preparation of a less than adequate presentence report. People v. Blas, 192 A.D.2d 540, 596 N.Y.S.2d 438 (2d Dept.), *lv. denied,* 82 N.Y.2d 751 (1993).

—Court's imposition of sentence without benefit of presentence report as to one of three incidents for which defendant was sentenced did not require remand where sentence was the result of a negotiated plea and defense counsel specifically agreed to proceed to sentence. People v. Kryminski, 154 A.D.2d 549, 546 N.Y.S.2d 389 (2d Dept. 1989).

—On appeal, defendant may not complain that the probation report was incomplete where prior to the imposition of sentence defense counsel read the report, which stated that it could not be completed because the defendant had absconded, and he did not raise any objection. People v. Morales, 127 A.D.2d 797, 512 N.Y.S.2d 194 (2d Dept. 1987).

—Defendant's contention that the sentencing court erred in imposing sentence based upon an incomplete sentencing report was not preserved for appellate review where the defendant did not raise the claim at sentencing. People v. Marin, 157 A.D.2d 804, 550 N.Y.S.2d 407 (2d Dept. 1990).

—Court erred in sentencing defendant to prison without the benefit of an updated presentence investigation report covering the 56 months during which defendant was on probation; sentence vacated and remitted for resentencing after preparation and review of an updated presentence report. People v. Klinkowski, 281 A.D.2d 972, 723 N.Y.S.2d 777 (4th Dept. 2001).

Presumption of regularity.—The absence of any reference to a presentence report in the record is insufficient to rebut the presumption of regularity accorded to judicial proceedings; a presentence report was ordered by the court and prepared by the Department of Probation prior to the sentencing date, and it is presumed that the defendant was lawfully sentenced on the basis of this report. People v. Nazario, 253 A.D.2d 726, 679 N.Y.S.2d 362 (1st Dept. 1998).

—In view of the presumption of regularity, and in the absence of proof to the contrary, it was concluded that the court had access to a presentence report prior to sentencing the defendant in absentia. People v. Hurd. 200 A.D.2d 521, 606 N.Y.S.2d 670 (1st Dept.), *lv. denied*, 83 N.Y.2d 854 (1994).

—A defendant may not presume by the record's silence that the trial court did not review the presentence report or that defense counsel was not afforded the opportunity to argue from it; judicial proceedings enjoy a presumption of regularity that may be overcome only by affirmative proof sufficient to rebut its effectiveness. People v. Marcano, 199 A.D.2d 86, 605 N.Y.S.2d 51 (1st Dept. 1993).

—The court is not obligated to make reference to the presentence report on the record, and the law mandates only that it receive the presentence report before pronouncing sentence (CPL § 390.20[1]). People v. Carmello, 114 A.D.2d 965, 495 N.Y.S.2d 230 (2d Dept. 1985).

—Judicial proceedings are entitled to a presumption of regularity and in the absence of affirmative proof to the contrary, it may be presumed that the sentencing court acted in accordance with its duty to consider the presentence report which had been prepared and was available before sentencing, notwithstanding the absence of any explicit reference to the report. People v. Kalakowski, 120 A.D.2d 763, 501 N.Y.S.2d 499 (3d Dept. 1986).

Waiver.—When both defendant and his attorney declined to challenge the presentence report at his sentencing to a negotiated sentence, defendant waived claim that the report was too incomplete to be relied upon at sentencing. People v. Smallwood, 212 A.D.2d 449, 622 N.Y.S.2d 939 (1st Dept. 1995).

—Defendant's failure to cooperate with Department of Probation did not result in the forfeiture of the requirement for a presentence report. People v. Villegas, 146 A.D.2d 228, 540 N.Y.S.2d 777 (1st Dept. 1989).

—Where defendant refused to be interviewed by the probation department, he could not argue on appeal that the presentence report was incomplete. People v. Greene, 209 A.D.2d 541, 619 N.Y.S.2d 74 (2d Dept. 1994), *lv. denied*, 85 N.Y.2d 909 (1995).

—A presentence report is not necessary if the minimum authorized sentence is imposed or the sentence is a bargained one and the defendant waives the presentence investigation requirement. People v. Goon, 124 A.D.2d 347, 507 N.Y.S.2d 288 (3d Dept. 1986), *lv. denied*, 69 N.Y.2d 711 (1987).

—A presentence report is waivable by the defendant; it may not withdrawn absent the existence of such factors as would support an application to withdraw a guilty plea itself. People v. Powell, 108 Misc. 2d 610, 438 N.Y.S.2d 220 (Crim Ct. N.Y. Co. 1981).

§ 390.30. Scope of pre-sentence investigation and report.

1. The investigation. The pre-sentence investigation consists of the gathering of information with respect to the circumstances attending the commission of the offense, the defendant's history of delinquency or criminality, and the defendant's social history, employment history, family situation, economic status, education, and personal habits. Such investigation may also include any other matter which the agency conducting the investigation deems relevant to the question of sentence, and must include any matter the court directs to be included.

2. Physical and mental examinations. Whenever information is available with respect to the defendant's physical and mental condition, the pre-sentence investigation must include the gathering of such information. In the case of a felony or a class A misdemeanor, or in any case where a person under the age of twenty-one is convicted of a crime, the court may order that the defendant undergo a thorough physical or mental examination in a designated facility and may further order

that the defendant remain in such facility for such purpose for a period not exceeding thirty days.

3. The report and victim impact statement. (a) The report of the pre-sentence investigation must contain an analysis of as much of the information gathered in the investigation as the agency that conducted the investigation deems relevant to the question of sentence. The report must also include any other immformation * that the court directs to be included and the material required by paragraph (b) of this subdivision which shall be considered part of the report.

(b) The report shall also contain a victim impact statement, unless it appears that such information would be of no relevance to the recommendation or court disposition, which shall include an analysis of the victim's version of the offense, the extent of injury or economic loss and the actual out-of-pocket loss to the victim and the views of the victim relating to disposition including the amount of restitution and reparation sought by the victim after the victim has been informed of the right to seek restitution and reparation, subject to the availability of such information. In the case of a homicide or where the victim is unable to assist in the preparation of the victim impact statement, the information may be acquired from the victim's family. The victim impact statement shall be made available to the victim by the prosecutor pursuant to subdivision two of section 390.50 of this article. Nothing contained in this section shall be interpreted to require that a victim supply information for the preparation of this report.

4. Abbreviated investigation and short form report. In lieu of the procedure set forth in subdivisions one, two and three, where the conviction is of a misdemeanor the scope of the pre-sentence investigation may be abbreviated and a short form report may be made. The use of abbreviated investigations and short form reports, the matters to be covered therein and the form of the reports shall be in accordance with the general rules regulating methods and procedures in the administration of probation as adopted from time to time by the state director of probation and correctional alternatives pursuant to the provisions of article twelve of the executive law. No such rule, however, shall be construed so as to relieve the agency conducting the investigation of the duty of investigating and reporting upon:

(a) the extent of the injury or economic loss and the actual out-of-pocket loss to the victim including the amount of restitution and reparation sought by the victim, after the victim has been informed of the right to seek restitution and reparation, or

(b) any matter relevant to the question of sentence that the court directs to be included in particular cases. Investigating agencies under this article shall be responsible for the collection, and transmission to the state division of probation, of data on the number of victim impact statements prepared, pursuant to regulations of the division. Such information shall be transmitted to the crime victims board and included in the board's annual report pursuant to subdivision twenty of section six hundred twenty-three of the executive law.

6. Interim probation supervision. In any case where the court determines that a defendant is eligible for a sentence of probation, the court, after consultation with the prosecutor and upon the consent of the defendant, may adjourn the sentencing to a specified date and order that the defendant be placed on interim probation supervision. In no event may the sentencing be adjourned for a period exceeding one year from the date the conviction is entered. When ordering that the defendant be placed on interim probation supervision, the court shall impose all of the conditions relating to supervision specified in subdivision three of section 65.10 of the penal law and may impose any or all of the conditions relating to conduct and rehabilitation specified in subdivisions two, four and five of section 65.10 of such law; provided, however, that the defendant must receive a written copy of any such conditions at the time he or she is placed on interim probation supervision. The defendant's record of compliance with such conditions, as well as any other relevant information, shall be included in the presentence report, or updated presentence report, prepared pursuant to this section, and the court must consider such record and information when pronouncing sentence.

* As originally enacted.

Amended by L. 1971, Ch. 450; L. 1982, Ch. 612; L. 1985, Ch. 14; L. 1985, Ch. 134; L. 1991, Ch. 530; L. 1992, Ch. 618; L. 1998, Ch. 159, § 1, eff. Oct. 5, 1998; L. 1999, Ch. 216, eff. Oct. 4, 1999, amending subd. 6.

ANNOTATIONS

Miranda **warnings unnecessary from probation officer.**—Presentence interview by probation officer does not constitute the type of custodial interrogation requiring *Miranda* warnings, because although a probation officer is a peace officer, when performing a presentence interview she is not an agent of the prosecutor or the police, but rather, an arm of the court; "[i]t is precisely because of a probation officer's nonadversarial position that it is unnecessary for her to advise defendant of his *Miranda* warnings." People v. Cortijo, 179 Misc. 2d 178, 684 N.Y.S.2d 435 (Sup. Ct. N.Y. Co. 1998).

Mental, medical examination.—Court rejected defendant's contention that a mental evaluation, in aid of sentence under CPL § 390.30 (2), must comply with the procedures for determining whether a defendant is fit to proceed to trial under CPL § 730.20, which includes, in part, the appointment of two examining psychiatrists. People v. Glover, 128 A.D.2d 636, 513 N.Y.S.2d 31 (2d Dept. 1987), *lv. denied*, 70 N.Y.2d 711 (1988).

—Court did not err in failing to order a medical examination of defendant prior to imposing sentence where neither defendant nor defense counsel ever raised the issue of defendant's health, nor did they controvert the assertion in the pre-sentence report that the defendant was in good health. People v. Smith, 171 A.D.2d 1060, 569 N.Y.S.2d 243 (4th Dept.), *lv. denied*, 78 N.Y.2d 927 (1991).

Timing.—The defendant may request a presentence report before the plea is accepted where it may be desirable to have a firm sentence commitment in advance of sentence. People v. Selikoff, 35 N.Y.2d 227, 360 N.Y.S.2d 623, 318 N.E.2d 784, *cert. denied*, 419 U.S. 1122 (1974).

Victim's statement.—Court denied application by counsel

for the parents of murder victim to make an oral statement at sentencing holding that clear import of CPL § 390.30 is that the Legislature contemplated the victim impact statement as a written document. People v. McCarthy, 136 Misc. 2d 623, 519 N.Y.S.2d 118 (St. Lawrence Co. Ct. 1987).

Defendant's statement.—There is no statutory requirement that a statement by the defendant be included in the presentence report. People v. Davila, 238 A.D.2d 625, 655 N.Y.S.2d 698 (3d Dept. 1997).

§ 390.40. Defendant's or prosecutor's pre-sentence memorandum.

1. Either the defendant or prosecutor may, at any time prior to the pronouncement of sentence, file with the court a written memorandum setting forth any information he may deem pertinent to the question of sentence. Such memorandum may include information with respect to any of the matters described in section 390.30. The defendant may annex written statements by others in support of facts alleged in the memorandum.

2. The memorandum of the prosecutor shall be served on the defendant's attorney at least ten days prior to the date fixed for sentence.

Amended by L. 1984, Ch. 263.

ANNOTATIONS

Factual dispute; presentence report.—Since there was a factual dispute about statements in the presentence report, the defendant should have been offered an opportunity to submit his own presentence memorandum, and the court could hold a presentence conference to resolve any factual disputes. People v. Ranieri, 43 A.D.2d 1012, 352 N.Y.S.2d 313 (4th Dept. 1974).

Resentencing.—The resentencing court was not required to grant an adjournment for the purpose of allowing defendant's counsel an opportunity to prepare a presentence memorandum. People v. Pennington, 50 A.D.2d 609, 375 N.Y.S.2d 384 (2d Dept. 1975).

§ 390.50. Confidentiality of pre-sentence reports and memoranda.

1. In general. Any pre-sentence report or memorandum submitted to the court pursuant to this article and any medical, psychiatric or social agency report or other information gathered for the court by a probation department, or submitted directly to the court, in connection with the question of sentence is confidential and may not be made available to any person or public or private agency except where specifically required or permitted by statute or upon specific authorization of the court. For purposes of this section, any report, memorandum or other information forwarded to a probation department within this state from a probation agency outside this state is governed by the same rules of confidentiality. Any person, public or private agency receiving material must retain it under the same conditions of confidentiality as apply to the probation department that made it available.

2. Pre-sentence report; disclosure, victim access to impact statements; general principles. (a) Not less than one court day prior to sentencing, unless such time requirement is waived by the parties, the pre-sentence report or

memorandum shall be made available by the court for examination and for copying by the defendant's attorney, the defendant himself, if he has no attorney, and the prosecutor. In its discretion, the court may except from disclosure a part or parts of the report or memoranda which are not relevant to a proper sentence, or a diagnostic opinion which might seriously disrupt a program of rehabilitation, or sources of information which have been obtained on a promise of confidentiality, or any other portion thereof, disclosure of which would not be in the interest of justice. In all cases where a part or parts of the report or memoranda are not disclosed, the court shall state for the record that a part or parts of the report or memoranda have been excepted and the reasons for its action. The action of the court excepting information from disclosure shall be subject to appellate review. The pre-sentence report shall be made available by the court for examination and copying in connection with any appeal in the case, including an appeal under this subdivision.

(b) The victim impact statement prepared pursuant to subdivision three of section 390.30 of this article shall be made available by the prosecutor prior to sentencing to the victim or victim's family in accordance with his responsibilities under subdivision one of section 60.27 of the penal law and sections six hundred forty-one and six hundred forty-two of the executive law. The district attorney shall also give at least twenty-one days notice to the victim's family of the date of sentencing and of the rights of the victim pursuant to subdivision two of section 380.50 of this chapter, including the victim or victim's family's obligation to inform the court of its intention, at least ten days prior to the sentencing date, to make a statement at sentencing. If the victim has not received timely notice pursuant to this paragraph, the court may proceed with sentencing if it determines that the victim and the defendant have received reasonable notice or may adjourn sentencing for no more than seven days in order to afford such reasonable notice. Failure to give notice shall not affect the validity of any sentence imposed.

3. Public agencies within this state. A probation department must make available a copy of its pre-sentence report and any medical, psychiatric or social agency report submitted to it in connection with its pre-sentence investigation or its supervision of a defendant, to any court, or to the probation department of any court, within this state that subsequently has jurisdiction over such defendant for the purpose of pronouncing or reviewing sentence and to any state agency to which the defendant is subsequently committed or certified or under whose care and custody or jurisdiction the defendant subsequently is placed upon the official request of such court or agency therefor. In any such case, the court or agency receiving such material must retain it under the same conditions of confidentiality as apply to the probation department that made it available.

4. Public agencies outside this state. Upon official request of any probation, parole or public institutional agency outside this state, a probation department may make any information in its files available to such agency. Any such release of information shall be conditioned upon the agreement of the receiving agency to retain it under the same conditions of confidentiality as apply to the probation department that made it available.

5. Division of criminal justice services. Nothing contained in this section may be construed to prevent the voluntary submission by a probation department of data in its files to the division of criminal justice services.

6. Professional licensing agencies. Probation departments shall provide a copy of pre-sentence reports prepared in the case of individuals who are known to be licensed pursuant to title eight of the education law to the state department of health if the licensee is a physician, a specialist's assistant or a physician's assistant, and to the state education department with respect to all other such licensees. Such reports shall be accumulated and forwarded every three months, shall be in writing, and shall contain the following information:

(a) the name of the licensee and the profession in which licensure is held,

(b) the date of the conviction and the nature thereof,

(c) the index or other identifying file number.

In any such case, the state department receiving such material must retain it under the same conditions of confidentiality as apply to the probation department that made it available.

Amended by L. 1972, Ch. 399; L. 1975, Ch. 310; L. 1980, Ch. 866; L. 1981, Ch. 581; L. 1982, Ch. 157; L. 1984, Ch. 132; L. 1985, Ch. 14; L. 1986, Chs. 224, 369; L. 1992, Ch. 307.

ANNOTATIONS

Co-defendant's presentence reports.—Court rejected defendant's contention that he was denied his right to cross-examination by the County Court's refusal to provide him with the presentence reports of his four co-defendants, because those reports are confidential, and defendant failed to make a sufficient showing of need for the information in the reports. People v. Summers, 242 A.D.2d 868, 662 N.Y.S.2d 911 (4th Dept. 1997).

Disclosure to defense.—Refusal to disclose presentence reports did not violate defendant's constitutional rights although fundamental fairness and appearance of fairness may best be accomplished by disclosure of presentence reports. However, in certain instances denial of disclosure might constitute an abuse of discretion, particularly where no legitimate public interest is achieved by nondisclosure. People v. Perry, 36 N.Y.2d 114, 365 N.Y.S.2d 518, 324 N.E.2d 878 (1975).

—Reports prepared by the Probation Department in connection with the testifying co-indictee were not *Rosario* material because they were confidential documents not within the possession or control of the People. People v. Figueroa, 258 A.D.2d 280, 685 N.Y.S.2d 53 (1st Dept. 1999).

—Inmate's bare assertion, without more, that he required the presentence report in order to properly prepare for an appearance before the Board of Parole was insufficient; at the very least, petitioner must demonstrate that he has been given notice of an impending hearing before the Board of Parole. Kilgore

v. New York, 274 A.D.2d 636, 710 N.Y.S.2d 690 (3d Dept. 2000).

—Petitioner failed to cite any statutory provision or other authority which would entitle him to a copy of the presentence report, and statute requiring access in any appeal was inapplicable to administrative appeals of Parole Board decisions. Allen v. People, 243 A.D.2d 1039, 663 N.Y.S.2d 455 (3d Dept. 1997).

—The sentencing judge, familiar with the report and with whatever parts thereof were redacted, if any, is the proper court to entertain an application for release of presentence reports for examination by appellate counsel and for use on a parole board hearing. Legal Aid Bureau of Buffalo v. Armer, 74 A.D.2d 737, 425 N.Y.S.2d 706 (4th Dept. 1980).

—In the absence of a statutory right to disclosure, CPL § 390.50(1) permits disclosure of a presentence report in collateral proceedings upon a proper factual showing that it is needed. Although the defendant had made the showing here, he is not automatically entitled to an unredacted copy. People v. Delatorre, 2 Misc. 2d 385, 767 N.Y.S.2d 766 (Co. Ct. Westchester Co. 2003).

Potential capital case.—Both the People and the defense demonstrated a legitimate basis for disclosure, in a potential death penalty case, of any pre-sentence investigation report to assist the District Attorney in determining whether to seek the death penalty, and for the defense to dissuade the District Attorney from making such a determination. However, disclosure was limited in that it would not include sealed records arising out of any youthful offender adjudication of the defendant. People v. Owens, 183 Misc. 2d 208, 703 N.Y.S.2d 881 (Co. Ct. Monroe Co. 1999).

Use of confidential statements.—Trial court did not err in permitting the People to use defendant's statements contained in a presentence report prepared in connection with an earlier matter in which defendant had pleaded guilty to impeach him; the use of those statements for impeachment did not violate public policy. People v. Cohen, 201 A.D.2d 494, 607 N.Y.S.2d 374 (2d Dept.), *lv. denied*, 84 N.Y.2d 824 (1994).

§ 390.60. Copy of reports to accompany defendant sentenced to imprisonment.

1. Cases where copy of report is required. Whenever a person is sentenced to a term of imprisonment, a copy of any pre-sentence report prepared, a copy of any pre-sentence memoran-dum filed by the defendant and a copy of any medical, psychiatric or social agency report submitted to the court or to the probation department in connection with the question of sentence must be delivered to the person in charge of the correctional or division for youth facility to which the defendant is committed at the time the defendant is delivered thereto. When a person is committed to any hospital operated by the office of mental health or referred to any program established pursuant to section four hundred one of the correction law, from a correctional facility or division for youth facility, the person in charge of the correctional facility or division for youth facility shall ensure that a copy of any pre-sentence report concerning such person, a copy of any pre-sentence memorandum filed by such person, and a copy of any medical, psychiatric or social agency report submitted to the court or to the probation department in connection with the question of sentence is provided to such hospital or program.

2. Effect of failure to deliver required report. A commitment is not void by reason of failure to comply with the provisions of subdivision one, but the person in charge of the correctional facility to which the defendant has been delivered in execution of the sentence is authorized to refuse to accept custody of such person until the required report is delivered.

Amended by L. 1984, Ch. 560; L. 1986, Ch. 62; L. 1995, Ch. 181, § 1, amending subd. 1, eff. July 10, 1995.

ANNOTATION

Right to challenge.—A defendant may not challenge the contents of a presentence report subsequent to sentence despite its potential effect on post-sentence events such as parole release. Gayle v. Lewis, 212 A.D.2d 919, 622 N.Y.S.2d 626 (3d Dept. 1995).

ARTICLE 400—PRE-SENTENCE PROCEEDINGS

LexisNexis Cross References

New York Criminal Practice (2d ed.), Vol. 4, Ch. 41, Pre-sentence Reports and Proceedings; *Criminal Practice Handbook (2d ed.),* Ch. 10, Disposition Alternatives Including Sentencing Issues.

§ 400.10. Pre-sentence conference.

1. Authorization and purpose. Before pronouncing sentence, the court, in its discretion, may hold one or more pre-sentence conferences in open court or in chambers in order to (a) resolve any discrepancies between the pre-sentence report, or other information the court has received, and the defendant's or prosecutor's pre-sentence memorandum submitted pursuant to section 390.40, or (b) assist the court in its consideration of any matter relevant to the sentence to be pronounced.

2. Attendance. Such conference may be held with the prosecutor and defense counsel in the absence of the defendant, or the court may direct that the defendant attend. The court may also direct that any person who has furnished or who can furnish information to the court concerning sentence attend. Reasonable notice of the conference must be given to the prosecutor and the defense counsel, who must be afforded an opportunity to participate therein.

3. Procedure at conference. The court may advise the persons present at the conference of the factual contents of any report or memorandum it has received and afford any of the participants an opportunity to controvert or to comment upon any fact. The court may also conduct a summary hearing at the conference on any matter relevant to sentence and may take testimony under oath. In the discretion of the court, all or any part of the proceedings at the conference may be recorded by a court stenographer and the transcript made part of the pre-sentence report.

4. Pre-sentence conditions. After conviction and prior sentencing the court may adjourn sentencing to a subsequent date and order the defendant to comply with any of the conditions contained in paragraphs (a) through (f) and paragraph (1) of subdivision two of section 65.10 of the penal law. In imposing sentence, the court shall take into consideration the defendant's record of compliance with pre-sentence conditions ordered by the court.

Amended by L. 1984, Ch. 263; **Amended** by L. 1994, Ch. 509, § 1, adding subd. 4.

ANNOTATIONS

Denial of pre-sentence conference.—Court properly denied defendant's requests for a pre-sentence conference and to call witnesses and subpoena records because defendant's sentence did not turn on any factual disputes requiring further exploration. People v. Yomtov, 19 A.D.3d 147, 796 N.Y.S.2d 348 (1st Dept. 2005).

Purpose.—The addition of subdivision 4 to CPL § 400.10 was enacted "specifically to correct the problem created by the Second Department's decision in People v. Johnson (197 A.D.2d 638) which erroneously concluded that [plea agreements conditioned on successful completion of a drug treatment program] constituted illegal interim probation.' " People v. Avery, 85 N.Y.2d 503, 626 N.Y.S.2d 726, 650 N.E.2d 384 (1995).

Postponing sentence.—The trial court neither exceeded its authority nor placed defendant on "interim probation" by postponing defendant's sentence after her plea of guilty and placing her with a private drug treatment program. People v. Smith, 85 N.Y.2d 919, 626 N.Y.S.2d 751, 650 N.E.2d 409 (1995).

§ 400.15. Procedure for determining whether defendant is a second violent felony offender.

1. Applicability. The provisions of this section govern the procedure that must be followed in any case where it appears that a defendant who stands convicted of a violent felony offense as defined in subdivision one of section 70.02 of the penal law has previously been subjected to a predicate violent felony conviction as defined in paragraph (b) of subdivision one of section 70.04 of the penal law and may be a second violent felony offender.

2. Statement to be filed. When information available to the court or to the people prior to sentencing for a violent felony offense indicates that the defendant may have previously been subjected to a predicate violent felony conviction, a statement must be filed by the prosecutor before sentence is imposed setting forth the date and place of each alleged predicate violent felony conviction. Where the provisions of subparagraph (v) of paragraph (c) of subdivision one of section 70.04 of the penal law apply, such statement also shall set forth the date of commencement and the date of termination as well as the place of imprisonment for each period of incarceration to be used for tolling of the ten year limitation set forth in subparagraph (iv) of paragraph (b) of such subdivision.

3. Preliminary examination. The defendant must be given a copy of such statement and the court must ask him whether he wishes to controvert any allegation made therein. If the defendant wishes to controvert any allegation in the statement, he must specify the particular allegation or allegations he wishes to controvert. Uncontroverted allegations in the statement shall be deemed to have been admitted by the defendant.

4. Cases where further hearing is not required. Where the uncontroverted allegations in the statement are sufficient to support a finding that the defendant has been subjected to a predicate violent felony conviction the court must enter such finding and when imposing sentence must sentence the defendant in accordance with the provisions of section 70.04 of the penal law.

5. Cases where further hearing is required. Where the defendant controverts an allegation in the statement and the uncontroverted allegations in such statement are not sufficient to support a finding that the defendant has been subjected to a predicate violent felony conviction the court must proceed to hold a hearing.

6. Time for hearing. In any case where a copy of the statement was not received by the defendant at least two days prior to the preliminary examination, the court must upon request of the defendant grant an adjournment of at least two days before proceeding with the hearing.

7. Manner of conducting hearing.

(a) A hearing pursuant to this section must be before the court without jury. The burden of proof is upon the people and a finding that the defendant has been subjected to a predicate violent felony conviction must be based upon proof beyond a reasonable doubt by evidence admissible under the rules applicable to a trial of the issue of guilt.

(b) A previous conviction in this or any other jurisdiction which was obtained in violation of the rights of the defendant under the applicable provisions of the constitution of the United States must not be counted in determining whether the defendant has been subjected to a predicate violent felony conviction. The defendant may, at any time during the course of the hearing hereunder controvert an allegation with respect to such conviction in the statement on the grounds that the conviction was unconstitutionally obtained. Failure to challenge the previous conviction in the manner provided herein constitutes a waiver on the part of the defendant of any allegation of unconstitutionality unless good cause be shown for such failure to make timely challenge.

(c) At the conclusion of the hearing the court must make a finding as to whether or not the defendant has been subjected to a predicate violent felony conviction.

8. Subsequent use of predicate violent felony conviction finding. Where a finding has been entered pursuant to this section, such finding shall be binding upon that defendant in any future proceeding in which the issue may arise.

Added by L. 1978, Ch. 481.

ANNOTATIONS

Tolling provision.—The requirement that the predicate violent felony information must plead the tolling of the 10-year limitation where a predicate felony more than 10 years old is to be used is mandatory. Failure to so plead required that defendant's sentence be vacated and the matter remanded for resentencing. People v. Johnson, 196 A.D.2d 408, 601 N.Y.S.2d 103 (1st Dept.), *lv. denied,* 82 N.Y.2d 806 (1993).

Resentencing required.—Defendant had to be resentenced where sentencing court failed to substantially comply with procedures set forth in the second violent felony offender statute. People v. Colon, 122 A.D.2d 150, 504 N.Y.S.2d 528 (2d Dept. 1986).

Waiver.—Defendant's failure to challenge the constitutionality of a prior felony conviction at a prior second violent felony conviction hearing constitutes a waiver of his right to challenge its use as a predicate for its subsequent as a predicate for finding defendant a persistent violent felony offender. People v. Dickerson, 202 A.D.2d 247, 608 N.Y.S.2d 463 (1st Dept.), *lv. denied,* 83 N.Y.2d 966 (1994).

§ 400.16. Procedure for determining whether defendant is a persistent violent felony offender.

1. Applicability. The provisions of this section govern the procedure that must be followed in any case where it appears that a defendant who stands convicted of a violent felony offense as defined in subdivision one of section 70.02 of the

penal law has previously been subjected to two or more predicate violent felony convictions as defined in paragraph (b) of subdivision one of section 70.04, and may be a persistent violent felony offender as defined in section 70.08 of the penal law.

2. Statement; preliminary examination; hearing; subsequent use of predicate violent felony conviction finding. The requirements set forth in subdivisions two, three, four, five, six, seven and eight of section 400.15 with respect to the statement to be filed, preliminary examination, hearing and subsequent use of a predicate violent felony conviction finding in the case of a second violent felony offender, shall also apply to a determination of whether a defendant has been subjected to two or more violent predicate felony convictions and is a persistent violent felony offender.

Added by L. 1978, Ch. 481.

ANNOTATIONS

Out-of-state predicates.—Defendant was improperly sentenced as a persistent violent felony offender since it was possible to violate the New Jersey statute, which was one of the necessary predicate convictions for invocation of that sentencing law, under circumstances which would not constitute a violent felony in New York. People v. Tilman, 114 A.D.2d 799, 495 N.Y.S.2d 50 (1st Dept. 1985).

Double jeopardy implications.—Defendant was properly resentenced as a persistent violent felony offender after his first sentence had been vacated; allowing the People to include in the new persistent felony offender statement a conviction not raised in the original statement did not violate the prohibition against double jeopardy. People v. Sanchez, 131 A.D.2d 605, 516 N.Y.S.2d 502 (2d Dept. 1987).

Right to a hearing.—Where defendant challenged his prior felony conviction on constitutional grounds, sentencing court was required to ascertain the nature of his challenge and conduct a hearing. People v. Katz, 214 A.D.2d 586, 625 N.Y.S.2d 71 (2d Dept. 1995).

—Where defendant elected to stand mute when arraigned on the second violent felony offender statement, the claim that it was error that no hearing was conducted on his status as a second violent felony offender was rejected. People v. Zagarella, 158 A.D.2d 636, 551 N.Y.S.2d 605 (2d Dept. 1990).

Defendant's right to be present.—It is proper to adjudge a defendant a second violent felony offender in absentia. People v. Santiago, 158 A.D.2d 629, 551 N.Y.S.2d 600 (2d Dept. 1990).

Sequentiality requirement.—Defendant was not properly adjudicated a persistent violent felony offender, since he was sentenced for both of the subject New Jersey armed robberies on the same day. People v. Stewart, 123 A.D.2d 566, 507 N.Y.S.2d 7 (1st Dept. 1986).

—As the defendant was sentenced on the same day for both of the violent felonies upon which the People relied in seeking to have the defendant adjudicated as a persistent felony offender, these two convictions may only count as one predicate felony for the purpose of PL § 70.08. People v. Ellison, 121 A.D.2d 462, 503 N.Y.S.2d 424 (2d Dept. 1986).

—Defendant was improperly sentenced as a persistent violent felony offender based upon two violent felony convictions rendered the same day; each of the two or more predicate violent felony convictions other than the first must be for a felony which occurred after sentence had been imposed for the conviction which preceded it. People v. Gonzalez, 114 A.D.2d 972, 495 N.Y.S.2d 417 (2d Dept. 1985).

§ 400.19. Procedure for determining whether defendant is a second child sexual assault felony offender.

1. Applicability. The provisions of this section govern the procedure that must be followed in any case where it appears that a defendant who stands convicted of a felony offense for a sexual assault upon a child as defined in section 70.07 of the penal law has previously been convicted of a predicate felony for a sexual assault upon a child.

2. When information available to the people prior to the trial of a felony offense for a sexual assault against a child indicates that the defendant may have previously been subjected to a predicate felony conviction for a sexual assault against a child, a statement may be filed by the prosecutor at any time before trial commences setting forth the date and place of each alleged predicate felony conviction for a sexual assault against a child and a statement whether the defendant was eighteen years of age or older at the time of the commission of the predicate felony. Where the provisions of subparagraph (v) of paragraph (b) of subdivision one of section 70.06 of the penal law apply, such statement also shall set forth the date of commencement and the date of termination as well as the place of imprisonment for each period of incarceration to be used for tolling of the ten year limitation set forth in subparagraph (iv) of paragraph (b) of such subdivision.

3. Preliminary examination. The defendant must be given a copy of such statement and the court must ask him whether he wishes to controvert any allegation made therein. If the defendant wishes to controvert any allegation in the statement, he must specify the particular allegation or allegations he wishes to controvert. Uncontroverted allegations in the statement shall be deemed to have been admitted by the defendant.

4. Cases where further hearing is not required. Where the uncontroverted allegations in the statement are sufficient to support a finding that the defendant has been subjected to a predicate felony conviction for a sexual assault upon a child and that the defendant was 18 years of age or older at the time of the commission of the predicate felony, the court must enter such finding and when imposing sentence must sentence the defendant in accordance with the provisions of section 70.07 of the penal law.

5. Cases where further hearing is required. Where the defendant controverts an allegation in the statement, the court must proceed to hold a hearing.

6. Manner of conducting hearing. (a) A hearing pursuant to this section must be before the court without jury. The burden of proof is upon the people and a finding that the defendant has

been subjected to a predicate felony conviction for a sexual assault against a child as defined in subdivision two of section 70.07 of the penal law and that the defendant was 18 years of age or older at the time of the commission of the predicate felony must be based upon proof beyond a reasonable doubt by evidence admissible under the rules applicable to a trial of the issue of guilt.

(b) Regardless of whether the age of the victim is an element of the alleged predicate felony offense, where the defendant controverts an allegation that the victim of an alleged sexual assault upon a child was less than fifteen years old, the people may prove that the child was less than fifteen years old by any evidence admissible under the rules applicable to a trial of the issue of guilt. For purposes of determining whether a child was less than fifteen years old, the people shall not be required to prove that the defendant knew the child was less than fifteen years old at the time of the alleged sexual assault.

(c) A previous conviction in this or any other jurisdiction which was obtained in violation of the rights of the defendant under the applicable provisions of the constitution of the United States must not be counted in determining whether the defendant has been subjected to a predicate felony conviction for a sexual assault upon a child. The defendant may, at any time during the course of the hearing hereunder, controvert an allegation with respect to such conviction in the statement on the grounds that the conviction was unconstitutionally obtained. Failure to challenge the previous conviction in the manner provided herein constitutes a waiver on the part of the defendant of any allegation of unconstitutionality unless good cause be shown for such failure to make timely challenge.

(d) At the conclusion of the hearing the court must make a finding as to whether or not the defendant has been subjected to a predicate felony conviction for a sexual assault against a child as defined in subdivision two of section 70.07 of the penal law and whether the defendant was 18 years of age or older at the time of the commission of the predicate felony.

7. Subsequent use of predicate felony conviction finding. Where a finding has been entered pursuant to this section, such finding shall be binding in any future proceeding in which the issue may arise.

Added by L. 2000, Ch. 1, eff. Feb. 1, 2001; L. 2003, Ch. 264, § 45, eff. Nov. 1, 2003, amending subds. 2, 4, and 6.

§ 400.20. Procedure for determining whether defendant should be sentenced as a persistent felony offender.

1. Applicability. The provisions of this section govern the procedure that must be followed in order to impose the persistent felony offender sentence authorized by subdivision two of section 70.10 of the penal law. Such sentence may not be imposed unless, based upon evidence in the record of a hearing held pursuant to this section, the court (a) has found that the defendant is a persistent felony offender as defined in subdivision one of section 70.10 of the penal law, and (b) is of the opinion that the history and character of the defendant and the nature and circumstances of his criminal conduct are such that extended incarceration and lifetime supervision of the defendant are warranted to best serve the public interest.

2. Authorization for hearing. When information available to the court prior to sentencing indicates that the defendant is a persistent felony offender, and when, in the opinion of the court, the available information shows that a persistent felony offender sentence may be warranted, the court may order a hearing to determine (a) whether the defendant is in fact a persistent felony offender, and (b) if so, whether a persistent felony offender sentence should be imposed.

3. Order directing a hearing. An order directing a hearing to determine whether the defendant should be sentenced as a persistent felony offender must be filed with the clerk of the court and must specify a date for the hearing not less than twenty days from the date the order is filed. The court must annex to and file with the order a statement setting forth the following:

(a) The dates and places of the previous convictions which render the defendant a persistent felony offender as defined in subdivision one of section 70.10 of the penal law; and

(b) The factors in the defendant's background and prior criminal conduct which the court deems relevant for the purpose of sentencing the defendant as a persistent felony offender.

4. Notice of hearing. Upon receipt of the order and statement of the court, the clerk of the court must send a notice of hearing to the defendant, his counsel and the district attorney. Such notice must specify the time and place of the hearing and the fact that the purpose of the hearing is to determine whether or not the defendant should be sentenced as a persistent felony offender. Each notice required to be sent hereunder must be accompanied by a copy of the statement of the court.

5. Burden and standard of proof; evidence. Upon any hearing held pursuant to this section the burden of proof is upon the people. A finding that the defendant is a persistent felony offender, as defined in subdivision one of section 70.10 of the penal law, must be based upon proof beyond a reasonable doubt by evidence admissible under the rules applicable to the trial of the issue of guilt. Matters pertaining to the defendant's history and character and the nature and circumstances of his criminal conduct may be established by any

relevant evidence, not legally privileged, regardless of admissibility under the exclusionary rules of evidence, and the standard of proof with respect to such matters shall be a preponderance of the evidence.

6. Constitutionality of prior convictions. A previous conviction in this or any other jurisdiction which was obtained in violation of the rights of the defendant under the applicable provisions of the Constitution of the United States may not be counted in determining whether the defendant is a persistent felony offender. The defendant may, at any time during the course of the hearing hereunder controvert an allegation with respect to such conviction in the statement of the court on the grounds that the conviction was unconstitutionally obtained. Failure to challenge the previous conviction in the manner provided herein constitutes a waiver on the part of the defendant of any allegation of unconstitutionality unless good cause be shown for such failure to make timely challenge.

7. Preliminary examination. When the defendant appears for the hearing the court must ask him whether he wishes to controvert any allegation made in the statement prepared by the court, and whether he wishes to present evidence on the issue of whether he is a persistent felony offender or on the question of his background and criminal conduct. If the defendant wishes to controvert any allegation in the statement of the court, he must specify the particular allegation or allegations he wishes to controvert. If he wishes to present evidence in his own behalf, he must specify the nature of such evidence. Uncontroverted allegations in the statement of the court are deemed evidence in the record.

8. Cases where further hearing is not required. Where the uncontroverted allegations in the statement of the court are sufficient to support a finding that the defendant is a persistent felony offender and the court is satisfied that (a) the uncontroverted allegations with respect to the defendant's background and the nature of his prior criminal conduct warrant sentencing the defendant as a persistent felony offender, and (b) the defendant either has no relevant evidence to present or the facts which could be established through the evidence offered by the defendant would not affect the court's decision, the court may enter a finding that the defendant is a persistent felony offender and sentence him in accordance with the provisions of subdivision two of section 70.10 of the penal law.

9. Cases where further hearing is required. Where the defendant controverts an allegation in the statement of the court and the uncontroverted allegations in such statement are not sufficient to support a finding that the defendant is a persistent felony offender as defined in subdivision one of section 70.10 of the penal law, or where the uncontroverted allegations with respect to the

defendant's history and the nature of his prior criminal conduct do not warrant sentencing him as a persistent felony offender, or where the defendant has offered to present evidence to establish facts that would affect the court's decision on the question of whether a persistent felony offender sentence is warranted, the court may fix a date for a further hearing. Such hearing shall be before the court without a jury and either party may introduce evidence with respect to the controverted allegations or any other matter relevant to the issue of whether or not the defendant should be sentenced as a persistent felony offender. At the conclusion of the hearing the court must make a finding as to whether or not the defendant is a persistent felony offender and, upon a finding that he is such, must then make such findings of fact as it deems relevant to the question of whether a persistent felony offender sentence is warranted. If the court both finds that the defendant is a persistent felony offender and is of the opinion that a persistent felony offender sentence is warranted, it may sentence the defendant in accordance with the provisions of subdivision two of section 70.10 of the penal law.

10. Termination of hearing. At any time during the pendency of a hearing pursuant to this section, the court may, in its discretion, terminate the hearing without making any finding. In such case, unless the court recommences the proceedings and makes the necessary findings, the defendant may not be sentenced as a persistent felony offender.

ANNOTATIONS

Constitutionality.—New York's discretionary offender sentencing scheme is unconstitutional under Apprendi v. New Jersey, 530 U.S. 466, 120 S. Ct. 2348, 147 L. Ed. 2d 435, contrary to People v. Rosen, 96 N.Y.2d 329, 728 N.Y.S.2d 407, 752 N.E.2d 844, *cert. denied*, 534 U.S. 899 (2001). People v. West, 2 Misc. 3d 332, 768 N.Y.S.2d 802 (Sup. Ct. N.Y. Co. 2003).

Procedure.—Where the sentencing court completely failed to follow the statutory procedures for imposing a persistent felony offender sentence, defendant's sentence must be vacated. People v. Hunter, 210 A.D.2d 11, 619 N.Y.S.2d 27 (1st Dept. 1994), *lv. denied*, 85 N.Y.2d 863 (1995).

—Where there was no indication that the sentencing court followed the procedures under CPL § 400.20 for imposing a persistent felony offender sentence, the error was preserved for review, despite defendant's failure to object at sentencing. People v. Vasquez, 189 A.D.2d 578, 592 N.Y.S.2d 34 (1st Dept. 1993), *modified on other grounds*, 83 N.Y.2d 269 (1994).

—County Court did not abuse its discretion in finding that defendant should be sentenced as a persistent felony offender, and giving the sentence it did where defendant had a multifarious criminal history which began as a youth, includes adult convictions, and shows defendant's hostility to reside in the community without running afoul of the law. People v. Batista, 235 A.D.2d 631, 652 N.Y.S.2d 645 (3d Dept. 1997).

—New York's discretionary offender scheme follows the approach in which prior convictions, combined with other factors, raise the sentencing range. Defendant was convicted of rape and sodomy in the first degree, and the trial court properly determined that defendant had previous convictions People v. West, 2 Misc. 3d 332, 768 N.Y.S.2d 802 (Sup. Ct. N.Y. Co. 2003).

Defendant's right to challenge predicate convictions.— The court did not err by refusing to entertain defendant's constitutional challenge to his prior convictions at the persistent felony offender hearing where defendant did not allege, pursuant to CPL § 400.20, that the prior convictions were "unconstitutionally obtained" within the meaning of that section. People v. Luciano, 46 N.Y.2d 767, 413 N.Y.S.2d 651, 386 N.E.2d 259 (1978).

—Even if defendant was not apprised of his statutory right to attack the constitutionality of his two predicate felony convictions at the time of his resentencing, he was not entitled to be resentenced, or, alternatively, to a hearing where his petition lacked factual allegations to support his claim of unconstitutionality of his predicate felony convictions. People v. Spencer, 32 N.Y.2d 446, 346 N.Y.S.2d 225, 299 N.E.2d 651 (1973).

—A defendant resentenced in accordance with *Montgomery* may upon such resentencing, challenge the constitutionality of a prior felony conviction relied upon as a predicate for multiple offender treatment. People v. Wilkins, 28 N.Y.2d 213, 321 N.Y.S.2d 87, 269 N.E.2d 803 (1971).

—A hearing was required where defendant was sentenced as a persistent felony offender since he contested the constitutionality of one of the two predicate convictions; the principle of double jeopardy does not bar the resentencing of the defendant as either a persistent or second felony offender. People v. Drummond, 87 A.D.2d 828, 448 N.Y.S.2d 758 (2d Dept. 1982).

Factors to be considered.—It was not error to sentence defendant as a persistent felony offender based upon a 1973 conviction for robbery in the third degree for which he was sentenced to the Narcotic Addiction Control Commission rather than to a term of imprisonment in excess of one year as required by the persistent-felony-offender statute since the Penal Law provision designates commitment to a drug abuse facility as a "sentence" and the legislature did not exclude such a sentence from the statute's application. People v. Johnson, 107 A.D.2d 763, 484 N.Y.S.2d 129 (2d Dept. 1985).

—Defendant was improperly sentenced as a persistent felony offender where the court based its determination solely upon defendant's criminal conduct and failed to consider defendant's "history and character" as required by CPL § 400.20(1)(b). People v. Perry, 161 A.D.2d 1156, 555 N.Y.S.2d 515 (4th Dept. 1990).

—Unless there is evidence that an invalid confession was obtained for the express purpose of increasing the sentence, CPL § 400.20(5) allows the Court to consider a confession obtained in violation of *Miranda* in a persistent felony offender proceeding as evidence of defendant's history and character that would warrant extended incarceration. People v. Wright, 104 Misc. 2d 911, 429 N.Y.S.2d 993 (Sup. Ct. N.Y. Co. 1980).

Sequentiality requirement.—Defendant was improperly found to be a persistent felony offender where his status was based upon two prior convictions for which he was sentenced, on the same day, to concurrent terms of imprisonment. People v. Battle, 133 A.D.2d 593, 520 N.Y.S.2d 155 (1st Dept. 1987).

§ 400.21. Procedure for determining whether defendant is a second felony offender or a second felony drug offender.

1. Applicability. The provisions of this section govern the procedure that must be followed in any case where it appears that a defendant who stands convicted of a felony has previously been convicted of a predicate felony and may be a second felony offender as defined in section 70.06 of the penal law or a second felony drug offender as defined in either paragraph (b) of subdivision one of section 70.70 of the penal law, or paragraph (b) of subdivision one of section 70.71 of the penal law.

2. Statement to be filed. When information available to the court or to the people prior to sentencing for a felony indicates that the defendant may have previously been subjected to a predicate felony conviction, a statement must be filed by the prosecutor before sentence is imposed

setting forth the date and place of each alleged predicate felony conviction and whether the predicate felony conviction was a violent felony as that term is defined in subdivision one of section 70.02 of the penal law, or in any other jurisdiction of an offense which includes all of the essential elements of any such felony for which a sentence to a term of imprisonment in excess of one year or death was authorized and is authorized in this state regardless of whether such sentence was imposed. Where the provisions of subparagraph (v) of paragraph (b) of subdivision one of section 70.06 of the penal law apply, such statement also shall set forth the date of commencement and the date of termination as well as the state or local incarcerating agency for each period of incarceration to be used for tolling of the ten year limitation set forth in subparagraph (iv) of paragraph (b) of such subdivision.

3. Preliminary examination. The defendant must be given a copy of such statement and the court must ask him or her whether he or she wishes to controvert any allegation made therein. If the defendant wishes to controvert any allegation in the statement, he must specify the particular allegation or allegations he wishes to controvert. Uncontroverted allegations in the statement shall be deemed to have been admitted by the defendant.

4. Cases where further hearing is not required. Where the uncontroverted allegations in the statement are sufficient to support a finding that the defendant has been subjected to a predicate felony conviction the court must enter such finding, including a finding that the predicate felony conviction was of a violent felony as that term is defined in subdivision one of section 70.02 of the penal law, or in any other jurisdiction of an offense which includes all of the essential elements of any such felony for which a sentence to a term of imprisonment in excess of one year or death was authorized and is authorized in this state regardless of whether such sentence was imposed, and when imposing sentence must sentence the defendant in accordance with the applicable provisions of section 70.06, 70.70 or 70.71 of the penal law.

5. Cases where further hearing is required. Where the defendant controverts an allegation in the statement and the uncontroverted allegations in such statement are not sufficient to support a finding that the defendant has been subjected to such a predicate felony conviction the court must proceed to hold a hearing.

6. Time for hearing. In any case where a copy of the statement was not received by the defendant at least two days prior to the preliminary examination, the court must upon request of the defendant grant an adjournment of at least two days before proceeding with the hearing.

7. Manner of conducting hearing. (c) A hearing pursuant to this section must be before the

court without jury. The burden of proof is upon the people and a finding that the defendant has been subjected to such a predicate felony conviction must be based upon proof beyond a reasonable doubt by evidence admissible under the rules applicable to a trial of the issue of guilt.

(b) A previous conviction in this or any other jurisdiction which was obtained in violation of the rights of the defendant under the applicable provisions of the constitution of the United States must not be counted in determining whether the defendant has been subjected to such a predicate felony conviction. The defendant may, at any time during the course of the hearing hereunder controvert an allegation with respect to such conviction in the statement on the grounds that the conviction was unconstitutionally obtained. Failure to challenge the previous conviction in the manner provided herein constitutes a waiver on the part of the defendant of any allegation of unconstitutionality unless good cause be shown for such failure to make timely challenge.

(c) At the conclusion of the hearing the court must make a finding as to whether or not the defendant has been subjected to a predicate felony conviction, including a finding as to whether or not the predicate felony conviction was of a violent felony as that term is defined in subdivision one of section 70.02 of the penal law, or in any other jurisdiction of an offense which includes all of the essential elements of any such felony for which a sentence to a term of imprisonment in excess of one year or death was authorized and is authorized in this state regardless of whether such sentence was imposed.

8. Subsequent use of predicate felony conviction finding. Where a finding has been entered pursuant to this section, such finding shall be binding upon that defendant in any future proceeding in which the issue may arise.

Added by L. 1973, Ch. 277; **Amended** by L. 1973, Ch. 1051; L. 2004, Ch. 738, § 18, eff. Jan. 13, 2005, and shall apply to crimes committed on or after that date.

ANNOTATIONS

Constitutionality of prior conviction.—A predicate conviction arising out of a guilty plea will not be deemed defective simply because the trial judge did not specifically enumerate all of the rights to which the defendant was entitled and which he might be relinquishing as a result of the guilty plea. People v. Moore, 71 N.Y.2d 1002, 530 N.Y.S.2d 94, 525 N.E.2d 740 (1988).

—A predicate conviction arising out of a guilty plea is not defective merely because a judge failed to enumerate all the rights to which a defendant is entitled. People v. Barry, 159 A.D.2d 353, 553 N.Y.S.2d 1 (1st Dept. 1990).

—A claim of inadequacy of a factual recitation is to be distinguished from a challenge based on constitutional grounds and may not properly be raised for the first time in a second felony offender adjudication hearing. People v. Meadows, 134 A.D.2d 374, 520 N.Y.S.2d 851 (2d Dept. 1987).

—Defendant's contention that his previous felony conviction by plea of guilty was tainted because the court failed to apprise him of his waiver of his right to remain silent during plea allocution is without merit since defendant had long experience with the criminal justice system, and he failed to allege any prejudice as a result of the purportedly defective allocution.

People v. Rickenbacker, 114 A.D.2d 982, 495 N.Y.S.2d 236 (2d Dept. 1985).

—Defendant who challenged his adjudication as a second felony offender on the basis that his plea allocution was deficient and that he was denied effective assistance of counsel, was not deprived of a fair assessment of the event which transpired at that plea proceeding because the transcript had been destroyed since the court was able to reconstruct those events. People v. DeVorce, 115 A.D.2d 553, 496 N.Y.S.2d 233 (2d Dept. 1985).

—Court should have conducted a hearing on the constitutionality of defendant's prior robbery conviction before adjudging him a prior felony offender and imposing sentence accordingly, where defendant admitted pleading guilty to prior felony, but referred the sentencing court to his trial testimony that the guilty plea had been obtained through prison officials' refusal to give him necessary medical treatment. People v. Frett, 79 A.D.2d 991, 434 N.Y.S.2d 481 (2d Dept. 1981).

—Defendant had no right to be advised of increased subsequent sentence at the time of the entry of the original plea as there is no duty on the court to advise defendant of all possible collateral consequences. People v. Jackson, 105 Misc. 2d 437, 432 N.Y.S.2d 309 (Sup. Ct. N.Y. Co. 1980).

Procedure.—The prosecution may conduct more than one second felony hearing in the same sentencing proceeding after failing to prove the underlying conviction or convictions. People v. Hunt, 162 A.D.2d 782, 557 N.Y.S.2d 694 (3d Dept. 1990), aff'd for the reasons stated below, 78 N.Y.2d 932, 574 N.Y.S.2d 178, 579 N.E.2d 208 (1991), cert. denied, 112 S. Ct. 432.

—CPL § 400.21 does not mandate a "catechism" of questioning prior to imposition of a sentence as a predicate felony offender; the procedure is sufficient if defendant admits that he was previously convicted of a felony and was subject to sentencing as a second felony offender. People v. Harris, 132 A.D.2d 570, 517 N.Y.S.2d 552 (2d Dept. 1987).

—Once the prosecution establishes the fact of a prior felony conviction and such conviction is admitted by the defendant, the burden then falls upon the defendant to allege and prove facts underlying any claim of unconstitutionality regarding such conviction. People v. Adams, 111 A.D.2d 381, 489 N.Y.S.2d 362 (2d Dept. 1985).

—The People satisfied their burden of proof at defendant's predicate felony hearing by establishing beyond a reasonable doubt the existence of defendant's predicate felony conviction; once the fact of the prior conviction was established, the burden is on the defendant to allege and prove facts supporting any claim that the prior conviction was unconstitutionally obtained. People v. Anderson, 100 A.D.2d 937, 474 N.Y.S.2d 846 (2d Dept. 1984).

—The use by the People of a different predicate felony at the defendant's resentencing does not constitute double jeopardy. People v. Maldonado, 82 A.D.2d 576, 442 N.Y.S.2d 567 (2d Dept. 1981).

—There was insufficient compliance with the meticulous safeguards mandated by the statute, where notwithstanding fact that sentencing court referred to matter not contained in the information which undoubtedly established that defendant was a second felony offender, prosecutor listed, in the predicate felony information, as defendant's predicate felony conviction, an erroneous extract from the minutes of the court showing another person's conviction. People v. Bush, 74 A.D.2d 927, 426 N.Y.S.2d 92 (2d Dept. 1980).

—Procedure for determining second felony offender status was sufficiently complied with where court, at time of plea, informed the defendant that he would be sentenced as a predicate felon and the defendant, after consulting with his attorney, stated that he understood and pleaded guilty voluntarily. People v. Traynor, 114 A.D.2d 643, 494 N.Y.S.2d 483 (3d Dept. 1985).

—There was insufficient compliance with the procedure required for defendant to be sentenced as a second felony offender where defendant had no opportunity to controvert the allegation of the second felony offender statement, never waived his opportunity to challenge his status as a second felony offender and never admitted the allegations underlying the predicate felony. People v. Snyder, 105 A.D.2d 553, 482 N.Y.S.2d 54 (3d Dept. 1984).

—Procedure did not prejudice defendant where the court conducted the inquiry to determine second felony offender status prior to conviction by way of plea to second charge. People v. Topping, 74 A.D.2d 703, 426 N.Y.S.2d 116 (3d Dept. 1980).

—Court was not required to ask the defendant whether he was the person convicted of the prior crime or whether he wished to controvert the constitutionality thereof even though without doing so he waived his right, as defendant was represented by counsel, and the record shows that he was fully informed of the facts of the prior felony upon which his sentence as a second felony offender was to be predicated. People v. English, 75 A.D.2d 981, 429 N.Y.S.2d 98 (4th Dept. 1980).

—Proposition that a ritualistic catechism of pleading defendant's constitutional rights is not required is not only applicable to attempts to directly set aside a current conviction but also to the context of a predicate felony sentencing hearing. People v. Davis, 133 Misc. 2d 606, 507 N.Y.S.2d 577 (Sup. Ct. N.Y. Co. 1986), *modified on other grounds*, 128 A.D.2d 450, 513 N.Y.S.2d 144 (1st Dept. 1987), *aff'd*, 71 N.Y.2d 1002 (1988).

Procedure; predicate felony statement.—People's failure to file a predicate felony statement was harmless error where the statutory purposes of such statement were otherwise satisfied in that the court was apprised of the prior conviction and the defendant was provided with reasonable notice and opportunity to be heard; the defendant admitted in open court and in the presence of counsel the existence and nature of his prior conviction and informed the court that he understood and intended to accept the plea agreement, which included the imposition of the sentence in question. People v. Bouyea, 64 N.Y.2d 1140, 490 N.Y.S.2d 724, 480 N.E.2d 338 (1985).

—Where People failed to file a predicate felony statement at the time of sentence, the court should have granted the prosecution's motion to resentence the defendant upon a predicate felony offender statement filed prior to resentencing. People v. Scarborough, 66 N.Y.2d 673, 496 N.Y.S.2d 409, 487 N.E.2d 266 (1985).

—Sentence vacated and remanded for imposition of a lawful sentence, where People failed to file a predicate felony statement and defendant had never affirmatively admitted the fact of prior convictions, nor explicitly waived the opportunity to challenge such a statement. People v. Davis, 240 A.D.2d 309, 659 N.Y.S.2d 437 (1st Dept. 1997).

—The People's failure to file a predicate felony statement was harmless where the court was apprised of the prior conviction and defendant was provided with reasonable notice and an opportunity to be heard and defendant stated we would decline to challenge the statement. People v. Nails, 196 A.D.2d 439, 601 N.Y.S.2d 280 (1st Dept. 1993).

—Since the court was required to resentence defendant as a second felony offender, it was of no consequence that the prosecution did not file the prior felony conviction statement until the commencement of the resentencing proceeding. People v. Cahill, 190 A.D.2d 744, 593 N.Y.S.2d 537 (2d Dept.), *lv. denied*, 81 N.Y.2d 883 (1993).

—Sentence and adjudication as second felony offender were reversed where prosecutor did not serve the required predicate felony information and court did not advise defendant of his right to receive a copy of it or his right to controvert the allegation that he had previously been convicted of a felony; defendant's admission in open court, made without any opportunity to consult with counsel, that he had been subjected to a predicate felony, conviction cannot construed as a knowing, intelligent and voluntary waiver of his rights under the statute. People v. Morrison, 100 A.D.2d 976, 475 N.Y.S.2d 115 (2d Dept. 1984).

Out-of-state convictions.—In making the determination as to whether a prior out-of-state conviction is a predicate felony, the court should analyze the relevant foreign statute in light of the comparable New York statute; the court may refer to the allegation of the accusatory instrument to clarify the statutory charge and to limit or narrow the basis for the conviction; but the instrument may not be used to enlarge or expand the crime charged. People v. Gonzalez, 61 N.Y.2d 586, 475 N.Y.S.2d 358, 463 N.E.2d 1210 (1984).

—In determining whether a foreign conviction constitutes a felony in New York, a court may scrutinize the accusatory instrument to determine, if possible, for which act under the foreign statute the defendant was convicted. People v. Jackson, 118 A.D.2d 469, 499 N.Y.S.2d 749 (1st Dept. 1986).

—Defendant's prior federal conviction under a federal statute prohibiting the receiving of "any firearm or ammunition which has been shipped or transported in interstate or foreign commerce" was not a predicate felony conviction upon which the defendant could be sentenced as a second felony offender; the allegedly analogous New York statute does not prohibit the possession or receipt of ammunition and the acts covered by the federal statute would therefore not be a felony in New York. People v. Falcone, 107 A.D.2d 587, 483 N.Y.S.2d 318 (1st Dept. 1985).

—Defendant was not a second felony offender when his prior federal conviction was under a statute which significantly differed from a New York State statute in that it encompassed drug crimes which could be either misdemeanors or felonies in New York; defendant's failure to raise this objection at sentence could not act as a waiver since the sentence itself was improper. People v. Williams, 100 A.D.2d 760, 474 N.Y.S.2d 307 (1st Dept. 1984).

—Defendant failed to demonstrate that his Canadian guilty plea was unconstitutionally obtained; since the Canadian offense was equivalent to a New York felony. People v. Adams, 164 A.D.2d 546, 565 N.Y.S.2d 821 (2d Dept.), *lv. denied*, 77 N.Y.2d 957 (1991).

—The defendant was improperly adjudicated a second felony offender based on a federal conviction for transporting narcotics as the statute under which he stood convicted included acts which are both misdemeanors and felonies under New York law. People v. Lopez, 121 A.D.2d 472, 503 N.Y.S.2d 430 (2d Dept. 1986).

—Defendant's previous conviction for bank robbery wherein he had been sentenced to probation under the Federal Youth Corrections Act 18 U.S.C. § 5010(a) made him a second felony offender since the instant offense took place at a time prior to his unconditional discharge from federal probation; and defendant was never issued a certificate vacating his federal convictions. People v. Moskowitz, 103 A.D.2d 784, 477 N.Y.S.2d 422 (2d Dept. 1984).

—Defendant's prior felony conviction as an adult offender in the State of Indiana at the age of 17 does not preclude his sentencing as a predicate felon merely because in New York he would have been eligible for youthful offender treatment. People v. Hamilton, 104 A.D.2d 1048, 481 N.Y.S.2d 116 (2d Dept. 1984).

—Defendant was improperly sentenced as a predicate felon on the basis of an earlier federal conviction relating to the interstate transportation of a forged instrument; as the federal statute does not require that there be knowledge that the instrument is forged; such offense would not necessarily be punishable as a felony in New York. People v. Giraldo, 106 A.D.2d 401, 482 N.Y.S.2d 320 (2d Dept. 1984).

—Sentence as second felony offender was vacated where defendant claimed that plea of guilty in prior case was unconstitutionally obtained through coercion and neither the plea or sentencing minutes of such conviction were provided by the prosecutor at the hearing despite his indication that he would do so. People v. Ferebee, 98 A.D.2d 751, 469 N.Y.S.2d 461 (2d Dept. 1983).

—In order to determine whether a foreign crime is equivalent to a New York felony, and thus a prior felony conviction, the court must examine the elements of the foreign statute and compare them to the analogous New York statute; the foreign crime cannot be extended or enlarged by allegations in the indictment or by referring to evidence at trial; the allegations of the original accusatory instrument may, however, be referred to when necessary to clarify the statutory charge. People v. Gill, 109 A.D.2d 419, 491 N.Y.S.2d 524 (3d Dept. 1985).

—Though prior court martial convictions may be used to impose enhanced sentences upon convicted felons, defendant's prior military conviction for "constructive force" rape could not serve as a predicate felony since "constructive force" does not mean the same thing as the "forcible compulsion" element of the New York State felony of rape. People v. Scaife, 133 Misc. 2d 460, 507 N.Y.S.2d 141 (Sup. Ct. Erie Co. 1986).

—Defendant who was previously sentenced under the Federal Youth Corrections Act on her plea of guilty could be sentenced as a second felony offender on a plea of guilty despite her eligibility for discharge and issuance of a certificate vacating her conviction under the Youth Corrections Act. People v. Celli, 105 Misc. 2d 1005, 430 N.Y.S.2d 949 (Westchester Co. Ct. 1980).

Resentencing required.—Where the sentencing minutes fail to reflect that a judicial finding of a prior predicate felony had been made by the court and the defendant did not admit the existence of a prior felony conviction, there is plain error. People v. Meadows, 114 A.D.2d 1044, 495 N.Y.S.2d 484 (2d Dept. 1985).

Right to challenge predicate.—At sentencing, defendant, who was proceeding pro se, clearly stated that he had been coerced through ineffectiveness of counsel to plead guilty to the predicate offense; thus, he should have been given a hearing regarding the constitutionality of the prior plea. People v. Mack, 203 A.D.2d 131, 610 N.Y.S.2d 502 (1st Dept. 1994).

—Sentencing court improperly denied defendant's request for a hearing to consider his claim that his prior conviction had been unconstitutionally obtained through ineffective assistance of counsel. People v. Giersz, 207 A.D.2d 843, 616 N.Y.S.2d 555 (2d Dept.), lv. denied, 84 N.Y.2d 1011 (1994).

—Although the defendant was neither arraigned as a second felony offender nor provided with a predicate felony information, the defendant's election to "stand mute" concerning the prior conviction does not negate the opportunity accorded him to controvert it; there was sufficient compliance with the statutory requirements where the court advised the defendant that he was being sentenced as a predicate felon and had the right to contest that conviction. People v. Tumminia, 101 A.D.2d 605, 474 N.Y.S.2d 855 (3d Dept. 1984).

—There is no requirement that a court expressly advise a defendant of his right to contest the constitutional basis of a prior conviction; the statutory requirements were satisfied where a second felony information was filed, the defendant was asked by the court whether he wished to controvert the alleged predicate felony conviction and the defendant, being represented by counsel, declined such opportunity. People v. Collins, 100 A.D.2d 691, 474 N.Y.S.2d 644 (3d Dept. 1984).

—The trial court substantially complied with the requirements of this section where the record reflects that at all stages the defendant was represented by counsel and he was given the opportunity to controvert the prior felony conviction and failed to do so. People v. Queen, 84 A.D.2d 649, 444 N.Y.S.2d 497 (3d Dept. 1981).

—Where defendant explicitly challenged prior conviction on ground of ineffective assistance of counsel, court erred in denying defendant's request for a hearing on the constitutionality of the predicate conviction. People v. Nolley, 233 A.D.2d 925, 649 N.Y.S.2d 565 (4th Dept. 1996).

Sequentiality requirement.—Defendant was previously sentenced on two prior violent felonies on the same day could not be sentenced on the present conviction as a persistent violent felony offender since the sentence on the first prior violent felony must have been imposed before the commission of the second violent felony offense. People v. Little, 104 A.D.2d 766, 480 N.Y.S.2d 723 (1st Dept. 1984).

—Defendant was erroneously sentenced as a persistent violent felony offender where both of defendant's prior felony convictions were rendered on the same day; the predicate offenses must have been committed sequentially, that is, the second offense must have been committed after imposition of sentence on the first. People v. Taylor, 103 A.D.2d 853, 478 N.Y.S.2d 812 (2d Dept. 1984).

Substantial compliance.—Imposition, without objection, of a second felony offender sentence despite prosecutor's failure to file a predicate felony statement does not merit resentencing, because the sentencing court substantially complied with the statutory purposes of CPL § 400.21. People v. Nunez, 253 A.D.2d 685, 678 N.Y.S.2d 91 (1st Dept. 1998).

—There was substantial compliance with CPL 400.21, where defendant unequivocally indicated at the plea allocution that he understood he was pleading guilty to the instant crime as a second felony offender, and where defendant raised no challenge to the County Court's consideration of his prior conviction, and made no objection to being sentenced as a second felony offender. People v. Polanco, 232 A.D.2d 674, 648 N.Y.S.2d 56 (3d Dept. 1996).

Tolling requirement.—For purposes of the determining whether the 10-year limitation for the use of prior violent felony has been exceeded, a period of incarceration on a conviction which is subsequently vacated and the indictment dismissed cannot be used to toll the limitation period. People v. Dozier, 78 N.Y.2d 242, 573 N.Y.S.2d 427, 577 N.E.2d 1019 (1991).

—Defendant's NYSID sheet was insufficient proof of the period of defendant's prior incarceration during which the statute was

tolled. People v. Ortiz, 188 A.D.2d 292, 591 N.Y.S.2d 13 (1st Dept. 1992), lv. denied, 81 N.Y.2d 890 (1993).

Waiver.—Where defendant failed to controvert the allegations in the predicate felony statement, issue of whether defendant's prior federal kidnapping conviction is equivalent to a conviction of a felony in New York was not preserved for appellate review. People v. Smith, 73 N.Y.2d 961, 540 N.Y.S.2d 987, 538 N.E.2d 339 (1989).

—Where defendant had failed to challenge his prior conviction at an earlier sentencing or demonstrate good cause for such failure, he waived any future challenge to the constitutionality of the conviction for sentence enhancement purposes. People v. Crawford, 204 A.D.2d 203, 612 N.Y.S.2d 28 (1st Dept.), lv. denied, 84 N.Y.2d 906 (1994).

—While defendant did not contest his adjudication as a second felony offender, where it was subsequently discovered that the underlying crime was not a predicate felony conviction, the interests of justice required that the sentence imposed be vacated and the matter remitted for resentencing. People v. Fusillo, 94 A.D.2d 802, 463 N.Y.S.2d 51 (2d Dept. 1983).

—Defendant's acknowledgment at the time he entered his plea that he was to be sentenced as a predicate felony offender did not constitute a waiver of his right to controvert the predicate felony statement. People v. Corey, 88 A.D.2d 560, 450 N.Y.S.2d 487 (1st Dept. 1982).

—Since the defendant did not challenge his predicate felony status at his sentencing, he waived the right to later claim it could not be used as a predicate conviction. People v. Khatib, 166 A.D.2d 668, 561 N.Y.S.2d 88 (2d Dept. 1990).

—Defendant waived his right to a predicate felony hearing when counsel stated to the court that his research indicated that the defendant pled guilty to a felony, but that the defendant recalled only that he pled to a misdemeanor and there was no constitutional challenge to the prior felony conviction. People v. Williams, 106 A.D.2d 786, 484 N.Y.S.2d 255 (3d Dept. 1984).

—By failing to appear for sentencing as ordered, defendant waived his right to controvert the allegations of the predicate felony statement. People v. Diola, 239 A.D.2d 961, 659 N.Y.S.2d 599 (4th Dept. 1997).

—Defendant was not entitled to a hearing pursuant to CPL § 400.21 where at sentencing he did not controvert the facts in the prosecutor's statement alleging that he had previously been convicted of escape, second degree, and he did not challenge the conviction on constitutional grounds. People v. Alston, 83 A.D.2d 744, 443 N.Y.S.2d 499 (4th Dept. 1981).

§ 400.22. Evidence of imprisonment.

The certificate of the commissioner of correction or of the warden or other chief officer of any prison, or of the superintendent or other chief officer of any penitentiary under the seal of his office containing name of person, a statement of the court in which conviction was had, the date and term of sentence, length of time imprisoned, and date of discharge from prison or penitentiary, shall be prima facie evidence of the imprisonment and discharge of any person under the conviction stated and set forth in such certificate for the purposes of any proceeding under section 400.20.

Amended by L. 1984, Ch. 673; L. 1988, Ch. 190; L. 1989, Ch. 240.

§ 400.27. Procedure for determining sentence upon conviction for the offense of murder in the first degree.

1. Upon the conviction of a defendant for the offense of murder in the first degree as defined by section 125.27 of the penal law, the court shall promptly conduct a separate sentencing proceeding to determine whether the defendant shall be

sentenced to death or to life imprisonment without parole pursuant to subdivision five of section 70.00 of the penal law. Nothing in this section shall be deemed to preclude the people at any time from determining that the death penalty shall not be sought in a particular case, in which case the separate sentencing proceeding shall not be conducted and the court may sentence such defendant to life imprisonment without parole or to a sentence of imprisonment for the class A-I felony of murder in the first degree other than a sentence of life imprisonment without parole.

2. The separate sentencing proceeding provided for by this section shall be conducted before the court sitting with the jury that found the defendant guilty. The court may discharge the jury and impanel another jury only in extraordinary circumstances and upon a showing of good cause, which may include, but is not limited to, a finding of prejudice to either party. If a new jury is impaneled, it shall be formed in accordance with the procedures in article two hundred seventy of this chapter. Before proceeding with the jury that found the defendant guilty, the court shall determine whether any juror has a state of mind that is likely to preclude the juror from rendering an impartial decision based upon the evidence adduced during the proceeding. In making such determination the court shall personally examine each juror individually outside the presence of the other jurors. The scope of the examination shall be within the discretion of the court and may include questions supplied by the parties as the court deems proper. The proceedings provided for in this subdivision shall be conducted on the record; provided, however, that upon motion of either party, and for good cause shown, the court may direct that all or a portion of the record of such proceedings be sealed. In the event the court determines that a juror has such a state of mind, the court shall discharge the juror and replace the juror with the alternate juror whose name was first drawn and called. If no alternate juror is available, the court must discharge the jury and impanel another jury in accordance with article two hundred seventy of this chapter.

3. For the purposes of a proceeding under this section each subparagraph of paragraph (a) of subdivision one of section 125.27 of the penal law shall be deemed to define an aggravating factor. Except as provided in subdivision seven of this section, at a sentencing proceeding pursuant to this section the only aggravating factors that the jury may consider are those proven beyond a reasonable doubt at trial, and no other aggravating factors may be considered. Whether a sentencing proceeding is conducted before the jury that found the defendant guilty or before another jury, the aggravating factor or factors proved at trial shall be deemed established beyond a reasonable doubt at the separate sentencing proceeding and shall not be relitigated. Where the jury is to determine

sentences for concurrent counts of murder in the first degree, the aggravating factor included in each count shall be deemed to be an aggravating factor for the purpose of the jury's consideration in determining the sentence to be imposed on each such count.

4. The court on its own motion or on motion of either party, in the interest of justice or to avoid prejudice to either party, may delay the commencement of the separate sentencing proceeding.

5. Notwithstanding the provisions of article three hundred ninety of this chapter, where a defendant is found guilty of murder in the first degree, no presentence investigation shall be conducted; provided, however, that where the court is to impose a sentence of imprisonment, a presentence investigation shall be conducted and a presentence report shall be prepared in accordance with the provisions of such article.

6. At the sentencing proceeding the people shall not relitigate the existence of aggravating factors proved at the trial or otherwise present evidence, except, subject to the rules governing admission of evidence in the trial of a criminal action, in rebuttal of the defendant's evidence. However, when the sentencing proceeding is conducted before a newly impaneled jury, the people may present evidence to the extent reasonably necessary to inform the jury of the nature and circumstances of the count or counts of murder in the first degree for which the defendant was convicted in sufficient detail to permit the jury to determine the weight to be accorded the aggravating factor or factors established at trial. Whenever the people present such evidence, the court must instruct the jury in its charge that any facts elicited by the people that are not essential to the verdict of guilty on such count or counts shall not be deemed established beyond a reasonable doubt. Subject to the rules governing the admission of evidence in the trial of a criminal action, the defendant may present any evidence relevant to any mitigating factor set forth in subdivision nine of this section; provided, however, that the defendant shall not be precluded from the admission of reliable hearsay evidence. The burden of establishing any of the mitigating factors set forth in subdivision nine of this section shall be on the defendant, and must be proven by a preponderance of the evidence. The people shall not offer evidence or argument relating to any mitigating factor except in rebuttal of evidence offered by the defendant.

7. (a) The people may present evidence at the sentencing proceeding to prove that in the ten year period prior to the commission of the crime of murder in the first degree for which the defendant was convicted, the defendant has previously been convicted of two or more offenses committed on different occasions; provided, that each such offense shall be either (i) a class A felony offense other than one defined in article two

hundred twenty of the penal law, a class B violent felony offense specified in paragraph (a) of subdivision one of section 70.02 of the penal law, or a felony offense under the penal law a necessary element of which involves either the use or attempted use or threatened use of a deadly weapon or the intentional infliction of or the attempted intentional infliction of serious physical injury or death, or (ii) an offense under the laws of another state or of the united states punishable by a term of imprisonment of more than one year a necessary element of which involves either the use or attempted use or threatened use of a deadly weapon or the intentional infliction of or the attempted intentional infliction of serious physical injury or death. For the purpose of this paragraph, the term "deadly weapon" shall have the meaning set forth in subdivision twelve of section 10.00 of the penal law. In calculating the ten year period under this paragraph, any period of time during which the defendant was incarcerated for any reason between the time of commission of any of the prior felony offenses and the time of commission of the crime of murder in the first degree shall be excluded and such ten year period shall be extended by a period or periods equal to the time served under such incarceration. The defendant's conviction of two or more such offenses shall, if proven at the sentencing proceeding, constitute an aggravating factor.

(b) In order to be deemed established, an aggravating factor set forth in this subdivision must be proven by the people beyond a reasonable doubt and the jury must unanimously find such factor to have been so proven. The defendant may present evidence relating to an aggravating factor defined in this subdivision and either party may offer evidence in rebuttal. Any evidence presented by either party relating to such factor shall be subject to the rules governing admission of evidence in the trial of a criminal action.

(c) Whenever the people intend to offer evidence of an aggravating factor set forth in this subdivision, the people must within a reasonable time prior to trial file with the court and serve upon the defendant a notice of intention to offer such evidence. Whenever the people intend to offer evidence of the aggravating factor set forth in paragraph (a) of this subdivision, the people shall file with the notice of intention to offer such evidence a statement setting forth the date and place of each of the alleged offenses in paragraph (a) of this subdivision. The provisions of section 400.15 of this chapter, except for subdivisions one and two thereof, shall be followed.

8. Consistent with the provisions of this section, the people and the defendant shall be given fair opportunity to rebut any evidence received at the separate sentencing proceeding.

9. Mitigating factors shall include the following:

(a) The defendant has no significant history of

prior criminal convictions involving the use of violence against another person;

(b) The defendant was mentally retarded at the time of the crime, or the defendant's mental capacity was impaired or his ability to conform his conduct to the requirements of law was impaired but not so impaired in either case as to constitute a defense to prosecution;

(c) The defendant was under duress or under the domination of another person, although not such duress or domination as to constitute a defense to prosecution;

(d) The defendant was criminally liable for the present offense of murder committed by another, but his participation in the offense was relatively minor although not so minor as to constitute a defense to prosecution;

(e) The murder was committed while the defendant was mentally or emotionally disturbed or under the influence of alcohol or any drug, although not to such an extent as to constitute a defense to prosecution; or

(f) Any other circumstance concerning the crime, the defendant's state of mind or condition at the time of the crime, or the defendant's character, background or record that would be relevant to mitigation or punishment for the crime.

10. At the conclusion of all the evidence, the people and the defendant may present argument in summation for or against the sentence sought by the people. The people may deliver the first summation and the defendant may then deliver the last summation. Thereafter, the court shall deliver a charge to the jury on any matters appropriate in the circumstances. In its charge, the court must instruct the jury that with respect to each count of murder in the first degree the jury should consider whether or not a sentence of death should be imposed and whether or not a sentence of life imprisonment without parole should be imposed, and that the jury must be unanimous with respect to either sentence. The court must also instruct the jury that in the event the jury fails to reach unanimous agreement with respect to the sentence, the court will sentence the defendant to a term of imprisonment with a minimum term of between twenty and twenty-five years and a maximum term of life. Following the court's charge, the jury shall retire to consider the sentence to be imposed. Unless inconsistent with the provisions of this section, the provisions of sections 310.10, 310.20 and 310.30 shall govern the deliberations of the jury.

11. (a) The jury may not direct imposition of a sentence of death unless it unanimously finds beyond a reasonable doubt that the aggravating factor or factors substantially outweigh the mitigating factor or factors established, if any, and unanimously determines that the penalty of death should be imposed. Any member or members of

the jury who find a mitigating factor to have been proven by the defendant by a preponderance of the evidence may consider such factor established regardless of the number of jurors who concur that the factor has been established.

(b) If the jury directs imposition of either a sentence of death or life imprisonment without parole, it shall specify on the record those mitigating and aggravating factors considered and those mitigating factors established by the defendant, if any.

(c) With respect to a count or concurrent counts of murder in the first degree, the court may direct the jury to cease deliberation with respect to the sentence or sentences to be imposed if the jury has deliberated for an extensive period of time without reaching unanimous agreement on the sentence or sentences to be imposed and the court is satisfied that any such agreement is unlikely within a reasonable time. The provisions of this paragraph shall apply with respect to consecutive counts of murder in the first degree. In the event the jury is unable to reach unanimous agreement, the court must sentence the defendant in accordance with subdivisions one through three of section 70.00 of the penal law with respect to any count or counts of murder in the first degree upon which the jury failed to reach unanimous agreement as to the sentence to be imposed.

(d) If the jury unanimously determines that a sentence of death should be imposed, the court must thereupon impose a sentence of death. Thereafter, however, the court may, upon written motion of the defendant, set aside the sentence of death upon any of the grounds set forth in section 330.30. The procedures set forth in sections 330.40 and 330.50, as applied to separate sentencing proceedings under this section, shall govern the motion and the court upon granting the motion shall, except as may otherwise be required by subdivision one of section 330.50, direct a new sentencing proceeding pursuant to this section. Upon granting the motion upon any of the grounds set forth in section 330.30 and setting aside the sentence, the court must afford the people a reasonable period of time, which shall not be less than ten days, to determine whether to take an appeal from the order setting aside the sentence of death. The taking of an appeal by the people stays the effectiveness of that portion of the court's order that directs a new sentencing proceeding.

(e) If the jury unanimously determines that a sentence of life imprisonment without parole should be imposed the court must thereupon impose a sentence of life imprisonment without parole.

(f) Where a sentence has been unanimously determined by the jury it must be recorded on the minutes and read to the jury, and the jurors must be collectively asked whether such is their sentence. Even though no juror makes any declaration in the negative, the jury must, if either party makes such an application, be polled and each juror separately asked whether the sentence announced by the foreman is in all respects his or her sentence. If, upon either the collective or the separate inquiry, any juror answers in the negative, the court must refuse to accept the sentence and must direct the jury to resume its deliberation. If no disagreement is expressed, the jury must be discharged from the case.

12. (a) Upon the conviction of a defendant for the offense of murder in the first degree as defined in section 125.27 of the penal law, the court shall, upon oral or written motion of the defendant based upon a showing that there is reasonable cause to believe that the defendant is mentally retarded, promptly conduct a hearing without a jury to determine whether the defendant is mentally retarded. Upon the consent of both parties, such a hearing, or a portion thereof, may be conducted by the court contemporaneously with the separate sentencing proceeding in the presence of the sentencing jury, which in no event shall be the trier of fact with respect to the hearing. At such hearing the defendant has the burden of proof by a preponderance of the evidence that he or she is mentally retarded. The court shall defer rendering any finding pursuant to this subdivision as to whether the defendant is mentally retarded until a sentence is imposed pursuant to this section.

(b) In the event the defendant is sentenced pursuant to this section to life imprisonment without parole or to a term of imprisonment for the class A-I felony of murder in the first degree other than a sentence of life imprisonment without parole, the court shall not render a finding with respect to whether the defendant is mentally retarded.

(c) In the event the defendant is sentenced pursuant to this section to death, the court shall thereupon render a finding with respect to whether the defendant is mentally retarded. If the court finds the defendant is mentally retarded, the court shall set aside the sentence of death and sentence the defendant either to life imprisonment without parole or to a term of imprisonment for the class A-I felony of murder in the first degree other than a sentence of life imprisonment without parole. If the court finds the defendant is not mentally retarded, then such sentence of death shall not be set aside pursuant to this subdivision.

(d) In the event that a defendant is convicted of murder in the first degree pursuant to subparagraph (iii) of paragraph (a) of subdivision one of section 125.27 of the penal law, and the killing occurred while the defendant was confined or under custody in a state correctional facility or local correctional institution, and a sentence of death is imposed, such sentence may not be set aside pursuant to this subdivision upon the ground that the defendant is mentally retarded. Nothing in this paragraph or paragraph (a) of this subdivision shall preclude a defendant from presenting mitigating evidence of mental retardation at the separate sentencing proceeding.

(e) The foregoing provisions of this subdivision notwithstanding, at a reasonable time prior to the commencement of trial the defendant may, upon a written motion alleging reasonable cause to believe the defendant is mentally retarded, apply for an order directing that a mental retardation hearing be conducted prior to trial. If, upon review of the defendant's motion and any response thereto, the court finds reasonable cause to believe the defendant is mentally retarded, it shall promptly conduct a hearing without a jury to determine whether the defendant is mentally retarded. In the event the court finds after the hearing that the defendant is not mentally retarded, the court must, prior to commencement of trial, enter an order so stating, but nothing in this paragraph shall preclude a defendant from presenting mitigating evidence of mental retardation at a separate sentencing proceeding. In the event the court finds after the hearing that the defendant, based upon a preponderance of the evidence, is mentally retarded, the court must, prior to commencement of trial, enter an order so stating. Unless the order is reversed on an appeal by the people or unless the provisions of paragraph (d) of this subdivision apply, a separate sentencing proceeding under this section shall not be conducted if the defendant is thereafter convicted of murder in the first degree. In the event a separate sentencing proceeding is not conducted, the court, upon conviction of a defendant for the crime of murder in the first degree, shall sentence the defendant to life imprisonment without parole or to a sentence of imprisonment for the class A-I felony of murder in the first degree other than a sentence of life imprisonment without parole. Whenever a mental retardation hearing is held and a finding is rendered pursuant to this paragraph, the court may not conduct a hearing pursuant to paragraph (a) of this subdivision. For purposes of this subdivision and paragraph (b) of subdivision nine of this section, "mental retardation" means significantly subaverage general intellectual functioning existing concurrently with deficits in adaptive behavior which were manifested before the age of eighteen.

(f) In the event the court enters an order pursuant to paragraph (e) of this subdivision finding that the defendant is mentally retarded, the people may appeal as of right from the order pursuant to subdivision ten of section 450.20 of this chapter. Upon entering such an order the court must afford the people a reasonable period of time, which shall not be less than ten days, to determine whether to take an appeal from the order finding that the defendant is mentally retarded. The taking of an appeal by the people stays the effectiveness of the court's order and any order fixing a date for trial. Within six months

of the effective date of this subdivision, the court of appeals shall adopt rules to ensure that appeals pursuant to this paragraph are expeditiously perfected, reviewed and determined so that pretrial delays are minimized. Prior to adoption of the rules, the court of appeals shall issue proposed rules and receive written comments thereon from interested parties.

13. (a) As used in this subdivision, the term "psychiatric evidence" means evidence of mental disease, defect or condition in connection with either a mitigating factor defined in this section or a mental retardation hearing pursuant to this section to be offered by a psychiatrist, psychologist or other person who has received training, or education, or has experience relating to the identification, diagnosis, treatment or evaluation of mental disease, mental defect or mental condition.

(b) When either party intends to offer psychiatric evidence, the party must, within a reasonable time prior to trial, serve upon the other party and file with the court a written notice of intention to present psychiatric evidence. The notice shall include a brief but detailed statement specifying the witness, nature and type of psychiatric evidence sought to be introduced. If either party fails to serve and file written notice, no psychiatric evidence is admissible unless the party failing to file thereafter serves and files such notice and the court affords the other party an adjournment for a reasonable period. If a party fails to give timely notice, the court in its discretion may impose upon offending counsel a reasonable monetary sanction for an intentional failure but may not in any event preclude the psychiatric evidence. In the event a monetary sanction is imposed, the offending counsel shall be personally liable therefor, and shall not receive reimbursement of any kind from any source in order to pay the cost of such monetary sanction. Nothing contained herein shall preclude the court from entering an order directing a party to provide timely notice.

(c) When a defendant serves notice pursuant to this subdivision, the district attorney may make application, upon notice to the defendant, for an order directing that the defendant submit to an examination by a psychiatrist, licensed psychologist, or licensed clinical social worker designated by the district attorney, for the purpose of rebutting evidence offered by the defendant with respect to a mental disease, defect, or condition in connection with either a mitigating factor defined in this section, including whether the defendant was acting under duress, was mentally or emotionally disturbed or mentally retarded, or was under the influence of alcohol or any drug. If the application is granted, the district attorney shall schedule a time and place for the examination, which shall be recorded. Counsel for the people and the defendant shall have the right to be present at the examination. A transcript of the examination shall be made available to the defendant and the district attorney promptly after its conclusion. The district attorney shall promptly serve on the defendant a written copy of the findings and evaluation of the examiner. If the court finds that the defendant has wilfully refused to cooperate fully in an examination pursuant to this paragraph, it shall, upon request of the district attorney, instruct the jury that the defendant did not submit to or cooperate fully in such psychiatric examination. When a defendant is subjected to an examination pursuant to an order issued in accordance with this subdivision, any statement made by the defendant for the purpose of the examination shall be inadmissible in evidence against him in any criminal action or proceeding on any issue other than that of whether a mitigating factor has been established or whether the defendant is mentally retarded, but such statement is admissible upon such an issue whether or not it would otherwise be deemed a privileged communication.

14. (a) At a reasonable time prior to the sentencing proceeding or a mental retardation hearing:

(i) the prosecutor shall, unless previously disclosed and subject to a protective order, make available to the defendant the statements and information specified in subdivision one of section 240.45 and make available for inspection, photographing, copying or testing the property specified in subdivision one of section 240.20; and

(ii) the defendant shall, unless previously disclosed and subject to a protective order, make available to the prosecution the statements and information specified in subdivision two of section 240.45 and make available for inspection, photographing, copying or testing, subject to constitutional limitations, the reports, documents and other property specified in subdivision one of section 240.30.

(b) Where a party refuses to make disclosure pursuant to this section, the provisions of section 240.35, subdivision one of section 240.40 and section 240.50 shall apply.

(c) If, after complying with the provisions of this section or an order pursuant thereto, a party finds either before or during a sentencing proceeding or mental retardation hearing, additional material subject to discovery or covered by court order, the party shall promptly make disclosure or apply for a protective order.

(d) If the court finds that a party has failed to comply with any of the provisions of this section, the court may enter any of the orders specified in subdivision one of section 240.70.

15. The court of appeals shall formulate and adopt rules for the development of forms for use by the jury in recording its findings and determinations of sentence.

Added by L. 1995, Ch. 1, § 20, eff. Sept. 1, 1995; **Amended** by L. 2001, Ch. 300, §§ 6 and 7, amending subd. 7(d), repealing subd. 7(a), and relettering subd. 7(b), (c), and (d) to (a), (b), and (c), eff. Sept. 17, 2001; L. 2004, Ch. 230, § 2, amending subd. 13(c), eff. July 27, 2004.

ANNOTATIONS

Accessorial liability.—The legislature did intend to permit first degree murder convictions to rest on accessorial liability. People v. Reed, 265 A.D.2d 56, 705 N.Y.S.2d 592 (2d Dept. 2000).

Aggravating factors.—The law does not require or suggest that every aggravating factor be given the same weight in every case. In determining a sentence in a capital case, juries may consider any evidence properly admitted at trial that discloses and explains the nature and circumstances of the charged murder so as to permit the jury to make an informed decision about the weight to give the proven aggravating factors. Such evidence may include proof of uncharged crimes. The court rejected the defendant's broad proposition that New York's statutory structure categorically prohibits the introduction of uncharged crimes proof before a potential sentencing jury. People v. Taylor, 193 Misc. 2d 110, 747 N.Y.S.2d 318, *motion denied,* 192 Misc. 2d 786, 747 N.Y.S.2d 337 (Sup. Ct. Queens Co. 2002).

Altering statutory procedure; only where good cause shown.—The court is only allowed to alter the statutory procedure for jury selection in capital cases by impaneling a separate sentencing jury in extraordinary circumstances for good cause shown, none of which were present in the instant case. People v. Harris, 176 Misc. 2d 967, 675 N.Y.S.2d 740 (Sup. Ct. Kings Co. 1998).

Constitutionality of subd. 1.—The deadlock instruction required by CPL § 400.27(1) is unconstitutional under the state constitution because of the unacceptable risk that it may result in a coercive, arbitrary, and unreliable sentence. People v. LaValle, 3 N.Y.3d 88, 783 N.Y.S.2d 485, 817 N.E.2d 341 (2004).

Constitutionality of subd. 3.—CPL § 400.27(3) is constitutional, and defendant has no constitutional right to relitigate the aggravating factors in order to create a lingering doubt in the jurors' minds. People v. Harris, 177 Misc. 2d 165, 676 N.Y.S.2d 440 (Sup. Ct. Kings Co. 1998).

Constitutionality of subd. 9.—In light of Atkins v. Virginia, 536 U.S. 304, 122 S. Ct. 2242, 153 L. Ed. 2d 335, the court finds unconstitutional the portion of CPL 400.27(9)(b), which states that mitigating factors shall include that the defendant was mentally retarded at the time of the crime. The appropriate remedy here is a simple addition to the charge to the jury during the sentencing proceeding as follows: If you find by a preponderance of the evidence adduced at this hearing that the defendant is mentally retarded (as defined in CPL 400.27(12)(e)— then you must not direct a sentence of death. People v. Smith, 193 Misc. 2d 538, 753 N.Y.S.2d 809 (Sup. Ct. Erie Co. 2002).

Constitutionality of subd. 10.—Defendant failed to prove beyond a reasonable doubt that the anticipatory deadlock instruction of CPL § 400.27(10) is unconstitutional; the instruction correctly advises the jury that a non-unanimous verdict is a final verdict. People v. Owens, 187 Misc. 2d 944, 727 N.Y.S.2d 275 (Sup. Ct. Monroe Co. 2001).

—CPL § 400.27(10) is unconstitutional, because it has the potential of coercing a unanimous death sentence determination. People v. Harris, 177 Misc. 2d 160, 677 N.Y.S.2d 659 (Sup. Ct. Kings Co. 1998).

Constitutionality of subd. 11.—CPL § 400.27(11) is constitutional; court rejected defendant's arguments that CPL § 400.27(11)(a) undermines appellate review and risks the arbitrary and capricious imposition of death, as well as defendant's claims that CPL § 400.27(11)(a) injected uncertainty and unreliability into the sentencing proceeding. People v. Harris, 177 Misc. 2d 378, 676 N.Y.S.2d 458 (Sup. Ct. Kings Co. 1998); *see also* People v. McIntosh, 178 Misc. 2d 433, 682 N.Y.S.2d 795 (Co. Ct. Dutchess Co. 1998) (CPL 400.27[11] is constitutional).

Constitutionality of subd. 12.—The statutory procedure for the sentencing phase of death penalty cases involving mentally retarded defendants is constitutional, but portions are unconstitutional in light of Atkins v. Virginia, 536 U.S. 304, 122 S. Ct. 2242, 153 L. Ed. 2d 335, which prohibits the execution of mentally retarded criminals. While most parts of CPL § 400.27

are unaffected by Atkins, 400.27(12)(d) is. This part precludes mentally retarded inmates convicted of a capital crime from the exoneration of a potential death penalty sentence based upon their mental retardation. This portion appears to be stricken by *Atkins* as unconstitutional. People v. Smith, 193 Misc. 2d 538, 753 N.Y.S.2d 809 (Sup. Ct. Erie Co. 2002).

Constitutionality of statute in general.—Defendant's argument that CPL § 400.27 is unconstitutional as unduly coercive is based on unwarranted speculation that jurors who are otherwise disposed to a life sentence without parole will ignore the instructions which the court will give, forsake their life sentence positions, and instead vote for a death sentence, only to prevent what may be an unacceptable third alternative of an indeterminate sentence with eligibility for parole consideration after 20 or 25 years. In fact, the converse is more likely—that a juror who might otherwise favor a death sentence may be willing to accede to the lesser penalty of life in prison without parole in order to avoid the possibility of parole. Court refused to strike CPL § 400.27 as unconstitutional. People v. McIntosh, 178 Misc. 2d 427, 682 N.Y.S.2d 791 (Co. Ct. Dutchess Co. 1998).

Constitutionality; non-capital cases.—Court rejected defendant's contention that CPL § 400.27, as it pertains to sentencing in a noncapital case, deprives defendant of his state and federal guarantees of due process of law in that it does not provide for a separate sentencing hearing at which a non-capital offender may submit evidence of mitigating factors. Court found that New York's sentencing scheme clearly comported with due process. People v. Hansen, 99 N.Y.2d 339, 756 N.Y.S.2d 122, 786 N.E.2d 21 (2003).

Ex parte **subpoenas.**—In a capital case, defendant is entitled to judicial subpoenas seeking material to be used in sentencing mitigation phase, and defendant's application can be ex parte, under seal, and reviewed in camera; upon such review, a decision will be rendered on an individual basis as to whether notice should be given to the District Attorney. People v. Mateo, 173 Misc. 2d 70, 660 N.Y.S.2d 672 (Monroe Co. Ct. 1997).

Grand jury; mitigation evidence.—The mitigation evidence proffered by defendant in a capital case is not admissible in the grand jury because it has no bearing on defendant's guilt or innocence. People v. Harris, 173 Misc. 2d 248, 661 N.Y.S.2d 712 (Sup. Ct. Kings Co. 1997).

Hearing unnecessary when death penalty not sought.— Where district attorney elected in murder case not to seek the death penalty against defendant, court declined to conduct an evidentiary, fact-finding hearing like the one specified in CPL 400.27 for death penalty cases, to consider aggravating and mitigating circumstances, because court found that such a hearing was not statutorily authorized simply because defendant was originally exposed to the possibility of a death sentence. People v. Johnson, 171 Misc. 2d 674, 655 N.Y.S.2d 327 (Sup. Ct. Kings Co. 1997).

Motions decided before jury selection.—Capital defendants' motions addressed to constitutional issues, with the exception of lethal injection, are timely decided prior to jury selection. People v. Arroyo, 176 Misc. 2d 967, 683 N.Y.S.2d 788 (Schoharie Co. Ct. 1998).

Proceedings of sentencing phase.—If a defendant is convicted of a capital offense, the proceedings in the sentencing phase shall be conducted pursuant to CPL § 400.27, which does not include the right to an unsworn address by the defendant to the jury. People v. Arroyo, 178 Misc. 2d 658, 682 N.Y.S.2d 545 (Schoharie Co. Ct. 1998).

Sentencing; mitigation.—Capital murder defendant had the right to waive the opportunity to offer mitigating factors at his sentencing proceeding, and defendant in the instant case was competent to waive his right to offer mitigation. People v. Lavalle, 181 Misc. 2d 916, 697 N.Y.S.2d 241 (Sup. Ct. Suffolk Co. 1999), *later proceeding at/remitted for resentencing,* 2004 N.Y. LEXIS 1575 (June 24, 2004).

—Factors bearing on mitigation of sentence are relevant only in the sentencing stage of the proceeding. People v. Rodriguez, 168 Misc. 2d 219, 647 N.Y.S.2d 350 (Sup. Ct. N.Y. Co. 1996).

Subd. 13(b).—The language of CPL 400.27(13)(b) is mandatory, and a party must serve notice of intent to offer psychiatric evidence in a reasonable time prior to trial; this provision is related to CPL 250.10 which contemplates disclosure to promote procedural fairness and orderliness. People v. Santiago, 183 Misc. 2d 715, 705 N.Y.S.2d 843 (Co. Ct. Monroe Co. 2000).

—CPL § 400.27(13)(b) requires either party intending to offer psychiatric evidence to file a notice of that intent "within a reasonable time prior to trial." Where, as here, defendant has affirmatively stated that there will be no psychiatric evidence submitted by him during the guilt phase, the Court decided to defer the defense obligation to file a notice under CPL § 400.27(13) until the completion of the guilt phase of the capital trial. If notice were to be filed at that time, the court would give the People an adequate opportunity to have the defendant examined by a psychiatrist of their choosing and to prepare for the sentencing phase. People v. Mateo, 177 Misc. 2d 814, 676 N.Y.S.2d 903 (Monroe Co. Ct. 1998).

§ 400.30. Procedure for determining the amount of a fine based upon the defendant's gain from the offense.

1. Order directing a hearing. In any case where the court is of the opinion that the sentence should consist of or include a fine and that, pursuant to article eighty of the penal law, the amount of the fine should be based upon the defendant's gain from the commission of the offense, the court may order a hearing to determine the amount of such gain. The order must be filed with the clerk of the court and must specify a date for the hearing not less than ten days after the filing of the order.

2. Notice of hearing. Upon receipt of the order, the clerk of the court must send a notice of the hearing to the defendant, his counsel and the district attorney. Such notice must specify the time and place of the hearing and the fact that the purpose thereof is to determine the amount of the defendant's gain from the commission of the offense so that an appropriate fine can be imposed.

3. Hearing. When the defendant appears for the hearing the court must ask him whether he wishes to make any statement with respect to the amount of his gain from the commission of the offense. If the defendant does make a statement, the court may accept such statement and base its finding thereon. Where the defendant does not make a statement, or where the court does not accept the defendant's statement, it may proceed with the hearing.

4. Burden and standard of proof; evidence. At any hearing held pursuant to this section the burden of proof rests upon the people. A finding as to the amount of the defendant's gain from the commission of the offense must be based upon a preponderance of the evidence. Any relevant evidence, not legally privileged, may be received regardless of its admissibility under the exclusionary rules of evidence.

5. Termination of hearing. At any time during the pendency of a hearing pursuant to this section the court may, in its discretion, terminate the hearing without making any finding.

ANNOTATIONS

Sufficiency of evidence.—The evidence at the hearing was legally sufficient to establish the victim's loss from the commission of these offenses by a fair preponderance of the evidence. People v. David N., 140 A.D.2d 460, 527 N.Y.S.2d 871 (2d Dept. 1988).

—The victim's sworn testimony concerning his wages, which was specific and was credited by County Court, was sufficient to establish his out-of-pocket losses by a preponderance of the evidence at the CPL § 400.30 hearing. People v. Morales, 256 A.D.2d 729, 682 N.Y.S.2d 681 (3d Dept. 1998).

—Matter remitted for resentencing where court imposed $50,000 fine on corporation without making any finding as to the amount of defendant's gain from the crime. People v. Brown and Ross Int'l Distribs. Inc., 131 A.D.2d 960, 516 N.Y.S.2d 541 (3d Dept. 1987).

Right to a hearing.—Defendant's failure at the time of sentencing to request a hearing does not constitute a forfeiture of his right of appellate review, since the failure to accord him a hearing constitutes a departure from the "essential nature" of the right to be sentenced as provided by law. People v. James, 186 A.D.2d 679, 588 N.Y.S.2d 634 (2d Dept. 1992).

—A colloquy between the court and counsel, and a review of an insurance company bill did not satisfy the requirement that the court conduct a hearing and determine the amount of the victim's loss and the manner of payment. People v. Mela, 172 A.D.2d 630, 568 N.Y.S.2d 432 (2d Dept. 1991).

—CPL § 400.30(4) is applicable to restitution hearings. People v. David N., 140 A.D.2d 460, 527 N.Y.S.2d 871 (2d Dept. 1988).

§ 400.40. Procedure for determining prior convictions for the purpose of sentence in certain cases.

1. Applicability. Where a conviction is entered for an unclassified misdemeanor or for a traffic infraction and the authorized sentence depends upon whether the defendant has a previous judgment of conviction for an offense, or where a conviction is entered for a violation defined outside the penal law and the amount of the fine authorized by the law defining such violation depends upon whether the defendant has a previous judgment of conviction for an offense, such issue is determined as provided in this section.

2. Statement to be filed. If it appears that the defendant has a previous judgment of conviction and if the court is required, or in its discretion desires, to impose a sentence that would not be authorized in the absence of such previous judgment, a statement must be filed after conviction and before sentence setting forth the date and place of the previous judgment or judgments and the court must conduct a hearing to determine whether the defendant is the same person mentioned in the record of such judgment or judgments. In any case where an increased sentence is mandatory, the statement may be filed by the court or by the prosecutor. In any case where an increased sentence is discretionary, the statement may be filed only by the court.

3. Preliminary examination. The defendant must be given a copy of such statement and the court must ask him whether he admits or denies such prior judgment or judgments. If the defendant denies the same or remains mute, the court may proceed with the hearing and, where the increased sentence is mandatory, it must impose such.

4. Time for hearing. In any case where a copy of the statement was not received by the defendant at least two days prior to the preliminary examination, the court must upon request of the defendant grant an adjournment of at least two days before proceeding with the hearing.

5. Manner of conducting hearing. A hearing pursuant to this section must be before the court without a jury. The burden of proof is upon the people and a finding that the defendant has been convicted of any offense alleged in the statement must be based upon proof beyond a reasonable doubt by evidence admissible under the rules applicable to trial of the issue of guilt.

ARTICLE 410—SENTENCES OF PROBATION, CONDITIONAL DISCHARGE AND PAROLE SUPERVISION

LexisNexis Cross References

Criminal Defense Techniques, Vol. 2, Ch. 47, Probation, Parole and Other Forms of Conditional Release; *New York Criminal Practice (2d ed.),* Vol. 4, Ch. 42, Classification of Offenses, Authorized Dispositions and Punishment.

§ 410.10. Specification of conditions of the sentence.

1. When the court pronounces a sentence of probation or of conditional discharge it must specify as part of the sentence the conditions to be complied with. Where the sentence is one of probation, the defendant must be given a written copy of the conditions at the time sentence is imposed. In any case where the defendant is given a written copy of the conditions, a copy thereof must be filed with and become part of the record of the case, and it is not necessary to specify the conditions orally.

2. Commission of an additional offense, other than a traffic infraction, after imposition of a sentence of probation or of conditional discharge, and prior to expiration or termination of the period of the sentence, constitutes a ground for revocation of such sentence irrespective of whether such fact is specified as a condition of the sentence.

3. When the court pronounces a sentence of probation or conditional discharge for a specified crime defined in paragraph (e) of subdivision one of section six hundred thirty-two-a of the executive law, in addition to specifying the conditions of the sentence, the court shall provide written notice to such defendant concerning any requirement to report to the crime victims board funds of a convicted person as defined in section six hundred thirty-two-a of the executive law, the procedures for such reporting and any potential penalty for a failure to comply.

Amended by L. 2001, Ch. 62, § 12, adding subd. 3, eff. June 25, 2001.

ANNOTATIONS

Additional offenses.—Evidence that the defendant violated probation held sufficient where it was shown that defendant wrote a letter to the victim and displayed harassing conduct toward the victim. Defendant was guilty of committing aggravated harassment; an additional offense warranting revocation of defendant's probation. People v. Johnson, 208 A.D.2d 1051, 617 N.Y.S.2d 577 (3d Dept. 1994).

—The commission of an additional offense justified revocation of defendant's probation even though defendant was later acquitted of those charges. People v. Britton, 158 A.D.2d 932, 551 N.Y.S.2d 718 (4th Dept. 1990).

Grave illness; probation rather than imprisonment warranted.—Seventy-three-year-old defendant's sentence was modified by imposing parole in lieu of imprisonment where fines and restitution had largely compensated for defendant's grand larceny and imprisonment would probably have resulted in defendant's death due to his peculiar and serious urological condition, complicated by diabetes and cardiac dysfunction, which could only be treated in a hospital by one doctor and where the alternative of furloughs from prison for treatment was impractical and would not have benefitted the community. People v. Notey, 72 A.D.2d 279, 423 N.Y.S.2d 947 (2d Dept. 1980).

Knowledge of probation conditions.—Defendant was held to possess knowledge of his probation conditions where defendant signed a copy of the conditions, received a copy, and subsequently reviewed the conditions with his probation officer. People v. Hurst, 197 A.D.2d 730, 602 N.Y.S.2d 244 (3d Dept. 1993).

—Where the defendant knew the exact conditions of his probation, the sentence was not rendered invalid where the sentencing court failed to supply defendant with a written copy of the conditions. Defendant was read the conditions upon sentencing by the court and defendant later reviewed the conditions with his probation officer. The defendant was held to possess knowledge as required by CPL § 410.10. People v. Nazarian, 150 A.D.2d 923, 541 N.Y.S.2d 262 (3d Dept. 1989).

—Defendant's probation was properly revoked even though defendant was not given a written copy of the conditions of his probation at the imposition of his sentence. Defendant was cognizant of the specific probation condition which he violated. People v. Davey. 193 A.D.2d 1108, 598 N.Y.S.2d 637 (4th Dept. 1993).

—Defendant was held to possess knowledge of his probation conditions where defendant was informed of the conditions at sentencing and was presented the conditions in writing, which he signed. People v. Bernstein, 163 A.D.2d 842, 559 N.Y.S.2d 71 (4th Dept. 1990).

§ 410.20. Modification or enlargement of conditions.

1. The court may modify or enlarge the conditions of a sentence of probation or of conditional discharge at any time prior to the expiration or termination of the period of the sentence. Such action may not, however, be taken unless the defendant is personally present, except that the defendant need not be present if the modification consists solely of the elimination or relaxation of one or more conditions. Whenever the defendant has not been present, the court shall notify the defendant in writing within twenty days of such modification specifying the nature of the elimination or relaxation of such condition or conditions and the effective date thereof. In any such case the modification or enlargement may be specified in the same manner as the conditions originally imposed and becomes part of the sentence.

2. The procedure set forth in this section applies to the imposition of an additional period of conditional discharge as authorized by subdivision three of section 65.05 of the penal law.

Amended by L. 1973, Ch. 127; L. 1976, Ch. 640.

ANNOTATIONS

Notice.—Defendant must be given notice of proceedings against the defendant or his co-defendant which affect a condition of defendant's probation, such as restitution. People v. Turco, 130 A.D.2d 785, 515 N.Y.S.2d 853 (2d Dept. 1987).

—Since defendant was not present for modification of his probation conditions, defendant's conviction for violating the amended condition of probation must be reversed. People v. LaFrance, 133 A.D.2d 521, 519 N.Y.S.2d 893 (4th Dept. 1987).

Court's discretion.—Judge exceeded his statutory powers when he vacated the unserved portion of inmate's jail sentence and substituted a term of home confinement with electronic monitoring; inasmuch as the jail sentence was separate from and independent of the probationary term, CPL § 410.20 did not furnish authority to vacate the former, and the judge was bound by the no-modification rule of CPL § 430.10. Pirro v. Angiolillo, 89 N.Y.2d 351, 653 N.Y.S.2d 237, 675 N.E.2d 1189 (1996).

§ 410.30. Declaration of delinquency.

If at any time during the period of a sentence of probation or of conditional discharge the court has reasonable cause to believe that the defendant has violated a condition of the sentence, it may declare the defendant delinquent and file a written declaration of delinquency. Upon such filing, the court must promptly take reasonable and appropriate action to cause the defendant to appear before it for the purpose of enabling the court to make a final determination with respect to the alleged delinquency.

ANNOTATIONS

Arrest of defendant for new offense.—Delinquency of the defendant was not established solely on the basis of the defendant's arrest for a new offense. Reasonable cause to hold the defendant delinquent was established where the defendant left the assigned facility, did not report to his probation officer, and was subsequently arrested; all acts violated the conditions of his probation. People v. Diaz, 101 A.D.2d 841, 475 N.Y.S.2d 504 (2d Dept. 1984).

—Where the Department of Probation failed to supervise the defendant, who subsequently committed an additional crime, the department was allowed to seek prosecution of the defendant for violating his probation terms. Given the defendant's location in another state, the department acted with due diligence upon learning of defendant's subsequent criminal conviction. People v. Brooks, 87 A.D.2d 718, 448 N.Y.S.2d 906 (3d Dept. 1982).

—Declaration of delinquency and termination of defendant's probation were vacated and annulled where defendant had been arrested six times under his true name since the declaration of delinquency and the warrant in the present case was never brought before the Court; such failure by the Department of Probation to exercise due diligence revoked the tolling effect of the declaration of delinquency on the running of the probationary term (PL § 65.15) and the term expired of its own force. People v. Roesler, 102 Misc. 2d 858, 424 N.Y.S.2d 643 (Crim. Ct. N.Y. Co. 1980).

Delinquent behavior.—The court acted properly in declaring defendant delinquent where the defendant failed to report to his probation officer and failed to report a change of address. Defendant had previously failed to attend several weekends of imprisonment, required as part of his probation terms. People v. Rivera, 130 Misc. 2d 326, 496 N.Y.S.2d 669 (Sup. Ct. Queens Co. 1985).

§ 410.40. Notice to appear, warrant.

1. Notice to appear. The court may at any time order that a person who is under a sentence of probation or of conditional discharge appear before it. Such order may be in the form of a written notice, specifying the time and place of appearance, mailed to or served personally upon the defendant as the court may direct. When the order is in the form of such a notice, failure to appear as ordered without reasonable cause therefor constitutes a violation of the conditions of the sentence irrespective of whether such requirement is specified as a condition thereof.

2. Warrant. If at any time during the period of a sentence of probation or of conditional discharge the court has reasonable grounds to believe that the defendant has violated a condition of the sentence, the court may issue a warrant to a police officer or to an appropriate peace officer directing him or her to take the defendant into custody and bring the defendant before the court without unnecessary delay; provided, however, if the court in which the warrant is returnable is a superior court, and such court is not available, and the warrant is addressed to a police officer or appropriate probation officer certified as a peace officer, such executing officer may bring the defendant to the local correctional facility of the county in which such court sits, to be detained there until not later than the commencement of the next session of such court occurring on the next business day; or if the court in which the warrant is returnable is a local criminal court, and such court is not available, and the warrant is addressed to a police officer or appropriate probation officer certified as a peace officer, such executing officer must without unnecessary delay bring the defendant before an alternate local criminal court, as provided in subdivision five of section 120.90. A court which issues such a

warrant may attach thereto a summary of the basis for the warrant. In any case where a defendant arrested upon the warrant is brought before a local criminal court other than the court in which the warrant is returnable, such local criminal court shall consider such summary before issuing a securing order with respect to the defendant.

Amended by L. 1980, Ch. 843; L. 1993, Ch. 161; L. 1996, Ch. 115, § 1, amending subd. 2, eff. June 4, 1996.

ANNOTATIONS

Notice to appear.—Where the Probation Department had just cause to believe that the defendant was in violation of the conditions of his probation, the department properly filed the petition with the court holding defendant delinquent. Defendant was given notice to appear. People v. Silkworth, 142 Misc. 2d 752, 538 N.Y.S.2d 692 (Crim. Ct. N.Y. Co. 1989).

Defects in notice to appear.—A purely technical defect in the notice does not prevent a court from finding a violation of probation and determining whether probation should be revoked. People v. Simone, 2 Misc. 3d 469, 771 N.Y.S.2d 304 (Sup. Ct. N.Y. Co. 2003), aff'd, 13 A.D.3d 71, 785 N.Y.S.2d 82 (1st Dept. 2004).

Warrant.—Issuance of a warrant acceptable where the defendant, while on probation, failed to report to his probation officer, left the assigned treatment facility, and was subsequently arrested in another county. The evidence was sufficient to establish that the defendant violated the conditions of his probation. People v. Diaz, 101 A.D.2d 841, 475 N.Y.S.2d 506 (2d Dept. 1984).

—Upon the issuance of a warrant pursuant to CPL § 410.40, the Department of Probation must act with diligence in the execution of the warrant. The defendant must be given notice of the proceedings and not be subjected to unreasonable probation termination procedures. People v. Roessler, 102 Misc. 2d 858, 424 N.Y.S.2d 643 (Crim. Ct. N.Y. Co. 1980)

§ 410.50. Custody and supervision of probationers.

1. Custody. A person who is under a sentence of probation is in the legal custody of the court that imposed it pending expiration or termination of the period of the sentence.

2. Supervision. The probation department serving the court that imposed a sentence of probation has the duty of supervising the defendant during the period of such legal custody.

3. Search order. If at any time during the period of probation the court has reasonable cause to believe that the defendant has violated a condition of the sentence, it may issue a search order. Such order must be directed to a probation officer and may authorize such officer to search the person of the defendant and/or any premises in which he resides or any real or personal property which he owns or which is in his possession.

4. Taking custody without warrant. When a probation officer has reasonable cause to believe that a person under his supervision pursuant to a sentence of probation has violated a condition of the sentence, such officer may, without a warrant, take the probationer into custody and search his person.

5. Assistance by police officer. In executing a search order, or in taking a person into custody,

pursuant to this section, a probation officer may be assisted by a police officer.

ANNOTATIONS

Conditions of probation; unreasonableness.—In the fairness of the law, a defendant must not be subjected to compulsory blood alcohol tests and unreasonable, unannounced searches of defendant's residence. Such conditions of probation are prohibited. People v. Brown, 177 A.D.2d 981, 578 N.Y.S.2d 3 (4th Dept. 1991).

Probation department role.—Following a sentence of probation, and not before this point, the probation department becomes the supervisor of those persons convicted of a crime. However, the defendant is still subject to the custody of the court's jurisdiction for the length of the probation term. People v. Rodney E., 77 N.Y.2d 672, 569 N.Y.S.2d 920, 572 N.E.2d 603 (1991).

Probationer; search.—As a condition of his plea agreement in which he received a sentence of probation, defendant consented to searches of his home for illegal drugs, and this consent was not coerced. People v. Hale, 93 N.Y.2d 454, 692 N.Y.S.2d 649, 714 N.E.2d 861 (1999).

—A probationer who has not previously violated the conditions of his sentence should not be subject to a complete search of his person and property whenever his probation officer receives an anonymous phone call. People v. Jackson, 46 N.Y.2d 171, 412 N.Y.S.2d 884, 385 N.E.2d 621 (1978).

—Unless a search order pursuant to CPL § 410.50(3) is first obtained, when there is no waiver and no exigent circumstances, a probation officer may not search a probationer's personal property, except as incident to arrest. People v. Brown, 114 A.D.2d 1035, 495 N.Y.S.2d 474 (2d Dept. 1985).

—The Fourth Amendment rights of a probationer are not the same as others possess and hence a probation officer's search of defendant's home, based on a police tip and grounded on a prior judicial determination of reasonable cause, in granting the search warrant, was valid and not to be considered a "police" search even though police officers aided the probation officer in the search. People v. Dawson, 73 A.D.2d 979, 423 N.Y.S.2d 554 (3d Dept. 1980).

—A probationer is protected by CPL Article 410 for his proposed violations of probation. The probationer's constitutional rights are not similar to the rights possessed by others. People v. Smythe, 155 Misc. 2d 961, 591 N.Y.S.2d 322 (Westchester Co. 1992).

Search; immediacy.—A probation officer's warrantless search of defendant's home must be supported by exigent circumstances and immediacy. Without the factor of immediacy, the matter must first be submitted to the court upon the showing of probation violations. People v. Suttell, 109 A.D.2d 249, 492 N.Y.S.2d 192 (4th Dept. 1985).

§ 410.60. Appearance before court.

A person who has been taken into custody pursuant to section 410.40 or section 410.50 for violation of a condition of a sentence of probation or a sentence of conditional discharge must forthwith be brought before the court that imposed the sentence. If the court has reasonable cause to believe that such person has violated a condition of the sentence, it may commit him to the custody of the sheriff or fix bail or release such person on his own recognizance for future appearance at a hearing to be held in accordance with section 410.70. If the court does not have reasonable cause to believe that such person has violated a condition of the sentence, it must direct that he be released.

§ 410.70. Hearing on violation.

1. In general. The court may not revoke a sentence of probation or a sentence of conditional

discharge unless (a) the court has found that the defendant has violated a condition of the sentence and (b) the defendant has had an opportunity to be heard. The defendant is entitled to a hearing in accordance with this section promptly after the court has filed a declaration of delinquency or has committed him or has fixed bail pursuant to this article.

2. Statement; preliminary examination. The court must file or cause to be filed with the clerk of the court a statement setting forth the condition or conditions of the sentence violated and a reasonable description of the time, place and manner in which the violation occurred. The defendant must appear before the court and the court must advise him of the contents of the statement and furnish him with a copy thereof. At the time of such appearance the court must ask the defendant whether he wishes to make any statement with respect to the violation. If the defendant makes a statement, the court may accept it and base its decision thereon. If the court does not accept it, or if the defendant does not make a statement, the court must proceed with the hearing. Provided, however, that upon request, the court must grant a reasonable adjournment to the defendant to enable him to prepare for the hearing.

3. Manner of conducting hearing. The hearing must be a summary one by the court without a jury and the court may receive any relevant evidence not legally privileged. The defendant may cross-examine witnesses and may present evidence on his own behalf. A finding that the defendant has violated a condition of his sentence must be based upon a preponderance of the evidence.

4. Counsel. The defendant is entitled to counsel at all stages of any proceeding under this section and the court must advise him of such right at the outset of the proceeding.

5. Revocation; modification; continuation. At the conclusion of the hearing the court may revoke, continue or modify the sentence of probation or conditional discharge. Where the court revokes the sentence, it must impose sentence as specified in subdivisions three and four of section 60.01 of the penal law. Where the court continues or modifies the sentence, it must vacate the declaration of delinquency and direct that the defendant be released. If the alleged violation is sustained and the court continues or modifies the sentence, it may extend the sentence up to the period of interruption specified in subdivision two of section 65.15 of the penal law, but any time spent in custody in any correctional institution pursuant to section 410.60 of this article shall be credited against the term of the sentence.

Amended by L. 1977, Ch. 355; L. 1985, Ch. 112.

ANNOTATIONS

Adjournment.—Court's refusal to further adjourn probation revocation hearing pending receipt of plea minutes on charges that underlay the revocation was proper, as the fact of the guilty pleas made out a *prima facie* case for revocation, and it was then incumbent on the defendant to assert that he pleaded guilty for reasons other than actual guilt. People v. Rosado, 74 A.D.2d 883, 426 N.Y.S.2d 22 (2d Dept. 1980).

Conditions of probation.—Defendant held in violation of his probation where defendant failed to report to his probation officer, failed to inform the officer of his location, and failed to complete the drug treatment program to which he was assigned. People v. Offley, 210 A.D.2d 262, 619 N.Y.S.2d 970 (2d Dept. 1994).

Conditional discharge; revocation hearing.—Revocation of conditional discharge after conviction of violating New York City's Noise Code did not deprive the defendant of an opportunity to be heard where, even though complainant failed to provide exact date defendant violated condition of his sentence "to maintain his music at reasonable level," she was reasonably specific as to time period involved. People v. Stefanik, 103 Misc. 2d 539, 430 N.Y.S.2d 190 (1st Dept., App. Term 1980).

Decision to revoke probation.—The decision to revoke defendant's probation consists of a determination whether the defendant actually violated the probation terms and whether the violations warrant revocation. The court properly included a statement of its reasons for revoking the defendant's probation within the sentencing minutes. People v. McCloud, 205 A.D.2d 1024, 614 N.Y.S.2d 72 (3d Dept. 1994).

District Attorney.—By participating as counsel in presenting violations at revocation hearings, the Department of Probation is not usurping authority vested exclusively in the District Attorney under County Law § 927. Darvin v. Jacobs, 69 N.Y.2d 957, 516 N.Y.S.2d 641, 509 N.E.2d 336 (1987).

Generally.—Whether a sentence for a violation of probation should be concurrent or consecutive with the sentence on the underlying crime or crimes that formed the basis for the violation rests in the sound discretion of the sentencing court. People v. Santana, 191 A.D.2d 655, 595 N.Y.S.2d 220 (2d Dept. 1993).

—The decision of the sentencing court to impose a consecutive sentence to be served with two concurrent terms stemming from prior convictions was proper. People v. Baucom, 154 A.D.2d 688, 546 N.Y.S.2d 676 (2d Dept. 1989).

—Fact that probation and suppression hearings were held jointly did not warrant reversal of the violation of probation. People v. Mallory, 191 A.D.2d 970, 595 N.Y.S.2d 266 (4th Dept. 1993).

Probation hearing on violation.—The purpose of the probation hearing was not to find that defendant committed a crime, rather, it was to determine whether defendant's acts violated his probation terms. The violation must be proven by a preponderance of the evidence; not beyond a reasonable doubt. People v. Davis, 161 Misc. 2d 533, 615 N.Y.S.2d 252 (Sup. Ct. Queens Co. 1994).

Probation revocation; hearsay evidence.—Defendant's claim that the probation violation hearing was improperly based upon hearsay evidence was not preserved for appellate review. During a hearing, the court is allowed to receive any evidence which is relevant even if such evidence is not legally privileged. People v. Park, 203 A.D.2d 596, 612 N.Y.S.2d 938 (2d Dept. 1994).

—Probation revocation must not be supported solely by hearsay evidence. The record must contain credible evidence establishing that the defendant violated a condition of his probation. The testimony of the director of the clinic and a discharge report from the clinic were held as credible evidence; not merely hearsay. People v. Raleigh, 184 A.D.2d 869, 585 N.Y.S.2d 118 (3d Dept. 1992).

Probation violation; sufficiency of evidence.—Contrary to defendant's contention, there is no inherent contradiction between a determination that the defendant violated his probation and a verdict acquitting him of criminal offenses which formed the basis of the violation inasmuch as the two matters are subject to different standards of proof. People v. Brown, 268 A.D.2d 592, 704 N.Y.S.2d 88 (2d Dept. 2000).

—Defendant was properly found to be in violation of his probation even though the verdict acquitted defendant of the offense which resulted in the probation violation. The hearing testimony supported defendant's violation by a preponderance of the evidence. People v. Powell, 209 A.D.2d 645, 619 N.Y.S.2d 123 (2d Dept. 1994).

—Testimony of witness and complainant establishing that defendant was on the premises of complainant's home was sufficient evidence allowing revocation of defendant's probation. People v. Rennie, 190 A.D.2d 830, 593 N.Y.S.2d 829 (2d Dept. 1993).

—Probation violation was supported by the testimony of the probation officer stating that defendant was not punctual for and often failed to attend appointments. The testimony also established that defendant attempted to threaten and bribe the officer. Defendant's numerous arrests provided additional support for finding defendant in violation of his probation. People v. Morillo, 159 A.D.2d 310, 552 N.Y.S.2d 589 (2d Dept. 1990).

—While affidavit of defendant's probation officer was admissible under the broad rules governing violation hearings, it did not qualify as competent evidence under the business record exception to the hearsay rule. People v. Usher, 80 A.D.2d 730, 437 N.Y.S.2d 156 (4th Dept. 1981).

Revocation.—Inconsistent statements in the testimony of the witness and the victim did not provide a basis for reevaluating the decision of the court to revoke defendant's probation. The testimony sufficiently established that the defendant violated his probation. People v. Mitchell, 201 A.D.2d 507, 607 N.Y.S.2d 417 (2d Dept. 1994).

—Probation may be revoked even though there has been an acquittal or dismissal of criminal charges. People v. Conway, 263 A.D.2d 548, 695 N.Y.S.2d 137 (3d Dept. 1999).

Right of defendant to notice and opportunity to be heard.—A probation revocation hearing is a summary, informal procedure, for which statutory and due process requirements are met as long as defendant is given formal notice of the charges and an opportunity to be heard and to confront the witnesses against her through cross-examination. People v. Ebert, 18 A.D.3d 963, 794 N.Y.S.2d 733 (3d Dept. 2005).

—The petition and letter supplied to defendant containing People's intent to factually prove that defendant violated his probation provided defendant with notice of the charged violation. People v. Schneider, 188 A.D.2d 754, 591 N.Y.S.2d 550 (3d Dept. 1992).

—Revocation of defendant's probation was proper where defendant was brought before the court and informed that the conviction for petit larceny provided the basis of the court's decision to revoke probation. Defendant was held to have received both notice and the opportunity to be heard. People v. Halaby, 77 A.D.2d 717, 430 N.Y.S.2d 717 (3d Dept. 1980).

Sentence after probation revocation.—The sentence received by defendant after revocation of his probation was not excessive where testimony established that defendant did not report an arrest nor did the defendant attend the scheduled meetings with the probation officer. People v. Morales, 178 A.D.2d 562, 577 N.Y.S.2d 469 (2d Dept. 1991).

Updated presentence report; functional equivalent acceptable.—The testimony and documentary evidence produced at the revocation hearing as well as defendant's own presentence memoranda provided the court with the functional equivalent of an updated presentence report. People v. Bennett, 269 A.D.2d 401, 704 N.Y.S.2d 95 (2d Dept. 2000).

§ 410.80. Transfer of supervision of probationers.

1. Authority to transfer supervision. In any case where a sentence of probation is pronounced, if the defendant resides or desires to reside in a place other than one within the jurisdiction of the probation department that serves the sentencing court, such court may designate any other probation department within the state to perform the duties of probation supervision and may transfer supervision of the defendant thereto. Any such designation must be in accordance with rules adopted by the director of the state division of probation and correctional alternatives.

2. Transfer of powers. Where supervision of

a probationer is transferred pursuant to subdivision one, the probation department and probation officers to which the duties of probation supervision have been transferred have the same powers and duties as otherwise would have been possessed by those serving the sentencing court. Unless the sentencing court indicates otherwise at the time of transfer, the court served by the probation department to which supervision is transferred shall assume the powers and duties of the sentencing court and shall have sole jurisdiction in the case including jurisdiction over matters specified in article twenty-three of the correction law. Where jurisdiction has been transferred, the sentencing court shall immediately forward its entire case record to the receiving court.

The sentencing court may retain its power and duties with respect to the supervision of said probationer. Unless the sentencing court indicates otherwise at the time of transfer the court served by the probation department to which supervision is transferred has the powers specified in sections 410.20, 410.30, 410.40, subdivision three of section 410.50, and section 410.60. If it appears that the defendant has violated a condition of his sentence, such court also has the power to:

(a) Commit the defendant to the custody of the sheriff, and direct such official to bring the defendant promptly before the court that imposed the sentence; or

(b) Conduct a hearing on the violation pursuant to subdivisions one through four of section 410.70 and make findings of fact. In such case, the court may then either (i) continue or modify the sentence, or (ii) commit the defendant as provided in paragraph (a) and send a certified copy of the transcript of the hearings and its findings to the court that imposed the sentence.

In transfers involving a defendant sentenced to probation upon conviction of a felony, the court served by the probation department to which supervision is transferred shall be the superior court within the jurisdiction of the probation department. In transfers involving a defendant sentenced to probation upon conviction of a misdemeanor, the court served by the probation department to which supervision is transferred shall be the appropriate local criminal court within the jurisdiction of the probation department. The probation department that serves the sentencing court shall consult with the probation department to which supervision will be transferred and recommend the appropriate local criminal court to receive the case.

3. Procedure upon return of the defendant. When a defendant is returned to the court that imposed the sentence the transfer is terminated and such court must proceed in accordance with the provisions of sections 410.60 and 410.70. In any case where a hearing was conducted pursuant to paragraph (b) of subdivision two, the hearing and findings have the same effect as a hearing

conducted by and findings made by the sentencing court. No person who has been returned to such court may be transferred back to supervision in the county that returned him without consent of the court that returned him.

4. Costs of returning a probationer. The costs incurred by a county in returning a probationer transferred thereto, including any costs necessary for a hearing conducted in such county, are charges upon the county in which the sentencing court is located.

5. Interstate compact. Nothing contained in this section affects or limits the provisions of section two hundred fifty-nine-m of the executive law relating to out-of-state probation supervision.

6. Federal transfer of custody and supervision. Notwithstanding the provisions of any other law, the court served by the probation department may consent to the transfer of custody and supervision of a probationer to the United States Department of Justice pursuant to the Witness Security Act of nineteen hundred eighty-four.

Amended by L. 1972, Ch. 545; L. 1978, Ch. 501; L. 1980, Ch. 201; L. 1981, Ch. 755; L. 1985, Ch. 134; L. 1986, Ch. 24; L. 1988, Ch. 430; L. 1993, Ch. 137.

ANNOTATIONS

Hearing on violation of probation; transfer of jurisdiction.—An order transferring supervision of defendant's probation failed to contain the receiving court's name and address. The error was held to be ministerial and did not affect the jurisdiction of the receiving court. The sentencing court did not specifically indicate that it would retain jurisdiction over the matter. People v. Perry, 188 A.D.2d 909, 591 N.Y.S.2d 867 (3d Dept. 1992).

—The sentencing court is permitted to transfer probation of the defendant to the probation department in defendant's residential county. Intercounty transfers of probation are permissible. People v. Mitchell, 137 Misc. 2d 450, 521 N.Y.S.2d 639 (Montgomery Co. Ct. 1987).

—Although the sentencing court failed to forward the case record to the receiving court, the receiving court's jurisdiction was unaffected. Without specific indication of the retention of jurisdiction, the receiving court assumes jurisdiction upon the transfer of the case to the probation department. People v. Buyce, 134 Misc. 2d 31, 509 N.Y.S.2d 701 (Hamilton Co. Ct. 1986).

Power of the receiving court.—CPL § 410.80 does not grant the receiving court the power to correct an illegal sentence. The receiving court is permitted specific power as possessed by the sentencing court such as the enlargement or modification of probation conditions according to CPL § 410.20. Stitham v. City of New York, Dept. of Probation, 127 Misc. 2d 906, 487 N.Y.S.2d 523 (Sup. Ct. N.Y. Co. 1985).

Probation department.—The probation department does not have the power or authority to construct a schedule for payment of restitution by the defendant. People v. DeFranseco, 136 A.D.2d 561, 523 N.Y.S.2d 557 (2d Dept. 1988).

§ 410.90. Termination of sentence.

1. The court may at any time terminate either a period of probation, other than a period of lifetime probation, for conviction to a crime or a period of conditional discharge for an offense.

2. The court may terminate a period of probation for a person who is subject to lifetime probation and who has been on unrevoked probation for at least five consecutive years.

3. (a) The court shall grant a request for termination of a sentence of probation under this section when, having regard to the conduct and condition of the probationer, the court is of the opinion that:

(i) the probationer is no longer in need of such guidance, training or other assistance which would otherwise be administered through probation supervision;

(ii) the probationer has diligently complied with the terms and conditions of the sentence of probation; and

(iii) the termination of the sentence of probation is not adverse to the protection of the public.

No such termination shall be granted unless the court is satisfied that the probationer, who is otherwise financially able to comply with an order of restitution or reparation, has made a good faith effort to comply therewith.

(b) The court shall grant a request for termination of a sentence of conditional discharge under this section when, having regard to the conduct and condition of the defendant, the court is of the opinion that:

(i) the defendant has diligently complied with the terms and conditions of the sentence of conditional discharge; and

(ii) termination of the sentence of conditional discharge is not adverse to protection of the public.

Amended by L. 1973, Ch. 278; L. 1979, Ch. 410; L. 1980, Ch. 238; L. 1982, Ch. 782; L. 1992, Ch. 618, eff. Nov. 1, 1992, amending subd. 3(a).

ANNOTATIONS

Termination; generally.—The prosecution of the defendant for probation violation was proper even though the probation department failed to supervise the defendant. The court has the power to terminate defendant's probation on the basis of a criminal conviction of the defendant. People v. Brooks, 87 A.D.2d 718, 448 N.Y.S.2d 906 (3d Dept. 1982).

—Termination of probation need not be afforded notice or hearings under CPL § 410.90. People v. Roesler, 102 Misc. 2d 858, 424 N.Y.S.2d 643 (Crim. Ct. N.Y. Co. 1980).

"Interim probation."—There is no express statutory authority for interim probation after conviction but before sentencing. People v. Rodney E., 77 N.Y.2d 672, 569 N.Y.S.2d 920, 572 N.E.2d 603 (1991).

§ 410.91. Sentence of parole supervision.

[Effective until Sept. 1, 2009.]

1. A sentence of parole supervision is an indeterminate sentence of imprisonment which may be imposed upon an eligible defendant, as defined in subdivision two of this section. Such sentence shall have a minimum term and a maximum term within the ranges specified by subdivisions three and four of section 70.06 of the penal law. Provided, however, if the court directs that the sentence be executed as a sentence of parole supervision, it shall remand the defendant for immediate delivery to a reception center operated

by the state department of correctional services, in accordance with section 430.20 of this chapter and six hundred one of the correction law, for a period not to exceed ten days. An individual who receives such a sentence shall be placed under the immediate supervision of the state division of parole and must comply with the conditions of parole, which shall include an initial placement in a drug treatment campus for a period of ninety days at which time the defendant shall be released therefrom.

2. A defendant is an "eligible defendant" for purposes of a sentence of parole supervision when such defendant is a second felony offender convicted of a specified offense or offenses as defined in subdivision five of this section, who stands convicted of no other felony offense, who has not previously been convicted of either a violent felony offense as defined in section 70.02 of the penal law, a class A felony offense or a class B felony offense, and is not subject to an undischarged term of imprisonment.

3. When an indeterminate sentence of imprisonment is imposed upon an eligible defendant for a specified offense, as defined in subdivision five of this section, the court may direct that such sentence be executed as a sentence of parole supervision if the court finds (i) that the defendant has a history of controlled substance dependence that is a significant contributing factor to such defendant's criminal conduct; (ii) that such defendant's controlled substance dependence could be appropriately addressed by a sentence of parole supervision; and (iii) that imposition of such a sentence would not have an adverse effect on public safety or public confidence in the integrity of the criminal justice system.

4. If the sentence is for a specified offense that is a class D felony, the court may not impose a sentence of parole supervision without the consent of the people. If the conviction is as a result of a plea of guilty, the people must communicate their consent, or lack thereof, at the time of the plea. If the conviction is not as a result of a plea of guilty, the people must communicate their consent, or lack thereof, at least ten days before sentencing. In either case, if the people do not consent, they must state on the record or in writing the reason or reasons for their opposition.

5. For the purposes of this section, a "specified offense" is an offense defined by any of the following provisions of the penal law: criminal mischief in the third degree as defined in section 145.05, criminal mischief in the second degree as defined in section 145.10, grand larceny in the fourth degree as defined in subdivision one, two, three, four, five, six, eight, nine or ten of section 155.30, grand larceny in the third degree as defined in section 155.35 (except where the property consists of one or more firearms, rifles or shotguns), unauthorized use of a vehicle in the second degree as defined in section 165.06, criminal possession of stolen property in the fourth

degree as defined in subdivision one, two, three, five or six of section 165.45, criminal possession of stolen property in the third degree as defined in section 165.50 (except where the property consists of one or more firearms, rifles or shotguns), forgery in the second degree as defined in section 170.10, criminal possession of a forged instrument in the second degree as defined in section 170.25, unlawfully using slugs in the first degree as defined in section 170.60, or an attempt to commit any of the aforementioned offenses if such attempt constitutes a felony offense; or any class D or class E controlled substance or marihuana felony offense as defined in article two hundred twenty or two hundred twenty-one.

6. Upon delivery of the defendant to the reception center, he or she shall be given a copy of the conditions of parole by a representative of the division of parole and shall acknowledge receipt of a copy of the conditions in writing. The conditions shall be established in accordance with article twelve-b of the executive law and the rules and regulations of the division of parole. Thereafter and while the parolee is participating in the intensive drug treatment program provided at the drug treatment campus, the division of parole shall assess the parolee's special needs and shall develop an intensive program of parole supervision that will address the parolee's substance abuse history and which shall include periodic urinalysis testing. Unless inappropriate, such program shall include the provision of treatment services by a community-based substance abuse service provider which has a contract with the division of parole.

7. Upon completion of the drug treatment program at the drug treatment campus, a parolee will be furnished with money, clothing and transportation in a manner consistent with section one hundred twenty-five of the correction law to permit the parolee's travel from the drug treatment campus to the county in which the parolee's supervision will continue.

8. If the parole officer having charge of a person sentenced to parole supervision pursuant to this section has reasonable cause to believe that such person has violated the conditions of his or her parole, the procedures of subdivision three of section two hundred fifty-nine-I of the executive law shall apply to the issuance of a warrant and the conduct of further proceedings; provided, however, that a parole violation warrant issued for a violation committed while the parolee is being supervised at a drug treatment campus shall constitute authority for the immediate placement of the parolee into a correctional facility operated by the department of correctional services, which to the extent practicable shall be reasonably proximate to the place at which the violation occurred, to hold in temporary detention pending completion of the procedures required by subdivision three of section two hundred fifty-nine-I of the executive law.

Added by L. 1995, Ch. 3, § 34, eff. Oct. 1, 1995, repealed Sept. 30, 2005, pursuant to L. 1995, Ch. 3, § 74, paragraph (a); L. 2005, Ch. 56, Part D, § 20, eff. Apr. 1, 2005, extending repeal date to Sept. 1, 2009.

ANNOTATIONS

Termination.—Probation may be terminated at any time for the conviction of a crime. People v. Brooks, 87 A.D.2d 718, 448 N.Y.S.2d 906 (3d Dept. 1982).

Constitutionality.—While CPL § 410.91(4) limits a court's discretion to the extent of requiring the prosecutor's consent prior to the imposition of a parole supervision sentence, it does not constrain a court to sentence a defendant in any particular way. Thus, court rejected defendant's claim that the consent provision of CPL § 410.91(4) unconstitutionally violates the separation of powers doctrine by improperly delegating judicial authority to the executive branch. People v. Schehr, 1 A.D.3d 719, 766 N.Y.S.2d 642 (3d Dept. 2003).

—Defendant argued that the sentencing option of parole supervision for a defendant with a controlled substance dependency deprived her of equal protection because she was not drug-dependent, but court rejected defendant's equal protection challenge to CPL § 410.91. People v. Lewis, 261 A.D.2d 648, 690 N.Y.S.2d 294 (3d Dept. 1999).

—CPL § 410.91, which creates the sentencing option of parole supervision for eligible individuals with a history of controlled substance dependence, is not unconstitutional as applied to defendant, who claims to have problem with alcohol and nonnarcotic drugs. People v. Kinch, 237 A.D.2d 830, 655 N.Y.S.2d 191 (3d Dept. 1997).

—Legislature's exclusion of the crime of scheme to defraud in the first degree from the list of specified offenses in CPL 410.91(5) for which one may receive an alternative sentence of drug treatment and parole supervision is not violative of defendant's right to due process or equal protection. People v. Ralston, 303 A.D.2d 1014, 757 N.Y.S.2d 414 (4th Dept. 2003).

Parolee; search.—In evaluating the reasonableness of a search or seizure, defendant's status as a parolee is always relevant and critical. People v. Huntley, 43 N.Y.2d 175, 401 N.Y.S.2d 31, 371 N.E.2d 794 (1977).

—Defendant consented to home entries and searches by parole officers as a condition of his parole; in any event, the apartment where defendant was seized was not the home in which he was permitted to reside. People v. Lopez, 288 A.D.2d 70, 733 N.Y.S.2d 154 (1st Dept. 2001).

—The Fourth Amendment protection afforded to parolees is significantly less than that which is afforded to ordinary citizens. People v. Dyla, 142 A.D.2d 423, 536 N.Y.S.2d 799 (2d Dept. 1988).

ARTICLE 420—FINES, RESTITUTION AND REPARATION

Section

LexisNexis Cross References

New York Criminal Practice (2d ed.), Vol. 4, Ch. 42, Classification of Offenses, Authorized Dispositions and Punishment.

§ 420.05. Payment of fines, mandatory surcharges and fees by credit card.

When the court imposes a fine, mandatory surcharge or fee upon an individual who stands convicted of any offense, such individual may pay such fine, mandatory surcharge or fee by credit card or similar device. In such event, notwithstanding any other provision of law, he or she also may be required to pay a reasonable administrative fee. The amount of such administrative fee and the time and manner of its payment shall be in accordance with the system established by the chief administrator of the courts pursuant to paragraph (j) of subdivision two of section two hundred twelve of the judiciary law.

Added by L. 1987, Ch. 805; **Amended** by L. 2003, Ch. 537, § 1, eff. Sept. 17, 2003; L. 2005, Ch. 457, § 3, eff. Aug. 9, 2005, and to expire and be deemed repealed five years after such date.

§ 420.10. Collection of fines, restitution or reparation.

1. Alternative methods of payment. When the court imposes a fine upon an individual, it shall designate the official other than the district attorney to whom payment is to be remitted. When the court imposes restitution or reparation and requires that the defendant pay a designated surcharge thereon pursuant to the provisions of subdivision eight of section 60.27 of the penal law, it shall designate the official or organization other than the district attorney, selected pursuant to subdivision eight of this section, to whom payment is to be remitted.

(a) The court may direct:

(i) That the defendant pay the entire amount at the time sentence is pronounced;

(ii) That the defendant pay the entire amount at some later date; or

(iii) That the defendant pay a specified portion at designated periodic intervals.

(b) When the court imposes both (i) a fine and (ii) restitution or reparation and such designated surcharge upon an individual and imposes a schedule of payments, the court shall also direct that payment of restitution or reparation and such designated surcharge take priority over the payment of the fine.

(c) Where the defendant is sentenced to a period of probation as well as a fine, restitution or reparation and such designated surcharge, the court may direct that payment of the fine, restitution or reparation and such designated surcharge be a condition of the sentence.

(d) When a court requires that restitution or reparation and such designated surcharge be made it must direct that notice be given to a person or persons to whom it is to be paid of the conditions under which it is to be remitted; the name and address of the public official or organization to whom it is to be remitted for payment and the amount thereof; and the availability of civil proceedings for collection under subdivision six of this section. An official or organization designated to receive payment under this subdivision must report to the court any failure to comply with the order and shall cooperate with the district attorney pursuant to his responsibilities under subdivision six of this section.

(e) Where cash bail has been posted by the defendant as the principal and is not forfeited or assigned, the court at its discretion may order that bail be applied toward payment of any order of restitution or reparation or fine. If the court so orders, the bail proceeds shall be applied to payment first of the restitution or reparation and then of the fine.

2. Death of victim. In the event that the individual to whom restitution or reparation is to be made dies prior to completion of said restitution or reparation, the remaining payments shall be made to the estate of the deceased.

3. Imprisonment for failure to pay. Where the court imposes a fine, restitution or reparation, the

sentence may provide that if the defendant fails to pay the fine, restitution or reparation in accordance with the direction of the court, the defendant must be imprisoned until the fine, restitution or reparation is satisfied. Such provision may be added at the time sentence is pronounced or at any later date while the fine, restitution or reparation or any part thereof remains unpaid; provided, however, that if the provision is added at a time subsequent to the pronouncement of sentence the defendant must be personally present when it is added. In any case where the defendant fails to pay a fine, restitution or reparation as directed the court may issue a warrant directing a peace officer, acting pursuant to his special duties, or a police officer, to take him into custody and bring him before the court; provided, however, if the court in which the warrant is returnable is a city, town or village court, and such court is not available, and the warrant is addressed to a police officer, such executing police officer must without unnecessary delay bring the defendant before an alternate local criminal court, as provided in subdivision five of section 120.90 of this chapter; or if the court in which the warrant is returnable is a superior court, and such court is not available, and the warrant is addressed to a police officer, such executing police officer may bring the defendant to the local correctional facility of the county in which such court sits, to be detained there until not later than the commencement of the next session of such court occurring on the next business day. Such warrant may also be delegated in the same manner as a warrant pursuant to section 530.70 of this chapter. Where a sentence provides that the defendant be imprisoned for failure to pay a fine, the court shall advise the defendant that if he is unable to pay such fine, he has a right, at any time, to apply to the court to be resentenced as provided in subdivision five of this section.

4. Period of imprisonment. When the court directs that the defendant be imprisoned until the fine, restitution or reparation be satisfied, it must specify a maximum period of imprisonment subject to the following limits:

(a) Where the fine, restitution or reparation is imposed for a felony, the period may not exceed one year;

(b) Where the fine, restitution or reparation is imposed for a misdemeanor, the period may not exceed one-third of the maximum authorized term of imprisonment;

(c) Where the fine, restitution or reparation is imposed for a petty offense, the period may not exceed fifteen days; and

(d) Where a sentence of imprisonment as well as a fine, restitution or reparation is imposed, the aggregate of the period and the term of the sentence may not exceed the maximum authorized term of imprisonment.

(e) Jail time and good behavior time shall be credited against the full period of imprisonment, if served, as provided in section 70.30 of the penal law for definite sentences.

5. Application for resentence. In any case where the defendant is unable to pay a fine, restitution or reparation imposed by the court he may at any time apply to the court for resentence. In such case, if the court is satisfied that the defendant is unable to pay the fine, restitution or reparation it must:

(a) Adjust the terms of payment; or

(b) Lower the amount of the fine, restitution or reparation; or

(c) Where the sentence consists of probation or imprisonment and a fine, restitution or reparation, revoke the portion of the sentence imposing the fine, restitution or reparation; or

(d) Revoke the entire sentence imposed and resentence the defendant.

Upon such resentence the court may impose any sentence it originally could have imposed, except that the amount of any fine, restitution or reparation imposed may not be in excess of the amount the defendant is able to pay.

In any case where the defendant applies for resentencing with respect to any condition of the sentence relating to restitution or reparation the court must order that notice of such application and a reasonable opportunity to be heard be given to the person or persons given notice pursuant to subdivision one of this section. If the court grants the defendant's application by changing the original order for restitution or reparation in any manner, the court must place the reasons therefor on the record.

For the purposes of this subdivision, the court shall not determine that the defendant is unable to pay the fine, restitution or reparation ordered solely because of such defendant's incarceration but shall consider all the defendant's sources of income including, but not limited to, moneys in the possession of an inmate at the time of his admission into such facility, funds earned by him in a work release program as defined in subdivision four of section one hundred fifty of the correction law, funds earned by him as provided for in section one hundred eighty-seven of the correction law and any other funds received by him or on his behalf and deposited with the superintendent or the municipal official of the facility where the person is confined.

6. Civil proceeding for collection. (a) A fine, restitution or reparation imposed or directed by the court shall be imposed or directed by a written order of the court containing the amount thereof required to be paid by the defendant. The court's order also shall direct the district attorney to file a certified copy of such order with the county clerk of the county in which the court is situate except where the court which issues such order is the supreme court in which case the order itself

shall be filed by the clerk of the court acting in his or her capacity as the county clerk of the county in which the court is situate. Such order shall be entered by the county clerk in the same manner as a judgment in a civil action in accordance with subdivision (a) of rule five thousand sixteen of the civil practice law and rules. Even if the defendant was imprisoned for failure to pay such fine, restitution or reparation, or has served the period of imprisonment imposed, such order after entry thereof pursuant to this subdivision may be collected in the same manner as a judgment in a civil action by the victim, as defined in paragraph (b) of subdivision four of section 60.27 of the penal law, to whom restitution or reparation was ordered to be paid, the estate of such person or the district attorney. The entered order shall be deemed to constitute a judgment-roll as defined in section five thousand seventeen of the civil practice law and rules and immediately after entry of the order, the county clerk shall docket the entered order as a money judgment pursuant to section five thousand eighteen of such law and rules. Wherever appropriate, the district attorney shall file a transcript of the docket of the judgment with the clerk of any other county of the state. Such a restitution or reparation order, when docketed shall be a first lien upon all real property in which the defendant thereafter acquires an interest, having preference over all other liens, security interests, and encumbrances whatsoever, except:

(i) a lien or interest running to the benefit of the government of the United States or the state of New York, or any political subdivision or public benefit corporation thereof; or

(ii) a purchase money interest in any property.

(b) The district attorney may, in his or her discretion, and must, upon order of the court, institute proceedings to collect such fine, restitution or reparation.

7. Undisbursed restitution payments. Where a court requires that restitution or reparation be made by a defendant, the official or organization to whom payments are to be remitted pursuant to subdivision one of this section may place such payments in an interest-bearing account. The interest accrued and any undisbursed payments shall be designated for the payment of restitution orders that have remained unsatisfied for the longest period of time. For the purposes of this subdivision, the term "undisbursed restitution payments" shall mean those payments which have been remitted by a defendant but not disbursed to the intended beneficiary and such payment has gone unclaimed for a period of one year and the location of the intended beneficiary cannot be ascertained by such official or organization after using reasonable efforts.

8. Designation of restitution agency. (a) The chief elected official in each county, and in the city of New York the mayor, shall designate an official or organization other than the district attorney to be responsible for the collection and administration of restitution and reparation payments under provisions of the penal law and this chapter; provided, however, that where the state division of probation and correctional alternatives provides for and delivers probation services pursuant to the provisions of section two hundred forty-seven of the executive law the state division of probation and correctional alternatives shall have the first option of designating such agency as the restitution agency for such county. This official or organization shall be eligible for the designated surcharge provided for by subdivision eight of section 60.27 of the penal law.

(b) The restitution agency, as designated by paragraph (a) of this subdivision, shall be responsible for the collection of data on a monthly basis regarding the numbers of restitution and reparation orders issued, the numbers of satisfied restitution and reparation orders and information concerning the types of crimes for which such orders were required. A probation department designated as the restitution agency shall then forward such information to the director of the state division of probation and correctional alternatives within the first ten days following the end of each month who shall transmit such information to the division of criminal justice services. In all other cases the restitution agency shall report to the division of criminal justice services directly. The division of criminal justice services shall compile and review all such information and make recommendations to promote the use of restitution and encourage its enforcement.

Amended by L. 1977, Ch. 694; L. 1980, Chs. 290, 584, 843; L. 1983, Ch. 515; L. 1984, Ch. 335; L. 1984, Ch. 965; L. 1985, Ch. 134; L. 1985, Ch. 233; L. 1985, Ch. 506; L. 1992, Ch. 378, eff. Nov. 1, 1992, amending subd. 3; L. 1992, Ch. 618, eff. Nov. 1, 1992, amending subd. 1(e), (5), and (6).

ANNOTATIONS

Court's failure to advise defendant of right to resentencing.—It was not error of court in failing to specifically advise defendant of his right to apply for resentencing if he was unable to pay his fines, since defendant's ability to pay was thoroughly explored at hearing requiring defendant to show cause why his failure to pay the fine, imposed in judgment of conviction, should not result in conviction. People v. Shields, 238 A.D.2d 759, 656 N.Y.S.2d 486 (3d Dept. 1997).

Fines; no reduction warranted.—Defendant is not entitled to an adjustment, reduction, or revocation of a $16,000 fine imposed on her $8,000 fraud of welfare system where she had an equity in her home and a separate lot of about $36,000, especially since a substantial part of the proceeds of the fraud was invested in the property and there was no constitutional infirmity in defendant's imprisonment for failure to pay the fine where the equity showed she had the means to pay, but refused to. People v. McArdle, 55 N.Y.2d 639, 446 N.Y.S.2d 256, 430 N.E.2d 1309 (1981).

—In prosecution for the offense of driving while ability is impaired, the court rejected defendant's contention that as a full-time student he was unable to pay $1000 fine; the defendant had a 10-year history of drunken driving, was a college graduate who had twice been employed with highly respected employers, and he did not enroll in school as a full-time student until after completion of his jail sentence. People v. Myers, 123 A.D.2d 474, 506 N.Y.S.2d 383 (3d Dept. 1986).

Hearing not required.—A hearing on the defendant's

ability to pay the fine imposed by the court was not required where the defendant admitted that he stole a specific amount of money from the bank. If the defendant is unable to meet the payments, he may move for resentencing in the future. People v. Foster, 216 A.D.2d 115, 628 N.Y.S.2d 643 (1st Dept. 1995).

Imprisonment in lieu of fine.—A sentence imposing an additional jail term rather than a fine and a surcharge was proper where defendant was a repeat offender of driving while intoxicated and the defendant had not received the maximum jail sentence. People v. Alleyne, 214 A.D.2d 575, 625 N.Y.S.2d 77 (2d Dept. 1995).

—Defendant may not be punished in the form of imposing additional imprisonment time for the failure to pay the fines imposed by the court where the defendant was already sentenced to the maximum time for his conviction. Any additional time imposed was held illegal. People v. Laurino, 205 A.D.2d 556, 613 N.Y.S.2d 206 (2d Dept. 1994).

—Defendant's sentence was legal where additional jail time served by the defendant for failure to pay the fine did not exceed the maximum term allowed for the convicted offense. People v. Romero, 204 A.D.2d 496, 614 N.Y.S.2d 173 (2d Dept. 1994).

Restitution.—Town court was empowered to make restitution a condition of defendant's sentence of probation, and when defendant failed to make restitution, he was properly sentenced to one year in jail; where a probationer willfully refuses to pay restitution when he or she can pay, the state is justified in revoking probation and using imprisonment as an appropriate penalty for the offense. People v. Amorosi, 96 N.Y.2d 180, 726 N.Y.S.2d 339, 750 N.E.2d 41 (2001).

—The court may not order restitution to be paid as part of the terms of defendant's probation or beyond the term of defendant's probation. The court may not order defendant to pay both restitution and the mandatory surcharge. People v. Meade, 195 A.D.2d 756, 600 N.Y.S.2d 353 (3d Dept. 1993).

—Statute authorizes court to direct restitution to be paid within a time less than that imposed as the term of probation, including the entire amount at the time of sentencing and thus there is no merit to defendant's contention that court erred in failing to ascertain his ability to pay restitution within three years. People v. Christman, 265 A.D.2d 856, 696 N.Y.S.2d 594 (4th Dept. 1999).

Undue hardship; payment of fines.—The defendant's claim of undue hardship must properly be filed according to CPL § 420.10, thus, allowing the defendant to move for resentencing. Since defendant is incarcerated, defendant's claim is premature. People v. Valesquez, 198 A.D.2d 25, 603 N.Y.S.2d 127 (1st Dept. 1993).

§ 420.20. Collection of fines, restitution or reparation imposed upon corporations.

Where a corporation is sentenced to pay a fine, restitution or reparation, the fine, restitution or reparation must be paid at the time sentence is imposed. If the fine, restitution or reparation is not so paid, it may be collected in the same manner as a judgment in a civil action, and if execution issued upon such judgment be returned unsatisfied an action may be brought in the name of the people of the state of New York to procure a judgment sequestering the property of the corporation, as provided by the business corporation law. It is the duty of the attorney general in all criminal proceedings prosecuted by him, and, in all other proceedings, the county attorney for counties outside the city of New York, and, in the city of New York the corporation counsel of the city of New York, to institute proceedings to collect such fine, restitution or reparation.

Amended by L. 1973, Ch. 488; L. 1980, Ch. 290.

ANNOTATIONS

Generally.—The court maintains authority over the

disposition of monies to be used for restitution. The court may appoint an official, a person other than the District Attorney, to receive payments and to direct payments. Stuhler v. State of New York, 127 Misc. 2d 390, 485 N.Y.S.2d 957 (Sup. Ct. N.Y. Co. 1985).

Obscene material.—The court directed the Sheriff to alter, deface or shred the obscene materials seized in satisfaction of a judgment in a criminal action so as to render it salable as scrap paper, and then sell it and apply the proceeds towards a partial satisfaction of the outstanding fine levied against the corporation after conviction for violating PL § 235.05(1). People v. Lo Ji Sales, Inc., 93 Misc. 2d 1012, 403 N.Y.S.2d 181 (Oneida Co. Ct. 1978).

§ 420.30. Remission of fines, restitution or reparation.

1. Applicability. The procedure specified in this section governs remission of fines, restitution or reparation in all cases not covered by subdivision four of section 420.10.

2. Procedure. (a) Any superior court which has imposed a fine, restitution or reparation for any offense may, in its discretion, on five days notice to the district attorney of the county in which such fine, restitution or reparation was imposed and to each person otherwise required to be given notice of restitution or reparation pursuant to subdivision one of section 420.10, remit such fine, restitution or reparation or any portion thereof. In case of a fine, restitution or reparation imposed by a local criminal court for any offense, a superior court holding a term in the county in which the fine, restitution or reparation was imposed may, upon like notice, remit such fine, restitution or reparation or any portion thereof.

(b) The court shall give each person given notice a reasonable opportunity to be heard on the question of remitting an order of restitution or reparation. If the court remits such restitution or reparation, or any part thereof, the reasons therefor shall be placed upon the record.

3. Restrictions. In no event shall a mandatory surcharge, sex offender registration fee, DNA databank fee or crime victim assistance fee be remitted provided, however, that a court may waive the crime victim assistance fee if such defendant is an eligible youth as defined in subdivision two of section 720.10 of this chapter, and the imposition of such fee would work an unreasonable hardship on the defendant, his or her immediate family, or any other person who is dependent on such defendant for financial support.

Amended by L. 1980, Ch. 290; L. 1992, Ch. 618, amending subd. 2, eff. Nov. 1, 1992; L. 1992, Ch. 794, adding subds. 3 and 4, eff. Aug. 7, 1992; L. 1993, Ch. 260; L. 1995, Ch. 3, § 65, eff. July 1, 1995, and amendment applies only when the acts constituting the offense for the conviction of which a mandatory surcharge may be imposed occurred on or after July 1, 1995, pursuant to L. 1995, Ch. 3, § 74, paragraph (i); L. 2003, Ch. 62, Part F, § 6, eff. May 15, 2003, amending subd. 3; L. 2004, Ch. 56, Part F, § 5, eff. Feb. 16, 2005, amending subd. 3.

ANNOTATIONS

Notice to defendant.—It was proper for the court to hold the defendant fully responsible for the victim's loss. However, defendant must be given notice of any other proceeding which would affect the payment of restitution to the victims. People v. Turco, 130 A.D.2d 785, 515 N.Y.S.2d 853 (2d Dept. 1987).

Restitution.—Where defendant, who was a lawyer, was convicted for having stolen funds from a client's estate, and failed to make restitution, the court increased the jail term of one year to 2½ to 7 years, and ordered the District Attorney to initiate civil proceedings against the defendant on the ground that he owned an expensive home which he could sell to cover the amount of restitution due. People v. Bertucci, 132 Misc. 2d 1051, 506 N.Y.S.2d 399 (Sup. Ct. Queens Co. 1986).

Waiver of surcharge.—CPL § 420.30(4) as amended requires the court to make an actual statement disclosing its reasoning for deciding to waive the mandatory surcharge. The court may not waive the surcharge on the sole basis that the defendant is serving a lengthy jail term. People v. Santiago, 160 Misc. 2d 349, 609 N.Y.S.2d 544 (Sup. Ct. Kings Co. 1994).

§ 420.35. Mandatory surcharge and crime victim assistance fee; applicability to sentences mandating payment of fines.

1. The provisions of section 420.10 of this article governing the collection of fines and the provisions of section 420.40 of this article governing deferral of mandatory surcharges, sex offender registration fees, DNA databank fees and financial hardship hearings and the provisions of section 430.20 of this chapter governing the commitment of a defendant for failure to pay a fine shall be applicable to a mandatory surcharge, sex offender registration fee, DNA databank fee and a crime victim assistance fee imposed pursuant to subdivision one of section 60.35 of the penal law, subdivision twenty-a of section three hundred eighty-five of the vehicle and traffic law, subdivision nineteen-a of section four hundred one of the vehicle and traffic law, or a mandatory surcharge imposed pursuant to section eighteen hundred nine of the vehicle and traffic law or section 27.10 of the parks, recreation and historic preservation law. When the court directs that the defendant be imprisoned until the mandatory surcharge, sex offender registration fee or DNA databank fee is satisfied, it must specify a maximum period of imprisonment not to exceed fifteen days; provided, however, a court may not direct that a defendant be imprisoned until the mandatory surcharge, sex offender registration fee, or DNA databank fee is satisfied or otherwise for failure to pay the mandatory surcharge, sex offender registration fee or DNA databank fee unless the court makes a contemporaneous finding on the record, after according defendant notice and an opportunity to be heard, that the payment of the mandatory surcharge, sex offender registration fee or DNA databank fee upon defendant will not work an unreasonable hardship upon him or her or his or her immediate family.

2. Under no circumstances shall the mandatory surcharge, sex offender registration fee, DNA databank fee or the crime victim assistance fee be waived provided, however, that a court may waive the crime victim assistance fee if such defendant is an eligible youth as defined in subdivision two of section 720.10 of this chapter, and the imposition of such fee would work an unreasonable hardship on the defendant, his or her immediate family, or any other person who is dependent on such defendant for financial support.

3. It shall be the duty of a court of record or administrative tribunal to report to the division of criminal justice services on the disposition and collection of mandatory surcharges, sex offender registration fees or DNA databank fees and crime victim assistance fees. Such report shall include, for all cases, whether the surcharge, sex offender registration fee, DNA databank fee or crime victim assistance fee levied pursuant to subdivision one of section 60.35 of the penal law or section eighteen hundred nine of the vehicle and traffic law has been imposed pursuant to law, collected, or is to be collected by probation or corrections or other officials. The form, manner and frequency of such reports shall be determined by the commissioner of the division of criminal justice services after consultation with the chief administrator of the courts and the commissioner of the department of motor vehicles.

Added by L. 1982, Ch. 55; **Amended** by L. 1983, Ch. 15; L. 1990, Chs. 190, 696; L. 1991, Ch. 166; L. 1992, Ch. 55; L. 1992, Ch. 794, eff. Aug. 7, 1992, renumbering subds. 3, 4 to 4, 5 and adding new subd. 3; L. 1993, Ch. 260; L. 1995, Ch. 3, § 66, amending heading and subd. 1; L. 1995, Ch. 3, § 67, repealing subds. 2, 3, and 5, eff. July 1, 1995; L. 1995, Ch. 3, § 68, renumbering subd. 4 to 2, and amending it; L. 1995, Ch. 3, § 69, renumbering subd. 6 to 3, and amending it. All amendments in Ch. 3, §§ 66-69 apply only when the acts constituting the offense for the conviction of which a mandatory surcharge may be imposed occurred on or after July 1, 1995; L. 2003, Ch. 62, Part F, § 7, eff. May 15, 2003, amending subds. 1–3; L. 2004, Ch. 56, Part F, § 6, eff. Feb. 16, 2005, amending subd. 2.

ANNOTATIONS

Penalties are reasonable.—It has been repeatedly held that Penal Law § 60.35 and CPL § 420.35 treat all persons convicted of Penal Law offenses similarly, and that the penalties imposed pursuant to those sections bear a reasonable relationship to the State's legitimate interest in raising revenues. People v. Dunn, 254 A.D.2d 511, 680 N.Y.S.2d 125 (3d Dept. 1998), *cert. denied*, 527 U.S. 1024 (1999).

Unreasonable hardship.—Evidence of unreasonable hardship upon the defendant or the defendant's family must be demonstrated before the court will consider whether the mandatory surcharge was improperly imposed. People v. Wilkins, 214 A.D.2d 449, 625 N.Y.S.2d 507 (1st Dept. 1995).

—Court did not abuse its discretion in imposing mandatory surcharge where there was no showing that the payment of the surcharge would work an unreasonable hardship upon the defendant; if at the end of his imprisonment the defendant finds himself unable to pay the surcharge, he may then move for a waiver. People v. Lewis, 134 A.D.2d 286, 520 N.Y.S.2d 455 (2d Dept. 1987).

—Court did not abuse its discretion in imposing a mandatory surcharge upon the defendant in accordance with Penal Law § 60.35, since there was no showing that the payment of the surcharge would work an unreasonable hardship on the defendant or her immediate family. People v. Brown, 133 A.D.2d 463, 519 N.Y.S.2d 678 (2d Dept. 1987).

Waiver of surcharge; application.—Defendant is not denied equal protection or due process where the court refuses to permit the defendant to move for waiver of the mandatory surcharge until defendant's prison term is complete. Defendant is not being held because of his difficulty in satisfying the payment of the surcharge. People v. Ramirez, 208 A.D.2d 381, 617 N.Y.S.2d 13 (1st Dept. 1994).

—An application to waive the mandatory surcharge is considered premature where the defendant files the application while presently incarcerated. People v. Perez, 179 A.D.2d 690, 579 N.Y.S.2d 905 (2d Dept. 1992).

Restitution and surcharge.—A sentencing court can simultaneously impose a sentence of restitution to the crime victim along with the mandatory surcharge/crime victim assistance fee, provided the defendant has not yet made restitution. People v. Quinones, 95 N.Y.2d 349, 717 N.Y.S.2d 86, 740 N.E.2d 231 (2000).

§ 420.40. Deferral of a mandatory surcharge; financial hardship hearings.

1. Applicability. The procedure specified in this section governs the deferral of the obligation to pay all or part of a mandatory surcharge, sex offender registration fee or DNA databank fee imposed pursuant to subdivision one of section 60.35 of the penal law and financial hardship hearings relating to mandatory surcharges.

2. On an appearance date set forth in a summons issued pursuant to subdivision three of section 60.35 of the penal law, section eighteen hundred nine of the vehicle and traffic law or section 27.10 of the parks, recreation and historic preservation law, a person upon whom a mandatory surcharge, sex offender registration fee or DNA databank fee was levied shall have an opportunity to present on the record credible and verifiable information establishing that the mandatory surcharge, sex offender registration fee or DNA databank fee should be deferred, in whole or in part, because, due to the indigence of such person the payment of said surcharge, sex offender registration fee or DNA databank fee would work an unreasonable hardship on the person or his or her immediate family.

3. In assessing such information the superior court shall be mindful of the mandatory nature of the surcharge, sex offender registration fee and DNA databank fee, and the important criminal justice and victim services sustained by such fees.

4. Where a court determines that it will defer part or all of a mandatory surcharge, sex offender registration fee or DNA databank fee imposed pursuant to subdivision one of section 60.35 of

the penal law, a statement of such finding and of the facts upon which it is based shall be made part of the record.

5. A court which defers a person's obligation to pay a mandatory surcharge, sex offender registration fee or DNA databank fee imposed pursuant to subdivision one of section 60.35 of the penal law shall do so in a written order. Such order shall not excuse the person from the obligation to pay the surcharge, sex offender registration fee or DNA databank fee. Rather, the court's order shall direct the filing of a certified copy of the order with the county clerk of the county in which the court is situate except where the court which issues such order is the supreme court in which case the order itself shall be filed by the clerk of the court acting in his or her capacity as the county clerk of the county in which the court is situate. Such order shall be entered by the county clerk in the same manner as a judgment in a civil action in accordance with subdivision (a) of rule five thousand sixteen of the civil practice law and rules. The order shall direct that any unpaid balance of the mandatory surcharge, sex offender registration fee or DNA databank fee may be collected in the same manner as a civil judgment. The entered order shall be deemed to constitute a judgment-roll as defined in section five thousand seventeen of the civil practice law and rules and immediately after entry of the order, the county clerk shall docket the entered order as a money judgment pursuant to section five thousand eighteen of such law and rules.

Added by L. 1995, Ch. 3, § 70, eff. July 1, 1995, but applying only when the acts constituting the offense for the conviction of which a mandatory surcharge may be imposed occurred on or after July 1, 1995, pursuant to L. 1995, Ch. 3, § 74, paragraph (i); L. 2003, Ch. 62, Part F, § 8, eff. May 15, 2003, amending subds. 1–5.

ANNOTATION

Deferment denied.—The court balanced the considerations of CPL § 420.40(2) and determined that defendant had failed to assert facts sufficient to warrant a deferment, because he did not distinguish his situation from that of any other inmate who was unemployed prior to his incarceration and has no friends or family to give him extra money while incarcerated. Defendant also failed to establish that he is in any way responsible for the support of any immediate family member who has been adversely affected by deferment of his mandatory surcharge. People v. Parker, 183 Misc. 2d 737, 704 N.Y.S.2d 790 (Sup. Ct. Kings Co. 2000).

ARTICLE 430—SENTENCES OF IMPRISONMENT

Section
430.10   Sentence of imprisonment not to be changed after commencement.
430.20   Commitment of defendant.
430.30   Duty to deliver defendant.

LexisNexis Cross References

Criminal Defense Techniques, Vol. 1B, Ch. 40A, Sentencing Considerations in Computer Crime Cases; Vol. 3A, Ch. 74, Criminal Sentencing Reform—Time to End the Lottery; Vol. 6, Ch. 121, Sentencing; *New York Criminal Practice (2d ed.),* Vol. 4, Ch. 42, Classification of Offenses, Authorized Dispositions and Punishment; *Prosecution and Defense of Sex Crimes,* Ch. 13, Sentencing.

§ 430.10. Sentence of imprisonment not to be changed after commencement.

Except as otherwise specifically authorized by law, when the court has imposed a sentence of imprisonment and such sentence is in accordance with law, such sentence may not be changed, suspended or interrupted once the term or period of the sentence has commenced.

ANNOTATIONS

Commencement of sentence.—Court acted properly where it modified the defendant's sentence within 7 days of pronouncing the original sentence. The defendant had not yet been delivered to the designated institution for commitment. People v. Johnson, 208 A.D.2d 1175, 617 N.Y.S.2d 939 (3d Dept. 1994).

—A defendant who was in medical isolation prior to his transfer to the state authorities was held to not have commenced his sentence. The court was allowed to change the defendant's sentence due to the medical circumstances involved. People v. Baghai-Kermani, 165 Misc. 2d 1, 626 N.Y.S.2d 378 (Sup. Ct. N.Y. Co. 1995).

—Jail facilities of the court and the Department of Corrections are agents of the State. The prisoner receives credit for time spent in one facility awaiting transfer to the other. Thus, the prisoner is under State custody and his sentence has commenced. People v. Ladone, 147 Misc. 2d 269, 556 N.Y.S.2d 215 (Sup. Ct. Queens Co. 1990).

Motions to stay or suspend the execution of judgment pending an appeal from a criminal court.—The court has the power to suspend judgment even where the defendant is currently serving the imposed sentence. People v. Blaho, 162 Misc. 2d 618, 617 N.Y.S.2d 1019 (Sup. Ct. Queens Co. 1994).

Illegal sentence.—The court was not allowed to reverse its holding that defendant was a youthful offender in order to correct an illegally imposed sentence. The court has no authority to revoke its finding once the proceeding has terminated. People v. Calderon, 79 N.Y.2d 61, 580 N.Y.S.2d 163, 588 N.E.2d 61 (1992).

—The defendant's sentence was legal where defendant sentenced upon two prior felony convictions, one of which was reversed. Defendant's sentence was in accordance with the law, and thus, the court lacked the power to reduce defendant's sentence. People v. Taveras, 158 Misc. 2d 358, 601 N.Y.S.2d 256 (Sup. Ct. Queens Co. 1993).

Inadvertent release; remedy.—Defendant's inadvertent release from custody prior to service of his full sentence did not divest courts of jurisdiction to order his reincarceration, and violation of statute is remedied by computing defendant's remaining term on the basis of his original sentence and date of imprisonment and by granting him credit for both such time

and such time as is attributable to the authorities error in releasing him. People v. Cavelli, 50 N.Y.2d 919, 431 N.Y.S.2d 450, 409 N.E.2d 924 (1980).

Resentence.—Neither defendant's constitutional rights under the double jeopardy clause nor the statutory prohibitions under CPL § 430.10 were violated when the court which mistakenly sentenced him to three years, instead of eight as agreed at the time of plea, corrected its error a few months later. People v. Minaya, 54 N.Y.2d 360, 445 N.Y.S.2d 690, 429 N.E.2d 1161 (1981), *cert. denied,* 455 U.S. 1024 (1982).

—Where the appellate court had returned the case to the sentencing court for a proper determination of the gain from gambling activities and imposition of a proper fine pursuant to PL § 80.00, it was improper to resentence defendants, who had served the term initially imposed and had been released, to longer periods of imprisonment. People v. Yannicelli, 40 N.Y.2d 598, 389 N.Y.S.2d 290, 357 N.E.2d 947 (1976).

—When a court's original sentence is defective, it has the inherent power to correct its own error by resentencing the defendant. People v. Ford, 143 A.D.2d 522, 533 N.Y.S.2d 35 (4th Dept. 1988).

—A federal conviction and incarceration of a defendant on a sentence to run consecutive to the state sentence while he was on bail pending appeal in the state court is not a suspension or interruption of that sentence and upon completion of the federal sentence he must serve the balance of the time owed the state. People *ex rel.* Shargel v. Coughlin, 105 Misc. 2d 827, 432 N.Y.S.2d 1004 (Sup. Ct. N.Y. Co. 1980).

No modification rule.—The authority to modify a lawful sentence that has commenced is limited to situations where the record in the case clearly indicates the presence of judicial oversight based on an accidental mistake of fact or an inadvertent misstatement that creates ambiguity in the record. CPL § 430.10 precluded the alteration of defendant's sentence, and the court improperly modified its original sentence to run consecutive to an undischarged term of imprisonment on an unrelated conviction, where the court did not specify whether the sentence was to run consecutively or concurrently to the undischarged term. People v. Richardson, 100 N.Y.2d 847, 767 N.Y.S.2d 384, 799 N.E.2d 607 (2003).

—Judge exceeded his statutory powers when he vacated the unserved portion of inmate's jail sentence and substituted a term of home confinement with electronic monitoring; inasmuch as the jail sentence was separate from and independent of the probationary term, CPL § 410.20 did not furnish authority to vacate the former, and the judge was bound by the no-modification rule of CPL § 430.10. Pirro v. Angiolillo, 89 N.Y.2d 351, 653 N.Y.S.2d 237, 675 N.E.2d 1189 (1996).

—After a defendant has begun serving a sentence of incarceration, a court has the power to correct an illegal sentence or a sentence that was imposed based on an inadvertent error or misstatement that creates an ambiguity in the record. A court may not alter a validly imposed sentence once it is being served. People v. Carpenter, 19 A.D.3d 730, 796 N.Y.S.2d 730 (3d Dept. 2005).

Sentence; authority to vacate.—The court did not have the authority to vacate the defendant's sentence where the defendant failed to uphold his vow to truthfully testify at the trial of the co-defendant. Defendant's actions did not constitute fraud, thus, the court lacked the power to vacate. People v. Smalls, 162 A.D.2d 642, 556 N.Y.S.2d 957 (2d Dept. 1990).

Sentence; interruption of.—Where the Appellate court found that the defendant was a second felony offender, vacated his sentence, and ordered resentencing, defendant's sentence was held to be interrupted. Anderson v. Kirk, 72 N.Y.2d 995, 534 N.Y.S.2d 369, 530 N.E.2d 1289 (1988).

—Defendant's sentence was not interrupted where the defendant was released from Federal custody and subsequently, after a lengthy time of liberty, was sent to a state correctional facility. Defendant was not allowed to credit the time spent at liberty toward the state sentence. Franks v. Koehler, 159 A.D.2d 213, 552 N.Y.S.2d 203 (1st Dept. 1990).

Sentence; narcotics.—Sentence was reduced to the one originally negotiated for where a misinterpretation of the law prevented defendant from receiving the bargained-for sentence of one to three years following a plea of guilty to the criminal sale of a controlled substance in the third degree. People v. Rivera, 82 A.D.2d 760, 440 N.Y.S.2d 206 (1st Dept. 1981).

§ 430.20. Commitment of defendant.

1. **In general.** When a sentence of imprisonment is pronounced, or when [*] sentence consists of a fine and the court has directed that the defendant be imprisoned until it is satisfied, the defendant must forthwith be committed to the custody of the appropriate public servant and detained until the sentence is complied with.

2. [*Repealed Sept. 1, 2009.*] Indeterminate and determinate sentences. In the case of an indeterminate or determinate sentence of imprisonment, commitment must be to the custody of the state department of correctional services as provided in subdivision one of section 70.20 of the penal law. The order of commitment must direct that the defendant be delivered to an institution designated by the commissioner of correctional services in accordance with the provisions of the correction law.

2. [*Effective Sept. 1, 2009.*] Indeterminate and reformatory sentences. In the case of an indeterminate or reformatory sentence of imprisonment, commitment must be to the custody of the state department of correctional services as provided in subdivision one of section 70.20 and section 75.05 of the penal law. The order of commitment must direct that the defendant be delivered to an institution designated by the commissioner of correctional services in accordance with the provisions of the correction law.

3. **Definite and intermittent sentences.** In the case of a definite or intermittent sentence of imprisonment, commitment must be as follows:

(a) In counties contained within New York City or in any county that has a county department of correction, commitment must be to the custody of the department of correction of such city or county;

(b) In any other case, commitment must be to the county jail, workhouse or penitentiary, or to a penitentiary outside the county and the order of commitment must specify the institution to which the defendant is to be delivered.

4. [*Repealed Sept. 1, 2009.*] Certain resentences. When a sentence of imprisonment that has been imposed on a defendant is vacated and a new sentence is imposed on such defendant for the same offense, or for an offense based upon the same act, if the term of the new definite or determinate sentence or the maximum term of the new indeterminate sentence so imposed is less than or equal to that of the vacated sentence:

(a) where the time served by the defendant on the vacated sentence is equal to or greater than the term or maximum term of the new sentence, the new sentence shall be deemed to be served in its entirety and the defendant shall not be committed to a correctional facility pursuant to said sentence; and

(b) where the defendant was under the supervision of a local conditional release commission or the division of parole at the time the sentence was vacated, then the commitment shall direct that said conditional release or parole be recommenced, and the defendant shall not be committed to a correctional facility pursuant to said sentence, except as a result of revocation of parole or of conditional release; and

(c) where the defendant was not under the supervision of the division of parole at the time the indeterminate or determinate sentence was vacated, but would immediately be eligible for conditional release from the new indeterminate or determinate sentence, the court shall ascertain from the department of correctional services whether the defendant has earned a sufficient amount of good time under the vacated sentence so as to require the conditional release of the defendant under the new sentence; in the event the defendant has earned a sufficient amount of good time, the court shall stay execution of sentence until the defendant surrenders at a correctional facility pursuant to the direction of the department of correctional services, which shall occur no later than sixty days after imposition of sentence; upon said stay of execution, the court clerk shall immediately mail to the commissioner of correctional services a certified copy of the commitment reflecting said stay of execution and the name, mailing address and telephone number of the defendant's legal representative; in the event the defendant fails to surrender as directed by the department of correctional services, the department shall notify the court which shall thereafter remand the defendant to custody pursuant to section 430.30 of this article; and

(d) upon the resentence of a defendant as described in this subdivision, the court clerk shall immediately mail a certified copy of the commitment to the commissioner of correctional services if the vacated sentence or the new sentence is an indeterminate or determinate sentence and no mailing is required by paragraph (c) of this subdivision; additionally, the court clerk shall immediately mail a certified copy of the new commitment to the head of the appropriate local correctional facility if the vacated sentence or the new sentence is a definite sentence.

4. [*Effective Sept. 1, 2009.*] Certain resentences. When a sentence of imprisonment that has been imposed on a defendant is vacated and a new sentence is imposed on such defendant for the same offense, or for an offense based upon the same act, if the term of the new definite sentence or the maximum term of the new indeterminate sentence so imposed is less than or equal to that of the vacated sentence:

(a) where the time served by the defendant on the vacated sentence is equal to or greater than the term or maximum term of the new sentence, the new sentence shall be deemed to be served in its entirety and the defendant shall not be committed to a correctional facility pursuant to said sentence; and

(b) where the defendant was under the supervision of a local conditional release commission or the division of parole at the time the sentence was vacated, then the commitment shall direct that said conditional release or parole be recommenced, and the defendant shall not be committed to a correctional facility pursuant to said sentence, except as a result of revocation of parole or of conditional release; and

(c) where the defendant was not under the supervision of the division of parole at the time the indeterminate sentence was vacated, but would immediately be eligible for conditional release from the new indeterminate sentence, the court shall ascertain from the department of correctional services whether the defendant has earned a sufficient amount of good time under the vacated sentence so as to require the conditional release of the defendant under the new sentence; in the event the defendant has earned a sufficient amount of good time, the court shall stay execution of sentence until the defendant surrenders at a correctional facility pursuant to the direction of the department of correctional services, which shall occur no later than sixty days after imposition of sentence; upon said stay of execution, the court clerk shall immediately mail to the commissioner of correctional services a certified copy of the commitment reflecting said stay of execution and the name, mailing address and telephone number of the defendant's legal representative; in the event the defendant fails to surrender as directed by the department of correctional services, the department shall notify the court which shall thereafter remand the defendant to custody pursuant to section 430.30 of this article; and

(d) upon the resentence of a defendant as described in this subdivision, the court clerk shall immediately mail a certified copy of the commitment to the commissioner of correctional services if the vacated sentence or the new sentence is an indeterminate sentence and no mailing is required

by paragraph (c) of this subdivision; additionally, the court clerk shall immediately mail a certified copy of the new commitment to the head of the appropriate local correctional facility if the vacated sentence or the new sentence is a definite sentence.

5. Commitment for failure to pay fine. Where the sentence consists of a fine and the court has directed that the defendant be imprisoned until it is satisfied, commitment must be as follows:

(a) If the sentence also includes a term of imprisonment, commitment must be to the same institution as is designated for service of the term of imprisonment, and the period of commitment commences (i) when the term of imprisonment is satisfied, or (ii) with the approval of the state board of parole, when the defendant becomes eligible for parole, or (iii) when the defendant becomes eligible for conditional release, whichever occurs first; provided, however, that the court may direct that the period of imprisonment for the fine run concurrently with the term of imprisonment; and

(b) In any other case, commitment must be to the agency or institution that would be designated in the case of a definite sentence.
* As originally enacted.

Amended by L. 1971, Ch. 788; L. 1994, Ch. 370, § 1, eff. July 20, 1994, amending subd. 4; L. 1995, Ch. 3, § 35, amending subds. 2 and 4, eff. Oct. 1, 1995, and amendments repealed Sept. 1, 2009, pursuant to L. 1995, Ch. 3, § 74, paragraph (d), as amended. The amendments in subds. 2 and 4, changing the word "reformatory" to "determinate" and adding the phrase "or determinate" after the word "indeterminate" apply only to offenses committed on or after Oct. 1, 1995, and offenses committed before Oct. 1, 1995 will be governed by the provisions of law in effect at the time the offense was committed, pursuant to L. 1995, Ch. 3, § 74, paragraph (e); L. 2005, Ch. 56, Part D, § 20, eff. Apr. 1, 2005, extending repeal date of subds. 2 and 4 to Sept. 1, 2009.

ANNOTATIONS

Acceptance of inmates; delay not allowed.—The State is responsible for accepting inmates from local facilities who are committed to the custody of the Department of Correctional Services. The State cannot delay accepting the inmates on the claim that the state and local facilities are overcrowded. James R. Ayers v. Coughlin, 72 N.Y.2d 346, 533 N.Y.S.2d 849, 530 N.E.2d 373 (1988).

—The Correctional Services Department must comply with an order requiring it to receive "state-ready" inmates who were already in custody for more than 14 days subsequent to their sentences. The department's delay of 7 months in complying with the order was not acceptable; thus, subjecting the department to civil contempt. Norwood E. Jackson v. New York State Dept. of Correctional Servs., 173 A.D.2d 467, 570 N.Y.S.2d 91 (2d Dept. 1991).

Generally.—CPL § 430.20 must be read in conjunction with § 70.30(1) of the Penal Law, which designates the date upon which defendant's sentence begins as the date on which the defendant is received at the institution. Franks v. Koehler, 159 A.D.2d 213, 552 N.Y.S.2d 203 (1st Dept. 1990).

Release of the defendant.—The release of the defendant to the custody of federal authorities subsequent to his commitment in State custody was not authorized. Defendant was entitled to receive credit towards the state sentence for his time spent in federal prison. Musto v. Sielaff, 194 A.D.2d 491, 599 N.Y.S.2d 563 (1st Dept. 1993).

—The transportation of the parole violators to a correctional institution of the State is equivalent to the transportation of newly sentenced defendants. Thus, the sheriff is held responsible for the transportation. Broome County v. State, 152 A.D.2d 160, 547 N.Y.S.2d 461 (3d Dept. 1989).

—Because relator received an indeterminate sentence, he is entitled to release only when he serves the maximum term of his new sentence. The court properly denied his petition because he has not served the maximum term of his new sentence. A hearing was not necessary because there was no triable issue of fact. People ex rel. Hill v. Kelly, 269 A.D.2d 851, 704 N.Y.S.2d 761 (4th Dept. 2000).

Standing to compel transfer.—Inmates who are sentenced to state prison and who have an interest in seeking admission to SHOCK, work release, education and rehabilitation programs, or release on parole, are within the "zone of interests" protected by CPL § 430.20, and therefore, state prisoners have standing to compel their transfer under § CPL 430.20. People ex rel. Perdue v. Jablonsky, 174 Misc. 2d 604, 665 N.Y.S.2d 827 (Sup. Ct. Nassau Co. 1997).

§ 430.30. Duty to deliver defendant.

In counties contained within New York City and in counties that have a commissioner of correction who is responsible for detention of defendants in criminal actions, it is the duty of the commissioner of correction of such city or county to deliver the defendant forthwith to the proper institution in accordance with the commitment. In all other counties it is the duty of the sheriff to deliver the defendant forthwith to the proper institution in accordance with the commitment.

ANNOTATIONS

Generally.—The Executive Law authorizes the sheriff to assume responsibility for the transportation of parole violators to the appropriate state facilities from the local jails. Broome County v. State of New York, 152 A.D.2d 160, 547 N.Y.S.2d 461 (3d Dept. 1989).

—"Forthwith" delivery of the defendant was held to mean within a reasonable time and with promptness, taking into consideration the circumstances involved in the case. County of Onondaga v. New York State Dept. of Correctional Servs., 97 A.D.2d 957, 468 N.Y.S.2d 760 (4th Dept. 1983).

—Where petitioner was returned to the federal authorities rather than being transferred to a state prison to commence his state sentence, petitioner was not delivered "forthwith" to the appropriate institution pursuant to CPL § 430.30. Rodriguez v. McMikens, 133 Misc. 2d 154, 506 N.Y.S.2d 646 (Sup. Ct. N.Y. Co. 1986).

TITLE M—PROCEEDINGS AFTER JUDGMENT

ARTICLE 440—POST-JUDGMENT MOTIONS

Section

LexisNexis Cross References

Criminal Defense Techniques, Vol. 2, Ch. 43, State Post-Conviction Remedies; Vol. 2, Ch. 44, Federal Habeas Corpus for State Prisoners, Vol. 6, Ch. 122, Appeals and Post-Conviction Remedies; Vol. 6, Ch. 123, Miscellaneous Motions; *New York Criminal Practice (2d ed.),* Vol. 4, Ch. 43, Post-Judgment Motions.

§ 440.10. Motion to vacate judgment.

1. At any time after the entry of a judgment, the court in which it was entered may, upon motion of the defendant, vacate such judgment upon the ground that:

(a) The court did not have jurisdiction of the action or of the person of the defendant; or

(b) The judgment was procured by duress, misrepresentation or fraud on the part of the court or a prosecutor or a person acting for or in behalf of a court or a prosecutor; or

(c) Material evidence adduced at a trial resulting in the judgment was false and was, prior to the entry of the judgment, known by the prosecutor or by the court to be false; or

(d) Material evidence adduced by the people at a trial resulting in the judgment was procured in violation of the defendant's rights under the constitution of this state or of the United States; or

(e) During the proceedings resulting in the judgment, the defendant, by reason of mental disease or defect, was incapable of understanding or participating in such proceedings; or

(f) Improper and prejudicial conduct not appearing in the record occurred during a trial resulting in the judgment which conduct, if it had appeared in the record, would have required a reversal of the judgment upon an appeal therefrom; or

(g) New evidence has been discovered since the entry of a judgment based upon a verdict of guilty after trial, which could not have been produced by the defendant at the trial even with due diligence on his part and which is of such character as to create a probability that had such evidence been received at the trial the verdict would have been more favorable to the defendant; provided that a motion based upon such ground must be made with due diligence after the discovery of such alleged new evidence; or

(h) The judgment was obtained in violation of a right of the defendant under the constitution of this state or of the United States.

2. Notwithstanding the provisions of subdivision one, the court must deny a motion to vacate a judgment when:

(a) The ground or issue raised upon the motion was previously determined on the merits upon an appeal from the judgment, unless since the time of such appellate determination there has been a retroactively effective change in the law controlling such issue; or

(b) The judgment is, at the time of the motion, appealable or pending on appeal, and sufficient facts appear on the record with respect to the ground or issue raised upon the motion to permit adequate review thereof upon such an appeal; or

(c) Although sufficient facts appear on the record of the proceedings underlying the judgment to have permitted, upon appeal from such judgment, adequate review of the ground or issue raised upon the motion, no such appellate review or determination occurred owing to the defendant's unjustifiable failure to take or perfect an appeal during the prescribed period or to his unjustifiable failure to raise such ground or issue upon an appeal actually perfected by him; or

(d) The ground or issue raised relates solely to the validity of the sentence and not to the validity of the conviction.

3. Notwithstanding the provisions of subdivision one, the court may deny a motion to vacate a judgment when:

(a) Although facts in support of the ground or issue raised upon the motion could with due diligence by the defendant have readily been made to appear on the record in a manner providing adequate basis for review of such ground or issue upon an appeal from the judgment, the defendant unjustifiably failed to adduce such matter prior to sentence and the ground or issue in question was not subsequently determined upon appeal. This paragraph does not apply to a motion based upon deprivation of the right to counsel at the trial or upon failure of the trial court to advise the defendant of such right; or

(b) The ground or issue raised upon the motion was previously determined on the merits upon a prior motion or proceeding in a court of this state, other than an appeal from the judgment, or upon a motion or proceeding in a federal court; unless since the time of such determination there has been a retroactively effective change in the law controlling such issue; or

(c) Upon a previous motion made pursuant to this section, the defendant was in a position adequately to raise the ground or issue underlying the present motion but did not do so.

Although the court may deny the motion under any of the circumstances specified in this subdivision, in the interest of justice and for good cause shown it may in its discretion grant the motion if it is otherwise meritorious and vacate the judgment.

4. If the court grants the motion, it must, except as provided in subdivision five, vacate the judgment, and must dismiss the accusatory instrument, or order a new trial, or take such other action as is appropriate in the circumstances.

5. Upon granting the motion upon the ground, as prescribed in paragraph (g) of subdivision one, that newly discovered evidence creates a probability that had such evidence been received at the trial the verdict would have been more favorable to the defendant in that the conviction would have been for a lesser offense than the one contained in the verdict, the court may either:

(a) Vacate the judgment and order a new trial; or

(b) With the consent of the people, modify the judgment by reducing it to one of conviction for such lesser offense. In such case, the court must re-sentence the defendant accordingly.

6. Upon a new trial resulting from an order vacating a judgment pursuant to this section, the indictment is deemed to contain all the counts and to charge all the offenses which it contained and charged at the time the previous trial was commenced, regardless of whether any count was dismissed by the court in the course of such trial,

except (a) those upon or of which the defendant was acquitted or deemed to have been acquitted, and (b) those dismissed by the order vacating the judgment, and (c) those previously dismissed by an appellate court upon an appeal from the judgment, or by any court upon a previous post-judgment motion.

7. Upon an order which vacates a judgment based upon a plea of guilty to an accusatory instrument or a part thereof, but which does not dismiss the entire accusatory instrument, the criminal action is, in the absence of an express direction to the contrary, restored to its prepleading status and the accusatory instrument is deemed to contain all the counts and to charge all the offenses which it contained and charged at the time of the entry of the plea, except those subsequently dismissed under circumstances specified in paragraphs (b) and (c) of subdivision six. Where the plea of guilty was entered and accepted, pursuant to subdivision three of section 220.30, upon the condition that it constituted a complete disposition not only of the accusatory instrument underlying the judgment vacated but also of one or more other accusatory instruments against the defendant then pending in the same court, the order of vacation completely restores such other accusatory instruments; and such is the case even though such order dismisses the main accusatory instrument underlying the judgment.

ANNOTATIONS

Scope of section.—CPL § 440.10 is designed and delineates the grounds for vacating a judgment of conviction and does not include a situation where the defendant is essentially seeking an extension of time for taking an appeal via resentencing rather than a vacatur of his conviction; this latter relief is provided for in CPL § 460.30. People v. Corso, 40 N.Y.2d 578, 388 N.Y.S.2d 886, 357 N.E.2d 357 (1976).

—CPL § 440.10 was intended to encompass contentions that formerly could have been raised on an application for post conviction relief in the nature of coram nobis, a post conviction application for a new trial upon the ground of newly discovered evidence, and those which may be raised in State and Federal habeas corpus proceedings, as well as other contentions. People v. Crimmins, 38 N.Y.2d 407, 381 N.Y.S.2d 1, 343 N.E.2d 719 (1975).

—A motion to vacate judgment pursuant to CPL § 440.10 is within the sole discretion of the court addressing the motion. The court has the discretion to vacate the judgment or to hold a hearing on the matter. People v. Robinson, 211 A.D.2d 733, 622 N.Y.S.2d 69 (2d Dept. 1995).

—Defendant's post-judgment motion relating to the insufficiency of his allocution providing the substantive basis for his guilty plea was not preserved for appellate review where it was first raised two years after sentences were imposed, and not raised, as required, "by motion in the court of first instance prior to conviction." People v. McKenzie, 88 A.D.2d 646, 450 N.Y.S.2d 218 (2d Dept. 1982).

Appeal limited to issues in notice of appeal.—Court would not address on appeal an argument that did not relate to the sentence imposed, because defendant's notice of appeal limited the scope of appeal to the sentence imposed. People v. Popson, 262 A.D.2d 989, 694 N.Y.S.2d 541 (4th Dept. 1999).

Coram nobis.—Defendant's motion to vacate judgment on the claim that his constitutional rights were violated must be supported by evidence. Defendant's opportunity to procure such evidence was not impaired. People v. Fox, 172 A.D.2d 218, 567 N.Y.S.2d 723 (1st Dept. 1991).

Coram nobis; change in deportation law.—Defendant was not entitled to a writ of *coram nobis* to obtain relief against a judgment because of a defense arising subsequent to rendition of the judgment; the change in the federal deportation law did not deprive defendant of due process, as deportation is a collateral consequence of defendant's criminal conviction and not within the control of the court system. People v. Agero, 234 A.D.2d 94, 651 N.Y.S.2d 430 (1st Dept. 1996).

Coram nobis; bad faith of D.A.; reduced charge for co-defendant.—There was no indication that co-defendant made deal with D.A. to plead guilty to second degree manslaughter rather than face first degree murder charges in exchange for testimony against defendant but rather a possible arrangement between the D.A. and the Court, uncommunicated to the co-defendant. Defendant was not denied a fair trial as a result. People v. Edwards, 39 A.D.2d 522, 330 N.Y.S.2d 469 (1st Dept. 1972), *aff'd,* 32 N.Y.2d 846, 346 N.Y.S.2d 271, 299 N.E.2d 683, *modified,* 33 N.Y.2d 639, 347 N.Y.S.2d 586, 301 N.E.2d 554 (1973).

Coram nobis; hearing discretionary.—No hearing required where defendant's coram nobis application included affidavits from three co-defendants stating that a prosecutor had threatened them with increased charges if they testified on behalf of defendant, no hearing was warranted since the affidavits did not contain the nature of any testimony that the co-defendants could offer or how it could be of value to the defendant. People v. Session, 34 N.Y.2d 254, 357 N.Y.S.2d 409, 313 N.E.2d 728 (1974).

Coram nobis; petition; knowledge of right to appeal.—One sentenced to 10-20 years on plea of guilty to first degree manslaughter in settlement of murder 1st indictment, on parole, and seeking coram nobis relief, must in addition to asserting that he was not advised by anyone of his right to appeal allege that he did not know of that right and if he had he would have exercised it, and further that the sentence was excessive. People v. Rodriguez, 40 A.D.2d 463, 336 N.Y.S.2d 335 (1st Dept. 1972), *aff'd,* 33 N.Y.2d 527, 347 N.Y.S.2d 433, 301 N.E.2d 421 (1973).

Coram nobis—ineffective assistance of counsel.—In the typical case it would be better, and in some cases essential, that an appellate attack on the effectiveness of counsel be bottomed on an evidentiary exploration by collateral or post conviction proceeding. People v. Brown, 45 N.Y.2d 852, 410 N.Y.S.2d 287, 382 N.E.2d 1149 (1978).

—Defendant was not denied effective assistance of counsel where it was established the defendant rejected all options proposed by the attorney in regard to alibi witnesses. The attorney acted diligently in issuing subpoenas for the witnesses. People v. Williams, 206 A.D.2d 331, 615 N.Y.S.2d 23 (1st Dept. 1994).

—Since ineffectiveness of counsel is usually not demonstrable on the main record it is advisable to bottom such an attack on an evidentiary hearing exploration proceeding brought under CPL § 440.10 to show that counsel's performance was deficient, that counsel made errors so serious that counsel was not functioning and that the errors deprived defendant of a fair trial and a reliable result. People v. Norris, 108 A.D.2d 760, 484 N.Y.S.2d 917 (2d Dept. 1985).

—Defendant's constitutional rights were not violated where the court decided that the defendant was provided with meaningful representation by counsel. Defendant's contentions did not suggest to the court that substitution of counsel was mandated. People v. Frayer, 215 A.D.2d 862, 627 N.Y.S.2d 107 (3d Dept. 1995).

—Ineffective assistance of counsel was not established from the record where the record disclosed the use of a reasonable trial strategy. People v. Cutting, 210 A.D.2d 791,621 N.Y.S.2d 149 (3d Dept. 1994).

Brady and Rosario material.—Even if documents constituted *Rosario* or *Brady* material, there is no reasonable possibility that the People's failure to turn over documents at trial affected the verdict, where the documents were generated after the witness had testified and were entirely consistent with the witness's testimony regarding his agreement with the prosecution. People v. Mancuso, 232 A.D.2d 659, 649 N.Y.S.2d 447 (2d Dept. 1996).

—Conviction reinstated; Supreme Court erred in vacating defendant's judgment of conviction based on the People's failure to disclose the criminal record of their key witness, where testimony regarding witness's regular participation in illegal gambling activity and his unlawful possession of a loaded

weapon was elicited during cross-examination at the defendant's trial, and there was no reasonable possibility that the failure to disclose the witness's criminal record contributed to the verdict. People v. Santos, 232 A.D.2d 508, 648 N.Y.S.2d 660 (2d Dept. 1996).

Duress.—Motion to vacate was denied even though defendant was under great pressure in entering her plea as she had been convicted of a felony previously, had small children, no knowledge of whether bail would be granted and what sentence would be imposed if convicted, however, all of these factors were fully discussed with her attorney and with full knowledge of all the circumstances she determined not to risk a trial and entered a plea. People v. Parker, 85 A.D.2d 565, 445 N.Y.S.2d 443 (1st Dept. 1981).

Prisoner certified to Dannemora; application for post-conviction relief; prior sanity hearing; procedure.—In bringing an application for post-conviction relief on behalf of a prisoner certified to Dannemora, the petitioner must first have a hearing to determine his mental capacity to prosecute and participate in a post-conviction proceeding. The papers for such sanity hearing must contain factual allegations that the prisoner-inmate is competent enough to warrant his examination and a hearing, without regard to time limitations imposed by Correction Law § 408 upon the periodic reviews there provided. The papers must also contain factual allegations sufficient to demonstrate, *prima facie,* the inmate's right to post-conviction relief. If the court finds, upon sufficient papers that: (1) such right has been shown prima facie and (2) the right to a competency hearing has been demonstrated, it shall direct and conduct such a hearing. If it finds that the inmate is competent to understand and participate in a post-conviction hearing, it shall direct that the application for this hearing be made to the court in which the conviction was obtained. People v. Aponte, 28 N.Y.2d 343, 321 N.Y.S.2d 871, 270 N.E.2d 700 (1971), *cert. denied,* 404 U.S. 859 (1972).

Prisoner certified to Dannemora; application for post-conviction remedy to challenge conviction; prior sanity hearing required.—A prisoner certified to Dannemora State Hospital as mentally ill, and who wishes to attack his conviction by application for post-conviction remedy, must first apply to the Supreme Court, within the county of the Hospital's situs, for a prior determination of the prisoner's competency to prosecute and participate in a proceeding for post-conviction relief. People v. Aponte, 28 N.Y.2d 343, 321 N.Y.S.2d 871, 270 N.E.2d 700 (1971), *cert. denied,* 404 U.S. 859 (1972).

Purpose of coram nobis hearing pursuant to People v. Montgomery.—Purpose of a coram nobis hearing under *People v. Montgomery,* 24 N.Y.2d 130, 299 N.Y.S.2d 156, 247 N.E.2d 130, is for limited purpose of determining whether defendant should be resentenced *nunc pro tunc* in order for time to appeal to run anew. The prior finding of guilt cannot be attacked. People v. Bennett, 35 A.D.2d 1000, 318 N.Y.S.2d 111 (2d Dept. 1970), *aff'd,* 29 N.Y.2d 494 (1971).

Adequate aid of counsel; conflict of interest.—Reversible error was committed where the trial court made no inquiry to ascertain whether the defendant was aware of the potential risks inherent in defense counsel's joint representation of defendant and a co-defendant where there was a "significant possibility" of conflict of interest between defendant and co-defendant. People v. Crump, 53 N.Y.2d 824, 440 N.Y.S.2d 170, 422 N.E.2d 815 (1981); *see also* People v. Burwell, 53 N.Y.2d 849, 440 N.Y.S.2d 177, 422 N.E.2d 822 (1981).

Failure to present adequate defense.—Where the record revealed a complete lack of investigation and preparation on part of defense counsel so as to amount to a total failure to present cause of the defendant in any fundamental respect, reversal of the conviction is required. People v. LaBree, 34 N.Y.2d 257, 357 N.Y.S.2d 412, 313 N.E.2d 730 (1974).

Coercion of guilty plea; hearing.—Defendant's claim that his plea was induced by coercion was unfounded where the record established that the defendant knowingly and voluntarily agreed to the plea. People v. Ross, 182 A.D.2d 1022, 583 N.Y.S.2d 34 (3d Dept. 1992).

Defendant's absence when jury note was read.—CPL § 440.10 motion is proper vehicle for defendant's claim that reversal was required because he was not present when jury note was read. People v. DePillo, 262 A.D.2d 996, 693 N.Y.S.2d 376 (4th Dept. 1999).

Double jeopardy.—Defendant's motion to vacate judgment of conviction should not have been denied without a hearing where defendant, who pleaded guilty to certain State charges, contended that she was deprived of effective assistance of counsel since lawyer failed to inform her of her right to impose statutory claim of former jeopardy, under CPL § 40.20 and 40.30, for prior prosecution for same offense in Federal Court. People v. Dodson, 79 A.D.2d 976, 434 N.Y.S.2d 453 (2d Dept. 1981).

Effective assistance of counsel.—A motion to vacate judgment under CPL § 440.10(1)(h) does not include the claim of ineffective assistance of appellate counsel and to force the fit would constitute legislation by judicial fiat. People v. Bachert, 69 N.Y.2d 593, 516 N.Y.S.2d 623, 625, 509 N.E.2d 318 (1987).

—Defendant's attorney's suspension on the ground of mental disability, subsequent to his representation of defendant at his guilty plea proceeding, did not warrant vacatur. "[A]n attorney's suspension on the ground of mental disability does not itself establish that every representation of a criminal defendant by that attorney during the time period giving rise to the suspension was necessarily ineffective, regardless of all other circumstances." People v. Lopez, 298 A.D.2d 114, 747 N.Y.S.2d 498 (1st Dept. 2002).

—Court properly denied defendant's ineffective assistance claim, which was based primarily on counsel's failure to utilize purported impeachment material that was undisputedly in counsel's possession, because it raised no issue that could not be resolved on the trial record, and the record established that defendant received meaningful representation. People v. Orr, 240 A.D.2d 213, 659 N.Y.S.2d 1 (1st Dept. 1997).

—The evidence adduced at the CPL § 440.10 hearing overwhelmingly demonstrated the defense counsel's lack of preparation and his failure to understand the applicable law, communicate with the defendant, investigate the facts of the case, and prepare the defendant to testify, thereby depriving defendant of effective assistance of counsel. People v. Smith, 237 A.D.2d 388, 655 N.Y.S.2d 416 (2d Dept. 1997).

—Representation by attorney was not ineffective simply because he failed to call defendant's landlady as a witness. People v. Kirby, 133 A.D.2d 652, 519 N.Y.S.2d 761 (2d Dept. 1987).

—A CPL § 440.10 motion is not an appropriate method for raising a claim of ineffective assistance of appellate counsel. People v. Byrne, 133 A.D.2d 485, 519 N.Y.S.2d 279 (3d Dept. 1987).

—It is a perfectly acceptable strategy for counsel to concede defendant's guilt of a lesser included charge during opening and closing statements in the hope that the jury would then be more receptive to the claim that the defendant was innocent of the far more serious charge. The concession was not the equivalent of entering a guilty plea for the defendant and did not constitute ineffective assistance of counsel, which would warrant vacatur of conviction. People v. Washington, 19 A.D.3d 1180, 796 N.Y.S.2d 500 (4th Dept. 2005).

Effective assistance of counsel; exception to procedural bar.—Although a defendant is precluded from seeking to vacate a judgment through a 440.10 motion where the grounds alleged in that motion were previously decided on the merits by a prior appeal (440.10[2][a]), an exception exists where, as here, the claim of ineffective assistance of counsel is based on an alleged failure to provide proper advice concerning sentencing exposure. People v. Reynolds, 309 A.D.2d 976, 766 N.Y.S.2d 142 (3d Dept. 2003).

Failure to make motion to vacate.—The defendant convicted of robbery in the first degree who was in possession of an inoperable weapon should have moved to vacate the conviction on that ground and not raise the issue on appeal. People v. Pellegrino, 91 A.D.2d 942, 458 N.Y.S.2d 556 (1st Dept. 1983), aff'd, 60 N.Y.2d 636, 467 N.Y.S.2d 355, 454 N.E.2d 938 (1983).

Greater sentence after retrial; no grounds for.—It was error for the court to have imposed a greater sentence following the retrial in the absence of objective information appearing affirmatively on the record concerning identifiable conduct on the part of the defendant occurring after the time of the original sentence which would justify the imposition of a harsher sentence and a hearing should be held on the defendant's application to vacate the judgment. People v. Simone, 78 A.D.2d 685, 432 N.Y.S.2d 248 (2d Dept. 1980).

Habeas corpus.—Court properly dismissed inmate's habeas petition where the inmate's claims of ineffective assistance of counsel and deprivation of the right to testify to the grand jury,

could be addressed upon direct appeal from the judgment. People ex rel. Gasper v. Sullivan, 164 A.D.2d 926, 559 N.Y.S.2d 585 (2d Dept. 1990).

—Defendant was denied habeas corpus relief on his claim of excessive sentencing. Defendant's sentence did not exceed the statutorily authorized penalty. Defendant's allegations should have been addressed pursuant to a CPL motion. People ex rel. Cotton II v. Senkowski 187 A.D.2d 850, 589 N.Y.S.2d 947 (3d Dept. 1992).

—Where there exists an independent basis for petitioner's detention, an application for habeas corpus relief will be denied. People ex rel. Hodge v. Wells, 133 A.D.2d 497, 519 N.Y.S.2d 423, 425 (3d Dept. 1987).

—Failure to file motion to vacate conviction precludes collateral attack by habeas corpus proceeding. People ex rel. Evans v. Fogg, 77 A.D.2d 750, 431 N.Y.S.2d 196 (3d Dept. 1980).

Harmless error.—The evidence of the defendant's guilt was so overwhelming that the alleged error in the admission of his co-defendant's confession was harmless beyond a reasonable doubt. Furthermore, no exception was taken to the charge, and no request was made for any limiting instructions. Accordingly, the application for a writ of error coram nobis was correctly denied. People v. Walker, 31 N.Y.2d 970, 341 N.Y.S.2d 111, 293 N.E.2d 257 (1973).

—Where the court did not instruct the jury about a missing witness, the action of the court was held as harmless error. The defendant was charged under acting in concert and his guilt was established by overwhelming evidence. People v. Lucas, 177 A.D.2d 599, 576 N.Y.S.2d 170 (2d Dept. 1991).

Hearing.—The court acted within its discretion in denying defendant's motion to vacate his 1959 judgment of conviction without an evidentiary hearing where the merits of the "newly discovered evidence" issue raised in the collateral proceeding were previously decided on a prior CPL § 440.10 motion. People v. Glinton, 74 N.Y.2d 779, 545 N.Y.S.2d 93, 543 N.E.2d 736 (1989).

—Court erred in summarily denying motion to vacate judgment where defendant's moving papers set forth material facts which if established would have entitled the defendant to the relief sought. People v. Ferreras, 70 N.Y.2d 630, 518 N.Y.S.2d 780, 512 N.E.2d 301 (1987).

—In the course of plea discussions, the prosecutor and the court misapprehended defendant's status for sentencing purposes, mistakenly believing him to be a persistent violent felony offender. Because defense counsel failed to ascertain and correct the misapprehension, counsel's conduct fell below the requirements of reasonably effective assistance. Defendant is entitled to a hearing to determine whether it is reasonably probable that an acceptable plea bargain would have been reached but for counsel's failure. People v. Garcia, 19 A.D.3d 17, 795 N.Y.S.2d 216 (1st Dept. 2005).

—Court properly denied defendant's motion to vacate the judgment of conviction without an evidentiary hearing where the defendant failed to show that facts dehors the record were material and would entitle him to vacatur. People v. Buckley, 139 A.D.2d 589, 527 N.Y.S.2d 83 (2d Dept. 1988).

—Failure to show actual prejudice resulting from the court's delay on its decision to vacate judgment denies the defendant any relief. People v. Valenti, 175 A.D.2d 489, 572 N.Y.S.2d 766 (3d Dept. 1991).

—Court properly denied defendant's CPL Article 440 motion without a hearing since sufficient facts appeared on the record with respect to the ground raised. People v. Hill, 146 A.D.2d 823, 536 N.Y.S.2d 566 (3d Dept. 1989).

—In order to be entitled to a hearing on a CPL § 440.10 motion based upon a claim of ineffectiveness of counsel, a defendant must show that the nonrecord facts sought to be established are material and would entitle him to relief. People v. Kittle, 154 A.D.2d 782, 546 N.Y.S.2d 233 (3d Dept. 1989).

—Once a defendant establishes through a sworn affidavit that his claim that he was denied a constitutional right, pursuant to CPL § 440, is not incredible on its face and is not shown to be false by unquestionable documentary proof, a full hearing is required to explore the issue raised. People v. Alexander, 136 Misc. 2d 573, 518 N.Y.S.2d 872 (Sup. Ct. Bronx Co. 1987).

Insanity; fitness to proceed; burden of proof.—Defendant brought a writ of error coram nobis to vacate the judgment against him. His contention that the People had the burden of proving his competency to stand trial was not sustained by the Court of Appeals. People v. Von Braunsberg, 31 N.Y.2d 842, 340 N.Y.S.2d 161, 292 N.E.2d 303 (1972).

Matters dehors the record.—Speedy trial or ineffective assistance of counsel claims based on matters outside the record are best reviewable by way of a CPL article 440 motion, which can be used to develop a record focused on those issues. People v. Obert, 1 A.D.3d 631, 766 N.Y.S.2d 264 (3d Dept. 2003).

—Where defendant's appellate claim rested on alleged conversations between defendant and his former attorneys, the matters were dehors the record and more appropriately raised in a 440.10 motion. People v. Magee, 263 A.D.2d 763, 695 N.Y.S.2d 166 (3d Dept. 1999).

Motion to vacate judgment; failure to appeal.—A court must deny a motion to vacate judgment where a defendant could have but did not raise an issue on direct appeal, despite a subsequent retroactively effective change in the law controlling that issue. People v. Cunningham, 104 Misc. 2d 298, 428 N.Y.S.2d 183 (Sup. Ct. Bronx Co. 1980).

—Where sufficient facts appear on the record, dismissal of a motion pursuant to CPL § 440 is required notwithstanding that by failing to perfect his *pro se* direct appeal defendant had lost that avenue of review. People v. Cooks, 67 N.Y.2d 100, 500 N.Y.S.2d 503, 491 N.E.2d 676 (1986).

Plea bargaining; bad faith by D.A.—Defendant's motion to vacate judgment of conviction under two different indictments for criminal sale of a controlled substance was granted and a full evidentiary hearing was ordered to determine the validity of defendant's allegation of an agreement by prosecutors to permit defendant to plead to a lesser offense and recommend a ten-year sentence in exchange for defendant's information about the sources of supply of morphine in India. People v. Yash Pal Gupta, 80 A.D.2d 743, 437 N.Y.S.2d 175 (4th Dept. 1981).

Motion to vacate judgment.—Defendant's motion to vacate judgment was properly denied where the defendant's allegations that the courtroom was closed were refuted by the court record. The defendant's wife was not allowed in the court room because she was a possible witness. People v. Santana, 180 A.D.2d 537, 580 N.Y.S.2d 254 (1st Dept. 1992).

—A sufficient basis to vacate judgment did not exist where the defendant could not establish that the co-defendant's statements affected the verdict against the defendant where those statements were not offered into evidence. People v. Eastman, 195 A.D.2d 572, 601 N.Y.S.2d 834 (2d Dept. 1993).

—Coram nobis or a motion pursuant to CPL § 440.10 is not available where a motion could have been made preconviction but was not made. People v. Coles, 141 Misc. 2d 965, 535 N.Y.S.2d 897, 901 (Sup. Ct. Kings Co. 1988).

Motion to vacate judgment; scope.—Court acted properly in denying defendant's motion to vacate judgment where the defendant's arguments were rebutted by the record and the evidence. People v. Franco, 192 A.D.2d 719, 596 N.Y.S.2d 860 (2d Dept. 1993).

Motion to vacate conviction; mental disease or defect.—Defendant, who pleaded guilty to killing his former wife while under the influence of extreme emotional disturbance, presented sufficient proof to require a hearing on his motion to vacate prior conviction of manslaughter, first degree where defendant denied remembering or understanding the plea or sentencing proceedings and record indicated that, less than two months after judgment was entered, defendant was diagnosed as suffering from psychosis associated with brain trauma. People v. Fixter, 79 A.D.2d 861, 434 N.Y.S.2d 484 (4th Dept. 1980).

New trial required; error in court's charge and prosecutorial misconduct.—A new trial was warranted in the interest of justice based upon errors in the court's charge coupled with improper remarks by the prosecutor, notwithstanding the failure to preserve such errors for review, where the complainants' limited opportunity to view the perpetrator raised "strong doubts" concerning their ability to make an accurate identification. People v. Torres, 111 A.D.2d 885, 490 N.Y.S.2d 793 (2d Dept. 1985).

Newly discovered evidence.—The power to vacate a criminal conviction and grant a new trial for newly discovered evidence rests within the unlimited discretion of the lower courts and is beyond review of the Court of Appeals. People v. Baxley, 84 N.Y.2d 208, 616 N.Y.S.2d 7, 639 N.E.2d 746 (1994).

—Where the defendant's conviction was vacated on the basis of newly discovered evidence, defendant was not subject to the tolling statute for second felony offenders. People v. Dozier, 78 N.Y.2d 242, 573 N.Y.S.2d 427, 577 N.E.2d 1019 (1991).

—Whether or not a hearing should be held on a motion to vacate judgment upon the ground of newly discovered evidence (CPL § 440.10[1][g]) is discretionary with the court to which the motion is addressed. People v. Crimmins, 38 N.Y.2d 407, 367 N.Y.S.2d 213, 326 N.E.2d 787 (1975).

—Newly discovered evidence that, prior to the defendant's trial for assaulting corrections officers, the complainant, a Department of Corrections Captain, had been charged with assaulting prisoners and falsifying records to conceal those assaults, went to the heart of the defendant's trial defense, and accordingly, defendant's motion to vacate was granted. People v. Santos, 306 A.D.2d 197, 761 N.Y.S.2d 641 (1st Dept.), *aff'd*, 1 N.Y.3d 548, 775 N.Y.S.2d 770, 807 N.E.2d 881 (2003).

—CPL § 440.10 motion based on newly discovered evidence was properly denied because defendant did not establish that evidence of the arresting officer's perjury in unrelated matters would probably have affected the result of the defendant's trial; the evidence merely tended to impeach the officer's credibility in general. People v. Roberson, 276 A.D.2d 446, 716 N.Y.S.2d 43 (1st Dept. 2000).

—Judgment properly set aside where complainant was the only eyewitness, her testimony contained material inconsistencies, and following defendant's conviction, defendant learned that complainant had a long-standing history of mental illness and violent assaultive behavior that predated her testimony at defendant's trial. People v. Collins, 250 A.D.2d 379, 673 N.Y.S.2d 76 (1st Dept. 1998).

—Defendant's motion to vacate judgment against him on the basis of newly discovered evidence required a hearing with respect thereto, where co-defendant, who testified and was acquitted at a separate trial but refused to take the stand at defendant's trial, now expresses a willingness to testify at a retrial of defendant. People v. Pollock, 67 A.D.2d 608, 412 N.Y.S.2d 12 (1st Dept. 1979), *aff'd*, 50 N.Y.2d 547, 429 N.Y.S.2d 628, 407 N.E.2d 472 (1980).

—Where defendant's newly discovered evidence consisted entirely of his own hearsay allegation that an acquaintance of his recently confessed to putting a drug-filled suitcase on a plane in defendant's name, court properly denied CPL § 440 motion without a hearing. People v. West, 237 A.D.2d 470, 655 N.Y.S.2d 570 (2d Dept. 1997).

—Police officer's failure to recall certain details did not constitute newly discovered evidence warranting a new trial; in order to constitute such evidence it must do more than merely impeach or contradict the former evidence. People v. Pineda, 207 A.D.2d 915, 616 N.Y.S.2d 660 (2d Dept. 1994).

—There is no form of proof so unreliable as recanting testimony. People v. Rodriguez, 201 A.D.2d 683, 608 N.Y.S.2d 255, 256 (2d Dept. 1994).

—Newly discovered evidence to support a motion to vacate a judgment of conviction pursuant to CPL § 440.10 must be such as will probably change the result if a new trial is granted, must have been discovered since trial, must be such as could not have been discovered before the trial by the exercise of due diligence, must not merely impeach or contradict the former evidence, must be based upon sworn allegations, and must be proven by a preponderance of the evidence. People v. Balan, 107 A.D.2d 811, 484 N.Y.S.2d 648 (2d Dept. 1985).

—Court erred when it refused to order a hearing on defendant's post-trial motion to set aside verdict on the ground of newly discovered evidence, where prior to sentencing, the defendant was for the first time able to locate and obtain affidavits from two individuals who claimed they overheard a supposed look-a-like of defendant admit that he had the committed crime for which defendant had been arrested. People v. Harris, 74 A.D.2d 879, 426 N.Y.S.2d 26 (2d Dept. 1980).

—Where defendant, who had been convicted of murder made a motion to set aside the judgment on the ground of newly discovered evidence which consisted of cellmate's confession, court improperly precluded cross-examination of defendant as to whether he saw cellmate on the night of the crime, which was pertinent to the issue of whether he exercised due diligence to discover the alleged new evidence. People v. Bridget, 73 A.D.2d 291, 426 N.Y.S.2d 285 (2d Dept. 1980).

—To support his newly discovered evidence claim, defendant proffered affidavits of seven inmates, each of whom allegedly witnessed stabbing, and averred that defendant was not the perpetrator. Where six of the seven affidavits were obtained more than four years before defendant filed this motion, defendant's delay in bringing forth this evidence, the cumulative nature of the evidence, and the absence of any convincing proof that it could not have been discovered prior to the trial through the exercise of due diligence, County Court cannot be faulted for rejecting it. People v. Wong, 256 A.D.2d 724, 682 N.Y.S.2d 689 (3d Dept. 1998).

—Defendant's motion to vacate judgment, based on newly discovered evidence, was denied where such evidence would not have resulted in a different verdict for the defendant. People v. Bryce, 210 A.D.2d 816, 620 N.Y.S.2d 579 (3d Dept. 1994).

—Defendant's motion to vacate was denied where the record refuted defendant's claims of newly discovered evidence establishing prosecutorial misconduct in failing to disclose material evidence at trial. People v. Gates, 189 A.D.2d 934, 592 N.Y.S.2d 284 (3d Dept. 1993).

—Defendant's motion to set aside her conviction of second degree murder (PL § 125.25) on the ground of newly discovered evidence was denied because the evidence, consisting of expert testimony, would not result in a more favorable verdict and because the defendant's condition as a battered woman was known and considered by the jury and hence evidence on this point would be cumulative to the issue previously considered. People v. Powell, 102 Misc. 2d 775, 424 N.Y.S.2d 626 (Tompkins Co. Ct. 1980), aff'd, 83 A.D.2d 719, 442 N.Y.S.2d 645 (3d Dept. 1981).

—Six-year delay in furnishing affidavit in support of motion to vacate judgment warranted denial of motion. People v. Mancuso, 141 Misc. 2d 382, 532 N.Y.S.2d 643 (Sup. Ct. Kings Co. 1988).

Newly discovered evidence; insufficient to require new trial.—Defendant, convicted and sentenced in 1988, brought newly discovered evidence claim based on 1996 conviction of police officer who had testified at defendant's hearing; evidence of officer's conviction was not newly discovered, because it was not material to defendant's case and only constituted general impeachment material. People v. Reyes, 167 A.D.2d 116, 680 N.Y.S.2d 493 (1st Dept. 1998).

—Alleged "newly discovered evidence" in the form of testimony by a convicted accomplice that he alone committed the burglary was insufficient to set aside the defendant's conviction of the crime; this evidence merely contradicted the victims' testimony that there were two perpetrators and provided only a possibility not the necessary probability, that the verdict would have been different. People v. Suarez, 98 A.D.2d 678, 469 N.Y.S.2d 752 (1st Dept. 1983).

—Defendant's motion pursuant to CPL § 440.10(1)(g) based on newly discovered evidence was properly denied, where defendant did not establish in his motion papers or at the hearing that the proffered evidence created the probability of a more favorable verdict or that the evidence could not have been produced by him at trial by the exercise of due diligence. May v. Stover, 254 A.D.2d 377, 678 N.Y.S.2d 734 (2d Dept. 1998).

—A defendant who withholds evidence during the trial is not entitled to a new trial on the basis of the evidence withheld. People v. Rivera, 118 A.D.2d 877, 500 N.Y.S.2d 181 (2d Dept. 1986).

—Vacatur of a judgment of conviction based on newly discovered evidence is expressly conditioned upon a verdict of guilt after trial; defendant's plea of guilty therefore foreclosed relief on this ground. People v. Sides, 242 A.D.2d 750, 661 N.Y.S.2d 863 (3d Dept. 1997).

—A motion for new trial should be denied where newly discovered evidence is merely contradictory and impeaching of testimony presented at trial, and it is not of such a character that it is probable the jury would have returned a verdict more favorable to defendant. People v. Powell, 96 A.D.2d 610, 464 N.Y.S.2d 611 (3d Dept. 1983).

—Since hospital records of rape victim were in existence prior to trial they did not constitute newly discovered evidence. People v. Holmes, 127 A.D.2d 993, 513 N.Y.S.2d 45 (4th Dept. 1987).

—Court rejected defendant's claim of newly discovered evidence where it was unsubstantiated by affidavits or other documentary evidence. People v. Fappiano, 134 Misc. 2d 693, 512 N.Y.S.2d 301, 304 (Sup. Ct. Kings Co. 1987).

Pretrial show up; due process.—Although pretrial show

up identification may be impermissibly suggestive or conducted out of presence of counsel, it was for defendant to show that it tainted the in-court identification and that existing procedure denied defendant an opportunity to assert claim of fundamental unfairness in violation of due process in order for coram nobis relief to be warranted. People v. Bennett, 30 N.Y.2d 283, 332 N.Y.S.2d 867, 283 N.E.2d 747 (1972).

Procedural bars to collateral review.—If an apparent error lies in defendant's plea allocution the defendant must raise the issue of that error on direct appeal. People v. Angelakos, 70 N.Y.2d 670, 518 N.Y.S.2d 785, 512 N.E.2d 305 (1987).

—Defendant's silence and delay in making a motion based on the judge's sleeping through portions of voir dire preclude the attack he now makes more than six years after he was sentenced. Motion denied pursuant to CPL § 440.10(3)(a). The prejudice defendant claims to have suffered by reason of judicial inattention during voir dire did not result in the seating of any juror whose impartiality defendant has impugned. People v. Degondea, 3 A.D.3d 148, 769 N.Y.S.2d 490 (1st Dept. 2003).

—Court properly denied defendant's ineffective assistance claim, which was based primarily on counsel's failure to utilize purported impeachment material that was undisputedly in counsel's possession, because it raised no issue that could not be resolved on the trial record, and the record established that defendant received meaningful representation. People v. Orr, 240 A.D.2d 213, 659 N.Y.S.2d 1 (1st Dept. 1997).

—Defendant was not entitled to vacatur of judgment where the court denied defendant's access to the records of his wife's case. Defendant's motion warranted denial on procedural grounds for lack of merit. People v. McMillan, 212 A.D.2d 445, 622 N.Y.S.2d 935 (1st Dept. 1995).

—Defendant's motion to vacate was properly denied where the defendant's claim contained issues warranting consideration on direct appeal. People v. Jones, 210 A.D.2d 91, 620 N.Y.S.2d 948 (1st Dept. 1994), aff'd, 90 N.Y.2d 835, 660 N.Y.S.2d 549, 683 N.E.2d 14 (1997).

—Court properly denied defendant's CPL § 440.10 motion on the ground that defendant did not raise the jury note issue in his previous CPL § 440.10 motion, although in a position to do so. People v. Moolenaar, 207 A.D.2d 711, 616 N.Y.S.2d 590 (1st Dept. 1994).

—Where the record clearly presented sufficient facts from which the defendant could have raised his present claims on appeal, it could not be raised on the CPL 440 motion. People v. Jossiah, 2 A.D.3d 877, 769 N.Y.S.2d 743 (2d Dept. 2003).

—Defendant's motion to set aside his judgment of conviction, pursuant to CPL § 440.10, was properly denied since the ground raised by the defendant was or could have been raised on direct appeal; was conclusively refuted by unquestionable documentary proof; and was contradicted by a court record. People v. Hargrove, 138 A.D.2d 741, 526 N.Y.S.2d 838 (2d Dept. 1988).

—Claims that were raised and rejected on a direct appeal may not form the basis for a CPL § 440.10 motion. People v. Sayles, 17 A.D.3d 924, 794 N.Y.S.2d 160 (3d Dept. 2005).

—Court properly denied defendant's post-conviction motion to vacate judgment or set aside sentence because all of the allegations of error appeared on the record and could have or had been raised on direct appeal. People v. Pham, 287 A.D.2d 789, 731 N.Y.S.2d 254 (3d Dept. 2001).

—Much of defendant's motion was properly denied on the ground that it raised issues which could and should have been raised by defendant on direct appeal, which defendant never pursued. People v. Barber, 280 A.D.2d 691, 720 N.Y.S.2d 223 (3d Dept. 2001).

—Defendant's motion to vacate judgment, pursuant to CPL § 440.10(1)(g), was premature where it was made prior to sentencing. People v. Ketchmore, 132 A.D.2d 889, 518 N.Y.S.2d 234 (3d Dept. 1987).

—There is not time limit on claims pursuant to CPL § 550.10; a defendant may move at nisi prius to vacate the judgment at any time. People v. Perez, 162 Misc. 2d 750, 616 N.Y.S.2d 928 (Sup. Ct. Kings Co. 1994).

—Defendant's failure to raise ineffective assistance of counsel claims based on counsel's alleged failure to raise an entrapment defense, when he could have raised it on his direct appeal, precludes him from raising it in the motion pursuant to CPL § 440.10(2)(a). He is also precluded from raising the issue pursuant to CPL § 440.10(3)(c) because he could have raised it in his prior motions. People v. Dover, 294 A.D.2d 594, 743 N.Y.S.2d 501 (2d Dept. 2002).

—Because the issue of whether defendant was denied his right to testify before the grand jury was previously raised on the direct appeal from his judgment of conviction, and found lacking in merit, it is not subject to review under CPL § 440.10(2)(a). People v. Saunders, 301 A.D.2d 869, 753 N.Y.S.2d 620 (3d Dept. 2003).

—Defendant argued that his rights against compulsory self-incrimination to due process, fair trial, and effective assistance of counsel were violated when the prosecution was permitted to call a judge to testify to establish defendant's prior conviction. Defendant challenged the propriety of that testimony on direct appeal, arguing that it exceeded what was necessary to prove his prior conviction. The present arguments should have been raised on his direct appeal as sufficient facts appear in the trial record to have permitted adequate review of these issues, but defendant failed to raise them. Accordingly, these issues are not subject to review in the CPL § 440.10 motion. People v. Saunders, 301 A.D.2d 869, 753 N.Y.S.2d 620 (3d Dept. 2003).

—Because defendant's claim involving an allegedly deficient plea allocution could have been raised but was not on direct appeal, the motion was properly denied. People v. Lindsey, 302 A.D.2d 128, 755 N.Y.S.2d 118 (3d Dept. 2003).

Prosecutor's awareness of false testimony.—Where defendant presented evidence that the People's expert witness gave false testimony at trial about his credentials, while the evidence might have affected jury's assessment of witness's credibility, nothing in the record indicated that prosecution was aware or should be charged with knowledge that witness was misrepresenting his credentials; vacatur not warranted under CPL § 440.10(1)(c). People v. Drake, 256 A.D.2d 1159, 684 N.Y.S.2d 102 (4th Dept. 1998).

Prosecutorial misconduct; when hearing is required.—Mere conclusory allegations of prosecutorial misconduct are alone insufficient to require a trial court to conduct an evidentiary hearing for the purpose of resolving those accusations; to raise a triable issue some actual evidence of knowledge on the part of the prosecution that a witness' testimony was false must be submitted to the court. People v. Brown, 56 N.Y.2d 242, 451 N.Y.S.2d 693, 436 N.E.2d 1295 (1982).

—A hearing was required where defendant alleged the existence of a conflict of interest between his counsel and the witness for the prosecution. Defendant was never informed of the conflict. People v. Gonzalez, 160 A.D.2d 724, 554 N.Y.S.2d 48 (2d Dept. 1990).

—Where the defendant failed to submit an affidavit support of his claim of prosecutorial misconduct, the court dismissed defendant's motion to vacate judgment. People v. Portalatin, 132 A.D.2d 581, 517 N.Y.S.2d 301 (2d Dept. 1987).

—Where defendant submitted papers containing questions of fact relating to the false use of evidence, defendant was granted a hearing on his motion to vacate judgment. People v. Bates, 535 N.Y.S.2d 571 (4th Dept. 1988).

Recantation by prosecution witness.—Recantation was totally unreliable, because the witness's account of the incident was incredible, and the affidavit was made ten years after defendant's conviction and after the witness had become an inmate of the same prison system in which the defendant is incarcerated; thus, the court did not deprive defendant of due process by summarily denying his 440.10 motion. People v. Cintron, 306 A.D.2d 151, 763 N.Y.S.2d 11 (1st Dept. 2003).

—Child victim's recantation merely impeached or contradicted the defendant's testimony and her former testimony and thus failed to constitute "newly discovered" evidence within the meaning of CPL 440.10(1)(g). People v. Cassels, 260 A.D.2d 392, 687 N.Y.S.2d 681 (2d Dept. 1999).

—Court properly denied defendant's motion to vacate his conviction pursuant to CPL § 440.10 without a hearing since the application was based upon a recanting inmate witness who had testified for the prosecution and then had become dissatisfied with the end result of his cooperation. People v. Donald, 107 A.D.2d 818, 484 N.Y.S.2d 651 (2d Dept. 1985).

Receipt of improper evidence.—It was reversible error for the hearing court to consider as evidence in defendant's motion to vacate judgment of conviction an affidavit of the former district attorney who was the prosecutor at defendant's murder

trial since the affidavit was clearly hearsay and was never formally received into evidence. People v. Klein, 75 A.D.2d 857, 427 N.Y.S.2d 842 (2d Dept. 1980).

Right to counsel.—Court rejected claim of incompetent counsel where defense counsel made numerous motions, effectively cross-examined the People's witnesses at trial, presented a cogent summation, continued to advocate the defendant's interests through sentencing and procured an extremely beneficial plea bargain for the defendant in a separate prosecution. People v. Lorenzo, 123 A.D.2d 886, 507 N.Y.S.2d 664 (2d Dept. 1986).

—Counsel's failure to request a *Wade* hearing without more does not constitute a basis for a finding of ineffectiveness. People v. Brown, 122 A.D.2d 546, 505 N.Y.S.2d 474 (4th Dept. 1986).

—Where defense counsel vigorously attacked the People's case and elicited inconsistencies in the testimony of the People's witnesses, his mere failure to request a *Mapp* hearing did not, in and of itself, constitute ineffective assistance of counsel. People v. Jenkins, 123 A.D.2d 884, 507 N.Y.S.2d 663 (2d Dept. 1986).

—Counsel at plea not deemed incompetent merely by virtue of his failure to ask for a recommendation against deportation or a certificate of relief from civil disabilities, or because he failed to inform the defendant of the possible immigration consequences of the plea. People v. Dor, 132 Misc. 2d 568, 505 N.Y.S.2d 317 (Sup. Ct. Kings Co. 1986).

Right to counsel; competency of counsel; insanity defense.—Where defendant charged with 1st degree robbery had history of mental instability and confinement, failure of his assigned counsel to investigate background as aid to defense of insanity demonstrated incompetency of counsel and deprived defendant of fundamental right to fair trial. People v. Bennett, 29 N.Y.2d 462, 329 N.Y.S.2d 801, 280 N.E.2d 637 (1972).

Right to effective aid of counsel; conflict of interest between defendants.—Defendant who was convicted of assault together with co-defendant, and both were acquitted of murder arising out of fight following a crap game, did not have conflict of interest with co-defendant as both sought to discredit prosecution witnesses and establish self defense as a defense. Record shows that attorney who represented both pressed favorable arguments of defendant even though he also represented gun wielding co-defendant. People v. Gonzalez, 30 N.Y.2d 28, 330 N.Y.S.2d 54, 280 N.E.2d 882, *cert. denied,* 409 U.S. 859 (1972).

Rosario **material; prosecution.**—*Rosario* claims raised by way of CPL § 440.10 motions made before direct appeal is exhausted should be rejected unless the violation prejudiced defendant. People v. Machado, 90 N.Y.2d 187, 659 N.Y.S.2d 242, 681 N.E.2d 409 (1997).

—Actual prejudice must be demonstrated on the claim that the prosecution failed to turn over *Rosario* material. Defendant must also demonstrate that the trial was affected by "improper and prejudicial conduct." People v. Jackson, 78 N.Y.2d 638, 578 N.Y.S.2d 483, 585 N.E.2d 795 (1991).

—Motion to vacate denied pursuant to CPL § 440.10(3)(a), where defendant's purported *Rosario* claim could, with due diligence, have been placed on the record and was thus not the proper subject of a motion to vacate judgment. People v. Blake, 232 A.D.2d 288, 648 N.Y.S.2d 910 (1st Dept. 1996).

—Defendant's motion to vacate was denied as unfounded where defendant's claim that the prosecution's failure to provide an interview report constituted withholding of *Rosario* material. The prosecution did not know the report existed until the trial had ended. People v. White, 210 A.D.2d 447, 620 N.Y.S.2d 437 (2d Dept. 1994).

—Defendant's motion to vacate judgment, made 4 years after the judgment, was properly denied where the defendant failed to establish that the verdict was affected by the People's failure to provide *Rosario* material. The defendant was aware of these documents at the time of the trial. People v. Adorno, 202 A.D.2d 439, 608 N.Y.S.2d 678 (2d Dept. 1994).

—Defendant's motion to vacate was granted where the prosecution failed to provide the defense with *Rosario* material. The statements of the witness possessed impeachment value and thus, the defense was entitled to access. People v. Palmer, 137 A.D.2d 881, 524 N.Y.S.2d 564 (3d Dept. 1988).

Shackling of defendant.—Motion to vacate judgment, predicated upon shackling of defendant in the presence of the jury, denied where defendant failed to object to the shackling at trial or to take steps to ameliorate the prejudice resulting therefrom. People v. Craft, 123 A.D.2d 481, 506 N.Y.S.2d 492 (2d Dept. 1986).

Speculative claims insufficient.—Where defendant's original and renewed CPL § 440.10 motions added nothing of significance to speculative claims he previously raised, those motions were properly denied. People v. Yuen Pang, 254 A.D.2d 101, 680 N.Y.S.2d 206 (1st Dept. 1998).

—County Court properly denied defendant's motion pursuant to CPL § 440.10 without a hearing, where the Justice determining the motion presided at the trial and the *Mapp* and *Huntley* hearings, and defendant's motion was based on speculative and conclusory allegations. People v. Turcotte, 252 A.D.2d 818, 675 N.Y.S.2d 443 (3d Dept. 1998).

Subd. 1(h).—Fact that a convicted felon who should have been disqualified from sitting on the jury pursuant to Judiciary Law § 510(3) does not require a new trial, but defendant is entitled to an evidentiary hearing at which he may attempt to establish that the juror's failure to disclose his conviction resulted in actual bias. People v. Mercado, 290 A.D.2d 237, 735 N.Y.S.2d 125 (1st Dept. 2002).

Summary denial improper.—Ordinarily a complete record adduced through a motion to vacate judgment of conviction pursuant to CPL § 440.10, which includes an affidavit from trial counsel explaining his or her trial tactics, is necessary for proper evaluation of an ineffective assistance of counsel claim. Here, however, defendant provided a viable explanation for his counsel's failure to include an affidavit—specifically, counsel's disbarment prior to defendant's bringing the motion. Thus, it was an abuse of discretion for the court to summarily deny defendant's 440 motion on the basis of this procedural deficiency. People v. Gil, 285 A.D.2d 7, 729 N.Y.S.2d 121 (1st Dept. 2001).

Sworn allegations required.—Court properly denied defendant's motion pursuant to CPL § 440.10 without a hearing since he failed to submit sworn allegations substantiating or tending to substantiate all essential facts necessary to support his claim. People v. Wells, 265 A.D.2d 589, 696 N.Y.S.2d 893 (2d Dept. 1999).

—The unsworn, undated statement of a social worker that defendant suffers from posttraumatic stress disorder did not constitute sworn allegations of fact supporting defendant's contention. People v. Comfort, 278 A.D.2d 872, 718 N.Y.S.2d 751 (4th Dept. 2000).

§ 440.20. Motion to set aside sentence; by defendant.

1. At any time after the entry of a judgment, the court in which the judgment was entered may, upon motion of the defendant, set aside the sentence upon the ground that it was unauthorized, illegally imposed or otherwise invalid as a matter of law. Where the judgment includes a sentence of death, the court may also set aside the sentence upon any of the grounds set forth in paragraph (b), (c), (f), (g) or (h) of subdivision one of section 440.10 as applied to a separate sentencing proceeding under section 400.27, provided, however, that to the extent the ground or grounds asserted include one or more of the aforesaid paragraphs of subdivision one of section 440.10, the court must also apply subdivisions two and three of section 440.10, other than paragraph (d) of subdivision two of such section, in determining the motion. In the event the court enters an order granting a motion to set aside a sentence of death under this section, the court must either direct a new sentencing proceeding in accordance with section 400.27 or, to the extent that the defendant cannot be resentenced to death consistent with the laws of this state or the constitution of this state or of the united states,

resentence the defendant to life imprisonment without parole or to a sentence of imprisonment for the class A-I felony of murder in the first degree other than a sentence of life imprisonment without parole. Upon granting the motion upon any of the grounds set forth in the aforesaid paragraphs of subdivision one of section 440.10 and setting aside the sentence, the court must afford the people a reasonable period of time, which shall be not less than ten days, to determine whether to take an appeal from the order setting aside the sentence of death. The taking of an appeal by the people stays the effectiveness of that portion of the court's order that directs a new sentencing proceeding.

2. Notwithstanding the provisions of subdivision one, the court must deny such a motion when the ground or issue raised thereupon was previously determined on the merits upon an appeal from the judgment or sentence, unless since the time of such appellate determination there has been a retroactively effective change in the law controlling such issue.

3. Notwithstanding the provisions of subdivision one, the court may deny such a motion when the ground or issue raised thereupon was previously determined on the merits upon a prior motion or proceeding in a court of this state, other than an appeal from the judgment, or upon a prior motion or proceeding in a federal court, unless since the time of such determination there has been a retroactively effective change in the law controlling such issue. Despite such determination, however, the court in the interest of justice and for good cause shown, may in its discretion grant the motion if it is otherwise meritorious.

4. An order setting aside a sentence pursuant to this section does not affect the validity or status of the underlying conviction, and after entering such an order the court must resentence the defendant in accordance with the law.

Amended by L. 1995, Ch. 1, § 21.

ANNOTATIONS

Scope of sections.—CPL § 440.20 will apply only if defendant asserts an issue which concerns the propriety of the sentence. If such an issue is not raised, defendant's motion must be denied. People v. Cooks, 67 N.Y.2d 100, 500 N.Y.S.2d 503, 491 N.E.2d 676 (1986).

—A defendant is allowed to move to set aside a sentence as invalid any time subsequent to the judgment. The one year time limit in CPL § 440.40 is a restriction on the ability of the People, not the defendant, to set aside a sentence. CPL § 440.20 and CPL § 440.40 are to be considered together. People v. Wright, 56 N.Y.2d 613, 450 N.Y.S.2d 473, 435 N.E.2d 1088 (1982).

—Defendant's allegation that sentencing court failed to consider certain factors in imposing sentence were insufficient to trigger relief under CPL § 440.20. People v. Meredith, 172 A.D.2d 364, 568 N.Y.S.2d 622, 623 (1st Dept. 1991).

—Defendant must be resentenced "in accordance with the law" following the court's decision to grant the motion to set aside the sentence. Thus, defendant must be present at the time of resentencing pursuant to CPL § 380.40(1). People v. Brown, 155 A.D.2d 608, 547 N.Y.S.2d 664 (2d Dept. 1989).

—Trial court's denial of defendant's CPL § 440.20 motion was proper since the issue raised had previously been raised and determined on the defendant's appeal from the judgment of conviction. People v. Simmons, 143 A.D.2d 153, 531 N.Y.S.2d 927 (2d Dept. 1988).

—Defendant is not entitled to be reheard on the issue of propriety of his sentence where defendant previously raised the issue pursuant to PL § 70.10 on direct appeal. Thus, the court must deny defendant's motion pursuant to CPL § 440.20. People v. Chapman, 115 A.D.2d 911, 496 N.Y.S.2d 589 (3d Dept. 1985).

—Courts are permitted to set aside a sentence on the motion of the People where the sentence is invalid as a matter of law. People v. Lewis, 138 Misc. 2d 822, 525 N.Y.S.2d 761, 762 (Sup. Ct. Kings Co. 1988).

Court decision of another state.—A legal sentence proceeding in one state cannot be made legally insufficient by a sentence imposed in another state. Court held defendant's sentence was legal where defendant was required to serve a sentence imposed in New York prior to a sentence of death imposed in Oklahoma. Defendant was not entitled to have his New York sentence set aside in order to remain in Oklahoma. People v. Grasso, 162 Misc. 2d 84, 616 N.Y.S.2d 156 (Sup. Ct. 1994).

Coram nobis application; motion for resentence in order to appeal.—Defendant, who made a coram nobis application for resentence in order to appeal on the ground that he was not advised of his right to appeal when judgement was entered upon his plea of guilty, must be granted a resentencing. Defendant must be resentenced so that he may appeal because at the hearing he established that he had not been advised of his right to appeal and he alleged a viable appealable issue: excessive sentence. The Appellate Division erred in denying defendant's application for resentence after deciding that his ground for appeal was not meritorious. People v. Santiago, 32 N.Y.2d 546, 347 N.Y.S.2d 16, 300 N.E.2d 399 (1973).

Coram nobis; right to challenge predicate convictions; hearing.—Even if defendant was not apprised of his statutory right to attack the constitutionality of his two predicate felony convictions at the time of his resentencing, he was not entitled to be resentenced, or, alternatively, to a hearing where his petition lacked factual allegations to support his claim of unconstitutionality of his predicate felony convictions. People v. Spencer, 32 N.Y.2d 446, 346 N.Y.S.2d 225, 299 N.E.2d 651 (1973).

—Defendant was not allowed to claim that his prior conviction was not constitutionally valid where that issue was previously dealt with on defendant's direct appeal from that prior conviction. Defendant's motion to set aside his sentence was properly denied. People v. Tirado, 192 A.D.2d 755, 596 N.Y.S.2d 183 (3d Dept. 1993).

—Defendant's motion to set aside his sentence was denied where defendant failed to raise the issue of the constitutionality of his predicate felony conviction, and where defendant failed to display good cause for not raising the issue at the time of sentencing. Defendant's claim that the sentence was illegal was properly precluded. People v. Crutchfield, 115 A.D.2d 189, 495 N.Y.S.2d 257 (3d Dept. 1985).

Delay in bringing motion.—The trial court did not abuse its discretion when it failed to provide a hearing where the proceeding was brought three years after sentencing with no explanation for the delay other than a statement by counsel that he was busy working on defendant's appeal and there was no disclosure of when he learned of the alleged coercive tactics of the prosecutor. People v. Friedgood, 58 N.Y.2d 467, 462 N.Y.S.2d 406, 448 N.E.2d 1317 (1983).

—The court's power to correct a sentence which is challenged as illegal is statutory in nature. The court must not act, sua sponte, two years subsequent to the judgment on the basis of a non-discernible error. People v. Riggins, 164 A.D.2d 797, 559 N.Y.S.2d 535 (1st Dept. 1990).

Hearing required.—A hearing was required where defense counsel at the time of sentencing noted the pressure placed on the court to impose a sentence greater than the off-the-record five year sentence which the court during plea negotiations thought fair although no firm commitment as to sentence had been made and the court imposed an eight year sentence. People v. Spencer, 86 A.D.2d 842, 447 N.Y.S.2d 451 (1st Dept. 1982).

Hearing not required.—Court properly denied defendant's motion to set aside his sentence holding that defendant's claim

of a harsh and excessive sentence was unfounded. The court was not required to hold a hearing on defendant's motion. People v. Brais, 209 A.D.2d 796, 618 N.Y.S.2d 601 (3d Dept. 1994).

Illegal sentence.—Defendant's sentence must be set aside for illegality, however, defendant's conviction is not affected. The defendant is entitled to a lawful resentence for the conviction. The court may not revoke defendant's status as a youthful offender in order to correct the illegitimate sentence. People v. Calderon, 79 N.Y.2d 61, 580 N.Y.S.2d 163, 588 N.E.2d 61 (1992).

—Although defendant's plea and sentence were illegal, once defendant received judgment, his plea could not be changed due to mutual mistake of the parties. Defendant should be resentenced according to the misdemeanor plea. Kisloff v. Covington, 73 N.Y.2d 445, 541 N.Y.S.2d 737, 539 N.E.2d 565 (1989).

Illegal sentence; confinement of person in need of supervision to institution for juvenile delinquents.—Defendant had been adjudged a person in need of supervision and later, upon recommendation of the Probation Department, was confined in an institution for juvenile delinquents by order of the Family Court. Defendant must be released from the institution as the Family Court Act provides for "confinement" as a possible treatment only for persons adjudged to be juvenile delinquents and not for persons in need of supervision. The purpose of the Family Court Act: to enhance the welfare of the children within its jurisdiction, would be defeated by confining persons in need of supervision to institutions for juvenile delinquents. Ellery C. v. Norman Redlich, 32 N.Y.2d 588, 347 N.Y.S.2d 51, 300 N.E.2d 424 (1973).

Jurisdictional defect.—Defendant's sentence as a second felony offender must be set aside where the underlying previous conviction was jurisdictionally defective. Defendant's status as a second felony offender is without basis. People v. Johnson, 187 A.D.2d 990, 591 N.Y.S.2d 275 (4th Dept. 1992).

Motion to set aside sentence; requirements.—Court properly held defendant's one year sentence of imprisonment invalid where the maximum allowable sentence was six months. The People failed to file a second crime offender statement before the trial or the plea is entered, as required pursuant to CPL § 400.14. People v. Harp, 134 A.D.2d 937, 521 N.Y.S.2d 945 (4th Dept. 1987).

Prior felony convictions.—Defendant may raise the issue of prior felony convictions where that issue was not considered by the Appellate Division upon defendant appealing from the judgment of the present case. Defendant's sentence was held valid even though two prior felony convictions, rather than one, were considered when imposing sentence upon the defendant. People v. Taveras, 158 Misc. 2d 358, 601 N.Y.S.2d 256 (Sup. Ct. Queens Co. 1993).

Retroactivity.—Defendant's motion to set aside his sentence as invalid was properly denied where the court refused to apply the "new rule" of People v. Van Pelt, 76 N.Y.2d 156, 556 N.Y.S.2d 984, 556 N.E.2d 423, retroactively to defendant's case. The presumption of vindictiveness issue would not affect defendant's case since defendant's case was final on the day Van Pelt was decided. People v. Alvarez, 152 Misc. 2d 697, 573 N.Y.S.2d 592 (Sup. Ct. Kings Co. 1991).

Reduction in sentence.—Thirty-one-year old defendant's motion to reduce his sentence was denied where he claimed that his problems including heroin addiction stemmed from a difficult childhood in which he was raised in substandard economic and emotional conditions. People v. Brailsford, 84 A.D.2d 581, 443 N.Y.S.2d 423 (2d Dept. 1981).

Resentence; court's failure to abide by plea bargain.—Defendant must be resentenced to a term of four years as the trial court had failed to abide by the plea bargain and did not inform the defendant that the bargain could not be kept. Defendant's failure to remind the court of the bargain was not an intelligent and intentional waiver. People v. Esposito, 32 N.Y.2d 291, 347 N.Y.S.2d 70, 300 N.E.2d 438 (1973).

Second felony offender status.—Court was not required to set aside defendant's guilty plea on defendant's claim that he was not aware his new term of imprisonment would be served consecutively with time not yet served for a prior conviction. The court held that defendant's sentence was statutorily mandated as per his second felony offender status. People v. Johnson, 183 A.D.2d 573, 584 N.Y.S.2d 5 (1st Dept. 1992).

Sentence; agreement on term.—Court granted defendant's

motion to vacate his sentence on the basis that the defendant did not receive the sentence agreed upon by the court. Upon resentencing, defendant opted to not withdraw his plea and was resentenced to consecutive sentences; not in accordance with the court's original promise. The court's actions were held proper pursuant to CPL § 70.25(2-b). People v. Todd, 173 A.D.2d 385, 570 N.Y.S.2d 15 (1st Dept. 1991).

—Although defendant waived his right to appeal, defendant did not waive his right to claim that his guilty plea was involuntarily given. The defendant was not given the chance to withdraw his guilty plea as the court had previously agreed defendant would be given such an opportunity. Thus, defendant's motion to vacate was granted. People v. Acevedo, 211 A.D.2d 802, 621 N.Y.S.2d 924 (2d Dept. 1995).

—Where defendant agreed to plead guilty in Nassau County in exchange for concurrent imprisonment terms, the court was not required to allow defendant to withdraw his guilty plea where defendant did not fulfill the condition of the plea. Further, the defendant agreed to consecutive terms, not concurrent, upon pleading guilty in Nassau. People v. Boyd, 179 A.D.2d 815, 579 N.Y.S.2d 696 (2d Dept. 1992).

—Defendant's sentence was properly vacated and changed where an agreement existed between the defense counsel and the prosecutor providing that defendant would be assigned to probation rather than incarceration. The court was not aware of the agreement until the time of sentencing. People v. Harper, 171 A.D.2d 468, 567 N.Y.S.2d 359 (2d Dept. 1991).

—Court properly vacated defendant's sentence where defendant was originally promised "zip to ten" years but received 3 to 10 years as his sentence. People v. Rodriguez, 142 Misc. 2d 403, 536 N.Y.S.2d 928 (Sup. Ct. Bronx Co. 1988).

Sentence enhancement.—Where defendant was absent at the sentencing proceeding, defendant may challenge the validity of the enhanced sentence received. Defendant may move to set aside the enhanced sentence. People v. Villegas, 146 A.D.2d 228, 540 N.Y.S.2d 777 (1st Dept. 1989).

—Court acted properly in enhancing defendant's sentence following defendant's arrest for violating a protection order. Defendant's motion to set aside the enhanced sentence was properly denied. The court was released from its original promise to defendant and a hearing was not necessary for the enhancement of the sentence. People v. Kessner, 181 A.D.2d 1044, 582 N.Y.S.2d 585 (4th Dept. 1992).

Sentence; plea bargaining.—Defendant's sentence for burglary was sustained where after the judge sentenced him in accordance with the plea agreement, the court was informed by the department of corrections that because of his prior felony offender status defendant could not legally be sentenced to a term to run concurrently with any prior undischarged term and the court offered the defendant the opportunity to withdraw his guilty plea and he refused and the court sentenced him to the mandatory minimum sentence to run consecutive to the prior undischarged term. People v. Bullard, 84 A.D.2d 845, 444 N.Y.S.2d 171 (2d Dept. 1981).

Sentence; reformatory; youthful offender; equal protection of the laws.—To sentence a defendant of the youthful offender age group, but not afforded offender treatment, to a reformatory term of imprisonment upon his plea of guilty to a Class A misdemeanor even though the same sentence could not be imposed on a youthful offender, does not violate statute or constitution where sentencing judge took into account unrehabilitative character of defendant. People v. De Perez, 70 Misc. 2d 982, 335 N.Y.S.2d 526 (Ontario Co. Ct. 1972), aff'd, 32 N.Y.2d 880, 346 N.Y.S.2d 533, 299 N.E.2d 898 (1973).

Underlying felony conviction.—Court must vacate defendant's sentence as a second felony offender pursuant to defendant's motion. Defendant's previous conviction for burglary in California is not the equivalent of a felony conviction in New York. People v. Lee, 194 A.D.2d 559, 599 N.Y.S.2d 980 (2d Dept. 1993).

—Defendant's sentence was vacated pursuant to CPL § 440.20 where a Federal felony conviction for possession of firearms was the same as a felony under New York law. Defendant's status as a persistent felon cannot be established without specific evidence of the type of firearm defendant possessed. Defendant was entitled to resentencing. People v. Trudo, 153 A.D.2d 993, 545 N.Y.S.2d 437 (3d Dept. 1989).

§ 440.30. Motion to vacate judgment and to set aside sentence; procedure.

1. A motion to vacate a judgment pursuant to section 440.10 and a motion to set aside a sentence pursuant to section 440.20 must be made in writing and upon reasonable notice to the people. Upon the motion, a defendant who is in a position adequately to raise more than one ground should raise every such ground upon which he intends to challenge the judgment or sentence. If the motion is based upon the existence or occurrence of facts, the motion papers must contain sworn allegations thereof, whether by the defendant or by another person or persons. Such sworn allegations may be based upon personal knowledge of the affiant or upon information and belief, provided that in the latter event the affiant must state the sources of such information and the grounds of such belief. The defendant may further submit documentary evidence or information supporting or tending to support the allegations of the moving papers. The people may file with the court, and in such case must serve a copy thereof upon the defendant or his counsel, if any, an answer denying or admitting any or all of the allegations of the motion papers, and may further submit documentary evidence or information refuting or tending to refute such allegations. After all papers of both parties have been filed, and after all documentary evidence or information, if any, has been submitted, the court must consider the same for the purpose of ascertaining whether the motion is determinable without a hearing to resolve questions of fact.

1-a. (a) Where the defendant's motion requests the performance of a forensic DNA test on specified evidence, and upon the court's determination that any evidence containing deoxyribonucleic acid ("DNA") was secured in connection with the trial resulting in the judgment, the court shall grant the application for forensic DNA testing of such evidence upon its determination that if a DNA test had been conducted on such evidence, and if the results had been admitted in the trial resulting in the judgment, there exists a reasonable probability that the verdict would have been more favorable to the defendant.

(b) In conjunction with the filing of a motion under this subdivision, the court may direct the people to provide the defendant with information in the possession of the people concerning the current physical location of the specified evidence and if the specified evidence no longer exists or the physical location of the specified evidence is unknown, a representation to that effect and information and documentary evidence in the possession of the people concerning the last known physical location of such specified evidence. If there is a finding by the court that the specified evidence no longer exists or the physical location of such specified evidence is unknown, such information in and of itself shall not be a factor from which any inference unfavorable to the people may be drawn by the court in deciding a motion under this section. The court, on motion of the defendant, may also issue a subpoena duces tecum directing a public or private hospital, laboratory or other entity to produce such specified evidence in its possession and/or information and documentary evidence in its possession concerning the location and status of such specified evidence.

2. If it appears by conceded or uncontradicted allegations of the moving papers or of the answer, or by unquestionable documentary proof, that there are circumstances which require denial thereof pursuant to subdivision two of section 440.10 or subdivision two of section 440.20, the court must summarily deny the motion. If it appears that there are circumstances authorizing, though not requiring, denial thereof pursuant to subdivision three of section 440.10 or subdivision three of section 440.20, the court may in its discretion either (a) summarily deny the motion, or (b) proceed to consider the merits thereof.

3. Upon considering the merits of the motion, the court must grant it without conducting a hearing and vacate the judgment or set aside the sentence, as the case may be, if:

(a) The moving papers allege a ground constituting legal basis for the motion; and

(b) Such ground, if based upon the existence or occurrence of facts, is supported by sworn allegations thereof; and

(c) The sworn allegations of fact essential to support the motion are either conceded by the people to be true or are conclusively substantiated by unquestionable documentary proof.

4. Upon considering the merits of the motion, the court may deny it without conducting a hearing if:

(a) The moving papers do not allege any ground constituting legal basis for the motion; or

(b) The motion is based upon the existence or occurrence of facts and the moving papers do not contain sworn allegations substantiating or tending to substantiate all the essential facts, as required by subdivision one; or

(c) An allegation of fact essential to support the motion is conclusively refuted by unquestionable documentary proof; or

(d) An allegation of fact essential to support the motion (i) is contradicted by a court record or other official document, or is made solely by the defendant and is unsupported by any other affidavit or evidence, and (ii) under these and all the other circumstances attending the case, there is no reasonable possibility that such allegation is true.

5. If the court does not determine the motion pursuant to subdivisions two, three or four, it must conduct a hearing and make findings of fact essential to the determination thereof. The defendant has a right to be present at such hearing but may waive such right in writing. If he does not so waive it and if he is confined in a prison or other institution of this state, the court must cause him to be produced at such hearing.

6. At such a hearing, the defendant has the burden of proving by a preponderance of the evidence every fact essential to support the motion.

7. Regardless of whether a hearing was conducted, the court, upon determining the motion, must set forth on the record its findings of fact, its conclusions of law and the reasons for its determination.

Amended by L. 1994, Ch. 737, § 2, eff. Aug. 2, 1994, adding subd. 1-a; L. 2004, Ch. 138, § 2, eff. Nov. 1, 2004, amending subd. 1-a.

Editor's Note: L. 2000, Ch. 8, § 2, eff. Mar. 6, 2000, deemed eff. Dec. 1, 1999, provides:

In the case of a motion pursuant to subdivision 1-a of section 440.30 of the criminal procedure law that was determined prior to December 1, 1999, an appeal to the intermediate appellate court may be taken by the filing and service of a notice of appeal on or before September 1, 2000 or thirty days after service upon such party of a copy of the order from which the appeal is taken, whichever is later.

Notwithstanding the provisions of any other law, if there shall be a case involving a motion pursuant to subdivision 1-a of section 440.30 of the criminal procedure law determined prior to December 1, 1999 that was appealed to an intermediate appellate court and such appeal was determined by such intermediate appellate court prior to May 1, 2000, an application for a certificate granting leave to appeal to the court of appeals from such determination of the intermediate appellate court in such case may be filed on or before September 1, 2000 or thirty days after service upon such party of a copy of the order sought to be appealed, whichever is later.

ANNOTATIONS

Coram nobis; excessiveness of sentence; not advised of right to appeal.—A coram nobis proceeding brought nine years after sentencing, seeking to obtain resentencing for purposes of taking an appeal and wherein the defendant claims he was not advised of the right to appeal and the sentence was excessive must be denied where the defendant pleaded guilty; a defendant who has been sentenced to less than the maximum allowable sentence cannot claim excessiveness of sentence. People v. Melton, 35 N.Y.2d 327, 361 N.Y.S.2d 877, 320 N.E.2d 622 (1974).

Coram nobis; ineffective counsel.—A hearing was required on defendant's claim that he was denied effective counsel as a result of a contingency fee agreement. The defendant claimed that the agreement was prejudicial to the counsel's representation. Without proof of such prejudice submitted by the People, defendant's motion should not have been granted without a hearing. People v. Winkler, 74 N.Y.2d 704, 543 N.Y.S.2d 381, 541 N.E.2d 409 (1989).

—Where the record reveals that defendant's claim of ineffective counsel is impossible, defendant is not entitled to a hearing pursuant to his motion to vacate judgment. People v. Walker, 200 A.D.2d 367, 608 N.Y.S.2d 69 (1st Dept. 1994).

—Defendant's claim of ineffective counsel did not require a hearing where there was no proof of prejudice. The record indicated that counsel's actions comprised part of the trial strategy. People v. Leka, 209 A.D.2d 723, 619 N.Y.S.2d 144 (2d Dept. 1994).

—Defendant was not entitled to a hearing on defendant's motion claiming that a conflict of interest existed from counsel representing the co-defendant. Four times prior to trial, defendant was warned of the potential conflict. However, defendant insisted on continuing the use of counsel. People v. Valenti, 175 A.D.2d 489, 572 N.Y.S.2d 766 (3d Dept. 1991).

Coram nobis; prosecutor's promise to help prosecution witness.—Since defendant did not testify at hearing in coram nobis proceeding concerning his ignorance that prosecutor's promise to help prosecution witness when concealed was fundamental error and his attorney conceded that he knew of such promise, vacatur of judgment of conviction would be reversed on law alone since facts were undisputed. People v. Washington, 39 A.D.2d 726, 331 N.Y.S.2d 880 (2d Dept. 1972), aff'd, 32 N.Y.2d 401, 345 N.Y.S.2d 520, 298 N.E.2d 665 (1973).

Coram nobis; resentence; withdrawal of plea.—Defendant who failed to move to withdraw his plea and who made four post judgment motions, none challenging the adequacy of his plea arrangement, failed to preserve the issue of his plea's adequacy for appellate review. People v. Nowak, 155 A.D.2d 995, 547 N.Y.S.2d 793 (4th Dept. 1989).

Coram nobis; right to counsel.—Defendant's motion for a hearing was properly denied where the court held that the defendant could have acted with diligence and raised the matters of right to counsel, unrelated charges, and knowledge of prior arrests, at an earlier time. Defendant's opportunity was not impaired or denied. People v. Donovon, 107 A.D.2d 433, 487 N.Y.S.2d 345 (2d Dept. 1985).

Coram nobis; right to appeal.—Defendant's claim that his waiver of the right to appeal was due to coercion was not supported in the record. Defendant persisted in accepting the waiver while the prosecutor displayed reluctance. Defendant's claims were invalidated by the voluntary acceptance of the waiver. People v. Seaberg, 139 A.D.2d 53, 530 N.Y.S.2d 278 (2d Dept. 1988).

Defendant's burden.—Court is not permitted to deny defendant's motion to vacate judgment solely because the court finds defendant may only have a remote chance of meeting the required burden. People v. Hughes, 181 A.D.2d 912, 581 N.Y.S.2d 839 (2d Dept. 1992).

Hearing; authority to issue subpoenas.—The CPL does not authorize the use of compulsory process to obtain evidence prior to the court's ordering a hearing on a post-conviction motion. Rather, CPL § 440.30 requires that the court receiving the motion determine, after its submission, whether or not an evidentiary hearing on the allegations is warranted. People v. Diaz, 195 Misc. 2d 337, 756 N.Y.S.2d 838 (Sup. Ct. Bronx Co. 2003).

Hearing; necessity thereof.—Court rejects notion that where a post-judgment motion is made under CPL § 440.10 that a hearing to develop additional background facts is invariably necessary; a court will in the first instance determine on written submissions whether the motion can be decided without a hearing. People v. Satterfield, 66 N.Y.2d 796, 497 N.Y.S.2d 903, 488 N.E.2d 834 (1985).

—Court was not allowed to refuse the affidavit of the co-defendant which established defendant's lack of knowledge of cocaine presence. The affidavit was not refuted by documented proof. The court should have conducted a hearing to determine the credibility of the affidavit at issue. People v. Beach, 186 A.D.2d 935, 589 N.Y.S.2d 626 (3d Dept. 1992).

Hearing not required.—Court properly denied defendant's motion without a hearing where defendant failed to provide the court with proof that the newly discovered evidence was unable to be produced with diligence at trial. People v. Hamilton, 213 A.D.2d 423, 624 N.Y.S.2d 864 (2d Dept. 1995).

—Court did not err in summarily denying defendant's CPL § 440.10 motion where alleged inconsistencies in police laboratory paperwork were easily reconciled and raised no genuine issue as to accuracy of analysis or integrity of chain of custody; defendant failed to come forward with competent evidence supporting ground for vacatur and, thus, summary denial was proper. People v. Alexander, 255 A.D.2d 708, 681 N.Y.S.2d 109 (3d Dept. 1998).

—Court properly denied defendant's CPL § 440.10 motion without a hearing, because defendant failed to comply with the requirements of CPL § 440.30(1), in that defendant did not submit an affidavit and his attorneys' affidavit did not disclose the basis for their conclusions that defendant had been coerced into a guilty plea. People v. Jackson, 240 A.D.2d 946, 659 N.Y.S.2d 532 (3d Dept. 1997).

—Hearing was not required where defendant could not establish that his plea of guilty resulted from prosecutor misconduct or coercion. Defendant's claims of coercion were conclusory assertions, unsupported by the record. People v. Ross, 182 A.D.2d 1022, 583 N.Y.S.2d 34 (3d Dept. 1992).

—Defendant's motion was properly denied without a hearing where it was predicated upon accomplice recanting testimony when called as a prosecution witness. People v. Allison, 119 A.D.2d 1005, 500 N.Y.S.2d 888 (4th Dept. 1986).

Hearing required.—Defendant was entitled to a hearing on his motion where defendant claimed one informant's statement impeached another informant's testimony. The statements were not refuted by documented proof or the record. The People failed to concede that the informant's statements were true. People v. Baxley, 84 N.Y.2d 208, 616 N.Y.S.2d 7, 639 N.E.2d 746 (1984).

—A hearing was required on defendant's post-judgment motion to vacate his conviction where the defendant alleged that the People failed to supply him with a statement made by another person admitting the shooting of the grocer at the same time and placed as the victim and the People admit that the statement exists. People v. Ausserau, 77 A.D.2d 152, 432 N.Y.S.2d 940 (4th Dept. 1980).

Hearing required; waiver of jury.—Defendant who supplied the court a transcript of his statements which indicated that defendant had waived a jury trial in the presence of an attorney was entitled to a hearing to decide whether the defendant's waiver of a jury was executed in open court. The transcript satisfied the requirement that the defendant submit "evidentiary facts." People v. McDaniel, 168 A.D.2d 926, 565 N.Y.S.2d 334 (4th Dept. 1990).

DNA testing; defendant's burden.—CPL § 440.30(1-a) does not impose on defendants a due diligence requirement limiting the time within which to make a CPL § 440.30(1-a) motion. There is no time limit for bringing a post-conviction motion requesting the performance of forensic DNA testing, and the defendant does not bear the burden of showing that the specified DNA evidence exists and is available for testing. People v. Pitts, 4 N.Y.3d 303, 795 N.Y.S.2d 151, 828 N.E.2d 67 (2005).

—Where DNA testing was conducted prior to defendant's trial, the testing was flawed, the results were unreliable, and retesting was not permitted. Thus, this is not a case where defendant has failed to avail himself of the opportunity for DNA testing prior to trial, and defendant demonstrated a reasonable probability of a favorable verdict if the test results negate the proof of guilt. DNA testing should be permitted if the evidence still exists in sufficient quantities for testing. People v. Keene, 4 A.D.3d 536, 772 N.Y.S.2d 337 (2d Dept. 2004).

—When a defendant brings a motion for DNA testing, it is incumbent upon the defendant to show that the evidence to be tested still exists and is available in quantities sufficient to make testing feasible at this late date; defendant failed to do so in this 17-year-old case. People v. Ahlers, 285 A.D.2d 664, 728 N.Y.S.2d 246 (3d Dept. 2001).

Ineffective assistance.—Court properly denied defendant's ineffective assistance claim, which was based primarily on counsel's failure to utilize purported impeachment material that was undisputedly in counsel's possession, because it raised no issue that could not be resolved on the trial record, and the record established that defendant received meaningful representation. People v. Orr, 240 A.D.2d 213, 659 N.Y.S.2d 1 (1st Dept. 1997).

Motion to set aside sentence; mental disability.—Without a substantive basis to support the claim that defendant was incapacitated, the court may properly refuse to grant defendant's motion without a hearing. There was no reason to find defendant mentally incapacitated at the time defendant entered his plea of guilty. People v. Elliott, 187 A.D.2d 666, 590 N.Y.S.2d 257 (2d Dept. 1992).

—Defendant's motion was properly denied without a hearing where the record was void of any evidence establishing that defendant did not understand the plea proceedings. Defendant stated in court that he did not possess a mental disability and that his Alzheimer's disease did not adversely affect his plea. People v. Edison, 192 A.D.2d 789, 596 N.Y.S.2d 493 (3d Dept. 1993).

Unsupported allegation; no hearing required.—Where pleading minutes indicated detailed promise that defendant would receive a sentence from three to 10 years, no hearing was required when defendant and his counsel averred that judge, off-the-record, had promised that he would not sentence defendant for more than four years. People v. Selikoff, 35 N.Y.2d 227, 360 N.Y.S.2d 623, 318 N.E.2d 784, *cert. denied,* 419 U.S. 1122 (1974).

—A bare allegation that a defendant was not informed of his right to appeal after trial is insufficient in law to warrant a hearing when the allegation (1) is not confirmed by the recorded facts and (2) is contrary to the conduct of the defendant and his attorney. People v. Williams, 37 A.D.2d 353, 325 N.Y.S.2d 220 (4th Dept. 1971), *aff'd,* 29 N.Y.2d 649, 342 N.Y.S.2d 854, 295 N.E.2d 653 (1973).

—Where defendant's main allegation was contradicted by the plea and sentencing minutes, no hearing was required. The minutes specifically note that defendant was informed that his sentences would run consecutively. Thus, defendant's claim was unsupported. People v. Trammell, 211 A.D.2d 527, 622 N.Y.S.2d 439 (1st Dept. 1995).

—Court acted properly in denying defendant's motion to vacate judgment. The moving papers contained conclusory and unsupported allegations claiming that the witness did not identify defendant. The court held that the allegations must be sworn and supportive of the claim. People v. Lake, 213 A.D.2d 494, 623 N.Y.S.2d 904 (2d Dept. 1995).

—Defendant's motion to vacate must be based upon sworn allegations. The defendant must support his motion with facts proven by a preponderance of the evidence. Defendant's production of a new police report satisfied this burden. Thus, the court has discretion to grant an order for a new trial. People v. Gurley, 197 A.D.2d 534, 602 N.Y.S.2d 185 (2d Dept. 1993).

—Pursuant to CPL § 440.30(4)(d), court properly denied CPL § 440.10 motion without a hearing where the minutes of the plea proceedings and other circumstances indicated that defendant was not intoxicated, as he claimed and as claimed in the affidavit by defendant's brother. People v. Varno, 297 A.D.2d 873, 747 N.Y.S.2d 261 (3d Dept. 2002).

Motion to vacate; prosecutorial misconduct.—Defendant's motion to vacate judgment was properly denied where defendant submitted documentation that did not support his claim of prosecutorial fraud or misrepresentation. Defendant's claim that the prosecutor knowingly used false testimony was not properly submitted by affidavit. People v. Portalatin, 132 A.D.2d 581, 517 N.Y.S.2d 301 (2d Dept. 1987).

—Hearing was not required on defendant's claims of prosecutorial misconduct and selective prosecution. Defendant did not request a venue change nor did he make a motion pursuant to his claims. The court found there was no possibility of truth in defendant's allegations. People v. Walton, 214 A.D.2d 805, 625 N.Y.S.2d 313 (3d Dept. 1995).

People's delay.—People's delay, if any, in serving and filing a response to defendant's section 440 motion did not entitle defendant to have his motion granted on default. People v. Russell, 235 A.D.2d 364, 652 N.Y.S.2d 977 (1st Dept. 1997).

Sentence; fourth felony; burden of proof in post conviction proceeding.—Defendant assumes burden of proving that prior felony conviction which was basis for sentencing as 4th felony offender was constitutionally invalid on grounds that he was not represented by counsel in face of documentary record indicating the appointment of counsel. People v. Lasky, 31 N.Y.2d 146, 335 N.Y.S.2d 266, 286 N.E.2d 712 (1972).

§ 440.40. Motion to set aside sentence; by people.

1. At any time not more than one year after the entry of a judgment, the court in which it was entered may, upon motion of the people, set aside the sentence upon the ground that it was invalid as a matter of law.

2. Notwithstanding the provisions of subdivision one, the court must summarily deny the motion when the ground or issue raised thereupon was previously determined on the merits upon an appeal from the judgment or sentence, unless since the time of such appellate determination there has been a retroactively effective change in the law controlling such issue.

3. Notwithstanding the provisions of subdivision one, the court may summarily deny such a motion when the ground or issue raised thereupon was previously determined on the merits upon a prior motion or proceeding in a court of this state, other than an appeal from the judgment or sentence, unless since the time of such determination there has been a retroactively effective change in the law controlling such issue. Despite such circumstance, however, the court, in the interests of justice and for good cause shown, may in its discretion grant the motion if it is otherwise meritorious.

4. The motion must be made upon reasonable notice to the defendant and to the attorney if any who appeared for him in the last proceeding which occurred in connection with the judgment or sentence, and the defendant must be given adequate opportunity to appear in opposition to the motion. The defendant has a right to be present at such proceeding but may waive such right in writing. If he does not so waive it and if he is confined in a prison or other institution of this state, the court must cause him to be produced at the proceeding upon the motion.

5. An order setting aside a sentence pursuant to this section does not affect the validity or status of the underlying conviction, and after entering such an order the court must resentence the defendant in accordance with the law.

6. Upon a resentence imposed pursuant to subdivision five, the terms of which are more severe than those of the original sentence, the defendant's time for taking an appeal from the judgment is automatically extended in the manner prescribed in subdivision four of section 450.30.

ANNOTATIONS

Motion for resentencing; illegality.—Court has the authority to set aside a sentence based on illegality, however, the conviction itself must not be affected. Here, the court was not allowed to alter its finding that defendant was a youthful offender in order to correct an illegally imposed sentence. The court must sentence defendant according to the conviction. People v. Calderon, 79 N.Y.2d 61, 580 N.Y.S.2d 163, 588 N.E.2d 61 (1992).

—Although the People did not timely appeal defendant's sentence, defendant's resentence was proper. Defendant's original sentence of 3 and one-half to 7 years was not valid under the law. People v. Johnson, 215 A.D.2d 258, 626 N.Y.S.2d 775 (1st Dept. 1995).

—People's application to correct an illegal sentence must be made within one year following the entry of the judgment. The court acted, sua sponte, two years post judgment. Such action is not supported statutorily and the alleged mistake in defendant's sentence was not discernible from the record. People v. Riggins, 164 A.D.2d 797, 559 N.Y.S.2d 535 (1st Dept. 1990).

Prior felony convictions.—Although the People failed to file a predicate felony statement pursuant to CPL § 400.21, the court was authorized to sentence defendant as a second felony offender. Both the People and the court possessed information prior to defendant's sentencing which disclosed that defendant most likely had a prior felony conviction. People v. Scarbrough, 66 N.Y.2d 673, 496 N.Y.S.2d 409, 487 N.E.2d 266 (1985).

—Where defendant utilized alias names to prevent the discovery of his prior offenses, thus failing to disclose his second felony offender status, the People's motion to invalidate defendant's sentence was properly granted. Defendant should be resentenced as a second felony offender. People v. Barnes, 160 A.D.2d 342, 553 N.Y.S.2d 413 (1st Dept. 1990).

Inadvertent sentencing error.—It was within the court's power to correct an inadvertent sentencing error *sua sponte* where the court had incorrectly imposed a sentence to run concurrently with time the defendant owed on a prior conviction and the district attorney brought to the court's attention that the sentence should run consecutively. People v. Wright, 56 N.Y.2d 613, 450 N.Y.S.2d 473, 435 N.E.2d 1088 (1982).

Issue previously determined.—Where court composed a memorandum holding defendant's sentence cruel and unusual punishment and both sides were allowed to argue the propriety of the sentence, the issue was held as previously determined on the merits. Thus, the People's motion to set aside defendant's sentence was improper. People v. Frangiamone, 99 A.D.2d 842, 472 N.Y.S.2d 447 (2d Dept. 1984).

—The court may deny a motion to set aside a sentence where the ground or issue was previously determined on the merits; the court correctly exercised its discretion where the people moved to have the defendant resentenced as a second violent felony offender, that motion was denied and no notice of appeal from that order or from the original order was filed. People v. Jordan, 88 A.D.2d 922, 450 N.Y.S.2d 561 (2d Dept. 1982).

§ 440.50. Notice to crime victims of case disposition.

1. Upon the request of a victim of a crime, or in any event in all cases in which the final disposition includes a conviction of a violent felony offense as defined in section 70.02 of the penal law or a felony defined in article one hundred twenty-five of such law, the district attorney shall, within sixty days of the final disposition of the case, inform the victim by letter of such final disposition. If such final disposition results in the commitment of the defendant to the custody of the department of correctional services for an indeterminate sentence, the notice provided to the crime victim shall also inform the victim of his or her right to submit a written, audiotaped, or videotaped victim impact statement to the state division of parole or to meet personally with a member of the state board of parole at a time and place separate from the personal interview between a member or members of the board and the inmate and make such a statement, subject to procedures and limitations contained in rules of the board, both pursuant to subdivision two of section two hundred fifty-nine-i of the executive law. The right of the victim under this subdivision to submit a written victim impact statement or to meet personally with a member of the state board of parole applies to each personal interview between a member or members of the board and the inmate.

2. As used in this section, "victim" means any person alleged or found, upon the record, to have sustained physical or financial injury to person or property as a direct result of the crime charged or a person alleged or found to have sustained, upon the record, an offense under article one hundred thirty of the penal law, or in the case of a homicide or minor child, the victim's family.

3. As used in this section, "final disposition"

means an ultimate termination of the case at the trial level including, but not limited to, dismissal, acquittal, or imposition of sentence by the court, or a decision by the district attorney, for whatever reason, to not file the case.

Added by L. 1978, Ch. 496; **Amended** by L. 1985, Chs. 14, 78; L. 1994, Ch. 559, § 1, eff. Nov. 1, 1994, amending subd. 1; L. 1998, Ch. 367, § 1, eff. July 14, 1998, and Ch. 611, § 1, eff. Oct. 6, 1998, amending subd. 1; L. 2005, Ch. 186, § 3, amending subd. 1, eff. Sept. 1, 2005.

ANNOTATION

Victim.—Plaintiffs sustained no direct injury to their persons or property as a result of the crime, or the actions upon which defendant's conviction was predicated—his intentional misrepresentation of critical facts on his income tax returns—and hence the plaintiffs cannot be considered victims of his crime. Boice v. Burnett, 245 A.D.2d 980, 667 N.Y.S.2d 100 (3d Dept. 1997).

§ 440.55. Notice to education department where a licensed professional has been convicted of a felony.

The district attorney shall give written notification to the department of education upon the conviction of a felony of any person holding a license pursuant to title eight of the education law. In addition, the district attorney shall give written notification to the department upon the vacatur or reversal of any felony conviction of any such person.

Added by L. 1996, Ch. 134, eff. Aug. 10, 1996.

§ 440.60. Notification of invalid sentences of probation.

Whenever it shall appear to the satisfaction of the appropriate director of the probation department that a person sentenced pursuant to article sixty of the penal law has received a sentence which is invalid as a matter of law, it shall become his duty to notify the district attorney of the county in which such person was convicted. Upon such notification, the district attorney shall immediately investigate the matter and if such sentence of probation is in fact invalid as a matter of law, the district attorney shall immediately move to set aside such sentence pursuant to section 440.40 of this chapter.

Added by L. 1984, Ch. 214.

ANNOTATIONS

Procedure.—Upon discovery of defendant's previous felony conviction under an undisclosed alias, the People moved to set aside defendant's sentence of 168 days incarceration and 5 years of probation as invalid as a matter of law. The People's motion was proper and timely. People v. Holley, 168 A.D.2d 992, 565 N.Y.S.2d 351 (4th Dept. 1990).

—Probation Department's contention that defendant's sentence was invalid as a matter of law was properly reported to the district attorney. However, the court's decision to split defendant's sentence, upon resentencing, was held valid under article 60 of the Penal Law. People v. Krawcyk, 130 Misc. 2d 253, 495 N.Y.S.2d 646 (Orange Co. Ct. 1985).

—Where probation department received defendant's condition of probation order and realized it was not signed by the defendant, the department should have notified the prosecutorial authorities of the potentially illegal sentence. Thus, an investigation would have ensued. Stitham v. City of New York, Dept. of Probation, 127 Misc. 2d 906, 487 N.Y.S.2d 523 (Sup. Ct. N.Y. Co. 1985).

ARTICLE 450—APPEALS—IN WHAT CASES AUTHORIZED AND TO WHAT COURTS TAKEN

LexisNexis Cross References

Criminal Constitutional Law, Vol. 3, Ch. 15, Appeals; *Bender's New York Evidence—CPLR,* Vol. 6, Ch. 31, Appellate Review; *Business Crime,* Vol. 4, Ch. 15, Appellate Practice; *Defense of Drunk Driving Cases,* Vol. 4, Ch. 52, Appeals; *Criminal Defense Techniques,* Vol. 2, Ch. 48, Criminal Appeals; *New York Criminal Practice (2d ed.),* Vol. 4, Ch. 44, Appeals; *see generally New York Appellate Practice,* Vol. 1, Ch. 2, Preservation of Error for Review; Vol. 1, Ch. 7, Preparation of the Appellate Brief; Vol. 1, Ch. 8, Argument of the Appeal; Vol. 2, Ch. 13, Criminal Appeals; *Prosecution and Defense of Sex Crimes,* Ch. 17, Appeals in Sex Crimes Cases; *New York Suppression Manual,* Ch. 4, Harmless Error; Ch. 27, Appealing Suppression Orders; *Criminal Practice Handbook (2d ed.),* Ch. 12, Direct Appeal.

§ 450.10. Appeal by defendant to intermediate appellate court; in what cases authorized as of right.

An appeal to an intermediate appellate court may be taken as of right by the defendant from the following judgment, sentence and order of a criminal court:

1. A judgment other than one including a sentence of death, unless the appeal is based solely upon the ground that a sentence was harsh or excessive when such sentence was predicated upon entry of a plea of guilty and the sentence imposed did not exceed that which was agreed to by the defendant as a condition of the plea and set forth on the record or filed with the court as required by subdivision five of section 220.50 or subdivision four of section 340.20;

2. A sentence other than one of death, as prescribed in subdivision one of section 450.30, unless the appeal is based solely upon the ground that a sentence was harsh or excessive when such sentence was predicated upon entry of a plea of guilty and the sentence imposed did not exceed that which was agreed to by the defendant as a condition of the plea and set forth in the record or filed with the court as required by subdivision five of section 220.50 or subdivision four of section 340.20;

3. A sentence including an order of criminal forfeiture entered pursuant to section 460.30 of the penal law with respect to such forfeiture order.

4. An order, entered pursuant to section 440.40, setting aside a sentence other than one of death, upon motion of the People.

5. An order denying a motion, made pursuant to subdivision one-a of section 440.30, for forensic DNA testing of evidence.

Amended by L. 1971, Chs. 671, 788; L. 1984, Ch. 671; L. 1986, Ch. 516; L. 1999, Ch. 560, § 7, adding subd. 5, eff. Dec. 1, 1999.

Editor's Note: L. 2000, Ch. 8, § 2, eff. Mar. 6, 2000, deemed eff. Dec. 1, 1999, provides:

Paragraph (b) shall apply to designated offenders convicted on or after December 1, 1999, is also further provided an appeal pursuant to subdivision (5) of section 450.10.

In the case of a motion pursuant to subdivision 1-a of section 440.30 of the criminal procedure law that was determined prior to December 1, 1999, an appeal to the intermediate appellate court may be taken by the filing and service of a notice of appeal on or before September 1, 2000 or thirty days after service upon such party of a copy of the order from which the appeal is taken, whichever is later.

Notwithstanding the provisions of any other law, if there shall be a case involving a motion pursuant to subdivision 1-a of section 440.30 of the criminal procedure law determined prior to December 1, 1999 that was appealed to an intermediate appellate court and such appeal was determined by such intermediate appellate court prior to May 1, 2000, an application for a certificate granting leave to appeal to the court of appeals from such determination of the intermediate appellate court in such case may be filed on or before September 1, 2000 or thirty days after service upon such party of a copy of the order sought to be appealed, whichever is later.

ANNOTATIONS

Appealability of order.—Permanent orders of protection are appealable. However, an appeal is neither the only nor the best means for resolving an expiration date issue. Because sentencing courts are in the best position to amend orders of protection, the best practice is for a defendant seeking an adjustment to request relief from the issuing court in the first instance, resorting to appellate courts only if necessary. People v. Nieves, 2 N.Y.3d 310, 778 N.Y.S.2d 751, 811 N.E.2d 13 (2004).

—CPL § 450.10 confers upon the defendant a fundamental right to appeal his conviction. People v. Harrison, 85 N.Y.2d 794, 628 N.Y.S.2d 939, 652 N.E.2d 638 (1995).

—CPL § 450.10 does not deprive the defendant from appealing the court's order denying defendant's motion pursuant to CPL § 440.10. Thus, CPL § 450.10 is constitutional. People v. Farrell, 85 N.Y.2d 60, 623 N.Y.S.2d 550, 647 N.E.2d 762 (1995).

—No appeal lay from the order of the Extraordinary Special and Trial Term of the Supreme Court denying petitioner's application to compel the Special State Prosecutor to inquire of Federal authorities as to whether they had conducted electronic surveillance of him and for the prosecutor to state whether the questions asked him before the Grand Jury were the product of any such surveillance. In re Santangello, 38 N.Y.2d 536, 381 N.Y.S.2d 472, 344 N.E.2d 404 (1976).

—In criminal cases, the right to appeal is purely statutory, and no appeal lies, either as of right or by permission, from an order denying a defendant's request to obtain a copy of his probation report. People v. Wright, 206 A.D.2d 337, 614 N.Y.S.2d 732, 733 (1st Dept. 1994).

—The right of review by appeal in criminal matters is determined exclusively by statute. People v. Ainsworth, 145 A.D.2d 74, 537 N.Y.S.2d 798, 799 (1st Dept. 1989).

—"Oral Bench subpoena," in which the court directed the county attorney to produce certain written documents was not appealable. People v. McIntosh, 199 A.D.2d 540, 606 N.Y.S.2d 248, 249 (2d Dept. 1993).

—The defendant does not have the statutory right to appeal from an intermediate order denying defendant's motion to dismiss a felony complaint. People v. Harlan, 177 A.D.2d 931, 575 N.Y.S.2d 1022 (3d Dept. 1991).

Subd. 1.—Subdivision as amended by the Laws of 1984 (Ch. 671), which purports to disallow an appeal as of right to the Appellate Division where the sole issue raised is the excessiveness of a negotiated sentence imposed by a judgment rendered upon a guilty plea, imposes a limitation or condition on the jurisdiction of the Appellate Division of Supreme Court in contravention of the N.Y. Constitution, article VI, section 4(k). People v. Pollenz, 125 A.D.2d 715, 509 N.Y.S.2d 786 (2d Dept.), aff'd, 67 N.Y.2d 264, 502 N.Y.S.2d 417, 493 N.E.2d 541 (1986).

Competency.—Court declined to exercise its discretion to hold the appeal in abeyance pending a further hearing to establish defendant's competence to take part in his appeal. People v. Christopher, 170 A.D.2d 1020, 566 N.Y.S.2d 167, 168 (4th Dept. 1991).

Denial of motion to suppress; final order; appealability.—A final order denying a motion to suppress evidence may be reviewed on an appeal from an ensuing judgment of conviction, notwithstanding that the conviction resulted from a plea of guilty. People v. Taylor, 102 A.D.2d 944, 477 N.Y.S.2d 805 (3d Dept. 1984), aff'd, 65 N.Y.2d 1, 489 N.Y.S.2d 152, 478 N.E.2d 755 (1985).

Effect of guilty plea.—A defendant's plea of guilty does not forfeit his right to raise on appeal a challenge to the constitutionality of the statute under which he was convicted. People v. Lee, 58 N.Y.2d 491, 462 N.Y.S.2d 417, 448 N.E.2d 1328 (1983).

—Defendant may not appeal from a sentence which was agreed upon as a condition of the defendant pleading guilty to the charges of attempted sodomy. People v. Ames, 120 A.D.2d 804, 501 N.Y.S.2d 546 (3d Dept. 1986).

—Defendant did not have the right to appeal a sentence on the basis that the sentence was harsh and excessive where the defendant agreed that he would plead guilty in exchange for a sentence not exceeding 1-3 years. People v. Barris, 120 A.D.2d 773, 501 N.Y.S.2d 232 (3d Dept. 1986).

Generally.—The Appellate Division has the constitutional duty to entertain all appeals from criminal case judgments. The defendant has the right to such an appeal pursuant to CPL § 450.109(1). Mosher v. State, 80 N.Y.2d 273, 590 N.Y.S.2d 53, 604 N.E.2d 108 (1992).

—Defendant's claim on appeal must be reviewed pursuant to the state of the law at the time of the appeal. People v. Brown, 171 A.D.2d 1038, 569 N.Y.S.2d 526, 527 (4th Dept. 1991).

Guilty plea.—Defendant may not litigate for the first time on appeal issues of whether his guilty plea should be vacated because the court failed to elicit a sufficient factual basis or question him about a defense, or because of the effectiveness of counsel at the time of the plea; rather, these issues should have been litigated in a post-conviction motion pursuant to CPL § 440.10 prior to the imposition of sentence. People v. Lowry, 107 A.D.2d 716, 484 N.Y.S.2d 71 (2d Dept. 1985).

Habeas corpus.—Habeas corpus does not lie to permit review of claimed errors already considered on a direct appeal. People v. Abrams, 114 A.D.2d 481, 494 N.Y.S.2d 395 (2d Dept. 1985).

—Habeas corpus is not available to petitioner whose judgment of conviction was affirmed on appeal since that writ is not a substitute for appeal, does not lie to permit review of errors considered on appeal, and, in any event, is an improper remedy in this case since a finding of error would merely result in a suppression of evidence and a new trial rather than immediate release from custody. People ex rel. Williams, 107 A.D.2d 729, 484 N.Y.S.2d 90 (2d Dept. 1985).

Hearsay; can't be raised for first time on appeal.—A defendant who failed to object to the court's charges as to hearsay, cannot for the first time on remittal to the Appellate Division raise the issue. People v. Berkowitz, 78 A.D.2d 621, 432 N.Y.S.2d 701 (1st Dept. 1980).

Ineffective counsel.—Defendant's rights were not violated where the court limited defendant's motion to vacate the judgment on the claim of ineffective counsel. Such a motion is an intermediate order which is, by statute, subject to limited review. People v. Ghee, 153 A.D.2d 954, 545 N.Y.S.2d 760 (2d Dept. 1989).

Issue must be preserved by plea of guilty.—A guilty plea entered on condition that the denial of defendant's motion to dismiss the indictment based on the alleged insufficiency of the evidence before the grand jury was preserved for appellate review must be vacated and the defendant be allowed to plead anew because of the Appellate Divisions policy of withholding appellate review of issues not preserved by a plea of guilty. People v. Jordan, 78 A.D.2d 878, 433 N.Y.S.2d 25 (2d Dept. 1980).

Loss of trial exhibit; effect of;—The loss of a trial exhibit did not deprive defendant of effective appellate review. The court could not conclude that the actual tape recording that was lost, of a phone call from the complainant to the defendant, which had been admitted into evidence, was necessary for effective appellate review of the legal sufficiency of the evidence. However, the Court ordered the case to be remitted to allow the parties to both brief and argue the need for the tape recording in order to accomplish effective appellate review. People v. Yavru-Sakuk, 98 N.Y.2d 56, 745 N.Y.S.2d 787, 772 N.E.2d 1145 (2002), on remand, 3 Misc. 3d 36, 779 N.Y.S.2d 329 (App. T. 2d Dept. 2004).

Motion to quash subpoena; no appeal.—An order by a trial court determining a motion to quash a subpoena for the production of police reports, issued in the course of a criminal proceeding, is not subject to direct appellate review. People v. Santos, 64 N.Y.2d 702, 485 N.Y.S.2d 524, 474 N.E.2d 1192 (1984).

Orders; not appealable.—Although no criminal action had been commenced against the individuals concerned, no appeal lay from orders of the Supreme Court directing one to provide handwriting exemplars at the District Attorney's office and directing another to appear in a lineup to be held at the District Attorney's office. Alphonso C. v. Morgenthau, 38 N.Y.2d 923, 382 N.Y.S.2d 980, 346 N.E.2d 819 (1976).

—Where the court refused to provide the defendant with a copy of his probation report, defendant did not have a statutory right to appeal the decision. People v. Wright, 206 A.D.2d 337, 614 N.Y.S.2d 732 (1st Dept. 1994).

Motion by assigned counsel to be relieved.—Assigned counsel has an obligation to investigate and inquire as to the possible merit of all appealable issues and he is required to make reference in the brief to all matters in the record which might arguably support the appeal. People v. Lowery, 86 A.D.2d 537, 445 N.Y.S.2d 992 (1st Dept. 1982).

Registration requirement for sex offenders; appealability.—The registration requirement imposed upon defendant convicted of sex offense was a condition of his probation and was part of his sentence and, therefore, was subject to challenge on direct appeal from the conviction. People v. Grice, 254 A.D.2d 710, 679 N.Y.S.2d 771 (4th Dept. 1998).

Right to counsel in appeal.—The Due Process clause of the 14th Amendment guarantees a criminal defendant the effective assistance of counsel on his first appeal where such appeal is provided as of right. Evitts v. Lucey, 469 U.S. 387, 105 S. Ct. 830, 83 L. Ed. 2d 821 (1985).

Suppression ruling; waiver.—A defendant who pleads guilty during a suppression hearing which is then terminated without a ruling, and who simultaneously waives his right to continue and conclude that hearing, cannot ask the appellate court to suppress his inculpatory statements. People v. Lucas, 106 A.D.2d 821, 484 N.Y.S.2d 220 (3d Dept. 1984).

Sentence; credit received.—CPL § 450.10 does not grant the defendant the right to seek credit towards his sentence through the direct appeal of his conviction. Defendant must utilize Article 78 proceedings. People v. Curtis, 143 A.D.2d 1030, 533 N.Y.S.2d 582 (2d Dept. 1988).

Waiver.—Because the waiver was never explicitly reviewed or considered by the trial court, so far as the record discloses, the appellate court did not have a sufficient basis for concluding the defendant's waiver of his right to appeal was knowing, intelligent, or voluntary, and the Appellate Division should not have given automatic effect to the waiver. People v. Calvi, 89 N.Y.2d 868, 653 N.Y.S.2d 89, 675 N.E.2d 843 (1996).

—Where there was no effort to conceal error and defendant was fully aware of what the appealable issues were, and chose to accept a lighter sentence rather than risk the delay and outcome of an appeal or new trial, there was no reason for the Court of Appeals to interfere with waiver of the right to appeal. People v. Holman, 89 N.Y.2d 876, 653 N.Y.S.2d 93, 675 N.E.2d 847 (1996).

—In view of defendant's deportation to England the appeal was dismissed. People v. Ragsdale, 144 A.D.2d 708, 535 N.Y.S.2d 63, 64 (2d Dept. 1988).

—Defendant's contention that his waiver of the right to appeal was invalid because the court failed to conduct an adequate inquiry before accepting the waiver was without merit where the record established that the waiver was part of a negotiated plea bargain and was voluntarily and knowingly made, and that defendant fully understood the consequences of the waiver. People v. Maurizio, 170 A.D.2d 905, 567 N.Y.S.2d 323, 324 (3d Dept. 1991).

§ 450.15. Appeal by defendant to intermediate appellate court; in what cases authorized by permission.

If an appeal by defendant is not authorized as of right pursuant to section 450.10, the defendant may appeal from the following orders of a criminal court, provided that a certificate granting leave to appeal is issued pursuant to section 460.15:

1. An order denying a motion, made pursuant to section 440.10, to vacate a judgment other than one including a sentence of death;

2. An order denying a motion by the defendant made pursuant to section 440.20, to set aside a sentence other than one of death;

3. A sentence which is not otherwise appealable as of right pursuant to subdivision one or two of section 450.10.

Added by L. 1971, Ch. 671; **Amended** by L. 1984, Ch. 671.

ANNOTATIONS

Appeal; resentencing.—Where the defendant is appealing from resentencing, the defendant may not raise issues from a prior appeal seeking to vacate the judgment of resentence. People v. Drummond, 104 A.D.2d 825, 480 N.Y.S.2d 48 (2d Dept. 1984).

—Defendant's motion for resentencing was not allowed where the defendant failed to obtain permission to appeal. People v. Sweeter, 125 A.D.2d 841, 509 N.Y.S.2d 949 (3d Dept. 1986).

Appeal; order denying motion to set aside sentence.—Where the defendant did not seek the permission from the Appellate Division, defendant could not appeal the denial of his motion to set aside the sentence. People v. Ramsey, 104 A.D.2d 388, 478 N.Y.S.2d 715 (2d Dept. 1984).

—Where defendant's motion to set aside the sentence on the basis that defendant was incorrectly sentenced as a second felony offender was denied, defendant must seek permission to appeal. People v. Thayer, 210 A.D.2d 977, 621 N.Y.S.2d 987 (4th Dept. 1994).

—Where defendant failed to obtain leave to appeal from the denial of his CPL § 440.20 motion, he could not raise the issue contained therein on direct appeal. People v. Kihm, 143 A.D.2d 199, 532 N.Y.S.2d 11 (2d Dept. 1988).

Generally.—Where defendant's failed to appeal their convictions, the court is not authorized to review the County Court's decision refusing to dismiss the defendant's indictments. People v. Taylor, 99 A.D.2d 820, 472 N.Y.S.2d 155 (2d Dept. 1984).

Sentence; reformatory; youthful offender; equal protection of the laws.—To sentence a defendant of the youthful offender age group, but not afforded youthful offender treatment, to a reformatory term of imprisonment upon his plea of guilty to a Class A misdemeanor even though the same sentence could not be imposed on a youthful offender, does not violate statute or constitution where sentencing judge took into account unrehabilitative character of defendant. People v. De Perez, 70 Misc. 2d 982, 335 N.Y.S.2d 526 (Ontario Co. Ct. 1972), aff'd, 32 N.Y.2d 880, 346 N.Y.S.2d 533, 299 N.E.2d 898 (1973).

Statutory authorization.—Where defendant's right to appeal a sentence as harsh or excessive where that sentence was received as a result of a negotiated guilty plea is abrogated by statute, the defendant must be granted permission to appeal. People v. Hickman, 111 A.D.2d 959, 490 N.Y.S.2d 281 (3d Dept. 1985).

§ 450.20. Appeal by people to intermediate appellate court; in what cases authorized.

An appeal to an intermediate appellate court may be taken as of right by the people from the following sentence and orders of a criminal court:

1. An order dismissing an accusatory instrument or a count thereof, entered pursuant to section 170.30, 170.50 or 210.20, or an order terminating a prosecution pursuant to subdivision four of section 180.85;

1-a. An order reducing a count or counts of an indictment or dismissing an indictment and directing the filing of a prosecutor's information, entered pursuant to subdivision one-a of section 210.20;

2. An order setting aside a verdict and dismissing an accusatory instrument or a count thereof, entered pursuant to paragraph (b) of subdivision one of section 290.10 or 360.40;

3. An order setting aside a verdict, entered pursuant to section 330.30 or 370.10;

4. A sentence other than one of death, as prescribed in subdivisions two and three of section 450.30;

5. An order, entered pursuant to section 440.10, vacating a judgment other than one including a sentence of death;

6. An order, entered pursuant to section 440.20, setting aside a sentence other than one of death;

7. An order denying a motion by the people, made pursuant to section 440.40, to set aside a sentence other than one of death;

8. An order suppressing evidence, entered before trial pursuant to section 710.20; provided that the people file a statement in the appellate court pursuant to section 450.50.

9. An order entered pursuant to section 460.30 of the penal law setting aside or modifying a verdict of forfeiture.

10. An order, entered pursuant to paragraph (e) of subdivision twelve of section 400.27, finding that the defendant is mentally retarded.

11. An order granting a motion, made pursuant to subdivision one-a of section 440.30, for forensic DNA testing of evidence.

Amended by L. 1983, Ch. 170; L. 1986, Ch. 516; L. 1995, Ch. 1, § 22, eff. Sept. 1, 1995, adding subd. 10; L. 1999, Ch. 560, § 8, adding subd. 11, eff. Dec. 1, 1999; L. 2004, Ch. 518, §3, eff. Nov. 1, 2004.

Editor's Note: L. 2000, Ch. 8, § 2, eff. Mar. 6, 2000, deemed eff. Dec. 1, 1999, provides:

Paragraph (b) shall apply to designated offenders convicted on or after December 1, 1999, is also further provided an appeal pursuant to subdivision 11 of section 450.20 of the criminal law.

In the case of a motion pursuant to subdivision 1-a of section 440.30 of the criminal procedure law that was determined prior to December 1, 1999, an appeal to the intermediate appellate court may be taken by the filing and service of a notice of appeal on or before September 1, 2000 or thirty days after service upon such party of a copy of the order from which the appeal is taken, whichever is later.

Notwithstanding the provisions of any other law, if there shall be a case involving a motion pursuant to subdivision 1-a of section 440.30 of the criminal procedure law determined prior to December 1, 1999 that was appealed to an intermediate appellate court and such appeal was determined by such intermediate appellate court prior to May 1, 2000, an application for a certificate granting leave to appeal to the court of appeals from such determination of the intermediate appellate court in such case may be filed on or before September 1, 2000 or thirty days after service upon such party of a copy of the order sought to be appealed, whichever is later.

ANNOTATIONS

Appeal; inapplicable.—CPL § 450.20 does not allow the People to appeal from a sua sponte order of a trial court setting aside a verdict pursuant to Judiciary Law § 2-b(3); instead, this challenge must be made in a CPLR Article 78 proceeding. People v. Dunn, 4 N.Y.3d 495, 796 N.Y.S.2d 331, 829 N.E.2d 295 (2005).

—People may not seek review by direct appeal on a motion to quash a subpoena arising during a criminal proceeding. People v. Santo, 64 N.Y.2d 702, 485 N.Y.S.2d 524, 474 N.E.2d 1192 (1984).

—The five year delay between the conviction and the granting of a new trial on appeal did not violate the defendant's right to a speedy appeal or retrial as CPL § 30.30 does not apply to appeals. People v. Cousart, 58 N.Y.2d 62, 458 N.Y.S.2d 507, 444 N.E.2d 971 (1982).

—Where the court ordered the Clerk of Property to return property to the defendant, the clerk lacked the statutory authority to appeal the court's order. People v. Reville-Oviedo, 178 A.D.2d 442, 577 N.Y.S.2d 301 (2d Dept. 1991).

—People are not statutorily authorized to appeal from an order which requires the People to succumb to inspection of a breathalyser machine. Yet, a remedy will exist where the court decision has exceeded its powers. Shay v. Mullen, 215 A.D.2d 935, 626 N.Y.S.2d 580 (3d Dept. 1995).

Defendant's right to counsel on People's appeal.—A defendant has vital interests at stake on People's appeal, and defendant has the right to appellate counsel of defendant's choice and the right to seek appointment of counsel upon proof of indigency; where defendant was unrepresented on appeal, absent record evidence that defendant was informed of his right to counsel and that he waived that right, court should not have proceeded to consider and decide People's appeal. People v. Garcia, 93 N.Y.2d 42, 687 N.Y.S.2d 601, 710 N.E.2d 247 (1999).

Dismissal of perjury prosecution for insufficiency of evidence.—CPL § 450.20(2), providing that the People may appeal a trial order of dismissal entered pursuant to CPL § 290.10, is unconstitutional as violative of the right not to be placed twice in jeopardy for the same offense if "further proceedings of some sort, devoted to the resolution of factual issues going to the elements of the offense charged, would have been required upon reversal and remand." People v. Brown, 40 N.Y.2d 381, 386 N.Y.S.2d 848, 353 N.E.2d 811 (1976), *cert. denied*, 433 U.S. 913 (1977).

Dismissal of indictment; appeal by People.—People may immediately appeal the decision of the court dismissing an indictment. The court must allow a reasonable time for the completion of the appeal. People v. Cortes, 80 N.Y.2d 201, 590 N.Y.S.2d 9, 604 N.Y.S.2d 71 (1992).

—A pretrial dismissal of an indictment in accordance with CPL § 210.20 is reviewable on direct appeal. Holtzman v. Goldman, 71 N.Y.2d 564, 528 N.Y.S.2d 21, 523 N.E.2d 297 (1988).

—A pretrial order dismissing the indictment (CPL § 450.20[1]) is appealable by the People even though the order was entered on the court's own motion and not upon motion of the defendant. People v. Edwards, 78 A.D.2d 582, 432 N.Y.S.2d 567 (4th Dept. 1980), *aff'd*, 64 N.Y.2d 658, 485 N.Y.S.2d 252, 474 N.E.2d 612 (1984).

—People were authorized to appeal the court's decision dismissing defendant's indictment. The court acted properly in granting the People the right to seek a conviction on lesser charges. People v. Ainsworth, 145 A.D.2d 74, 537 N.Y.S.2d 798 (1989).

Double jeopardy.—Where the motion to dismiss the information because of a deficiency is discoverable and capable of being made prior to trial, the right to assert the defense of double jeopardy when the motion is made during trial should be deemed waived. People v. Key, 87 Misc. 2d 262, 391 N.Y.S.2d 781 (App. Term 9-10 Jud. Dist. 1976), aff'd, 45 N.Y.2d 111, 408 N.Y.S.2d 16, 379 N.E.2d 1147 (1978).

—The People may appeal the court's order, setting aside the convictions of the defendants, without subjecting the defendants to double jeopardy. People v. Foster, 143 A.D.2d 56, 532 N.Y.S.2d 127 (1st Dept. 1988).

Further prosecution.—Where, pursuant to CPL § 450.20(8), the People take an appeal from an order suppressing evidence and such appeal proves unsuccessful, CPL § 440.50(2) prohibits subsequent prosecutions of the same defendant upon either the same or a superseding accusatory instrument for the crimes charged in the original instrument, at least in the absence of extraordinary circumstances. Forte v. Supreme Court of the State of New York, 48 N.Y.2d 179, 422 N.Y.S.2d 26, 397 N.E.2d 717 (1979).

Erroneous trial order of dismissal; appealable.—The People may take an appeal from an erroneous trial order of dismissal. People v. Gallo, 75 A.D.2d 148, 431 N.Y.S.2d 1009 (1st Dept. 1980).

Generally.—The right of the People to appeal in a criminal case is statutorily determined and the statutes conferring such right must be strictly construed. People v. Brummel, 136 A.D.2d 322, 526 N.Y.S.2d 823, 824 (1st Dept. 1988).

—The People's authority to appeal to an intermediate appellate court in a criminal case is strictly the product of statute. People v. Rodriguez, 178 A.D.2d 1019, 578 N.Y.S.2d 774 (4th Dept. 1991).

—Absent any error of law, the People have no right to appeal and the Appellate Division may not interfere with a court's decision to impose concurrent terms. People v. Santiago, 181 A.D.2d 460, 581 N.Y.S.2d 298, 299 (1st Dept.), aff'd, 80 N.Y.2d 916, 589 N.Y.S.2d 302, 602 N.E.2d 1118 (1992).

—The People do not have the right to appeal preclusion orders issued pursuant to CPL § 710.30. People v. Laing, 79 N.Y.2d 166, 581 N.Y.S.2d 149, 589 N.E.2d 372 (1992).

Order dismissing indictment; appealability.—A trial court order, pursuant to CPL § 210.20(1)(h) and (i), which dismissed the indictment for the failure of the people to state a *prima facie* case in their opening address to the jury, should have been reviewed by the intermediate appellate court notwithstanding the fact that the trial court's reliance on the statute may have been misplaced; any inquiry into the court's reliance on CPL § 210.20 should have been considered on the merits. People v. Coppa, 45 N.Y.2d 244, 408 N.Y.S.2d 365, 380 N.E.2d 195 (1978).

Order modifying verdict; appealability.—CPL § 330.30, referring to an order setting aside a verdict, also includes an order which modifies a verdict in part or in whole. Thus, the People have the authority to appeal an order pursuant to CPL § 330.30 which modifies the verdict. People v. McDonald, 68 N.Y.2d 1, 505 N.Y.S.2d 824, 496 N.E.2d 844 (1986).

Prosecutor's appeal; trial order of dismissal.—CPL § 450.20(2) allowing the prosecutor to appeal a trial order of dismissal (CPL § 290.10) is unconstitutional. People v. Brown, 40 N.Y.2d 381, 386 N.Y.S.2d 848, 353 N.E.2d 811 (1976).

Sentence invalid.—Court acted properly in ordering the resentencing of the defendant as a second felony offender following the People's appeal of defendant's sentence as invalid. Anderson v. Kirk 72 N.Y.2d 995, 534 N.Y.S.2d 369, 530 N.E.2d 1289 (1988).

—Where the defendant was incorrectly sentenced without taking into account defendant's status as a second felony offender, the People were authorized to appeal the illegality of the sentence. People v. Kuyal, 155 A.D.2d 901, 547 N.Y.S.2d 731 (4th Dept. 1989).

Suppression orders; appeal.—The People can appeal to an intermediate appellate court to challenge a trial court's ruling suppressing the results of a consented-to chemical test; the People's appeal options under CPL § 450.20(8) incorporate the whole of CPL § 710.20. People v. Ayala, 89 N.Y.2d 874, 653 N.Y.S.2d 92, 675 N.E.2d 846 (1996).

—Where the People's case cannot proceed due to the suppressed evidence, the People are authorized to appeal the order. People v. McIntosh, 80 N.Y.2d 87, 587 N.Y.S.2d 568, 600 N.E.2d 199 (1992).

—Where the People are in possession of evidence legally sufficient to convict the defendant, the People's appeal of a suppression order must be dismissed. Here, the People's complaining witness was available to testify. People v. Robinson, 171 A.D.2d 475, 567 N.Y.S.2d 401 (1st Dept. 1991).

—People are authorized to appeal the suppression order of an accusatory instrument containing charges which were affected by the suppression order, although, at one time, it contained charges which were unaffected by the suppression order. People v. Salgado, 207 A.D.2d 918, 616 N.Y.S.2d 657 (2d Dept. 1994).

—An order precluding identification evidence is not appealable where the order was entered subsequent to the impaneling and swearing in of the jury. Further, the People failed to serve the defendant with notice of this identification evidence. People v. Austin, 208 A.D.2d 990, 618 N.Y.S.2d 115 (3d Dept. 1994).

—Where the court's suppression order was not pursuant to CPL § 710.20, the People could not appeal the order. The People were allowed to appeal the suppression of the statements made to the officers by the defendant. People v. Weaver, 177 A.D.2d 809, 576 N.Y.S.2d 424 (3d Dept. 1991).

Trial order of dismissal; dismissal of appeal to intermediate appellate court; double jeopardy.—Trial order of dismissal pursuant to CPL § 290.10 based partly upon evidence and partly on the court's interpretation of the law could not be appealed from by the People because of the double jeopardy clause of the Fifth Amendment of the United States Constitution and Article 1, Section 6 of the New York State Constitution. People v. Brown, 48 A.D.2d 95, 368 N.Y.S.2d 171 (1st Dept. 1975), aff'd, 40 N.Y.2d 381, 386 N.Y.S.2d 848, 353 N.E.2d 811 (1976).

§ 450.30. Appeal from sentence.

1. An appeal by the defendant from a sentence, as authorized by subdivision two of section 450.10, may be based upon the ground that such sentence either was (a) invalid as a matter of law, or (b) harsh or excessive. A sentence is invalid as a matter of law not only when the terms thereof are unauthorized but also when it is based upon an erroneous determination that the defendant had a previous valid conviction for an offense or, in the case of a resentence following a revocation of a sentence of probation or conditional discharge, upon an improper revocation of such original sentence. An appeal by the defendant from a sentence, as authorized by subdivision three of section 450.15, may be based upon the ground that such sentence was harsh or excessive.

2. An appeal by the people from a sentence, as authorized by subdivision four of section 450.20, may be based only upon the ground that such sentence was invalid as a matter of law.

3. An appeal from a sentence, within the meaning of this section and sections 450.10 and 450.20, means an appeal from either the sentence originally imposed or from a resentence following an order vacating the original sentence. For purposes of appeal, the judgment consists of the conviction and the original sentence only, and when a resentence occurs more than thirty days after the original sentence, a defendant who has not previously filed a notice of appeal from the judgment may not appeal from the judgment, but only from the resentence.

4. When as a result of a successful appeal by the people from a sentence, the defendant receives

a resentence the terms of which are more severe than those of the original or reversed sentence, the defendant, if he has not taken an appeal from the judgment, may, even though the period for doing so as prescribed in section 460.10 has expired, take such an appeal by filing and serving a notice of appeal, or an affidavit of errors as the case may be, within thirty days after imposition of the resentence. Upon such an appeal, only the conviction is reviewable; and any appellate challenge to the resentence must be made upon a separate appeal therefrom.

Amended by L. 1984, Ch. 671.

ANNOTATIONS

Appeals from resentence; timeliness.—Where defendant failed to appeal his original judgment, defendant was not entitled to a reconstruction hearing on the original proceeding upon his appeal for resentencing. People v. Williams, 192 A.D.2d 322, 595 N.Y.S.2d 449 (1st Dept. 1993).

—Where the defendant failed to file a timely notice of appeal from the original judgment, defendant could not challenge a ruling from the original judgment upon his appeal from resentencing. People v. Anderson, 151 A.D.2d 684, 542 N.Y.S.2d 743 (2d Dept. 1989).

—Defendant's motion appealing a fine imposed at his original sentence was held to be untimely where the defendant made such a motion at the time of resentencing for violating probation. People v. Rutnik, 198 A.D.2d 617, 603 N.Y.S.2d 642 (3d Dept. 1993).

—Court properly held defendant's motion to set aside the verdict as untimely where the motion was made prior to resentencing rather than the original sentencing. People v. Ferrin, 197 A.D.2d 882, 602 N.Y.S.2d 289 (4th Dept. 1993).

Excessiveness, outstanding background of defendant.— Sentence of 8 to 25 years after entry of a guilty plea to the crime of first degree manslaughter was excessive in light of the defendants' background. Defendant had no prior conflicts with the law, had a background described by the sentencing judge as outstanding and at the sentence proceeding, defendant expressed extreme remorse for the incident and its impact upon the victim's family. Accordingly, the court reduced the sentence to 5 to 15 years. People v. Medina, 95 A.D.2d 696, 464 N.Y.S.2d 2 (1st Dept. 1983).

Grounds for; unavailability of testimony.—Availability of trial testimony is irrelevant for an appeal pursuant to CPL § 450.30 subsequent to defendant's resentencing. The underlying conviction is not reviewable. People v. Johnson, 509 N.Y.S.2d 789 (4th Dept. 1986).

Reduction in the interest of justice.—Defendant, an illegal alien had his sentence reduced in the interests of justice from, not less than seven years nor more than 22 and a half, to not less than four nor more than 12, where he had no previous criminal record and he had a wife and children living abroad. People v. Campbell, 82 A.D.2d 766, 440 N.Y.S.2d 647 (1st Dept. 1981).

Sentence; equal protection of the laws.—It was not an abuse of discretion to sentence defendant, after conviction by jury on charges of murder, second degree, to 25 years to life even though co-defendants who had pleaded guilty received lighter sentences, since the defendant slightly over 16 years of age when the incident occurred, had been involved in numerous serious offenses while a juvenile; his willingness to participate in the crime was based on his desire for personal profit and he did not have any feelings or guilt or any sense of remorse. People v. Mendez, 75 A.D.2d 400, 430 N.Y.S.2d 57 (1st Dept. 1980).

Sentence; error of law.—A sentence of probation pursuant to PL § 70.02(2)(c)(I) may not be altered by the Appellate Court where there is no evidence the sentence was in error of law. People v. Alejandro, 195 A.D.2d 356, 600 N.Y.S.2d 635 (1st Dept. 1993).

—The trial court's determination that the defendant should be sentenced to probation may not be disturbed by the People or the Appellate Court unless the sentence is invalid. People v.

Washington, 175 A.D.2d 732, 573 N.Y.S.2d 180 (1st Dept. 1991).

—The court is not authorized under CPL § 450.30 to disturb a sentence based on the sentence being too lenient upon the defendant. People v. Williams, 164 A.D.2d 1, 560 N.Y.S.2d 1009 (1st Dept. 1990).

—Where the defendant reaffirmed his plea of guilty the court held that the defendant still possessed the right to challenge his sentence as invalid as a matter of law. Defendant did not waive the right upon the reaffirmation. People v. Holley, 168 A.D.2d 992, 565 N.Y.S.2d 351 (4th Dept. 1990).

Underlying conviction.—People were not authorized to appeal the decision of the trial court where the trial court accepted defendant's plea of guilty over the objection of the prosecution. The People were not authorized to challenge the underlying conviction. People v. Cosme, 80 N.Y.2d 790, 587 N.Y.S.2d 274, 599 N.E.2d 678 (1992).

Youthful offender adjudication; not predicate felony.— Defendant was improperly sentenced as a second felony offender since the predicate felony was the result of a youthful offender adjudication which is not a judgment of conviction. People v. Mitchell, 88 A.D.2d 982, 451 N.Y.S.2d 789 (2d Dept. 1982).

§ 450.40. Appeal by people from trial order of dismissal.

1. An appeal by the people from a trial order of dismissal, as authorized by subdivision two of section 450.20, may, as indicated by section 290.10, be based either (a) upon the ground that the evidence adduced at the trial was legally sufficient to support the count or counts of the accusatory instrument dismissed by the order, or (b) upon the ground that, though not legally sufficient, such evidence would have been legally sufficient had the court not erroneously excluded admissible evidence offered by the people.

2. If the appeal is based upon the ground specified in paragraph (b) of subdivision one, and if the appellate court determines that the evidence unsuccessfully offered by the people was improperly excluded, and if at the trial the people made on[*] offer of proof with respect thereto pursuant to subdivision three of section 290.10, the appellate court, in making its determination whether the people's evidence would have been legally sufficient had it not been for the improper exclusion, must treat the excluded evidentiary matter as it is summarized in the offer of proof as evidence constituting a part of the people's case.

[*] As originally enacted. Should probably be "an."

ANNOTATION

People have no right to appeal from trial order of dismissal.—People do not have a right to appeal from a trial order of dismissal granted in a jury trial at the close of the People's case. People v. Harding, 101 A.D.2d 221, 475 N.Y.S.2d 611 (3d Dept. 1984).

§ 450.50. Appeal by people from order suppressing evidence; filing of statement in appellate court.

1. In taking an appeal, pursuant to subdivision eight of section 450.20, to an intermediate appellate court from an order of a criminal court suppressing evidence, the people must file, in addition to a notice of appeal or, as the case may

be, an affidavit of errors, a statement asserting that the deprivation of the use of the evidence ordered suppressed has rendered the sum of the proof available to the people with respect to a criminal charge which has been filed in the court either (a) insufficient as a matter of law, or (b) so weak in its entirety that any reasonable possibility of prosecuting such charge to a conviction has been effectively destroyed.

2. The taking of an appeal by the people, pursuant to subdivision eight of section 450.20, from an order suppressing evidence constitutes a bar to the prosecution of the accusatory instrument involving the evidence ordered suppressed, unless and until such suppression order is reversed upon appeal and vacated.

ANNOTATIONS

Discretion of the People.—The prosecutor has the authority to appeal the order suppressing the evidence where the prosecution established that the remaining evidence was insufficient to proceed with the case. The defendant may not oppose the prosecutor's assessment. People v. Kates, 53 N.Y.2d 591, 444 N.Y.S.2d 446, 428 N.E.2d 852 (1981).

—The People may decide whether to proceed or not on the evidence which remains following an order suppressing evidence. People v. Smedman, 184 A.D.2d 600, 584 N.Y.S.2d 627 (2d Dept. 1992).

Filing of the statement.—Statement pursuant to CPL § 450.50 is not required to be filed with the notice of the appeal. The People may file the statement prior to the appeal. People v. Morales, 198 A.D.2d 129, 603 N.Y.S.2d 318 (1st Dept. 1993).

—Dismissal of the indictment simultaneously with the suppression of statements guarantees finality and renders the filing of a statement, pursuant to CPL § 450.50(1), unnecessary. People v. Townsend, 127 A.D.2d 505, 511 N.Y.S.2d 858, 860 (1st Dept. 1987).

Further prosecution.—Defendant may not be subsequently prosecuted for the crimes in the indictment where the People's appeal from an order suppressing evidence is unsuccessful. Forte v. Supreme Court of the State of New York, 48 N.Y.2d 179, 422 N.Y.S.2d 26, 397 N.E.2d 717 (1979).

—Court must dismiss an indictment where the People unsuccessfully appealed the suppression order. Defendant must not be subjected to further prosecution for the charges in the accusation. People v. Caruso, 174 A.D.2d 1051, 572 N.Y.S.2d 216 (4th Dept. 1991).

Search and seizure; mere suspicion insufficient.—Neither suspicious nor equivocal behavior alone justifies a search, and the fact that defendant was actually in possession of narcotics did not change the illegal search here into a legal one, because a search is bad or good when it starts, and is not made good by what is found. Since the defendant was not under arrest at the time of the search, it could not later be justified as incidental to a lawful arrest. People v. Munoz, 40 A.D.2d 337, 340 N.Y.S.2d 238 (1st Dept. 1973), aff'd, 33 N.Y.2d 998, 353 N.Y.S.2d 965, 309 N.E.2d 427 (1974).

Suppression order.—Court order precluding identification evidence was not appealable as a suppression order. The order was entered subsequent to the commencement of the trial. People v. Austin, 208 A.D.2d 990, 618 N.Y.S.2d 115 (3d Dept. 1994).

Withdrawal of appeal.—Indictment of defendant was properly upheld where the People withdrew the appeal, with the court's permission, from an order suppressing evidence. The People were not unsuccessful on the appeal nor was the appeal "taken" pursuant to CPL § 450.50(2). Rather, the withdrawn appeal was held to be null. People v. McIntosh, 80 N.Y.2d 87, 587 N.Y.S.2d 568, 600 N.E.2d 199 (1992).

§ 450.55. Appeal by people from order reducing a count of an indictment or directing the filing of a prosecutor's information.

In taking an appeal to an intermediate appellate court pursuant to subdivision one-a of section 450.20, the people shall file a notice of appeal. Upon request of either party, the hearing and determination of such appeal shall be conducted in an expeditious manner. The chief administrator of the courts, with the advice and consent of the administrative board of the courts, shall adopt rules for the expeditious briefing, hearing and determination of such appeals.

Added by L. 1990, Ch. 209.

§ 450.60. Appeal to intermediate appellate court; to what court taken.

The particular intermediate appellate courts to which appeals authorized by sections 450.10 and 450.20 must be taken are as follows:

1. An appeal from a judgment, sentence or order of the supreme court must be taken to the appellate division of the department in which such judgment, sentence or order was entered.

2. An appeal from a judgment, sentence or order of a county court must be taken to the appellate division of the department in which such judgment, sentence or order was entered.

3. An appeal from a judgment, sentence or order of a local criminal court located outside of New York City must, except as otherwise provided in this subdivision, be taken to the county court of the county in which such judgment, sentence or order was entered.

If the appellate division of the second, third or fourth department has established an appellate term of the supreme court for its department, it may direct that appeals from such judgments, sentences and orders of such local criminal courts, or of particular classifications of such local criminal courts, be taken to such appellate term of the supreme court instead of to the county court; and in such case such an appeal must be so taken.

4. An appeal from a judgment, sentence or order of the New York City criminal court must be taken, if such judgment, sentence or order was entered at a term of such court held in New York or Bronx county, to the appellate division of the first department, and, if entered at a term of such court held in Kings, Queens or Richmond county, to the appellate division of the second department; except that if the appellate division of either such department has established an appellate term of the supreme court for its department, it may direct that all such appeals be taken thereto; and in such case such an appeal must be so taken.

Amended by L. 1979, Ch. 74.

§ 450.70. Appeal by defendant directly to court of appeals; in what cases authorized.

An appeal directly to the court of appeals may be taken as of right by the defendant from the following judgment and orders of a superior court:

1. A judgment including a sentence of death;

2. An order denying a motion, made pursuant to section 440.10, to vacate a judgment including a sentence of death;

3. An order denying a motion, made pursuant to section 440.20, to set aside a sentence of death;

4. An order denying a motion, made pursuant to paragraph (d) of subdivision eleven of section 400.27, to set aside a sentence of death.

Amended by L. 1995, Ch. 1, § 23, eff. Sept. 1, 1995, amending subd. (3) and adding subd. (4).

§ 450.80. Appeal by people directly to court of appeals; in what cases authorized.

An appeal directly to the court of appeals may be taken as of right by the people from the following orders of a superior court:

1. An order, entered pursuant to section 440.10, vacating a judgment including a sentence of death;

2. An order, entered pursuant to section 440.20, setting aside a sentence of death;

3. An order, entered pursuant to paragraph (d) of subdivision eleven of section 400.27, setting aside a sentence of death;

4. An order, entered pursuant to subdivision twelve of section 400.27, setting aside a sentence of death.

Amended by L. 1995, Ch. 1, § 24, eff. Sept. 1, 1995, adding subds. 3 and 4.

ANNOTATION

Jurisdiction.—The jurisdiction of the Court of Appeals in criminal cases is limited to considering questions of law except in the instance of an appeal taken directly to the Court of Appeals pursuant to CPL §§ 450.70, 450.80. People v. Robinson, 36 N.Y.2d 224, 367 N.Y.S.2d 208, 326 N.E.2d 784 (1975).

§ 450.90. Appeal to court of appeals from order of intermediate appellate court; in what cases authorized.

1. Provided that a certificate granting leave to appeal is issued pursuant to section 460.20, an appeal may, except as provided in subdivision two, be taken to the court of appeals by either the defendant or the people from any adverse or partially adverse order of an intermediate appellate court entered upon an appeal taken to such intermediate appellate court pursuant to section 450.10, 450.15, or 450.20 or from an order granting or denying a motion to set aside an order of an intermediate appellate court on the ground of ineffective assistance or wrongful deprivation of appellate counsel. An order of an intermediate appellate court is adverse to the party who was the appellant in such court when it affirms the judgment, sentence or order appealed from, and is adverse to the party who was the respondent in such court when it reverses the judgment, sentence or order appealed from. An appellate court order which modifies a judgment or order appealed from is partially adverse to each party.

2. An appeal to the court of appeals from an order of an intermediate appellate court reversing or modifying a judgment, sentence or order of a criminal court may be taken only if:

(a) The court of appeals determines that the intermediate appellate court's determination of reversal or modification was on the law alone or upon the law and such facts which, but for the determination of law, would not have led to reversal or modification; or

(b) The appeal is based upon a contention that corrective action, as that term is defined in section 470.10, taken or directed by the intermediate appellate court was illegal.

Amended by L. 1971, Ch. 671; L. 1979, Ch. 651; L. 2002, Ch. 498, § 1, eff. Nov. 1, 2002, amending subd. 1.

ANNOTATIONS

Appeal.—An appeal of an issue to the Court of Appeals from a decision of the Appellate Court was permissible where that specific issue served as the basis for the Appellate Court's decision to reverse. People v. Diaz, 81 N.Y.2d 106, 595 N.Y.S.2d 940, 612 N.E.2d 298 (1993).

Appeal from appellate court based on the law and facts.—A determination by the Appellate Division that its decision to reverse was based "on the law" was a question of both law and fact. Thus, the Appellate Division's order was not appealable. People v. Hinton, 81 N.Y.2d 867, 597 N.Y.S.2d 927, 613 N.E.2d 958 (1993).

—Decision based on the law and the facts, that defendant was in custody at the time of his interrogation, was appealable on the Appellate Division's legal conclusion. People v. Albro, 52 N.Y.2d 619, 439 N.Y.S.2d 836, 422 N.E.2d 496 (1981).

Appeals; order adverse to party.—Order of the Appellate Division reversing defendant's conviction for one count of criminal possession of a weapon and ordering a new trial was held not to be adverse to the defendant. Thus, the order was not appealable pursuant to CPL § 450.90. The corrective action of the Appellate Division was not illegal. People v. Jackson, 80 N.Y.2d 112, 589 N.Y.S.2d 300, 602 N.E.2d 1116 (1992).

—Defendant was not "adversely affected" where the Appellate Court denied defendant's request to suppress evidence and dismiss the first count of the indictment. People v. Griminger, 71 N.Y.2d 635, 529 N.Y.S.2d 58 (1988).

—Defendant's appeal from order reversing his conviction must be dismissed as not "adverse" to him within the meaning of CPL § 450.90(1), despite the fact that defendant was "aggrieved" insofar as his request for suppression was granted only as to a weapon and not to his out-of-court statements to police. People v. Rolston, 50 N.Y.2d 1048, 431 N.Y.S.2d 701, 409 N.E.2d 1375 (1980).

Appeals; order for new trial; authority of Appellate Division.—Where the Appellate Division declined to exercise its interest of justice authority to review defendant's unpreserved challenge to the lack of proof of defendant's knowledge of the weight of the cocaine, the Court of Appeals held that the Appellate Division's exercise of its interest of justice jurisdiction was beyond the review power of the Court of Appeals. People v. Cooper, 88 N.Y.2d 1056, 651 N.Y.S.2d 7, 673 N.E.2d 1234 (1996).

—Power of Court of Appeals to review opinion for reason of intermediate appellate court's decision is limited to cases where the order of such court states that decision is on law alone and not where there is a recital as to factual or discretionary basis. Since opinion of Appellate Division indicates order was exercise of discretionary power, it is not reviewable, even though settled order deleted this reference and recited that decision was on law alone. People v. Williams, 31 N.Y.2d 151, 335 N.Y.S.2d 271, 286 N.E.2d 715 (1972).

ARTICLE 460—APPEALS—TAKING AND PERFECTION THEREOF AND STAYS DURING PENDENCY THEREOF

LexisNexis Cross References

Criminal Constitutional Law, Vol. 3, Ch. 15, Appeals; *Bender's New York Evidence—CPLR,* Vol. 6, Ch. 31, Appellate Review; *Criminal Defense Techniques,* Vol. 2, Ch. 48, Criminal Appeals; *Business Crime,* Vol. 4, Ch. 15, Appellate Practice; *Defense of Drunk Driving Cases,* Vol. 4, Ch. 52, Appeals; *New York Criminal Practice (2d ed.),* Vol. 4, Ch. 44, Appeals; *see generally New York Appellate Practice;* Vol. 1, Ch. 5, Taking and Perfecting the Appeal; Vol. 1, Ch. 6, Stays Pending Appeal; Vol. 1, Ch. 8, Argument of the Appeal; Vol. 1, Ch. 9, Disposition of the Appeal; Vol. 2, Ch. 13, Criminal Appeals; *Prosecution and Defense of Sex Crimes,* Ch. 17, Appeals in Sex Crimes Cases; *New York Suppression Manual,* Ch. 4, Harmless Error; Ch. 27, Appealing Suppression Orders; *Criminal Practice Handbook (2d ed.),* Ch. 12, Direct Appeal.

§ 460.10. Appeal; how taken.

1. Except as provided in subdivisions two and three, an appeal taken as of right to an intermediate appellate court or directly to the court of appeals from a judgment, sentence or order of a criminal court is taken as follows:

(a) A party seeking to appeal from a judgment or a sentence or an order and sentence included within such judgment, or from a resentence, or from an order of a criminal court, not included in a judgment, must, within thirty days after imposition of the sentence or, as the case may be, within thirty days after service upon such party of a copy of an order not included in a judgment, file with the clerk of the criminal court in which such sentence was imposed or in which such order was entered a written notice of appeal, in duplicate, stating that such party appeals therefrom to a designated appellate court.

(b) If the defendant is the appellant, he must, within such thirty day period, serve a copy of such notice of appeal upon the district attorney of the county embracing the criminal court in which the judgment or order being appealed was entered. If the appeal is directly to the court of appeals, the district attorney, following such service upon him, must immediately give written notice thereof

to the public servant having custody of the defendant.

(c) If the people are the appellant, they must, within such thirty day period, serve a copy of such notice of appeal upon the defendant or upon the attorney who last appeared for him in the court in which the order being appealed was entered.

(d) Upon filing and service of the notice of appeal as prescribed in paragraphs (a), (b) and (c), the appeal is deemed to have been taken.

(e) Following the filing with him of the notice of appeal in duplicate, the clerk of the court in which the judgment, sentence or order being appealed was entered or imposed, must endorse upon such instruments the filing date and must transmit the duplicate notice of appeal to the clerk of the court to which the appeal is being taken.

2. An appeal taken as of right to a county court or to an appellate term of the supreme court from a judgment, sentence or order of a local criminal court in a case in which the underlying proceedings were recorded by a court stenographer is taken in the manner provided in subdivision one; except that where no clerk is employed by such local criminal court the appellant must file the notice of appeal with the judge of such court, and

must further file a copy thereof with the clerk of the appellate court to which the appeal is being taken.

3. An appeal taken as of right to a county court or to an appellate term of the supreme court from a judgment, sentence or order of a local criminal court in a case in which the underlying proceedings were not recorded by a court stenographer is taken as follows:

(a) Within thirty days after entry or imposition in such local criminal court of the judgment, sentence or order being appealed, the appellant must file with such court either (i) an affidavit of errors, setting forth alleged errors or defects in the proceedings which are the subjects of the appeal, or (ii) a notice of appeal. Where a notice of appeal is filed, the appellant must serve a copy thereof upon the respondent in the manner provided in paragraphs (b) and (c) of subdivision one, and, within thirty days after the filing thereof, must file with such court an affidavit of errors.

(b) Not more than three days after the filing of the affidavit of errors, the appellant must serve a copy thereof upon the respondent or the respondent's counsel or authorized representative. If the defendant is the appellant, such service must be upon the district attorney of the county in which the local criminal court is located. If the people are the appellant, such service must be upon the defendant or upon the attorney who appeared for him in the proceedings in the local criminal court.

(c) Upon filing and service of the affidavit of errors as prescribed in paragraphs (a) and (b), the appeal is deemed to have been taken.

(d) Within ten days after the appellant's filing of the affidavit of errors with the local criminal court, such court must file with the clerk of the appellate court to which the appeal has been taken both the affidavit of errors and the court's return, and must deliver a copy of such return to each party or a representative thereof as indicated in paragraph (b). The court's return must set forth or summarize evidence, facts or occurrences in or adduced at the proceedings resulting in the judgment, sentence or order, which constitute the factual foundation for the contentions alleged in the affidavit of errors.

(e) If the local criminal court does not file such return within the prescribed period, or if it files a defective return, the appellate court, upon application of the appellant, must order such local criminal court to file a return or an amended return, as the case may be, within a designated time which such appellate court deems reasonable.

4. An appeal by a defendant to an intermediate appellate court by permission, pursuant to section 450.15, is taken as follows:

(a) Within thirty days after service upon the defendant of a copy of the order sought to be appealed, the defendant must make application, pursuant to section 460.15, for a certificate granting leave to appeal to the intermediate appellate court.

(b) If such application is granted and such certificate is issued, the defendant, within fifteen days after issuance thereof, must file with the criminal court in which the order sought to be appealed was rendered the certificate granting leave to appeal together with a written notice of appeal, or if the appeal is from a local criminal court in a case in which the underlying proceedings were not recorded by a court stenographer, either (i) an affidavit of errors, or (ii) a notice of appeal. In all other respects the appeal shall be taken as provided in subdivisions one, two and three.

5. An appeal to the court of appeals from an order of an intermediate appellate court is taken as follows:

(a) Within thirty days after service upon the appellant of a copy of the order sought to be appealed, the appellant must make application, pursuant to section 460.20, for a certificate granting leave to appeal to the court of appeals. The appellate division of each judicial department shall adopt rules governing the procedures for service of a copy of such order.

(b) If such application is granted, the issuance of the certificate granting leave to appeal shall constitute the taking of the appeal.

(c) [Repealed.]

(d) [Repealed.]

(e) [Repealed.]

6. Where a notice of appeal, an affidavit of errors, an application for leave to appeal to an intermediate appellate court, or an application for leave to appeal to the court of appeals is premature or contains an inaccurate description of the judgment, sentence or order being or sought to be appealed, the appellate court, in its discretion, may, in the interest of justice, treat such instrument as valid. Where an appellant files a notice of appeal within the prescribed period but, through mistake, inadvertence or excusable neglect, omits to serve a copy thereof upon the respondent within the prescribed period, the appellate court to which the appeal is sought to be taken may, in its discretion and for good cause shown, permit such service to be made within a designated period of time, and upon such service the appeal is deemed to be taken.

Amended by L. 1971, Ch. 671; L. 1977, Ch. 699; L. 1992, Ch. 85, eff. Aug. 15, 1992, amending subd. (1)(a); L. 1994, Ch. 137.

ANNOTATIONS

Appeal; competency of assigned counsel.—An indigent criminal defendant was deprived of effective assistance of counsel where the attorney appointed to handle his appeal filed a brief that summarized the evidence, stated that in the opinion of the writer there were no points to be raised on appeal, and set forth four point headings stating the points defendant wanted presented but advanced no argument in support of any point; affirmance of defendant's conviction was reversed and the case was remitted for *de novo* appeal. People v. Gonzalez, 47 N.Y.2d 606, 419 N.Y.S.2d 913, 393 N.E.2d 987 (1979).

Appeal; extension of time to file notice of appeal.—The requirement that a notice of appeal be filed and served within 15 days after a certificate granting leave to appeal has been issued under CPL § 460.20 is not jurisdictional, and the period for such filing and service may accordingly be extended by the Court of Appeals for good cause. People v. Sher, 35 N.Y.2d 310, 361 N.Y.S.2d 155, 319 N.E.2d 419 (1974).

—In order to be granted an extension of time to take an appeal, it is necessary that a defendant's moving papers contain sworn and specific allegations of fact establishing, for example, improper conduct or an inability to communicate; general allegations will not entitle a defendant to relief. People v. Kaczynski, 119 A.D.2d 927, 507 N.Y.S.2d 946 (3d Dept. 1986).

Appeal; failure to prosecute; failure to compel a return.—The fact that the attorney assigned to the case by the Public defender pursued the procedure under the CPL, rather than filing a return under the controlling CCP, did not reflect an egregious lack of competent representation for which relief could be granted. People v. Eldridge, 31 N.Y.2d 820, 339 N.Y.S.2d 673, 291 N.E.2d 719 (1972), *cert. denied,* 412 U.S. 909 (1973).

Appeal; notice.—The time within the People have to serve their notice of appeal begins running not from the date the order was entered, or the date the People received actual notice of the order, but rather from the date of "service" of a copy of the order; it has been held that service of the order must include notice of entry, but First Department found no basis for that requirement in CPL § 460.10(1a). People v. Washington, 209 A.D.2d 162, 618 N.Y.S.2d 32 (1st Dept. 1994).

—The Appellate Division may treat a premature notice of appeal as valid in its discretion in the interest of justice and hold the appeal in abeyance until a proper appealable order is entered. People v. Austin, 208 A.D.2d 990, 618 N.Y.S.2d 115, 117 (3d Dept. 1994).

—When a copy of the judgment from which defendant appeals is received by the defendant, defendant's time to apply to appeal begins to run. People v. Kendall, 214 A.D.2d 1051, 627 N.Y.S.2d 590 (4th Dept. 1995).

Appeal; timely notice.—The notice function is effectively accomplished by service of the order on the attorney, whose status as representative of the defendant continues through the filing of a timely application for leave to appeal and who is obligated to advise the defendant of his rights incident to the taking of an appeal and to make application for leave if the defendant informs him of his desire to do so. People v. Wooley, 40 N.Y.2d 699, 389 N.Y.S.2d 809, 358 N.E.2d 493 (1976).

—Defendant's allegation that he only understood Spanish, and that he was not informed of his right to appeal in writing either in Spanish or English, nor knew of his right, was conclusively refuted by the sentencing minutes which showed that defendant, his attorney, and an official interpreter were present; that the clerk advised defendant of his right to appeal, and that defendant was given a bilingual written copy of his right to appeal. People v. Salinas, 88 A.D.2d 553, 450 N.Y.S.2d 789 (1st Dept. 1982).

Appeal by People; timeliness.—Where People failed to act diligently in attempting to procure a copy of the written order, the People were charged with the delay. People v. Holmes, 206 A.D.2d 542, 615 N.Y.S.2d 52 (2d Dept. 1994).

Application.—When the application is submitted to the court, current law requires that it be made to the Chief Judge who "must then designate a judge of such court to determine the application" (CPL § 460.20[3][b]); the decision of the Judge so designated must be considered final. People v. Welcome, 37 N.Y.2d 811, 375 N.Y.S.2d 573, 338 N.E.2d 328 (1975).

Destruction of trial transcript and stenographic notes.—Defendant cannot be heard to complain of the destruction of his trial minutes where the stenographic notes were destroyed in accordance with the applicable law during defendant's willful and intentional five year absence from the jurisdiction of the trial court. People v. Smalls, 116 A.D.2d 675, 497 N.Y.S.2d 743 (2d Dept. 1986).

Dismissal required.—People's failure to serve notice of appeal within 30 days after service of a copy of the order sought to be reviewed required dismissal of People's appeal; no exception to or possibility of extension of that time constraint is

countenanced by CPL § 450.20. People v. Marsh, 127 A.D.2d 945, 512 N.Y.S.2d 545, 546 (3d Dept. 1987).

Due process.—Due process does not require the personal service of the People's briefs to the defendant. Defendant's interests are afforded sufficient protection pursuant to CPL § 460.10. People v. Ramos, 85 N.Y.2d 678, 628 N.Y.S.2d 27, 651 N.E.2d 895 (1995).

Electronic recording.—A transcript of an electronic recording of defendant's probation proceeding, filed with the county court, satisfied the requirement for the court's return pursuant to CPL § 460.10(3)(d). People v. Robinson, 72 N.Y.2d 989, 534 N.Y.S.2d 367, 530 N.E.2d 1287 (1988).

Expiration of time.—Defendant abandoned his right to appeal when he failed to perfect his appeal for more than 14 years and where he had been advised of his right to appeal. People v. West, 100 N.Y.2d 23, 759 N.Y.S.2d 437, 789 N.E.2d 615 (2003).

—Upon the expiration of the time to take an appeal, the property clerk may release the property on the basis that the proceedings are terminated. DeBellis v. New York City Property Clerk, 79 N.Y.2d 49, 580 N.Y.S.2d 157, 588 N.E.2d 55 (1992).

Filing; generally.—Defendant may not challenge the propriety of his plea where defendant did not file a notice of appeal from his indictment. People v. Maxwell, 156 A.D.2d 476, 548 N.Y.S.2d 763 (2d Dept. 1989).

—Defendant's claim that he was not afforded a speedy trial was properly denied where the defendant made no showing that he filed a notice of appeal after the Supreme Court denied a writ of habeas corpus. People v. Mena-Coss, 210 A.D.2d 745, 620 N.Y.S.2d 547 (3d Dept. 1994).

—Where the defendant failed to file a notice of appeal, defendant may not appeal the judgment. People v. Coble, 168 A.D.2d 982, 566 N.Y.S.2d 566 (4th Dept. 1990).

Death of defendant.—A prosecution in which the defendant dies prior to appeal is abated simply because there will be no appeal, and the reliability of the conviction will never be the subject of appellate scrutiny. People v. Pikul, 192 A.D.2d 259, 601 N.Y.S.2d 113 (1st Dept. 1993).

People's failure to provide affidavit of service.—Because the People failed to provide the court with an affidavit of service indicating that defendant was served with a copy of the County Court's order, the time to move for permission to appeal therefrom did not begin to run. People v. Walker, 237 A.D.2d 726, 655 N.Y.S.2d 112 (3d Dept. 1997).

Generally.—People failed to correctly file the notice of appeal where service was made upon the county judge and not the Clerk of Criminal Court. CPL § 460.10 provides no exceptions that would remedy the People's actions. People v. Doyne, 178 A.D.2d 870, 577 N.Y.S.2d 921 (3d Dept. 1991).

Justice Court; failure to file return.—The County Court acted properly in admitting defendant's allegations where the Justice Court failed to file a return. The County Court was under no obligation to warn the Justice Court of the admission of defendant's allegations upon failing to reply. People v. Feldes, 73 N.Y.2d 661, 543 N.Y.S.2d 34, 541 N.E.2d 34 (1989).

—The Justice Court fails to file a return within 30 days, the allegations of the affidavit of errors will be deemed admitted and the appellate court may decide the appeals on the merits of the affidavit of errors alone. People v. Greenbaum, 104 Misc. 2d 1012, 429 N.Y.S.2d 388 (Albany Co. Ct. 1980).

Record.—Court's credibility assessment, upon hearing testimony from the trial judge, the court clerk, and the prosecutor, each of whom testified that he believed the stenographic minutes to be in error, would not be disturbed. People v. Molina, 202 A.D.2d 521, 609 N.Y.S.2d 66 (2d Dept. 1994).

—The contention of the defendant that he was entitled to reversal or remittal for a hearing to reconstruct the record of certain side-bar conferences conducted during the trial in his absence lacked merit because defendant did not allege that his absence had an impact on his defense. People v. Spataro, 202 A.D.2d 1005, 612 N.Y.S.2d 699 (4th Dept. 1994).

—Courts possess inherent power to correct their records where the correction relates to mistakes, or errors, which may be termed clerical in their nature, or where it is made in order to conform the record to the truth. People v. Zohar, 158 Misc. 2d 1028, 607 N.Y.S.2d 209 (App. Term, 2d and 11th Jud. Dists. 1993).

Scope.—Appellate Division dismissed appeal from an order dismissing the indictment where the People had moved for reargument of that order and subsequently appealed from the order adhering to the original determination upon reargument; the original order was superseded by the order made upon reargument. People v. Collier, 131 A.D.2d 864, 517 N.Y.S.2d 224 (2d Dept. 1987), aff'd, 72 N.Y.2d 298, 532 N.Y.S.2d 718, 528 N.E.2d 1191 (1988).

—While CPL § 460.10(6) allows a court to excuse errors, such as premature filings or in the description of the judgment, sentence or order being or sought to be appealed, it does not permit a court to excuse non-compliance with CPL § 460.10(2). People v. Duggan, 69 N.Y.2d 931, 516 N.Y.S.2d 633, 509 N.E.2d 328 (1987).

—CPL § 460.10 requires that an appeal by the People from an oral order modifying a conviction must be taken at the latest within 30 days after the imposition of the sentence rather than within 30 days of the service or entry of that order. People v. Coaye, 68 N.Y.2d 857, 508 N.Y.S.2d 410, 501 N.E.2d 18 (1986).

Sufficiency of notice.—Where the defendant's location was unknown, service of the notice of appeal upon the defendant's counsel was held to be sufficient. People v. Hernandez, 210 A.D.2d 504, 621 N.Y.S.2d 810 (2d Dept. 1994).

Transcript of trial minutes lost.—Twenty-three years after conviction a defendant, who was not advised of his right to appeal at conviction and was subsequently resentenced *nunc pro tunc* to commence again the time in which to take an appeal, was entitled to a new trial because a transcript of the original trial no longer existed, even though an intermediate appellate decision held defendant had failed to raise any appealable issues with respect to the first trial. People v. Rivera, 39 N.Y.2d 519, 384 N.Y.S.2d 726, 349 N.E.2d 825 (1976).

Summation and Judge's charge.—Conviction affirmed notwithstanding loss of untranscribed stenographic notes covering the summations and the Judge's charge to jury where interval between trial and discovery of the loss was only months, alternative methods were available to provide an accurate record, and defendant failed to assert that any exception had been made at trial to charge or summation, thus making any alleged errors beyond ordinary scope of review. People v. Glass, 43 N.Y.2d 283, 401 N.Y.S.2d 189, 372 N.E.2d 24 (1977).

Right to appeal; severity of sentence.—Coram nobis lies where defendant seeks reimposition of judgment so as to revive his right to appeal where he has a viable claim that sentence he is still serving is excessive and he is entitled to proper review. People v. Coleman, 30 N.Y.2d 582, 330 N.Y.S.2d 797, 281 N.E.2d 845 (1972).

Defendant must be advised at sentencing.—The Appellate Division acted within the proper exercise of its discretion to control its own calendar when it denied defendant's motion to file a supplemental brief. People v. Fratta, 83 N.Y.2d 771, 610 N.Y.S.2d 947, 632 N.E.2d 1270 (1994).

Supplemental brief.—Defendant had no right to file a supplemental brief in the Appellate Division. People v. Perez, 74 N.Y.2d 637, 541 N.Y.S.2d 976, 539 N.E.2d 1104 (1989).

§ 460.15. Certificate granting leave to appeal to intermediate appellate court.

1. A certificate granting leave to appeal to an intermediate appellate court is an order of one judge or justice of the intermediate appellate court to which the appeal is sought to be taken granting such permission and certifying that the case involves questions of law or fact which ought to be reviewed by the intermediate appellate court.

2. An application for such a certificate must be made in a manner determined by the rules of the appellate division of the department in which such intermediate appellate court is located. Not more than one application may be made for such a certificate.

Added by L. 1971, Ch. 671.

ANNOTATIONS

Appeal application.—Absent permission from a Justice of the Appellate Court, defendant may not properly appeal an order denying his motion to vacate the judgment. People v. Cooper, 154 A.D.2d 612, 546 N.Y.S.2d 441 (2d Dept. 1989).

Due Process.—Defendant's right to appeal is not restricted by requiring defendant to obtain permission to appeal. Such a requirement is not violative of defendant's due process rights. People v. Ghee, 153 A.D.2d 954, 545 N.Y.S.2d 760 (2d Dept. 1989).

Status as youthful offender.—Where request for status as a youthful offender has been denied, permission to appeal may be granted. People v. Anderson, 493 N.Y.S.2d 985 (3d Dept. 1985).

§ 460.20. Certificate granting leave to appeal to court of appeals.

1. A certificate granting leave to appeal to the court of appeals from an order of an intermediate appellate court is an order of a judge granting such permission and certifying that the case involves a question of law which ought to be reviewed by the court of appeals.

2. Such certificate may be issued by the following judges in the indicated situations:

(a) Where the appeal sought is from an order of the appellate division, the certificate may be issued by (i) a judge of the court of appeals or (ii) a justice of the appellate division of the department which entered the order sought to be appealed.

(b) Where the appeal sought is from an order of an intermediate appellate court other than the appellate division, the certificate may be issued only by a judge of the court of appeals.

3. An application for such a certificate must be made in the following manner:

(a) An application to a justice of the appellate division must be made upon reasonable notice to the respondent;

(b) An application seeking such a certificate from a judge of the court of appeals must be made to the chief judge of such court by submission thereof, either in writing or first orally and then in writing, to the clerk of the court of appeals. The chief judge must then designate a judge of such court to determine the application. The clerk must then notify the respondent of the application and must inform both parties of such designation.

4. A justice of the appellate division to whom such an application has been made, or a judge of the court of appeals designated to determine such an application, may in his discretion determine it upon such papers as he may request the parties to submit, or upon oral argument, or upon both.

5. Every judge or justice acting pursuant to this section shall file with the clerk of the court of appeals, immediately upon issuance, a copy of every certificate granting or denying leave to appeal.

Amended by L. 1977, Ch. 699.

ANNOTATIONS

Appeal; assignment of counsel.—Upon application for an assignment of counsel to prosecute an appeal, the Appellate Term did not abuse its discretion in determining that the defendants did not satisfactorily demonstrate that they were at that time financially unable to obtain counsel. People v. Simmons, 31 N.Y.2d 997, 341 N.Y.S.2d 451, 293 N.E.2d 826 (1973).

Reapplication.—Motion pursuant to CPL § 460.20 may only be made once. Defendant's second motion for an extension of time to apply for permission to appeal was denied. People v. Spence, 82 N.Y.2d 671, 601 N.Y.S.2d 566, 619 N.E.2d 644 (1993).

—Denial of application for permission to appeal by judge or justice first applied to is final, and no new application may thereafter be made to any other judge or justice. People v. Bellamy, 259 A.D.2d 452, 688 N.Y.S.2d 132 (1st Dept. 1999); People v. Adames, 253 A.D.2d 704, 679 N.Y.S.2d 100 (1st Dept. 1998); People v. Hernandez, 253 A.D.2d 683, 680 N.Y.S.2d 74 (1st Dept. 1998) (same); People v. Bryan, 255 A.D.2d 247, 683 N.Y.S.2d 481 (1st Dept. 1998) (same).

§ 460.30. Extension of time for taking appeal.

1. Upon motion to an intermediate appellate court of a defendant who desires to take an appeal to such court from a judgment, sentence or order of a criminal court but has failed to file a notice of appeal, an application for leave to appeal, or, as the case may be, an affidavit of errors, with such criminal court within the prescribed period, or upon motion to the court of appeals of a defendant who desires to take an appeal to such court from an order of a superior court or of an intermediate appellate court, but has failed to make an application for a certificate granting leave to appeal to the court of appeals, or has failed to file a notice of appeal with the intermediate appellate court, within the prescribed period, such intermediate appellate court or the court of appeals, as the case may be, may order that the time for the taking of such appeal or applying for leave to appeal be extended to a date not more than thirty days subsequent to the determination of such motion, upon the ground that the failure to so file or make application in timely fashion resulted from (a) improper conduct of a public servant or improper conduct, death or disability of the defendant's attorney, or (b) inability of the defendant and his attorney to have communicated, in person or by mail, concerning whether an appeal should be taken, prior to the expiration of the time within which to take an appeal due to the defendant's incarceration in an institution and through no lack of due diligence or fault of the attorney or defendant. Such motion must be made with due diligence after the time for the taking of such appeal has expired, and in any case not more than one year thereafter.

2. The motion must be in writing and upon reasonable notice to the People and with opportunity to be heard. The motion papers must contain sworn allegations of facts claimed to establish the improper conduct, inability to communicate, or other facts essential to support the motion, and the People may file papers in opposition thereto. After all papers have been filed, the court must consider the same for the purpose of ascertaining whether the motion is determinable without a hearing to resolve issues of fact.

3. If the motion papers allege facts constituting a legal basis for the motion, and if the essential allegations are either conclusively substantiated by unquestionable documentary proof or are conceded by the People to be true, the court must grant the motion.

4. If the motion papers do not allege facts constituting a legal basis for the motion, or if an essential allegation is conclusively refuted by unquestionable documentary proof, the court may deny the motion.

5. If the court does not determine the motion pursuant to subdivision three or four, it must order the criminal court which entered or imposed the judgment, sentence or order sought to be appealed to conduct a hearing and to make and report findings of fact essential to the determination of such motion. Upon receipt of such report, the intermediate appellate court or the court of appeals, as the case may be, must determine the motion.

6. An order of an intermediate appellate court granting or denying a motion made pursuant to this section is appealable to the court of appeals if (a) such order states that the determination was made upon the law alone, and (b) a judge of the court of appeals, pursuant to procedure provided in section 460.20, of this chapter, issues a certificate granting leave to the appellant to appeal to the court of appeals.

Amended by L. 1971, Ch. 671; L. 1977, Ch. 699.

ANNOTATIONS

Attorney conduct.—Where an attorney advised the defendant of his right to appeal and defendant declined the opportunity to do so, the attorney's conduct was not improper. Thus, the defendant's request for an extension of time to take an appeal was denied. People v. Klem, 214 A.D.2d 1051, 627 N.Y.S.2d 590 (4th Dept. 1995).

—Where counsel submitted a form pursuant to rule 1022.11(a) containing the defendant's signed acknowledgment of his wish not to appeal, the counsel did not act improperly under CPL § 460.30. Wilson v. State, 172 A.D.2d 1074, 571 N.Y.S.2d 393 (4th Dept. 1991).

Authority.—Defendant's motion to extend time of appeal was denied by the Appellate Division for lack of authority. The Court of Appeals is vested with the authority to extend the time of appeal. People v. Robertson, 182 A.D.2d 1144, 583 N.Y.S.2d 710 (4th Dept. 1992).

Determination made upon the law alone.—An appeal from an order of an intermediate appellate court granting or denying an application for an extension of time in which to take an appeal may be entertained by Court of Appeals only if the order states that the determination was made upon the law alone. People v. Thomas, 44 N.Y.2d 759, 405 N.Y.S.2d 684, 376 N.E.2d 1329 (1978).

Extension of time for taking appeal; interests of justice.—Defendant's motion for an extension of time to take an appeal was denied where the defendant misrepresented the proceedings as a resentencing proceeding. The defendant was actually being remanded to commence a sentence which he never served. People v. Pabon, 175 A.D.2d 270, 572 N.Y.S.2d 381 (2d Dept. 1991).

Generally.—A motion pursuant to CPL § 460.30 limits the time for taking an appeal to 30 days from the imposition, not the execution, of the sentence. People v. Torres, 179 A.D.2d 358, 578 N.Y.S.2d 834 (1st Dept. 1992).

Montgomery hearing.—The hearing afforded to the defendant pursuant to People v. Montgomery, 24 N.Y.2d 130, 299 N.Y.S.2d 156, 247 N.E.2d 130, is now available pursuant to CPL § 460.30(5), which provides that, if the intermediate court determines that there are factual issues to be resolved in order for the motion to be decided, it must remit to the court which entered or imposed the judgment, sentence or order sought to be appealed from in order to make findings of fact, following which the appellate court may proceed to decide the motion. People v. Corso, 40 N.Y.2d 578, 388 N.Y.S.2d 886, 357 N.E.2d 357 (1976).

Timeliness.—Defendant's appeal was not barred where, although his conviction was imposed 23 years earlier, defendant made timely efforts to review that conviction. Because the State prevented the review of the defendant's conviction, defendant is not barred by the time limit set in CPL § 460.30. People v. Johnson, 69 N.Y.2d 339, 514 N.Y.S.2d 324, 506 N.E.2d 1177 (1987).

—Since the omissions on the part of the prosecutor, though no doubt made more critical by assigned counsel's less than assiduous performance, frustrated the good faith exercise of the defendant's right to the remedy of CPL § 460.30, the People should be stopped from invoking the bar of the one-year limit. People v. Thomas, 47 N.Y.2d 37, 416 N.Y.S.2d 573, 389 N.E.2d 1094 (1979).

—A motion pursuant to CPL § 460.30 must be made with due diligence and in any event may not be made more than one year after the time for taking an appeal has expired (CPL § 460.30[1]). People v. Corso, 40 N.Y.2d 578, 388 N.Y.S.2d 886, 357 N.E.2d 357 (1976).

—Where the defendant made a motion to extend the time for taking an appeal more than one year following the allowable time, the appeal was dismissed. People v. Valle, 184 A.D.2d 447,587 N.Y.S.2d 147 (1st Dept. 1992).

§ 460.40. Effect of taking of appeal upon judgment or order of courts below; when stayed.

1. The taking of an appeal by the defendant directly to the court of appeals, pursuant to subdivision one of section 450.70, from a superior court judgment including a sentence of death stays the execution of such sentence. Except as provided in subdivision two of this section, in no other case does the taking of an appeal, by either party, in and of itself stay the execution of any judgment, sentence or order of either a criminal court or an intermediate appellate court.

2. The taking of an appeal by the people to an intermediate appellate court pursuant to subdivision one-a of section 450.20, from an order reducing a count or counts of an indictment or dismissing an indictment and directing the filing of a prosecutor's information, stays the effect of such order. In addition, the taking of an appeal by the people to an intermediate appellate court pursuant to subdivision one of section 450.20, from an order dismissing a count or counts of an indictment charging murder in the first degree, stays the effect of such order.

3. Within six months of the effective date of this subdivision, the court of appeals shall adopt rules to ensure that a defendant is granted a stay of the execution of any death warrant issued pursuant to article twenty-two-b of the correction law to allow the defendant an opportunity to prepare and timely file an initial motion pursuant to section 440.10 or 440.20 seeking to set aside a sentence of death or vacate a judgment including a sentence of death and to allow the motion and any appeal from the denial thereof to be timely determined. The rules shall provide that in the event a defendant seeks to file any subsequent motion with respect to the judgment or sentence following a final determination of the defendant's initial motion pursuant to section 440.10 or 440.20, a motion for a stay of the execution of the death warrant may only be granted for good cause shown. The people and the defendant shall have a right to appeal to the court of appeals from orders granting or denying such stay motions and any rules adopted pursuant to this subdivision shall provide that the court of appeals may affirm such orders, reverse them or modify them upon such terms as the court deems appropriate and shall provide for the expeditious perfection and determination of such appeals. Prior to adoption of the rules, the court of appeals shall issue proposed rules and receive written comments thereon from interested parties.

Amended by L. 1990, Ch. 209; L. 1995, Ch. 1, § 25, eff. Sept. 1, 1995, amending subd. 2; L. 1995, Ch. 1, § 26, eff. Sept. 1, 1995, adding subd. 3.

§ 460.50. Stay of judgment pending appeal to intermediate appellate court.

1. Upon application of a defendant who has taken an appeal to an intermediate appellate court from a judgment or from a sentence of a criminal court, a judge designated in subdivision two may issue an order both (a) staying or suspending the execution of the judgment pending the determination of the appeal, and (b) either releasing the defendant on his own recognizance or fixing bail pursuant to the provisions of article five hundred thirty. That phase of the order staying or suspending execution of the judgment does not become effective unless and until the defendant is released, either on his own recognizance or upon the posting of bail.

2. An order as prescribed in subdivision one may be issued by the following judges in the indicated situations:

(a) If the appeal is to the appellate division from a judgment or a sentence of either the supreme court or the New York City criminal court, such order may be issued by (i) a justice of the appellate division of the department in which the judgment was entered, or (ii) a justice of the supreme court of the judicial district embracing the county in which the judgment was entered;

(b) If the appeal is to the appellate division from a judgment or a sentence of a county court, such order may be issued by (i) a justice of such appellate division, or (ii) a justice of the supreme court of the judicial district embracing the county in which the judgment was entered, or (iii) a judge of such county court;

(c) If the appeal is to an appellate term of the supreme court from a judgment or sentence of the New York City criminal court, such order may be issued by a justice of the supreme court of the judicial district embracing the county in which the judgment was entered;

(d) With respect to appeals to county courts from judgments or sentences of local criminal courts, and with respect to appeals to appellate terms of the supreme court from judgments or sentences of any criminal courts located outside of New York City, the judges who may issue such orders in any particular situation are determined by rules of the appellate division of the department embracing the appellate court to which the appeal has been taken.

3. An application for an order specified in this section must be made upon reasonable notice to the People, and the People must be accorded adequate opportunity to appear in opposition thereto. Not more than one application may be made pursuant to this section.

4. Notwithstanding the provisions of subdivision one, if within one hundred twenty days after the issuance of such an order the appeal has not been brought to argument in or submitted to the intermediate appellate court, the operation of such order terminates and the defendant must surrender himself to the criminal court in which the judgment was entered in order that execution of the judgment be commenced or resumed; except that this subdivision does not apply where the intermediate appellate court has (a) extended the time for argument or submission of the appeal to a date beyond the specified period of one hundred twenty days, and (b) upon application of the defendant, expressly ordered that the operation of the order continue until the date of the determination of the appeal or some other designated future date or occurrence.

5. Where the defendant is at liberty during the pendency of an appeal as a result of an order issued pursuant to this section, the intermediate appellate court, upon affirmance of the judgment, must by appropriate certificate remit the case to the criminal court in which such judgment was entered. The criminal court must, upon at least two days notice to the defendant, his surety and his attorney, promptly direct the defendant to surrender himself to the criminal court in order that execution of the judgment be commenced or resumed, and if necessary the criminal court may issue a bench warrant to secure his appearance.

6. Upon application of a defendant who has been granted a certificate granting leave to appeal pursuant to section 460.15 of this chapter, and in accordance with the procedures set forth in subdivisions three, four and five of this section, the

intermediate appellate court may issue an order both (a) staying or suspending the execution of the judgment pending the determination of the appeal, and (b) either releasing the defendant on his own recognizance or fixing bail pursuant to the provisions of article five hundred thirty. That phase of the order staying or suspending execution of the judgment does not become effective unless and until the defendant is released, either on his own recognizance or upon the posting of bail.

Amended by L. 1971, Ch. 884; L. 1981, Ch. 168.

ANNOTATIONS

Appeal; application.—Defendant must take an appeal from a judgment or sentence as a prerequisite to defendant's motion pursuant to CPL § 460.50. Without prerequisite appeal, defendant's application is void. People v. Clark, 86 N.Y.2d 824, 634 N.Y.S.2d 433, 258 N.E.2d 211 (1995).

Appeal dismissed; no action by People to remand.—A conditional discharge was the proper remedy where People took no action to remand the defendant for two years after his appeal was dismissed although he was readily available. People v. Healy, 76 A.D.2d 868, 428 N.Y.S.2d 499 (2d Dept. 1980).

Bail pending appeal.—Where the petitioner properly filed a brief on appeal within 120 days of the order granting the petitioner stay of judgment, the petitioner was entitled to exoneration of bail and release from custody. Artale v. Goodman, 90 A.D.2d 1006, 477 N.Y.S.2d 183 (2d Dept. 1984).

—Where the defendant was convicted and sentenced as a Class A felon, defendant was not entitled to be released on bail pending his appeal. People v. Murphy, 491 N.Y.S.2d 280 (3d Dept. 1985).

—A defendant convicted in the state court, while incarcerated obtained bail pending appeal, and while on bail, was convicted in the federal court and sentenced to nine years to run consecutively to the state sentence upon completion of the federal sentence he must serve the balance of the time owed on the state conviction, which had been affirmed, since he voluntarily secured bail pending appeal, the federal conviction and sentence continued the lawful interruption of the state sentence. People ex rel. Shargel v. Coughlin, 105 Misc. 2d 827, 432 N.Y.S.2d 1004 (Sup. Ct. N.Y. Co. 1980).

Denial of stay.—Where the court denied the defendant's motion to extend the stay of execution of his sentence, the defendant should have been placed into custody. People v. Marshall, 118 A.D.2d 735, 500 N.Y.S.2d 69 (2d Dept. 1986).

Extension of stay.—Any extensions of a stay of execution for a defendant who does not perfect his appeal within the 120 day period provided for in CPL § 460.50 must be obtained from the full intermediate Appellate Court upon motion by the defendant; should a defendant fail to bring the appeal to argument or submit such appeal to the Appellate Division to extend the stay, he has an affirmative obligation to surrender himself upon the expiration of the 120 days. People v. Clapper, 131 Misc. 2d 1079, 502 N.Y.S.2d 919 (Schoharie Co. Ct. 1986).

Issue to be resolved on stay application.—Although the defendant's sentence did not contain an imprisonment term, rather, the imposition of fines, the defendant was allowed to move for stay of the execution of the judgment. The issue was resolved at the judge's discretion. People v. Derham, 149 Misc. 2d 708, 567 N.Y.S.2d 573 (Sup. Ct. Nassau Co. 1991).

Jail credit for time at liberty.—Where the petitioner sought to receive jail time credit on his state sentence, it was not proper to petition the court pursuant to CPL § 460.50 where the petitioner was not seeking to stay judgment pending an appeal. Franks v. Koehler, 159 A.D.2d 213, 552 N.Y.S.2d 203 (1st Dept. 1990).

—Defendant was obligated to surrender to the authorities following the expiration of his stay of execution of the judgment. Where the defendant failed to surrender, he was not allowed to receive any jail time credit for the time after the stay expired. People v. Higgins, 177 A.D.2d 1052, 578 N.Y.S.2d 71 (4th Dept. 1991).

Judgment.—State properly enforced its judgment against

the defendant where the State notified the defendant that his State conviction was affirmed; thus, compelling his surrender. Because the defendant was incarcerated in Federal prison at that time, defendant's State sentence was held to be interrupted. People v. LeFevre, 100 A.D.2d 662, 473 N.Y.S.2d 849 (3d Dept. 1984).

Stay; application.—On the defense counsel's motion to stay the judgment and to fix bail, the defense counsel must prepare a notice of appeal before the judgment and complete and serve it following the judgment. People v. Shakur, 215 A.D.2d 184, 627 N.Y.S.2d 341 (1st Dept. 1995).

—It was proper for the judge chosen by the defendant to render a decision on defendant's application for stay of judgment. It was not required to be the decision of the judge who accepted the defendant's plea. Defendant has the right to choose any Supreme Court judge. People v. Meredith, 152 Misc. 2d 387, 578 N.Y.S.2d 79 (Sup. Ct. Kings Co. 1991).

Stay; prior application.—Defendant's application for a stay was a nullity where at the time it was made to the sentencing court, he had not filed a notice of appeal, therefore application to the Appellate Division was not barred by CPL § 460.50(3). People v. Garcia, 80 A.D.2d 924, 437 N.Y.S.2d 382 (2d Dept. 1981).

No stay of conviction by operation of CPL § 460.50(1).—A "judgment of conviction" is not a "conviction" but it is the "sentence" of the court as found in its minutes. A "conviction" is complete upon an adjudication of guilt or the entry of a plea of guilty and cannot be stayed or suspended by the operation of CPL 460.50(1). People v. Cunningham, 182 Misc. 790, 702 N.Y.S.2d 523 (Co. Ct. 1999), *modified*, 95 N.Y.2d 909, 717 N.Y.S.2d 68, 740 N.E.2d 213 (2000).

Supreme Court Justice; authority.—A Supreme Court Justice may stay the execution of defendant's sentence pending an appeal where the Justice lacks the authority to vacate the defendant's sentence. People v. Carthrens, 171 A.D.2d 387, 577 N.Y.S.2d 249 (1st Dept. 1991).

—Where the defendant moves to stay the execution of judgment and to be released on bail or upon his own recognizance, the judge must consider factors that will secure defendant's future court appearances. Such factors for consideration are contained in CPL § 510.30(2)(a) and (b). People v. Kern, 137 A.D.2d 862, 524 N.Y.S.2d 521(2d Dept. 1988).

—Where the defendant's history provided the court with confidence in the defendant's character, the court granted defendant's motion to stay judgment and fix bail. People v. Vasquez, 88 A.D.2d 667, 450 N.Y.S.2d 606 (2d Dept. 1982).

—Supreme Court judge had the authority to grant motion to suspend judgment while the defendant was imprisoned serving his sentence. The court based its decision on the likelihood of the reversal of the defendant's conviction. People v. Blaho, 162 Misc. 2d 618, 617 N.Y.S.2d 1019 (Sup. Ct. Queens Co. 1994).

§ 460.60. Stay of judgment pending appeal to court of appeals from intermediate appellate court.

1. (a) A judge who, pursuant to section 460.20 of this chapter, has received an application for a certificate granting a defendant leave to appeal to the court of appeals from an order of an intermediate appellate court affirming or modifying a judgment including a sentence of imprisonment, a sentence of imprisonment, or an order appealed pursuant to section 450.15 of this chapter, of a criminal court, may, upon application of such defendant-appellant issue an order both (i) staying or suspending the execution of the judgment pending the determination of the application for leave to appeal, and, if that application is granted, staying or suspending the execution of the judgment pending the determination of the appeal, and (ii) either releasing the defendant on his own recognizance or continuing bail as previously determined or fixing bail pursuant to the

provisions of article five hundred thirty. Such an order is effective immediately and that phase of the order staying or suspending execution of the judgment does not become effective unless and until the defendant is released, either on his own recognizance or upon the posting of bail.

(b) If the application for leave to appeal is denied, the stay or suspension pending the application automatically terminates upon the signing of the certificate denying leave. Upon such termination, the certificate denying leave must be sent to the criminal court in which the original judgment was entered, and the latter must proceed in the manner provided in subdivision five of section 460.50 of this chapter.

2. An application pursuant to subdivision one must be made upon reasonable notice to the people, and the people must be accorded adequate opportunity to appear in opposition thereto. Such an application may be made immediately after the entry of the order sought to be appealed or at any subsequent time during the pendency of the appeal. Not more than one application may be made pursuant to this section.

3. Notwithstanding the provisions of subdivision one, if within one hundred twenty days after the issuance of a certificate granting leave to appeal, the appeal or prospective appeal has not been brought to argument in or submitted to the court of appeals, the operation of an order issued pursuant to subdivision one of this section terminates and the defendant must surrender himself to the criminal court in which the original judgment was entered in order that execution of such judgment be commenced or resumed; except that this subdivision does not apply where the court of appeals has (a) extended the time for argument or submission of the appeal to a date beyond the specified period of one hundred twenty days and (b) upon application of the defendant expressly ordered that the operation of such order continue until the date of the determination of the appeal or some other designated future date or occurrence.

4. Where the defendant is at liberty during the pendency of an appeal as a result of an order issued pursuant to this section, the court of appeals, upon affirmance of the judgment or order, must, by appropriate certificate, remit the case to the criminal court in which the judgment was entered, and the latter must proceed in the manner provided in subdivision five of section 460.50 of this chapter.

Amended by L. 1977, Ch. 699; L. 1981, Ch. 168.

ANNOTATION

Jurisdiction of court.—Court had no jurisdiction to hear defendant's motion for a stay. Such a motion is within the jurisdiction of the Appellate Division. People v. Librie, 70 N.Y.2d 668, 518 N.Y.S.2d 961, 512 N.E.2d 544 (1987).

§ 460.70. Appeal; how perfected.

1. Except as provided in subdivision two, the

mode of and time for perfecting an appeal which has been taken to an intermediate appellate court from a judgement, sentence or order of a criminal court are determined by rules of the appellate division of the department in which such appellate court is located. Among the matters to be determined by such court rules are the times when the appeal must be noticed for and brought to argument, the content and form of the records and briefs to be served and filed, and the time when such records and briefs must be served and filed. When an appeal is taken by a defendant pursuant to section 450.10, a transcript shall be prepared and settled. The expense for such transcript and any reproduced copies of such transcript shall be paid by the defendant. Where the defendant is granted permission to proceed as a poor person by the appellate court, the court reporter shall promptly make and file with the criminal court a transcript of the stenographic minutes of such proceedings as the appellate court shall direct. The expense of transcripts and any reproduced copies of transcripts prepared for poor persons under this section shall be a state charge payable out of funds appropriated to the office of court administration for that purpose. The appellate court shall where such is necessary for perfection of the appeal, order that the criminal court furnish a reproduced copy of such transcript to the defendant or his counsel.

2. An appeal which has been taken to a county court or to an appellate term of the supreme court from a judgment, sentence or order of a local criminal court pursuant to subdivision three of section 460.10 is perfected as follows:

(a) After the local criminal court has, pursuant to paragraph (d) of subdivision three of section 460.10, filed its return with the clerk of the appellate court and delivered a copy thereof to the appellant, the appellant must file with such clerk, and serve a copy thereof upon the respondent, a notice of argument, noticing the appeal for argument at the term of such appellate court immediately following the term being held at the time of the appellant's receipt of the return. Upon motion of the appellant, however, such appellate court may for good cause shown enlarge the time to a subsequent term, in which case the appellant must notice the appeal for argument at such subsequent term;

(b) The appellant must further comply with all court rules applicable to the mode of perfecting such appeals;

(c) If the appellant does not file a notice of argument as provided in paragraph (a) or does not comply with all applicable court rules as provided in paragraph (b), the appellate court may, either upon motion of the respondent or upon its own motion, dismiss the appeal.

3. The mode of and time for perfecting any appeal which has been taken to the court of appeals are determined by the rules of the court of appeals. Among the matters to be determined by such court rules are the times when the appeal must be noticed for and brought to argument, the content, form and number of the records and briefs and copies thereof to be served and filed, and the times when such records and briefs must be served and filed.

When an appeal is taken by a defendant pursuant to section 450.70, the defendant shall cause to be prepared and printed or otherwise duplicated pursuant to rules of the court of appeals the record on appeal and the required number of copies thereof. If the defendant is granted permission to appeal as a poor person, the expense thereof shall be a state charge payable out of funds appropriated to the office of court administration for that purpose.

Amended by L. 1977, Ch. 695; L. 1995, Ch. 83.

ANNOTATIONS

Appeal; assignment of counsel.—Upon application for an assignment of counsel to prosecute an appeal, the Appellate Term did not abuse its discretion in determining that the defendants did not satisfactorily demonstrate that they were at that time financially unable to obtain counsel. People v. Simmons, 31 N.Y.2d 997, 341 N.Y.S.2d 451, 293 N.E.2d 826 (1973).

Appellate counsel.—The same standard—meaningful representation—that applies to claimed ineffective assistance of trial counsel applies in assessing the effectiveness of appellate counsel. People v. Stultz, 2 N.Y.3d 277, 778 N.Y.S.2d 431, 810 N.E.2d 883 (2004).

—The Appellate Division must assign new counsel where it determines there exists a nonfrivolous issue on appeal. People v. Davis, 73 N.Y.2d 864, 537 N.Y.S.2d 475, 534 N.E.2d 313 (1989).

—The procedure to be followed by appellate counsel when a client requests that several points be presented, some with merit and some without merit, is to argue the claim found meritorious and make no comment about claims considered frivolous. People v. Vasquez, 70 N.Y.2d l, 516 N.Y.S.2d 921, 509 N.E.2d 934 (1987).

—Defendant was deprived of effective assistance on the appeal where counsel merely submitted a brief consisting of a three-page summary of the facts, followed by a four-line conclusion in which she stated that she had not discovered any non-frivolous issues and requested that she be relieved. People v. Lopez, 158 A.D.2d 430, 552 N.Y.S.2d 5 (1st Dept. 1990).

—Where appellate counsel's brief neither discussed nor analyzed potential issues presented by the record, it was deficient and assignment of new counsel was warranted. People v. Bing, 144 A.D.2d 249, 533 N.Y.S.2d 720 (1st Dept. 1988).

—Defendant failed to meet his burden of establishing his claim of ineffective appellate counsel since he failed to identify a single issue that his appellate counsel failed to present. People v. De La Hoz, 131 A.D.2d 154, 520 N.Y.S.2d 386 (1st Dept. 1987).

—In submitting an *Anders* brief, the question is not whether any meritorious issues could be raised on appeal, but whether any issues raised would be "wholly frivolous"; where an *Anders* brief contained no reference to the facts and merely advised the court on the ultimate merits of defendant's appeal, it was insufficient. People v. Truss, 287 A.D.2d 750, 732 N.Y.S.2d 237 (2d Dept. 2001).

—Defendant was denied effective assistance of appellate counsel where the attorney appointed to handle his appeal filed a brief consisting of a one page "Digest of Essential Facts" and a one-and-a-half page argument. People v. Henry, 143 A.D.2d 277, 532 N.Y.S.2d 155 (2d Dept. 1988).

Appellate Division; authority.—Although the Appellate Division has the general authority providing for the "mode of and time for perfecting an appeal," the Appellate Division does not have the authority to require the People to personally serve the appellate brief to the defendant. People v. Ramos, 85 N.Y.2d 768, 628 N.Y.S.2d 27, 651 N.E.2d 895 (1995).

Failure to perfect.—Matter would be remitted for lower court to exercise its discretion where the lower court dismissed People's appeal due to failure to timely perfect the appeal based upon the erroneous belief that dismissal was mandatory under the Rules of Court, rather than discretionary. People v. Evans, 69 N.Y.2d 997, 517 N.Y.S.2d 904, 511 N.E.2d 48 (1987).

—Five-year delay on part of assigned counsel in perfecting the appeal did not deprive the defendant of effective assistance of counsel. People v. Gaines, 143 A.D.2d 520, 532 N.Y.S.2d 944 (4th Dept. 1988).

Generally.—District Attorneys are obligated by County Law § 700(1) to file a brief setting forth their positions with respect to a defendant's appeal. People v. Sawyer, 188 A.D.2d 939, 592 N.Y.S.2d 92 (3d Dept. 1992).

Dehors the record.—The defendant's claim that his attorney only met with him for 10 minutes, the day before the trial is dehors the record and may not be considered on appeal. People v. Otero, 201 A.D.2d 675, 608 N.Y.S.2d 260 (2d Dept. 1994).

—Matters dehors the record may not be raised on direct appeal. People v. Higgins, 170 A.D.2d 621, 566 N.Y.S.2d 394 (2d Dept. 1991).

—Since the claims raised in defendant's *pro se* supplemental brief relied on facts not contained in the record and they were not reviewable by the court. People v. Piparo, 134 A.D.2d 295, 520 N.Y.S.2d 621 (2d Dept. 1987).

—Court denied defendant's motion to expand the record on appeal to include information as to the defendant's activities after the imposition on the sentence. People v. Askinazi, 130 A.D.2d 665, 515 N.Y.S.2d 596 (2d Dept. 1987).

—While, as a general rule, the Appellate Division is bound by the certified record on appeal, it may consider documentary evidence for purposes of sustaining the underlying determination. People *ex rel.* Glidden v. Nemier, 133 A.D.2d 487, 519 N.Y.S.2d 287 (3d Dept. 1987).

Reply brief.—The practice of raising a new substantive issue in a reply brief at a time when an adversary can no longer respond to it is improper. People v. Minota, 137 A.D.2d 837, 525 N.Y.S.2d 300 (2d Dept. 1988).

—Argument raised to the first time in reply brief was not properly before the court; the practice of raising a new substantive issue in a reply brief at time when an adversary can no longer respond to it is improper. People v. Clanton, 204 A.D.2d 810, 612 N.Y.S.2d 83 (3d Dept. 1994).

Timeliness.—Although the People's briefs were untimely served and filed, where defendant was not prejudiced thereby, motion to strike the People's briefs would be denied. People v. Paz, 158 A.D.2d 1008, 550 N.Y.S.2d 975 (4th Dept. 1990).

Transcripts.—Where the records of the defendant's trial have been lost and neither reconstruction nor a new trial is possible, and defendant has raised appealable issues with possible merits, the only available remedy is vacatur of the conviction and dismissal of the indictment. People v. Johnson, 69 N.Y.2d 339, 514 N.Y.S.2d 324, 506 N.E.2d 1177 (1987).

—Defendant is not entitled to summary reversal based on the unavailability of plea minutes until he establishes that a reconstruction of those proceedings is impossible. People v. Grimmett, 127 A.D.2d 547, 512 N.Y.S.2d 371 (1st Dept. 1987).

—Loss of minutes of decision rendered after the suppression hearing did not deprive the defendant of his right to appellate review since the defendant failed to make an appropriate showing of the nature of the issues he might have raised on appeal had the minutes been available. People v. Torres, 145 A.D.2d 664, 536 N.Y.S.2d 176 (2d Dept. 1988).

—When a transcript is missing through no fault of the People, the burden is on the defendant to demonstrate that alternate methods of providing an adequate record cannot be utilized. People v. Suren, 131 A.D.2d 896, 517 N.Y.S.2d 251 (2d Dept. 1987).

—Court properly denied the defendant's motion to be provided with a free transcript of the suppression hearing where the defendant failed to submit any proof of indigency when given the opportunity to do so. People v. Gonzalez, 127 A.D.2d 787, 512 N.Y.S.2d 182 (2d Dept. 1987).

§ 460.80. Appeal; argument and submission thereof.

The mode of and procedure for arguing or otherwise litigating appeals in criminal cases are determined by rules of the individual appellate courts. Among the matters to be determined by such court rules are the circumstances in which oral argument is required and those in which the case may be submitted by either or both parties without oral argument; the consequences or effect of failure to present oral argument when such is required; the amount of time for oral argument allowed to each party; and the number of counsel entitled to be heard.

ANNOTATIONS

Appeal; mentally ill defendant.—The presence of defendant was not required; the appeal was decided solely on the record and briefs. The present mental state of the appellant did not require that his appeal be held in abeyance. People v. Laudati, 41 A.D.2d 552, 339 N.Y.S.2d 766 (2d Dept. 1973).

District Attorney's duty to submit brief on appeal.—"It is the duty of every District Attorney to conduct all prosecutions for crimes or offenses cognizable by the courts of the county for which he shall have been elected." (County Law § 700[1]). The Fourth Department feels that this duty requires that the District Attorney file a brief stating his position concerning an appeal taken by the defendant. People v. Pitsley, 37 A.D.2d 905, 325 N.Y.S.2d 451 (4th Dept. 1971).

ARTICLE 470—APPEALS—DETERMINATION THEREOF

LexisNexis Cross References

Criminal Constitutional Law, Vol. 3, Ch. 15, Appeals; *Bender's New York Evidence—CPLR,* Vol. 6, Ch. 31, Appellate Review; *Criminal Defense Techniques,* Vol. 1A, Ch. 14A, Effective Assistance of Counsel; Vol. 2, Ch. 48, Criminal Appeals; Vol. 6, Ch. 122, Appeals and Post-Conviction Remedies; *Business Crime,* Vol. 4, Ch. 15, Appellate Practice; *Defense of Drunk Driving Cases,* Vol. 4, Ch. 52, Appeals; *New York Criminal Practice (2d ed.),* Vol. 4, Ch. 44, Appeals; *see generally New York Appellate Practice;* Vol. 1, Ch. 5, Taking and Perfecting the Appeal; Vol. 1, Ch. 6, Stays Pending Appeal; Vol. 1, Ch. 8, Argument of the Appeal; Vol. 1, Ch. 9, Disposition of the Appeal; Vol. 1, Ch. 10, Motions for Reargument; Vol. 2, Ch. 13, Criminal Appeals; *Prosecution and Defense of Sex Crimes,* Ch. 17, Appeals in Sex Crimes Cases; *New York Suppression Manual,* Ch. 4, Harmless Error; Ch. 27, Appealing Suppression Orders; *Criminal Practice Handbook (2d ed.),* Ch. 12, Direct Appeal.

§ 470.05. Determination of appeals; general criteria.

1. An appellate court must determine an appeal without regard to technical errors or defects which do not affect the substantial rights of the parties.

2. For purposes of appeal, a question of law with respect to a ruling or instruction of a criminal court during a trial or proceeding is presented when a protest thereto was registered, by the party claiming error, at the time of such ruling or instruction or at any subsequent time when the court had an opportunity of effectively changing the same. Such protest need not be in the form of an "exception" but is sufficient if the party made his position with respect to the ruling or instruction known to the court, or if in reponse* to a protest by a party, the court expressly decided the question raised on appeal. In addition, a party who without success has either expressly or impliedly sought or requested a particular ruling or instruction, is deemed to have thereby protested the court's ultimate disposition of the matter or failure to rule or instruct accordingly sufficiently to raise a question of law with respect to such disposition or failure regardless of whether any actual protest thereto was registered.

* As originally enacted.

Amended by L. 1986, Ch. 798.

ANNOTATIONS

Appealable issue; question of law.—Defendant who consented to a post summation viewing of the crime scene after he had repeatedly objected to the change of conditions; protestations were sufficient to create a question of law. People v. White, 52 N.Y.2d 721, 439 N.Y.S.2d 333, 421 N.E.2d 825 (1981).

Appeals; order for new trial; authority of Appellate

Division.—Power of Court of Appeals to review opinion for reason of intermediate appellate court's decision is limited to cases where the order of such court states that decision is on law alone and not where there is a recital as to factual or discretionary basis. Since opinion of Appellate Division indicates order was exercise of discretionary power, it is not reviewable, even though settled order deleted this reference and recited that decision was on law alone. People v. Williams, 31 N.Y.2d 151, 335 N.Y.S.2d 271, 286 N.E.2d 715 (1972).

Conflict of interest.—Defense counsel's former employment at the District Attorney's Office does not establish a conflict of interest that constitutes good cause for substitution of counsel. People v. Smith, 242 A.D.2d 908, 662 N.Y.S.2d 878 (4th Dept. 1997).

Conflict of interest; joint representation.—Defendant did not demonstrate a conflict of interest or significant possibility thereof in the joint representation of defendant and his brother by the same attorney where the defenses defendant argued should have been raised were not necessarily in conflict. People v. Cruz, 63 N.Y.2d 848, 482 N.Y.S.2d 259, 472 N.E.2d 35 (1984).

Constitutional error.—To sustain a conviction, where the trial court has committed a constitutional error, it must be shown that there was no reasonable possibility that the jury would have acquitted defendant if the error had not been committed. People v. Ermo 61 A.D.2d 177, 401 N.Y.S.2d 831 (2d Dept. 1978), aff'd, 47 N.Y.2d 863, 419 N.Y.S.2d 65, 392 N.E.2d 1248 (1979).

Conviction upheld; failure of defense attorney to take exception or request charge.—General objections made by the defense counsel in relation to the prosecution's expert witness were not preserved for review. Counsel failed to provide the trial court with the basis of the objections. People v. Waugh, 189 A.D.2d 907, 592 N.Y.S.2d 789 (2d Dept. 1993).

—Issues were not properly preserved for review as a matter of law since no objection was raised to an allegedly improper charge to the jury or to an allegedly improper comment by the prosecutor and since an objection was taken to one of the prosecutor's comment which was sustained by the trial court and immediate curative instruction was given and there was no request for further instruction or mistrial. People v. Giles, 87 A.D.2d 636, 448 N.Y.S.2d 221 (2d Dept. 1982).

—Where defense counsel failed to object prior to the jury resuming its deliberation, after declining to have the cross examination read back, the matter was not reviewable as a matter of law. People v. Michem, 195 A.D.2d 1038, 600 N.Y.S.2d 528 (4th Dept. 1993).

Cumulative impact of several errors.—Cumulative effect of several errors deprived the defendant of his right to a fair trial although each error, taken individually, might not have amounted to a constitutional violation; such errors included the improper cross-examination of the defendant and his character witnesses by the prosecutor and the court's improper admonition to the jury regarding the trouble and expense to the taxpayers of not reaching a verdict. People v. Hudson, 104 A.D.2d 157, 483 N.Y.S.2d 215 (1st Dept. 1984).

—Court properly ordered a new a trial where the prosecutor's's conduct prejudiced the defendant. The defendant's trial was plagued with a sufficient amount of harmless errors warranting a new trial. People v. Jackson, 143 A.D.2d 363, 532 N.Y.S.2d 303 (2d Dept. 1988).

—Defendant was deprived of a fair trial because of the cumulative effect of the following errors: (1) prosecutor misconduct in compelling defendant to characterize police witnesses as lying, speaking untruths, wrong or mistaken; (2) two erroneous statements by the court advising the jury that sufficient evidence had been presented for them to reach a verdict and thus created the possibility that the stated opinion of the trial court or even the suggestion of an opinion might be seized upon by the jury and eventually prove decisive; (3) inclusion of a *Sandstrom* charge stating that a person intends the natural and probable consequences of his act. The court reversed the conviction as a matter of discretion and in the interest of justice. People v. Balkum, 94 A.D.2d 933, 464 N.Y.S.2d 63 (4th Dept. 1983).

Dismissal for insufficient evidence; acquittal.—A dismissal for insufficient evidence at the end of a prior trial is an acquittal for double jeopardy purposes. People v. Davis, 91 A.D.2d 948, 458 N.Y.S.2d 563 (1st Dept. 1983).

Error affecting mode of proceedings prescribed by law;

reviewability despite failure to object.—In a criminal prosecution, any error in improperly placing the burden of proof on the defendant goes to the essential validity of the proceedings and therefore such error is reviewable by Court of Appeals, notwithstanding the failure to object to the charge during the trial. People v. Patterson, 39 N.Y.2d 288, 383 N.Y.S.2d 573, 347 N.E.2d 898 (1976), aff'd, 432 U.S. 197, 97 S. Ct. 2319, 53 L. Ed. 2d 281 (1977).

Exception; proper objection.—Defense counsel's failure to object to the trial court's ban on "all meaningful communication between the defendant and his attorney during defendant's testimony" waived the question for appellate review as defense counsel was present at the time of the trespass on defendant's rights and his protest would have allowed the trial judge the opportunity to reverse his error. People v. Narayan, 54 N.Y.2d 106, 444 N.Y.S.2d 604, 429 N.E.2d 123 (1981).

—Defendant's failure to request a ruling in the court below; on whether the name of the informant who gave the police the information that led to his arrest could be disclosed, precluded him from raising the issue on appeal. People v. Medina, 53 N.Y.2d 951, 441 N.Y.S.2d 442, 424 N.E.2d 276 (1981).

—The failure of defendant to take appropriate exception or to request further clarification at a time "when the court had an opportunity of effectively changing" any instruction preserved no question of law in connection therewith reviewable by the court. People v. Gurley, 42 N.Y.2d 1086, 399 N.Y.S.2d 650, 369 N.E.2d 1183 (1977).

—Defendant's failure to object that the known substance relied on for comparative tests was not established as reliable by either of the testifying experts did not preserve the issue for appellate review. People v. Weeks, 84 A.D.2d 582, 443 N.Y.S.2d 421 (2d Dept. 1981).

—At trial the defendant failed to object to the protective orders upon the People's witnesses and he failed to claim he was prejudiced by the delayed receipt of *Rosario* material. Thus, the defendant's claims were not preserved for appellate review. People v. Morales, 216 A.D.2d 154, 628 N.Y.S.2d 284 (1st Dept. 1995).

Failure to except to charge; effect.—Error in charge of the trial judge was not preserved for review where defendant did not make "his position with respect to the . . . Instruction known to the court" at a "time when the court had an opportunity of effectively changing the same." People v. Rumph, 38 N.Y.2d 989, 384 N.Y.S.2d 436, 348 N.E.2d 912 (1976).

—Court held that the charge made to the jury did not mislead the jury nor did it deprive the defendant of a fair trial. The defendant had previously agreed to the charge given and thus, defendant's claim was not preserved for review. People v. Palmer, 214 A.D.2d 479, 625 N.Y.S.2d 522 (1st Dept. 1995).

—Where the defendant failed to object to the prosecutor's introduction of evidence of the defendant's prior robbery of the involved store, the defendant's claim was not reviewable. The evidence did not constitute inadmissible hearsay. People v. Diaz, 189 A.D.2d 574, 592 N.Y.S.2d 29 (1st Dept. 1993).

—Failure at trial to raise the issue of probable cause to arrest, was deemed a waiver of his right to raise it on appeal, under the doctrine of preservation of error. People v. Jones, 81 A.D.2d 22, 440 N.Y.S.2d 248 (2d Dept. 1981).

—By failing to object to jury charge, defendant failed to preserve his contentions for appellate review. People v. McNear, 265 A.D.2d 810, 696 N.Y.S.2d 611 (4th Dept. 1999).

Habeas corpus; denial of bail. —An order denying bail in a habeas corpus proceeding is not appealable. People ex rel. Smith v. Smith, 91 A.D.2d 1204, 459 N.Y.S.2d 198 (4th Dept. 1983).

Harmless error.—Although the People's case was entirely based upon circumstantial evidence, circumstantial evidence charge was not required where the evidence against defendant was overwhelming. Failure of the court to give such a charge was harmless error. People v. Brian, 84 N.Y.2d 887, 620 N.Y.S.2d 789, 644 N.E.2d 1345 (1994).

—Although defendant was entitled to a jury instruction on an alibi defense, court's failure to instruct did not warrant reversal where People's burden of proof was otherwise conveyed to jury. People v. Warren, 76 N.Y.2d 773, 559 N.Y.S.2d 954, 559 N.E.2d 648 (1990).

—Where co-defendant's statements were erroneously admitted against defendant, reversal was not required; such admission did not contribute to the outcome of defendant's case, as the evidence against the defendant was extremely persuasive. People v. Ayala 75 N.Y.2d 960, 554 N.Y.S.2d 412, 553 N.E.2d 960 (1990).

—Although the reading of the witness' grand jury testimony was not necessary to rebut any evidence introduced by the defense and therefore constituted improper bolstering, the error was harmless. People v. Tejeda, 73 N.Y.2d 958, 540 N.Y.S.2d 985, 538 N.E.2d 337 (1989).

—Although prosecutor committed error in affirmatively representing that the dead witness was alive and might be called as a witness, in view of the overwhelming evidence of guilt and the lack of any prejudice to the defendant by virtue of the misrepresentation, the error was harmless. People v. Rice, 69 N.Y.2d 781, 513 N.Y.S.2d 108, 109, 505 N.E.2d 618 (1987).

—To assess the impact of an error, the court must determine "likelihood that, if the error had not been committed, the outcome would have been different," taking into account the quantum and nature of the proof of guilt. People v. Wood, 66 N.Y.2d 374, 497 N.Y.S.2d 340, 488 N.E.2d 86 (1985).

—Where court precluded admission of defendant's statements at trial, fact that it may have erred in failing to suppress the statements prior to trial was not consequential. People v. Williams, 181 A.D.2d 503, 581 N.Y.S.2d 677 (1st Dept. 1992).

—In light of the overwhelming evidence of the defendant's guilt, there is no reasonable possibility that the admission into evidence of the confession by nontestifying co-defendant contributed to the conviction of the defendant. People v. Henry, 134 A.D.2d 370, 520 N.Y.S.2d 848 (2d Dept. 1987).

—Where proof of guilt was overwhelming, any error in not redacting a portion of the defendant's videotaped conversation with the prosecutor, in which the defendant exhibited behavior claimed by him to be prejudicial, was harmless beyond a reasonable doubt. People v. Morris, 130 A.D.2d 517, 515 N.Y.S.2d 96 (2d Dept. 1987).

—Although statements elicited from defendant in violation of his *Miranda* rights should have been suppressed, their admission into evidence constituted harmless error due to the overwhelming proof of guilt. People v. Nocella, 129 A.D.2d 653, 514 N.Y.S.2d 268 (2d Dept. 1987).

—In view of the overwhelming evidence of the defendant's guilt, the single reference to his post-arrest silence was harmless beyond a reasonable doubt. People v. Boyd, 128 A.D.2d 886, 513 N.Y.S.2d 809 (2d Dept. 1987).

—Where the court issued prompt curative instructions and proof of guilt was overwhelming, prosecutor's comment concerning the defendant—"Let her take the stand if she wants to"— amounted to harmless error. People v. Crociata, 123 A.D.2d 781, 507 N.Y.S.2d 255 (2d Dept. 1986).

—Wrongful admission of inculpatory statements of an accomplice, who did not testify, constituted harmless error due to the abundant evidence, independent of the accomplice's statements, which overwhelmingly established the guilt of the defendant. People v. Sheffield, 118 A.D.2d 882, 500 N.Y.S.2d 546 (2d Dept. 1986).

—Court's error in charging accessorial conduct only as to larceny and not as to the robbery was harmless since defendant could have been convicted as a principal or accessory in the robbery and larceny charges. People v. Kinsman, 144 A.D.2d 772, 534 N.Y.S.2d 756 (3d Dept. 1988).

—Although court erred in admitting testimony from two prosecution witnesses that improperly bolstered the victim's identification of defendant, the error was harmless in light of the victim's strong and unequivocal identification of the defendant, who resided in the same building as the victim. People v. Marks, 182 A.D.2d 1122, 583 N.Y.S.2d 331 (4th Dept. 1992).

Inadequacy of defendant's representation.—A defendant urging that a conviction should be overturned on account of counsel's relationship with a former client must show that "the conduct of the defense was in fact affected by the operation of the conflict of interest" or that the conflict "operated on the representation." People v. Ortiz, 76 N.Y.2d 652, 563 N.Y.S.2d 20, 564 N.E.2d 630 (1990).

Ineffective assistance of counsel; Article 440 motion proper.—Issue raised for the first time on appeal regarding trial counsel's failure to raise certain arguments will not constitute ineffective assistance of counsel when unsubstantiated by the record, and the appropriate vehicle for defendant's challenge

would be a proceeding pursuant to CPL Article 440. People v. Jones, 114 A.D.2d 974, 495 N.Y.S.2d 418 (2d Dept. 1985).

Law to be applied.—The validity of a conviction shall be determined as of the time it is entered; an unconstitutional conviction is, by definition, a conviction which was obtained in violation of the defendant's constitutional rights, i.e., his right as defined by the law existing at the time the conviction was obtained or by subsequent law applicable to the judgment under principles of retroactivity. People v. Catalanotte, 72 N.Y.2d 641, 536 N.Y.S.2d 16, 532 N.E.2d 1244 (1988), *cert. denied*, 493 U.S. 811 (1989).

Lost minutes; reconstruction hearing.—If a significant portion of the minutes of court proceedings has been lost, then a reconstruction hearing should normally be available for a defendant appealing his conviction after trial if the defendant has acted with reasonable diligence to mitigate the harm done by the mishap. However, a defendant who has pleaded guilty is entitled to a reconstruction hearing only if he can identify a ground for appeal that is based on something that occurred during the untranscribed proceeding. People v. Parris, 4 N.Y.3d 41, 790 N.Y.S.2d 421, 823 N.E.2d 827 (2004).

Mistrial; necessity for motion.—The failure of a defendant to move for a mistrial precluded a review of the issue presented by the prosecution's failure to produce a witness with it's opening statement. People v. DeTore, 34 N.Y.2d 199, 356 N.Y.S.2d 598, 313 N.E.2d 61, *cert. denied*, 419 U.S. 1025 (1974).

New trial when transcript unavailable.—Defendant's 22-year-old conviction was reversed and new trial ordered where he was denied his fundamental right to appeal since, at the time of his original conviction, he was not advised of his right to appeal, the transcript of the original trial minutes were unavailable, and a reconstruction hearing would have been insufficient. People v. Rivera, 39 N.Y.2d 519 384 N.Y.S.2d 726, 349 N.E.2d 825 (1976).

—Where defendant's counsel tried to obtain the trial transcript in order to perfect an appeal but court reporter failed to transcribe the minutes for three years, and when the trial transcript was turned over it was missing the summations, the jury instructions, and a readback of the charges, defendant was entitled to summary reversal and a new trial in the absence of an alternative method of providing an adequate record for appellate review. People v. Jacobs, 286 A.D.2d 404, 729 N.Y.S.2d 189 (2d Dept. 2001).

No valid issue on appeal.—Defendant's contention that the trial court erred in not issuing a pretrial ruling regarding admissibility of a knife at trial was unpreserved upon appellate review when his only motion for mistrial was grounded solely on People's inability to connect knife to defendant, and was not based on any claim of prejudice as a result of references to the knife. People v. Weston, 56 N.Y.2d 844, 453 N.Y.S.2d 167, 438 N.E.2d 873 (1982).

—Defense counsel did not seek a mistrial or request further curative instructions, so it must be assumed that the court's prompt intervention, and in some cases, express admonitions to the jury to disregard the statements, cured the defects to defendant's satisfaction. People v. Walters, 116 A.D.2d 757, 497 N.Y.S.2d 943 (2d Dept. 1986).

On summation.—Prosecutorial summation statements which went without objection were not preserved for review. People v. Williams, 46 N.Y.2d 1070, 416 N.Y.S.2d 792, 390 N.E.2d 299 (1979).

—Since no objection was made to the prosecutor's remarks in summation, including the comments expressing confidence, in the truthfulness of the police officers, they were not preserved for review by the Court of Appeals. People v. Utley, 45 N.Y.2d 908, 411 N.Y.S.2d 6, 383 N.E.2d 558 (1978).

—Defendant must raise timely objections to preserve the issues for review. However, the defendant's objections to the prosecution's summation did not warrant reversal of the conviction. The court held that although the summation was not completely void of misconduct, it was acceptable. People v. D'Allessandro, 184 A.D.2d 114, 591 N.Y.S.2d 1001 (1st Dept. 1992).

—Prosecutor's closing argument that it was only in the unlikely event there was one "nut" on the jury who might believe the "cock and bull story" presented by defense counsel that he bothered to sum up at all was a patently improper manner of advocacy by which the prosecutor presented his own belief as to lack of merit of the defense testimony. People v. Lee, 79 A.D.2d 641, 433 N.Y.S.2d 610 (2d Dept. 1980).

Preservation.—Defendant's motion for a mistrial and the trial court's denial of that motion sufficiently preserved the question of law for the Court of Appeals' review. People v. Smith, 97 N.Y.2d 324, 740 N.Y.S.2d 279, 766 N.E.2d 941 (2002).

—Where trial counsel joined in an objection made by counsel for a co-defendant, the issue was preserved for appellate review. People v. DeRosario, 81 N.Y.2d 801, 595 N.Y.S.2d 372, 611 N.E.2d 273 (1993).

—Where the defendant applied to attend sidebar conferences, but was denied attendance by the court, the issue was held to be preserved for review. The defendant made a specific application and the court made a specific ruling. People v. Rosen, 81 N.Y.2d 237, 597 N.Y.S.2d 914, 613 N.E.2d 946 (1993).

—The defendant must raise timely objections to the procedures employed by the court. Failure to make the objections results in forfeiture of the right to challenge these procedures upon appellate review. People v. Callahan, 80 N.Y.2d 273, 590 N.Y.S.2d 46, 604 N.E.2d 108 (1992).

—Defendant failed to object to any of the alleged instances of prosecutorial misconduct on summation and therefore failed to preserve the issue for appellate review. People v. Romanelli, 239 A.D.2d 940, 659 N.Y.S.2d 615 (4th Dept. 1997).

Prosecutor's opening statement.—When the People fail to produce a witness referred to in opening statements, "the general rule is that, absent bad faith or undue prejudice, a trial will not be undone." Here, defendant conceded that prosecutor did not act in bad faith, and there was overwhelming evidence against the defendant; thus, there is no significant probability that the jury would have acquitted him had it not heard the references to the witnesses. People v. Thompson, 276 A.D.2d 811, 716 N.Y.S.2d 397 (2d Dept. 2000).

—Where People's opening statement communicated that a witness had observed the shooting and identified the defendant in a lineup, defendant claimed it was reversible error that the witness was not produced; contention was unpreserved because defendant failed to move for a mistrial based on the witness' failure to testify and failed to object to the lineup testimony. People v. Seabrooks, 244 A.D.2d 514, 664 N.Y.S.2d 105 (2d Dept. 1997).

Prosecutorial misconduct.—Where prosecutor persistently disregarded trial court's rulings, the cumulative effect of such conduct subsequently prejudiced defendant's rights, and a new trial was ordered. People v. Calabria, 94 N.Y.2d 519, 706 N.Y.S.2d 691, 727 N.E.2d 1245 (2000).

—Among other errors, during opening statement, prosecutor told jury that defendant was a "parasite," and that "citizens like [them]selves indicted this defendant," and during direct examination of arresting officer, he elicited the fact that the defendant had remained silent after his arrest; defense counsel objected to the reference to defendant's post-arrest silence, but court compounded error by instructing defense counsel not to interrupt. Accordingly, defendant was denied a fair trial and conviction must be reversed. People v. Lippolis, 246 A.D.2d 557, 667 N.Y.S.2d 423 (2d Dept. 1998).

—Where the defendant was questioned by the prosecutor about a prior conviction, the court found the prosecutor's actions improper. However, the court held the error to be harmless due to the substantial amount of evidence establishing the defendant's guilt. People v. Bright, 190 A.D.2d 855, 594 N.Y.S.2d 651 (2d Dept. 1993).

—Prosecutor's introduction of hearsay evidence tending to connect the defendant to an unrelated killing, together with other prosecutorial misconduct, was so highly prejudicial that reversal was required in the interest of justice even though defense counsel failed to object thereto. People v. Woodhull, 105 A.D.2d 815, 481 N.Y.S.2d 749 (2d Dept. 1984).

—Conviction reversed where prosecutor repeatedly impeached his own witnesses with prior inconsistent statements and compounded the error when, on summation, he denigrated their credibility and called attention to the fact that he had impeached their testimony with prior statements. People v. Dowdall, 236 A.D.2d 836, 654 N.Y.S.2d 72 (4th Dept. 1997).

Squabbling between defense counsel and prosecutor; right to fair trial.—Defendant was not deprived of a fair trial despite repeated squabbling between defense counsel and prosecutor, which culminated in both being sworn and testifying. People v. Chapman, 48 A.D.2d 778, 369 N.Y.S.2d 1 (1st Dept.

1975), aff'd, 39 N.Y.2d 791, 385 N.Y.S.2d 287, 350 N.E.2d 618 (1976).

Trial; errors.—Whenever there is doubt as to whether a conviction is premised on an impermissible ground, the doubt must be resolved in the defendant's favor. People v. Velasquez, 151 A.D.2d 159, 547 N.Y.S.2d 6, 9 (1st Dept. 1989), aff'd, 76 N.Y.2d 905, 561 N.Y.S.2d 911, 563 N.E.2d 282 (1990).

—A reversal by the Appellate Division based on claimed trial error to which objection is not taken presents no questions of law for appellate review. People v. Dercole, 52 N.Y.2d 956, 437 N.Y.S.2d 966, 419 N.E.2d 869 (1981).

—Where proof of guilt is overwhelming, nonconstitutional trial error is prejudicial and, hence, reversible, only if, upon the People's evidence viewed by the fact finders as credible, there is a significant probability that the jury would have acquitted the defendant had it not been for the error which occurred. People v. Perez, 36 N.Y.2d 848, 370 N.Y.S.2d 914, 331 N.E.2d 691 (1975).

—Although the court held that the testimony of the investigator that the defendant was the subject of an investigation constituted an error, the court held that the error did not warrant reversal of the defendant's conviction. The testimony of the investigator was followed by curative instructions to the jury. People v. Roberts, 188 A.D.2d 735, 591 N.Y.S.2d 559 (3d Dept. 1992).

Waiver of appeal.—Where defendant knowingly and voluntarily pleads guilty, an appeal waiver encompasses issues relating to the sentence even where defendant has not received a specific sentence promise at the time of the plea colloquy and waiver. People v. Hidalgo, 91 N.Y.2d 733, 675 N.Y.S.2d 327, 698 N.E.2d 46 (1998); see also People v. Lococo, 92 N.Y.2d 825, 677 N.Y.S.2d 57, 699 N.E.2d 416; (1998) (same); People v. Garcia, 92 N.Y.2d 869, 677 N.Y.S.2d 772, 700 N.E.2d 311 (1998) (defendant's receipt of inaccurate information regarding his possible sentence exposure did not render his guilty plea involuntary, where the length of the sentence was one of many factors that defendant considered before accepting the plea, and where, as here, defendant could have received a consecutive sentence).

Waiver of error; generally.—A post-verdict motion made pursuant to CPL § 330.30 is not, by itself, ordinarily sufficient to preserve a question of law within the meaning of CPL § 470.05(2). People v. Padro, 75 N.Y.2d 820, 552 N.Y.S.2d 555, 551 N.E.2d 1233 (1990).

—The word "objection" alone is not sufficient to preserve a claim for appellate review. People v. Fleming, 70 N.Y.2d 947, 524 N.Y.S.2d 670, 519 N.E.2d 616 (1988).

—Defendant's generalized objections did not adequately alert the Trial Judge to defendant's arguments so as to preserve those issues for appellate review. People v. Ford, 69 N.Y.2d 775, 513 N.Y.S.2d 106, 505 N.E.2d 615 (1987).

—An unelaborated objection, general in nature, is not sufficient to alert the court to the specific claim of error. People v. Blow, 172 A.D.2d 366, 568 N.Y.S.2d 623 (1st Dept. 1991).

—An alleged violation assertedly of constitutional dimension must be preserved for appellate review. People v. Marel, 152 A.D.2d 97, 47 N.Y.S.2d 302 (1st Dept. 1989).

—Defendant's failure to raise specific objections to the court's deprivation of his right to be present did not preclude appellate review as a matter of law. People v. Cooper, 158 A.D.2d 465, 551 N.Y.S.2d 254 (2d Dept. 1990).

—Defendant's argument concerning the specificity of the allegations contained in the indictment could not be raised for the first time on appeal. People v. Andrews, 146 A.D.2d 787, 537 N.Y.S.2d 268 (2d Dept. 1989).

—Defense counsel's stating the one word "objection" was insufficient to preserve for appellate review the issue concerning the admission of alleged bolstering testimony. People v. McCorkle, 119 A.D.2d 700, 500 N.Y.S.2d 822 (2d Dept. 1986).

Waiver of error; amendment of indictment.—The claim by the defendant that the indictment was improperly amended during trial was not preserved for review since he argued only that the evidence did not warrant the amendment, not that the amendment was otherwise impermissible. People v. Montgomery, 124 A.D.2d 602, 507 N.Y.S.2d 745 (2d Dept. 1986).

Waiver of error; court's instructions or court's conduct.—By objecting to court's giving of cautionary instructions, defendant waived any claim he might have had regarding the need for cautionary instructions. People v. Stewart, 81 N.Y.2d 877, 597 N.Y.S.2d 634, 613 N.E.2d 540 (1993).

—Defendant failed to preserve his challenge by specific objection, to the court's refusal to read back opening and closing statements on the basis that they were not evidence. People v. Velasco, 160 A.D.2d 170, 553 N.Y.S.2d 331 (1st Dept. 1990), aff'd, 77 N.Y.2d 469, 568 N.Y.S.2d 721, 570 N.E.2d 1070 (1991).

—Where defendant did not request additional instructions following the issuance of the court's curative instructions, he may not complain of the insufficiency of the instructions given. People v. Jacquin, 124 A.D.2d 594, 507 N.Y.S.2d 736 (2d Dept. 1986), aff'd, 71 N.Y.2d 825, 527 N.Y.S.2d 728, 522 N.E.2d 1026 (1988).

—Any error by the court was not preserved for appellate review when during cross-examination the court sustained the People's objection to a question and defense counsel simply proceeded to another subject, never calling to the court's attention the purpose of that question, or disputing the People's claim that it was irrelevant, or in any way attempting to call the court's attention to the nature of the alleged error in sustaining the objection. People v. George, 67 N.Y.2d 817, 501 N.Y.S.2d 639, 492 N.E.2d 767 (1986).

—By failing to move for a mistrial, or to challenge the court's limiting instructions on the basis of a line of questioning during cross-examination of defendant, and a related comment on summation, defendant failed to preserve his claims for review. People v. McFadden, 196 A.D.2d 717, 602 N.Y.S.2d 3 (1st Dept. 1993).

—By failing to specifically object to the court's reasonable doubt charge, defendant failed to preserve any challenge to the charge for appellate review. People v. Lozada, 181 A.D.2d 430, 580 N.Y.S.2d 754 (1st Dept. 1992).

—Defendant failed to preserve the claim that the court's charge was error where he failed to make his position with respect to the instruction known to the court at the time the charge was given so as to afford the court an opportunity to issue a correct or curative instruction. People v. Rivera, 171 A.D.2d 488, 567 N.Y.S.2d 229 (1st Dept. 1991).

—Defendant failed to preserve any challenge to the lack of a hearsay instruction when he did not request an instruction or except to the lack of an instruction. People v. Tufino, 162 A.D.2d 161, 556 N.Y.S.2d 575 (1st Dept. 1990).

—Defendant failed to preserve claim that trial court improperly marshaled the evidence in the prosecution's favor, and, in any event, court is not required to explain all of the contents of both parties' evidence, or outline all inconsistencies in evidence, but rather, court must provide a sufficient statement of facts to explain, as far as practicable, the application of law to the facts. People v. Barren, 240 A.D.2d 586, 659 N.Y.S.2d 68 (2d Dept. 1997).

—The defendant waived his objections to the trial court's identification charge, since the charge was essentially given as requested and the defendant failed to alert the trial court that he was not satisfied with it. People v. Jakes, 181 A.D.2d 913, 582 N.Y.S.2d 445 (2d Dept. 1992).

—Defendant's failure to object to the trial court's marshaling of the evidence rendered the claim of error unpreserved for appellate review. People v. Beaumont, 170 A.D.2d 513, 566 N.Y.S.2d 651 (2d Dept. 1991).

—Defendant's belated objection, on appeal, to trial court's refusal to charge certain language requested by co-defendant was not preserved for appellate review in the absence of an exception by defendant himself. People v. Colon, 132 A.D.2d 563, 517 N.Y.S.2d 552 (2d Dept. 1987).

—Defendant failed to object to the court's additional instructions to the jury on reasonable doubt and thus failed to preserve any issue concerning that charge for appellate review. People v. Stokes, 198 A.D.2d 847, 605 N.Y.S.2d 712 (4th Dept. 1993).

Waiver of error; evidentiary issue.—People were precluded from raising evidentiary issue on appeal where they failed to raise the issue to the trial court. People v. Paulin, 70 N.Y.2d 685, 518 N.Y.S.2d 790, 512 N.E.2d 312 (1987).

—The defendant's objection to the receipt of evidence did not preserve his claim for appellate review since the objection did not specifically question the admissibility upon the ground of hearsay. People v. Martinez, 171 A.D.2d 760, 567 N.Y.S.2d 314 (2d Dept. 1991).

Waiver of error to prosecutor's comments or alleged prosecutorial misconduct.—Where defendant made only a general objection to prosecutor's comment, issue concerning propriety of that comment was not preserved for appellate review. People v. Dien, 77 N.Y.2d 885, 568 N.Y.S.2d 899, 571 N.E.2d 69 (1991).

—Where defense counsel merely registered general objection to prosecutor's comments in summation, issue was not preserved for appellate review. People v. Rivera, 73 N.Y.2d 941, 540 N.Y.S.2d 233, 537 N.E.2d 618 (1989).

—Where defense objections were sustained and adequate curative instructions were given, the issue concerning propriety of the prosecutor's summation remarks was not preserved for appellate review. People v. Tardbania, 72 N.Y.2d 852, 532 N.Y.S.2d 354, 528 N.E.2d 507 (1988).

—By failing to move for a mistrial, or to challenge the court's limiting instructions on the basis of a line of questioning during cross-examination of defendant, and a related comment on summation, defendant failed to preserve his claims for review. People v. McFadden, 196 A.D.2d 717, 602 N.Y.S.2d 3 (1st Dept. 1993).

—Where defense counsel failed to register an objection to the prosecutor's comment referring to a Jackie Gleason episode, the issue concerning the propriety of that remark was not preserved for appellate review. People v. Sanchez, 172 A.D.2d 340, 568 N.Y.S.2d 612 (1st Dept. 1991).

—Defendant waived claim of prosecutorial misconduct in view of his counsel's failure to elaborate on a one-word objection. People v. Torres, 160 A.D.2d 285, 553 N.Y.S.2d 382 (1st Dept. 1990).

—In the absence of an objection the prosecutor's error in placing the defendant in the position of having to accuse the police witnesses of perjury in order to maintain his innocence was not preserved for appellate review. People v. Hudson, 143 A.D.2d 682, 533 N.Y.S.2d 20 (2d Dept. 1988).

—Where defense counsel's objection to prosecutor's cross-examination of the defendant was sustained before the defendant could answer, and no curative instruction was requested, the error was not preserved for appellate review. People v. Samuel, 122 A.D.2d 285, 504 N.Y.S.2d 784 (2d Dept. 1986).

—Defendant's challenges to the People's summation were waived due to the failure to object at trial. People v. Murphy, 188 A.D.2d 742, 591 N.Y.S.2d 860 (3d Dept. 1992).

—Since they were not raised in the court below, defendant's arguments that failure of the police to maintain a "mug book" without change after it had been shown to the eyewitnesses, and failure of the People to furnish a fingerprint analysis report deprived him of Brady material, was not preserved for appellate review. People v. Griffin, 129 A.D.2d 975, 514 N.Y.S.2d 289 (4th Dept. 1987).

Waiver of error; privilege.—The prosecutor did not preserve his claim for appellate review where the claim that the requested documents were privileged was not raised before the trial court. People v. DeJesus, 69 N.Y.2d 855, 514 N.Y.S.2d 708, 507 N.E.2d 301 (1987).

Waiver of error; alleged police misconduct; warrantless arrest; probable cause.—While the defendant raised the issue during the suppression hearing of whether the police officer violated his Fourth Amendment rights by leaning into the car through an open window, the issue of whether his rights were violated by the officer's opening of the car door and reaching into the automobile to recover a weapon was not raised thus precluding appellate review of the latter issue. People v. Vasquez, 66 N.Y.2d 968, 498 N.Y.S.2d 788, 489 N.E.2d 757 (1985), cert. denied, 475 U.S. 1109 (1986).

—Defendant waived any contention as to the invalidity of his warrantless arrest, based on the prior filing of felony complaints charging him with the crimes for which he was arrested, by failing to raise such argument or objection either in written motions or at the suppression hearing. People v. Claudio, 64 N.Y.2d 858, 487 N.Y.S.2d 318, 476 N.E.2d 644 (1985).

—The defendant failed to preserve for appellate review the issue of probable cause for his arrest by failing to cross-examine the arresting officer as to the probable cause basis for his arrest, failing to mention the issue in his closing statement and failing to object when the hearing court's decision did not address the issue. People v. Jackson, 118 A.D.2d 731, 500 N.Y.S.2d 63 (2d Dept. 1986).

—A defendant may not assert for the first time on appeal standing to challenge a warrantless search where he testified at the suppression hearing that he was an invitee on the premises, thereby negating any privacy interest in the searched premises. People v. Bencevi, 111 A.D.2d 397, 489 N.Y.S.2d 364 (2d Dept. 1985).

—By failing to raise the issue before the trial court that his statement should be suppressed because he was arrested in his home without a warrant and in the absence of exigent circumstances, defendant did not preserve the issue for appellate review and under the circumstances presented, review of this issue was not warranted as a matter if discretion in the interest of justice. People v. Cornelius, 107 A.D.2d 757, 484 N.Y.S.2d 122 (2d Dept. 1985).

—Where defendant's contention that his arrest was illegal because it was accomplished without consent to enter his dwelling was not raised in his motion papers, it was not preserved for review. People v. Dickerson, 148 A.D.2d 970, 546 N.Y.S.2d 908 (4th Dept. 1989).

—Since they were not raised in the court below, defendant's arguments that failure of the police to maintain a "mug book" without change after it had been shown to the eyewitnesses, and failure of the People to furnish a fingerprint analysis report deprived him of *Brady* material, was not preserved for appellate review. People v. Griffin, 129 A.D.2d 975, 514 N.Y.S.2d 289 (4th Dept. 1987).

Waiver of error; identification procedures or testimony—Any error caused by a post-indictment line-up held without defendant's attorney present would not require reversal because of the sufficient independent source as to that line-up witness and the overwhelming evidence of guilt resulting from the properly admissible identification of other witnesses. People v. Meadows, 64 N.Y.2d 956, 488 N.Y.S.2d 643, 477 N.E.2d 1097, *cert. denied,* 474 U.S. 820 (1985).

Waiver of error; constitutionality of statute.—Defendant may not challenge the constitutionality of the persistent felony offender statute or the proceeding on appeal when he made no such objections at the hearing. People v. Oliver, 63 N.Y.2d 973, 483 N.Y.S.2d 992, 473 N.E.2d 242 (1984).

—Defendant's claim, raised for the first time on appeal, that the mandatory life sentence provided under the sentencing statute was unconstitutional as applied to him, was not preserved for appellate review. People v. Buffa, 139 A.D.2d 751, 527 N.Y.S.2d 501 (2d Dept. 1988).

Waiver of error; co-defendant's objections do not apply to defendant.—Defendant's contention that the court erred in denying a challenge to a prospective juror for cause has not been preserved for appellate review since co-defendant's counsel challenged the juror, and his own attorney did not join in the motion. People v. Colselby, 240 A.D.2d 227, 659 N.Y.S.2d 5 (1st Dept. 1997).

—Defendant's objection to the testimony of the arresting officer on hearsay grounds was insufficient to preserve his claim on appeal of prejudicial bolstering; defendant cannot rely on objections made by counsel for the co-defendant to preserve the issue for appellate review as a matter of law. People v. Hynes, 193 A.D.2d 516, 598 N.Y.S.2d 182 (1st Dept. 1993).

—For purposes of preservation, a defendant could not rely on his co-defendant's objection to the charge on intent. People v. Smith, 176 A.D.2d 615, 575 N.Y.S.2d 56 (1st Dept. 1991).

—Objection by co-defendant did not preserve *Cruz* violation issue for defendant. People v. Sennon, 170 A.D.2d 546, 566 N.Y.S.2d 327 (2d Dept. 1991).

—The objections made by the co-defendants did not preserve the allegations of error for the defendant. People v. Lopez, 158 A.D.2d 623, 551 N.Y.S.2d 606 (2d Dept. 1990).

Waiver of error; testimony—If a defendant fails to raise in a timely manner the claim that he was surprised and prejudiced by certain testimony, a post-summation claim based on that theory is not preserved for appellate review. People v. Jones, 188 A.D.2d 331, 591 N.Y.S.2d 159 (1st Dept. 1992).

—The defendant by failing to make an argument as to the admissibility of defense testimony after the People's objection precluded a resolution of the evidentiary question and failed to preserve her claim for appellate review. People v. Black, 138 A.D.2d 498, 526 N.Y.S.2d 32 (2d Dept. 1988).

—Issue of police hearsay testimony concerning complainant's statements made moments after the crime was not preserved for appellate review since no objection was made at trial. People v. Mitchell, 114 A.D.2d 978, 495 N.Y.S.2d 234 (2d Dept. 1985).

—Defendant's contention that the admission of his parole officer's rebuttal testimony required reversal because the voluntariness of defendant's statements to his parole officer was not established was not preserved, because at trial, defendant objected to the parole officer's testimony on a different ground. People v. Hobbs, 178 A.D.2d 1017, 578 N.Y.S.2d 773 (4th Dept. 1991).

—Issue was not preserved for appellate review where defendant failed to object to testimony concerning amount of money in his possession following his arrest. People v. McNeil, 132 A.D.2d 986, 518 N.Y.S.2d 516 (4th Dept. 1987).

Waiver of error; bolstering testimony.—Where the defendant failed to object to the admission of the challenged bolstering testimony, any error of law was not preserved for appellate review. People v. Foster, 182 A.D.2d 636, 582 N.Y.S.2d 250 (2d Dept. 1992).

—Because the defendant failed to object to the police officers' testimony specifically on the ground that it impermissibly bolstered the identification testimony given by the complainants, that claim was not preserved for review. People v. Jones, 124 A.D.2d 596, 507 N.Y.S.2d 738 (2d Dept. 1986).

Waiver of error; repugnancy claim.—By failing to raise a repugnancy claim prior to the jury's discharge, the defendant failed to preserve that claim as a matter of law. People v. Rodriguez, 179 A.D.2d 554, 579 N.Y.S.2d 652 (1st Dept. 1992).

—Contention that verdict was repugnant was not preserved for appellate review where it was not raised before the discharge of the jury. People v. Gross, 184 A.D.2d 1051, 584 N.Y.S.2d 705 (2d Dept. 1992).

Waiver of error; *Sandoval* ruling.—By failing to object to the *Sandoval* ruling, defendant waived appellate review of the issue as a matter of law. People v. Medina, 171 A.D.2d 559, 567 N.Y.S.2d 651 (1st Dept. 1991).

Waiver of error; dismissal motion.—The issue was not preserved for appellate review since defendant failed to move for dismissal of weapons charge at trial on the specific ground raised for the first time on appeal. People v. Patel, 132 A.D.2d 498, 518 N.Y.S.2d 384 (1st Dept. 1987).

—The issue of legal sufficiency was not preserved for appellate review since the defendant's motion for a trial order of dismissal was not specific. People v. Romano, 199 A.D.2d 433, 605 N.Y.S.2d 113 (2d Dept. 1993).

—The defendant failed to move for dismissal of the indictment on speedy trial grounds and therefore any claim of error with respect thereto was unpreserved for appellate review. People v. Bencosme, 191 A.D.2d 639, 595 N.Y.S.2d 221 (2d Dept. 1993).

—By failing to assert the claims in support of his argument for dismissal of a particular count of the indictment with specificity before the trial court, the defendant failed to preserved it for appellate review. People v. Blunt, 176 A.D.2d 741, 574 N.Y.S.2d 812 (2d Dept. 1991).

—Where defendant failed to move in the trial court for dismissal on the specific ground that the evidence corroborating the accomplice testimony was insufficient to support the conviction, the issue was not preserved for appellate review. People v. Coico, 176 A.D.2d 339, 574 N.Y.S.2d 775 (2d Dept. 1991).

—Issue concerning the sufficiency of the proof of the element of "serious physical injury" was not preserved where counsel did not raise it in his motion to dismiss at the conclusion of the evidence. People v. Davis, 172 A.D.2d 553, 568 N.Y.S.2d 410 (2d Dept. 1991).

Waiver of error; legal sufficiency; dismissal motion.—Defendant failed to preserve his claim that the convictions were based on legally insufficient evidence, where his motion for a trial order of dismissal failed to refer to any specific deficiency in the People's evidence. People v. Pitta, 266 A.D.2d 243, 697 N.Y.S.2d 655 (2d Dept. 1999).

—The issue of legal sufficiency was not preserved for appellate review since the defendant's motion for a trial order of dismissal was not specific. People v. Romano, 199 A.D.2d 433, 605 N.Y.S.2d 113 (2d Dept. 1993).

—By failing to raise the issue at trial the defendant's contention that the People failed to prove beyond a reasonable doubt that they possessed the fireworks was not preserved for appellate review as a matter of law. People v. Whitehead, 159 A.D.2d 741, 552 N.Y.S.2d 685 (2d Dept. 1990).

—Defendant's contention that the People failed to prove an

element of the crime was not preserved for appellate review as a matter of law. People v. Ruiz, 159 A.D.2d 656, 553 N.Y.S.2d 173 (2d Dept. 1990).

—Where defendant failed to raise contention that the People failed to adduce legally sufficient evidence on the element of intent in her motion to dismiss after the completion of the People's case the issue was not preserved for appellate review. People v. Randolph, 158 A.D.2d 722, 552 N.Y.S.2d 170 (2d Dept. 1990).

—In a nonjury case the defendant is not required to make a motion to dismiss the indictment on the ground that the evidence is legally insufficient in order to preserve the issue for appellate review. People v. Little, 157 A.D.2d 673, 549 N.Y.S.2d 773 (2d Dept. 1990).

—Defendant's contention that the People failed to prove his participation in the sales beyond a reasonable doubt was not preserved for appellate review since it was not raised with specificity in the trial court. People v. Vernon, 150 A.D.2d 407, 540 N.Y.S.2d 837 (2d Dept. 1989).

—Defendant failed to timely preserve for appellate review a challenge to the indictment where he failed to file a pretrial motion to dismiss the indictment pursuant to CPL §§ 210.20 and 210.25. People v. Tice, 147 A.D.2d 776, 537 N.Y.S.2d 648 (3d Dept. 1989).

Waiver of error; suppression; confessions.—Because defendant failed to argue before the hearing court that his statements to law enforcement authorities should be suppressed as the product of police coercion and abuse, the defendant's contention is unpreserved for appellate review. People v. Jackson, 241 A.D.2d 526, 663 N.Y.S.2d 988 (2d Dept. 1997), *cert. denied,* 523 U.S. 1061 (1998).

—The defendant failed to preserve the issue for appellate review by failing to specifically present to the hearing court the issue of whether the confession should be suppressed on the ground that it was coerced from him after he had invoked his right to remain silent. People v. Clink, 143 A.D.2d 838, 533 N.Y.S.2d 136 (2d Dept. 1988).

—By failing to raise the issue before the trial court that his statement should be suppressed because he was arrested in his home without a warrant and in the absence of exigent circumstances, defendant did not preserve the issue for appellate review and under the circumstances presented, review of this issue was not warranted as a matter if discretion in the interest of justice. People v. Cornelius, 107 A.D.2d 757, 484 N.Y.S.2d 122 (2d Dept. 1985).

—Where defendant failed to advance a particular factual claim before the suppression court, he was precluded from raising it on appeal. People v. Herr, 161 A.D.2d 1031, 557 N.Y.S.2d 599 (3d Dept. 1990).

Waiver of error; court interpreter.—Contention that the performance by the court interpreter was deficient was not preserved for appellate review since no objection was raised during the trial as to the adequacy of the translation during either direct or cross-examination. People v. Ko, 133 A.D.2d 850, 520 N.Y.S.2d 412 (2d Dept. 1987).

Waiver of error; untimely objection.—Defense counsel's belated motion for a mistrial made after the trial court struck the testimony in question from the record and gave the jury curative instructions and after the two additional witnesses, one of whom was a defense witness, had testified, was not timely made as required by CPL § 470.05(2). People v. Price, 120 A.D.2d 690, 502 N.Y.S.2d 278 (2d Dept. 1986).

—Defendant failed to timely preserve for appellate review a challenge to the indictment where he failed to file a pretrial motion to dismiss the indictment pursuant to CPL §§ 210.20 and 210.25. People v. Tice, 147 A.D.2d 776, 537 N.Y.S.2d 648 (3d Dept. 1989).

Waiver of error; confrontation.—Where defendant objected only to the good faith basis of the challenged cross-examination questions, he did not preserve the issue of a denial of his right to confront adverse witnesses. People v. Perone, 119 A.D.2d 838, 501 N.Y.S.2d 464 (2d Dept. 1986).

Waiver of error; guilty plea.—Defendant who failed to raise the factual sufficiency of his guilty plea allocution to the court wherein the plea was made failed to preserve that claim for appellate review. People v. Johnson, 107 A.D.2d 713, 484 N.Y.S.2d 85 (2d Dept. 1985).

—A defendant who fails to make a postallocution motion

challenging the sufficiency of a plea allocution can still challenge the plea on direct appeal, if the trial court accepted the plea after defendant's factual recitation negated an essential element of the crime, thereby casting significant doubt on defendant's guilt. Here, defendant's factual allocution negated an essential element of each offense to which he pleaded guilty, and thus, judgments were reversed. People v. Pangburn, 298 A.D.2d 989, 747 N.Y.S.2d 672 (4th Dept. 2002).

Waiver of error; sentence.—A defendant's challenge to the legality of the sentence cannot be waived. People v. Nephew, 200 A.D.2d 799, 606 N.Y.S.2d 452 (3d Dept. 1994).

Waiver of error; excusal of juror.—By consenting to the excusal of a sworn juror during jury selection, defendant failed to preserve any issue for review concerning the removal of the juror. People v. Parker, 168 A.D.2d 917, 565 N.Y.S.2d 333 (4th Dept. 1990).

Waiver of error; immunity.—A claim of statutory immunity is waived if it is not raised in a motion to dismiss the indictment before trial or before sentencing. People v. Haggins, 148 A.D.2d 987, 538 N.Y.S.2d 967 (4th Dept. 1989).

Waiver of error; orders of protection.—Defendant's contention that the duration of the final orders of protection failed to take into account his jail-time credit was not preserved for appellate review because defendant did not raise this issue at sentencing, nor did he move to amend the final orders of protection on this ground. People v. Allums, 18 A.D.3d 768, 795 N.Y.S.2d 697 (2d Dept. 2005); People v. Jackson, 18 A.D.3d 574, 795 N.Y.S.2d 310 (2d Dept. 2005).

Waiver not found despite absence of protest.—An issue may be raised on appeal, even in the absence of an objection on the specific ground proffered, if the trial court expressly decided the question so raised. People v. Johnson, 144 A.D.2d 490, 534 N.Y.S.2d 207 (2d Dept. 1988).

—A claimed deprivation of the State constitutional right to counsel may be raised for the first time on appeal. People v. Bayer, 133 A.D.2d 374, 519 N.Y.S.2d 554 (2d Dept. 1987).

—No objection is required in order to preserve for appeal a claimed deprivation of the State constitutional right to counsel provided there exists a factual record sufficient to permit appellate review. People v. Leonard, 113 A.D.2d 258, 497 N.Y.S.2d 28 (2d Dept. 1985).

—Court's failure to instruct jury that shackling of defendant should be disregarded and should not bear on their determination as to defendant's guilt or innocence required reversal despite defendant's failure to request such an instruction. People v. Neu, 124 A.D.2d 885, 508 N.Y.S.2d 652 (3d Dept. 1986).

§ 470.10. Determination of appeals; definitions of terms.

The following definitions are applicable to this article:

1. "Reversal" by an appellate court of a judgment, sentence or order of another court means the vacating of such judgment, sentence or order.

2. "Modification" by an appellate court of a judgment or order of another court means the vacating of a part thereof and affirmance of the remainder.

3. "Corrective action" means affirmative action taken or directed by an appellate court upon reversing or modifying a judgment, sentence or order of another court, which disposes of or continues the case in a manner consonant with the determinations and principles underlying the reversal or modification.

§ 470.15. Determination of appeals by intermediate appellate courts; scope of review.

1. Upon an appeal to an intermediate appellate

court from a judgment, sentence or order of a criminal court, such intermediate appellate court may consider and determine any question of law or issue of fact involving error or defect in the criminal court proceedings which may have adversely affected the appellant.

2. Upon such an appeal, the intermediate appellate court must either affirm or reverse or modify the criminal court judgment, sentence or order. The ways in which it may modify a judgment include, but are not limited to, the following:

(a) Upon a determination that the trial evidence adduced in support of a verdict is not legally sufficient to establish the defendant's guilt of an offense of which he was convicted but is legally sufficient to establish his guilt of a lesser included offense, the court may modify the judgment by changing it to one of conviction for the lesser offense;

(b) Upon a determination that the trial evidence is not legally sufficient to establish the defendant's guilt of all the offenses of which he was convicted but is legally sufficient to establish his guilt of one or more of such offenses, the court may modify the judgment by reversing it with respect to the unsupported counts and otherwise affirming it;

(c) Upon a determination that a sentence imposed upon a valid conviction is illegal or unduly harsh or severe, the court may modify the judgment by reversing it with respect to the sentence and by otherwise affirming it.

3. A reversal or a modification of a judgment, sentence or order must be based upon a determination made:

(a) Upon the law; or

(b) Upon the facts; or

(c) As a matter of discretion in the interest of justice; or

(d) Upon any two or all three of the bases specified in paragraphs (a), (b) and (c).

4. The kinds of determinations of reversal or modification deemed to be upon the law include, but are not limited to, the following:

(a) That a ruling or instruction of the court, duly protested by the defendant, as prescribed in subdivision two of section 470.05, at a trial resulting in a judgment, deprived the defendant of a fair trial;

(b) That evidence adduced at a trial resulting in a judgment was not legally sufficient to establish the defendant's guilt of an offense of which he was convicted;

(c) That a sentence was unauthorized, illegally imposed or otherwise invalid as a matter of law.

5. The kinds of determinations of reversal or modification deemed to be on the facts include, but are not limited to, a determination that a verdict of conviction resulting in a judgment was, in whole or in part, against the weight of the evidence.

6. The kinds of determinations of reversal or modification deemed to be made as a matter of discretion in the interest of justice include, but are not limited to, the following:

(a) That an error or defect occurring at a trial resulting in a judgment, which error or defect was not duly protested at trial as prescribed in subdivision two of section 470.05 so as to present a question of law, deprived the defendant of a fair trial;

(b) That a sentence, though legal, was unduly harsh or severe.

ANNOTATIONS

Appeals; order for new trial; authority of appellate division.—Power of Court of Appeals to review opinion for reason of intermediate appellate court's decision is limited to cases where the order of such court states that decision is on law alone and not where there is a recital as to factual or discretionary basis. Since opinion of Appellate Division indicates order was exercise of discretionary power, it is not reviewable, even though settled order deleted this reference and recited that decision was on law alone. People v. Williams, 31 N.Y.2d 151, 335 N.Y.S.2d 271, 286 N.E.2d 715 (1972).

Appellate Division bound by Court of Appeals' decision.—In the absence of a United States Supreme Court decision declaring the statute unconstitutional, a New York Court of Appeals' decision holding that the statute is constitutional is binding on all courts in New York even though an intermediate federal court has held the statute is unconstitutional. People v. Sierra, 85 A.D.2d 546, 445 N.Y.S.2d 2 (1st Dept. 1981).

Charge; failure to submit to jury lesser degrees of crime.—A defendant who, prior to his conviction for second degree assault, failed to request a charge as to the lesser included offense of attempted assault cannot raise this issue on appeal. People v. Roberts, 91 A.D.2d 1099, 458 N.Y.S.2d 355 (3d Dept. 1983).

Cross-examination of prosecution witness.—Even though an important prosecution witness falsely and insistently testified on cross-examination that he had no reason to expect leniency in return for his testifying for prosecution and that prosecutor, who had made promises of leniency did not inform the court regarding the truth, a reversal of conviction was not required, where defendant and his counsel with knowledge of the facts stood silently by and did nothing to remedy the situation. People v. Washington, 32 N.Y.2d 401, 345 N.Y.S.2d 520, 298 N.E.2d 665 (1973).

Credibility; minor inconsistencies.—The existence of an inconsistency between the police officer's testimony before the Grand Jury and before the trial jury did not render the officer's testimony incredible. People v. Bristol, 187 A.D.2d 403, 589 N.Y.S.2d 886 (1st Dept. 1992).

—Minor inconsistencies in the testimony of a witness are acceptable and are not, in and of themselves, sufficient to show that a witness is not credible as a matter of law. People v. Wilson, 190 A.D.2d 835, 593 N.Y.S.2d 824 (2d Dept. 1993); People v. Jennings, 188 A.D.2d 552, 591 N.Y.S.2d 452 (2d Dept. 1992); People v. Stackhouse, 201 A.D.2d 686, 608 N.Y.S.2d 252 (2d Dept. 1994).

Credibility determined by jury.—It is well established that issues of credibility are to be determined by the jury, which had the opportunity to observe the witness. People v. Bell, 176 A.D.2d 659, 575 N.Y.S.2d 315 (1st Dept. 1991); People v. Simmons, 176 A.D.2d 189, 574 N.Y.S.2d 314 (1st Dept. 1991); People v. Maisonet, 172 A.D.2d 274, 568 N.Y.S.2d 96 (1st Dept. 1991); People v. Ventura, 171 A.D.2d 553, 567 N.Y.S.2d 439 (1st Dept. 1991); People v. Almonte, 170 A.D.2d 267, 566 N.Y.S.2d 10 (1st Dept. 1991); People v. Lozado, 157 A.D.2d 630, 550 N.Y.S.2d 649 (1st Dept. 1990); People v. Burns, 155 A.D.2d 292, 547 N.Y.S.2d 55 (1st Dept. 1989); People v. Ward, 191 A.D.2d 661, 595 N.Y.S.2d 224 (2d Dept 1993); People v.

Attanasio, 191 A.D.2d 447, 594 N.Y.S.2d 299 (2d Dept. 1993); People v. Neary, 189 A.D.2d 828, 592 N.Y.S.2d 464 (2d Dept. 1993); People v. Hartley, 188 A.D.2d 615, 591 N.Y.S.2d 503 (2d Dept. 1992); People v. Gayle, 178 A.D.2d 431, 577 N.Y.S.2d 294 (2d Dept. 1991); People v. Hill, 176 A.D.2d 755, 574 N.Y.S.2d 819 (2d Dept. 1991); People v. Hall, 175 A.D.2d 879, 573 N.Y.S.2d 726 (2d Dept. 1991); People v. Huber, 156 A.D.2d 469, 548 N.Y.S.2d 570 (2d Dept. 1989); People v. Martinez, 149 A.D.2d 438, 539 N.Y.S.2d 781 (2d Dept. 1989); People v. Wright, 206 A.D.2d 750, 614 N.Y.S.2d 818 (3d Dept. 1994); People v. Rising, 289 A.D.2d 1069, 735 N.Y.S.2d 680 (4th Dept. 2001).

Credibility; drug use or unsavory character of witness.— Fact that victim had history of drug use and mental illness did not warrant disturbing jury's finding that witness was credible. People v. Blanco, 158 A.D.2d 347, 551 N.Y.S.2d 38 (1st Dept. 1990).

—The character of the witnesses, the effect of their drug use on their perceptions, and any minor inconsistencies in their testimony presented nothing more than questions of credibility for the jury. People v. Carter, 155 A.D.2d 276, 547 N.Y.S.2d 38 (1st Dept. 1989).

—The facts that the complainant was a crack cocaine addict at the time of the robbery and had been drinking the night of the crime were insufficient to make his testimony incredible as a matter of law. People v. Sierra, 191 A.D.2d 657, 595 N.Y.S.2d 222 (2d Dept. 1993).

—Jury could accept the testimony of the eyewitness even though she was an admitted drug user. People v. Campell, 187 A.D.2d 442, 589 N.Y.S.2d 539 (2d Dept. 1992).

—The unsavory character of the only witness to identify both defendants, the witness's previous recantation of that identification, and the fact that he testified pursuant to a plea agreement, did not necessarily render his testimony incredible. People v. Royall, 172 A.D.2d 703, 568 N.Y.S.2d 830 (2d Dept. 1991).

—Jury was free to credit testimony of complainant even though she was high on cocaine the morning of the incident. People v. Greco, 154 A.D.2d 391, 545 N.Y.S.2d 780 (2d Dept. 1989).

—Witness' use of drugs and her condition at the time of the crime did not render her testimony incompetent but were factors to be considered by the jury on the issue of her credibility. People v. Goddard, 153 A.D.2d 758, 545 N.Y.S.2d 42 (2d Dept. 1989).

—Resolution of issues of credibility, as well as the weight to be accorded to the evidence presented, are primarily questions to be determined by the jury, even where the witnesses have criminal histories and prior involvement with illegal drugs. People v. Bossett, 145 A.D.2d 639, 536 N.Y.S.2d 478 (2d Dept. 1988).

—It was within the province of the jury to believe the prosecution witness despite his drug addiction. People v. Vierra, 144 A.D.2d 603, 534 N.Y.S.2d 440 (2d Dept. 1988).

Credibility; weight to be accorded to the evidence.— Resolution of issues of credibility, as well as the weight to be accorded the evidence presented, are primarily to be determined by the jury, which saw and heard the witnesses. People v. Stapleton, 204 A.D.2d 580, 612 N.Y.S.2d 178 (2d Dept. 1994); People v. Tomlinson, 199 A.D.2d 352, 605 N.Y.S.2d 100 (2d Dept. 1993); People v. Robson, 197 A.D.2d 602, 602 N.Y.S.2d 422 (2d Dept. 1993).

Credibility; expert testimony.—Where conflicting expert testimony is presented, the question of sanity is primarily for the jury; the jury has the right to accept or reject the opinion of any expert and where there is no serious flaw in the testimony of the People's experts, there is no basis for disturbing the jury's findings. People v. Han, 200 A.D.2d 780, 607 N.Y.S.2d 365 (2d Dept. 1994).

Credibility; alibi witnesses.—The jury is free to disregard the testimony of any witness, including that of an alibi witness. People v. Hickman, 194 A.D.2d 555, 598 N.Y.S.2d 571 (2d Dept. 1993).

—Alibi testimony, though uncontroverted, is subject to credibility evaluation by the jury. People v. Brewington, 149 A.D.2d 852, 540 N.Y.S.2d 364 (3d Dept. 1989).

Credibility; weight to accord jury's assessment on appeal.—Determination of a jury should be accorded great weight on appeal and should not be disturbed unless clearly unsupported by the evidence. People v. Fetter, 201 A.D.2d 500, 607

N.Y.S.2d 381 (2d Dept. 1994); People v. Persaud, 188 A.D.2d 559, 591 N.Y.S.2d 455 (2d Dept. 1992); People v. James M., 170 A.D.2d 696, 567 N.Y.S.2d 111 (2d Dept. 1991); People v. Kelly, 155 A.D.2d 692, 548 N.Y.S.2d 259 (2d Dept. 1989); People v. Forgione, 145 A.D.2d 639, 536 N.Y.S.2d 119 (2d Dept. 1988).

Court's comments about credibility of complainant.— Upon reversing, the Appellate Division directed that the retrial take place before another judge on the basis of the trial judge's comments as to the credibility of the complainant. People v. Stewart, 153 A.D.2d 706, 544 N.Y.S.2d 875 (2d Dept. 1989).

Credibility; miscellaneous.—Mere fact that the arresting police officer was accused, during the course of an unrelated trial, of participating in corrupt police practices, did not render his testimony incredible as a matter of law. People v. Barnes, 144 A.D.2d 371, 533 N.Y.S.2d 923 (2d Dept. 1988).

—Fact that the prosecutor discussed the case with the witness in front of the complainant did not create a basis for reversal but rather created an issue of credibility for the jury. People v. Lane, 139 A.D.2d 534, 526 N.Y.S.2d 855 (2d Dept. 1988).

Credibility; bias of witness.—In the case of bias on the part of a witness it is for the trier of fact to determine the weight to be given the witness's testimony. People v. Emil "XX," 191 A.D.2d 895, 594 N.Y.S.2d 465, 466 (3d Dept. 1993).

Cruel and unusual punishment.—Ceasing to supply inmate with multivitamins did not involve a violation of his Eighth Amendment rights where there was no allegation that prison officials were deliberately indifferent to petitioner's medical needs. Abdullah v. Coughlin, 129 A.D.2d 699, 514 N.Y.S.2d 462 (2d Dept. 1987).

—Overcrowding, in and of itself, is not a violation of the Eighth Amendment prohibition against cruel and unusual punishment. George v. Goldrick, 136 Misc. 2d 258, 518 N.Y.S.2d 582 (Sup. Ct. Rockland Co. 1987).

Erroneous advice on sentencing does not require reversal. —The fact that counsel's advice to defendant at the time of plea as to the crediting of "good time" against defendant's minimum sentence was erroneous did not require reversal or remand for an evidentiary hearing inasmuch as defense counsel's erroneous advice was not placed on the record at the time of the plea and therefor is not entitled to judicial recognition. People v. Ramos, 63 N.Y.2d 640, 479 N.Y.S.2d 510, 468 N.E.2d 692 (1984).

Evidence legally sufficient.—Where the evidence convicting the defendant of robbery in the first degree and robbery in the second degree was legally sufficient, the court, in reviewing the facts, held that the verdict was in accord with the evidence. People v. Blas, 196 A.D.2d 878, 603 N.Y.S.2d 761 (2d Dept. 1993).

—The testimony of a single eyewitness is legally sufficient to support a conviction. People v. Williams, 187 A.D.2d 547, 589 N.Y.S.2d 604 (2d Dept. 1992).

Evidentiary ruling, failure to object, waiver.—Defendant failed to preserve objection to evidentiary ruling by failing to raise such objections at second trial, although objections were made and *overruled,* at first trial; evidentiary rulings made at one trial are normally not binding in a subsequent trial. People v. Malizia, 62 N.Y.2d 755, 476 N.Y.S.2d 825, 465 N.E.2d 364, *cert. denied,* 469 U.S. 932 (1984).

Failure to raise issue at sentence; waiver.—Where such point was not brought to court's attention at time of sentence, defendant waived contention that court, in sentencing him to consecutive terms of imprisonment, misunderstood the effect of such sentencing upon defendant's ability to obtain parole release. People v. Lemon, 62 N.Y.2d 745, 476 N.Y.S.2d 824, 465 N.E.2d 363 (1984).

Harmless error analysis did not apply where guilty plea taken after erroneous denial of suppression motion.—When defendant pleaded guilty after erroneous denial of his motion to suppress statements, conviction must be reversed since harmless error rules were designed to review trial verdicts and are difficult to apply to guilty pleas; People's contention that denial of the motion did not influence defendant to plead guilty is unsupported since there is no statement to that effect on the record, and there was no waiver by defendant of his right to appeal with regard to the denial of his motion. People v. Coles, 62 N.Y.2d 908, 479 N.Y.S.2d 1, 467 N.E.2d 885 (1984).

Juror; hallucinations.—Alleged incapacity of a juror did not warrant reversal where the reporting doctor concluded that, though the juror suffered from hallucinations, he was nonetheless competent to make a judgment on the merits of the case presented to him in court. People v. Sullivan, 48 A.D.2d 398, 369 N.Y.S.2d 744 (1st Dept. 1975), aff'd, 39 N.Y.2d 903, 386 N.Y.S.2d 399, 352 N.E.2d 586 (1976).

No relitigation of Article 78 claims on appeal—Defendant's double jeopardy claims, which are based on the fact that his guilt of the instant crime was established as an aggravating factor during the penalty phase of his federal prosecution for a capital crime, have been fully litigated before this court in his unsuccessful article 78 proceeding and thus may not properly be relitigated on appeal. In any event, there was no previous prosecution within the meaning of CPL § 40.30. People v. Sullivan, 265 A.D.2d 241, 697 N.Y.S.2d 592 (1st Dept. 1999).

Restriction of appealable issue.—In an appeal from a resentencing appellant cannot raise as an issue the propriety of his original conviction and sentence. People v. Manino, 90 A.D.2d 777, 455 N.Y.S.2d 282 (2d Dept. 1982).

Retroactivity.—When a decision of the court merely applies settled precedents to new and different factual situations, the decision is generally accorded retroactivity because it has not altered the rule of the earlier case in any material way. People v. Catalanotte, 137 A.D.2d 697, 524 N.Y.S.2d 788 (2d Dept.), aff'd, 72 N.Y.2d 641, 536 N.Y.S.2d 16, 532 N.E.2d 1244 (1988), cert. denied, 493 U.S. 811 (1989).

Subd. 1

Appellant adversely affected.—Where the trial court improperly set aside the verdict, the issues involved were reviewable as "adversely affecting" the appellant: the People. People v. Carthrens, 171 A.D.2d 387, 577 N.Y.S.2d 249 (1st Dept. 1991).

—Where the trial court refused to dismiss the charges against the defendant, the action was held not reviewable on appeal. The appellant (the People) was not adversely affected by the trial court's ruling. People v. Westbrook, 180 A.D.2d 772, 580 N.Y.S.2d 399 (2d Dept. 1992).

Appellate Division; authority.—The Appellate Division did not have the authority to review issues of possible prosecutorial prejudice upon an appeal by the People. The Appellate Division is subject to the limitations imposed by the CPL. People v. Karp, 76 N.Y.2d 1006, 565 N.Y.S.2d 751, 566 N.E.2d 1156 (1990).

—The Appellate Division may not review the issue of sufficiency of evidence upon an appeal by the People. The defendant must make a motion on direct appeal. People v. Clausell, 182 A.D.2d 132, 587 N.Y.S.2d 672 (2d Dept. 1992).

Court of Appeals review.—Where a sentence was not unlawful and was within legal limits, defendant may not appeal to the Court of Appeals to reduce a sentence. People v. Discala, 45 N.Y.2d 38, 407 N.Y.S.2d 660, 379 N.E.2d 187 (1978).

Defendant adversely affected.—Where the trial court stated that it did not decide the defendant's case on the issue of sufficiency of evidence, the only issue to be addressed on appeal must be an issue which is adverse to the defendant. People v. Smith, 183 A.D.2d 653, 584 N.Y.S.2d 795 (1st Dept. 1992).

—The defendant was held not to be "adversely affected" upon his claim that his plea of guilty was in violation of CPL § 220.15. People v. Gray, 181 A.D.2d 831, 583 N.Y.S.2d 162 (2d Dept. 1992).

Jurisdiction.—Judges are under the duty to review suppression motions fairly and impartially. Furthermore, the Appellate Division has the authority to provide further review of the suppression orders. People v. Tambe, 71 N.Y.2d 492, 527 N.Y.S.2d 372, 522 N.E.2d 448 (1988).

—Failure to object to the adequacy of the plea or to move to withdraw the plea bars the defendant from raising the issue on appeal as a matter of law. People v. Vicks, 91 A.D.2d 1052, 458 N.Y.S.2d 654 (2d Dept. 1983).

People's summation; improper and prejudicial statements.—Prosecutor improperly raised the issue of race-based identification for the first time on summation, and the error was compounded by the court's failure to give a curative instruction or otherwise rectify the situation. Because the proof of defendant's guilt was not overwhelming, the error was not harmless, and a new trial was ordered. People v. Alexander, 94 N.Y.2d 382, 705 N.Y.S.2d 551, 727 N.E.2d 109 (1999).

—Patently improper remarks in prosecutor's summation did not warrant a reversal of conviction where, given the strong nature of the case against the defendant, such misconduct could not be said to have deprived the defendant of a fair trial. People v. Roopchand, 107 A.D.2d 35, 485 N.Y.S.2d 332 (2d Dept. 1985), aff'd, 65 N.Y.2d 837, 493 N.Y.S.2d 129, 482 N.E.2d 924 (1985).

—Court should not reverse conviction in the interest of justice on the ground that the prosecutor made prejudicial remarks, where the challenged remarks were not so prejudicial as to have deprived defendant of a fair trial. People v. Sim, 53 A.D.2d 992, 386 N.Y.S.2d 114 (3d Dept. 1976), aff'd, 44 N.Y.2d 758, 405 N.Y.S.2d 686, 376 N.E.2d 1331 (1978).

—While it was improper for the prosecutor to comment on testimony which the jury had previously been instructed to disregard, the court sustained an objection to the comment and gave a curative instruction which was sufficient to eliminate any prejudice that might have been caused by the brief reference to negative identification testimony. People v. Lee, 206 A.D.2d 390, 614 N.Y.S.2d 57 (2d Dept. 1994).

—Inflammatory comments and expressions of opinion concerning the veracity of witnesses are improper in the summations of either prosecutor or defense counsel and where defense counsel's summation opened the door to such comment, the response by the prosecutor was harmless error. People v. Mitchell, 114 A.D.2d 978, 495 N.Y.S.2d 234 (2d Dept. 1985).

—Although prosecutor made improper remarks concerning the presumption of innocence, the court's immediate curative instructions were sufficient to dispel the prejudicial effect; moreover, since the defendant did not request additional instructions or seek a mistrial, the court must be deemed to have cured the error to defendant's satisfaction. People v. Jalah, 107 A.D.2d 762, 484 N.Y.S.2d 116 (2d Dept. 1985).

—Prosecutor's remarks in summation that there was no evidence to support defense that defendant did not knowingly or voluntarily participate in the crime of larceny were fair comment on the evidence where defendant did not testify, and, in any event, the failure of counsel to object did not preserve the issue for appellate review. People v. Baldo, 107 A.D.2d 751, 484 N.Y.S.2d 114 (2d Dept. 1985).

Prosecutorial misconduct; effect thereof.—In homicide prosecution involving death of defendant's child, prosecutor's comment that defendant was not hysterical and did not voice concern during rescue attempts by paramedics was not improper comment on defendant's pretrial silence; remark was made in response to defense summation and was more of a behavioral characterization than an attempt to impeach defendant by reference to his pretrial silence. People v. Balls, 118 A.D.2d 887, 499 N.Y.S.2d 454 (3d Dept.), aff'd, 69 N.Y.2d 641, 511 N.Y.S.2d 586, 503 N.E.2d 1017 (1986).

—Reversal was warranted where the prosecutor impugned defense counsel's integrity, implicitly commented on the defendant's failure to testify, mischaracterized the defense, suggested that the defendant had an obligation to call witnesses and sought to appeal to the sympathies and fears of the jurors. People v. Ortiz, 116 A.D.2d 531, 497 N.Y.S.2d 678 (1st Dept. 1986).

—While reversal is an ill-suited remedy for prosecutorial misconduct, where the misconduct was so persuasive, so egregious and results in violation of fundamental due process rights, and where the prosecutor disregards court rulings and warnings, reversal is warranted. People v. Sandy, 115 A.D.2d 27, 499 N.Y.S.2d 75 (1st Dept. 1986).

—In a trial concerning a stabbing that occurred in an establishment characterized by defense counsel as a "motorcycle bar," the prosecutor's single question to a defense witness as to her membership in a motorcycle club known as "Satan's Soldiers" although an improper one, did not constitute drastic misconduct warranting a reversal. People v. Locicero, 119 A.D.2d 699, 500 N.Y.S.2d 821 (2d Dept. 1986).

—Where the defense witness indicated to the court and the jury that she did not go to the police because she believed that her efforts to exonerate the defendant would be futile, prosecutor's inquiry concerning her failure to provide law enforcement authorities with exculpatory information prior to trial was proper notwithstanding the failure to lay a foundation or to conduct a bench conference prior to such inquiry. People v. Mullins, 118 A.D.2d 737, 500 N.Y.S.2d 70 (2d Dept. 1986).

—Where defense counsel invited the jury to speculate as to the reason for the lack of certain evidence, the comment of the prosecutrix whereby she implied to the jury that she was precluded by evidentiary rules from presenting additional inculpatory evidence merely was technically improper. People v. Scatliffe, 117 A.D.2d 827, 499 N.Y.S.2d 148 (2d Dept. 1986).

Sentence; defendant's background and character.—In manslaughter prosecution, 28-year-old defendant's negotiated sentence was reduced where he had never been in trouble with the law before, he had a credible employment record and a strong family life with a fully supportive wife, and he had compiled an extraordinary record of academic and service achievement during the period from his arrest to the time of sentencing. People v. Chambers, 123 A.D.2d 270, 506 N.Y.S.2d 173 (1st Dept. 1986).

—The fact that a defendant is HIV positive is not a sufficient reason to modify an otherwise lawful sentence of imprisonment. People v. Clark, 176 A.D.2d 1206, 576 N.Y.S.2d 704 (4th Dept. 1991).

Sentence; legality.—People concede that defendant's sentence of 10 to 20 years confinement was illegal and must be vacated because the crime of attempted murder in the second degree is not a class B armed felony. People v. Lucas, 119 A.D.2d 700, 501 N.Y.S.2d 116 (2d Dept. 1986).

Sentence not excessive.—Where defendant merely served as a lookout during robbery in which victim was killed, his sentence of 20 years to life was reduced to 15 years to life. People v. Rivera, 133 A.D.2d 24, 518 N.Y.S.2d 619 (1st Dept. 1987), aff'd, 71 N.Y.2d 705, 530 N.Y.S.2d 52, 525 N.E.2d 698 (1988).

—Given the brutality of the defendant's acts against his wife and his subsequent attempts to protect himself by hiding his culpability, the sentence of 25 years to life for murder was a proper exercise of sentencing court's discretion. People v. Guevara, 134 A.D.2d 518, 521 N.Y.S.2d 292 (2d Dept. 1987).

—Defendant's sentence, which was the statutory minimum, could not be characterized as unduly harsh or excessive particularly considering that the sentence imposed was that which was promised when the guilty plea was accepted. People v. May, 129 A.D.2d 589, 513 N.Y.S.2d 1003 (2d Dept. 1987).

Waiver.—Defendant waived his right to review the issue of the illegality of the initial seizure on arrest where he failed to raise the question at the suppression hearing and the evidence at the hearing did not address the issue. People v. Johnson, 84 A.D.2d 715, 444 N.Y.S.2d 5 (1st Dept. 1981).

Subd. 2

Intermediate appellate court; scope.—It is reversible error when the Appellate Division manifestly avoids its exclusive statutory authority to review the weight of the evidence in criminal cases. People v. Bleakley, 69 N.Y.2d 490, 515 N.Y.S.2d 761, 508 N.E.2d 672 (1987).

—If an error of law is committed by the hearing court which directly causes the People to fail to offer potentially critical evidence a rehearing should be ordered so that the evidence may be presented. People v. Crandall, 69 N.Y.2d 459, 515 N.Y.S.2d 745, 508 N.E.2d 657 (1987).

—When the court improperly adjudicated defendant a second felony offender, remand was unnecessary since imposition of minimum sentence would be consistent with sentencing court's intent. People v. Lawrence, 130 A.D.2d 383, 515 N.Y.S.2d 31 (1st Dept. 1987).

—There was no need to remit for resentencing on modified charges where defendant had already served the maximum time to which he could have been sentenced on those charges. People v. Oliphant, 127 A.D.2d 802, 512 N.Y.S.2d 200 (2d Dept. 1987).

Issue not preserved.—Where the court, on a single instance, referred to reasonable doubt as "reasonable certainty," there was no reason to reverse the defendant's conviction. Additionally, the issue was not preserved for review. People v. McGill, 183 A.D.2d 730, 583 N.Y.S.2d 470 (2d Dept. 1992).

Legal sufficiency claim unpreserved.—Defendant's contention that the evidence was legally insufficient to establish his guilt is unpreserved for appellate review since his attorney failed to make the argument with specificity before the trial court. People v. Butler, 265 A.D.2d 487, 697 N.Y.S.2d 633 (2d Dept. 1999).

Lesser included offense; appellate court's modification of judgment.—Appellate court acted properly where it dismissed first count of indictment for insufficiency of the evidence

and ordered a new trial on the remaining counts instead of modifying the judgment by changing it to one of conviction for a lessor included offense. People v. Holmes, 52 N.Y.2d 976, 438 N.Y.S.2d 284, 420 N.E.2d 82 (1981).

—Where the evidence was not legally sufficient to support the trial court's judgment convicting defendants of conspiracy in the second degree, but was logically sufficient to support a conviction of conspiracy in the third degree, the appellate court modified the trial court's judgment to the lesser included offense of conspiracy in the third degree, and remitted the matter for resentencing. People v. Dowling, 42 A.D.2d 958, 348 N.Y.S.2d 568 (1st Dept. 1973), aff'd, 37 N.Y.2d 913, 378 N.Y.S.2d 386 340 N.E.2d 747 (1975).

—Where the defendant did not request the court to charge the jury with the lesser offense, the defendant could not appeal the court's failure to inform the jury of the matter. People v. Valentin, 185 A.D.2d 865, 587 N.Y.S.2d 371 (2d Dept. 1992).

—Reversal of murder, second degree, conviction by the Appellate Division was modified by the Court of Appeals to reflect a conviction for the lesser included offense of attempted murder, second degree, since, although the evidence was legally insufficient to support the homicide conviction it was sufficient for the jury to conclude that defendant thought that the victim was alive and established the attempt to commit the crime of murder, second degree. People v. Dlugash, 41 N.Y.2d 725, 395 N.Y.S.2d 419, 363 N.E.2d 1155 (1977).

—Where the People failed to prove an essential element of the defendant's crime, the court properly reduced defendant's conviction upon the finding of legally sufficient evidence to support a lesser charge. People v. Wager, 199 A.D.2d 642, 604 N.Y.S.2d 1008 (3d Dept. 1993).

—Court was authorized to reduce the defendant's sentence from guilty of attempted robbery in the first degree, to attempted robbery in the third degree where the evidence was insufficient to support the conviction on the former charge. People v. Miller, 201 A.D.2d 109, 615 N.Y.S.2d 172 (4th Dept. 1994).

Subd. 3

Accused deprived of fair and impartial trial.—Reversal required "as a matter of discretion and in the interests of justice" where the prosecutor bolstered by hearsay the testimony of a witness, questioned defendant as to his frequent change of address, use of marihuana and in summation vouched for the credibility of the peoples witnesses even though the defendant failed to object. People v. Bolden, 82 A.D.2d 757, 440 N.Y.S.2d 202 (1st Dept. 1981).

—Although the defendant failed to preserve for appeal the fact that the verdict sheet submitted to the jury contained portions of the indictment, the error warranted reversal on the defendant's conviction in the interest of justice. People v. Pymm, 188 A.D.2d 561, 591 N.Y.S.2d 458 (2d Dept. 1992).

—Although the defendant did not timely object to the trial judge's wife as a juror, the defendant was entitled to reversal of his conviction as a matter in the interest of justice. The defendant must be tried by a fair and impartial jury. People v. Hartson, 160 A.D.2d 1046, 553 N.Y.S.2d 537 (3d Dept. 1990).

—Defendant's conviction must be reversed in the interest of justice where the court's error resulted in the People's burden being lessened. Thus, the defendant was deprived of a fair trial. People v. Towndrow, 187 A.D.2d 194, 594 N.Y.S.2d 469 (4th Dept. 1993).

Appellate court; authority.—While the appellate court can modify a sentence in the interest of justice, sentencing is a matter primarily for the trial court's discretion. Because of the defendant's criminal history and because the defendant ordered the killing of a woman for giving unfavorable grand jury testimony, the appellate court would not substitute its sentence for the trial court's sentence. People v. Kornegay, 180 A.D.2d 759, 580 N.Y.S.2d 77 (2d Dept. 1992).

Egregious comments of District Attorney requiring reversal.—Absent curative instructions to the jury, a district attorney's irrelevant and inflammatory conclusions and comments, including comments on defendant's failure to testify, were so egregious, that the strong likelihood existed that the prejudicial summation tainted the jury verdict and deprived defendant of his right to a fair trial, requiring reversal. People v. Brewer, 94 A.D.2d 812, 463 N.Y.S.2d 297 (3d Dept. 1983).

Exclusion of co-defense counsel from participating in

case.—Trial court abused its discretion in excluding one of defendant's two attorneys from participating in his case, where nothing in the record contradicted defense counsel's statements that the excluded attorney's participating was sought in good faith to provide co-counsel with assistance in conducting the defense, and where court improperly stated that the excluded attorney had been sought to evoke sympathy from the jury by seeking the assistance of an African-American attorney. People v. Knowles, 88 N.Y.2d 763, 650 N.Y.S.2d 617, 673 N.E.2d 902 (1996).

Ineffective assistance of counsel.—Defendant was not provided meaningful representation where defense counsel embarked on an inexplicably prejudicial course by raising the defense of entrapment that enabled the prosecution to introduce highly damaging evidence on cross examination. People v. Zaborski, 59 N.Y.2d 863, 465 N.Y.S.2d 927, 452 N.E.2d 1255 (1983).

—Defendant was denied effective assistance of counsel at the preliminary hearing where defense counsel's concession that the police were entitled to seize contraband found on the bed in defendant's room because they were in plain view from the hallway in a residential hotel was apparently made based on his misapprehension of the plain view doctrine, and it could not be viewed as a strategic decision. People v. Vega, 276 A.D.2d 414, 714 N.Y.S.2d 291 (1st Dept. 2000).

—Defendant's allegations that trial counsel failed to effectuate his right to testify before the grand jury and failed to make a timely dismissal motion pursuant to CPL § 190.50(5)(c) would not constitute ineffective assistance of counsel, and defendant has not demonstrated that the result of the grand jury proceeding would have been any different had defendant testified. People v. Hook, 246 A.D.2d 470, 668 N.Y.S.2d 183 (1st Dept. 1998).

—Defendant, who testified at a jury trial in which credibility was crucial, did not receive effective assistance of counsel where after achieving exclusion of a prior conviction following a *Sandoval* hearing, counsel inexplicably elicited from the defendant the existence of the previously suppressed conviction. People v. Ofunniyin, 114 A.D.2d 1045, 495 N.Y.S.2d 485 (2d Dept. 1985).

—Conviction for robbery in the second degree was reversed due to ineffective assistance of counsel at trial where counsel failed to request a *Huntley* hearing, failed to seek preclusion of statements which had not been properly noticed, failed to object to damaging hearsay testimony, failed to object to improper prosecutorial comments in summation, and failed to object to an improper charge by the court on the issue of intent. People v. Andrew S., 108 A.D.2d 935, 485 N.Y.S.2d 828 (2d Dept. 1985).

—Effective assistance of counsel was denied where the defense attorney failed to raise a valid insanity defense, call any witnesses and failed to prepare any defense. People v. Angellilo, 91 A.D.2d 666, 457 N.Y.S.2d 118 (2d Dept. 1982).

—Court rejected defendant's claim of ineffective assistance of counsel where counsel made omnibus motion requesting various hearings and discovery material, delivered effective opening and closing statements, adequately cross-examined witnesses, made appropriate objections to testimony, pursued a viable defense strategy, and requested that County Court charge lesser included offenses. People v. Kelly, 256 A.D.2d 1133, 684 N.Y.S.2d 715 (4th Dept. 1998).

Preservation of issue.—Defendant failed to preserve for review the matter of the court's mistake in explaining reasonable doubt by failing to object. However, the court's error did not warrant reversal because the weight of the evidence against the defendant was overwhelming. People v. Hardy, 136 A.D.2d 915, 524 N.Y.S.2d 919 (4th Dept. 1988).

Prosecutorial misconduct.—Defendant was entitled to a new trial based upon prosecutorial misconduct, both in cross-examination designed primarily to disparage the defendant's character and in a summation where he ridiculed and attacked the defendant's credibility and the sincerity of defense counsel and vouched for the credibility of the People's witnesses. People v. Hicks, 102 A.D.2d 173, 478 N.Y.S.2d 256 (1st Dept. 1984).

—Prosecutor is obligated to correct misstatements of a witness regarding the consideration given for the witness's testimony; if such misstatements are not corrected and are in any way relevant to the case, a guilty verdict will not be permitted to stand. People v. Schwartz, 240 A.D.2d 600, 659 N.Y.S.2d 51 (2d Dept. 1997).

—Conviction reversed due to prosecutor's misconduct, where prosecutor improperly asked defendant if he refused the polygraph because "you knew that you had done it, and they could tell you were lying on a polygraph," and prosecutor improperly commented on summation that defendant did not take the polygraph "because he had something to hide." People v. Uriah, 261 A.D.2d 848, 691 N.Y.S.2d 216 (4th Dept. 1999).

Reduction of sentence; rehabilitation.—Defendant's sentence was not improper where the record did not reflect that a promise was made by the court, at the time defendant's guilty plea was accepted, with respect to the length of the sentence to be imposed, although the court noted that the prosecutor had recommended a lesser sentence, the record was manifestly clear that the court explained to the defendant at the plea taking that no promise concerning sentence was being made and specifically stated that the recommendation would be followed only "If your probation report shows that you . . . deserve a break." People v. Roman, 84 A.D.2d 851, 444 N.Y.S.2d 167 (2d Dept. 1981).

Reversal in interests of justice; issue first raised on appeal.—Reversal of conviction by the Appellate Division on a ground not raised at the suppression hearing was made as a matter of discretion in the interests of justice and was therefore not appealable to Court of Appeals. People v. Figueroa, 62 N.Y.2d 727, 476 N.Y.S.2d 817, 465 N.E.2d 356 (1984).

Reversal in interest of justice; weak identification and credible alibi.—Court reversed defendant's conviction on the facts and in the interest of justice where the prosecution's identification evidence was extremely weak and the defendant presented a credible alibi defense. People v. Crudup, 100 A.D.2d 938, 474 N.Y.S.2d 827 (2d Dept. 1984).

Right to counsel; issue on appeal.—The right to counsel is sufficiently critical that a claim of deprivation may be raised for the first time on appeal as long as there is a sufficient basis in the record for reviewing the issue. People v. Howard, 106 A.D.2d 663, 482 N.Y.S.2d 917 (2d Dept. 1984).

Sandoval motion.—Trial court failed to discharge its obligation to exercise its discretionary power in striking a balance between the probative worth of evidence of prior specific criminal, vicious and immoral acts on the issue of the defendants' credibility versus the risk of unfair prejudice to the defendant. People v. Coe, 95 A.D.2d 685, 463 N.Y.S.2d 795 (1st Dept. 1983).

Subd. 4

Authority of court.—The defendant is not required to request for the Appellate Division to review or modify the judgment due to insufficient evidence. The court has the authority to act pursuant to CPL § 470.15(4)(b). People v. Cooper, 204 A.D.2d 24, 618 N.Y.S.2d 257 (1st Dept. 1994).

Defendant's right to present witnesses.—The refusal to grant the accused an adjournment to secure the attendance of two alibi witnesses was an abuse of discretion requiring a new trial. While a trial court is not required to grant an adjournment to allow pursuit of an elusive witness whose name and address are unknown, when a witness has been identified to the court and is within the jurisdiction, a request for a short adjournment should not be denied if some diligence and good faith have been shown; such a denial would be a deprivation of defendant's fundamental right to present witnesses in his own behalf. People v. Foy, 32 N.Y.2d 473, 346 N.Y.S.2d 245, 299 N.E.2d 664 (1973).

Excessive participation of judge.—While a trial judge has a duty to clarify issues for the jury and to facilitate or expedite the orderly progress of the trial, where incriminatory testimony was elicited by the court's own questioning, the court assumes a prosecutorial role which seriously prejudices the defendant's right to a fair trial and requires a reversal. People v. Cooper, 96 A.D.2d 866, 465 N.Y.S.2d 755 (2d Dept. 1983).

Fair trial.—Defendant was not deprived of a fair trial where the court excluded parts of defendant's conversation with an informant. The defendant's defense of entrapment was not hindered by the exclusion. People v. Black, 180 A.D.2d 806, 580 N.Y.S.2d 444 (2d Dept. 1992).

—The defendant was deprived of a fair trial where the trial court allowed the jury to consider the illegal actions of the defendant's family in considering the defendant's guilt. The court properly reversed the defendant's conviction due to the prejudicial impact of the information. People v. Cheatham, 158 A.D.2d 934, 550 N.Y.S.2d 961 (4th Dept. 1990).

Fair trial; failure to object to prosecutor's statements.—Defendant could not contend that he was deprived of a fair trial where he failed to object to allegedly prejudicial statements made by prosecutor in his opening and closing statements and prosecutor's remarks were not so prejudicial as to require a reversal in the court's discretion in the interests of justice. People v. Sim, 53 A.D.2d 992, 386 N.Y.S.2d 114 (3d Dept. 1976), aff'd, 44 N.Y.2d 758, 405 N.Y.S.2d 686, 376 N.E.2d 1331 (1978).

Failure of People to preserve material evidence.—The dismissal of the indictment was required where the detective willfully destroyed the complainant's blood-stained pants. The People have a duty to preserve such material evidence and the failure to do so violates the defendant's due process rights. People v. McCann, 115 Misc. 2d 1025, 455 N.Y.S.2d 212 (Sup. Ct. Queens Co. 1982).

Fair trial; prosecutor's summation to jury.—The assault victim had been found abandoned in a gas station, unconscious after a night of drinking with defendant, suffering from a skull fracture due to a heavy blow, and covered with blood and with tooth marks about her breasts and genitalia, and the prosecutor had characterized the defendant as a liar, an "animal," and a "beast." Because in this case it was at most only arguable that the prosecutor's misconduct could have produced a greater adverse effect on the jury than did the bizarre facts of the crime and the overwhelming evidence of defendant's culpability, the objectionable summation did not, on balance, require a new trial. People v. Brosnan, 32 N.Y.2d 254, 344 N.Y.S.2d 900, 298 N.E.2d 78 (1973).

Fair trial; due process; gagging of disruptive defendant.—Noting that a trial court attempting to deal with a disruptive or stubbornly defiant defendant may bind and gag him, cite him for contempt, or exclude him from the courtroom, the Court of Appeals ruled that in view of the warning given the defendant, the short duration of the gagging, and the prompt removal of the gag upon defendant's agreeing to observe reasonable and responsible courtroom procedures, the trial court did not abuse its discretion in the method used to restore order to the courtroom. The court further noted that the trial court had properly instructed the jury to disregard the incident and to arrive at no unwarranted inferences from it. People v. Palermo, 32 N.Y.2d 222, 344 N.Y.S.2d 874, 298 N.E.2d 61 (1973).

Insufficient instruction on identification.—Where the issue of identification is paramount, it is incumbent upon the trial court to give an appropriate charge. The real issue in many identification cases is not the veracity of the witness, but whether or not the witness is honestly mistaken. An appropriate charge should instruct the jury to focus upon "accuracy as well as veracity, weighing all the facts and circumstances surrounding the giving of two different descriptions, one of a stranger, the other of defendant." The court's failure to so instruct the jury, in a case where the defendant's guilt was not overwhelming, was reversible error requiring a new trial. People v. Knowell, 94 A.D.2d 255, 464 N.Y.S.2d 525 (2d Dept. 1983), rev'd, 127 A.D.2d 794, 512 N.Y.S.2d 190 (2d Dept. 1987).

Joint representation.—Defendant's conviction was reversed where the court failed to ascertain whether defendant and co-defendant were aware of the risks in being represented by the same attorney. People v. Cabrera, 108 A.D.2d 819, 485 N.Y.S.2d 102 (2d Dept. 1985).

Preservation of the issue.—Where the defendant moved to dismiss the charge at the end of the People's case, the issue of the legal sufficiency of the evidence was preserved and reviewable. People v. Watson, 163 A.D.2d 253, 558 N.Y.S.2d 537 (1st Dept. 1990).

—The defendant must raise his argument before the hearing court in order to preserve the issue. The court will not review the issue if defendant fails to raise timely arguments. People v. Vernon, 157 A.D.2d 542, 549 N.Y.S.2d 730 (1st Dept. 1990).

Right to counsel of own choice.—At a sentencing hearing which required an adjournment so that a predicate felony hearing could take place, defense counsel moved for a substitution of counsel. Where there was no indication that the substitution would have resulted in any delay, the court's denial was improper and deprived the defendant of his right to counsel of his own choice. People v. Walker, 92 A.D.2d 905, 460 N.Y.S.2d 101 (2d Dept. 1983).

Subd. 5

Admissibility of uncharged crimes.—The trial court was correct in admitting evidence of prior uncharged crimes where the victim of a robbery was unable to identify her assailant and had previously been involved in crimes involving the cutting of the girls' hair, a pattern similar to the present case. People v. Rossman, 95 A.D.2d 873, 463 N.Y.S.2d 891 (3d Dept. 1983).

Appellate Court.—The Appellate Court must correctly and efficiently utilize its authority to review the facts and consider issues in the interest of justice. People v. Autry, 75 N.Y.2d 836, 552 N.Y.S.2d 908, 552 N.E.2d 156 (1990).

Bolstering; harmless error.—Although the admission of the victim's statement regarding her prior identification of the defendant to the doctor was improper bolstering, in view of the overwhelming evidence of guilt it was harmless error. People v. Randall, 91 A.D.2d 838, 458 N.Y.S.2d 394 (4th Dept. 1982).

Effectiveness of counsel.—Defendant was not deprived of his constitutional right to effective assistance of counsel because defense counsel conceded in summation that the line-up was fair since counsel also argued that the photo identification was suggestive and tainted the line-up. People v. Morris, 64 N.Y.2d 803, 486 N.Y.S.2d 920, 476 N.E.2d 319 (1985).

—Trial counsel was not ineffective and did provide meaningful assistance, and it could not be said that counsel's performance produced a conviction that resulted from a breakdown in the adversary process rendering the resultant conviction unreliable. People v. Harris, 107 A.D.2d 761, 484 N.Y.S.2d 127 (2d Dept. 1985).

—Defendant was not denied effective assistance of counsel where she and her fianc were represented on drug charges by one attorney, in spite of a significant possibility of actual conflict, since defendant was sufficiently warned about the risks of joint representation by both the trial court and her attorney. People v. Medina, 106 A.D.2d 756, 484 N.Y.S.2d 177 (3d Dept. 1984).

Evidence.—The trial court may set aside the verdict if, on appeal, the conviction would be modified or reversed. Questions regarding the weight of the evidence are questions of fact. People v. Land, 193 A.D.2d 438, 604 N.Y.S.2d 146 (2d Dept. 1993).

—Where the verdict was supported by evidence and the defendant's alibi was directly refuted by testimony, the defendant's claim lacked merit. People v. Brockington, 199 A.D.2d 570, 604 N.Y.S.2d 361 (3d Dept. 1993).

Role of jury.—Defendant's claims that the court allowed vague testimony and that the jury did not take into account the testimony of a defense witness, were unsupported by the record. It is the duty of the jury to decide on the issues of credibility. People v. Johnson, 215 A.D.2d 589, 627 N.Y.S.2d 931 (2d Dept. 1995).

Self-representation.—Although a defendant has a right to represent himself, it is incumbent upon the court to determine that his decision to forego counsel is knowing and intelligent. Therefore, the court must undertake a searching inquiry of defendant to be reasonably certain that the dangers and disadvantages of giving up the right to counsel have been impressed on the defendant and where the court's inquiry is inadequate, the conviction must be reversed. People v. Williams, 96 A.D.2d 740, 465 N.Y.S.2d 332 (4th Dept. 1983).

Subd. 6

Excessive sentence.—A sentence of 20 years to life for the criminal sale of a controlled substance in the first degree is unduly harsh and must be modified in the interests of justice to 15 years to life where the defendant was 27 years old at the time, with one previous criminal involvement for possession of a weapon for which he received a conditional discharge. People v. Lopez, 79 A.D.2d 531, 433 N.Y.S.2d 782 (1st Dept. 1980).

Improper charge; knowledge and intent.—In prosecution for criminal possession of a forged instrument, court's charge that "the law says that possession of a forged instrument if you find it was forged is enough to permit the inference that the defendant here knew it was forged if it was on his person" and pertaining to intent the court's charge that "a person presumed to intend the natural and probable consequences of his act so accordingly if the consequences are natural and probable he will not be heard to say that he didn't intend them" was erroneous as it shifted to the defendant the burden of proof on a crucial element of the crime charged. People v. Harris, 77 A.D.2d 804, 430 N.Y.S.2d 753 (4th Dept. 1980).

Interests of justice.—Reversal in the interests of justice was required even though some of the prosecutor's comments were not objected to, where the summation was inflammatory, bore no relationship to the issues in the case and went beyond a fair response to defense counsel's summation. People v. Stewart, 92 A.D.2d 226, 459 N.Y.S.2d 853 (2d Dept. 1983).

—Court declined to reverse the defendant's conviction in the interest of justice where, although the County Court erred in its jury charge, the defendant was not prejudiced by the charge. People v. Ryan, 184 A.D.2d 24, 591 N.Y.S.2d 218 (3d Dept. 1992).

—The court properly reversed the defendant's conviction in the interest of justice where the People's burden of proof was reduced as a result of the trial court's jury instructions. The defendant did not receive a fair trial. People v. Banks, 193 A.D.2d 1051, 598 N.Y.S.2d 1014 (4th Dept. 1993).

Prosecutorial misconduct.—Reversal of a conviction of first degree conspiracy was required because of the "deliberate and pervasive pattern of prosecutorial misconduct at defendant's trial" resulting in defendant being denied his fundamental right to a fair trial. People v. Mott, 94 A.D.2d 415, 465 N.Y.S.2d 307 (4th Dept. 1983).

§ 470.20. Determination of appeals by intermediate appellate courts; corrective action upon reversal or modification.

Upon reversing or modifying a judgment, sentence or order of a criminal court, an intermediate appellate court must take or direct such corrective action as is necessary and appropriate both to rectify any injustice to the appellant resulting from the error or defect which is the subject of the reversal or modification and to protect the rights of the respondent. The particular corrective action to be taken or directed is governed in part by the following rules:

1. Upon a reversal of a judgment after trial for error or defect which resulted in prejudice to the defendant or deprived him of a fair trial, the court must, whether such reversal be on the law or as a matter of discretion in the interest of justice, order a new trial of the accusatory instrument and remit the case to the criminal court for such action.

2. Upon a reversal of a judgment after trial for legal insufficiency of trial evidence, the court must dismiss the accusatory instrument.

3. Upon a modification of a judgment after trial for legal insufficiency of trial evidence with respect to one or more but not all of the offenses of which the defendant was convicted, the court must dismiss the count or counts of the accusatory instrument determined to be legally unsupported and must otherwise affirm the judgment. In such case, it must either reduce the total sentence to that imposed by the criminal court upon the counts with respect to which the judgment is affirmed or remit the case to the criminal court for re-sentence upon such counts; provided that nothing contained in this paragraph precludes further sentence reduction in the exercise of the appellate court's discretion pursuant to subdivision six.

4. Upon a modification of a judgment after trial which reduces a conviction of a crime to one for a lesser included offense, the court must remit the case to the criminal court with a direction that the latter sentence the defendant accordingly.

5. Upon a reversal or modification of a judgment after trial upon the ground that the verdict, either in its entirety or with respect to a particular count or counts, is against the weight of the trial evidence, the court must dismiss the accusatory instrument or any reversed count.

6. Upon modifying a judgment or reversing a sentence as a matter of discretion in the interest of justice upon the ground that the sentence is unduly harsh or severe, the court must itself impose some legally authorized lesser sentence.

ANNOTATIONS

Dismissal.—Dismissal is not warranted based on trial error. However, dismissal will be warranted where the court finds that the evidence is legally insufficient. People v. Perkins, 189 A.D.2d 830, 592 N.Y.S.2d 752 (2d Dept. 1993).

Generally.—When case is remitted to lower court for purposes of a hearing, it is error to venture into area and issues beyond the scope of the remittal order. People v. Wiggins, 197 A.D.2d 802, 603 N.Y.S.2d 81 (3d Dept. 1993).

—Where the court established that the evidence was legally sufficient to support the defendant's conviction the court properly ordered a new trial. People v. Moss, 168 A.D.2d 960, 565 N.Y.S.2d 935 (4th Dept. 1990).

Insufficient evidence.—Examination of all evidence against defendant did not establish guilt beyond a reasonable doubt. The statements and behavior attributed to defendant were at best equivocal and certainly not incriminatory. People v. Hudson, 95 A.D.2d 688, 463 N.Y.S.2d 799 (1st Dept. 1983).

Modification of judgment.—The bench which decided the original appeal and the bench which has received the remittitur from the Court of Appeals are not courts of coordinate jurisdiction but constitute the same bench although one of the original judges is no longer a member of the court and this panel can render a different decision. People v. Palumbo, 79 A.D.2d 518, 433 N.Y.S.2d 770 (1st Dept. 1980), aff'd, 53 N.Y.2d 894, 440 N.Y.S.2d 633, 423 N.E.2d 56 (1981).

Subd. 2

Corrective action.—Court properly took corrective action in remitting the case for full consideration based on the review of the evidence. People v. Bleakley, 69 N.Y.2d 490, 515 N.Y.S.2d 761, 508 N.E.2d 672 (1987).

Double jeopardy, modification by appellate court; retrial for higher degree of crime.—Where Appellate Division modified murder second degree conviction to one of manslaughter, first degree because decisional law barred inculpatory statements of defendant and federal Court of Appeals later ruled that modification was improper, the second trial court lacked the power to try defendant for murder, second degree and the Appellate court properly modified by reducing the conviction to manslaughter, first degree, setting the murder conviction aside on double jeopardy grounds. People v. Graham, 36 N.Y.2d 633, 370 N.Y.S.2d 888, 331 N.E.2d 673 (1975).

Evidence legally insufficient for conviction; dismissal.—If the evidence adduced at the trial was legally insufficient to warrant the conviction, the indictment must be dismissed. People v. Lagana, 43 A.D.2d 834, 350 N.Y.S.2d 747 (2d Dept. 1974); see also People v. Crimmins, 36 N.Y.2d 230, 367 N.Y.S.2d 213, 326 N.E.2d 787 (1975); People v. Mackell, 40 N.Y.2d 59, 386 N.Y.S.2d 37, 351 N.E.2d 684 (1976).

—Defendant's conviction was properly reversed where the evidence did not support the conviction. The evidence involved was circumstantial and thus, legally insufficient. People v. Williams, 198 A.D.2d 804, 604 N.Y.S.2d 390 (4th Dept. 1993).

—Because it is the duty of the jury to determine the factual issues, it was improper to allow an investigator to interpret defendant's conversations. Thus, the defendant's conviction cannot stand. The admission of lay opinion testimony warrants dismissal of the indictment. People v. Vizzini, 183 A.D.2d 302, 591 N.Y.S.2d 281 (4th Dept. 1992).

Presumption of sanity.—Where defendant introduced the opinion testimony of a qualified psychiatrist that he was suffering from severe schizophrenic reaction, together with evidence of ten years of mental illness requiring four commitments prior to arraignment and commitment thereafter, the prosecutor could not rely on the presumption of sanity and was required to meet this challenge with contradictory proof. People v. Silver, 33 N.Y.2d 475, 354 N.Y.S.2d 915, 310 N.E.2d 520 (1974).

Subd. 3

Conviction on remaining counts.—Where the indictment of the defendant was insufficient on all counts of grand larceny, the court was authorized to modify and reduce the defendant's sentence. People v. Sanchez, 84 N.Y.2d 440, 618 N.Y.S.2d 887, 643 N.E.2d 509 (1994).

—Although one count of the defendant's conviction was vacated and dismissed, defendant was properly sentenced in accordance with the remaining count. People v. Porter, 177 A.D.2d 1001, 578 N.Y.S.2d 22 (4th Dept. 1991).

Subd. 4

Insufficient evidence.—Defendant's sentence was properly reduced where the evidence did not support the defendant's conviction for possession of a controlled substance. The evidence did not establish that the defendant knew the weight of the substance involved. People v. Lewis, 213 A.D.2d 1065, 625 N.Y.S.2d 982 (4th Dept. 1995).

—The court acted properly in reducing defendant's conviction where the evidence was insufficient to establish that the victim was subjected to pain or physical impairment. People v. Hunt, 187 A.D.2d 981, 591 N.Y.S.2d 107 (4th Dept. 1992).

Lesser included offense; appellate court's modification of judgment.—Where the evidence was not legally sufficient to support the trial court's judgment convicting defendants of conspiracy in the second degree, but was legally sufficient to support a conviction of conspiracy in the third degree, the appellate court modified the trial court's judgment to the lesser included offense of conspiracy in the third degree, and remitted the matter for resentencing. People v. Dowling, 42 A.D.2d 958, 348 N.Y.S.2d 568 (1st Dept. 1973), aff'd, 37 N.Y.2d 913, 378 N.Y.S.2d 386, 340 N.E.2d 747 (1975).

—Reduction in defendant's sentence was warranted where the court failed to explain and clarify the difference between first and second degree assault to the jury. People v. Thomas, 178 A.D.2d 363, 577 N.Y.S.2d 812 (1st Dept. 1991).

Subd. 5

Evidence; sufficiency of.—The Appellate Court is authorized to determine whether the jury afforded the evidence the proper weight. It is within the discretion of the court to determine the legal sufficiency of the evidence involved. People v. Wagner, 178 A.D.2d 679, 577 N.Y.S.2d 332 (3d Dept. 1991).

Reversal in the interests of justice.—A conviction for robbery in the second degree must be reversed and the indictment dismissed in the interests of justice even though the verdict was not against the weight of the evidence where the complainant recognized the defendant on the street two days after the incident; the complainant stopped to take a close look at him; defendant had been working at a job that required him to get up early in the morning; incident occurred around midnight when he would usually be asleep; and defendant was mentally retarded. People v. Kidd, 76 A.D.2d 665, 431 N.Y.S.2d 542 (1st Dept. 1980).

Subd. 6

Modification of sentence; interest of justice.—Where the court finds the imposed sentence is excessive, the court has the authority to modify the sentence in the interest of justice. Thus, the court had the authority to impose concurrently running sentences upon the defendant to reduce the time of incarceration. People v. Tortorice, 142 A.D.2d 916, 531 N.Y.S.2d 414 (3d Dept. 1988).

—Where the defendant claims the sentence should be reduced in the interest of justice, there must be an indication that the

sentencing court acted in abuse of its discretion. People v. Paige, 122 A.D.2d 494, 505 N.Y.S.2d 733 (3d Dept. 1986).

Modification of sentence; original sentence excessive.—The Appellate Division was authorized to reduce the defendant's sentence where the court concluded the sentence was excessive. The court was not required to give the People an opportunity to withdraw their consent to plea. People v. Thompson, 60 N.Y.2d 513, 470 N.Y.S.2d 551, 458 N.E.2d 1228 (1983).

—Sentence was reduced to 1 to 4 years where the record established that the trial court did not originally intend to impose a custodial sentence upon the defendant. However, when the court discovered that the defendant had lied during the trial, it doubled the sentence. People v. Hernandez, 86 A.D.2d 618, 446 N.Y.S.2d 90 (2d Dept. 1982).

Sentence; no reduction warranted.—Defendant was not entitled to sentence reduction where the court imposed the minimum legal sentence upon the defendant. People v. Compton, 157 A.D.2d 903, 550 N.Y.S.2d 148 (3d Dept. 1990).

§ 470.25. Determination of appeals by intermediate appellate courts; form and content of order.

1. An order of an intermediate appellate court which affirms a judgment, sentence or order of a criminal court need only state such affirmance.

2. An order of an intermediate appellate court which reverses or modifies a judgment, sentence or order of a criminal court must contain the following:

(a) A statement of whether the determination was upon the law or upon the facts or as a matter of discretion in the interest of justice, or upon any specified two or all three of such bases; and

(b) If the decision is rendered without opinion, a brief statement of the specific grounds of the reversal or modification; and

(c) A statement of the corrective action taken or directed by the court; and

(d) If the determination is exclusively upon the law, a statement of whether or not the facts upon which the criminal court's judgment, sentence or order is based have been considered and determined to have been established. In the absence of such a statement, it is presumed that the intermediate appellate court did not consider or make any determination with respect to such facts.

ANNOTATIONS

Opinions; intermediate appellate court; recital of grounds of reversal or modification.—Failure of County Court to recite grounds for reversal was improper, but not so fatal as to justify remand of case for formal implementation. People v. Hanley, 30 N.Y.2d 863, 335 N.Y.S.2d 298, 286 N.E.2d 734 (1972).

Remittance of case.—Where the evidence strongly indicated that the defendant created a situation of grave risk of death to the victim, it was proper for the court to remit the case for consideration of the facts. People v. Chrysler, 85 N.Y.2d 413, 626 N.Y.S.2d 18, 649 N.E.2d 1162 (1995).

—Where the Appellate Division is found not to have reviewed the facts, but made its decision on the law, the case will be remitted for consideration of the facts. People v. Jenkins, 163 A.D.2d 259, 559 N.Y.S.2d 685 (1st Dept. 1990).

Standard of review for intermediate appellate court.—The issue for an intermediate appellate court involves only a legal assessment of whether inferences of guilt could be rationally drawn from proven facts, and not a substituted fact-finding reassessment of the persuasiveness of the evidence. People v. Taylor, 94 N.Y.2d 910, 707 N.Y.S.2d 618, 729 N.E.2d 337 (2000).

§ 470.30. Determination by court of appeals of appeals taken directly thereto from judgments and orders of criminal courts.

1. Wherever appropriate, the rules set forth in sections 470.15 and 470.20, governing the consideration and determination by intermediate appellate courts of appeals thereto from judgments and orders of criminal courts, and prescribing their scope of review and the corrective action to be taken by them upon reversal or modification, apply equally to the consideration and determination by the court of appeals of appeals taken directly thereto, pursuant to sections 450.70 and 450.80, from judgments and orders of superior criminal courts.

2. Whenever a sentence of death is imposed, the judgment and sentence shall be reviewed on the record by the court of appeals. Review by the court of appeals pursuant to subdivision one of section 450.70 may not be waived.

3. With regard to the sentence, the court shall, in addition to exercising the powers and scope of review granted under subdivision one of this section, determine:

(a) whether the sentence of death was imposed under the influence of passion, prejudice, or any other arbitrary or legally impermissible factor including whether the imposition of the verdict or sentence was based upon the race of the defendant or a victim of the crime for which the defendant was convicted;

(b) whether the sentence of death is excessive or disproportionate to the penalty imposed in similar cases considering both the crime and the defendant. In conducting such review the court, upon request of the defendant, in addition to any other determination, shall review whether the sentence of death is excessive or disproportionate to the penalty imposed in similar cases by virtue of the race of the defendant or a victim of the crime for which the defendant was convicted; and

(c) whether the decision to impose the sentence of death was against the weight of the evidence.

4. The court shall include in its decision: (a) the aggravating and mitigating factors established in the record on appeal; and (b) those similar cases it took into consideration.

5. In addition to exercising any other corrective action pursuant to subdivision one of this section, the court, with regard to review of a sentence of death, shall be authorized to:

(a) affirm the sentence of death; or

(b) set the sentence aside and remand the case for resentencing pursuant to the procedures set forth in section 400.27 for a determination as to whether the defendant shall be sentenced to death, life imprisonment without parole or to a term of imprisonment for the class A-I felony of murder in the first degree other than a sentence of life imprisonment without parole; or

(c) set the sentence aside and remand the case for resentencing by the court for a determination as to whether the defendant shall be sentenced to life imprisonment without parole or to a term of imprisonment for the class A-I felony of murder in the first degree other than a sentence of life imprisonment without parole.

Amended by L. 1995, Ch. 1, § 27, eff. Sept. 1, 1995, amending subds. 1 and 2, and adding subds. 3, 4, and 5.

ANNOTATION

Death sentence.—Whenever sentence of death is imposed, Court of Appeals is mandated to review judgment and sentence. Scope of review includes determining whether death sentence was imposed under influence of passion, prejudice, or any other arbitrary or legally impermissible factor, including race of victim or defendant, and whether death sentence is excessive or disproportionate to penalty imposed in similar cases, considering the circumstances of the crime and of the defendant. People v. Arroyo, 178 Misc. 2d 653, 683 N.Y.S.2d 788 (Schoharie Co. Ct. 1998).

§ 470.35. Determination by court of appeals of appeals from orders of intermediate appellate courts; scope of review.

1. Upon an appeal to the court of appeals from an order of an intermediate appellate court affirming a judgment, sentence or order of a criminal court, the court of appeals may consider and determine not only questions of law which were raised or considered upon the appeal to the intermediate appellate court, but also any question of law involving alleged error or defect in the criminal court proceedings resulting in the original criminal court judgment, sentence or order, regardless of whether such question was raised, considered of determined upon the appeal to the intermediate appellate court.

2. Upon an appeal to the court of appeals from an order of an intermediate appellate court reversing or modifying a judgment, sentence or order of a criminal court, the court of appeals may consider and determine:

(a) Any question of law which was determined by the intermediate appellate court and which, as so determined, constituted a basis for such court's order of reversal or modification; and

(b) Any other question of law involving alleged or possible error or defect in the criminal court proceedings resulting in the original judgment, sentence or order which may have adversely affected the party who was appellant in the intermediate appellate court and who is respondent in the court of appeals. The court of appeals is not precluded from considering and determining such a question by the circumstance that it was not considered or determined by the intermediate appellate court, or that it did not constitute a basis for such court's reversal or modification, or that the party who may have been adversely affected thereby is the respondent rather than the appellant in the court of appeals; and the court of appeals, even though rejecting the intermediate appellate court's reasons for its order of reversal or modification, may affirm or modify such order upon the basis of such other questions; and

(c) Any question concerning the legality of the corrective action taken by the intermediate appellate court.

3. Upon such an appeal, the court must affirm, reverse or modify the intermediate appellate court order.

ANNOTATIONS

Appellate term holding not appealable; mixed question of law and fact.—Appellate Term holding that evidence seized was not in plain view involved a mixed question of law and fact not subject to further review as it was supported by evidence in the record. People v. McLaren, 62 N.Y.2d 730, 476 N.Y.S.2d 818, 465 N.E.2d 357 (1984).

—A double jeopardy defense based on the State and Federal Constitutions poses a question of law reviewable in the Court of Appeals despite the failure to raise it at the trial level. People v. Michael, 48 N.Y.2d 1, 420 N.Y.S.2d 371, 394 N.E.2d 1134 (1979).

Credibility of witness.—Credibility of a witness is a factual issue which is not generally within the competence of Court of Appeal review. People v. Concepcion, 38 N.Y.2d 211, 379 N.Y.S.2d 399, 341 N.E.2d 823 (1975).

Deficient record.—Court of Appeals declined to remit case for hearing to determine whether items never disclosed constituted duplicative equivalents of the materials made available to defense counsel at trial; if the People intended to raise this issue to justify the nondisclosure, they should have included those items in the trial court record so that the point could be resolved on appeal in the normal course. People v. Quinones, 73 N.Y.2d 988, 540 N.Y.S.2d 993, 994, 538 N.E.2d 345 (1989).

—Defendant's conviction for burglary was affirmed where if the specific arrangement for a one-year sentence had been made it would have been reflected in the statements signed by defendant with his attorney's approval. People v. De Crescente, 53 N.Y.2d 995, 441 N.Y.S.2d 664, 424 N.E.2d 551, *cert. denied,* 454 U.S. 857 (1981).

—Defendant's conviction of robbery in the first degree was affirmed where the evidence was not insufficient as a matter of law; the Court of Appeals does not have the power to assess the credibility of the witnesses or the weight of the evidence. People v. Thomas, 53 N.Y.2d 983, 441 N.Y.S.2d 664, 424 N.E.2d 551 (1981).

—The Court of Appeals has for a long time and still does review a record in a criminal action as a whole and is empowered and obliged to conclude on a deficient record that guilt has not been established beyond a reasonable doubt as a matter of law. People v. Santos, 38 N.Y.2d 173, 379 N.Y.S.2d 41, 341 N.E.2d 554 (1975).

Double jeopardy applicable in juvenile proceedings.—Double jeopardy is applicable in juvenile proceedings and that bar precludes appellate review of factual determinations which have been resolved in accused's favor by the original trier of facts. *In re* Tony M., 44 N.Y.2d 899, 407 N.Y.S.2d 634, 379 N.E.2d 162 (1978).

Direct appeal to Court of Appeals.—Direct appeal to Court of Appeals does not lie where questions other than the constitutional validity of a statutory provision are involved (N.Y. Const., Art. VI, § 3[b][2], § 5[b]; CPLR 5601[b][2]. People v. Rosario, 38 N.Y.2d 1006, 384 N.Y.S.2d 442, 348 N.E.2d 918 (1976).

Destruction of tapes.—Since, at trial, defendant made no inquiry at all with respect to the tapes, made no request for their production, failed to request any charge regarding them and made no post-trial motions concerning them, court refused on the appeal to review the propriety of the police conduct in destroying the tape recordings of various conversations with the defendant based upon their independent judgment that the tapes were inaudible and contained no exculpatory material. People v. Johnson, 42 N.Y.2d 841, 397 N.Y.S.2d 380, 366 N.E.2d 80 (1977).

Failure to raise constitutional issue.—Defendants contention that the seizure of an incriminatory handwritten note from her apartment violated her rights under the search and seizure provisions of the federal and state constitution, could not be raised on appeal when the issue was not raised at the suppression hearing. People v. Dancey, 57 N.Y.2d 1033, 457 N.Y.S.2d 782, 444 N.E.2d 32 (1982).

—Defendant's contention that the questioning by the police was conducted while the defendant was being held on less than probable cause cannot be raised on appeal where the record shows that this issue was not properly raised in the suppression court. People v. Adams, 57 N.Y.2d 1035, 457 N.Y.S.2d 783, 444 N.E.2d 33 (1982).

Federal constitutional error.—Federal constitutional error in a criminal case may be harmless only if it is "harmless beyond a reasonable doubt," that is, if there is no reasonable possibility that the erroneously admitted evidence contributed to the conviction; the test is concededly stricter than the one applied to nonconstitutional error in New York. People v. Almestica, 42 N.Y.2d 222, 397 N.Y.S.2d 709, 366 N.E.2d 799 (1977).

Judicial misconduct.—Since a sharp issue of credibility was involved, reversal was required where the court demeaned defense counsel, cast a pall of suspicion over his case, and interjected extraneous considerations unfairly burdening the defendant with the obligation of not only rebutting the proof of the People, but also of countering the implications imputed by the court. People v. DeJesus, 42 N.Y.2d 519, 399 N.Y.S.2d 196, 369 N.E.2d 752 (1977).

Jurisdiction.—Whether the particular circumstances in a case give rise to reasonable suspicion is a mixed question of law and fact beyond Court of Appeals review if there is, as here, support in the record for the Appellate Division's conclusion that reasonable suspicion existed justifying the pursuit. People v. Pines, 99 N.Y.2d 525, 752 N.Y.S.2d 266, 782 N.E.2d 62 (2002).

—Court of Appeals' review of an order pursuant to CPL § 210.40(1) dismissing indictments in the interest of justice is limited to the questions of whether the dismissal was an abuse of discretion as a matter of law. People v. Herman L., 83 N.Y.2d 958, 615 N.Y.S.2d 865, 639 N.E.2d 404 (1994).

—Whether the circumstances known to the police in a particular case give rise to reasonable suspicion is a mixed question of law and fact beyond review of the Court of Appeals unless there is no evidence in the record to support the determination of the lower courts. People v. Sierra, 83 N.Y.2d 928, 615 N.Y.S.2d 310, 638 N.E.2d 955 (1994).

—The Appellate Division's determination that defendant abandoned the property was a mixed question of law and fact that was supported by the record and thus not subject to further review by the Court of Appeals. People v. Reyes, 83 N.Y.2d 945, 615 N.Y.S.2d 316, 638 N.E.2d 961, *cert. denied,* 115 S. Ct. 492 (1994).

—While the order of the Appellate Division appealed from stated that its reversal was based solely "on the law," that recital was not binding on the Court of Appeals. People v. Hinton, 81 N.Y.2d 867, 597 N.Y.S.2d 926, 613 N.E.2d 958 (1993).

—Court of Appeals is not authorized to grant relief to the party who is not appealing. Where the defendant appealed from a reversal of a suppression motion, the court could not entertain People's issue on the *Darden* examination. People v. Carpenito, 80 N.Y.2d 65, 587 N.Y.S.2d 264, 599 N.E.2d 668 (1992).

—Ordinarily questions of attenuation are mixed questions of law and fact that Court of Appeals may review only to ascertain whether there is support in the record for the determination of the lower courts. People v. Harris, 72 N.Y.2d 614, 536 N.Y.S.2d 1, 532 N.E.2d 1229 (1988), *rev'd,* 495 U.S. 14, 110 S. Ct. 1640, 109 L. Ed. 2d 13 (1990), *rev'd,* 77 N.Y.2d 434, 568 N.Y.S.2d 702, 570 N.E.2d 1051 (1991).

—Prosecution's objection to providing the defense with a

witness' prior statement could not be review by the Court of Appeals. The prosecution failed to assert these objections in the trial court. People v. DeJesus, 69 N.Y.2d 855, 514 N.Y.S.2d 708, 507 N.E.2d 301 (1987).

—While questions of attenuation generally present mixed questions of law and fact, where the lower court applied an incorrect legal standard, an issue of law reviewable by the Court of Appeals was presented. People v. Borges, 69 N.Y.2d 1031, 517 N.Y.S.2d 914, 511 N.E.2d 58 (1987).

—Although probable cause determinations that involve questions of fact, or mixed questions of law or fact, are generally beyond the scope of review of the Court of Appeals, where the issue is the minimum showing necessary to establish probable cause, a question of law is presented. People v. Edwards, 69 N.Y.2d 814, 513 N.Y.S.2d 960, 506 N.E.2d 530 (1987).

—Suppression court's findings that entry into defendant's apartment was consensual and that the subsequent warrantless arrest inside the apartment was lawful involved mixed questions of law and fact, and because there was evidence in the record to support the hearing court's findings, review by Court of Appeals was barred. People v. Jones, 69 N.Y.2d 853, 514 N.Y.S.2d 706, 708, 507 N.E.2d 299 (1987).

—The Court of Appeals has no jurisdiction to find error in charge where no objection to the charge was made at trial. People v. Jones, 55 N.Y.2d 771, 447 N.Y.S.2d 242, 431 N.E.2d 967 (1981).

—In a noncapital case, it is in the discretion of the trial court and the intermediate appellate court to grant a motion for a new trial on the ground of newly discovered evidence; denial of such a motion raises no question of law reviewable by the Court of Appeals. People v. Monroe, 40 N.Y.2d 1096, 392 N.Y.S.2d 393, 360 N.E.2d 1076 (1977).

—The jurisdiction of the Court of Appeals in criminal cases is limited to considering questions of law except in the instance of an appeal taken directly to the Court of Appeals pursuant to CPL §§ 450.70, 450.80. People v. Robinson, 36 N.Y.2d 224, 367 N.Y.S.2d 208, 326 N.E.2d 784 (1975).

Matter of law.—Trial court abused its discretion as a matter of law when it abruptly refused, on calendar call, to allow an adjournment until 2 P.M. of the day previously set for trial. People v. DeRosa, 42 N.Y.2d 872, 397 N.Y.S.2d 780, 366 N.E.2d 868 (1977).

Mistrial; necessity for motion.—The failure of a defendant to move for a mistrial precluded a review of the issue presented by the prosecution's failure to produce a witness with its opening statement. People v. De Tore, 34 N.Y.2d 199, 356 N.Y.S.2d 598, 313 N.E.2d 61, *cert. denied,* 419 U.S. 1025 (1974).

Plea of guilty.—Appellate review of statements sought to be suppressed is precluded where the defendant plead guilty before the trial and did not make a motion to suppress the statements. People v. Charleston, 54 N.Y.2d 622, 442 N.Y.S.2d 493, 425 N.E.2d 881 (1981)

Power of review limited to legal insufficiency.—The Court of Appeals power of review is limited to legal insufficiency of the conviction and no trial errors of law in rulings or charge to the jury were claimed by the defendant; the conviction was accordingly affirmed. People v. Bland, 37 N.Y.2d 858, 378 N.Y.S.2d 42, 340 N.E.2d 475 (1975).

—Defendant's failure to object to the admission of evidence on the ground that it violated his Fourth Amendment rights; the questions of the propriety of defendant's detention and the admissibility of the resulting evidence, are now beyond the Court of Appeals' scope of review. People v. Miguel, 53 N.Y.2d 920, 440 N.Y.S.2d 923, 423 N.E.2d 400 (1981).

Probable cause determination; beyond review.—A probable cause determination, involving mixed questions of law and fact, is beyond the review powers of the Court of Appeals in those instances where conflicting inferences may be drawn from the evidence. People v. Ortiz, 64 N.Y.2d 997, 489 N.Y.S.2d 46, 478 N.E.2d 187 (1985).

Sentence.—Although the Court of Appeals is not permitted to review the appropriateness of a sentence, a question of law reviewable by it is presented where the issue is one of the power of the court below to impose the particular sentence. People v. Jones, 39 N.Y.2d 694, 385 N.Y.S.2d 525, 350 N.E.2d 913 (1976).

Suppression of statements; mixed question of law and

fact.—An appeal to the Court of Appeals did not lie from an Appellate Division finding that two statements by the defendant were the result of such continuous interrogation that the subsequently administered *Miranda* warnings were insufficient to protect his rights; such determination was a mixed question of law and fact and was not based upon the law alone or upon the law and such facts which, but for the determination of law, would not have led to reversal. People v. Mayorga, 64 N.Y.2d 864, 487 N.Y.S.2d 548, 476 N.E.2d 993 (1985).

—The finding that the statements in question were not sufficiently attenuated from the initial unlawful search presented a mixed question of law and fact that was beyond the scope of review of the Court of Appeals. People v. Benthall, 65 N.Y.2d 679, 491 N.Y.S.2d 617, 481 N.E.2d 249 (1985).

Trial court errors.—Reversal was required where trial court prohibited defendants from conferring with their attorney during trial and denied counsel's request to be removed as defendants counsel when he was required to testify as a witness at the trial. People v. Smith, 34 N.Y.2d 758, 358 N.Y.S.2d 135, 314 N.E.2d 875 (1974).

§ 470.40. Determination by court of appeals of appeals from intermediate appellate courts; corrective action upon reversal or modification.

1. Upon reversing or modifying an order of an intermediate appellate court affirming a criminal court judgment, sentence or order, the court of appeals must take or direct such corrective action as the intermediate appellate court would, pursuant to section 470.20, have been required or authorized to take or direct had it reversed or modified the criminal court judgment, sentence or order upon the same ground or grounds.

2. Upon reversing an order of an intermediate appellate court reversing or modifying a criminal court judgment, sentence or order upon the ground that questions of law were erroneously determined by the intermediate appellate court in favor of the party appellant therein, the court of appeals must take or direct corrective action as follows:

(a) If the facts underlying the original criminal court judgment, sentence or order were considered and determined to have been established by the intermediate appellate court, the court of appeals must reinstate and affirm the original criminal court judgment, sentence or order and remit the case to such criminal court for whatever further proceedings may be necessary to complete the action or proceedings therein; provided, however, that where such facts were applied to an erroneous determination of law, the court of appeals may remit the case to the intermediate appellate court for a further determination of the facts;

(b) If the facts underlying the original criminal court judgment, sentence or order were not, or are presumed not to have been, considered and determined by the intermediate appellate court, the court of appeals must remit the case to such intermediate appellate court for determination of the facts.

3. Upon modifying an intermediate appellate

court order reversing or modifying a criminal court judgment or order, upon the ground that corrective action taken or directed by the intermediate appellate court was illegal, the court of appeals must either (a) itself take or direct the appropriate corrective action or (b) remit the case to the intermediate appellate court for appropriate corrective action by the latter.

Amended by L. 1979, Ch. 651.

ANNOTATIONS

Case required to be remitted to appellate division pursuant to statute.—Charge of criminal possession of a weapon, second degree, which was factually related to murder charge, was required to first be remitted to the appellate division pursuant to CPL § 470.40 where murder conviction was reversed. People v. Cohen, 50 N.Y.2d 908, 431 N.Y.S.2d 446, 409 N.E.2d 921 (1980), *cert. denied,* 461 U.S. 930 (1983).

Facts.—The Court of Appeals is without power to review determinations of fact unless it can be said, as a matter of law, that they are unsupported, or that they are incredible. People v. Gruttola, 43 N.Y.2d 116, 400 N.Y.S.2d 788, 371 N.E.2d 506 (1977).

New trial based on Appellate Division holding.—A new trial was ordered where defendant was convicted on charges that grew out of two separate criminal incidents, two days apart, and the Appellate Division dismissed the counts relating to the first episode and remanded for resentencing since the evidence on the dismissed counts would not have been admitted against defendant on the second charge if he had been tried on that count alone. People v. Castillo, 47 N.Y.2d 270, 417 N.Y.S.2d 915, 391 N.E.2d 997 (1979).

Reversal on law alone.—Case was remitted to the Appellate Division for determination of the facts where reversal at the Appellate Division was on the law alone; also, since disposition at the Appellate Division was predicated on the erroneous resolution of a single issue of law, on remittal, the Appellate Division should consider any other legal issues the defendant may be entitled and choose to raise. People v. Coonan, 48 N.Y.2d 772, 423 N.Y.S.2d 914, 399 N.E.2d 944 (1979).

Review power.—The Appellate Court's use of its evidence review power must be present, although it is not required to be in writing. Where the Court of Appeals finds that the Appellate Court did not use its review power, the court will remit the case. People v. Bleakley, 69 N.Y.2d 490, 515 N.Y.S.2d 761, 508 N.E.2d 672 (1987).

Standard of review for intermediate appellate court.—The issue for an intermediate appellate court involves only a legal assessment of whether inferences of guilt could be rationally drawn from proven facts, and not a substituted fact-finding reassessment of the persuasiveness of the evidence. People v. Taylor, 94 N.Y.2d 910, 707 N.Y.S.2d 618, 729 N.E.2d 337 (2000).

§ 470.45. Remission of case by appellate court to criminal court upon reversal or modification of judgment; action by criminal court.

Upon reversing or modifying a judgment and directing corrective action, an appellate court must remit the case to the criminal court in which the judgment was entered. Such criminal court must execute the direction of the appellate court and must, depending upon the nature of such direction, either discharge the defendant from custody, exonerate his bail or issue a securing order.

§ 470.50. Reargument of appeal; motion and criteria for.

1. After its determination of an appeal taken pursuant to article four hundred fifty, an appellate court, in the interest of justice and for good cause shown, may in its discretion, upon motion of a party adversely affected by its determination, or upon its own motion, order a reargument or reconsideration of the appeal. Upon such an order the court may either direct further oral argument by the parties or confine its reconsideration to re-examination of the issues as previously argued or submitted upon the appeal proper. Upon ordering a reargument or reconsideration of an appeal, the court must again determine the appeal pursuant to the provisions of this article.

2. The court of appeals may promulgate rules limiting the time within which a motion for reargument of appeals determined by such court may be made, and the appellate division of each department may similarly promulgate such rules with respect to appeals determined by such appellate division and appeals determined by the other intermediate appellate courts located within such department. In the absence of any such rule of limitation, a motion for reargument may be made at any time.

ANNOTATIONS

Coram nobis.—Defendant's motion for reargument based on his claim of ineffective counsel was not properly made before the court. Defendant's motion warranted review pursuant to coram nobis proceedings. People v. Bachert, 69 N.Y.2d 593, 516 N.Y.S.2d 623, 509 N.E.2d 318 (1987).

Generally.—Where defendant's counsel failed to timely object to the court's charge to the jury and to the jury requests, the issues were not reviewable by the court. People v. Williams, 171 A.D.2d 551, 567 N.Y.S.2d 263 (1st Dept. 1991).

—Motion for reargument may not encompass new questions which were not addressed in the parties' briefs. Rather, where the court overlooks or misconstrues a point, the party may move to reargue. People v. Ramos, 108 A.D.2d 209, 488 N.Y.S.2d 762 (2d Dept. 1985).

§ 470.55. Status of accusatory instrument upon order of new trial or restoration of action to pre-pleading status.

1. Upon a new trial of an accusatory instrument resulting from an appellate court order reversing a judgment and ordering such new trial, such accusatory instrument is deemed to contain all the counts and to charge all the offenses which it contained and charged at the time the previous trial was commenced, regardless of whether any count was dismissed by the court in the course of such trial, except (a) those upon or of which the defendant was acquitted or deemed to have been acquitted, and (b) those dismissed upon appeal or upon some other post-judgment order.

2. Upon an appellate court order which reverses a judgment based upon a plea of guilty to an accusatory instrument or a part thereof, but

which does not dismiss the entire accusatory instrument, the criminal action is, in the absence of express appellate court direction to the contrary, restored to its pre-pleading status and the accusatory instrument is deemed to contain all the counts and to charge all the offenses which it contained and charged at the time of the entry of the plea, except those dismissed upon appeal or upon some other post-judgment order. Where the plea of guilty was entered and accepted, pursuant to subdivision three of section 220.30, upon the condition that it constituted a complete disposition and dismissal not only of the accusatory instrument underlying the judgment reversed but also of one or more other accusatory instruments against the defendant then pending in the same court, the appellate court order of reversal completely restores such other accusatory instruments; and such is the case even where the order of reversal dismisses the entire accusatory instrument underlying the judgment reversed.

ANNOTATIONS

Defendant could not be retried for manslaughter after acquittal on murder charge.—Defendant could not be retried on manslaughter charges where he was indicted for murder in the second degree, was acquitted of that charge but convicted on lesser included charge of manslaughter, and where appellate court reversed such manslaughter conviction; indictment as to murder charge had to be dismissed because of jury acquittal and there was no other charge remaining that would support further prosecution for manslaughter. People v. Gonzalez, 61 N.Y.2d 633, 471 N.Y.S.2d 847, 459 N.E.2d 1285 (1983).

Dismissal of count; after verdict.—Where the trial court dismissed the charges of criminal possession of a weapon and reckless endangerment against the defendant, the defendant may be tried on all counts during his new trial. The defendant was not acquitted of the charges. People v. Jamerson, 99 A.D.2d 816, 472 N.Y.S.2d 148 (2d Dept. 1984).

Retrial.—Upon retrial, the defendant was treated as if the first trial had not occurred. Thus, the People were obligated to provide alleged *Rosario* material to the defense. People v. Watkins, 189 A.D.2d 623, 592 N.Y.S.2d 347 (1st Dept. 1993).

—Following the reversal of a case, the trial court must adhere to the Appellate Division's instructions relating to retrial and prior rulings. People v. Baba-Ali, 154 Misc. 2d 389, 585 N.Y.S.2d 298 (Sup. Ct. Queens Co. 1992).

§ 470.60. Dismissal of appeal.

1. At any time after an appeal has been taken and before determination thereof, the appellate court in which such appeal is pending may, upon motion of the respondent or upon its own motion, dismiss such appeal upon the ground of mootness, lack of jurisdiction to determine it, failure of timely prosecution or perfection thereof, or other substantial defect, irregularity or failure of action by the appellant with respect to the prosecution or perfection of such appeal.

2. Such motion must be made upon reasonable notice to the appellant and with opportunity to be heard. If the people are the appellant, such notice must be served upon the appropriate district attorney either personally or by ordinary mail. If the appellant is a defendant, such notice must be served upon him by ordinary mail at his last known place of residence or, if he is imprisoned, at the institution in which he is confined, and similar notice must be served upon the attorney, if any, who last appeared for him. Upon determination of the motion, a copy of the order entered thereon must similarly be served.

3. Provided that a certificate granting leave to appeal is issued pursuant to this subdivision, an appeal may be taken, in the manner prescribed in subdivision four of section 460.10, to the court of appeals from an order of an intermediate appellate court dismissing an appeal thereto. Such appeal may be based either upon the ground that the dismissal was invalid as a matter of law or upon the ground that it constituted an abuse of discretion. A certificate granting leave to appeal from such an order of dismissal may be issued only by a judge of the court of appeals upon an application made in the manner prescribed in paragraph (b) of subdivision three of section 460.20. Upon such an appeal, the court of appeals must either affirm or reverse the intermediate appellate court order.

ANNOTATIONS

Motion to dismiss; permission.—Motion to quash a subpoena involved in a criminal proceeding is not reviewable on direct appeal. A judge of the Court of Appeals must give permission to appeal from the order of the Appellate Division. People v. Santos, 64 N.Y.2d 702, 485 N.Y.S.2d 524, 474 N.E.2d 1192 (1984).

—Where the Appellate Division orders dismissal of an appeal, the Court of Appeals judge is authorized to issue a certificate granting leave to appeal the Appellate Division's order. People v. Garofalo, 49 N.Y.2d 879, 427 N.Y.S.2d 990, 405 N.E.2d 233 (1980).

Prompt prosecution.—People are not required to personally serve their brief upon the defendant. Defendant and his counsel may be served through ordinary mail service at the last known address. People v. Ramos, 85 N.Y.2d 678, 628 N.Y.S.2d 27, 651 N.E.2d 895 (1995).

—Defendant is allowed to move to dismiss an appeal for lack of prosecution. The People are primarily responsible for ensuring that the defendant is promptly prosecuted. People v. Rothman, 118 A.D.2d 738, 500 N.Y.S.2d 270 (2d Dept. 1986).

—Defendant was not denied his constitutional rights to a speedy trial and due process where, although the People were allegedly tardy, defendant had the opportunity to move to dismiss the appeal due to lack of prosecution. People v. Finley, 107 A.D.2d 709, 484 N.Y.S.2d 63 (2d Dept. 1985).

PART THREE—SPECIAL PROCEEDINGS AND MISCELLANEOUS PROCEDURES

TITLE P—PROCEDURES FOR SECURING ATTENDANCE AT CRIMINAL ACTIONS AND PROCEEDINGS OF DEFENDANTS AND WITNESSES UNDER CONTROL OF COURT—RECOGNIZANCE BAIL AND COMMITMENT

ARTICLE 500—RECOGNIZANCE, BAIL AND COMMITMENT— DEFINITIONS OF TERMS

Section
500.10   Recognizance, bail and commitment; definitions of terms.

LexisNexis Cross References

Criminal Law Advocacy, Vol. 1, Ch. 5, Bail; *Criminal Defense Techniques,* Vol. 1, Ch. 1, The Bail Reform Act of 1984; Vol. 5, Ch. 102, Bail; *New York Criminal Practice (2d ed.),* Vol. 1, Ch. 13, Bail, Recognizance and Commitment; *Criminal Practice Handbook (2d ed.),* Ch. 2, Bail, Arraignment, and Lower Court Practice.

§ 500.10. Recognizance, bail and commitment; definitions of terms.

As used in this title, and in this chapter generally, the following terms have the following meanings:

1. "Principal" means a defendant in a criminal action or proceeding, or a person adjudged a material witness therein, or any other person so involved therein that he may by law be compelled to appear before a court for the purpose of having such court exercise control over his person to secure his future attendance at the action or proceeding when required, and who in fact either is before the court for such purpose or has been before it and been subjected to such control.

2. "Release on own recognizance." A court releases a principal on his own recognizance when, having acquired control over his person, it permits him to be at liberty during the pendency of the criminal action or proceeding involved upon condition that he will appear threat whenever his attendance may be required and will at all times render himself amenable to the orders and processes of the court.

3. "Fix bail." A court fixes bail when, having acquired control over the person of a principal, it designates a sum of money and stipulates that, if bail in such amount is posted on behalf of the principal and approved, it will permit him to be at liberty during the pendency of the criminal action or proceeding involved.

4. "Commit to the custody of the sheriff." A court commits a principal to the custody of the sheriff when, having acquired control over his person, it orders that he be confined in the custody of the sheriff during the pendency of the criminal action or proceeding involved.

5. "Securing order" means an order of a court committing a principal to the custody of the sheriff, or fixing bail, or releasing him on his own recognizance.

6. "Order of recognizance or bail" means a securing order releasing a principal on his own recognizance or fixing bail.

7. "Application for recognizance or bail" means an application by a principal that the court, instead of committing him to or retaining him in the custody of the sheriff, either release him on his own recognizance or fix bail.

8. "Post bail" means to deposit bail in the amount and form fixed by the court, with the court or with some other authorized public servant or agency.

9. "Bail" means cash bail or a bail bond.

10. "Cash bail" means a sum of money, in the amount designated in an order fixing bail, posted by a principal or by another person on his behalf with a court or other authorized public servant or agency, upon the condition that such money will become forfeit to the people of the state of New York if the principal does not comply with the directions of a court requiring his attendance at the criminal action or proceeding involved or does not otherwise render himself amenable to the orders and processes of the court.

11. "Obligor" means a person who executes a bail bond on behalf of a principal and thereby

assumes the undertaking described therein. The principal himself may be an obligor.

12. "Surety" means an obligor who is not a principal.

13. "Bail bond" means a written undertaking, executed by one or more obligors, that the principal designated in such instrument will, while at liberty as a result of an order fixing bail and of the posting of the bail bond in satisfaction thereof, appear in a designated criminal action or proceeding when his attendance is required and otherwise render himself amenable to the orders and processes of the court, and that in the event that he fails to do so the obligor or obligors will pay to the people of the state of New York a specified sum of money, in the amount designated in the order fixing bail.

14. "Appearance bond" means a bail bond in which the only obligor is the principal.

15. "Surety bond" means a bail bond in which the obligor or obligors consist of one or more sureties or of one or more sureties and the principal.

16. "Insurance company bail bond" means a surety bond, executed in the form prescribed by the superintendent of insurance, in which the surety-obligor is a corporation licensed by the superintendent of insurance to engage in the business of executing bail bonds.

17. "Secured bail bond" means a bail bond secured by either:

(a) Personal property which is not exempt from execution and which, over and above all liabilities and encumbrances, has a value equal to or greater than the total amount of the undertaking; or

(b) Real property having a value of at least twice the total amount of the undertaking. For purposes of this paragraph, value of real property is determined by dividing the last assessed value of such property by the last given equalization rate or in a special assessing unit, as defined in article eighteen of the real property tax law, the appropriate class ratio established pursuant to section twelve hundred two of such law of the assessing municipality wherein the property is situated and by deducting from the resulting figure the total amount of any liens or other encumbrances upon such property.

18. "Partially secured bail bond" means a bail bond secured only by a deposit of a sum of money not exceeding ten percent of the total amount of the undertaking.

19. "Unsecured bail bond" means a bail bond, other than an insurance company bail bond, not secured by any deposit of or lien upon property.

20. "Court" includes, where appropriate, a judge authorized to act as described in a particular statute, though not as a court.

Amended by L. 1992, Ch. 316, eff. Nov. 1, 1992, amending subd.(17)(b).

ANNOTATIONS

Bail; class action; constitutionality.—There was no proper basis here for bringing a class action charging that present bail laws are unconstitutional, since every bail application is determined on an individual basis. Bellamy v. Judges & Justices of the N.Y.C., Crim. Ct., 41 A.D.2d 196, 342 N.Y.S.2d 137 (1st Dept.), *aff'd*, 32 N.Y.2d 886, 346 N.Y.S.2d 812, 300 N.E.2d 153 (1973).

Bail; remittance.—Parents and grandparent of the defendant held to be indemnitors where those individuals merely posted the security rather than actually executed a bail bond. Thus, bail is not required to be remitted. Van Deusen v. People, 97 A.D.2d 924, 470 N.Y.S.2d 770 (3d Dept. 1983).

Bond; sufficiency.—Where the defendant is ordered to file a "fully secured surety company bond" for a certain amount, the bond must be secured by property worth twice that amount. Failure to do so renders that bond insufficient. People v. Sherman, 132 Misc. 2d 15, 502 N.Y.S.2d 914 (Sup. Ct. N.Y. Co. 1986).

Constitutionality.—The requirement that the value of real property must be worth twice the amount of undertaking, when real property is used as a security, is not unconstitutional. The differential treatment of real property and personal property is rational. People *ex rel.* Hardy v. Sielaff, 79 N.Y.2d 618, 584 N.Y.S.2d 742, 595 N.E.2d 817 (1992).

Denial of bail; likelihood of flight.—Bail may be denied where Court determines that defendant, if released on bail, would be likely to flee the jurisdiction, especially after consideration of the nature of the offense wherein an unusually large amount of drugs and money are involved, the probability of conviction and resulting severity of sentence. People *ex rel.* Parker v. Hasenauer, 62 N.Y.2d 777, 477 N.Y.S.2d 320, 465 N.E.2d 1256 (1984).

ARTICLE 510—RECOGNIZANCE, BAIL AND COMMITMENT— DETERMINATION OF APPLICATION FOR RECOGNIZANCE OR BAIL, ISSUANCE OF SECURING ORDERS, AND RELATED MATTERS

LexisNexis Cross References

Criminal Law Advocacy, Vol. 1, Ch. 5, Bail; *Criminal Defense Techniques,* Vol. 1, Ch. 1, The Bail Reform Act of 1984; Vol. 5, Ch. 102, Bail; *New York Criminal Practice (2d ed.),* Vol. 1, Ch. 13, Bail, Recognizance and Commitment; *Criminal Practice Handbook (2d ed.),* Ch. 2, Bail, Arraignment, and Lower Court Practice.

§ 510.10. Securing order; when required.

When a principal, whose future court attendance at a criminal action or proceeding is or may be required, initially comes under the control of a court, such court must, by a securing order, either release him on his own recognizance, fix bail or commit him to the custody of the sheriff. When a securing order is revoked or otherwise terminated in the course of an uncompleted action or proceeding but the principal's future court attendance still is or may be required and he is still under the control of a court, a new securing order must be issued. When the court revokes or otherwise terminates a securing order which committed the principal to the custody of the sheriff, the court shall give written notification to the sheriff of such revocation or termination of the securing order.

Amended by L. 1984, Ch. 459.

ANNOTATIONS

Production; principle.—The City of Yonkers law enforcement officials are required to perform any legal mandates or criminal processes issued by the city court, and no exception regarding orders affecting the transportation of principals appears. *In re* Delaney, 75 A.D.2d 642, 427 N.Y.S.2d 284 (2d Dept. 1980).

Transportation; principle.—When a motion for change of venue has been granted, the order must include a provision for transfer of custody by the sheriff or other appropriate public servant. The purpose of this requirement is to enable the public servant of the transferee county to carry out the statutory duty of transporting and producing the defendant in that country's superior court. People v. Boudin, 100 A.D.2d 266, 474 N.Y.S.2d 70 (2d Dept. 1984).

Custody; principle.—The sheriff is mandated to retain custody of lawfully remanded prisoners, as the court's functions do not entail retaining custody of prisoners. Howell v. McGinity, 129 A.D.2d 60, 516 N.Y.S.2d 694 (2d Dept. 1987).

§ 510.15. Commitment of principal under sixteen.

1. When a principal who is under the age of sixteen is committed to the custody of the sheriff the court must direct that the principal be taken to and lodged in a place certified by the state division for youth as a juvenile detention facility for the reception of children. Where such a direction is made the sheriff shall deliver the principal in accordance therewith and such person shall although lodged and cared for in a juvenile detention facility continue to be deemed to be in the custody of the sheriff. No principal under the age of sixteen to whom the provisions of this section may apply shall be detained in any prison, jail, lockup, or other place used for adults convicted of a crime or under arrest and charged with the commission of a crime without the approval of the state division for youth in the case of each principal and the statement of its reasons therefor. The sheriff shall not be liable for any acts done to or by such principal resulting from negligence in the detention of and care for such principal, when the principal is not in the actual custody of the sheriff.

2. Except upon consent of the defendant or for good cause shown, in any case in which a new securing order is issued for a principal previously committed to the custody of the sheriff pursuant to this section, such order shall further direct the sheriff to deliver the principal from a juvenile detention facility to the person or place specified in the order.

Added by L. 1978, Ch. 481; **Amended** by L. 1979, Ch. 411; L. 1980, Ch. 359.

§ 510.20. Application for recognizance or bail; making and determination thereof in general.

1. Upon any occasion when a court is required to issue a securing order with respect to a principal, or at any time when a principal is confined in the custody of the sheriff as a result of a previously issued securing order, he may make an application for recognizance or bail.

2. Upon such application, the principal must be accorded an opportunity to be heard and to contend that an order of recognizance or bail must or should issue, that the court should release him on his own recognizance rather than fix bail, and that if bail is fixed it should be in a suggested amount and form.

ANNOTATIONS

Bail; determination.—The County court's determination of bail constituted an exercise of discretion with a rational basis, and should not have been disturbed. People *ex rel.* Moore v. Bednosky, 198 A.D.2d 251, 604 N.Y.S.2d 807 (2d Dept. 1993).

Bail; parolee detainer warrant.—Statute authorizes release on bail only in criminal action or proceeding and parolee arrested on warrant for retaking and detaining prior to revocation hearing is neither involved in criminal action nor proceeding so that court could not release him on bail. People v. *ex rel.* Gatti v. Amico, 39 A.D.2d 826, 333 N.Y.S.2d 103 (4th Dept.), *app. dismissed,* 30 N.Y.2d 955, 335 N.Y.S.2d 705, 287 N.E.2d 394 (1972).

§ 510.30. Application for recognizance or bail; rules of law and criteria controlling determination.

1. Determinations of applications for recognizance or bail are not in all cases discretionary but are subject to rules, prescribed in article five hundred thirty and other provisions of law relating to specific kinds of criminal actions and proceedings, providing (a) that in some circumstances such an application must as a matter of law be granted, (b) that in others it must as a matter of law be denied and the principal committed to or retained in the custody of the sheriff, and (c) that in others the granting or denial thereof is a matter of judicial discretion.

2. To the extent that the issuance of an order of recognizance or bail and the terms thereof are matters of discretion rather than of law, an application is determined on the basis of the following factors and criteria:

(a) With respect to any principal, the court must consider the kind and degree of control or restriction that is necessary to secure his court attendance when required. In determining that matter, the court must, on the basis of available information, consider and take into account:

(i) The principal's character, reputation, habits and mental condition;

(ii) His employment and financial resources; and

(iii) His family ties and the length of his residence if any in the community; and

(iv) His criminal record if any; and

(v) His record of previous adjudication as a juvenile delinquent, as retained pursuant to section 354.2 of the family court act, or, of pending cases where fingerprints are retained pursuant to section 306.1 of such act, or a youthful offender, if any; and

(vi) His previous record if any in responding to court appearances when required or with respect to flight to avoid criminal prosecution; and

(vii) If he is a defendant, the weight of the evidence against him in the pending criminal action and any other factor indicating probability or improbability of conviction; or, in the case of an application for bail or recognizance pending appeal, the merit or lack of merit of the appeal; and

(viii) If he is a defendant, the sentence which may be or has been imposed upon conviction.

(b) Where the principal is a defendant-appellant in a pending appeal from a judgment of conviction, the court must also consider the likelihood of ultimate reversal of the judgment. A determination that the appeal is palpably without merit alone justifies, but does not require, a denial of the application, regardless of any determination made with respect to the factors specified in paragraph (a).

3. When bail or recognizance is ordered, the court shall inform the principal, if he is a defendant charged with the commission of a felony, that the release is conditional and that the court may revoke the order of release and commit the principal to the custody of the sheriff in accordance with the provisions of subdivision two of section 530.60 of this chapter if he commits a subsequent felony while at liberty upon such order.

Amended by L. 1977, Ch. 447; L. 1979, Ch. 411; L. 1981, Ch. 788; L. 1982, Ch. 920.

ANNOTATIONS

Bail; discretion.—City court judge was disbarred for misconduct, including a pattern of setting exorbitant and punitive bail and jailing defendants in lieu of bail for offenses that rarely, if at all, carry jail sentences upon conviction. *In re* Bauer, 3 N.Y.3d 158, 785 N.Y.S.2d 372, 818 N.E.2d 1113 (2004).

—The court acted within its discretion in denying bail to a foreign defendant and by setting bail at $150,000 to another defendant based upon the likelihood of conviction and their links to a terrorist organization. People *ex rel.* Lazer v. Warden, New York County Men's House of Detention, 79 N.Y.2d 839, 580 N.Y.S.2d 183, 588 N.E.2d 81 (1992).

—Judge was removed from office where, among other misconduct, he arbitrarily required defendants to post bail without inquiry or reference to the statutory standards. Sardino v. State Commission on Judicial Conduct, 58 N.Y.2d 286, 461 N.Y.S.2d 229, 448 N.E.2d 83 (1983).

—The court did not exceed its discretion by denying bail to defendant based upon the potential sentence, defendant's status as a repeat felon, alleged ties to organized crime, and defendant's's accessability to an ample amount of monetary resources. People *ex rel.* Capparelli v. McGrane, 189 A.D.2d 561, 592 N.Y.S.2d 15 (1st Dept. 1993).

—A court may not undertake a de novo determination of bail in collateral proceedings. People *ex rel.* Siegel v. Sielaff, 182 A.D.2d 389, 582 N.Y.S.2d 131 (1st Dept. 1992).

—The court was within its discretion by conditioning bail to a defendant, by requiring his presence in the jurisdiction and weekly reports to a supervisor program, based upon defendant's community ties, record of employment, and lack of a criminal record. State *ex rel.* Ray v. Warden, Brooklyn House of Detention for Men, 184 A.D.2d 477, 585 N.Y.S.2d 424 (1st Dept. 1992).

—The trial court was within its discretion in setting conditional bail of $500,000 based upon defendant's involvement in a drug smuggling operation, defendant's failure to present any feasible defenses, and the inability of the court to determine the defendant's past United States residence or ties to the community. People *ex rel.* Washer v. Freckelton, 187 A.D.2d 406, 590 N.Y.S.2d 203 (1st Dept. 1992).

—The court abused its discretion in denying bail, in the sum of $300,000, to defendant who was charged with murder with depraved indifference because of defendant's close community ties, minimal record, defendant's surrendering of his passport, and daily reporting to the police. People *ex rel.* Tannuzzo v. New York City, 174 A.D.2d 446, 571 N.Y.S.2d 231 (1st Dept. 1991).

—The court exceeded its discretion in setting bail based upon the likelihood of defendant being convicted, rather than focusing upon the great probability of defendant appearing in court. People *ex rel.* Benton v. Warden: New York City House of Detention for Men, East Elmhurst, New York, 118 A.D.2d 443, 499 N.Y.S.2d 738 (1st Dept. 1986).

—Court did not abuse its discretion in revoking defendant's bail, which had been set for a previous offense, after his rearrest, in light of the seriousness of the crimes with which defendant was charged and the probability of his conviction. People *ex rel.* Ortiz v. Commissioner of Corrections, 76 A.D.2d 818, 429 N.Y.S.2d 26 (1st Dept. 1980).

—The court is within its discretion by rationally setting bail based upon the offenses, possibility of flight, and probability and severity of conviction. Moreover, a habeas court may not substitute its own discretion and reduce the set bail. Mascia v. Jacquin, 184 A.D.2d 542, 586 N.Y.S.2d 901 (2d Dept. 1992); People *ex rel.* Brown v. Bednosky, 190 A.D.2d 836, 593 N.Y.S.2d 859 (2d Dept. 1993).

—The court has the discretion to set bail at $50,000 for a defendant accused of a Class D felony, when the defendant had a criminal record, faced possible conviction as a second felony criminal, and was free on bail, for a different charge, at the time the crime was committed. People *ex rel.* Robinson v. Campbell, 184 A.D.2d 988, 585 N.Y.S.2d 604 (3d Dept. 1992).

—The re-setting of bail in the amount of $10,000 after initially set at $4,500 was an arbitrary abuse of discretion, as the record does not sufficiently demonstrate the factors used in determining the amount required for bail. As the purpose of bail is to assure defendant's appearance, the prosecution must demonstrate a rational need for a higher bail. People *ex rel.* Ryan v. Infante, 108 A.D.2d 987, 485 N.Y.S.2d 852 (3d Dept. 1985).

Bail; defendant's finances.—The court is required to take into account the defendant's financial situation, along with the other factors enumerated in the CPL in setting bail. People *ex rel.* Mordkofsky v. Stancari, 93 A.D.2d 826, 460 N.Y.S.2d 830 (2d Dept. 1983).

Bail; re-setting.—The court is estopped from re-setting bail solely because the defendant objected to the condition of finding her co-defendant brother. People *ex rel.* Ryan v. Infante, 108 A.D.2d 987, 485 N.Y.S.2d 852 (3d Dept. 1985).

Bail; record.—The court is required to state, in the record, its reasons for increasing bail, as per the factors set forth in the CPL. People *ex rel.* Meyer v. Commissioner of the Dept. of Correction of the City of New York, 119 A.D.2d 472, 500 N.Y.S.2d 684 (1st Dept. 1986).

Bail; secured appearance.—The court acted arbitrarily in denying bail as the defendant had always appeared for past court dates because the only concern in making bail determinations is securing the defendant's presence at trial. People *ex rel.* Masselli v. Levy, 126 A.D.2d 501, 511 N.Y.S.2d 236 (1st Dept. 1987).

—Where the defendant displays suicidal tendencies, the court is prohibited from equating this with an intent to not appear in court. People *ex rel.* Bryce v. Infante, 144 A.D.2d 898, 535 N.Y.S.2d 215 (3d Dept. 1988).

Bail; non-felony.—In some cases, the court improperly denied bail based on defendant's inability to establish his identity because the CPL does not mandate denial of bail based upon failure to establish one's identity in a non-felony case. In re Labelle, 79 N.Y.2d 350, 582 N.Y.S.2d 970, 591 N.E.2d 1156 (1992).

Bail; preventive detention.—The county court violated the standard set by the CPL by denying bail for preventive detention, as it is not one of the factors in § 510.30. Monquin v. Infante, 134 A.D.2d 764, 521 N.Y.S.2d 581 (3d Dept. 1987).

Bail; defendant's burden.—The trial court erred in reducing bail to $25,000 as defendant failed to demonstrate that bail in the amount of $105,000 was excessive. In determining bail, the court must factor in the defendant's illegal alien status, a possible sentence of 15 years to life if convicted, and the fact that defendant had fled after posting bail on three separate occasions. People *ex rel.* Morales v. Warden, 166 A.D.2d 626, 561 N.Y.S.2d 587 (2d Dept. 1990)

Bail; appeal.—Upon granting a stay of execution, the court should consider the likelihood of a reversal on appeal in setting or allowing bail. People v. Kern, 137 A.D.2d 862, 524 N.Y.S.2d 521 (2d Dept 1988).

Bail; alternatives.—The court may impose a condition on defendant to attend a drug rehabilitation program in lieu of bail. People v. Ellis, 162 A.D.2d 701, 558 N.Y.S.2d 82 (2d Dept. 1990).

§ 510.40. Application for recognizance or bail; determination thereof, form of securing order and execution thereof.

1. An application for recognizance or bail must be determined by a securing order which either:

(a) Grants the application and releases the principal on his own recognizance; or

(b) Grants the application and fixes bail; or

(c) Denies the application and commits the principal to, or retains him in, the custody of the sheriff.

2. Upon ordering that a principal be released on his own recognizance, the court must direct him to appear in the criminal action or proceeding involved whenever his attendance may be required and to render himself at all times amenable to the orders and processes of the court. If such principal is in the custody of the sheriff or at liberty upon bail at the time of the order, the court must direct that he be discharged from such custody or, as the case may be, that his bail be exonerated.

3. Upon the issuance of an order fixing bail, and upon the posting thereof, the court must examine the bail to determine whether it complies with the order. If it does, the court must, in the absence of some factor or circumstance which in law requires or authorizes disapproval thereof, approve the bail and must issue a certificate of release, authorizing the principal to be at liberty, and, if he is in the custody of the sheriff at the time, directing the sheriff to discharge him therefrom. If the bail fixed is not posted, or is not

approved after being posted, the court must order that the principal be committed to the custody of the sheriff.

ANNOTATIONS

Application; denial.—The court may mandate that the defendant be remanded into the custody of the sheriff, who is required to enforce and abide by the city court's mandate. City of Newburgh v. County of Orange, 105 Misc. 2d 986, 430 N.Y.S.2d 537 (Sup. Ct. Orange Co. 1980).

Release; recognizance.—Although the court is estopped from dismissing felony charges, the court may release the defendant on his own recognizance and exonerate the bail. People v. Leonardo, 141 Misc. 2d 526, 533 N.Y.S.2d 660 (Sup. Ct. Greene Co. 1988).

Bail; post and release.—County Court is authorized to examine both bail bond or cash bail posted to determine whether it complies with the court order of bail and to approve or disapprove the same; if approved, the court must issue a certificate of release, and if the defendant is in custody of the sheriff at the time, the court must direct the sheriff to discharge the defendant. People v. Pullara, 172 Misc. 2d 63, 656 N.Y.S.2d 832 (Nassau Co. Ct. 1997).

—The court must determine if the posted bail is for the stated amount and if so, then it issues a certificate that allows for the release of the principle from custody. In re Rayls, 156 Misc. 2d 268, 592 N.Y.S.2d 572 (Co. Ct. 1992).

§ 510.50. Enforcement of securing order.

When the attendance of a principal confined in the custody of the sheriff is required at the criminal action or proceeding at a particular time and place, the court may compel such attendance by directing the sheriff to produce him at such time and place. If the principal is at liberty on his own recognizance or on bail, his attendance may be achieved or compelled by various methods, including notification and the issuance of a bench warrant, prescribed by law in provisions governing such matters with respect to the particular kind of action or proceeding involved.

ANNOTATIONS

Principal; attendance.—The CPL places a statutory duty upon a public servant to transport and produce the principal. People v. Boudin, 100 A.D.2d 266, 474 N.Y.S.2d 70 (2d Dept. 1984).

—When the principal is required to appear before the court, the court may order the sheriff to compel such attendance by producing the principal. In re Delaney, 75 A.D.2d 642, 427 N.Y.S.2d 284 (2d Dept. 1980).

ARTICLE 520—BAIL AND BAIL BONDS

LexisNexis Cross References

Criminal Law Advocacy, Vol. 1, Ch. 5, Bail; *Criminal Defense Techniques,* Vol. 1, Ch. 1, The Bail Reform Act of 1984; Vol. 5, Ch. 102, Bail; *New York Criminal Practice (2d ed.),* Vol. 1, Ch. 13, Bail, Recognizance and Commitment; *Criminal Practice Handbook (2d ed.),* Ch. 2, Bail, Arraignment, and Lower Court Practice.

§ 520.10. Bail and bail bonds; fixing of bail and authorized forms thereof.

1. The only authorized forms of bail are the following:

(a) Cash bail.

(b) An insurance company bail bond.

(c) A secured surety bond.

(d) A secured appearance bond.

(e) A partially secured surety bond.

(f) A partially secured appearance bond.

(g) An unsecured surety bond.

(h) An unsecured appearance bond.

(i) [*Effective until Jan. 1, 2006.*] Credit card or similar device where the principal is charged with a violation under the vehicle and traffic law; provided, however, notwithstanding any other provision of law, any person posting bail by credit card or similar device also may be required to pay a reasonable administrative fee. The amount of such fee and the time and manner of its payment shall be in accordance with the system established pursuant to subdivision four of section 150.30 of this chapter or paragraph (i) of subdivision two of section two hundred twelve of the judiciary law, as appropriate.

(i) [*Effective Jan. 1, 2006, and repealed Aug. 9, 2010.*] Credit card or similar device; provided, however, that notwithstanding any other provision of law, any person posting bail by credit card or similar device also may be required to pay a reasonable administrative fee. The amount of such administrative fee and the time and manner of its payment shall be in accordance with the system established pursuant to subdivision four of section 150.30 of this chapter or paragraph (j) of subdivision two of section two hundred twelve of the judiciary law, as appropriate.

2. The methods of fixing bail are as follows:

(a) A court may designate the amount of the bail without designating the form or forms in which it may be posted. In such case, the bail may be posted in either of the forms specified in paragraphs (g) and (h) of subdivision one;

(b) The court may direct that the bail be posted in any one of two or more of the forms specified in subdivision one, designated in the alternative, and may designate different amounts varying with the forms;*

* Punctuation as originally enacted.

Amended by L. 1972, Ch. 784; L. 1986, Ch. 708; L. 1987, Ch. 805; L. 2005, Ch. 457, § 4, amending subd. 1(i), eff. Jan. 1, 2006, and amendment to expire five years after such date.

ANNOTATIONS

Bail; review on writ of habeas corpus.—The action of the bail-fixing court is nonappealable, but may be reviewed in a habeas corpus proceeding "if it appears that the constitutional or statutory standards inhibiting excessive bail or the arbitrary refusal of bail are violated"; the review is limited to the record before the *nisi prius* court. People *ex rel.* Rosenthal v. Wolfson, 48 N.Y.2d 230, 422 N.Y.S.2d 55, 397 N.E.2d 745 (1979).

Resetting bail improper.—Court reversed dismissal of petition for writ of habeas corpus where there was insufficient reason for resetting bail at $10,000 after initially setting it at $4,500; bail had been improperly raised when defendant objected to the requirement that she find and bring her co-defendant brother to court as a condition for the lower bail. People *ex rel.* Ryan v. Infante, 108 A.D.2d 987, 485 N.Y.S.2d 852 (3d Dept. 1985).

Bail; class action; constitutionality.—There was no proper basis here for bringing a class action charging that present bail laws are unconstitutional, since every bail application is determined on an individual basis. Bellamy v. Judges & Justices of the N.Y.C. Crim. Ct., 41 A.D.2d 196, 342 N.Y.S.2d 137 (1st Dept.), *aff'd,* 32 N.Y.2d 886, 346 N.Y.S.2d 812, 300 N.E.2d 153 (1973).

Bail; judicial review.—Since the legislature has allowed for stay of judgment pending appeal to intermediate court in certain instances, there is no legal basis for the claim that the bail system in New York fails to provide a prompt and meaningful procedure for judicial review of a bail determination. Bellamy v. Judges & Justices of the N.Y.C. Crim. Ct., 41 A.D.2d 196, 342 N.Y.S.2d 137 (1st Dept.), *aff'd,* 32 N.Y.2d 886, 346 N.Y.S.2d 812, 300 N.E.2d 153 (1973).

§ 520.15. Bail and bail bonds; posting of cash bail.

1. Where a court has fixed bail pursuant to subdivision two of section 520.10, at any time after the principal has been committed to the custody of the sheriff pending the posting thereof, cash bail in the amount designated in the order fixing bail may be posted even though such bail was not specified in such order. Cash bail may be deposited with (a) the county treasurer of the county in which the criminal action or proceeding is pending or, in the city of New York with the commissioner of finance, or (b) the court which issued such order, or (c) the sheriff in whose custody the principal has been committed. Upon proof of the deposit of the designated amount the principal must be forthwith released from custody.

2. The person posting cash bail must complete and sign a form which states (a) the name, residential address and occupation of each person posting cash bail; and (b) the title of the criminal action or proceeding involved; and (c) the offense or offenses which are the subjects of the action or proceeding involved, and the status of such action or proceeding; and (d) the name of the principal and the nature of his involvement in or connection with such action or proceeding; and (e) that the person or persons posting cash bail undertake that the principal will appear in such action or proceeding whenever required and will at all times render himself amenable to the orders and processes of the court; and (f) the date of the principal's next appearance in court; and (g) an acknowledgment that the cash bail will be forfeited if the principal does not comply with any requirement or order of process to appear in court; and (h) the amount of money posted as cash bail.

3. Money posted as cash bail is and shall remain the property of the person posting it unless forfeited to the court.

Amended by L. 1978, Ch. 655; L. 1984, Ch. 384.

ANNOTATIONS

Bail; financial records.—The District Attorney must be supplied with records that demonstrates the account from where the funds were withdrawn in order to post bail, whereby it may be determined if the money was obtained from an illegal activity. People v. Esquivel, 158 Misc. 2d 726, 601 N.Y.S.2d 541 (Sup. Ct. N.Y. Co. 1993).

Bail; release.—The sheriff, who may receive the bail, may not release the defendant upon deposit of the bail without the court's approval, because the sheriff is unable to set the defendant's next court date. In re Rayls, 156 Misc. 2d 268, 592 N.Y.S.2d 572 (Montgomery Co. Ct. 1992).

Bail; return.—Since the open court does not issue an order of appearance, the bail is to be returned to the party who posted the bail originally. People v. Salabarria, 121 A.D.2d 438, 503 N.Y.S.2d 411 (2d Dept. 1986).

Posted bail properly disapproved.—Court acted within its authority in disapproving the posted bail where the record was completely devoid of any testimony or evidence of how the two individuals posting bail would ensure the petitioner's appearance for all future court dates, which is the purpose of bail. People v. Baker, 188 Misc. 2d 821, 729 N.Y.S.2d 580 (Sup. Ct. N.Y. Co. 2001).

CPL § 510.40(3).—Any interpretation of CPL § 520.15(1) requiring forthwith release of the defendant prior to court approval would be inconsistent with CPL § 510.40(3); since both statutes are integral parts of the bail provision of the CPL, both sections must be read together and harmonized, if possible, to achieve a result giving effect to each one. People v. Pullara, 172 Misc. 2d 63, 656 N.Y.S.2d 832 (Nassau Co. Ct. 1997).

§ 520.20. Bail and bail bonds; posting of bail bond and justifying affidavits; form and contents thereof.

1. (a) Except as provided in paragraph (b) when a bail bond is to be posted in satisfaction of bail, the obligor or obligors must submit to the court a bail bond in the amount fixed, executed in the form prescribed in subdivision two, accompanied by a justifying affidavit of each obligor, executed in the form prescribed in subdivision four.

(b) When a bail bond is to be posted in satisfaction of bail fixed for a defendant charged by information or simplified information or prosecutor's information with one or more traffic infractions and no other offense, the defendant may submit to the court, with the consent of the court, an insurance company bail bond covering the amount fixed, executed in a form prescribed by the superintendent of insurance.

2. Except as provided in paragraph (b) of subdivision one, a bail bond must be subscribed and sworn to by each obligor and must state:

(a) The name, residential address and occupation of each obligor; and

(b) The title of the criminal action or proceeding involved; and

(c) The offense or offenses which are the subjects of the action or proceeding involved, and the status of such action or proceeding; and

(d) The name of the principal and the nature of his involvement in or connection with such action or proceeding; and

(e) That the obligor, or the obligors jointly and severally, undertake that the principal will appear in such action or proceeding whenever required and will at all times render himself amenable to the orders and processes of the court; and

(f) That in the event that the principal does not comply with any such requirement, order or process, such obligor or obligors will pay to the people of the state of New York a designated sum of money fixed by the court.

3. A bail bond posted in the course of a criminal action is effective and binding upon the obligor or obligors until the imposition of sentence or other termination of the action, regardless of whether the action is dismissed in the local criminal court after an indictment on the same charge or charges by a superior court, and regardless of whether such action is partially conducted

or prosecuted in a court or courts other than the one in which the action was pending when such bond was posted, unless prior to such termination such order of bail is vacated or revoked or the principal is surrendered, or unless the terms of such bond expressly limit its effectiveness to a lesser period; provided, however, the effectiveness of such bond may only be limited to a lesser period if the obligor or obligors submit notice of the limitation to the court and the district attorney not less than fourteen days before effectiveness ends.

4. A justifying affidavit must be subscribed and sworn to by the obligor-affiant and must state his name, residential address and occupation. Depending upon the kind of bail bond which it justifies, such affidavit must contain further statements as follows:

(a) An affidavit justifying an insurance company bail bond must state:

(i) The amount of the premium paid to the obligor; and

(ii) All security and all promises of indemnity received by the surety-obligor in connection with its execution of the bond, and the name, occupation and residential and business addresses of every person who has given any such indemnifying security or promise.

An action by the surety-obligor against an indemnitor, seeking retention of security deposited by the latter with the former or enforcement of any indemnity agreement of a kind described in this sub-paragraph, will not lie except with respect to agreements and security specified in the justifying affidavit.

(b) An affidavit justifying a secured bail bond must state every item of personal property deposited and of real property pledged as security, the value of each such item, and the nature and amount of every lien or encumbrance thereon.

(c) An affidavit justifying a partially secured bail bond or an unsecured bail bond must state the place and nature of the obligor-affiant's business or employment, the length of time he has been engaged therein, his income during the past year, and his average income over the past five years.

Amended by L. 1973, Ch. 927; L. 1974, Ch. 425; L. 1981, Chs. 145, 268.

ANNOTATIONS

Bail; improper judicial order.—The court's order to transfer bail without issuing a securing order is improper in form, but valid, and therefore remains binding in its force and effect. People v. Spampinato, 70 A.D.2d 647, 416 N.Y.S.2d 665 (2d Dept. 1979).

Bail; bondsman.—Bail bondsman are required to provide "posters" of the bail bonds in order to guarantee the defendant's attendance in court. People v. Castro, 119 Misc. 2d 787, 464 N.Y.S.2d 650 (Sup. Ct. Kings Co. 1983).

§ 520.30. Bail and bail bonds; examination as to sufficiency.

1. Following the posting of a bail bond and the justifying affidavit or affidavits or the posting of cash bail, the court may conduct an inquiry for the purpose of determining the reliability of the obligors or person posting cash bail, the value and sufficiency of any security offered, and whether any feature of the undertaking contravenes public policy; provided that before undertaking an inquiry, of a person posting cash bail the court, after application of the district attorney, must have had reasonable cause to believe that the person posting cash bail is not in rightful possession of money posted as cash bail or that such money constitutes the fruits of criminal or unlawful conduct. The court may inquire into any matter stated or required to be stated in the justifying affidavits, and may also inquire into other matters appropriate to the determination, which include but are not limited to the following:

(a) The background, character and reputation of any obligor, and, in the case of an insurance company bail bond, the qualifications of the surety-obligor and its executing agent; and

(b) The source of any money or property deposited by any obligor as security, and whether any such money or property constitutes the fruits of criminal or unlawful conduct; and

(c) The source of any money or property delivered or agreed to be delivered to any obligor as indemnification on the bond, and whether any such money or property constitutes the fruits of criminal or unlawful conduct; and

(d) The background, character and reputation of any person who has indemnified or agreed to indemnify an obligor upon the bond; and whether any such indemnitor, not being licensed by the superintendent of insurance in accordance with the insurance law, has within a period of one month prior to such indemnity transaction given indemnification or security for like purpose in more than two cases not arising out of the same transaction; and

(e) The source of any money posted as cash bail, and whether any such money constitutes the fruits of criminal or unlawful conduct; and

(f) The background, character and reputation of the person posting cash bail.

2. Upon such inquiry, the court may examine, under oath or otherwise, the obligors and any other persons who may possess material information. The district attorney has a right to attend such inquiry, to call witnesses and to examine any witness in the proceeding. The court may, upon application of the district attorney, adjourn the proceeding for a reasonable period to allow him to investigate the matter.

3. At the conclusion of the inquiry, the court

must issue an order either approving or disapproving the bail.

Amended by L. 1984, Ch. 384.

ANNOTATIONS

Denial of bail reduction.—The court's denial of a motion for bail reduction does not preempt a judge from conducting a hearing on the sufficiency of the collateral for the bail. People ex rel. Morales v. Warden, 166 A.D.2d 626, 561 N.Y.S.2d 587 (2d Dept. 1990).

Bail; purpose of.—Court acted within its authority in disapproving the posted bail where the record was completely devoid of any testimony or evidence of how the two individuals posting bail would ensure the petitioner's appearance for all future court dates, which is the purpose of bail. People v. Baker, 188 Misc. 2d 821, 729 N.Y.S.2d 580 (Sup. Ct. N.Y. Co. 2001).

Bail; source of.—The court is within its discretion to deny bail based upon its proposed surety and if the possibility exists that the funds were gained through illegal means. Furthermore, the court may deny bail based upon a transformation of a previously denied cash bond into a bail bond through payment of a premium. Johnson v. Crane, 171 A.D.2d 537, 568 N.Y.S.2d 22 (1st Dept. 1991).

Sufficiency hearing.—The court has the authority pursuant to CPL § 520.30 to order a sufficiency hearing for the purposes of determining the reliability of the obligor's securing the bail bond or the person posting cash bail, the value of sufficiency of any security offered, and whether any feature of the undertaking contravenes public policy. People v. Pullara, 172 Misc. 2d 63, 656 N.Y.S.2d 832 (Nassau Co. Ct. 1997).

Surety; transfer restriction.—The court denied use of property as collateral for bail, when a federal court order prohibited transfer of the property in question. People ex rel.

School v. Commissioner, New York City Dept. of Corrections; People ex rel. Hatch v. Commissioner, New York City Dept. of Corrections, 172 A.D.2d 432, 569 N.Y.S.2d 10 (1st Dept. 1991).

§ 520.40. Transfer of cash bail from local criminal to superior court.

When a local criminal court acquires control over the person of an accused and such court designates the amount of bail that the accused may post and such bail is posted in cash and subsequently the accused is arraigned in superior court where bail is fixed by such court, the accused may request that the cash bail posted in the local criminal court be transferred to the superior court. Notice of such request must be given to the person who posted cash bail. Upon such a request the superior court shall make an order directing the local criminal court to transfer the cash bail that it holds to the superior court for use in the superior court. If there is an overage, the superior court shall order it be paid over to the person who posted the cash bail in the local criminal court. If there is a deficiency, the accused shall post additional bail as directed by the superior court.

Added by L. 1974, Ch. 219; **Amended** by L. 1984, Ch. 384.

ARTICLE 530—ORDERS OF RECOGNIZANCE OR BAIL WITH RESPECT TO DEFENDANTS IN CRIMINAL ACTIONS AND PROCEEDINGS—WHEN AND BY WHAT COURTS AUTHORIZED

LexisNexis Cross References

Criminal Law Advocacy, Vol. 1, Ch. 5, Bail; *Criminal Defense Techniques,* Vol. 1, Ch. 1, The Bail Reform Act of 1984; Vol. 5, Ch. 102, Bail; *New York Criminal Practice (2d ed.),* Vol. 1, Ch. 13, Bail, Recognizance and Commitment; *Criminal Practice Handbook (2d ed.),* Ch. 2, Bail, Arraignment, and Lower Court Practice.

§ 530.10. Order of recognizance or bail; in general.

Under circumstances prescribed in this article, a court, upon application of a defendant charged with or convicted of an offense, is required or authorized to order bail or recognizance for the release or prospective release of such defendant during the pendency of either:

1. A criminal action based upon such charge; or

2. An appeal taken by the defendant from a judgment of conviction or a sentence or from an order of an intermediate appellate court affirming or modifying a judgment of conviction or a sentence.

ANNOTATIONS

Bail; parolee detainer warrant.—Statute authorizes release on bail only in criminal action or proceeding and parolee arrested on warrant for retaking and detaining prior to revocation hearing is neither involved in criminal action nor proceeding so that court could not release him on bail. People *ex rel.* Gatti v. Amico, 39 A.D.2d 826, 333 N.Y.S.2d 103 (4th Dept.), *app. dismissed,* 30 N.Y.2d 955, 335 N.Y.S.2d 705, 287 N.E.2d 394 (1972).

Bail; application.—Although the CPL requires that the bail application is to be made by the defendant, a third party may apply for bail, for an incarcerated party, if the judge is satisfied that the statutory procedures had been performed and that it was on behalf of the incarcerated party. People v. Tyler, 62 A.D.2d 146, 404 N.Y.S.2d 370 (2d Dept. 1978).

—Upon the introduction of an application the court is required to review and possibly grant the application. People v. Meredith, 152 Misc. 2d 387, 578 N.Y.S.2d 79 (Sup. Ct. Kings Co. 1991).

Bail; required.—Any time during a criminal investigation, the court may order a defendant to be held with or without bail. People v. McLees, 166 Misc. 2d 260, 631 N.Y.S.2d 990 (1st Dist. Suffolk Co. 1995).

§ 530.11. Procedures for family offense matters.

1. Jurisdiction. The family court and the criminal courts shall have concurrent jurisdiction over any proceeding concerning acts which would constitute disorderly conduct, harassment in the first degree, harassment in the second degree, aggravated harassment in the second degree, stalking in the first degree, stalking in the second degree, stalking in the third degree, stalking in the fourth degree, menacing in the second degree, menacing in the third degree, reckless endangerment, assault in the second degree, assault in the third degree or an attempted assault between spouses or former spouses, or between parent and child or between members of the same family or household except that if the respondent would not

be criminally responsible by reason of age pursuant to section 30.00 of the penal law, then the family court shall have exclusive jurisdiction over such proceeding. Notwithstanding a complainant's election to proceed in family court, the criminal court shall not be divested of jurisdiction to hear a family offense proceeding pursuant to this section. For purposes of this section, "disorderly conduct" includes disorderly conduct not in a public place. For purposes of this section, "members of the same family or household" with respect to a proceeding in the criminal courts shall mean the following:

(a) persons related by consanguinity or affinity;

(b) persons legally married to one another;

(c) persons formerly married to one another; and

(d) persons who have a child in common, regardless whether such persons have been married or have lived together at any time.

2. Information to petitioner or complainant. The chief administrator of the courts shall designate the appropriate probation officers, warrant officers, sheriffs, police officers, district attorneys or any other law enforcement officials, to inform any petitioner or complainant bringing a proceeding under this section before such proceeding is commenced, of the procedures available for the institution of family offense proceedings, including but not limited to the following:

(a) That there is concurrent jurisdiction with respect to family offenses in both family court and the criminal courts;

(b) That a family court proceeding is a civil proceeding and is for the purpose of attempting to stop the violence, end family disruption and obtain protection. That referrals for counseling, or counseling services, are available through probation for this purpose;

(c) That a proceeding in the criminal courts is for the purpose of prosecution of the offender and can result in a criminal conviction of the offender;

(d) That a proceeding or action subject to the provisions of this section is initiated at the time of the filing of an accusatory instrument or family court petition, not at the time of arrest, or request for arrest, if any;

(e) [Repealed by L. 1994, Ch. 222, § 35, eff. Jan. 1, 1995.]

(f) That an arrest may precede the commencement of a family court or a criminal court proceeding, but an arrest is not a requirement for commencing either proceeding.

(g) [Repealed by L. 1997, Ch. 186, § 7, eff. July 8, 1997.]

(h) At such time as the complainant first appears before the court on a complaint or information, the court shall advise the complainant that the complainant may: continue with the proceeding in criminal court; or have the allegations contained therein heard in a family court proceeding; or proceed concurrently in both criminal and family court. Notwithstanding a complainant's election to proceed in family court, the criminal court shall not be divested of jurisdiction to hear a family offense proceeding pursuant to this section;

(i) Nothing herein shall be deemed to limit or restrict complainant's rights to proceed directly and without court referral in either a criminal or family court, or both, as provided for in section one hundred fifteen of the family court act and section 100.07 of this chapter;

(j) [Repealed by L. 1997, Ch. 186, § 9, eff. July 8, 1997.]

2-a. Upon the filing of an accusatory instrument charging a crime or violation described in subdivision one of this section between members of the same family or household, as such terms are defined in this section, or as soon as the complainant first appears before the court, whichever is sooner, the court shall advise the complainant of the right to proceed in both the criminal and family courts, pursuant to section 100.07 of this chapter.

3. Official responsibility. No official or other person designated pursuant to subdivision two of this section shall discourage or prevent any person who wishes to file a petition or sign a complaint from having access to any court for that purpose.

4. When a person is arrested for an alleged family offense or an alleged violation of an order of protection or temporary order of protection or arrested pursuant to a warrant issued by the supreme or family court, and the supreme or family court, as applicable, is not in session, such person shall be brought before a local criminal court in the county of arrest or in the county in which such warrant is returnable pursuant to article one hundred twenty of this chapter. Such local criminal court may issue any order authorized under subdivision eleven of section 530.12 of this article, section one hundred fifty-four-d or one hundred fifty-five of the family court act or subdivision three-b of section two hundred forty or subdivision two-a of section two hundred fifty-two of the domestic relations law, in addition to discharging other arraignment responsibilities as set forth in this chapter. In making such order, the local criminal court shall consider the bail recommendation, if any, made by the supreme or family court as indicated on the warrant or certificate of warrant. Unless the petitioner or complainant requests otherwise, the court, in addition to scheduling further criminal proceedings, if any, regarding such alleged family offense or violation allegation, shall make such matter returnable in

the supreme or family court, as applicable, on the next day such court is in session.

5. Filing and enforcement of out-of-state orders of protection. A valid order of protection or temporary order of protection issued by a court of competent jurisdiction in another state, territorial or tribal jurisdiction shall be accorded full faith and credit and enforced as if it were issued by a court within the state for as long as the order remains in effect in the issuing jurisdiction in accordance with sections two thousand two hundred sixty-five and two thousand two hundred sixty-six of title eighteen of the United States Code.

(a) An order issued by a court of competent jurisdiction in another state, territorial or tribal jurisdiction shall be deemed valid if:

(i) the issuing court had personal jurisdiction over the parties and over the subject matter under the law of the issuing jurisdiction;

(ii) the person against whom the order was issued had reasonable notice and an opportunity to be heard prior to issuance of the order; provided, however, that if the order was a temporary order of protection issued in the absence of such person, that notice had been given and that an opportunity to be heard had been provided within a reasonable period of time after the issuance of the order; and

(iii) in the case of orders of protection or temporary orders of protection issued against both a petitioner, plaintiff or complainant and respondent or defendant, the order or portion thereof sought to be enforced was supported by: (A) a pleading requesting such order, including, but not limited to, a petition, cross-petition or counter-claim; and (B) a judicial finding that the requesting party is entitled to the issuance of the order which may result from a judicial finding of fact, judicial acceptance of an admission by the party against whom the order was issued or judicial finding that the party against whom the order was issued had given knowing, intelligent and voluntary consent to its issuance.

(b) Notwithstanding the provisions of article fifty-four of the civil practice law and rules, an order of protection or temporary order of protection issued by a court of competent jurisdiction in another state, territorial or tribal jurisdiction, accompanied by a sworn affidavit that upon information and belief such order is in effect as written and has not been vacated or modified, may be filed without fee with the clerk of the court, who shall transmit information regarding such order to the statewide registry of orders of protection and warrants established pursuant to section two hundred twenty-one-a of the executive law; provided, however, that such filing and registry entry shall not be required for enforcement of the order.

6. Notice. Every police officer, peace officer or district attorney investigating a family offense under this article shall advise the victim of the availability of a shelter or other services in the community, and shall immediately give the victim written notice of the legal rights and remedies available to a victim of a family offense under the relevant provisions of the criminal procedure law, the family court act and the domestic relations law. Such notice shall be prepared in Spanish and English and if necessary, shall be delivered orally, and shall include but not be limited to the following statement:

"If you are the victim of domestic violence, you may request that the officer assist in providing for your safety and that of your children, including providing information on how to obtain a temporary order of protection. You may also request that the officer assist you in obtaining your essential personal effects and locating and taking you, or assist in making arrangements to take you, and your children to a safe place within such officer's jurisdiction, including but not limited to a domestic violence program, a family member's or a friend's residence, or a similar place of safety. When the officer's jurisdiction is more than a single county, you may ask the officer to take you or make arrangements to take you and your children to a place of safety in the county where the incident occurred. If you or your children are in need of medical treatment, you have the right to request that the officer assist you in obtaining such medical treatment. You may request a copy of any incident reports at no cost from the law enforcement agency. You have the right to seek legal counsel of your own choosing and if you proceed in family court and if it is determined that you cannot afford an attorney, one must be appointed to represent you without cost to you.

You may ask the district attorney or a law enforcement officer to file a criminal complaint. You also have the right to file a petition in the family court when a family offense has been committed against you. You have the right to have your petition and request for an order of protection filed on the same day you appear in court, and such request must be heard that same day or the next day court is in session. Either court may issue an order of protection from conduct constituting a family offense which could include, among other provisions, an order for the respondent or defendant to stay away from you and your children. The family court may also order the payment of temporary child support and award temporary custody of your children. If the family court is not in session, you may seek immediate assistance from the criminal court in obtaining an order of protection.

The forms you need to obtain an order of protection are available from the family court and the local criminal court (the addresses and telephone numbers shall be listed). The resources available in this community for information relating to domestic violence, treatment of injuries, and places of safety and shelters can be accessed by calling the following 800 numbers (the state-wide English and Spanish language 800 numbers shall be listed and space shall be provided for local domestic violence hotline telephone numbers).

Filing a criminal complaint or a family court petition containing allegations that are knowingly false is a crime."

The division of criminal justice services in consultation with the state office for the prevention of domestic violence shall prepare the form of such written notice consistent with provisions of this section and distribute copies thereof to the appropriate law enforcement officials pursuant to subdivision nine of section eight hundred forty-one of the executive law.

Additionally, copies of such notice shall be provided to the chief administrator of the courts to be distributed to victims of family offenses through the criminal court at such time as such persons first come before the court and to the state department of health for distribution to all hospitals defined under article twenty-eight of the public health law. No cause of action for damages shall arise in favor of any person by reason of any failure to comply with the provisions of this subdivision except upon a showing of gross negligence or willful misconduct.

7. Rules of court regarding concurrent jurisdiction. The chief administrator of the courts, pursuant to paragraph (e) of subdivision two of section two hundred twelve of the judiciary law, shall promulgate rules to facilitate record sharing and other communication between the criminal and family courts, subject to applicable provisions of this chapter and the family court act pertaining to the confidentiality, expungement and sealing of records, when such courts exercise concurrent jurisdiction over family offense proceedings.

Added by L. 1980, Ch. 530; **Amended** by L. 1981, Ch. 416; L. 1983, Ch. 925; L. 1984, Ch. 948; L. 1986, Ch. 847; L. 1990, Ch. 667; L. 1992, Ch. 345, eff. Nov. 1, 1992; L. 1994, Ch. 222, § 34, eff. Jan. 1, 1995, amending subd. 1; L. 1994, Ch. 222, § 35, eff. Jan. 1, 1995, repealing subds. 2(e) and (4); L. 1994, Ch. 222, § 36, eff. Jan. 1, 1995, adding subd. 2(g), (h), (i), (j); L. 1994, Ch. 222, § 37, eff. Jan. 1, 1995, adding subd. 2-a; L. 1994, Ch. 222, § 38, and Ch. 224, § 7, eff. Jan. 1, 1995, amending subd. 6; L. 1994, Ch. 222, § 39, eff. Jan. 1, 1995, adding subd. 7; L. 1995, Ch. 349, § 5, repealing subd. 5, eff. July 28, 1995; L. 1995, Ch. 440, § 2, amending subd. 1, eff. Nov. 1, 1995; L. 1997, Ch. 186, § 7, repealing subd. 2(g), § 8, adding subd. 4, and § 9, repealing subd. 2(j), eff. July 8, 1997; L. 1998, Ch. 597, § 11, eff. Dec 22, 1998, adding subd. 5; L. 1999, Ch. 125, eff. June 29, 1999, amending subds. 1 and 2(h), and Ch. 635, § 3, amending subd. 1, eff. Dec. 1, 1999.

ANNOTATIONS

Divorce decree; peace order.—A prior divorce decree granting the father visitation with his son does not bar the criminal court from issuing a peace order barring the father from seeing the son when the father is charged with assaulting the son. People v. Duignan, 104 Misc. 2d 351, 432 N.Y.S.2d 291 (Crim. Ct. Bronx Co. 1980).

Jurisdiction; transfer.—In the event that family court decides it is an inappropriate forum for resolving an assault charge, it is within the court's discretion to transfer the matter to criminal court, as their jurisdictions run concurrently. People v. Brown, 80 A.D.2d 902, 437 N.Y.S.2d 22 (2d Dept. 1981).

—Failure of the court to provide the complainant with the information, required by the statute, to make an informed decision as to forum is not a reversible error mandated by jurisdictional defect. People v. Munck, 190 A.D.2d 963, 599 N.Y.S.2d 77 (3d Dept. 1993).

Plea; defective procedure.—By entering a guilty plea, defendant waives any cause of action or defense that resulted from the trial court's failure to adhere to the procedures as mandated by the CPL. People v. Holdin, 150 A.D.2d 726, 541 N.Y.S.2d 595 (2d Dept. 1989).

§ 530.12. Protection for victims of family offenses.

1. When a criminal action is pending involving a complaint charging any crime or violation between spouses, former spouses, parent and child, or between members of the same family or household, as members of the same family or household are defined in subdivision one of section 530.11 of this article, the court, in addition to any other powers conferred upon it by this chapter may issue a temporary order of protection as a condition of any order of recognizance or bail or an adjournment in contemplation of dismissal. In addition to any other conditions, such an order may require the defendant:

(a) to stay away from the home, school, business or place of employment of the family or household member or of any designated witness, provided that the court shall make a determination, and shall state such determination in a written decision or on the record, whether to impose a condition pursuant to this paragraph, provided further, however, that failure to make such a determination shall not affect the validity of such temporary order of protection. In making such determination, the court shall consider, but shall not be limited to consideration of, whether the temporary order of protection is likely to achieve its purpose in the absence of such a condition, conduct subject to prior orders of protection, prior incidents of abuse, past or present injury, threats, drug or alcohol abuse, and access to weapons;

(b) to permit a parent, or a person entitled to visitation by a court order or a separation agreement, to visit the child at stated periods;

(c) to refrain from committing a family offense, as defined in subdivision one of section 530.11 of this article, or any criminal offense against the child or against the family or household member or against any person to whom custody of the child is awarded, or from harassing, intimidating or threatening such persons;

(d) to refrain from acts of commission or omission that create an unreasonable risk to the health, safety and welfare of a child, family or household member's life or health;

(e) to permit a designated party to enter the residence during a specified period of time in order to remove personal belongings not in issue in this proceeding or in any other proceeding or action under this chapter, the family court act or the domestic relations law.

2. Notwithstanding any other provision of law, a temporary order of protection issued or continued by a family court pursuant to section eight hundred thirteen of the family court act shall continue in effect, absent action by the appropriate criminal court pursuant to subdivision three of this section, until the defendant is arraigned upon an accusatory instrument filed pursuant to section eight hundred thirteen of the family court act in such criminal court.

3. The court may issue a temporary order of protection ex parte upon the filing of an accusatory instrument and for good cause shown. When a family court order of protection is modified, the criminal court shall forward a copy of such modified order to the family court issuing the original order of protection; provided, however, that where a copy of the modified order is transmitted to the family court by facsimile or other electronic means, the original copy of such modified order and accompanying affidavit shall be forwarded immediately thereafter.

3-a. Emergency powers when family court not in session; issuance of temporary orders of protection. Upon the request of the petitioner, a local criminal court may on an ex parte basis issue a temporary order of protection pending a hearing in family court, provided that a sworn affidavit, verified in accordance with subdivision one of section 100.30 of this chapter, is submitted: (i) alleging that the family court is not in session; (ii) alleging that a family offense, as defined in subdivision one of section eight hundred twelve of the family court act and subdivision one of section 530.11 of this article, has been committed; (iii) alleging that a family offense petition has been filed or will be filed in family court on the next day the court is in session; and (iv) showing good cause. Upon appearance in a local criminal court, the petitioner shall be advised that he or she may continue with the proceeding either in family court or upon the filing of a local criminal court accusatory instrument in criminal court or both. Upon issuance of a temporary order of protection where petitioner requests that it be returnable in family court, the local criminal court shall transfer the matter forthwith to the family court and shall make the matter returnable in family court on the next day the family court is in session, or as soon thereafter as practicable, but in no event more than four calendar days after issuance of the order. The local criminal court, upon issuing a temporary order of protection returnable in family court pursuant to this subdivision, shall immediately forward, in a manner designed to insure arrival before the return date set in the order, a copy of the temporary order of protection and sworn affidavit to the family court and shall provide a copy of such temporary order of protection to the petitioner; provided,

however, that where a copy of the temporary order of protection and affidavit are transmitted to the family court by facsimile or other electronic means, the original order and affidavit shall be forwarded to the family court immediately thereafter. Any temporary order of protection issued pursuant to this subdivision shall be issued to the respondent, and copies shall be filed as required in subdivisions six and eight of this section for orders of protection issued pursuant to this section. Any temporary order of protection issued pursuant to this subdivision shall plainly state the date that such order expires which, in the case of an order returnable in family court, shall be not more than four calendar days after its issuance, unless sooner vacated or modified by the family court. A petitioner requesting a temporary order of protection returnable in family court pursuant to this subdivision in a case in which a family court petition has not been filed shall be informed that such temporary order of protection shall expire as provided for herein, unless the petitioner files a petition pursuant to subdivision one of section eight hundred twenty-one of the family court act on or before the return date in family court and the family court issues a temporary order of protection or order of protection as authorized under article eight of the family court act. Nothing in this subdivision shall limit or restrict the petitioner's right to proceed directly and without court referral in either a criminal or family court, or both, as provided for in section one hundred fifteen of the family court act and section 100.07 of this chapter.

3-b. Emergency powers when family court not in session; modifications of orders of protection or temporary orders of protection. Upon the request of the petitioner, a local criminal court may on an ex parte basis modify a temporary order of protection or order of protection which has been issued under article four, five, six or eight of the family court act pending a hearing in family court, provided that a sworn affidavit verified in accordance with subdivision one of section 100.30 of this chapter is submitted: (i) alleging that the family court is not in session and (ii) showing good cause, including a showing that the existing order is insufficient for the purposes of protection of the petitioner, the petitioner's child or children or other members of the petitioner's family or household. The local criminal court shall make the matter regarding the modification of the order returnable in family court on the next day the family court is in session, or as soon thereafter as practicable, but in no event more than four calendar days after issuance of the modified order. The court shall immediately forward a copy of the modified order, if any, and sworn affidavit to the family court and shall provide a copy of such modified order, if any, and affidavit to the petitioner; provided, however, that where copies of such modified order and affidavit are transmitted to the family court by facsimile or other electronic means, the original copies of such modified order and affidavit shall be forwarded to the family court immediately thereafter. Any modified temporary order of protection or order of protection issued pursuant to this subdivision shall be issued to the respondent and copies shall be filed as required in subdivisions six and eight of this section for orders of protection issued pursuant to this section.

4. The court may issue or extend a temporary order of protection ex parte or on notice simultaneously with the issuance of a warrant for the arrest of defendant. Such temporary order of protection may continue in effect until the day the defendant subsequently appears in court pursuant to such warrant or voluntarily or otherwise.

5. [*Effective until Sept. 1, 2009.*] Upon conviction of any crime or violation between spouses, parent and child, or between members of the same family or household, the court may in addition to any other disposition, including a conditional discharge or youthful offender adjudication, enter an order of protection. Where a temporary order of protection was issued, the court shall state on the record the reasons for issuing or not issuing an order of protection. The duration of such an order shall be fixed by the court and, in the case of a felony conviction, shall not exceed the greater of: (i) five years from the date of such conviction, or (ii) three years from the date of the expiration of the maximum term of an indeterminate or the term of a determinate sentence of imprisonment actually imposed; or in the case of a conviction for a class A misdemeanor, shall not exceed three years from the date of such conviction; or in the case of a conviction for any other offense, shall not exceed one year from the date of conviction. For purposes of determining the duration of an order of protection entered pursuant to this subdivision, a conviction shall be deemed to include a conviction that has been replaced by a youthful offender adjudication. In addition to any other conditions, such an order may require the defendant:

5. [*Effective Sept. 1, 2009.*] Upon conviction of any crime or violation between spouses, parent and child, or between members of the same family or household, the court may in addition to any other disposition, including a conditional discharge or youthful offender adjudication, enter an order of protection. Where a temporary order of protection was issued, the court shall state on the record the reasons for issuing or not issuing an order of protection. The duration of such an order shall be fixed by the court and, in the case of a felony conviction, shall not exceed the greater of: (i) five years from the date of such conviction, or (ii) three years from the date of the expiration of the maximum term of an indeterminate sentence of imprisonment actually imposed; or in the case of a conviction for a class A misdemeanor, shall not exceed three years from the date of such conviction; or in the case of a conviction for any

other offense, shall not exceed one year from the date of conviction. For purposes of determining the duration of an order of protection entered pursuant to this subdivision, a conviction shall be deemed to include a conviction that has been replaced by a youthful offender adjudication. In addition to any other conditions, such an order may require the defendant:

(a) to stay away from the home, school, business or place of employment of the family or household member, the other spouse or the child, or of any witness designated by the court, provided that the court shall make a determination, and shall state such determination in a written decision or on the record, whether to impose a condition pursuant to this paragraph, provided further, however, that failure to make such a determination shall not affect the validity of such order of protection. In making such determination, the court shall consider, but shall not be limited to consideration of, whether the order of protection is likely to achieve its purpose in the absence of such a condition, conduct subject to prior orders of protection, prior incidents of abuse, extent of past or present injury, threats, drug or alcohol abuse, and access to weapons;

(b) to permit a parent, or a person entitled to visitation by a court order or a separation agreement, to visit the child at stated periods;

(c) to refrain from committing a family offense, as defined in subdivision one of section 530.11 of this article, or any criminal offense against the child or against the family or household member or against any person to whom custody of the child is awarded, or from harassing, intimidating or threatening such persons; or

(d) to refrain from acts of commission or omission that create an unreasonable risk to the health, safety and welfare of a child, family or household member's life or health;

(e) to permit a designated party to enter the residence during a specified period of time in order to remove personal belongings not in issue in this proceeding or in any other proceeding or action under this chapter, the family court act or the domestic relations law.

6. An order of protection or a temporary order of protection issued pursuant to subdivision one, two, three, four or five of this section shall bear in a conspicuous manner the term "order of protection" or "temporary order of protection" as the case may be and a copy shall be filed by the clerk of the court with the sheriff's office in the county in which the complainant resides, or, if the complainant resides within a city, with the police department of such city. The absence of such language shall not affect the validity of such order. A copy of such order of protection or temporary order of protection may from time to time be filed by the clerk of the court with any other police department or sheriff's office having

jurisdiction of the residence, work place, and school of anyone intended to be protected by such order. A copy of the order may also be filed by the complainant at the appropriate police department or sheriff's office having jurisdiction. Any subsequent amendment or revocation of such order shall be filed in the same manner as herein provided. Such order of protection shall plainly state the date that such order expires.

6-a. The court shall inquire as to the existence of any other orders of protection between the defendant and the person or persons for whom the order of protection is sought.

7. A family offense subject to the provisions of this section which occurs subsequent to the issuance of an order of protection under this chapter shall be deemed a new offense for which the complainant may seek to file a new accusatory instrument and may file a family court petition under article eight of the family court act as provided for in section 100.07 of this chapter.

8. In any proceeding in which an order of protection or temporary order of protection or a warrant has been issued under this section, the clerk of the court shall issue to the complainant and defendant and defense counsel and to any other person affected by the order a copy of the order of protection or temporary order of protection. The presentation of a copy of such order or a warrant to any peace officer acting pursuant to his special duties or police officer shall constitute authority for him to arrest a person who has violated the terms of such order and bring such person before the court and, otherwise, so far as lies within his power, to aid in securing the protection such order was intended to afford.

9. If no warrant, order or temporary order of protection has been issued by the court, and an act alleged to be a family offense as defined in section 530.11 of this chapter is the basis of the arrest, the magistrate shall permit the complainant to file a petition, information or accusatory instrument and for reasonable cause shown, shall thereupon hold such respondent or defendant, admit to, fix or accept bail, or parole him for hearing before the family court or appropriate criminal court as the complainant shall choose in accordance with the provisions of section 530.11 of this chapter.

10. Punishment for contempt based on a violation of an order of protection or temporary order of protection shall not affect the original criminal action, nor reduce or diminish a sentence upon conviction for the original crime or violation alleged therein or for a lesser included offense thereof.

11. If a defendant is brought before the court for failure to obey any lawful order issued under this section, or an order of protection issued by a court of competent jurisdiction in another state, territorial or tribal jurisdiction, and if, after hearing, the court is satisfied by competent proof that the defendant has willfully failed to obey any such order, the court may:

(a) revoke an order of recognizance or revoke an order of bail or order forfeiture of such bail and commit the defendant to custody; or

(b) restore the case to the calendar when there has been an adjournment in contemplation of dismissal and commit the defendant to custody or impose or increase bail pending a trial of the original crime or violation; or

(c) revoke a conditional discharge in accordance with section 410.70 of this chapter and impose probation supervision or impose a sentence of imprisonment in accordance with the penal law based on the original conviction; or

(d) revoke probation in accordance with section 410.70 of this chapter and impose a sentence of imprisonment in accordance with the penal law based on the original conviction. In addition, if the act which constitutes the violation of the order of protection or temporary order of protection is a crime or a violation the defendant may be charged with and tried for that crime or violation.

12. The chief administrator of the courts shall promulgate appropriate uniform temporary orders of protection and orders of protection forms to be used throughout the state. Such forms shall be promulgated and developed in a manner to ensure the compatibility of such forms with the statewide computerized registry established pursuant to section two hundred twenty-one-a of the executive law.

13. Notwithstanding the foregoing provisions, an order of protection, or temporary order of protection when applicable, may be entered against a former spouse and persons who have a child in common, regardless whether such persons have been married or have lived together at any time.

14. The People shall make reasonable efforts to notify the complainant alleging a crime constituting a family offense when the people have decided to decline prosecution of such crime, to dismiss the criminal charges against the defendant or to enter into a plea agreement. The People shall advise the complainant of the right to file a petition in the family court pursuant to section 100.07 of this chapter and section one hundred fifteen of the family court act.

In any case where allegations of criminal conduct are transferred from the family court to the criminal court pursuant to paragraph (ii) of subdivision (b) of section eight hundred forty-six of the family court act, the People shall advise the family court making the transfer of any decision to file an accusatory instrument against the family court respondent and shall notify such court of the disposition of such instrument and the sentence, if any, imposed upon such respondent.

Release of a defendant from custody shall not be delayed because of the requirements of this subdivision.

15. Any motion to vacate or modify an order of protection or temporary order of protection shall be on notice to the non-moving party, except as provided in subdivision three-b of this section.

Added by L. 1977, Ch. 449; **Amended** by L. 1978, Chs. 628, 629; L. 1980, Ch. 530; L. 1981, Chs. 143, 416; L. 1982, Ch. 516; L. 1984, Chs. 388, 948; L. 1985, Ch. 672; L. 1986, Chs. 620, 794; L. 1988, Ch. 702; L. 1989, Ch. 164; L. 1990, Ch. 454; L. 1993, Ch. 498; L. 1994, Ch. 222, § 41; L. 1994, Ch. 222, § 40; L. 1994, Ch. 222, § 42; L. 1994, Ch. 222, § 43; L. 1994, Ch. 222, § 44; L. 1994, Ch. 224, § 14; L. 1994, Ch. 222, § 45; L. 1995, Ch. 3, § 36, and amendments repealed Sept. 1, 2009; L. 1995, Ch. 483, § 15, amending subds. 1(b), (c), and (d), and adding subd. 1(e), eff. Nov. 1, 1995; L. 1995, Ch. 483, § 16, amending subds. 5(b), (c), and (d), and adding subd. 5(e), eff. Nov. 1, 1995; L. 1996, Ch. 511, amending subd. 1, eff. Nov. 6, 1996; L. 1996, Ch. 644, §§ 1 and 2, amending subd. 11(d) and repealing subd. 11(e), respectively, effective Nov. 1, 1996; L. 1997, Ch. 186, § 10, amending subd. 3, § 11, adding subds. 3-a and 3-b, and § 12 amending subd. 15, and Ch. 589, § 1, eff. Sept. 1, 1997, amending subd. 4; L. 1998, Ch. 597, § 12, eff. Dec. 22, 1998, amending subd. 11, and Ch. 610, § 1, eff. Oct. 6, 1998, amending subd. 5(a) by adding "or of any witness designated by the court," and amendment shall apply to orders of protection issued on or after Oct. 6, 1998; L. 2001, Ch. 384, eff. Nov. 1, 2001, and deemed repealed on the same date that section 36 of chapter 3 of the laws of 1995 is deemed repealed pursuant to subdivision d of section 74 of such chapter of the laws of 1995, as from time to time amended; L. 2005, Ch. 56, Part D, § 20, eff. Apr. 1, 2005, extending repeal date of subd. 5 to Sept. 1, 2009.

ANNOTATIONS

Constitutionality.—CPL § 530.12 is constitutional and its provision authorizing issuance of a temporary order of protection without a prior hearing was not a denial of defendant's due process rights. People v. Faieta, 109 Misc. 2d 841, 440 N.Y.S.2d 1007 (1st Dist. Ct. Nassau Co. 1981).

Double jeopardy implications.—Defendant's ex-wife obtained two orders of protection, one through City Court and one through Family Court, and defendant was later found guilty in Family Court of violating the order of protection. Thereafter, defendant was indicted for first degree criminal contempt, second degree aggravated harassment, and first degree harassment. Defendant's conviction of criminal contempt was reversed, and remaining counts were dismissed on double jeopardy grounds. People v. Wood, 95 N.Y.2d 509, 719 N.Y.S.2d 639, 742 N.E.2d 114 (2000).

Violation; intent.—Defendant does not need to be served a copy of the protective order, so long as defendant has knowledge of the court's action. However, the prosecution must demonstrate that the defendant willfully disobeyed the court's order in respect to the protected party. People v. Said, 120 A.D.2d 961, 502 N.Y.S.2d 840 (4th Dept. 1986).

Violation; burden of proof.—The state does not need to meet the trial standard of proving that the defendant was issued an order of protection when bail was revoked for violating the order. People v. Stevens, 133 Misc. 2d 407, 506 N.Y.S.2d 995 (City Ct. Oswego Co. 1986).

Temporary order; review.—A review of a securing order may be undertaken only in the event that there are new facts relevant to the order and it may not be reviewed nunc pro tunc. People v. Forman, 145 Misc. 2d 115, 546 N.Y.S.2d 755 (N.Y. City Crim. Ct. 1989).

Temporary order; procedure.—A court may issue a temporary order of protection as long as the action is pending when the order is issued. People v. Lewis, 184 Misc. 2d 399, 710 N.Y.S.2d 515 (Co. Ct. Monroe Co. 2000).

—A continuance of a temporary order is warranted upon proof of a husband's violent conduct and resulting injury to his wife. Danger or threat of injury is the standard for issuing a temporary order of protection as a condition for allowing bail. However, upon presentation of the facts and law, defendant must be afforded an opportunity to present the opposing facts and law

in order to contest the continuance of the temporary order. People v. Forman, 145 Misc. 2d 115, 546 N.Y.S.2d 755 (N.Y. City Crim. Ct. 1989).

Order of protection; scope of.—Where defendant pleaded guilty to sexual abuse in the first degree and attempted sexual abuse in the first degree based on incidents involving his infant son, and sexual misconduct for an incident involving his wife, and an order of protection was issued prohibiting defendant from any contact with his wife and all three of his children, the court rejected defendant's contention that the scope of the order had to be limited to the two victims of defendant's crimes or that the duration of the order as it pertains to his wife is limited to three years from the date of his conviction. "When a crime has been committed between members of the same family or household, an order of protection may be issued in favor of the victim of such crime and members of the family or household of the victim." People v. Goodband, 291 A.D.2d 584, 737 N.Y.S.2d 680 (3d Dept. 2002).

Order of protection; amendment of.—The court is within its discretion to amend an order of protection, so long as the defendant is convicted prior to its issuance. Therefore, the court is not limited in issuing at the time of sentencing. People v. Garris, 159 Misc. 2d 586, 605 N.Y.S.2d 818 (1st Dist. Nassau Co. 1993).

Family offense; forum.—Complainant reserves the right to decide between family court or criminal court as the initial forum when a family court order is violated and, moreover, defendant is unable to object. People v. Jhon, 150 Misc. 2d 842, 570 N.Y.S.2d 427 (N.Y.C. Crim. Ct. 1991).

§ 530.13. Protection of victims of crimes, other than family offenses.

1. When any criminal action is pending, and the court has not issued a temporary order of protection pursuant to section 530.12 of this article, the court, in addition to the other powers conferred upon it by this chapter, may for good cause shown issue a temporary order of protection as a condition of a pre-trial release, or as a condition of release on bail or an adjournment in contemplation of dismissal. In addition to any other conditions, such an order may require that the defendant:

(a) stay away from the home, school, business or place of employment of the victims of, or designated witnesses to, the alleged offense;

(b) refrain from harassing, intimidating, threatening or otherwise interfering with the victims of the alleged offense and such members of the family or household of such victims or designated witnesses as shall be specifically named by the court in such order.

2. The court may issue a temporary order of protection under this section *ex parte* upon the filing of an accusatory instrument and for good cause shown.

3. The court may issue or extend a temporary order of protection under this section ex parte simultaneously with the issuance of a warrant for the arrest of the defendant. Such temporary order of protection may continue in effect until the day the defendant subsequently appears in court pursuant to such warrant or voluntarily or otherwise.

4. [*Effective until Sept. 1, 2009.*] Upon conviction of any offense, where the court has not issued an order of protection pursuant to section 530.12 of this article, the court may, in addition to any

other disposition, including a conditional discharge or youthful offender adjudication, enter an order of protection. Where a temporary order of protection was issued, the court shall state on the record the reasons for issuing or not issuing an order of protection. The duration of such an order shall be fixed by the court and, in the case of a felony conviction, shall not exceed the greater of: (i) five years from the date of such conviction, or (ii) three years from the date of the expiration of the maximum term of an indeterminate or the term of a determinate sentence of imprisonment actually imposed; or in the case of a conviction for a class A misdemeanor, shall not exceed three years from the date of such conviction; or in the case of a conviction for any other offense, shall not exceed one year from the date of conviction. For purposes of determining the duration of an order of protection entered pursuant to this subdivision, a conviction shall be deemed to include a conviction that has been replaced by a youthful offender adjudication. In addition to any other conditions such an order may require that the defendant:

4. [*Effective Sept. 1, 2009.*] Upon conviction of any offense, where the court has not issued an order of protection pursuant to section 530.12 of this article, the court may, in addition to any other disposition, including a conditional discharge or youthful offender adjudication, enter an order of protection. Where a temporary order of protection was issued, the court shall state on the record the reasons for issuing or not issuing an order of protection. The duration of such an order shall be fixed by the court and, in the case of a felony conviction, shall not exceed the greater of: (i) five years from the date of such conviction, or (ii) three years from the date of the expiration of the maximum term of an indeterminate sentence of imprisonment actually imposed; or in the case of a conviction for a class A misdemeanor, shall not exceed three years from the date of such conviction; or in the case of a conviction for any other offense, shall not exceed one year from the date of conviction. For purposes of determining the duration of an order of protection entered pursuant to this subdivision, a conviction shall be deemed to include a conviction that has been replaced by a youthful offender adjudication. In addition to any other conditions such an order may require that the defendant:

(a) stay away from the home, school, business or place of employment of the victim or victims, or of any witness designated by the court, of such offense;

(b) refrain from harassing, intimidating, threatening or otherwise interfering with the victim or victims of the offense and such members of the family or household of such victim or victims as shall be specifically named by the court in such order.

5. The court shall inquire as to the existence of any other orders of protection between the defendant and the person or persons for whom the order of protection is sought. An order of protection issued under this section shall plainly state the date that such order expires. Orders of protection issued to protect victims of domestic violence, as defined in section four hundred fifty-nine-a of the social services law, shall be on uniform statewide forms that shall be promulgated by the chief administrator of the courts in a manner to ensure the compatibility of such forms with the statewide registry of orders of protection and warrants established pursuant to section two hundred twenty-one-a of the executive law. A copy of an order of protection or a temporary order of protection issued pursuant to subdivision one, two, three, or four of this section shall be filed by the clerk of the court with the sheriff's office in the county in which such victim or victims reside, or, if the victim or victims reside within a city, with the police department of such city. A copy of such order of protection or temporary order of protection may from time to time be filed by the clerk of the court with any other police department or sheriff's office having jurisdiction of the residence, work place, and school of anyone intended to be protected by such order. A copy of the order may also be filed by the victim or victims at the appropriate police department or sheriff's office having jurisdiction. Any subsequent amendment or revocation of such order shall be filed in the same manner as herein provided.

6. In any proceeding in which an order of protection or temporary order of protection or a warrant has been issued under this section, the clerk of the court shall issue to the victim and the defendant and to any other person affected by the order, a copy of the order of protection or temporary order of protection. The presentation of a copy of such order or a warrant to any police officer or peace officer acting pursuant to his special duties shall constitute authority for him to arrest a person who has violated the terms of such order and bring such person before the court and, otherwise, so far as lies within his power, to aid in securing the protection such order was intended to afford.

7. Punishment for contempt based upon a violation of an order or [*] protection or temporary order of protection issued under this section shall not affect a pending criminal action, nor reduce or diminish a sentence upon conviction for any other crimes or offenses.

8. If a defendant is brought before the court for failure to obey any lawful order issued under this section and if, after hearing, the court is satisfied by competent proof that the defendant has willfully failed to obey any such order, the court may:

(a) revoke an order of recognizance or bail and commit the defendant to custody; or

(b) restore the case to the calendar when there has been an adjournment in contemplation of dismissal and commit the defendant to custody or impose or increase bail pending a trial of the original crime or violation; or

(c) revoke a conditional discharge in accordance with section 410.70 of this chapter and impose probation supervision or impose a sentence of imprisonment in accordance with the penal law based on the original conviction; or

(d) revoke probation in accordance with section 410.70 of this chapter and impose a sentence of imprisonment in accordance with the penal law based on the original conviction. In addition, if the act which constitutes the violation of the order of protection or temporary order of protection is a crime or a violation the defendant may be charged with and tried for that crime or violation.

9. The chief administrator of the courts shall promulgate appropriate uniform temporary order of protection and order of protection forms to be used throughout the state.

* As originally enacted. Should probably be "of."

Added by L. 1981, Ch. 575; **Amended** by L. 1984, Ch. 388; L. 1985, Ch. 672; L. 1986, Chs. 620, 794; L. 1990, Ch. 454; L. 1995, Ch. 3, § 37, amending subd. 4, eff. Oct. 1, 1995, amendment repealed Sept. 1, 2009 pursuant to L. 1995, Ch. 3, § 74, paragraph (d), as amended, and amendment applies only to offenses committed on or after Oct. 1, 1995, pursuant to L. 1995, Ch. 3, § 74, paragraph (e); L. 1997, Ch. 589, § 2, eff. Sept. 17, 1997; L. 1998, Ch. 610, § 2, eff. Oct. 6, 1998, amending subd. 4(a) by adding "or of any witness designated by the court," and amendment shall apply to orders of protection issued on or after Oct. 6, 1998; L. 2001, Ch. 384, eff. Nov. 1, 2001, and deemed repealed on the same date that section 37 of chapter 3 of the laws of 1995 is deemed repealed pursuant to subdivision d of section 74 of such chapter of the laws of 1995, as from time to time amended; L. 2002, Ch. 462, § 1, amending subd. 5, eff. Nov. 18, 2002, and amendment shall apply to all petitions filed on or after such date; L. 2005, Ch. 56, Part D, § 20, eff. Apr. 1, 2005, extending repeal date of subd. 4 to Sept. 1, 2009.

ANNOTATIONS

Court's authority to issue order.—The issuance of a temporary order of protection is predicated upon the court's continuing jurisdiction over the accused and its concomitant desire to exercise a modicum of control over the defendant's actions and behaviors; once a defendant is acquitted or sentenced, the criminal action is no longer pending and the temporary order of protection becomes a nullity. People v. Bleau, 276 A.D.2d 131, 718 N.Y.S.2d 453 (3d Dept. 2001).

—District Court's authority to issue a temporary order of protection ex parte is limited to those factual allegations as are set forth within accusatory instrument on file; if new facts are available since the filing of the accusatory instrument that would necessitate an ex parte order protection, a new complaint or information should be processed, a new arrest should be made, and the defendant should be brought before the court for issuance of an order of protection. People v. Tullo, 176 Misc. 2d 972, 675 N.Y.S.2d 787 (Dist. Ct. Nassau Co. 1998).

Order; appealability of.—Permanent orders of protection are appealable. However, an appeal is neither the only nor the best means for resolving an expiration date issue. Because sentencing courts are in the best position to amend orders of protection, the best practice is for a defendant seeking an adjustment to request relief from the issuing court in the first instance, resorting to appellate courts only if necessary. People v. Nieves, 2 N.Y.3d 310, 778 N.Y.S.2d 751, 811 N.E.2d 13 (2004).

Order; notice.—When defendant's release is conditioned upon an order of protection, oral notification in court is insufficient notice because the defendant must be told orally or in writing the contents of the order and the conduct it prohibits. People v. McCowan, 85 N.Y.2d 985, 629 N.Y.S.2d 163, 652 N.E.2d 909 (1995).

Order; application.—The order of protection issued to the defendant was valid as applied to the alleged victim of the assault, his son. People v. Adib, 120 A.D.2d 961, 502 N.Y.S.2d 840 (4th Dept. 1986).

Order; constitutionality.—A order of protection survives constitutional scrutiny if sufficient evidence exists, as defendant possesses no right to confrontation prior to the trial. People v. Hayday, 144 A.D.2d 207, 534 N.Y.S.2d 521 (3d Dept. 1988).

Order; duration of.—County Court's determination of the duration of the order of protection issued at sentencing pursuant to 530.13(4) should have taken into account his jail-time credit. A new determination was required. People v. Serrano, 309 A.D.2d 822, 765 N.Y.S.2d 662 (2d Dept. 2003).

Order; probation.—Revocation of probation need not be based on defendant's violation of the protection order, which was incorporated into the conditions of probation; there was sufficient evidence to support a finding of second degree aggravated harassment, which is a ground for revocation. People v. Johnson, 208 A.D.2d 1051, 617 N.Y.S.2d 577 (3d Dept. 1994).

Order; sanction.—County court had power to sanction a defendant who violated a temporary order of protection previously issued in a criminal action, even one issued by a local criminal court, because it assumes jurisdiction over all conditions of defendant's release when it divests the local criminal court of jurisdiction. People v. Taylor, 176 Misc. 2d 30, 670 N.Y.S.2d 732 (Greene Co. Ct. 1998).

Order; violation of.—Once duly served an individual violating an order of protection may be prosecuted for criminal contempt with jurisdiction vesting within any of the 62 counties of New York, based on the geographic location in which such violation is committed. People v. Perez, 189 Misc. 2d 516, 734 N.Y.S.2d 398 (Co. Ct. Nassau Co. 2001).

Plea agreement.—An order of protection may be issued independent of a plea agreement. People v. Peters, 232 A.D.2d 432, 648 N.Y.S.2d 447 (2d Dept. 1996).

Subject and length of order.—The purpose of fixing expiration dates in orders of protection is to provide certainty for defendants, the protected victims, witnesses, and law enforcement who may be called to enforce the orders. The expiration date established here, of 100 years after the date of sentencing, fulfills the purpose of the expiration date and also allows the court to exercise its discretion to issue a lifetime order of protection, affording the victim the utmost safety and peace of mind. People v. McClemore, 4 N.Y.3d 821, 797 N.Y.S.2d 351, 830 N.E.2d 249 (2005).

—Although court did not improvidently exercise its discretion in signing order of protection, it erred in setting expiration date of order as twelve years after the conviction. Since defendant was sentenced to a determinate sentence of seven years, the maximum duration of the order of protection was ten years. People v. Wheeler, 268 A.D.2d 448, 701 N.Y.S.2d 442 (2d Dept. 2000).

—An order of protection issued in favor of a person who was a witness, rather than a victim, did not necessarily render the order invalid. However, it must be a witness "designated by the court, of such offense" of which the defendant was convicted. Insofar as the order here was issued in favor of a witness to the unrelated murder, and not to the burglary, the offense for which defendant was convicted as a result of his plea, the order of protection was not authorized and is invalid. Another order, issued in favor of the burglary victims, was deficient insofar as it did not specifically name the family members related to those victims to whom it extended, and the matter was remitted to remedy the defect. People v. Creighton, 754 N.Y.S.2d 370 (3d Dept. 2002).

—Court properly issued order of protection in favor of grand larceny victim's daughter, and the fact that the victim's daughter was in jail at the time of the defendant's sentencing does not remove her from the scope of the statute. People v. Fisher, 19 A.D.3d 1034, 796 N.Y.S.2d 475 (4th Dept. 2005).

—An order of protection entered upon a conviction of a violation shall not exceed one year from the date of conviction.

People v. Jones, 277 A.D.2d 928, 716 N.Y.S.2d 495 (4th Dept. 2000).

—An order of protection may run in favor of the victim or victims of the offense and members of the family or household of such victim or victims, and the order of protection may extend until three years from the date of the expiration of the maximum term of an indeterminate prison sentence. People v. Debo, 234 A.D.2d 944, 652 N.Y.S.2d 174 (4th Dept. 1996).

—Order of protection was invalid because it only directed the defendant to stay away from a specific address; while an order of protection may include a directive to stay away from the home, school, business, or place of employment of a victim or designated witness, provision in the statute authorizes the issuance of an order of protection in favor of a place. Orders of protection are explicitly for the protection of victims and designated witnesses. People v. Smith, 4 Misc. 3d 909, 782 N.Y.S.2d 596 (Crim. Ct. N.Y. Co. 2004).

§ 530.14. Suspension and revocation of a license to carry, possess, repair or dispose of a firearm or firearms pursuant to section 400.00 of the penal law and ineligibility for such a license; order to surrender firearms.

1. Mandatory and permissive suspension of firearms license and ineligibility for such a license upon issuance of temporary order of protection. Whenever a temporary order of protection is issued pursuant to subdivision one of section 530.12 or subdivision one of section 530.13 of this article:

(a) the court shall suspend any such existing license possessed by the defendant, order the defendant ineligible for such a license and order the immediate surrender of any or all firearms owned or possessed where the court receives information that gives the court good cause to believe that (i) the defendant has a prior conviction of any violent felony offense as defined in section 70.02 of the penal law; (ii) the defendant has previously been found to have willfully failed to obey a prior order of protection and such willful failure involved (A) the infliction of serious physical injury, as defined in subdivision ten of section 10.00 of the penal law, (B) the use or threatened use of a deadly weapon or dangerous instrument as those terms are defined in subdivisions twelve and thirteen of section 10.00 of the penal law, or (C) behavior constituting any violent felony offense as defined in section 70.02 of the penal law; or (iii) the defendant has a prior conviction for stalking in the first degree as defined in section 120.60 of the penal law, stalking in the second degree as defined in section 120.55 of the penal law, stalking in the third degree as defined in section 120.50 of the penal law or stalking in the fourth degree as defined in section 120.45 of such law; and

(b) the court may where the court finds a substantial risk that the defendant may use or threaten to use a firearm unlawfully against the person or persons for whose protection the temporary order of protection is issued, suspend any such existing license possessed by the defendant, order the defendant ineligible for such a license and order the immediate surrender of any or all firearms owned or possessed.

2. Mandatory and permissive revocation or suspension of firearms license and ineligibility for such a license upon issuance of an order of protection. Whenever an order of protection is issued pursuant to subdivision five of section 530.12 or subdivision four of section 530.13 of this article:

(a) the court shall revoke any such existing license possessed by the defendant, order the defendant ineligible for such a license and order the immediate surrender of any or all firearms owned or possessed where such action is required by section 400.00 of the penal law; and

(b) the court may where the court finds a substantial risk that the defendant may use or threaten to use a firearm unlawfully against the person or persons for whose protection the order of protection is issued,

(i) revoke any such existing license possessed by the defendant, order the defendant ineligible for such a license and order the immediate surrender of any or all firearms owned or possessed or

(ii) suspend or continue to suspend any such existing license possessed by the defendant, order the defendant ineligible for such a license and order the immediate surrender of any or all firearms owned or possessed.

3. Mandatory and permissive revocation or suspension of firearms license and ineligibility for such a license upon a finding of a willful failure to obey an order of protection. Whenever a defendant has been found pursuant to subdivision eleven of section 530.12 or subdivision eight of section 530.13 of this article to have willfully failed to obey an order of protection issued by a court of competent jurisdiction in this state or another state, territorial or tribal jurisdiction, in addition to any other remedies available pursuant to subdivision eleven of section 530.12 or subdivision eight of section 530.13 of this article:

(a) the court shall revoke any such existing license possessed by the defendant, order the defendant ineligible for such a license and order the immediate surrender of any or all firearms owned or possessed where the willful failure to obey such order involved

(i) the infliction of serious physical injury, as defined in subdivision ten of section 10.00 of the penal law,

(ii) the use or threatened use of a deadly weapon or dangerous instrument as those terms are defined in subdivisions twelve and thirteen of section 10.00 of the penal law,

(iii) behavior constituting any violent felony

offense as defined in section 70.02 of the penal law; or

(iv) behavior constituting stalking in the first degree as defined in section 120.60 of the penal law, stalking in the second degree as defined in section 120.55 of the penal law, stalking in the third degree as defined in section 120.50 of the penal law or stalking in the fourth degree as defined in section 120.45 of such law; and

(b) the court may where the court finds a substantial risk that the defendant may use or threaten to use a firearm unlawfully against the person or persons for whose protection the order of protection was issued,

(i) revoke any such existing license possessed by the defendant, order the defendant ineligible for such a license and order the immediate surrender of any or all firearms owned or possessed or

(ii) suspend any such existing license possessed by the defendant, order the defendant ineligible for such a license and order the immediate surrender of any or all firearms owned or possessed.

4. Suspension. Any suspension order issued pursuant to this section shall remain in effect for the duration of the temporary order of protection or order of protection, unless modified or vacated by the court.

5. Surrender.

(a) Where an order to surrender one or more firearms has been issued, the temporary order of protection or order of protection shall specify the place where such firearms shall be surrendered, shall specify a date and time by which the surrender shall be completed and, to the extent possible, shall describe such firearms to be surrendered, and shall direct the authority receiving such surrendered firearms to immediately notify the court of such surrender.

(b) The prompt surrender of one or more firearms pursuant to a court order issued pursuant to this section shall be considered a voluntary surrender for purposes of subparagraph (f) of paragraph one of subdivision a of section 265.20 of the penal law. The disposition of any such firearms shall be in accordance with the provisions of subdivision six of section 400.05 of the penal law.

(c) The provisions of this section shall not be deemed to limit, restrict or otherwise impair the authority of the court to order and direct the surrender of any or all pistols, revolvers, rifles, shotguns or other firearms owned or possessed by a defendant pursuant to sections 530.12 or 530.13 of this article.

6. Notice.

(a) Where an order of revocation, suspension or ineligibility has been issued pursuant to this section, any temporary order of protection or order of protection issued shall state that such firearm license has been suspended or revoked or that the defendant is ineligible for such license, as the case may be.

(b) The court revoking or suspending the license, ordering the defendant ineligible for such a license, or ordering the surrender of any firearm shall immediately notify the duly constituted police authorities of the locality concerning such action and, in the case of orders of protection and temporary orders of protection issued pursuant to section 530.12 of this article, shall immediately notify the statewide registry of orders of protection.

(c) The court revoking or suspending the license or ordering the defendant ineligible for such a license shall give written notice thereof without unnecessary delay to the division of state police at its office in the city of Albany.

(d) Where an order of revocation, suspension, ineligibility or surrender is modified or vacated, the court shall immediately notify the statewide registry of orders of protection and the duly constituted police authorities of the locality concerning such action and shall give written notice thereof without unnecessary delay to the division of state police at its office in the city of Albany.

7. Hearing. The defendant shall have the right to a hearing before the court regarding any revocation, suspension, ineligibility or surrender order issued pursuant to this section, provided that nothing in this subdivision shall preclude the court from issuing any such order prior to a hearing. Where the court has issued such an order prior to a hearing, it shall commence such hearing within fourteen days of the date such order was issued.

8. Nothing in this section shall delay or otherwise interfere with the issuance of a temporary order of protection or the timely arraignment of a defendant in custody.

Added by L. 1996, Ch. 644, § 3, effective Nov. 1, 1996; **Amended** by L. 1998, Ch. 597, § 13, eff. Dec. 22, 1998, amending subd. 3; L. 1999, Ch. 635, § 4, eff. Dec. 1, 1999; L. 2000, Ch. 434, § 1, eff. Oct. 20, 2000, amending subd. 1(a).

§ 530.20. Order of recognizance or bail; by local criminal court when action is pending therein.

When a criminal action is pending in a local criminal court, such court, upon application of a defendant, must or may order recognizance or bail as follows:

1. When the defendant is charged, by information, simplified information, prosecutor's information or misdemeanor complaint, with an offense or offenses of less than felony grade only, the court must order recognizance or bail.

2. When the defendant is charged, by felony complaint, with a felony, the court may, in its

discretion, order recognizance or bail except as otherwise provided in this subdivision:

(a) A city court, a town court or a village court may not order recognizance or bail when (i) the defendant is charged with a class A felony, or (ii) it appears that the defendant has two previous felony convictions;

(b) No local criminal court may order recognizance or bail with respect to a defendant charged with a felony unless and until:

(i) The district attorney has been heard in the matter or, after knowledge or notice of the application and reasonable opportunity to be heard, has failed to appear at the proceeding or has otherwise waived his right to do so; and

(ii) The court has been furnished with a report of the division of criminal justice services concerning the defendant's criminal record if any or with a police department report with respect to the defendant's prior arrest record. If neither report is available, the court, with the consent of the district attorney, may dispense with this requirement; provided, however, that in an emergency, including but not limited to a substantial impairment in the ability of such division or police department to timely furnish such report, such consent shall not be required if, for reasons stated on the record, the court deems it unnecessary. When the court has been furnished with any such report or record, it shall furnish a copy thereof to counsel for the defendant or, if the defendant is not represented by counsel, to the defendant.

Amended by L. 1971, Ch. 762; L. 1972, Chs. 399, 661; L. 1975, Ch. 531; L. 1979, Ch. 218.

ANNOTATIONS

Bail or recognizance.—The local criminal court is required to order bail or recognizance when the charge against the defendant is for a non-felony offense, because defendant is entitled to bail. *In re* LaBelle, 79 N.Y.2d 350, 582 N.Y.S.2d 970, 591 N.E.2d 1156 (1992).

Bail; defendant's interest.—The court is required to set a nominal bail, regardless of the fact that the accused may receive better care in jail or may wish to remain incarcerated. *In re* LaBelle, 79 N.Y.2d 350, 582 N.Y.S.2d 970, 591 N.E.2d 1156 (1992).

Bail; discretion.—The court has the discretion as to granting or denying bail or recognizance when a defendant is charged with a felony offense. People v. Burton, 148 Misc. 2d 716, 561 N.Y.S.2d 328 (Sup. Ct. Bronx Co. 1990).

—The city court is prohibited from granting bail to a defendant charged with a Class A felony or any other felony, if the defendant has two prior felony convictions. People v. Torres, 112 Misc. 2d 145, 446 N.Y.S.2d 969 (Sup. Ct. N.Y. Co. 1981).

§ 530.30. Order of recognizance or bail; by superior court judge when action is pending in local criminal court.

1. When a criminal action is pending in a local criminal court, other than one consisting of a superior court judge sitting as such, a judge of a superior court holding a term thereof in the

county, upon application of a defendant, may order recognizance or bail when such local criminal court:

(a) Lacks authority to issue such an order, pursuant to paragraph (a) of subdivision two of section 530.20; or

(b) Has denied an application for recognizance or bail; or

(c) Has fixed bail which is excessive. In such case, such superior court judge may vacate the order of such local criminal court and release the defendant on his own recognizance or fix bail in a lesser amount or in a less burdensome form.

2. Notwithstanding the provisions of subdivision one, when the defendant is charged with a felony in a local criminal court, a superior court judge may not order recognizance or bail unless and until the district attorney has had an opportunity to be heard in the matter and such judge has been furnished with a report as described in subparagraph (ii) of paragraph (b) of subdivision two of section 530.20.

3. Not more than one application may be made pursuant to this section.

Amended by L. 1971, Ch. 762.

ANNOTATIONS

Order of Protection; temporary.—The CPL does not authorize a review of temporary protection order, even if it needs to be vacated in order to grant the defendant release on his own recognizance. People v. Forman, 145 Misc. 2d 115, 546 N.Y.S.2d 755 (N.Y.C. Crim. Ct. 1989).

Change in bail; courts of concurrent jurisdiction; issuance of bench warrant.—The issuance of a bench warrant may not be an arbitrary decision by a judge of equal authority, and should be based on new facts. While judges of concurrent jurisdiction may not overrule each other, it is within their power to make new orders in ambulatory interlocutory situations, where new matter is presented to them in the regular course of their judicial duties. A judge of concurrent jurisdiction may also increase or lower bail upon a showing of new facts. People v. Gruttola, 72 Misc. 2d 295, 339 N.Y.S.2d 178 (Crim. Ct. N.Y. Co. 1972).

§ 530.40. Order of recognizance or bail; by superior court when action is pending therein.

When a criminal action is pending in a superior court, such court, upon application of a defendant, must or may order recognizance or bail as follows:

1. When the defendant is charged with an offense or offenses of less than felony grade only, the court must order recognizance or bail.

2. When the defendant is charged with a felony, the court may, in its discretion, order recognizance or bail. In any such case in which an indictment (a) has resulted from an order of a local criminal court holding the defendant for the action of the grand jury, or (b) was filed at a time when a felony complaint charging the same conduct was pending in a local criminal court, and in which such local criminal court or a superior

court judge has issued an order of recognizance or bail which is still effective, the superior court's order may be in the form of a direction continuing the effectiveness of the previous order.

3. Notwithstanding the provisions of subdivision two, a superior court may not order recognizance or bail, or permit a defendant to remain at liberty pursuant to an existing order, after he has been convicted of either: (a) a class A felony or (b) any class B or class C felony defined in article one hundred thirty of the penal law committed or attempted to be committed by a person eighteen years of age or older against a person less than eighteen years of age. In either case the court must commit or remand the defendant to the custody of the sheriff.

4. Notwithstanding the provisions of subdivision two, a superior court may not order recognizance or bail when the defendant is charged with a felony unless and until the district attorney has had an opportunity to be heard in the matter and such court has been furnished with a report as described in subparagraph (ii) of paragraph (b) of subdivision two of section 530.20.

Amended by L. 1971, Ch. 762; L. 2000, Ch. 1, Feb. 1, 2001; L. 2003, Ch. 264, § 46, eff. Nov. 1, 2003, amending subd. 3.

ANNOTATIONS

Bail; parolee detainer warrant.—Statute authorizes release on bail only in criminal action or proceeding and parolee arrested on warrant for retaking and detaining prior to revocation hearing is neither involved in criminal action nor proceeding so that court could not release him on bail. People *ex rel.* Gatti v. Amico, 39 A.D.2d 826, 333 N.Y.S.2d 103 (4th Dept.), *app. dismissed,* 30 N.Y.2d 955, 335 N.Y.S.2d 705, 287 N.E.2d 394 (1972).

Bail; application.—Pending submission of the case to the Grand Jury, the county court is required to grant a securing order and either release the defendant upon his own recognizance, set bail, or place him in the sheriff's custody. People v. Murphy, 148 A.D.2d 715, 539 N.Y.S.2d 376 (2d Dept. 1989)

—The Supreme Court is the proper jurisdiction for bail applications, after a defendant has been held pursuant to an order for a Grand Jury. People v. Daniel P. (Anonymous), 94 A.D.2d 83, 463 N.Y.S.2d 838 (2d Dept. 1983).

Bail; continuation.—After indictment, a county court is not required to abide by the previous order of a criminal court and may therefore require a new bail application be filed. People *ex rel.* Bauer v. McGreay, 147 Misc. 2d 213, 555 N.Y.S.2d 581 (Sup. Ct. Rensselaer Co. 1990).

Bail; remanded.—A defendant who was released on bail may be remanded on an A-II felony conviction. People v. Insignares, 109 A.D.2d 221, 491 N.Y.S.2d 166 (1st Dept. 1985).

Bail properly denied.—Defendant was charged with possession of marihuana, and sought an order setting bail. Court denied defendant's bail application, because in a situation wholly unrelated to the marihuana charge, defendant had threatened to shoot certain individuals at his former place of employment, and then to shoot himself after the killings. Court found that in reaching bail determination, there was no requirement that the dangerousness posed to the community and violence of the defendant be related to the conduct charged in the indictment. People v. Bosco, 175 Misc. 2d 166, 668 N.Y.S.2d 331 (Co. Ct. N.Y. Co. 1997).

Plea; agreement.—The formal acceptance of a plea bargain, which requires the defendant's bail to be revoked and any agreement to defer acceptance of the plea, so as to allow limited liberty, does not diminish the enforceability of the plea bargain. People v. D'Amico, 179 A.D.2d 671, 578 N.Y.S.2d 610 (2d Dept. 1992).

Plea; felony.—The entrance of a guilty plea for an A-II

felony requires immediate incarceration until the court sentences the defendant. People v. D'Amico, 147 Misc. 2d 731, 556 N.Y.S.2d 456 (Sup. Ct. Suffolk Co. 1990).

§ 530.45. Order of recognizance or bail; after conviction and before sentence.

1. When the defendant is at liberty in the course of a criminal action as a result of a prior order of recognizance or bail and the court revokes such order and then either fixes no bail or fixes bail in a greater amount or in a more burdensome form than was previously fixed and remands or commits defendant to the custody of the sheriff, a judge designated in subdivision two, upon application of the defendant following conviction of an offense other than a class A felony or a class B or class C felony offense defined in article one hundred thirty of the penal law committed or attempted to be committed by a person eighteen years of age or older against a person less than eighteen years of age, and before sentencing, may issue a securing order and either release defendant on his own recognizance, or fix bail, or fix bail in a lesser amount or in a less burdensome form than fixed by the court in which the conviction was entered.

2. An order as prescribed in subdivision one may be issued by the following judges in the indicated situations:

(a) If the criminal action was pending in supreme court or county court, such order may be issued by a justice of the appellate division of the department in which the conviction was entered.

(b) If the criminal action was pending in a local criminal court, such order may be issued by a judge of a superior court holding a term thereof in the county in which the conviction was entered.

3. An application for an order specified in this section must be made upon reasonable notice to the people, and the people must be accorded adequate opportunity to appear in opposition thereto. Not more than one application may be made pursuant to this section. Defendant must allege in his application that he intends to take an appeal to an intermediate appellate court immediately after sentence is pronounced.

4. Notwithstanding the provisions of subdivision one, if within thirty days after sentence the defendant has not taken an appeal to an intermediate appellate court from the judgment or sentence, the operation of such order terminates and the defendant must surrender himself to the criminal court in which the judgment was entered in order that execution of the judgment be commenced.

5. Notwithstanding the provisions of subdivision one, if within one hundred twenty days after the filing of the notice of appeal such appeal has not been brought to argument in or submitted to the intermediate appellate court, the operation of

such order terminates and the defendant must surrender himself to the criminal court in which the judgment was entered in order that execution of the judgment be commenced or resumed; except that this subdivision does not apply where the intermediate appellate court has (a) extended the time for argument or submission of the appeal to a date beyond the specified period of one hundred twenty days, and (b) upon application of the defendant, expressly ordered that the operation of the order continue until the date of the determination of the appeal or some other designated future date or occurrence.

6. Where the defendant is at liberty during the pendency of an appeal as a result of an order issued pursuant to this section, the intermediate appellate court, upon affirmance of the judgment, must by appropriate certificate remit the case to the criminal court in which such judgment was entered. The criminal court must, upon at least two days notice to the defendant, his surety and his attorney, promptly direct the defendant to surrender himself to the criminal court in order that execution of the judgment be commenced or resumed, and if necessary the criminal court may issue a bench warrant to secure his appearance.

Added by L. 1974, Ch. 435; L. 2000, Ch. 1, eff. Feb. 1, 2001; L. 2003, Ch. 246, § 47, eff. Nov. 1, 2003, amending subd. 1.

ANNOTATIONS

Bail; convictions.—Following a conviction, defendant may forego bail between conviction and sentencing as to accumulate time to credit towards the upcoming sentence. *In re* LaBelle, 79 N.Y.2d 350, 582 N.Y.S.2d 970, 591 N.E.2d 1156 (1992).

—Defendant's ability to obtain bail between the date of conviction and date of sentencing expires upon the date of sentencing. Morgenthau v. Rosenberger, 217 A.D.2d 478, 630 N.Y.S.2d 55 (1st Dept.), *aff'd*, 86 N.Y.2d 826, 633 N.Y.S.2d 473, 657 N.E.2d 494 (1995).

—Defendant's application for bail, following his conviction, pending appeal was denied as defendant was convicted of criminally negligent homicide. People v. Laezza, 143 A.D.2d 424, 533 N.Y.S.2d 3 (2d Dept. 1988).

§ 530.50. Order of recognizance or bail; during pendency of appeal.

A judge who is otherwise authorized pursuant to section 460.50 or section 460.60 to issue an order of recognizance or bail pending the determination of an appeal, may do so unless the defendant received a class A felony sentence or a sentence for any class B or class C felony offense defined in article one hundred thirty of the penal law committed or attempted to be committed by a person eighteen years of age or older against a person less than eighteen years of age.

Amended by L. 2000, Ch. 1, eff. Feb. 1, 2001; L. 2003, Ch. 264, § 48, eff. Nov. 1, 2003.

ANNOTATIONS

Class of sentence controls.—A stay of execution may be granted where a class A felony is subsequently modified pursuant to statute because it is not the grade of conviction but rather the class of the sentence that controls. People v. Vasquez, 88 A.D.2d 667, 450 N.Y.S.2d 606 (2d Dept. 1982).

CPL § 530.50 is constitutional.—Gold v. Shapiro, 62

A.D.2d 62, 403 N.Y.S.2d 906 (2d Dept.), *aff'd*, 45 N.Y.2d 849, 410 N.Y.S.2d 68, 382 N.E.2d 767 (1978).

Bail; conviction.—Defendant's conviction on a class A-II felony mandates imprisonment and prohibits the granting of bail pending appeal. Lanza v. New York, 130 A.D.2d 872, 515 N.Y.S.2d 928 (3d Dept. 1987).

—Defendant was denied bail pending appeal because the CPL prohibits granting bail to a defendant convicted of a class A felony. People v. McGuire, 101 A.D.2d 914, 476 N.Y.S.2d 28 (3d Dept. 1984); People v. Murphy, 491 N.Y.S.2d 280 (3d Dept. 1985).

§ 530.60. Order of recognizance or bail; revocation thereof.

1. Whenever in the course of a criminal action or proceeding a defendant is at liberty as a result of an order of recognizance or bail issued pursuant to this article, and the court considers it necessary to review such order, it may, and by a bench warrant if necessary, require the defendant to appear before the court. Upon such appearance, the court, for good cause shown, may revoke the order of recognizance or bail. If the defendant is entitled to recognizance or bail as a matter of right, the court must issue another such order. If he is not, the court may either issue such an order or commit the defendant to the custody of the sheriff.

2. (a) Whenever in the course of a criminal action or proceeding a defendant charged with the commission of a felony is at liberty as a result of an order of recognizance or bail issued pursuant to this article it shall be grounds for revoking such order that the court finds reasonable cause to believe the defendant committed one or more specified class A or violent felony offenses or intimidated a victim or witness in violation of sections 215.15, 215.16 or 215.17 of the penal law while at liberty. Before revoking an order of recognizance or bail pursuant to this subdivision, the court must hold a hearing and shall receive any relevant, admissible evidence not legally privileged. The defendant may cross-examine witnesses and may present relevant, admissible evidence on his own behalf. Such hearing may be consolidated with, and conducted at the same time as, a felony hearing conducted pursuant to article one hundred eighty of this chapter. A transcript of testimony taken before the grand jury upon presentation of the subsequent offense shall be admissible as evidence during the hearing. The district attorney may move to introduce grand jury testimony of a witness in lieu of that witness' appearance at the hearing.

(b) Revocation of an order of recognizance or bail and commitment pursuant to this subdivision shall be for the following periods, either:

(i) For a period not to exceed ninety days exclusive of any periods of adjournment requested by the defendant; or

(ii) Until the charges contained within the accusatory instrument have been reduced or dismissed such that no count remains which charges the defendant with commission of a felony; or

(iii) Until reduction or dismissal of the charges contained within the accusatory instrument charging the subsequent offense such that no count remains which charges the defendant with commission of a class A or violent felony offense.

Upon expiration of any of the three periods specified within this paragraph, whichever is shortest, the court may grant or deny release upon an order of bail or recognizance in accordance with the provisions of this article. Upon conviction to an offense the provisions of article five hundred thirty of this chapter shall apply.

(c) Notwithstanding the provisions of paragraph (a) of this subdivision a defendant, against whom a felony complaint has been filed which charges the defendant with commission of a class A or violent felony offense committed while he was at liberty as specified therein, may be committed to the custody of the sheriff pending a revocation hearing for a period not to exceed seventy-two hours. An additional period not to exceed seventy-two hours may be granted by the court upon application of the district attorney upon a showing of good cause or where the failure to commence the hearing was due to the defendant's request or occurred with his consent. Such good cause must consist of some compelling fact or circumstance which precluded conducting the hearing within the initial prescribed period.

Amended by L. 1981, Ch. 788; L. 1986, Ch. 794.

ANNOTATIONS

Bail revocation hearing.—Petitioner's writ of habeas corpus was improperly dismissed since, at petitioner's prior bail revocation hearing, the hearing court refused to permit the defense to examine the grand jury minutes which were used in lieu of a witness' appearance, pursuant to statute. People *ex rel.* Ryan v. Warden of H.D.M., 113 A.D.2d 116, 495 N.Y.S.2d 373 (1st Dept. 1985).

Bail; appearance.—The court is mandated to fix bail upon a non-felony charge, regardless of the fact that the court believes that incarceration is necessary to secure the defendant's appearance before the court. *In re* LaBelle, 79 N.Y.2d 350, 582 N.Y.S.2d 970, 591 N.E.2d 1156 (1992).

Bail; revocation.—The court acted within its discretion in revoking defendant's bail and placing defendant in police custody, upon discovering that defendant had threatened a witness for the prosecution. People v. Bowers, 128 A.D.2d 541, 512 N.Y.S.2d 473 (2d Dept. 1987).

—Revocation of bail pursuant to CPL § 530.60(1) must be "based on some factor that has a material bearing upon the probability of defendants future attendance," which must be determined in a summary hearing, and the court must consider the factors outlined in CPL § 530.60(2)(a); here, the chain of related criminal acts furnished good cause to believe that they would have a material bearing upon the probability of defendant's future attendance. People v. McDonnell, 177 Misc. 2d 610, 677 N.Y.S.2d 700 (Sup. Ct. Queens Co. 1998).

—Revocation of defendant's bail requires a reasonable belief that defendant committed a class A or violent felony. The burden is not sustained upon allegations of an assault, when no indictments were imposed, no charge filed, and where the evidence is mainly hearsay. People v. Silvestri, 132 Misc. 2d 1015, 506 N.Y.S.2d 251 (Sup. Ct. Kings Co. 1986).

—The court's discretion in revoking bail is limited to the CPL in a case where it is reasonable to believe that defendant committed a violent or class A felony. However, revocation is prohibited in situations such as non-violent felonies, intimidation of witnesses, or non-criminal, but anti-social, acts. People

v. Saulnier, 129 Misc. 2d 151, 492 N.Y.S.2d 897 (Sup. Ct. N.Y. Co. 1985).

§ 530.70. Order of recognizance or bail; bench warrant.

1. A bench warrant issued by a superior court, by a district court, by the New York City criminal court or by a superior court judge sitting as a local criminal court may be executed anywhere in the state. A bench warrant issued by a city court, a town court or a village court may be executed in the county of issuance or any adjoining county; and it may be executed anywhere else in the state upon the written endorsement thereon of a local criminal court of the county in which the defendant is to be taken into custody. When so endorsed, the warrant is deemed the process of the endorsing court as well as that of the issuing court.

2. A bench warrant may be addressed to: (a) any police officer whose geographical area of employment embraces either the place where the offense charged was allegedly committed or the locality of the court by which the warrant is issued; or (b) any uniformed court officer for a court in the city of New York, the county of Nassau, the county of Suffolk or the county of Westchester that is part of the unified court system of the state for execution in the building wherein such court officer is employed or in the immediate vicinity thereof. A bench warrant must be executed in the same manner as a warrant of arrest, as provided in section 120.80, and following the arrest, such executing police officer or court officer must without unnecessary delay bring the defendant before the court in which it is returnable; provided, however, if the court in which the bench warrant is returnable is a city, town or village court, and such court is not available, and the bench warrant is addressed to a police officer, such executing police officer must without unnecessary delay bring the defendant before an alternate local criminal court, as provided in subdivision five of section 120.90; or if the court in which the bench warrant is returnable is a superior court, and such court is not available, and the bench warrant is addressed to a police officer, such executing police officer may bring the defendant to the local correctional facility of the county in which such court sits, to be detained there until not later than the commencement of the next session of such court occurring on the next business day.

2-a. A court which issues a bench warrant may attach thereto a summary of the basis for the warrant. In any case where, pursuant to subdivision two of this section, a defendant arrested upon a bench warrant is brought before a local criminal court other than the court in which the warrant is returnable, such local criminal court shall consider such summary before issuing a securing order with respect to the defendant.

3. A bench warrant may be executed by (a) any officer to whom it is addressed, or (b) any other police officer delegated to execute it under circumstances prescribed in subdivisions four and five.

4. The issuing court may authorize the delegation of such warrant. Where the issuing court has so authorized, a police officer to whom a bench warrant is addressed may delegate another police officer to whom it is not addressed to execute such warrant as his agent when:

(a) He has reasonable cause to believe that the defendant is in a particular county other than the one in which the warrant is returnable; and

(b) The geographical area of employment of the delegated police officer embraces the locality where the arrest is to be made.

5. Under circumstances specified in subdivision four, the police officer to whom the bench warrant is addressed may inform the delegated officer, by telecommunication, mail or any other means, of the issuance of the warrant, of the offense charged in the underlying accusatory instrument and of all other pertinent details, and may request him to act as his agent in arresting the defendant pursuant to such bench warrant. Upon such request, the delegated police officer is to the same extent as the delegating officer, authorized to make such arrest pursuant to the bench warrant within the geographical area of such delegated officer's employment. Upon so arresting the defendant, he must without unnecessary delay deliver the defendant or cause him to be delivered to the custody of the police officer by whom he was so delegated, and the latter must then without unnecessary delay bring the defendant before the court in which such bench warrant is returnable.

6. A bench warrant may be executed by an officer of the state division of parole or a probation officer when the person named within the warrant is under the supervision of the division of parole or a department of probation and the probation officer is authorized by his probation director, as the case may be. The warrant must be executed upon the same conditions and in the same manner as is otherwise provided for execution by a police officer.

Amended by L. 1976, Ch. 265; L. 1979, Ch. 492; L. 1981, Chs. 456, 463; L. 1988, Ch. 565; L. 1990, Ch. 681; L. 1991, Ch. 352, eff. Nov. 1, 1991, amending subd. 2.

ANNOTATIONS

Bench warrant; issuance.—The city court of Yonkers properly issued a bench warrant as it was executed in Rockland County which adjoins Westchester County, the county of issuance. People v. Ennis, 186 A.D.2d 145, 587 N.Y.S.2d 722 (2d Dept. 1992).

—The issuance of a bench warrant is performed pursuant to defendant's failure to appear in court. People v. Pappas, 128 A.D.2d 556, 512 N.Y.S.2d 493 (2d Dept. 1987).

Bench warrant; prosecution.—During the time between the issuance of the bench warrant, due to the defendant's absence in court, until the time defendant appears in the court, the People's case must be in a state of preparation. People v. Luperon, 85 N.Y.2d 71, 623 N.Y.S.2d 735, 647 N.E.2d 1243 (1995).

§ 530.80. Order of recognizance or bail; surrender of defendant.

1. At any time before the forfeiture of a bail bond, an obligor may surrender the defendant in his exoneration, or the defendant may surrender himself, to the court in which his case is pending or to the sheriff to whose custody he was committed at the time of giving bail, in the following manner:

(a) A certified copy of the bail bond must be delivered to the sheriff, who must detain the defendant in his custody thereon, as upon a commitment. The sheriff must acknowledge the surrender by a certificate in writing, and must forthwith notify the court in which the case is pending that such surrender has been made.

(b) Upon the bail bond and the certificate of the sheriff, or upon the surrender to the court in which the case is pending, such court must, upon five days notice to the district attorney, order that the bail be exonerated. On filing such order, the bail is exonerated accordingly.

2. For the purpose of surrendering the defendant, an obligor or the person who posted cash bail for the defendant may take him into custody at any place within the state, or he may, by a written authority indorsed on a certified copy of the bail bond, empower any person over twenty years of age to do so.

3. At any time before the forfeiture of cash bail, the defendant may surrender himself or the person who posted bail for the defendant may surrender the defendant in the manner prescribed in subdivision one. In such case, the court must order a return of the money to the person who posted it, upon producing the certificate of the sheriff showing the surrender, and upon a notice of five days to the district attorney.

Amended by L. 1984, Ch. 384.

ARTICLE 540—FORFEITURE OF BAIL AND REMISSION THEREOF

Section

LexisNexis Cross Reference

Criminal Law Advocacy, Vol. 1, Ch. 5, Bail.

§ 540.10. Forfeiture of bail; generally.

1. If, without sufficient excuse, a principal does not appear when required or does not render himself amenable to the orders and processes of the criminal court wherein bail has been posted, the court must enter such facts upon its minutes and the bail bond or the cash bail, as the case may be, is thereupon forfeited.

2. If the principal appears at any time before the final adjournment of the court, and satisfactorily excuses his neglect, the court may direct the forfeiture to be discharged upon such terms as are just. If the forfeiture is not so discharged and the forfeited bail consisted of a bail bond, the district attorney, within one hundred twenty days after the adjournment of the court at which such bond was directed to be forfeited, must proceed against the obligor or obligors who executed such bond, in the manner prescribed in subdivision three. If the forfeited bail consisted of cash bail, the county treasurer with whom it is deposited shall give written notice of the forfeiture to the person who posted cash bail for the defendant may at any time after the final adjournment of the court or forty-five days after notice of forfeiture required herein has been given, whichever comes later, apply the money deposited to the use of the county.

3. A bail bond or cash bail, upon being forfeited, together with a certified copy of the order of the court forfeiting the same, must be filed by the district attorney in the office of the clerk of the county wherein such order was issued. Such clerk must docket the same in the book kept by him for docketing of judgments and enter therein a judgment against the obligor or obligors who executed such bail bond for the amount of the penalty of said bond or against the person who posted the cash bail for the amount of the cash bail, and the bond and the certified copy of the order of the court forfeiting the bond or the cash bail constitutes the judgment roll. Such judgment constitutes a lien on the real estate of the obligor or obligors who executed such bail bond from the time of the entry of the judgment. An execution may be issued to collect the amount of said bail bond in the same form and with the same effect as upon a judgment recovered in an action in said county upon a debt in favor of the people of the state of New York against such obligor or obligors.

Amended by L. 1984, Ch. 384; L. 1998, Ch. 427, § 1, eff. Oct. 20, 1998, amending subd. 2, extending the time in which the district attorney must proceed to 120 days.

ANNOTATIONS

Forfeiture of bail; procedure.—CPL § 540.10 mandates that the People take action to enforce a bail bond forfeiture order within a specified period of time. The time requirement is triggered when the Supreme Court finds a defendant's absence is unexcused and makes a determination on the record directing forfeiture of the bail bond. People v. Nicholas, 97 N.Y.2d 24, 734 N.Y.S.2d 557, 760 N.E.2d 345 (2001).

—In cases involving bail bonds the People must act in a timely manner when filing an order for forfeiture for non-appearance as the legislature mandated a sixty day period that commences after the adjournment of the court. The use of the term "must" in the CPL is interpreted as a mandatory provision. However, in cases where cash bail has been posted the People are permitted to appropriate the funds "at any time." People v. Schonfeld, 74 N.Y.2d 324, 547 N.Y.S.2d 266, 546 N.E.2d 395 (1989).

—Failure of the People to move for forfeiture of bail in a timely manner will preclude the state from recovery. Only the legislature has the ability to amend CPL § 540.10 in order to allow recovery if the People fail to act within the sixty day period mandated by the statute. International Fidelity Ins. Co. v. People, 208 A.D.2d 838, 618 N.Y.S.2d 399 (2d Dept. 1994).

—District Attorney's failure to file certified copy of forfeiture order rendered the underlying debt unenforceable, but did not affect the validity of the order. People v. Santiago, 175 Misc. 2d 268, 668 N.Y.S.2d 878 (Westchester Co. Ct. 1998).

Forfeiture of bail; burden of proof.—Unless the People can demonstrate competent proof of the bail being forfeited, the bail must be returned to the defendant. People v. Signorite, 538 N.Y.S.2d 487 (2d Dept. 1989).

Forfeiture of bail; court's discretion.—Once a bail forfeiture has been reduced to a judgment, it can only be set aside upon a motion for remission, which must be made within one year after the forfeiture of bail is declared. Here, defendant's motion for remission of bail was time-barred. Furthermore, it was a proper exercise of the court's discretion to conclude that defendant's incarceration, which was the result of crimes he committed while released on bail, did not constitute an exceptional circumstance, and was the result of his willful conduct. People v. Cotto, 262 A.D.2d 138, 693 N.Y.S.2d 98 (1st Dept. 1999).

—The court acted within its discretion in forfeiting bail because the defendant did not appear in court upon the specified date because the medical evidence presented to explain defendant's absence had no factual basis and was merely a conclusion. Indemnity Ins. Co. Of N. Am. v. People, 133 A.D.2d 345, 519 N.Y.S.2d 244 (2d Dept. 1987).

—If the court does not order the defendant to appear in court upon a specified date, any forfeiture of bail posted by the defendant is illegal and an abuse of the court's discretion. People v. Salabarria, 121 A.D.2d 438, 503 N.Y.S.2d 411 (2d Dept. 1986).

Forfeiture of bail; date.—The court may forfeit the

defendant's bail on the exact date that the defendant failed to make his scheduled court appearance. People v. Jackson, 179 A.D.2d 825, 579 N.Y.S.2d 159 (2d Dept. 1992).

§ 540.20. Forfeiture of bail; certain local criminal courts.

Notwithstanding the provisions of section 540.10, when bail has been posted in a city court, town court or village court in connection with a local criminal court accusatory instrument, other than a felony complaint, and thereafter such bail is forfeited, the following rules are applicable:

1. If such bail consists of a bail bond, the financial officer of such city, town or village must promptly commence an action for the recovery of the sum of money specified in such bond, and upon collection thereof shall pay the same over to the treasurer or financial officer of the city, the supervisor of the town or the treasurer of the village. Any amount recovered in such action, unless otherwise provided by law, shall be the property of the city, town or village in which the offense charged is alleged to have been committed.

2. If such bail consists of cash bail, the local criminal court must:

(a) If it is a city court, pay the forfeited bail to the treasurer or other financial officer of the city. Such forfeited bail, unless otherwise provided by law, is the property of such city.

(b) If it is a town court or a village court, pay the forfeited bail to the state comptroller on or before the tenth day of the month next succeeding such forfeiture. Such forfeited bail, unless otherwise provided by law is the property of the town or village in which the offense charged is alleged to have been committed; provided, however, that when (i) a single amount of bail is posted for more than a single offense charged, and (ii) the town or village justice court does not attribute a specific amount of bail to each offense, and (iii) forfeited bail for at least two of the offenses would be the property of different governmental entities, the entire amount of forfeited bail shall be the property of the town or village in which the offenses charged are alleged to have been committed, except that, when forfeited bail for at least one of the offenses would be the property of the state, the entire amount of forfeited bail shall be the property of the state.

Amended by L. 1991, ch. 460, eff. Nov. 1, 1991, amending subd. 2.

ANNOTATION

Disposition of forfeited bail posted pursuant to CPL § 460.50.—Bail pending appeal posted to the County Commissioner of Finance pursuant to CPL § 460.50 is not to be remitted to the local criminal court under CPL § 540.20; CPL § 540.10 governs the disposition of such bail. People v. Ali, 82 Misc. 2d 75, 368 N.Y.S.2d 771 (Sup. Ct. Orange Co. 1975).

§ 540.30. Remission of forfeiture.

1. After the forfeiture of a bail bond or cash

bail, as provided in section 540.10, an application for remission of such forfeiture may be made to a court as follows:

(a) If the forfeiture has been ordered by a superior court, the application must be made in such court;

(b) If the forfeiture has been ordered by a local criminal court, the application must be made to a superior court in the county, except that if the local criminal court which ordered the forfeiture was a district court, the application may alternatively be made to that district court.

2. The application must be made within one year after the forfeiture of the bail is declared upon at least five days notice to the district attorney and service of copies of the affidavits and papers upon which the application is founded. The court may grant the application and remit the forfeiture or any part thereof, upon such terms as are just. The application may be granted only upon payment of the costs and expenses incurred in the proceedings for the enforcement of the forfeiture.

Amended by L. 1980, Ch. 248.

ANNOTATIONS

Bail granted on erroneous criminal record.—The newly discovered fact that the principal's record of prior convictions before the court at the time bail was granted was erroneous cannot serve to invalidate a court order granting bail. People v. Public Serv. Mutual Ins. Co., 43 A.D.2d 961, 352 N.Y.S.2d 651 (2d Dept.), aff'd, 32 N.Y.2d 901, 346 N.Y.S.2d 818, 300 N.E.2d 157 (1973).

Remission of bail forfeiture; standing to seek.—County Court correctly held that petitioners have no standing to seek remission or exoneration of a forfeited bail since they were not sureties, but rather stood merely as indemnitors to the surety which was an insurance company which actually posted the bond in question. In re Leonard Van Deusen, 97 A.D.2d 924, 470 N.Y.S.2d 770 (3d Dept. 1983), app. dismissed, 64 N.Y.2d 1110 (1985).

Remission of bail forfeiture properly denied.—People's failure to extradite defendant, who did not meet the U.S. Justice Department's criteria for seeking extradition, does not entitle appellant to remission of bail. People v. Jaquez, 309 A.D.2d 635, 765 N.Y.S.2d 621 (1st Dept. 2003).

—It was a proper exercise of court's discretion to deny the motion for remission since defendant's incarceration, after committing a crime while out on bail, did not constitute an exceptional circumstance and was the result of willful conduct. People v. Shell, 266 A.D.2d 28, 698 N.Y.S.2d 214 (1st Dept. 1999).

—Remission of bail forfeiture was properly denied where it appeared that the defendant left his residence and lived in another state under an assumed name and there was no denial that defense counsel, three days before the surrender date, telephoned defendant's residence and left a message as to said date. People v. Scalise, 105 A.D.2d 869, 482 N.Y.S.2d 362 (3d Dept.), app. dismissed, 62 N.Y.2d 915 (1984).

Remission of bail forfeiture; court's discretion.—It is within the court's discretion whether or not to grant an application for remission in the event bail is forfeited. This application is granted only in the interest of promoting justice and in exceptional circumstances. Indemnity Ins. Co. of N. Am. v. People, 133 A.D.2d 345, 519 N.Y.S.2d 244 (2d Dept. 1987).

Remission of bail forfeiture; statute of limitations.—The one year statute of limitations for an application for remission of bail is inapplicable when the bail is accepted illegally or if defendant claims the forfeiture is illegal or void. People v. Salabarria, 121 A.D.2d 438, 503 N.Y.S.2d 411 (2d Dept. 1986).

—When the court exonerates the bail, the one year statute of limitations is inapplicable because there is no need to direct the county treasurer to release the bail, when it should no longer be in the county's possession. People v. Morales, 108 A.D.2d 827, 485 N.Y.S.2d 30 (2d Dept. 1985).

—The legislature drafted the remission statute to secure defendant's appearance in court, therefore at the conclusion of a one year period remission is precluded because the state's interests have become irreparably damaged. People v. Schonfeld, 145 A.D.2d 741, 535 N.Y.S.2d 479 (3d Dept. 1988).

—The courts are mandated to interpret the time limit, as set in the CPL, strictly, so the construction of the CPL shall remain uniform. People v. Schonfeld, 145 A.D.2d 741, 535 N.Y.S.2d 479 (3d Dept. 1988).

Sufficient excuse for principal's failure to appear.—The defendant or surety must demonstrate that the non-appearance was not deliberate or willful and the non-appearance did not prejudice or deprive the people of any rights. Therefore, a medically excused non-appearance requires an affidavit demonstrating that the illness either disabled the defendant or made it dangerous for the defendant to appear before the court. Indemnity Ins. Co. of N. Am. v. People, 133 A.D.2d 345, 519 N.Y.S.2d 244 (2d Dept. 1987).

Forfeiture of bail; court's discretion.—When the defendant, who owns the funds posted as bail, flees prior to the termination of the criminal proceedings, the court may act within its discretion by directing a forfeiture of the bail. People v. Lee, 179 A.D.2d 829, 579 N.Y.S.2d 159 (2d Dept. 1992).

TITLE Q—PROCEDURES FOR SECURING ATTENDANCE AT CRIMINAL ACTIONS AND PROCEEDINGS OF DEFENDANTS NOT SECURABLE BY CONVENTIONAL MEANS—AND RELATED MATTERS

ARTICLE 550—SECURING ATTENDANCE OF DEFENDANTS—IN GENERAL

Section
550.10 Securing attendance of defendants; in general.

LexisNexis Cross Reference

New York Criminal Practice (2d ed.), Vol. 1, Ch. 7, Securing Attendance of Defendants for Arraignment and Prosecution.

§ 550.10. Securing attendance of defendants; in general.

Depending upon the status of a criminal action pending against a defendant, the geographical location of the defendant at the time and other factors, his attendance thereat for purposes of arraignment or prosecution may be secured by the following methods:

1. If the defendant has never been arraigned in the action, and if he is at liberty within the state, his attendance may, under given circumstances, be secured by a warrant of arrest, as prescribed in article one hundred twenty, a superior court warrant of arrest, as prescribed in subdivision three of section 210.10, or a summons, as prescribed in article one hundred thirty.

2. If the defendant has been arraigned in the action and, by virtue of a securing order, is either in the custody of the sheriff or at liberty within the state on his own recognizance or on bail, his attendance may be secured as follows:

(a) If the defendant is confined in the custody of the sheriff, the court may direct the sheriff to produce him;

(b) If the defendant is at liberty within the state as a result of an order releasing him on his own recognizance or on bail, the court may secure his attendance by notification or by the issuance of a bench warrant.

3. If the defendant's attendance cannot be secured by methods described in subdivisions one and two, either because he is outside the state or because he is confined in an institution within the state as a result of an order issued in some other action, proceeding or matter, his attendance may, under indicated circumstances, be secured by procedures prescribed in the ensuing articles of this title.

ANNOTATIONS

Bail; class action; constitutionality.—There was no proper basis here for bringing a class action charging that present bail laws are unconstitutional, since every bail application is determined on an individual basis. Bellamy v. Judges & Justices of the N.Y.C. Crim. Ct., 41 A.D.2d 196, 342 N.Y.S.2d 137 (1st Dept.), *aff'd,* 32 N.Y.2d 886, 346 N.Y.S.2d 812, 300 N.E.2d 153 (1973).

Bail; judicial review.—Since the legislature has allowed for stay of judgment pending appeal to intermediate court in certain instances, there is no legal basis for the claim that the bail system in New York fails to provide a prompt and meaningful procedure for judicial review of a bail determination. Bellamy v. Judges & Justices of the N.Y.C. Crim. Ct., 41 A.D.2d 196, 342 N.Y.S.2d 137 (1st Dept. 1973).

Production of defendant.—The CPL places a statutory duty upon the appropriate public official to produce the defendant to the superior court, whether the defendant is incarcerated or at liberty. People v. Boudin, 100 A.D.2d 266, 474 N.Y.S.2d 70 (2d Dept. 1984).

—Generally, when a securing order is issued committing the custody of a principal to the sheriff, it is the latter who will be called upon to transport the principal to the appropriate jail, and similarly, when the court requires the attendance of a principal committed to the custody of the sheriff, the court in which attendance is required may compel such attendance by directing the sheriff to produce him. *In re* Delaney, 75 A.D.2d 642, 427 N.Y.S.2d 284 (2d Dept. 1980).

—The court retains the exclusive discretion in designating a public official to produce the defendant, but a refusal to produce does not allow for recovery of damages for costs incurred in the transportation of the defendant. Town of Poughkeepsie v. Town of Dutchess, 129 Misc. 2d 312, 492 N.Y.S.2d 1009 (Sup. Ct. Dutchess Co. 1985).

ARTICLE 560—SECURING ATTENDANCE OF DEFENDANTS CONFINED IN INSTITUTIONS WITHIN THE STATE

Section
560.10   Securing attendance of defendants confined in institutions within the state.

LexisNexis Cross Reference

New York Criminal Practice (2d ed.), Vol. 1, Ch. 7, Securing Attendance of Defendants for Arraignment and Prosecution.

§ 560.10. Securing attendance of defendants confined in institutions within the state.

1. When a criminal action is pending against a defendant who is confined in an institution within the state pursuant to a court order issued in a different action, proceeding or matter, the following courts and judges may, under the indicated circumstances, order that the defendant be produced in the court in which the criminal action is pending for purposes of arraignment or prosecution therein:

(a) If the action is pending in a superior court or with a superior court judge sitting as a local criminal court, or in a district court or the New York City criminal court, such court may, upon application of the district attorney, order the production therein of a defendant confined in any institution within the state.

(b) If the action is pending in a city court or a town court or a village court, such court may, upon application of the district attorney, order production therein of a defendant confined in a county jail of such county. Production therein of a defendant confined in any other institution within the state may, upon application of the district attorney, be ordered by a judge of a superior court holding a term thereof in the county in which the action is pending.

2. An application by a district attorney, pursuant to subdivision one, for production of a defendant confined in an institution located in another county in connection with a criminal action or proceeding pending in such other county, must be made upon reasonable notice to the district attorney of such other county and to the attorney representing such defendant in or in connection with the action or proceeding pending therein, and the court or judge must accord them reasonable opportunity to be heard in the matter. If such court or judge determines that production of the defendant would result in an unreasonable interference with the conduct of the action in such other county, it must deny the application. If an order of production is issued, a justice of the appellate division, of either the department embracing the county of issuance thereof or of the department embracing the county of the defendant's confinement, upon application of the district attorney of the county of confinement or of the attorney representing the defendant in or in connection with the action pending therein, may for good cause shown vacate such order of production.

ANNOTATIONS

Production of defendant.—The state's duty to exercise due diligence in securing the defendant's appearance in court is satisfied by following the statutory provisions of the CPL. People v. Bryant, 139 A.D.2d 750, 527 N.Y.S.2d 500 (2d Dept. 1988)

—The District Attorney must present sufficient evidence to demonstrate that the state abided by the standards set by the CPL in ensuring that defendant would be in attendance in court when defendant was confined in a different county within the state. People v. Billups, 105 A.D.2d 795, 481 N.Y.S.2d 430 (2d Dept. 1984).

—The state prosecutor is responsible for issuing a petition to the court to order the production of the defendant for an arraignment or prosecution. People v. Greenwaldt, 103 A.D.2d 933, 479 N.Y.S.2d 781 (3d Dept. 1984).

Return of defendant.—Defendant was returned to New York City pursuant to an outstanding bench warrant because the Nassau County authorities failed to assure defendant's presence as mandated by the CPL. People v. Cropper, 202 A.D.2d 603, 609 N.Y.S.2d 288 (2d Dept 1994).

ARTICLE 570—SECURING ATTENDANCE OF DEFENDANTS WHO ARE OUTSIDE THE STATE BUT WITHIN THE UNITED STATES—RENDITION TO OTHER JURISDICTIONS OF DEFENDANTS WITHIN THE STATE— UNIFORM CRIMINAL EXTRADITION ACT

LexisNexis Cross Reference

New York Criminal Practice (2d ed.), Vol. 1, Ch. 7, Securing Attendance of Defendants for Arraignment and Prosecution.

§ 570.02. Short title.

This article may be cited and referred to as the uniform criminal extradition act.

ANNOTATIONS

Jurisdiction.—Petitioner's claims supporting her resistance to extradition to North Carolina, under the necessities of our Federal system and the requirements of the Uniform Criminal Extradition Act must be presented to the courts of North Carolina or in the Federal courts. People *ex rel.* Little v. Ciuros,

61 A.D.2d 1053, 403 N.Y.S.2d 291 (2d Dept.), *aff'd,* 44 N.Y.2d 825, 406 N.Y.S.2d 449, 370 N.E.2d 980 (1978).

Appeal.—Petitioner who argues against an order of extradition is limited in the scope of issues that can be raised in a habeas corpus proceeding, that specifically excludes raising the issue of laches. People *ex rel.* Quarterman v. Commissioner of the N.Y.C. Dept. of Corrections, 183 A.D.2d 763, 583 N.Y.S.2d 297 (2d Dept. 1992).

Extradition; charges.—Once the trial court ascertains the identity of the person and determines that the extradition papers are in order, a court cannot inquire into the merits of the charges pending against the person named in the extradition warrant issued by the Governor. Fitzpatrick v. Cunningham, 193 A.D.2d 1109, 598 N.Y.S.2d 639 (4th Dept. 1993).

§ 570.04. Definitions.

As used in this article, the following terms have the following meanings:

1. "Governor" includes any person performing the functions of governor by authority of the law of this state.

2. "Executive authority" includes the governor, and any person performing the functions of governor in a state other than this state.

3. "State," when referring to a state other than this state, includes any other state or territory, organized or unorganized, of the United States of America.

§ 570.06. Fugitives from justice; duty of governor.

Subject to the provisions of this article, the provisions of the constitution of the United States controlling, and any and all acts of congress enacted in pursuance thereof, it is the duty of the governor of this state to have arrested and delivered up to the executive authority of any other state of the United States any person charged in that state with treason, felony, or other crime, who has fled from justice and is found in this state.

ANNOTATIONS

Collateral estoppel.—The doctrine of collateral estoppel is virtually nullified in extradition cases; collateral estoppel did not bar the instant extradition request because of the lack of identity of issues. People ex rel. Schank v. Gerace, 231 A.D.2d 380, 661 N.Y.S.2d 403 (4th Dept. 1997).

Extradition; rationale.—The constitution, federal statutes, and CPL all order the implementation of extradition as to prevent states from providing sanctuary from the law. Strachen v. Colon, Warden of Manhattan House of Detention, 77 N.Y.2d 499, 568 N.Y.S.2d 895, 571 N.E.2d 65 (1991).

Extradition; Governor's discretion.—When the court rules that an individual is a fugitive the Governor of the deciding state is mandated to extradite the fugitive. People ex rel. Peterkin v. Warden of the House of Detention for Men, 199 A.D.2d 560, 608 N.Y.S.2d 110 (2d Dept. 1993).

—When a prisoner is not a "fugitive from justice," it is at the Governor's discretion to involuntarily remove the prisoner. However, there is a mandatory duty to extradite when the prisoner is a "fugitive from justice." People ex rel. Richardson v. McMickens, 115 A.D.2d 786, 496 N.Y.S.2d 559 (2d Dept. 1985).

Extradition; presence within the state.—The return of a fugitive, whether of his own volition or not, to the state who ordered the extradition and where the offense was committed does not relieve the defendant of his fugitive status. All the state needs to demonstrate is that at the moment the extradition order was issued the "fugitive from justice" was in a different state. People ex rel. Quarterman v. Commissioner of the N.Y.C. Dept. of Corrections, 183 A.D.2d 736, 583 N.Y.S.2d 297 (2d Dept. 1992).

§ 570.08. Demand; form.

No demand for the extradition of a person charged with crime in another state shall be recognized by the governor unless in writing alleging that the accused was present in the

demanding state at the time of the commission of the alleged crime, and that thereafter he fled from the state, except in cases arising under section 570.14 or 570.16, and accompanied by a copy of an indictment found or by information supported by an affidavit in the state having jurisdiction of the crime, or by a copy of an affidavit made before a magistrate there, together with a copy of any warrant which was issued thereon, or by a copy of a judgment of conviction or of a sentence imposed in execution thereof, together with a statement by the executive authority of the demanding state that the person claimed has escaped from confinement or has broken the terms of his bail, probation or parole. The indictment, information or affidavit made before the magistrate must substantially charge the person demanded with having committed a crime under the law of that state; and the copy of the indictment, information, affidavit, judgment of conviction or sentence must be authenticated by the executive authority making the demand.

ANNOTATIONS

Extradition hearing.—In accordance with limited purpose and scope of extradition hearing, jury is permitted to weigh evidence presented before them. This purpose is limited to the identification of the charged party and to establish that the defendant was present in the state when the crime was committed. People v. Birden, 86 A.D.2d 774, 448 N.Y.S.2d 66 (4th Dept. 1982).

Copy of demanding state's statutes.—CPL Article 570 does not require that a copy of the applicable statutes of the demanding state be included among the supporting papers for extradition. People ex rel. Donohoe v. Andrews, 104 Misc. 2d 384, 428 N.Y.S.2d 384 (Sup. Ct. Broome Co. 1979).

Extradition; conspiracy.—The court may allow extradition to South Carolina if one act of the conspiracy occurred in Florida, but the indictment charge stated that other activities of the conspiracy occurred in South Carolina, so long as the charge is sufficient to allow for extradition even if the accused was not in South Carolina on the date of the crime. People ex rel. Mikulec v. Braun, 112 A.D.2d 803, 492 N.Y.S.2d 305 (4th Dept. 1985).

Sufficiency of demand.—The demanding state must "substantially charge" the party to be extradited with the crime and the local magistrate must determine that there is probable cause to charge the defendant with the commission of the crime. People ex rel. Kotch v. District Attorney, Kings County, 170 A.D.2d 632, 566 N.Y.S.2d 404 (2d Dept. 1991).

—The court shifts the burden of proof to the defendant to demonstrate that he was not in the state at the time the crime was committed, so long as the state established a prima facie case through the introduction of an application for extradition and a warrant that was issued by the Governor of the state of New York. People ex rel. O'Connell v. Sheriff of County of Putnam, 160 A.D.2d 828, 554 N.Y.S.2d 79 (2d Dept. 1990).

—The Connecticut request for extradition was invalid because the accused was in a different state on the date the crime was committed. People ex rel. Hayden v. Phillips, 96 A.D.2d 912, 466 N.Y.S.2d 95 (2d Dept. 1983).

—County courts are limited, in the extent, they may examine an Alabama request for extradition, so long as the request, on its face, is in order. The request must be in writing, allege defendant's presence in the state at the time the crime was committed, and that defendant fled the state following the commission of the crime. The request must be accompanied by an affidavit issued before a magistrate of the state of Alabama, a copy of the arrest warrant, and authentication by the executive branch of the state of Alabama. People ex rel. Deschamps v. Knowlton, 112 A.D.2d 689, 491 N.Y.S.2d 858 (3d Dept. 1985).

—Where Florida Governor's requisition and supporting papers sufficiently show probable cause for appellant's arrest and substantially charge him with having committed the crime of escape together with appellant's apprehension in New York State, there is sufficient support for a Warrant of Extradition. People *ex rel.* Davis v. Skinner, 38 A.D.2d 673, 327 N.Y.S.2d 124 (4th Dept. 1971), *aff'd*, 30 N.Y.2d 564, 330 N.Y.S.2d 620, 281 N.E.2d 561 (1972); *see also* People *ex rel.* O'Dell v. Quinlan, 81 Misc. 2d 271, 366 N.Y.S.2d 531 (Dutchess Co. Ct. 1975).

§ 570.10. Investigation by governor.

When a demand shall be made upon the governor of this state by the executive authority of another state for the surrender of a person so charged with crime, the governor may call upon the attorney general or any district attorney in this state to investigate or assist in investigating the demand, and to report to him the situation and circumstances of the person so demanded, and whether he ought to be surrendered.

ANNOTATION

Extradition; Governor's duty.—The Governor of the state of Alabama is bound to issue an order of extradition, upon making a determination as to whether the accused is a fugitive from justice, as defined by the CPL. People *ex rel.* Harris v. Mattoney, 152 Misc. 2d 799, 579 N.Y.S.2d 582 (Sup. Ct. Suffolk Co. 1991).

§ 570.12. Extradition of persons imprisoned or awaiting trial in another state.

When it is desired to have returned to this state a person charged in this state with a crime and such person is imprisoned or is held under criminal proceedings then pending against him in another state, the governor of this state may agree with the executive authority of such other state for the extradition of such person before the conclusion of his term of sentence in such other state, upon condition that such person be returned to such other state at the expense of this state as soon as the prosecution in this state is terminated.

ANNOTATION

Extradition; agreement.—The CPL sets forth the procedure required for extradition, in which the Governor of the state who seeks extradition must reach an agreement with the Governor of the state where the defendant is imprisoned. People v. Reilly, 136 A.D.2d 355, 527 N.Y.S.2d 234 (2d Dept. 1988).

§ 570.14. Extradition of persons who left the demanding state under compulsion.

The governor of this state may also surrender, on demand of the executive authority of any other state, any person in this state who is charged in the manner provided in section 570.08 with having violated the laws of the state whose executive authority is making the demand, even though such person left the demanding state involuntarily.

ANNOTATIONS

Extradition; Governor's discretion.—A non-fugitive is entitled to the state Governor's discretionary power, in the

determining whether to issue an order of extradition. Neufeld v. Commissioner of the N.Y.C. Dept. of Corrections, 71 N.Y.2d 881, 527 N.Y.S.2d 762, 522 N.E.2d 1060 (1988).

—The CPL is interpreted broadly, therefore the court shall allow a prisoner to be involuntarily removed from the state where the crime was committed, because the removal falls within the discretionary powers of the Governor. People *ex rel.* Richardson v. McMickens, 115 A.D.2d 786, 496 N.Y.S.2d 559 (2d Dept. 1985).

—The state Governor's discretionary power of issuing an extradition warrant must be in accord with the discretionary extradition provisions if the charged party is not fugitive from justice. People *ex rel.* Hayden v. Phillips, 96 A.D.2d 912, 466 N.Y.S.2d 95 (2d Dept. 1983).

Extradition; fugitive from justice.—Prisoner who escaped jail because of numerous beatings conducted by prison officials is fugitive and his status does not change to an involuntary transferred prisoner in order to be covered by the discretionary provisions of CPL § 570.14. People *ex rel.* Neufeld v. Commissioner, New York City Dept. Of Corrections, 71 N.Y.2d 881, 527 N.Y.S.2d 762, 522 N.E.2d 1060 (1988).

§ 570.16. Extradition of persons not present in demanding state at time of commission of crime.

The governor of this state may also surrender, on demand of the executive authority of any other state, any person in this state charged in such other state in the manner provided in section 570.08 with committing an act in this state or in a third state, intentionally resulting in a crime in the state whose executive authority is making the demand, when the acts for which extradition is sought would be punishable by the laws of this state, if the consequences claimed to have resulted therefrom in the demanding state had taken effect in this state; and the provisions of this article not otherwise inconsistent, shall apply to such cases, even though the accused was not in that state at the time of the commission of the crime, and has not fled therefrom; provided, however, that the governor of this state may, in his discretion, make any such surrender conditional upon agreement by the executive authority of the demanding state, that the person so surrendered will be held to answer no criminal charges of any nature except those set forth in the requisition upon which such person is so surrendered, at least until such person has been given reasonable opportunity to return to this state after his acquittal, if he shall be acquitted, or if he shall be convicted, after he shall be released from confinement. Nothing in this section shall apply to the crime of libel.

ANNOTATIONS

Habeas corpus; extradition; insufficiency of demand.—Extradition demand of Governor of California was defective where it alleged that the defendant committed an act in New York intentionally resulting in crime in California but failed to contain an evidentiary showing that the alleged act would also have been crime in New York State if it had its effect there. People v. Hinton, 40 N.Y.2d 345, 386 N.Y.S.2d 703, 353 N.E.2d 617 (1976).

—The state must demonstrate in non-fugitive extradition case that prima facie case had been established by showing that the accused would have violated the laws of the state if the consequences of the act had been felt in the state. People *ex rel.* v. Allen v. Dooley, 156 A.D.2d 406, 548 N.Y.S.2d 530 (2d Dept. 1989).

Sufficiency of demand.—The state seeking extradition must establish that even though the accused was not within the borders of the demanding state, that both the laws of the demanding state and the state where the accused is being charged would be able to punish the accused for the commission of the crime. People *ex rel.* Allen v. Dooley, 156 A.D.2d 406, 548 N.Y.S.2d 530 (2d Dept. 1989).

—The requirements of CPL § 570.16 were satisfied where the petitioner, although not in Pennsylvania at the time the crimes were committed, was charged with theft and passing bad checks, crimes which were punishable in New York. The evidence before the Philadelphia grand jury showed the acts were knowingly and intentionally committed and his own testimony confirmed that he knew with whom he was dealing and therefore, must have known that his acts would result in crimes in Pennsylvania. People *ex rel.* Grillo v. Holtzman, 91 A.D.2d 983, 457 N.Y.S.2d 575 (2d Dept.), *aff'd,* 58 N.Y.2d 934, 460 N.Y.S.2d 533, 447 N.E.2d 81 (1983).

—Defendant's overt acts that were conducted in New York, while being in Maryland, contributed to the furtherance of conspiracy and therefore the extradition was valid. People *ex rel.* Orucle v. Coughlin, 165 A.D.2d 933, 561 N.Y.S.2d 96 (3d Dept. 1990).

§ 570.18. Issuance of warrant of arrest by governor; recitals therein.

If the governor decides that the demand should be complied with, he shall sign a warrant of arrest, which shall be sealed with the state seal, and be directed to any police officer or other person whom he may think fit to entrust with the execution thereof. The warrant must substantially recite the facts necessary to the validity of its issuance.

ANNOTATIONS

Governor's grant of extradition prima facie evidence of validity.—Governor's grant of extradition is prima facie evidence that the constitutional and statutory requirements have been met, and once the governor has granted extradition, court considered extradition can do no more than decide (a) whether the extradition documents on their face are in order; (b) whether the petitioner has been charged with crime in the demanding state; (c) whether the petitioner is the person named in the request for extradition and (d) whether the petitioner is fugitive. People *ex rel.* Coster v. Andrews, 104 Misc. 2d 506, 428 N.Y.S.2d 594 (Sup. Ct. Broome Co. 1980).

Extradition; warrant.—The state Governor's warrant for extradition must be, on its face, prima facie true and state that the defendant was in the state when the crime was committed and then fled the jurisdiction. People *ex rel.* Glidden v. Nemier, 133 A.D.2d 487, 519 N.Y.S.2d 217 (3d Dept. 1987).

§ 570.20. Execution of warrant; manner and place thereof.

Such warrant shall authorize the police officer or other person to whom directed to arrest the accused at any time and any place where he may be found within the state and to command the aid of all police officers or other persons in the execution of the warrant, and to deliver the accused, subject to the provisions of this article to the duly authorized agent of the demanding state.

§ 570.22. Authority of arresting officer.

Every such police officer or other person empowered to make the arrest, shall have the same authority, in arresting the accused to command assistance therein, as police officers have by law in the execution of any criminal process directed to them, with like penalties against those who refuse their assistance.

§ 570.24. Rights of accused person: application for writ of habeas corpus.

No person arrested upon such warrant shall be delivered over to the agent whom the executive authority demanding him shall have appointed to receive him unless he shall first be taken forthwith before a justice or judge of a court of record in this state, who shall inform him of the demand made for his surrender and of the crime with which he is charged, and that he has the right to demand and procure legal counsel; and if the prisoner or his counsel shall state that he or they desire to test the legality of his arrest, the justice or judge of such court of record shall fix a reasonable time to be allowed within which to apply for a writ of habeas corpus. When such writ is applied for, notice thereof, and of the time and place of hearing thereon, shall be given to the district attorney of the county in which the arrest is made and in which the accused is in custody, and to the said agent of the demanding state.

ANNOTATIONS

Incompetency; no bar to extradition.—The question of the fugitive's competency cannot be used to deny his return to the demanding state. People v. Faustino, 105 Misc. 2d 641, 432 N.Y.S.2d 782 (Crim. Ct. Queens Co. 1980).

Proof of absence from demanding state; crimes of continuing nature.—Where the indictment charged crimes of continuing nature which allegedly took place throughout the entire period covered by the indictment, it was incumbent upon the petitioner to prove his absence from the demanding State throughout the entire period, in order to successfully fight extradition. People *ex rel.* Pata v. Lindemann, 75 A.D.2d 654, 427 N.Y.S.2d 445 (2d Dept. 1980).

—Habeas corpus relief is generally available only to challenge an unlawful detention, but it may apply where the manner and circumstances of detention are such as to extend beyond that which is authorized by judgment and commitment order. People *ex rel.* Jacobson v. Warden, Brooklyn House of Detention, 77 A.D.2d 937, 431 N.Y.S.2d 114 (2d Dept. 1980).

Scope of inquiry.—The application was denied where relator commenced habeas corpus proceeding to resist her extradition to North Carolina contending that if forced to return her constitutional rights would be violated and she would be subjected to cruel and inhuman treatment by correctional officials, since one alleging present of future improper activity in another state is under the necessity of seeking redress in accordance with law and in the forum in which the alleged improprieties will occur. People *ex rel.* Little v. Ciuros, 44 N.Y.2d 825, 406 N.Y.S.2d 449, 377 N.E.2d 980 (1978).

—Habeas corpus relief is generally available only to challenge an unlawful detention, but it may apply where the manner and circumstances of detention are such as to extend beyond that which is authorized by judgment and commitment order. People *ex. rel.* Jacobson v. Warden, Brooklyn House of Detention, 77 A.D.2d 937, 431 N.Y.S.2d 114 (2d Dept. 1980).

—In extradition proceedings, surrender is not to be interfered with in the asylum state by the summary process of habeas corpus upon speculations as to what ought to be the result of trial in the demanding state where the Constitution provides for it to take place. California v. Superior Court of California, 482 U.S. 400, 107 S. Ct. 2433, 96 L. Ed. 2d 332 (1987).

Use of writ of habeas corpus.—Habeas corpus may not be utilized to review errors already passed upon in an earlier appeal, nor may it be used to collaterally attack judgment on constitutional grounds. Sales v. LeFevre, 93 A.D.2d 945, 463 N.Y.S.2d 58 (3d Dept. 1983).

Habeas corpus; hearings.—Defendant may petition for release through habeas corpus hearing and the court has the discretion to set bail for the accused, even though the CPL does not explicitly provide for bail in extradition hearings. Strachan v. Soloff; People ex rel. Sirachon v. Colon, 157 A.D.2d 122, 554 N.Y.S.2d 565 (1st Dept. 1990).

—Prior to the extradition to the demanding state, judicial proceeding is conduct in which the accused has the right to counsel and the right to challenge the extradition order. Welkes v. Brennan, 79 A.D.2d 644, 433 N.Y.S.2d 817 (2d Dept. 1980).

—The court may conduct hearing for an application for writ of habeas corpus, upon an oral request by the defendant after defendant was arrested and arraigned for demand of extradition. People ex rel. Glidden v. Nemier, 133 A.D.2d 487, 519 N.Y.S.2d 287 (3d Dept. 1987).

—The court is required to honor an extradition order on the basis of conflicting evidence, if the petitioner is unable to prove conclusively to the court that he was not present in the state at the time the crime was committed. People ex rel. Dragon v. Trombley, 79 A.D.2d 768, 435 N.Y.S.2d 60 (3d Dept. 1980).

—Although habeas corpus writ is utilized, traditionally, to appeal an order of extradition, it is only applicable to incarcerated parties and may not be utilized by parties who are not illegally deprived of their liberty rights. Edelbaun v. Cumo, 122 Misc. 2d 1029, 472 N.Y.S.2d 302 (Sup. Ct. Crim. Term, Queens Co. 1984).

—The court where the accused is contesting the demanding state's extradition order may only inquire as to certain matters in habeas corpus proceeding. The court may investigate whether the accused is the party addressed by the warrant, whether the accused was in the demanding state at the time the crime was committed, and if the accused is charged with crime in the demanding state. People ex rel. Fuscow v. Sera, 123 Misc. 2d 19, 472 N.Y.S.2d 564 (Sup. Ct. Bronx Co. 1984).

Habeas corpus; Uniform Extradition Act.—The accused retains the right to petition the court for an extraordinary writ and habeas corpus relief because extradition will result in the accused being deprived of their liberty rights. State ex rel. Rudin v. Word, 112 Misc. 2d 62, 445 N.Y.S.2d 1002 (Sup. Ct. N.Y. Co. 1981).

§ 570.26. Noncompliance with preceding section; penalties for violation.

Any officer who shall deliver to the agent for extradition of the demanding state a person in his custody under the governor's warrant, in disobedience of the preceding section, shall be guilty of a felony.

§ 570.28. Confinement of the accused in jail when necessary.

The officer or persons executing the governor's warrant of arrest, or the agent of the demanding state to whom the prisoner may have been delivered may, when necessary, confine the prisoner in the jail of any county or city through which he may pass; and the keeper of such jail must receive and safely keep the prisoner until the officer or person having charge of him is ready to proceed on his route, such officer or person, however, being chargeable with the expense of keeping.

§ 570.30. Confinement of extradited persons passing through this state.

The officer or agent of a demanding state to whom a prisoner may have been delivered following extradition proceedings in another state, or to whom a prisoner may have been delivered after waiving extradition in such other state, and who is passing through this state with such a prisoner for the purpose of immediately returning such prisoner to the demanding state may, when necessary, confine the prisoner in the jail of any county or city through which he may pass; and the keeper of such jail must receive and safely keep the prisoner until the officer or agent having charge of him is ready to proceed on his route, such officer or agent, however, being chargeable with the expense of keeping, provided, however, that such officer or agent shall produce and show to the keeper of such jail satisfactory written evidence of the fact that he is actually transporting such prisoner to the demanding state after a requisition by the executive authority of such demanding state or waiver thereof. Such person shall not be entitled to demand a new requisition while in this state.

§ 570.32. Arrest of accused before making of requisition.

Whenever any person within this state shall be charged on the oath of any credible person before any local criminal court of this state with the commission of any crime in any other state and, except in cases arising under section 570.14 or 570.16, with having fled from justice, or, with having been convicted of a crime in that state and having escaped from confinement, or having broken the terms of his bail, probation or parole, or, whenever complaint shall have been made before any local criminal court in this state setting forth on the affidavit of any credible person in another state that a crime has been committed in such other state and that the accused has been charged in such other state with the commission of the crime, and, except in cases arising under section 570.14 or 570.16, has fled from justice, or with having been convicted of a crime in that state and having escaped from confinement or having broken the terms of his bail, probation or parole and is believed to be in this state, the local criminal court shall issue a warrant directed to any police officer directing him to apprehend the person named therein, wherever he may be found in this state, and to bring him before the same or any other local criminal court which may be available in or convenient of access to the place where the arrest may be made, to answer the charge or complaint and affidavit, and a certified copy of the sworn charge or complaint and affidavit upon which the warrant is issued shall be attached to such warrant.

ANNOTATION

Detainer warrant; extradition; due process.—Vacatur of detainer warrant lodged with custodial officials did not preclude the prosecuting state (in this case, Rhode Island) from seeking extradition in New York for the underlying criminal act, pursuant to the appropriate statute. Rhode Island is a signatory to the Uniform Criminal Extradition Act, and can request extradition of such a petitioner while he is imprisoned in this state. Failure by a state to request extradition may constitute a denial of due process, despite the fact that one of the states involved is not a signatory to the Agreement on Detainers. Failure to request extradition promptly adversely affects a prisoner's present condition and his ability to defend himself in the future. Baker v. Schubin, 72 Misc. 2d 413, 339 N.Y.S.2d 360 (Sup. Ct. Westchester Co. 1972).

§ 570.34. Arrest of accused without warrant therefor.

The arrest of a person in this state may be lawfully made also by any police officer or a private person, without a warrant, upon reasonable information that the accused stands charged in the courts of another state with a crime punishable by death or imprisonment for a term exceeding one year; but when so arrested the accused must be taken before a local criminal court with all practicable speed and complaint must be made against him under oath setting forth the ground for the arrest as in the preceding section; and, thereafter, his answers shall be heard as if he had been arrested on a warrant.

ANNOTATIONS

Arrest; out-of-state warrant.—The sparse case law available indicates that only an officer specially authorized to make arrests in New York can execute a federal warrant in New York for New York prosecution purposes; out-of-state police officers may be authorized to make arrests in New York, but generally only when they are in hot pursuit, which did not occur in the instant case. People v. LaFontaine, 92 N.Y.2d 470, 682 N.Y.S.2d 671, 705 N.E.2d 663 (1998).

—The CPL grants law enforcement officials the authority to arrest fugitives with out-of-state warrants. People v. McDermott, 150 A.D.2d 805, 542 N.Y.S.2d 41 (2d Dept. 1989).

—A law enforcement official may arrest a suspect without an arrest warrant if the suspect is a fugitive from another state. After the arrest an extradition hearing may be commenced. People ex rel. Deschamps v. Knowlton, 112 A.D.2d 689, 491 N.Y.S.2d 858 (3d Dept. 1985).

§ 570.36. Commitment to await requisition; bail.

If from the examination before the local criminal court it appears that the person held is the person charged with having committed the crime alleged, and, except in cases arising under section 570.14 or 570.16, that he has fled from justice, the local criminal court must, by a warrant reciting the accusation, commit him to the county jail for such a time not exceeding thirty days and specified in the warrant, as will enable the arrest of the accused to be made under a warrant of the governor on a requisition of the executive authority of the state having jurisdiction of the offense, unless the accused gives bail as provided in the next section, or until he shall be legally discharged.

ANNOTATIONS

Detention beyond 30 days.—An accused party may request for a release from detention, if the Governor seeking extradition fails to issue a warrant within the thirty day time limit mandated by the CPL. However, any violation of this section does not bar future extradition, so long as the accused is not detained

indefinitely. People ex rel. Brandolino v. Hastings, 72 A.D.2d 821, 421 N.Y.S.2d 893 (2d Dept. 1979)

Extradition; custody.—The courts may arraign and incarcerate a fugitive from justice so long as extradition is not waived upon defendant's release from jail. People ex rel. McKinnon v. Infante, 108 A.D.2d 1026, 485 N.Y.S.2d 583 (3d Dept. 1985).

Extradition; arrests.—Following the issuance of an order of extradition, the court may enforce an arrest of parties who are fugitives from justice, as defined by the CPL. People ex rel. Deschamps v. Knowlton, 112 A.D.2d 689, 491 N.Y.S.2d 851 (3d Dept. 1985).

§ 570.38. Bail; in what cases; conditions of bond.

Unless the offense with which the prisoner is charged is shown to be an offense punishable by death or life imprisonment under the laws of the state in which it was committed, a justice of the supreme court or county judge in this state may admit the person arrested to bail by bond or undertaking, with sufficient sureties, and in such sum as he deems proper, conditioned for his appearance before him at a time specified in such bond or undertaking but not later than thirty days after the examination referred to in section 570.36 and for his surrender, to be arrested upon the warrant of the governor of this state.

ANNOTATION

Bail; murder.—Although the CPL prohibits bail for crimes that could receive life imprisonment or death, this section does not prohibit bail if an extradition order is filed and accepted. Bail may be determined and set following the issuance of a warrant. People ex rel. Strachan v. Soloff; People ex rel. Strachan v. Colon, 157 A.D.2d 122, 554 N.Y.S.2d 565 (1st Dept. 1990).

§ 570.40. Extension of time of commitment; adjournment.

If the accused is not arrested under warrant of the governor by the expiration of the time specified in the warrant, bond or undertaking, a local criminal court may discharge him or may recommit him for a further period of sixty days, or for further periods not to exceed in the aggregate sixty days, or a supreme court justice or county judge may again take bail for his appearance and surrender, as provided in section 570.38 but within a period not to exceed sixty days after the date of such new bond or undertaking.

ANNOTATIONS

Expiration; 90 days.—Although CPL §§ 570.36 and 570.40 allows an accused who has not been arrested pursuant to a Governor's warrant within 90 days of his detention, to demand his release, it does not immunize him from extradition and upon receipt of a Governors warrant CPL §§ 570.36 and 570.40 lose all effect and cannot interfere with the court's obligation to comply with the requisition. People ex. rel. Brondolino v. Hastings, 72 A.D.2d 821, 421 N.Y.S.2d 893 (2d Dept. 1979).

—The defendant's commitment may be extended an additional sixty days, following the accused being arraigned and incarcerated. However, following this additional time period, if the demanding Governor's warrant is insufficient or not forthcoming, the accused shall be released, but is still classified as a fugitive from justice. People ex rel. McKinnon v. Infante, 108 A.D.2d 1026, 485 N.Y.S.2d 583 (3d Dept. 1985).

Previous release; failure to issue warrant.—Even though petitioner had been previously released because the Governor failed to issue a warrant within 90 days of his detention, he remained a fugitive from justice within meaning of the Federal Constitution and the statutes permitting extradition and could be detained upon subsequent receipt of the Governor's warrant. People v. Warden, Rikers Island Adolescent Detention Ctr., 51 A.D.2d 756, 379 N.Y.S.2d 502 (2d Dept. 1976). *See also* Jones v. People, 94 Misc. 2d 304, 404 N.Y.S.2d 525 (Rockland Co. Ct. 1978).

§ 570.42. Bail; when forfeited.

If the prisoner is admitted to bail, and fails to appear and surrender himself according to the conditions of his bond or undertaking, the justice of the supreme court or county judge, by proper order, shall declare the bond forfeited and order his immediate arrest without warrant if he be within this state. Recovery may be had on such bond or undertaking in the name of the state as in the case of other bonds or undertakings given by the accused in criminal proceedings within this state.

§ 570.44. Persons under criminal prosecution in this state at time of requisition.

If a criminal prosecution has been instituted against such person under the laws of this state and is still pending, the governor, in his discretion, may either surrender him on demand of the executive authority of another state or hold him until he has been tried and discharged or convicted and punished in this state.

ANNOTATION

Criminal prosecution; Governor's discretion.—Under the CPL, the Governor has the discretion whether or not to grant extradition if the accused is already a party to a criminal prosecution, unless the defendant waives extradition. People v. Santos, 135 Misc.2d 51, 514 N.Y.S.2d 854 (Sup. Ct. N.Y. Co. 1987).

§ 570.46. Guilt or innocence of accused; when inquired into.

The guilt or innocence of the accused as to the crime with which he is charged may not be inquired into by the governor, or in any proceeding after the demand for extradition accompanied by a charge of crime in legal form as above provided shall have been presented to the governor, except as it may be involved in identifying the person held as the person charged with the crime.

ANNOTATIONS

Requirement of personal knowledge.—The affidavit in support of the extradition proceeding does not have to be based on personal knowledge. People *ex rel.* Donohoe v. Andrews, 104 Misc. 2d 384, 428 N.Y.S.2d 384 (Sup. Ct. Broome Co. 1979).

Appellate review.—The appellate division is permitted to inquire into the identity of the party charged in the extradition order, but they are prohibited from conducting an investigation as to the guilt of the accused party. People *ex rel.* Kotch v. District Attorney, Kings County, 170 A.D.2d 632, 566 N.Y.S.2d 404 (2d Dept. 1991).

Affidavits; hearsay.—The courts are permitted to admit hearsay evidence because affidavits made without personal

knowledge may be used to support an extradition order and, therefore, witnesses are not required to testify in court. People *ex rel.* Semexant v. Warden of Corrections of the City of New York, Brooklyn House of Detentions, 133 Misc. 2d 202, 506 N.Y.S.2d 812 (Sup. Ct. Kings Co. 1986).

§ 570.48. Alias warrant of arrest.

The governor may recall his warrant of arrest or may issue another warrant whenever he deems proper.

ANNOTATION

Limit on discontinuances.—Legislature did not intend the CPLR limit on discontinuances to apply to extradition proceedings. People *ex rel.* Witty v. Warden, Riker's Island, 248 A.D.2d 333, 670 N.Y.S.2d 472 (1st Dept. 1998).

§ 570.50. Written waiver of extradition proceedings.

Any person arrested in this state charged with having committed any crime in another state or alleged to have escaped from confinement, or broken the terms of his bail, probation or parole, may waive the issuance and service of the warrant provided for in sections 570.18 and 570.20 and all other procedure incidental to extradition proceedings by executing or subscribing in the presence of a judge of any court of record within this state a writing which states that he consents to return to the demanding state, provided, however, that before such waiver shall be executed or subscribed by such person it shall be the duty of such judge to inform such person of his rights to the issuance and service of a warrant of extradition and to obtain a writ of habeas corpus as provided for in section 570.24.

If and when such consent has been duly executed it shall forthwith be forwarded to the office of the secretary of state of this state and filed therein. The judge shall direct the officer having such person in custody to deliver forthwith such person to the duly accredited agent or agents of the demanding state, and shall deliver or cause to be delivered to such agent or agents a copy of such consent. Provided, however, that nothing in this section shall be deemed to limit the rights of the accused person to return voluntarily and without formality to the demanding state, nor shall this waiver procedure be deemed to be an exclusive procedure or to limit the powers, rights or duties of the officers of the demanding state or of this state.

ANNOTATION

Procedures.—The statutory procedures of CPL § 570 are not exclusive, and waivers of extradition need not conform strictly to the procedures set forth in the Uniform Criminal Extradition Act. People v. Gordon, 176 Misc. 2d 46, 672 N.Y.S.2d 631 (Sup. Ct. Queens Co. 1998) (triple homicide case).

§ 570.52. Fugitives from this state; duty of governor.

Whenever the governor of this state shall demand a person charged with crime or with escaping from confinement or breaking the terms of his bail, probation or parole in this state from the executive authority of any other state, or from the chief justice or an associate justice of the supreme court of the District of Columbia authorized to receive such demand under the laws of the United States, he shall issue a warrant under the seal of this state to some agent commanding him to receive the person so charged, if delivered to him, and convey him to the proper officer of the county in this state in which the offense was committed.

§ 570.54. Application for issuance of requisition; by whom made; contents.

1. When the return to this state of a person charged with crime in this state is required, the district attorney of the county in which the offense was committed, or, if the offense is one which is cognizable by him, the attorney general shall present to the governor his written application for a requisition for the return of the person charged, in which application shall be stated the name of the person so charged, the crime charged against him, the approximate time, place and circumstances of its commission, the state in which he is believed to be, including the location of the accused therein at the time the application is made and certifying that, in the opinion of the said district attorney or attorney general the ends of justice require the arrest and return of the accused to this state for trial and that the proceeding is not instituted to enforce a private claim.

2. When there is required the return to this state of a person who has been convicted of a crime in this state and has escaped from confinement or broken the terms of his bail, probation or parole, the district attorney of the county in which the offense was committed, the parole board, or the warden of the institution or sheriff of the county, from which escape was made, or the commissioner of the state department of correctional services or his designee shall present to the governor a written application for a requisition for the return of such person, in which application shall be stated the name of the person, the crime of which he was convicted, the circumstances of his escape from confinement or of the breach of the terms of his bail, probation or parole, the state in which he is believed to be, including the location of the person therein at the time the application is made.

3. The application shall be verified by affidavit, shall be executed in duplicate and shall be accompanied by two certified copies of the accusatory instrument stating the offense with which the accused is charged, or of the judgment of conviction or of the sentence. The district attorney, attorney general, parole board, warden, sheriff or the commissioner of the state department of correctional services or his designee may also attach such further affidavits and other documents in duplicate as he shall deem proper to be submitted with such application. One copy of the application, with the action of the governor indicated by endorsement thereon, and one of the certified copies of the accusatory instrument, or of the judgment of conviction or the sentence shall be filed in the office of the secretary of state to remain of record in that office. The other copies of all papers shall be forwarded with the governor's requisition.

Amended by L. 1980, Ch. 2.

§ 570.56. Expense of extradition.

The expenses of extradition must be borne by the county from which the application for a requisition comes or, where the application is made by the attorney general, by the county in which the offense was committed. In the case of extradition of a person who has been convicted of a crime in this state and has escaped from a state prison or reformatory, the expense of extradition shall be borne by the department of correctional services. Where a person has broken the terms of his parole from a state prison or reformatory, the expense of extradition shall be borne by the state division of parole. Where a person has broken the terms of his bail or probation, the expense of extradition shall be borne by the county. Where a person has been convicted but not yet confined to a prison, or has been sentenced for a felony to a county jail or penitentiary and escapes, the expenses of extradition shall be charged to the county from whose custody the escape is effected. Nothing in this section shall preclude a county, the department of correctional services or the state division of parole, as the case may be, from collecting the expenses involved in extradition from the person who was extradited.

Amended by L. 1995, Ch. 193, § 1, eff. Nov. 1, 1995.

ANNOTATION

Defendant ordered to pay extradition cost.—County Court was authorized to order defendant, who agreed as part of his plea bargain, to pay the cost of extraditing him from California to New York. People v. Perry, 261 A.D.2d 650, 690 N.Y.S.2d 298 (3d Dept. 1999).

§ 570.58. Immunity from service of process in certain civil actions.

A person brought into this state on or after waiver of extradition based on a criminal charge shall not be subject to service of personal process in civil actions arising out of the same facts as the criminal proceeding to answer which he is being or has been returned until he has been convicted in the criminal proceeding, or if acquitted, until he has had reasonable opportunity to return to the state from which he was extradicted. *

* As originally enacted.

§ 570.60. No immunity from other criminal prosecution while in this state.

After a person has been brought back to this state by extradition proceedings, he may be tried in this state for other offenses which he may be charged with having committed here as well as that specified in the requisition for his extradition.

§ 570.62. Non-waiver by this state.

Nothing in this article contained shall be deemed to constitute a waiver by this state of its right, power or privilege to try such demanded person for offenses committed within this state, or of its right, power or privilege to regain custody of such person by extradition proceedings or otherwise for the purpose of trial, sentence or punishment for any offense committed within this state, nor shall any proceedings had under this article which result in, or fail to result in, extradition be deemed a waiver by this state of any of its rights, privileges or jurisdiction in any way whatsoever.

§ 570.64. Interpretation.

The provisions of this article shall be so interpreted and construed as to effectuate its general purposes to make uniform the law of those states which enact it.

ANNOTATION

Limit on discontinuances.—Legislature did not intend the CPLR limit on discontinuances to apply to extradition proceedings. People *ex rel.* Witty v. Warden, Riker's Island, 248 A.D.2d 333, 670 N.Y.S.2d 472 (1st Dept. 1998).

§ 570.66. Constitutionality.

If any part of this article is for any reason declared void, such invalidity shall not affect the validity of the remaining portions thereof.

ARTICLE 580—SECURING ATTENDANCE OF DEFENDANTS CONFINED AS PRISONERS IN INSTITUTIONS OF OTHER JURISDICTIONS OF THE UNITED STATES—RENDITION TO OTHER JURISDICTIONS OF PERSONS CONFINED AS PRISONERS IN THIS STATE—AGREEMENT ON DETAINERS

§ 580.10. Securing attendance of defendants confined as prisoners in institutions of other jurisdictions of the United States; methods.

The attendance in a criminal action pending in a court of this state of a defendant confined as a prisoner in an institution of another jurisdiction of the United States may, under prescribed circumstances, be secured pursuant to:

1. Section 570.12 of article five hundred seventy, known as the uniform criminal extradition act; or

2. Section 580.20, known as the agreement on detainers; or

3. Section 580.30.

ANNOTATIONS

Attendance; procedures.—The CPL requires a detainer to be formulated as mandated by the Interstate Agreement on Detainers in order to compel defendant's attendance. People v. Chan, 81 A.D.2d 765, 439 N.Y.S.2d 112 (1st Dept. 1981).

—The CPL lists the three sole methods of compelling the attendance of a defendant who may be incarcerated in another state or by the federal government. People v. Reilly, 136 A.D.2d 355, 527 N.Y.S.2d 234 (2d Dept. 1988).

Extradition hearing; new evidence.—In view of the truncated notice of the first hearing, in which the relator's presentation of proof was curtailed, and in view of new evidence received in a related proceeding, the court ruled that the interests of justice mandated a new hearing. People ex rel. Harris v. Warden, 42 A.D.2d 549, 345 N.Y.S.2d 29 (1st Dept. 1973).

§ 580.20. Agreement on detainers.

The agreement on detainers is hereby enacted into law and entered into by this state with all other jurisdictions legally joining therein in the form substantially as follows:

TEXT OF THE AGREEMENT ON DETAINERS

The contracting states solemnly agree that:

ARTICLE I

The party states find that charges outstanding against a prisoner, detainers based on untried indictments, informations or complaints, and difficulties in securing speedy trial of persons already incarcerated in other jurisdictions, produce uncertainties which obstruct programs of prisoner treatment and rehabilitation. Accordingly, it is the policy of the party states and the purpose of this agreement to encourage the expeditious and orderly disposition of such charges and determination of the proper status of any and all detainers based on untried indictments, informations or complaints. The party states also find that proceedings with reference to such charges and detainers, when emanating from another jurisdiction, cannot properly be had in the absence of cooperative procedures. It is the further purpose of this agreement to provide such cooperative procedures.

ARTICLE II

As used in this agreement:

(a) "State" shall mean a state of the United States; the United States of America; a territory or possession of the United States; the District of Columbia; the Commonwealth of Puerto Rico.

(b) "Sending state" shall mean a state in which a prisoner is incarcerated at the time that he initiates a request for final disposition pursuant to Article III hereof or at the time that a request for custody or availability is initiated pursuant to Article IV hereof.

(c) "Receiving state" shall mean the state in which trial is to be had on an indictment, information or complaint pursuant to Article III or Article IV hereof.

ARTICLE III

(a) Whenever a person has entered upon a term of imprisonment in a penal or correctional institution of a party state, and whenever during the continuance of the term of imprisonment there is pending in any other party state any untried indictment, information or complaint on the basis of which a detainer has been lodged against the prisoner, he shall be brought to trial within one hundred eighty days after he shall have caused to be delivered to the prosecuting officer and the appropriate court of the prosecuting officer's jurisdiction written notice of the place of his imprisonment and his request for a final disposition to be made of the indictment, information or complaint; provided that for good cause shown in open court, the prisoner or his counsel being present, the court having jurisdiction of the matter may grant any necessary or reasonable continuance. The request of the prisoner shall be accompanied by a certificate of the appropriate official having custody of the prisoner, stating the term of commitment under which the prisoner is being held, the time already served, the time remaining to be served on the sentence, the amount of good time earned, the time of parole eligibility of the prisoner, and any decisions of the state parole agency relating to the prisoner.

(b) The written notice and request for final disposition referred to in paragraph (a) hereof shall be given or sent by the prisoner to the warden, commissioner of correction or other official having custody of him, who shall promptly forward it together with the certificate to the appropriate prosecuting official and court by registered or certified mail, return receipt requested.

(c) The warden, commissioner of correction or other official having custody of the prisoner shall promptly inform him of the source and contents of any detainer lodged against him and shall also inform him of his right to make a request for final disposition of the indictment, information or complaint on which the detainer is based.

(d) Any request for final disposition made by a prisoner pursuant to paragraph (a) hereof shall operate as a request for final disposition of all untried indictments, informations or complaints on the basis of which detainers have been lodged against the prisoner from the state to whose prosecuting official the request for final disposition is specifically directed. The warden, commissioner of correction or other official having custody of the prisoner shall forthwith notify all appropriate prosecuting officers and courts in the several jurisdictions within the state to which the prisoner's request for final disposition is being sent of the proceeding being initiated by the prisoner. Any notification sent pursuant to this paragraph shall be accompanied by copies of the prisoner's written notice, request, and the certificate. If trial is not had on any indictment, information or complaint contemplated hereby prior to the return of the prisoner to the original place of imprisonment, such indictment, information or complaint shall not be of any further force or effect, and the court shall enter an order dismissing the same with prejudice.

(e) Any request for final disposition made by a prisoner pursuant to paragraph (a) hereof shall also be deemed to be a waiver of extradition with respect to any charge or proceeding contemplated thereby or included therein by reason of paragraph (d) hereof, and a waiver of extradition to the receiving state to serve any sentence there imposed upon him, after completion of his term of imprisonment in the sending state. The request for final disposition shall also constitute a consent by the prisoner to the production of his body in any court where his presence may be required in order to effectuate the purposes of this agreement and a further consent voluntarily to be returned to the original place of imprisonment in accordance with the provisions of this agreement. Nothing in this paragraph shall prevent the imposition of a concurrent sentence if otherwise permitted by law.

(f) Escape from custody by the prisoner subsequent to his execution of the request for final disposition referred to in paragraph (a) hereof shall void the request.

ARTICLE IV

(a) The appropriate officer of the jurisdiction in which an untried indictment, information or complaint is pending shall be entitled to have a prisoner against whom he has lodged a detainer and who is serving a term of imprisonment in any party state made available in accordance with Article V (a) hereof upon presentation of a written request for temporary custody or availability to the appropriate authorities of the state in which the prisoner is incarcerated; provided that the court having jurisdiction of such indictment, information or complaint shall have duly approved, recorded and transmitted the request; and provided further that there shall be a period of thirty days after receipt by the appropriate authorities before the request be honored, within which period the governor of the sending state may disapprove the request for temporary custody or availability, either upon his own motion or upon motion of the prisoner.

(b) Upon receipt of the officer's written request as provided in paragraph (a) hereof, the appropriate authorities having the prisoner in custody shall furnish the officer with a certificate stating the term of commitment under which the prisoner is being held, the time already served, the time remaining to be served on the sentence, the amount of good time earned, the time of parole eligibility of the prisoner, and any decisions of the state parole agency relating to the prisoner. Said authorities simultaneously shall furnish all other officers and appropriate courts in the receiving state who have lodged detainers against the prisoner with similar certificates and with notices informing them of the request for custody or availability and of the reasons therefor.

(c) In respect of any proceeding made possible by this Article, trial shall be commenced within one hundred twenty days of the arrival of the prisoner in the receiving state, but for good cause shown in open court, the prisoner or his counsel being present, the court having jurisdiction of the matter may grant any necessary or reasonable continuance.

(d) Nothing contained in this Article shall be construed to deprive any prisoner of any right which he may have to contest the legality of his delivery as provided in paragraph (a) hereof but such delivery may not be opposed or denied on the ground that the executive authority of the sending state has not affirmatively consented to or ordered such delivery.

(e) If trial is not had on any indictment, information or complaint contemplated hereby prior to the prisoner's being returned to the original place of imprisonment pursuant to Article V (e) hereof, such indictment, information or complaint shall not be of any further force or effect, and the court shall enter an order dismissing the same with prejudice.

ARTICLE V

(a) In response to a request made under Article III or Article IV hereof, the appropriate authority in a sending state shall offer to deliver temporary custody of such prisoner to the appropriate authority in the state where such indictment, information or complaint is pending against such person in order that speedy and efficient prosecution may be had. If the request for final disposition is made by the prisoner, the offer of temporary custody shall accompany the written notice provided for in Article III of this agreement. In the case of a federal prisoner, the appropriate authority in receiving state shall be entitled to temporary custody as provided by this agreement or to the prisoner's presence in federal custody at the place for trial, whichever custodial arrangement may be approved by the custodian.

(b) The officer or other representative of a state accepting an offer of temporary custody shall present the following upon demand:

(1) Proper identification and evidence of his authority to act for the state into whose temporary custody the prisoner is to be given.

(2) A duly certified copy of the indictment, information or complaint on the basis of which the detainer has been lodged and on the basis of which the request for temporary custody of the prisoner has been made.

(c) If the appropriate authority shall refuse or fail to accept temporary custody of said person, or in the event that an action on the indictment, information or complaint on the basis of which the detainer has been lodged is not brought to trial within the period provided in Article III or Article IV hereof, the appropriate court of the jurisdiction where the indictment, information or complaint has been pending shall enter an order dismissing the same with prejudice, and any detainer based thereon shall cease to be of any force or effect.

(d) The temporary custody referred to in this agreement shall be only for the purpose of permitting prosecution on the charge or charges contained in one or more untried indictments, informations or complaints which form the basis of the detainer or detainers or for prosecution on any other charge or charges arising out of the same transaction. Except for his attendance at court and while being transported to or from any place at which his presence may be required, the prisoner shall be held in a suitable jail or other facility regularly used for persons awaiting prosecution.

(e) At the earliest practicable time consonant with the purposes of this agreement, the prisoner shall be returned to the sending state.

(f) During the continuance of temporary custody or while the prisoner is otherwise being made available for trial as required by this agreement, time being served on the sentence shall continue to run but good time shall be earned by the prisoner only if, and to the extent that, the law and practice of the jurisdiction which imposed the sentence may allow.

(g) For all purposes other than that for which temporary custody as provided in this agreement is exercised, the prisoner shall be deemed to remain in the custody of and subject to the jurisdiction of the sending state and any escape from temporary custody may be dealt with in the same manner as an escape from the original place of imprisonment or in any other manner permitted by law.

(h) From the time that a party state receives custody of a prisoner pursuant to this agreement until such prisoner is returned to the territory and custody of the sending state, the state in which the one or more untried indictments, informations or complaints are pending or in which trial is being had shall be responsible for the prisoner and shall also pay all costs of transporting, caring for, keeping and returning the prisoner. The provisions of this paragraph shall govern unless the states concerned shall have entered into a supplementary agreement providing for a different allocation of costs and responsibilities as between or among themselves. Nothing herein contained shall be construed to alter or affect any internal relationship among the departments, agencies and officers of and in the government of a party state, or between a party state and its subdivisions, as to the payment of costs, or responsibilities therefor.

ARTICLE VI

(a) In determining the duration and expiration dates of the time periods provided in Articles III and IV of this agreement, the running of said time periods shall be tolled whenever and for as long as the prisoner is unable to stand trial, as determined by the court having jurisdiction of the matter.

(b) No provision of this agreement, and no

remedy made available by this agreement, shall apply to any person who is adjudged to be mentally ill.

ARTICLE VII

Each state party to this agreement shall designate an officer who, acting jointly with like officers of other party states, shall promulgate rules and regulations to carry out more effectively the terms and provisions of this agreement, and who shall provide, within and without the state, information necessary to the effective operation of this agreement.

ARTICLE VIII

This agreement shall enter into full force and effect as to a party state when such state has enacted the same into law. A state party to this agreement may withdraw herefrom by enacting a statute repealing the same. However, the withdrawal of any state shall not affect the status of any proceedings already initiated by inmates or by state officers at the time such withdrawal takes effect, nor shall it affect their rights in respect thereof.

ARTICLE IX

1. This agreement shall be liberally construed so as to effectuate its purposes. The provisions of this agreement shall be severable and if any phrase, clause, sentence or provision of this agreement is declared to be contrary to the constitution of any party state or of the United States or the applicability thereof to any government, agency, person or circumstance is held invalid, the validity of the remainder of this agreement and the applicability thereof to any government, agency, person or circumstance shall not be affected thereby. If this agreement shall be held contrary to the constitution of any state party hereto, the agreement shall remain in full force and effect as to the remaining states and in full force and effect as to the state affected as to all severable matters.

2. The phrase "appropriate court" as used in the agreement on detainers shall, with reference to the courts of this state, mean any court with criminal jurisdiction.

3. All courts, departments, agencies, officers and employees of this state and its political subdivisions are hereby directed to enforce the agreement on detainers and to cooperate with one another and with other party states in enforcing the agreement and effectuating its purposes.

4. Escape from custody while in another state pursuant to the agreement on detainers shall constitute an offense against the laws of this state

to the same extent and degree as an escape from the institution in which the prisoner was confined immediately prior to having been sent to another state pursuant to the provisions of the agreement on detainers and shall be punishable in the same manner as an escape from said institution.

5. It shall be lawful and mandatory upon the warden or other official in charge of a penal or correctional institution in this state to give over the person of any inmate thereof whenever so required by the operation of the agreement on detainers.

6. The governor is hereby authorized and empowered to designate an administrator who shall perform the duties and functions and exercise the powers conferred upon such person by Article VII of the agreement on detainers.

7. In order to implement Article IV (a) of the agreement on detainers, and in furtherance of its purposes, the appropriate authorities having custody of the prisoner shall, promptly upon receipt of the officer's written request, notify the prisoner and the governor in writing that a request for temporary custody has been made and such notification shall describe the source and contents of said request. The authorities having custody of the prisoner shall also advise him in writing of his rights to counsel, to make representations to the governor within thirty days, and to contest the legality of his delivery.

ANNOTATIONS

Agreement on detainers; when dismissal of indictment is appropriate.—Indictment pending against defendant in New York must be dismissed where defendant, who was being held in custody in California, was not brought to trial within the 180-day period mandated by the Interstate Agreement on Detainers; the adverse effect of the California sheriff's failure to properly notify the New York County district attorney's office of defendant's request that he be brought to trial on the New York indictment must be charged to the prosecution. People v. Diaz, 94 Misc. 2d 1010, 406 N.Y.S.2d 239 (Sup. Ct. N.Y. Co. 1978).

Applicability.—The court is under a duty, independent of the Agreement on Detainers, to comply with the statutory requirement of a speedy trial. People v. Santos, 68 N.Y.2d 859, 508 N.Y.S.2d 411, 501 N.E.2d 19 (1986).

—The appellate court should grant defendant's motion to dismiss based on the prosecution's failure to commence the trial within the 180-day period following defendant's request for final disposition as mandated by the Interstate Agreement on Detainers. People v. Torres, 60 N.Y.2d 119, 468 N.Y.S.2d 606, 456 N.E.2d 497 (1983).

—The Interstate Agreement on Detainers applies only to "untried" charges, and is inapplicable where, as here, defendant has been convicted but not sentenced. People v. Peterson, 264 A.D.2d 574, 695 N.Y.S.2d 550 (1st Dept. 1999), *cert. denied,* 531 U.S. 831 (2000).

—People's failure to bring defendant to trial after his request pursuant to CPL § 580.20 (Interstate Agreement on Detainers) and within 180 days was not excused by a superseding indictment since the People may not avoid the operation of time limitations under either CPL § 30.30 or CPL § 580.20 simply by the expedient of procuring another indictment, whether it arises out of the discovery of new evidence or otherwise. People v. C'Allah, 100 A.D.2d 754, 474 N.Y.S.2d 305 (1st Dept. 1984).

—CPL § 580.20 applies where an out-of-state prisoner has a pending untried indictment, information or complaint in New York, not where guilt has been established and defendant is awaiting sentencing. People v. Nosek, 236 A.D.2d 892, 654 N.Y.S.2d 63 (4th Dept. 1997).

Detainers; tolling the statute of limitations.—The court is mandated to toll the 180-day limitation of disposition of defendant's indictments pending in New York, because it was defendant's own actions that led to his unavailability, as defendant was being prosecuted for federal crimes. People v. Urlaku, 73 N.Y.2d 800, 537 N.Y.S.2d 24, 533 N.E.2d 1053 (1988).

Detainer; waiver of rights.—Defendant waived his contention that he was denied a speedy trial pursuant to the Interstate Agreement on Detainers because he failed to raise this contention before his trial or his sentencing. People v. Madden, 234 A.D.2d 394, 651 N.Y.S.2d 549 (2d Dept. 1996).

—Defendant's waiver of a right to a speedy trial under the Interstate Agreement on Detainers is binding, even though defense counsel did not attempt to obtain consent from the defendant because defendant was conscious of the time limits and did not object to the delays in his trial. People v. Sacco, 199 A.D.2d 288, 604 N.Y.S.2d 971 (2d Dept. 1993).

—In the event that defendant neglects to raise issue during the trial that the state violated the Agreement on Detainers shall constitute a waiver on the part of the defendant and precludes appeal for failure to preserve the issue. People v. Palumb, 433 N.Y.S.2d 997 (2d Dept. 1980).

—By pleading guilty to superior court information, defendant waived his contention that the proceeding was untimely commenced in violation of CPL § 580.20. People v. Zak, 242 A.D.2d 895, 662 N.Y.S.2d 654 (4th Dept. 1997).

—Defendant's guilty plea constituted a waiver of any appeal or claims arising under CPL § 580.20. People v. Nelson, 79 A.D.2d 1093, 435 N.Y.S.2d 836 (4th Dept. 1981).

Detainers; credit towards incarceration.—Defendant is not entitled to receive credit towards sentencing in New York for time spent imprisoned for a separate conviction in Connecticut. Hagerman v. Henderson, 79 A.D.2d 1112, 435 N.Y.S.2d 864 (4th Dept. 1981)

Detainer; inserted into records.—Petitioner's failure to comply with the Interstate Agreement on Detainers coupled with his refusal to waive extradition offsets the state's failure to commence proceedings within the 180-day period and allows for the insertion of a detainer into the petitioner's prison records. Hill v. E. W. Jones, 94 A.D.2d 904, 463 N.Y.S.2d 655 (3d Dept. 1993).

Interstate Compact.—The Interstate Agreement on Detainers, entered in to between signatories, preserves a defendant's right to a speedy trial, even if the defendant is incarcerated in a different jurisdiction. However, defendant retains the right to waive any benefits that may accrue from the use of the agreement. Amiger v. Long, 101 A.D.2d 616, 474 N.Y.S.2d 852 (3d Dept. 1984).

Delay by the defendant.—Defendant's omnibus motion to the court did not deny his right to a speedy trial, because the 21-day delay was attributed to the transcription and production of Grand Jury minutes that were required in order to entertain defendant's motion. People v. Torres, 111 A.D.2d 281, 489 N.Y.S.2d 115 (2d Dept. 1985).

Preservation for appellate review.—In addition to defendant entering a plea of guilty, defendant's delinquency in presenting the issue of the state failing to abide by the Interstate Agreement on Detainers and the time limits placed upon the proceedings precluded appellate review of the case. People v. Gooden, 151 A.D.2d 773, 542 N.Y.S.2d 757 (2d Dept. 1989).

—Defendant is required to move for dismissal of the indictment if his right to a speedy trial, as mandated by the CPL, is denied and failure to do so precludes his right to appeal the issue. People v. Harden, 543 N.Y.S.2d 947 (2d Dept. 1989).

—Defendant preserved the issue of CPL compliance, in regard to his rights being violated, by presenting the issue to the court prior to a guilty verdict being entered to the county court. Furthermore, the court had assured the defendant that a plea of guilty would not waive his right to appeal. Therefore defendant's plea of guilty is not construed as a waiver of his rights as granted by the CPL. People v. Fargher, 112 A.D.2d 599, 492 N.Y.S.2d 123 (3d Dept. 1985).

Ineffective assistance of counsel.—Defendant claimed that he received ineffective assistance of counsel in that his attorney failed to pursue a speedy trial violation predicated on the Interstate Agreement on Detainers; it was not ineffective assistance of counsel, because record contained no writing, as required by CPL § 580.20 indicating that defendant was invoking the 180-day time limit. People v. Gamez, 241 A.D.2d 693, 660 N.Y.S.2d 196 (3d Dept. 1997).

Federal preemption.—The state court is preempted from forcing the defendant to appear in court, in accordance with the Interstate Agreement on Detainers, when the defendant has federal charges against him and has not commenced a term of imprisonment. People v. Brown, 136 A.D.2d 715, 523 N.Y.S.2d 911 (2d Dept. 1988).

Detainers; preclusion of state courts.—New York courts are precluded from dismissing an out-of-town detainer motion unless the Interstate Agreement on Detainers is violated. However, the Detainers are limited to untried indictments, information, or complaints. Epps v. Hunt, 167 A.D.2d 789, 563 N.Y.S.2d 347 (3d Dept. 1990).

Art. I

Interstate Agreement on Detainers; purpose.—The Agreement on Detainers was developed in order to expedite and dispose of out-of-state criminal charges and ascertain the status of all detainers that deal with "untried indictments, information, or complaints." People v. Warder, 119 A.D.2d 526, 501 N.Y.S.2d 664 (1st Dept. 1986).

Art. III

Detainer; 180-day limit.—The state must bring the defendant to trial within the 180-day time limit; however, the state may request a reasonable continuance. Failure of the state to make a request for a continuance coupled with an opportunity to do so results in a dismissal of the charges. People v. Reilly, 136 A.D.2d 355, 527 N.Y.S.2d 234 (2d Dept. 1988); People v. Walker, 113 A.D.2d 448, 496 N.Y.S.2d 871 (4th Dept. 1985).

—The failure to afford defendant a trial within 180 days after he properly demanded one by invoking the procedures set forth in CPL § 580.20 requires dismissal of the indictment.—People v. Conway, 74 A.D.2d 582, 424 N.Y.S.2d 304 (2d Dept. 1980).

Art. III(a)

Detainers; tolling.—The 180-day time period was tolled for New York state indictments, because the defendant's own actions led to federal prosecution in New York, which rendered him unavailable for trial in Richmond County. People v. Vrlaku, 73 N.Y.2d 800, 537 N.Y.S.2d 24, 533 N.E.2d 1053 (1988).

Final disposition; request.—Defendant, if incarcerated in a different state, is required to submit a written notice and request for final disposition in a "timely fashion," however, the court will take any actions by the prison officials that caused any delay into consideration. Amiger v. Long, 101 A.D.2d 616, 474 N.Y.S.2d 852 (3d Dept. 1984).

—The CPL requires that defendants send a written request for final disposition to the prosecutor's jurisdiction and a certificate to the official who is maintaining custody of the defendant. Hill v. Jones, 94 A.D.2d 904, 463 N.Y.S.2d 656 (3d Dept. 1983)

Constitutional guarantees.—By entering a plea of guilty, defendant waived any claim under the CPL that his trial did not commence within the 180-day requisite period. Defendant is not adversely affected because his plea waived his rights and the Agreement on Detainers is neither a constitutional nor fundamental guarantee. People v. Cusick, 111 A.D.2d 251, 489 N.Y.S.2d 96 (2d Dept. 1985).

Trial; continuance.—The CPL mandates that the state shall commence court proceedings against the defendant in 180-days. Although the court may grant a continuance, failure of the state to obtain one shall result in a dismissal of charges. People v. Walker, 113 A.D.2d 448, 496 N.Y.S.2d 871 (4th Dept. 1985).

Art. III(d)

Detainers; speedy trial.—The purpose of the Interstate Agreement on Detainers is to protect an individual's right to a speedy trial and expedite matters so that a defendant is able to undergo treatment and begin his rehabilitation. People ex rel. Capalongo v. Howard, 87 A.D.2d 242, 453 N.Y.S.2d 45 (3d Dept. 1982).

Interstate Agreement on Detainers; violation.—The court held that returning the defendant to Maryland following his arraignment in New York, prior to trial, was a violation of the Interstate Agreement on Detainers and required dismissal of the charges. People v. Fargher, 112 A.D.2d 599, 492 N.Y.S.2d 123 (3d Dept. 1985).

Art. IV

Chain of custody.—Defendant's use of article IV is erroneous because, even though the charges against the defendant were dismissed and the agreement on detainers requires dismissal of the complaint, article IV sanctions are inappropriate as there was never a break in the federal chain of custody. People v. Sorenson, 80 A.D.2d 878, 436 N.Y.S.2d 745 (2d Dept. 1981).

Delay; motion to dismiss indictment.—In entertaining a motion to dismiss due to delay, the court must determine the date the defendant first arrived in the state and if there was good cause or "reasonable contingencies" for any delay between defendant's arrival and the start of the trial. People v. Rivera, 84 A.D.2d 541, 443 N.Y.S.2d 106 (2d Dept. 1981).

Art. IV(a)

Detainer; appellate review.—The statute requires a period of 30-days in which time the defense and prosecution have the opportunity to answer the detainer. Even though the People did not abide by the 120-day requirement, defendant is precluded from appellate review because he did not raise the issue prior to the appeal. This is necessary in order to allow the People to introduce new evidence that could feasibly overcome the challenge. People v. Mucciolo, 104 A.D.2d 905, 480 N.Y.S.2d 516 (2d Dept. 1984).

Interstate Agreement on Detainers; procedures.—In order to be granted temporary custody of a prisoner it must be shown to the court that the accused is actually serving a prison term, "a detainer must previously have been lodged against the prisoner", the state in which the charges are pending must have approved the request, and the Governor of the sending state must have had, at least, a 30-day period where he could have refused to release the prisoner. People v. Reilly, 136 A.D.2d 355, 527 N.Y.S.2d 234 (2d Dept. 1988).

Art. IV(c)

120-day period tolled.—CPL § 580.20 (iv) was not violated where the delay in proceeding to trial was occasioned by defense counsel who represented another defendant whose case had priority on which he was on standby. People v. Lambert, 92 A.D.2d 550, 459 N.Y.S.2d 120 (2d Dept. 1983), aff'd, 61 N.Y.2d 978, 475 N.Y.S.2d 280, 463 N.E.2d 621 (1984).

Art. IV(e)

Interstate Agreement on Detainers; waiver.—Defendant waived his right to claim that the Interstate Agreement on Detainers was violated, even though defendant was given incorrect information by the United States Parole Commission. Defendant relied on these facts in requesting to be returned to his original place of incarceration. But, because defendant and his counsel did not relay these facts to the county or prosecutor, after discovering the error, defendant waived his right to contest these actions under the CPL. People v. Quamina, 176 A.D. 2d 1208, 576 N.Y.S.2d 706 (4th Dept. 1991).

Art. V(f)

Detainers; time credited.—Petitioner, who was transferred to New York on detainers, was properly credited 365 days towards his Connecticut, the sending state, sentence. However, the court properly denied petitioner credit towards his New York, the receiving state, sentence. Hagerman v. Henderson, 79 A.D.2d 1112, 435 N.Y.S.2d 864 (4th Dept. 1981).

Art. VI(a)

Tolling.—Defendant was not entitled to a commencement of tolling because of the inability to commence with his trial in Queens County, due to the fact that Suffolk County authorities precipitated the delays in the proceedings. People v. Torres, 60 N.Y.2d 119, 468 N.Y.S.2d 606, 456 N.E.2d 497 (1983).

Waiver.—Defendant waived his rights under CPL § 580.20 when, represented by counsel, he pleaded guilty and did not raise his CPL § 580.20 claim until he appealed. People v. Primmer, 59 A.D.2d 221, 399 N.Y.S.2d 478 (3d Dept. 1977), aff'd, 46 N.Y.2d 1048, 416 N.Y.S.2d 548, 389 N.E.2d 1070 (1979). See also People v. Vidal, 85 A.D.2d 701, 445 N.Y.S.2d 479 (2d Dept. 1981).

—The CPL allows for tolling of the statutory period "when the defendant is unable to stand trial," but this does not apply when defendant is without counsel. Defendant's actions do not constitute a waiver of his rights, when neither his rights nor motions that could be made are explained to him. People v. Walker, 113 A.D.2d 448, 496 N.Y.S.2d 871 (4th Dept. 1985).

Art. IX(7)

Notice; burden.—The CPL mandates that the state who receives the request for extradition bears the burden of notifying the inmate and any failure to do so will not bear upon the petition made by the requesting state. People ex rel. Ortiz v. Warden, 119 A.D.2d 526, 501 N.Y.S.2d 667 (1st Dept. 1986).

§ 580.30. Securing attendance of defendants confined in federal prisons.

1. A defendant against whom a criminal action is pending in a court of record of this state, and who is confined in a federal prison or custody either within or outside the state, may, with the consent of the attorney general of the United States, be produced in such court for the purpose of criminal prosecution, pursuant to the provisions of:

(a) Section four thousand eighty-five of title eighteen of the United States Code; or

(b) Subdivision two of this section.

2. When such a defendant is in federal custody as specified in subdivision one, a superior court, at a term held in the county in which the criminal action against him is pending, may, upon application of the district attorney of such county, issue a certificate, known as a writ of habeas corpus ad prosequendum, addressed to the attorney general of the United States, certifying that such defendant has been charged by the particular accusatory instrument filed against him in the specified court with the offense or offenses alleged therein, and that attendance of the defendant in such court for the purpose of criminal prosecution thereon is necessary in the interest of justice, and requesting the attorney general of the United States to cause such defendant to be produced in such court, under custody of a federal public servant, upon a designated date and for a period of time necessary to complete the prosecution. Upon issuing such a certificate, the court may deliver it, or cause or authorize it to be delivered, together with a certified copy of the accusatory instrument upon which it is based, to the attorney general of the United States or to his representative authorized to entertain the request.

ANNOTATIONS

Writ of habeas corpus ad prosequendum.—Where the People made repeated requests for defendant's production and were unequivocally advised by federal prosecutor that defendant would not be released before his federal trial, it was not necessary for People to make obviously futile gesture of obtaining writ of habeas corpus ad prosequendum pursuant to CPL § 580.30, which would not have been binding on the Department of Justice. People v. Gonzalez, 235 A.D.2d 366, 653 N.Y.S.2d 321 (1st Dept. 1997).

—The use of a writ of habeas corpus ad prosequendum may be utilized only in respect to federal prisoners and is a viable alternative to use of the Interstate Agreement on Detainers. Moreover, the issuance of such a writ by the state is equivalent to the conveyance of a "written request for temporary custody." People v. Reilly, 136 A.D.2d 355, 527 N.Y.S.2d 234 (2d Dept. 1988).

ARTICLE 590—SECURING ATTENDANCE OF DEFENDANTS WHO ARE OUTSIDE THE UNITED STATES

Section

590.10   Securing attendance of defendants who are outside the United States.

§ 590.10. Securing attendance of defendants who are outside the United States.

1. When a criminal action for an offense committed in this state is pending in a criminal court of this state against a defendant who is in a foreign country with which the United States has an extradition treaty, and when the accusatory instrument charges an offense which is declared in such treaty to be an extraditable one, the district attorney of the county in which such offense was allegedly committed may make an application to the Governor, requesting him to make an application to the President of the United States to institute extradition proceedings for the return of the defendant to this country and state for the purpose of prosecution of such action. The district attorney's application must comply with rules, regulations and guidelines established by the Governor for such applications and must be accompanied by all the accusatory instruments, affidavits and other documents required by such rules, regulations and guidelines.

2. Upon receipt of the district attorney's application, the Governor, if satisfied that the defendant is in the foreign country in question, that the offense charged is an extraditable one pursuant to the treaty in question, and that there are no factors or impediments which in law preclude such an extradition, may in his discretion make an application, addressed to the secretary of state of the United States, requesting that the President of the United States institute extradition proceedings for the return of the defendant from such foreign country. The Governor's application must comply with rules, regulations and guidelines established by the secretary of state for such applications and must be accompanied by all the accusatory instruments, affidavits and other documents required by such rules, regulations and guidelines.

3. If the Governor's application is granted and the extradition is achieved or attempted, all expenses incurred therein must be borne by the county from which the application emanated.

4. The provisions of this section apply equally to extradition or attempted extradition of a person who is a fugitive following the entry of a judgment of conviction against him in a criminal court of this state.

ARTICLE 600—SECURING ATTENDANCE OF CORPORATE DEFENDANTS AND RELATED MATTERS

Section

§ 600.10. Corporate defendants; securing attendance.

1. The court attendance of a corporation for purposes of commencing or prosecuting a criminal action against it may be accomplished by the issuance and service of a summons or an appearance ticket if such action has been or is about to be commenced in a local criminal court, and by a corporate summons if such action has been commenced in a superior court. Such process must be served upon the corporation by delivery thereof to an officer, director, managing or general agent, or cashier or assistant cashier of such corporation or to any other agent of such corporation authorized by appointment or by law to receive service of process.

2. A "corporate summons" is a process issued by a superior court directing a corporate defendant designated in an indictment to appear before it at a designated future time in connection with such indictment. A corporate summons must be generally in the form of a summons as prescribed in subdivision two of section 130.10. A corporate summons may be served by a public servant designated by the issuing court, and may be served anywhere in the state.

ANNOTATIONS

Books or records of corporation.—It is settled law that one who has custody or control of the books or records of a corporation may not object to their production pursuant to a valid subpoena on the ground that the documents may tend to incriminate that individual personally. People v. Carassavas, 103 Misc. 2d 562, 426 N.Y.S.2d 437 (Sup. Ct. Saratoga Co. 1980).

Service of process; what is proper.—Personal delivery to the Secretary of State at the office of the Department of State in Albany constitutes proper service. The office should then forward a copy of the appearance ticket via certified mail, on the same day, to defendant corporation. People v. Sage Realty Corp., 155 Misc. 2d 832, 590 N.Y.S.2d 660 (Crim. Ct. N.Y. Co. 1992).

—In both civil and criminal actions, the legislature intended that the Secretary of State serve as a valid agent for service of process against corporations. People v. New York Paving, Inc., 155 Misc. 2d 934, 591 N.Y.S.2d 318 (Crim. Ct. Queens Co. 1992).

—Corporate defendants' appearance tickets do not confer jurisdiction because serving appearance tickets by mail is improper and contrary to CPL §600.10(1). People v. Neuberger, 149 Misc. 2d 1, 570 N.Y.S.2d 256 (Crim. Ct. N.Y. Co. 1991).

§ 600.20. Corporate defendants; prosecution thereof.

At all stages of a criminal action, from the commencement thereof through sentence, a corporate defendant must appear by counsel. Upon failure of appearance at the time such defendant is required to enter a plea to the accusatory instrument, the court may enter a plea of guilty and impose sentence.

ANNOTATIONS

Appearance before the court.—Once a defendant has appeared before the court, any defect in the issuance of a judicial summons is irrelevant. Accordingly, the defendant corporation, having appeared by its counsel, has satisfied the general prerequisites for jurisdiction. People v. Benjamin Dev. Co., 155 Misc. 2d 528, 589 N.Y.S.2d 144 (Crim. Ct. Queens Co. 1992).

Corporate vs. non-corporate status.—Inasmuch as a corporation appears only through its counsel, it is not exposed to the same degree of threat to liberty as an individual defendant. Therefore, defendant corporation is not entitled to the same due process "notice protection" afforded to a non-corporate defendant. People v. Sage Realty Corp., 155 Misc. 2d 832, 590 N.Y.S.2d 660 (Crim. Ct. N.Y. Co. 1992).

Default judgment.—A default judgment may be entered against a corporation that fails to appear through counsel. People v. Erin Const. Corp., 136 Misc. 2d 807, 519 N.Y.S.2d 466, 469 (Crim. Ct. N.Y. Co. 1987), *modified on other grounds,* 560 N.Y.S.2d 728 (1st Dept. 1990).

TITLE R—PROCEDURES FOR SECURING ATTENDANCE OF WITNESSES IN CRIMINAL ACTIONS

ARTICLE 610—SECURING ATTENDANCE OF WITNESSES BY SUBPOENA

LexisNexis Cross Reference

New York Criminal Practice (2d ed.), Vol. 3, Ch. 31, Securing Attendance of Non-Prisoner Witnesses.

§ 610.10. Securing attendance of witnesses by subpoena; in general.

1. Under circumstances prescribed in this article, a person at liberty within the state may be required to attend a criminal court action or proceeding as a witness by the issuance and service upon him of a subpoena.

2. A "subpoena" is a process of a court directing the person to whom it is addressed to attend and appear as a witness in a designated action or proceeding in such court, on a designated date and any recessed or adjourned date of the action or proceeding. If the witness is given reasonable notice of such recess or adjournment, no further process is required to compel his attendance on the adjourned date.

3. As used in this article, "subpoena" includes a "subpoena duces tecum." A subpoena duces tecum is a subpoena requiring the witness to bring with him and produce specified physical evidence.

ANNOTATIONS

Bank records.—Since bank records are the business records of the bank and not the personal property of the depositor, requiring their production by the bank did not constitute a denial of depositor's privilege against self-incrimination. Cappetta v. Santucci, 42 N.Y.2d 1066, 399 N.Y.S.2d 638, 369 N.E.2d 1172 (1977).

Compelling a witness to testify.—The right to compel witnesses to testify is not absolute. Even where testimony would be relevant to the defense, such testimony will be excluded where there is a showing of bad faith. People v. King, 148 Misc. 2d 859, 561 N.Y.S.2d 395 (Crim. Ct. N.Y. Co. 1990).

Defendant proceeding pro se; failure of court to assist in production of witness to whom defendant confessed.—Failure of trial court to assist defendant who was defending pro se, in producing at the trial the person to whom defendant

initially confessed was reversible error. People v. Reade, 29 N.Y.2d 493, 323 N.Y.S.2d 969, 272 N.E.2d 481 (1971).

Grand Jury subpoena duces tecum.—Grand Jury subpoena duces tecum issued by the Special Prosecutor does not authorize the Special Prosecutor to seize or impound the records produced; if the circumstances warrant, the prosecutor may apply for an order of impoundment or inspection, which is within the inherent power of court to grant. Heisler v. Hynes, 42 N.Y.2d 250, 397 N.Y.S.2d 727, 366 N.E.2d 817 (1977).

Issuance of a subpoena.—Neither a court nor an attorney can issue a subpoena where there is no action of issue before it. Court held that seeking the current address of an involved party is enforceable where there is a proceeding pending before the court. People v. Jones, 160 Misc. 2d 246, 608 N.Y.S.2d 795 (Crim. Ct. Kings Co. 1994).

Newsmen; Shield Law (Civil Rights Law § 79-h).—The court denied a motion by the author of a book on an alleged crime family to quash a subpoena duces tecum covering tape recordings and notes made during interviews with a witness who testified before the grand jury and who was expected to testify at trial on the grounds that (1) the Shield Law (Civil Rights Law § 79-h) applied to journalists and newscasters only and (2) the information was no longer confidential in nature as a result of the witness's grand jury testimony. People v. LeGrand, 67 A.D. 446, 415 N.Y.S.2d 252 (2d Dept. 1979).

Patient's dental records.—The defendant, a dentist, charged with sexually abusing several of his patients, cannot rely upon the privilege against compulsory self-incrimination to avoid producing patient's records which are in his possession in a representative capacity, even if these records might incriminate him personally. People v. Cohen, 98 Misc. 2d 874, 414 N.Y.S.2d 642 (Dist. Ct. Nassau Co. 1979).

Personnel records of police officers.—The trial court should have conducted an in camera proceeding to determine the relevancy and materiality of the police personnel records sought since the People introduced, on direct examination, evidence of the medals and departmental commendations received by the arresting officers, one of whom was dismissed from the department after his conviction for shaking down narcotic dealers. People v. Vasquez, 49 A.D.2d 590, 370 N.Y.S.2d 144 (2d Dept. 1975).

Records of school custodian.—School records maintained by school custodian were records of the Board of Education, the employing institution, and were not custodian's personal property subject to his personal privilege against self-incrimination; the custodian was required to maintain the records with respect to public moneys received and disbursed by him. Cappetta v. Santucci, 42 N.Y.2d 1066, 399 N.Y.S.2d 638, 369 N.E.2d 1172 (1977).

Subpoena duces tecum; massive seizures.—The subpoena duces tecum is generally used to obtain production of evidence not in control of the party seeking to use it, and it is authorized for use in criminal matters by CPL § 610.10(3). Where massive seizures have been held to violate First Amendment rights, and these wrongs have been rectified by the return of the seized materials, the procedure for the government to follow to secure evidence for use in trials in the state courts would be either issuance of a subpoena duces tecum or the obtaining of a court order. People v. Brown, 72 Misc. 2d 526, 339 N.Y.S.2d 470 (Dist. Ct. Suffolk Co. 1972).

Subpoena duces tecum.—Public Service Commission (PSC) order involved activities which were beyond the reach of PSC jurisdiction where it sought to compel notification in advance by the telephone company to a subscriber that his records were being subpoenaed by an investigative body unless a court order provided otherwise. City of New York v. Public Serv. Comm'n, 53 A.D.2d 164, 385 N.Y.S.2d 634 (3d Dept. 1976), aff'd, 42 N.Y.2d 916, 397 N.Y.S.2d 1005, 366 N.E.2d 1359 (1977).

—A subpoena duces tecum is not the equivalent of a search warrant for which a showing of probable cause is required; to sustain the subpoena it is sufficient to show that the inquiry is lawfully and properly authorized and the description of the materials sought is reasonably definite; the question is one of relevance not of probable cause. Hynes v. Lefkowitz, 62 A.D.2d 365, 405 N.Y.S.2d 56 (1st Dept. 1978).

Subpoena duces tecum; appeal.—The denial of a motion to quash a subpoena duces tecum issued during a criminal trial is final and appealable. People v. Marin, 86 A.D.2d 40, 448 N.Y.S.2d 748 (2d Dept. 1982).

Subpoena duces tecum; records of amounts received from attorneys' clients.—Only substantive matters have protection of lawyer-client privilege; privilege does not extent to amounts billed and received from attorneys' clients, subject of subpoena duces tecum. People v. Cook, 82 Misc. 2d 875, 372 N.Y.S.2d 10 (Monroe Co. Ct. 1975).

Subpoena duces tecum; cross-examination concerning collateral matters.—The court refused to grant the defendant a subpoena duces tecum as to police department personnel files to enable the defendant to acquire evidence of misconduct by certain police officers in order to impeach their credibility as witnesses. The court held that the defendant could not use extrinsic evidence (i.e., any record of misconduct) to refute the witnesses' answers on collateral matters. People v. Fraiser, 75 Misc. 2d 756, 348 N.Y.S.2d 529 (Nassau Co. Ct. 1973).

Subpoena; immunity.—The court quashed the subpoena for the production of the adult coperpetrator of the robbery since it knew that his testimony was privileged and that the coperpetrator intended to make use of his privilege. In re Tyrone S., 91 Misc. 2d 1055, 399 N.Y.S.2d (Fam Ct. N.Y. Co. 1977).

Subpoena of property; adversary hearing.—An adversary hearing may be required in an obscenity prosecution prior to police seizure of an allegedly obscene film. In this case, there being no seizure, and only the issuance of a subpoena, no adversary hearing was required. People v. Modern Amusement Co., 72 Misc. 2d 950, 340 N.Y.S.2d 748 (Crim. Ct. N.Y. Co. 1973).

Use of subpoena duces tecum for purpose of discovery.— While a subpoena duces tecum may be employed by defense counsel to compel the production of documents to be used in connection with the testimony given by a witness at trial, it cannot be employed for the purpose of discovery or to ascertain the existence of evidence. People v. Chambers, 134 Misc. 2d 688, 512 N.Y.S.2d 631 (Sup. Ct. N.Y. Co. 1987).

—Although historically the subpoena duces tecum was not intended to provide a means of discovery, the more enlightened view, held by the federal courts for many years, is that properly subpoenaed materials should be produced before trial at a specific time and place for inspection by the moving party who, in order to obtain a subpoena for such purposes must show: (1) the materials are relevant and evidentiary; (2) the request is specific; (3) the materials are not otherwise procurable reasonably in advance of trial by the exercise of due diligence; (4) the party cannot properly prepare for trial without such production and inspection in advance of trial and the failure to obtain such information may tend unreasonably to delay the

trial; and (5) the application is made in good faith and is not intended as a general fishing expedition. People v. Price, 100 Misc. 2d 372, 419 N.Y.S.2d 415 (Sup. Ct. Bronx Co. 1979).

§ 610.20. Securing attendance of witnesses by subpoena; when and by whom subpoena may be issued.

1. Any criminal court may issue a subpoena for the attendance of a witness in any criminal action or proceeding in such court.

2. A district attorney, or other prosecutor where appropriate, as an officer of a criminal court in which he is conducting the prosecution of a criminal action or proceeding, may issue a subpoena of such court, subscribed by himself, for the attendance in such court or a grand jury thereof of any witness whom the people are entitled to call in such action or proceeding.

3. An attorney for a defendant in a criminal action or proceeding, as an officer of a criminal court, may issue a subpoena of such court, subscribed by himself, for the attendance in such court of any witness whom the defendant is entitled to call in such action or proceeding. An attorney for a defendant may not issue a subpoena duces tecum of the court directed to any department, bureau or agency of the state or of a political subdivision thereof, or to any officer or representative thereof. Such a subpoena duces tecum may be issued in behalf of a defendant upon order of a court pursuant to the rules applicable to civil cases as provided in section twenty-three hundred seven of the civil practice law and rules.

ANNOTATIONS

Alibi witness.—There is no statute conferring upon a prosecutor of this State the right to subpoena a citizen for the purpose of compelling him to visit the prosecutor's office for questioning about a pending investigation; no inference should be drawn from a person not going to the police or a District Attorney upon learning that a defendant has been arrested for a crime committed at a time when that person can provide alibi testimony. People v. Hamlin, 58 A.D.2d 631, 395 N.Y.S.2d 679 (2d Dept. 1977).

—A witness subject to a subpoena ad testificandum cannot raise an issue of privilege until he has actually appeared and been questioned. People v. Doe, 61 A.D.2d 426, 403 N.Y.S.2d 375 (4th Dept. 1978).

Capital case.—In capital murder case, prosecution can issue subpoenas duces tecum to third parties without notifying defendant. People v. Owens, 188 Misc. 2d 200, 727 N.Y.S.2d 266 (Sup. Ct. Monroe Co. 2001).

Criminal records.—An appeal lies from the denial of the motion to quash the subpoena if the subpoena for the material comes during preparation for trial, and therefore does not interfere with the course of the trial. Morgenthau v. 9X Hopes, 55 A.D.2d 255, 390 N.Y.S.2d 109 (1st Dept. 1977).

District attorney (or other prosecutor); code of conduct.— District attorney acts as an "officer of the court" when authorized to issue subpoenas; therefore, he has a "solemn responsibility... to act with honor and due respect towards the judiciary." People v. Warmus, 148 Misc. 2d 374, 561 N.Y.S.2d 11 (Westchester Co. Court 1990).

District attorney (or other prosecutor); when allowed to issue subpoenas duces tecum.—District attorney has no power to issue a subpoena for the purpose of conducting his own criminal investigation when, in fact, no grand jury has been convened. Rodrigues v. City of New York, 193 A.D.2d 79, 602 N.Y.S.2d 337 (1st Dept. 1993); People v. Carkner, 213 A.D.2d 735, 623 N.Y.S.2d 350 (3d Dept. 1995).

—Attorney general is authorized to issue an office subpoena to require recipient to appear before the court; but, he can only use the subpoena to compel witnesses to appear at a grand jury or court where a proceeding or action is in progress. Kuriansky v. Patel, 144 Misc. 2d 59, 542 N.Y.S.2d 906 (Sup. Ct. Bronx Co. 1989).

Failure to obey command of a subpoena.—Neither reliance on the assurance of counsel nor hardship is reasonable cause to disobey a subpoena. People v. Forsyth, 109 Misc. 2d 234, 439 N.Y.S.2d 808 (Sup. Ct. N.Y. Co. 1981).

Improper use of subpoena.—Cable television records were improperly obtained through the use of a grand jury subpoena duces tecum, where no grand jury proceeding was pending and the records were possessed by the police without statutory authority, but the court properly refused to suppress the records since defendant lacked standing, having no possessory or proprietary interest in such records. People v. MacGilfrey, 288 A.D.2d 554, 733 N.Y.S.2d 254 (3d Dept. 2001).

Judge's discretion.—Judge did not act in excess of his authority by issuing subpoena to witness because (CPL § 610.20[1]) grants a criminal court such authority. Cohen v. Demakos, 144 A.D.2d 605, 534 N.Y.S.2d 1022 (2d Dept. 1988).

No exception for police reports.—The plain language of CPL § 610.20(3) authorizes a court-ordered subpoena to "any department, bureau or agency of the state or of a political subdivision thereof"—and there is no exception for police reports. People v. Bagley, 183 Misc. 2d 523, 705 N.Y.S.2d 488 (Sup. Ct. N.Y. Co. 1999).

Personnel records of police officers.—A subpoena duces tecum may not be used "in the hope of finding something helpful to [the] defense"; defendant's motion for personnel records of four uniformed court officers who are complainants against him in impending trial was denied where defendant made no showing that personnel records would likely yield known evidence relevant to trial. People v. Magliore, 178 Misc. 2d 489, 679 N.Y.S.2d 267 (Crim. Ct. Kings Co. 1998).

Post-conviction hearing; authority to issue subpoenas.—The filing of a post-judgment motion pursuant to CPL § 440.10 does not create a right to an evidentiary proceeding in which defendant is entitled to call witnesses or present evidence. Rather, CPL § 440.30 requires that the court receiving the motion determine, after its submission, whether or not an evidentiary hearing on the allegations is warranted. The CPL does not authorize the use of compulsory process to obtain such evidence prior to the court's ordering a hearing on the motion. Accordingly, defendant's request that the court authorize and/or order the issuance of the three subpoenas is denied. People v. Diaz, 195 Misc. 2d 337, 756 N.Y.S.2d 838 (Sup. Ct. Bronx Co. 2003).

Production of physical evidence.—District attorneys may compel witnesses to produce physical evidence by subpoena only before the grand jury or court where the proceeding is pending. People v. Natal, 75 N.Y.2d 379, 553 N.E.2d 239, 553 N.Y.S.2d 650 (1990).

Records; Commissioner of Social Services.—Defense attorney, representing juveniles accused of robbery, second degree, could apply to Supreme Court for a subpoena duces tecum, pursuant to CPL § 610.20(3), directing the New York City Commissioner of Social Services to disclose to the Criminal Court records relating to defendants' recent placement as Persons In Need of Supervision ("PINS") (Fam. Court Act Art. 7). The Crim. Ct. could inspect the documents in camera and redact all entries which were irrelevant or immaterial to the issues sub judici and then disclose the redacted records to both defense and prosecution so that the interests of both the juvenile and the State could be adequately represented. In re Roman, 97 Misc. 2d 782, 412 N.Y.S.2d 325 (Sup. Ct. N.Y. Co. 1979).

State Commission on Judicial Conduct.—The State Commission on Judicial Conduct may issue its own subpoena for records of a district attorneys office. In re Hendley, 116 Misc. 2d 1044, 457 N.Y.S.2d 165 (Sup. Ct. Warren Co. 1982).

Subpoena duces tecum; motion to quash.—Once a subpoena duces tecum is issued and a witness feels that all of the documents sought are validly privileged, he is, in effect, challenging the validity of the subpoena itself and the proper remedy

is a motion to quash since such a motion is limited in scope, challenging only the validity of the subpoena or the jurisdiction of the issuing authority. Such motion should be made promptly and prior to the return date. Hynes v. Doe, 101 Misc. 2d 350, 420 N.Y.S.2d 978 (Queens Co. 1979).

§ 610.25. Securing attendance of witness by subpoena; possession of physical evidence.

1. Where a subpoena duces tecum is issued on reasonable notice to the person subpoenaed, the court or grand jury shall have the right to possession of the subpoenaed evidence. Such evidence may be retained by the court, grand jury or district attorney on behalf of the grand jury.

2. The possession shall be for a period of time, and on terms and conditions, as may reasonably be required for the action or proceeding. The reasonableness of such possession, time, terms, and conditions shall be determined with consideration for, among other things, (a) the good cause shown by the party issuing the subpoena or in whose behalf the subpoena is issued, (b) the rights and legitimate needs of the person subpoenaed and (c) the feasibility and appropriateness of making copies of the evidence. The cost of reproduction and transportation incident thereto shall be borne by the person or party issuing the subpoena unless the court determines otherwise in the interest of justice. Nothing in this article shall be deemed to prohibit the designation of a return date for a subpoena duces tecum prior to trial. Where physical evidence specified to be produced will be sought to be retained in custody, notice of such fact shall be given the subpoenaed party. In any case where the court receives or retains evidence prior to trial, it may, as may otherwise be authorized by law, grant the issuing party a reasonable opportunity to inspect such evidence.

Added by L. 1977, Ch. 451; **Amended** by L. 1979, Ch. 413.

ANNOTATIONS

Contempt sanctions for failure to comply.—Trial court which had ordered the production of certain subpoenaed records improperly held a law firm in criminal contempt since the mandate of commitment violated Section 752 of the Judiciary Law by failing to set forth the particular circumstances of the offense. In re Law Firm of Daniel P. Foster, P.C., 115 A.D.2d 375, 495 N.Y.S.2d 403 (1st Dept. 1985), app. dismissed, 67 N.Y.2d 828, 492 N.E.2d 786, 501 N.Y.S.2d 658 (1986).

Custody.—The prosecutor need only serve a subpoena duces tecum to initiate an effort to secure custody of the subpoenaed records; the subpoena should provide the entity subpoenaed with reasonable notice that custody of the evidence is sought (CPL § 610.25[1]); only with such notice can the entity subpoenaed endeavor to invoke in court by motion the safeguards provided for in CPL § 610.25[2]). In re Long Beach Grandell Nursing Home & Health Related Facility, 93 Misc. 2d 117, 402 N.Y.S.2d 308 (Nassau Co. Ct.), modified on other grounds, 94 Misc. 2d 222, 404 N.Y.S.2d 524 (1978).

Grand Jury subpoena duces tecum.—Once an indictment is issued, a Grand Jury subpoena duces tecum may not be used for the sole or dominant purpose of preparing the pending indictment for trial; however, where the purpose of the Grand Jury investigation is directed to other offenses, its scope should not be circumscribed and any collateral or incidental evidence from bona fide inquiries may be used by the prosecutor against the defendant at the trial of the pending indictment. Hynes v. Lerner, 44 N.Y.2d 329, 405 N.Y.S.2d 649, 376 N.E.2d 1294, *app. dismissed*, 439 U.S. 888 (1978).

No right to E-mail communications.—After in camera review of all E-mail communications sent to and received by complainant for four-month period, court determined that production of E-mails to defendant was unwarranted because defendant failed to establish that material sought contained evidence and that he could not obtain information in E-mails from other sources. People v. Jovanovic, 176 Misc. 2d 729, 676 N.Y.S.2d 392 (Sup. Ct. N.Y. Co. 1997).

No right to names and addresses of prosecution's witnesses.—The names and addresses of prosecution witnesses cannot be obtained as a matter of right pursuant to a subpoena issued under CPL § 610.25. People v. Miranda, 115 Misc. 2d 533, 455 N.Y.S.2d 247 (Sup. Ct. Bronx Co. 1982), *dismissed*, 102 A.D.2d 742, 477 N.Y.S.2d 291 (1st Dept. 1984).

Order of impoundment.—An order of impoundment is necessary to retain records obtained by subpoena duces tecum but which were never actually introduced into evidence before the Grand Jury and the prosecutor must show "special circumstances" in order to prevail. People v. Fairview Nursing Home, 92 Misc. 2d 694, 401 N.Y.S.2d 390 (Sup. Ct. Queens Co. 1977).

Placement of subpoenaed materials.—It is the court's duty, and not the prosecutor's, to determine where subpoenaed materials should be deposited and to settle any disputes concerning production of evidence. People v. Natal, 75 N.Y.2d 379, 553 N.E.2d 239, 553 N.Y.S.2d 650, *cert. denied*, 498 U.S. 862 (1990).

§ 610.30. Securing attendance of witnesses by subpoena; where subpoena may be served.

1. A subpoena of any criminal court, issued pursuant to section 610.20, may be served anywhere in the county of issuance or anywhere in an adjoining county.

2. A subpoena of a superior court or of a superior court judge sitting as a local criminal court, issued pursuant to section 610.20, may be served anywhere in the state.

3. A subpoena of a district court or of the New York City criminal court, issued pursuant to section 610.20, may be served anywhere in the state; provided that, if such subpoena is issued by a prosecutor or by an attorney for a defendant, it may be served in a county other than the county of issuance or an adjoining county only if such court, upon application of such prosecutor or attorney, endorses upon such subpoena an order for the attendance of the witness.

4. A subpoena of a city court or a town court or a village court, issued pursuant to section 610.20, may be served in a county other than the one of issuance or an adjoining county if a judge of a superior court, upon application of the issuing court or the district attorney or an attorney for the defendant, endorses upon such subpoena an order for the attendance of the witness.

ANNOTATION

Prisoner; doctor-patient privilege.—Prospective witness' medical and psychiatric records were not sought in connection with the issue of defendant's guilt or innocence, but merely on a collateral issue of credibility of the witness. Accordingly, the court would not (without patient waiver) strike down the statutory doctor-patient privilege conferred upon the witness by the Legislature. People v. Dodge, 73 Misc. 2d 80, 341 N.Y.S.2d 471 (Nassau Co. Ct. 1973).

§ 610.40. Securing attendance of witnesses by subpoena; how and by whom subpoena may be served.

A subpoena may be served by any person more than eighteen years old. Service must be made in the manner provided by the civil practice law and rules for the service of subpoenas in civil cases.

§ 610.50. Securing attendance of witness by subpoena; fees.

1. A witness subpoenaed by the people in a criminal action is entitled to the same fees and mileage as a witness in a civil action, payable by the treasurer of the county upon the certificate of the court or the clerk thereof, stating the number of days the witness actually attended and the number of miles traveled by him in order to attend. In any such action, the court may, by order, direct the county treasurer to pay to such witness a further reasonable sum for expenses, to be specified in the order, and the county treasurer, upon the production of the order or a certified copy thereof, must pay the witness the sum specified therein out of the county treasury. Such certificates shall only be issued by the court or the clerk thereof, upon the production of the affidavit of the witness, stating that he attended as such either on subpoena or request of the district attorney, the number of miles necessarily traveled and the duration of attendance. An officer in any state department who attends as a witness under this section in his official capacity, or in consequence of any official action taken by him, and who receives a fixed sum in lieu of expenses, or who is entitled to receive the actual expenses incurred by him in the discharge of his official duties, is not entitled to the compensation herein provided.

2. A witness subpoenaed by the defendant in a criminal action is not entitled as of right to witness and mileage fees, but the court may in its discretion, by order, direct the county treasurer to pay to such a witness a reasonable sum for expenses, to be specified in the order. Upon the production of the order or a certified copy thereof, the county treasurer must pay the witness the sum specified therein, out of the county treasury.

ANNOTATIONS

Subpoena of witness; fee.—In a criminal case, witness fees are paid upon appropriate application after a witness has appeared in court. People v. Modern Amusement Co., 72 Misc. 2d 950, 340 N.Y.S.2d 748 (Crim. Ct. N.Y. Co. 1973).

—Payment of witness and mileage fees need only be made by the Treasurer of the county after appearances before the Grand Jury. People v. Ruggiano, 92 Misc. 2d, 876, 401 N.Y.S.2d 729 (Sup. Ct. Suffolk Co. 1978).

ARTICLE 620—SECURING ATTENDANCE OF WITNESSES BY MATERIAL WITNESS ORDER

LexisNexis Cross Reference

New York Criminal Practice (2d ed.), Vol. 3, Ch. 31, Securing Attendance of Non-Prisoner Witnesses.

§ 620.10. Material witness order; defined.

A material witness order is a court order (a) adjudging a person a material witness in a pending criminal action and (b) fixing bail to secure his future attendance thereat.

§ 620.20. Material witness order; when authorized; by what courts issuable; duration thereof.

1. A material witness order may be issued upon the ground that there is reasonable cause to believe that a person whom the people or the defendant desire to call as a witness in a pending criminal action:

(a) Possesses information material to the determination of such action; and

(b) Will not be amenable or responsive to a subpoena at a time when his attendance will be sought.

2. A material witness order may be issued only when:

(a) An indictment has been filed in a superior court and is currently pending therein; or

(b) A grand jury proceeding has been commenced and is currently pending; or

(c) A felony complaint has been filed with a local criminal court and is currently pending therein.

3. The following courts may issue material witness orders under the indicated circumstances:

(a) When an indictment has been filed, or a grand jury proceeding has been commenced, or a defendant has been held by a local criminal court for the action of a grand jury, a material witness order may be issued only by the superior court in which such indictment is pending or by which such grand jury has been or is to be impaneled;

(b) When a felony complaint is currently pending in a district court or in the New York City criminal court or before a superior court judge sitting as a local criminal court, a material witness order may be issued either by such court or by the superior court which would have jurisdiction of the case upon a holding of the defendant for the action of the grand jury;

(c) When a felony complaint is currently pending in a city court or a town court or a village court, a material witness order may be issued only by the superior court which would have jurisdiction of the case upon a holding of the defendant for the action of the grand jury.

4. Unless vacated pursuant to section 620.60, a material witness order remains in effect during the following periods of time under the indicated circumstances:

(a) An order issued by a superior court under the circumstances prescribed in paragraph (a) of subdivision three remains in effect during the pendency of the criminal action in such superior court;

(b) An order issued by a district court or the New York City criminal court or a superior court judge siting as a local criminal court, under circumstances prescribed in paragraph (b) of subdivision three, remains in effect (i) until the disposition of the felony complaint pending in such court, and (ii) if the defendant is held for the action of a grand jury, during the pendency of the grand jury proceeding, and (iii) if an indictment results, for a period of ten days following the filing of such indictment, and (iv) if within such ten day period such order is indorsed by the superior court in which the indictment is pending, during the pendency of the action in such superior court. Upon such indorsement, the order is deemed to be that of the superior court.

(c) An order issued by a superior court under circumstances prescribed in paragraph (c) of subdivision three remains in effect (i) until the disposition of the felony complaint pending in the city, town or village court, and (ii) if the defendant is held for the action of the grand jury, during the pendency of the action in the superior court.

ANNOTATION

Denial of material witness order.—Court properly denied defendant's application for a material witness order because defendant did not, in his written or oral application, establish that there was reasonable cause to believe that the proffered witness possessed information material to the determination of the action. The court offered to reconsider the application, but the defendant provided no additional information. Court's ruling did not undermine defendant's right to present a defense because defendant's claims about the exculpatory value of the witness were speculative. People v. Parsons, 18 A.D.3d 317, 795 N.Y.S.2d 37 (1st Dept. 2005).

§ 620.30. Material witness order; commencement of proceeding by application; procurement of appearance of prospective witness.

1. A proceeding to adjudge a person a material witness must be commenced by application to the appropriate court, made in writing and subscribed and sworn to by the applicant, demonstrating reasonable cause to believe the existence of a facts, as specified in subdivision one of section 620.20, warranting the adjudication of such person as a material witness.

2. If the court is satisfied that the application is well founded, the prospective witness may be compelled to appear in response thereto as follows:

(a) The court may issue an order directing him to appear therein at a designated time in order that a determination may be made whether he should be adjudged a material witness, and, upon personal service of such order or a copy thereof within the state, he must so appear.

(b) If in addition to the allegations specified in subdivision one, the application contains further allegations demonstrating to the satisfaction of the court reasonable cause to believe that (i) the witness would be unlikely to respond to such an order, or (ii) after previously having been served with such an order, he did not respond thereto, the court may issue a warrant addressed to a police officer, directing such officer to take such prospective witness into custody within the state and to bring him before the court forthwith in order that a proceeding may be conducted to

determine whether he is to be adjudged a material witness.

ANNOTATIONS

District Attorney as originator of Family Court proceeding.—FCA § 158 which provides for Family Court protective custody of material witnesses under sixteen, includes situations where the pending case is in another court; the District Attorney may be considered a person directed by the court to bring in child protective proceedings under Fam. Ct. Act § 1032. People v. Louise D., 82 Misc. 2d 68, 368 N.Y.S.2d 746 (Fam. Ct. Bronx Co. 1975).

Generally.—In order to justify granting an application for a material witness order, the moving party must satisfy the burden of establishing that the testimony of the witness is relevant, material or necessary to the issues raised in the case. People v. Bragg, 176 A.D.2d 464, 574 N.Y.S.2d 546, 547 (1st Dept. 1991).

§ 620.40. Material witness order; arraignment.

1. When the prospective witness appears before the court, the court must inform him of the nature and purpose of the proceeding, and that he is entitled to a prompt hearing upon the issue of whether he should be adjudged a material witness. The prospective witness possesses all the rights, and is entitled to all the court instructions, with respect to right to counsel, opportunity to obtain counsel and assignment of counsel in case of financial inability to retain such, which, pursuant to subdivisions three through five of section 180.10, accrue to a defendant arraigned upon a felony complaint in a local criminal court.

2. If the proceeding is adjourned at the prospective witness' instance, for the purpose of obtaining counsel or otherwise, the court must order him to appear upon the adjourned date. The court may further fix bail to secure his appearance upon such date or until the proceeding is completed and, upon default thereof, may commit him to the custody of the sheriff for such period.

§ 620.50. Material witness order; hearing, determination and execution of order.

1. The hearing upon the application must be conducted as follows:

(a) The applicant has the burden of proving by a preponderance of the evidence all facts essential to support a material witness order, and any testimony so adduced must be given under oath;

(b) The prospective witness may testify under oath or may make an unsworn statement;

(c) The prospective witness may call witnesses in his behalf, and the court must cause process to be issued for any such witness whom he reasonably wishes to call, and any testimony so adduced must be given under oath;

(d) Upon the hearing, evidence tending to demonstrate that the prospective witness does or does not possess information material to the criminal action in issue, or that he will or will not be amenable or respond to a subpoena at the time his attendance will be sought, is admissible even though it consists of hearsay.

2. If the court is satisfied after such hearing that there is reasonable cause to believe that the prospective witness (a) possesses information material to the pending action or proceeding, and (b) will not be amenable or respond to a subpoena at a time when his attendance will be sought, it may issue a material witness order, adjudging him a material witness and fixing bail to secure his future attendance.

3. A material witness order must be executed as follows:

(a) If the bail is posted and approved by the court, the witness must, as provided in subdivision three of section 510.40, be released and be permitted to remain at liberty; provided that, where the bail is posted by a person other than the witness himself, he may not be so released except upon his signed written consent thereto;

(b) If the bail is not posted, or if though posted it is not approved by the court, the witness must, as provided in subdivision three of section 510.40, be committed to the custody of the sheriff.

§ 620.60. Material witness order; vacation, modification and amendment thereof.

1. At any time after a material witness order has been issued the court must, upon application of such witness, with notice to the party upon whose application the order was issued, and with opportunity to be heard, make inquiry whether by reason of new or changed facts or circumstances the material witness order is no longer necessary or warranted, or, if it is, whether the original bail currently appears excessive. Upon making any such determination, the court must vacate the order. If its determination is that the order is no longer necessary or warranted, it must, as the situation requires, either discharge the witness

from custody or exonerate the bail. If its determination is that the bail is excessive, it must issue a new order fixing bail in a lesser amount or on less burdensome terms.

2. At any time when a witness is at liberty upon bail pursuant to a material witness order, the court may, upon application of the party upon whose application the order was issued, with notice to the witness if possible and to his attorney if any and opportunity to be heard, make inquiry whether, by reason of new or changed facts or circumstances, the original bail is no longer sufficient to secure the future attendance of the witness at the pending action. Upon making such a determination, the court must vacate the order and issue a new order fixing bail in a greater amount or on terms more likely to secure the future attendance of the witness.

§ 620.70. Material witness order; compelling attendance of witness who fails to appear.

If a witness at liberty on bail pursuant to a material witness order cannot be found or notified at the time his appearance as a witness is required, or if after notification he fails to appear in such action or proceeding as required, the court may issue a warrant, addressed to a police officer, directing such officer to take such witness into custody anywhere within the state and to bring him to the court forthwith.

§ 620.80. Material witness order; witness fee.

A witness held in the custody of the sheriff as a result of a material witness order must be paid the sum of three dollars per day for each day of confinement in such custody. Such compensation is a county charge and is payable upon release of such material witness from custody or, in the discretion of the court, at any designated times or intervals during the confinement as the court may deem appropriate.

ARTICLE 630—SECURING ATTENDANCE AS WITNESSES OF PERSONS CONFINED IN INSTITUTIONS WITHIN THE STATE

Section

630.10   Securing attendance of witnesses confined in institutions within the state; in general.

630.20   Securing attendance of witnesses confined in institutions within the state; when and by what courts order may be issued.

LexisNexis Cross Reference

New York Criminal Practice (2d ed.), Vol. 3, Ch. 32, Production As Witnesses of Prisoners and Persons Confined Inside and Outside New York State.

§ 630.10. Securing attendance of witnesses confined in institutions within the state; in general.

Under circumstances prescribed in this article, a person confined in an institution within this state pursuant to a court order may, upon application of a party to a criminal action or proceeding, demonstrating reasonable cause to believe that such person possesses information material thereto, be produced by court order and compelled to attend such action or proceeding as a witness.

ANNOTATION

Third party involvement.—Where witness admitted he knew that a third party was personally involved in the fabrication of evidence against defendant, such witness possesses "material" information and should be compelled to testify. People v. Prentice, 208 A.D.2d 1064, 617 N.Y.S.2d 570 (3d Dept. 1994), *app. dismissed,* 623 N.Y.S.2d 193 (1995).

§ 630.20. Securing attendance of witnesses confined in institutions within the state; when and by what courts order may be issued.

The following courts and judges may, under the indicated circumstances, order production as witnesses of persons confined by court order in institutions within the state.

1. If the criminal action or proceeding is one pending in a superior court or with a superior court judge sitting as a local criminal court, such court may, except as provided in subdivision four, order the production as a witness therein of a person confined in any institution in the state.

2. If the criminal action or proceeding is one pending in a district court or the New York City criminal court, such court may order the production as a witness therein of a person confined in any institution within the state other than a state prison. Production therein of a prospective witness confined in a state prison may, except as provided in subdivision four, be ordered, upon application of the party desiring to call him, by a judge of a superior court holding a term thereof in the county in which the action or proceeding is pending.

3. If the criminal action or proceeding is one pending in a city court or a town court or a village court, such court may order the production as a witness therein of a person confined in a county jail of such county. Production therein of a prospective witness confined in any other institution within the state may, except as provided in subdivision four, be ordered, upon application of the party desiring to call him, by a judge of a superior court holding a term thereof in the county in which the action or proceeding is pending.

4. Regardless of the court in which the criminal action or proceeding is pending, production as a witness therein of a prisoner who has been sentenced to death may be ordered, upon application of the party desiring to call him, only by a justice of the appellate division of the department in which the action or proceeding is pending. The application for such order, if made by the defendant, must be upon notice to the district attorney of the county in which the action or proceeding is pending, and an application made by either party must be based upon a showing that the prisoner's attendance is clearly necessary in the interests of justice. Upon issuing such an order, the appellate division justice may fix and include therein any terms or conditions which he deems appropriate for execution thereof.

ARTICLE 640—SECURING ATTENDANCE AS WITNESSES OF PERSONS AT LIBERTY OUTSIDE THE STATE—RENDITION TO OTHER JURISDICTIONS OF WITNESSES AT LIBERTY WITHIN THE STATE—UNIFORM ACT TO SECURE ATTENDANCE OF WITNESSES FROM WITHOUT THE STATE IN CRIMINAL CASES

Section

640.10 Securing attendance of witnesses from within and without the state in criminal proceedings.

LexisNexis Cross Reference

New York Criminal Practice (2d ed.), Vol. 3, Ch. 31, Securing Attendance of Non-Prisoner Witnesses.

§ 640.10. Securing attendance of witnesses from within and without the state in criminal proceedings.

1. As used in this section the following words shall have the following meanings unless the context requires otherwise.

"Witness" shall include a person whose testimony is desired in any proceeding or investigation by a grand jury or in a criminal action, prosecution or proceeding.

"State" shall include any territory of the United States and the District of Columbia.

"Subpoena" shall include a summons in any state where a summons is used in lieu of a subpoena.

2. Subpoenaing witness in this state to testify in another state. If a judge of a court of record in any state which by its laws has made provision for commanding persons within that state to attend and testify in this state certifies under the seal of such court that there is a criminal prosecution pending in such court, or that a grand jury investigation has commenced or is about to commence, that a person being within this state is a material witness in such prosecution, or grand jury investigation, and that his presence will be required for a specified number of days, upon presentation of such certificate to a justice of the supreme court or a county judge in the county in which such person is, such justice or judge shall fix a time and place for a hearing, and shall make an order directing the witness to appear at a time and place certain for the hearing.

If at such hearing the justice or judge determines that the witness is material and necessary, that it will not cause undue hardship to the witness to be compelled to attend and testify in the prosecution or a grand jury investigation in the other state, and that the laws of the state in which the prosecution is pending, or grand jury investigation has commenced or is about to commence, will give to him protection from arrest and the service of civil and criminal process, he shall issue a subpoena, with a copy of the certificate attached, directing the witness to attend and testify in the court where the prosecution is pending, or where a grand jury investigation has commenced or is about to commence at a time and place specified in the subpoena. In any such hearing the certificate shall be prima facie evidence of all the facts stated therein.

If said certificate recommends that the witness be taken into immediate custody and delivered to an officer of the requesting state to assure his attendance in the requesting state such justice or judge may, in lieu of notification of the hearing, direct that such witness be forthwith brought before him for said hearing; and the justice or judge at the hearing being satisfied of the desirability of such custody and delivery, for which determination the certificate shall be prima facie proof of such desirability may, in lieu of issuing subpoena, order that said witness be forthwith taken into custody and delivered to an officer of the requesting state.

If the witness, who is subpoenaed as above provided, after being paid or tendered by some properly authorized person the sum of ten cents a mile for each mile and five dollars for each day that he is required to travel and attend as a witness fails without good cause to attend and testify as directed in the subpoena, he shall be punished in the manner provided for the punishment of any witness who disobeys a subpoena issued from a court of record in this state.

3. Witness from another state subpoenaed to testify in this state. If a person in any state, which by its laws has made provision for commanding persons within its borders to attend and testify in criminal prosecutions, or grand jury investigations commenced or about to commence, in this state, is a material witness in a prosecution pending in a court of record in this state, or in a grand jury investigation which has commenced or is about to commence, a judge of such court may issue a certificate under the seal of the court stating these facts and specifying the number of days the

witness will be required. This certificate shall be presented to a judge of a court of record in the county in which the witness is found.

If said certificate recommends that the witness be taken into immediate custody and delivered to an officer of this state to assure his attendance in this state, such judge may direct that such witness be forthwith brought before him; and the judge being satisfied of the desirability of such custody and delivery, for which determination said certificate shall be prima facie proof, may order that said witness be forthwith taken into custody and delivered to an officer of this state, which order shall be sufficient authority to such officer to take such witness into custody and hold him unless and until he may be released by bail, recognizance, or order of the judge issuing the certificate.

If the witness is summoned to attend and testify in this state he shall be tendered the sum of ten cents a mile for each mile and five dollars for each day that he is required to travel and attend as a witness. Such fees shall be a proper charge upon the county in which such criminal prosecution or grand jury investigation is pending. A witness who has appeared in accordance with the provisions of the subpoena shall not be required to remain within this state a longer period of time than the period mentioned in the certificate, unless otherwise ordered by the court. If such witness fails without good cause to attend and testify as directed in this subpoena, he shall be punished in the manner provided for the punishment of any witness who disobeys a subpoena issued from a court of record in this state.

4. Exemption from arrest and service of process. If a person comes into this state in obedience to a subpoena directing him to attend and testify in this state he shall not while in this state pursuant to such subpoena or order be subject to arrest or the service of process, civil or criminal, in connection with matters which arose before his entrance into this state under the subpoena.

If a person passes through this state while going to another state in obedience to a subpoena or order to attend and testify in that state or while returning therefrom, he shall not while so passing through this state be subject to arrest or the service of process, civil or criminal, in connection with matters which arose before his entrance into this state under the subpoena or order.

5. Uniformity of interpretation. This section shall be so interpreted and construed as to effectuate its general purpose to make uniform the law of the states which enact it.

6. Short title. This section may be cited as "Uniform act to secure the attendance of witnesses from without the state in criminal cases."

7. Constitutionality. If any part of this section is for any reason declared void, such invalidity shall not affect the validity of the remaining portions thereof.

ANNOTATIONS

Appealability.—Although New York trial court, pursuant to CPL § 640.10(2), held that two Virginia residents were material witnesses, the Virginia court did not agree, and consequently denied a petition ordering the presence of either witness in New York. Indeed, if defendant was dissatisfied with the Virginia court's determination, then he should have appealed the decision in Virginia, not New York. People v. Jones, 147 A.D.2d 983, 537 N.Y.S.2d 364 (4th Dept. 1989).

Defendant's right to present witnesses.—The refusal to grant the accused an adjournment to secure the attendance of two alibi witnesses was an abuse of discretion requiring a new trial. While a trial court is not required to grant an adjournment to allow pursuit of an elusive witness whose name and address are unknown, when a witness has been identified to the court and is within the jurisdiction, a request for a short adjournment should not be denied if some diligence and good faith have been shown; such denial would be a deprivation of defendant's fundamental right to present witnesses in his own behalf. People v. Foy, 32 N.Y.2d 473, 346 N.Y.S.2d 245, 299 N.E.2d 664 (1973).

Due diligence to produce witness; lack of.—Prosecution's failure to even try to produce robbery victim for trial, when he was stationed with the armed forces in Europe, rendered invalid a videotaped conditional examination made of the witness; prosecutor must use due diligence to try to get absent witness to testify before relying on other, substitute examinations. People v. McDowell, 88 A.D.2d 522, 449 N.Y.S.2d 981 (1st Dept. 1982).

Evidence of materiality and necessity of appellant's appearance.—Police officers acting pursuant to the "fellow officer rule," who make an arrest at the direction of another law enforcement officer, are not deemed "material" witnesses under this section. People v. Clark, 216 A.D.2d 919, 629 N.Y.S.2d 700 (4th Dept. 1995).

Requirements.—The party who seeks to secure the presence of an out-of-state witness should present evidence in the form of an affidavit of the witness or otherwise show that the testimony of the desired witness is admissible, material and necessary; the burden of showing materiality is upon the party seeking to compel the attendance of an out-of-state witness. People v. McCartney, 38 N.Y.2d 618, 381 N.Y.S.2d 855, 345 N.E.2d 326 (1976).

—Prosecutorial immunity did not extend to District Attorney's failure to follow the procedure provided by CPL 640.10(3) with respect to securing a certificate from a New York Judge and dispatching it to an out-of-state judge before the arrest of an out-of-state material witness; the prosecutor's obligation to comply with the prescribed procedural steps involved no evaluation of evidence, nor exercise of discretion, and instead resembled an administrative duty. Broughton v. City of New York, 91 Misc. 2d 543, 398 N.Y.S.2d 397 (Civil Ct. N.Y.C. 1977).

Subpoena duces tecum.—Certificate of New Jersey Superior Court Judge and supporting affidavits established a sufficient factual predicate for the finding of materiality and need for documents consisting of notes taken by respondent, a newspaper reporter, in the course of interviews with persons who have subsequently testified for the prosecution. Superior Court v. Farber, 94 Misc. 2d 886, 405 N.Y.S.2d 989 (Sup. Ct. N.Y. Co. 1978).

ARTICLE 650—SECURING ATTENDANCE AS WITNESSES OF PRISONERS CONFINED IN INSTITUTIONS OF OTHER JURISDICTIONS OF THE UNITED STATES—RENDITION TO OTHER JURISDICTIONS OF PRISONERS CONFINED IN INSTITUTIONS WITHIN THE STATE

LexisNexis Cross Reference

New York Criminal Practice (2d ed.), Vol. 3, Ch. 32, Production As Witnesses of Prisoners and Persons Confined Inside and Outside New York State.

§ 650.10. Securing attendance of prisoner in this state as witness in proceeding without the state.

If a judge of a court of record in any other state, which by its laws has made provision for commanding a prisoner within that state to attend and testify in this state, certifies under the seal of that court that there is a criminal prosecution pending in such court or that a grand jury investigation has commenced, and that a person confined in a New York state correctional institution or prison within the department of correction, other than a person confined as criminally mentally ill, or as a defective delinquent, or confined in the death house awaiting execution, is a material witness in such prosecution or investigation and that his presence is required for a specified number of days, upon presentment of such certificate to a judge of a superior court in the county where the person is confined, upon notice to the attorney general, such judge, shall fix a time and place for a hearing and shall make an order directed to the person having custody of the prisoner requiring that such prisoner be produced at the hearing.

If at such hearing the judge determines that the prisoner is a material and necessary witness in the requesting state, the judge shall issue an order directing that the prisoner attend in the court where the prosecution or investigation is pending, upon such terms and conditions as the judge prescribes, including among other things, provision for the return of the prisoner at the conclusion of his testimony, proper safeguards on his custody, and proper financial reimbursement or other payment by the demanding jurisdiction for all expenses incurred in the production and return of the prisoner.

The attorney general is authorized as agent for the state of New York, when in his judgment it is necessary, to enter into such agreements with the appropriate authorities of the demanding jurisdiction as he determines necessary to ensure proper compliance with the order of the court.

Amended by L. 1978, Ch. 550.

§ 650.20. Securing attendance of prisoner outside the state as witness in criminal action in the state.

1. When (a) a criminal action is pending in a court of record of this state, or a grand jury proceeding has been commenced, and (b) there is reasonable cause to believe that a person confined in a correctional institution or prison of another state, other than a person awaiting execution of a sentence of death or one confined as mentally ill or as a defective delinquent, possesses information material to such criminal action or proceeding, and (c) the attendance of such person as a witness in such action or proceeding is desired by a party thereto, and (d) the state in which such person is confined possesses a statute equivalent to section 650.10, the court in which such action or proceeding is pending may issue a certificate under the seal of such court, certifying all such facts and that the attendance of such person as a witness in such court is required for a specified number of days.

2. Such certificate may be issued upon application, of either the people or a defendant, demonstrating all the facts specified in subdivision one.

3. Upon issuing such a certificate, the court may deliver it, or cause or authorize it to be delivered, to a judge or a court of such other state who or which, pursuant to the laws thereof, is authorized to initiate or undertake legal action for the delivery of such prisoners to this state as witnesses.

§ 650.30. Securing attendance of prisoner in federal institution as witness in criminal action in the state.

1. When (a) a criminal action is pending in a court of record of this state by reason of the filing therewith of an accusatory instrument, or a grand jury proceeding has been commenced, and (b) there is reasonable cause to believe that a person confined in a federal prison or other federal custody, either within or outside this state, possesses information material to such criminal action or proceeding, and (c) the attendance of such person as a witness in such action or proceeding is desired by a party thereto, a superior court, at a term held in the county in which such action

or proceeding is pending, may issue a certificate, known as a writ of habeas corpus ad testificandum, addressed to the attorney general of the United States, certifying all such facts and requesting the attorney general of the United States to cause the attendance of such person as a witness in such court for a specified number of days under custody of a federal public servant.

2. Such a certificate may be issued upon application of either the people or a defendant, demonstrating all the facts specified in subdivision one.

3. Upon issuing such certificate, the court may deliver it, or cause or authorize it to be delivered, to the attorney general of the United States or to his representative authorized to entertain the request.

TITLE S—PROCEDURES FOR SECURING TESTIMONY FOR FUTURE USE, AND FOR USING TESTIMONY GIVEN IN A PRIOR PROCEEDING

ARTICLE 660—SECURING TESTIMONY FOR USE IN A SUBSEQUENT PROCEEDING—EXAMINATION OF WITNESSES CONDITIONALLY

§ 660.10. Examination of witnesses conditionally; in general.

After a defendant has been arraigned upon an accusatory instrument, and under circumstances prescribed in this article, a criminal court may, upon application of either the people or a defendant, order that a witness or prospective witness in the action be examined conditionally under oath in order that such testimony may be received into evidence at subsequent proceedings in or related to the action.

Amended by L. 1980, Ch. 291.

ANNOTATIONS

Completion of cross-examination by videotape.—The completion of cross-examination of a witness who suffered severe respiratory failure at the beginning of his cross-examination, by means of a videotaped conditional examination in the hospital, was permissible under CPL §§ 660.10 and 660.30, and in any event, the claim was meritless because the court struck the offending testimony. People v. Association of Trade Waste Removers, 267 A.D.2d 137, 701 N.Y.S.2d 12 (1st Dept. 1999), cert. denied, 531 U.S. 918 (2000).

Court's discretion.—Court properly granted People's application to take a particular witness's testimony at a conditional examination, because the testimony was material on the issue of identity and there was reasonable cause to believe that due the witness's extremely poor health, he would be unavailable for trial. People v. Balazs, 258 A.D.2d 658, 685 N.Y.S.2d 782 (2d Dept. 1999).

Discovery requirements.—Since Art. 660 provides that the conditional examination may be utilized in place of and instead of an actual appearance of the victim at trial with prescribed safeguards, it follows that the timing of the disclosure requirements contained in 240.45 of the CPL are triggered by the granting of the 660.10 examination. The material must be disclosed in toto at the outset of the prosecution's case, and not just in piecemeal fashion immediately prior to the particular witness testifying. People v. Coyne, 192 Misc. 2d 507, 748 N.Y.S.2d 206 (County Ct. Onondaga Co. 2002).

Witnesses; promise of leniency; new trial required.—While there was no explicit promise of leniency from the district attorney, there was a possibility here that the witnesses believed they would be rewarded for testifying. Under this circumstance, it was incumbent upon the assistant district attorney to inform the court and the jury of all the facts and circumstances surrounding the pretrial conversations with the key prosecution witnesses. In such a situation, a new trial is required in the interests of justice; this goes to the credibility of the witnesses. People v. Ford, 41 A.D.2d 550, 339 N.Y.S.2d 620 (2d Dept. 1973).

§ 660.20. Examination of witnesses conditionally; grounds for order.

An order directing examination of a witness conditionally must be based upon the ground that there is reasonable cause to believe that such witness:

1. Possesses information material to the criminal action or proceeding in issue; and

2. Will not be amenable or responsive to legal process or available as a witness at a time when his testimony will be sought, either because he is:

(a) About to leave the state and not return for a substantial period of time; or

(b) Physically ill or incapacitated.

§ 660.30. Examination of witnesses conditionally; when and to what courts application may be made.

1. An application to examine a witness conditionally may be made at any time after the defendant has been arraigned upon an accusatory instrument and before termination of the action, or of a proceeding therein or related thereto, in which the witness's testimony is sought.

2. Such application must be made to and determined by the following courts under the indicated circumstances:

(a) If the action is pending in a local criminal court as a result of an accusatory instrument filed therewith, the application must be made to and determined by such local criminal court;

(b) If the defendant has been held by a local criminal court for the action of a grand jury on the basis of a felony complaint, or if an indictment has been filed against him, the application must be made to and determined by the superior court by which the grand jury was or is to be impaneled or in which the indictment is pending. If the superior court by which the grand jury is to be impaneled is the supreme court, the motion may, in the alternative, be made in the county court of the county in which the action is pending.

Amended by L. 1973, Ch. 221.

ANNOTATIONS

Application.—Defendants, accused of conspiracy, were not entitled to conditional examination of witness, dying of cancer, where the affidavits in support of the motion were purely conclusory and contained no allegations of fact which would demonstrate reasonable cause to believe the witness possessed information material to the crime in issue. People v. Darienzo, 79 Misc. 2d 977, 362 N.Y.S.2d 694 (Sup. Ct. Bronx Co. 1974).

Completion of cross-examination by videotape.—The completion of cross-examination of a witness who suffered severe respiratory failure at the beginning of his cross-examination, by means of a videotaped conditional examination in the hospital, was permissible under CPL §§ 660.10 and 660.30, and in any event, the claim was meritless because the court struck the offending testimony. People v. Association of Trade Waste Removers, 267 A.D.2d 137, 701 N.Y.S.2d 12 (1st Dept. 1999), *cert. denied,* 531 U.S. 918 (2000).

§ 660.40. Examination of witnesses conditionally; application and notice.

1. An application to examine a witness conditionally must be made in writing, must be subscribed and sworn to, and must contain:

(a) The title of the action, the offense or offenses charged, the nature and status of the action, and the name and residential address of the witness sought to be examined; and

(b) A statement that there is reasonable cause to believe that grounds for such an examination, as specified in section 660.20, exist, together with allegations of fact supporting such statement. Such allegations of fact may be those of the applicant, or those of another person in an accompanying deposition, or of both. They may be based either upon personal knowledge of the deponent or upon information and belief, provided that in the latter event the sources of such information and the grounds of such belief are stated.

2. The application may also contain a request that the examination, in addition to its being recorded in the same manner as would be required were the witness testifying at trial, also be recorded by videotape or other photographic method approved by and subject to standards and administrative policies promulgated pursuant to section twenty-eight of article six of the constitution.

3. A copy of the application, with reasonable notice and opportunity to be heard, must be served upon the other party to the action. If the defendant is the applicant, such service must be upon the district attorney. If the people are the applicant, such service must be upon the defendant and upon his attorney if any. The respondent party may file and serve a sworn written answer to the application.

Amended by L. 1980, Ch. 291.

§ 660.50. Examination of witnesses conditionally; determination of application.

1. Before ruling upon the application, the court may, in addition to examining the papers and hearing oral argument, make any inquiry it deems appropriate for the purpose of making findings of fact essential to the determination. For such purpose, it may examine witnesses, under oath or otherwise, subpoena or call witnesses and authorize the attorneys for the parties to do so.

2. If the court is satisfied that grounds for the application exist, it must order an examination of the witness conditionally at a designated time and place. Such examination must be conducted by the same court; except that, if it is to be held in another county, it may be conducted by a designated superior court of such other county.

3. The court must order that the examination be recorded in the same manner as would be required were the witness testifying at trial, and the court may, in addition, order that the examination also be recorded by videotape or other photographic method approved by and subject to standards and administrative policies promulgated pursuant to section twenty-eight of article six of the constitution.

4. Upon ordering the examination, the court must direct the party securing the order of examination to serve a copy of the order upon the respondent party and, if a defendant be such, upon his attorney also, and must either issue a subpoena for the witness' attendance thereat or authorize the applicant party's attorney to do so.

Amended by L. 1975, Ch. 181; L. 1980, Ch. 291.

ANNOTATION

Videotape.—Court granted motion of District Attorney to videotape the deposition of complainant, who had enlisted in the army for three-years and was to leave for Oklahoma, subject to District Attorney obtaining the permission of the Presiding Justice of the Appellate Division, First Judicial Department, and also recording the testimony in the conventional manner by an official Court Reporter and having a transcript made. People v. Winborne, 90 Misc. 2d 71, 394 N.Y.S.2d 769 (Sup. Ct. Bronx Co. 1977).

§ 660.60. Examination of witnesses conditionally; the examination proceeding.

1. The examination proceeding must be conducted in the same manner as would be required were the witness testifying at a trial, and must be recorded in such fashion as the court has directed pursuant to subdivision three of section 660.50 of this chapter. The witness must testify under oath. The applicant party must first examine the witness and the respondent party may then cross-examine him, with each party entitled to register objections and to receive rulings of the court thereon.

2. Upon conclusion of the examination, a

transcript and any videotape or photographic recording thereof must be certified and filed with the court which ordered the examination.

Amended by L. 1980, Ch. 291.

ANNOTATIONS

General.—The trial court properly admitted the conditional examinations where the People satisfied their obligation under CPL § 660.60(2) by filing the tapes and transcripts before the start of the trial. People v. Cray, 195 A.D.2d 303, 600 N.Y.S.2d 7 (1st Dept. 1993), aff'd, 84 N.Y.2d 874, 620 N.Y.S.2d 782, 644 N.E.2d 1338 (1994).

Videotape.—Motion for an order to have eyewitness examined conditionally and on videotape must be denied since the Criminal Procedure Law does not vest the trial court with the discretion to order the recording of such examination by any means other than stenographic. People v. Lamberty, 94 Misc. 2d 636, 405 N.Y.S.2d 599 (Sup. Ct. Bronx Co. 1978).

ARTICLE 670—USE IN A CRIMINAL PROCEEDING OF TESTIMONY GIVEN IN A PREVIOUS PROCEEDING

Section

670.10   Use in a criminal proceeding of testimony given in a previous proceeding; when authorized.

670.20   Use in a criminal proceeding of testimony given in a previous proceeding; procedure.

§ 670.10. Use in a criminal proceeding of testimony given in a previous proceeding; when authorized.

1. Under circumstances prescribed in this article, testimony given by a witness at (a) a trial of an accusatory instrument, or (b) a hearing upon a felony complaint conducted pursuant to section 180.60, or (c) an examination of such witness conditionally, conducted pursuant to article six hundred sixty, may, where otherwise admissible, be received into evidence at a subsequent proceeding in or relating to the action involved when at the time of such subsequent proceeding the witness is unable to attend the same by reason of death, illness or incapacity, or cannot with due diligence be found, or is outside the state or in federal custody and cannot with due diligence be brought before the court. Upon being received into evidence, such testimony may be read and any videotape or photographic recording thereof played. Where any recording is received into evidence, the stenographic transcript of that examination shall also be received.

2. The subsequent proceedings at which such testimony may be received in evidence consist of:

(a) Any proceeding constituting a part of a criminal action based upon the charge or charges which were pending against the defendant at the time of the witness's testimony and to which such testimony related; and

(b) Any post-judgment proceeding in which a judgment of conviction upon a charge specified in paragraph (a) is challenged.

Amended by L. 1971, Ch. 884; L. 1980, Ch. 291.

ANNOTATIONS

Admissions; independently admissible.—People were not required to satisfy the requirements of CPL § 670.10 where evidence included admissions by defendant and was independently admissible under that exception to the hearsay rule. People v. Gardner, 237 A.D.2d 895, 654 N.Y.S.2d 924 (4th Dept. 1997).

Fifth Amendment; unavailability.—Prosecution's witnesses at the retrial who asserted their Fifth Amendment privilege were unavailable for the purpose of introducing their former testimony at the first trial into evidence. People v. Ortiz, 209 A.D.2d 332, 619 N.Y.S.2d 12 (1st Dept. 1994).

—Trial court properly admitted the sworn testimony of witness since witness's Fifth Amendment privilege rendered him an unavailable witness. People v. Varsos, 182 A.D.2d 508, 582 N.Y.S.2d 193 (1st Dept. 1992).

—Testimony of robbery victim given at the earlier trial of co-defendant violated defendant's constitutional right to confrontation, and consequently, a new trial was ordered as to those specific counts. People v. Scott, 197 A.D.2d 646, 602 N.Y.S.2d 684 (2d Dept. 1993).

—Trial court erred in denying defendant's application to admit his former co-defendant's prior felony hearing testimony into evidence because 1) witness was unavailable, and 2) the testimony was otherwise admissible under CPL § 670.10. People v. Hinds, 183 A.D.2d 783, 583 N.Y.S.2d 512 (2d Dept. 1992).

—There was no error in admitting in evidence the previous trial testimony of witness because defense counsel did not object to the admission of that testimony, and he did not assert that the testimony was inadmissible pursuant to CPL § 670.10. People v. Briggs, 190 A.D.2d 995, 593 N.Y.S.2d 622 (4th Dept. 1993).

Grand Jury testimony.—Although the grand jury testimony of an unavailable eyewitness is inadmissible as evidence-in-chief, this case is an exception to the rule because defendant procured the witness's unavailability by threatening him. People v. Geraci, 85 N.Y.2d 359, 625 N.Y.S.2d 469, 649 N.E.2d 817 (1995), *limited by* 654 N.Y.S.2d 1004, 1007.

—The Grand Jury testimony of an eyewitness to the crime, who identified defendant as one of the perpetrators, did not fall within the classes of prior testimony rendered admissible in criminal proceedings by CPL § 670.10. People v. Green, 78 N.Y.2d 1029, 1030, 576 N.Y.S.2d 75, 581 N.E.2d 1330 (1991).

—Where there was no evidence that defendant or someone acting on his behalf tampered with the People's witness, the trial court committed reversible error by allowing the People to introduce, as part of its case-in-chief at trial, the Grand Jury testimony of that witness. People v. Hamilton, 70 N.Y.2d 987, 526 N.Y.S.2d 421, 521 N.E.2d 428 (1988).

—Court erred in admitting grand jury testimony of store owner in place of her live testimony at trial because the People failed to establish that the witness's unavailability was procured by the defendant, and all of the threats warning the store owner not to testify were made by a suspected accomplice, not defendant; however, error was harmless. People v. Perkins, 289 A.D.2d 940, 735 N.Y.S.2d 273 (4th Dept. 2001).

Locating witness; due diligence.—The People did not exercise due diligence in attempting to secure witness's presence at trial, where the state officials who telephoned the witness to ask him to return to the United States to testify neither addressed him in his native language of Spanish nor employed an interpreter, despite their awareness of his difficulty communicating in English. People v. Diaz, 97 N.Y.2d 109, 735 N.Y.S.2d 885, 761 N.E.2d 577 (2001).

—The testimony of the complainant at the preliminary hearing was admissible at the trial where the complainant disappeared the day before the trial and the district attorney exercised due diligence in attempting to locate her by repeatedly telephoning her apartment, sending the police to the apartment on several occasions, questioning neighbors, contacting the Missing Persons Bureau and the local welfare office where she picked up her checks. People v. Arroyo, 54 N.Y.2d 567, 446 N.Y.S.2d 910, 431 N.E.2d 27, *cert. denied*, 456 U.S. 979 (1982).

—Prior testimony may be admitted upon a showing that the witness "cannot with due diligence be found, or is outside the state or in federal custody and cannot with due diligence be brought before the court." Here, People failed to make any showing of due diligence to justify admission of the officer's prior testimony, and the People made no attempt to locate the witness; thus, court erred in admitting testimony. People v. Combo, 272 A.D.2d 992, 708 N.Y.S.2d 781 (4th Dept. 2000).

—Court properly admitted into evidence the testimony of a witness from defendant's first trial after determining that the People exercised due diligence but could not locate that witness. People v. Koberstein, 261 A.D.2d 849, 691 N.Y.S.2d 214 (4th Dept. 1999).

Pretrial testimony admissible at trial.—Hearing court has recourse to robbery victim's pretrial testimony at trial, where victim could not be found with "due diligence" in state and there was nothing to raise a doubt that victim's trial testimony would have differed. People v. Martin, 38 A.D.2d 536, 327 N.Y.S.2d 53 (1st Dept. 1971), aff'd, 32 N.Y.2d 771, 344 N.Y.S.2d 957, 298 N.E.2d 119 (1973).

—Court properly permitted People to read into evidence the felony hearing testimony of a missing witness pursuant to CPL § 670.10. At the hearing on the admissibility of the testimony, two officers testified about the extensive efforts made to locate the witness who had escaped from police custody and remained a fugitive, and court was satisfied that it was very unlikely that any additional efforts would have resulted in locating the witness. People v. Hernandez, 259 A.D.2d 763, 688 N.Y.S.2d 170 (2d Dept. 1999).

Suppression hearing testimony.—Testimony given at suppression hearing is inadmissible because hearing was not a trial of an accusatory instrument within the meaning of the statute. People v. Ayala, 75 N.Y.2d 422, 554 N.Y.S.2d 412, 553 N.E.2d 960 (1990).

—Court properly refused to permit defendant to introduce the suppression hearing testimony of a defense witness who had died between the hearing and the trial. Suppression hearing testimony is not one of the categories of prior testimony that may be received pursuant to CPL § 670.10, and such testimony is therefore inadmissible as hearsay. People v. Rosa, 302 A.D.2d 231, 754 N.Y.S.2d 279 (1st Dept. 2003).

—Even if the presentment agency had established that the complainant were unavailable to testify at the *Sirois* hearing, the Family Court erred in ruling that the officer's *Wade* hearing testimony be admitted as evidence in chief at the fact-finding hearing. *In re* Duane F., 309 A.D.2d 265, 764 N.Y.S.2d 434 (1st Dept. 2003).

Testimony at preliminary hearing.—Where the opportunity for cross-examination of the victim on the identification issue was unduly restricted by the court at the preliminary hearing, the use of that testimony at trial was precluded by the confrontation clauses of the United States and New York State Constitutions. People v. Simmons, 36 N.Y.2d 126, 365 N.Y.S.2d 812, 325 N.E.2d 139 (1975).

Transcript of testimony from previous trial.—Trial court correctly allowed prosecution to present a transcript of witness's testimony at the second trial inasmuch as the prosecution made a good faith effort to locate witness by conducting a thorough investigation as to his whereabouts. People v. Wiggins, 189 A.D.2d 908, 593 N.Y.S.2d 62 (2d Dept. 1992).

—Prosecution properly permitted to read into evidence testimony of witness from defendant's first trial where the witness failed to appear at the trial, a material witness order was issued, and an investigator from the prosecutor's office made extensive efforts to locate witness including visiting her home several times, questioning her neighbors and checking other locations where she might be found. People v. Nettles, 118 A.D.2d 875, 500 N.Y.S.2d 361 (2d Dept. 1986).

—Defendant's cousin, Evans, who was present at murder and assisted in disposing of body, testified at the first trial but refused to testify at the second trial. Evans was held in contempt because of his persistent refusal, and the court then determined that Evans was unavailable. Court properly admitted that testimony pursuant to CPL § 670.10. People v. Barber, 2 A.D.3d 1290, 770 N.Y.S.2d 537 (4th Dept. 2003).

§ 670.20. Use in a criminal proceeding of testimony given in a previous proceeding; procedure.

1. In any criminal action or proceeding other than a grand jury proceeding, a party thereto who desires to offer in evidence testimony of a witness given in a previous action or proceeding as provided in section 670.10, must so move, either in writing or orally in open court, and must submit to the court, and serve a copy thereof upon the adverse party, an authenticated transcript of the testimony and any videotape or photographic recording thereof sought to be introduced. Such moving party must further state facts showing that personal attendance of the witness in question is precluded by some factor specified in subdivision one of section 670.10. In determining the motion, the court, with opportunity for both parties to be heard, must make inquiry and conduct a hearing to determine whether personal attendance of the witness is so precluded. If the court determines that such is the case and grants the motion, the moving party may introduce the transcript in evidence and read into evidence the testimony contained therein. In such case, the adverse party may register any objection or protest thereto that he would be entitled to register were the witness testifying in person, and the court must rule thereon.

2. Without obtaining any court order or authorization, a district attorney may introduce in evidence in a grand jury proceeding testimony of a witness given in a previous action or proceeding specified in subdivision one of section 670.10, provided that a foundation for such evidence is laid by other evidence demonstrating that personal attendance of such witness is precluded by some factor specified in subdivision one of section 670.10.

Amended by L. 1980, Ch. 291.

ANNOTATION

Objection to testimony.—A defendant can register any objection or protest to the testimony that he would be entitled to were the witness testifying in person, but he cannot waive reading the cross-examination testimony. People v. Reingold, 44 A.D.2d 191, 353 N.Y.S.2d 978 (4th Dept. 1974).

ARTICLE 680—SECURING TESTIMONY OUTSIDE THE STATE FOR USE IN PROCEEDING WITHIN THE STATE— EXAMINATION OF WITNESSES ON COMMISSION

LexisNexis Cross Reference

New York Criminal Practice (2d ed.), Vol. 3, Ch. 31, Securing Attendance of Non-Prisoner Witnesses.

§ 680.10. Examination of witnesses on commission; in general.

1. Under circumstances prescribed in this article, testimony material to a trial or pending trial of an accusatory instrument which charges a crime, may be taken by "examination on a commission" outside the state and received in evidence at such trial.

2. A "commission" is a process issued by a superior court designating one or more persons as commissioners and authorizing them to conduct a recorded examination of a witness or witnesses under oath, primarily on the basis of interrogatories annexed to the commission, and to remit to the issuing court the transcript of such examination.

ANNOTATIONS

Denial of application.—Where the defendant moved to commission his former wife, an out of state and unavailable witness, the court denied the motion on the grounds that commissions do not apply to pre-trial motions to suppress evidence. Commissions apply to information to be utilized at the trial. People v. Moore, 216 A.D.2d 218, 629 N.Y.S.2d 405 (1st Dept. 1995).

—The defendant was prejudiced by the denial of his application for commission of a witness. The defendant's witness possessed material evidence supporting the defendant's theory. Failure to obtain the testimony of the witness hindered the defendant's defense. People v. Zlochevsky, 196 A.D.2d 701, 603 N.Y.S.2d 433 (1st Dept. 1993).

Discretion of court.—Court did not abuse its discretion in denying commission where defendant's supporting papers furnished little more than a very brief conclusional summary, without differentiation as to the person named rather than a "brief summary of facts" supporting a statement that the witnesses possess "information material to the action which in the interest of justice should be disclosed at the trial." People v. Carter, 37 N.Y.2d 234, 371 N.Y.S.2d 905, 333 N.E.2d 177 (1975).

§ 680.20. Examination of witnesses on commission; when commission issuable; form and content of application.

1. Upon a pre-trial application of a defendant who has pleaded not guilty to an indictment or other accusatory instrument which charges a crime, the superior court in which such indictment is pending, or a superior court in the county in which such other accusatory instrument is pending, may issue a commission for examination of a designated person as a witness in the action, at a designated place outside this state, if it is satisfied that (a) such person possesses information material to the action which in the interest of justice should be disclosed at the trial, and (b) resides outside the state.

2. The application and moving papers must be in writing and must be subscribed and sworn to by the defendant or his attorney. A copy thereof must be served on the district attorney, with reasonable notice and opportunity to be heard. The moving papers must allege:

(a) The offense or offenses charged; and

(b) The status of the action; and

(c) The name of the prospective witness; and

(d) A statement that such prospective witness resides outside the state, and his address in the jurisdiction in which the examination sought is to occur; and

(e) A statement that he possesses information material to the action which in the interest of justice should be disclosed at the trial, together with a brief summary of the facts supporting such statement.

3. An application for issuance of a commission may request examination pursuant thereto of more than one person residing in the particular jurisdiction. In such case, it must contain allegations specified in subdivision two with respect to each such person, and the court must make separate rulings as to each.

ANNOTATIONS

Discretion of the court.—It is within the discretion of the court to determine if the witness sought to be obtained through commission, possesses information which should be procured in the interest of justice. People v. Moore, 216 A.D.2d 218, 629 N.Y.S.2d 405 (1st Dept. 1995).

—Exceptional circumstances existed for granting a commission where the witness could not attend the trial due to incarceration in Israel. The witness possessed material evidence for the defendant. Thus, the commission should have been granted. People v. Zlochevsky, 196 A.D.2d 701, 603 A.D.2d 433 (1st Dept. 1993).

Failure to obtain witness.—The defendant was denied effective counsel where counsel failed to procure the attendance of a physician who possessed material information supporting the defendant's theory. People v. Baba-Ali, 179 A.D.2d 725, 578 N.Y.S.2d 633 (2d Dept. 1992).

Generally.—The People are not afforded a remedy under Article 680 for commission of a witness unless it is the defendant who is initiating the process. People v. Craig, 151 Misc. 2d 442, 581 N.Y.S.2d 987 (Sup. Ct. Bronx Co. 1992).

§ 680.30. Examination of witnesses on commission; application by people for examination of witnesses.

1. Upon granting the defendant's application for issuance of a commission, the court may, upon application of the people, determine that the commission shall also authorize examination of a person or persons designated by the people, who reside in the jurisdiction in which the examination proceeding is to occur, if it is satisfied that such person or persons possess material information, reside outside the state and otherwise meet the standards for examination of witnesses on a commission as prescribed in subdivision one of section 680.20.

2. Such application and the moving papers must be in writing, must be subscribed and sworn to by the district attorney, and copies thereof must be served upon the defendant and his attorney, with reasonable notice and opportunity to be heard. The moving papers must contain all of the allegations required upon a defendant's application, as specified in subdivision two of section 680.20.

§ 680.40. Examination of witnesses on commission; when commission issuable upon application of people.

When a commission has been issued upon application of a defendant pursuant to section 680.20, the court may, upon application of the people, issue another commission for examination, either in the same or another jurisdiction, of a person designated by the people, under the same conditions as prescribed in said section 680.20. In such case, the court may, upon application of the defendant, determine, in the manner provided in section 680.30, that such commission shall also authorize examination of a person or persons designated by the defendant.

§ 680.50. Examination of witnesses on commission; interrogatories.

1. Following an order for the issuance of a commission and the court's designation of the witnesses to be examined thereon, each party must prepare interrogatories or questions to be asked of each witness who is to be examined upon his or its request, and must submit the same to the court and serve a copy thereof upon the other party. Following such submission and service, such other party may in the same manner submit and serve cross-interrogatories or questions, to be asked of the witness following his examination upon the direct inquiry.

2. After all such interrogatories and cross-interrogatories have been submitted and served, the court may examine them and, with opportunity for counsel to be heard, exclude and strike any question which it considers irrelevant, incompetent or otherwise improper or violative of the rules of evidence which prevail at a criminal trial.

§ 680.60. Examination of witnesses on commission; form and content of the commission.

1. The commission must be subscribed by the court and must contain:

(a) The name and address of each witness to be examined; and

(b) The name, or a descriptive title, of a commissioner or commissioners who, pursuant to subdivision two, are authorized to conduct the examination; and

(c) A statement authorizing such commissioner or commissioners to administer the oath to witnesses; and

(d) A direction that, upon completion of such examination, such commissioner or commissioners cause it to be transcribed and remit to the court the transcript, the commission, the interrogatories and all other pertinent instruments and documents.

2. The following persons may be designated commissioners:

(a) If the examination is to occur within the United States or any territory thereof, any attorney authorized to practice law in the specified jurisdiction or any person authorized to administer oaths therein;

(b) If the examination is to occur in a foreign country, any diplomatic or consular agent or representative of the United States employed in such capacity in such country, or any commissioned officer of the armed forces.

3. The court must cause the commission to be delivered to a commissioner designated therein, together with a copy of this article.

§ 680.70. Examination of witnesses on commission; the examination.

The examination on the commission must be conducted as follows:

1. Each witness must testify under oath, and the examination must be recorded and transcribed.

2. Each witness must first be asked all the questions contained in the interrogatories submitted by the party requesting his examination. He must then be asked all the questions contained in the cross-interrogatories, if any, submitted by the other party.

3. The defendant has a right to be represented by counsel at the examination, and the district attorney also has a right to be present, but both such rights may be waived. Upon the conclusion of the questioning of a witness upon the written interrogatories, he may be further examined by the attorney or representative of the party who requested his examination, and may then be cross-examined by the attorney or representative of the adverse party. Each such attorney or representative may register objections to the authority or qualifications of the commissioner, to the manner in which the examination is conducted, and to the admissibility of evidence, and all such objections must be recorded and transcribed.

4. Documentary or other physical evidence may be produced and submitted by a witness.

Such evidence must be subscribed or otherwise identified by the witness, and certified by a commissioner and annexed to the transcript of the examination as a part of the record.

5. After the examination is transcribed, the commissioner or commissioners must subscribe and certify the transcript as an accurate record of the proceedings, and must then remit such transcript and all other pertinent instruments, documents and evidence to the court which issued the commission, in accordance with the directions thereof.

§ 680.80. Examination of witnesses on commission; use at trial of transcript of examination.

1. When the transcript and record of the examination on commission are received by the superior court which issued the commission, they must be filed therewith if such court be the trial court, and, if not, transmitted to the trial court. A copy of the transcript must be delivered by the trial court to each party.

2. Upon the trial of the action, either party may, subject to the provisions of subdivision three, introduce and read into evidence the transcript or that portion thereof containing the testimony of a witness examined on the commission.

3. At any time prior to the introduction of such evidence, the trial court may examine the transcript and, upon according both parties opportunity to be heard and to register objections, may exclude and strike therefrom irrelevant, incompetent or otherwise inadmissible testimony. While the transcript or any portion thereof is being read into evidence at the trial by a party, the other party may register any objection or protest thereto that he would be entitled to register were the witness testifying in person, regardless of whether such protest has previously been raised and passed upon by the court, and the court must rule thereon.

TITLE T—PROCEDURES FOR SECURING EVIDENCE BY MEANS OF COURT ORDER AND FOR SUPPRESSING EVIDENCE UNLAWFULLY OR IMPROPERLY OBTAINED

ARTICLE 690—SEARCH WARRANTS

LexisNexis Cross References

Defense of Narcotics Cases, Vol. 1, Ch. 3B, Searches Pursuant to Warrants; *New York Suppression Manual,* Ch. 9, Search Warrants; *Courtroom Criminal Evidence (3d ed.),* Vol. 1, Ch. 19, Probable Cause and Warrants.

§ 690.05. Search warrants; in general; definition.

1. Under circumstances prescribed in this article, a local criminal court may, upon application of a police officer, a district attorney or other public servant acting in the course of his official duties, issue a search warrant.

2. A search warrant is a court order and process directing a police officer to conduct:

(a) a search of designated premises, or of a designated vehicle, or of a designated person, for the purpose of seizing designated property or kinds of property, and to deliver any property so obtained to the court which issued the warrant.

(b) a search of a designated premises for the purpose of searching for and arresting a person who is the subject of:

(i) a warrant of arrest issued pursuant to this chapter, a superior court warrant of arrest issued pursuant to this chapter, or a bench warrant for a felony issued pursuant to this chapter, where the designated premises is the dwelling of a third party who is not the subject of the arrest warrant; or

(ii) a warrant of arrest issued by any other state or federal court for an offense which would constitute a felony under the laws of this state, where the designated premises is the dwelling of a third party who is not the subject of the arrest warrant.

Amended by L. 1980, Ch. 843; L. 1991, Ch. 504, eff. Nov. 1, 1991, amending subd. 2; L. 1998, Ch. 424, § 9, eff. Jan. 1, 1999, amending subd. 2.

ANNOTATIONS

Justice Court.—Although a warrant to seize films was issued by a Supreme Court Justice, the Justice Court was authorized to hear a motion to suppress the films and to evaluate the probable cause supporting the warrant. People v. P.J. Video, Inc., 65 N.Y.2d 566, 493 N.Y.S.2d 988, 483 N.E.2d 1120 (1985).

—Since a Justice Court may not issue a search warrant unless it has geographic, but not necessarily trial, jurisdiction, the affidavits which form the basis for issuance of the search warrant must allege that an offense was committed within its jurisdiction. People v. Hickey, 40 N.Y.2d 761, 390 N.Y.S.2d 42, 358 N.E.2d 868 (1976).

Organized Crime Task Force Attorney.—Where an OCTF attorney applies for a search warrant in County Court without the requisite approval of the Governor and local District Attorney, it is inappropriate to recognize that attorney as a "District Attorney" for the purpose of CPL § 690.05(1). B.T. Productions, Inc. v. Barr, 54 A.D.2d 315, 388 N.Y.S.2d 483 (4th Dept. 1976), *aff'd,* 44 N.Y.2d 226, 405 N.Y.S.2d 9, 376 N.E.2d 171 (1978).

—While a State Police officer has the authority to apply for a search warrant in pursuance of his police duties, he does not have such power to obtain the warrant on behalf of the State Organized Crime Task Force, a State agency which does not itself have that authority. B.T. Productions, Inc. v. Barr, 44 N.Y.2d 226, 405 N.Y.S.2d 9, 376 N.E.2d 171 (1978).

Probable cause.—In order for a warrant to be issued, a police officer must believe that probable cause exists. Upon the issuance of the warrant, a search can proceed. People v. Burr, 70 N.Y.2d 354, 520 N.Y.S.2d 739, 514 N.E.2d 1363 (1987).

—Application for a warrant was granted on the grounds that probable cause existed from the content of a nine year old child's statement. A police officer's sworn statement was based on the statement of the child. People v. Hetrick, 175 A.D.2d 491, 572 N.Y.S.2d 768 (3d Dept. 1991).

Procedure.—Where a search warrant application was made pursuant to the CPL, such search was subject to the standards of a criminal search. The purpose of the search was the investigation of possible criminal conduct. Town of East Hampton v. Omabuild USA No. 1, Inc., 215 A.D.2d 746, 627 N.Y.S.2d 723 (2d Dept. 1995).

—The issuance of a search warrant is usually performed without notice to the suspect involved. However, when a warrant is issued upon a person, that person must be given an opportunity to be heard. Dist. Atty. of Erie County v. Corlett, 140 Misc. 2d 162, 530 N.Y.S.2d 462 (Sup. Ct. Erie Co. 1988).

Search warrant; issuance.—Court held that a search warrant issued to a police officer, a member of a subsequently organized drug task force, was proper. The officer applied for the warrant as a police officer and pursuant to his duties. People v. Martin, 163 A.D.2d 536, 558 N.Y.S.2d 192 (2d Dept. 1990).

State Investigation Commission.—State Investigation Commission lacked the power to apply for a search warrant, and thus, evidence seized pursuant to a search warrant obtained by the Commission was suppressed. People v. DiLorenzo, 103 Misc. 2d 1098, 427 N.Y.S.2d 396 (Co. Ct. Montgomery Co. 1980), aff'd, 80 A.D.2d 952, 438 N.Y.S.2d 37 (3d Dept. 1981).

Tip; probable cause needed.—Since a "tip" does not disclose any circumstances from which it may be concluded that illegal activity was taking place, police observations must be relied on to sustain the warrant and the mere observance of a man entering the building on two occasions with a brown paper bag does not constitute probable cause. People v. Germano, 91 A.D.2d 1137, 458 N.Y.S.2d 713 (3d Dept. 1983).

§ 690.10. Search warrants; property subject to seizure thereunder.

Personal property is subject to seizure pursuant to a search warrant if there is reasonable cause to believe that it:

1. Is stolen; or

2. Is unlawfully possessed; or

3. Has been used, or is possessed for the purpose of being used, to commit or conceal the commission of an offense against the laws of this state or another state, provided however, that if such offense was against the laws of another state, the court shall only issue a warrant if the conduct comprising such offense would, if occurring in this state, constitute a felony against the laws of this state; or

4. Constitutes evidence or tends to demonstrate that an offense was committed in this state or another state, or that a particular person participated in the commission of an offense in this state or another state, provided however, that if such offense was against the laws of another state, the court shall only issue a warrant if the conduct comprising such offense would, if occurring in this state, constitute a felony against the laws of this state.

Amended by L. 1994, Ch. 612, § 1, eff. July 26, 1994, amending subds. 3 and 4.

ANNOTATIONS

Issuance of warrant.—Where three informants supplied detailed factual information to the police officer, it was proper to issue a search warrant upon the officer's application. The omission of certain details did not establish that the officer knowingly falsified the statements. People v. Jenkins, 184 A.D.2d 585, 584 N.Y.S.2d 643 (2d Dept. 1992).

Probable cause.—Court held that a blood sample taken from the defendant pursuant to a search warrant issued under CPL

§ 690.10 was proper. The issuance of the warrant was based on probable cause. People v. Casadei, 66 N.Y.2d 846, 498 N.Y.S.2d 357, 489 N.E.2d 244 (1985).

—Probable cause must be determined by a neutral magistrate upon consideration of all the facts. The magistrate must act with independent judgment and exactness. People v. P.J. Video, 65 N.Y.2d 566, 493 N.Y.S.2d 988, 483 N.E.2d 1120 (1985).

Property seized; grounds for seizure.—Where the police officer considered the blood stained sneaker to be evidence in the murder of the defendant's girlfriend, the officer was authorized to seize the sneakers. The officer's determination that the blood stain constituted evidence was justified. People v. Thomas, 188 A.D.2d 569, 591 N.Y.S.2d 464 (2d Dept. 1992).

Validity of warrant.—Where the search warrant failed to specify that there was reasonable cause to believe that certain clothing being sought was actually in defendant's dormitory room, the court did not invalidate the warrant. The court held that reasonable inferences are allowed in the execution of the warrant. People v. Robinson, 68 N.Y.2d 485, 510 N.Y.S.2d 837, 503 N.E.2d 485 (1986).

—Warrant which permitted video surveillance was valid under CPL § 690.10(4). People v. Teicher, 52 N.Y.2d 638, 439 N.Y.S.2d 846, 422 N.E.2d 506 (1981).

§ 690.15. Search warrants; what and who are subject to search thereunder.

1. A search warrant must direct a search of one or more of the following:

(a) A designated or described place or premises;

(b) A designated or described vehicle, as that term is defined in section 10.00 of the penal law;

(c) A designated or described person.

2. A search warrant which directs a search of a designated or described place, premises or vehicle, may also direct a search of any person present thereat or therein.

ANNOTATIONS

Description.—Misdescription of premises to be searched did not render search warrant invalid. People v. Eldridge, 173 A.D.2d 975, 569 N.Y.S.2d 482 (3d Dept. 1991).

Proper seizure of gun not described in warrant.—Where search warrant was issued upon probable cause seizure of revolver was proper during inventory search of defendant's unlocked and open suitcase despite fact that gun was not particularly described in warrant. People v. Matos, 94 A.D.2d 950, 464 N.Y.S.2d 76 (4th Dept. 1983).

Search warrant; authorizing search of vehicle.—Court suppressed the evidence found in the van when the tax investigators, who had a search warrant for the van but not the garage, entered the garage after the drivers had left and no exigent circumstances existed to validate their action. People v. Sciacca, 57 A.D.2d 846, 393 N.Y.S.2d 999 (2d Dept. 1977), aff'd, 45 N.Y.2d 122, 408 N.Y.S.2d 22, 379 N.E.2d 1153 (1978).

—Authority to search a vehicle does not include authority to enter private premises to effect a search of a vehicle within those premises; the constitutional mandate that a warrant particularly describe the place to be searched may not be circumvented by implication and the entry into a private garage was not permissible under a warrant to search a particular van. People v. Sciacca, 45 N.Y.2d 122, 408 N.Y.S.2d 22, 379 N.E.2d 1153 (1978).

—Where there was sufficient probable cause that the defendant was transporting drugs in his vehicle, a search warrant authorizing a search of the entire vehicle was proper. People v. Avery, 129 A.D.2d 852, 513 N.Y.S.2d 883 (3d Dept. 1987).

Search warrant; authorizing search of premises and persons found therein.—The search authority requested and granted was limited to the premises where the contraband was believed to be and extended only to those individuals, including the occupant, who were found therein and might reasonably be expected to conceal the contraband on their persons, but it did not authorize a search of any person seen casually leaving the premises prior to the execution of the warrant. People v. Green, 33 N.Y.2d 496, 354 N.Y.S.2d 933, 310 N.E.2d 533 (1974).

Search warrant; authorizing search of premises only.— Where the search warrant authorized a premises search only, the police officers were not allowed to search the occupants without probable cause. Furthermore, the occupants could be arrested only if the officers had sufficient probable cause. *In re* Kronberg, 95 A.D.2d 714, 464 N.Y.S.2d 466 (1st Dept. 1988).

Search warrants; authorizing search of premises; named individual and any other persons occupying said premises.—A warrant to search each and every occupant of a bar and restaurant for policy slips is too broad, as there was no probable cause to believe that any person in the premises might be in possession of illegal gambling records at the time of the search; the fact that only three persons were present when warrant was executed and all possessed contraband was not determinative of the warrant's validity. People v. Nieves, 36 N.Y.2d 396, 369 N.Y.S.2d 50, 330 N.E.2d 26 (1975).

—In a prosecution for robbery in the first degree, search warrants obtained to search two apartments of the defendants were properly issued pursuant to the police officer's application to the court describing and detailing the probable cause based upon the officer's knowledge that the defendants were the alleged perpetrators, continually were in one another's company, moved freely between the apartments and the manner and method of their operations which allegedly involved moving and/or dividing the stolen property in the two apartments. People v. Alaxanian, 76 A.D.2d 187, 430 N.Y.S.2d 884 (3d Dept. 1980), *aff'd,* 54 N.Y.2d 725, 442 N.Y.S.2d 979, 426 N.E.2d 473 (1981).

—Court properly issued a search warrant to search the defendant's boyfriend, his apartment, and his automobile where the informants established that defendant was involved with the criminal possession of controlled substances. People v. Vanderpool, 217 A.D.2d 716, 629 N.Y.S.2d 307 (3d Dept. 1995).

Search of person leaving apartment.—The warrant authorized the search of a named person and his apartment, as well as "of any other person who may be found to have such property (heroin and narcotic implements) in his possession," which validates search by the police officers of the defendants in the hallway of the building immediately after they left the apartment and before the officers had entered or searched the apartment. People v. Easterbrook, 43 A.D.2d 719, 350 N.Y.S.2d 442 (2d Dept. 1973), *aff'd,* 35 N.Y.2d 913, 364 N.Y.S.2d 899, 324 N.E.2d 367 (1974), *cert. denied,* 421 U.S. 965 (1975).

§ 690.20. Search warrants; where executable.

1. A search warrant issued by a district court, the New York City criminal court or a superior court judge sitting as a local criminal court may be executed pursuant to its terms anywhere in the state.

2. A search warrant issued by a city court, a town court or a village court may be executed pursuant to its terms only in the county of issuance or an adjoining county.

ANNOTATIONS

CPL § 690.20(2).—Police Justice of the City of Albany authorized to issue a search warrant for search of person or premises located in the Town of Colonie, outside the geographical limits of the City. People v. Fishman, 48 A.D.2d 726, 367 N.Y.S.2d 608 (3d Dept. 1975), *aff'd,* 40 N.Y.2d 858, 387 N.Y.S.2d 1003, 356 N.E.2d 475 (1976).

Jurisdiction.—The town justice lacked the authority to issue a search warrant because there was no proof that the alleged criminal act occurred within the geographic jurisdiction of the Justice Court. People v. Hickey, 40 N.Y.2d 761, 390 N.Y.S.2d 42, 358 N.E.2d 868 (1976).

Search warrant; address.—The CPL requires that a search

warrant be addressed to a police officer, however, when dealing with a blood sample it is reasonable to extend the statute to allow the doctor to procure the sample. Jon L. v. District Attorney, New York Co., 81 A.D.2d 362, 440 N.Y.S.2d 928 (1st Dept. 1981).

§ 690.25. Search warrants; to whom addressable and by whom executable.

1. A search warrant must be addressed to a police officer whose geographical area of employment embraces or is embraced or partially embraced by the county of issuance. The warrant need not be addressed to a specific police officer but may be addressed to any police officer of a designated classification, or to any police officer of any classification employed or having general jurisdiction to act as a police officer in the county.

2. A police officer to whom a search warrant is addressed, as provided in subdivision one, may execute it pursuant to its terms anywhere in the county of issuance or an adjoining county, and he may execute it pursuant to its terms in any other county of the state in which it is executable if (a) his geographical area of employment embraces the entire county of issuance or (b) he is a member of the police department or force of a city located in such county of issuance.

3. [*Repealed pursuant to L. 1998, Ch. 424, § 10, eff. Jan. 1, 1999.*]

Amended by L. 1980, Ch. 843; L. 1998, Ch. 424, § 10, eff. Jan. 1, 1999, repealing subd. 3.

ANNOTATIONS

Civilian participation in execution.—Civil participation in the execution of a search warrant, although not expressly provided for in the statute, is not prohibited. People v. Boyd, 123 Misc. 2d 634, 474 N.Y.S.2d 661 (Sup. Ct. N.Y. Co. 1984).

Search warrant; issuance and execution.—Search warrant was properly issued to a police officer who was a member of a drug task force not yet in existence at the time the warrant was issued. The officer applied for the warrant pursuant to his duties as a police officer. People v. Martin, 163 A.D.2d 536, 558 N.Y.S.2d 192 (2d Dept. 1990).

—Police officer who served the search warrant upon the defendant was not in violation of the warrant where he did not conduct the search. The officer was allowed to procure the assistance of the deputy warden in searching the defendant's prison cell. People v. Gamble, 122 Misc. 2d 960, 472 N.Y.S.2d 580 (Sup. Ct. Bronx Co. 1984).

§ 690.30. Search warrants; when executable.

1. A search warrant must be executed not more than ten days after the date of issuance and it must thereafter be returned to the court without unnecessary delay.

2. A search warrant may be executed on any day of the week. It may be executed only between the hours of 6:00 A.M. and 9:00 P.M., unless the warrant expressly authorizes execution thereof at any time of the day or night, as provided in subdivision five of section 690.45.

ANNOTATIONS

Motion to suppress; search and seizure.—Narcotics seized pursuant to a no-knock search after 9 p.m. were admissible as evidence, even where the affidavit authorizing the warrant was alleged to be insufficient to allow a nighttime search of the premises. People v. Rose, 31 N.Y.2d 1036, 342 N.Y.S.2d 66, 294 N.E.2d 852 (1973).

—Court held that searches which properly commence prior to 9:00 p.m. are not required to stop merely because the search continues past that time. The testimony established that the warrant was proper and the search commenced at 8:50 p.m.. People v. Vara, 117 A.D.2d 1013, 499 N.Y.S.2d 296 (4th Dept. 1986).

Physical possession of warrant.—Once a warrant has been issued by neutral magistrate, physical possession of the warrant at the time of entry is not required. People v. Mahoney, 58 N.Y.2d 475, 462 N.Y.S.2d 410, 448 N.E.2d 1321 (1983).

Reissuance of warrant.—If the court deems the information upon which the search warrant is based as not stale, the court may reissue a search warrant without requiring a new application where the previous warrant was never executed. A ten day delay between the issuance and the execution did not warrant the need for a new application. People v. Moon, 168 A.D.2d 110, 571 N.Y.S.2d 580 (3d Dept. 1991).

Search warrant; invalidation.—Failure to return the search warrant to the court following the execution of the warrant is a ministerial error. If the warrant is valid then it will not be held invalid because of the failure to return it without "unnecessary delay." People v. Frange, 109 A.D.2d 802, 486 N.Y.S.2d 315 (2d Dept. 1985).

—Where two months passed between the information upon which the warrant was based was received and the issuance of the warrant, the court held that the search warrant was invalid. A time lapse is difficult to justify for an isolated activity. It was not established that the defendant was engaged in continual criminal activity over that period of time. People v. Acevedo, 175 A.D.2d 323, 572 N.Y.S.2d 101 (3d Dept. 1991).

—Where criminal activity underlying the issuance of a search warrant is of a continuing nature, a greater time lapse is justified before the information becomes stale than where the offense is an isolated one. People v. Mallory, 234 A.D.2d 913, 651 N.Y.S.2d 793 (4th Dept. 1996).

Typographical error in warrant.—Apparent typographical error in search warrant with respect to time when warrant could be executed does not invalidate the search where there was no indication that the issuing magistrate intended to restrict execution to three-hour period between 6:00 p.m. and 9:00 p.m. People v. Shetler, 256 A.D.2d 1234, 682 N.Y.S.2d 784 (4th Dept. 1998).

§ 690.35. Search warrants; the application.

1. An application for a search warrant may be in writing or oral. If in writing, it must be made, subscribed and sworn to by a public servant specified in subdivision one of section 690.05. If oral, it must be made by such a public servant and sworn to and recorded in the manner provided in section 690.36.

2. The application shall be made to:

(a) A local criminal court, as defined in section 10.10 of this chapter, having preliminary jurisdiction over the underlying offense, or geographical jurisdiction over the location to be searched when the search is to be made for personal property of a kind or character described in section 690.10 of this article except that:

(i) if a town court has such jurisdiction but is not available to issue the search warrant, the warrant may be issued by the local criminal court of any village within such town or, any adjoining town, village embraced in whole or in part by such adjoining town, or city of the same county;

(ii) if a village court has such jurisdiction but is not available to issue the search warrant, the warrant may be issued by the town court of the town embracing such village or any other village court within such town, or, if such town or village court is not available either, before the local criminal court of any adjoining town, village embraced in whole or in part by such adjoining town, or city of the same county; and

(iii) if a city court has such jurisdiction but is not available to issue the search warrant, the warrant may be issued by the local criminal court of any adjoining town or village, or village court embraced by an adjoining town, within the same county as such city.

(b) A local criminal court, as defined in section 10.10 of this chapter, with geographical jurisdiction over the location where the premises to be searched is located, or which issued the underlying arrest warrant, when the search warrant is sought pursuant to paragraph (b) of subdivision two of section 690.05 of this article, for the purpose of arresting a wanted person.

Any search warrant issued pursuant to this section shall be subject to the territorial limitations provided by section 690.20 of this article.

3. The application must contain:

(a) The name of the court and the name and title of the applicant; and

(b) A statement that there is reasonable cause to believe that property of a kind or character described in section 690.10 may be found in or upon a designated or described place, vehicle or person; or, in the case of an application for a search warrant as defined in paragraph (b) of subdivision two of section 690.05, a statement that there is reasonable cause to believe that the person who is the subject of the warrant of arrest may be found in the designated premises; and,

(c) Allegations of fact supporting such statement. Such allegations of fact may be based upon personal knowledge of the applicant or upon information and belief, provided that in the latter event the sources of such information and the grounds of such belief are stated. The applicant may also submit depositions of other persons containing allegations of fact supporting or tending to support those contained in the application; and

(d) A request that the court issue a search warrant directing a search for and seizure of the property or person in question; and

(e) In the case of an application for a search warrant as defined in paragraph (b) of subdivision two of section 690.05, a copy of the warrant of arrest and the underlying accusatory instrument.

4. The application may also contain:

(a) A request that the search warrant be made executable at any time of the day or night, upon the ground that there is reasonable cause to believe that (i) it cannot be executed between the hours of 6:00 A.M. and 9:00 P.M., or (ii) the property sought will be removed or destroyed if not seized forthwith, or (iii) in the case of an application for a search warrant as defined in paragraph (b) of subdivision two of section 690.05, the person sought is likely to flee or commit another crime, or may endanger the safety of the executing police officers or another person if not seized forthwith or between the hours of 9 P.M. and 6 A.M.;

(b) A request that the search warrant authorize the executing police officer to enter premises to be searched without giving notice of his authority and purpose, upon the ground that there is reasonable cause to believe that (i) the property sought may be easily and quickly destroyed or disposed of, or (ii) the giving of such notice may endanger the life or safety of the executing officer or another person, or (iii) in the case of an application for a search warrant as defined in paragraph (b) of subdivision two of section 690.05 for the purpose of searching for and arresting a person who is the subject of a warrant for a felony, the person sought is likely to commit another felony, or may endanger the life or safety of the executing officer or another person.

Amended by L. 1980, Ch. 843; L. 1982, Ch. 679; L. 1991, Ch. 504, eff. Nov. 1, 1991, amending subds. 2 & 3; L. 1992, Ch. 815, eff. Nov. 1, 1992, renumbering subds. 2, 3 to 3, and 4 and adding new subd. 2; L. 1992, Ch. 816, eff. Nov. 1, 1992, amending subd. 2; L. 1998, Ch. 424, § 11, eff. Jan. 1, 1999, amending subd. 4(b).

ANNOTATIONS

Affidavit; perjury.—Despite false statement in affidavit in support of search warrant, the search warrant was valid where it contained sufficient other facts to establish probable cause. People v. Villalba, 208 A.D.2d 782, 618 N.Y.S.2d 40 (2d Dept. 1994).

Application; sufficiency.—Substantial compliance with CPL 690.35 was found even though the signature of the Magistrate was absent from the search warrant application. The Magistrate noted that the police officer must have signed the affidavit in the presence of the Magistrate in order to procure the warrant. People v. Rodriguez, 150 A.D.2d 622, 541 N.Y.S.2d 491 (2d Dept. 1989).

—Application for the search warrant was valid even though the warrant did not possess a provision specifying that the wiretaps would cease upon the completion of the investigation's objective. The defendant was not prejudiced by a failure to include the provision. People v. Campagni, 151 A.D.2d 1010, 542 N.Y.S.2d 449 (4th Dept. 1989).

Corroboration.—Court rejects the "totality of the circumstances" test articulated by the United States Supreme Court in *Illinois v. Gates,* 462 U.S. 213, 103 S. Ct. 2317, 76 L. Ed. 2d 527 (1985) and reaffirms its support for the reliability requirement of the *Aguilar-Spinelli* rule; court distinguished the *Gates* scenario on the ground that it involved a search warrant with a determination of probable cause being made by a detached and neutral magistrate, as opposed to a warrantless arrest and search scenario. People v. Johnson, 66 N.Y.2d 398, 497 N.Y.S.2d 618, 488 N.E.2d 439 (1985).

—Corroboration supplied by a police officer's independent investigation can establish the credibility of an informant's information. People v. Loewel, 50 A.D.2d 483, 378 N.Y.S.2d 521 (4th Dept. 1976), *aff'd,* 41 N.Y.2d 609, 394 N.Y.S.2d 591, 363 N.E.2d 316 (1977).

—Where independent observation of a police officer sufficiently corroborated a significant portion of the information provided by a police informer, this constituted sufficient independent verification to establish the reliability of the informer and to support the issuance of a search warrant. People v. Alaimo, 34 N.Y.2d 187, 356 N.Y.S.2d 591, 313 N.E.2d 55 (1974).

—Reliability of the informants' information, upon which a search warrant had been granted, was established by the fact that the informants were not merely reporting rumors, but actually participated in the illegal activity. People v. Santana, 106 A.D.2d 523, 483 N.Y.S.2d 60 (2d Dept. 1984).

Defective affidavit requesting search warrant.—The warrant was invalid when the affidavits utterly failed to show that the information was current; an affidavit that fails to mention times or dates might nonetheless set forth other facts and circumstances which make it obvious that the information is fresh. People v. Loewel, 50 A.D.2d 483, 378 N.Y.S.2d 521 (4th Dept. 1976), *aff'd,* 41 N.Y.2d 609, 394 N.Y.S.2d 591, 363 N.E.2d 316 (1977).

—There was no probable cause to issue the search warrant where the affidavit failed to disclose any of the underlying circumstances from which the informant concluded that the defendant, a known criminal, was engaged in gambling activities and the subsequent police observations of defendant's conduct were susceptible of an interpretation of innocent activity. People v. Wirchansky, 41 N.Y.2d 130, 391 N.Y.S.2d 70, 359 N.E.2d 666 (1976).

—Affidavit was defective when it omitted the underlying basis for informant's statement that suspect had received a pistol from identified source. Informant's statement was hearsay, not of affiant's personal knowledge, and therefore cognizable only upon a showing of both the informant's veracity and the basis for his statements. People v. Wright, 37 N.Y.2d 88, 371 N.Y.S.2d 460, 332 N.E.2d 331 (1975).

Generally.—It was not necessary for the judge who issued the search warrant to conduct an inquiry into whether the search warrant applications were supported by affidavits. The judge found that reasonable cause existed and issued the warrant. People v. Israel, 161 A.D.2d 730, 555 N.Y.S.2d 865 (2d Dept. 1990).

—Fact that time stated in the supporting affidavit for the time of pre-execution sale was incorrect did not serve to invalidate the warrant. People v. Casado, 199 A.D.2d 845, 606 N.Y.S.2d 366 (3d Dept. 1993).

—Application for search warrant was upheld as valid where it was accompanied by a sworn affidavit. Further, the court is allowed to make all reasonable inferences in considering a search warrant application. People v. Morelock, 187 A.D.2d 756, 589 N.Y.S.2d 673 (3d Dept. 1993).

Immediate search necessary.—Town Justice who signed warrant properly considered that search would be conducted after defendant was arrested at his workplace, and that an "immediate search was reasonably necessary because . . . the potential loss of evidence was a real concern, and the recovery of that evidence was essential to the continued progress of the investigation." People v. Younis, 265 A.D.2d 931, 696 N.Y.S.2d 324 (4th Dept. 1999).

Jurisdiction.—CPL § 690.35 authorizes a town justice to sign search warrants to be executed in jurisdictions where the justice has preliminary or geographic jurisdiction. The location of the execution of the warrant is the crucial jurisdictional issue, and not where the justice happened to be when he signed it. People v. Cobb, 192 Misc. 2d 309, 745 N.Y.S.2d 895 (Co. Ct. Dutchess Co. 2002).

Motion to suppress; nighttime warrant.—Motion to suppress was granted where there was no showing of necessity for nighttime execution and the property sought to be seized was not likely to be removed. People v. Miller, 109 Misc. 2d 276, 439 N.Y.S.2d 983 (Crim. Ct. N.Y. Co. 1981).

Motion to suppress; search and seizure.—New York State Commission of Investigation has no powers except investigative and there is no specific grant of power to seek warrants in aid of its investigations. People v. Cardillo, 80 A.D.2d 952, 438 N.Y.S.2d 37 (3d Dept. 1981).

Oral application to court.—CPL § 690.35(1) was complied with when the officer's application was orally presented to the Judge and his sworn statements were recorded by a court reporter. People v. Brown, 40 N.Y.2d 183, 386 N.Y.S.2d 359, 352 N.E.2d 545 (1976).

Out-of-state search warrant; choice of law.—Defendant had no cause to expect that a search of his Michigan residence would comply with New York's procedural law, and neither the core purpose of the exclusionary rule nor New York's interests would be served by invoking it in these circumstances. People v. Vega, 225 A.D.2d 890, 639 N.Y.S.2d 511 (3d Dept.), *app. denied,* 88 N.Y.2d 943 (1996).

Reliability of informant; reliability of information.— Probable cause necessary for the issuance of a search warrant is lacking where the application for the warrant is supported by the affidavit of a confidential informant who has not been questioned by the issuing court and whose reliability has not been established. People v. Martinez, 80 N.Y.2d 549, 592 N.Y.S.2d 628, 629, 607 N.E.2d 775 (1992).

—When an affidavit in support of a search warrant relies on hearsay information supplied by an informer, the affidavit must show (1) that the informant is reliable, and (2) that the underlying circumstances as to how the informant came by his information demonstrates sufficient probability of credibility to allow the search of the premises. People v. Loewel, 50 A.D.2d 483 378 N.Y.S.2d 521 (4th Dept. 1976), *aff'd,* 41 N.Y.2d 609, 394 N.Y.S.2d 591, 363 N.E.2d 316 (1977).

—An informant's reliability can be corroborated by details concerning dress, mannerisms, route or conveyance to be used by the subject of the information, which in themselves are wholly unsuggestive of crime. People v. Torres, 155 A.D.2d 231, 546 N.Y.S.2d 848 (1st Dept. 1989).

—The reliability of the undercover officer's information, as recounted in the affidavit of another office (in support of the search warrant) is presumed to be reliable. People v. Salgado, 207 A.D.2d 918, 616 N.Y.S.2d 657 (2d Dept. 1994).

—A finding of reliability may be based upon corroboration of the informant's statement with information obtained independently during the course of a police investigation. People v. Fowler, 153 A.D.2d 865, 545 N.Y.S.2d 384 (2d Dept. 1989).

—A search warrant may be validly based upon hearsay information found to be reliable. People v. Londono, 148 A.D.2d 753, 539 N.Y.S.2d 484 (2d Dept. 1989).

—Information provided by two identifiable victims of a crime with actual knowledge of the events was clearly reliable and served as basis for issuance of search warrant. People v. Lentini, 120 A.D.2d 548, 501 N.Y.S.2d 738 (2d Dept. 1986).

Reliability of informant; satisfaction of *Aguilar* test.—The warrant application contained sufficient indicia of the co-defendant's reliability, because the co-defendant admitted to participation in some of the crimes and the information provided was against his penal interest. People v. McCann, 202 A.D.2d 968, 609 N.Y.S.2d 495 (4th Dept. 1994), *aff'd,* 85 N.Y.2d 951, 626 N.Y.S.2d 1006, 650 N.E.2d 853 (1995).

—The search warrant was valid where the informer's reliability had been previously demonstrated and the informer was a runner in the policy operation and had called in policy wagers to the telephone under surveillance. People v. Seidita, 49 N.Y.2d 755, 426 N.Y.S.2d 463, 403 N.E.2d 169 (1980).

—When the information furnished the court came directly from the citizen informer's sworn affidavit, without the benefit of filtering by the police the *Aguilar-Spinelli* test was inappropriate since the court knew who the informer was, how he came by the information and exactly what the informer had to offer; the sworn statements of private citizens, who report crime in an honest and forthright manner, may and should be relied upon by the police and the courts as a basis for further action. People v. Hicks, 38 N.Y.2d 90, 378 N.Y.S.2d 660, 341 N.E.2d 227 (1975).

—Statement of the informant, which was made by her after she was arrested for unlawful possession of a hypodermic needle and informed of her rights, to the effect that she was a heavy narcotics user and that defendant was her supplier, was a statement against the informant's own penal interest, made under circumstances which seemed to imply the needed reliability under the *Aguilar* test sufficient to create probable cause to issue a search warrant. People v. Barcia, 37 N.E.2d 612, 323 N.Y.S.2d 517 (2d Dept. 1971), *dismissed,* 30 N.Y.2d 873, 335 N.Y.S.2d 305, 286 N.E.2d 738 (1972).

—Where the information that served as the basis for the warrant came from the confidential informant's sworn statement, rather than from the hearsay information relayed by a police officer, the *Aguilar-Spinelli* test is not applicable. People v. Deliz, 172 A.D.2d 877, 568 N.Y.S.2d 181, 182 (3d Dept. 1991).

—Although the suppression court improperly used the *Gates* standard in upholding the validity of the search warrant, the order was nonetheless upheld where the warrant application was sufficient to satisfy the requirements of the *Aguilar-Spinelli* test. People v. Maldonado, 154 A.D.2d 890, 546 N.Y.S.2d 50, 51 (4th Dept. 1989).

—In the absence of a showing of the informant's reliability, from evidence of prior reports from him found to be reliable or from notes by the issuing magistrate demonstrating reliability, the mere fact that the informant's statement to the police might have been against his penal interest is not enough to establish probable cause for issuance of the warrant. People v. Lewis, 73 A.D.2d 1032, 425 N.Y.S.2d 436 (4th Dept. 1980).

—In seeking the issuance of a search warrant based upon information supplied by an informant it was necessary that the issuing court be informed of the underlying circumstances from which the informant concluded that there were illegal drugs where he claimed they were, and also of the circumstances from which the officer concluded that the informant was reliable. People v. Reaves, 73 A.D.2d 1032, 425 N.Y.S.2d 396 (4th Dept. 1980).

Search warrant; validity of.—In reviewing validity of warrant, court must focus on circumstances known to magistrate at time of its issuance, and not those that existed at time of its execution. People v. Gilmore, 6 A.D.3d 748, 776 N.Y.S.2d 327 (3d Dept. 2004).

Subd. 2

Application.—Where oral testimony was the basis for a search warrant application, the application was held to be a written application. It was a written formal document which was accompanied by the police officer's sworn statement and a deposition. People v. Taylor, 73 N.Y.2d 683, 543 N.Y.S.2d 357, 541 N.E.2d 386 (1989).

—The defendant did not establish that the detective made knowingly false statements upon his application for the search warrant. Where the shooter was identified and the detective previously visited the shooter's home, information contained in the application was sufficient to issue a search warrant. People v. Jenkins, 184 A.D.2d 585, 584 N.Y.S.2d 643 (2d Dept. 1992).

Application defective.—Search warrant application was defective where the police officer's information which he supplied to the Magistrate was not based upon first hand knowledge. Thus, the Magistrate was misled in determining whether probable cause existed so as to issue the warrant. People v. Fromen, 125 A.D.2d 987, 510 N.Y.S.2d 384 (4th Dept. 1986).

Application; interpretation of.— Search warrant applications should be interpreted in a common-sense manner. Where the affidavit provided information sufficient to support a reasonable belief that evidence of a crime would be found in the defendant's apartment, the court erred in suppressing the physical evidence seized and the defendant's statement to law enforcement authorities. People v. Harvey, 298 A.D.2d 527, 748 N.Y.S.2d 785 (2d Dept. 2002).

Citizen; credibility.—Where a citizen provides first hand knowledge information to the police the reliability of the citizen need not be established to apply for a search warrant. The search warrant application was upheld as valid. People v. Slater, 173 A.D.2d 1024, 570 N.Y.S.2d 691 (3d Dept. 1991).

—Where the citizen established that the information given to the police was not a rumor, the affirmation of the information was considered to constitute a deposition by the police officer. Reliability is sufficiently established by citizen status. People v. Simon, 107 A.D.2d 196, 486 N.Y.S.2d 118 (4th Dept. 1985).

Informer; credibility.—The Judge was able to assess the credibility of the informer when the informer personally appeared before the court and was examined under circumstances where his unrecorded and unsworn statement, if false, would subject him to possible criminal sanctions. People v. Brown, 40 N.Y.2d 183, 386 N.Y.S.2d 359, 352 N.E.2d 545 (1976).

Procedure.—Search warrant was held valid where it was issued by the County Court. A County Court Judge may receive applications for search warrants pursuant to CPL § 690.35. People v. Carson, 216 A.D.2d 965, 629 N.Y.S.2d 366 (4th Dept. 1995).

Search warrant based on information provided by informant.—The affidavit for the search warrant was valid where it was based upon information disclosed by a named informant whose statement was against his own penal interest and detailed his own participation in the purchase of drugs from the defendant inside the subject premises. People v. Harwood, 90 A.D.2d 923, 457 N.Y.S.2d 940 (3d Dept. 1982).

Search warrant; reasonable cause.—Where reasonable cause exists to believe that a vehicle dismantler has processed stolen auto parts on a continuous basis, the likelihood that other stolen auto parts may be on the premises is sufficient to justify issuance of a warrant. People v. Teribury, 91 A.D.2d 815, 458 N.Y.S.2d 85 (3d Dept. 1982).

Search warrant; probable cause.—There was probable cause for issuance of a search warrant where an informer, without any marijuana on his person, had entered the premises where defendant resided and left the premises carrying a plastic bag which appeared on field examination to contain marijuana and said that he had purchased the alleged marijuana from defendant. People v. Garzia, 44 N.Y.2d 867, 407 N.Y.S.2d 475, 387 N.E.2d 1045 (1978), cert. denied, 439 U.S. 930 (1978).

—The pattern of behavior described in the affidavit amounted to probable cause to believe that the defendant committed the crime charged and justified the issuance of a search warrant. People v. Giammarino, 53 A.D.2d 871, 385 N.Y.S.2d 343 (2d Dept. 1976), aff'd, 42 N.Y.2d 1090, 399 N.Y.S.2d 658, 369 N.E.2d 1191 (1977).

—The existence of probable cause is a determination solely for the Magistrate and should only be made when probable cause has been demonstrated as a matter of fact in the manner prescribed by statute (CPL Art. 690) and decisional law. People v. Hanlon, 36 N.Y.2d 549, 369 N.Y.S.2d 677, 330 N.E.2d 631 (1975).

—Without regard to information obtained by a "pen register" used without judicial authorization, there was adequate evidence to establish probable cause for the defendant's arrest and for the seizure of his briefcase during a search of his two apartments. People v. Magaril, 31 N.Y.2d 802, 339 N.Y.S.2d 458, 291 N.E.2d 583 (1972).

—A search pursuant to a warrant is valid even where some of the information included in the warrant application has been obtained while an officer was illegally trespassing on defendant's property; such a search will be upheld if the application contained sufficient untainted information to constitute probable cause. People v. Vonderhyde, 114 A.D.2d 479, 494 N.Y.S.2d 393 (2d Dept. 1985).

—Probable cause for the issuance of a warrant existed where a detective who was an expert in illegal gambling observed "repeated and regularly timed behavior engaged in by known gamblers consistent with an illegal policy scheme," coupled with a confidential informant's tip and the defendant's criminal reputation. People v. Weygant, 79 A.D.2d 667, 433 N.Y.S.2d 848 (2d Dept. 1980).

—Where the informant's reliability was insured by having the informant testify and submit an affidavit, such a procedure may be utilized in a determination on the existence of probable cause. People v. Bradley, 181 A.D.2d 316, 586 N.Y.S.2d 119 (1st Dept. 1992).

—Probable cause required for the issuance of an eavesdropping warrant is the same as that required for a search warrant. People v. Ianniello, 156 A.D.2d 469, 548 N.Y.S.2d 755 (2d Dept. 1989).

—Informant who had previously provided reliable information and who was presently under indictment, was held to be reliable. The phone conversation tapes between the defendant and the informant were properly used to establish the existence of probable cause in order to issue the search warrant. People v. Seager, 147 A.D.2d 932, 537 N.Y.S.2d 392 (4th Dept. 1989).

—Search warrant was supported by probable cause, where a photography laboratory technician had called the police after developing some of the defendant's child pornographic photographs, and the warrant specified all material related to child pornography; the items recovered were not beyond the scope of the warrant. People v. Burke, 287 A.D.2d 512, 731 N.Y.S.2d 467 (2d Dept. 2001).

Subd. 3

Destruction of evidence; immediacy of search.—Warrant was held to be valid even though the search was conducted at night. Information revealed the necessity of an immediate search to recover the evidence. The search warrant authorized the entry into defendant's apartment at night. People v. Silverstein, 74 N.Y.2d 768, 545 N.Y.S.2d 86, 543 N.E.2d 729 (1989).

—Where information established that the evidence which was sought through the search warrant may be destroyed or removed from the premises, it was proper to allow a search to be conducted at night. People v. Conklin, 139 A.D.2d 156, 531 N.Y.S.2d 374 (3d Dept. 1988).

"No knock."—There was a demonstrated necessity for a "no knock" entry when the court was apprised that there were guns in the apartment. People v. Brown, 46 A.D.2d 590, 364 N.Y.S.2d 512 (1st Dept. 1975), aff'd, 40 N.Y.2d 183, 386 N.Y.S.2d 359, 352 N.E.2d 545 (1976).

—Where the judge received information revealing possible harm to the police officers and destruction of the property to be seized, the judge acted properly in placing both a nighttime entry provision and a no knock provision in the search warrant. People v. Israel, 161 A.D.2d 730, 555 N.Y.S.2d 865 (2d Dept. 1990).

—The "anytime" and "no knock" provisions of the search warrant were justified by the police assertions that the items to be seized were drugs which could be easily and quickly disposed of, and that the occupants of the house were known as "hunters" and might possess firearms. People v. Garzia, 56 A.D.2d 635, 391 N.Y.S.2d 697 (2d Dept. 1977), aff'd, 44 N.Y.2d 867, 407 N.Y.S.2d 475, 378 N.E.2d 1045, cert. denied, 493 U.S 930 (1978).

—Warrant application requested that it be made executable at any time of the day or night and that it authorize a search without notice, because the property sought as evidence could be removed, destroyed or disposed of if not seized forthwith; application as a whole set forth sufficient facts to justify the issuance of a no-knock, all-hours warrant. People v. Ackerman, 237 A.D.2d 849, 654 N.Y.S.2d 876 (3d Dept. 1997).

Warrant; upheld.—Police search of defendant's apartment was proper where the warrant was based upon information from the defendant's roommate who possessed personal knowledge of the information. An earlier search of the defendant's apartment corroborated the roommate's statements. People v. Kane, 175 A.D.2d 881, 573 N.Y.S.2d 729 (2d Dept. 1991).

§ 690.36. Search warrants; special provisions governing oral applications therefor.

1. An oral application for a search warrant may be communicated to a judge by telephone, radio or other means of electronic communication.

2. Where an oral application for a search warrant is made, the applicant therefor must identify himself and the purpose of his communication. After being sworn as provided in subdivision three of this section, the applicant must also make the statement required by paragraph (b) of subdivision two of section 690.35 and provide the same allegations of fact required by paragraph (c) of such subdivision; provided, however, persons, properly identified, other than the applicant may also provide some or all of such allegations of fact directly to the court. Where appropriate, the applicant may also make a request specified in subdivision three of section 690.35.

3. Upon being advised that an oral application for a search warrant is being made, a judge shall place under oath the applicant and any other person providing information in support of the application. Such oath or oaths and all of the remaining communication must be recorded, either by means of a voice recording device or verbatim stenographic or verbatim longhand notes. If a voice recording device is used or a stenographic record made, the judge must have

the record transcribed, certify to the accuracy of the transcription and file the original record and transcription with the court within twenty-four hours of the issuance of a warrant. If longhand notes are taken, the judge shall subscribe a copy and file it with the court within twenty-four hours of the issuance of a warrant.

Added by L. 1982, Ch. 679.

ANNOTATIONS

Application; process.—Where the written application was preserved for the defense, the written application need not be filed with the court that issued the search warrant. People v. Dodge, 177 A.D.2d 1025, 578 N.Y.S.2d 43 (4th Dept. 1991).

Statutory compliance.—Where the Magistrate failed to technically comply with CPL § 690.36 by failing to certify that the transcript was accurate, the court did not reverse. The court held that the filing of the original tape within 24 hours after issuing the warrant was sufficient compliance. People v. Brinson, 177 A.D.2d 1019, 578 N.Y.S.2d 38 (4th Dept. 1991).

§ 690.40. Search warrants; determination of application.

1. In determining an application for a search warrant the court may examine, under oath, any person whom it believes may possess pertinent information. Any such examination must be either recorded or summarized on the record by the court.

2. If the court is satisfied that there is reasonable cause to believe that property of a kind or character referred to in section 690.10, and described in the application, may be found in or upon the place, premises, vehicle or person designated or described in the application, or, in the case of an application for a search warrant as defined in paragraph (b) of subdivision two of section 690.05, that there is reasonable cause to believe that the person who is the subject of a warrant of arrest, a superior court warrant of arrest, or a bench warrant for a felony may be found at the premises designated in the application, it may grant the application and issue a search warrant directing a search of the said place, premises, vehicle or person and a seizure of the described property or the described person. If the court is further satisfied that grounds, described in subdivision four of section 690.35, exist for authorizing the search to be made at any hour of the day or night, or without giving notice of the police officer's authority and purpose, it may make the search warrant executable accordingly.

3. When a judge determines to issue a search warrant based upon an oral application, the applicant therefor shall prepare the warrant in accordance with section 690.45 and shall read it, verbatim, to the judge.

Amended by L. 1980, Ch. 843; L. 1982, Ch. 679; L. 1991, Ch. 504, eff. Nov. 1, 1991, amending subd. 2; L. 1998, Ch. 424, § 12, eff. Jan. 1, 1999, amending subd. 2.

ANNOTATIONS

Substantial compliance with statute required.—In upholding validity of warrant without reading transcript of informant's testimony, suppression court failed to determine that there had been substantial compliance with the requirements of CPL § 690.40(1); suppression court must find that there was substantial compliance with CPL § 690.40(1) in order to provide an "assurance of the regularity of the of the application process . . . and . . . preservation for appellate review of the grounds upon which a search warrant is issued." Case remitted for new suppression hearing. People v. Serrano, 93 N.Y.2d 73, 688 N.Y.S.2d 90, 710 N.E.2d 655 (1999).

Defective warrant.—Search warrant was invalid where it was not based upon the personal knowledge of the police officer but was based on an informant not regularly used by the police. Further, the judge, upon issuing the warrant, failed to make a record of the informant's examination. People v. Blair, 155 A.D.2d 676, 547 N.Y.S.2d 897 (2d Dept. 1989).

—Evidence which was seized pursuant to a defective warrant was properly suppressed by the court. People v. Isenberg, 188 A.D.2d 1042, 592 N.Y.S.2d 1006 (4th Dept. 1992).

—The defendant who was illegally arrested pursuant to an illegal search of his home was entitled to the dismissal of the indictment. Because the search warrant was not conveyed to the judge in a verbatim manner over the phone, the warrant was invalid. People v. Farmer, 188 A.D.2d 1063, 591 N.Y.S.2d 911 (4th Dept. 1992).

No appellate review available.—The defendant's claim that the court erred in failing to keep a record of an interview by an informant could not be reviewed. The defendant failed to state his claim before the suppression court at the appropriate time. People v. Naranjo, 174 A.D.2d 546, 571 N.Y.S.2d 718 (1st Dept. 1991).

Obscene films; necessity of viewing by judge.—Allegedly obscene video cassette movies were seized on less than probable cause and the warrant application and supporting affidavits were defective where the magistrate issuing the search warrant did not view the videos, but relied upon affidavits partially describing them, thereby failing to consider the films as a whole and whether their predominant appeal was to the prurient interest. People v. P.J. Video, Inc., 65 N.Y.2d 566, 493 N.Y.S.2d 988, 483 N.E.2d 1120 (1985), rev'd, 475 U.S. 868 (1986).

Oral synopsis of application.—Detective's oral synopsis of the contents of a search warrant application for the judge did not violate CPL § 690.40, and detective's inability to recall whether the judge asked her any questions did not indicate that the search warrant was issued on other than the contents of her sworn affidavit. People v. Valdez-Rodrigues, 235 A.D.2d 627, 652 N.Y.S.2d 797 (3d Dept. 1997).

Reliability of informant.—Where an informant is considered by the police officer to be reliable and the officer also is knowledgeable of the facts given by the informant, probable cause may be established from such information. People v. Hetrick, 80 N.Y.2d 344, 590 N.Y.S.2d 183, 604 N.E.2d 732 (1992).

Search warrant; based on determination of another judge.—A magistrate could not issue a search warrant for the seizure of allegedly obscene materials when he had personally viewed these materials and the supporting affidavits of the police officers requesting the warrant stated that another judge had determined the materials to be obscene. People v. Potwora, 95 Misc. 2d 350, 407 N.Y.S.2d 99 (Sup. Ct. Erie Co. 1977). aff'd, 48 N.Y.2d 91, 421 N.Y.S.2d 850, 397 N.E.2d 361 (1979).

Search warrant; motion to suppress; perjury in underlying affidavit.—Where search warrants were based on probable cause would be admitted but defendants were entitled to a hearing on the claim of perjury in underlying affidavit of police officer in view of questionable conduct of arresting policeman involved in Knapp, Commission inquiry into police corruption. People v. Cameron, 40 A.D.2d 1034, 339 N.Y.S.2d 12 (2d Dept. 1972), cert. denied, 419 U.S. 1049 (1974).

Search warrant; probable cause for issuance.—The fact that detective related unsworn, unwritten and unrecorded details of investigation to Town Justice at the time he issued search warrant on an affidavit which only obliquely suggested that evidence of crime could be found at defendant's premises and set forth what little could be considered probative in the most conclusory terms did not overcome defective affidavit. People v. Lalli, 43 N.Y.2d 729, 401 N.Y.S.2d 489, 372 N.E.2d 330 (1977).

—Reversal was necessary where the affidavit on which the warrant was issued did not indicate the sources of the informant's belief—whether on personal knowledge or otherwise.

People v. Sutton, 32 N.Y.2d 923, 347 N.Y.S.2d 192, 300 N.E.2d 726 (1973).

—A search warrant application should not be read in a hypertechnical manner and should be considered in the clear light of everyday experience and accorded all reasonable inference. People v. Kane, 175 A.D.2d 881, 573 N.Y.S.2d 729 (2d Dept. 1991).

—Affidavits may establish probable cause. Thus, a judge was not required to conduct an examination upon the complainants where the judge held that the affidavits were sufficient to establish probable cause. People v. Israel, 161 A.D.2d 730, 555 N.Y.S.2d 865 (2d Dept. 1990).

—Where the police investigator had personal knowledge of the facts surrounding the defendant's dealing in drugs through tapped telephone conversations, the investigator's knowledge was sufficient to establish probable cause and issue the warrant. People v. St. Louis, 177 A.D.2d 882, 576 N.Y.S.2d 466 (3d Dept. 1991).

—The trial judge may look beyond a police investigator's affidavit to the sworn in camera testimony of a confidential informant to determine if the search warrant was issued upon probable cause. People v. Brown, 110 Misc. 2d 1050, 443 N.Y.S.2d 363 (Sup. Ct. Erie Co. 1981).

Search warrant; probable cause; suppression.—An affidavit of experienced narcotics policeman with detailed observations of surreptitious and suspicious activities of known narcotic activists was sufficient to establish probable cause to justify the issuance of a search warrant. People v. Calvo, 40 A.D.2d 982, 338 N.Y.S.2d 453 (2d Dept. 1972); see also People v. Christofara, 43 A.D.2d 766, 350 N.Y.S.2d 772 (3d Dept. 1973), cert. denied, 419 U.S. 867 (1974).

Staleness.—Information upon which search warrant was predicated was not stale; the observations of the police, made over a five-month period, the last one only four days before the application, were sufficient to support a reasonable belief that an ongoing drug enterprise existed and that evidence of illegal drug activity would be present at the time and the place of the search. People v. Munoz, 205 A.D.2d 452, 613 N.Y.S.2d 892 (1st Dept. 1994).

—The three-week gap between the date of the last transaction mentioned in the warrant application and the date of the issuance of the warrant did not render the information stale since it was clear from the application that the defendant's drug-dealing activities were ongoing and continuous. People v. Telesco, 207 A.D.2d 920, 616 N.Y.S.2d 773 (2d Dept. 1994).

—Court rejected defendants' contention that the search warrant was based on stale information because defendants' failure to provide sustenance to animals was of a continuing nature, justifying a greater lapse of time between the acquisition of the information supporting the search warrant application and the issuance of the search warrant. People v. Gilfus, 4 A.D.3d 788, 772 N.Y.S.2d 164 (4th Dept. 2004).

Subd. (1); compliance.—The issuing magistrate was presented with a search warrant application consisting of a sworn affidavit from the investigating officer, a search and seizure inventory form and a proposed search warrant. The magistrate took sworn testimony from the presenting police officer and confidential informant, and made notes summarizing the essential points of testimony. These notes were adequate to comply with CPL § 690.40(1). People v. Mendoza, 5 A.D.3d 810, 773 N.Y.S.2d 152 (3d Dept. 2004).

Testimony recorded.—Where the informant's statement was attached to the search warrant application, the court was held to have recorded the testimony of the informant as required in considering to issue the warrant. People v. McGourty, 188 A.D.2d 679, 591 N.Y.S.2d 533 (3d Dept. 1992).

Warrant valid; ministerial error.—The search warrant was valid even though the audiotapes for the warrant application were not filed for two days. The filing of the tapes on the next business day subsequent to the search was held to be admissible. People v. Camarre, 171 A.D.2d 1003, 569 N.Y.S.2d 224 (4th Dept. 1991).

§ 690.45. Search warrants; form and content.

A search warrant must contain:

1. The name of the issuing court and, except where the search warrant has been obtained on an oral application, the subscription of the issuing judge; and

2. Where the search warrant has been obtained on an oral application, it shall so indicate and shall state the name of the issuing judge and the time and date on which such judge directed its issuance.

3. The name, department or classification of the police officer to whom it is addressed; and

4. A description of the property which is the subject of the search or, in the case of a search warrant as defined in paragraph (b) of subdivision two of section 690.05, a description of the person to be searched for; and

5. A designation or description of the place, premises or person to be searched, by means of address, ownership, name or any other means essential to identification with certainty; and

6. A direction that the warrant be executed between the hours of 6:00 A.M. and 9:00 P.M., or, where the court has specially so determined, an authorization for execution thereof at any time of the day or night; and

7. An authorization, where the court has specially so determined, that the executing police officer enter the premises to be searched without giving notice of his authority and purpose; and

8. A direction that the warrant and any property seized pursuant thereto be returned and delivered to the court without unnecessary delay; and

9. In the case of a search warrant as defined in paragraph (b) of subdivision two of section 690.05, a copy of the warrant of arrest and the underlying accusatory instrument.

Amended by L. 1980, Ch. 843; L. 1982, Ch. 679; L. 1991, Ch. 504, eff. Nov. 1, 1991, amending subds. 4 & 8 and adding subd. 9; L. 1998, Ch. 424, § 13, eff. Jan. 1, 1999, amending subds. 3 and 7.

ANNOTATIONS

Absence of name from warrant.—The absence of defendant's name from the search warrant did not require the granting of his motion to suppress where the defendant had a close association with the drug transaction going on in the premises named in the warrant and with the two people named in the warrant. People v. Soler, 92 A.D.2d 280, 460 N.Y.S.2d 537 (1st Dept. 1983).

Description of premises; technical errors.—The description of the premises in the search warrant survived constitutional and statutory scrutiny because the warrant was worded so the officer who was executing the warrant could reasonably identify the property to be searched, even though the warrant incorrectly stated the defendant's name and incorrectly identified the number of levels in the home. Haberman v. Sobol, 138 A.D.2d 838, 525 N.Y.S.2d 950 (3d Dept. 1988).

Impermissibly broad.—Warrant authorizing police to seize "8 mm films cut and uncut depicting males and females in various positions of sexual intercourse, sodomy and masturbation" was impermissibly broad in scope since it permitted the exercise of a "wide police discretion without judicial supervision." People v. S & L Processing Lab., Inc., 33 N.Y.2d 851, 352 N.Y.S.2d 196, 307 N.E.2d 255 (1973).

Jurat not signed; warrant valid.—The statutory procedure for issuance of a search warrant was sufficiently conformed with where the issuing magistrate testified that the warrant application was sworn to by a police officer, notwithstanding that the jurat was not signed; the jurat is simply evidence that the oath was properly taken and its absence was cured by the testimony. People v. Zimmer, 112 A.D.2d 500, 490 N.Y.S.2d 912 (3d Dept. 1985).

Nighttime execution.—Motion to controvert the search warrant was denied where facts established affiant requested a nighttime search and there was a good faith basis to justify the request, even though the warrant lacked the traditional phrase "nighttime execution." People v. Arnow, 108 Misc. 2d 128, 436 N.Y.S.2d 950 (Sup. Ct. N.Y. Co. 1981).

Overbroad warrant.—The search warrant was valid and not overbroad even though it specified a search for other controlled substance other that the type found because there was a continuous flow of drug dealing. Different types were therefore allowable. People v. Germaine, 87 A.D.2d 848, 449 N.Y.S.2d 508 (2d Dept. 1982).

Probable cause.—The use of a trained dog by California police to sniff defendant's luggage at the airport constituted probable cause to obtain a search warrant and the passing of this information to the New York police gave them probable cause to obtain a search warrant in New York. People v. Price 78 A.D.2d 484, 434 N.Y.S.2d 834 (4th Dept. 1981), aff'd, 54 N.Y.2d 557, 446 N.Y.S.2d 906, 431 N.E.2d 267 (1981).

—The affidavit for the search warrant was valid where it was based upon information disclosed by a named informant whose statement was against his own penal interest and detailed his own participation in the purchase of drugs from the defendant inside the subject premises. People v. Harwood, 90 A.D.2d 923, 457 N.Y.S.2d 940 (3d Dept. 1982).

Probable cause; oath or affirmation requirement.—A warrant issued on the basis of a statement which, while not sworn to, contained a form notice to the effect that false statements are punishable under PL § 210.45 satisfies the "oath or affirmation" aspect of the probable cause requirement. People v. Sullivan, 56 N.Y.2d 378, 452 N.Y.S.2d 373, 437 N.E.2d 1130 (1982).

Procedure.—The CPL mandates that the warrant is read back to the judge and failure to do so invalidates the application process because the judge is required to focus on the specific descriptions identified on the warrant. People v. Price, 204 A.D.2d 753, 611 N.Y.S.2d 675 (3d Dept. 1994).

Return of property.—The failure of an officer to return property seized pursuant to a warrant, along with the warrant, is insufficient grounds for the invalidation of the warrant or the search. People v. Davis, 93 A.D.2d 970, 463 N.Y.S.2d 67 (3d Dept. 1993).

Search warrant; reasonable cause.—Although the "basis of knowledge" test was not satisfied by the officers averment that the informant had told him that he had observed stolen cars on the premises without any statement of facts relied on by the informant, it was satisfied in an alternative manner by the personal observations of the officer, a member of the auto crime unit, in the course of his independent investigation. People v. Maldonado, 80 A.D.2d 563, 435 N.Y.S.2d 344 (2d Dept. 1981).

Search warrant; motion to suppress; particularity of description of property to be seized; grounds for seizure.—Although the "basis of knowledge" test was not satisfied by the officers averment that the informant had told him that he had observed stolen cars on the premises without any statement of facts relied on by the informant, it was satisfied in an alternative manner by the personal observations of the officer, a member of the auto crime unit, in the course of his independent investigation. People v. Maldonado, 80 A.D.2d 563, 435 N.Y.S.2d 344 (2d Dept. 1981).

Search warrant; standing to contest.—Defendant, who was not charged with an offense that included, as an essential element, possession of the evidence seized, at the time of the search lacked standing to contest the validity of the search warrant. People v. Dwyer, 80 A.D.2d 561, 435 N.Y.S.2d 347 (2d Dept. 1981).

Substantial compliance.—The search warrant was valid because it substantially complied with the statutory requirements that mandates the inclusion of the name of the issuing court, even though the warrant only stated the court's venue and the signature of the county court judge. People v. Smythe, 172 A.D.2d 108, 569 N.Y.S.2d 287 (4th Dept. 1991).

Sufficiency of description.—The search warrant merely has to describe the outer appearance of the building identified in the warrant, and there is not requirement to identify any illegal conversion in the warrant. People v. Germaine, 87 A.D.2d 848, 449 N.Y.S.2d 508 (2d Dept. 1982).

§ 690.50. Search warrants; execution thereof.

1. In executing a search warrant directing a search of premises or a vehicle, a police officer must, except as provided in subdivision two, give, or make reasonable effort to give, notice of his authority and purpose to an occupant thereof before entry and show him the warrant or a copy thereof upon request. If he is not thereafter admitted, he may forcibly enter such premises or vehicle and may use against any person resisting his entry or search thereof as much physical force, other than deadly physical force, as is necessary to execute the warrant; and he may use deadly physical force if he reasonably believes such to be necessary to defend himself or a third person from what he reasonably believes to be the use or imminent use of deadly physical force.

2. In executing a search warrant directing a search of premises or a vehicle, a police officer need not give notice to anyone of his authority and purpose, as prescribed in subdivision one, but may promptly enter the same if:

(a) Such premises or vehicle are at the time unoccupied or reasonably believed by the officer to be unoccupied; or

(b) The search warrant expressly authorizes entry without notice.

3. In executing a search warrant directing or authorizing a search of a person, a police officer must give, or make reasonable effort to give, such person notice of his authority and purpose and show him the warrant or a copy thereof upon request. If such person, or another, thereafter resists or refuses to permit the search, the officer may use as much physical force, other than deadly physical force, as is necessary to execute the warrant; and he may use deadly physical force if he reasonably believes such to be necessary to defend himself or a third person from what he reasonably believes to be the use or imminent use of deadly physical force.

4. Upon seizing property pursuant to a search warrant, a police officer must write and subscribe a receipt itemizing the property taken and containing the name of the court by which the warrant was issued. If property is taken from a person, such receipt must be given to such person. If property is taken from premises or a vehicle, such receipt must be given to the owner, tenant or other person in possession thereof if he is present; or if he is not, the officer must leave such a receipt in the premises or vehicle from which the property was taken.

5. Upon seizing property pursuant to a search

warrant, a police officer must without unnecessary delay return to the court the warrant and the property, and must file therewith a written inventory of such property, subscribed and sworn to by such officer.

6. Upon arresting a person during a search for him or her pursuant to a search warrant as defined in paragraph (b) of subdivision two of section 690.05, a police officer shall comply with the terms of the warrant of arrest, superior court warrant of arrest, or bench warrant for a felony, and shall proceed in the manner directed by this chapter. Upon arresting such person, the police officer shall also, without unnecessary delay, file a written statement with the court which issued the search warrant, subscribed and sworn to by such officer, setting forth that the person has been arrested and duly brought before the appropriate court, return to the court the warrant and the property seized in the course of its execution, and file therewith a written inventory of any such property, subscribed and sworn to by such officer.

Amended by L. 1980, Ch. 843; L. 1991, Ch. 504, eff. Nov. 1, 1991, adding subd. 6; L. 1998, Ch. 424, § 14, eff. Jan. 1, 1999.

ANNOTATIONS

Different property seized than that listed in warrant.— The failure of the detective to seize the property particularized in the search warrant obtained by the detective was not merely a ministerial defect, but as a matter of law a substantial deviation from the statute; thus, all information obtained by the People during the execution of the warrant must be suppressed. People v. Ciccarelli, 104 Misc. 2d 287, 428 N.Y.S.2d 150 (Crim. Ct. Kings Co. 1980).

Entry.—The police officers were authorized to forcible open the defendant's apartment door after the defendant announced that his key was lost. The police officers properly identified themselves, indicating that they possessed a warrant to search the premises. The force utilized upon entry into the apartment was not excessive. People v. Gomez, 193 A.D.2d 882, 597 N.Y.S.2d 815 (3d Dept. 1993).

—Actions of the police officers did not violate CPL §§ 690.45 and 690.50 where undercover officer, posing as a prostitute, gained entry into the apartment for which police had a search warrant and later the "back-up" team intercepted the apartment occupant and the undercover officer outside the door of the apartment, while they were exiting, and then re-entered apartment and executed the search warrant. People v. King, 104 Misc. 2d 213, 428 N.Y.S.2d 166 (Sup. Ct. N.Y. Co. 1980).

Error; ministerial.—The court held that the police officer's error to be ministerial where the officer did not return an inventory of the evidence seized for five months following the execution of the warrant. The defendant was not entitled to suppression of the seized evidence. People v. Nelson, 144 A.D.2d 714, 535 N.Y.S.2d 132 (3d Dept. 1988).

Execution of search warrant; hearing.—Where the defendant's attorney agreed with both the co-defendant's attorney and the court that a hearing on the search warrant's execution was not necessary, the defendant was not entitled to a hearing on the matter. All parties were in agreement. People v. Ramirez, 168 A.D.2d 908, 565 N.Y.S.2d 659 (4th Dept. 1990).

Photographs.—Photographs taken of defendant's apartment at the time of the execution of the search warrant were admissible although the search warrant did not specifically authorize the taking of photographs; the photographs were nothing more than a permissible representation of a crime scene depicting contraband seized pursuant to a valid warrant or found in plain view. People v. Nelson, 144 A.D.2d 714, 535 N.Y.S.2d 132 (3d Dept. 1988).

Return of warrant.—The defendant was not entitled to the suppression of evidence where the defendant claimed there was

an unnecessary delay in the return of the search warrant. The court held that the requirement is ministerial and not a sufficient basis to render the search invalid. People v. Hernandez, 131 A.D.2d 509, 516 N.Y.S.2d 254 (2d Dept. 1987).

—Delay in returning the warrant to the issuing court or providing a copy thereof to the court did not require suppression of the evidence obtained since those requirements are ministerial and there was no prejudice to defendant by delay in compliance therewith. People v. Earl, 138 A.D.2d 839, 525 N.Y.S.2d 952 (3d Dept. 1988).

—The seizure of the drugs was upheld as valid even though the warrant was not returned within three days of the search. The court held the error to be ministerial in nature. People v. Camarre, 171 A.D.2d 1003, 569 N.Y.S.2d 224 (4th Dept. 1991).

Seizure of items at scene; not enumerated in warrant.— Suppression was required since it was inconceivable that the County Court Judge could have examined the thousands of other items seized on the premises and not presented to him in the original warrant application, with sufficiently close scrutiny given the limited duration of his inquiry. Monserrate v. Upper Court St. Bookstore Inc., 49 N.Y.2d 306, 425 N.Y.S.2d 304, 401 N.E.2d 414 (1980).

Search valid.—The search of the premises was upheld as valid even though the police officers conducting the search failed to leave a receipt for the seized controlled substances. The police officer's error was ministerial in nature and did not affect the validity of the search. People v. Morgan, 162 A.D.2d 723, 558 N.Y.S.2d 88 (2d Dept. 1990).

Substantial compliance with search warrant statute.— Substantial compliance with the provisions of CPL § 690.50 constitutes a valid execution of a search warrant. Where the law enforcement authorities knocked on the door of defendant's room and identified themselves, waited 30 seconds before using a pass key, handed defendant the search warrant to read and thereafter commenced the search which disclosed certain controlled substances, the procedure utilized was valid and the motion to suppress the seized evidence was properly denied. People v. Drapala, 93 A.D.2d 956, 463 N.Y.S.2d 70 (3d Dept. 1983).

Warrant not presented.—Where the defendant failed to claim to have asked the officers to view the search warrant authorizing the search, the officers were not required to present the defendant with the warrant. The record was devoid of evidence establishing that the officers did not inform the defendant that their search was being conducted pursuant to a warrant. People v. Cotroneo, 199 A.D.2d 670, 604 N.Y.S.2d 979 (3d Dept. 1993).

—Where, upon the defendant's request to view the warrant, the police officers failed to be in possession of the warrant, it was allowable for the officers to procure a copy of the warrant from the police car. The court held that the officer's actions were statutorily compliant. People v. Mikolasko, 144 A.D.2d 760, 535 N.Y.S.2d 167 (3d Dept. 1988).

§ 690.55. Search warrants; disposition of seized property.

1. Upon receiving property seized pursuant to a search warrant, the court must either:

(a) Retain it in the custody of the court pending further disposition thereof pursuant to subdivision two or some other provision of law; or

(b) Direct that it be held in the custody of the person who applied for the warrant, or of the police officer who executed it, or of the governmental or official agency or department by which either such public servant is employed, upon condition that upon order of such court such property be returned thereto or delivered to another court.

2. A local criminal court which retains custody of such property must, upon request of another criminal court in which a criminal action

involving or relating to such property is pending, cause it to be delivered thereto.

Amended by L. 1980, Ch. 843; L. 1998, Ch. 424, § 15, eff. Jan. 1, 1999.

ARTICLE 700—EAVESDROPPING AND VIDEO SURVEILLANCE WARRANTS

LexisNexis Cross References

Criminal Defense Techniques, Vol. 1, Ch. 5, Electronic Surveillance Under Federal Law; *Defense of Narcotics Cases,* Vol. 1, Ch. 3E, Wiretapping and Other Forms of Electronic Eavesdropping; *New York Suppression Manual,* Ch. 19, Electronic Surveillance; *New York Criminal Practice (2d ed.),* Vol. 2, Ch. 22, Electronic Eavesdropping; *Courtroom Criminal Evidence (3d ed.),* Vol. 1, Ch. 18, Search or Seizure.

§ 700.05. Eavesdropping and video surveillance warrants; definitions of terms.

As used in this article, the following terms have the following meanings:

1. "Eavesdropping" means "wiretapping," "mechanical overhearing of coversation," or the "intercepting or accessing of an electronic communication," as those terms are defined in section 250.00 of the penal law, but does not include the use of a pen register or trap and trace device when authorized pursuant to article 705 of this chapter.

2. "Eavesdropping warrant" means an order of a justice authorizing or approving eavesdropping.

3. "Intercepted communication" means (a) a telephonic or telegraphic communication which was intentionally overheard or recorded by a person other than the sender or receiver thereof, without the consent of the sender or receiver, by means of any instrument, device or equipment, or (b) a conversation or discussion which was intentionally overheard or recorded, without the consent of at least one party thereto, by a person not present thereat, by means of any instrument, device or equipment; or (c) an electronic communication which was intentionally intercepted or accessed, as that term is defined in section 250.00 of the penal law. The term "contents," when used with respect to a communication, includes any information concerning the identity of the parties to such communications, and the existence, substance, purport, or meaning of that communication. The term "communication" includes conversation and discussion.

3-a. "Telephonic communication," "electronic communication," and "intentionally intercepted or accessed" have the meanings given to those terms by subdivisions three, five, and six respectively, of section 250.00 of the penal law.

4. "Justice," except as otherwise provided herein, means any justice of an appellate division of the judicial department in which the eavesdropping warrant is to be executed, or any justice of the supreme court of the judicial district in which the eavesdropping warrant is to be executed, or any county court judge of the county in which the eavesdropping warrant is to be executed. When the eavesdropping warrant is to authorize the interception of oral communications occurring in a vehicle or wire communications occurring over a telephone located in a vehicle, "justice" means any justice of the supreme court of the judicial department or any county court judge of

the county in which the eavesdropping device is to be installed or connected or of any judicial department or county in which communications are expected to be intercepted. When such a justice issues such an eavesdropping warrant, such warrant may be executed and such oral or wire communications may be intercepted anywhere in the state.

5. "Applicant" means a district attorney or the attorney general or if authorized by the attorney general, the deputy attorney general in charge of the organized crime task force. If a district attorney or the attorney general is actually absent or disabled, the term "applicant" includes that person designated to act for him and perform his official function in and during his actual absence or disability.

6. "Law enforcement officer" means any public servant who is empowered by law to conduct an investigation of or to make an arrest for a designated offense, and any attorney authorized by law to prosecute or participate in the prosecution of a designated offense.

7. "Exigent circumstances" means conditions requiring the preservation of secrecy, and whereby there is a reasonable likelihood that a continuing investigation would be thwarted by alerting any of the persons subject to surveillance to the fact that such surveillance had occurred.

8. "Designated offense" means any one or more of the following crimes:

(a) A conspiracy to commit any offense enumerated in the following paragraphs of this subdivision, or an attempt to commit any felony enumerated in the following paragraphs of this subdivision which attempt would itself constitute a felony;

(b) Any of the following felonies: assault in the second degree as defined in section 120.05 of the penal law, assault in the first degree as defined in section 120.10 of the penal law, reckless endangerment in the first degree as defined in section 120.25 of the penal law, promoting a suicide attempt as defined in section 120.30 of the penal law, criminally negligent homicide as defined in section 125.10 of the penal law, manslaughter in the second degree as defined in section 125.15 of the penal law, manslaughter in the first degree as defined in section 125.20 of the penal law, murder in the second degree as defined in section 125.25 of the penal law, murder in the first degree as defined in section 125.27 of the penal law, abortion in the second degree as defined in section 125.40 of the penal law, abortion in the first degree as defined in section 125.45 of the penal law, rape in the third degree as defined in section 130.25 of the penal law, rape in the second degree as defined in section 130.30 of the penal law, rape in the first degree as defined in section 130.35 of the penal law, criminal sexual act in the third degree as defined in section 130.40

of the penal law, criminal sexual act in the second degree as defined in section 130.45 of the penal law, criminal sexual act in the first degree as defined in section 130.50 of the penal law, sexual abuse in the first degree as defined in section 130.65 of the penal law, unlawful imprisonment in the first degree as defined in section 135.10 of the penal law, kidnapping in the second degree as defined in section 135.20 of the penal law, kidnapping in the first degree as defined in section 135.25 of the penal law, custodial interference in the first degree as defined in section 135.50 of the penal law, coercion in the first degree as defined in section 135.65 of the penal law, criminal trespass in the first degree as defined in section 140.17 of the penal law, burglary in the third degree as defined in section 140.20 of the penal law, burglary in the second degree as defined in section 140.25 of the penal law, burglary in the first degree as defined in section 140.30 of the penal law, criminal mischief in the third degree as defined in section 145.05 of the penal law, criminal mischief in the second degree as defined in section 145.10 of the penal law, criminal mischief in the first degree as defined in section 145.12 of the penal law, criminal tampering in the first degree as defined in section 145.20 of the penal law, arson in the fourth degree as defined in section 150.05 of the penal law, arson in the third degree as defined in section 150.10 of the penal law, arson in the second degree as defined in section 150.15 of the penal law, arson in the first degree as defined in section 150.20 of the penal law, grand larceny in the fourth degree as defined in section 155.30 of the penal law, grand larceny in the third degree as defined in section 155.35 of the penal law, grand larceny in the second degree as defined in section 155.40 of the penal law, grand larceny in the first degree as defined in section 155.42 of the penal law, robbery in the third degree as defined in section 160.05 of the penal law, robbery in the second degree as defined in section 160.10 of the penal law, robbery in the first degree as defined in section 160.15 of the penal law, unlawful use of secret scientific material as defined in section 165.07 of the penal law, criminal possession of stolen property in the fourth degree as defined in section 165.45 of the penal law, criminal possession of stolen property in the third degree as defined in section 165.50 of the penal law, criminal possession of stolen property in the second degree as defined by section 165.52 of the penal law, criminal possession of stolen property in the first degree as defined by section 165.54 of the penal law, trademark counterfeiting in the first degree as defined in section 165.73 of the penal law, forgery in the second degree as defined in section 170.10 of the penal law, forgery in the first degree as defined in section 170.15 of the penal law, criminal possession of a forged instrument in the second degree as defined in section 170.25 of the penal law, criminal possession of a forged instrument in the first degree as defined in section 170.30 of the penal law, criminal possession of forgery devices as defined in section 170.40 of the penal law, falsifying business records in the first degree as defined in section 175.10 of the penal law, tampering with public records in the first degree as defined in section 175.25 of the penal law, offering a false instrument for filing in the first degree as defined in section 175.35 of the penal law, issuing a false certificate as defined in section 175.40 of the penal law, criminal diversion of prescription medications and prescriptions in the second degree as defined in section 178.20 of the penal law, criminal diversion of prescription medications and prescriptions in the first degree as defined in section 178.25 of the penal law, escape in the second degree as defined in section 205.10 of the penal law, escape in the first degree as defined in section 205.15 of the penal law, absconding from temporary release in the first degree as defined in section 205.17 of the penal law, promoting prison contraband in the first degree as defined in section 205.25 of the penal law, hindering prosecution in the second degree as defined in section 205.60 of the penal law, hindering prosecution in the first degree as defined in section 205.65 of the penal law, criminal possession of a weapon in the third degree as defined in subdivisions two, three, four and five of section 265.02 of the penal law, criminal possession of a weapon in the second degree as defined in section 265.03 of the penal law, criminal possession of a dangerous weapon in the first degree as defined in section 265.04 of the penal law, manufacture, transport, disposition and defacement of weapons and dangerous instruments and appliances defined as felonies in subdivisions one, two, and three of section 265.10 of the penal law, sections 265.11, 265.12 and 265.13 of the penal law, or prohibited use of weapons as defined in subdivision two of section 265.35 of the penal law, relating to firearms and other dangerous weapons;

(c) Criminal possession of a controlled substance in the seventh degree as defined in section 220.03 of the penal law, criminal possession of a controlled substance in the fifth degree as defined in section 220.06 of the penal law, criminal possession of a controlled substance in the fourth degree as defined in section 220.09 of the penal law, criminal possession of a controlled substance in the third degree as defined in section 220.16 of the penal law, criminal possession of a controlled substance in the second degree as defined in section 220.18 of the penal law, criminal possession of a controlled substance in the first degree as defined in section 220.21 of the penal law, criminal sale of a controlled substance in the fifth degree as defined in section 220.31 of the penal law, criminal sale of a controlled substance in the fourth degree as defined in section 220.34 of the penal law, criminal sale of a controlled substance in the third degree as

defined in section 220.39 of the penal law, criminal sale of a controlled substance in the second degree as defined in section 220.41 of the penal law, criminal sale of a controlled substance in the first degree as defined in section 220.43 of the penal law, criminally possessing a hypodermic instrument as defined in section 220.45 of the penal law, criminal possession of methamphetamine manufacturing material in the second degree as defined in section 220.70 of the penal law, criminal possession of methamphetamine manufacturing material in the first degree as defined in section 220.71 of the penal law, criminal possession of precursors of methamphetamine as defined in section 220.72 of the penal law, unlawful manufacture of methamphetamine in the third degree as defined in section 220.73 of the penal law, unlawful manufacture of methamphetamine in the second degree as defined in section 220.74 of the penal law, unlawful manufacture of methamphetamine in the first degree as defined in section 220.75 of the penal law, unlawful disposal of methamphetamine laboratory material as defined in section 220.76 of the penal law, criminal possession of marihuana in the first degree as defined in section 221.30 of the penal law, criminal sale of marihuana in the first degree as defined in section 221.55 of the penal law, promoting gambling in the second degree as defined in section 225.05 of the penal law, promoting gambling in the first degree as defined in section 225.10 of the penal law, possession of gambling records in the second degree as defined in section 225.15 of the penal law, possession of gambling records in the first degree as defined in section 225.20 of the penal law, and possession of a gambling device as defined in section 225.30 of the penal law;

(d) Commercial bribing, commercial bribe receiving, bribing a labor official, bribe receiving by a labor official, sports bribing and sports bribe receiving, as defined in article one hundred eighty of the penal law;

(e) Criminal usury, as defined in article one hundred ninety of the penal law;

(f) Bribery, in the third degree, bribery, in the second degree, bribery in the first degree, bribe receiving in the third degree, bribe receiving in the second degree, bribe receiving in the first degree, bribe giving for public office and bribe receiving for public office, as defined in article two hundred of the penal law;

(g) Bribing a witness, bribe receiving by a witness, bribing a juror and bribe receiving by a juror, as defined in article two hundred fifteen of the penal law;

(h) Promoting prostitution in the first degree, as defined in section 230.32 of the penal law, promoting prostitution in the second degree, as defined by subdivision one of section 230.30 of the penal law;

(i) Riot in the first degree and criminal

anarchy, as defined in article two hundred forty of the penal law;

(j) Eavesdropping, as defined in article two hundred fifty of the penal law;

(k) Any of the acts designated as felonies in subdivisions two and four of section four hundred eighty-one of the tax law, which section relates to penalties under the tax on cigarettes imposed by article twenty of such law, and any of the acts designated as felonies in subdivision c of section 11-1317 of the administrative code of the city of New York, which section relates to penalties under the cigarette tax imposed by chapter thirteen of title eleven of such code.

(l) Scheme to defraud in the first degree as defined in article one hundred ninety of the penal law.

(m) Any of the acts designated as felonies in section three hundred fifty-two-c of the general business law.

(n) Any of the acts designated as felonies in title twenty-seven of article seventy-one of the environmental conservation law.

(o) Money laundering in the first degree, as defined in section 470.20 of the penal law, money laundering in the second degree as defined in section 470.15 of the penal law, money laundering in the third degree as defined in section 470.10 of such law, and money laundering in the fourth degree as defined in section 470.05 of such law, where the property involved represents or is represented to be the proceeds of specified criminal conduct which itself constitutes a designated offense within the meaning of this subdivision.

(p) Stalking in the second degree as defined in section 120.55 of the penal law, and stalking in the first degree as defined in section 120.60 of the penal law.

(q) Soliciting or providing support for an act of terrorism in the second degree as defined in section 490.10 of the penal law, soliciting or providing support for an act of terrorism in the first degree as defined in section 490.15 of the penal law, making a terroristic threat as defined in section 490.20 of the penal law, crime of terrorism as defined in section 490.25 of the penal law, hindering prosecution of terrorism in the second degree as defined in section 490.30 of the penal law, hindering prosecution of terrorism in the first degree as defined in section 490.35 of the penal law, criminal possession of a chemical weapon or biological weapon in the third degree as defined in section 490.37 of the penal law, criminal possession of a chemical weapon or biological weapon in the second degree as defined in section 490.40 of the penal law, criminal possession of a chemical weapon or biological weapon in the first degree as defined in section 490.45 of the penal law, criminal use of a chemical weapon or biological weapon in the third degree as defined in section 490.47 of the penal

law, criminal use of a chemical weapon or biological weapon in the second degree as defined in section 490.50 of the penal law, and criminal use of a chemical weapon or biological weapon in the first degree as defined in section 490.55 of the penal law.

(r) Falsely reporting an incident in the second degree as defined in section 240.55 of the penal law, falsely reporting an incident in the first degree as defined in section 240.60 of the penal law, placing a false bomb in the second degree as defined in section 240.61 of the penal law, placing a false bomb in the first degree as defined in section 240.62 of the penal law, and placing a false bomb in a sports stadium or arena, mass transportation facility or enclosed shopping mall as defined in section 240.63 of the penal law.

(s) Identity theft in the second degree, as defined in section 190.79 of the penal law, identity theft in the first degree, as defined in section 190.80 of the penal law, unlawful possession of personal identification information in the second degree, as defined in section 190.82 of the penal law, and unlawful possession of personal identification information in the first degree, as defined in section 190.83 of the penal law.

9. "Video surveillance" means the intentional visual observation by law enforcement of a person by means of a television camera or other electronic device that is part of a television transmitting apparatus, whether or not such observation is recorded on film or video tape, without the consent of that person or another person thereat and under circumstances in which such observation in the absence of a video surveillance warrant infringes upon such person's reasonable expectation of privacy under the constitution of this state or of the United States.

10. "Video surveillance warrant" means an order of a justice authorizing or approving video surveillance.

Amended by L. 1972, Ch. 586; L. 1973, Ch. 276; L. 1978, Ch. 22; L. 1979, Ch. 410; L. 1981, Ch. 565; L. 1983, Chs. 105, 646; L. 1984, Ch. 919; L. 1985, Ch. 611; L. 1986, Ch. 671; L. 1988, Ch. 744; L. 1990, Ch. 154; L. 1991, Ch. 496, eff. Nov. 1, 1991; L. 1992, Ch. 490, amending subd. 8(b), eff. Nov. 1, 1992; L. 1995, Ch. 1, § 28, eff. Sept. 1, 1995; L. 1998, Ch. 2, § 40, eff. Nov. 1, 1998; L. 1999, Ch. 635, § 5, adding subd. 8(p), eff. Dec. 1, 1999; L. 2000, Ch. 489, § 2, eff. Nov. 1, 2000, amending subd. 8(o); L. 2001, Ch. 300, § 8, adding subd. 8(q), Ch. 301, § 9, adding subd. 8(r), and Ch. 302, § 4, amending subd. 8(r), eff. Sept. 17, 2001; L. 2002, Ch. 619, § 6, adding subd. 8(s), eff. Nov. 1, 2002; L. 2003, Ch. 264, § 49, eff. Nov. 1, 2003, amending subd. 8(b); L. 2004, Ch. 1, § 3 (Part A), eff. July 23, 2004, amending subd. 8(q); L. 2005, Ch. 394, § 6, amending subd. 8(c), eff. Oct. 1, 2005.

ANNOTATIONS

Authority to issue warrant. —An acting Supreme Court Justice designated to sit in a special narcotics part of Supreme Court located in one judicial district of the City of New York has the authority to issue an eavesdropping warrant which is to be executed in another judicial district in that city. People v. Rodriquez, 58 N.Y.2d 327, 461 N.Y.S.2d 248, 448 N.E.2d 102 (1983), *cert. denied,* 469 U.S. 818 (1984).

Consent of a party.—It is unnecessary to superimpose the admissibility requirements of CPL Article 700 on consensual recordings; in consensual recordings a foundation may be established by a participant to the conversation who testifies that the conversation has been accurately and fairly reproduced and proof that the evidence has not been altered may be established in a similar fashion. People v. McGee, 49 N.Y.2d 48, 424 N.Y.S.2d 157, 399 N.E.2d 1177 (1979), cert. denied, 446 U.S. 942 (1980).

—One party's consent to the taping of a telephone conversation removes such a taped conversation from the purview of CPL § 700.05 and its warrant requirements. People v. Tabora, 139 A.D.2d 540, 527 N.Y.S.2d 36, 39 (2d Dept. 1988).

—Defendant does not have standing to challenge the interception of the third party conversations involved. People v. Marans, 127 A.D.2d 795, 512 N.Y.S.2d 192, 193 (2d Dept. 1987).

—Constitutional rights are not implicated where one party to a telephone conversation consents to the tape recording of that conversation, notwithstanding that the second party to the conversation has no knowledge that he or she is being recorded. People v. Paulo, 115 A.D.2d 185, 495 N.Y.S.2d 531 (3d Dept. 1985).

Crimes.—The federal statute did not authorize wiretapping by state officials under the authority of a warrant issued out of a state court for the crime of criminal conspiracy in restraint of trade, an unclassified misdemeanor (General Business Law § 341). People v. Schipani, 56 A.D.2d 126, 391 N.Y.S.2d 875 (2d Dept. 1977).

Eavesdropping warrants; pen registers.—Police need not obtain an eavesdropping warrant before making a record of defendant's telephone calls by use of a pen register since the same records are available from the telephone company and therefore the defendant has no legitimate expectation of privacy. People v. Guerra, 65 N.Y.2d 60, 489 N.Y.S.2d 718, 478 N.E.2d 1319 (1985).

Foundation for admission of recording at trial; consent of party.—A foundation for admission at trial of a recording not within the purviews of CPL § 700 may be established by the testimony of a participant to the conversation or of one who heard the simultaneous transmission thereof to the effect that the conversation has been "accurately and fairly reproduced"; where the only foundation for admission of recording into evidence was testimony by officers monitoring conversation, who either could not specifically recall the conversation or stated that the sound "faded in and out" and was at times inaudible, this was insufficient to establish that tapes "accurately and fairly reproduced" conversation between defendant and police informant, and therefore defendant's conviction was reversed. People v. Rodriguez, 78 A.D.2d 769, 433 N.Y.S.2d 650 (4th Dept. 1980), cert. denied, 469 U.S. 818 (1984).

Justice; not sitting in district.—Warrant was not defective where justice was sitting in the first judicial district when he issued a warrant that was to be executed in the eleventh judicial district; this section is to be liberally construed. People v. Paz, 109 Misc. 2d 832, 441 N.Y.S.2d 183 (Sup. Ct. N.Y. Co. 1981), aff'd, 58 N.Y.2d 327, 461 N.Y.S.2d 248, 448 N.E.2d 102 (1983).

Toll billing records.—Telephone Company Toll records contain no personal conversations of the subscriber but only the places and telephone numbers outside his area called by him and the charges therefor; as such, toll calls are merely records kept in the due course of telephone company business for billing purposes and are as disclosable as any ordinary business record so kept. City of New York v. Public Service Comm'n, 84 Misc. 2d 1058, 379 N.Y.S.2d 987 (Sup. Ct. Albany Co. 1976), aff'd, 53 A.D.2d 164, 385 N.Y.S.2d 634 (3d Dept 1976).

Usury; extortion.—A state wiretap order for usury does not violate the federal statute which bars the wiretapping of consensual conduct where the informant borrower was told, "We're not doctors—we're not lawyers. If you don't pay things happen," which statements also constitute extortion, a nonconsensual crime. People v. Ardito, 106 Misc. 2d 100, 431 N.Y.S.2d 311 (Sup. Ct. Bronx Co. 1980).

Violations of sealing requirements; consequences.—CPL § 700.05(3) and § 700.65(3) explicitly require that, when People violate sealing requirements, they are barred from offering into evidence not only the substance of the intercepted communications, but also testimony about the very existence of the conversation. People v. Huang, 248 A.D.2d 73, 682 N.Y.S.2d 146 (1st Dept. 1998).

Wiretapping; warrant; intercepted conversations with another.—Defendant pleaded guilty to possession of gambling records after denial of suppression motion, which court held to be proper because the eavesdropping warrant authorized interception of the telephone conversations of Nellis Slayka concerning gambling and therefore all persons, though not named in the warrant, conversing about gambling with Slayka were searched with probable cause, without requiring amendment of warrant. People v. Zorn, 38 A.D.2d 359, 329 N.Y.S.2d 592 (1st Dept.), aff'd, 31 N.Y.2d 134, 335 N.Y.S.2d 257, 286 N.E.2d 706, cert. denied, 410 U.S. 943 (1972).

§ 700.10. Eavesdropping and video surveillance warrants; in general.

1. Under circumstances prescribed in this article, a justice may issue an eavesdropping warrant or a video surveillance warrant upon ex parte application of an applicant who is authorized by law to investigate, prosecute or participate in the prosecution of the particular designated offense which is the subject of the application.

2. No eavesdropping or video surveillance warrant may authorize or approve the interception of any communication or the conducting of any video surveillance for any period longer than is necessary to achieve the objective of the authorization, or in any event longer than thirty days. Such thirty day period shall begin on the date designated in the warrant as the effective date, which date may be no later than ten days after the warrant is issued.

Amended by L. 1988, Ch. 744.

ANNOTATIONS

Application for wiretap order; statement of authority.—The required statement of the applicant's authority to apply for a wiretap order (eavesdropping warrant) is sufficient if it provides: "I am the Acting District Attorney" and cites the relevant statutory provisions (CPL §§ 700.10, 700.05[5]) which give the applicant authority to apply for wiretap orders. People v. Fusco, 75 Misc. 2d 981, 348 N.Y.S.2d 858 (Nassau Co. Ct. 1973).

Eavesdropping warrant; duration.—Where wiretap warrant was issued for full statutory term of 30 days through affidavit indicated incriminating conversations would be repeated often daily and there was nothing to support provision that "a conspiracy was involved," it would be suppressed since legislative purpose was to allow tap for no longer than absolutely necessary to accomplish legitimate purpose and not to unreasonably invade privacy. People v. Pieri, 69 Misc. 2d 1085, 332 N.Y.S.2d 786 (Erie Co. Ct. 1972).

Prejudice to defendant.—Absent a showing of prejudice to the defendant, the fruits of electronic surveillance need not be suppressed simply because the original eavesdropping order did not contain a directive that interception of communications must terminate upon achievement of the authorized objective. People v. Scarnati, 133 Misc. 2d 795, 508 N.Y.S.2d 365 (Nassau Co. Ct. 1986).

Sufficient nexus with the county.—Where the subpoenaed telephone records indicated that a number of telephone calls had been made to correction officers at various facilities from a bar in Bronx County, the contacts were sufficient to permit the Bronx County District Attorney to investigate certain crimes, and authorized him to seek issuance of wiretap orders in Bronx county. People v. DiPasquale, 47 N.Y.2d 764, 417 N.Y.S.2d 678, 391 N.E.2d 710 (1979).

Wiretap order; thirty-day time limit.—A wiretap order issued to investigate gambling for thirty days, the maximum length of time for surveillance provided by statute (CPL § 700.10[2]), is not unreasonable. People v. Fusco, 75 Misc. 2d 981, 348 N.Y.S.2d 858 (Nassau Co. Ct. 1973).

Wiretap; duration; progress reports.—While the statute is clear that a wiretap should not last any longer than is necessary to achieve its objectives, and in no event longer than 30 days (CPL § 700.10[2]), the time during which a wiretap continues must reasonably relate to the kind of conversations being sought and the crime involved. It might be a better practice to use the provision of CPL 700.50(1), which requires periodic progress reports; this would inhibit 24-hour-a-day, 30-day warrants from turning into the general warrants frowned upon by the Fourth Amendment. People v. Castania, 73 Misc. 2d 166, 340 N.Y.S.2d 829 (Monroe Co. Ct. 1973).

§ 700.15. Eavesdropping and video surveillance warrants; when issuable.

An eavesdropping or video surveillance warrant may issue only:

1. Upon an appropriate application made in conformity with this article; and

2. Upon probable cause to believe that a particularly described person is committing, has committed, or is about to commit a particular designated offense; and

3. Upon probable cause to believe that particular communications concerning such offense will be obtained through eavesdropping, or upon probable cause to believe that particular observations concerning such offense will be obtained through video surveillance; and

4. Upon a showing that normal investigative procedures have been tried and have failed, or reasonably appear to be unlikely to succeed if tried, or to be too dangerous to employ; and

5. Upon probable cause to believe that the facilities from which, or the place where, the communications are to be intercepted or the video surveillance is to be conducted, are being used, or are about to be used, in connection with the commission of such offense, or are leased to, listed in the name of, or commonly used by such person.

Amended by L. 1988, Ch. 744.

ANNOTATIONS

Consent.—An eavesdropping warrant was not required for the audiotape in light of the fact that the person wearing the body wire from which the audiotape was obtained consented to the recording of the conversation with defendant. People v. Erwin, 236 A.D.2d 787, 653 N.Y.S.2d 990 (4th Dept. 1997).

Crime forming basis for warrant.—A criminal scheme to circumvent the regulation requirements for valid operators' licenses and motor vehicle inspections falls within the category of "other crimes dangerous to life, limb, or property" under 18 U.S.C. § 2512(2) and is sufficient to sustain an application for electronic eavesdropping. People v. Principe, 65 N.Y.2d 33, 489 N.Y.S.2d 463, 478 N.E.2d 979 (1985).

Satisfying requirements for warrant.—To satisfy requirements for issuance of eavesdropping warrant, applicant need not make a showing that every conceivable method of investigation has been tried and failed, but needs to establish the nature and progress of the investigation and the difficulties inherent in the use of normal law enforcement methods, which were met in this case, in which the normal procedures had proved ineffective, and an attorney's affidavit showed that the police were unable to infiltrate the distribution network without the eavesdropping warrant. People v. Brown, 233 A.D.2d 764, 650 N.Y.S.2d 836 (3d Dept. 1996).

—CPL § 700.15(4) requires the applicant to make a showing that normal investigative procedures have been tried and have failed or reasonably appear to be unlikely to succeed if tried or to be too dangerous to employ. Neither New York nor federal law requires that any particular investigative procedure be exhausted before wiretapping may be authorized. The objective is to ensure that wiretapping is not routinely employed as the initial step in a criminal investigation. Requirements for issuance of warrant were satisfied here, where the application was made after numerous normal investigative techniques had been used. People v. Adams, 2 Misc. 3d 166, 766 N.Y.S.2d 765 (Co. Ct. Niagara Co. 2003).

Lack of probable cause.—Defendant who had a prior criminal record for assault and robbery and one unresolved charge of gambling, was entitled to suppression of tapes of conversations obtained from a wiretap of his home phone on the ground that the fact that he met regularly with persons who also had criminal records including some gambling convictions, sometimes at his home though mostly at a restaurant, where on one occasion, one or more of the persons was seen carrying brown paper bags, newspapers or brief cases, did not constitute probable cause to believe that defendant was engaged in gambling or that a wiretap on his home phone would yield evidence of illegal gambling. People v. Pomponio, 47 N.Y.2d 918, 419 N.Y.S.2d 486, 393 N.E.2d 480 (1979).

Probable cause; background and other factors.—Probable cause for an eavesdropping warrant was shown by description of defendants' criminal background combined with such other indications as numerous similar burglaries in the area in which the defendants rented a house, police observations of one defendant as he "cased" various homes, and other similar factors. People v. Seney, 34 N.Y.2d 817, 359 N.Y.S.2d 49, 316 N.E.2d 335 (1974).

§ 700.20. Eavesdropping and video surveillance warrants; application.

1. An *ex parte* application for an eavesdropping or video surveillance warrant must be made to a justice in writing, except as provided in section 700.21 of this article, and must be subscribed and sworn to by an applicant.

2. The application must contain:

(a) The identity of the applicant and a statement of the applicant's authority to make such application; and

(b) A full and complete statement of the facts and circumstances relied upon by the applicant, to justify his belief that an eavesdropping or video surveillance warrant should be issued, including (i) a statement of facts establishing probable cause to believe that a particular designated offense has been, is being, or is about to be committed, (ii) a particular description of the nature and location of the facilities from which or the place where the communication is to be intercepted or the video surveillance is to be conducted, (iii) a particular description of the type of the communications sought to be intercepted or of the observations sought to be made, and (iv) the identity of the person, if known, committing such designated offense and whose communications are to be intercepted or who is to be the subject of the video surveillance; and

(c) A statement that such communications or observations are not otherwise legally privileged; and

(d) A full and complete statement of facts

establishing that normal investigative procedures have been tried and have failed or reasonably appear to be unlikely to succeed if tried or to be too dangerous to employ, to obtain the evidence sought; and

(e) A statement of the period of time for which the eavesdropping or video surveillance is required to be maintained. If the nature of the investigation is such that the authorization for eavesdropping or video surveillance should not automatically terminate when the described type of communication has been first obtained or when the described type of observation has been first made, a particular description of facts establishing probable cause to believe that additional communications or observations of the same type will occur thereafter; and

(f) A full and complete statement of the facts concerning all previous applications, known to the applicant, for an eavesdropping or video surveillance warrant involving any of the same persons, facilities or places specified in the application, and the action taken by the justice on each such application.

3. Allegations of fact in the application may be based either upon the personal knowledge of the applicant or upon information and belief. If the applicant personally knows the facts alleged, it must be so stated. If the facts stated in the application are derived in whole or part from the statements of persons other than the applicant, the sources of such facts must be either disclosed or described, and the application must contain facts establishing the existence and reliability of the informants or the reliability of the information supplied by them. The application must also state, so far as possible, the basis of the informant's knowledge or belief. Affidavits of persons other than the applicant may be submitted in conjunction with the application if they tend to support any fact or conclusion alleged therein. Such accompanying affidavits may be based either on personal knowledge of the affiant, or information and belief with the source thereof, and the reason therefor specified.

Amended by L. 1988, Ch. 744.

ANNOTATIONS

Admission of evidence; electronic surveillance.—The standard of proof to be applied when determining whether evidence sought to be admitted was the fruit of an unlawful electronic surveillance or was discovered from independent sources is the clear and convincing evidence test. People v. Pobliner, 32 N.Y.2d 356, 345 N.Y.S.2d 482, 298 N.E.2d 637 (1973), *cert. denied*, 416 U.S. 905 (1974).

Person not named in order.—Failure to include the defendant's name in the search warrant where his name was not ascertained until after execution of the warrant was not error and the intercepted conversations may be used against him. People v. Germaine, 87 A.D.2d 848, 449 N.Y.S.2d 508 (2d Dept. 1982).

—There were no grounds for suppressing the conversations, where the failure to include the defendants' names in the eavesdropping application was not a deliberate attempt to mislead the court, and the exclusion of the names could not conceivably have affected the issuance of the warrant itself,

People v. Watkins, 63 A.D.2d 1033, 406 N.Y.S.2d 343 (2d Dept.), *cert. denied* 439 U.S. 984 (1978).

—Where an order authorized interception of "telephone conversations relating to bets and wagers placed by . . . unknown persons with a . . . person known as 'Sal,' " and "the supervision of persons involved in these activities," it was proper to intercept the conversation of defendant, not named in warrant, when overheard on target telephone accepting wagers. People v. Palozzi, 44 A.D.2d 224, 353 N.Y.S.2d 987 (4th Dept. 1974).

Information based upon prior tainted warrant.—Where the information for an eavesdropping warrant came from a prior warrant tainted by illegality, the subsequent tapes and information will be suppressed, not only pursuant to the fruit of the poisonous tree doctrine, but more importantly because violations of eavesdropping statutes have the potential for abuse. People v. Gallina, 66 N.Y.2d 52, 495 N.Y.S.2d 9, 485 N.E.2d 216 (1985).

Intercepted communications authorized despite new telephone number.—The change in telephone number did not change the particularized description in the eavesdropping warrant application because the new number remained the sole telephone line assigned to the same person at the same address and because the description and identity never changed, there is no basis to conclude that the change in telephone number rendered the intercepted communications unauthorized. People v. Darling, 95 N.Y.2d 530, 720 N.Y.S.2d 82, 742 N.E.2d 596 (2000), *affirming* 263 A.D.2d 61, 700 N.Y.S.2d 312 (4th Dept. 1999). *See also* People v. Vaccaro, 272 A.D.2d 871, 707 N.Y.S.2d 280 (4th Dept. 2000), *aff'd*, People v. Darling, 95 N.Y.2d 530, 720 N.Y.S.2d 82, 742 N.Y.S.2d 596 (2000) (same).

Normal investigative procedures.—Issuance of the eavesdropping warrant was justified where, in application for warrant, the detective noted that previous attempts to infiltrate the conspiracy had proven unsuccessful, that the targets of the investigation were not vulnerable by way of conventional techniques, many had criminal records and were careful and evasive, the buildings involved did not lend themselves to simple physical surveillance, and the execution of search warrants had not revealed the information sought. People v. Versace, 73 A.D.2d 304, 426 N.Y.S.2d 61 (2d Dept. 1980).

—Where the applications in support of the eavesdropping warrants failed to establish that normal investigative techniques had been tried without success or that they would be unlikely to succeed if tried, all evidence obtained from the eavesdropping must be suppressed. People v. Viscomi, 113 A.D.2d 76, 495 N.Y.S.2d 298 (4th Dept. 1985).

Privileged communications.—The obvious import of CPL § 700.20(2)(c) is that privileged communications may not be intercepted and if this minimization requirement is not observed, the ensuing conversations and information derived therefrom may not be used as part of the evidence-in-chief by the People. People v. Watkins, 89 Misc. 2d 870, 393 N.Y.S.2d 283 (Sup. Ct. Suffolk Co. 1977), *cert. denied,* 439 U.S. 984 (1978).

Reviewability of warrant by trial court.—The law of the case doctrine does not prevent the court at a subsequent suppression hearing from reviewing the sufficiency of the probable cause determination of the judge who issued an eavesdropping warrant; the warrant is an *ex parte* order which was issued without the defendant having an opportunity to litigate the matter. People v. Guerra, 65 N.Y.2d 60, 489 N.Y.S.2d 718, 478 N.E.2d 1319 (1985).

Satisfying requirements for warrant.—To satisfy requirements for issuance of eavesdropping warrant, applicant need not make a showing that every conceivable method of investigation has been tried and failed, but needs to establish the nature and progress of the investigation and the difficulties inherent in the use of normal law enforcement methods, which were met in this case, in which the normal procedures had proved ineffective, and an attorney's affidavit showed that the police were unable to infiltrate the distribution network without the eavesdropping warrant. People v. Brown, 233 A.D.2d 764, 650 N.Y.S.2d 836 (3d Dept. 1996).

—A warrant may not be issued unless the application contains a complete statement of facts establishing that normal investigative procedures reasonably appear unlikely to succeed. The eavesdropping and video surveillance warrants were supported by probable cause where video surveillance was the only way to determine fully how the defendant, a matrimonial judge, would react to the offer of money and what he would do with it. People v. Garson, 4 Misc. 3d 258, 775 N.Y.S.2d 827 (Sup.

Ct. Kings Co. 2004), *aff'd,* 17 A.D.3d 695, 793 N.Y.S.2d 539 (2d Dept. 2005).

Search and seizure; eavesdropping warrant; intercepted conversations as probable cause for search warrant.—Where eavesdropping warrants were issued upon probable cause within limits of the statute, intercepted communications could be used as basis for probable cause for search warrant against "person sought but not named" without obtaining amendment of eavesdropping warrant. People v. Gnozzo, 31 N.Y.2d 134, 335 N.Y.S.2d 257, 286 N.E.2d 706 (1972), *cert. denied,* 410 U.S. 943 (1973).

§ 700.21. Temporary authorization for eavesdropping or video surveillance in emergency situations.

1. In an emergency situation where imminent danger of death or serious physical injury exists and, under the circumstances, it is impractical for the applicant to prepare a written application without risk of such death or injury occurring, an application for an eavesdropping or video surveillance warrant need not be in writing but may be communicated to a justice by telephone, radio or other means of electronic communication.

2. Where an oral application for an eavesdropping or video surveillance warrant is made, the applicant therefor must identify himself and the purpose of his communication or observation, after being sworn as provided in subdivision three of this section. The application must meet the requirements of section 700.20 of this article and provide the same allegations of fact required by that section.

3. Upon being advised that an oral application for an eavesdropping or video surveillance warrant is being made, a justice shall place under oath the applicant and any other person providing information in support of the application. Such oath or oaths and all of the remaining communication must be recorded, either by means of a voice recording device or verbatim stenographic or verbatim longhand notes. If a voice recording device is used or a stenographic record made, the justice must have the record transcribed, certify to the accuracy of the transcription and file the original record and transcription with the court within twenty-four hours of the issuance of a warrant. If longhand notes are taken, the justice shall subscribe a copy and file it with the court within twenty-four hours of the issuance of a warrant.

4. Upon oral application, the court may, where it finds that an emergency situation exists and that the requirements of section 700.15 of this article have been satisfied, issue a temporary eavesdropping or video surveillance warrant authorizing eavesdropping or video surveillance for a period not to exceed twenty-four hours. Such eavesdropping or video surveillance warrant shall be executed in the manner prescribed by this article. The twenty-four hour period may not be extended nor may a temporary warrant be renewed except by

written application in conformity with the requirements of this article.

Amended by L. 1988, Ch. 744.

§ 700.25. Eavesdropping warrants; determination of application.

1. If the application conforms to section 700.20, the justice may require the applicant to furnish additional testimony or documentary evidence in support of the application. He may examine, under oath, any person for the purpose of determining whether grounds exist for the issuance of the warrant pursuant to section 700.15. Any such examination must be either recorded or summarized in writing.

2. If the justice determines on the basis of the facts submitted by the applicant that grounds exist for the issuance of an eavesdropping warrant pursuant to section 700.15, the justice may grant the application and issue an eavesdropping warrant, in accordance with section 700.30.

3. If the application does not conform to section 700.20, or if the justice is not satisfied that grounds exist for the issuance of an eavesdropping warrant, the application must be denied.

ANNOTATION

Recording; consent of one party.—Private parties had a legal right to tape record their conversation with defendant and violated none of his rights in so doing, and such evidence was properly presented to the grand jury and admitted at trial. People v. Hochberg, 62 A.D.2d 239, 404 N.Y.S.2d 161 (1978).

§ 700.30. Eavesdropping and video surveillance warrants; form and content.

An eavesdropping or video surveillance warrant must contain:

1. The name of the applicant, date of issuance, and the subscription and title of the issuing justice; and

2. The identity of the person, if known, whose communications are to be intercepted or who is to be the subject of video surveillance; and

3. The nature and location of the communications facilities as to which, or the place where, authority to intercept or conduct video surveillance is granted; and

4. A particular description of the type of communications sought to be intercepted or of the type of observations to be made, and a statement of the particular designated offense to which it relates; and

5. The identity of the law enforcement agency authorized to intercept the communications or conduct the video surveillance; and

6. The period of time during which such interception or observation is authorized, including a statement as to whether or not the interception

or video surveillance shall automatically terminate when the described communication has been first obtained or the described observation has been first made; and

7. A provision that the authorization to intercept or conduct video surveillance shall be executed as soon as practicable, shall be conducted in such a way as to minimize the interception of communications or the making of observations not otherwise subject to eavesdropping or video surveillance under this article, and must terminate upon attainment of the authorized objective, or in any event in thirty days; and

8. An express authorization to make secret entry upon a private place or premises to install an eavesdropping or video surveillance device, if such entry is necessary to execute the warrant; and

9. An order authorizing eavesdropping or video surveillance may direct that providers of wire or electronic communication services furnish the applicant information, facilities, or technical assistance necessary to accomplish the interception unobtrusively and with a minimum of interference with the services that the service provider accords the party whose communications are to be intercepted. The order shall not direct the service providers to perform the intercept or use the premises of the service provider for such activity.

Amended by L. 1988, Ch. 744.

ANNOTATIONS

CPLR Article 78; review eavesdropping warrant.—The Supreme Court had no power or jurisdiction to entertain a CPLR Article 78 proceeding to review the legality of an eavesdropping warrant signed by a County Court Judge pursuant to CPL § 700.30. Watson v. Kurlander, 87 Misc. 2d 1083, 386 N.Y.S.2d 946 (Sup. Ct. Monroe Co. 1976).

Eavesdropping warrant; absence of provisions.—The eavesdrop warrant was null and void because it did not contain minimization provisions; the identity of the person, if known, whose communications were to be intercepted; or a particular description of the type of communications to be intercepted and a statement of the particular designated offense to which it relates. People v. Sturgis, 96 Misc. 2d 1053, 352 N.Y.S.2d 942 (Sup. Ct. N.Y. Co. 1973).

Eavesdropping warrant; duration.—Request for a warrant for thirty days because gambling is of continuing nature and that much time was necessary to learn the identity of other conspirators and participants in the bookmaking operation presented sufficient factual basis for issuing such order. People v. Palozzi, 44 A.D.2d 224, 353 N.Y.S.2d 987 (4th Dept. 1974).

—Where wiretap warrant was issued for full statutory term of 30 days though affidavit indicated incriminating conversations would be repeated often daily and there was nothing to support provision that "a conspiracy was involved," it would be suppressed since legislative purpose was to allow tap for no longer than absolutely necessary to accomplish legitimate purpose and not to unreasonably invade privacy. People v. Pieri, 69 Misc. 2d 1085, 332 N.Y.S.2d 786 (Erie Co. Ct. 1972), aff'd, 346 N.Y.S.2d 213 (4th Dept. 1973).

Evidence gained by "bug" suppressed when only wiretap ordered.—Suppression was granted where evidence was obtained by installation of a "bug" inside a residence, capable of picking up non-telephonic communications since the eavesdropping warrant only authorized the interception of telephone calls. People v. Frank, 85 A.D.2d 109, 447 N.Y.S.2d 558 (4th Dept. 1982).

Intercepted communications; minimization rule; suppression.—Where defendants sought to assert standing to attack minimization procedures relating to the interception of conversations other than their own, they failed to meet the burden of establishing a legitimate expectation of privacy where they had no colorable interest in the premises where the wiretaps were installed. People v. Edelstein, 98 Misc. 2d 1018, 415 N.Y.S.2d 366 (Sup. Ct. N.Y. Co. 1979), aff'd, 54 N.Y.2d 308, 445 N.Y.S.2d 125, 429 N.E.2d 803 (1981).

—The defendant's constitutional rights were flagrantly violated and total suppression of all monitored conversations and of the tainted fruits thereof was mandated where the eavesdropping taping machines operated automatically and were continuously operated during the 20 days of tapping. People v. Brenes, 53 A.D.2d 78, 385 N.Y.S.2d 530 (1st Dept. 1976), aff'd, 42 N.Y.2d 41, 396 N.Y.S.2d 629, 364 N.E.2d 1322 (1977).

Minimization requirement.—The People have the burden "of going forward to show the legality of the police conduct in the first instance"; it may be satisfied by demonstrating that procedures were established to minimize interception of non-pertinent communications and that a conscientious effort was made to follow such procedures. People v. Floyd, 41 N.Y.2d 245, 392 N.Y.S.2d 257, 360 N.E.2d 935 (1976).

—Since authorities may monitor the initial portion of any conversation to determine its pertinency and the act of dialing is necessarily at the beginning of any out-going call, New Jersey authorities, acting under valid eavesdropping warrant, properly intercepted and recorded the sound of the clicks made when dialing the tapped phone. People v. Estrada, 97 Misc. 2d 127, 410 N.Y.S.2d 757 (Sup. Ct. Queens Co. 1978).

Subd. 5

Failure to identify law enforcement agency.—Failure to identify the law enforcement agency was not a substantial violation of CPL § 700.30(5) where the warrant was narrowly drawn and carefully sought to limit incursions on defendant's rights by setting out procedures as to method and scope of eavesdropping well within the limits mandated by the statute and the U.S. Supreme Court, and the district attorney was named as the person applying for the warrant, and the application and supporting papers indicated that the Buffalo Police Department would execute it at a specific address, and language identifying them was inadvertently deleted from a handwritten draft, and such police in fact executed the warrant. People v. Zendano, 62 A.D.2d 537, 405 N.Y.S.2d 347 (4th Dept. 1978).

Search and seizure; eavesdropping warrant; intercepted conversations as probable cause for search warrant.—Where eavesdropping warrants were issued upon probable cause within limits of the statute, intercepted communications could be used as basis for probable cause for search warrant against "person sought but not named" without obtaining amendment of eavesdropping warrant. People v. Gnozzo, 31 N.Y.2d 134, 335 N.Y.S.2d 257, 286 N.E.2d 706 (1972), cert. denied, 410 U.S. 943 (1973).

Standing to contest.—The right to object to the "use of intercepted conversations obtained through eavesdropping devices is personal and limited to a party to the conversation or whose premises are involved." People v. Sardegna, 91 A.D.2d 671, 457 N.Y.S.2d 123 (2d Dept. 1982).

Subd. 8

Time of commencement.—A provision in an eavesdropping warrant that interception shall commence as soon as practicable is not specific enough to change the general rule that the 30-day period commences when the warrant is issued. People v. Paluska, 109 A.D.2d 389, 491 N.Y.S.2d 999 (3d Dept. 1985).

§ 700.35. Eavesdropping and video surveillance warrants; manner and time of execution.

1. An eavesdropping or video surveillance warrant must be executed according to its terms by a law enforcement officer who is a member of the law enforcement agency authorized in the warrant to intercept the communications or conduct the video surveillance.

2. Upon termination of the authorization in the warrant, eavesdropping or video surveillance must cease and as soon as practicable thereafter any device installed for such purpose either must be removed or must be permanently inactivated as soon as practicable by any means approved by the issuing justice. Entry upon a private place or premise for the removal or permanent inactivation of such device is deemed to be authorized by the warrant.

3. The contents of any communication intercepted or of any observation made by any means authorized by this article must, if possible, be recorded on tape or wire or other comparable device. The recording of the contents of any such communication or observation must be done in such way as will protect the recording from editing or other alterations.

4. In the event an intercepted communication is in a code or foreign language, and the services of an expert in that foreign language or code cannot reasonably be obtained during the interception period, where the warrant so authorizes and in a manner specified therein, the minimization required by subdivision seven of section 700.30 of this article may be accomplished as soon as practicable after such interception.

5. A good faith reliance by a provider of a wire or electronic communication service upon the validity of a court order issued pursuant to this article is a complete defense against any civil cause of action or criminal action based solely on a failure to comply with this article.

Amended by L. 1988, Ch. 744.

ANNOTATIONS

Destruction of tapes.—Since, at the trial, the defendant made no inquiry at all with respect to the tapes; made no request for their production; failed to request any charge regarding them and made no post trial motions concerning them, the court refused on the appeal to review the propriety of the police conduct in destroying the tape recordings of various conversations with the defendant based upon their independent judgment that the tapes were inaudible and contained no exculpatory material. People v. Johnson, 42 N.Y.2d 841, 397 N.Y.S.2d 380, 366 N.E.2d 80 (1977).

"Live" conversations not covered. —An eavesdropping warrant authorizing the monitoring of telephone conversations did not permit the monitoring of conversations carried on within the home where the telephone was located which became audible when the telephone receiver was left off the hook; the "plain view" doctrine did not apply because it was apparent to the officers from the nature of the system that no telephone conversation was in progress. People v. Basilicato, 64 N.Y.2d 103, 485 N.Y.S.2d 7, 474 N.E.2d 215 (1984).

Termination.—Simply turning off eavesdropping equipment does not meet the requirement that upon termination of the warrant such equipment must be removed or permanently inactivated, since the equipment could easily be turned on again by anyone with access. People v. Gallina, 66 N.Y.2d 52, 495 N.Y.S.2d 9, 485 N.E.2d 216 (1985).

—Reversal of the conviction and suppression of the evidence was required where the People failed to furnish defendant with a copy of eavesdropping warrant and accompanying application which authorized interception within 15 days after defendant's arraignment (CPL § 700.70); failed to serve defendant with written notice of fact and date of issuance within 90 days after its termination CPL § 700.50(3);and continued the eavesdropping for at least two days after they had achieved the objective

of the eavesdrop (CPL § 700.10[2]). People v. Mark, 68 A.D.2d 315, 417 N.Y.S.2d 149 (4th Dept. 1979).

§ 700.40. Eavesdropping and video surveillance warrants; order of extension.

At any time prior to the expiration of an eavesdropping or video surveillance warrant, the applicant may apply to the issuing justice, or, if he is unavailable, to another justice, for an order of extension. The period of extension shall be no longer than the justice deems necessary to achieve the purposes for which it was granted and in no event longer than thirty days. The application for an order of extension must conform in all respects to the provisions of section 700.20 and, in addition, must contain a statement setting forth the results thus far obtained from the interception, or a reasonable explanation of the failure to obtain such results. The provisions of sections 700.15 and 700.25 are applicable in the determination of such application. The order of extension must conform in all respects to the provisions of section 700.30. In the execution of such order of extension the provisions of section 700.35 are applicable.

Amended by L. 1988, Ch. 744.

ANNOTATIONS

Extension; time for application.—An application for an order of extension of an eavesdropping warrant must be made prior to the expiration of the original eavesdropping warrant. People v. Gallina, 66 N.Y.2d 52, 495 N.Y.S.2d 9, 485 N.E.2d 216 (1985).

Renewal.—Where the extension warrant was obtained prior to the obligation to seal the original tapes arose, the subsequent warrant was free from taint at the time it was acquired and was not rendered invalid when the original tapes were not properly sealed. People v. Versace, 73 A.D.2d 304, 426 N.Y.S.2d 61 (2d Dept. 1980).

Search and seizure; eavesdropping warrant; intercepted conversations as probable cause for search warrant.—Where eavesdropping warrants were issued upon probable cause within limits of the statute, intercepted communications could be used as basis for probable cause for search warrant against "person sought but not named" without obtaining amendment of eavesdropping warrant. People v. Gnozzo, 31 N.Y.2d 134, 335 N.Y.2d 257, 286 N.E.2d 706 (1972), cert. denied, 410 U.S. 943 (1973).

§ 700.50. Eavesdropping and video surveillance warrants; progress reports and notice.

1. An eavesdropping or video surveillance warrant may require reports to be made to the issuing justice showing what progress has been made toward achievement of the authorized objective and the need for continued eavesdropping or video surveillance. Such reports shall be made at such intervals as the justice may require.

2. Immediately upon the expiration of the period of an eavesdropping or video surveillance warrant, the recordings of communications or observations made pursuant to subdivision three of section 700.35 must be made available to the issuing justice and sealed under his directions.

3. Within a reasonable time, but in no case later than ninety days after termination of an eavesdropping or video surveillance warrant, or expiration of an extension order, except as otherwise provided in subdivision four, written notice of the fact and date of the issuance of the eavesdropping or video surveillance warrant, and of the period of authorized eavesdropping or video surveillance, and of the fact that during such period communications were or were not intercepted or observation * were or were not made, must be served upon the person named in the warrant and such other parties to the intercepted communications or subjects of the video surveillance as the justice may determine in his discretion is in the interest of justice. Service reasonably calculated to give affected parties the notice required by this subdivision shall be effected within the time limits provided herein and in a manner prescribed by the justice. The justice, upon the filing of a motion by any person served with such notice, my in his discretion make available to such person or his counsel for inspection such portions of the intercepted communications or video surveillance, applications and warrants as the justice determines to be in the interest of justice.

4. On a showing of exigent circumstances to the issuing justice, the service of the notice required by subdivision three may be postponed by order of the justice for a reasonable period of time. Renewals of an order of postponement may be obtained on a new showing of exigent circumstances.

* As originally enacted.

Amended by L. 1988, Ch. 744.

ANNOTATIONS

Eavesdropping warrant; expiration of.—Eavesdropping warrants expire either on the expiration date set forth in the warrant or on attainment of the authorized objective. Because there were many targets of the investigation, the People had not completely achieved the investigative objectives of the warrant at the time of defendant's arrest. Thus, court found that the defendant failed to demonstrate the success of his motion to vacate based on counsel's failure to move for suppression of the eavesdropping tapes. People v. Peterson, 19 A.D.3d 1015, 796 N.Y.S.2d 796 (4th Dept. 2005).

Eavesdropping warrant; suppression.—Although defendant was not entitled to suppression hearing during grand jury proceedings, he was so entitled after indictment for criminal contempt and notice of eavesdropping in spite of his failure to object to sources of grand jury questions. The mere fact that eavesdropping warrant was pursuant to judicial scrutiny does not preclude defendant from contesting the validity of the court permission. People v. Mulligan, 40 A.D.2d 165, 338 N.Y.S.2d 488 (1st Dept. 1972).

Grand jury; eavesdropping motion to suppress.—Defendant, served subsequent to his grand jury appearance with notice that he had been subjected to prior electronic surveillance, was not entitled to a suppression hearing during pendency of the grand jury proceedings; and failure of the prosecutor, during proceedings prior to trial, to answer defendant's questions concerning the surveillance was no defense to his contempt charge for refusal to answer questions, since he had been granted "transactional immunity." People v. Breindel, 73 Misc. 2d 734, 342 N.Y.S.2d 428 (Sup. Ct. N.Y. Co. 1973), aff'd, 45 A.D.2d 691, 356 N.Y.S.2d 626, aff'd, 35 N.Y.2d 929, 365 N.Y.S.2d 163, 324 N.E.2d 545 (1974).

Grand jury; immunity.—Where defendant testified in a grand jury proceeding that he understood the concepts of immunity, perjury, and contempt, as well as the scope of the immunity he was not permitted to avail himself (in a prosecution for criminal contempt) of the defense that the explanation of "transactional immunity" was inadequate, especially where defendant was represented and advised by counsel. People v. Breindel, 73 Misc. 2d 734, 342 N.Y.S.2d 428 (Sup. Ct. N.Y. Co. 1973), aff'd, 45 A.D.2d 691, 356 N.Y.S.2d 626 (1974), aff'd, 35 N.Y.2d 929, 365 N.Y.S.2d 163, 324 N.E.2d 545 (1974).

Search and seizure; eavesdropping warrant; intercepted conversations as probable cause for search warrant.—Where eavesdropping warrants were issued upon probable cause within limits of the statute, intercepted communications could be used as basis for probable cause for search warrant against "person sought but not named" without obtaining amendment of eavesdropping warrant. People v. Gnozzo, 31 N.Y.2d 134, 335 N.Y.S.2d 257, 286 N.E.2d 706 (1972), cert. denied, 410 U.S. 943 (1973).

Wiretap; duration; progress reports.—Absent a showing of prejudice to the defendant, the failure of the district attorney to comply with the court direction to file interim progress reports during the pendency of a wiretap did not necessitate the suppression of the tapes obtained pursuant to the warrant. People v. Marino, 49 N.Y.2d 774, 426 N.Y.S.2d 474, 403 N.E.2d 179 (1980).

—The better practice is for the Judge to require progress reports, especially where the surveillance extends over a rather long period of time as in this case (120 day interval). People v. Floyd, 41 N.Y.2d 245, 392 N.Y.S.2d 257, 360 N.E.2d 935 (1976).

—The failure of the issuing judge and district attorney to supervise electronic surveillance procedures did not require suppression of the tape recordings of telephone conversations where daily log sheets were delivered to the issuing judge and district attorney, and the record shows that conscientious and reasonable efforts were made to comply with the spirit of the law. People v. Calogero, 75 A.D.2d 455, 429 N.Y.S.2d 970 (4th Dept. 1980).

Subd. 2

Monitored conversation; consent of one party.—A monitored conversation to which one of the parties has consented to the overhearing of the conversation by persons not present, has been held not to violate the right of privacy protected by the Fourth Amendment and the tapes of these conversations are not required to be sealed; the tapes are admissible in evidence when the chain of custody has been established and it is shown that the tapes have not been tampered with or altered. People v. Smith, 58 A.D.2d 1005, 396 N.Y.S.2d 949 (4th Dept. 1977).

Eavesdropping evidence suppressed; independent source.—Where the questioning of defendants before the Grand Jury emanated from wiretaps of conversations, the contents of which have been suppressed for failure to timely seal, it loses potency as a predicate for punishing defendants for contempt by refusing to answer because such questioning constitutes evidence derived from the use or disclosure of the contents of the intercepted conversations, however, if the questioning of the defendants before the Grand Jury has a source or basis independent of the wiretaps then it is admissible evidence at the trial of the contempt indictments. People v. DeMartino, 71 A.D.2d 477, 422 N.Y.S.2d 949 (1st Dept. 1979).

Eavesdropping; sealing of recordings.—A one-day delay in sealing the tapes resulting from an eavesdropping warrant may be excused, even absent an explanation, but any additional delay, if not satisfactorily explained, requires suppression. People v. Gallina, 66 N.Y.2d 52, 495 N.Y.S.2d 9, 485 N.E.2d 216 (1985).

—The statutory requirement that eavesdropping tapes be sealed "immediately upon the expiration of the period" for the warrant was not satisfied where there was a six-day delay in sealing such tapes that could not be satisfactorily explained; the defendant has no burden to show actual tampering. People v. Basilicato, 64 N.Y.2d 103, 485 N.Y.S.2d 7, 474 N.E.2d 215 (1984).

—The requirement that recordings obtained pursuant to eavesdropping warrants be sealed is to be strictly construed, and a failure to seal such recordings, in the absence of a satisfactory explanation, resulted in rendering such tape recordings inadmissible as evidence. People v. Nicoletti, 34 N.Y.2d 249, 356 N.Y.S.2d 855, 313 N.E.2d 336 (1974).

—The actual or assumed unavailability of the court does not excuse a delay in the sealing of tapes more than one day; even if the issuing judge is unavailable, efforts must be made to contact an available judge. Here, unexcused delay in sealing tapes required suppression of certain intercepts and tangible evidence seized pursuant to warrant issued on date after obligation to seal arose. People v. Fonville, 247 A.D.2d 115, 681 N.Y.S.2d 420 (4th Dept. 1998).

—The sealing procedure was proper where after the tapes were brought before the Judge and he ordered them sealed they were taken by a Deputy to the Monroe County Sheriff's office and sealed in two boxes found at that office. People v. Portanova, 56 A.D.2d 265, 392 N.Y.S.2d 123 (4th Dept. 1977).

—The evidence derived from the tapes was suppressed since there was no reasonable basis in the statute which permitted the police to keep the recordings for fourteen days after the expiration of the wiretap order before making them available to the issuing judge for sealing. People v. Scaccia, 55 A.D.2d 444, 390 N.Y.S.2d 743 (4th Dept. 1977).

CPL § 700.50(2) mandates sealing upon expiration of each original and extension order.—Search warrant, issued as result of information concerning a new crime overheard during wiretapping and for which wiretap order was amended, was not required to be suppressed because the wiretap warrant it upon termination, since the evidence obtained under the search warrant was not contaminated by the failure to seal the tapes. People v. Iucci, 61 A.D.2d 1, 401 N.Y.S.2d 823 (2d Dept. 1978).

Failure to seal wiretap tapes.—Failure to timely seal renders inadmissible both the tapes and any evidence seized pursuant to a search warrant issued after the obligation to seal arose and based on information gleaned from the tapes, however, evidence acquired pursuant to a warrant obtained prior to the time when sealing was required is not precluded. People v. Weiss, 48 N.Y.2d 988, 425 N.Y.S.2d 543, 401 N.E.2d 901 (1980).

Recordings; delivery to issuing judge.—The obligation to seal tapes arises at the expiration of the 30-day period of the warrant and at the close of each extension thereafter granted; an unexplained delay of 36 days in sealing the tapes obtained pursuant to the initial warrant and a similarly unexplained delay of 8 days in sealing the tapes obtained pursuant to the extension order require suppression of both recordings. People v. Weiss, 63 A.D.2d 662, 404 N.Y.S.2d 392 (2d Dept. 1978), aff'd, 48 N.Y.2d 988, 425 N.Y.S.2d 543, 401 N.E.2d 901 (1980).

—The police must present recordings of overheard communications for sealing immediately upon the expiration of the specific warrant or extension covering the period when they were intercepted. People v. Washington, 46 N.Y.2d 116, 412 N.Y.S.2d 854, 385 N.E.2d 593 (1978).

—Since tape recordings of intercepted telephone communications resulting from the issuance of an eavesdropping warrant should have been sealed immediately upon expiration of that warrant and were not, such tapes, as well as those gathered pursuant to the extension of the warrant and any and all other evidence garnered as a result of such intercepted communications must be suppressed. People v. Portanova, 66 A.D.2d 487, 413 N.Y.S.2d 753 (2d Dept. 1979).

—The transcription of the 120 reels of intercepted communications did not constitute a satisfactory explanation for the 39-day hiatus between the expiration of the last extension of the eavesdropping warrant and the date upon which the original tapes were presented for sealing. People v. Washington, 55 A.D.2d 609, 389 N.Y.S.2d 382 (2d Dept. 1976).

—Unexplained ten-day delay in sealing records after the last of three 30-day extensions of the original eavesdropping warrant violated CPL § 700.50(2) and required suppression of the tape recordings. People v. Winograd, 62 A.D.2d 954, 404 N.Y.S.2d 102 (1978).

—The prohibition against the use of tapes which have not been sealed pursuant to CPL § 700.50(2) applies to their use or the disclosure of their contents while giving testimony under oath in any criminal proceeding (CPL § 700.65[3]). People v. Canarrozzo, 64 A.D.2d 1018, 409 N.Y.S.2d 466 (4th Dept. 1978).

Search warrant; obtained as result of eavesdropping.— The failure to seal recordings pursuant to CPL § 700.50(2) which results in their suppression does not necessitate the suppression of evidence obtained pursuant to a valid search

warrant where such warrant was obtained before any obligation to seal the tapes arose. People v. Weiss, 63 A.D.2d 662, 404 N.Y.S.2d 392 (2d Dept. 1978).

Search warrant.—Evidence acquired pursuant to the search warrant was admissible where the intercepts upon which the search warrant was based were obtained before sealing of tapes was required. People v. Seidita, 49 N.Y.2d 755, 426 N.Y.S.2d 463, 403 N.E.2d 169 (1980).

§ 700.55. Eavesdropping and video surveillance warrants; custody of warrants, applications and recordings.

1. Applications made and warrants issued under this article shall be sealed by the justice. Any eavesdropping or video surveillance warrant, together with a copy of papers upon which the application is based, shall be delivered to and retained by the applicant as authority for the eavesdropping or video surveillance authorized therein. A copy of such eavesdropping or video surveillance warrant, together with all the original papers upon which the application was based, must be retained by the justice issuing the same, and, in the event of the denial of an application for such an eavesdropping or video surveillance warrant, a copy of the papers upon which the application was based must be retained by the justice denying the same. Such applications and warrants may be disclosed only upon a showing of good cause before a court and may not be destroyed except on order of the issuing or denying justice, and in any event must be kept for ten years.

2. Custody of the recordings made pursuant to subdivision three of section 700.35 may be wherever the justice orders. They may not be destroyed except upon an order of the justice who issued the warrant and in any event must be kept for ten years. Duplicate recordings may be made for use or disclosure pursuant to the provisions of subdivisions one and two of section 700.65 for investigations.

Amended by L. 1988, Ch. 744.

ANNOTATION

Eavesdropping warrants; failure to file supporting affidavits, warrants and transcripts in accordance with CPL 700.55.—Unless the defendants show that failure to comply with CPL 700.55 resulted in some type of tampering with the records, a motion to suppress will not be granted. The requirements of the statute are ministerial and do not affect substantial rights. The failure to perform a required subsequent act does not void prior lawful acts. People v. Sher, 68 Misc. 2d 917, 329 N.Y.S.2d 2 (Greene Co. Ct. 1972).

§ 700.60. Eavesdropping warrants; reports to the administrative office of the United States courts.

1. Within thirty days after the termination of an eavesdropping warrant or the expiration of an extension order, the issuing or denying justice must submit such report to the administrative

office of the United States courts as is required by federal law.

2. In January of each year, the attorney general and each district attorney must submit such report to the administrative office of the United States courts as is required by federal law.

Amended by L. 1974, Ch. 615; L. 1985, Ch. 421.

§ 700.65. Eavesdropping and video surveillance warrants; disclosure and use of information; order of amendment.

1. Any law enforcement officer who, by any means authorized by this article, has obtained knowledge of the contents of any intercepted communication or video surveillance, or evidence derived therefrom, may disclose such contents to another law enforcement officer to the extent that such disclosure is appropriate to the proper performance of the official duties of the officer making or receiving the disclosure.

2. Any law enforcement officer who, by any means authorized by this article, has obtained knowledge of the contents of any intercepted communication or video surveillance, or evidence derived therefrom, may use such contents to the extent such use is appropriate to the proper performance of his official duties.

3. Any person who has received, by any means authorized by this article, any information concerning a communication or video surveillance, or evidence derived therefrom, intercepted or conducted in accordance with the provisions of this article, may disclose the contents of that communication or video surveillance, or such derivative evidence, while giving testimony under oath in any criminal proceeding in any court, in any grand jury proceeding or in any action commenced pursuant to article thirteen-A or thirteen-B of the civil practice law and rules; provided, however, that the presence of the seal provided for by subdivision two of section 700.50, or a satisfactory explanation of the absence thereof, shall be a prerequisite for the use or disclosure of the contents of any communication or video surveillance, or evidence derived therefrom; and provided further, however, that where a criminal court of competent jurisdiction has ordered exclusion or suppression of the contents of an intercepted communication or video surveillance, or evidence derived therefrom, such determination shall be binding in an action commenced pursuant to article thirteen-A or thirteen-B of the civil practice law and rules.

4. When a law enforcement officer, while engaged in intercepting communications or conducting video surveillance in the manner authorized by this article, intercepts a communication or makes an observation which was not otherwise sought and which constitutes evidence of any crime that has been, is being or is about to be committed, the contents of such communications or observation, and evidence derived therefrom, may be disclosed or used as provided in subdivisions one and two. Such contents and any evidence derived therefrom may be used under subdivision three when a justice amends the eavesdropping or video surveillance warrant to include such contents. The application for such amendment must be made by the applicant as soon as practicable by giving notice to the court of the interception of the communication or the making of the observation and of the contents of such interception or observation; provided that during the period in which the eavesdropping or video surveillance is continuing, such notice must be given within ten days after probable cause exists to believe that a crime not named in the warrant has been, is being, or is about to be committed, or at the time an application for an order of extension is made pursuant to section 700.40 of this article, if such probable cause then exists, whichever is earlier. If the justice finds that such contents were otherwise intercepted in accordance with the provisions of this article, he may grant the application.

Amended by L. 1988, Ch. 744.

ANNOTATIONS

Eavesdropping warrants; timely application for amendment.—Where conversation, unrelated to the crime or persons for which an eavesdropping warrant was authorized, was overheard, a failure to make a timely application to amend the eavesdropping warrant so as to include the newly discovered crime required the suppression of testimony concerning such conversation as well as a related conversation occurring eleven days later. People v. Distefano, 45 A.D.2d 56, 356 N.Y.S.2d 316 (1st Dept. 1974). *See also* People v. O'Meara, 70 A.D.2d 890, 417 N.Y.S.2d 95 (2d Dept. 1979) *aff'd*, 52 N.Y.2d 990, 438 N.Y.S.2d 287, 420 N.E.2d 85 (1981).

Eavesdropping warrants; persons not named in original warrant but named in amended warrant.—Telephone conversations that were inadvertently overheard by the police who had the phone tapped pursuant to order are admissible under the plain view doctrine. People v. DiStefano, 38 N.Y.2d 640, 382 N.Y.S.2d 5, 345 N.E.2d 548 (1976).

Retroactive amendment not necessary.—Amendment of a warrant for a wiretap for usury is not necessary when evidence of extortion is also obtained because the crimes overlap and the defendant was indicted for usury and extortion. People v. Lagano, 105 Misc. 2d 665, 432 N.Y.S.2d 798 (Sup. Ct. Bronx Co. 1980).

Search & seizure; eavesdropping warrant; intercepted conversations as probable cause for search warrant.—Where eavesdropping warrants were issued upon probable cause within limits of the statute, intercepted communications could be used as basis for probable cause for search warrant against "person sought but not named" without obtaining amendment of eavesdropping warrant. People v. Gnozzo, 31 N.Y.2d 134, 335 N.Y.S.2d 257, 286 N.E.2d 706 (1972), *cert. denied*, 410 U.S. 943 (1973).

Unsealed tapes.—The prohibition against the use of tapes which have not been sealed does not extend to disclosure of the contents of unsealed tapes to other law enforcement personnel for purposes of assisting their investigation or for establishing probable cause for the issuance of other warrants. People v. Canarrozzo, 64 A.D.2d 1018, 409 N.Y.S.2d 466 (4th Dept. 1978).

Unsealing of tapes.—The failure of the prosecutor to obtain judicial approval for the unsealing of the tapes for trial preparation and the absence of judicial supervision over the unsealing process violated the procedure clearly mandated by the Federal and State statutes and required exclusion of the wiretap recordings and the evidence derived therefrom. People v. Sher, 38 N.Y.2d 600, 381 N.Y.S.2d 843, 345 N.E.2d 314 (1976).

—CPL § 700.05(3) and § 700.65(3) explicitly require that, when People violate sealing requirements, they are barred from offering into evidence not only the substance of the intercepted communications, but also testimony about the very existence of the conversation. People v. Huang, 248 A.D.2d 73, 682 N.Y.S.2d 146 (1st Dept. 1998).

Wiretapping; warrant; intercepted conversations with another.—Defendant pleaded guilty to possession of gambling records after denial of suppression motion, which court held to be proper because the eavesdropping warrant authorized interception of telephone conversations of Nellis Slayka concerning gambling and therefore all persons, though not named in the warrant conversing about gambling with Slayka were searched with probable cause, without requiring amendment of warrant. People v. Zorn, 38 A.D.2d 359, 329 N.Y.S.2d 592 (1st Dept. 1972), aff'd, 31 N.Y.2d 134, 335 N.Y.S.2d 257, 286 N.E.2d 706 (1972), cert. denied, 410 U.S. 943 (1973).

—Amendment of the eavesdropping warrant to include defendant's name was not untimely because the inculpatory conversations intercepted was between the defendant and a named suspect and, therefore, no amendment was necessary. People v. Penna, 53 A.D.2d 941, 385 N.Y.S.2d 400 (3d Dept. 1976).

Wiretap warrant; intercepted conversations; use against person not named in warrant.—There was no merit in defendant's contention that his conversations on tape were suppressible, because he was not named in the original warrant application, nor was the crime he was convicted for either enumerated in the original warrant or a crime for which an eavesdropping warrant may issue originally; defendant's call to the warrant target, and the inadvertent discovery of the subject conversation renders it admissible, consistent with the "plain view" exception to the warrant requirement. People v. Calogero, 84 A.D.2d 667, 446 N.Y.S.2d 615 (4th Dept. 1982).

§ 700.70. Eavesdropping warrants; notice before use of evidence.

The contents of any intercepted communication, or evidence derived therefrom, may not be received in evidence or otherwise disclosed upon a trial of a defendant unless the people, within fifteen days after arraignment and before the commencement of the trial, furnish the defendant with a copy of the eavesdropping warrant, and accompanying application, under which interception was authorized or approved. This fifteen day period may be extended by the trial court upon good cause shown if it finds that the defendant will not be prejudiced by the delay in receiving such papers.

Amended by L. 1976, Ch. 194.

Arraignment.—The 15 day period contained in CPL § 700.70 in which the People must serve a defendant with a copy of the eavesdropping warrant and accompanying application runs from the date of the arraignment in the Supreme Court, rather than the arraignment in Criminal Court. People v. Penasso, 142 A.D.2d 691, 531 N.Y.S.2d 291 (2d Dept. 1988).

Failure of prosecutor to serve notice; sanctions. —Evidence derived from an intercepted communication must be suppressed where there has been a failure to comply with the notice provision of CPL § 700.70, and where there has been neither an application for an extension of time within the 15 days provided in that statute nor a showing of good cause for noncompliance and lack of prejudice to defendant. People v. Schulz, 67 N.Y.2d 144, 501 N.Y.S.2d 12, 492 N.E.2d 120 (1986).

—Suppression of the eavesdropping tapes was required where the prosecution failed to serve the defendants with copies of the warrant and application within 15 days of arraignment and offered no "good cause" for such delay. People v. Basilicato, 64 N.Y.2d 103, 485 N.Y.S.2d 7, 474 N.E.2d 215 (1984).

Suppression hearing; wiretapping; duty of prosecutor.—A defendant at a suppression hearing is entitled to the assistance of the prosecutor in learning whether he has been the subject of a wiretapping, even though the People have given no notice of intention to use wiretap evidence at trial, as long as defendant has a reasonable belief that wiretapping has occurred. People v. Trasso, 109 Misc. 2d 438, 440 N.Y.S.2d 504 (Crim. Ct. N.Y. Co. 1981).

Tapes prepared by undercover officer cannot be used. —It was improper for the trial court to permit the jury to use transcripts of Spanish language tapes of three alleged drugs sales which were essentially prepared by the undercover officer who participated in the taped conversations as an aid to listening to the tapes and it was also improper to permit the undercover officer to supplement the transcripts used by the jury. People v. Colon, 87 A.D.2d 826, 449 N.Y.S.2d 11 (2d Dept. 1982).

Transcript of tape.—Although special problems may arise in consequence of the introduction, on trial or at a hearing, of tape recordings without transcription, and recognizing that practical difficulties may attend such practice, especially in instances of their extended use, it does not follow that use of untranscribed tape recordings for which a proper foundation has been laid is necessarily or even unusually suspect. People v. Savino, 44 N.Y.2d 669, 405 N.Y.S.2d 35, 376 N.E.2d 196 (1978).

—The trial court properly admitted into evidence transcripts of the taped telephone conversation for the limited purpose of aiding the jury in understanding the tapes when played, but the jury was not allowed to use the transcripts in its deliberations. People v. Campbell, 55 A.D.2d 688, 389 N.Y.S.2d 146 (3d Dept. 1976).

—Court rejected argument that the People's failure to provide defendant with a copy of one page out of a total of approximately 700 pages of material constituted a failure to comply with the strict compliance requirement of CPL § 700.70. People v. Packies, 156 Misc. 2d 710, 594 N.Y.S.2d 599, 605 (Sup. Ct. Suffolk Co. 1993).

ARTICLE 705—PEN REGISTERS AND TRAP AND TRACE DEVICES

LexisNexis Cross References

New York Suppression Manual, Ch. 19, Electronic Surveillance; *New York Criminal Practice (2d ed.),* Vol. 2, Ch. 22, Electronic Eavesdropping.

§ 705.00. Definitions.

As used in this article, the following terms have the following meanings:

1. "Pen register" means a device which records or decodes electronic or other impulses which identify the numbers dialed or otherwise transmitted on the telephone line to which such device is attached, but such term does not include any device used by a provider or customer of a wire or electronic communication service for billing, or recording as an incident to billing, for communications services provided by such provider or any device used by a provider or customer of a wire communication service for cost accounting or other like purposes in the ordinary course of its business.

2. "Trap and trace device" means a device which captures the incoming electronic or other impulses which identify the originating number of an instrument or device from which a wire or electronic communication was transmitted.

3. "Applicant" means a district attorney, an assistant district attorney, and when empowered by law to conduct an investigation of or to prosecute or participate in the prosecution of a designated crime, the attorney general, an assistant attorney general, the deputy attorney general in charge of the statewide organized crime task force, or an assistant deputy attorney general of such task force.

4. "Law enforcement agency" means any agency which is empowered by law to conduct an investigation or to make an arrest for a felony, and any agency which is authorized by law to prosecute or participate in the prosecution of a felony.

5. "Designated crime" means any crime included within the definition of a "designated

offense" in subdivision eight of section 700.05 of this chapter, any criminal act as defined in subdivision one of section 460.10 of the penal law, bail jumping in the first and second degree as defined in sections 215.57 and 215.56 of such law, or aggravated harassment as defined in subdivisions one and two of section 240.30 of such law.

6. "Justice" means justice as defined in subdivision four of section 700.05 of this chapter.

§ 705.05. Pen register and trap and trace authorizations; in general.

Under circumstances prescribed in this article, a justice may issue an order authorizing the use of a pen register or a trap and trace device upon *ex parte* application of an applicant who is authorized by law to investigate, prosecute or participate in the prosecution of the designated crimes which are the subject of the application.

ANNOTATIONS

Generally.—Without strict adherence to the guidelines set forth in CPL § 705.05, any evidence procured would be inadmissible. The use of wiretaps must be authorized to prevent any interceptions from being illegal, thus, rendering the evidence inadmissible. People v. Capolongo, 85 N.Y.2d 151, 623 N.Y.S.2d 778, 647 N.E.2d 1286 (1995).

Pen registers.—The *Bialostok* rule should be applied only prospectively. People v. Martello, 93 N.Y.2d 525, 695 N.Y.S.2d 526, 717 N.E.2d 684 (1999).

—Disablement of a pen register's audio function is insufficient to remove it from ambit of eavesdropping statute; where a pen register has the additional capacity to monitor conversations, evidence obtained from it must be suppressed unless a warrant is obtained. People v. Bialostok, 80 N.Y.2d 738, 594 N.Y.S.2d 701, 703, 610 N.E.2d 374 (1993).

—Court properly determined that *People v. Bialostok,* 80 N.Y.2d 738, should be applied prospectively only and does not apply to pen register orders or electronic eavesdropping warrants in this case, all of which were issued and/or extended prior to date of *Bialostok* decision, because *Bialostok* is subject to New York's flexible approach to retroactivity rather than the federal rule of automatic retroactivity to pending cases. People v. Martello, 251 A.D.2d 187, 675 N.Y.S.2d 33 (1st Dept. 1998), aff'd, 93 N.Y.2d 645, 695 N.Y.S.2d 525, 717 N.E.2d 684 (1999).

—*People v. Martello*, 93 N.Y.2d 645, 695 N.Y.S.2d 525, 717 N.E.2d 684 (1999), can be applied retroactively to the instant case, which was pending at the time that *Martello* was decided, and applying *Martello*, court found that motion to suppress pen register and wire tap evidence should be denied because the surveillance was conducted in compliance with the statutory requirements of CPL article 705. People v. Kramer, 267 A.D.2d 328, 701 N.Y.S.2d 78 (2d Dept. 1999).

—No warrant is required to be obtained by the police prior to installing a pen register. However, there must be a judicial order permitting the installation. Where the pen register intercepts conversations, the police must then obtain a warrant pursuant to probable cause in order to use such an "eavesdropping device." People v. LaMendola, 206 A.D.2d 207, 619 N.Y.S.2d 901 (4th Dept. 1994).

—Where the record established that the pen register was not in use against the defendants, the defendants could not challenge the use of the pen register. The defendants' conversations were not intercepted nor were the defendants the owners of the telephone involved. Thus, the defendants failed to establish standing. People v. Varacilli, 154 Misc. 2d 805, 596 N.Y.S.2d 346 (Sup. Ct. Kings Co. 1993).

§ 705.10. Orders authorizing the use of a pen register or a trap and trace device; when issuable.

An order authorizing the use of a pen register or a trap and trace device may issue only:

1. Upon an appropriate application made in conformity with this article; and

2. Upon a determination that an application sets forth specific, articulable facts, warranting the applicant's reasonable suspicion that a designated crime has been, is being, or is about to be committed and demonstrating that the information likely to be obtained by use of a pen register or trap and trace device is or will be relevant to an ongoing criminal investigation of such designated crime.

§ 705.15. Application for an order authorizing the use of a pen register or a trap and trace device.

1. An *ex parte* application for an order or an extension of an order authorizing the use of a pen register or a trap and trace device must be made to a justice in writing, and must be subscribed and sworn to by the applicant.

2. The application must contain:

(a) The identity of the applicant and the identity of the law enforcement agency conducting the investigation; and

(b) A statement of facts and circumstances sufficient to justify the applicant's belief that an order authorizing the use of a pen register or a trap and trace device should be issued, including (i) a statement of the specific facts on the basis of which the applicant reasonably suspects that the designated crime has been, is being, or is about to be committed and demonstrating that the

information likely to be obtained by use of a pen register or a trap and trace device is or will be relevant to an ongoing criminal investigation of such designated offense, (ii) the identity, if known, of the person to whom is leased or in whose name is listed the telephone line to which the pen register or trap and trace device is to be attached, (iii) the identity, if known, of the person who is the subject of the criminal investigation, (iv) the number and, if known, the physical location of the telephone line to which the pen register or trap and trace device is to be attached and, in the case of a trap and trace, the geographic limits of the trap and trace order, and (v) a statement of the designated crime or crimes to which the information likely to be obtained by the use of the pen register or trap and trace device relates; and

(c) A statement of the period of time for which the authorization for the use of a pen register or a trap and trace device is required; and

(d) A statement of the facts concerning all previous applications, known to the applicant, for an order authorizing the use of a pen register or a trap and trace device involving any of the same persons or facilities specified in the application, and the action taken by the justice on each such application.

3. Allegations of fact in the application may be based either upon the personal knowledge of the applicant or upon information and belief. If the applicant personally knows the facts alleged, it must be so stated. If the facts stated in the application are derived in whole or in part from the statements of persons other than the applicant, the sources of such facts must be either disclosed or described.

§ 705.20. Orders authorizing the use of a pen register or a trap and trace device; determination of application.

1. If the justice determines on the basis of the facts submitted by the applicant that grounds exist for the issue of an order authorizing the use of a pen register or a trap and trace device pursuant to section 705.10 of this article, the justice shall grant the application and issue an order authorizing the use of a pen register or a trap and trace device, in accordance with subdivision three of this section.

2. If the application does not conform to section 705.15 of this article, or if the justice is not satisfied that grounds exist for the issuance of an order authorizing the use of a pen register or a trap and trace device, the application must be denied.

3. An order issued under this section must contain:

(a) the name of the applicant, date of issuance,

and the subscription and title of the issuing justice; and

(b) the identity, if known, of the person to whom is leased or in whose name is listed the telephone line to which the pen register or trap and trace device is to be attached; and

(c) the identity, if known, of the person who is the subject of the criminal investigation; and

(d) the number and, if known, the physical location of the telephone line to which the pen register or trap and trace device is to be attached and, in the case of a trap and trace device, the geographic limits of the trap and trace order; and

(e) a statement of the designated crime or crimes to which the information likely to be obtained by the pen register or trap and trace device relates.

4. An order issued under this section shall direct, upon the request of the applicant, the furnishing of information, facilities, and technical assistance necessary to accomplish the installation of the pen register or trap and trace device under section 705.25 of this article.

ANNOTATION

Standing.—Defendants had no standing to challenge the propriety of the pen register order because they were not the target of the pen register order, nor were they identified or referred to in the papers submitted in that order. People v. Fiore, 246 A.D.2d 664, 668 N.Y.S.2d 625 (2d Dept. 1998), *modified,* 267 A.D.2d 321, 702 N.Y.2d 80 (1999).

§ 705.25. Pen register or trap and trace device orders; time period and extensions.

1. An order issued under this section shall authorize the installation and use of a pen register or a trap and trace device for a period not to exceed sixty days.

2. Extensions of such an order may be granted, but only upon an application for an order under section 705.05 of this article and upon the judicial finding required by subdivision one of section 705.10 of this article. The period of extension shall be for a period not to exceed sixty days.

§ 705.30. Nondisclosure of existence of pen register or a trap and trace device.

An order authorizing or approving the installation and use of a pen register or a trap and trace device shall direct that:

1. the order be sealed until otherwise ordered by the court; and

2. the person owning or leasing the line to which the pen register or a trap and trace device is attached, or who has been ordered by the court to provide assistance to the applicant, not disclose the existence of the pen register or trap and trace device or the existence of the investigation to the listed subscriber, or to any other person, unless or until otherwise ordered by the court.

§ 705.35. Assistance in installation and use of a pen register or a trap and trace device.

1. Upon the request of an applicant authorized to use a pen register under this article, a provider of a wire or electronic communication service, landlord, custodian, or other person shall furnish such applicant, or his agent, forthwith all information, facilities and technical assistance necessary to accomplish the installation of the pen register unobtrusively and with a minimum of interference with the services that the person so ordered by the court accords the party with respect to whom the installation and use is to take place, if such assistance is directed by a court order provided in section 705.10 of this article.

2. Upon the request of an applicant authorized to receive the results of a trap and trace device under this article, a provider of a wire or electronic communication service, landlord, custodian, or other person shall install such device forthwith on the appropriate line and shall furnish such applicant forthwith all information, facilities and technical assistance including installation and operation of the device unobtrusively and with a minimum of interference with the services that the person so ordered by the court accords the party with respect to whom the installation and use is to take place, if such installation and assistance is directed by the court order as provided in section 705.10 of this article. Unless otherwise ordered by the court, the results of the trap and trace device shall be furnished to the applicant, or his agent, at reasonable intervals during regular business hours for the duration of the order.

3. A provider of a wire or electronic communication service, landlord, custodian, or other person who furnishes facilities or technical assistance pursuant to this section shall be reasonably compensated for such reasonable expenses incurred in providing such facilities and assistance.

4. No cause of action shall lie in any court against any provider of a wire or electronic communication service, its officers, employees, agents or other specified persons for providing information, facilities or assistance in accordance with the terms of a court order under this article. A good faith reliance by a provider of a wire or electronic communication service upon the validity of a court order issued pursuant to this article is a complete defense against any civil cause of action or criminal action based entirely on a failure to comply with this article.

ARTICLE 710—MOTION TO SUPPRESS EVIDENCE

Section

710.10 Motion to suppress evidence; definitions of terms.
710.20 Motion to suppress evidence; in general; grounds for.
710.30 Motion to suppress evidence; notice to defendant of intention to offer evidence.
710.40 Motion to suppress evidence; when made and determined.
710.50 Motion to suppress evidence; in what courts made.
710.60 Motion to suppress evidence; procedure.
710.70 Motion to suppress evidence; orders of suppression; effects of orders and of failure to make motion.

LexisNexis Cross References

New York Criminal Practice (2d ed.), Vol. 2, Ch. 18, Motion to Suppress Evidence; *Defense of Narcotics Cases,* Vol. 1, Ch. 3A, Motions to Suppress in Narcotics Cases; *New York Suppression Manual,* Ch. 28, The Suppression Motion—Preliminary Considerations; Ch. 29, Instituting the Suppression Process; Ch. 30, Litigating the Suppression Motion; *Criminal Evidentiary Foundations,* Ch. 12, Motions to Suppress Evidence; *Courtroom Criminal Evidence (3d ed.),* Vol. 1, Ch. 18, Search or Seizure.

§ 710.10. Motion to suppress evidence; definitions of terms.

As used in this article, the following terms have the following meanings:

1. "Defendant" means a person who has been charged by an accusatory instrument with the commission of an offense.

2. "Evidence," when referring to matter in the possession of or available to a prosecutor, means any tangible property or potential testimony which may be offered in evidence in a criminal action.

3. "Potential testimony" means information or factual knowledge of a person who is or may be available as a witness.

4. "Eavesdropping" means "wiretapping", "mechanical overhearing of a conversation," or "intercepting or accessing of an electronic communication", as those terms are defined in section 250.00 of the penal law.

5. "Aggrieved." An "aggrieved person" includes, but is in no wise limited to, an "aggrieved person" as defined in subdivision two of section forty-five hundred six of the civil practice law and rules.

6. "Video surveillance" has the meaning given to that term by section 700.05 of this chapter.

7. "Pen register" and "trap and trace device" have the meanings given to those terms by subdivisions one and two respectively of section 705.00 of this chapter.

Amended by L. 1988, Ch. 744.

ANNOTATIONS

Burden of proof at suppression hearing.—Defendant bears the burden of proof at the suppression hearing. People v. Perez 149 A.D.2d 344, 539 N.Y.S.2d 750 (1st Dept. 1989).

Eavesdropping; consent of one party.—It is not unlawful to eavesdrop on a telephone conversation with the consent of one of the parties to the conversation. People v. Lasher, 58 N.Y.2d 962, 460 N.Y.S.2d 522, 447 N.E.2d 70 (1983).

Evidence.—Evidence unconnected with an alleged illegal detention need not be suppressed when it is not the fruit of the illegal detention. People v. Woodward, 127 A.D.2d 929, 512 N.Y.S.2d 513, 515 (3d Dept. 1987).

—The trial court has inherent power to determine evidentiary matters even if there is no specific statutory authorization for the hearing; thus, a court has the right to decide defendant's motion to suppress an infant witness' statement to a physician as the product of a suggestive interview. People v. Michael M., 162 Misc. 2d 803, 618 N.Y.S.2d 171 (Sup. Ct. Kings Co. 1994).

Hearing; no statutory authorization.—Even if no specific statutory authorization exists, trial courts should hold hearings to determine if a witness' statements are the product of coercive or unduly suggestive questioning thereby rendering that witness' testimony unreliable. People v. Michael M., 162 Misc. 2d 803, 618 N.Y.S.2d 171 (Sup. Ct. Kings Co. 1994).

Hearing; witnesses.—Prosecutor was not required to produce at the suppression hearing the officer who sent a radio transmission of a burglary in progress, resulting in defendant's arrest, where defendant never specifically challenged the reliability of such transmission. People v. Makedon, 108 A.D.2d 826, 485 N.Y.S.2d 103 (2d Dept. 1985).

Juvenile entitled to pretrial suppression hearing.—In Family Court, a juvenile respondent in a designated felony case is entitled to the same procedural right to a pretrial hearing afforded his adult and juvenile offender counterparts in criminal court; the same judge who will preside over fact finding can preside over the pre-trial hearing. In re James A., 102 Misc. 2d 670, 424 N.Y.S.2d 334 (Family Ct. Bronx Co. 1980).

Matter for suppression hearing.—Evidence need not be suppressed if it is gathered in a manner consistent with the Federal Constitution and merely in violation of some state law or ordinance. People v. Dyla, 142 A.D.2d 423, 536 N.Y.S.2d 799 (2d Dept. 1988).

Motion to suppress.—Court did not err in permitting the witness, who had not participated in any pretrial identification procedures, to make an in-court identification of the defendant. People v. Merced, 137 A.D.2d 562, 524 N.Y.S.2d 108 (2d Dept. 1988).

Motion to suppress; infant witnesses.—A civilian physician's questioning of an infant witness is not a ground for suppression nor is it a specifically authorized ground for a hearing on a motion to suppress. People v. Michael M., 162 Misc. 2d 803, 618 N.Y.S.2d 171 (Sup. Ct. Kings Co. 1994).

Motion to suppress; standing.—The mere fact that a defendant is charged with constructive possession does not endow him with automatic standing. People v. Wesley, 73 N.Y.2d 351, 540 N.Y.S.2d 757, 538 N.E.2d 76 (1989).

—Despite the fact that defendant had allegedly stayed over at the apartment several times, he lacked standing where his only relationship with the apartment was that his drug supplier resided there and he had gone to the apartment for the sole purpose of obtaining heroin. People v. Rodriguez, 69 N.Y.2d 159, 513 N.Y.S.2d 75, 505 N.E.2d 586 (1987).

—The defendant had no standing to challenge a search of his co-defendant. People v. Paige, 154 A.D.2d 318, 546 N.Y.S.2d 607, 608 (1st Dept. 1989).

—It was not necessary for defendant to assert a proprietary interest in the gun seized from him where it was clear that defendant's person had been subjected to search and seizure. People v. Lee, 130 A.D.2d 400, 515 N.Y.S.2d 260 (1st Dept. 1987).

—Defendant did not have standing where the evidence showed that he was merely a transient in his grandfather's house, who had no expectation of privacy in the "baby boy's room." People v. Walker, 150 A.D.2d 740, 540 N.Y.S.2d 838 (2d Dept. 1989).

—Defendant lacked standing where, by his own admission, he did not reside in the apartment in which the drugs were found and he did not possess a key to the apartment. People v. Daniel, 152 A.D.2d 742, 544 N.Y.S.2d 194 (2d Dept. 1989).

—Defendant lacked standing to contest seizure of drugs where they were found hidden under a rear tire of a parked car and behind the license plate of the car. People v. Jackson, 143 A.D.2d 471, 532 N.Y.S.2d 808 (3d Dept. 1988).

—For movant to have standing to contest an illegal pen register, that person must have a proprietary interest in the premises or telephone wiretapped, have had conversation(s) intercepted, or be the subject of the wiretap. People v. Varacalli, 154 Misc. 2d 805, 596 N.Y.S.2d 346 (Sup. Ct. Kings Co. 1993).

—To have standing to ask for suppression of eavesdropping evidence, the government must have listened to movant's conversation or have tapped his telephone. People v. Wakefield Financial Corp., 155 Misc. 2d 775, 590 N.Y.S.2d 382 (Sup. Ct. N.Y. Co. 1992).

Retroactivity.—Supreme Court of the United States decision in *Dunaway v. New York* (442 U.S. 200) is not retroactive. People v. Wise, 104 Misc. 2d 77, 427 N.Y.S.2d 691 (Sup. Ct. Kings Co. 1980), *aff'd,* 82 A.D.2d 869, 440 N.Y.S.2d 266 (2d Dept. 1981).

Waiver of *Dunaway.*—Defendant waived his right to a hearing based on Dunaway v. New York, 442 U.S. 200, 99 S. Ct. 2248, 60 L. Ed. 2d 824, where his arguments at the original *Huntley* hearing were directed solely to the alleged violations of defendant's fifth amendment rights. People v. Cappiello, 85 A.D.2d 608, 444 N.Y.S.2d 681 (2d Dept. 1981).

***Wade* hearings.**—*See* People v. Dixon, 85 N.Y.2d 218, 623 N.Y.S.2d 813, 647 N.E.2d 1321 (1995).

—The court properly denied a "Wade" hearing because identity was not an issue; therefore, suggestiveness was not a concern. People v. Frederick, 196 A.D.2d 91, 602 N.Y.S.2d 107 (1st Dept. 1993).

§ 710.20. Motion to suppress evidence; in general; grounds for.

Upon motion of a defendant who (a) is aggrieved by unlawful or improper acquisition of evidence and has reasonable cause to believe that such may be offered against him in a criminal action, or (b) claims that improper identification testimony may be offered against him in a criminal action, a court may, under circumstances prescribed in this article, order that such evidence be suppressed or excluded upon the ground that it:

1. Consists of tangible property obtained by means of an unlawful search and seizure under circumstances precluding admissibility thereof in a criminal action against such defendant; or

2. Consists of a record or potential testimony reciting or describing declarations, conversations, or other communications overheard, intercepted, accessed, or recorded by means of eavesdropping, or observations made by means of video surveillance, obtained under circumstances precluding admissibility thereof in a criminal action against such defendant; or

3. Consists of a record or potential testimony reciting or describing a statement of such defendant involuntarily made, within the meaning of section 60.45; or

4. Was obtained as a result of other evidence obtained in a manner described in subdivisions one, two and three; or

5. Consists of a chemical test of the defendant's blood administered in violation of the provisions of subdivision three of section eleven hundred ninety-four of the vehicle and traffic law, subdivision eight of section forty-nine-a of the navigation law, subdivision seven of section 25.24 of the parks, recreation and historic preservation law, or any other applicable law; or

6. Consists of potential testimony regarding an observation of the defendant either at the time or place of the commission of the offense or upon some other occasion relevant to the case, which potential testimony would not be admissible upon the prospective trial of such charge owing to an improperly made previous identification of the defendant by the prospective witness.

7. Consists of information obtained by means of a pen register or trap and trace device installed or used in violation of the provisions of article seven hundred five of this chapter.

Amended by L. 1976, Ch. 8; L. 1982, Ch. 214; L. 1983, Ch. 481; L. 1988, Chs. 47, 744; L. 1992, Ch. 805, eff. Nov. 1, 1992, amending subd. 5; L. 1998, Ch. 629, eff. Nov. 1, 1999, amending subd. 5.

ANNOTATIONS

SEARCH AND SEIZURE

Abandonment of property.—Property is deemed abandoned when the defendant gives up the expectation of privacy in the object or place searched by voluntarily and knowingly discarding the property. A court will find defendant's intention to relinquish an expectation of privacy if the circumstances reveal a purposeful divestment of possession of the item searched. People v. Ramirez-Portoreal, 88 N.Y.2d 99, 643 N.Y.S.2d 502, 666 N.E.2d 207 (1996).

—The throwing or dropping of the property after an illegal detention is not an intentional abandonment and a warrantless search is impermissible. People v. Howard, 50 N.Y.2d 583, 430 N.Y.S.2d 578, 408 N.E.2d 908, *cert. denied,* 449 U.S. 1023 (1980).

—Defendant's suppression motion was properly denied without a hearing, where defendant expressly disputed the People's allegation that he had dropped a bag of cocaine to the ground, and disclaimed that the drugs had ever been in his possession. People v. Ramirez, 281 A.D.2d 332, 723 N.Y.S.2d 13 (1st Dept. 2001).

—Although the police improperly used a ruse to remove defendant from the privacy of his home to effect a warrantless arrest, the admission into evidence of the ring found in the police vehicle was proper since the defendant's abandonment of the ring attenuated the due process violation. People v. Bannister, 208 A.D.2d 467, 617 N.Y.S.2d 324 (1st Dept. 1994).

—The deliberate and immediate flight from the scene by the defendant and his companion constituted an abandonment of the property left behind; property which has in fact been abandoned is outside the protection of constitutional provisions. People v. Bloomfield, 156 A.D.2d 572, 549 N.Y.S.2d 78 (2d Dept. 1989).

—Trial court properly denied defendant's motion to suppress where the evidence indicated that the defendant had abandoned the property prior to its retrieval by the police. People v. Fraumani, 108 A.D.2d 756, 485 N.Y.S.2d 100 (2d Dept. 1985).

—Suppression unwarranted where transit authority police officer noticed two people on platform carrying packages, and when he approached them they dropped everything and ran up the stairs. Property seized at station was abandoned by defendants prior to their arrest and officer was well within his authority to approach for purpose of inquiry since the abandonment raised suspicion to the level of probable cause to arrest. People v. Chestnut, 91 A.D.2d 981, 457 N.Y.S.2d 573 (2d Dept. 1983).

—An abandonment occurs when the act of discarding property is an independent act involving a calculated risk, as opposed to a spontaneous reaction to a sudden and unexpected confrontation with the police. People v. Martinez, 206 A.D.2d 693, 614 N.Y.S.2d 787 (3d Dept. 1994).

—Where police had probable cause to arrest defendant, his disposal of bag containing marijuana during chase constituted a valid abandonment. People v. Stone, 132 A.D.2d 902, 518 N.Y.S.2d 461 (3d Dept. 1987).

—Radar detectors thrown from the car windows during police pursuit were abandoned and not seized as the product of any illegal police activity because the police had a right to stop and check defendant's car. People v. Buckley, 147 A.D.2d 898, 537 N.Y.S.2d 356 (4th Dept. 1989), aff'd, 75 N.Y.2d 843, 552 N.Y.S.2d 912, 552 N.E.2d 160.

Administrative inspection; motion denied.—A search conducted, pursuant to VTL § 415(n)(a)(5), clearly falls within the well-established exception to the warrant requirement for administrative inspections of "closely regulated" business. New York v. Burger, 482 U.S. 691, 107 S. Ct. 2636, 96 L. Ed. 2d 601 (1987).

—Routine search of an inmate's cell and person was a reasonable procedure for the purpose of maintaining security at a correctional institution, and was not a search in violation of any constitutional right to the expectation of privacy. People v. Frye, 144 A.D.2d 714, 534 N.Y.S.2d 735 (3d Dept. 1988).

— Vague suspicions of criminality should not confer immunity from regulatory inspections upon the subject premises; all premises, shady ones and clean ones, should be treated alike and subject to bona fide regulatory inspections. People v. Brigante, 131 Misc. 2d 708, 501 N.Y.S.2d 583 (Sup. Ct. Kings Co. 1986).

—Stopping the defendant's tow truck which was towing an automobile that had no visible damage to it, in a high crime area, did not violate the defendant's fourth amendment rights; since the towing truck business has been closely regulated, the owners consent to the stop by advance knowledge and submission to the license requirements and there is the presence of exigent circumstances, therefore, it qualifies as an exception to the warrant requirement of the fourth amendment. People v. Velez, 109 Misc. 2d 853, 441 N.Y.S.2d 176 (N.Y. Crim. Ct. 1981).

Administrative search; entry.—Where a warrantless search of defendant's automobile salvage yard was not undertaken for administrative purposes, the evidence obtained must be suppressed. People v. Pace, 65 N.Y.2d 684, 491 N.Y.S.2d 618, 481 N.E.2d 250 (1985).

—Since there is no suggestion in the record that officer's warrantless entry into defendant's auto junkyard was for a purpose other than to inspect the premises pursuant to the statutory scheme set forth in the Vehicle and Traffic Law and the New York City Charter, the subsequent arrest of defendant and seizure of stolen property was proper and lawful. People v. Cusumano, 108 A.D.2d 752, 484 N.Y.S.2d 909 (2d Dept. 1985).

—Defendant was entitled to reopen the suppression hearing to determine whether the ostensible administrative search of a junkyard was merely a pretext to disguise a search for evidence where counsel first learned during the trial that the sergeant who led the search might have had prior knowledge of criminal activity at the junkyard. People v. Brigante, 115 A.D.2d 547, 496 N.Y.S.2d 70 (2d Dept. 1985).

Administrative proceeding.—Evidence that is the product of an unlawful search by police and is suppressed in a criminal prosecution may be used in an administrative proceeding commenced by the Division of State Police. Boyd v. Constantine, 81 N.Y.2d 189, 597 N.Y.S.2d 605, 613 N.E.2d 511 (1993).

Anonymous call; motion to suppress.—Defendant's motion to suppress was denied where the police responded to an anonymous call stating that two men armed with guns were standing in front of a building; upon arriving at the scene the officers observed two men standing at the location and while frisking the defendant the officer observed a shopping bag about twelve inches from defendant's leg, looking inside the bag without touching it, the officer observed glassine envelopes with rubber bands around them; under the circumstances the defendants had no reasonable or legitimate expectation of privacy with respect to the shopping bag. People v. George, 84 A.D.2d 731, 444 N.Y.S.2d 84 (1st Dept. 1981).

—Defendant's motion to suppress was denied where the anonymous tip was sufficient to trigger the police officers right of inquiry, since once on the scene, they observed a car the same type and color of the informant's tip except that one letter of the registration was wrong and officers approached with their guns unholstered, it was not unreasonable because the informant told the police that the occupants were armed and the subsequent seizure of the gun from under the front seat, after the officer observed one defendant lean forward was justified. People v. Foster, 83 A.D.2d 282, 443 N.Y.S.2d 835 (1st Dept. 1981).

—Defendant's motion to suppress was denied where police received a radio run advising that a "male, black, wearing brown shorts, shirt with purple polka dots and a white towel around his neck was firing a gun," and one of the people standing near that location as the officers responded to the call was the defendant who fit the description of the man described in the radio run; as the officers approached the defendant, they observed him take a vinyl bag which he had been carrying and place it on top of a garbage bin, at which point a man seated on top of the bin pushed it behind him toward the back of the bin; the frisk of the defendant and the subsequent retrieval and search of the bag was proper in order to protect the officers. People v. Lambert, 84 A.D.2d 849, 444 N.Y.S.2d 168 (2d Dept. 1981).

—Defendant's motion to suppress was denied where an anonymous caller stated that three Hispanic men, seated in a brown Pontiac, at a certain location and identified the license plate number, were passing around guns and a computer check of the plate number revealed that the license plate was registered to a gold Chevrolet and upon arrival at the scene the car was placed under surveillance and the police observed only one man in the car; then upon seeing the defendant and a friend enter the car, police approached the car with their guns drawn and defendant was ordered out of the car; when he exited, police saw a bulge on defendant's left side near his waistband and a pat down revealed a weapon. The police had probable cause for the search and the arrest. People v. Dominquez, 84 A.D.2d 820, 444 N.Y.S.2d 120 (2d Dept. 1981).

Appeal.—The People can appeal to an intermediate appellate court to challenge a trial court's ruling suppressing the results of a consented-to chemical test; the People's appeal options under CPL 450.20(8) incorporate the whole of CPL § 710.20. People v. Ayala, 89 N.Y.2d 874, 653 N.Y.S.2d 92, 553 N.E.2d 960 (1996).

Blood samples.—The fact that the defendant was incapable of consenting to the taking of a blood sample does not violate his privilege against self-incrimination. People v. Kates, 77 A.D.2d 417, 433 N.Y.S.2d 938 (4th Dept. 1980), aff'd, 53 N.Y.2d 591, 444 N.Y.S.2d 446, 428 N.E.2d 852 (1981).

Body cavity search.—The body cavity search of defendant incident to his arrest was unreasonable and invalid because the People failed to offer any evidence of exigent circumstances to justify dispensing with the warrant requirement and the record is devoid of any evidence from which an officer might reasonably have believed he was confronted with an emergency. People v. More, 97 N.Y.2d 209, 738 N.Y.S.2d 667, 764 N.E.2d 967 (2002).

—A visual body cavity search usually means visual inspection of a naked body, including genitals and anus, without any contact, and it is more invasive than a strip search. While a visual body cavity search might be necessary to preserve order or security in situations in which a defendant is about to enter a jail, a prison, or a cell with other detainees, these considerations were not present at the time of the body cavity search of the defendant, who had not yet been charged, arraigned, or sent to central booking for processing and who was not lodged in a courthouse with other arrestees. People v. Barnville, 7 Misc. 3d 688, 794 N.Y.S.2d 847 (Sup. Ct. Bronx Co. 2005).

Border.—Where search was the functional equivalent of a border search, it was not necessary that the suspicion justifying the pat-down search rise to the level of that which must support a stop and frisk in a domestic situation. People v. Silva, 178 A.D.2d 446, 577 N.Y.S.2d 123 (2d Dept. 1991).

Commercial premises; no expectation of privacy.—A police officer who observed an apparent commercial operation with a light on and the door unlocked was justified in entering the premises and after observing illegal gambling therein arresting the defendants and they could not claim a reasonable expectation of privacy merely because their ineffectual subterfuge of a seemingly innocent business operation failed to achieve its purpose. People v. Perez, 78 A.D.2d 703, 432 N.Y.S.2d 497 (2d Dept. 1980).

Common-carrier employee.—The prior search and seizure of a parcel accomplished in another city by an airline employee, which parcel was turned over to the police who found it contained illicit drugs and marked it and returned it to the carrier for shipment to New York, the warrantless police search and seizure of the parcel addressed to defendant at the parcel's airport destination was not constitutionally offensive as the act of the airline employee was private conduct. People v. Adler, 50 N.Y.2d 730, 431 N.Y.S.2d 412, 409 N.E.2d 888, *cert. denied,* 449 U.S. 1014 (1980).

Curtilage.—Where police officer, while observing a building used as headquarters for a motorcycle gang preparing to engage in a gang war, observed two members deposit a package at the rear of a garage unattached to the clubhouse, his subsequent seizure of the package was lawful since the clubhouse was not defendant's place of residence nor did he individually have any proprietary interest therein. People v. Doerbecker, 48 A.D.2d 120, 367 N.Y.S.2d 976 (2d Dept. 1975), *aff'd,* 39 N.Y.2d 448, 384 N.Y.S.2d 400, 348 N.E.2d 875 (1976).

—Trial court should have held an in camera examination of the informant even though defendant did not request it where apart from the information given to the arresting officer by the informant, there was insufficient evidence to justify the detention and frisk of the defendant. People v. Fulton, 83 A.D.2d 856, 441 N.Y.S.2d 736 (2d Dept. 1981).

Consent.—Defendant's girlfriend had actual and apparent authority to consent to the search of an apartment; although she did not have a key, she, defendant, and their child lived at the one-room apartment on weekends, and the baby's clothing, carriage, and crib were in the apartment. People v. Lopez, 291 A.D.2d 279, 738 N.Y.S.2d 308 (1st Dept. 2002).

—Fact that police officers pretended to be parole officers when they spoke with defendant's wife did not vitiate consent to the search. People v. Entzminger, 163 A.D.2d 138, 558 N.Y.S.2d 525 (1st Dept. 1990).

—The burden of proof rests upon the People to establish that the consent was freely and voluntarily given; consent by person with whom defendant shared the apartment given in the presence of armed police officers using walkie-talkies is not voluntary. People v. Benitez, 77 A.D.2d 537, 430 N.Y.S.2d 287 (1st Dept. 1980). *See also* People v. Brown, 76 A.D.2d 196, 430 N.Y.S.2d 303 (1st Dept. 1980).

—Absent proof that the person who consented to the police entry had common authority over the box based on mutual use or joint access, the warrantless seizure of the box was improper. Furthermore, the seizure of the box could not be justified pursuant to the plain view doctrine because the discovery of the box by the police was not inadvertent. People v. Coston, 271 A.D.2d 694, 706 N.Y.S.2d 732 (2d Dept. 2000).

—Search violated Fourth Amendment since estranged husband had no authority to consent to search of defendant wife's apartment especially in light of fact that husband needed police assistance to gain admittance to apartment because locks had been changed in an apparent effort to exclude him. People v. Yalti, 76 A.D.2d 847, 428 N.Y.S.2d 330 (2d Dept. 1980).

—The voluntariness of a consent to search is not vitiated, *per se,* by the failure to give *Miranda* warnings to an accused while subject to custodial interrogation as there is no requirement that specific fourth amendment warnings be given to a suspect in custody. People v. Tremblay, 77 A.D.2d 807, 430 N.Y.S.2d 757 (3d Dept. 1980).

—Police entered defendant's residence with the voluntary consent of a guest who had been living there for about one week, and thus, there is no merit to defendant's contention that the court should have suppressed his statement to the police as the product of an unlawful arrest of defendant in his home. People v. Lewis, 277 A.D.2d 1010, 716 N.Y.S.2d 204 (4th Dept. 2000).

—Voluntary consent of defendant's girlfriend to a search of the premises and removal of the guns rendered the warrantless search valid. People v. Kemp, 273 A.D.2d 806, 708 N.Y.S.2d 542 (4th Dept. 2000), *cert. denied,* 532 U.S. 977 (2001).

—Court properly denied defendant's motion to suppress physical evidence seized from his grandfather's home because the grandfather consented to the search and the defendant had no legitimate expectation of privacy in the duffel bag belonging to his girlfriend. People v. Gatti, 277 A.D.2d 1041, 716 N.Y.S.2d 182 (4th Dept. 2000).

—In obtaining consent, it is not necessarily an improper tactic for the police to capitalize on the reluctance of a defendant to involve his family in a pending investigation, especially where the police have a legal basis to carry out their threats to arrest the defendant's family members. People v. LaDuke, 206 A.D.2d 859, 614 N.Y.S.2d 851 (4th Dept. 1994).

—By statute, consent to a blood test is implied as to an unconscious operator. People v. Grant, 192 A.D.2d 798, 596 N.Y.S.2d 529 (3d Dept. 1993).

Consent for police to enter room.—Question of whether defendant's wife voluntarily consented to the search of their apartment presented a mixed question of law and fact which was beyond review by the Court of Appeals. People v. Thatch, 71 N.Y.2d 906, 528 N.Y.S.2d 527, 523 N.E.2d 814 (1988).

—Where defendant voluntarily consented to a search of his person by two undercover police officers by responding to inquiry as to whether he had brought any drugs back with him from New York City, "no, you can check if you want," his action in suddenly becoming evasive and attempting to conceal a gold-colored pin on his underwear during the search did not effect a repudiation of consent. People v. Meredith, 49 N.Y.2d 1038, 429 N.Y.S.2d 555, 407 N.E.2d 402 (1980).

—Consent of female, who shared apartment with defendant, provided the police with sufficient authority to conduct a warrantless search of the bedroom closet in defendant's apartment even though defendant was present and refused to give his consent. People v. Cosme, 48 N.Y.2d 286, 422 N.Y.S.2d 652, 397 N.E.2d 1319 (1979).

—The consent of the defendant's sister was sufficient predicate for lawful police presence in the hallway from which the observations were made; the mere fact that the consent was limited to entry for purposes of discussion and not for a search could not logically limit the proximity of the consent to only a location where the defendant was located for it would defy common sense to require police officers to close their eyes to anything except the immediate subject which formed the predicate for the consensual entry. People v. Lawrence, 177 A.D.2d 348, 576 N.Y.S.2d 120 (1st Dept. 1991).

—Police had the requisite consent to enter the premises when defendant's uncle, a person with ostensible authority on the premises, effectively consented to the police presence, if not explicitly, then tacitly, by failing to direct them to leave, or in any other fashion indicating that they did not have his permission to remain. People v. Schof, 136 A.D.2d 578, 523 N.Y.S.2d 179 (2d Dept. 1988).

—Defendant's consent to search was not vitiated by the failure to advise the defendant of his right to refuse consent. People v. Conklin, 139 A.D.2d 156, 531 N.Y.S.2d 374 (3d Dept. 1988).

Search and seizure; roommate's authority to consent.—Defendant's roommate had authority to consent to police entry into the motel room they shared; such consent, even if given while roommate was in custody and in violation of the roommate's Fourth Amendment rights, would be valid as against the defendant. People v. Brown, 95 A.D.2d 569, 469 N.Y.S.2d 159 (3d Dept. 1983).

Consent to search; voluntariness.—Appellate Division erred in holding, as a matter of law, that defendant's wife's consent to enter their apartment was involuntary; it is not possible to state that under no view of the evidence could the entry be found to be voluntary; the case was remitted for a factual determination since Court of Appeals' power to review is limited to questions of law. People v. Rivera, 60 N.Y.2d 910, 470 N.Y.S.2d 577, 458 N.E.2d 1254 (1983).

—Defendant's wife voluntarily consented to the search of the apartment for a gun; the consent was in writing and was obtained in a calm, non-coercive atmosphere, and the consent encompassed any location where a gun might have been secreted, including a down jacket. People v. Bruno, 294 A.D.2d 179, 743 N.Y.S.2d 401 (1st Dept. 2002).

Drug detection by trained dog not search.—Police dogs which sniff out drugs on a person or his luggage do nothing more than smell air surrounding that person which is not a search since there is no intrusion or search of person or luggage and there is no right to privacy for odors emanating from luggage checked with a commercial airline. People v. Price, 54 N.Y.2d 557, 446 N.Y.S.2d 906, 431 N.E.2d 267 (1981).

—The canine sniff of the exterior of the defendant's apartment did not infringe upon any legitimate and reasonable expectation of privacy and thus did not constitute a search within the meaning of the Fourth Amendment of the United States Constitution or New York Constitution. People v. Dunn, 155 A.D.2d 75, 553 N.Y.S.2d 257, 265 (4th Dept. 1990).

Exclusionary rule inapplicable.—The exclusionary rule does not apply to the discovery of evidence in response to the untainted information gained from an independent source. Here, although police initially discovered defendant's possession of gold chain during an unlawful search, they did not go to defendant's cell and inquiry about the chain until after they learned that the chain had been stolen from the victim. People v. Coste, 272 A.D.2d 205, 708 N.Y.S.2d 376 (1st Dept. 2000).

Hallway.—The internal hallway area of a rooming house was part of the defendant's home for Fourth Amendment purposes. People v. Garriga, 189 A.D.2d 236, 596 N.Y.S.2d 25 (1st Dept. 1993).

Hypnosis evidence.—Arkansas *per se* rule excluding all posthypnosis testimony infringes impermissibly on the right of the defendant to testify on his or her own behalf; in this case, the defective condition of the gun corroborated the details defendant remembered about the shooting, the tape recordings of the hypnosis session provided some means to evaluate the hypnosis, the trial judge concluded that the doctor did not suggest responses by asking leading questions, and thus an argument for admissibility of defendant's testimony was presented which must be considered by the trial court. Rock v. Arkansas, 483 U.S. 44, 107 S. Ct. 2704, 97 L. Ed. 2d 37 (1987).

Hypnosis evidence; inadmissible.—Testimony hypnotically produced may not be used at trial because hypnosis has not gained general acceptance in the scientific community. People v. Hughes, 88 A.D.2d 17, 452 N.Y.S.2d 929 (4th Dept. 1982), *aff'd,* 59 N.Y.2d 523, 466 N.Y.S.2d 255, 453 N.E.2d 484 (1983), *cert. denied,* 492 U.S. 908 (1989).

Arrest warrant; search incidental thereto.—Untaxed cartons of cigarettes seized from defendant's garage by Tax Department investigators were not suppressed since the investigators were lawfully on defendant's property to execute a warrant for his arrest for cigarette tax offenses, and the cartons in question were observed by the investigators in defendant's garage while they were at the threshold of the garage executing the warrant. People v. Grande, 45 N.Y.2d 717, 408 N.Y.S.2d 469, 380 N.E.2d 295 (1978).

—A search for and seizure of defendant's shotgun was not invalid where police, under a prior arrest warrant issued for defendant, responded to informant's tip that defendant was at his mother's house and was armed with a shotgun; the fact that the informant's information was partially verified when police found defendant justified careful search of house on basis that defendant might be armed; the court emphasized that police discovered the shotgun in the course of their search for the defendant. People v. Etcheverry, 39 N.Y.2d 252, 383 N.Y.S.2d 292, 347 N.E.2d 654 (1976).

Arrest warrant; validity of.—Court rejected defendant's argument that physical evidence at the time of his arrest should have been suppressed because the arrest warrant was invalid, since the defendant offered no proof that the Judiciary Law was violated by the issuance of the warrant or that actual bias influenced the court's determination of probable cause. People v. Roberts, 6 A.D.3d 942, 775 N.Y.S.2d 424 (3d Dept. 2004).

Defendant charged with possession.—New York follows United States v. Salvucci, 448 U.S. 83, 100 S. Ct. 2547, 65 L. Ed. 2d 619 (1980), which holds that a defendant charged with a possessory crime may only contest an allegedly illegal search and seizure if he had a "legitimate expectation of privacy" in the area searched and to the extent this decision is in conflict with People v. Waddy, 63 A.D.2d 492, 407 N.Y.S.2d 522, the latter is overruled. People v. McCloud, 81 A.D.2d 645, 438 N.Y.S.2d 151 (2d Dept. 1981).

Federal court; motion; effect.—The denial of a motion to suppress in the United States District Court was an intermediate determination, and was not binding on the county court considering a similar motion. People v. Rizzo, 31 N.Y.2d 998, 341 N.Y.S.2d 452, 293 N.E.2d 827 (1973).

Generally.—Random drug screening constitutes a search and seizure within the meaning of the Federal and State Constitutions. Delabara v. Nassau County Police Dept., 83 N.Y.2d 367, 610 N.Y.S.2d 928, 632 N.E.2d 1251 (1994).

—The requirement that searches and seizures be reasonable limits the police use of unnecessarily frightening or offensive methods of investigation. People v. Henry, 185 A.D.2d 1, 591 N.Y.S.2d 1018 (1st Dept. 1992).

—Where evidence was found by a private citizen, no Fourth Amendment considerations were implicated. People v. Lawton, 159 A.D.2d 302, 552 N.Y.S.2d 580 (1st Dept. 1990).

—Officer's use of a flashlight did not constitute an unreasonable intrusion. People v. Wallace, 153 A.D.2d 59, 549 N.Y.S.2d 515, 517 (2d Dept. 1990).

—Searches and seizures inside a home without a warrant are presumptively unreasonable, absent a showing of probable cause and exigent circumstances. People v. Stockman, 159 Misc. 2d 730, 606 N.Y.S.2d 864 (Justice Ct. Erie Co. 1994).

Good faith.—Court declined, on State constitutional grounds, to apply the good-faith exception the United States Supreme court enunciated in *United States v. Leon,* (104 S. Ct. 3405, 82 L. Ed. 2d 677 [1984]), where under the facts of the case before the Court, its application would completely frustrate the exclusionary rule since the police did not have probable cause for the warrantless arrest. People v. Bigelow, 66 N.Y.2d 417, 497 N.Y.S.2d 630, 488 N.E.2d 451 (1985).

Hearing transcript; timely demand.—The request for a transcript followed closely upon the conclusion of the pretrial suppression hearing, and ample justification was shown for defense counsel's brief delay in making the request. Although the jury had meanwhile been drawn, no other trial proceedings had as yet taken place, and the demand was held timely. People v. Sanders, 31 N.Y.2d 463, 341 N.Y.S.2d 305, 293 N.E.2d 555 (1973).

Inevitable discovery.—People are entitled to an initial determination by suppression court of factual questions raised by their invocation of inevitable discovery rule, which they rely on in asserting that absent a consent search of rental van, a constitutionally valid inventory search would have been conducted and would have revealed the dead body and murder weapon in steamer trunk; case remitted to Supreme Court for further proceedings. People v. Turriago, 90 N.Y.2d 77, 659 N.Y.S.2d 183, 681 N.E.2d 350 (1997).

—The theory of inevitable discovery is essentially a safety valve for the exclusionary rule to be used when the constitutional violation is of technical dimension and could not be used to countenance the breaking into a locked garage by administrative investigators. People v. Sciacca, 45 N.Y.2d 122, 408 N.Y.S.2d 22, 379 N.E.2d 1153 (1978).

—The inevitable discovery rule cannot be relied upon where the testimony at the suppression does not establish to a very high degree of probability that the evidence in question would have been obtained independently of the tainted source. People v. Walker, 198 A.D.2d 785, 605 N.Y.S.2d 726 (1st Dept. 1993).

—Suppression of cocaine seized in the car was properly denied even though the unlawful arrest tainted the evidence as it would be admissible under the doctrine of "inevitable discovery" in that the officers would "inevitably" have impounded the car and found the cocaine. People v. Buffardi, 92 A.D.2d 899, 459 N.Y.S.2d 893 (2d Dept. 1983).

Invitee.—An invitee must confine himself to such parts of the premises as are included within an express or implied invitation and may not without further invitation go to out-of-the-way places on the premises wholly disconnected from and in no way pertaining to the business in hand; the invitation extends to those parts of the premises which are so arranged as to lead an invitee reasonably to think that they are open to him. *See* People v. Johnson, 105 Misc. 2d 561, 432 N.Y.S.2d 608 (Sup. Ct. N.Y. Co. 1980).

Motion to suppress; erroneous suppression.—Court erroneously suppressed pliers which had been abandoned by defendants on the ground that they were not introduced into evidence at suppression hearing; at a suppression hearing, the judge may order the exclusion or suppression of evidence only on any one of the six grounds contained in CPL § 240.70. People v. Sharrieff, 117 A.D.2d 635, 497 N.Y.S.2d 959 (2d Dept. 1986).

New hearing; exigent circumstances.—The People are entitled to a new hearing on a motion to suppress after the Supreme Court of the United States held that the statute under which the police officers entered and searched the defendant's apartment, without a warrant, to make a felony arrest was declared unconstitutional and the trial court at the original suppression hearing in reliance on the statute barred any testimony as to exigent circumstances; the People should be given an opportunity to submit proof of exigent circumstances, if any, at a new hearing. People v. Payton, 51 N.Y.2d 169, 433 N.Y.S.2d 61, 412 N.E.2d 1288 (1980).

—Defendant's conviction for criminal possession of a weapon was reversed and he was entitled to a hearing on his motion to suppress where there was no forfeiture of his constitutional right to challenge the seizure of evidence which was the result of a police chase that had no justification from the start. People v. Glover, 82 A.D.2d 43, 441 N.Y.S.2d 242 (1st Dept. 1981).

Motion to suppress breathalyzer results.—Court properly denied the defendant's application to file a motion addressing the integrity of the ampoules used in a breathalyzer test because the motion was not a motion to suppress. People v. Nania, 177 A.D.2d 1015, 578 N.Y.S.2d 34 (4th Dept. 1991).

—Results of breathalyzer suppressed because it was administered, without court order, more than two hours after defendant's arrest. People v. Ali, 151 Misc. 2d 742, 573 N.Y.S.2d 575 (Crim. Ct. N.Y. Co. 1991).

—Because the Legislature did not state that breathalyzer tests were grounds upon which evidence could be suppressed, People could not appeal from the trial court's order to suppress defendant's breathalyzer results. People v. Cardenas, 165 Misc. 2d 587, 632 N.Y.S.2d 937 (App. Term, 1st Dept. 1995).

—When defendant's request to phone his attorney was denied, his right to counsel was violated and breathalyzer test that was administered in mobile van, with phone booth 5 minutes away, was suppressed. People v. Rinaldi, 107 Misc. 2d 916, 436 N.Y.S.2d 156 (Monroe Co. Ct. 1981).

Motion to suppress; search and seizure.—Narcotics seized pursuant to a no-knock search after 9 p.m. were admissible as evidence, even where the affidavit authorizing the warrant was alleged to be insufficient to allow a nighttime search of the premises. People v. Rose, 31 N.Y.2d 1036, 342 N.Y.S.2d 66, 294 N.E.2d 852 (1973).

Motion to suppress; search warrant based on prior illegal search.—Because the application for a warrant to search defendant's apartment was based on a prior search and seizure which a court had ruled illegal, evidence seized form defendant's residence had to be suppressed as fruit of the poisonous tree. People v. Cirrincione, 207 A.D.2d 1031, 617 N.Y.S.2d 94 (4th Dept. 1994).

Open fields.—An owner does not have a reasonable expectation of privacy in open fields and woods where no precautions have been taken to exclude the public from entry. People v. Reynolds, 71 N.Y.2d 552, 528 N.Y.S.2d 15, 17 523 N.E.2d 291 (1988).

—The warrantless helicopter surveillance by police of an open field on defendant's property did not violate defendant's Fourth Amendment rights. People v. Abbot, 105 A.D.2d 1029, 483 N.Y.S.2d 452 (3d Dept. 1984).

Plain view.—Defendant's conviction was sustained where an investigating detective while viewing the crime scene to better understand the statements given him, saw on a dresser a note in plain view addressed to defendant's husband which incriminated her; the seizure was lawful because the initial police presence on the scene was proper and the note was in plain view. People v. Dancey, 84 A.D.2d 763, 443 N.Y.S.2d 776 (2d Dept. 1981), *aff'd,* 57 N.Y.2d 1033, 457 N.Y.S.2d 782, 444 N.E.2d 32 (1982).

—Absent evidence of intent to exclude the public, the entry way

to a person's house offers implied permission to approach and knock on the front door; thus where police utilized an unobstructed access to defendant's home for the purpose of making inquiry, no warrant required. People v. Kozlowski, 69 N.Y.2d 769, 513 N.Y.S.2d 101, 505 N.E.2d 611 (1987).

—Defendant waived his expectation of privacy and his motion to suppress was denied where upon seeing the police, two men, including the defendant, quickly entered the house and immediately, thereafter, a gun was thrown out the door and landed on the front lawn. People v. Ford, 82 A.D.2d 923, 440 N.Y.S.2d 676 (2d Dept. 1981).

—Court rejected the proposed extension of the plain view exception and concluded that justifying the warrantless search on the basis of the items felt during a protective pat-down would be contrary to both the State and Federal Constitutions; the "plain touch" exception is rejected. People v. Diaz, 81 N.Y.2d 106, 595 N.Y.S.2d 940, 941, 612 N.E.2d 298 (1993).

—Defendant's suppression motion was denied when the police entered his apartment, with his consent, to view the crime scene from his back window and while in the apartment they observed in plain view a tennis shoe lying on its side on the floor in a nearby open doorway; the tread of the tennis shoe resembled the footprint discovered earlier at the scene of the crime and after comparing the shoe to a photograph made of that footprint were justified in arresting the defendant. People v. Houle, 85 A.D.2d 751, 445 N.Y.S.2d 255 (3d Dept. 1981).

Presence of victim at execution of search warrant does not require suppression of evidence seized.—Evidence seized pursuant to a valid search warrant need not be suppressed because a crime victim, or other civilian with relevant knowledge concerning the items being sought, is present during the search and assists the police in the execution of the warrant by identifying stolen goods or other evidence of a crime; with regard to the sighting by such a civilian of items not specified in the warrant, the rules regarding plain view findings by the police should govern. People v. Boyd, 123 Misc. 2d 634, 474 N.Y.S.2d 661 (Sup. Ct. N.Y. Co. 1984).

Reasonableness of search and seizure; inquiry required.—In determining whether a search and seizure is reasonable, courts must undertake a dual inquiry: whether the officer's action was justified at its inception, and whether it was reasonably related in scope to the circumstances which justified the interference in the first place. People v. William II, 98 N.Y.2d 93, 745 N.Y.S.2d 792, 772 N.E.2d 1150 (2002).

Search by private person.—The action of the hotel security guard was not subject to Fourth Amendment challenge. People v. Bezear, 208 A.D.2d 446, 617 N.Y.S.2d 717 (1st Dept. 1994).

—An unauthorized search or seizure by private individuals does not render the evidence inadmissible at subsequent civil or criminal proceedings; therefore, the private search did not preclude the subsequent consensual and valid search by the police based upon the information discovered as a result of the prior private search. People v. Rhodes, 107 A.D.2d 769, 484 N.Y.S.2d 135 (2d Dept. 1985).

—Computer repairman's private search of defendant's computer, which led to the discovery of images of child pornography, cannot be the subject of suppression because the repairman was a private individual, not acting as an agent of the government. People v. Emerson, 196 Misc. 2d 716, 766 N.Y.S.2d 482 (Sup. Ct. Monroe Co. 2003).

—The provisions of the Fourth Amendment are inapplicable to the conduct of private parties. People v. LaFontaine, 159 Misc. 2d 751, 760 n.7, 603 N.Y.S.2d 660, 666 n.7 (Sup. Ct. N.Y. Co. 1993).

—Suppression of evidence will not result from a search initiated and performed by a landlord, acting on his own initiative, because of the lack of state action. People v. Segna, 158 Misc. 2d 35, 600 N.Y.S.2d 615 (Sup. Ct. Kings Co. 1993).

—A private security guard, securing an area that is publicly owned, is not working closely with the police department or any other governmental law enforcement agency, and is not subject to the restrictions of the Fourth Amendment. People v. Huff, 159 Misc. 2d 366, 604 N.Y.S.2d 1024 (Crim. Ct. Kings Co. 1993).

—Objects obtained from defendant's employer, who had received them from defendant two days before any contact with the police, were not suppressible. People v. Bonneau, 140 Misc. 2d 938, 531 N.Y.S.2d 1013 (Westchester Co. Ct. 1988).

Search warrant.—The search of defendant's apartment was

pursuant to a validly executed search warrant; since the more onerous requirements of a search warrant had been satisfied, there was no constitutional infirmity in the failure to also secure a warrant of arrest. People v. Battista, 197 A.D.2d 486, 602 N.Y.S.2d 865 (1st Dept. 1993).

—Since the task force members were police officers from participating municipalities, they had the authority to secure a warrant and arrest the defendant based upon his illegal drug activity, notwithstanding that the agreement authorizing the task force was not executed before this activity. People v. Pearson, 179 A.D.2d 786, 579 N.Y.S.2d 150 (2d Dept. 1992).

—The failure to comply with the procedural requirements for obtaining a nighttime search warrant does not justify the suppression of the evidence where there exists a basis for the nighttime search. People v. Acevedo, 179 A.D.2d 813, 579 N.Y.S.2d 156 (2d Dept. 1992).

—It was proper for the court to have sealed the affidavit supporting the search warrant in order to protect the anonymity of the confidential informant and to protect him from danger, in light of the defendant's prior record and the nature of his present activities; it is well known that violence is typically associated with narcotics trafficking. People v. Woolnough, 180 A.D.2d 837, 580 N.Y.S.2d 776 (2d Dept. 1992).

—The error in the description of the premises to be searched did not invalidate the warrant; the premises intended to be searched were identifiable and there was no reasonable probability that a search would be made of premises other than the one intended to be searched under the warrant. People v. Guerrero, 181 A.D.2d 1030, 582 N.Y.S.2d 576 (4th Dept. 1992).

—The reliability prong of the *Aguilar-Spinelli* test does not apply in cases of sworn oral testimony, where the issuing magistrate can evaluate veracity to determine whether probable cause exists. People v. Drake, 178 A.D.2d 929, 578 N.Y.S.2d 796 (4th Dept. 1991).

—A defendant is entitled to challenge a search warrant on the ground that there is no facial showing of probable cause or that there was perjury on the part of the affiant. People v. Marte, 153 Misc. 2d 18, 579 N.Y.S.2d 820 (Crim. Ct. N.Y. Co. 1991).

—To date New York has not adopted the *Illinois v. Gates* "totality of circumstances" test to determine whether there exists probable cause supportive of a search warrant. People v. Seychel, 136 Misc. 2d 310, 518 N.Y.S.2d 754 (Sup. Ct. N.Y. Co. 1987).

Search warrant; evidence seized before execution.—The search warrant was issued for seizure of package of marijuana and other illicit trafficking paraphernalia; although the package was seized at another location before the warrant was employed, it was proper to execute the warrant since the search was conducted in conformity with its terms. People v. Singer, 44 A.D.2d 730, 354 N.Y.S.2d 178 (3d Dept. 1974), *aff'd*, 36 N.Y.2d 1006, 374 N.Y.S.2d 612, 337 N.E.2d 126 (1975).

Search warrant application; interpretation.—Search warrant applications should be interpreted in a common-sense manner. Where the affidavit provided information sufficient to support a reasonable belief that evidence of a crime would be found in the defendant's apartment, the court erred in suppressing the physical evidence seized and the defendant's statement to law enforcement authorities. People v. Harvey, 298 A.D.2d 527, 748 N.Y.S.2d 785 (2d Dept. 2002).

—The underlying documents in support of an application for a search warrant should be interpreted in a common-sense manner rather than hypertechnically; an application that was less than ideal in its description of the property sought, in failing to name the officers who made the observations giving rise to the application and in other ways was, nevertheless, sufficient to provide a substantial basis for issuance of the warrant. People v. Sinatra, 102 A.D.2d 189, 476 N.Y.S.2d 913 (2d Dept. 1984).

Search warrant; failure to examine recovered property.—Trial court suppressed evidence of contraband recovered in a precinct house search because the officers, who had a general description of the alleged drug seller and who knew that she had four different bottles of prescription pills, failed to examine the contents of the bottles or whether defendant was the ultimate user. People v. Quianes, 179 A.D.2d 577, 579 N.Y.S.2d 63 (1st Dept. 1992).

Securing apartment; not a seizure.—The unlawful act of securing a apartment does not automatically constitute a "seizure" of any contraband in the apartment and contraband subsequently seized pursuant to a valid search warrant is admissible. People v. Arnau, 58 N.Y.2d 27, 457 N.Y.S.2d 763, 444 N.E.2d 13 (1982).

Security guard; search by.—Motion to suppress gun was properly denied where search had been conducted by a private security guard at a hospital, and guard was not acting as agent for police, the police did not participate in the search, and it was conducted by a private employee on hospital premises in accordance with hospital procedures to protect patients and visitors on hospital property. People v. Martin, 240 A.D.2d 434, 658 N.Y.S.2d 105 (2d Dept. 1997).

Search; unconstitutional statute.—It is immaterial if an officer approaches a suspect on the basis of a probable unconstitutional statute if there are existing circumstances that create an objective, credible reason for the approach. People v. Melton, 152 Misc. 2d 649, 578 N.Y.S.2d 377 (Sup. Ct. Monroe Co. 1990).

Statement of apology; subject to suppression.—The defendant's statement of apology for the rape, given after he had been brought to the police station, bleeding and in handcuffs, after being rescued by police officers from an agitated crowd which had set upon him following accusations of the mother that he raped her daughter should have been suppressed, as the apology was in response to a statement by a police officer. People v. Lange, 77 A.D.2d 632, 430 N.Y.S.2d 370 (2d Dept. 1980).

Suppression hearing; free transcript.—An indigent defendant has a fundamental constitutional right to a free transcript of the minutes of a pretrial suppression hearing, and its denial requires a reversal of the judgment of conviction, even though no prejudice has been shown and regardless of the nature and quantum of proof against him. People v. Sanders, 31 N.Y.2d 463, 341 N.Y.S.2d 305, 293 N.E.2d 555 (1973).

Undercover officer; testimony necessary.—An undercover officer who supplied the information to the arresting officer and is available to testify must do so or else the People have failed to show probable cause. People v. Delgado, 79 A.D.2d 976, 434 N.Y.S.2d 454 (2d Dept. 1980).

Unlawful entry; lack of purposeful exploitation.—Since police officers were present only to locate a homicide suspect, even assuming their entry was unlawful, it lacked the element of purposeful exploitation which would taint discovery of defendant's weapon as defendant's dropping the gun was not a direct response to police conduct but an independent act calculated to rid himself of incriminating evidence. People v. Green, 81 A.D.2d 621, 437 N.Y.S.2d 698 (2d Dept. 1981).

Use of informant; corroboration by independent observation.—Probable cause for a warrantless entry into the apartment existed where police acting on a tip from an anonymous informant and a reasonable belief of the imminent removal of the goods proceeded to an apartment building, pushed open the apartment door and encountered defendant with goods from the burglary. People v. Coley, 83 A.D.2d 640, 441 N.Y.S.2d 522 (2d Dept. 1981).

Validity of search executed pursuant to invalid warrant; existence of probable cause independent of warrant.—Where police officers in executing warrant for search of premises used in connection with heroin distribution, viewed occurrences and articles which gave them probable cause for a search independent of the warrant, the warrant's invalidity did not render the ensuing search and seizure invalid. People v. Powell, 36 A.D.2d 177, 319 N.Y.S.2d 485 (1st Dept. 1971), *aff'd*, 30 N.Y.2d 634, 331 N.Y.S.2d 445, 282 N.E.2d 333 (1972).

Waiver.—Defendant, by failing to challenge the reliability of the radio transmission upon which probable cause was based, failed to preserve for appellate review any question regarding the basis of the sending officer's information and the issue of the failure of the People to produce the sending officer at the suppression hearing. People v. Reddick, 107 A.D.2d 721, 484 N.Y.S.2d 78 (2d Dept. 1985).

STANDING

Automatic standing.—Fact that defendant had automatic standing with respect to certain property due to reliance by People on statutory presumption did not confer standing upon the defendant as to property that was not the subject of the statutory presumption. People v. Tejada, 81 N.Y.2d 861, 597 N.Y.S.2d 626, 613 N.E.2d 532 (1993).

—Since the criminal possession charges were not rooted solely in a statutory presumption attributing possession to the defendant, the hearing court erred in conferring automatic standing on him; moreover, the People may first raise on appeal the issue of standing. People v. Jackson, 207 A.D.2d 805, 616 N.Y.S.2d 530 (2d Dept. 1994).

—The doctrine of "automatic standing" no longer exists in New York; New York now follows the rule set forth in *United States v. Salvucci*, 448 U.S. 83, 100 S. Ct. 2547, 65 L. Ed. 2d 619 (1980), *i.e.*, whether or not the defendant had a legitimate expectation of privacy so that his own Fourth Amendment rights were violated by the search. People v. Johnson, 105 Misc. 2d 561, 432 N.Y.S.2d 608 (Sup. Ct. N.Y. Co. 1980).

—One charged with possession of a controlled substance has automatic standing to challenge the search and seizure; the prosecution can not allege possession as part of the crime charged and yet deny that there was possession sufficient for standing purposes. *See* People v. Calo, 102 Misc. 2d 1115, 425 N.Y.S.2d 239 (Bronx Co. Crim. Ct. 1980).

Homeless shelter; standing.—Defendant, a resident of a homeless shelter, expressly consented to search of his locker conducted by peace officer with the shelter's consent by signing a contract agreeing to keep the locker in an orderly and sanitary condition and agreeing that the shelter would have unlimited right to inspect the locker. People v. Alston, 16 A.D.3d 358, 792 N.Y.S.2d 73 (1st Dept. 2005).

—Defendant had no reasonable expectation of privacy in his assigned room at a homeless shelter, given the semi-public nature of the room, and the defendant could not create any expectation of privacy by placing clothes over the wire mesh to block visual access to the room or by locking the door with a broomstick handle. People v. Gaffney, 308 A.D.2d 598, 764 N.Y.S.2d 727 (2d Dept. 2003).

—Defendant was arrested without a warrant at a public homeless shelter in Brooklyn. The supervisor of the shelter consented to the arresting officer's entry and the shelter's supervising guard escorted the detective to the room and bed where defendant had been assigned. There were no locks or doors preventing entry onto the floors or rooms. Warrantless arrest of defendant at homeless shelter was proper. Defendant could not show actual expectation of privacy in his room or bed, given the semi-public nature of the living area. People v. Robinson, 300 A.D.2d 511, 751 N.Y.S.2d 543 (2d Dept. 2002).

Standing to assert illegality of search.—A defendant is not required to testify in order to sustain his or her burden of proving standing; the claim of standing may be supported with evidence adduced from the People's case. People v. Whitfield, 81 N.Y.2d 904, 597 N.Y.S.2d 641, 613 N.E.2d 547 (1993).

—People's imputation of constructive possession of weapon to defendant as the predicate for the crime with which he was charged constituted a sufficient basis for defendant to challenge the police conduct in searching the passenger compartment in the taxicab. People v. Millan, 69 N.Y.2d 514, 516 N.Y.S.2d 168, 508 N.E.2d 903 (1987).

—Neither co-defendant nor defendant had standing to assert illegality of the search when, at the time of the search, the car was in the actual possession of a repairman, and in the constructive possession of a finance company; co-defendant's right to redeem the car was not a possessory but an ownership interest, and a contingent one not sufficient to continue co-defendant's right to privacy with respect to automobile he once owned and possessed as a conditional purchase. People v. Russ, 37 N.Y.2d 935, 380 N.Y.S.2d 646, 343 N.E.2d 286 (1975).

—Standing to object to a search of a residence generally requires a showing of some combination of the following factors: defendant's status (visitor, overnight guest, relative); length, purpose, and frequency of defendant's stays at the premises; possession of a key; and presence of any belongings or contribution to expenses. Under all the circumstances here, defendant's possession of a key merely showed that he had temporary access to the apartment; there was no evidence explaining how he came into possession of the key or even that he had permission to have it. People v. Jose, 252 A.D.2d 401, 676 N.Y.S.2d 545 (1st Dept. 1998), *aff'd*, 94 N.Y.2d 844, 702 N.Y.S.2d 574, 724 N.E.2d 366 (1999).

—Court properly denied defendant's suppression motion because defendant lacked standing to challenge the search of the grate on the street into which the police had seen him drop the narcotics; defendant lacked any reasonable expectation of privacy in the grate, which was visible and accessible to the public, and defendant had no right to exclude others. People v. Fabelo, 277 A.D.2d 130, 717 N.Y.S.2d 98 (1st Dept. 2000).

—Defendant had no legitimate expectation of privacy in a hallway outside of his apartment. People v. Coppin, 202 A.D.2d 279, 608 N.Y.S.2d 661 (1st Dept. 1994).

—At a suppression hearing, defendant has the burden of establishing standing by demonstrating a personal, legitimate expectation of privacy and, this burden may be buttressed by evidence reduced from the People's case. People v. Corona, 206 A.D.2d 305, 614 N.Y.S.2d 722 (1st Dept. 1994).

—Defendant had standing where he was a guest in the co-defendant's apartment. People v. Delgado, 192 A.D.2d 318, 595 N.Y.S.2d 467 (1st Dept. 1993).

—Defendant had no standing in dumpster in which a gun was found. People v. Brown, 182 A.D.2d 451, 582 N.Y.S.2d 177 (1st Dept. 1992).

—Where the defendant told his trial counsel that the police had not recovered any incriminating property from him, the defendant did not have standing to bring a motion to suppress. People v. Cruz, 165 A.D.2d 205, 566 N.Y.S.2d 608 (1st Dept. 1991).

—Defendant had standing where the People relied on the "room presumption." People v. Tejada, 171 A.D.2d 585, 567 N.Y.S.2d 464 (1st Dept. 1991).

—Defendant lacked a sufficient expectation of privacy to challenge seizure of the gun from someone else's jacket. People v. Ochsner, 159 A.D.2d 435, 553 N.Y.S.2d 136 (1st Dept. 1990).

—Since defendant sufficiently alleged that the brown bag was unlawfully seized from her person, no proprietary interest in the automobile needed to be asserted in order to establish standing. People v. Zarate, 160 A.D.2d 466, 554 N.Y.S.2d 137 (1st Dept. 1990).

—Defendant failed to demonstrate any legitimate expectation of privacy in the hallway of the apartment building, because it was accessible to all tenants and their invitees. People v. Washington, 287 A.D.2d 752, 732 N.Y.S.2d 241 (2d Dept. 2001).

—The evidence failed to show that the defendant had any reasonable expectation of privacy in the bag that was recovered from inside the telephone pole. People v. Meredith, 201 A.D.2d 674, 607 N.Y.S.2d 979 (2d Dept. 1994).

—Since one has no legitimate expectation of privacy in locations within a car which are observable to a passerby, an officer's simply peering into an automobile will not constitute a search; however, where an action is undertaken so as to expose an area in the car which is not readily observable from the outside, then the action does constitute a search within the meaning of the Fourth Amendment. People v. Young, 207 A.D.2d 465, 615 N.Y.S.2d 767 (2d Dept. 1994).

—Defendant failed to establish standing to seek suppression of the narcotics discovered during a search of the bag that he was carrying, where the hearing testimony demonstrated that the defendant repeatedly insisted that the bag did not belong to him, that he did not know what it contained, and that he was merely transporting its contents from one city to another for someone else. People v. Alvaranga, 198 A.D.2d 286, 603 N.Y.S.2d 568 (2d Dept. 1993), *aff'd*, 84 N.Y.2d 985, 622 N.Y.S.2d 500, 646 N.E.2d 802.

—The defendant had no expectation of privacy with respect to individuals making observations of the car from the driveway leading to his home; absent evidence of an intent to exclude the public, the entryway to a person's home offers implied permission to approach. People v. Warmuth, 187 A.D.2d 473, 589 N.Y.S.2d 522 (2d Dept. 1992).

—Where defendant stated that he was holding pillowcases for his brother, he constituted a bailee of the pillowcases and therefore did not have standing to contest the legality of the search of the pillowcases. People v. Gatling, 133 A.D.2d 465, 519 N.Y.S.2d 681 (2d Dept. 1987).

—Defendant lacks standing to seek the suppression of the prerecorded buy money utilized in making the drug purchase since it was obtained from the person of an accomplice. People v. Morales, 117 A.D.2d 714, 498 N.Y.S.2d 739 (2d Dept. 1986).

—Where defendant failed to introduce evidence of his privacy interest at a suppression hearing and thus failed to establish his standing to challenge the search, evidence relating to standing subsequently introduced at trial could not be used to undermine the suppression ruling. People v. Wilkerson, 108 A.D.2d 832, 485 N.Y.S.2d 107 (2d Dept. 1985).

—Defendant failed to establish his standing to challenge the warrantless entry by police into his girlfriend's apartment to effectuate his arrest where he did not demonstrate that he had a reasonable expectation of privacy in the premises. People v. DeMoss, 106 A.D.2d 395, 482 N.Y.S.2d 313 (2d Dept. 1984).

—Where the proceeds of a crime committed the day before the arrest were found on the person of the defendant's companion, defendant lacked standing to contest the seizure from the person of his companion. People v. Cyrus, 76 A.D.2d 842, 428 N.Y.S.2d 325 (2d Dept. 1980).

—Where defendant's written consent was expressly limited to a computer in his bedroom, defendant had a privacy interest in the other computer in his home and thus he had standing to challenge the seizure of the other computer. People v. O'Brien, 2 A.D.3d 1222, 769 N.Y.S.2d 654 (3d Dept. 2003).

—Defendant lacked standing to raise issue based on a violation of his co-defendant's Fourth Amendment rights. People v. Eaddy, 200 A.D.2d 896, 606 N.Y.S.2d 928 (3d Dept. 1994).

—Court rejected defendant's attempt to buttress standing argument with facts derived from the trial testimony. People v. Maye, 206 A.D.2d 755, 615 N.Y.S.2d 94 (3d Dept. 1994).

—Defendant, as a mere passenger in the automobile, failed to meet his burden of establishing standing to contest the search of the vehicle. People v. McElroy, 202 A.D.2d 810, 609 N.Y.S.2d 109 (3d Dept. 1994).

—Defendant had no expectation of privacy with respect to narcotics found in police car used to transport the defendant. People v. Fernandez, 193 A.D.2d 896, 597 N.Y.S.2d 778 (3d Dept. 1993).

—Because defendant had moved out of the victim's townhouse prior to the search, he lacked standing to challenge the warrantless search, and thus court properly refused to suppress items of physical evidence obtained there. People v. Bradley, 17 A.D.3d 1050, 794 N.Y.S.2d 201 (4th Dept. 2005).

—Murder defendant lacked standing to challenge police entry into common hallway area accessible to all tenants and their invitees. People v. Muldrow, 273 A.D.2d 814, 711 N.Y.S.2d 649 (4th Dept. 2000).

—Court properly determined that defendant lacked standing to contest warrantless search of victim's apartment where court credited victim's testimony that defendant did not live with her, but merely stayed overnight occasionally and kept a few personal items at the victim's home, but did not have a key. People v. Conway, 277 A.D.2d 1020, 716 N.Y.S.2d 223 (4th Dept. 2000).

—The People may raise for the first time on appeal the issue of standing. People v. Rivera, 206 A.D.2d 832, 615 N.Y.S.2d 196 (4th Dept. 1994); People v. Jones, 182 A.D.2d 1066, 582 N.Y.S.2d 868 (4th Dept. 1992); People v. Sanchez-Reyes, 172 A.D.2d 1034, 569 N.Y.S.2d 539 (4th Dept. 1991).

—Although defendant did not have any proprietary interest in the apartment searched, he still had standing to challenge the search because a prior illegal search of defendant led to the search of the apartment. People v. Polanco, 203 A.D.2d 942, 611 N.Y.S.2d 403 (4th Dept. 1994).

—Defendant had standing to contest the search of an automobile in which he was a passenger where the owner of the vehicle had entrusted it to defendant's possession several days earlier for needed repairs. People v. Castrechino, 105 A.D.2d 1089, 482 N.Y.S.2d 191 (4th Dept. 1984).

—As a mere visitor to the premises, defendant lacked standing to complain of a search of someone else's apartment. People v. Thompson, 160 Misc. 2d 579, 610 N.Y.S.2d 743 (Sup. Ct. Kings Co. 1994).

—The defendant had standing where the People relied on the statutory presumption of possession found in Penal Law § 220.25(2). People v. Davis, 156 Misc. 2d 926, 595 N.Y.S.2d 287 (Sup. Ct. Bronx Co. 1993).

—While an employee can have a legitimate expectation of privacy in his or her workplace, not all areas of a person's business office are encompassed within the ambit of an objective zone of privacy. People v. Holland, 155 Misc. 2d 964, 591 N.Y.S.2d 744 (Crim. Ct. Richmond Co. 1992).

Pen register orders.—Defendant who is aggrieved by the unlawful or improper acquisition of evidence by means of a pen register or trap and trace device can move to suppress that evidence; in the instant case, all appellants had statutory standing to challenge the respective pen register and trap and trace

orders. People v. Kramer, 92 N.Y.2d 529, 683 N.Y.S.2d 743, 706 N.E.2d 731 (1998).

Stolen vehicles; standing.—A passenger in a stolen vehicle has standing to challenge the stop of the vehicle and the subsequent search of his person, but he waived the right to review the legality of the stop. People v. Dugard, 192 A.D.2d 418, 596 N.Y.S.2d 394 (1st Dept. 1993).

—Defendant had no legitimate expectation of privacy with respect to the vehicle that was owned by and stolen from another individual; therefore defendant lacked standing to object to the search of the vehicle. People v. Strunkey, 202 A.D.2d 610, 609 N.Y.S.2d 255 (2d Dept. 1994).

Rental car.—Defendant lacked standing to challenge the search of the parked rental car which was conducted at the time of his arrest. The defendant did not have a reasonable expectation of privacy in the rental car, which had been rented by another individual and was parked on the street in front of the residence the defendant was caught burglarizing. The fact that defendant possessed keys that fit the car did not establish his right to drive or possess the vehicle, that he had a legitimate expectation of privacy in it, or that he had standing to dispute the validity of its search. People v. Miller, 298 A.D.2d 467, 748 N.Y.S.2d 768 (2d Dept. 2002).

—Defendant had no standing to move to suppress cocaine found in a police search of a jeep he rented for the purpose of cocaine storage, since he was unable to prove that he had a legitimate expectation of privacy in the jeep where its doors were unlocked at the time of the search, defendant did not possess the keys to the jeep, and the owner of the jeep and his wife had free access to the vehicle. People v. Cacioppo, 104 A.D.2d 559, 479 N.Y.S.2d 264 (2d Dept. 1984).

No standing; end of rental term at hotel.—Motion to suppress the stolen goods was properly denied where defendant whose rental term of a hotel room had expired no longer had a legitimate expectation of privacy in the room and the owner had the right to enter the room and remove the defendant's belongings. People v. Lerhinan, 90 A.D.2d 74, 455 N.Y.S.2d 822 (2d Dept. 1982).

—Defendant lacked standing to challenge the search of a stolen vehicle in which she was a passenger that was abandoned after a high speed chase for speeding and when the police officer entered the vehicle to shut off the ignition saw in "plain view" furs on hangers with the retail sales slips attached. People v. Traynham, 85 A.D.2d 748, 445 N.Y.S.2d 256 (3d Dept. 1981).

Defendant not lawfully on premises; standing.—Court properly found that defendant failed to meet his burden of establishing a legitimate expectation of privacy in the premises, where defendant's claim that he was an "overnight guest" in the apartment was unsupported by the record; defendant's connection to the apartment was entirely that of a trespasser, notwithstanding his claimed relationship with a former tenant. People v. Francis, 253 A.D.2d 704, 679 N.Y.S.2d 2 (1st Dept. 1998).

—Defendant, arriving at an illegal gambling house in Chinatown just after the execution of a search warrant had begun, lacked standing to controvert the warrant. People v. Tsang, 173 A.D.2d 173, 569 N.Y.S.2d 78 (1st Dept. 1991).

—The police do not need a search warrant to enter an apartment in an abandoned building owned by the city; contraband seized is admissible because the occupants had no right to privacy as they were trespassers. People v. Sumlin, 105 Misc. 2d 134, 431 N.Y.S.2d 967 (Sup N.Y. Co. 1980).

Parolees, probationers, and fugitives; standing.—Parolee does not surrender his constitutional right against unreasonable search and seizure, but his parole status is always relevant in evaluating reasonableness, and his parole officer has the right to conduct a warrantless search of the parolee's residence where it is rationally and reasonably related to the performance of his duty. People v. Huntley, 43 N.Y.2d 175, 401 N.Y.S.2d 31, 371 N.E.2d 794 (1977).

—Search of an apartment in defendant's absence could not be justified by terms of defendant's parole agreement, where evidence revealed that he was not the tenant and did not exercise such control over the apartment as to limit or control the ingress or egress of others, nor did he have the power or authority to manage the apartment. People v. Gambino, 35 N.Y.2d 932, 365 N.Y.S.2d 164, 324 N.E.2d 546 (1974).

—Defendant consented to home entries and searches by parole officers as a condition of his parole; in any event, the apartment where defendant was seized was not the home in which he was permitted to reside. People v. Lopez, 288 A.D.2d 70, 733 N.Y.S.2d 154 (1st Dept. 2001).

—Where defendant absconded from a prisoner's work-release program, and police learned that defendant was staying at his brother's apartment, defendant had no legitimate expectation of privacy in his brother's apartment, and had no standing to assert that the search of the apartment was illegal. People v. Hernandez, 218 A.D.2d 167, 639 N.Y.S.2d 423 (2d Dept.), *app. denied,* 88 N.Y.2d 1068 (1996); *see also* United States v. Roy, 734 F.2d 108, 111 (2d Cir. 1984) (defendant's presence at scene of search was wrongful, because he was a prison escapee, and thus, a "trespasser on society").

—Defendant's arrest on a parole violation warrant was lawful, and did not render the consensual search illegal; however, defendant did demonstrate that he had standing to challenge the search, because he resided at the premises at least part of the time with his father and had a bedroom there. People v. Adams, 244 A.D.2d 897, 665 N.Y.S.2d 991 (4th Dept. 1997).

—Motion to suppress physical evidence obtained in a search of a parolee's apartment should be granted when the search of parolee's apartment was not related to the detection or prevention of parole violation but was made after the parole officer offered his assistance in a rape investigation because he knew parolees in the neighborhood and then accompanied officers on their search of defendant's apartment. Parolee who signs an authorization for searches of his person, residence and property extends this authority to warrantless searches only if there is a reason to suspect that the defendant has violated his condition of parole and is not an unrestrictive consent to any and all searches. People v. Mackie, 77 A.D.2d 778, 430 N.Y.S.2d 733 (4th Dept. 1980).

—Where defendant absconded from work release program, thereby violating conditions of his parole, and fled to Chicago, court upheld the search as reasonable following a lawful arrest, finding that "defendant's liberty interest in the place of arrest . . . was severely limited by reason of his parole and fugitive status." People v. Diaz, 163 Misc. 2d 103, 618 N.Y.S.2d 1000 (Sup. Ct. Richmond Co. 1994).

SEARCH WITHOUT WARRANT

Anonymous radio description not sufficiently specific; physical evidence suppressed.—Suppression of physical evidence was affirmed where anonymous radio ran description that formed basis for police investigation and pat down of the defendant was insufficiently specific to single out the defendant, there was no furtive or suspicious activity on the part of the defendant and there was no basis for the police to reasonably believe they were in danger. People v. Vincent, 100 A.D.2d 789, 474 N.Y.S.2d 511 (1st Dept.), *aff'd,* 63 N.Y.2d 745, 480 N.Y.S.2d 202, 469 N.E.2d 523 (1984).

Arrest and search; motion to suppress.—Suppression was granted where defendant was stopped because the officer noticed that his clothes were untidy and that his hair was "frizzled up" and upon questioning the officer found that he was carrying a radio, whose brand name he did not know, and other items that he allegedly found in the trash; there was no justification for detaining the defendant when the police initiated the confrontation because the defendant's behavior was innocuous. People v. Carrasquillo, 54 N.Y.2d 248, 445 N.Y.S.2d 97, 429 N.E.2d 775 (1981).

—Motion to suppress was granted where police, who were in complete control of the house went into the bedroom without a search warrant and seized contraband after the defendant was under arrest. People v. Knapp, 52 N.Y.2d 689, 439 N.Y.S.2d 871, 422 N.E.2d 531 (1981).

Arrest; probable cause.—Where the observed acts of the defendant were susceptible of various innocent interpretations, even if involving a person with a narcotics background, where the behavior was at most equivocal and suspicious, and where there was no supplementation by any additional behavior raising the level of inference from suspicion to probable cause, more must be shown to form the basis for a warrantless arrest and an incidental search. People v. Davis, 36 N.Y.2d 280, 367 N.Y.S.2d 256, 326 N.E.2d 818, *cert. denied,* 423 U.S. 876 (1975).

—The lack of probable cause to sustain the custodial detention and transportation of one defendant operates to vitiate his ensuing consent to the search of the defendant's apartment and the evidence seized in the apartment should therefore be suppressed as to that defendant. People v. Henley, 53 N.Y.2d 403, 442 N.Y.S.2d 428, 425 N.E.2d 816 (1981).

—The police had probable cause to arrest defendant for burglary where they observed the shattered storefront in a high crime area, saw that property had been taken from the store, observed an unmarked closed van, the only vehicle on the street, halt momentarily some 200 feet from the scene of the burglary where an unidentified man suddenly appeared and hurriedly entered the front of the van as a passenger, and after they stopped the car to make inquiries, defendant gave evasive answers while the van's other known occupant began to flee on foot and upon search of the van discovered two men hiding, burglar's tools and the proceeds of the burglary. People v. Marner, 47 N.Y.2d 982, 419 N.Y.S.2d 963, 393 N.E.2d 1036, *cert. denied,* 444 U.S. 971 (1979).

—The search was proper and the failure of the officer to obtain the eyewitness' identity did not require suppression, where the eyewitness to an attempted robbery while informing the officer again saw the perpetrator and pointed him out to the officer, who grabbed him with one hand, spun him around patted him down, and found a gun. People v. Green, 35 N.Y.2d 193, 360 N.Y.S.2d 243, 318 N.E.2d 464 (1974).

—The contents of an attache case in the defendant's possession when arrested and taken into custody for criminal trespass without a warrant is admissible as the fruits of a lawful custodial arrest, since the authority to search clearly includes those personal effects of the arrestee that are "ready to hand." People v. Weintraub, 35 N.Y.2d 351, 361 N.Y.S.2d 897, 320 N.E.2d 636 (1974).

—Where defendant was arrested and searched on insufficient probable cause, the fact that the search was successful in producing contraband did not vitiate the unlawfulness of the arrest. People v. Martin, 32 N.Y.2d 123, 343 N.Y.S.2d 343, 296 N.E.2d 245 (1973).

—Because of the innocuous nature of the pestle, a club-like cooking utensil, which was under the driver's seat of defendant's car, the police did not have the requisite probable cause to arrest and search defendant, and the drugs should have been suppressed. People v. Buhagiar, 185 Misc. 2d 203, 713 N.Y.S.2d 114 (App. Term, 2d Dept. 2000).

—It was incumbent upon the people to produce, at a suppression hearing, the undercover officer who relayed information to the arresting officer, was available to testify and whose reliability had been called into question; the undercover officer, a member of a "buy and bust" narcotics team, told the backup officer that he had just bought narcotics from defendant. People v. Green, 87 A.D.2d 892, 449 N.Y.S.2d 524 (2d Dept. 1982).

Arrest; probable cause; rehearing denied.—At the time of the arrest defendant was holding a briefcase in his hand, large enough to contain a weapon. Its contents were readily accessible to him, he had just committed a crime and was wearing a bulletproof vest. The arrest and search of the briefcase were for all practical purposes conducted at the same time and place and accordingly the search was reasonable. People v. Smith, 59 N.Y.2d 454, 465 N.Y.S.2d 896, 452 N.E.2d 1224 (1983).

—Rehearing was denied where the sending and receiving police officers were members of the same police department and the sending officer who relayed the information to the arresting officer was available to testify at the hearing but the prosecutor chose only to offer the testimony of the arresting officer. People v. Jones, 80 A.D.2d 876 436 N.Y.S.2d 783 (2d Dept. 1981).

Arrest without warrant; search.—Motion to suppress was reversed where the police officer was of sufficient experience in narcotics, working in an area with a high number of narcotics trafficking, observed defendant and another in conversation, saw defendant reach into a brown paper bag and withdraw a glassine envelope which he handed to his companion and when defendant and his companion turned and faced the patrol car, they registered a "look of surprise or shock in their face," the police officers had probable cause to arrest. People v. Alston, 84 A.D.2d 737, 444 N.Y.S.2d 76 (1st Dept. 1981).

Arrest and search based on police computer.—Defendant's motion to suppress was granted where a computer-generated police alarm falsely indicated that the automobile was stolen, even though, it was in fact returned three days after the initial report was filed therefore, the arrest and seizure of evidence was unlawful because the police had failed to update the computer and were aware that 20% of the police alarms were mistakes and failed to consider the driver's claim that the automobile was not stolen. People v. Jones, 110 Misc. 2d 875, 443 N.Y.S.2d 298 (Crim. Ct. N.Y. Co. 1981).

Blood sample may be taken from unconscious defendant.—Where defendant was convicted of criminally negligent homicide as a result of an automobile crash which killed his passenger, the taking of a blood sample from defendant while he was unconscious without a court order was permissible since the police had reasonable cause to believe he was intoxicated, the sample was taken at a hospital within two hours of arrest, and consent to take the blood sample is implied under VTL § 1194; further, the issue of the suppressibility of the blood test taken without a court order and used in a Penal Law prosecution was not preserved for appeal since defendant did not raise the argument at the suppression hearing. People v. Hall, 61 N.Y.2d 834, 473 N.Y.S.2d 959, 462 N.E.2d 136 (1984).

Blood samples.—VTL § 1194(1), which requires chemical testing of a motor vehicle operator's breath, blood, urine or saliva to be administered "at the direction" of a police officer, does not preclude the police officer who determines that testing is warranted from administering the test as well. People v. Evers, 68 N.Y.2d 658, 505 N.Y.S.2d 68, 496 N.E.2d 227 (1986).

Collateral estoppel.—Defendant who refused to testify at pretrial suppression hearing on issue of consent to search, was not estopped from testifying regarding that issue at a subsequent pre-trial suppression hearing based on unrelated charges, even though it arose from the same nucleus of facts. People v. Plevy, 52 N.Y.2d 58, 436 N.Y.S.2d 224, 417 N.E.2d 518 (1980).

Common-carrier employee.—Where the search of personal property is made by an employee of a common carrier in pursuit of the private interests of the employer and in furtherance of the common carrier's common law right to inspect goods presented for shipment, it is not constitutionally proscribed. People v. DeSantis, 59 A.D.2d 257, 399 N.Y.S.2d 514 (4th Dept. 1977), aff'd, 46 N.Y.2d 82, 412 N.Y.S.2d 838, 385 N.E.2d 577 (1978), cert. denied, 443 U.S. 912 (1979).

Illegal stop.—Defendant's DMV records were suppressible as fruit of the poisonous tree if they were gotten because of an illegal stop. People v. Thomas, 164 Misc. 2d 721, 626 N.Y.S.2d 405 (Crim. Ct. N.Y. 1995).

Involuntary consent.—Conviction on narcotics charges was reversed where court found that defendants' consent to have their apartment searched was induced by overbearing official conduct and was not a free exercise of the will; among the factors considered by the court in making this finding was the number of agents present in the small apartment, the youth of the defendants, the separation and handcuffing of the defendants (who were newlyweds), the removal of the defendants' relatives from the scene, and the circumstances of the arrest. People v. Gonzalez, 39 N.Y.2d 122, 383 N.Y.S.2d 215, 347 N.E.2d 575 (1976).

—Defendant's motion to suppress was denied where an undercover police officer purchased cocaine from a co-defendant, inside the apartment of both defendants and one week later, an informant advised a narcotics division officer that he was in the apartment when a quantity of cocaine was delivered to the defendant and later that day the undercover officer returned to the apartment and purchased cocaine from the defendant; an officer went for a search warrant and when he returned with it the apartment was searched. The search was justified on the doctrine of independent origin, since it was conducted pursuant to a valid search warrant based on information already known before they entered the apartment. People v. Lee, 83 A.D.2d 311, 444 N.Y.S.2d 100 (1st Dept. 1981), aff'd, 58 N.Y.2d 771, 459 N.Y.S.2d 38, 445 N.E.2d 214 (1982), cert. denied, 460 U.S. 1044 (1983).

—The People have the heavy burden of proving the voluntariness of a defendant's consent to a search and the prosecution must "demonstrate that the consent was in fact voluntarily given and not the result of duress or coercion, express or implied." People v. Springer, 92 A.D.2d 209, 460 N.Y.S.2d 86 (2d Dept. 1983).

Consent.—Mere presence of three police officers at defendant's apartment door did not support defendant's contention that his will to refuse the officers entrance into his apartment was overborne; rather, it was only one factor in the determination of whether consent to enter was voluntarily given. People v. Phiefer, 43 N.Y.2d 719, 401 N.Y.S.2d 483, 372 N.E.2d 323 (1977).

—Where one person alone occupies a room in a hotel or an apartment in an apartment house, he is deemed to have exclusive possession and control over those premises—at least with regard to search and seizure in the criminal law, and no third party may consent to the premises' being entered or searched by the police. People v. Wood, 31 N.Y.2d 975, 341 N.Y.S.2d 310, 293 N.E.2d 559 (1973).

—The bedroom which was searched in this instance was actually being shared by the defendant and his landlady's 10-year-old son. Since that room was not set aside for the defendant's exclusive possession or use, it followed that he could have no reasonable expectation of privacy, and that the landlady, who had a right to enter her son's bedroom, was privileged to give consent to the search. People v. Wood, 31 N.Y.2d 975, 341 N.Y.S.2d 310, 293 N.E.2d 559 (1973).

—Motion to suppress was granted due to involuntary consent where the evidence showed that before the police officers requested the defendant to open the trunk of the car, to which he acceded, the police had questioned him with regard to the car registration, removed from him a leather pouch which was searched revealing bullets, had searched the car finding marijuana, asked the defendant to step out of the car and then frisked him. People v. Falu, 85 A.D.2d 501, 444 N.Y.S.2d 108 (1st Dept. 1981).

—Warrantless search and removal of guns and ammunition from a closet in defendant's apartment was held proper after defendant had fired shots at an officer where police were directed to the apartment by defendant's girlfriend, a sometime resident of the apartment, who let them in with her key and directed the officers to the exact spot where the gun was located. People v. Adams, 72 A.D.2d 156, 423 N.Y.S.2d 936 (1st Dept. 1980), aff'd, 53 N.Y.2d 1, 439 N.Y.S.2d 877, 422 N.E.2d 537 (1981).

—Totality of circumstances indicated that defendant's consent to search of his home for narcotics was not voluntarily given where: (1) there were seven police officers in the house at the time of defendant's consent; (2) defendant had no prior criminal record; and (3) defendant was faced with intense and unjustified psychological pressure to consent to warrantless search of bedroom at risk of losing his two-month-old baby to a child welfare shelter. People v. Litt, 71 A.D.2d 926, 419 N.Y.S.2d 726 (2d Dept. 1979).

—The use of deception does not per se destroy the voluntariness of a consent unless the deception is so fundamentally unfair as to deny due process. People v. Esposito, 191 A.D.2d 176, 594 N.Y.S.2d 424 (3d Dept. 1993).

—Troopers were not obligated to expressly warn defendant of his right to refuse consent to search his vehicle. People v. Bapp, 149 A.D.2d 804, 539 N.Y.S.2d 592, 593 (3d Dept. 1989).

Consent to search obtained after defendant requested an attorney.—Motion to suppress physical evidence granted where police officer, who had defendant in custody, obtained defendant's consent to search his premises after defendant had requested an attorney but before one arrived; the fact that consent was voluntarily given and that the attorney, when he later arrived, raised no objection did not validate the unconstitutional search. People v. Johnson, 48 N.Y.2d 565, 423 N.Y.S.2d 905, 399 N.E.2d 936 (1979).

Evidence suppressed where police had opportunity to obtain warrant. —Contraband found in defendant's automobile during a warrantless search must be suppressed when police had adequate time to obtain a search warrant for the car, which was parked in a private garage under circumstances permitting the police to guard the car until the warrant was obtained; it was irrelevant that money, criminally obtained, was used to purchase the car. People v. Ready, 61 N.Y.2d 790, 473 N.Y.S.2d 389, 461 N.E.2d 875 (1984).

Exigent circumstances.—Evidence that defendant was armed and was planning to commit another armed robbery in the immediate future gave rise to exigent circumstances supporting warrantless entry into the apartment. People v. Mathis, 132 A.D.2d 626, 517 N.Y.S.2d 780 (2d Dept. 1987).

Exigent circumstances; information on gun insufficient.—Information that the defendant had committed a robbery and that he had a gun in his apartment did not constitute "exigent circumstances" justifying a warrantless entry into defendant's apartment without defendant's consent; suppression of gun, drugs and victim's property found inside defendant's apartment was therefore required. People v. Lott, 102 A.D.2d 506, 478 N.Y.S.2d 193 (4th Dept. 1984).

Motion to suppress granted; no authority to seize physical evidence without warrant.—Warrantless search defendant's apartment, after he admitted weapons were in his apartment and after he was arrested on street, was not justified by exigent circumstances absent showing that weapons were likely to be removed from premises or destroyed, especially where police had probable cause and opportunity to obtain search warrant. Kwok T. v. Mauriello, 43 N.Y.2d 213, 401 N.Y.S.2d 52, 371 N.E.2d 814 (1977).

Parole officer.—The motion to suppress evidence seized from the defendant's apartment by his parole officer after the defendant's arrest on a parole violation warrant was properly denied as being "in furtherance of parole purposes" where the officer had substantial information relating to the defendant's involvement in other crimes. People v. Johnson, 63 N.Y.2d 888, 483 N.Y.S.2d 201, 472 N.E.2d 1029 (1984).

Preliminary search valid; warrant required for later searches.—When a constitutionally protected area becomes the scene of a crime, the police may subject the premises to a preliminary search and inspection whose scope and duration must be limited by and reasonably related to the exigencies of the situation and once that preliminary investigation has come to an end, no further searches may be conducted unless authorized by a warrant; where police conducted an exhaustive top to bottom search without a warrant after having left the apartment after the preliminary investigation in reference to a shooting without maintaining a continuing police presence and without returning for eight hours, the evidence seized must be suppressed. People v. Cohen, 87 A.D.2d 77, 450 N.Y.S.2d 497 (2d Dept. 1982), aff'd, 58 N.Y.2d 844, 460 N.Y.S.2d 18, 446 N.E.2d 774, cert. denied, 461 U.S. 930 (1983).

Proper stop but improper frisk.—Car was legally stopped based on suspected involvement in a reported larceny at a car wash, but defendant was improperly frisked because defendant was not suspected of a serious or violent crime or a crime involving potentially dangerous instruments and the deputy failed to articulate a reason justifying the frisk, and thus, the court granted the motion to suppress the evidence seized during the frisk. People v. DelVecchio, 277 A.D.2d 927, 716 N.Y.S.2d 256 (4th Dept. 2000).

Search and seizure; "emergency doctrine."—Pursuant to the emergency exception, no warrant was required because police were responding to an emergency, namely, a neighbor's complaints about an overwhelming odor emanating from the defendant's apartment. Police tried and considered several unsuccessful means of entry before ordering maintenance personnel to pry the door open. People v. Molnar, 98 N.Y.2d 328, 746 N.Y.S.2d 673, 774 N.E.2d 738 (2002).

—Where police, attempting to locate a missing hotel maid, proceeded to search all the rooms in the hotel and found the maid's body in the defendant's room, the court upheld the validity of the search as being within the right of the police to enter and investigate in an emergency; the basic elements involved in such emergency searches were enumerated by the court as (1) a reasonable belief on the part of the police that there is an emergency, (2) the search must not be primarily motivated by intent to arrest and seize evidence, and (3) there must be a reasonable basis to associate the emergency with the place to be searched. People v. Mitchell, 39 N.Y.2d 173, 383 N.Y.S.2d 246, 347 N.E.2d 607 (1976).

—For warrantless entry to be justified on basis of emergency exception, three conditions must be met: (1) police must have reasonable grounds to believe that there is an emergency at hand and an immediate need for their assistance for the protection of life or property; (2) the search must not be primarily motivated by intent to arrest and seize evidence; and (3) there must be some reasonable basis, approximating probable cause, to associate the emergency with the area or place to be searched. People v. Thatcher, 9 A.D.3d 682, 779 N.Y.S.2d 818 (3d Dept. 2004).

—Warrantless search may be conducted under the emergency doctrine, where there is substantial threat of imminent danger to either life, health, or property, and the protection of animals which constitute property may be included within the emergency exception. People v. Rogers, 184 Misc. 2d 419, 708 N.Y.S.2d 795 (App. Term 2d Dept. 2000).

—"Emergency" doctrine exception to search warrant requirement applied where detective, shortly after homicide, followed trail of blood from victim into a social club located about 150 feet away and seized physical evidence that was found there

in plain view. People v. Taper, 105 A.D.2d 813, 481 N.Y.S.2d 745 (2d Dept. 1984).

—Warrantless police entry into defendant's apartment was proper since they were responding to an emergency, namely to locate and give aid to the reported victim of a serious assault, and, once lawfully within the apartment and observing signs of violence therein, they had a right to question defendant as part of their investigation. People v. Gaudet, 115 A.D.2d 183, 495 N.Y.S.2d 253 (3d Dept. 1985).

—Police officer's seizure of crack cocaine from a pantry shelf in plain view in defendant's apartment was proper pursuant to emergency exception, where the People established at the suppression hearing that when no one responded to their knocking, firefighters forcibly entered defendant's apartment to determine whether a fire in the apartment below had spread to defendant's apartment. A police officer went into defendant's apartment after being advised that firefighters had forcibly entered. People v. Crawford, 298 A.D.2d 850, 747 N.Y.S.2d 618 (4th Dept. 2002).

Search and seizure; illegal arrest; collateral source.—Evidence does not need to be suppressed simply because it was discovered subsequent to an illegal arrest; the prosecution must have somehow exploited or benefitted from its illegal conduct to such an extent that there is a connection between the violation of the constitutional right and the derivative evidence obtained by the police. People v. Jones, 2 N.Y.3d 235, 778 N.Y.S.2d 133, 810 N.E.2d 415 (2004).

Search and seizure; waiver.—Defendants failed to preserve search and seizure issues for review where they relied upon doctrine of "automatic standing" in trial court at a time when that doctrine was in serious question. People v. Cofresi, 60 N.Y.2d 728, 469 N.Y.S.2d 75, 456 N.E.2d 1198 (1983).

Search; stop and frisk; lack of consent; probable cause.—Police officer had a reasonable suspicion basis to instruct the defendant to place a plastic bag on the ground and to then search such bag where the defendant was a passenger on a moped which was being operated without license plates at 2:30 a.m. in a high crime area and neither the defendant nor the driver could produce identification and the officer further noted a heavy bulge in the bottom of the bag after the defendant implied that it contained only a pair of pants. People v. Davis, 64 N.Y.2d 1143, 490 N.Y.S.2d 725, 480 N.E.2d 339 (1985).

—A police officer, responding to a radio report of a man with a gun on a particular corner and who observed the defendant emerge from a building on that corner carrying a packet of white envelopes which he put into a black plastic bag upon seeing the officer, was justified in approaching and questioning the defendant, but not in searching the bag, and the evidence found in the bag should have been suppressed. People v. McNutt, 65 N.Y.2d 1046, 494 N.Y.S.2d 297, 484 N.E.2d 660 (1985).

—When police officers learned of the existence of a small handgun, the officers were clearly justified in searching those areas of the apartment where such a weapon might be found. People v. Golob, 154 A.D.2d 709, 547 N.Y.S.2d 69, 71 (2d Dept. 1989).

School authorities.—Evidence was suppressed, where defendant, a student in the high school, who had been suspected of dealing in drugs by the faculty for six months, was observed by the school coordinator of security twice entering a toilet room with a fellow student and exiting within 10 seconds, and was then taken to the Principal's office and search there at revealed drugs on his person; more than equivocal suspicion is required to justify a search of a school student by school authorities. People v. D., 34 N.Y.2d 483, 358 N.Y.S.2d 403, 315 N.E.2d 466 (1974).

Search of students by school officials; requirements.—Although the Fourth Amendment's prohibition against unreasonable searches and seizures applies to searches of students by public school officials, the requirement of a warrant is not suited to the school environment and need not be obtained before searching a student; additionally, the search need not be based upon probable cause to believe that the student is violating the law, but may be based upon reasonable grounds for suspecting that the search will discover evidence that the student has violated or is violating either the law or rules of the school providing that the scope of the search is reasonably related to its objectives, the nature of the infraction and the student's age and sex. New Jersey v. T.L.O., 469 U.S. 325, 105 S. Ct. 733, 83 L. Ed. 2d 720 (1985).

Hijacking (aircraft piracy) statutes do not authorize

search without probable cause.—Where the danger to the public is evident, the governmental interest so overwhelming, and the intrusion into personal privacy so minimal, the use of a magnetometer to search a prospective passenger is reasonable and constitutionally permissible. Once the magnetometer is "triggered," indicating the presence of metal upon a person, a further personal search or frisk of the passenger is not authorized unless the passenger consents. People v. Kuhn, 33 N.Y.2d 303, 351 N.Y.S.2d 649, 306 N.E.2d 777 (1973).

***Payton v. New York* retroactive.**—*Payton v. New York,* 445 U.S. 573, 100 S. Ct. 1371, 63 L. Ed. 2d 639, is retroactive to all convictions not final at the time of the decision. People v. Graham, 90 A.D.2d 198, 457 N.Y.S.2d 962 (3d Dept. 1982), *cert. denied,* 464 U.S. 896, *reh'g denied,* 464 U.S. 1005 (1983).

Violation of *Payton* rule.—The police officers' warrantless and nonconsensual entry into defendant's bedroom violated Payton v. New York, 445 U.S. 573, 100 S. Ct. 1371, 63 L. Ed. 2d 639, and therefore, the confession must be suppressed. People v. King, 92 A.D.2d 922, 460 N.Y.S.2d 140 (2d Dept. 1983), *aff'd,* 61 N.Y.2d 969, 475 N.Y.S.2d 275, 463 N.E.2d 616 (1984).

Suppression of evidence; lawful search and seizure.—At a $75,000 drug sale the police could reasonably expect an arsenal of weapons present; accordingly they had probable cause to search anyone they reasonably believed was connected to the transaction. People v. Castro, 80 A.D.2d 535, 436 N.Y.S.2d 22 (1st Dept. 1981), *aff'd,* 53 N.Y.2d 1046, 442 N.Y.S.2d 500, 425 N.E.2d 888 (1981).

Search by school official away from school grounds; reasonable suspicion valid basis.—A school official who had reasonable suspicion that a student was in possession of contraband materials had a right to pursue the student, after the latter ran from the school, and to search him upon apprehension, even though the search occurred away from school property. People v. Jackson, 65 Misc. 2d 909, 319 N.Y.S.2d 731 (App. Term, 1st Dept. 1971), *aff'd,* 30 N.Y.2d 734, 333 N.Y.S.2d 167, 284 N.E.2d 153 (1972).

Suppression hearing; probable cause for arrest; waiver.—Defendant, who argued at suppression hearing that sole issue was the involuntary nature of his statements due to his intoxication at the time such statements were made waived any argument that the statements should have been suppressed due to the lack of probable cause for defendant's arrest. People v. Albert, 98 A.D.2d 725, 469 N.Y.S.2d 136 (2d Dept. 1983).

Suppression of evidence; credibility of police testimony.—Suppression of evidence was required where photographs demonstrated that it was impossible for police officer to have seen a bag protruding from under the driver's seat of an automobile as he had testified at the suppression hearing. People v. Feingold, 106 A.D.2d 583, 482 N.Y.S.2d 857 (2d Dept. 1984).

Surveillance from public area.—Police officer who was engaged in surveillance of premises suspected of being a "chop shop" and from a public sidewalk was entitled to kneel down and peer through a three-inch gap beneath defendant's garage door. People v. Alberti, 111 A.D.2d 860, 490 N.Y.S.2d 261 (2d Dept. 1985).

Unlawful arrest.—Police lacked reasonable cause to justify defendant's arrest for criminally using drug paraphernalia in second degree (PL § 220.50(2)), where there was no evidence that defendant owned or regularly occupied the apartment in which the police were executing a search warrant to find drug paraphernalia, and where the evidence was insufficient to establish that defendant "exercised dominion or control over the property by a sufficient level of control over the area in which the contraband [was] found." Because search of defendant was not incident to a lawful arrest, the fruits of the search must be suppressed. People v. Williams, 298 A.D.2d 964, 747 N.Y.S.2d 664 (4th Dept. 2002).

Unlawful stop.—Unlawful police stop of defendant required suppression of a weapon found in defendant's waistband since the defendant's action in reaching into the waistband was spontaneous and precipitated by the illegality rather than being a calculated act not provoked by the unlawful police activity. People v. Wilkerson, 64 N.Y.2d 749, 485 N.Y.S.2d 981, 475 N.E.2d 448 (1984).

—Where police approach a suspect on the street and question him pursuant to the common law right to inquire, even a suspect's obvious falsehoods cannot justify further police intrusion without some other conduct which provides probable cause

or a reasonable fear that the officer is in danger of physical injury. People v. Meachem, 115 A.D.2d 370, 495 N.Y.S.2d 667 (1st Dept. 1985).

Voluntary surrender of contraband.—Where officer properly frisked defendant and found no weapons pursuant to a *Terry* stop, the officer had no right to examine a folded packet of papers in defendant's pocket which when opened were found to contain gambling records; neither the "plain view" exception nor the "inevitable discovery" exception were applicable. People v. Roth, 66 N.Y.2d 688, 496 N.Y.S.2d 413, 487 N.E.2d 270 (1985).

—Police officers who had reasonable grounds to fear for their safety were justified in drawing their guns when they approached defendant in his automobile and also were justified in patting defendant's chest area and, upon feeling a hard object, reaching into defendant's jacket to retrieve it. People v. Woods, 64 N.Y.2d 736, 485 N.Y.S.2d 975, 475 N.E.2d 442 (1984).

Warrantless search incident to arrest.—A duffel bag that is within the immediate control or "grabbable area" of a suspect at the time of his arrest may not be subjected to a warrantless search incident to the arrest unless the circumstances leading to the arrest support a reasonable belief that the suspect may gain possession of a weapon or be able to destroy evidence located in the bag. People v. Gokey, 60 N.Y.2d 309, 469 N.Y.S.2d 618, 457 N.E.2d 723 (1983).

Warrantless entry into home—Payton v. New York, 445 U.S. 573, 100 S. Ct. 1371, 63 L. Ed 2d 639 not retroactive; *see also* People v. Rosencrants, 77 A.D.2d 768, 431 N.Y.S.2d 216 (3d Dept. 1980).

SEARCH OF AUTOMOBILE

Arrest without a warrant; seizure of evidence.—Where the defendant showed his panel truck to police investigating an assault, and the police saw a woman's shoe, a pair of glasses, and a bloodstained dashboard, the victim's acquaintance with the defendant and the condition of his truck completed the incriminating circle; and the seizure of the evidence, as incident to the arrest or independently, was justified. Furthermore, because the seizure of the truck was simultaneous with the arrest of the defendant, the seizure was made under the classic exception to the general requirement that otherwise reasonable searches must be performed on warrant obtained from a magistrate or on probable cause. People v. Brosnan, 32 N.Y.2d 254, 344 N.Y.S.2d 900, 298 N.E.2d 78 (1973).

—"While the stop of the cab may have been justified, given the traffic infraction and the alleged erratic behavior, after defendant was removed from cab and frisked without recovering anything, the search of the cab was unlawful . . . [g]iven the unlawfulness of the search, the plain view doctrine does not apply." People v. Olivo, 271 A.D.2d 345, 707 N.Y.S.2d 406 (1st Dept. 2000).

—Probable cause exists under the so-called "automobile exception" to the warrant requirement of the fourth amendment where there was no advance opportunity to obtain a warrant prior to seizure of the vehicle, the truck was stopped on a public highway, there was a reasonable possibility that a search of the vehicle would produce the weapon used to commit the crime and the police had a description of the assailant from the victim who identified him at the scene, and no weapon was found when he was frisked. People v. Hill, 79 A.D.2d 616, 433 N.Y.S.2d 479 (2d Dept. 1980).

Arrest; search of automobile on premises.—Search of truck incidental to arrest on unrelated charge was unlawful; property instead, a warrant was necessary because police knew that the trucks were in rear of defendant's business premises for four months, no license plates were on the trucks and there was no fear they would be spirited away. People v. Spinelli, 35 N.Y.2d 77, 358 N.Y.S.2d 743, 315 N.E.2d 792 (1974).

Automobile exception to search warrant requirement.—Under the "narrow" automobile exception to the State and Federal Constitutions' requirement of a search warrant, police officers having probable cause to believe that contraband is located in a motor vehicle may conduct a warrantless search of the entire vehicle, including any compartments or closed containers located therein. People v. Langen, 60 N.Y.2d 170, 469 N.Y.S.2d 44, 456 N.E.2d 1167 (1983), *cert. denied,* 465 U.S. 108 (1984).

—The search of an automobile is lawful when it is limited to those areas in which a weapon may be placed or hidden and the police officer possesses a reasonable belief, based on specific and articulable facts, which reasonably warrant him to believe the suspect is dangerous. People v. McClane, 143 A.D.2d 848, 533 N.Y.S.2d 326 (2d Dept. 1988).

Flashlight; vehicle.—Where there was no basis for suspicion other than defendant's prior presence in a rented car and his walking about the block, the police use of a flashlight to illuminate the interior of the car was an unwarranted intrusion into the interior of the vehicle and the firearm and the drugs discovered were suppressed. People v. Smith, 42 N.Y.2d 961, 398 N.Y.S.2d 142, 367 N.E.2d 648 (1977).

Inevitable discovery.—In applying the inevitable discovery rule, it is necessary to exclude wrongfully obtained primary evidence notwithstanding that such evidence would inevitably have been recovered lawfully through subsequent police activity. People v. Stith, 69 N.Y.2d 313, 514 N.Y.S.2d 201, 506 N.E.2d 911 (1987).

—The doctrine of inevitable discovery may not be used to excuse unlawful police actions by admitting what was obtained as a direct result of the misconduct. People v. Burr, 70 N.Y.2d 354, 520 N.Y.S.2d 739, 742 n.3, 514 N.E.2d 1363 (1987).

—Suppression of cocaine seized in the car was properly denied even though the unlawful arrest tainted the evidence as it would be admissible under the doctrine of "inevitable discovery" in that the officers would "inevitably" have impounded the car and found the cocaine. People v. Buffardi, 92 A.D.2d 899, 459 N.Y.S.2d 893 (2d Dept. 1983).

—Even though search warrant was invalid, the discovery of evidence in defendant's vehicle was inevitable because the car was stuck in a ditch and abandoned by its occupants, making it destined for impoundment and a permissible inventory search under normal police procedures, which would have revealed the physical evidence from the burglaries. People v. Ladd, 16 A.D.3d 972, 792 N.Y.S.2d 246 (3d Dept. 2005).

—Court properly refused to suppress evidence recovered during unlawful search of truck where computer check which commenced prior to unlawful search later revealed that the truck was stolen and the vehicle could and would have been searched pursuant to normal State Police procedure in any event. People v. Stith, 124 A.D.2d 342, 507 N.Y.S.2d 283 (3d Dept. 1986).

Roadblocks.—The suspicionless roadblock stop of defendant's vehicle contravened the fourth amendment because the hearing testimony of the officers who set up and operated the roadblock pointed to a series of unprioritized purposes, i.e., to reduce crime, educate cab drivers, prevent cab robberies and carjackings, and interdict drugs and guns. Many of these objectives were related only to general crime control and the evidence seized was properly suppressed. People v. Jackson, 99 N.Y.2d 125, 752 N.Y.S.2d 271, 782 N.E.2d 67 (2002).

—Defendant's motion to suppress should have been granted, where defendant was arrested as the result of a suspicionless stop of the livery cab in which he was a passenger at a police roadblock similar to the one found unconstitutional in People v. Jackson, 99 N.Y.2d 125, 752 N.Y.S.2d 271, 782 N.E.2d 67. People v. Williams, 309 A.D.2d 648, 765 N.Y.S.2d 629 (1st Dept. 2003).

—No prior empirical evidence of alcohol related arrests or accidents at a particular site is required before that site can be used for a sobriety checkpoint. People v. Sears, 2 Misc. 3d 447, 769 N.Y.S.2d 708 (Justice Ct. Monroe Co. 2003).

—The State has a substantial interest in curbing drunk driving and road blocks are permissible to achieve that result provided they are operated in a nondiscriminatory and nonarbitrary manner. People v. Snead, 160 Misc. 2d 466, 609 N.Y.S.2d 520 (Nassau Co. Dist. Ct. 1994).

Seizure of evidence.—After defendant's arrest at 4 a.m. at the crime site and seizure of his auto, it was reasonable for the police to defer further search of the vehicle until later that morning at the sheriff's parking lot. People v. Fustanio, 35 N.Y.2d 196, 360 N.Y.S.2d 245, 318 N.E.2d 466 (1974).

—Officer observed three foot long bar with hook on end in the trunk of defendant's car when he opened it for the officer; later at the scene of the burglary, defendant's passenger was positively identified as the burglar and there than existed probable cause to arrest defendant for possession of burglar's tools and seize the automobile. People v. Fustanio, 35 N.Y.2d 196, 360 N.Y.S.2d 245, 318 N.E.2d 466 (1974).

—A warrantless opening of a clothing box is valid after it had previously been shown to an undercover police officer in the car and contained cocaine as this was not personal luggage, was in plain view on the floor of the car, could be opened by merely lifting the lid, and there was no expectation of privacy in the contents of the box. People v. Maldanado, 76 A.D.2d 691, 431 N.Y.S.2d 580 (2d Dept. 1980).

Search; border crossing; probable cause.—In absence of defendant's proof that customs search was unconstitutional, marijuana found in car is admissible in evidence and fact that inspectors' observation of anti-draft literature prompted search is irrelevant. People v. Dworkin, 30 N.Y.2d 706, 332 N.Y.S.2d 645, 283 N.E.2d 620 (1972).

Evidence uncovered during inventory search of car.—Where police towed away an illegally parked car and conducted an inventory search pursuant to police regulations, a gun discovered in a briefcase in the car was not the product of an unlawful search and seizure. People v. Sullivan, 29 N.Y.2d 69, 323 N.Y.S.2d 945, 272 N.E.2d 464 (1971).

Border search of vehicle; no probable cause or even suspicion required.—Customs officials have the right to stop and examine any vehicle, person or baggage at a border search without probable cause. Moreover, no suspicion of the presence of contraband is necessary to make a border search reasonable, since "the mere fact that a person crosses the border is sufficient to subject him to a border search of his baggage, vehicle or personal effect." People v. Dworkin, 36 A.D.2d 313, 321 N.Y.S.2d 263 (4th Dept. 1971), aff'd, 30 N.Y.2d 706, 332 N.Y.S.2d 645, 283 N.E.2d 620 (1972).

Drug-sniffing canine.—Where defendant's vehicle had been stopped in connection with a traffic violation, and the arresting officer observed a glass pipe used to smoke crack cocaine with cocaine residue, these observations, together with the driver's inability to produce a valid registration or driver's license, provided the police with probable cause to arrest and to believe the vehicle contained contraband; accordingly, use of drug-sniffing canine was proper. People v. Rives, 237 A.D.2d 312, 654 N.Y.S.2d 797 (2d Dept. 1997).

Inventory search.—Where the police department policy governing the inventory search failed to generate a meaningful inventory of the vehicle's contents and allowed the officer undue discretion, it violated both the State and Federal Constitutions. People v. Galak, 80 N.Y.2d 715, 594 N.Y.S.2d 689, 610 N.E.2d 362 (1993).

—Where purpose of an inventory search of an automobile was to preserve property and not to discover evidence of crime, under the parameters of the reasonableness standard applied to administrative inventory search after lawful arrests, police should be permitted to inventory contents of all closed containers located by them within an automobile during such an inventory search. People v. Gonzalez, 62 N.Y.2d 386, 477 N.Y.S.2d 103, 465 N.E.2d 823 (1984).

—Inventory search does include the right to open or search packages, or other items found in the vehicle. People v. Roman, 53 N.Y.2d 39, 439 N.Y.S.2d 894, 422 N.E.2d 554 (1981).

—Cocaine found in a crumpled up paper bag suspended by a wire from the dashboard of a car which was seized after defendant had been arrested for driving with a suspended license and was discovered in the course of an inventory search was admissible. People v. Gonzalez, 92 A.D.2d 512, 459 N.Y.S.2d 281 (1st Dept. 1983), aff'd, 62 N.Y.2d 386, 477 N.Y.S.2d 103, 465 N.E.2d 823 (1984).

—Police were authorized to conduct warrantless inventory search of car where defendant was stopped for speeding and, in the course of a routine, noncustodial roadside interrogation, defendant admitted that her Florida driver's license had been suspended, which the police confirmed by radio; further, defendant's passenger was not licensed to drive the car. People v. Kearney, 288 A.D.2d 398, 733 N.Y.S.2d 460 (2d Dept. 2001).

—People alleged that two separate quantities of marihuana were seized from defendant's car pursuant to an inventory search, but there was nothing in the suppression hearing record to indicate that the police were acting pursuant to any standardized procedure, and no inventory report was generated. Thus, the marihuana should have been suppressed and the convictions based on the possession of marihuana had to be vacated. People v. Minto, 272 A.D.2d 558, 708 N.Y.S.2d 434 (2d Dept. 2000).

Plain view; automobiles.—The motion to suppress physical evidence was granted after the officer testified that he had seen the stock of the shotgun under the car seat because he was looking for a weapon since the element of inadvertence was absent and the discovery of the weapon must be deemed the product of a search. People v. Earley, 76 A.D.2d 335, 430 N.Y.S.2d 641 (2d Dept. 1980).

—Although initial stop of vehicle driven by defendant was lawful, and pipe was in plain view, officer's search of vehicle was not lawful, in view of fact that it was not immediately apparent that pipe was either evidence or contraband. People v. Richie, 77 A.D.2d 667, 430 N.Y.S.2d 154 (2d Dept. 1980).

—Where defendant's garage was open to the public, the police officer, as any other citizen, was free to enter the premises and observe the vehicles in "plain view." People v. Ciardullo, 74 A.D.2d 580, 424 N.Y.S.2d 301 (2d Dept. 1980).

—Contraband is not in plain view when the police officer, in response to an anonymous tip, had to jump up in the air and shine his flashlight into a window of a garage to see the contraband. People v. Sciacca, 78 A.D.2d 545, 432 N.Y.S.2d 90 (2d Dept. 1980).

—When an inventory search is challenged, the People have the burden of establishing that it was conducted pursuant to standardized procedures. People v. Rhodes, 206 A.D.2d 710, 614 N.Y.S.2d 641 (3d Dept. 1994).

—To satisfy the constitutional standard of reasonableness, an inventory search of an impounded vehicle must be conducted pursuant to a standard procedure that is designed to meet the legitimate objectives of the search, and which clearly limits the discretion exercisable by officers in the field. People v. Walker, 194 A.D.2d 92, 604 N.Y.S.2d 631 (3d Dept. 1993).

—Sergeant's use of a flashlight to illuminate the interior of defendant's vehicle, which resulted in discovery of the handgun, did not constitute a search. People v. Harris, 173 Misc. 2d 49, 660 N.Y.S.2d 792 (Sup. Ct. Monroe Co. 1997).

—Police officers may seize contraband in plain view inside an automobile, provided that observation is made from a lawfully-obtained vantage point. People v. Beriguette, 199 A.D.2d 515, 605 N.Y.S.2d 759 (2d Dept. 1993), aff'd, 84 N.Y.2d 978, 622 N.Y.S.2d 497, 646 N.E.2d 799 (1994).

Probable cause; search of automobile.—Once defendant and other occupants had been lawfully removed from the vehicle, police could commit the greater intrusion of reaching into the vehicle, because the officer observed that defendant wore bulletproof vest and bent down to hide something underneath the seat as the officer approached. People v. Carvey, 89 N.Y.2d 707, 657 N.Y.S.2d 879, 680 N.E.2d 150 (1997).

—The authority of the police to search an automobile usually arises when there is probable cause to believe that it contains weapons, contraband or evidence, and there is ordinarily no requirement that the police delay their search until they obtain a warrant, even where the vehicle has been reduced to their control. People v. Milerson, 51 N.Y.2d 919, 434 N.Y.S.2d 980, 415 N.E.2d 968 (1980).

—The use of coat hangers to open defendant's car and search it when it was a few feet from the police station and a woman in the station had accused the defendant of menacing her with a gun and had seen it and defendant stated he had thrown away the keys to his expensive car was valid as probable cause existed. People v. Cabral, 91 A.D.2d 944, 458 N.Y.S.2d 559 (1st Dept.), dismissed, 59 N.Y.2d 704, 463 N.Y.S.2d 439, 450 N.E.2d 245 (1983).

—Policeman who had been informed by defendant's father that defendant had a gun and who saw the defendant was wearing a shoulder holster had probable cause to search the person of the defendant as well as the car from which he had just exited. People v. Caldwell, 107 A.D.2d 62, 437 N.Y.S.2d 829 (1st Dept. 1981).

—Defendant's motion to suppress the gun was denied in view of all the circumstances particularly the defendant's peculiar and suspicious action of bending forward when the police officer approached the car, the hour of the night, and the neighborhood, the actions of the officer in shining his flashlight and looking into the car was entirely reasonable. People v. Simmons, 83 A.D.2d 79, 443 N.Y.S.2d 378 (1st Dept. 1981).

Probable cause for arrest.—Where defendant's vehicle had been stopped in connection with a traffic violation, and the arresting officer observed a glass pipe used to smoke crack cocaine with cocaine residue, these observations, together with the driver's inability to produce a valid registration or driver's license, provided the police with probable cause to arrest and to believe the vehicle contained contraband; accordingly, use

of drug-sniffing canine was proper. People v. Rives, 237 A.D.2d 312, 654 N.Y.S.2d 797 (2d Dept. 1997).

—Probable cause existed to arrest defendant and seize his packages when an experienced officer, with 50 heroin arrests and with having watched 8-10 heroin packaging processes, observed defendant with three very tight, square shaped bundles of newspaper. People v. Germany, 157 Misc. 2d 932, 599 N.Y.S.2d 416 (Sup. Ct. Bronx Co. 1993).

Probable cause to search for further evidence.—A Belton search can be justified on grounds other than those that initially prompted police to stop the vehicle. People v. Galak, 81 N.Y.2d 463, 600 N.Y.S.2d 185, 616 N.E.2d 842 (1993).

—Where police found a live bullet in the defendant's pocket after lawfully stopping him in his automobile for a traffic infraction and frisking him prior to removal to station house for issuance of a summons, they had probable cause to believe a gun was inside the car and could search it and its contents including, but not limited to, the locked glove compartment in which the weapon was found after being forced open by the police at the scene of the stop. People v. Ellis, 62 N.Y.2d 393, 477 N.Y.S.2d 106, 465 N.E.2d 826 (1984).

—Where police forcibly detained defendant, who was a passenger, following a stop for a traffic violation and searched the defendant when he attempted to leave, such conduct exceeded that permissible during a normal traffic stop, as there was no showing of a reasonable suspicion on the part of the police that the defendant was committing, had committed, or was about to commit a crime. People v. Antelmi, 196 A.D.2d 658, 601 N.Y.S.2d 634 (2d Dept. 1993).

—The actions of the police officers in detaining the vehicle and ordering the occupants out was supported by their receipt of a radio transmission regarding a suspicious white van bearing the same license number and by their personal observation that the van's driver committed several dangerous traffic infractions. People v. Sprinkler, 198 A.D.2d 313, 603 N.Y.S.2d 550 (2d Dept. 1993).

—Observation of a .32 caliber cartridge in the back seat of a car that had been stopped for traveling more than a mile in the left passing lane of the New York State Thruway did not constitute probable cause to search the entire vehicle; the presence of the cartridge, in the absence of any indication of criminal activity, was susceptible of innocent interpretation. People v. Savona, 112 A.D.2d 328, 491 N.Y.S.2d 779 (2d Dept. 1985).

—Court properly suppressed pistol found in glove compartment of defendant's car because police, after being given the car's keys by unidentified men who found them in the trunk lock, could have identified the owner of the vehicle by less intrusive means. People v. Perez, 107 A.D.2d 825, 484 N.Y.S.2d 664 (2d Dept. 1985).

—Police officers, who had received reliable information as to a "contract" to kill a particular individual, had a reasonable suspicion to believe that the occupants of a vehicle were involved in criminal activity based upon information that the vehicle had been operated in a suspicious manner over a period of time on the street where the intended victim resided and the officers acted properly in stopping the vehicle and seizing weapons in "plain view" under the front seat of the vehicle. People v. Evans, 106 A.D.2d 527, 483 N.Y.S.2d 339 (2d Dept. 1984).

Motion to suppress; probable cause; search of automobile independent of misdemeanor arrest.—Motion to suppress was denied where the search of the parolee's residence bore a substantially rational and reasonable relation to the officer's duty. People v. Fridell, 81 A.D.2d 869, 438 N.Y.S.2d 884 (2d Dept. 1981), dismissed, 56 N.Y.2d 642, 450 N.Y.S.2d 787, 436 N.E.2d 193 (1982).

—Police request to search the car was justified upon their founded suspicion that criminal activity was afoot based on the obvious spurious response to the inquiry about the origin and destination of the trip. People v. Carter, 199 A.D.2d 817, 606 N.Y.S.2d 786 (3d Dept. 1994).

—Search of a vehicle cannot be justified solely on the basis of a lawful stop of the vehicle for speeding. People v. Sora, 176 A.D.2d 1172, 575 N.Y.S.2d 970 (3d Dept. 1991).

—An officer is authorized to arrest a person for driving a car without ownership papers and upon that arrest may impound the car and drive it to the precinct to protect it while the ownership can be checked out; an officer may also take a car to the precinct after arresting the driver for an offense not related to the car. People v. Berry, 158 Misc. 2d 202, 600 N.Y.S.2d 1018 (Sup. Ct. Kings Co. 1993).

Routine traffic check; illegal search.—The Fourth Amendment does not prohibit the police from employing a roving roadblock in a uniform and nondiscriminatory manner in a sparsely populated area where a rash of burglaries occurred, and where the roving patrol was limited to stopping vehicles in the region where there had been many burglaries. People v. John B., 56 N.Y.2d 482, 453 N.Y.S.2d 158, 438 N.E.2d 864 (1982), cert. denied, 459 U.S. 1010 (1982).

—Except for routine checks to enforce automobile regulations, the stopping of an automobile by the police constitutes an impermissible seizure absent at least a reasonable suspicion that its occupants had been, are then, or are about to be, engaged in conduct in violation of law. People v. Sobotker, 43 N.Y.2d 559, 402 N.Y.S.2d 993, 373 N.E.2d 1218 (1978).

—Stopping of auto to conduct a routine traffic check constituted an illegal seizure of auto and contraband found upon search could not be used as evidence where defendant's 23-year-old auto was in apparently excellent condition, had no visible signs of defective equipment and defendant was not in violation of any traffic laws, and state trooper had no information concerning defendant or his auto. People v. Ingle, 36 N.Y.2d 413, 369 N.Y.S.2d 67, 330 N.E.2d 39 (1975).

—The arresting officers had probable cause to arrest defendants and seize the contraband on the following facts; the area was a high crime area and a known narcotics area, the officers reasonably suspected violations of the Vehicle and Traffic laws which were open and notorious and when they approached the car they observed a clear plastic bag containing white powder, tinfoil packets and glassine envelopes on the seat between the defendants and the officers had extensive training in narcotics. People v. Cabot, 88 A.D.2d 556, 450 N.Y.S.2d 489 (1st Dept. 1982).

—Checkpoint stop of defendant's car was unconstitutional, despite its non-discretionary implementation pursuant to written checkpoint guidelines, because its primary purpose was to advance the general interest in crime control, and not within the types of checkpoint programs that have been recognized, i.e., ones designed to serve purposes closely related to the problems of policing the border or the necessity of ensuring roadway safety. People v. Pope, 190 Misc. 2d 508, 738 N.Y.S.2d 543 (Sup. Ct. Bronx Co. 2002).

Search of automobile proper; incident to lawful arrest.—Search of automobile was proper as incident to a lawful custodial arrest where the officer, who stopped the automobile, had knowledge that a robbery had been committed, had positive identification of the car and positive identification of the defendant prior to the search. People v. Appel, 103 A.D.2d 860, 477 N.Y.S.2d 915 (3d Dept. 1984).

Search of vehicle; delay has no effect.—Where police have probable cause to make a warrantless search of a lawfully stopped vehicle and, under United States v. Ross, any container found therein that may conceal the object of the search, the search of the containers need not take place immediately nor while such containers are still in the vehicle and a warrantless search of packages three days after their removal from a vehicle pursuant to such a search was reasonable and proper. United States v. Johns, 469 U.S. 478, 105 S. Ct. 881, 83 L. Ed. 2d 890 (1985).

Search and seizure; general or exploratory search improper even where incident to a lawful arrest.—General or exploratory searches are condemned even when they are incident to lawful arrests; and where a defendant has produced his license and registration and there has been no showing that he was not able to answer satisfactorily questions concerning the identification number of his automobile, mere violation of a provision of the Vehicle and Traffic Law pertaining to an identification number which has been destroyed, removed, or defaced, without more, will not sustain a search of defendant's person. People v. Adams, 32 N.Y.2d 451, 346 N.Y.S.2d 229, 299 N.E.2d 653 (1973).

Seizure of evidence.—A lawful arrest authorizes the search of a vehicle and of closed containers visible in the passenger compartment of the vehicle when the circumstances give reason to believe that the vehicle or its visible contents may be related to the crime for which the arrest is made, or there is reason to believe a weapon may be discovered; the discovery of the odor of marihuana and marihuana made it reasonable to believe

auto might contain other drugs, and justified warrantless search and seizure of cocaine found in defendant's jacket in back seat of car, after occupants of car arrested. People v. Belton, 55 N.Y.2d 49, 447 N.Y.S.2d 873, 432 N.E.2d 745 (1982).

Standing to object.—Defendant, as a passenger in the taxicab, had standing to contest the legality of the stop of the taxicab. People v. Patterson, 129 A.D.2d 527, 514 N.Y.S.2d 378 (1st Dept. 1987).

—A mere passenger in a car does not have standing to challenge the search of a lawfully stopped vehicle. People v. Ballard, 16 A.D.3d 697, 794 N.Y.S.2d 60 (2d Dept. 2005); People v. Bell, 9 A.D.3d 492, 780 N.Y.S.2d 373 (2d Dept. 2004).

—Defendant had no standing to challenge the search and seizure of two cars in a used car lot where the defendant had no connection with the lot nor a legitimate expectation of privacy in the vehicles seized, People v. Boylan, 111 A.D.2d 928, 491 N.Y.S.2d 37 (2d Dept. 1985).

—The defendant had standing to object to the search of his daughter's car which he had been driving with her consent. People v. Zimmerman, 117 Misc. 2d 121, 458 N.Y.S.2d 468 (Sup. Ct. Suffolk Co. 1982).

Probable cause; consent.—Court erred in granting defendant's suppression motion since the police officer was lawfully on defendant's business premises when he observed in open view a tampered vehicle identification plate on the dashboard of the automobile in question; thus, the observation involved no Fourth Amendment search. People v. Salamino, 107 A.D.2d 827, 484 N.Y.S.2d 666 (2d Dept. 1985).

Traffic stop.—Frisk of defendant was justified, where it was undertaken only after defendant's unusual movement immediately following the valid traffic stop, the defendant's evasive denials about his bulletproof vest, and the officer's observation of what his personal experience taught him was a bulletproof vest on a person. People v. Batista, 88 N.Y.2d 650, 649 N.Y.S.2d 356, 672 N.E.2d 581 (1996).

—The stop of the cab in which the defendant was a passenger was justified by the officers' observation that the cab's brake lights were not functioning. People v. Robbins, 196 A.D.2d 699, 601 N.Y.S.2d 617 (1st Dept. 1993).

—The stop of the vehicle in which defendant was a passenger was justified by the police officer's observation of a defective headlight. People v. Clemente, 195 A.D.2d 300, 600 N.Y.S.2d 12 (1st Dept. 1993).

—A routine traffic stop may be made on a minimal degree of suspicion of a vehicle violation. People v. Perez, 149 A.D.2d 344, 539 N.Y.S.2d 750 (1st Dept. 1989).

—The police may not use traffic violations as mere pretext to investigate the defendant on an unrelated matter. People v. Lewis, 195 A.D.2d 523, 600 N.Y.S.2d 272 (2d Dept. 1993).

—Since the rear lights of the van were not operating, offering reasonable grounds to suspect a violation of the Vehicle and Traffic Law, a police stop of the vehicle was justified. People v. Harvey, 146 A.D.2d 585, 536 N.Y.S.2d 507 (2d Dept. 1989).

—Search of vehicle cannot be based solely upon a violation of the Vehicle and Traffic Law. People v. Banks, 202 A.D.2d 902, 609 N.Y.S.2d 420 (3d Dept. 1994).

—State trooper's observation of the speed offense provided a reasonable basis to stop the car. People v. Carter, 199 A.D.2d 817, 606 N.Y.S.2d 786 (3d Dept. 1993), aff'd, 86 N.Y.2d 721, 631 N.Y.S.2d 116, 655 N.E.2d 157 (1995).

—The police can stop a vehicle when they reasonably suspect a violation of the Vehicle and Traffic Law, and there is no requirement that the violation be substantial. People v. Durgey, 186 A.D.2d 899, 589 N.Y.S.2d 631 (3d Dept. 1992).

—A driver's inability to produce a license authorizes an officer to detain the car and driver for further investigation. People v. Williams, 158 Misc. 2d 933, 602 N.Y.S.2d 314, 317 (Crim. Ct. Queens Co. 1993).

Warrantless search of private property; probable cause for subsequent search of auto.—Information obtained as a result of a trespass by police may not be used to justify subsequent warrantless stop and search of an auto and seizure of incriminating evidence discovered during earlier trespass. People v. Gleeson, 36 N.Y.2d 462, 369 N.Y.S.2d 113, 330 N.E.2d 72 (1975).

INFORMANTS

Darden hearing.—When information obtained from a

confidential informant is necessary to establish probable cause, it would be "fair and wise" for the People "to be required to make the informer available for interrogation before the Judge" in an ex parte hearing. People v. Darden, 34 N.Y.2d 177, 356 N.Y.S.2d 582, 313 N.E.2d 49 (1974).

—A *Darden* hearing is a requirement rather than a matter of discretion. People v. Edwards, 95 N.Y.2d 486, 719 N.Y.S.2d 202, 741 N.E.2d 876 (2000).

Frisk; unidentified informer.—Policeman, having been told by an unidentified citizen on the street, in a high-crime area, that defendant was carrying a concealed weapon, acted reasonably in conducting a limited search. People v. Bronk, 31 N.Y.2d 995, 341 N.Y.S.2d 450, 293 N.E.2d 826 (1973).

Probable cause for warrantless search; substantiation of informer.—When an arrest or intrusion into a constitutionally protected premises is based on the accusation of an informer the police are under a duty to substantiate the informer's information. This substantiation "can come either from the informer's own character and reputation or from the separate objective check of the tale he tells." People v. Sullivan, 37 A.D.2d 559, 323 N.Y.S.2d 1 (1st Dept. 1971), *dism'd,* 29 N.Y.2d 937, 329 N.Y.S.2d 325, 280 N.E.2d 98 (1972).

Unknown man's report of gun does not warrant search.—When there is only the information from an unknown person that one of two men walking west on 112th Street, wearing a brown army jacket, had a gun, but had not been reported as having done anything of a suspicious nature, there were no exigent circumstances warranting the officer to take drastic action of searching the man and seizing a gun. People v. Bronk, 66 Misc. 2d 932, 323 N.Y.S.2d 134 (1st Dept. 1971), *aff'd,* 31 N.Y.2d 995, 341 N.Y.S.2d 450, 293 N.E.2d 826 (1973).

Disclosure of informant's identity or communications; when required and purposes of disclosure.—Prosecutor's refusal to disclose the name and address of informant prior to trial did not present a reviewable question of law, where defendant failed to demonstrate his need for the information during pretrial proceedings and disclosure was in fact ordered as soon as it appeared that informant's testimony might be relevant. People v. Maneiro, 49 N.Y.2d 769, 426 N.Y.S.2d 471, 403 N.E.2d 176 (1980).

Arrest; probable cause established; corroboration of informant's information.—Where reliable prior informant, manager of rooming house, observed addicts going in and out of defendant's room to purchase drugs and police thereafter personally observed four persons, including two known narcotics' addicts, in 15-minute period separately enter and leave room, with one holding two bills in his hand, police properly could enter room with key provided by manager based on probable cause a felony had been committed, confiscate gun being held by defendant, search and find 22 glassine envelopes on his person and thereupon arrest him. Exigent circumstances, including established recited facts and possibility of destruction of the contraband, justified unannounced entry into room without a warrant as exception to Code Cr. Proc. § 178. People v. Richardson, 36 A.D.2d 603, 318 N.Y.S.2d 891 (1st Dept.), *aff'd,* 29 N.Y.2d 802, 327 N.Y.S.2d 364, 277 N.E.2d 412 (1972).

—Information from an unidentified informant that defendant had a gun was insufficient, without more, to justify a gunpoint search of that defendant and the gun found pursuant to such search should have been suppressed. People v. Francis, 108 A.D.2d 322, 489 N.Y.S.2d 166 (1st Dept. 1985).

—A warrantless search may be based upon information from an informant which is hearsay especially where the person giving the information to the informant was a participant in the crime as this constituted a declaration against penal interest; what is required is information of such quality, considering its source and the circumstances in which it came into possession of the informant, that a reasonable observer would be warranted in determining that the basis of the informants knowledge was such that it led logically to the conclusion that a crime had been or was about to be committed. People v. Restrepo, 87 A.D.2d 320, 451 N.Y.S.2d 144 (1st Dept. 1982).

—People satisfied veracity component of *Aguilar-Spinelli* by showing that the police independently verified significant details of the information provided by the informants. People v. Smalls, 271 A.D.2d 754, 707 N.Y.S.2d 245 (3d Dept. 2000).

—The reliability of the informant was satisfactorily established by the Investigator's attestation to the past instances of the informant's reliability leading to the arrest and conviction of other persons on drug related charges, and the reliability of the information supplied by the informant was sufficiently supported where a police investigator verified informer's information that defendant had parked his car in the Albany Airport and took a flight to Miami, where informer said defendant would buy cocaine. People v. Kilmer, 87 A.D.2d 949, 451 N.Y.S.2d 244 (3d Dept. 1982).

Reliability of informant; corroboration by observation.—Although general trustworthiness of informant was not established, the fact that the information given by the informant was against his penal interest and that his information concerning cocaine in the defendant's home was corroborated by police observations of the informant visiting the defendant's home and the discovery thereafter of a large amount of cocaine on informant's person provided a sufficient basis to consider the specific tip to be credible. People v. Conforto, 62 N.Y.2d 725, 476 N.Y.S.2d 815, 465 N.E.2d 354 (1984).

—Where defendant was arrested for criminal trespass, a violation or a misdemeanor, it was proper for the police officer to search the attache case he was carrying at the time. People v. Weintraub, 35 N.Y.2d 351, 361 N.Y.S.2d 897, 320 N.E.2d 636 (1974).

Reneging on cooperation agreements.—Defendant's statements made under a cooperation agreement could be used against him for impeachment or rebuttal purposes but the prosecutor must show at a hearing that the defendant reneged on the promises contained in the agreement. People v. Stokes, 165 Misc. 2d 934, 630 N.Y.S.2d 634 (Sup. Ct. Monroe Co. 1995).

Informant's disclosure required.—The People should not be penalized when the informant has, on his or her own initiative, effectively disappeared after relinquishment of government control. People v. Maneiro, 49 N.Y.2d 769, 426 N.Y.S.2d 471, 403 N.E.2d 176 (1980).

In camera hearing on probable cause.—When probable cause is the issue, as opposed to guilt, defendant's rights are amply protected by an *in camera* examination by the hearing judge. People v. Singletary, 37 N.Y.2d 310, 372 N.Y.S.2d 68, 333 N.E.2d 369 (1975).

—Defendant is not entitled to a *Franks* hearing to challenge the veracity of a citizen informant whose *in camera* testimony before the issuing magistrate provided the probable cause necessary to support the issuance of a search warrant. People v. Grisafi, 192 A.D.2d 147, 601 N.Y.S.2d 737 (4th Dept. 1993).

NOTICE PROCEDURES

Pretrial identification; tainted identifications.—Court ruled a witness' description of the perpetrator admissible because there was no pretrial identification procedure to taint the description. People v. Ptah, 149 Misc. 2d 488, 565 N.Y.S.2d 397 (Sup. Ct. Bronx Co. 1990).

Failure to give notice for inculpatory statements; admissibility.—If the defense attorney opens the door to introduce statements through cross-examination, the People can introduce defendant's inculpatory statements without notice where there is no indication that the People knew of the statements or intended to offer them. People v. Purdie, 165 A.D.2d 720, 564 N.Y.S.2d 257 (1st Dept. 1990).

Failure to give notice for inculpatory statements; reversal.—Prosecutor's failure to give notice of intent to introduce defendant's prior testimony did not require reversal because there is not notice requirement for statements made as a witness in a prior trial and there was overwhelming proof of defendant's guilt. People v. Thorton-Bay, 180 A.D.2d 610, 580 N.Y.S.2d 321 (1st Dept. 1992).

Insufficient chain of custody.—The fact that People did not offer a knife, seized from defendant at the time of arrest for robbery, due to insufficient chain of custody did not establish grounds for a suppression hearing for the knife. People v. Moore, 185 A.D.2d 825, 586 N.Y.S.2d 647 (2d Dept. 1992).

HEARINGS

Refusal of officer to testify concerning conduct following seizure.—Where the officer at the suppression hearing was questioned in great detail about the contents of his affidavit and answered all questions, his refusal to answer questions concerning his conduct following the seizure did not warrant suppression of the seized evidence. People v Cameron, 44 A.D.2d 721, 355 N.Y.S.2d 19 (2d Dept.), cert. denied, 419 U.S. 1049 (1974).

Identification; defendant known to victim.—If whether the victim knew the defendant and whether their prior relationship was fleeting and distant is at issue, then a *Wade* hearing should be held with respect to the victim's previous identification. People v. Williams, 182 A.D.2d 490, 582 N.Y.S.2d 406 (1st Dept. 1992).

—A *Wade* hearing is not necessary when the victim and defendant are known to each other because there can be no suggestive identification. People v. Williams, 182 A.D.2d 490, 582 N.Y.S.2d 406 (1st Dept. 1992).

—Defendant was entitled to a hearing on admissibility of prior identification because the form that stated that the victim knew the defendant failed to state the period of time victim knew defendant. People v. Williams, 182 A.D.2d 490, 582 N.Y.S.2d 406 (1st Dept. 1992).

Pretrial taint hearing.—Although there is no express statutory authority for a pretrial taint hearing, in which the court determines whether suggestive questioning tainted the testimony of child witnesses, a court may direct a pretrial taint hearing on a proper showing of undue suggestion. People v. Nickel, 14 A.D.3d 869, 788 N.Y.S.2d 274 (3d Dept. 2005).

Suggestive viewings.—No need for a hearing for a second photographic viewing that occurs ten months after the first since the viewing is not inherently suggestive. People v. Bussey, 155 Misc. 2d 916, 591 N.Y.S.2d 916 (Sup. Ct. Monroe Co. 1992).

—A photographic viewing was not suggestive even though the witness had viewed the same photographic array a second time the day before trial; the prosecutor did not lead the witness nor did the second viewing taint the witness' prior positive identification. People v. Bussey, 155 Misc. 2d 916, 591 N.Y.S.2d 916 (Sup. Ct. Monroe Co. 1992).

MISCELLANEOUS

Burden of proof on defendant.—The defendant carries the burden of proof when he challenges the legality of a search and seizure. People v. Dworkin, 36 A.D.2d 430, 321 N.Y.S.2d 263 (4th Dept. 1971), aff'd, 30 N.Y.2d 706, 332 N.Y.S.2d 645, 283 N.E.2d 620 (1972).

Crime committed in presence of police.—The exclusionary rule does not require suppression of evidence of defendant's commission of a new crime in the presence of the arresting officer. People v. Van Duser, 277 A.D.2d 1034, 716 N.Y.S.2d 197 (4th Dept. 2000).

Eavesdropping evidence.—Nothing prevents the judge issuing an eavesdropping warrant from entertaining a motion to suppress evidence seized pursuant to it. People v. Tambre, 71 N.Y.2d 372, 527 N.Y.S.2d 372, 522 N.E.2d 448 (1988).

Incredible testimony by officers; binoculars.—Officer's identification through binoculars of a two-inch crack vial from an observation point at least 200 feet above the street in the dusk, officer's inexplicable decision to take a dinner break instead of arresting a suspected drug seller leaving the area, his spontaneous post-dinner identification of the defendant as a participant in drug sales viewed two hours earlier from a great distance, and a steep angle, and his well-rehearsed claim that he approached the defendant merely to exercise a common law right of inquiry, present a combination of circumstances that are so contrary to experience as to strain the officer's credibility beyond the breaking point; motion to suppress should be granted and indictment dismissed. People v. Carmona, 233 A.D.2d 142, 649 N.Y.S.2d 432 (1st Dept. 1996).

Evidence; plain view.—Plain view alone is never enough to justify a warrantless search and seizure; moreover, the object must have come into plain view inadvertently. People v. Spinelli, 35 N.Y.2d 77, 358 N.Y.S.2d 743, 315 N.E.2d 792 (1974).

—Absent proof that the person who consented to the police entry had common authority over the box based on mutual use or joint access, the warrantless seizure of the box was improper. Furthermore, the seizure of the box could not be justified pursuant to the plain view doctrine because the discovery of the box by the police was not inadvertent. People v. Coston, 271 A.D.2d 694, 706 N.Y.S.2d 732 (2d Dept. 2000).

—Where officer observed defendant slumped over the wheel of a parked car it was proper for the officer to ask defendant to get out of the car after he did not respond to questions concerning his well-being, however, there was no basis upon which to detain him, require that he furnish a registration for the car or identify himself in the absence of a reasonable suspicion that the defendant was engaged in criminal activity and the gun subsequently found was not properly seized under the "plain view" doctrine because there was no justification for the intrusion into the car. People v. Engle, 74 A.D.2d 583, 424 N.Y.S.2d 306 (2d Dept. 1980).

"In custody" factors.—Absent obvious restraint, a court will consider four factors in determining if a custody situation is present: (1) was there probable cause for arrest; (2) what was the subjective intent of the interrogation; (3) what was the suspect's subjective belief as to his freedom; and (4) was the investigation focused on the suspect. People v. Medvecky, 95 A.D.2d 921, 463 N.Y.S.2d 947 (3d Dept. 1983).

Search, property in police custody.—No warrant was required to subsequently remove evidence, consisting of slips showing names of victims, from police property envelope containing items obtained from defendant during search following his abortion arrest. People v. Perel, 34 N.Y.2d 462, 358 N.Y.S.2d 383, 315 N.E.2d 452 (1974).

Search of private ship at sea.—Motion to suppress physical evidence was properly denied where Coast Guard officials expressed an articulable reason for boarding the sailboat, i.e., for a safety check based on their observations of defective exterior navigation lighting on the subject vessel, observations that the vessel was lying low or heavy in the water, together with the fact that at one time in the not too distant past it had been on the "Suspect Vessel Lookout List" and probable cause to search the vessel accrued when one official smelled marijuana shortly after the boarding. People v. Van Horn, 76 A.D.2d 378, 430 N.Y.S.2d 646 (2d Dept. 1980).

Strip searches.—Strip search of defendant in public view on a street was not reasonable, and the glassine envelopes of cocaine should have been suppressed. A strip search, conducted in a public place, regardless of whether it includes a search of the arrested person's body cavities, is not justified or reasonable, absent the most compelling circumstances. People v. Mitchell, 2 A.D.3d 145, 768 N.Y.S.2d 204 (1st Dept. 2003).

—"[S]trip searches of arrestees charged with misdemeanors or other minor offenses violate the Fourth Amendment . . . unless there is a reasonable suspicion that the arrestee is concealing weapons or contraband based on the crime charged, the particular characteristics of the arrestee, or the circumstances of the arrest." The search of defendant's person conducted incident to his arrest for the unlawful possession of marijuana, a violation under PL § 221.05, was illegal, because at no point during the suppression hearing did the police officers claim that the strip search was anything other than part of the investigation of the bag of marijuana or that they suspected the defendant was concealing weapons or other contraband on his person. People v. Jennings, 297 A.D.2d 644, 747 N.Y.S.2d 235 (2d Dept. 2002).

—Repeated scanner readings evincing defendant's continued secretion of an object, coupled with his intransigent conduct, support the reasonableness of the strip search. People v. Pagan, 304 A.D.2d 980, 759 N.Y.S.2d 226 (3d Dept. 2003).

—Persons who are charged with misdemeanors or other minor offenses and are held in a local correctional facility have a right to be free from warrantless strip searches unless the officials have a reasonable suspicion that the arrestee is concealing weapons or other contraband. People v. Kelley, 306 A.D.2d 699, 762 N.Y.S.2d 438 (3d Dept. 2003).

CONFESSIONS

Admissions; *Miranda* warnings; lack of counsel.—Admissions made by defendant to the arresting officers before the *Miranda* warnings were given, and the statement made to the interrogator at the police barracks (after warnings had been given, but in the absence of an attorney), were all deemed voluntary. People v. Coons, 31 N.Y.2d 800, 339 N.Y.S.2d 458, modf'd 31 N.Y.2d 961, 341 N.Y.S.2d 105, 293 N.E.2d 253 (1972), cert. denied, 410 U.S. 988 (1974).

Admissibility of confession at joint trial.—The fact that the co-defendant did not testify does not bar the admission of her confession at a joint trial where the defendant had made a full and voluntary confession virtually identical to the co-defendant's confession. People v. Close, 90 A.D.2d 562, 456 N.Y.S.2d 152 (3d Dept. 1982).

Admissibility of confession; probable cause for arrest based on police alarm.—Where motion to suppress was directed to the sufficiency of the evidence and did not attack the underlying basis of reliability for the police alarm, the presumption of probable cause to issue it remained and the People were not called upon to rebut the presumption by an evidentiary showing and the subsequent confession was not the fruit of an unlawful arrest. People v. Jenkins, 47 N.Y.2d 722, 417 N.Y.S.2d 57, 390 N.E.2d 775 (1979).

Attenuation.—Even if defendant's second statement was ruled inadmissible, his third statement, made about four hours after his second statement and preceded by the administration and waiver of *Miranda* rights was sufficiently attenuated so that defendant would properly be considered to have been no longer under the influence of the prior questioning. People v. Hotchkiss, 260 A.D.2d 241, 691 N.Y.S.2d 3 (1st Dept. 1999).

—Court should have suppressed initial statement, made before the administration of *Miranda* warnings, as well as the subsequent statements defendant made after the administration of *Miranda* warnings but without a pronounced break from the initial statement; the later videotaped statement, made after the readministration of *Miranda* warnings, was admissible because it was sufficiently attenuated from the initial taint. People v. Vachet, 5 A.D.3d 700, 773 N.Y.S.2d 455 (2d Dept. 2004).

Custody; test.—The mere fact that the defendant was questioned at the police barracks for approximately 6 hours did not establish that he was in custody. People v. Macklin, 202 A.D.2d 445, 608 N.Y.S.2d 509 (2d Dept. 1994).

—Mere fact that defendant was at station house for three hours did not mean that he was in custody; *Miranda* warnings were not required. People v. Petrovich, 202 A.D.2d 523, 609 N.Y.S.2d 248 (2d Dept. 1994).

—In determining whether a defendant was in custody when he made a statement, the court should consider: (1) the amount of time the defendant spent with the police; (2) whether his freedom was restricted in any significant manner; (3) the location and atmosphere in which the defendant was questioned; (4) the degree of cooperation exhibited by the defendant; (5) whether he was apprised of his constitutional rights; and (6) whether the questioning was investigatory or accusatory in nature. People v. Lunderman, 19 A.D.3d 1067, 796 N.Y.S.2d 481 (4th Dept. 2005).

—The mere fact that a guilty person may feel threatened or restrained in the presence of police, not because of objective police conduct but because of secret guilty knowledge, does not render the situation custodial. People v. Johnson, 91 A.D.2d 327, 458 N.Y.S.2d 775 (4th Dept. 1983), *aff'd,* 61 N.Y.2d 932, 474 N.Y.S.2d 967, 463 N.E.2d 368 (1984).

Defendant familiar with *Miranda* warnings.—A *Miranda* warning given at the scene of the crime was valid even though the officer failed to inform the defendant that he had the right to have an attorney actually present at the questioning, since the defendant had two prior arrests and presumably had some familiarity with *Miranda* warnings. People v. Clee, 89 A.D.2d 188, 455 N.Y.S.2d 8 (1st Dept. 1982), *dism'd,* 61 N.Y.2d 899, 474 N.Y.S.2d 482, 462 N.E.2d 1200 (1984).

Defendants over 16 years old; presence of parents not required.—Police were under no obligation to tell the 20-year-old defendant's parents of his whereabouts while he was being questioned. People v. Myers, 17 A.D.3d 699, 793 N.Y.S.2d 537 (2d Dept. 2005).

—Police were not required to provide 18-year-old defendant with access to his grandmother during his interrogation because defendant was an adult, capable of waiving or invoking his *Miranda* rights. People v. Wells, 18 A.D.3d 1022, 795 N.Y.S.2d 383 (3d Dept. 2005).

—A 16-year-old is legally an adult, and the police are under no obligation to allow friends or family to communicate with a competent adult while he or she is in custody; defendant's claim that his oral and written statements should have been suppressed because the police isolated him from his family and used deceit and trickery to prevent his parents from having contact with him during the interrogation rejected. People v. Insonia, 277 A.D.2d 819, 716 N.Y.S.2d 791 (3d Dept. 2000).

—At the time of defendant's arrest, he was 17 years old and legally an adult; thus, there was no requirement that his parents be present during the police questioning. People v. Lewis, 277 A.D.2d 1010, 716 N.Y.S.2d 204 (4th Dept. 2000).

Determination; whether statement was made.—No persuasive reason has been advanced to expand the intended scope of a suppression hearing to require the determination of whether an accused in fact made the alleged confession; such a determination is peculiarly a function of credibility and absent any question of improper conduct in obtaining a confession, there are no compelling reasons for excluding a statement purportedly made by an accused since this is a question to be resolved by the jury. People v. Washington, 68 A.D.2d 90, 416 N.Y.S.2d 626 (2d Dept. 1979), *aff'd,* 51 N.Y.2d 214, 433 N.Y.S.2d 745, 413 N.E.2d 1159 (1980).

—The use of deception and trickery by the police need not result in a finding of involuntariness unless there is some showing that the deception was so fundamentally unfair as to deny due process. People v. Hassell, 180 A.D.2d 819, 580 N.Y.S.2d 773 (2d Dept. 1992).

—To determine whether a defendant's statements are the product of coercion, the focus is on the belief of the defendant. People v. Crawford, 152 Misc. 2d 763, 578 N.Y.S.2d 814, 819 (Sup. Ct. N.Y. Co. 1991).

Confession; *Miranda* warnings.—Defendant's rights against compulsory self-incrimination and to the assistance of counsel were not violated by his change in status from complainant to suspect since defendant was properly Mirandized at the time of the status change and the police investigation was conducted without deception. People v. Winchell, 64 N.Y.2d 826, 486 N.Y.S.2d 930, 476 N.E.2d 329 (1985).

—Where a defendant arrested for murder was twice given the *Miranda* warnings and confessed to police officers and to the District Attorney, his confession was properly admitted, even though he once expressed reservations about confessing if the victim were dead and one of the police officers present knew the victim was dead and did not so inform the defendant. People v. Solari, 43 A.D.2d 610, 349 N.Y.S.2d 31 (3d Dept. 1973), *aff'd,* 35 N.Y.2d 876, 363 N.Y.S.2d 953, 323 N.E.2d 191 (1974).

—Questions asked of a suspect in an opening criminal investigation that are designed to clarify the situation rather than coerce a statement are not considered part of the interrogation process to which *Miranda* requirement is applicable. People v. Jones, 118 A.D.2d 86, 503 N.Y.S.2d 740 (1st Dept. 1986).

—The order of suppression was reversed where the court improperly suppressed defendant's statements in the hospital because he was so agitated and excited that he could not voluntarily, intelligently, and knowingly waive his rights however this would appear to be a normal reaction for a person who had just been arrested for homicide. People v. Lee, 85 A.D.2d 577, 445 N.Y.S.2d 451 (1st Dept. 1981).

—An illiterate defendant may validly waive his rights so long as it is established that he understands the immediate meaning of the warnings. People v. Crant, 183 A.D.2d 846, 584 N.Y.S.2d 93, 94 (2d Dept. 1992).

—Defendant understood the *Miranda* warnings although he was mildly retarded. People v. Forbes, 182 A.D.2d 829, 583 N.Y.S.2d 14 (2d Dept. 1992).

—With the numerous people and children in the immediate area, the question posed to the defendant as to the whereabouts of the gun was more for the purpose of ascertaining for safety reasons the location of the gun, than to secure evidence of a crime. People v. Melvin, 188 A.D.2d 555, 591 N.Y.S.2d 454 (2d Dept. 1992).

—Police inquiries posed to defendant at time of their arrival at scene of homicide of "Who shot him?" and "Where was the murder weapon?" did not constitute interrogation but were merely a threshold inquiry designed to clarify the nature of the situation, thus the answers were admissible without *Miranda* warnings. People v. Alling, 118 A.D.2d 960, 500 N.Y.S.2d 186 (2d Dept. 1986).

—Police officer's inquiries of the defendant concerning whether he had shot alleged shooting victim and the location of the weapon, made prior to the administration of *Miranda* warnings, were proper; inquiries were made to clarify a volatile situation rather than to elicit evidence of a crime and were also proper under the public safety exception to the *Miranda* rule. People v. Chatman, 122 A.D.2d 148, 504 N.Y.S.2d 703 (2d Dept. 1986).

—Policeman's asking the defendant what he was doing hiding in a confessional was merely designed to clarify the situation and did not constitute custodial interrogation, thus the resulting statement was admissible notwithstanding the failure to forewarn the defendant of his *Miranda rights*. People v. Albano, 124 A.D.2d 739, 508 N.Y.S.2d 243 (2d Dept. 1986).

—Previous *Miranda* warnings issued to the defendant while undergoing custodial questioning by police officers with whom he presumably had not established an ongoing law enforcement relationship, could not suffice to provide the required assurance that the defendant's inculpatory statements made to his parole officer were the product of a voluntary and informed waiver of the right to remain silent. People v. Alston, 77 A.D.2d 906, 431 N.Y.S.2d 82 (2d Dept. 1980).

—A defendant's impaired intelligence is but one factor to be considered in deciding whether the accused understood the *Miranda* waiver. The inquiry focuses on defendant's ability to grasp the basic concepts that he or she could refuse to talk to an investigator or could ask to speak to a lawyer. People v. Comfort, 6 A.D.3d 871, 775 N.Y.S.2d 127 (3d Dept. 2004).

—One with subnormal intelligence may waive the *Miranda* rights as long as it is established that the immediate meaning of the warnings was understood. People v. Orlando LL, 188 A.D.2d 685, 591 N.Y.S.2d 211 (3d Dept. 1992).

—Statements which defendant made after having received his *Miranda* warnings would not be suppressed where probable cause to arrest the defendant without a warrant had been established by a police investigator. People v. Hall, 115 A.D.2d 138, 495 N.Y.S.2d 524 (3d Dept. 1985).

—The fact that defendant did not sign the *Miranda* rights waiver did not preclude a finding that his waiver was adequate and proper. People v. McDowell, 202 A.D.2d 1012, 609 N.Y.S.2d 985 (4th Dept. 1994).

—The officer's question regarding whether defendant had been drinking constituted a noncustodial investigatory inquiry for which *Miranda* warnings were not required. People v. Baker, 188 A.D.2d 1012, 592 N.Y.S.2d 161 (4th Dept. 1992).

—Suppression of defendant's incriminating oral statements was required where there was no attempt to "scrupulously honor" the defendant's assertion of *Miranda* rights and where, in fact, the conscious objective of the police was to elicit statements in clear violation of his rights to counsel and silence—they continued to question him after he asserted his right to counsel. People v. Nelson, 189 Misc. 2d 362, 731 N.Y.S.2d 593 (Monroe Co. Ct. 2001)

Custodial interrogation.—Questioning of an inmate is not per se custodial in nature. People v. Alls, 83 N.Y.2d 94, 608 N.Y.S.2d 139, 629 N.E.2d 1018 (1994).

—A person who is subjected to a frisk is not, as a matter of law, thereafter in custody for the purposes of administration of *Miranda* warnings; questioning after a frisk, without more, does not constitute custodial interrogation. People v. Morales, 65 N.Y.2d 997, 494 N.Y.S.2d 95, 484 N.E.2d 124 (1985).

—Defendant was not in custody when he made statements to the police where defendant went voluntarily to the police station to discuss an incident in which he had been shot, he was not handcuffed or restrained in any way, he was left alone in an unlocked room for an extended period of time with the officers occasionally inquiring as to his welfare, and all of the police actions were consistent with interviewing a crime victim, as opposed to a suspect. People v. Burns, 18 A.D.3d 397, 795 N.Y.S.2d 574 (1st Dept. 2005).

—Police brought defendant, who was seriously injured, to the hospital by ambulance, and although the police officer patted defendant down for her safety, she was unaware whether defendant was a suspect or victim. Unsure if defendant would die, a detective questioned defendant in the trauma room. The questioning was investigatory, not accusatory. During questioning defendant admitted that he had kidnapped the victim, who was later shot to death. A reasonable person, innocent of any crime would not have believed he was in custody and defendant was not entitled to suppression of the statement based on an absence of *Miranda* warnings. People v. Gren, 285 A.D.2d 612, 729 N.Y.S.2d 489 (2d Dept. 2001).

—The defendant was in custody and should have been advised of his *Miranda* rights after the police observed contraband in plain view in the defendant's room, drew their weapons and directed the occupants to stand against the wall; accordingly, defendant's reply to police questions about the location of a gun were inadmissible, as was physical evidence seized as a result of defendant's reply. People v. Cesar, 111 A.D.2d 707,

491 N.Y.S.2d 319 (1st Dept. 1985), *dismissed,* People v. Martinez, 67 N.Y.2d 752, 500 N.Y.S.2d 101, 490 N.E.2d 1227 (1985).

—*Miranda* warnings were not required since defendant was not in custody; while at home, he moved freely about the apartment, and was asked politely to go to the precinct house, and thereafter, he was at no point deprived of food, sleep, or outside contacts. People v. Almodovar, 196 A.D.2d 718, 601 N.Y.S.2d 914 (1st Dept. 1993), *cert. denied,* 114 S. Ct. 2143 (1994).

—The *Miranda* warnings are required when a person's freedom of movement is restrained and the questioning is designed to elicit incriminating evidence. People v. Chappell, 189 A.D.2d 695, 592 N.Y.S.2d 713 (1st Dept. 1993).

—Defendant's presence at the precinct for nearly two days was not determinative of the custody issue. People v. Wright, 188 A.D.2d 272, 591 N.Y.S.2d 3 (1st Dept. 1992).

—Defendant was not in custody when the police, believing that they were responding to the scene of a terrible accident, simply asked defendant what had happened in an attempt to clarify the situation. People v. McKenzie, 183 A.D.2d 631, 584 N.Y.S.2d 13 (1st Dept. 1992).

—The fact that questioning takes place in a police station, or that a person is read his or her rights, does not automatically transform investigatory questioning into a custodial interrogation, even if that person is a "suspect." People v. Nolcox, 190 A.D.2d 824, 593 N.Y.S.2d 835 (2d Dept. 1993).

—The test of whether an individual is in custody is determined not by what the defendant thought, but what a reasonable person, innocent of any crime, would have thought in the defendant's position. People v. Mosley, 196 A.D.2d 893, 601 N.Y.S.2d 1021 (2d Dept. 1993); People v. Perkins, 189 A.D.2d 830, 592 N.Y.S.2d 752 (2d Dept. 1993); People v. Ash, 191 A.D.2d 739, 594 N.Y.S.2d 366 (3d Dept. 1993).

Confession; voluntariness; admissibility of.—Unwarranted delay in arraignment is but one of the many factors bearing on the question of the voluntariness, and admissibility of a defendant's inculpatory statements. People v. Dairsaw, 46 N.Y.2d 739, 413 N.Y.S.2d 640, 386 N.E.2d 249 (1978), *cert. denied,* 440 U.S. 985 (1979).

—Where the People failed to call as a witness the police officer who interrogated the defendant, and the defendant's uncontradicted testimony that he was mentally and physically abused during interrogation went unchallenged, it was reversible error for the trial court to rule that the confession was voluntary beyond a reasonable doubt. People v. Valerius, 31 N.Y.2d 51, 334 N.Y.S.2d 871, 286 N.E.2d 254 (1972), *rev'g,* 36 A.D.2d 671, 318 N.Y.S.2d 883 (3d Dept. 1971).

—Generally, prearraignment interrogation does not deprive a defendant of his right to counsel except where police have caused an undue or unreasonable delay in arraigning defendant for the purpose of depriving him of his right to counsel; three and one half hour delay was not unreasonable. People v. Ortlieb, 201 A.D.2d 865, 607 N.Y.S.2d 786 (4th Dept. 1994).

Due process.—Although the police falsely informed the defendant, before obtaining his confession, that the co-perpetrator had implicated the defendant in the crime, the ruse was not so fundamentally unfair as to deny the defendant due process of law. People v. Ingram, 208 A.D.2d 561, 616 N.Y.S.2d 780 (2d Dept. 1994).

Evidence disclosed by inadmissible statement.—Physical evidence whose existence was disclosed by an inadmissible oral statement must be suppressed; defendant was improperly asked about the whereabouts of a rifle after he was arrested but before the *Miranda* warnings had been given. People v. Ross, 88 A.D.2d 729, 451 N.Y.S.2d 887 (3d Dept. 1982).

Failure to give defendant notice.—It was reversible error for a trial court to allow the prosecutor to elicit testimony regarding defendant's statements where the prosecution failed to inform the defendant of the existence of those statements. People v. Hoover, 57 N.Y.2d 908, 456 N.Y.S.2d 756, 442 N.E.2d 1267 (1982).

Fifth Amendment.—A statement made under threat of dismissal is protected by the privilege against self incrimination and is automatically immunized from use in criminal proceedings. People v. Corrigan, 80 N.Y.2d 326, 590 N.Y.S.2d 174, 604 N.E.2d 723 (1992).

General.—Defendant's right against self incrimination was not violated by the prosecution's use, as evidence in chief, of defendant's testimony in an earlier contempt proceeding it had brought against the defendant, since defendant was not compelled in any manner to testify at the contempt proceeding. People v. Lehrman, 200 A.D.2d 540, 606 N.Y.S.2d 701 (1st Dept. 1994).

Grand jury testimony.—Defendant's grand jury testimony relating to his admissions to a police officer following his arrest was not tainted by the officer's failure to give *Miranda* warnings. People v. Benson, 114 A.D.2d 506, 494 N.Y.S.2d 727 (2d Dept. 1985).

Guilty plea; waiver.—Defendant failed to preserve the suppression issue for appellate review by pleading guilty after the court ordered a *Huntley* hearing but prior to hearing itself and the decision on the motion. People v. Ruiz, 107 A.D.2d 770, 484 N.Y.S.2d 136 (2d Dept. 1985).

Hearing required.—Defendant was entitled to a hearing where his motion papers alleged that his confession was given in violation of his *Miranda* rights and as the result of threatening conduct by the police despite the People's contention that the statement was spontaneously made after his apprehension while fleeing from the crime scene and did not result from any interrogation. People v. Benitez, 70 A.D.2d 883, 417 N.Y.S.2d 106 (2d Dept. 1979).

Impeachment; suppressed statements.—Defendant's voluntary statements, although obtained in violation of his right to counsel, could be used for impeachment purposes. People v. Maerling, 64 N.Y.2d 134, 485 N.Y.S.2d 23, 474 N.E.2d 231 (1984).

—The People may impeach a defendant with his or her voluntary statement even if it is obtained in violation of his or her right to counsel. People v. Palmer, 192 A.D.2d 803, 596 N.Y.S.2d 522 (3d Dept. 1993).

Inconsistent statements; indirect use of.—Prior inconsistent statements secured in disregard of constitutional safeguards may not be used, directly or indirectly, to establish the people's case. People v. Ricco, 56 N.Y.2d 320, 452 N.Y.S.2d 340, 437 N.E.2d 1097 (1982).

Interlocking statements by co-defendants.—Statements of the defendant and a co-defendant which are substantially identical or which interlock may be fully admitted into evidence at a joint trial without violating the *Bruton* rule or the defendant's right to confrontation, notwithstanding that they may differ in reliability, because one was videotaped and the other was given to a lay witness who did not record it and testified from memory. People v. Cruz, 66 N.Y.2d 61, 495 N.Y.S.2d 14, 485 N.E.2d 221 (1985).

Interrogation over counsel's alleged objections not reversible error.—Contention of defendant that trial court committed reversible error when it permitted a police officer to testify to an admission made by defendant to the officer after defendant's attorney had allegedly instructed the officer not to question him was not allowed. People v. McCormick, 31 N.Y.2d 807, 339 N.Y.S.2d 460, 291 N.E.2d 584 (1972).

Intoxication; voluntariness.—For a statement to be suppressed because the defendant was intoxicated when it was made, the degree of inebriation must have risen to the level of "mania." People v. O'Keefe, 191 A.D.2d 464, 594 N.Y.S.2d 265 (2d Dept. 1993).

—Intoxication alone does not require suppression of statements made to the police without a showing that the defendant was so intoxicated as to be unable to comprehend the meaning of his words. People v. Dobronski, 112 A.D.2d 541, 491 N.Y.S.2d 478 (3d Dept. 1985).

—Court rejected defendant's claim that the trial court erred in denying his motion to suppress statements he made to police because he was intoxicated when he made those statements; although there was evidence that defendant may have been under the influence of a drug during police questioning, there was no evidence that defendant was "intoxicated to the degree of mania, or of being unable to understand the meaning of his statements." People v. Jackson, 288 A.D.2d 939, 732 N.Y.S.2d 524 (4th Dept. 2001).

Involuntary confession; police brutality.—Reversible error was committed when the court denied defendant's request for a *Huntley* hearing to suppress his confession in view of the defendant's allegation of police brutality and the submission of medical records in support of his claim, he "was entitled to full inquiry into the voluntary nature of his purported confession even though he denied having made any confession." People

v. Armioia, 92 A.D.2d 549, 459 N.Y.S.2d 118 (2d Dept.), *aff'd,* 96 A.D.2d 514, 464 N.Y.S.2d 993 (2d Dept. 1983).

Juvenile.—Where a juvenile defendant claims that he was isolated from those supportive adults who attempted to see him, a showing that the isolation resulted from official deception or trickery is required before suppression becomes available. People v. Salaam, 83 N.Y.2d 51, 607 N.Y.S.2d 899, 629 N.E.2d 371 (1994).

—Police were not obligated to refrain from questioning 16-year-old defendant in his mother's absence. People v. Chung, 287 A.D.2d 575, 731 N.Y.S.2d 494 (2d Dept. 2001).

Miranda.—After declining to answer questions, a defendant may not within a short period of time thereafter and without a fresh set of warnings be importuned to speak about the same suspected crime. People v. Jacobs, 196 A.D.2d 831, 601 N.Y.S.2d 635 (2d Dept. 1993).

Miranda warnings; capital case.—State constitution does not extend beyond the parameters of federal constitutional guarantees even in the context of a capital case, and federal due process does not mandate that police electronically record *Miranda* warnings. People v. Owens, 185 Misc. 2d 661, 713 N.Y.S.2d 452 (Sup. Ct. Monroe Co. 2000).

Miranda warnings; oral or written.—It is not essential that *Miranda* warnings be given in oral rather than written form. People v. Warren, 2 A.D.3d 1317, 770 N.Y.S.2d 266 (4th Dept. 2003).

Motion to suppress; Miranda rights.—Although defendant was not in custody at the time he was interviewed by officers, the officers should have given defendant his *Miranda* warnings because they had enough information before questioning to arrest and would have arrested defendant had he tried to leave. People v. Weaver, 177 A.D.2d 809, 576 N.Y.S.2d 424 (3d Dept. 1991).

Overheard statements.—Statements suppressed where it could not be concluded that statements made by defendant were truly "overheard" by police; rather the police attempted to subtly maneuver the defendant into a situation in which their interception of his statements was assured. People v. Jackson, 202 A.D.2d 689, 609 N.Y.S.2d 320 (2d Dept. 1994).

Public safety exception to Miranda—The public safety exception to *Miranda* was inappropriate in a case where police questioned defendants about a child born to them while using heroin, because the questions did not address dangers posed to the public at large, and police did not begin to question the defendants to learn about the child's whereabouts until 11 days after the child was born and four hours after defendant's arrest. However, the rescue doctrine, or private safety exception was applicable, because the officer's sole motive in questioning the defendants was to locate the baby and ascertain his medical condition. People v. Swoboda, 190 Misc. 2d 214, 737 N.Y.S.2d 821 (Crim. Ct. Queens Co. 2002).

Pre-arraignment right to counsel.—Police did not violate defendant's right to counsel by obtaining the defendant's statement after the victim had signed the felony complaint; the right to counsel attaches once the action is commenced by the filing of the accusatory instrument, such as the felony complaint, not merely by the signing of it. People v. Lane, 64 N.Y.2d 1047, 489 N.Y.S.2d 704, 478 N.E.2d 1305 (1985).

—Court rejected argument that delay caused by the investigation into charges unrelated to defendant's pre-arraignment detention was unnecessary or calculated to prevent attachment of defendant's right to counsel. People v. Caldwell, 198 A.D.2d 178, 604 N.Y.S.2d 75 (1st Dept. 1993).

—An attorney's presence was not required for defendant's waiver of his *Miranda* rights where such waiver occurred prior to formal arraignment, notwithstanding that it took place after the issuance of a search warrant following the defendant's arrest; even if the issuance of the search warrant constituted sufficient judicial activity to trigger the critical stage right to counsel, such right, prior to arraignment, is not indelible. People v. Coleman, 115 A.D.2d 488, 496 N.Y.S.2d 41 (2d Dept. 1985).

—Reversal of conviction for murder was necessary where defendant's incriminating statements should have been suppressed since they were made after an arrest warrant had been obtained; since the issuance of a warrant must be preceded by the filing of an accusatory instrument, the right to counsel had therefore attached and could not be waived without counsel being present. People v. Howard, 106 A.D.2d 663, 482 N.Y.S.2d 917 (2d Dept. 1984).

Right to counsel.—Defendant's right to counsel did not attach when his father informed a detective that an attorney was en route to the police station. While it is conceivable that a third party could reliably impart knowledge of counsel's involvement to the police, it would be unreasonable to require the police to cease a criminal investigation and begin a separate inquiry to verify whether defendant is actually represented by counsel. People v. Grice, 100 N.Y.2d 318, 763 N.Y.S.2d 227, 794 N.E.2d 9 (2003).

—The mere passage of time, standing alone, does not strip the defendant of the right to counsel once that right has indelibly attached. People v. West, 81 N.Y.2d 370, 599 N.Y.S.2d 484, 615 N.E.2d 968 (1993).

—A defendant who voluntarily appeared and who informed the police during questioning that he had arranged for an appointment with an attorney did not establish as a matter of law the indelible attachment of the right to counsel. People v. Hartley, 65 N.Y.2d 703, 492 N.Y.S.2d 1, 481 N.E.2d 541 (1985).

—Although the People concede that the detectives deliberately failed to secure an arrest warrant before speaking with defendant in order to avoid triggering his right to counsel, such action did not warrant suppression of his statement. People v. Caviano, 194 A.D.2d 429, 599 N.Y.S.2d 251 (1st Dept. 1993).

—Defendant's question to detective concerning whether he should call his lawyer, after he showed the detective his lawyer's business card, did not constitute an unequivocal invocation of the right to counsel which would prevent further police interrogation. People v. Thompson, 271 A.D.2d 555, 706 N.Y.S.2d 136 (2d Dept. 2000).

—Where defendant made it quite clear that she did not wish to extend her relationship with attorney previously retained for her in other cases, detectives did not interfere with defendant's relationship with attorney, and did not impede her opportunity to receive counsel; county court correctly concluded that defendant's right to counsel had not attached at time she made inculpatory statements. Decision to retain counsel rests with defendant. People v. Lennon, 243 A.D.2d 495, 662 N.Y.S.2d 821 (2d Dept. 1997).

—Request of the New York City Police Department for cooperation with the Philadelphia police was not the equivalent of an arrest warrant and did not cause the defendant's right to counsel to attach. People v. Fisher, 121 A.D.2d 655, 504 N.Y.S.2d 45 (2d Dept. 1986).

—Defendant did not make an unequivocal request for counsel when he said "maybe I better call somebody" in response to the interrogating officer's explanation of his rights, and the officer placed a call to somebody in the Public Defender's office on his behalf. A few minutes later, however, while waiting for a return call form the Public Defender's office, defendant made an incriminating statement. Although defendant considered seeking the advice of counsel and was given ample opportunity to decide, he never made an unequivocal request for counsel and thus his right to counsel did not attach. People v. Wade, 296 A.D.2d 720, 745 N.Y.S.2d 306 (3d Dept. 2002).

—An inquiry about whether or not one should contact an attorney does not, without more, constitute an unequivocal invocation of the right to counsel. People v. Hurd, 279 A.D.2d 892, 719 N.Y.S.2d 752 (3d Dept. 2001).

—Defendant's inquiry concerning whether he can ask for an attorney during the course of questioning was not sufficient to trigger the right to counsel. People v. Snickles, 206 A.D.2d 675, 614 N.Y.S.2d 805 (3d Dept. 1994).

—Taped conversation between defendant and accomplice, who was acting on behalf of police, did not violate defendant's right to counsel though he had retained counsel on a prior unrelated charge, since at the time of the conversation he was not in custody. People v. Jewell, 123 A.D.2d 463, 506 N.Y.S.2d 236 (3d Dept. 1986).

—Defendant's response of "Yes" to cohort's remark, "Don't say anything until we see a lawyer" did not constitute a request for counsel. People v. Bacalocostantis, 121 A.D.2d 812, 504 N.Y.S.2d 560 (3d Dept. 1986).

—By his statement, "maybe I need an attorney," the defendant did not unequivocally assert his right to counsel. People v. Davis, 193 A.D.2d 1142, 598 N.Y.S.2d 622 (4th Dept. 1993).

—Defendant's inquiry—"can I call a lawyer"—did not invoke his right to counsel. People v. Dehmler, 188 A.D.2d 1056, 591 N.Y.S.2d 918 (4th Dept. 1992).

—The issuance of a search warrant did not trigger defendant's indelible right to counsel. People v. Antinore, 154 A.D.2d 920, 545 N.Y.S.2d 873 (4th Dept. 1989).

Right to counsel; call to attorney who did not enter proceedings.—The oral and written confessions, as well as the inculpatory statements made by defendant must be suppressed; the suppression issue was not affected by the fact that the lawyer whom defendant called did not actually enter the proceedings on her behalf because that call did not afford defendant the right to counsel. People v. King, 89 A.D.2d 571, 452 N.Y.S.2d 218 (2d Dept. 1982).

Right to counsel during interrogation at scene of homicide.—Defendant's right to counsel not violated during interrogation by police officer at scene of homicide where there was uncontradicted testimony by officer that he did not know that a certain person was defendant's attorney until questioning was concluded, and nothing in the record to indicate that, prior to that time that the attorney had communicated with the police for purpose of representing the defendant; nor was right to counsel denied where a second trooper, arriving at the scene, walked directly into kitchen, saw the events and asked "Who did this?" and defendant, voluntarily and in the presence of witnesses, stated that she did, and trooper immediately placed her under arrest and advised her as to her rights. People v. Coons, 36 A.D.2d 116, 318 N.Y.S.2d 559 (3d Dept. 1971), *aff'd*, 31 N.Y.2d 800, 339 N.Y.S.2d 458, 291 N.E.2d 582, *modified*, 31 N.Y.2d 961, 341 N.Y.S.2d 105, 293 N.E.2d 253 (1972) *cert. denied*, 410 U.S. 988 (1973).

Right to counsel; representation in unrelated case.—While defendant was incarcerated at county jail on rape charges, for which he had counsel, investigators met with him in the absence of counsel concerning an unrelated murder, even though the investigators knew that defendant had counsel on the pending rape case. Defendant was advised of his *Miranda* rights, and he gave a statement regarding his involvement in the murder, and later signed a written statement. Because defendant was represented by counsel on the rape case, he could not be interrogated while in custody in the absence of counsel, on any matter. People v. Burdo, 91 N.Y.2d 146, 667 N.Y.S.2d 970, 690 N.E.2d 854 (1997).

—The interference with an existing attorney-client relationship in violation of defendant's State and constitutional rights was flagrant and intentional, and the officers' testimony at the suppression hearing demonstrates that the questioning regarding one incident was purposely exploitive and designed to elicit incriminating statements regarding another crime, and designed to add pressure to defendant to confess; motion to suppress statements should be granted. People v. Cohen, 90 N.Y.2d 632, 665 N.Y.S.2d 30, 687 N.E.2d 1313 (1997).

—Although defendant's right to counsel had attached on sexual abuse charges, where defendant neither retained nor requested an attorney on those charges, suppression of statements concerning unrelated homicide was not required. People v. Ruff, 81 N.Y.2d 330, 599 N.Y.S.2d 221, 615 N.E.2d 611 (1993).

—Properly Mirandized defendant's right to counsel was not violated by state police questioning of her without an attorney present after the issuance of a federal arrest warrant and the filing of a federal complaint but prior to the commencement of a state criminal action. People v. Ridgeway, 64 N.Y.2d 952, 488 N.Y.S.2d 641, 477 N.E.2d 1095 (1985).

—Police did not violate defendant's right to counsel by questioning him about a crime when they knew that he had been arrested several months earlier on minor unrelated charges but were unaware that such charges were still pending and that defendant was represented by counsel; it was reasonable for the police to assume, given the minor nature of the earlier charges and the time that had elapsed since defendant's arrest thereon, that they were no longer pending. People v. Bertolo, 65 N.Y.2d 111, 490 N.Y.S.2d 475, 480 N.E.2d 61 (1985).

—Where police are aware that defendant has an unrelated pending charge, they have a duty to inquire whether the defendant had obtained representation on that pending charge prior to questioning on the unrelated case, and if police fail to make that inquiry, they are chargeable with whatever it would have disclosed. People v. Rosa, 65 N.Y.2d 380, 492 N.Y.S.2d 542, 482 N.E.2d 21 (1985).

—The rule prohibiting police interrogation where an individual is actually represented by counsel on a pending charge and that representation is known, shall not be applied to criminal cases on appeal. People v. Colwell, 65 N.Y.2d 883, 493 N.Y.S.2d 298, 482 N.E.2d 1214 (1985).

—Where defendant made statements to New York police while in custody in New Jersey on charges unrelated to the instant charges, at the time of questioning defendant was not represented by counsel and had not requested counsel, and under New Jersey law, no right to counsel attached to New Jersey charges, defendant's rights regarding the pending New Jersey charges were not violated and suppressing those statements would not serve any purpose in New York. People v. Fiber, 261 A.D.2d 484, 692 N.Y.S.2d 396 (2d Dept. 1999).

—Defendant's claim that post-arrest statement should have been suppressed because of the failure of the arresting officer to inquire as to whether the defendant had representation in any pending cases prior to taking the statement was rejected since defendant failed to establish that he in fact had representation in any pending cases, or that the arresting officer had knowledge of those pending cases, or that the officer otherwise acted in bad faith. People v. Hardwick, 122 A.D.2d 165, 504 N.Y.S.2d 541 (2d Dept. 1986).

—Where police officer was unaware of prior pending charge against defendant, and there is no indication in the record that the defendant had actually been represented by, or that he had already been assigned counsel on pending charge, the police were not foreclosed from interrogating the defendant concerning the instant charges. People v. Thomas, 122 A.D.2d 962, 506 N.Y.S.2d 108 (2d Dept. 1986).

—Although the anti-crime unit officer had arrested the defendant earlier on unrelated charges, there was no showing that the interaction between the officer and the detective was so close as to render their work a joint investigation, the court refused to impute to the detective the officer's knowledge of the prior arrest. People v. Woolard, 124 A.D.2d 723, 508 N.Y.S.2d 259 (2d Dept. 1986).

—Where defendant proceeded *pro se* following his arraignment on one charge, he could effectively waive his right to counsel when he was questioned by police on another charge three weeks later; the protection against questioning outside of counsel's presence exists only when a defendant is actually represented by an attorney on the prior pending charge. People v. Abdullah, 108 A.D.2d 817, 485 N.Y.S.2d 330 (2d Dept.), *cert. denied*, 474 U.S. 919 (1985).

—Defendant was not entitled to a new suppression hearing on the ground that the interrogating detectives knew or should have known that he was represented by counsel on a pending unrelated matter where the issue was raised at the original hearing and no evidence was offered as to the detective's knowledge. People v. Sepe, 108 A.D.2d 941, 485 N.Y.S.2d 833 (2d Dept. 1985).

—Defendant was not entitled to suppression of statements made to an interrogating detective on the ground that he was represented by counsel on another case where the detective had no knowledge of the unrelated matter and where the defendant answered "no" when asked if he had a lawyer. People v. Alver, 111 A.D.2d 339, 489 N.Y.S.2d 323 (2d Dept. 1985).

—In the absence of any actual knowledge of a prior, presently pending and unrelated charge, the police before questioning the defendant were under no obligation to inquire whether defendant was represented by counsel. People v. Williams, 114 A.D.2d 870, 494 N.Y.S.2d 902 (2d Dept. 1985).

—A suspect under interrogation does not have a derivative right to counsel based on representation on prior, totally unrelated charges, and thus, can validly waive the right to counsel outside the presence of counsel. People v. Lawrence, 1 A.D.3d 625, 766 N.Y.S.2d 261 (3d Dept. 2003).

—The limited inquiry by police regarding defendant's pending weapon charge in New York City went no further than to elicit the fact that it existed, which the Schenectady police already knew, and the police elicited the most damaging information without any reference to the New York City charge. Court held under the circumstances that the questioning was not in violation of the principles of *People v. Cohen*, 90 N.Y.2d 632, 665 N.Y.S.2d 30, 687 N.E.2d 1313 (1997). People v. Grant, 260 A.D.2d 860, 690 N.Y.S.2d 139 (3d Dept. 1999).

—While defendant was being held by Toledo police on charge stemming from homicide committed in Ohio, he waived his *Miranda* rights and was not represented by counsel in connection with that charge. Defendant thereafter confessed to the Ohio homicide; subsequently, New York police officers were dispatched to Ohio, where defendant waived his *Miranda* rights

again and confessed to the New York police about a New York homicide. Defendant was represented by counsel on a pending grand larceny charge in New York, but he was not in custody on that charge, it was unrelated to the homicides, and the attorney did not represent defendant in connection with either homicide. Thus, no derivative right of counsel attached prohibiting the custodial interrogation of defendant about the New York homicide, and defendant's voluntary waiver of *Miranda* rights with respect to the New York murder charge was valid, notwithstanding the absence of counsel. People v. Tenace, 256 A.D.2d 928, 682 N.Y.S.2d 279 (3d Dept. 1998), *cert. denied,* 530 U.S. 1217 (2000).

—Defendant's statements were not obtained in violation of his right to counsel where the police could reasonably believe the defendant's statement that he was not represented by counsel in a pending New Jersey case. People v. Mehan, 112 A.D.2d 482, 490 N.Y.S.2d 897 (3d Dept. 1985).

—By failing to raise the issue at the *Huntley* hearing, the defendant did not preserve the contention that his statement at the police station should have been suppressed because he was represented by counsel on an unrelated case who was not present during the questioning. People v. Cook, 112 A.D.2d 522, 491 N.Y.S.2d 466 (3d Dept. 1985).

—When there has been questioning of a suspect after waiver of *Miranda* rights where there is a prior pending case investigated by a separate police agency in which the suspect is represented by counsel, the suppression court must determine whether there was a joint investigation or an intent to evade interrogation limitations requiring the constructive imputation of knowledge of counsel from one agency to another. People v. Miles, 106 A.D.2d 822, 484 N.Y.S.2d 218 (3d Dept. 1984).

Silence admissible; where credibility involved.—Where a police officer was convicted of extortion and attempted extortion and he testified that he agreed to being corrupted so that he could later arrest the complainant for bribery but such testimony was in direct conflict with that of the prosecution witnesses, the prosecutor on cross-examination can ask about non-utterances or silence when such silence is patently inconsistent with the defense asserted. There is a patent obligation to speak, for a law enforcement officer is required to promptly report any bribe or attempted bribe to his superiors, and to protest and reveal such an alleged scheme after his arrest. People v. Rothschild, 35 N.Y.2d 355, 361 N.Y.S.2d 901, 320 N.E.2d 639 (1974).

Spontaneous statements.—Police officer's question, "Where's all this blood coming from?" was not interrogation, but was intended to clarify the situation, including defendant's physical condition, where his clothes were bloody and he stated that he had been shot, and court properly denied defendant's motion to suppress his statements. People v. Valderas, 7 A.D.3d 265, 776 N.Y.S.2d 41 (1st Dept. 2004).

—There is no basis for suppression of a spontaneous, incriminating statement made by defendant in the presence of a crowd of news media reporters and photographers as he was being moved from one police station to another, because the police did not arrange for the presence on a public street of the reporters, and there was no police conduct that could be viewed as the functional equivalent of interrogation. People v. Arthur, 290 A.D.2d 387, 738 N.Y.S.2d 15 (1st Dept. 2002).

—"When, during processing at the police station, one officer asked another, within earshot of defendant, what type of weapon was recovered, this did not constitute the functional equivalent of interrogation and defendant's unsolicited spontaneous responses were not subject to suppression." People v. Atkins, 273 A.D.2d 12, 708 N.Y.S.2d 109 (1st Dept. 2000).

—Limited exception to rule that once an individual in custody requests counsel, he or she may not be questioned without counsel is made for spontaneous statements, but where, as here, none of defendant's statements were genuinely spontaneous, they should not have been admitted into evidence, and the erroneous admission was not harmless error because the prosecution relied on them to show consciousness of guilt. People v. Facciolo, 288 A.D.2d 392, 734 N.Y.S.2d 179 (2d Dept. 2001).

—Assigned detective's inquiry to defendant, "Do you know who I am?" did not constitute a remark or conduct likely to elicit an incriminating remark, thus defendant's ensuring statement was deemed spontaneous. People v. Rios, 123 A.D.2d 404, 506 N.Y.S.2d 602 (2d Dept. 1986).

—Testimony of a police officer as to spontaneous comments

between the co-defendants during the felony hearing which he unavoidably overheard from his position four to six feet behind the defendants was properly admitted at the trial; as the officer's presence was visible to defendants and counsel in the courtroom and the comments were not made to counsel or in furtherance of a common defense, neither the right to counsel nor the attorney-client privilege were implicated. People v. Borcsok, 107 A.D.2d 42, 485 N.Y.S.2d 766 (2d Dept. 1985).

—Defendant's disclosures to police were spontaneous and not the result of police questioning or conduct. The police are not required to silence a chatterbox. People v. Taylor, 1 A.D.3d 623, 766 N.Y.S.2d 266 (3d Dept. 2003).

—Defendant's statement to police as he was being placed in handcuffs at the scene of the arrest was spontaneous, and therefore defendant's motion to suppress was properly denied in spite of the fact that he had been Mirandized at that time. People v. Martin, 115 A.D.2d 178, 495 N.Y.S.2d 247 (3d Dept. 1985).

Statements after waiver of counsel; defendants represented by counsel on unrelated charge.—Where defendants charged with robbery and murder waived their rights to counsel but had been assigned counsel for purposes of an arraignment on an unrelated charge, which was not a sham, statements made by them in connection with robbery and murder were not rendered inadmissible on ground they were elicited in absence of counsel representing defendants on unrelated charge. People v. Taylor, 27 N.Y.2d 327, 318 N.Y.S.2d 1, 266 N.E.2d 630 (1971).

Statements after polygraph examination.—Court rejected defendant's contention that his confession was involuntary based on unfair interrogation tactics, such as informing him that he failed a polygraph examination, because defendant did not show that the deception was accompanied by a promise or threat that could induce a false confession. People v. Serrano, 14 A.D.3d 874, 788 N.Y.S.2d 272 (3d Dept. 2005).

—The fact that the police called the defendant, drove him to the polygraph test and told him after the test that he failed does not by itself make the inculpatory statements made the result of coercion and suppressible. People v. Knighton, 91 A.D.2d 1077, 458 N.Y.S.2d 320 (3d Dept. 1983).

—Although the use of a polygraph examination is a factor in determining whether a statement is voluntary, there was no fundamental unfairness in connection with the polygraph examiner's falsely informing the defendant prior to administering the test that the police took her sneakers and matched them to the prints at the scene of the crime, which prompted the defendant to say "You've got me" and provide details of the crime. People v. Voorhees, 2 A.D.3d 1447, 770 N.Y.S.2d 529 (4th Dept. 2003).

—Defendant was not in custody during polygraph examination or during the post-examination interview in which he made admissions, but in any event, defendant was given timely *Miranda* warnings before he took the polygraph examination and he knowingly and voluntarily waived his rights before he agreed to take the examination and speak to the officers. People v. Macri, 244 A.D.2d 970, 665 N.Y.S.2d 158 (4th Dept. 1997).

Statement made to person who is not agent of law enforcement.—Court rejected defendant's contention that the inculpatory statement he made to the victim's mother should have been suppressed on the ground that she was acting as an agent of the police in violation of his *Miranda* rights where her action was neither instigated nor supervised by the police. People v. Lewis, 273 A.D.2d 254, 709 N.Y.S.2d 572 (2d Dept. 2000).

—Hearing testimony did not establish that defendant's stepfather was acting as agent of police, because testimony showed that the stepfather voluntarily spoke with defendant after defendant committed the murder, and stepfather was not instructed to or encouraged to pick defendant up in Atlantic City; accordingly, defendant was not entitled to constitutional protections when he admitted to his stepfather that he beat the victim or when he provided the stepfather with the victim's wallet. People v. Del Duco, 247 A.D.2d 487, 668 N.Y.S.2d 704 (2d Dept. 1998).

Statement to foreign military police.—Defendant's statement to Vietnamese military police, after being arrested in Vietnam at the request of American officials, was suppressed because defendant could not waive his right to counsel without the actual presence of an attorney. People v. Nguyen, 177 Misc. 2d 16, 675 N.Y.S.2d 799 (Sup. Ct. Monroe Co. 1998).

Suppression; no inquiry as to counsel.—Motion to suppress was granted where the interrogating detective knew of defendant's arrest 16 days earlier and failed to inquire if he was represented by counsel. People v. Patterson, 85 A.D.2d 698, 445 N.Y.S.2d 474 (2d Dept. 1981).

Suppression of confession; effect of illegal arrest.—Illegal arrest does not automatically bar confession. It is a circumstance to be considered in determining voluntariness. People v. Zakrezewski, 36 A.D.2d 646, 318 N.Y.S.2d 94 (3d Dept. 1971).

Miranda **warnings; interrogation following request for counsel.**—In a murder prosecution the defendant's confession should have been suppressed where, within ten minutes after being informed of his rights and requesting the presence of an attorney, the defendant was convinced by the attending police officer to answer the District Attorney's questions without the benefit of counsel. People v. Grant, 45 N.Y.2d 358, 408 N.Y.S.2d 429, 380 N.E.2d 257 (1978). *See also* People v. Munlin, 45 N.Y.2d 427, 408 N.Y.S.2d 461, 380 N.E.2d 288 (1978).

Miranda **warnings; promise by detective.**—Not every promise made by police poses the threat of inducing a defendant to make a false incriminating statement, and a statement given after *Miranda* warnings will be suppressed only if there is some indication in the record that a promise made by police created a risk that the defendant might be prompted to falsely admit to a crime. People v. Taber, 115 A.D.2d 126, 495 N.Y.S.2d 529 (3d Dept. 1985).

—A private store detective was not required to administer *Miranda* warnings to a shoplifting suspect where there was insufficient state involvement to create a police-dominated custodial atmosphere. People v. Ray, 65 N.Y.2d 282, 491 N.Y.S.2d 283, 480 N.E.2d 1065 (1985).

—Court properly denied defendant's motion to suppress his statements to department store personnel since the store personnel were not acting as government agents. People v. Basir, 141 A.D.2d 745, 529 N.Y.S.2d 841 (2d Dept. 1988).

No notice to police to conclude questioning.—Statement made after defendant's oral confession and just prior to the taking of his written confession that "I don't feel like doing much more" did not rise to the level of a request to stop the interview and was not sufficient notice that the interview must cease. People v. Davis, 91 A.D.2d 1191, 459 N.Y.S.2d 178 (4th Dept. 1983).

Spontaneous declaration; no subtle maneuvering.—Defendant's statement "No man. I didn't stab nobody" in response to officer informing defendant that the basis of his arrest was a warrant for attempted murder, was admissible as a spontaneous statement and was not the product of "subtle maneuvering" by the police. People v. Bell, 94 A.D.2d 894, 463 N.Y.S.2d 646 (3d Dept. 1983), *aff'd*, 63 N.Y.2d 796, 481 N.Y.S.2d 324, 471 N.E.2d 137 (1984).

Voluntariness.—"Defendant's claim that his statements were physically coerced is belied by his appearance in his arrest photo and his appearance and demeanor during his videotaped statement." People v. Chapman, 277 A.D.2d 392, 717 N.Y.S.2d 211 (2d Dept. 2000).

—The fact that police showed the defendant the statement of the co-defendant during questioning did not render his ensuing statement the product of psychological coercion. People v. Vila, 208 A.D.2d 781, 617 N.Y.S.2d 495 (2d Dept. 1994).

—Defendant had been interrogated by the alleged victim's family, severely beaten for his denials, and held by them against his will in excess of an hour, and upon arrest, this 17-year-old defendant with no criminal record had been placed alone in an interrogation room for two hours. During ensuing interrogation, police ignored defendant's complaints of a headache and possible broken nose, denied him access to his family, and promised he would be let go if he cooperated. Because County Court's decision to suppress the statements as involuntary was grounded in the record, court did not err in finding that the statements were involuntarily made. People v. Miller, 244 A.D.2d 828, 666 N.Y.S.2d 281 (3d Dept. 1997).

—Where defendant voluntarily turned over tape to police, its admission did not contravene his right against self-incrimination because that right only applies to compelled testimony. People v. Marks, 198 A.D.2d 542, 603 N.Y.S.2d 243 (3d Dept. 1993).

—Deceptive practices by the police are permissible as long as they are not fundamentally unfair or likely to produce a false confession. People v. Finkle, 192 A.D.2d 783, 596 N.Y.S.2d 549 (3d Dept. 1993).

—The statement by one of the officers that, if defendant cooperated, such cooperation would help him, if anything, in the long run, did not constitute a promise that rendered the statement involuntary. People v. Engert, 202 A.D.2d 1023, 609 N.Y.S.2d 979 (4th Dept. 1994).

—Assurance that defendant would not be arrested "at this time" did not create a substantial risk that the defendant might falsely incriminate himself. People v. Richardson, 202 A.D.2d 958, 609 N.Y.S.2d 981 (4th Dept. 1994).

—A defendant's statement is admissible at trial only where its voluntariness is established by the People beyond a reasonable doubt. People v. Pena, 156 Misc. 2d 791, 594 N.Y.S.2d 586 (Schenectady Co. Ct. 1993), aff'd, 209 A.D.2d 744, 618 N.Y.S.2d 149 (1994).

Admissions after indictment; waiver of rights.—A defendant who had been indicted, but did not know it, and who was not told of the indictment by the arresting officers, was not entitled to suppression of statements made to the arresting officers after he had signed a waiver of his rights. He was not represented by counsel when the waiver was made. People v. Lopez, 28 N.Y.2d 23, 319 N.Y.S.2d 825, 268 N.E.2d 628, cert. denied, 404 U.S. 840 (1971).

Suppression of statements made to police agent.— Suppression was required of statements made by defendant to his employer who was acting as an informer and therefore as an agent of the police after defendant's attorney had advised the police that the defendant was not to be questioned further in relation to the crime. People v. Knapp, 57 N.Y.2d 161, 455 N.Y.S.2d 539, 441 N.E.2d 1057 (1982), cert. denied, 462 U.S. 1106 (1983).

—There was no error in the hearing court's denial of the defendant's motion pursuant to CPL § 710.30 to suppress various statements overheard by a police officer that were made by the defendant and a co-defendant while the two were conversing in the police station holding cell; not only were the contested statements voluntarily made, they were not made to the police or to one of their agents. People v. Stewart, 160 A.D.2d 966, 554 N.Y.S.2d 687, 688 (2d Dept. 1990).

Defendant proceeding pro se; failure of court to assist in production of witness to whom defendant confessed.— Failure of trial court to assist defendant who was defending pro se, in producing at the trial the person to whom defendant initially questioned defendant about ownership of a car, without giving him confessed was reversible error. People v. Reade, 29 N.Y.2d 493, 323 N.Y.S.2d 969, 272 N.E.2d 481 (1971).

Rosario material; inspection.—Defendant was not deprived of a full and fair hearing where the prosecutor, during the *Huntley* hearing, offered his file to the trial court for an *in camera* inspection after the detective testified but defendant's counsel insisted that he be allowed to personally inspect the file and the trial court's then refused to examine the file. People v. Poole, 48 N.Y.2d 144, 422 N.Y.S.2d 5, 397 N.E.2d 697 (1979).

Suppression; binding on Court of Appeals—When the County Court suppressed certain oral and written statements and the determination was affirmed by the Appellate Division, the findings were binding upon the Court of Appeals. People v. Yarter, 41 N.Y.2d 830, 393 N.Y.S.2d 393, 361 N.E.2d 1041, cert. denied, 433 U.S. 910 (1977).

IDENTIFICATION EVIDENCE

Accidental viewings.—Victim's accidental viewing of defendant's photograph was the unavoidable product of the victim's unexpected arrival at the police station; thus, defendant's motion to suppress the identification testimony was denied. People v. Curry, 287 A.D.2d 252, 731 N.Y.S.2d 1 (1st Dept. 2001).

—Court properly allowed the in-court identification by the robbery victim notwithstanding that he saw a photograph of defendant while waiting to testify the morning of the trial, where the viewing occurred accidentally and was not police arranged, and where identity was not seriously contested at trial. People v. Colon, 138 A.D.2d 392, 525 N.Y.S.2d 675 (2d Dept. 1988).

—Complainant's identification of the defendant as he was led to a patrol car by police, who were not aware that the complainant was amidst the crowd of people that had assembled in front of the home in which the defendant was apprehended, resulted from an inadvertent observation rather than a police-arranged showup and was therefore properly admissible. People v. Brown, 123 A.D.2d 875, 507 N.Y.S.2d 476 (2d Dept. 1986).

—Witness' observation of the defendant in the police ambulance would not be suppressed since no police activity was involved. People v. Lopez, 118 A.D.2d 873, 500 N.Y.S.2d 359 (2d Dept. 1986).

—Accidental observation of the defendant by an eyewitness when the defendant was brought to the precinct several hours after the incident was not unnecessarily or impermissibly suggestive, since it was unavoidable and not due to any fault of law enforcement officials. People v. Bookhard, 117 A.D.2d 739, 498 N.Y.S.2d 466 (2d Dept. 1986).

—When the witness's viewing of defendant, sitting in the police car, was spontaneous and accidental it was admissible. People v. Slaughter, 138 A.D.2d 835, 525 N.Y.S.2d 942, 943 (3d Dept. 1988).

Attenuation.—Where lineup was held more than five months after the photographic identification procedure it was sufficiently attenuated in time from it to nullify any possible taint. People v. Smith, 154 A.D.2d 633, 546 N.Y.S.2d 457 (2d Dept. 1989).

Aural identification.—The federal constitution does not require that counsel be present when an aural identification of a suspect is made, as it does when, in the absence of special circumstances, a visual identification is made during a critical stage of the proceedings however an aural identification must be surrounded by the same procedural safeguards as a visual identification. People v. Collins, 84 A.D.2d 35, 445 N.Y.S.2d 168 (2d Dept. 1981), aff'd, 60 N.Y.2d 214, 469 N.Y.S.2d 65, 456 N.E.2d 1188 (1983).

Blind judge; inability to evaluate photograph.—A blind judge who, because of his inability to see, was unable to evaluate a critical lineup photograph without calling upon another person to describe it to him abused his discretion in denying defendant's request that he excuse himself. People v. Brown, 62 N.Y.2d 743, 476 N.Y.S.2d 823, 465 N.E.2d 362 (1984).

Bolstering; *Trowbridge* rule.—Where police officers did not testify that the complainant had identified the defendant, there was no violation of the *Trowbridge* rule, especially where the circumstances of defendant's apprehension by the police had been previously testified to by the complainant. People v. Brown, 115 A.D.2d 485, 495 N.Y.S.2d 716 (2d Dept. 1985).

—Defendant failed to object to the testimony of the victim's fiance with respect to the lineup on the ground that it constituted impermissible bolstering and thus has failed to preserve the claim that the court erred in admitting the testimony on that ground. In any event, the People were properly allowed to present the testimony as evidence in chief. People v. Davis, 294 A.D.2d 936, 742 N.Y.S.2d 758 (4th Dept. 2002).

Court directed lineup.—Where defendant is incarcerated pending trial on one charge and he is compelled by judicial order of removal to participate in a lineup held in relation to a wholly unrelated investigation, the right to counsel attaches, but it may be waived if it is shown that the waiver is voluntarily and intelligently made. People v. Coleman, 43 N.Y.2d 222, 401 N.Y.S.2d 57, 371 N.E.2d 819 (1977). *See also* People v. Lloyd Winston G. (Anonymous), 45 N.Y.2d 962, 412 N.Y.S.2d 135, 384 N.E.2d 681 (1978).

Confirmatory identification.—Where 26 days elapsed between undercover officer's drug transaction with defendant and subsequent identification, defendant was entitled to a *Wade* hearing. People v. Mato, 83 N.Y.2d 406, 611 N.Y.S.2d 92, 633 N.E.2d 446 (1994).

—In order to establish that an identification is merely confirmatory, the People must show that the witness and the defendant are known to one another. People v. Rodriguez, 79 N.Y.2d 445, 583 N.Y.S.2d 814, 593 N.E.2d 268 (1992).

—Identification by undercover police officer, who purchased drugs on November 27, 1984, but did not view defendant until December 7 when he was at the station-house and handcuffed to two other defendants, was suppressed. People v. Gordon, 76 N.Y.2d 595, 561 N.Y.S.2d 903, 563 N.E.2d 274 (1990).

—While the initial showup at the subway station occurred two days after the robbery, it occurred shortly after the victim had independently recognized his assailant without police involvement. Thus, the showup was merely confirmatory, as was the subsequent showup at the precinct, and the court properly denied defendant's motion to suppress identification testimony. People v. McCray, 298 A.D.2d 203, 748 N.Y.S.2d 722 (1st Dept. 2002).

—Undercover officer's identification of defendant's photograph one month after drug buy was confirmatory rather than an initial confrontation. People v. Perez, 139 A.D.2d 477, 527 N.Y.S.2d 231 (1st Dept. 1988).

—Identification by detective 7 months after the drug sale could not be deemed confirmatory. People v. Castagna, 207 A.D.2d 902, 616 N.Y.S.2d 665 (2d Dept. 1994).

—Prosecution's reliance on Grand Jury testimony of two witnesses to support claim that identifications were confirmatory was inappropriate. People v. Bryan, 206 A.D.2d 434, 614 N.Y.S.2d 542 (2d Dept. 1994).

—Viewing by undercover officer of defendant's mugshot photo four days after one of a number of meetings with the defendant was confirmatory. People v. Harewood, 206 A.D.2d 437, 614 N.Y.S.2d 544 (2d Dept. 1994).

—Given that the victim indicated that she knew the defendant from high school, the identification procedure using the school yearbook was confirmatory in nature and the issue of suggestiveness was not relevant. People v. Anaya, 206 A.D.2d 380, 614 N.Y.S.2d 59 (2d Dept. 1994)

—Identification procedure conducted approximately 10 minutes after the drug transaction was confirmatory, and thus no *Wade* hearing was required. People v. Liddell, 189 A.D.2d 896, 592 N.Y.S.2d 792 (2d Dept. 1993).

—Issue of suggestiveness of the precinct identification of the defendant, made by two witnesses to the crime, was of minimal relevance, if any, since the testimony was more in the nature of a confirmation than an identification, where the witnesses knew the defendant for four years and 1-1/2 years, respectively, prior to the incident. People v. Hixon, 130 A.D.2d 508, 515 N.Y.S.2d 89 (2d Dept. 1987).

—Where the defendant was already known to the correction officer prior to the riot, the photo arrays merely confirmed the officer's identification of the defendant. People v. Jackson. 201 A.D.2d 840, 608 N.Y.S.2d 540 (3d Dept. 1994).

—Identification procedure was simply used to connect a name to a face, since witness had prior familiarity with the defendant. People v. Cherry, 179 A.D.2d 938, 579 N.Y.S.2d 204 (3d Dept. 1992).

—Single photo identification procedure was not unduly suggestive where the police officer's identification of defendant from the photo two hours after observing defendant in a face-to-face drug transaction was merely confirmatory. People v. Lewis, 277 A.D.2d 1037, 716 N.Y.S.2d 188 (4th Dept. 2000).

—Court rejected claim that prosecutor's act of showing the complainant a photograph of the lineup and asking her if she remembered the lineup and which number she had selected constituted an identification procedure; the court, however, cautioned prosecutors not to use photographs of a defendant to refresh the recollections of witnesses prior to their trial testimony. People v. Herner, 201 A.D.2d 954, 607 N.Y.S.2d 822 (4th Dept. 1994), *aff'd,* 85 N.Y.S.2d 877, 626 N.Y.S.2d 54, 649 N.E.2d 1198 (1995).

—No *Wade* hearing was required where the witness was acquainted with the defendant. People v. Allen, 159 A.D.2d 953, 552 N.Y.S.2d 788 (4th Dept. 1990).

Generally.—The hearing court properly permitted eyewitnesses to the incident to make an in-court identification of the defendant at the trial; the witnesses' prior failure to identify the defendant in a photographic array related to the weight, and not the admissibility of the testimony. People v. Finley, 190 A.D.2d 859, 593 N.Y.S.2d 876 (2d Dept. 1993).

—Notwithstanding the training and experience which distinguishes the police from the public at large, they have never been considered incapable of making a mistaken identification; consequently, there is no "trained police officer" exception to necessary sanctions against a tainted identification. People v. Waring, 183 A.D.2d 271, 590 N.Y.S.2d 506 (2d Dept. 1992).

—The dangers of misidentification are greatly reduced when the person who views the suspect is a law enforcement officer who is trained to be both accurate and objective in his observations. People v. Stokes, 188 A.D.2d 627, 591 N.Y.S.2d 200 (2d Dept. 1992).

Identification; spontaneous declaration; juvenile delinquency proceeding.—Testimony by arresting officer at Family Court fact finding hearing that victim cried "that's him" upon seeing defendant, who was brought back to the scene of the robbery by the officer, was properly admissible as a spontaneous declaration; CPL § 60.25 does not alter the rule recognizing the admissibility of such evidence in criminal prosecutions or similar proceedings as an exception to the hearsay rule. *In re* Danny R., 50 N.Y.2d 1026, 431 N.Y.S.2d 687, 409 N.E.2d 1361 (1980).

Identification; independent basis; due process.—Although it would have been preferable for the hearing court to have more clearly articulated its determination, the absence of an explicit finding by the hearing judge that the in-court identification of defendant at trial had been shown by clear and convincing evidence not to have been tainted does not deny defendant due process. People v. Bamberg, 51 N.Y.2d 868, 433 N.Y.S.2d 1013, 414 N.E.2d 394 (1980).

Identification valid despite officer's remark.—Identification procedures did not become unduly suggestive either because of officer's pre-identification remark to witness that he had a suspect in custody, or because of officer's display of a single photo after the witness had chosen a black-and-white photo of the defendant from a photo array. People v. Rodriguez, 64 N.Y.2d 738, 485 N.Y.S.2d 976, 475 N.E.2d 443 (1984).

—While it is impermissible for the police to indicate the correctness of a lineup identification, court could not conclude that detective's comment following the complainant's first lineup identification was an endorsement or confirmation of the complainant's selection. People v. Bier, 16 A.D.3d 698, 794 N.Y.S.2d 61 (2d Dept. 2005).

—Lineup was not tainted simply because a police officer, approximately two months before the lineup, had told the complainant that it would probably be necessary for him to view a lineup of the persons whose photographs he selected as having been two of the three perpetrators of robbery. People v. Reddy, 124 A.D.2d 835, 508 N.Y.S.2d 554 (2d Dept. 1986).

Identification at or near scene of crime.—Even if the brief canvass was viewed as police-initiated, the complainant's identification of defendant was not the product of police suggestiveness, where complainant led the officers in the direction of defendant's flight, and, without any prompting from the officers, pointed defendant out a half block from the crime scene within minutes after the robbery. People v. Spruill, 232 A.D.2d 278, 649 N.Y.S.2d 11 (1st Dept. 1996).

—Show-up approximately two to three blocks from the scene of the crime and within 20 minutes thereafter was not unduly suggestive. People v. Manners, 120 A.D.2d 680, 502 N.Y.S.2d 99 (2d Dept. 1986).

—Show-up identification of defendant while he sat in rear of unmarked police car was not unduly suggestive when it was conducted within 2 hours of the crime, the witness had not left the crime scene, and it was the witness' detailed description of the perpetrators which led to the defendant's arrest. People v. Nimmons, 123 A.D.2d 648, 506 N.Y.S.2d 912 (2d Dept. 1986).

—Where police officers were uncertain of the nature and extent of the defendant's involvement in the crime and the seriousness of the complainant's injuries, they were fully justified in exhibiting the defendant to the complainant at the hospital some 15 to 20 minutes after the stabbing. People v. Castillo, 123 A.D.2d 878, 507 N.Y.S.2d 657 (2d Dept. 1986).

—Identification testimony of resident of burglarized dwelling was admissible where he had an opportunity to observe the burglar for about 10 minutes at close range, under excellent lighting conditions. Accordingly, there was an adequate basis for his identification of the defendant and his testimony was not tainted in any way by his prior identification at the scene of the crime when the police presented defendant as a suspect approximately 30 minutes after the incident. People v. Bonds, 93 A.D.2d 951, 463 N.Y.S.2d 62 (3d Dept. 1983).

Identification; pretrial viewing, presence of counsel.—If a suspect already has counsel, his attorney may not be excluded from the lineup proceedings. People v. La Clere, 76 N.Y.2d 670, 563 N.Y.S.2d 30 564 N.E.2d 640 (1990).

—Where hearing disclosed that victim had ample opportunity to observe defendant at close quarters during crime and had accurately described defendant, his gun and clothing, absence of counsel at pretrial viewing was at most harmless error. People v. Hill, 38 A.D.2d 919, 329 N.Y.S.2d 847 (1st Dept. 1972), *aff'd,* 33 N.Y.2d 889, 352 N.Y.S.2d 446, 307 N.E.2d 562 (1973).

Identification as a result of private citizens' action.—Eyewitness' pre-trial identification of defendant was not tainted by appearance of defendant's photograph in a newspaper article prior to the lineup since the eyewitness did not see the newspaper article and photograph, and there was not showing to indicate that the photograph published in the newspaper was supplied by law enforcement officials. People v. Pauley, 125 A.D.2d 341, 508 N.Y.S.2d 610 (2d Dept. 1986).

In court identification valid.—The complainant's in-court identification of the defendant was not tainted by a suggestive confrontation while testifying at the identification suppression hearing since the hearing Judge found that the complainant's identification was the product of her own independent recollection. People v. Ramos, 42 N.Y.2d 834, 397 N.Y.S.2d 375, 366 N.E.2d 76 (1977).

—When record revealed that defendant sustained unexplained injuries, while in police custody, voluntariness of his consent to search of his apartment was not sufficiently established to permit introduction of evidence seized pursuant to such search. People v. Jackson, 77 A.D.2d 630, 430 N.Y.S.2d 126 (2d Dept. 1980).

In-court identification; physical characteristics.—An identification is not precluded merely because the witness did not see the facial features of the perpetrator. *In re* Ryan W., 143 A.D.2d 435, 532 N.Y.S.2d 575 (2d Dept. 1988).

Independent basis.—Absence of counsel at earlier lineups rendered pretrial identifications inadmissible, but an independent source hearing determined that the witnesses had an independent source for the in-court identifications. People v. Massie, 2 N.Y.3d 179, 777 N.Y.S.2d 794, 809 N.E.2d 1102 (2004).

—The complainant's in-court identification of the defendant had an independent source and was not tainted by any suggestive identification at the station house where the complainant had ample opportunity to observe the defendant at the time of the burglary. People v. Ramos, 42 N.Y.2d 834, 397 N.Y.S.2d 375, 366 N.E.2d 76 (1977).

—Independent source was found where the witnesses viewed defendant at close range for approximately two minutes in a well-lighted area during the attempted robbery. People v. Santos, 202 A.D.2d 258, 608 N.Y.S.2d 645 (1st Dept. 1994).

—"A witness may identify the perpetrator of a crime as part of his or her in-court testimony notwithstanding the existence of a procedurally-defective pretrial identification procedure, provided that the People establish by clear and convincing evidence that the in-court identification is based on the witness's independent observation of defendant." People v. Radcliffe, 273 A.D.2d 483, 711 N.Y.S.2d 436 (2d Dept. 2000).

—Following a robbery on Halloween, where defendants' faces were covered or disguised and the complainant identified them only by their coats, that could not establish that the in-court identification was come at by means sufficiently distinguishable to be purged of the primary taint, and therefore, trial court properly denied People's application for an independent source hearing and properly suppressed complainant's in-court identification testimony. People v. Underwood, 239 A.D.2d 366, 658 N.Y.S.2d 629 (2d Dept. 1997).

—Where the defendant failed to meet his burden of establishing that the pretrial photographic array shown to the victim was unduly suggestive, it was not necessary for the People to show that an independent source existed for the complainant's in-court identification. People v. Hayes, 191 A.D.2d 644, 595 N.Y.S.2d 239 (2d Dept. 1993).

—Independent source was established where area in which crime took place was well illuminated, and the witness had a clear and unobstructed view of the defendant's face for 40 to 60 seconds. People v. Rodriguez, 137 A.D.2d 847, 525 N.Y.S.2d 312 (2d Dept. 1988).

—Hearing court correctly found that the identifying witness had an independent source for his identification where the witness viewed the defendant from a distance of inches, under very good lighting conditions, for two to three minutes during the robbery which took place inside a subway token booth. People v. Daniels, 128 A.D.2d 631, 513 N.Y.S.2d 29 (2d Dept. 1987).

—Independent basis properly found where complainant observed the defendant for over 5 minutes before and during the robbery at close range and in good light. People v. Johnson, 129 A.D.2d 739, 514 N.Y.S.2d 383 (2d Dept. 1987).

—An independent basis was found where witness viewed the defendant on three distinct occasions during the two to three minute course of the robbery. People v. Grant, 130 A.D.2d 589, 515 N.Y.S.2d 525 (2d Dept. 1987).

—Witness had an independent basis for lineup identification where she viewed the defendant for 5 to 10 minutes in a well-lit store from close proximity. People v. Grate, 130 A.D.2d 590, 515 N.Y.S.2d 525 (2d Dept. 1987).

—Where police were led by husband-complainant to defendant on street and arrested him for a prior burglary of complainant's home, and thereafter illegally permitted defendant to be viewed by complainant's wife, the in-court identification by the wife was not error since she had adequate opportunity to observe the burglar and recall specific features including a distinctive facial scar. People v. Friday, 114 A.D.2d 970, 495 N.Y.S.2d 415 (2d Dept. 1985).

—Although the single photograph identification procedure employed was impermissibly suggestive, suppression of all identification evidence is not required if the identification has a separate, independent basis. Here, an adequate independent basis existed for the in-court identification of defendant because the transaction in question took place in the middle of the afternoon in a well-lit area, each of the three identifying witnesses observed the defendant for up to 20 minutes, and one of the witnesses had prior dealings with the defendant. People v. Rockwell, 18 A.D.3d 969, 794 N.Y.S.2d 726 (3d Dept. 2005).

—Period of time the victim spent with defendant during the crime, over an hour, provided an independent basis for the victim's in-court identification of defendant as the robber, regardless of the manner in which the show-up occurred. People v. Roberts, 122 A.D.2d 436, 505 N.Y.S.2d 452 (3d Dept. 1986).

—Although photo and lineup procedures were defective, identification testimony in court was proper because there was an independent source for the identification, where the witness had a clear and unobstructed view of the defendant under well-lit conditions for a 15-second period. People v. Brown, 293 A.D.2d 686, 741 N.Y.S.2d 791 (4th Dept. 2002).

Investigatory lineup; no right to counsel.—There is no automatic entitlement to counsel at pre-accusatory investigatory lineups, including in the context of juvenile delinquency proceedings. People v. Mitchell, 2 N.Y.3d 272, 778 N.Y.S.2d 427, 810 N.E.2d 879 (2004).

Lineup; age discrepancies.—"[A]n age discrepancy between a defendant and the fillers in a lineup, without more, is not 'sufficient to create a substantial likelihood that the defendant would be singled out for identification.'" People v. Jackson, 98 N.Y.2d 555, 750 N.Y.S.2d 561, 780 N.E.2d 162 (2002).

—Although an age disparity existed among the participants in the lineup, that factor did not present a substantial risk of misidentification. People v. Middleton, 128 A.D.2d 554, 512 N.Y.S.2d 489 (2d Dept. 1987); People v. Mattocks, 133 A.D.2d 89, 518 N.Y.S.2d 436 (2d Dept. 1987).

—While two of the subjects in the lineup appeared to be in their mid-twenties and three of the subjects appeared to be in their late teens or early twenties, since defendant appeared older than his stated (17) the lineup constituted a "fairly representative panel." People v. Gairy, 116 A.D.2d 733, 497 N.Y.S.2d 775 (2d Dept. 1986).

Lineup; clothing discrepancies.—Fact that defendant was the only one in the lineup wearing a white shirt was not so unduly suggestive of his identity as to create a substantial likelihood of irreparable misidentification because there is no evidence that defendant's clothing figured prominently in the complainant's description of the perpetrator. People v. Torres, 309 A.D.2d 823, 765 N.Y.S.2d 650 (2d Dept. 2003).

—Lineup was suggestive where defendant was the only participant wearing a red shirt, which had figured prominently in the victim's description of the perpetrator. People v. Brady, 202 A.D.2d 440, 608 N.Y.S.2d 679 (2d Dept. 1994).

—The mere fact that the defendant was the only one wearing an "Hawaiian shirt" in the lineup did not serve to draw the viewer's attention to the defendant or to indicate that the police had made a particular selection. People v. Chalmers, 163 A.D.2d 528, 559 N.Y.S.2d 27 (2d Dept. 1990).

Lineup; hair discrepancies.—Although defendant's ponytail figured prominently in the witness's descriptions, the evidence at the hearing established that defendant and the fillers were positioned in a way that obscured defendant's ponytail and two of the fillers had some long hair in the back; accordingly, the fact that defendant was the only participant in the lineup with a ponytail did not render the lineup unduly suggestive. People v. Mena, 287 A.D.2d 394, 731 N.Y.S.2d 451 (1st Dept. 2001).

—Lineup was deemed suggestive where defendant was only person in lineup with distinctive flattop haircut, particularly since that physical characteristic was prominent in the description of perpetrator. People v. Carolina, 184 A.D.2d 520, 584 N.Y.S.2d 185 (2d Dept. 1992).

—The lineup was not unduly suggestive because the police took reasonable steps to conceal the defendant's distinctive hairstyle by requiring the lineup participants to wear caps to cover their hair. People v. Meatley, 162 A.D.2d 721, 557 N.Y.S.2d 421 (2d Dept. 1990).

Lineup; facial hair discrepancies.—Differences in facial hair did not render lineup unduly suggestive given that the stand-ins were similar to defendant in height and color and all had facial hair. People v. Evans, 202 A.D.2d 377, 610 N.Y.S.2d 192 (1st Dept. 1994).

—Defendant's contention that the lineup was unduly suggestive because he was the only person with a goatee was without merit because his facial hair was not a characteristic emphasized by the two eyewitnesses. People v. Herrera, 198 A.D.2d 9, 603 N.Y.S.2d 142 (1st Dept. 1993).

—Fact that the defendant was only person in lineup with hazel eyes and stringy hair did not render lineup suggestive. People v. Jacobi, 159 A.D.2d 308, 552 N.Y.S.2d 587 (1st Dept. 1990).

—Although defendant was the only lineup participant wearing a mustache, the lineup was nonetheless not tainted where the victim had described the assailant as being clean shaven. People v. Bunting, 134 A.D.2d 646, 521 N.Y.S.2d 330 (3d Dept. 1987).

—Lineup was not unduly suggestive just because the defendant was the only person with any gray hairs in his beard because all of the participants in the lineup were African-American males with dark skin, short hair, and some facial hair. People v. Diggs, 19 A.D.3d 1098, 796 N.Y.S.2d 802 (4th Dept. 2005).

Lineup; facial discepancies.—Fact that the defendant was only person in lineup with hazel eyes and stringy hair did not render lineup suggestive. People v. Jacobi, 159 A.D.2d 308, 552 N.Y.S.2d 587 (1st Dept. 1990).

—Since the lineup participants possessed the same general physical characteristics as those of the defendant, the fact that the defendant has facial birthmarks did not render the lineup impermissibly suggestive. People v. Nolan, 277 A.D.2d 400, 717 N.Y.S.2d 193 (2d Dept. 2000).

—That one witness recalled that the defendant's lips appeared swollen did not render the lineups unduly suggestive. People v. Brathwaite, 163 A.D.2d 402, 558 N.Y.S.2d 125 (2d Dept. 1990).

—Lineup was not rendered unduly suggestive by the injuries to the defendant's face where all of the other participants in the lineup were approximately the same age, height, weight and build as the defendant and had similar skin tones and hairstyles. People v. Phillips, 145 A.D.2d 656, 536 N.Y.S.2d 171 (2d Dept. 1988).

Lineup; right to participate.—A criminal defendant does not have a constitutional right to participate in a lineup whenever he requests one; in any event, the defendant's application to participate in a lineup, which was brought in the middle of the trial, was untimely. People v. Bradley, 154 A.D.2d 609, 546 N.Y.S.2d 437 (2d Dept. 1989).

—Court properly permitted eyewitness, who had not participated in any pretrial identification procedures, to identify handcuffed defendant in open court since a defendant does not have a constitutional right to have a lineup conducted whenever he requests one; court's action particularly proper where defense counsel rejected option of having witness view defendant in a holding pen with other black male inmates prior to the in-court identification. People v. Simpson, 125 A.D.2d 347, 508 N.Y.S.2d 613 (2d Dept. 1986).

—It is clear that a suspect may be compelled to appear in a lineup. People v. Webb, 161 A.D.2d 1147, 555 N.Y.S.2d 507 (4th Dept. 1990).

—The defendant may be compelled to conform his appearance at a lineup to his appearance at the time of the crime. People v. Ayala, 151 A.D.2d 1028, 542 N.Y.S.2d 91 (4th Dept. 1989).

—Defendant opposes a traditional lineup but consents to a "double blind and sequential" lineup in which the law enforcement officer conducting the sequential lineup (eyewitness views members of the pool, one at a time) does not know which member of the pool is the suspect. But a defendant has no constitutional right to be placed in a lineup and, accordingly, no right to choose the type of lineup he appeared in. People v. Aspinall, 194 Misc. 2d 630, 756 N.Y.S.2d 397 (Sup. Ct. Richmond Co. 2003).

—There is no constitutional requirement that a defense requested in-court lineup be conducted or that a request to vary the traditional courtroom seating arrangements be granted, nor is there authority to compel a third party to participate in an in-court lineup or to sit in the courtroom during the trial. People v. Grady, 133 A.D.2d 211, 506 N.Y.S.2d 922 (Sup. Ct. Bronx Co. 1986).

Lineup; unique features.—Lineup was not tainted simply because the defendant was the only filler with a bandage on his head. People v. Green, 159 A.D.2d 325, 552 N.Y.S.2d 602 (1st Dept. 1990).

Lineup; height and weight discrepancies.—Lineup was not impermissibly suggestive by a minor weight discrepancy where the perpetrator's weight was not a factor in the identification. People v. Chaparro, 303 A.D.2d 277, 758 N.Y.S.2d 608 (1st Dept. 2003).

—Lineup was not unduly suggestive, where the record supports the court's finding that the body size difference between defendant and other lineup participants was effectively concealed by the use of cardboard screens. People v. Murphy, 1 A.D.3d 184, 767 N.Y.S.2d 82 (1st Dept. 2003).

—Although some of the stand-ins were taller and heavier than the defendant, this was effectively hidden by the fact that all of the participants were seated. People v. Harris, 187 A.D.2d 530, 589 N.Y.S.2d 598 (2d Dept. 1992).

—Though defendant was 6 feet 7 inches tall and weighed 275 pounds, lineup was not suggestive where all of the participants were seated so as to diminish any size discrepancies. People v. Wiley, 137 A.D.2d 735, 524 N.Y.S.2d 821 (2d Dept. 1988).

Lineup; complainant's knowledge that suspect is in it.— Knowledge by complainant that the suspect is in a lineup does not, in itself, taint the lineup. People v. Ferrer, 205 A.D.2d 305, 613 N.Y.S.2d 865 (1st Dept. 1994); People v. Brito, 179 A.D.2d 666, 578 N.Y.S.2d 607 (2d Dept. 1992); People v. Smith, 140 A.D.2d 647. 528 N.Y.S.2d 872 (2d Dept. 1988).

—While the police told the complainant that they had "caught somebody that matched her description of the man that mugged her," this did not automatically contaminate her identification at the lineup. People v. Dabdaub, 186 A.D.2d 481, 589 N.Y.S.2d 407 (1st Dept. 1992).

—Any indication to the complaining witness by the officer, who arranged the lineup in the matter, that a suspect was in custody did not contaminate the lineup procedure. People v. Black, 170 A.D.2d 383, 566 N.Y.S.2d 273 (1st Dept. 1991); People v. Adams, 178 A.D.2d 536, 577 N.Y.S.2d 637 (2d Dept. 1991); People v. Shaw, 145 A.D.2d 515, 535 N.Y.S.2d 450 (2d Dept. 1988); People v. Buxton, 189 A.D.2d 996, 593 N.Y.S.2d 87 (3d Dept. 1993).

—Statement that those viewing the lineup would see the person "who did something" to the complainant did not render the otherwise proper lineup unduly suggestive. People v. Council, 162 A.D.2d 293, 556 N.Y.S.2d 641 (1st Dept. 1990).

—Fact that witness, prior to the lineup, was informed by a detective that the person whose photograph he had picked out of a photographic array was going to be in the lineup did not taint the lineup. People v. Martinez, 151 A.D.2d 786, 543 N.Y.S.2d 116 (2d Dept. 1989); People v. Wiredo, 138 A.D.2d 652, 526 N.Y.S.2d 235 (2d Dept. 1988); People v. Hammond, 131 A.D.2d 876, 517 N.Y.S.2d 232 (2d Dept. 1987); People v. Thomas, 133 A.D.2d 867, 520 N.Y.S.2d 421 (2d Dept. 1987).

Lineup; number of participants.—A five-man lineup is not constitutionally impermissible. People v. Odom, 278 A.D.2d 344, 717 N.Y.S.2d 314 (2d Dept. 2000).

—The fact that witness knew some of the fillers in the lineup did not render the lineup unduly suggestive; there is no *per se* requirement regarding the numerical composition of lineups. People v. Green, 143 A.D.2d 768, 533 N.Y.S.2d 474 (2d Dept. 1988).

—Since there is no *per se* requirement regarding the numerical composition of lineups, the mere fact that the viewer knew a police officer, who served as a filler, did not require suppression of the lineup identification. People v. Rodriguez, 124 A.D.2d 611, 507 N.Y.S.2d 756 (2d Dept. 1986).

—Although only five persons appeared in the lineup and unbeknownst to the police, the victim was previously acquainted with two of them, court held that the attendant circumstances demonstrated that the lineup was not impermissibly suggestive. People v. Norris, 122 A.D.2d 82, 504 N.Y.S.2d 491 (2d Dept. 1986).

—When defense counsel inadvertently placed into the defendant's lineup three of the stand-ins from his co-defendant's lineup which the complainant had just viewed, in effect converting a five-man lineup into a three-man lineup, the totality of the circumstances supported the hearing court's finding of no undue suggestiveness. People v. Johnson, 122 A.D.2d 812, 505 N.Y.S.2d 451 (2d Dept. 1986).

Lineup; propriety of.—Lineup is deemed fair where the fillers are of such reasonably similar appearance that there is no substantial likelihood that defendant would be singled out for identification. People v. Figueroa, 611 N.Y.S.2d 526, 204 A.D.2d 103 (1st Dept. 1994).

—There is no requirement that a defendant in a lineup be surrounded by people nearly identical in appearance. People v. Tyler, 199 A.D.2d 102, 605 N.Y.S.2d 65 (1st Dept. 1993); People v. Peterson, 183 A.D.2d 450, 583 N.Y.S.2d 419 (1st Dept. 1992); People v. Rudolph, 161 A.D.2d 115, 554 N.Y.S.2d 843 (1st Dept. 1990); People v. Baptiste, 201 A.D.2d 659, 608 N.Y.S.2d 266 (2d Dept. 1994); People v. Valdez, 204 A.D.2d 369, 611 N.Y.S.2d 566 (2d Dept. 1994); People v. Waters, 195 A.D.2d 613, 600 N.Y.S.2d 746 (2d Dept. 1993); People v. Morris, 192 A.D.2d 518, 595 N.Y.S.2d 56 (2d Dept. 1993); People v. Christenson, 188 A.D.2d 659, 591 N.Y.S.2d 507 (2d Dept. 1992); People v. Herrin, 187 A.D.2d 670, 590 N.Y.S.2d 523 (2d Dept. 1992); People v. Livieri, 171 A.D.2d 815, 567 N.Y.S.2d 522 (2d Dept. 1991); People v. Dobbins, 155 A.D.2d 551, 547 N.Y.S.2d 408 (2d Dept. 1989).

—The complainant's identification was not impugned merely because of her request, after the lineup, for a voice identification, without any prompting by the police. People v. Liggins, 159 A.D.2d 443, 553 N.Y.S.2d 329 (1st Dept. 1990).

—Failure of the police detective to ask the complainant if she was aware of where she had just seen the defendant did not transform an inherently fair lineup procedure into an unduly suggestive one, particularly in view of the absence of a legal requirement for such an inquiry. People v. Howard, 130 A.D.2d 384, 515 N.Y.S.2d 246 (1st Dept. 1987).

—Concealing the identity of a lineup witness by use of a curtain at the lineup, though not a mode to be followed, did not violate the defendant's rights where the concealed witness was questioned at a subsequent hearing and at the trial. People v. Andriani; People v. Doyle, 73 A.D.2d 864, 423 N.Y.S.2d 671 (1st Dept. 1980).

—As a general rule, a criminal defendant does not have a constitutional right to be placed in a lineup. People v. Medina, 208 A.D.2d 771, 617 N.Y.S.2d 491 (2d Dept. 1994).

—When a lineup occurs before an accusatory instrument is filed and is merely investigatory in nature, the defendant's right to counsel does not attach. People v. Shepherd, 176 A.D.2d 369, 574 N.Y.S.2d 596 (2d Dept. 1991).

—Where the defendant created the conditions which caused the unusual method of lineup identification he waived his right to claim error as a result. People v. Cobb, 161 A.D.2d 721, 555 N.Y.S.2d 859 (2d Dept. 1990).

—Tainted photo array did not taint subsequent lineup where approximately two months elapsed between the two identification procedures. People v. Watts, 130 A.D.2d 695, 515 N.Y.S.2d 619 (2d Dept. 1987).

—Court rejected defendant's challenge to the lineup identification made by three witnesses on the ground that, prior to the lineup, one of the witnesses could have communicated to the other witness a description of what he was wearing since the contention was purely speculative and unsupported by the hearing record. People v. Morales, 134 A.D.2d 292, 520 N.Y.S.2d 618 (2d Dept. 1987).

—Where eyewitness and complainant both knew the defendant and saw him on a daily basis, and correctly identified his accomplice, contention that their identifications of defendant were unreliable was rejected. People v. Murray, 124 A.D.2d 603, 507 N.Y.S.2d 746 (2d Dept. 1986).

—Although the victims of other crimes in which the defendant was a suspect shared experiences with complainant, the record is clear that the victim viewed the photo arrays and lineups independently and did not rely on her consultations with others to form a mental picture of her assailant. People v. Badely, 122 A.D.2d 63, 505 N.Y.S.2d 433 (2d Dept. 1986).

—Even if defendant's arrest had been found to be unlawful, suppression of the victim's identification testimony would not be warranted since there was sufficient independent basis for both the in-court and line-up identifications. People v. Ennis, 107 A.D.2d 707, 484 N.Y.S.2d 61 (2d Dept. 1985).

—Motion to suppress identification testimony was properly denied despite taint from suggestive photo array where the two witnesses had ample opportunity to observe the defendant for various periods over the course of an hour or more, in good light, from distances of three to twelve feet and where both witnesses specifically claimed that they had concentrated on the defendant's face so that they could later describe him. People v. Ruder, 112 A.D.2d 255, 491 N.Y.S.2d 464 (2d Dept. 1985).

—Defendant who was identified in two line-ups, which lineups used two stand-ins whose skin shades differed from defendant's to some extent and three others whose descriptions fit those previously given by victims to the police, was properly identified in that is was not "highly likely" that the identifications were made by suggestion. People v. Scott, 114 A.D.2d 915, 495 N.Y.S.2d 84 (2d Dept. 1985).

Line-up; compelled wearing of wig.—A criminal defendant who is represented by counsel and who specifically requests the assistance of his attorney at an investigatory lineup may not be subjected to such a lineup by the police without defendant's lawyer being notified of the impending lineup and afforded an opportunity to appear. People v. Coates, 74 N.Y.2d 244, 544 N.Y.S.2d 992, 543 N.E.2d 440 (1989).

—Since a removal order had been issued to secure defendant's presence at the pretrial identification procedures, the defendant had a right to the presence of counsel during the lineups. People v. Jackson, 74 N.Y.2d 787, 545 N.Y.S.2d 95, 96, 543 N.E.2d 738 (1989).

—It was not error to compel defendant to conform his appearance at the lineup to his appearance at the time of the crime by wearing artificial head and facial hairs. People v. Cwikla, 46 N.Y.2d 434, 414 N.Y.S.2d 102, 386 N.E.2d 1070 (1979).

Line-up; presence of counsel.—Exclusionary rule did not bar People's use of lineup identifications that were conducted in absence of counsel and made subsequent to the arrest in violation of *Payton* doctrine. People v. Jones, 2 N.Y.3d 235, 778 N.Y.S.2d 133, 810 N.E.2d 415 (2004).

—Court-ordered lineup in the absence of counsel violated defendant's Sixth Amendment right to counsel, and the admission of the tainted lineup in this single eyewitness case was not harmless beyond a reasonable doubt; the case was reversed and remanded to determine whether the in-court identification testimony had an independent source. People v. Rodriquez, 95 N.Y.2d 497, 719 N.Y.S.2d 208, 741 N.E.2d 882 (2000).

—A defendant has no right to counsel for an investigatory lineup. People v. Leidinger, 196 A.D.2d 688, 601 N.Y.S.2d 301 (1st Dept. 1993).

—It was not error to place defendant in a prearraignment lineup, even though the defendant informed the police that he was represented by an attorney on an unrelated pending matter. People v. Rodriguez, 148 A.D.2d 759, 539 N.Y.S.2d 491 (2d Dept. 1989).

—Counsel for the defendant was not required at the lineup since it was conducted at an investigatory stage of the proceedings and before adversarial proceedings had commenced. People v. Carreras, 133 A.D.2d 643, 519 N.Y.S.2d 752 (2d Dept. 1987).

—Although a suspect is not entitled to counsel at a lineup held before the initiation of formal judicial proceedings, an attorney who is present and available may not be excluded from the lineup proceedings; where the attorney is excluded the lineup identification must be suppressed. People v. Drummond, 134 A.D.2d 276, 520 N.Y.S.2d 607 (2d Dept. 1987).

—Defendant was not denied his constitutional right to counsel when he was compelled to stand in a pre-arraignment lineup, without his attorney present, despite the arresting officer's knowledge as to pending, unrelated charges involving the defendant. People v. Rodriguez, 121 A.D.2d 660, 504 N.Y.S.2d 53 (2d Dept. 1986).

—When the defendant did not request his attorney's presence, the police had no duty to provide for the presence of the defendant's attorney at the preindictment investigatory lineup. People v. Earley, 118 A.D.2d 868, 500 N.Y.S.2d 353 (2d Dept. 1986).

—It was not error to place defendant in a prearraignment lineup despite his representation by an attorney in connection with other unrelated charges pending at the time of his arrest. People v. Cunningham, 116 A.D.2d 585, 497 N.Y.S.2d 442 (2d Dept. 1986).

—The issuance of an *ex parte* order directing a suspect, who was incarcerated and represented by counsel on an unrelated matter, to appear for a lineup is comparable to the filing of an accusatory instrument which triggers a defendant's right to counsel; reversal required when proof of guilt rested heavily on identification at a lineup conducted absent a valid waiver of the defendant's right to counsel. People v. Smith, 120 A.D.2d 118, 508 N.Y.S.2d 460 (2d Dept. 1986).

—Where defendant had been represented by counsel on an unrelated charge, counsel's presence at a line-up conducted in the investigative stages of the proceedings and before an adversary proceeding had been commenced was not mandated. People v. Jones, 114 A.D.2d 974, 495 N.Y.S.2d 418 (2d Dept. 1985).

—The only person having a right to counsel at a lineup is the suspect or defendant who is to be identified; defendant did not have the right to have counsel present at the lineup of the co-defendant. People v. Gianfrate, 192 A.D.2d 970, 596 N.Y.S.2d 933 (3d Dept. 1992).

Lineup; witness's acquaintance or familiarity with fillers.—The fact that one witness knew two fillers in the lineup did not render the lineup unduly suggestive, considering that six witnesses selected the defendant from the lineup. People v. Diggs, 19 A.D.3d 1098, 796 N.Y.S.2d 802 (4th Dept. 2005).

Lineup following *Payton* violation.—The state constitution does not require the suppression of evidence of a lineup identification made after an arrest based on probable cause, but in violation of *Payton*. People v. Jones, 2 N.Y.3d 235, 778 N.Y.S.2d 133, 810 N.E.2d 415 (2004).

Loss of lineup photo.—Acknowledging that the original lineup photo is far preferable, the Court of Appeals held that the loss of the original photo of the lineup did not prevent proper appellate review in this case, where the court was able to review the photocopy of the missing photo, which had been introduced at trial without objection. People v. Jackson, 98 N.Y.2d 555, 750 N.Y.S.2d 561, 780 N.E.2d 162 (2002).

—Loss of lineup photo did not deprive defendant of his right to appeal or preclude meaningful appellate review. People v. Carroll, 303 A.D.2d 200, 759 N.Y.S.2d 443 (1st Dept. 2003).

—Loss of lineup photo sometime after trial does not give rise to an inference that the lineup was suggestive where the hearing court had the opportunity to view the photo and determined that it was not suggestive. People v. Cain, 271 A.D.2d 542, 708 N.Y.S.2d 413 (2d Dept. 2000).

No risk of mistaken voice identification.—Trial court's conclusion that there was no impermissible police suggestion or risk of irreparable mistaken identification in a voice identification by a witness was supported, even though the witness saw the defendant at the station house prior to making the identification, where the witness did not know the defendant and had been arrested for making threatening phone calls and was well acquainted with the defendant and could identify her voice on the basis of prior conversations in person and on the phone. People v. Collins, 60 N.Y.2d 214, 469 N.Y.S.2d 65, 456 N.E.2d 1188 (1983).

Photographic identification; preservation of array.—At the *Wade* hearing, the failure to produce the photographs of the defendant, previously identified by the complainant, did not mandate suppression of the in-court identification, since the complainant had viewed drawers containing hundreds of photographs and the volume and scope of the procedure militated against the presence of suggestiveness. People v. Ludwigser, 128 A.D.2d 810, 513 N.Y.S.2d 513 (2d Dept. 1987).

—Failure of the police to preserve a photographic array creates a presumption that the array was impermissibly suggestive. People v. Bratton, 133 A.D.2d 408, 519 N.Y.S.2d 401 (2d Dept. 1987).

—Although we strongly disapprove of the failure of the police to preserve the photo array shown to the complainant, the inference of suggestiveness arising from that failure was sufficiently rebutted by the circumstances surrounding the identification procedure employed and by the volume of pictures shown to the complainant. People v. Lynch, 117 A.D.2d 823, 499 N.Y.S.2d 143 (2d Dept. 1986).

—Although it is ordinarily incumbent upon the People to preserve a photo array so that a court might determine its suggestiveness, the fact that the complainant came to the precinct within hours of the crime and was shown approximately 1,000 photographs over a two-day period militated against suggestiveness and the undue burden of preserving and producing such an array at the *Wade* hearing. People v. Jerome, 111 A.D.2d 874, 490 N.Y.S.2d 790 (2d Dept. 1985).

Photographic identification; suggestibility.—Court rejected claim that defendant's planned defense, revolving around discrepancy between witness's description of perpetrator and defendant's appearance, was impaired when the People's identifying witness saw a photograph of defendant during a meeting with police on the morning she was scheduled to testify at trial; the fact that police actions may have deprived counsel of the added opportunity to catch the witness by surprise with respect to the discrepancy was not the type of prejudice that should have led to reversal. People v. Horonzy, 81 N.Y.2d 853, 597 N.Y.S.2d 622, 613 N.E.2d 528 (1993).

—Police officer's statements to witness upon handing him photographs, "I got photos. We got the guy who hold (sic) you up," did not taint photographic identification procedure. People v. Hernandez, 70 N.Y.2d 833, 523 N.Y.S.2d 442, 517 N.E.2d 1328 (1987).

—Showing 10-year-old witness, who had been unable to make an in-court identification of the defendant who had shaved his beard since his arrest, a single photograph of the defendant taken at the time of his arrest constituted reversible error. People v. Powell, 67 N.Y.2d 661, 499 N.Y.S.2d 669, 490 N.E.2d 536 (1986).

—Investigator's sequential display of a group of photographs including defendant's was not unduly suggestive, even though, years earlier, the witness had selected the same photograph of defendant from another photo array. People v. Wager, 19 A.D.3d 263, 796 N.Y.S.2d 615 (1st Dept. 2005).

—Single photograph identification procedure was not basis for suppression where conducted by person not acting as agent of the police. People v. Stephenson, 202 A.D.2d 280, 608 N.Y.S.2d 662 (1st Dept. 1994).

—There was no impermissible suggestion in the fact that defendant's photo was the only one in the array with a height chart rather than a white background, a difference that could not have directed the identifying witness to the defendant. People v. Mendez, 208 A.D.2d 358, 617 N.Y.S.2d 5 (1st Dept. 1994). *Accord* People v. Chaparro, 303 A.D.2d 277, 758 N.Y.S.2d 608 (1st Dept. 2003).

—Although the photographic array contained a photograph of a person known to the complainant, this did not render the array unduly suggestive. People v. Vargas, 194 A.D.2d 499, 599 N.Y.S.2d 289 (1st Dept. 1993).

—Where witness's viewing of defendant's photograph in the newspaper was fortuitous there was no due process violation. People v. Brown, 159 A.D.2d 411, 553 N.Y.S.2d 322 (1st Dept. 1990).

—Procedures employed by private individuals provide no basis for suppression, including single photo procedures employed by private security. People v. Alexander, 162 A.D.2d 164, 556 N.Y.S.2d 576 (1st Dept. 1990).

—Defendant's claim that the People improperly failed to produce the photograph binders from which the victim identified her was unpreserved because defendant failed to raise it at *Wade* hearing. In any event, the record established that the complainant selected the defendant's photo from binders containing over 100 photos of black females that had not been compiled specifically for this case and, under these circumstances, the sheer volume and scope of the procedure militates against any suggestiveness. People v. Hunte, 276 A.D.2d 717, 714 N.Y.S.2d 331 (2d Dept. 2000).

—The mere presence of the defendant's photo in both the 1976 and 1995 arrays did not render the latter array per se impermissibly suggestive, where the second photo procedure took place 19 years after the first and was sufficiently attenuated in time to nullify any possible taint. People v. Galletti, 239 A.D.2d 598, 658 N.Y.S.2d 80 (2d Dept. 1997).

—Procedures involving the repeated display of a single photograph in successive arrays until a positive identification is obtained are viewed with great caution by the courts. People v. Carroll, 202 A.D.2d 630, 606 N.Y.S.2d 734 (2d Dept. 1994).

—The detective's comment to the eyewitness that he believed that the police had arrested the same individual she had selected from the photographic array did not render the lineup unduly suggestive. People v. Simmonds, 182 A.D.2d 650, 582 N.Y.S.2d 236 (2d Dept. 1992).

—While there was some testimony that the complainants sat together for up to 20 minutes after they first viewed the photographic array, and failed to identify any of the photographs, suppression was not required since there was no evidence that the two witnesses consulted with or influenced each other. People v. Bates, 147 A.D.2d 707, 538 N.Y.S.2d 318 (2d Dept. 1989).

—Photographic array was not suggestive *per se* merely because it consisted of five photographs. People v. Campbell, 149 A.D.2d 719, 540 N.Y.S.2d 327 (2d Dept. 1989).

—Photo array was not suggestive despite fact defendant was the only man who wore a beard. People v. Callace, 143 A.D.2d 1027, 533 N.Y.S.2d 745 (2d Dept. 1988).

—The mere fact that the defendant was the only one depicted in a photographic array with a swollen eye did not indicate that his picture stood out from the rest. People v. Mullen, 143 A.D.2d 849, 533 N.Y.S.2d 320 (2d Dept. 1988).

—Photo array was not unduly suggestive although it contained four photographs of men with noticeably darker skin tone than the defendant. People v. Dubois, 140 A.D.2d 619, 528 N.Y.S.2d 660, 663 (2d Dept. 1988).

—After the witness's unequivocal identification of the defendant as her assailant, it was proper for the police to display the defendant's photograph to her a second time in an array which included a photograph of the defendant's brother who bore a resemblance to him. People v. Ballard, 140 A.D.2d 529, 528 N.Y.S.2d 615 (2d Dept. 1988).

—Photographic identification was not tainted by fact that before the complainant viewed the photographic array a detective told her that one of the photographs was one of the suspect. People v. Aufiero, 139 A.D.2d 656, 527 N.Y.S.2d 431 (2d Dept. 1988).

—Photographic identification procedure was not unduly suggestive where it consisted of the complainant viewing 219 photographic slides. People v. Azzara, 138 A.D.2d 495, 525 N.Y.S.2d 890 (2d Dept. 1988).

—Prosecution's failure to preserve the photographic array, from which the complaining witness identified the defendant, did not render the identification impermissibly suggestive where the array contained some fifty photos which had not been compiled specifically for the case. People v. Mason, 138 A.D.2d 411, 525 N.Y.S.2d 694 (2d Dept. 1988).

—The fact that the photographic array shown the eyewitnesses was apparently lost some time after the trial does not give rise to an inference that the array was suggestive since the hearing court had the opportunity to view the array and determined that it was not suggestive. People v. Eleby, 137 A.D.2d 707, 525 N.Y.S.2d 53 (2d Dept. 1988).

—Procedure of employing two different photographic arrays, each containing a photograph of the defendant was not improper. People v. Bowers, 128 A.D.2d 541, 512 N.Y.S.2d 473 (2d Dept. 1987).

—Separate showing of three different photographs of the defendant was not so impermissibly suggestive as to give a very substantial likelihood of irreparable misidentification. People v. Brown, 133 A.D.2d 733, 520 N.Y.S.2d 166 (2d Dept. 1987).

—Despite the fact that the witness was shown a single photograph of the defendant on two separate occasions, the trial court properly determined that she had an independent basis for her identification since she had seen the defendant numerous times in her neighborhood. People v. Kolomick, 132 A.D.2d 677, 518 N.Y.S.2d 46 (2d Dept. 1987).

—The fact that the birth dates appeared on the backs of the photographs was not relevant as the witnesses did not view the backs of the photographs. People v. Golliver, 132 A.D.2d 618, 517 N.Y.S.2d 572 (2d Dept. 1987).

—The fact that the defendant's photograph showed him with

a ponytail did not constitute a "characteristic of one picture [that] draws the viewer's attention, indicating that the police have made a particular selection," particularly since the other photos showed individuals of similar height, build, hair length and hair color as the defendant. People v. Olkoski, 131 A.D.2d 706, 517 N.Y.S.2d 35 (2d Dept. 1987).

—Where no photographs of the defendant were presented in the first array, and the second array, though containing two non-identical photographs of the defendant, contained 128 pictures, the identification procedures were not impermissibly suggestive. People v. Stroud, 121 A.D.2d 484, 503 N.Y.S.2d 816 (2d Dept. 1986).

—Where it was not alleged that the defendant's photograph was distinctive, the use of an array of six photographs provided a fair and constitutionally adequate sample for the identification procedure, even where the photograph of more than one perpetrator of the crime was utilized within the array. People v. Cicero, 119 A.D.2d 687, 500 N.Y.S.2d 809 (2d Dept. 1986).

—The photographic array shown to the rape victim was not unduly suggestive though it did contain at least two different pictures of the defendant. People v. Prendergast, 118 A.D.2d 602, 499 N.Y.S.2d 206 (2d Dept. 1986).

—Although each of the witnesses were in the same room while the other was viewing photographs, since they were separated by at least 10 feet and neither saw nor heard the other make a selection, the identification procedure was not suggestive. People v. Magee, 122 A.D.2d 226, 504 N.Y.S.2d 758 (2d Dept. 1986).

—While the practice of eliciting photographic identifications from more than one witness at a time has been condemned as unduly suggestive, it cannot be said that this procedure alone constitutes reversible error. People v. Byrd, 183 A.D.2d 773, 583 N.Y.S.2d 849 (3d Dept. 1992).

—While the sole inclusion of a single suspect's photograph in successive arrays is not a practice to be encouraged, it does not *per se* invalidate the identification procedures. People v. Cordilone, 159 A.D.2d 864, 553 N.Y.S.2d 514 (3d Dept. 1990).

—Where correction officer witnesses were familiar with the defendant-inmates, viewing of photographs by these officers did not constitute an identification procedure which warranted a suppression hearing. People v. Cuevas, 133 A.D.2d 504, 519 N.Y.S.2d 430 (3d Dept. 1987).

—The photographic identification procedure was not unduly suggestive although the defendant's photograph, unlike the six others, was not taken against a white background; the defendant was not unusually dressed, his appearance and pose did not differ greatly from those of the other men in the other photographs, and each man, including the defendant, had a beard and mustache. People v. Emmons, 123 A.D.2d 475, 506 N.Y.S.2d 485 (3d Dept. 1986).

—Repeated showing of a picture of defendant in a number of photographic arrays, which also contained the repeated pictures of at least one other individual, was not impermissibly suggestive, particularly where the general physical characteristics of the pictured individuals were well matched. People v. Hughes, 124 A.D.2d 344, 507 N.Y.S.2d 285 (3d Dept. 1986).

mdash;The fact that a witness viewed the photo array while a second witness was in the room did not taint the witness's identification of defendant's photograph in the photo array, because there was no communication between the two witnesses while the first witness viewed the photo array and identified defendant's photograph. People v. Rodriguez, 17 A.D.3d 1127, 794 N.Y.S.2d 543 (4th Dept. 2005).

—Defendant failed to preserve his contention that the photo array was unduly suggestive because he was the only person in it with protruding eyes and, in any event, there was no testimony at the suppression hearing that the witnesses had described defendant as having protruding eyes. People v. Bell, 19 A.D.3d 1074, 796 N.Y.S.2d 464 (4th Dept. 2005).

—Where all six subjects in the photo array were similar age, weight, coloring, had similar hairstyles, and all were wearing eyeglasses, there was no substantial likelihood that defendant would be singled out for identification by the fact that his eyeglasses shone with a brighter reflection than those of the other subjects, that defendant wore a patterned shirt while the others did not, or that some of the other subjects wore eyeglasses larger than his. People v. Porter, 2 A.D.3d 1429, 768 N.Y.S.2d 905 (4th Dept. 2003).

—Although the hairstyles of the women depicted in the photo

array were not identical, the "viewer's attention is not drawn to defendant's photo in such a way as to indicate that the police were urging a particular selection" and, thus, it was not unduly suggestive. People v. Levy, 281 A.D.2d 984, 723 N.Y.S.2d 300 (4th Dept. 2001).

—Fact that defendant was photographed at a closer range than the others depicted in the photo array does not render the array unduly suggestive. People v. Ivey, 272 A.D.2d 883, 708 N.Y.S.2d 767 (4th Dept. 2000).

—Joint identification by two witnesses of defendant's photograph out of a series of mugshots was not proper. People v. Gonzalez, 145 A.D.2d 923, 536 N.Y.S.2d 297 (4th Dept. 1988).

—Even though the photos used were not preserved, the large volume of photographs viewed—an array of approximately 300 photographs—mitigated against the presence of suggestiveness. People v. Jackson, 161 Misc. 2d 45, 613 N.Y.S.2d 1018 (Sup. Ct. Bronx Co. 1994).

—Multiple photographic identification procedures are not inherently suggestive. People v. Bussey, 155 Misc. 2d 916, 591 N.Y.S.2d 291 (Sup. Ct. Monroe Co. 1992).

Pretrial show-up at hospital.—Hospital show-up was not inherently improper where defendant was in handcuffs and bleeding from the head when witness identified him; witness had abdominal wound, and a prompt identification was necessary. People v. Blanche, 90 N.Y.2d 821, 660 N.Y.S.2d 375, 682 N.E.2d 976 (1997).

—Show-up at hospital where defendant was being treated was justified by the need for a prompt identification. People v. Gillard, 271 A.D.2d 318, 708 N.Y.S.2d 368 (1st Dept. 2000).

—The procedure was not unduly suggestive although defendant was the only black and the only male in the hospital emergency room at the time of the show-up. People v. Thompson, 129 A.D.2d 655, 514 N.Y.S.2d 270 (2d Dept. 1987).

Pretrial show-up at scene.—Show-up at the scene of the crime was valid where the police had probable cause to arrest the defendant for burglary and it occurred 10 minutes after the burglary and the complainant identified his clothing and body characteristics. People v. Wilmer, 90 A.D.2d 918, 457 N.Y.S.2d 934 (3d Dept. 1982).

Preliminary hearing; ground for reversal.—Failure to provide pretrial minutes on timely demand is a ground for reversal without a showing of prejudice, and presumably may not be treated as harmless error. In this case, the guilt of the defendant had been established in part by identification by the victim; however, the victim's description at trial of defendant's facial hair differed from his earlier description at the hearing. People v. Peacock, 31 N.Y.2d 907, 340 N.Y.S.2d 642, 292 N.E.2d 785 (1972).

Private action.—Witnesses' viewings of a high school yearbook were not unduly suggestive where there was no evidence that the yearbook displayed the defendant's photograph in an unduly suggestive manner. People v. Burris, 171 A.D.2d 668, 567 N.Y.S.2d 150 (2d Dept. 1991).

Show-up.—Whether a crime scene showup is unduly suggestive is a mixed question of law and fact, and where, as here, the evidence supports the determination below that the procedures used were reasonable under the circumstances, the Court of Appeals' review is at an end. People v. Brisco, 99 N.Y.2d 596, 758 N.Y.S.2d 262, 788 N.E.2d 611 (2003).

—Show-up conducted hours after the crime, with both the complainant and the defendant transported to the crime scene, was improper. People v. Johnson, 81 N.Y.2d 828, 595 N.Y.S.2d 385, 611 N.E.2d 286 (1993).

—While show-up identifications are generally suspect and disfavored, at-the-scene-civilian show-up identifications are not presumptively infirm. People v. Duuvon, 77 N.Y.2d 541, 569 N.Y.S.2d 346, 571 N.E.2d 654 (1991).

—Investigatory detention for the purpose of immediate on-the-scene identification was warranted, and the ensuing identification procedure, conducted in extremely close temporal and spatial proximity to the crime, was not rendered unduly suggestive by the fact that multiple witnesses viewed defendant simultaneously. People v. Brown, 288 A.D.2d 152, 733 N.Y.S.2d 182 (1st Dept. 2001).

—Where the show-up occurred near the scene of the crime and shortly after it, and where the police asked the victim to look at somebody to determine whether or not that person was involved with what happened, it was not unduly suggestive.

People v. Smith, 200 A.D.2d 428, 606 N.Y.S.2d 225 (1st Dept. 1994).

—Court properly refused to grant motion to suppress show-up identification, even where it took place a week after the crime, since complainant had independently recognized defendant approximately 20 minutes before as the robber, the show-up was merely confirmatory. People v. Martindale, 202 A.D.2d 158, 608 N.Y.S.2d 183 (1st Dept. 1994).

—Court rejected claim that merely because the police had probable cause to arrest, they should have conducted a lineup rather than a show-up. People v. Harris, 203 A.D.2d 98, 610 N.Y.S.2d 216 (1st Dept. 1994).

—Evidence of prompt show-up identifications involving three eyewitnesses conducted 40 minutes after the armed robbery, at the crime scene, was admissible. People v. Horn, 197 A.D.2d 420, 602 N.Y.S.2d 390 (1st Dept. 1993).

—The arresting officer's statement that he "knew the defendant" did not obviate the need to produce the defendant before the victims for a show-up identification. People v. Dorsett, 182 A.D.2d 507, 582 N.Y.S.2d 191 (1st Dept. 1992).

—Show-up identifications, although inherently suggestive, are permissible when held in close proximity to that of the crime. People v. Cruz, 173 A.D.2d 320, 575 N.Y.S.2d 661 (1st Dept. 1991).

—Show-up was proper where it was conducted minutes after the robbery and only two blocks away from the scene of the crime. People v. Ramirez, 198 A.D.2d 310, 603 N.Y.S.2d 554 (2d Dept. 1993).

—Prompt, on the scene identification by witnesses following a defendant's arrest at or near the crime scene are generally allowed and are not categorically or presumptively condemned. People v. Sturgis, 199 A.D.2d 549, 606 N.Y.S.2d 241 (2d Dept. 1993).

—The fact that the defendant was identified while sitting in the rear portion of an unmarked police vehicle and in the presence of recovered property did not required suppression of the identification. People v. Hawkins, 188 A.D.2d 616, 591 N.Y.S.2d 75 (2d Dept. 1992).

—Accidental or unarranged show-ups at the police station are not unnecessarily suggestive when they are unavoidable and not attributable to any misconduct on the part of the police or the prosecutor. People v. Santiago, 163 A.D.2d 539, 559 N.Y.S.2d 25 (2d Dept. 1990); People v. Sims, 150 A.D.2d 402, 540 N.Y.S.2d 834 (2d Dept. 1989).

—Show-up conducted at initiation of complainant's employer and another bystander was not a police-arranged confrontation for purposes of establishing the identity of the criminal actor and therefore there was no need to confront an identification hearing. People v. Samuels, 162 A.D.2d 559, 556 N.Y.S.2d 747 (2d Dept. 1990).

—Mere fact defendant was viewed together with co-defendant did not render show-up suggestive. People v. Colson, 148 A.D.2d 626, 539 N.Y.S.2d 89 (2d Dept. 1989).

—The dangers of misidentification are minimal where law enforcement officials, trained in making careful observations, view the defendant in a show-up procedure for purposes of confirming that the correct person has been apprehended. People v. Richardson, 137 A.D.2d 846, 525 N.Y.S.2d 310 (2d Dept. 1988).

—Show-up which took place within a few blocks of the crime and within 20 minutes thereof was proper. People v. Redd, 137 A.D.2d 770, 524 N.Y.S.2d 841, 843 (2d Dept. 1988).

—A show-up identification is not *per se* improper and may be sustained where the witness is shown the suspect within a relatively short time after the incident. People v. Henley, 145 A.D.2d 570, 535 N.Y.S.2d 754 (2d Dept. 1988).

—The dangers of misidentification are minimal where law enforcement officials, trained in making careful observations, view the defendant in a show-up procedure for purposes of confirming that the correct person has been apprehended. People v. Richardson, 137 A.D.2d 846, 525 N.Y.S.2d 310 (2d Dept. 1988).

—The fact that defendant was in custody when identified did not render the show-up unduly suggestive. People v. Jordan, 178 A.D.2d 1009, 578 N.Y.S.2d 764 (4th Dept. 1991).

—The mere fact that the police may have referred to defendant as "suspect" or "someone fitting the description" does not, without more, render the show-up unnecessarily suggestive. People v. Nettles, 154 A.D.2d 925, 547 N.Y.S.2d 163 (4th Dept. 1989).

—Show-up of defendants sitting in police car was not tainted by presence of the victim's property on dashboard of the police vehicle since the victim did not see her property until after the identification. People v. Brown, 143 A.D.2d 524, 533 N.Y.S.2d 354 (4th Dept. 1988).

Show-up; defendant in handcuffs.—Show-up identification was not tainted by the fact that the defendant was handcuffed in the backseat of a police car when he was identified by both victims simultaneously. People v. Burns, 133 A.D.2d 642, 519 N.Y.S.2d 751 (2d Dept. 1987).

—Show-up was not unduly suggestive where the defendant was standing handcuffed among many uniformed police officers and the witness testified that he recognized the defendant prior to observing that the defendant was handcuffed. People v. Lewis, 123 A.D.2d 716, 507 N.Y.S.2d 80 (2d Dept. 1986).

—Fact that defendant was in handcuffs and standing next to a police vehicle during the show-up does not render the procedure unduly suggestive. People v. Libbett, 289 A.D.2d 961, 737 N.Y.S.2d 708 (4th Dept. 2001).

—Show-up identifications were not unduly suggestive when they occurred in close geographic and temporal proximity to the crime, and the fact that defendant was identified while handcuffed, in the presence of uniformed officers, and while he had blood on him, did not render the identification unduly suggestive. People v. Anthony, 249 A.D.2d 102, 671 N.Y.S.2d (1st Dept. 1998).

—That the defendant was detained handcuffed in a patrol car did not render the show-up identifications per se unduly suggestive; the hearing court properly found that the consecutive show-up identifications made by two complainants constituted acceptable police procedure, as proximate in time and place to the crime. People v. Aquino, 202 A.D.2d 261, 608 N.Y.S. 2d 643 (1st Dept. 1994).

—Mere fact that defendant was handcuffed and seated in a police car did not taint show-up. People v. Muhammad, 159 A.D.2d 266, 552 N.Y.S.2d 267 (1st Dept. 1990); People v. Smith, 203 A.D.2d 396, 610 N.Y.S.2d 81 (2d Dept. 1994); In re Sharrod J., 205 A.D.2d 628, 613 N.Y.S.2d 262 (2d Dept. 1994); People v. Grassia, 195 A.D.2d 607, 601 N.Y.S.2d 124 (2d Dept. 1993); People v. Carbonaro, 162 A.D.2d 459, 556 N.Y.S.2d 158 (2d Dept. 1990).

—Show-up not impermissibly suggestive despite fact defendant was in handcuffs and in the presence of police when the identification was made. People v. Jones, 149 A.D.2d 970, 540 N.Y.S.2d 105 (4th Dept. 1989).

—The fact that defendant was handcuffed, in the rear of a police car did not, of and in itself, render the show-up infirm. People v. Rutkowski, 161 Misc. 2d 930, 615 N.Y.S.2d 635 (Nassau Co. Ct. 1994).

Show-up identification; denial of due process.—Show-up identification procedure held after defendant was already identified by another robbery victim, thereby negating any exigent circumstances, and while defendant was handcuffed and seated alone in police vehicle, was so unnecessarily and impermissibly suggestive as to amount to a denial of due process. People v. Ford, 100 A.D.2d 941, 474 N.Y.S.2d 831 (2d Dept. 1984).

Show-up identification; illegal arrest; causal connection.—Although initial arrest was without probable cause, information received moments later via radio was sufficient to provide probable cause and was of such significance that it broke any causal connection between the illegal arrest and a show-up identification conducted after the new information was received. People v. Johnson, 102 A.D.2d 616, 478 N.Y.S.2d 987 (4th Dept. 1984).

Show-up and photo identification.—A show-up identification procedure and a photo array in which defendant was identified by one of the victims of an armed robbery, were not impermissibly suggestive, as neither procedure could have tainted the later in-court identification, which was shown to have an independent basis. People v. Battee, 94 A.D.2d 935, 463 N.Y.S.2d 954 (4th Dept. 1983).

Show-up unduly suggestive.—Show-up was unduly suggestive where unrestrained defendant was flanked by plainclothes police officers, and the arresting officer told the witness to look in the general direction of defendant while a spotlight described as a "take-down" or "alley" light was shining on him. People

v. Dubinsky, 289 A.D.2d 415, 734 N.Y.S.2d 245 (2d Dept. 2001).

Store videotape; identification.—In case involving the robbery of convenience store clerk, defendant contended that showing the clerk the composite of stills from the surveillance video was unduly suggestive and tainted the subsequent lineup and in-court identification; court found that treating the viewing of surveillance or security photos or videos as a police-arranged identification procedure, and forbidding a witness from viewing such depictions of the crime itself in furtherance of the police investigation would be tantamount to rewarding defendant for his own hubris in committing the crime on camera; the viewing did not constitute an identification procedure, and not an unnecessarily suggestive one. People v. Gee, 286 A.D.2d 62, 730 N.Y.S.2d 810 (4th Dept. 2001), aff'd, 99 N.Y.2d 158, 753 N.Y.S.2d 19, 782 N.E.2d 1155 (2002), reargument denied, 99 N.Y.2d 652, 760 N.Y.S.2d 105, 790 N.E.2d 279 (2003).

—Court properly permitted civilian witnesses to identify defendant in store videotape of robbery, which identifications were particularly appropriate in light of fact that defendant had changed his appearance after the crime was committed. People v. Sampson, 289 A.D.2d 1022, 735 N.Y.S.2d 283 (4th Dept. 2001).

Suppression of identification; lineup following illegal arrest.—Where defendant was identified in a lineup following an illegal arrest, it was error to admit evidence of the lineup identification at trial. People v. Dodt, 61 N.Y.2d 408, 474 N.Y.S.2d 441, 462 N.E.2d 1159 (1984).

Testimony as to extrajudicial identification of defendant's photograph.—A witness may not testify as to an extrajudicial identification of a photograph of the defendant. People v. Griffin 29 N.Y.2d 91, 323 N.Y.S.2d 964, 272 N.E.2d 477 (1971).

—Witnesses generally may not testify to an extra-judicial identification of a photograph of the defendant, but such testimony may be appropriate when the People introduce it to remedy some misapprehension created by the defense upon cross-examination. People v. Jackson, 240 A.D.2d 680, 659 N.Y.S.2d 479 (2d Dept. 1997).

Testimony on direct case that identifying witness cooperated in producing composite sketch.—It was error for trial court, over objection, to allow testimony on people's direct case, from identifying witness that four days after robbery she had cooperated with police artist in producing composite sketch of defendant which was introduced into evidence. People v. Griffin 29 N.Y.2d 91, 323 N.Y.S.2d 964, 272 N.E.2d 477 (1971).

Use of composite sketch; when allowed.—A composite sketch may be used in suppression hearing where issue is probable cause for arrest or reasonable suspicion for a stop. It may also be introduced by defendant on cross-examination to show inconsistencies between courtroom identification and prior description as recorded in sketch. People v. Griffin 29 N.Y.2d 91, 323 N.Y.S.2d 964, 272 N.E.2d 477 (1971).

Suppression; effect of.—The trial court did not violate the pretrial ruling prohibiting the witness from making an in-court identification; by allowing the witness to testify at trial as to his observations at the scene of the crime, including his description of the person he saw in the hallway with a gun; the witness gave his description to the police prior to the suggestive identification procedures at the station house, and thus the description itself was not tainted by those procedures. People v. Sanders, 66 N.Y.2d 906, 498 N.Y.S.2d 774, 489 N.E.2d 743 (1985).

Testimony concerning identification by other party.—It was permissible for a third party to testify concerning a prior identification made by a witness where the witness is unable to make an in-court identification. People v. Ponton, 90 A.D.2d 799, 455 N.Y.S.2d 409 (2d Dept. 1982).

Voice identification.—Court rejected defendant's contention that the lack of a tape recording of the vocal aspect of the lineup required suppression. The People met their burden of showing that the identification procedure was not unduly suggestive, where each witness was able to identify defendant before hearing the lineup participants speak a phrase used in the crime, the voice lineup was conducted merely as a secondary procedure, none of the lineup participants had accents, and there was no indication that the description given by either witness included anything distinctive about defendant's voice. People v. Wallington, 271 A.D.2d 384, 708 N.Y.S.2d 60 (1st Dept. 2000).

—The voice identification procedure was not rendered unduly suggestive merely because the defendant had occupied the same position in both the visual and voice lineups. People v. Parnell, 182 A.D.2d 840, 582 N.Y.S.2d 796 (2d Dept. 1992).

—Court properly denied suppression of the robbery victim's voice identification of the defendant because the identification was not the result of any suggestive police procedures, but, rather, was the result of the defendant's spontaneous outburst. People v. Elmore, 19 A.D.3d 1046, 796 N.Y.S.2d 470 (4th Dept. 2005).

Wade hearing; identifying witnesses.—There is no requirement that the People produce the undercover drug purchaser at the suppression hearing in order to establish probable cause. People v. Stokes, 271 A.D.2d 237, 708 N.Y.S.2d 54 (1st Dept. 2000).

—Defendant had no absolute right to call the eyewitness at a Wade hearing. People v. Ortiz, 171 A.D.2d 407, 566 N.Y.S.2d 633 (1st Dept. 1991); People v. Mitchell, 270 A.D.2d 859, 706 N.Y.S.2d 799 (4th Dept. 2000), amended, 2000 N.Y. App. LEXIS 14171 (4th Dept. June 16, 2000).

—There was no evidence of an abuse of discretion by the hearing court in denying defendant's request to call the complainant at the Wade hearing as defendant's offer of proof regarding the need to call that witness was purely speculative. People v. Dancy, 176 A.D.2d 597, 575 N.Y.S.2d 41 (1st Dept. 1991).

—Court properly declined to reopen the Wade hearing when it was revealed at trial that the complainants had viewed numerous photographs without making any identification, because these facts could not have had any effect on the suppression issue. People v. Ferguson, 237 A.D.2d 187, 655 N.Y.S.2d 15 (1st Dept. 1997).

—Wade hearing is not required where, as here, defendant and witness are known to each other, and the issue of police suggestiveness is not a concern because the identification is merely confirmatory. People v. Vera, 235 A.D.2d 509, 653 N.Y.S.2d 360 (2d Dept. 1997).

—There is no general requirement that the complainant testify at a Wade hearing. People v. Green, 170 A.D.2d 692, 567 N.Y.S.2d 107 (2d Dept. 1991); People v. Reid, 137 A.D.2d 844, 525 N.Y.S.2d 307 (2d Dept. 1988); People v. Monroe, 135 A.D.2d 741, 522 N.Y.S.2d 643 (2d Dept. 1987).

—People were not required to call identifying witnesses at a Wade hearing since they merely have the burden of initially going forward and would be required to call their identification witnesses only when the defense has established that a pretrial identification was so impermissibly suggestive as to deny the defendant due process of law; whereupon the burden shifts to the People to demonstrate by clear and convincing evidence that the eyewitness's in-court identification was based upon a source independent of the tainted procedure. People v. Jackson, 108 A.D.2d 757, 484 N.Y.S.2d 913 (2d Dept. 1985).

—No Wade hearing was required where both eyewitnesses were acquainted with the defendant prior to the crime and recognized the defendant the moment he entered the apartment where the murder took place. People v. Parson, 112 A.D.2d 250, 491 N.Y.S.2d 699 (2d Dept. 1985).

Waiver.—Defendant waived any challenge of his in-court identification by an undercover officer on the ground that it was the fruit of an unlawful arrest by failing to raise such issue either during the pretrial proceedings or at the trial itself. People v. Carolina, 112 A.D.2d 244, 491 N.Y.S.2d 459 (2d Dept. 1985).

—Although the defendant had moved to suppress identification testimony on the ground that the photographic show-up employed by the police was unduly suggestive, which motion was denied, he waived the contention, raised for the first time on appeal, that his identification was obtained as a result of his illegal arrest by failing to raise such issue at the time of the original hearing. People v. Rose, 112 A.D.2d 252, 491 N.Y.S.2d 461 (2d Dept. 1985).

Waiver by guilty plea.—By pleading guilty, a defendant waives his right to challenge a conviction on the ground that identification testimony or evidence of prior statements is inadmissible due to the failure of the prosecution to provide timely notice of the intention to offer such evidence at trial. People v. Taylor 65 N.Y.2d 1, 489 N.Y.S.2d 152, 478 N.E.2d 755 (1985).

OBSCENITY

Tape of conversation which occurred after conspiracy;

admissible for identification.—The admission of a taped conversation found by the trial court to have occurred after the expiration of the conspiracy charged as a declaration against penal interests was error but a harmless error, if any; the defendant's participation in the criminal act was confirmed by an earlier tape which had been properly admitted, all the disputed tape added was a specific identification of the defendant as the third party concerned with the division of the property so it was improbable that this evidence affected the jury's verdict. People v. Schmotzer, 87 A.D.2d 792, 449 N.Y.S.2d 717 (1st Dept. 1982).

Fruit of the poisonous tree; evidence obtained as result of illegal wiretap.—Where police uncovered a witness' identity by means of an illegal wiretap of defendant's phone, and then obtained a search warrant based on information furnished by witness, who later became the complainant in an abortion prosecution against defendant, the evidence seized pursuant to the warrant was not fruit of the poisonous tree, especially where the witness was not aware of the wiretap. People v. Mendez, 28 N.Y.2d 94, 320 N.Y.S.2d 39, cert. denied, 404 U.S. 911 (1971).

—Physical evidence obtained as the result of the defendant's oral confession made after a valid waiver of Miranda rights was not tainted by the fact that a subsequent written confession, identical in all material respects, was suppressed because it was made in the absence of defendant's counsel who had already entered the proceeding. People v. Garafolo, 46 N.Y.2d 592, 415 N.Y.S.2d 810, 389 N.E.2d 123 (1979).

TRANSCRIPT OF HEARING

Failure to supply defendant with minutes of Huntley hearing.—Failure to supply defendant with free minutes of "Huntley Hearing" was reversible error. People v. West, 29 N.Y.2d 728, 326 N.Y.S.2d 388, 276 N.E.2d 226 (1971).

Remittitur based on insufficient record.—Remittitur was required where the absence of a record impeded any review regarding the correctness of a Sandoval ruling made during an unreported pretrial conference. People v. Henderson, 95 A.D.2d 875, 464 N.Y.S.2d 44 (3d Dept. 1983).

Search and seizure; standing to test constitutionality.—It was of no consequence that the defendant, absent from his apartment when a search was made, failed to claim a proprietary interest in the premises at the hearing on his motion to suppress evidence seized. Charged with possessory crimes, he had standing conferred on him on the simple showing that the People sought to use the contraband evidence against him. However, the court held that defendant's arrest for loitering, on the day of the search of his apartment, did not constitute an illegal pretext for conducting a search of his person. People v. Gonzalez, 31 N.Y.2d 787, 339 N.Y.S.2d 112, 291 N.E.2d 391 (1972), cert. denied, 410 U.S. 988 (1973).

Search warrant; probable cause.—Without regard to information obtained by a "pen register" used without judicial authorization, there was adequate evidence to establish probable cause for the defendant's arrest and for the seizure of his briefcase during a search of his two apartments. People v. Magaril, 31 N.Y.2d 802, 339 N.Y.S.2d 458, 291 N.E.2d 583 (1972).

§ 710.30. Motion to suppress evidence; notice to defendant of intention to offer evidence.

1. Whenever the people intend to offer at a trial (a) evidence of a statement made by a defendant to a public servant, which statement if involuntarily made would render the evidence thereof suppressible upon motion pursuant to subdivision three of section 710.20, or (b) testimony regarding an observation of the defendant either at the time or place of the commission of the offense or upon some other occasion relevant to the case, to be given by a witness who has previously identified him as such, they must serve upon the defendant a notice of such intention, specifying the evidence intended to be offered.

2. Such notice must be served within fifteen days after arraignment and before trial, and upon such service the defendant must be accorded reasonable opportunity to move before trial, pursuant to subdivision one of section 710.40, to suppress the specified evidence. For good cause shown, however, the court may permit the people to serve such notice thereafter and in such case it must accord the defendant reasonable opportunity thereafter to make a suppression motion.

3. In the absence of service of notice upon a defendant as prescribed in this section, no evidence of a kind specified in subdivision one may be received against him upon trial unless he has, despite the lack of such notice, moved to suppress such evidence and such motion has been denied and the evidence thereby rendered admissible as prescribed in subdivision two of section 710.70.

Amended by L. 1976, Chs. 8, 194.

ANNOTATIONS

Public servant; definition.—Court declined to interpret reference to "public servants" in CPL § 710.30(1)(a) to require notice of the statements made by defendant to an employee of the Administration for Children's Services because the caseworker here was not acting as an agent of the police in obtaining either the arrest or confession of defendant, but was acting as an interpreter and investigating a child's claims of sexual abuse. People v. Batista, 277 A.D.2d 141, 717 N.Y.S.2d 113 (1st Dept. 2000).

—A high school Dean of Boys is not a "public servant" for purposes of CPL § 710.30(1)(a). People v. Irving County, 103 Misc. 2d 980, 427 N.Y.S.2d 371 (Crim. Ct. Queens Co. 1980).

Actual notice.—Where defense counsel had been made aware of the possible use of the voice identification, a CPL § 710.30 violation did not warrant granting of a mistrial. People v. Anthony, 172 A.D.2d 322, 568 N.Y.S.2d 395 (1st Dept. 1991).

Amending notice.—People could amend timely notice that listed an identification witness incorrectly because the error was in good faith and the amendment did not change the theory or substance of the notice nor prejudice the defendant. People v. Ocasio, 146 Misc. 2d 688, 552 N.Y.S.2d 514 (Sup. Ct. Kings Co. 1990).

Arraignment.—Notice, pursuant to CPL § 710.30, must be served within 15 days of arraignment in the Supreme Court, not within 15 days of the arraignment in Criminal Court. People v. Hylton, 139 Misc. 2d 645, 529 N.Y.S.2d 412, 415 (Sup. Ct. Nassau Co. 1988).

Appeals.—Trial orders that bar the introduction of identification evidence because the prosecutor failed to comply with the notice requirement in a timely fashion are not appealable. People v. Laing, 79 N.Y.2d 166, 581 N.Y.S.2d 149, 589 N.E.2d 372 (1992).

Back-up officer identification.—A back-up officer who was present at a buy and bust drug operation could give identification testimony without pre-trial notice. People v. Newball, 158 A.D.2d 553, 551 N.Y.S.2d 324 (2d Dept. 1990).

Brady **material.**—Uncertain identification of another perpetrator by decedent's nine-year-old son was not exculpatory material, in light of defendant's admission that he struck the deceased. People v. Mosher, 81 A.D.2d 684, 438 N.Y.S.2d 392 (3d Dept. 1981).

Compliance.—If prosecutor attached police report containing defendant's statement to the notice, the prosecutor is in compliance; if the statement was not attached, the notice directing the defendant to "see attached statements" should have alerted him that the statement was missing and it was for the defendant to inform the People about the missing statement. People v. Manzi, 162 A.D.2d 955, 558 N.Y.S.2d 337 (4th Dept. 1990).

—State satisfied notice requirement by serving a copy of the written notice at the arraignment and by stating on record at the arraignment the details of defendant's statement even though the details were not in the notice. People v. Schoendorf, 148 Misc. 2d 76, 559 N.Y.S.2d 768 (Sup. Ct. Suffolk Co. 1989).

—A notice of statement which does not state sum and substance does not comply with the People's requirement to give notice to defendant; even if two statements are almost the same, the court must preclude late notice statements if the People make no showing of good cause. People v. Olds, 140 Misc. 2d 458, 531 N.Y.S.2d 479 (Sup. Ct. Bronx Co. 1988).

Delinquency proceeding.—No notice of intent to offer evidence was necessary where the complainant and respondent were known to one another and the complainant merely relayed the identity of the respondent to a police officer. In re Darrold D., 111 Misc. 2d 189, 443 N.Y.S.2d 810 (Fam. Ct. N.Y. Co. 1981).

Evidence; suppression hearing on improper pretrial identification.—It is necessary to afford defendant a hearing to determine whether the in-court identification has been tainted by improper pretrial identification, absent a finding by the court that testimony during the main trial on pretrial identification would not be prejudicial. The order was modified and the case remitted to county court for pretrial hearing. People v. Harrington, Jr., 31 N.Y.2d 785, 339 N.Y.S.2d 110, 291 N.E.2d 390 (1972).

—Remand for *Wade* hearing was required where during trial, witness testified that two detectives had come to her home and showed her pictures and asked if she could pick out the person whom she saw, and no notice had been served pursuant to CPL § 710.30 prior to trial to afford defendant an opportunity to suppress in-court identification testimony based on any suggestive pretrial identification procedure employed. People v. Hand, 74 A.D.2d 909, 425 N.Y.S.2d 851 (2d Dept. 1980).

Family Court; delinquency. —It was reversible error for the trial court to admit defendant's confession into evidence where the People had authorization, there was adequate evidence not given defendant pretrial notice as required by CPL § 710.30; nor was good cause for filing a late notice established by the failure of the arresting officer to inform the prosecutor before the trial that defendant had made inculpatory statements at the time of his arrest. People v. Spruill, 47 N.Y.2d 869, 419 N.Y.S.2d 69, 392 N.E.2d 1252 (1979).

—It was reversible error for the court to allow prosecution's witness to testify that he had previously identified defendant at a preliminary hearing where the prosecution had failed to give the requisite notice that it intended to present such testimony and no good cause was shown for its failure to give such notice. People v. Cruz, 88 A.D.2d 621, 450 N.Y.S.2d 37 (2d Dept. 1982).

—Fundamental fairness require that a juvenile respondent be given notice prior to a fact-finding hearing of petitioner's intention to introduce evidence of respondent's prior statements to a public servant or identification testimony by a witness who has previously identified respondent. In re Albert B., 79 A.D.2d 251 436 N.Y.S.2d 653 (2d Dept. 1981).

—Although not constituting reversible error in and of itself, the prosecutor should have properly and timely served an accurate and truthful statement of intention to utilize a defendant's statement, even if such statement was only to be utilized for the limited purpose of cross-examination. People v. Barrie, 74 A.D.2d 576, 424 N.Y.S.2d 477 (2d Dept. 1980).

—Failure of district attorney to file notice of intention to offer testimony at trial by complaining witness as to identification of defendant did not bar admission, where defendant moved to suppress, hearing was held and the motion denied. People v. Banks, 77 A.D.2d 742, 431 N.Y.S.2d 202 (3d Dept. 1980).

Generally.—The fact that the People mistakenly appended a copy of the co-defendant's confession to the defendant's CPL § 710.30 notice did not violate the notice requirements of that section. People v. Mejia-Cruz, 187 A.D.2d 935, 590 N.Y.S.2d 623 (4th Dept. 1992).

—In calculating the 15 day time period in CPL § 710.30, the day of arraignment is not to be included. People v. Morales, 159 Misc. 2d 745, 610 N.Y.S.2d 720 (Crim. Ct. Kings Co. 1994).

—The People are permitted to serve CPL § 710.30 notice prior to the Supreme Court arraignment, and such notice is effective. People v. Korang, 160 Misc. 2d 604, 610 N.Y.S.2d 730, 731 (Sup. Ct. Queens Co. 1994).

—CPL § 710.30 notice served prior to arraignment is still

timely served. People v. Alcindor, 157 Misc. 2d 725, 598 N.Y.S.2d 449, 452 (Crim. Ct. Kings Co. 1993).

Good cause.—"Lack of continuity" or other office failure in the prosecutor's office did not constitute good cause for a failure to give the required notice before trial and the inculpatory statements were not admissible. People v. Briggs, 38 N.Y.2d 319, 379 N.Y.S.2d 779, 342 N.E.2d 557 (1975).

—Although court erroneously admitted a homicide eyewitness' testimony despite the People's failure to show good cause, the error was harmless because of overwhelming proof of defendant's guilt. People v. Jones, 182 A.D.2d 708, 582 N.Y.S.2d 476 (2d Dept. 1992).

—Office failure does not constitute good cause for failure to provide timely notice of intent. People v. Sian, 167 A.D.2d 435, 561 N.Y.S.2d 791 (2d Dept. 1990).

—The good cause requirement contained in CPL § 710.30 is strictly construed and is satisfied only on a demonstration of unusual circumstances. People v. Showers, 200 A.D.2d 864, 606 N.Y.S.2d 816, 817 (3d Dept. 1994).

—The good cause requirement of CPL 710.30 is strictly construed and is satisfied only upon a demonstration of unusual circumstances. People v. Showers, 200 A.D.2d 864, 606 N.Y.S.2d 816 (3d Dept. 1994).

Grand jury testimony.—Where the statement consists of the defendant's grand jury testimony the People are not required to give notice, pursuant to CPL § 710.30, of intention to offer such statement at trial. People v. Steele, 134 Misc. 2d 629, 512 N.Y.S.2d 298 (Sup. Ct. N.Y. Co. 1987).

Hypnosis.—Notice and presence of defense counsel was not required where the prosecution had an eyewitness to the crime examined under hypnosis, since she knew defendant prior to the offense and merely gave a statement of her recollection of the events as she recalled them and this did not qualify as an "identification procedure," however, when hypnosis is utilized, by either the People or the defense, upon witnesses to be called upon the trial, notice that such hypnosis has been utilized upon a named witness should be given within a reasonable time prior to trial so that either party may properly prepare any appropriate motions relative to such testimony. People v. McDowell, 103 Misc. 2d 831, 427 N.Y.S.2d 181 (Sup. Ct. Onondaga Co. 1980).

Impeachment.—Defendant is not entitled to notice of an incriminating statement if the People use the statement for impeachment purposes on rebuttal and if the defendant opened the door to its admission. People v. Connor, 157 A.D.2d 739, 550 N.Y.S.2d 34 (2d Dept. 1990).

Inadequate notice.—To meet the requisite specificity of CPL § 710. 30 (1)(b) notices of intention to use identification evidence at trial must contain, at a minimum, the name of the witness who made the previous identification, and the manner in which the identification was conducted. People v. Fort, 109 Misc. 2d 990, 441 N.Y.S.2d 357 (City Ct. Syracuse 1981).

Juvenile delinquency; notice required.—CPL § 710.30(1), requiring notice within fifteen days after arraignment, applies to juvenile proceedings and prejudice to the defendant by failure to do so need not be shown. In re Damon R., 105 Misc. 2d 380, 432 N.Y.S.2d 80 (Fam. Ct. Kings Co. 1980).

Late notice of statement.—In view of overwhelming proof of guilt the prosecutor's violation of the requirements of CPL § 710.30 constituted harmless error. People v. Lubarska, 143 A.D.2d 1048, 533 N.Y.S.2d 576 (2d Dept. 1988).

—People's failure to provide requisite notice, pursuant to CPL § 710.30, did not require reversal where both direct and circumstantial evidence overwhelmingly established the defendant's guilt. People v. Pinney, 136 A.D.2d 573, 523 N.Y.S.2d 567 (2d Dept. 1988).

—Defendant was not prejudiced by late notice of the People's intent to introduce at trial a statement made by the defendant where six months elapsed between the People's motion for an order allowing them to serve a late notice of intention to offer the statement and the commencement of trial, thus providing defense counsel with an opportunity to prepare a defense. People v. O'Doherty, 121 A.D.2d 570, 503 N.Y.S.2d 618 (2d Dept. 1986).

—People's delay in furnishing defendant notice of existence of taped recorded statement did not require exclusion of statement where defense counsel declined court's offer to adjourn or recess the suppression hearing. People v. Wilder, 124 A.D.2d 846, 508 N.Y.S.2d 562 (2d Dept. 1986).

—Suppression was denied even though notice of the people's intent to introduce at trial the defendant's statement was not made within 15 days of his arraignment, as required by CPL § 710.30(2), since the defendant nonetheless received ample pretrial notice. People v. Brown, 92 A.D.2d 939, 460 N.Y.S.2d 365 (2d Dept. 1983).

Law of the case.—Court's determination that identification testimony could not be used at trial due to CPL § 710.30 violation constituted the law of the case and was binding on the judge who tried the case. People v. Broome, 151 A.D.2d 995, 542 N.Y.S.2d 433 (4th Dept. 1989).

Oral statements; exact recitation.—A notice of intent to offer an oral statement need not provide a verbatim recitation nor state each damaging statement defendant allegedly made; notice is sufficient if it gives defendant an opportunity to challenge admissibility and if it apprises defendant generally of statement made. People v. Cooper, 158 A.D.2d 743, 550 N.Y.S.2d 947 (3d Dept. 1990).

Notice; miscellaneous.—The provisions of CPL § 710.30 do not apply to judicially supervised identifications which occur when a defendant is represented by counsel. People v. White, 73 N.Y.2d 468, 541 N.Y.S.2d 749, 539 N.E.2d 577 (1989).

—When the arresting officer momentarily lost sight of the defendant and then saw him again in the custody of other officers, this did not constitute an "identification" requiring notice under CPL § 710.30 or a Wade hearing. People v. Oliveras, 204 A.D.2d 226, 612 N.Y.S.2d 41 (1st Dept. 1994).

—§ 710.30 notice as to lineup identification did not have to include notice that the victim had also identified defendant's voice at the lineup. People v. McRae, 195 A.D.2d 180, 607 N.Y.S.2d 624 (1st Dept. 1994).

—Oral notice defendant received at his arraignment on the felony complaint of a prior photographic identification was sufficient to comply with CPL § 710.30; it was consistent with the purpose of the statute to allow a defendant an opportunity to challenge identification procedures at a Wade hearing. People v. Santana, 191 A.D.2d 174, 594 N.Y.S.2d 189 (1st Dept. 1993).

—Any alleged deficiency in CPL § 710.30 notice provided by the People is irrelevant, where defendant was afforded open file discovery, and received a full hearing and a determination on the admissibility of the showup identification before trial. People v. Sigue, 300 A.D.2d 414, 752 N.Y.S.2d 71 (2d Dept. 2002).

—It is well settled that where there has been a violation of the mandatory disclosure provision of CPL § 710.30, both the out-of-court and in-court identifications must be excluded regardless of the existence of an independent basis for the identification. People v. Perez, 177 A.D.2d 657, 576 N.Y.S.2d 359 (2d Dept. 1991).

—The CPL § 710.30 violation was rendered harmless in light of the overwhelming evidence of the defendant's guilt. People v. Miller, 171 A.D.2d 697, 567 N.Y.S.2d 163 (2d Dept. 1991).

—Where identity was not at issue, the notice and hearing procedures of Article 710 of the Criminal Procedure Law did not come into play. People v. Mitchem, 171 A.D.2d 888, 567 N.Y.S.2d 814 (2d Dept. 1991).

—Where complainant's identification of the defendant was arranged by a private security, the defendant's due process rights were not violated. People v. Taylor, 123 A.D.2d 893, 507 N.Y.S.2d 668 (2d Dept. 1986).

Notice of identification; adequacy of notice.—Notice of intent to offer show-up identification was adequate because it stated the date of the identification and that two eyewitnesses made the identification. People v. Bae, 164 Misc. 2d 669, 625 N.Y.S.2d 883 (Sup. Ct. Queens Co. 1995).

Notice of intention to offer identification evidence; failure to give.—The requirement that the People give notice of intent to offer identification testimony from a witness is excused when a defendant moves for suppression of the identification testimony; because defendant here moved to suppress the identification testimony and received a full hearing on the fairness of the identification procedure, any alleged deficiency in the notice provided by the People was irrelevant. People v. Kirkland, 89 N.Y.2d 903, 653 N.Y.S.2d 256, 675 N.E.2d 1208 (1996).

—Where one of the police investigator's pretrial photo identifications of defendant was not confirmatory, the notice required by CPL 710.30 should have been provided, but the error was harmless in light of other compelling proof. People v. Thompson, 306 A.D.2d 758, 763 N.Y.S.2d 109 (3d Dept. 2003).

—Where the defendant moved to suppress the show-up identification evidence, despite the lack of notice, and the motion to suppress was denied, such evidence was admissible although the People failed to notify defendant of the show-up identification. People v. Jones, 69 A.D.2d 912, 415 N.Y.S.2d 124 (3d Dept. 1979), aff'd, 51 N.Y.2d 915, 434 N.Y.S.2d 978, 415 N.E.2d 967 (1980)

—CPL § 710.30 was inapplicable to a photo identification procedure conducted three days after officer participated in an undercover operation to purchase narcotics. People v. McQuiller, 202 A.D.2d 978, 609 N.Y.S.2d 490 (4th Dept. 1994).

—Showing a witness a trial exhibit, one of which was a forged photo identification that defendant had displayed to the witness during the course of the crime, did not require service of § 710.30 notice. People v. Clark, 203 A.D.2d 935, 611 N.Y.S.2d 387 (4th Dept. 1994).

—The requirements of CPL § 710.30 do not apply to inadvertent and casual observations made on a public street by one who previously observed defendant during the transaction at issue. People v. Rose, 152 A.D.2d 924, 543 N.Y.S.2d 836 (4th Dept. 1989).

—The failure to name the identifying witness in a § 710.30 notice does not necessarily render such notice defective. People v. Cox, 161 Misc. 2d 1011, 615 N.Y.S.2d 983 (Sup. Ct. Queens Co. 1994).

—Failure of People to delineate nature of identification procedure utilized did not vitiate CPL § 710.30 notice. People v. Lane, 144 Misc. 2d 90, 543 N.Y.S.2d 862 (Sup. Ct. Bronx Co. 1989).

Notice of intention to offer statements.—Although prosecutor had timely served the notice of intent to use at trial oral statement made by the defendant to a police officer, such notice was ineffective where it was withdrawn and not served again until after the requisite time period. People v. Boughton, 70 N.Y.2d 854, 523 N.Y.S.2d 454, 517 N.E.2d 1340 (1987).

—People's service of notice to offer identification testimony did not change the confirmatory nature of officer's viewing. People v. Allen, 162 A.D.2d 538, 556 N.Y.S.2d 7334 (2d Dept. 1990).

—People's CPL § 710.30 notice was sufficient where the notice served on the defendant and the version testified to at trial did not differ in any appreciable respect; the notice contained the sum and substance of the challenged statement and adequately provided the defendant with the opportunity to contest its voluntariness. People v. Miller, 154 A.D.2d 717, 546 N.Y.S.2d 692 (2d Dept. 1989).

—Court properly denied defendant's motion to suppress a witness' identification testimony despite the People's failure to give the proper statutory notice of an intention to offer such testimony at trial, where a full and fair Wade hearing was held prior to the trial after which the suppression motion was denied. People v. White, 118 A.D.2d 886, 500 N.Y.S.2d 549 (2d Dept. 1986).

—Where defendant participated in Huntley hearing during the trial, concerning the admissibility of his oral statement to a police officer, but held before the officer testified, any failure of the People to serve a notice pursuant to CPL § 710.30 was statutorily excused. People v. Quesnel, 238 A.D.2d 725, 656 N.Y.S.2d 772 (3d Dept. 1997).

—Where defendant had actual knowledge that People intended to use statement of defendant, failure to comply in timely fashion with CPL § 710.30 did not prejudice the defendant. People v. Willsey, 148 A.D.2d 764, 538 N.Y.S.2d 342 (3d Dept. 1989).

—The single CPL § 710.30 notice was adequate to provide the defendant with an opportunity to contest the voluntariness of the admission where the defendant's oral and written statements were virtually the same. People v. Wilson, 144 A.D.2d 980, 534 N.Y.S.2d 617 (4th Dept. 1988).

—Even if two statements by a defendant are the same in content, CPL § 710.30 requires preclusion of the late-noticed one. People v. Olds, 140 Misc. 2d 458, 531 N.Y.S.2d 479 (Sup. Ct. Bronx Co. 1988).

—The fact that the People's notice of intention to use defendant's statement did not contain an exact or full report of the defendant's statement did not negate the sufficiency of the notice. People v. Grandenetti, 139 Misc. 2d 614, 528 N.Y.S.2d 303 (Sup. Ct. N.Y. Co. 1988).

Notice of statement.—The issue was not properly preserved for appellate review, since defense counsel initially failed to not given defendant pretrial notice as required object to testimony concerning defendant's statement on the ground that notice pursuant to CPL § 710.30 had not been given, then later, during the testimony of a second witness, objected on this ground but subsequently abandoned the objection. People v. Clark, 41 N.Y.2d 612, 394 N.Y.S.2d 593, 363 N.E.2d 319, cert. denied, 434 U.S. 864 (1977).

—The purpose of CPL § 710.20 is to afford a defendant adequate time in preparing his case in respect to the voluntariness of a confession or admission and where the notice of intention served by the prosecutor did not include any reference to an admission by defendant that he did not know the victim's name, it was reversible error for the trial court to deny defense counsel's request for a suppression hearing and to permit the police officer to testify to the statement. People v. Greer, 42 N.Y.2d 170, 397 N.Y.S.2d 613, 366 N.E.2d 273 (1977).

—Notice sufficed despite the fact that at pretrial hearing and at trial the officer told slightly different version of defendant's statement because the officer's testimony gave a consistent version and the People disclosed the substance of the statement. People v. Bowman, 211 A.D.2d 590, 622 N.Y.S.2d 22 (1st Dept. 1995).

—The People's failure to give defendant pretrial notice of their intention to use statements specified in CPL § 710.30(1) or prove "good cause" for failure to give such notice is not reviewable in the absence of any objection on the ground of involuntariness of defendant's oral statement (CPL §§ 470.05(2); 470.15(1)), and the court found no sound reason to consider this point when raised for the first time on appeal (CPL § 470.15[3][c]; [6][a]). People v. Travison, 59 A.D.2d 404, 400 N.Y.S.2d 188 (3d Dept. 1977), aff'd, 46 N.Y.2d 758, 413 N.Y.S.2d 648, 386 N.E.2d 256, cert. denied, 441 U.S. 949 (1979).

—Defendant's statement to public servant admissible even though the statement was not attached to the notice because the People independently gave the information to the defendant and his counsel did not object to the failure to attach the statement. People v. Black, 177 A.D.2d 1040, 578 N.Y.S.2d 54 (4th Dept. 1991).

—CPL § 710.30 does not require the prosecution to furnish the defense with a verbatim report containing the complete oral statement in their § 710.30 notice. People v. Lucas, 161 Misc. 2d 954, 615 N.Y.S.2d 838 (Dist. Ct. Suffolk Co. 1994).

No notice required; identification.—In court identification of defendant accused of selling narcotics, based on officer's viewing her on the night of the sale, was admissible even though the prosecutor did not provide pretrial notice to defendant of subsequent viewing of the defendant by officers at the time of her arrest; such viewings did not constitute a previous identification of the defendant within the intendment of the CPL § 710.30(1)(b). People v. Gissendanner, 48 N.Y.2d 543, 423 N.Y.S.2d 893, 399 N.E.2d 924 (1979).

—Defendant was not entitled to notice regarding testimony of complainant who identified the defendant from his driver's license which he left at the crime scene because the identification was chance and not police arranged. People v. Kavanaugh, 207 A.D.2d 719, 625 N.Y.S.2d 1 (1st Dept. 1994).

—Defendant was not entitled to CPL § 710.30 notice as to the identification of an officer who identified the defendant at the scene. People v. Manick, 190 A.D.2d 624, 594 N.Y.S.2d 14 (1st Dept. 1993).

—An eyewitness identification of defendant does not require notice if the eyewitness' station house viewing of defendant is purely chance and not police arranged. People v. Richardson, 212 A.D.2d 743, 622 N.Y.S.2d 966 (2d Dept. 1995).

—Defendant was not entitled to CPL § 710.30 notice as to photographic identification where the witness was able to describe the defendant in detail and knew the defendant's name and address; the identification was deemed confirmatory. People v. Breland, 191 A.D.2d 500, 594 N.Y.S.2d 789, 791 (2d Dept. 1993), aff'd, 83 N.Y.2d 286, 609 N.Y.S.2d 571, 631 N.E.2d 577 (1994).

—Defendant was not entitled to CPL § 710.30 notice where the officer's identification of the defendant was merely confirmatory in nature and therefore not within the scope of pretrial identifications necessitating such notice. People v. Williams, 191 A.D.2d 527, 594 N.Y.S.2d 352, 353 (2d Dept. 1993).

—An undercover agent's inadvertent observation of defendant while checking through defendant's police file does not fall within the meaning of "previously identified" so notice is not necessary. People v. Moon, 180 A.D.2d 652, 580 N.Y.S.2d 362 (2d Dept. 1992).

—No notice to defendant is necessary when an employee of a robbed jewelry store looks at a photo array but does not make an identification. People v. Paden, 158 A.D.2d 554, 551 N.Y.S.2d 325 (2d Dept. 1990).

—An officer's show-up identification of defendant, made within minutes of defendant's arrest and not long after officer had ended pursuit, was merely confirmatory and did not require notice. People v. Jackson, 167 A.D.2d 420, 561 N.Y.S.2d 828 (2d Dept. 1990).

—Where viewing by police was confirmatory the People were not required to give notice pursuant to CPL § 710.30. People v. Duffy, 152 A.D.2d 704, 544 N.Y.S.2d 162 (2d Dept. 1989).

—Where the witness made no previous identification of the defendant, notice pursuant to CPL § 710.30 is not required. People v. Dozier, 150 A.D.2d 483, 541 N.Y.S.2d 224 (2d Dept. 1989).

—Eyewitness testimony of a defendant's participation in a crime, where the eyewitness has not previously made any out-of-court, police-initiated identification of the defendant in connection with that crime, does not require CPL § 710.30 notice. People v. Butler, 16 A.D.3d 915, 791 N.Y.S.2d 723 (3d Dept. 2005).

—CPL § 710.30 notice was not necessary because the witness's out-of-court identification did not arise from a police arranged procedure but resulted from the mere happenstance that the witness saw a "wanted" poster featuring defendant. People v. Guilbault, 256 A.D.2d 632, 681 N.Y.S.2d 180 (3d Dept. 1998).

—CPL § 710.30 does not apply to happenstance encounters with a defendant. People v. Dobbs, 194 A.D.2d 996, 599 N.Y.S.2d 883, 885 (3d Dept. 1993).

—Where sole purpose of the photographic identification was "to put a name to the face" that the victims already knew, there was no identification within the meaning of CPL § 710.30. People v. Cherny, 179 A.D.2d 938, 579 N.Y.S.2d 204 (3d Dept. 1991).

—Court did not err in determining, after Wade hearing, that there was an independent basis for the in-court identification of defendant, because the People established that the witness had an opportunity to view the defendant in well-lit conditions, and that the witness focused on the defendant because of his unusual mode of dress. People v. O'Connor, 242 A.D.2d 908, 662 N.Y.S.2d 951 (4th Dept. 1997).

—When a trained undercover officer saw defendant in a face to face drug transaction and knew that defendant would soon be arrested, the identification was confirmatory; thus, the People's notice, which failed to state place and manner of identification, was not fatal. Defendant was not entitled to a Wade hearing. People v. Ramirez, 164 Misc. 2d 342, 624 N.Y.S.2d 552 (Sup. Ct. Queens Co. 1995).

No notice required; statement.—Prosecution did not have to provide notice pursuant to 710.30(1)(a) of a statement made by defendant in the course of unrelated drug transaction. Although this admission was a statement of fact, it was made in the course of the commission of a crime and there was no question of voluntariness. People v. Garcia-Lopez, 308 A.D.2d 366, 764 N.Y.S.2d 264 (1st Dept. 2003), cert. denied, 124 S. Ct. 2424, 158 L. Ed. 2d 991 (2004).

—Notice of intent is not required when the statement is made to a private party even if the defendant addresses the question to a witness at a show up scene. People v. Rivera, 173 A.D.2d 360, 570 N.Y.S.2d 5 (1st Dept. 1991).

—Court allowed officer's testimony concerning defendant's statement volunteered at the murder scene even though no notice was given; the officer had testified to the statement in an earlier trial. People v. Simmons, 170 A.D.2d 15, 573 N.Y.S.2d 960 (1st Dept. 1991).

—Defendant's statement was admissible, notwithstanding People's failure to provide notice of it, where the information was elicited by both the People and the defense during the Huntley hearing, and the testimony at the pretrial suppression hearing was sufficient to put the defendant on notice of the People's intent to use the statement. People v. Schnugg, 257 A.D.2d 669, 684 N.Y.S.2d 581 (2d Dept. 1999).

—Hearing court properly denied defendant's motion to suppress evidence that he opened a locked safe found in the apartment during the execution of the search warrant, because defendant's conduct in opening the safe was not a statement intended to communicate any information, and therefore no CPL § 710.30 notice was required. People v. Morales, 248 A.D.2d 731, 670 N.Y.S.2d 591 (2d Dept.), appeal denied, 92 N.Y.2d 902 (1998).

—People were not required to serve § 710.30 notice as to defendant's answer, "Sales," made in response to the arresting officer's question, "What do you do for a living," since the information was of a pedigree nature. People v. Rodney, 203 A.D.2d 394, 610 N.Y.S.2d 83 (2d Dept. 1994).

—There was not § 710.30 violation where the challenged statement was merely a small part of a lengthy confession, the sum and substances of which the defendant received notice and actually sought to suppress; given that the challenged statement did not materially augment or differ from the noticed confession, and the defendant received a full and fair opportunity to contest the admissibility of that confession, there was no violation. People v. Figueras, 199 A.D.2d 409, 606 N.Y.S.2d 237 (2d Dept. 1994).

—No notice required when a police officer testifies to statements he overheard while defendant and co-defendant were talking. People v. Stewart, 160 A.D.2d 966, 554 N.Y.S.2d 687 (2d Dept. 1990).

—No notice required if a police officer witness volunteers a statement defendant made to him and if the People did not intend to elicit the statement. People v. Jones, 159 A.D.2d 589, 552 N.Y.S.2d 447 (2d Dept. 1990).

—Defendant is not entitled to notice of an incriminating statement if the People use the statement for impeachment purposes on rebuttal and if the defendant opened the door to its admission. People v. Connor, 157 A.D.2d 739, 550 N.Y.S.2d 34 (2d Dept. 1990).

—Defendant's statements, made during an altercation with the correction officers, were properly admitted at trial, and they did not necessitate CPL § 710.30 notice because defendant was not in custody when he made the statements, they were not in response to police questioning, and their voluntariness was not at issue. People v. Hennigan, 19 A.D.3d 1102, 796 N.Y.S.2d 478 (4th Dept. 2005).

—Because the statement was not used as evidence-in-chief, but only on cross-examination to impeach defendant's testimony, CPL § 710.30 notice was not required. People v. Sanzotta, 191 A.D.2d 1032, 595 N.Y.S.2d 152 (4th Dept. 1993).

—Statements defendant makes when waiving his Miranda rights, that he understood his rights and was willing to talk without counsel are not subject to notice. People v. Grimes, 162 A.D.2d 1031, 557 N.Y.S.2d 815 (4th Dept. 1990).

—When there is no question as to the voluntariness of a defendant's statements, as in the case of res gestae statements, notice to the defendant of the intention to offer such statements into evidence is not required. People v. Abedi, 156 Misc. 2d 904, 595 N.Y.S.2d 1011 (Sup. Ct. N.Y. Co. 1993).

No notice required; rebuttal.—CPL § 710.30 notice was not required as to statement that People did not intend to offer at trial and that was only offered to rebut contention advanced by defense counsel. People v. Degrijze, 194 A.D.2d 801, 599 N.Y.S.2d 634 (2d Dept. 1993).

—Section 710.30 notice does not require notice where the use of the evidence is solely for rebuttal purposes. People v. Robinson, 205 A.D.2d 836, 613 N.Y.S.2d 284 (3d Dept. 1994).

—People were not required to serve § 710.30 notice as to statement which they only intended to use upon rebuttal for impeachment purposes, even though they were aware of the statement prior to that time. People v. Spinks, 205 A.D.2d 842, 613 N.Y.S.2d 288 (3d Dept. 1994).

No notice required; surveillance tape viewing.—In viewing a surveillance videotape, a convenience store clerk did not previously identify the defendant within the meaning of CPL § 710.30(1), because there was no suggestiveness involved in the clerk's viewing of the tape—the only people on the tape were the witness and the robbers. "Inasmuch as it was the robber shown on the videotape (as opposed to a police-acquired photograph or other depiction of defendant), there is no danger that the clerk identified defendant by unduly suggestive means" and thus defendant was not entitled to notice of the surveillance tape viewing. People v. Gee, 99 N.Y.2d 158, 753 N.Y.S.2d 19, 782 N.E.2d 1155 (2002), reargument denied, 99 N.Y.2d 652,

760 N.Y.S.2d 105, 790 N.E.2d 279 (2003), *reargument denied,* 99 N.Y.2d 652, 760 N.Y.S.2d 105, 790 N.E.2d 279 (2003).

Notice of statement; not required when given to non-police officer.—CPL § 710.30 does not apply to statements made to civilian witnesses. People v. Velez, 168 A.D.2d 207, 562 N.Y.S.2d 91 (1st Dept. 1990).

—When defendant makes statements to the complainant and the complainant is not a public servant nor acting as an agent of law enforcement, notice is not necessary. People v. Bell, 161 A.D.2d 772, 556 N.Y.S.2d 118 (2d Dept. 1990).

—The People were not required to provide notice of defendant's statements to his brother, who could not be considered an agent of the police where the police gave the brother no instructions, offered no assistance in obtaining the inculpatory statements, and the brief mention of the fund for confidential information was, at most, "generalized encouragement." People v. Johnson, 303 A.D.2d 830, 758 N.Y.S.2d 687 (3d Dept. 2003).

—CPL § 710.30 notice was not required as to statements made to off-duty police officers. People v. Socia, 150 Misc. 2d 518, 568 N.Y.S.2d 864 (Sup. Ct. Bronx Co. 1991).

Preclusion.—Court ruled both in and out court identification inadmissible whether or not an independent basis for the identification existed because the prosecutor failed to give notice. People v. Perez, 177 A.D.2d 657, 576 N.Y.S.2d 359 (2d Dept. 1991).

—Preclusion did not lie where defendant's statement was not attached to the CPL § 710.30 notice since defense counsel had otherwise been provided a copy of the defendant's statement; additionally, when defense counsel discovered that the statement was not attached to the CPL § 710.30 notice, he should have immediately informed the People or the court of the deficiency. People v. Black, 177 A.D.2d 1040, 578 N.Y.S.2d 53 (4th Dept. 1991).

—While identification evidence is generally precluded if notice of intent is not given or is delayed without good cause, such identification will not be precluded when the victim and witness initiated the identification; nor did the fact that police asked the victim and witness to come to the precinct house to identify the defendants preclude the evidence since the purpose was to clarify the role each defendant played. People v. Little, 149 Misc. 2d 860, 566 N.Y.S.2d 837 (Sup. Ct. Bronx Co. 1991).

—A victim's description of the perpetrator will be admissible, even if the in-court identification is precluded, if the description is not tainted by an out of court identification. People v. Ptah, 149 Misc. 2d 488, 565 N.Y.S.2d 397 (Sup. Ct. Bronx Co. 1990).

Prejudice.—Lack of prejudice to the defendant resulting from People's delay in filing notice pursuant to CPL § 710.30 does not obviate the need for the People to meet the statutory requirement of good cause before they may be permitted to serve a late notice. People v. O'Doherty, 70 N.Y.2d 479, 522 N.Y.S.2d 498, 517 N.E.2d 213 (1987).

Prior notification of intent to offer identification testimony required. —Trial court erred in permitting a witness present at the crime to testify to an identification made by him shortly after the defendant's arrest since the People failed prior to hearing and trial to notify the defense of their intent to offer such testimony as required by CPL § 710.30. People v. McKeever, 104 A.D.2d 608, 479 N.Y.S.2d 545 (2d Dept. 1984).

Pedigree questions.—There was no obligation for the People to give defendant pretrial notice of a pedigree statement that they did not introduce on their direct case, because the statement fell within the pedigree exception, the People had no intent to introduce it, and the People did not introduce it until the defendant opened the door. People v. Carione, 244 A.D.2d 274, 664 N.Y.S.2d 297 (1st Dept. 1997).

—Pedigree information provided by a defendant to police during processing—*e.g.,* fact that defendant was not employed—is not subject to suppression under CPL § 60.45 and it is not subject to the notice requirements of CPL § 710.30. People v. Thomas, 195 A.D.2d 301, 600 N.Y.S.2d 11 (1st Dept. 1993).

—Defendant's statement regarding his nickname fell within the pedigree exception to *Miranda;* furthermore, the People were not required to give notice of the defendant's statement. People v. Ennis, 197 A.D.2d 404, 602 N.Y.S.2d 374 (1st Dept. 1993).

—Defendant was wanted on a murder charge; prison officials later intercepted one of defendant's letters to an inmate which described the murder and made specific reference to defendant's brother, Delroy; three years later, defendant was traced Florida, arrested, and taken to the station house where as part of his pedigree information he stated he had a brother named Delroy; the court ruled that defendant was not entitled to notice because the information was pedigree. People v. Scott, 215 A.D.2d 699, 628 N.Y.S.2d 300 (2d Dept. 1995).

—No notice required when prosecutor offers into evidence defendant's answer to pedigree questions. People v. Stewart, 160 A.D.2d 966, 554 N.Y.S.2d 687 (2d Dept. 1990).

—People were not required to serve the defendant with notice of their intent to offer into evidence testimony that the defendant gave a fictitious name to the arresting officers, since such information was of a pedigree nature and therefore not properly subject to a motion to suppress. People v. Miller, 123 A.D.2d 721, 507 N.Y.S.2d 409 (2d Dept. 1986).

—Pedigree statement was not subject to suppression because the People were entitled to make reasonable inquiry concerning an arrested person's identity, including his name and address, without the necessity of formal warnings; the People had provided defendant with CPL § 710.30 notice that was not required because the statement was in response to routine pedigree questions. People v. Perez, 198 A.D.2d 540, 603 N.Y.S.2d 197 (3d Dept. 1993).

—Defendant's statement that he used an alias does not require notice of intent because that statement was made for processing purposes and because it fell within the pedigree exception to *Miranda.* People v. Haddock, 174 A.D.2d 773, 570 N.Y.S.2d 719 (3d Dept. 1991).

—Pedigree information is not generally subject to suppression challenges. People v. Alhadi, 151 A.D.2d 873, 543 N.Y.S.2d 175 (3d Dept. 1989); People v. Vaccarella, 177 A.D.2d 990, 578 N.Y.S.2d 11 (4th Dept. 1991).

—CPL § 710.30 notice was not required where statement in question was merely utilized for purposes of cross-examination. People v. Mitche, 155 A.D.2d 879, 547 N.Y.S.2d 486 (4th Dept. 1989).

"Res gestae" statement.—No CPL § 710.30 notice was required where the defendant's statements to the confidential informant were both spontaneous in nature and part of the res gestae. People v. Copes, 200 A.D.2d 680, 606 N.Y.S.2d 751 (2d Dept. 1994).

—The People were not required to serve 710.30 notice where the defendant's statements to the confidential informant was both spontaneous in nature and part of the res gestae. People v. Copes, 200 A.D.2d 680, 606 N.Y.S.2d 751 (2d Dept. 1994).

—Statements made by the defendant within two minutes after he struck a correction officer with a chair were spontaneous declarations or excited utterances intimately connected with the defendant's act of hitting the correction officer and were part of the *res gestae* and the statements do not come within the notice requirement of CPL § 710.30 because they were not made to a "public servant" and/or are not of such a nature as to be subject to a question of voluntariness. People v. Holloway, 77 A.D.2d 122, 432 N.Y.S.2d 905 (3d Dept. 1980).

—Statements that are spontaneous in nature and part of the *res gestae* do not require notice of intent to use. People v. Early, 85 A.D.2d 752, 445 N.Y.S.2d 252 (3d Dept. 1981).

Sealing of notice; not required.—In highly publicized murder case, defendant moved for an order sealing from the public the contents of the CPL § 710.30 notice, arguing that the unrestricted public access to the contents of the oral and written statements contained in her notice would prejudice her right to an impartial jury. Court denied defendant's request, holding that a court may not close a *Huntley* hearing on a possibility that there might be tainted, nonpublic evidence that might impair the selection of an impartial jury. People v. DeBeer, 3 Misc. 3d 515, 774 N.Y.S.2d 314 (Co. Ct. Ontario Co. 2004).

Section not applicable where no real issue of identification.—Since it is undisputed that the defendant was the person brought to the precinct after a citizen's arrest by the witness and the victim, their identification of defendant after he was put in a separate room was not a show-up within the meaning of CPL § 710.30; that section is applicable only where there is a real issue of identification predicated upon "police arranged confrontation between a defendant and an eyewitness, typically involving the use of line ups, show ups or photographs, for the purpose of establishing the identity of object to testimony concerning the criminal actor." *In re* Leo T., 87 A.D.2d 297, 451 N.Y.S.2d 147 (1st Dept. 1982).

Spontaneous.—Court properly denied defendant's motion to suppress statements he made while in a holding cell at the police precinct, because the record reflects that the statements were not the result of custodial interrogation, but were spontaneous. People v. Reese, 248 A.D.2d 411, 669 N.Y.S.2d 643 (2d Dept. 1998).

—Compliance with CPL § 710.30 is not necessary where a statement is clearly spontaneous. People v. Pulido, 138 A.D.2d 641, 526 N.Y.S.2d 224 (2d Dept. 1988).

—Spontaneous statements and statements that are not the product of police conduct or its equivalent are not subject to notice. People v. Murphy, 163 A.D.2d 425, 558 N.Y.S.2d 327 (3d Dept. 1990).

—Statements by a defendant which are clearly spontaneous or are in response to a request for "pedigree" information, and identification procedures employed in cases where the parties knew each other before the incident, or which are essentially confirmatory in nature, or an identification by a witness that was initiated by him and not the police, do not require a suppression hearing. People v. Little, 149 Misc. 2d 860, 566 N.Y.S.2d 837 (Sup. Ct. Bronx Co. 1991).

Unnamed identifying witness.—Identification notice that did not name identifying witness was sufficient because the complaint, which named the complainant as the source of accusation, accompanied the notice and complainant was the only identification witness at trial. People v. Hilton, 147 Misc. 2d 200, 555 N.Y.S.2d 550 (Sup. Ct. Queens Co. 1990).

Untimely notice.—Court imposed the proper remedy for the prosecutor's failure to provide timely CPL § 710.30 notice with respect to photo identification, namely, preclusion of that evidence, leaving unaffected the lineup identification, which had been properly noticed and was a valid basis for the in-court identification. People v. Alvarado, 235 A.D.2d 237, 653 N.Y.S.2d 295 (1st Dept. 1997).

—No error in admitting statement for which untimely notice was given because the statement was not very damaging and there was overwhelming evidence of guilt. People v. Howard, 162 A.D.2d 615, 556 N.Y.S.2d 940 (2d Dept. 1990).

—Court correctly precluded prosecution from using defendant's inculpatory statements when the prosecutor attached the wrong inculpatory statement to the notice and the notice did not otherwise convey the substance of the statement. People v. Sian, 167 A.D.2d 435, 561 N.Y.S.2d 791 (2d Dept. 1990).

—Because the prosecutor failed to give timely notice of identification testimony, the assault victim's testimony had to be suppressed even though the defendant was not prejudiced by the prosecutor's omission. People v. Miles, 163 A.D.2d 330, 557 N.Y.S.2d 163 (2d Dept. 1990).

—An undercover officer's identification testimony was still admissible even though the prosecutor failed to serve timely notice that the officer had a made a prior photo identification since the identification was merely confirmatory. People v. Veale, 169 A.D.2d 939, 565 N.Y.S.2d 252 (3d Dept. 1991).

—Prosecutor could elicit witness' testimony despite a failure to give timely notice because the prosecutor avoided asking the witness identification questions. People v. Laurez, 163 A.D.2d 742, 558 N.Y.S.2d 327 (3d Dept. 1990).

—Defendant granted a new trial because the People failed to provide timely notice of their intention to elicit line up and in-court identification testimony from a witness; additionally, the trial transcript was lost leaving the Appellate Division unable to determine if the defendant had raised timely objections or if the court permitted untimely service of notice because the People made a good faith showing. People v. Briggs, 162 A.D.2d 1006, 557 N.Y.S.2d 797 (4th Dept. 1990).

—A witness' description of defendant was not excluded for lack of timely notice because the witness gave the description before the police conducted the identification procedure; therefore, the identification was not tainted. People v. Jones, 163 A.D.2d 911, 558 N.Y.S.2d 774 (4th Dept. 1990).

—Identification that is not police arranged is exempt from notice requirements; a witness identification is non-exempt and considered police arranged when defendant waits outside the crime scene while officers talk to complaining witness, the witness sees defendant and then spontaneously identifies defendant. People v. Mora, 149 Misc. 2d 446, 565 N.Y.S.2d 382 (Sup. Ct. Kings Co. 1990).

Voice identification testimony.—Court properly denied suppression of a voice identification by a cab company dispatcher who recognized defendant's voice as a that of a very frequent customer; voice identification was confirmatory. People v. Watkins, 288 A.D.2d 151, 733 N.Y.S.2d 70 (1st Dept. 2001).

—Court properly ruled that the officers' voice identifications of defendant were confirmatory and not subject to notice requirements of CPL § 710.30, where each officer had spent hours listening to and transcribing intercepted telephone conversations of defendant—some of them only hours before the arrest—and defendant's voice had a distinctive whiny quality. People v. Deleon, 273 A.D.2d 27, 709 N.Y.S.2d 529 (1st Dept. 2000).

—Notice of voice identification testimony was not required here, where witnesses and defendant know one another, because in such a case, there is little or no risk that any suggestiveness in the procedure could lead to misidentification. People v. Van Wallendael, 259 A.D.2d 716, 688 N.Y.S.2d 166 (2d Dept. 1999).

—Identification of defendant's voice by a trained police officer who had become familiar with it while monitoring over 150 phone calls over a 20-day period was confirmatory and therefore not subject to the notice requirement of CPL § 710.30. People v. Morentino, 281 A.D.2d 928, 722 N.Y.S.2d 841 (4th Dept. 2001).

Suppression improperly granted.—County Court erred in suppressing identification evidence as a sanction against the People for their including an inaccurate date in their CPL § 710.30 notice; Appellate Division granted People's motion for leave to amend the notice to include the correct date. People v. Williams, 238 A.D.2d 914, 661 N.Y.S.2d 131 (4th Dept. 1997).

Voluntary statement; notice not required.—Notice of intention to use the statement need not be served on the defendant where there is no question of the voluntariness of the statements. People v. Balschweit, 91 A.D.2d 1127, 458 N.Y.S.2d 730 (3d Dept. 1983).

Waiver of defective notice.—The mere making of a suppression motion does not result in a waiver of the right to advance a claim pursuant to CPL § 710.30. People v. Bernier, 73 N.Y.2d 1006, 541 N.Y.S.2d 760, 539 N.E.2d 588 (1989).

—Failure to object to a notice that failed to state the contents of the statement and the circumstances under which it was made constituted a waiver and the issue cannot be raised on appeal. People v. Rivera, 53 N.Y.2d 1005, 442 N.Y.S.2d 475, 425 N.E.2d 863 (1981).

—Defendant did not waive his right to object to admitting statement for which there was untimely notice when he sought to suppress any and all statements; trial court committed reversible error by letting the People introduce statements not contained in the voluntary disclosure form even though the court held a hearing on voluntariness of all defendant's statements and had denied defendant's motion to suppress. People v. St. Martine, 160 A.D.2d 35, 559 N.Y.S.2d 697 (1st Dept. 1990).

—Once defendant has received a notice of intent to use statements and has moved to suppress those statements, the defendant cannot argue that notice was not sufficiently specific. People v. Holmes, 170 A.D.2d 534, 566 N.Y.S.2d 93 (2d Dept. 1991).

—By pleading guilty, defendant waives all claims of untimely notice. People v. McBayne, 160 A.D.2d 735, 555 N.Y.S.2d 609 (2d Dept. 1990).

Waiver of untimely notice.—Defendant did not waive his right to preclude identification testimony because of untimely notice when the court denied his suppression motion following a defacto *Wade* hearing. People v. Miles, 163 A.D.2d 330, 557 N.Y.S.2d 163 (2d Dept. 1990).

—Fact that defendant moved for a *Wade* hearing after he protested the timeliness of the CPL § 710.30 notice did not act as a waiver of his objection to the notice. People v. Mole, 147 A.D.2d 714, 538 N.Y.S.2d 325 (2d Dept. 1989).

—Where defendant, after his arrest in New York for robbery, gave no statements and absconded while on bail, and later was arrested in Virginia and purportedly gave a statement concerning the robbery at that time, the District Attorney's notice should have included the substance of this alleged statement together with the circumstances under which it was made. People v. Couch, 74 A.D.2d 582, 424 N.Y.S.2d 304 (2d Dept. 1980).

—Defendant waived his § 710.30 claim where he moved for a suppression hearing, which was held and resulted in a ruling of admissibility, prior to lodging any complaint about the sufficiency of the § 710.30 notice. People v. Jackson, 606 N.Y.S.2d 147 (3d Dept. 1994).

—Even if it was accepted that under the facts of the case the People were required to notify the defendant of the identification evidence they intended to use against him, his suppression motion on this question waived any objection concerning the timeliness of such notice. People v. LiCastro, 180 A.D.2d 840, 579 N.Y.S.2d 245 (3d Dept. 1992).

—Prosecution's violation of CPL § 710.30 was not preserved for appellate review in the absence of a timely objection; in any event the error was harmless since two of the identifications could have been made by independent evidence at trial. People v. Leary, 145 A.D.2d 732, 535 N.Y.S.2d 471 (3d Dept. 1988).

—Reversible error was not committed by the failure of the people to include in the notice to defendant under CPL § 710.30 their intent to use a certain statement since the statement was made known to defendant and fully explored during a suppression hearing held some time before trial, and he thus had the opportunity to excise the statement but failed to do so and there was overwhelming evidence of defendant's guilt and the court gave a strong curative instruction regarding the statement. People v. Thornton, 87 A.D.2d 991, 450 N.Y.S.2d 125 (4th Dept. 1982).

§ 710.40. Motion to suppress evidence; when made and determined.

1. A motion to suppress evidence must be made after the commencement of the criminal action in which such evidence is allegedly about to be offered, and, except as otherwise provided in section 710.30 and in subdivision two of this section, it must be made within the period provided in subdivision one of section 255.20.

2. The motion may be made for the first time when, owing to unawareness of facts constituting the basis thereof or to other factors, the defendant did not have reasonable opportunity to make the motion previously, or when the evidence which he seeks to suppress is of a kind specified in section 710.30 and he was not served by the people, as provided in said section 710.30, with a pre-trial notice of intention to offer such evidence at the trial.

3. When the motion is made before trial, the trial may not be commenced until determination of the motion.

4. If after a pre-trial determination and denial of the motion the court is satisfied, upon a showing by the defendant, that additional pertinent facts have been discovered by the defendant which he could not have discovered with reasonable diligence before the determination of the motion, it may permit him to renew the motion before trial or, if such was not possible owing to the time of the discovery of the alleged new facts, during trial.

Amended by L. 1974, Ch. 763; L. 1976, Ch. 194; L. 1977, Ch. 273.

ANNOTATIONS

Burden on prosecution to show probable cause.—The methadone bottle upon which the people base their claim of probable cause must be produced by the people at the new suppression hearing along with the officers memo book, arrest report and incident report and defense counsel must be allowed to cross-examine as to these items. People v. Shephard, 77 A.D.2d 502, 430 N.Y.S.2d 61 (1st Dept. 1980).

Determination during course of trial.—A mid-trial determination of a motion to suppress under CPL § 710.40(3) involves no constitutional infirmity unless substantial actual prejudice in the particular circumstances of the individual case can be demonstrated. People v. Lawrence, 39 N.Y.2d 956, 386 N.Y.S.2d 885, 353 N.E.2d 849 (1976).

—Court committed reversible error by compelling defense counsel to commence jury selection prior to the conclusion of the suppression hearing. People v. Blowe, 130 A.D.2d 668, 515 N.Y.S.2d 812 (2d Dept. 1987).

Demand for transcript; future requirements.—The court held that in the future a defendant should not only proceed with the requisite reasonable diligence in making his pretrial suppression motion, but should also make his request for a transcript of the minutes of any pretrial hearing prior to its conclusion. People v. Sanders, 31 N.Y.2d 463, 341 N.Y.S.2d 305, 293 N.E.2d 555 (1973).

Deviation in procedure.—Although general suppression issues should be decided prior to trial, court may deviate from that procedure where, as here, defendant consents to it. People v. Yousef, 236 A.D.2d 868, 654 N.Y.S.2d 82 (4th Dept. 1997).

Wade **hearings.**—*Wade* hearings are not part of a trial itself because CPL § 710.40 requires that motions to suppress evidence must be made and determined before trial. People v. Ayala, 75 N.Y.2d 422, 554 N.Y.S.2d 412, 553 N.E.2d 960 (1990).

Evidence; suppression hearing on improper pretrial identification.—It is necessary to afford defendant a hearing to determine whether the in-court identification has been tainted by improper pretrial identification, absent a finding by the court that testimony during the main trial on pretrial identification would not be prejudicial. The order was modified and the case remitted to county court for pretrial hearing. People v. Harrington, Jr., 31 N.Y.2d 784, 339 N.Y.S.2d 110, 291 N.E.2d 289 (1972).

Late motions.—Because defendant's motion to go pro se was filed more than 45 days after arraignment, trial court properly denied the motion. People v. Harvey, 198 A.D.2d 828, 605 N.Y.S.2d 1011 (4th Dept. 1993).

Motion to suppress.—Harmless error to start jury selection before deciding defendant's suppression motion because defendant was not prejudiced. People v. Gonzalez, 214 A.D.2d 451, 625 N.Y.S.2d 203 (1st Dept. 1995).

—Defendant was not entitled to a pretrial determination of his motion to suppress statement on the grounds that it was coerced because the prosecution had agreed to use the statement for impeachment purposes should the defendant choose to testify. People v. Whitney, 167 A.D.2d 254, 561 N.Y.S.2d 254 (1st Dept. 1990).

—Motion to suppress was untimely because the defendant signed a written consent to search and failed to state good cause as to why 300 days had elapsed before defendant contended the search was unlawful. People v. Kasparek, 174 A.D.2d 9780, 572 N.Y.S.2d 129 (4th Dept. 1991).

Motion to suppress; when determined.—A defendant failed to preserve on appeal his claim that the court should have ruled on his motion to suppress before jury selection because his lawyer consented to the court's suggestion to go ahead with jury selection. People v. Orkabi, 160 A.D.2d 644, 559 N.Y.S.2d 261 (1st Dept. 1990).

Renewal of motion.—Trial court did not abuse its discretion when it denied defendant's request to reopen the *Wade* hearing where the defendant failed to disclose any pertinent facts which would justify such a motion. People v. Fuentes, 53 N.Y.2d 892, 440 N.Y.S.2d 625, 423 N.E.2d 48 (1981).

—Since defendant made no application to reopen the *Mapp* hearing during trial, the court was under no obligation to reopen the hearing *sua sponte*. People v. Freeman, 253 A.D.2d 692, 679 N.Y.S.2d 360 (1st Dept. 1998).

—Inconsistent testimony about whether the on-scene identification was police arranged did not raise additional pertinent facts warranting a reopening of the *Wade* hearing. People v. Adams, 231 A.D.2d 447, 648 N.Y.S.2d 4 (1st Dept. 1996).

—Arresting officer's contradictory suppression hearing and trial testimony entitled defendant to a reopening of the suppression hearing. People v. Figliolo, 207 A.D.2d 679, 616 N.Y.S.2d 367 (1st Dept. 1994).

—Trial court should have reopened defendant's *Wade* hearing when complainant and friend testified that, contrary to office testimony and prosecutorial representation, other officers escorted them to the show up scene to identify those who had been apprehended; however, trial court's denial was harmless error due to overwhelming evidence of guilt. People v. Villanova, 179 A.D.2d 381, 578 N.Y.S.2d 1515 (1st Dept. 1992).

—Because eyewitness was credible and defendant's introduction of photos confirmed rather than contradicted the eyewitness' testimony, the trial court properly denied defendant's midtrial request to reopen the suppression hearing because of additional pertinent facts. People v. Robinson, 183 A.D.2d 420, 583 N.Y.S.2d 394 (1st Dept. 1992).

—A trial court need only reopen a hearing during trial where defendant makes a showing that additional pertinent facts have been discovered which could not have been discovered with reasonable diligence before the determination of the original suppression motion. Here, the alleged new facts were the circumstances surrounding defendant's arrest, of which he is presumed to have knowledge. People v. Hankins, 265 A.D.2d 572, 697 N.Y.S.2d 144 (2d Dept. 1999).

—Though the People did not properly preserve for appellate review the issue of the propriety of reopening the *Mapp/Huntley* hearing, court reached it in the interests of justice, where hearing should not have been reopened, because People had no obligation to turn over the information involved to defendant, and defendant could have learned about the summonses at issue during the initial hearing by asking pertinent questions of the witnesses. People v. Lester, 232 A.D.2d 427, 648 N.Y.S.2d 615 (2d Dept. 1996).

—Contradictory evidence will not suffice to reopen suppression hearing when defendant was aware of "new" facts from the outset. People v. Taylor, 206 A.D.2d 904, 616 N.Y.S.2d 116 (4th Dept. 1994).

—The court properly denied the defendant's request for a hearing to suppress physical evidence because it was untimely (made at the beginning of trial), unwritten, and had no supporting sworn allegations. People v. Massimi, 191 A.D.2d 969, 595 N.Y.S.2d 341 (4th Dept. 1993).

—Defendant's motion to reopen suppression hearing on the basis of newly discovered evidence should not have been granted when the new evidence was two eyewitness affidavits describing defendant's arrest which contradicted arresting officers' testimony; defendant knew the facts surrounding his arrest, and therefore, those facts are not newly discovered; defendant did not attempt to locate witnesses for the first hearing. People v. Mitchell-Benetiz, 168 A.D.2d 994, 564 N.Y.S.2d 936 (4th Dept. 1990).

Reopened hearing.—Court properly denied defendant's application to testify at the reopened suppression hearing, since he had the opportunity at the original hearing but declined to do so, and the hearing was reopened only for the purpose of allowing counsel to utilize previously unavailable grand jury testimony on further cross-examination of a prosecution witness. People v. Peterson, 6 A.D.3d 363, 777 N.Y.S.2d 48 (1st Dept. 2004).

Search and seizure; motion to suppress; retroactivity.—The rule of Chimel v. California (395 U.S. 752, 89 S. Ct. 2034, 23 L. Ed. 2d 685) applies in those cases involving the admissibility of evidence seized in searches occurring after June 23, 1969. People v. Buia, 34 N.Y.2d 529, 354 N.Y.S.2d 98, 309 N.E.2d 869 (1974).

Untimely motion.—County Court properly denied defendant's motion to suppress items of physical evidence without conducting a hearing where motion was made at the beginning of trial, was untimely, and was not made in writing or supported by sworn allegations of fact. People v. Adams, 252 A.D.2d 980, 676 N.Y.S.2d 361 (4th Dept. 1998).

Waiver of hearing.—Defendant waived his right to a pretrial suppression hearing by proceeding to trial without a hearing and failing to object to the admission of his statements. By waiving the hearing, defendant failed to preserve the merits of the suppression claims for review. People v. Murray, 7 A.D.3d 828, 776 N.Y.S.2d 368 (3d Dept. 2004).

§ 710.50. Motion to suppress evidence; in what courts made.

1. The particular courts in which motions to suppress evidence must be made are as follows:

(a) If an indictment is pending in a superior court, or if the defendant has been held by a local criminal court for the action of a grand jury, the motion must be made in the superior court in which such indictment is pending or which impaneled or will impanel such grand jury. If the superior court which will impanel such grand jury is the supreme court, the motion may, in the alternative, be made in the county court of the county in which the action is pending;

(b) If a currently undetermined felony complaint is pending in a local criminal court, the motion must be made in the superior court which would have trial jurisdiction of the offense or offenses charged were an indictment therefor to result;

(c) If an information, a simplified information, a prosecutor's information or a misdemeanor complaint is pending in a local criminal court, the motion must be made in such court.

2. If after a motion has been made in and determined by a superior court a local criminal court acquires trial jurisdiction of the action by reason of an information, a prosecutor's information or a misdemeanor complaint filed therewith, such superior court's determination is binding upon such local criminal court. If, however, the motion has been made in but not yet determined by the superior court at the time of the filing of such information, prosecutor's information or misdemeanor complaint, the superior court may not determine the motion but must refer it to the local criminal court of trial jurisdiction.

Amended by L. 1972, Ch. 661; L. 1973, Ch. 221.

ANNOTATIONS

Collateral estoppel.—A prior criminal court adjudication that the search warrant was invalid because it was overbroad in that it provided for the search of 25 apartments cannot be relitigated by the people after indictment in the Supreme Court because of collateral estoppel. People v. Nieves, 106 Misc. 2d 395, 431 N.Y.S.2d 892 (Sup. Ct. Bronx Co. 1980).

Motion to suppress.—CPL § 710.50 does not require that a suppression hearing be held before the indictment. Burse v. Bristol, 203 A.D.2d 962, 612 N.Y.S.2d 990 (4th Dept. 1994).

—An application to bar administrative proceedings to revoke a mortgage license until the motion to suppress illegally seized evidence was heard did not have to be brought in the county where the grand jury convened because it was unclear if any indictments would be handed down. Gouiran Holdings v. Miller, 140 Misc. 2d 142, 531 N.Y.S.2d 441 (Sup. Ct. Kings Co. 1989).

Review of motion to suppress by co-equal court.—When a motion to suppress evidence obtained under a warrant is made on the ground of insufficiency of the factual showing in the papers before the issuing judge, another judge of that same court, though having jurisdiction, should not entertain the motion in the absence of a showing of fact in addition to those presented on the application for the warrant. People v. Romney, 77 A.D.2d 482, 433 N.Y.S.2d 941 (4th Dept. 1980).

Search & seizure; suppression; jurisdiction to hear motion.—County Court had jurisdiction to hear motion to suppress after indictment of defendant for gambling and possession of weapons and City Court order denying motion was a nullity as it did not have jurisdiction of the matter after indictment even though it issued the search warrant. People v. Kelly, 40 A.D.2d 624, 336 N.Y.S.2d 514 (4th Dept. 1972).

Wiretap warrant; intercepted conversations; use against person not named in warrant.—Wiretap warrant that named one Roth and resulted in intercepted phone calls of defendant who was not named in warrant could not be used against defendant as statute authorizing judicially supervised wiretapping as exception to inviolability of privacy, must be strictly construed, and only an amendment to wiretap warrant would justify use of conversations against defendant. People v. Ferrandino, 69 Misc. 2d 508, 330 N.Y.S.2d 114 (Albany Co. Ct. 1972).

§ 710.60. Motion to suppress evidence; procedure.

1. A motion to suppress evidence made before trial must be in writing and upon reasonable notice to the people and with opportunity to be heard. The motion papers must state the ground or grounds of the motion and must contain sworn allegations of fact, whether of the defendant or of another person or persons, supporting such grounds. Such allegations may be based upon personal knowledge of the deponent or upon information and belief, provided that in the latter event the sources of such information and the grounds of such belief are stated. The people may file with the court, and in such case must serve a copy thereof upon the defendant or his counsel, an answer denying or admitting any or all of the allegations of the moving papers.

2. The court must summarily grant the motion if:

(a) The motion papers comply with the requirements of subdivision one and the people concede the truth of allegations of fact therein which support the motion; or

(b) The people stipulate that the evidence sought to be suppressed will not be offered in evidence in any criminal action or proceeding against the defendant.

3. The court may summarily deny the motion if:

(a) The motion papers do not allege a ground constituting legal basis for the motion; or

(b) The sworn allegations of fact do not as a matter of law support the ground alleged; except that this paragraph does not apply where the motion is based upon the ground specified in subdivision three or six of section 710.20.

4. If the court does not determine the motion pursuant to subdivisions two or three, it must conduct a hearing and make findings of fact essential to the determination thereof. All persons giving factual information at such hearing must testify under oath, except that unsworn evidence pursuant to subdivision two of section 60.20 of this chapter may also be received. Upon such hearing, hearsay evidence is admissible to establish any material fact.

5. A motion to suppress evidence made during trial may be in writing and may be litigated and determined on the basis of motion papers as provided in subdivisions one through four, or it may, instead, be made orally in open court. In the latter event, the court must, where necessary, also conduct a hearing as provided in subdivision four, out of the presence of the jury if any, and make findings of fact essential to the determination of the motion.

6. Regardless of whether a hearing was conducted, the court, upon determining the motion, must set forth on the record its findings of fact, its conclusions of law and the reasons for its determination.

Amended by L. 1975, Ch. 39; L. 1986, Ch. 776.

ANNOTATIONS

Adjournment; *Huntley* hearing.—As a general matter of policy, requests for brief adjournments to secure witnesses should be granted where the witness is identified, is within the court's jurisdiction and there is a showing of some diligence and good faith. People v. Brown, 78 A.D.2d 861, 432 N.Y.S.2d 630 (2d Dept. 1980).

Adjournment; refusal to grant.—Court did not abuse its discretion when it denied the defendant's request for an adjournment of the *Wade* hearing based upon the defendant's ear infection, which he claimed affected his ability to hear, since the defendant supplied no medical documentation, responded to questions posed by the court without assistance, and did not demonstrate an inability to comprehend the proceedings or consult with his attorney. People v. Green, 127 A.D.2d 788, 512 N.Y.S.2d 183 (2d Dept. 1987).

—The court did not abuse its discretion in refusing to grant defendant an adjournment of a suppression hearing where one prior adjournment had been granted to the defendant during which time defendant failed to serve a witness with subpoena and where the evidence from said witness could be obtained from other witnesses immediately available. People v. Africk, 107 A.D.2d 700, 484 N.Y.S.2d 55 (2d Dept. 1985).

Burden of proof.—The fact that the People have the burden of proving voluntariness beyond a reasonable doubt, does not mean that the People are mandated to produce all police officers who had contact with the defendant from arrest to the time that the challenged statements were elicited. People v. Witherspoon, 66 N.Y.2d 973, 498 N.Y.S.2d 789, 489 N.E.2d 758 (1985).

—The People have the burden at a *Wade* hearing of proving by clear and convincing evidence that any in-court identification of the defendant will not be traceable to suggestive police identification procedures. People v. Foster, 200 A.D.2d 196, 613 N.Y.S.2d 616, 620 n.6 (1st Dept. 1994).

—On a motion to suppress evidence claimed to have been unlawfully obtained, the prosecution bears the burden of going forward to show the legality of the police conduct in the first instance. People v. Whitfield, 178 A.D.2d 334, 577 N.Y.S.2d 800 (1st Dept. 1991).

—Absent some showing of impermissible suggestiveness, there is no burden upon the People nor any need to demonstrate that a source independent of the pretrial identification procedure exists for the witness's in-court identification. *In re* Raymond A., 178 A.D.2d 134, 577 N.Y.S.2d 795 (1st Dept. 1991).

—On a motion to suppress evidence, it is the accused, not the People, who bear the ultimate burden of proof. People v. Perez, 149 A.D.2d 344, 539 N.Y.S.2d 750 (1st Dept. 1989).

—There is no automatic requirement that the complainant testify at a *Wade* hearing. People v. McGovern, 158 A.D.2d 551, 551 N.Y.S.2d 321, 323 (2d Dept. 1990).

—Court did not err in not requiring the production of the identifying non-police witnesses at the *Wade* hearing. People v. Geames, 157 A.D.2d 744, 550 N.Y.S.2d 39 (2d Dept. 1990).

—On a motion to suppress evidence a defendant challenging the legality of a search and seizure bears the ultimate burden of proving illegality, but the People bear the burden of going forward in the first instance to show the lawfulness of the police conduct. People v. Burton, 130 A.D.2d 675, 515 N.Y.S.2d 601 (2d Dept. 1987).

—The record of the suppression hearing contained no evidence concerning the circumstances of the seizure of the physical property, nor evidence of what was seized; because the People failed to present any witness with first-hand knowledge of the police conduct, the proof was insufficient to meet their burden of coming forward with evidence showing the legality of the police conduct. People v. DeFrain, 204 A.D.2d 1002, 613 N.Y.S.2d 303 (4th Dept. 1994).

—The People are not obligated to produce any particular witness at a suppression hearing provided they sustain their burden of coming forward with evidence showing that there was probable cause for the arrest; they are not required to produce the detaining officer. People v. Lucas, 162 Misc. 2d 326, 616 N.Y.S.2d 708 (Sup. Ct. Queens Co. 1994).

—In a motion to suppress physical evidence, the People have the initial burden of going forward to show the legality of the police conduct; once the People have met this burden, the defendant must prove by a preponderance of the credible evidence that the physical evidence should be suppressed. People v. Del Gizzo, 156 Misc. 2d 720, 594 N.Y.S.2d 583 (Sup. Ct. N.Y. Co. 1993).

—On a motion to suppress physical evidence, the prosecution has the burden of going forward in the first instance to show the legality of the police conduct. People v. Sanchez, 151 Misc. 2d 431, 579 N.Y.S.2d 825 (Sup. Ct. Kings Co. 1991).

Defendant's burden of proof.—The sufficiency of the defendant's factual allegations in a suppression motion should be evaluated by the face of the pleadings, assessed in conjunction with the context of the motion, and defendant's access to information. People v. Mendoza, 82 N.Y.2d 415, 604 N.Y.S.2d 922, 624 N.E.2d 1017 (1993).

—Defendant's untimely and unsupported oral application for a *Dunaway* hearing, made at the start of a *Huntley* hearing, was properly denied by the suppression court. People v. Fuller, 200 A.D.2d 498, 606 N.Y.S.2d 640 (1st Dept. 1993).

—Defendant has the burden of establishing the suggestiveness of an identification procedure. People v. Faust, 178 A.D.2d 352, 577 N.Y.S.2d 403 (1st Dept. 1991).

—Where defendant's moving papers alleged only that he was standing in a public street when placed under arrest by officers who had not seen him engaged in any criminal activity, these vague and conclusory allegations did not warrant a *Dunaway* hearing. People v. Alers, 234 A.D.2d 310, 651 N.Y.S.2d 537 (2d Dept. 1996).

—It is the defendant who bears the ultimate burden of proving that the identification procedure was unduly suggestive. People v. Sanchez, 178 A.D.2d 567, 577 N.Y.S.2d 653 (2d Dept. 1991).

—Testimony of additional officers was not required where defendant failed to sustain his burden of presenting a *bona fide* factual predicate which demonstrated that they possessed material evidence on the issue of whether the oral statements were coerced. People v. Wilson, 143 A.D.2d 786, 533 N.Y.S.2d 313 (2d Dept. 1988).

—Where defendant failed in his initial obligation to allege the illegality of his arrest as a ground for the suppression motion, People were not required to submit proof that the arrest was supported by probable cause. People v. Smith, 252 A.D.2d 737, 676 N.Y.S.2d 288 (3d Dept. 1998).

Dunaway rule.—The defendant was entitled to a rehearing on the matter of the legality or illegality of the defendant's arrest after the trial court erroneously ruled that the legality or illegality of defendant's arrest is not determinative of the fundamental issue in the *Huntley* hearing. People v. Burns, 75 A.D.2d 899, 428 N.Y.S.2d 60 (2d Dept. 1980).

Exclusion of public and press.—Reporter's rights and those of his employer were violated by court's refusal to allow reporter's counsel to advance arguments after reporter was excluded from the suppression hearing concerning tape recordings and their audibility. Merola v. Warner, 74 A.D.2d 287, 427 N.Y.S.2d 808 (1st Dept. 1980).

General.—People were deprived of adequate notice where they were served with suppression motion one day before the suppression hearing. People v. Zimmerman, 157 Misc. 2d 293, 596 N.Y.S.2d 307 (Monroe Co. 1993).

Grand jury minutes.—Defendant was denied due process of law and a new suppression hearing was ordered where the prosecutor failed to disclose the grand jury testimony of the police officer which was contradictory to the testimony of the parole officer as the evidence was of a material nature which if disclosed could have affected the suppression decision. People v. Geaslen, 54 N.Y.2d 510, 446 N.Y.S.2d 227, 430 N.E.2d 1280 (1981).

Hearing required before suppression of evidence.—Whether a store security guard's search of defendant was a state action was an issue of fact entitling defendant to a suppression hearing. People v. Mendoza, 82 N.Y.2d 415, 604 N.Y.S.2d 922, 624 N.E.2d 1017 (1993).

—Defendant's assertion in motion papers that the arresting officer was not standing near defendant at the time of the alleged drug exchange, that the exchange would have appeared as a handshake to the officer, and that a handshake is innocent and insufficient to support probable cause were sufficient to entitle defendant to a suppression hearing. People v. Altruz, 198 A.D.2d 423, 604 N.Y.S.2d 134 (2d Dept. 1993).

—The court should have held a hearing to determine the nature and extent of defendant's prior dealings with a witness informant; the informant's knowledge of defendant stemmed only from a few street encounters. People v. Sydney, 195 A.D.2d 763, 600 N.Y.S.2d 358 (3d Dept. 1993).

—Trial court improperly ordered the suppression of a blood test, without holding a hearing, after determining that defendant was incapable of giving an informal consent at the time of the request for a blood sample based upon an *in camera* inspection of the minutes of the Grand Jury; a hearing is required before any evidence can be suppressed. People v. Cole, 97 A.D.2d 886, 470 N.Y.S.2d 705 (3d Dept. 1983).

Hearing not required.—Court properly denied, without a hearing, defendant's motion to suppress physical evidence because defense counsel's affirmation failed to identify the source of information, failed to address the information available to defendant, and defendant did not avail himself of the opportunity provided by the court to correct these defects. People v. Anderson, 253 A.D.2d 636, 678 N.Y.S.2d 315 (1st Dept. 1998).

Juvenile.—Court properly denied juvenile's motion which did not give any facts relating to the juvenile's conduct or specifically deny juvenile's illegal conduct; rather, the motion merely denied involvement in illegal conduct at the time of seizure. People v. Mendoza, 82 N.Y.2d 415, 604 N.Y.S.2d 922, 624 N.E.2d 1017 (1993).

Motion to suppress; grounds.—Court did not err in refusing to permit the defense to raise the issue of entrapment at the suppression hearing since it was in all respects irrelevant to the issues raised—that is, the existence of probable cause for defendant's arrest and whether he voluntarily consented to a search of his home—and even if present did not vitiate or negate a finding of probable cause. People v. Cline, 192 A.D.2d 957, 596 N.Y.S.2d 925 (3d Dept. 1993).

—Court properly denied suppression motion without a hearing where the court had sufficient information before it to conclude, as a matter of law, that the confrontation between the witness and defendant was either unarranged, or was arranged independently of the police. People v. Omaro, 201 A.D.2d 324, 607 N.Y.S.2d 44 (1st Dept. 1994).

—Court properly denied defendant's suppression motion without a hearing where his papers were vague and conclusory; defendant merely stated that he did not sell or possess drugs, and that the police violated his Fourth Amendment rights by arresting him, which did not refute the People's detailed statements relating to the officer's observation of defendant and codefendant selling narcotics. People v. Hightower, 206 A.D.2d 253, 614 N.Y.S.2d 407 (1st Dept. 1994), *modified and aff'd,* 85 N.Y.2d 988, 629 N.Y.S.2d 164, 652 N.E.2d 910 (1995).

—Because defendant did not contest that the witness was his friend, summary denial of the defense motion for a *Wade* hearing was proper. People v. Dominguez, 207 A.D.2d 715, 616 N.Y.S.2d 502 (1st Dept. 1994).

—The bare assertion of innocence and the conclusory allegation that evidence has been illegally recovered are insufficient to warrant a suppression hearing. People v. Marte, 207 A.D.2d 314, 615 N.Y.S.2d 678 (1st Dept. 1994).

—An affirmation containing only legal conclusions instead of the sworn allegations of fact required by statutory law is insufficient to warrant a suppression hearing. People v. Coleman, 191 A.D.2d 390, 595 N.Y.S.2d 431 (1st Dept.), *aff'd,* 82 N.Y.2d 415, 604 N.Y.S.2d 922, 624 N.E.2d 1017 (1993).

Motion to suppress; necessity of hearing.—When the trial court denies a motion to suppress, the judge must explain why the motion was denied; however, if neither the People nor the motion court identify a deficiency in the motion to suppress, the appellate court cannot later find a deficiency to uphold the denied motion. People v. Bonilla, 82 N.Y.2d 825, 604 N.Y.S.2d 937, 624 N.E.2d 1032 (1993).

—Court properly denied the application for a *Mapp* hearing where the defense failed to allege sufficient facts to warrant a hearing. People v. Cameron, 189 A.D.2d 628, 592 N.Y.S.2d 351 (1st Dept. 1993).

—Before a court may summarily deny a *Wade* hearing, it must conclude as a matter of law that no degree of police suggestiveness could possibly have tainted the identification. People v. Lawhorn, 192 A.D.2d 359, 595 N.Y.S.2d 777 (1st Dept. 1993).

—Spontaneous identifications, unarranged by police, are not subject to suppression. People v. Fernandez, 182 A.D.2d 431, 582 N.Y.S.2d 161 (1st Dept. 1992).

—Defendant's suppression motion was properly summarily denied where defendant simply claimed in his moving papers that he was acting innocently when he was seized. People v. Murray, 172 A.D.2d 437, 569 N.Y.S.2d 12 (1st Dept. 1991).

—CPL Article 710 does not permit a suppression hearing merely to serve as a fishing expedition. People v. Holder, 149 A.D.2d 325, 539 N.Y.S.2d 747 (1st Dept. 1989).

—Contradictory factual allegations concerning the circumstances of the defendant's arrest clearly raise a question of fact mandating a suppression hearing. People v. Acosta, 150 A.D.2d 166, 540 N.Y.S.2d 439 (1st Dept. 1989).

—Where the undercover officer identified the defendant at the station house approximately two hours after the drug transaction, no *Wade* hearing was required. People v. Jackson, 171 A.D.2d 756, 567 N.Y.S.2d 310 (2d Dept. 1991).

—The offhand remark made by the defendant's trial attorney during colloquy, to the effect that an "interesting question of whether or not there was an illegal search" had arisen, did not constitute an oral motion to suppress evidence. People v. Luperena, 159 A.D.2d 727, 553 N.Y.S.2d 208 (2d Dept. 1990).

—The defendant's request for a hearing to determine whether his arrest was supported by probable cause was properly denied since his supporting papers were conclusory and failed to state sufficient facts to warrant such a hearing. People v. Gonzalez, 153 A.D.2d 592, 544 N.Y.S.2d 632 (2d Dept. 1989).

—Viewing by undercover officer at precinct seven hours after drug transaction constituted a confirmatory procedure, and no *Wade* hearing was required. People v. Hill, 147 A.D.2d 500, 537 N.Y.S.2d 594 (2d Dept. 1989).

—There must be a hearing whenever the defendant claims his statements were involuntary no matter what facts he puts in support of that claim. People v. Bingham, 144 A.D.2d 682, 535 N.Y.S.2d 70 (2d Dept. 1988).

—It was error for court to summarily deny the defendant's suppression motion without conducting a hearing where the defendant's papers were sufficient to entitle him to a hearing and the People conceded that a show-up identification procedure had been conducted; and also since the court made no findings of fact and conclusions of law and gave no reasons for its determination. People v. Vitetta, 118 A.D.2d 885, 500 N.Y.S.2d 547 (2d Dept. 1986).

—Pursuant to CPL § 710.60, a hearing is required on a suppression motion whenever the People, in their motion papers, refuse to concede the truth of the facts alleged by the defendant. People v. Wilsey, 301 A.D.2d 755, 753 N.Y.S.2d 232 (3d Dept. 2003).

—The sufficiency of the factual allegations in a suppression motion should be evaluated by the face of the pleadings, the context of the motion, and the defendant's access to information. People v. Fagan, 203 A.D.2d 933, 611 N.Y.S.2d 389 (4th Dept. 1994).

—Since the bank security investigator's conduct was not a police arranged confrontation between defendant and a victim, the court properly ruled that there was no need to conduct a *Wade* hearing. People v. Dunnigan, 188 A.D.2d 1052, 592 N.Y.S.2d 207 (4th Dept. 1992).

—An affidavit of defendant's counsel which merely contains conclusory allegations that an unconstitutional search had been conducted at the time of defendant's arrest is insufficient to raise a factual issue that would require a hearing. People v. Robinson, 154 A.D.2d 931, 546 N.Y.S.2d 502 (4th Dept. 1989).

—Court's summary rejection of suppression motion was proper where the moving papers in support of the motion to suppress physical evidence contained only conclusory assertions of legal grounds and failed to allege any evidentiary facts to support

it. People v. Vega, 145 A.D.2d 924, 535 N.Y.S.2d 855 (4th Dept. 1988).

—Court summarily denied motion to suppress physical evidence where defendant, in his moving papers, merely asserted there was no "probable cause" to arrest him. People v. Brown, 142 Misc. 2d 76, 535 N.Y.S.2d 907 (Sup. Ct. Kings Co. 1988).

Motion to suppress; seizure of pistols.—The Court of Appeals affirmed an order of the Appellate Division which reversed a trial order to suppress pistols. The court held that police acted reasonably when, upon noticing a parked rented automobile with its motor running with four male occupants in a high incident crime area, they inquired as to who threw a six-inch blade hunting knife from the vehicle and upon receiving no answer conducted a contemporaneous search of the vehicle which led to discovery of the pistols. The officer had probable cause to believe defendants had committed a crime and the search was reasonable to protect the safety of the searching officer and his fellow officers. People v. Rosello, 29 N.Y.2d 838, 327 N.Y.S.2d 852, 277 N.E.2d 785 (1971).

Motion to suppress statements; reopening of hearing based on new evidence.—Where new evidence was discovered during a non-jury trial relating to the defendant's motion to suppress statements, which motion had previously been denied after a hearing, the trial court should have granted defendant's motion to reopen hearing on ground that a potentially illegal arrest without probable cause caused the defendant to make an otherwise spontaneous statement. People v. Perez, 104 A.D.2d 454, 478 N.Y.S.2d 968 (2d Dept. 1984).

Motion to suppress; sufficiency.—The sufficiency of defendant's suppression motion should be decided upon by evaluating the face of the pleadings, the context of the motion, and the defendant's access to information. People v. Mendoza, 82 N.Y.2d 415, 604 N.Y.S.2d 922, 624 N.E.2d 1017 (1993).

—Court properly denied defendant's suppression motion because it was an untimely, unsupported oral application for a *Dunaway* hearing made at the beginning of a *Wade* hearing. People v. Fuller, 200 A.D.2d 498, 606 N.Y.S.2d 640 (1st Dept. 1994).

Motion to suppress; summary denial.—Although the hearing court improperly considered certain video and audiotapes to decide the issue of probable cause, its summary denial of defendant's motion to suppress physical evidence was proper because the defense attorney's affirmation contained conclusory allegations insufficient to raise a triable issue of fact. People v. Holden, 198 A.D.2d 435, 605 N.Y.S.2d 912 (2d Dept. 1993).

Refusal to reopen suppression hearing proper.—Trial court did not abuse its discretion in denying defendant's motion to reopen suppression hearing based upon a recent U.S. Supreme Court decision where the evidence at the hearing and the papers submitted in support of the motion to reopen did not establish a factual predicate to support defendant's contention that his rights were violated. People v. Mercado, 62 N.Y.2d 866, 478 N.Y.S.2d 253, 466 N.E.2d 845 (1984).

—A trial court has the authority to reopen a suppression hearing based on evidence adduced at trial which indicates that substantial rights of a defendant may have been affected. People v. Figlioli, 207 A.D.2d 679, 616 N.Y.S.2d 367 (1st Dept. 1994).

—Court denied the People's motion to reopen the suppression hearing where the People failed to adduce evidence, at the hearing, explaining the delay in the defendant's hearing. People v. Moore, 134 Misc. 2d 822, 512 N.Y.S.2d 999, 1000 (Sup. Ct. Queens Co. 1987), *modified*, 159 A.D.2d 491, 552 N.Y.S.2d 956 (1st Dept. 1990).

—Court did not err in denying defendant's request to reopen the suppression hearing where the request was made nearly five months after the hearing was conducted, and defense counsel failed to offer an adequate explanation as to why the request could not have been made sooner. People v. Anderson, 201 A.D.2d 658, 608 N.Y.S.2d 267 (2d Dept. 1994).

Reopening hearing.—Court should have granted defendant's renewed request for a *Wade* hearing where it was shown, at trial, that the witness did not in fact know the person he identified as the perpetrator prior to the crime. People v. Jackson, 150 A.D.2d 491, 541 N.Y.S.2d 226 (2d Dept. 1989).

—The court properly exercised its discretion in denying the People's motion to reopen the suppression hearing; there was no justification to afford the People a second chance to succeed where once they had tried and failed. People v. Lopez, 206 A.D.2d 894, 615 N.Y.S.2d 158 (4th Dept. 1994).

Right to counsel.—Defendant's right to the assistance of counsel as well as his fundamental right to confront and cross-examine prosecution witnesses were necessarily violated when the hearing court ordered that the suppression hearing proceed despite the fact that the defendant's counsel was not present in the courtroom and notwithstanding the consent of the prosecutor to adjourn the proceeding pending the appearance of counsel. People v. Spellner, 133 A.D.2d 865, 520 N.Y.S.2d 418, 419 (2d Dept. 1987).

Right to waive presence at preliminary hearing; *Wade* motion.—Defendant, who was improperly denied the right to waive his presence at a preliminary hearing, should have had his Wade motion to suppress the witness's in-court identification granted; however, the error was harmless in light of testimony of an untainted identification witness who was not present at the hearing and because there was additionally an independent basis for both identifications which clearly was established at trial. People v. Lyde, 104 A.D.2d 957, 480 N.Y.S.2d 734 (2d Dept. 1984).

Search; border crossing; probable cause.—In absence of defendant's proof that customs search was unconstitutional, marijuana found in car is admissible in evidence and fact that inspectors observation of anti-draft literature prompted search is irrelevant. People v. Dworkin, 30 N.Y.2d 706, 332 N.Y.S.2d 645, 283 N.E.2d 620 (1972).

Suppression hearings; grounds; sworn allegations of fact.—Reference by defense counsel in moving papers supporting suppression motion to an allegation in the felony complaint that the evidence was found "in defendant's apartment" was insufficient as a factual assertion that defendant had an expectation of privacy in the area searched. People v. Gomez, 67 N.Y.2d 843, 501 N.Y.S.2d 650, 492 N.E.2d 778 (1986).

—Defendant's application for a suppression hearing regarding certain physical evidence allegedly seized from him was properly denied because his supporting papers were conclusory and failed to state any facts in support of the motion. People v. Stevens, 129 A.D.2d 749, 514 N.Y.S.2d 509 (2d Dept. 1987).

—Defense counsel satisfied his statutory obligation to support his suppression motion with sworn allegations of fact where he supported his motion with an affirmation made upon information and belief and generally, though not specifically, set forth his sources. People v. Marshall, 122 A.D.2d 283, 504 N.Y.S.2d 782 (2d Dept. 1986).

—Defense counsel's affidavit, which did not state the sources of counsel's information and which merely contains conclusory allegations that an unconstitutional search had been conducted at the time of defendant's arrest, was insufficient to raise a factual issue that would require a hearing. People v. Lofton, 129 A.D.2d 970, 514 N.Y.S.2d 577 (4th Dept. 1987).

Suppression hearing improperly reopened after 12 days; no extraordinary circumstances.—It was improper for the trial court to reopen a suppression hearing 12 days after both sides rested to permit the People to present evidence concerning statements by two of the defendant's companions since the People had every opportunity to present their evidence at the original hearing and there were no extraordinary or extenuating circumstances which would have warranted such reopening. People v. Robinson, 100 A.D.2d 945, 474 N.Y.S.2d 836 (2d Dept. 1984).

Untimely motion summarily denied.—County Court properly denied defendant's motion to suppress items of physical evidence without conducting a hearing where the motion was made at the beginning of trial, was untimely, and was not made in writing or supported by sworn allegations of fact. People v. Adams, 252 A.D.2d 980, 676 N.Y.S.2d 361 (4th Dept. 1998).

Wade hearing; necessity of presence of witness.—Defendant was not denied due process by the denial of his request to call the complainant at the *Wade* hearing, since he failed to demonstrate some indicia of suggestiveness of the identification procedures employed. People v. Jones, 188 A.D.2d 364, 591 N.Y.S.2d 172 (1st Dept. 1992).

—A defendant does not have an unqualified right to call the complaining or identifying witness at a *Wade* hearing; that right is generally only triggered when the hearing record raises substantial issues as to the constitutionality of the identification procedure. People v. Ford, 188 A.D.2d 613, 591 N.Y.S.2d 504 (2d Dept. 1992).

—Hearing court did not err in failing to compel the People to produce the complaining witness, since there is no automatic

rule requiring that a complainant testify at a pretrial hearing. People v. Davis, 123 A.D.2d 640, 506 N.Y.S.2d 783 (2d Dept. 1986).

—There is no absolute right to call an identifying witness at a Wade hearing. People v. Griffiths, 202 A.D.2d 1003, 609 N.Y.S.2d 486 (4th Dept. 1994).

Subd. 3

Withdrawal of motion before determination.—Defendant's waiver of a court determination at the conclusion of his suppression hearing as a precondition to the offer of a reduced plea was valid. People v. Esajerre, 35 N.Y.2d 463, 363 N.Y.S.2d 931, 323 N.E.2d 175 (1974).

Motion to suppress based on Fourth Amendment grounds.—A motion to suppress based on Fourth, as distinguished from Fifth Amendment grounds, must be supported by sworn allegations of fact. People v. Egan, 72 A.D.2d 239, 424 N.Y.S.2d 546 (4th Dept. 1980).

Summary denial.—Defendant's oral motion to suppress physical evidence was properly denied since it did not comply with the requirements of CPL § 710.60(1). People v. LaBron, 172 A.D.2d 462, 568 N.Y.S.2d 807 (1st Dept. 1991).

—Defendant's moving papers were deficient where the factual allegations therein merely claimed that at the time of defendant's arrest, and immediately subsequent thereto he was not engaged in any illegal activity or in open possession of contraband. People v. Rodriguez, 172 A.D.2d 191, 567 N.Y.S.2d 714, 715 (1st Dept. 1991).

—The lapse of one week between the drug sale and the subsequent viewing of the defendant was not a significant passage of time giving rise to "special circumstances" warranting a *Wade* Hearing. People v. Hunter, 173 A.D.2d 321, 575 N.Y.S.2d 460 (1st Dept. 1991).

—Court erred in summarily denying suppression motion where prosecution's version of the facts as to the legality of the stop was inadequate to establish legality as a matter of law. People v. Ramos, 130 A.D.2d 439, 515 N.Y.S.2d 472 (1st Dept. 1987).

—It was error to deny that portion of defendant's omnibus pretrial motion which sought the suppression of certain potential identification evidence without court conducting a hearing where the moving papers sufficiently complied with CPL § 710.60(1). People v. De Vaughn, 81 A.D.2d 924, 439 N.Y.S.2d 180 (2d Dept. 1981).

—A court may, but is not required to, deny a suppression motion where the pleadings are deficient. People v. Cooper, 162 Misc. 2d 192, 616 N.Y.S.2d 442, 445 (Justice Ct. Monroe Co. 1994).

—A court may summarily deny a motion to suppress identification testimony where the viewing consists of an undercover officer's "confrontation" to ascertain whether the right person had been arrested. People v. Doherty, 136 Misc. 2d 164, 518 N.Y.S.2d 78 (Sup. Ct. N.Y. Co. 1987).

—Request for a *Wade* hearing was properly denied since the defendant failed to make any factual showing that the pretrial identification was suggested or that the procedure was suggestive. People v. Seymour, 104 Misc. 2d 482, 428 N.Y.S.2d 796 (Suffolk Co. Ct. 1980).

Voice identification.—Trial court did not err in denying defendant's motion without holding a *Wade* hearing pursuant to CPL § 710.60 to determine whether a voice identification made at the station house was unduly suggestive since there was no factual support in the record for the contention that the identification procedure was suggestive. People v. Allweiss, 48 N.Y.2d 40, 421 N.Y.S.2d 341, 396 N.E.2d 735 (1979).

Waiver.—When defendant withdrew his motion to suppress physical evidence and failed to renew it, he waived his right to suppress physical evidence seized during the search of his home. People v. Rodrick, 205 A.D.2d 841, 613 N.Y.S.2d 445 (3d Dept. 1994), *cert. denied*, 115 S. Ct. 1409 (1995).

Subd. 4

Admissions; *Huntley* hearing; burden of proof; voluntariness.—A *Huntley* hearing must be held where it is alleged that the district attorney threatened the defendants with a murder indictment if they did not sign waivers of immunity and testify before the grand jury and failed to advise them of their right to counsel, since the issue is the voluntariness of a statement and no factual showing is needed. People v. Richard MM, 75 A.D.2d 389, 430 N.Y.S.2d 695 (3d Dept. 1980).

Cross-examination.—Defendant was not entitled to a directive limiting the prosecutor's cross-examination of him at the suppression hearing. People v. Walden, 148 A.D.2d 971, 539 N.Y.S.2d 206 (4th Dept. 1989).

Demand for transcript; future requirements.—The court held that in the future a defendant should not only proceed with the requisite reasonable diligence in making his pretrial suppression motion, but should also make his request for a transcript of the minutes of any pretrial hearing prior to its conclusion. People v. Sanders, 31 N.Y.2d 463, 341 N.Y.S.2d 305, 293 N.E.2d 555 (1973).

Discovery.—Trial court could and properly did deny defendant discovery of search warrant and supporting documents and properly held suppression hearing in camera without defendant's participation. People v. Castillo, 80 N.Y.2d 578, 592 N.Y.S.2d 945, 607 N.E.2d 1050 (1992), *cert. denied*, 507 U.S. 1033 (1993).

Hearing transcript; timely demand.—The request for a transcript followed closely upon the conclusion of the pretrial suppression hearing, and ample justification was shown for defense counsel's brief delay in making the request. Although the jury had meanwhile been drawn, no other trial proceedings had as yet taken place, and the demand was held timely. People v. Sanders, 31 N.Y.2d 463, 341 N.Y.S.2d 305, 293 N.E.2d 555 (1973).

Hearsay.—The rule of *Petralia* is not limited to undercover officer situations; also, double hearsay is permitted at suppression hearings. People v. Parris, 83 N.Y.2d 342, 610 N.Y.S.2d 464, 468, 632 N.E.2d 870 (1994).

—Hearing court did not err in allowing the police officer to characterize the area as a drug-prone location for such testimony was not hearsay but rather was based upon the officer's personal knowledge and experience. People v. Riviezzo, 124 A.D.2d 837, 508 N.Y.S.2d 566 (2d Dept. 1986).

—Hearsay evidence is admissible at a suppression hearing for the purpose of establishing material facts. People v. Kinner, 147 A.D.2d 742, 537 N.Y.S.2d 337 (3d Dept. 1989).

***Huntley* hearing granted; *Mapp* hearing should also be granted.** —It was an error for the court to deny defendant's request for a *Mapp* hearing to suppress a gun taken from him by police in an alleged illegal search and seizure since the court granted defendant a *Huntley* hearing to suppress statements he claimed he made in consequence of the illegal search and seizure; since the two requests sprang from the same ground, a factual showing sufficient to warrant one hearing should have ensured the other. People v. Dugan, 88 A.D.2d 549, 450 N.Y.S.2d 485 (1st Dept. 1982).

***Huntley-Wade* hearing; probable cause.**—Suppression of confession was required where, defendant's motion to suppress contended it was the aftermath of an unlawful arrest and the prosecution failed to come forward with any evidence that the arrest was supported by probable cause. People v. Bouton, 50 N.Y.2d 130, 428 N.Y.S.2d 218, 405 N.E.2d 699 (1980).

—The matter was remitted for a hearing and appropriate findings on the issue where the court, after the combined *Huntley* and *Wade* hearings, made no factual findings and arrived at no conclusions on defendant's contention that his arrest lacked probable cause. People v. Davis, 74 A.D.2d 714, 425 N.Y.S.2d 671 (4th Dept. 1980).

Motion to suppress.—People's failure to contest the facts alleged in the motion papers does not require the granting of the motion to suppress; the court must summarily grant the motion only if "the people concede the truth of allegations of fact therein which support the motion." People v. Helstrom, 50 A.D.2d 685, 375 N.Y.S.2d 189 (3d Dept. 1975), *aff'd*, 40 N.Y.2d 914, 389 N.Y.S.2d 366, 357 N.E.2d 1021 (1976).

Motion to suppress confession; *Huntley* hearing.—Evidence adduced at a *Huntley* hearing on a motion to suppress the admissibility of defendant's confession conclusively established that defendant knowingly and intelligently waived his right to counsel and his right to remain silent. The Court of Appeals held that defendant was not deprived of a full and fair hearing. People v. Ramsey, 29 N.Y.2d 832, 327 N.Y.S.2d 850, 277 N.E.2d 783 (1971).

—If deception concerning the results of a polygraph test were used in an attempt to induce a confession, the accuracy of the polygraph machine and the validity of the conclusions reached were relevant areas of inquiry at a suppression hearing. People

v. Cavagnara, 88 A.D.2d 938, 450 N.Y.S.2d 870 (2d Dept. 1982).

Pretrial suppression hearing; closure.—To avoid becoming a link in the chain of prejudicial disclosures, the trial court has the power to exclude the public from pretrial suppression hearings at the defendant's request; in so doing the courts should afford interested members of the news media an opportunity to be heard, not in the context of a full evidentiary hearing, but in a preliminary proceeding adequate to determine the magnitude of any genuine public interest; the public interest can be fully satisfied, consonant with constitutional free press guarantees, by affording the media access to transcripts redacted to exclude matters ruled inadmissible during the closed suppression hearing. Gannett Company, Inc. v. De Pasquale, 43 N.Y.2d 370, 401 N.Y.S.2d 756, 372 N.E.2d 544, *aff'd*, 443 U.S. 368, 99 S. Ct. 2898, 61 L. Ed. 2d 608 (1977).

—Where there is a risk that public attendance at a pretrial hearing will jeopardize a defendant's right to a fair trial in the community and closure is granted, the public interest which reporting fosters may be preserved by making the transcript available to the media as soon as the danger of prejudice to the defendant has passed. Westchester Rockland Newspapers, Inc. v. Leggett, 48 N.Y.2d 430, 423 N.Y.S.2d 630, 399 N.E.2d 518 (1979).

Privileged communications.—There is no Fourth Amendment prohibition against using privileged communications as a basis for a finding of probable cause to search. People v. Lifreiri, 157 Misc. 2d 598, 597 N.Y.S.2d 580 (Sup. Ct. Kings Co. 1993).

Re-hearing.—The People should not be deprived of one full opportunity to present evidence of the dispositive issues involved at the suppression hearing, and if an error of law is committed by the hearing court which directly causes the People to fail to offer potentially critical evidence, a rehearing should be ordered so that the evidence may be presented; however where no contention is made that the People had not had a full opportunity to present evidence there is no justification to afford the People a second chance to succeed where once they had tried and failed. People v. Havelka, 45 N.Y.2d 636, 412 N.Y.S.2d 345, 384 N.E.2d 1269 (1978).

Remand; further findings of fact.—Case was remanded where the record did not serve as a sufficient basis for review of the decision of the hearing judge as the testimony of the witnesses, a police officer and defendant, conflicted, and the determination as to their credibility may affect the application of the legal principals involved. People v. Clements, 84 A.D.2d 707, 444 N.Y.S.2d 69 (1st Dept. 1981).

Suppression; necessity for hearing.—CPL § 710.60(4) requires a hearing whenever the defendant claims his statement was involuntary no matter what facts he puts forth in support of that claim and the People do not concede the facts or stipulate not to use the evidence. People v. Weaver, 49 N.Y.2d 1012, 429 N.Y.S.2d 399, 406 N.E.2d 1335 (1980).

—A *Mapp* hearing was warranted where defendant specifically denied his participation in the buy and bust transaction that led to his arrest; a moving defendant does not need to raise an issue of fact as to every factual allegation put forth by the prosecution for a hearing to be ordered. People v. Bennett, 240 A.D.2d 292, 659 N.Y.S.2d 260 (1st Dept. 1997).

—Where court had sufficient information to conclude as a matter of law that confrontation between the witness and the defendant either had not been arranged, or had been arranged independently of the police, it was proper to deny summarily the *Wade* motion. People v. Omaro, 201 A.D.2d 324, 607 N.Y.S.2d 44 (1st Dept. 1994).

—Since the pretrial encounter between one of the police officers and the defendant was not a police arranged confrontation but rather a mere happenstance, suppression of the officer's identification testimony was properly denied. People v. Rodriguez, 194 A.D.2d 634, 599 N.Y.S.2d 46 (2d Dept. 1993).

Suppression hearing; free transcript.—An indigent defendant has a fundamental constitutional right to a free transcript of the minutes of a pretrial suppression hearing, and its denial requires a reversal of the judgment of conviction, even though no prejudice has been shown and regardless of the nature and quantum of proof against him. People v. Sanders, 31 N.Y.2d 463, 341 N.Y.S.2d 305, 293 N.E.2d 555 (1973).

Suppression hearing; informant need not be present.—People's non-production of informant for a *Darden* hearing did not damage defendant's right of confrontation, since it is well established that hearsay evidence can suffice for a finding of adequate cause for police searches and seizures, and defendant was not precluded from challenging the informant's existence or the content of her tip through cross-examination of the officers testifying at the suppression hearing. People v. Fleet, 88 A.D.2d 538, 450 N.Y.S.2d 392 (1st Dept. 1982).

Testimony; suppression.—Court did not err in denying defendant's request to call a police witness at the suppression hearing, supported as it was only by defendant's conjecture that the proposed witness would have raised an issue as to whether defendant was read his *Miranda* warnings or voluntarily answered questions. People v. Sierra, 192 A.D.2d 475, 596 N.Y.S.2d 418 (1st Dept. 1993).

—A defendant has no absolute right to call a complainant as a witness at a pretrial *Wade* hearing. People v. Harrell, 194 A.D.2d 502, 599 N.Y.S.2d 812 (1st Dept. 1993).

—Defendant's suppression motion was appropriately denied since there was no ground to find the testimony of the police witnesses patently tailored to nullify constitutional objections. People v. Elleby, 194 A.D.2d 312, 598 N.Y.S.2d 242 (1st Dept. 1993).

—Court rejected the defendant's contention that the People were required to produce at the suppression hearing the officer who relayed the description of the perpetrator to the arresting officers, since the reliability of that information was sufficiently established by the testimony of the arresting officer. People v. Parris, 190 A.D.2d 593 N.Y.S.2d 865 (2d Dept. 1993).

—Under *Petralia* rule, People were not required to call officer who observed the defendant engage in several narcotics transactions. People v. Illescas, 197 A.D.2d 637, 602 N.Y.S.2d 677 (2d Dept. 1993).

—Hearing court is vested with the authority to regulate the taking of oral testimony and to manage the conduct of the examination of witnesses. People v. Harrison, 151 A.D.2d 778, 543 N.Y.S.2d 108 (2d Dept. 1989).

Subd. 6

Denial of suppression motion; no findings of fact or conclusions of law.—Court erred in denying defendant's motion to suppress identification testimony without placing its findings of fact and conclusions of law upon the record as required by CPL § 710.60(6); however, defendant nonetheless had a full and fair hearing on his suppression motion and the record permits review of the court's determination. People v. Smith, 179 A.D.2d 1022, 580 N.Y.S.2d 119 (4th Dept. 1992).

Findings of fact.—The motion court's decision denying the suppression motion without explanation not only transgressed CPL § 710.60(6), which requires the court to set forth the reasons for its determination, but also effectively precluded informed appellate review. People v. Bonilla, 82 N.Y.2d 825, 604 N.Y.S.2d 937, 624 N.E.2d 1032 (1993).

—Where the suppression court made no finding as to when, in relation to police questioning, the police actually placed handcuffs on the defendant, remittal to the suppression court was necessary to resolve that material question of fact. People v. Tirado, 69 N.Y.2d, 863, 514 N.Y.S.2d 713, 507 N.E.2d 306 (1987).

—A hearing court's findings of fact are entitled to great weight. People v. Rosa, 179 A.D.2d 538, 579 N.Y.S.2d 43 (1st Dept. 1992).

—The hearing court's determination as to credibility are afforded great weight on appeal and should not be disturbed unless clearly unsupported by the evidence. People v. Olivo, 189 A.D.2d 786, 592 N.Y.S.2d 394 (2d Dept. 1993).

—The hearing court's determination is accorded great weight on appeal and will not be disturbed unless it is clearly unsupported by the record. People v. Cinatus, 188 A.D.2d 477, 590 N.Y.S.2d 536 (2d Dept. 1992).

—Testimony of officer that at one point he observed the handle of the gun protruding half-way out of the defendant's jacket pocket was not incredible as a matter of law. People v. Higgins, 179 A.D.2d 778, 578 N.Y.S.2d 656 (2d Dept. 1992).

—The hearing court's determinations as to credibility are afforded great weight on appeal and should not be disturbed unless clearly unsupported by the evidence. People v. Boone, 183 A.D.2d 721, 583 N.Y.S.2d 299 (2d Dept. 1992).

—The fact-finding of the hearing court, which has the

opportunity to observe the demeanor of the witnesses and hear their testimony, should be accorded great weight. People v. Falciglia, 153 A.D.2d 795, 545 N.Y.S.2d 149 (1st Dept.), aff'd, 75 N.Y.2d 938, 555 N.Y.S.2d 681, 554 N.E.2d 1269 (1989), cert. denied, 489 U.S. 833 (1990).

—Findings of hearing court are entitled to great deference and should not be set aside unless clearly erroneous. People v. Sinclair, 148 A.D.2d 647, 539 N.Y.S.2d 394 (2d Dept. 1989); see also People v. Alleyne, 154 A.D.2d 473, 545 N.Y.S.2d 943 (2d Dept. 1989).

—The hearing court's determination must be afforded great deference because the court had the opportunity to see and hear the witnesses. People v. Flores, 153 A.D.2d 585, 544 N.Y.S.2d 630 (2d Dept. 1989).

—Court rejected argument that identification testimony of two witnesses should have been suppressed due to inconsistencies in their hearing testimony. People v. Brown, 148 A.D.2d 742, 539 N.Y.S.2d 475 (2d Dept. 1989).

—Matter was remitted to the hearing court since the court failed to make findings of fact and conclusions of law as to each of the two identification procedures in the case. People v. McCalla, 133 A.D.2d 280, 519 N.Y.S.2d 70 (2d Dept. 1987).

—Assessing the credibility of witnesses at a *Huntley* hearing is the responsibility of the judge conducting the hearing. People v. Donson, 147 A.D.2d 815, 537 N.Y.S.2d 904 (3d Dept. 1989).

Reargument or rehearing.—Defendant's challenge to the admissibility of police lab reports was asserted for the first time in his renewal motion and is subject to the interdiction that a motion to renew or reargue does not afford an unsuccessful party with an opportunity to advance arguments different from those proffered in the original application. People v. Lopez, 235 A.D.2d 496, 653 N.Y.S.2d 130 (2d Dept. 1997).

—The decision to grant reargument of the suppression rested in the sound discretion of the hearing court. People v. Harrington, 193 A.D.2d 756, 597 N.Y.S.2d 723 (2d Dept. 1993).

Review on appeal.—Great weight must be accorded to the determination of the suppression hearing court, which saw and heard the witnesses; its determination should not be disturbed on appeal unless it is clearly unsupported by the record. People v. Hines, 18 A.D.3d 882, 796 N.Y.S.2d 652 (2d Dept. 2005).

—The propriety of the denial of a suppression motion must be judged on the evidence before the suppression court. People v. Denny, 177 A.D.2d 589, 576 N.Y.S.2d 304 (2d Dept. 1991).

—Trial testimony may not be considered in reviewing a hearing court's denial of a defendant's motion to suppress evidence. People v. Braithwaite, 172 A.D.2d 548, 568 N.Y.S.2d 135 (2d Dept. 1991).

—Evidence adduced at trial may not be used to correct omissions or fill gaps in pretrial hearings. People v. Bajraktari, 154 A.D.2d 542, 546 N.Y.S.2d 384, (2d Dept. 1989).

—In ruling upon the propriety of the trial court's determination denying suppression, the Appellate Division may not resort to the trial evidence. People v. Whitney, 149 A.D.2d 748, 540 N.Y.S.2d 531 (2d Dept. 1989).

—In view of trial court's erroneous determination with respect to the issue of suggestiveness, the People are entitled to a reopened *Wade* hearing where they will be afforded the opportunity to demonstrate that the witness' identification of the defendant was based on an independent source. People v. Moore, 143 A.D.2d 1056, 533 N.Y.S.2d 602 (2d Dept. 1988).

—Trial testimony cannot be used in reviewing the ruling of the suppression court. People v. Bolling, 142 A.D.2d 733, 531 N.Y.S.2d 118 (2d Dept. 1988).

—The Appellate Division can make the necessary findings where a fair and full hearing on the motion to suppress produces an adequate record despite the hearing court's failure to state its findings of fact and conclusions of law as is required by CPL § 710.60(4)(6). People v. Acosta, 74 A.D.2d 640, 425 N.Y.S.2d 40 (2d Dept. 1980).

—Where defendant's suppression motion was based on a ground different from that argued on appeal, defendant's contention is not preserved for appellate review. People v. Wallace, 270 A.D.2d 823, 706 N.Y.S.2d 539 (4th Dept. 2000).

—Where an appellate court, after suppressing an out-of-court identification, directs a new *Wade* hearing to determine an "independent source" for an in-court identification, it would be unreasonable for a trial court making a similar determination not to direct a new *Wade* hearing. People v. Malcolm, 139 Misc. 2d 140, 526 N.Y.S.2d 888, 892 (Sup. Ct. Kings Co. 1988).

§ 710.70. Motion to suppress evidence; orders of suppression; effects of orders and of failure to make motion.

1. Upon granting a motion to suppress evidence, the court must order that the evidence in question be excluded in the criminal action pending against the defendant. When the order is based upon the ground specified in subdivision one of section 710.20 and excludes tangible property unlawfully taken from the defendant's possession, and when such property is not otherwise subject to lawful retention, the court may, upon request of the defendant, further order that such property be restored to him.

2. An order finally denying a motion to suppress evidence may be reviewed upon an appeal from an ensuing judgment of conviction notwithstanding the fact that such judgment is entered upon a plea of guilty.

3. A motion to suppress evidence made pursuant to this article is the exclusive method of challenging the admissibility of evidence upon the grounds specified in section 710.20, and a defendant who does not make such a motion before or in the course of a criminal action waives his right to judicial determination of any such contention.

Nothing contained in this article, however, precludes a defendant from attempting to establish at a trial that evidence introduced by the people of a pre-trial statement made by him should be disregarded by the jury or other trier of the facts on the ground that such statement was involuntarily made within the meaning of section 60.45. Even though the issue of the admissibility of such evidence was not submitted to the court, or was determined adversely to the defendant upon motion, the defendant may adduce trial evidence and otherwise contend that the statement was involuntarily made. In the case of a jury trial, the court must submit such issue to the jury under instructions to disregard such evidence upon a finding that the statement was involuntarily made.

ANNOTATIONS

Appellate review.—By failing to join in co-defendant's application for a *Darden* hearing, defendant may not properly claim error in connection with determination of that issue, and in any event, any claim of error in connection with such a preliminary ruling does not survive a guilty plea. People v. Dunbar, 240 A.D.2d 275, 660 N.Y.S.2d 109 (1st Dept. 1997).

—Defendant did not waive, as part of his general waiver of appeal, his right to seek review of the denial of that branch of his omnibus motion that was to suppress statements made by him to law enforcement officials; defendant was never informed at the plea allocution that his plea was conditioned on his waiver of his statutory right to seek review of the suppression court's ruling. However, conviction was affirmed, because court properly denied suppression of the defendant's statements. People v. Woody, 240 A.D.2d 770, 660 N.Y.S.2d 31 (2d Dept. 1997).

—By statute, an order denying a motion to suppress may be reviewed upon appeal from a conviction even if the conviction results from a guilty plea. People v. Finger, 208 A.D.2d 645, 617 N.Y.S.2d 358 (2d Dept. 1994).

—The propriety of the denial of a defendant's suppression motion should be judged on the evidence before the suppression court. People v. Sumpter, 192 A.D.2d 628, 596 N.Y.S.2d 158 (2d Dept. 1993).

—Since it was not raised before the suppression court the defendant's contention that the identification should have been suppressed because it resulted from an arrest made without probable cause had not been preserved for appellate review. People v. Kennedy, 128 A.D.2d 549, 512 N.Y.S.2d 483 (2d Dept. 1987).

—Where defendant did not raise the propriety of the search warrant at the suppression hearing, he was properly precluded from raising the issue for the first time on the third day of trial and was properly denied the opportunity to call as a witness the judge who issued the search warrant against him. People v. Ragsdale, 198 A.D.2d 721, 604 N.Y.S.2d 626 (3d Dept. 1993).

—Defendant did not preserve for appellate review the county court's failure to instruct on voluntariness of the pretrial statement because the defendant failed to object specifically to the instruction of the statement on voluntariness grounds, failed to ask for the charge, and failed to object to the charge as given. People v. Esposito, 191 A.D.2d 746, 594 N.Y.S.2d 424 (3d Dept. 1993).

—While the judge failed to instruct the jury that the defendant's statement to the police was involuntary if defendant had asserted his right to counsel or to remain silent, the defendant did not object and failed to preserve the issue for review. People v. Maddox, 198 A.D.2d 804, 605 N.Y.S.2d 1014 (4th Dept. 1993).

Credibility.—It is for the hearing court to resolve any questions of credibility and its resolution will not be disturbed on appeal. People v. Elleby, 194 A.D.2d 312, 598 N.Y.S.2d 242 (1st Dept. 1993).

—A hearing court's findings of fact are entitled to great weight. People v. Rosa, 179 A.D.2d 538, 579 N.Y.S.2d 43 (1st Dept. 1992).

—Where the hearing court is presented with conflicting evidence of competency, great deference will be accorded its findings. People v. Cox, 196 A.D.2d 596, 601 N.Y.S.2d 175 (2d Dept. 1993).

—It is well-settled that much weight must be accorded to the determination of the suppression court with its peculiar advantages of having seen and heard the witnesses. People v. Rumph, 199 A.D.2d 434, 605 N.Y.S.2d 338 (2d Dept. 1993); People v. Hoe, 176 A.D.2d 963, 575 N.Y.S.2d 570 (2d Dept. 1991); People v. Alvarado, 130 A.D.2d 663, 515 N.Y.S.2d 593 (2d Dept. 1987).

—As the trier-of-fact, the hearing court's determination is entitled to great weight on appeal and should not be disturbed unless clearly unsupported by the record. *In re* Ronnie H., 198 A.D.2d 415, 603 N.Y.S.2d 579 (2d Dept. 1993); People v. Diaz, 170 A.D.2d 620, 566 N.Y.S.2d 391 (2d Dept. 1991).

—The fact that defendant's testimony at the suppression hearing contradicted that of the People's witness merely presented a credibility question for the hearing court to resolve, a determination which was not disturbed since it was supported by the record. People v. Wood, 196 A.D.2d 908, 601 N.Y.S.2d 969 (3d Dept. 1993).

—Any conflict in suppression testimony merely presents a credibility question for the suppression court and its determination will only be rejected by the court on appeal if unsupported as a matter of law. People v. Grimes, 191 A.D.2d 745, 594 N.Y.S.2d 392 (3d Dept. 1993).

—The findings of fact made by the suppression court, which had the opportunity to observe the demeanor of the witnesses and to assess their credibility, are entitled to great weight and will not be disturbed unless clearly erroneous. People v. May, 191 A.D.2d 1011, 595 N.Y.S.2d 165 (4th Dept. 1993).

—At the hearing stage, it is the court that weighs the credibility of witnesses and any adverse inference from the loss of or destruction of *Rosario* material; dismissal of the indictment or preclusion of a witness for failure to provide *Rosario* material at a hearing is an extreme penalty and should not be used unless prejudice to a defendant is apparent. People v. Richards, 152 Misc. 2d 775, 578 N.Y.S.2d 380 (Sup. Ct. Kings Co. 1991).

Defendant's voluntary statements.—Notwithstanding an adverse pretrial ruling, a defendant may at trial establish that his statement was involuntary. People v. Luis, 189 A.D.2d 657, 592 N.Y.S.2d 357 (1st Dept. 1993).

—The fact that the defendant disputed the statement's existence at trial did not warrant an instruction that the People had to prove the existence of the statement beyond a reasonable doubt. People v. Lopez, 187 A.D.2d 383, 590 N.Y.S.2d 199 (1st Dept. 1992).

—A court's refusal to instruct the jury on the issue of voluntariness of defendant's statements, as mandated by CPL § 710.70(3) after a request by defendant, is not harmless error and requires a reversal on the law. People v. Iglesia, 96 A.D.2d 515, 464 N.Y.S.2d 557 (2d Dept. 1983).

Denial of motion; plea to lesser offense.—Court acted properly where after denying motion to suppress defendant's statements, it accepted his plea to a lesser offense. (Also discusses effect of defendant's waiver of right to appeal orders denying suppression). People v. Williams, 43 A.D.2d 884, 351 N.Y.S.2d 761 (4th Dept. 1974), aff'd, 36 N.Y.2d 829, 370 N.Y.S.2d 904, 331 N.E.2d 684, cert. denied, 423 U.S. 873 (1975).

Failure to move to suppress evidence; no ineffective assistance of counsel.—Defendant's right to effective assistance of counsel was not violated when counsel failed to move to suppress certain physical evidence in defendant's possession in view of the uncertain state of the law as to standing at the time the motion could have been made, defendant's denial of possession to counsel, and the fact that counsel could have reasonably concluded that defendant abandoned a portion of the property, the gun, by throwing it as he was pursued by the police. People v. Barshai, 100 A.D.2d 253, 474 N.Y.S.2d 288 (1st Dept.), cert. denied, 469 U.S. 885 (1984).

Flashlight; vehicle.—Where there was no basis for suspicion other than defendant's prior presence in a rented car and his walking about the block, the police use of a flashlight to illuminate the interior of the car was an unwarranted intrusion into the interior of the vehicle and the firearm and the drugs discovered were suppressed. People v. Smith, 42 N.Y.2d 961, 398 N.Y.S.2d 142, 367 N.E.2d 648 (1977).

Generally.—A motion pursuant to Article 710 is the exclusive means of challenging the admissibility of evidence upon the ground that it was obtained as the result of an illegal seizure or arrest. People v. Lancaster, 272 A.D.2d 719, 708 N.Y.S.2d 182 (3d Dept. 2000).

Guilty plea; appeal from denial of motion to suppress; harmless error doctrine inapplicable.—Defendant's act of pleading guilty before the hearing on his suppression motions precluded the making of a record and foreclosed the possibility of appellate review of his challenge to the admissibility of the People's evidence; that the defendant may have believed his plea would not result in such forfeiture is irrelevant, because, even if communicated to the court, a subjective belief cannot permit evasion of what otherwise would be the consequences of the plea. People v. Fernandez, 67 N.Y.2d 686, 499 N.Y.S.2d 919, 490 N.E.2d 838 (1986).

—Defendant's guilty plea should be vacated and his conviction reversed where it was determined on appeal that the lower court's denial of defendant's motion to suppress a confession should be reversed. People v. Grant, 45 N.Y.2d 366, 408 N.Y.S.2d 429, 380 N.E.2d 257 (1978).

—The defendant waived his right to appellate review where he pleaded guilty prior to determination of his suppression motion. People v. Simmons, 121 A.D.2d 483, 504 N.Y.S.2d 12 (2d Dept. 1986).

Order not appealable until after judgment.—An intermediate order denying a motion to suppress evidence is reviewable only on appeal from the judgment of conviction. People v. Boyd, 91 A.D.2d 1045, 458 N.Y.S.2d 643 (2d Dept. 1983).

Plea of guilty before motion to suppress.—Defendant forfeited any right to appellate review of the suppression issues by pleading guilty before the conclusion of the suppression hearing. People v. Henderson, 130 A.D.2d 789, 515 N.Y.S.2d 120, 122 (3d Dept. 1987).

—An appeal from a judgment of conviction on a plea of guilty in one criminal action does not necessarily bring up for review the denial of a suppression motion in another criminal action in which no judgment is rendered but which is covered by a plea in the judgment appealed from. People v. Davis, 80 A.D.2d 767, 436 N.Y.S.2d 716 (1st Dept. 1981).

Plea of guilty after motion to suppress.—Defendant did not waive his right to appeal the denial of his motion to suppress by pleading guilty to a reduced charge prior to the entry of the court's formal order denying the motion. People v. Gambino, 35 N.Y.2d 932, 365 N.Y.S.2d 164, 324 N.E.2d 546 (1974).

—Defendant waived his right to appellate review of the denial of any suppression motions where, as a condition of the plea, he withdrew all motions. People v. Sackel, 130 A.D.2d 525, 515 N.Y.S.2d 104 (2d Dept. 1987).

—Where defendant failed to move to vacate his plea or to set aside his conviction, he failed to preserve the issue of whether he knowingly waived his right to appeal from the denial of his motion to suppress, having withdrawn all pretrial motions, pending and decided, as part of the plea agreement. People v. Ricciardi, 121 A.D.2d 407, 502 N.Y.S.2d 530 (2d Dept. 1986).

—A defendant may properly waive his statutory right to appeal the denial of a suppression motion as a condition of a plea bargain, where the waiver had been knowingly and voluntarily made. People v. Moore, 123 A.D.2d 363, 506 N.Y.S.2d 375 (2d Dept. 1986).

—Defendant waived his claim that his confession was coerced and obtained in violation of his right to counsel when, prior to entering his plea of guilty, he withdrew his motion to suppress confession (CPL § 710.30[3]). People v. Waggoner, 76 A.D.2d 847, 428 N.Y.S.2d 329 (2d Dept. 1980).

Record on appeal.—The propriety of a denial of a motion to suppress must be judged on the evidence before the suppression court. People v. Smith, 134 A.D.2d 382, 520 N.Y.S.2d 859 (2d Dept. 1987).

—Appellate Court did not consider the claim where defendant's allegation of impermissible police conduct during the interrogation was erroneously based upon his trial testimony which was not presented to the hearing court. People v. Morris, 172 A.D.2d 574, 571 N.Y.S.2d 554 (2d Dept. 1987).

Reliability of evidence.—Defendant has the right to contest the reliability of an incriminating statement during the trial. People v. Pagan, 211 A.D.2d 532, 622 N.Y.S.2d 9 (4th Dept. 1995).

—Defendant's assertion that his statements to police were hypnosis generated went to the reliability of the statements not the voluntariness. People v. Sterling, 209 A.D.2d 1006, 619 N.Y.S.2d 449 (4th Dept. 1994).

Right to appellate review of an order denying an application for permission to make a late motion to suppress is forfeited by a guilty plea.—An order denying an application for permission to make a late motion to suppress, as distinguished from an order denying a motion to suppress on the merits does not come within the scope of CPL § 710.70(2); and accordingly the right to appellate review thereof is forfeited by a guilty plea. People v. Petgen, 55 N.Y.2d 529, 450 N.Y.S.2d 299, 435 N.E.2d 669 (1982).

Transcript.—Reversal was required where the defendant was forced to proceed to trial without the transcript of the suppression hearing, where the request for the transcript was made 8 months before the trial. People v. Coleman, 81 N.Y.2d 826, 595 N.Y.S.2d 384, 385, 611 N.E.2d 285 (1993).

Voluntariness; failure to charge.—Notwithstanding the denial of defendant's motion to suppress his statements, the defendant was entitled to attempt to show at trial that his inculpatory statements should be disregarded by the jury because they were involuntarily. People v. Aparicio, 137 A.D.2d 540, 524 N.Y.S.2d 280 (2d Dept. 1988).

—Any error involved in court's failure to permit the defendant to place before the jury the issue of the voluntariness of his statement to the police was harmless error where there was no evidentiary support for the defendant's attack on the voluntariness of the statement. People v. Bakker, 133 A.D.2d 161, 518 N.Y.S.2d 680 (2d Dept. 1987).

—Notwithstanding the denial of his motion to suppress, the defendant was entitled to contend at trial that evidence of his confessions should be disregarded by the trier of fact on the ground that they were involuntarily made. People v. Casiono, 123 A.D.2d 712, 507 N.Y.S.2d 406 (2d Dept. 1986).

—Defendant was not entitled to a charge on voluntariness where he did not object to the introduction of the statement at trial, did not contest the voluntariness of the statement and his defense counsel never requested the issue go before the jury. People v. Faber, 83 A.D.2d 883, 442 N.Y.S.2d 113 (2d Dept. 1981).

Wade hearing; motion to reopen during trial.—Defendant, who chose not to call two identifying witnesses at the _Wade_ hearing could not move during trial to reopen the _Wade_ hearing to examine their capacity to make an untainted identification, absent some special or compelling circumstance. People v. Fuentes, 74 A.D.2d 753, 425 N.Y.S.2d 589 (1st Dept. 1980), _aff'd,_ 53 N.Y.2d 892, 440 N.Y.S.2d 625, 423 N.E.2d 48 (1981).

Warrantless search; insufficient excuse.—The gun found "in plain view" was suppressed where it was found after anti-crime officers had approached a double parked vehicle with their guns drawn and ordered the occupants to debark, since the subsequent finding of the contraband and its seizure was based on nothing but a mere "whim or caprice." People v. Allende, 39 N.Y.2d 474, 384 N.Y.S.2d 416, 348 N.E.2d 891 (1976).

ARTICLE 715—DESTRUCTION OF DANGEROUS DRUGS

Section

LexisNexis Cross References

See generally Defense of Narcotics Cases; *New York Suppression Manual,* Ch. 3, Derivative Evidence; Ch. 6, Probable Cause; Ch. 12, Exigent Circumstances and the Emergency Doctrine; Ch. 18, Consent Searches.

§ 715.05. Dangerous drugs; definition.

"Dangerous drugs" means any substance listed in schedule I, II, III, IV or V of section thirty-three hundred six of the public health law.

Added by L. 1984, Ch. 851.

§ 715.10. Pretrial motion to destroy dangerous drugs.

1. Subject to the limitations in paragraph (b) of subdivision two hereof a district attorney may move in a superior court for an order of destruction of the dangerous drugs in felony cases involving the possession or sale of such drugs.

2. A motion for an order of destruction of dangerous drugs shall be in writing, have attached thereto a copy of the report of analysis and shall be made in the following manner:

(a) Ex parte; where no defendants have been arrested in connection with seizure of such drugs and a showing is made upon affidavit that the likelihood of any future arrest in connection therewith is nonexistent; or

(b) Upon notice, when a defendant has been arraigned in a superior court upon an indictment charging him with a felony involving the possession or sale of a dangerous drug and the dangerous drugs sought to be destroyed are material to the prosecution of said indictment.

3. When such motion is ex parte, the court may order the destruction of all or part of the subject drugs.

4. When such motion is upon notice, further proceedings shall be had as provided in section 715.20 hereof.

Added by L. 1973, Ch. 750.

ANNOTATION

Inadvertent destruction; effect thereof.—Good faith inadvertent destruction of drugs was of no impact where defendant, who had moved for an independent inspection of the substance one month prior to its destruction, made no attempt to analyze the evidence during the pendency of the criminal proceeding until the commencement of the trial, a period of 13 months. People v. Henderson, 123 A.D.2d 883, 507 N.Y.S.2d 662 (2d Dept. 1986).

§ 715.20. Proceedings on motion upon notice.

1. When such motion is on notice, a hearing thereon shall be held by the court before which it is returnable not later than thirty days after the return date and the defendant shall be present at such hearing.

2. A hearing held pursuant to this section shall be conducted and recorded in the same manner as would be required were the witnesses testifying at trial. The district attorney shall establish by competent evidence the nature and quantity of the dangerous drugs which are the subject of the motion. Each party shall have the right to call and cross examine witnesses and to register objections and to receive rulings of the court thereon.

3. If the court finds upon the conclusion of the hearing that neither the prosecution nor the defendant will be prejudiced thereby it may grant the motion and may make such order as it may deem appropriate for the destruction of part or all of such drugs.

4. A defendant may waive such hearing and consent to the granting of the motion and entry of an order of destruction either by sworn affidavit or by personal appearance in court and declaration on the record of such waiver and consent.

Added by L. 1973, Ch. 750.

§ 715.30. Orders of the court.

1. In any proceeding brought pursuant to this article, the court may grant or deny any motion made hereunder or the relief requested therein in whole or in part and issue any order thereon as it may deem proper and as the interests of justice may require in order to effectuate the provisions of this article.

2. An order of destruction of a dangerous drug issued by the court pursuant to this article shall state the time within which the provisions of such order are to be complied with. It shall direct the person having custody of the drug to make provision for the destruction thereof in the presence of at least two witnesses, at least one of whom shall be a police officer.

Added by L. 1973, Ch. 750.

§ 715.40. Affidavit of destruction.

An affidavit attesting to the date, time, place and manner of destruction of a dangerous drug pursuant to an order therefor and identifying the same by reference to the report of analysis or by other identifying number or system and the order of the court issued thereon, shall be filed with the court by the person who destroyed the drugs and by each of the witnesses required to be present by subdivision two of section 715.30 of this article.

Added by L. 1973, Ch. 750.

§ 715.50. Analysis of dangerous drugs.

1. On and after September first, nineteen hundred seventy-three, in every felony case involving the possession or sale of a dangerous drug, the head of the agency charged with custody of such drugs, or his designee, shall within forty-five days after receipt thereof perform or cause to be performed an analysis of such drugs, such analysis to include qualitative identification; weight and quantity where appropriate.

2. Within ten days after the report of such analysis is received by such agency, the head thereof or his designee shall forward a copy thereof to the appropriate district attorney and inform him of the location where the subject drugs are being held.

3. The failure to have an analysis made or to forward a copy thereof within the time specified in subdivisions one and two of this section shall not be deemed or construed to bar the making or granting of a motion pursuant to this article or to the prosecution of a case involving such drugs.

Added by L. 1973, Ch. 750.

ANNOTATIONS

Applicability.—CPL § 715.50 applies to drugs seized by or in the custody of the police. Where, as here, the pills in question were never in the custody of the police, the People's failure to perform an analysis did not preclude their proffering testimony as to the nature and amount of that substance where the absence of the substance at trial was not the result of bad faith. People v. Czarnowski, 268 A.D.2d 701, 702 N.Y.S.2d 398 (3d Dept. 2000).

45-day requirement.—Police department did not deliver purported substance to state police lab for analysis until more than 45 days beyond its receipt, but absent bad faith or prejudice to defendant due to the delay, the People may still present evidence regarding the nature and amount of the drugs. People v. Coleman, 306 A.D.2d 549, 760 N.Y.S.2d 263 (3d Dept. 2003).

TITLE U—SPECIAL PROCEEDINGS WHICH REPLACE, SUSPEND OR ABATE CRIMINAL ACTIONS

ARTICLE 720—YOUTHFUL OFFENDER PROCEDURE

LexisNexis Cross Reference

New York Criminal Practice (2d ed.), Vol. 1, Ch. 8, Juvenile Offender Proceedings.

§ 720.10. Youthful offender procedure; definition of terms.

As used in this article, the following terms have the following meanings:

1. "Youth" means a person charged with a crime alleged to have been committed when he was at least sixteen years old and less than nineteen years old or a person charged with being a juvenile offender as defined in subdivision forty-two of section 1.20 of this chapter.

2. "Eligible youth" means a youth who is eligible to be found a youthful offender. Every youth is so eligible unless:

(a) the conviction to be replaced by a youthful offender finding is for (i) a class A-I or class A-II felony, or (ii) an armed felony as defined in subdivision forty-one of section 1.20, except as provided in subdivision three, or (iii) rape in the first degree, sodomy in the first degree, or aggravated sexual abuse, except as provided in subdivision three, or

(b) such youth has previously been convicted and sentenced for a felony, or

(c) such youth has previously been adjudicated a youthful offender following conviction of a felony or has been adjudicated on or after September first, nineteen hundred seventy-eight a juvenile delinquent who committed a designated felony act as defined in the family court act.

3. Notwithstanding the provisions of subdivision two, a youth who has been convicted of an armed felony offense or of rape in the first degree, criminal sexual act in the first degree, or aggravated sexual abuse is an eligible youth if the court determines that one or more of the following factors exist: (i) mitigating circumstances that bear directly upon the manner in which the crime was committed; or (ii) where the defendant was not the sole participant in the crime, the defendant's participation was relatively minor although

not so minor as to constitute a defense to the prosecution. Where the court determines that the eligible youth is a youthful offender, the court shall make a statement on the record of the reasons for its determination, a transcript of which shall be forwarded to the state division of criminal justice services, to be kept in accordance with the provisions of subdivision three of section eight hundred thirty-seven-a of the executive law.

4. "Youthful offender finding" means a finding, substituted for the conviction of an eligible youth, pursuant to a determination that the eligible youth is a youthful offender.

5. "Youthful offender sentence" means the sentence imposed upon a youthful offender finding.

6. "Youthful offender adjudication." A youthful offender adjudication is comprised of a youthful offender finding and the youthful offender sentence imposed thereon and is completed by imposition and entry of the youthful offender sentence.

Added by L. 1971, Ch. 981; **Amended** by L. 1975, Ch. 832; L. 1978, Ch. 481; L. 1979, Ch. 411; L. 1986, Ch. 416; L. 2003, Ch. 264, § 50, eff. Nov. 1, 2003, amending subd. 3.

ANNOTATIONS

Determination of age.—Right to youthful offender treatment is based on the age of the defendant at the time of the commission of the crime in question and not upon the age at the time of indictment or conviction. People v. Revells, 71 A.D.2d 985, 420 N.Y.S.2d 380 (1st Dept. 1979).

Eligible youth.—A double plea to a weapons charge and to burglary does not bar the defendant from being determined an "eligible youth" as he had not previously been adjudicated a youthful offender. People v. Cecil Z, 57 N.Y.2d 899, 456 N.Y.S.2d 753, 442 N.E.2d 1264 (1982).

—Youths who are charged with crimes alleged to have been committed when they were 16 to 19 years old and persons charged as juvenile offenders are, with some exceptions, eligible for youthful offender status. *In re* Dillon, 171 Misc. 2d 665, 655 N.Y.S.2d 322 (N.Y. Co. Ct. 1997).

Eligibility.—Defendant could not be considered for youthful offender treatment where he and an accomplice robbed the complainant and defendant held a knife to the victim's throat as required mitigating factors were not present. People v. Mason, 85 A.D.2d 673, 445 N.Y.S.2d 197 (2d Dept. 1981).

—County Court did not abuse its discretion in refusing to sentence defendant as a youthful offender, because a defendant convicted of an armed felony is generally ineligible for sentencing as a youthful offender. People v. O'Hanlon, 252 A.D.2d 670, 675 N.Y.S.2d 404 (3d Dept. 1998); *see also* People v. Boyd, 254 A.D.2d 740, 679 N.Y.S.2d 768 (4th Dept. 1998) (no youthful offender status for armed felons unless court determined that mitigating circumstances existed).

Eligibility provisions; constitutionality.—The limitations in CPL § 720.10 conditioning eligibility for youthful offender treatment on the highest count of the indictment violates due process of law and are unconstitutional; such limitations make the privileged penal sanction to be imposed depend solely upon an accusation, however formal, rather than an adjudication, however, informal, in the adversarial criminal process. People v. Drummond, 40 N.Y.2d 990, 391 N.Y.S.2d 67, 359 N.E.2d 663 (1976), *cert. denied*, 431 U.S. 908 (1977).

Juvenile delinquency process distinguished.—A juvenile delinquent adjudication is not the result of a criminal process, as is the youthful offender procedure, but, rather, is a proceeding in which the needs and best interests of the infant are balanced in family court and in which the Criminal Procedure Law does not apply. Niver v. New York, 1 Misc. 3d 579, 770 N.Y.S.2d 577 (N.Y. Ct. Cl. 2003), *aff'd*, 12 A.D.3d 51, 784 N.Y.S.2d 201 (3d Dept. 2004).

Mitigating circumstances.—The defendant was eligible for youthful offender status where at the time of crime he was sixteen and the shooting was "hasty and thoughtless, rather than intentional or calculated." People v. Davis, 81 A.D.2d 510, 437 N.Y.S.2d 352 (1st Dept. 1981).

Severity of sentence.—The severest possible sentence was not too harsh because the defendant had been convicted of the first degree sodomy and sexual abuse of boys, had shown no remorse or mitigating factors. People v. Gutkaiss, 206 A.D.2d 54, 614 N.Y.S.2d 462 (3d Dept. 1994).

Youthful offender treatment not mandatory; even though eligible.—Eligibility alone does not mandate youthful offender treatment; the granting of such benefit lies wholly within the discretion of the Court. People v. Williams, 78 A.D.2d 642, 432 N.Y.S.2d 120 (2d Dept. 1980).

Subd. 2

Prior felony conviction.—Even though defendant had been convicted in Florida as a youthful offender, the trial court could sentence the defendant as a second-felony offender because Florida youthful offender status deals with conditions of sentence but does not vitiate the underlying conviction; moreover, the defendant would have been too old to qualify for youthful offender status under New York law. People v. Cahill, 190 A.D.2d 744, 593 N.Y.S.2d 537 (2d Dept. 1993).

—Inasmuch as the defendant had been previously adjudicated as youthful offender following his conviction of a felony, he was ineligible for youthful offender treatment following his subsequent conviction of the crime of attempted burglary in the third degree. People v. Green, 75 A.D.2d 625, 427 N.Y.S.2d 44 (2d Dept. 1980).

—Defendant is eligible for youthful offender treatment unless he was previously convicted and sentenced for a felony before conviction. People v. Mosley, 88 A.D.2d 520, 450 N.Y.S.2d 17 (1st Dept. 1982).

Subd. 3

Mitigating circumstances.—The fact alone that in the commission of an armed felony, the defendant used a starter pistol incapable of inflicting harm does not provide the requisite "mitigating circumstances that bear directly upon the manner in which the crime was committed" so as to permit the court to consider the minor eligible for youthful offender treatment under CPL § 720.10(3)(i). People v. O'Neill, 86 A.D.2d 213, 449 N.Y.S.2d 515 (2d Dept. 1982).

—A youth convicted of armed robbery is eligible for youthful offender status only if there are mitigating circumstances. People v. Smalls, 219 A.D.2d 865, 632 N.Y.S.2d 1004 (4th Dept. 1995).

—Unless there are mitigating circumstances, a youth convicted of first degree sodomy is ineligible for youthful offender status.

People v. Moore, 209 A.D.2d 1041, 619 N.Y.S.2d 1002 (4th Dept. 1994).

—A defendant who pleads guilty to burglary in the first degree is not eligible for youthful offender status if the burglary is an armed felony, there are no mitigating factors, and the defendant's role was not minor. People v. Patterson, 195 A.D.2d 976, 600 N.Y.S.2d 877 (4th Dept. 1993).

§ 720.15. Youthful offender procedure; sealing of accusatory instrument; privacy of proceedings; preliminary instructions to jury.[*]

1. When an accusatory instrument against an apparently eligible youth is filed with a court, the court, with the defendant's consent, must order that it be filed as a sealed instrument, though only with respect to the public.

2. When a youth is initially arraigned upon an accusatory instrument, such arraignment and all proceedings in the action thereafter may, in the discretion of the court and with the defendant's consent, be conducted in private.

3. The provisions of subdivisions one and two of this section requiring or authorizing the accusatory instrument filed against a youth to be sealed, and the arraignment and all proceedings in the action to be conducted in private shall not apply in connection with a pending charge of committing any felony offense as defined in the penal law. The provisions of subdivision one requiring the accusatory instrument filed against a youth to be sealed shall not apply where such youth has previously been adjudicated a or convicted of a crime.

[*] Provisions for preliminary instructions to the jury were repealed by L. 1972, Ch. 937.

Added L. 1971, Ch. 981; **Amended** by L. 1972, Ch. 937; L. 1975, Ch. 832; L. 1978, Ch. 481; L. 1979, Ch. 411; L. 1985, Ch. 774.

ANNOTATIONS

Sealing the record.—CPL § 720.15 does not apply to felony offenses and therefore the court does not have the broad discretion to close youthful offender proceedings. Daily Gazette v. Harrigan, 209 A.D.2d 767, 618 N.Y.S.2d 469 (3d Dept. 1994).

—Sealing the record does not mandate physical exclusion of the press and certainly does not authorize an order, in prospectus, restraining the press from reporting the case. People v. Gomez, 103 Misc. 2d 352, 425 N.Y.S.2d 776 (Ontario Co. Ct. 1980).

§ 720.20. Youthful offender determination; when and how made; procedure thereupon.

1. Upon conviction of an eligible youth, the court must order a presentence investigation of the defendant. After receipt of a written report of the investigation and at the time of pronouncing sentence the court must determine whether or not the eligible youth is a youthful offender. Such determination shall be in accordance with the following criteria:

(a) If in the opinion of the court the interest of justice would be served by relieving the eligible youth from the onus of a criminal record and by not imposing an indeterminate term of imprisonment of more than four years, the court may, in its discretion, find the eligible youth is a youthful offender; and

(b) Where the conviction is had in a local criminal court and the eligible youth had not prior to commencement of trial or entry of a plea of guilty been convicted of a crime or found a youthful offender, the court must find he is a youthful offender.

2. Where an eligible youth is convicted of two or more crimes set forth in separate counts of an accusatory instrument or set forth in two or more accusatory instruments consolidated for trial purposes, the court must not find him a youthful offender with respect to any such conviction pursuant to subdivision one of this section unless it finds him a youthful offender with respect to all such convictions.

3. Upon determining that an eligible youth is a youthful offender, the court must direct that the conviction be deemed vacated and replaced by a youthful offender finding; and the court must sentence the defendant pursuant to section 60.02 of the penal law.

4. Upon determining that an eligible youth is not a youthful offender, the court must order the accusatory instrument unsealed and continue the action to judgment pursuant to the ordinary rules governing criminal prosecutions.

Added by L. 1971, Ch. 981; **Amended** by L. 1974, Ch. 652; L. 1980, Ch. 471

ANNOTATIONS

Appeals.—When a court applies an incorrect legal standard in imposing a sentence, the Court of Appeals has jurisdiction to review a court's decision not to sentence the defendant as a youthful offender. People v. Thiessen, 76 N.Y.2d 816, 559 N.Y.S.2d 970, 559 N.E.2d 664 (1990).

Determination at sentencing.—A decision to deny youthful offender status must appear distinctly in the sentencing minutes and cannot be assumed from the fact that a conventional sentence was imposed; the court should first rule on youthful offender status and give its reasons. People v. LaGrange, 115 A.D.2d 149, 495 N.Y.S.2d 511 (3d Dept. 1985).

Classification.—The classification in CPL § 720.20 is based on the gravity of the crime with which a youth is charged and there is no invidious discrimination in a legislative decision that those individuals who, on preliminary investigation, are believed to have committed felonies should not automatically be endowed with the benefit of youthful offender status and that in these cases youthful offender status should be conferred only in the court's discretion upon due consideration of the youth's background and prior history of involvement with the law. People v. Drayton, 39 N.Y. 580, 385 N.Y.S.2d 1, 350 N.E.2d 377 (1976).

Discretion of court.—The court abused its discretion when it denied a juvenile offender youthful offender status because it was not part of the plea negotiations. People v. Pabon, 80 A.D.2d 525, 436 N.Y.S.2d 5 (1st Dept. 1981).

—Youthful offender treatment was properly denied in light of defendant's commission of another crime while awaiting sentencing for the instant offense. People v. Roger, 287 A.D.2d 747, 732 N.Y.S.2d 250 (2d Dept. 2001).

—Youthful offender treatment is a privilege accorded to a youth, not a constitutional right. People v. Drayton, 47 A.D.2d 952, 367 N.Y.S.2d 506 (2d Dept. 1975), aff'd, 39 N.Y.2d 580, 385 N.Y.S.2d 1, 350 N.E.2d 377 (1976).

—Court did not abuse its discretion in denying defendant youthful offender treatment, given defendant's criminal history, his disruptive behavior in jail during trial, and his lack of remorse for his crimes. People v. Montcrieft, 296 A.D.2d 718, 745 N.Y.S.2d 602 (3d Dept. 2002).

—Court properly denied youthful offender status to defendant based on the gravity of the crime (sexual abuse in the first degree), the manner in which it was committed (victim was 13 years old), and lack of mitigating circumstances. People v. Ferguson, 285 A.D.2d 901, 729 N.Y.S.2d 799 (3d Dept. 2001).

—Court did not abuse discretion by denying youthful offender status. Despite defendant's age of seventeen at the time these misdemeanors were committed and her lack of a prior criminal record, the court reasonably concluded that, in view of the violent and intentional nature of these crimes perpetrated against her own infant, defendant was not an appropriate candidate for such treatment. People v. Watrous, 270 A.D.2d 651, 704 N.Y.S.2d 707 (3d Dept. 2000).

—Given the serious nature of the crime, defendant's lack of remorse and his disrespect for the law as is evident because the instant offense was committed while he was awaiting sentencing on another conviction for which he received youthful offender treatment, court did not err in denying him youthful offender status in this case. People v. Wamsganz, 245 A.D.2d 919, 666 N.Y.S.2d 860 (3d Dept. 1997).

—The determination of youthful offender status is a matter within the sound discretion of the sentencing court and will not be disturbed where, as in the instant case, there was no abuse of such discretion. People v. Wagoner, 234 A.D.2d 831, 651 N.Y.S.2d 668 (3d Dept. 1996).

—County Court could deny a 17-year-old youthful offender status because the youth had been convicted of two counts of second degree robbery and the mitigating circumstances were in the presentence report the judge reviewed before denying youthful offender status. People v. Carter, 158 A.D.2d 851, 551 N.Y.S.2d 644 (3d Dept. 1990).

Grand Jury.—Presenting grand jury minutes to the court as part of sentencing procedure was proper because the judge used the minutes to determine whether there were any mitigating factors. People v. Thomas, 206 A.D.2d 708, 614 N.Y.S.2d 643 (3d Dept. 1994).

Guilty plea; conditioned on youthful offender finding.—The trial court was required to either adjudicate defendant a youthful offender or allow him to withdraw his guilty plea where a promise to that effect was made by the court in order to induce the defendant's plea. People v. Torres, 45 N.Y.2d 751, 408 N.Y.S.2d 487, 380 N.E.2d 313 (1978).

Sentence reformatory; youthful offender; equal protection of the laws.—CPL § 720.20 does not violate defendant's equal protection rights because it vests only a superior court with the discretion to give a defendant youthful offender treatment; the original indictment supported multiple felony charges which are properly heard only by a superior court. People v. Curtis, 160 Misc. 2d 508, 610 N.Y.S.2d 441 (Dutchess Co. Court 1993).

—To sentence a defendant of the youthful offender age group, but not afforded youthful offender treatment, to a reformatory term of imprisonment upon his plea of guilty to a class A misdemeanor even though the same sentence could not be imposed on a youthful offender, does not violate statute or constitution where sentencing judge took into account unrehabilitative character of defendant. People v. De Perez, 70 Misc. 2d 982, 335 N.Y.S.2d 526 (Ontario Co. Ct. 1972), aff'd, 32 N.Y.2d 880, 346 N.Y.S.2d 533, 299 N.E.2d 898 (1973).

Timeliness.—The determination as to whether an eligible youth is to be treated as a youthful offender is to be made after conviction, after the receipt of a written report of presentence investigation and at the time of pronouncing sentence. People v. Gina M.M., 40 N.Y.2d 595, 388 N.Y.S.2d 899, 357 N.E.2d 370 (1976).

Waiver.—Since defendant made no assertion at the time of sentence that he was entitled to an adjudication of his youthful offender status, his right thereto was waived; the statute did not require the court to alert the defendant or his lawyer to his rights or the detriment he may suffer. People v. McGowen, 42 N.Y.2d 905, 397 N.Y.S.2d 993, 366 N.E.2d 1347 (1977).

—Where defendant made no assertion at time of sentencing that he was entitled to be adjudicated a youthful offender, he waived his right to such sentencing. People v. Pagano, 253 A.D.2d 500, 676 N.Y.S.2d 508 (2d Dept. 1998).

—Defendant, who was 16 when he committed each crime, waived his right to be considered for youthful offender treatment by failing to request it at sentencing. People v. Rogers, 5 A.D.3d 871, 774 N.Y.S.2d 93 (3d Dept. 2004).

Youthful offender status; sentencing.—Sentencing court has statutory obligation to determine on the record whether a defendant should be afforded youthful offender treatment; when this issue is properly raised before the sentencing court, the court must determine whether the defendant is a youthful offender, and the requirement may not be ignored. People v. Miles, 244 A.D.2d 433, 664 N.Y.S.2d 79 (2d Dept. 1997).

—By failing to assert entitlement to youthful offender treatment at sentencing, defendant waived the issue for appellate review. People v. Williams, 133 A.D.2d 871, 520 N.Y.S.2d 424, 425 (2d Dept. 1987).

—Appellate Division vacated sentence where record raised a serious question whether defense counsel and the court were aware that defendant was eligible for youthful offender treatment; matter remitted to County Court to determine whether defendant should be granted youthful offender treatment. People v. Torres, 238 A.D.2d 933, 661 N.Y.S.2d 153 (4th Dept. 1997).

—Defendant's right to an adjudication of his youthful offender status was not waived where at the plea the court, defense counsel, and the district attorney agreed that the defendant was eligible for youthful offender treatment and a presentence investigation was ordered and the record was sealed but at the time of pronouncing sentence substitute attorneys represented the defendant and the district attorney and no claim of defendant's eligibility for adjudication of his youthful offender status was then asserted and no determination of his status was made. People v. Stein, 80 A.D.2d 728, 437 N.Y.S.2d 153 (4th Dept. 1981).

—Defendant should have been accorded youthful offender status on all charges under CPL § 720.20(2) where trial court determined, after a plea of guilty, that defendant was not a youthful offender on a count of driving while intoxicated, but was a youthful offender on two counts of criminally negligent homicide. People v. Huther, 78 A.D.2d 1011, 433 N.Y.S.2d 665 (4th Dept. 1980).

§ 720.30. Youthful offender adjudication; post-judgment motions and appeal.

The provisions of this chapter, governing the making and determination of post-judgment motions and the taking and determination of appeals in criminal cases, apply to post-judgment motions and appeals with respect to youthful offender adjudications wherever such provisions can reasonably be so applied.

Added by L. 1971, Ch. 981.

§ 720.35. Youthful offender adjudication; effect thereof; records.

1. A youthful offender adjudication is not a judgment of conviction for a crime or any other offense, and does not operate as a disqualification of any person so adjudged to hold public office or public employment or to receive any license granted by public authority but shall be deemed a conviction only for the purposes of transfer of supervision and custody pursuant to section two hundred fifty-nine-m of the executive law.

2. Except where specifically required or permitted by statute or upon specific authorization of the court, all official records and papers, whether on file with the court, a police agency or the division of criminal justice services, relating to a case involving a youth who has been adjudicated a youthful offender, are confidential and may not be made available to any person or public or private agency, other than the designated educational official of the public or private elementary or secondary school in which the youth is enrolled as a student provided that such local educational official shall only have made available a notice of such adjudication and shall not have access to any other official records and papers, such youth or such youth's designated agent (but only where the official records and papers sought are on file with a court and request therefor is made to that court or to a clerk thereof), an institution to which such youth has been committed, the division of parole and a probation department of this state that requires such official records and papers for the purpose of carrying out duties specifically authorized by law; provided, however, that information regarding an order of protection or temporary order of protection issued pursuant to section 530.12 of this chapter or a warrant issued in connection therewith may be maintained on the statewide automated order of protection and warrant registry established pursuant to section two hundred twenty-one-a of the executive law during the period that such order of protection or temporary order of protection is in full force and effect or during which such warrant may be executed. Such confidential information may be made available pursuant to law only for purposes of adjudicating or enforcing such order of protection or temporary order of protection and, where provided to a designated educational official, as defined in section 380.90 of this chapter, for purposes related to the execution of the student's educational plan, where applicable, successful school adjustment and re-entry into the community. Such notification shall be kept separate and apart from such student's school records and shall be accessible only by the designated educational official. Such notification shall not be part of such student's permanent school record and shall not be appended to or included in any documentation regarding such student and shall be destroyed at such time as such student is no longer enrolled in the school district. At no time shall such notification be used for any purpose other than those specified in this subdivision.

3. If a youth who has been adjudicated a youthful offender is enrolled as a student in a public or private elementary or secondary school the court that has adjudicated the youth as a youthful offender shall provide notification of such adjudication to the designated educational official of the school in which such youth is enrolled as a student. Such notification shall be used by the designated educational official only for purposes related to the execution of the student's educational plan, where applicable,

successful school adjustment and reentry into the community. Such notification shall be kept separate and apart from such student's school records and shall be accessible only by the designated educational official. Such notification shall not be part of such student's permanent school record and shall not be appended to or included in any documentation regarding such student and shall be destroyed at such time as such student is no longer enrolled in the school district. At no time shall such notification be used for any purpose other than those specified in this subdivision.

Added by L. 1971, Ch. 981; **Amended** by L. 1972, Ch. 399; L. 1980, Ch. 189; L. 1992, Ch. 452; L. 1996, Ch. 217, amending subd. 2, eff. June 25, 1996; L. 2000, Ch. 181, §§ 15 and 16, amending subd. 2 and adding subd. 3, eff. Nov. 1, 2000; L. 2001, Ch. 412, amending subd. 2, eff. Nov. 1, 2001.

ANNOTATIONS

Intent in issue; prior confession.—Where intent to commit burglary was in issue, defendant's prior confession to burglary which resulted in youthful offender adjudication, was admissible subject to proper instructions limiting that proof to the issue of intent. People v. Gross, 74 A.D.2d 701, 426 N.Y.S.2d 118 (3d Dept. 1980).

Effect of prior convictions in other states.—Because Florida youthful offender statute allows a prior youthful offender conviction to be used as a predicate, New York could use defendant's prior conviction for first degree burglary as a predicate. People v. Kuey, 83 N.Y.2d, 609 N.Y.S.2d 568, 631 N.E.2d 574 (1994).

—The practical effect of a Pennsylvania juvenile adjudication is almost indistinguishable from a youthful offender adjudication in New York. People v. Negron, 160 Misc. 2d 333, 608 N.Y.S.2d 1020 (Sup. Ct. N.Y. Co. 1994).

Photo from prior conviction.—Court properly rejected defendant's claim that her photo, obtained after an earlier arrest which ended in a youthful offender conviction, could not be used for identification and should be suppressed as part of her sealed, confidential record. People v. Morris, 220 A.D.2d 808, 632 N.Y.S.2d 231 (3d Dept. 1995).

Unsealing.—Applicant homeowners insurance carrier of youths did not prove by clear and convincing evidence that the criminal records of the youths were required to be unsealed, where there was other evidence available to State Farm; the goal of restoring youth to the status that he or she held after successful termination of a criminal proceeding or after being adjudicated a youthful offender far outweighs any pecuniary or economic consideration. People v. John F., 174 Misc. 2d 540, 665 N.Y.S.2d 822 (Nassau Ct. Dist. Ct. 1997).

ARTICLE 725—REMOVAL OF PROCEEDING AGAINST JUVENILE OFFENDER TO FAMILY COURT

[Added by L. 1978, ch. 481, eff. Sept. 1, 1978.]

Section

LexisNexis Cross Reference

New York Criminal Practice (2d ed.), Vol. 1, Ch. 8, Youthful Offender Proceedings.

§ 725.00. Applicability

The provisions of this article apply in any case where a court directs that an action or charge is to be removed to the family court under section 180.75, 190.71, 210.43, 220.10, 310.85 or 330.25 of this chapter.

Added by L. 1978, Ch. 481; **Amended** by L. 1979, Ch. 411.

§ 725.05. Order of removal.

When a court directs that an action or charge is to be removed to the family court the court must issue an order of removal in accordance with this section. Such order must be as follows:

1. It must provide that the action or charge is to be removed to the family court of the county in which such action or charge was pending, and it must specify the section pursuant to which the removal is authorized.

2. Where the direction is authorized pursuant to paragraph (b) of subdivision three of section 180.75 of this chapter, it must specify the act or acts it found reasonable cause to believe the defendant did.

3. Where the direction is authorized pursuant to subdivision four of section 180.75 of this chapter, it must specify the act or acts it found reasonable cause to allege.

4. Where the direction is authorized pursuant to section 190.71 of this chapter, the court shall annex to the order as part thereof a certified copy of the grand jury request.

4-a. Where the direction is authorized pursuant to subdivision seven of section 210.30 of this chapter, it must specify the act or acts for which there was sufficient evidence to believe that defendant did.

5. Where the direction is authorized pursuant to section 220.10, 310.85 or 330.25 of this chapter, it must specify the act or acts for which a plea or verdict of guilty was rendered or accepted and entered.

6. Where a securing order has not been made, the order of removal must provide that the police officer or peace officer who made the arrest or some other proper officer forthwith and with all reasonable speed take the juvenile to the designated family court or, where that cannot be done, it must provide for release or detention in the same manner as provided for a family court proceeding pursuant to section 320.5 of the family court act.

7. Whether or not a securing order has been made, the order of removal must specify a date certain within ten days from the date of the order of removal for the defendant's appearance in the family court and where the defendant is in detention or in the custody of the sheriff that date must be not later than the next day the family court is in session.

8. The order of removal must direct that all of the pleadings and proceedings in the action, or a certified copy of same be transferred to the designated family court and be delivered to and filed with the clerk of that court. For the purposes of this subdivision the term "pleadings and proceedings" includes the minutes of any hearing inquiry or trial held in the action, the minutes of any grand jury proceeding and the minutes of any plea accepted and entered.

9. The order of removal must be signed by a judge or justice of the court that directed the removal.

Added by L. 1978, Ch. 481; **Amended** by L. 1980, Chs. 136, 843; L. 1982, Ch. 920; L. 1990, Ch. 223.

ANNOTATIONS

Forwarding records.—"Pleadings and proceedings" transferred by an order of removal to the family court must include the grand jury minutes. *In re* Glenford S., 78 A.D.2d 350, 435 N.Y.S.2d 292 (2d Dept. 1981).

Jurisdictional defect.—Petition to adjudicate a defendant as a juvenile delinquent was not jurisdictionally defective because the hearsay complaint and nonhearsay supporting deposition were unsworn. People v. Galarza, 206 A.D.2d 387, 614 N.Y.S.2d 433 (2d Dept. 1994).

Family Court; sentencing.—A juvenile defendant's plea to a nondesignated felony must be sentenced in Family Court. People v. Statton, 156 Misc. 2d 778, 594 N.Y.S.2d 580 (Nassau County Court 1992).

§ 725.10. Removal of action.

1. When an order of removal is filed with the family court a proceeding pursuant to article three of the family court act must be originated. The family court thereupon must assume jurisdiction and proceed to render such judgment as the circumstances require, in the manner and to the extent provided by law.

2. Upon the filing of an order of removal in a criminal court the criminal action upon which the order is based shall be terminated, and there shall be no further criminal proceedings in any criminal court as defined in section 10.10 of this chapter with respect to the offense or offenses charged in the accusatory instrument which was the subject of removal. All further proceedings including motions and appeals shall be in accordance with laws appertaining to the family court and for this purpose all findings, determinations, verdicts and orders other than the order of removal, shall be deemed to have been made by the family court.

Added by L. 1978, Ch. 481; **Amended** by L. 1979, Ch. 411; L. 1982, Ch. 920.

ANNOTATIONS

Order of removal; general effect.—When juvenile petitioner has not made a fraudulent misrepresentation to obtain a removal order, and in the absence of extraordinary circumstances, removal from Supreme Court to Family Court is final. John G. v. Dubin, 89 A.D.2d 839, 452 N.Y.S.2d 907 (2d Dept. 1982).

Statutory purpose.—CPL § 725.10 was added to handle cases that were deemed appropriate to transfer to Family Court; absent a removal order issued by criminal court pursuant to CPL § 725.10, the respondent cannot be a juvenile delinquent within the meaning of the Family Court Act. *In re* Nick C., 172 Misc. 2d 739, 659 N.Y.S.2d 969 (Fam. Ct. Bronx Co. 1997).

§ 725.15. Sealing of records.

Except where specifically required or permitted by statute or upon specific authorization of the court that directed removal of an action to the family court all official records and papers of the action up to and including the order of removal, whether on file with the court, a police agency or the division of criminal justice services, are confidential and must not be made available to any person or public or private agency, provided however that availability of copies of any such records and papers on file with the family court shall be governed by provisions that apply to family court records.

Added by L. 1978, Ch. 481.

§ 725.20. Record of certain actions removed.

1. The provisions of this section shall apply in any case where an order of removal to the family court is entered pursuant to a direction authorized by subdivision four of section 180.75, or section 210.43, or subparagraph (iii) of paragraph (h) of subdivision five of section 220.10 of this chapter, or section 330.25 of this chapter.

2. When such an action is removed the court that directed the removal must cause the following additional records to be filed with the clerk of the county court or in the city of New York with the clerk of the supreme court of the county wherein the action was pending and with the division of criminal justice services:

(a) A certified copy of the order of removal;

(b) Where the direction is one authorized by subdivision four of section 180.75 of this chapter, a copy of the statement of the district attorney made pursuant to paragraph (b) of subdivision six of section 180.75 of this chapter;

(c) Where the direction is authorized by section 180.75, a copy of the portion of the minutes containing the statement by the court pursuant to paragraph (a) of subdivision six of such section 180.75;

(d) Where the direction is one authorized by subparagraph (iii) of paragraph (h) of subdivision five of section 220.10 or section 330.25 of this chapter, a copy of the minutes of the plea of guilty, including the minutes of the memorandum submitted by the district attorney and the court;

(e) Where the direction is one authorized by subdivision one of section 210.43 of this chapter, a copy of that portion of the minutes containing the statement by the court pursuant to paragraph (a) of subdivision five of section 210.43;

(f) Where the direction is one authorized by paragraph (b) of subdivision one of section 210.43 of this chapter, a copy of that portion of the minutes containing the statement of the district attorney made pursuant to paragraph (b) of subdivision five of section 210.43; and

(g) In addition to the records specified in this subdivision, such further statement or submission of additional information pertaining to the proceeding in criminal court in accordance with standards established by the commissioner of the division of criminal justice services, subject to the provisions of subdivision three of this section.

3. It shall be the duty of said clerk to maintain a separate file for copies of orders and minutes filed pursuant to this section. Upon receipt of such orders and minutes the clerk must promptly delete such portions as would identify the defendant, but the clerk shall nevertheless maintain a separate confidential system to enable correlation of the documents so filed with identification of the defendant. After making such deletions the orders and minutes shall be placed within the file and must be available for public inspection. Information permitting correlation of any such record with the identity of any defendant shall not be divulged to any person except upon order of a

justice of the supreme court based upon a finding that the public interest or the interests of justice

warrant disclosure in a particular cause for a particular case or for a particular purpose or use.

Added by L. 1978, Ch. 481; **Amended** by L. 1979, Ch. 411.

ARTICLE 730—MENTAL DISEASE OR DEFECT EXCLUDING FITNESS TO PROCEED

LexisNexis Cross Reference

New York Criminal Practice (2d ed.), Vol. 1, Ch. 14, Mental Disease or Defect Precluding Fitness to Proceed.

§ 730.10. Fitness to proceed; definitions.

As used in this article, the following terms have the following meanings:

1. "Incapacitated person" means a defendant who as a result of mental disease or defect lacks capacity to understand the proceedings against him or to assist in his own defense.

2. "Order of examination" means an order issued to an appropriate director by a criminal court wherein a criminal action is pending against a defendant or by a family court pursuant to section 322.1 of the family court act wherein a juvenile delinquency proceeding is pending against a juvenile, directing that such person be examined for the purpose of determining if he is an incapacitated person.

3. "Commissioner" means the state commissioner of mental health or the state commissioner of mental retardation and developmental disabilities.

4. "Director" means (a) the director of a state hospital operated by the office of mental health or the director of a developmental center operated by the office of mental retardation and developmental disabilities, or (b) the director of a hospital operated by any local government of the state that has been certified by the commissioner as having adequate facilities to examine a defendant to determine if he is an incapacitated person, or (c) the director of community mental health services.

5. "Qualified psychiatrist" means a physician who:

(a) is a diplomate of the American board of psychiatry and neurology or is eligible to be certified by that board; or,

(b) is certified by the American osteopathic board of neurology and psychiatry or is eligible to be certified by that board.

6. "Certified psychologist" means a person who is registered as a certified psychologist under article one hundred fifty-three of the education law.

7. "Psychiatric examiner" means a qualified psychiatrist or a certified psychologist who has been designated by a director to examine a defendant pursuant to an order of examination.

8. "Examination report" means a report made by a psychiatric examiner wherein he sets forth his opinion as to whether the defendant is or is not an incapacitated person, the nature and extent of his examination and, if he finds that the defendant is an incapacitated person, his diagnosis and prognosis and a detailed statement of the reasons for his opinion by making particular reference to those aspects of the proceedings wherein the defendant lacks capacity to understand or to assist in his own defense. The state administrator and the commissioner must jointly adopt the form of the examination report; and the state administrator shall prescribe the number of copies thereof that must be submitted to the court by the director.

Amended by L. 1973, Ch. 195; L. 1974, Chs. 615, 629; L. 1976, Ch. 435; L. 1987, Ch. 440; L. 1994, Ch. 566, § 1, eff. July 26, 1994, amending subd. 2.

ANNOTATIONS

Generally.—Article 730's procedure for determining whether a criminal defendant is incapacitated is not a determination of mental illness, and is completely unrelated to issues associated with the insanity defense and its concern with the defendant's mental capacity at the time of the commission of the crime. People v. Severance, 184 Misc. 2d 232, 708 N.Y.S.2d 258 (St. Lawrence Co. Ct. 2000).

Amnesia.—The capacity to stand trial is the same as that required to waive the right to be represented by counsel and to act as one's own attorney. People v. Reason, 37 N.Y.2d 351, 372 N.Y.S.2d 614, 334 N.E.2d 572 (1975).

—The inability to recall the events charged because of amnesia does not constitute mental incapacity to stand trial. People v. Francabandera, 33 N.Y.2d 429, 354 N.Y.S.2d 609, 310 N.E.2d 292 (1974).

—Even a defendant who suffers from amnesia and lacks any recollection of the crucial events underlying an offense may be found fit to stand trial. Mollen v. Mathews, 269 A.D.2d 42, 710 N.Y.S.2d 399 (3d Dept. 2000).

Appeal; mentally ill defendant.—An individual is considered fit until adjudicated otherwise since there is a presumption of competency. People v. Gelikkaya, 197 A.D.2d 405, 602 N.Y.S.2d 372 (1st Dept. 1993).

—In the absence of any basis in the record to conclude that the defendant lacked the capacity to understand the proceedings or to assist in his defense, defense counsel was not ineffective for failing to request a competency hearing. People v. Rivas, 206 A.D.2d 549, 614 N.Y.S.2d 753 (2d Dept. 1994).

—A defendant is not entitled to an evaluation as to his competency or capacity to stand trial; for a court to order a 730 examination there must be some reasonable ground for believing that the defendant may be incapable of understanding the charges against him or aiding in his defense. People v. Idlet, 208 A.D.2d 649, 617 N.Y.S.2d 489 (2d Dept. 1994).

—A defendant is not entitled, as a matter of right, to have the question of her capacity to stand trial passed on before the commencement of the trial, if the court is satisfied from the available information that there is no proper basis for questioning the defendant's sanity. People v. Parker, 191 A.D.2d 717, 595 N.Y.S.2d 519 (2d Dept. 1993).

—The presence of defendant was not required; the appeal was decided solely on the record and briefs. The present mental state of the appellant did not require that his appeal be held in abeyance. People v. Laudati, 41 A.D.2d 552, 339 N.Y.S.2d 766 (2d Dept. 1973), aff'd, 35 N.Y.2d 696, 361 N.Y.S.2d 347, 319 N.E.2d 708 (1974).

—Finding that defendant was fit to proceed to trial was supported by conclusions of a psychiatrist and a psychologist and by *pro se* motions made by the defendant which evidenced his understanding of the criminal process and his ability to actively participate in his defense. People v. Thomas, 129 A.D.2d 910, 514 N.Y.S.2d 817 (3d Dept. 1987).

Appropriate facility.—An appropriate facility for a defendant committed as unfit to stand criminal trial is one that provides "care and treatment" for the committee, and does so in the least restrictive manner; court can be guided by the way that the Legislature has mandated care and custody of insanity acquittees under CPL Art. 330. People v. Betances, 176 Misc. 2d 66, 671 N.Y.S.2d 930 (Sup. Ct. N.Y. Co. 1998).

Court's discretion to request informal examination.—Court's decision to request an informal evaluation by a psychiatrist was within its discretion and did not automatically require the court to issue an order of examination or otherwise comply with CPL article 730. People v. Conforti, 263 A.D.2d 513, 695 N.Y.S.2d 99 (2d Dept. 1999).

Competency determinations; court's discretion.—Court properly found defendant competent to stand trial, where, at the competency hearing, the court heard testimony of two psychiatrists who had examined defendant and both agreed that while defendant suffered from a delusional disorder, he had a factual understanding of the charges against him, logistics of the judicial process, and he would be able to rationally assist in his defense as long as he continued with his antipsychotic medication. People v. Ciborowski, 302 A.D.2d 620, 755 N.Y.S.2d 113 (3d Dept. 2003).

—Deliberate refusal of defendant to cooperate with defense counsel is not a valid basis for his contention that he lacked the ability to consult with defense counsel and to assist defense counsel in his defense, and thus, the court rejected defendant's contention that he was mentally incompetent to stand trial. People v. Hinton, 302 A.D.2d 1008, 755 N.Y.S.2d 548 (4th Dept. 2003).

Competency presumed.—A defendant is presumed to be competent, and a defendant's history of psychiatric illness does not in itself call into question defendant's competence to stand trial. People v. Tortorici, 92 N.Y.2d 757, 686 N.Y.S.2d 346, 709 N.E.2d 87, *cert. denied,* 528 U.S. 834 (1999).

—A defendant is presumed to be competent and is not entitled, as a matter of law, to a competency hearing unless the court has reasonable grounds to believe that, because of mental disease or defect, the defendant is incapable of assisting in his/her own defense or of understanding the proceedings against him. People v. Planty, 238 A.D.2d 806, 657 N.Y.S.2d 109 (3d Dept. 1997).

Defendant's refusal to resort to insanity plea.—Defendant,

before trial and before sentencing, was examined by psychiatrists and found competent to understand the charges and to cooperate in his defense, and his refusal to permit an appeal on the question of his competency did not deny his constitutional right to the effective assistance of counsel. People v. Reason, 44 A.D.2d 533, 353 N.Y.S.2d 449 (1st Dept. 1974), aff'd, 37 N.Y.2d 351, 372 N.Y.S.2d 614, 334 N.E.2d 572 (1975).

Discretion to commit.—Although defense counsel failed to seek relief from an order of committal by application to confirm the fitness examination findings, the court could commit defendant on its own motion and at the request of the probation and prosecution department. People v. Panesga, 160 Misc. 2d 1063, 612 N.Y.S.2d 299 (Sup. Ct. Queens Co. 1994).

District attorney; examination by defendant's psychiatrist.—District attorney is not entitled to be present during examination of defendant by his own psychiatrist appointed pursuant to Art. 18 B of the County Law. People v. Thomas, 77 Misc. 2d 1095, 355 N.Y.S.2d 909 (Sup. Ct. N.Y. Co. 1974).

Incompetent as matter of law.—Where record disclosed prior repeated psychiatric testimony of defendant's serious mental incapacity and possibility of non-cooperation with his attorney, it establishes that he was incompetent as a matter of law. People v. Jordan, 35 N.Y.2d 577, 364 N.Y.S.2d 474, 324 N.E.2d 131 (1974).

Fitness to proceed.—Court erred in finding defendant competent because the defendant was not present at the proceeding; further it is impossible to analyze the required factors and reach an independent conclusion as to the defendant's competency if defendant is not present. People v. Williams, 204 A.D.2d 77, 611 N.Y.S.2d 849 (1st Dept. 1994).

—Defendant, who had an IQ of 85, was competent to stand trial. People v. Hart, 205 A.D.2d 943, 613 N.Y.S.2d 762 (3d Dept. 1994).

—Although defendant was mentally retarded, his level of intellectual capacity was sufficient to render him competent to stand trial. People v. Schwartz, 204 A.D.2d 937, 614 N.Y.S.2d 948 (4th Dept. 1994).

—A trial court holding a probation violation proceeding can order a competency examination for defendant between arraignment and sentence even though the statute expressly authorizes the exam to occur during criminal pendency. People v. Panesga, 160 Misc. 2d 1063, 612 N.Y.S.2d 299 (Sup. Ct. Queens Co. 1994).

—Whether to order a CPL Article 730 examination is within the trial court's discretion in deciding whether a defendant is competent to proceed; the court is to take into consideration available medical proof coupled with all other evidence and its own observations of the defendant. People v. Chisholm, 162 A.D.2d 267, 556 N.Y.S.2d 625 (1st Dept. 1990).

—Fact that defendant was deemed incapacitated and committed to an institution two months after being found competent to proceed was irrelevant; defendant's fitness to proceed must be judged at the time of the original competency hearing. People v. Colon, 128 A.D.2d 422, 512 N.Y.S.2d 809 (1st Dept. 1987).

—Defendant was competent to stand trial despite caveat in the psychiatric report that he "might disorganize under the stress of incarceration and require psychiatric attention." People v. Sullivan, 48 A.D.2d 398, 369 N.Y.S.2d 744 (1st Dept. 1975), aff'd, 39 N.Y.2d 903, 369 N.Y.S.2d 386, 352 N.E.2d 586 (1976).

—When the court is satisfied from the available information that there is no proper basis to question the defendant's sanity, the defendant is not entitled, as a matter of right, to have his capacity to stand trial passed upon. People v. Carbone, 159 A.D.2d 511, 552 N.Y.S.2d 380 (2d Dept. 1990).

—Defendant does not have to be competent, independent of medication, before he can be found fit to stand trial. People v. Williams, 144 A.D.2d 402, 533 N.Y.S.2d 963 (2d Dept. 1988).

—Procedures outlined in CPL Article 730 apply only to persons who are unfit to stand trial as a result of "mental imbalance"; they do not apply to those who merely claim that their physical problems make it difficult for them to assist in their defense. People v. Bisnett, 144 A.D.2d 567, 534 N.Y.S.2d 424 (2d Dept. 1988).

Insanity; fitness to proceed; burden of proof.—Defendant brought a writ of error *coram nobis* to vacate the judgment against him. His contention that the People had the burden of proving his competency to stand trial was not sustained by the Court of Appeals. People v. Von Braunsberg, 31 N.Y.2d 842, 340 N.Y.S.2d 161, 292 N.E.2d 303 (1972).

—A defendant, whose most recent psychiatric examination found him fit to stand trial, had no basis to support his contention that he lacked capacity to understand when he entered his guilty plea. People v. Santiago, 205 A.D.2d 565, 614 N.Y.S.2d 269 (2d Dept. 1994).

No reason for competency exam.—There was no merit to defendant's contention that County Court should have, *sua sponte*, ordered a competency examination, where nothing in the record indicated that defendant had any difficulty communicating with defense counsel, or that defendant was incapable of assisting in his own defense, nor was there any indication that defendant engaged in bizarre behavior. People v. Charnock, 239 A.D.2d 933, 659 N.Y.S.2d 613 (4th Dept. 1997).

Pro se.—Where a defendant is deemed competent to stand trial, he is also competent to proceed pro se. People v. Schoolfield, 196 A.D.2d 111, 608 N.Y.S.2d 413, 417 (1st Dept. 1994)

Physical defect; hearing problem.—A defect which impairs the defendant's reason, comprehension or hampers his ability to effectively consult with his counsel may be physical as well as mental; where defendant has a hearing problem and a mistrial had already been granted because of this, the second trial should be adjourned and an otolaryngologist appointed to examine the defendant. People v. Jackson, 88 A.D.2d 604, 449 N.Y.S.2d 759 (2d Dept. 1982).

Refused examination by the People's psychiatrist.—The trial court properly held that the defendant could not submit expert testimony in support of his defense of a mental defect impairing his memory unless he afforded the People an opportunity to examine him so that they may submit evidence of similar quality. People v. Segal, 54 N.Y.2d 58, 444 N.Y.S.2d 588, 429 N.E.2d 107 (1981).

—Where defendant on seven separate occasions refused to submit to a psychiatric examination, he could not maintain that his rights to a hearing were violated. People v. Torres, 194 A.D.2d 488, 599 N.Y.S.2d 561 (1st Dept. 1993).

Retrospective competency determinations.—Procedures of article 730 do not apply to retrospective competency determinations. People v. Sanabria, 266 A.D.2d 41, 698 N.Y.S.2d 622 (1st Dept. 1999).

—Article 730 applies prospectively to defendant's competency for sentencing; there is no case law requiring adherence to the procedures of Article 730 in connection with a retrospective competency determination, which focuses on any contemporaneous evidence of defendants condition at the time of trial rather than the results of a new mental examination. People v. Pena, 251 A.D.2d 26, 675 N.Y.S.2d 330 (1st Dept. 1998).

Right to counsel.—Where a defendant is unable to assist in his or her own defense due to a mental impairment or disability, such defendant is not competent to waive his or her right to counsel in deciding whether to submit to questioning by law enforcement. People v. Newton, 175 Misc. 2d 887, 671 N.Y.S.2d 601 (Sup. Ct. Bronx Co. 1998).

Right to second competency hearing.—Court did not abuse its discretion in denying application of defense counsel for a second competency hearing after defendant's prior psychiatric examination revealed that he was fit to proceed but was intentionally trying to give a contrary impression, and defense counsel could not particularize his claim that defendant was out of touch with reality, and the court further found that defendant's courtroom demeanor indicated that he was fit to proceed and his later participation in the trial substantiated the finding he was fit. People v. Rodriguez, 79 A.D.2d 576, 434 N.Y.S.2d 347 (1st Dept.), *aff'd*, 56 N.Y.2d 557, 449 N.Y.S.2d 962, 434 N.E.2d 1340 (1980).

***Rosario* doctrine.**—The *Rosario* doctrine applies to competency hearings. People v. McPhee, 161 Misc. 2d 660, 614 N.Y.S.2d 884 (Sup. Ct. Queens Co. 1994).

—The examining psychiatrists' notes were *Rosario* material which were to be disclosed to the defendant for the purpose of a confidentiality hearing; however, once the notes were written into formal reports, there was no issue of confidentiality. People v. McPhee, 161 Misc. 2d 660, 614 N.Y.S.2d 884 (Sup. Ct. Queens Co. 1994).

Unable to proceed due to amnesia.—Where defendant claimed inability to stand trial due to genuine amnesia, the court approved use of CPL § 730.10 motion to determine whether,

under all the circumstances and with regard to the nature of the crime and the availability of evidence to the defendant, it is likely he could receive a fair trial. If the decision is that defendant is not incapacitated then the defendant can choose either to proceed to trial, after which he can move for evaluation of the fairness of the trial, or he can plead guilty. People v. Francabandera, 33 N.Y.2d 429, 354 N.Y.S.2d 609, 310 N.E.2d 292 (1974).

Waiver of defendant's competency.—Counsel's attempt to waive defendant's presence at competency proceedings both after the order confirming the psychiatric reports and after the cases were adjourned was ineffective. People v. Williams, 204 A.D.2d 77, 611 N.Y.S.2d 849 (1st Dept. 1994).

§ 730.20. Fitness to proceed; generally.

1. The appropriate director to whom a criminal court issues an order of examination must be determined in accordance with rules jointly adopted by the judicial conference and the commissioner. Upon receipt of an examination order, the director must designate two qualified psychiatric examiners, of whom he may be one, to examine the defendant to determine if he is an incapacitated person. In conducting their examination, the psychiatric examiners may employ any method which is accepted by the medical profession for the examination of persons alleged to be mentally ill or mentally defective. The court may authorize a psychiatrist or psychologist retained by the defendant to be present at such examination.

2. When the defendant is not in custody at the time a court issues an order of examination, because he was theretofore released on bail or on his own recognizance, the court may direct that the examination be conducted on an out-patient basis, and at such time and place as the director shall designate. If, however, the director informs the court that hospital confinement of the defendant is necessary for an effective examination, the court may direct that the defendant be confined in a hospital designated by the director until the examination is completed.

3. When the defendant is in custody at the time a court issues an order of examination, the examination must be conducted at the place where the defendant is being held in custody. If, however, the director determines that hospital confinement of the defendant is necessary for an effective examination, the sheriff must deliver the defendant to a hospital designated by the director and hold him in custody therein, under sufficient guard, until the examination is completed.

4. Hospital confinement under subdivisions two and three shall be for a period not exceeding thirty days, except that, upon application of the director, the court may authorize confinement for an additional period not exceeding thirty days if it is satisfied that a longer period is necessary to complete the examination. During the period of hospital confinement, the physician in charge of the hospital may administer or cause to be administered to the defendant such emergency psychiatric, medical or other therapeutic treatment as in his judgment should be administered.

5. Each psychiatric examiner, after he has completed his examination of the defendant, must promptly prepare an examination report and submit it to the director. If the psychiatric examiners are not unanimous in their opinion as to whether the defendant is or is not an incapacitated person, the director must designate another qualified psychiatric examiner to examine the defendant to determine if he is an incapacitated person. Upon receipt of the examination reports, the director must submit them to the court that issued the order of examination. The court must furnish a copy of the reports to counsel for the defendant and to the district attorney.

6. When a defendant is subjected to examination pursuant to an order issued by a criminal court in accordance with this article, any statement made by him for the purpose of the examination or treatment shall be inadmissible in evidence against him in any criminal action on any issue other than that of his mental condition, but such statement is admissible upon that issue whether or not it would otherwise be deemed a privileged communication.

7. A psychiatric examiner is entitled to his reasonable traveling expenses, a fee of fifty dollars for each examination of a defendant and a fee of fifty dollars for each appearance at a court hearing or trial but not exceeding two hundred dollars in fees for examination and testimony in any one case; except that if such psychiatric examiner be an employee of the state of New York he shall be entitled only to reasonable travelling expenses, unless such psychiatric examiner makes the examination or appears at a court hearing or trial outside his hours of state employment in a county in which the director of community mental health services certifies to the fiscal officer thereof that there is a shortage of qualified psychiatrists available to conduct examinations under the criminal procedure law in such county, in which event he shall be entitled to the foregoing fees and reasonable traveling expenses. Such fees and traveling expenses and the costs of sending a defendant to another place of detention or to a hospital for examination, of his maintenance therein and of returning him shall, when approved by the court, be a charge of the county in which the defendant is being tried.

Amended by L. 1971, Ch. 884; L. 1972, Ch. 692; L. 1989, Ch. 693, eff. July 22, 1989, amending subds. (1) and (5).

ANNOTATIONS

CPL § 730.20(1) requires an examination of defendant by two qualified psychiatrists.—Although court-ordered psychiatric examination denied defendant's statutory right to two psychiatric examinations, the denial could be cured by remitting the matter for a reconstruction hearing. People v. Gray, 201 A.D.2d 961, 607 N.Y.S.2d 828 (4th Dept. 1994).

—A court ordered examination of a defendant to determine his mental capacity to stand trial was not satisfied by an examination and report by a single psychiatrist; it is mandatory that a defendant be examined by two psychiatrists as required by statute. People v. Vallelunga, 101 A.D.2d 603, 474 N.Y.S.2d 857 (3d Dept. 1984).

Mental capacity to stand trial; defendant's burden of proof—Prosecution met its burden of proof showing that the defendant, who had dissociative personality disorder, was competent to stand trial, where three psychiatrists all independently reached the same conclusion. Court declined to hold that any defendant with dissociative personality disorder is incompetent as a matter of law. People v. Mendez, 1 N.Y.3d 15, 769 N.Y.S.2d 162, 801 N.E.2d 382 (2003).

Mental capacity to stand trial; People's burden of proof.—Error caused by the court's failure to abide by the provisions of CPL § 730.20 may be remedied by ordering the People to prove, at a hearing held during the pendency of this appeal, that the defendant was, in fact, competent at the time he was made to stand trial. People v. Duggins, 137 A.D.2d 613, 524 N.Y.S.2d 503 (2d Dept. 1988).

Psychiatric reports.—Although the psychiatrists were not unanimous in their diagnoses of the defendant, there was ample evidence in the record supporting the court's determination that the defendant was competent to stand trial. People v. Allen, 135 A.D.2d 823, 522 N.Y.S.2d 926 (2d Dept. 1987).

—During the course of an interview by two psychiatrists, defendant was cooperative and responded appropriately when asked about his background and the reason for his current incarceration, but refused to answer any further questions once he learned that the purpose of the interview was to determine his competency to stand trial. Both psychiatrists concluded that defendant knowingly declined to discuss the charges against him, that he would be able to testify, and that he understood the judicial process sufficiently to proceed. Based on these reports, the trial court properly determined that defendant was fit to proceed. People v. Jeffrey, 277 A.D.2d 714, 715 N.Y.S.2d 781 (3d Dept. 2000).

Required forms.—The statute was not violated when two psychiatrists did not submit their evaluations on forms referred to in the statute because the reports contained the required information. People v. Carkner, 213 A.D.2d 735, 623 N.Y.S.2d 350 (3d Dept. 1995).

Reconstruction hearing regarding mental status.—Where it is possible to reconstruct the defendant's mental status at the time of the commencement of trial, once the issue of defendant's competency has reasonably been raised, the court is required to hold a reconstruction hearing in which the People have the burden of proving the defendant's mental competency at that prior time by a fair preponderance of the evidence. People v. Arnold, 113 A.D.2d 101, 495 N.Y.S.2d 537 (4th Dept. 1985).

Recommendation of psychiatrist.—A recommendation that psychiatric treatment be pursued is not necessarily indicative of incompetence. People v. Perrotti, 257 A.D.2d 776, 685 N.Y.S.2d 116 (3d Dept. 1999).

§ 730.30. Fitness to proceed; order of examination.

1. At any time after a defendant is arraigned upon an accusatory instrument other than a felony complaint and before the imposition of sentence, or at any time after a defendant is arraigned upon a felony complaint and before he is held for the action of the grand jury, the court wherein the criminal action is pending must issue an order of examination when it is of the opinion that the defendant may be an incapacitated person.

2. When the examination reports submitted to the court show that each psychiatric examiner is of the opinion that the defendant is not an incapacitated person, the court may, on its own motion, conduct a hearing to determine the issue of capacity, and it must conduct a hearing upon motion therefor by the defendant or by the district attorney. If no motion for a hearing is made, the criminal action against the defendant must proceed. If, following a hearing, the court is satisfied that the defendant is not an incapacitated person,

the criminal action against him must proceed; if the court is not so satisfied, it must issue a further order of examination directing that the defendant be examined by different psychiatric examiners designated by the director.

3. When the examination reports submitted to the court show that each psychiatric examiner is of the opinion that the defendant is an incapacitated person, the court may, on its own motion, conduct a hearing to determine the issue of capacity and it must conduct such hearing upon motion therefor by the defendant or by the district attorney.

4. When the examination reports submitted to the court show that the psychiatric examiners are not unanimous in their opinion as to whether the defendant is or is not an incapacitated person, or when the examination reports submitted to the superior court show that the psychiatric examiners are not unanimous in their opinion as to whether the defendant is or is not a dangerous incapacitated person, the court must conduct a hearing to determine the issue of capacity or dangerousness.

Amended by L. 1974, Ch. 629.

ANNOTATIONS

Capacity to stand trial; determination.—Trial court abused its discretion by denying several applications for a psychiatric examination of defendant after he made several incoherent outbursts during the trial, which, taken together, placed his competence in doubt. People v. Peterson, 40 N.Y.S.2d 1014, 391 N.Y.S.2d 530, 359 N.E.2d 1325 (1976).

—The fact that the defendant began a pattern of strange behavior only after the competency hearing was requested provided particular support for the court's conclusion that the defendant was feigning mental illness. People v. Catlett, 254 A.D.2d 198, 681 N.Y.S.2d 230 (1st Dept. 1998).

—It is only when the court is of the opinion that the defendant may be an incapacitated person that a psychiatric examination may be ordered. People v. Salladeen, 50 A.D.2d 765, 377 N.Y.S.2d 63 (1st Dept. 1975), aff'd, 42 N.Y.2d 914, 397 N.Y.S.2d 994, 366 N.E.2d 1348 (1977).

—It is within the trial court's discretion to make the determination as to whether a competency hearing is required. People v. King, 187 A.D.2d 612, 590 N.Y.S.2d 110 (2d Dept. 1992).

—Despite the fact that two psychiatrists issued reports opining that defendant was not competent to stand trial because of schizophrenic disorder, both the prosecutor and defense counsel asked the court to find the defendant competent after the competency hearing at which defendant testified. Court did not abuse its discretion in concluding that defendant's delusional thoughts did not render him incapable of proceeding or assisting in his defense because defendant demonstrated at the hearing that he understood the judicial process and knew the charges against him and the sentence that would be imposed as a result of his plea. People v. Dewey, 18 A.D.3d 894, 795 N.Y.S.2d 111 (3d Dept. 2005).

Competency examination not required.—The trial court was not obligated to order, sua sponte, a competency hearing where defendant apparently dozed at times during the trial. People v. Davis, 231 A.D.2d 474, 648 N.Y.S.2d 6 (1st Dept. 1996).

—Although the information before the court revealed that the defendant experienced emotional difficulty at the time of trial, there was no evidence of any impairment on the defendant's part to assist and cooperate in her defense. Consequently, court did not err in not issuing an order directing a competency examination; motion to vacate on these grounds was properly denied. People v. Harris, 109 A.D.2d 351, 491 N.Y.S.2d 678 (2d Dept. 1985).

—It was not incumbent upon court to order a competency

evaluation in light of defendant's rational participation in and evident comprehension of the proceedings. People v. Wheeler, 249 A.D.2d 774, 672 N.Y.S.2d 155 (3d Dept. 1998).

—Trial court did not err in accepting defendant's plea without sua sponte ordering a competency examination, where defendant exhibited no delusional behavior at the plea or at sentencing, and defense counsel did not raise the issue of defendant's fitness to proceed or request an examination pursuant to CPL § 730.30(2). People v. Carbonel, 296 A.D.2d 858, 745 N.Y.S.2d 367 (4th Dept. 2002).

Error to accept guilty plea without hearing.—The court erred in permitting defendant to plead guilty without first holding a hearing as to defendant's competency where psychiatric examinations were in conflict as to defendant's competency; where there is conflict there must be a hearing. People v. McCabe, 87 A.D.2d 852, 449 N.Y.S.2d 245 (2d Dept. 1982).

Public and press; exclusion of.—Order which excluded public and press from a pretrial mental competency hearing in a rape case should not have been granted where there was no showing that there would be testimony describing the sexual acts specified in the Judiciary Law, Section 4, nor any showing of the need for the court to exercise its inherent power to exclude the public. Westchester Rockland Newspapers, Inc. v. Leggett, 48 N.Y.2d 430, 423 N.Y.S.2d 630, 399 N.E.2d 518 (1979).

Failure to request examination; ineffective assistance of counsel.—Where record revealed that both trial court and counsel had doubts as to defendant's competency to stand trial and the presentence report revealed that defendant was possibly mentally retarded, counsel's failure to obtain a psychiatric examination constituted ineffective assistance of counsel and, in any event, the court should have ordered an examination on its own motion. People v. Frazier, 114 A.D.2d 1038, 495 N.Y.S.2d 478 (2d Dept. 1985).

Finding of "dangerous incapacity" without jury trial; commitment requires jury review.—Despite the report the court had from two psychiatrists that the defendant did not lack the capacity to aid in his own defense, it was error for the trial court to accept the defendant's plea of guilty to a reduced charge of arson in the fourth degree without a capacity hearing when the defendant displayed a past history of mental defect as evidenced by a prior acquittal on the basis of mental disease and/or defect and the defendant had been institutionalized most of his life. People v. Bradt, 77 A.D.2d 795, 430 N.Y.S.2d 742 (4th Dept. 1980).

Mental examination required.—Trial court has an independent obligation to assess competency and can conduct its own hearing although two psychiatrists agree defendant is competent. People v. Williams, 204 A.D.2d 77, 616 N.Y.S.2d 849 (1st Dept. 1994).

—If, at any time before final judgment in a criminal action, it shall appear to the court that there is reasonable ground for believing that a defendant is in such a state of idiocy, imbecility or insanity that he is incapable of understanding the charges, the indictment or the proceedings, or in assisting his defense, it is the duty of the court to direct, sua sponte, a mental examination. People v. Arnold, 113 A.D.2d 101, 495 N.Y.S.2d 537 (4th Dept. 1985).

Presumption of competency.—Notwithstanding defendant's asserted history of psychiatric illness, defendant was properly presumed to be competent where he demonstrated at his arraignment that he understood the charges against him and he gave coherent and informed answers during the plea colloquy. People v. Woodard, 17 A.D.3d 929, 793 N.Y.S.2d 622 (3d Dept. 2005).

Statements of defendant; inadmissible at trial.—Statements made by a defendant at his competency hearing are not admissible at trial on the People's direct case. People v. Angelillo, 105 Misc. 2d 338, 432 N.Y.S.2d 127 (Co. Ct. Suffolk Co. 1980).

Subd. 2

Hearing.—Where a most recent hospital psychiatric report concluded the defendant was competent the court was not required sua sponte to conduct a competency hearing despite doubts about defendant's competency. People v. Gensler, 72 N.Y.2d 239, 532 N.Y.S.2d 72, 527 N.E.2d 1209 (1988).

—The court should consider the defendant's history of irrational behavior, demeanor (including statements and appearance), and previous medical opinions in determining whether to hold a sua sponte competency hearing. People v. Williams, 204 A.D.2d 77, 611 N.Y.S.2d 849 (1st Dept. 1994).

—Although defendant had a history of substance abuse, psychiatric problems, and had been diagnosed as a paranoid schizophrenic, there was no basis in the record to support the conclusion that the defendant was incompetent at the time of his plea proceedings. People v. Hollis, 204 A.D.2d 569, 614 N.Y.S.2d 211 (2d Dept. 1994).

—Where reports revealed defendant was mildly retarded and suffered from significant psychiatric disorders, court was not required to order a competency hearing since both examining psychiatrists found him competent to stand trial and neither defense counsel nor the District Attorney moved for a hearing. People v. Bronson, 115 A.D.2d 484, 495 N.Y.S.2d 716 (2d Dept. 1985).

—Defendant was aware, responsive to the court's questioning, understood the proceedings and charges against him, and was capable of assisting in his defense; thus, the county court was not required to determine whether the defendant was fit to stand trial. People v. Sims, 217 A.D.2d 912, 629 N.Y.S.2d 923 (4th Dept. 1995).

Hearing; right to present expert testimony.—A defendant found to lack capacity to participate in his own defense and committed for care and treatment, who is thereafter determined by the superintendent of the institution to which he is committed to be no longer incapacitated, has the right to present expert testimony during the hearing held following the report, and the court had no authority to refuse to hear expert testimony other than that of defendant's treating psychiatrist. People v. Christopher, 65 N.Y.2d 417, 492 N.Y.S.2d 566, 482 N.E.2d 45 (1985).

Incapacitated person; burden of proof.—Once the procedure mandated by CPL Art. 730 had been invoked, the defendant was entitled to a full and impartial determination of his mental capacity and the trial court's failure to secure the second psychiatric report, pursuant to CPL § 730.20 could hardly be viewed as an insubstantial error in light of defendant's prior history of mental illness. People v. Armlin, 37 N.Y.2d 167, 371 N.Y.S.2d 691, 332 N.E.2d 870 (1975).

—At a hearing to determine defendant's fitness to proceed to trial, the People are required to prove competency by a fair preponderance of the credible evidence, and in a case where the hearing court is presented with conflicting evidence of competency, its findings will be accorded great deference. People v. Breeden, 115 A.D.2d 484, 495 N.Y.S.2d 715 (2d Dept. 1985).

Subd. 4

Defendant's right to confront witnesses.—Where evaluation reports submitted to trial court show lack of unanimity between two psychiatric examiners as to defendant's dangerousness or capacity to stand trial, the court must conduct a hearing, under CPL § 730.30(4), to determine those issues, with due regard for defendant's fundamental constitutional right to be confronted by and to cross-examine witnesses testifying against his interest; trial court's finding of defendant's competency based upon written report of third psychiatrist, submitted after formal competency hearing was concluded and outside of the hearing record, was improper and should be reversed. People v. Charette, 78 A.D.2d 567, 431 N.Y.S.2d 733 (3d Dept. 1980).

§ 730.40. Fitness to proceed; local criminal court accusatory instrument.

1. When a local criminal court, following a hearing conducted pursuant to subdivision three or four of section 730.30, is satisfied that the defendant is not an incapacitated person, the criminal action against him must proceed. If it is satisfied that the defendant is an incapacitated person, or if no motion for such a hearing is made, such court must issue a final or temporary order of observation committing him to the custody of the commissioner for care and treatment in an appropriate institution for a period not to exceed ninety days from the date of the order. When a local criminal court accusatory instrument other than a felony complaint has been filed against the defendant, such court must issue a final order of observation; when a felony complaint has been filed against the defendant, such court must issue a temporary order of observation, except that, with the consent of the district attorney, it may issue a final order of observation.

2. When a local criminal court has issued a final order of observation, it must dismiss the accusatory instrument filed in such court against the defendant and such dismissal constitutes a bar to any further prosecution of the charge or charges contained in such accusatory instrument. When the defendant is in the custody of the commissioner at the expiration of the period prescribed in a temporary order of observation, the proceedings in the local criminal court that issued such order shall terminate for all purposes and the commissioner must promptly certify to such court and to the appropriate district attorney that the defendant was in his custody on such expiration date. Upon receipt of such certification, the court must dismiss the felony complaint filed against the defendant.

3. When a local criminal court has issued an order of examination or a temporary order of observation, and when the charge or charges contained in the accusatory instrument are subsequently presented to a grand jury, such grand jury need not hear the defendant pursuant to section 190.50 unless, upon application by defendant to the superior court that impaneled such grand jury, the superior court determines that the defendant is not an incapacitated person.

4. When an indictment is filed against a defendant after a local criminal court has issued an order of examination and before it has issued a final or temporary order of observation, the defendant must be promptly arraigned upon the indictment, and the proceedings in the local criminal court shall thereupon terminate for all purposes. The district attorney must notify the local criminal court of such arraignment, and such court must thereupon dismiss the accusatory instrument filed in such court against the defendant. If the director has submitted the examination reports to the local criminal court, such court must forward them to the superior court in which the indictment was filed. If the director has not submitted such reports to the local criminal court, he must submit them to the superior court in which the indictment was filed.

5. When an indictment is timely filed against the defendant after the issuance of a temporary order of observation or after the expiration of the period prescribed in such order, the superior court in which such indictment is filed must direct the sheriff to take custody of the defendant at the institution in which he is confined and bring him before the court for arraignment upon the indictment. After the defendant is arraigned upon the

indictment, such temporary order of observation or any order issued pursuant to the mental hygiene law after the expiration of the period prescribed in the temporary order of observation shall be deemed nullified. Notwithstanding any other provision of law, an indictment filed in a superior court against a defendant for a crime charged in the felony complaint is not timely for the purpose of this subdivision if it is filed more than six months after the expiration of the period prescribed in a temporary order of observation issued by a local criminal court wherein such felony complaint was pending. An untimely indictment must be dismissed by the superior court unless such court is satisfied that there was good cause for the delay in filing such indictment.

ANNOTATIONS

Amendment.—The defendant's motion to dismiss the indictment was granted where after the court had granted a Final Order of Observation, the District Attorney, two days later, without notice to any of the parties, issued an amended order stating that the defendant was held on a Temporary Order of Observation and subsequently obtained the indictment. People v. Paulides, 88 Misc. 2d 1061, 389 N.Y.S.2d 1018 (Nassau Co. Ct. 1976).

Constitutionality; subd. 3.—The fact that the right to testify before the grand jury is an important one does not mean that it is a fundamental right; CPL § 730.40(3) dos not violate the equal protection or due process. People v. Fox, 175 Misc. 2d 333, 669 N.Y.S.2d 470 (Nassau Co. Ct. 1997).

Incapacitated defendant's right to be a witness.—Where defendant, who had been arraigned in the Crim. Ct. on a felony complaint, was indicted more than 90 days after issuance of a temporary order of observation committing her to custody for no more than 90 days, the district attorney was not obliged to notify defendant of the pending grand jury proceeding and accord defendant time to exercise her right to appear as witness in grand jury because there was no longer a currently undisposed of felony complaint pending since it had been dismissed pursuant to CPL § 730.40(2). People v. Moss, 99 Misc. 2d 534, 416 N.Y.S.2d 741 (Sup. Ct. Queens Co. 1979).

§ 730.50. Fitness to proceed; indictment.

1. When a superior court, following a hearing conducted pursuant to subdivision three or four of section 730.30, is satisfied that the defendant is not an incapacitated person, the criminal action against him must proceed. If it is satisfied that the defendant is an incapacitated person, or if no motion for such a hearing is made, it must adjudicate him an incapacitated person, and must issue a final order of observation or an order of commitment. When the indictment does not charge a felony or when the defendant has been convicted of an offense other than a felony, such court (a) must issue a final order of observation committing the defendant to the custody of the commissioner for care and treatment in an appropriate institution for a period not to exceed ninety days from the date of such order and (b) must dismiss the indictment filed in such court against the defendant, and such dismissal constitutes a bar to any further prosecution of the charge or charges contained in such indictment. When the indictment charges a felony or when the defendant has been convicted of a felony, it must issue an order of commitment committing the defendant to the custody of the commissioner for care and treatment in an appropriate institution for a period not to exceed one year from the date of such order. Upon the issuance of an order of commitment, the court must exonerate the defendant's bail if he was previously at liberty on bail.

2. When a defendant is in the custody of the commissioner immediately prior to the expiration of the period prescribed in a temporary order of commitment and the superintendent of the institution wherein the defendant is confined is of the opinion that the defendant continues to be an incapacitated person, such superintendent must apply to the court that issued such order for an order of retention. Such application must be made within sixty days prior to the expiration of such period on forms that have been jointly adopted by the judicial conference and the commissioner. The superintendent must give written notice of the application to the defendant and to the mental hygiene legal service. Upon receipt of such application, the court may, on its own motion, conduct a hearing to determine the issue of capacity, and it must conduct such hearing if a demand therefor is made by the defendant or the mental hygiene legal service within ten days from the date that notice of the application was given them. If, at the conclusion of a hearing conducted pursuant to this subdivision, the court is satisfied that the defendant is no longer an incapacitated person, the criminal action against him must proceed. If it is satisfied that the defendant continues to be an incapacitated person, or if no demand for a hearing is made, the court must adjudicate him an incapacitated person and must issue an order of retention which shall authorize continued custody of the defendant by the commissioner for a period not to exceed one year.

3. When a defendant is in the custody of the commissioner immediately prior to the expiration of the period prescribed in the first order of retention, the procedure set forth in subdivision two shall govern the application for and the issuance of any subsequent order of retention, except that any subsequent orders of retention must be for periods not to exceed two years each; provided, however, that the aggregate of the periods prescribed in the temporary order of commitment, the first order of retention and all subsequent orders of retention must not exceed two-thirds of the authorized maximum term of imprisonment for the highest class felony charged in the indictment or for the highest class felony of which he was convicted.

4. When a defendant is in the custody of the commissioner at the expiration of the authorized period prescribed in the last order of retention, the criminal action pending against him in the superior court that issued such order shall terminate for all purposes, and the commissioner must promptly certify to such court and to the appropriate district attorney that the defendant was in his custody on such expiration date. Upon receipt of

such certification, the court must dismiss the indictment, and such dismissal constitutes a bar to any further prosecution of the charge or charges contained in such indictment.

5. When, on the effective date of this subdivision, * any defendant remains in the custody of the commissioner pursuant to an order issued under former code of criminal procedure section six hundred sixty-two-b, the superintendent or director of the institution where such defendant is confined shall, if he believes that the defendant continues to be an incapacitated person, apply forthwith to a court of record in the county where the institution is located for an order of retention. The procedures for obtaining any order pursuant to this subdivision shall be in accordance with the provision of subdivisions two, three and four of this section, except that the period of retention pursuant to the first order obtained under this subdivision shall be for not more than one year and any subsequent orders of retention must be for periods not to exceed two years each; provided, however, that the aggregate of the time spent in the custody of the commissioner pursuant to any order issued in accordance with the provisions of former code of criminal procedure section six hundred sixty-two-b and the periods prescribed by the first order obtained under this subdivision and all subsequent orders of retention must not exceed two-thirds of the authorized maximum term of imprisonment for the highest class felony charged in the indictment or the highest class felony of which he was convicted.

* June 2, 1972.

Amended by L. 1972, Ch. 810; L. 1974, Ch. 629; L. 1985, Ch. 789.

ANNOTATIONS

"Dangerousness"; burden of proof.—The burden of proof in a hearing to determine dangerousness following a finding that a defendant was not responsible for charged crimes is on the People and the standard is a preponderance of the credible evidence. People v. Simowitz, 124 Misc. 2d 431, 477 N.Y.S.2d 956 (Sup. Ct. N.Y. Co. 1984).

Defendant not entitled to dismissal of indictment.—Not every custodial retention of an indicted defendant by the Commissioner of Mental Health for two-thirds of the authorized imprisonment is sufficient for dismissal under CPL § 730.50(3) and (4); only custodial periods under superior court orders qualify toward dismissal. Court rejected defendant's request for a more expansive interpretation of CPL § 730.50(3) to include defendants who were civilly committed under the Mental Hygiene Law, finding that he had not asserted any basis to require heightened scrutiny for purposes of equal protection analysis, and denied defendant's motion to dismiss the indictment. People v. Lewis, 95 N.Y.2d 539, 720 N.Y.S.2d 87, 742 N.E.2d 601 (2000).

Retention hearing; dangerous mental disorder; burden of proof.—Prosecutor's statutory burden of proof in a retention hearing—"to the satisfaction of the court"—is fulfilled when People establish by a fair preponderance of the credible evidence that the defendant suffers from a dangerous mental disorder or is mentally ill; proof by a "clear and convincing evidence" standard is not required. People v. Escobar, 61 N.Y.2d 431, 474 N.Y.S.2d 453, 462 N.E.2d 1171 (1984).

Subsequent hearings; who conducts.—The court that issued the original order of commitment is to conduct any subsequent hearing on an application for an order of retention and erred when it granted a motion for a change of venue. *In*

re Thomas C., 196 A.D.2d 393, 609 N.Y.S.2d 936 (2d Dept. 1994).

Order of commitment.—The trial court is required to issue an order commitment once the defendant was found incompetent to stand trial. People v. Schaffer, 207 A.D.2d 421, 615 N.Y.S.2d 733 (2d Dept. 1994).

§ 730.60. Fitness to proceed; procedure following custody by commissioner.

1. When a local criminal court issues a final or temporary order of observation or an order of commitment, it must forward such order and a copy of the examination reports and the accusatory instrument to the commissioner, and, if available, a copy of the pre-sentence report. Upon receipt thereof, the commissioner must designate an appropriate institution operated by the department of mental hygiene in which the defendant is to be placed. The sheriff must hold the defendant in custody pending such designation by the commissioner, and when notified of the designation, the sheriff must deliver the defendant to the superintendent of such institution. The superintendent must promptly inform the appropriate director of the mental hygiene legal service of the defendant's admission to such institution. If a defendant escapes from the custody of the commissioner, the escape shall interrupt the period prescribed in any order of observation, commitment or retention, and such interruption shall continue until the defendant is returned to the custody of the commissioner.

2. Except as otherwise provided in subdivisions four and five, when a defendant is in the custody of the commissioner pursuant to a temporary order of observation or an order of commitment or an order of retention, the criminal action pending against the defendant in the court that issued such order is suspended until the superintendent of the institution in which the defendant is confined determines that he is no longer an incapacitated person. In that event, the court that issued such order and the appropriate district attorney must be notified, in writing, by the superintendent of his determination. The court must thereupon proceed in accordance with the provisions of subdivision two of section 730.30 of this chapter; provided, however, if the court is satisfied that the defendant remains an incapacitated person, and upon consent of all parties, the court may order the return of the defendant to the institution in which he had been confined for such period of time as was authorized by the prior order of commitment or order of retention. Upon such return, the defendant shall have all rights and privileges accorded by the provisions of this article.

3. When a defendant is in the custody of the commissioner pursuant to an order issued in accordance with this article, the commissioner may transfer him to any appropriate institution operated by the department of mental hygiene.

The commissioner may discharge a defendant in his custody under a final order of observation at any time prior to the expiration date of such order, or otherwise treat or transfer such defendant in the same manner as if he were a patient not in confinement under a criminal court order.

4. When a defendant is in the custody of the commissioner pursuant to an order of commitment or an order of retention, he may make any motion authorized by this chapter which is susceptible of fair determination without his personal participation. If the court denies any such motion it must be without prejudice to a renewal thereof after the criminal action against the defendant has been ordered to proceed. If the court enters an order dismissing the indictment and does not direct that the charge or charges be resubmitted to a grand jury, the court must direct that such order of dismissal be served upon the commissioner.

5. When a defendant is in the custody of the commissioner pursuant to an order of commitment or an order of retention, the superior court that issued such order may, upon motion of the defendant, and with the consent of the district attorney, dismiss the indictment when the court is satisfied that (a) the defendant is a resident or citizen of another state or country and that he will be removed thereto upon dismissal of the indictment, or (b) the defendant has been continuously confined in the custody of the commissioner for a period of more than two years. Before granting a motion under this subdivision, the court must be further satisfied that dismissal of the indictment is consistent with the ends of justice and that custody of the defendant by the commissioner pursuant to an order of commitment or an order of retention is not necessary for the protection of the public and that care and treatment can be effectively administered to the defendant without the necessity of such order. If the court enters an order of dismissal under this subdivision, it must set forth in the record the reasons for such action, and must direct that such order of dismissal be served upon the commissioner. The dismissal of an indictment pursuant to this subdivision constitutes a bar to any further prosecution of the charge or charges contained in such indictment.

6. (a) Notwithstanding any other provision of law, no person committed to the custody of the commissioner pursuant to this article, or continuously thereafter retained in such custody, shall be discharged, released on condition or placed in any less secure facility or on any less restrictive status, including, but not limited to vacations, furloughs and temporary passes, unless the commissioner shall deliver written notice, at least four days, excluding Saturdays, Sundays and holidays, in advance of the change of such committed person's facility or status, to all of the following:

(1) The district attorney of the county from which such person was committed;

(2) The superintendent of state police;

(3) The sheriff of the county where the facility is located;

(4) The police department having jurisdiction of the area where the facility is located;

(5) Any person who may reasonably be expected to be the victim of any assault or any violent felony offense, as defined in the penal law, which would be carried out by the committed person; and

(6) Any other person the court may designate.

Said notice may be given by any means reasonably calculated to give prompt actual notice.

(b) The notice required by this subdivision shall also be given immediately upon the departure of such committed person from the commissioner's actual custody, without proper authorization. Nothing in this subdivision shall be construed to impair any other right or duty regarding any notice or hearing contained in any other provision of law.

(c) Whenever a district attorney has received the notice described in this subdivision, and the defendant is in the custody of the commissioner pursuant to a final order of observation or an order of commitment, he may apply within three days of receipt of such notice to a superior court, for an order directing a hearing to be held to determine whether such committed person is a danger to himself or others. Such hearing shall be held within ten days following the issuance of such order. Such order may provide that there shall be no further change in the committed person's facility or status until the hearing. Upon a finding that the committed person is a danger to himself or others, the court shall issue an order to the commissioner authorizing retention of the committed person in the status existing at the time notice was given hereunder, for a specified period, not to exceed six months. The district attorney and the committed person's attorney shall be entitled to the committed person's clinical records in the commissioner's custody, upon the issuance of an order directing a hearing to be held.

(d) Nothing in this subdivision shall be construed to impair any other right or duty regarding any notice or hearing contained in any other provision of law.

Amended by L. 1973, Ch. 195; L. 1974, Ch. 629; L. 1980, Ch. 549; L. 1981, Ch. 791; L. 1984, Ch. 57; L. 1985, Ch. 789; L. 1987, Ch. 440.

ANNOTATIONS

Appeal; mentally ill defendant.—The presence of defendant was not required; the appeal was decided solely on the record and briefs. The present mental state of the appellant did not require that his appeal be held in abeyance. People v. Laudati, 41 A.D.2d 552, 339 N.Y.S.2d 766 (2d Dept. 1973), aff'd, 35 N.Y.2d 696, 361 N.Y.S.2d 347, 319 N.E.2d 708 (1974).

Requirement of notification.—Only when the defendant is found competent is the superintendent of the facility required to notify the court and the district attorney. People v. Lebron,

211 A.D.2d 208, 628 N.Y.S.2d 54 (1st Dept. 1995), *aff'd,* 88 N.Y.2d 891, 644 N.Y.S.2d 915, 667 N.E.2d 925 (1996).

§ 730.70. Fitness to proceed; procedure following termination of custody by commissioner.

When a defendant is in the custody of the commissioner on the expiration date of a final or temporary order of observation or an order of commitment, or on the expiration date of the last order of retention, or on the date an order dismissing an indictment is served upon the commissioner, the superintendent of the institution in which the defendant is confined may retain him for care and treatment for a period of thirty days from such date.

If the superintendent determines that the defendant is so mentally ill or mentally defective as to require continued care and treatment in an institution, he may, before the expiration of such thirty day period, apply for an order of certification in the manner prescribed in section 31.33 of the mental hygiene law.

Amended by L. 1973, Ch. 195; L. 1974, Ch. 629.

ANNOTATION

Dangerous incapacitated person; right to jury trial; retention by department of correction.—Defendant who was indicted for attempted murder but untried due to finding that he was "dangerously incapacitated person" and was confined to Matteawan was entitled to jury trial on issue of his status relative to retention by Matteawan so as to render statute constitutional, conferring equal rights to all persons confined under it. People v. Metesky, 71 Misc. 2d 519, 336 N.Y.S.2d 581 (Sup. Ct. Kings Co. 1972).

STATE OF NEW YORK

PENAL LAW

AN ACT providing for the punishment of offenses, constituting chapter forty of the consolidated laws.

Became a law July 20, 1965 (in effect Sept. 1, 1967) with the approval of the Governor. Passed, three-fifths being present.

The People of the State of New York, represented in Senate and Assembly, do enact as follows:

CHAPTER 40 OF THE CONSOLIDATED LAWS

PENAL LAW
SYNOPSIS OF ARTICLES

(*See also* other statutes of the Consolidated Laws for the definition and substance of crimes not set forth in the Penal Law.)

PL

PART ONE—GENERAL PROVISIONS

TITLE A—GENERAL PURPOSES, RULES OF CONSTRUCTION, AND DEFINITIONS

ARTICLE 1—GENERAL PURPOSES

Section

1.00   Short title.

1.05   General purposes.

§ 1.00. Short title.

This chapter shall be known as the "Penal Law."

§ 1.05. General purposes.

The general purposes of the provisions of this chapter are:

1. To proscribe conduct which unjustifiably and inexcusably causes or threatens substantial harm to individual or public interests;

2. To give fair warning of the nature of the conduct proscribed and of the sentences authorized upon conviction;

3. To define the act or omission and the accompanying mental state which constitute each offense;

4. To differentiate on reasonable grounds between serious and minor offenses and to prescribe proportionate penalties therefor;

5. To provide for an appropriate public response to particular offenses, including consideration of the consequences of the offense for the victim, including the victim's family, and the community; and

6. To insure the public safety by preventing the commission of offenses through the deterrent influence of the sentences authorized, the rehabilitation of those convicted, and their confinement when required in the interests of public protection.

Amended by L. 1982, Ch. 612.

ANNOTATIONS

Generally.—Generally, criminal prosecutions must be based on clear and unambiguous regulation or prohibition of conduct such that reasonable persons would be on notice that their conduct is criminally punishable. People v. Allied Health Care Prods., 81 N.Y.2d 27, 595 N.Y.S.2d 713, 611 N.E.2d 752 (1993).

—The standard for criminal liability is higher than that required for civil liability. People v. Roth, 80 N.Y.2d 239, 590 N.Y.S.2d 30, 604 N.E.2d 92 (1992).

—Maximum sentence of nine years to life of juvenile offender convicted of second degree murder appropriately balanced the competing values of "societal protection, rehabilitation and deterrence" given defendant's brutal strangulation and bludgeoning of the four-year-old victim. People v. Smith, 217 A.D.2d 221, 635 N.Y.S.2d 824 (4th Dept. 1995).

—Impossibility of commission is no defense so long as there was the requisite intent and the belief by the defendant that the attendant circumstances allowed for commission of the crime. People v. Acosta, 172 A.D.2d 103, 578 N.Y.S.2d 525 (1st Dept. 1992).

—Defining a crime in terms of a willful violation of a duly-promulgated regulation is clearly permissible under decisional law. People v. Allied Health Care Prods., 174 A.D.2d 246, 578 N.Y.S.2d 937 (3d Dept. 1992).

—A person is not responsible for an omission unless a duty is imposed by law. People v. Galatro, 153 Misc. 2d 54, 579 N.Y.S.2d 860 (Sup. Ct. Kings Co. 1992).

Prosecutorial discretion.—The law gives the prosecutor discretion as to whether to prosecute in the first instance. People v. Esposito, 144 Misc. 2d 919, 545 N.Y.S.2d 468, 474 (Sup. Ct. N.Y. Co. 1989).

ARTICLE 5—GENERAL RULES OF CONSTRUCTION AND APPLICATION

§ 5.00. Penal law not strictly construed.

The general rule that a penal statute is to be strictly construed does not apply to this chapter, but the provisions herein must be construed according to the fair import of their terms to promote justice and effect the objects of the law.

ANNOTATIONS

Vagueness.—The fact that a key word is not precisely defined in a statute does not mean that it becomes constitutionally defective if the plain meaning of the word can be ascertained. People v. Fulvio, 135 Misc. 2d 93, 514 N.Y.S.2d 594 (Crim. Ct. Bronx Co. 1987).

Condemning strained construction.—Provisions of the Penal Law must be construed according to the fair import of their terms to promote justice and effect the objects of the law; here the arrest was complete at the time the defendant was taken into custody. People v. Hasenflue, 169 Misc. 2d 766, 648 N.Y.S.2d 254 (Sup. Ct. Ulster Co. 1996).

—In the context of a discussion concluding that entrance into a subway station without paying the fare does not constitute trespass, the court notes that the Court of Appeals has traditionally and consistently condemned the strained construction of penal statutes; penal statutes are to be read according to the fair import of their terms in order to promote justice and effect the objects of the law. People v. Pratt, 164 Misc. 2d 498, 625 N.Y.S.2d 869 (Crim. Ct. N.Y. Co. 1995).

§ 5.05. Application of chapter to offenses committed before and after enactment.

1. The provisions of this chapter shall govern the construction of and punishment for any offense defined in this chapter and committed after the effective date hereof, as well as the construction and application of any defense to a prosecution for such an offense.

2. Unless otherwise expressly provided, or unless the context otherwise requires, the provisions of this chapter shall govern the construction of and punishment for any offense defined outside of this chapter and committed after the effective date thereof, as well as the construction and application of any defense to a prosecution for such an offense.

3. The provisions of this chapter do not apply to or govern the construction of and punishment for any offense committed prior to the effective date of this chapter, or the construction and application of any defense to a prosecution for such an offense. Such an offense must be construed and punished according to the provisions of law existing at the time of the commission thereof in the same manner as if this chapter had not been enacted.

ANNOTATION

Ex post facto.—The Ex Post Facto Clause of the United States Constitution does not preclude application of statute which repealed the statutory provisions requiring corroboration of the victim's testimony in certain sex crime prosecutions involving underage victims to prosecutions for crimes occurring before its effective date. People v. Hudy, 73 N.Y.2d 40, 538 N.Y.S.2d 197, 535 N.E.2d 250 (1988).

§ 5.10. Other limitations on applicability of this chapter.

1. Except as otherwise provided, the procedure governing the accusation, prosecution, conviction and punishment of offenders and offenses is not regulated by this chapter but by the criminal procedure law.

2. This chapter does not affect any power conferred by law upon any court-martial or other military authority or officer to prosecute and punish conduct and offenders violating military codes or laws.

3. This chapter does not bar, suspend, or otherwise affect any right or liability to damages, penalty, forfeiture or other remedy authorized by law to be recovered or enforced in a civil action, regardless of whether the conduct involved in such civil action constitutes an offense defined in this chapter.

4. Sections 120.45, 120.50, 120.55, 120.60 and 240.25, subdivisions two and three of section 240.26, and sections 240.70 and 240.71 of this chapter (a) do not apply to conduct which is otherwise lawful under the provisions of the National Labor Relations Act as amended, the National Railway Labor Act as amended, or the Federal Employment Labor Management Act as amended, and (b) do not bar any conduct, including, but not limited to, peaceful picketing or other peaceful demonstration, protected from legal prohibition by the federal and state constitutions.

Amended by L. 1999, Ch. 635, § 12, adding subd. 4, eff. Dec. 1, 1999; L. 2000, Ch. 434, § 6, eff. Oct. 20, 2000, amending subd. 4.

ARTICLE 10—DEFINITIONS

Section

10.00   Definitions of terms of general use in this chapter.

§ 10.00. Definition of terms of general use in this chapter.

Except where different meanings are expressly specified in subsequent provisions of this chapter, the following terms have the following meanings:

1. "Offense" means conduct for which a sentence to a term of imprisonment or to a fine is provided by any law of this state or by any law, local law or ordinance of a political subdivision of this state, or by any order, rule or regulation of any governmental instrumentality authorized by law to adopt the same.

2. "Traffic infraction" means any offense defined as "traffic infraction" by section one hundred fifty-five of the vehicle and traffic law.

3. "Violation" means an offense, other than a "traffic infraction," for which a sentence to a term of imprisonment in excess of fifteen days cannot be imposed.

4. "Misdemeanor" means an offense, other than a "traffic infraction," for which a sentence to a term of imprisonment in excess of fifteen days may be imposed, but for which a sentence to a term of imprisonment in excess of one year cannot be imposed.

5. "Felony" means an offense for which a sentence to a term of imprisonment in excess of one year may be imposed.

6. "Crime" means a misdemeanor or a felony.

7. "Person" means a human being, and where appropriate, a public or private corporation, an unincorporated association, a partnership, a government or a governmental instrumentality.

8. "Possess" means to have physical possession or otherwise to exercise dominion or control over tangible property.

9. "Physical injury" means impairment of physical condition or substantial pain.

10. "Serious physical injury" means physical injury which creates a substantial risk of death, or which causes death or serious and protracted disfigurement, protracted impairment of health or protracted loss or impairment of the function of any bodily organ.

11. "Deadly physical force" means physical force which, under the circumstances in which it is used, is readily capable of causing death or other serious physical injury.

12. "Deadly weapon" means any loaded weapon from which a shot, readily capable of producing death or other serious physical injury, may be discharged, or a switchblade knife, gravity knife, pilum ballistic knife, metal knuckle knife, dagger, billy, blackjack, or metal knuckles.

13. "Dangerous instrument" means any instrument, article or substance, including a "vehicle" as that term is defined in this section, which, under the circumstances in which it is used, attempted to be used or threatened to be used, is readily capable of causing death or other serious physical injury.

14. "Vehicle" means a "motor vehicle", "trailer" or "semi-trailer," as defined in the vehicle and traffic law, any snowmobile as defined in the parks and recreation law, any aircraft, or any vessel equipped for propulsion by mechanical means or by sail.

15. "Public servant" means (a) any public officer or employee of the state or of any political subdivision thereof or of any governmental instrumentality within the state, or (b) any person exercising the functions of any such public officer or employee. The term public servant includes a person who has been elected or designated to become a public servant.

16. "Juror" means any person who is a member of any jury, including a grand jury, impaneled by any court in this state or by any public servant authorized by law to impanel a jury. The term juror also includes a person who has been drawn or summoned to attend as a prospective juror.

17. "Benefit" means any gain or advantage to the beneficiary and includes any gain or advantage to a third person pursuant to the desire or consent of the beneficiary.

18. "Juvenile offender" means (1) a person thirteen years old who is criminally responsible for acts constituting murder in the second degree as defined in subdivisions one and two of section 125.25 of this chapter; and (2) a person fourteen or fifteen years old who is criminally responsible for acts constituting the crimes defined in subdivisions one and two of section 125.25 (murder in the second degree) and in subdivision three of such section provided that the underlying crime for the murder charge is one for which such person is criminally responsible; section 135.25 (kidnapping in the first degree); 150.20 (arson in the first degree); subdivisions one and two of section 120.10 (assault in the first degree); 125.20 (manslaughter in the first degree); subdivisions one and two of section 130.35 (rape in the first degree); subdivisions one and two of section 130.50 (criminal sexual act in the first degree); 130.70 (aggravated sexual abuse in the first degree); 140.30 (burglary in the first degree); subdivision one of section 140.25 (burglary in the second degree); 150.15 (arson in the second

degree); 160.15 (robbery in the first degree); subdivision two of section 160.10 (robbery in the second degree) of this chapter; subdivision four of section 265.02 of this chapter, where such firearm is possessed on school grounds, as that phrase is defined in subdivision fourteen of section 220.00 of this chapter; or section 265.03 of this chapter, where such machine gun or such firearm is possessed on school grounds, as that phrase is defined in subdivision fourteen of section 220.00 of this chapter; or defined in this chapter as an attempt to commit murder in the second degree or kidnapping in the first degree.

19. For the purposes of section 260.30 and 120.01 of this chapter the term "child day care provider" shall be defined as provided for in section three hundred ninety of the social services law.

Amended by L. 1967, Ch. 791; L. 1968, Ch. 73; L. 1975, Ch. 686; L. 1978, Ch. 481; L. 1979, Ch. 411; L. 1980, Ch. 295; L. 1981, Ch. 335; L. 1986, Ch. 328; L. 1995, Ch. 219, amending subd. 12, eff. Nov. 1, 1995; L. 1998, Ch. 435, § 3, eff. Nov. 1, 1998, amending subd. 18, and Ch. 600, § 4, eff. Nov. 1, 1998, adding sub. 19; L. 2003, Ch. 264, § 1, eff. Nov. 1, 2003, amending subd. 18(2).

ANNOTATIONS

Subd. 3

Violation defined.—Town's ordinance which charged defendant with a "violation" but which permitted sentences of up to 30 days jail time triggered defendant's statutory right to jury trial and town prosecutor committed prejudicial, material, and non-harmless error by representing to presiding Justice, a non-attorney, that defendant was not entitled to a jury trial. People v. Brown, 170 Misc. 2d 266, 648 N.Y.S.2d 283 (Allegany Co. Ct. 1996).

Subd. 7

Person defined.—Infant was a "person" from the moment of birth, notwithstanding that defendant may have perpetrated the act that caused the injury prior to her birth. People v. Hayat, 235 A.D.2d 287, 653 N.Y.S.2d 305 (1st Dept. 1997).

Unincorporated association.—Statute clearly states legislative intent that an unincorporated association such as a labor union may be prosecuted and held criminally liable under New York law. People v. Newspaper & Mail Deliverers, 170 Misc. 2d 790, 649 N.Y.S.2d 760 (Sup. Ct. N.Y. Co. 1996).

Subd. 8

Constructive possession.—A defendant may constructively possess drugs if he has dominion and control over them as a result of his authority over the person who actually possesses them, rather than through his access to or control over the place where the drugs are kept. People v. Manini, 79 N.Y.2d 561, 584 N.Y.S.2d 282, 289, 594 N.E.2d 563 (1992).

—While access to a vehicle by others does not necessarily foreclose a finding of constructive possession, lack of any direct evidence linking defendant to the marihuana in trunk placed a "heavy burden" on the People to establish possession element; evidence of defendant's mere presence in vehicle where drugs are found is not sufficient evidence of constructive possession. People v. Burns, 17 A.D.3d 709, 792 N.Y.S.2d 700 (3d Dept. 2005).

—Evidence that defendant was found asleep alone in a bedroom containing her property (social security card, driver's license, completed application for public assistance, and a utility bill addressed to her at that address) along with female clothing was sufficient for jury to conclude that defendant exercised dominion and control over the bedroom and thus was in constructive possession of the cocaine secreted in the closet of that bedroom. People v. Tarver, 292 A.D.2d 110, 741 N.Y.S.2d 130 (3d Dept. 2002).

Dominion and control.—The defendant may physically be elsewhere, even in another state, but as long as he exercised dominion and control over locations where subject drugs were discovered or over subordinates who were physically in possession of drugs, possession is established. People v Roque, 99 N.Y.2d 50, 54, 751 N.Y.S.2d 165, 780 N.E.2d 976 (2002); *see also* People v. Carvajal, 14 A.D.3d 165, 786 N.Y.S.2d 450 (1st Dept. 2004), *appeal granted,* 4 N.Y.3d 762, 792 N.Y.S.2d 6, 825 N.E.2d 138 (2005), *motion denied,* 4 N.Y.3d 825, 796 N.Y.S.2d 578, 829 N.E.2d 671 (2005).

—Court's instruction that, if the defendant threw away a black object, he had possession of that black object within the meaning of Penal Law § 10.00(8) was an accurate statement of the law, albeit confusing. People v. Leung, 68 N.Y.2d 320, 506 N.Y.S.2d 320, 497 N.E.2d 687 (1986).

—Ample evidence was presented to support defendants' conviction of criminal possession of a weapon in the first degree where defendants admitted living in apartment in which hand grenade simulator was found, both hung their clothes in the bedroom where the simulator was found, and additionally, a photograph of one of defendants was found in the suitcase in which the simulator was located. People v. Watson, 56 N.Y.2d 632, 450 N.Y.S.2d 784, 436 N.E.2d 190 (1982).

—Although mere presence as a passenger in a stolen vehicle, without more, is insufficient to establish possession, here, minutes before the fatal accident, defendant was seen driving the vehicle thus providing sufficient evidence for his conviction of criminal possession of stolen property in the third degree. People v. Mitchell, 223 A.D.2d 655, 637 N.Y.S.2d 176 (2d Dept. 1996).

Possession.—Criminal possession of a weapon requires proof of possession of weapon, either actual or constructive; if constructive, the proof must establish that defendant exercised dominion and control over the weapon or the area in which it was found. People v. Kirby, 280 A.D.2d 775, 721 N.Y.S.2d 130 (3d Dept. 2001).

—Fact that defendant's guest brought gun into defendant's house weeks before his arrest for unlawful possession does not alone establish the defense of temporary and lawful possession; once unlawful possession is established, the possessory crime is complete. People v. Myers, 265 A.D.2d 598, 697 N.Y.S.2d 178 (3d Dept. 1999).

Subd. 9

Physical injury.—Information was factually sufficient to satisfy "physical injury" element of offense where information described a physical attack by defendant and another for the purposes of stealing the motor scooter victim was riding at the time of the attack; the kicks the victim received in the course of the attack, which resulted in contusions and swelling and caused the victim substantial pain, were more substantial than the "petty slaps [or] shoves delivered out of meanness," which were specifically excluded by the Legislature in its notes. People v. Henderson, 92 N.Y.2d 677, 708 N.E.2d 165, 685 N.Y.S.2d 409 (1998).

—Conviction for assault, second degree, was reversed where testimony showed that victim only suffered a one centimeter cut above her lip; this was insufficient to show that victim suffered either "substantial pain" or "impairment of physical condition." People v. Jimenez, 55 N.Y.2d 895, 449 N.Y.S.2d 22, 433 N.E.2d 1270 (1982).

—Physical injury element was established through testimony of complainant that he suffered substantial pain when defendant pulled on his thick gold neck chain until it broke, and the pain and red marks lasted for several weeks after the incident. People v. Arroyo, 270 A.D.2d 386, 720 N.Y.S.2d 33 (1st Dept. 2001), *rev'd on other grounds,* 98 N.Y.2d 101, 772 N.E.2d 1154, 745 N.Y.S.2d 796 (2002).

—Physical injury includes the pain suffered by a child as a result of being struck. People v. Wilkins, 239 A.D.2d 105, 657 N.Y.S.2d 599 (1st Dept. 1997).

—Legally sufficient proof of physical injury existed even though victim did not seek medical attention where victim testified that he was struck on the head, neck and shoulder with a wooden stick and with such force that the stick slightly broke and that when he collapsed to the ground, defendant kicked him. As a result, the victim sustained bruises and discoloration in those areas and stated that he suffered pain for three weeks. In addition, a detective corroborated that there was swelling to the victim's head and face immediately after the incident. People v. Jackson, 232 A.D.2d 193, 647 N.Y.S.2d 764 (1st Dept. 1996).

—Victim sustained physical injury within the meaning of the statute when she was kicked in the eye by the defendant. People v. Hansen, 267 A.D.2d 474, 700 N.Y.S.2d 759 (2d Dept. 1999), appeal denied, 95 N.Y.2d 797 (2000).

—Insufficient evidence was presented to establish "physical injury" where complainant did not testify and the only evidence as to the extent of complainant's injury was a witness who saw complainant bleeding and then cleaning the cut with peroxide. People v. Saunders, 245 A.D.2d 471, 666 N.Y.S.2d 663 (2d Dept. 1997).

—Testimony was sufficient where, as a result of defendant's repeated beatings, victim sustained bruises on her face, a black eye, and abrasions that lasted for about one and a half weeks, required painkillers, and continued to have headaches as a result. People v. Morales, 245 A.D.2d 467, 666 N.Y.S.2d 660 (2d Dept. 1997), app. denied, 92 N.Y.2d 902, 680 N.Y.S.2d 66, 702 N.E.2d 851 (1998).

—Testimony by complainant that he experienced pain, headaches, and blurred vision and that he sought medical attention and missed one week of school as a result of the appellant's hitting him in the face with a lock was sufficient to establish that the complainant suffered a physical injury. In re Manuel G., 215 A.D.2d 558, 626 N.Y.S.2d 859 (2d Dept. 1995).

—People successfully proved that defendant caused physical injury to a police officer where proof showed that officer suffered a sharp pain in his hand, was treated for a broken bone in his hand, and missed three weeks of work while his hand was in a case. People v. Brooks, 215 A.D.2d 491, 626 N.Y.S.2d 825 (2d Dept. 1995).

—No merit found in defendant's contention that victim did not suffer physical injury where victim and treating physician testified that victim sustained a swollen and bruised upper eyelid and cuts to the mouth, and where victim alone stated that he suffered back pain and headaches and missed one week of work. People v. Callaghan, 220 A.D.2d 609, 633 N.Y.S.2d 46 (2d Dept. 1995).

—Physical injury was established where the victim received a bruised or blackened eye, red marks on her neck, a swollen face, and a constant headache and sought medical treatment. People v. Sloan, 202 A.D.2d 525, 609 N.Y.S.2d 67 (2d Dept. 1994).

—Physical injury element was satisfied where officer testified that, approximately 14 months after the injuries were first sustained, he still experienced pain in his knees. People v. Daniels, 199 A.D.2d 332, 605 N.Y.S.2d 106 (2d Dept. 1994).

—"Physical injury" was not established where one victim suffered a bloody lip, and the other merely cried upon being struck, and neither victim requested or received medical treatment. People v. Wainright, 123 A.D.2d 894, 507 N.Y.S.2d 669 (2d Dept. 1986).

—Evidence that one victim sustained a non-life threatening gunshot wound for which he was treated when he arrived at the emergency room fully conscious and responsive and second victim's bullet wound to the neck was treated without surgery did not support assault in the first degree conviction, these were physical injuries not serious physical injuries, no medical evidence about health risks to victim with fragments left in place introduced. People v. Horton, 9 A.D.3d 503, 780 N.Y.S.2d 654 (3d Dept. 2004).

—Evidence established presence of "physical injury" by medical testimony of pain at specific points on the victim's head upon palpation, a diagnosis of a mild concussion, victim's testimony of severe pain, and her reporting of residual problems for which she sought further treatment and medicine, including recurring severe headaches caused after defendant struck her in the head with a novelty baseball bat. People v. Hines, 9 A.D.3d 507, 780 N.Y.S.2d 419 (3d Dept. 2004).

—Where after five-month old child was left alone in defendant's care, and when she was returned to her mother she had black and blue marks on her cheeks, nose and lip and under her eyes, physician who treated victim testified that child's injuries were consistent with child abuse, and that child could not have sustained her injuries through her own actions and, in his opinion, injuries would have caused her substantial pain at the time of infliction, this physical injury supported defendant's conviction under §120.05(8). People v. Tompkins, 8 A.D.3d 901, 780 N.Y.S.2d 387 (3d Dept. 2004).

—Victim's testimony that as a result of defendant's assault, his hand was "quite sore," swollen, and black and blue, that he could not flex his wrist, and, when he tried to move it, he felt sharp pain established presence of a physical injury, broken bones were not necessary, victim wore a support brace for three days and worked light duty for approximately one week. People v. Ellis, 8 A.D.3d 826, 778 N.Y.S.2d 555 (3d Dept. 2004).

—Parole officer's injuries sustained when defendant repeatedly jabbed him in the eye with a metal rod to the extent that "he almost lost [his] eyeball" constituted a physical injury within the meaning of the statute. People v. Colantonio, 277 A.D.2d 498, 715 N.Y.S.2d 764 (3d Dept. 2000), appeal denied, 96 N.Y.2d 781 (2001).

—Fact that complainant did not seek medical attention for injuries sustained as a result of defendant's attack was not dispositive of the presence of "physical injury." People v. Andrews, 236 A.D.2d 735, 654 N.Y.S.2d 53 (3d Dept. 1997).

—Evidence of an unspecified degree of pain and slight swelling on the right cheek falls short of the required objective level of proof to establish physical injury. People v. McCummings, 203 A.D.2d 656, 610 N.Y.S.2d 634 (3d Dept. 1994).

—"Pain" criteria of physical injury element was satisfied by robbery victim's testimony that he experienced pain in his shoulder for 5 months after the crime. People v. James, 133 A.D.2d 507, 519 N.Y.S.2d 578 (3d Dept. 1987).

—Testimony that defendant and his codefendants struck victim in the head with a blunt instrument and kicked and "stomped on" the victim's body and face, that victim was covered in blood when police arrived and had cuts and bruises all over his body, he was admitted to the trauma unit for several days following the incident and still suffers from headaches, established a physical injury, conviction for assault affirmed. People v. Carter, 6 A.D.3d 1174, 776 N.Y.S.2d 403 (4th Dept. 2004).

—"Impairment of physical condition" was established by testimony that police officer was out of work for a week to ten days, had to take muscle relaxants and pain killers, and wore a sling for several days after altercation with defendant. People v. Sekoll, 254 A.D.2d 797, 679 N.Y.S.2d 225 (4th Dept. 1998), review denied, 92 N.Y.2d 1053, 685 N.Y.S.2d 432, 708 N.E.2d 189 (2000).

—Physical injury was established by police officer's testimony of pain experienced as defendant hit him with a wooden bat or club and description of pain and swelling that continued for some time. People v. Sylvester, 254 A.D.2d 711, 677 N.Y.S.2d 865 (4th Dept. 1998).

—Defendant's conviction for assault in the second degree was reduced to assault in the third degree upon appellate court's determination that physical injury sustained by victim when defendant shot him in the foot did not rise to the level of serious physical injury which would have supported the original charge. People v. Bodford, 238 A.D.2d 928, 661 N.Y.S.2d 158 (4th Dept.1997).

—Evidence that defendant repeatedly hit victim with a stick or pipe which caused blunt force bruises and abrasions to the victim's face, back and legs established that the victim suffered "substantial pain." People v. Young, 236 A.D.2d 808, 653 N.Y.S.2d 879 (4th Dept. 1997).

Subd. 10

Serious physical injury.—Victim's testimony, corroborated by medical evidence that victim did not have full use of her arm, in addition to the permanent scar visible for the jury to observe and treating physician's testimony that the wounds created a substantial risk of death, established "serious physical injury." People v. McDuffie, 293 A.D.2d 287, 740 N.Y.S.2d 48 (1st Dept. 2002).

—Victim of assault who suffered multiple gunshot wounds suffered serious physical injury. People v. Foster, 278 A.D.2d 241, 717 N.Y.S.2d 303 (2d Dept. 2000), appeal denied, 96 N.Y.2d 734 (2001).

—Serious physical injury was not established by head wound which required stitches but was not life threatening or caused a protracted or serious impairment or disfigurement. People v. Mack, 268 A.D.2d 599, 707 N.Y.S.2d 105 (2d Dept.), appeal denied, 94 N.Y.2d 904 (2000).

—Defendant's actions of repeatedly hitting victim in the head and body with a stick until victim fell to the ground is sufficient to establish that the victim sustained serious physical injury.

People v. Foxx, 240 A.D.2d 430, 658 N.Y.S.2d 392 (2d Dept. 1997).

—Evidence was legally sufficient to establish defendant's guilt of assault in the first degree: victim testified that as a result of the beating by defendant she still suffered some loss of vision in her right eye nine months later at the time of trial, thus there was sufficient evidence of "protracted impairment of the function of a bodily organ." People v. Hirschhorn, 231 A.D.2d 591, 648 N.Y.S.2d 34 (2d Dept. 1996).

—Serious physical injury requires death or serious and protracted loss or injury of a bodily organ, and serious physical injury element was not satisfied by testimony that victim sustained a fractured jaw at the hands of the defendant. People v. Phillip, 279 A.D.2d 802, 718 N.Y.S.2d 727 (3d Dept. 2001).

—Conviction for robbery in the first degree was supported by evidence of serious physical injury; defendant participated in beating the victim which resulted in head injuries and severe facial lacerations from which victim would have bled to death if left unattended. People v. Jeanty, 268 A.D.2d 675, 702 N.Y.S.2d 194 (3d Dept.), *appeal denied,* 94 N.Y.2d 949 (2000).

—Defendant's actions of squeezing three-month-old infant so hard as to break 20 ribs, while a severe injury, was not a serious physical injury since it was not life threatening. People v. Parrotte, 267 A.D.2d 884, 702 N.Y.S.2d 137 (3d Dept. 1999), *appeal denied,* 95 N.Y.2d 801 (2000).

—Injuries complainant suffered when defendant attacked her with a brick while she was sleeping, including cuts on her head requiring sutures, a broken hand, bruises on her shoulder, arms leg and feet, supported jury's determination that she had sustained "serious physical injury." People v. Quesnel, 238 A.D.2d 725, 656 N.Y.S.2d 772 (3d Dept. 1997).

Subd. 11

Deadly physical force.—Juvenile's use of deadly physical force, *i.e.,* stabbing complainant in the head and back with a kitchen knife, was justified where respondent was being held on the ground, kicked by complainant about the body, head and face and surrounded by 10 to 15 people who urged the beating to continue, and respondent was without anyone in the area to help her. *In re* Y.K., 87 N.Y.2d 430, 639 N.Y.S.2d 1000, 663 N.E.2d 313 (1996).

—Deadly physical force was established when evidence showed defendant assaulted complainant with knife; force used was "readily capable of causing death or other serious physical injury," regardless of degree of injury he actually intended or inflicted. People v. Steele, 19 A.D.3d 175, 798 N.Y.S.2d 391 (1st Dept. 2005).

Subd. 12

Deadly weapon.—Record did not support finding of physical injury necessary to prove assault in the third degree; although testimony did support finding of neglect based on evidence that defendant hit 13-month-old victim and left red finger marks on his face, that is not sufficient to establish that the victim suffered a physical injury. *In re* Mary P., 278 A.D.2d 750, 718 N.Y.S.2d 442 (3d Dept. 2000).

Subd. 13

Dangerous instrument.—A human body part is not a "dangerous instrument" within the meaning of the statute; indictment charging defendant with burglary in the first degree as well as other counts with aggravating factors based upon the use of his teeth to bite complainant's finger was properly dismissed or reduced. People v. Owusu, 93 N.Y.2d 398, 690 N.Y.S.2d 863, 712 N.E.2d 1228 (1999).

—Sufficient proof existed to establish guilt of second degree assault under § 120.05(2): a wad of paper towels that defendant used to gag his 10-year-old victim during an assault was a dangerous instrument within the meaning of § 10.00(13). The wad of towels was wadded up with rubber bands to create a "dense ball that was shoved into the victim's mouth with sufficient force to break a tooth," the victim's hands were bound thereby preventing her from removing the towels and therefore the wad was capable of causing serious physical injury. People v. Vasquez, 88 N.Y.2d 561, 647 N.Y.S.2d 697, 670 N.E.2d 1328 (1996).

—Where defendant using his hands, struck victim's head against sidewalk, the sidewalk was used as a "dangerous

instrument" thereby excluding a charge of assault in the third degree as lesser included. People v. Galvin, 65 N.Y.2d 761, 492 N.Y.S.2d 25, 481 N.E.2d 565 (1985).

—Defendant's shoe constituted a dangerous instrument within meaning of section by virtue of manner in which it was used—to kick a fallen victim in elbow, dislocating it and causing severe damage to it. People v. Edwards, 16 A.D.3d 226, 792 N.Y.S.2d 394 (1st Dept. 2005).

—In a case of road rage, evidence that defendant used a car door as a dangerous weapon when he slammed victim's face into the car door and caused injury supported a conviction of second degree. assault People v. Izquierdo, 292 A.D.2d 247, 739 N.Y.S.2d 78 (1st Dept. 2002).

—Wire handle of flyswatter used to strike 5-year-old child on the back over her clothing was capable of causing serious physical injury. People v. Wade, 232 A.D.2d 290, 648 N.Y.S.2d 563 (1st Dept. 1996).

—The People failed to present sufficient evidence to establish pepper spray was a "dangerous instrument." People v. Sinatra, 302 A.D.2d 615, 755 N.Y.S.2d 312 (2d Dept. 2003).

—As no evidence was offered that the stun gun "under the circumstances in which it [was] used, attempted to be used or threatened to be used, [was] readily capable of causing death or other serious physical injury," conviction for first degree robbery should be reversed. People v. Nelson, 292 A.D.2d 397, 738 N.Y.S.2d 603 (2d Dept. 2002). *See also* People v. Maio Ni, 293 A.D.2d 552, 742 N.Y.S.2d 61 (2d Dept. 2002) (conviction for second degree assault reversed where People failed to present sufficient evidence that stun gun was a "dangerous instrument")

—Boots defendant was wearing when he kicked victim in the eye were dangerous instruments. People v. Hansen, 267 A.D.2d 474, 700 N.Y.S.2d 759 (2d Dept. 1999), *appeal denied,* 95 N.Y.2d 797 (2000).

—The jury could have reasonably concluded from evidence that, where defendant smashed victim in the face with a plate and received injuries, the plate was readily capable of causing serious physical injury. People v. Zabala, 290 A.D.2d 578, 735 N.Y.S.2d 244 (3d Dept. 2002).

—Fire in common usage qualifies as a "substance" readily capable of causing death or other serious physical injury within the meaning of PL § 10.00(13) when used to damage a building, regardless of actor's intent or whether the building was occupied; serious risk of harm was created to those called upon to extinguish the fire. Holloway v. Travis, 289 A.D.2d 821, 735 N.Y.S.2d 628 (3d Dept. 2001).

—Broken B.B. gun, not used in any violent capacity in the course of the crime, cannot be characterized as a "dangerous weapon." People v. Espinoza, 253 A.D.2d 983, 680 N.Y.S.2d 122 (3d Dept. 1998).

—Tree limb used by defendant to cause physical injury constituted a deadly weapon or dangerous instrument; defendant used the limb as a club to strike the victim about the face and head, and the victim suffered a broken nose, eye damage, and various contusions and abrasions. People v. Ross, 200 A.D.2d 853, 607 N.Y.S.2d 149 (3d Dept. 1994).

—Where defendant repeatedly punched and kicked the victim into a comatose state, the rubber boots which defendant was wearing at the time were properly found to have been a "dangerous instrument." People v. Carter, 73 A.D.2d 986, 423 N.Y.S.2d 559 (3d Dept. 1980), *aff'd,* 52 N.Y.2d 113, 440 N.Y.S.2d 607, 423 N.E.2d 30 (1981).

—Tire iron that was used to strike victim repeatedly in the head and caused open wounds requiring stitches was a dangerous instrument capable of causing serious physical injury. People v. Saunders, 292 A.D.2d 780, 738 N.Y.S.2d 785 (4th Dept. 2002).

—Either a hammer or a screwdriver can be a dangerous instrument when used in a manner that "is readily capable of causing death or other serious physical injury." People v. Holmes, 9 A.D.3d 689, 780 N.Y.S.2d 96 (3d Dept. 2004).

Subd. 17

Benefit.—"Benefit" is broadly defined "to include any gain or advantage." People v. Reynolds, 174 Misc. 2d 812, 667 N.Y.S.2d 591 (Sup. Ct. N.Y. Co. 1997).

TITLE B—PRINCIPLES OF CRIMINAL LIABILITY

ARTICLE 15—CULPABILITY

LexisNexis Cross Reference

New York Criminal Practice (2d ed.), Vol. 5, Ch. 49, Criminal Liability, Culpability and Capacity.

§ 15.00. Culpability; definitions of terms.

The following definitions are applicable to this chapter:

1. "Act" means a bodily movement.

2. "Voluntary act" means a bodily movement performed consciously as a result of effort or determination, and includes the possession of property if the actor was aware of his physical possession or control thereof for a sufficient period to have been able to terminate it.

3. "Omission" means a failure to perform an act as to which a duty of performance is imposed by law.

4. "Conduct" means an act or omission and its accompanying mental state.

5. "To act" means either to perform an act or to omit to perform an act.

6. "Culpable mental state" means "intentionally" or "knowingly" or "recklessly" or with "criminal negligence," as these terms are defined in section 15.05.

ANNOTATION

Voluntary act; weapons possession.—The corpus delecti of weapons possession is the voluntary, aware act of the possession of a weapon with the additional feature of operability of a firearm; "possession" in this context includes the penal law component of a "voluntary act" which incorporates the attribute of awareness of the possession or control. People v. Saunders, 85 N.Y.2d 339, 624 N.Y.S.2d 568, 648 N.E.2d 1331 (1995).

§ 15.05. Culpability; definitions of culpable mental states.

The following definitions are applicable to this chapter:

1. "Intentionally." A person acts intentionally with respect to a result or to conduct described by a statute defining an offense when his conscious objective is to cause such result or to engage in such conduct.

2. "Knowingly." A person acts knowingly with respect to conduct or to a circumstance described by a statute defining an offense when he is aware that his conduct is of such nature or that such circumstance exists.

3. "Recklessly." A person acts recklessly with respect to a result or to a circumstance described by a statute defining an offense when he is aware of and consciously disregards a substantial and unjustifiable risk that such result will occur or that such circumstance exists. The risk must be of such nature and degree that disregard thereof constitutes a gross deviation from the standard of conduct that a reasonable person would observe in the situation. A person who creates such a risk but is unaware thereof solely by reason of voluntary intoxication also acts recklessly with respect thereto.

4. "Criminal negligence." A person acts with criminal negligence with respect to a result or to a circumstance described by a statute defining an offense when he fails to perceive a substantial and unjustifiable risk that such result will occur or that such circumstance exists. The risk must be of such nature and degree that the failure to perceive it constitutes a gross deviation from the standard of care that a reasonable person would observe in the situation.

ANNOTATIONS

Generally.—A person cannot commit a single homicidal act while entertaining two inconsistent mental states. People v. Tankleff, 199 A.D.2d 550, 606 N.Y.S.2d 707 (2d Dept. 1994).

Knowledge.—The people may prove knowledge circumstantially by conduct or directly by admission or indirectly by contradictory statements from which guilt may be inferred; knowledge may be implied based on all the surrounding circumstances. People v. Cadbury Beverages, Inc., 203 A.D.2d 918, 614 N.Y.S.2d 82 (4th Dept. 1994).

Criminal negligence.—Where defendant's information that the copper-colored flat-topped bullets he loaded into the revolver before pointing and firing it at the victim was third-hand, and defendant did not test them or otherwise verify their nature, his belief that they were blanks and could cause no harm was unreasonable and a gross deviation from the standard of conduct a reasonable person would have observed. Defendant's mistaken belief that the bullets were harmless was not based on a known fact regarding their nature and therefore was not a "factual mistake" which would excuse his conduct. People v. Reynoso, 231 A.D.2d 454, 647 N.Y.S.2d 208 (1st Dept. 1996).

—Evidence was sufficient to try defendant on criminally negligent homicide count where allegations, if accepted as true, established that defendant passed other stopped vehicles to go through a red light that had been red for six seconds in medium to heavy traffic on a highway with three lanes in either direction, without braking or blowing his horn; defendant's conduct clearly constituted a gross deviation from the standard of care that a reasonable person would have observed. People v. Mitchell, 213 A.D.2d 562, 624 N.Y.S.2d 187 (2d Dept. 1995).

—Defendant was guilty of criminally negligent homicide by way of driving while intoxicated was established by evidence defendant and victim had been drinking beer and shots of alcohol for hours, defendant put severely intoxicated victim in back seat of his car and proceeded to drive away and off road, instead of getting assistance for victim in rear of car or allowing others to help, defendant spent over 30 minutes trying to extricate car from ditch, victim died of "Aspiration gastric contents due to Concussion due to Motor vehicle accident Alcoholic intoxication." People v. Prue, 8 A.D.3d 894, 779 N.Y.S.2d 271 (3d Dept. 2004).

—Evidence supported conviction of corporation of criminally negligent homicide and reckless endangerment in the second degree. Executive director of corporation was high managerial agent of corporation whose wrongdoing could form the basis for corporate liability and director failed to obtain valid state inspection of vehicle, failed to conduct any steps to evaluate vehicle's safety which would have revealed unsafe conditions of tires and director permitted youthful driver with little automotive knowledge to operate vehicle. People v. Congregation Khal Chaisidiei, 232 A.D.2d 919, 649 N.Y.S.2d 499 (3d Dept. 1996).

—Criminal negligence is defined as failing to perceive a substantial and unjustifiable risk which is of such a degree that the failure to perceive it constitutes a gross deviation from the standard of care that a reasonable person would observe under the circumstances; some culpable "risk creation" is essential; the defendant must have engaged in some blameworthy conduct creating or contributing to a substantial or unjustifiable risk. People v. Labar, 221 A.D.2d 783, 633 N.Y.S.2d 423 (3d Dept. 1995).

—Defendant's unexplained failure to see the pedestrians that she hit while traveling 10 to 15 miles per hour below the speed limit on a slushy road, even when coupled with evidence that defendant's car drifted onto the shoulder of the road and that she did not apply brakes prior to impact, without more, did not establish that defendant acted with criminal negligence. People v. Maloof, 254 A.D.2d 766, 678 N.Y.S.2d 175 (4th Dept.), app. denied, 92 N.Y.2d 1035, 684 N.Y.S.2d 500, 70 N.E.2d 455 (1998).

Proof of criminal intent.—The intent to commit a crime may be implied by the act itself, or it may be established by the defendant's conduct and the surrounding circumstances. People v. McGee, 204 A.D.2d 353, 611 N.Y.S.2d 261 (2d Dept. 1994).

Recklessness.—In a fatal excavation accident, where reasonable safety precautions were taken to ensure the safety of workers, the proof offered to the grand jury was insufficient to establish the foreseeability of the victim's death; there was no evidence that the defendants "consciously disregard[ed] a substantial and unjustifiable risk" and no recklessness established. People v. Reagan, 94 N.Y.2d 804, 701 N.Y.S.2d 306, 723 N.E.2d 55 (1999).

—Defendant's mistaken belief that bullets he loaded into gun were blanks was based on third hand information and never tested or verified by defendant before he pointed and fired at victim. Defendant's conduct was reckless; he disregarded the possibility that the bullets were live was a gross deviation from the conduct a reasonable person would have observed. People v. Reynoso, 231 A.D.2d 454, 647 N.Y.S.2d 208 (1st Dept. 1996).

—Proof of driving in excess of the speed limit, without more, is insufficient to establish criminal negligence. People v. Paris, 138 A.D.2d 534, 525 N.Y.S.2d 913, 916 (2d Dept. 1988).

—Proof of intoxication may be offered to negate the mens rea element of an intentional crime, but it will not negate the presence of a reckless mental state. People v. Johnson, 277 A.D.2d 702, 717 N.Y.S.2d 668 (3d Dept. 2000), appeal denied, 96 N.Y.2d 831 (2001).

—Recklessness was established where defendant drove at an excessive rate of speed under the influence of marijuana, which he knew dulled the reflexes and minimized his concentration, passed cars in a no-passing lane, acknowledged that he heard his passengers ask him to pull over, but instead elected to continue to speed to avoid the pursuing police car, and lost control of the car, where resulting crash killed two passengers and injured three others. People v. Crandall, 255 A.D.2d 616, 681 N.Y.S.2d 99 (3d Dept. 1998).

—The evidence was sufficient to establish that respondent acted recklessly where petitioner presented proof that respondent struck a teacher when he swung his arm, with a closed fist, intending to deliver a "roundhouse" blow to a fellow student. In re Robert W., 212 A.D.2d 1005, 622 N.Y.S.2d 405 (4th Dept. 1995).

—A person is chargeable with "recklessness" when he is aware of a designated risk and consciously disregards it, while he is only criminally negligent if he fails to perceive the risk. People v. Figueroa, 164 Misc. 2d 814, 625 N.Y.S.2d 839 (Crim. Ct. Kings Co. 1995).

Inference of culpable mental state.—Defendant held criminally liable for death of police officer who fell to his death while pursuing defendant across darkened roof, even though defendant did not actually push the officer to his death. People v. Matos, 150 Misc. 2d 499, 568 N.Y.S.2d 683 (Sup. Ct. N.Y. Co. 1991).

Evidence.—A conviction for manslaughter in the second degree may be sustained by evidence that the defendant was driving northbound in a southbound lane, passed several cars going in the opposite direction and when she stopped at the last intersection before the crash two cars faced hers, one of which was directly in front of her since the jury could infer that she was aware of the risk or unaware of it solely by reason of impairment of her judgment due to the consumption of alcohol. People v. Schaffer, 80 A.D.2d 865, 436 N.Y.S.2d 749 (2d Dept. 1981).

Failure to perceive risk.—It was proper for the court to charge criminally negligent homicide as a lesser included offense of manslaughter in the second degree since the jury could have reasonably found that the defendant did not perceive the risk that the victim would be killed; the record indicated that defendant drew his gun to coerce the victim to give up his weapon and to scare him and, in addition, that the defendant was somewhat intoxicated when he aimed and cocked the gun. People v. Murphy, 88 A.D.2d 1000, 451 N.Y.S.2d 838 (2d Dept. 1982).

Intentional Murder.—Evidence that defendant walked up to victim and fired point blank ten times did not support depraved indifference murder, it only supported a charge of intentional murder, error to submit to depraved indifference to jury. People v. Gonzales, 1 N.Y.3d 464, 775 N.Y.S.2d 224, 807 N.E.2d 273 (2004).

§ 15.10. Requirements for criminal liability in general and for offenses of strict liability and mental culpability.

The minimal requirement for criminal liability is the performance by a person of conduct which includes a voluntary act or the omission to perform an act which he is physically capable of performing. If such conduct is all that is required for commission of a particular offense, or if an offense or some material element thereof does not require a culpable mental state on the part of the actor, such offense is one of "strict liability." If a culpable mental state on the part of the actor is required with respect to every material element of an offense, such offense is one of "mental culpability."

§ 15.15. Construction of statutes with respect to culpability requirements.

1. When the commission of an offense defined in this chapter, or some element of an offense, requires a particular culpable mental state, such mental state is ordinarily designated in the statute defining the offense by use of the terms "intentionally," "knowingly," "recklessly" or "criminal negligence," or by use of terms, such as "with intent to defraud" and "knowing it to be false," describing a specific kind of intent or knowledge. When one and only one of such terms appears in a statute defining an offense, it is presumed to apply to every element of the offense unless an intent to limit its application clearly appears.

2. Although no culpable mental state is expressly designated in a statute defining an offense, a culpable mental state may nevertheless be required for the commission of such offense, or with respect to some or all of the material elements thereof, if the proscribed conduct necessarily involves such culpable mental state. A statute defining a crime, unless clearly indicating a legislative intent to impose strict liability, should be construed as defining a crime of mental culpability. This subdivision applies to offenses defined both in and outside this chapter.

ANNOTATIONS

Strict liability.—There is no bar to a criminal prosecution of attempted robbery in the first degree; because strict liability attaches to an aggravating circumstance rather than the proscribed result, a robber charged with attempted robbery in the first degree is not being punished for an unintended criminal act. People v. Miller, 87 N.Y.2d 211, 638 N.Y.S.2d 577, 661 N.E.2d 1358 (1995).

Culpable mental state; inference from facts.—Where defendant was a bailee in charge of the care of a horse, and neglected to feed it adequately, he could be found guilty of the misdemeanor of failure to provide proper sustenance for an animal in his care (Section 353 of the Agriculture and Market Law), and the culpable mental state required for conviction could be inferred from the fact that he knew the diet was inadequate yet failed to provide more or to return the horse to the bailors. People v. Aridicano, 75 Misc. 2d 294, 347 N.Y.S.2d 850 (Dist. Ct. Suffolk Co. 1973), aff'd, 79 Misc. 2d 242, 360 N.Y.S.2d 156 (Sup Ct, App. Term, 9th and 10th Jud. Dists. 1974).

§ 15.20. Effect of ignorance or mistake upon liability.

1. A person is not relieved of criminal liability for conduct because he engages in such conduct under a mistaken belief of fact, unless:

(a) Such factual mistake negatives the culpable mental state required for the commission of an offense; or

(b) The statute defining the offense or a statute related thereto expressly provides that such factual mistake constitutes a defense or exemption; or

(c) Such factual mistake is of a kind that supports a defense of justification as defined in article thirty-five of this chapter.

2. A person is not relieved of criminal liability for conduct because he engages in such conduct under a mistaken belief that it does not, as a matter of law, constitute an offense, unless such mistaken belief is founded upon an official statement of the law contained in (a) a statute or other enactment, or (b) an administrative order or grant of permission, or (c) a judicial decision of a state or federal court, or (d) an interpretation of the statute or law relating to the offense, officially made or issued by a public servant, agency or body legally charged or empowered with the responsibility or privilege of administering, enforcing or interpreting such statute or law.

3. Notwithstanding the use of the term "knowingly" in any provision of this chapter defining an offense in which the age of a child is an element thereof, knowledge by the defendant of the age of such child is not an element of any such offense and it is not, unless expressly so provided, a defense to a prosecution therefor that the defendant did not know the age of the child or believed such age to be the same as or greater than that specified in the statute.

4. Notwithstanding the use of the term "knowingly" in any provision of this chapter defining an offense in which the aggregate weight of a controlled substance or marihuana is an element, knowledge by the defendant of the aggregate weight of such controlled substance or marihuana is not an element of any such offense and it is not, unless expressly so provided, a defense to a prosecution therefor that the defendant did not know the aggregate weight of the controlled substance or marihuana.

Amended by L. 1995, Ch. 75, § 19, adding subd. 4, eff. June 10, 1995, and offenses committed before that date will be governed by laws in effect at the time the offenses were committed, pursuant to L. 1995, Ch. 75, § 20.

ANNOTATIONS

Knowledge of age; sale to person under 18 years of age.—When the term "knowingly" appears in a section in which the age of a child is an element, knowledge of such age is not an element of the offense and the defendant may not assert a lack thereof as a defense (PL § 15.20(3)). People v. Wenzel, 77 A.D.2d 715, 430 N.Y.S.2d 431 (3d Dept. 1980).

Mistaken belief.—Where defendant's information that the copper-colored flat-topped bullets he loaded into the revolver before pointing and firing it at the victim was third-hand, and defendant did not test them or otherwise verify their nature, his belief that they were blanks and could cause no harm was unreasonable and a gross deviation from the standard of conduct a reasonable person would have observed. Defendant's mistaken belief that the bullets were harmless was not based on a known fact regarding their nature and therefore was not a "factual mistake" which would excuse his conduct. People v. Reynoso, 231 A.D.2d 454, 647 N.Y.S.2d 208 (1st Dept. 1996).

—Defendant was not entitled to mistake of fact charge, even though he claimed he did not know the men chasing him were police officers, where defendant broke into the victim's home unlawfully and grabbed and held a child in an attempt to avoid the men chasing him. People v. Gibbs, 245 A.D.2d 1124, 666 N.Y.S.2d 530 (4th Dept. 1997).

§ 15.25. Effect of intoxication upon liability.

Intoxication is not, as such, a defense to a

criminal charge; but in any prosecution for an offense, evidence of intoxication of the defendant may be offered by the defendant whenever it is relevant to negative an element of the crime charged.

ANNOTATIONS

Charge.—Intoxication instruction to jury was not warranted where "evidence of intoxication is so minimal that no reasonable person would have entertained a doubt as to the element of intent on that basis." People v. Salco, 302 A.D.2d 613, 755 N.Y.S.2d 309 (2d Dept. 2003).

—In a prosecution for murder in the second degree and manslaughter in the first degree, after intoxication had been raised by the defense, it was reversible error for the court in its charge to merely read Pen. Law 15.25 to the jury with little elaboration. People v. Lawrence, 78 A.D.2d 702, 432 N.Y.S.2d 508 (2d Dept. 1980).

—Rejecting defendant's argument that court erred in submitting to the jury the charge of arson in the fourth degree because, if at all, defendant intentionally started fire: evidence of defendant's intoxication was sufficient to negate the element of intent and permit a finding of recklessness, leaving to the jury the factual question of whether the extent of intoxication acted to negate the element of intent. People v. Borst, 232 A.D.2d 727, 648 N.Y.S.2d 720 (3d Dept. 1996).

—Where evidence of intoxication was not limited to negating only the element of intent, but relevant to defendant's knowing possession of a firearm and that the firearm was loaded, jury should have received a charge on issue of intoxication. People v. Ressler, 302 A.D.2d 921, 754 N.Y.S.2d 485 (4th Dept. 2003).

—Court properly declined to charge jury on intoxication to negate element of intent where the record contained no evidence of the number of alcoholic beverages defendant consumed over what period of time, and the resulting effect that may have had on him; evidence that defendant appeared to be passed out in the rear of the patrol car was not enough to warrant charge to jury. People v. Hill, 255 A.D.2d 969, 681 N.Y.S.2d 919 (4th Dept. 1998).

—Court properly refused intoxication charge where defendant testified that although he had consumed alcoholic beverages on the night in question he was not intoxicated, and the record was devoid of evidence that at the time defendant committed the rape, drugs or alcohol affected his behavior. People v. Brown, 226 A.D.2d 1108, 642 N.Y.S.2d 145 (4th Dept. 1996).

Effect of intoxication on confession.—The record did not support the defendant's assertion that his degree of intoxication impaired his ability to give a knowing and intelligent waiver of his *Miranda* rights where although the detective to whom the waiver had been given thought that the defendant had been drinking, defendant denied any complicity in the holdup, refused to sign a statement, and did not make inculpatory statements until he was informed he would be put in a lineup. People v. Nolan, 75 A.D.2d 828, 427 N.Y.S.2d 467 (2d Dept. 1980).

Effect of intoxication on plea.—Court was not required to advise defendant of effect of intoxication on criminal liability where defendant's plea was knowing and voluntary, and his allocution sufficiently established that his mental state during the course of his criminal conduct was unaffected by the intoxication. People v. Wheeler, 251 A.D.2d 86, 672 N.Y.S.2d 728 (1st Dept. 1998).

Evidentiary hearing.—When defendant sought to withdraw his guilty plea, an evidentiary hearing was required to determine if the defendant, as claimed, was intoxicated at the time the crime was committed since intent was an essential element of the crime of coercion, first degree, and there was nothing of an evidentiary nature in the People's opposition papers that refuted defendant's claim of innocence because of lack of intent. People v. Parizo, 78 A.D.2d 863, 432 N.Y.S.2d 627 (2d Dept. 1980).

Grand jury instructions.—A grand jury must be instructed as to exculpatory defenses that may result in avoiding an unwarranted prosecution; however, it need not be instructed in the case of a mitigating defense, such as intoxication, which only reduces the severity of an offense by negating an element of that offense. People v. Harris, 98 N.Y.2d 452, 749 N.Y.S.2d 766, 779 N.E.2d 705 (2002).

Intent.—Where the evidence of the specific intake of alcohol by defendant was meager but there was ample evidence that large quantities of alcoholic beverages had been disposed of by the male participants at the party prior to the homicide, the defendant was entitled to a charge on the potential effect of intoxication upon intent. People v. Costello, 73 A.D.2d 901, 424 N.Y.S.2d 215 (1st Dept. 1980).

—Intoxication alone is not a complete defense to a crime of intent, an intoxicated person can form the requisite criminal intent to commit a crime, and it is a jury question as to whether the extent of the intoxication acted to negate the element of intent. People v. Gonzalez, 6 A.D.3d 457, 773 N.Y.S.2d 889 (2d Dept. 2004).

—Whether a defendant was so intoxicated as to be unable to form the requisite intent for a given crime presents a question of fact for the jury to resolve. People v. Goodman, 152 A.D.2d 705, 544 N.Y.S.2d 163 (2d Dept. 1989).

—Testimony that defendant was often in an intoxicated condition in the past is not admissible to show that he was intoxicated at the time of the incident. People v. Westergard, 113 A.D.2d 640, 497 N.Y.S.2d 65 (2d Dept. 1985).

—Proof of intoxication may be offered to negate the mens rea element of an intentional crime, but it will not negate the presence of a reckless mental state. People v. Johnson, 277 A.D.2d 702, 717 N.Y.S.2d 668 (3d Dept. 2000), *appeal denied,* 96 N.Y.2d 831 (2001).

—There was insufficient basis to allow the jury to conclude that the defendant was too intoxicated to formulate specific intent where the only evidence of the defendant's intoxication was his own testimony that, at the time of the burglary, he had been on a two-day drinking spree and was unable to recall whether he was in the victim's apartment. People v. Enderle, 114 A.D.2d 693, 494 N.Y.S.2d 555 (3d Dept. 1985).

PL

ARTICLE 20—PARTIES TO OFFENSES AND LIABILITY THROUGH ACCESSORIAL CONDUCT

Section
20.00 Criminal liability for conduct of another.
20.05 Criminal liability for conduct of another; no defense.
20.10 Criminal liability for conduct of another; exemption.
20.15 Convictions for different degrees of offense.
20.20 Criminal liability of corporations.
20.25 Criminal liability of an individual for corporate conduct.

LexisNexis Cross Reference

New York Criminal Practice (2d ed.), Vol. 5, Ch. 51, Acting in Concert and Other Issues of Joint liability, Vol. 7, Ch. 68, Fraudulent Schemes and Loansharking.

§ 20.00. Criminal liability for conduct of another.

When one person engages in conduct which constitutes an offense, another person is criminally liable for such conduct when, acting with the mental culpability required for the commission thereof, he solicits, requests, commands, importunes, or intentionally aids such person to engage in such conduct.

ANNOTATIONS

Acting in concert.—It is not necessary to prove that the defendant fired the fatal shot if the evidence is sufficient to establish that the defendant was acting in concert with another who did fire the fatal shot and that the defendant was acting with the mental culpability required for the commission of the crime. People v. Boyd, 164 A.D.2d 800, 560 N.Y.S.2d 15 (1st Dept. 1990).

Accessorial liability.—Accessorial liability for first degree felony murder, PL § 125.27(1)(a)(vii), available only when theory proved by prosecution is that defendant commanded the killing, the defendant "need not commit the final, fatal act to be culpable for causing death." People v. Mateo, 2 N.Y.3d 383, 779 N.Y.S.2d 399, 811 N.E.2d 1053, *cert. denied,* 542 U.S. 946 (2004).

—Accessorial liability is not limited for the other 12 subdivisions of the first degree murder statute, only for first degree murder. People v. Cahill, 2 N.Y.3d 14, 777 N.Y.S.2d 332, 809 N.E.2d 561 (2003).

—The word "commands," as used in the statute to establish accomplice liability, is not impermissibly vague, and charge for first degree murder based upon defendant's command of a fellow gang member to kill a material witness was proper. People v. Couser, 94 N.Y.2d 631, 709 N.Y.S.2d 155, 730 N.E.2d 953 (2000).

—Where three defendants accepted each other's challenge, and all participated in a gun battle during which an innocent bystander was killed, court properly charged jury with accomplice liability in the depraved indifference murder of the victim. The fact that ballistic test on the fatal bullet was inconclusive, and the shooter among the three defendants was never identified, was irrelevant. People v. Russell, 91 N.Y.2d 280, 670 N.Y.S.2d 166, 693 N.E.2d 193 (1998).

—Court's charge to the jury, which included the instruction that acting in concert liability requires acting with the mental culpability required for the commission of the crime charged, was sufficient to protect the defendant from being found guilty of felony murder and robbery without first establishing that defendant had the requisite intent to commit robbery. People v. Slacks, 90 N.Y.2d 850, 660 N.Y.S.2d 863, 683 N.E.2d 769 (1997).

—The trial court did not err in permitting the prosecutor to pursue an accessorial liability theory at trial where the indictment charged the defendant only as the principal actor; "the key to understanding accessorial liability is that whether one is the actual perpetrator of the offense or an accomplice is, with respect to criminal liability for the offense, irrelevant." (Citations omitted). People v. Rivera, 84 N.Y.2d 766, 622 N.Y.S.2d 671, 646 N.E.2d 1098 (1995).

—Proof of defendant's role as a look out in a robbery is sufficient to establish accessorial liability. People v. Coulter, 240 A.D.2d 756, 660 N.Y.S.2d 43 (2d Dept. 1997).

—Clause in PL § 125.27(1)(a), which provides that PL § 20.00 is not applicable to that degree of felony murder "unless the defendant's criminal liability . . . is based upon the defendant having commanded another person to cause the death of the victim or intended victim," is not unconstitutionally vague. People v. Couser, 258 A.D.2d 74, 695 N.Y.S.2d 781 (4th Dept. 1999), *aff'd,* 94 N.Y.2d 631, 709 N.Y.S.2d 155, 730 N.E.2d 953 (2000).

—Whether the defendant acted as the principal perpetrator or as an accomplice is irrelevant with respect to his criminal liability as charged in the indictment. People v. Bell, 162 A.D.2d 989, 557 N.Y.S.2d 784 (4th Dept. 1990).

—The fact that an indictment accuses a defendant as a principal does not preclude his conviction as an accessory and a charge based on accessorial conduct is not grounds for reversal. People v. Kimbrough, 155 A.D.2d 933, 547 N.Y.S.2d 756 (4th Dept. 1989).

—Where defendant instigated the drag race, which resulted in fatal crash, conviction for manslaughter affirmed, that decedent voluntarily participated in drag race, and no evidence that defendant's car came into contact with the decedent's car nor forced it into oncoming traffic, not relevant for criminal responsibility to attach; a defendant's actions must have been an actual contributory cause of death, that defendant set in motion the events which ultimately result in the victim's death but, defendant's acts need not be the sole cause of death, and defendant need not commit final fatal act. People v. Hart, 8 A.D.3d 402, 778 N.Y.S.2d 94 (2d Dept. 2004).

Evidence.—Evidence was legally sufficient to establish accessorial liability; facts that defendant knew of the shooter's plan, rode with the shooter to the scene, accepted the murder weapon from the shooter and secreted it on his body, and left with the shooter established "community of purpose." People v. Carter, 293 A.D.2d 484, 741 N.Y.S.2d 546 (2d Dept. 2002).

—Although there was no testimony that the defendant helped or encouraged a co-defendant, who assaulted and robbed the victim, evidence that the defendant stood directly behind the victim during the incident, thus discouraging escape or resistance, was sufficient to establish accessorial conduct such that the defendant was liable for the co-defendant's conduct. People v. Dorsey, 112 A.D.2d 536, 491 N.Y.S.2d 473 (3d Dept. 1985).

Accomplice.—Where "defendant's guilt is premised upon a theory of accomplice liability . . . defendant can be guilty of depraved indifference murder only if he intentionally aided co-defendant in commission of the crime and shared the co-defendant's culpable mental state." People v. Hafeez, 100 N.Y.2d 253, 762 N.Y.S.2d 572, 792 N.E.2d 1060 (2003).

—A witness may be an accomplice for corroboration purposes even though such witness is not criminally liable for the offense being tried, an accomplice witness must however "be in some manner implicated in, and possibly subject to, prosecution for the general conduct or factual transaction on trial." People v. Caban, 4 A.D.3d 274, 772 N.Y.S.2d 675 (1st Dept. 2004), aff'd, 5 N.Y.3d 143, 800 N.Y.S.2d 70, 833 N.E.2d 213 (2005).

—People established that defendant intentionally aided his co-defendant in the sale of drugs when defendant, in response to undercover officer's question as to whether anyone was working, replied, "Yeah. My boy right here will hook you up." Defendant then directed the officer to his co-defendant standing 15 feet away where the undercover officer then purchased drugs. People v. Johnson, 238 A.D.2d 267, 657 N.Y.S.2d 27 (1st Dept. 1997).

—Even though a defendant may not have physical possession of the drugs, evidence that he was an accomplice to a coperpetrator who did have possession of the drugs is legally sufficient to uphold a conviction of criminal possession of a controlled substance. People v. Dean, 200 A.D.2d 582, 606 N.Y.S.2d 290 (2d Dept. 1994).

—The question of whether a particular person is an accomplice is a question of fact for the jury where different inferences can be reasonably drawn from the evidence produced at trial. People v. Jeffries, 122 A.D.2d 281, 504 N.Y.S.2d 781 (2d Dept. 1986).

—Though witness made false statements to police, was present while evidence of the murder was destroyed, and actually participated in the destruction of the evidence by removing the license plate from the car in which the victim was abducted and driven to the scene of the crime, he was not an accomplice to the murder for he was not implicated in the murder itself. People v. Vataj, 121 A.D.2d 756, 504 N.Y.S.2d 677 (2d Dept. 1986).

—Witness' act of dropping a machete or butcher knife down to the boys involved in the fight, which resulted in the victim's death by shooting, did not make her an accomplice and require corroboration of her testimony. People v. Maldanado, 123 A.D.2d 788, 507 N.Y.S.2d 415 (2d Dept. 1986).

—Defendant's assertion of the affirmative defense of extreme emotional disturbance will not insulate him from culpability under an aider and abettor theory of liability. People v. Motter, 235 A.D.2d 582, 653 N.Y.S.2d 378 (3d Dept. 1997).

—Conviction of robbery in the second degree upheld where there was proof that defendant lured victim to apartment and co-defendant forcibly removed jewelry and stole money from the victim. Although co-defendant may have demanded victim's money and jewelry, defendant was present and in a position to aid in the forcible taking of the victim's property. People v. Brown, 232 A.D.2d 750, 649 N.Y.S.2d 51 (3d Dept. 1996).

Charge.—The trial judge committed error when, in a trial in which defendant was charged with first and second degree riot and with first and second degree unlawful imprisonment, he read PL 20.00 to the jury, but refused to instruct them, as required by PL 20.15, that the degree of guilt is determined by the mental state of the defendant and each defendant's individual accountability for an aggravating fact or circumstance. People v. Castro, 55 N.Y.2d 972, 449 N.Y.S.2d 184, 434 N.E.2d 253 (1982).

—Trial court's charge, which essentially qyoted PL § 20.00, properly instructed jury on standard for accessorial liability. People v. Leach, 293 A.D.2d 760, 741 N.Y.S.2d 443 (2d Dept. 2002).

—Trial court committed reversible error with regard to the issue of accessorial liability when it failed to instruct the jury to consider the evidence of guilt or innocence separately as to each defendant, and improperly charged the jury by failing to indicate that each defendant had to act with the mental culpability required for the commission of each crime. People v. Ortiz, 107 A.D.2d 824, 484 N.Y.S.2d 661 (2d Dept. 1985).

Drug possession.—The fact that neither the prerecorded buy money nor drugs were found on defendant did not negate her accessorial liability under Penal Law 20.00. People v. Davis 202 A.D.2d 325, 609 N.Y.S.2d 212 (1st Dept. 1994).

—That a passenger in the car pleaded guilty to possession of the heroin found in the car did not preclude a finding that the defendant and the passenger possessed the heroin jointly. People v. Lovett, 200 A.D.2d 421, 606 N.Y.S.2d 218 (1st Dept. 1994).

Intent.—Evidence presented established that defendant, half owner of the business that was destroyed by arson, had the requisite mens rea for each element of the arson to support a conviction under accessorial liability. People v. Grassi, 92 N.Y.2d 695, 708 N.E.2d 976, 685 N.Y.S.2d 903 (1999).

—It is not required that a defendant personally possess and use a weapon in the course of a robbery; here, the evidence clearly established that the defendant intentionally aided others who seized one victim's gun and used it against both victims in stealing property. People v. Rivera, 221 A.D.2d 193, 633 N.Y.S.2d 166 (1st Dept. 1995).

—Accessorial liability requires that the defendant have the mental culpability required for the crimes charged and that the conduct was knowing and intentional. People v. Latchman, 251 A.D.2d 683, 676 N.Y.S.2d 471 (2d Dept. 1998).

—An accessory is required to share the intent of the principal actor in order to be held liable for the crime. People v. Tomasello, 189 A.D.2d 903, 593 N.Y.S.2d 65 (2d Dept. 1993).

—The defendant's acts of holding closed and then releasing the door to the booth while one of his accomplices displayed what appeared to be a gun, amply supported the finding that the defendant aided his cohort and that he shared the intent to commit a robbery. People v. Suarez, 157 A.D.2d 757, 550 N.Y.S.2d 50 (2d Dept. 1990).

—In order to hold an accessory criminally liable for acts committed by his principal, the people must establish, beyond a reasonable doubt, that the accessory possessed the requisite mental culpability for the crime charged. People v. Hayes, 117 A.D.2d 621, 498 N.Y.S.2d 163 (2d Dept. 1986).

—Defendant's allocution did not establish the mental culpability necessary to satisfy robbery in the first degree since defendant stated that he thought his co-defendants, who entered the house, while he remained outside, went to complete a drug transaction; he did not know they intended to rob the victim. People v. Ocasio, 265 A.D.2d 675, 697 N.Y.S.2d 368 (3d Dept. 1999).

—Defendant's robbery, assault, and criminal mischief convictions were supported by evidence that defendant participated in the robbery and assault of victims as part of a group as well as by evidence that he alone assaulted one victim with the intent to steal property. People v. Morris, 267 A.D.2d 1032, 700 N.Y.S.2d 897 (4th Dept. 1999), appeal denied, 96 N.Y.2d 800 (2000).

—Defendant observed a larceny in progress and while asportation of the goods was continuing, assisted the perpetrator in completing the larceny; the jury could reasonably have inferred that, by reason of his conduct, defendant had the requisite intent to commit a larceny. People v. Farmer, 156 A.D.2d 1003, 549 N.Y.S.2d 288 (4th Dept. 1989).

Culpability.—An order adjudging the respondent a juvenile delinquent for, inter alia, acting in concert with his companions was reversed where the court found that even if one of the respondent's companions had committed the criminal act (throwing a bottle), there was no evidence that the respondent shared the mental culpability of his companions or solicited, commanded, requested, importuned, or intentionally aided his companion to throw the bottle. In re Paris M., 218 A.D.2d 554, 630 N.Y.S.2d 732 (1st Dept. 1995).

—Defendant's conviction for criminal possession of a weapon affirmed; the evidence clearly established that the defendant possessed the mental culpability necessary to commit the crime charged (i.e., to possess a gun and use it unlawfully against another) and that he intentionally aided his accomplices in furtherance of that crime. People v. Breeden, 220 A.D.2d 761, 632 N.Y.S.2d 849 (2d Dept. 1995).

—In order to hold an individual liable for the conduct of another, the prosecution must show that the individual acted with the mental culpability required to commit the crimes charged. In re Joseph J., 205 A.D.2d 777, 614 N.Y.S.2d 39 (2d Dept. 1994).

§ 20.05. Criminal liability for conduct of another; no defense.

In any prosecution for an offense in which the

criminal liability of the defendant is based upon the conduct of another person pursuant to section 20.00, it is no defense that:

1. Such other person is not guilty of the offense in question owing to criminal irresponsibility or other legal incapacity or exemption, or to unawareness of the criminal nature of the conduct in question or of the defendant's criminal purpose or to other factors precluding the mental state required for the commission of the offense in question; or

2. Such other person has not been prosecuted for or convicted of any offense based upon the conduct in question, or has previously been acquitted thereof, or has legal immunity from prosecution therefor; or

3. The offense in question, as defined, can be committed only by a particular class or classes of persons, and the defendant, not belonging to such class or classes, is for that reason legally incapable of committing the offense in an individual capacity.

ANNOTATION

Offering false instrument for filing.—The crime of offering a false instrument for filing may be accomplished through an intermediary; however, the guilty part must, at a minimum, contemplate or understand that a writing of some sort will be involved. People v. Shu, 216 A.D.2d 46, 627 N.Y.S.2d 657 (1st Dept. 1995).

§ 20.10. Criminal liability for conduct of another; exemption.

Notwithstanding the provisions of sections 20.00 and 20.05, a person is not criminally liable for conduct of another person constituting an offense when his own conduct, though causing or aiding the commission of such offense, is of a kind that is necessarily incidental thereto. If such conduct constitutes a related but separate offense upon the part of the actor, he is liable for that offense only and not for the conduct or offense committed by the other person.

§ 20.15. Convictions for different degrees of offense.

Except as otherwise expressly provided in this chapter, when, pursuant to section 20.00, two or more persons are criminally liable for an offense which is divided into degrees, each person is guilty of such degree as is compatible with his own culpable mental state and with his own accountability for an aggravating fact or circumstance.

§ 20.20. Criminal liability of corporations.

1. As used in this section:

(a) "Agent" means any director, officer or employee of a corporation, or any other person who is authorized to act in behalf of the corporation.

(b) "High managerial agent" means an officer of a corporation or any other agent in a position of comparable authority with respect to the formulation of corporate policy or the supervision in a managerial capacity of subordinate employees.

2. A corporation is guilty of an offense when:

(a) The conduct constituting the offense consists of an omission to discharge a specific duty of affirmative performance imposed on corporations by law; or

(b) The conduct constituting the offense is engaged in, authorized, solicited, requested, commanded, or recklessly tolerated by the board of directors or by a high managerial agent acting within the scope of his employment and in behalf of the corporation; or

(c) The conduct constituting the offense is engaged in by an agent of the corporation while acting within the scope of his employment and in behalf of the corporation, and the offense is (i) a misdemeanor or a violation, (ii) one defined by a statute which clearly indicates a legislative intent to impose such criminal liability on a corporation or (iii) any offense set forth in title twenty-seven of article seventy-one of the environmental conservation law.

Amended by L. 1981, Ch. 719; L. 1986, Ch. 671.

ANNOTATION

High managerial agent.—Evidence supported conviction of corporation of criminally negligent homicide and reckless endangerment in the second degree. Executive director of corporation was high managerial agent of corporation whose wrongdoing could form basis for criminal liability of corporation and director failed to obtain valid state inspection of vehicle, failed to conduct any steps to evaluate vehicle's safety which would have revealed unsafe conditions of tires, and permitted youthful driver with little automotive knowledge to operate vehicle. People v. Congregation Khal Chaisidiei, 232 A.D.2d 919, 649 N.Y.S.2d 499 (3d Dept. 1996).

§ 20.25. Criminal liability of an individual for corporate conduct.

A person is criminally liable for conduct constituting an offense which he performs or causes to be performed in the name of or in behalf of a corporation to the same extent as if such conduct were performed in his own name or behalf.

ANNOTATIONS

Issuing a bad check; Penal Law § 190.05.—Defendant was criminally responsible under Penal Law § 20.25 for acts of drawer corporation because he caused the check to be issued in the name of the corporation. People v. Dean, 48 A.D.2d 223, 368 N.Y.S.2d 349 (4th Dept. 1975).

Purpose.—This section eliminates the possibility that a culpable defendant might evade criminal responsibility simply because he was acting in a corporate capacity or in the interests of a corporation; the corporate veil can be pierced, if appropriate, in criminal as well as civil cases. People v. Aquarian Age 2000 Inc., 85 Misc. 2d 504, 380 N.Y.S.2d 545 (Sup. Ct. Queens Co. 1976).

TITLE C—DEFENSES

ARTICLE 25—DEFENSES IN GENERAL

Section
25.00   Defenses; burden of proof.

LexisNexis Cross References

Defense of Narcotics Cases, Vol. 3, Ch. 13, Drug-Induced Intoxication as a Defense to Criminal Liability; *New York Criminal Practice (2d ed.),* Vol. 5, Ch. 52, General Defenses.

§ 25.00. Defenses; burden of proof.

1. When a "defense," other than an "affirmative defense," defined by statute is raised at a trial, the people have the burden of disproving such defense beyond a reasonable doubt.

2. When a defense declared by statute to be an "affirmative defense" is raised at a trial, the defendant has the burden of establishing such defense by a preponderance of the evidence.

ANNOTATIONS

Alibi.—Defendant's conviction was reversed where the trial judge erroneously charged that the jurors must be satisfied as to the truth of the alibi and it was their duty to determine whether or not the alibi could be believed, as the People have the burden to disprove the alibi defense. People v. Acevedo, 83 A.D.2d 813, 442 N.Y.S.2d 56 (1st Dept. 1981).

—While a defendant may, in attempting to establish an affirmative defense, rely upon the prosecution's evidence, the components of a statutory defense are peculiarly within the knowledge of the defendant and are matters upon which he may be fairly required to adduce supporting evidence. People v. Jackson, 208 A.D.2d 862, 618 N.Y.S.2d 57 (2d Dept. 1994).

—Alibi testimony does not have to show that it would have been impossible for the defendant to have committed the crime and need not cover the whole time of the transaction in question; to support an alibi charge it is enough that it renders guilt merely improbable. People v. Wiley, 120 A.D.2d 66, 507 N.Y.S.2d 928 (4th Dept. 1986).

Charge; burden of proof.—Reversal was required where the court failed to instruct the jury that it was the burden of the People to disapprove the defense beyond a reasonable doubt. People v. Lediard, 80 A.D.2d 237, 438 N.Y.S.2d 540 (1st Dept. 1981).

—Trial court erred, where defendant presented an alibi, by failing to charge that the People have the burden of disproving the alibi beyond a reasonable doubt and by charging the jury that they must carefully scrutinize alibi testimony but failing to give similar instructions with respect to the identification testimony. People v. Chestnut, 99 A.D.2d 515, 470 N.Y.S.2d 685 (2d Dept. 1984).

Duress.—The appellate court rejected the defendant's contention that the indictment should be dismissed because the prosecutor failed to present to the grand jury, in its entirety, a videotaped confession containing statements that supported the defendant's affirmative defense of duress. The prosecutor had no duty to present the entire videotaped statement merely because it contained statements that could be construed to support the affirmative defense of duress; the prosecutor met or exceeded his obligations by eliciting a summary of the videotape from a police witness and by delivering a duress charge. People v. Black, 220 A.D.2d 604, 632 N.Y.S.2d 823 (2d Dept. 1995).

—Threats and violence emanating from the person to the defendant after the incident were irrelevant to the duress defense because they could not have affected defendant's mind set at the time of the crime. People v. Cornwell, 160 A.D.2d 1175, 555 N.Y.S.2d 188 (3d Dept. 1990).

Entrapment.—Whether defendant met his burden of establishing the affirmative defense of entrapment was a question of fact for the jury. People v. Beach, 188 A.D.2d 1079, 592 N.Y.S.2d 184 (4th Dept. 1992).

Extreme emotional disturbance.—Affirmative defense of extreme emotional disturbance can be charged only if evidence presented contained requisite proof to establish the defense; to charge the jury regardless of evidence adduced at trial would encourage impermissible speculation by the jury. People v. Roche, 98 N.Y.2d 70, 745 N.Y.S.2d 775, 772 N.E.2d 1133 (2002).

—Defendant's assertion that he "acted under the influence of extreme emotional disturbance for which there was a reasonable explanation or excuse" was not an affirmative defense to second degree murder. People v. Morrison, 95 A.D.2d 868, 464 N.Y.S.2d 245 (3d Dept. 1983).

Inconsistent defenses.—Where the facts supporting the defense of agency were adduced during the People's case, the defendant's assertion of the inconsistent defense of alibi did not preclude him from requesting a charge on the defense of agency. People v. Cierzniewski, 141 A.D.2d 828, 529 N.Y.S.2d 886 (2d Dept. 1988).

Infancy.—If infancy defense raised at trial, People must disprove it by reasonable doubt. People v. Holmes, 220 A.D.2d 109, 645 N.Y.S.2d 115 (3d Dept. 1996).

Intoxication.—Intoxication is not a defense but merely a matter to be considered by the fact-finder in determining whether it negates an element of the crime charged. People v. Mercado, 200 A.D.2d 424, 606 N.Y.S.2d 223 (1st Dept. 1994).

—The general rule is that an intoxicated person may form the required intent to commit a crime, and it is for the jury to decide if the extent of the intoxication acted to negate the element of intent. People v. Dorst, 194 A.D.2d 622, 598 N.Y.S.2d 800 (2d Dept. 1993).

—Whether a defendant is so intoxicated as to be unable to form the requisite intent for a given crime presents a question of fact for the trier of fact. People v. Robinson, 161 A.D.2d 676, 555 N.Y.S.2d 448 (2d Dept. 1990).

—Defendant's allegation that he was intoxicated at the time of the offense did not constitute a defense to the crime of sodomy in the first degree based upon an act of deviate sexual intercourse with a person under the age of 11, since intent is not an element thereof. People v. Washington, 156 A.D.2d 496, 548 N.Y.S.2d 771 (2d Dept. 1989).

—Intent as an element of the crime is an issue to be decided by the trier of fact; intoxication does not automatically negate specific intent for it is merely a factor to be considered by the fact finder. People v. Piscitelli, 156 A.D.2d 596, 549 N.Y.S.2d 104 (2d Dept. 1989).

—The mental element of recklessness in depraved indifference murder cannot be negated by evidence of intoxication. People v. Zebrowski, 198 A.D.2d 716, 604 N.Y.S.2d 622 (3d Dept. 1993).

—Intoxication is not a defense to criminality; although it may be offered to negate an element of a charged crime, because the issue of whether one's conduct occurred under circumstances evidencing a depraved indifference to human life is not an element in the traditional sense but rather a definition of the factual setting in which the risk creating conduct must occur, it is well established that depraved indifference cannot be negated by evidence of a defendant's intoxication. People v. Ward, 192 A.D.2d 880, 597 N.Y.S.2d 178 (3d Dept. 1993).

Justification.—Viewing the evidence in the light most favorable to the prosecution, it was legally sufficient to disprove the defense of justification beyond a reasonable doubt. People v. Webb, 215 A.2d 610, 626 N.Y.S.2d 561 (2d Dept. 1995).

—It was reversible error when the court failed to instruct the jury that the prosecution had the burden of proving the defense of justification beyond a reasonable doubt where defendant presented evidence sufficient to entitle him to submission of this issue to the jury. People v. Burns, 78 A.D.2d 1009, 433 N.Y.S.2d 667 (4th Dept. 1980).

Mistake.—Defense of mistake of law was not available to a Federal corrections officer arrested in a Manhattan social club for possession of a .38 caliber automatic pistol who claimed he mistakenly believed he was entitled to carry a handgun without a permit as a police officer. People v. Marrero, 69 N.Y.2d 382, 515 N.Y.S.2d 212, 507 N.E.2d 1068 (1987).

When required to charge.—Court properly refused to charge affirmative defense where defendant failed to present any evidence at trial that established any element of the affirmative defense requested. People v. Crump, 254 A.D.2d 742, 680 N.Y.S.2d 765 (4th Dept. 1998).

ARTICLE 30—DEFENSE OF INFANCY

Section
  30.00   **Infancy.**

LexisNexis Cross References

Criminal Defense Techniques, Vol. 1B, Ch. 32, Diminished Capacity; *New York Criminal Practice (2d ed.),* Vol. 5, Ch. 53, Defenses of Mental Disease or Defect and Post-Judgment Procedures.

§ 30.00. Infancy.

1. Except as provided in subdivision two of this section, a person less than sixteen years old is not criminally responsible for conduct.

2. A person thirteen, fourteen or fifteen years of age is criminally responsible for acts constituting murder in the second degree as defined in subdivisions one and two of section 125.25 and in subdivision three of such section provided that the underlying crime for the murder charge is one for which such person is criminally responsible; and a person fourteen or fifteen years of age is criminally responsible for acts constituting the crimes defined in section 135.25 (kidnapping in the first degree); 150.20 (arson in the first degree); subdivisions one and two of section 120.10 (assault in the first degree); 125.20 (manslaughter in the first degree); subdivisions one and two of section 130.35 (rape in the first degree); subdivisions one and two of section 130.50 (criminal sexual act in the first degree); 130.70 (aggravated sexual abuse in the first degree); 140.30 (burglary in the first degree); subdivision one of section 140.25 (burglary in the second degree); 150.15 (arson in the second degree); 160.15 (robbery in the first degree); subdivision two of section 160.10 (robbery in the second degree) of this chapter; subdivision four of section 265.02 of this chapter, where such firearm is possessed on school grounds, as that phrase is defined in subdivision fourteen of section 220.00 of this chapter; or section 265.03 of this chapter, where such machine gun or such firearm is possessed on school grounds, as that phrase is defined in subdivision fourteen of section 220.00 of this chapter; or defined in this chapter as an attempt to commit murder in the second degree or kidnapping in the first degree.

3. In any prosecution for an offense, lack of criminal responsibility by reason of infancy, as defined in this section, is a defense.

Amended by L. 1978, Ch. 481; L. 1979, Ch. 411; L. 1981, Ch. 335; L. 1998, Ch. 435, § 4, eff. Nov. 1, 1998; L. 2003, Ch. 264, § 2, eff. Nov. 1, 2003, amending subd. 2.

ANNOTATIONS

Constitutionality.—The defendant's constitutional challenge to PL § 30.00 was deemed unpreserved for appeal; however, the court did state that the defendant's claim that the statute violated due process and equal protection by relying on chronological age had no merit. People v. Mayfield, 208 A.D.2d 391, 618 N.Y.S.2d 208 (1st Dept. 1994).

Enumerated crimes.—As a juvenile offender, the defendant cannot be held criminally responsible for felony murder where underlying felony, attempted robbery, is a crime for which he cannot be held criminally responsible; therefore, plea to murder in second degree must be vacated. People v. Stowe, 15 A.D.3d 597, 790 N.Y.S.2d 521 (2d Dept. 2005).

—Pursuant to PL § 30.00, person who is 15 years of age is not responsible as an adult for criminal conduct, except for acts constituting those crimes explicitly stated; defendant was convicted of attempted robbery in the first degree and conspiracy in the fourth degree, neither of which are included in that section; therefore, defendant cannot be held criminally responsible for them, nor can criminal liability for felony murder predicated upon convictions for those crimes be imposed. People v. Faith QQ., 20 A.D.3d 584, 798 N.Y.S.2d 217 (3d Dept. 2005).

Presumption of infancy.—The presumption of infancy is inapplicable in delinquency cases. *In re* Robert M., 110 Misc. 2d 113, 441 N.Y.S.2d 860 (Fam. Ct. N.Y. Co. 1981).

Endangering the welfare of a child.—A youthful offender is not criminally responsible by reason of infancy of the crime of endangering the welfare of a child. People v. Lester B, 84 A.D.2d 791, 444 N.Y.S.2d 20 (2d Dept. 1981).

Impeachment value of youthful offender/delinquency adjudication.—Youthful offender or juvenile delinquency adjudications may not be used for impeachment purposes because such adjudications are not criminal convictions; however, the prosecutor may inquire into the acts underlying the adjudications. People v. Gray, 84 N.Y.2d 709, 622 N.Y.S.2d 223, 646 N.E.2d 444 (1995).

New trial.—New trial was the proper remedy where an error in the charge to the jury made it impossible to determine whether the defendant's conviction of felony murder was based on the commission of an offense for which he could be held criminally responsible. People v. Smith, 220 A.D.2d 547, 632 N.Y.S.2d 591 (2d Dept. 1995).

Jurisdiction.—A defendant less than 16 years of age was properly tried in Bronx Supreme Court for a combination of different crimes; however, upon his conviction for felony murder, for which he could not have been criminally responsible since the underlying crime was for attempted first degree robbery and appellant was not 16 years old at the time of the crime, the matter was then properly transferred to Family Court for disposition. *In re* Equcon M., 291 A.D.2d 332, 737 N.Y.S.2d 622 (1st Dept. 2002).

—Family court and criminal justice system have concurrent original jurisdiction over designated felony offenses specified in Family Court Act, including first degree rape, and District Attorney's decision not to prosecute juvenile offender did not preclude prosecution of case in family court as designated felony. *In re* Meleick H., 170 Misc. 2d 230, 647 N.Y.S.2d 669 (Fam. Ct. Kings Co. 1996).

ARTICLE 35—DEFENSE OF JUSTIFICATION

LexisNexis Cross Reference

New York Criminal Practice (2d ed.), Vol. 5, Ch. 54, Defense of Justification.

§ 35.00. Justification; a defense.

In any prosecution for an offense, justification, as defined in sections 35.05 through 35.30, is a defense.

§ 35.05. Justification; generally.

Unless otherwise limited by the ensuing provisions of this article defining justifiable use of physical force, conduct which would otherwise constitute an offense is justifiable and not criminal when:

1. Such conduct is required or authorized by law or by a judicial decree, or is performed by a public servant in the reasonable exercise of his official powers, duties or functions; or

2. Such conduct is necessary as an emergency measure to avoid an imminent public or private injury which is about to occur by reason of a situation occasioned or developed through no fault of the actor, and which is of such gravity that, according to ordinary standards of intelligence and morality, the desirability and urgency of avoiding such injury clearly outweigh the desirability of avoiding the injury sought to be prevented by the statute defining the offense in issue. The necessity and justifiability of such conduct may not rest upon considerations pertaining only to the morality and advisability of the statute, either in its general application or with respect to its application to a particular class of cases arising thereunder. Whenever evidence relating to the defense of justification under this subdivision is offered by the defendant, the court shall rule as a matter of law whether the claimed facts and circumstances would, if established, constitute a defense.

ANNOTATIONS

Generally.—The conduct referred to in Penal Law § 35.05(2) bears both on the nature of the conduct to be justified and the harm to be avoided; the conduct must be necessary as an emergency measure to avoid an imminent public or private injury which is about to occur. People v. Craig, 78 N.Y.2d 616, 578 N.Y.S.2d 471, 585 N.E.2d 783 (1991).

—Defendant was entitled to justification charge at trial for escape and criminal mischief where defendant claimed that he kicked out the back of the police car in which he was being transported and then ran because the officers had taunted and beat him in the patrol car. People v. Mercer, 267 A.D.2d 1019, 701 N.Y.S.2d 551 (4th Dept. 1999) (mem.).

Burden of proof.—The evidence was legally sufficient to disprove the defense of justification beyond a reasonable doubt; the jury could have concluded that the defendant did not reasonably believe that the decedent was committing or attempting to commit a burglary. People v. Webb, 215 A.D.2d 610, 626 N.Y.S.2d 561 (2d Dept. 1995).

Charge.—In criminal trespass prosecution, court properly refused to charge defense of justification, pursuant to PL § 35.05(1), where the defense rested upon defendant's belief that his conduct was authorized rather than a claim that "such conduct is required or authorized by law or by a judicial decree." People v. Cardone, 68 N.Y.2d 829, 508 N.Y.S.2d 169, 500 N.E.2d 867 (1986).

—Justification will not be charged where no reasonable view of evidence presented demonstrated imminent or unavoidable harm or where defendant's decision not to treat complainant could be viewed as an emergency measure or a necessary choice over alternative legal choice of action. People v. Anyalora, 238 A.D.2d 216, 656 N.Y.S.2d 253 (1st Dept. 1997).

—Reversible error was not committed when trial court charged jury to apply the "ordinary prudent man" standard since the defendant did not object and the defense of justification was not properly placed in issue. People v. Gonzalez, 80 A.D.2d 543, 436 N.Y.S.2d 293 (1st Dept. 1981).

—The defendant contended that the trial court erred in failing to charge the defense of justification; there was no reasonable view of the evidence that would support a finding that the defendant slashed the complainant's tire in order to avoid imminent injury. People v. Bolton, 213 A.D.2d 660, 624 N.Y.S.2d 210 (2d Dept. 1995).

—Defendant's claim that he took the actions he did for the protection of himself and his passengers warranted a charge on justification despite defense counsel's failure to request it. People v. Zurita, 76 A.D.2d 871, 428 N.Y.S.2d 495 (2d Dept. 1980).

Justification no defense to certain crimes.—Justification based on self-defense, PL § 35.15, pertains only to the use of physical force; there are no circumstances when justification (PL § 35.15) can be a defense to the crime of criminal possession of a weapon because such offense does not involve the use of physical force. People v. Pons, 68 N.Y.2d 264, 608 N.Y.S.2d 403, 501 N.E.2d 11 (1986).

—Justification is not a defense to a charge of criminal

possession of a weapon in the second degree. People v. Wooten, 149 A.D.2d 751, 540 N.Y.S.2d 533 (2d Dept. 1989).

—The justification defense is inapplicable to the misdemeanor of endangering the welfare of a child. People v. Fields, 134 A.D.2d 365, 520 N.Y.S.2d 842 (2d Dept. 1987).

—Promoting prison contraband in the first degree does not involve the use of physical force so justification is no defense to that crime. People v. Diaz, 145 A.D.2d 833, 535 N.Y.S.2d 819 (3d Dept. 1988).

—Justification is not a defense to illegal possession of a weapon. People v. Faison, 154 A.D.2d 923, 546 N.Y.S.2d 67 (4th Dept. 1989).

—One cannot use the necessity defense to justify unlawful action intended to limit the advancement of ideas contrary to one's own; one's moral convictions alone can never be the basis for a justification defense. People v. Anderson, 144 Misc. 2d 133, 540 N.Y.S.2d 948 (Crim. Ct. N.Y. Co. 1989).

Evidence.—A defendant who testifies in support of his justification defense that stab wounds on his body were inflicted by the decedent does not thereby waive the psychologist-client privilege and it was, therefore, error to permit a hospital psychologist, who interviewed the defendant to determine if he was suicidal, to testify over objection and claim of privilege that defendant had stated to him that the wounds were self-inflicted. People v. Wilkins, 65 N.Y.2d 172, 490 N.Y.S.2d 759, 480 N.E.2d 373 (1985).

§ 35.10. Justification; use of physical force generally.

The use of physical force upon another person which would otherwise constitute an offense is justifiable and not criminal under any of the following circumstances:

1. A parent, guardian or other person entrusted with the care and supervision of a person under the age of twenty-one or an incompetent person, and a teacher or other person entrusted with the care and supervision of a person under the age of twenty-one for a special purpose, may use physical force, but not deadly physical force, upon such person when and to the extent that he reasonably believes it necessary to maintain discipline or to promote the welfare of such person.

2. A warden or other authorized official of a jail, prison or correctional institution may, in order to maintain order and discipline, use such physical force as is authorized by the correction law.

3. A person responsible for the maintenance of order in a common carrier of passengers, or a person acting under his direction, may use physical force when and to the extent that he reasonably believes it necessary to maintain order, but he may use deadly physical force only when he reasonably believes it necessary to prevent death or serious physical injury.

4. A person acting under a reasonable belief that another person is about to commit suicide or to inflict serious physical injury upon himself may use physical force upon such person to the extent that he reasonably believes it necessary to thwart such result.

5. A duly licensed physician, or a person acting under a physician's direction, may use physical force for the purpose of administering a recognized form of treatment which he or she reasonably believes to be adapted to promoting the physical or mental health of the patient if (a) the treatment is administered with the consent of the patient or, if the patient is under the age of eighteen years or an incompetent person, with the consent of the parent, guardian or other person entrusted with the patient's care and supervision, or (b) the treatment is administered in an emergency when the physician reasonably believes that no one competent to consent can be consulted and that a reasonable person, wishing to safeguard the welfare of the patient, would consent.

6. A person may, pursuant to the ensuing provisions of this article, use physical force upon another person in self-defense or defense of a third person, or in defense of premises, or in order to prevent larceny of or criminal mischief to property, or in order to effect an arrest or prevent an escape from custody. Whenever a person is authorized by any such provision to use deadly physical force in any given circumstance, nothing contained in any other such provision may be deemed to negate or qualify such authorization.

Amended by L. 1968, Ch. 73; L. 1974, Ch. 930; L. 2004, Ch. 511, § 1, eff. Sept. 28, 2004.

ANNOTATIONS

Evidence.—Court erred by refusing to charge jury with justification defense where reasonable view of evidence supported defendant's version that he drove his car into a crowd to defend his out numbered friends from an armed gang; victim, part of the armed gang, was injured when he was thrown from the car after defendant stopped short. People v. Minaya, 6 A.D.3d 728, 775 N.Y.S.2d 367(2d Dept. 2004).

—Since defendant, in claiming justification, never denied using a knife to cause the victim's injuries, ownership by the defendant of a knife was never a material issue in the case and therefore wrongful admission concerning a second knife allegedly owned by the defendant constituted harmless error. People v. Medina, 123 A.D.2d 331, 506 N.Y.S.2d 226 (2d Dept. 1986).

Use of force believed necessary to discipline child.—The court erred in dismissing the indictment where the prosecutor instructed the jury that §35.10 "in no way [permits] the cruel beating of children" and that "the law recognizes that a parent may use some physical force in disciplining their children, but it has to be reasonable. . ."; prosecutor's statement was consistent with case law and was not so egregious as to impair the integrity of the grand jury proceeding or render it invalid. People v. Prue, 219 A.D.2d 873, 632 N.Y.S.2d 347 (4th Dept. 1995).

§ 35.15. Justification; use of physical force in defense of a person.

1. A person may, subject to the provisions of subdivision two, use physical force upon another person when and to the extent he or she reasonably believes such to be necessary to defend himself, herself or a third person from what he or she reasonably believes to be the use or imminent use of unlawful physical force by such other person, unless:

(a) The latter's conduct was provoked by the actor with intent to cause physical injury to another person; or

(b) The actor was the initial aggressor; except that in such case the use of physical force is nevertheless justifiable if the actor has withdrawn from the encounter and effectively communicated such withdrawal to such other person but the latter persists in continuing the incident by the use or threatened imminent use of unlawful physical force; or

(c) The physical force involved is the product of a combat by agreement not specifically authorized by law.

2. A person may not use deadly physical force upon another person under circumstances specified in subdivision one unless:

(a) The actor reasonably believes that such other person is using or about to use deadly physical force. Even in such case, however, the actor may not use deadly physical force if he or she knows that with complete personal safety, to oneself and others he or she may avoid the necessity of so doing by retreating; except that the actor is under no duty to retreat if he or she is:

(i) in his or her dwelling and not the initial aggressor; or

(ii) a police officer or peace officer or a person assisting a police officer or a peace officer at the latter's direction, acting pursuant to section 35.30; or

(b) He or she reasonably believes that such other person is committing or attempting to commit a kidnapping, forcible rape, forcible criminal sexual act or robbery; or

(c) He or she reasonably believes that such other person is committing or attempting to commit a burglary, and the circumstances are such that the use of deadly physical force is authorized by subdivision three of section 35.20.

Added by L. 1968, Ch. 73; Amended by L. 1980, Ch. 843; L. 2003, Ch. 264, § 3, eff. Nov. 1, 2003, amending subd. 2(b); L. 2004, Ch. 511, § 2, eff. Sept. 28, 2004.

ANNOTATIONS

Generally.—To determine whether a defendant's conduct was justified under PL § 35.15, a two step jury inquiry is required: (1) whether the defendant actually believed that deadly physical force was necessary, and if the People fail to meet their burden of proving that the defendant did not actually believe that the use of deadly physical force was necessary, then (2) the jury must move to the second step of the inquiry and assess the reasonableness of this belief. People v. Wesley, 76 N.Y.2d 555, 561 N.Y.S.2d 707, 563 N.E.2d 21 (1990).

—The defense of justification is as much of a defense to reckless conduct as it is to intentional conduct, and thus justification may be charged as a defense to a crime regardless of the mens rea involved. People v. Felder, 178 A.D.2d 936, 579 N.Y.S.2d 247, 248 (4th Dept. 1991).

Deadly force.—Before using deadly physical force in self-defense, a defendant, standing in doorway between his apartment and common hallway of multiple unit dwelling, has a duty under PL § 35.15 to retreat into his home when he can safely do so. People v. Aiken, 4 N.Y.3d 324, 795 N.Y.S.2d 158, 828 N.E.2d 74 (2005)

—Even though defendant's wife was initial aggressor and threatened him with a knife, once defendant wrestled the knife away from her, he was no longer facing use of imminent use of deadly force, and any action by the defendant after that could not be protected by the defense of justification. People v. Bennett, 279 A.D.2d 585, 719 N.Y.S.2d 281 (2d Dept. 2001).

—Trial court properly instructed jury that it could find that defendant was justified in his actions if it found that he reasonably believed victim was using or was about to use deadly physical force against him and if the average person would have had the same belief under the same circumstances. People v. Santos, 280 A.D.2d 251, 720 N.Y.S.2d 384 (2d Dept. 2001).

—People successfully disproved justification defense where defendant, although able to safely retreat, sought out victim with loaded shotgun and shot back in retaliation, shooting victim several times. People v. Nurse, 277 A.D.2d 256, 715 N.Y.S.2d 863 (2d Dept. 2000), *appeal denied,* 96 N.Y.2d 737, 722 N.Y.S.2d 804, 745 N.E.2d 1027 (2001).

—The distinction between the use of deadly physical force to resist the imminent use of deadly force (§ 35.15(2)(a)) and the use of deadly physical force to aver an attempted robbery (§ 35.15(2)(b)) may be critical; a defendant may use deadly physical force to resist a robbery even though the victim has threatened the use of physical force and not deadly physical force. People v. Wang, 164 Misc. 2d 413, 625 N.Y.S.2d 413 (Sup. Ct. N.Y. Co. 1995).

Dwelling.—Defendant was not entitled to a "no duty to retreat" justification charge under PL § 35.15(2)(a)(i) in connection with an attack that occurred in the lobby area of the six-story apartment building where defendant resided; the lobby and common stairwell were not under defendant's "exclusive possession and could not fairly be characterized as defendant's living quarters," and thus were not part of defendant's dwelling. People v. Hernandez, 98 N.Y.2d 175, 746 N.Y.S.2d 434, 774 N.E.2d 198 (2002).

Excessive force.—Defendant's use of a dangerous weapon against an unarmed individual cannot be viewed as anything but excessive use of force, which precludes defense of justification. People v. Vecchio, 240 A.D.2d 854, 658 N.Y.S.2d 720 (3d Dept. 1997).

Reasonableness.—Juvenile's use of deadly physical force, i.e., stabbing complainant in the head and back with a kitchen knife, was justified where respondent was being held on the ground, kicked by complainant about the body, head and face, and was surrounded by 10 to 15 people who urged the beating to continue, and respondent was without anyone in the area to help her. In re Y.K., 87 N.Y.2d 430, 639 N.Y.S.2d 1000, 663 N.E.2d 313 (1996).

—A determination of reasonableness for purposes of § 35.15 is both subjective and objective; the "critical focus must be placed on the particular defendant and the circumstances actually confronting him at the time of the incident, and what a reasonable person in those circumstances and having defendant's background and experiences would conclude..." In re Ismael S., 213 A.D.2d 169, 623 N.Y.S.2d 571 (1st Dept. 1995).

Evidence.—Were the court to review defendant's unpreserved justification claim on appeal, it would have rejected it. Where defendant accepted opponent's challenge to a gun fight, left the scene, and returned armed to engage in a gun battle, the defense of justification was not established, and the fact that defendant's opponent fired first was of no consequence. People v. Rosario, 292 A.D.2d 324, 740 N.Y.S.2d 23 (1st Dept. 2002).

—Appellate court will not disturb jury's rejection of defendant's justification defense where evidence supported their conclusion that victim did not present a imminent threat of deadly physical force. People v. Colon, 267 A.D.2d 125, 701 N.Y.S.2d 10 (1st Dept. 1999), *appeal denied,* 95 N.Y.2d 794 (2000).

—It is a question for the jury to determine whether defendant reasonably believed in the necessity of the degree of force he employed. People v. Mojica, 264 A.D.2d 693, 696 N.Y.S.2d 30 (1st Dept. 1999), *appeal denied,* 94 N.Y.2d 905 (2000).

—The evidence presented was legally sufficient to disprove the defense of justification beyond a reasonable doubt. People v. Nelson, 215 A.D.2d 783, 627 N.Y.S.2d 975 (2d Dept. 1995).

—Justification defense was disproved by evidence that decedent was unarmed and that the defendant shot him six times at close range, five of the shots being fired while the victim was lying on the floor. People v. Tinedo, 144 A.D.2d 507, 533 N.Y.S.2d 979 (2d Dept. 1988).

—Although justification may be available to a defendant who is the initial aggressor, where defendant shot his 15-year-old niece in the face with a shot gun, seriously wounding her, evidence that she may have had a knife sometime during the altercation did not warrant the conclusion that she was "using or about to use deadly physical force on him." People v. Benson, 265 A.D.2d 814, 697 N.Y.S.2d 222 (4th Dept. 2000).

Expert evidence.—Trial court properly excluded psychiatric testimony offered to support justification defense as to defendant's delusional belief that at the time of the attack defendant thought victim was going to rob him of thousands of dollars of jewels; "[a]s a general rule, the admissibility and limits of expert testimony lie primarily in the sound discretion of the trial court." People v. Williams, 97 N.Y.2d 735, 742 N.Y.S.2d 597, 769 N.E.2d 343 (2002).

Possibility of retreat.—Exception to duty to retreat exists when person attacked is in his dwelling and he or she is not the initial aggressor, and even when assailant and victim share the same dwelling, there is no duty to retreat. People v. Jones, 3 N.Y.3d 491, 788 N.Y.S.2d 651, 821 N.E.2d 955 (2004).

—Where victim was innocent bystander caught in cross fire between defendants, defense of justification was not available since there was evidence that, regardless of who fired the first shot, defendants could have safely retreated but instead reciprocated with deadly physical force. People v. Russell, 91 N.Y.2d 280, 670 N.Y.S.2d 166, 693 N.E.2d 193 (1998).

—Defendant's own version of events contained no indication that he reasonably believed that victim was about to use deadly physical force on him, furthermore, defendant never availed himself of opportunity to retreat from situation. People v. Cavers, 237 A.D.2d 192, 655 N.Y.S.2d 369 (1st Dept. 1997).

—Defense of justification of use of deadly force was not established where, although three men appeared poised to lunge at defendant, there was no basis to conclude that no avenue of escape existed before defendant fired his weapon. In addition, lower court found defendant's testimony that he believed that deceased had a gun, thereby prompting defendant to fire, to be fabricated. People v. Roldan, 222 A.D.2d 132, 647 N.Y.S.2d 179 (1st Dept. 1996).

—Where evidence presented reveals defendant had an opportunity to retreat and that defendant could not have believed victim was about to use deadly physical force, justification defense was disproved beyond a reasonable doubt. People v. Narine, 240 A.D.2d 763, 660 N.Y.S.2d 994 (2d Dept. 1997).

—The prosecutor did not have to charge the grand jury with the defense of justification where the other evidence presented clearly established that the defendant was the initial aggressor, he could have retreated with complete safety, and his use of deadly physical force was not necessary to avert imminent use of such force (CPL § 35.15). People v. Spinelli, 165 A.D.2d 888, 560 N.Y.S.2d 358 (2d Dept. 1990).

—Court did not err in refusing to charge jury with the home exception of the duty to retreat, encounter occurred in home shared by defendant and the victim and in which defendant's justification defense raised no question with respect to who was the initial aggressor, the appellate court agreed that in order to avoid any confusion on the part of the jury, it was better not to mention the duty to retreat at all, as opposed to mentioning a general duty to retreat and then qualifying that duty by delineating the applicable home exception. People v. Jones, 4 A.D.3d 853, 772 N.Y.S.2d 778 (4th Dept.), aff'd, 3 N.Y.3d 491, 788 N.Y.S.2d 651, 821 N.E.2d 955 (2004).

Physical force.—Complainant's use of voodoo was not relevant to defendant's justification defense since voodoo is not "physical force" as defined under Penal Law § 35.15. People v. Morgan, 172 A.D.2d 414, 568 N.Y.S.2d 788 (1st Dept. 1991).

—Dazed victim's actions of hitting or merely taking a "whack" at defendant is not the "unlawful physical force" required for defendant to employ the defense of justification. This ineffective strike which did not phase defendant did not justify defendant's response of picking victim up and throwing him to the concrete, head first. People v. Lane, 241 A.D.2d 763, 660 N.Y.S.2d 890 (3d Dept. 1997).

Charge.—Charge of justification was warranted where victim of assault had previously pulled a gun out of his pocket and pointed it at close range in defendant's face during an argument, evidence that during this argument with defendant, victim again went to put his hand in his pocket, supported defendant's belief that victim was about to use deadly physical force against him, defendant was under no duty to retreat since argument took place by his apartment door. People v. Arzu, 7 A.D.3d 458, 777 N.Y.S.2d 485 (1st Dept. 2004).

—The trial court's error in not instructing the jury on justification was critical and merited reversal even though defense

counsel failed to request a justification charge or object to the charge provided; reversal was required in the interests of justice since the jury could have found, based on a reasonable view of the evidence, that the defendant's actions were justified. People v. Copeland, 216 A.D.2d 55, 627 N.Y.S.2d 653 (1st Dept. 1995).

—To be entitled to a charge on justification, there must be evidence that the defendant reasonably believed that another person was using deadly physical force or was about to use deadly physical force against him, or that another person was committing or attempting to commit, inter alia, a robbery; no reasonable view of the evidence in this case supported any such finding. People v. Mitchell, 216 A.D.2d 331, 627 N.Y.S.2d 771 (2d Dept. 1995).

—A trial court need not charge the jury on justification where no reasonable view of the evidence establishes the basic elements of the defense; no reasonable view of the evidence in this case would support a finding that the defendant reasonably believed that the use of physical force was necessary to defend himself from what he reasonably believed was the use or imminent use of illegal force against him. People v. Flores, 213 A.D.2d 670, 624 N.Y.S.2d 941 (2d Dept. 1995).

—Defendant failed to preserve for appeal his claim that the trial court erred in failing to charge the jury on the defense of justification where the defendant neither requested such a charge at trial nor objected to the charge given by the court. People v. Perez, 218 A.D.2d 754, 630 N.Y.S.2d 777 (2d Dept. 1995).

Defendant's state of mind.—Trial court's ruling was not erroneously restrictive where it excluded testimony relative to decedent's propensities for violence except to the extent that it might bear on defendant's state of mind. In re Robert S., 52 N.Y.2d 1046, 438 N.Y.S.2d 509, 420 N.E.2d 390 (1981).

Privileged information.—It was reversible error for the district attorney to question the defendant regarding confidential discussion concerning his justification defense which he had with his attorney and which was the principal issue in the case. People v. Glenn, 52 N.Y.2d 880, 437 N.Y.S.2d 298, 418 N.E.2d 1316 (1981).

Relevance of testimony to defense.—Court rejected contention that trial court erred in precluding defendant from testifying in support of his justification defense that he previously had been beaten by police officers since defendant had failed to make a clear and unambiguous offer of proof to indicate that his prospective testimony would be relevant to a justification defense. People v. Baxter, 177 A.D.2d 1003, 578 N.Y.S.2d 23 (4th Dept. 1991).

§ 35.20. Justification; use of physical force in defense of premises and in defense of a person in the course of burglary.

1. Any person may use physical force upon another person when he or she reasonably believes such to be necessary to prevent or terminate what he or she reasonably believes to be the commission or attempted commission by such other person of a crime involving damage to premises. Such person may use any degree of physical force, other than deadly physical force, which he or she reasonably believes to be necessary for such purpose, and may use deadly physical force if he or she reasonably believes such to be necessary to prevent or terminate the commission or attempted commission of arson.

2. A person in possession or control of any premises, or a person licensed or privileged to be thereon or therein, may use physical force upon another person when he or she reasonably believes such to be necessary to prevent or terminate what he or she reasonably believes to be the commission or attempted commission by such

other person of a criminal trespass upon such premises. Such person may use any degree of physical force, other than deadly physical force, which he or she reasonably believes to be necessary for such purpose, and may use deadly physical force in order to prevent or terminate the commission or attempted commission of arson, as prescribed in subdivision one, or in the course of a burglary or attempted burglary, as prescribed in subdivision three.

3. A person in possession or control of, or licensed or privileged to be in, a dwelling or an occupied building, who reasonably believes that another person is committing or attempting to commit a burglary of such dwelling or building, may use deadly physical force upon such other person when he or she reasonably believes such to be necessary to prevent or terminate the commission or attempted commission of such burglary.

4. As used in this section, the following terms have the following meanings:

(a) The terms "premises," "building" and "dwelling" have the meanings prescribed in section 140.00;

(b) Persons "licensed or privileged" to be in buildings or upon other premises include, but are not limited to:

(i) police officers or peace officers acting in the performance of their duties; and

(ii) security personnel or employees of nuclear powered electric generating facilities located within the state who are employed as part of any security plan approved by the federal operating license agencies acting in the performance of their duties at such generating facilities. For purposes of this subparagraph, the term "nuclear powered electric generating facility" shall mean a facility that generates electricity using nuclear power for sale, directly or indirectly, to the public, including the land upon which the facility is located and the safety and security zones as defined under federal regulations.

Added by L. 1968, Ch. 73; **Amended** by L. 1980, Ch. 843; L. 2004, Ch. 393, § 1, eff. Aug. 17, 2004, amending subd. 4(b); L. 2004, Ch. 511, § 3, eff. Sept. 28, 2004, amending subds. 1, 2, & 3.

ANNOTATIONS

Charge.—Defendant-owner was entitled to a jury charge of justification where evidence established that victim re-entered grocery store unlawfully after being directed to leave the premises/owner, and that victim was highly intoxicated, violent, and threatened to kill defendant and his brother. People v. Deis, 97 N.Y.2d 717, 740 N.Y.S.2d 284, 766 N.E.2d 946 (2002).

—Where no reasonable view of evidence could support justification defense, court's refusal to charge jury as defendant requested was not error; no rational view of evidence supported defendant's contention that the use of deadly force was justified. People v. Cox, 92 N.Y 2d 1002, 707 N.E.2d 428, 684 N.Y.S.2d 473 (1998).

—Reversible error for failure to grant request to charge defense, where bar employee presented evidence that he had repeatedly asked victims to leave bar prior to altercation, this supported finding that he reasonably believed victims were committing

a criminal trespass and that physical force was necessary to protect the premises. People v. Gavigan, 2 A.D.3d 748, 768 N.Y.S.2d 652 (2d Dept. 2003).

—The trial court did not err in refusing defendant's justification charge where there was no reasonable view of the evidence from which the jury could conclude that the victim was attempting to commit, or was committing, a robbery or burglary. People v. Bertone, 213 A.D.2d 417, 624 N.Y.S.2d 879 (2d Dept. 1995).

—Defendant was not entitled to a justification charge where no reasonable view of evidence at trial would support conclusion that deadly physical force was necessary. People v. Savage, 267 A.D.2d 968, 700 N.Y.S.2d 608 (4th Dept. 1999), *review denied,* 94 N.Y.2d 906 (2000).

—The trial court erred in refusing the defendant's justification charge; a reasonable view of the evidence would have permitted the jury to find that the defendant reasonably believed that the victim was committing a burglary and that deadly force was necessary in response. People v. Wynn, 212 A.D.2d 969, 623 N.Y.S.2d 460 (4th Dept. 1995).

Dwelling.—Defendant was not entitled to a "no duty to retreat" justification charge under PL § 35.15(2)(a)(i) in connection with an attack that occurred in the lobby area of the six-story apartment building where defendant resided; the lobby and common stairwell were not under defendant's "exclusive possession and could not fairly be characterized as defendant's living quarters," and thus were not part of defendant's dwelling. People v. Hernandez, 98 N.Y.2d 175, 746 N.Y.S.2d 434, 774 N.E.2d 198 (2002).

§ 35.25. Justification; use of physical force to prevent or terminate larceny or criminal mischief.

A person may use physical force, other than deadly physical force, upon another person when and to the extent that he or she reasonably believes such to be necessary to prevent or terminate what he or she reasonably believes to be the commission or attempted commission by such other person of larceny or of criminal mischief with respect to property other than premises.

Added by L. 1968, Ch. 73; **Amended** by L. 2004, Ch. 511, § 4, eff. Sept. 28, 2004.

§ 35.27. Justification; use of physical force in resisting arrest prohibited.

A person may not use physical force to resist an arrest, whether authorized or unauthorized, which is being effected or attempted by a police officer or peace officer when it would reasonably appear that the latter is a police officer or peace officer.

Added by L. 1968, Ch. 73; **Amended** by L. 1980, Ch. 843.

ANNOTATION

Resisting an unauthorized arrest.—PL § 35.27 was intended to take effect only in those cases where the police officer involved had effectuated a valid arrest and was not designed to prohibit totally, any resistance at any time to a police officer. *In re* Musso, 102 Misc. 2d 934, 424 N.Y.S.2d 855 (Fam. Ct. Monroe Co. 1980).

§ 35.30. Justification; use of physical force in making an arrest or in preventing an escape.

1. A police officer or a peace officer, in the course of effecting or attempting to effect an

arrest, or of preventing or attempting to prevent the escape from custody, of a person whom he or she reasonably believes to have committed an offense, may use physical force when and to the extent he or she reasonably believes such to be necessary to effect the arrest, or to prevent the escape from custody, or in self-defense or to defend a third person from what he or she reasonably believes to be the use or imminent use of physical force; except that deadly physical force may be used for such purposes only when he or she reasonably believes that:

(a) The offense committed by such person was:

(i) a felony or an attempt to commit a felony involving the use or attempted use or threatened imminent use of physical force against a person; or

(ii) kidnapping, arson, escape in the first degree, burglary in the first degree or any attempt to commit such a crime; or

(b) The offense committed or attempted by such person was a felony and that, in the course of resisting arrest therefor or attempting to escape from custody, such person is armed with a firearm or deadly weapon; or

(c) Regardless of the particular offense which is the subject of the arrest or attempted escape, the use of deadly physical force is necessary to defend the police officer or peace officer or another person from what the officer reasonably believes to be the use or imminent use of deadly physical force.

2. The fact that a police officer or a peace officer is justified in using deadly physical force under circumstances prescribed in paragraphs (a) and (b) of subdivision one does not constitute justification for reckless conduct by such police officer or peace officer amounting to an offense against or with respect to innocent persons whom he or she is not seeking to arrest or retain in custody.

3. A person who has been directed by a police officer or a peace officer to assist such police officer or peace officer to effect an arrest or to prevent an escape from custody may use physical force, other than deadly physical force, when and to the extent that he or she reasonably believes such to be necessary to carry out such police officer's or peace officer's direction, unless he or she knows that the arrest or prospective arrest is not or was not authorized and may use deadly physical force under such circumstances when:

(a) He or she reasonably believes such to be necessary for self-defense or to defend a third

person from what he or she reasonably believes to be the use or imminent use of deadly physical force; or

(b) He or she is directed or authorized by such police officer or peace officer to use deadly physical force unless he or she knows that the police officer or peace officer is not authorized to use deadly physical force under the circumstances.

4. A private person acting on his or her own account may use physical force, other than deadly physical force, upon another person when and to the extent that he or she reasonably believes such to be necessary to effect an arrest or to prevent the escape from custody of a person whom he or she reasonably believes to have committed an offense and who in fact has committed such offense; and may use deadly physical force for such purpose when he or she reasonably believes such to be necessary to:

(a) Defend himself, herself or a third person from what he or she reasonably believes to be the use or imminent use of deadly physical force; or

(b) Effect the arrest of a person who has committed murder, manslaughter in the first degree, robbery, forcible rape or forcible criminal sexual act and who is in immediate flight therefrom.

5. A guard, police officer or peace officer who is charged with the duty of guarding prisoners in a detention facility, as that term is defined in section 205.00, or while in transit to or from a detention facility, may use physical force when and to the extent that he or she reasonably believes such to be necessary to prevent the escape of a prisoner from a detention facility or from custody while in transit thereto or therefrom.

Added by L. 1968, Ch. 73; Amended by L. 1972, Ch. 598; L. 1973, Ch. 676; L. 1975, Ch. 667; L. 1980, Chs. 471, 843; L. 2003, Ch. 264, § 4, eff. Nov. 1, 2003, amending subd. 4(b); L. 2004, Ch. 511, § 5, eff. Sept. 28, 2004.

ANNOTATIONS

No civil liability.—A violation of the justification defenses found in PL § 35.30 can not be the sole basis for recovery under N.Y. General Municipal Law § 205-e, which allows police officers to bring tort claims for most work injuries that occur in the line of duty and in those instances where the law violated mandates a reasonably defined and precedentially developed standard of care, § 35.30 "does not establish a standard of care upon which a civil cause of action can be based, but rather a defense." Williams v. City of New York, 2 N.Y.3d 352, 779 N.Y.S.2d 449, 811 N.E.2d 1103 (2004).

Suspect's post-arrest statement.—The police are not prohibited from taking a statement from a suspect who is still suffering from injuries sustained at the time of his arrest, even if those injuries are the result of excessive force, as long as there is no causal connection between the statement and the injuries. People v. Nieves, 205 A.D.2d 173, 617 N.Y.S.2d 751 (1st Dept. 1994), aff'd, 88 N.Y.2d 618, 648 N.Y.S.2d 863, 671 N.E.2d 1260 (1996).

ARTICLE 40—OTHER DEFENSES INVOLVING LACK OF CULPABILITY

LexisNexis Cross References

Criminal Defense Techniques, Vol. 1B, Ch. 31, The Insanity Defense; Vol. 1B, Ch. 32, Diminished Capacity; *New York Criminal Practice (2d ed.),* Vol. 1, Ch. 14, Mental Disease or Defect Precluding Fitness to Proceed; Vol. 5, Ch. 53, Defenses of Mental Disease or Defect and Post-Judgment Procedures; *see generally The Entrapment Defense (2d ed.).*

§ 40.00. Duress.

1. In any prosecution for an offense, it is an affirmative defense that the defendant engaged in the proscribed conduct because he was coerced to do so by the use or threatened imminent use of unlawful physical force upon him or a third person, which force or threatened force a person of reasonable firmness in his situation would have been unable to resist.

2. The defense of duress as defined in subdivision one of this section is not available when a person intentionally or recklessly places himself in a situation in which it is probable that he will be subjected to duress.

ANNOTATIONS

Abuse.—Court properly denied defendant's request to charge jury on the affirmative defense of duress where defendant claimed husband's abusiveness constituted duress; record did not contain evidence of acts or threats of abuse at time of crimes, and post-crime threats and force are irrelevant as a matter of law; prior threats coupled with assault may give rise to a claim of duress, but only if combined with present and immediate compulsion. People v. Staffieri, 251 A.D.2d 998, 674 N.Y.S.2d 885 (4th Dept. 1998).

Burden of proof.—The trial court erred in refusing the defendant's duress charge where the evidence showed, inter alia, that: (1) the defendant, who was not quite 15 years old at the time of the crime, participated in the crime at the behest of an older co-defendant, who had shot and critically wounded the defendant three years prior to the crime; (2) the co-defendant threatened to shoot the defendant if he refused to participate in the crime; and (3) the co-defendant allegedly exploited other youths in order to insulate himself from liability for criminal acts. People v. Jenkins, 214 A.D.2d 584, 625 N.Y.S.2d 70 (2d Dept. 1995).

—The jury properly rejected the defendant's duress defense where the evidence failed to establish that the defendant was coerced to escape from prison by the use or threatened imminent use of unlawful physical force against him. People v. Christopher R., 220 A.D.2d 781, 633 N.Y.S.2d 191 (2d Dept. 1995).

—Defendant failed to prove the defense of duress by a preponderance of the evidence where, based upon his own admissions, he, after allegedly being compelled through the use of physical force to drive the three other perpetrators to the scene of the crime, chose to remain in his vehicle and wait for them for 15 to 25 minutes. People v. Ramjohn, 128 A.D.2d 904, 513 N.Y.S.2d 830, 831 (2d Dept. 1987).

—The trial court properly denied the defendant's request for a duress charge; in the absence of proof of an imminent threat, there is no reasonable view of the evidence to support the

defense. People v. Cox, 207 A.D.2d 995, 617 N.Y.S.2d 690 (4th Dept. 1994).

Constitutionality.—Penal Law § 40.00, which denominates duress an affirmative defense, is constitutional. People v. Bastidas, 67 N.Y.2d 1006, 503 N.Y.S.2d 315, 316 N.E.2d 446 (1986).

§ 40.05. Entrapment.

In any prosecution for an offense, it is an affirmative defense that the defendant engaged in the proscribed conduct because he was induced or encouraged to do so by a public servant, or by a person acting in cooperation with a public servant, seeking to obtain evidence against him for purpose of criminal prosecution, and when the methods used to obtain such evidence were such as to create a substantial risk that the offense would be committed by a person not otherwise disposed to commit it. Inducement or encouragement to commit an offense means active inducement or encouragement. Conduct merely affording a person an opportunity to commit an offense does not constitute entrapment.

ANNOTATIONS

Entrapment defense; jury issue.—Whether defendant established his entrapment defense by a preponderance of the evidence presented an issue of credibility that the trier of fact was authorized to resolve against the defendant. People v. Cuozzo, 199 A.D.2d 966, 605 N.Y.S.2d 600 (4th Dept. 1993).

Evidence.—Court properly declined to charge jury with entrapment defense where no reasonable view of the evidence supported assertion that defendant was actively induced to engage in criminal activity, rather than merely being afforded an opportunity to do so. People v. Moultrie, 5 A.D.3d 241, 773 N.Y.S.2d 287 (1st Dept. 2004).

—Undercover building inspector's overstatement of building violations did not support a defense of entrapment to defendant building owner's conviction of third degree bribery. People v. Chou, 292 A.D.2d 199, 738 N.Y.S.2d 210 (1st Dept. 2002).

—Testimony that undercover officer merely asked defendant to bring along gun to a meeting was insufficient to support an affirmative defense of entrapment; evidence was insufficient to establish defendant was induced or encouraged by undercover to commit the crimes for which he was being tried. People v. Skervin, 17 A.D.3d 771, 792 N.Y.S.2d 716 (3d Dept. 2005).

—Asking a defendant to commit a crime, in and of itself, is not such an inducement or encouragement to constitute entrapment. People v. Delaney, 309 A.D.2d 968, 765 N.Y.S.2d 696 (3d Dept. 2003).

—Where there is no reasonable view of the evidence which

could support the conclusion that the defendant's criminal conduct was "induced or encouraged by the police," no entrapment charge is warranted. People v. Minckler, 265 A.D.2d 799 695 N.Y.S.2d 843 (4th Dept. 1999), *review denied,* 94 N.Y.2d 882 (2000).

Production of informant.—Reversal was required although defendant made no formal motion for production of informer whose testimony the people knew or should have known would be material and relevant to the defense and for whom the People had inadequately searched and the record disclosed that defense counsel requested the court to order the production of the informant by the People, and this was equivalent to a formal demand where informant was the only witness who could shed light on the circumstances of the alleged crime and would likely have supported defendant's entrapment defense. People v. Brown, 84 A.D.2d 910, 446 N.Y.S.2d 664 (4th Dept. 1981).

Waiver.—The defense of entrapment is waived by a plea of guilty. People v. Ottomanelli, 74 A.D.2d 653, 424 N.Y.S.2d 38 (2d Dept. 1980).

§ 40.10. Renunciation.

1. In any prosecution for an offense, other than an attempt to commit a crime, in which the defendant's guilt depends upon his criminal liability for the conduct of another person pursuant to section 20.00, it is an affirmative defense that, under circumstances manifesting a voluntary and complete renunciation of his criminal purpose, the defendant withdrew from participation in such offense prior to the commission thereof and made a substantial effort to prevent the commission thereof.

2. In any prosecution for criminal facilitation pursuant to article one hundred fifteen, it is an affirmative defense that, prior to the commission of the felony which he facilitated, the defendant made a substantial effort to prevent the commission of such felony.

3. In any prosecution pursuant to section 110.00 for an attempt to commit a crime, it is an affirmative defense that, under circumstances manifesting a voluntary and complete renunciation of his criminal purpose, the defendant avoided the commission of the crime attempted by abandoning his criminal effort and, if mere abandonment was insufficient to accomplish such avoidance, by taking further and affirmative steps which prevented the commission thereof.

4. In any prosecution for criminal solicitation pursuant to article one hundred or for conspiracy pursuant to article one hundred five in which the crime solicited or the crime contemplated by the conspiracy was not in fact committed, it is an affirmative defense that, under circumstances manifesting a voluntary and complete renunciation of his criminal purpose, the defendant prevented the commission of such crime.

5. A renunciation is not "voluntary and complete" within the meaning of this section if it is motivated in whole or in part by (a) a belief that circumstances exist which increase the probability of detection or apprehension of the defendant or another participant in the criminal enterprise, or which render more difficult the accomplishment of the criminal purpose, or (b) a decision to postpone the criminal conduct until another time or to transfer the criminal effort to another victim or another but similar objective.

ANNOTATIONS

Evidence of renunciation.—Renunciation requires more than merely withdrawal from a conspiracy, and there must be a demonstration that a substantial effort was made to prevent the commission of the conspiracy. People v. Ozarowski, 38 N.Y.2d 481, 381 N.Y.S.2d 438, 344 N.E.2d 370 (1976).

—Evidence of defendant's withdrawal from the commission of the crime but no effort to prevent the commission of that crime does not establish the affirmative defense of renunciation. People v. Curry, 294 A.D.2d 608, 741 N.Y.S.2d 324 (3d Dept. 2002).

Attempt.—Renunciation does not negate the commission of the inchoate crime of attempt, as renunciation applies only when "the defendant avoided the commission of the crime attempted." People v. Johnson, 87 A.D.2d 703, 448 N.Y.S.2d 902 (3d Dept. 1982).

Charge.—The trial court did not err in refusing the defendant's renunciation charge; no reasonable view of the evidence would support the conclusion that the defendant voluntarily and completely withdrew from participation in the crime prior to commission and that he made a substantial effort to prevent the crime. People v. Montes, 211 A.D.2d 687, 622 N.Y.S.2d 468 (2d Dept. 1995).

§ 40.15. Mental disease or defect.

In any prosecution for an offense, it is an affirmative defense that when the defendant engaged in the proscribed conduct, he lacked criminal responsibility by reason of mental disease or defect. Such lack of criminal responsibility means that at the time of such conduct, as a result of mental disease or defect, he lacked substantial capacity to know or appreciate either:

1. The nature and consequences of such conduct; or

2. That such conduct was wrong.

Added by L. 1984, Ch. 668

ANNOTATIONS

Constitutionality.—Penal Law § 40.15, which defines affirmative defense of mental disease or defect, does not violate the state constitutional due process clause even though it places the burden of proving all defenses by a preponderance of the evidence on defendants. People v. Kohl, 72 N.Y.2d 191, 532 N.Y.S.2d 45, 527 N.E.2d 1182 (1988).

—Prosecutor's showing that defendant invoked his right to remain silent after being given the *Miranda* warnings as evidence of sanity in case where defendant raised insanity defense violated due process and required reversal of defendant's conviction. Wainwright v. Greenfield, 474 U.S. 284, 106 S. Ct. 634, 88 L. Ed. 2d 623 (1985).

Burden of proof.—The defendant must prove the defense (under Penal Law §40.15) by a preponderance of the evidence. People v. Mawhinney, 163 Misc. 2d 329, 622 N.Y.S.2d 182 (Sup. Ct. Bronx Co. 1994).

Standard of proof.—Jury verdict which found defendant guilty of attempted murder in the second degree, thereby rejecting defendant's expert witness's testimony that he lack the requisite mental capacity to commit this crime, and accepting People's witness who stated that defendant knew right from wrong and could control his violent impulses, will not be disturbed absent a "serious flaw" in expert's testimony. People v. Irizarry, 238 A.D.2d 940, 661 N.Y.S.2d 147 (4th Dept. 1997).

—Trial court's supplemental instruction to the jury on the insanity defense which used the "knowing right from wrong" standard was in error and, together with other instructions, confusing, thereby requiring reversal. People v. Young, 65 N.Y.2d 103, 490 N.Y.S.2d 179, 479 N.E.2d 815 (1985).

—Penal law § 40.15 involves a cognitive rather than volitional test; the defendant must prove that (1) at the time of the offense he suffered from a mental disease or defect; and (2) the disease or defect cause him to lack substantial capacity to know or appreciate the nature and consequences of his conduct, or that it was wrong. People v. Mawhinney, 163 Misc. 2d 329, 622 N.Y.S.2d 182 (Sup. Ct. Bronx Co. 1994).

Experts.—The question of sanity is for the jury where conflicting expert testimony is presented; the jury has the right to accept or reject the opinion of any expert and where there is an absence of a serious flaw in the testimony of the People's experts, the jury's finding of sanity will not be disturbed. People v. Jandelli, 118 A.D.2d 656, 499 N.Y.S.2d 962 (2d Dept. 1986).
—Jury was entitled to reject expert testimony that defendant was delusional on night he committed crimes underlying his conviction; on appeal, great deference was given to jury decision to credit People's expert testimony that, despite operating under delusions, defendant was able to understand that he was firing 59 shots at police and neighbors and that his conduct was wrong. People v. Stoffel, 17 A.D.3d 992, 794 N.Y.S.2d 230 (4th Dept. 2005).

Irresistible impulse. —PL § 40.15 does not immunize a defendant from criminal liability due to a defendant's irresistible impulse to commit a crime, but presents a "cognitive test" instead—whether defendant lacked "substantial capacity to know and appreciate either the nature and consequences of his or her conduct or that such conduct is wrong." People v. Goldstein,14 A.D.3d 32, 786 N.Y.S.2d 428 (1st Dept. 2004), *appeal granted,*4 N.Y.3d 798, 795 N.Y.S.2d 174, 828 N.E.2d 90, *motion granted,* 4 N.Y.3d 810, 796 N.Y.S.2d 31, 828 N.E.2d 988 (2005).

Presumption.—There is a presumption of sanity which a defendant must rebut and which alone can sustain the People's burden of proof of sanity when the defendant's proof is weak. People v. Rison, 151 A.D.2d 879, 542 N.Y.S.2d 852 (3d Dept. 1989).

Extreme emotional disturbance distinguished.—Trial court committed reversible error in prosecution for second degree murder by submitting affirmative defense of extreme emotional disturbance over defendant's objection. Defendant asserted the defense of not responsible by reason of a mental disease or defect which was clearly incompatible with the affirmative defense of extreme emotional disturbance which would have necessarily involved a temporary loss of control by a person who was otherwise capable of appreciating the nature and consequences of his actions. People v. Bradley, 88 N.Y.2d 901, 646 N.Y.S.2d 657, 669 N.E.2d 815 (1996).

PART TWO—SENTENCES

TITLE E—SENTENCES

ARTICLE 55—CLASSIFICATION AND DESIGNATION OF OFFENSES

LexisNexis Cross Reference

New York Criminal Practice (2d ed.), Vol. 4, Ch. 42, Classification of Offenses, Authorized Dispositions and Punishment.

§ 55.00. Applicability of article.

The provisions of this article govern the classification and designation of every offense, whether defined within or outside of this chapter.

§ 55.05. Classifications of felonies and misdemeanors.

1. Felonies. Felonies are classified, for the purpose of sentence, into five categories as follows:

(a) Class A felonies;

(b) Class B felonies;

(c) Class C felonies;

(d) Class D felonies; and

(e) Class E felonies.

Class A felonies are subclassified, for the purpose of sentence, into two categories as follows: subclass I and subclass II, to be known as class A-I and class A-II felonies, respectively.

2. Misdemeanors. Misdemeanors are classified, for the purpose of sentence, into three categories as follows:

(a) Class A misdemeanors;

(b) Class B misdemeanors; and

(c) Unclassified misdemeanors.

Amended by L. 1973, Ch. 276; L. 1979, Ch. 410.

§ 55.10. Designation of offenses.

1. Felonies.

(a) The particular classification or subclassification of each felony defined in this chapter is expressly designated in the section or article defining it.

(b) Any offense defined outside this chapter which is declared by law to be a felony without specification of the classification thereof, or for which a law outside this chapter provides a sentence to a term of imprisonment in excess of one year, shall be deemed a class E felony.

2. Misdemeanors.

(a) Each misdemeanor defined in this chapter is either a class A misdemeanor or a class B misdemeanor, as expressly designated in the section or article defining it.

(b) Any offense defined outside this chapter which is declared by law to be a misdemeanor without specification of the classification thereof or of the sentence therefor shall be deemed a class A misdemeanor.

(c) Except as provided in paragraph (b) of subdivision three, where an offense is defined outside this chapter and a sentence to a term of imprisonment in excess of fifteen days but not in excess of one year is provided in the law or ordinance defining it, such offense shall be deemed an unclassified misdemeanor.

3. Violations. Every violation defined in this chapter is expressly designated as such. Any offense defined outside this chapter which is not expressly designated a violation shall be deemed a violation if:

(a) Notwithstanding any other designation specified in the law or ordinance defining it, a sentence to a term of imprisonment which is not in excess of fifteen days is provided therein, or the only sentence provided therein is a fine; or

(b) A sentence to a term of imprisonment in excess of fifteen days is provided for such offense in a law or ordinance enacted prior to the effective date of this chapter but the offense was not a crime prior to that date.

4. Traffic infraction. Notwithstanding any other provision of this section, an offense which is defined as a "traffic infraction" shall not be deemed a violation or a misdemeanor by virtue of the sentence prescribed therefor.

Amended by L. 1967, Ch. 791; L. 1973, Ch. 276; L. 1978, Ch. 104.

ANNOTATIONS

Defining violation.—Town's ordinance which charged defendant with a "violation" but which permitted sentence of up to 30 days jail time triggered defendant's statutory right to jury trial, and town prosecutor committed prejudicial, material, and non-harmless error by representing to presiding Justice, a non-attorney, that defendant was not entitled to a jury trial. People v. Brown, 170 Misc. 2d 266, 648 N.Y.S.2d 283 (Allegany Co. Ct. 1996).

Jurisdiction of court.—The court was empowered to hear matter where defendant was charged with misdemeanors; before conducting business other than preliminary matters, the court must be satisfied that the accusatory instrument states a crime, and that the defendant is subject to the court's jurisdiction. People v. Causeway Constr. Co., 164 Misc. 2d 393, 625 N.Y.S.2d 856 (Crim. Ct. Bronx Co. 1995).

ARTICLE 60—AUTHORIZED DISPOSITIONS OF OFFENDERS

§ 60.00. Applicability of provisions.

1. The sentences prescribed by this article shall apply in the case of every offense, whether defined within or outside of this chapter.

2. The sole provision of this article that shall apply in the case of an offense committed by a juvenile offender is section 60.10 of this article and no other provisions of this article shall be deemed or construed to apply in any such case.

Amended by L. 1978, Ch. 481.

§ 60.01. Authorized dispositions; generally.

1. Applicability. Except as otherwise specified in this article, when the court imposes sentence upon a person convicted of an offense, the court must impose a sentence prescribed by this section.

2. Revocable dispositions.

(a) The court may impose a revocable sentence as herein specified:

(i) the court, where authorized by article sixty-five, may sentence a person to a period of probation or to a period of conditional discharge as provided in that article; or

(ii) the court, where authorized by article eighty-five, may sentence a person to a term of intermittent imprisonment as provided in that article.

(b) A revocable sentence shall be deemed a tentative one to the extent that it may be altered or revoked in accordance with the provisions of the article under which it was imposed, but for all other purposes shall be deemed to be a final judgment of conviction.

(c) In any case where the court imposes a sentence of probation, conditional discharge, or a sentence of intermittent imprisonment, it may also impose a fine authorized by article eighty.

(d) In any case where the court imposes a sentence of imprisonment not in excess of sixty days, for a misdemeanor or not in excess of six months for a felony or in the case of a sentence of intermittent imprisonment not in excess of four months, it may also impose a sentence of probation or conditional discharge provided that the term of probation or conditional discharge together with the term of imprisonment shall not exceed the term of probation or conditional discharge authorized by article sixty-five of this chapter. The sentence of imprisonment shall be a condition of and run concurrently with the sentence of probation or conditional discharge.

3. Other dispositions. When a person is not

sentenced as specified in subdivision two, or when a sentence specified in subdivision two is revoked, the sentence of the court must be as follows:

(a) A term of imprisonment; or

(b) A fine authorized by article eighty, provided, however, that when the conviction is of a class B felony or of any felony defined in article two hundred twenty, the sentence shall not consist solely of a fine; or

(c) Both imprisonment and a fine; or

(d) Where authorized by section 65.20, unconditional discharge as provided in that section; or

(e) Following revocation of a sentence of conditional discharge imposed pursuant to section 65.05 of this chapter or paragraph (d) of subdivision two of this section, probation as provided in section 65.00 of this chapter or to the sentence of imprisonment and probation as provided for in paragraph (d) of subdivision two of this section.

4. In any case where a person has been sentenced to a period of probation imposed pursuant to section 65.00 of this chapter, if the part of the sentence that provides for probation is revoked, the court must sentence such person to imprisonment or to the sentence of imprisonment and probation as provided for in paragraph (d) of subdivision two of this section.

Amended by L. 1970, Ch. 477; L. 1972, Ch. 157; L. 1973, Chs. 276, 277; L. 1974, Chs. 652, 835; L. 1978, Ch. 274; L. 1980, Ch. 86; L. 1982, Ch. 65; L. 1984, Ch. 548.

ANNOTATIONS

Cruel and unusual punishment.—Mere speculation that due to his medical condition the defendant might suffer unspecified harm if incarcerated does not suffice to warrant modification of the sentence imposed to only a term of probation. People v. Kelsky, 144 A.D.2d 386, 533 N.Y.S.2d 962 (2d Dept. 1988).

—Fact that defendant suffered from Acquired Immune Deficiency Syndrome (AIDS) was not, in and of itself, a ground for reducing the negotiated sentence. People v. Napolitano, 138 A.D.2d 414, 525 N.Y.S.2d 698 (2d Dept. 1988).

Restitution; condition of probation only.—Restitution can only be required as a condition of probation and cannot be made a condition of the sentence. People v. Cappetta, 86 A.D.2d 876, 447 N.Y.S.2d 293 (2d Dept. 1982).

Modification of sentence in the interest of justice.—Youthful offender sentence was modified as a matter of discretion in the interest of justice where defendant's criminal conduct was not part of a life-pattern, but a shocking departure from an otherwise law abiding lifestyle, and he was genuinely remorseful for the offense. People v. Herbert, 82 A.D.2d 924, 440 N.Y.S.2d 675 (2d Dept. 1981).

§ 60.02. Authorized disposition; youthful offender.

When a person is to be sentenced upon a youthful offender finding, the court must impose a sentence as follows:

(1) If the sentence is to be imposed upon a youthful offender finding which has been substituted for a conviction of an offense other than a felony, the court must impose a sentence authorized for the offense for which the youthful offender finding was substituted, except that if the youthful offender finding was entered pursuant to paragraph (b) of subdivision one of section 720.20 of the criminal procedure law, the court must not impose a definite or intermittent sentence of imprisonment with a term of more than six months; or

(2) If the sentence is to be imposed upon a youthful offender finding which has been substituted for a conviction for any felony, the court must impose a sentence authorized to be imposed upon a person convicted of a class E felony provided, however, that the court must not impose a sentence of conditional discharge or unconditional discharge if the youthful offender finding was substituted for a conviction of a felony defined in article two hundred twenty of this chapter.

(3) The provisions of section 60.35 of this article shall apply to a sentence imposed upon a youthful offender finding and the amount of the mandatory surcharge and crime victim assistance fee which shall be levied at sentencing shall be equal to the amount specified in such section for the offense of conviction for which the youthful offender finding was substituted.

Added L. 1979, Ch. 411; Amended by L. 1980, Ch. 471; L. 2004, Ch. 56, § 1 (Part F), eff. Aug. 20, 2004, adding subd. 3.

ANNOTATIONS

Maximum sentence.—Upon adjudication of defendant, as a youthful offender, court could not impose three indeterminate terms of imprisonment, each with a maximum of four years, to be served consecutively; if the sentencing court believed that defendant should be imprisoned for a maximum period of 12 years, it should not have afforded him youthful offender treatment. People v. Matthew John G., 60 A.D.2d 919, 401 N.Y.S.2d 575 (2d Dept. 1978).

Youthful offender; maximum sentence.—The imposition of two consecutive terms on defendant granted youthful offender status each with a maximum of four years, is inconsistent with the underlying concept of youthful offender treatment and it is unrealistic to conclude that one eligible for such treatment requires prolonged confinement to achieve the objective of the legislation; if one requires imprisonment for more than four years, he is not eligible for youthful offender treatment. People v. David H., 70 A.D.2d 205, 420 N.Y.S.2d 519 (3d Dept. 1979).

§ 60.04. Authorized disposition; controlled substances and marihuana felony offenses.

1. Applicability. Notwithstanding the provisions of any law, this section shall govern the dispositions authorized when a person is to be sentenced upon a conviction of a felony offense defined in article two hundred twenty or two hundred twenty-one of this chapter or when a person is to be sentenced upon a conviction of such a felony as a multiple felony offender as defined in subdivision five of this section.

2. Class A felony. Every person convicted of a class A felony must be sentenced to imprisonment in accordance with section 70.71 of this title, unless such person is convicted of a class A-II

felony and is sentenced to probation for life in accordance with section 65.00 of this title.

3. Class B felonies. Every person convicted of a class B felony must be sentenced to imprisonment in accordance with the applicable provisions of section 70.70 of this title, unless such person is convicted of a class B felony and is sentenced to probation in accordance with section 65.00 of this title.

4. Alternative sentence. Where a sentence of imprisonment or a sentence of probation as an alternative to imprisonment is not required to be imposed pursuant to subdivision two, three or five of this section, the court may impose any other sentence authorized by section 60.01 of this article, provided that when the court imposes a sentence of imprisonment, such sentence must be in accordance with section 70.70 of this title. Where the court imposes a sentence of imprisonment in accordance with this section, the court may also impose a fine authorized by article eighty of this title and in such case the sentence shall be both imprisonment and a fine.

5. Multiple felony offender. Where the court imposes a sentence upon a second felony drug offender, as defined in paragraph (b) of subdivision one of section 70.70 of this title, it must sentence such offender to imprisonment in accordance with the applicable provisions of section 70.70 of this title.

6. Substance abuse treatment. When the court imposes a sentence of imprisonment which requires a commitment to the state department of correctional services upon a person who stands convicted of a controlled substance or marihuana offense, the court may, upon motion of the defendant in its discretion, issue an order directing that the department of correctional services enroll the defendant in the comprehensive alcohol and substance abuse treatment program in an alcohol and substance abuse correctional annex as defined in subdivision eighteen of section two of the correction law, provided that the defendant will satisfy the statutory eligibility criteria for participation in such program. Notwithstanding the foregoing provisions of this subdivision, any defendant to be enrolled in such program pursuant to this subdivision shall be governed by the same rules and regulations promulgated by the department of correctional services, including without limitation those rules and regulations establishing requirements for completion and those rules and regulations governing discipline and removal from the program. No such period of court ordered corrections based drug abuse treatment pursuant to this subdivision shall be required to extend beyond the defendant's conditional release date.

Added by L. 2004, Ch. 738, § 20, eff. Jan. 13, 2005, and shall apply to crimes committed on or after the effective date, with the exception of subd. 6.

§ 60.05. Authorized dispositions; other class A, B, certain C and D felonies and multiple felony offenders.

1. Applicability. Except as provided in section 60.04 of this article governing the authorized dispositions applicable to felony offenses defined in article two hundred twenty or two hundred twenty-one of this chapter, this section shall govern the dispositions authorized when a person is to be sentenced upon a conviction of a class A felony, a class B felony or a class C, class D or class E felony specified here in, or when a person is to be sentenced upon a conviction of a felony as a multiple felony offender.

2. Class A felony. Except as provided in subdivisions three and four of section 70.06 of this chapter, every person convicted of a class A felony must be sentenced to imprisonment in accordance with section 70.00 of this title, unless such person is convicted of murder in the first degree and is sentenced in accordance with section 60.06 of this article.

3. Class B felony. Except as provided in subdivision six of this section, every person convicted of a class B violent felony offense as defined in subdivision one of section 70.02 of this title, must be sentenced to imprisonment in accordance with such section 70.02; and, except as provided in subdivision six of this section, every person convicted of any other class B felony must be sentenced to imprisonment in accordance with section 70.00 of this title.

4. Certain class C felonies. Except as provided in subdivision six, every person convicted of a class C violent felony offense as defined in subdivision one of section 70.02 of this title, must be sentenced to imprisonment in accordance with section 70.02 of this title; and, except as provided in subdivision six of this section, every person convicted of the class C felonies of: attempt to commit any of the class B felonies of bribery in the first degree as defined in section 200.04, bribe receiving in the first degree as defined in section 200.12, conspiracy in the second degree as defined in section 105.15 and criminal mischief in the first degree as defined in section 145.12; criminal usury in the first degree as defined in section 190.42, rewarding official misconduct in the first degree as defined in section 200.22, receiving reward for official misconduct in the first degree as defined in section 200.27, attempt to promote prostitution in the first degree as defined in section 230.32, promoting prostitution in the second degree as defined in section 230.30, arson in the third degree as defined in section 150.10 of this chapter, must be sentenced to imprisonment in accordance with section 70.00 of this title.

5. Certain class D felonies. Except as provided in subdivision six of this section, every

person convicted of the class D felonies of assault in the second degree as defined in section 120.05 or attempt to commit a class C felony as defined in section 230.30 of this chapter, must be sentenced in accordance with section 70.00 or 85.00 of this title.

6. Multiple felony offender. When the court imposes sentence upon a second violent felony offender, as defined in section 70.04, or a second felony offender, as defined in section 70.06, the court must impose a sentence of imprisonment in accordance with section 70.04 or 70.06, as the case may be, unless it imposes a sentence of imprisonment in accordance with section 70.08 or 70.10.

7. Fines. Where the court imposes a sentence of imprisonment in accordance with this section, the court also may impose a fine authorized by article eighty and in such case the sentence shall be both imprisonment and a fine.

Added by L. 1973, Ch. 277; **Amended** by L. 1973, Chs. 278, 1051; L. 1974, Chs. 367, 1041; L. 1976, Ch. 424; L. 1977, Ch. 22; L. 1978, Chs. 481, 627; L. 1979, Ch. 410; L. 1980, Ch. 233; L. 1981, Ch. 711; L. 1995, Ch. 1, § 1, eff. Sept. 1, 1995, amending subd. 2; L. 2004, Ch. 738, § 24, eff. Jan. 13, 2005, amending section heading and subds. 1 through 5.

ANNOTATIONS

Mandatory indeterminate term.—Where defendant was convicted of several violent offenses, pursuant to Penal Law Sections 60.05 and 70.02, an indeterminate term of imprisonment was mandatory and the court was not permitted to consider sentencing alternatives. People v. Wallis, 147 A.D.2d 821, 537 N.Y.S.2d 910, 911 (3d Dept. 1989).

—Court imposed a determinate term of imprisonment based upon its misunderstanding that such a sentence is mandatory for assault in the second degree, however a determinate term of imprisonment is authorized sentence for that offense, but it is not required and, although some imprisonment is mandatory a definite term of imprisonment of one year or less under § 70.00 or an intermittent term of imprisonment under §§ 60.05 and 85.00 is also authorized as is a split sentence of imprisonment and probation, appellate court vacated sentence and remanded for resentence. People v. Endresz, 1 A.D.3d 888, 767 N.Y.S.2d 732 (4th Dept. 2003).

Second felony offender.—Where the defendant had been convicted of the felony of criminal possession of a weapon in the third degree prior to commission of the offense at bar, his contention on appeal that he was improperly sentenced as a second felony offender was meritless. People v. Britton, 208 A.D.2d 761, 619 N.Y.S.2d 571 (2d Dept. 1994).

§ 60.06. Authorized disposition; murder in the first degree offenders; certain murder in the second degree offenders; certain terrorism offenders; criminal possession of a chemical weapon or biological weapon offenders; criminal use of a chemical weapon or biological weapon offenders.

When a defendant is convicted of murder in the first degree as defined in section 125.27 of this chapter, the court shall, in accordance with the provisions of section 400.27 of the criminal procedure law, sentence the defendant to death, to life imprisonment without parole in accordance with subdivision five of section 70.00 of this title, or to a term of imprisonment for a class A-I felony other than a sentence of life imprisonment without parole, in accordance with subdivisions one through three of section 70.00 of this title. When a person is convicted of murder in the second degree as defined in subdivision five of section 125.25 of this chapter, the court shall sentence the defendant to life imprisonment without parole in accordance with subdivision five of section 70.00 of this title. When a defendant is convicted of the crime of terrorism as defined in section 490.25 of this chapter, and the specified offense the defendant committed is a class A-I felony offense, or when a defendant is convicted of the crime of criminal possession of a chemical weapon or biological weapon in the first degree as defined in section 490.45 of this chapter, or when a defendant is convicted of the crime of criminal use of a chemical weapon or biological weapon in the first degree as defined in section 490.55 of this chapter, the court shall sentence the defendant to life imprisonment without parole in accordance with subdivision five of section 70.00 of this title; provided, however, that nothing in this section shall preclude or prevent a sentence of death when the defendant is also convicted of murder in the first degree as defined in section 125.27 of this chapter.

Added by L. 1974, Ch. 367; **Amended** by L. 1995, Ch. 1, § 2, eff. Sept. 1, 1995; L. 2004, Ch. 1, § 4 (Part A), deemed in full force and effect on Apr. 1, 2004; L. 2004, Ch. 459, eff. Nov. 1, 2004.

§ 60.07. Authorized disposition; criminal attack on operators of for-hire vehicles.

1. Notwithstanding any other provision of law to the contrary, when a court has found, pursuant to the provisions of section 200.61 of the criminal procedure law, both that a person has been convicted of a specified offense as defined in subdivision two of this section and the victim of such offense was operating a for-hire vehicle in the course of providing for-hire vehicle services at the time of the commission of such offense, the sentence of imprisonment imposed upon conviction for such offense shall be the sentence authorized by the applicable provisions of article seventy of this chapter, provided, however, that the minimum term of an indeterminate sentence or minimum determinate sentence shall be not less than three years nor more than five years greater than the minimum term or sentence otherwise required to be imposed pursuant to such provisions. The provisions of this subdivision shall not apply where the court, having regard to the nature and circumstances of the crime and the history and character of the defendant, finds on the record that such additional term or sentence would be

unduly harsh and that not imposing such additional term or sentence would be consistent with the public safety and would not deprecate the seriousness of the crime.

2. For purposes of this section:

(a) the term "specified offense" shall mean an attempt to commit murder in the second degree as defined in section 125.25 of this chapter, gang assault in the first degree as defined in section 120.07 of this chapter, gang assault in the second degree as defined in section 120.06 of this chapter, assault in the first degree as defined in section 120.10 of this chapter, manslaughter in the first degree as defined in section 125.20 of this chapter, manslaughter in the second degree as defined in section 125.15 of this chapter, robbery in the first degree as defined in section 160.15 of this chapter, robbery in the second degree as defined in section 160.10 of this chapter, or the attempted commission of any of the following offenses: gang assault in the first degree as defined in section 120.07, assault in the first degree as defined in section 120.10, manslaughter in the first degree as defined in section 125.20 or robbery in the first degree as defined in section 160.15;

(b) the term "for-hire vehicle" shall mean a vehicle designed to carry not more than five passengers for compensation and such vehicle is a taxicab, as defined in section one hundred forty-eight-a of the vehicle and traffic law, a livery, as such term is defined in section one hundred twenty-one-e of the vehicle and traffic law, or a "black car", as such term is defined in paragraph (g) of this subdivision;

(c) the term "livery car base" shall mean a central facility, wherever located, that dispatches a livery operator to both pick-up and discharge passengers in the state;

(d) "for-hire vehicle services" shall mean:

(i) with respect to a taxicab, the transport of passengers pursuant to a license or permit issued by a local authority by a person duly authorized to operate such taxicab;

(ii) with respect to a livery, the transport of passengers by a livery operator while affiliated with a livery car base; or

(iii) with respect to a "black car", the transport of passengers by a "black car operator" pursuant to dispatches from or by a central dispatch facility regardless of where the pick-up and discharge occurs, and, with respect to dispatches from or by a central dispatch facility located outside the state, all dispatches involving a pick-up in the state, regardless of where the discharge occurs.

(e) "livery operator" shall mean the registered owner of a livery, as such term is defined in section one hundred twenty-one-e of the vehicle and traffic law, or a driver designated by such registered owner to operate the registered owner's

livery as the registered owner's authorized designee, where such registered owner or driver provides services while affiliated with a livery car base;

(f) "black car operator" shall mean the registered owner of a "black car" or a driver designated by such registered owner to operate the registered owner's black car as the registered owner's authorized designee; and

(g) "black car" shall mean a for-hire vehicle dispatched from a central facility, which has certified to the satisfaction of the department of state pursuant to article six-F of the executive law that more than ninety percent of the central facility's for-hire business is on a payment basis other than direct cash payment by a passenger.

Added by L. 2000, Ch. 148, § 9, eff. Nov. 1, 2000, and shall apply to offenses committed on or after such date.

§ 60.08. Authorized dispositions; resentencing of certain controlled substance offenders.

Any person convicted of an offense and sentenced to prison for an indeterminate sentence, the minimum of which was at least one year and the maximum of which was life imprisonment, which sentence was imposed pursuant to chapter two hundred seventy-six, two hundred seventy-seven, two hundred seventy-eight, or ten hundred fifty-one of the laws of nineteen hundred seventy-three, and for which such sentence was imposed upon conviction of the crime of criminal possession of a controlled substance in the first degree, criminal possession of a controlled substance in the second degree, criminal possession of a controlled substance in the third degree, criminal sale of a controlled substance in the first degree, criminal sale of a controlled substance in the second degree, or criminal sale of a controlled substance in the third degree, and the sole controlled substance involved was methadone, may apply, upon notice to the appropriate district attorney, for resentencing in the court which originally imposed sentence.

Such resentencing shall, unless substantial justice dictates otherwise, be pursuant to the current provisions of the penal law, and shall include credit for any jail time incurred upon the subject conviction as well as credit for any period of incarceration incurred pursuant to the sentence originally imposed.

In cases where the proof before the court is not available or is not sufficiently reliable to determine the amount of methadone present in any preparation, compound, mixture or substance containing methadone, there shall exist a rebuttable presumption that each ounce of the preparation, compound, mixture or substance containing methadone, there shall exist a rebuttable presumption that each ounce of the preparation, compound, mixture or substance contained sixty milligrams of methadone.

Added by L. 1975, Ch. 783.

§ 60.09. Authorized dispositions; resentencing of certain persons convicted of specific controlled substance offenses.

a. Any person convicted of an offense as defined in section 115.05, 220.16, 220.18, 220.39 or 220.41 of this chapter or of an attempt thereof, for an act committed on or after September first, nineteen hundred seventy-three but prior to the date on which the provisions of this section become effective, may, upon notice to the appropriate district attorney, apply for resentencing in the court which originally imposed sentence. Such resentencing shall be in accordance with the provisions of subdivision (b) of this section and shall include credit for any jail time incurred upon the subject conviction as well as credit for any period of incarceration incurred pursuant to the sentence originally imposed

b. A court, upon an application specified in subdivision (a) of this section may resentence a person as follows:

(i) if the conviction was for a class A-III offense the court may impose a new maximum term which shall be no less than three times the amount of the minimum term imposed in the original sentence and no more than twenty-five years;

(ii) if the conviction was for a class A-II offense the court may impose a new minimum term which shall be no less than three years imprisonment and no more than eight and one-third years;

(iii) upon resentence of a person as specified in paragraph (i) of this subdivision the court shall resentence the person to the same minimum term previously imposed;

(iv) upon resentence of a person as specified in paragraph (ii) of this subdivision the court shall impose a maximum term of life imprisonment;

(v) if the conviction was for an offense as specified in section 115.05 of this chapter and the offense which was the object of the criminal facilitation was a class A-III felony then the court shall set aside the conviction and substitute it with a conviction for violation of section 115.01 or 115.00 of this chapter, whichever is appropriate under the facts of the case, and impose a sentence in accordance with those provisions.

c. Upon resentence as provided in this section the court may not impose a sentence greater than the sentence previously imposed.

Added by L. 1979, Ch. 410.

ANNOTATIONS

Appeal.—The decision to grant the application for resentencing is discretionary and there is no statutory provision for an appeal. People v. DeJesus, 54 N.Y.2d 447, 446 N.Y.S.2d 201, 430 N.E.2d 1254 (1981).

Curative relief.—PL § 60.09 should be construed as providing curative relief and such relief should be granted liberally unless compelling factors dictate the contrary. People v. Sea, 102 Misc. 2d 901, 424 N.Y.S.2d 670 (Dutchess Co. Ct. 1980).

Resentence invalid.—The statute permits the sentencing court to deny an application for resentencing outright and thus maintain the original sentence, but if the court does exercise its discretion to resentence the defendant, it must do so within the limitations of the resentencing structure contained in PL § 60.09. People v. Aken, 83 A.D.2d 617, 441 N.Y.S.2d 285 (2d Dept. 1981).

People's request for minimum sentence.—Trial court was not constrained by People's insistence on a minimum sentence of two and one-third years, but, rather, court had sentencing scope from one year to life, in proceeding in which the defendant pled guilty to criminal possession of a controlled substance in the third degree. People v. Best, 77 A.D.2d 836, 431 N.Y.S.2d 24 (1st Dept. 1980).

§ 60.10. Authorized disposition; juvenile offender.

1. When a juvenile offender is convicted of a crime, the court shall sentence the defendant to imprisonment in accordance with section 70.05 or sentence him upon a youthful offender finding in accordance with section 60.02 of this chapter.

2. Subdivision one of this section shall apply when sentencing a juvenile offender notwithstanding the provisions of any other law that deals with the authorized sentence for persons who are not juvenile offenders. Provided, however, that the limitation prescribed by this section shall not be deemed or construed to bar use of a conviction of a juvenile offender, other than a juvenile offender who has been adjudicated a youthful offender pursuant to section 720.20 of the criminal procedure law, as a previous or predicate felony offender under section 70.04, 70.06, 70.08 or 70.10, when sentencing a person who commits a felony after he has reached the age of sixteen.

Added by L. 1978, Ch. 481; Amended by L. 1979, Ch. 411.

§ 60.11. Authorized dispositions; criminal possession of a weapon in the fourth degree.

When a person is to be sentenced upon a conviction of the crime of criminal possession of a weapon in the fourth degree as defined in subdivision one of section 265.01 as a result of a plea of guilty entered in satisfaction of an indictment or count thereof charging the defendant with the class D violent felony offense of criminal possession of a weapon in the third degree as defined in subdivision four of section 265.02, the court must sentence the defendant in accordance with the provisions of section 70.15.

Added by L. 1980, Ch. 233.

§ 60.12. Authorized disposition; alternative indeterminate sentence of imprisonment; domestic violence cases.

1. Notwithstanding any other provision of law, where a court is imposing sentence pursuant to section 70.02 upon a conviction for an offense enumerated in subdivision one of such section, other than an offense defined in article one hundred thirty of this chapter, and is authorized or required pursuant to such section to impose a determinate sentence of imprisonment for such offense, the court, upon a determination following a hearing that (a) the defendant was the victim of physical, sexual or psychological abuse by the victim or intended victim of such offense, (b) such abuse was a factor in causing the defendant to commit such offense and (c) the victim or intended victim of such offense was a member of the same family or household as the defendant as such term is defined in subdivision one of section 530.11 of the criminal procedure law, may, in lieu of imposing such determinate sentence of imprisonment, impose an indeterminate sentence of imprisonment in accordance with subdivisions two and three of this section.

2. The maximum term of an indeterminate sentence imposed pursuant to subdivision one of this section must be fixed by the court as follows:

(a) For a class B felony, the term must be at least six years and must not exceed twenty-five years;

(b) For a class C felony, the term must be at least four and one-half years and must not exceed fifteen years;

(c) For a class D felony, the term must be at least three years and must not exceed seven years; and

(d) For a class E felony, the term must be at least three years and must not exceed four years.

3. The minimum period of imprisonment under an indeterminate sentence imposed pursuant to subdivision one of this section must be fixed by the court at one-half of the maximum term imposed and must be specified in the sentence.

Added by L. 1998, Ch. 1, § 1, eff. Aug. 6, 1998, and shall apply to offenses committed on or after Sept. 1, 1998. Offenses committed prior to Sept. 1, 1998 shall be governed by the provisions of law in effect at the time the offense was committed; provided, however, that nothing contained herein shall be deemed to affect the application, qualification, expiration, reversion or repeal of any provision of law amended by any section of L. 1998, Ch. 1 and the provisions of L. 1998, Ch. 1 shall be applied or qualified or shall expire or revert or be deemed repealed in the same manner, to the same extent and on the same date as the case may be as otherwise provided by law.

§ 60.20. Authorized dispositions; traffic infraction.

1. When a person is convicted of a traffic infraction, the sentence of the court shall be as follows:

(a) A period of conditional discharge, as provided in article sixty-five; or

(b) Unconditional discharge as provided in section 65.20; or

(c) A fine or a sentence to a term of imprisonment, or both, as prescribed in and authorized by the provision that defines the infraction; or

(d) A sentence of intermittent imprisonment, as provided in article eighty-five.

2. Where a sentence of conditional discharge is imposed for a traffic infraction, all incidents of the sentence shall be the same as would be applicable if the sentence were for a violation.

Amended by L. 1970, Ch. 477.

§ 60.25. Authorized dispositions; corporation.

When a corporation is convicted of an offense, the sentence of the court shall be as follows:

(a) A fine authorized by section 80.10; or

(b) Where authorized by section 65.05, a period of conditional discharge as provided in that section; or

(c) Where authorized by section 65.20, unconditional discharge as provided in that section.

In any case where a corporation has been sentenced to a period of conditional discharge and such sentence is revoked, the court shall sentence the corporation to pay a fine.

ANNOTATION

Jury trial; penalty of forfeiture.—Defendant, a mercantile corporation charged with violating Sabbath Laws was entitled to a jury trial because the statute authorized the trial court to declare a forfeiture of all property on sale in violation of Sabbath Law and Constitution of N.Y. State conferred right to jury trial in such a case. People v. Witherill, 29 N.Y.2d 446, 328 N.Y.S.2d 668, 278 N.E.2d 905 (1972).

§ 60.27. Restitution and reparation.

1. In addition to any of the dispositions authorized by this article, the court shall consider restitution or reparation to the victim of the crime and may require restitution or reparation as part of the sentence imposed upon a person convicted of an offense, and after providing the district attorney with an opportunity to be heard in accordance with the provisions of this subdivision, require the defendant to make restitution of the fruits of his or her offense or reparation for the actual out-of-pocket loss caused thereby and, in the case of a violation of section 190.78, 190.79, 190.80, 190.82 or 190.83 of this chapter, any costs or losses incurred due to any adverse action taken against the victim. The district attorney shall where appropriate, advise the court at or before the time of sentencing that the victim seeks restitution or reparation, the extent of injury

or economic loss or damage of the victim, and the amount of restitution or reparation sought by the victim in accordance with his or her responsibilities under subdivision two of section 390.50 of the criminal procedure law and article twenty-three of the executive law. The court shall hear and consider the information presented by the district attorney in this regard. In that event, or when the victim impact statement reports that the victim seeks restitution or reparation, the court shall require, unless the interests of justice dictate otherwise, in addition to any of the dispositions authorized by this article that the defendant make restitution of the fruits of the offense and reparation for the actual out-of-pocket loss and, in the case of a violation of section 190.78, 190.79, 190.80, 190.82 or 190.83 of this chapter, any costs or losses incurred due to any adverse action, caused thereby to the victim. In the event that restitution or reparation are not ordered, the court shall clearly state its reasons on the record. Adverse action as used in this subdivision shall mean and include actual loss incurred by the victim and the consequential financial losses from such action.

2. Whenever the court requires restitution or reparation to be made, the court must make a finding as to the dollar amount of the fruits of the offense and the actual out-of-pocket loss to the victim caused by the offense. In making this finding, the court must consider any victim impact statement provided to the court. If the record does not contain sufficient evidence to support such finding or upon request by the defendant, the court must conduct a hearing upon the issue in accordance with the procedure set forth in section 400.30 of the criminal procedure law.

3. The provisions of sections 420.10, 420.20 and 420.30 of the criminal procedure law shall apply in the collection and remission of restitution and reparation.

4. For purposes of the imposition, determination and collection of restitution or reparation, the following definitions shall apply:

(a) the term "offense" shall include the offense for which a defendant was convicted, as well as any other offense that is part of the same criminal transaction or that is contained in any other accusatory instrument disposed of by any plea of guilty by the defendant to an offense.

(b) the term "victim" shall include the victim of the offense, the representative of a crime victim as defined in subdivision six of section six hundred twenty-one of the executive law, an individual whose identity was assumed or whose personal identifying information was used in violation of section 190.78, 190.79 or 190.80 of this chapter, or any person who has suffered a financial loss as a direct result of the acts of a defendant in violation of section 190.78, 190.79, 190.80, 190.82 or 190.83 of this chapter, a good

samaritan as defined in section six hundred twenty-one of the executive law and the crime victims' board or other governmental agency that has received an application for or has provided financial assistance or compensation to the victim.

5. (a) Except upon consent of the defendant or as provided in paragraph (b) of this subdivision, or as a condition of probation or conditional discharge as provided in paragraph (g) of subdivision two of section 65.10 of this chapter, the amount of restitution or reparation required by the court shall not exceed fifteen thousand dollars in the case of a conviction for a felony, or ten thousand dollars in the case of a conviction for any offense other than a felony.

(b) The court in its discretion may impose restitution or reparation in excess of the amounts specified in paragraph (a) of this subdivision, provided however that the amount in excess must be limited to the return of the victim's property, including money, or the equivalent value thereof; and reimbursement for medical expenses actually incurred by the victim prior to sentencing as a result of the offense committed by the defendant.

6. Any payment made as restitution or reparation pursuant to this section shall not limit, preclude or impair any liability for damages in any civil action or proceeding for an amount in excess of such payment.

7. In the event that the court requires restitution or reparation to be made to a person and that person dies prior to the completion of said restitution or reparation, the remaining payments shall be made to the estate of the deceased.

8. The court shall in all cases where restitution or reparation is imposed direct as part of the disposition that the defendant pay a designated surcharge of five percent of the entire amount of a restitution or reparation payment to the official or organization designated pursuant to subdivision eight of section 420.10 of the criminal procedure law. The designated surcharge shall not exceed five percent of the amount actually collected. Upon the filing of an affidavit of the official or organization designated pursuant to subdivision eight of section 420.10 of the criminal procedure law demonstrating that the actual cost of the collection and administration of restitution or reparation in a particular case exceeds five percent of the entire amount of the payment or the amount actually collected, as the case may be, the court shall direct that the defendant pay an additional surcharge of not more than five percent of the entire amount of a restitution or reparation payment to such official or organization, or the actual cost of collection or administration, whichever is less unless, upon application of the defendant, the court determines that imposition of such additional surcharge would cause undue hardship to the defendant, or any other person who is financially supported by the defendant, or would otherwise not be in the interest of justice. Such

additional surcharge, when added to the initial five percent surcharge, shall not exceed ten percent of the amount actually collected.

9. If the offense of which a person is convicted is a class A, class B, class C, or class D felony involving the sale of a controlled substance, as defined in article two hundred twenty of this chapter, and no other victim who is a person is seeking restitution in the case, the term "victim" as used in this section, in addition to its ordinary meaning shall mean any law enforcement agency of the state of New York or any subdivision thereof which has expended funds in the purchase of any controlled substance from such person or his agent as part of the investigation leading to such conviction. Any restitution which may be required to be made to a law enforcement agency pursuant to this section shall be limited to the amount of funds expended in the actual purchase of such controlled substance by such law enforcement agency, less the amount of any funds which have been or will be recovered from any other source, and shall not include a designated surcharge pursuant to subdivision eight of this section. Any law enforcement agency seeking restitution pursuant to this section shall file with the court and the district attorney an affidavit stating that funds expended in the actual purchase of a controlled substance for which restitution is being sought have not been and will not be recovered from any other source or in any other civil or criminal proceeding. Any law enforcement agency receiving restitution pursuant to this section shall promptly transmit to the commissioner of the division of criminal justice services a report stating the dollar amount of the restitution received.

10. If the offense of which a person is convicted is defined in section 150.10, 150.15 or 150.20 of this chapter, and no other victim who is a person is seeking restitution in the case, the term "victim" as used in this section, in addition to its ordinary meaning, shall mean any municipality which has expended funds or will expend funds for the purpose of restoration, rehabilitation or clean-up of the site of the arson. Any restitution which may be required to be made to a municipality pursuant to this section shall be limited to the amount of funds reasonably expended or to be expended for the purpose of restoration, rehabilitation or clean-up of the site of the arson, less the amount of any funds which have been or will be recovered from any other source, and shall not include a designated surcharge pursuant to subdivision eight of this section. Any municipality seeking restitution pursuant to this section shall file with the court, district attorney and defense counsel an affidavit stating that the funds reasonably expended or to be expended for which restitution is being sought have not been and will not be recovered from any other source or in any other civil or criminal proceeding.

11. * Notwithstanding any other provision of this section to the contrary, when a person is convicted of harming an animal trained to aid a person with a disability in the second degree as defined in section 195.11 of this chapter, or harming an animal trained to aid a person with a disability in the first degree as defined in section 195.12 of this chapter, the court, in addition to any other sentence, shall order the payment of restitution to the person with a disability who was aided by such animal. [*Added by L. 1999, Ch. 160.*]

11. * If the offense of which a person is convicted is defined in section 240.50, subdivision one or two of section 240.55, section 240.60 or section 240.61 of this chapter, and no other victim who is a person is seeking restitution in the case, the term "victim" as used in this subdivision, in addition to the ordinary meaning, shall mean any school, municipality, fire district, fire company, fire corporation, ambulance association, ambulance corporation, or other legal or public entity engaged in providing emergency services which has expended funds for the purpose of responding to a false report of an incident or false bomb as defined in section 240.50, subdivision one or two of section 240.55, section 240.60 or section 240.61 of this chapter. Any restitution which may be required to be made to a victim pursuant to this subdivision shall be limited to the amount of funds reasonably expended for the purpose of responding to such false report of incident or false bomb, less the amount of any funds which have been or will be recovered from any other source and shall not include a designated surcharge pursuant to subdivision eight of this section. Any victim seeking restitution pursuant to this subdivision shall file with the court, district attorney and defense counsel an affidavit stating that the funds reasonably expended for which restitution is being sought have not been and will not be recovered from any other source or in any other civil or criminal proceeding, except as provided for by section 3-112 of the general obligations law. [*Added by L. 1999, Ch. 207.*]

12. [*Effective Mar. 1, 2004.*] If the offense of which a person is convicted is defined in section 155.25, 155.30, 155.35, 155.40 or 155.42 of this chapter, and the property taken is timber, the court may upon conviction, in addition to any other sentence, direct the defendant to pay the rightful owner of such timber an amount equal to treble the stumpage value of the timber stolen as defined in section 71-0703 of the environmental conservation law and for any permanent and substantial damage caused to the land or the improvements thereon as a result of such violation. Such reparations shall be of such kind, nature and extent as will reasonably restore the lands affected by the violation to their condition immediately before the violation and may be made by physical restoration of such lands and/or by the assessment of monetary payment to make such restoration.

* **Editor's Note:** The 1999 Legislature added two versions of subdivision 11 to § 60.27, each without reference to each other.

Added by L. 1980, Ch. 290; **Amended** by L. 1983, Chs. 397, 468; L. 1984, Chs. 335, 965; L. 1985, Chs. 14, 187, 233, 506; L. 1986, Ch. 615; L. 1991, Ch, 363, amending subd. 8; L. 1991, Ch. 545; L. 1992, Ch. 618, amending subds. 1, 2, 4 and 5(a); L. 1996, Ch. 310, adding subd. 10, effective Nov. 1, 1996; L. 1999, Chs. 160, eff. Nov. 1, 1999, and Ch. 207, eff. July 6, 1999, each adding a subd. 11; L. 2002, Ch. 619, §§ 1 and 2, amending subds. 1 and 4(b), eff. Nov. 1, 2002; L. 2003, Ch. 602, § 14, eff. Mar. 1, 2004, adding subd. 12.

ANNOTATIONS

Necessity of a hearing.—Absent a request by defendant, a hearing to determine out-of-pocket expenses is necessary only where record does not contain sufficient evidence of loss. Where the presentence report contains a fully detailed and documented list of medical expenses, including itemized provider medical expense reports whose accuracy is uncontested, no hearing is required. People v. Kim, 91 N.Y.2d 407, 671 N.Y.S.2d 420, 694 N.E.2d 421 (1998).

—Defendant's claim of error relating to the court's failure to hold a hearing on the restitution issue was not preserved for appeal. In any case, there was no error since the defendant and his counsel consented to the restitution ordered. In addition, the court did not err in relying on two letters from the victim in determining restitution; the defendant's experience in numismatics and his position as a benefactor of the victim provided him with an understanding of the damages that arose from his theft of numerous coins from the victim. People v. Suros, 209 A.D.2d 203, 618 N.Y.S.2d 532 (1st Dept. 1994).

—The sentencing court did not err in directing the defendant to make restitution in the amount of $258 without first conducting a hearing, inasmuch as the defendant had consented to pay the restitution as part of the plea agreement, and the record was otherwise adequate to support the amount of money directed to be paid. People v. Oliver, 182 A.D.2d 716, 582 N.Y.S.2d 265 (2d Dept. 1992).

—A hearing with respect to the proper amount of restitution is warranted unless the defendant explicitly admits the amount of the victim's monetary loss. People v. Kade, 153 A.D.2d 907, 545 N.Y.S.2d 609 (2d Dept. 1989).

—Necessity of hearing was obviated where defendant agreed to amount of restitution during allocution and record contained evidence of victim's medical costs and itemized damages to police vehicles, which supported amount ordered. People v. Drew, 16 A.D.3d 840, 792 N.Y.S.2d 639 (3d Dept. 2005).

—Sworn testimony of victim, which included itemized listing of damages, including expenses to replace damaged items, medical expenses, and lost wages, was sufficient to support restitution award. People v. Periard, 15 A.D.3d 693, 788 N.Y.S.2d 725 (3d Dept. 2005).

—Although defendant did not request a hearing, one should have been held because the plea minutes and record did not contain sufficient evidence to support the finding of the amount of restitution ordered. People v. Harrington, 3 A.D.3d 737, 770 N.Y.S.2d 792 (3d Dept. 2004).

—The court erred in failing to hold a hearing on the restitution issue where defendant's counsel requested a hearing; there was no express consent to, or admission of, the victim's monetary loss. People v. Spry, 214 A.D.2d 771, 625 N.Y.S.2d 98 (3d Dept. 1995).

—Court should have conducted a hearing to determine the amount of restitution, the manner of payment, and the defendant's financial ability to pay and should not have relied exclusively on information supplied by the police department; the matter was remitted to the county court for a hearing, but this was not a sufficient reason for vacatur of the defendant's sentence in its entirety. People v. Frisco, 221 A.D.2d 779, 633 N.Y.S.2d 422 (3d Dept. 1995).

—Since the record contained neither consent, admission nor evidence of the victims' losses, the matter had to be remitted for a hearing to determine the proper amount of restitution. People v. Jody M., 208 A.D.2d 1019, 618 N.Y.S.2d 587 (3d Dept. 1994).

—Matter remitted for restitution hearing notwithstanding the purported waiver of the hearing by defendant's failure to request

it. People v. Bohart, 153 A.D.2d 963, 545 N.Y.S.2d 613 (3d Dept. 1989).

—Evidentiary hearing to determine victim's out-of-pocket expenses is not required where the record contains sufficient documentation to establish amount of expenses and defendant did not request a hearing. People v. Gahrey, M.O., 231 A.D.2d 909, 647 N.Y.S.2d 626 (4th Dept. 1996).

—The court did not err in imposing restitution without a hearing to determine the amount of restitution in violation of § 60.27 because: (1) defendant was represented by counsel and knowingly and voluntarily waived her right to counsel and stipulated to the amount of restitution; and (2) defendant failed to demonstrate that her waiver of the hearing constituted a departure from the "essential nature" of her right to be sentenced in accordance with the law. People v. Hill, 207 A.D.2d 1029, 617 N.Y.S.2d 676 (4th Dept. 1994).

—The court erred when it directed defendant to pay $800.00 in restitution without first conducting a hearing on the amount of the restitution to be paid. People v. Gettys, 162 A.D.2d 963, 559 N.Y.S.2d 50 (4th Dept. 1990).

—Where court ordered restitution without holding a hearing and relied solely upon the probation report, the provision for restitution was deleted. People v. Cheatum, 148 A.D.2d 986, 539 N.Y.S.2d 222 (4th Dept. 1989).

—Restitution hearing not necessary where the court based its findings that the fruits of the crime amounted to $900 from the entire record, which included the victim's sworn statement to that effect. People v. Welsher, 154 A.D.2d 915, 545 N.Y.S.2d 870, 871 (4th Dept. 1989).

Amount of restitution.—Sentencing court acted properly in requiring the defendant to make restitution to Nassau County for costs that resulted from injuries caused by defendant to a police officer, where the county became legally obligated to incur expenses for medical costs and sick leave because of injuries sustained by the officer, who was attempting to arrest the defendant for burglary. People v. Cruz, 81 N.Y.2d 996, 599 N.Y.S.2d 533, 615 N.E.2d 1017 (1993).

—Imposition of a mandatory surcharge and a crime victim's assistance fee pursuant to section 60.35 is inconsistent with the requirement that a defendant pay restitution pursuant to section 60.27. People v. Espola, 238 A.D.2d 281, 656 N.Y. S.2d 268 (1st Dept. 1997).

—Court erred when it ordered the defendant to make restitution to the Rockland County Narcotics Task Force for the money that the agency expended in the sales with the defendant. People v. Wilson, 182 A.D.2d 734, 582 N.Y.S.2d 462 (2d Dept. 1992).

—In directing a judgment of restitution, the sum cannot exceed the amount alleged to have been misappropriated. People v. Smith, 146 A.D.2d 722, 537 N.Y.S.2d 65 (2d Dept. 1989).

—Restitution or reparation is not limited to dollar amount included in indictment; court can order actual repayment of "out-of-pocket losses caused by the offense for which defendant was convicted or any other offense that is part of the same criminal transaction." People v. Melino, 16 A.D.3d 908,791 N.Y.S.2d 718 (3d Dept. 2005).

—Defendant's waiver of appeal precluded court from considering his objection to the amount of restitution ordered for those crimes related to his plea, however, court could consider argument that a portion of the restitution award was not authorized by law, an objection to the legality of a sentence may not be waived. People v. Casiano, 8 A.D.3d 761, 779 N.Y.S.2d 259 (3d Dept. 2004).

—Restitution order was vacated where record was unclear as to whether the restitution was intended to compensate for uncharged crimes or for those charged in the indictment. People v. Miller, 251 A.D.2d 747, 674 N.Y.S.2d 471 (3d Dept. 1998).

—Court erred in requiring defendant to make restitution to the county to cover the expense of transporting the arresting officer from Nebraska for trial. People v. Stacey, 173 A.D.2d 960, 569 N.Y.S.2d 470 (3d Dept. 1991).

—In determining the proper amount of restitution the court is entitled to consider hearsay testimony such as the damage estimate report prepared by an adjustor on the victim's behalf. People v. Francis L.M., 278 A.D.2d 919, 718 N.Y.S.2d 669 (4th Dept. 2000).

—Consideration of victim impact statement alone is an insufficient basis upon which to determine the amount of restitution without a hearing. People v. Lynch, 255 A.D.2d 1001, 681 N.Y.S.2d 183 (4th Dept. 1998).

—Where defendant pleaded guilty to grand larceny in the first degree, court was not required to consider defendant's ability to pay; based on proof received at restitution hearing, restitution in excess of one million dollars was proper. People v. Emmi, 254 A.D.2d 840, 679 N.Y.S.2d 484 (4th Dept. 1998).

Consent.—There was no error in directing the defendant to pay restitution to the police department where the defendant and his counsel expressly agreed to the amount of restitution, even though the police department failed to file an affidavit as required by § 60.27(9). People v. Serafini, 213 A.D.2d 1066, 624 N.Y.S.2d 328 (4th Dept. 1995).

Joint and several liability.—The restitution order properly imposed joint and several liability for the full amount of the medical expenses among all the defendants, rather than dividing the amount equally among defendant and accomplices and assigning each a portion of the restitution amount. People v. Kim, 91 N.Y.2d 407, 671 N.Y.S.2d 420, 694 N.E.2d 421 (1998).

Appeal.—An error which results in an illegal sentence of restitution can be reviewed on appeal as a question of law. People v. Zinke, 147 A.D.2d 106, 541 N.Y.S.2d 986 (1st Dept. 1989).

Who may be a "victim."—Neither a county nor its District Attorney is a "victim" as defined in Penal Law § 60.27 such that either might be qualified to receive restitution for "public monies . . . expended in the pursuit of solving crimes." People v. Snow, 180 A.D.2d 698, 579 N.Y.S.2d 714 (2d Dept. 1992).

—Defendant, a physician and sole shareholder, officer, and director of a medical services corporation, convicted on misdemeanor charges of failure to file corporate tax returns (Tax Law § 1801(b)), was appropriately required to personally pay restitution for the loss to the taxing authority, specifically, the corporate taxes for the years returns were not filed. People v. Brigham, 261 A.D.2d 43, 702 N.Y.S.2d 119 (3d Dept. 1999), *appeal withdrawn,* 94 N.Y.2d 901 (2000).

—The cost to extradite defendant, who moved to California and against whom bail jumping charges were never filed, did not constitute "actual out of pocket loss" for the extradicting county, so county was not a "victim"; restitution for defendant's return from California was not proper. People v. La Fave, Jr., 265 A.D.2d 740, 698 N.Y.S.2d 733 (3d Dept. 1999), *appeal denied,* 94 N.Y.2d 881 (2000).

—For the purposes of restitution, business tenant of a building vandalized by defendant constituted a "victim"; defendant broke windows in the building and damaged a computer used by the tenant in his business, resulting in an "out-of-pocket" loss to victim. People v. Christman, 265 A.D.2d 856, 696 N.Y.S.2d 594 (4th Dept. 1999).

—Court erred in ordering defendant to pay restitution to reimburse Sheriff for monies expended to secure defendant's return to New York on a warrant issued for the defendant's failure to appear on a DWI charge; defendant had not committed an "offense" within the meaning of the Penal Law, and the Sheriff was not a "victim," since the expenditure of public monies by the Sheriff to return defendant to the jurisdiction for prosecution was part of its normal law enforcement operating costs. People v. Watson, 197 A.D.2d 880, 602 N.Y.S.2d 471 (4th Dept. 1993).

Restitution as condition of probation.—The court erred in ordering the payment of restitution as a term and condition of defendant's probation beyond the period of probation. People v. Meade, 195 A.D.2d 756, 600 N.Y.S.2d 353 (3d Dept. 1993).

—Judgment of conviction could not be modified to include restoration and reparation after the sentence had been imposed where no notice had been given by the People prior to sentencing that restoration and reparation were going to be sought. People v. Kevin C., 265 A.D.2d 828, 697 N.Y.S.2d 217 (4th Dept. 1999).

Legality of restitution order.—"Because there is no statutory limitation on the types of criminal conduct that can support a sentence of restitution or reparation, restitution is a viable sentence for any crime provided there is a recognizable victim who has suffered 'actual out of pocket loss' or there are discernible 'fruits of the offense.' " Restitution was appropriate sentence for defendant who was convicted of offering a false instrument for filing and and who received social security overpayments. People v. Horne, 97 N.Y.2d 404, 740 N.Y.S.2d 675, 767 N.E.2d 132 (2002).

—PL § 60.27(8) "unequivocally and unconditionally entitles a crime victim to receive restitution, within the context of a criminal matter, if the court orders it." Where portions of a plea agreement are illegal, as in this case, where the court impermissibly conditioned victims' right to receive restitution on their execution of releases, court was able to excise illegal portions of restitution order without allowing defendant to withdraw his plea. People v. Wein, 294 A.D.2d 78, 743 N.Y.S.2d 439 (1st Dept. 2002).

—Court's failure to issue restitution order setting out specific amount at sentencing does not preclude the court from subsequently issuing the order as long as the record is clear that the defendant knew that restitution was part of the sentence at the time of sentencing. People v. Knowles, 293 A.D.2d 770, 740 N.Y.S.2d 151 (3d Dept. 2002).

Reliance on evidence in record.—Since there was adequate trial evidence of the total amount that the defendant took from investors in his scheme, and since there was no request for a hearing, the trial court did not err in determining restitution. People v. Barr, 212 A.D.2d 485, 623 N.Y.S.2d 207 (1st Dept. 1995).

—Since the victim's trial testimony supported the court's determination of the amount of restitution, no hearing was required. People v. Generoso, 219 A.D.2d 670, 631 N.Y.S.2d 722 (2d Dept. 1995).

—Because the record supported the court's conclusion regarding the total amount of money stolen by defendant, the court did not err in determining the amount of restitution without first conducting a hearing. People v. Gustke, 201 A.D.2d 923, 607 N.Y.S.2d 771 (4th Dept. 1994).

§ 60.28. Authorized disposition; making graffiti and possession of graffiti instruments.

When a person is convicted of an offense defined in section 145.60 or 145.65 of this chapter, or of an attempt to commit such offense, and the sentence imposed by the court for such conviction includes a sentence of probation or conditional discharge, the court shall, where appropriate, include as a condition of such sentence the defendant's successful participation in a graffiti removal program pursuant to paragraph (h) of subdivision two of section 65.10 of this chapter.

Added by L. 1995, Ch. 536, § 1, eff. Nov. 1, 1995.

§ 60.29. Authorized disposition; cemetery desecration.

When a person is convicted of an offense defined in section 145.22 or 145.23 of this chapter or of an attempt to commit such an offense, and the sentence imposed by the court for such conviction includes a sentence of probation or conditional discharge, such sentence shall, where appropriate, be in accordance with paragraph (h) of subdivision two of section 65.10 of this article as such section relates to cemetery crime.

Added by L. 1997, Ch. 165, § 4, eff. Nov. 11, 1997.

§ 60.30. Civil penalties.

This article does not deprive the court of any authority conferred by law to decree a forfeiture of property, suspend or cancel a license, remove a person from office, or impose any other civil penalty and any appropriate order exercising such authority may be included as part of the judgment of conviction.

ANNOTATION

Generally.—Because of the differing degrees of proof, even a criminal acquittal would not necessarily prevent a subsequent forfeiture. People v. Milone, 158 Misc. 2d 316, 600 N.Y.S.2d 1010 (Crim. Ct. Bronx Co. 1993).

§ 60.35. Mandatory surcharge, sex offender registration fee, DNA databank fee, supplemental sex offender victim fee and crime victim assistance fee required in certain cases.

1. (a) Except as provided in section eighteen hundred nine of the vehicle and traffic law and section 27.12 of the parks, recreation and historic preservation law, whenever proceedings in an administrative tribunal or a court of this state result in a conviction for a felony, a misdemeanor, or a violation, as these terms are defined in section 10.00 of this chapter, there shall be levied at sentencing a mandatory surcharge, sex offender registration fee, DNA databank fee and a crime victim assistance fee in addition to any sentence required or permitted by law, in accordance with the following schedule:

(i) a person convicted of a felony shall pay a mandatory surcharge of two hundred fifty dollars and a crime victim assistance fee of twenty dollars;

(ii) a person convicted of a misdemeanor shall pay a mandatory surcharge of one hundred forty dollars and a crime victim assistance fee of twenty dollars;

(iii) a person convicted of a violation shall pay a mandatory surcharge of seventy-five dollars and a crime victim assistance fee of twenty dollars;

(iv) a person convicted of a sex offense as defined by subdivision two of section one hundred sixty-eight-a of the correction law or a sexually violent offense as defined by subdivision three of section one hundred sixty-eight-a of the correction law shall, in addition to a mandatory surcharge and crime victim assistance fee, pay a sex offender registration fee of fifty dollars.

(v) a person convicted of a designated offense as defined by subdivision seven of section nine hundred ninety-five of the executive law shall, in addition to a mandatory surcharge and crime victim assistance fee, pay a DNA databank fee of fifty dollars.

(b) When the felony or misdemeanor conviction in subparagraphs (i), (ii) or (iv) of paragraph (a) of this subdivision results from an offense contained in article one hundred thirty of this chapter, incest as defined in section 255.25 of this chapter or an offense contained in article two hundred sixty-three of this chapter, the person convicted shall pay a supplemental sex offender victim fee of one thousand dollars in addition to the mandatory surcharge and any other fee.

2. Where a person is convicted of two or more crimes or violations committed through a single act or omission, or through an act or omission which in itself constituted one of the crimes or violations and also was a material element of the other, the court shall impose a mandatory surcharge and a crime victim assistance fee, and where appropriate a supplemental sex offender victim fee, in accordance with the provisions of this section for the crime or violation which carries the highest classification, and no other sentence to pay a mandatory surcharge, crime victim assistance fee or supplemental sex offender victim fee required by this section shall be imposed. Where a person is convicted of two or more sex offenses or sexually violent offenses, as defined by subdivisions two and three of section one hundred sixty-eight-a of the correction law, committed through a single act or omission, or through an act or omission which in itself constituted one of the offenses and also was a material element of the other, the court shall impose only one sex offender registration fee. Where a person is convicted of two or more designated offenses, as defined by subdivision seven of section nine hundred ninety-five of the executive law, committed through a single act or omission, or through an act or omission which in itself constituted one of the offenses and also was a material element of the other, the court shall impose only one DNA databank fee.

3. The mandatory surcharge, sex offender registration fee, DNA databank fee, crime victim assistance fee, and supplemental sex offender victim fee provided for in subdivision one of this section shall be paid to the clerk of the court or administrative tribunal that rendered the conviction. Within the first ten days of the month following collection of the mandatory surcharge, crime victim assistance fee, and supplemental sex offender victim fee, the collecting authority shall determine the amount of mandatory surcharge, crime victim assistance fee, and supplemental sex offender victim fee collected and, if it is an administrative tribunal, or a town or village justice court, it shall then pay such money to the state comptroller who shall deposit such money in the state treasury pursuant to section one hundred twenty-one of the state finance law to the credit of the criminal justice improvement account established by section ninety-seven-bb of the state finance law. Within the first ten days of the month following collection of the sex offender registration fee and DNA databank fee, the collecting authority shall determine the amount of the sex offender registration fee and DNA databank fee collected and, if it is an administrative tribunal, or a town or village justice court, it shall then pay such money to the state comptroller who shall deposit such money in the state treasury pursuant to section one hundred twenty-one of the state finance law to the credit of the general fund. If such collecting authority is any other court of the unified court system, it shall, within such period, pay such

money attributable to the mandatory surcharge or crime victim assistance fee to the state commissioner of taxation and finance to the credit of the criminal justice improvement account established by section ninety-seven-bb of the state finance law. If such collecting authority is any other court of the unified court system, it shall, within such period, pay such money attributable to the sex offender registration fee and the DNA databank fee to the state commissioner of taxation and finance to the credit of the general fund.

4. Any person who has paid a mandatory surcharge, sex offender registration fee, DNA databank fee, a crime victim assistance fee or a supplemental sex offender victim fee under the authority of this section based upon a conviction that is subsequently reversed or who paid a mandatory surcharge, sex offender registration fee, DNA databank fee, a crime victim assistance fee or supplemental sex offender victim fee under the authority of this section which is ultimately determined not to be required by this section shall be entitled to a refund of such mandatory surcharge, sex offender registration fee, DNA databank fee, crime victim assistance fee or supplemental sex offender victim fee upon application to the state comptroller. The state comptroller shall require such proof as is necessary in order to determine whether a refund is required by law.

5. [*Effective until Sept 1, 2007.*]

(a) When a person who is convicted of a crime or violation and sentenced to a term of imprisonment has failed to pay the mandatory surcharge, sex offender registration fee, DNA databank fee, crime victim assistance fee or supplemental sex offender victim fee required by this section, the clerk of the court that rendered the conviction shall notify the superintendent or the municipal official of the facility where the person is confined. The superintendent or the municipal official shall cause any amount owing to be collected from such person during his or her term of imprisonment from moneys to the credit of an inmates' fund or such moneys as may be earned by a person in a work release program pursuant to section eight hundred sixty of the correction law. Such moneys attributable to the mandatory surcharge or crime victim assistance fee shall be paid over to the state comptroller to the credit of the criminal justice improvement account established by section ninety-seven-bb of the state finance law and such moneys attributable to the sex offender registration fee or DNA databank fee shall be paid over to the state comptroller to the credit of the general fund, except that any such moneys collected which are surcharges, sex offender registration fees, DNA databank fees, crime victim assistance fees or supplemental sex offender victim fees levied in relation to convictions obtained in a town or village justice court shall be paid within thirty days after the receipt thereof by the superintendent or municipal official of the facility to the justice of the court in which

the conviction was obtained. For the purposes of collecting such mandatory surcharge, sex offender registration fee, DNA databank fee, crime victim assistance fee, and supplemental sex offender victim fee, the state shall be legally entitled to the money to the credit of an inmates' fund or money which is earned by an inmate in a work release program. For purposes of this subdivision, the term "inmates' fund" shall mean moneys in the possession of an inmate at the time of his or her admission into such facility, funds earned by him or her as provided for in section one hundred eighty-seven of the correction law and any other funds received by him or her or on his or her behalf and deposited with such superintendent or municipal official.

(b) The incarceration fee provided for in subdivision two of section one hundred eighty-nine of the correction law shall not be assessed or collected if any order of restitution or reparation, fine, mandatory surcharge, sex offender registration fee, DNA databank fee, crime victim assistance fee or supplemental sex offender victim fee remains unpaid. In such circumstances, any monies which may lawfully be withheld from the compensation paid to a prisoner for work performed while housed in a general confinement facility in satisfaction of such an obligation shall first be applied toward satisfaction of such obligation.

5. [*Effective Sept. 1, 2007.*] When a person who is convicted of a crime or violation and sentenced to a term of imprisonment has failed to pay the mandatory surcharge, sex offender registration fee, DNA databank fee, crime victim assistance fee or supplemental sex offender victim fee required by this section, the clerk of the court that rendered the conviction shall notify the superintendent or the municipal official of the facility where the person is confined. The superintendent or the municipal official shall cause any amount owing to be collected from such person during his or her term of imprisonment from moneys to the credit of an inmates' fund or such moneys as may be earned by a person in a work release program pursuant to section eight hundred sixty of the correction law. Such moneys attributable to the mandatory surcharge or crime victim assistance fee shall be paid over to the state comptroller to the credit of the criminal justice improvement account established by section ninety-seven-bb of the state finance law and such moneys attributable to the sex offender registration fee or DNA databank fee shall be paid over to the state comptroller to the credit of the general fund, except that any such moneys collected which are surcharges, sex offender registration fees, DNA databank fees, crime victim assistance fees or supplemental sex offender victim fees levied in relation to convictions obtained in a town or village justice court shall be paid within thirty days after the receipt thereof by the superintendent or municipal official of the facility to the

justice of the court in which the conviction was obtained. For the purposes of collecting such mandatory surcharge, sex offender registration fee, DNA databank fee, crime victim assistance fee and supplemental sex offender victim fee, the state shall be legally entitled to the money to the credit of an inmates' fund or money which is earned by an inmate in a work release program. For purposes of this subdivision, the term "inmates' fund" shall mean moneys in the possession of an inmate at the time of his or her admission into such facility, funds earned by him or her as provided for in section one hundred eighty-seven of the correction law and any other funds received by him or her or on his or her behalf and deposited with such superintendent or municipal official.

6. Notwithstanding any other provision of this section, where a person has made restitution or reparation pursuant to section 60.27 of this article, such person shall not be required to pay a mandatory surcharge or a crime victim assistance fee.

7. Notwithstanding the provisions of subdivision one of section 60.00 of this article, the provisions of subdivision one of this section shall not apply to a violation under any law other than this chapter.

8. Subdivision one of section 130.10 of the criminal procedure law notwithstanding, at the time that the mandatory surcharge, sex offender registration fee or DNA databank fee, crime victim assistance fee or supplemental sex offender victim fee is imposed a town or village court may, and all other courts shall, issue and cause to be served upon the person required to pay the mandatory surcharge, sex offender registration fee or DNA databank fee, crime victim assistance fee or supplemental sex offender victim fee, a summons directing that such person appear before the court regarding the payment of the mandatory surcharge, sex offender registration fee or DNA databank fee, crime victim assistance fee or supplemental sex offender victim fee, if after sixty days from the date it was imposed it remains unpaid. The designated date of appearance on the summons shall be set for the first day court is in session falling after the sixtieth day from the imposition of the mandatory surcharge, sex offender registration fee or DNA databank fee, crime victim assistance fee or supplemental sex offender victim fee. The summons shall contain the information required by subdivision two of section 130.10 of the criminal procedure law except that in substitution for the requirement of paragraph (c) of such subdivision the summons shall state that the person served must appear at a date, time and specific location specified in the summons if after sixty days from the date of issuance the mandatory surcharge, sex offender registration fee or DNA databank fee, crime victim assistance fee or supplemental sex offender victim fee remains unpaid. The court shall not issue a summons under this subdivision to a person who is being sentenced to a term of confinement in excess of sixty days in jail or in the department of correctional services. The mandatory surcharges, sex offender registration fee and DNA databank fees, crime victim assistance fees and supplemental sex offender victim fees for those persons shall be governed by the provisions of section 60.30 of this article.

9. Notwithstanding the provisions of subdivision one of this section, in the event a proceeding is in a town or village court, such court shall add an additional five dollars to the surcharges imposed by such subdivision one.

10. The provisions of this section shall apply to sentences imposed upon a youthful offender finding.

Added by L. 1982, Ch. 55; **Amended** by L. 1983, Chs. 15, 16; L. 1985, Ch. 59; L. 1989, Ch. 62; L. 1990, Ch. 190; L. 1991, Ch. 166, eff. June 12, 1991; L. 1992, Ch. 55, eff. Apr. 10, 1992, amending subd. 1 and shall be deemed to have been in full force and effect on and after Apr. 1, 1992; L. 1995, Ch. 3, § 56, amending subd. 5, eff. June 10, 1995, amendment expires Sept. 1, 1997 pursuant to L. 1995, Ch. 3, § 74, paragraph (h), and reverts back to the previous version of subd. 5. The previous version of subd. 5 contained only the existing 5(a), but was labeled 5, and 5(b) was not included; L. 1995, Ch. 3, § 71, adding subd. 8, eff. July 1, 1995, which applies only when the acts constituting the offense for the conviction of which a mandatory surcharge may be imposed occurred on or after July 1, 1995; L. 1997, Ch. 452, § 1, eff. Jan, 1, 1998, and Ch. 435, § 53, extending expiration date to Sept. 1, 1999, eff. Aug. 20, 1997; L. 1999, Ch. 452, eff. Sept. 1, 1999, extending effective date of subd. 5 as amended by L. 1995, Ch. 3 § 56; L. 1999, Ch. 385, § 2, amending subd. 5(a) as amended by L. 1995, Ch. 3, § 56, eff. July 27, 1999, and § 3, amending subd. 5, eff. July 27, 1999; L. 2000, Ch. 57, Part L, § 1, amending subd. 1, eff. May 15, 2000, deemed eff. Apr. 1, 2000; L. 2001, Ch. 95, § 9, extending eff. date of subd. 5, eff. July 13, 2001; L. 2003, Ch. 16, § 9, extending expiration date until Sept. 1, 2005; Ch. 62, Part F, §§ 1, 2, eff. May 15, 2003, amending section heading, subds. 1–5, 8.; Ch. 62, Part M, § 1, amending subd. 1, eff. Nov. 11, 2003; L. 2004, Ch. 56, §§ 1 & 2 (Part E), deemed in full force and effect Apr. 1, 2004, and § 2 (Part F), eff. Feb. 16, 2005, adding subd. 10.

Editor's Note: Section 3 of L. 2004, Ch. 56, Part E, provides: "This act shall take effect immediately and shall be deemed to have been in full force and effect on and after April 1, 2004; provided, however, that the amendments to subdivision 5 of section 60.35 of the penal law, made by section one of this act shall be subject to the expiration and reversion of such subdivision pursuant to section 74 of chapter 3 of the laws of 1995, as amended, when upon such date the provisions of section two of this act shall take effect."

ANNOTATIONS

Constitutionality.—The procedure which allows a defendant, at the end of his term of imprisonment, to move for a waiver of the mandatory surcharge if he is unable to pay at that time does not violate the defendant's due process and equal protection rights since he is not being imprisoned or kept from release because of an inability to pay the surcharge. People v. Ramirez, 208 A.D.2d 381, 617 N.Y.S.2d 13 (1st Dept. 1994).

—Court rejected defendant's allegation that statute violated Equal Protection Clause because it discriminated against indigent inmates who are incarcerated for more than 60 months; the penalties imposed bear a reasonable relationship to the state's legitimate interest in raising revenue. People v. Dunn, 254 A.D.2d 511, 680 N.Y.S.2d 125 (3d Dept. 1998), cert. denied, 527 U.S. 1024 (1999).

Effective date.—Where defendant committed crime before the effective date of the amendment which raised the crime victim assistance fee from two dollars to five dollars, the fee which applies upon sentencing is two dollars. People v. Fabela, 240 A.D.2d 677, 659 N.Y.S.2d 1018 (2d Dept. 1997)

Time for waiver application.—An application for waiver

of the mandatory surcharge on the ground of unreasonable hardship is premature until the end of the defendant's term of imprisonment. People v. Ramirez, 208 A.D.2d 381, 617 N.Y.S.2d 13 (1st Dept. 1994).

—Defendant's claim that the mandatory surcharge pursuant to Penal Law § 60.35 should be waived because it would cause him undue hardship was premature; should defendant, at the end of his prison term, find himself unable to pay the surcharge, he may move for a waiver at that time; the procedure for raising a claim of undue hardship is to move for resentencing pursuant to CPL § 420.10(5). People v. Velasquez, 198 A.D.2d 25, 603 N.Y.S.2d 126 (1st Dept. 1993).

—Since defendant was still incarcerated and failed to move for resentencing on the basis of his alleged inability to pay the mandatory surcharge, his application in respect thereto was deemed premature. People v. Lewis, 182 A.D.2d 453, 582 N.Y.S.2d 177 (1st Dept. 1992).

Restitution.—Sentencing court may simultaneously impose a sentence of restitution to the crime victim along with the mandatory surcharge/crime victim assistance fee. People v. Quinones, 95 N.Y.2d 349, 717 N.Y.S.2d 86, 740 N.E.2d 231 (2000).

—Imposition of a mandatory surcharge and a crime victim's assistance fee pursuant to section 60.35 is inconsistent with the requirement that a defendant pay restitution pursuant to section 60.27. People v. Espola, 238 A.D.2d 281, 656 N.Y. S.2d 268 (1st Dept. 1997).

—Court properly imposed a mandatory surcharge on defendant for each of the six counts of first degree robbery where each count involved a separate and distinct act of taking property from a separate victim. People v. Leung, 279 A.D.2d 480, 718 N.Y.S.2d 863 (2d Dept. 2001).

—The court erred in ordering the defendant to pay restitution and pay a mandatory surcharge; the imposition of the surcharge was inconsistent with the requirement that the defendant pay restitution. People v. Bauer, 229 A.D.2d 502, 645 N.Y.S.2d 323 (2d Dept. 1996).

—Penal Law § 60.35(6) prevents the court from imposing a mandatory surcharge where restitution has been ordered. People v. Allen, 236 A.D.2d 653, 654 N.Y.S.2d 194 (3d Dept. 1997).

Youthful offender status.—Restitution would not preclude sentencing court from adjudicating defendant a youthful offender, but mandatory surcharge would. People v. Cruz, 229 A.D.2d 321, 645 N.Y.S.2d 25 (1st Dept. 1996).

ARTICLE 65—SENTENCES OF PROBATION, CONDITIONAL DISCHARGE AND UNCONDITIONAL DISCHARGE

LexisNexis Cross Reference

New York Criminal Practice (2d ed.), Vol. 4, Ch. 42, Classification of Offenses, Authorized Dispositions and Punishment.

§ 65.00. Sentence of probation.

1. Criteria. (a) Except as otherwise required by section 60.04 or 60.05 of this title, and except as provided by paragraph (b) hereof, the court may sentence a person to a period of probation upon conviction of any crime if the court, having regard to the nature and circumstances of the crime and to the history, character and condition of the defendant, is of the opinion that:

(i) Institutional confinement for the term authorized by law of the defendant is or may not be necessary for the protection of the public;

(ii) the defendant is in need of guidance, training or other assistance which, in his case, can be effectively administered through probation supervision; and

(iii) such disposition is not inconsistent with the ends of justice.

(b) The court, with the concurrence of either the administrative judge of the court or of the judicial district within which the court is situated or such administrative judge as the presiding justice of the appropriate appellate division shall designate, may sentence a person to a period of probation upon conviction of a class A-II felony or a class B felony defined in article two hundred twenty if the prosecutor either orally on the record or in a writing filed with the indictment recommends that the court sentence such person to a period of probation upon the ground that such person has or is providing material assistance in the investigation, apprehension or prosecution of any person for a felony defined in article two hundred twenty or the attempt or the conspiracy to commit any such felony, and if the court, having regard to the nature and circumstances of the crime and to the history, character and condition of the defendant is of the opinion that:

(i) Institutional confinement of the defendant is not necessary for the protection of the public;

(ii) The defendant is in need of guidance, training or other assistance which, in his case, can be effectively administered through probation supervision;

(iii) The defendant has or is providing material assistance in the investigation, apprehension or prosecution of a person for a felony defined in article two hundred twenty or the attempt or conspiracy to commit any such felony; and

(iv) Such disposition is not inconsistent with the ends of justice.

[*Effective until Sept. 1, 2009.*] Provided, however, that the court shall not, except to the extent authorized by paragraph (d) of subdivision two of section 60.01 of this chapter, impose a sentence of probation in any case where it sentences a defendant for more than one crime and imposes a sentence of imprisonment for any one of the crimes, or where the defendant is subject to an undischarged indeterminate or determinate sentence of imprisonment which was imposed at a previous time by a court of this state and has more than one year to run.

[*Effective Sept. 1, 2009.*] Provided, however, that the court shall not, except to the extent authorized by paragraph (d) of subdivision two of section 60.01 of this chapter, impose a sentence of probation in any case where it sentences a defendant for more than one crime and imposes a sentence of imprisonment for any one of the crimes, or where the defendant is subject to an undischarged indeterminate or reformatory sentence of imprisonment which was imposed at a previous time by a court of this state and has more than one year to run.

2. Sentence. When a person is sentenced to a period of probation the court shall, except to the extent authorized by paragraph (d) of subdivision two of section 60.01 of this chapter, impose the period authorized by subdivision three of this section and shall specify, in accordance with section 65.10, the conditions to be complied with. The court may modify or enlarge the conditions or, if the defendant commits an additional offense or violates a condition, revoke the sentence at any

time prior to the expiration or termination of the period of probation.

3. Periods of probation. Unless terminated sooner in accordance with the criminal procedure law, the period of probation shall be as follows:

(a) (i) For a felony, other than a class A-II felony or a class B felony defined in article two hundred twenty of this chapter or a sexual assault, the period of probation shall be five years;

(ii) For a class A-II felony controlled substance offender as defined in paragraph (a) of subdivision one of section 70.71 of this chapter or a class B second felony drug offender as defined in paragraph (b) of subdivision one of section 70.70 of this chapter, the period of probation shall be life, and for a class B felony drug offender as defined in paragraph (a) of subdivision one of section 70.70 of this chapter, the period of probation shall be twenty-five years;

(iii) For a felony sexual assault, the period of probation shall be ten years.

(b) (i) For a class A misdemeanor, other than a sexual assault, the period of probation shall be three years;

(ii) For a class A misdemeanor sexual assault, the period of probation shall be six years.

(c) For a class B misdemeanor, the period of probation shall be one year;

(d) For an unclassified misdemeanor, the period of probation shall be three years if the authorized sentence of imprisonment is in excess of three months, otherwise the period of probation shall be one year.

For the purposes of this section, the term "sexual assault" means an offense defined in article one hundred thirty or two hundred sixty-three, or in section 255.25 of this chapter, or an attempt to commit any of the foregoing offenses.

4. In any case where a court pursuant to its authority under subdivision four of section 60.01 of this chapter revokes probation and sentences such person to imprisonment and probation, as provided in paragraph (d) of subdivision two of section 60.01 of this chapter, the period of probation shall be the remaining period of the original probation sentence or one year whichever is greater.

Amended by L. 1971, Ch. 1097; L. 1973, Chs. 276, 277, 278, 676, 1051; L. 1974, Ch. 835; L. 1979, Ch. 410; L. 1980, Ch. 471; L. 1985, Ch. 79; L. 1995, Ch. 3, § 1-a, amending closing paragraph of subd. 1, eff. Oct. 1, 1995, amendment repealed Sept. 30, 2005, and amendment applies only to offenses committed on or after Oct. 1, 1995 pursuant to L. 1995, Ch. 3, § 74, paragraph (e); L. 2000, Ch. 1, eff. Feb. 1, 2001; L. 2003, Ch. 264, § 5, eff. Nov. 1, 2003, amending subd. 3; L. 2004, Ch. 738, § 25, amending subd. 1(a) opening paragraph, eff. Jan. 13, 2005, and § 26, amending subd. 3(a)(ii), eff. Dec. 27, 2004; L. 2005, Ch. 56, Part D, § 20, extending repeal date of amendment to Sept. 1, 2009.

ANNOTATIONS

Conditions of probation.—Where evidence indicates that defendant acted in good faith in attempt to carry out the condition of her probation that she undergo psychiatric treatment, the refusal of State hospital to accept her as a patient did not indicate a violation of probation. People v. Bowman, 73 A.D.2d 921, 423 N.Y.S.2d 242 (2d Dept. 1980).

Effect of defendants' cooperation in investigations.— Defendants were not entitled to outright dismissal of their indictments, in the interest of justice, of felony drug offenses, even though they had cooperated in investigation, as enforcement of probation promise would not guarantee the necessary approval by sentencing court and administrative judge. People v. Kaufman, 77 A.D.2d 924, 431 N.Y.S.2d 102 (2d Dept. 1980)

Incarceration and probation.—When a court sentences a defendant for more than one crime and one of the crimes is a felony for which a sentence of imprisonment in excess of six months is imposed, it cannot also sentence him to a term of probation for another crime. People v. McIntyre, 135 A.D.2d 920, 522 N.Y.S.2d 688 (3d Dept. 1987).

—The defendant's sentence of five years of probation was authorized by § 65.00[3][a][i]; the defendant's sentence of four months in prison had to be construed to run concurrently with the term of probation; thus, the sentence was lawful. People v. Youngs, 212 A.D.2d 1001, 622 N.Y.S.2d 835 (4th Dept. 1995).

Lifetime probation.—Sentence of lifetime probation was invalid where prosecutor failed to recommend either orally on the record or in a writing filed with the indictment that defendant be sentenced to a term of probation. People v. Edwards, 148 A.D.2d 923, 539 N.Y.S.2d 163 (4th Dept. 1989).

Revocation of probation.—Failure of defendant to make any restitution payments as required by his conditions of probation, despite his full-time employment, was sufficient to support the revocation of such probation notwithstanding defendant's testimony that his pay was low and his probation officer told him that he could pay when he was able to. People v. Ray, 105 A.D.2d 988, 482 N.Y.S.2d 133 (3d Dept. 1984).

—The commission of a crime is sufficient ground for revocation of probation. People v. Willi, 77 A.D.2d 711, 430 N.Y.S.2d 428 (3d Dept. 1980).

§ 65.05. Sentence of conditional discharge.

1. Criteria. (a) Except as otherwise required by section 60.05, the court may impose a sentence of conditional discharge for an offense if the court, having regard to the nature and circumstances of the offense and to the history, character and condition of the defendant, is of the opinion that neither the public interest nor the ends of justice would be served by a sentence of imprisonment and that probation supervision is not appropriate.

(b) When a sentence of conditional discharge is imposed for a felony, the court shall set forth in the record the reasons for its action.

2. Sentence. Except to the extent authorized by paragraph (d) of subdivision two of section 60.01 of this chapter, when the court imposes a sentence of conditional discharge the defendant shall be released with respect to the conviction for which the sentence is imposed without imprisonment or probation supervision but subject, during the period of conditional discharge, to such conditions as the court may determine. The court shall impose the period of conditional discharge authorized by subdivision three of this section and shall specify, in accordance with section 65.10, the conditions to be complied with. If a defendant is sentenced pursuant to paragraph (e) of subdivision two of section 65.10 of this chapter, the court

shall require the administrator of the program to provide written notice to the court of any violation of program participation by the defendant. The court may modify or enlarge the conditions or, if the defendant commits an additional offense or violates a condition, revoke the sentence at any time prior to the expiration or termination of the period of conditional discharge.

3. Periods of conditional discharge. Unless terminated sooner in accordance with the criminal procedure law, the period of conditional discharge shall be as follows:

(a) Three years in the case of a felony; and

(b) One year in the case of a misdemeanor or a violation.

Where the court has required, as a condition of the sentence, that the defendant make restitution of the fruits of his or her offense or make reparation for the loss caused thereby and such condition has not been satisfied, the court, at any time prior to the expiration or termination of the period of conditional discharge, may impose an additional period. The length of the additional period shall be fixed by the court at the time it is imposed and shall not be more than two years. All of the incidents of the original sentence, including the authority of the court to modify or enlarge the conditions, shall continue to apply during such additional period.

Amended by L. 1971, Ch. 1097; L. 1972, Ch. 157; L. 1973, Chs. 276, 277, 1051; L. 1974, Ch. 835; L. 1980, Ch. 471; L. 1981, Ch. 742; L. 1992, Ch. 618, eff. Nov. 1, 1992, amending subd. (3).

§ 65.10. Conditions of probation and of conditional discharge.

1. In general. The conditions of probation and of conditional discharge shall be such as the court, in its discretion, deems reasonably necessary to insure that the defendant will lead a law-abiding life or to assist him to do so.

2. Conditions relating to conduct and rehabilitation. When imposing a sentence of probation or of conditional discharge, the court shall, as a condition of the sentence, consider restitution or reparation and may, as a condition of the sentence, require that the defendant:

(a) Avoid injurious or vicious habits;

(b) Refrain from frequenting unlawful or disreputable places or consorting with disreputable persons;

(c) Work faithfully at a suitable employment or faithfully pursue a course of study or of vocational training that will equip him for suitable employment;

(d) Undergo available medical or psychiatric treatment and remain in a specified institution, when required for that purpose;

(e) Participate in an alcohol or substance abuse program or an intervention program approved by the court after consultation with the local probation department having jurisdiction, or such other public or private agency as the court determines to be appropriate;

(f) Support his dependents and meet other family responsibilities;

(g) Make restitution of the fruits of his or her offense or make reparation, in an amount he can afford to pay, for the actual out-of-pocket loss caused thereby. When restitution or reparation is a condition of the sentence, the court shall fix the amount thereof, the manner of performance, specifically state the date when restitution is to be paid in full prior to the expiration of the sentence of probation and may establish provisions for the early termination of a sentence of probation or conditional discharge pursuant to the provisions of subdivision three of section 410.90 of the criminal procedure law after the restitution and reparation part of a sentence of probation or conditional discharge has been satisfied. The court shall provide that in the event the person to whom restitution or reparation is to be made dies prior to the completion of said restitution or reparation, the remaining payments shall be made to the estate of the deceased.

(h) Perform services for a public or not-for-profit corporation, association, institution or agency, including but not limited to services for the division of substance abuse services, services in an appropriate community program for removal of graffiti from public or private property, including any property damaged in the underlying offense, or services for the maintenance and repair of real or personal property maintained as a cemetery plot, grave, burial place or other place of interment of human remains. Provided however, that the performance of any such services shall not result in the displacement of employed workers or in the impairment of existing contracts for services, nor shall the performance of any such services be required or permitted in any establishment involved in any labor strike or lockout. The court may establish provisions for the early termination of a sentence of probation or conditional discharge pursuant to the provisions of subdivision three of section 410.90 of the criminal procedure law after such services have been completed. Such sentence may only be imposed upon conviction of a misdemeanor, violation, or class D or class E felony, or a youthful offender finding replacing any such conviction, where the defendant has consented to the amount and conditions of such service;

(i) If a person under the age of twenty-one years, (i) resides with his parents or in a suitable foster home or hostel as referred to in section two hundred forty-four of the executive law, (ii) attends school, (iii) spends such part of the period of the sentence as the court may direct, but not exceeding two years, in a facility made available by the division for youth pursuant to article nineteen-G of the executive law, provided that admission to such facility may be made only with the prior consent of the division for youth, (iv) attend a non-residential program for such hours and pursuant to a schedule prescribed by the court as suitable for a program of rehabilitation of youth, (v) contribute to his own support in any home, foster home or hostel;

(j) Post a bond or other security for the performance of any or all conditions imposed;

(k) Observe certain specified conditions of conduct as set forth in an order of protection issued pursuant to section 530.12 or 530.13 of the criminal procedure law.

(k-1) Install and maintain a functioning ignition interlock device, as that term is defined in section one hundred nineteen-a of the vehicle and traffic law, in any vehicle owned or operated on a regular basis by the defendant if the court in its discretion determines that such a condition is necessary to ensure the public safety. The court may require such condition only where a person has been convicted of a violation of subdivision two or three of section eleven hundred ninetytwo of the vehicle and traffic law, or any crime defined by the vehicle and traffic law or this chapter of which an alcohol-related violation of any provision of section eleven hundred ninety-two of the vehicle and traffic law is an essential element.

(l) Satisfy any other conditions reasonably related to his rehabilitation.

3. Conditions relating to supervision. When imposing a sentence of probation the court, in addition to any conditions imposed pursuant to subdivision two of this section, shall require as conditions of the sentence, that the defendant:

(a) Report to a probation officer as directed by the court or the probation officer and permit the probation officer to visit him at his place of abode or elsewhere;

(b) Remain within the jurisdiction of the court unless granted permission to leave by the court or the probation officer; and

(c) Answer all reasonable inquiries by the probation officer and notify the probation officer prior to any change in address or employment.

4. Electronic monitoring. When imposing a sentence of probation the court may, in addition to any conditions imposed pursuant to subdivisions two and three of this section, require the defendant to submit to the use of an electronic monitoring device and/or to follow a schedule that governs the defendant's daily movement. Such condition may be imposed only where the court, in its discretion, determines that requiring the defendant to comply with such condition will advance public safety, probationer control or probationer surveillance. Electronic monitoring

shall be used in accordance with uniform procedures developed by the division of probation and correctional alternatives.

4-a. Mandatory condition for sex offenders. When imposing a sentence of probation or conditional discharge upon a person convicted of an offense defined in article one hundred thirty, two hundred thirty-five or two hundred sixty-three of this chapter, or section 255.25 of this chapter, and the victim of such offense was under the age of eighteen at the time of such offense, the court shall require, as a mandatory condition of such sentence, that such sentenced offender shall refrain from knowingly entering into or upon any school grounds, as that term is defined in paragraph (a) of subdivision fourteen of section 220.00 of this chapter, or any other facility or institution primarily used for the care or treatment of persons under the age of eighteen while one or more of such persons under the age of eighteen are present, provided however, that when such sentenced offender is a registered student or participant or an employee of such facility or institution or entity contracting therewith or has a family member enrolled in such facility or institution, such sentenced offender may, with the written authorization of his or her probation officer or the court and the superintendent or chief administrator of such facility, institution or grounds, enter such facility, institution or upon such grounds for the limited purposes authorized by the probation officer or the court and superintendent or chief officer. Nothing in this subdivision shall be construed as restricting any lawful condition of supervision that may be imposed on such sentenced offender.

5. Other conditions. When imposing a sentence of probation the court may, in addition to any conditions imposed pursuant to subdivisions two, three and four of this section, require that the defendant comply with any other reasonable condition as the court shall determine to be necessary or appropriate to ameliorate the conduct which gave rise to the offense or to prevent the incarceration of the defendant.

Amended by L. 1973, Ch. 676; L. 1974, Ch. 930; L. 1975, Ch. 667; L. 1978, Ch. 500; L. 1980, Ch. 270, Ch. 284, Ch. 471, Ch. 530; L. 1981, Chs. 583, 742; L. 1982, Ch. 782, L. 1984, Chs. 335, 417; L. 1985, Ch. 672; L. 1986, Ch. 552; L. 1989, Ch. 443; L. 1992, Ch. 465, Jan. 14, 1993, amending subd. (2)(i)(iii) and shall apply to all persons placed in or committed to the custody of the division for youth on or after such date; L. 1992, Ch. 618, eff. Nov. 1, 1992, amending subd. (2)(g); L. 1995, Ch. 536, § 2, amending subd. (2)(h), eff. Nov. 1, 1995; L. 1996, Ch. 186, § 1, amending subd. (2)(h), eff. Nov. 1, 1996; L. 1996, Ch. 653, § 1, adding subds. 4 and 5, eff. Sept. 18, 1996; L. 1997, Ch. 181, § 1, adding subparagraph 2(k-1), eff. July 8, 1997; L. 2000, Ch. 1, eff. Feb. 1, 2001; L. 2001, Ch. 508, amending subd. 2(h), eff. Jan. 20, 2002.

ANNOTATIONS

Community service.—Where community service is imposed after a misdemeanor conviction, the record must explicitly reflect that the defendant agrees to the amount and conditions of the service, or a remand will be necessary. People v. Tice, 267 A.D.2d 504, 699 N.Y.S.2d 745 (3d Dept. 1999).

Conditions.—The sentencing court was not authorized to

create a new penalty and require the defendant, who had been convicted of six alcohol-related driving offenses since 1971, to attach florescent signs to his license plates saying "CONVICTED DWI" in the event that driving privileges were restored to the defendant prior to the end of his probationary period; the creation of such a penalty usurped the legislative prerogative and could not be validated under the "catch-all" provisions contained in § 65.10(2)(l). People v. Letterlough, 86 N.Y.2d 259, 631 N.Y.S.2d 105, 655 N.E.2d 148 (1995).

—Court's imposition of a condition of probation that prohibited defendant from associating with prison inmate for whom defendant was convicted of attempted smuggling of prison contraband was a proper exercise of court's discretion to set terms of probation designed to ensure that the "defendant will lead a law-abiding life or to assist him [or her] to do so." People v. Swenson, 12 A.D.3d 948, 785 N.Y.S.2d 175 (3d Dept. 2004).

—Condition of probation that required defendant to notify his probation officer of any contact with law enforcement officials was not improper and did not infringe on defendant's privilege against self-incrimination. People v. Murray, 12 A.D.3d 838, 784 N.Y.S.2d 674 (3d Dept. 2004).

—Defendant, who had pleaded guilty to third degree grand larceny resulting from the misappropriation of third party funds, and who was sentenced to probation and terms of probation prohibited him from working in a business or occupation involving the solicitation or handling of money, was guilty of violating the terms of his probation when he worked as a public insurance claims adjuster and once again misappropriated funds. People v. Suib, 289 A.D.2d 871, 734 N.Y.S.2d 516 (3d Dept. 2001).

—Conditions placed on probation must be "primarily rehabilitative in nature"; court's requirement that defendant participate in a sex offender rehabilitation program and abide by the rules of its "contract" was within the court's authority under section 65.10. People v. Griffith, 239 A.D.2d 705, 657 N.Y.S.2d 823 (3d Dept. 1997).

—Court properly found defendant had violated terms of probation which required defendant, a convicted sex offender, to have a mental health evaluation and to follow all treatments; defendant failed to keep mental health appointments and refused to take medication. People v. Brogan, 292 A.D.2d 781, 738 N.Y.S.2d 784 (4th Dept. 2002).

Restitution.—Where the company has reimbursed its own customer for the loss suffered by reason of its employee's conduct, a court may order a security guard convicted of attempted arson and criminal mischief, as a condition of probation, to make restitution to the security company that employed her. People v. Hall-Wilson, 69 N.Y.2d 154, 513 N.Y.S.2d 73, 505 N.E.2d 584 (1987).

—Hearing court properly relied upon hearsay evidence to establish the value of stolen items for determining the proper amount of restitution. People v. David N., 140 A.D.2d 460, 527 N.Y.S.2d 871 (2d Dept. 1988).

—Inasmuch as the statute authorizing a 5% surcharge on restitution became effective following the date of the crimes committed by the defendant, the surcharge imposed by the court was vacated. People v. Pani, 138 A.D.2d 532, 525 N.Y.S.2d 912 (2d Dept. 1988).

—Sentencing court erred in imposing a mandatory surcharge in addition to restitution. People v. Dublar, 136 A.D.2d 727, 524 N.Y.S.2d 65 (2d Dept. 1988).

—Remittitur was required where the court improperly delegated to the Department of Probation the task of fixing the amount of restitution. People v. Minutoli, 128 A.D.2d 813, 513 N.Y.S.2d 517 (2d Dept. 1987).

—Court had no authority to impose a conditional discharge with full restitution a condition, without first holding a hearing to determine the appropriate restitution, assess defendant's financial ability to pay the restitution and establish a payment schedule. People v. Landes, 238 A.D.2d 804, 656 N.Y.S.2d 517 (3d Dept. 1997).

—Whether or not encompassed in a plea bargain, a sentencing court must consider according restitution to crime victims. People v. Jackson, 143 A.D.2d 473, 532 N.Y.S.2d 590 (3d Dept. 1988).

—Adhering to the statutory directive that restitution be ordered in an amount representing the loss or damage caused by the defendant's offense, the court ordered the defendant to pay 25% of the damage, suffered by accident victim. People v. Crossley,

134 Misc. 2d 742, 512 N.Y.S.2d 756 (Dist. Ct. Suffolk Co. 1987).

Reparation.—While the amounts of a victim's out-of-pocket loss and the "fruits of the offense" are determined without respect to the defendant's ability to pay, any order of reparation must be in an amount that the defendant can afford to pay. People v. Young, 163 Misc. 2d 72, 618 N.Y.S.2d 983 (Sup. Ct. N.Y. Co. 1994).

Unauthorized sentence for VOP.—Where the violation of probation is predicated upon an unauthorized sentence, prison sentence imposed for the violation of probation must be vacated and the defendant resentenced. People v. Maynard, 295 A.D.2d 805, 743 N.Y.S.2d 912 (3d Dept. 2002).

§ 65.15. Calculation of periods of probation and of conditional discharge.

1. A period of probation or a period or additional period of conditional discharge commences on the day it is imposed. Multiple periods, whether imposed at the same or at different times, shall run concurrently.

2. When a person has violated the conditions of his probation or conditional discharge and is declared delinquent by the court, the declaration of delinquency shall interrupt the period of the sentence as of the date of the delinquency and such interruption shall continue until a final determination as to the delinquency has been made by the court pursuant to a hearing held in accordance with the provisions of the criminal procedure law.

3. [*Effective until Sept. 1, 2009.*] In any case where a person who is under a sentence of probation or of conditional discharge is also under an indeterminate or determinate sentence of imprisonment, imposed for some other offense by a court of this state the service of the sentence of imprisonment shall satisfy the sentence of probation or of conditional discharge unless the sentence of probation or of conditional discharge is revoked prior to the next to occur of parole or conditional release under, or satisfaction of, the sentence of imprisonment. Provided, however, that the service of an indeterminate or determinate sentence of imprisonment shall not satisfy a sentence of probation if the sentence of probation was imposed at a time when the sentence of imprisonment had one year or less to run.

3. [*Effective Sept. 1, 2009.*] In any case where a person who is under a sentence of probation or of conditional discharge is also under an indeterminate sentence of imprisonment, or a reformatory sentence of imprisonment authorized by section 75.00, imposed for some other offense by a court of this state the service of the sentence of imprisonment shall satisfy the sentence of probation or of conditional discharge unless the sentence of probation or of conditional discharge is revoked prior to the next to occur of parole or conditional release under, or satisfaction of, the sentence of imprisonment. Provided, however, that the service of an indeterminate or a reformatory sentence of imprisonment shall not satisfy

a sentence of probation if the sentence of probation was imposed at a time when the sentence of imprisonment had one year or less to run.

Amended by L. 1971, Ch. 1097; L. 1995, Ch. 3, § 1-b, amending subd. 3, eff. Oct. 1, 1995, amendment repealed Sept. 30, 2005 pursuant to L. 1995, Ch. 3, § 74, paragraph (d), and amendment applies only to offenses committed on or after Oct. 1, 1995 pursuant to L. 1995, Ch. 3, § 74, paragraph (e); L. 2005, Ch. 56, Part D, § 20, extending repeal date of amendment to Sept. 1, 2009.

ANNOTATIONS

Violation of probation.—Filing of a declaration of delinquency, which resulted from a violation of probation, tolls an earlier imposed, but yet unfulfilled, probationary sentence. People v. Douglas, 94 N.Y.2d 807, 701 N.Y.S.2d 305, 723 N.E.2d 54 (1999).

—Filing of declaration of delinquency tolled the expiration of a probationary sentence based on a prior conviction, and therefore court had authority to adjudicate defendant to be in violation of probation based on his commission of armed robberies. People v. Douglas, 254 A.D.2d 300, 680 N.Y.S.2d 551 (2d Dept. 1998), *aff'd,* 94 N.Y.2d 807, 701 N.Y.S.2d 305, 723 N.E.2d 54 (1999).

—An amended sentence imposed upon defendant for conviction of violating the terms of probation could be made to run consecutively to the sentence imposed on conviction of the crime which formed the predicate for the probation violation. People v. Jackson, 106 A.D.2d 93, 483 N.Y.S.2d 725 (2d Dept. 1984).

—When an individual has violated conditions of probation and is declared delinquent by the court, the probation sentence is tolled until a final determination concerning the delinquency is made. People v. Blatt, 229 A.D.2d 903, 645 N.Y.S.2d 675 (4th Dept. 1996).

Time for filing violation of probation.—Violation of probation filed five years and 59 days after the defendant had been sentenced to 60 days' imprisonment plus five years' probation was not timely filed since the court only had the power to include the 60-day term of imprisonment within the five-year term of probation and not in addition thereto and the violation was required to be filed prior to the expiration of the five-year term of probation. People v. Montgomery, 115 A.D.2d 102, 494 N.Y.S.2d 913 (3d Dept. 1985).

Commencement of probation.—Probation should have commenced on the date of sentencing and not upon defendant's release from prison for a prior unrelated conviction. People v. Barnett, 232 A.D.2d 170, 647 N.Y.S.2d 474 (1st Dept. 1996).

§ 65.20. Sentence of unconditional discharge.

1. Criteria. The court may impose a sentence of unconditional discharge in any case where it is authorized to impose a sentence of conditional discharge under section 65.05 if the court is of the opinion that no proper purpose would be served by imposing any condition upon the defendant's release.

When a sentence of unconditional discharge is imposed for a felony, the court shall set forth in the record the reasons for its action.

2. Sentence. When the court imposes a sentence of unconditional discharge, the defendant shall be released with respect to the conviction for which the sentence is imposed without imprisonment, fine or probation supervision. A sentence of unconditional discharge is for all purposes a final judgment of conviction.

ARTICLE 70—SENTENCES OF IMPRISONMENT

LexisNexis Cross References

Criminal Defense Techniques, Vol. 6, Ch. 121, Sentencing; *New York Criminal Practice (2d ed.),* Vol. 4, Ch. 42, Classification of Offenses, Authorized Dispositions and Punishment; *Prosecution and Defense of Sex Crimes,* Ch. 13, Sentencing.

§ 70.00. Sentence of imprisonment for felony.

1. [*Effective until Sept. 1, 2009.*] Indeterminate sentence. Except as provided in subdivisions four, five and six of this section, a sentence of imprisonment for a felony, other than a felony defined in article two hundred twenty or two hundred twenty-one of this chapter, shall be an indeterminate sentence. When such a sentence is imposed, the court shall impose a maximum term in accordance with the provisions of subdivision two of this section and the minimum period of imprisonment shall be as provided in subdivision three of this section.

1. [*Effective Sept. 1, 2009.*] Indeterminate sentence. Except as provided in subdivisions four and five of this section, a sentence of imprisonment for a felony, other than a felony defined in article two hundred twenty or two hundred twenty-one of this chapter, shall be an indeterminate sentence. When such a sentence is imposed, the court shall impose a maximum term in accordance with the provisions of subdivision two of this section and the minimum period of imprisonment shall be as provided in subdivision three of this section.

2. Maximum term of sentence. The maximum term of an indeterminate sentence shall be at least three years and the term shall be fixed as follows:

(a) For a class A felony, the term shall be life imprisonment;

(b) For a class B felony, the term shall be fixed by the court, and shall not exceed twenty-five years;

(c) For a class C felony, the term shall be fixed by the court, and shall not exceed fifteen years;

(d) For a class D felony, the term shall be fixed by the court, and shall not exceed seven years; and

(e) For a class E felony, the term shall be fixed by the court, and shall not exceed four years.

3. Minimum period of imprisonment. The minimum period of imprisonment under an indeterminate sentence shall be at least one year and shall be fixed as follows:

(a) In the case of a class A felony, the minimum period shall be fixed by the court and specified in the sentence.

(i) For a class A-I felony, such minimum period shall not be less than fifteen years nor more than twenty-five years; provided, however, that (A) where a sentence, other than a sentence of death or life imprisonment without parole, is imposed upon a defendant convicted of murder in the first degree as defined in section 125.27 of this chapter such minimum period shall be not less than twenty years nor more than twenty-five years, and, (B) where a sentence is imposed upon a defendant convicted of murder in the second degree as defined in subdivision five of section 125.25 of this chapter the sentence shall be life imprisonment without parole.

(ii) For a class A-II felony, such minimum period shall not be less than three years nor more than eight years four months.

(b) For a class B felony, the minimum period shall be fixed by the court and specified in the sentence and shall be not less than one year nor more than one-third of the maximum term imposed.

4. Alternative definite sentence for class D and E felonies. When a person, other than a second or persistent felony offender, is sentenced for a class D or class E felony, and the court, having regard to the nature and circumstances of the crime and to the history and character of the defendant, is of the opinion that a sentence of imprisonment is necessary but that it would be unduly harsh to impose an indeterminate or determinate sentence, the court may impose a definite sentence of imprisonment and fix a term of one year or less.

5. Life imprisonment without parole. Life imprisonment without parole. Notwithstanding any other provision of law, a defendant sentenced to life imprisonment without parole shall not be or become eligible for parole or conditional release. For purposes of commitment and custody, other than parole and conditional release, such sentence shall be deemed to be an indeterminate sentence. A defendant may be sentenced to life imprisonment without parole upon conviction for the crime of murder in the first degree as defined in section 125.27 of this chapter and in accordance with the procedures provided by law for imposing a sentence for such crime. A defendant must be sentenced to life imprisonment without parole upon conviction for the crime of murder in the second degree as defined in subdivision five of section 125.25 of this chapter. A defendant must be sentenced to life imprisonment without parole upon conviction for the crime of terrorism as defined in section 490.25 of this chapter, where the specified offense the defendant committed is a class A-I felony; the crime of criminal possession of a chemical weapon or biological weapon in the first degree as defined in section 490.45 of this chapter; or the crime of criminal use of a chemical weapon or biological weapon in the first degree as defined in section 490.55 of this chapter; provided, however, that nothing in this subdivision shall preclude or prevent a sentence of death when the defendant is also convicted of the crime of murder in the first degree as defined in section 125.27 of this chapter.

6. [*Effective until Sept. 1, 2009.*] Determinate sentence. Except as provided in subdivision four of this section and subdivisions two and four of section 70.02, when a person is sentenced as a violent felony offender pursuant to section 70.02 or as a second violent felony offender pursuant to section 70.04 or as a second felony offender on a conviction for a violent felony offense pursuant to section 70.06, the court must impose a determinate sentence of imprisonment in accordance with the provisions of such sections and such sentence shall include, as a part thereof, a period of post-release supervision in accordance with section 70.45.

Amended by L. 1973, Chs. 276, 277; L. 1976, Ch. 480; L. 1978, Ch. 481; L. 1979, Ch. 410; L. 1980, Ch. 873; L. 1983, Ch. 238; L. 1986, Ch. 280; L. 1995, Ch. 1, § 3, § 4, and § 5, eff. Sept. 1, 1995, amending, respectively, subds. (1), (3)(a)(i), and adding subd. (5); L. 1995, Ch. 3, § 1-c, amending subd. (1), eff. Oct. 1, 1995, amendment repealed Sept. 30. 2005 pursuant to L. 1995, Ch. 3, § 74, paragraph (d), and amendment applies only to offenses committed on or after Oct. 1, 1995 pursuant to L. 1995, Ch. 3, § 74, paragraph (e); L. 1995, Ch. 3, § 2, amending subd. (3)(b), eff. Oct. 1, 1995, amendment repealed Sept. 30, 2005 pursuant to L. 1995, Ch. 3, § 74, paragraph (d), and amendment applies only to offenses committed on or after Oct. 1, 1995 pursuant to L. 1995, Ch. 3, § 74, paragraph (e); L. 1995, Ch. 3, § 3, adding subd. (6), eff. Oct. 1, 1995, amendment repealed Sept. 30, 2005 pursuant to L. 1995, Ch. 3, § 74, paragraph (d), and amendment applies only to offenses committed on or after Oct. 1, 1995 pursuant to L. 1995, Ch. 3, § 74, paragraph (e); L. 1998, Ch. 1, §§ 2–4, eff. Aug. 6, 1998, and shall apply to offenses committed on or after Sept. 1, 1998. Offenses committed prior to Sept. 1, 1998 shall be governed by the provisions of law in effect at the time the offense was committed; provided, however, that nothing contained herein shall be deemed to affect the application, qualification, expiration, reversion or repeal of any provision of law amended by any section of L. 1998, Ch. 1 and the provisions of L. 1998, Ch. 1 shall be applied or qualified or shall expire or revert or be deemed repealed in the same manner, to the same extent and on the same date as the case may be as otherwise provided by law; L. 2004, Ch. 1, § 5 (Part A), eff. July 23, 2004; L. 2004, Ch. 459, § 3, eff. Nov. 1, 2004, amending subds. 3(a)(i) and 5; L. 2004, Ch. 738, §§ 28 and 29, eff. Dec. 14, 2004, amending subds. 1 through 4; L. 2005, Ch. 56, Part D, § 20, extending repeal of amendments to Sept. 1, 2009.

ANNOTATIONS

Constitutionality.—Mandatory sentence for a class A-felony of a minimum term of 15 to 25 years and a maximum term of life is not unconstitutional. People v. Lamberto, 151 A.D.2d 503, 542 N.Y.S.2d 292 (2d Dept. 1989).

—Mandatory maximum sentence of life incarceration for persons convicted of class A felony drug offenses is constitutional. People v. Buckmaster, 139 A.D.2d 659, 527 N.Y.S.2d 297 (2d Dept. 1988).

Excessive sentence.—Sentence of two to six years of imprisonment for grand larceny in the fourth degree was illegal since it exceeded the maximum term authorized by law; sentence was reduced to 1 1/3 to four years of imprisonment. People v. Dominguez, 210 A.D.2d 249, 620 N.Y.S.2d 257 (2d Dept. 1994).

—Sentence imposed upon the defendant, which was the minimum prescribed by law, was clearly not excessive. People v. Abdurrahman, 135 A.D.2d 721, 522 N.Y.S.2d 621 (2d Dept. 1987).

Sentence after retrial.—When a greater sentence is imposed after successful appeal and retrial than was originally imposed, a presumption of vindictiveness arises which may be overcome by evidence that the higher sentence rests upon a legitimate and reasoned basis. People v. Miller, 65 N.Y.2d 502, 493 N.Y.S.2d 96, 482 N.E.2d 892 (1985).

—Defendant could properly be sentenced to a longer term of imprisonment following retrial on a rape charge after an appellate reversal of his original conviction based upon a plea bargain where one of the considerations in the original plea bargain was that the rape victim would not have to testify. People v. Miller, 103 A.D.2d 808, 477 N.Y.S.2d 688 (2d Dept. 1984), aff'd, 65 N.Y.2d 502, 493 N.Y.S.2d 96, 482 N.E.2d 892, cert. denied, 474 U.S. 951 (1985).

Applicable law.—Defendant was entitled to be sentenced under the law in effect at the time the crimes were committed. People v. Corrigan, 139 A.D.2d 918, 527 N.Y.S.2d 907 (4th Dept. 1988).

Minimum sentence.—Although the court did not condone the failure to set forth in the record the reasons for imposing a minimum sentence, it did not remit the matter since the reasons which impelled the minimum terms were obvious from the record which was also more than adequate for a review by the Appellate Division of any question as to excessiveness of the sentence. People v. Esteves, 41 N.Y.2d 826, 393 N.Y.S.2d 389, 361 N.E.2d 1037 (1977).

—Upon conviction of grand larceny in the second degree as a first felony offender, an indeterminate term ranging from one to three to five to fifteen years is mandated by statute, a sentence of one year is available only for class C drug felonies. People v. Furman, 280 A.D.2d 385 721 N.Y.S.2d 229 (2d Dept. 2001).

—Given that sentence of 15 years to life is the minimum permitted under § 70.00[2][a], [3][a][i] for attempted murder in the first degree, sentence could not be modified in the exercise of interest of justice jurisdiction. People v. Beverly, 229 A.D.2d 970, 645 N.Y.S.2d 689 (4th Dept. 1996).

—Defendant's sentence of one to four years of imprisonment for falsifying business records was lawful; the minimum term of the sentence was not less than one year and not more than one third of the maximum term imposed. People v. Thomas, 209 A.D.2d 1047, 619 N.Y.S.2d 1007 (4th Dept. 1994).

Effect of plea.—A sentencing court is not bound to impose the sentence agreed upon as part of a plea bargain, but may, in its discretion, impose a lesser sentence; however, when it acts outside the terms of the plea arrangement, the prosecutor should be given the opportunity to withdraw his consent to the plea. People v. Martinez, 124 A.D.2d 505, 508 N.Y.S.2d 180 (1st Dept. 1986).

—General written waiver of right to appeal offered and accepted as part of valid and negotiated plea bargain to a charge of criminal possession of a controlled substance in the second degree, to which defendant received seven years to life, also included a waiver of defendant's claim on appeal that sentence was harsh and excessive. People v. Brathwaite, 263 A.D.2d 89, 703 N.Y.S.2d 191 (2d Dept. 2000)

—The fact that the sentence imposed after trial is greater than that offered as part of a plea bargain does not automatically establish that in determining the sentence, the trial court improperly increased the defendant's punishment solely for asserting his right to a trial. People v. Durkin, 132 A.D.2d 668, 518 N.Y.S.2d 38, 39 (2d Dept. 1987).

Reduction/modification of sentence.—Term of three and one third to 10 years imposed for each conviction of rape in the second degree was not a lawful sentence for that class D felony, appellate court did not remand rather replaced illegal sentence with a legal term of two and one third to seven years leaving the aggregate sentence unchanged. People v. Barriento, 5 A.D.3d 220, 772 N.Y.S.2d 824 (1st Dept. 2004).

—The court rejected the defendant's contention that his sentence was harsh and excessive; the sentence was within the statutory range and less than the harshest permissible sentence, and the defendant failed to present any extraordinary circumstances or abuse of discretion which would warrant modification. People v. Dexheimer, 214 A.D.2d 898, 625 N.Y.S.2d 719 (3d Dept. 1995).

—Where the defendant's sentence is within statutory limits, the sentence should not be disturbed absent a showing of a clear abuse of discretion on the part of the sentencing court, or extraordinary circumstances warranting modification. People v. Parson, 209 A.D.2d 882, 619 N.Y.S.2d 372 (3d Dept. 1994).

—Court imposed a determinate term of imprisonment based upon its misunderstanding that such a sentence is mandatory for assault in the second degree, however a determinate term of imprisonment is authorized sentence for that offense, but it is not required and, although some imprisonment is mandatory, a definite term of imprisonment of one year or less under § 70.00 or an intermittent term of imprisonment under §§ 60.05 and 85.00 is also authorized as is a split sentence of

imprisonment and probation, appellate court vacated sentence and remanded for resentence. People v. Endresz, 1 A.D.3d 888, 767 N.Y.S.2d 732 (4th Dept. 2003).

§ 70.02. Sentence of imprisonment for a violent felony offense.

1. Definition of a violent felony offense. A violent felony offense is a class B violent felony offense, a class C violent felony offense, a class D violent felony offense, or a class E violent felony offense, defined as follows:

(a) Class B violent felony offenses: an attempt to commit the class A-I felonies of murder in the second degree as defined in section 125.25, kidnapping in the first degree as defined in section 135.25, and arson in the first degree as defined in section 150.20; manslaughter in the first degree as defined in section 125.20, rape in the first degree as defined in section 130.35, criminal sexual act in the first degree as defined in section 130.50, aggravated sexual abuse in the first degree as defined in section 130.70, course of sexual conduct against a child in the first degree as defined in section 130.75; assault in the first degree as defined in section 120.10, kidnapping in the second degree as defined in section 135.20, burglary in the first degree as defined in section 140.30, arson in the second degree as defined in section 150.15, robbery in the first degree as defined in section 160.15, criminal possession of a dangerous weapon in the first degree as defined in section 265.04, criminal use of a firearm in the first degree as defined in section 265.09, criminal sale of a firearm in the first degree as defined in section 265.13, aggravated assault upon a police officer or a peace officer as defined in section 120.11, gang assault in the first degree as defined in section 120.07, intimidating a victim or witness in the first degree as defined in section 215.17, hindering prosecution of terrorism in the first degree as defined in section 490.35, criminal possession of a chemical weapon or biological weapon in the second degree as defined in section 490.40, and criminal use of a chemical weapon or biological weapon in the third degree as defined in section 490.47.

(b) Class C violent felony offenses: an attempt to commit any of the class B felonies set forth in paragraph (a); aggravated sexual abuse in the second degree as defined in section 130.67, assault on a peace officer, police officer, fireman or emergency medical services professional as defined in section 120.08, gang assault in the second degree as defined in section 120.06, burglary in the second degree as defined in section 140.25, robbery in the second degree as defined in section 160.10, criminal possession of a weapon in the second degree as defined in section 265.03, criminal use of a firearm in the second degree as defined in section 265.08, criminal sale of a firearm in the second degree as defined in section 265.12, criminal sale of a firearm with the aid of a minor as defined in section 265.14, soliciting or providing support for an act of terrorism in the first degree as defined in section 490.15, hindering prosecution of terrorism in the second degree as defined in section 490.30, and criminal possession of a chemical weapon or biological weapon in the third degree as defined in section 490.37.

(c) Class D violent felony offenses: an attempt to commit any of the class C felonies set forth in paragraph (b); assault in the second degree as defined in section 120.05, stalking in the first degree, as defined in subdivision one of section 120.60, sexual abuse in the first degree as defined in section 130.65, course of sexual conduct against a child in the second degree as defined in section 130.80, aggravated sexual abuse in the third degree as defined in section 130.66, criminal possession of a weapon in the third degree as defined in subdivision four, five, six, seven or eight of section 265.02, intimidating a victim or witness in the second degree as defined in section 215.16, soliciting or providing support for an act of terrorism in the second degree as defined in section 490.10, and making a terroristic threat as defined in section 490.20, falsely reporting an incident in the first degree as defined in section 240.60, placing a false bomb in the first degree as defined in section 240.62, placing a false bomb in a sports stadium or arena, mass transportation facility, enclosed shopping mall as defined in section 240.63, and aggravated unpermitted use of indoor pyrotechnics in the first degree as defined in section 405.18.

(d) Class E violent felony offenses: an attempt to commit any of the felonies of criminal possession of a weapon in the third degree as defined in subdivision four, five, six, seven or eight of section 265.02 as a lesser included offense of that section as defined in section 220.20 of the criminal procedure law, falsely reporting an incident in the second degree as defined in section 240.55 and placing a false bomb in the second degree as defined in section 240.61.

2. Authorized sentence.

(a) [*Effective until Sept. 1, 2009.*] Except as provided in subdivision six of section 60.05, the sentence imposed upon a person who stands convicted of a class B or class C violent felony offense must be a determinate sentence of imprisonment which shall be in whole or half years. The term of such sentence must be in accordance with the provisions of subdivision three of this section.

(a) [*Effective Sept. 1, 2009.*] The sentence imposed upon a person who stands convicted of a class B or class C violent felony offense must be an indeterminate sentence of imprisonment. Except as provided in subdivision five of section 60.05, the maximum term of such sentence must be in accordance with the provisions of subdivision three of this section and the minimum period of imprisonment under such sentence must be in accordance with subdivision four of this section.

(b) Except as provided in subdivision six of section 60.05 and subdivision four of this section, the sentence imposed upon a person who stands convicted of a class D violent felony offense, other than the offense of criminal possession of a weapon in the third degree as defined in subdivision four, five, seven or eight of section 265.02, must be in accordance with the applicable provisions of this chapter relating to sentencing for class D felonies provided, however, that where a sentence of imprisonment is imposed which requires a commitment to the state department of correctional services, such sentence shall be a determinate sentence in accordance with paragraph (c) of subdivision three of this section.

(c) Except as provided in subdivision six of section 60.05, the sentence imposed upon a person who stands convicted of the class D violent felony offenses of criminal possession of a weapon in the third degree as defined in subdivision four, five, seven or eight of section 265.02 or the class E violent felonies of attempted criminal possession of a weapon in the third degree as defined in subdivision four, five, seven or eight of section 265.02 must be a sentence to a determinate period of imprisonment, or, in the alternative, a definite sentence of imprisonment for a period of no less than one year, except that:

(i) The court may impose any other sentence authorized by law upon a person who has not been previously convicted in the five years immediately preceding the commission of the offense for a class A misdemeanor defined in this chapter, if the court having regard to the nature and circumstances of the crime and to the history and character of the defendant, finds on the record that such sentence would be unduly harsh and that the alternative sentence would be consistent with public safety and does not deprecate the seriousness of the crime; and

(ii) the court may apply the provisions of paragraphs (b) and (c) of subdivision four of this section when imposing a sentence upon a person who has previously been convicted of a class A misdemeanor defined in this chapter in the five years immediately preceding the commission of the offense.

3. Term of sentence. The term of a determinate sentence for a violent felony offense must be fixed by the court as follows:

(a) For a class B felony, the term must be at least five years and must not exceed twenty-five years;

(b) For a class C felony, the term must be at least three and one-half years and must not exceed fifteen years;

(c) For a class D felony, the term must be at least two years and must not exceed seven years; and

(d) For a class E felony, the term must be at

least one and one-half years and must not exceed four years.

4. (a) Except as provided in paragraph (b) of this subdivision, where a plea of guilty to a class D violent felony offense is entered pursuant to section 220.10 or 220.30 of the criminal procedure law in satisfaction of an indictment charging the defendant with an armed felony, as defined in subdivision forty-one of section 1.20 of the criminal procedure law, the court must impose a determinate sentence of imprisonment.

(b) In any case in which the provisions of paragraph (a) of this subdivision or the provisions of subparagraph (ii) of paragraph (c) of subdivision two of this section apply, the court may impose a sentence other than a determinate sentence of imprisonment, or a definite sentence of imprisonment for a period of no less than one year, if it finds that the alternate sentence is consistent with public safety and does not depreciate the seriousness of the crime and that one or more of the following factors exist:

(i) Mitigating circumstances that bear directly upon the manner in which the crime was committed; or

(ii) where the defendant was not the sole participant in the crime, the defendant's participation was relatively minor although not so minor as to constitute a defense to the prosecution; or

(iii) possible deficiencies in proof of the defendant's commission of an armed felony.

(c) The defendant and the district attorney shall have an opportunity to present relevant information to assist the court in making a determination pursuant to paragraph (b) of this subdivision, and the court may, in its discretion, conduct a hearing with respect to any issue bearing upon such determination. If the court determines that a determinate sentence of imprisonment should not be imposed pursuant to the provisions of such paragraph (b), it shall make a statement on the record of the facts and circumstances upon which such determination is based. A transcript of the court's statement, which shall set forth the recommendation of the district attorney, shall be forwarded to the state division of criminal justice services along with a copy of the accusatory instrument.

Amended by L. 1980, Chs. 233, 234, 583; L. 1981, Ch. 175; L. 1986, Ch. 124; L. 1988, Ch. 450; L. 1991, Ch. 521, eff. Nov. 1, 1991, amending subd. (1)(c); L. 1991, Ch. 496, eff. Nov. 1, 1991, amending subd. (1)(b) & (c); L. 1993, Ch. 291; L. 1995, Ch. 3, § 4, amending subds. (2)(a) and (4), eff. Oct. 1, 1995, amendment repealed Sept. 30, 2005 pursuant to L. 1995, Ch. 3, § 74, paragraph (d), and amendment applies only to offenses committed on or after Oct. 1, 1995 pursuant to L. 1995, Ch. 3, § 74, paragraph (e); L. 1996, Ch. 122, § 2, amending subds. 1(a) and (c), eff. Aug. 1, 1996; L. 1996, Ch. 181, § 1, amending subds. 1(c), eff. Nov. 1, 1996; L. 1996, Ch. 646, § 1, amending subds. 1(a) and (b), eff. Nov. 1, 1996; L. 1996, Ch. 647, § 1, amending subds. 1(a) and (b), eff. Nov. 1, 1996; L. 1996, Ch. 632, § 1, amending subd. 1(b), eff. Nov. 1, 1996; L. 1998, Ch. 1, §§ 5 through 9, eff. Aug. 6, 1998, and shall apply to offenses committed on or after Sept. 1, 1998. Offenses committed prior to Sept. 1, 1998 shall be governed by the provisions of law in effect at the time the offense was committed; provided, however, that nothing contained herein shall be deemed to affect the application, qualification, expiration, reversion or repeal of any provision of law amended by any section of L. 1998, Ch. 1 and the provisions of L. 1998, Ch. 1 shall be applied or qualified or shall expire or revert or be deemed repealed in the same manner, to the same extent and on the same date as the case may be as otherwise provided by law; and L. 1998, Ch. 378, § 2, eff. Nov. 1, 1998; L. 1999, Ch. 33, eff. Nov. 1, 1999, amending subds. 1 and 2, and Ch. 635, § 10, eff. Dec. 1, 1999, amending subd. 1(c); L. 2000, Ch. 189, §§ 6 and 7, eff. Nov. 1, 2000, amending subds. 1 and 2; L. 2001, Ch. 300, § 2, amending subd. 1(a), (b), and (c), and Ch. 301, § 8, amending subd. 1(c) and (d), eff. Sept. 17, 2001; L. 2003, Ch. 264, § 6, eff. Nov. 1, 2003, amending subd. 1(a); L. 2003, Ch. 584, § 3, eff. Nov. 1, 2003, "provided that any state agency and any political subdivision of the state are authorized to promulgate any and all rules and regulations and take any other measures necessary to implement this act on its effective date on or before such date," amending subd. 1(c); L. 2004, Ch. 1, § 6, eff. July 23, 2004, amending subd. 1(a) & (b); L. 2005, Ch. 56, Part D, § 20, extending repeal of amendments to Sept. 1, 2009.

ANNOTATIONS

Appeal.—Any failure of the sentencing court to exercise the full scope of its discretion or to take into consideration all relevant factors in sentencing a defendant, pursuant to PL § 70.02[5] can be remedied by the exercise of the unfettered discretion of the Appellate Court. People v. Felix, 87 A.D.2d 529, 447 N.Y.S.2d 945 (1st Dept. 1982), aff'd, 58 N.Y.2d 156, 460 N.Y.S.2d 1, 446 N.E.2d 757, dismissed, 464 U.S. 802 (1983).

Constitutionality.—There is no due process infirmity under either the federal or the state constitution in the requirement of PL § 70.02(5) that a defendant who has been charged with an armed felony and permitted in satisfaction of the indictment to plead guilty to a class D violent felony must receive an indeterminate sentence of one to three years unless the court finds that factors specified in the section warrant imposition of less than an indeterminate sentence. People v. Felix, 58 N.Y.2d 156, 460 N.Y.S.2d 1, 446 N.E.2d 757, dismissed, 464 U.S. 802 (1983).

—Defendant's claim that the sentence imposed upon convictions for first degree burglary and petit larceny was cruel and unusual and unduly harsh was meritless; the sentence was within the permissible statutory range and neither defendant's youth nor the lesser sentences received by his accomplices required a different result. People v. Hoyle, 211 A.D.2d 973, 621 N.Y.S.2d 756 (3d Dept. 1995).

Excessive sentence.—Maximum penalty imposed for a conviction of sexual abuse in the first degree is double, not triple, the minimum sentence; therefore, defendant's sentence was reduced from 2 to 6 years consecutive sentence to run on each count to 2 to 4 years on each count. People v. Ocean, 292 A.D.2d 545, 739 N.Y.S.2d 735 (2d Dept. 2002).

—The sentence imposed was not excessive in light of the violent nature of the crimes committed. People v. Barrales, 221 A.D.2d 348, 633 N.Y.S.2d 368 (2d Dept. 1995).

Improper sentence.—Defendant was improperly sentenced as a persistent violent felony offender upon his conviction of grand larceny in the second degree as this offense is included within the definition of a violent felony. People v. Ford, 279 A.D.2d 588, 719 N.Y.S.2d 677 (2d Dept.), appeal denied, 96 N.Y.2d 828 (2001).

—Minimum term of imprisonment for a violent felony offense under this section prior to amendment in 1995 was one-third the maximum term; therefore defendant's sentence for a conviction prior to the 1995 amendment should be reduced from $12\frac{1}{2}$ years to $8\frac{1}{3}$ years. People v. Foster, 235 A.D.2d 490, 652 N.Y.S.2d 620 (2d Dept. 1997).

—Where defendant was not adjudicated a second felony offender, it was error to fix the minimum term of imprisonment at one-half the maximum term. People v. Faulkner, 220 A.D.2d 525, 632 N.Y.S.2d 189 (2d Dept. 1995).

—Sentence for conviction of robbery in the first degree was illegal since the crime is not an "armed felony"; court modified sentence by reducing the minimum term to one-third, rather than one-half, the maximum term. People v. Agramonte, 228 A.D.2d 607, 644 N.Y.S.2d 632 (2d Dept. 1996).

—Since attempted murder in the second degree is not, by definition, an armed felony offense, and since defendant was a first felony offender, the court erred in imposing a minimum sentence of one-half the maximum term of imprisonment. People v. Bernard, 214 A.D.2d 576, 625 N.Y.S.2d 78 (2d Dept. 1995).

—County court failed to impose a sentence which conformed to the minimum term required by law at the time defendant committed the offense; sentence vacated and remanded for resentencing. People v. Ward, 236 A.D.2d 886, 654 N.Y.S.2d 704 (4th Dept. 1997).

—Indeterminate sentence of imprisonment of five to fifteen years for assault in the second degree was illegal given that maximum sentence for offense committed before October 1, 1995 is two and one-third to seven years. People v. Bates, 233 A.D.2d 937, 649 N.Y.S.2d 878 (4th Dept. 1996).

Mitigating circumstances.—Factors directly flowing from and relating to defendant's conduct while committing the crime qualify as mitigating circumstances. People v. Garcia, 84 N.Y.2d 336, 618 N.Y.S.2d 621, 642 N.E.2d 1077 (1994).

—Mitigating circumstances under Penal Law § 70.02(5)(b)(i) must relate to defendant's conduct in committing the crime, not to the conduct of the police in effecting the arrest. People v. Williams, 79 N.Y.2d 281, 582 N.Y.S.2d 71, 590 N.E.2d 1199 (1992).

—Defendant, who was convicted of armed felonies, was eligible for youthful offender treatment only if the court found mitigating circumstances bearing directly on the manner in which the crime was committed. People v. Smalls, 219 A.D.2d 865, 632 N.Y.S.2d 1004 (4th Dept. 1995).

Notice.—Despite defendant's contentions, the language of the indictment put defendant on notice that he was being charged with an armed felony whose sentencing would be governed by Penal Law § 70.02. People v. Colman, 235 A.D.2d 928, 653 N.Y.S.2d 423 (3d Dept. 1997).

Persistent violent felony offender.—The court erred in sentencing the defendant as a persistent violent felony offender because criminal possession of a weapon in the third degree is not defined as a violent felony offense in § 70.02(1)(c). People v. Maynard, 211 A.D.2d 505, 621 N.Y.S.2d 557 (1st Dept. 1995).

—Defendant, who had prior judgments of conviction for robbery in the second degree and assault in the second degree, was properly adjudicated to be a persistent violent felony offender upon his second conviction for robbery in the second degree. People v. Davis, 212 A.D.2d 724, 622 N.Y.S.2d 805 (2d Dept. 1995).

§ 70.04. Sentence of imprisonment for second violent felony offender.

1. Definition of second violent felony offender.

(a) A second violent felony offender is a person who stands convicted of a violent felony offense as defined in subdivision one of section 70.02 after having previously been subjected to a predicate violent felony conviction as defined in paragraph (b) of this subdivision.

(b) For the purpose of determining whether a prior conviction is a predicate violent felony conviction the following criteria shall apply:

(i) The conviction must have been in this state of a class A felony (other than one defined in article two hundred twenty) or of a violent felony offense as defined in subdivision one of section 70.02, or of an offense defined by the penal law in effect prior to September first, nineteen hundred sixty-seven, which includes all of the essential elements of any such felony, or in any other jurisdiction of an offense which includes all of

the essential elements of any such felony for which a sentence to a term of imprisonment in excess of one year or a sentence of death was authorized and is authorized in this state irrespective of whether such sentence was imposed;

(ii) Sentence upon such prior conviction must have been imposed before commission of the present felony;

(iii) Suspended sentence, suspended execution of sentence, a sentence of probation, a sentence of conditional discharge or of unconditional discharge, and a sentence of certification to the care and custody of the division of substance abuse services, shall be deemed to be a sentence;

(iv) Except as provided in subparagraph (v) of this paragraph, sentence must have been imposed not more than ten years before commission of the felony of which the defendant presently stands convicted;

(v) In calculating the ten year period under subparagraph (iv), any period of time during which the person incarcerated * for any reason between the time of commission of the previous felony and the time of commission of the present felony shall be excluded and such ten year period shall be extended by a period or periods equal to the time served under such incarceration;

(vi) An offense for which the defendant has been pardoned on the ground of innocence shall not be deemed a predicate violent felony conviction.

2. [*Effective until Sept. 1, 2009.*] Authorized sentence. When the court has found, pursuant to the provisions of the criminal procedure law, that a person is a second violent felony offender the court must impose a determinate sentence of imprisonment which shall be in whole or half years. Except where sentence is imposed in accordance with the provisions of section 70.10, the term of such sentence must be in accordance with the provisions of subdivision three of this section.

2. [*Effective Sept. 1, 2009.*] Authorized sentence. When the court has found, pursuant to the provisions of the criminal procedure law, that a person is a second violent felony offender the court must impose an indeterminate sentence of imprisonment. Except where sentence is imposed in accordance with the provisions of section 70.10, the maximum term of such sentence must be in accordance with the provisions of subdivision three of this section and the minimum period of imprisonment under such sentence must be in accordance with subdivision four of this section.

3. [*Effective until Sept. 1, 2009.*] Term of sentence. The term of a determinate sentence for a second violent felony offender must be fixed by the court as follows:

(a) For a class B felony, the term must be at least ten years and must not exceed twenty-five years;

(b) For a class C felony, the term must be at least seven years and must not exceed fifteen years; and

(c) For a class D felony, the term must be at least five years and must not exceed seven years.

(d) For a class E felony, the term must be at least three years and must not exceed four years.

3. [*Effective Sept. 1, 2009.*] Maximum term of sentence. The maximum term of an indeterminate sentence for a second violent felony offender must be fixed by the court as follows:

(a) (a) For a class B felony, the term must be at least twelve years and must not exceed twenty-five years;

(b) For a class C felony, the term must be at least eight years and must not exceed fifteen years; and

(c) For a class D felony, the term must be at least five years and must not exceed seven years.

(d) For a class E felony, the term must be at least four years.

* As originally enacted.

Added by L. 1978, Ch. 481; **Amended** by L. 1980, Chs. 233, 471; L. 1995, Ch. 3, § 5, amending subds. 2-4, eff. Oct. 1, 1995, amendments repealed Sept. 30, 2005, pursuant to L. 1995, Ch. 3, § 74, paragraph (d), and amendments apply only to offenses committed on or after Oct. 1, 1995 pursuant to L. 1995, Ch. 3, § 74, paragraph (e); L. 2005, Ch. 56, Part D, § 20, extending repeal date of amendments to Sept. 1, 2009.

ANNOTATIONS

Calculating the time of the prior and prior felony offense.—Although over 12 years passed between date of prior conviction and the commission of the crimes for which defendant appealed his convictions and his adjudication as a second felony offender, the six years he was incarcerated on the prior conviction tolls the 10-year calculation; therefore, defendant was properly sentenced. People v. Ehrenberg, 236 A.D.2d 420, 653 N.Y.S.2d 137 (2d Dept. 1997).

Constitutionality.—PL §§ 70.02 and 70.04 do not violate the *ex post facto* clause of Article 1 (Sections 9, 10) of the United States Constitution. People v. Aiello, 93 A.D.2d 864, 461 N.Y.S.2d 370 (2d Dept. 1983).

Persistent violent felony offenders.—Mandatory sentence for second violent felony offender convicted of a class E felony is now a determinate term of 3, 3½, or 4 years; where defendant agreed to a sentence of 4 to life and 4 years is a lawful sentence, court will not disturb sentence. People v. Tolbert, 251 A.D.2d 44, 674 N.Y.S.2d 13 (1st Dept.), *aff'd*, 93 N.Y.2d 86, 688 N.Y.S.2d 105, 710 N.E.2d 669 (1999).

—Defendant was improperly sentenced as a persistent violent felony offender upon his conviction of grand larceny in the second degree, as this offense is not included within the definition of violent felony. People v. Ford, 279 A.D.2d 588, 719 N.Y.S.2d 677 (2d Dept.), *appeal denied*, 96 N.Y.2d 828 (2001).

—Defendant, who had prior judgments of conviction for robbery in the second degree and assault in the second degree, was properly adjudicated to be a persistent violent felony offender upon his second conviction for robbery in the second degree. People v. Davis, 212 A.D.2d 724, 622 N.Y.S.2d 805 (2d Dept. 1995).

—PL § 70.04 permits the use of a prior felony conviction as a predicate violent felony conviction, if, at the time the present violent felony offense was committed, the prior crime was designated a violent felony offense under PL § 70.02. People v. Balfour, 95 A.D.2d 812, 463 N.Y.S.2d 859 (2d Dept. 1983).

—Defendant, an inmate who was convicted of assault after punching a hearing officer in the face, was properly sentenced

to a seven-year consecutive term to begin running after the term he was serving as a violent felony offender in light of his extensive criminal record with a propensity for violent behavior while incarcerated. People v. Bernier, 279 A.D.2d 701, 719 N.Y.S.2d 186 (3d Dept.), *appeal denied*, 96 N.Y.2d 797 (2001).

§ 70.05. Sentence of imprisonment for juvenile offender.

1. Indeterminate sentence. A sentence of imprisonment for a felony committed by a juvenile offender shall be an indeterminate sentence. When such a sentence is imposed, the court shall impose a maximum term in accordance with the provisions of subdivision two of this section and the minimum period of imprisonment shall be as provided in subdivision three of this section. The court shall further provide that where a juvenile offender is under placement pursuant to article three of the family court act, any sentence imposed pursuant to this section which is to be served consecutively with such placement shall be served in a facility designated pursuant to subdivision four of section 70.20 of this article prior to service of the placement in any previously designated facility.

2. Maximum term of sentence. The maximum term of an indeterminate sentence for a juvenile offender shall be at least three years and the term shall be fixed as follows:

(a) For the class A felony of murder in the second degree, the term shall be life imprisonment;

(b) For the class A felony of arson in the first degree, or for the class A felony of kidnapping in the first degree the term shall be fixed by the court, and shall be at least twelve years but shall not exceed fifteen years;

(c) For a class B felony, the term shall be fixed by the court, and shall not exceed ten years;

(d) For a class C felony, the term shall be fixed by the court, and shall not exceed seven years; and

(e) For a class D felony, the term shall be fixed by the court and shall not exceed four years.

3. Minimum period of imprisonment. The minimum period of imprisonment under an indeterminate sentence for a juvenile offender shall be specified in the sentence as follows:

(a) For the class A felony of murder in the second degree, the minimum period of imprisonment shall be fixed by the court and shall be not less than five years but shall not exceed nine years provided, however, that where the sentence is for an offense specified in subdivision one or two of section 125.25 of this chapter and the defendant was fourteen or fifteen years old at the time of such offense, the minimum period of imprisonment shall be not less than seven and one-half years but shall not exceed fifteen years;

(b) For the class A felony of arson in the first

degree, or for the class A felony of kidnapping in the first degree, the minimum period of imprisonment shall be fixed by the court and shall be not less than four years but shall not exceed six years; and

(c) For a class B, C or D felony, the minimum period of imprisonment shall be fixed by the court at one-third of the maximum term imposed.

Added by L. 1978, Ch. 481; **Amended** by L. 1981, Ch. 303; L. 1984, Ch. 615; L. 1998, Ch. 435, §§ 5 and 6, eff. Nov. 1, 1998; L. 2003, Ch. 174, § 1, eff. Nov. 1, 2003, amending subd. 3(a).

ANNOTATION

Robbery.—Defendant's guilty plea was vacated where defendant was erroneously informed that the minimum sentence for robbery in the first degree was 25 years imprisonment; defendant, a juvenile offender, could not have received such a sentence. People v. Hurd, 220 A.D.2d 454, 631 N.Y.S.2d 871 (2d Dept. 1995).

§ 70.06. Sentence of imprisonment for second felony offender.

1. Definition of second felony offender.

(a) A second felony offender is a person, other than a second violent felony offender as defined in section 70.04, who stands convicted of a felony defined in this chapter, other than a class A-I felony, after having previously been subjected to one or more predicate felony convictions as defined in paragraph (b) of this subdivision.

(b) For the purpose of determining whether a prior conviction is a predicate felony conviction the following criteria shall apply:

(i) The conviction must have been in this state of a felony, or in any other jurisdiction of an offense for which a sentence to a term of imprisonment in excess of one year or a sentence of death was authorized and is authorized in this state irrespective of whether such sentence was imposed;

(ii) Sentence upon such prior conviction must have been imposed before commission of the present felony;

(iii) Suspended sentence, suspended execution of sentence, a sentence of probation, a sentence of conditional discharge or of unconditional discharge, and a sentence of certification to the care and custody of the division of substance abuse services, shall be deemed to be a sentence;

(iv) Except as provided in subparagraph (v) of this paragraph, sentence must have been imposed not more than ten years before commission of the felony of which the defendant presently stands convicted;

(v) In calculating the ten year period under subparagraph (iv), any period of time during which the person was incarcerated for any reason between the time of commission of the previous felony and the time of commission of the present felony shall be excluded and such ten year period

shall be extended by a period or periods equal to the time served under such incarceration;

(vi) An offense for which the defendant has been pardoned on the ground of innocence shall not be deemed a predicate felony conviction.

2. [*Effective until Sept. 1, 2009.*] Authorized sentence. Except as provided in subdivision five or six of this section, when the court has found, pursuant to the provisions of the criminal procedure law, that a person is a second felony offender the court must impose an indeterminate sentence of imprisonment. The maximum term of such sentence must be in accordance with the provisions of subdivision three of this section and the minimum period of imprisonment under such sentence must be in accordance with subdivision four of this section.

2. [*Effective Sept. 1, 2009.*] Authorized sentence. Except as provided in subdivision five of this section, when the court has found, pursuant to the provisions of the criminal procedure law, that a person is a second felony offender the court must impose an indeterminate sentence of imprisonment. The maximum term of such sentence must be in accordance with the provisions of subdivision three of this section and the minimum period of imprisonment under such sentence must be in accordance with subdivision four of this section.

3. [*Effective until Sept. 1, 2009.*] Maximum term of sentence. Except as provided in subdivision five or six of this section, the maximum term of an indeterminate sentence for a second felony offender must be fixed by the court as follows:

(a) For a class A-II felony, the term must be life imprisonment;

(b) For a class B felony, the term must be at least nine years and must not exceed twenty-five years;

(c) For a class C felony, the term must be at least six years and must not exceed fifteen years;

(d) For a class D felony, the term must be at least four years and must not exceed seven years; and

(e) For a class E felony, the term must be at least three years and must not exceed four years; provided, however, that where the sentence is for the class E felony offense specified in section 240.32 of this chapter, the maximum term must be at least three years and must not exceed five years.

3. [*Effective Sept. 1, 2009.*] Maximum term of sentence. Except as provided in subdivision five of this section, the maximum term of an indeterminate sentence for a second felony offender must be fixed by the court as follows:

(a) For a class A-II felony, the term must be life imprisonment;

(b) For a class B felony, the term must be at

least nine years and must not exceed twenty-five years;

(c) For a class C felony, the term must be at least six years and must not exceed fifteen years;

(d) For a class D felony, the term must be at least four years and must not exceed seven years; and

(e) For a class E felony, the term must be at least three years and must not exceed four years.

4. Minimum period of imprisonment. (a) The minimum period of imprisonment for second felony offender convicted of a class A-II felony must be fixed by the court at no less than six years and not to exceed twelve and one-half years and must be specified in the sentence.

(b) Except as provided in paragraph (a), the minimum period of imprisonment under an indeterminate sentence for a second felony offender must be fixed by the court at one-half of the maximum term imposed and must be specified in the sentence.

5. [Repealed.]

6. [Effective until Sept. 1, 2009.] Determinate sentence. When the court has found, pursuant to the provisions of the criminal procedure law, that a person is a second felony offender and the sentence to be imposed on such person is for a violent felony offense, as defined in subdivision one of section 70.02, the court must impose a determinate sentence of imprisonment the term of which must be fixed by the court as follows:

(a) For a class B violent felony offense, the term must be at least eight years and must not exceed twenty-five years;

(b) For a class C violent felony offense, the term must be at least five years and must not exceed fifteen years;

(c) For a class D violent felony offense, the term must be at least three years and must not exceed seven years; and

(d) For a class E violent felony offense, the term must be at least two years and must not exceed four years.

7. [Effective until Sept. 1, 2009.] Notwithstanding any other provision of law, in the case of a person sentenced for a specified offense or offenses as defined in subdivision five of section 410.91 of the criminal procedure law, who stands convicted of no other felony offense, who has not previously been convicted of either a violent felony offense as defined in section 70.02 of this article, a class A felony offense or a class B felony offense, and is not under the jurisdiction of or awaiting delivery to the department of correctional services, the court may direct that such sentence be executed as a parole supervision sentence as defined in and pursuant to the procedures prescribed in section 410.91 of the criminal procedure law.

Added by L. 1973, Ch. 277; **Amended** by L. 1973, Chs. 278, 1051; L. 1975, Chs. 667, 784; L. 1978, Ch. 481; L. 1979, Ch. 410; L. 1980, Ch. 471; L. 1995, Ch. 3, § 6, amending subds. 2 and 3, eff. Oct. 1, 1995, amendments repealed Sept. 30, 2005 pursuant to L. 1995, Ch. 3, § 74, paragraph (d); L. 1995, Ch. 3, § 7, adding subds. 6 and 7, eff. Oct. 1, 1995, additions repealed Sept. 30, 2005 pursuant to L. 1995, Ch. 3, § 74, paragraph (d), and additions apply only to offenses committed on or after Oct. 1, 1995 pursuant to L. 1995, Ch. 3, § 74, paragraph (e); L. 1996, Ch. 92, § 1, amending subd. 3(e), eff. Jun. 5, 1996, amendment repealed Sept. 30, 2005 pursuant to L. 1996, Ch. 92 § 5; L. 2004, Ch. 738, §§ 31 & 32, eff. Dec. 14, 2004, repealing subd. 5 and amending subd. 7; L. 2005, Ch. 56, Part D, § 20, extending repeal dates until Sept. 1, 2009.

ANNOTATIONS

Constitutionality.—PL § 70.06 (1)(b)(i) does not violate the Equal Protection Clause.—People v. Pacheco, 53 N.Y.2d 663, 438 N.Y.S.2d 994, 421 N.E.2d 114 (1981).

—Defendant's predicate felony sentence does not violate the rule against *ex post facto* laws even though his prior conviction took place before passage and enactment of the predicate felony offender sentencing law, since the increased punishment was inflicted for the present crime only and not as an additional penalty for the prior offense. People v. Pendergrass, 115 A.D.2d 497, 495 N.Y.S.2d 721 (2d Dept. 1985).

Effect of conviction in other jurisdiction.—Sentencing court improperly accepted an out-of-state conviction as a predicate felony where intent requirement of out-of-state offense was equivalent to a class A misdemeanor, not a felony, in New York. People v. Rota, 245 A.D.2d 133, 665 N.Y.S.2d 661 (1st Dept. 1997).

—The court properly relied on defendant's prior military conviction for cocaine distribution as a predicate felony; the elements of the military crime of narcotics distribution are equivalent to those of the New York felony of sale of a controlled substance in the third degree. People v. Sanchez, 211 A.D.2d 537, 621 N.Y.S.2d 345 (1st Dept. 1995).

—Defendant's prior conviction in Utah of third degree forgery could be used as predicate offense to sentence defendant as second felony offender, since equivalent offense under New York law, forgery in the second degree, authorizes a prison term in excess of one year. People v. Wicks, 232 A.D.2d 680, 648 N.Y.S.2d 713 (3d Dept. 1996).

—Court erred in sentencing defendant as a second felony offender based upon two prior California convictions where neither constituted a predicate felony conviction pursuant to § 70.06. People v. Francis, 231 A.D.2d 839, 647 N.Y.S.2d 885 (4th Dept. 1996).

—Defendant was properly sentenced as a second felony offender where she entered a plea of no contest in North Carolina for solicitation to commit murder since, under North Carolina law, acceptance of that plea constituted a conviction; the elements of the North Carolina crime of solicitation to commit murder are equivalent to those of the New York felony of criminal solicitation in the second degree. People v. Long, 207 A.D.2d 988, 617 N.Y.S.2d 97 (4th Dept. 1994).

—A foreign conviction is a predicate felony when the statute underlying the foreign conviction and a comparable New York statute are equivalent as to their elements, and each authorizes a sentence of more than one year. People v. Leacock, 163 Misc. 2d 95, 619 N.Y.S.2d 514 (Sup. Ct. Kings Co. 1994).

Illegal sentence.—Defendant was improperly sentenced as a second felony offender because the "predicate" felony occurred after the commission of the instant felonies. People v. Ortega, 245 A.D.2d 213, 666 N.Y.S.2d 634 (1st Dept. 1997).

—Where defendant was not sentenced on prior convictions before he committed the present felonies, he was improperly adjudicated a second felony offender. People v. Acevedo, 292 A.D.2d 538, 739 N.Y.S.2d 582 (2d Dept. 2002).

—Conviction for criminal possession of stolen property in the third degree that occurred ten months after the burglary for which defendant was being sentenced could not properly form the basis for sentencing defendant as a second felony offender. People v. Mariano, 268 A.D.2d 671, 701 N.Y.S.2d 512 (3d Dept. 2000).

—Defendant was improperly sentenced as a second felony offender since the predicate felony conviction was obtained after the commission of the instant offenses. People v. Rogner, 265 A.D.2d 688, 697 N.Y.S.2d 363 (3d Dept. 1999).

—Defendant was not illegally sentenced as a second felony offender because his prior conviction did not actually result in a sentence to a term of imprisonment in excess of one year. There is no such requirement under § 70.06(1)(b)(i), and it is sufficient that the prior conviction was for a New York felony. (Distinguishing the persistent felony offender statute (§ 70.10(1)(b)(i)). People v. Parmer, 231 A.D.2d 867, 648 N.Y.S.2d 61 (4th Dept. 1996).

DWI as prior offense.—The express language of PL § 70.06(1)(b)(i) does not require that the prior felony be one defined by the Penal Law; the legislature intended to include any prior felony conviction, including a Vehicle and Traffic Law felony, as a predicate felony to enhance the severity of punishment. People v. Shannon, 89 N.Y.2d 1000, 679 N.E.2d 633, 657 N.Y.S.2d 394 (1997).

—Defendant may not be sentenced to a term of two to four years as a second felony offender under PL § 70.06, since the statute only applies to second felonies which are of a class specifically defined by PL § 70.06, and driving while intoxicated is not so defined. People v. Morris, 86 A.D.2d 763, 448 N.Y.S.2d 82 (4th Dept. 1982).

Effect of constitutional error in prior conviction.—First felony conviction obtained in violation of constitutional rights not a predicate felony under Penal Law § 70.06. People v. Bennett, 86 A.D.2d 674, 446 N.Y.S.2d 381 (2d Dept. 1982).

—Court was not obligated to expressly advise defendant of his right to contest the constitutionality of the prior conviction. People v. Smith, 121 A.D.2d 771, 503 N.Y.S.2d 183 (3d Dept. 1986).

Predicate felony.—A defendant can only be adjudged a second felony offender if the sentence for the crime which is to serve as the predicate for the adjudication was imposed prior to the commission of the present felony. People v. Young, 91 A.D.2d 965, 458 N.Y.S.2d 586 (1st Dept. 1983).

—Defendant's contention that PL § 70.06 was inapplicable to one who escapes from custody while serving a sentence on a prior felony conviction was without merit; the fact that imprisonment for the predicate felony was an element of the second felony does not change the nature of the second felony nor does the fact that the sentence for the second felony comprehends a longer period of incarceration because the prior felony conviction is an element thereof. People v. Lloyd, 87 A.D.2d 899, 449 N.Y.S.2d 365 (3d Dept. 1982).

—Criminal possession of a weapon in the third degree under §265.02(4) is a violent felony offense, where defendant has been found to be a second felony offender and the crime is a violent felony, the court "must" impose a determinate sentence. People v. Goston, 9 A.D.3d 905, 779 N.Y.S.2d 699 (4th 2004).

Resentencing; error in sentence.—An error as to the sentence of a defendant may be corrected by the court even though the resentence is greater. People v. Finnerty, 78 A.D.2d 554, 432 N.Y.S.2d 19 (2d Dept. 1980).

Time of sentencing for predicate felony.—A felony upon which defendant was not sentenced until eleven months after the commission of the present felony cannot be used as a predicate felony. People v. Mickle, 91 A.D.2d 920, 457 N.Y.S.2d 807 (1st Dept. 1983).

—Defendant was properly sentenced as a second felony offender even though his predicate felony offense occurred almost 13 years before this subsequent felony; it is the date of sentencing in the prior felony which starts the 10-year clock running. Additionally, the statute contains a tolling provision for the period of incarceration because the prior felony. People v. Faust, 235 A.D.2d 430, 652 N.Y.S.2d 120 (2d Dept. 1997).

—Defendant was properly sentenced as a second felony offender where he was sentenced on the earlier conviction within 10 years of the commission of the second felony; the people were not required to set forth the period and places of defendant's incarceration in the second felony offender statement because they were not relying on the tolling provision contained in § 70.06(1)(b)(v). People v. Merriweather, 212 A.D.2d 1061, 623 N.Y.S.2d 32 (4th Dept. 1995).

Effect of uncontested predicate felony conviction.—While defendant did not contest his adjudication as a second felony offender, where it was subsequently discovered that the underlying crime was not a predicate felony conviction, the interests of justice required that the sentence imposed be vacated and

the matter remitted for resentencing. People v. Fusillo, 94 A.D.2d 802, 463 N.Y.S.2d 51 (2d Dept. 1983).

Waiver.—The court ruled correctly in refusing to permit the defendant to challenge, at his sentencing or resentencing, the constitutionality of earlier convictions relied upon in adjudicating the defendant a second felony offender since the defendant failed to raise that challenge at his earlier sentencing on unrelated charges; such failure constituted a waiver of the defendant's right to raise such a challenge which waiver was binding on any future proceedings in which the issue may arise. People v. Evans, 123 A.D.2d 328, 506 N.Y.S.2d 221 (2d Dept. 1986).

Tolling.—Rejecting defendant's contention that a period of pretrial detention should not have been included in the toll of § 70.06(1)(b)(v). People v. Cortez, 231 A.D.2d 450, 647 N.Y.S.2d 206 (1st Dept. 1996).

§ 70.07. Sentence of imprisonment for second child sexual assault felony offender.

1. A person who stands convicted of a felony offense for a sexual assault against a child, having been subjected to a predicate felony conviction for a sexual assault against a child, must be sentenced in accordance with the provisions of subdivision four or five of this section.

2. A "sexual assault against a child" means a felony offense, other than persistent sexual abuse as defined in section 130.53 of this chapter, (a) the essential elements of which include the commission or attempted commission of sexual conduct, as defined in subdivision ten of section 130.00 of this chapter, (b) committed or attempted to be committed against a child less than fifteen years old.

3. For purposes of determining whether a person has been subjected to a predicate felony conviction under this section, the criteria set forth in paragraph (b) of subdivision one of section 70.06 shall apply provided however that for purposes of this subdivision, the terms "ten year" or "ten years", as provided in subparagraphs (iv) and (v) of paragraph (b) of subdivision one of such section 70.06, shall be "fifteen year" or "fifteen years". The provisions of section 400.19 of the criminal procedure law shall govern the procedures that must be followed to determine whether a person who stands convicted of a sexual assault against a child has been previously subjected to a predicate felony conviction for such a sexual assault and whether such offender was eighteen years of age or older at the time of the commission of the predicate felony.

4. Where the court has found pursuant to subdivision three of this section that a person who stands convicted of a felony offense defined in article one hundred thirty of this chapter for the commission or attempted commission of a sexual assault against a child has been subjected to a predicate felony conviction for a sexual assault against a child, the court shall sentence the defendant as follows:

(a) where the defendant stands convicted of such sexual assault against a child and such conviction is for a class B felony offense, and the predicate conviction for such sexual assault against a child is for a class B or class C felony offense, the court shall impose an indeterminate sentence of imprisonment, the maximum term of which shall be life and the minimum period of which shall be at least fifteen years and no more than twenty-five years;

(b) where the defendant stands convicted of such sexual assault against a child and the conviction is for a class C felony offense, and the predicate conviction for such sexual assault against a child is for a class B or class C felony offense, the court shall impose a determinate sentence of imprisonment, the term of which must be at least twelve years and must not exceed thirty years; provided however, that if the court determines that a longer sentence is warranted, the court shall set forth on the record the reasons for such determination and, in lieu of imposing such sentence of imprisonment, may impose an indeterminate sentence of imprisonment, the maximum term of which shall be life and the minimum period of which shall be at least fifteen years and no more than twenty-five years;

(c) where the defendant stands convicted of such sexual assault against a child and the conviction is for a class B felony offense, and the predicate conviction for such sexual assault against a child is for a class D or class E felony offense, the court shall impose a determinate sentence of imprisonment, the term of which must be at least twelve years and must not exceed thirty years;

(d) where the defendant stands convicted of such sexual assault against a child and the conviction is for a class C felony offense, and the predicate conviction for such sexual assault against a child is for a class D or class E felony offense, the court shall impose a determinate sentence of imprisonment, the term of which must be at least ten years and must not exceed twenty-five years;

(e) where the defendant stands convicted of such sexual assault against a child and the conviction is for a class D felony offense, and the predicate conviction for such sexual assault against a child is for a felony offense, the court shall impose a determinate sentence of imprisonment, the term of which must be at least five years and must not exceed fifteen years; and

(f) where the defendant stands convicted of such sexual assault against a child and the conviction is for a class E felony offense, and the predicate conviction for such sexual assault against a child is for a felony offense, the court shall impose a determinate sentence of imprisonment, the term of which must be at least four years and must not exceed twelve years.

5. Notwithstanding subdivision four of this section, where the court has found pursuant to subdivision three of this section that a person: (a)

stands convicted of a felony offense defined in article one hundred thirty of this chapter for the commission or attempted commission of a sexual assault against a child; and (b) has been subjected to a predicate felony conviction for sexual assault against a child as defined in subdivision two of this section; and (c) who was under the age of eighteen years at the time of the commission of such predicate felony offense, then the court may, in lieu of the sentence authorized by subdivision four of this section, sentence the defendant to a term of imprisonment in accordance with the sentence authorized for the instant felony offense pursuant to subdivision three of section 70.04 of this article. The court shall set forth on the record the reasons for such determination.

Added by L. 2000, Ch. 1, eff. Feb. 1, 2001; L. 2003, Ch. 264, §§ 7–9, eff. Nov. 1, 2003, amending subds. 1, 2, 3, 4(b) and adding subd 5.

§ 70.08. Sentence of imprisonment for persistent violent felony offender; criteria.

1. Definition of persistent violent felony offender.

(a) A persistent violent felony offender is a person who stands convicted of a violent felony offense as defined in subdivision one of section 70.02 after having previously been subjected to two or more predicate violent felony convictions as defined in paragraph (b) of subdivision one of section 70.04.

(b) For the purpose of determining whether a person has two or more predicate violent felony convictions, the criteria set forth in paragraph (b) of subdivision one of section 70.04 shall apply.

2. Authorized sentence. When the court has found, pursuant to the provisions of the criminal procedure law, that a person is a persistent violent felony offender the court must impose an indeterminate sentence of imprisonment, the maximum term of which shall be life imprisonment. The minimum period of imprisonment under such sentence must be in accordance with subdivision three of this section.

3. [Effective until Sept. 1, 2009.] Minimum period of imprisonment. The minimum period of imprisonment under an indeterminate life sentence for a persistent violent felony offender must be fixed by the court as follows:

(a) For a class B felony, the minimum period must be at least twenty years and must not exceed twenty-five years;

(b) For a class C felony, the minimum period must be at least sixteen years and must not exceed twenty-five years;

(c) For a class D felony, the minimum period must be at least twelve years and must not exceed twenty-five years.

3. [Effective Sept. 1, 2009.] Minimum period

of imprisonment. The minimum period of imprisonment under an indeterminate life sentence for a persistent violent felony offender must be fixed by the court as follows: (a) For a class B felony, the minimum period must be at least ten years and must not exceed twenty-five years;

(b) For a class C felony, the minimum period must be at least eight years and must not exceed twenty-five years;

(c) For a class D felony, the minimum period must be at least six years and must not exceed twenty-five years.

Added by L. 1978, Ch. 481, eff. Sept. 1, 1978; L. 1995, Ch. 3, § 8, amending subd. 3, eff. Oct. 1, 1995, amendments repealed Sept. 30, 2005, pursuant to L. 1995, Ch. 3, § 74, paragraph (d); L. 2005, Ch. 56, Part D, § 20, extending repeal date to Sept. 1, 2009.

ANNOTATIONS

Constitutionality.—Penal Law § 70.08 does not violate the constitutional prohibition against *ex post facto* law by enhancing the sentences for crimes committed before its enactment. People v. Mullady, 180 A.D.2d 408, 579 N.Y.S.2d 365 (1st Dept. 1992).

—Persistent violent felony offender mandatory sentencing scheme is not unconstitutional as being cruel and unusual punishment nor does it violate due process rights by preventing the sentencing court from considering a particular defendant's character and past record. People v. Brabham, 104 A.D.2d 1043, 481 N.Y.S.2d 111 (2d Dept. 1984).

Two or more predicate violent felony convictions.—Defendant was not eligible for sentence as a persistent violent felony offender; although defendant had two prior convictions for criminal possession of a weapon, his plea to attempted criminal possession of a weapon in the third degree constituted a Class E violent felony offense only if his conviction of this charge was as a lesser included offense under an indictment charging a greater offense. People v. Dickerson, 85 N.Y.2d 870, 626 N.Y.S.2d 50, 649 N.E.2d 1194 (1995).

—Reckless endangerment in the first degree, a violation of § 120.25, is not a violent felony offense, therefore defendant's adjudication as a persistent violent felony offender based upon his two prior violent felony convictions and his conviction for the instant offense of reckless endangerment in the first degree was improper. People v. Carrion, 265 A.D.2d 564, 697 N.Y.S.2d 638 (2d Dept. 1999).

§ 70.10. Sentence of imprisonment for persistent felony offender.

1. Definition of persistent felony offender.

(a) A persistent felony offender is a person, other than a persistent violent felony offender as defined in section 70.08, who stands convicted of a felony after having previously been convicted of two or more felonies, as provided in paragraphs (b) and (c) of this subdivision.

(b) A previous felony conviction within the meaning of paragraph (a) of this subdivision is a conviction of a felony in this state, or of a crime in any other jurisdiction, provided:

(i) that a sentence to a term of imprisonment in excess of one year, or a sentence to death, was imposed therefor; and

(ii) that the defendant was imprisoned under sentence for such conviction prior to the commission of the present felony; and

(iii) that the defendant was not pardoned on the ground of innocence; and

(iv) that such conviction was for a felony offense other than persistent sexual abuse, as defined in section 130.53 of this chapter.

(c) For the purpose of determining whether a person has two or more previous felony convictions, two or more convictions of crimes that were committed prior to the time the defendant was imprisoned under sentence for any of such convictions shall be deemed to be only one conviction.

2. Authorized sentence. When the court has found, pursuant to the provisions of the criminal procedure law that a person is a persistent felony offender, and when it is of the opinion that the history and character of the defendant and the nature and circumstances of his criminal conduct indicate that extended incarceration and life-time supervision will best serve the public interest, the court, in lieu of imposing the sentence of imprisonment authorized by section 70.00, 70.02, 70.04 or 70.06 for the crime of which such person presently stands convicted, may impose the sentence of imprisonment authorized by that section for a class A-I felony. In such event the reasons for the court's opinion shall be set forth in the record.

Amended by L. 1971, Ch. 1097; L. 1973, Chs. 277, 1051; L. 1978, Ch. 481; L. 2003, Ch. 264, §§ 69 and 70, amending subd. 1(b)(iii) and adding subd. 1(b)(iv).

ANNOTATIONS

Constitutionality. —Constitutionality of the persistent felony offender statutes (PL § 70.10 and CPL § 400.20(5)) was sustained in the face of a challenge pursuant to *Blakely v Washington,* 542 U.S. 296, 124 S. Ct. 2531, 159 L. Ed. 2d 403 (2004), since no "facts beyond those essential to the jury's verdict (other than prior convictions or admissions) were necessary for the trial judge to impose the persistent felony offender sentence." People v. Rivera, 5 N.Y.3d 61, 800 N.Y.S.2d 51, 833 N.E.2d 194 (2005).

—Constitutionality of the persistent felony offender statutes, PL § 70.10 and CPL § 400.20(5) was sustained, since determination whether defendant is a persistent felony offender is based solely on whether defendant had two prior felony convictions; therefore, resulting sentence is outside scope of violation present in *Apprendi v New Jersey,* 530 U.S. 466, 120 S. Ct. 2348, 147 L. Ed. 2d 435 (2000). People v. Rosen 96 N.Y.2d 329, 728 N.Y.S.2d 407, 752 N.E.2d 844, *cert denied,* 534 U.S. 899 (2001).

—U. S. Supreme Court's decisions in *Blakely v Washington,* 542 U.S. 296, 124 S. Ct. 2531, 159 L. Ed. 2d 403 (2004), and *Ring v Arizona* 536 U.S. 584, 122 S. Ct. 2428, 153 L. Ed. 2d 556 (2002), which apply the rule set forth in *Apprendi v New Jersey,* 530 U.S. 466, 120 S. Ct. 2348, 147 L. Ed. 2d 435 (2000), do not invalidate New York State's persistent felony offender statute; both *Blakely* and *Ring* allow for enhancement of sentence based on a prior conviction; defendant's prior felony convictions are sole determinant "of whether a defendant is subject to enhanced sentencing as a persistent felony offender." People v. Conger, 19 A.D.3d 938, 798 N.Y.S.2d 169 (3d Dept. 2005).

Improper underlying conviction.—Defendant was improperly adjudicated a persistent felony offender where the record indicated that at the time of one of his two underlying convictions, the defendant was unaware of his rights and the alternatives available to him. Thus, for the purposes of sentencing only, one of his convictions may stand, and he should be resentenced as a second-felony offender. People v. Foley, 96 A.D.2d 866, 465 N.Y.S.2d 754 (2d Dept. 1983).

Persistent felony sentencing; discretionary.—The court did not err in denying the defendant's motion to withdraw his pleas; the court did misstate the potential sentences defendant could receive as a persistent felony offender by quoting sentences for persistent violent felony offender. However, the court correctly informed defendant of the possibility of a maximum sentence of 25 years to life if it exercised its discretion under § 75.10(2) and there was no evidence that the court's misstatement had any effect on the defendant's decision to take the pleas. People v. Burnett, 221 A.D.2d 355, 633 N.Y.S.2d 365 (2d Dept. 1995).

—Sentencing court properly exercised its discretion in sentencing defendant as a persistent felony offender; however, sentence was excessive under all the circumstances, including that fact that the prosecutor recommended a lesser sentence. People v. Quinitchett, 210 A.D.2d 438,620 N.Y.S.2d 430 (2d Dept. 1994).

—Court properly exercised its discretion in sentencing defendant as a persistent felony offender based on his two predicate felonies and his lengthy criminal record, which included a number of violent offenses. People v. Ward, 233 A.D.2d 899, 649 N.Y.S.2d 865 (4th Dept. 1996).

Reasons for sentence.—Mandates of this section were adequately fulfilled where sentencing court stated on the record reasons, based on history and character of defendant and nature and circumstances of his criminal conduct, why it believed incarceration and lifetime supervision would best serve the public. People v. Garcia, 280 A.D.2d 682, 721 N.Y.S.2d 545 (2d Dept. 2001), *appeal denied,* 96 N.Y.2d 797 (2001).

—Sentencing court must include reasons that the "history and character of the defendant and the nature and circumstances of the criminal conduct" require extended incarceration and lifetime supervision; failure to include these reasons will result in remittal for resentencing. People v. Garcia, 267 A.D.2d 247, 700 N.Y.S.2d 44 (2d Dept. 1999), *appeal denied,* 94 N.Y.2d 945 (2000).

—Procedure for determining whether or not a defendant may be subjected to increased punishment as a persistent felony offender mandates a "two-pronged analysis," i.e., whether defendant has been convicted of at least two felonies, and whether the "history and characteristics of the defendant and the nature and circumstances of his criminal conduct are such that extended incarceration and lifetime supervision of the defendant are warranted to best serve the public interest." Here, the court's conclusory recitation at sentencing that the court had reviewed defendant's presentence report and criminal record was insufficient to fulfill the statute's requirement that the court set on the record the reasons why the second element is present. People v. Smith, 232 A.D.2d 586, 649 N.Y.S.2d 444 (2d Dept. 1996).

—Court's conclusory recitation at sentencing that it had reviewed the defendant's record was insufficient to comply with requirement of PL § 70.10(2) that the court set forth its reasons for sentencing defendant as a persistent felony offender. People v. Gaines, 136 A.D.2d 731, 524 N.Y.S.2d 70 (2d Dept. 1988).

Prior felonies; order of commission.—When making persistent felony determination, only sentences sequentially imposed may be used as predicate in calculating number of felonies in defendant's record. People v. King, 120 A.D.2d 338, 502 N.Y.S.2d 3 (1st Dept. 1986).

—Defendant was improperly sentenced as a persistent violent felony offender since his three previous convictions were pursuant to guilty pleas, all taken on the same day; the persistent violent felony sentencing provision is applicable only when each of the two or more predicate violent felony convictions, other than the first, are for crimes occurring subsequent to the imposition of the sentence on the preceding conviction. People v. Santana, 107 A.D.2d 922, 483 N.Y.S.2d 860 (1st Dept. 1985).

—Where defendant committed his second felony while on probation for his first felony conviction, court erroneously sentenced defendant as a persistent felony offender instead of a second felony offender; the two prior felonies count as one conviction for the purposes of persistent felony status in sentencing. People v. Nelson, 237 A.D.2d 626, 655 N.Y.S.2d 642 (2d Dept. 1997).

Reformatory sentence as predicate.—A reformatory sentence pursuant to sections 75.00(2) and 75.10(1) of the Penal Law, repealed in 1974, can serve as the predicate for a persistent felony offender sentence under section 70.10(1)(b)(i) of the Penal Law, which defines a previous felony conviction as one for which a sentence to a term of imprisonment in excess of

one year was imposed. People v. Williams, 66 N.Y.2d 629, 495 N.Y.S.2d 355, 485 N.E.2d 1020 (1985).

§ 70.15. Sentences of imprisonment for misdemeanors and violation.

1. Class A misdemeanor. A sentence of imprisonment for a class A misdemeanor shall be a definite sentence. When such a sentence is imposed the term shall be fixed by the court, and shall not exceed one year; provided, however, that a sentence of imprisonment imposed upon a conviction of criminal possession of a weapon in the fourth degree as defined in subdivision one of section 265.01 must be for a period of no less than one year when the conviction was the result of a plea of guilty entered in satisfaction of an indictment or any count thereof charging the defendant with the class D violent felony offense of criminal possession of a weapon in the third degree as defined in subdivision four of section 265.02, except that the court may impose any other sentence authorized by law upon a person who has not been previously convicted in the five years immediately preceding the commission of the offense for a felony or a class A misdemeanor defined in this chapter, if the court having regard to the nature and circumstances of the crime and to the history and character of the defendant, finds on the record that such sentence would be unduly harsh and that the alternative sentence would be consistent with public safety and does not deprecate the seriousness of the crime.

2. Class B misdemeanor. A sentence of imprisonment for a class B misdemeanor shall be a definite sentence. When such a sentence is imposed the term shall be fixed by the court, and shall not exceed three months.

3. Unclassified misdemeanor. A sentence of imprisonment for an unclassified misdemeanor shall be a definite sentence. When such a sentence is imposed the term shall be fixed by the court, and shall be in accordance with the sentence specified in the law or ordinance that defines the crime.

4. Violation. A sentence of imprisonment for a violation shall be a definite sentence. When such a sentence is imposed the term shall be fixed by the court, and shall not exceed fifteen days.

In the case of a violation defined outside this chapter, if the sentence is expressly specified in the law or ordinance that defines the offense and consists solely of a fine, no term of imprisonment shall be imposed.

Amended by L. 1980, Ch. 233; L. 1981, Ch. 175; L. 1984, Ch. 673; L. 1987, Ch. 727; L. 1988, Ch. 190; L. 1989, Ch. 240; L. 1990, Ch. 305; L. 1993, Ch. 291.

ANNOTATIONS

Maximum permissible sentence.—Maximum term of imprisonment to be imposed on defendant convicted of leaving the scene of an accident was 3 months absent proof that the defendant committed the same crime in the past. People v. Saporita, 132 A.D.2d 713, 518 N.Y.S.2d 625 (2d Dept. 1987).

Time for trial.—Where the defendant is charged with a Class A misdemeanor, punishable by a term of more than three months imprisonment, the People must be ready for trial within 90 days of the commencement of the action. People v. Han, 166 Misc. 2d 246, 632 N.Y.S.2d 748 (Crim. Ct. Bronx Co. 1995).

§ 70.20. Place of imprisonment.

1. (a) [*Effective until Sept. 1, 2009.*] Indeterminate or determinate sentence. Except as provided in subdivision four of this section, when an indeterminate or determinate sentence of imprisonment is imposed, the court shall commit the defendant to the custody of the state department of correctional services for the term of his or her sentence and until released in accordance with the law; provided, however, that a defendant sentenced pursuant to subdivision seven of section 70.06 shall be committed to the custody of the state department of correctional services for immediate delivery to a reception center operated by the department.

(a) [*Effective Sept. 1, 2009.*] Indeterminate sentence. Except as provided in subdivision four of this section, when an indeterminate sentence of imprisonment is imposed, the court shall commit the defendant to the custody of the state department of correctional services for the term of his or her sentence and until released in accordance with the law.

(b) The court in committing a defendant who is not yet eighteen years of age to the department of correctional services shall inquire as to whether the parents or legal guardian of the defendant, if present, will grant to the minor the capacity to consent to routine medical, dental and mental health services and treatment.

(c) Notwithstanding paragraph (b) of this subdivision, where the court commits a defendant who is not yet eighteen years of age to the custody of the department of correctional services in accordance with this section and no medical consent has been obtained prior to said commitment, the commitment order shall be deemed to grant the capacity to consent to routine medical, dental and mental health services and treatment to the person so committed.

(d) Nothing in this subdivision shall preclude a parent or legal guardian of an inmate who is not yet eighteen years of age from making a motion on notice to the department of correctional services pursuant to article twenty-two of the civil practice law and rules and section one hundred forty of the correction law, objecting to routine medical, dental or mental health services and treatment being provided to such inmate under the provisions of paragraph (b) of this subdivision.

(e) Nothing in this section shall require that consent be obtained from the parent or legal guardian, where no consent is necessary or where the defendant is authorized by law to consent on his or her own behalf to any medical, dental, and mental health service or treatment.

2. Definite sentence. Except as provided in subdivision four of this section, when a definite sentence of imprisonment is imposed, the court shall commit the defendant to the county or regional correctional institution for the term of his sentence and until released in accordance with the law.

2-a. Sentence of life imprisonment without parole. When a sentence of life imprisonment without parole is imposed, the court shall commit the defendant to the custody of the state department of correctional services for the remainder of the life of the defendant.

3. [*Effective until Sept. 1, 2009.*] Undischarged imprisonment in other jurisdiction. Undischarged imprisonment in other jurisdiction. When a defendant who is subject to an undischarged term of imprisonment, imposed at a previous time by a court of another jurisdiction, is sentenced to an additional term or terms of imprisonment by a court of this state to run concurrently with such undischarged term, as provided in subdivision four of section 70.25, the return of the defendant to the custody of the appropriate official of the other jurisdiction shall be deemed a commitment for such portion of the term or terms of the sentence imposed by the court of this state as shall not exceed the said undischarged term. The defendant shall be committed to the custody of the state department of correctional services if the additional term or terms are indeterminate or determinate or to the appropriate county or regional correctional institution if the said term or terms are definite for such portion of the term or terms of the sentence imposed as shall exceed such undischarged term or until released in accordance with law. If such additional term or terms imposed shall run consecutively to the said undischarged term, the defendant shall be committed as provided in subdivisions one and two of this section.

3. [*Effective Sept. 1, 2009.*] Undischarged imprisonment in other jurisdiction. When a defendant who is subject to an undischarged term of imprisonment, imposed at a previous time by a court of another jurisdiction, is sentenced to an additional term or terms of imprisonment by a court of this state to run concurrently with such undischarged term, as provided in subdivision four of section 70.25, the return of the defendant to the custody of the appropriate official of the other jurisdiction shall be deemed a commitment for such portion of the term or terms of the sentence imposed by the court of this state as shall not exceed the said undischarged term. The defendant shall be committed to the custody of the state department of correctional services if the additional term or terms are indeterminate or to the appropriate county or regional correctional institution if the said term or terms are definite for such portion of the term or terms of the sentence

imposed as shall exceed such undischarged term or until released in accordance with law. If such additional term or terms imposed shall run consecutively to the said undischarged term, the defendant shall be committed as provided in subdivisions one and two of this section.

4. (a) Notwithstanding any other provision of law to the contrary, a juvenile offender, or a juvenile offender who is adjudicated a youthful offender and given an indeterminate or a definite sentence, shall be committed to the custody of the director of the division for youth who shall arrange for the confinement of such offender in secure facilities of the division. The release or transfer of such offenders from the division for youth shall be governed by section five hundred eight of the executive law.

(b) The court in committing a juvenile offender and youthful offender to the custody of the division for youth shall inquire as to whether the parents or legal guardian of the youth, if present, will consent for the division to provide routine medical, dental and mental health services and treatment.

(c) Notwithstanding paragraph (b) of this subdivision, where the court commits an offender to the custody of the division for youth in accordance with this section and no medical consent has been obtained prior to said commitment, the commitment order shall be deemed to grant consent for the division for youth to provide for routine medical, dental and mental health services and treatment to the offender so committed.

(d) Nothing in this subdivision shall preclude a parent or legal guardian of an offender who is not yet eighteen years of age from making a motion on notice to the division for youth pursuant to article twenty-two of the civil practice law and rules objecting to routine medical, dental or mental health services and treatment being provided to such offender under the provisions of paragraph (b) of this subdivision.

(e) Nothing in this section shall require that consent be obtained from the parent or legal guardian, where no consent is necessary or where the offender is authorized by law to consent on his or her own behalf to any medical, dental and mental health service or treatment.

5. Subject to regulations of the department of health, routine medical, dental and mental health services and treatment is defined for the purposes of this section to mean any routine diagnosis or treatment, including without limitation the administration of medications or nutrition, the extraction of bodily fluids for analysis, and dental care performed with a local anesthetic. Routine mental health treatment shall not include psychiatric administration of medication unless it is part of an ongoing mental health plan or unless it is otherwise authorized by law.

Amended by L. 1975, Ch. 782; l. 1978, Ch. 268; L. 1981, Ch. 303; L. 1992, Ch. 479, eff. July 17, 1992, amending subd. 4; L. 1992, Ch. 465, eff. Jan. 14, 1993, amending subd. 4 relating to Executive Law § 508, and shall apply to all persons placed in or committed to the custody of the division for youth on or after such date; L. 1995, Ch. 1, § 6, adding subd. 2-a, eff. Sept. 1, 1995; L. 1995, Ch. 3, § 9, amending subds. 1 and 3, eff. Oct. 1, 1995, amendments repealed Sept. 30, 2005, pursuant to L. 1995, Ch. 3, § 74, paragraph (d); L. 1995, Ch. 516, § 2, amending subd. 1, eff. Aug. 2, 1995; L. 1995, Ch. 516, § 3, renumbering subd. 4(d) to subd. 5, and relettering subds. 4(e) and 4(f) to 4(d) and 4(e), eff. Aug. 2, 1995; L. 2005, Ch. 56, Part D, § 20, extending repeal dates to Sept. 1, 2009.

ANNOTATION

Generally.—Defendant had no right to select the facility where he was incarcerated; the decision to transfer inmates is within the broad discretionary powers of the Department of Corrections. Martin v. Coughlin, 207 A.D.2d 932, 616 N.Y.S.2d 416 (3d Dept. 1994).

§ 70.25. Concurrent and consecutive terms of imprisonment.

1. Except as provided in subdivisions two, two-a and five of this section, when multiple sentences of imprisonment are imposed on a person at the same time, or when a person who is subject to any undischarged term of imprisonment imposed at a previous time by a court of this state is sentenced to an additional term of imprisonment, the sentence or sentences imposed by the court shall run either concurrently or consecutively with respect to each other and the undischarged term or terms in such manner as the court directs at the time of sentence. If the court does not specify the manner in which a sentence imposed by it is to run, the sentence shall run as follows:

(a) [*Effective until Sept. 1, 2009.*] An indeterminate or determinate sentence shall run concurrently with all other terms; and

(a) [*Effective Sept. 1, 2009.*] An indeterminate sentence shall run concurrently with all other terms; and

(b) A definite sentence shall run concurrently with any sentence imposed at the same time and shall be consecutive to any other term.

2. When more than one sentence of imprisonment is imposed on a person for two or more offenses committed through a single act or omission, or through an act or omission which in itself constituted one of the offenses and also was a material element of the other, the sentences, except if one or more of such sentences is for a violation of section 270.20 of this chapter, must run concurrently.

2-a. [*Effective until Sept. 1, 2009.*] When an indeterminate or determinate sentence of imprisonment is imposed pursuant to section 70.04, 70.06, 70.08, 70.10, subdivision three or four of section 70.70 or subdivision three or four of section 70.71 of this article, and such person is subject to an undischarged indeterminate or determinate sentence of imprisonment imposed prior to the date on which the present crime was committed, the court must impose a sentence to run consecutively with respect to such undischarged sentence.

2-a. [*Effective Sept. 1, 2009.*] When an indeterminate or determinate sentence of imprisonment is imposed pursuant to section 70.04, 70.06, 70.08, 70.10, subdivision three or four of section 70.70 or subdivision three or four of section 70.71 of this article, and such person is subject to an undischarged indeterminate sentence of imprisonment imposed prior to the date on which the present crime was committed, the court must impose a sentence to run consecutively with respect to such undischarged sentence.

2-b. [*Effective until Sept. 1, 2009.*] When a person is convicted of a violent felony offense committed after arraignment and while released on recognizance or bail, but committed prior to the imposition of sentence on a pending felony charge, and if an indeterminate or determinate sentence of imprisonment is imposed in each case, such sentences shall run consecutively. Provided, however, that the court may, in the interest of justice, order a sentence to run concurrently in a situation where consecutive sentences are required by this subdivision if it finds either mitigating circumstances that bear directly upon the manner in which the crime was committed or, where the defendant was not the sole participant in the crime, the defendant's participation was relatively minor although not so minor as to constitute a defense to the prosecution. The defendant and the district attorney shall have an opportunity to present relevant information to assist the court in making this determination and the court may, in its discretion, conduct a hearing with respect to any issue bearing upon such determination. If the court determines that consecutive sentences should not be ordered, it shall make a statement on the record of the facts and circumstances upon which such determination is based.

2-b. [*Effective Sept. 1, 2009.*] When a person is convicted of a violent felony offense committed after arraignment and while released on recognizance or bail, but committed prior to the imposition of sentence on a pending felony charge, and if an indeterminate sentence of imprisonment is imposed in each case, such sentences shall run consecutively. Provided, however, that the court may, in the interest of justice, order a sentence to run concurrently in a situation where consecutive sentences are required by this subdivision if it finds either mitigating circumstances that bear directly upon the manner in which the crime was committed or, where the defendant was not the sole participant in the crime, the defendant's participation was relatively minor although not so minor as to constitute a defense to the prosecution. The defendant and the district attorney shall have an opportunity to present relevant information to assist the court in making this determination and the court may, in its discretion, conduct a hearing with respect to any issue bearing upon

such determination. If the court determines that consecutive sentences should not be ordered, it shall make a statement on the record of the facts and circumstances upon which such determination is based.

2-c. When a person is convicted of bail jumping in the second degree as defined in section 215.56 or bail jumping in the first degree as defined in section 215.57 committed after arraignment and while released on recognizance or bail in connection with a pending indictment or information charging one or more felonies, at lease one of which he is subsequently convicted, and if an indeterminate sentence of imprisonment is imposed in each case, such sentences shall run consecutively. Provided, however, that the court may, in the interest of justice, order a sentence to run concurrently in a situation where consecutive sentences are required by this subdivision if it finds mitigating circumstances that bear directly upon the manner in which the crime was committed. The defendant and the district attorney shall have an opportunity to present relevant information to assist the court in making this determination and the court may, in its discretion, conduct a hearing with respect to any issue bearing upon such determination. If the court determines that consecutive sentences should not be ordered, it shall make a statement on the record of the facts and circumstances upon which such determination is based.

2-d. When a person is convicted of escape in the second degree as defined in section 205.10 or escape in the first degree as defined in section 205.15 committed after issuance of a securing order, as defined in subdivision five of section 500.10 of the criminal procedure law, in connection with a pending indictment or information charging one or more felonies, at least one of which he is subsequently convicted, and if an indeterminate sentence of imprisonment is imposed in each case, such sentences shall run consecutively. Provided, however, that the court may, in the interest of justice, order a sentence to run concurrently in a situation where consecutive sentences are required by this subdivision if it finds mitigating circumstances that bear directly upon the manner in which the crime was committed. The defendant and the district attorney shall have an opportunity to present relevant information to assist the court in making this determination and the court may, in its discretion, conduct a hearing with respect to any issue bearing upon such determination. If the court determines that consecutive sentences should not be ordered, it shall make a statement on the record of the facts and circumstances upon which such determination is based.

2-e. Whenever a person is convicted of course of sexual conduct against a child in the first degree as defined in section 130.75 or course of sexual conduct against a child in the second degree as defined in section 130.80 and any other crime under article one hundred thirty committed against the same child and within the period charged under section 130.75 or 130.80, the sentences must run concurrently.

2-f. Whenever a person is convicted of facilitating a sex offense with a controlled substance as defined in section 130.90 of this chapter, the sentence imposed by the court for such offense may be ordered to run consecutively to any sentence imposed upon conviction of an offense defined in article one hundred thirty of this chapter arising from the same criminal transaction.

2-g. Whenever a person is convicted of unlawful manufacture of methamphetamine in the third degree as defined in section 220.73 of this chapter, unlawful manufacture of methamphetamine in the second degree as defined in section 220.74 of this chapter, or unlawful manufacture of methamphetamine in the first degree as defined in section 220.75 of this chapter, or any attempt to commit any of such offenses, and such person is also convicted, with respect to such unlawful methamphetamine laboratory, of unlawful disposal of methamphetamine laboratory material as defined in section 220.76 of this chapter, the sentences must run concurrently.

3. Where consecutive definite sentences of imprisonment are not prohibited by subdivision two of this section and are imposed on a person for offenses which were committed as parts of a single incident or transaction, the aggregate of the terms of such sentences shall not exceed one year.

4. When a person, who is subject to any undischarged term of imprisonment imposed at a previous time by a court of another jurisdiction, is sentenced to an additional term or terms of imprisonment by a court of this state, the sentence or sentences imposed by the court of this state, subject to the provisions of subdivisions one, two and three of this section, shall run either concurrently or consecutively with respect to such undischarged term in such manner as the court directs at the time of sentence. If the court of this state does not specify the manner in which a sentence imposed by it is to run, the sentence or sentences shall run consecutively.

5. (a) [*Effective until Sept. 1, 2009.*] Except as provided in paragraph (c) of this subdivision, when a person is convicted of assault in the second degree, as defined in subdivision seven of section 120.05 of this chapter, any definite, indeterminate or determinate term of imprisonment which may be imposed as a sentence upon such conviction shall run consecutively to any undischarged term of imprisonment to which the defendant was subject and for which he was confined at the time of the assault.

(a) [*Effective Sept. 1, 2009.*] Except as provided in paragraph (c) of this subdivision, when

a person is convicted of assault in the second degree, as defined in subdivision seven of section 120.05 of this chapter, any definite or indeterminate term of imprisonment which may be imposed as a sentence upon such conviction shall run consecutively to any undischarged term of imprisonment to which the defendant was subject and for which he was confined at the time of the assault.

(b) [*Effective until Sept. 1, 2009.*] Except as provided in paragraph (c) of this subdivision, when a person is convicted of assault in the second degree, as defined in subdivision seven of section 120.05 of this chapter, any definite, indeterminate or determinate term of imprisonment which may be imposed as a sentence upon such conviction shall run consecutively to any term of imprisonment which was previously imposed or which may be prospectively imposed where the person was confined within a detention facility at the time of the assault upon a charge which culminated in such sentence of imprisonment.

(b) [*Effective Sept. 1, 2009.*] Except as provided in paragraph (c) of this subdivision, when a person is convicted of assault in the second degree, as defined in subdivision seven of section 120.05 of this chapter, any definite or indeterminate term of imprisonment which may be imposed as a sentence upon such conviction shall run consecutively to any term of imprisonment which was previously imposed or which may be prospectively imposed where the person was confined within a detention facility at the time of the assault upon a charge which culminated in such sentence of imprisonment.

(c) Notwithstanding the provisions of paragraphs (a) and (b) of this subdivision, a term of imprisonment imposed upon a conviction to assault in the second degree as defined in subdivision seven of section 120.05 of this chapter may run concurrently to any other term of imprisonment, in the interest of justice, provided the court sets forth in the record its reasons for imposing a concurrent sentence. Nothing in this section shall require the imposition of a sentence of imprisonment where it is not otherwise required by law.

Amended by L. 1975, Ch. 782; L. 1978, Ch. 481; L. 1981, Ch. 372; L. 1982, Ch. 559; L. 1984, Ch. 56; L. 1986, Ch. 795; L. 1995, Ch. 3, § 10, amending subd. 1(a), § 11, amending subds. 2-a and 2-b, and § 12, amending subds. 5(a) and (b), amendments eff. Oct. 1, 1995, repealed Sept. 30, 2005 pursuant to L. 1995, Ch. 3, § 74, paragraph (d); L. 1996, Ch. 122, § 3, adding subd. 2-e, eff. Aug. 1, 1996; L. 2000, Ch. 1, eff. Feb. 1, 2001; L. 2004, Ch. 738, § 33 & 34, eff. Dec. 14, 2004, amending subd. 2-a; L. 2005, Ch. 394, § 5, adding subd. 2-g, eff. Oct. 1, 2005; L. 2005, Ch. 56, Part D, § 20, extending repeal dates to Sept. 1, 2009.

ANNOTATIONS

Ambiguity of sentence.—Sentence will run concurrently by operation of law where court does not specify that sentence is to be consecutive with existing undischarged term. People v. Pitts, 75 A.D.2d 719, 426 N.Y.S.2d 993 (4th Dept. 1980).

Correction of illegal sentence.—Trial court has inherent authority to correct improper sentence and properly resentenced defendant, after his plea and over his objection, to two to four years in prison to run consecutively from the undischarged portion of an earlier sentence, even though this extended his time in prison; corrected sentence was within the range initially stated by the court. People v. DeValle, 94 N.Y.2d 870, 704 N.Y.S.2d 924, 726 N.E.2d 476 (2000).

Court's silence.—Defendant's sentence mandating consecutive sentences was improperly altered after its service began: by operation of statute, court's failure to state how sentences on certain counts are to run in relation to each other meant that sentences were to be concurrent. People v. Vasquez, 88 N.Y.2d 561, 647 N.Y.S.2d 697, 670 N.E.2d 1328 (1996).

—Where the state court does not specify the manner in which an additional term of imprisonment is to run for a defendant presently serving a federal sentence, the new term will run consecutively. Cachoian v. New York State Dept. of Corrections, 239 A.D.2d 118, 656 N.Y.S.2d 635 (1st Dept. 1997).

—Where sentencing court is silent as to whether in-state sentence should run concurrently or consecutively with unrelated out-of-state sentence, sentences are to run concurrently. People v. Garcia, 268 A.D.2d 595, 702 N.Y.S.2d 834 (2d Dept. 2000).

—Court's failure to specify whether or not sentences are concurrent or consecutive does not render sentence invalid; the statute directs that where the court does not specify the manner in which the sentences should run, indeterminate and determinate sentences run concurrently with all other terms. People v. Haynes, 251 A.D.2d 595, 674 N.Y.S.2d 765 (2d Dept. 1998).

—Where defendant is sentenced as a second felony offender for his conviction of attempted criminal sale of a controlled substance in the third degree before his first sentence has been completed, the sentence for the subsequent conviction must be served consecutively to the petitioner's undischarged sentence, regardless of whether or not the court is silent on this issue. Santiago v. Van Zandt, 236 A.D.2d 728, 654 N.Y.S.2d 421 (3d Dept. 1997).

—Where sentences for robbery and criminal use of a firearm while on parole were required by statute to run consecutively to time remaining on defendant's prior undischarged sentence for robbery, sentencing court's silence on issue was not determinative. Jackson v. Wolford, 232 A.D.2d 795, 649 N.Y.S.2d 59 (3d Dept. 1996).

Concurrent sentences.—Court erred by imposing consecutive sentences for weapons possession with sentences for manslaughter and assault; where weapon in defendant's possession was used to commit manslaughter and assault and weapons charge was not separate and apart from shootings, concurrent sentences should have been imposed. People v. Hamilton, 4 N.Y.3d 654, 797 N.Y.S.2d 408, 830 N.E.2d 306 (2005).

—If an act violates one statute and constitutes a legal component of a second crime, then the first offense would be a material element of the second and only single (i.e., concurrent) punishment would be permissible. People v. Day, 73 N.Y.2d 208, 538 N.Y.S.2d 785, 535 N.E.2d 1325 (1989).

—Court should have imposed concurrent sentences for attempted rape and sexual abuse where the the acts constituting the sexual abuse were "an integral part of the [attempted] rape." People v. Jones, 295 A.D.2d 243, 745 N.Y.S.2d 15 (1st Dept. 2002).

—Where robbery was a predicate for felony murder, sentence for both murder and robbery should run concurrently; however, where intentional murder was distinct from second degree murder, which did not require injury to the murder victim, consecutive sentences were warranted. People v. Slater, 268 A.D.2d 260, 701 N.Y.S.2d 371 (1st Dept. 2000).

—Concurrent sentences for leaving the scene of an accident without reporting and vehicular assault in the second degree were not required; each crime has one element in common—that victim sustained a serious physical injury. People v. Chambers, 257 A.D.2d 418, 683 N.Y.S.2d 238 (1st Dept. 1999).

—Since the weapons possession conviction and the reckless endangerment conviction arose out of a single act, the sentences for those convictions had to run concurrently. People v. Cruz, 194 A.D.2d 488, 599 N.Y.S.2d 808 (1st Dept. 1993).

—An assault conviction based upon physical injury to the complainant during the course of the rape was a material element of the rape; thus, the sentences must run concurrently. People v. Bolden, 83 A.D.2d 921, 442 N.Y.S.2d 777 (1st Dept.

1981), aff'd, 58 N.Y.2d 741, 459 N.Y.S.2d 22, 445 N.E.2d 198 (1982).

—Sentences on all counts relating to arson fire set on same day should run concurrently. People v. Ruiz, 291 A.D.2d 418, 738 N.Y.S.2d 59 (2d Dept. 2001).

—Where defendant's conviction for burglary in the first degree was the basis for a felony murder conviction, sentences for burglary in the first degree and murder should run concurrently. People v. Roman, 279 A.D.2d 485, 719 N.Y.S.2d 583 (2d Dept.), appeal denied, 96 N.Y.2d 806 (2001).

—Convictions for assault in the second degree and kidnapping in the first degree based on the same act should have run concurrently. People v. Lin, 267 A.D.2d 249, 701 N.Y.S.2d 77 (2d Dept. 1999), appeal denied, 94 N.Y.2d 949 (2000); People v. Zheng, 267 A.D.2d 257, 699 N.Y.S.2d 295 (2d Dept. 1999), appeal denied, 94 N.Y.2d 951 (2000).

—Where convictions for attempted kidnapping in the first degree and murder in the second degree arose from the same factual circumstances, the sentences should run concurrently. People v. Fullan, 267 A.D.2d 323, 699 N.Y.S.2d 876 (2d Dept. 1999).

—Where each assault was a distinct and separate act, the imposition of consecutive sentences for each count of assault arising from defendant's altercation with six different guards in the course of their attempt to move him from his cell was proper. People v. Coulanges, 264 A.D.2d 853, 696 N.Y.S.2d 466 (2d Dept. 1999).

—Concurrent sentences were not mandated where robberies were part of the same extended criminal transaction but were not committed by a single act; each robbery involved a separate act and a different victim, and the robbery of one victim was not a material element of the robbery of another victim. People v. Watts, 251 A.D.2d 687, 676 N.Y.S.2d 475 (2d Dept. 1998).

—Court erred in imposing consecutive sentences for defendant's convictions for burglary in the first degree and robbery in the first degree arising out of the same acts; defendant's acts underlying the crimes for which he was convicted cannot be considered separate and distinct acts, sentences should have run concurrently. People v. Roberts, 251 A.D.2d 431, 674 N.Y.S.2d 117 (2d Dept. 1998).

—Court properly imposed concurrent sentences where there were two separate robberies and the robbery of one victim was not a material element of the robbery of the other victim. People v. Hill, 245 A.D.2d 464, 666 N.Y.S.2d 644 (2d Dept. 1997).

—Court has discretion to impose concurrent terms of imprisonment. People v. Walls, 240 A.D.2d 686, 659 N.Y.S.2d 1019 (2d Dept.), aff'd, 91 N.Y.2d 987, 663 N.Y.S.2d 524, 686 N.E.2d 236 (1997).

—Court erred in imposing consecutive sentences for intentional murder and robbery in the first degree where those convictions are based on the same acts; sentence modified for imposition of concurrent sentences. People v. Fullan, 237 A.D.2d 619, 655 N.Y.S.2d 644 (2d Dept. 1997), modified and affirmed, 92 N.Y.2d 690, 685 N.Y.S.2d 901, 708 N.E.2d 974 (1999).

—Since defendant's convictions of rape in the first degree and incest resulted from a single act, the sentences imposed had to run concurrently. People v. Respass, 213 A.D.2d 430, 623 N.Y.S.2d 337 (2d Dept. 1995).

—Where defendant's possession of a gun and shooting of the victim were both committed through a single act, the sentence imposed for the crime of criminal possession of a weapon should run concurrently with the manslaughter sentence. People v. Tabb, 208 A.D.2d 780, 617 N.Y.S.2d 787 (2d Dept. 1994).

—Concurrent sentences for criminal possession of a weapon in the second degree and criminal possession of a weapon in the third degree should have been imposed; the defendant's possession of a loaded weapon and the shooting of the victim occurred in a single act. People v. Bernard, 210 A.D.2d 419, 620 N.Y.S.2d 414 (2d Dept. 1994).

—Sentences imposed from criminal possession of a weapon and manslaughter must run concurrently; defendant's possession of a gun and shooting of the victim occurred in a single act. People v. Doczy, 210 A.D.2d 425, 620 N.Y.S.2d 408 (2d Dept. 1994).

—Concurrent sentences were mandated where defendant's driving while under the influence was an element of first degree aggravated unlicensed operation, and both offenses occurred at the same date, time, and place, and both served as basis of revocation of defendant's license. People v. De Maio, 304 A.D.2d 988, 760 N.Y.S.2d 558 (3d Dept. 2003).

—Where defendant was convicted of felony murder of one victim and first degree robbery and assault as a result of the severe beating of another, concurrent sentences on the robbery and assault convictions and consecutive sentence on the murder conviction was proper. People v. Jeanty, 268 A.D.2d 675, 702 N.Y.S.2d 194 (3d Dept.), *appeal denied,* 94 N.Y.2d 949 (2000).

—Defendant's possession of two guns at the same time and at the same place with the intent to use them against the same victim required the imposition of concurrent sentences since the offenses arose out of the same act. People v. Cleveland, 236 A.D.2d 802, 653 N.Y.S.2d 472 (4th Dept. 1997).

—Concurrent sentences should have been imposed for criminal possession of a controlled substance in the second degree and criminal possession of a controlled substance in the third degree since both offenses arose from the possession of a quantity of cocaine; sentences must run concurrently for two or more offenses committed through a single act. People v. Smith, 209 A.D.2d 996, 622 N.Y.S.2d 163 (4th Dept. 1994).

Consecutive sentences.—Continuous possession of a weapon throughout the duration of defendant's criminal acts does not, in and of itself, dictate whether the resulting sentences for convictions on the criminal acts committed during that time will run consecutively or concurrently. Because the crime of possession of a weapon was separate and apart from the act of murder, consecutive sentences were properly imposed. People v. Salcedo, 92 N.Y.2d 1019, 684 N.Y.S.2d 480, 707 N.E.2d 435 (1998).

—Consecutive sentences for robbery and burglary in the first degree were upheld; crime of burglary was complete as soon as defendant entered victim's office with a firearm and with the intent to commit a crime, and the actions on which the conviction for robbery were based constituted separate acts. People v. Yong Yun Lee, 92 N.Y.2d 987, 684 N.Y.S.2d 161, 703 N.E.2d 1185 (1998).

—Consecutive sentences were properly imposed on defendant for possession of a defaced weapon and aiding and abetting a co-defendant's possession of a defaced weapon. The "actus reas" of one charge is possession and the other is aiding and abetting, and as these are two separate and distinct acts, consecutive sentences are appropriate. People v. Bryant, 92 N.Y.2d 216, 677 N.Y.S.2d 286, 699 N.E.2d 910 (1998).

—Consecutive sentences could not be imposed upon defendant who was charged with manslaughter as a result of killing a teenage girl by striking her with his car and with leaving the scene of the accident; the manslaughter was a material element of the charge of leaving the scene. People v. Catone, 65 N.Y.2d 1003, 494 N.Y.S.2d 97, 484 N.E.2d 126 (1985).

—Consecutive sentences are authorized where the crimes charged are not the result of a single act but instead emanate from separate successive acts. People v. Walsh, 44 N.Y.2d 631, 407 N.Y.S.2d 472, 378 N.E.2d 1041 (1978).

—Where proof was adequate to show that defendant held up a taxicab driver, and then, after the robbery was completed and while the driver offered no resistance, shot and killed the driver, the crimes committed were not part of a single act, and consecutive sentences were permissible. People v. Tanner, 30 N.Y.2d 103, 331 N.Y.S.2d 1, 282 N.E.2d 98 (1972).

—Consecutive terms were properly imposed for defendant's convictions for felony murder and burglary in the first degree, since the felony underlying the felony murder charge was robbery in the first degree, and the murder and burglary charges were based on separate acts. People v. Tucker, 278 A.D.2d 38, 717 N.Y.S.2d 151 (1st Dept. 2000), *appeal denied,* 96 N.Y.2d 788 (2001).

—Consecutive sentences were appropriate where defendant committed successive acts of stealing a car in New York and bringing the stolen car into New Jersey where other crimes were then committed; acts were distinct and separate. People v. Garland, 254 A.D.2d 111, 679 N.Y.S.2d 111 (1st Dept. 1998).

—Court properly imposed consecutive sentences where defendant was convicted of simultaneous attempted robberies of two victims and then accomplice liability of co-defendant's act of attempting to take property, an act separate and apart from his own criminal conduct. People v. Bellamy, 254 A.D.2d 188, 680 N.Y.S.2d 481 (1st Dept. 1998).

—Consecutive sentences were authorized because the shooting of two victims constituted separate and distinct acts. People v. Perez, 221 A.D.2d 169, 633 N.Y.S.2d 284 (1st Dept. 1995).

—The imposition of consecutive sentences after defendant

pleaded guilty to manslaughter in the second degree and criminal possession of a weapon in the third degree was proper; defendant pleaded to two distinct and separate crimes that do not contain common material elements. People v. Higdon, 214 A.D.2d 488, 625 N.Y.S.2d 224 (1st Dept. 1995).

—The imposition of consecutive sentences for rape, sodomy and robbery was proper; the victim's testimony clearly showed that the offenses committed by the defendant (robbery in an elevator, sodomy in one area of a terrace and rape in another area of the terrace) were separate and distinct acts. People v. Whitley, 211 A.D.2d 528, 621 N.Y.S.2d 336 (1st Dept. 1995).

—Plea bargain which provided consecutive sentences for manslaughter and weapons charges was proper; the possession of the weapon and the use of the weapon were separate, successive acts. People v. Simpson, 209 A.D.2d 281, 619 N.Y.S.2d 259 (1st Dept. 1994).

—Consecutive sentences were legally imposed, the jury having found that defendant had tried to kill two officers; each attempted killing, which involved the firing of separate shots, constituted distinct acts perpetrated against the separate victims. People v. Ramos, 205 A.D.2d 404, 613 N.Y.S.2d 879 (1st Dept. 1994).

—Defendant was properly sentenced to consecutive terms for his convictions of reckless endangerment and robbery, since acts that formed the basis of each conviction were separate and distinct acts. People v. Stallone, 279 A.D.2d 592, 719 N.Y.S.2d 293 (2d Dept. 2001).

—Consecutive sentences for convictions of three counts of sodomy in the first degree were appropriate where each count involved a separate sexual act constituting a distinct offense. People v. Gersten, 280 A.D.2d 487, 719 N.Y.S.2d 900 (2d Dept. 2001).

—As a second felony offender, sentencing court has no discretion to impose concurrent sentence for new offenses with term defendant is currently serving; consecutive sentences must be imposed. People v. Hansen, 267 A.D.2d 474, 700 N.Y.S.2d 759 (2d Dept. 1999), *appeal denied,* 95 N.Y.2d 797 (2000).

—Terms of incarceration for crimes committed on two separate occasions properly run as consecutive sentences. People v. Byers, 254 A.D.2d 494, 679 N.Y.S.2d 838 (2d Dept. 1998), *appeal denied,* 93 N.Y.2d 1043 (1999).

—Evidence at trial revealed that defendant's subsequent act of killing victim was separate offense from the robbery which began the encounter, as such, the sentence imposed for robbery in the first degree ran consecutively to the sentence for intentional murder in the second degree. People v. Jackson, 237 A.D.2d 620, 656 N.Y.S.2d 276 (2d Dept. 1997).

—Defendant's motion or withdrawal of a conditional plea based on mutual mistake was granted where the conditional plea was accepted on the mistaken belief of the court and all the parties that the Division of Parole had the authority to run any undischarged sentence with the new sentence imposed by the terms of the plea bargain, when in fact, the sentences had to run consecutively. People v. Scott, 237 A.D.2d 543, 565 N.Y.S.2d 908 (2d Dept. 1997).

—Sentence imposed for conviction of criminal possession of a weapon in the second degree should have been made concurrent to sentences imposed for robbery convictions since possession of the weapon constituted a "material element" of the robbery offenses. People v. Jenkins, 232 A.D.2d 504, 648 N.Y.S.2d 352 (2d Dept. 1996).

—Sentences for defendant's possession of a weapon relating to two weapons used by defendant's accomplices during a hostage incident should have run concurrently instead of consecutively to sentence imposed on the felony murder count. People v. Vidal, 231 A.D.2d 655, 648 N.Y.S.2d 109 (2d Dept. 1996).

—Even though offenses were part of continuous course of conduct, imposition of consecutive sentences for intentional murder, burglary and robbery was lawful where the intentional murders were separate and distinct from burglary and robbery offenses and conduct constituting burglary was separate and distinct from conduct constituting robbery. People v. Hladky, 229 A.D.2d 400, 645 N.Y.S.2d 74 (2d Dept. 1996).

—Sentencing court did not err in imposing consecutive sentences for manslaughter and criminal possession of a weapon; from the facts presented, the jury could reasonably have found that the defendant possessed a gun with the intent to use it illegally against another, and that the gun possession was prior to and separate from the ultimate act of homicide. People v. James, 211 A.D.2d 824, 622 N.Y.S.2d 95 (2d Dept. 1995).

—Consecutive sentences for burglary, criminal possession of stolen property, and third and fourth degree criminal possession of a weapon were proper; defendant's possession of a weapon in the car and his accomplice's possession of a knife while committing the burglary in another location were not a single act. People v. Messina, 209 A.D.2d 642, 619 N.Y.S.2d 135 (2d Dept. 1994).

—It was error to impose consecutive sentences for defendant's convictions of manslaughter, attempted robbery and criminal possession of a weapon since all three crimes arose out of a single incident; the mere fact that the defendant possessed the weapon immediately prior to the shooting is insufficient to establish proof of a separate and distinct act. People v. Banks, 208 A.D.2d 759, 617 N.Y.S.2d 796 (2d Dept. 1994).

—It is well settled that a court may not impose consecutive sentences where all of the counts in a multicount indictment arise out of the same act; where manslaughter and weapon possession charges arose out of the same act, consecutive sentences could not be imposed. People v. McInnis, 179 A.D.2d 781, 579 N.Y.S.2d 144 (2d Dept. 1992).

—Imposition of consecutive terms of imprisonment for the rape and the sodomy committed by the defendant was improper. People v. Chamberlin, 140 A.D.2d 579, 527 N.Y.S.2d 851 (2d Dept. 1988).

—Court did not err in imposing consecutive sentences for the crimes of attempted murder in the second degree and robbery in the first degree since the crimes, which were based on the same transaction, nonetheless involved disparate or separate acts. People v. Galloway, 138 A.D.2d 735, 526 N.Y.S.2d 549 (2d Dept. 1988).

—Where the imposition of consecutive sentences for crimes committed by separate acts is proper, the imposition of a surcharge as to each crime arising from a disparate and separate act is also lawful. People v. Higgins, 137 A.D.2d 620, 524 N.Y.S.2d 508 (2d Dept. 1988).

—Imposition of consecutive terms of imprisonment on convictions for rape, sodomy, and burglary was proper despite the fact that the crimes took place over a continuous course of activity where the crimes constituted separate and distinct acts, and none of the completed offenses was a material element of another offense. People v. Boyce, 133 A.D.2d 164, 518 N.Y.S.2d 827 (2d Dept. 1987).

—Court properly imposed consecutive sentences for the defendant's conviction of manslaughter, first degree, and criminal possession of a weapon, second degree, since there was sufficient proof adduced at the trial that the offenses were separate and distinct acts, although arising out of the same transaction; while a weapon was used in the course of the commission of the manslaughter, nevertheless possession of a deadly weapon or the display of a firearm is not a material element of manslaughter in the first degree. People v. Robbins, 118 A.D.2d 820, 500 N.Y.S.2d 177 (2d Dept. 1986).

—Maximum consecutive sentences were properly imposed for the intentional murder of one victim and the attempted murder of another; although the acts were successive, they were separate and distinct. People v. Walker, 279 A.D.2d 696, 719 N.Y.S.2d 322 (3d Dept. 2001).

—Concurrent sentences were improperly imposed on a defendant as a result of a conviction of two counts of incest committed on the same day; two distinct acts required consecutive sentences. People v. Otero, 268 A.D.2d 615, 701 N.Y.S.2d 457 (3d Dept. 2000).

—Consecutive sentences imposed for separate and distinct criminal acts was appropriate; moreover, sentencing as a second felony offender was appropriate in where prior convictions were for sexual abuse of children arising out of sexual contact with children of friends and her own children and her lack of insight into harm caused by her actions warranted modification of her sentence. People v. Guillery, 267 A.D.2d 781, 701 N.Y.S.2d 150 (3d Dept. 1999), *appeal denied,* 94 N.Y.2d 920 (2000).

—Consecutive sentences for assault and resisting arrest convictions were authorized where defendant's act of punching his son, the basis of the assault charge, had been accomplished before defendant struck the police officer, giving rise to the resisting arrest charge. People v. O'Neil, 116 A.D.2d 853, 498 N.Y.S.2d 173 (3d Dept. 1986).

—Court properly imposed consecutive sentences for

defendant's convictions for two counts of petit larceny where "[e]ach offense was a separate crime committed at a discrete time by a distinct act." People v. Mainella, 251 A.D.2d 1000, 675 N.Y.S.2d 580 (4th Dept. 1998).

—The defendant's possession of a rifle and the firing of that rifle were separate and distinct acts authorizing the imposition of consecutive sentences; however, the imposition of two consecutive one year sentences was proscribed because the acts were committed as part of a single incident or transaction. People v. Frazier, 212 A.D.2d 976, 623 N.Y.S.2d 459 (4th Dept. 1995).

—Defendant's consecutive sentences for burglary in the second degree and grand larceny in the third degree were proper. People v. Miller, 212 A.D.2d 966, 623 N.Y.S.2d 673 (4th Dept. 1995).

—The sentencing court erred in imposing consecutive sentences for robbery and burglary; the offenses were both committed through a single act. People v. Nguyen, 210 A.D.2d 871, 621 N.Y.S.2d 973 (4th Dept. 1994).

Consecutive sentences exceeding 30 years.—Consecutive sentences which exceed the aggregate maximum limitation of 30 years of Penal Law § 70.30 are not illegal or void, but should be "deemed" to be equal to that limitation and "reduced" accordingly. People v. Moore, 61 N.Y.2d 575, 475 N.Y.S.2d 354, 436 N.E.2d 1206 (1984).

Discretionary authority.—The sentencing discretion afforded by § 70.25 devolves upon the last judge in the sentencing chain. Murray v. Goord, 1 N.Y.3d 29, 769 N.Y.S.2d 165, 801 N.E.2d 385 (2003).

—The existence of discretionary consecutive authority does not compel consecutive sentencing. People v. Brown, 80 N.Y.2d 361, 590 N.Y.S.2d 422, 604 N.E.2d 1353 (1992).

—Sentencing court's findings that defendant did not use a weapon in one of the robberies committed, and that the other robbery did not result in injuries were properly deemed mitigating circumstances authorizing the use of the court's narrow discretion in imposing concurrent rather than consecutive sentence for violent felonies committed when defendant was free on bail. People v. Reyes, 221 A.D.2d 202, 633 N.Y.S.2d 307 (1st Dept. 1995).

—The decision of whether to impose consecutive or concurrent sentences is within the discretion of the sentencing court; the trial court here erroneously concluded that it was required to impose consecutive sentences for two burglaries defendant committed. People v. Crosby, 221 A.D.2d 357, 633 N.Y.S.2d 364 (2d Dept. 1995).

—Court's erroneous belief that it did not have the discretion to direct that sentences run concurrently under the limited circumstances provided for in § 70.25(2-b) required that the sentence be vacated and remanded for resentencing. People v. Broadbent, 245 A.D.2d 1114, 666 N.Y.S.2d 534 (4th Dept. 1997).

Preservation for appeal.—Defendant's failure to object to imposition of consecutive sentences at time of sentence rendered that objection waived and unpreserved for appellate review. People v. Fernandez, 251 A.D.2d 142, 673 N.Y.S.2d 312 (1st Dept. 1998).

Waiver of provisions of subdivision (3); guilty plea.—The provisions of Penal Law § 70.25(3) cannot be waived even if the waiver is the result of a plea bargain in which defendant agrees to consecutive sentences for different offenses arising out of one transaction. People v. Lopez, 28 N.Y.2d 148, 320 N.Y.S.2d 235, 269 N.E.2d 28 (1971).

Concurrent and consecutive sentences.—Court has no authority to impose concurrent sentences where the statute mandates that the sentence must run consecutively with respect to an undischarged sentence. People v. Ramon, 239 A.D.2d 198, 657 N.Y.S.2d 172 (1st Dept. 1997).

—Imposition of consecutive sentences on the convictions of assault in the first degree and murder in the second degree was within the court's discretion since each firing of defendant's gun constituted a separate act. However, defendant's sentence for criminal possession of a weapon should have run concurrently with the above two sentences since the convictions arose out of a single incident. People v. Reyes, 239 A.D.2d 524, 658 N.Y.S.2d 353 (2d Dept. 1997).

—Defendant, convicted of two counts of offering a false instrument for filing and one count of larceny by false pretenses was properly sentenced to two consecutive terms of imprisonment, one for each of the two separate filings, and a sentence for larceny which was to run concurrently with the two consecutive sentences. People v. Starks, 238 A.D.2d 621, 656 N.Y.S.2d 399 (3d Dept. 1997).

—A sentence split so that it is half concurrent and half consecutive is not within the parameters of Penal Law § 70.25(l). People v. Bakalocostantis, 148 A.D.2d 842, 539 N.Y.S.2d 115, 117 (3d Dept. 1989).

§ 70.30. Calculation of terms of imprisonment.

1. [*Effective until Sept. 1, 2007.*] Indeterminate or determinate sentences. An indeterminate or determinate sentence of imprisonment commences when the prisoner is received in an institution under the jurisdiction of the state department of correctional services. Where a person is under more than one indeterminate or determinate sentence, the sentences shall be calculated as follows:

(a) If the sentences run concurrently, the time served under imprisonment on any of the sentences shall be credited against the minimum periods of all the concurrent indeterminate sentences and against the terms of all the concurrent determinate sentences. The maximum term or terms of the indeterminate sentences and the term or terms of the determinate sentences shall merge in and be satisfied by discharge of the term which has the longest unexpired time to run;

(b) If the defendant is serving two or more indeterminate sentences which run consecutively, the minimum periods of imprisonment are added to arrive at an aggregate minimum period of imprisonment equal to the sum of all the minimum periods, and the maximum terms are added to arrive at an aggregate maximum term equal to the sum of all the maximum terms, provided, however, that both the aggregate maximum term and the aggregate minimum period of imprisonment shall be subject to the limitations set forth in paragraphs (e) and (f) of this subdivision, where applicable;

(c) If the defendant is serving two or more determinate sentences of imprisonment which run consecutively, the terms of the determinate sentences are added to arrive at an aggregate maximum term of imprisonment, provided, however, that the aggregate maximum term of imprisonment shall be subject to the limitations set forth in paragraphs (e) and (f) of this subdivision, where applicable.

(d) If the defendant is serving one or more indeterminate sentences of imprisonment and one or more determinate sentence of imprisonment which run consecutively, the minimum term or terms of the indeterminate sentence or sentences and the term or terms of the determinate sentence or sentences are added to arrive at an aggregate maximum term of imprisonment, provided, however, (i) that in no event shall the aggregate maximum so calculated be less than the term or maximum term of imprisonment of the sentence

which has the longest unexpired time to run; and (ii) that the aggregate maximum term of imprisonment shall be subject to the limitations set forth in paragraphs (e) and (f) of this subdivision, where applicable.

(e) (i) Except as provided in subparagraph (ii), (iii), (iv), (v), (vi) or (vii) of this paragraph, the aggregate maximum term of consecutive sentences, all of which are indeterminate sentences or all of which are determinate sentences, imposed for two or more crimes, other than two or more crimes that include a class A felony, committed prior to the time the person was imprisoned under any of such sentences shall, if it exceeds twenty years, be deemed to be twenty years, unless one of the sentences was imposed for a class B felony, in which case the aggregate maximum term shall, if it exceeds thirty years, be deemed to be thirty years. Where the aggregate maximum term of two or more indeterminate consecutive sentences is reduced by calculation made pursuant to this paragraph, the aggregate minimum period of imprisonment, if it exceeds one-half of the aggregate maximum term as so reduced, shall be deemed to be one-half of the aggregate maximum term as so reduced;

(ii) Where the aggregate maximum term of two or more consecutive sentences, one or more of which is a determinate sentence and one or more of which is an indeterminate sentence, imposed for two or more crimes, other than two or more crimes that include a class A felony, committed prior to the time the person was imprisoned under any of such sentences, exceeds twenty years, and none of the sentences was imposed for a class B felony, the following rules shall apply:

(A) if the aggregate maximum term of the determinate sentence or sentences exceeds twenty years, the defendant shall be deemed to be serving to [serving a]* a determinate sentence of twenty years.

* The bracketed words have been inserted by the Publisher.

(B) if the aggregate maximum term of the determinate sentence or sentences is less than twenty years, the defendant shall be deemed to be serving an indeterminate sentence the maximum term of which shall be deemed to be twenty years. In such instances, the minimum sentence shall be deemed to be ten years or six-sevenths of the term or aggregate maximum term of the determinate sentence or sentences, whichever is greater.

(iii) Where the aggregate maximum term of two or more consecutive sentences, one or more of which is a determinate sentence and one or more of which is an indeterminate sentence, imposed for two or more crimes, other than two or more crimes that include a class A felony, committed [committed]* prior to the time the person was imprisoned under any of such sentences, exceeds thirty years, and one of the sentences was imposed for a class B felony, the following rules shall apply:

* The bracketed word has been inserted by the Publisher.

(A) if the aggregate maximum term of the determinate sentence or sentences exceeds thirty years, the defendant shall be deemed to be serving a determinate sentence of thirty years;

(B) if the aggregate maximum term of the determinate sentence or sentences is less than thirty years, the defendant shall be deemed to be serving an indeterminate sentence the maximum term of which shall be deemed to be thirty years. In such instances, the minimum sentence shall be deemed to be fifteen years or six-sevenths of the term or aggregate maximum term of the determinate sentence or sentences, whichever is greater.

(iv) Notwithstanding subparagraph (i) of this paragraph, the aggregate maximum term of consecutive sentences, all of which are indeterminate sentences or all of which are determinate sentences, imposed for the conviction of two violent felony offenses committed prior to the time the person was imprisoned under any of such sentences and one of which is a class B violent felony offense, shall, if it exceeds forty years, be deemed to be forty years;

(v) Notwithstanding subparagraphs (ii) and (iii) of this paragraph, where the aggregate maximum term of two or more consecutive sentences, one or more of which is a determinate sentence and one or more of which is an indeterminate sentence, and where such sentences are imposed for the conviction of two violent felony offenses committed prior to the time the person was imprisoned under any such sentences and where one of which is a class B violent felony offense, the following rules shall apply:

(A) if the aggregate maximum term of the determinate sentence or sentences exceeds forty years, the defendant shall be deemed to be serving a determinate sentence of forty years;

(B) if the aggregate maximum term of the determinate sentence or sentences is less than forty years, the defendant shall be deemed to be serving an indeterminate sentence the maximum term of which shall be deemed to be forty years. In such instances, the minimum sentence shall be deemed to be twenty years or six-sevenths of the term or aggregate maximum term of the determinate sentence or sentences, whichever is greater.

(vi) Notwithstanding subparagraphs (i) and (iv) of this paragraph, the aggregate maximum term of consecutive sentences, all of which are indeterminate or all of which are determinate sentences, imposed for the conviction of three or more violent felony offenses committed prior to the time the person was imprisoned under any of such sentences and one of which is a class B violent felony offense, shall, if it exceeds fifty years, be deemed to be fifty years;

(vii) Notwithstanding subparagraphs (ii), (iii)

and (v) of this paragraph, where the aggregate maximum term of two or more consecutive sentences, one or more of which is a determinate sentence and one or more of which is an indeterminate sentence, and where such sentences are imposed for the conviction of three or more violent felony offenses committed prior to the time the person was imprisoned under any such sentences and one of which is a class B violent felony offense, the following rules shall apply:

(A) if the aggregate maximum term of the determinate sentence or sentences exceeds fifty years, the defendant shall be deemed to be serving a determinate sentence of fifty years.

(B) if the aggregate maximum term of the determinate sentence or sentences is less than fifty years, the defendant shall be deemed to be serving an indeterminate sentence the maximum term of which shall be deemed to be fifty years. In such instances, the minimum sentence shall be deemed to be twenty-five years or six-sevenths of the term or aggregate maximum term of the determinate sentence or sentences, whichever is greater.

(viii) Notwithstanding any provision of this subdivision to the contrary where a person is serving two or more consecutive sentences, one or more of which is an indeterminate sentence and one or more of which is a determinate sentence, and if he would be eligible for a reduction provision pursuant to this subdivision if the maximum term or aggregate maximum term of the indeterminate sentence or sentences were added to the term or aggregate maximum term of the determinate sentence or sentences, the person shall be deemed to be eligible for the applicable reduction provision and the rules set forth in this subdivision shall apply.

(f) The aggregate maximum term of consecutive sentences imposed upon a juvenile offender for two or more crimes, not including a class A felony, committed before he has reached the age of sixteen, shall, if it exceeds ten years, be deemed to be ten years. If consecutive indeterminate sentences imposed upon a juvenile offender include a sentence for the class A felony of arson in the first degree or for the class A felony of kidnapping in the first degree, then the aggregate maximum term of such sentences shall, if it exceeds fifteen years, be deemed to be fifteen years. Where the aggregate maximum term of two or more consecutive sentences is reduced by a calculation made pursuant to this paragraph, the aggregate minimum period of imprisonment, if it exceeds one-half of the aggregate maximum term as so reduced, shall be deemed to be one-half of the aggregate maximum term as so reduced.

1. [*Effective Sept. 1, 2007.*] Indeterminate sentences. An indeterminate or determinate sentence of imprisonment commences when the prisoner is received in an institution under the jurisdiction of the state department of correctional services. Where a person is under more than one

indeterminate sentence, the sentences shall be calculated as follows:

(a) If the sentences run concurrently, the time served under imprisonment on any of the sentences shall be credited against the minimum periods of all the concurrent sentences, and the maximum terms merge in and are satisfied by discharge of the term which has the longest unexpired time to run;

(b) If the sentences run consecutively, the minimum periods of imprisonment are added to arrive at an aggregate minimum period of imprisonment equal to the sum of all the minimum periods, and the maximum terms are added to arrive at an aggregate maximum term equal to the sum of all the maximum terms, provided, however, that both the aggregate maximum term and the aggregate minimum period of imprisonment shall be subject to the limitations set forth in paragraphs (c) and (d) of this subdivision, where applicable;

(c) (i) Except as provided in subparagraph (ii) or (iii) of this paragraph, the aggregate maximum term of consecutive sentences imposed for two or more crimes, other than two or more crimes that include a class A felony, committed prior to the time the person was imprisoned under any of such sentences shall, if it exceeds twenty years, be deemed to be twenty years, unless one of the sentences was imposed for a class B felony, in which case the aggregate maximum term shall, if it exceeds thirty years, be deemed to be thirty years. Where the aggregate maximum term of two or more consecutive sentences is reduced by calculation made pursuant to this paragraph, the aggregate minimum period of imprisonment, if it exceeds one-half of the aggregate maximum term as so reduced, shall be deemed to be one-half of the aggregate maximum term as so reduced;

(ii) Notwithstanding subparagraph (i) of this paragraph, the aggregate maximum term of consecutive sentences imposed for the conviction of two violent felony offenses committed prior to the time the person was imprisoned under any of such sentences and one of which is a class B violent felony offense, shall, if it exceeds forty years, be deemed to be forty years;

(iii) Notwithstanding subparagraphs (i) and (ii) of this paragraph, the aggregate maximum term of consecutive sentences imposed for the conviction of three or more violent felony offenses committed prior to the time the person was imprisoned under any of such sentences and one of which is a class B violent felony offense, shall, if it exceeds fifty years, be deemed to be fifty years;

(d) The aggregate maximum term of consecutive sentences imposed upon a juvenile offender for two or more crimes, not including a class A felony, committed before he has reached the age of sixteen, shall, if it exceeds ten years, be deemed

to be ten years. If consecutive indeterminate sentences imposed upon a juvenile offender include a sentence for the class A felony of arson in the first degree or for the class A felony of kidnapping in the first degree, then the aggregate maximum term of such sentences shall, if it exceeds fifteen years, be deemed to be fifteen years. Where the aggregate maximum term of two or more consecutive sentences is reduced by a calculation made pursuant to this paragraph, the aggregate minimum period of imprisonment, if it exceeds one-half of the aggregate maximum term as so reduced, shall be deemed to be one-half of the aggregate maximum term as so reduced.

2. Definite sentences. A definite sentence of imprisonment commences when the prisoner is received in the institution named in the commitment. Where a person is under more than one definite sentence, the sentences shall be calculated as follows:

(a) If the sentences run concurrently and are to be served in a single institution, the terms merge in and are satisfied by discharge of the term which has the longest unexpired time to run;

(b) If the sentences run consecutively and are to be served in a single institution, the terms are added to arrive at an aggregate term and are satisfied by discharge of such aggregate term, or by service of two years imprisonment plus any term imposed for an offense committed while the person is under the sentences, whichever is less;

(c) If the sentences run concurrently and are to be served in more than one institution, the term of each such sentence shall be credited with the portion of any concurrent term served after that sentence was imposed;

(d) If the sentences run consecutively and are to be served in more than one institution, the aggregate of the time served in all of the institutions shall not exceed two years plus any term imposed for an offense committed while the person is under the sentences.

2-a. Undischarged imprisonment in other jurisdiction. Where a person who is subject to an undischarged term of imprisonment imposed at a previous time by a court of another jurisdiction is sentenced to an additional term or terms of imprisonment by a court of this state, to run concurrently with such undischarged term, such additional term or terms shall be deemed to commence when the said person is returned to the custody of the appropriate official of such other jurisdiction where the undischarged term of imprisonment is being served. If the additional term or terms imposed shall run consecutively to the said undischarged term, such additional term or terms shall commence when the prisoner is received in the appropriate institution as provided in subdivisions one and two of this section. The term or terms of such imprisonment shall be calculated and such other pertinent provisions of this section applied in the same manner as where a person is under more than one sentence in this state as provided in this section.

3. [*Effective until Sept. 1, 2009.*] Jail time. The term of a definite sentence, a determinate sentence, or the maximum term of an indeterminate sentence imposed on a person shall be credited with and diminished by the amount of time the person spent in custody prior to the commencement of such sentence as a result of the charge that culminated in the sentence. In the case of an indeterminate sentence, if the minimum period of imprisonment has been fixed by the court or by the board of parole, the credit shall also be applied against the minimum period. The credit herein provided shall be calculated from the date custody under the charge commenced to the date the sentence commences and shall not include any time that is credited against the term or maximum term of any previously imposed sentence or period of post-release supervision to which the person is subject. Where the charge or charges culminate in more than one sentence, the credit shall be applied as follows:

(a) If the sentences run concurrently, the credit shall be applied against each such sentence;

(b) If the sentences run consecutively, the credit shall be applied against the aggregate term or aggregate maximum term of the sentences and against the aggregate minimum period of imprisonment.

In any case where a person has been in custody due to a charge that culminated in a dismissal or an acquittal, the amount of time that would have been credited against a sentence for such charge, had one been imposed, shall be credited against any sentence that is based on a charge for which a warrant or commitment was lodged during the pendency of such custody.

3. [*Effective Sept. 1, 2009.*] Jail time. The term of a definite sentence or the maximum term of an indeterminate sentence imposed on a person shall be credited with and diminished by the amount of time the person spent in custody prior to the commencement of such sentence as a result of the charge that culminated in the sentence. In the case of an indeterminate sentence, if the minimum period of imprisonment has been fixed by the court or by the board of parole, the credit shall also be applied against the minimum period. The credit herein provided shall be calculated from the date custody under the charge commenced to the date the sentence commences and shall not include any time that is credited against the term or maximum term of any previously imposed sentence to which the person is subject. Where the charge or charges culminate in more than one sentence, the credit shall be applied as follows:

(a) If the sentences run concurrently, the credit shall be applied against each such sentence;

(b) If the sentences run consecutively, the credit shall be applied against the aggregate term or aggregate maximum term of the sentences and against the aggregate minimum period of imprisonment.

In any case where a person has been in custody due to a charge that culminated in a dismissal or an acquittal, the amount of time that would have been credited against a sentence for such charge, had one been imposed, shall be credited against any sentence that is based on a charge for which a warrant or commitment was lodged during the pendency of such custody.

4. [*Effective until Sept. 1, 2009.*] Good behavior time. Time allowances earned for good behavior, pursuant to the provisions of the correction law, shall be computed and applied as follows:

(a) In the case of a person serving an indeterminate or determinate sentence, the total of such allowances shall be calculated as provided in section eight hundred three of the correction law and the allowances shall be applied as provided in paragraph (b) of subdivision one of section 70.40;

(b) In the case of a person serving a definite sentence, the total of such allowances shall not exceed one-third of his term or aggregate term and the allowances shall be applied as a credit against such term.

4. [*Effective Sept. 1, 2009.*] Good behavior time. Time allowances earned for good behavior, pursuant to the provisions of the correction law, shall be computed and applied as follows:

(a) In the case of a person serving an indeterminate sentence, the total of such allowances shall not exceed one-third of his maximum or aggregate maximum term and the allowances shall be applied as provided in subdivision one (b) of section 70.40;

(b) In the case of a person serving a definite sentence, the total of such allowances shall not exceed one-third of his term or aggregate term and the allowances shall be applied as a credit against such term.

5. Time served under vacated sentence. When a sentence of imprisonment that has been imposed on a person is vacated and a new sentence is imposed on such person for the same offense, or for an offense based upon the same act, the new sentence shall be calculated as if it had commenced at the time the vacated sentence commenced, and all time credited against the vacated sentence shall be credited against the new sentence. In any case where a vacated sentence also includes a period of post-release supervision, all time credited against the period of post-release supervision shall be credited against the period of post-release supervision included with the new sentence. In the event a period of post-release supervision is not included with the new sentence,

such period shall be credited against the new sentence.

6. Escape. When a person who is serving a sentence of imprisonment escapes from custody, the escape shall interrupt the sentence and such interruption shall continue until the return of the person to the institution in which the sentence was being served or, if the sentence was being served in an institution under the jurisdiction of the state department of correctional services, to an institution under the jurisdiction of that department. Any time spent by such person in custody from the date of escape to the date the sentence resumes shall be credited against the term or maximum term of the interrupted sentence, provided:

(a) That such custody was due to an arrest or surrender based upon the escape; or

(b) That such custody arose from an arrest on another charge which culminated in a dismissal or an acquittal; or

(c) That such custody arose from an arrest on another charge which culminated in a conviction, but in such case, if a sentence of imprisonment was imposed, the credit allowed shall be limited to the portion of the time spent in custody that exceeds the period, term or maximum term of imprisonment imposed for such conviction.

7. [*Expires Sept. 1, 2007.*] Absconding from temporary release or furlough program. When a person who is serving a sentence of imprisonment is permitted to leave an institution to participate in a program of work release or furlough program as such term is defined in section six hundred thirty-one of the correction law, or in the case of an institution under the jurisdiction of the state department of correctional services or a facility under the jurisdiction of the state division for youth to participate in a program of temporary release, fails to return to the institution or facility at or before the time prescribed for his return, such failure shall interrupt the sentence and such interruption shall continue until the return of the person to the institution in which the sentence was being served or, if the sentence was being served in an institution under the jurisdiction of the state department of correctional services or a facility under the jurisdiction of the state division for youth to an institution under the jurisdiction of that department or a facility under the jurisdiction of that division. Any time spent by such person in an institution from the date of his failure to return to the date his sentence resumes shall be credited against the term or maximum term of the interrupted sentence, provided:

(a) That such incarceration was due to an arrest or surrender based upon the failure to return; or

(b) That such incarceration arose from an arrest on another charge which culminated in a dismissal or an acquittal; or

(c) That such custody arose from an arrest on another charge which culminated in a conviction, but in such case, if a sentence of imprisonment was imposed, the credit allowed shall be limited to the portion of the time spent in custody that exceeds the period, term or maximum term of imprisonment imposed for such conviction.

Amended by L. 1972, Ch. 339; L. 1974, Chs. 465, 966; L. 1975, Ch. 782; L. 1976, Chs. 21, 145, 471; L. 1977, Ch. 691; L. 1978, Chs. 481, 691; L. 1979, Chs. 485, 648; L. 1980, Chs. 176, 296; L. 1981, Ch. 495; L. 1982, Ch. 137; L. 1983, Chs. 199, 460, 519; L. 1985, Ch. 573; L. 1986, Ch. 395, L. 1987, Ch. 261; L. 1988, Ch. 292; L. 1991, Ch. 511, eff. July 19, 1991; L. 1992 Ch. 55, eff. Apr. 10, 1992, extending the expiration date of subd. 7 to Sept. 1, 1994; L. 1994, Ch. 61, § 8, extending expiration date of subd. 7; L. 1995, Ch. 3, § 13, amending subds. 1(a), 1(b), 1(c), 1(d), by relettering 1(c) to (e) and 1(d) to (f), and adding new subds. (c) and (d); L. 1995, § 14, amending subd. 1(e); L. 1995, § 15, amending subd. (3); L. 1995, § 16, amending subd. 4. The preceding amendments contained in L. 1995, Ch. 3, are effective Oct. 1, 1995, repealed Sept. 30, 2005 pursuant to L. 1995, Ch. 3, § 74, paragraph (d); L. 1995, § 50, extending expiration date of subd. 7 to Sept. 1, 1997; L. 1997, Ch. 435, § 50, extending expiration date of subd. (7) to Sept. 1, 1999; L. 1998, Ch. 1, §§ 10 and 11, eff. Aug. 6, 1998, and shall apply to offenses committed on or after Sept. 1, 1998. Offenses committed prior to Sept. 1, 1998 shall be governed by the provisions of law in effect at the time the offense was committed; provided, however, that nothing contained herein shall be deemed to affect the application, qualification, expiration, reversion or repeal of any provision of law amended by any section of L. 1998, Ch. 1 and the provisions of L. 1998, Ch. 1 shall be applied or qualified or shall expire or revert or be deemed repealed in the same manner, to the same extent and on the same date as the case may be as otherwise provided by law; L. 1999, Ch. 452, § 4, extending expiration date of subd. 7 to Sept. 1, 2001; L. 2001, Ch. 95, § 6, extending expiration date of subd. 7 to Sept. 1, 2003; L. 2003, Ch. 16, § 6, eff. Mar. 31, 2003, extending expiration date of subd. 7 to Sept. 1, 2005; L. 2005, Ch. 56, Part D, §§ 6 & 20, extending expiration dates.

ANNOTATIONS

Aggregate consecutive sentences; persistent felony offender.—The limitations on aggregate consecutive sentences set forth in Penal Law § 70.30 do not apply where a defendant has received a lifetime maximum sentence as a persistent felony offender. Roballo v. Smith, 63 N.Y.2d 485, 483 N.Y.S.2d 178, 472 N.E.2d 1006 (1984).

Aggregate maximum term.—There was no impropriety in imposing an aggregate maximum prison term of 40 years upon defendant, who was convicted of three counts of robbery in the second degree. People v. Sutton, 208 A.D.2d 574, 617 N.Y.S.2d 63 (2d Dept. 1994).

—Appellate court is not required to modify a sentence where the aggregate sentence imposed exceeds the maximum aggregate term set forth in PL § 70.30(1)(e)(vi); the determination of the maximum allowable statutory limit is left to the Department of Correctional Services. People v. Printup, 255 A.D.2d 1000, 681 N.Y.S.2d 182 (4th Dept. 1998).

Aggregate minimum term.—Minimum aggregate terms of two or more consecutive indeterminate sentences is calculated by adding minimum periods of each sentence. Viserto v. Coombe, 238 A.D.2d 646, 656 N.Y.S.2d 958 (3d Dept. 1997).

Jail time credit.—PL § 70.30 does not contemplate place of detention as a factor DOCS should consider in computing jail time credit, out-of-state and federal detention should be extended same jail time credit as custody in New York. Guido v. Goord, 1 N.Y.3d 345, 774 N.Y.S.2d 113, 806 N.E.2d 138 (2004).

—For purposes of calculating jail time credit, PL §70.30 makes no distinction between detention in New York and detention by federal government and/or sister states. Chang v. Goord, 1 N.Y.3d 603, 776 N.Y.S.2d 534, 808 N.E.2d 854 (2004).

—Defendant was not entitled to sentence credit for period during which he was free from incarceration between the reversal of his conviction by the intermediate appellate court and reinstatement of the conviction by the Court of Appeals.

Licitra v. Coughlin, 61 N.Y.2d 450, 474 N.Y.S.2d 685, 463 N.E.2d 11 (1984).

—Since defendant was being held seven months while awaiting the disposition of a weapons charge and a prior unrelated misdemeanor and later a one and a half to three year's sentence was imposed on the weapons charge, defendant's jail time should have been credited to that sentence because the jail time was not a "previously imposed sentence" within the meaning of subd. 3 of § 70.30 of the Penal Law. People *ex rel.*Davis v. Arnette, 44 N.Y.2d 877, 407 N.Y.S.2d 629, 379 N.E.2d 157 (1978).

—Jail time already credited on a prior conviction cannot be credited against a subsequent conviction to reduce a sentence, even if the two sentences were to run concurrently. People v. Endee, 268 A.D.2d 823, 702 N.Y.S.2d 224 (3d Dept. 2000).

—Where defendant forfeited five years of good time as a result of penalties imposed at disciplinary hearings, the determinations of which he did not challenge, those years were properly subtracted from the jail time credit he received in determining his actual time of incarceration. Porter v. Senkowski, 245 A.D.2d 919, 666 N.Y.S.2d 853 (3d Dept. 1997).

—Defendant was entitled to and received credit for time spent in county jail on charges which culminated in a sentence; however, he was not entitled to credit for that jail time against a prior undischarged term that was interrupted when he was declared delinquent by the parole board. People v. Hanna, 219 A.D.2d 792, 631 N.Y.S.2d 787 (3d Dept. 1995).

—Defendant/petitioner was not entitled to have time served under a federal sentence applied to his state sentence because he was never returned to the actual custody of the federal jurisdiction. People *ex rel.* Fredricks v. Mann, 219 A.D.2d 763, 631 N.Y.S.2d 199 (3d Dept. 1994).

—Where defendant spent some 36 days in custody for the charge upon which he was subsequently convicted and sentenced to a five year period of probation, the first 60 days of which were to be served in jail, the trial court improperly extended the period of imprisonment authorized under PL § 60.01(2)(d) by failing to credit defendant with the period of time already spent in custody. People v. Didio, 78 A.D.2d 970, 433 N.Y.S.2d 682 (4th Dept. 1980).

—Defendant who received intermittent sentence was entitled to receive credit for jail time actually served, rejecting argument that he should be credited with seven days for each of the eighteen weekends he was incarcerated instead of the actual three days confinement each weekend. People *ex rel.* Bailey v. Netzel, 169 Misc. 2d 623, 647 N.Y.S.2d 343 (Sup. Ct. Erie Co. 1996).

Limitation on court's direction.—Sentencing court can direct that state time be served concurrently with the undischarged portion of an existing federal sentence; however, it cannot direct that state time be served first. Jones v. Portundo, 268 A.D.2d 807, 702 N.Y.S.2d 227 (3d Dept.), *appeal denied,* 95 N.Y.2d 754 (2000).

Recalculation.—Where court exceeded statutory limit in imposing sentence of 9 to 45 years for conviction on five counts of sale of controlled substance in the third degree, sentence would be recalculated administratively by the Dept. of Corr. Services to 30 years and court was not required to vacate sentence as illegal. People v. Leigh, 232 A.D.2d 904, 649 N.Y.S.2d 503 (3d Dept. 1996).

Sentence interruption.—Penal Law § 70.30(7) unambiguously provides for sentence interruption whenever a person on temporary release fails to return regardless of whether the failure is intentional. Pughe v. Parrott, 302 A.D.2d 823, 758 N.Y.S.2d 404 (3d Dept. 2003).

"Under the sentence of."—Defendant, who committed a crime while awaiting sentencing on prior offenses, would have a release dated calculated on a two-year aggregate term. Defendant was not "under the sentence" of the prior offense at the time the subsequent offense was committed since he had not yet been sentenced on those prior charges. Serfaty v. Jablonsky, 236 A.D. 413, 653 N.Y.S.2d 371 (2d Dept. 1997).

§ 70.35. Merger of certain definite and indeterminate or determinate sentences. [*Effective until Sept. 1, 2009.*]

The service of an indeterminate or determinate sentence of imprisonment shall satisfy any definite sentence of imprisonment imposed on a person for an offense committed prior to the time the indeterminate or determinate sentence was imposed, except as provided in paragraph (b) of subdivision five of section 70.25 of this article. A person who is serving a definite sentence at the time an indeterminate or determinate sentence is imposed shall be delivered to the custody of the state department of correctional services to commence service of the indeterminate or determinate sentence immediately unless the person is serving a definite sentence pursuant to paragraph (b) of subdivision five of section 70.25 of this article. In any case where the indeterminate or determinate sentence is revoked or vacated, the person shall receive credit against the definite sentence for each day spent in the custody of the state department of correctional services.

§ 70.35. Merger of certain definite and indeterminate sentences. [*Effective Sept. 1, 2009.*]

The service of an indeterminate sentence of imprisonment shall satisfy any definite sentence of imprisonment imposed on a person for an offense committed prior to the time the indeterminate sentence was imposed, except as provided in paragraph (b) of subdivision five of section 70.25 of this article. A person who is serving a definite sentence at the time an indeterminate sentence is imposed shall be delivered to the custody of the state department of correctional services to commence service of the indeterminate sentence immediately unless the person is serving a definite sentence pursuant to paragraph (b) of subdivision five of section 70.25 of this article. In any case where the indeterminate sentence is revoked or vacated, the person shall receive credit against the definite sentence for each day spent in the custody of the state department of correctional services.

Amended by L. 1981, Ch. 372; L. 1989, Ch. 527; L. 1995, Ch. 3, § 18, adding the phrase "or determinate" to the heading and throughout the subd., eff. Oct. 1, 1995, amendment repealed Sept. 30, 2005, pursuant to L. 1995, Ch. 3, § 74, paragraph (d); L. 2005, Ch. 56, Part D, § 20, extending repeal date.

ANNOTATIONS

Concurrent sentence.—Penal Law § 70.35 contemplates that definite and indefinite sentences will be served concurrently; the appellate division correctly modified the defendant's sentences to run concurrently rather than consecutively since criminal mischief was committed by defendant prior to imposition of an indeterminate sentence for driving while intoxicated. People v. Leabo, 84 N.Y.2d 952, 620 N.Y.S.2d 821, 644 N.E.2d 1376 (1994).

—Where the defendant was sentenced to a one-year determinate sentence prior to the imposition of an indeterminate sentence for a related offense, the one-year determinate sentence should run concurrently with the indeterminate sentence. People v. Dottin, 238 A.D.2d 604, 657 N.Y.S.2d 76 (2d Dept. 1997).

§ 70.40. Release on parole; conditional release; presumptive release.

1. Indeterminate sentence.

(a) [*Expires and repealed Sept. 1, 2007.*] A person who is serving one or more than one indeterminate sentence of imprisonment may be paroled from the institution in which he is confined at any time after the expiration of the minimum or the aggregate minimum period of imprisonment of the sentence or sentences or after the successful completion of a shock incarceration program, as defined in article twenty-six-A of the correction law, or at any time on medical parole pursuant to section two hundred fifty-nine-r of the executive law, whichever is sooner. Release on parole shall be in the discretion of the state board of parole, and such person shall continue service of his sentence or sentences while on parole, in accordance with and subject to the provisions of the executive law.

(a) [*Effective until Sept. 1, 2009.*] Release on parole shall be in the discretion of the state board of parole, and such person shall continue service of his sentence or sentences while on parole, in accordance with and subject to the provisions of the executive law.

(i) [*Expires and repealed Sept. 1, 2007.*] A person who is serving one or more than one indeterminate sentence of imprisonment may be paroled from the institution in which he is confined at any time after the expiration of the minimum or the aggregate minimum period of the sentence or sentences or, where applicable, the minimum or aggregate minimum period reduced by the merit time allowance granted pursuant to paragraph (d) of subdivision one of section eight hundred three of the correction law.

(i) [*Effective Sept. 1, 2007.*] A person who is serving one or more than one indeterminate sentence of imprisonment may be paroled from the institution in which he is confined at any time after the expiration of the minimum or the aggregate minimum period of the sentence or sentences or, where applicable, the minimum or aggregate minimum period reduced by the merit time allowance granted pursuant to paragraph (d) of subdivision one of section eight hundred three of the correction law.

(ii) A person who is serving one or more than one determinate sentence of imprisonment shall be ineligible for discretionary release on parole.

(iii) A person who is serving one or more than one indeterminate sentence of imprisonment and one or more than one determinate sentence of imprisonment which run concurrently may be paroled at any time after the expiration of the minimum period of imprisonment of the indeterminate sentence or sentences, or upon the expiration of six-sevenths of the term of imprisonment of the determinate sentence or sentences, whichever is later.

(iv) A person who is serving one or more than one indeterminate sentence of imprisonment and one or more than one determinate sentence of imprisonment which run consecutively may be paroled at any time after the expiration of the sum of the minimum or aggregate minimum period of the indeterminate sentence or sentences and six-sevenths of the term or aggregate term of imprisonment of the determinate sentence or sentences.

(v) Notwithstanding any other subparagraph of this paragraph, a person may be paroled from the institution in which he is confined at any time on medical parole pursuant to section two hundred fifty-nine-r of the executive law or for deportation pursuant to paragraph (d) of subdivision two of section two hundred fifty-nine-i of the executive law or after the successful completion of a shock incarceration program pursuant to article twenty-six-A of the correction law.

(a) [*Effective Sept. 1, 2009.*] A person who is serving one or more than one indeterminate sentence of imprisonment may be paroled from the institution in which he is confined at any time after the expiration of the minimum or the aggregate minimum period of imprisonment of the sentence or sentences or after the successful completion of a shock incarceration program, as defined in article twenty-six-A of the correction law, or at any time on medical parole pursuant to section two hundred fifty-nine-r of the executive law, whichever is sooner. Release on parole shall be in the discretion of the state board of parole, and such person shall continue service of his sentence or sentences while on parole, in accordance with and subject to the provisions of the executive law.

(b) [*Effective until Sept. 1, 2009.*] A person who is serving one or more than one indeterminate or determinate sentence of imprisonment shall, if he so requests, be conditionally released from the institution in which he is confined when the total good behavior time allowed to him, pursuant to the provisions of the correction law, is equal to the unserved portion of his term, maximum term or aggregate maximum term; provided, however, that (i) in no event shall a person serving one or more indeterminate sentence of imprisonment and one or more determinate sentence of imprisonment which run concurrently be conditionally released until serving at least six-sevenths of the determinate term of imprisonment which has the longest unexpired time to run and (ii) in no event shall a person be conditionally released prior to the date on which such person is first eligible for discretionary parole release. The conditions of release, including those governing post-release supervision, shall be such as may be imposed by the state board of parole in accordance with the provisions of the executive law.

Every person so released shall be under the supervision of the state board of parole for a period equal to the unserved portion of the term, maximum term, aggregate maximum term, or period of post-release supervision.

(b) [*Effective Sept. 1, 2009.*] A person who is serving one or more than one indeterminate sentence of imprisonment shall, if he so requests, be conditionally released from the institution in which he is confined when the total good behavior time allowed to him, pursuant to the provisions of the correction law, is equal to the unserved portion of his maximum or aggregate maximum term. The conditions of release shall be such as may be imposed by the state board of parole in accordance with the provisions of the executive law.

Every person so released shall be under the supervision of the state board of parole for a period equal to the unserved portion of the maximum or aggregate maximum term.

(c) A person who is serving one or more than one indeterminate sentence of imprisonment shall, if he or she so requests, be released from the institution in which he or she is confined if granted presumptive release pursuant to section eight hundred six of the correction law. The conditions of release shall be such as may be imposed by the state board of parole in accordance with the provisions of the executive law. Every person so released shall be under the supervision of the state board of parole for a period equal to the unserved portion of his or her maximum or aggregate maximum term unless discharged in accordance with law.

2. [*Expires and repealed Sept. 1, 2007.*] Definite sentence. A person who is serving one or more than one definite sentence of imprisonment with a term or aggregate term in excess of ninety days may, if he so requests, be conditionally released from the institution in which he is confined at any time after service of sixty days of that term, exclusive of credits allowed under subdivisions four and six of section 70.30. In computing service of sixty days, the credit allowed for jail time under subdivision three of section 70.30 shall be calculated as time served. Conditional release from such institution shall be in the discretion of the local conditional release commission, and shall be upon such conditions as may be imposed by that commission, in accordance with the provisions of the correction law.

Conditional release shall interrupt service of the sentence or sentences and the remaining portion of the term or aggregate term shall be held in abeyance. Every person so released shall be under the supervision of a local probation department and in the custody of the local conditional release commission in accordance with article

twelve of the correction law for a period of one year. The local probation department shall cause complete records to be kept of every person released to its supervision pursuant to this subdivision. The division of parole may supply to a local probation department and the local condition [conditional] * release commission custody information and records maintained on persons under the supervision of such local probation department to aid in the performance of its supervision responsibilities. Compliance with the conditions of release during the period of supervision shall satisfy the portion of the term or aggregate term that has been held in abeyance.

* The bracketed word has been inserted by the Publisher.

2. [*Effective Sept. 1, 2007.*] Definite sentence. A person who is serving one or more than one definite sentence of imprisonment with a term or aggregate term in excess of ninety days may, if he so requests, be conditionally released from the institution in which he is confined at any time after service of sixty days of that term, exclusive of credits allowed under subdivisions four and six of section 70.30. In computing service of sixty days, the credit allowed for jail time under subdivision three of section 70.30 shall be calculated as time served. Conditional release from such institution shall be in the discretion of the parole board, and shall be upon such conditions as may be imposed by that board, in accordance with the provisions of the executive law.

Conditional release shall interrupt service of the sentence or sentences and the remaining portion of the term or aggregate term shall be held in abeyance. Every person so released shall be under the supervision of the parole board for a period of one year. Compliance with the conditions of release during the period of supervision shall satisfy the portion of the term or aggregate term that has been held in abeyance.

3. Delinquency.

(a) When a person is alleged to have violated the terms of presumptive release or parole and the state board of parole has declared such person to be delinquent, the declaration of delinquency shall interrupt the person's sentence as of the date of the delinquency and such interruption shall continue until the return of the person to an institution under the jurisdiction of the state department of correctional services.

(b) [*Expires and repealed Sept. 1, 2007.*] When a person is alleged to have violated the terms of his conditional release or post-release supervision and has been declared delinquent by the board having supervision over such person or the local conditional release commission, the declaration of delinquency shall interrupt the period of supervision or post-release supervision as of the date of the delinquency. For a conditional releasee, such interruption shall continue until the return of the person to the local correctional facility located in the jurisdiction of the commission having custody of such person or, if he was released from an institution under the jurisdiction of the state department of correctional services, to an institution under the jurisdiction of that department. Upon such return, the person shall resume service of his sentence. For a person released to post-release supervision, the provisions of section 70.45 shall apply.

(b) [*Effective Sept. 1, 2007.*] When a person has violated the terms of his conditional release and has been declared delinquent by the board or commission having supervision over him, the declaration of delinquency shall interrupt the period of supervision as of the date of the delinquency and such interruption shall continue until the return of the person to the institution from which he was released or, if he was released from an institution under the jurisdiction of the state department of correction, to an institution under the jurisdiction of that department. Upon such return, the person shall resume service of his sentence.

(c) Any time spent by a person in custody from the time of delinquency to the time service of the sentence resumes shall be credited against the term or maximum term of the interrupted sentence, provided:

(i) that such custody was due to an arrest or surrender based upon the delinquency; or

(ii) that such custody arose from an arrest on another charge which culminated in a dismissal or an acquittal; or

(iii) that such custody arose from an arrest on another charge which culminated in a conviction, but in such case, if a sentence of imprisonment was imposed, the credit allowed shall be limited to the portion of the time spent in custody that exceeds the period, term or maximum term of imprisonment imposed for such such conviction.

Amended by L. 1967, Ch. 324; L. 1971, Ch. 425; L. 1972, Ch. 295; L. 1973, Chs. 468, 478; L. 1975, Ch. 148; L. 1978, Ch. 481; L. 1979, Ch. 467; L. 1987, Ch. 261; L. 1989, Ch. 79; L. 1990, Ch. 117; L. 1992, Ch. 55, eff. Apr. 10, 1992, amending subd. 1(a), and shall apply to all persons released on medical parole prior to Mar. 31, 1994, and shall expire and be of no further effect 2 years following the date on which it shall have become a law; L. 1994, Ch. 61, § 3, extending expiration date of subd. 1(a) to Apr. 10, 1996, and also extending "applicable to persons" date to Apr. 10, 1996; L. 1994, Ch. 61, § 6, extending repeal date of amendments to subd. 2 and 3(b) to May 1, 1997; L. 1995, Ch. 3, §§ 18 and 19, amending subds. 1(a) and (b), respectively, eff. Oct. 1, 1995, amendment repealed Sept. 30, 2005 pursuant to L. 1995, Ch. 3, § 74, paragraph (d); L. 1997, Chs. 57, 117, 145, 162, 194, 211, and 264, extending expiration date of subd. 2 and subparagraph 3(b) to Aug. 1, 1997, eff. July 23, 1997, in full force and effect Apr. 1, 1997, and Ch. 435, § 45, eff. Aug. 20, 1997, amending subd. (1)(a)(i), expiring Sept. 1, 2002, and § 54, eff. Aug. 20, 1997, extending the repeal date of subds. 2 and 3 to Sept. 1, 1999; any provision of this subd. which expired prior to Aug. 20, 1997 shall be revived and shall be deemed to have been in full force and effect from and after the date of the applicable expiration; L. 1998, Ch. 38, § 1, eff. Apr. 8, 1998, extending the expiration date of amendment to subd. (1)(a) by L. 1992, Ch. 55 to Apr. 10, 2000, and L. 1998, Ch. 1, §§ 12–14, eff. Aug. 6, 1998, and shall apply to offenses committed on or after Sept. 1, 1998. Offenses committed prior to Sept. 1, 1998 shall be governed by the provisions of law in effect at the time the offense was committed; provided, however, that nothing contained herein shall be deemed to affect the application, qualification, expiration, reversion or repeal of any provision of law amended by any section of L. 1998, Ch. 1 and the provisions of L. 1998, Ch. 1 shall be applied or qualified or shall expire or revert or be deemed repealed in the same manner, to the same extent and on the same date as the case may be as otherwise provided by law; L. 1999, Ch. 452, § 8, eff. Sept. 1, 1999, extending expiration dates of subds. 2 and 3(b) to Sept. 1, 2001; L. 2000, Ch. 16, § 1, eff. Mar. 30, 2000, extending expiration date of subd. 1(a) to Sept. 1, 2001; L. 2001, Ch. 95, § 12, eff. July 13, 2001, extending expiration date of subd. 1(a) to Sept. 1, 2003; L. 2002, Ch. 81, Part D § 1, eff. May 29, 2002, extending expiration date of subd. 1(a)(i) to Sept. 1, 2003; L. 2003, Ch. 16, §§ 10, 17 and 19, eff. Mar. 31, 2003, extending expiration date to Sept. 1, 2005; L. 2003, Ch. 62, Part E, §§ 12–14, amending section heading, subds. 1(c) and 3(a), eff. May 15, 2003 and deemed in full force and effect Apr. 1, 2003; L. 2005, Ch. 56, Part D, §§ 15, 17, 20, extending repeal dates.

ANNOTATIONS

Revocation hearing; evidence.—Although parole violation report could be admitted into evidence at parole revocation hearing as a business record, the use of the record in the preparer's absence as the sole evidence against the defendant deprived the defendant of his due process right of confrontation where no good cause for preparer's absence was found. People ex rel. McGee v. Walters, 62 N.Y.2d 317, 476 N.Y.S.2d 803, 465 N.E.2d 342 (1984).

Revocation hearings; procedures.—An Article 78 proceeding commenced over three years after revocation of parole is time barred by the four-month period of limitation prescribed by CPLR 217, notwithstanding the fact that petitioner's revocation hearing did not take place within 90 days of the probable cause determination required by statute. Soto v. State Board of Parole, 107 A.D.2d 693, 484 N.Y.S.2d 49 (2d Dept. 1985).

—Where petitioner is not entitled to an immediate release from custody, the remedy of habeas corpus is not available to review parole revocation proceedings; any challenge must be by Article 78 petition. Soto v. State Board of Parole, 107 A.D.2d 693, 484 N.Y.S.2d 49 (2d Dept. 1985).

—Habeas corpus relief was not available to relator who was not subject to immediate release where condition of release requiring that relator reside in a residence approved by state parole division was not met; although the court had the power to convert the petition to an article 78 proceeding, relator did not request such relief and it was not appropriate based upon the record presented. People ex rel. Travis v. Coombe, 219 A.D.2d 881, 632 N.Y.S.2d 340 (4th Dept. 1995).

Rescission.—The Board of Parole has the power to rescind a parole grant either prior to its effective date or thereafter and because a rescission proceeding generally arises when it is discovered that the parole was granted in error and the authorities are attempting to terminate a release to which the parolee was never rightfully entitled, the petitioner is not entitled to a prompt hearing on the matter as he would be in a revocation proceeding. Trimarco v. New York State Board of Parole, 87 A.D.2d 114, 450 N.Y.S.2d 544 (2d Dept. 1982), dismissed, 58 N.Y.2d 968, 460 N.Y.S.2d 535, 447 N.E.2d 83 (1983).

§ 70.45. Determinate sentence; post-release supervision.

1. **In general.** Each determinate sentence also includes, as a part thereof, an additional period of post-release supervision. Such period shall commence as provided in subdivision five of this section and a violation of any condition of supervision occurring at any time during such period of post-release supervision shall subject the defendant to a further period of imprisonment of at least six months and up to the balance of the remaining period of post-release supervision, not to exceed five years. Such maximum limits shall not preclude a longer period of further imprisonment for a violation where the defendant is

subject to indeterminate and determinate sentences.

2. Period of post-release supervision. The period of post-release supervision for a determinate sentence shall be five years except that:

(a) such period shall be one year whenever a determinate sentence of imprisonment is imposed pursuant to subdivision two of section 70.70 of this article upon a conviction of a class D or class E felony offense;

(b) such period shall be not less than one year nor more than two years whenever a determinate sentence of imprisonment is imposed pursuant to subdivision two of section 70.70 of this article upon a conviction of a class B or class C felony offense;

(c) such period shall be not less than one year nor more than two years whenever a determinate sentence of imprisonment is imposed pursuant to subdivision three or four of section 70.70 of this article upon conviction of a class D or class E felony offense;

(d) such period shall be not less than one and one-half years nor more than three years whenever a determinate sentence of imprisonment is imposed pursuant to subdivision three or four of section 70.70 of this article upon conviction of a class B felony or class C felony offense;

(e) such period shall be not less than one and one-half years nor more than three years whenever a determinate sentence of imprisonment is imposed pursuant to subdivision three of section 70.02 of this article upon a conviction of a class D or class E violent felony offense;

(f) such period shall be not less than two and one-half years nor more than five years whenever a determinate sentence of imprisonment is imposed pursuant to subdivision three of section 70.02 of this article upon a conviction of a class B or class C violent felony offense.

3. Conditions of post-release supervision. The board of parole shall establish and impose conditions of post-release supervision in the same manner and to the same extent as it may establish and impose conditions in accordance with the executive law upon persons who are granted parole or conditional release; provided that, notwithstanding any other provision of law, the board of parole may impose as a condition of post-release supervision that for a period not exceeding six months immediately following release from the underlying term of imprisonment the person be transferred to and participate in the programs of a residential treatment facility as that term is defined in subdivision six of section two of the correction law. Upon release from the underlying term of imprisonment, the person shall be furnished with a written statement setting forth the conditions of post-release supervision in sufficient detail to provide for the person's conduct and supervision.

4. Revocation of post-release supervision. An alleged violation of any condition of post-release supervision shall be initiated, heard and determined in accordance with the provisions of subdivisions three and four of section two hundred fifty-nine-i of the executive law.

5. Calculation of service of period of post-release supervision. A period or periods of post-release supervision shall be calculated and served as follows:

(a) A period of post-release supervision shall commence upon the person's release from imprisonment to supervision by the division of parole and shall interrupt the running of the determinate sentence or sentences of imprisonment and the indeterminate sentence or sentences of imprisonment, if any. The remaining portion of any maximum or aggregate maximum term shall then be held in abeyance until the successful completion of the period of post-release supervision or the person's return to the custody of the department of correctional services, whichever occurs first.

(b) Upon the completion of the period of post-release supervision, the running of such sentence or sentences of imprisonment shall resume and only then shall the remaining portion of any maximum or aggregate maximum term previously held in abeyance be credited with and diminished by such period of post-release supervision. The person shall then be under the jurisdiction of the division of parole for the remaining portion of such maximum or aggregate maximum term.

(c) When a person is subject to two or more periods of post-release supervision, such periods shall merge with and be satisfied by discharge of the period of post-release supervision having the longest unexpired time to run; provided, however, any time served upon one period of post-release supervision shall not be credited to any other period of post-release supervision except as provided in subdivision five of section 70.30 of this article.

(d) When a person is alleged to have violated a condition of post-release supervision and the division of parole has declared such person to be delinquent: (i) the declaration of delinquency shall interrupt the period of post-release supervision; (ii) such interruption shall continue until the person is restored to post-release supervision; (iii) if the person is restored to post-release supervision without being returned to the department of correctional services, any time spent in custody from the date of delinquency until restoration to post-release supervision shall first be credited to the maximum or aggregate maximum term of the sentence or sentences of imprisonment, but only to the extent authorized by subdivision three of section 70.40 of this article. Any time spent in custody solely pursuant to such delinquency after completion of the maximum or aggregate maximum term of the sentence or sentences of imprisonment shall be credited to the period of post-release supervision, if any; and (iv) if the person is ordered returned to the department of correctional services, the person shall be required to serve a time assessment of at least six months before being re-released to post-release supervision. In the event the balance of the remaining period of post-release supervision is six months or less, such time assessment shall be six months unless a longer period is authorized pursuant to subdivision one of this section. The time assessment shall commence upon the issuance of a determination after a final hearing that the person has violated one or more conditions of supervision. While serving such assessment, the person shall not receive any good behavior allowance pursuant to section eight hundred three of the correction law. Any time spent in custody from the date of delinquency until return to the department of correctional services shall first be credited to the maximum or aggregate maximum term of the sentence or sentences of imprisonment, but only to the extent authorized by subdivision three of section 70.40 of this article. The maximum or aggregate maximum term of the sentence or sentences of imprisonment shall run while the person is serving such time assessment in the custody of the department of correctional services. Any time spent in custody solely pursuant to such delinquency after completion of the maximum or aggregate maximum term of the sentence or sentences of imprisonment shall be credited to the period of post-release supervision, if any.

(e) Notwithstanding paragraph (d) of this subdivision, in the event a person is sentenced to one or more additional indeterminate or determinate term or terms of imprisonment prior to the completion of the period of post-release supervision, such period of post-release supervision shall be held in abeyance and the person shall be committed to the custody of the department of correctional services in accordance with the requirements of the prior and additional terms of imprisonment.

(f) When a person serving a period of post-release supervision is returned to the department of correctional services pursuant to an additional consecutive sentence of imprisonment and without a declaration of delinquency, such period of post-release supervision shall be held in abeyance while the person is in the custody of the department of correctional services. Such period of post-release supervision shall resume running upon the person's re-release.

Added by L. 1998, Ch. 1, § 15, and shall apply to offenses committed on or after Sept. 1, 1998. Offenses committed prior to Sept. 1, 1998 shall be governed by the provisions of law in effect at the time the offense was committed; provided, however, that nothing contained herein shall be deemed to affect the application, qualification, expiration, reversion or repeal of any provision of law amended by any section of L. 1998, Ch. 1 and the provisions of L. 1998, Ch. 1 shall be applied or qualified or shall expire or revert or be deemed repealed in the same manner, to the same extent and on the same date as the case may be as otherwise provided by law. Amended by L. 2004, Ch. 738, § 35, eff. Jan. 13, 2005, amending subd. 2.

ANNOTATIONS

Post-release supervision.—As a second felony offender, defendant's sentence included a mandatory period of five years' post-release supervision, and failure of sentencing court to advise defendant of this direct consequence of his plea required that plea be vacated. People v. Catu, 4 N.Y.3d 242, 792 N.Y.S.2d 887, 825 N.E.2d 1081 (2005).

—Imposition of determinate sentence without the post-release supervision would violate Penal Law 70.45, rendering it illegal, and such requested relief may not be granted. People v. Rawdon, 296 A.D.2d 599, 744 N.Y.S.2d 573 (3d Dept. 2002).

—"The failure to inform a defendant of the post-release supervision component of a sentence does not, in and of itself, provide a basis for modifying the sentence." People v. Housman, 291 A.D.2d 665, 737 N.Y.S.2d 699 (3d Dept. 2002).

—A period of post-release supervision is an automatic and requisite part of every determinate sentence and is a "significant putative component" of that sentence; court's failure to inform defendant of post-release supervision during the plea required that defendant be allowed to withdraw the plea. People v. Jachimowicz, 292 A.D.2d 688, 738 N.Y.S.2d 770 (3d Dept. 2002).

—Where County Court's failure to advise defendant that he was subject to a mandatory five-year period of post-release supervision, and evidence showed that parties and County Court specifically agreed that defendant would waive indictment, be prosecuted upon a superior court information charging assault in the second degree, agree to a nonjury trial on stipulated facts, all with the expectation that defendant would be found guilty and sentenced to no more than a four-year determinate prison sentence, the arrangement was functionally equivalent to a guilty plea, and defendant was entitled to have his conviction reversed and remitted for futher proceedings. People v. Harler, 296 A.D.2d 712, 744 N.Y.S.2d 916 (3d Dept. 2002).

§ 70.70. Sentence of imprisonment for felony drug offender other than a class A felony.

1. 1. For the purposes of this section, the following terms shall mean:

(a) "Felony drug offender" means a defendant who stands convicted of any felony, defined in article two hundred twenty or two hundred twenty-one of this chapter other than a class A felony.

(b) "Second felony drug offender" means a second felony offender as that term is defined in subdivision one of section 70.06 of this article, who stands convicted of any felony, defined in article two hundred twenty or two hundred twenty-one of this chapter other than a class A felony.

(c) "Violent felony" shall have the same meaning as that term is defined in subdivision one of section 70.02 of this article.

2. Except as provided in subdivision three or four of this section, a sentence of imprisonment for a felony drug offender shall be a determinate sentence as provided in paragraph (a) of this subdivision.

(a) Term of determinate sentence. Except as provided in paragraph (b) or (c) of this subdivision, the court shall impose a determinate term of imprisonment upon a felony drug offender which shall be imposed by the court in whole or half years, which shall include as a part thereof a period of post-release supervision in accordance with section 70.45 of this article. The terms of imprisonment authorized for such determinate sentences are as follows:

(i) for a class B felony, the term shall be at least one year and shall not exceed nine years, except that for the class B felony of criminal sale of a controlled substance in or near school grounds as defined in subdivision two of section 220.44 of this chapter, the term shall be at least two years and shall not exceed nine years;

(ii) for a class C felony, the term shall be at least one year and shall not exceed five and one-half years;

(iii) for a class D felony, the term shall be at least one year and shall not exceed two and one-half years; and

(iv) for a class E felony, the term shall be at least one year and shall not exceed one and one-half years.

(b) Probation. Notwithstanding any other provision of law, the court may sentence a defendant convicted of a class B, class C, class D or class E felony offense defined in article two hundred twenty or two hundred twenty-one of this chapter to probation in accordance with the provisions of section 65.00 of this chapter.

(c) Alternative definite sentence for class C, class D, and class E felonies. If the court, having regard to the nature and circumstances of the crime and to the history and character of the defendant, is of the opinion that a sentence of imprisonment is necessary but that it would be unduly harsh to impose a determinate sentence upon a person convicted of a class C, class D or class E felony offense defined in article two hundred twenty or two hundred twenty-one of this chapter, the court may impose a definite sentence of imprisonment and fix a term of one year or less.

3. Sentence of imprisonment for second felony drug offender.

(a) Applicability. This subdivision shall apply to a second felony drug offender whose prior felony conviction was not a violent felony.

(b) Authorized sentence. Except as provided in paragraph (c) or (d) of this subdivision, when the court has found pursuant to the provisions of section 400.21 of the criminal procedure law that a defendant is a second felony drug offender who stands convicted of a class B, class C, class D or class E felony offense defined in article two hundred twenty or two hundred twenty-one of this chapter the court shall impose a determinate sentence of imprisonment. Such determinate sentence shall include as a part thereof a period of post-release supervision in accordance with section 70.45 of this article. The terms of such determinate sentence shall be imposed by the court in whole or half years as follows:

(i) for a class B felony, the term shall be at least three and one-half years and shall not exceed twelve years;

(ii) for a class C felony, the term shall be at least two years and shall not exceed eight years;

(iii) for a class D felony, the term shall be at least one and one-half years and shall not exceed four years; and

(iv) for a class E felony, the term shall be at least one and one-half years and shall not exceed two years.

(c) Lifetime probation. Notwithstanding any other provision of law, the court may sentence a defendant convicted of a class B felony defined in article two hundred twenty of this chapter to lifetime probation in accordance with the provisions of section 65.00 of this chapter.

(d) Sentence of parole supervision. In the case of a person sentenced for a specified offense or offenses as defined in subdivision five of section 410.91 of the criminal procedure law, who stands convicted of no other felony offense, who has not previously been convicted of either a violent felony offense as defined in section 70.02 of this article, a class A felony offense or a class B felony offense, and is not under the jurisdiction of or awaiting delivery to the department of correctional services, the court may direct that a determinate sentence imposed pursuant to this subdivision shall be executed as a parole supervision sentence as defined in and pursuant to the procedures prescribed in section 410.91 of the criminal procedure law.

4. Sentence of imprisonment for second felony drug offender previously convicted of a violent felony.

(a) Applicability. This subdivision shall apply to a second felony drug offender whose prior felony conviction was a violent felony.

(b) Authorized sentence. When the court has found pursuant to the provisions of section 400.21 of the criminal procedure law that a defendant is a second felony drug offender whose prior felony conviction was a violent felony, who stands convicted of a class B, class C, class D or class E felony offense defined in article two hundred twenty or two hundred twenty-one of this chapter, the court shall impose a determinate sentence of imprisonment. Such determinate sentence shall include as a part thereof a period of post-release supervision in accordance with section 70.45 of this article. The terms of such determinate sentence shall be imposed by the court in whole or half years as follows:

(i) for a class B felony, the term shall be at least six years and shall not exceed fifteen years;

(ii) for a class C felony, the term shall be at least three and one-half years and shall not exceed nine years;

(iii) for a class D felony, the term shall be at

least two and one-half years and shall not exceed four and one-half years; and

(iv) for a class E felony, the term shall be at least two years and shall not exceed two and one-half years.

Added by L. 2004, Ch. 738, § 36, eff. Jan. 13, 2005.

§ 70.71. Sentence of imprisonment for a class A felony drug offender.

1. For the purposes of this section, the following terms shall mean:

(a) "Felony drug offender" means a defendant who stands convicted of any class A felony as defined in article two hundred twenty of this chapter.

(b) "Second felony drug offender" means a second felony offender as that term is defined in subdivision one of section 70.06 of this article, who stands convicted of and is to be sentenced for any class A felony as defined in article two hundred twenty of this chapter.

(c) "Violent felony offense" shall have the same meaning as that term is defined in subdivision one of section 70.02 of this article.

2. Sentence of imprisonment for a first felony drug offender.

(a) Applicability. Except as provided in subdivision three or four of this section, this subdivision shall apply to a person convicted of a class A felony as defined in article two hundred twenty of this chapter.

(b) Authorized sentence. The court shall impose a determinate term of imprisonment which shall be imposed by the court in whole or half years and which shall include as a part thereof a period of post-release supervision in accordance with section 70.45 of this article. The terms authorized for such determinate sentences are as follows:

(i) for a class A-I felony, the term shall be at least eight years and shall not exceed twenty years;

(ii) for a class A-II felony, the term shall be at least three years and shall not exceed ten years.

(c) Lifetime probation. Notwithstanding any other provision of law, the court may sentence a defendant convicted of a class A-II felony defined in article two hundred twenty of this chapter to lifetime probation in accordance with the provisions of section 65.00 of this chapter.

3. Sentence of imprisonment for a second felony drug offender.

(a) Applicability. This subdivision shall apply to a second felony drug offender whose prior felony conviction or convictions did not include one or more violent felony offenses.

(b) Authorized sentence. When the court has found pursuant to the provisions of section 400.21 of the criminal procedure law that a defendant is a second felony drug offender who stands convicted of a class A felony as defined in article two hundred twenty or two hundred twenty-one of this chapter, the court shall impose a determinate sentence of imprisonment. Such determinate sentence shall include as a part thereof a period of post-release supervision in accordance with section 70.45 of this article. Such determinate sentence shall be imposed by the court in whole or half years as follows:

(i) for a class A-I felony, the term shall be at least twelve years and shall not exceed twenty-four years;

(ii) for a class A-II felony, the term shall be at least six years and shall not exceed fourteen years.

(c) Lifetime probation. Notwithstanding any other provision of law, the court may sentence a defendant convicted of a class A-II felony defined in article two hundred twenty of this chapter to lifetime probation in accordance with the provisions of section 65.00 of this chapter.

4. Sentence of imprisonment for a second felony drug offender previously convicted of a violent felony offense.

(a) Applicability. This subdivision shall apply to a second felony drug offender whose prior felony conviction was a violent felony.

(b) Authorized sentence. When the court has found pursuant to the provisions of section 400.21 of the criminal procedure law that a defendant is a second felony drug offender whose prior felony conviction was a violent felony, who stands convicted of a class A felony as defined in article two hundred twenty or two hundred twenty-one of this chapter, the court shall impose a determinate sentence of imprisonment. Such determinate sentence shall include as a part thereof a period of post-release supervision in accordance with section 70.45 of this article. Such determinate sentence shall be imposed by the court in whole or half years as follows:

(i) for a class A-I felony, the term shall be at least fifteen years and shall not exceed thirty years;

(ii) for a class A-II felony, the term shall be at least eight years and shall not exceed seventeen years.

Added by L. 2004, Ch. 738, § 36, eff. Jan. 13, 2005.

Note: L. 2004, Ch. 738, § 23 provides: "Notwithstanding any contrary provision of law, any person in the custody of the department of correctional services convicted of a class A-I felony offense defined in article 220 of the penal law which was committed prior to the effective date of this section [Dec. 14, 2004], and sentenced thereon to an indeterminate term of imprisonment with a minimum period not less than fifteen years pursuant to provisions of the law in effect prior to the effective date of this section, may, upon notice to the appropriate district attorney, apply to be resentenced in accordance with section 70.71 of the penal law in the court which imposed the original sentence. Such application shall be referred for determination to the judge or justice who imposed the original sentence upon such person. If at the time of the application the original sentencing judge or justice is a judge or justice of a court of competent jurisdiction, but such court is not the court in which the original sentence was imposed, then the application shall be randomly assigned to another judge or justice of the court in which the original sentence was imposed, provided that the district attorney and applicant may agree that the application be referred to the original sentencing judge. If the original sentencing judge is no longer a judge or justice of a court of competent jurisdiction, then the application shall be randomly assigned to another judge or justice of the court. If the court determines that such person does not stand convicted of such a class A-I felony offense, it shall issue an order denying the application. If the court determines that such person does stand convicted of such a class A-I felony offense, it may consider any facts or circumstances relevant to the imposition of a new sentence which are submitted by such person or the people and may, in addition, consider the institutional record of confinement of such person, but shall not order a new pre-sentence investigation and report or entertain any matter challenging the underlying basis of the subject conviction. The court shall offer an opportunity for a hearing and bring the applicant before it. The court may also conduct a hearing, if necessary, to determine whether such person qualifies to be resentenced or to determine any controverted issue of fact relevant to the issue of sentencing. Upon its review of the submissions and the findings of fact made in connection with the application, the court shall, unless substantial justice dictates that the application should be denied, in which event the court shall issue an order denying the application, specify and inform such person of the term of a determinate sentence of imprisonment it would impose upon such conviction, as authorized for a class A-I felony by and in accordance with section 70.71 of the penal law, in the event of a resentence and shall enter an order to that effect. The court shall notify the person that, unless he or she withdraws the application or appeals from such order, the court will enter an order vacating the sentence originally imposed and imposing a determinate sentence of imprisonment authorized to be imposed upon such conviction by section 70.71 of the penal law; provided that the term thereof shall be the same as the court previously specified. Any order issued by a court pursuant to this section must include written findings of fact and the reasons for such order. An appeal may be taken as of right in accordance with applicable provisions of the criminal procedure law: (a) from an order denying resentencing; or (b) from a new sentence imposed under this provision and may be based on the grounds that (i) the term of the new sentence is harsh or excessive; or (ii) that the term of the new sentence is unauthorized as a matter of law. An appeal in accordance with the applicable provisions of the criminal procedure law may also be taken as of right by the defendant from an order specifying and informing such person of the term of the determinate sentence the court would impose upon resentencing on the ground that the term of the proposed sentence is harsh or excessive; upon remand to the sentencing court following such appeal the defendant shall be given an opportunity to withdraw an application for resentencing before any resentence is imposed. Subdivision 1 of section 717 and subdivision 4 of section 722 of the county law and the related provisions of article 18-A of such law shall apply to the preparation of and proceedings on applications pursuant to this section. In calculating the term of imprisonment to be served by the person pursuant to the determinate sentence imposed, such person shall be credited for any jail time credited towards the subject conviction as well as any period of incarceration credited toward the sentence originally imposed."

ARTICLE 80—FINES

§ 80.00. Fine for felony.

1. A sentence to pay a fine for a felony shall be a sentence to pay an amount, fixed by the court, not exceeding the higher of

a. five thousand dollars; or

b. double the amount of the defendant's gain from the commission of the crime; or

c. if the conviction is for any felony defined in article two hundred twenty or two hundred twenty-one of this chapter, according to the following schedule:

(i) for A-I felonies, one hundred thousand dollars;

(ii) for A-II felonies, fifty thousand dollars;

(iii) for B felonies, thirty thousand dollars;

(iv) for C felonies, fifteen thousand dollars.

When imposing a fine pursuant to the provisions of this paragraph, the court shall consider the profit gained by defendant's conduct, whether the amount of the fine is disproportionate to the conduct in which defendant engaged, its impact on the victims, and defendant's economic circumstances, including the defendant's ability to pay, the effect of the fine upon his or her immediate family or any other persons to whom the defendant owes an obligation of support.

2. As used in this section the term "gain" means the amount of money or the value of property derived from the commission of the crime, less the amount of money or the value of property returned to the victim of the crime or seized by or surrendered to lawful authority prior to the time sentence is imposed.

3. When the court imposes a fine for a felony pursuant to paragraph b of subdivision one of this section, the court shall make a finding as to the amount of the defendant's gain from the crime. If the record does not contain sufficient evidence to support such a finding or to permit adequate consideration of the matters specified in paragraph c of subdivision one of this section, the court may conduct a hearing upon such issues.

4. Exception. The provisions of this section shall not apply to a corporation.

5. All moneys in excess of five thousand dollars received or collected in payment of a fine imposed pursuant to paragraph c of subdivision one of this section are the property of the state and the state comptroller shall deposit all such fines to the rehabilitative alcohol and substance treatment fund established pursuant to section ninety-seven-cc of the state finance law.

6. Notwithstanding any inconsistent provision of subdivision one of this section a sentence to pay a fine for a felony set forth in the vehicle and traffic law shall be a sentence to pay an amount fixed by the court in accordance with the provisions of the law that defines the crime.

7. When the court imposes a fine pursuant to section 145.22 or 145.23 of this chapter, the court shall direct that no less than ten percent of such fine be credited to the state cemetery vandalism restoration and administration fund created pursuant to section ninety-seven-r of the state finance law.

Amended by L. 1977, Ch. 352; L. 1989, Ch. 338; L. 1990, Ch. 892; L. 1997, Ch. 165, § 3, adding subd. 7, eff. Nov. 1, 1997.

ANNOTATIONS

Restitution distinguished.—The restitution statute focuses on making the crime victim whole; to the extent that the defendant has gained from the commission of the crime, the gain is governed by the fine statute; any gain is subtracted from the amount of money or value of property returned to the victim. People v. Young, 163 Misc. 2d 72, 618 N.Y.S.2d 983 (Sup. Ct. N.Y. Co. 1994).

Resentence.—Where the appellate court had returned the case to the sentencing court for a proper determination of the gain from gambling activities and imposition of a proper fine pursuant to PL § 80.00, it was improper to resentence defendants, who had served the term initially imposed and had been released, to longer periods of imprisonment. People v. Yannicelli, 40 N.Y.2d 598, 389 N.Y.S.2d 290, 357 N.E.2d 947 (1976).

Ability to pay irrelevant.—The determination of the amount of a fine, unlike restitution or reparation, is not based upon the defendant's ability to pay; the fine statute does not require a finding of such ability at the time the fine is imposed. People v. Young, 163 Misc. 2d 72, 618 N.Y.S.2d 983 (Sup. Ct. N.Y. Co. 1994).

Findings required by court.—It was error to impose a fine without considering the profit gained by defendant's conduct, whether the amount of the fine is disproportionate to the defendant's conduct, and the defendant's economic circumstances; the People's argument that these considerations were unnecessary because defendant was convicted of a felony defined in Penal Law Articles 220 and 110 rather than Article 220 was meritless. People v. Colburn, 213 A.D.2d 746, 622 N.Y.S.2d 1003 (3d Dept. 1995).

§ 80.05. Fines for misdemeanors and violations.

1. Class A misdemeanor. A sentence to pay a fine for a class A misdemeanor shall be a sentence to pay an amount, fixed by the court, not exceeding one thousand dollars, provided, however, that a sentence imposed for a violation of section 215.80 of this chapter may include a

fine in an amount equivalent to double the value of the property unlawfully disposed of in the commission of the crime.

2. Class B misdemeanor. A sentence to pay a fine for a class B misdemeanor shall be a sentence to pay an amount, fixed by the court, not exceeding five hundred dollars.

3. Unclassified misdemeanor. A sentence to pay a fine for an unclassified misdemeanor shall be a sentence to pay an amount, fixed by the court, in accordance with the provisions of the law or ordinance that defines the crime.

4. Violation. A sentence to pay a fine for a violation shall be a sentence to pay an amount, fixed by the court, not exceeding two hundred fifty dollars.

In the case of a violation defined outside this chapter, if the amount of the fine is expressly specified in the law or ordinance that defines the offense, the amount of the fine shall be fixed in accordance with that law or ordinance.

5. Alternative sentence. If a person has gained money or property through the commission of any misdemeanor or violation then upon conviction thereof, the court, in lieu of imposing the fine authorized for the offense under one of the above subdivisions, may sentence the defendant to pay an amount, fixed by the court, not exceeding double the amount of the defendant's gain from the commission of the offense; provided, however, that the amount fixed by the court pursuant to this subdivision upon a conviction under section 11-1904 of the environmental conservation law shall not exceed five thousand dollars. In such event the provisions of subdivisions two and three of section 80.00 shall be applicable to the sentence.

6. Exception. The provisions of this section shall not apply to a corporation.

Amended by L. 1977, Ch. 352; L. 1984, Ch. 669; L. 1999, Ch. 210, eff. Nov. 1, 1999, amending subd. 5.

ANNOTATION

Generally.—The Penal Law provides for the imposition of a fine not to exceed double the amount of defendant's gain from the commission of the crime. People v. Young, 163 Misc. 2d 72, 618 N.Y.S.2d 983 (Sup. Ct. N.Y. Co. 1994).

§ 80.10. Fines for corporations.

1. In general. A sentence to pay a fine, when imposed on a corporation for an offense defined in this chapter or for an offense defined outside this chapter for which no special corporate fine is specified, shall be a sentence to pay an amount, fixed by the court, not exceeding:

(a) Ten thousand dollars, when the conviction is of a felony;

(b) Five thousand dollars, when the conviction is of a class A misdemeanor or of an unclassified

misdemeanor for which a term of imprisonment in excess of three months is authorized;

(c) Two thousand dollars, when the conviction is of a class B misdemeanor or of an unclassified misdemeanor for which the authorized term of imprisonment is not in excess of three months;

(d) Five hundred dollars, when the conviction is of a violation;

(e) Any higher amount not exceeding double the amount of the corporation's gain from the commission of the offense.

2. Exception. In the case of an offense defined outside this chapter, if a special fine for a corporation is expressly specified in the law or ordinance that defines the offense, the fine fixed by the court shall be as follows:

(a) An amount within the limits specified in the law or ordinance that defines the offense; or

(b) Any higher amount not exceeding double the amount of the corporation's gain from the commission of the offense.

3. Determination of amount or value. When the court imposes the fine authorized by paragraph (e) of subdivision one or paragraph (b) of subdivision two for any offense the provisions of subdivision three of section 80.00 shall be applicable to the sentence.

ANNOTATION

"Special fine."—Court was authorized to sentence corporation to $2,000 maximum fine for each unclassified misdemeanor violation of city transportation code, where Code did not provide special corporate fine for violation of its terms. People v. Causeway Constr. Corp., 169 Misc. 2d 70, 649 N.Y.S.2d 630 (1st Dept. 1996).

§ 80.15. Multiple offenses.

Where a person is convicted of two or more offenses committed through a single act or omission, or through an act or omission which in itself constituted one of the offenses and also was a material element of the other, and the court imposes a sentence of imprisonment or a fine or both for one of the offenses, a fine shall not be imposed for the other. The provisions of this section shall not apply to any offense or offenses set forth in the vehicle and traffic law.

Amended by L. 1990, Ch. 892.

ANNOTATIONS

Maximum fines.—Where defendant was fined $10,000 on each of two counts of criminally negligent homicide and $5,000 for each of seven counts of reckless endangerment in the second degree, fines merged into a maximum fine of $10,000. People v. Congregation Khal Chaisidiei, 232 A.D.2d 919, 649 N.Y.S.2d 499 (3d Dept. 1996).

—Where two counts of vehicular manslaughter were committed through a single act, the imposition of two fines was improper. People v. Atwood, 2 A.D.3d 1331, 768 N.Y.S.2d 918 (4th Dept. 2003).

ARTICLE 85—SENTENCE OF INTERMITTENT IMPRISONMENT

Section

85.00   Sentence of intermittent imprisonment.

85.05   Modification and revocation of sentences of intermittent imprisonment.

85.10   Commitment; notifications; warrants.

85.15   Subsequent sentences.

§ 85.00. Sentence of intermittent imprisonment.

1. Definition. A sentence of intermittent imprisonment is a revocable sentence of imprisonment to be served on days or during certain periods of days, or both, specified by the court as part of the sentence. A person who receives a sentence of intermittent imprisonment shall be incarcerated in the institution to which he is committed at such times as are specified by the court in the sentence.

2. Authorization for use of sentence. The court may impose a sentence of intermittent imprisonment in any case where:

(a) the court is imposing sentence, upon a person other than a second or persistent felony offender, for a class D or class E felony or for any offense that is not a felony; and

(b) the court is not imposing any other sentence of imprisonment upon the defendant at the same time; and

(c) the defendant is not under any other sentence of imprisonment with a term in excess of fifteen days imposed by any other court; and

(d) [*Repealed.*]

3. Duration of sentence. A sentence of intermittent imprisonment may be for any term that could be imposed as a definite sentence of imprisonment for the offense for which such sentence is imposed. The term of the sentence shall commence on the day it is imposed and shall be calculated upon the basis of the duration of its term, rather than upon the basis of the days spent in confinement, so that no person shall be subject to any such sentence for a period that is longer than a period that commences on the date the sentence is imposed and ends on the date the term of the longest definite sentence for the offense would have expired, after deducting the credit that would have been applicable to a definite sentence for jail time but without regard to any credit authorized to be allowed against the term of a definite sentence for good behavior. The provisions of section five hundred-l of the correction law shall not be applicable to a sentence of intermittent imprisonment.

4. Imposition of sentence.

(a) When the court imposes a sentence of intermittent imprisonment the court shall specify in the sentence:

(i) that the court is imposing a sentence of intermittent imprisonment;

(ii) the term of such sentence;

(iii) the days or parts of days on which the sentence is to be served, but except as provided in paragraph (iv) hereof such specification need not include the dates on which such days fall; and

(iv) the first and last dates on which the defendant is to be incarcerated under the sentence.

(b) The court, in its discretion, may specify any day or days or parts thereof on which the defendant shall be confined and may specify a period to commence at the commencement of the sentence and not to exceed fifteen days during which the defendant is to be continuously confined.

Amended by L. 1973, Chs. 277, 523; L. 1987, Ch 304.

ANNOTATIONS

Weekend sentences.—The length of an intermittent sentence is measured from the first day of confinement to the last day of confinement rather than counting the number of days actually spent in jail. Since the sentence imposed by Family Court here spans 90 weekends and thus exceeds six months, the sentence is illegal and must be reversed. De Ruzzio v. De Ruzzio, 288 A.D.2d 725, 733 N.Y.S.2d 276 (3d Dept. 2001).

—Sentence imposed upon a defendant, who was convicted of trespass, to spend the next 52 weekends in the county jail violated PL § 85.00 by extending the incarceration of the defendant beyond the period of one year from the date of sentence. People v. White, 83 A.D.2d 668, 442 N.Y.S.2d 186 (3d Dept. 1981).

—Defendant, who had been sentenced to a year of weekends but was informed that if he violated any conditions of the sentence he would be resentenced to straight time, could not be resentenced to a 4 year indeterminate term of imprisonment upon being found guilty of violating the terms of the original sentence; the matter was remitted for resentencing in accordance with the promise made and full credit was to be afforded for time already served. People v. Murdie, 73 A.D.2d 1008, 424 N.Y.S.2d 63 (3d Dept. 1980).

—Defendant who received intermittent sentence was entitled to receive credit for jail time actually served, rejecting argument that he should be credited with seven days for each of the eighteen weekends he was incarcerated instead of the actual three days confinement each weekend. People ex rel. Bailey v. Netzel, 169 Misc. 2d 623, 647 N.Y.S.2d 343 (Sup. Ct. Erie Co. 1996).

§ 85.05. Modification and revocation of sentences of intermittent imprisonment.

1. Authorization. A sentence of intermittent imprisonment may be modified by the court in its discretion upon application of the defendant; and the court on its own motion may modify or revoke any such sentence if:

(a) the court is satisfied during the term of the sentence that the defendant has committed another offense during such term;

(b) the defendant has failed to report to the institution to which he has been committed, or to the institution designated by the head of the agency to which he has been committed, on a day or dates specified in the commitment and is unable or unwilling to furnish a reasonable and acceptable explanation for such failure; or

(c) the defendant has violated a rule or regulation of the institution or agency to which he has been committed and the head of such institution or agency or someone delegated by him has reported such violation in writing to the court.

2. Interruption of sentence. In any case where the defendant fails to report to the institution or to an institution of the agency to which he has been committed, the term of the sentence shall be interrupted and such interruption shall continue until the defendant either reports to such institution or appears before the court that imposed the sentence, whichever occurs first. If the defendant reports to the institution before he appears before the court, he shall be brought before the court.

3. Action by court. The court shall not modify or revoke a sentence of intermittent imprisonment unless the defendant has been afforded an opportunity to be heard. Any modification of a sentence of intermittent imprisonment:

(a) may provide (i) for different or additional or fewer days or parts of days on which the defendant is to be confined, or (ii) where the defendant has failed to report as specified in the sentence, an extension of the term of the sentence for the period during which it was interrupted, or (iii) for both; and

(b) shall be by written order of the court and shall be delivered and filed in the same manner as the original sentence, as specified in subdivision two of section 85.10 of this article.

4. Jail time. Where a sentence of intermittent imprisonment is revoked and a sentence of imprisonment is imposed in its place for the same offense, time spent in confinement under the sentence of intermittent imprisonment shall be calculated as jail time under subdivision three of section 70.30 of this chapter and shall be added to any jail time accrued against such sentence prior to imposition thereof.

Added by L. 1970, Ch. 477.

ANNOTATION

Resentence.—Defendant, who had been sentenced to a year of weekends but was informed that if he violated any conditions of the sentence he would be resentenced to straight time, could not be resentenced to a 4 year indeterminate term of imprisonment upon being found guilty of violating the terms of the original sentence; the matter was remitted for resentencing in accordance with the promise made and full credit was to be afforded for time already served. People v. Murdie, 73 A.D.2d 1008, 424 N.Y.S.2d 63 (3d Dept. 1980).

§ 85.10. Commitment; notifications; warrants.

1. Commitment. Commitment under a sentence of intermittent imprisonment and execution of the judgment shall be in accordance with the procedure applicable to a definite sentence of imprisonment, except that: (a) detention of the defendant under the judgment shall be executed during the times specified in the sentence; and (b) the court may provide that the defendant is to report to a specified institution on a specified date at a specified time to commence service of the sentence and in such case the defendant need not be taken into or retained in custody when sentence is imposed.

2. Notifications. A written copy of the sentence imposed by the court signed by the judge who imposed the sentence shall be delivered to the defendant and shall be annexed to the commitment and to each copy of the commitment required to be delivered or filed. When the defendant is not taken into or retained in custody at the time sentence is imposed, the commitment and copy of the sentence shall forthwith be delivered to the person whose duty it is to execute the judgment. If at any time the defendant fails to report for confinement as provided in the sentence the officer in charge of the institution or department to which such commitment is made or someone designated by such officer shall forthwith notify the court in writing of such failure to report.

3. Warrants. Upon receipt of any such notification the court may issue a warrant to an appropriate police officer or peace officer directing him to take the defendant into custody and bring him before the court. The court may then commit such person to custody or fix bail or release him on his own recognizance for future appearance before the court.

Added by L. 1970, Ch. 477; L. 1980, Ch. 843.

§ 85.15. Subsequent sentences.

1. [*Effective until Sept. 1, 2009.*] Indeterminate and determinate sentences. The service of an indeterminate or a determinate sentence of imprisonment shall satisfy any sentence of intermittent imprisonment imposed on a person for an offense committed prior to the time the indeterminate or determinate sentence was imposed. A person who is serving a sentence of intermittent imprisonment at the time an indeterminate or a determinate sentence of imprisonment is imposed shall be delivered to the custody of the state department of correctional services to commence service of the indeterminate or determinate sentence immediately.

1. [*Effective Sept. 1, 2009.*] Indeterminate and determinate sentences. Indeterminate and reformatory sentences. The service of an indeterminate or a reformatory sentence of imprisonment shall

satisfy any sentence of intermittent imprisonment imposed on a person for an offense committed prior to the time the indeterminate or reformatory sentence was imposed. A person who is serving a sentence of intermittent imprisonment at the time an indeterminate or a reformatory sentence of imprisonment is imposed shall be delivered to the custody of the state department of correction to commence service of the indeterminate or reformatory sentence immediately.

2. Definite sentences. If a definite sentence of imprisonment is imposed on a person who is under a previously imposed sentence of intermittent imprisonment, such person shall commence service of the definite sentence immediately.

Where such definite sentence is for a term in excess of thirty days, the service of such sentence shall satisfy the sentence of intermittent imprisonment unless the sentence of intermittent imprisonment is revoked, or a warrant is issued pursuant to subdivision three of section 85.10 of this article and prior to satisfaction of, or conditional release under, such definite sentence of imprisonment.

Added by L. 1970, Ch. 477; **Amended** by L. 1995, Ch. 3, § 20, amending subd. 1 by changing the word "reformatory" to "determinate" throughout the subd., and changing "state department of correction" to "state department of correctional services." The amendment is eff. Oct. 1, 1995, repealed on Sept. 30, 2005 pursuant to L. 1995, Ch. 3, § 74, paragraph (d); L. 2005, Ch. 56, Part D, § 20, extending repeal date of amendment.

PART THREE—SPECIFIC OFFENSES

TITLE G—ANTICIPATORY OFFENSES

ARTICLE 100—CRIMINAL SOLICITATION

§ 100.00. Criminal solicitation in the fifth degree.

A person is guilty of criminal solicitation in the fifth degree when, with intent that another person engage in conduct constituting a crime, he solicits, requests, commands, importunes or otherwise attempts to cause such other person to engage in such conduct.

Criminal solicitation in the fifth degree is a violation.

Amended by L. 1978, Ch. 422.

ANNOTATIONS

Generally.—"The basic statutory definition of criminal solicitation is that with intent that another person shall 'engage in conduct constituting a crime' the accused 'solicits, requests, commands, importunes or otherwise attempts to cause such other person to engage in such conduct.' This basic definitory language is continued through three grades of solicitation, the gravity depending on what crime the conduct sought to be induced would effectuate." People v. Lubow, 29 N.Y.2d 58, 323 N.Y.S.2d 829, 272 N.E.2d 331 (1971).

"If the conduct would be 'a crime,' it is criminal solicitation in the third degree, a 'violation' (§ 100.00); if the conduct would be 'a felony' it is criminal solicitation in the second degree, a class A misdemeanor (§ 100.05); and if the conduct would be murder or kidnapping in the first degree it is criminal solicitation in the first degree, a class D felony (§ 100.10)." People v. Lubow, 29 N.Y.2d 58, 323 N.Y.S.2d 829, 272 N.E.2d 331 (1971).

—The gravamen of the crime of criminal solicitation is the request or other attempt by the defendant to get the person solicited to engage in criminal conduct; it is not necessary the person solicited engage in any criminal activity or even any preparation for criminal activity. People v. Agnello, 165 Misc. 2d 855, 630 N.Y.S.2d 614 (Rochester City Ct. Monroe Co. 1995).

§ 100.05. Criminal solicitation in the fourth degree.

A person is guilty of criminal solicitation in the fourth degree when:

1. with intent that another person engage in conduct constituting a felony, he solicits, requests, commands, importunes or otherwise attempts to cause such other person to engage in such conduct; or [~~more than one way to do it~~]

2. being over eighteen years of age, with intent that another person under sixteen years of age engage in conduct that would constitute a crime, he solicits, requests, commands, importunes or otherwise attempts to cause such other person to engage in such conduct.

Criminal solicitation in the fourth degree is a class A misdemeanor.

Amended by L. 1978, Ch. 422.

ANNOTATIONS

Corpus delicti of solicitation.—The communication itself, with intent the other person engage in the unlawful conduct is enough; it needs no corroboration, and nothing need be done in furtherance of the communication ("solicits, commands, importunes") to constitute the offense. People v. Lubow, 29 N.Y.2d 58, 323 N.Y.S.2d 829, 272 N.E.2d 331 (1971).

—Crime of solicitation is complete when the communication is made with the intent that the other person commit the intended crime; no overt acts to effectuate the underlying crime are necessary. People v. Cheathem, 239 A.D.2d 595, 658 N.Y.S.2d 84 (2d Dept. 1997).

—Criminal solicitation in the fourth degree was supported by evidence that, although defendant did not solicit the witness to impersonate a claimant in a worker's compensation case, he did not intercede and stop and fraud when he became aware that the witness was perjuring herself. In re Hobika, 271 A.D.2d 12, 707 N.Y.S.2d 279 (4th Dept. 2000).

§ 100.08. Criminal solicitation in the third degree.

A person is guilty of criminal solicitation in the third degree when, being over eighteen years of age, with intent that another person under sixteen years of age engage in conduct that would constitute a felony, he solicits, requests, commands, importunes or otherwise attempts to cause such other person to engage in such conduct.

Criminal solicitation in the third degree is a class E felony.

Added by L. 1978, Ch. 422.

§ 100.10. Criminal solicitation in the second degree.

A person is guilty of criminal solicitation in the second degree when, with intent that another person engage in conduct constituting a class A felony, he solicits, requests, commands, importunes or otherwise attempts to cause such other person to engage in such conduct.

Criminal solicitation in the second degree is a class D felony.

Amended by L. 1972, Ch. 292; L. 1978, Ch. 422.

ANNOTATIONS

Generally.—The jury properly convicted the defendant of criminal solicitation in the second degree where the defendant solicited an undercover police officer to kill three witnesses who defendant knew were planning to testify against him. People v. Blair, 144 A.D.2d 972, 534 N.Y.S.2d 616, 617 (2d Dept. 1988).

Sentence.—Defendant was properly sentenced as a second felony offender; defendant's first felony, solicitation to commit murder, was committed in North Carolina, and the North Carolina crime was equivalent to the New York crime of criminal solicitation in the second degree. People v. Long, 207 A.D.2d 988, 617 N.Y.S.2d 97 (4th Dept. 1994).

§ 100.13. Criminal solicitation in the first degree.

A person is guilty of criminal solicitation in the first degree when, being over eighteen years of age, with intent that another person under sixteen years of age engage in conduct that would constitute a class A felony, he solicits, requests, commands, importunes or otherwise attempts to cause such other person to engage in such conduct.

Criminal solicitation in the first degree is a class C felony.

Added by L. 1978, Ch. 422.

§ 100.15. Criminal solicitation; no defense.

It is no defense to a prosecution for criminal solicitation that the person solicited could not be guilty of the crime solicited owing to criminal irresponsibility or other legal incapacity or exemption, or to unawareness of the criminal nature of the conduct solicited or of the defendant's criminal purpose or to other factors precluding the mental state required for the commission of the crime in question.

§ 100.20. Criminal solicitation; exemption.

A person is not guilty of criminal solicitation when his solicitation constitutes conduct of a kind that is necessarily incidental to the commission of the crime solicited. When under such circumstances the solicitation constitutes an offense other than criminal solicitation which is related to but separate from the crime solicited, the actor is guilty of such related and separate offense only and not of criminal solicitation.

ANNOTATIONS

Exemption provision.—In a sting operation conducted by police in which undercover officers posed as street drug dealers to lure would-be buyers of "marihuana" (in this case oregano), the criminal sale of marihuana could not have occurred but for the would-be buyers' direct participation; therefore, their conduct was necessarily incidental to the commission of the completed crime and the statutory exemption for criminal solicitation applied. People v. Allen, 92 N.Y.2d 378, 681 N.Y.S.2d 216, 703 N.E.2d 1229 (1998).

Necessarily incidental.—Section 100.20 mandates that a person is not guilty of criminal solicitation when that person's conduct in the solicitation is necessarily incidental to the commission of the crime solicited; the defendants' requests to undercover police officers in this case to sell them marijuana were necessarily incidental to the sale of marijuana, since it was the sale that was alleged to be the conduct that the defendants were trying to get another person to engage in. People v. Agnello, 630 N.Y.S.2d 614 (Rochester City Ct. Monroe Co. 1995).

ARTICLE 105—CONSPIRACY

LexisNexis Cross References

Criminal Defense Techniques, Vol. 3, Ch. 59, Defense of a Conspiracy Case; *New York Criminal Practice (2d ed.),* Vol. 6, Ch. 56, Attempt, Solicitation, Conspiracy and Facilitation; *see generally Prosecution and Defense of Criminal Conspiracy Cases.*

§ 105.00. Conspiracy in the sixth degree.

A person is guilty of conspiracy in the sixth degree when, with intent that conduct constituting a crime be performed, he agrees with one or more persons to engage in or cause the performance of such conduct.

Conspiracy in the sixth degree is a class B misdemeanor.

Added by L. 1973, Ch. 1051; **Amended** by L. 1978, Ch. 422.

ANNOTATION

Evidence.—Prima facie case of conspiracy requires evidence "that a person, with intent that conduct constituting a crime be performed, agrees with one or more persons to engage or cause the performance of such conduct," here non-hearsay evidence established a clear nexus between the defendant and the murder which included defendant's admission that he offered to pay $5,000 for the murder of Ortiz to any one of several associates present at the meeting. People v. Caban, 4 A.D.3d 274, 772 N.Y.S.2d 675 (1st Dept. 2004), *aff'd,* 5 N.Y.3d 143, 800 N.Y.S.2d 70, 833 N.E.2d 213 (2005).

—Although evidence established that only one person used knife that inflicted stab wounds, defendant was part of a group of at least four people who acted with a community of purpose; since there is "no distinction between liability as a principal and criminal culpability as an accessory," conviction for assault in the third degree was affirmed. People v. Staples, 19 A.D.3d 1096, 796 N.Y.S.2d 209 (4th Dept. 2005).

Two or more persons required.—Article 105 of the Penal Law deals with the classic "anticipatory offenses" which are distinguished by a corrupt agreement by two or more persons to commit a specific "object crime." People v. Csabon, 79 A.D.2d 609, 433 N.Y.S.2d 487 (2d Dept. 1980).

§ 105.05. Conspiracy in the fifth degree.

A person is guilty of conspiracy in the fifth degree when, with intent that conduct constituting:

1. a felony be performed, he agrees with one or more persons to engage in or cause the performance of such conduct; or

2. a crime be performed, he, being over eighteen years of age, agrees with one or more persons under sixteen years of age to engage in or cause the performance of such conduct.

Conspiracy in the fifth degree is a class A misdemeanor.

Added by L. 1973, Ch. 1051; **Amended** by L. 1978, Ch. 422.

ANNOTATIONS

Corresponding federal crime.—Conspiracy in the fifth degree corresponds to the federal crime of conspiracy to defraud the United States in violation of 18 U.S.C. § 371. *In re* Papworth, 208 A.D.2d 69, 622 N.Y.S.2d 407 (4th Dept. 1995).

Evidence.—Verdict convicting defendants of scheme to defraud but acquitting them of conspiracy in the fifth degree was not a repugnant verdict since defendants can act in concert without forming a conspiracy. People v. Kronberg, 277 A.D.2d 182, 716 N.Y.S.2d 653 (1st Dept. 2000), *appeal denied,* 96 N.Y.2d 785 (2001).

—Agreement to reveal confidential and privileged information acquired in the course of attorney/client relationship and to testify falsely in future court proceedings was sufficient to establish existence of a conspiracy. People v. Canale, 268 A.D.2d 699, 704 N.Y.S.2d 151 (3d Dept. 2000).

§ 105.10. Conspiracy in the fourth degree.

A person is guilty of conspiracy in the fourth degree when, with intent that conduct constituting:

1. a class B or class C felony be performed, he or she agrees with one or more persons to engage in or cause the performance of such conduct; or

2. a felony be performed, he or she, being over eighteen years of age, agrees with one or more persons under sixteen years of age to engage in or cause the performance of such conduct; or

3. the felony of money laundering in the third

degree as defined in section 470.10 of this chapter, be performed, he or she agrees with one or more persons to engage in or cause the performance of such conduct.

Conspiracy in the fourth degree is a class E felony.

Added by L. 1973, Ch. 1051; **Amended** by L. 1978, Ch. 422; L. 2000, Ch. 489, § 1, eff. Nov. 1, 2000.

ANNOTATIONS

Charge to jury.—The instruction that the jury could not convict one defendant and not the other on the conspiracy charge was error in light of the present wording of PL § 105.10 and the expressed provision in PL § 105.30; however, an exception to the charge on that ground must be made to preserve the error for review by the appellate court. People v. Teeter, 47 N.Y.2d 1002, 420 N.Y.S.2d 217, 394 N.E.2d 286 (1979).

Corresponding federal crime.—Conspiring to commit bank fraud in violation of 18 U.S.C. § 371 is tantamount to the New York crime of conspiracy to commit grand larceny in the second degree which, in New York, is conspiracy in the fourth degree. In re Kim, 209 A.D.2d 127, 625 N.Y.S.2d 490 (1st Dept. 1995).

—Federal conspiracy and wire fraud convictions in violation of 18 U.S.C. § 371 and 1343 were essentially similar to conspiracy in the fourth degree to commit grand larceny in the second degree. In re Levy, 211 A.D.2d 10, 626 N.Y.S.2d 247 (2d Dept. 1995).

Sufficiency of evidence.—The requirements of Penal Law § 105.10(1) were satisfied by evidence that defendant, with another, planned and did cause "serious physical injury to the victim through an attack with a deadly weapon" (a concealed knife), a class B felony of assault in the first degree. People v. Hafeez, 100 N.Y.2d 253, 762 N.Y.S.2d 572, 792 N.E.2d 1060 (2003).

§ 105.13. Conspiracy in the third degree.

A person is guilty of conspiracy in the third degree when, with intent that conduct constituting a class B or a class C felony be performed, he, being over eighteen years of age, agrees with one or more persons under sixteen years of age to engage in or cause the performance of such conduct.

Conspiracy in the third degree is a class D felony.

Added by L. 1978, Ch. 422.

ANNOTATION

Conspiracy; crime.—The crime of conspiracy is an offense separate from the crime that is the object of the conspiracy and once an illicit agreement is shown the overt act of any conspirator may be attributed to other conspirators to establish the offense of conspiracy; the overt act itself is not the crime in the conspiracy prosecution, but merely an element that has as its basis the agreement. People v. McGee, 49 N.Y.2d 48, 424 N.Y.S.2d 157, 399 N.E.2d 1177 (1979), cert. denied, 446 U.S. 942 (1980).

§ 105.15. Conspiracy in the second degree.

A person is guilty of conspiracy in the second degree when, with intent that conduct constituting a class A felony be performed, he agrees with one or more persons to engage in or cause the performance of such conduct.

Conspiracy in the second degree is a class B felony.

Added by L. 1973, Ch. 1051; **Amended** by L. 1978, Ch. 422.

ANNOTATIONS

Evidence.—Where a defendant is convicted of conspiracy to commit murder, it is not relevant to the validity of the conviction that the murder was carried out, or even that the defendant had no intent to commit the crime, as long as he believed he had entered into the agreement; the acceptance of the invitation to commit murder is a "verbal act which rendered defendant and his co-conspirators culpable for the inchoate crime of conspiracy, even if the planned substantive crime never came to fruition." People v. Caban, 5 N.Y.3d 143, 800 N.Y.S.2d 70, 833 N.E.2d 213 (2005).

—Defendant's agreement with his employer to procure an individual to carry out two murders was an agreement to cause the performance of conduct constituting a class A felony; adequate proof of defendant's guilt of conspiracy in the second degree was presented. People v. Ayala, 216 A.D.2d 7, 627 N.Y.S.2d 374 (1st Dept. 1995).

—Viewed in the light most favorable to the People, the evidence was sufficient to convict the defendant of conspiracy in the second degree. People v. Smith, 209 A.D.2d 996, 622 N.Y.S.2d 163 (4th Dept. 1994); People v. Morgan, 209 A.D.2d 952, 619 N.Y.S.2d 983 (4th Dept. 1994).

§ 105.17. Conspiracy in the first degree.

A person is guilty of conspiracy in the first degree when, with intent that conduct constituting a class A felony be performed, he, being over eighteen years of age, agrees with one or more persons under sixteen years of age to engage in or cause the performance of such conduct.

Conspiracy in the first degree is a class A-1 felony.

Added by L. 1978, Ch. 422.

ANNOTATIONS

Conspiracy must be established before statements in furtherance of the conspiracy are admissible.—A conviction for conspiracy in the first degree must be reversed where hearsay statements in furtherance of the conspiracy were admitted without the People first proving that a conspiracy existed at the time the statements were made. People v. Malagon, 50 N.Y.2d 954, 431 N.Y.S.2d 460, 409 N.E.2d 934 (1980).

Conspiring with a minor.—The legislature intentionally raised penalties for those adults who commit criminal facilitation, solicitation or conspiracy by involving juveniles; the age factor does not require that the juvenile be the person to engage in or cause the performance of the object crime. People v. Austin, 9 A.D.3d 369, 780 N.Y.S.2d 23 (2d Dept. 2004).

§ 105.20. Conspiracy; pleading and proof; necessity of overt act.

A person shall not be convicted of conspiracy unless an overt act is alleged and proved to have been committed by one of the conspirators in furtherance of the conspiracy.

ANNOTATIONS

Charge.—It was reversible error where, although defendant was neither indicted nor tried for conspiracy, the court in its charge explained the crime of conspiracy in great detail in an attempt to explain the distinct crime of aiding and abetting. People v. Hentschel, 80 A.D.2d 943, 438 N.Y.S.2d 32 (3d Dept. 1981), aff'd, 54 N.Y.2d 740, 442 N.Y.S.2d 995, 426 N.E.2d 489 (1981).

Acts of co-conspirators.—Where two or more persons have entered into an illicit agreement to commit a crime, each of them to some extent may be deemed to speak as an agent for the others with respect to statements made in furtherance of and in the course of that conspiracy; once a prima facie case of conspiracy has been made out, such statements are admissible against each conspirator. People v. Berkowitz, 50 N.Y.2d 927, 428 N.Y.S.2d 927, 406 N.E.2d 783 (1980).

—The acts and declarations of one co-conspirator which occur while the conspiracy is in progress and which are in furtherance of the common scheme are admissible and provable as to all other co-conspirators as part of the res gestae and as a recognized exception to the hearsay rule. People v. Rastelli, 37 N.Y.2d 240, 371 N.Y.S.2d 911, 333 N.E.2d 182 (1975), cert. denied, 423 U.S. 995, 96 S. Ct. 421, 40 L. Ed. 2d 369 (1976).

Prima facie case.—No prima facie showing of a conspiracy to commit criminal usury was shown where defendant's taped conversations with informant in themselves were merely "vague and suspicious," and where there was no testimony that defendant was present during the transfer of usurious loan funds. People v. Ardito, 86 A.D.2d 144, 449 N.Y.S.2d 202 (1st Dept.), aff'd, 58 N.Y.2d 842, 460 N.Y.S.2d 22, 446 N.E.2d 778 (1983).

Overt act.—The overt acts of any conspirator may be attributable to other conspirators to establish the offense of conspiracy. People v. Leisner, 73 N.Y.2d 140, 538 N.Y.S.2d 517, 535 N.E.2d 647 (1989).

—The overt act merely provides corroboration of the existence of the agreement, and conspiracy in the first degree applies to any agreement between an adult and a juvenile to commit or cause the commission of a class A felony, regardless of the age of the person who is to commit or cause the commission of the class A felony. People v. Austin, 9 A.D.3d 369, 780 N.Y.S.2d 23 (2d Dept. 2004).

—An overt act in furtherance of a conspiracy was satisfied by evidence of $400 payment for confidential and privileged information acquired from an attorney in breach of his attorney/client privilege. People v. Canale, 268 A.D.2d 699, 704 N.Y.S.2d 151 (3d Dept. 2000).

—Defendant co-conspirator's offer of cash to a third person to commit a murder would be considered an overt act in furtherance of a conspiracy where the third person was an undercover police functionary who lacked necessary criminal intent to be a conspirator; there was evidence that defendant gave the undercover agent bullets, a gun and money to commit the murder; therefore, the jury could clearly find that defendant committed overt acts. People v. Lakomec, 86 A.D.2d 77, 449 N.Y.S.2d 71 (3d Dept. 1982).

—A meeting to discuss plans is not an overt act done in furtherance of the conspiracy, but is only part of the agreement itself, and an indictment pursuant to PL § 105.20 that fails to allege an overt act is jurisdictionally defective. People v. Menache, 110 Misc. 2d 987, 443 N.Y.S.2d 204 (Co. Ct. Westchester Co. 1981), aff'd, 98 A.D.2d 335, 470 N.Y.S.2d 171 (2d Dept. 1983).

Specific intent to commit substantive crime.—Conviction for conspiracy in New York requires that the defendant have an intent to commit a substantive crime, and where that specific intent is missing as to an element of the substantive crime, it cannot be supplied by acts and declarations of conspiracy. People v. Joyce, 100 A.D.2d 343, 474 N.Y.S.2d 337 (2d Dept. 1984).

Sentence.—Defendant was properly sentenced to consecutive terms for possession of drugs and conspiracy to possess those drugs; although the possession could be viewed as closely related to the overt acts necessary to prove the conspiracy, the crimes of conspiracy and possession were not committed through a single act. People v. Cordoba, 208 A.D.2d 420, 617 N.Y.S.2d 305 (1st Dept. 1994).

§ 105.25. Conspiracy; jurisdiction and venue.

1. A person may be prosecuted for conspiracy in the county in which he entered into such conspiracy or in any county in which an overt act in furtherance thereof was committed.

2. An agreement made within this state to engage in or cause the performance of conduct in another jurisdiction is punishable herein as a conspiracy only when such conduct would constitute a crime both under the laws of this state if performed herein and under the laws of the other jurisdiction if performed therein.

3. An agreement made in another jurisdiction to engage in or cause the performance of conduct within this state, which would constitute a crime herein, is punishable herein only when an overt act in furtherance of such conspiracy is committed within this state. Under such circumstances, it is no defense to a prosecution for conspiracy that the conduct which is the objective of the conspiracy would not constitute a crime under the laws of the other jurisdiction if performed therein.

ANNOTATION

Corroboration; elements of offense.—Corroboration is not an "element" of the crime of conspiracy, and its absence does not preclude finding a prima facie case. People v. King, 48 A.D.2d 457, 370 N.Y.S.2d 52 (1st Dept. 1975).

§ 105.30. Conspiracy; no defense.

It is no defense to a prosecution for conspiracy that, owing to criminal irresponsibility or other legal incapacity or exemption, or to unawareness of the criminal nature of the agreement or the object conduct or of the defendant's criminal purpose or to other factors precluding the mental state required for the commission of conspiracy or the object crime, one or more of the defendant's co-conspirators could not be guilty of conspiracy or the object crime.

ANNOTATIONS

Generally.—Even if a defendant's sole co-conspirator is legally irresponsible or has feigned agreement, defendant's conviction on conspiracy charge will stand provided the evidence is otherwise legally sufficient. People v. Macklowitz, 135 Misc. 2d 232, 514 N.Y.S.2d 883 (Sup. Ct. N.Y. Co. 1987).

Instruction to jury.—The instruction that the jury could not convict one defendant and not the other on the conspiracy charge was error in light of the present wording of PL § 105.10 and the expressed provision in PL § 105.30; however, an exception to the charge on that ground must be made to preserve the error for appellate review. People v. Teeter, 47 N.Y.2d 1002, 420 N.Y.S.2d 217, 394 N.E.2d 286 (1979).

Unilateral approach.—The legislature by PL § 105.30 adopts the unilateral rather than the bilateral approach to conspiracy. People v. Schwimmer, 47 N.Y.2d 1004, 420 N.Y.S.2d 218, 394 N.E.2d 288 (1979); see also People v. Villetto, 47 N.Y.2d 1006, 420 N.Y.S.2d 219, 394 N.E.2d 288 (1979).

Renunciation.—Renunciation requires more than merely withdrawal from a conspiracy and there must be a demonstration, inter alia, that a "substantial effort" was made to "prevent the commission" of the conspiracy. People v. Ozerowski, 38 N.Y.2d 481, 381 N.Y.S.2d 438, 344 N.E.2d 370 (1976).

§ 105.35. Conspiracy; enterprise corruption; applicability.

For purposes of this article, conspiracy to commit the crime of enterprise corruption in violation of section 460.20 of this chapter shall not constitute an offense.

Added by L. 1986, Ch. 516.

ARTICLE 110—ATTEMPT

Section
  110.00 Attempt to commit a crime.
  110.05 Attempt to commit a crime; punishment.
  110.10 Attempt to commit a crime; no defense.

LexisNexis Cross Reference

New York Criminal Practice (2d ed.), Vol. 6, Ch. 56, Attempt, Solicitation, Conspiracy and Facilitation.

§ 110.00. Attempt to commit a crime.

A person is guilty of an attempt to commit a crime when, with intent to commit a crime, he engages in conduct which tends to effect the commission of such crime.

ANNOTATIONS

Impossibility.—Attempted unlicensed operation of a vehicle and attempted driving while intoxicated are not crimes. People v. Prescott, 95 N.Y.2d 655, 722 N.Y.S.2d 778, 745 N.E.2d 1000 (2001).

—Where the possession of a weapon would have been an intentional and knowing one rather than one based on a statutory presumption, an attempt to commit criminal possession is not a legal possibility. People v. Saunders, 200 A.D.2d 640, 606 N.Y.S.2d 744 (2d Dept. 1994), aff'd, 85 N.Y.2d 339, 624 N.Y.S.2d 568, 648 N.E.2d 1331 (1995).

Attempted arson.—The court properly accepted the plea where the defendant stated that he intentionally aided and abetted another in setting the fire and that he knew or should have known the building in question was occupied at the time. People v. Paige, 92 A.D.2d 653, 460 N.Y.S.2d 147 (3d Dept. 1983).

Attempted assault.—A person cannot attempt to commit an assault by engaging in reckless conduct. People v. Karp, 158 A.D.2d 378, 551 N.Y.S.2d 503, 504 (1st Dept. 1990).

—To commit attempted second degree assault, a defendant need not cause any physical injury; rather, he must merely attempt to harm another. People v. Jackson, 211 A.D.2d 495, 621 N.Y.S.2d 328 (2d Dept. 1995).

—Neither evidence of serious physical injury nor physical injury is required to support a conviction for attempted assault. People v. Koufomichalis, 2 A.D.3d 987, 768 N.Y.S.2d 246 (3d Dept. 2003).

Attempted murder.—Attempted murder in the second degree is not an "armed felony offense" by definition because possession, use, or display of a weapon is not a statutory element of the crime. People v. Roye, 255 A.D.2d 464, 682 N.Y.S.2d 862 (2d Dept. 1998).

Attempted rape.—It is no defense to a charge of attempted rape that the victim was dead if the defendant believed the victim was alive at the time of the attempted rape. People v. Gorman, 150 A.D.2d 797, 542 N.Y.S.2d 225, 226 (2d Dept. 1989).

—Courts have distinguished between punishable attempts and mere preparations to commit a crime, between those remote acts and those which are proximate and very near to accomplishing the crime; there is no need to commit the final act towards committing the crime to be guilty of attempt, allegations that defendant touched 13-year-old victim's breasts and vaginal area and told the victim that he was going to have sex with her, if established at trial, do constitute an attempt. People v. Spagnualo, 5 A.D.3d 995, 774 N.Y.S.2d 223 (4th Dept. 2004).

Attempted robbery.—Where defendants planned a robbery and were in the process of undertaking it when a gun belonging to one accidentally discharged and killed a third person, the abandonment of the robbery, because of such killing, occurred too late in the stage of preparation to indicate that no attempt

occurred. People v. Mirenda, 23 N.Y.2d 439, 297 N.Y.S.2d 532, 245 N.E.2d 194 (1969).

Attempted weapons possession.—A person can criminally attempt to possess a weapon; an attempt prosecution for the crime of weapons possession is not legally impossible; notwithstanding the strict liability nature of the crime of weapons possession, a defendant may logically attempt to possess a weapon. People v. Saunders, 85 N.Y.2d 339, 624 N.Y.S.2d 568, 648 N.E.2d 1331 (1995).

Acts constituting attempts.—The change in the statutory definition of "attempt" so as not to require a failure to effect the commission of a crime in an attempt crime did not entitle defendant to an instruction to the jury that they might find him guilty of an attempt to commit grand larceny where there was evidence only of a consummated grand larceny. People v. Richette, 33 N.Y.2d 42, 349 N.Y.S.2d 65, 303 N.E.2d 857 (1973).

—To make out an attempted crime, a defendant's conduct must come "very near," indeed, "dangerously near" consummation of the criminal act. People v. Acosta, 197 A.D.2d 448, 602 N.Y.S.2d 845 (1st Dept. 1993).

—In an attempted insurance fraud prosecution based on an attempt to arrange a car theft, defendant's acts of plotting out substantive crime, obtaining the keys to a co-conspirators car and transferring them to a third party who was to arrange for disposal of the vehicle, and advising the co-conspirator that he had disposed of the car and that it should be reported stolen to the insurance company, constituted the requisite overt acts to establish the crime charged; that an insurance claim was neither prepared nor filed is not controlling. People v. Vastaro, 117 A.D.2d 637, 498 N.Y.S.2d 87 (2d Dept. 1986).

—A telephone conversation may constitute an overt act in furtherance of a conspiracy, provided it is an independent act which tends to carry out the conspiracy and is not simply a conversation in which the agreement is reached. People v. Bongarzone, 116 A.D.2d 164, 500 N.Y.S.2d 532 (2d Dept. 1986).

—To establish an attempt, the act tending to effect the commission of the crime need not be the final one toward the completion of the offense, but it must carry the project forward within dangerous proximity to be commission of the crime. People v. Colp, 147 A.D.2d 964, 537 N.Y.S.2d 715 (4th Dept. 1989).

—Merely because the police uncover a plan to commit a crime and take steps to prevent its completion does not preclude the liability of those involved for the crime of attempt. People v. Sanoguet, 157 Misc. 2d 771, 597 N.Y.S.2d 854 (Sup. Ct. Bronx Co. 1993).

Charge.—Even though trial court departed from statutory language by using the phrase "substantial contributing cause" in its charge on attempt, phrase did not dilute the effect of the charge which repeatedly and accurately conveyed to the jury the concept of attempt. People v. Callender, 232 A.D.2d 650, 649 N.Y.S.2d 448 (2d Dept. 1996).

—Trial court did not err in refusing to charge attempted robbery in the third degree as a lesser included offense of attempted robbery in the first degree; no reasonable view of the evidence supported a finding that defendant attempted to steal property forcibly but did not use or threaten immediate use of a dangerous instrumentality. People v. Johnson, 219 A.D.2d 809, 632 N.Y.S.2d 357 (4th Dept. 1995).

Evidence.—If the evidence was insufficient to establish the necessary mens rea for criminal sale of a controlled substance, it would also have been insufficient to sustain a conviction for attempt, which is a specific intent crime. People v. Flores, 84 N.Y.2d 957, 620 N.Y.S.2d 823, 644 N.E.2d 1379 (1994).

—Viewing the evidence in the light most favorable to the People, a reasonable juror could find beyond a reasonable doubt that defendant intended to cause injury to the victim by tapping, slapping, smacking, and punching; thus, the elements of attempted assault in the third degree were established. *In re Marvin D.*, 208 A.D.2d 360, 617 N.Y.S.2d 157 (1st Dept. 1994).

—Conviction for attempted burglary in the second degree was affirmed; defendant's admission that he went to the apartment with the intent to commit burglary coupled with his action of trying the locked door was sufficient to support the conviction. People v. Hissen, 267 A.D.2d 599, 699 N.Y.S.2d 773 (3d Dept. 1999), *appeal denied,* 94 N.Y.2d 921 (2000).

Intent.—It must first be established that the defendant acted with a specific intent; that is, that he intended to commit specific crime. People v. Bracey, 41 N.Y.2d 296, 392 N.Y.S.2d 412, 360 N.E.2d 1094 (1977).

—There must be proof of intent to commit a specific crime to make out an attempt. People v. Wager, 199 A.D.2d 642, 604 N.Y.S.2d 1008 (3d Dept. 1993).

§ 110.05. Attempt to commit a crime; punishment.

An attempt to commit a crime is a:

1. Class A-I felony when the crime attempted is the A-I felony of murder in the first degree, criminal possession of a controlled substance in the first degree, criminal sale of a controlled substance in the first degree, criminal possession of a chemical or biological weapon in the first degree or criminal use of a chemical or biological weapon in the first degree;

2. Class A-II felony when the crime attempted is a class A-II felony;

3. Class B felony when the crime attempted is a class A-I felony except as provided in subdivision one hereof;

4. Class C felony when the crime attempted is a class B felony;

5. Class D felony when the crime attempted is a class C felony;

6. Class E felony when the crime attempted is a class D felony;

7. Class A misdemeanor when the crime attempted is a class E felony;

8. Class B misdemeanor when the crime attempted is a misdemeanor.

Amended by L. 1970, Ch. 112; L. 1972, Ch. 292; L. 1973, Ch. 276; L. 1974, Ch. 367; L. 1979, Ch. 410; L. 2004, Ch. 1, § 11 (Part A), eff. July 23, 2004.

L. 1979, Ch. 410, § 29 provides:

Except as provided in section three of this act, the provisions of this act do not apply to or govern the construction of and punishment for any offense committed prior to the effective date of this act, or the construction and application of any defense to a prosecution for such an offense. Such an offense must be construed and punished according to the provisions of law existing at the time of the commission thereof in the same manner as if this act had not been enacted.

ANNOTATION

Sentence.—Although sentence imposed on defendant convicted of attempted robbery in the first degree was within the statutory guidelines for a class C persistent violent felony offender, the minimum sentence which could have been imposed was a lesser sentence; because the sentence may have been based on the sentencing court's misapprehension of the law, the matter was remitted for resentencing. People v. Jiminez, 209 A.D.2d 719, 620 N.Y.S.2d 963 (2d Dept. 1994).

§ 110.10. Attempt to commit a crime; no defense.

If the conduct in which a person engages otherwise constitutes an attempt to commit a crime pursuant to section 110.00, it is no defense to a prosecution for such attempt that the crime charged to have been attempted was, under the attendant circumstances, factually or legally impossible of commission, if such crime could have been committed had the attendant circumstances been as such person believed them to be.

ANNOTATIONS

Attempted sale of a controlled substance.—Defendant could properly be indicted for criminal sale of a controlled substance, although the substance sold proved to be aspirin; nothing in the grand jury minutes established that defendant knew the white powder was aspirin, and if he believed that it was cocaine he could be found guilty of criminal sale of a controlled substance. People v. Culligan, 79 A.D.2d 875, 434 N.Y.S.2d 546 (4th Dept. 1980).

Attempted murder.—A person is guilty of an attempted murder when, with intent to commit the crime, he engages in conduct which tends to effect the commission of such crime (PL § 110.10); it is no defense that, under the attendant circumstances, the crime was factually or legally impossible of commission "if such crime could have been committed had the attendant circumstances been as such person believed them to be" (PL § 110.10); if defendant believed the victim to be alive at the time of the shooting, it is no defense to the charge of attempted murder that the victim may have been dead. People v. Dlugash, 41 N.Y.2d 725, 395 N.Y.S.2d 419, 363 N.E.2d 1155 (1977).

Reckless endangerment.—Factual impossibility is a defense to reckless endangerment inasmuch as that crime is defined in terms of the risk produced by the defendant's conduct rather than by intent. People v. Galatro, 84 N.Y.2d 160, 615 N.Y.S.2d 650, 639 N.E.2d 7 (1994).

ARTICLE 115—CRIMINAL FACILITATION

LexisNexis Cross Reference

New York Criminal Practice (2d ed.), Vol. 6, Ch. 56, Attempt, Solicitation, Conspiracy and Facilitation.

§ 115.00. Criminal facilitation in the fourth degree.

A person is guilty of criminal facilitation in the fourth degree when, believing it probable that he is rendering aid:

1. to a person who intends to commit a crime, he engages in conduct which provides such person with means or opportunity for the commission thereof and which in fact aids such person to commit a felony; or

2. to a person under sixteen years of age who intends to engage in conduct which would constitute a crime, he, being over eighteen years of age, engages in conduct which provides such person with means or opportunity for the commission thereof and which in fact aids such person to commit a crime.

Criminal facilitation in the fourth degree is a class A misdemeanor.

Amended by L. 1978, Ch. 422.

ANNOTATIONS

Time of commission of crime.—The criminal facilitation statute contemplates that the facilitated crime must occur in the future, after the intervention of the facilitator. People v. Llanos, 151 A.D.2d 128, 546 N.Y.S.2d 584 (1st Dept. 1989).

Facilitation as lesser included offense.—Appellate Division, after concluding that facilitation is not a lesser included offense of criminal sale of a controlled substance, properly overturned a conviction on a facilitation charge which had, over objection, been submitted to the jury as a lesser included offense of a drug sale; however, appellate division erred in reducing the invalid facilitation conviction to possession, because possession is not a lesser included charge of facilitation, and the conviction could not be so reduced. People v. Luther, 61 N.Y.2d 724, 472 N.Y.S.2d 614, 460 N.E.2d 1099 (1984).

—Criminal facilitation is not a lesser included offense of criminal sale of a controlled substance. People v. Armstrong, 160 A.D.2d 206, 553 N.Y.S.2d 169, 170 (1st Dept. 1990).

Possession of a dangerous drug.—Defendant could not have believed it probable that he was helping an undercover narcotics agent who was intending to commit a crime and did commit a crime; the undercover agent was told by defendant that he could probably get marijuana from a certain person, and the agent did so. People v. Gordon, 32 N.Y.2d 62, 343 N.Y.S.2d 103, 295 N.E.2d 777 (1973).

§ 115.01. Criminal facilitation in the third degree.

A person guilty[*] of criminal facilitation in the third degree, when believing it probable that he is rendering aid to a person under sixteen years of age who intends to engage in conduct that would constitute a felony, he, being over eighteen years of age, engages in conduct which provides such person with means or opportunity for the commission thereof and which in fact aids such person to commit a felony.

Criminal facilitation in the third degree is a class E felony.

[*] As originally enacted.

Added by L. 1978, Ch. 422.

§ 115.05. Criminal facilitation in the second degree.

A person is guilty of criminal facilitation in the second degree when, believing it probable that he is rendering aid to a person who intends to commit a class A felony, he engages in conduct which provides such person with means or opportunity for the commission thereof and which in fact aids such person to commit such class A felony.

Criminal facilitation in the second degree is a class C felony.

Amended by L. 1972, Ch. 292; L. 1978, Ch. 422.

ANNOTATION

Evidence.—Defendant's conviction of criminal facilitation in the second degree reversed where evidence revealed that defendant had no contact with the person he was accused of aiding to commit crime of bribe receiving in the second degree until after the crime had been consummated; defendant did not provide means or opportunity for person to receive bribe. People v. Arcadi, 79 A.D.2d 845, 434 N.Y.S.2d 507 (4th Dept.), *aff'd*, 54 N.Y.2d 981, 446 N.Y.S.2d 39, 430 N.E.2d 915 (1981).

§ 115.08. Criminal facilitation in the first degree.

A person is guilty of criminal facilitation in the first degree when, believing it probable that he is rendering aid to a person under sixteen years of age who intends to engage in conduct that would constitute a class A felony, he, being over eighteen years of age, engages in conduct which provides such person with means or opportunity for the commission thereof and which in fact aids such person to commit such a class A felony.

Criminal facilitation in the first degree is a class B felony.

Added by L. 1978, Ch. 422.

§ 115.10. Criminal facilitation; no defense.

It is no defense to a prosecution for criminal facilitation that:

1. The person facilitated was not guilty of the underlying felony owing to criminal irresponsibility or other legal incapacity or exemption, or to unawareness of the criminal nature of the conduct in question or to other factors precluding the mental state required for the commission of such felony; or

2. The person facilitated has not been prosecuted for or convicted of the underlying felony, or has previously been acquitted thereof; or

3. The defendant himself is not guilty of the felony which he facilitated because he did not act with the intent or other culpable mental state required for the commission thereof.

§ 115.15. Criminal facilitation; corroboration.

A person shall not be convicted of criminal facilitation upon the testimony of a person who has committed the felony charged to have been facilitated unless such testimony be corroborated by such other evidence as tends to connect the defendant with such facilitation.

TITLE H—OFFENSES AGAINST THE PERSON INVOLVING PHYSICAL INJURY, SEXUAL CONDUCT, RESTRAINT AND INTIMIDATION

ARTICLE 120—ASSAULT AND RELATED OFFENSES

LexisNexis Cross Reference

New York Criminal Practice (2d ed.), Vol. 6, Ch. 57, Assault and Related Offenses.

§ 120.00. Assault in the third degree.

A person is guilty of assault in the third degree when:

1. With intent to cause physical injury to another person, he causes such injury to such person or to a third person; or

2. He recklessly causes physical injury to another person; or

3. With criminal negligence, he causes physical injury to another person by means of a deadly weapon or a dangerous instrument.

Assault in the third degree is a class A misdemeanor.

ANNOTATIONS

Constitutionality.—PL § 120.00 is constitutional and the showing of either substantial pain or impairment of physical condition will sustain a conviction. People v. Gordon, 107 A.D.2d 248, 438 N.Y.S.2d 184 (1st Dept. 1981).

Charge; reckless assault.—It was error for the trial court to refuse to charge reckless assault, where the witnesses testified to the presence of alcohol on defendant's breath and that he appeared very intoxicated. People v. Collins, 86 A.D.2d 616, 446 N.Y.S.2d 93 (2d Dept. 1981).

Deadly weapon.—The People failed to prove that the gun found at the scene was a "deadly weapon" where it failed to fire four times when directed toward its intended victim and where no tests were conducted of the bullets in the gun to determine if they were live. People v. Shaffer, 66 N.Y.2d 663, 495 N.Y.S.2d 965, 486 N.E.2d 823 (1985).

Intent.—Trial judge's failure in assault prosecution to reiterate the requirements of the particular intent as to charge of assault in third degree in supplementary charge was not prejudicial where defendant was convicted of assault in the second degree. People v. Jones, 27 N.Y.2d 222, 316 N.Y.S.2d 617, 265 N.E.2d 446 (1970).

—Evidence was insufficient to establish defendant's intent to cause physical injury to the complaining witness where the defendant was out of the door of the restaurant when the coperpetrator, standing in the restaurant approximately 20 feet from the door, suddenly turned and fired his gun at the complaining witness. People v. Padgett, 145 A.D.2d 443, 535 N.Y.S.2d 414, 415 (2d Dept. 1988).

Evidence.—A rational trier of fact could find beyond a reasonable doubt that the defendant intended to cause injury to the victim by tapping, slapping, smacking and punching the victim; thus, the elements of attempted assault in the third degree were established. In re Marvin D., 208 A.D.2d 360, 617 N.Y.S.2d 157 (1st Dept. 1994).

—Evidence that defendant and decedent together engaged in a drag race which caused a fatal crash between decedent's car and a third car which killed the driver and injured the passenger, supported a conviction for assault of the passenger on the theory of accessorial liability in that he intentionally aided decedent in reckless conduct. People v. Hart, 8 A.D.3d 402, 778 N.Y.S.2d 94 (2d Dept. 2004).

—No reasonable view of the evidence supported defendant's request to charge assault in the third degree where at trial testimony of the victim revealed that defendant intentionally, as opposed to recklessly, beat the victim with a wooden crutch and a metal pipe and caused physical injury. People v. Sudan, 298 A.D.2d 620, 748 N.Y.S.2d 415 (3d Dept. 2002).

—Although evidence established that only one person used the knife that inflicted the stab wounds, defendant was part of a group of at least four people who acted with a community of purpose; since there is "no distinction between liability as a principal and criminal culpability as an accessory," conviction for assault in the third degree was affirmed. People v. Staples, 19 A.D.3d 1096, 796 N.Y.S.2d 209 (4th Dept. 2005).

—Defendant's unexplained failure to see the pedestrians she hit while traveling 10 to 15 miles per hour below the speed limit on a slushy road, even when coupled with evidence that defendant's car drifted onto the shoulder of the road and she did not apply her brakes prior to impact, without more, did not establish that defendant acted with criminal negligence. People v. Maloof, 254 A.D.2d 766, 678 N.Y.S.2d 175 (4th Dept. 1998).

Physical injury.—Information established prima facie case for assault in the third degree where it described the victim's "physical injury" as contusions and swelling that caused the victim substantial pain and were sustained as a result of a physical attack on the victim by defendant and another for the purposes of stealing the motor scooter the victim was riding at the time of the attack; the prima facie requirement is not the same as the burden of proof required to obtain and sustain a conviction. People v. Henderson, 92 N.Y.2d 677, 685 N.Y.S.2d 409, 708 N.E.2d 165 (1998).

—The evidence that complainant had been hit, that it caused him pain, caused him to cry out and caused a real mark was held not to be within the definition of "substantial pain" as required to establish "physical injury." (PL § 10.00(9)). In re Philip A., 49 N.Y.2d 198, 424 N.Y.S.2d 418, 400 N.E.2d 358 (1980).

—The complainant's testimony that he experienced pain, headaches, blurred vision, and that he sought medical attention and missed one week of school as a result of being hit in the face with a lock by the defendant was sufficient to establish a physical injury. In re Manuel G., 215 A.D.2d 558, 626 N.Y.S.2d 859 (2d Dept. 1995).

—Proof of physical injury was lacking where the complainant did not testify as to how long any of her injuries persisted or whether and in what manner those injuries impaired her physical functions or ability to work. People v. Bruce, 162 A.D.2d 604, 556 N.Y.S.2d 782 (2d Dept. 1990).

—Victim's testimony that he suffered pain for about three weeks as a result of beating was sufficient proof of physical injury even though victim did not quantify or describe the pain he suffered. People v. McNair, 147 A.D.2d 593, 537 N.Y.S.2d 888 (2d Dept. 1989).

—Record did not support finding of physical injury necessary to prove assault in the third degree, although testimony supported a finding of neglect based on evidence that the defendant hit the 13-month-old victim and left red finger marks on his face. In re Mary P., 278 A.D.2d 750, 718 N.Y.S.2d 442 (3d Dept. 2000).

—Evidence that complainant's jaw was swollen and caused him pain for two weeks was sufficient to establish "physical injury." People v. Washington, 148 A.D.2d 952, 539 N.Y.S.2d 190 (4th Dept. 1989).

—Whether the element of physical injury necessary to support

a conviction of assault in the second degree has been proven is generally a question of fact. People v. Maturexitz, 149 A.D.2d 908, 540 N.Y.S.2d 44 (4th Dept. 1989).

—Allegation that defendant's kick to woman, who was eight months pregnant, caused her stomach pains was sufficient allegation of physical injury for third degree assault. People v. Moorehead, 170 Misc. 2d 35, 648 N.Y.S.2d 528 (Just. Ct. Monroe Co. 1996).

Assault as lesser included offense.—Court properly refused to charge assault in the third degree as a lesser included offense of assault in the second degree, since the evidence proved that defendant either intended to cause or did cause physical injury to victim with the use of a dangerous or deadly weapon, a razor. People v. Smith, 235 A.D.2d 558, 653 N.Y.S.2d 931 (2d Dept. 1997).

—Trial court did not err in refusing to instruct the jury on assault in the third degree as a lesser included offense of depraved indifference murder; no reasonable view of the evidence would support the conclusion that defendant committed the crime of assault in the third degree but did not, by the same conduct, cause the victim's death. People v. Feldman, 219 A.D.2d 665, 631 N.Y.S.2d 720 (2d Dept. 1995).

—Defendant's conviction for depraved indifference assault in the first degree was reduced to assault in the third degree because of the lack of medical testimony that the victims' injuries exposed them to a grave risk of death. People v. Murphy, 235 A.D.2d 933, 654 N.Y.S.2d 187 (3d Dept. 1997).

—"In the absence of evidence of injuries caused by anything other than a dangerous instrument, there is no reasonable view of the evidence that would support a finding that defendant committed the lesser offense but not the greater," and the trial court therefore did not err by refusing defendant's request to charge the lesser included offense of assault in the third degree. People v. Saunders, 292 A.D.2d 780, 738 N.Y.S.2d 785 (4th Dept. 2002).

—Appellate court modified defendant's conviction for assault in the second degree to assault in the third degree based upon its determination that victim's injury after being shot in the foot by defendant was not a "serious physical injury, but only a "physical injury." People v. Bodford, 238 A.D.2d 928, 661 N.Y.S.2d 158 (4th Dept. 1997).

Harassment as lesser included offense of assault.— Harassment requires an intent to harass, annoy or alarm, which is not included in or required by the language of Penal Law 120.00, which defines assault; thus, harassment is not a lesser included offense of assault for purposes of conviction after verdict. People v. Moyer, 27 N.Y.2d 252, 317 N.Y.S.2d 9 (1970).

Corroboration.—Corroboration of assault complainant's testimony, where she also claimed a consummated rape, was not required since the third degree assaults of which defendant was convicted were subsequent to and separate and apart from the alleged act of rape. People v. Peters, 26 N.Y.2d 774, 309 N.Y.S.2d 209, 257 N.E.2d 655 (1970).

§ 120.01. Reckless assault of a child by a child day care provider.

A person is guilty of reckless assault of a child when, being a child day care provider or an employee thereof, he or she recklessly causes serious physical injury to a child under the care of such provider or employee who is less than eleven years of age.

Reckless assault of a child by a child day care provider is a class E felony.

Added by L. 1998, Ch. 600, § 3, eff. Nov. 1, 1998.

§ 120.03. Vehicular assault in the second degree.

A person is guilty of vehicular assault in the second degree when he or she causes serious physical injury to another person, and either:

(1) operates a motor vehicle in violation of subdivision two, three or four of section eleven hundred ninety-two of the vehicle and traffic law or operates a vessel or public vessel in violation of paragraph (b), (c), (d) or (e) of subdivision two of section forty-nine-a of the navigation law, and as a result of such intoxication or impairment by the use of a drug, operates such motor vehicle, vessel or public vessel in a manner that causes such serious physical injury to such other person, or

(2) operates a motor vehicle with a gross vehicle weight rating of more than eighteen thousand pounds which contains flammable gas, radioactive materials or explosives in violation of subdivision one of section eleven hundred ninety-two of the vehicle and traffic law, and such flammable gas, radioactive materials or explosives is the cause of such serious physical injury, and as a result of such intoxication or impairment by the use of a drug, operates such motor vehicle in a manner that causes such serious physical injury to such other person, or

(3) operates a snowmobile in violation of paragraph (b), (c) or (d) of subdivision one of section 25.24 of the parks, recreation and historic preservation law or operates an all terrain vehicle as defined in paragraph (a) of subdivision one of section twenty-two hundred eighty-one of the vehicle and traffic law and in violation of subdivision two, three, or four of section eleven hundred ninety-two of the vehicle and traffic law, and as a result of such intoxication or impairment by the use of a drug, operates such snowmobile or all terrain vehicle in a manner that causes such serious physical injury to such other person.

If it is established that the person operating such motor vehicle, vessel, public vessel, snowmobile or all terrain vehicle caused such serious physical injury while unlawfully intoxicated or impaired by the use of a drug, then there shall be a rebuttable presumption that, as a result of such intoxication or impairment by the use of a drug, such person operated the motor vehicle, vessel, public vessel, snowmobile or all terrain vehicle in a manner that caused such serious physical injury, as required by this section.

Vehicular assault in the second degree is a class E felony.

Added by L. 1983, Ch. 298, eff. Sept. 1, 1983; **Amended** by L. 1985, Ch. 507, eff. Nov. 1, 1985, reclassifying offense as second degree; L. 1989, Ch. 393, eff. Nov. 1, 1989; L. 1990, Ch. 173, eff. Aug. 19, 1990, amending subd. 2 and adding subd. 3; L. 1990, Ch. 452, eff. Nov. 1, 1990, amending subd. 2; L. 1992, Ch. 427, eff. Nov. 1, 1992, amending subd. 3; L. 1992, Ch. 805, eff. Nov. 1, 1992, amending subd. 2; L. 1998, Ch. 629, eff. Nov. 1, 1999, amending subd. 3; L. 2005, Ch. 39, § 2, eff. Nov. 1, 2005.

ANNOTATION

Constitutionality.—In finding, PL § 120.03 constitutional, court reaffirmed proposition that it is not violative of the Constitution to base a crime upon a finding that a defendant acted with criminal negligence rather than a more highly culpable mental state. People v. Librie, 130 A.D.2d 593, 515 N.Y.S.2d 302 (2d Dept. 1987).

§ 120.04. Vehicular assault in the first degree.

A person is guilty of vehicular assault in the first degree when he or she:

(1) commits the crime of vehicular assault in the second degree as defined in section 120.03, and

(2) commits such crime while knowing or having reason to know that: (a) his or her license or his or her privilege of operating a motor vehicle in another state or his or her privilege of obtaining a license to operate a motor vehicle in another state is suspended or revoked and such suspension or revocation is based upon a conviction in such other state for an offense which would, if committed in this state, constitute a violation of any of the provisions of section eleven hundred ninety-two of the vehicle and traffic law; or (b) his or her license or his or her privilege of operating a motor vehicle in the state or his or her privilege of obtaining a license issued by the commissioner of motor vehicles is suspended or revoked and such suspension or revocation is based upon either a refusal to submit to a chemical test pursuant to section eleven hundred ninety-four of the vehicle and traffic law or following a conviction for a violation of any of the provisions of section eleven hundred ninety-two of the vehicle and traffic law.

If it is established that the person operating such motor vehicle caused such serious physical injury while unlawfully intoxicated or impaired by the use of a drug, then there shall be a rebuttable presumption that, as a result of such intoxication or impairment by the use of a drug, such person operated the motor vehicle in a manner that caused such serious physical injury, as required by this section.

Vehicular assault in the first degree is a class D felony.

Added by L. 1985, Ch. 507, eff. Nov. 1, 1985; **Amended** by L. 1996, Ch. 528, § 1, amending subd. 2, eff. Nov. 1, 1996; L. 2005, Ch. 39, § 3, eff. Nov. 1, 2005.

§ 120.05. Assault in the second degree.

A person is guilty of assault in the second degree when:

1. With intent to cause serious physical injury to another person, he causes such injury to such person or to a third person; or

2. With intent to cause physical injury to another person, he causes such injury to such person or to a third person by means of a deadly weapon or a dangerous instrument; or

3. With intent to prevent a peace officer, police officer, a fireman, including a fireman acting as a paramedic or emergency medical technician administering first aid in the course of performance of duty as such fireman, an emergency medical service paramedic or emergency

medical service technician, or medical or related personnel in a hospital emergency department, from performing a lawful duty, by means including releasing or failing to control an animal under circumstances evincing the actor's intent that the animal obstruct the lawful activity of such peace officer, police officer, fireman, paramedic or technician, he causes physical injury to such peace officer, police officer, fireman, paramedic, technician or medical or related personnel in a hospital emergency department; or

4. He recklessly causes serious physical injury to another person by means of a deadly weapon or a dangerous instrument; or

5. For a purpose other than lawful medical or therapeutic treatment, he intentionally causes stupor, unconsciousness or other physical impairment or injury to another person by administering to him, without his consent, a drug, substance or preparation capable of producing the same; or

6. In the course of and in furtherance of the commission or attempted commission of a felony, other than a felony defined in article one hundred thirty which requires corroboration for conviction, or of immediate flight therefrom, he, or another participant if there be any, causes physical injury to a person other than one of the participants; or

7. Having been charged with or convicted of a crime and while confined in a correctional facility, as defined in subdivision three of section forty of the correction law, pursuant to such charge or conviction, with intent to cause physical injury to another person, he causes such injury to such person or to a third person; or

8. Being eighteen years old or more and with intent to cause physical injury to a person less than eleven years old, the defendant recklessly causes serious physical injury to such person; or

9. Being eighteen years old or more and with intent to cause physical injury to a person less than seven years old, the defendant causes such injury to such person; or

10. Acting at a place the person knows, or reasonably should know, is on school grounds and with intent to cause physical injury, he or she:

(a) causes such injury to an employee of a school or public school district; or

(b) not being a student of such school or public school district, causes physical injury to another, and such other person is a student of such school who is attending or present for educational purposes. For purposes of this subdivision the term "school grounds" shall have the meaning set forth in subdivision fourteen of section 220.00 of this chapter.

11. With intent to cause physical injury to a train operator, ticket inspector, conductor, bus operator or station agent employed by any transit agency, authority or company, public or private, whose operation is authorized by New York state or any of its political subdivisions, he or she causes physical injury to such train operator, ticket inspector, conductor, bus operator or station agent while such employee is performing an assigned duty on, or directly related to, the operation of a train or bus.

Assault in the second degree is a class D felony.

Amended by L. 1967, Ch. 791; L. 1968, Ch. 37; L. 1972, Ch. 598; L. 1974, Chs. 239, 660; L. 1975, Chs. 134, 667; L. 1980, Chs. 471, 843; L. 1981, Ch. 372; L. 1984, Ch. 284; L. 1985, Ch. 262; L. 1990, Ch. 477; L. 1996, Ch. 122, § 4, amending subd. 8, and adding subd. 9, both eff. Aug. 1, 1996; L. 1998, Ch. 269, § 1, and Ch. 287, § 1, both eff. Nov. 1, 1998; L. 2000, Ch. 181, § 13, eff. Nov. 1, 2000; L. 2002, Ch. 598, § 1, eff. Nov. 1, 2002, adding subd. 11; L. 2003, Ch. 607, § 1, eff. Nov. 1, 2003, amending subd. 11.

ANNOTATIONS

Constitutionality.—PL § 120.05(6) is constitutional. People v. Fonseca, 36 N.Y.2d 133, 365 N.Y.S.2d 818, 325 N.E.2d 143 (1975).

—PL § 120.05(3) upheld as constitutional; term "physical injury" is not vague and overbroad. People v. Cortez, 143 A.D.2d 464, 532 N.Y.S.2d 585 (3d Dept. 1988).

Intent.—Jury's request that court explain "the *difference* between first, second and third degree assault" did not require a full reiteration of all of the elements of each of the crimes charged; specific intent is a necessary element in all three degrees; thus, the element of intent is not a difference requiring clarification. People v. Jones, 27 N.Y.2d 222, 316 N.Y.S.2d 617, 265 N.E.2d 446 (1970).

—Where the People failed to establish that defendant intended to cause serious physical injury, the conviction must be reversed. People v. Aruz, 253 A.D.2d 592, 677 N.Y.S.2d 322 (1st Dept. 1998).

—Verdict of guilty of assault, second degree (PL § 125.05), was not repugnant to a verdict of acquittal of criminal possession of a weapon, second degree (PL § 165.03), since the elements of the crimes are not identical and the jury may have concluded that the defendant possessed the weapon initially without any intent to use it unlawfully but, in the course of the altercation, decided to and did use the weapon offensively, that is, beyond the lawful bounds of self defense. People v. Garcia, 72 A.D.2d 356, 424 N.Y.S.2d 697 (1st Dept.), aff'd, 52 N.Y.2d 716, 436 N.Y.S.2d 273, 417 N.E.2d 567 (1980).

Second and third degree assault; distinctions.—The trial court committed reversible error in refusing to charge the jury on assault in the third degree, a lesser included offense of assault in the second degree where defendants conceded that the victim suffered serious physical injury, but did not concede that they intended to cause it. People v. Hall, 56 N.Y.2d 547, 449 N.Y.S.2d 960, 434 N.E.2d 1338 (1982).

—No reasonable view of the evidence supported defendant's request to charge assault in the third degree where at trial testimony of the victim revealed that defendant intentionally, as opposed to recklessly, beat the victim with a wooden crutch and a metal pipe and caused physical injury. People v. Sudan, 298 A.D.2d 620, 748 N.Y.S.2d 415 (3d Dept. 2002).

—Appellate court modified defendant's conviction for assault in the second degree to assault in the third degree based upon their determination that victim's injury after being shot in the foot by defendant was not a "serious physical injury, but rather only a physical injury." People v. Bodford, 238 A.D.2d 928, 661 N.Y.S.2d 158 (4th Dept. 1997).

—Defendant's conviction for assault in the second degree was affirmed where, although the wound victim suffered at hands of defendant were not fatal, the wound was still serious. People v. Young, 236 A.D.2d 808, 653 N.Y.S.2d 879 (4th Dept. 1997).

Attempt.—Attempted assault under Penal Law 120.05(3) is an impossibility because the section imposes criminal responsibility for an unintended injury and one cannot be convicted of the crime of attempting to bring about an unintended result. People v. Campell, 72 N.Y.2d 602, 535 N.Y.S.2d 580, 532 N.E.2d 86 (1988).

—A defendant can plead guilty to a nonexistent crime, for example, attempted assault in the second degree, in satisfaction of an indictment charging a crime for which a greater penalty may be imposed. People v. Daniels, 237 A.D.2d 298, 654 N.Y.S.2d 799 (2d Dept. 1997).

—A defendant cannot be convicted of attempted assault in the second degree because it is a legal impossibility. People v. Perez, 218 A.D.2d 754, 630 N.Y.S.2d 777 (2d Dept. 1995).

Physical injury.—Defendant was properly convicted of assault in the second degree by means of gunshot where jury found victim suffered substantial pain—proof of which would be inferred from a bullet wound, treatment of the wound and the doctor's testimony that the injury would have caused pain, notwithstanding the fact that victim gave no testimony concerning degree of pain he felt. People v. Rojay, 61 N.Y.2d 726, 472 N.Y.S.2d 615, 460 N.E.2d 1100 (1984).

—Conviction for assault, second degree, was reversed where testimony showed that victim only suffered a one centimeter cut above her lip; this was inadequate to show that victim suffered either "substantial pain" or "impairment of a physical condition." People v. Jimenez, 55 N.Y.2d 895, 449 N.Y.S.2d 22, 433 N.E.2d 1270 (1982).

—Evidence was insufficient to support conviction where the only evidence of injury to another was witness' testimony that he saw complainant bleeding and wash the cut with peroxide; the complainant did not seek medical attention and did not testify as to how he was injured or who injured him. People v. Sanders, 245 A.D.2d 472, 666 N.Y.S.2d 465 (2d Dept. 1997).

—People adequately proved that defendant caused physical injury to a police officer where the proof established that the officer suffered a sharp pain in his hand, that he was treated for a broken bone in his hand, and that he missed three weeks of work while his hand was in a cast. People v. Brooks, 215 A.D.2d 491, 626 N.Y.S.2d 825 (2d Dept. 1995).

—Evidence established presence of "physical injury" by medical testimony of pain at specific points on the victim's head upon palpation, a diagnosis of a mild concussion, the victim's testimony of severe pain, and her reporting of residual problems for which she sought further treatment and medicine, including recurring severe headaches caused after defendant struck her in the head with a novelty baseball bat. People v. Hines, 9 A.D.3d 507, 780 N.Y.S.2d 419 (3d Dept. 2004).

—Victim's testimony that as a result of defendant's assault, his hand was "quite sore," swollen, and black and blue, that he could not flex his wrist, and, when he tried to move it, he felt sharp pain, established presence of a physical injury; broken bones were not necessary, victim wore a support brace for three days and worked light duty for approximately one week. People v. Ellis, 8 A.D.3d 826, 778 N.Y.S.2d 555 (3d Dept. 2004).

—Parole officer's injuries sustained when defendant repeatedly jabbed him in the eye with a metal rod to the extent that "he almost lost [his] eyeball" constituted a physical injury within the meaning of the statute. People v. Colantonio, 277 A.D.2d 498, 715 N.Y.S.2d 764 (3d Dept. 2000), *appeal denied,* 96 N.Y.2d 781 (2001).

—Testimony that defendant repeatedly hit victim and fractured his jaw, nasal bone, and maxillary sinus area was legally sufficient to support a conviction of assault in the second degree. People v. Lane, 241 A.D.2d 763, 660 N.Y.S.2d 890 (3d Dept. 1997).

—Conviction for assault in the second degree supported where police officer received cut lip, abrasions, choke marks around his throat, scraped knee and suffered severe back pain as a result of altercation. People v. Cancer, 232 A.D.2d 875, 649 N.Y.S.2d 492 (3d Dept. 1996).

—Evidence was sufficient to support conviction for assault in the second degree: defendant and accomplices challenged victim to fight and although victim agreed to "fair fight" before fight began, defendant jumped on victim from behind and struck victim with a hammer. People v. Trichilo, 230 A.D.2d 926, 646 N.Y.S.2d 898 (3d Dept. 1996).

—Testimony that defendant and his co-defendants struck victim in the head with a blunt instrument and kicked and "stomped on" the victim's body and face, that victim was covered in blood when police arrived and had cuts and bruises all over his body, he was admitted to the trauma unit for several days following the incident and still suffers from headaches, established a physical injury, conviction for assault affirmed. People v. Carter, 6 A.D.3d 1174, 776 N.Y.S.2d 403 (4th Dept. 2004).

—Physical injury was established when police officer testified as to the pain experienced when defendant hit him with a

wooden bat or club and described the pain and swelling which continued for some time. People v. Sylvester, 254 A.D.2d 711, 677 N.Y.S.2d 865 (4th Dept. 1998).

—Evidence established second degree assault conviction where defendant slashed victim's face, thigh and back with a box cutter. People v. Walos, 229 A.D.2d 953, 645 N.Y.S.2d 695 (4th Dept. 1996).

Serious physical injury.—Conviction for assault in the second degree not supported by evidence; serious physical injury not established by head wound which required stitches but was not life threatening or caused a protracted or serious impairment or disfigurement. People v. Mack, 268 A.D.2d 599, 707 N.Y.S.2d 105 (2d Dept.), *appeal denied,* 94 N.Y.2d 904 (2000).

—Defendant's conviction for assault in the second degree was supported by evidence that he beat the mother of his minor children in their presence from which she sustained a fractured jaw in three places, facial contusions and lacerations, and two ruptured eardrums. People v. Spickerman, 307 A.D.2d 774, 762 N.Y.S.2d 470 (4th Dept. 2003).

Peace officer, police officer or fireman.—Proof defendant intended to prevent officer from performing his official duties and caused physical injury to the arresting officer was established by the officer's testimony that he was injured in the course of a chase with defendant which ensued after the officer told the defendant he was going to be arrested. People v. Coulanges, 264 A.D.2d 853, 696 N.Y.S.2d 466 (2d Dept. 1999).

—Injuries accidentally sustained by prison guard while defendant intentionally resisted being moved from one cell to another by that guard in the course of his official duties was sufficient to support conviction for assault in the second degree. People v. Harmon, 264 A.D.2d 941, 695 N.Y.S.2d 758 (3d Dept. 1999).

Uncharged sex offenses.—The fact that the evidence revealed that defendant might have been guilty of an uncharged sex offense as well as of assault imposed no additional burden on the People; the argument that the victim's testimony must be corroborated whenever it indicates that the defendant has committed, or might have committed, any sex offenses requiring corroboration, is not supported by current law. People v. Colclough, 32 N.Y.2d 227, 344 N.Y.S.2d 880, 298 N.E.2d 64 (1973).

—A defendant's failure to take an exception or request a charge that corroboration of assault with intent to commit rape is necessary where evidence of an actual rape is received "precludes review of the question" by an appellate court. People v. Reynolds, 25 N.Y.2d 489, 307 N.Y.S.2d 201, 255 N.E.2d 548 (1969).

Defense.—It is no defense to an assault second degree conviction that an arrest may not have been authorized. People v. Winslow, 153 A.D.2d 965, 545 N.Y.S.2d 405 (3d Dept. 1989).

Dangerous instrument.—Sufficient proof existed to establish guilt of second degree assault: a wad of paper towels that defendant used to gag his 10-year-old victim during an assault was a dangerous instrument where the wad of towels was wadded up with rubber bands to create a "dense ball that was shoved into the victim's mouth with sufficient force to break a tooth," victim's hands were bound, preventing her from removing towels, and therefore, wad was capable of causing serious physical injury. People v. Vasquez, 88 N.Y.2d 561, 647 N.Y.S.2d 697, 670 N.E.2d 1328 (1996).

—In a case of road rage, evidence that punched victim when he got out of his car and slammed victim's face into the car door, causing injury, supported a conviction of second degree assault. People v. Izquierdo, 292 A.D.2d 247, 739 N.Y.S.2d 78 (1st Dept. 2002).

—Wire handle of flyswatter used to strike 5-year-old child on the back over her clothing was capable of causing serious physical injury. People v. Wade, 232 A.D.2d 290, 648 N.Y.S.2d 563 (1st Dept. 1996).

—A child's toy bat, under the circumstances of its use in this case, was readily capable of causing serious physical injury; thus, it satisfied the definition of "dangerous instrument" for purposes of determining the sufficiency of the second degree assault charge. People v. Torres, 211 A.D.2d 509, 621 N.Y.S.2d 340 (1st Dept. 1995).

—"The use by the average layperson of the hand to strike a blow is insufficient proof of assault in the second degree, which requires causing physical injury to another by use of a dangerous instrument." People v. Nealy, 254 A.D.2d 505, 681 N.Y.S.2d 33 (2d Dept. 1998).

—Defendant's admitted use of either a hammer or a screwdriver to hit victim over head in order to gain access to apartment supported conviction for assault in the second degree, either tool can be a dangerous instrument when used in a manner that "is readily capable of causing death or other serious physical injury." People v. Holmes, 9 A.D.3d 689, 780 N.Y.S.2d 96 (3d Dept. 2004).

—Evidence that defendant smashed victim in the face with a plate, an instrument readily capable of causing serious physical injury, and caused a laceration, supported a conviction for assault in the second degree. People v. Zabala, 290 A.D.2d 578, 735 N.Y.S.2d 244 (3d Dept. 2002).

—Conviction for assault in the second degree was supported by evidence that defendant used a tire iron to hit victim repeatedly in the head, inflicting serious physical injury. People v. Saunders, 292 A.D.2d 780, 738 N.Y.S.2d 785 (4th Dept. 2002).

Evidence.—The People's failure to establish that the assault was committed in furtherance of the underlying felonies, criminal possession of a weapon in the second or third degree, required reversal of the conviction. People v. Williams, 255 A.D.2d 610, 682 N.Y.S.2d 60 (2d Dept. 1998).

—Four-month old victim sustained bruised face, ribs, back, and neck after being left alone in defendant's care; treating doctor testified that injuries caused victim pain and were not consistent with accidental injury, as defendant had claimed; victim also had many fractured ribs and a broken arm, all in various stages of healing, which was indicative of a pattern of abuse; conviction for assault in second degree was affirmed. People v. Jennings, 20 A.D.3d 777, 798 N.Y.S.2d 597 (3d Dept. 2005).

—Where after five-month old child was left alone in defendant's care, when she was returned to her mother she had black and blue marks on her cheeks, nose and lip and under her eyes, physician who treated victim testified that injuries were consistent with child abuse, and that child could not have sustained her injuries through her own actions and, in his opinion, the injuries would have caused her substantial pain at the time of infliction, supported defendant's conviction under §120.05(8). People v. Tompkins, 8 A.D.3d 901, 780 N.Y.S.2d 387 (3d Dept. 2004).

—The evidence, viewed in the light most favorable to the People, was sufficient to support a conviction for assault in the second degree. People v. Puckett, 212 A.D.2d 1041, 623 N.Y.S.2d 444 (4th Dept. 1995).

Family court jurisdiction.—An assault charge based on defendant's attack of his eleven-year-old daughter with the intent to commit incest should have been heard by the family court because the prosecution of any assault within the enumerated family group, of any degree or purpose, must begin in the family court (Family Court Act 813-a); thus, an assault conviction in county court was reversed and the case transferred to family court. People v. Nuernberger, 25 N.Y.2d 179, 303 N.Y.S.2d 74, 250 N.E.2d 352 (1969).

—Since the family court has jurisdiction over assault offenses between spouses and since the assault and nonassault charges were so inextricably related, the transaction lay, in the first instance, within the jurisdiction of the family court where defendant was charged with attempted assault of his wife, burglary, and felonious possession of a dangerous weapon. However, where a husband assaults his divorced wife, the crime is not within the jurisdiction of the family court because the use of violence is no longer the symptom of a failing family relationship capable of being salvaged or made tolerable by family court intervention. Therefore, the Supreme Court had original jurisdiction over the crime charged and could convict defendant. People v. Williams 24 N.Y.2d 274, 300 N.Y.S.2d 89, 248 N.E.2d 8 (1969).

—Defendant appealed conviction for assault on his uncle on the ground that the matter should have been submitted to the family court; the Court of Appeals held that because the assault arose to a greater extent out of a landlord-tenant relationship between defendant and his uncle, rather than an intimate family relationship, the criminal court properly exercised jurisdiction. People v. Williams, 24 N.Y.2d 274, 200 N.Y.S.2d 89, 248 N.E.2d 8 (1969).

Felony assault.—Court rejected proposition that the felony assault statute may be analogized to a felony murder where

acquittal of the underlying felony is not deemed inconsistent with a felony murder conviction. People v. Sanchez, 128 A.D.2d 377, 512 N.Y.S.2d 389 (1st Dept. 1987).

No completed felony necessary.—Defendant's conviction for assault in the second degree was not repugnant; there is no requirement that the defendant be found guilty of a completed felony in order to be convicted of assault in the second degree. People v. Ladson, 209 A.D.2d 640, 619 N.Y.S.2d 133 (2d Dept. 1994).

Lesser included offenses.—it was proper exercise of discretion for court, sua sponte, to submit assault in the second degree as a lesser included offense of assault in the first degree over objections of both defense and People; decision was supported by a reasonable view of evidence that defendant intended to cause physical injury, but not serious physical injury, and there was no surprise in submission nor prejudice to defense. People v. Edwards, 16 A.D.3d 226, 792 N.Y.S.2d 394 (1st Dept. 2005).

—Court properly refused to charge the jury with the offense of attempted assault in the second degree along with attempted assault in the first degree because no reasonable view of the evidence supported any conclusion other than defendant intended to cause serious physical injury with a deadly weapon where defendant aimed a gun at the victim and fired, then pursued him while firing three more times. People v. Brooks, 278 A.D.2d 501, 718 N.Y.S.2d 402 (2d Dept. 2000), *appeal denied,* 96 N.Y.2d 781 (2001).

—Evidence that one victim sustained a non-life threatening gunshot wound for which he was treated when he arrived at the emergency room fully conscious and responsive and second victim's bullet wound to the neck was treated without surgery did not support assault in the first degree conviction, these were physical injuries not serious physical injuries, no medical evidence about health risks to victim with fragments left in place introduced; lesser included offense of assault in the second degree established. People v. Horton, 9 A.D.3d 503, 780 N.Y.S.2d 654 (3d Dept. 2004).

—Assault in the second degree is a lesser included offense of assault in the first degree when a gun is involved. People v. Watson, 277 A.D.2d 593, 715 N.Y.S.2d 543 (3d Dept. 2000), *appeal denied,* 96 N.Y.2d 764 (2001).

—Defendant was not denied effective assistance of counsel by reason of counsel's failure to request that court consider assault in the second degree and reckless endangerment in the second degree as lesser included offenses of attempted murder in the first degree since neither is a lesser included offense of attempted murder. People v. Beverly, 229 A.D.2d 970, 645 N.Y.S.2d 689 (4th Dept. 1996).

§ 120.06. Gang assault in the second degree.

A person is guilty of gang assault in the second degree when, with intent to cause physical injury to another person and when aided by two or more other persons actually present, he causes serious physical injury to such person or to a third person.

Gang assault in the second degree is a class C felony.

Added by L. 1996, Ch. 647, § 2, eff. Nov. 1, 1996.

ANNOTATIONS

Nature of crime.—On appeal, court determined that jury could reasonably have inferred that defendant and codefendant were in a position to render immediate assistance to their accomplice and, therefore, posed a sufficient threat of additional violence so as to satisfy aggravating element necessary to sustain conviction of gang assault in second degree. People v. Williams, 14 A.D.3d 519, 787 N.Y.S.2d 399 (2d Dept. 2005).

—Gang assault, a violent felony, is a serious charge, typically allowing a longer delay in prosecution. People v. Magar, 8 A.D.3d 689, 777 N.Y.S.2d 786 (3d Dept. 2004).

—Where evidence showed that group of four defendants decided to attack previously unknown victim from behind by hitting him with a wooden object in back of the head, and once victim was down, accomplice and codefendants punched and kicked him, and 17-year-old victim sustained fractured skull and injury to the brain requiring surgery and had no memory of unprovoked attack, conviction was affirmed. People v. Rimmen, 17 A.D.3d 1078, 794 N.Y.S.2d 246 (4th Dept. 2005).

—Court properly found the testimony of the victim that respondent, along with several other young men, attacked him outside the school they all attended, that victim obtained medical treatment at two hospitals and was hospitalized for six nights, his eye was swollen shut and he was unable to move it from side to side for approximately one week, and that his eyesight was still impaired well over a month after the attack supported a finding of serious physical injury, and gang assault in the second degree. *In re* Timothy S., 1 A.D.3d 908, 767 N.Y.S.2d 190 (4th Dept. 2004).

—Gang assault in the second degree is a violent crime involving an intent to cause physical injury when aided by two or more people and recognizes the threat to public safety posed by gang attacks. People v. Johnson, 191 Misc. 2d 105, 742 N.Y.S.2d 482 (Sup. Ct. Bronx Co. 2002).

§ 120.07. Gang assault in the first degree.

A person is guilty of gang assault in the first degree when, with intent to cause serious physical injury to another person and when aided by two or more other persons actually present, he causes serious physical injury to such person or to a third person.

Gang assault in the first degree is a class B felony.

Added by L. 1996, Ch. 647, § 2, eff. Nov. 1, 1996.

§ 120.08. Assault on a peace officer, police officer, fireman or emergency medical services professional.

A person is guilty of assault on a peace officer, police officer, fireman or emergency medical services professional when, with intent to prevent a peace officer, police officer, a fireman, including a fireman acting as a paramedic or emergency medical technician administering first aid in the course of performance of duty as such fireman, or an emergency medical service paramedic or emergency medical service technician, from performing a lawful duty, he causes serious physical injury to such peace officer, police officer, fireman, paramedic or technician.

Assault on a peace officer, police officer, fireman or emergency medical services professional is a class C felony.

Added by L. 1996, Ch. 632, § 2, eff. Nov. 1, 1996.

§ 120.10. Assault in the first degree.

A person is guilty of assault in the first degree when:

1. With intent to cause serious physical injury to another person, he causes such injury to such person or to a third person by means of a deadly weapon or a dangerous instrument; or

2. With intent to disfigure another person seriously and permanently, or to destroy, amputate or disable permanently a member or organ of his body, he causes such injury to such person or to a third person; or

3. Under circumstances evincing a depraved indifference to human life, he recklessly engages in conduct which creates a grave risk of death to another person, and thereby causes serious physical injury to another person; or

4. In the course of and in furtherance of the commission or attempted commission of a felony or of immediate flight therefrom, he, or another participant if there be any, causes serious physical injury to a person other than one of the participants.

Assault in the first degree is a class B felony.

Amended by L. 1967, Ch. 791; L. 1996, Ch. 646, § 2, amending closing para., eff. Nov. 1, 1996.

ANNOTATIONS

Evidence.—Evidence that defendant shot two people, killing one of them, supported conviction for manslaughter in the first degree, assault in the first degree, and a weapons charge; sentencing for weapons charge should have run concurrently with manslaughter and assault charges, since weapon was involved in shootings and jury found defendant guilty of second-degree weapon possession for having possessed a pistol "with intent to use it unlawfully against another," namely, the two shooting victims. People v. Hamilton, 4 N.Y.3d 654, 797 N.Y.S.2d 408, 830 N.E.2d 306 (2005).

—Evidence was legally sufficient to establish defendant's guilt of assault in the first degree: victim testified that as a result of the beating by defendant she still suffered some loss of vision in her right eye nine months later at the time of trial, thus there was sufficient evidence of "protracted impairment of the function of a bodily organ." People v. Hirschhorn, 231 A.D.2d 591, 648 N.Y.S.2d 34 (2d Dept. 1996).

—Conviction for attempted assault in the first degree sustained based on evidence at trial that included repeated threats by defendant to kill victim, stabbing her with knives, and beating her with a table leg. People v. Elliot, 299 A.D.2d 731, 751 N.Y.S.2d 331 (3d Dept. 2002), *appeal after remand*, 757 N.Y.S. 807 (3d Dept. 2003).

—Circumstantial evidence can be used to establish that defendant used a dangerous instrument to inflict injuries on victim. The type of wound sustained by the victim, in this case a ten-inch long laceration to the chest which penetrated the sternum, proved that the assault was committed with a dangerous instrument. People v. Wilson, 240 A.D.2d 774, 658 N.Y.S.2d 524 (3d Dept. 1997).

—Evidence viewed in light most favorable to the People supports conviction for first degree assault and endangering the welfare of a child; evidence also established the "absence of accident or mistake." People v. Brewer, 295 A.D.2d 1013, 743 N.Y.S.2d 920 (4th Dept. 2002).

—An intent to inflict serious physical injury was readily inferable from defendant's admissions concerning the beating of his wife, where defendant admitted that he took an ash tray and struck her at least three times, causing severe injuries. People v. Smallwood, 162 A.D.2d 1004, 557 N.Y.S.2d 214 (4th Dept. 1990).

Lesser included offense.—Where "verdict is comprised of inclusory concurrent counts, a verdict of guilty on the greatest count is deemed a dismissal of every lesser count"; thus here, where defendant was convicted of both assault in the first degree and assault in the second degree based on the same incident, the conviction for assault in the second degree was vacated and that count of the indictment was dismissed. People v. Ashman, 280 A.D.2d 483, 720 N.Y.S.2d 524 (2d Dept.), *appeal denied*, 96 N.Y.2d 781 (2001).

—Court properly refused to charge the jury with the offense of attempted assault in the second degree along with attempted assault in the first degree because no reasonable view of the evidence supported any conclusion other than defendant intended to cause serious physical injury with a deadly weapon where defendant aimed a gun at the victim and fired, then pursued him while firing three more times. People v. Brooks, 278 A.D.2d 501, 718 N.Y.S.2d 402 (2d Dept. 2000), *appeal denied*, 96 N.Y.2d 781 (2001).

—Assault in the second degree is a lesser included offense of assault in the first degree when a gun is involved. People v. Watson, 277 A.D.2d 593, 715 N.Y.S.2d 543 (3d Dept. 2000), *appeal denied,* 96 N.Y.2d 764 (2001).

—Defendant's conviction on assault in the first degree is dismissed as a lesser included offense of robbery in the first degree. People v. Miles, 236 A.D.2d 786, 654 N.Y.S.2d 57 (4th Dept. 1997).

Serious physical injury.—Evidence legally sufficient to establish that defendant, "with intent to disfigure another person seriously and permanently," caused a serious physical injury by repeatedly punching and kicking the victim, causing, among other things, a permanent and noticeable change in the shape of his face. People v. McLaughlin, 8 A.D.3d 146, 780 N.Y.S.2d 119 (1st Dept. 2004).

—Conviction for assault in the first degree was sufficiently supported by evidence that assault victim suffered serious physical injury, specifically, multiple gunshot wounds. People v. Foster, 278 A.D.2d 241, 717 N.Y.S.2d 303 (2d Dept. 2000).

—Evidence that one victim sustained a non-life threatening gunshot wound for which he was treated when he arrived at the emergency room fully conscious and responsive and second victim's bullet wound to the neck was treated without surgery did not support assault in the first degree conviction, these were physical injuries not serious physical injuries, no medical evidence about health risks to victim with fragments left in place introduced; lesser included offense of assault in the second degree established. People v. Horton, 9 A.D.3d 503, 780 N.Y.S.2d 654 (3d Dept. 2004).

—Conviction for assault in the first degree supported by evidence of serious physical injury; defendant participated in beating of victim which resulted in head injuries and severe facial lacerations from which victim would have bled to death if left unattended. People v. Jeanty, 268 A.D.2d 675, 702 N.Y.S.2d 194 (3d Dept.), *appeal denied,* 94 N.Y.2d 949 (2000).

—Defendant's actions of squeezing three-month-old infant so hard as to break 20 ribs, although a severe injury, was not a serious physical injury since it was not life threatening, and therefore could not support a charge under this section. People v. Parrotte, 267 A.D.2d 884, 702 N.Y.S.2d 137 (3d Dept. 1999), *appeal denied,* 95 N.Y.2d 801 (2000).

—"Serious physical injury" within the meaning of this section was established by the testimony of four witnesses to the attack, as well as medical records documenting the severe injuries victim sustained as a result of the beating. People v. Jau Kud Su, 239 A.D.2d 703, 657 N.Y.S.2d 483 (3d Dept. 1997).

—Medical evidence established victim lost two liters of blood when stabbed before he was attended to by emergency medical personnel, and thus jury properly could concluded that if the "injuries had been left untreated [the victim] could have bled to death." People v. Irwin, 5 A.D.3d 1122, 774 N.Y.S.2d 237 (4th Dept. 2004).

—Where defendant fired gun into crowded bar and shot two patrons, evidence was insufficient to support conviction of assault in the first degree where there was no evidence that victims sustained serious physical injury; however, evidence was sufficient to sustain attempted assault in the first degree. People v. Pross, 302 A.D.2d 895, 754 N.Y.S.2d 792 (4th Dept. 2003).

Dangerous instrument.—Where defendant repeatedly punched and kicked the victim into a comatose state, the rubber boots which defendant was wearing at the time were properly found to have been a "dangerous instrument." People v. Carter, 73 A.D.2d 986, 423 N.Y.S.2d 559 (3d Dept. 1980), *aff'd,* 53 N.Y.2d 113, 440 N.Y.S.2d 607, 423 N.E.2d 30 (1981).

Depraved indifference.—Testimony that defendant stabbed his ex-girlfriend's brother as the brother tried to defend her from defendant's assault, defendant stabbed his victim in the back, causing a two and one-half inch deep wound under his left armpit and a collapsed lung, coupled with physician's testimony that wound could have been fatal, supported conclusion of defendant's depraved indifference to human life and that his reckless infliction of serious physical injury on his victim which created a grave risk of death. People v. Bentley, 7 A.D.3d 414, 777 N.Y.S.2d 431 (1st Dept. 2004).

—Depraved indifference to human life refers to the wantonness of a defendant's conduct; the focus is on an objective determination of the degree of risk presented by the defendant's reckless

conduct. People v. Jackson, 211 A.D.2d 644, 620 N.Y.S.2d 486 (2d Dept. 1995).

§ 120.11. Aggravated assault upon a police officer or a peace officer.

A person is guilty of aggravated assault upon a police officer or a peace officer when, with intent to cause serious physical injury to a person whom he knows or reasonably should know to be a police officer or a peace officer engaged in the course of performing his official duties, he causes such injury by means of a deadly weapon or dangerous instrument.

Aggravated assault upon a police officer or a peace officer is a class B felony.

Added by L. 1980, Ch. 233; **Amended** by L. 1981, Ch. 175.

ANNOTATIONS

Performing official duties.—Defendant's conviction for aggravated assault under PL § 120.11 was affirmed where defendant rammed his car at 70 miles per hour into a police car backing up down a road and police officer was performing official duties in assisting state police in setting up roadblock to help capture a fleeing fugitive (defendant); whether injured officer could have made a lawful arrest is separate, but irrelevant, inquiry in this case. People v. Glanda, 18 A.D.3d 956,794 N.Y.S.2d 712 (3d Dept. 2005).

—People did not need to establish that defendant intended to cause crash between his van and police car which was involved in a high speed chase after defendant refused an order to stop, conviction only required that defendant intended to prevent police officer from performing a lawful duty and serious injuries resulted. People v. Bridges, 16 A.D.3d 911, 791 N.Y.S.2d 228 (3d Dept. 2005).

§ 120.12. Aggravated assault upon a person less than eleven years old.

A person is guilty of aggravated assault upon a person less than eleven years old when being eighteen years old or more the defendant commits the crime of assault in the third degree as defined in section 120.00 of this article upon a person less than eleven years old and has been previously convicted of such crime upon a person less than eleven years old within the preceding three years.

Aggravated assault upon a person less than eleven years old is a class E felony.

Added by L. 1990, Ch. 477.

§ 120.13. Menacing in the first degree.

A person is guilty of menacing in the first degree when he or she commits the crime of menacing in the second degree and has been previously convicted of the crime of menacing in the second degree within the preceding ten years.

Menacing in the first degree is a class E felony.

Added by L. 1992, Ch. 345, eff. Nov. 1, 1992.

§ 120.14. Menacing in the second degree.

A person is guilty of menacing in the second degree when:

1. He or she intentionally places or attempts

to place another person in reasonable fear of physical injury, serious physical injury or death by displaying a deadly weapon, dangerous instrument or what appears to be a pistol, revolver, rifle, shotgun, machine gun or other firearm; or

2. He or she repeatedly follows a person or engages in a course of conduct or repeatedly commits acts over a period of time intentionally placing or attempting to place another person in reasonable fear of physical injury, serious physical injury or death; or

3. He or she commits the crime of menacing in the third degree in violation of that part of a duly served order of protection, or such order which the defendant has actual knowledge of because he or she was present in court when such order was issued, pursuant to article eight of the family court act, section 530.12 of the criminal procedure law, or an order of protection issued by a court of competent jurisdiction in another state, territorial or tribal jurisdiction, which directed the respondent or defendant to stay away from the person or persons on whose behalf the order was issued.

Menacing in the second degree is a class A misdemeanor.

Added by L. 1992, Ch. 345, eff. Nov. 1, 1992; **Amended** by L. 1994, Ch. 222, § 46, eff. Jan. 1, 1995; L. 1998, Ch. 597, § 14, eff. Dec. 22, 1998, amending subd. 3.

ANNOTATIONS

Evidence.—Defendant displayed and threatened to use his handgun to shoot the engine of an all-terrain vehicle used by two 14-year-old girls who trespassed on his property, he spotted the girls in the distance on his property without permission and after they failed to respond to his yells to leave, he fired a warning shot, threatened to shoot out their engine and told them they were under arrest. Manne v. Main, 8 A.D.3d 790, 778 N.Y.S.2d 210 (3d Dept. 2004).

—Evidence did not support charge of menacing in the second degree where basis of charge was defendant's telephone conversation with a third party in which he stated he intended to harm two classmates; there was no evidence that those threats were ever communicated to the intended victims, and defendant thus did not put them in "reasonable fear of physical injury." In re Kyle L., 268 A.D.2d 836, 701 N.Y.S.2d 525 (3d Dept. 2000).

—"Intent can be inferred from the act itself or from the defendant's conduct and the surrounding circumstances"; conviction was supported by evidence from which jury could find that defendant intended to place victim in reasonable fear of physical injury when, among other things, he displayed a tire iron during confrontation. People v. Bryant, 13 A.D.3d 1170, 787 N.Y.S.2d 540 (4th Dept. 2004).

—Uncontroverted evidence that defendant, a part-time patrolman employed by the local police department, displayed his firearm while trying to talk to the complainant on a friend's behalf about custody of his daughter, established probable cause to support the charge. Quigley v. City of Auburn, 267 A.D.2d 978, 701 N.Y.S.2d 580 (4th Dept. 1999).

Lesser included offense.—Harassment in the second degree is not a lesser included offense of menacing in the second degree. People v. Bartkow, 96 N.Y.2d 770, 725 N.Y.S.2d 589, 749 N.E.2d 158 (2001).

§ 120.15. Menacing in the third degree.

A person is guilty of menacing in the third degree when, by physical menace, he or she intentionally places or attempts to place another

person in fear of death, imminent serious physical injury or physical injury.

Menacing in the third degree is a class B misdemeanor.

Amended by L. 1992, Ch. 345, eff. Nov. 1, 1992.

ANNOTATIONS

Menacing as lesser included offense.—The crime of menacing does not constitute a lesser degree of any of the following crimes: (1) riot (Penal Law § 240.05), (2) reckless endangerment (Penal Law § 120.20) and resisting arrest (Penal Law § 205.30). People v. Weixel, 28 N.Y.2d 738, 321 N.Y.S.2d 119, 269 N.E.2d 827 (1971).

Sufficiency of allegation.—Allegation that defendant displayed a handgun and punched and struck an informant about the body with a nightstick was sufficient to establish the charge of menacing. People v. Gore, 143 Misc. 2d 106, 540 N.Y.S.2d 147 (Crim. Ct. Kings Co. 1989).

Evidence.—The elements of this crime, which include physical rather than merely verbal menace, were established by evidence, appellant and three other students approached their former teacher on a subway platform, surrounded her and blocked her path, one of the youths told her she was not going anywhere since she had failed them, that appellant said "Why don't we throw her on the tracks? A train is coming," and that appellant reached toward her as she escaped. In re Pedro H., 308 A.D.2d 374, 764 N.Y.S.2d 274 (1st Dept. 2003).

—There was ample evidence presented to find, beyond a reasonable doubt, that the respondent, acting with another, attempted to forcibly steal property from the complainant by using gestures and the threatened use of a gun that caused the complainant to fear death or serious physical injury; these actions, if committed by an adult, would constitute the crimes of robbery in the third degree and menacing in the third degree. In re William A., 219 A.D.2d 494, 631 N.Y.S.2d 314 (1st Dept. 1995).

—Evidence was sufficient to establish menacing in the third degree where there was testimony that respondent pointed gun at witness and pumped it twice, and that witness was frightened because he thought he was going to die. In re David P., 211 A.D.2d 995, 621 N.Y.S.2d 742 (3d Dept. 1995).

§ 120.16. Hazing in the first degree.

A person is guilty of hazing in the first degree when, in the course of another person's initiation into or affiliation with any organization, he intentionally or recklessly engages in conduct which creates a substantial risk of physical injury to such other person or a third person and thereby causes such injury.

Hazing in the first degree is a class A misdemeanor.

Added by L. 1983, Ch. 716; **Amended** by L. 1988, Ch. 86.

ANNOTATION

Sufficiency of evidence.—The coercive effect of the initiation ritual and related issues of culpable conduct, including the decedent's action, are questions of fact for the jury to resolve. Thoja v. Grand Ch. of Theta Chi Fraternity, 174 Misc. 2d 966, 667 N.Y.S.2d 650 (Sup. Ct. Tompkins Co. 1997).

§ 120.17. Hazing in the second degree.

A person is guilty of hazing in the second degree when, in the course of another person's initiation or affiliation with any organization, he intentionally or recklessly engages in conduct which creates a substantial risk of physical injury to such other person or a third person.

Hazing in the second degree is a violation.

Added by L. 1988, Ch. 86.

§ 120.20. Reckless endangerment in the second degree.

A person is guilty of reckless endangerment in the second degree when he recklessly engages in conduct which creates a substantial risk of serious physical injury to another person.

Reckless endangerment in the second degree is a class A misdemeanor.

ANNOTATIONS

Evidence.—In a fatal excavation accident, where reasonable safety precautions were taken to ensure safety of workers, proof offered to the grand jury was insufficient to establish the foreseeability of the victim's death; there was no evidence that the defendant's "consciously disregard[ed] a substantial and unjustifiable risk," and no recklessness established. People v. Reagan, 94 N.Y.2d 804, 701 N.Y.S.2d 306, 723 N.E.2d 55 (1999).

—Evidence was legally sufficient to establish defendant's guilt of reckless endangerment beyond a reasonable doubt; evidence established that defendant/doctor was aware of and consciously disregarded a substantial risk of serious physical injury to nursing home patient by delaying her transfer to a hospital, and that the defendant's conduct deviated from that which a reasonable person would have observed in the same situation. People v. Einaugler, 208 A.D.2d 946, 618 N.Y.S.2d 414 (2d Dept. 1994).

—The conviction of reckless endangerment in the second degree was supported by evidence that defendant started a fire in the apartment she shared with a friend by splashing rubbing alcohol about and then igniting it. People v. Canty, 135 A.D.2d 721, 522 N.Y.S.2d 622 (2d Dept. 1987).

—People did not need to establish that defendant intended to cause crash between his van and police car that was involved in a high speed chase after defendant refused an order to stop; conviction only required that defendant's conduct created substantial risk of serious physical injury to another person. People v. Bridges, 16 A.D.3d 911, 791 N.Y.S.2d 228 (3d Dept. 2005).

—Evidence supported conviction of corporation of criminally negligent homicide and reckless endangerment in the second degree where defendant failed to obtain valid state inspection of vehicle, failed to conduct any steps to evaluate vehicle's safety which would have revealed unsafe conditions of tires and permitted youthful driver with little automotive knowledge to operate vehicle. People v. Congregation Khal Chaisidiei, 232 A.D.2d 919, 649 N.Y.S.2d 499 (3d Dept. 1996).

—Evidence that defendant drove a vehicle that swerved into the opposing lane of traffic and nearly collided with two vehicles before eventually colliding with a third vehicle, killing the driver of that vehicle, defendant's passenger was intoxicated and repeatedly grabbed the steering wheel, however, defendant continued driving despite her passenger's repeated interference with her driving, continued to speed, and did not slow down or apply brakes before collision or near collisions, supported conviction under this section. People v. Botting, 8 A.D.3d 1064, 778 N.Y.S.2d 824 (4th Dept. 2004).

Intent.—Conviction must be reversed where the defendant was a passenger in an automobile that stopped several times behind the complainant's truck, making it difficult for the complainant to move the truck, as there was no showing that defendant intentionally aided the driver of the car to engage in such conduct. People v. Perniciaro, 58 N.Y.2d 751, 459 N.Y.S.2d 20, 445 N.E.2d 196 (1982).

Lesser included offenses.—It was error for court not to charge reckless endangerment in the second degree as a lesser included offense of reckless endangerment in the first degree where evidence showed that defendant shot at victims' house from a distance of 50 yards, using birdshot as ammunition, court noting "reasonable view of the evidence that defendant's conduct created a substantial risk of serious physical injury to each victim but did not create a grave risk of death." People v. Dann, 17 A.D.3d 1152, 793 N.Y.S.2d 852 (4th Dept. 2005).

—Defendant was not denied effective assistance of counsel by reason of counsel's failure to request that court consider assault in the second degree and reckless endangerment in the second degree as lesser included offenses of attempted murder in the first degree since neither is a lesser included offense of attempted murder. People v. Beverly, 229 A.D.2d 970, 645 N.Y.S.2d 689 (4th Dept. 1996).

§ 120.25. Reckless endangerment in the first degree.

A person is guilty of reckless endangerment in the first degree when, under circumstances evincing a depraved indifference to human life, he recklessly engages in conduct which creates a grave risk of death to another person.

Reckless endangerment in the first degree is a class D felony.

ANNOTATIONS

Evidence.—Evidence of defendant's conduct was legally sufficient to sustain conviction for first degree reckless endangerment; proof showed that defendant physically restrained complainant by her hair, placed handgun to her temple, and cocked weapon, and reasonable trier of fact could conclude that by creating this situation, where a sudden movement could readily have resulted in the accidental discharge of the weapon, the defendant recklessly created a grave risk of death under circumstances evidencing a depraved mind. People v. Chrysler, 85 N.Y.2d 413, 626 N.Y.S.2d 18, 649 N.E.2d 1162 (1995).

—Crime of reckless endangerment is committed based on actor's conduct whether directed at one person or several people; the counts of reckless endangerment reflect the conduct, not the number of individuals affected. People v. Stockholm, 279 A.D.2d 704, 719 N.Y.S.2d 330 (3d Dept. 2001), *appeal denied*, 96 N.Y.2d 802 (2001).

—Defendant's actions of squeezing three-month-old infant so hard as to break 20 ribs evidenced a depraved indifference to human life as well as creating a grave risk of death to another and was sufficient to support a charge under this section. People v. Parrotte, 267 A.D.2d 884, 702 N.Y.S.2d 137 (3d Dept. 1999), *appeal denied*, 95 N.Y.2d 797 (2000).

—Evidence that defendant fired a semiautomatic weapon at two uniformed police officers who stopped his vehicle for traffic violations, could not support both convictions for attempted murder in the first degree and reckless endangerment in the first degree (one intentional act and one unintentional act, respectively), verdicts were reversed on appeal with instruction to trial court that on retrial, these two counts had to be presented to the jury in the alternative. People v. Robinson, 8 A.D.3d 1028, 778 N.Y.S.2d 808 (4th Dept. 2004), *aff'd sub nom.* People v. Daniels, 5 N.Y.3d 738, 800 N.Y.S.2d 369, 833 N.E.2d 704 (2005).

Nature of offense.—Reckless endangerment in the first degree is not a violent felony offense, and defendant's adjudication as a persistent violent felony offender based upon his two prior violent felony convictions and his conviction for the instant offense of reckless endangerment in the first degree was improper. People v. Carrion, 265 A.D.2d 564, 697 N.Y.S.2d 638 (2d Dept. 1999).

Nonslayer defense.—Jury was within provence to reject nonslayer defense, which would mean that defendant did not in any way cause or aid in victim's death; evidence established that defendant assisted assailants by leaving access window open for robbery, helped bind and move victim who later died. People v. Jeanty, 268 A.D.2d 675, 702 N.Y.S.2d 194 (3d Dept.), *appeal denied*, 94 N.Y.2d 949 (2000).

No outcome or injury necessary.—The reckless endangerment statute does not proscribe a particular outcome or injury. The risk created by an actor's conduct is what it seeks to prevent and what is criminalized by the statute. People v. Chrysler, 85 N.Y.2d 413, 626 N.Y.S.2d 18, 649 N.E.2d 1162 (1995).

Lesser included offense.—Defendant charged with reckless endangerment in the first degree was not entitled to a charge of reckless endangerment in the second degree since there was no reasonable view of the evidence from which the jury could have found that the defendant committed the lesser crime;

evidence showed that a pistol, which had been pointed by defendant at a police officer's chest, discharged during the resulting struggle, causing the officer powder burn injuries, and thereby creating a grave risk of death and not merely a substantial risk of serious physical injury. People v. Vincent, 115 A.D.2d 179, 495 N.Y.S.2d 249 (3d Dept. 1985).

—Defendant was entitled to charge of reckless endangerment in the second degree as a lesser included offense of reckless endangerment of in the first degree where evidence showed that defendant shot at victims' house from a distance of 50 yards, using birdshot as ammunition, court noting "reasonable view of the evidence that defendant's conduct created a substantial risk of serious physical injury to each victim but did not create a grave risk of death." People v. Dann, 17 A.D.3d 1152, 793 N.Y.S.2d 852 (4th Dept. 2005).

Sentence.—Consecutive sentences were properly imposed for convictions of reckless endangerment in the first degree and criminal possession of a weapon in the second degree due to lack of overlapping statutory elements. People v. Woodruff, 237 A.D.2d 548, 656 N.Y.S.2d 32 (2d Dept. 1997).

Sufficiency of Evidence.—Evidence was legally insufficient to support conviction for reckless endangerment in the first degree; there was no evidence that defendant possessed a weapon at time of crime, was aware of robbery plan, or shared intent of the co-defendants or aided them in any way; mere presence cannot support a conviction. People v. Eldridge, 302 A.D.2d 934, 755 N.Y.S.2d 193 (4th Dept. 2003).

§ 120.30. Promoting a suicide attempt.

A person is guilty of promoting a suicide attempt when he intentionally causes or aids another person to attempt suicide.

Promoting a suicide attempt is a class E felony.

§ 120.35. Promoting a suicide attempt; when punishable as attempt to commit murder.

A person who engages in conduct constituting both the offense of promoting a suicide attempt and the offense of attempt to commit murder may not be convicted of attempt to commit murder unless he causes or aids the suicide attempt by the use of duress or deception.

§ 120.40. Definitions.

For purposes of sections 120.45, 120.50, 120.55 and 120.60 of this article:

1. "Kidnapping" shall mean a kidnapping crime defined in article one hundred thirty-five of this chapter.

2. "Unlawful imprisonment" shall mean an unlawful imprisonment felony crime defined in article one hundred thirty-five of this chapter.

3. "Sex offense" shall mean a felony defined in article one hundred thirty of this chapter, sexual misconduct, as defined in section 130.20 of this chapter, sexual abuse in the third degree as defined in section 130.55 of this chapter or sexual abuse in the second degree as defined in section 130.60 of this chapter.

4. "Immediate family" means the spouse, former spouse, parent, child, sibling, or any other person who regularly resides or has regularly resided in the household of a person.

5. "Specified predicate crime" means:

a. a violent felony offense;

b. a crime defined in section 130.20, 130.25, 130.30, 130.40, 130.45,130.55, 130.60, 130.70 or 255.25;

c. assault in the third degree, as defined in section 120.00; menacing in the first degree, as defined in section 120.13; menacing in the second degree, as defined in section 120.14; coercion in the first degree, as defined in section 135.65; coercion in the second degree, as defined in section 135.60; aggravated harassment in the second degree, as defined in section 240.30; harassment in the first degree, as defined in section 240.25; menacing in the third degree, as defined in section 120.15; criminal mischief in the third degree, as defined in section 145.05; criminal mischief in the second degree, as defined in section 145.10, criminal mischief in the first degree, as defined in section 145.12; criminal tampering in the first degree, as defined in section 145.20; arson in the fourth degree, as defined in section 150.05; arson in the third degree, as defined in section 150.10; criminal contempt in the first degree, as defined in section 215.51; endangering the welfare of a child, as defined in section 260.10; or

d. stalking in the fourth degree, as defined in section 120.45; stalking in the third degree, as defined in section 120.50; stalking in the second degree, as defined in section 120.55; or

e. an offense in any other jurisdiction which includes all of the essential elements of any such crime for which a sentence to a term of imprisonment in excess of one year or a sentence of death was authorized and is authorized in this state irrespective of whether such sentence was imposed.

Added by L. 1999, Ch. 635, § 13, eff. Dec. 1, 1999.

§ 120.45. Stalking in the fourth degree.

A person is guilty of stalking in the fourth degree when he or she intentionally, and for no legitimate purpose, engages in a course of conduct directed at a specific person, and knows or reasonably should know that such conduct:

1. Is likely to cause reasonable fear of material harm to the physical health, safety or property of such person, a member of such person's immediate family or a third party with whom such person is acquainted; or

2. Causes material harm to the mental or emotional health of such person, where such conduct consists of following, telephoning or initiating communication or contact with such person, a member of such person's immediate family or a third party with whom such person is acquainted, and the actor was previously clearly informed to cease that conduct; or

3. Is likely to cause such person to reasonably fear that his or her employment, business or career

is threatened, where such conduct consists of appearing, telephoning or initiating communication or contact at such person's place of employment or business, and the actor was previously clearly informed to cease that conduct.

Stalking in the fourth degree is a class B misdemeanor.

Added by L. 1999, Ch. 635, § 13, eff. Dec. 1, 1999.

ANNOTATIONS

Constitutionality.—The anti-stalking statute is neither unconstitutionally vague on its face nor as applied; the "failure of an as-applied challenge to the constitutionality of a statute on vagueness grounds automatically constitutes failure of a facial challenge as well." People v. Stuart, 100 N.Y.2d 412, 765 N.Y.S.2d 1, 797 N.E.2d 28 (2003).

—The term "legitimate purpose" does not render the statute void for vagueness; "[t]he legislative use of inherently imprecise language does not render a statute fatally vague where, as here, that language 'conveys sufficiently definite warning as to the proscribed conduct when measured by common understanding and practices.' " People v. Stuart, 191 Misc. 2d 541, 742 N.Y.S.2d 767 (App. T. 1st Dept. 2002).

Evidence.—Verdict was not against the weight of the evidence where, every day for over five weeks, defendant, a stranger to victim, stared at her and followed her around her neighborhood and school, circling around victim and darting in and out of buildings to avoid detection, after she had rejected his offers of candy and flowers on Valentine's Day. People v. Stuart, 191 Misc. 2d 541, 742 N.Y.S.2d 767 (App. T. 1st Dept. 2002).

§ 120.50. Stalking in the third degree.

A person is guilty of stalking in the third degree when he or she:

1. Commits the crime of stalking in the fourth degree in violation of section 120.45 of this article against three or more persons, in three or more separate transactions, for which the actor has not been previously convicted; or

2. Commits the crime of stalking in the fourth degree in violation of section 120.45 of this article against any person, and has previously been convicted, within the preceding ten years of a specified predicate crime, as defined in subdivision five of section 120.40 of this article, and the victim of such specified predicate crime is the victim, or an immediate family member of the victim, of the present offense; or

3. With intent to harass, annoy or alarm a specific person, intentionally engages in a course of conduct directed at such person which is likely to cause such person to reasonably fear physical injury or serious physical injury, the commission of a sex offense against, or the kidnapping, unlawful imprisonment or death of such person or a member of such person's immediate family; or

4. Commits the crime of stalking in the fourth degree and has previously been convicted within the preceding ten years of stalking in the fourth degree.

Stalking in the third degree is a class A misdemeanor.

Added by L. 1999, Ch. 635, § 13, eff. Dec. 1, 1999.

§ 120.55. Stalking in the second degree.

A person is guilty of stalking in the second degree when he or she:

1. Commits the crime of stalking in the third degree as defined in subdivision three of section 120.50 of this article and in the course of and in furtherance of the commission of such offense: (i) displays, or possesses and threatens the use of, a firearm, pistol, revolver, rifle, shotgun, machine gun, electronic dart gun, electronic stun gun, cane sword, billy, blackjack, bludgeon, metal knuckles, chuka stick, sand bag, sandclub, slingshot, slungshot, shirken, "Kung Fu Star", dagger, dangerous knife, dirk, razor, stiletto, imitation pistol, dangerous instrument, deadly instrument or deadly weapon; or (ii) displays what appears to be a pistol, revolver, rifle, shotgun, machine gun or other firearm; or

2. Commits the crime of stalking in the third degree in violation of subdivision three of section 120.50 of this article against any person, and has previously been convicted, within the preceding five years, of a specified predicate crime as defined in subdivision five of section 120.40 of this article, and the victim of such specified predicate crime is the victim, or an immediate family member of the victim, of the present offense; or

3. Commits the crime of stalking in the fourth degree and has previously been convicted of stalking in the third degree as defined in subdivision four of section 120.50 of this article against any person; or

4. Being twenty-one years of age or older, repeatedly follows a person under the age of fourteen or engages in a course of conduct or repeatedly commits acts over a period of time intentionally placing or attempting to place such person who is under the age of fourteen in reasonable fear of physical injury, serious physical injury or death; or

5. Commits the crime of stalking in the third degree, as defined in subdivision three of section 120.50 of this article, against ten or more persons, in ten or more separate transactions, for which the actor has not been previously convicted.

Stalking in the second degree is a class E felony.

Added by L. 1999, Ch. 635, § 13, eff. Dec. 1, 1999; **Amended** by L. 2000, Ch. 434, § 4, eff. Oct. 20, 2000, amending subd. 1; L. 2003, Ch. 598, eff. Nov. 1, 2003, adding subd. 5.

ANNOTATIONS

Constitutional challenge .—Letters to victim are not constitutionally protected speech; threatening conduct that causes fear of physical harm is not protected speech, and a criminal statute proscribing such activity does not implicate the First and Fourteenth Amendments of the U.S. Constitution or N.Y. Const. art. I, § 8. People v. Brown, 13 A.D.3d 667, 786 N.Y.S.2d 592 (3d Dept. 2004).

§ 120.60. Stalking in the first degree.

A person is guilty of stalking in the first degree when he or she commits the crime of stalking in the third degree as defined in subdivision three of section 120.50 or stalking in the second degree as defined in section 120.55 of this article and, in the course and furtherance thereof, he or she:

1. intentionally or recklessly causes physical injury to the victim of such crime; or

2. commits a class A misdemeanor defined in article one hundred thirty of this chapter, or a class E felony defined in section 130.25, 130.40 or 130.85 of this chapter, or a class D felony defined in section 130.30 or 130.45 of this chapter.

Stalking in the first degree is a class D felony.

Added by L. 1999, Ch. 635, § 13, eff. Dec. 1, 1999; **Amended** by L. 2000, Ch. 434, § 5, eff. Oct. 20, 2000.

ARTICLE 125—HOMICIDE, ABORTION AND RELATED OFFENSES

LexisNexis Cross References

Defense of Speeding, Reckless Driving and Vehicular Homicide, Vol. 2, Ch. 16, Elements of Vehicular Homicide; Vol. 2, Ch. 17, Pretrial Preparation of a Vehicular Homicide Case; Vol. 2, Ch. 18, Trial Considerations in a Vehicular Homicide Case; Vol. 2, Ch. 19, Jury Selection in a Vehicular Homicide Case; *Criminal Defense Techniques,* Vol. 2, Ch. 50, Defense of Homicide Cases; Vol. 3, Ch. 55A, Defense of Capital Cases; *New York Criminal Practice (2d ed.),* Vol. 6, Ch. 58, Homicide and Abortion; *Police Investigation Handbook,* Ch. 26, Criminal Death Investigations; *see generally Investigation and Prosecution of DWI and Vehicular Homicide.*

§ 125.00. Homicide defined.

Homicide means conduct which causes the death of a person or an unborn child with which a female has been pregnant for more than twenty-four weeks under circumstances constituting murder, manslaughter in the first degree, manslaughter in the second degree, criminally negligent homicide, abortion in the first degree or self-abortion in the first degree.

ANNOTATIONS

Motive.—It was proper to introduce evidence that a charge for assaulting the victim was pending against defendant at the time of the homicide since the evidence went to establish the motive and intent of the defendant including motive to avoid punishment for the prior crime; it was also proper for the court to instruct the jury that it was not to consider the prior charge as indicative of guilt or innocence of the crime charged. People v. Mees, 47 N.Y.2d 997, 420 N.Y.S.2d 214, 394 N.E.2d 283 (1979).

Removal of life sustaining device as homicide.—Conduct which results in the death of a human being who is medically alive implicates the homicide statutes, and such conduct may take the form of an act, or an omission where an affirmative duty to act is imposed by law, and the actor's motive, no matter how kindly, is legally irrelevant; this remains true notwithstanding the fact that the consent of the deceased had been obtained, or that the actor firmly believed his conduct to be morally justified as euthanasia, and any physician who, acting on his own, removes a life-sustaining respirator arguably commits some form of homicide. Eichner v. Dillon, 73 A.D.2d 431, 426

N.Y.S.2d 517 (2d Dept.), *modified,* 52 N.Y.2d 363, 438 N.Y.S.2d 266, 420 N.E.2d 64, *cert. denied,* 454 U.S. 858 (1981).

§ 125.05. Homicide, abortion and related offenses; definitions of terms.

The following definitions are applicable to this article:

1. "Person," when referring to the victim of a homicide, means a human being who has been born and is alive.

2. "Abortional act" means an act committed upon or with respect to a female, whether by another person or by the female herself, whether she is pregnant or not, whether directly upon her body or by the administering, taking or prescription of drugs or in any other manner, with intent to cause a miscarriage of such female.

3. "Justifiable abortional act." An abortional act is justifiable when committed upon a female with her consent by a duly licensed physician acting (a) under a reasonable belief that such is necessary to preserve her life, or, (b) within twenty-four weeks from the commencement of her pregnancy. A pregnant female's commission of an abortional act upon herself is justifiable when she acts upon the advice of a duly licensed

physician (1) that such act is necessary to preserve her life, or, (2) within twenty-four weeks from the commencement of the pregnancy. The submission by a female to an abortional act is justifiable when she believes that it is being committed by a duly licensed physician, acting under a reasonable belief that such act is necessary to preserve her life, or, within twenty-four weeks from the commencement of her pregnancy.

Amended by L. 1970, Ch. 127.

ANNOTATIONS

Abortion; constitutionality.—A fetus is not a legal person unless conferred as such by the Constitution and accorded attendant rights and privileges by the legislature; limited abortion statute providing less than full protection to fetus is not unconstitutional and the issue is not justiciable. Byrn v. New York City Health & Hosps. Corp., 31 N.Y.2d 194, 335 N.Y.S.2d 390, 286 N.E.2d 887 (1972), *dismissed,* 410 U.S. 949, 93 S. Ct. 1414, 35 L. Ed. 2d 683 (1973), *reh'g denied,* 411 U.S. 940, 93 S. Ct. 1889, 36 L. Ed. 2d 404 (1973).

Abortion; state law preempts local ordinance.—Where the state legislature, in the exercise of its police power for the "protection and promotion of the health" of its citizens, and to regulate the practice of medicine, preempts the field of abortion regulation, a local ordinance seeking to limit justifiable abortions to duly licensed hospitals is prohibited. Robin v. Incorporated Village of Hempstead, 30 N.Y.2d 347, 334 N.Y.S.2d 129, 285 N.E.2d 285 (1972).

§ 125.10. Criminally negligent homicide.

A person is guilty of criminally negligent homicide when, with criminal negligence, he causes the death of another person.

Criminally negligent homicide is a class E felony.

ANNOTATIONS

Constitutionality.—The statute is not unconstitutionally vague. People v. Kealey, 33 N.Y.2d 897, 352 N.Y.S.2d 449, 307 N.E.2d 564 (1973).

—Because the depraved mind murder statute is sufficiently definite to notify an individual of the conduct forbidden and provides specific standards for the jury to apply, it passes constitutional muster. People v. Cole, 202 A.D.2d 988, 609 N.Y.S.2d 469 (4th Dept. 1994).

Defendant's awareness/perception of risk.—Corporate and individual defendants could not be held criminally liable for deaths of employees, on theory of either reckless or negligent conduct, where such deaths were occasioned by an explosion of which the triggering cause was neither foreseen nor foreseeable, even though there was a broad, undifferentiated risk of an explosion arising from procedures employed at factory. People v. Warner-Lambert Co., 51 N.Y.2d 295, 434 N.Y.S.2d 159, 414 N.E.2d 660 (1980), *cert. denied,* 450 U.S. 1031 (1981).

—Defendant's awareness of the risk determines the degree of culpability, if he fails to perceive the substantial and unjustified risk of death inherent in his act, he is guilty of criminally negligent homicide (PL § 125.10), but if he is aware of the grave risk of death and acts in disregard of it, he acts recklessly and is guilty of manslaughter, second degree (PL § 125.15(1)). People v. Montanez, 41 N.Y.2d 53, 390 N.Y.S.2d 861, 359 N.E.2d 371 (1976).

—Defendant, a leader of a religious sect that believed in "mind over matter" was granted a reversal of his second degree manslaughter conviction where facts indicated that there was a reasonable basis upon which the jury could have found that the defendant failed to perceive the risk inherent in his actions when he plunged a knife into the chest of one of his followers with the intent not to cause injury; court erred in not submitting, as requested, the lesser charge of criminally negligent homicide. People v. Strong, 37 N.Y.2d 568, 376 N.Y.S.2d 87, 338 N.E.2d 602 (1975).

—Evidence supported conviction of corporation of criminally negligent homicide and reckless endangerment in the second degree. Executive director of corporation was high managerial agent of corporation whose wrongdoing could form basis for criminal liability of corporation and director failed to obtain valid state inspection of vehicle, failed to conduct any steps to evaluate vehicle's safety which would have revealed unsafe conditions of tires, and permitted youthful driver with little automotive knowledge to operate vehicle. People v. Congregation Khal Chaisidiei, 232 A.D.2d 919, 649 N.Y.S.2d 499 (3d Dept. 1996).

Admission of expert medical testimony.—The decision to admit expert medical testimony on the "battered child syndrome" in a prosecution for criminally negligent homicide is within the discretion of the trial court. People v. Hensen, 33 N.Y.2d 63, 349 N.Y.S.2d 657, 304 N.E.2d 358 (1973).

Evidence.—Defendant's request that court submit criminally negligent homicide, a lesser included offense of depraved indifference murder, to jury, waived defendant's right to argue that conviction for depraved indifference murder was bared by statute of limitations. People v. Mills, 1 N.Y.3d 269, 772 N.Y.S.2d 228, 804 N.E.2d 392 (2003).

—Evidence of parents-defendants' prior conduct toward victim-child was admissible in a prosecution for criminally negligent homicide. People v. Hensen, 33 N.Y.2d 63, 349 N.Y.S.2d 657, 304 N.E.2d 358 (1973).

—Blood samples taken from the defendant (who was arrested for driving while intoxicated) two hours after his arrest and while unconscious were admissible as his consent to the taking of blood was implied under VTL § 1194. People v. Hall, 91 A.D.2d 1002, 457 N.Y.S.2d 580 (2d Dept. 1983), *aff'd,* 61 N.Y.2d 834, 473 N.Y.S.2d 959, 462 N.E.2d 136 (1984).

—Reversing defendant's convictions for vehicular manslaughter in the second degree and criminally negligent homicide; although defendant's blood-alcohol level of 0.117 met the legal presumption of intoxication, admission of a six-year-old wedding photograph of the decedent, in spite of the parties' stipulation as to her identity, may have impermissibly played to the jury's emotions. People v. Donohue, 229 A.D.2d 396, 645 N.Y.S.2d 60 (2d Dept. 1996).

—"Criminally negligent homicide involves 'a failure to perceive a risk of death, [and] some serious blameworthiness in the conduct that caused it. The risk involved must have been "substantial and unjustifiable," and the failure to perceive that risk must have been a "gross deviation" from reasonable care.'" People v. Prue, 8 A.D.3d 894, 779 N.Y.S.2d 271 (3d Dept. 2004) (citation omitted).

—The elements of the federal crime of involuntary manslaughter are equivalent to the New York felonies of criminally negligent homicide and vehicular manslaughter in the second degree, therefore, defendant's federal conviction supported his disbarment in New York. *In re* Smalls, 7 A.D.3d 877, 776 N.Y.S.2d 626 (3d Dept. 2004).

—Minor victim died while in the baby-sitting care of defendant, who locked victim in her room and ignored her cries for help; where victim died in her locked bedroom due to excessive heat caused by a faulty furnace, even though defendant failed to help her by unlocking the bedroom door or attempting to reduce heat, court determined that the evidence did not establish that defendant's acts and omissions were "committed under circumstances which evidenced a wanton indifference to human life or a depravity of mind." People v. Baker, 4 A.D.3d 606, 771 N.Y.S.2d 607 (3d Dept. 2004).

—Defendant's unexplained failure to see the pedestrians she hit while traveling 10 to 15 miles per hour below the speed limit on a slushy road, even when coupled with evidence that defendant's car drifted onto the shoulder of the road and she did not apply her brakes prior to impact, without more, did not establish that defendant acted with criminal negligence. People v. Maloof, 254 A.D.2d 766, 678 N.Y.S.2d 175 (4th Dept. 1998).

Prima facie case.—Proof that decedent was struck by defendant's car at intersection, that defendant failed to stop for a red light and was traveling at a high rate of speed just before and at impact, and that there was no visual obstruction to the sighting of decedent, constitutes a prima facie case of criminally negligent homicide. People v. Haney, 30 N.Y.2d 328, 333 N.Y.S.2d 403, 284 N.E.2d 564 (1972).

Criminally negligent homicide as lesser included offense.—The Court of Appeals affirmed an order of the appellate division which reversed judgment and dismissed an indictment on the ground that criminally negligent homicide is not a lesser included offense in an indictment which charged manslaughter in the first degree and an intent to injure. People v. Wall, 29 N.Y.2d 863, 328 N.Y.S.2d 170, 278 N.E.2d 341 (1971).

—Trial court erred in refusing to charge criminally negligent homicide in addition to, *inter alia*, manslaughter as a lesser included offense of murder in the second degree; jury could find, from defendant's statements to law enforcement officials, that defendant did not intend to fire the gun in question and that it discharged accidentally, and it was for jury to determine whether defendant intentionally caused the victim's death, perceived the risk of harm and consciously disregarded it, or negligently failed to perceive the risk. People v. Irizarry, 213 A.D.2d 425, 623 N.Y.S.2d 611 (2d Dept. 1995).

—Defendant was not entitled to charge of criminally negligent homicide as a lesser included offense of murder in the second degree; no reasonable view of the evidence could support conclusion that defendant committed the lesser crime but not the greater. People v. Gil-Cabrera, 213 A.D.2d 1065, 624 N.Y.S.2d 327 (4th Dept. 1995).

Liability for failure to act.—Parents have an affirmative duty to provide their children with adequate medical care and, under certain circumstances, the failure to perform that duty can form the basis of a homicide charge. People v. Wong, 81 N.Y.2d 600, 601 N.Y.S.2d 440, 619 N.E.2d 377 (1993).

—Defendant's four-year-old son died because defendant failed to seek medical care for his peritonitis, which set in after his broken rib punctured his intestine, a condition which was curable if treated timely, parents have a non-delegable affirmative duty to provide their children with adequate medical care, and a parent's failure to fulfill that duty can form the basis of a homicide charge, jury found defendant criminally negligent for failing to obtain medical care for her child, who was suffering for hours before his death. People v. Mayo, 4 A.D.3d 827, 771 N.Y.S.2d 627 (4th Dept. 2004).

Proximate cause.—Although defendant charged with criminally negligent homicide argued that medical procedures performed on the victim were done negligently, at trial he made no showing of the gross negligence that is required to establish the existence of a superseding intervening act between the shooting of the victim and the victim's death. People v. Dickerson, 171 A.D.2d 422, 567 N.Y.S.2d 2 (1st Dept. 1991).

§ 125.12. Vehicular manslaughter in the second degree.

A person is guilty of vehicular manslaughter in the second degree when he or she causes the death of another person, and either:

(1) operates a motor vehicle in violation of subdivision two, three or four of section eleven hundred ninety-two of the vehicle and traffic law or operates a vessel or public vessel in violation of paragraph (b), (c), (d) or (e) of subdivision two of section forty-nine-a of the navigation law, and as a result of such intoxication or impairment by the use of a drug, operates such motor vehicle, vessel or public vessel in a manner that causes the death of such other person, or

(2) operates a motor vehicle with a gross vehicle weight rating of more than eighteen thousand pounds which contains flammable gas, radioactive materials or explosives in violation of subdivision one of section eleven hundred ninety-two of the vehicle and traffic law, and such flammable gas, radioactive materials or explosives is the cause of such death, and as a result of such intoxication or impairment by the use of a drug, operates such motor vehicle in a manner that causes the death of such other person, or

(3) operates a snowmobile in violation of paragraph (b), (c) or (d) of subdivision one of section 25.24 of the parks, recreation and historic preservation law or operates an all terrain vehicle as defined in paragraph (a) of subdivision one of section twenty-two hundred eighty-one of the vehicle and traffic law in violation of subdivision two, three, or four of section eleven hundred ninety-two of the vehicle and traffic law, and as a result of such intoxication or impairment by the use of a drug, operates such snowmobile or all terrain vehicle in a manner that causes the death of such other person.

If it is established that the person operating such motor vehicle, vessel, public vessel, snowmobile or all terrain vehicle caused such death while unlawfully intoxicated or impaired by the use of a drug, then there shall be a rebuttable presumption that, as a result of such intoxication or impairment by the use of a drug, such person operated the motor vehicle, vessel, public vessel, snowmobile or all terrain vehicle in a manner that caused such death, as required by this section.

Vehicular manslaughter in the second degree is a class D felony.

Added by L. 1983, Ch. 298, eff. Sept. 1, 1983; **Amended** by L. 1985, Ch. 507; L. 1989, Ch. 393; L. 1990, Chs. 173, 452; L. 1992, Ch. 427, eff. Nov. 1, 1992, amending subd. 3; L. 1992, Ch. 805, eff. Nov. 1, 1992; L. 1998, Ch. 629, eff. Nov. 1, 1999, amending subd. 3; L. 2005, Ch. 39, § 4, eff. Nov. 1, 2005.

ANNOTATIONS

Evidence.—Reversing defendant's convictions for vehicular manslaughter in the second degree and criminally negligent homicide; although defendant's blood alcohol level of 0.117 met the legal presumption of intoxication, admission of a six-year-old wedding photograph of the decedent in spite of the parties stipulation as to her identity may have impermissibly played to the jury's emotions. People v. Donohue, 229 A.D.2d 396, 645 N.Y.S.2d 60 (2d Dept. 1996).

—Evidence that defendant hit victim's van after crossing double yellow line and never applied his brakes before impact, together with results of breathalyzer test, testimony of prior drinking, and other witnesses' accounts of the accident, supported conviction for vehicular manslaughter. People v. Curkendall, 12 A.D.3d 710, 783 N.Y.S.2d 707 (3d Dept. 2004).

—Vehicular manslaughter in the second degree (criminally negligent homicide in which the death is caused by an operator who is driving while intoxicated) conviction affirmed, evidence established criminal negligence and that defendant's conduct caused the victim's death, defendant driving with a BAC of 0.17%, was involved in a single car accident, failed to get immediate help for victim who died of "aspiration gastric contents due to concussion due to Motor vehicle accident Alcoholic intoxication," defendant instead spent over one half hour trying to get his car out of a ditch and prevented others from helping victim. People v. Prue, 8 A.D.3d 894, 779 N.Y.S.2d 271 (3d Dept. 2004).

—The elements of the federal crime of involuntary manslaughter are equivalent to the New York felonies of criminally negligent homicide and vehicular manslaughter in the second degree, therefore, defendant's federal conviction supported his disbarment in New York. In re Smalls, 7 A.D.3d 877, 776 N.Y.S.2d 626 (3d Dept. 2004).

—Defendant's conduct was sufficiently blameworthy to support a finding of criminal negligence; jury could reasonably conclude based on evidence of defendant's intoxication, his failure to maintain control of his vehicle for no apparent reason, and his failure to take any corrective action despite the opportunity to do so, that defendant's conduct grossly deviated from the standard of care of a reasonable person presented with the same circumstances. People v. Carkner, 213 A.D.2d 735, 623 N.Y.S.2d 350 (3d Dept. 1995).

—Defendant's convictions for vehicular manslaughter in the second degree and driving while impaired by drugs were supported by evidence that defendant was negligent in driving an all terrain vehicle at dusk without a helmet at a speed that was too fast to be safe with a passenger and under the influence of marijuana. People v. Roth, 256 A.D.2d 1206, 683 N.Y.S.2d 358 (4th Dept. 1998).

Penalty.—Where two counts of vehicular manslaughter were committed through a single act, the imposition of two fines was improper. People v. Atwood, 2 A.D.3d 1331, 768 N.Y.S.2d 918 (4th Dept. 2003)

§ 125.13. Vehicular manslaughter in the first degree.

A person is guilty of vehicular manslaughter in the first degree when he or she:

(1) commits the crime of vehicular manslaughter in the second degree as defined in section 125.12, and

(2) commits such crime while knowing or having reason to know that: (a) his or her license or his or her privilege of operating a motor vehicle in another state or his or her privilege of obtaining a license to operate a motor vehicle in another state is suspended or revoked and such suspension or revocation is based upon a conviction in such other state for an offense which would, if committed in this state, constitute a violation of any of the provisions of section eleven hundred ninety-two of the vehicle and traffic law; or (b) his or her license or his or her privilege of operating a motor vehicle in the state or his or her privilege of obtaining a license issued by the commissioner of motor vehicles is suspended or revoked and such suspension or revocation is based upon either a refusal to submit to a chemical test pursuant to section eleven hundred ninety-four of the vehicle and traffic law or following a conviction for a violation of any of the provisions of section eleven hundred ninety-two of the vehicle and traffic law.

If it is established that the person operating such motor vehicle caused such death while unlawfully intoxicated or impaired by the use of a drug, then there shall be a rebuttable presumption that, as a result of such intoxication or impairment by the use of a drug, such person operated the motor vehicle in a manner that caused such death, as required by this section.

Vehicular manslaughter in the first degree is a class C felony.

Added by L. 1985, Ch. 507; **Amended** L. 1993, Ch. 678; L. 1996, Ch. 528, § 2, amending subd. 2, eff. Nov. 1, 1996; L. 2005, Ch. 39, § 5, eff. Nov. 1, 2005.

§ 125.15. Manslaughter in the second degree.

A person is guilty of manslaughter in the second degree when:

1. He recklessly causes the death of another person; or

2. He commits upon a female an abortional act which causes her death, unless such abortional act is justifiable pursuant to subdivision three of section 125.05; or

3. He intentionally causes or aids another person to commit suicide.

Manslaughter in the second degree is a class C felony.

ANNOTATIONS

Awareness of risk.—Defendant's awareness of the risk determines the degree of culpability, if he fails to perceive the substantial and unjustified risk of death in his act, he is guilty of criminally negligent homicide (PL § 125.10), but if he is aware of the grave risk of death and acts in disregard of it, he acts recklessly and is guilty of manslaughter, second degree (PL § 125.15(1)). People v. Montanez, 41 N.Y.2d 53, 390 N.Y.S.2d 861, 359 N.E.2d 371 (1976).

—Defendant acted recklessly within the meaning of PL § 125.15 when at the time he administered the fatal injection, he knew deceased was already "completely bombed out on downs" and had lost the capacity to "walk or talk straight" and there was a substantial possibility that a further injection could cause her death. People v. Cruciani, 36 N.Y.2d 304, 367 N.Y.S.2d 758, 327 N.E.2d 803 (1975).

Blood samples.—Motion to suppress was granted where the results of a blood test which was taken over the defendant's objection while he was under arrest for driving while intoxicated could not be used in defendant's trial for manslaughter because of the prohibition in § 1194 of the Vehicle & Traffic law. People v. Wolter, 83 A.D.2d 187, 444 N.Y.S.2d 331 (4th Dept. 1981), aff'd, 57 N.Y.2d 97, 454 N.Y.S.2d 292, 439 N.E.2d 1235 (1982).

Charge.—Failure to charge jury, as requested by defendant, that defendant could not be responsible for the killing of an innocent bystander unless he knew of the danger to him and consciously disregarded it constituted reversible error. People v. Sierra, 231 A.D.2d 907, 647 N.Y.S.2d 891 (4th Dept. 1996).

—By affirmatively requesting that court charge manslaughter in the second degree as a lesser included offense, defendant waived any claim of error in connection with the submission of that offense to the jury. People v. Alvarado, 213 A.D.2d 1013, 624 N.Y.S.2d 489 (4th Dept. 1995).

Lesser included offenses.—Trial court did not err in rejecting requests for manslaughter lesser included offenses to be charged; in light of the circumstances of this case, including the nature and brutality of the crime, no lesser included offense instruction was compelled; the crime was intentional murder in the second degree or nothing, under the law and under the instructions that were given. People v. Butler, 84 N.Y.2d 627, 620 N.Y.S.2d 775, 644 N.E.2d 1331 (1994).

—Evidence of the quantity of alcohol consumed by the defendant during the afternoon prior to the crime, and of the fact that he was continuing to drink immediately prior to the shooting, was sufficient to require that the court charge the jury to consider manslaughter in the second degree as a lesser included offense of intentional murder, as requested by defense counsel. People v. Brantley, 209 A.D.2d 272, 618 N.Y.S.2d 342 (1st Dept. 1994).

—Manslaughter in the second degree is not a lesser included offense of murder in the second degree, as creating a grave risk of physical injury is an element of murder but not of manslaughter. People v. Robinson, 278 A.D.2d 798, 723 N.Y.S.2d 277 (4th Dept. 2000), appeal denied, 96 N.Y.2d 762 (2001).

Recklessness.—Defendant was properly convicted of manslaughter in the Second Degree under a theory of recklessness where the proof showed the defendant was speeding in an unregistered vehicle, tailgating a van and then, while attempting to pass the van, crossed the center line and drove onto a safety island, killing two pedestrians; evidence permitted the jury to find that defendant was aware of and consciously disregarded a substantial and unjustifiable risk that his actions would cause the death of another. People v. Heinsohn, 61 N.Y.2d 855, 473 N.Y.S.2d 968, 462 N.E.2d 145 (1984).

—Brutal beatings of a three-year-old child warranted murder conviction of defendant based on a degree of recklessness, which although without specific homicidal intent, evinced a depraved kind of wantonness and indifference to human life within the statutory definition. People v. Poplis, 30 N.Y.2d 85, 330 N.Y.S.2d 365, 281 N.E.2d 167 (1972).

—Recklessness was established where the record revealed that defendant was driving at an excessive rate of speed, under the influence of marijuana, which he knew dulled the reflexes and minimized his concentration, passed cars in a no-passing lane, acknowledged that he heard his passengers ask him to pull over but instead elected to continue to speed to avoid the pursuing police car, and lost control of the car; convictions for manslaughter in the second degree affirmed. People v. Crandall, 255 A.D.2d 616, 681 N.Y.S.2d 99 (3d Dept. 1998).

—Charge of manslaughter in the second degree could not be supported where evidence established that defendant was negligent but not reckless in his operation of an all terrain vehicle under the influence of marijuana without a helmet and at an unsafe speed which caused the death of his passenger, who was also riding without a helmet, when defendant lost control of the vehicle. People v. Roth, 256 A.D.2d 1206, 683 N.Y.S.2d 358 (4th Dept. 1998).

Reversibly inconsistent or repugnant verdicts.—The court refused reversal where defendant was acquitted of the weapons charge and found guilty of manslaughter, where the record was utterly devoid of any indication that the jury's acquittal on the weapons charge, an essential element of which was intent to use unlawfully, represented a finding of lack of intent to use the gun unlawfully at the time of the shootings, and instead clearly showed that the jury merely misunderstood the possession element of the weapons charge; the verdicts were rationally reconcilable. People v. Haymes, 34 N.Y.2d 639, 355 N.Y.S.2d 376, 311 N.E.2d 509 (1974), *cert. denied*, 419 U.S. 1003 (1974).

Second degree manslaughter and criminally negligent homicide; distinguished.—Defendant, a leader of a religious sect that believed in "mind over matter" was granted a reversal of his manslaughter, second degree, conviction where facts indicated that there was a reasonable basis upon which the jury could have found that the defendant failed to perceive the risk inherent in his actions when he plunged a knife into the chest of one of his followers with the intent not to cause injury; court erred in not submitting, as requested, the lesser charge of criminally negligent homicide. People v. Strong, 37 N.Y.2d 568, 376 N.Y.S.2d 87, 338 N.E.2d 602 (1975).

Evidence.—Where the record indicated that defendant removed a loaded revolver from his belt area, swung it across his body with his finger on the trigger, allowed the barrel to point in the direction of another person barely three feet away whereupon the gun discharged striking his wife in the head, the evidence was sufficient to convict defendant of second degree manslaughter, PL § 125.15; although the shooting may well have been unintentional, the jury was entitled to consider whether the risk created by defendant's actions was substantial and unjustifiable and constituted a gross deviation from the standard of conduct that a reasonable person would have observed. People v. Licitra, 47 N.Y.2d 554, 419 N.Y.S.2d 461, 393 N.E.2d 456 (1979).

—Evidence that defendant and decedent together engaged in a drag race which caused a fatal crash between decedent's car and a third car which killed the driver of the third car and the decedent, supported defendant's conviction for two counts of manslaughter on the theory of accessorial liability in that he intentionally aided decedent in reckless conduct which caused two deaths. People v. Hart, 8 A.D.3d 402, 778 N.Y.S.2d 94 (2d Dept. 2004).

—Conviction for manslaughter in the second degree was sustained where the defendant, in order to pass a car in front of him, drove onto a safety island and killed two people; People were not required to show that the defendant actually had been aware that there were people on the safety island; rather, the People need only show that death was caused by consciously disregarding a substantial and unjustifiable risk of which he was aware. People v. Heinsohn, 92 A.D.2d 574, 459 N.Y.S.2d 329 (2d Dept. 1983), *aff'd*, 61 N.Y.2d 855, 473 N.Y.S.2d 968, 462 N.E.2d 145 (1984).

—Although evidence was sufficient to establish that defendant acted recklessly by failing to replace left front tire on truck after repeated notice of problems with the tire, evidence was insufficient for conviction of manslaughter in the second degree given that the People failed to prove that the blowout of the tire resulted from defendant's inaction rather than an unrelated condition such as a puncture. People v. Phippen, 232 A.D.2d 790, 649 N.Y.S.2d 191 (3d Dept. 1996).

—Evidence that defendant drove a vehicle that swerved into the opposing lane of traffic and nearly collided with two vehicles before eventually colliding with a third vehicle, killing the driver of that vehicle, defendant's passenger was intoxicated and repeatedly grabbed the steering wheel, however, defendant continued driving despite her passenger's repeated interference with her driving, continued to speed, and did not slow down or apply brakes before collision or near collisions, supported conviction under this section. People v. Botting, 8 A.D.3d 1064, 778 N.Y.S.2d 824 (4th Dept. 2004).

Suicide.—A person may be found guilty of manslaughter in the second degree for causing or aiding a suicide only when he or she acts intentionally. People v. Duffy, 171 A.D.2d 900, 566 N.Y.S.2d 768 (3d Dept. 1991).

§ 125.20. Manslaughter in the first degree.

A person is guilty of manslaughter in the first degree when:

1. With intent to cause serious physical injury to another person, he causes the death of such person or of a third person; or

2. With intent to cause the death of another person, he causes the death of such person or of a third person under circumstances which do not constitute murder because he acts under the influence of extreme emotional disturbance, as defined in paragraph (a) of subdivision one of section 125.25. The fact that homicide was committed under the influence of extreme emotional disturbance constitutes a mitigating circumstance reducing murder to manslaughter in the first degree and need not be proved in any prosecution initiated under this subdivision; or

3. He commits upon a female pregnant for more than twenty-four weeks an abortional act which causes her death, unless such abortional act is justifiable pursuant to subdivision three of section 125.05; or

4. Being eighteen years old or more and with intent to cause physical injury to a person less than eleven years old, the defendant recklessly engages in conduct which creates a grave risk of serious physical injury to such person and thereby causes the death of such person.

Manslaughter in the first degree is a class B felony.

Amended by L. 1990, Ch. 477.

ANNOTATIONS

Attempt.—The crime of attempted manslaughter in the first degree is a non-existent crime except in those instances where a defense of extreme emotional disturbance is interposed to reduce a charge of attempted murder. People v. Robinson, 143 A.D.2d 376, 532 N.Y.S.2d 411 (2d Dept. 1988).

Causation.—The manslaughter, first degree, conviction was modified to assault, first degree, when the testimony of the medical examiner indicated that after the operating surgeons repaired the stab wound in the victim's abdomen inflicted by the defendant they also performed other unrelated surgical repair, and the medical examiner indicated that he believed the victim would have survived the operation if the latter procedure had not been performed, and he also acknowledged that there was some evidence the anesthesiologist could have caused the death. People v. Stewart, 40 N.Y.2d 692, 389 N.Y.S.2d 804, 358 N.E.2d 487 (1976).

—Criminal liability for death resulting from a felonious assault is not relieved by such contributing factors as a victim's pre-existing health condition or medical intervention in the form of improper treatment. People v. Bowie, 200 A.D.2d 511, 607 N.Y.S.2d 248 (1st Dept. 1994).

Extreme emotional disturbance.—Placing the burden upon the defendant as to proof of extreme emotional disturbance does not violate due process. People v. Patterson, 39 N.Y.2d 288, 383 N.Y.S.2d 573, 347 N.E.2d 898, *aff'd,* 432 U.S. 197, 97 S. Ct. 2319, 53 L. Ed. 2d 281 (1976).

—An action influenced by extreme emotional disturbance need not be spontaneous since, unlike former "heat of passion" defense, it does not negate intent; the purpose of the extreme emotional disturbance defense is to permit defendant to show that his actions were caused by a mental infirmity not rising to the level of insanity, and that he is less culpable for having committed them. People v. Patterson, 39 N.Y.2d 288, 383 N.Y.S.2d 573, 347 N.E.2d 898, *aff'd,* 432 U.S. 197, 97 S. Ct. 2319, 53 L. Ed. 2d 281 (1976).

—Neither the defendant's jealousy and anger over the complainant's new boyfriend, nor the evidence that he had been drinking on the date of the stabbing constituted a reasonable explanation or excuse for the proffered emotional disturbance defense. People v. Feris, 144 A.D.2d 691, 535 N.Y.S.2d 17 (2d Dept. 1988).

Intent.—It was reversible error where the defendant was convicted of manslaughter, but the prosecution failed to prove beyond a reasonable doubt that the defendant shared in his co-defendant's intent to cause serious physical injury to the decedent. People v. Igoe, 82 A.D.2d 812, 439 N.Y.S.2d 401 (2d Dept. 1981).

—Defendant's conviction for manslaughter in the first degree was supported by reasonable view of evidence; whether defendant's intent was to kill or cause serious physical injury is a question for the jury. People v. Owens, 251 A.D.2d 898, 674 N.Y.S.2d 847 (3d Dept. 1998).

—Although defendant admitted he intended to hit victim, he did not intend to cause serious physical injury, however, a defendant may be presumed to intend the natural and probable consequences of his actions and "intent may be inferred from the totality of conduct of the accused," conviction affirmed. People v. Mahoney, 6 A.D.3d 1104, 776 N.Y.S.2d 402 (4th Dept. 2004).

Lesser included offense.—Court's decision that evidence could not support conviction for intentional murder, and subsequent refusal to submit charge to jury was a dismissal of the charge and double jeopardy prevented retrial on charges of manslaughter in the first degree, since it precludes consecutive prosecutions for greater and lesser included offenses where, "the lesser offense. . .requires no proof beyond that which is required for conviction of the greater. " People v. Biggs, 1 N.Y.3d 225, 771 N.Y.S.2d 49, 803 N.E.2d 370. (2003).

—Trial court properly denied the defendant's request to charge manslaughter in the first degree as a lesser-included offense of murder in the second degree since there was no reasonable view of the evidence, when viewed in the light most favorable to the defendant, to support a finding that he intended only to cause serious physical injury rather than to kill victim, where defendant shot victim in the head at point blank range. People v. Maldonado, 5 A.D.3d 505, 772 N.Y.S.2d 583 (2d Dept. 2004).

Sentence.—Plea bargain providing that sentence for first degree manslaughter was to run consecutively with sentence on weapons counts was not improper; possession of the weapon and its subsequent use were separate, successive acts allowing for the imposition of consecutive sentences. People v. Simpson, 209 A.D.2d 281, 619 N.Y.S.2d 259 (1st Dept. 1994).

§ 125.25. Murder in the second degree.

A person is guilty of murder in the second degree when:

1. With intent to cause the death of another person, he causes the death of such person or of a third person; except that in any prosecution under this subdivision, it is an affirmative defense that:

(a) The defendant acted under the influence of extreme emotional disturbance for which there was a reasonable explanation or excuse, the reasonableness of which is to be determined from the viewpoint of a person in the defendant's situation under the circumstances as the defendant believed them to be. Nothing contained in this paragraph shall constitute a defense to a prosecution for, or preclude a conviction of, manslaughter in the first degree or any other crime; or

(b) The defendant's conduct consisted of causing or aiding, without the use of duress or deception, another person to commit suicide. Nothing contained in this paragraph shall constitute a defense to a prosecution for, or preclude a conviction of, manslaughter in the second degree or any other crime; or

2. Under circumstances evincing a depraved indifference to human life, he recklessly engages in conduct which creates a grave risk of death to another person, and thereby causes the death of another person; or

3. Acting either alone or with one or more other persons, he commits or attempts to commit robbery, burglary, kidnapping, arson, rape in the first degree, criminal sexual act in the first degree, sexual abuse in the first degree, aggravated sexual abuse, escape in the first degree, or escape in the second degree, and, in the course of and in furtherance of such crime or of immediate flight therefrom, he, or another participant, if there be any, causes the death of a person other than one of the participants; except that in any prosecution under this subdivision, in which the defendant was not the only participant in the underlying crime, it is an affirmative defense that the defendant:

(a) Did not commit the homicidal act or in any way solicit, request, command, importune, cause or aid the commission thereof; and

(b) Was not armed with a deadly weapon, or any instrument, article or substance readily capable of causing death or serious physical injury and of a sort not ordinarily carried in public places by law-abiding persons; and

(c) Had no reasonable ground to believe that any other participant was armed with such a weapon, instrument, article or substance; and

(d) Had no reasonable ground to believe that any other participant intended to engage in conduct likely to result in death or serious physical injury.

4. Under circumstances evincing a depraved indifference to human life, and being eighteen years old or more the defendant recklessly engages in conduct which creates a grave risk of serious physical injury or death to another person less than eleven years old and thereby causes the death of such person; or

5. Being eighteen years old or more, while in the course of committing rape in the first, second or third degree, criminal sexual act in the first, second or third degree, sexual abuse in the first degree, aggravated sexual abuse in the first, second, third or fourth degree, or incest as defined in section 255.25 of this chapter, against a person less than fourteen years old, he or she intentionally causes the death of such person.

Murder in the second degree is a class A-I felony.

Amended by L. 1973, Ch. 276; L. 1974, Ch. 367; L. 1984, Ch. 210; L. 1990, Ch. 477; L. 2003, Ch. 264, § 10, eff. Nov. 1, 2003, amending subd. 3 opening paragraph; L. 2004, Ch. 459, § 4, eff. Nov. 1, 2004, adding subd. 5.

ANNOTATIONS

Constitutionality.—In murder case, placing burden of persuasion on defendant concerning defense of acting under influence of extreme emotional distress so as to reduce homicide to less culpable crime of first degree manslaughter did not violate defendant's due process rights; *Mullaney* not controlling since under New York law the prosecution is at all times required to prove, beyond a reasonable doubt, the facts bearing on the defendant's intent. People v. Patterson, 39 N.Y.2d 288, 383 N.Y.S.2d 573, 347 N.E.2d 898 (1976).

—Defendant contended that the statutory affirmative defenses under this section violated his constitutional privilege against self incrimination to the extent that it required him to take the witness stand and disprove any connection with the killing. In upholding the statute, the court concluded that while the defendant has the burden of going forward with some evidence making the defense one of the issues in the case, the burden of persuasion remains upon the People, upon the whole case, to negate the defense beyond a reasonable doubt. People v. Bornholdt, 33 N.Y.2d 75, 350 N.Y.S.2d 369, 305 N.E.2d 461 (1973), *cert. denied,* 416 U.S. 905 (1974).

Age of defendant.—Reliance on the jury's observation of a defendant to establish the necessary element of age does not satisfy the People's obligation of proof. People v. Blodgett, 160 A.D.2d 1105, 553 N.Y.S.2d 897 (3d Dept. 1990).

Attempt.—Attempted murder in the second degree is not an "armed felony offense" by definition because possession, use, or display of a weapon is not a statutory element of the crime. People v. Roye, 255 A.D.2d 464, 682 N.Y.S.2d 862 (2d Dept. 1998).

—Evidence that defendant, from whom victim had a standing order of protection, entered her home with a large carving knife yelling that he was going to kill the victim and her children, and stabbed the victim in the head and knee before police intervened, was sufficient to support the conviction for attempted murder. People v. King, 293 A.D.2d 815, 740 N.Y.S.2d 500 (3d Dept. 2002).

Causation.—Expert's testimony that victim died of myocardial infarction precipitated by the stress of finding a burglar in his home was sufficient to sustain felony-murder conviction. People v. Ingram, 67 N.Y.2d 897, 501 N.Y.S.2d 804, 492 N.E.2d 1220 (1986).

—Convictions for felony murder and manslaughter were supported by evidence that robberies of elderly victims by defendants, and the injuries inflicted on such victims, contributed to the fatal heart failures suffered by the victims some days after the crimes, even where there were other possible causes of the heart attacks. *In re* Anthony M., 63 N.Y.2d 270, 481 N.Y.S.2d 675, 471 N.E.2d 447 (1984).

—Mere fact that alcohol and cocaine ingested by victim could have caused his death did not preclude the jury's finding that the defendant's act of shooting the deceased was the direct cause of death. People v. Spencer, 146 A.D.2d 817, 537 N.Y.S.2d 550, 551 (2d Dept. 1989).

—Where burglary victim suffered a fatal intracerebral hemorrhage as a result of the stress of defendant's burglary of her home, evidence was sufficient to sustain a conviction for murder. The ultimate harm was something that could have been foreseen as being reasonably related to the defendant's acts;

"where the necessary causative link is established, other causes, such as a victim's preexisting condition, will not relieve the defendant of responsibility for homicide." People v. Lapan, 289 A.D.2d 698, 734 N.Y.S.2d 648 (3d Dept. 2001).

—Proof that the victim dies from a heart attack sustained during the course of the burglary provided adequate factual support for the charge of felony murder. People v. Hayes, 208 A.D.2d 1054, 617 N.Y.S.2d 574 (3d Dept. 1994).

—If multiple injuries cause death together, each participant is criminally liable for the death if his actions were factors in the victim's death; when a secondary and intervening event occurs between the initial injury and resulting death, the intervening event operates as a defense to criminal liability only where the death is solely attributable to the secondary agency and is not at all induced by the primary one. People v. Velez, 159 Misc. 2d 38, 602 N.Y.S.2d 758 (Sup. Ct. Bronx Co. 1993).

—Defendant's conviction of murder, second degree (PL § 125.25(2)) was affirmed where the evidence of injuries suffered by the child victim linked the defendant to those injuries and the medical testimony relating to the cause of the victim's death corroborated defendant's admission since it was sufficient to establish that the victim's death resulted from conduct on the part of the defendant which evinced a depraved indifference to human life. People v. Arca, 72 A.D.2d 205, 424 N.Y.S.2d 569 (4th Dept. 1980), *affd,* 51 N.Y.2d 476, 434 N.Y.S.2d 947, 415 N.E.2d 936.

Defendant's understanding of conduct.—The trial court adequately charged the degree of understanding required to comply with former Penal Law § 1120 (which is restated in Revised Penal Law § 30.05) when it charged a murder first degree jury that defendant could be held criminally responsible only if it were proven beyond a reasonable doubt that she had "some understanding as opposed to surface understanding" of the legal and moral import of the conduct involved. People v. Adams, 26 N.Y.2d 129, 309 N.Y.S.2d 145, 257 N.E.2d 610 (1970), *cert. denied,* 399 U.S. 931 (1970).

Evidence.—Evidence, when viewed as a whole, although circumstantial in nature, was sufficient to support a conviction for second degree murder where it was established that the defendant was the last person to see his former girlfriend alive, that he had disposed of her belongings the following day and fled New York for the West coast, dramatically altered his appearance and had made inconsistent and false statements to the police. People v. Lewis, 64 N.Y.2d 1111, 490 N.Y.S.2d 166, 479 N.E.2d 802 (1985).

—Defendant's conviction for murder was supported by his statements to police that he was at the scene, was looking for the victim and saw the stabbing, together with co-defendant's testimony that defendant had previously threatened to kill the victim and had threatened to kill the co-defendant if he did not testify that defendant was not at the scene. People v. Foster, 64 N.Y.2d 1144, 490 N.Y.S.2d 726, 480 N.E.2d 340 (1985).

—The proscription of CPL § 60.50 against conviction solely upon evidence of a confession or admission without proof that the offense charged has been committed does not require direct proof, other than the confession or admission, of death or criminal agency. Although the body of the victim was never found and there was no direct evidence, other than the confession, that the defendant caused the victim's death, a jury question was presented by circumstantial evidence calculated to suggest that the victim was dead and implicated the defendant as the criminal agency, the key to which was furnished by the confession as admission. People v. Lipsky, 57 N.Y.2d 560, 457 N.Y.S.2d 451, 443 N.E.2d 925 (1982).

—The *corpus delicti* may be established by circumstantial evidence and *People v. Ruloff,* 18 N.Y. 179 is no longer the law. People v. Lipsky, 57 N.Y.2d 560, 457 N.Y.S.2d 451, 443 N.E.2d 925 (1982).

—The admission into evidence of an extra-judicial confession of a co-defendant who never took the stand and thus was not available for cross-examination was an error since the confession added substantially to the case and impermissibly deprived the defendant of his right to confront the witness against him; the defect was not waived where defendant's attorney participated in a redaction process because the attorney continued to object to the entire procedure. People v. Smalls, 55 N.Y.2d 407, 449 N.Y.S.2d 696, 434 N.E.2d 1063 (1982).

—Where through conflicting testimony presented to grand jury, defendant's actions could be interpreted as either intentional or reckless, even if evidence is circumstantial, the decision is for the grand jury to make, not for the judge on a motion to dismiss indictment prior to trial. People v. Molloy, 235 A.D.2d 48, 664 N.Y.S.2d 17 (1st Dept. 1997).

—Defendant's conviction for second degree murder affirmed where evidence was sufficient to disprove defense of justification and there was no merit to defendant's argument that the verdict was against the weight of the evidence; any error in admitting the opinion testimony of an emergency medical technician as to the time of death was harmless. People v. Davis, 209 A.D.2d 954, 620 N.Y.S.2d 21 (4th Dept. 1994).

Insanity defense.—Trial court committed reversible error in prosecution for second degree murder by submitting affirmative defense of extreme emotional disturbance over defendant's objection. Defendant asserted the defense of not responsible by reason of a mental disease or defect which was clearly incompatible with the affirmative defense of extreme emotional disturbance which would have necessarily involved a temporary loss of control by a person who was otherwise capable of appreciating the nature and consequences of his actions. People v. Bradley, 88 N.Y.2d 901, 646 N.Y.S.2d 657, 669 N.E.2d 815 (1996).

—Defendant requested the trial judge to instruct the jury that if they found defendant not guilty of murder by reason of insanity, she would be turned over to the Commissioner of Mental Health for further processing in accordance with the laws of this State. The court of Appeals held that it would be improper to give the instruction requested since consideration of punishment or disposition of the defendant is beyond the province of the jury. People v. Adams, 26 N.Y.2d 129, 309 N.Y.S.2d 145, 257 N.E.2d 610, *cert. denied,* 399 U.S. 931 (1970).

Victim not alive at time of crime; attempted murder.— Defendant's conviction of murder could not stand when the People failed to prove beyond a reasonable doubt that victim had been alive at the time he was shot by defendant. People v. Dlugash, 51 A.D.2d 974, 380 N.Y.S.2d 315 (2d Dept. 1976), *modified,* 41 N.Y.2d 725, 395 N.Y.S.2d 419, 363 N.E.2d 1155.

—A person is guilty of an attempted murder when, with intent to commit the crime, he engages in conduct which tends to effect the commission of such crime (PL § 110.00); it is no defense that, under the attendant circumstances, the crime was factually or legally impossible of commission "if such crime could have been committed had the attendant circumstances been as such person believed them to be" (PL § 110.10) and if defendant believed the victim to be alive at the time of the shooting, it is no defense to the charge of attempted murder that the victim may have been dead. People v. Dlugash, 41 N.Y.2d 725, 395 N.Y.S.2d 419, 363 N.E.2d 1155 (1977).

Depraved indifference.—Defendant who went to the deceased's home armed with a twelve-gauge shotgun and shot him at point-blank range did not commit depraved indifference murder. People v. Payne, 3 N.Y.3d 266, 786 N.Y.S.2d 116, 819 N.E.2d 634 (2004).

—Depraved indifference differs from intentional murder in that it does not result from a specific conscious intent to cause death but from a depraved indifference to disregard to the risks attending defendant's conduct; evidence that defendant walked up to victim and fired point blank ten times did not support depraved indifference murder, error to submit to jury. People v. Gonzales, 1 N.Y.3d 464, 775 N.Y.S.2d 224, 807 N.E.2d 273 (2004).

—The "heightened recklessness" required for depraved indifference murder was not present where the co-defendant planned and lured the victim alone into insolated area where he attacked at close range by a knife concealed in the sleeve of a co-defendant. People v. Hafeez, 100 N.Y.2d 253, 762 N.Y.S.2d 572, 792 N.E.2d 1060 (2003).

—Defendant's act of firing a gun at point blank range directly at the victim's chest manifested a clear intent to kill the victim; it did not have to be shown beyond a reasonable doubt that defendant harbored a particularly evil intent toward the victim, but only that he engaged in conduct creating a grave risk of death to the victim and thereby caused his death. People v. Sanchez, 98 N.Y.2d 373, 748 N.Y.S.2d 312, 777 N.E.2d 204 (2002).

—Where defendants all engaged in gun battle in a grassy thoroughfare of a housing complex in the middle of the day, during which the victim, an innocent bystander, was killed in the crossfire, evidence supported jury's decision to convict defendants of murder with depraved indifference. People v. Russell, 91 N.Y.2d 280, 670 N.Y.S.2d 166, 693 N.E.2d 193 (1998).

—Evidence of the defendant's mental state is not pertinent to a determination of the additional element required for depraved indifference murder; i.e., whether the objective circumstances bearing on the nature of a defendant's reckless conduct are such that the conduct creates a very substantial risk of death. People v. Roe, 74 N.Y.2d 20, 544 N.Y.S.2d 297, 542 N.E.2d 610 (1989).

—Evidence that defendant drove his car at a high rate of speed on a busy New York City street and the sidewalk adjacent thereto for a distance of several blocks and refused to apply the brakes when requested by another occupant of the vehicle, thereby killing two children and endangering several other pedestrians, was sufficient to support conviction for two counts of "depraved mind" murder. People v. Gomez, 65 N.Y.2d 9, 489 N.Y.S.2d 156, 478 N.E.2d 759 (1985).

—Evidence that defendant actively participated in a robbery and ensuing shootout in which a coperpetrator was killed, though not by defendant, was sufficient to support a conviction for depraved indifference murder under an "acting in concert" theory. People v. Braithwaite, 63 N.Y.2d 839, 482 N.Y.S.2d 253, 472 N.E.2d 29 (1984).

—Evidence was legally sufficient to convict defendant of "depraved indifference" murder where it was established that the defendant entered a crowded bar with a loaded gun, several times said words to the effect that he was "going to kill somebody tonight," and ultimately fired the gun three times in the "packed" barroom, resulting in the death of the victim. People v. Register, 60 N.Y.2d 270, 469 N.Y.S.2d 599, 457 N.E.2d 704 (1983).

—Evidence that defendant knowingly and deliberately fired a pistol through a door leading into small enclosed place in which the victim and another stood, then called the bar where the shooting took place to ask "Did I hit anyone?" and responded "good" when he was told he did, supported the verdict under a depraved indifference theory. People v. Mannix, 302 A.D.2d 297, 754 N.Y.S.2d 33 (1st Dept. 2003).

—Whether or not defendant knew the gun was loaded was irrelevant where, after an argument with victim, defendant picked up a sawed-off shot gun, pointed it at victim's head, and pulled the trigger. People v. Smith, 255 A.D.2d 404, 680 N.Y.S.2d 556 (2d Dept. 1998).

—Assessment of the objective circumstances which establish the actor's depraved indifference to human life is a "qualitative judgment" for the jury. People v. Soto, 240 A.D.2d 768, 660 N.Y.S.2d 49 (2d Dept. 1997).

—Pathologist's testimony that decedent had been stabbed four times in the abdomen and twice in the back with one stab wound to the abdomen piercing decedent's heart which was fatal, whether or not medical treatment was available, coupled with testimony that defendant struck the first blow, was sufficient to sustain conviction of depraved indifference murder. People v. Stewart, 239 A.D.2d 614, 658 N.Y.S.2d 998 (2d Dept. 1997).

—Evidence was legally sufficient to establish that defendant acted with a depraved indifference to human life where the defendant admitted to whirling around and firing one shot in the direction of a group of people following closely behind him. People v. Thompson, 215 A.D.2d 514, 627 N.Y.S.2d 395 (2d Dept. 1995).

—Guilt of depraved mind murder proven where defendant, sitting approximately 10 feet away from the victim, aimed his gun at the victim's chest and pulled the trigger three times. People v. Dellemand, 205 A.D.2d 551, 613 N.Y.S.2d 195 (2d Dept. 1994).

—Conviction for depraved indifference murder was affirmed where defendant helped beat the victim, did nothing as the victim was stabbed with a screwdriver 25 times by co-defendants, and helped another co-defendant carry victim to the river and dump his body even though defendant told police he knew victim was still alive, but unconscious. People v. Fink, 251 A.D.2d 751, 674 N.Y.S.2d 793 (3d Dept. 1998).

—Evidence was legally sufficient to support defendant's conviction where jury could have rationally concluded beyond a reasonable doubt that defendant's conduct in repeatedly punching a 23-month-old child in the stomach, failing to summon emergency aid, and knowing that his previous assault of the child had necessitated hospital treatment, created a grave risk of death evidencing a depraved indifference to human life. People v. Dexheimer, 214 A.D.2d 898, 625 N.Y.S.2d 719 (3d Dept. 1995).

Extreme emotional disturbance.—Defense requires both proof of subjective element that defendant under an extreme emotional disturbance and objective element that there was a reasonable explanation or excuse for the emotional disturbance, defendant's explanation that she was affected by the long-standing relationship with deceased could not support defense. People v. Smith, 1 N.Y.3d 610, 776 N.Y.S.2d 198, 808 N.E.2d 333 (2004).

—Extreme emotional disturbance can be established without psychiatric testimony, however, defendant can not establish defense without evidence he suffered from a mental infirmity which did not rise to level of insanity at the time of homicide, typically manifested by a loss of self-control. People v. Roche, 98 N.Y.2d 70, 745 N.Y.S.2d 775, 772 N.E.2d 1133 (2002).

—Court erred by refusing to charge jury with the affirmative defense of extreme emotional disturbance where evidence demonstrated that defendant killed his long-time friend with a machete and, with the help of his lover, decapitated and dismembered the victim's body, put the body parts in garbage bags, and discarded them, because he was provoked to rage over the emotionally charged subject of his lover's past and potential future infidelity with the victim; conviction reversed and new trial ordered. People v. Harris, 95 N.Y.2d 316, 717 N.Y.S.2d 82, 740 N.E.2d 227 (2000).

—Trial court committed reversible error in prosecution for second degree murder by submitting affirmative defense of extreme emotional disturbance over defendant's objection. Defendant asserted the defense of not responsible by reason of a mental disease or defect which was clearly incompatible with the affirmative defense of extreme emotional disturbance which would have necessarily involved a temporary loss of control by a person who was otherwise capable of appreciating the nature and consequences of his actions. People v. Bradley, 88 N.Y.2d 901, 646 N.Y.S.2d 657, 669 N.E.2d 815 (1996).

—Defendant charged with the crime of murder in the second degree was not entitled to a charge of the affirmative defense that he acted under the influence of extreme emotional disturbance where the evidence at trial showed that he acted out of anger or embarrassment, or both, without any indication of mental infirmity not rising to the level of insanity. People v. Walker, 64 N.Y.2d 741, 485 N.Y.S.2d 978, 475 N.E.2d 445 (1984).

—It was not error for the trial court to refuse to permit testimony by the psychologist regarding the interpretation of tests administered to the defendant as these tests applied to the defendant's mental condition and the witnesses' expertise in interpretations of this nature had not been satisfactorily established. People v. Diaz, 51 N.Y.2d 841, 433 N.Y.S.2d 751, 413 N.E.2d 1166 (1980).

—The determination whether there was reasonable explanation or excuse for a particular emotional disturbance should be made by viewing the subjective, internal situation in which the defendant found himself and the external circumstances as he perceived them at the time, however inaccurate that perception may have been, and assessing from that standpoint whether the explanation or excuse for his emotional disturbance was reasonable, so as to entitle him to a reduction of the crime charged from murder in the second degree to manslaughter in the first degree. People v. Casassa, 49 N.Y.2d 688, 427 N.Y.S.2d 769, 404 N.E.2d 1310 (1980), *cert. denied,* 449 U.S. 842 (1980).

—An action influenced by extreme emotional disturbance need not be spontaneous since, unlike former "heat of passion" defense, it does not negate intent; the purpose of the extreme emotional disturbance defense is to permit defendant to show that his actions were caused by a mental infirmity not arising to the level of insanity, and that he is less culpable for having committed them. People v. Patterson, 39 N.Y.2d 288, 383 N.Y.S.2d 573, 347 N.E.2d 898, *aff'd,* 432 U.S. 197, 97 S. Ct. 2319, 53 L. Ed. 2d 281 (1976).

—Evidence supported finding that defendant acted under extreme emotional disturbance justifying reducing conviction of murder in the second degree to manslaughter in the first degree and conviction of attempted murder in the second degree to attempted manslaughter in the first degree. Defendant was familiar with violent gang activities in the area, was summoned by a hysterical security guard screaming that someone had just been killed, once at the scene defendant recognized the "troublemakers" who outnumbered him three to one standing over an apparently dead man lying in a pool of blood, defendant believed the three had just killed defendant's partner, and the entire incident involving defendant's shooting unfolded in a matter of seconds. People v. Roldan, 222 A.D.2d 132, 647 N.Y.S.2d 179 (1st Dept. 1996).

—Trial court properly refused to charge defense of extreme emotional disturbance where the subjective element of this defense was negated by the evidence, supplied largely in defendant's confession, that a week before the murder the defendant told the victim's mother that he would kill the victim if he failed to return a loaned gun to the defendant, and that, on the day of the shooting, the defendant lured the victim, who was rumored to have called the defendant a "sucker," to a rooftop, and shot him in the back of his head and stomach. People v. Pagan, 210 A.D.2d 126, 620 N.Y.S.2d 54 (1st Dept. 1994).

—Defendant's request to charge defense of extreme emotional disturbance properly denied by court, viewing evidence in light most favorable to defendant. The elements of defense were not established, the shooting of the victim had no " 'reasonable explanation or excuse' and was not 'an understandable human response deserving of mercy.' " People v. Gehy, 238 A.D.2d 354, 656 N.Y.S.2d 58 (2d Dept. 1997).

—Applicability of extreme emotional disturbance defense is a matter left to the sound discretion of the jury. Here, the jury was presented with conflicting experts, one which supported defendant's defense and one whom did not. The jury was entitled to credit the expert it found most credible and discount the other. People v. Gabrielle, 241 A.D.2d 835, 661 N.Y.S.2d 306 (3d Dept. 1997).

—Trial court did not err in refusing to charge defense of extreme emotional disturbance; while evidence established that defendant may have been upset at the prospect of having been infected with a sexually transmitted disease by the victim as per the victim's statement to the defendant, the evidence did not support the conclusion that the defendant acted with a complete loss of control. People v. Matthews, 220 A.D.2d 822, 632 N.Y.S.2d 298 (3d Dept. 1995).

—No ineffective assistance of counsel where counsel raised defense of extreme emotional distress and succeeded in having this defense charged to jury on the facts as he knew them where defense counsel claimed that defendant was reluctant to confide in him about abuse by her husband; counsel was persuaded to emphasize the defense of justification over the defense of extreme emotional defense since the former would legally excuse the defendant's conduct while the latter would merely result in a reduction in the degree of the crime. People v. Cutting, 210 A.D.2d 791, 621 N.Y.S.2d 149 (3d Dept. 1994).

—Although prosecutor's statement that defendant claiming extreme emotional disturbance as affirmative defense was required to prove reasonable explanation for action rather than reasonable cause or excuse for extreme emotional disturbance was error, where defendant objected and court gave curative instruction, defendant was not denied a fair trial. People v. Hetherington, 229 A.D.2d 916, 645 N.Y.S.2d 679 (4th Dept. 1996).

Intent.—Evidence that defendant fired a rifle through a wooden door at a height of four feet immediately after the victim pushed the rifle away and slammed the door between them was sufficient to support a conviction for attempted murder in the second degree. People v. Perez, 64 N.Y.2d 868, 487 N.Y.S.2d 550, 476 N.E.2d 995 (1985).

—Defendant's argument that the crime of attempted murder in the second degree under a theory of transferred intent is a nonexistent crime because it imposes liability for an unintended result, and it is impossible to attempt to cause the death of an unintended victim, is without merit; although the victim was unintended, this crime does contain an element of strict liability with respect to the result of the crime—an intended death. People v. Fernandez, 215 A.D.2d 234, 626 N.Y.S.2d 191 (1st Dept. 1995), *aff'd,* 650 N.Y.S.2d 625 (1996).

—Where defendant fired a weapon into a group of people resulting in the death of one victim, it was not error for court to permit testimony from witness that defendant had threatened him with a gun one week prior to the shooting. Testimony of the uncharged crime was probative in establishing defendant's intent and motive. People v. Seeley, 231 A.D.2d 653, 648 N.Y.S.2d 111 (2d Dept. 1996).

—Evidence that victim died of 17 separate stab wounds, three of which were to the chest and one of which pierced his heart, was sufficient to prove an intent to kill. People v. Savage, 140 A.D.2d 553, 538 N.Y.S.2d 880 (2d Dept. 1989).

—Proof of intoxication may be offered to negate the mens rea element of an intentional crime, but it will not negate the presence of a reckless mental state. People v. Johnson, 277 A.D.2d 702, 717 N.Y.S.2d 668 (3d Dept. 2000), *appeal denied,* 96 N.Y.2d 831 (2001).

—Evidence supported conviction for attempted murder in the second degree where jury could rationally find that defendant was not so intoxicated so as to negate intent. Although defendant claimed he had consumed eight beers and had no recollection of the attack, police described him as not being intoxicated, defendant showered after the assault, stuffed the knife used in the crime in a pillow of a chair, changed clothes and attempted to clean up the victim's blood. People v. Gagliardi, 232 A.D.2d 879, 649 N.Y.S.2d 214 (3d Dept. 1996).

—Fact that defendant engages in intentional conduct causing victim's death does not preclude finding that defendant's conduct was also reckless, so as to support a conviction for depraved indifference murder. People v. Meehan, 229 A.D.2d 715, 646 N.Y.S.2d 716 (3d Dept. 1996).

—Proof of defendant's intent to kill was demonstrated by evidence that victim was found with ten .22 caliber bullet wounds to her head, face, breast, ribs, shoulders and neck. People v. DeGraw, 140 A.D.2d 984, 529 N.Y.S.2d 656 (4th Dept. 1988).

Immunity from prosecution.—Although a grand jury may grant immunity from prosecution for conspiracy to commit murder, it cannot grant such immunity for murder. However, once the immunity is granted for the former crime, the witness who has been granted the immunity is protected from prosecution based on any testimony he may give concerning the crime of murder. Gold v. Menna, 25 N.Y.2d 475, 307 N.Y.S.2d 33, 255 N.E.2d 235 (1969).

Felony murder.—A conviction of felony murder under Penal Law 125.25(3) should be sustained where the homicide victim, a police officer, was shot not by one of the defendants but by a fellow officer during a gun battle following defendant's attempted robbery. People v. Hernandez, 82 N.Y.2d 309, 604 N.Y.S.2d 524, 624 N.E.2d 661 (1993).

—The underlying felony in a felony murder charge is not a lesser included offense which merges in the conviction for which it was the predicate since, in felony murder, the underlying felony is not so much an element of the crime but instead functions as a replacement for the *mens rea* or intent necessary for common-law murder. People v. Berzups, 49 N.Y.2d 417, 426 N.Y.S.2d 253, 402 N.E.2d 1155 (1980).

—Defendant's conviction affirmed where defendant failed to prove affirmative defense to felony murder; evidence was overwhelming that defendant aided in commission of homicidal act and that he had reasonable ground to believe that another participant was armed with a deadly weapon. People v. Carpenter, 209 A.D.2d 246 619 N.Y.S.2d 537 (1st Dept. 1994).

—Felony murder does not require that the underlying felony take place in this state; rather, it is sufficient that one of the elements of the offense takes place in New York State. People v. Nieves, 205 A.D.2d 173, 617 N.Y.S.2d 751 (1st Dept. 1994), *aff'd,* 88 N.Y.2d 618, 648 N.Y.S.2d 863, 671 N.E.2d 1260 (1996).

—Trial court committed error when it concluded that the predicate sodomy count was a lesser included count of felony murder and failed to sentence the defendant on the sodomy count. People v. Santana, 82 A.D.2d 784, 440 N.Y.S.2d 668 (1st Dept. 1981), *aff'd,* 55 N.Y.2d 673, 446 N.Y.S.2d 944, 431 N.E.2d 305 (1981).

—Defendant could be convicted of felony murder notwithstanding his acquittal on the underlying felony. People v. Crum, 160 A.D.2d 892, 554 N.Y.S.2d 324 (2d Dept. 1990).

—The intent required to establish felony murder is not the intent to commit the murder; the People need only establish the defendant's intent to commit the designated felony. People v. Curry, 294 A.D.2d 608, 741 N.Y.S.2d 324 (3d Dept. 2002).

—In a felony murder prosecution, the pertinent inquiry is not whether the defendant intended to kill the victim, but whether he acted with the requisite mental state to commit the underlying crime. People v. Stevens, 153 A.D.2d 768, 544 N.Y.S.2d 889, 890 (3d Dept. 1989).

—Conviction of felony murder was affirmed; intent to burglarize home supported intent for murder conviction, even though defendant might not have intended to kill victim. People v. Couser, 12 A.D.3d 1040, 785 N.Y.S.2d 212 (4th Dept. 2004).

—"[F]elony murder is a strict liability offense, and the killer's subjective intent or motive is not relevant." People v. Williams, 239 A.D.2d 922, 659 N.Y.S.2d 597 (4th Dept. 1997).

—Pursuant to felony-murder statute, the death need only be caused by the commission of the crime; it need not occur at the time of the commission of the crime. People v. Zane, 152 A.D.2d 976, 543 N.Y.S.2d 777 (4th Dept. 1989).

—Robbery is not a lesser included offense of felony murder, nor are the elements of the crime the same. People v. Ponder, 77 A.D.2d 223, 433 N.Y.S.2d 288 (4th Dept. 1980), *aff'd,* 54 N.Y.2d 951, 445 N.Y.S.2d 143, 429 N.E.2d 821 (1981).

Reckless endangerment.—Evidence was factually insufficient to establish that defendant, recklessly or otherwise, created a grave risk of death to another where there was testimony that defendant fired a gun into the air near a group of people and that, approximately 20 minutes after this shooting, defendant's brother shot and wounded another, and where there was no evidence that the police recovered the weapon discharged by the defendant or any bullets or casings traceable to that weapon. People v. Abney, 211 A.D.2d 801, 622 N.Y.S.2d 85 (2d Dept. 1995).

—Evidence that defendant entered a barbershop, then left with one person before returning and shooting the victim from six to seven feet away, then fired at point blank range, supported intentional murder only; no evidence supported recklessness. People v. Gonzalez, 302 A.D.2d 870, 755 N.Y.S.2d 146 (4th Dept. 2003), *appeal granted,* 99 N.Y.2d 659, 760 N.Y.S.2d 124, 790 N.E.2d 292 (2003).

Lesser included offenses.—New trial was required where trial court refused to charge manslaughter, second degree, although there was evidence that defendant was too intoxicated at the time he stabbed victim to have intended either to kill her or to cause her serious physical injury and defendant was convicted of murder, first degree. People v. Lee, 35 N.Y.2d 826, 362 N.Y.S.2d 860, 35 N.E.2d 826 (1974).

—Trial court properly denied defendant's request to charge manslaughter in the first degree as a lesser-included offense of murder in the second degree; there was no reasonable view of the evidence, when viewed in the light most favorable to the defendant, to support a finding that he intended only to cause serious physical injury rather than to kill victim, defendant shot victim in he head at point blank range. People v. Maldonado, 5 A.D.3d 505, 772 N.Y.S.2d 583 (2d Dept. 2004).

—Felony murder is not, as a matter of law, a lesser included offense of first degree murder. People v. Hildreth, 279 A.D.2d 791, 719 N.Y.S.2d 339 (3d Dept. 2001).

—Manslaughter in the second degree is not a lesser included offense of murder in the second degree, as creating a grave risk of physical injury is an element of murder but not of manslaughter. People v. Robinson, 278 A.D.2d 798, 723 N.Y.S.2d 277 (4th Dept. 2000), *appeal denied,* 96 N.Y.2d 762 (2001).

—Criminal possession of a weapon with intent to use unlawfully is not an inclusory concurrent count of murder in the second degree. People v. Ryan, 105 Misc. 2d 837, 433 N.Y.S.2d 394 (Sup. Ct. Queens Co. 1980).

Sentence.—Sentencing court erred in imposing minimum term of imprisonment that was half the maximum term upon defendant's conviction of attempted second degree murder; defendant was a first felony offender, and the offense was not, by definition, an armed felony offense. People v. Bernard, 214 A.D.2d 576, 625 N.Y.S.2d 78 (2d Dept. 1995).

Sufficiency of Evidence.—Court's decision that evidence could not support conviction for intentional murder, and subsequent refusal to submit charge to jury was a dismissal of the charge and double jeopardy prevented retrial on charges of manslaughter in the first degree, since it precludes consecutive prosecutions for greater and lesser included offenses where, "the lesser offense. . .requires no proof beyond that which is required for conviction of the greater. " People v. Biggs, 1 N.Y.3d 225, 771 N.Y.S.2d 49, 803 N.E.2d 370 (2003).

—Evidence was legally insufficient to support conviction for second degree murder; there was no evidence that defendant possessed a weapon at the time of the crime, was aware of the robbery plan, or shared the intent of the co-defendants or aided them in any way; mere presence cannot support a conviction.

People v. Eldridge, 302 A.D.2d 934, 755 N.Y.S.2d 193 (4th Dept. 2003).

§ 125.27. Murder in the first degree.

A person is guilty of murder in the first degree when:

1. With intent to cause the death of another person, he causes the death of such person or of a third person; and

(a) Either:

(i) the intended victim was a police officer as defined in subdivision 34 of section 1.20 of the criminal procedure law who was at the time of the killing engaged in the course of performing his official duties, and the defendant knew or reasonably should have known that the intended victim was a police officer; or

(ii) the intended victim was a peace officer as defined in paragraph a of subdivision twenty-one, subdivision twenty-three, twenty-four or sixty-two (employees of the division for youth) of section 2.10 of the criminal procedure law who was at the time of the killing engaged in the course of performing his official duties, and defendant knew or reasonably should have known that the intended victim was such a uniformed court officer, parole officer, probation officer, or employee of the division for youth; or

(iii) the intended victim was an employee of a state correctional institution or was an employee of a local correctional facility as defined in subdivision two of section forty of the correction law, who was at the time of the killing engaged in the course of performing his official duties, and the defendant knew or reasonably should have known that the intended victim was an employee of a state correctional institution or a local correctional facility; or

(iv) at the time of the commission of the killing, the defendant was confined in a state correctional institution or was otherwise in custody upon a sentence for the term of his natural life, or upon a sentence commuted to one of natural life, or upon a sentence for an indeterminate term the minimum of which was at least fifteen years and the maximum of which was natural life, or at the time of the commission of the killing, the defendant had escaped from such confinement or custody while serving such a sentence and had not yet been returned to such confinement or custody; or

(v) the intended victim was a witness to a crime committed on a prior occasion and the death was caused for the purpose of preventing the intended victim's testimony in any criminal action or proceeding whether or not such action or proceeding had been commenced, or the intended victim had previously testified in a criminal action or proceeding and the killing was committed for the purpose of exacting retribution for such prior testimony, or the intended victim

was an immediate family member of a witness to a crime committed on a prior occasion and the killing was committed for the purpose of preventing or influencing the testimony of such witness, or the intended victim was an immediate family member of a witness who had previously testified in a criminal action or proceeding and the killing was committed for the purpose of exacting retribution upon such witness for such prior testimony. As used in this subparagraph "immediate family member" means a husband, wife, father, mother, daughter, son, brother, sister, stepparent, grandparent, stepchild or grandchild; or

(vi) the defendant committed the killing or procured commission of the killing pursuant to an agreement with a person other than the intended victim to commit the same for the receipt, or in expectation of the receipt, of anything of pecuniary value from a party to the agreement or from a person other than the intended victim acting at the direction of a party to such agreement; or

(vii) the victim was killed while the defendant was in the course of committing or attempting to commit and in furtherance of robbery, burglary in the first degree or second degree, kidnapping in the first degree, arson in the first degree or second degree, rape in the first degree, criminal sexual act in the first degree, sexual abuse in the first degree, aggravated sexual abuse in the first degree or escape in the first degree, or in the course of and furtherance of immediate flight after committing or attempting to commit any such crime or in the course of and furtherance of immediate flight after attempting to commit the crime of murder in the second degree; provided however, the victim is not a participant in one of the aforementioned crimes and, provided further that, unless the defendant's criminal liability under this subparagraph is based upon the defendant having commanded another person to cause the death of the victim or intended victim pursuant to section 20.00 of this chapter, this subparagraph shall not apply where the defendant's criminal liability is based upon the conduct of another pursuant to section 20.00 of this chapter; or

(viii) as part of the same criminal transaction, the defendant, with intent to cause serious physical injury to or the death of an additional person or persons, causes the death of an additional person or persons; provided, however, the victim is not a participant in the criminal transaction; or

(ix) prior to committing the killing, the defendant had been convicted of murder as defined in this section or section 125.25 of this article, or had been convicted in another jurisdiction of an offense which, if committed in this state, would constitute a violation of either of such sections; or

(x) the defendant acted in an especially cruel and wanton manner pursuant to a course of conduct intended to inflict and inflicting torture upon the victim prior to the victim's death. As used in this subparagraph, "torture" means the intentional and depraved infliction of extreme physical pain; "depraved" means the defendant relished the infliction of extreme physical pain upon the victim evidencing debasement or perversion or that the defendant evidenced a sense of pleasure in the infliction of extreme physical pain; or

(xi) the defendant intentionally caused the death of two or more additional persons within the state in separate criminal transactions within a period of twenty-four months when committed in a similar fashion or pursuant to a common scheme or plan; or

(xii) the intended victim was a judge as defined in subdivision twenty-three of section 1.20 of the criminal procedure law and the defendant killed such victim because such victim was, at the time of the killing, a judge; or

(xiii) the victim was killed in furtherance of an act of terrorism, as defined in paragraph (b) of subdivision one of section 490.05 of this chapter; and

(b) the defendant was more than eighteen years old at the time of the commission of the crime.

2. In any prosecution under subdivision one, it is an affirmative defense that:

(a) The defendant acted under the influence of extreme emotional disturbance for which there was a reasonable explanation or excuse, the reasonableness of which is to be determined from the viewpoint of a person in the defendant's situation under the circumstances as the defendant believed them to be. Nothing contained in this paragraph shall constitute a defense to a prosecution for, or preclude a conviction of, manslaughter in the first degree or any other crime except murder in the second degree; or

(b) The defendant's conduct consisted of causing or aiding, without the use of duress or deception, another person to commit suicide. Nothing contained in this paragraph shall constitute a defense to a prosecution for, or preclude a conviction of, manslaughter in the second degree or any other crime except murder in the second degree.

Murder in the first degree is a class A-I felony.

Added by L. 1974, Ch. 367; L. 1995, Ch. 1, § 7, amending subd. 1, eff. Sept. 1, 1995; L. 2001, Ch. 300, § 3, amending subd. 1(a)(xii) and adding subd. 1(a)(xiii), eff. Sept. 17, 2001; L. 2003, Ch. 264, § 11, eff. Nov. 1, 2003, amending subd. 1(a)(vii).

ANNOTATIONS

Accessorial liability.—Accessorial liability is not limited for the other 12 subdivisions of the first degree murder statute, only for first degree murder. People v. Cahill, 2 N.Y.3d 14, 777 N.Y.S.2d 332, 809 N.E.2d 561 (2003).

Affirmative defense of extreme emotional disturbance.— Defendant was precluded from having the jury consider the affirmative defense of extreme emotional disturbance where he failed to advance this position during the trial but maintained that he did not commit the acts charged. People v. Adams, 72 A.D.2d 156, 423 N.Y.S.2d 936 (1st Dept. 1980), affd, 53 N.Y.2d 1, 439 N.Y.S.2d 877, 422 N.E.2d 537 (1981).

—When the defendant offers evidence of extreme emotional disturbance for which there is a reasonable explanation or cause, the grand jury should be instructed that extreme emotional disturbance constitutes an affirmative defense which precludes a charge of murder in the first degree. People v. Prater, 170 A.D.2d 327, 648 N.Y.S.2d 228 (Sup. Ct. Kings Co. 1996).

Age.—The language "more than 18 years old" contained in Penal Law 125.27 includes persons who have reached their eighteenth birthday. People v. Carr, 159 Misc. 2d 1093, 608 N.Y.S.2d 48 (Sup. Ct. Kings Co. 1994).

Commands.—Accessorial liability for first degree felony murder under PL §125.27(1)(a)(vii) is available only when theory proved by prosecution is that defendant commanded the killing. People v. Mateo, 2 N.Y.3d 383, 779 N.Y.S.2d 399, 811 N.E.2d 1053, cert. denied, 542 U.S. 946 (2004).

Constitutionality.—Constitutional challenge alleging statutory meaning of word "commands" in terms of accomplice liability aggregating factor was impermissibly vague, is rejected; charge of indictment alleging defendant was guilty of murder in the first degree, based upon his command of a fellow gang member to kill a material witness against him, was proper. People v. Couser, 94 N.Y.2d 631, 709 N.Y.S.2d 155, 730 N.E.2d 953 (2000).

—Defendant who had been properly convicted of the intentional murder of a correction officer while serving a life sentence could not be sentenced to death since the New York statute requiring a mandatory death sentence for such a conviction is unconstitutional in that it violates the eighth and fourteenth Amendments by excluding consideration of mitigating circumstances by the sentencing authority. People v. Smith, 63 N.Y.2d 41, 479 N.Y.S.2d 706, 468 N.E.2d 879 (1984), cert. denied, 469 U.S. 1227 (1985).

—Although New York's death penalty statute has been declared unconstitutional, the crime of murder in the first degree has not. People v. Edgehill, 130 A.D.2d 761, 516 N.Y.S.2d 55, 56 (2d Dept. 1987).

Intent.—In a prosecution for first degree burglary and capital murder, it is not enough for the prosecution to establish that "the burglar intended only murder, that intent cannot be used both to define the burglary and at the same time bootstrap the second degree (intentional) murder to a capital crime." People v. Cahill, 2 N.Y.3d 14, 777 N.Y.S.2d 332, 809 N.E.2d 561 (2003).

—Where defendant shot through the door of his apartment about five and one-half feet above the ground at police who first identified themselves and then tried to gain access to defendant's apartment to execute a search warrant, evidence was legally sufficient to establish that defendant intended to cause the death of another person and that he knew or reasonably should have known that such person was a police officer engaged in the course of performing his official duties. People v. Rocker, 5 A.D.3d 1106, 773 N.Y.S.2d 318 (4th Dept. 2004).

—Evidence that defendant fired a semiautomatic weapon at two uniformed police officers who stopped his vehicle for traffic violations, could not support both convictions for attempted murder in the first degree and reckless endangerment in the first degree (one intentional act and one unintentional act, respectively), verdicts were reversed on appeal with instruction to trial court that on retrial, these two counts had to be presented to the jury in the alternative. People v. Robinson, 8 A.D.3d 1028, 778 N.Y.S.2d 808 (4th Dept. 2004), aff'd sub nom. People v. Daniels, 5 N.Y.3d 738, 800 N.Y.S.2d 369, 833 N.E.2d 704 (2005).

—Intent "is an issue of fact that often must be determined only on the basis of the criminal act and the circumstances surrounding its commission." People v. Parker, 304 A.D.2d 146, 755 N.Y.S.2d 521 (4th Dept. 2003).

Legally insufficient.—Requirement that murders of two or more people within a 24-month period be "committed in a similar fashion" was not met where, although it was uncontroverted that defendant killed each victim with a firearm, each scenario was unique in that each of the victims had different ethnic and racial backgrounds, they varied in age from 16 to 20, and the motive for each was different, as was the setting and circumstances under which each was killed. People v. Mateo, 93 N.Y.2d 327, 690 N.Y.S.2d 527, 712 N.E.2d 692 (1999).

—Where there was evidence that incarcerated defendant shared a community of purpose with coconspirators to kill complaining witness, but entire record at trial was consistent with spontaneously formed decision by his coconspirators, upon finding witness not there, to instead shoot family members of complaining witness, a decision in which defendant took no part, conviction for murder in first degree was not supported. People v. Couser, 12 A.D.3d 1040, 785 N.Y.S.2d 212 (4th Dept. 2004).

Lesser included offense.—Defendant's request that court submit to jury criminally negligent homicide, a lesser included offense of depraved indifference murder, waived defendant's right to argue that conviction for depraved indifference murder was bared by statute of limitations. People v. Mills, 1 N.Y.3d 269, 772 N.Y.S.2d 228, 804 N.E.2d 392 (2003).

—Trial court did not err in refusing to charge jury that attempted aggravated assault on a police officer was a lesser included offense of attempted first degree murder since, at the time defendant was tried the aggravated assault crime required a firearm while the murder crime did not; thus, at the time defendant was tried it was possible to commit the crime of attempted murder in the first degree without also committing attempted aggravated assault upon a police officer. People v. Van Buren, 213 A.D.2d 504, 623 N.Y.S.2d 907 (2d Dept. 1995).

—Felony murder is not, as a matter of law, a lesser included offense of first degree murder. People v. Hildreth, 279 A.D.2d 791, 719 N.Y.S.2d 339 (3d Dept. 2001).

Performing official duties.—In prosecution for attempted murder, first degree, and aggravated assault upon a police officer, it was proper for the court to admit evidence that the police officers were looking for the defendant just prior to the crimes in order to arrest him; such evidence was necessary to establish the element that the victim officer was engaged in the course of performing his official duties. People v. Simon, 118 A.D.2d 883, 500 N.Y.S.2d 367 (2d Dept. 1986).

Same criminal transaction. —Evidence was legally sufficient to establish that defendant killed multiple victims during same criminal transaction where two victims were killed within 90 minutes within small area of housing project because he believed them to be part of a rival gang who were intending to kill him; "criminal transaction" should be interpreted in accordance with technical definition contained in CPL § 40.10(2). People v. Duggins, 3 N.Y.3d 522, 788 N.Y.S.2d 638, 821 N.E.2d 942 (2004).

Sufficiency of indictment.—Where indictment charged defendant with two counts of murder in the first degree and cited § 125.27(1)(a)(vii), all necessary elements of the counts were incorporated by reference even if they were not explicitly listed in the indictment; indictment was not jurisdictionally defective. People v. Rivera, 182 Misc. 2d 235, 697 N.Y.S.2d 831 (Sup. Ct. Bronx Co. 1999).

§ 125.40. Abortion in the second degree.

A person is guilty of abortion in the second degree when he commits an abortional act upon a female, unless such abortional act is justifiable pursuant to subdivision three of section 125.05.

Abortion in the second degree is a class E felony.

Actions not within statute—The abortion provision of the homicide statutes does not protect the defendant, who was properly convicted of homicide where he shot a pregnant woman and the infant was born alive but died 36 hours after the emergency delivery. People v. Hall, 158 A.D.2d 69, 557 N.Y.S.2d 879 (1st Dept. 1990).

§ 125.45. Abortion in the first degree.

A person is guilty of abortion in the first degree when he commits upon a female pregnant for more than twenty-four weeks an abortional act which causes the miscarriage of such female, unless such abortional act is justifiable pursuant to subdivision three of section 125.05.

Abortion in the first degree is a class D felony.

§ 125.50. Self-abortion in the second degree.

A female is guilty of self-abortion in the second degree when, being pregnant, she commits or submits to an abortional act upon herself, unless such abortional act is justifiable pursuant to subdivision three of section 125.05.

Self-abortion in the second degree is a class B misdemeanor.

§ 125.55. Self-abortion in the first degree.

A female is guilty of self-abortion in the first degree when, being pregnant for more than twenty-four weeks, she commits or submits to an abortional act upon herself which causes her miscarriage, unless such abortional act is justifiable pursuant to subdivision three of section 125.05.

Self-abortion in the first degree is a class A misdemeanor.

§ 125.60. Issuing abortional articles.

A person is guilty of issuing abortional articles when he manufactures, sells or delivers any instrument, article, medicine, drug or substance with intent that the same be used in unlawfully procuring the miscarriage of a female.

Issuing abortional articles is a class B misdemeanor.

ARTICLE 130—SEX OFFENSES

LexisNexis Cross References

Criminal Defense Techniques, Vol. 2, Ch. 53, Defense of Sex Crimes; Vol. 2, Ch. 53A, Defense of a Rape Case; *New York Criminal Practice (2d ed.),* Vol. 6, Ch. 59, Sex Offenses and Offenses Against Marriage; *Sexual Assault Trials (2d ed.),* Vol. 1, Ch. 7, Consent; *Police Investigation Handbook,* Ch. 25, Rape and Other Sexual Offenses; *see generally Prosecution and Defense of Sex Crimes.*

§ 130.00. Sex offenses; definitions of terms.

The following definitions are applicable to this article:

1. "Sexual intercourse" has its ordinary meaning and occurs upon any penetration, however slight.

2. (a) "Oral sexual conduct" means conduct between persons consisting of contact between the mouth and the penis, the mouth and the anus, or the mouth and the vulva or vagina.

(b) "Anal sexual conduct" means conduct between persons consisting of contact between the penis and anus.

3. "Sexual contact" means any touching of the sexual or other intimate parts of a person not married to the actor for the purpose of gratifying sexual desire of either party. It includes the touching of the actor by the victim, as well as the touching of the victim by the actor, whether directly or through clothing.

4. For the purposes of this article "married" means the existence of the relationship between the actor and the victim as spouses which is recognized by law at the time the actor commits an offense proscribed by this article against the victim.

5. "Mentally disabled" means that a person suffers from a mental disease or defect which renders him or her incapable of appraising the nature of his or her conduct.

6. "Mentally incapacitated" means that a person is rendered temporarily incapable of

appraising or controlling his conduct owing to the influence of a narcotic or intoxicating substance administered to him without his consent, or to any other act committed upon him without his consent.

7. "Physically helpless" means that a person is unconscious or for any other reason is physically unable to communicate unwillingness to an act.

8. "Forcible compulsion" means to compel by either:

a. use of physical force; or

b. a threat, express or implied, which places a person in fear of immediate death or physical injury to himself, herself or another person, or in fear that he, she or another person will immediately be kidnapped.

9. "Foreign object" means any instrument or article which, when inserted in the vagina, urethra, penis or rectum, is capable of causing physical injury.

10. "Sexual conduct" means sexual intercourse, oral sexual conduct, anal sexual conduct, aggravated sexual contact, or sexual contact.

11. "Aggravated sexual contact" means inserting, other than for a valid medical purpose, a foreign object in the vagina, urethra, penis or rectum of a child, thereby causing physical injury to such child.

12. "Health care provider" means any person who is, or is required to be, licensed or registered or holds himself or herself out to be licensed or registered, or provides services as if he or she were licensed or registered in the profession of medicine, chiropractic, dentistry or podiatry under any of the following: article one hundred thirty-one, one hundred thirty-two, one hundred thirty-three, or one hundred forty-one of the education law.

13. "Mental health care provider" shall mean a licensed physician, licensed psychologist, registered professional nurse, licensed clinical social worker or a licensed master social worker under the supervision of a physician, psychologist or licensed clinical social worker.

Amended by L. 1977, Ch. 692; L. 1978, Ch. 723, Ch. 735; L. 1981, Ch. 696; L. 1982, Ch. 560; L. 1983, Ch. 449; L. 1984, Ch. 650; L. 1996, Ch. 122, § 5, adding subds. 10 and 11, eff. Aug. 1, 1996; L. 2000, Ch. 1, eff. Feb. 1, 2001; L. 2003, Ch. 264, § 12, eff. Nov. 1, 2003, amending subds. 2, 4, and 10; L. 2004, Ch. 230, § 25, eff. July 27, 2004, amending subd. 13.

ANNOTATIONS

Sexual contact.—"Sexual contact" is defined broadly. People v. Watson, 171 A.D.2d 529, 567 N.Y.S.2d 529, 530 (2d Dept. 1991).

—Requirement of "contact" between mouth and penis does not also require penetration. People v. May, 263 A.D.2d 215, 702 N.Y.S.2d 393 (3d Dept.), *appeal denied,* 94 N.Y.2d 950 (2000).

Sexual intercourse.—Evidence was legally insufficient to establish defendant's guilt of rape in the first degree; the evidence did not show beyond a reasonable doubt that the defendant had sexual intercourse with the complainant at the times in question. People v. Palmer, 212 A.D.2d 742, 632 N.Y.S.2d 157 (2d Dept. 1995).

—Rape conviction affirmed; medical evidence corroborated complainant's testimony that penetration, "however slight," had occurred. People v. Velez, 212 A.D.2d 819, 623 N.Y.S.2d 271 (2d Dept. 1995).

Forcible compulsion.—Forcible compulsion as defined in PL § 130.00(8) is not unconstitutionally vague. People v. Beam, 57 N.Y.2d 241, 455 N.Y.S.2d 575, 441 N.E.2d 1093 (1982).

—The existence of "forcible compulsion" need not be corroborated by medical evidence. People v. Agard, 199 A.D.2d 401, 606 N.Y.S.2d 239 (2d Dept. 1993).

—Forcible compulsion element was met even though victim permitted defendant to kiss her and fondle her; victim, who weighed 140 pounds, was assaulted by defendant, who stood over six feet tall and weighed 270 pounds, and in light of overwhelming size advantage, victim need not have struggled or tried to cry out to establish forcible compulsion. People v. Smith, 302 A.D.2d 677, 756 N.Y.S.2d 290 (3d Dept. 2003).

—Forcible compulsion to engage in deviate sexual intercourse was not established by the testimony of the complainant, who described the incident without detailing the defendant's use of physical force and only with the conclusory statement that she was forced to engage in these sexual acts. The record included the testimony of the defendant who conceded the sexual took place, but argued it was consensual, along with other witnesses who testified that complainant told them that no physical force was used and that she did not feel threatened. People v. Mirabel, 278 A.D.2d 526, 717 N.Y.S.2d 404 (3d Dept. 2000).

—Testimony of defendant's 12-year-old stepdaughter established that the defendant had threatened to harm the child's mother if the child refused his advances and that defendant used physical force to ensure her compliance. People v. Nailor, 268 A.D.2d 695, 701 N.Y.S.2d 476 (3d Dept. 2000).

—It was error for the court to charge the jury with a definition of "forcible compulsion" which included both physical force and threats, express or implied, when the indictment and bill of particulars only alleged physical force. People v. Norfleet, 267 A.D.2d 881, 704 N.Y.S.2d 146 (3d Dept. 1999), *appeal denied,* 95 N.Y.2d 801 (2000).

—Sufficient evidence existed to support conviction for sexual abuse in the first degree where 13-year-old victim testified that prior to being abused by victim's 31-year-old live-in companion, he told her that he wanted to rape her, have a baby with her, and that he would kill her whole family if she told anyone: element of "forcible compulsion" was met. People v. Archer, 232 A.D.2d 820, 649 N.Y.S.2d 204 (3d Dept. 1996).

—Threats to "blow [complainant's] head off" if she did not submit, as well as dragging her down the street was sufficient to constitute forcible compulsion even though complainant had not been bruised or battered. People v. Walton, 171 A.D.2d 954, 567 N.Y.S.2d 899, 900 (3d Dept. 1991).

Earnest resistance.—Complainant's testimony that defendant grabbed her hair and arms and punched her in the jaw, which was corroborated by other witnesses who testified to complainant's bruised appearance immediately after the incident and the testimony of the attending physician who treated complainant sufficiently established complainant's "earnest resistance" to defendant's "forcible compulsion" and supported defendant's conviction for rape. People v. Turner, 99 A.D.2d 615, 472 N.Y.S.2d 159 (3d Dept. 1984).

Physically helpless.—Evidence was legally sufficient to support defendant's convictions for sodomy and rape in the first degree where record contained substantial testimony regarding victim's intoxication and supported jury's finding that victim was physically helpless and lacked the mental capacity to consent due to intoxication. People v. Ferrer, 250 A.D.2d 860, 672 N.Y.S.2d 795 (2d Dept. 1998).

—A person is physically helpless when he or she is unable to communicate by reason of voluntary intoxication. People v. Himmel, 252 A.D.2d 273, 686 N.Y.S.2d 504 (3d Dept. 1999).

—"Physically helpless" is broadly defined so as to cover a sleeping victim. People v. Smith, 16 A.D.3d 1033, 790 N.Y.S.2d 805 (4th Dept. 2005).

—Conviction, based on jury's conclusion that victim was physically helpless, was supported by evidence that victim was incapable of consent because she was unconscious at the time defendant committed the acts of sexual abuse. People v. Brandel, 306 A.D.2d 860, 762 N.Y.S.2d 468 (4th Dept. 2003).

—Natural uninduced sleep constitutes being in a physically helpless condition from which one may be deemed incapable of consenting to deviate sexual intercourse. People v. Copp, 169 Misc. 2d 757, 648 N.Y.S.2d 492 (City Ct. Monroe Co. 1996).

Charge.—A failure to give unnecessarily expanded, meticulous instructions with respect to the meaning and application of the concept of "forcible compulsion" in rape cases may be less significant than might otherwise be true and does not mandate reversal. People v. Yanik, 43 N.Y.2d 97, 400 N.Y.S.2d 778, 371 N.E.2d 497 (1977).

—The charge was proper where the court employed the current language of PL § 130.00(8), which included the newly inserted definition of resistance. People v. Walstatter, 73 A.D.2d 175, 425 N.Y.S.2d 623 (2d Dept. 1980), aff'd, 53 N.Y.2d 871, 440 N.Y.S.2d 615, 423 N.E.2d 38 (1981).

§ 130.05. Sex offenses; lack of consent.

1. Whether or not specifically stated, it is an element of every offense defined in this article that the sexual act was committed without consent of the victim.

2. Lack of consent results from:

(a) Forcible compulsion; or

(b) Incapacity to consent; or

(c) Where the offense charged is sexual abuse or forcible touching, any circumstances, in addition to forcible compulsion or incapacity to consent, in which the victim does not expressly or impliedly acquiesce in the actor's conduct; or

(d) Where the offense charged is rape in the third degree as defined in subdivision three of section 130.25, or criminal sexual act in the third degree as defined in subdivision three of section 130.40, in addition to forcible compulsion, circumstances under which, at the time of the act of intercourse, oral sexual conduct or anal sexual conduct, the victim clearly expressed that he or she did not consent to engage in such act, and a reasonable person in the actor's situation would have understood such person's words and acts as an expression of lack of consent to such act under all the circumstances.

3. A person is deemed incapable of consent when he or she is:

(a) less than seventeen years old; or

(b) mentally disabled; or

(c) mentally incapacitated; or

(d) physically helpless; or

(e) committed to the care and custody of the state department of correctional services or a hospital, as such term is defined in subdivision two of section four hundred of the correction law, and the actor is an employee, not married to such person, who knows or reasonably should know that such person is committed to the care and custody of such department or hospital. For purposes of this paragraph, "employee" means

(i) an employee of the state department of correctional services who performs professional duties in a state correctional facility consisting of providing custody, medical or mental health services, counseling services, educational programs, or vocational training for inmates;

(ii) an employee of the division of parole who performs professional duties in a state correctional facility and who provides institutional parole services pursuant to section two hundred fifty-nine-e of the executive law; or

(iii) an employee of the office of mental health who performs professional duties in a state correctional facility or hospital, as such term is defined in subdivision two of section four hundred of the correction law, consisting of providing custody, or medical or mental health services for such inmates; or

(f) committed to the care and custody of a local correctional facility, as such term is defined in subdivision two of section forty of the correction law, and the actor is an employee, not married to such person, who knows or reasonably should know that such person is committed to the care and custody of such facility. For purposes of this paragraph, "employee" means an employee of the local correctional facility where the person is committed who performs professional duties consisting of providing custody, medical or mental health services, counseling services, educational services, or vocational training for inmates; or

(g) committed to or placed with the office of children and family services and in residential care, and the actor is an employee, not married to such person, who knows or reasonably should know that such person is committed to or placed with such office of children and family services and in residential care. For purposes of this paragraph, "employee" means an employee of the office of children and family services or of a residential facility who performs duties consisting of providing custody, medical or mental health services, counseling services, educational services, or vocational training for persons committed to or placed with the office of children and family services and in residential care; or

(h) a client or patient and the actor is a health care provider or mental health care provider charged with rape in the third degree as defined in section 130.25, criminal sexual act in the third degree as defined in section 130.40, aggravated sexual abuse in the fourth degree as defined in section 130.65-a, or sexual abuse in the third degree as defined in section 130.55, and the act of sexual conduct occurs during a treatment session, consultation, interview, or examination.

Amended by L. 1965, Ch. 1038; L. 1996, Ch. 266, § 1, amending subd. 3(e), and adding subd. 3(f), eff. Aug. 1, 1996; L. 2000, Ch. 1, eff. Feb. 1, 2001; L. 2003, Ch. 264, §§ 13, 14, eff. Nov. 1, 2003, amending subds. 1, 2(c), 2(d) and 3(h); L. 2004, Ch. 40, § 1, eff. April 20, 2004, amending subd. 2(d).

ANNOTATIONS

Forcible compulsion.—The charge on sexual abuse in the first degree should have made clear that a conviction required a finding that the victim's lack of consent resulted from forcible compulsion and no reference should be made to factors which could in other cases result in lack of consent. People v. Mott, 77 A.D.2d 606, 429 N.Y.S.2d 916 (2d Dept. 1980).

Lack of consent.—When the lack of consent results solely from an incapacity to consent because of the age of victim, there must be evidence in addition to victim's testimony to: (a) establish that an attempt was made to engage the alleged victim in sexual contact and (b) connect defendant with the commission of the offense. People v. St. John, 74 A.D.2d 85, 426 N.Y.S.2d 863 (3d Dept. 1980).

—Evidence was insufficient to support third degree rape conviction where it failed to establish that crack cocaine ingested by the victim was administered without her consent and rendered her incapable of appraising or controlling her conduct; proof failed to show that victim was incapable of consent because she was mentally incapacitated. People v. Thomas, 210 A.D.2d 992, 620 N.Y.S.2d 692 (4th Dept. 1994).

—PL § 130.05(2)(c) does not apply to the crime of forcible touching (PL § 130.52); information charging violation of that section must contain specific allegations addressing lack of consent by either forcible compulsion or incapacity to consent. People v. Parbhu, 191 Misc. 2d 473, 743 N.Y.S.2d 660 (Crim. Ct. N.Y. Co. 2002).

—Natural uninduced sleep constitutes being in a physically helpless condition from which one may be deemed incapable of consenting to deviate sexual intercourse. People v. Copp, 169 Misc. 2d 757, 648 N.Y.S.2d 492 (City Ct. Monroe Co. 1996).

§ 130.10. Sex offenses; limitation; defenses.

1. In any prosecution under this article in which the victim's lack of consent is based solely upon his or her incapacity to consent because he or she was mentally disabled, mentally incapacitated or physically helpless, it is an affirmative defense that the defendant, at the time he or she engaged in the conduct constituting the offense, did not know of the facts or conditions responsible for such incapacity to consent.

2. Conduct performed for a valid medical or mental health care purpose shall not constitute a violation of any section of this article in which incapacity to consent is based on the circumstances set forth in paragraph (h) of subdivision three of section 130.05 of this article.

3. In any prosecution for the crime of rape in the third degree as defined in section 130.25, criminal sexual act in the third degree as defined in section 130.40, aggravated sexual abuse in the fourth degree as defined in section 130.65-a, or sexual abuse in the third degree as defined in section 130.55 in which incapacity to consent is based on the circumstances set forth in paragraph (h) of subdivision three of section 130.05 of this article it shall be an affirmative defense that the client or patient consented to such conduct charged after having been expressly advised by the health care or mental health care provider that such conduct was not performed for a valid medical purpose.

4. In any prosecution under this article in which the victim's lack of consent is based solely on his or her incapacity to consent because he or she was less than seventeen years old, mentally disabled, or a client or patient and the actor is a health care provider, it shall be a defense that the defendant was married to the victim as defined in subdivision four of section 130.00 of this article.

Amended by L. 2000, Ch. 1, eff. Feb. 1, 2001; L. 2003, Ch. 264, § 15, eff. Nov. 1, 2003, amending subd. 3 and adding subd. 4.

§ 130.16. Sex offenses; corroboration.

A person shall not be convicted of any offense defined in this article of which lack of consent is an element but results solely from incapacity to consent because of the victim's mental defect, or mental incapacity, or an attempt to commit the same, solely on the testimony of the victim, unsupported by other evidence tending to:

(a) Establish that an attempt was made to engage the victim in sexual intercourse, oral sexual conduct, anal sexual conduct, or sexual contact, as the case may be, at the time of the occurrence; and

(b) Connect the defendant with the commission of the offense or attempted offense.

Added by L. 1974, Ch. 14; **Amended** by L. 1984, Ch. 89; L. 2003, Ch. 264, § 16, eff. Nov. 1, 2003, amending opening par. and subd. (a).

ANNOTATIONS

Age of victim.—Pursuant to PL § 130.16, corroboration is no longer required in cases where the incapacity to consent results solely from the victim's age. People v. Bolden, 194 A.D.2d 834, 598 N.Y.S.2d 603, 605 (3d Dept. 1993).

—No corroboration was required for victim's sworn testimony of sex act to which victim is deemed incapable of consent due to age. People v. Lamphier, 302 A.D.2d 864, 754 N.Y.S.2d 482 (4th Dept. 2003).

Lesser included offense.—Corroboration is required to prove a charge of sexual abuse in the second degree; insufficient evidence to sustain a finding of sexual abuse in the second degree did however, sustain a finding of the lesser included offense. People v. Jones, 107 Misc. 2d 1082, 436 N.Y.S.2d 145 (Nassau Co. Dist. Ct. 1981).

Evidence.—Victim's vague recollection as to feeling "pressure between [her] legs and inside [her] vagina," when she testified that she never saw defendant's penis and did not remember any other details about the incidents such as what the "pressure" felt like, whether it hurt, and whether she and defendant were clothed or unclothed, was not sufficient to corroborate penetration when coupled with the lack of physical evidence supporting penetration. People v. Carroll, 95 N.Y.2d 375, 718 N.Y.S.2d 10, 740 N.E.2d 1084 (2000).

—At trial of defendant for rape, sodomy and incest on complaint of his eleven-year-old daughter, the corroborative value of the photographs depicting the acts was properly submitted to the jury where testimony showed the negatives, from which the prints were made, were seized in defendant's home, the photographic expert testified that the negatives had not been altered and prints were accurate reproductions, and mother identified subjects as daughter and husband. People v. Byrnes, 33 N.Y.2d 343, 352 N.Y.S.2d 913, 308 N.E.2d 435 (1974).

—"[M]edical evidence of one type of sexual abuse is sufficiently corroborative of unsworn testimony concerning another type of sexual abuse committed as part of the same overall criminal transaction"; court properly accepted medical testimony consistent with sexual abuse of a three-year-old girl to corroborate the victim's testimony that the defendant had her touch his penis with her hand. People v. Lowe, 289 A.D.2d 705, 733 N.Y.S.2d 555 (3d Dept. 2001).

Sufficiency of corroboration.—The complainant's testimony was sufficiently corroborated where evidence was presented as to the presence of sperm on clothing worn by the complainant on the day of the incident, the complainant's supervisor testified that she noticed nothing unusual about the complainant's appearance on that day just prior to the incident, there was unsworn witness testimony that the complainant and the defendant were alone in a van, the complainant's mother testified as to the complainant's appearance upon arriving home in the van immediately after the incident, and the complainant's outcry after the incident; this evidence tended to establish sexual contact and also to connect the defendant with the commission of the offense. People v. Novak, 212 A.D.2d 740, 622 N.Y.S.2d 783 (2d Dept. 1995).

—Sister's testimony to the effect that she saw her father touching the victim's legs, backside and genitals provided sufficient corroboration in sodomy prosecution. People v. Shabala, 117 A.D.2d 924, 498 N.Y.S.2d 926 (3d Dept. 1986).

—In a prosecution for sodomy, sexual abuse, obscenity and endangering the welfare of a child, the corroboration requirement of § 130.16 of the Penal Law was satisfied by the general testimony of the children as to the sexual acts of defendant, notwithstanding the fact that they could not corroborate with specificity the testimony of each other. People v. Ahlers, 98 A.D.2d 821, 470 N.Y.S.2d 483 (3d Dept. 1983).

—Testimony of the mentally retarded victim with respect to each count of the indictment was sufficiently corroborated by taped telephone conversations between defendant and victim; statute's corroboration requirement "is satisfied when the victim's testimony is supported by evidence tending to establish that a crime was committed and that the defendant committed it." People v. Jordal, 294 A.D.2d 953, 742 N.Y.S.2d 760 (4th Dept. 2002).

§ 130.20. Sexual misconduct.

A person is guilty of sexual misconduct when:

1. he or she engages in sexual intercourse with another person without such person's consent; or

2. He or she engages in oral sexual conduct or anal sexual conduct with another person without such person's consent; or

3. he or she engages in sexual conduct with an animal or a dead human body.

Sexual misconduct is a class A misdemeanor.

Amended by L. 2001, Ch. 1, eff. Feb. 1, 2001; L. 2003, Ch. 264, § 17, eff. Nov. 1, 2003, amending subd. 2.

ANNOTATIONS

Constitutionality.—The sexual misconduct statute is unconstitutional because of its underinclusion of females. However, the appropriate remedy is to strike the statute's gender exemption in order to preserve the statute; dismissal of the charge against the defendant was not warranted or required by the striking of the statute's gender exemption, but was warranted under court's discretionary power since conviction or prosecution of defendant would be unjust under the circumstances presented. People v. M.K.R., 166 Misc. 2d 456, 632 N.Y.S.2d 382 (Justice Ct. Delaware Co. 1995).

Lesser included offense.—Defendant's argument that sexual misconduct is a lesser included offense of rape in the first degree rejected; no reasonable view of the evidence supported defendant's claim that he committed the lesser offense of sexual misconduct and, based on the record, it was theoretically impossible for defendant to have committed the greater crime of rape without, by the same conduct, committing sexual misconduct. People v. Cole, 212 A.D.2d 822, 622 N.Y.S.2d 354 (3d Dept. 1995).

—Proof was insufficient to establish rape in the third degree, but was sufficient to establish sexual misconduct since it showed that defendant engaged in sexual intercourse with the victim without her consent; prior judgment modified to reduce rape conviction to sexual misconduct conviction. People v. Thomas, 210 A.D.2d 992, 620 N.Y.S.2d 693 (4th Dept. 1994).

Evidence.—Defendant's acts ripened into the crime of sexual misconduct upon contact between the defendant's penis and the complainant's anus. People v. Copp, 169 Misc. 2d 757, 648 N.Y.S.2d 492 (City Ct. Monroe Co. 1996).

§ 130.25. Rape in the third degree.

A person is guilty of rape in the third degree when:

1. He or she engages in sexual intercourse with another person who is incapable of consent by reason of some factor other than being less than seventeen years old;

2. Being twenty-one years old or more, he or she engages in sexual intercourse with another person less than seventeen years old; or

3. He or she engages in sexual intercourse with another person without such person's consent where such lack of consent is by reason of some factor other than incapacity to consent.

Rape in the third degree is a class E felony.

Amended by L. 1987, Ch. 510; L. 2000, Ch. 1, eff. Feb. 1, 2001.

ANNOTATIONS

Constitutionality.—Statute will be upheld where, as here, it is supported by unrefuted, plausible, and constitutionally sufficient justification; statute does not violate equal protection by making distinctions based on gender as gender distinctions are necessary to: (1) prevent psychological injury to young women; (2) prevent physical damage; and (3) prevent deleterious consequences of pregnancy in minors. People v. Whidden, 51 N.Y.2d 457, 434 N.Y.S.2d 937, 415 N.E.2d 927 (1980).

—PL § 130.25 does not violate the equal protection of the laws and is constitutional. People v. Dozier, 72 A.D.2d 478, 424 N.Y.S.2d 1010 (1st Dept.), aff'd, 52 N.Y.2d 781, 436 N.Y.S.2d 620, 417 N.E.2d 1008 (1980).

—PL §130.25 is not unconstitutional because it subjects adults over the age of 21, but not between the ages of 18 and 21, to punishment; the age distinction serves a rational and legitimate state interest in the imposition of sanctions based upon differences in maturity between these age groups. People v. White, 211 A.D.2d 982, 621 N.Y.S.2d 728 (3d Dept. 1995).

—PL § 130.25(2) does not violate the equal protection clause of the state and federal constitutions. People v. Whidden, 71 A.D.2d 367, 423 N.Y.S.2d 512 (3d Dept. 1979), aff'd, 51 N.Y.2d 457, 434 N.Y.S.2d 936, 415 N.E.2d 927 (1980).

Elements.—The crime of rape is completed once there is any unlawful penetration, however slight. People v. Hobot, 200 A.D.2d 586, 606 N.Y.S.2d 277 (2d Dept. 1994).

Multiple rapes.—Multiple rapes of the same victim do not constitute a continuing offense; each act of intercourse is a separate and distinct offense. People v. Pries, 81 A.D.2d 1039, 440 N.Y.S.2d 116 (4th Dept. 1981).

§ 130.30. Rape in the second degree.

A person is guilty of rape in the second degree when:

1. being eighteen years old or more, he or she engages in sexual intercourse with another person less than fifteen years old; or

2. he or she engages in sexual intercourse with another person who is incapable of consent by reason of being mentally disabled or mentally incapacitated.

It shall be an affirmative defense to the crime

of rape in the second degree as defined in subdivision one of this section that the defendant was less than four years older than the victim at the time of the act.

Rape in the second degree is a class D felony.

Amended by L. 2000, Ch. 1, eff. Feb. 1, 2001.

ANNOTATIONS

Age.—Rape victim's testimony that she was 14 at the time of the crime was sufficient to prove her age at that time; moreover, the jury had the opportunity at trial to observe the victim and determine her age from her physical appearance at the trial. People v. Jackson, 148 A.D.2d 930, 539 N.Y.S.2d 168 (4th Dept. 1989).

—Proof that defendant was over 21 years old was satisfied by testimony given regarding his age by his two teenage daughters. People v. White, 149 A.D.2d 939, 540 N.Y.S.2d 72 (4th Dept. 1989).

Evidence.—Evidence which established that defendant had sexual intercourse with his daughter who was less than 14 years of age satisfied the charges of rape in the second degree. People v. Chapin, 265 A.D.2d 738, 697 N.Y.S.2d 713 (3d Dept. 1999), *appeal denied*, 94 N.Y.2d 917 (2000).

—Defendant's conviction of rape in the second degree affirmed; no merit to his claims that jury "selectively dissected" victim's testimony or that her testimony was not credible as a matter of law. People v. Green, 219 A.D.2d 856, 632 N.Y.S.2d 352 (4th Dept. 1995).

Jury charge.—Court did not err by failing to inform jury that a defense to rape in the second degree is that the defendant and the victim were married; not only was claim unpreserved for appeal, but there was no evidence to suggest that defendant and victim were married when the rape occurred. People v. Hackney, 293 A.D.2d 757, 741 N.Y.S.2d 441 (2d Dept. 2002).

Lesser included offense.—Just as it is possible to commit the crimes of rape in the first degree and sodomy in the first degree without concomitantly, by the same conduct, committing sexual abuse in the first degree, by analogous reasoning it is possible to commit rape in the second degree and sodomy in the second degree without also committing sexual abuse in the second degree; sexual abuse in the second degree is not a lesser included offense of second degree rape or second degree sodomy. People v. Gibson, 2 A.D.3d 969, 768 N.Y.S.2d 511 (3d Dept. 2003).

§ 130.35. Rape in the first degree.

A person is guilty of rape in the first degree when he or she engages in sexual intercourse with another person:

1. By forcible compulsion; or

2. Who is incapable of consent by reason of being physically helpless; or

3. Who is less than eleven years old; or

4. Who is less than thirteen years old and the actor is eighteen years old or more.

Rape in the first degree is a class B felony.

Amended by L. 2000, Ch. 1, eff. Feb. 1, 2001.

ANNOTATIONS

Constitutionality.—The court found that the New York rape statute (PL § 130.35) was unconstitutional because it exempted females from criminal liability for forcible rape; the court declared that the statute covers forcible rape by both males and females, rather than striking it down in its entirety. People v. Liberta, 64 N.Y.2d 152, 485 N.Y.S.2d 207, 474 N.E.2d 567 (1984).

—Marital exemption for rape is unconstitutional as there is no rational basis for distinguishing between marital rape and nonmarital rape; statute, rather than being stricken, was declared to include marital rape. People v. Liberta, 64 N.Y.2d 152, 485 N.Y.S.2d 207, 474 N.E.2d 567 (1984).

Elements.—Defendant's acquittal of rape in the first degree but conviction of sexual abuse in the first degree was not repugnant where the jury could have found that forcible compulsion was employed but penetration was not achieved, a necessary element of rape in the first degree. People v. Burns, 83 A.D.2d 639, 441 N.Y.S.2d 525 (2d Dept. 1981).

—Physical injury, screaming, and crying out are not necessary components of first degree rape; forcible compulsion can be inferred from the facts leading up to the rape or sodomy. *In re* Dakota EE, 209 A.D.2d 782, 618 N.Y.S.2d 133 (3d Dept. 1994).

Attempted rape.—Where a defendant is charged with attempted rape, a jury may infer defendant's intent to rape from his conduct and the surrounding circumstances and may find that defendant acted to carry the project forward within dangerous proximity to the criminal end to be attained. People v. Pereau, 64 N.Y.2d 1055, 489 N.Y.S.2d 872, 479 N.E.2d 217 (1985).

—Legally sufficient evidence was presented to support attempted rape conviction where testimony revealed defendant viciously assaulted victim when she refused his advances and he almost completed the rape of victim. People v. Urbina, 248 A.D.2d 123, 669 N.Y.S.2d 804 (1st Dept. 1998).

—Conviction for attempted rape in first degree was affirmed; forcible compulsion was established where defendant, who stood 6'2" and was 35 years older than 13-year-old victim, came into her bedroom at night and tried to rape her and victim testified that she could not move because defendant's body was on top of her and his hand was over her mouth. People v. Oglesby, 12 A.D.3d 857, 787 N.Y.S.2d 401 (3d Dept. 2004).

Physically helpless.—Where both indictment and bill of particulars as well as People's opening advanced the theory that defendant hit the victim over the head, thus rendering her unconscious, but medical testimony and People's summation instead attributed victim's physical helplessness to "dissociative amnesia" and "psychoneurological shock," this mid-trial variance in prosecution denied the defendant the right to a fair notice of charges against him. People v. Chin, 267 A.D.2d 404, 700 N.Y.S.2d 477 (2d Dept. 1999), *appeal denied*, 95 N.Y.2d 799 (2000).

—Evidence was legally sufficient to support defendant's convictions for sodomy and rape in the first degree where record contained substantial testimony regarding victim's intoxication and supported jury's finding that victim was physically helpless and lacked the mental capacity to consent due to intoxication. People v. Ferrer, 250 A.D.2d 860, 672 N.Y.S.2d 795 (2d Dept. 1998).

—A person is physically helpless when he or she is unable to communicate by reason of voluntary intoxication. People v. Himmel, 252 A.D.2d 273, 686 N.Y.S.2d 504 (3d Dept. 1999).

Evidence.—The victim's inability to testify with respect to penetration is not conclusive if other evidence exists from which that fact may be established, but where there was no physical evidence to support penetration, such as significant tearing and bleeding, the conviction for rape could not be sustained. People v. Carroll, 95 N.Y.2d 375, 718 N.Y.S.2d 10, 740 N.E.2d 1084 (2000).

—It was error for the trial court, where the crucial issue at trial was the complainant's lack of consent, to refuse to admit the redacted portion of the hospital record which indicated an absence of any scratches on complainant's neck and to allow testimony by the YMCA supervisor concerning defendant's practice of karate which, when viewed in conjunction with the court's minimal instruction to the jury as to the element of forcible compulsion, was highly prejudicial since there was a significant probability that the jury would have acquitted the defendant had it not been for these errors. People v. Dabney, 52 N.Y.2d 974, 438 N.Y.S.2d 283, 420 N.E.2d 81 (1981).

—Proof that defendant had type A blood and that the semen found within the victim was emitted from a male with blood of that type should not have been admitted, in view of the large proportion of the general population having blood of that type. People v. Macedonio, 42 N.Y.2d 944, 397 N.Y.S.2d 1002, 366 N.E.2d 1355 (1977).

—Evidence that defendant grabbed a two-year-old child away from the child's adult relative and walked quickly with the child into a crowded street was sufficient to establish the defendant's intent to abduct. People v. Cassano, 254 A.D.2d 92, 681 N.Y.S.2d 1 (1st Dept. 1998).

—Evidence was legally sufficient to support defendant's convictions for sodomy and rape in the first degree where record contained substantial testimony regarding victim's intoxication and supported jury's finding that victim was physically helpless and lacked the mental capacity to consent due to intoxication. People v. Ferrer, 250 A.D.2d 860, 672 N.Y.S.2d 795 (2d Dept. 1998).

—Evidence was insufficient to establish defendant's guilt; the evidence was legally insufficient to establish beyond a reasonable doubt that the defendant had sexual intercourse with the victim. People v. Palmer, 212 A.D.2d 742, 623 N.Y.S.2d 157 (2d Dept. 1995).

—Conviction under this section was affirmed where defendant admitted punishing seven-year-old stepdaughter over a period of one and one-half years by pushing his finger or penis into her rectum, putting his penis into her mouth, or placing his finger in her vagina. People v. Munroe, 307 A.D.2d 588, 763 N.Y.S.2d 691 (3d Dept. 2003).

—While a defendant may not be convicted solely on the basis of a confession without corroborating evidence under this section, victim's testimony describing the sexual contact in similar terms to those set forth in defendant's confession, the police officer's description of defendant's demeanor and physical manifestations of guilt while giving the statement, right after the statement, as well as the subsequent telephone call with his parents about the incident, provided sufficient corroboration. People v. Nolan, 2 A.D.3d 1221; 768 N.Y.S.2d 853 (3d Dept. 2003).

—Verdict finding defendant guilty of first degree rape was not against the weight of the evidence; in any event, defendant failed to preserve for appeal the issue of whether legally sufficient evidence on forcible compulsion was presented. People v. Hryckewicz, 221 A.D.2d 990, 634 N.Y.S.2d 297 (4th Dept. 1995).

Charge.—A failure to give unnecessarily expanded, meticulous instructions with respect to the meaning and application of the concept of "forcible compulsion" in rape cases may be less significant than might otherwise be true and does not mandate reversal. People v. Yanik, 43 N.Y.2d 97, 400 N.Y.S.2d 778, 371 N.E.2d 497 (1977).

Corroboration.—In the absence of any statutory requirement for corroboration, the sworn testimony of a 12-year-old complainant need not be corroborated in a prosecution for her forcible rape. People v. Fuller, 50 N.Y.2d 628, 431 N.Y.S.2d 357, 409 N.E.2d 834 (1980).

—The corroboration required to support a rape conviction involving a 16-year-old victim was sufficiently provided by the victim's testimony that she was naked when she regained consciousness, felt pain and was bleeding from the vagina, and had never previously engaged in intercourse, and the hospital finding that she was nonvirginal when subsequently examined at a hospital. People v. Ploss, 105 A.D.2d 1031, 483 N.Y.S.2d 449 (3d Dept. 1984).

Forcible compulsion.—Neither physical injury nor screaming or crying out is required for a conviction of first degree rape. In addition, corroboration is not required to establish rape or other Article 130 offenses that include forcible compulsion as an element. People v. Alford, 287 A.D.2d 884, 731 N.Y.S.2d 563 (2d Dept. 2001).

—The existence of forcible compulsion need not be corroborated by medical evidence. People v. Agard, 199 A.D.2d 401, 606 N.Y.S.2d 239 (2d Dept. 1994).

—Forcible compulsion can be inferred from the facts leading up to the rape and/or sodomy. People v. Gonzalez, 136 A.D.2d 735, 524 N.Y.S.2d 73 (2d Dept. 1988).

Merger.—The merger doctrine applies to preclude conviction for unlawful imprisonment where any restraint the defendant imposed upon the victim was clearly wholly incidental to and inseparable from the substantive crime of rape. People v. Stoesser, 92 A.D.2d 650, 460 N.Y.S.2d 371 (3d Dept. 1983).

Lesser included offenses.—Sexual abuse in the second degree which involves lack of consent based upon the victim being under 14 years of age is not a lesser included offense of rape in the first degree which is based upon forcible compulsion. In re John D., 91 A.D.2d 962, 458 N.Y.S.2d 581 (1st Dept.), dism'd, 60 N.Y.2d 925, 471 N.Y.S.2d 82, 459 N.E.2d 191 (1983).

—A defendant who was acquitted of a charge of rape in the first degree could not be convicted of coercion in the second degree as a lesser included offense of the rape count; it is theoretically possible to commit rape in the first degree without committing coercion in the second degree as rape does not require proof of the victim's fear of injury as is required for the coercion charge. People v. Tiedmann, 111 A.D.2d 280, 489 N.Y.S.2d 279 (2d Dept. 1985).

—Just as it is possible to commit the crimes of rape in the first degree and sodomy in the first degree without concomitantly, by the same conduct, committing sexual abuse in the first degree, by analogous reasoning it is possible to commit rape in the second degree and sodomy in the second degree without also committing sexual abuse in the second degree; sexual abuse in the second degree is not a lesser included offense of second degree rape or second degree sodomy. People v. Gibson, 2 A.D.3d 969, 768 N.Y.S.2d 511 (3d Dept. 2003).

—Defendant's conviction of two counts of sexual abuse first degree was dismissed since the counts of sexual abuse first degree were lesser included offenses of crimes of rape first degree and sodomy first degree, for which defendant was also convicted. People v. Greenhagen, 78 A.D.2d 964, 433 N.Y.S.2d 683 (4th Dept. 1980).

Bill of particulars.—Bill of particulars supplied by people in response to defendant's request was sufficient in that it stated the date, time and place of the alleged rape and that forcible compulsion consisted of the use of either force or express or implied threats, or both; defendant was properly apprised of the theory to be advanced by the People at trial and was not entitled to information as to the evidence to be used to prove that theory. People v. Earl, 220 A.D.2d 899, 632 N.Y.S.2d 689 (3d Dept. 1995).

§ 130.38. Repealed pursuant to L. 2000, Ch. 1, § 6, eff. Feb. 1, 2001.

§ 130.40. Criminal sexual act in the third degree.

A person is guilty of criminal sexual act in the third degree when:

1. He or she engages in oral sexual conduct or anal sexual conduct with a person who is incapable of consent by reason of some factor other than being less than seventeen years old;

2. Being twenty-one years old or more, he or she engages in oral sexual conduct or anal sexual conduct with a person less than seventeen years old; or

3. He or she engages in oral sexual conduct or anal sexual conduct with another person without such person's consent where such lack of consent is by reason of some factor other than incapacity to consent.

Criminal sexual act in the third degree is a class E felony.

Amended by L. 2000, Ch. 1, eff. Feb. 1, 2001; L. 2003, Ch. 264, § 18, eff. Nov. 1, 2003.

ANNOTATIONS

Consent.—Court concluded, in regard to Penal Law § 130.40(2), that setting the age of consent at 17 years is a rational way for New York to protect minors from the unpropitious consequences of consensual sexual acts. People v. Halm, 180 A.D.2d 841, 579 N.Y.S.2d 765 (3d Dept. 1992).

—Where the victim was the mentally retarded daughter of defendant's live-in companion, resided in a group home for mentally retarded adults, and was unable to consent to sexual contact as a result of her mental retardation, evidence that defendant subjected the victim to sexual contact without her consent is legally sufficient to support the charges. People v. Jordal, 294 A.D.2d 953, 742 N.Y.S.2d 760 (4th Dept. 2002).

Details.—The court erred in permitting the mother of the 14-year-old sodomy victim to testify as what her son told her of the details of what occurred at the time of the attack, however, it was proper for her to testify that when the victim returned home, fifteen minutes after the attack, he told her that defendant had "raped" him and that she observed that her son was trembling and visibly upset. People v. Mackley, 60 A.D.2d 791, 400 N.Y.S.2d 658 (4th Dept. 1977).

§ 130.45. Criminal sexual act in the second degree.

A person is guilty of criminal sexual act in the second degree when:

1. being eighteen years old or more, he or she engages in oral sexual conduct or anal sexual conduct with another person less than fifteen years old; or

2. he or she engages in oral sexual conduct or anal sexual conduct with another person who is incapable of consent by reason of being mentally disabled or mentally incapacitated.

It shall be an affirmative defense to the crime of criminal sexual act in the second degree as defined in subdivision one of this section that the defendant was less than four years older than the victim at the time of the act.

Criminal sexual act in the second degree is a class D felony.

Amended by L. 2000, Ch. 1, eff. Feb. 1, 2001; L. 2003, Ch. 264, § 19, eff. Nov. 1, 2003.

ANNOTATIONS

Indictment.—Where the indictment contained all the elements of the crimes of sodomy, third degree, and second degree, it was not defective although it did not describe the exact nature of the deviate sexual intercourse. People v. Setford, 67 A.D.2d 1060, 413 N.Y.S.2d 775 (3d Dept. 1979).

Modification of sentence after conviction of sodomy.—Although there was nothing in the record to mitigate the seriousness of defendant's conduct in committing sodomy with a person less than fourteen years old, the Appellate Division modified defendant's sentence because the probation report revealed that the 60-year-old defendant was industrious, had a good job, conscientiously supported his family, was of sound mind, and not a danger to the community. People v. Cerio, 34 A.D.2d 1095, 312 N.Y.S.2d 596 (4th Dept. 1970).

§ 130.50. Criminal sexual act in the first degree.

A person is guilty of criminal sexual act in the first degree when he or she engages in oral sexual conduct or anal sexual conduct with another person:

1. By forcible compulsion; or

2. Who is incapable of consent by reason of being physically helpless; or

3. Who is less than eleven years old; or

4. Who is less than thirteen years old and the actor is eighteen years old or more.

Criminal sexual act in the first degree is a class B felony.

Amended by L. 2000, Ch. 1, eff. Feb. 1, 2001; L. 2003, Ch. 264, § 20, eff. Nov. 1, 2003.

ANNOTATIONS

Corroboration.—Defendant's confession to the sodomy of a 7-year-old child was corroborated by the unsworn testimony of the child and the child's statement was corroborated by the defendant's admissions. Such cross-corroboration is permitted where the corroboration requirements of each statement are set forth in different statutes for different reasons. People v. Philipp, 106 A.D.2d 681, 484 N.Y.S.2d 138 (3d Dept. 1984).

Elements.—Although inartfully drawn, the indictment charging sodomy, first degree, which contained all the elements of the crime was not defective since any ambiguity with respect to the precise nature of the deviate sexual intercourse alleged could be clarified by the bill of particulars. People v. Jackson, 46 N.Y.2d 720, 413 N.Y.S.2d 369, 385 N.E.2d 1296 (1978).

—Penetration is not an element of the crime of sodomy. People v. May, 263 A.D.2d 215, 702 N.Y.S.2d 393 (3d Dept.), *appeal denied*, 94 N.Y.2d 950 (2000); People v. Ramos, 203 A.D.2d 599, 611 N.Y.S.2d 216, 217 (2d Dept. 1994); People v. Francis, 153 A.D.2d 901, 545 N.Y.S.2d 607 (2d Dept. 1989).

Evidence.—It was proper for the trial court to admit evidence of a previous assault by the defendant against another prisoner as to the issue of consent by the complaining witness and force used against him. People v. Tas, 51 N.Y.2d 915, 434 N.Y.S.2d 978, 415 N.E.2d 967 (1980).

—Conviction for sodomy in the first degree affirmed where defendant admitted punishing seven-year-old stepdaughter over a period of one and one-half years by pushing his finger or penis into her rectum, putting his penis into her mouth, or placing his finger in her vagina. People v. Munroe, 305 A.D.2d 588, 763 N.Y.S.2d 691 (3d Dept. 2003).

Forcible compulsion.—Forcible compulsion in conviction for first degree sodomy was established by testimony of 12-year-old stepdaughter that defendant threatened to harm mother if child refused his advances and defendant used physical force to ensure her compliance. People v. Nailor, 268 A.D.2d 695, 701 N.Y.S.2d 476 (3d Dept. 2000).

—Evidence was sufficient to establish forcible compulsion where it established the location of the incident on a sparsely populated dirt road, and where the complainant testified as to facts causing her to fear for her life, that defendant stated that the truck that he and the complainant were travelling in "died for a reason," and that defendant was going to "get something out of this"; the relevant inquiry is not what the defendant would or could have done, but what the victim feared he would or could do if the victim did not comply with his demands. People v. Sweezey, 215 A.D.2d 910, 626 N.Y.S.2d 584 (3d Dept. 1995).

Charge.—It was reversible error for the court to charge, over defendant's objection, that they could find him guilty whether he used physical force or a threat placing the victim in fear of immediate death or physical injury where the indictment accused defendant of first degree sodomy "by means of physical force which overcame earnest resistance." People v. Kaminski, 58 N.Y.2d 886, 460 N.Y.S.2d 495, 447 N.E.2d 43 (1983).

Lesser included offenses.—Sexual abuse in the second degree which involves lack of consent based upon the victim being under 14 years of age is not a lesser included offense of sodomy in the first degree which is based upon forcible compulsion. *In re* John S., 91 A.D.2d 962, 458 N.Y.S.2d 581 (1st Dept.), *dism'd*, 60 N.Y.2d 925, 471 N.Y.S.2d 82, 459 N.E.2d 191 (1983).

§ 130.52. Forcible touching.

A person is guilty of forcible touching when such person intentionally, and for no legitimate purpose, forcibly touches the sexual or other intimate parts of another person for the purpose of degrading or abusing such person; or for the purpose of gratifying the actor's sexual desire.

For the purposes of this section, forcible touching includes squeezing, grabbing or pinching.

Forcible touching is a class A misdemeanor.

Added by L. 2000, Ch. 1, eff. Feb. 1, 2001; **Amended** by L. 2003, Ch. 264, § 21, eff. Nov. 1, 2003.

ANNOTATIONS

Evidence.—PL § 130.05(2)(c) does not apply to the crime of forcible touching, and victim's lack of consent cannot be established by surrounding circumstances; information charging violation of that section must contain specific allegations addressing lack of consent by either forcible compulsion or incapacity to consent. People v. Parbhu, 191 Misc. 2d 473, 743 N.Y.S.2d 660 (Crim. Ct. N.Y. Co. 2002).

—The term "sexual abuse" contained in P.L. § 130.05(2)(c) must be read to encompass the term "forcible touching" contained in P.L. § 130.52 in order to give effect to the legislative intent. Lack of consent can be established directly through the affidavit of a complainant or by circumstantial evidence. People v. Soto, 192 Misc. 2d 161, 745 N.Y.S.2d 880 (N.Y.C. Crim.Ct. 2002).

§ 130.53. Persistent sexual abuse.

A person is guilty of persistent sexual abuse when he or she commits the crime of forcible touching, as defined in section 130.52 of this article, sexual abuse in the third degree, as defined in section 130.55 of this article, or sexual abuse in the second degree, as defined in section 130.60 of this article, and, within the previous ten year period, has been convicted two or more times, in separate criminal transactions for which sentence was imposed on separate occasions, of forcible touching, as defined in section 130.52 of this article, sexual abuse in the third degree as defined in section 130.55 of this article, sexual abuse in the second degree, as defined in section 130.60 of this article, or any offense defined in this article, of which the commission or attempted commission thereof is a felony.

Persistent sexual abuse is a class E felony.

Added by L. 2000, Ch. 1, eff. Feb. 1, 2001; **Amended** by L. 2003, Ch. 264, § 22, eff. Nov. 1, 2003.

§ 130.55. Sexual abuse in the third degree.

A person is guilty of sexual abuse in the third degree when he or she subjects another person to sexual contact without the latter's consent; except that in any prosecution under this section, it is an affirmative defense that (a) such other person's lack of consent was due solely to incapacity to consent by reason of being less than seventeen years old, and (b) such other person was more than fourteen years old, and (c) the defendant was less than five years older than such other person.

Sexual abuse in the third degree is a class B misdemeanor.

Amended by L. 2000, Ch. 1, eff. Feb. 1, 2001.

ANNOTATIONS

Evidence of intent.—Sufficient evidence of intent was shown where the defendant put his body atop that of the victim for several minutes, his forearm across her breast, pulled the bedclothes off her nude body, gagged her with an item of clothing and removed the gag and sought to substitute another. People v. Shealy, 51 N.Y.2d 933, 434 N.Y.S.2d 986, 415 N.E.2d 974 (1980).

Lesser included offense.—Sexual abuse in the third degree is a lesser included offense of sexual abuse in the second degree; the lack of consent may be shown by age or non-acquiescence. People v. Jones, 107 Misc. 2d 1082, 436 N.Y.S.2d 657 (1st Dist. Ct. Nassau Co. 1981).

Actors.—The crime of sexual abuse may encompass the causing of a third party to touch the victim. People v. Jones, 165 A.D.2d 103, 566 N.Y.S.2d 590 (1st Dept. 1991).

Charge.—Court's charge correctly apprised jury of standards to apply in deciding whether defendant was guilty of sexual abuse in the third degree; court's instruction that jury had to find that defendant intentionally, and "not by accident," subjected the victim to sexual contact, did not shift the burden of proof or otherwise prejudice the defendant. People v. Yates, 165 Misc. 2d 375, 630 N.Y.S.2d 449 (Yates Co. Ct. 1995).

§ 130.60. Sexual abuse in the second degree.

A person is guilty of sexual abuse in the second degree when he or she subjects another person to sexual contact and when such other person is:

1. Incapable of consent by reason of some factor other than being less than seventeen years old; or

2. Less than fourteen years old.

Sexual abuse in the second degree is a class A misdemeanor.

Amended by L. 2000, Ch. 1, eff. Feb. 1, 2001.

ANNOTATION

Lesser included offense.—In a nonjury trial, the court must notify counsel, prior to summation, of its intent to consider a lesser included offense; trial court erred in failing to notify defendant that it would consider sexual abuse in the second degree as a lesser included offense of the first degree crimes charged in the indictment. People v. Hughes, 220 A.D.2d 529, 632 N.Y.S.2d 585 (2d Dept. 1995).

—Just as it is possible to commit the crimes of rape in the first degree and sodomy in the first degree without concomitantly, by the same conduct, committing sexual abuse in the first degree, by analogous reasoning it is possible to commit rape in the second degree and sodomy in the second degree without also committing sexual abuse in the second degree; sexual abuse in the second degree is not a lesser included offense of second degree rape or second degree sodomy. People v. Gibson, 2 A.D.3d 969, 768 N.Y.S.2d 511 (3d Dept. 2003).

§ 130.65. Sexual abuse in the first degree.

A person is guilty of sexual abuse in the first degree when he or she subjects another person to sexual contact:

1. By forcible compulsion; or

2. When the other person is incapable of consent by reason of being physically helpless; or

3. When the other person is less than eleven years old.

Sexual abuse in the first degree is a class D felony.

Amended by L. 2000, Ch. 1, eff. Feb. 1, 2001.

ANNOTATIONS

Concurrent/continuous crimes.—Defendant's conviction for sexual abuse was reversed where court found that the acts forming the basis of the sexual abuse charge were part and parcel of the continuous conduct culminating in the rape of the complainant for which the defendant was also convicted. People v. Grant, 108 A.D.2d 823, 485 N.Y.S.2d 299 (2d Dept. 1985).

—Where defendant was convicted of attempted rape in the first degree and attempted sexual abuse in the first degree, the sexual abuse crime constituted an inclusory concurrent count of the rape charge and the finding of guilt upon the greater count mandated a dismissal of the lesser count. People v. Timothy, 96 A.D.2d 875, 465 N.Y.S.2d 739 (2d Dept. 1983).

Lesser included offense.—Under the facts of this case, the two counts of sexual abuse in the first degree were not inclusory counts of sodomy in the first degree. People v. Napolitano, 82 A.D.2d 840, 439 N.Y.S.2d 661 (2d Dept. 1981).

—Sexual abuse in the third degree based on incapacity to consent by reason of age, etc., is not a lesser included offense of sexual abuse in the first degree by forcible compulsion since it requires proof of an element which need not be proved in a prosecution for the higher offense. People v. Mott, 77 A.D.2d 606, 429 N.Y.S.2d 916 (2d Dept. 1980).

Consent.—Victim who was a police decoy did not implicitly consent to the physical touching because she voluntarily placed herself in a position to incur abuse. People v. Teicher, 52 N.Y.2d 638, 439 N.Y.S.2d 846, 422 N.E.2d 506 (1981).

Elements.—Defendant's acquittal of rape in the first degree but conviction of sexual abuse in the first degree was not repugnant where the jury could have found that forcible compulsion was employed but penetration, a necessary element of rape in the first degree, was not achieved. People v. Burns, 83 A.D.2d 639, 441 N.Y.S.2d 525 (2d Dept. 1981).

Sexual contact.—Sexual contact occurs when the defendant forces the victim to touch his sexual or intimate parts. People v. Ditta, 52 N.Y.2d 657, 439 N.Y.S.2d 855, 422 N.E.2d 515 (1981).

—Sexual contact, as an element of sexual abuse in the first degree, does not require touching with hands. People v. Johnson, 102 A.D.2d 895, 477 N.Y.S.2d 57 (2d Dept. 1984).

—Defendant's conviction for sodomy was reversed as the elements of the lesser included offense of sexual abuse were established where there was evidence that the complainant's anus was touched but the record did not reflect that it was defendant's penis which touched the complainant's anus. People v. Stroman, 84 A.D.2d 851, 444 N.Y.S.2d 166 (2d Dept. 1981).

Evidence.—Defendant's act of placing his patient's hand against his genitals constituted sexual abuse. People v. Teicher, 52 N.Y.2d 638, 439 N.Y.S.2d 846, 422 N.E.2d 506 (1981).

—Evidence was legally sufficient to establish defendant's guilt beyond a reasonable doubt; complainant's testimony was logical and consistent and established that defendant committed acts constituting sexual abuse in the first degree. In re Tyrik H., 207 A.D.2d 485, 616 N.Y.S.2d 240 (2d Dept. 1994).

—Photographs mother took of her six-year-old daughter squatting naked as an adult's hands spread the child's buttocks apart supported a charge of sexual abuse in the first degree; jury could reasonably infer sexual gratification from defendant's conduct. People v. Pinkoski, 300 A.D.2d 834, 752 N.Y.S.2d 421 (3d Dept. 2002).

—Sufficient evidence existed to support conviction for sexual abuse in the first degree where 13-year-old victim testified that prior to being abused by her aunt's 31-year-old live-in companion, he told her that he wanted to rape her, have a baby with her, and that he would kill her whole family if she told anyone: element of "forcible compulsion" was met. People v. Archer, 232 A.D.2d 820, 649 N.Y.S.2d 204 (3d Dept. 1996).

Collateral estoppel.—State is not collaterally estopped from prosecuting the defendant for sexual abuse in the first degree following a probation revocation hearing for the same charge that terminated in his favor. People v. Hilton, 95 N.Y.2d 950, 722 N.Y.S.2d 461, 745 N.E.2d 381 (2000).

§ 130.65-a. Aggravated sexual abuse in the fourth degree.

1. A person is guilty of aggravated sexual abuse in the fourth degree when:

(a) He or she inserts a foreign object in the vagina, urethra, penis or rectum of another person and the other person is incapable of consent by reason of some factor other than being less than seventeen years old; or

(b) He or she inserts a finger in the vagina, urethra, penis or rectum of another person causing physical injury to such person and such person is incapable of consent by reason of some factor other than being less than seventeen years old.

2. Conduct performed for a valid medical purpose does not violate the provisions of this section.

Aggravated sexual abuse in the fourth degree is a class E felony.

Added by L. 2000, Ch. 1, eff. Feb. 1, 2001.

§ 130.66. Aggravated sexual abuse in the third degree.

1. A person is guilty of aggravated sexual abuse in the third degree when he inserts a foreign object in the vagina, urethra, penis or rectum of another person:

(a) by forcible compulsion; or

(b) when the other person is incapable of consent by reason of being physically helpless; or

(c) when the other person is less than eleven years old.

2. A person is guilty of aggravated sexual abuse in the third degree when he or she inserts a foreign object in the vagina, urethra, penis or rectum of another person causing physical injury to such person and such person is incapable of consent by reason of being mentally disabled or mentally incapacitated.

3. Conduct performed for a valid medical purpose does not violate the provisions of this section.

Aggravated sexual abuse in the third degree is a class D felony.

Added by L. 1996, Ch. 181, eff. Nov. 1, 1996; L. 2000, Ch. 1, eff. Feb. 1, 2001.

§ 130.67. Aggravated sexual abuse in the second degree.

1. A person is guilty of aggravated sexual abuse in the second degree when he inserts a finger in the vagina, urethra, penis, or rectum of another person causing physical injury to such person:

(a) By forcible compulsion; or

(b) When the other person is incapable of consent by reason of being physically helpless; or

(c) When the other person is less than eleven years old.

2. Conduct performed for a valid medical purpose does not violate the provisions of this section.

Aggravated sexual abuse in the second degree is a class C felony.

Added by L. 1988, Ch. 450.

ANNOTATION

Findings by family court.—Family court's failure to specify particular sex offense allegedly committed by respondent did not violate respondent's due process rights, as this error neither affected the respondent's ability to make an effective appeal or undermine the court's ability to engage in appellate review; the appellate court could make the finding that the family court should have made, and the specific sex offense that should have been identified was aggravated sexual abuse in the second degree. *In re* Nichole L., 213 A.D.2d 750, 622 N.Y.S.2d 1006 (3d Dept. 1995).

§ 130.70. Aggravated sexual abuse in the first degree.

1. A person is guilty of aggravated sexual abuse in the first degree when he inserts a foreign object in the vagina, urethra, penis or rectum of another person causing physical injury to such person:

(a) By forcible compulsion; or

(b) When the other person is incapable of consent by reason of being physically helpless; or

(c) When the other person is less than eleven years old.

2. Conduct performed for a valid medical purpose does not violate the provisions of this section.

Aggravated sexual abuse in the first degree is a class B felony.

Added by L. 1978, Ch. 723; **Amended** by L. 1981, Ch. 696; L. 1988, Ch. 450.

ANNOTATIONS

Merger; kidnapping.—The merger doctrine is intended to preclude conviction for kidnapping based on acts which are so much the part of another substantive crime that the substantive crime could not have been committed without such acts and that independent criminal responsibility may not fairly be attributed to them, however, if the kidnapping aspect is aggravated by the particular means or manner of the abduction it may then support a separate prosecution. People v. Cassidy, 40 N.Y.2d 763, 390 N.Y.S.2d 45, 358 N.E.2d 870 (1976).

—Where defendant was convicted of four counts of rape in the first degree, four counts of sexual abuse in the first degree, three counts of sodomy in the first degree, kidnapping in the second degree, assault in the third degree and menacing, the conviction for kidnapping could not stand because the evidence revealed that any detention of the victim was incidental to the crimes of rape and sexual abuse. People v. Ruiz, 96 A.D.2d 603, 465 N.Y.S.2d 297 (2d Dept. 1983).

§ 130.75. Course of sexual conduct against a child in the first degree.

1. A person is guilty of course of sexual conduct against a child in the first degree when, over a period of time not less than three months in duration:

(a) he or she engages in two or more acts of sexual conduct, which includes at least one act of sexual intercourse, oral sexual conduct, anal sexual conduct or aggravated sexual contact, with a child less than eleven years old; or

(b) he or she, being eighteen years old or more, engages in two or more acts of sexual conduct, which include at least one act of sexual intercourse, oral sexual conduct, anal sexual conduct or aggravated sexual contact, with a child less than thirteen years old.

2. A person may not be subsequently prosecuted for any other sexual offense involving the same victim unless the other charged offense occurred outside the time period charged under this section.

Course of sexual conduct against a child in the first degree is a class B felony.

Added by L. 1996, Ch. 122, eff. Aug. 1, 1996; **Amended** by L. 2000, Ch. 1, eff. Feb. 1, 2001; L. 2003, Ch. 264, § 23, eff. Nov. 1, 2003, amending subds. 1(a), (b).

ANNOTATION

Period of time.—Where there was no evidence in record as to time period over which sexual abuse had occurred, conviction must be vacated. People v. Juara, 279 A.D.2d 479, 719 N.Y.S.2d 102 (2d Dept.), *appeal denied*, 96 N.Y.2d 831 (2001).

§ 130.80. Course of sexual conduct against a child in the second degree.

1. A person is guilty of course of sexual conduct against a child in the second degree when, over a period of time not less than three months in duration:

(a) he or she engages in two or more acts of sexual conduct with a child less than eleven years old; or

(b) he or she, being eighteen years old or more, engages in two or more acts of sexual conduct with a child less than thirteen years old.

2. A person may not be subsequently prosecuted for any other sexual offense involving the same victim unless the other charged offense occurred outside the time period charged under this section.

Course of sexual conduct against a child in the second degree is a class D felony.

Added by L. 1996, Ch. 122, eff. Aug. 1, 1996; **Amended** by L. 2000, Ch. 1, eff. Feb. 1, 2001.

§ 130.85. Female genital mutilation.

1. A person is guilty of female genital mutilation when:

(a) a person knowingly circumcises, excises, or infibulates the whole or any part of the labia majora or labia minora or clitoris of another person who has not reached eighteen years of age; or

(b) being a parent, guardian or other person legally responsible and charged with the care or custody of a child less than eighteen years old, he or she knowingly consents to the circumcision, excision or infibulation of whole or part of such child's labia majora or labia minora or clitoris.

2. Such circumcision, excision, or infibulation is not a violation of this section if such act is:

(a) necessary to the health of the person on whom it is performed, and is performed by a person licensed in the place of its performance as a medical practitioner; or

(b) performed on a person in labor or who has just given birth and is performed for medical purposes connected with that labor or birth by a person licensed in the place it is performed as a medical practitioner, midwife, or person in training to become such a practitioner or midwife.

3. For the purposes of paragraph (a) of subdivision two of this section, no account shall be taken of the effect on the person on whom such procedure is to be performed of any belief on the part of that or any other person that such procedure is required as a matter of custom or ritual.

Female genital mutilation is a class E felony.

Added by L. 1997, Ch. 618, eff. Dec. 1, 1997.

§ 130.90. Facilitating a sex offense with a controlled substance.

A person is guilty of facilitating a sex offense with a controlled substance when he or she:

1. knowingly and unlawfully possesses a controlled substance or any preparation, compound, mixture or substance that requires a prescription to obtain and administers such substance or preparation, compound, mixture or substance that requires a prescription to obtain to another person without such person's consent and with intent to commit against such person conduct constituting a felony defined in this article; and

2. commits or attempts to commit such conduct constituting a felony defined in this article.

Facilitating a sex offense with a controlled substance is a class D felony.

Added by L. 2000, Ch. 1, eff. Feb. 1, 2001; **Amended** by L. 2003, Ch. 264, § 24, eff. Nov. 1, 2003, amending subds. 1 and 2.

PL

ARTICLE 135—KIDNAPPING, COERCION AND RELATED OFFENSES

LexisNexis Cross Reference

New York Criminal Practice (2d ed.), Vol. 6, Ch. 60, Kidnapping, Coercion and Custodial Interference.

§ 135.00. Unlawful imprisonment, kidnapping and custodial interference; definitions of terms.

The following definitions are applicable to this article:

1. "Restrain" means to restrict a person's movements intentionally and unlawfully in such manner as to interfere substantially with his liberty by moving him from one place to another, or by confining him either in the place where the restriction commences or in a place to which he has been moved, without consent and with knowledge that the restriction is unlawful. A person is so moved or confined "without consent" when such is accomplished by (a) physical force, intimidation or deception, or (b) any means whatever, including acquiescence of the victim, if he is a child less than sixteen years old or an incompetent person and the parent, guardian or other person or institution having lawful control or custody of him has not acquiesced in the movement or confinement.

2. "Abduct" means to restrain a person with intent to prevent his liberation by either (a) secreting or holding him in a place where he is not likely to be found, or (b) using or threatening to use deadly physical force.

3. "Relative" means a parent, ancestor, brother, sister, uncle or aunt.

ANNOTATIONS

Evidence.—Evidence supported defendant's conviction for kidnapping of 13-year-old child, where there was ample proof that for religious purposes, defendant and his followers moved the child from one place to another secreting him from his parents and the authorities. The fact that the child acquiesced to such restraint was of no moment since under § 135.00 a child under the age of 16 is incapable of providing consent. People v. Helbrans, 228 A.D.2d 612, 645 N.Y.S.2d 307 (2d Dept. 1996).

—Defendant failed to preserve for appellate review the issue of whether the People established the element of "abduction"; in any event, the evidence was sufficient to establish that the victim was secreted or held in a place in which she was not likely to be found. People v. Connor, 219 A.D.2d 664, 631 N.Y.S.2d 402 (2d Dept. 1995); People v. Wagstaff, 219 A.D.2d 690, 631 N.Y.S.2d 410 (2d Dept. 1995).

—Evidence which established that: (1) victim was abducted at gunpoint and threatened with physical harm if he did "anything stupid"; (2) victim's requests for release were ignored; and (3) defendant or his accomplice were with victim through entire course of 12-hour car ride sufficiently established that victim was "abducted" and "restrained." People v. Moon, 219 A.D.2d 817, 631 N.Y.S.2d 958 (4th Dept. 1995).

Relative.—Biological mother of an adopted child is not a relative within the meaning of this section and can be charged under this section. People v. Brown, 264 A.D.2d 12, 702 N.Y.S.2d 739 (4th Dept. 2000).

§ 135.05. Unlawful imprisonment in the second degree.

A person is guilty of unlawful imprisonment in the second degree when he restrains another person.

Unlawful imprisonment in the second degree is a class A misdemeanor.

ANNOTATION

Intent.—The fact that defendant, by threats of shooting, compelled a father and son to drive him from Utica to Syracuse did not bring this case within the former Penal Law provisions (§ 1250) to establish beyond a reasonable doubt that he kidnapped the complainants with an intent that they be "confined or imprisoned" or "kept or detained." The compulsion to provide transportation had no such relationship to detention as to constitute a true kidnapping under the former statute; the new Penal Law defines more precisely the scope of kidnapping and related crimes. People v. Miles, 31 N.Y.2d 918, 340 N.Y.S.2d 647, 292 N.E.2d 788 (1972).

§ 135.10. Unlawful imprisonment in the first degree.

A person is guilty of unlawful imprisonment in the first degree when he restrains another person under circumstances which expose the latter to a risk of serious physical injury.

Unlawful imprisonment in the first degree is a class E felony.

ANNOTATIONS

Merger.—Where a robbery was fully consummated before the victim was forced at gunpoint to embark on an hour-long drive, two separate crimes, first the robbery and then the unlawful imprisonment, were committed and, as the criminal conduct at the root of the two crimes was different, the merger doctrine, even if available, could have no application. People v. Smith, 47 N.Y.2d 83, 416 N.Y.S.2d 784, 390 N.E.2d 291 (1979).

—Assailants' actions in binding the victims' mouths, hands and feet with tape, placing a plastic bag over one victim's head, and placing the other victim inside a cardboard box, were not necessary and integral to, or inseparable from, the assault, but did establish elements of first-degree unlawful imprisonment. People v. Peters, 1 A.D.3d 270, 767 N.Y.S.2d 433 (1st Dept. 2003).

—Defendant's contention that unlawful imprisonment offense merged into higher assault offense was not preserved for appeal. People v. Knapp, 213 A.D.2d 740, 623 N.Y.S.2d 355 (3d Dept. 1995).

Lesser included offense.—Court properly refused request to charge unlawful imprisonment in the first degree as a lesser included offense of kidnapping in the second degree because no reasonable view of the evidence supported defendant's claim that he committed the lesser but not the greater offense. People v. Linderberry, 222 A.D.2d 731, 634 N.Y.S.2d 571 (3d Dept. 1995).

§ 135.15. Unlawful imprisonment; defense.

In any prosecution for unlawful imprisonment, it is an affirmative defense that (a) the person restrained was a child less than sixteen years old, and (b) the defendant was a relative of such child, and (c) his sole purpose was to assume control of such child.

§ 135.20. Kidnapping in the second degree.

A person is guilty of kidnapping in the second degree when he abducts another person.

Kidnapping in the second degree is a class B felony.

ANNOTATIONS

Evidence.—Evidence supported defendant's conviction for kidnapping of 13-year-old child, where there was ample proof that for religious purposes, defendant and his followers moved the child from one place to another secreting him from his parents and the authorities. The fact that the child acquiesced to such restraint was of no moment since under PL § 135.00 a child under the age of 16 is incapable of providing consent. People v. Helbrans, 228 A.D.2d 612, 645 N.Y.S.2d 307 (2d Dept. 1996).

—Defendant's threats to kill his wife with a starter pistol were sufficient to establish abduction with the threat of deadly force

and kidnapping in the second degree. People v. Govan, 268 A.D.2d 689, 701 N.Y.S.2d 474 (3d Dept.), *appeal denied,* 94 N.Y.2d 920 (2000).

—Biological mother of an adopted child is not a relative within the meaning of this section and can be charged with kidnapping. People v. Brown, 264 A.D.2d 12, 702 N.Y.S.2d 739 (4th Dept. 2000).

Merger.—Defendant's kidnapping convictions were dismissed pursuant to the merger doctrine which precludes conviction for kidnapping and related offenses based on acts which are so much the part of another substantive crime that the substantive crime could not have been committed without those acts and independent criminal responsibility may not be fairly attributed to them. People v. Burgess, 107 A.D.2d 703, 484 N.Y.S.2d 58 (2d Dept. 1985).

§ 135.25. Kidnapping in the first degree.

A person is guilty of kidnapping in the first degree when he abducts another person and when:

1. His intent is to compel a third person to pay or deliver money or property as ransom, or to engage in other particular conduct, or to refrain from engaging in particular conduct; or

2. He restrains the person abducted for a period of more than twelve hours with intent to:

(a) Inflict physical injury upon him or violate or abuse him sexually; or

(b) Accomplish or advance the commission of a felony; or

(c) Terrorize him or a third person; or

(d) Interfere with the performance of a governmental or political functions; or

3. The person abducted dies during the abduction or before he is able to return or to be returned to safety. Such death shall be presumed, in a case where such person was less than sixteen years old or an incompetent person at the time of the abduction, from evidence that his parents, guardians or other lawful custodians did not see or hear from him following the termination of the abduction and prior to trial and received no reliable information during such period persuasively indicating that he was alive. In all other cases, such death shall be presumed from evidence that a person whom the person abducted would have been extremely likely to visit or communicate with during the specified period were he alive and free to do so did not see or hear from him during such period and received no reliable information during such period persuasively indicating that he was alive.

Kidnapping in the first degree is a class A-I felony.

Amended by L. 1967, Ch. 791; L. 1973, Ch. 276.

ANNOTATIONS

Attempt.—Attempted kidnapping is a cognizable crime. The core crime in kidnapping in the first degree is the abduction of another person; conduct tending to affect the abduction constitutes the attempt. People v. Fullan, 92 N.Y.2d 690, 685 N.Y.S.2d 901, 708 N.E.2d 974 (1999)

Constitutionality.—Defendant's constitutional challenge to the statute was rejected; the statute does not predicate a conviction on a mere disappearance, and the statutory presumption of death operates only in limited circumstances to provide strong protection against arbitrary enforcement. People v. Thibodeau, 267 A.D.2d 952, 700 N.Y.S.2d 621 (4th Dept. 1999).

Merger.—Where defendants transported their victim in the trunk of an automobile for a number of hours, over an extended area, in connection with an attempt to murder him, and such transportation was for purposes connected with, but not directly instrumental to, the attempted murder, the Court of Appeals held inapplicable the rule that asportation of a victim in connection with another crime is part of that crime and not necessarily the separate crime of kidnapping. People v. Miles, 23 N.Y.2d 527, 297 N.Y.S.2d 913, 245 N.E.2d 688 (1969), *dismissed,* 28 N.Y.2d 583, 319 N.Y.S.2d 1029, *cert. denied,* 395 U.S. 948 (1969).

Intent.—Defendants alleged that they could not be found guilty of kidnapping because their restraint of the victim was for the purpose of disposing of his body (because they believed he was dead); thus, they could not have formed an intent to kidnap the victim. The Court of Appeals held that the trial court's failure to charge the jury concerning the defendants' lack of intent was not prejudicial in the absence of a request to so charge. People v. Miles, 23 N.Y.2d 527, 297 N.Y.S.2d 913, 245 N.E.2d 688 (1969).

Evidence.—The evidence at trial sufficiently established that the victim, a car salesman, was abducted and restrained against his will for a period of more than 12 hours during a lengthy car trip; the victim was abducted at gunpoint while on a test drive and threatened not to do "anything stupid," his requests for release were ignored, and he was constantly accompanied by either the defendant or an accomplice. People v. Moon, 219 A.D.2d 817, 631 N.Y.S.2d 958 (4th Dept. 1995).

Lesser included offense.—Reversing defendant's conviction where trial court erred when it submitted unlawful imprisonment in the first degree as a lesser included offense of kidnapping in the first degree. It is theoretically possible for a person to be guilty of kidnapping in the first degree without exposing the victim to serious physical injury as required for a conviction of unlawful imprisonment. People v. Ahedo, 229 A.D.2d 588, 646 N.Y.S.2d 520 (2d Dept. 1996).

Order of protection.—After defendant entered plea of guilty, court properly imposed indeterminate term of imprisonment of 15 years to life and entered order of protection in favor of kidnapping victim that had an expiration date of 100 years after the date of sentencing; certainty in sentencing for defendant and for protection of victim are paramount concerns and were achieved. People v. McClemore, 4 N.Y.3d 821, 797 N.Y.S.2d 351, 830 N.E.2d 249 (2005).

§ 135.30. Kidnapping; defense.

In any prosecution for kidnapping, it is an affirmative defense that (a) the defendant was a relative of the person abducted, and (b) his sole purpose was to assume control of such person.

§ 135.45. Custodial interference in the second degree.

A person is guilty of custodial interference in the second degree when:

1. Being a relative of a child less than sixteen years old, intending to hold such child permanently or for a protracted period, and knowing that he has no legal right to do so, he takes or entices such child from his lawful custodian; or

2. Knowing that he has no legal right to do so, he takes or entices from lawful custody any incompetent person or other person entrusted by authority of law to the custody of another person or institution.

Custodial interference in the second degree is a class A misdemeanor.

Lawful custodian.—The identity of a child's lawful custodian and whether the individual who took the child acted with knowledge that he or she lacked the legal right to do so are not essential elements in a prosecution under Penal Law Sections 135.45 and 135.50. People v. Morel, 164 A.D.2d 677, 566 N.Y.S.2d 653, 656 (2d Dept. 1991).

Persons entitled to claim defense.—Defendant, the biological mother of an adopted child, charged with kidnapping in the second degree, is not a relative of the child within the meaning of § 135.00 and so was not entitled to claim defense. People v. Brown, 264 A.D.2d 12, 702 N.Y.S.2d 739 (4th Dept. 2000).

Protracted period.—The term "protracted period" means a lengthy or unusually long time under the circumstances and is constitutional; a father's taking of his daughters from their mother, the lawful custodian, without her consent, for eight days, during school term, was a protracted period. People v. Obertance, 105 Misc. 2d 558, 432 N.Y.S.2d 475 (Crim. Ct. Bronx Co. 1980).

§ 135.50. Custodial interference in the first degree.

A person is guilty of custodial interference in the first degree when he commits the crime of custodial interference in the second degree:

1. With intent to permanently remove the victim from this state, he removes such person from the state; or

2. Under circumstances which expose the victim to a risk that his safety will be endangered or his health materially impaired.

It shall be an affirmative defense to a prosecution under subdivision one of this section that the victim had been abandoned or that the taking was necessary in an emergency to protect the victim because he has been subjected to or threatened with mistreatment or abuse.

Custodial interference in the first degree is a class E felony.

Amended by L. 1981, Ch. 785.

§ 135.55. Substitution of children.

A person is guilty of substitution of children when, having been temporarily entrusted with a child less than one year old and intending to deceive a parent, guardian or other lawful custodian of such child, he substitutes, produces or returns to such parent, guardian or custodian a child other than the one entrusted.

Substitution of children is a class E felony.

§ 135.60. Coercion in the second degree.

A person is guilty of coercion in the second degree when he compels or induces a person to engage in conduct which the latter has a legal right to abstain from engaging in, or to abstain from engaging in conduct in which he has a legal right to engage, by means of instilling in him a fear that, if the demand is not complied with, the actor or another will:

1. Cause physical injury to a person; or

2. Cause damage to property; or

3. Engage in other conduct constituting a crime; or

4. Accuse some person of a crime or cause criminal charges to be instituted against him; or

5. Expose a secret or publicize an asserted fact, whether true or false, tending to subject some person to hatred, contempt or ridicule; or

6. Cause a strike, boycott or other collective labor group action injurious to some person's business; except that such a threat shall not be deemed coercive when the act or omission compelled is for the benefit of the group in whose interest the actor purports to act; or

7. Testify or provide information or withhold testimony or information with respect to another's legal claim or defense; or

8. Use or abuse his position as a public servant by performing some act within or related to his official duties, or by failing or refusing to perform an official duty, in such manner as to affect some person adversely; or

9. Perform any other act which would not in itself materially benefit the actor but which is calculated to harm another person materially with respect to his health, safety, business, calling, career, financial condition, reputation or personal relationships.

Coercion in the second degree is a class A misdemeanor.

ANNOTATIONS

Constitutionality.—Fact that statute making first-degree coercion a felony had exactly the same elements as were required for second-degree coercion, a misdemeanor, did not violate constitutional guarantees of due process and equal protection even where choice of charge is solely in discretion of prosecutor. People v. Eboli, 34 N.Y.2d 281, 357 N.Y.S.2d 435, 313 N.E.2d 746 (1974).

Lesser included offense.—Coercion in the second degree is not a lesser included offense of rape in the first degree. People v. Greaves, 1 A.D.3d 979, 767 N.Y.S.2d 530 (4th Dept. 2003).

§ 135.65. Coercion in the first degree.

A person is guilty of coercion in the first degree when he commits the crime of coercion in the second degree, and when:

1. He commits such crime by instilling in the victim a fear that he will cause physical injury to a person or cause damage to property; or

2. He thereby compels or induces the victim to:

(a) Commit or attempt to commit a felony; or

(b) Cause or attempt to cause physical injury to a person; or

(c) Violate his duty as a public servant.

Coercion in the first degree is a class D felony.

ANNOTATIONS

Constitutionality.—Fact that statute making first-degree coercion a felony had exactly the same elements as were required for second-degree coercion, a misdemeanor, did not violate constitutional guarantees of due process and equal protection even where choice of charge is solely in discretion of prosecutor. People v. Eboli, 34 N.Y.2d 281, 357 N.Y.S.2d 435, 313 N.E.2d 746 (1974).

Lesser included offense.—In a prosecution for attempted coercion in the first degree, trial court should submit the lesser included offense of attempted coercion in the second degree if the People had established coercion by threat of personal physical injury without showing the heinousness ordinarily associated with this manner of commission of the crime. People v. Discala, 45 N.Y.2d 38, 407 N.Y.S.2d 660, 379 N.E.2d 187 (1978).

Threats.—Reversal was required when, in prosecution for coercion first degree, the court's general charge may well have caused the jury to conclude that it could convict based upon the threats voiced by defendant against persons other than the complainant; although these threats were admissible to show a general scheme to compel the complainant's intercession on his behalf, strict instructions were required in order that the jury be made aware that it was fear of injury to the complainant which was alleged to have constituted the coercion. People v. Hertz, 77 A.D.2d 885, 430 N.Y.S.2d 665 (2d Dept. 1980).

§ 135.70. Coercion; no defense.

The crimes of (a) coercion and attempt to commit coercion, and (b) bribe receiving by a labor official as defined in section 180.20, and bribe receiving as defined in section 200.05, are not mutually exclusive, and it is no defense to a prosecution for coercion or an attempt to commit coercion that, by reason of the same conduct, the defendant also committed one of such specified crimes of bribe receiving.

§ 135.75. Coercion; defense.

In any prosecution for coercion committed by instilling in the victim a fear that he or another person would be charged with a crime, it is an affirmative defense that the defendant reasonably believed the threatened charge to be true and that his sole purpose was to compel or induce the victim to take reasonable action to make good the wrong which was the subject of such threatened charge.

TITLE I—OFFENSES INVOLVING DAMAGE TO AND INTRUSION UPON PROPERTY

ARTICLE 140—BURGLARY AND RELATED OFFENSES

LexisNexis Cross References

Criminal Defense Techniques, Vol. 2, Ch. 50A, Defense of a Burglary Case; *New York Criminal Practice (2d ed.),* Vol. 6, Ch. 61, Burglary and Criminal Trespass; *Police Investigation Handbook,* Ch. 24, Property Crimes: Theft and Burglary Investigations.

§ 140.00. Criminal trespass and burglary; definitions of terms.

The following definitions are applicable to this article:

1. "Premises" includes the term "building," as defined herein, and any real property.

2. "Building," in addition to its ordinary meaning, includes any structure, vehicle or watercraft used for overnight lodging of persons, or used by persons for carrying on business therein, or used as an elementary or secondary school, or an inclosed motor truck, or an inclosed motor truck trailer. Where a building consists of two or more units separately secured or occupied, each unit shall be deemed both a separate building in itself and a part of the main building.

3. "Dwelling" means a building which is usually occupied by a person lodging therein at night.

4. "Night" means the period between thirty minutes after sunset and thirty minutes before sunrise.

5. "Enter or remain unlawfully." A person "enters or remains unlawfully" in or upon premises when he is not licensed or privileged to do so. A person who, regardless of his intent, enters or remains in or upon premises which are at the time open to the public does so with license and privilege unless he defies a lawful order not to enter or remain, personally communicated to him by the owner of such premises or other authorized person. A license or privilege to enter or remain in a building which is only partly open to the public is not a license or privilege to enter or remain in that part of the building which is not open to the public. A person who enters or remains upon unimproved and apparently unused land, which is neither fenced nor otherwise enclosed in a manner designed to exclude intruders, does so with license and privilege unless notice against trespass is personally communicated to him by the owner of such land or other authorized person, or unless such notice is given by posting in a conspicuous manner. A person who enters or remains in or about a school building without written permission from someone authorized to issue such permission or without a legitimate reason which includes a relationship involving custody of or responsibility for a pupil or student enrolled in the school or without legitimate business or a purpose relating to the operation of the school does so without license and privilege.

Amended by L. 1967, Ch. 791; L. 1969, Ch. 1151; L. 1979, Ch. 698.

ANNOTATIONS

Building.—Defendant's two convictions for burglary did not violation double jeopardy, he first entered a secured part of a store, returned to a public part and then entered a separate and different secured area, this constituted entry into two separate buildings for the purposes of the burglary statute. People v. Felder, 2 A.D.3d 365, 769 N.Y.S.2d 539 (1st Dept. 2003).

—A Con Ed manhole is a building within the meaning of the statute, as it is the structure within which Con Ed workers remain while performing many work-related duties. People v. Edmonds, 267 A.D.2d 51, 699 N.Y.S.2d 673 (1st Dept. 1999), *appeal denied,* 94 N.Y.2d 947 (2000).

—Defendant, who was stopped by police while on a fence and in possession of burglar's tools, could not be charged with crimes involving a "building" within meaning of § 140.00(2). People v. Feliciano, 253 A.D.2d 664, 680 N.Y.S.2d 79 (1st Dept. 1998).

—A van with a 1½ ton capacity, used to transport cargo to and from the city's airports, constituted a "building" under burglary statute. People v. Silva, 122 A.D.2d 750, 506 N.Y.S.2d 55 (1st Dept. 1986).

—In prosecution for burglary in the second degree, a nurse's station situated within a prison as a separately secured enclosed structure, with one separate door that was always locked, constituted a building as defined in subdivision (2) of § 140.00 of the Penal Law. People v. Pringle, 96 A.D.2d 873, 465 N.Y.S.2d 742 (2d Dept. 1983).

Dwelling.—Structure, a one-family residence, retained its character as a "dwelling" despite the death of the sole occupant three days before the burglary; fully furnished with working utilities, it could have been occupied overnight, as decedent's property was still in the house, including food in the refrigerator. People v. Barney, 99 N.Y.2d 367, 756 N.Y.S.2d 132, 786 N.E.2d 31 (2003).

—Defendant was not entitled to a "no duty to retreat" justification charge under PL § 35.15(2)(a)(i) in connection with an attack that occurred in the lobby area of the six-story apartment building where defendant resided; the lobby and common stairwell were not under defendant's "exclusive possession and could not fairly be characterized as defendant's living quarters," and thus were not part of defendant's dwelling. People v. Hernandez, 98 N.Y.2d 175, 746 N.Y.S.2d 434, 774 N.E.2d 198 (2002).

—"Dwelling" does not encompass a school building in which an office contains a bed that is used for an occasional overnight stay and a chair that can be used for sleeping. Where the facilities were rarely used for overnight accommodations, perhaps 20 to 30 times a year, and there was no one using the overnight accommodations at the time of the burglary, such use was too infrequent to transform the school into a dwelling. People v. Quattlebaum, 91 N.Y.2d 744, 675 N.Y.S.2d 585, 698 N.E.2d 421 (1998).

—Vestibule of a building was a "dwelling" within the meaning of the statute where it was located beyond the entrance and separated from the outside by two doors, one of which was ordinarily locked. In re Ryan R., 254 A.D.2d 49, 678 N.Y.S.2d 324 (1st Dept. 1998).

—Trial court properly advised jury that a vestibule could be considered part of a dwelling. People v. Rios, 215 A.D.2d 509, 626 N.Y.S.2d 515 (2d Dept. 1995).

—There was insufficient evidence to establish that an unoccupied residential building was a dwelling where the building's owner lived elsewhere and neither of the two apartments were rented to tenants. People v. Murray, 278 A.D.2d 898, 718 N.Y.S.2d 554 (4th Dept. 2000), *appeal denied,* 96 N.Y.2d 804 (2001).

Elements.—The People need only show a knowing entry with intent to commit a crime therein, and it is not necessary to establish what particular crime the intruder intended to commit, or that in fact any crime was committed. People v. Mackey, 49 N.Y.2d 274, 425 N.Y.S.2d 288, 401 N.E.2d 398 (1980).

Insufficient evidence.—Where store defendant entered was open to the public, and there was no evidence that defendant defied a lawful order not to enter or remain, a conviction for trespass cannot be sustained, regardless of defendant's intent upon entering. People v. Casey, 245 A.D.2d 295, 667 N.Y.S.2d 374 (2d Dept. 1997).

Permission to enter.—Defendant's conviction was reversed where he had free access to the apartment by permission of the tenant-occupant, and no evidence was adduced to show that such permission was ever revoked. People v. Miles, 85 A.D.2d 610, 444 N.Y.S.2d 678 (2d Dept. 1981).

—Defendant failed to establish that he was "licensed or privileged" to enter homeowner's residence; upon knocking to gain entrance, defendant did not give anyone a chance to open the door and broke it down without invitation or permission; although defendant was asked by homeowner to come over, he only had permission to turn handle and enter if door was unlocked. People v, Hargett, 11 A.D.3d 812, 784 N.Y.S.2d 197 (3d Dept. 2004).

—Greeting card sent by victim to defendant was not an invitation to defendant to enter victim's home and could not be construed as a license permitting the defendant to enter; court properly refused to allow greeting card into evidence. People v. Whitney, 211 A.D.2d 838, 621 N.Y.S.2d 222 (3d Dept. 1995).

—Information charging defendant with trespass in the third

degree on the basis of alleged subway fare evasion is strained and untenable; a public transportation facility implies a license to enter and a prosecution for trespass in a subway station premised solely on allegations of fare evasion is insufficient as a matter of law. People v. Pratt, 164 Misc. 2d 498, 625 N.Y.S.2d 869 (Crim. Ct. NY Co. 1995).

Remain unlawfully.—A person "enters or remains unlawfully' in or upon premises when he is not licensed or privileged to do so," that lack of a license or privilege to be in or upon premises may be proven by circumstantial evidence. *In re* Quanel M., 8 A.D.3d 386,777 N.Y.S.2d 726 (2d Dept. 2004).

—Since the intent of the burglary statute is to protect habitation rights, the security of the occupant is paramount, therefore, under certain circumstances "an owner can properly be convicted of burglarizing premises he owns but which are occupied by another." People v. Glanda, 5 A.D.3d 945, 774 N.Y.S.2d 576 (3d Dept. 2004).

—Although defendant had spent four nights at the complainant's apartment with the complainant's permission, defendant had no reasonable basis for believing that he had a possessory interest in the premises after the complainant had asked him to leave the premises approximately one week earlier. People v. Maycumber, 8 A.D.3d 1071, 778 N.Y.S.2d 254 (4th Dept. 2004).

Sentence.—Imposition of a probationary sentence for a class D felony is authorized by statute as is the imposition of a definite term of imprisonment; however, although authorized, an indeterminate term of imprisonment with a maximum of three years and a minimum of one year for attempted burglary was harsh and excessive and, in the interests of justice, should be reduced to imprisonment for 60 days and 5 years probation. People v. DePetris, 87 A.D.2d 827, 448 N.Y.S.2d 755 (2d Dept. 1982).

Unlawful entry.—Evidence that defendant passed a sign unequivocally warning that visitors were not licensed to proceed beyond the lobby of the building unless they signed in, and defendant failed to sign in before proceeding beyond lobby was sufficient to establish unlawful entry; less than consistent enforcement of the rule did not diminish effect of the notice. People v. Mason, 292 A.D.2d 294, 739 N.Y.S.2d 257 (1st Dept. 2002).

—Defendant failed to preserve for appeal issue of whether court should have further defined unlawful entry as it relates to premises otherwise open to the public; any error was harmless beyond a reasonable doubt where evidence showed that defendant disregarded a lawful order to stay off premises and overcame physical resistance to entry while harboring an intent to commit an assaultive crime on premises. People v. Amrani, 214 A.D.2d 445, 625 N.Y.S.2d 513 (1st Dept. 1995).

§ 140.05. Trespass.

A person is guilty of trespass when he knowingly enters or remains unlawfully in or upon premises.

Trespass is a violation.

Amended by L. 1969, Ch. 341; L. 1971, Ch. 307.

ANNOTATIONS

Area not open to the public.—The area behind the counter in the grocery store where the cash register is kept is a non-public area; there is no requirement that this area be separately secured or occupied. People v. Canady, 235 A.D.2d 290, 653 N.Y.S.2d 2 (1st Dept. 1997).

Constitutionality.—CPL § 140.05 is constitutional. People v. Bush, 82 Misc. 2d 50, 365 N.Y.S.2d 125 (App. Term 9-10 Judicial Dist. 1975), *aff'd,* 39 N.Y.2d 529, 384 N.Y.S.2d 733, 349 N.E.2d 832 (1976).

Justification defense.—Defendant, who participated in a mass demonstration at a nuclear power plant and who climbed a fence in order to halt construction and was charged with trespass, could not utilize a justification defense, despite his sincere belief that his act was moral and justified. People v. Chachere, 104 Misc. 2d 521, 428 N.Y.S.2d 781 (Suffolk County Dist. Ct. 1980).

First amendment defense.—Picketing by union members on private property in front of store selling their employer's products was not protected under the first amendment; accordingly, arrest of those picketing and their conviction for trespass was affirmed; New York jurisdiction over such offense is not preempted by federal labor law. People v. Bush, 39 N.Y.2d 529, 384 N.Y.S.2d 733, 349 N.E.2d 832 (1976).

—First amendment defense was not available to defendant, a judicial candidate, who was charged with violation of PL § 140.05 for distributing campaign literature in a church parking lot during the church's annual feast; the defendant failed to show a significant degree of state involvement in the church feast to support a finding that the allegedly unconstitutional conduct of the church and its representatives constituted state action. People v. Raab, 163 Misc. 2d 382, 621 N.Y.S.2d 440 (Dist. Ct. Nassau Co. 1994).

Easement.—Defendant, grantor of an easement to the State Power Authority, did not violate PL § 140.05, where, in protest of appropriation of right-of-way from him by the Authority, he entered and remained on the right of way as a construction crew attempted to use such right of way. People v. Munafo, 50 N.Y.2d 326, 428 N.Y.S.2d 924, 406 N.E.2d 780 (1980).

Knowingly entering premises.—In a prosecution for trespass in violation of PL § 140.05 it must be proved that the person "knowingly" entered the premises without license or privilege and, therefore, a person who enters upon premises accidentally, or who honestly believes that he is licensed or privileged to enter, is not guilty of any degree of criminal trespass. People v. Basch, 36 N.Y.2d 154, 365 N.Y.S.2d 836, 365 N.E.2d 156 (1975).

Knowingly remaining after request to leave.—Defendant who knowingly remained upon the premises after having been forbidden to do so by the person in lawful control is subject to the sanction of the trespass statute. People v. Hedeman, 107 A.D.2d 241, 438 N.Y.S.2d 172 (1st Dept. 1981).

Loitering/soliciting.—Defendant could be liable for criminal trespass where he was observed by police officer for approximately ten minutes approaching several people going through the exits of the an airport's international arrivals building, and was ordered by the officer not to enter or remain upon the sidewalk areas of the international arrivals building; the police officer's order was lawful in that it was issued by an officer with authority based upon observations which provided information sufficient to establish probable cause for arrest. People v. Nunez, 106 Misc. 2d 236, 431 N.Y.S.2d 650 (Crim. Ct. Queens Co. 1980), aff'd, 114 Misc. 2d 573, 454 N.Y.S.2d 290 (Sup. Ct. App. Term 1982).

Remains unlawfully.—Although victim originally entered defendant/owner's store lawfully as a licensee, his entry became unlawful when he defied defendant's order to leave the premises. People v. Deis, 97 N.Y.2d 717, 740 N.Y.S.2d 284, 766 N.E.2d 946 (2002).

§ 140.10. Criminal trespass in the third degree.

A person is guilty of criminal trespass in the third degree when he knowingly enters or remains unlawfully in a building or upon real property

(a) which is fenced or otherwise enclosed in a manner designed to exclude intruders; or

(b) where the building is utilized as an elementary or secondary school or a children's overnight camp as defined in section one thousand three hundred ninety-two of the public health law or a summer day camp as defined in section one thousand three hundred ninety-two of the public health law in violation of conspicuously posted rules or regulations governing entry and use thereof; or

(c) located within a city with a population in excess of one million and where the building or real property is utilized as an elementary or secondary school in violation of a personally communicated request to leave the premises from

a principal, custodian or other person in charge thereof; or

(d) located outside of a city with a population in excess of one million and where the building or real property is utilized as an elementary or secondary school in violation of a personally communicated request to leave the premises from a principal, custodian, school board member or trustee, or other person in charge thereof; or

(e) where the building is used as a public housing project in violation of conspicuously posted rules or regulations governing entry and use thereof; or

(f) where a building is used as a public housing project in violation of a personally communicated request to leave the premises from a housing police officer or other person in charge thereof; or

(g) where the property consists of a right-of-way or yard of a railroad or rapid transit railroad which has been designated and conspicuously posted as a no-trespass railroad zone, pursuant to section eighty-three-b of the railroad law, by the city or county in which such property is located.

Criminal trespass in the third degree is a class B misdemeanor.

Amended by L. 1969, Ch. 341; L. 1979, Ch. 698; L. 1983, Ch. 813; L. 1987, Ch. 192; L. 1992, Ch. 434, eff. Nov. 1, 1992, amending subd. (d) and adding subd. (e) and (f); L. 1997, Ch. 338, §§ 2 and 3, eff. Nov. 1, 1997, amending subd. (f) and adding subd. (g); L. 2000, Ch. 533, § 1, eff. Oct. 4, 2000, amending subd. (b); L. 2001, Ch. 350, § 1, eff. Sept. 19, 2001, amending subd. (b).

ANNOTATIONS

Lesser included offense.—The critical distinction between burglary and trespass is that a trespass in a building or dwelling is complete when a person knowingly enters or remains unlawfully in those premises; burglary requires that the trespasser intends to commit a separate crime when entering or remaining unlawfully in a building; burglary is thus an aggravated form of criminal trespass, in which the aggravating factor is the trespasser's intent to commit a separate crime. People v. Cahill, 2 N.Y.3d 14, 777 N.Y.S.2d 332, 809 N.E.2d 561 (2003).

—Criminal trespass in the third degree is a lesser included offense of burglary, third degree. People v. Henderson, 41 N.Y.2d 233, 391 N.Y.S.2d 563, 359 N.E.2d 1357 (1976).

Building.—Judgment was reversed on the law where defendant entered a locked meter closet which was utilized by the complainant to store jewelry; the statute's meaning of "building" does not include such a structure. People v. O'Keefe, 80 A.D.2d 923, 437 N.Y.S.2d 385 (2d Dept. 1981).

Fenced or otherwise enclosed.—An information that failed to allege that campus defendant entered was fenced or otherwise enclosed in a manner designed to exclude intruders was facially insufficient to establish criminal trespass. People v. Moore, 5 N.Y.3d 725, 800 N.Y.S.2d 49, 833 N.E.2d 192 (2005).

—The phrase "which is fenced or otherwise enclosed in a manner designed to exclude intruders" modifies both the words "building" and "real property." People v. Santos, 182 Misc. 2d 764, 700 N.Y.S.2d 381 (Crim. Ct. N.Y. Co. 1999).

Reentry onto premises after prior order to vacate.—Defendant was guilty of criminal trespass where he entered a racetrack after having previously been issued a notice ordering him to leave and not to enter or remain on the premises at any time; fact that the second entry was pursuant to an admission ticket is irrelevant. People v. Licata, 28 N.Y.2d 113, 320 N.Y.S.2d 53, 268 N.E.2d 787 (1971).

Entry by teacher into locked school.—Teacher has no

"license" or "privilege" to open school locked during teacher's strike by surreptitious entry and force, but had to resort to assistance of superiors, police and courts to open school, or gain entry; and where he entered through basement window resulting in struggle with custodial employee and physically resisted arrest by police, he was guilty of Class A & B misdemeanors. People v. Horelick, 30 N.Y.2d 453, 334 N.Y.S.2d 623, 285 N.E.2d 864 (1972), *cert. denied,* 410 U.S. 943 (1973).

Public housing.—Since simply being in the lobby of a housing project can subject someone to a criminal trespass violation, defendant's unauthorized presence in the building provided probable cause that a crime had been committed. People v. Carter, 169 Misc. 2d 248, 645 N.Y.S.2d 725 (Crim. Ct. Kings Co. 1996).

Squatter in city owned building.—A squatter and his guest in a city owned abandoned building are both trespassers. People v. Sumlin, 105 Misc. 2d 134, 431 N.Y.S.2d 967 (Sup. Ct. N.Y. Co. 1980).

§ 140.15. Criminal trespass in the second degree.

A person is guilty of criminal trespass in the second degree when he knowingly enters or remains unlawfully in a dwelling.

Criminal trespass in the second degree is a Class A misdemeanor.

Amended by L. 1969, Ch. 341.

ANNOTATIONS

Evidence.—Although it could not be reasonably established from the evidence that defendant intended to commit a crime when he entered complainant's residence, evidence did support a conviction for criminal trespass in the second degree. People v. Person, 239 A.D.2d 612, 658 N.Y.S.2d 372 (2d Dept. 1997).

—Evidence viewed in light most favorable to the People was sufficient to establish all the elements of criminal trespass in the second degree. People v. Lamb, 213 A.D.2d 1023, 625 N.Y.S.2d 976 (4th Dept. 1995).

Lesser included offense.—The trial court did not err in refusing to instruct jury on the lesser included offense of criminal trespass in the second degree during defendant's trial for, *inter alia,* burglary in the first degree; while defendant met his burden of showing that criminal trespass in the second degree was a lesser included offense of the crime of burglary in the first degree, no reasonable view of the evidence supported defendant's contention that he committed the lesser crime but not the greater one. People v. Hoyle, 211 A.D.2d 973, 621 N.Y.S.2d 756 (3d Dept. 1995).

§ 140.17. Criminal trespass in the first degree.

A person is guilty of criminal trespass in the first degree when he knowingly enters or remains unlawfully in a building, and when, in the course of committing such crime, he:

1. Possesses, or knows that another participant in the crime possesses, an explosive or a deadly weapon; or

2. Possesses a firearm, rifle or shotgun, as those terms are defined in section 265.00, and also possesses or has readily accessible a quantity of ammunition which is capable of being discharged from such firearm, rifle or shotgun; or

3. Knows that another participant in the crime possesses a firearm, rifle or shotgun under circumstances described in subdivision two.

Criminal trespass in the first degree is a class D felony.

Amended by L. 1969, Ch. 341.

§ 140.20. Burglary in the third degree.

A person is guilty of burglary in the third degree when he knowingly enters or remains unlawfully in a building with intent to commit a crime therein.

Burglary in the third degree is a class D felony.

ANNOTATIONS

Attempt.—There was sufficient proof to support defendant's conviction of attempted burglary, third degree, after defendant and another individual were observed within five feet of the doorway of a business building then closed for the night, located in a rather desolate area; then fled as the police approached and hid across the street beneath a nearby car, and after they were apprehended the officers found evidence of a broken door at the premises where they were first observed. People v. Mitteager, 44 N.Y.2d 927, 408 N.Y.S.2d 9, 379 N.E.2d 1139 (1978).

—Defendant was properly convicted of attempted burglary, third degree, after he was observed breaking in the front door of a liquor store in the early morning hours; defendant's intent to commit a crime on entering the building could be inferred beyond a reasonable doubt from the circumstances of the breaking. People v. Gilligan, 42 N.Y.2d 969, 398 N.Y.S.2d 269, 367 N.E.2d 867 (1977).

Intent.—It is not necessary for the prosecution in a burglary trial to demonstrate the exact crime that the defendant intended to commit while unlawfully in the building. People v. Barnes, 50 N.Y.2d 375, 429 N.Y.S.2d 178, 406 N.E.2d 1071 (1980).

—The jury rejected the defendant's contention that he had entered the premises to panhandle or request a job; the jury could properly have inferred that the defendant's entry without the permission of the owner was with the intent to commit a crime therein. People v. McCrea, 194 A.D.2d 742, 600 N.Y.S.2d 84 (2d Dept. 1993).

—The evidence concerning the defendant's forcible entry into the premises in question was sufficient to permit the jury to infer that the defendant harbored an intent to commit a crime while inside the building. People v. Johnson, 155 A.D.2d 555, 547 N.Y.S.2d 410 (2d Dept. 1989).

—Intent may be inferred from the circumstances. People v. Misevis, 155 A.D.2d 729, 547 N.Y.S.2d 439 (3d Dept. 1989).

—In burglary prosecution, court rejected defendant's claim that his due process rights were violated when the jury was permitted to consider that the defendant may have intended to commit a crime other than those charged in the indictment upon his lawful entry. People v. Goldsmith, 127 A.D.2d 293, 515 N.Y.S.2d 321 (3d Dept. 1987).

—In burglary prosecution, there is no requirement that the People allege or prove what particular crime was intended, or that the intended crime actually be committed. People v. Collier, 204 A.D.2d 1064, 614 N.Y.S.2d 83 (4th Dept. 1994).

Evidence.—Victim's unlawful re-entry into defendant's store after being directed to leave, coupled with his violent conduct and threats to kill defendant and his brother, supported a finding of burglary required as a predicate for a jury instruction of justification. People v. Deis, 97 N.Y.2d 717, 740 N.Y.S.2d 284, 766 N.E.2d 946 (2002).

—Defendant's conviction for burglary in the second degree was modified to burglary in the third degree upon the court's determination that the school that was the target of defendant's break-in was not a "dwelling" within the meaning of the statute, despite the presence of a bed in one of the offices, which was rarely used for overnight accommodations and which was not used on the night of the crime. People v. Quattlebaum, 91 N.Y.2d 744, 675 N.Y.S.2d 585, 698 N.E.2d 421 (1998).

—Evidence was sufficient to support defendant's conviction of burglary in the third degree; contrary to defendant's argument, a passenger train car is a "building" for purposes of the statute because it is a structure or vehicle used by persons for the carrying on of business therein. People v. Marino, 208 A.D.2d 564, 617 N.Y.S.2d 26 (2d Dept. 1994).

—Defendant's guilt of burglary was established by proof that the police found the defendant inside a grocery store when the store was locked and closed; the only way the defendant could have entered the store was through a two-foot wide hole, 11 feet above the ground, that had been made by bending back a metal sign above the awning; and the store appeared to have been ransacked. People v. Gilmore, 199 A.D.2d 410, 605 N.Y.S.2d 109 (2d Dept. 1994).

—People need not establish what crime the defendant intended to commit when he unlawfully entered the victim's home or that the crime he intended to commit was actually committed; intent can be inferred from the circumstances. People v. Richards, 290 A.D.2d 584, 734 N.Y.S.2d 746 (3d Dept. 2002).

—Where affirmative proof offered by the defense on its direct case showed that the defendant did not intend to commit larceny when he entered the garage, this proof made the intent element equivocal and permitted the prosecutor to introduce proof of other burglaries to negate the proof offered of lack of criminal intent subject to proper instructions limiting that proof to the issue of intent. People v. Gross, 74 A.D.2d 701, 426 N.Y.S.2d 118 (3d Dept. 1980).

—There was insufficient evidence to establish that an unoccupied residential building was a dwelling where the building's owner lived elsewhere and neither of the two apartments were rented to tenants. People v. Murray, 278 A.D.2d 898, 718 N.Y.S.2d 554 (4th Dept. 2000), appeal denied, 96 N.Y.2d 804 (2001).

—In burglary prosecution, court rejected contention that court erred in permitting the complainants to testify that they considered the room from which their radio was stolen to be part of their "home"; the room adjoined their apartment and was exclusively occupied and used by them as an "art room" and for the storage of personal belongings. People v. Figueroa, 204 A.D.2d 972, 613 N.Y.S.2d 301 (4th Dept. 1994).

Charge.—It was not reversible error to refuse to charge that the People had to show, in addition to the entry of the premises, that defendants intended to commit a "Felony or a misdemeanor" therein. People v. Borrello, 52 N.Y.2d 947, 437 N.Y.S.2d 965, 419 N.E.2d 868 (1981).

Probable cause for arrest.—Experienced police officers who observed defendants engaging in furtive behavior for one half hour at night on a street where no businesses were open and there were no residential buildings had probable cause to arrest defendants for burglary where, even though garbage obstructed their view of the sidewalk grating, the officers could have fairly inferred that the defendants had opened the grating and entered the basement, since one of them disappeared from sight and subsequently reappeared with two boxes in his hand. People v. Valdez, 78 A.D.2d 449, 437 N.Y.S.2d 671 (1st Dept. 1981).

Acting in concert.—Defendant could be convicted of burglary even though he was in the apartment by invitation; defendant could properly be held criminally responsible for the burglary on the basis of an unlawful entry upon the premises by the person with whom he was acting in concert. People v. Palmer, 176 A.D.2d 995, 574 N.Y.S.2d 853 (3d Dept. 1991).

—Lack of knowledge that a co-participant in the burglary is armed is never a defense to second degree burglary. People v. Mann, 102 Misc. 2d 1101, 424 N.Y.S.2d 1022 (Sup. Ct. Erie Co. 1980).

Felony-murder.—Where the defendant went to an apartment with a knife and spray can and, when the door was opened, attacked two people, killing one, there was sufficient evidence for the jury to find that the defendant committed the crime of burglary, despite defendant's claim that the crime of assault was the underlying felony. People v. Miller, 32 N.Y.2d 157, 344 N.Y.S.2d 342, 297 N.E.2d 85 (1973).

Lesser included offense.—Court properly declined to charge jury with burglary in the third degree where structure burglarized was a "dwelling" within the meaning of Penal Law § 140.00. People v. Barney, 99 N.Y.2d 367, 756 N.Y.S.2d 132, 786 N.E.2d 31 (2003).

Sentencing.—Florida burglary statute included conduct, i.e., a noncriminal violation, that is not a felony under its closest New York felony analog, § 140.20, thus defendant's prior Florida conviction should not have been used as a basis for a predicate felon adjudication. People v. Fermin, 231 A.D.2d 436, 647 N.Y.S.2d 202 (1st Dept. 1996).

§ 140.25. Burglary in the second degree.

A person is guilty of burglary in the second

degree when he knowingly enters or remains unlawfully in a building with intent to commit a crime therein, and when:

1. In effecting entry or while in the building or in immediate flight therefrom, he or another participant in the crime:

(a) Is armed with explosives or a deadly weapon; or

(b) Causes physical injury to any person who is not a participant in the crime; or

(c) Uses or threatens the immediate use of a dangerous instrument; or

(d) Displays what appears to be a pistol, revolver, rifle, shotgun, machine gun or other firearm; or

2. The building is a dwelling.

Burglary in the second degree is a class C felony.

Amended by L. 1967, Ch. 791; L. 1969, Ch. 1012; L. 1973, Ch. 374; L. 1981, Ch. 361.

ANNOTATIONS

Armed co-participants.—The People do not have to prove beyond a reasonable doubt that a defendant had prior knowledge that his accomplices were armed with deadly weapons as an element of the offense of burglary in the second degree. People v. Gomez, 87 A.D.2d 829, 449 N.Y.S.2d 10 (2d Dept. 1982).

Evidence.—Structure, a one-family residence, retained its character as a "dwelling" despite the death of the sole occupant three days before the burglary; the residence was fully furnished with working utilities, and it could have been occupied overnight, as decedent's property was still in the house, including food in the refrigerator. People v. Barney, 99 N.Y.2d 367, 756 N.Y.S.2d 132, 786 N.E.2d 31 (2003).

—Apprehension of the defendant in possession of the fruits of a burglary near the scene may be established by circumstantial evidence. People v. Borrero, 26 N.Y.2d 430, 311 N.Y.S.2d 475, 259 N.E.2d 902 (1970).

—Evidence was insufficient to show that defendant knowingly entered a building with the intent to commit a crime therein; evidence that defendant was in the building's vestibule and tampered with but did not enter a locked inner door did not establish unlawful entry, and an unlocked vestibule was not necessarily closed to the public. People v. Sanchez, 209 A.D.2d 265, 618 N.Y.S.2d 770 (1st Dept. 1994).

—People did not need to prove that defendant intended to commit a particular crime once inside the dwelling in question; however, where the People specified in the bill of particulars that defendant intended to commit larceny, failure to prove that larceny should have reduced defendant's conviction to the lesser included offense of criminal trespass in the second degree. People v. Kolempear, 267 A.D.2d 327, 701 N.Y.S.2d 92 (2d Dept. 1999), appeal denied, 95 N.Y.2d 799 (2000).

—Court properly refused defendant's request for dismissal at the close of the People's case; a rational jury could have concluded that the defendant unlawfully entered an apartment that he had been evicted from intending to commit a crime therein, and was not bound to accept the defendant's stated purpose of getting his own door back in unlawfully entering the apartment. People v. Giannizzero, 209 A.D.2d 635, 619 N.Y.S.2d 307 (2d Dept. 1994).

—Although defendant lawfully entered the apartment building in order to remove a boiler from the basement, while in the building he unlawfully entered victim's apartment by breaking down victim's door and, while assaulting the victim, damaged victim's property; this was sufficient to support defendant's conviction for, inter alia, second degree burglary. People v. Zabala, 290 A.D.2d 578, 735 N.Y.S.2d 244 (3d Dept. 2002).

—Evidence that resident of a four-unit apartment building who left her apartment empty, and heard noises emanating from that apartment, then heard a door close and the bells on her door ring, then immediately thereafter saw defendant in the hallway of the apartment carrying a bag filled with electronic equipment, who could not offer a reasonable explanation for his presence in the building and who assaulted the resident's boyfriend before fleeing the building, supported a conviction for burglary in the second degree. People v. Board, 268 A.D.2d 795, 702 N.Y.S.2d 201 (3d Dept. 2000).

—Conviction for burglary in second degree was reversed; defendant initially had permission to enter girlfriend's apartment and spend the night before argument and assault occurred, and even her repeated requests to leave her home did not convert his status from licensee to trespasser who "remains unlawfully" on the premises within the meaning of the burglary statute. People v. Bowen, 17 A.D.3d 1054, 794 N.Y.S.2d 203 (4th Dept. 2005).

—The evidence, which included the arresting officer's testimony identifying defendant as the first man to emerge from the burglarized premises, was legally sufficient to establish defendant's participation as a principal in the burglary. People v. Stephens, 288 A.D.2d 837, 732 N.Y.S.2d 313 (4th Dept. 2001).

—Evidence could not support a conviction of robbery in the first degree where People failed to establish that the gun defendant possessed during robbery was both operational and loaded with live ammunition. People v. Adams, 278 A.D.2d 920, 719 N.Y.S.2d 428 (4th Dept. 2000), *appeal denied,* 96 N.Y.2d 825 (2001).

—There was insufficient evidence to establish that an unoccupied residential building was a dwelling where the building's owner lived elsewhere and neither of the two apartments were rented to tenants. People v. Murray, 278 A.D.2d 898, 718 N.Y.S.2d 554 (4th Dept. 2000), *appeal denied,* 96 N.Y.2d 804 (2001).

"Inside" a building.—Trespassing on the roof and fire escape of an adjoining building, even assuming intent to commit a crime in the subject building, cannot be defined as being "inside" a building. People v. Diaz, 170 A.D.2d 202, 565 N.Y.S.2d 101 (1st Dept. 1991).

Lesser included offense.—Defendant's convictions for two counts of robbery in the second degree and burglary in the second degree were dismissed as they were lesser included offenses of the crimes of robbery in the first degree and burglary in the first degree; defendant could not have committed the greater offenses without also committing the lesser offenses. People v. Skinner, 211 A.D.2d 979, 621 N.Y.S.2d 733 (3d Dept. 1995).

§ 140.30. Burglary in the first degree.

A person is guilty of burglary in the first degree when he knowingly enters or remains unlawfully in a dwelling with intent to commit a crime therein and when, in effecting entry or while in the dwelling or in immediate flight therefrom, he or another participant in the crime:

1. Is armed with explosives or a deadly weapon; or

2. Causes physical injury to any person who is not a participant in the crime; or

3. Uses or threatens the immediate use of a dangerous instrument; or

4. Displays what appears to be a pistol, revolver, rifle, shotgun, machine gun or other firearm; except that in any prosecution under this subdivision, it is an affirmative defense that such pistol, revolver, rifle, shotgun, machine gun or other firearm was not a loaded weapon from which a shot, readily capable of producing death or other serious physical injury, could be discharged. Nothing contained in this subdivision shall constitute a defense to a prosecution for, or

preclude a conviction of, burglary in the second degree, burglary in the third degree or any other crime.

Burglary in the first degree is a class B felony.

Amended by L. 1967, Ch. 791; L. 1969, Ch. 1012; L. 1973, Ch. 374; L. 1981, Ch. 361.

ANNOTATIONS

Charge.—Trial court properly charged jury that it could determine defendant's guilt under either theory of unlawful entry or unlawful remaining; court rejected defendant's contention that the trial court should not have charged the jury on the portion of the statute which imposes liability for unlawful remaining since People's case rested solely on theory that defendant unlawfully entered a dwelling. People v. Lafond, 213 A.D.2d 678, 624 N.Y.S.2d 951 (2d Dept. 1995).

Consent to search.—The bedroom which was searched in this instance was actually being shared by the defendant and his landlady's 10-year-old son; since that room was not set aside for the defendant's exclusive possession or use, it followed that he could have no reasonable expectation of privacy, and that the landlady, who had a right to enter her son's bedroom, was privileged to give consent to the search. People v. Wood, 31 N.Y.2d 975, 341 N.Y.S.2d 310, 293 N.E.2d 559 (1973).

—Where one person alone occupies a room in a hotel or an apartment in an apartment house, he is deemed to have exclusive possession and control over those premises—at least with regard to search and seizure in the criminal law, and no third party may consent to the premises being entered or searched by the police. People v. Wood, 31 N.Y.2d 975, 341 N.Y.S.2d 310, 293 N.E.2d 559 (1973).

Dangerous instrument.—Testimony that defendant pointed a large kitchen knife at complainant and threatened to kill her during the burglary was sufficient to establish burglary in the first degree. People v. Brown, 255 A.D.2d 686, 681 N.Y.S.2d 616 (3d Dept. 1998).

Deadly weapon.—Evidence could not support a conviction of robbery in the first degree where People failed to establish that the gun defendant possessed during robbery was both operational and loaded with live ammunition. People v. Adams, 278 A.D.2d 920, 719 N.Y.S.2d 428 (4th Dept. 2000), *appeal denied,* 96 N.Y.2d 825 (2001).

Dwelling.—Bedroom of a cotenant, which was independent of the rest of the house, constituted a separate dwelling within a building; fact that the defendant was properly in the common areas of the house did not give him a license to enter the locked room of another tenant. People v. Smith, 144 A.D.2d 600, 534 N.Y.S.2d 1021 (2d Dept. 1988).

Effect of acquittal.—Acquittal of robbery and burglary charges did not negate defendant's intent to use a knife recovered from his person and thereby make his conviction of criminal possession of a weapon in the fourth degree repugnant; the crimes of which defendant was acquitted contain elements that are not a part of the crime of criminal possession of a weapon in the fourth degree. People v. Tyson, 220 A.D.2d 708, 632 N.Y.S.2d 664 (2d Dept. 1995).

Family court jurisdiction.—Defendant was charged with attempted assault of his wife, burglary, and felonious possession of a dangerous weapon. Since the family court has jurisdiction over assault offenses between spouses, and since the assault and non-assault charges were so inextricably related, the transaction lay in the first instance within the jurisdiction of the Family Court. People v. Williams, 24 N.Y.2d 274, 300 N.Y.S.2d 89, 248 N.E.2d 8 (1969).

Mens rea.—In a prosecution for first degree burglary and capital murder, it is not enough for the prosecution to establish that "the burglar intended only murder, that intent cannot be used both to define the burglary and at the same time bootstrap the second degree (intentional) murder to a capital crime." People v. Cahill, 2 N.Y.3d 14, 777 N.Y.S.2d 332, 809 N.E.2d 561 (2003).

Physical injury.—Subjective testimony by complainant that the defendant had hurt her and that she had screamed in pain, without additional evidence, was insufficient to establish beyond a reasonable doubt that the victim had sustained either impairment of physical condition or substantial pain. People v. Cicciari, 90 A.D.2d 853, 456 N.Y.S.2d 103 (2d Dept. 1982).

PL

—Evidence of physical injury was sufficient to sustain charge of burglary in the first degree where photograph of victim showed that she sustained several bruises around her nose and eyes and she testified as to pain and recurring headaches. People v. Bramble, 103 A.D.2d 1019, 478 N.Y.S.2d 399 (4th Dept. 1984).

Possession of stolen goods.—A person may not be convicted of burglary and larceny merely because he has exclusive and recent possession of stolen goods, unless such possession is unexplained. People v. Cefaro, 21 N.Y.2d 252, 287 N.Y.S.2d 371, 234 N.E.2d 423 (1967), *modified,* 23 N.Y.2d 283, 296 N.Y.S.2d 345, 244 N.E.2d 42 (1968).

Proof.—"[C]rime of burglary in the first degree was complete when defendant entered the [doctor's] office with a firearm with the intent to commit a crime." People v. Yong Yun Lee, 92 N.Y.2d 987, 684 N.Y.S.2d 161, 703 N.E.2d 1185 (1998).

—Conviction for burglary in the first degree was affirmed; defendant was told to come get the victim inside homeowner's residence, but after knocking, defendant did not give anyone a chance to open the door, but instead broke down door without invitation or permission and threatened to stab both victim and homeowner with knife he was holding. People v, Hargett, 11 A.D.3d 812, 784 N.Y.S.2d 197 (3d Dept. 2004).

Sentence.—Trial court erred in imposing consecutive sentences for robbery in the first degree and burglary in the first degree convictions; the offenses in this case were committed through a single act and all other sentences were concurrent. People v. Nguyen, 210 A.D.2d 871, 621 N.Y.S.2d 973 (4th Dept. 1994).

§ 140.35. Possession of burglar's tools.

A person is guilty of possession of burglar's tools when he possesses any tool, instrument or other article adapted, designed or commonly used for committing or facilitating offenses involving forcible entry into premises, or offenses involving larceny by a physical taking, or offenses involving theft of services as defined in subdivisions four, five and six of section 165.15, under circumstances evincing an intent to use or knowledge that some person intends to use the same in the commission of an offense of such character.

Possession of burglar's tools is a class A misdemeanor.

ANNOTATIONS

Tools.—Jury was free to conclude from the circumstantial evidence that the two flashlights, assorted tools, and two pairs of gloves, in defendant's attache case were burglar's tools. People v. Hernandez, 127 A.D.2d 790, 512 N.Y.S.2d 185, 188 (2d Dept. 1987).

—Defendant was properly convicted of possession of burglar's tools in a case involving an ordinary brick which had been used to break a window, since the question of whether a brick could be considered to be a burglar's tool was submitted to the jury.

People v. Jones, 115 A.D.2d 495, 495 N.Y.S.2d 719 (2d Dept. 1985).

—A reversal of conviction for possession of burglar's tools was required where the tools consisted of a duplicate room key stolen from the building manager; a key is not adapted or designed for criminal purposes and cannot be said to be commonly used for committing or facilitating offenses involving larceny by physical taking. People v. Baer, 96 A.D.2d 717, 465 N.Y.S.2d 368 (4th Dept. 1983).

—Possession of a scanner programmed to intercept cellular telephone code information and of digital audio tape recorder adapted to record such data met statutory definition of possession of burglar's tools. People v. Garcia, 170 Misc. 2d 543, 647 N.Y.S.2d 355 (Westchester Co. Ct. 1996).

Proof; entry into vehicle.—In cases where the defendant is observed inserting a wire into a car window, or prying a car window with a screwdriver, it is preferable practice for the prosecution to introduce direct proof of another's ownership of the subject vehicle, but failure to do so is not necessarily fatal to the People's case. The defendant's lack of ownership may be inferred from the surrounding circumstances. People v. Borrero, 26 N.Y.2d 430, 311 N.Y.S.2d 475, 258 N.E.2d 902 (1970).

—In a burglar's tools prosecution, there is sufficient circumstantial evidence of a defendant's lack of ownership of a vehicle to support a conviction where defendant was: (1) observed looking into several parked cars with another; (2) they had attempted to enter a car containing merchandise; (3) they fled upon the approach of the individuals who had keys to the car. People v. Borrero, 26 N.Y.2d 430, 311 N.Y.S.2d 475, 259 N.E.2d 902 (1970).

Evidence.—The element of intent to use a tool unlawfully may be established by circumstantial evidence; the nature of the tool used in this case (a box cutter) along with detailed circumstantial factual allegations regarding damage to a vehicle, were sufficient to support the charged violation of PL § 140.35. People v. Givens, 164 Misc. 2d 463, 624 N.Y.S.2d 790 (Crim. Ct. N.Y. Co. 1995).

§ 140.40. Unlawful possession of radio devices.

As used in this section, the term "radio device" means any device capable of receiving a wireless voice transmission on any frequency allocated for police use, or any device capable of transmitting and receiving a wireless voice transmission. A person is guilty of unlawful possession of a radio device when he possesses a radio device with the intent to use that device in the commission of robbery, burglary, larceny, gambling or a violation of any provision of article two hundred twenty of the penal law.

Unlawful possession of a radio device is a class B misdemeanor.

Amended by L. 1970, Ch. 754.

ARTICLE 145—CRIMINAL MISCHIEF AND RELATED OFFENSES

LexisNexis Cross Reference

New York Criminal Practice (2d ed.), Vol. 6, Ch. 62, Criminal Mischief and Related Offenses.

§ 145.00. Criminal mischief in the fourth degree.

A person is guilty of criminal mischief in the fourth degree when, having no right to do so nor any reasonable ground to believe that he has such right, he:

1. Intentionally damages property of another person; or

2. Intentionally particpates * in the destruction of an abandoned building as defined in section one thousand nine hundred seventy-one-a of the real property actions and proceedings law; or

3. Recklessly damages property of another person in an amount exceeding two hundred fifty dollars.

Criminal mischief in the fourth degree is a class A misdemeanor.

* As originally enacted.

Amended by L. 1967, Ch. 791; L. 1971, Ch. 961; L. 1983, Ch. 496.

ANNOTATIONS

Evidence.—While the extent of damage necessary to sustain a conviction for fourth degree criminal mischief is slight, *some* amount of damage is required; thus, where in the course of a boundary dispute with a neighbor defendant pulled out of the ground a surveyor's stake marking the property line and threw it on the neighbor's property, no damage was established, and the conviction must be reversed. People v. Hills, 95 N.Y.2d 947, 722 N.Y.S.2d 460, 745 N.E.2d 379 (2000).

—Defendant can not be charged with criminal mischief in the fourth degree or petit larceny for stealing or damaging property in which he has an equitable interest. People v. Person, 239 A.D.2d 612, 658 N.Y.S.2d 372 (2d Dept. 1997).

—Failure to establish the amount of damages caused exceeded $250 required that defendant's conviction for criminal mischief in the third degree be reduced to criminal mischief in the fourth degree, which requires no proof of monetary value for the damages. People v. Duran, 238 A.D.2d 351, 656 N.Y.S.2d 56 (2d Dept. 1997).

—Although there is no definition of "damages" included within the statute, court properly charged jury that "damages" is an injury or harm to property which reduces its value or usefulness; "slight" damage is sufficient to satisfy the statute. People v. Collins, 288 A.D.2d 756, 733 N.Y.S.2d 289 (3d Dept. 2001).

Intent.—Where defendant fired weapon at victim and several bullets struck car being driven by victim, evidence was legally sufficient to establish mens rea of intent to damage property. People v. Bodine, 231 A.D.2d 840, 648 N.Y.S.2d 394 (4th Dept. 1996).

Justification defense.—Defense of justification was available to defendant on trial on charges of escape and criminal mischief where he claimed he kicked out the back of the police car in which he was being transported after his arrest on a parole violation charge and ran was because the officers taunted him and beat him in the patrol car. People v. Mercer, 267 A.D.2d 1019, 701 N.Y.S.2d 551 (4th Dept. 1999) (mem.).

Lesser included offense.—Trial court erred in refusing to charge criminal mischief in the fourth degree as a lesser included offense of criminal mischief in the third degree; a reasonable view of the evidence supported a finding that defendant acted recklessly rather than intentionally in damaging his girlfriend's car after consuming alcoholic beverages prior to and during a party. People v. Young, 207 A.D.2d 1011, 617 N.Y.S.2d 255 (4th Dept. 1994).

Ownership of destroyed property.—Proof that the property which was damaged is owned by a person other than the defendant is an essential element of the crime of criminal mischief in the fourth degree. People v. Person, 239 A.D.2d 612, 658 N.Y.S.2d 372 (2d Dept. 1997).

—Defendant found guilty of attempted criminal mischief where he had no ownership interest in car and "did not believe and could not reasonably have believed that he had a right to destroy the car." People v. Brown, 185 Misc. 2d 326, 711 N.Y.S.2d 707 (N.Y.C. Crim. Ct. 2000).

—Although it is reasonable to interpret "property of another" under this statute to include property which another, in addition to the defendant, owns, court is compelled to follow Second Department's interpretation of statute; because the defendant has an equitable interest in the items he was charged with damaging, he could not be charged with criminal mischief in damaging or destroying the property. People v. Kheyfets, 174 Misc. 2d 516, 665 N.Y.S.2d 802 (Sup. Ct. Kings Co. 1997).

§ 145.05. Criminal mischief in the third degree.

A person is guilty of criminal mischief in the third degree when, with intent to damage property of another person, and having no right to do so nor any reasonable ground to believe that he or she has such right, he or she:

1. damages the motor vehicle of another person, by breaking into such vehicle when it is locked with the intent of stealing property, and within the previous ten year period, has been convicted three or more times, in separate criminal transactions for which sentence was imposed on separate occasions, of criminal mischief in the fourth degree as defined in section 145.00, criminal mischief in the third degree as defined in this section, criminal mischief in the second degree as defined in section 145.10, or criminal mischief in the first degree as defined in section 145.12 of this article; or

2. damages property of another person in an amount exceeding two hundred fifty dollars.

Criminal mischief in the third degree is a class E felony.

Amended by L. 1971, Ch. 961; L. 2003, Ch. 276, § 1, eff. Nov. 1, 2003.

ANNOTATIONS

Evidence.—Evidence that defendant made a hole in a pane of glass and bent protective bars was sufficient to support a conviction of criminal mischief in the fourth degree, intentional damage to the property of another person. People v. Cunningham, 95 A.D.2d 680, 463 N.Y.S.2d 470 (1st Dept. 1983).

—Evidence was sufficient to establish that defendant caused damage to complainant's property in excess of $250.00. People v. Glusko, 213 A.D.2d 557, 624 N.Y.S.2d 815 (2d Dept. 1995).

—Evidence was sufficient to establish arson in the second degree and criminal mischief in the second and third degrees. Defendant had a motive and an opportunity to set fire to a trailer from which his estranged girlfriend had asked him to move, defendant had argued with the girlfriend the night before the fire, three witnesses heard and observed defendant's car at the scene immediately before the fire started, a butane lighter and several books of matches were found in defendant's car and an expert testified that no accidental cause for the fire existed. People v. Brown, 231 A.D.2d 956, 648 N.Y.S.2d 198 (4th Dept. 1996).

—Evidence was sufficient to support defendant's conviction; possession of the damaged property is not an element of the crime. People v. Funderburk, 214 A.D.2d 990, 627 N.Y.S.2d 495 (4th Dept. 1995).

Intent.—Testimony that defendant was "combative" after he was arrested for violating an order of protection from his former

wife and, while handcuffed in the police car, broke the backseat side window of the patrol car by hitting it with his head and feet, supported conclusion that defendant intended to cause damage to car which ran in excess of $250. People v. De Chellis, 265 A.D.2d 735, 697 N.Y.S.2d 711 (3d Dept. 1999).

—Evidence of other similar incidents in close temporal proximity were properly admitted to establish defendant's intent to force door open on vending machine so as to secure money and soda located inside. People v. Normile, 229 A.D.2d 627, 645 N.Y.S.2d 337 (3d Dept. 1996).

Value of property.—Evidence could only support conviction for criminal mischief in the third degree where proof at trial established that reasonable cost of repairs to complainant's automobile exceeded $250.00 but not $1,500.00 People v. Betts, 232 A.D.2d 258, 648 N.Y.S.2d 301 (1st Dept. 1996).

—Failure to establish the amount of damages caused exceeded $250 required that defendant's conviction for criminal mischief in the third degree be reduced to criminal mischief in the fourth degree which requires no proof of monetary value for the damages. People v. Duran, 238 A.D.2d 351, 656 N.Y.S.2d 56 (2d Dept. 1997).

—In prosecutions for criminal mischief, it is sufficient to define the value of the property and to prove it in terms of the cost of repairing the damage to the property in instances where the property can be repaired. People v. Katovich, 238 A.D.2d 751, 656 N.Y.S.2d 499 (3d Dept. 1997).

§ 145.10. Criminal mischief in the second degree.

A person is guilty of criminal mischief in the second degree when with intent to damage property of another person, and having no right to do so nor any reasonable ground to believe that he has such right, he damages property of another person in an amount exceeding one thousand five hundred dollars.

Criminal mischief in the second degree is a class D felony.

Amended by L. 1971, Ch. 961.

ANNOTATIONS

Elements.—The crimes of criminal mischief in the second degree (PL § 145.10) and arson in the third degree (§ 150.10) do not have identical elements, hence a verdict of guilty on the criminal mischief count was not repugnant to a dismissal of the arson count where the prosecution's proof failed to establish that the damaged property constituted a building, which proof was not necessary for the criminal mischief conviction. People v. Hollis, 73 A.D.2d 994, 424 N.Y.S.2d 31 (3d Dept. 1980).

Evidence.—Evidence that defendant sprayed the front of the court house with chicken excrement, which destroyed a commemorative banner and permeated the facade of the building with a putrid odor and required power washing in freezing temperatures that, in turn, caused structural damage to the steps of the building, was legally sufficient to establish that defendant caused "damage." People v. Collins, 288 A.D.2d 756, 733 N.Y.S.2d 289 (3d Dept. 2001).

—Evidence was sufficient to establish arson in the second degree and criminal mischief in the second and third degrees. Defendant had a motive and an opportunity to set fire to a trailer from which his estranged girlfriend had asked him to move, defendant had argued with the girlfriend the night before the fire, three witnesses heard and observed defendant's car at the scene immediately before the fire started, a butane lighter and several books of matches were found in defendant's car and an expert testified that no accidental cause for the fire existed. People v. Brown, 231 A.D.2d 956, 648 N.Y.S.2d 198 (4th Dept. 1996).

Intent.—Intent to damage property can be inferred from the act itself or from the defendant's conduct and the surrounding circumstances; defendant's act of driving his SUV through the glass entranceway of the movie theatre was sufficient to establish the element of intent. People v. Douglas, 291 A.D.2d 455, 737 N.Y.S.2d 545 (2d Dept. 2002).

Value of property.—Evidence could only support conviction for criminal mischief in the third degree where proof at trial established that reasonable cost of repairs to complainant's automobile exceeded $250.00 but not $1,500.00 People v. Betts, 232 A.D.2d 258, 648 N.Y.S.2d 301 (1st Dept. 1996).

—Testimony of complainant, standing alone, was insufficient to establish value of damaged property, no expert testified as to value of the damaged property and no documentary proof as to the cost of repair or replacement was introduced, conviction for criminal mischief in the second degree, reduced to criminal mischief in the fourth degree. People v. Deolall, 7 A.D.3d 635, 777 N.Y.S.2d 173 (2d Dept. 2004).

—Although the court erred in admitting receipts and an insurance check payable to the victim without a proper foundation, the error was harmless; victim's testimony that the cost to repair the property exceeded $1,500 was sufficient to support the conviction under this section. People v. Singleton, 291 A.D.2d 869, 737 N.Y.S.2d 728 (4th Dept. 2002).

—A reversal of conviction was required despite the fact that defendant slashed the tires of nine different cars, owned by nine different people, within a short period of time and the slashings may have been the product of a single intent and design; the defendant's acts were separate acts against various owners and therefore could not be considered together to constitute a single crime of criminal mischief in the second degree, a conviction could only be sustained if the value of the damaged property of *one* individual exceeded $1,500. People v. Bornstein, 96 A.D.2d 722, 465 N.Y.S.2d 361 (4th Dept. 1983).

§ 145.12. Criminal mischief in the first degree.

A person is guilty of criminal mischief in the first degree when with intent to damage property of another person, and having no right to do so nor any reasonable ground to believe that he has such right, he damages property of another person by means of an explosive.

Criminal mischief in the first degree is a class B felony.

Added by L. 1971, Ch. 961.

§ 145.14. Criminal tampering in the third degree.

A person is guilty of criminal tampering in the third degree when, having no right to do so nor any reasonable ground to believe that he has such right, he tampers with property of another person with intent to cause substantial inconvenience to such person or to a third person.

Criminal tampering in the third degree is a class B misdemeanor.

Added by L. 1978, Ch. 420.

§ 145.15. Criminal tampering in the second degree.

A person is guilty of criminal tampering in the second degree when, having no right to do so nor any reasonable ground to believe that he has such right, he tampers or makes connection with property of a gas, electric, sewer, steam or water-works corporation, telephone or telegraph corporation, common carrier, or public utility operated by a municipality or district; except that in any prosecution under this section, it is an affirmative defense that the defendant did not engage in such conduct for a larcenous or otherwise unlawful or wrongful purpose.

Criminal tampering in the second degree is a class A misdemeanor.

Amended by L. 1969, Ch. 862; L. 1978, Ch. 420.

ANNOTATION

Tampering.—Tampering conviction was supported by evidence that defendant was observed pushing a metal rod up and down in a subway turnstile token slot. People v. Gittens, 279 A.D.2d 291, 719 N.Y.S.2d 230 (1st Dept. 2001), *appeal denied*, 96 N.Y.2d 829 (2001).

§ 145.20. Criminal tampering in the first degree.

A person is guilty of criminal tampering in the first degree when, with intent to cause a substantial interruption or impairment of a service rendered to the public, and having no right to do so nor any reasonable ground to believe that he has such right, he damages or tampers with property of a gas, electric, sewer, steam or water-works corporation, telephone or telegraph corporation, common carrier, or public utility operated by a municipality or district, and thereby causes such substantial interruption or impairment of service.

Criminal tampering in the first degree is a class D felony.

Amended by L. 1969, Ch. 861.

ANNOTATION

Bridge maintained by the city.—A municipal bridge does not come within the common conception of a public utility nor does the statute indicate that it is to be considered as such. People v. Gibson, 77 Misc. 2d 49, 354 N.Y.S.2d 273 (Sup. Ct. Bronx Co. 1974).

§ 145.22. Cemetery desecration in the second degree.

A person is guilty of cemetery desecration in the second degree when with intent to damage property of another person, and having no right to do so nor any reasonable ground to believe that he has such right, he damages any real or personal property maintained as a cemetery plot, grave, burial place or other place of interment of human remains.

Cemetery desecration in the second degree is a class A misdemeanor.

Added by L. 1997, Ch. 165, § 2, eff. Nov. 1, 1997.

§ 145.23. Cemetery desecration in the first degree.

A person is guilty of cemetery desecration in the first degree when with intent to damage property of another person, and having no right to do so nor any reasonable ground to believe that he has such right, he:

(a) damages any real or personal property maintained as a cemetery plot, grave, burial place or other place of interment of human remains in an amount exceeding two hundred fifty dollars; or

(b) commits the crime of cemetery desecration

in the second degree as defined in section 145.22 of this article and has been previously convicted of the crime of cemetery desecration in the second degree within the preceding five years.

Cemetery desecration in the first degree is a class E felony.

Added by L. 1997, Ch. 165, § 2, eff. Nov. 1, 1997.

§ 145.25. Reckless endangerment of property.

A person is guilty of reckless endangerment of property when he recklessly engages in conduct which creates a substantial risk of damage to the property of another person in an amount exceeding two hundred fifty dollars.

Reckless endangerment of property is a class B misdemeanor.

§ 145.30. Unlawfully posting advertisements.

1. A person is guilty of unlawfully posting advertisements when, having no right to do so nor any reasonable ground to believe that he has such right, he posts, paints or otherwise affixes to the property of another person any advertisement, poster, notice or other matter designed to benefit a person other than the owner of the property.

2. Where such matter consists of a commercial advertisement, it shall be presumed that the vendor of the specified product, service or entertainment is a person who placed such advertisement or caused it to be placed upon the property.

Unlawfully posting advertisements is a violation.

ANNOTATION

Juvenile delinquent; Family Court has jurisdiction where act charged would be a crime if committed by an adult.— Defendant allegedly defaced a wall in a subway station, and was charged with criminal mischief in the fourth degree; the act charged would have been a crime if committed by an adult. The Family Court therefore had jurisdiction. The court did not accept defendant's argument that he was only unlawfully posting "advertisements" (a mere violation) and that the Family Court thus did not have jurisdiction over the matter. *In re* Charles W., 72 Misc. 2d 370, 339 N.Y.S.2d 193 (Fam. Ct. N.Y. Co. 1972).

§ 145.35. Tampering with a consumer product; consumer product defined.

For the purposes of sections 145.40 and 145.45 of this article, "consumer product" means any drug, food, beverage or thing which is displayed or offered for sale to the public, for administration into or ingestion by a human being or for application to any external surface of a human being.

Added by L. 1986, Ch. 359.

§ 145.40. Tampering with a consumer product in the second degree.

A person is guilty of tampering with a consumer product in the second degree when, having no right to do so nor any reasonable ground to believe that he has such right, and with intent to cause physical injury to another or with intent to instill in another a fear that he will cause such physical injury, he alters, adulterates or otherwise contaminates a consumer product.

Tampering with a consumer product in the second degree is a class A misdemeanor.

Added by L. 1986, Ch. 359.

§ 145.45. Tampering with a consumer product in the first degree.

A person is guilty of tampering with a consumer product in the first degree when, having no right to do so nor any reasonable ground to believe that he has such right, and with intent to cause physical injury to another or with intent to instill in another a fear that he will cause such physical injury, he alters, adulterates or otherwise contaminates a consumer product and thereby creates a substantial risk of serious physical injury to one or more persons.

Tampering with a consumer product in the first degree is a class E felony.

Added by L. 1986, Ch. 359.

§ 145.50. Penalties for littering on railroad tracks and rights-of-way.

1. No person shall throw, dump, or cause to be thrown, dumped, deposited or placed upon any railroad tracks, or within the limits of the rights-of-way of any railroad, any refuse, trash, garbage, rubbish, litter or any nauseous or offensive matter.

2. Where a highway or road lies in whole or part within a railroad rights-of-way, nothing in this section shall be construed as prohibiting the use in a reasonable manner of ashes, sand, salt or other material for the purpose of reducing the hazard of, or providing traction on snow, ice or sleet situated on such highway or road.

3. A violation of the provisions of subdivision one of this section shall be punishable by a fine not to exceed two hundred fifty dollars and/or a requirement to perform services for a public or not for profit corporation, association, institution or agency not to exceed eight hours and for any second or subsequent violation by a fine not to exceed five hundred dollars and/or a requirement to perform services for a public or not-for-profit corporation, association, institution or agency not to exceed eight hours.

4. Nothing in this section shall be deemed to apply to a railroad or its employees when matter

deposited by them on the railroad tracks or rights-of-way is done pursuant to railroad rules, regulations or procedures.

Added by L. 1987, Ch. 266; **Amended** by L. 1991, Ch. 186, eff. Nov. 1, 1991, amending subd. (3).

§ 145.60. Making graffiti.

1. For purposes of this section, the term "graffiti" shall mean the etching, painting, covering, drawing upon or otherwise placing of a mark upon public or private property with intent to damage such property.

2. No person shall make graffiti of any type on any building, public or private, or any other property real or personal owned by any person, firm or corporation or any public agency or instrumentality, without the express permission of the owner or operator of said property.

Making graffiti is a class A misdemeanor.

Added by L. 1992, Ch. 458, eff. Nov. 1, 1992.

§ 145.65. Possession of graffiti instruments.

A person is guilty of possession of graffiti instruments when he possesses any tool, instrument, article, substance, solution or other compound designed or commonly used to etch, paint, cover, draw upon or otherwise place a mark upon a piece of property which that person has no permission or authority to etch, paint, cover, draw

upon or otherwise mark, under circumstances evincing an intent to use same in order to damage such property.

Possession of graffiti instruments is a class B misdemeanor.

Added by L. 1992, Ch. 458, eff. Nov. 1, 1992.

§ 145.70. Criminal possession of a taximeter accelerating device.

1. For purposes of this section, a "taximeter" means an instrument or device that automatically calculates and displays the charge to a passenger in a vehicle that is licensed to transport members of the public for hire pursuant to local law.

2. For purposes of this section, a "taximeter accelerating device" means an instrument or device that causes a taximeter to increase the charge displayed by such taximeter to an amount greater than the maximum amount permitted by local law.

3. A person is guilty of criminal possession of a taximeter accelerating device when he knowingly possesses, with intent to use unlawfully, a taximeter accelerating device. If such a device is knowingly possessed there is a rebuttable presumption that it is intended to be used unlawfully.

Criminal possession of a taximeter accelerating device is a class A misdemeanor.

Added by L. 1999, Ch. 603, eff. Nov. 9, 1999.

ARTICLE 150—ARSON

Section

LexisNexis Cross Reference

New York Criminal Practice (2d ed.), Vol. 6, Ch. 63, Arson.

§ 150.00. Arson; definitions.

As used in this article, 1. "Building," in addition to its ordinary meaning, includes any structure, vehicle or watercraft used for overnight lodging of persons, or used by persons for carrying on business therein. Where a building consists of two or more units separately secured or occupied, each unit shall not be deemed a separate building.

2. "Motor vehicle," includes every vehicle operated or driven upon a public highway which is propelled by any power other than muscular power, except (a) electrically-driven invalid chairs being operated or driven by an invalid, (b) vehicles which run only upon rails or tracks, and (c) snowmobiles as defined in article forty-seven of the vehicle and traffic law.

Amended by L. 1979, Ch. 225.

ANNOTATION

Building.—Conviction for arson in the second degree affirmed, make-shift shelter used by homeless individuals for overnight shelter for several months constituted a "building" within the meaning of the arson statute. People v. Fox, 3 A.D.3d 577, 771 N.Y.S.2d 156 (2d Dept. 2004).

Generally.—It was proper to convict defendant of three counts of arson even though she set only one fire, since the arson resulted in serious physical injury to three separate persons, two of whom died. People v. Perez, 173 A.D.2d 162, 569 N.Y.S.2d 72 (1st Dept. 1991).

§ 150.01. Arson in the fifth degree.

A person is guilty of arson in the fifth degree when he or she intentionally damages property of another without consent of the owner by intentionally starting a fire or causing an explosion. Arson in the fifth degree is a class A misdemeanor.

Added by L. 2001, Ch. 224, § 1, eff. Nov. 1, 2001.

§ 150.05. Arson in the fourth degree.

1. A person is guilty of arson in the fourth degree when he recklessly damages a building or motor vehicle by intentionally starting a fire or causing an explosion.

2. In any prosecution under this section, it is an affirmative defense that no person other than the defendant had a possessory or proprietary interest in the building or motor vehicle.

Arson in the fourth degree is a class E felony.

Amended by L. 1971, Ch. 961; L. 1979, Ch. 225.

ANNOTATIONS

Evidence.—It is not necessary that a building burn in order for there to be arson in the fourth degree; the slightest damage to a building caused by a fire which is intentionally set is sufficient to establish the damage element of this crime and the smoke and heat damage did so in this case. People v. Fleming, 164 A.D.2d 942, 560 N.Y.S.2d 50 (2d Dept. 1990).

—Rejecting defendant's argument that court erred in submitting to the jury charge of arson in the fourth degree because, if at all, defendant intentionally started fire: evidence of defendant's intoxication was sufficient to negate the element of intent and permit a finding of recklessness, leaving to the jury the factual question whether the extent of intoxication acted to negate the element of intent. People v. Borst, 232 A.D.2d 727, 648 N.Y.S.2d 720 (3d Dept. 1996).

Lesser included offense.—Fact that counts of arson in the third degree and arson in the fourth degree submitted to the jury required demonstration of different culpable mental states did not preclude a finding that the latter was a lesser included offense of the former. People v. Borst, 232 A.D.2d 727, 648 N.Y.S.2d 720 (3d Dept. 1996).

§ 150.10. Arson in the third degree.

1. A person is guilty of arson in the third degree when he intentionally damages a building or motor vehicle by starting a fire or causing an explosion.

2. In any prosecution under this section, it is an affirmative defense that (a) no person other than the defendant had a possessory or proprietary interest in the building or motor vehicle, or if other persons had such interests, all of them consented to the defendant's conduct, and (b) the defendant's sole intent was to destroy or damage the building or motor vehicle for a lawful and proper purpose, and (c) the defendant had no reasonable ground to believe that his conduct might endanger the life or safety of another person or damage another building or motor vehicle.

Arson in the third degree is a class C felony.

Amended by L. 1971, Ch. 961; L. 1979, Ch. 225.

ANNOTATIONS

Evidence.—Acquittal was required where the circumstantial evidence connecting the defendant with the actual commission of the arson did not negate a reasonable and innocent explanation. People v. Piazza, 48 N.Y.2d 151, 422 N.Y.S.2d 9, 397 N.E.2d 700 (1979).

—Where evidence indicated that on the day of the fire, defendant's employee closed the store and left the premises, but that contrary to the usual practice of the defendant, the latter remained in the store, and was observed a few minutes later in the back of the store throwing cartons, and expert testimony supported the view that the fire had its source in the store, the evidence established motive and opportunity to commit the crime and excluded any reasonable hypothesis that the fire was innocent in nature. People v. Feuerstein, 74 A.D.2d 853, 425 N.Y.S.2d 379 (2d Dept. 1980).

—Evidence presented at trial was sufficient to support conviction for arson in the third degree where two fire investigators testified that evidence was consistent with a fire intentionally started in two areas of the house, not accidentally in the kitchen, as defendant had claimed. People v. Venkatesan, 295 A.D.2d 635, 743 N.Y.S.2d 615 (3d Dept. 2002).

Expert testimony.—Although it was improper for fire investigator to give his opinion that fire was arson, taken with totality of evidence presented to grand jury that fire was intentionally started, admission of that improper opinion was not fatal, and dismissal of the arson count was not required. People v. Smith, 289 A.D.2d 597, 735 N.Y.S.2d 813 (2d Dept. 2001).

—It was improper to allow an expert witness to testify as to his opinion as to whether a fire was incendiary in origin; such expert's testimony should have been limited to his observations at the scene. People v. Abreu, 114 A.D.2d 853, 494 N.Y.S.2d 762 (2d Dept. 1985).

Lesser included offense.—Fact that counts of arson in the third degree and arson in the fourth degree submitted to the jury required demonstration of different culpable mental states did not preclude a finding that the latter was a lesser included offense of the former. People v. Borst, 232 A.D.2d 727, 648 N.Y.S.2d 720 (3d Dept. 1996).

§ 150.15. Arson in the second degree.

A person is guilty of arson in the second degree when he intentionally damages a building or motor vehicle by starting a fire, and when (a) another person who is not a participant in the crime is present in such building or motor vehicle at the time, and (b) the defendant knows that fact or the circumstances are such as to render the presence of such a person therein a reasonable possibility.

Arson in the second degree is a class B felony.

Amended by L. 1967, Ch. 791; l. 1971, Ch. 961; L. 1979, Ch. 225.

ANNOTATIONS

Arson; prejudicial error to allow presentence statement of co-defendant.—Defendant's arson conviction was reversed and a new trial ordered, where co-defendant made a presentence statement that he was covering up for the defendant, since it was prejudicial to the defendant because the district attorney's statement regarding the conversation with the co-defendant afforded the defendant no chance to cross-examine or rebut the statement. People v. Epstein, 42 A.D.2d 1, 344 N.Y.S.2d 4 (1st Dept. 1973).

Arson; proof.—In arson cases, proof of criminal agency is usually only circumstantial, because, more often than not, the fire destroys and consumes all evidence of its origin. People v. Trippoda, 40 A.D.2d 388, 341 N.Y.S.2d 66 (3d Dept. 1973).

—Evidence was sufficient to establish arson in the second degree and criminal mischief in the second and third degrees. Defendant had a motive and an opportunity to set fire to a trailer from which his estranged girlfriend had asked him to move, defendant had argued with the girlfriend the night before the fire, three witnesses heard and observed defendant's car at the scene immediately before the fire started, a butane lighter and several books of matches were found in defendant's car and an expert testified that no accidental cause for the fire existed. People v. Brown, 231 A.D.2d 956, 648 N.Y.S.2d 198 (4th Dept. 1996).

Expert testimony.—Court's admission of expert testimony was not error even though based in part on hearsay; "an expert may rely upon out-of-court material that would otherwise be inadmissible hearsay where, as here, 'it is of a kind accepted in the profession as reliable in forming a professional opinion.' " Moreover, the hearsay evidence only confirmed what the expert had determined independently. People v. Mana, 738 N.Y.S.2d 796, 292 A.D.2d 863 (4th Dept. 2002).

Damage.—Evidence of damage to building need not be significant to satisfy statute; "slightest damage to a building" is enough; presence of burn pattern and charring sufficient to establish damage element of statute. People v. Jackson, 265 A.D.2d 343, 696 N.Y.S.2d 75 (2d Dept. 1999), *rehearing denied*, 94 N.Y.2d 824 (2000).

Inhabited building.—Conviction for arson in the second degree affirmed, make-shift shelter used by homeless individuals for overnight shelter for several months constituted a "building" within the meaning of the arson statute. People v. Fox, 3 A.D.3d 577; 771 N.Y.S.2d 156 (2d Dept. 2004).

—The defendant was properly charged with Arson, second degree, when he was accused of setting fire to an uninhabited building and the fire spread to an adjacent inhabited building, since the spreading of the fire was a foreseeable consequence of the original act without any supervening cause. People v. Davis, 89 Misc. 2d 535, 392 N.Y.S.2d 195 (Sup. Ct. Kings Co. 1977).

§ 150.20. Arson in the first degree.

1. A person is guilty of arson in the first degree when he intentionally damages a building or motor vehicle by causing an explosion or a fire and when (a) such explosion or fire is caused by an incendiary device propelled, thrown or placed inside or near such building or motor vehicle; or when such explosion or fire is caused by an explosive; or when such explosion or fire either (i) causes serious physical injury to another person other than a participant, or (ii) the explosion or fire was caused with the expectation or receipt of financial advantage or pecuniary profit by the actor; and when (b) another person who is not a participant in the crime is present in such building or motor vehicle at the time; and (c) the defendant knows that fact or the circumstances are such as to render the presence of such person therein a reasonable possibility.

2. As used in this section, "incendiary device" means a breakable container designed to explode or produce uncontained combustion upon impact, containing flammable liquid and having a wick or a similar device capable of being ignited.

Arson in the first degree is a class A-I felony.

Added by L. 1980, Ch. 152; **Amended** by L. 1981, Ch. 71; L. 1984, Ch. 950.

ANNOTATIONS

Evidence.—Accomplice and non-accomplice witnesses provided sufficient corroboration to support finding that the explosion and fire were caused with expectation of financial gain by defendant. People v. Gelman, 240 A.D.2d 181, 658 N.Y.S.2d 872 (1st Dept. 1997), *aff'd*, 93 N.Y.2d 314, 690 N.Y.S.2d 520, 712 N.E.2d 686 (1999).

—Circumstantial evidence was sufficient to support conviction of attempted arson in the first degree. People v. Wigfall, 207 A.D.2d 973, 617 N.Y.S.2d 672 (4th Dept. 1994).

TITLE J—OFFENSES INVOLVING THEFT

ARTICLE 155—LARCENY

LexisNexis Cross Reference

New York Criminal Practice (2d ed.), Vol. 6, Ch. 64, Larceny.

§ 155.00. Larceny; definitions of terms.

The following definitions are applicable to this title:

1. "Property" means any money, personal property, real property, computer data, computer program, thing in action, evidence of debt or contract, or any article, substance or thing of value, including any gas, steam, water or electricity, which is provided for a charge or compensation.

2. "Obtain" includes, but is not limited to, the bringing about of a transfer or purported transfer of property or of a legal interest therein, whether to the obtainer or another.

3. "Deprive." To "deprive" another of property means (a) to withhold it or cause it to be withheld from him permanently or for so extended a period or under such circumstances that the major portion of its economic value or benefit is lost to him, or (b) to dispose of the property in such manner or under such circumstances as to render it unlikely that an owner will recover such property.

4. "Appropriate." To "appropriate" property of another to oneself or a third person means (a) to exercise control over it, or to aid a third person to exercise control over it, permanently or for so extended a period or under such circumstances as to acquire the major portion of its economic value or benefit, or (b) to dispose of the property for the benefit of oneself or a third person.

5. "Owner." When property is taken, obtained or withheld by one person from another person, an "owner" thereof means any person who has a right to possession thereof superior to that of the taker, obtainer or withholder.

A person who has obtained possession of property by theft or other illegal means shall be deemed to have a right of possession superior to that of a person who takes, obtains or withholds it from him by larcenous means.

A joint or common owner of property shall not be deemed to have a right of possession thereto superior to that of any other joint or common owner thereof.

In the absence of a specific agreement to the contrary, a person in lawful possession of property shall be deemed to have a right of possession superior to that of a person having only a security interest therein, even if legal title lies with the holder of the security interest pursuant to a conditional sale contract or other security agreement.

6. "Secret scientific material" means a sample, culture, micro-organism, specimen, record, recording, document, drawing or any other article, material, device or substance which constitutes, represents, evidences, reflects, or records a scientific or technical process, invention or formula or any part or phase thereof, and which is not, and is not intended to be, available to anyone other than the person or persons rightfully in possession thereof or selected persons having access thereto with his or their consent, and when it accords or may accord such rightful possessors an advantage over competitors or other persons who do not have knowledge or the benefit thereof.

7. "Credit card" means any instrument or article defined as a credit card in section five hundred eleven of the general business law.

7-a. "Debit card" means any instrument or article defined as a debit card in section five hundred eleven of the general business law.

7-b. "Public benefit card" means any medical assistance card, food stamp assistance card, public assistance card, or any other identification, authorization card or electronic access device issued by the state or a social services district as defined in subdivision seven of section two of the social services law, which entitles a person to obtain public assistance benefits under a local, state or federal program administered by the state, its political subdivisions or social services districts.

7-c. "Access device" means any telephone calling card number, credit card number, account number, mobile identification number, electronic serial number or personal identification number that can be used to obtain telephone service.

8. "Service" includes, but is not limited to, labor, professional service, a computer service, transportation service, the supplying of hotel accommodations, restaurant services, entertainment, the supplying of equipment for use, and the supplying of commodities of a public utility nature such as gas, electricity, steam and water. A ticket or equivalent instrument which evidences a right to receive a service is not in itself service but constitutes property within the meaning of subdivision one.

9. "Cable television service" means any and all services provided by or through the facilities of any cable television system or closed circuit coaxial cable communications system, or any microwave or similar transmission service used in connection with any cable television system or other similar closed circuit coaxial cable communications system.

Amended by L. 1967, Ch. 791; L. 1969, Ch. 115; L. 1975, Ch. 530; L. 1978, Ch. 420; L. 1986, Ch. 514; L. 1987, Ch. 556; L. 1992, Ch. 41, eff. Apr. 2, 1992, adding subd. 7-b; L. 1992, Ch. 491, eff. Nov. 1, 1992, adding subd. 7-c; L. 1993, Ch. 171; L. 1995, Ch. 81, § 169, repealing subd. 7-b and adding a new subd. 7-b, eff. Nov. 1, 1995.

ANNOTATIONS

Charge.—Defendant's conviction for petit larceny was reversed and new trial ordered because the charge to the jury was insufficient as the court failed to read the statutory definitions of "deprive" and "appropriate" and the court did not distinguish between an intent to permanently deprive and an intent to temporarily deprive; had the jury been instructed more thoroughly they might have found that the defendant was only joking and did not intend to permanently deprive. People v. Albanese, 88 A.D.2d 603, 449 N.Y.S.2d 765 (2d Dept. 1982).

—Court committed reversible error when, in its charge, it omitted from its definition the statutory requirement that the withholding of the property be permanent or for so extended a period of time that the major portion of its economic value is lost. People v. Johnson, 75 A.D.2d 585, 426 N.Y.S.2d 570 (2d Dept. 1980).

Multiple larcenies.—Multiple larcenies may be considered as a single offense where the property is taken from the same owner by a series of acts that are pursuant to a single intent and in execution of a common fraudulent scheme. People v. Cantarella, 160 Misc. 2d 8, 606 N.Y.S.2d 942 (Sup. Ct. N.Y. Co. 1993).

Completed crime.—Defendant was not guilty of larceny where he first became involved the day after the theft of a car when, knowing the car to be stolen, he helped his friends remove its wheels and tires; transportation had ceased and the larceny had been completed when dominion and control of the car were assumed prior to the time defendant became involved. People

v. Robinson, 60 N.Y.2d 982, 471 N.Y.S.2d 258, 459 N.E.2d 483 (1984).

—Evidence that defendant forcibly took a van from the victim and that defendant intended to deprive the victim of his van or to appropriate it to himself was sufficient to support his conviction for larceny. People v. Velez, 1 A.D.3d 290, 767 N.Y.S.2d 592 (1st Dept. 2003).

—Taking of complainant's hat and throwing it upon roof of store established intent to deprive complainant of his property. In re Nehial W., 232 A.D.2d 152, 647 N.Y.S.2d 512 (1st Dept. 1996).

Owner.—Withdrawals by a successor attorney from the special account did not constitute larceny since the predecessor attorney did not, by reason of the order fixing the amount of his fee, have property in or ownership of the money held by the successor attorney; the terms "property" and "owner" are defined by PL § 155.00, and the fact that the proceeds were in a special or "attorney's" account did not make them trust funds held for the benefit of the predecessor attorney. People v. Keefe, 50 N.Y.2d 149, 428 N.Y.S.2d 446, 405 N.E.2d 1012 (1980).

—Defendant's lack of ownership of property may be inferred from the circumstances. People v. Stafford, 173 A.D.2d 233, 569 N.Y.S.2d 441, 442 (1st Dept. 1991).

—Larceny was established even though the people did not call the owner of the car but rather called garage attendant of garage in which the pushcart had been stored; the attendant qualified as an "owner" within the meaning of Penal Law § 155.00(5). People v. Polanco, 172 A.D.2d 276, 568 N.Y.S.2d 99 (1st Dept. 1991).

—Evidence was sufficient to establish defendant's guilt where complainant, an accountant working in a client's office, had a right to possession of the office equipment stolen by defendant and was the "owner" of the property within the meaning of the statute. People v. Marshall, 293 A.D.2d 629, 740 N.Y.S.2d 245 (2d Dept. 2002).

—Defendant who has an equitable interest in property is an "owner" and cannot be charged with criminal mischief in the fourth degree or petit larceny for stealing or damaging that property. People v. Person, 239 A.D.2d 612, 658 N.Y.S.2d 372 (2d Dept. 1997).

Property.—Torn pieces of currency taken by the defendant constituted property. People v. Freeman, 148 A.D.2d 467, 538 N.Y.S.2d 619 (2d Dept. 1989).

Credit cards.—Theft of "decoy" credit card issued by credit card company to undercover police officer under imaginary name was sufficient to support defendant's conviction for grand larceny in the fourth degree; in fact, "criminal liability with regard to credit cards can arise even with respect to non-activated, expired or canceled cards." People v. Thompson, 99 N.Y.2d 38, 751 N.Y.S.2d 162, 780 N.E.2d 973 (2002).

§ 155.05. Larceny; defined.

1. A person steals property and commits larceny when, with intent to deprive another of property or to appropriate the same to himself or to a third person, he wrongfully takes, obtains or withholds such property from an owner thereof.

2. Larceny includes a wrongful taking, obtaining or withholding of another's property, with the intent prescribed in subdivision one of this section, committed in any of the following ways:

(a) By conduct heretofore defined or known as common law larceny by trespassory taking, common law larceny by trick, embezzlement, or obtaining property by false pretenses;

(b) By acquiring lost property.

A person acquires lost property when he exercises control over property of another which he knows to have been lost or mislaid, or to have been delivered under a mistake as to the identity of the recipient or the nature or amount of the property, without taking reasonable measures to return such property to the owner;

(c) By committing the crime of issuing a bad check, as defined in section 190.05;

(d) By false promise.

A person obtains property by false promise when, pursuant to a scheme to defraud, he obtains property of another by means of a representation, express or implied, that he or a third person will in the future engage in particular conduct, and when he does not intend to engage in such conduct or, as the case may be, does not believe that the third person intends to engage in such conduct.

In any prosecution for larceny based upon a false promise, the defendant's intention or belief that the promise would not be performed may not be established by or inferred from the fact alone that such promise was not performed. Such a finding may be based only upon evidence establishing that the facts and circumstances of the case are wholly consistent with guilty intent or belief and wholly inconsistent with innocent intent or belief, and excluding to a moral certainty every hypothesis except that of the defendant's intention or belief that the promise would not be performed;

(e) By extortion.

A person obtains property by extortion when he compels or induces another person to deliver such property to himself or to a third person by means of instilling in him a fear that, if the property is not so delivered, the actor or another will:

(i) Cause physical injury to some person in the future; or

(ii) Cause damage to property; or

(iii) Engage in other conduct constituting a crime; or

(iv) Accuse some person of a crime or cause criminal charges to be instituted against him; or

(v) Expose a secret or publicize an asserted fact, whether true or false, tending to subject some person to hatred, contempt or ridicule; or

(vi) Cause a strike, boycott or other collective labor group action injurious to some person's business; except that such a threat shall not be deemed extortion when the property is demanded or received for the benefit of the group in whose interest the actor purports to act; or

(vii) Testify or provide information or withhold testimony or information with respect to another's legal claim or defense; or

(viii) Use or abuse his position as a public servant by performing some act within or related to his official duties, or by failing or refusing to perform an official duty, in such manner as to affect some person adversely; or

(ix) Perform any other act which would not in itself materially benefit the actor but which is calculated to harm another person materially with respect to his health, safety, business, calling, career, financial condition, reputation or personal relationships.

ANNOTATIONS

Intent.—The intent to deprive or appropriate element of the crime is satisfied by the exertion of permanent or virtually permanent control over the property taken. People v. Jensen, 86 N.Y.2d 248, 630 N.Y.S.2d 989, 654 N.E.2d 1237 (1995).

—Taking of complainant's hat and throwing it upon roof of store established intent to deprive complainant of his property. In re Nehial W., 232 A.D.2d 152, 647 N.Y.S.2d 512 (1st Dept. 1996).

—The people established defendant's intent to permanently deprive another of his money beyond a reasonable doubt; the evidence showed that defendant intended not merely to borrow another's money, but that he had concocted a plan to divest another of his money and use it for the payment of his own debts. People v. Generoso, 219 A.D.2d 670, 631 N.Y.S.2d 722 (2d Dept. 1995).

—Evidence was sufficient to support defendant's conviction of grand larceny in the third degree and to demonstrate that defendant had the requisite intent to commit this crime; the people presented evidence that defendant wrongfully deprived an owner of property valued at more than $3,000 with the specific intent to permanently deprive the owner of the property. People v. Johnson, 213 A.D.2d 791, 623 N.Y.S.2d 418 (3d Dept. 1995).

—"Proof of intent in false promise cases is rarely direct and, therefore, must be inferred from all of the facts and circumstances," here fact that defendant was a director, board member, and secretary of New York Amazons corporation (Amazons) and was a signatory on the corporate bank account of Amazons which purported to be a premier high school-aged girls' basketball program with additional educational and community service benefits, coupled with fact that defendant and co-defendant collected fees but failed to deliver on promises made in connection with the program, established that they were running a fraudulent enterprise. People v. Kowallis, 1 A.D.3d 1026, 767 N.Y.S.2d 183 (4th Dept. 2003).

Transportation.—There is nothing in PL § 155.05 which states that transportation is an essential element of larceny in all cases; the primary element is the exercise of dominion and control adverse to that of the owner. People v. Gasparik, 102 A.D.2d 487, 425 N.Y.S.2d 936 (1st Dept. 1980), aff'd, 52 N.Y.2d 309, 438 N.Y.S.2d 242, 420 N.E.2d 40 (1981).

Larceny of automobile.—Where an automobile is entered, the culprit positions himself behind the wheel, starts the engine, turns on the lights, and starts to move the car or is about to do so, the completed larceny of the auto is accomplished since moving of the vehicle is not necessary. People v. Alamo, 34 N.Y.2d 453, 358 N.Y.S.2d 375, 315 N.E.2d 446 (1974).

Larceny by embezzlement.—The failure to pay full refunds to the residents of a nursing home did not constitute larceny by embezzlement where the residents had a contractual right to receive refunds from the operator of the home equal to the fuel amount they had previously paid him, but the money from which defendant was required to make the payments belonged to him. People v. Yannett, 49 N.Y.2d 296, 425 N.Y.S.2d 300, 401 N.E.2d 410 (1980).

Larceny by extortion.—Although intangible, an advantageous business relationship may constitute the sort of property which may be obtained through extortion. People v. Spatarella, 34 N.Y.2d 157, 356 N.Y.S.2d 566, 313 N.E.2d 38 (1974).

—Fear of future economic harm is sufficient to establish extortion under the statute. People v. Capparelli, 158 Misc. 2d 996, 603 N.Y.S.2d 99 (Sup. Ct. N.Y. Co. 1993).

—Extortion requires an intent to create a fear that the victim's business will be harmed if the demands are not met, and a threat to prevent an award of a future contract qualifies as a threat to harm a business. People v. Kacer, 113 Misc. 2d 338, 448 N.Y.S.2d 1002 (Sup. Ct. N.Y. Co. 1982).

Larceny by false promise.—The proof was insufficient to establish the defendant's guilt where it only disclosed that defendant had entered into three contracts for which he received substantial down payments and that he failed to complete performance; the inferences to be drawn did not exclude to a moral certainty every hypothesis but that at the time he entered into the contracts he had no intention of meeting his obligations; equally strong was the inference that defendant was simply an inexperienced, uneducated tyro whose talents of salesmanship surpassed his ability to manage a business. People v. Churchill, 47 N.Y.2d 151, 417 N.Y.S.2d 221, 390 N.E.2d 1146 (1979).

—In the context of the crime of larceny by false promise, the inference of intent must overcome to a moral certainty any implication of mere civil wrong. People v. Ryan, 41 N.Y.2d 634, 394 N.Y.S.2d 609, 363 N.E.2d 334 (1977); *see also* People v. Churchill, 47 N.Y.2d 151, 417 N.Y.S.2d 221, 390 N.E.2d 1146 (1979).

—While the crime of scheme to defraud requires an intent to defraud more than one person, the scheme to defraud element of larceny by false promise contains no such requirement. People v. Omrami, 155 A.D.2d 369, 548 N.Y.S.2d 158 (1st Dept. 1990).

—Court's charge on false promise and intent clearly protected defendant by outlining the elements of false promise and by reminding the jury that the intent not to perform could not be found from the fact alone that the promise was not performed. People v. Beecher, 122 A.D.2d 407, 505 N.Y.S.2d 222 (3d Dept. 1986).

Lesser included offenses.—The count of the indictment for crime of issuing a bad check should be dismissed where, upon the facts submitted, it was impossible for defendant to have committed the crime of larceny without concomitantly committing the crime of issuing a bad check, and therefore the latter charge was a lesser included offense of larceny. People v. Barbuto, 106 Misc. 2d 542, 434 N.Y.S.2d 120 (Sup. Ct. Suffolk Co. 1980).

Evidence.—Evidence was legally insufficient to support a conviction for grand larceny by false pretenses where record failed to establish that defendant made a false, material statement about a past or presently existing fact. People v. Hart, 100 N.Y.2d 550, 763 N.Y.S.2d 806, 795 N.E.2d 31 (2003).

—Evidence was sufficient to sustain a conviction for larceny where defendant looked furtively up and down an aisle before secreting a book in his attaché case. People v. Spatzier, 52 N.Y.2d 309, 438 N.Y.S.2d 242, 420 N.E.2d 40 (1981).

—A person may be guilty of larceny before leaving a store depending on the circumstances of each case; some of the factors in determining whether the evidence is sufficient to support a conviction are concealment of the goods under clothing or in a container, furtive or unusual behavior on the part of defendant, proximity or movement toward the store's exits, or possession of a known shoplifting device. People v. Olivo, 52 N.Y.2d 309, 438 N.Y.S.2d 242, 420 N.E.2d 40 (1981).

—Evidence was sufficient to support a larceny conviction where defendant removed the price tag and sensor device from a jacket, abandoned his own garment, put on the jacket and headed for the main floor. People v. Gasparik, 52 N.Y.2d 309, 438 N.Y.S.2d 242, 420 N.E.2d 40 (1981).

—Evidence that defendant deliberately misrepresented the contents of a package which he sold and falsely promised to return with three more packages in exchange for the money that he had already received supported conviction for larceny by false pretenses. People v. Overton, 309 A.D.2d 571, 765 N.Y.S.2d 344 (1st Dept. 2003).

—Stolen property can include property stolen by common law trespassory taking or by acquiring another's lost property. People v. Meador, 279 A.D.2d 327, 718 N.Y.S.2d 351 (1st Dept. 2001).

—Evidence was sufficient to establish defendant's guilt where complainant, an accountant working in a client's office, had a right to possession of the office equipment stolen by defendant and was the "owner" of the property within the meaning of the statute. People v. Marshall, 293 A.D.2d 629, 740 N.Y.S.2d 245 (2d Dept. 2002).

Wrongful withholding of taxes.—A person who wrongfully obtains or withholds personal income and sales tax revenues belonging to the state can be indicted for larceny. People v. Lyon, 82 A.D.2d 516, 442 N.Y.S.2d 538 (2d Dept. 1981).

§ 155.10. Larceny; no defense.

The crimes of (a) larceny committed by means of extortion and an attempt to commit the same, and (b) bribe receiving by a labor official as defined in section 180.20, and bribe receiving as defined in section 200.05, are not mutually exclusive, and it is no defense to a prosecution for larceny committed by means of extortion or for an attempt to commit the same that, by reason of the same conduct, the defendant also committed one of such specified crimes of bribe receiving.

§ 155.15. Larceny; defenses.

1. In any prosecution for larceny committed by trespassory taking or embezzlement, it is an affirmative defense that the property was appropriated under a claim of right made in good faith.

2. In any prosecution for larceny by extortion committed by instilling in the victim a fear that he or another person would be charged with a crime, it is an affirmative defense that the defendant reasonably believed the threatened charge to be true and that his sole purpose was to compel or induce the victim to take reasonable action to make good the wrong which was the subject of such threatened charge.

ANNOTATIONS

Claim of right.—Though a good-faith claim of right negates larcenous intent in certain thefts, it does not negate the intent to commit robbery by a defendant who uses force to recover cash allegedly owed him. People v. Reid, 69 N.Y.2d 469, 515 N.Y.S.2d 750, 508 N.E.2d 661 (1987).

Burden of proof.—An assertion that payments were made in good faith by the defendant from a law firm's special trust account to those whom he believed to be creditors who had advanced funds for construction of a project is the obverse of the contention that the payments were made with the intent to deprive another of property and to appropriate it to a third person; to apply PL § 155.15 which places the burden of proof on the defendant to establish the defense, by a preponderance of the evidence, in consequence of Lien Law § 79-e(2) would be a constitutionally impermissible shift in the burden. People v. Chesler, 50 N.Y.2d 203, 428 N.Y.S.2d 639, 406 N.E.2d 455 (1980).

§ 155.20. Larceny; value of stolen property.

For the purposes of this title, the value of property shall be ascertained as follows:

1. Except as otherwise specified in this section, value means the market value of the property at the time and place of the crime, or if such cannot be satisfactorily ascertained, the cost of replacement of the property within a reasonable time after the crime.

2. Whether or not they have been issued or delivered, certain written instruments, not including those having a readily ascertainable market value such as some public and corporate bonds and securities, shall be evaluated as follows:

(a) The value of an instrument constituting an

evidence of debt, such as a check, draft or promissory note, shall be deemed the amount due or collectable thereon or thereby, such figure ordinarily being the face amount of the indebtedness less any portion thereof which has been satisfied.

(b) The value of a ticket or equivalent instrument which evidences a right to receive a transportation, entertainment or other service shall be deemed the price stated thereon, if any; and if no price is stated thereon the value shall be deemed the price of such ticket or equivalent instrument which the issuer charges the general public.

(c) The value of any other instrument which creates, releases, discharges or otherwise affects any valuable legal right, privilege or obligation shall be deemed the greatest amount of economic loss which the owner of the instrument might reasonably suffer by virtue of the loss of the instrument.

3. Where the property consists of gas, steam, water or electricity, which is provided for charge or compensation, the value shall be the value of the property stolen in any consecutive twelve-month period.

4. When the value of property cannot be satisfactorily ascertained pursuant to the standards set forth in subdivisions one and two of this section, its value shall be deemed to be an amount less than two hundred fifty dollars.

Amended by L. 1969, Ch. 115; L. 1978, Ch. 420.

ANNOTATIONS

Market value.—The market value of a stolen item is gauged by the price the thief would have had to pay had he purchased the stolen object. The price for which an item sells in a particular store is some evidence of its value when stolen from that store; however, such evidence is not conclusive. People v. Harold, 22 N.Y.2d 443, 293 N.Y.S.2d 96, 239 N.E.2d 727 (1968).

—Market value or replacement cost, not the original cost of stolen property is required to sustain conviction. People v. Van Etten, 94 A.D.2d 953, 464 N.Y.S.2d 77 (4th Dept. 1983).

Proof of value.—An unsupported statement of value by an owner is not legally sufficient evidence on the issue of value; rather, a victim must provide a basis of knowledge for her statement of value. People v. Kirkwood, 200 A.D.2d 409, 606 N.Y.S.2d 612 (1st Dept. 1994).

—People, by presenting at trial only the complainant's testimony as to the value of a stolen television set which had been received as a gift three or four years before, failed to comply with the statutory requirement that in a larceny prosecution the People must prove either the market value or the cost of replacement within a reasonable time after the crime. People v. Moore, 114 A.D.2d 765, 495 N.Y.S.2d 34 (1st Dept. 1985).

—Jewelry store clerk's testimony as to the value, as reflected on the price tag, of the two gold chains that the defendant attempted to "purchase" with a stolen credit card was sufficient to prove the value of the items. People v. Solomon, 124 A.D.2d 840, 508 N.Y.S.2d 557 (2d Dept. 1986).

—Proof of market or replacement value of stolen property at the time and place of the crime must be established by the People. Defendant successfully argued that the value of stolen property was far less than the $3,000 required for a conviction for possession of stolen property in the third degree since the property would have been sold at discount outlets for half of its original price. Conviction reduced to criminal possession of stolen property in the third degree. People v. Holley, 237 A.D.2d 642, 654 N.Y.S.2d 462 (3d Dept. 1997).

—Evidence was not insufficient to support conviction of grand larceny in the third degree because people did not establish value of property at more than $3,000; record contained sufficient proof that defendant took property worth more than $3,000 from supermarket, as verified by market's head bookkeeper. People v. Hill, 217 A.D.2d 803, 629 N.Y.S.2d 544 (3d Dept. 1995).

—Defendant was improperly convicted of grand larceny for failing to report pension benefits while receiving public assistance because the prosecution failed to prove what amount of public assistance benefits she would have been entitled to, if any, had her pension income been reported. People v. Bently, 106 A.D.2d 825, 484 N.Y.S.2d 222 (3d Dept. 1984).

—"In the absence of legally sufficient proof of the value of the [stolen] van, its value shall be deemed less than $250." People v. Smith, 289 A.D.2d 1056, 735 N.Y.S.2d 693 (4th Dept. 2001).

Evidence.—Before a defendant could be convicted of grand larceny second degree, under the former Penal Law for stealing a pump purchased for over $100 five days after its owner purchased it and after it had been damaged, there had to be evidence of the effect of the damage on the pump's value, and the trial court had to consider that the pump was not new when it was stolen. People v. Harold, 22 N.Y.2d 443, 293 N.Y.S.2d 96, 239 N.E.2d 727 (1968).

—At the trial it was not incumbent upon the people to produce the tag and the sensormatic device and the jacket from which they were taken; the oral testimony of the people's witnesses was adequate to convince the trier of the fact of their version of the incident. People v. Gasparik, 102 A.D.2d 487, 425 N.Y.S.2d 936 (1st Dept. 1980), aff'd, 52 N.Y.2d 309, 438 N.Y.S.2d 242, 420 N.E.2d 40 (1981).

—Proof of value of property stolen must be proved by legally sufficient evidence. People v. Archer, 236 A.D.2d 478, 654 N.Y.S.2d 591 (2d Dept. 1997).

—Under certain circumstances an owner is considered competent to testify respecting the value of property. People v. Funchess, 137 A.D.2d 831, 525 N.Y.S.2d 293 (2d Dept. 1988).

—Legally sufficiency of value is not supplied by the opinion testimony of a victim who is not qualified to testify as an expert. People v. Stein, 172 A.D.2d 1060, 569 N.Y.S.2d 552 (4th Dept. 1991).

—Court erred in admitting two store receipts as evidence of the value of a stolen VCR and television; since no foundation was laid by a qualified custodian to establish that these receipts were made in the ordinary course of business, the evidence constituted inadmissible hearsay. People v. Teague, 145 A.D.2d 911, 536 N.Y.S.2d 293 (4th Dept. 1988).

Lesser included offense.—Even in the absence of proof of the value of the property stolen the defendant can be convicted of the lesser included offense of petit larceny if the evidence supports such a conviction. People v. Clark, 91 A.D.2d 1102, 458 N.Y.S.2d 360 (3d Dept. 1983).

§ 155.25. Petit larceny.

A person is guilty of petit larceny when he steals property.

Petit larceny is a class A misdemeanor.

ANNOTATIONS

Generally.—A person is guilty of petit larceny when he steals property; a person steals property when he wrongfully takes, obtains or withholds property from its owner with intent to deprive the owner of the property or to appropriate the property to himself or a third person. People v. Jensen, 86 N.Y.2d 248, 630 N.Y.S.2d 989, 654 N.E.2d 1237 (1995).

—Defendant cannot be charged with criminal mischief in the fourth degree or petit larceny for stealing or damaging property in which he has an equitable interest. People v. Person, 239 A.D.2d 612, 658 N.Y.S.2d 372 (2d Dept. 1997).

Lesser included offense.—Court properly declined to charge petit larceny as a lesser included offense of grand larceny in the fourth degree where no reasonable view of the evidence supported defendant's interpretation that defendant did not steal victim's wallet, but instead only acquired lost property after victim's wallet fell out of his pocket. People v. Washington, 21 A.D.3d 253, 799 N.Y.S.2d 217 (1st Dept. 2005).

—Although there was insufficient proof to support the charge of grand larceny, the fact that there was sufficient proof to support the lesser included offense of petit larceny precluded the court from issuing a trial order of dismissal. People v. Johnson, 76 A.D.2d 983, 429 N.Y.S.2d 281 (3d Dept. 1980).

Grand larceny distinguished.—Defendant, who purchased a television set by issuing check drawn on an account which he knew contained no funds, was guilty of petit larceny, and not third degree grand larceny (which requires proof of value in excess of $250) since the selling price of the item was less than $250, notwithstanding that defendant's check, which included sales tax, was drawn for an amount in excess of $250; the "market value" of an item is its selling price, exclusive of any statute or local sales taxes. People v. Barbuto, 106 Misc. 2d 542, 434 N.Y.S.2d 120 (Sup. Ct. Suffolk Co. 1980).

§ 155.30. Grand larceny in the fourth degree.

A person is guilty of grand larceny in the fourth degree when he steals property and when:

1. The value of the property exceeds one thousand dollars; or

2. The property consists of a public record, writing or instrument kept, filed or deposited according to law with or in the keeping of any public office or public servant; or

3. The property consists of secret scientific material; or

4. The property consists of a credit card or debit card; or

5. The property, regardless of its nature and value, is taken from the person of another; or

6. The property, regardless of its nature and value, is obtained by extortion; or

7. The property consists of one or more firearms, rifles or shotguns, as such terms are defined in section 265.00 of this chapter; or

8. The value of the property exceeds one hundred dollars and the property consists of a motor vehicle, as defined in section one hundred twenty-five of the vehicle and traffic law, other than a motorcycle, as defined in section one hundred twenty-three of such law; or

9. The property consists of a scroll, religious vestment, vessel or other item of property having a value of at least one hundred dollars kept for or used in connection with religious worship in any building or structure used as a place of religious worship by a religious corporation, as incorporated under the religious corporations law or the education law.

10. The property consists of an access device which the person intends to use unlawfully to obtain telephone service.

11. The property consists of anhydrous ammonia or liquified ammonia gas and the actor intends to use, or knows another person intends to use, such anhydrous ammonia or liquified ammonia gas to manufacture methamphetamine.

Grand larceny in the fourth degree is a class E felony.

Amended by L. 1967, Ch. 791; L. 1969, Chs. 115, 352; L.

1982, Ch. 234; L. 1986, Ch. 515; L. 1987, Ch. 556; L. 1990, Ch. 450; L. 1992, Ch. 491, eff. Nov. 1, 1992, adding subd. 10; L. 2005, Ch. 394, § 1, adding subd. 11, eff. Oct. 1, 2005.

ANNOTATIONS

Amendment to accusatory instrument.—Where there has been an incomplete amendment to the accusatory instrument charging defendant with the crime of attempted grand larceny in the third degree, but containing a factual portion which described attempted grand larceny in the fourth degree, the factual portion of the accusatory instrument controls. Therefore, defendant could not have been convicted of the greater crime of attempted grand larceny in the third degree. People v. Duran, 238 A.D.2d 351, 656 N.Y.S.2d 56 (2d Dept. 1997).

Application of amendment increasing value of property stolen.—The amendment to Penal Law § 155.30(1), increasing the minimum value of the property stolen required for the crime of grand larceny, third degree, is an ameliorative change which should be applied retroactively to a defendant who had not yet been sentenced at the time of the amendment's effective date. People v. Behlog, 74 N.Y.2d 237, 544 N.Y.S.2d 804, 543 N.E.2d 69 (1989).

—Judgment modified by reducing defendant's conviction of grand larceny in the second degree to grand larceny in the fourth degree where jury was charged to render a guilty verdict if it found that defendant stole money in excess of $1,500; defendant was entitled to benefit of amendment to PL § 155.40 increasing minimum value of property required for second degree of crime to $50,000. People v. Quinney, 213 A.D.2d 1069, 625 N.Y.S.2d 984 (4th Dept), *cert. denied,* 516 U.S. 1030 (1995).

—The defendant is entitled to the benefit of the ameliorative amendment of the larceny statute and his grand larceny conviction must be reduced to petit larceny. People v. Davis, 166 A.D.2d 928, 560 N.Y.S.2d 580 (4th Dept. 1990).

Charge.—It was reversible error in a trial on a charge of attempted larceny in the third degree for the court to charge the jury that the value of the property was irrelevant in that the law requires that the property be valued in excess of $250 to support such charge. People v. Stack, 60 N.Y.2d 771 469 N.Y.S.2d 673, 457 N.E.2d 779 (1983).

Lesser included offense.—It is impossible to commit robbery without also committing grand larceny, third degree, pursuant to PL § 155.30(5), and the larceny in these instances is a lesser included offense of the robbery. People v. Acevedo, 40 N.Y.2d 701, 389 N.Y.S.2d 811, 358 N.E.2d 495 (1976).

—Court properly declined to charge petit larceny as a lesser included offense of grand larceny in the fourth degree where no reasonable view of the evidence supported defendant's interpretation that defendant did not steal victim's wallet, but instead only acquired lost property after the victim's wallet fell out of his pocket. People v. Washington, 21 A.D.3d 253, 799 N.Y.S.2d 217 (1st Dept. 2005).

—Defendant's request to submit "grand larceny from the person" to the jury did not constitute a request to submit also a charge of petit larceny as a lesser included offense, since no evidence received at trial could view the offense as a "nonforcible taking." People v. Collins, 255 A.D.2d 120, 678 N.Y.S.2d 897 (1st Dept. 1998).

—Grand larceny in the fourth degree "from the person of another" is not a lesser included offense of grand larceny in the third degree. People v. Reynolds, 240 A.D.2d 210, 658 N.Y.S.2d 596 (1st Dept. 1997).

—It was proper for the court to refuse to charge the jury on petit larceny as a lesser included offense of grand larceny, third degree, where the jury, in analyzing the evidence, could have found either that the money was taken from the wallet on the person of the police decoy thus constituting the crime of grand larceny, third degree, or that as defendant claimed, he found the money on the subway step, which action would not constitute a crime. People v. Salters, 75 A.D.2d 901, 428 N.Y.S.2d 293 (2d Dept. 1980), *aff'd,* 52 N.Y.2d 1061, 438 N.Y.S.2d 520, 420 N.E.2d 401 (1981).

—PL § 155.30(8) is *not* a lesser included offense of PL § 155.35, because it is possible to steal property, other than a motor vehicle, worth more than $ 3,000 without also committing the crime of grand larceny in the fourth degree under section 155.30. People v. Williams, 295 A.D.2d 968, 743 N.Y.S.2d 353 (4th Dept. 2002).

—Criminal possession of stolen property in the second degree is not a lesser included offense of grand larceny in the third degree. People v. Robinson, 90 A.D.2d 249, 457 N.Y.S.2d 347 (4th Dept. 1982), aff'd, 60 N.Y.2d 982, 471 N.Y.S.2d 258, 459 N.E.2d 483 (1983).

Evidence.—To sustain a conviction of grand larceny, third degree, in public assistance fraud cases, the prosecution must present proof establishing that the defendant received public assistance to which he was not entitled, together with showing that the specific value of this assistance was in excess of $ 250. People v. Hunter, 34 N.Y.2d 432, 358 N.Y.S.2d 360, 315 N.E.2d 436 (1974).

—Although it was error to receive into evidence, during the people's case-in-chief, that portion of the defendant's grand jury testimony in which he acknowledged a prior conviction, such portion of the transcript could have been redacted and the error avoided if defense counsel had brought this matter to the attention of the trial court by means of a specific objection; the absence of a specific objection to the introduction of the prior conviction prevented this court from reviewing the issue. People v. Rullo, 31 N.Y.2d 894, 340 N.Y.S.2d 405, 292 N.E.2d 674 (1972).

—There was no valid line of reasoning and permissible inferences from which a reasonable person could conclude that every element of fourth degree grand larceny was proved beyond a reasonable doubt. "The People introduced no direct evidence that established when or how defendant came into possession of the wallet, that he took it or knew that it had been taken from the complaining witness, or that the wallet indeed was stolen, rather than lost. The only circumstantial evidence of defendant's guilt was his possession of the wallet at the time of his arrest." People v, Moore, 291 A.D.2d 336, 738 N.Y.S.2d 332 (1st Dept. 2002).

—Testimony that defendant took the property of victim was legally sufficient to establish grand larceny in the fourth degree. People v. Evans, 232 A.D.2d 170, 648 N.Y.S.2d 11 (1st Dept. 1996).

Property stolen "from the person."—Evidence that defendant stole complainant's purse, which was hanging on the back of the chair in which she was seated, was sufficient to establish the "from the person" element of section 155.30(5). People v. Haynes, 91 N.Y.2d 966, 672 N.Y.S.2d 845, 695 N.E.2d 714 (1998).

—Where the shoulder bag was "more or less hanging" on the victim's back at the time of the theft, the billfold taken from the bag was stolen "from the person" of the victim. People v. Cunningham, 73 A.D.2d 976, 424 N.Y.S.2d 240 (2d Dept. 1980).

§ 155.35. Grand larceny in the third degree.

A person is guilty of grand larceny in the third degree when he steals property and when the value of the property exceeds three thousand dollars.

Grand larceny in the third degree is a class D felony.

Amended by L. 1986, Ch. 515.

ANNOTATIONS

Consistent counts.—Defendant's argument that he could not consistently be convicted of both grand larceny in the second degree and unauthorized use of a vehicle was rejected. People v. Kirnon, 31 N.Y.2d 877, 340 N.Y.S.2d 183, 292 N.E.2d 319 (1972).

Failure to pay out insurance proceeds.—The failure of an armored courier to pay out the full amount of insurance proceeds to two companies it was required to reimburse for funds stolen from its possession would constitute grand larceny in the second degree. People v. Jennings, 111 A.D.2d 678, 490 N.Y.S.2d 496 (1st Dept. 1985).

Evidence.—Although it was error to receive into evidence, during the people's case-in-chief, that portion of the defendant's grand jury testimony in which he acknowledged a prior conviction, such portion of the transcript could have been redacted and the error avoided if defense counsel had brought this matter

to the attention of the trial court by means of a specific objection; The absence of a specific objection to the introduction of the prior conviction prevented this court from reviewing the issue. People v. Rullo, 31 N.Y.2d 894, 340 N.Y.S.2d 405, 292 N.E.2d 674 (1972).

—The evidence was insufficient to establish the crime of grand larceny where it showed that the complainant lent money to the defendant to purchase a grocery store and the defendant did not purchase the store or repay the loan. People v. Duda, 79 A.D.2d 712, 434 N.Y.S.2d 255 (2d Dept. 1980).

—Evidence that defendant made misrepresentations to an insurance company in which he stated he had not worked in any capacity during the last six months to one year and received $34,000 in benefits, when in fact he had only stopped working at one of his two jobs during that time, was sufficient to support convictions for grand larceny in the third degree and insurance fraud in the third degree. People v. Hade, 255 A.D.2d 769, 682 N.Y.S.2d 468 (3d Dept. 1998).

—"The market value of property stolen from a consumer is the price of the item reduced for any depreciation or change in its condition which affected its value at the time of the crime." People failed to satisfy statutory threshold where victim testified as to the original purchase price and age of stolen items, he gave no substantive testimony as to the condition of these items at the time of the crime to enable the jury to reasonably infer, rather than merely speculate, that the value of the stolen goods exceeded the statutory threshold. People v. Vanderberg, 254 A.D.2d 532, 681 N.Y.S.2d 359 (3d Dept. 1998).

—Submitting false Medicaid claims provided basis for conviction. People v. Scotti, 232 A.D.2d 755, 649 N.Y.S.2d 55 (3d Dept. 1996).

Value.—Value of stolen property was properly established through testimony of owners as to cost and condition and introduction of items into evidence. People v. McGlotten, 278 A.D.2d 936, 718 N.Y.S.2d 770 (4th Dept. 2000), appeal denied, 96 N.Y.2d 761 (2001).

Extortion.—Extortion is a form of larceny under New York law; where respondent's demands for payment ranged in amount from $5,000 up to $400,000, the crime for which she was convicted was essentially similar to grand larceny in the second degree or grand larceny in the third degree. In re Walter, 207 A.D.2d 247, 621 N.Y.S.2d 691 (2d Dept. 1995).

Lesser included offense.—PL § 155.30(8) is not a lesser included offense of PL § 155.35, because it is possible to steal property, other than a motor vehicle, worth more than $ 3,000 without also committing the crime of grand larceny in the fourth degree under section 155.30. People v. Williams, 295 A.D.2d 968, 743 N.Y.S.2d 353 (4th Dept. 2002).

—Evidence that defendant promised two women, one of whom was an undercover officer, that he would make their DWI charges "disappear" in exchange for a fee and was paid fees by the undercover officer for both women at the same time and at the same place, a conviction under this section was supported; "where the larceny occurred at the same time and place and pursuant to a single intent and common plan, aggregation of the amount taken by defendant [is] permissible." People v. Bastian, 294 A.D.2d 882, 743 N.Y.S.2d 217 (4th Dept. 2002).

Sufficiency of indictment.—Where there has been incomplete amendment to the accusatory instrument charging defendant with the crime of attempted grand larceny in the third degree, but containing a factual portion which described attempted grand larceny in the fourth degree, the factual portion of the accusatory instrument controls. Therefore, defendant could not have been convicted of the greater crime of attempted grand larceny in the third degree. People v. Duran, 238 A.D.2d 351, 656 N.Y.S.2d 56 (2d Dept. 1997).

—Indictment charging police officer with offering false instrument for filing, attempted grand larceny and grand larceny and defrauding the government provided fair notice of the charges which were based on defendant's falsely claiming to be permanently disabled and of improperly collecting money from Nassau County. People v. Patino, 170 Misc. 2d 284, 648 N.Y.S.2d 241 (Nassau Co. Ct. 1996).

Value of property.—"In the absence of legally sufficient proof of the value of the [stolen] van, its value shall be deemed less than $250." People v. Smith, 289 A.D.2d 1056, 735 N.Y.S.2d 693 (4th Dept. 2001).

§ 155.40. Grand larceny in the second degree.

A person is guilty of grand larceny in the second degree when he steals property and when:

1. The value of the property exceeds fifty thousand dollars; or

2. The property, regardless of its nature and value, is obtained by extortion committed by instilling in the victim a fear that the actor or another person will (a) cause physical injury to some person in the future, or (b) cause damage to property, or (c) use or abuse his position as a public servant by engaging in conduct within or related to his official duties, or by failing or refusing to perform an official duty, in such manner as to affect some person adversely.

Grand larceny in the second degree is a class C felony.

Amended by L. 1986, Ch. 515.

ANNOTATIONS

Possession of stolen goods.—A person may not be convicted of burglary and larceny merely because he has exclusive and recent possession of stolen goods, unless such possession is unexplained. People v. Cefaro, 21 N.Y.2d 252, 287 N.Y.S.2d 371, 234 N.E.2d 423 (1967), *modified,* 23 N.Y.2d 283, 296 N.Y.S.2d 345, 244 N.E.2d 42 (1968).

Receiving stolen property.—Larceny and receiving stolen property are mutually exclusive crimes. People v. Cefaro, 21 N.Y.2d 252, 287 N.Y.S.2d 371, 234 N.E.2d 423 (1967), *modified,* 23 N.Y.2d 283, 296 N.Y.S.2d 345, 244 N.E.2d 42 (1968).

Evidence.—Jury verdict finding defendants guilty of grand larceny in the second degree and offering a false instrument for filing but which acquitted defendants on charges of violating Tax Law § 1817(b)(1) was not repugnant where People established that, as a result of underreporting sales, defendants collected $200,000 in sales tax which was not remitted. Jury could have found that defendants offered the false returns for filing but did not "make and subscribe" them. People v. Filacouris, 95 N.Y.2d 940, 722 N.Y.S.2d 459, 745 N.E.2d 378 (2000).

—The evidence of the defendant's guilt was so overwhelming that the alleged error in the admission of his co-defendant's confession was harmless beyond a reasonable doubt; furthermore, no exception was taken to the charge, and no request was made for any limiting instructions. People v. Walker, 31 N.Y.2d 970, 341 N.Y.S.2d 111, 293 N.E.2d 257 (1973).

—Evidence that through the use of forged documents and other fraudulent devices defendants inflated the cost of renovating a building over $50, 000 and obtained reimbursement in excess of their contractual entitlement was sufficient to support their conviction of grand larceny in the second degree. People v. Dicarlo, 293 A.D.2d 279, 741 N.Y.S.2d 508 (1st Dept. 2002).

—Evidence that defendant understood the public charge regulation and yet created schemes to conceal his violation of it by creating two separate price schedules—$12 per hour for public care, which was accurate and actually charged to the clients, and $15.25 per hour, which he reported to Medicaid officials—supported defendant's conviction for grand larceny in the second degree and six counts of offering a false instrument for filing in the first degree. People v. Rubin, 271 A.D.2d 759; 706 N.Y.S.2d 225 (3d Dept. 2000).

Entrapment defense.—The burden of proving entrapment is on the defendant; where defendants initiated extortion by phone call, subsequent use of bug by police and victim required defendants to show that they were enticed to commit a crime which they otherwise would not have committed. People v.

Laietta, 30 N.Y.2d 68, 330 N.Y.S.2d 351, 281 N.E.2d 157 (1972), *cert. denied,* 407 U.S. 923 (1972).

Essentially similar crimes.—Bank fraud, in violation of 18 U.S.C. § 1344, is "essentially similar" to the New York crime of grand larceny in the second degree. *In re* Kelly, 205 A.D.2d 56, 618 N.Y.S.2d 390 (2d Dept. 1994).

—The federal offense of mail fraud is "essentially similar" to grand larceny in the second degree. *In re* Sinker, 209 A.D.2d 85, 625 N.Y.S.2d 1083 (4th Dept. 1995).

§ 155.42. Grand larceny in the first degree.

A person is guilty of grand larceny in the first degree when he steals property and when the value of the property exceeds one million dollars.

Grand larceny in the first degree is a class B felony.

Added by L. 1986, Ch. 515.

ANNOTATION

Disbarment.—Respondent's admissions in plea allocution, when considered in conjunction with counts of the information, were sufficient to satisfy the elements of § 155.42; thus, they constituted a predicate for immediate disbarment under the Judiciary Law. *In re* Benson, 207 A.D.2d 81, 621 N.Y.S.2d 30 (1st Dept. 1995).

§ 155.45. Larceny; pleading and proof.

1. Where it is an element of the crime charged that property was taken from the person or obtained by extortion, an indictment for larceny must so specify. In all other cases, an indictment, information or complaint for larceny is sufficient if it alleges that the defendant stole property of the nature or value required for the commission of the crime charged without designating the particular way or manner in which such property was stolen or the particular theory of larceny involved.

2. Proof that the defendant engaged in any conduct constituting larceny as defined in section 155.05 is sufficient to support any indictment, information or complaint for larceny other than one charging larceny by extortion. An indictment charging larceny by extortion must be supported by proof establishing larceny by extortion.

ANNOTATIONS

Intent.—"[W]here intention to defraud is an essential element of the crime charged, . . . evidence competent to establish criminal intention is not a collateral matter with respect to cross-examination." People v. Schwartzman, 24 N.Y.2d 241, 299 N.Y.S.2d 817, 247 N.E.2d 642 (1969), *cert. denied,* 396 U.S. 846 (1970).

—A conviction of larceny requires that intent must be proven with respect to every element of the crime. People v. Ricchiuti, 93 A.D.2d 842, 461 N.Y.S.2d 67 (2d Dept. 1983).

Indictment.—Indictment which tracked language of statute was not defective; prosecution was not required to plead criminal intent or larceny by false pretenses. People v. Duffy, 231 A.D.2d 586, 647 N.Y.S.2d 275 (2d Dept. 1996).

—The people are not required to allege any particular "theory of larceny" in the indictment. People v. Pillich, 207 A.D.2d 1004, 617 N.Y.S.2d 607 (4th Dept. 1994).

ARTICLE 156—OFFENSES INVOLVING COMPUTERS; DEFINITION OF TERMS

LexisNexis Cross Reference

Criminal Defense Techniques, Vol. 4, Ch. 84, Computer Crime.

§ 156.00. Offenses involving computers; definition of terms.

The following definitions are applicable to this chapter except where different meanings are expressly specified:

1. "Computer" means a device or group of devices which, by manipulation of electronic, magnetic, optical or electrochemical impulses, pursuant to a computer program can automatically perform arithmetic, logical, storage or retrieval operations with or on computer data, and includes any connected or directly related device, equipment or facility which enables such computer to store, retrieve or communicate to or from a person, another computer or another device the results of computer operations, computer programs or computer data.

2. "Computer program" is property and means an ordered set of data representing coded instructions or statements that, when executed by computer, cause the computer to process data or direct the computer to perform one or more computer operations or both and may be in any form, including magnetic storage media, punched cards, or stored internally in the memory of the computer.

3. "Computer data" is property and means a representation of information, knowledge, facts, concepts or instructions which are being processed, or have been processed in a computer and may be in any form, including magnetic storage media, punched cards, or stored internally in the memory of the computer.

4. "Computer service" means any and all services provided by or through the facilities of any computer communication system allowing the input, output, examination, or transfer, of computer data or computer programs from one computer to another.

5. "Computer material" is property and means any computer data or computer program which:

(a) contains records of the medical history or medical treatment of an identified or readily identifiable individual or individuals. This term shall not apply to the gaining access to or duplication solely of the medical history or medical treatment records of a person by that person or by another specifically authorized by the person whose records are gained access to or duplicated; or

(b) contains records maintained by the state or any political subdivision thereof or any governmental instrumentality within the state which contains any information concerning a person, as defined in subdivision seven of section 10.00 of this chapter, which because of name, number. symbol, mark or other identifier, can be used to identify the person and which is otherwise prohibited by law from being disclosed. This term shall not apply to the gaining access to or duplication solely of records of a person by that person or by another specifically authorized by the person whose records are gained access to or duplicated; or

(c) is not and is not intended to be available to anyone other than the person or persons rightfully in possession thereof or selected persons having access thereto with his or their consent and which accords or may accord such rightful possessors an advantage over competitors or other persons who do not have knowledge or the benefit thereof.

6. "Uses a computer or computer service without authorization" means the use of a computer or computer service without the permission of, or in excess of the permission of, the owner or lessor or someone licensed or privileged by the owner or lessor after notice to that effect to the

user of the computer or computer service has been given by:

(a) giving actual notice in writing or orally to the user; or

(b) prominently posting written notice adjacent to the computer being utilized by the user; or

(c) a notice that is displayed on, printed out on or announced by the computer being utilized by the user. Proof that the computer is programmed to automatically display, print or announce such notice or a notice prohibiting copying, reproduction or duplication shall be presumptive evidence that such notice was displayed, printed or announced.

7. "Felony" as used in this article means any felony defined in the laws of this state or any offense defined in the laws of any other jurisdiction for which a sentence to a term of imprisonment in excess of one year is authorized in this state.

§ 156.05. Unauthorized use of a computer.

A person is guilty of unauthorized use of a computer when he knowingly uses or causes to be used a computer or computer service without authorization and the computer utilized is equipped or programmed with any device or coding system, a function of which is to prevent the unauthorized use of said computer or computer system.

Unauthorized use of a computer is a class A misdemeanor.

ANNOTATION

Unauthorized use.—Mere allegation that defendant gained access to computer without owner's authority is insufficient to establish a violation of P.L. § 156.05. People v. Angeles, 180 Misc. 2d 146, 687 N.Y.S.2d 884 (Crim. Ct. N.Y. Co. 1999).

§ 156.10. Computer trespass.

A person is guilty of computer trespass when he knowingly uses or causes to be used a computer or computer service without authorization and:

1. he does so with an intent to commit or attempt to commit or further the commission of any felony; or

2. he thereby knowingly gains access to computer material.

Computer trespass is a class E felony.

§ 156.20. Computer tampering in the fourth degree.

A person is guilty of computer tampering in the fourth degree when he uses or causes to be used a computer or computer service and having no right to do so he intentionally alters in any manner or destroys computer data or a computer program of another person.

Computer tampering in the fourth degree is a class A misdemeanor.

Amended by L. 1993, Ch. 89.

ANNOTATION

Elements.—Defendant "altered" programs within the meaning of Penal Law § 156.20 when he activated existing instructions that commanded the computers to shut down; defendant was guilty for he changed the instructions being received in the computers and thereby prevented the computers from performing their intended functions. People v. Versaggi, 83 N.Y.2d 123, 608 N.Y.S.2d 155, 629 N.E.2d 1034 (1994).

§ 156.25. Computer tampering in the third degree.

A person is guilty of computer tampering in the third degree when he commits the crime of computer tampering in the fourth degree and:

1. he does so with an intent to commit or attempt to commit or further the commission of any felony; or

2. he has been previously convicted of any crime under this article or subdivision eleven of section 165.15 of this chapter; or

3. he intentionally alters in any manner or destroys computer material; or

4. he intentionally alters in any manner or destroys computer data or a computer program so as to cause damages in an aggregate amount exceeding one thousand dollars.

Computer tampering in the third degree is a class E felony.

Amended by L. 1993, Ch. 89; L. 1997, Ch. 376, § 1, eff. Nov. 1, 1997.

§ 156.26. Computer tampering in the second degree.

A person is guilty of computer tampering in the second degree when he commits the crime of computer tampering in the fourth degree and he intentionally alters in any manner or destroys computer data or a computer program so as to cause damages in an aggregate amount exceeding three thousand dollars.

Computer tampering in the second degree is a class D felony.

Added by L. 1993, Ch. 89.

§ 156.27. Computer tampering in the first degree.

A person is guilty of computer tampering in the first degree when he commits the crime of computer tampering in the fourth degree and he intentionally alters in any manner or destroys computer data or a computer program so as to cause damages in an aggregate amount exceeding fifty thousand dollars.

Computer tampering in the first degree is a class C felony.

Added by L. 1993, Ch. 89.

§ 156.30. Unlawful duplication of computer related material.

A person is guilty of unlawful duplication of computer related material when having no right to do so, he copies, reproduces or duplicates in any manner:

1. any computer data or computer program and thereby intentionally and wrongfully deprives or appropriates from an owner thereof an economic value or benefit in excess of two thousand five hundred dollars; or

2. any computer data or computer program with an intent to commit or attempt to commit or further the commission of any felony.

Unlawful duplication of computer related material is a class E felony.

ANNOTATIONS

Evidence.—Taping of cellular computer data with the intention of furthering the "cloning" of cellular telephones constitutes offense of unlawful duplication of computer related material as well as criminal possession of computer related material. People v. Garcia, 170 Misc. 2d 543, 647 N.Y.S.2d 355 (Westchester Co. Ct. 1996).

Reproduced data.—Charge that defendant printed specific information through the computer system of another without the owner's authority is sufficient to satisfy the requirement that defendant "reproduced" data in question. People v. Angeles, 180 Misc. 2d 146, 687 N.Y.S.2d 884 (Crim. Ct. N.Y. Co. 1999).

§ 156.35. Criminal possession of computer related material.

A person is guilty of criminal possession of computer related material when having no right to do so, he knowingly possesses, in any form, any copy, reproduction or duplicate of any computer data or computer program which was copied, reproduced or duplicated in violation of section 156.30 of this article, with intent to benefit himself or a person other than an owner thereof.

Criminal possession of computer related material is a class E felony.

ANNOTATIONS

Evidence.—Criminal possession of stolen computer data with intent to benefit another person will satisfy requirements of P.L. § 156.35. People v. Angeles, 180 Misc. 2d 146, 687 N.Y.S.2d 884 (Crim. Ct. N.Y. Co. 1999).

—Taping of cellular computer data with the intention of furthering the "cloning" of cellular telephones constitutes offense of unlawful duplication of computer related material as well as criminal possession of computer related material. People v. Garcia, 170 Misc. 2d 543, 647 N.Y.S.2d 355 (Westchester Co. Ct. 1996).

§ 156.50. Offenses involving computers; defenses.

In any prosecution:

1. under section 156.05, 156.10, 156.25 or 156.27 of this article, it shall be a defense that the defendant had reasonable grounds to believe that he had authorization to use the computer;

2. under section 156.20 or 156.25 of this article it shall be a defense that the defendant had reasonable grounds to believe that he had the right to alter in any manner or destroy the computer data or the computer program;

3. under section 156.30 of this article it shall be a defense that the defendant had reasonable grounds to believe that he had the right to copy, reproduce or duplicate in any manner the computer data or the computer program.

Amended by L. 1993, Ch. 89.

ANNOTATION

Procedure.—CPL §250.10 requires a defendant to serve upon the people a notice of intention to invoke any of the defenses specified in §156.50. People v. Fulton, 162 Misc. 2d 360, 616 N.Y.S.2d 881 (Sup. Ct. Monroe Co. 1994).

ARTICLE 158—WELFARE FRAUD

Section

LexisNexis Cross Reference

Criminal Defense Techniques, Vol. 4, Ch. 85, Essentials for the Prosecution and Defense of Federal Program Fraud.

§ 158.00. Definitions; presumption; limitation.

1. Definitions. The following definitions are applicable to this article:

(a) "Public benefit card" means any medical assistance card, food stamp assistance card, public assistance card, or any other identification, authorization card or electronic access device issued by the state or a social services district, as defined in subdivision seven of section two of the social services law, which entitles a person to obtain public assistance benefits under a local, state, or federal program administered by the state, its political subdivisions, or social services districts.

(b) "Fraudulent welfare act" means knowingly and with intent to defraud, engaging in an act or acts pursuant to which a person:

(1) Offers, presents or causes to be presented to the state, any of its political subdivisions or social services districts, or any employee or agent thereof, an oral or written application or request for public assistance benefits or for a public benefit card with knowledge that the application or request contains a false statement or false information, and such statement or information is material, or

(2) Holds himself or herself out to be another person, whether real or fictitious, for the purpose of obtaining public assistance benefits, or

(3) Makes a false statement or provides false information for the purpose of (i) establishing or maintaining eligibility for public assistance benefits or (ii) increasing or preventing reduction of public assistance benefits, and such statement or information is material.

(c) "Public assistance benefits" means money, property or services provided directly or indirectly through programs of the federal government, the state government or the government of any political subdivision within the state and administered by the department of social services or social services districts.

2. Rebuttable presumption. (a) A person who possesses five or more public benefit cards in a name or names other than his or her own is presumed to possess the same with intent to defraud, deceive or injure another.

(b) The presumption established by this subdivision shall not apply to:

(1) Any employee or agent of the department of social services to the extent that he or she possesses such cards in the course of his or her official duties; or

(2) Any person to the extent that he she possesses a public benefit card or cards issued to a member or members of his or her immediate family or household with the consent of the cardholder; or

(3) Any person providing home health services or personal care services pursuant to title eleven of article five of the social services law, or any agent or employee of a congregate care or residential treatment facility or foster care provider, to the extent that in the course of his or her duties, he or she possesses public assistance cards issued to persons under his or her care.

(c) The presumption established by this subdivision is rebuttable by evidence tending to show that the defendant did not possess such public benefit card or cards with intent to defraud, deceive or injure another. In any action tried before a jury, the jury shall be so instructed.

(d) The foregoing presumption shall apply to

prosecutions for criminal possession of public benefit cards.

3. Limitation. Nothing contained in this article shall be construed to prohibit a recipient of public assistance benefits from pledging his or her public assistance benefits or using his or her public benefit card as collateral for a loan.

Added by L. 1995, Ch. 81, § 168, eff. Nov. 1, 1995.

§ 158.05. Welfare fraud in the fifth degree.

A person is guilty of welfare fraud in the fifth degree when he or she commits a fraudulent welfare act and thereby takes or obtains public assistance benefits.

Welfare fraud in the fifth degree is a class A misdemeanor.

Added by L. 1995, Ch. 81, § 168, eff. Nov. 1, 1995.

§ 158.10. Welfare fraud in the fourth degree.

A person is guilty of welfare fraud in the fourth degree when he or she commits a fraudulent welfare act and thereby takes or obtains public assistance benefits, and when the value of the public assistance benefits exceeds one thousand dollars.

Welfare fraud in the fourth degree is a class E felony.

Added by L. 1995, Ch. 81, § 168, eff. Nov. 1, 1995.

§ 158.15. Welfare fraud in the third degree.

A person is guilty of welfare fraud in the third degree when he or she commits a fraudulent welfare act and thereby takes or obtains public assistance benefits, and when the value of the public assistance benefits exceeds three thousand dollars.

Welfare fraud in the third degree is a class D felony.

Added by L. 1995, Ch. 81, § 168, eff. Nov. 1, 1995.

§ 158.20. Welfare fraud in the second degree.

A person is guilty of welfare fraud in the second degree when he or she commits a fraudulent welfare act and thereby takes or obtains public assistance benefits, and when the value of the public assistance benefits exceeds fifty thousand dollars.

Welfare fraud in the second degree is a class C felony.

Added by L. 1995, Ch. 81, § 168, eff. Nov. 1, 1995.

§ 158.25. Welfare fraud in the first degree.

A person is guilty of welfare fraud in the first degree when he or she commits a fraudulent welfare act and thereby takes or obtains public assistance benefits, and when the value of the public assistance benefits exceeds one million dollars.

Welfare fraud in the first degree is a class B felony.

Added by L. 1995, Ch. 81, § 168, eff. Nov. 1, 1995.

§ 158.30. Criminal use of a public benefit card in the second degree.

A person is guilty of criminal use of a public benefit card in the second degree when he or she knowingly:

1. Loans money or otherwise provides property or services on credit, and accepts a public benefit card as collateral or security for the repayment of such loan or for the provision of such property or services;

2. Obtains a public benefit card in exchange for a benefit; or

3. Transfers or delivers a public benefit card to another (a) In exchange for money or a controlled substance as defined in subdivision five of section 220.00, or (b) For the purpose of committing an unlawful act.

Criminal use of a public benefit card in the second degree is a class A misdemeanor.

Added by L. 1995, Ch. 81, § 168, eff. Nov. 1, 1995.

§ 158.35. Criminal use of a public benefit card in the first degree.

A person is guilty of criminal use of a public benefit card in the first degree when he or she, pursuant to an act or a series of acts, knowingly (i) obtains three or more public benefit cards from another or others in exchange for a benefit, or (ii) transfers or delivers three or more public benefit cards to another or others in exchange for money or a controlled substance as defined in subdivision five of section 220.00 of this chapter.

Criminal use of a public benefit card in the first degree is a class E felony.

Added by L. 1995, Ch. 81, § 168, eff. Nov. 1, 1995.

§ 158.40. Criminal possession of public benefit cards in the third degree.

A person is guilty of criminal possession of public benefit cards in the third degree when he or she with intent to defraud, deceive or injure another, knowingly possesses five or more public benefit cards in a name or names other than the person's own name.

Criminal possession of public benefit cards in the third degree is a class E felony.

Added by L. 1995, Ch. 81, § 168, eff. Nov. 1, 1995.

§ 158.45. Criminal possession of public benefit cards in the second degree.

A person is guilty of criminal possession of public benefit cards in the second degree when he or she with intent to defraud, deceive or injure another, knowingly possesses ten or more public benefit cards in a name or names other than the person's own name.

Criminal possession of public benefit cards in the second degree is a class D felony.

Added by L. 1995, Ch. 81, § 168, eff. Nov. 1, 1995.

§ 158.50. Criminal possession of public benefit cards in the first degree.

A person is guilty of criminal possession of public benefit cards in the first degree when he or she with intent to defraud, deceive or injure another, knowingly possesses twenty-five or more public benefit cards in a name or names other than the person's own name.

Criminal possession of public benefit cards in the first degree is a class C felony.

Added by L. 1995, Ch. 81, § 168, eff. Nov. 1, 1995.

PL

ARTICLE 160—ROBBERY

Section
  160.00 Robbery; defined.
  160.05 Robbery in the third degree.
  160.10 Robbery in the second degree.
  160.15 Robbery in the first degree.

LexisNexis Cross References

New York Criminal Practice (2d ed.), Vol. 6, Ch. 65, Robbery; *Police Investigation Handbook,* Ch. 28, Robbery Investigations.

§ 160.00. Robbery; defined.

Robbery is forcible stealing. A person forcibly steals property and commits robbery when, in the course of committing a larceny, he uses or threatens the immediate use of physical force upon another person for the purpose of:

1. Preventing or overcoming resistance to the taking of the property or to the retention thereof immediately after the taking; or

2. Compelling the owner of such property or another person to deliver up the property or to engage in other conduct which aids in the commission of the larceny.

ANNOTATIONS

Elements.—The particular nature of the property stolen is not, by statute, a material element of the crime of robbery; trial court could correctly charge jury that they could find defendant guilty of robbery even if they found that defendant had stolen illegal drugs from complainant instead of the "money or jewelry" specified in the indictment, where the nature of the crime and the underlying facts of victim, time, place, and date were the same. People v. Spann, 56 N.Y.2d 469, 452 N.Y.S.2d 869, 438 N.E.2d 402 (1982).

—In order to sustain a charge of robbery, the People must show not only the taking of property, but that the taking was accomplished by means of the use or threatened immediate use of physical force. People v. Woods, 41 N.Y.2d 279, 392 N.Y.S.2d 400, 360 N.E.2d 1082 (1977).

—Evidence supported jury's view that defendant was not just running from store, "but was attempting to prevent a store employee from recovering the stolen goods that defendant had secreted in his jacket." People v. Williams, 12 A.D.3d 317, 784 N.Y.S.2d 867 (1st Dept. 2004).

—It was not necessary for defendant to have actual, physical possession of complainant's property at the time he threatened the immediate use of physical force, especially given that he demonstrated his continued dominion of the change purse by offering to return it in exchange for dropping charges against him. People v. Smith, 233 A.D.2d 124, 649 N.Y.S.2d 418 (1st Dept. 1996).

—Robbery conviction was affirmed where forcible taking was established by victim's testimony that defendant grabbed her, scratching her neck, and demanded money in the course of crime, and photographs of injuries taken after crime were submitted at trial. People v. Reyes, 15 A.D.3d 505, 790 N.Y.S.2d 492 (2d Dept. 2005).

—The particular nature of the property stolen during the commission of a robbery is not by statute a material element of that crime. People v. Clark, 159 A.D.2d 629, 553 N.Y.S.2d 27 (2d Dept. 1990).

Force.—Defendant's possession of stolen property while engaged in the use of force to defeat a security guard's efforts to recover the property entitled the jury to infer that his purpose

in use of force was to retain control over the stolen property. People v. Brandley, 254 A.D.2d 185, 680 N.Y.S.2d 212 (1st Dept. 1998).

—Where defendant engaged in a tug of war with victim over items stolen, threatened to kill victim, and physically prevented victim from calling police, the use of force to overcome victim's resisting to taking was clearly established. People v. Ross, 251 A.D.2d 235, 675 N.Y.S.2d 342 (1st Dept. 1998).

—Crime of robbery did not occur when defendant slapped complainant and defendant's companion snatched radio which belonged to the defendant and which had been found by the complainant. In re Monroe, 157 A.D.2d 608, 550 N.Y.S.2d 626 (1st Dept. 1990).

—Defendant's threat to use the knife was a threat of "the immediate use of physical force" so shortly after the taking as to constitute the use of physical force "immediately after the taking" to overcome the victim's resistance to the defendant's retention of the property. People v. Dekle, 83 A.D.2d 522, 441 N.Y.S.2d 261 (1st Dept. 1981), aff'd, 56 N.Y.2d 835, 452 N.Y.S.2d 568, 438 N.E.2d 101 (1982).

—Evidence insufficient to sustain conviction for robbery in the second degree where People did not establish that defendant used or threatened the immediate use of force in taking or retaining the property. People v. Lowery, 203 A.D.2d 893, 680 N.Y.S.2d 253 (2d Dept. 1998).

—Evidence was sufficient for robbery in the third degree where victim testified she suffered pain in her neck and suffered a scratch when defendant ripped two chains from around her neck, one of the chains broke in two, and defendant was found with the chains in his possession. People v. Dixon, 232 A.D.2d 653, 648 N.Y.S.2d 1009 (2d Dept. 1996).

—Evidence was legally sufficient to show that defendant forcibly stole property where it was established that defendant grabbed, twisted, and pulled the complainant; the defendant used physical force to prevent the complainant's resistance or compel the complainant to turn over property or engage in conduct aiding in the commission of a larceny. People v. Johnson, 215 A.D.2d 590, 626 N.Y.S.2d 567 (2d Dept. 1995).

—It is the rule in New York that a purse snatching unaccompanied by any resistance does not constitute a robbery; where there was no evidence adduced at purse snatching trial to show aggravating factors such as defendant's knocking down, striking, injuring, or intimidating the complainant, the prosecution failed to prove the element of force and the defendant's robbery conviction had to be dismissed. People v. Middleton, 212 A.D.2d 809, 623 N.Y.S.2d 298 (2d Dept. 1995).

Taking of property.—Defendant's conviction was sustained where the jury found that his taking of the property was a continuous act where he removed the item from the showcase, removed its price tag in the adjacent department, and removed it from the store. People v. Dekle, 83 A.D.2d 522, 441 N.Y.S.2d 261 (1st Dept. 1981), aff'd, 56 N.Y.2d 835, 452 N.Y.S.2d 568, 438 N.E.2d 101 (1982).

Merger.—Where a robbery was fully consummated before the victim was forced, at gunpoint, to embark on an hour-long drive, two separate crimes were committed: first, robbery and then, unlawful imprisonment; the criminal conduct at the root of the two crimes was different, and the merger doctrine, even if available, could have no application. People v. Smith, 46 N.Y.2d 83, 416 N.Y.S.2d 784, 390 N.E.2d 291 (1979).

Immediate use of force.—Where roobery victim awoke minutes after his property had been taken and demanded its return, at which time co-defendant used the threat of force to retain the property, the element of immediacy was satisfied. People v. Carr-El, 99 N.Y.2d 546, 754 N.Y.S.2d 198, 784 N.E.2d 71 (2002).

—Defendant was properly adjudicated a second felony offender based upon a prior Texas robbery conviction; the use of the word "imminent" in the Texas statute was equivalent to the use of the word "immediate" in the New York statute. People v. Moore, 213 A.D.2d 242, 624 N.Y.S.2d 19 (1st Dept. 1994).

—Statement "do as I tell you and you won't get hurt," involved threat of "immediate use of physical force." People v. Vidal, 231 A.D.2d 655, 648 N.Y.S.2d 109 (2d Dept. 1996).

—Court rejects argument that the threatened use of force was not sufficiently proximate in time to the taking to constitute threatening the immediate use of physical force upon another "immediately after the taking." People v. Wiley, 213 A.D.2d 1075, 625 N.Y.S.2d 987 (4th Dept. 1995).

Resistance; use of deadly force.—Whether a person may legally use deadly force to resist a robbery attempt depends upon whether, under the circumstances known to that person, he reasonably believed that the robber was about to use immediate physical force to compel the surrender of property, and that the use of deadly force was necessary to avert the robbery. People v. Wang, 164 Misc. 2d 707, 625 N.Y.S.2d 413 (Sup. Ct. N.Y. Co. 1995).

§ 160.05. Robbery in the third degree.

A person is guilty of robbery in the third degree when he forcibly steals property.

Robbery in the third degree is a class D felony.

ANNOTATIONS

Elements.—Robbery could not have occurred unless, as an essential element of the crime, there had been a larceny in some degree. People v. Carbonell, 40 N.Y.2d 948, 390 N.Y.S.2d 409, 358 N.E.2d 1034 (1976).

Evidence.—Evidence which showed that respondent, acting in concert with another, attempted to forcibly steal property from another using gestures and threatening the use of a gun, and that he caused the complainant to fear serious physical injury or death, established that respondent committed acts which, if committed by an adult, would constitute attempted robbery in the third degree. In re William A., 219 A.D.2d 494, 631 N.Y.S.2d 314 (1st Dept. 1995).

—Where there was insufficient evidence presented to establish that defendant caused a physical injury to another, robbery in the second degree was properly reduced to robbery in the third degree, which requires no proof of physical injury. People v. Sanders, 245 A.D.2d 472, 666 N.Y.S.2d 465 (2d Dept. 1997).

—Evidence was sufficient for robbery in the third degree where victim testified she suffered pain in her neck and suffered a scratch when defendant ripped two chains from around her neck, one of the chains broke in two, and defendant was found with the chains in his possession. People v. Dixon, 232 A.D.2d 653, 648 N.Y.S.2d 1009 (2d Dept. 1996).

—Evidence at trial supported jury's view that defendant used force to retain physical control over stolen property, not to defend himself or to leave, record reflected defendant struggled with the store's loss prevention officer and threatened to cut him if officer did not let him go. People v. Jones, 4 A.D.3d 622, 771 N.Y.S.2d 613 (3d Dept. 2004).

—Failure to request a charge on the affirmative defense that gun was inoperable waived the argument on appeal that trial court erred in failing to charge jury on that defense. People v. Fair, 254 A.D.2d 768, 678 N.Y.S.2d 759 (4th Dept. 1998).

Lesser included offense.—In the absence of proof that a firearm was displayed, the defendant could only be convicted of attempted robbery in the third degree, conviction for robbery in the first degree reduced. People v. Martin, 7 A.D.3d 640, 776 N.Y.S.2d 499 (2d Dept. 2004).

Prima facie case.—Juvenile delinquency petition established a prima facie case of robbery as the allegations contained therein established each element of the crime; the complainant stated during deposition that the respondent not only blocked her

escape while others took her property, but also that he demanded that she surrender property and such actions are sufficient to establish "in-concert" liability for robbery. In re Eric R., 213 A.D.2d 310, 624 N.Y.S.2d 164 (1st Dept. 1995).

Right to speedy trial.—A delay of 51 months in bringing defendant to trial after filing of felony information in prosecution for robbery in first degree was a denial of defendant's right to a speedy trial; defendant's "waiver" of right to speedy trial by accepting the district attorney's offer to allow him to plead guilty to robbery in the third degree rather than be tried for robbery in the first degree, which was conditioned on the fact that defendant accept offer before a decision was rendered on his motion to dismiss for failure to afford a speedy trial, was product of coercion. People v. White, 32 N.Y.2d 393, 345 N.Y.S.2d 513, 298 N.E.2d 659 (1973).

Analogous crimes.—Defendant was properly adjudicated a second felony offender based upon a prior Texas conviction for robbery; the Texas statute's use of the word "imminent" was equivalent to the New York statute's use of the word "immediate." The crime was analogous at least to robbery in the third degree. People v. Moore, 213 A.D.2d 242, 624 N.Y.S.2d 19 (1st Dept. 1995).

§ 160.10. Robbery in the second degree.

A person is guilty of robbery in the second degree when he forcibly steals property and when:

1. He is aided by another person actually present; or

2. In the course of the commission of the crime or of immediate flight therefrom, he or another participant in the crime:

(a) Causes physical injury to any person who is not a participant in the crime; or

(b) Displays what appears to be a pistol, revolver, rifle, shotgun, machine gun or other firearm; or

3. The property consists of a motor vehicle, as defined in section one hundred twenty-five of the vehicle and traffic law.

Robbery in the second degree is a class C felony.

Amended by L. 1969, Ch. 1012; L. 1973, Ch. 374; L. 1995, Ch. 308, § 1, amending subd. 2(b) and adding subd. 3.

ANNOTATIONS

Elements.—The proof of "aid" and "actual presence" of an associate under PL § 160.10 are not identical with elements that must be proved under PL § 160.15. People v. Acevedo 40 N.Y.2d 701, 389 N.Y.S.2d 811, 358 N.E.2d 495 (1976).

—Complainant's injuries sustained during the course of the robbery, when he was pushed down by co-defendant trying to help defendant escape, supported charge of robbery in the second degree; the injury to the complainant was something that defendant should have reasonably foreseen as a result of his actions. People v. Brown, 235 A.D.2d 303, 653 N.Y.S.2d 301 (1st Dept. 1997).

—A defendant who conceals his hand in such a manner as to give the impression he has a gun even though he does not is guilty of robbery second degree. People v. Knowles, 79 A.D.2d 116, 436 N.Y.S.2d 25 (2d Dept. 1981).

—Element of being "aided by another person actually present" was established; testimony of eyewitness stated that co-defendant approached victim, who was walking with two friends, and asked for money and when victim refused, co-defendant pointed object toward victim and pushed him into doorway, where he searched victim's pockets and grabbed wallet, and while that occurred, defendant restrained victim's friends, saying, "it will be over soon," and co-defendant and defendant then fled. People v. Cyrus, 18 A.D.3d 1020, 794 N.Y.S.2d 755 (3d Dept. 2005).

Sentence.—Defendant's contention that the court abused its discretion by sentencing him to an indeterminate term of imprisonment rather than certifying him to the care and custody of the Narcotic Addiction Control Commission was not allowed. People v. Fowler, 31 N.Y.2d 806, 339 N.Y.S.2d 460, 291 N.E.2d 584 (1972).

Evidence.—Evidence established that defendant was "aided by another person actually present" where defendant and another unidentified co-defendant took up a position about ten feet away from where a second co-defendant was robbing complainant, visible and ready to lend assistance if the other co-defendant required. People v. Stokes, 278 A.D.2d 18, 716 N.Y.S.2d 666 (1st Dept. 2000), *appeal denied*, 96 N.Y.2d 763 (2001).

—Defendant's removal of victim's wallet from his person completed the crime;it was of no import that the victim immediately grabbed it back. People v. Jones, 265 A.D.2d 159, 696 N.Y.S.2d 38 (1st Dept. 1999).

—Evidence that defendant and another surrounded victim while on subway platform, tore at his clothes, while they took his property, then punched and kicked him resulting in his fall to the platform, subsequent bruises, pain and dizziness which lasted for a month, all supported conviction of robbery in the second degree. People v. Simmons, 265 A.D.2d 200, 697 N.Y.S.2d 251 (1st Dept. 1999), *appeal denied*, 94 N.Y.2d 885 (2000).

—Evidence that accomplice manned the get away car and drove the car towards the armed complainant to facilitate their escape was sufficient to establish that defendant was aided by another who was "actually present." People v. Sanders, 267 A.D.2d 171, 700 N.Y.S.2d 811 (1st Dept. 1999), *appeal denied*, 94 N.Y.2d 906 (2000).

—Co-defendant's actions before, during, and after crime supported finding that defendant was "aided by another person actually present." People v. Reynolds, 240 A.D.2d 210, 658 N.Y.S.2d 596 (1st Dept. 1997).

—Evidence established robbery in the second degree where defendant or co-defendant pushed victim into third man who punched victim in the mouth and took money from his pocket as two others stood by menacingly with the suggestion that they possessed weapons in their pockets and victim's lip bled a great deal and was swollen and painful for several days. People v. Spry, 232 A.D.2d 232, 648 N.Y.S.2d 86 (1st Dept. 1996).

—Evidence that defendant, acting in concert with co-defendant, smashed glass jewelry case, struggled with jewelry store proprietor, and used force against a uniformed police officer who attempted to prevent defendant's escape from jewelry store constituted overwhelming evidence of defendant's guilt of robbery in the second degree. People v. Culp, 211 A.D.2d 501, 621 N.Y.S.2d 334 (1st Dept. 1995).

—Evidence that defendant acted as a lookout while co-defendant slashed victim's pants with razor to steal his beeper and warned co-defendant of victim's return when he sought to get his property back supported defendant's conviction. People v. Carr-El, 287 A.D.2d 731, 732 N.Y.S.2d 256 (2d Dept. 2001).

—Robbery in the second degree established where appellant and two others approached victim, demanded his bicycle, and took it from him after beating him. *In re* Jemel T., 231 A.D.2d 730, 647 N.Y.S.2d 992 (2d Dept. 1996).

—Complainant's testimony that appellant was among group of youths who beat him and stole his money was sufficient to establish that appellant, acting in concert with other youths, committed acts which, if committed by an adult, would constitute, *inter alia* robbery in the second degree. *In re* Kawame C., 213 A.D.2d 634, 624 N.Y.S.2d 249 (2d Dept. 1995).

—Defendant's use of force to overcome store employee's efforts to regain property defendant had taken from the store established the "forcibly" element of the crime. People v. Tetreault, 12 A.D.3d 722, 783 N.Y.S.2d 433 (3d Dept. 2004).

—Evidence that while victim was pinned down by another while in the midst of a heated discussion, defendant ripped victim's chain off his neck, did not support conviction for robbery in the third degree, nothing in the record indicated that third person held the victim down so as to enable defendant to steal or that the third person even knew "that it was probable that his own assaultive conduct would prompt or assist defendant in committing his own crime against the victim." People v. Coleman, 5 A.D.3d 956, 773 N.Y.S.2d 747(3d Dept. 2004).

—Although defendant lawfully entered the apartment building in order to remove a boiler from the basement, while in the

building he unlawfully entered victim's apartment by breaking down victim's door and, while assaulting the victim, damaged victim's property; this was sufficient to support defendant's conviction for, inter alia, second degree robbery. People v. Zabala, 290 A.D.2d 578, 735 N.Y.S.2d 244 (3d Dept. 2002).

—Regardless of reason why co-defendant took money from victim, testimony that defendant used physical force to restrain victim by holding a knife to victim's throat while co-defendant removed money from victim's pocket supported finding that defendant acted with co-defendant with the conscious objective of taking the money, thereby satisfying all elements of the statute. People v. Hughes, 280 A.D.2d 694, 720 N.Y.S.2d 586 (3d Dept.), *appeal denied*, 96 N.Y.2d 801 (2001).

—Conviction of robbery in the second degree upheld where there was proof that defendant lured victim to apartment, and co-defendant forcibly removed jewelry and stole money from the victim. Although co-defendant may have demanded victim's money and jewelry, defendant was present and in a position to aid in the forcible taking of the victim's property. People v. Brown, 232 A.D.2d 750, 649 N.Y.S.2d 51 (3d Dept. 1996).

Lesser included offense.—Court erred in setting aside verdict on count charging robbery in the second degree: robbery in the second degree is not an inclusory concurrent count of robbery in the first degree. People v. Hayes, 228 A.D.2d 611, 645 N.Y.S.2d 492 (2d Dept. 1996).

—Jury's verdict of not guilty to charge of assault in the third degree was not inconsistent with the finding of guilt on the charge of robbery in the second degree and should have been recorded. People v. Brown, 76 A.D.2d 932, 429 N.Y.S.2d 727 (2d Dept. 1980).

—Defendant's conviction for robbery in the second degree dismissed; robbery in the second degree is a lesser included count of robbery in the first degree since the defendant could not have committed the greater crime without also committing the lesser crime. People v. Skinner, 211 A.D.2d 979, 621 N.Y.S.2d 733 (3d Dept. 1995).

—Grand larceny in the third degree is not a lesser included offense of robbery in the second degree. People v. Harris, 92 A.D.2d 738, 461 N.Y.S.2d 95 (4th Dept. 1983).

—Criminal possession of stolen property is a lesser included offense in the crime of robbery where the defendant wrongfully took property from the complainant's business premises. People v. Hayes, 43 A.D.2d 99, 349 N.Y.S.2d 869 (4th Dept. 1973), *aff'd*, 35 N.Y.2d 907, 364 N.Y.S.2d 897, 324 N.E.2d 365 (1974).

Plea.—Defendant's plea of guilty was defective and reversal was required where in allocution he declined to admit the offense in the words of the indictment and denied that his co-defendant was present at the time of the crime. People v. Brundage, 83 A.D.2d 579, 441 N.Y.S.2d 120 (2d Dept. 1981).

Intent.—The element of intent, which is an indispensable ingredient of the crime of robbery, must independently be established beyond a reasonable doubt. People v. Ramos, 83 A.D.2d 817, 442 N.Y.S.2d 61 (1st Dept. 1981).

Physical injury.—Physical injury element was established through complainant's testimony that he suffered substantial pain when defendant pulled on his thick gold neck chain until it broke, and that the pain and red marks lasted for several weeks after the incident. People v. Arroyo, 270 A.D.2d 386, 720 N.Y.S.2d 33 (1st Dept. 2001), *rev'd on other grounds*, 98 N.Y.2d 101, 772 N.E.2d 1154, 745 N.Y.S.2d 796 (2002).

—Testimony of the victim that she suffered pain in the course of the robbery was purely subjective and did not reach the objective level required to be "substantial" under second degree robbery. People v. Contreras, 108 A.D.2d 627, 485 N.Y.S.2d 261 (1st Dept. 1985).

—Defendant's conviction was reversed where the victim's testimony that he received blows to the side of the head and to the bridge of his nose resulting in bruises, a headache and minor pain was insufficient to prove impairment of physical condition or substantial pain. People v. Reed, 83 A.D.2d 566, 441 N.Y.S.2d 10 (2d Dept. 1981).

Repugnant verdict.—Defendant's acquittal of grand larceny in the third degree is repugnant to his conviction of robbery in the second degree, thus the charge of robbery in the second degree was dismissed. People v. Littlejohn, 83 A.D.2d 856, 441 N.Y.S.2d 735 (2d Dept. 1981).

—Defendant's conviction of robbery in the second degree on

the theory of being aided by other persons actually present was repugnant to the co-defendant's acquittal of robbery since it entailed a finding that the co-defendants did not aid or abet the defendant in the commission of the robbery. People v. Fallon, 78 A.D.2d 659, 432 N.Y.S.2d 225 (2d Dept. 1980).

§ 160.15. Robbery in the first degree.

A person is guilty of robbery in the first degree when he forcibly steals property and when, in the course of the commission of the crime or of immediate flight therefrom, he or another participant in the crime:

1. Causes serious physical injury to any person who is not a participant in the crime; or

2. Is armed with a deadly weapon; or

3. Uses or threatens the immediate use of a dangerous instrument; or

4. Displays what appears to be a pistol, revolver, rifle, shotgun, machine gun or other firearm; except that in any prosecution under this subdivision, it is an affirmative defense that such pistol, revolver, rifle, shotgun, machine gun or other firearm was not a loaded weapon from which a shot, readily capable of producing death or other serious physical injury, could be discharged. Nothing contained in this subdivision shall constitute a defense to a prosecution for, or preclude a conviction of, robbery in the second degree, robbery in the third degree or any other crime.

Robbery in the first degree is a class B felony.

Amended L. 1967, Ch. 791; by L. 1969, Ch. 1012; L. 1973, Ch. 374.

ANNOTATIONS

Constitutionality.—PL § 160.15(4) is constitutional. People v. Coleman, 42 N.Y.2d 837, 397 N.Y.S.2d 378, 366 N.E.2d 78 (1977).
—Affirmative defense contained in PL § 160.15(4) is constitutional. People v. Clark, 41 N.Y.2d 612, 394 N.Y.S.2d 593, 363 N.E.2d 319 (1977).

Elements.—The proof of "aid" and "actual presence" of an associate under PL § 160.10 are not identical with any element that must be proved under PL § 160.15. People v. Acevedo, 40 N.Y.2d 701, 389 N.Y.S.2d 811, 358 N.E.2d 495 (1976).
—Evidence of forcible taking of property of another coupled with aggravating factors of a participant in the crime armed with a deadly weapon supported a conviction under this section; defendant's knowledge or lack of knowledge that a gun would be used is immaterial. People v. Garcia, 302 A.D.2d 474, 753 N.Y.S.2d 754 (2d Dept. 2003).

Charge.—Defendant was entitled to a charge of second degree robbery where his tape recorded confession stated that the pistol he used was unloaded. People v. Kranenburg, 89 A.D.2d 509, 453 N.Y.S.2d 9 (1st Dept. 1982).

Sentence.—The crime of robbery in the first degree is defined as an "armed felony"; as such, court properly imposed a minimum term of imprisonment of one-half the maximum term. People v. Rodney, 237 A.D.2d 541, 655 N.Y.S.2d 577 (2d Dept. 1997).
—Sentence for conviction of robbery in the first degree was illegal since the crime is not an "armed felony"; court modified sentence by reducing the minimum term to one-third, rather than one-half, the maximum term. People v. Agramonte, 228 A.D.2d 607, 644 N.Y.S.2d 632 (2d Dept. 1996).
—Court erred in imposing consecutive sentences for convictions of robbery in the first degree and burglary in the first degree; under the circumstances presented, court found that both crimes

were committed through a single act. People v. Nguyen, 210 A.D.2d 871, 621 N.Y.S.2d 973 (4th Dept. 1994).

Affirmative defense.—Reversible error was committed where trial court refused to charge jury regarding affirmative defense where there was some evidence weapon was not a gun; without benefit of charge jury may have believed that it was their duty to find defendant guilty of robbery in the 1st degree. People v. Lockwood, 52 N.Y.2d 790, 436 N.Y.S.2d 703, 417 N.E.2d 1244 (1980).
—The defense need not present evidence in support of affirmative defense to robbery in the first degree; it may, as well, emerge in the course of the People's case. People v. Watts, 151 A.D.2d 307, 542 N.Y.S.2d 576 (1st Dept. 1989).
—Where court failed to charge the jury on the affirmative defense contained in Penal Law § 160.15(4), defendant's first degree robbery conviction would be reduced to robbery in the second degree. People v. Bailey, 148 A.D.2d 327, 538 N.Y.S.2d 811 (1st Dept. 1989).
—Defendant successfully established affirmative defense that the weapon used was a BB gun, not a firearm, and therefore his conviction for robbery in the first degree could not stand. People v. Layton, 302 A.D.2d 408, 754 N.Y.S.2d 552 (2d Dept. 2003).
—The court is required to point out the availability of an affirmative defense which, if established, would subject the defendant to a lower sentence in a case where the defendant made a statement at the time he entered his plea of guilty that he used a toy gun to commit the crime; however, the error was not preserved for review because defendant failed to move to withdraw his plea waiving his right to assert this deficiency on appeal. People v. Ebron, 87 A.D.2d 653, 448 N.Y.S.2d 514 (2d Dept. 1982).
—It is an affirmative defense that the gun defendant possessed during the robbery was not operable or loaded; defendant's guilty plea must be vacated as the colloquy did not reflect defendant's knowledge of this defense and that it was being knowingly and voluntarily waived by the plea. People v. Powell, 278 A.D.2d 848, 718 N.Y.S.2d 748 (4th Dept. 2000).

Abandonment of crime.—Where defendants planned a robbery and were in the process of undertaking it, when a gun belonging to one accidentally discharged and killed a third person, the abandonment of the robbery, because of such killing, occurred too late in the stage of preparation to indicate that no attempt occurred. People v. Mirenda, 23 N.Y.2d 439, 297 N.Y.S.2d 532, 245 N.E.2d 194 (1969).

Intent.—Acquittal of defendant on charges of robbery (first and second degree) and burglary (first degree) did not negate his alleged intention to use or threaten to use a knife so as to make conviction for criminal possession of a weapon in the fourth degree repugnant; the charges upon which defendant was acquitted contain elements not contained in the weapons offense. People v. Tyson, 220 A.D.2d 708, 632 N.Y.S.2d 664 (2d Dept. 1995).
—Defendant's allocution did not establish the mental culpability necessary to satisfy robbery in the first degree since defendant stated that he thought his co-defendants, who entered the house while he remained outside, went to complete a drug transaction; he did not know they intended to rob the victim. People v. Ocasio, 265 A.D.2d 675, 697 N.Y.S.2d 368 (3d Dept. 1999).

Attempt.—Conviction of attempted robbery in first degree pursuant to section 160.15(1) and acquittal of attempted robbery in the first degree pursuant to section 160.15(3) was not inconsistent under the facts of this case. People v. Foxx, 240 A.D.2d 430, 658 N.Y.S.2d 392 (2d Dept. 1997).
—Defendant's guilty plea to the crime of robbery in the first degree was lawful and properly accepted, despite defendant's contentions about the impossibility of such a plea. People v. Jamerson, 215 A.D.2d 404, 626 N.Y.S.2d 973 (2d Dept. 1995).
—Defendant's contention that attempted robbery in the first degree is a nonexistent crime is without merit. People v. Durden, 219 A.D.2d 605, 631 N.Y.S.2d 862 (2d Dept. 1995).

Evidence.—The evidence of the defendant's guilt was so overwhelming that the alleged error in the admission of his co-defendant's confession was harmless beyond a reasonable doubt. Furthermore, no exception was taken to the charge, and no request was made for any limiting instructions. Accordingly, the application for a writ of error *coram nobis* was correctly denied. People v. Walker, 31 N.Y.2d 970, 341 N.Y.S.2d 111, 243 N.E.2d 257 (1973).

—Robbery committed in connection with a rape is a crime totally unrelated to the rape, and a conviction for the robbery need not be based on evidence corroborating its commission. People v. Moore, 23 N.Y.2d 565, 297 N.Y.S.2d 944, 245 N.E.2d 710, *cert. denied,* 394 U.S. 1006 (1969).

—People need not establish that defendant was armed with a deadly weapon during the robbery; it is sufficient that defendant shared the intent to rob the complainant with his co-defendants and that one of them was armed with a deadly weapon. People v. Murdough, 278 A.D.2d 434, 717 N.Y.S.2d 377 (2d Dept. 2000), *appeal denied,* 96 N.Y.2d 803 (2001).

—Conviction under P.L. § 160.15(2) could not be sustained where People introduced evidence that defendant displayed a weapon during the robbery; there was no evidence that weapon was a "deadly weapon." People v. Ferguson, 255 A.D.2d 598, 688 N.Y.S.2d 154 (2d Dept. 1998).

—PL § 160.15(4) does not require the People to introduce into evidence the gun used in the robbery or to present evidence that it was loaded. People v. Harper, 136 A.D.2d 736, 524 N.Y.S.2d 75, 76 (2d Dept. 1988).

—Defendant's guilt of robbery, first degree, was established by complainant's testimony that the defendant threatened to cut her and that she felt a cold hard object, which she did not see, next to her body. People v. Lawrence, 124 A.D.2d 597, 507 N.Y.S.2d 739 (2d Dept. 1986).

—Regardless of reason why co-defendant took money from victim, testimony that defendant used physical force to restrain victim by holding a knife to victim's throat while co-defendant removed money from victim's pocket supported finding that defendant acted with co-defendant with the conscious objective of taking the money, thereby satisfying all elements of the statute. People v. Hughes, 280 A.D.2d 694, 720 N.Y.S.2d 586 (3d Dept.), *appeal denied,* 96 N.Y.2d 801 (2001).

—Conviction for robbery in the first degree supported by evidence of serious physical injury; defendant participated in beating of victim which resulted in head injuries and severe facial lacerations from which victim would have bled to death if left unattended. People v. Jeanty, 268 A.D.2d 675, 702 N.Y.S.2d 194 (3d Dept.), *appeal denied,*, 94 N.Y.2d 949 (2000).

—Evidence that in the course of forcibly stealing property defendant used and threatened the immediate use of a dangerous instrument was sufficient to support robbery conviction; proof that defendant inflicted serious physical injury is not an element of the crime. People v. Todd, 280 A.D.2d 906, 719 N.Y.S.2d 913 (4th Dept.), *appeal denied,* 96 N.Y.2d 836 (2001).

Sufficiency of Evidence—Testimony of a single witness was sufficient to support defendant's conviction; waitress testified that she was alone after closing when defendant walked in, asked for change of a bill, and, when she opened the cash register, told her to give him all the money and added, with his hand in his jacket pocket motioning as if with a gun, "Don't make me shoot you." People v. Mills, 20 A.D.3d 779, 798 N.Y.S.2d 595 (3d Dept. 2005).

—Evidence was sufficient to support conviction where there was testimony from accomplices that while they were lookouts, defendant and armed co-defendant walked into store, grabbed one of the clerks by the neck, pistol-whipped him, and put the gun to his head, then demanded money and took an undetermined amount of cash from store and fired shots as they both left, and those shots hit no one. People v. Harris, 19 A.D.3d 871, 797 N.Y.S.2d 614 (3d Dept. 2005).

—Evidence was legally insufficient to support conviction for attempted robbery in the first degree; there was no evidence that defendant possessed weapon at time of crime, was aware of robbery plan, or shared intent of the co-defendants or aided them in any way; mere presence cannot support a conviction. People v. Eldridge, 302 A.D.2d 934, 755 N.Y.S.2d 193 (4th Dept. 2003).

Dangerous instrument.—In order to convict the defendant for a violation of PL § 160.15(3), the jury must find that the defendant actually possessed a dangerous instrument at the time of the commission of the crime. People v. Pena, 50 N.Y.2d 400, 429 N.Y.S.2d 410, 406 N.E.2d 1347, *cert. denied,* 449 U.S. 1037 (1980).

—Subway train was a "dangerous instrument" for purposes of first degree robbery, notwithstanding the defendant's failure to "possess" that instrumentality. People v. Pagan, 160 A.D.2d 284, 553 N.Y.S.2d 380, 381 (1st Dept. 1990).

—Convictions for attempted robbery in the first degree and criminal possession of a weapon in the fourth degree were vacated where People presented insufficient evidence to establish that pepper spray was a dangerous instrument. People v. Sinatra, 302 A.D.2d 615, 755 N.Y.S.2d 312 (2d Dept. 2003).

—Conviction for robbery was reversed where there was no evidence in the record that the stun gun displayed during the robbery was a dangerous instrument. People v. Nelson, 292 A.D.2d 397, 738 N.Y.S.2d 603 (2d Dept. 2002). *See also* People v. Maio Ni, 293 A.D.2d 552, 742 N.Y.S.2d 61 (2d Dept. 2002) (conviction for assault in the second degree reversed where no evidence offered to show that stun gun is a dangerous instrument).

—In order for the People to sustain burden of proving that the defendant actually used an instrument during the crime which was "readily capable of causing death or other serious physical injury," it was not necessary for the victim to actually see the weapon or instrument to prove this element of the crime. People v. Hallums, 157 A.D.2d 800, 550 N.Y.S.2d 401 (2d Dept. 1990).

—Conviction of robbery in the first degree based upon defendant's use or threatened immediate use of a "dangerous instrument" could not be sustained when the evidence at trial failed to establish that the object actually possessed by the defendant during the commission of the robbery was employed by him in such a manner as to render it a "dangerous instrument" within the purview of PL § 10.00(13). People v. Siler, 76 A.D.2d 938, 429 N.Y.S.2d 461 (2d Dept. 1980).

—Allocution did not provide sufficient factual basis to support conviction for P.L. § 160.15(3) where weapon utilized was a broken B.B. gun used in connection with a robbery; defendant can challenge sufficiency of plea because an essential element of crime, namely, "uses or threatens to use a dangerous instrument," was missing. People v. Espinoza, 253 A.D.2d 982, 680 N.Y.S.2d 122 (3d Dept. 1998).

—Defendant was properly charged with robbery and attempted robbery in the first degree where he significantly and deliberately added to the force available to him as an individual the force of a moving train, a dangerous instrument, simply by timing his own movements to coincide with the train's. People v. Cephas, 110 Misc. 2d 1075, 443 N.Y.S.2d 558 (Sup. Ct. N.Y. Co. 1981).

"Display" of weapon.—An object can be "displayed" without actually being seen by the victim even in outline; all that is required is that the defendant, by his actions, consciously manifest the presence of an object to the victim in such a way that the victim reasonably perceives that the defendant has a gun. People v. Lopez, 73 N.Y.2d 214, 538 N.Y.S.2d 788, 792, 535 N.E.2d 1328 (1989).

—Defendant's reference to a gun, combined with his demands upon the complainant while keeping his hand in his jacket pocket, constituted sufficient evidence of the display of what appeared to be a firearm, to support that element of both robbery in the first degree and burglary in the first degree. People v. Butts, 181 A.D.2d 432, 580 N.Y.S.2d 758 (1st Dept. 1992).

—Defendant's display of a concealed gun to give the victim the impression that he was threatening her with the gun was legally sufficient to establish robbery. People v. Frazier, 156 A.D.2d 198, 548 N.Y.S.2d 456, 457 (1st Dept. 1989).

—The fact that the complainants never actually saw a gun is not determinative of whether the defendant was guilty of robbery in the first degree. People v. Cromwell, 163 A.D.2d 410, 559 N.Y.S.2d 18 (2d Dept. 1990).

—It was error to reduce the count of the indictment charging robbery in the first degree to robbery in the third degree; by placing her hand in her jacket pocket in a position that was "up over her heart" and keeping her hand concealed throughout the robbery, defendant consciously conveyed the impression that she held something that could reasonably have been believed to be a firearm. People v. Van Voorhis, 207 A.D.2d 1023, 617 N.Y.S.2d 257 (4th Dept. 1994).

Threatened use of a weapon.—A threat to immediately use a dangerous object in the course of a robbery need not be accompanied by a verbalization; defendant's conduct in grabbing for his sheathed knife when the complainant refused to surrender his property was sufficient to establish the threat. People v. Di Girolamo, 108 A.D.2d 755, 485 N.Y.S.2d 98 (2d Dept. 1985).

—The threatened use of a dangerous instrument was established for the purposes of a conviction of robbery in the first degree (PL § 160.15(3)) where the evidence indicated that victim began screaming when confronted by the robbers and that one of them, in an effort to silence her, told her to "shut up" while brandishing a knife for her to see. People v. Bullock, 73 A.D.2d 1006, 424 N.Y.S.2d 61 (3d Dept. 1980).

Weapon inoperable or incapable of causing death or serious physical injury.—The defendant, who was convicted of robbery in the first degree, and who was in possession of an inoperable weapon, should have moved to vacate the conviction on that ground and not raise the issue on appeal. People v. Pellegrino, 91 A.D.2d 942, 458 N.Y.S.2d 556 (1st Dept.), aff'd, 60 N.Y.2d 636, 467 N.Y.S.2d 355, 454 N.E.2d 938 (1983).

—A guilty plea to robbery in the first degree must be vacated in the interests of justice where during the colloquy the defendant stated that he had possessed a "cap gun" during the robbery. People v. Hernandez, 78 A.D.2d 816, 433 N.Y.S.2d 131 (1st Dept. 1980).

—Although defense counsel stipulated that the ballistic expert, if called as a witness, would testify that the subject gun was tested and found to be operable, such stipulation merely encompassed what the expert would state in his testimony, and was not a concession that the expert's conclusions were accurate or that the gun, in fact, was operable, and the court should have granted defense request to charge that the "jury must find beyond a reasonable doubt that the pistol was in fact operable." People v. Fivilo, 47 A.D.2d 727, 365 N.Y.S.2d 194 (1st Dept. 1975).

Acquittal of robbery in the second degree.—Defendant's acquittal of second degree robbery, on theory of being aided by another person actually present, is not repugnant with verdict of guilty of first degree robbery, on theory of use or threatened immediate use of a dangerous instrument. People v. Delgado, 79 A.D.2d 975, 434 N.Y.S.2d 455 (2d Dept. 1981).

Lesser included offense.—The trial court erred in refusing defendant's request to charge the jury on the lesser included offense of robbery in the second degree where defendant's confession stated that he used a toy gun; this provided a reasonable basis for jury to conclude that the firearm displayed by defendant "was not a loaded weapon . . . readily capable of producing death or serious physical injury." People v. Smith, 55 N.Y.2d 888, 449 N.Y.S.2d 19, 433 N.E.2d 1267 (1982).

—Court properly refused to charge jury with robbery in third degree as a lesser included offense of robbery in the first degree where victim testified he was certain that defendant threatened him with a box cutter, and no evidence that defendant obtained the victim's money by "using or threatening the immediate use" of any other kind of physical force. People v. Scott, 5 A.D.3d 250 773 N.Y.S.2d 291 (1st Dept. 2004).

—Defendant was not entitled to a charge of robbery third degree where no "reasonable view" of the evidence would support a finding that he committed robbery in the third degree even though no gun was found where the two prosecution witnesses both testified to seeing the defendant holding a gun in his hand. People v. Rice, 81 A.D.2d 515, 446 N.Y.S.2d 47 (1st Dept. 1981).

—Court erred in setting aside verdict on count charging robbery in the second degree: robbery in the second degree is not an inclusory concurrent count of robbery in the first degree. People v. Hayes, 228 A.D.2d 611, 645 N.Y.S.2d 492 (2d Dept. 1996).

—Defendant's request for a charge on the lesser included offense of robbery in the third degree was properly denied; while proof of all of the elements of the crime of robbery in the third degree is required for proof of guilt of robbery in the first degree, a reasonable view of the evidence would not support a finding that defendant committed the crime without the display of a gun, and he therefore could not have committed the lesser crime. People v. Ruiz, 220 A.D.2d 466, 631 N.Y.S.2d 779 (2d Dept. 1995).

—Defendant's failure to assert affirmative defense to robbery in the first degree, that gun was unloaded or inoperable at trial, properly resulted in court's refusal to charge the lesser included of offense of robbery in the second degree. People v. Bell, 265 A.D.2d 813, 696 N.Y.S.2d 610 (4th Dept. 1999), appeal denied, 94 N.Y.2d 916 (2000).

—Defendant's conviction for felony assault in the first degree dismissed as a lesser included offense of robbery in the first degree. People v. Miles, 236 A.D.2d 786, 654 N.Y.S.2d 57 (4th Dept. 1997).

—Trial court erred in refusing defendant's request that jury be instructed on the crime of petit larceny as a lesser included offense of robbery in the first degree as it is impossible to commit robbery in the first degree without also committing petit larceny and a reasonable view of the evidence would support a finding that the defendant committed the lesser but not the greater offense; however, defendant's conviction of first degree robbery implied jury's rejection of lesser included offenses of second and third degree robbery, thus there was no reversible error. People v. Smith, 214 A.D.2d 971, 626 N.Y.S.2d 915 (4th Dept. 1995).

—Where the People proved beyond a reasonable doubt that defendant displayed what appeared to be a pistol and forcibly stole a sum of money from the victim and defendant was convicted of robbery, first degree, and criminal possession of a weapon, fourth degree, the latter count was dismissed as it was a lesser included offense of the robbery, first degree. People v. Johnson, 103 Misc. 2d 798, 426 N.Y.S.2d 994 (Sup. Ct. Bronx Co. 1980).

Plea.—Where defendant moved, at sentencing, to withdraw his plea of guilty to robbery in the first degree on the ground that he falsely admitted use or threatened use of a weapon in the course of commission of the crime, it was error for the court not to assign new counsel to the defendant, as he was denied effective assistance of counsel when his attorney, who recommended the plea, was forced to take a position adverse to the defendant. People v. Welsh, 207 A.D.2d 1025, 617 N.Y.S.2d 107 (4th Dept. 1994).

ARTICLE 165—OTHER OFFENSES RELATING TO THEFT

LexisNexis Cross Reference

New York Criminal Practice (2d ed.), Vol. 6, Ch. 66, Other Offenses Related to Theft, Computer Crimes and Trademark Counterfeiting.

§ 165.00. Misapplication of property.

1. A person is guilty of misapplication of property when, knowingly possessing personal property of another pursuant to an agreement that the same will be returned to the owner at a future time,

(a) he loans, leases, pledges, pawns or otherwise encumbers such property without the consent of the owner thereof in such manner as to create a risk that the owner will not be able to recover it or will suffer pecuniary loss; or

(b) he intentionally refuses to return personal property valued in excess of one hundred dollars to the owner pursuant to the terms of the rental agreement provided that the owner shall have made a written demand for the return of such personal property in person or by certified mail at an address indicated in the rental agreement and he intentionally refuses to return such personal property for a period of thirty days after such demand has been received by him. Such written demand shall state: (i) the date and time at which the personal property was to have been returned under the rental agreement; (ii) that the owner does not consent to the continued withholding or retaining of such personal property and demands its return; and (iii) that the continued withholding or retaining of the property may constitute a class a misdemeanor punishable by a fine of up to one thousand dollars or by a sentence to a term of imprisonment for a period of up to one year or by both such fine and imprisonment.

(c) as used in paragraph (b) of this subdivision and in subdivision three of this section, the terms owner, personal property, and rental agreement shall be defined as in subdivision one of section three hundred ninety-nine-w of the general business law.

2. In any prosecution under paragraph (a) of subdivision one of this section, it is a defense that, at the time the prosecution was commenced, (a) the defendant had recovered possession of the property, unencumbered as a result of the unlawful disposition, and (b) the owner had suffered no material economic loss as a result of the unlawful disposition.

3. In any prosecution under paragraph (b) of subdivision one of this section, it is a defense that at the time the prosecution was commenced, (a) the owner had recovered possession of the personal property and suffered no material economic loss as a result of the unlawful retention; or (b) the defendant is unable to return such personal property because it has been accidentally destroyed or stolen; or (c) the owner failed to comply with the provisions of section three hundred ninety-nine-w of the general business law.

Misapplication of property is a class A misdemeanor.

Amended by L. 1995, Ch. 81, § 372, eff. Nov. 1, 1995.

§ 165.05. Unauthorized use of a vehicle in the third degree.

A person is guilty of unauthorized use of a vehicle in the third degree when:

1. Knowing that he does not have the consent of the owner, he takes, operates, exercises control over, rides in or otherwise uses a vehicle. A person who engages in any such conduct without the consent of the owner is presumed to know that he does not have such consent; or

2. Having custody of a vehicle pursuant to an agreement between himself or another and the owner thereof whereby he or another is to perform for compensation a specific service for the owner involving the maintenance, repair or use of such vehicle, he intentionally uses or operates the same, without the consent of the owner, for his own purposes in a manner constituting a gross deviation from the agreed purpose; or

3. Having custody of a vehicle pursuant to an agreement with the owner thereof whereby such vehicle is to be returned to the owner at a specified time, he intentionally retains or withholds possession thereof, without the consent of the owner, for so lengthy a period beyond the specified time as to render such retention or possession a gross deviation from the agreement.

For purposes of this section "a gross deviation from the agreement" shall consist of, but not be limited to, circumstances wherein a person who having had custody of a vehicle for a period of fifteen days or less pursuant to a written agreement retains possession of such vehicle for at least seven days beyond the period specified in the agreement and continues such possession for a

period of more than two days after service or refusal of attempted service of a notice in person or by certified mail at an address indicated in the agreement stating (i) the date and time at which the vehicle was to have been returned under the agreement; (ii) that the owner does not consent to the continued withholding or retaining of such vehicle and demands its return; and that continued withholding or retaining of the vehicle may constitute a class A misdemeanor punishable by a fine of up to one thousand dollars or by a sentence to a term of imprisonment for a period of up to one year or by both such fine and imprisonment.

Unauthorized use of a vehicle in the third degree is a class A misdemeanor.

Amended by L. 1978, Ch. 626; L. 1981, Ch. 602; L. 1982, Ch. 413.

ANNOTATIONS

Constitutionality.—The statutory presumption that a person who takes, operates, exercises control over, rides in or otherwise uses a vehicle without the owner's consent does so with the knowledge that he lacks such consent, is constitutional. People v. McCaleb, 25 N.Y.2d 394, 306 N.Y.S.2d 889, 255 N.E.2d 136 (1969).

Consistent counts; grand larceny.—The Court of Appeals rejected defendant's argument that he could not consistently be convicted of both grant larceny and unauthorized use of a vehicle. People v. Kirnon, 31 N.Y.2d 877, 340 N.Y.S.2d 183 (1972), aff'd, 31 N.Y.2d 877, 340 N.Y.S.2d 183, 292 N.E.2d 319 (1972).

Jury instructions; judge's comments.—Although § 165.05(1) creates the presumption that a person operating a motor vehicle without the owner's consent knows that he does not have such consent, the presumption is not conclusive, and the trial court's failure to charge the jury that the presumption may be destroyed by rebuttal evidence constituted fatal error. People v. Simmons, 32 N.Y.2d 250, 344 N.Y.S.2d 897 (1973).

—Where a trial judge, in summarizing the facts for the jury, remarked that defendant had unexplained possession of stolen property, but he had advised the jury twice that Code Crim. Proc. § 393 prevented them from drawing an inference against defendant because he had not testified, the defendant's rights were not abridged by the fact that an inference could arise from his unexplained possession of stolen property. People v. Moro, 23 N.Y.2d 496, 297 N.Y.S.2d 578, 245 N.E.2d 226 (1969).

—Defendant was not deprived of a fair trial even though the court failed to expressly state that the statutory presumptions of PL §§ 165.05(1) and 165.55(1) were rebuttable, since it conveyed to the jury that they had an obligation to weigh the evidence of defendant's intoxication in determining if the People had sustained their burden of proving defendant's guilt beyond a reasonable doubt. People v. McIntosh, 93 A.D.2d 947, 463 N.Y.S.2d 271 (3d Dept. 1983).

Lesser included counts.—Unauthorized use of a vehicle is a lesser included offense of criminal possession of stolen property in the first degree. People v. Tuozzo, 82 A.D.2d 813, 439 N.Y.S.2d 400 (2d Dept. 1981).

Evidence.—Conviction was valid even though the motor was not running and there was no key in the ignition. People v. Roby, 39 N.Y.2d 69, 382 N.Y.S.2d 739, 346 N.E.2d 540 (1976).

—Owner's deposition, stating that the defendant did not have his consent to operate the car could be considered together with the information and was sufficient to establish, by non-hearsay allegations, every element of the offense charged (PL § 165.05). People v. Shipp, 35 N.Y.2d 982, 365 N.Y.S.2d 530, 324 N.E.2d 887 (1975).

—Testimony by a state trooper that defendant had committed prior similar crimes was allowed. People v. Pickney, 31 N.Y.2d 789, 339 N.Y.S.2d 113, 291 N.E.2d 392 (1972).

—Defendants who were found in parked stolen automobiles could be presumed to have known that they used the automobile without the owner's consent, and were, therefore, subject to conviction under Revised Penal Law § 165.05 even though in one case the defendant was in the back seat and in the other the defendant was asleep in the front seat. People v. McCaleb, 25 N.Y.2d 394, 306 N.Y.S.2d 889, 255 N.E.2d 136 (1969).

—Evidence was sufficient to support finding that respondent committed acts constituting a violation of § 165.05 where it established that respondent was in the driver's seat of a stolen vehicle when arrested, and that the owner of the vehicle had not given respondent or anyone else permission to use the vehicle. In re Curtis H., 216 A.D.2d 173, 629 N.Y.S.2d 402 (1st Dept. 1995).

—Evidence that defendant "purchased" the vehicle, which the complainant had bought just a few months earlier for $65,000, for $16,000 in cash, without a bill of sale or title and had no way of contacting the seller after the transaction was completed, was legally sufficient to establish that he was guilty of criminal possession of stolen property in the third degree and unauthorized use of a vehicle in the third degree. People v. Derrell, 6 A.D.3d 625, 774 N.Y.S.2d 805 (2d Dept. 2004).

—Judge justifiably relied upon statutory presumption that appellant knew he lacked owner's consent to drive his automobile. In re John R., 229 A.D.2d 442, 645 N.Y.S.2d 294 (2d Dept. 1996).

Sufficiency of indictment.—Indictment did not adequately allege that defendant's delay in returning leased vehicle was so lengthy so as to constitute "gross deviation" from rental agreement, where indictment alleged that defendant was found behind wheel of vehicle 10 days from when it was expected to be returned, but was silent as to length of rental agreement. People v. Johnson, 169 Misc. 2d 746, 647 N.Y.S.2d 685 (Crim. Ct. N.Y. Co. 1996).

—Respondent's presence in a car that she did not own, which had been stolen two days earlier, coupled with evidence that she knew she lacked owner's consent, was sufficient to establish acts which if committed by an adult, would constitute the crime of unauthorized use of a vehicle in the third degree. In re Katrina W., 277 A.D.2d 949, 715 N.Y.S.2d 815 (4th Dept. 2000).

Statutory presumption.—Family Court correctly applied the statutory presumption, contained in Penal Law § 165.05(1), that a person who "rides in or otherwise uses a vehicle.without the consent of the owner is presumed to know that he does not have such consent"; presumption is permissive and "allows, but does not require, the trier of fact to accept the presumed fact, and does not shift to the defendant the burden of proof." In re Raquel M., 99 N.Y.2d 92, 752 N.Y.S.2d 268, 782 N.E.2d 64 (2003).

§ 165.06. Unauthorized use of a vehicle in the second degree.

A person is guilty of unauthorized use of a vehicle in the second degree when:

He commits the crime of unauthorized use of a vehicle in the third degree as defined in subdivision one of section 165.05 of this article and has been previously convicted of the crime of unauthorized use of a vehicle in the third degree as defined in subdivision one of section 165.05 or second degree within the preceding ten years.

Unauthorized use of a vehicle in the second degree is a class E felony.

Added by L. 1981, Ch. 602; **Amended** by L. 1982, Ch. 413.

ANNOTATIONS

Evidence.—Evidence established that the vehicle at issue was driven without the owner's consent sufficient to support conviction under this section. People v. Tate, 9 A.D.3d 29, 779 N.Y.S.2d 380 (4th Dept. 2004).

Sentence.—In light of defendant's history of criminality and antisocial behavior, sentencing defendant as persistent felony offender to two concurrent indeterminate terms of 15 years to life imprisonment for convictions of unauthorized use of a vehicle in the second degree and criminal possession of stolen property was not an abuse of discretion. People v. Woods, 219 A.D.2d 840, 632 N.Y.S.2d 1013 (4th Dept. 1995).

§ 165.07. Unlawful use of secret scientific material.

A person is guilty of unlawful use of secret scientific material when, with intent to appropriate to himself or another the use of secret scientific material, and having no right to do so and no reasonable ground to believe that he has such right, he makes a tangible reproduction or representation of such secret scientific material by means of writing, photographing, drawing, mechanically or electronically reproducing or recording such secret scientific material.

Unlawful use of secret scientific material is a class E felony.

§ 165.08. Unauthorized use of a vehicle in the first degree.

A person is guilty of unauthorized use of a vehicle in the first degree when knowing that he does not have the consent of the owner, he takes, operates, exercises control over, rides in or otherwise uses a vehicle with the intent to use the same in the course of or the commission of a class A, class B, class C or class D felony or in the immediate flight therefrom. A person who engages in any such conduct without the consent of the owner is presumed to know he does not have such consent.

Unauthorized use of a vehicle in the first degree is a class D felony.

Added by L. 1982, Ch. 413.

ANNOTATION

Evidence.—Circumstantial evidence of defendant's knowledge that vehicle was stolen along with testimony of accomplice were sufficient to support defendant's conviction. People v. Dixon, 216 A.D.2d 915, 629 N.Y.S.2d 556 (4th Dept. 1995).

§ 165.09. Auto stripping in the third degree.

A person is guilty of auto stripping in the third degree when:

1. He or she removes or intentionally destroys or defaces any part of a vehicle, other than an abandoned vehicle, as defined in subdivision one of section one thousand two hundred twenty-four of the vehicle and traffic law, without the permission of the owner; or

2. He or she removes or intentionally destroys or defaces any part of an abandoned vehicle, as defined in subdivision one of section one thousand two hundred twenty-four of the vehicle and traffic law, except that it is a defense to such charge that such person was authorized to do so pursuant to law or by permission of the owner.

Auto stripping in the third degree is a class A misdemeanor.

Added by L. 1984, Ch. 390; **Amended** by L. 1996, Ch. 494, eff. Nov. 1, 1996.

§ 165.10. Auto stripping in the second degree.

A person is guilty of auto stripping in the second degree when:

1. He or she commits the offense of auto stripping in the third degree and when he or she has been previously convicted within the last five years of having violated the provisions of section 165.09 or this section; or

2. He or she removes or intentionally destroys, defaces, disguises, or alters any part of two or more vehicles, other than abandoned vehicles, as defined in subdivision one of section one thousand two hundred twenty-four of the vehicle and traffic law, without the permission of the owner, and the value of the parts of vehicles removed, destroyed, defaced, disguised, or altered exceeds an aggregate value of one thousand dollars.

Auto stripping in the second degree is a class E felony.

Added by L. 1984, Ch. 390; **Amended** by L. 1996, Ch. 494, eff. Nov. 1, 1996.

ANNOTATION

Generally.—Statute is not limited in application to those who remove parts from automobiles for resale, but also covers removal of, intentional damage to, or defacement of any part of a vehicle. People v. Robinson, 95 N.Y.2d 179, 711 N.Y.S.2d 148, 733 N.E.2d 220 (2000).

§ 165.11. Auto stripping in the first degree.

A person is guilty of auto stripping in the first degree when he or she removes or intentionally destroys, defaces, disguises, or alters any part of three or more vehicles, other than abandoned vehicles, as defined in subdivision one of section one thousand two hundred twenty-four of the vehicle and traffic law, without the permission of the owner, and the value of the parts of vehicles removed, destroyed, defaced, disguised, or altered exceeds an aggregate value of three thousand dollars.

Auto stripping in the first degree is a class D felony.

Added by L. 1996, Ch. 494, eff. Nov. 1, 1996.

§ 165.15. Theft of services.

A person is guilty of theft of services when:

1. He obtains or attempts to obtain a service, or induces or attempts to induce the supplier of a rendered service to agree to payment therefor on a credit basis, by the use of a credit card or debit card which he knows to be stolen.

2. With intent to avoid payment for restaurant services rendered, or for services rendered to him as a transient guest at a hotel, motel, inn, tourist cabin, rooming house or comparable establishment, he avoids or attempts to avoid such payment by unjustifiable failure or refusal to pay, by stealth, or by any misrepresentation of fact which he knows to be false. A person who fails or refuses to pay for such services is presumed to have intended to avoid payment therefor; or

3. With intent to obtain railroad, subway, bus, air, taxi or any other public transportation service without payment of the lawful charge therefor, or to avoid payment of the lawful charge for such transportation service which has been rendered to him, he obtains or attempts to obtain such service or avoids or attempts to avoid payment therefor by force, intimidation, stealth, deception or mechanical tampering, or by unjustifiable failure or refusal to pay; or

4. With intent to avoid payment by himself or another person of the lawful charge for any telecommunications service, including, without limitation, cable television service, or any gas, steam, sewer, water, electrical, telegraph or telephone service which is provided for a charge or compensation, he obtains or attempts to obtain such service for himself or another person or avoids or attempts to avoid payment therefor by himself or another person by means of (a) tampering or making connection with the equipment of the supplier, whether by mechanical, electrical, accoustical or other means, or (b) offering for sale or otherwise making available, to anyone other than the provider of a telecommunications service for such service provider's own use in the provision of its service, any telecommunications decoder or descrambler, a principal function of which defeats a mechanism of electronic signal encryption, jamming or individually addressed switching imposed by the provider of any such telecommunications service to restrict the delivery of such service, or (c) any misrepresentation of fact which he knows to be false, or (d) any other artifice, trick, deception, code or device. For the purposes of this subdivision the telecommunications decoder or descrambler described in paragraph (b) above or the device described in paragraph (d) above shall not include any non-decoding and non-descrambling channel frequency converter or any television receiver-type accepted by the federal communications commission. In any prosecution under this subdivision, proof that telecommunications equipment, including, without limitation, any cable television converter, descrambler, or related equipment, has been tampered with or otherwise intentionally prevented from performing its functions of control of service delivery without the consent of the supplier of the service, or that telecommunications equipment, including, without limitation, any cable television converter, descrambler, receiver, or related equipment, has been connected to the equipment of the supplier of the service without the consent of the supplier of the service, shall be presumptive evidence that the resident to whom the service which is at the time being furnished by or through such equipment has, with intent to avoid payment by himself or another

person for a prospective or already rendered service, created or caused to be created with reference to such equipment, the condition so existing. A person who tampers with such a device or equipment without the consent of the supplier of the service is presumed to do so with intent to avoid, or to enable another to avoid, payment for the service involved. In any prosecution under this subdivision, proof that any telecommunications decoder or descrambler, a principal function of which defeats a mechanism of electronic signal encryption, jamming or individually addressed switching imposed by the provider of any such telecommunications service to restrict the delivery of such service, has been offered for sale or otherwise made available by anyone other than the supplier of such service shall be presumptive evidence that the person offering such equipment for sale or otherwise making it available has, with intent to avoid payment by himself or another person of the lawful charge for such service, obtained or attempted to obtain such service for himself or another person or avoided or attempted to avoid payment therefor by himself or another person; or

5. With intent to avoid payment by himself or another person of the lawful charge for any telephone service which is provided for a charge or compensation he (a) sells, offers for sale or otherwise makes available, without consent, an existing, canceled or revoked access device; or (b) uses, without consent, an existing, canceled or revoked access device; or (c) knowingly obtains any telecommunications service with fraudulent intent by use of an unauthorized, false, or fictitious name, identification, telephone number, or access device. For purposes of this subdivision access device means any telephone calling card number, credit card number, account number, mobile identification number, electronic serial number or personal identification number that can be used to obtain telephone service.

6. With intent to avoid payment by himself or another person for a prospective or already rendered service the charge or compensation for which is measured by a meter or other mechanical device, he tampers with such device or with other equipment related thereto, or in any manner attempts to prevent the meter or device from performing its measuring function, without the consent of the supplier of the service. In any prosecution under this subdivision, proof that a meter or related equipment has been tampered with or otherwise intentionally prevented from performing its measuring function without the consent of the supplier of the service shall be presumptive evidence that the person to whom the service which is at the time being furnished by or through such meter or related equipment has, with intent to avoid payment by himself or another person for a prospective or already rendered service, created or caused to be created with reference to such meter or related equipment, the

condition so existing. A person who tampers with such a device or equipment without the consent of the supplier of the service is presumed to do so with intent to avoid, or to enable another to avoid, payment for the service involved; or

7. He knowingly accepts or receives the use and benefit of service, including gas, steam or electricity service, which should pass through a meter but has been diverted therefrom, or which has been prevented from being correctly registered by a meter provided therefor, or which has been diverted from the pipes, wires, or conductors of the supplier thereof. In any prosecution under this subdivision proof that service has been intentionally diverted from passing through a meter, or has been intentionally prevented from being correctly registered by a meter provided therefor, or has been intentionally diverted from the pipes, wires or conductors of the supplier thereof, shall be presumptive evidence that the person who accepts or receives the use and benefit of such service has done so with knowledge of the condition so existing; or

8. With intent to obtain, without the consent of the supplier thereof, gas, electricity, water, steam or telephone service, he tampers with any equipment designed to supply or to prevent the supply of such service either to the community in general or to particular premises; or

9. With intent to avoid payment of the lawful charge for admission to any theatre or concert hall, or with intent to avoid payment of the lawful charge for admission to or use of a chair lift, gondola, rope-tow or similar mechanical device utilized in assisting skiers in transportation to a point of ski arrival or departure, he obtains or attempts to obtain such admission without payment of the lawful charge therefor.

10. Obtaining or having control over labor in the employ of another person, or of business, commercial or industrial equipment or facilities of another person, knowing that he is not entitled to the use thereof, and with intent to derive a commercial or other substantial benefit for himself or a third person, he uses or diverts to the use of himself or a third person such labor, equipment or facilities.

11. With intent to avoid payment by himself or another person of the lawful charge for use of any computer or computer service which is provided for a charge or compensation he uses, causes to be used or attempts to use a computer or computer service and avoids or attempts to avoid payment therefor. In any prosecution under this subdivision proof that a person overcame or attempted to overcome any device or coding system a function of which is to prevent the unauthorized use of said computer or computer service shall be presumptive evidence of an intent to avoid payment for the computer or computer service.

Theft of services is a class A misdemeanor,

provided, however, that theft of cable television service as defined by the provisions of paragraphs (a), (c) and (d) of subdivision four of this section, and having a value not in excess of one hundred dollars by a person who has not been previously convicted of theft of services under subdivision four of this section is a violation, that theft of services under subdivision nine of this section by a person who has not been previously convicted of theft of services under subdivision nine of this section is a violation and provided further, however, that theft of services of any telephone service under paragraph (a) or (b) of subdivision five of this section having a value in excess of one thousand dollars or by a person who has been previously convicted within five years of theft of services under paragraph (a) of subdivision five of this section is a class E felony.

Amended by L. 1967, Ch. 791; L. 1969, Ch. 115; L. 1975, Ch. 530; L. 1976, Ch. 768; L. 1978, Ch. 420; L. 1983, Chs. 521, 522; L. 1986, Chs. 15, 514; L. 1987, Chs. 556, 753; L. 1992, Ch. 41, eff. Apr. 2, 1991, amending subd. 1; L. 1992, Ch. 491, eff. Nov. 1, 1992, renumbered subds. 5 through 10 to subds. 6 through 11, added subd. 5, and amended the last paragraph; L. 1993, Ch. 171; L. 1995, Ch. 81, § 170, amending subd. 1, eff. Nov. 1, 1995; L. 1996, Ch. 357, § 2, amended subd. 5, eff. Nov. 1, 1996.

ANNOTATIONS

Entry into subway.—Conduct consisting of the entry into a subway station without paying the fare unquestionably constitutes the crime of theft of services. People v. Pratt, 164 Misc. 2d 498, 625 N.Y.S.2d 869 (Crim. Ct. N.Y. Co. 1995).

Exiting taxi without paying fare.—Police officer's observation that defendant, sole passenger in a taxi, was attempting to leave the vehicle too quickly to have paid the fare, in violation of §165.15, allowed the officer to temporarily detain defendant to determine if fare had been paid. People v. Yates, 3 N.Y.3d 625, 782 N.Y.S.2d 395, 816 N.E.2d 184 (2004).

Rebuttable presumptions.—Failure to instruct grand jury that presumptions set forth in each of the subdivisions is rebuttable impaired the integrity of the grand jury and required dismissal of those counts of the indictment. People v. Pezzimenti, 245 A.D.2d 1030, 666 N.Y.S.2d 64 (4th Dept. 1997).

§ 165.16. Unauthorized sale of certain transportation services.

1. A person is guilty of unauthorized sale of certain transportation services when, with intent to avoid payment by another person to the metropolitan transportation authority, New York city transit authority or a subsidiary or affiliate of either such authority of the lawful charge for transportation services on a railroad, subway, bus or mass transit service operated by either such authority or a subsidiary or affiliate thereof, he or she, in exchange for value, sells access to such transportation services to such person, without authorization, through the use of an unlimited farecard or doctored farecard. This section shall apply only to such sales that occur in a transportation facility, as such term is defined in subdivision two of section 240.00 of this chapter, operated by such metropolitan transportation authority, New York city transit authority or subsidiary or affiliate of such authority, when public notice of the prohibitions of its section and the exemptions thereto appears on the face of the farecard or is conspicuously posted in transportation facilities operated by such metropolitan transportation authority, New York city transit authority or such subsidiary or affiliate of such authority.

2. It shall be a defense to a prosecution under this section that a person, firm, partnership, corporation, or association: (a) selling a farecard containing value, other than a doctored farecard, relinquished all rights and privileges thereto upon consummation of the sale; or (b) sold access to transportation services through the use of a farecard, other than a doctored farecard, when such sale was made at the request of the purchaser as an accommodation to the purchaser at a time when a farecard was not immediately available to the purchaser, provided, however, that the seller lawfully acquired the farecard and did not, by means of an unlawful act, contribute to the circumstances that caused the purchaser to make such request.

3. For purposes of this section:

(a) "farecard" means a value-based, magnetically encoded card containing stored monetary value from which a specified amount of value is deducted as payment of a fare;

(b) "unlimited farecard" means a farecard that is time-based, magnetically encoded and which permits entrance an unlimited number of times into facilities and conveyances for a specified period of time; and

(c) "doctored farecard" means a farecard that has been bent or manipulated or altered so as to facilitate a person's access to transportation services without paying the lawful charge.

Unauthorized sale of transportation service is a class B misdemeanor.

Added by L. 2005, Ch. 57, Part T, § 1, eff. July 11, 2005.

§ 165.17. Unlawful use of credit card, debit card or public benefit card.

A person is guilty of unlawful use of credit card, debit card or public benefit card when in the course of obtaining or attempting to obtain property or a service, he uses or displays a credit card, debit card or public benefit card which he knows to be revoked or cancelled. Unlawful use of a credit card, debit card or public benefit card is a class A misdemeanor.

Added by L. 1969, Ch. 115; Amended by L. 1987, Ch. 556; L. 1992, Ch. 41, eff. Apr. 2, 1992; L. 1995, Ch. 81, § 171, eff. Nov. 1, 1995.

§ 165.20. Fraudulently obtaining a signature.

A person is guilty of fraudulently obtaining a signature when, with intent to defraud or injure another or to acquire a substantial benefit for himself or a third person, he obtains the signature of a person to a written instrument by means of any misrepresentation of fact which he knows to be false.

Fraudulently obtaining a signature is a class A misdemeanor.

§ 165.25. Jostling.

A person is guilty of jostling when, in a public place, he intentionally and unnecessarily:

1. Places his hand in the proximity of a person's pocket or handbag; or

2. Jostles or crowds another person at a time when a third person's hand is in the proximity of such person's pocket or handbag.

Jostling is a class A misdemeanor.

ANNOTATIONS

Defendant's act not jostling.—Act of pulling or dragging victim down the stairs did not constitute jostling. People v. Thomas, 36 N.Y.2d 514, 369 N.Y.S.2d 645, 330 N.E.2d 609 (1975).

Intent.—Larcenous intent is not an element of the crime of jostling. People v. Booker, 69 N.Y.2d 941, 516 N.Y.S.2d 640, 509 N.E.2d 335 (1987).

Evidence.—It is not necessary to produce the victim at trial, as a conviction for jostling requires only that the defendant's hand be placed in the proximity of "another's pocket or handbag" and jostling is thus basically an inchoate theft offense. People v. Rivera, 105 Misc. 2d 285, 431 N.Y.S.2d 970 (Crim. Ct. N.Y. Co. 1980).

§ 165.30. Fraudulent accosting.

1. A person is guilty of fraudulent accosting when he accosts a person in a public place with intent to defraud him of money or other property by means of a trick, swindle or confidence game.

2. A person who, either at the time he accosts another in a public place or at some subsequent time or at some other place, makes statements to him or engages in conduct with respect to him of a kind commonly made or performed in the perpetration of a known type of confidence game, is presumed to intend to defraud such person of money or other property.

Fraudulent accosting is a class A misdemeanor.

Amended by L. 1971, Ch. 772.

ANNOTATION

Supporting allegations.—Where it is alleged that the dealer in a three-card monte game has acted fraudulently and employed deception or trickery, the perpetrator may be charged with fraudulent accosting. People v. Hunt, 162 Misc. 2d 70, 616 N.Y.S.2d 168 (Crim. Ct. N.Y. Co. 1994).

§ 165.35. Fortune telling.

A person is guilty of fortune telling when, for a fee or compensation which he directly or indirectly solicits or receives, he claims or pretends to tell fortunes, or holds himself out as being able, by claimed or pretended use of occult powers, to answer questions or give advice on personal matters or to exorcise, influence or affect evil spirits or curses; except that this section does not

apply to a person who engages in the aforedescribed conduct as part of a show or exhibition solely for the purpose of entertainment or amusement.

Fortune telling is a class B misdemeanor.

ANNOTATION

Time of offense.—The People's characterization of fortune telling as a continuing offense was rejected since the crime is completed each time a person uses claimed occult powers to answer questions or give advice of a personal nature or exorcise, influence or affect evil spirits or curses; defendant's conviction for fortune telling as a continuing crime were reversed as the five-year time periods alleged were unreasonably broad. People v. Sanchez, 84 N.Y.2d 440, 618 N.Y.S.2d 887, 643 N.E.2d 509 (1994).

§ 165.40. Criminal possession of stolen property in the fifth degree.

A person is guilty of criminal possession of stolen property in the fifth degree when he knowingly possesses stolen property, with intent to benefit himself or a person other than an owner thereof or to impede the recovery by an owner thereof.

Criminal possession of stolen property in the fifth degree is a class A misdemeanor.

Amended by L. 1986, Ch. 515.

ANNOTATIONS

Double jeopardy.—By pleading guilty to criminal possession of stolen property in the third degree, defendant did not preclude later prosecution for robbery arising out of the same transaction, since robbery required proof of forcible stealing, which was not required for conviction of possession of stolen property, and possession of stolen property required proof of intent to benefit possessor or person other than the owner which was not required for robbery conviction. People v. Artis, 74 A.D.2d 644, 425 N.Y.S.2d 142 (2d Dept. 1980).

Effect of conviction.—Revocation of petitioner's pistol license based on conviction of two counts of criminal possession of stolen property in the fifth degree was supported by substantial evidence notwithstanding that the crime is not defined as a "serious offense" mandating automatic revocation of license; there was ample evidence in record that petitioner lacked good moral character, and revocation decision was not arbitrary or capricious. Davi v. Cosgrove, 211 A.D.2d 788, 621 N.Y.S.2d 386 (2d Dept. 1995).

Evidence.—Failure to prove the underlying theft in a prosecution for possession of stolen property will result in a dismissal of the charge. People v. Smith, 21 N.Y.2d 853, 288 N.Y.S.2d 1007, 236 N.E.2d 162 (1968).

—Allegation that defendant illegally took computer-generated information from owner without consent is sufficient to satisfy the statute. People v. Angeles, 180 Misc. 2d 146, 687 N.Y.S.2d 884 (Crim. Ct. N.Y. Co. 1999).

—The mere presence of defendant in a non-moving vehicle does not establish control and dominion over it; if the ignition had been wired, the engine running or a key available, the court may have reason to find otherwise. People v. Velez, 149 Misc. 2d 592, 565 N.Y.S.2d 950 (Crim. Ct. Kings Co. 1990).

Knowledge.—Generally, possession suffices to permit the inference that the possessor knows what he possesses, especially but not exclusively if it is in his hands, on his person, in his vehicle or on his premises. People v. Chavel, 161 A.D.2d 413, 555 N.Y.S.2d 132 (1st Dept. 1990).

Relationship to crime of larceny.—Larceny and receiving stolen property are mutually exclusive crimes. People v. Cefaro, 21 N.Y.2d 252, 287 N.Y.S.2d 371, 234 N.E.2d 423 (1967), *modified,* 23 N.Y.2d 283, 296 N.Y.S.2d 345, 244 N.E.2d 42 (1968).

§ 165.45. Criminal possession of stolen property in the fourth degree.

A person is guilty of criminal possession of stolen property in the fourth degree when he knowingly possesses stolen property, with intent to benefit himself or a person other than an owner thereof or to impede the recovery by an owner thereof, and when:

1. The value of the property exceeds one thousand dollars; or

2. The property consists of a credit card, debit card or public benefit card; or

3. He is a collateral loan broker or is in the business of buying, selling or otherwise dealing in property; or

4. The property consists of one or more firearms, rifles and shotguns, as such terms are defined in section 265.00 of this chapter; or

5. The value of the property exceeds one hundred dollars and the property consists of a motor vehicle, as defined in section one hundred twenty-five of the vehicle and traffic law, other than a motorcycle, as defined in section one hundred twenty-three of such law; or

6. The property consists of a scroll, religious vestment, vessel or other item of property having a value of at least one hundred dollars kept for or used in connection with religious worship in any building or structure used as a place of religious worship by a religious corporation, as incorporated under the religious corporations law or the education law.

7. The property consists of anhydrous ammonia or liquified ammonia gas and the actor intends to use, or knows another person intends to use, such anhydrous ammonia or liquified ammonia gas to manufacture methamphetamine.

Criminal possession of stolen property in the fourth degree is a class E felony.

Amended by L. 1969, Chs. 115, 354; L. 1979, Ch. 329; L. 1983, Ch. 321; L. 1986, Ch. 515; L. 1987, Ch. 556; L. 1990, Ch. 450; L. 1995, Ch. 81, § 172, amending subd. 2, eff. Nov. 1, 1995; L. 2005, Ch. 394, § 2, adding subd. 7, eff. Oct. 1, 2005.

ANNOTATIONS

Generally.—The legislative history and context of the language used in Penal Law § 165.45 demonstrate that the gravamen of the offense is the knowing possession of stolen property and the character of the act is not affected by the fact that the property may have belonged to several owners rather than one. People v. Buckley, 75 N.Y.2d 843, 552 N.Y.S.2d 912, 913, 552 N.E.2d 160 (1990).

Charge; value of property.—The trial court properly instructed the jury to consider the market value of the property first, and only if they concluded that such was unascertainable, could they consider replacement value, and that to convict they would have to conclude that this alternative measure of value exceeded $1,000. People v. Vientos, 164 A.D.2d 122, 561 N.Y.S.2d 443 (1st Dept. 1990).

—It is reversible error for the trial court to fail to charge the jury as to the proper method of assessing the value of the stolen item such as the market value of the typewriter at the time of the theft or at the time it was sold by the defendant to the police

so that the degree of the crime committed could properly be determined. People v. McKay, 79 A.D.2d 665, 433 N.Y.S.2d 845 (2d Dept. 1980).

Improper charge; guilty knowledge.—Conviction of criminal possession of stolen property in the second degree (PL 165.45) was reversed and a new trial ordered where, after evidence established that the defendant had presented stolen property to a fencing operation, the trial court instructed the jurors that they could find that defendant had guilty knowledge if they believed that "all the facts and circumstances surrounding the receipt of the goods would require a reasonable man to make inquiry, and that defendant failed to follow up the inquiry for fear that he would learn the truth and know the goods were stolen;" such instruction under the circumstances was improper because it allowed the jurors to impose upon defendant a statutory presumption which is limited to pawnbrokers and persons in the business of buying, selling or otherwise dealing in property. (PL § 165.55, subd. 2). People v. Barrie, 74 A.D.2d 576, 424 N.Y.S.2d 477 (2d Dept. 1980).

Evidence.—There was no valid line of reasoning and permissible inferences from which a reasonable person could conclude that every element of fourth degree grand larceny was proved beyond a reasonable doubt. "The People introduced no direct evidence that established when or how defendant came into possession of the wallet, that he took it or knew that it had been taken from the complaining witness, or that the wallet indeed was stolen, rather than lost. The only circumstantial evidence of defendant's guilt was his possession of the wallet at the time of his arrest." People v. Moore, 291 A.D.2d 336, 738 N.Y.S.2d 332 (1st Dept. 2002).

—Accomplice's testimony combined with circumstantial evidence of defendants' knowledge that vehicle was stolen were sufficient to support conviction of, *inter alia*, criminal possession of stolen property. People v. Dixon, 216 A.D.2d 915, 629 N.Y.S.2d 556 (4th Dept. 1995).

Credit card.—Theft of "decoy" credit card issued by credit card company to undercover police officer under imaginary name was sufficient to support defendant's conviction for grand larceny in the fourth degree; in fact, "criminal liability with regard to credit cards can arise even with respect to nonactivated, expired or canceled cards." People v. Thompson, 99 N.Y.2d 38, 751 N.Y.S.2d 162, 780 N.E.2d 973 (2002).

—The court's instruction that an expired credit card was a "credit card" within the meaning of § 165.45(2) was proper as this issue was one of law for the court, while the issue of whether the particular card in evidence was a "credit card" was properly left to the jury; the proof was sufficient to establish the defendant's criminal possession of stolen property in the fourth degree. People v. Johnson, 214 A.D.2d 478, 625 N.Y.S.2d 521 (1st Dept. 1995).

Lesser included offense.—Criminal possession of stolen property in the second degree is not a lesser included offense of grand larceny in the third degree. People v. Robinson, 90 A.D.2d 249, 457 N.Y.S.2d 347 (4th Dept. 1982), *aff'd*, 60 N.Y.2d 982, 471 N.Y.S.2d 258, 459 N.E.2d 483 (1983).

Analogous crimes.—New Hampshire conviction for felony of receiving stolen property was analogous to New York crime of criminal possession of stolen property in the fourth degree; both statutes make felonious the knowing possession of stolen property with the intent to deprive the owner of the property. *In re* Wong, 212 A.D.2d 863, 622 N.Y.S.2d 356 (3d Dept. 1995).

Possession.—Possession of keys that unlocked door and started engine of stolen car is legally sufficient to establish "dominion and control" element of criminal possession of stolen property in the fourth degree. People v. Bell, 265 A.D.2d 813, 696 N.Y.S.2d 610 (4th Dept. 1999), *appeal denied*, 94 N.Y.2d 916 (2000).

§ 165.50. Criminal possession of stolen property in the third degree.

A person is guilty of criminal possession of stolen property in the third degree when he knowingly possesses stolen property, with intent to benefit himself or a person other than an owner thereof or to impede the recovery by an owner thereof, and when the value of the property exceeds three thousand dollars.

Criminal possession of stolen property in the third degree is a class D felony.

Amended by L. 1986, Ch. 515.

ANNOTATIONS

Evidence.—Evidence that defendant "purchased" the vehicle, which the complainant had bought just a few months earlier for $65,000, for $16,000 in cash, without a bill of sale or title and had no way of contacting the seller after the transaction was completed, was legally sufficient to establish that he was guilty of criminal possession of stolen property in the third degree and unauthorized use of a vehicle in the third degree. People v. Derrell, 6 A.D.3d 625, 774 N.Y.S.2d 805 (2d Dept. 2004).

—Defendant was properly convicted of criminal possession of stolen property in the third degree, where the complainant car dealer's testimony that he purchased a car for $3,110 five days before it was stolen, combined with the bill of receipt, were sufficient to show that the stolen car exceeded the statutory minimum of $3,000, despite the fact that the car dealer was never qualified as an expert witness. People v. Cosme, 228 A.D.2d 515, 644 N.Y.S.2d 310 (2d Dept. 1996).

—Where defendant was convicted of, *inter alia*, criminal possession of stolen property in the third degree based on evidence that he obtained more than $20,000 for the purchase of a "log home kit" from a customer and failed to deliver the kit, court properly admitted evidence of similar transactions between the defendant and other customers to show intent and a common plan or scheme. People v. Norman, 217 A.D.2d 902, 629 N.Y.S.2d 920 (4th Dept. 1995).

Accomplice testimony.—The testimony of defendant's girlfriend, who was an accomplice as a matter of law, required corroboration to support defendant's conviction of criminal possession of stolen property. People v. McGlotten, 278 A.D.2d 936, 718 N.Y.S.2d 770 (4th Dept. 2000), *appeal denied,* 96 N.Y.2d 761 (2001).

§ 165.52. Criminal possession of stolen property in the second degree.

A person is guilty of criminal possession of stolen property in the second degree when he knowingly possesses stolen property, with intent to benefit himself or a person other than an owner thereof or to impede the recovery by an owner thereof, and when the value of the property exceeds fifty thousand dollars.

Criminal possession of stolen property in the second degree is a class C felony.

Added by L. 1986, Ch. 515.

§ 165.54. Criminal possession of stolen property in the first degree.

A person is guilty of criminal possession of stolen property in the first degree when he knowingly possesses stolen property, with intent to benefit himself or a person other than an owner thereof or to impede the recovery by an owner, and when the value of the property exceeds one million dollars.

Criminal possession of stolen property in the first degree is a class B felony.

Added by L. 1986, Ch. 515.

§ 165.55. Criminal possession of stolen property; presumptions.

1. A person who knowingly possesses stolen property is presumed to possess it with intent to benefit himself or a person other than an owner thereof or to impede the recovery by an owner thereof.

2. A collateral loan broker or a person in the business of buying, selling or otherwise dealing in property who possesses stolen property is presumed to know that such property was stolen if he obtained it without having ascertained by reasonable inquiry that the person from whom he obtained it had a legal right to possess it.

3. A person who possesses two or more stolen credit cards, debit cards or public benefit cards is presumed to know that such credit cards, debit cards or public benefit cards were stolen.

4. A person who possesses three or more tickets or equivalent instrument for air transportation service, which tickets or instruments were stolen by reason of having been obtained from the issuer or agent thereof by the use of one or more stolen or forged credit cards, is presumed to know that such tickets or instruments were stolen.

Amended by L. 1969, Ch. 115; L. 1983, Ch. 321; L. 1987, Ch. 556; L. 1995, Ch. 81, § 173, amending subd. 3, eff. Nov. 1, 1995.

ANNOTATIONS

Accomplice.—Defendant's girlfriend, who testified that she knew the property was stolen when she took it to a pawn shop while the defendant waited outside, then gave him the proceeds after which they bought her a wedding dress, was an accomplice as a matter of law, not a "fence," whose uncorroborated testimony could not support a conviction of criminal possession of stolen property. People v. McGlotten, 278 A.D.2d 936, 718 N.Y.S.2d 770 (4th Dept. 2000), *appeal denied,* 96 N.Y.2d 761 (2001).

Constitutionality.—The presumption in PL § 165.55 that a person who possesses two or more stolen credit cards knows that such credit cards are stolen does not violate due process by requiring a lesser standard than "beyond a reasonable doubt," since there is a rational relation between the possession of the stolen cards and the ultimate fact to be inferred: knowledge that the cards were stolen. People v. Baveghems, 107 A.D.2d 815, 484 N.Y.S.2d 652 (2d Dept. 1985).

Credit cards.—The presumption that one who possesses two or more stolen credit cards is presumed to know that the cards were stolen was properly charged where defendant was charged in the indictment with two counts of possession of a stolen credit card, only one of which was submitted to the jury; the evidence that the defendant possessed a second card was sufficient for purposes of the presumption and proof beyond a reasonable doubt was not necessary for this purpose. People v. Harrell, 208 A.D.2d 365, 616 N.Y.S.2d 739 (1st Dept. 1994). *See also* People v. White, 251 A.D.2d 157, 673 N.Y.S.2d 905 (1st Dept. 1998).

Improper charge; judge's comments.—In a prosecution for possession of stolen property, the judge's comment that defendant had unexplained possession of a stolen car did not violate the defendant's privilege against self-incrimination. The inference to be drawn from such possession continues only until some evidence is presented to explain the possession. Such evidence need not come from defendant's testimony and, therefore, the inference is not sustainable merely because the defendant does not testify. Therefore, the inference in no way requires the defendant to rebut it, and it does not prevent him from exercising his right not to testify in his own behalf. People v.

Moro, 23 N.Y.2d 496, 297 N.Y.S.2d 578, 245 N.E.2d 226 (1969).

—Reversible error was committed when the court refused to charge that the presumption regarding the knowing possession of stolen property was rebuttable where rebuttal evidence was presented. People v. Ornstein, 91 A.D.2d 788, 458 N.Y.S.2d 87 (3d Dept. 1982).

Evidence.—Knowledge may be shown circumstantially by conduct or directly by admission or indirectly by contradictory statements from which guilt may be inferred. People v. Von Werne, 41 N.Y.2d 584, 394 N.Y.S.2d 183, 362 N.E.2d 982 (1977).

§ 165.60. Criminal possession of stolen property; no defense.

In any prosecution for criminal possession of stolen property, it is no defense that:

1. The person who stole the property has not been convicted, apprehended or identified; or

2. The defendant stole or participated in the larceny of the property; or

3. The larceny of the property did not occur in this state.

Amended by L. 1976, Ch. 375.

ANNOTATIONS

Robbery prosecution after guilty plea.—By pleading guilty to criminal possession of stolen property in the third degree, defendant did not preclude later prosecution for robbery arising out of the same transaction, since robbery required proof of forcible stealing, which was not required for conviction of possession of stolen property, and possession of stolen property required proof of intent to benefit possessor or person other than the owner, which was not required for robbery conviction. People v. Artis, 74 A.D.2d 644, 425 N.Y.S.2d 1142 (2d Dept. 1980).

Robbery conviction.—Since at the time of the instant offense there was no statutory prohibition against convicting a defendant of both the crimes of larceny and the crime of criminal possession of stolen property with respect to the same property, defendant's convictions of both robbery in the second degree (of which larceny is a element), and criminal possession of stolen property in the third degree should stand. People v. Grant, 113 A.D.2d 311, 497 N.Y.S.2d 23 (2d Dept. 1985).

§ 165.65. Criminal possession of stolen property; corroboration.

1. A person charged with criminal possession of stolen property who participated in the larceny thereof may not be convicted of criminal possession of such stolen property solely upon the testimony of an accomplice in the larceny unsupported by corroborative evidence tending to connect the defendant with such criminal possession.

2. Unless inconsistent with the provisions of subdivision one of this section, a person charged with criminal possession of stolen property may be convicted thereof solely upon the testimony of one from whom he obtained such property or solely upon the testimony of one to whom he disposed of such property.

Amended by L. 1971, Ch. 1097.

§ 165.70. Definitions.

As used in sections 165.71, 165.72, 165.73 and 165.74, the following terms have the following definitions:

1. The term "trademark" means (a) any word, name, symbol, or device, or any combination thereof adopted and used by a person to identify goods made by a person and which distinguish them from those manufactured or sold by others which is in use and which is registered, filed or recorded under the laws of this state or of any other state or is registered in the principal register of the united states patent and trademark office; or (b) the symbol of the International Olympic Committee, consisting of five interlocking rings; the emblem of the United States Olympic Committee, consisting of an escutcheon having a blue chief and vertically extending red and white bars on the base with five interlocking rings displayed on the chief; any trademark, trade name, sign, symbol, or insignia falsely representing association with, or authorization by, the International Olympic Committee or the United States Olympic Committee; or the words "Olympic," "Olympiad," "Citius Altius Fortius," or any combination thereof tending to cause confusion, to cause mistake, to deceive, or to falsely suggest a connection with the United States Olympic Committee or any International Olympic Committee or United States Olympic Committee activity.

2. The term "counterfeit trademark" means a spurious trademark or an imitation of a trademark that is:

(a) used in connection with trafficking in goods; and

(b) used in connection with the sale, offering for sale or distribution of goods that are identical with or substantially indistinguishable from a trademark as defined in subdivision one of this section.

The term "counterfeit trademark" does not include any mark used in connection with goods for which the person using such mark was authorized to use the trademark for the type of goods so manufactured or produced by the holder of the right to use such mark or designation, whether or not such goods were manufactured or produced in the United States or in another country, and does not include imitations of trade dress or packaging such as color, shape and the like unless those features have been registered as trademarks as defined in subdivision one of this section.

3. The term "traffic" means to transport, transfer, or otherwise dispose of, to another, as consideration for anything of value, or to obtain control of with intent to so transport, transfer, or otherwise dispose of.

4. The term "goods" means any products, services, objects, materials, devices or substances which are identified by the use of a trademark.

Added by L. 1992, Ch. 490; **Amended** by L. 1993, Ch. 155.

§ 165.71. Trademark counterfeiting in the third degree.

A person is guilty of trademark counterfeiting in the third degree when, with the intent to deceive or defraud some other person or with the intent to evade a lawful restriction on the sale, resale, offering for sale, or distribution of goods, he or she manufactures, distributes, sells, or offers for sale goods which bear a counterfeit trademark, or possesses a trademark knowing it to be counterfeit for the purpose of affixing it to any goods.

Trademark counterfeiting in the third degree is a class A misdemeanor.

Added by L. 1992, Ch. 490, eff. Nov. 1, 1992.

ANNOTATIONS

Sufficiency of Information.—Misdemeanor information dismissed as facially insufficient where accusatory instrument failed to contain a clear description of the of the trademark in question. People v. Ensley, 183 Misc. 2d 141, 702 N.Y.S.2d 752 (Crim. Ct. N.Y. Co. 1999).

Value.—Liability is imposed for trademark counterfeiting in the first or second degree based on the value of the trademark to the goods passed off as genuine or the incremental value added to the goods by the affixing of the counterfeit mark; since there was no testimony before the grand jury as to the value of the trademark to the counterfeit goods, those counts of the indictment charging trademark counterfeiting in the first and second degrees were reduced to trademark counterfeiting in the third degree, which requires no proof of value. People v. Kim, 163 Misc. 2d 451, 621 N.Y.S.2d 479 (Sup. Ct. N.Y. Co. 1994).

§ 165.72. Trademark counterfeiting in the second degree.

A person is guilty of trademark counterfeiting in the second degree when, with the intent to deceive or defraud some other person or with the intent to evade a lawful restriction on the sale, resale, offering for sale, or distribution of goods, he or she manufactures, distributes, sells, or offers for sale goods which bear a counterfeit trademark, or possesses a trademark knowing it to be counterfeit for the purpose of affixing it to any goods, and the retail value of all such goods bearing counterfeit trademarks exceeds one thousand dollars.

Trademark counterfeiting in the second degree is a class E felony.

Added by L. 1992, Ch. 490, eff. Nov. 1, 1992; **Amended** by L. 1995, Ch. 535, § 1, eff. Nov. 1, 1995.

ANNOTATION

Value.—Liability is imposed for trademark counterfeiting in the first or second degree based on the value of the trademark to the goods passed off as genuine or the incremental value added to the goods by the affixing of the counterfeit mark; since there was no testimony before the grand jury as to the value of the trademark to the counterfeit goods, those counts of the indictment charging trademark counterfeiting in the first and second degrees were reduced to trademark counterfeiting in the

third degree, which requires no proof of value. People v. Kim, 163 Misc. 2d 451, 621 N.Y.S.2d 479 (Sup. Ct. N.Y. Co. 1994).

§ 165.73. Trademark counterfeiting in the first degree.

A person is guilty of trademark counterfeiting in the first degree when, with the intent to deceive or defraud some other person, or with the intent to evade a lawful restriction on the sale, resale, offering for sale, or distribution of goods, he or she manufactures, distributes, sells, or offers for sale goods which bear a counterfeit trademark, or possesses a trademark knowing it to be counterfeit for the purpose of affixing it to any goods, and the retail value of all such goods bearing counterfeit trademarks exceeds one hundred thousand dollars.

Trademark counterfeiting in the first degree is a class C felony.

Added by L. 1992, Ch. 490, eff. Nov. 1, 1992; **Amended** by L. 1995, Ch. 535, § 2, eff. Nov. 1, 1995.

ANNOTATION

No proof of value necessary.—Liability is imposed for trademark counterfeiting in the first or second degree based on the value of the trademark to the goods passed off as genuine or the incremental value added to the goods by the affixing of the counterfeit mark; since there was no testimony before the grand jury as to the value of the trademark to the counterfeit goods, those counts of the indictment charging trademark counterfeiting in the first and second degrees were reduced to trademark counterfeiting in the third degree, which requires no proof of value. People v. Kim, 163 Misc. 2d 451, 621 N.Y.S.2d 479 (Sup. Ct. N.Y. Co. 1994).

§ 165.74. Seizure and destruction of goods bearing counterfeit trademarks.

Any goods manufactured, sold, offered for sale, distributed or produced in violation of this article may be seized by any police officer. The magistrate must, within forty-eight hours after arraignment of the defendant, determine whether probable cause exists to believe that the goods had been manufactured, sold, offered for sale, distributed or produced in violation of this article, and upon a finding that probable cause exists to believe that the goods had been manufactured, sold, offered for sale, distributed, or produced in violation of this article, the court shall authorize such articles to be retained as evidence pending the trial of the defendant. Upon conviction of the defendant, the articles in respect whereof the defendant stands convicted shall be destroyed. Destruction shall not include auction, sale or distribution of the items in their original form.

Added by L. 1992, Ch. 490, eff. Nov. 1, 1992; **Amended** by L. 1995, Ch. 535, § 3, eff. Nov. 1, 1995.

TITLE K—OFFENSES INVOLVING FRAUD

ARTICLE 170—FORGERY AND RELATED OFFENSES

LexisNexis Cross Reference

New York Criminal Practice (2d ed.), Vol. 6, Ch. 66, Other Offenses Related to Theft, Computer Crimes and Trademark Counterfeiting; Vol. 7, Ch. 67, Forgery and False Written Statements.

§ 170.00. Forgery; definitions of terms.

1. "Written instrument" means any instrument or article, including computer data or a computer program, containing written or printed matter or the equivalent thereof, used for the purpose of reciting, embodying, conveying or recording information, or constituting a symbol or evidence of value, right, privilege or identification, which is capable of being used to the advantage or disadvantage of some person.

2. "Complete written instrument" means one which purports to be a genuine written instrument fully drawn with respect to every essential feature thereof. An endorsement, attestation, acknowledgment or other similar signature or statement is deemed both a complete written instrument in itself and a part of the main instrument in which it is contained or to which it attaches.

3. "Incomplete written instrument" means one which contains some matter by way of content or authentication but which requires additional matter in order to render it a complete written instrument.

4. "Falsely make." A person "falsely makes" a written instrument when he makes or draws a complete written instrument in its entirety, or an incomplete written instrument, which purports to be an authentic creation of its ostensible maker or drawer, but which is not such either because the ostensible maker or drawer is fictitious or because, if real, he did not authorize the making or drawing thereof.

5. "Falsely complete." A person "falsely completes" a written instrument when, by adding, inserting or changing matter, he transforms an incomplete written instrument into a complete one, without the authority of anyone entitled to grant it, so that such complete instrument appears or purports to be in all respects an authentic creation of or fully authorized by its ostensible maker or drawer.

6. "Falsely alter." A person "falsely alters" a written instrument when, without the authority of anyone entitled to grant it, he changes a written instrument, whether it be in complete or incomplete form, by means of erasure, obliteration, deletion, insertion of new matter, transposition of matter, or in any other manner, so that such instrument in its thus altered form appears or purports to be in all respects an authentic creation

of or fully authorized by its ostensible maker or drawer.

7. "Forged instrument" means a written instrument which has been falsely made, completed or altered.

8. "Electronic access device" means a mobile identification number or electronic serial number that can be used to obtain telephone service.

Amended by L. 1986, Ch. 514; L. 1996, Ch. 357, § 4, added subd. 8, eff. Nov. 1, 1996.

ANNOTATIONS

Falsely make.—The People must establish that defendant signed another's name without that person's authorization in order to establish necessary elements of forgery; People failed to submit proof that defendant forged two checks where checks were issued directly to mother, who signed and endorsed both checks in the presence of a bank employee. People v. Friedman, 14 A.D.3d 713, 789 N.Y.S.2d 250 (2d Dept. 2005).

Fully authorized.—An instrument is not "fully authorized" when it is made in excess of maker's authority, by someone other than the maker altering the amount of the check or completing the amount when they did not have the authority to do so. Where maker filled out all portions of the check except for the payee's name, which was left blank, defendant's actions of simply filling in the payee's name is not forgery. The document remained authentic. People v. Adkins, 236 A.D.2d 850, 653 N.Y.S.2d 1007 (4th Dept. 1997).

Signing own name.—Defendant's act of signing her own name on three money orders cannot provide the basis for the crime of forgery, as she signed the orders in the capacity of what is considered "purchaser"; defendant was not the actual drawer of the money orders and could only be the agent of the drawer, and since such agency was not indicated on the face of the money orders at the time defendant signed them, she must be viewed as the ostensible and actual agent of the drawer. People v. Johnson, 88 A.D.2d 922, 450 N.Y.S.2d 560 (2d Dept. 1982).

Use of assumed name.—Where defendant merely used an assumed name to secure a temporary motor vehicle operator's permit and to apply for a permanent license, and did not simulate, alter, erase, or obliterate someone else's signature, he was not guilty of criminal possession of a forged instrument. People v. Briggins, 50 N.Y.2d 302, 428 N.Y.S.2d 909, 406 N.E.2d 766 (1980).

—A genuine document, even though it bears a false (assumed) name, is not a forgery within the meaning of PL § 170.00. People v. Augustin, 11 A.D.3d 290, 782 N.Y.S.2d 718 (1st Dept. 2004).

Written instrument.—Defendant's admissions of preparing bank withdrawal slips and then signing her mother's name to the slips without authorization and using them to obtain funds from her mother's accounts along with a note purportedly authorizing the withdrawals to which she also signed her mother's name constituted forgery. People v. Seavey, 305 A.D.2d 937, 762 N.Y.S.2d 435 (3d Dept. 2003).

—Cloned cellular telephone is "written instrument" for purposes of statute. People v. Lawrence, 169 Misc. 2d 752, 647 N.Y.S.2d 675 (Sup. Ct. Kings Co. 1996); People v. Garcia, 170 Misc. 2d 543, 647 N.Y.S.2d 355 (Westchester Co. Ct. 1996).

§ 170.05. Forgery in the third degree.

A person is guilty of forgery in the third degree when, with intent to defraud, deceive or injure another, he falsely makes, completes or alters a written instrument.

Forgery in the third degree is a class A misdemeanor.

§ 170.10. Forgery in the second degree.

A person is guilty of forgery in the second

degree when, with intent to defraud, deceive or injure another, he falsely makes, completes or alters a written instrument which is or purports to be, or which is calculated to become or to represent if completed:

1. A deed, will, codicil, contract, assignment, commercial instrument, credit card, as that term is defined in subdivision seven of section 155.00, or other instrument which does or may evidence, create, transfer, terminate or otherwise affect a legal right, interest, obligation or status; or

2. A public record, or an instrument filed or required or authorized by law to be filed in or with a public office or public servant; or

3. A written instrument officially issued or created by a public office, public servant or governmental instrumentality; or

4. Part of an issue of tokens, public transportation transfers, certificates or other articles manufactured and designed for use as symbols of value usable in place of money for the purchase of property or services; or

5. A prescription of a duly licensed physician or other person authorized to issue the same for any drug or any instrument or device used in the taking or administering of drugs for which a prescription is required by law.

Forgery in the second degree is a class D felony.

Amended by L. 1984, Ch. 949.

ANNOTATIONS

Evidence.—Defendant's conviction for forgery in the second degree was reversed on appeal, having no authority to sign a check on behalf of the corporation, defendant signed his own name to a corporate check, however, because he signed his own name and was the actual maker of the check, he was not guilty of forgery, although the court left open the possibility that defendant was guilty of some form of larceny. People v. Cunningham, 2 N.Y.3d 593, 780 N.Y.S.2d 750, 813 N.E.2d 891 (2004).

—Evidence that defendant completed a driver's license application renewal which contained his own name, his own social security number, his signature, but contained an incorrect date of birth was not sufficient to establish that the defendant "falsely made" the application, or affected the genuineness of the document for its stated purpose. People v. Asaro, 94 N.Y.2d 792, 699 N.Y.S.2d 706, 721 N.E.2d 950 (1999) (mem.).

Written instrument.—Cloned cellular telephone is "written instrument" for purposes of statute. People v. Lawrence, 169 Misc. 2d 752, 647 N.Y.S.2d 675 (Sup. Ct. Kings Co. 1996); People v. Garcia, 170 Misc. 2d 543, 647 N.Y.S.2d 355 (Westchester Co. Ct. 1996).

—A counterfeit handbag cannot be considered a written instrument as defined by the statute; since forgery in the second degree requires alteration of a written instrument, the forgery count of the indictment was dismissed. People v. Vu, 161 Misc. 2d 692, 616 N.Y.S.2d 718 (Sup. Ct. N.Y. Co. 1994).

Use of assumed name.—Defendant who signed an application for automobile insurance with the assumed name of "John E. Zopp" was not guilty of forgery since he was the same person as John E. Zopp and did not intend to assume the identity of another. People v. Wesley, 238 A.D.2d 939, 661 N.Y.S.2d 148 (4th Dept. 1997).

Credit card voucher; receipt; application.—A defendant who signs a voucher, receipt or other paper in the name of the card owner is guilty of forgery in the second degree. People v. LeGrand, 81 A.D.2d 945, 439 N.Y.S.2d 695 (3d Dept. 1981).

—The evidence was sufficient to convict the defendant of forgery in the second degree where it revealed that the name the defendant used on his credit application was the name of a real person who had a good credit rating and that the person did not give the defendant authority to use his name. People v. Ramirez, 168 A.D.2d 907, 565 N.Y.S.2d 658 (4th Dept. 1990).

Deeds.—Since defendant was both the actual and the ostensible drawer of the deeds in question, she did not commit a forgery and the fact that the defendant was not the real owner of the property did not change the situation; although the deeds contained false information they were not falsely made. People v. Levitan, 49 N.Y.2d 87, 424 N.Y.S.2d 179, 399 N.E.2d 1199 (1980).

Charge.—In prosecution for criminal possession of a forged instrument, court's charge that "the law says that possession of a forged instrument if you find it was forged is enough to permit the inference that the defendant here knew it was forged if it was on his person" and that "a person is presumed to intend the natural and probable consequences of his act so accordingly if the consequences are natural and probable he will not be heard to say that he didn't intend them" was erroneous; it shifted to the defendant the burden of proof on a crucial element of the crime charged. People v. Harris, 77 A.D.2d 804, 430 N.Y.S.2d 753 (4th Dept. 1980).

§ 170.15. Forgery in the first degree.

A person is guilty of forgery in the first degree when, with intent to defraud, deceive or injure another, he falsely makes, completes or alters a written instrument which is or purports to be, or which is calculated to become or to represent if completed:

1. Part of an issue of money, stamps, securities or other valuable instruments issued by a government or governmental instrumentality; or

2. Part of an issue of stock, bonds or other instruments representing interests in or claims against a corporate or other organization or its property.

Forgery in the first degree is a class C felony.

ANNOTATION

Requisite intent but valid instrument.—Defendant who sold goods to confidential informant on a credit card that defendant knew did not belong to the informant did not commit forgery in the first degree by falsely completing the credit card slip; although defendant acted with the requisite intent, the informant, who was participating in a credit card investigation conducted jointly by various banks, the district attorney and the police department, was authorized to use the card, thus making it legally impossible for defendant to have committed forgery in the first degree. People v. Babits, 122 Misc. 2d 6, 469 N.Y.S.2d 537 (Sup. Ct. Queens Co. 1983).

§ 170.20. Criminal possession of a forged instrument in the third degree.

A person is guilty of criminal possession of a forged instrument in the third degree when, with knowledge that it is forged and with intent to defraud, deceive or injure another, he utters or possesses a forged instrument.

Criminal possession of a forged instrument in the third degree is a class A misdemeanor.

ANNOTATIONS

Evidence.—Evidence was legally sufficient beyond a reasonable doubt to show that defendants committed crime of criminal

possession of a forged instrument in the third degree; while knowledge that an instrument is forged may not be imputed to a defendant solely by the fact of his possession or presentment of the instrument, the circumstantial evidence presented in this case established defendants' knowledge that certain signatures were forged; the jury could conclude from the evidence that the defendants possessed the forged instruments (medical examination forms) with an intent to deceive or defraud the state. People v. Mathis, 218 A.D.2d 817, 630 N.Y.S.2d 793 (2d Dept. 1995).

Written instrument.—Cloned cellular telephone is "written instrument" for purposes of statute. People v. Lawrence, 169 Misc. 2d 752, 647 N.Y.S.2d 675 (Sup. Ct. Kings Co. 1996); People v. Garcia, 170 Misc. 2d 543, 647 N.Y.S.2d 355 (Westchester Co. Ct. 1996).

§ 170.25. Criminal possession of a forged instrument in the second degree.

A person is guilty of criminal possession of a forged instrument in the second degree when, with knowledge that it is forged and with intent to defraud, deceive or injure another, he utters or possesses any forged instrument of a kind specified in section 170.10.

Criminal possession of a forged instrument in the second degree is a class D felony.

ANNOTATIONS

Written instrument.—Cloned cellular telephone is "written instrument" for purposes of statute. People v. Lawrence, 169 Misc. 2d 752, 647 N.Y.S.2d 675 (Sup. Ct. Kings Co. 1996); People v. Garcia, 170 Misc. 2d 543, 647 N.Y.S.2d 355 (Westchester Co. Ct. 1996).

—The crime of criminal possession of a forged instrument in the second degree requires the alteration of a written instrument; since a counterfeit handbag cannot be considered a written instrument as defined by the statute, the count of the indictment charging criminal possession of a forged instrument was dismissed. People v. Vu, 161 Misc. 2d 692, 616 N.Y.S.2d 718 (Sup. Ct. N.Y. Co. 1994).

Evidence.—Possession of a driver's license on which maker misrepresented the birth date, but where all the other information was correct and the holder was entitled to possess such a document, did not support a conviction under this section. People v. Asaro, 94 N.Y.2d 792, 699 N.Y.S.2d 706, 721 N.E.2d 950 (1999).

—Defendant was properly convicted of criminal possession of a forged instrument where the evidence showed that he had attempted more than once to cash a check which had a forged endorsement and the check was later found in a garbage can, notwithstanding the fact that no witness was able to testify that he had seen the forged endorsement of payee's name at the times the defendant had attempted to cash the check. People v. Loughlin, 66 N.Y.2d 633, 495 N.Y.S.2d 357, 485 N.E.2d 1022 (1985).

—In order to find the defendant guilty beyond a reasonable doubt, other evidentiary factors must be present such as the defendant's access to the instrument and his opportunity or ability to forge the instrument, because mere possession of a forged instrument cannot establish a presumption of guilty knowledge. People v. Johnson, 65 N.Y.2d 556, 493 N.Y.S.2d 445, 483 N.E.2d 120 (1985).

—There was insufficient proof, as a matter of law, where there was no finding that the defendant had knowledge that the check was forged. People v. Green, 53 N.Y.2d 651, 438 N.Y.S.2d 992, 421 N.E.2d 112 (1981).

—Evidence was not sufficient to sustain conviction for possession of a forged instrument where it was not shown that the check involved was fraudulently endorsed at the time it was presented by the defendant, nor was it shown that defendant knew endorsement was forged. People v. Loughlin, 105 A.D.2d 846, 482 N.Y.S.2d 42 (2d Dept. 1984).

—It was reversible error to admit into evidence 10 stolen credit cards found in the car in which defendant was riding as well as testimony concerning their ownership. The cards were not the subject of any of the counts in the indictment and their probative value was outweighed by its potential for confusion and prejudice. People v. Zeldes, 78 A.D.2d 865, 432 N.Y.S.2d 714 (2d Dept. 1980).

—Evidence of defendant's possession of a "forged instrument purporting to be a New Jersey automobile operator's license," which was used as supporting document for "identification purposes" to cash bogus checks, was legally sufficient to support her conviction. People v. Edmunds, 21 A.D.3d 578, 799 N.Y.S.2d 338 (3d Dept. 2005).

—Evidence did not support the charge of criminal possession of a forged instrument in the second degree where the defendant obtained a check for the benefit of the Girl Scouts and then tried to use it for her personal benefit, since the check was not a forgery. People v. Seavey, 305 A.D.2d 937, 762 N.Y.S.2d 435 (3d Dept. 2003).

—Evidence that defendant obtained the drug percodan from various drug stores by using false names and addresses on prescriptions in which the doctor's signature had been forged, testimony by six pharmacists that they filled defendant's forged prescriptions, descriptions of seven such transactions, and evidence of the doctor's signature on his application for a medical license, was sufficient to support defendant's conviction for criminal possession of a forged instrument in the second degree. People v. Tagliamonte, 78 A.D.2d 565, 431 N.Y.S.2d 738 (3d Dept. 1980).

—In court identification of defendant by four witnesses who testified that he was the person who presented the forged checks was sufficient to establish defendant's guilt. People v. O'Neill, 79 A.D.2d 202, 437 N.Y.S.2d 202 (4th Dept. 1981).

Indictment.—The indictment and bill of particulars charging defendant with knowingly possessing a forged birth certificate and a forged driver's license with intent to defraud others contained all the essential elements of criminal possession of a forged instrument in the second degree. People v. Terpolilli, 80 A.D.2d 973, 438 N.Y.S.2d 614 (3d Dept. 1981).

§ 170.27. Criminal possession of a forged instrument in the second degree; presumption.

A person who possesses two or more forged instruments, each of which purports to be a credit card or debit card, as those terms are defined in subdivisions seven and seven-a of section 155.00, is presumed to possess the same with knowledge that they are forged and with intent to defraud, deceive or injure another.

Added by L. 1969, Ch. 115; **Amended** by L. 1987, Ch. 556.

§ 170.30. Criminal possession of a forged instrument in the first degree.

A person is guilty of criminal possession of a forged instrument in the first degree when, with knowledge that it is forged and with intent to defraud, deceive or injure another, he utters or possesses any forged instrument of a kind specified in section 170.15.

Criminal possession of a forged instrument in the first degree is a class C felony.

ANNOTATION

Lottery ticket.—Tampering with a lottery agent's number on the reverse side of a lottery ticket constituted the crime of forgery. People v. Canfield, 70 A.D.2d 706, 416 N.Y.S.2d 688 (3d Dept. 1979).

§ 170.35. Criminal possession of a forged instrument; no defense.

In any prosecution for criminal possession of a forged instrument, it is no defense that the defendant forged or participated in the forgery of the instrument in issue; provided that a person may not be convicted of both criminal possession of a forged instrument and forgery with respect to the same instrument.

ANNOTATIONS

Different instruments.—There was no violation of PL § 170.35 where the record established that defendant's conviction arose from the possession of a check drawn on a credit union account of two individuals and endorsed by a third individual, and the forgery of a credit union draft; there was no question that two instruments were involved, and convictions for criminal possession of a forged instrument in the second degree and forgery in the second degree were upheld. People v. Jacot, 210 A.D.2d 979, 621 N.Y.S.2d 999 (1994).

Evidence.—After being injured on the job, defendant executed recertification forms attesting that he had not received any income; however, defendant had begun to receive worker's compensation benefits as a result of his permanent partial disability during this time. Proof at trial established that defendant received an overpayment as a result of his failure to disclose the disability payments, and was sufficient to support a conviction under this section. People v. Starks, 238 A.D.2d 621, 656 N.Y.S.2d 399 (3d Dept. 1997).

—Making a false written statement to the government contains the same elements as offering a false instrument for filing in the first degree. In re Trammell, 240 A.D.2d 90, 667 N.Y.S.2d 965 (4th Dept. 1998).

Federal law.—Conviction under 18 U.S.C. § 1001 is analogous to a conviction under Penal Law § 175.35; defendant's conviction under the federal statute was the basis for his disbarment. In re Gottlieb, 240 A.D.2d 81, 669 N.Y.S.2d 363 (2d Dept. 1998).

Prosecutorial Jurisdiction—Prosecutorial jurisdiction was not established where defendants, accused of filing allegedly false New York State and New York City tax returns, were prosecuted in New York County based on location of bank accounts and agencies which process the returns and remit payment o the City; "in a prosecution whose gravamen is the deprivation of revenue from New York City-the location of the City agencies and bank accounts is alone insufficient to establish a particular effect on the county in which they happen to be located." Taub v. Altman, 3 N.Y.3d 30, 781 N.Y.S.2d 492, 814 N.E.2d 799 (2004).

Sentencing.—Court erred by not imposing concurrent sentences for defendant's convictions for offering a false instrument for filing in the first degree and larceny by false pretenses, where both crimes arose out of the single act of offering a false statement for filing. People v. Starks, 238 A.D.2d 621, 656 N.Y.S.2d 399 (3d Dept. 1997).

§ 170.40. Criminal possession of forgery devices.

A person is guilty of criminal possession of forgery devices when:

1. He makes or possesses with knowledge of its character any plate, die or other device, apparatus, equipment, or article specifically designed for use in counterfeiting or otherwise forging written instruments; or

2. With intent to use, or to aid or permit another to use, the same for purposes of forgery, he makes or possesses any device, apparatus, equipment or article capable of or adaptable to such use.

Criminal possession of forgery devices is a class D felony.

§ 170.45. Criminal simulation.

A person is guilty of criminal simulation when:

1. With intent to defraud, he makes or alters any object in such manner that it appears to have an antiquity, rarity, source or authorship which it does not in fact possess; or

2. With knowledge of its true character and with intent to defraud, he utters or possesses an object so simulated.

Criminal simulation is a class A misdemeanor.

ANNOTATIONS

Independent inference; effect on right to remain silent.—A defendant's right to remain silent is unimpaired by the fact that an independent inference may arise from his unexplained possession of the fruits of a crime. People v. Wheeler, 40 A.D.2d 348, 340 N.Y.S.2d 196 (2d Dept. 1973), *cert. denied,* 412 U.S. 931 (1973).

Silence; no inference of guilt proper.—The defense did not object to the court's questioning a witness, in front of the jury, on the defendant's refusal to be interrogated in the absence of counsel. Furthermore, the court stated in its charge to the jury that no inference could or should be drawn from the defendant's silence. Defendant's confession, made after his refusal to answer questions, rendered harmless any prejudice resulting from the testimony that the defendant had wished to remain silent. People v. Wheeler, 40 A.D.2d 348, 340 N.Y.S.2d 196 (2d Dept.), *cert. denied,* 412 U.S. 931 (1973).

Simulation; necessary ingredient—The people must show the object meets the necessary element of antiquity, rarity, source, or authorship, to obtain a conviction. People v. James, 79 Misc. 2d 805, 361 N.Y.S.2d 255 (Dist. Ct. Nassau Co. 1974).

§ 170.47. Criminal possession of an anti-security item.

A person is guilty of criminal possession of an anti-security item, when with intent to steal property at a retail mercantile establishment as defined in article twelve-B of the general business law, he knowingly possesses in such an establishment an item designed for the purpose of overcoming detection of security markings or attachments placed on property offered for sale at such an establishment.

Criminal possession of an anti-security item is a class B misdemeanor.

Added by L. 1983, Ch. 580.

§ 170.50. Unlawfully using slugs; definitions of terms.

The following definitions are applicable to sections 170.55 and 170.60:

1. "Coin machine" means a coin box, turnstile, vending machine or other mechanical or electronic device or receptacle designed (a) to receive a coin or bill or a token made for the purpose, and (b) in return for the insertion or deposit thereof, automatically to offer, to provide, to assist in providing or to permit the acquisition of some property or some service.

2. "Slug" means an object or article which, by virtue of its size, shape or any other quality, is capable of being inserted or deposited in a coin machine as an improper substitute for a genuine coin, bill or token.

3. "Value" of a slug means the value of the coin, bill or token for which it is capable of being substituted.

§ 170.55. Unlawfully using slugs in the second degree.

A person is guilty of unlawfully using slugs in the second degree when:

1. With intent to defraud the owner of a coin machine, he inserts or deposits a slug in such machine; or

2. He makes, possesses or disposes of a slug with intent to enable a person to insert or deposit it in a coin machine.

Unlawfully using slugs in the second degree is a class B misdemeanor.

ANNOTATION

Independent inference; effect on right to remain silent.—A defendant's right to remain silent is unimpaired by the fact that an independent inference may arise from his unexplained possession of the fruits of a crime. People v. Wheeler, 40 A.D.2d 348, 340 N.Y.S.2d 196 (2d Dept.), *cert. denied,* 412 U.S. 931 (1973).

§ 170.60. Unlawfully using slugs in the first degree.

A person is guilty of unlawfully using slugs in the first degree when he makes, possesses or disposes of slugs with intent to enable a person to insert or deposit them in a coin machine, and the value of such slugs exceeds one hundred dollars.

Unlawfully using slugs in the first degree is a class E felony.

§ 170.65. Forgery of a vehicle identification number.

A person is guilty of forgery of a vehicle identification number when:

(1) He knowingly destroys, covers, defaces, alters or otherwise changes the form or appearance of a vehicle identification number on any vehicle or component part thereof, except tires; or

(2) He removes any such number from a vehicle or component part thereof, except as required by the provisions of the vehicle and traffic law; or

(3) He affixes a vehicle identification number to a vehicle, except in accordance with the provisions of the vehicle and traffic law.

Forgery of a vehicle identification number is a class E felony.

Added by L. 1970, Ch. 880; Amended by L. 1977, Ch. 488.

§ 170.70. Illegal possession of a vehicle identification number.

A person is guilty of illegal possession of a vehicle identification number when:

(1) He knowingly possesses a vehicle identification number label, sticker or plate which has been removed from the vehicle or vehicle part to which such label, sticker or plate was affixed by the manufacturer in accordance with 49 U.S.C. section 32101, et seq. and regulations promulgated thereunder or in accordance with the provisions of the vehicle and traffic law; or

(2) He knowingly possesses a vehicle or vehicle part to which is attached a vehicle identification number label, sticker or plate or on which is stamped or embossed a vehicle identification number which has been destroyed, covered, defaced, altered or otherwise changed, or a vehicle or vehicle part from which a vehicle identification number label, sticker or plate has been removed, which label, sticker or plate was affixed in accordance with 49 U.S.C. section 32101, et seq. or regulations promulgated thereunder, except when he has complied with the provisions of the vehicle and traffic law and regulations promulgated thereunder; or

(3) He knowingly possesses a vehicle, or part of a vehicle to which by law or regulation must be attached a vehicle identification number, either (a) with a vehicle identification number label, sticker, or plate which was not affixed by the manufacturer in accordance with 49 U.S.C. section 32101, et seq. or regulations promulgated thereunder, or in accordance with the provisions of the vehicle and traffic law or regulations promulgated thereunder, or

(b) on which is affixed, stamped or embossed a vehicle identification number which was not affixed, stamped or embossed by the manufacturer, or in accordance with 49 U.S.C. section 32101, et seq. or regulations promulgated thereunder or in accordance with the provisions of the vehicle and traffic law or regulations promulgated thereunder.

Illegal possession of a vehicle identification number is a class E felony.

Added by L. 1970, Ch. 880; Amended by L. 1977; Ch. 488; L. 1981, Ch. 976; L. 1984, Ch. 81; L. 1992, Ch. 317, eff. Nov. 1, 1992; L. 2001, Ch. 540, eff. Nov. 1, 2002.

ANNOTATIONS

Evidence.—If the prosecution intends to rely on testimony as to a confidential VIN, cross-examination must be unrestricted; if, however, the defendant's conviction is based on other proof, a mere inconsequential reference to the confidential VIN may not open the door to unlimited cross-examination. People v. Silver, 39 N.Y.2d 99, 382 N.Y.S.2d 972, 346 N.E.2d 811 (1976).

Corroboration.—Defendant's motion for dismissal of an information charging him with attempted possession of an illegal vehicle identification number (VIN) was denied; the court rejected defendant's claim that the information was fatally flawed for lack of the vehicle owner's corroborating affidavit, finding that the defendant's actions wee inconsistent with lawful ownership and that direct proof of lack of the owner's permission and/or authority was unnecessary. Moreover, the court stated that the unlawful possession of the VIN was established by the mere fact of the attachment of the VIN to a dashboard which obviously had been removed from an automobile, and which the defendant was carrying. People v. Codrington, 165 Misc. 2d 215, 629 N.Y.S.2d 369 (Crim. Ct. Queens Co. 1995).

§ 170.71. Illegal possession of a vehicle identification number; presumptions.

(1) A person is presumed to knowingly possess a vehicle or vehicle part in violation of subdivision two of section 170.70, when he possesses any combination of five such whole vehicles or individual vehicle parts, none of which are attached to or contained in the same vehicle.

(2) A person is presumed to knowingly possess a vehicle or vehicle part in violation of subdivision three of section 170.70, when he possesses any combination of five such whole vehicles or individual vehicle parts, none of which are attached to or contained in the same vehicle.

Added by L. 1984, Ch. 81, eff. Nov. 1, 1984; Amended by L. 1984, Ch. 576, eff. Nov. 1, 1984.

§ 170.75. Fraudulent making of an electronic access device in the second degree.

A person is guilty of fraudulent making of an electronic access device in the second degree when, with intent to defraud, deceive or injure another, he falsely makes, completes or alters two or more electronic access devices, as that term is defined in subdivision eight of section 170.00 of this article.

Fraudulent making of an electronic access device in the second degree is a class D felony.

Added by l. 1996, Ch. 357, eff. Nov. 1, 1996.

ARTICLE 175—OFFENSES INVOLVING FALSE WRITTEN STATEMENTS

Section

175.00   Definitions of terms.

175.05   Falsifying business records in the second degree.

175.10   Falsifying business records in the first degree.

175.15   Falsifying business records; defense.

175.20   Tampering with public records in the second degree.

175.25   Tampering with public records in the first degree.

175.30   Offering a false instrument for filing in the second degree.

175.35   Offering a false instrument for filing in the first degree.

175.40   Issuing a false certificate.

175.45   Issuing a false financial statement.

§ 175.00. Definitions of terms.

The following definitions are applicable to this article:

1. "Enterprise" means any entity of one or more persons, corporate or otherwise, public or private, engaged in business, commercial, professional, industrial, eleemosynary, social, political or governmental activity.

2. "Business record" means any writing or article, including computer data or a computer program, kept or maintained by an enterprise for the purpose of evidencing or reflecting its condition or activity.

3. "Written instrument" means any instrument or article, including computer data or a computer program, containing written or printed matter or the equivalent thereof, used for the purpose of reciting, embodying, conveying or recording information, or constituting a symbol or evidence of value, right, privilege or identification, which is capable of being used to the advantage or disadvantage of some person.

Amended by L. 1978, Ch. 233; L. 1986, Ch. 514.

ANNOTATIONS

"Business record."—Where the business record referred to in the indictment was a "transition piece," which is a section of manhole cover marked by the manufacturer with identifying markings, the fact that inspectors hired by the county referred to those markings in their daily log and inspection records did not render the transition piece and its markings a public or business record. People v. W.D. Boccard & Sons, Inc., 74 A.D.2d 654, 425 N.Y.S.2d 130 (2d Dept. 1980).

Enterprise.—Petitioner's medical practice was an enterprise within the meaning of PL § 175.00(1), and medical records were not personal records but those of the entity. Momah v. Rogers, 93 N.Y.2d 864, 689 N.Y.S.2d 13, 711 N.E.2d 198 (1999).

Kept or maintained.—Forged documents created by defendant to prevent the Securities and Exchange Commission from discovering the true owners of offshore corporations were not business records under the statute, since the letters were held by an attorney, and not "kept or maintained" by those offshore corporations (the enterprise). People v. Bloomfield, 15 A.D.3d 302, 790 N.Y.S.2d 443 (1st Dept. 2005).

Written instrument.—Document given by defendant to parole officer which falsely stated that criminal charges against defendant had been dismissed by grand jury was a "written instrument" within the meaning of PL article 175. People v. Sinclair, 208 A.D.2d 573, 617 N.Y.S.2d 45 (2d Dept. 1994).

—An employment application is a written instrument within the

meaning of Penal Law § 175.00(3). People v. Armitt, 195 Misc. 2d 879, 762 N.Y.S.2d 222 (Sup. Ct. App. T. 2003).

§ 175.05. Falsifying business records in the second degree.

A person is guilty of falsifying business records in the second degree when, with intent to defraud, he:

1. Makes or causes a false entry in the business records of an enterprise; or

2. Alters, erases, obliterates, deletes, removes or destroys a true entry in the business records of an enterprise; or

3. Omits to make a true entry in the business records of an enterprise in violation of a duty to do so which he knows to be imposed upon him by law or by the nature of his position; or

4. Prevents the making of a true entry or causes the omission thereof in the business records of an enterprise.

Falsifying business records in the second degree is a class A misdemeanor.

ANNOTATIONS

Evidence.—Although it was error to receive into evidence during the People's case-in-chief that portion of the defendant's grand jury testimony in which he acknowledged a prior conviction, such portion of the transcript could have been redacted and the error avoided if defense counsel had brought this matter to the attention of the trial court by means of a specific objection. The absence of a specific objection to the introduction of the prior conviction prevented this court from reviewing the issue. People v. Rullo, 31 N.Y.2d 894, 340 N.Y.S.2d 405, 292 N.E.2d 674 (1972).

—Requirements of statute were satisfied by evidence that defendant called power corporation on 13 separate occasions representing himself to be another person or that person's daughter and requesting that the power be shut off, the billing address changed, or an investigation commenced upon his report of a gas leak, knowing that false records were being created as a result of these calls. People v. Fushino, 278 A.D.2d 657, 719 N.Y.S.2d 152 (3d Dept. 2000), *appeal denied*, 96 N.Y.2d 800 (2001).

§ 175.10. Falsifying business records in the first degree.

A person is guilty of falsifying business records in the first degree when he commits the crime of falsifying business records in the second degree, and when his intent to defraud includes an intent to commit another crime or to aid or conceal the commission thereof.

Falsifying business records in the first degree is a class E felony.

ANNOTATIONS

Motor vehicle records.—Evidence that defendant falsified forms which county automobile bureau was required to prepare in order to account to state department of motor vehicles for missing or mutilated registration plates or validation stickers and to account for transactions taking place at county auto bureau was sufficient to support guilty verdict for falsifying business records. People v. Davis, 49 N.Y.2d 910, 428 N.Y.S.2d 195, 405 N.E.2d 677 (1980).

Evidence.—Evidence was sufficient to establish defendant's commission of the crime of falsifying business records in the first degree where it was shown that defendant gave parole officer a document which falsely stated that criminal charges against him had been dismissed by grand jury, that the parole officer placed the document in defendant's parole file; the fact that the defendant did not ask for the return of the document permitted the jury to infer that he knew that the document was to become part of his parole file. People v. Sinclair, 208 A.D.2d 573, 617 N.Y.S.2d 45 (2d Dept. 1994).

Sentence.—Defendant was properly sentenced to a term of 1 to 4 years following conviction of falsifying business records in the first degree; the sentence was lawful as the minimum term of the sentence was not less than one year and not more than one third of the maximum term imposed. People v. Thomas, 209 A.D.2d 1047, 619 N.Y.S.2d 1007 (4th Dept. 1994).

§ 175.15. Falsifying business records; defense.

In any prosecution for falsifying business records, it is an affirmative defense that the defendant was a clerk, bookkeeper or other employee who, without personal benefit, merely executed the orders of his employer or of a superior officer or employee generally authorized to direct his activities.

§ 175.20. Tampering with public records in the second degree.

A person is guilty of tampering with public records in the second degree when, knowing that he does not have the authority of anyone entitled to grant it, he knowingly removes, mutilates, destroys, conceals, makes a false entry in or falsely alters any record or other written instrument filed with, deposited in, or otherwise constituting a record of a public office or public servant.

Tampering with public records in the second degree is a class A misdemeanor.

§ 175.25. Tampering with public records in the first degree.

A person is guilty of tampering with public records in the first degree when, knowing that he does not have the authority of anyone entitled to grant it, and with intent to defraud, he knowingly removes, mutilates, destroys, conceals, makes a false entry in or falsely alters any record or other written instrument filed with, deposited in, or otherwise constituting a record of a public office or public servant.

Tampering with public records in the first degree is a class D felony.

§ 175.30. Offering a false instrument for filing in the second degree.

A person is guilty of offering a false instrument for filing in the second degree when, knowing that a written instrument contains a false statement or false information, he offers or presents it to a public office or public servant with the knowledge or belief that it will be filed with, registered or recorded in or otherwise become a part of the records of such public office or public servant.

Offering a false instrument for filing in the second degree is a class A misdemeanor.

ANNOTATION

Evidence.—Defendant's submission of an employment application to Nassau County District Attorney's office for position as attorney's assistant in which she indicated that she had never been convicted of a crime, when she had been convicted of a felony in 1991, was sufficient to support a conviction under this section. People v. Armitt, 195 Misc. 2d 879, 762 N.Y.S.2d 222 (Sup. Ct. Nassau Co. 2003).

§ 175.35. Offering a false instrument for filing in the first degree.

A person is guilty of offering a false instrument for filing in the first degree when, knowing that a written instrument contains a false statement or false information, and with intent to defraud the state or any political subdivision, public authority or public benefit corporation of the state, he offers or presents it to a public office, public servant, public authority or public benefit corporation with the knowledge or belief that it will be filed with, registered or recorded in or otherwise become a part of the records of such public office, public servant, public authority or public benefit corporation.

Offering a false instrument for filing in the first degree is a class E felony.

Amended by L. 1998, Ch. 99, § 1, eff. Nov. 1, 1998, and shall only apply when acts constituting the offenses added by this act occurred on or after Nov. 1, 1998.

ANNOTATIONS

Instrument.—Application for a certificate of occupancy is not an "instrument" within the contemplation of PL § 175.35. People v. Gottlieb, 36 N.Y.2d 629, 370 N.Y.S.2d 884, 331 N.E.2d 670 (1975).

—Evidence that defendant submitted false collection reports and equipment sign-out sheets to his employer to conceal his theft of proceeds from parking meters satisfied the statutory requirement that the potential benefit to defendant flows from the fraudulent nature of the documents in question. People v. Ravenell, 154 A.D.2d 51, 680 N.Y.S.2d 196 (1st Dept. 1998).

—A written contract for sale of a tavern to police officers conducting investigation which stated that price of such tavern was $15,000, even though the actual price was $75,000 with $60,000 to be paid under the table, was a "written instrument" containing false statement or false information which was filed with the office of Alcoholic Beverage Control Board, and was an instrument contemplated in PL § 175.35. People v. Kase,

76 A.D.2d 532, 431 N.Y.S.2d 531 (1st Dept. 1980), *aff'd*, 53 N.Y.2d 989, 441 N.Y.S.2d 671, 424 N.E.2d 558 (1981).

—County resolution is not instrument within the meaning of PL § 175.35 as that term was defined before the enactment of PL § 175.00(3). People v. Gothainer, 80 A.D.2d 922, 437 N.Y.S.2d 386 (2d Dept.), *aff'd*, 55 N.Y.2d 765, 447 N.Y.S.2d 246, 431 N.E.2d 971 (1981).

Evidence.—Jury verdict finding defendants guilty of grand larceny in the second degree and offering a false instrument for filing but which acquitted defendants on charges of violating Tax Law § 1817(b)(1) was not repugnant where People established that, as a result of underreporting sales, defendants collected $200,000 in sales tax which was not remitted. Jury could have found that defendants offered the false returns for filing but did not "make and subscribe" them. People v. Filacouris, 95 N.Y.2d 940, 722 N.Y.S.2d 459, 745 N.E.2d 378 (2000).

—Evidence was sufficient to establish defendant's commission of the crime of offering a false instrument for filing in the first degree where it was shown that defendant gave parole officer a document which falsely stated that criminal charges against him had been dismissed by grand jury, and that the parole officer placed the document in defendant's parole file; the fact that the defendant did not ask for the return of the document permitted the jury to infer that he knew that the document was to become part of his parole file. People v. Sinclair, 208 A.D.2d 573, 617 N.Y.S.2d 45 (2d Dept. 1994).

—Defendant's submissions of fraudulently inflated Medicaid claim forms with the intent to defraud in order to obtain monies and properties to which he was not entitled supported both convictions of grand larceny in the second degree and offering a false instrument for filing the first degree. People v. Rubin, 286 A.D.2d 555, 729 N.Y.S.2d 561 (3d Dept. 2001).

—Evidence that defendant understood the public charge regulation and yet created schemes to conceal his violation of it by creating two separate price schedules—$12 per hour for public care, which was accurate and actually charged to the clients, and $15.25 per hour, which he reported to Medicaid officials—supported defendant's conviction for grand larceny in the second degree and six counts of offering a false instrument for filing in the first degree. People v. Rubin, 271 A.D.2d 759; 706 N.Y.S.2d 225 (3d Dept. 2000).

—Rejecting defendant's argument that filing of claims for reimbursement with a private concern could not form the basis for charge of offering a false instrument for filing. People v. Scotti, 232 A.D.2d 775, 649 N.Y.S.2d 55 (3d Dept. 1996).

—Evidence showing that the defendant had not reported income of household members and that the department of social services had relied upon the information supplied by the defendant was sufficient to establish guilt on the charge of offering a false instrument for filing in the first degree. People v. Layman, 112 A.D.2d 530, 491 N.Y.S.2d 468 (3d Dept. 1985).

—Conviction for offering a false instrument for filing was supported by sufficient evidence of intent to defraud, specifically that defendant indicated on the recertification form that his daughter resided with him when he knew that she did not. People v. Scutt, 19 A.D.3d 1131, 796 N.Y.S.2d 816 (4th Dept. 2005).

Prosecutorial Jurisdiction—Prosecutorial jurisdiction was not established where defendants, accused of filing allegedly false New York State and New York City tax returns, were prosecuted in New York County based on location of bank accounts and agencies which process the returns and remit

payment to the City; "in a prosecution whose gravamen is the deprivation of revenue from New York City-the location of the City agencies and bank accounts is alone insufficient to establish a particular effect on the county in which they happen to be located." Taub v. Altman, 3 N.Y.3d 30, 781 N.Y.S.2d 492, 814 N.E.2d 799 (2004).

Sufficiency of indictment.—Indictment charging police officer with offering false instrument for filing, attempted grand larceny and grand larceny and defrauding the government provided fair notice of the charges which were based on defendant's falsely claiming to be permanently disabled and of improperly collecting money from Nassau County. People v. Patino, 170 Misc. 2d 284, 648 N.Y.S.2d 241 (Nassau Co. Ct. 1996).

Restitution.—Defendant's sentence of restitution after a conviction for filing a false instrument in the first degree resulting from her failure to disclose accurate income information to social security was an appropriate sentence, even though defendant was acquitted of grand larceny and welfare fraud charges; identifiable victim sustained monetary losses due to her criminal conduct. People v. Horne, 97 N.Y.2d 404, 740 N.Y.S.2d 675, 767 N.E.2d 132 (2002).

§ 175.40. Issuing a false certificate.

A person is guilty of issuing a false certificate when, being a public servant authorized by law to make or issue official certificates or other official written instruments, and with intent to defraud, deceive or injure another person, he issues such an instrument, or makes the same with intent that it be issued, knowing that it contains a false statement or false information.

Issuing a false certificate is a class E felony.

§ 175.45. Issuing a false financial statement.

A person is guilty of issuing a false financial statement when, with intent to defraud:

1. He knowingly makes or utters a written instrument which purports to describe the financial condition or ability to pay of some person and which is inaccurate in some material respect; or

2. He represents in writing that a written instrument purporting to describe a person's financial condition or ability to pay as of a prior date is accurate with respect to such person's current financial condition or ability to pay, whereas he knows it is materially inaccurate in that respect.

Issuing a false financial statement is a class A misdemeanor.

ARTICLE 176—INSURANCE FRAUD

§ 176.00. Insurance fraud; definition of terms.

The following definitions are applicable to the article.

1. "Insurance policy" has the meaning assigned to insurance contract by subsection (a) of section one thousand one hundred one of the insurance law except it shall include reinsurance contracts, purported insurance policies and purported reinsurance contracts.

2. "Statement" includes, but is not limited to, any notice, proof of loss, bill of lading, invoice, account, estimate of property damages, bill for services, diagnosis, prescription, hospital or doctor records, x-ray, test result, and other evidence of loss, injury or expense.

3. "Person" includes any individual, firm, association or corporation.

4. "Personal insurance" means a policy of insurance insuring a natural person against any of the following contingencies:

(a) loss of or damage to real property used predominantly for residential purposes and which consists of not more than four dwelling units, other than hotels, motels and rooming houses;

(b) loss of or damage to personal property which is not used in the conduct of a business;

(c) losses or liabilities arising out of the ownership, operation, or use of a motor vehicle, predominantly used for non-business purposes;

(d) other liabilities for loss of, damage to, or injury to persons or property, not arising from the conduct of a business;

(e) death, including death by personal injury, or the continuation of life, or personal injury by accident, or sickness, disease or ailment, excluding insurance providing disability benefits pursuant to article nine of the workers' compensation law.

A policy of insurance which insures any of the contingencies listed in paragraphs (a) through (e) of this subdivision as well as other contingencies shall be personal insurance if that portion of the annual premium attributable to the listed contingencies exceeds that portion attributable to other contingencies.

5. "Commercial insurance" means insurance other than personal insurance, and shall also include insurance providing disability benefits pursuant to article nine of the workers' compensation law, insurance providing workers' compensation benefits pursuant to the provisions of the workers' compensation law and any program of self insurance providing similar benefits.

Amended by L. 1984, Ch. 805; L. 1996, Ch. 635, § 24, amending subd. 5, eff. Sept. 10, 1996.

ANNOTATIONS

Statement.—A written statement within the meaning of PL § 176.00(2) may consist of one materially false or misleading document or multiple documents collectively submitted to the insurer to advance a single fraudulent claim. People v. Aksoy, 84 N.Y.2d 912, 620 N.Y.S.2d 806, 644 N.E.2d 1362 (1994).

Evidence.—Evidence that defendant knowingly submitted false information to his insurance company, including that fire which caused damage was not accidental, that same property had been previously insured by defendant, and that a few years earlier it had sustained substantial fire damage in the same manner and that defendant received a large settlement, was sufficient to establish insurance fraud. People v. Chase, 299 A.D.2d 597, 750 N.Y.S.2d 182 (3d Dept. 2002).

§ 176.05. Insurance fraud; defined.

1. A fraudulent insurance act is committed by any person who, knowingly and with intent to defraud presents, causes to be presented, or prepares with knowledge or belief that it will be presented to or by an insurer, self insurer, or purported insurer, or purported self insurer, or any agent thereof, any written statement as part of, or in support of, an application for the issuance of, or the rating of a commercial insurance policy, or certificate or evidence of self insurance for commercial insurance or commercial self insurance, or a claim for payment or other benefit pursuant to an insurance policy or self insurance program for commercial or personal insurance which he knows to: (i) contain materially false information concerning any fact material thereto; or (ii) conceal, for the purpose of misleading, information concerning any fact material thereto.

2. A fraudulent health care insurance act is committed by any person who, knowingly and with intent to defraud, presents, causes to be presented, or prepares with knowledge or belief

that it will be presented to, or by, an insurer or purported insurer or self-insurer, or any agent thereof, any written statement or other physical evidence as part of, or in support of, an application for the issuance of a health insurance policy, or a policy or contract or other authorization that provides or allows coverage for, membership or enrollment in, or other services of a public or private health plan, or a claim for payment, services or other benefit pursuant to such policy, contract or plan, which he knows to:

(a) contain materially false information concerning any material fact thereto; or

(b) conceal, for the purpose of misleading, information concerning any fact material thereto. Such policy or contract or plan or authorization shall include, but not be limited to, those issued or operating pursuant to any public or governmentally-sponsored or supported plan for health care coverage or services or those otherwise issued or operated by entities authorized pursuant to the public health law. For purposes of this subdivision an "application for the issuance of a health insurance policy" shall not include (A) any application for a health insurance policy or contract approved by the superintendent of insurance pursuant to the provisions of sections three thousand two hundred sixteen, four thousand three hundred four, four thousand three hundred twenty-one or four thousand three hundred twenty-two of the insurance law or any other application for a health insurance policy or contract approved by the superintendent of insurance in the individual or direct payment market; and (B) any application for a certificate evidencing coverage under a self-insured plan or under a group contract approved by the superintendent of insurance.

Amended by L. 1996, Ch. 635, § 23, eff. Sept. 10, 1996; L. 1998, Ch. 2, § 42, eff. Nov. 1, 1998, adding subd. 2.

ANNOTATION

Elements.—The criminal act which constitutes the offense encompasses both the filing of the false documents and the making of a false claim for payment. People v. Aksoy, 84 N.Y.2d 912, 644 N.E.2d 1362, 620 N.Y.S.2d 806 (1994).

§ 176.10. Insurance fraud in the fifth degree.

A person is guilty of insurance fraud in the fifth degree when he commits a fraudulent insurance act.

Insurance fraud in the fifth degree is a class A misdemeanor.

Amended by L. 1986, Ch. 515.

§ 176.15. Insurance fraud in the fourth degree.

A person is guilty of insurance fraud in the fourth degree when he commits a fraudulent insurance act and thereby wrongfully takes, obtains or withholds, or attempts to wrongfully take,

obtain or withhold property with a value in excess of one thousand dollars.

Insurance fraud in the fourth degree is a class E felony.

Amended by L. 1986, Ch. 515.

§ 176.20. Insurance fraud in the third degree.

A person is guilty of insurance fraud in the third degree when he commits a fraudulent insurance act and thereby wrongfully takes, obtains or withholds, or attempts to wrongfully take, obtain or withhold property with a value in excess of three thousand dollars.

Insurance fraud in the third degree is a class D felony.

Amended by L. 1986, Ch. 515.

ANNOTATIONS

Evidence.—Evidence that defendant made misrepresentations to an insurance company in which he stated he had not worked in any capacity during the last six months to one year and received $34,000 in benefits, when in fact he had only stopped working at one of his two jobs during that time, was sufficient to support convictions for grand larceny in the third degree and insurance fraud in the third degree. People v. Hade, 255 A.D.2d 769, 682 N.Y.S.2d 468 (3d Dept. 1998).

—Evidence was sufficient to sustain conviction where proof at trial was overwhelming that defendant was fully aware that fire was set intentionally to collect insurance proceeds, and that she presented materially false sworn proofs of loss to insurer; proof also established that defendant attempted to wrongfully obtain property valued in excess of $3,000 where defendant's sworn proofs of loss sought recovery of $50,000 in damages to the building and $25,000 in damages to its contents. People v. Michael, 210 A.D.2d 874, 620 N.Y.S.2d 637 (4th Dept. 1994).

§ 176.25. Insurance fraud in the second degree.

A person is guilty of insurance fraud in the second degree when he commits a fraudulent insurance act and thereby wrongfully takes, obtains or withholds, or attempts to wrongfully take, obtain or withhold property with a value in excess of fifty thousand dollars.

Insurance fraud in the second degree is a class C felony.

Added by L. 1986, Ch. 515.

ANNOTATION

Evidence.—Where defendant obtained an insurance settlement in excess of $50,000 for water and fire damage to his home, and People failed to introduce evidence as to which portion of the proceeds were attributable to the water damage, which was a legitimate claim, and which portion to fire damage, which was established at trial to be the fraudulent claim, the conviction under this section could not stand. People v. Chase, 299 A.D.2d 597, 750 N.Y.S.2d 182 (3d Dept. 2002).

§ 176.30. Insurance fraud in the first degree.

A person is guilty of insurance fraud in the first degree when he commits a fraudulent insurance act and thereby wrongfully takes, obtains or withholds, or attempts to wrongfully take, obtain or withhold property with a value in excess of one million dollars.

Insurance fraud in the first degree is a class B felony.

Added by L. 1986, Ch. 515.

§ 176.35. Aggravated insurance fraud.

A person is guilty of aggravated insurance fraud in the fourth degree when he commits a fraudulent insurance act, and has been previously convicted within the preceding five years of any offense, an essential element of which is the commission of a fraudulent insurance act.

Aggravated insurance fraud in the fourth degree is a class D felony.

Added by L. 1996, Ch. 635, § 21, eff. Sept. 10, 1996.

ARTICLE 178—CRIMINAL DIVERSION OF PRESCRIPTION MEDICATIONS AND PRESCRIPTIONS

LexisNexis Cross Reference

Defense of Narcotics Cases, Vol. 1, Ch. 1, Narcotic Crimes.

§ 178.00. Criminal diversion of prescription medications and prescriptions; definitions.

The following definitions are applicable to this article:

1. "Prescription medication or device" means any article for which a prescription is required in order to be lawfully sold, delivered or distributed by any person authorized by law to engage in the practice of the profession of pharmacy.

2. "Prescription" means a direction or authorization by means of a written prescription form or an oral prescription which permits a person to lawfully obtain a prescription medication or device from any person authorized to dispense such prescription medication or device.

3. "Criminal diversion act" means an act or acts in which a person knowingly:

(a) Transfers or delivers, in exchange for anything of pecuniary value, a prescription medication or device with knowledge or reasonable grounds to know that the recipient has no medical need for it; or

(b) Receives, in exchange for anything of pecuniary value, a prescription medication or device with knowledge or reasonable grounds to know that the seller or transferor is not authorized by law to sell or transfer such prescription medication or device; or

(c) Transfers or delivers a prescription in exchange for anything of pecuniary value; or

(d) Receives a prescription in exchange for anything of pecuniary value.

Added by L. 1995, Ch. 81, § 94, eff. Nov. 1, 1995.

§ 178.05. Criminal diversion of prescription medications and prescriptions; limitation.

1. The provisions of this article shall not apply to:

(a) A duly licensed physician or other person authorized to issue a prescription acting in good faith in the lawful course of his or her profession; or

(b) A duly licensed pharmacist acting in good faith in the lawful course of the practice of pharmacy; or

(c) A person acting in good faith seeking treatment for a medical condition or assisting another person to obtain treatment for a medical condition.

2. No provision of this article relating to the sale of a prescription medication or device shall be deemed to authorize any act prohibited by article thirty-three of the public health law or article two hundred twenty of this chapter.

Added by L. 1995, Ch. 81, § 94, eff. Nov. 1, 1995.

§ 178.10. Criminal diversion of prescription medications and prescriptions in the fourth degree.

A person is guilty of criminal diversion of prescription medications and prescriptions in the fourth degree when he or she commits a criminal diversion act.

Criminal diversion of prescription medications and prescriptions in the fourth degree is a class A misdemeanor.

Added by L. 1995, Ch. 81, § 94, eff. Nov. 1, 1995.

§ 178.15. Criminal diversion of prescription medications and prescriptions in the third degree.

A person is guilty of criminal diversion of prescription medications and prescriptions in the third degree when he or she:

1. Commits a criminal diversion act, and the value of the benefit exchanged is in excess of one thousand dollars; or

2. Commits the crime of criminal diversion of prescription medications and prescriptions in the fourth degree, and has previously been convicted of the crime of criminal diversion of prescription medications and prescriptions in the fourth degree.

Criminal diversion of prescription medications and prescriptions in the third degree is a class E felony.

Added by L. 1995, Ch. 81, § 94, eff. Nov. 1, 1995.

§ 178.20. Criminal diversion of prescription medications and prescriptions in the second degree.

A person is guilty of criminal diversion of prescription medications and prescriptions in the second degree when he or she commits a criminal diversion act, and the value of the benefit exchanged is in excess of three thousand dollars.

Criminal diversion of prescription medications and prescriptions in the second degree is a class D felony.

Added by L. 1995, Ch. 81, § 94, eff. Nov. 1, 1995.

§ 178.25. Criminal diversion of prescription medications and prescriptions in the first degree.

A person is guilty of criminal diversion of prescription medications and prescriptions in the first degree when he or she commits a criminal diversion act, and the value of the benefit exchanged is in excess of fifty thousand dollars.

Criminal diversion of prescription medications and prescriptions in the first degree is a class C felony.

Added by L. 1995, Ch. 81, § 94, eff. Nov. 1, 1995.

ARTICLE 180—BRIBERY NOT INVOLVING PUBLIC SERVANTS, AND RELATED OFFENSES

LexisNexis Cross Reference

New York Criminal Practice (2d ed.), Vol. 7, Ch. 69, Bribery Not Involving Public Servants and Related Offenses.

§ 180.00. Commercial bribing in the second degree.

A person is guilty of commercial bribing in the second degree when he confers, or offers or agrees to confer, any benefit upon any employee, agent or fiduciary without the consent of the latter's employer or principal, with intent to influence his conduct in relation to his employer's or principal's affairs.

Commercial bribing in the second degree is a class A misdemeanor.

Amended by L. 1976, Ch. 458; L. 1983, Ch. 577.

ANNOTATIONS

Commercial bribery; constitutionality.—Clear warning not to offer or pay anything to another's employee with intent to influence his conduct in relation to his employer's affairs without consent of employer is not constitutionally vague because it does not specifically condemn improper influence. People v. Axel, 69 Misc. 2d 216, 329 N.Y.S.2d 992 (1st Dept. 1971).

Commercial bribing; applicability.—Unlike § 439 of the former Penal Law, the present commercial bribing statute does not apply only to private business, but may also be applied to nonbusiness entities, such as local conservation and ecological organizations. People v. Tuttle, 45 A.D.2d 750, 356 N.Y.S.2d 652 (2d Dept. 1974).

Evidence.—Defendant's participation in a bribery attempt to expedite an insurance settlement was sufficient to support a conviction of commercial bribery in the second degree and, in turn, constitute a "serious crime" basis for charges of professional misconduct. The fact that the scheme was thwarted by the intervention of the District Attorney's office does not reduce the seriousness of defendant's actions. *In re* Pomerantz, 235 A.D.2d 36, 663 N.Y.S.2d 75 (2d Dept. 1997).

§ 180.03. Commercial bribing in the first degree.

A person is guilty of commercial bribing in the first degree when he confers, or offers or agrees to confer, any benefit upon any employee, agent or fiduciary without the consent of the latter's employer or principal, with intent to influence his conduct in relation to his employer's or principal's affairs, and when the value of the benefit conferred or offered or agreed to be conferred exceeds one thousand dollars and causes economic harm to the employer or principal in an amount exceeding two hundred fifty dollars.

Commercial bribing in the first degree is a class E felony.

Added by L. 1976, Ch. 458; **Amended** by L. 1983, Ch. 577.

ANNOTATIONS

Affirmative defense.—There is no affirmative defense created by statute available to defendant charged with either commercial bribery or commercial bribe receiving in the first degree based on fact that there was no economic harm to the employer or principal. People v. Reynolds, 174 Misc. 2d 812, 667 N.Y.S.2d 591 (Sup. Ct. N.Y. Co. 1997).

Economic harm.—Evidence of a kickback in and of itself is not sufficient to establish economic harm—the People must prove that the company incurred economic harm in excess of $250 as a result of defendant's bribery of the employees; where the settlement negotiations remained unchanged despite the payment of the kickback, the case remained with the same honest adjuster who had no knowledge of the kickback and engaged in a typically protracted negotiation before a settlement acceptable to all parties was reached. People v. Wolf, 98 N.Y.2d 105, 745 N.Y.S.2d 766, 772 N.E.2d 1124 (2002).

—Where an employee accepts "kickbacks," the amount of monies paid is usually the amount of the economic harm suffered. People v. Reynolds, 174 Misc. 2d 812, 667 N.Y.S.2d 591 (Sup. Ct. N.Y. Co. 1997).

Intent to influence employee's conduct.—If an adjuster accepts a "benefit" to expedite the settlement of a case, whether or not it is his or her job to do so, the receipt of the payment has influenced the conduct of the employee in his or her employment. People v. Reynolds, 174 Misc. 2d 812, 667 N.Y.S.2d 591 (Sup. Ct. N.Y. Co. 1997).

RICO predicate.—Commercial bribery can constitute a civil cause of action; in this case one of many underlying causes of action in a Civil RICO action. Niagra Mohawk Power Corp. v. Freed, 265 A.D.2d 938, 696 N.Y.S.2d 600 (4th Dept. 1999).

§ 180.05. Commercial bribe receiving in the second degree.

An employee, agent or fiduciary is guilty of commercial bribe receiving in the second degree when, without the consent of his employer or principal, he solicits, accepts or agrees to accept any benefit from another person upon an agreement or understanding that such benefit will influence his conduct in relation to his employer's or principal's affairs.

Commercial bribe receiving in the second degree is a class A misdemeanor.

Amended by L. 1976, Ch. 458; L. 1983, Ch. 577.

Commercial bribery; constitutionality.—Clear warning not to offer or pay anything to another's employee with intent to influence his conduct in relation to his employer's affairs without consent of employer is not constitutionally vague because it does not specifically condemn improper influence. People v. Axel, 69 Misc. 2d 216, 329 N.Y.S.2d 992 (1st Dept. 1971).

§ 180.08. Commercial bribe receiving in the first degree.

An employee, agent or fiduciary is guilty of commercial bribe receiving in the first degree when, without the consent of his employer or principal, he solicits, accepts or agrees to accept any benefit from another person upon an agreement or understanding that such benefit will influence his conduct in relation to his employer's or principal's affairs, and when the value of the benefit solicited, accepted or agreed to be accepted exceeds one thousand dollars and causes economic harm to the employer or principal in an amount exceeding two hundred fifty dollars.

Commercial bribe receiving in the first degree is a class E felony.

Added by L. 1976, Ch. 458; **Amended** by L. 1983, Ch. 577.

Affirmative defense.—A lack of economic harm is not an affirmative defense under this section. People v. Reynolds, 174 Misc. 2d 812, 667 N.Y.S.2d 591 (Sup. Ct. N.Y. Co. 1997).

Economic harm.—Where an employee accepts "kickbacks," the amount of monies paid is usually the amount of the economic harm suffered. People v. Reynolds, 174 Misc. 2d 812, 667 N.Y.S.2d 591 (Sup. Ct. N.Y. Co. 1997).

Intent to influence employee's conduct.—If an adjuster accepts a "benefit" to expedite the settlement of a case, whether or not it is his or her job to do so, the receipt of the payment has influenced the conduct of the employee in his or her employment. People v. Reynolds, 174 Misc. 2d 812, 667 N.Y.S.2d 591 (Sup. Ct. N.Y. Co. 1997).

§ 180.10. Bribery of labor official; definition of term.

As used in this article, "labor official" means any duly appointed representative of a labor organization or any duly appointed trustee or representative of an employee welfare trust fund.

§ 180.15. Bribing a labor official.

A person is guilty of bribing a labor official when, with intent to influence a labor official in respect to any of his acts, decisions or duties as such labor official, he confers, or offers or agrees to confer, any benefit upon him.

Bribing a labor official is a class D felony.

§ 180.20. Bribing a labor official; defense.

In any prosecution for bribing a labor official, it is a defense that the defendant conferred or agreed to confer the benefit involved upon the labor official as a result of conduct of the latter constituting larceny committed by means of extortion, or an attempt to commit the same, or coercion, or an attempt to commit coercion.

§ 180.25. Bribe receiving by a labor official.

A labor official is guilty of bribe receiving by a labor official when he solicits, accepts or agrees to accept any benefit from another person upon an agreement or understanding that such benefit will influence him in respect to any of his acts, decisions, or duties as such labor official.

Bribe receiving by a labor official is a class D felony.

§ 180.30. Bribe receiving by a labor official; no defense.

The crimes of (a) bribe receiving by a labor official, and (b) larceny committed by means of extortion, attempt to commit the same, coercion or attempt to commit coercion, are not mutually exclusive, and it is no defense to a prosecution for bribe receiving by a labor official that, by reason of the same conduct, the defendant also committed one of such other specified crimes.

§ 180.35. Sports bribery and tampering; definitions of terms.

As used in this article:

1. "Sports contest" means any professional or amateur sport or athletic game or contest viewed by the public.

2. "Sports participant" means any person who participates or expects to participate in a sports contest as a player, contestant or member of a team, or as a coach, manager, trainer or other person directly associated with a player, contestant or team.

3. "Sports official" means any person who acts or expects to act in a sports contest as an umpire, referee, judge or otherwise to officiate at a sports contest.

4. "Pari-mutuel betting" is such betting as is authorized under the provisions of the pari-mutuel revenue law as set forth in chapter 254 of the laws of 1940 * with amendments.

5. "Pari-mutuel horse race" means any horse race upon which betting is conducted under the provisions of the pari-mutuel revenue law as set forth in chapter 254 of the laws of 1940. *

  * Repealed.

Amended by L. 1982, Ch. 382.

§ 180.40. Sports bribing.

A person is guilty of sports bribing when he:

1. Confers, or offers or agrees to confer, any benefit upon a sports participant with intent to influence him not to give his best efforts in a sports contest; or

2. Confers, or offers or agrees to confer, any benefit upon a sports official with intent to influence him to perform his duties improperly.

Sports bribing is a class D felony.

§ 180.45. Sports bribe receiving.

A person is guilty of sports bribe receiving when:

1. Being a sports participant, he solicits, accepts or agrees to accept any benefit from another person upon an agreement or understanding that he will thereby be influenced not to give his best efforts in a sports contest; or

2. Being a sports official, he solicits, accepts or agrees to accept any benefit from another person upon an agreement or understanding that he will perform his duties improperly.

Sports bribe receiving is a class E felony.

§ 180.50. Tampering with a sports contest in the second degree.

A person is guilty of tampering with a sports contest when, with intent to influence the outcome of a sports contest, he tampers with any sports participant, sports official or with any animal or equipment or other thing involved in the conduct or operation of a sports contest in a manner contrary to the rules and usages purporting to govern such a contest.

Tampering with a sports contest in the second degree is a class A misdemeanor.

Amended by L. 1982, Ch. 382.

ANNOTATIONS

Attempt.—When defendant, a jockey, appeared in paddock area shortly before post time, where he was to mount his horse for the race with an electrical device, his actions constituted an attempt to tamper with a sporting event. People v. Hernandez, 85 Misc. 2d 26, 378 N.Y.S.2d 879 (9th-10th Jud. Dist. 1975).

Constitutionality.—PL § 180.50 is constitutional. People v. Hernandez, 85 Misc. 2d 26, 378 N.Y.S.2d 879 (9th-10th Jud. Dist. 1975).

§ 180.51. Tampering with a sports contest in the first degree.

A person is guilty of tampering with a sports contest in the first degree when, with intent to influence the outcome of a pari-mutuel horse race:

1. He affects any equine animal involved in the conduct or operation of a pari-mutuel horse race by administering to the animal in any manner whatsoever any controlled substance listed in section thirty-three hundred six of the public health law; or

2. He knowingly enters or furnishes to another person for entry or brings into this state for entry into a pari-mutuel horse race, or rides or drives in any pari-mutuel horse race any running, trotting or pacing horse, mare, gelding, colt or filly under an assumed name, or deceptively out of its proper class, or that has been painted or disguised or represented to be any other or different horse, mare, gelding, colt or filly from that which it actually is; or

3. He knowingly and falsely registers with the jockey club, United States trotting association, American quarterhorse association or national steeplechase and hunt association a horse, mare, gelding, colt or filly previously registered under a different name; or

4. He agrees with one or more persons to enter such misrepresented or drugged animal in a pari-mutuel horse race. A person shall not be convicted of a violation of this subdivision unless an overt act is alleged and proved to have been committed by one of said persons in furtherance of said agreement.

Tampering with a sports contest in the first degree is a class E felony.

Added by L. 1982, Ch. 382.

§ 180.52. Impairing the integrity of a pari-mutuel betting system in the second degree.

A person is guilty of impairing the integrity of a pari-mutuel betting system in the second degree when, with the intent to obtain either any payment for himself or for a third person or with the intent to defraud any person he:

1. Alters, changes or interferes with any equipment or device used in connection with pari-mutuel betting; or

2. Causes any false, inaccurate, delayed or unauthorized data, impulse or signal to be fed into, or transmitted over, or registered in or displayed upon any equipment or device used in connection with pari-mutuel betting.

Impairing the integrity of a pari-mutuel betting system in the second degree is a class E felony.

Added by L. 1982, Ch. 382.

§ 180.53. Impairing the integrity of a pari-mutuel betting system in the first degree.

A person is guilty of impairing the integrity of a pari-mutuel betting system in the first degree when, with the intent to obtain either any payment for himself or for a third person or with the intent to defraud any person, and when the value of the payment exceeds one thousand five hundred dollars he:

1. Alters, changes or interferes with any equipment or device used in connection with pari-mutuel betting; or

2. Causes any false, inaccurate, delayed or unauthorized data, impulse or signal to be fed into, or transmitted over, or registered in or displayed upon any equipment or device used in connection with pari-mutuel betting.

Impairing the integrity of a pari-mutuel betting system in the first degree is a class D felony.

Added by L. 1982, Ch. 382.

§ 180.54. Rent gouging; definition of term.

As used in this article, "lawful rental and other lawful charges" means registered, reported or contracted for rent pursuant to chapter four hundred three of the laws of nineteen hundred eighty-three, article two of the private housing finance law or section eight of the federal housing act of nineteen hundred sixty-eight, or, rent contained in a court approved stipulation of settlement, even if such rent or charges are subsequently decreased by order of the department of housing and community renewal or a court of competent jurisdiction.

Added by L. 1991, Ch. 584, eff. Nov. 1, 1991.

§ 180.55. Rent gouging in the third degree.

A person is guilty of rent gouging in the third degree when, in connection with the leasing, rental or use of real property, he solicits, accepts or agrees to accept from a person some consideration of value, less than two hundred fifty dollars in addition to lawful rental and other lawful charges, upon an agreement or understanding that the furnishing of such consideration will increase the possibility that any person may obtain or renew the lease, rental or use of such property, or that a failure to furnish it will decrease the possibility that any person may obtain or renew the same.

Rent gouging in the third degree is a class B misdemeanor.

Amended by L. 1991, Ch. 584, eff. Nov. 1, 1991.

§ 180.56. Rent gouging in the second degree.

A person is guilty of rent gouging in the second degree when, in connection with the leasing, rental or use of real property, he solicits, accepts or agrees to accept from a person some consideration of value, of two hundred fifty dollars or more, in addition to lawful rental and other lawful charges, upon agreement or understanding that the furnishing of such consideration will increase the possibility that any person may obtain or renew the lease, rental or use of such property, or that a failure to furnish it will decrease the possibility that any person may obtain or renew the same.

Rent gouging in the second degree is a class A misdemeanor.

Added by L. 1991, Ch. 584, eff. Nov. 1, 1991.

§ 180.57. Rent gouging in the first degree.

A person is guilty of rent gouging in the first degree when, in the course of a scheme constituting a systematic ongoing course of conduct in connection with the leasing, rental or use of three or more apartment units, the rental price of which is regulated pursuant to the provisions of federal, state or local law, he solicits, accepts or agrees to accept from one or more persons in three separate transactions some consideration of value, knowing that such consideration is in addition to lawful rental and other lawful charges established pursuant to the provisions of such federal, state or local law, and upon an agreement or understanding that the furnishing of such consideration will increase the possibility that any person may obtain or renew the lease, rental or use of such property, or that a failure to furnish it will decrease the possibility that any person may obtain or renew same, and thereby obtains such consideration from one or more persons.

Rent gouging in the first degree is a class E felony.

Added by L. 1991, Ch. 584, eff. Nov. 1, 1991.

ANNOTATION

Sufficiency of indictment.—Sufficient evidence existed to support indictment for rent gouging in the first degree where tenants and real estate brokers testified that over a period of three years, defendant demanded contributions to political campaigns in regard to rent stabilized apartments as a condition of obtaining leases. People v. Koeppel, 169 Misc. 2d 795, 646 N.Y.S.2d 1007 (Sup. Ct. N.Y. Co. 1995).

ARTICLE 185—FRAUDS ON CREDITORS

LexisNexis Cross Reference

New York Criminal Practice (2d ed.), Vol. 7, Ch. 68, Fraudulent Schemes and Loansharking.

§ 185.00. Fraud in insolvency.

1. As used in this section, "administrator" means an assignee or trustee for the benefit of creditors, a liquidator, a receiver or any other person entitled to administer property for the benefit of creditors.

2. A person is guilty of fraud in insolvency when, with intent to defraud any creditor and knowing that proceedings have been or are about to be instituted for the appointment of an administrator, or knowing that a composition agreement or other arrangement for the benefit of creditors has been or is about to be made, he

(a) conveys, transfers, removes, conceals, destroys, encumbers or otherwise disposes of any part of or any interest in the debtor's estate; or

(b) obtains any substantial part of or interest in the debtor's estate; or

(c) presents to any creditor or to the administrator any writing or record relating to the debtor's estate knowing the same to contain a false material statement; or

(d) misrepresents or fails or refuses to disclose to the administrator the existence, amount or location of any part of or any interest in the debtor's estate, or any other information which he is legally required to furnish to such administrator.

Fraud in insolvency is a class A misdemeanor.

ANNOTATION

Analogous crimes.—Federal crime of fraudulently concealing assets from bankruptcy trustee corresponds to New York crime of fraud in insolvency. *In re* Pelland, 208 A.D.2d 71, 623 N.Y.S.2d 31 (4th Dept. 1995).

§ 185.05. Fraud involving a security interest.

A person is guilty of fraud involving a security interest when, having executed a security agreement creating a security interest in personal property securing a monetary obligation owed to a secured party, and:

1. Having under the security agreement both the right of sale or other disposition of the property and the duty to account to the secured party for the proceeds of disposition, he sells or otherwise disposes of the property and wrongfully fails to account to the secured party for the proceeds of disposition; or

2. Having under the security agreement no right of sale or other disposition of the property, he knowingly secretes, withholds or disposes of such property in violation of the security agreement.

Fraud involving a security interest is a class A misdemeanor.

§ 185.10. Fraudulent disposition of mortgaged property.

A person is guilty of fraudulent disposition of mortgaged property when, having theretofore executed a mortgage of real or personal property or any instrument intended to operate as such, he sells, assigns, exchanges, secretes, injures, destroys or otherwise disposes of any part of the property, upon which the mortgage or other instrument is at the time a lien, with intent thereby to defraud the mortgagee or a purchaser thereof.

Fraudulent disposition of mortgaged property is a class A misdemeanor.

ANNOTATION

Sufficiency of the evidence.—Defendant's conviction was sustained where he executed mortgages to premises that were neither owned by him or his corporation and upon acquisition of such property he conveyed it without satisfying the mortgages. People v. Prince, 110 Misc. 2d 55, 441 N.Y.S.2d 586 (Sup. Ct. Queens Co. 1981).

§ 185.15. Fraudulent disposition of property subject to a conditional sale contract.

A person is guilty of fraudulent disposition of property subject to a conditional sale contract when, prior to the performance of the condition of a conditional sale contract and being the buyer or any legal successor in interest of the buyer, he sells, assigns, mortgages, exchanges, secretes, injures, destroys or otherwise disposes of the goods subject to the conditional sale contract under claim of full ownership, with intent thereby to defraud another.

Fraudulent disposition of property subject to a

conditional sale contract is a class A misdemeanor.

ARTICLE 190—OTHER FRAUDS

LexisNexis Cross Reference

New York Criminal Practice (2d ed.), Vol. 7, Ch. 68, Fraudulent Schemes and Loansharking.

§ 190.00. Issuing a bad check; definitions of terms.

The following definitions are applicable to this article:

1. "Check" means any check, draft or similar sight order for the payment of money which is not post-dated with respect to the time of utterance.

2. "Drawer" of a check means a person whose name appears thereon as the primary obligor, whether the actual signature be that of himself or of a person purportedly authorized to draw the check in his behalf.

3. "Representative drawer" means a person who signs a check as drawer in a representative capacity or as agent of the person whose name appears thereon as the principal drawer or obligor.

4. "Utter." A person "utters" a check when, as a drawer or representative drawer thereof, he delivers it or causes it to be delivered to a person who thereby acquires a right against the drawer with respect to such check. One who draws a check with intent that it be so delivered is deemed to have uttered it if the delivery occurs.

5. "Pass." A person "passes" a check when, being a payee, holder or bearer of a check which previously has been or purports to have been drawn and uttered by another, he delivers it, for a purpose other than collection, to a third person who thereby acquires a right with respect thereto.

6. "Funds" means money or credit.

7. "Insufficient funds." A drawer has "insufficient funds" with a drawee to cover a check when he has no funds or account whatever, or funds in an amount less than that of the check; and a

check dishonored for "no account" shall also be deemed to have been dishonored for "insufficient funds."

§ 190.05. Issuing a bad check.

A person is guilty of issuing a bad check when:

1. (a) As a drawer or representative drawer, he utters a check knowing that he or his principal, as the case may be, does not then have sufficient funds with the drawee to cover it, and

(b) he intends or believes at the time of utterance that payment will be refused by the drawee upon presentation, and

(c) payment is refused by the drawee upon presentation; or

2. (a) He passes a check knowing that the drawer thereof does not have sufficient funds with the drawee to cover it, and

(b) he intends or believes at the time the check is passed that payment will be refused by the drawee upon presentation, and

(c) payment is refused by the drawee upon presentation.

Issuing a bad check is a class B misdemeanor.

ANNOTATIONS

Acceptance of replacement checks; commencement of civil suit.—Neither the acceptance of replacement checks nor the institution of a civil action based on the bad checks is a bar to a criminal prosecution for the issuance of the bad checks. People v. Goldstein, 79 Misc. 2d 996, 361 N.Y.S.2d 994 (Crim. Ct. N.Y. Co. 1974).

Liability of individual for corporate conduct; Penal Law § 20.25.—Defendant was criminally responsible under Penal Law § 20.25 for acts of drawer corporation because he caused the check to be issued in the name of the corporation. People v. Dean, 48 A.D.2d 223, 368 N.Y.S.2d 349 (4th Dept. 1975).

Evidence.—Convictions for larceny and attempted larceny supported by evidence that at time defendant passed bad checks, he intended or believed that the drawee banks, where defendant had opened accounts with other worthless checks, would refuse payment upon presentation. People v. Barreau, 232 A.D.2d 238, 648 N.Y.S.2d 544 (1st Dept. 1996).

§ 190.10. Issuing a bad check; presumptions.

1. When the drawer of a check has insufficient funds with the drawee to cover it at the time of utterance, the subscribing drawer or representative drawer, as the case may be, is presumed to know of such insufficiency.

2. A subscribing drawer or representative drawer, as the case may be, of an ultimately dishonored check is presumed to have intended or believed that the check would be dishonored upon presentation when:

(a) The drawer had no account with the drawee at the time of utterance; or

(b) (i) The drawer had insufficient funds with the drawee at the time of utterance, and

(ii) the check was presented to the drawee for

payment not more than thirty days after the date of utterance, and

(iii) the drawer had insufficient funds with the drawee at the time of presentation.

3. Dishonor of a check by the drawee and insufficiency of the drawer's funds at the time of presentation may properly be proved by introduction in evidence of a notice of protest of the check, or of a certificate under oath of an authorized representative of the drawee declaring the dishonor and insufficiency, and such proof shall constitute presumptive evidence of such dishonor and insufficiency.

ANNOTATION

Evidence.—Convictions for larceny and attempted larceny supported by evidence that at time defendant passed bad checks, he intended or believed that the drawee banks, where defendant had opened accounts with other worthless checks, would refuse payment upon presentation. People v. Barreau, 232 A.D.2d 238, 648 N.Y.S.2d 544 (1st Dept. 1996).

§ 190.15. Issuing a bad check; defenses.

In any prosecution for issuing a bad check, it is an affirmative defense that:

1. The defendant or a person acting in his behalf made full satisfaction of the amount of the check within ten days after dishonor by the drawee; or

2. The defendant, in acting as a representative drawer, did so as an employee who, without personal benefit, merely executed the orders of his employer or of a superior officer or employee generally authorized to direct his activities.

§ 190.20. False advertising.

A person is guilty of false advertising when, with intent to promote the sale or to increase the consumption of property or services, he makes or causes to be made a false or misleading statement in any advertisement or publishes any advertisement in violation of chapter three of the act of congress entitled "Truth in Lending Act" and the regulations thereunder, as such act and regulations may from time to time be amended, addressed to the public or to a substantial number of persons; except that, in any prosecution under this section, it is an affirmative defense that the allegedly false or misleading statement was not knowingly or recklessly made or caused to be made.

False advertising is a class A misdemeanor.

Amended by L. 1968, Chs. 1072, 1073; L. 1969, Ch. 1141.

ANNOTATION

"Bait and switch advertising."—Both the PL § 190.20 and the General Business Law § 396 proscribe the same promotional practice known as "bait and switch advertising," "bait advertising," or "fictitious bargain claims," with the latter law giving the Attorney General the right to seek a civil injunction against the alleged false advertising. People v. Block & Kleaver, Inc., 103 Misc. 2d 758, 427 N.Y.S.2d 133 (Monroe Co. Ct. 1980).

§ 190.23. False personation.

A person is guilty of false personation when after being informed of the consequences of such act, he or she knowingly misrepresents his or her actual name, date of birth or address to a police officer or peace officer with intent to prevent such police officer or peace officer from ascertaining such information.

False personation is a class B misdemeanor.

Added by L. 1997, Ch. 69, § 1, eff. Jan. 1, 1998.

ANNOTATIONS

Generally—Evidence that defendant had falsely identified himself to police while they were in the midst of an investigation provided probable cause to support an arrest for false personation. People v. Isidro, 6 A.D.3d 1234, 776 N.Y.S.2d 669 (4th Dept. 2004).

§ 190.25. Criminal impersonation in the second degree.

A person is guilty of criminal impersonation in the second degree when he:

1. Impersonates another and does an act in such assumed character with intent to obtain a benefit or to injure or defraud another; or

2. Pretends to be a representative of some person or organization and does an act in such pretended capacity with intent to obtain a benefit or to injure or defraud another; or

3. (a) Pretends to be a public servant, or wears or displays without authority any uniform, badge, insignia or facsimile thereof by which such public servant is lawfully distinguished, or falsely expresses by his words or actions that he is a public servant or is acting with approval or authority of a public agency or department; and

(b) so acts with intent to induce another to submit to such pretended official authority, to solicit funds or to otherwise cause another to act in reliance upon that pretense.

Criminal impersonation in the second degree is a class A misdemeanor.

Amended by L. 1980, Ch. 27.

ANNOTATIONS

Continuing offense.—Criminal impersonation can constitute a continuing offense, and one can impersonate another with an intent to defraud with a single act or a series of acts; the defendant in this case allegedly impersonated an FBI agent for the entire five-year period during which he knew the complainant. People v. Sanchez, 84 N.Y.2d 440, 618 N.Y.S.2d 887, 643 N.E.2d 509 (1994).

Evidence.—In order to be found guilty under this section, the People must prove that defendant impersonated a real person; "to 'impersonate' is to pass oneself off as another having a certain identity." People v. Sadiq, 236 A.D.2d 638, 654 N.Y.S.2d 35 (2d Dept. 1997).

—Seventeen-year-old boy's use of his older brother's identification in order to buy alcoholic beverages was a crime under this section. N.Y. Cent. Mut. Fire Ins. Co. v. Nationwide Mut. Ins. Co., 307 A.D.2d 449, 761 N.Y.S.2d 730 (3d Dept. 2003).

Generally—Evidence that defendant had falsely identified himself to police while they were in the midst of an investigation provided probable cause to support an arrest for false

personation. People v. Isidro, 6 A.D.3d 1234, 776 N.Y.S.2d 669 (4th Dept. 2004).

§ 190.26. Criminal impersonation in the first degree.

A person is guilty of criminal impersonation in the first degree when he:

1. Pretends to be a police officer, or wears or displays without authority, any uniform, badge or other insignia or facsimile thereof, by which such police officer is lawfully distinguished or expresses by his words or actions that he is acting with the approval or authority of any police department; and

2. So acts with intent to induce another to submit to such pretended official authority or otherwise to act in reliance upon said pretense and in the course of such pretense commits or attempts to commit a felony; or

3. Pretending to be a duly licensed physician or other person authorized to issue a prescription for any drug or any instrument or device used in the taking or administering of drugs for which a prescription is required by law, communicates to a pharmacist an oral prescription which is required to be reduced to writing pursuant to section thirty-three hundred thirty-two of the public health law.

Criminal impersonation in the first degree is a class E felony.

Added by L. 1980, Ch. 27; **Amended** by L. 1998, Ch. 2, § 41, eff. Nov. 1, 1998.

§ 190.27. Criminal sale of a police uniform.

A person is guilty of criminal sale of a police uniform when he or she sells or offers for sale the uniform of any police officer to any person, unless presented with a valid photo identification card showing the purchaser to be a member of the police department which has authorized the requested uniform or an authorization to purchase specified uniforms signed by the police chief or the police commissioner of such police department accompanied by a personal photo identification. For purposes of this section, "police officer" shall include federal law enforcement officers, as defined in section 2.15 of the criminal procedure law; and "uniform" shall include all or any part of the uniform which identifies the wearer as a member of a police department, such as the uniform, shield, badge, numbers or other identifying insignias or emblems.

Criminal sale of a police uniform is a class A misdemeanor.

Added by L. 1994, Ch. 99.

§ 190.30. Unlawfully concealing a will.

A person is guilty of unlawfully concealing a will when, with intent to defraud, he conceals, secretes, suppresses, mutilates or destroys a will, codicil or other testamentary instrument.

Unlawfully concealing a will is a class E felony.

§ 190.35. Misconduct by corporate official.

A person is guilty of misconduct by corporate official when:

1. Being a director of a stock corporation, he knowingly concurs in any vote or act of the directors of such corporation, or any of them, by which it is intended:

(a) To make a dividend except in the manner provided by law; or

(b) To divide, withdraw or in any manner pay to any stockholder any part of the capital stock of the corporation except in the manner provided by law; or

(c) To discount or receive any note or other evidence of debt in payment of an installment of capital stock actually called in and required to be paid, or with intent to provide the means of making such payment; or

(d) To receive or discount any note or other evidence of debt with intent to enable any stockholder to withdraw any part of the money paid in by him on his stock; or

(e) To apply any portion of the funds of such corporation, directly or indirectly, to the purchase of shares of its own stock, except in the manner provided by law; or

2. Being a director or officer of a stock corporation:

(a) He issues, participates in issuing, or concurs in a vote to issue any increase of its capital stock beyond the amount of the capital stock thereof, duly authorized by or in pursuance of law; or

(b) He sells, or agrees to sell, or is directly or indirectly interested in the sale of any share of stock of such corporation, or in any agreement to sell the same, unless at the time of such sale or agreement he is an actual owner of such share, provided that the foregoing shall not apply to a sale by or on behalf of an underwriter or dealer in connection with a bona fide public offering of shares of stock of such corporation.

Misconduct by corporate official is a class B misdemeanor.

Amended by L. 1967, Ch. 791.

§ 190.40. Criminal usury in the second degree.

A person is guilty of criminal usury in the second degree when, not being authorized or permitted by law to do so, he knowingly charges, takes or receives any money or other property as interest on the loan or forbearance of any money or other property, at a rate exceeding twenty-five per centum per annum or the equivalent rate for a longer or shorter period.

Criminal usury in the second degree is a class E felony.

Added by L. 1967, Ch. 791; Amended by L. 1976, Ch. 424.

ANNOTATIONS

Effect of plea.—A defendant who pleaded guilty to criminal usury in the second degree cannot contest the constitutionality of another statute, criminal usury in the first degree, under which he was indicted but which is irrelevant to his conviction. People v. DiRaffaele, 55 N.Y.2d 234, 448 N.Y.S.2d 448, 433 N.E.2d 513 (1982).

Indictment.—The indictments charging criminal usury fulfilled the statutory and constitutional mandates for a valid indictment where they charged each and every element of the crime of criminal usury and alleged that the defendant committed the acts which constituted that crime at a specified place during a specified time period. People v. Iannone, 45 N.Y.2d 589, 412 N.Y.S.2d 110, 384 N.E.2d 656 (1978).

§ 190.42. Criminal usury in the first degree.

A person is guilty of criminal usury in the first degree when, not being authorized or permitted by law to do so, he knowingly charges, takes or receives any money or other property as interest on the loan or forbearance of any money or other property, at a rate exceeding twenty-five per centum per annum or the equivalent rate for a longer or shorter period and either the actor had previously been convicted of the crime of criminal usury or of the attempt to commit such crime, or the actor's conduct was part of a scheme or business of making or collecting usurious loans.

Criminal usury in the first degree is a class C felony.

Added by L. 1976, Ch. 424.

ANNOTATIONS

Constitutionality.—PL § 190.42 is constitutional. People v. DiRaffaeli, 100 Misc. 2d 634, 420 N.Y.S.2d 109 (Sup. Ct. Suffolk Co. 1979).

Purchase of accounts receivable at a discount.—Where the defendant purchased a funeral home's accounts receivable at a discount, paying 92% of face value, subject to a provision for repurchase by the assignor within 60 days or failing that to pay an additional 6% service charge for each 60 days the account remained unpaid, and no notice was given to account debtors, the transactions constituted loans subject to the usury law. People v. The Serv. Inst., 101 Misc. 2d 549, 421 N.Y.S.2d 325 (Suffolk Co. 1979).

§ 190.45. Possession of usurious loan records.

A person is guilty of possession of usurious loan records when, with knowledge of the contents thereof, he possesses any writing, paper, instrument or article used to record criminally usurious transactions prohibited by section 190.40.

Possession of usurious loan records is a class A misdemeanor.

Added by L. 1967, Ch. 791.

§ 190.50. Unlawful collection practices.

A person is guilty of unlawful collection practices when, with intent to enforce a claim or judgment for money or property, he knowingly sends, mails or delivers to another person a notice, document or other instrument which has no judicial or official sanction and which in its format or appearance, simulates a summons, complaint, court order or process, or an insignia, seal or printed form of a federal, state, or local government or an instrumentality thereof, or is otherwise calculated to induce a belief that such notice, document or instrument has a judicial or official sanction.

Unlawful collection practices is a class B misdemeanor.

Added by L. 1968, Ch. 739.

ANNOTATION

Restraining notice.—The issuance of a second restraining notice by a court officer in violation of CPLR 5222(b) was not an act proscribed by PL § 190.50 (Unlawful Collection practices). Finkelstein v. McGuirk, 90 Misc. 2d 649, 395 N.Y.S.2d 377 (Sup. Ct. Orange Co. 1977).

§ 190.55. Making a false statement of credit terms.

A person is guilty of making a false statement of credit terms when he knowingly and wilfully violates the provisions of chapter two of the act of congress entitled "Truth in Lending Act" and the regulations thereunder, as such act and regulations may from time to time be amended, by understating or failing to state the interest rate required to be disclosed, or by failing to make or by making a false or inaccurate or incomplete statement of other credit terms in violation of such act.

Making a false statement of credit terms is a class A misdemeanor.

Added by L. 1968, Ch. 1072; **Amended** by L. 1968, Ch. 1073; L. 1969, Ch. 1141; L. 1982, Ch. 674.

§ 190.60. Scheme to defraud in the second degree.

1. A person is guilty of a scheme to defraud in the second degree when he engages in a scheme constituting a systematic ongoing course of conduct with intent to defraud more than one person or to obtain property from more than one person by false or fraudulent pretenses, representations or promises, and so obtains property from one or more of such persons.

2. In any prosecution under this section, it shall be necessary to prove the identity of at least one person from whom the defendant so obtained property, but it shall not be necessary to prove the identity of any other intended victim.

Scheme to defraud in the second degree is a class A misdemeanor.

Added by L. 1976, Ch. 384; **Amended** by L. 1992. Ch. 491, eff. Nov. 1, 1992, amending subd. 1; L. 1993, Ch. 171; L. 1996, Ch. 357, § 3, amending subd. 1, eff. Nov. 1, 1996.

ANNOTATIONS

Sufficiency of indictment.—Time is not a substantive element of scheme to defraud, so an indictment is legally sufficient if the time span alleged is not so long that it prevents preparation of a defense. A one-year time period is not so excessive as to prevent defendant from answering charges and preparing a defense. People v. O'Connor, 240 A.D.2d 764, 660 N.Y.S.2d 140 (2d Dept. 1997).

Property.—Securities broker-dealer licenses and registrations fraudulently obtained did not constitute "property" within the meaning of the scheme to defraud statute, since they were not the "property" of the regulatory agencies, only a representation of the regulatory interest that the agencies issued to the defendants, albeit as a result of their fraud. People v. Cohen, 187 Misc. 2d 435, 720 N.Y.S.2d 731 (Sup. Ct. N.Y. Co. 2001).

Evidence.—It is not necessary to establish the victim's state of mind when property was transferred to defendant; it is enough that the victim was a person whom the defendant/schemer sought to defraud. People v. Taylor, 304 A.D.2d 434, 758 N.Y.S.2d 634 (1st Dept. 2003).

§ 190.65. Scheme to defraud in the first degree.

1. A person is guilty of a scheme to defraud in the first degree when he: (a) engages in a scheme constituting a systematic ongoing course of conduct with intent to defraud ten or more persons or to obtain property from ten or more persons by false or fraudulent pretenses, representations or promises, and so obtains property from one or more of such persons; or (b) engages in scheme constituting a systematic ongoing course of conduct with intent to defraud more than one person or to obtain property from more than one person by false or fraudulent pretenses, representations or promises, and so obtains property with a value in excess of one thousand dollars from one or more such persons.

2. In any prosecution under this section, it shall be necessary to prove the identity of at least one person from whom the defendant so obtained property, but it shall not be necessary to prove the identity of any other intended victim.

Scheme to defraud in the first degree is a class E felony.

Added by L. 1976, Ch. 384; L. 1986, Ch. 515.

ANNOTATIONS

Evidence.—Verdict convicting defendants of scheme to defraud but acquitting them of conspiracy in the fifth degree was not repugnant since defendants can act in concert without forming a conspiracy. People v. Kronberg, 277 A.D.2d 182, 716 N.Y.S.2d 653 (1st Dept. 2000), *appeal denied,* 96 N.Y.2d 785 (2001).

—Evidence that defendant engaged in an ongoing pattern of fraudulent conduct involving logging agreements with more than 10 elderly property owners (or their representatives) in Sullivan County, where defendant removed logs from their property, left the property in disarray, and never paid the landowners for the logs taken, supported conviction under PL § 190.65. People v. Houghaling, 14 A.D.3d 879,787 N.Y.S.2d 733 (3d Dept. 2005).

—Evidence that defendant promised two women, one of whom was an undercover officer, that he would make their DWI charges "disappear" in exchange for a fee was sufficient to support a conviction under PL § 190.65; evidence of prior similar crimes was properly admitted to establish defendant's fraudulent intent. People v. Bastian, 294 A.D.2d 882, 743 N.Y.S.2d 217 (4th Dept. 2002).

—Securities broker-dealer licenses and registrations fraudulently obtained did not constitute "property" within the meaning of the scheme to defraud statute since they were not the "property" of the regulatory agencies, only a representation of the regulatory interest that the agencies issued to the defendants, albeit as a result of their fraud. People v. Cohen, 187 Misc. 2d 435, 720 N.Y.S.2d 731 (Sup. Ct. N.Y. Co. 2001).

—A violation of PL § 190.65 may be proven by circumstantial evidence, and fraudulent intent may be inferred from all the facts and circumstances, from the *modus operandi*, from the dealings between the parties and from the losses sustained by the victims. People v Block & Kleaver, Inc., 103 Misc. 2d 758, 427 N.Y.S.2d 133 (Monroe Co. Ct. 1980).

Applicability of section.—Scheme to defraud is not limited in its application to consumer fraud; the framers based the statute on the federal mail fraud statute which has been applied in a wide variety of fraudulent practices well beyond the scope of consumer fraud. People v. Reynolds, 174 Misc. 2d 812, 667 N.Y.S.2d 591 (Sup. Ct. N.Y. Co. 1997).

"Bad check" schemes.—Defendant who issued the bad checks to ten different businesses over a period of four months was guilty of scheme to defraud in the first degree. People v. Palmer, 108 A.D.2d 545, 490 N.Y.S.2d 293 (3d Dept. 1985).

—Defendants, who obtained property from more than 10 persons by engaging in bad check scheme constituting systematic ongoing course of conduct with intent to defraud and thereby obtain property, may properly be prosecuted under PL § 190.65 as a scheme to defraud, even though the same conduct may constitute a larceny offense under Title J, since property was actually obtained by means of the fraud. People v. Lennon, 107 Misc. 2d 329, 434 N.Y.S.2d 95 (Broome Co. Ct. 1980).

Essentially similar crimes.—The federal crime of bank fraud is essentially similar to the New York crime of scheme to defraud in the first degree. *In re* Kim, 209 A.D.2d 127, 625 N.Y.S.2d 490 (1st Dept. 1995).

—The federal crime of bank fraud is essentially similar to the New York crime of scheme to defraud in the first degree. *In re* Kelly, 205 A.D.2d 56, 618 N.Y.S.2d 390 (2d Dept. 1994).

§ 190.70. Scheme to defraud the state by unlawfully selling prescriptions.

A person is guilty of a scheme to defraud the state by unlawfully selling prescriptions when he or she engages, with intent to defraud the state, in a scheme constituting a systematic, ongoing course of conduct to make, sell, deliver for sale or offer for sale one or more prescriptions and so obtains goods or services from the state with a value in excess of one thousand dollars or causes the state to reimburse another in excess of one thousand dollars for the delivery of such goods or services.

Scheme to defraud the state by unlawfully selling prescriptions is a class A misdemeanor.

Added by L. 1992, Ch. 41, eff. Apr. 2, 1992.

§ 190.75. Criminal use of an access device in the second degree.

A person is guilty of criminal use of an access device in the second degree when he knowingly uses an access device without consent of an owner thereof with intent to unlawfully obtain telecommunications services on behalf of himself or a third person. As used in this section, access device shall have the meaning set forth in subdivision seven-c of section 155.00 of this chapter.

Criminal use of an access device in the second degree is a class A misdemeanor.

Added by L. 1996, Ch. 357, eff. Nov. 1, 1996.

§ 190.76. Criminal use of an access device in the first degree.

A person is guilty of criminal use of an access device in the first degree when he knowingly uses an access device without consent of an owner thereof with intent to unlawfully obtain telecommunications services on behalf of himself or a third person, and so obtains such services with a value in excess of one thousand dollars. As used in this section, access device shall have the meaning set forth in subdivision seven-c of section 155.00 of this chapter.

Criminal use of an access device in the first degree is a class E felony.

Added by L. 1996, Ch. 357, eff. Nov. 1, 1996.

§ 190.77. Offenses involving theft of identity; definitions.

1. For the purposes of sections 190.78, 190.79 and 190.80 of this article "personal identifying information" means a person's name, address, telephone number, date of birth, driver's license number, social security number, place of employment, mother's maiden name, financial services account number or code, savings account number or code, checking account number or code, brokerage account number or code, credit card account number or code, debit card number or code, automated teller machine number or code, taxpayer identification number, computer system password, signature or copy of a signature, electronic signature, unique biometric data that is a fingerprint, voice print, retinal image or iris image of another person, telephone calling card number, mobile identification number or code, electronic serial number or personal identification number, or any other name, number, code or information that may be used alone or in conjunction with other such information to assume the identity of another person.

2. For the purposes of sections 190.78, 190.79, 190.80, 190.81, 190.82 and 190.83 of this article:

a. "electronic signature" shall have the same meaning as defined in subdivision three of section one hundred two of the state technology law.

b. "personal identification number" means any number or code which may be used alone or in conjunction with any other information to assume the identity of another person or access financial resources or credit of another person.

Added by L. 2002, Ch. 619, § 3, eff. Nov. 1, 2002.

§ 190.78. Identity theft in the third degree.

A person is guilty of identity theft in the third

degree when he or she knowingly and with intent to defraud assumes the identity of another person by presenting himself or herself as that other person, or by acting as that other person or by using personal identifying information of that other person, and thereby:

1. obtains goods, money, property or services or uses credit in the name of such other person or causes financial loss to such person or to another person or persons; or

2. commits a class A misdemeanor or higher level crime.

Identity theft in the third degree is a class A misdemeanor.

Added by L. 2002, Ch. 619, § 3, eff. Nov. 1, 2002.

§ 190.79. Identity theft in the second degree.

A person is guilty of identify theft in the second degree when he or she knowingly and with intent to defraud assumes the identity of another person by presenting himself or herself as that other person, or by acting as that other person or by using personal identifying information of that other person, and thereby:

1. obtains goods, money, property or services or uses credit in the name of such other person in an aggregate amount that exceeds five hundred dollars; or

2. causes financial loss to such person or to another person or persons in an aggregate amount that exceeds five hundred dollars; or

3. commits or attempts to commit a felony or acts as an accessory to the commission of a felony; or

4. commits the crime of identity theft in the third degree as defined in section 190.78 of this article and has been previously convicted within the last five years of identity theft in the third degree as defined in section 190.78, identity theft in the second degree as defined in this section, identity theft in the first degree as defined in section 190.80, unlawful possession of personal identification information in the third degree as defined in section 190.81, unlawful possession of personal identification information in the second degree as defined in section 190.82, unlawful possession of personal identification information in the first degree as defined in section 190.83, grand larceny in the fourth degree as defined in section 155.30, grand larceny in the third degree as defined in section 155.35, grand larceny in the second degree as defined in section 155.40 or grand larceny in the first degree as defined in section 155.42 of this chapter.

Identity theft in the second degree is a class E felony.

Added by L. 2002, Ch. 619, § 3, eff. Nov. 1, 2002.

§ 190.80. Identity theft in the first degree.

A person is guilty of identity theft in the first degree when he or she knowingly and with intent to defraud assumes the identity of another person by presenting himself or herself as that other person, or by acting as that other person or by using personal identifying information of that other person, and thereby:

1. obtains goods, money, property or services or uses credit in the name of such other person in an aggregate amount that exceeds two thousand dollars; or

2. causes financial loss to such person or to another person or persons in an aggregate amount that exceeds two thousand dollars; or

3. commits or attempts to commit a class D felony or higher level crime or acts as an accessory in the commission of a class D or higher level felony; or

4. commits the crime of identity theft in the second degree as defined in section 190.79 of this article and has been previously convicted within the last five years of identity theft in the third degree as defined in section 190.78, identity theft in the second degree as defined in section 190.79, identity theft in the first degree as defined in this section, unlawful possession of personal identification information in the third degree as defined in section 190.81, unlawful possession of personal identification information in the second degree as defined in section 190.82, unlawful possession of personal identification information in the first degree as defined in section 190.83, grand larceny in the fourth degree as defined in section 155.30, grand larceny in the third degree as defined in section 155.35, grand larceny in the second degree as defined in section 155.40 or grand larceny in the first degree as defined in section 155.42 of this chapter.

Identity theft in the first degree is a class D felony.

Added by L. 2002, Ch. 619, § 3, eff. Nov. 1, 2002.

§ 190.81. Unlawful possession of personal identification information in the third degree.

A person is guilty of unlawful possession of personal identification information in the third degree when he or she knowingly possesses a person's financial services account number or code, savings account number or code, checking account number or code, brokerage account number or code, credit card account number or code, debit card number or code, automated teller machine number or code, personal identification number, mother's maiden name, computer system password, electronic signature or unique biometric data that is a fingerprint, voice print, retinal image or iris image of another person knowing such information is intended to be used in furtherance of the commission of a crime defined in this chapter.

Unlawful possession of personal identification information in the third degree is a class A misdemeanor.

Added by L. 2002, Ch. 619, § 3, eff. Nov. 1, 2002.

§ 190.82. Unlawful possession of personal identification information in the second degree.

A person is guilty of unlawful possession of personal identification information in the second degree when he or she knowingly possesses two hundred fifty or more items of personal identification information of the following nature: a person's financial services account number or code, savings account number or code, checking account number or code, brokerage account number or code, credit card account number or code, debit card number or code, automated teller machine number or code, personal identification number, mother's maiden name, computer system password, electronic signature or unique biometric data that is a fingerprint, voice print, retinal image or iris image of another person knowing such information is intended to be used in furtherance of the commission of a crime defined in this chapter.

Unlawful possession of personal identification information in the second degree is a class E felony.

Added by L. 2002, Ch. 619, § 3, eff. Nov. 1, 2002.

§ 190.83. Unlawful possession of personal identification information in the first degree.

A person is guilty of unlawful possession of personal identification information in the first degree when he or she commits the crime of unlawful possession of personal identification information in the second degree and:

1. with intent to further the commission of identity theft in the second degree, he or she supervises more than three accomplices; or

2. he or she has been previously convicted within the last five years of identity theft in the third degree as defined in section 190.78, identity theft in the second degree as defined in section 190.79, identity theft in the first degree as defined in section 190.80, unlawful possession of personal identification information in the third degree as defined in section 190.81, unlawful possession of personal identification information in the second degree as defined in section 190.82, unlawful possession of personal identification information in the first degree as defined in this section, grand larceny in the fourth degree as defined in section 155.30, grand larceny in the third degree as defined in section 155.35, grand larceny in the second degree as defined in section 155.40 or grand larceny in the first degree as defined in section 155.42 of this chapter.

Unlawful possession of personal identification information in the first degree is a class D felony.

Added by L. 2002, Ch. 619, § 3, eff. Nov. 1, 2002.

§ 190.84. Defenses.

In any prosecution for identity theft or unlawful possession of personal identification information pursuant to this article, it shall be an affirmative defense that the person charged with the offense:

1. was under twenty-one years of age at the time of committing the offense and the person used or possessed the personal identifying or identification information of another solely for the purpose of purchasing alcohol;

2. was under eighteen years of age at the time of committing the offense and the person used or possessed the personal identifying or identification information of another solely for the purpose of purchasing tobacco products; or

3. used or possessed the personal identifying or identification information of another person solely for the purpose of misrepresenting the person's age to gain access to a place the access to which is restricted based on age.

Added by L. 2002, Ch. 619, § 3, eff. Nov. 1, 2002.

TITLE L—OFFENSES AGAINST PUBLIC ADMINISTRATION

ARTICLE 195—OFFICIAL MISCONDUCT AND OBSTRUCTION OF PUBLIC SERVANTS GENERALLY

LexisNexis Cross References

New York Criminal Practice (2d ed.), Vol. 7, Ch. 71, Official Misconduct and Obstruction of Government Operations.

§ 195.00. Official misconduct.

A public servant is guilty of official misconduct when, with intent to obtain a benefit or deprive another person of a benefit:

1. He commits an act relating to his office but constituting an unauthorized exercise of his official functions, knowing that such act is unauthorized; or

2. He knowingly refrains from performing a duty which is imposed upon him by law or is clearly inherent in the nature of his office.

Official misconduct is a class A misdemeanor.

Amended by L. 1990, Ch. 906.

ANNOTATION

Indictment.—An indictment charging a Judge with official misconduct is insufficient where the indictment, for the purpose of defining the "clearly inherent" duty allegedly violated, only incorporated by reference the provisions of the Code of Judicial Conduct; those provisions do not come within the ambit of one of the express provisions of the Penal Law and have never been adopted by the legislature. People v. La Carrubba, 46 N.Y.2d 658, 416 N.Y.S.2d 203, 389 N.E.2d 799 (1979).

Evidence.—Evidence that defendant falsified a prior memorandum of an assistant to the Mayor to make it appear as if he had received a $5,500 salary increase and a lump-sum back payment, supported his conviction under this section. *In re* Vasquez, 1 A.D.3d 16, 766 N.Y.S.2d 419 (1st Dept. 2003).

—Defendant's admission that while acting as town highway superintendent he used town gasoline and diesel fuel for his personal vehicles, used town license plates on his personal business equipment, and used town employees and town equipment to perform private work, supported his conviction. Grady v. Yeno, 302 A.D.2d 385, 754 N.Y.S.2d 562 (2d Dept. 2003).

§ 195.05. Obstructing governmental administration in the second degree.

A person is guilty of obstructing governmental administration when he intentionally obstructs, impairs or perverts the administration of law or other governmental function or prevents or attempts to prevent a public servant from performing an official function, by means of intimidation, physical force or interference, or by means of any independently unlawful act, or by means of interfering, whether or not physical force is involved, with radio, telephone, television or other telecommunications systems owned or operated by the state, or a county, city, town, village, fire district or emergency medical service or by means of releasing a dangerous animal under circumstances evincing the actor's intent that the animal obstruct governmental administration.

Obstructing governmental administration is a class A misdemeanor.

Amended by L. 1984, Ch. 956; L. 1998, Ch. 269, § 2, Nov. 1, 1998.

ANNOTATIONS

"Interference."—*Case* distinguished; here police activity was confined and defined, and "interference" was established through words and actions. Undercover police officers about to engage in "buy and bust" operation saw juvenile/respondent on his bicycle circling target location. The police approached him, identified themselves and specifically directed him to stay away from location and not to get involved. In response, respondent went to location and alerted the occupants to presence of the police. The "interference" required under the section was established since respondent's words and actions caused a physical reaction, in that the occupants of the location dispersed and increased the danger to police, occupants, and himself. *In re* Davan L., 91 N.Y.2d 88, 666 N.Y.S.2d 1015, 689 N.E.2d 909 (1997).

—"Interference" in PL § 195.05 means "physical interference." People v. Case, 42 N.Y.2d 98, 396 N.Y.S.2d 841, 365 N.E.2d 872 (1977).

—While the interference necessary to support the charge must be, at least in part, physical in nature, inappropriate or disruptive conduct at the scene of the performance of an official function is within the ambit of the statute even if no physical force is involved. Willinger v. City of New Rochelle, 212 A.D.2d 526, 622 N.Y.S.2d 321 (2d Dept. 1995).

Evidence.—Where a defendant was charged with obstructing an officer in the performance of his duty and the defense offered a television newsreel film depicting the commission of the alleged crime as proof of defendant's innocence, such proof was insufficient because counsel had stipulated at the trial that the film had been cut and spliced, and there was no testimony that the film was a complete record of the events leading to defendant's arrest. People v. Eisenberg, 22 N.Y.2d 99, 291 N.Y.S.2d 318, 238 N.E.2d 719 (1968).

—Evidence was sufficient to support defendant's conviction where it established that defendant's actions constituted a knowing physical interference with and disruption of an officer's official function. People v. Meath, 219 A.D.2d 838, 632 N.Y.S.2d 1014 (4th Dept. 1995).

—Defendant's refusal to be fingerprinted after her arrest for criminal trespass, whereby she pulled away from officer trying to fingerprint her, sat in a chair and refused to get up, all supported violation of this section. People v. Santos, 182 Misc. 2d 764, 700 N.Y.S2d 381 (Crim. Ct. N.Y. Co. 1999).

—Defendant's refusal to be fingerprinted and his attempts to leave the police station could not be grounds for resisting arrest, but could be for attempted escape in the third degree and obstructing governmental administration in the second degree. People v. Hasenflue, 169 A.D.2d 766, 648 N.Y.S.2d 254 (Sup. Ct. Ulster Co. 1996).

§ 195.06. Killing or injuring a police animal.

A person is guilty of killing or injuring a police animal when such person intentionally kills or injures any animal while such animal is in the performance of its duties and under the supervision of a police or peace officer.

Killing or injuring a police animal is a class A misdemeanor.

Added by L. 1986, Ch. 42.

§ 195.07. Obstructing governmental administration in the first degree.

A person is guilty of obstructing governmental administration in the first degree when he commits the crime of obstructing governmental administration in the second degree by means of interfering with a telecommunications system thereby causing serious physical injury to another person.

Obstructing governmental administration in the first degree is a class E felony.

Added by L. 1984, Ch. 956.

§ 195.08. Obstructing governmental administration by means of a self-defense spray device.

A person is guilty of obstructing governmental administration by means of a self-defense spray device when, with the intent to prevent a police officer or peace officer from performing a lawful duty, he causes temporary physical impairment to a police officer or peace officer by intentionally discharging a self-defense spray device, as defined in paragraph fourteen of subdivision a of section 265.20 of this chapter, thereby causing such temporary physical impairment.

Obstructing governmental administration by means of a self-defense spray device is a class D felony.

Added by L. 1996, Ch. 354, eff. Nov. 1, 1996.

§ 195.10. Refusing to aid a peace or a police officer.

A person is guilty of refusing to aid a peace or a police officer when, upon command by a peace or a police officer identifiable or identified to him as such, he unreasonably fails or refuses to aid such peace or a police officer in effecting an arrest, or in preventing the commission by another person of any offense.

Refusing to aid a peace or a police officer is a class B misdemeanor.

Amended by L. 1980, Ch. 843.

§ 195.11. Harming an animal trained to aid a person with a disability in the second degree.

A person is guilty of harming an animal trained to aid a person with a disability in the second degree when such person intentionally causes physical injury to such animal while it is in the performance of aiding a person with a disability, and thereby renders such animal incapable of providing such aid to such person, or to another person with a disability.

For purposes of this section and section 195.12 of this article, the term "disability" means "disability" as defined in subdivision twenty-one of section two hundred ninety-two of the executive law.

Harming an animal trained to aid a person with a disability in the second degree is a class B misdemeanor.

Added by L. 1989, Ch. 344.

§ 195.12. Harming an animal trained to aid a person with a disability in the first degree.

A person is guilty of harming an animal trained to aid a person with a disability in the first degree when such person:

1. intentionally causes physical injury to such animal while it is in the performance of aiding a person with a disability, and thereby renders such animal permanently incapable of providing

such aid to such person, or to another person with a disability; or

2. intentionally kills such animal while it is in the performance of aiding a person with a disability.

Harming an animal trained to aid a person with a disability in the first degree is a class A misdemeanor.

Added by L. 1989, Ch. 344.

§ 195.15. Obstructing firefighting operations.

A person is guilty of obstructing firefighting operations when he intentionally and unreasonably obstructs the efforts of any:

1. fireman in extinguishing a fire, or prevents or dissuades another from extinguishing or helping to extinguish a fire; or

2. fireman, police officer or peace officer in performing his duties in circumstances involving an imminent danger created by an explosion, threat of explosion or the presence of toxic fumes or gases.

Obstructing firefighting operations is a class A misdemeanor.

Amended by L. 1969, Ch. 314; L. 1981, Ch. 731.

ANNOTATION

Extinguishing a fire.—Defendant's actions in yelling obscenities and preventing the free movement of the firefighters through a multiple dwelling, where they were responding to a fire alarm and attempting to locate the fire, and where there clearly was a fire present on the premises, constituted a violation of this section. People v. Melendez, 180 Misc. 2d 48, 688 N.Y.S.2d 870 (Crim. Ct. Queens Co. 1999).

§ 195.16. Obstructing emergency medical services.

A person is guilty of obstructing emergency medical services when he or she intentionally and unreasonably obstructs the efforts of any service, technician, personnel, system or unit specified in section three thousand one of the public health law in the performance of their duties.

Added by L. 2003, Ch. 600, § 1, eff. Nov. 1, 2003.

§ 195.20. Defrauding the government.

A person is guilty of defrauding the government when, being a public servant or party officer, he:

(a) engages in a scheme constituting a systematic ongoing course of conduct with intent to defraud the state or a political subdivison of the state or a governmental instrumentality within the state or to obtain property from the state or a political subdivison of the state or a governmental instrumentality within the state by false or fraudulent pretenses, representations or promises and

(b) so obtains property with a value in excess of one thousand dollars from such state, political subdivison or governmental instrumentality.

Defrauding the government is a class E felony.

Added by L. 1986, Ch. 833.

ARTICLE 200—BRIBERY INVOLVING PUBLIC SERVANTS AND RELATED OFFENSES

LexisNexis Cross Reference

New York Criminal Practice (2d ed.), Vol. 7, Ch. 70, Bribery—Public Servants.

§ 200.00. Bribery in the third degree.

A person is guilty of bribery in the third degree when he confers, or offers or agrees to confer, any benefit upon a public servant upon an agreement or understanding that such public servant's vote, opinion, judgment, action, decision or exercise of discretion as a public servant will thereby be influenced.

Bribery in the third degree is a class D felony.

Amended by L. 1973, Ch. 276; L. 1986, Ch. 833.

ANNOTATIONS

No proof connecting defendants with payment of bribe necessary.—The proof need not tend to connect the defendant with the actual payment of the money as the crime of bribery is complete when the offer is made. People v. Potenza, 92 A.D.2d 21, 459 N.Y.S.2d 639 (4th Dept. 1983).

Evidence.—Evidence presented failed to establish either an agreement or an understanding; People had to prove both an understanding in the mind of the bribe maker that the receiver would "effectuate the proscribed corruption of public process and was affected to do so by the actus reus of this particular crime. The mere hope that the public servant would be influenced by the benefit offered or conferred is insufficient." People v. Canepa, 295 A.D.2d 247, 745 N.Y.S.2d 153 (1st Dept. 2002).

—Building owner's payment of $300 to an undercover building inspector with the intention that the inspector's actions on the buildings would be affected supported the conviction of third degree bribery. People v. Chou, 292 A.D.2d 199, 738 N.Y.S.2d 210 (1st Dept. 2002).

—"Understanding" entered into among two plumbers and a plumbing inspector that inspector would perform inspections and deliver inspection reports expeditiously, which was a matter of significant economic importance to the plumbers, was sufficient to support conviction; that there was no agreement to approve unsatisfactory work was not required. People v. Kitsos, 299 A.D.2d 291, 750 N.Y.S.2d 68 (1st Dept. 2002).

—On appeal, court reinstated count in indictment which charged defendant, a desk officer at a local police station, with a violation of this section, based on evidence that he took a complaint of suspected drug activity from two women, instead of referring them to the detectives, he called the mother of a suspect mentioned by the women and told her that her son's name had been mentioned in connection with drug activity and to keep him away from a certain location for a while. People v. Lucharelli, 300 A.D.2d 1013, 753 N.Y.S.2d 638 (4th Dept. 2002).

Essentially similar crimes.—Federal bribery conviction under 18 U.S.C. § 666(a)(2) is essentially similar to the New York crime under PL § 200.00; both statutes make felonious the bribing of a public servant. *In re* Castro, 216 A.D.2d 782, 628 N.Y.S.2d 850 (3d Dept. 1995).

§ 200.03. Bribery in the second degree.

A person is guilty of bribery in the second degree when he confers, or offers or agrees to confer, any benefit valued in excess of ten thousand dollars upon a public servant upon an agreement or understanding that such public servant's vote, opinion, judgment, action, decision or exercise of discretion as a public servant will thereby be influenced.

Bribery in the second degree is a class C felony.

Added by L. 1986, Ch. 833.

§ 200.04. Bribery in the first degree.

A person is guilty of bribery in the first degree when he confers, or offers or agrees to confer, any benefit upon a public servant upon an agreement or understanding that such public servant's vote, opinion, judgment, action, decision or exercise of discretion as a public servant will thereby be influenced in the investigation, arrest, detention, prosecution, or incarceration of any person for the commission or alleged commission of a class A felony defined in article two hundred twenty of the penal law or an attempt to commit any such class A felony.

Bribery in the first degree is a class B felony.

Added by L. 1973, Ch. 276.

§ 200.05. Bribery; defense.

In any prosecution for bribery, it is a defense that the defendant conferred or agreed to confer the benefit involved upon the public servant involved as a result of conduct of the latter constituting larceny committed by means of extortion, or an attempt to commit the same, or coercion, or an attempt to commit coercion.

ANNOTATIONS

Evidence.—Defense of extortion/coercion was not supported by evidence that a building inspector, who was paid $ 300 by defendant to affect his action on the buildings, overstated the scope of the building violations. People v. Chou, 292 A.D.2d 199, 738 N.Y.S.2d 210 (1st Dept. 2002).

Coerced bribe.—A person who pays a coerced bribe is not guilty of criminal conduct and cannot be an accomplice of the bribe receiver. People v. Manfredi, 166 A.D.2d 460, 560 N.Y.S.2d 679 (2d Dept. 1990).

§ 200.10. Bribe receiving in the third degree.

A public servant is guilty of bribe receiving in the third degree when he solicits, accepts or agrees to accept any benefit from another person upon an agreement or understanding that his vote, opinion, judgment, action, decision or exercise of discretion as a public servant will thereby be influenced.

Bribe receiving in the third degree is a class D felony.

Amended by L. 1973, Ch. 276; L. 1986, Ch. 833.

ANNOTATIONS

Defendant's ability to procure benefit.—Where defendant was a criminal court clerk who accepted a money bribe to dismiss a ticket, even though such dismissal could not be and was not procured by him, the bribe related to his "colorable" authority and was offered for a corrupt act which had some official relation to his powers and duties and receipt of the money was therefore proscribed. People v. Charles, 61 N.Y.2d 321, 473 N.Y.S.2d 941, 462 N.E.2d 118 (1984).

Intent.—Defendant's state of mind is controlling in determining whether there is an "agreement" or "understanding"; the results of the agreement or understanding are irrelevant, and no benefit need actually be conferred. People v. Souvenir, 209 A.D.2d 455, 618 N.Y.S.2d 447 (2d Dept. 1994).

Evidence.—Evidence of prior unconnected and uncharged receiving of bribes is inadmissible as proof relating to the receiving of a later bribe unless a common scheme or plan is established. People v. Fiore, 34 N.Y.2d 81, 356 N.Y.S.2d 38, 312 N.E.2d 174 (1974).

—Acceptance of the bribe is not required to establish the crime of bribe receiving in the third degree; the agreement to accept the bribe completes the crime. People v. Dowell, 236 A.D.2d 242, 654 N.Y.S.2d 126 (1st Dept. 1997).

—The People need not present any direct evidence of an agreement by a public official to accept a bribe; the evidence of such an agreement may be shown circumstantially. People v. Logan, 145 A.D.2d 437, 535 N.Y.S.2d 411 (2d Dept. 1988).

Attempt.—Defendant was not entitled to a charge of attempted bribe receiving since a person who solicits a bribe is guilty of the completed offense; there can be no attempt at a solicitation crime because the solicitation is itself an attempt. People v. Souvenir, 209 A.D.2d 455, 618 N.Y.S.2d 447 (2d Dept. 1994).

§ 200.11. Bribe receiving in the second degree.

A public servant is guilty of bribe receiving in the second degree when he solicits, accepts or agrees to accept any benefit valued in excess of ten thousand dollars from another person upon an agreement or understanding that his vote, opinion, judgment, action, decision or exercise of discretion as a public servant will thereby be influenced.

Bribe receiving in the second degree is a class C felony.

Added by L. 1986, Ch. 833.

ANNOTATION

Evidence—Respondent, an attorney was disbarred upon his plea of guilty to two counts of attempted bribe receiving in the second degree based on evidence that on two occasions, from approximately July 1999 to approximately January 2002, respondent acted in concert with State Assemblywoman Gloria Davis, a public servant, and others, in soliciting, accepting and agreeing to accept a benefit valued in excess of $10,000 in return for Gloria Davis's influence as a public servant. In re Jenkins, 309 A.D.2d 186, 765 N.Y.S.2d 246 (1st Dept. 2004).

§ 200.12. Bribe receiving in the first degree.

A public servant is guilty of bribe receiving in the first degree when he solicits, accepts or agrees to accept any benefit from another person upon an agreement or understanding that his vote, opinion, judgment, action, decision or exercise of discretion as a public servant will thereby be influenced in the investigation, arrest, detention, prosecution or incarceration of any person for the commission or alleged commission of a class A felony defined in article two hundred twenty of the penal law or an attempt to commit any such class A felony.

Bribe receiving in the first degree is a class B felony.

Added by L. 1973, Ch. 276.

ANNOTATIONS

Defendant's state of mind.—If the officers agreed to accept a benefit not to arrest the undercover officer, believing that he had in his possession an ounce or more of a controlled substance, then whether or not he in fact had one ounce or more of such drug in his possession, the jury could find them guilty of bribe receiving, first degree. People v. Holmes, 72 A.D.2d 1, 423 N.Y.S.2d 45 (1st Dept. 1979).

Inclusory count; unlawful gratuities.—A count of receiving unlawful gratuities is an inclusory concurrent count of the crimes of bribe receiving. People v. Williams, 52 A.D.2d 540, 382 N.Y.S.2d 86 (1st Dept. 1976).

§ 200.15. Bribe receiving; no defense.

1. The crimes of (a) bribe receiving, and (b)

larceny committed by means of extortion, attempt to commit the same, coercion and attempt to commit coercion, are not mutually exclusive, and it is no defense to a prosecution for bribe receiving that, by reason of the same conduct, the defendant also committed one of such other specified crimes.

2. It is no defense to a prosecution pursuant to the provisions of this article that the public servant did not have power or authority to perform the act or omission for which the alleged bribe, gratuity or reward was given.

Amended by L. 1986, Ch. 834.

§ 200.20. Rewarding official misconduct in the second degree.

A person is guilty of rewarding official misconduct in the second degree when he knowingly confers, or offers or agrees to confer, any benefit upon a public servant for having violated his duty as a public servant.

Rewarding official misconduct in the second degree is a class E felony.

Amended by L. 1973, Ch. 276.

§ 200.22. Rewarding official misconduct in the first degree.

A person is guilty of rewarding official misconduct in the first degree when he knowingly confers, or offers or agrees to confer, any benefit upon a public servant for having violated his duty as a public servant in the investigation, arrest, detention, prosecution, or incarceration of any person for the commission or alleged commission of a class A felony defined in article two hundred twenty of the penal law or the attempt to commit any such class A felony.

Rewarding official misconduct in the first degree is a class C felony.

Added by L. 1973, Ch. 276.

§ 200.25. Receiving reward for official misconduct in the second degree.

A public servant is guilty of receiving reward for official misconduct in the second degree when he solicits, accepts or agrees to accept any benefit from another person for having violated his duty as a public servant.

Receiving reward for official misconduct in the second degree is a class E felony.

Amended by L. 1973, Ch. 276.

ANNOTATION

Evidence.—Evidence of prior unconnected and uncharged receiving of bribes is inadmissible as proof relating to the receiving of a later bribe unless a common scheme or plan is established. People v. Fiore, 34 N.Y.2d 81, 356 N.Y.S.2d 38, 312 N.E.2d 174 (1974).

—"An indictment in which the defendant's duty as a public

servant, an essential element of the crime of receiving reward for official misconduct, is defined solely by reference to the Rules of Judicial Conduct, specifically, 22 NYCRR 100.2(C) and 100.3(B)(6) . . . is insufficient." People v. Garson, 17 A.D.3d 695, 793 N.Y.S.2d 539 (2d Dept. 2005) (citations omitted).

§ 200.27. Receiving reward for official misconduct in the first degree.

A public servant is guilty of receiving reward for official misconduct in the first degree when he solicits, accepts or agrees to accept any benefit from another person for having violated his duty as a public servant in the investigation, arrest, detention, prosecution, or incarceration of any person for the commission or alleged commission of a class A felony defined in article two hundred twenty of the penal law or the attempt to commit any such class A felony.

Receiving reward for official misconduct in the first degree is a class C felony.

Added by L. 1973, Ch. 276.

§ 200.30. Giving unlawful gratuities.

A person is guilty of giving unlawful gratuities when he knowingly confers, or offers or agrees to confer, any benefit upon a public servant for having engaged in official conduct which he was required or authorized to perform, and for which he was not entitled to any special or additional compensation.

Giving unlawful gratuities is a class A misdemeanor.

ANNOTATION

Lesser included offenses.—Giving unlawful gratuities is not a lesser included offense of bribery, second degree. People v. Graham, 57 A.D.2d 478, 394 N.Y.S.2d 982 (4th Dept. 1977), aff'd, 44 N.Y.2d 768, 406 N.Y.S.2d 36, 377 N.E.2d 480.

§ 200.35. Receiving unlawful gratuities.

A public servant is guilty of receiving unlawful gratuities when he solicits, accepts or agrees to accept any benefit for having engaged in official conduct which he was required or authorized to perform, and for which he was not entitled to any special or additional compensation.

Receiving unlawful gratuities is a class A misdemeanor.

ANNOTATIONS

Bribe receiving; receiving unlawful gratuities.—In bribe receiving a benefit must be conferred or offered or agreed to be conferred upon a public servant for the purpose of influencing his decision, whereas in receiving unlawful gratuities the benefit is conferred upon the public servant for having already engaged in official conduct which he was required or authorized to do and for which he was not entitled to additional compensation. People v. Hendy, 64 A.D.2d 407, 409 N.Y.S.2d 736 (1st Dept. 1978).

Conduct; official capacity of defendants.—Conviction for violating PL § 206.35 was reversed where defendants' official duties consisted of supervising, inspecting and licensing adult care institutions and the evidence presented revealed that defendant had accepted gratuities for negotiating with prospective lessees and providing counseling services in connection with the opening and staffing of an adult home since such services were not part of his official duties. People v. Zambuto, 73 A.D.2d 828, 423 N.Y.S.2d 770 (4th Dept. 1979).

§ 200.40. Bribe giving and bribe receiving for public office; definition of term.

As used in sections 200.45 and 200.50, "party officer" means a person who holds any position or office in a political party, whether by election, appointment or otherwise.

§ 200.45. Bribe giving for public office.

A person is guilty of bribe giving for public office when he confers, or offers or agrees to confer, any money or other property upon a public servant or a party officer upon an agreement or understanding that some person will or may be appointed to a public office or designated or nominated as a candidate for public office.

Bribe giving for public office is a class D felony.

§ 200.50. Bribe receiving for public office.

A public servant or a party officer is guilty of bribe receiving for public office when he solicits, accepts or agrees to accept any money or other property from another person upon an agreement or understanding that some person will or may be appointed to a public office or designated or nominated as a candidate for public office.

Bribe receiving for public office is a class D felony.

ARTICLE 205—ESCAPE AND OTHER OFFENSES RELATING TO CUSTODY

LexisNexis Cross Reference

New York Criminal Practice (2d ed.), Vol. 7, Ch. 72, Escape and Other Offenses Relating to Custody.

§ 205.00. Escape and other offenses relating to custody; definitions of terms.

The following definitions are applicable to this article:

1. "Detention Facility" means any place used for the confinement, pursuant to an order of a court, of a person (a) charged with or convicted of an offense, or (b) charged with being or adjudicated a youthful offender, person in need of supervision or juvenile delinquent, or (c) held for extradition or as a material witness, or (d) otherwise confined pursuant to an order of a court.

2. "Custody" means restraint by a public servant pursuant to an authorized arrest or an order of a court.

3. "Contraband" means any article or thing which a person confined in a detention facility is prohibited from obtaining or possessing by statute, rule, regulation or order.

4. "Dangerous contraband" means contraband which is capable of such use as may endanger the safety or security of a detention facility or any person therein.

Amended by L. 1972, Ch. 207.

ANNOTATIONS

Constitutionality.—Court rejected defendant's challenge to § 205.00[3] as unconstitutionally vague and as improper delegation of legislative authority. People v. Hughes, 212 A.D.2d 910, 623 N.Y.S.2d 167 (3d Dept. 1995).

Custody.—A defendant is deemed "in custody" for purposes of escape charges when he is in the courtroom, sentence is pronounced by the court, and a commitment order committing defendant to the custody of the sheriff has been signed by the court. People v. Neeley, 168 Misc. 2d 889, 645 N.Y.S.2d 283 (Monroe Co. Ct. 1996).

Dangerous contraband.—Defendant's possession of a razor blade attached to a handle by electrical tape constituted dangerous contraband, even if the razor was dull, since it was "capable of such use as may endanger the safety or security of a detention facility or any person therein." People v. Carralero, 9 A.D.3d 790, 780 N.Y.S.2d 245 (3d Dept. 2004).

—Possession of marijuana could not support a conviction under this section in this case, although there is precedent indicating that a controlled substance can constitute dangerous contraband in some circumstances review of this record fails to reveal competent and specific proof, even when viewed in the light most favorable to the prosecution, that defendant's possession of marihuana endangered safety or security at the St. Lawrence County facility. People v. Brown, 2 A.D.3d 1216, 769 N.Y.S.2d 657 (3d Dept. 2003).

—Marijuana is "dangerous contraband" within the meaning of PL § 205.00(4) because it is capable of "endangering the safety or security of a detention facility or any person therein." People v. McCrae, 297 A.D.2d 878, 747 N.Y.S.2d 399 (3d Dept. 2002).

—Certain items of contraband, such as weapons, by their very nature pose an apparent danger to a facility, but mere presence of a "very small amount of marihuana," standing alone, in the absence of specific proof as to how the marijuana possessed endangers the safety of a facility, will not support a conviction under PL § 205.00. People v. Stanley, 19 A.D.3d 1152, 796 N.Y.S.2d 767 (4th Dept. 2005).

Evidence.—Absent evidence in the record that defendant was prohibited from possessing a bat or weight bar in prison, evidence was insufficient to support a conviction of promoting prison contraband, namely a bat and weight bar. People v. Mathis, 278 A.D.2d 802, 718 N.Y.S.2d 523 (4th Dept. 2000), *appeal denied,* 96 N.Y.2d 785 (2001).

—Evidence was sufficient to establish that defendant had been charged with the crime of rape in the first degree and was in custody pursuant to a securing order on the date of the escape. People v. Richardson, 216 A.D.2d 915, 629 N.Y.S.2d 557 (4th Dept. 1995), *aff'd,* 88 N.Y.2d 1049, 650 N.Y.S.2d 633, 673 N.E.2d 918 (1996).

§ 205.05. Escape in the third degree.

A person is guilty of escape in the third degree when he escapes from custody.

Escape in the third degree is a class A misdemeanor.

ANNOTATION

Evidence.—Defendant's refusal to be fingerprinted and his attempts to leave the police station could not be grounds for resisting arrest but could be for attempted escape in the third degree and obstructing governmental administration in the second degree. People v. Hasenflue, 169 Misc. 2d 766, 648 N.Y.S.2d 254 (Sup. Ct. Ulster Co. 1996).

§ 205.10. Escape in the second degree.

A person is guilty of escape in the second degree when:

1. He escapes from a detention facility; or

2. Having been arrested for, charged with or convicted of a class C, class D or class E felony, he escapes from custody; or

3. Having been adjudicated a youthful offender, which finding was substituted for the conviction of a felony, he escapes from custody.

Escape in the second degree is a class E felony.

Amended by L. 1980, Ch. 118; L. 1983, Ch. 277.

ANNOTATIONS

Custody.—A defendant is deemed "in custody" for purposes of escape charges when he is in the courtroom, sentence is pronounced by the court, and a commitment order committing defendant to the custody of the sheriff has been signed by the court. People v. Neeley, 168 Misc. 2d 889, 645 N.Y.S.2d 283 (Monroe Co. Ct. 1996).

Justification defense.—Defense of justification was available to defendant on trial on charges of escape and criminal mischief where defendant claimed he kicked out the back of the police car in which he was being transported after his arrest on a parole violation charge and ran because the officers taunted and beat him in the patrol car. People v. Mercer, 267 A.D.2d 1019, 701 N.Y.S.2d 551 (4th Dept. 1999) (mem.).

Lesser included offense.—Since resisting arrest involves conduct occurring at the time of the arrest itself, and escape involves conduct subsequent to the arrest, the trial court properly refused to charge the jury on resisting arrest as a lesser included offense of second degree escape. People v. Becoats, 88 A.D.2d 766, 451 N.Y.S.2d 497 (4th Dept. 1982).

Non-secure facility.—The defendant could not be guilty of escape in the second degree for his escape from the Bronx Psychiatric Center since a non-secure facility does not constitute a detention facility within the meaning of Penal Law § 205.00(1). People v. Ortega, 69 N.Y.2d 763, 513 N.Y.S.2d 103, 505 N.E.2d 613 (1986).

—An alleged PINS who is held in a non-secure agency boarding home (9 N.Y.C.R.R. § 180.3(b)(2)) is not in "detention" for purposes of the criminal escape provisions of the Penal Law. In re Freeman, 103 Misc. 2d 649, 426 N.Y.S.2d 948 (Fam. Ct. Onondaga Co. 1980).

Unauthorized arrest.—Prosecution for escape cannot be based on an arrest procured without probable cause. People v. Allah, 111 Misc. 2d 516, 444 N.Y.S.2d 412 (Sup. Ct. N.Y. Co. 1981).

§ 205.15. Escape in the first degree.

A person is guilty of escape in the first degree when:

1. Having been charged with or convicted of a felony, he escapes from a detention facility; or

2. Having been arrested for, charged with or convicted of a class A or class B felony, he escapes from custody; or

3. Having been adjudicated a youthful offender, which finding was substituted for the conviction of a felony, he escapes from a detention facility.

Escape in the first degree in class D felony.

Amended by L. 1980, Ch. 118; L. 1983, Ch. 277.

ANNOTATIONS

Correctional facility.—The trial court properly denied defendant's motion to dismiss an indictment for escape in the first degree upon defendant's contention that, because he was working at a power house down the street from the wall of the Clinton correctional facility he was not escaping from the facility, since the power house was still a part of the correctional facility. People v. Blank, 87 A.D.2d 947, 451 N.Y.S.2d 242 (3d Dept. 1982).

Justification defense.—Without at least a tender of proof, the court could not reach the question whether conditions or treatment in a correctional facility can constitute proof of justification as a defense to the crime of escape. People v. Barkman, 34 N.Y.2d 624, 355 N.Y.S.2d 367, 311 N.E.2d 502 (1974).

§ 205.16. Absconding from temporary release in the second degree.
[Expires Sept. 1, 2007.]

A person is guilty of absconding from temporary release in the second degree when having been released from confinement in a correctional institution or division for youth facility to participate in a program of work release, he intentionally fails to return to the institution or facility of his confinement at or before the time prescribed for his return.

Absconding from temporary release in the second degree is a class A misdemeanor.

Added by L. 1969, Ch. 678; **Amended** by L. 1972, Ch. 339; L. 1974, Ch. 966; L. 1976, Ch. 471; L. 1979, Ch. 485; L. 1980, Ch. 296; L. 1981, Ch. 495; L. 1982, Ch. 137; L. 1983, Chs. 460, 519; L. 1984, Ch. 983; L. 1985, Ch. 573; L. 1986, Ch. 395; L. 1987, Ch. 261; L. 1991, Ch. 511, eff. July 19, 1991; extending expiration date to Sept. 1, 1994; L. 1997, Ch. 435, § 50, extending expiration date; L. 1999, Ch. 452, § 4, extending expiration date to Sept. 1, 2001, eff. Sept. 1, 1999; L. 2001, Ch. 95, § 6, July 13, 2001, extending expiration date to Sept. 1, 2003; L. 2003, Ch. 16, § 6, eff. Mar. 31, 2003, extending expiration date until Sept. 1, 2005; L. 2005, Ch. 56, Part D, § 6, extending expiration date to Sept. 1, 2007.

ANNOTATION

Distinction with PL § 205.17.—Court rejected defendant's contention that the distinction between PL § 205.16 and § 205.17 is unconstitutional. Additionally, no prosecutorial misconduct was found during summation, where the statements noted by the defendant were either rhetorical questions posed to the jury or statements made in response to defendant and his attorney's attempt to categorize him as an "angel." People v. Burke, 222 A.D.2d 837, 635 N.Y.S.2d 733 (3d Dept. 1995).

§ 205.17. Absconding from temporary release in the first degree. [Expires Sept. 1, 2007.]

A person is guilty of absconding from temporary release in the first degree when having been released from confinement in a correctional institution under the jurisdiction of the state department of correctional services or a facility under the jurisdiction of the state division for youth to participate in a program of temporary release, he intentionally fails to return to the institution or facility of his confinement at or before the time prescribed for his return.

Absconding from temporary release in the first degree is a class E felony.

Added by L. 1969, Ch. 472; **Amended** by L. 1972, Ch. 339; L. 1974, Ch. 966; L. 1976, Ch. 471; L. 1977, Ch. 691; L. 1978, Ch. 691; L. 1979, Ch. 485; L. 1980, Ch. 296; L. 1981, Ch. 495; L. 1982, Ch. 137; L. 1983, Chs. 460, 519; L. 1984, Ch. 983; L. 1985, Ch. 573; L. 1986, Ch. 395; L. 1987, Ch. 261; L. 1988, Ch. 661; L. 1989, Ch. 250; L. 1990, Ch. 193; L. 1991, Ch. 511; L. 1992, Ch. 55; L. 1993, Ch. 60, eff. Apr. 15, 1993, extending expiration date to July 1, 1994; L. 1997, Ch. 435, § 50, extending expiration date to Sept. 1, 1999; L. 1999, Ch. 452, § 4, extending expiration date to Sept. 1, 2001, eff. Sept. 1, 1999; L. 2001, Ch. 95, § 6, July 13, 2001, extending expiration date to Sept. 1, 2003; L. 2003, Ch. 16, § 6, eff. Mar. 31, 2003, extending expiration date to Sept. 1, 2005; L. 2005, Ch. 56, Part D, § 6, extending expiration date to Sept. 1, 2007.

ANNOTATIONS

Constitutionality.—Contention that PL § 205.17 is unconstitutional because it differentiates between escape from the custody of State prisons and escape from other institutions, and also that the punishment is excessive—"cruel and unusual"— found to have no merit. People v. James, 70 A.D.2d 706, 416 N.Y.S.2d 441 (3d Dept. 1979).

—PL § 205.17 is constitutional. People v. Scannelli, 49 A.D.2d 648, 370 N.Y.S.2d 254 (3d Dept. 1975).

Evidence—Evidence that defendant failed to return to the Rochester Correctional Facility after his temporary release from custody pursuant to a work release program supported a conviction under this section. People v. McCullough, 8 A.D.3d 1122, 778 N.Y.S.2d 333 (4th Dept. 2004).

§ 205.18. Absconding from a furlough program. [*Expires Sept. 1, 2007.*]

A person is guilty of absconding from a furlough program when, having been released from confinement in an institution under the jurisdiction of the commissioner of correction in a city having a population of one million or more or of a county which elects to have this article apply thereto to participate in a furlough program, he intentionally fails to return to the institution of his confinement at or before the time prescribed for his return.

Absconding from a furlough program is a class A misdemeanor.

Added by L. 1972, Ch. 886; **Amended** by L. 1973, Ch. 622; L. 1974, Ch. 299; L. 1986, Ch. 395; L. 1987, Ch. 261; L. 1991, Ch. 511, eff. July 19, 1991; L. 1992, Ch. 55, eff. Apr. 10, 1992, extending expiration date to Sept. 1, 1994; L. 1994, Ch. 61, § 9, extending expiration date until Sept. 1, 1995; L. 1995, Ch. 3, § 47, extending expiration date until Sept. 1, 1997; L. 1997, Ch. 435, § 50, extending expiration date to Sept. 1, 1999; L. 1999, Ch. 452, § 1, extending expiration date to Sept. 1, 2001, eff. Sept. 1, 1999; L. 2001, Ch. 95, § 3, extending expiration date to Sept. 1, 2003; L. 2003, Ch. 16, § 3, eff. Mar. 31, 2003, extending expiration date to Sept. 1, 2005; L. 2005, Ch. 56, Part D, § 3, extending expiration date to Sept. 1, 2007.

§ 205.19. Absconding from a community treatment facility. [*Expires Sept. 1, 2007.*]

A person is guilty of absconding from a community treatment facility when having been released from confinement from a correctional institution under the jurisdiction of the state department of correctional services by transfer to a community treatment facility, he leaves such facility without authorization or he intentionally fails to return to the community treatment facility at or before the time prescribed for his return.

Absconding from a community treatment facility is a class E felony.

Added by L. 1986, Ch. 554; **Amended** by L. 1997, Ch. 435, § 52, eff. Aug. 20, 1997; L. 1999, Ch. 452, § 6, extending expiration date to Sept. 1, 2001, eff. Sept. 1, 1999; L. 2001, Ch. 95, § 8, extending expiration date to Sept. 1, 2003; L. 2003, Ch. 16, § 8, eff. Mar. 31, 2003, extending expiration date until Sept. 1, 2005; L. 2005, Ch. 56, Part D, § 8, extending expiration date to Sept. 1, 2007.

§ 205.20. Promoting prison contraband in the second degree.

A person is guilty of promoting prison contraband in the second degree when:

1. He knowingly and unlawfully introduces any contraband into a detention facility; or

2. Being a person confined in a detention facility, he knowingly and unlawfully makes, obtains or possesses any contraband.

Promoting prison contraband in the second degree is a class A misdemeanor.

ANNOTATION

Possession of marijuana by prisoner.—Dangerous contraband means an article or substance likely to cause death or other serious injury, i.e., weapons, tools, explosives and items of such type, and accordingly marijuana is contraband. People v. Soto, 77 Misc. 2d 427, 353 N.Y.S.2d 375 (N.Y.C. Crim. Ct. 1974).

§ 205.25. Promoting prison contraband in the first degree.

A person is guilty of promoting prison contraband in the first degree when:

1. He knowingly and unlawfully introduces any dangerous contraband into a detention facility; or

2. Being a person confined in a detention facility, he knowingly and unlawfully makes, obtains or possesses any dangerous contraband.

Promoting prison contraband in the first degree is a class D felony.

ANNOTATIONS

Constitutionality—PL § 205.25(2) is not unconstitutionally vague. People v. Rivera, 221 A.D.2d 380, 633 N.Y.S.2d 507 (2d Dept. 1995).

—Court rejected challenges to PL § 205.25(2) for vagueness and improper delegation of legislative authority. People v. Hughes, 212 A.D.2d 910, 623 N.Y.S.2d 167 (3d Dept. 1995).

Dangerous contraband.—Heroin is dangerous contraband; its use may endanger the safety or security of detention facility or person therein. People v. Rivera, 221 A.D.2d 380, 633 N.Y.S.2d 507 (2d Dept. 1995).

—Defendant's possession of a razor blade attached to a handle by electrical tape constituted dangerous contraband, even if the razor was dull, since it was "capable of such use as may endanger the safety or security of a detention facility or any person therein." People v. Carralero, 9 A.D.3d 790, 780 N.Y.S.2d 245 (3d Dept. 2004).

—Testimony that during a prison melee officer saw defendant holding a steel rod, approximately eight and one-half inches long, with a point on one end supported this conviction. People v. Almarez, 2 A.D.3d 1151, 770 N.Y.S.2d 165 (3d Dept. 2003).

—"The distinction between the two degrees of promoting prison contraband would be nonexistent if every item of contraband could be considered dangerous contraband by merely speculating as to how such an item could endanger the safety of a facility. Specific proof is needed regarding how the particular marihuana that was possessed by each defendant endangered the safety of the facility"; absent that proof, conviction under PL § 205.25 cannot stand. People v. Stanley, 19 A.D.3d 1152, 796 N.Y.S.2d 767 (4th Dept. 2005). *But see* People v. McCrae, 297 A.D.2d 878, 747 N.Y.S.2d 399 (3d Dept. 2002) (marijuana is "dangerous contraband," and use of illegal drugs by inmates in correctional facilities has potential to cause disruptive and dangerous behavior among prison population).

Evidence.—Absent evidence in the record that defendant was prohibited from possessing a bat or weight bar in prison, evidence was insufficient to support a conviction of promoting prison contraband, namely a bat and weight bar. People v. Mathis, 278 A.D.2d 802, 718 N.Y.S.2d 523 (4th Dept. 2000), *appeal denied,* 96 N.Y.2d 785 (2001).

Selective Prosecution.—Defendants were not selectively prosecuted for promoting prison contraband where 61.5% of the cases prosecuted involved inmates similarly situated, i.e., inmates who were within three and one-half years of their maximum release date, and lower court erred in dismissing the indictments. People v. Blount, 231 A.D.2d 860, 647 N.Y.S.2d 888 (4th Dept. 1996).

Sufficiency of indictment.—People's failure to allege that the crime occurred while defendant was confined to a detention facility and to allege the location of that facility was not fatal; incorporating by reference the statute defining that crime " 'not only constituted an allegation of the elements of the crime charged, but also an allegation of the statutory definitions of those relevant elements.' " People v. Martin, 237 A.D.2d 746, 655 N.Y.S.2d 458 (3d Dept. 1997).

§ 205.30. Resisting arrest.

A person is guilty of resisting arrest when he intentionally prevents or attempts to prevent a police officer or peace officer from effecting an authorized arrest of himself or another person.

Resisting arrest is a class A misdemeanor.

Amended by L. 1980, Ch. 843.

ANNOTATIONS

Lawful arrest necessary.—An authorized arrest is a key element of the crime of resisting arrest; lawfulness includes a finding that the arrest was premised upon probable cause. People v. Jensen, 86 N.Y.2d 248, 630 N.Y.S.2d 989, 654 N.E.2d 1237 (1995).

Evidence.—Defendant's convictions for assault in the second degree, and resisting arrest arising from an incident during which he bit a deputy sheriff on the finger and punched him several times were supported by the record and affirmed on appeal. People v. Endresz, 1 A.D.3d 888, 767 N.Y.S.2d 732 (4th Dept. 2003).

—Defendant Eugene Bell's failure to stop running when officer yelled to him, "Freeze Eugene," is legally sufficient to support conviction for resisting arrest. People v. Bell, 265 A.D.2d 813, 696 N.Y.S.2d 610 (4th Dept. 1999), *appeal denied,* 94 N.Y.2d 916 (2000).

—For purposes of resisting arrest, defendant's arrest was complete when he was placed in the police vehicle and transported to the police station, and defendant's refusal to be fingerprinted and his attempts to leave the police station could not be grounds for resisting arrest but could be for attempted escape in the third degree and obstructing governmental administration in the second degree. People v. Hasenflue, 169 Misc. 2d 766, 648 N.Y.S.2d 254 (Sup. Ct. Ulster Co. 1996).

Intent.—Where defendant was obstructing traffic and was uncooperative with policeman who placed him under arrest to which he answered "No, for what," he evidenced verbal conduct clearly showing requisite intent for resisting properly authorized arrest and subsequent physical conduct was not self defense against excessive physical force. Refusal of court to answer jury's question as to difference between resisting arrest and self defense was proper, and defendant's failure to object that harassment was not lesser included crime of assault was waiver of that claim. People v. Stevenson, 31 N.Y.2d 108, 335 N.Y.S.2d 52, 286 N.E.2d 445 (1972).

—Defendant failed to present evidence to support contention that he lacked the requisite intent to resist arrest where hospital test results did not support defendant's contentions that he was suffering from a psychotic episode or that he was intoxicated. Whether defendant was intoxicated to the extent of being unable to form requisite intent is a question of fact and credibility for jury. People v. Clark, 241 A.D.2d 710, 660 N.Y.S.2d 200 (3d Dept. 1997).

Arrest of another.—Teacher who protested arrest of fellow teacher during strike and repeatedly opened door of police car where arrested teacher was confined did not commit crime of resisting arrest. People v. Adickes, 30 N.Y.2d 461, 334 N.Y.S.2d 629, 285 N.E.2d 868 (1972).

Indictment.—Indictment charging resisting arrest was erroneously dismissed; instructions to grand jury, which contained almost a verbatim reading of PL § 205.30 defining resisting arrest and a verbatim reading of PL § 15.05 defining intentional act, were adequate. People v. Cannon, 210 A.D.2d 764, 620 N.Y.S.2d 539 (3d Dept. 1994).

§ 205.50. Hindering prosecution; definition of term.

As used in sections 205.55, 205.60 and 205.65, a person "renders criminal assistance" when, with intent to prevent, hinder or delay the discovery or apprehension of, or the lodging of a criminal charge against, a person who he knows or believes has committed a crime or is being sought by law enforcement officials for the commission of a crime, or with intent to assist a person in profiting or benefiting from the commission of a crime, he:

1. Harbors or conceals such person; or

2. Warns such person of impending discovery or apprehension; or

3. Provides such person with money, transportation, weapon, disguise or other means of avoiding discovery or apprehension; or

4. Prevents or obstructs, by means of force, intimidation or deception, anyone from performing an act which might aid in the discovery or apprehension of such person or in the lodging of a criminal charge against him; or

5. Suppresses, by any act of concealment, alteration or destruction, any physical evidence which might aid in the discovery or apprehension of such person or in the lodging of a criminal charge against him; or

6. Aids such person to protect or expeditiously profit from an advantage derived from such crime.

§ 205.55. Hindering prosecution in the third degree.

A person is guilty of hindering prosecution in the third degree when he renders criminal assistance to a person who has committed a felony.

Hindering prosecution in the third degree is a class A misdemeanor.

ANNOTATION

Absence of element of crime in indictment.—The absence of allegation in the indictment that the person to whom assistance was rendered committed a class B or C felony, or any felony, makes ineffective any attempt to construe it as charging hindering prosecution in the second or third degree. People v. Clough, 43 A.D.2d 451, 353 N.Y.S.2d 260 (3d Dept. 1974).

§ 205.60. Hindering prosecution in the second degree.

A person is guilty of hindering prosecution in the second degree when he renders criminal assistance to a person who has committed a class B or class C felony.

Hindering prosecution in the second degree is a class E felony.

ANNOTATION

Hindering prosecution; mentally retarded defendant; intent.—In an appeal by a mentally retarded defendant, of a conviction for hindering prosecution in the second degree, it was held that mentally retarded defendant could be held liable for the acts of juveniles who affirmatively helped the mugger to escape if the defendant participated with mental culpability in those acts, or if he directed, planned or importuned those acts. People v. Grant, 42 A.D.2d 736, 345 N.Y.S.2d 673 (2d Dept. 1973).

§ 205.65. Hindering prosecution in the first degree.

A person is guilty of hindering prosecution in the first degree when he renders criminal assistance to a person who has committed a class A felony, knowing or believing that such person has engaged in conduct constituting a class A felony.

Hindering prosecution in the first degree is a class D felony.

Amended by L. 1970, Ch. 398.

ANNOTATIONS

Corroboration requirement.—People needed to provide corroboration for the defendant's confession that an underlying felony (murder) had occurred. Without a predicate felony upon which to base a hindering of prosecution case, there is no crime, regardless of defendant's belief and assistance to person thought to have committed the crime. People v. Chico, 90 N.Y.2d 585, 665 N.Y.S.2d 5, 687 N.E.2d 1288 (1997).

Dead body.—Count in indictment charging a violation of PL § 205.65 was upheld where it charged defendant hindered prosecution by moving a dead body immediately after the homicide. People v. Nicholas, 93 Misc. 2d 1037, 403 N.Y.S.2d 683 (Sup. Ct. N.Y. Co. 1978).

Elements necessary to constitute crime.—Three separate elements must coalesce to constitute the crime of hindering prosecution in the first degree (1) actor must render criminal assistance; (2) such assistance must be rendered to one who has committed a class A felony; and (3) actor must know or believe that such person has engaged in conduct constituting a class A felony. All such elements must be alleged in the indictment and failure to do so warrants dismissal of the indictment. People v. Clough, 43 A.D.2d 451, 353 N.Y.S.2d 260 (3d Dept. 1974).

Renders criminal assistance. —The plain language of § 205.65 "contemplates a continuing crime as well as a single act. The very essence of concealment is continuity for the period required to accomplish the desired result. The fact that there may be successive acts in aid of the concealment does not interrupt the continuity of the conduct which was directed to the accomplishment of a single purpose." People v. DeBeer, 4 Misc. 3d 466, 778 N.Y.S.2d 678 (Co. Ct. Ontario Co. 2004) (citation omitted).

Sufficiency of evidence.—A defendant who drove to the scene of a murder with the admitted intent to move the body for the purpose of hindering its discovery, but who turned around several hundred feet away from the victim's body without getting out of his car, did not commit acts sufficiently close to tampering with evidence or hindering prosecution to support convictions on those charges. People v. Ciardullo, 106 A.D.2d 14, 483 N.Y.S.2d 352 (2d Dept. 1984).

ARTICLE 210—PERJURY AND RELATED OFFENSES

LexisNexis Cross Reference

New York Criminal Practice (2d ed.), Vol. 7, Ch. 73, Perjury and Related Offenses.

§ 210.00. Perjury and related offenses; definitions of terms.

The following definitions are applicable to this article:

1. "Oath" includes an affirmation and every other mode authorized by law of attesting to the truth of that which is stated.

2. "Swear" means to state under oath.

3. "Testimony" means an oral statement made under oath in a proceeding before any court, body, agency, public servant or other person authorized by law to conduct such proceeding and to administer the oath or cause it to be administered.

4. "Oath required by law." An affidavit, deposition or other subscribed written instrument is one for which an "oath is required by law" when, absent an oath or swearing thereto, it does not or would not, according to statute or appropriate regulatory provisions, have legal efficacy in a court of law or before any public or governmental body, agency or public servant to whom it is or might be submitted.

5. "Swear falsely." A person "swears falsely" when he intentionally makes a false statement which he does not believe to be true (a) while giving testimony, or (b) under oath in a subscribed written instrument. A false swearing in a subscribed written instrument shall not be deemed complete until the instrument is delivered by its subscriber, or by someone acting in his behalf, to another person with intent that it be uttered or published as true.

6. "Attesting officer" means any notary public or other person authorized by law to administer oaths in connection with affidavits, depositions and other subscribed written instruments, and to certify that the subscriber of such an instrument has appeared before him and has sworn to the truth of the contents thereof.

7. "Jurat" means a clause wherein an attesting officer certifies, among other matters, that the subscriber has appeared before him and sworn to the truth of the contents thereof.

ANNOTATIONS

Entrapment.—Court rejected defendant's contention that he was a victim of a perjury and contempt trap set by the special prosecutor where the questions posed to the defendant were pertinent to the substance of the grand jury investigation and the prosecutor provided ample cues to stimulate his recollection. People v. Smith, 153 A.D.2d 764, 545 N.Y.S.2d 46 (2d Dept. 1989).

Witness.—A grand jury witness who is a possible defendant or target, and who has not received transactional immunity for a previously committed substantive offense, may be prosecuted for perjury on the basis of his testimony; since such a witness is afforded protection by the rule which forbids use of his compelled statements and any evidence derived therefrom in a prosecution against him for a previously committed substantive crime, he is not additionally protected from prosecution for giving perjured testimony before the grand jury. People v. Ianniello, 21 N.Y.2d 418, 288 N.Y.S.2d 462, 235 N.E.2d 439 (1968), *cert. denied,* 393 U.S. 827 (1968).

Proceeding.—Tape recorded sworn statements given in the District Attorney's office were not part of a criminal proceeding or given in a written instrument and could not form the basis for perjury in the first or second degree. A "proceeding necessarily envisions some eventual judicial or administrative intervention, where, under the authority of law, the public factual and legal resolution of interests is determined by a fact-finder" and, in this case, an oath was not required by law. People v. Uhrey, 169 Misc. 2d 1015, 647 N.Y.S.2d 910 (Sup. Ct. Kings Co. 1996).

Appeal.—Defendant's claim that his conviction for perjury was not supported by sufficient proof that he actually subscribed a written instrument for which an oath is required was not preserved for appellate review. People v. Young, 220 A.D.2d 872, 632 N.Y.S.2d 668 (3d Dept. 1995).

§ 210.05. Perjury in the third degree.

A person is guilty of perjury in the third degree when he swears falsely.

Perjury in the third degree is a class A misdemeanor.

ANNOTATIONS

Entrapment.—Indictment was properly dismissed where it was based on an answer given before a grand jury which was of little relevance to the subject matter of the investigation, and where it appeared the answer was made in response to a question that was intended to entrap the defendant into committing perjury. People v. Davis, 74 A.D.2d 801, 426 N.Y.S.2d 5 (1st Dept. 1980).

Evidence.—Testimony before a grand jury conducting an investigation into a murder could form the basis for perjury in the third degree. Although defendant received immunity for the subject matter of his testimony in the grand jury, nowhere during the grand jury presentation was defendant questioned about his previous false statement made by defendant in the District Attorney's office. People v. Uhrey, 169 Misc. 2d 1015, 647 N.Y.S.2d 910 (Sup. Ct. Kings Co. 1996).

§ 210.10. Perjury in the second degree.

A person is guilty of perjury in the second degree when he swears falsely and when his false statement is (a) made in a subscribed written instrument for which an oath is required by law, and (b) made with intent to mislead a public servant in the performance of his official functions, and (c) material to the action, proceeding or matter involved.

Perjury in the second degree is a class E felony.

ANNOTATION

Proceeding.—Tape recorded sworn statements given in the District Attorney's office were not part of a criminal proceeding or given in a written instrument and could not form the basis for perjury in the first or second degree. A "proceeding necessarily envisions some eventual judicial or administrative intervention, where, under the authority of law, the public factual and legal resolution of interests is determined by a fact-finder" and, in this case, an oath was not required by law. People v. Uhrey, 169 Misc. 2d 1015, 647 N.Y.S.2d 910 (Sup. Ct. Kings Co. 1996).

§ 210.15. Perjury in the first degree.

A person is guilty of perjury in the first degree when he swears falsely and when his false statement (a) consists of testimony, and (b) is material to the action, proceeding or matter in which it is made.

Perjury in the first degree is a class D felony.

ANNOTATIONS

Location of defendant when making statement.—A prosecution for perjury before the grand jury was not defective because the false testimony concerned an out-of-state meeting, arranged by the special prosecutor, between defendant and an out of-state nursing home operator who was working as an undercover agent. People v. Pomerantz, 46 N.Y.2d 240, 413 N.Y.S.2d 288, 385 N.E.2d 1218 (1978).

Proceeding.—Tape recorded sworn statements given in the District Attorney's office were not part of a criminal proceeding or given in a written instrument and could not form the basis for perjury in the first or second degree. A "proceeding necessarily envisions some eventual judicial or administrative intervention, where, under the authority of law, the public factual and legal resolution of interests is determined by a fact-finder" and, in this case, an oath was not required by law. People v. Uhrey, 169 Misc. 2d 1015, 647 N.Y.S.2d 910 (Sup. Ct. Kings Co. 1996).

Materiality of statement.—Defendant police officer's false testimony before a grand jury was material to its investigation and an indictment for perjury in the first degree was proper where the false testimony had the "natural effect or tendency to impede, influence or dissuade the grand jury from pursuing

its investigation." People v. Davis, 53 N.Y.2d 164, 440 N.Y.S.2d 864, 423 N.E.2d 341 (1981).

Ultimate issue for jury.—Ordinarily it is for the jury to determine the validity of a defendant's claim that his answers to questions asked were truthful because he ascribed a particular meaning to a word. People v. Neumann, 51 N.Y.2d 658, 435 N.Y.S.2d 956, 417 N.E.2d 69 (1980).

Evidence.—The defendant was guilty of perjury before a grand jury and the prosecutor, in questioning the defendant, did not limit his inquiry to peripheral details of an insignificant transaction; the recording of the encounter proved that a corrupt arrangement was discussed at a New Jersey meeting and would be memorable 10 months later, and the prosecutor's repetition and restatement provided ample cues to stimulate defendant's recollection. People v. Pomerantz, 46 N.Y.2d 240, 413 N.Y.S.2d 288, 385 N.E.2d 1218 (1978).

—Defendant, a former stockbroker, who was banned from future trading, was convicted under this section for swearing falsely before the National Association of Securities Dealers that he had not supervised retail sales of securities. People v. Cohen, 9 A.D.3d 71, 773 N.Y.S.2d 371 (1st Dept.), *cert. denied,* — U.S. —, 125 S. Ct. 316 (2004).

Jurisdiction.—New York State has the jurisdiction to prosecute perjury based on false testimony given under oath before the National Association of Securities Dealers. People v. Cohen, 187 Misc. 2d 117, 718 N.Y.S.2d 147 (Sup. Ct. N.Y. Co. 2000).

§ 210.20. Perjury; pleading and proof where inconsistent statements involved.

Where a person has made two statements under oath which are inconsistent to the degree that one of them is necessarily false, where the circumstances are such that each statement, if false, is perjuriously so, and where each statement was made within the jurisdiction of this state and within the period of the statute of limitations for the crime charged, the inability of the people to establish specifically which of the two statements is the false one does not preclude a prosecution for perjury, and such prosecution may be conducted as follows:

1. The indictment or information may set forth the two statements and, without designating either, charge that one of them is false and perjuriously made.

2. The falsity of one or the other of the two statements may be established by proof or a showing of their irreconcilable inconsistency.

3. The highest degree of perjury of which the defendant may be convicted is determined by hypothetically assuming each statement to be false and perjurious. If under such circumstances perjury of the same degree would be established by the making of each statement, the defendant may be convicted of that degree at most. If perjury of different degrees would be established by the making of the two statements, the defendant may be convicted of the lesser degree at most.

ANNOTATIONS

Oath.—In order to make a valid oath, for the falsity of which perjury would lie, there must be the presence of an officer authorized to administer it and an unequivocal act of the affiant consciously taking upon himself the obligation of an oath. Such form is required in order to distinguish between an oath and a bare assertion. The jurat is merely evidence that the oath was properly taken. It is no part of the oath, nor is it conclusive evidence of its proper administration; and it may be attacked and shown to be false. People v. Guer, 42 A.D.2d 803, 346 N.Y.S.2d 422 (3d Dept. 1973).

Perjury may also constitute contempt.—Perjury will also constitute a criminal contempt, when it is shown that the witness intended to obstruct the court in the performance of its duty. Holtzman v. Tobin, 78 Misc. 2d 8, 358 N.Y.S.2d 94 (Sup. Ct. App. Term 1974).

§ 210.25. Perjury; defense.

In any prosecution for perjury, it is an affirmative defense that the defendant retracted his false statement in the course of the proceeding in which it was made before such false statement substantially affected the proceeding and before it became manifest that its falsity was or would be exposed.

§ 210.30. Perjury; no defense.

It is no defense to a prosecution for perjury that:

1. The defendant was not competant to make the false statement alleged; or

2. The defendant mistakenly believed the false statement to be immaterial; or

3. The oath was administered or taken in an irregular manner or that the authority or jurisdiction of the attesting officer who administered the oath was defective, if such defect was excusable under any statute or rule of law.

§ 210.35. Making an apparently sworn false statement in the second degree.

A person is guilty of making an apparently sworn false statement in the second degree when (a) he subscribes a written instrument knowing that it contains a statement which is in fact false and which he does not believe to be true, and (b) he intends or believes that such instrument will be uttered or delivered with a jurat affixed thereto, and (c) such instrument is uttered or delivered with a jurat affixed thereto.

Making an apparently sworn false statement in the second degree is a class A misdemeanor.

ANNOTATIONS

Failure to make out a prima facie case.—Conviction under PL § 210.35 was reversed where defendants who submitted four affidavits to a lending institution in order to obtain construction advances left blank the space provided therein for notation of outstanding unpaid bills because the requisite intent to utter or publish as true was not shown where the testimony of the institution's mortgage officer indicated that both parties to the loan were aware that a portion of the construction advances would be used to pay existing debts owing to subcontractors and the instructions in the affidavits seemed to suggest that notation of pre-existing debts was required only where the institution was to make direct payments to third parties. People v. Rosano, 69 A.D.2d 643, 419 N.Y.S.2d 543 (2d Dept. 1979), *aff'd,* 50 N.Y.2d 1013, 431 N.Y.S.2d 683, 409 N.E.2d 1357 (1980).

§ 210.40. Making an apparently sworn false statement in the first degree.

A person is guilty of making an apparently sworn false statement in the first degree when he commits the crime of making an apparently sworn false statement in the second degree, and when (a) the written instrument involved is one for which an oath is required by law, and (b) the false statement contained therein is made with intent to mislead a public servant in the performance of his official functions, and (c) such false statement is material to the action, proceeding or matter involved.

Making an apparently sworn false statement in the first degree is a class E felony.

ANNOTATIONS

Witness statement.—A conviction based solely upon inconsistencies between defendant's sworn statement to the police and complainant's testimony before the grand jury required a reversal, as the defendant's statement was simply a witness statement, not subscribed under oath and made prior to the commencement of any legal proceedings against anyone; the necessary element of making the statement where "an oath is required by law" was missing. People v. Hart, 90 A.D.2d 856, 456 N.Y.S.2d 499 (3d Dept. 1982).

Appeal.—Defendant's argument that his conviction for making an apparently sworn false statement in the first degree was not supported by sufficient proof that he actually subscribed a written instrument for which an oath is required was not preserved for review on appeal. People v. Young, 220 A.D.2d 872, 632 N.Y.S.2d 668 (3d Dept. 1995).

§ 210.45. Making a punishable false written statement.

A person is guilty of making a punishable false written statement when he knowingly makes a false statement, which he does not believe to be true, in a written instrument bearing a legally authorized form notice to the effect that false statements made therein are punishable.

Making a punishable false written statement is a class A misdemeanor.

ANNOTATIONS

Verification by form notice.—Statement which contained warning that any falsities would be punishable as violation of PL § 210.45 served as procedural and functional equivalent of more traditional type of oath or affirmation; this section was enacted by legislature in order to provide a convenient method of assuring truthfulness of documents without requiring an oath before a notary. People v. Sullivan, 56 N.Y.2d 378, 452 N.Y.S.2d 373, 437 N.E.2d 1130 (1982).

Application of statute.—PL § 210.45 is only applicable to situations where a specific authorization exists for the use of an affirmation in place of a notarized form. People v. Guido, 114 Misc. 2d 470, 454 N.Y.S.2d 171 (App. Term 9th and 10th Dist. 1982).

Juvenile delinquency petition.—Delinquency petition not defective because police chemist's signature merely subscribed a form notice pursuant to PL § 210.45; form notice combined with subscription of deponent is the functional equivalent of a statement under oath and is sufficient to verify an instrument. *In re* Shermaine J., 208 A.D.2d 158, 622 N.Y.S.2d 694 (1st Dept. 1995).

—Police laboratory report signed by police chemist that certified only that report was true and full copy of original report, and stated that individual signing report was subject to penalties for violation of PL § 210.45, was insufficient basis for petition; chemist did not testify as to personal knowledge regarding who conducted test or results of test conducted, and therefore did not contain sufficient non-hearsay allegations. *In re* Kirk G., 208 A.D.2d 375, 617 N.Y.S.2d 24 (1st Dept. 1994).

—Juvenile delinquency petition not defective because supporting depositions were not sworn to; supporting depositions were based on deponents' first hand knowledge and contained warning that false statements made therein were punishable as violations of PL § 210.45 immediately above deponents' signatures. *In re* Michael F., 210 A.D.2d 758, 621 N.Y.S.2d 112 (3d Dept. 1994).

§ 210.50. Perjury and related offenses; requirement of corroboration.

In any prosecution for perjury, except a prosecution based upon inconsistent statements pursuant to section 210.20, or in any prosecution for making an apparently sworn false statement, or making a punishable false written statement, falsity of a statement may not be established by the uncorroborated testimony of a single witness.

ANNOTATIONS

Sufficient corroboration.—The indictment for perjury was sufficient where the People offered circumstantial evidence to corroborate the testimony of the single witness. People v. Ginsberg, 80 Misc. 2d 921, 364 N.Y.S.2d 260 (Nassau Co. Ct. 1974), *aff'd,* 50 A.D.2d 804, 375 N.Y.S.2d 855 (1976).

Perjury; sufficient corroboration.—In perjury prosecution based on defendant's denial of alleged theft of proceeds of salary check of another, indorsement by bartender who cashed check which consisted of name of employer company and its president constituted sufficient corroboration of police officer's testimony that he saw defendant cash check and pocket the proceeds, since it could be inferred that bartender would not have so indorsed check if payee had cashed it. People v. Fitzpatrick, 40 N.Y.2d 44, 386 N.Y.S.2d 28, 351 N.E.2d 675 (1976).

ARTICLE 215—OTHER OFFENSES RELATING TO JUDICIAL AND OTHER PROCEEDINGS

LexisNexis Cross Reference

New York Criminal Practice (2d ed.), Vol. 7, Ch. 74, Offenses Relating to Judicial and Other Proceedings.

§ 215.00. Bribing a witness.

A person is guilty of bribing a witness when he confers, or offers or agrees to confer, any benefit upon a witness or a person about to be called as a witness in any action or proceeding upon an agreement or understanding that (a) the testimony of such witness will thereby be influenced, or (b) such witness will absent himself from, or otherwise avoid or seek to avoid appearing or testifying at, such action or proceeding.

Bribing a witness is a class D felony.

ANNOTATIONS

Bribing a witness; generally.—This section was not intended to apply to cooperation agreements between prosecutors and witnesses. People v. Sease, 265 A.D.2d 176, 696 N.Y.S.2d 430 (1st Dept. 1999).

—Evidence was insufficient to establish that benefit conferred upon defendant's former clients was based upon agreement that their testimony would be influenced; witnesses testified they were never told they had to testify a certain way in order to receive fee. People v. Kramer, 132 A.D.2d 708, 518 N.Y.S.2d 189 (2d Dept. 1986), aff'd, 72 N.Y.2d 1003, 534 N.Y.S.2d 912, 531 N.E.2d 633 (1988).

§ 215.05. Bribe receiving by a witness.

A witness or a person about to be called as a witness in any action or proceeding is guilty of bribe receiving by a witness when he solicits, accepts or agrees to accept any benefit from another person upon an agreement or understanding that (a) his testimony will thereby be influenced, or (b) he will absent himself from, or otherwise avoid or seek to avoid appearing or testifying at, such action or proceeding.

Bribe receiving by a witness is a class D felony.

ANNOTATION

Sufficiency of evidence.—Evidence that defendant, an attorney, offered to provide certain information about the victim which he had obtained from her attorney in exchange for five hundred dollars was sufficient to support a conviction. People v. Canale, 240 A.D.2d 839, 658 N.Y.S.2d 715 (3d Dept. 1997).

§ 215.10. Tampering with a witness in the fourth degree.

A person is guilty of tampering with a witness when, knowing that a person is or is about to be called as a witness in an action or proceeding, (a) he wrongfully induces or attempts to induce such person to absent himself from, or otherwise to avoid or seek to avoid appearing or testifying at, such action or proceeding, or (b) he knowingly makes any false statement or practices any fraud or deceit with intent to affect the testimony of such person.

Tampering with a witness in the fourth degree is a class A misdemeanor.

Amended by L. 1982, Ch. 664.

ANNOTATION

Insufficient evidence.—There was insufficient evidence as a matter of law to establish defendant's commission of the crime of tampering with a witness where nothing in the proof adduced at trial indicated that defendant was aware of the fact that the person he had harassed was then a witness in a pending Family Court matter or revealed that the objective of his acts of harassment was to induce nonappearance. People v. Plummer, 44 A.D.2d 573, 353 N.Y.S.2d 51 (2d Dept. 1974), aff'd, 36 N.Y.2d 161, 365 N.Y.S.2d 842, 325 N.E.2d 161 (1975).

§ 215.11. Tampering with a witness in the third degree.

A person is guilty of tampering with a witness in the third degree when, knowing that a person is about to be called as a witness in a criminal proceeding:

1. He wrongfully compels or attempts to compel such person to absent himself from, or otherwise to avoid or seek to avoid appearing or testifying at such proceeding by means of instilling in him a fear that the actor will cause physical injury to such person or another person; or

2. He wrongfully compels or attempts to compel such person to swear falsely by means of instilling in him a fear that the actor will cause physical injury to such person or another person.

Tampering with a witness in the third degree is a class E felony.

Added by L. 1982, Ch. 664.

ANNOTATIONS

Evidence.—Defendant's attempt to instill fear in a witness need not be successful to satisfy this section. People v. Henderson, 265 A.D.2d 573, 705 N.Y.S.2d 589 (2d Dept. 1999).

—Evidence at trial established that defendant telephoned victim once and threatened her in a manner that instilled in her a fear that he would cause physical injury to her was sufficient to sustain this conviction. People v. Porter, 2 A.D.3d 1429, 768 N.Y.S.2d 905 (4th Dept. 2003).

§ 215.12. Tampering with a witness in the second degree.

A person is guilty of tampering with a witness in the second degree when he:

1. Intentionally causes physical injury to a person for the purpose of obstructing, delaying, preventing or impeding the giving of testimony in a criminal proceeding by such person or another person or for the purpose of compelling such person or another person to swear falsely; or

2. He intentionally causes physical injury to a person on account of such person or another person having testified in a criminal proceeding.

Tampering with a witness in the second degree is a class D felony.

Added by L. 1982, Ch. 664.

§ 215.13. Tampering with a witness in the first degree.

A person is guilty of tampering with a witness in the first degree when:

1. He intentionally causes serious physical injury to a person for the purpose of obstructing, delaying, preventing or impeding the giving of testimony in a criminal proceeding by such person or another person or for the purpose of compelling such person or another person to swear falsely; or

2. He intentionally causes serious physical injury to a person on account of such person or another person having testified in a criminal proceeding.

Tampering with a witness in the first degree is a class B felony.

Added by L. 1982, Ch. 664.

§ 215.14. Employer unlawfully penalizing witness or victim.

1. Any person who is the victim of an offense upon which an accusatory instrument is based or,

is subpoenaed to attend a criminal proceeding as a witness pursuant to article six hundred ten of the criminal procedure law or who exercises his rights as a victim as provided by section 380.50 or 390.30 of the criminal procedure law or subdivision two of section two hundred fifty-nine-i of the executive law and who notifies his employer or agent of his intent to appear as a witness, to consult with the district attorney, or to exercise his rights as provided in the criminal procedure law, the family court act and the executive law prior to the day of his attendance, shall not on account of his absence from employment by reason of such service be subject to discharge or penalty except as hereinafter provided. Upon request of the employer or agent, the party who sought the attendance or testimony shall provide verification of the employee's service. An employer may, however, withhold wages of any such employee during the period of such attendance. The subjection of an employee to discharge or penalty on account of his absence from employment by reason of his required attendance as a witness at a criminal proceeding or consultation with the district attorney or exercise of his rights as provided under law shall constitute a class B misdemeanor.

2. For purposes of this section, the term "victim" shall include the aggrieved party or the aggrieved party's next of kin, if the aggrieved party is deceased as a result of the offense, the representative of a victim as defined in subdivision six of section six hundred twenty-one of the executive law, a good samaritan as defined in subdivision seven of such law or a person pursuing an application or enforcement of an order of protection under the criminal procedure law or the family court act.

Added by L. 1982, Ch. 823; Amended by L. 1983, Ch. 101; L. 1985, Ch. 187; L. 1996, Ch. 331, eff. Nov. 1, 1996.

§ 215.15. Intimidating a victim or witness in the third degree.

A person is guilty of intimidating a victim or witness in the third degree when, knowing that another person possesses information relating to a criminal transaction and other than in the course of that criminal transaction or immediate flight therefrom, he:

1. Wrongfully compels or attempts to compel such other person to refrain from communicating such information to any court, grand jury, prosecutor, police officer or peace officer by means of instilling in him a fear that the actor will cause physical injury to such other person or another person; or

2. Intentionally damages the property of such other person or another person for the purpose of compelling such other person or another person to refrain from communicating, or on account of

such other person or another person having communicated, information relating to that criminal transaction to any court, grand jury, prosecutor, police officer or peace officer.

Intimidating a victim or witness in the third degree is a class E felony.

Added by L. 1985, Ch. 667.

ANNOTATIONS

Pending charge.—The crime of intimidating a victim or witness is not inapplicable to attempt to coerce a complainant to drop pending charges, or to instances where the complainant has already provided the authorities with a statement. *In re* Phillippa P., 221 A.D.2d 159, 633 N.Y.S.2d 287 (1st Dept. 1995).

—The crime of intimidating a victim or witness can occur by demand that victim or witness withdraw a pending charge. People v. Soper, 209 A.D.2d 829, 620 N.Y.S.2d 1014 (3d Dept. 1994).

Evidence.—Defendant was properly convicted of intimidating a witness in the third degree, where defendant went back to his former workplace a week after injuring a co-worker there, held the victim captive in an elevator and yelled at him that the defendant had not assaulted the victim. At the same time, the defendant's brother stood next to the defendant, shaking his fist at the victim's head and demanding that he not say anything contrary to anyone. People v. Wu, 225 A.D.2d 358, 639 N.Y.S.2d 21 (1st Dept. 1996).

—Evidence supported conviction where testimony established that respondent choked complainant, hit her in head or neck, and threatened to kill her if she did not drop pending charges, and where other testimony established prior assault on complainant by respondent. *In re* Phillippa P., 221 A.D.2d 159, 633 N.Y.S.2d 287 (1st Dept. 1995).

—Defendant's statement that he accompanied co-defendants to apartment of victim/witness because one of his co-defendants was worried about the victim/witness testifying and wanted to "squash" the "robbery thing," coupled with evidence that victim/witness was murdered, supported defendant's conviction under this section. People v. Lyons, 4 A.D.3d 549, 771 N.Y.S.2d 585 (3d Dept. 2004).

—Evidence that defendant assaulted complainant in July 2001 and went to her home two months later in violation of an order of protection, attempting to compel her to give false testimony in his favor supported his conviction under this section. People v. Roach, 1 A.D.3d 963, 767 N.Y.S.2d 326 (4th Dept. 2003), *cert. denied,* — U.S. —, 125 S. Ct. 298 (2004).

§ 215.16. Intimidating a victim or witness in the second degree.

A person is guilty of intimidating a victim or witness in the second degree when, other than in the course of that criminal transaction or immediate flight therefrom, he:

1. Intentionally causes physical injury to another person for the purpose of obstructing, delaying, preventing or impeding the communication by such other person or another person of information relating to a criminal transaction to any court, grand jury, prosecutor, police officer or peace officer or for the purpose of compelling such other person or another person to swear falsely; or

2. Intentionally causes physical injury to another person on account of such other person or another person having communicated information relating to a criminal transaction to any court, grand jury, prosecutor, police officer or peace officer; or

3. Recklessly causes physical injury to another person by intentionally damaging the property of such other person or another person, for the purpose of obstructing, delaying, preventing or impeding such other person or another person from communicating, or on account of such other person or person or another person having communicated, information relating to a criminal transaction to any court, grand jury, prosecutor, police officer or peace officer.

Intimidating a victim or witness in the second degree is a class D felony.

Added by L. 1985, Ch. 667.

§ 215.17. Intimidating a victim or witness in the first degree.

A person is guilty of intimidating a victim or witness in the first degree when, other than in the course of that criminal transaction or immediate flight therefrom, he:

1. Intentionally causes serious physical injury to another person for the purpose of obstructing, delaying, preventing or impeding the communication by such other person or another person of information relating to a criminal transaction to any court, grand jury, prosecutor, police officer or peace officer or for the purpose of compelling such other person or another person to swear falsely; or

2. Intentionally causes serious physical injury to another person on account of such other person or another person having communicated information relating to a criminal transaction to any court, grand jury, prosecutor, police officer or peace officer.

Intimidating a victim or witness in the first degree is a class B felony.

Added by L. 1985, Ch. 667.

§ 215.19. Bribing a juror.

A person is guilty of bribing a juror when he confers, or offers or agrees to confer, any benefit upon a juror upon an agreement or understanding that such juror's vote, opinion, judgment, decision or other action as a juror will thereby be influenced.

Bribing a juror is a class D felony.

Amended by L. 1985, Ch. 667.

ANNOTATIONS

Amending an indictment.—The People moved to amend the indictment charging attempted bribery, so that the reason for the alleged bribe would be changed from not arresting the defendant to releasing the already-arrested defendant. Since such an amendment does not change the theory of the prosecution as reflected in the evidence before the grand jury, and since the defendant did not show prejudice, the motion was granted. People v. Salley, 72 Misc. 2d 521, 339 N.Y.S.2d 702 (Nassau Co. Ct. 1972).

Witness; application to "cancel and vacate" subpoenas.—A witness may not delay the Grand Jury proceedings by an application to "cancel and vacate" a Grand Jury subpoena but must await the formal accusation of contempt and service of the required notice. Then he may appropriately inquire whether the questions asked by the Grand Jury were based upon an improperly issued electronic surveillance order and if they were, he cannot be convicted for his refusal to answer. *In re* O'Brien, 76 Misc. 2d 303, 350 N.Y.S.2d 498 (Rockland Co. Ct. 1973).

§ 215.20. Bribe receiving by a juror.

A juror is guilty of bribe receiving by a juror when he solicits, accepts or agrees to accept any benefit from another person upon an agreement or understanding that his vote, opinion, judgment, decision or other action as a juror will thereby be influenced.

Bribe receiving by a juror is a class D felony.

§ 215.22. Providing a juror with a gratuity.

A person is guilty of providing a juror with a gratuity when he or she, having been a party in a concluded civil or criminal action or proceeding or having been a person with regard to whom a grand jury has taken action pursuant to any subdivision of section 190.60 of the criminal procedure law (or acting on behalf of such a party or such a person), directly or indirectly confers, offers to confer or agrees to confer upon a person whom he or she knows has served as a juror in such action or proceeding or on such grand jury any benefit with intent to reward such person for such service.

Providing a juror with a gratuity is a class A misdemeanor.

Added by L. 2001, Ch. 42, § 2, eff. Nov. 1, 2001.

§ 215.23. Tampering with a juror in the second degree.

A person is guilty of tampering with a juror in the second degree when, prior to the discharge of the jury, he:

1. confers, or offers or agrees to confer, any payment or benefit upon a juror or upon a third person acting on behalf of such juror, in consideration for such juror or third person supplying information in relation to an action or proceeding pending or about to be brought before such juror; or

2. acting on behalf of a juror, accepts or agrees to accept any payment or benefit for himself or for such juror, in consideration for supplying any information in relation to an action or proceeding pending or about to be brought before such juror and prior to his discharge.

Tampering with a juror in the second degree is a class B misdemeanor.

Added by L. 1990, Ch. 305.

§ 215.25. Tampering with a juror in the first degree.

A person is guilty of tampering with a juror

in the first degree when, with intent to influence the outcome of an action or proceeding, he communicates with a juror in such action or proceeding, except as authorized by law.

Tampering with a juror in the first degree is a class A misdemeanor.

Amended by L. 1990, Ch. 305.

§ 215.28. Misconduct by a juror in the second degree.

A person is guilty of misconduct by a juror in the second degree when, in relation to an action or proceeding pending or about to be brought before him and prior to discharge, he accepts or agrees to accept any payment or benefit for himself or for a third person in consideration for supplying any information concerning such action or proceeding.

Misconduct by a juror in the second degree is a violation.

Added by L. 1990, Ch. 305.

§ 215.30. Misconduct by a juror in the first degree.

A juror is guilty of misconduct by a juror in the first degree when, in relation to an action or proceeding pending or about to be brought before him, he agrees to give a vote, opinion, judgment, decision or report for or against any party to such action or proceeding.

Misconduct by a juror in the first degree is a class A misdemeanor.

Amended by L. 1990, Ch. 305.

§ 215.35. Tampering with physical evidence; definitions of terms.

The following definitions are applicable to section 215.40:

1. "Physical evidence" means any article, object, document, record or other thing of physical substance which is or is about to be produced or used as evidence in an official proceeding.

2. "Official proceeding" means any action or proceeding conducted by or before a legally constituted judicial, legislative, administrative or other governmental agency or official, in which evidence may properly be received.

ANNOTATION

Evidence.—Defendant police officer's conviction for tampering with physical evidence affirmed; evidence was legally sufficient to establish defendant's guilt beyond a reasonable doubt, and it could readily be contemplated under the circumstances of the case that a prescription for a controlled substance that a police doctor had written for the defendant would be received as evidence as a prospective official proceeding. People v. Porpiglia, 215 A.D.2d 784, 627 N.Y.S.2d 720 (2d Dept. 1995).

§ 215.40. Tampering with physical evidence.

A person is guilty of tampering with physical evidence when:

1. With intent that it be used or introduced in an official proceeding or a prospective official proceeding, he (a) knowingly makes, devises or prepares false physical evidence, or (b) produces or offers such evidence at such a proceeding knowing it to be false; or

2. Believing that certain physical evidence is about to be produced or used in an official proceeding or a prospective official proceeding, and intending to prevent such production or use, he suppresses it by any act of concealment, alteration or destruction, or by employing force, intimidation or deception against any person.

Tampering with physical evidence is a class E felony.

ANNOTATIONS

Official proceeding.—Defendant's conviction for tampering with physical evidence affirmed; evidence of an actual or prospective official proceeding was unnecessary since it could readily have been contemplated under the circumstances, and there is no requirement that an official proceeding be commenced at the time of trial. People v. Johnson, 219 A.D.2d 865, 632 N.Y.S.2d 1003 (4th Dept. 1995).

Advice of attorney.—If an attorney affirmatively advises his client to conceal or dispose of a dead body, he is counselling the commission of a crime (PL § 215.40(2)), impeding the discovery of evidence, and violating the Code of Professional Responsibility (DR 1-102A(4)(5)); he may thus destroy the attorney client privilege itself. People v. Fentress, 103 Misc. 2d 179, 425 N.Y.S.2d 485 (Dutchess Co. Ct. 1980).

Sufficiency of evidence.—Conviction was properly supported by evidence that "defendant believed that co-defendant intended to discard the weapon used in the stabbing and acquiesced in the request to stop his van to give his friend an opportunity to toss what remained of the knife into a sewer." People v. Hafeez, 100 N.Y.2d 253, 762 N.Y.S.2d 572, 792 N.E.2d 1060 (2003).

§ 215.45. Compounding a crime.

1. A person is guilty of compounding a crime when:

(a) He solicits, accepts or agrees to accept any benefit upon an agreement or understanding that he will refrain from initiating a prosecution for a crime; or

(b) He confers, or offers or agrees to confer, any benefit upon another person upon an agreement or understanding that such other person will refrain from initiating a prosecution for a crime.

2. In any prosecution under this section, it is an affirmative defense that the benefit did not exceed an amount which the defendant reasonably believed to be due as restitution or indemnification for harm caused by the crime.

Compounding a crime is a class A misdemeanor.

ANNOTATION

Affirmative defense.—The indictment was dismissed when

certain evidence before the Grand Jury established an affirmative defense but the District Attorney failed to charge the jurors as to such affirmative defense. People v. Ferrara, 82 Misc. 2d 270, 370 N.Y.S.2d 356 (Nassau Co. Ct. 1975).

§ 215.50. Criminal contempt in the second degree.

A person is guilty of criminal contempt in the second degree when he engages in any of the following conduct:

1. Disorderly, contemptuous, or insolent behavior, committed during the sitting of a court, in its immediate view and presence and directly tending to interrupt its proceedings or to impair the respect due to its authority; or

2. Breach of the peace, noise, or other disturbance, directly tending to interrupt a court's proceedings; or

3. Intentional disobedience or resistance to the lawful process or other mandate of a court except in cases involving or growing out of labor disputes as defined by subdivision two of section seven hundred fifty-three-a of the judiciary law; or

4. Contumacious and unlawful refusal to be sworn as a witness in any court proceeding or, after being sworn, to answer any legal and proper interrogatory; or

5. Knowingly publishing a false or grossly inaccurate report of a court's proceeding; or

6. Intentional failure to obey any mandate, process or notice, issued pursuant to articles sixteen, seventeen,* eighteen,* or eighteen-a* of the judiciary law, or to rules adopted pursuant to any such statute or to any special statute establishing commissioners of jurors and prescribing their duties or who refuses to be sworn as provided therein; or

7. On or along a public street or sidewalk within a radius of two hundred feet of any building established as a courthouse, he calls aloud, shouts, holds or displays placards or signs containing written or printed matter, concerning the conduct of a trial being held in such courthouse or the character of the court or jury engaged in such trial or calling for or demanding any specified action or determination by such court or jury in connection with such trial.

Criminal contempt in the second degree is a class A misdemeanor.

* Repealed.

Amended by L. 1967, Ch. 791; L. 1970, Ch. 734; L. 1972, Ch. 702.

ANNOTATIONS

Constitutionality of underlying order.—Contempt conviction for failing to provide voice exemplars could not stand because the mandate requiring the exemplars ignored due process requirements, where the defendant was orally ordered by the court during trial to submit to the test, since no prior notice of the prosecution's intention to apply for that relief was given to the defendant, the necessity for the relief was not established on any papers served on the defendant, and the defendant was not afforded the opportunity to controvert the grounds for the application. People v. Giglio, 74 A.D.2d 348, 428 N.Y.S.2d 27 (2d Dept. 1980).

Grand jury witness.—Since statements elicited by compulsion from a grand jury witness who is also a possible defendant may not be used against him in a later prosecution for a previously committed substantive crime, such witness is protected sufficiently even without expressly being granted transactional immunity, and he may be charged with contempt for giving answers which are so evasive as to equal no answers at all. People v. Ianniello, 21 N.Y.2d 418, 288 N.Y.S.2d 462, 235 N.E.2d 439, *cert. denied,* 393 U.S. 827 (1968).

Double jeopardy.—Defendant's punishment for contempt of court pursuant to the Judiciary Law was for "criminal" contempt; defendant's subsequent indictment for the same offense under section 600 of the former Penal Law was barred by the double jeopardy clause of the federal Constitution. People v. Colombo, 31 N.Y.2d 947, 341 N.Y.S.2d 97 (1972).

Defendant's failure to respond to question.—Where defendant before the grand jury initially answered the district attorney's question, his alleged failure to respond unequivocally to rephrased questions on the same subject did not obstruct the grand jury proceedings. People v. Renaghan, 33 N.Y.2d 991, 353 N.Y.S.2d 962, 309 N.E.2d 425 (1974).

—The statement of a witness who has been granted immunity that he will not answer questions relative to a specific subject constitutes one act of contempt, regardless of the number of questions he is asked concerning the subject. People v. Chestnut, 26 N.Y.2d 481, 311 N.Y.S.2d 853, 260 N.E.2d 501 (1970).

False and evasive answers.—Contempt of the grand jury is committed when a defendant's answer is "so false and evasive as to be equivalent to no answer at all." People v. Ianniello, 21 N.Y.2d 418, 288 N.Y.S.2d 462, 235 N.E.2d 469, *cert. denied,* 393 U.S. 827 (1968).

"Other mandate of court."—The plain meaning of the phrase "other mandate of court" includes a temporary order of protection; thus, defendant was properly charged with criminal contempt in the second degree for a violation of such an order. People v. Halper, 209 A.D.2d 637, 619 N.Y.S.2d 308 (2d Dept. 1994).

Evidence.—Defendant's actions of leaving threatening voice mail messages on the answering machines of specific individuals who had obtained an order of protection based on earlier harassment supported a conviction under this section. People v. D'Angelo, 98 N.Y.2d 733, 750 N.Y.S.2d 811, 780 N.E.2d 496 (2002).

—This section is not limited to protecting victims only after they acquire witness status in a criminal proceeding; further, defendant's attempt to instill fear in a witness need not be successful to satisfy this section. People v. Henderson, 265 A.D.2d 573, 705 N.Y.S.2d 589 (2d Dept. 1999).

—Complainant's testimony regarding order of protection was properly admitted into evidence because it constituted the factual predicate for the defendant being charged with criminal contempt in the second degree. People v. Murrell, 220 A.D.2d 780, 633 N.Y.S.2d 329 (2d Dept. 1995).

—Where there was a valid order of protection directing defendant to stay away from the complainant, the failure of the accusatory instrument to include the distance the defendant was from the complainant during the encounter was not fatal and did not require dismissal of the indictment. People v. Nawaz, 183 Misc. 2d 195, 702 N.Y.S.2d 520 (Crim. Ct. Kings Co. 1999).

Lesser included offense—Evidence that complainant was not home when defendant violated order of protection was legally insufficient to establish defendant's guilt of criminal contempt in the first degree under PL § 215.15, but was legally sufficient to support a conviction of the lesser-included offense of criminal contempt in the second degree, a violation of PL § 215.50. People v. DeWall, 15 A.D.3d 498, 790 N.Y.S.2d 182 (2d Dept. 2005).

Sufficiency of information.—Presence of defendant's name on signature line of order of protection adequately supports allegation that defendant knew of contents of order. People v. Inserra, 4 N.Y.3d 30, 790 N.Y.S.2d 72, 823 N.E.2d 437 (2004).

§ 215.51. Criminal contempt in the first degree.

A person is guilty of criminal contempt in the first degree when:

(a) he contumaciously and unlawfully refuses to be sworn as a witness before a grand jury, or, when after having been sworn as a witness before a grand jury, he refuses to answer any legal and proper interrogatory; or

(b) in violation of a duly served order of protection, or such order of which the defendant has actual knowledge because he or she was present in court when such order was issued, or an order of protection issued by a court of competent jurisdiction in this or another state, territorial or tribal jurisdiction, he or she:

(i) intentionally places or attempts to place a person for whose protection such order was issued in reasonable fear of physical injury, serious physical injury or death by displaying a deadly weapon, dangerous instrument or what appears to be a pistol, revolver, rifle, shotgun, machine gun or other firearm or by means of a threat or threats; or

(ii) intentionally places or attempts to place a person for whose protection such order was issued in reasonable fear of physical injury, serious physical injury or death by repeatedly following such person or engaging in a course of conduct or repeatedly committing acts over a period of time; or

(iii) intentionally places or attempts to place a person for whose protection such order was issued in reasonable fear of physical injury, serious physical injury or death when he or she communicates or causes a communication to be initiated with such person by mechanical or electronic means or otherwise, anonymously or otherwise, by telephone, or by telegraph, mail or any other form of written communication; or

(iv) with intent to harass, annoy, threaten or alarm a person for whose protection such order was issued, repeatedly makes telephone calls to such person, whether or not a conversation ensues, with no purpose of legitimate communication; or

(v) with intent to harass, annoy, threaten or alarm a person for whose protection such order was issued, strikes, shoves, kicks or otherwise subjects such other person to physical contact or attempts or threatens to do the same; or

(vi) by physical menace, intentionally places or attempts to place a person for whose protection such order was issued in reasonable fear of death, imminent serious physical injury or physical injury.

(c) he or she commits the crime of criminal contempt in the second degree as defined in subdivision three of section 215.50 of this article by violating that part of a duly served order of protection, or such order of which the defendant has actual knowledge because he or she was present in court when such order was issued, under sections two hundred forty and two hundred fifty-two of the domestic relations law, articles four, five, six and eight of the family court act and section 530.12 of the criminal procedure law, or an order of protection issued by a court of competent jurisdiction in another state, territorial or tribal jurisdiction, which requires the respondent or defendant to stay away from the person or persons on whose behalf the order was issued, and where the defendant has been previously convicted of the crime of criminal contempt in the first or second degree for violating an order of protection as described herein within the preceding five years; or

(d) in violation of a duly served order of protection, or such order of which the defendant has actual knowledge because he or she was present in court when such order was issued, or an order issued by a court of competent jurisdiction in this or another state, territorial or tribal jurisdiction, he or she intentionally or recklessly damages the property of a person for whose protection such order was issued in an amount exceeding two hundred fifty dollars.

Criminal contempt in the first degree is a class E felony.

Added by L. 1970, Ch. 734; **Amended** by L. 1972, Ch. 702; L. 1994, Ch. 222, § 47, eff. Jan. 1, 1995; L. 1996, Ch. 353, § 1, repealing subd. (b), and adding new subd. (b), eff. Sept. 1, 1996; L. 1998, Ch. 597, § 15, eff. Dec. 22, 1998; L. 2003, Ch. 331, § 1, eff. Nov. 1, 2003, amending subd. (c).

ANNOTATIONS

Notice.—Notice is adequate to support a criminal prosecution stemming from a violation of a court order if given orally in court; however, simply informing a defendant that an order has been issued is insufficient, and the defendant must also be told, either orally or in writing, of the contents of the order and the conduct prohibited. People v. McCowan, 85 N.Y.2d 985, 629 N.Y.S.2d 163, 652 N.E.2d 909 (1995).

Intent.—Defendant was not entitled to a separate, explicit charge that among the essential elements of the crime of criminal contempt in the first degree which the prosecution was required to establish to obtain a conviction was an intent on defendant's part to obstruct the grand jury investigation. People v. Tantleff, 40 N.Y.2d 862, 387 N.Y.S.2d 1005, 356 N.E.2d 477 (1976).

Alleged illegal wiretap.—No witness has a license to testify evasively or falsely before the grand jury and such witness may not seek to avoid prosecution for criminal contempt by raising the defense of an illegal wiretap; by his own voluntary and independent act before the grand jury, an evasively contumacious witness dissipates any taint flowing from proscribed police conduct. People v. McGrath, 46 N.Y.2d 12, 412 N.Y.S.2d 801, 385 N.E.2d 541 (1978), *cert. denied,* 440 U.S. 972 (1979).

—When the witness raises the objection that the questions being asked during the grand jury proceeding are based on information obtained from illegal wiretapping, the prosecutor is not obligated to affirm or deny the underlying facts unless the witness requests to be brought before the court. People v. Einhorn, 35 N.Y.2d 948, 365 N.Y.S.2d 171, 324 N.E.2d 551 (1974).

Evasive testimony.—The essence of any conviction for evasive contempt is that the jury shall find beyond a reasonable doubt that the defendant's response was intended as no answer at all and was thus tantamount to a refusal to answer; for this purpose it is unnecessary to determine whether the underlying event, conversation or fact did nor did not occur. People v. Fischer, 53 N.Y.2d 170, 440 N.Y.S.2d 872, 423 N.E.2d 349 (1981).

Charge.—Although the legality and propriety of the questions put to a witness charged with contempt are questions of law, the court should charge the jury on that element as it does on any other question of law. People v. Ianniello, 36 N.Y.2d 137, 365 N.Y.S.2d 821, 325 N.E.2d 146, *cert. denied,* 423 U.S. 831 (1975).

Defendant's ability to recall transaction.—Defendant's conviction, for criminal contempt, first degree, was affirmed for it is not unreasonable to expect the defendant, an active businesswoman throughout her life, when called before a grand jury, to recall approximate dates and purpose of $1,000 payments made by her on loans taken out nine and four months earlier where the loans were critical to her business as a bail bond agent and the questioner provided more than enough cues through restatement and repetition to stimulate her recollection. People v. Schenkman, 46 N.Y.2d 232, 413 N.Y.S.2d 284, 385 N.E.2d 1214 (1978).

—The pivotal inquiry to be made is whether "the events of the details to be recalled were, on the record, significant and therefore memorable," therefore the conviction of the defendant must be affirmed because it is inconceivable that he could not recall whether lawyers, well known to him, and a law assistant, whom he had known for twenty years, had told him eight or eleven months earlier that money would be paid to influence the outcome of cases to be decided by the justice whom defendant served as a law secretary. People v. Roseman, 78 A.D.2d 878, 433 N.Y.S.2d 174 (2d Dept. 1980).

Purging of contempt.—When a defendant has been indicted for criminal contempt (for refusal to testify before the grand jury) he may not purge himself of the indictment by complying, belatedly, with the court order earlier disobeyed. People v. Leone, 44 N.Y.2d 315, 405 N.Y.S.2d 642, 376 N.E.2d 1287 (1978).

—The contempt must be vacated where the court refused to allow her to purge herself of the contempt. Additional Jan. Grand Jury v. Doe, 84 A.D.2d 588, 444 N.Y.S.2d 201 (3d Dept. 1981).

Repugnant verdicts; duplicitous counts.—Court reversed defendant's convictions for first degree criminal contempt (PL § 215.51) where defendants were found guilty based on their refusals to answer interrogatories concerning their acquaintance with certain individuals, but were found not guilty on counts which resulted from their refusals to answer questions about the criminal activities of the same persons; all questions were facets of a single basic inquiry and the refusals constituted a single contempt, hence there was a clear repugnancy between the findings of guilt and nonguilt. People v. Dercole, 72 A.D.2d 318, 424 N.Y.S.2d 459 (2d Dept. 1980).

Double jeopardy.—Defendant's phone calls to ex-wife on five separate occasions, in violation of an order of protection, which resulted in a contempt conviction under FCA § 846-a, was a lesser included offense of criminal contempt in the first degree, Penal Law § 215.51, and double jeopardy precluded further prosecution for these same phone calls under that section. People v. Wood, 260 A.D.2d 102, 698 N.Y.S.2d 122 (4th Dept. 1999), *aff'd,* 95 N.Y.2d 509, 719 N.Y.S.2d 639, 742 N.E.2d 114 (2000).

Temporary order of protection.—Defendant's actions of leaving threatening voice mail messages on the answering machines of specific individuals who had obtained an order of protection based on earlier harassment supported a conviction under this section. People v. D'Angelo, 98 N.Y.2d 733, 750 N.Y.S.2d 811, 780 N.E.2d 496 (2002).

—Evidence that defendant assaulted complainant in July 2001 and went to her home two months later in violation of an order of protection, attempting to compel her to give false testimony in his favor supported his conviction under this section. People v. Roach, 1 A.D.3d 963, 767 N.Y.S.2d 326 (4th Dept. 2003), *cert. denied,* — U.S. —, 125 S. Ct. 298 (2004).

—Evidence that defendant placed two threatening telephone calls to his wife in violation of an order of protection, was sufficient to support his convictions for harassment and criminal contempt even though she did not actually answer the phone and speak to defendant, it was enough that the answering machine recorded defendant's message. People v. Ruey Dei, 2 A.D.3d 1459, 769 N.Y.S.2d 772 (4th Dept. 2003).

§ 215.52. Aggravated criminal contempt.

A person is guilty of aggravated criminal contempt when in violation of a duly served order of protection, or such order of which the defendant has actual knowledge because he or she was present in court when such order was issued, or an order of protection issued by a court of competent jurisdiction in another state, territorial or tribal jurisdiction, he or she intentionally or recklessly causes physical injury or serious physical injury to a person for whose protection such order was issued.

Aggravated criminal contempt is a class D felony.

Added by L. 1996, Ch. 353, § 2, eff Sept. 1, 1996; **Amended** by L. 1998, Ch. 597, § 16, eff. Dec. 22, 1998.

ANNOTATION

Jurisdiction.—County court assumes jurisdiction over all conditions of a defendant's release once the case is transferred to that superior court. Temporary order of protection issued by local criminal court survives transfer to county court and can be enforced there. People v. Taylor, 176 Misc. 2d 30, 670 N.Y.S.2d 732 (Co. Ct. Greene Co. 1998).

§ 215.54. Criminal contempt; prosecution and punishment.

Adjudication for criminal contempt under subdivision A of section seven hundred fifty of the judiciary law shall not bar a prosecution for the crime of criminal contempt under section 215.50 based upon the same conduct but, upon conviction thereunder, the court, in sentencing the defendant shall take the previous punishment into consideration.

Amended by L. 1983, Ch. 277.

ANNOTATIONS

Necessity to bring witness before the court.—Although in the summary proceedings a witness must be brought before the court and directed to answer before he is held in contempt, it is not a prerequisite to a charge of criminal contempt before the Grand Jury (PL § 215.51); however, the taking of the witness before the court may reduce stalling tactics and expedite the proceeding. People v. Rappaport, 47 N.Y.2d 308, 418 N.Y.S.2d 306, 391 N.E.2d 1284 (1979).

Purging contempt.—Petitioners, complied with the opportunity to purge themselves provided by the prior decision of the court, when they took the stand and testified under oath and whether an answer at the continued hearing was false or equivocal did not bear on whether petitioners purged themselves of the previous adjudication of contempt. Marino v. Meyers, 64 A.D.2d 600, 407 N.Y.S.2d 151 (1st Dept. 1978), *aff'd,* 48 N.Y.2d 866, 424 N.Y.S.2d 432, 400 N.E.2d 371 (1979).

§ 215.55. Bail jumping in the third degree.

A person is guilty of bail jumping in the third degree when by court order he has been released from custody or allowed to remain at liberty, either upon bail or upon his own recognizance, upon condition that he will subsequently appear personally in connection with a criminal action or proceeding, and when he does not appear personally on the required date or voluntarily within thirty days thereafter.

Bail jumping in the third degree is a class A misdemeanor.

Added by L. 1983, Ch. 277.

ANNOTATION

Time.—Dismissal of bail jumping charge was proper; defendant may not be prosecuted for bail jumping when he is arrested before the expiration of 30 days following his failure to appear. People v. McLean, 162 Misc. 2d 270, 616 N.Y.S.2d 580 (New Rochelle City Ct. Westchester Co. 1994), aff'd, 168 Misc. 2d 140, 646 N.Y.S.2d 266 (App. Term 2d Dept. 1996).

§ 215.56. Bail jumping in the second degree.

A person is guilty of bail jumping in the second degree when by court order he has been released from custody or allowed to remain at liberty, either upon bail or upon his own recognizance, upon condition that he will subsequently appear personally in connection with a charge against him of committing a felony, and when he does not appear personally on the required date or voluntarily within thirty days thereafter.

Bail jumping in the second degree is a class E felony.

Added by L. 1968, Ch. 510; Amended by L. 1983, Ch. 277.

ANNOTATION

Required date.—When defendant fails to appear on a court-ordered adjourned date, but the court, in its discretion, stays the issuance of the warrant, defendant has not failed to appear on the statutory "required date," and a bail jumping charge will not be sustained. People v. Coppez, 93 N.Y.2d 249, 689 N.Y.S.2d 692, 711 N.E.2d 970 (1999).

§ 215.57. Bail jumping in the first degree.

A person is guilty of bail jumping in the first degree when by court order he has been released from custody or allowed to remain at liberty, either upon bail or upon his own recognizance, upon condition that he will subsequently appear personally in connection with an indictment pending against him which charges him with the commission of a class A or class B felony, and when he does not appear personally on the required date or voluntarily within thirty days thereafter.

Bail jumping in the first degree is a class D felony.

Amended by L. 1983, Ch. 277.

ANNOTATIONS

Effect of acquittal of underlying charge.—Acquittal on charge for which bail was originally granted does not obviate bail-jumping charge. People v. Holcombe, 89 A.D.2d 644, 453 N.Y.S.2d 126 (3d Dept. 1982).

Evidence.—Conviction of bail jumping must be reversed where basis of charge was defendant's failure to appear on last day of trial; defendant had repeatedly been told by his attorney and the court that he had the right to be present during the trial, but if he did not show up for trial, he waived that right; no further instructions were given. People v. Vigliotti, 277 A.D.2d 890, 715 N.Y.S.2d 267 (4th Dept. 2000).

Indictment not required at time of original release.—Conviction for bail jumping does not require that defendant be under indictment at the time of his original release. People v. Wilder, 251 A.D.2d 210, 675 N.Y.S.2d 30 (1st Dept.1998),

modified, aff'd, and remitted, 93 N.Y.2d 352, 712 N.E.2d 652, 690 N.Y.S.2d 483 (1999).

§ 215.58. Failing to respond to an appearance ticket.

1. A person is guilty of failing to respond to an appearance ticket when, having been personally served with an appearance ticket, as defined in subdivision two, based upon his alleged commission of a crime, he does not appear personally in the court in which such appearance ticket is returnable on the return date thereof or voluntarily within thirty days thereafter.

2. As used in this section, an appearance ticket means a written notice, whether referred to as a summons or by any other name, issued by a police officer, peace officer or other non-judicial public servant authorized by law to issue the same, directing a designated person to appear in a designated court at a designated future time in connection with a criminal action to be instituted in such court with respect to his alleged commission of a designated offense.

3. This section does not apply to any case in which an alternative to response to an appearance ticket is authorized by law and the actor complies with such alternative procedure.

Failing to respond to an appearance ticket is a violation.

Amended by L. 1980, Ch. 843; L. 1991, Ch. 378, eff. Nov. 1, 1991, amending subd. (1).

§ 215.59. Bail jumping and failing to respond to an appearance ticket; defense.

In any prosecution for bail jumping or failing to respond to an appearance ticket, it is an affirmative defense that:

1. The defendant's failure to appear on the required date or within thirty days thereafter was unavoidable and due to circumstances beyond his control; and

2. During the period extending from the expiration of the thirty day period to the commencement of the action, the defendant either:

(a) appeared voluntarily as soon as he was able to do so, or

(b) although he did not so appear, such failure of appearance was unavoidable and due to circumstances beyond his control.

ANNOTATION

Unavoidable circumstances.—Defendant was properly convicted of bail jumping in the first degree when, during his robbery trial, he was arrested in New Jersey for disorderly conduct and New Jersey agreed to dismiss the disorderly conduct charge if the defendant would waive extradition and he refused to do so; defendant failed to show that unavoidable circumstances prevented him from appearing. People v. Birden, 86 A.D.2d 774, 448 N.Y.S.2d 66 (4th Dept. 1982).

§ 215.60. Criminal contempt of the legislature.

A person is guilty of criminal contempt of the legislature when, having been duly subpoenaed to attend as a witness before either house of the legislature or before any committee thereof, he:

1. Fails or refuses to attend without lawful excuse; or

2. Refuses to be sworn; or

3. Refuses to answer any material and proper question; or

4. Refuses, after reasonable notice, to produce books, papers, or documents in his possession or under his control which constitute material and proper evidence.

Criminal contempt of the legislature is a class A misdemeanor.

§ 215.65. Criminal contempt of a temporary state commission.

A person is guilty of criminal contempt of a temporary state commission when, having been duly subpoenaed to attend as a witness at an investigation or hearing before a temporary state commission, he fails or refuses to attend without lawful excuse.

Criminal contempt of a temporary state commission is a class A misdemeanor.

Amended by L. 1970, Ch. 245.

§ 215.66. Criminal contempt of the state commission on judicial conduct.

A person is guilty of criminal contempt of the state commission on judicial conduct when, having been duly subpoenaed to attend as a witness at an investigation or hearing before the commission or a referee designated by the commission, he fails or refuses to attend without lawful excuse.

Criminal contempt of the state commission on judicial conduct is a class A misdemeanor.

Added by L. 1978, Ch. 156.

§ 215.70. Unlawful grand jury disclosure.

A person is guilty of unlawful grand jury disclosure when, being a grand juror, a public prosecutor, a grand jury stenographer, a grand jury interpreter, a police officer or a peace officer guarding a witness in a grand jury proceeding, or a clerk, attendant, warden or other public servant having official duties in or about a grand jury room or proceeding, or a public officer or public employee, he intentionally discloses to another the nature or substance of any grand jury testimony, or any decision, result or other matter attending a grand jury proceeding which is required by law to be kept secret, except in the proper discharge of his official duties or upon written order of the court. Nothing contained herein shall prohibit a witness from disclosing his own testimony.

Unlawful grand jury disclosure is a class E felony.

Amended by L. 1977, Ch. 451; 1980, Ch. 843

ANNOTATION

Prohibited disclosure.—CPL § 215.70 does not limit matters which are prohibited from disclosure to Grand Jury evidence and statements of grand jurors but includes statements of the prosecutor to the grand jurors and witnesses, and the names of witnesses who appear. Goldberg v. Extraordinary Special Grand Juries, Onondaga Co., 69 A.D.2d 1, 418 N.Y.S.2d 695 (4th Dept. 1979).

§ 215.75. Unlawful disclosure of an indictment.

A public servant is guilty of unlawful disclosure of an indictment when, except in the proper discharge of his official duties, he intentionally discloses the fact that an indictment has been found or filed before the accused person is in custody.

Unlawful disclosure of an indictment is a class B misdemeanor.

§ 215.80. Unlawful dispositions of assets subject to forfeiture.

Any defendant in a forfeiture action pursuant to article thirteen-A of the civil practice law and rules who knowingly and intentionally conceals, destroys, dissipates, alters, removes from the jurisdiction, or otherwise disposes of, property specified in a provisional remedy ordered by the court or in a judgment of forfeiture in knowing contempt of said order shall be guilty of a class A misdemeanor.

Added by L. 1984, Ch. 669.

TITLE M—OFFENSES AGAINST PUBLIC HEALTH AND MORALS

ARTICLE 220—CONTROLLED SUBSTANCES OFFENSES

Editor's Notes: L. 2004, Ch. 738, § 30, as amended, provides:

"1. Notwithstanding any contrary provision of law, any person convicted of a felony defined in article 220 or 221 of the penal law, other than a class A-I felony offense defined in article 220 of the penal law, which was committed prior to the effective date of this section [Jan. 13, 2005], and sentenced thereon to an indeterminate term of imprisonment pursuant to provisions of the law in effect prior to the effective date of this section and who meets the eligibility requirements of paragraph (d) of subdivision 1 of section 803 of the correction law as it existed on the effective date of this section, may receive an additional merit time allowance not to exceed one-sixth of the minimum term or period imposed by the court provided the inmate either: (i) successfully participates or has participated in two or more of the four program objectives set forth in paragraph (d) of subdivision 1 of section 803 of the correction law, or (ii) successfully participates in one of the program objectives set forth in paragraph (d) of subdivision 1 of section 803 of the correction law and successfully maintains employment while in a work release program or any other continuous temporary release program for a period of not less than three months.

"2. Such allowance shall be withheld for any serious disciplinary infraction or upon a judicial determination that the person, while an inmate, commenced or continued a civil action, proceeding or claim that was found to be frivolous as defined in subdivision (c) of section 8303-a of the civil practice law and rules, or an order of a federal court pursuant to Rule 11 of the federal rules of civil procedure imposing sanctions in an action commenced by a person, while an inmate, against a state agency, officer or employee."

L. 2005, Ch. 643, § 1 provides:

"Notwithstanding any contrary provision of law, any person in the custody of the department of correctional services convicted of a class A-II felony offense defined in article 220 of the penal law which was committed prior to the effective date of this section, and who was sentenced thereon to an indeterminate term of imprisonment with a minimum period not less than three years pursuant to provisions of the law in effect prior to the effective date of this section, and who is more than twelve months from being an eligible inmate as that term is defined in subdivision 2 of section 851 of the correction law, and who meets the eligibility requirements of paragraph (d) of subdivision 1 of section 803 of the correction law may, upon notice to the appropriate district attorney, apply to be resentenced in accordance with section 70.71 of the penal law in the court which imposed the original sentence. Such application shall be referred for determination to the judge or justice who imposed the original sentence upon such person. If at the time of the application the original sentencing judge or justice is a judge or justice of a court of competent jurisdiction, but such court is not the court in which the original sentence was imposed, then the application shall be randomly assigned to another judge or justice of the court in which the original sentence was imposed, provided that the district attorney and applicant may agree that the application be referred to the original sentencing judge. If the original sentencing judge is no longer a judge or justice of a court of competent jurisdiction, then the application shall be randomly assigned to another judge or justice of the court. If the court determines that such person does not stand convicted of such a class A-II felony offense, it shall issue an order denying the application. If the court determines that such person does stand convicted of such a class A-II felony offense, it may consider any facts or circumstances relevant to the imposition of a new sentence which are submitted by such person or the people and may, in addition, consider the institutional record of confinement of such person, but shall not order a new pre-sentence investigation and report or entertain any matter challenging the underlying basis of the subject conviction. The court shall offer an opportunity for a hearing and bring the applicant before it. The court may also conduct a hearing, if necessary, to determine whether such person qualifies to be resentenced or to determine any controverted issue of fact relevant to the issue of sentencing. Upon its review of the submissions and the findings of fact made in connection with the application, the court shall, unless substantial justice dictates that the application should be denied, in which event the court shall issue an order denying the application, specify and inform such person of the term of a determinate sentence of imprisonment it would impose upon such conviction, as authorized for a class A-II felony by and in accordance with section 70.71 of the penal law, in the event of a resentence and shall enter an order to that effect. The court shall notify the person that, unless he or she withdraws the application or appeals from such order, the court will enter an order vacating the sentence originally imposed and imposing a determinate sentence of imprisonment authorized to be imposed upon such conviction by section 70.71 of the penal law; provided that the term thereof shall be the same as the court previously specified. Any order issued by a court pursuant to this section must include written findings of fact and the reasons for such order. An appeal may be taken as of right in accordance with applicable provisions of the criminal procedure law: (a) from an order denying resentencing; or (b) from a new sentence imposed under this provision and may be based on the grounds that (i) the term of the new sentence is harsh or excessive; or (ii) that the term of the new sentence is unauthorized as a matter of law. An appeal in accordance with the applicable provisions of the criminal procedure law may also be taken as of right by the defendant from an order specifying and informing such person of the term of the determinate sentence the court would impose upon resentencing on the ground that the term of the proposed sentence is harsh or excessive; upon remand to the sentencing court following such appeal the defendant shall be given an opportunity to withdraw an application for resentencing before any resentence is imposed. Subdivision 1 of section 717 and subdivision 4 of section 722 of the county law and the related provisions of article 18-A of such law shall apply to the preparation of and proceedings on applications pursuant to this section. In calculating the term of imprisonment to be served by the person pursuant to the determinate sentence imposed, such person shall be credited for any jail time credited towards the subject conviction as well as any period of incarceration credited toward the sentence originally imposed."

LexisNexis Cross References

Criminal Defense Techniques, Vol. 1, Ch. 4A, The Drug Courier Profile; Vol. 3, Ch. 57, Defense of a Drug Abuse Case; *New York Criminal Practice (2d ed.),* Vol. 7, Ch. 75, Controlled Substances Offenses and Marijuana Offenses; *New York Suppression Manual,* Ch. 14, Automobile Searches; Ch. 15, Plain View; Ch. 16, Stop and Frisk; *Police Investigation Handbook,* Ch. 27, Drug Investigations.

§ 220.00. Controlled substances; definitions.

1. "Sell" means to sell, exchange, give or dispose of to another, or to offer or agree to do the same.

2. "Unlawfully" means in violation of article thirty-three of the public health law.

3. "Ounce" means an avoirdupois ounce as applied to solids or semisolids,* and a fluid ounce as applied to liquids.

4. "Pound" means an avoirdupois pound.

5. "Controlled substance" means any substance listed in schedule I, II, III, IV or V of section thirty-three hundred six of the public health law other than marihuana, but including concentrated cannabis as defined in paragraph (a) of subdivision four of section thirty-three hundred two of such law.

6. "Marihuana" means "marihuana" or "concentrated cannabis" as those terms are defined in section thirty-three hundred two of the public health law.

7. "Narcotic drug" means any controlled substance listed in schedule I(b), I(c), II(b) or II(c) other than methadone.

8. "Narcotic preparation" means any controlled substance listed in schedule III(d) or III(e).

9. "Hallucinogen" means any controlled substance listed in schedule I(d)(5), (18), (19), (20), (21) and (22).

10. "Hallucinogenic substance" means any controlled substance listed in schedule I(d) other than concentrated cannabis, lysergic acid diethylamide, or an hallucinogen.

11. "Stimulant" means any controlled substance listed in schedule I(f), II(d).

12. "Dangerous depressant" means any controlled substance listed in schedule I(e)(2), (3), II(e), III(c)(3) or IV(c)(2), (31), (32), (40).

13. "Depressant" means any controlled substance listed in schedule IV(c) except (c)(2), (31), (32), (40).

14. "School grounds" means (a) in or on or within any building, structure, athletic playing field, playground or land contained within the real property boundary line of a public or private elementary, parochial, intermediate, junior high,

vocational, or high school, or (b) any area accessible to the public located within one thousand feet of the real property boundary line comprising any such school or any parked automobile or other parked vehicle located within one thousand feet of the real property boundary line comprising any such school. For the purposes of this section an "area accessible to the public" shall mean sidewalks, streets, parking lots, parks, playgrounds, stores and restaurants.

15. "Prescription for a controlled substance" means a direction or authorization, by means of an official New York state prescription form, a written prescription form or an oral prescription, which will permit a person to lawfully obtain a controlled substance from any person authorized to dispense controlled substances.

16. For the purposes of sections 220.70, 220.71, 220.72, 220.73, 220.74, 220.75 and 220.76 of this article:

(a) "Precursor" means ephedrine, pseudoephedrine, or any salt, isomer or salt of an isomer of such substances.

(b) "Chemical reagent" means a chemical reagent that can be used in the manufacture, production or preparation of methamphetamine.

(c) "Solvent" means a solvent that can be used in the manufacture, production or preparation of methamphetamine.

(d) "Laboratory equipment" means any items, components or materials that can be used in the manufacture, preparation or production of methamphetamine.

(e) "Hazardous or dangerous material" means any substance, or combination of substances, that results from or is used in the manufacture, preparation or production of methamphetamine which, because of its quantity, concentration, or physical or chemical characteristics, poses a substantial risk to human health or safety, or a substantial danger to the environment.

* As originally enacted.

Added by L. 1973, Ch. 276; **Amended** by L. 1973, Ch. 1051; L. 1975, Ch. 785; L. 1977, Ch. 360; L. 1978, Ch. 772; L. 1981, Chs. 455, 474; L. 1985, Chs. 341, 664; L. 1986, Chs. 118, 280; L. 1994, Ch. 292, § 1, eff. Nov. 1, 1994, amending subd. 14; L. 1998, Ch. 537, § 13, eff. Nov. 1, 1998; L. 2005, Ch. 394, § 3, adding subd. 16, eff. Oct. 1, 2005.

ANNOTATIONS

Agency.—Evidence of agency can be used to find a defendant guilty of criminal possession of a controlled substance. People v. VanBuren, 188 A.D.2d 887, 591 N.Y.S.2d 627 (3d Dept. 1992).

—The agency defense does not apply to the offense of criminal possession of controlled substance in the seventh degree. People v. Wallace, 206 A.D.2d 825, 615 N.Y.S.2d 194 (4th Dept. 1994).

Attempted possession.—A person who orders illegal narcotics from a supplier, admits a courier into his or her home, examines the quality of the goods, and ultimately rejects them because of perceived defects in quality, has attempted to possess cocaine within the meaning of the Penal Law. People v. Acosta, 80 N.Y.2d 665, 593 N.Y.S.2d 978 609 N.E.2d 518 (1993).

Defense of agency; inconsistent verdicts.—Where the defendant raised the defense of agency, the jury, having accepted such defense, could not acquit defendant of the criminal sale and convict him of criminal possession of a controlled substance with intent to sell. People v. Rodriguez, 74 A.D.2d 858, 425 N.Y.S.2d 372 (2d Dept. 1980).

Jurisdiction to prosecute.—Jurisdiction to prosecute the defendant did lie in Richmond County, for although the actual exchange took place in New York County, the agreement to effectuate the transaction was reached in Richmond County, and an offer or agreement to sell is a "sale" within PL § 220.00. People v. Cousart, 74 A.D.2d 877, 426 N.Y.S.2d 295 (2d Dept. 1980).

Drug possession; total weight; sufficiency of proof.—Random sampling of 115 of the 161 vials seized from the defendant was sufficient to establish that each of the vials contained cocaine. People v. Thurman, 179 A.D.2d 382, 578 N.Y.S.2d 154 (1st Dept. 1992).

Evidence.—"[T]he proper way to determine whether a sale was 1000 feet or less from a school is by a straight-line or 'as the crow flies' method, and not as measured along the route a pedestrian would be required to travel, including detours around obstructions. The statute provides for a 1000-foot radius without regard to whether the geographic area is occupied by any obstructions to pedestrian traffic." People v. Robbins, 10 A.D.3d 570, 782 N.Y.S.2d 80 (1st Dept.), *appeal granted*, 4 N.Y.3d 747, 790 N.Y.S.2d 660, 824 N.E.2d 61 (2004), *motion granted*, 4 N.Y.3d 774, 792 N.Y.S.2d 893, 825 N.E.2d 1088 (2005).

—Evidence was legally sufficient to support indictment for criminal sale of controlled substance in or near school grounds where the police officer testified that the sale took place within 1000 feet of school property and "about a block away" from two schools. People v. Zelaya, 232 A.D.2d 261, 648 N.Y.S.2d 93 (1st Dept. 1996).

—Defendant cannot be convicted of criminal sale of a controlled substance when the item sold was not a controlled substance, even if defendant mistakenly believed it was. People v. Alameen, 264 A.D.2d 937, 697 N.Y.S.2d 173 (3d Dept. 1999).

—In situations where the illegal substance is not available for analysis, drug users who can demonstrate knowledge of the narcotic are competent to testify. People v. Christopher, 161 A.D.2d 896, 557 N.Y.S.2d 461 (3d Dept. 1990).

Proof.—That the defendant did not have the drugs or money on him approximately one-half hour after he was arrested did not negate his guilt. People v. Perez, 189 A.D.2d 562, 592 N.Y.S.2d 14 (1st Dept. 1993).

Sell.—Defendant-doctor who wrote false prescriptions, with the knowledge that they were to be used for illegal purposes, could not be convicted of criminal "sale" of a controlled substance since under Article 220 of the Penal Law "to prescribe" is not to "sell." People v. Lipton, 54 N.Y.2d 340, 445 N.Y.S.2d 430, 429 N.E.2d 1059 (1981).

—A defendant may be guilty as a seller even if he does not receive any consideration for the transfer of drugs to the buyer. People v. Herring, 83 N.Y.2d 780, 610 N.Y.S.2d 949, 950, 632 N.E.2d 1272 (1994).

Agency defense; jury instruction.—Where no reasonable view of the evidence would support a defense of agency the issue need not be submitted to the jury. People v. Ortiz, 76 N.Y.2d 446, 560 N.Y.S.2d 186, 560 N.E.2d 102 (1990).

—Defendant's right to a charge on agency defense was not preserved for review by the Court of Appeals since no request was made for a charge on an agency defense, no mention of it was made in the defense summation, and counsel took no exception at the conclusion of the court's charge which made no reference to the defense. People v. Darrisaw, 49 N.Y.2d 786, 426 N.Y.S.2d 728, 403 N.E.2d 450 (1980).

—Agency charge was required where defendant testified he had received no money and had merely, upon undercover officer's request for assistance in obtaining drugs, pointed out to him a person as someone who had heroin for sale. People v. Echols, 75 A.D.2d 531, 426 N.Y.S.2d 776 (1st Dept. 1980).

—Trial court's charge on agency defense that limited application to situations in which the seller's efforts to accommodate buyer were under circumstances utterly devoid of personal gain, may have deprived the defendant of due consideration of the agency defense, as defendant, who did not receive any part of the money paid in the transaction, did receive $20 from under-cover officer after the transaction was consummated. People v. Rivera, 74 A.D.2d 882, 426 N.Y.S.2d 515 (2d Dept. 1980).

§ 220.03. Criminal possession of a controlled substance in the seventh degree.

A person is guilty of criminal possession of a controlled substance in the seventh degree when he knowingly and unlawfully possesses a controlled substance.

Criminal possession of a controlled substance in the seventh degree is a class A misdemeanor.

Added by L. 1973, Ch. 276; **Amended** by L. 1978, Ch. 772; L. 1979, Ch. 410.

ANNOTATIONS

Lesser included offense.—Conviction on sale count does not require dismissal of possession counts, insofar as possession is not a lesser included offense of sale. People v. Perez, 139 A.D.2d 460, 527 N.Y.S.2d 230 (1st Dept. 1988).

—A defendant could be convicted of sale under circumstances where he did not necessarily possess the drugs; hence, criminal possession in the seventh degree would not be a lesser included offense of criminal sale in the third degree. People v. Scarincio, 95 A.D.2d 967, 464 N.Y.S.2d 311 (3d Dept. 1983).

Possession, not purchase, is prohibited.—The statute does not criminalize the purchase of a controlled substance, though once the purchased contraband comes into defendant's possession, a crime is committed. People v. Lam Lek Chong, 45 N.Y.2d 64, 407 N.Y.S.2d 674, 379 N.E.2d 200 (1978), *cert. denied,* 439 U.S. 935.

Possession is necessary element.—The People must prove that the defendant possessed the controlled substance, even though the possession may be constructive or actual, and that such possession was knowing. People v. Sierra, 45 N.Y.2d 56, 407 N.Y.S.2d 669, 379 N.E.2d 196 (1978); *but see* People v. Marshall, 72 A.D.2d 922, 422 N.Y.S.2d 187 (4th Dept. 1979) (defendant only briefly possessed drugs when co-defendant, in car with defendant and an undercover officer, asked defendant to hand them over to the putative buyer).

—People did not have to prove that defendant knew his possession was unlawful, but only that he knowingly possessed the controlled substance. People v. Georgens, 107 A.D.2d 820, 484 N.Y.S.2d 657 (2d Dept. 1985).

Constructive possession.—Defendant did not constructively possess controlled substance recovered from a car which he had driven on a prior occasion, but had not been seen driving the car when the drugs were recovered, possessed the registration and insurance card for the car, but did not own the car and did not possess the parking ticket for the lot in which the car was recovered; defendant was arrested as he walked toward the passenger seat, after a long meeting, and a third party was seated in driver's seat. People v. Francis, 79 N.Y.2d 925, 582 N.Y.S.2d 982, 591 N.E.2d 1168 (1992).

—Defendant was found in same apartment where drugs were recovered, which was an apartment associated with drug dealing activity; but there was no further evidence that he had dominion and control over the premises; not constructive possession. People v. Headley, 74 N.Y.2d 858, 547 N.Y.S.2d 827, 547 N.E.2d 82 (1989).

—When defendant was in custody, and handcuffed, and police had not found drugs during a patdown, drugs found on seat of patrol car were constructively possessed by defendant. People v. Turner, 173 A.D.2d 381, 570 N.Y.S.2d 11 (1st Dept. 1991).

—In order to prove constructive possession, the People need only prove that the drugs were within defendant's immediate reach and control. People v. Francis, 172 A.D.2d 342, 569 N.Y.S.2d 403 (1st Dept.), *rev'd on other grounds,* 79 N.Y.2d 925, 582 N.Y.S.2d 982, 591 N.E.2d 1168 (1991).

—Defendant was sitting, intoxicated, in a car in which cocaine was recovered, constituting his constructive possession. People v. Jenkins, 216 A.D.2d 193, 628 N.Y.S.2d 669 (3d Dept.1995).

—Defendant constructively possessed the drugs which were recovered from a bedroom which he shared with co-defendant; theory of possession not defeated by opportunity for other persons, also present, to have placed the drugs in that location. People v. Rosenholm, 181 A.D.2d 943, 581 N.Y.S.2d 466 (3d Dept. 1992).

—Defendant's presence in bedroom where cocaine, a ledger, and a bundle of cash was located, about fifteen feet away, was constructive possession. People v. Westbrook, 177 A.D.2d 1039, 578 N.Y.S.2d 52 (4th Dept. 1991); *accord* People v. Shuron W., 185 A.D.2d 852, 587 N.Y.S.2d 357 (2d Dept. 1992).

—Drugs found in filing cabinet in a garage while defendant was present, when only defendant had the keys to the cabinet, were constructively possessed by defendant. People v. Rowell, 163 A.D.2d 833, 558 N.Y.S.2d 367 (4th Dept. 1990).

Knowing possession.—Reversing court's reduction of criminal possession of controlled substance in third and fifth degrees to seventh degree where evidence was sufficient to support defendant's knowledge of the weight of contraband in question. Knowledge can be shown by inferences drawn from circumstances attendant to defendant's possession such as the amount of the controlled substance possessed, uniform packaging of the substance, defendant's handling of the substance and "saleslike conduct." People v. Litwa, 230 A.D.2d 638, 646 N.Y.S.2d 329 (1st Dept. 1996).

Defense.—Agency defense is not available for a charge of mere possession. People v. Jackson, 155 A.D.2d 479, 547 N.Y.S.2d 139 (2d Dept. 1989).

Personal possession not constitutionally protected right.—It is inappropriate for a court to remove marijuana from the legislature's consideration by classifying its personal possession as a constitutionally protected right, thus possession of marijuana plants in the home is not a constitutionally protected right. People v. Shepard, 50 N.Y.2d 640, 431 N.Y.S.2d 363, 409 N.E.2d 840 (1980).

Possession of narcotics and paraphernalia by addict.—Imposition of criminal penalties on a narcotic addict who possesses narcotics and associated instruments for his own was never in possession of controlled use does not violate Federal and State constitutional proscriptions against cruel and unusual punishment. People v. Davis, 33 N.Y.2d 221, 351 N.Y.S.2d 663, 306 N.E.2d 787, *cert. denied,* 416 U.S. 973 (1974).

Prescription.—Defendant's possession of a controlled substance was unlawful in violation of PL 220.03 where the drugs were prescribed for the defendant but he intended to sell, not to use them. People v. Garthaffner, 103 Misc. 2d 671, 426 N.Y.S.2d 955 (Crim. Ct. N.Y. Co. 1980).

Presumption.—Unlawful possession was not proved beyond a reasonable doubt by prosecutor's introduction into evidence of two vials of controlled substances marked with the dispensing agency's name and a pink card identifying defendant as a patient in the agency's program, since the People's evidence did not controvert the possibility that the defendant was a patient entitled to possess the methadone. People v. Rodriguez, 58 A.D.2d 612, 395 N.Y.S.2d 222 (2d Dept. 1977).

§ 220.06. Criminal possession of a controlled substance in the fifth degree.

A person is guilty of criminal possession of a controlled substance in the fifth degree when he knowingly and unlawfully possesses:

1. a controlled substance with intent to sell it; or

2. one or more preparations, compounds, mixtures or substances containing a narcotic preparation and said preparations, compounds, mixtures or substances are of an aggregate weight of one-half ounce or more; or

3. phencyclidine and said phencyclidine weighs fifty milligrams or more; or

4. one or more preparations, compounds,

mixtures or substances containing concentrated cannabis as defined in paragraph (a) of subdivision four of section thirty-three hundred two of the public health law and said preparations, compounds, mixtures or substances are of an aggregate weight of one-fourth ounce or more; or

5. Cocaine and said cocaine weighs five hundred milligrams or more;

6. ketamine and said ketamine weighs more than one thousand milligrams; or

7. ketamine and has previously been convicted of possession or the attempt to commit possession of ketamine in any amount; or

8. one or more preparations, compounds, mixtures or substances containing gamma hydroxybutyric acid, as defined in paragraph four of subdivision (e) of schedule I of section thirty-three hundred six of the public health law, and said preparations, compounds, mixtures or substances are of an aggregate weight of twenty-eight grams or more.

Criminal possession of a controlled substance in the fifth degree is a class D felony.

Added by L. 1973, Ch. 276; **Amended** by L. 1973, Ch. 1051; L. 1977, Ch. 360; L. 1978, Ch. 772; L. 1979, Ch. 410; L. 1985, Ch. 341; L. 1988, Ch. 178; L. 1995, Ch. 75, § 1, eff. June 10, 1995, and applying only to offenses committed on or after that date, pursuant to L. 1995, Ch. 75, § 20; L. 1997, Ch. 635, eff. Jan. 22, 1998, adding subds. 6 and 7; L. 1998, Ch. 537, § 14, eff. Nov. 1, 1998; L. 2003, Ch. 264, § 25, eff. Nov. 1, 2003, amending subd. 7 and adding subd. 8.

ANNOTATIONS

Knowing possession.—Defendant's knowledge that he possesses a controlled substance may be proved directly as well as circumstantially; guilt may be inferred from evasive conduct or contradictory statements. People v. Reisman, 29 N.Y.2d 278, 327 N.Y.S.2d 342, 277 N.E.2d 396 (1971), cert. denied, 405 U.S. 1041.

—Although defendant's theory was one of his mere presence, and that he did not have knowing possession when he removed package containing drugs from garbage, evidence established that defendant had been given package, and the inconsistencies in his witness's testimony supported the inference of defendant's knowing possession. People v. Elizondo, 168 A.D.2d 295, 562 N.Y.S.2d 516 (1st Dept. 1990).

—Defendant, denying knowledge of drugs found in his vehicle, had participated in similar recent drug transactions; evidence admissible on issue of knowledge. People v. Sbraccia, 92 A.D.2d 628, 459 N.Y.S.2d 921 (3d Dept. 1983).

Knowledge of weight.—Failure to prove defendant's knowledge of weight for aggregate weight count does not preclude reduction to criminal possession in the seventh degree, which lacks a weight element. People v. Gordan, 86 N.Y.2d 10, 629 N.Y.S.2d 173, 652 N.E.2d 919 (1995), rev'g 204 A.D.2d 22, 618 N.Y.S.2d 261 (1st Dept. 1994); accord People v. Lawrence, 204 A.D.2d 969, 614 N.Y.S.2d 84 (4th Dept. 1994).

—When drugs were contained in vials, knowledge of weight could be inferred. People v. Sanchez, 86 N.Y.2d 27, 629 N.Y.S.2d 179, 652 N.E.2d 925 (1995).

—When defendant is tried on a theory that he possessed in excess of a statutory weight requirement, the People must prove beyond a reasonable doubt that defendant knew the weight which he possessed; knowledge, though, can be proved by inference. People v. Ryan, 82 N.Y.2d 497, 605 N.Y.S.2d 235, 626 N.E.2d 51 (1993).

—When aggregate weight is charged, defendant's handling of the controlled substance may support an inference of knowledge of the weight. People v. Ryan, 82 N.Y.2d 497, 605 N.Y.S.2d 235, 626 N.E.2d 51 (1993); accord People v. Sanchez, 86 N.Y.2d 27, 629 N.Y.S.2d 179, 652 N.E.2d 925 (1995).

—Negotiations by defendant concerning price, quantity or quality could support an inference that he knew the weight which he sold possessed with intent to sell. People v. Ryan, 82 N.Y.2d 497, 605 N.Y.S.2d 235, 626 N.E.2d 51 (1993); accord People v. Hill, 85 N.Y.2d 256, 624 N.Y.S.2d 79, 648 N.E.2d 455 (1995).

—Reversing court's reduction of criminal possession of controlled substance in third and fifth degrees to seventh degree where evidence was sufficient to support defendant's knowledge of the weight of contraband in question. Knowledge can be shown by inferences drawn from circumstances attendant to defendant's possession such as the amount of the controlled substance possessed, uniform packaging of the substance, defendant's handling of the substance and "saleslike conduct." People v. Litwa, 230 A.D.2d 638, 646 N.Y.S.2d 329 (1st Dept. 1996).

Possession is necessary element.—The People must prove that the defendant possessed the controlled substance, even though the possession may be constructive or actual, and that such possession was knowing. People v. Sierra, 45 N.Y.2d 56, 407 N.Y.S.2d 669, 379 N.E.2d 196 (1978).

—People did not have to prove that defendant knew his possession was unlawful, but only that he knowingly possessed the controlled substance. People v. Georgens, 107 A.D.2d 820, 484 N.Y.S.2d 657 (2d Dept. 1985).

Constructive possession.—Defendant was found in same apartment where drugs were recovered, which was an apartment associated with drug dealing activity; but there was no further evidence that he had dominion and control over the premises; not constructive possession. People v. Headley, 74 N.Y.2d 858, 547 N.Y.S.2d 827, 547 N.E.2d 82 (1989).

—Defendant was in kitchen of premises where a vial of crack was recovered; several other vials of crack also were recovered on the premises, a shelter for runaway children; evidence insufficient to establish defendant's constructive possession. In re Dallas L., 183 A.D.2d 897, 584 N.Y.S.2d 588 (2d Dept. 1992).

—Defendant was sitting, intoxicated, in a car in which cocaine was recovered, constituting his constructive possession. People v. Jenkins, 216 A.D.2d 193, 628 N.Y.S.2d 669 (3d Dept. 1995).

—Defendant constructively possessed the drugs which were recovered from a bedroom which he shared with co-defendant; theory of possession not defeated by opportunity for other persons, also present, to have placed the drugs in that location. People v. Rosenholm, 181 A.D.2d 943, 581 N.Y.S.2d 466 (3d Dept. 1992).

—Defendant's presence in bedroom where cocaine, a ledger, and a bundle of cash was located, about fifteen feet away, was constructive possession. People v. Westbrook, 177 A.D.2d 1039, 578 N.Y.S.2d 52 (4th Dept. 1991).

—Drugs found in filing cabinet in a garage while defendant was present, when only defendant had the keys to the cabinet, were constructively possessed by defendant. People v. Rowell, 163 A.D.2d 833, 558 N.Y.S.2d 367 (4th Dept. 1990).

Aggregate weight distinguished from pure weight.—Where court was charged with criminal possession in the fifth degree under a pure weight theory for 500 milligrams of cocaine, but court instructed jury to evaluate the evidence on an aggregate weight standard, conviction reversed. People v. Paul, 212 A.D.2d 1020, 623 N.Y.S.2d 50 (4th Dept. 1995).

Closing courtroom to public absent compelling necessity; reversible error.—Defendant's conviction of criminal possession of a controlled substances in the fifth degree reversed since trial court, without proper inquiry, closed the courtroom to the public during testimony of undercover police officer who was no longer assigned to undercover work, and such closing of trial to public without a factual showing of compelling necessity is, per se, reversible error. People v. Brown, 79 A.D.2d 659, 434 N.Y.S.2d 445 (2d Dept. 1980), aff'd, 56 N.Y.2d 242, 451 N.Y.S.2d 693, 436 N.E.2d 1295 (1982).

Cross-examination of defendant; prior treatment for drug addiction.—Decision by trial court to permit cross-examination of defendant on past treatment for drug addiction while forbidding questioning on prior drug conviction was not an abuse of discretion; fact that defendant was charged with drug offense, which presented special risk of impermissible prejudice, does not necessarily prohibit questioning concerning defendant's prior activities of a similar nature. People v. Hill, 79 A.D.2d 641, 433 N.Y.S.2d 611 (2d Dept. 1980).

§ 220.09. Criminal possession of a controlled substance in the fourth degree.

A person is guilty of criminal possession of a controlled substance in the fourth degree when he knowingly and unlawfully possesses:

1. one or more preparations, compounds, mixtures or substances containing a narcotic drug and said preparations, compounds, mixtures or substances are of an aggregate weight of one-eighth ounce or more; or

2. one or more preparations, compounds, mixtures or substances containing methamphetamine, its salts, isomers or salts of isomers and said preparations, compounds, mixtures or substances are of an aggregate weight of one-half ounce or more; or

3. one or more preparations, compounds, mixtures or substances containing a narcotic preparation and said preparations, compounds, mixtures or substances are of an aggregate weight of two ounces or more; or

4. a stimulant and said stimulant weighs one gram or more; or

5. lysergic acid diethylamide and said lysergic acid diethylamide weighs one milligram or more; or

6. a hallucinogen and said hallucinogen weighs twenty-five milligrams or more; or

7. a hallucinogenic substance and said hallucinogenic substance weighs one gram or more; or

8. a dangerous depressant and such dangerous depressant weighs ten ounces or more; or

9. a depressant and such depressant weighs two pounds or more; or

10. one or more preparations, compounds, mixtures or substances containing concentrated cannabis as defined in paragraph (a) of subdivision four of section thirty-three hundred two of the public health law and said preparations, compounds, mixtures or substances are of an aggregate weight of one ounce or more; or

11. phencyclidine and said phencyclidine weighs two hundred fifty milligrams or more; or

12. methadone and said methadone weighs three hundred sixty milligrams or more; or

13. phencyclidine and said phencyclidine weighs fifty milligrams or more with intent to sell it and has previously been convicted of an offense defined in this article or the attempt or conspiracy to commit any such offense; or

14. ketamine and said ketamine weighs four thousand milligrams or more; or

15. one or more preparations, compounds, mixtures or substances containing gamma hydroxybutyric acid, as defined in paragraph four of subdivision (e) of schedule I of section thirty-three hundred six of the public health law, and said preparations, compounds, mixtures or substances are of an aggregate weight of two hundred grams or more.

Criminal possession of a controlled substance in the fourth degree is a class C felony.

Added by L. 1973, Ch. 276; **Amended** by L. 1973, Ch. 1051; L. 1975, Ch. 785; L. 1977, Ch. 360; L. 1978, Ch. 772; L. 1979, Ch. 410; L. 1985, Ch. 341; L. 1995, Ch. 75, § 2, eff. June 10, 1995, and applying only to offenses committed on or after that date, pursuant to L. 1995, Ch. 75, § 20; L. 1997, Ch. 635, eff. Jan. 22, 1998, adding subd. 14; L. 1998, Ch. 537, § 15, eff. Nov. 1, 1998; L. 2003, Ch. 264, § 26, eff. Nov. 1, 2003, amending subd. 14 and adding subd. 15.

ANNOTATIONS

Possession is necessary element.—The People must prove that the defendant possessed the controlled substance, even though the possession may be constructive or actual, and that such possession was knowing. People v. Sierra, 45 N.Y.2d 56, 407 N.Y.S.2d 669, 379 N.E.2d 196 (1978).

—People did not have to prove that defendant knew his possession was unlawful, but only that he knowingly possessed the controlled substance. People v. Georgens, 107 A.D.2d 820, 484 N.Y.S.2d 657 (2d Dept. 1985).

Knowing possession.—Defendant's knowledge that he possesses a controlled substance may be proved directly as well as circumstantially; guilt may be inferred from evasive conduct or contradictory statements. People v. Reisman, 29 N.Y.2d 278, 327 N.Y.S.2d 342, 277 N.E.2d 396 (1971), cert. denied, 405 U.S. 1041.

—Although defendant's theory was one of his mere presence, and that he did not have knowing possession when he removed package containing drugs from garbage, evidence established that defendant had been given package, and the inconsistencies in his witness's testimony supported the inference of defendant's knowing possession. People v. Elizondo, 168 A.D.2d 295, 562 N.Y.S.2d 516 (1st Dept. 1990).

—Defendant, denying knowledge of drugs found in his vehicle, had participated in similar recent drug transactions; evidence admissible on issue of knowledge. People v. Sbraccia, 92 A.D.2d 628, 459 N.Y.S.2d 921 (3d Dept. 1983).

Constructive possession.—Defendant did not constructively possess controlled substance recovered from a car which he had driven on a prior occasion, but had not been seen driving the car when the drugs were recovered, possessed the registration and insurance card for the car, but did not own the car and did not possess the parking ticket for the lot in which the car was recovered; defendant was arrested as he walked toward the passenger seat, after a long meeting, and a third party was seated in driver's seat. People v. Francis, 79 N.Y.2d 925, 582 N.Y.S.2d 982, 591 N.E.2d 1168 (1992).

—Defendant was found in same apartment where drugs were recovered, which was an apartment associated with drug dealing activity; but there was no further evidence that he had dominion and control over the premises; not constructive possession. People v. Headley, 74 N.Y.2d 858, 547 N.Y.S.2d 827, 547 N.E.2d 82 (1989).

—Even though bag containing 203 vials of crack, sufficient to support prosecution for criminal possession in the fourth degree, was found in a part of a park removed from defendant, defendant had been acting in concert with co-defendant in connection with a sale count, and bag had been in proximity to co-defendant; defendant was deemed to exercise dominion and control over the bag. People v. Cann, 191 A.D.2d 290, 595 N.Y.S.2d 27 (1st Dept. 1993).

—When defendant was in custody, and handcuffed, and police had not found drugs during a patdown, drugs found on seat of patrol car were constructively possessed by defendant. People v. Turner, 173 A.D.2d 381, 570 N.Y.S.2d 11 (1st Dept. 1991).

—In order to prove constructive possession, the People need only prove that the drugs were within defendant's immediate reach and control. People v. Francis, 172 A.D.2d 342, 569 N.Y.S.2d 403 (1st Dept.), rev'd on other grounds, 79 N.Y.2d 925, 582 N.Y.S.2d 982, 591 N.E.2d 1168 (1991).

—Defendant's possession of stolen car, which he was driving, gave him dominion and control over 92 vials of crack found in the glove compartment. People v. Parks, 199 A.D.2d 426, 605 N.Y.S.2d 347 (2d Dept. 1993).

—Defendant was sitting, intoxicated, in a car in which cocaine was recovered, constituting his constructive possession. People v. Jenkins, 216 A.D.2d 193, 628 N.Y.S.2d 669 (3d Dept. 1995).

—Defendant constructively possessed the drugs which were recovered from a bedroom which he shared with co-defendant; theory of possession not defeated by opportunity for other persons, also present, to have placed the drugs in that location. People v. Rosenholm, 181 A.D.2d 943, 581 N.Y.S.2d 466 (3d Dept. 1992).

—Defendant was convicted of criminal possession in the fourth degree when he constructively possessed cocaine recovered from a bedroom which contained many of his personal effects and identification, even if he was not present at the time of the search. People v. Nevins, 203 A.D.2d 936, 611 N.Y.S.2d 69 (4th Dept. 1994).

—Defendant's presence in bedroom where cocaine, a ledger, and a bundle of cash was located, about fifteen feet away, was constructive possession. People v. Westbrook, 177 A.D.2d 1039, 578 N.Y.S.2d 52 (4th Dept. 1991); accord People v. Shuron W., 185 A.D.2d 852, 587 N.Y.S.2d 357 (2d Dept. 1992).

—Drugs found in filing cabinet in a garage while defendant was present, when only defendant had the keys to the cabinet, were constructively possessed by defendant. People v. Rowell, 163 A.D.2d 833, 558 N.Y.S.2d 367 (4th Dept. 1990).

Knowledge of weight.—When drugs were contained in vials, knowledge of weight could be inferred. People v. Sanchez, 86 N.Y.2d 27, 629 N.Y.S.2d 179, 652 N.E.2d 925 (1995).

—When defendant is tried on a theory that he possessed in excess of a statutory weight requirement, the People must prove beyond a reasonable doubt that defendant knew the weight which he possessed; knowledge, though, can be proved by inference. People v. Ryan, 82 N.Y.2d 497, 605 N.Y.S.2d 235, 626 N.E.2d 51 (1993).

—When aggregate weight is charged, defendant's handling of the controlled substance may support an inference of knowledge of the weight. People v. Ryan, 82 N.Y.2d 497, 605 N.Y.S.2d 235, 626 N.E.2d 51 (1993); accord People v. Sanchez, 86 N.Y.2d 27, 629 N.Y.S.2d 179, 652 N.E.2d 925 (1995).

—Negotiations by defendant concerning price, quantity or quality could support an inference that he knew the weight which he sold possessed with intent to sell. People v. Ryan, 82 N.Y.2d 497, 605 N.Y.S.2d 235, 626 N.E.2d 51 (1993); accord People v. Hill, 85 N.Y.2d 256, 624 N.Y.S.2d 79, 648 N.E.2d 455 (1995).

—Trial court erred in refusing to instruct jury that defendant must know the weight of the controlled substance as an element of the crime. People v. Warren, 232 A.D.2d 589, 648 N.Y.S.2d 670 (2d Dept. 1996).

—Rejecting contention that court erred in accepting defendant's guilty plea where court's inquiry was sufficient to establish that defendant knew that the cocaine he possessed weighed one-eighth ounce or more. People v. Madden, 231 A.D.2d 925, 648 N.Y.S.2d 363 (4th Dept. 1996).

—Failure to prove defendant's knowledge of weight for aggregate weight count does not preclude reduction to criminal possession in the seventh degree, which lacks a weight element. People v. Gordan, 86 N.Y.2d 10, 629 N.Y.S.2d 173, 652 N.E.2d 919, rev'g 204 A.D.2d 22, 618 N.Y.S.2d 261 (1st Dept. 1994); accord People v. Lawrence, 204 A.D.2d 969, 614 N.Y.S.2d 84 (4th Dept. 1994).

Testing methods for weight.—In an aggregate weight case, it was irrelevant whether testing by police chemists had reduced the weight of the cocaine by extracting water. People v. Francis, 172 A.D.2d 342, 569 N.Y.S.2d 403 (1st Dept. 1991), rev'd on other grounds 79 N.Y.2d 925, 582 N.Y.S.2d 982, 591 N.E.2d 1168 (1991).

—When defendant was charged with possession of in excess of ⅛ ounce of cocaine, the fact that his chemist's testing determined a lesser weight was not dispositive; the police chemists had used a different testing method, which satisfactorily established the requisite weight. People v. Nelson, 190 A.D.2d 823, 593 N.Y.S.2d 836 (2d Dept. 1993).

Constitutionality.—PL § 220.09 applies to cocaine and the section is constitutional. People v. Collier, 89 A.D.2d 1041, 456 N.Y.S.2d 119 (3d Dept. 1982).

Growing of mushrooms containing psilocybin.—Defendant was properly convicted of drug charges for growing mushrooms which naturally contained the proscribed hallucinogen, psilocybin; defendant's contention that he did not know possession and/or sale of psilocybin were unlawful constitute a mistake of law and not one of fact and will not relieve him of criminal liability. People v. Georgens, 107 A.D.2d 817, 484 N.Y.S.2d 654 (2d Dept. 1985).

Knowingly possesses.—Evidence was sufficient to sustain verdict where the defendant admitted he owned the car and he was the sole occupant at the time the contraband was found. People v. Roque, 108 Misc. 2d 965, 437 N.Y.S.2d 527 (Sup. Ct. N.Y. Co. 1981).

Inventory search.—Cocaine found in a crumpled up paper bag suspended by a wire from the dashboard of a car which was seized after defendant had been arrested for driving with a suspended license and was discovered in the course of an inventory search was admissible. People v. Gonzalez, 92 A.D.2d 512, 459 N.Y.S.2d 281 (1st Dept. 1983), aff'd, 62 N.Y.2d 386, 477 N.Y.S.2d 103, 465 N.E.2d 823 (1984).

Laboratory analysis.—Expert's testimony was admissible, although he made no use of comparative samples that constituted a reliable norm, where the expert's opinion that the vials contained cocaine was premised on tests which did not involve comparisons to a known standard. People v. Spence, 182 A.D.2d 845, 583 N.Y.S.2d 18, 19 (2d Dept. 1992).

—The police chemist's reliance on a colleague's test results was proper for evidentiary purposes because the colleague's findings were of a kind accepted in the profession as reliable. People v. Rosario, 179 A.D.2d 554, 579 N.Y.S.2d 63 (1st Dept. 1992).

Defenses available.—Court could instruct jury on defense of temporary innocent possession of a controlled substance modeled on defense available under Penal Law § 265.02, temporary innocent possession of a weapon, because under certain circumstances, possession of cocaine or any controlled substance is not unlawful if it is a temporary and incidental possession by a person assisting a public official in the course of official duties. People v. E.C., 195 Misc. 2d 680, 761 N.Y.S.2d 443 (Sup. Ct. Queens Co. 2003).

§ 220.16. Criminal possession of a controlled substance in the third degree.

A person is guilty of criminal possession of a controlled substance in the third degree when he knowingly and unlawfully possesses:

1. a narcotic drug with intent to sell it; or

2. a stimulant, hallucinogen, hallucinogenic substance, or lysergic acid diethylamide, with intent to sell it and has previously been convicted of an offense defined in article two hundred twenty or the attempt or conspiracy to commit any such offense; or

3. a stimulant with intent to sell it And said stimulant weighs one gram or more; or

4. lysergic acid diethylamide with intent to sell it and said lysergic acid diethylamide weighs one milligram or more; or

5. a hallucinogen with intent to sell it and said hallucinogen weighs twenty-five milligrams or more; or

6. a hallucinogenic substance with intent to sell it and said hallucinogenic substance weighs one gram or more; or

7. one or more preparations, compounds,

mixtures or substances containing methamphetamine, its salts, isomers or salts of isomers with intent to sell it and said preparations, compounds, mixtures or substances are of an aggregate weight of one-eighth ounce or more; or

8. a stimulant and said stimulant weighs five grams or more; or

9. lysergic acid diethylamide and said lysergic acid diethylamide weighs five milligrams or more; or

10. a hallucinogen and said hallucinogen weighs one hundred twenty-five milligrams or more; or

11. a hallucinogenic substance and said hallucinogenic substance weighs five grams or more; or

12. one or more preparations, compounds, mixtures or substances containing a narcotic drug and said preparations, compounds, mixtures or substances are of an aggregate weight of one-half ounce or more; or

13. phencyclidine and said phencyclidine weighs one thousand two hundred fifty milligrams or more.

Criminal possession of a controlled substance in the third degree is a class B felony.

Added by L. 1973, Ch. 276; **Amended** by L. 1973, Ch. 1051; L. 1979, Ch. 410; L. 1985, Ch. 341; L. 1995, Ch. 75, § 3, eff. June 10, 1995, and amendment applies only to offenses committed on or after that date, pursuant to L. 1995, Ch. 75, § 20.

ANNOTATIONS

Expert testimony. —Trial court properly admitted expert testimony by police officer as to quantity and packaging of the narcotics found on defendant, it was helpful to the jury in understanding the evidence and reaching a verdict, defense argued that possession of 14 glassine envelopes of heroin was for personal use, however average juror may not be aware of the quantity and packaging of heroin carried by someone who sells drugs, as opposed to someone who merely uses them; "Since the expert testimony was beyond the ken of the average juror, it matters not whether the testimony related to the ultimate issue in the case." People v. Hicks, 2 N.Y.3d 750, 778 N.Y.S.2d 745, 811 N.E.2d 7 (2004).

—Introduction of expert testimony is not proper in every drug sale case where a defendant asserts a misidentification defense, "the mere absence of drugs or marked money on the accused, however, cannot by itself serve 'as an automatic basis to introduce expert testimony addressing the general characteristics of street drug transactions,' " here trial court abused its discretion in permitting the introduction of the undercover officer's expert testimony on multi-individual street-level narcotics transactions because the evidence presented was that defendant acted alone, there was no evidence of accomplices. People v. Smith, 2 N.Y.3d 8, 776 N.Y.S.2d 209, 808 N.E.2d 344 (2004).

Intent to sell.—Sheer quantity of drug possessed (aggregate weight of 729 milligrams of cocaine) coupled with manner of preparation (11 equally weighted individual bags) justified conclusion that defendant possessed controlled substances with intent to sell. People v. Belo, 240 A.D.2d 964, 659 N.Y.S.2d 910 (3d Dept. 1997).

Possession is necessary element.—The People must prove that the defendant possessed the controlled substance, even though the possession may be constructive or actual, and that such possession was knowing. People v. Sierra, 45 N.Y.2d 56, 407 N.Y.S.2d 669, 379 N.E.2d 196 (1978).

—Even brief possession may be criminal. People v. Sierra, 45 N.Y.2d 56, 407 N.Y.S.2d 669, 379 N.E.2d 196 (1978); *but see* People v. Marshall, 72 A.D.2d 922, 422 N.Y.S.2d 187 (4th

Dept. 1979) (defendant only briefly possessed drugs when co-defendant, in car with defendant and an undercover officer, asked defendant to hand them over to the putative buyer).

—People did not have to prove that defendant knew his possession was unlawful, but only that he knowingly possessed the controlled substance. People v. Georgens, 107 A.D.2d 820, 484 N.Y.S.2d 657 (2d Dept. 1985).

Sufficiency of evidence.—Evidence of recent prior sale by defendant of identical glassine envelope that contained heroin, a controlled substance, to an undercover officer, was sufficient to make out a prima facie case of intent to sell the second glassine envelope. People v. Boone, 245 A.D.2d 102, 666 N.Y.S.2d 127 (1st Dept. 1997).

—Conviction was based on legally sufficient evidence where bag of cocaine containing 665 vials and with an estimated street value of $35,000 was found in defendant's apartment, the bag's owner had supplied defendant with cocaine, defendant was a known drug addict and had recently sold cocaine to a third person and defendant possessed drug paraphernalia. People v. Hardy, 232 A.D.2d 769, 649 N.Y.S.2d 58 (3d Dept. 1996).

Knowing possession.—Defendant's knowledge that he possesses a controlled substance may be proved directly as well as circumstantially; guilt may be inferred from evasive conduct or contradictory statements. People v. Reisman, 29 N.Y.2d 278, 327 N.Y.S.2d 342, 277 N.E.2d 396 (1971), *cert. denied,* 405 U.S. 1041.

—Although defendant's theory was one of his mere presence, and that he did not have knowing possession when he removed package containing drugs from garbage, evidence established that defendant had been given package, and the inconsistencies in his witness's testimony supported the inference of defendant's knowing possession. People v. Elizondo, 168 A.D.2d 295, 562 N.Y.S.2d 516 (1st Dept. 1990).

—Defendant, denying knowledge of drugs found in his vehicle, had participated in similar recent drug transactions; evidence admissible on issue of knowledge. People v. Sbraccia, 92 A.D.2d 628, 459 N.Y.S.2d 921 (3d Dept. 1983).

Constructive possession.—Defendant did not constructively possess controlled substance recovered from a car which he had driven on a prior occasion, but had not been seen driving the car when the drugs were recovered, possessed the registration and insurance card for the car, but did not own the car and did not possess the parking ticket for the lot in which the car was recovered; defendant was arrested as he walked toward the passenger seat, after a long meeting, and a third party was seated in driver's seat. People v. Francis, 79 N.Y.2d 925, 582 N.Y.S.2d 982, 591 N.E.2d 1168 (1992).

—Defendant was found in same apartment where drugs were recovered, which was an apartment associated with drug dealing activity; but there was no further evidence that he had dominion and control over the premises; not constructive possession. People v. Headley, 74 N.Y.2d 858, 547 N.Y.S.2d 827, 547 N.E.2d 82 (1989); *accord* People v. Williams, 135 A.D.2d 763, 522 N.Y.S.2d 667 (2d Dept. 1987) (defendant was not a resident of the apartment, nor was he the tenant, but had only slept on the porch on occasion; mere presence in room where drugs were recovered was insufficient to establish dominion and control).

—Even though bag containing 203 vials of crack, sufficient to support prosecution for criminal possession in the fourth degree, was found in a part of a park removed from defendant, defendant had been acting in concert with co-defendant in connection with a sale count, and bag had been in proximity to co-defendant; defendant was deemed to exercise dominion and control over the bag. People v. Cann, 191 A.D.2d 290, 595 N.Y.S.2d 27 (1st Dept. 1993).

—When defendant was in custody, and handcuffed, and police had not found drugs during a patdown, drugs found on seat of patrol car were constructively possessed by defendant. People v. Turner, 173 A.D.2d 381, 570 N.Y.S.2d 11 (1st Dept. 1991).

—In order to prove constructive possession, the People need only prove that the drugs were within defendant's immediate reach and control. People v. Francis, 172 A.D.2d 342, 569 N.Y.S.2d 403 (1st Dept. 1991), *rev'd on other grounds,* 79 N.Y.2d 925, 582 N.Y.S.2d 982, 591 N.E.2d 1168 (1991).

—Defendant's possession of stolen car, which he was driving, gave him dominion and control over 92 vials of crack found in the glove compartment. People v. Parks, 199 A.D.2d 426, 605 N.Y.S.2d 347 (2d Dept. 1993).

—Defendant was standing in the kitchen with a bag containing

17 vials of cocaine between her feet; she constructively possessed the cocaine. People v. Dawkins, 136 A.D.2d 726, 524 N.Y.S.2d 64 (2d Dept. 1988).

—When defendant directed co-defendant to give cocaine to the undercover officer, defendant constructively possessed cocaine extracted by co-defendant from a nearby hole in a wall. People v. Diaz, 112 A.D.2d 311, 491 N.Y.S.2d 758 (2d Dept. 1985).

—Evidence that defendant was found asleep alone in a bedroom containing her property (social security card, driver's license, completed application for public assistance, and a utility bill addressed to her at that address) along with female clothing was sufficient for jury to conclude that defendant exercised dominion and control over the bedroom and thus was in constructive possession of the cocaine secreted in the closet of that bedroom. People v. Tarver, 292 A.D.2d 110, 741 N.Y.S.2d 130 (3d Dept. 2002).

—Defendant was sitting, intoxicated, in a car in which cocaine was recovered, constituting his constructive possession. People v. Jenkins, 216 A.D.2d 193, 628 N.Y.S.2d 669 (3d Dept. 1995).

—Defendant constructively possessed the drugs which were recovered from a bedroom which he shared with co-defendant; theory of possession not defeated by opportunity for other persons, also present, to have placed the drugs in that location. People v. Rosenholm, 181 A.D.2d 943, 581 N.Y.S.2d 466 (3d Dept. 1992).

—Defendant constructively possessed cocaine recovered from a bedroom which contained many of his personal effects and identification, even if he was not present at the time of the search. People v. Nevins, 203 A.D.2d 936, 611 N.Y.S.2d 69 (4th Dept. 1994).

—Defendant's presence in bedroom where cocaine, a ledger, and a bundle of cash was located, about fifteen feet away, was constructive possession. People v. Westbrook, 177 A.D.2d 1039, 578 N.Y.S.2d 52 (4th Dept. 1991); *accord* People v. Shuron W., 185 A.D.2d 852, 587 N.Y.S.2d 357 (2d Dept. 1992).

—Drugs found in filing cabinet in a garage while defendant was present, when only defendant had the keys to the cabinet, were constructively possessed by defendant. People v. Rowell, 163 A.D.2d 833, 558 N.Y.S.2d 367 (4th Dept. 1990).

Knowledge of weight.—Failure to prove defendant's knowledge of weight for aggregate weight count does not preclude reduction to criminal possession in the seventh degree, which lacks a weight element. People v. Gordan, 86 N.Y.2d 10, 629 N.Y.S.2d 173, 652 N.E.2d 919, *rev'g* 204 A.D.2d 22, 618 N.Y.S.2d 261 (1st Dept. 1994); *accord* People v. Lawrence, 204 A.D.2d 969, 614 N.Y.S.2d 84 (4th Dept. 1994).

—When drugs were contained in vials, knowledge of weight could be inferred. People v. Sanchez, 86 N.Y.2d 27, 629 N.Y.S.2d 179, 652 N.E.2d 925 (1995).

—When defendant is tried on a theory that he possessed in excess of a statutory weight requirement, the People must prove beyond a reasonable doubt that defendant knew the weight which he possessed; knowledge, though, can be proved by inference. People v. Ryan, 82 N.Y.2d 497, 605 N.Y.S.2d 235, 626 N.E.2d 51 (1993).

—When aggregate weight is charged, defendant's handling of the controlled substance may support an inference of knowledge of the weight. People v. Ryan, 82 N.Y.2d 497, 605 N.Y.S.2d 235, 626 N.E.2d 51 (1993); *accord* People v. Sanchez, 86 N.Y.2d 27, 629 N.Y.S.2d 179, 652 N.E.2d 925 (1995).

—Negotiations by defendant concerning price, quantity or quality could support an inference that he knew the weight which he sold possessed with intent to sell. People v. Ryan, 82 N.Y.2d 497, 605 N.Y.S.2d 235, 626 N.E.2d 51 (1993); *accord* People v. Hill, 85 N.Y.2d 256, 624 N.Y.S.2d 79, 648 N.E.2d 455 (1995).

—Reversing court's reduction of criminal possession of controlled substance in third and fifth degrees to seventh degree where evidence was sufficient to support defendant's knowledge of the weight of contraband in question. Knowledge can be shown by inferences drawn from circumstances attendant to defendant's possession such as the amount of the controlled substance possessed, uniform packaging of the substance, defendant's handling of the substance and "saleslike conduct." People v. Litwa, 230 A.D.2d 638, 646 N.Y.S.2d 329 (1st Dept. 1996).

—Trial court erred in refusing to instruct jury that defendant must know the weight of the controlled substance as an element of the crime. People v. Warren, 232 A.D.2d 589, 648 N.Y.S.2d 670 (2d Dept. 1996).

Testing methods for weight.—In an aggregate weight case, it was irrelevant whether testing by police chemists had reduced the weight of the cocaine by extracting water. People v. Francis, 172 A.D.2d 342, 569 N.Y.S.2d 403 (1st Dept.), *rev'd on other grounds,* 79 N.Y.2d 925, 582 N.Y.S.2d 982, 591 N.E.2d 1168 (1991).

—When defendant was charged with possession of in excess of 1/8 ounce of cocaine, the fact that his chemist's testing determined a lesser weight was not dispositive; the police chemists had used a different testing method, which satisfactorily established the requisite weight. People v. Nelson, 190 A.D.2d 823, 593 N.Y.S.2d 836 (2d Dept. 1993).

Lesser included offense.—Conviction for criminal possession of a controlled substance in the third degree based upon possession of ½ ounce of a controlled substance containing cocaine, reversed and dismissed, it was an inclusory concurrent offense to criminal possession of a controlled substance in the first degree based on possession of more than 4 ounces of a substance containing cocaine. People v. Reyes, 264 A.D.2d 531, 696 N.Y.S.2d 462 (2d Dept. 1999).

Decided under former PL § 220.20

Inconsistent verdict.—The trial court could not have correctly found the defendant guilty of criminal possession of a controlled substance in the third degree with intent to sell when he was acquitted of a criminal sale count on the basis of his defense of agency. People v. Dixon, 87 A.D.2d 828, 448 N.Y.S.2d 756 (2d Dept. 1982).

Physical or constructive possession.—The location of narcotics on premises subject to defendant's control raises the inference of his possession and control of the contraband. People v. Martinez, 207 A.D.2d 695, 616 N.Y.S.2d 491, 494 (1st Dept. 1994)

—Where defendant was neither the lessee nor a resident of the apartment and, although he had slept on the front porch a few times, his mere presence in a room where contraband was located was not sufficient to support his conviction of drug crimes. People v. Willliams, 135 A.D.2d 763, 522 N.Y.S.2d 667, 668 (2d Dept. 1987).

Inconsistent verdicts.—Reversal was required where the jury found defendant guilty of criminal possession of a controlled substance in the third degree, but found him not guilty of criminal sale of a controlled substance in the first degree where the evidence conclusively established that a sale had taken place. People v. Lucas, 80 A.D.2d 836, 436 N.Y.S.2d 334 (2d Dept. 1981).

Intent to sell—The element of intent to sell may be established by proof that the defendant possessed a substantial quantity of drugs. People v. Sanchez, 205 A.D.2d 472, 613 N.Y.S.2d 912 (1st Dept. 1994).

—Mere possession of 45 vials was sufficient to establish an intent to sell. People v. Nelson, 189 A.D.2d 828, 592 N.Y.S.2d 466 (2d Dept. 1993).

1973 Drug Laws

Constitutionality

Penalties not unconstitutional.—A defendant was sentenced to an indeterminate term of imprisonment with a minimum of 7 years and a maximum of life. The penalties generally called for under the statutes are constitutional and do not violate the Eighth Amendment since, in view of the crime's seriousness, the required sentences do not constitute cruel and inhuman punishment. People v. Venable, 46 A.D.2d 73, 361 N.Y.S.2d 398 (3d Dept. 1974), *aff'd,* 37 N.Y.2d 100, 371 N.Y.S.2d 471, 332 N.E.2d 338 (1975).

Mandatory sentence not unconstitutional.—A mandatory indeterminate sentence with a maximum of life imprisonment upon conviction of Class A felonies, such as the drug offenses involved in the instant case, is not cruel and unusual punishment within the meaning of the Eighth Amendment. People v. Gardner, 78 Misc. 2d 744, 359 N.Y.S.2d 196 (Sup. Ct. Westchester Co. 1974).

Penalty.—The penalty imposed by the statute does not constitute cruel and unusual punishment nor deny defendant due process and equal protection of the law. People v. Winson, 79 Misc. 2d 557, 360 N.Y.S.2d 818 (Westchester Co. Sup. Ct. 1974).

Evidence Matters

Chain of custody.—Notwithstanding an apparent gap in the chain of custody of the recovered drugs, there was sufficient evidence to support defendant's conviction since the drugs were admitted based on reasonable assurances of their identity and unchanged condition; reasonable assurances of identity have been found where there are indications of continual police control over the evidence in issue. People v. Murray, 191 A.D.2d 397, 595 N.Y.S.2d 205 (1st Dept. 1993).

—Any change in the condition of the cocaine was adequately explained as a result of the chemist's analysis and therefore narcotics were properly introduced into evidence. People v. Luna, 191 A.D.2d 588, 594 N.Y.S.2d 804, 805 (2d Dept. 1993).

—Fact that narcotics were out of sight for three minutes until the police stopped the purchaser's car and found the packages in defendant's clenched right hand, merely went to the weight to be given the evidence rather than to its admissibility. People v. Streeter, 139 A.D.2d 786, 527 N.Y.S.2d 531, 531-532 (2d Dept. 1988).

—Where two basic requirements of proof, identity and unchanged condition, had been established, the alleged deficiencies in the chain of custody of the packet of cocaine the defendant sold to the undercover officer went to the weight of that evidence and not to its admissibility. People v. Rice, 137 A.D.2d 845, 525 N.Y.S.2d 309, 310 (2d Dept. 1988).

Evidence.—The undercover officer, properly qualified as an expert, was properly allowed to give expert testimony to explain the methodology of street drug sales. People v. Garcia, 196 A.D.2d 433, 601 N.Y.S.2d 482 (1st Dept.), aff'd, 83 N.Y.2d 817, 611 N.Y.S.2d 498, 633 N.E.2d 1094 (1993).

—Testimony that TNT teams target specific areas based on community complaints was not prejudicial to the defendant; also, testimony of officer concerning the normal buy and bust operation, the objectives of TNT, and the roles of each member was clearly admissible to enable the jurors to place the testimony of the other police witnesses in context. People v. Kelsey, 194 A.D.2d 248, 606 N.Y.S.2d 621, 624 (1st Dept. 1994).

—The money recovered from defendant at the time of his arrest was properly admitted at trial as relevant to the issue of intent to sell drugs. People v. Anderson, 191 A.D.2d 228, 595 N.Y.S.2d 1 (1st Dept. 1993).

—The failure to recover prerecorded buy money was not dispositive of the issue of guilt. People v. Padilla, 190 A.D.2d 639, 594 N.Y.S.2d 163, 164 (1st Dept. 1993).

—The court's instruction that the buy money was not an element of the crime and that the fact it was not recovered in no way lessens the culpability of defendant for the sale of narcotics was not error; the court had previously instructed the jury that in determining reasonable doubt they could consider the available evidence or the lack of evidence. People v. Covington, 191 A.D.2d 285, 595 N.Y.S.2d 32 (1st Dept. 1993).

—In prosecution for criminal sale and possession with intent to sell, the defendant's possession of a substantial amount of cash was probative of his possession of drugs with intent to sell. People v. Burgos, 192 A.D.2d 472, 596 N.Y.S.2d 418 (1st Dept. 1993).

—Since the People were required to prove that defendant possessed heroin with the specific intent to sell it, the $2,060 in cash recovered from him upon his arrest was properly admitted. People v. Valerio, 183 A.D.2d 487, 583 N.Y.S.2d 400 (1st Dept. 1992).

—In criminal sale prosecution, evidence that defendant possessed money in his pants pocket at the time of his arrest was relevant as it corroborated the police officer's testimony that after the sale, the defendant placed the money in that particular pocket. People v. Mitchell, 171 A.D.2d 403, 566 N.Y.S.2d 629 (1st Dept. 1991).

—Where defendant was charged with possession with intent to sell, in addition to criminal sale, the court properly permitted into evidence money recovered from the person to whom defendant handed the buy money. People v. Haynes, 172 A.D.2d 242, 567 N.Y.S.2d 736 (1st Dept. 1991).

—Evidence that a defendant handled a controlled substance, together with other circumstantial evidence, may give rise to an inference that the possessor knew the weight of the controlled substance which he or she possessed. People v. Okehoffurum, 201 A.D.2d 508, 607 N.Y.S.2d 695 (2d Dept. 1994).

—Court erred in admitting into evidence empty vials recovered from the co-defendant's person upon his arrest, since the vials had no probative value and served only to prejudice the defendant. People v. Diaz, 194 A.D.2d 688, 599 N.Y.S.2d 111 (2d Dept. 1993).

—Court did not abuse its discretion when it permitted expert testimony by the undercover police officer, who had observed the drug sale, concerning narcotics abuse, particularly of cocaine and its derivatives. People v. VanHuse, 187 A.D.2d 684, 590 N.Y.S.2d 520 (2d Dept. 1992).

—Court did not err in permitting testimony regarding money which was discovered on the defendant's person at the time of his arrest since defendant was charged with criminal possession of a controlled substance in the third degree. People v. Randolph, 157 A.D.2d 866, 550 N.Y.S.2d 741 (2d Dept. 1990).

—The court properly allowed expert testimony regarding the pricing and packaging of cocaine, since this subject is not within the knowledge of the average juror. People v. Vaughan, 187 A.D.2d 685, 590 N.Y.S.2d 246 (2d Dept. 1992).

—Evidence that defendant wore a beeper and expert testimony concerning its significance was permissible in a pure possession case. People v. Carpenter, 187 A.D.2d 519, 589 N.Y.S.2d 912, 915 (2d Dept. 1992).

Evidence concerning uncharged crime.—Defendant's conviction was affirmed and the admission into evidence of testimony from a police officer that he believed he observed defendant trafficking in cocaine was not prejudicial where the defense raised a general denial of guilt, as the prosecution had to prove every element of the crime, including intent. People v. Rose, 84 A.D.2d 645, 444 N.Y.S.2d 302 (3d Dept. 1981), aff'd, 57 N.Y.2d 837, 455 N.Y.S.2d 760, 442 N.E.2d 57 (1982).

—Court did not err in admitting $25 of non-buy money as relevant to whether defendant was acting in concert with his co-defendant who was apprehended with drugs and buy money in his possession, with the intent to sell drugs. People v. Bowen, 203 A.D.2d 204, 611 N.Y.S.2d 9 (1st Dept. 1994).

—Testimony that defendant had engaged in hand-to-hand exchanges, and references to the area as a drug-prone location, provided narrative information explaining why police targeted the defendant for observation. People v. Brown, 200 A.D.2d 416, 606 N.Y.S.2d 214 (1st Dept. 1994).

—Evidence concerning prior complaints of drug activity at building where drug transaction with officer transpired did not prejudice the defendant. People v. Gonzalez, 199 A.D.2d 65, 605 N.Y.S.2d 40 (1st Dept. 1994).

—Evidence of prior drug sales was admissible to rebut a claimed agency defense. People v. Askew, 194 A.D.2d 341, 598 N.Y.S.2d 484 (1st Dept. 1993).

—In sale prosecution, evidence of defendant's intent to sell drugs in the form of prior criminal acts is not permissible where intent may be easily inferred from the commission of the act itself. People v. Rodriguez, 194 A.D.2d 316, 598 N.Y.S.2d 236 (1st Dept. 1993).

—Evidence of defendant's unsuccessful sale to undercover officer (defendant believed potential buyer to be police officer) was properly admitted since its probative value on the issue of defendant's possession with intent to sell outweighed any potential for undue prejudice. People v. Garcia, 199 A.D.2d 50, 605 N.Y.S.2d 24 (1st Dept. 1993).

—The court properly admitted evidence of currency found on the defendant's person at the time of his arrest where the defendant was charged with possession of cocaine with the intent to sell it. People v. Wells, 144 A.D.2d 400, 533 N.Y.S.2d 936 (2d Dept. 1988).

—Since indictment charged defendant with criminal possession of cocaine and heroin with the intent to sell, evidence of the currency found on the defendant's person at the time of his arrest was properly found to be relevant to prove the crime charged. People v. Jones, 138 A.D.2d 405, 525 N.Y.S.2d 689 (2d Dept. 1988).

—In prosecution for criminal sale of a controlled substance in the third degree, the court did not err in permitting the People to offer direct evidence of defendant's prior drug sales. People v. Rubens, 190 A.D.2d 969, 594 N.Y.S.2d 82 (3d Dept. 1993).

—Where defendant was charged with possession with intent to sell evidence of prior sale by defendant to the informant was proper. People v. Taylor, 141 A.D.2d 982, 530 N.Y.S.2d 859 (3d Dept. 1988).

—In prosecution for criminal possession of a controlled

substance in the third degree the testimony concerning the prior sale of drugs by defendant was properly admitted to show defendant's intent to sell. People v. Atkinson, 141 A.D.2d 921, 530 N.Y.S.2d 606 (3d Dept. 1988).

—If a defendant is charged with drug possession or with one isolated drug sale, evidence that defendant possessed a large sum of money either at the time of the arrest or at the time of the sale is not admissible. People v. Whitfield, 144 A.D.2d 915, 534 N.Y.S.2d 25 (4th Dept. 1988).

Experts.—Expert testimony concerning drug transactions at the street level did not imply the defendant's involvement in extensive drug trafficking, especially since the court limited the testimony to the definition of the terms "hawker," "hand-to-hand" and "money man." People v. Garcia, 83 N.Y.2d 817, 611 N.Y.S.2d 490, 633 N.E.2d 1094 (1994).

—Testimony of undercover officer regarding general street level narcotics operations was admissible to explain why the police did not recover either additional drugs or prerecorded buy money from defendant. People v. Woney, 205 A.D.2d 480, 614 N.Y.S.2d 500 (1st Dept. 1994).

—The undercover officer's testimony regarding a typical buy and bust operation was appropriately limited to providing the jury with an understanding of the officer's actions. People v. Perez, 203 A.D.2d 123, 610 N.Y.S.2d 483 (1st Dept. 1994).

—Court did not err in allowing police witness to briefly testify as an expert about the practices and patterns of two and three drug-selling teams in order to explain why no drugs or money were found on the defendant at the time of arrest. People v. Applewhite, 202 A.D.2d 250, 608 N.Y.S.2d 634 (1st Dept. 1994).

—Limited background testimony as to methods used by drug dealers was properly received in prosecution for criminal sale of a controlled substance prosecution. People v. Graves, 202 A.D.2d 240, 608 N.Y.S.2d 443 (1st Dept. 1994), aff'd, 85 N.Y.2d 1024, 630 N.Y.S.2d 972, 654 N.E.2d 1220.

—Undercover officer was well qualified to give expert testimony as to the code words used in the drug trade, given his extensive experience as an undercover narcotics officer. People v. Rodriguez, 205 A.D.2d 328, 613 N.Y.S.2d 21 (1st Dept. 1994).

—Court properly permitted expert testimony about the tactics of drug dealers used to avoid being apprehended in possession of either the stash or cash. People v. Kelsey, 194 A.D.2d 248, 606 N.Y.S.2d 621 (1st Dept. 1994).

—Where the main objective of defense strategy in this buy and bust case was to persuade the jury that the nature of such an operation allows for manipulation of evidence and to discredit the testimony of the police witnesses for not using standard equipment that could have exculpated defendant, the People properly elicited background testimony from the officers describing the general mechanics of such an operation. People v. Salazar, 199 A.D.2d 103, 605 N.Y.S.2d 66 (1st Dept. 1993).

—The admission of background testimony of the police officers explaining generally what is a 'buy and bust'operation and the roles played by the police officers helped the jury understand the actions of the police which led to the defendant's arrest, to explain why no drugs or buy money was recovered from the defendant who was arrested shortly after the sale, and did not impermissibly imply that the defendant was involved in a large-scale operation. People v. Kane, 205 A.D.2d 480, 616 N.Y.S.2d 554 (2d Dept.), aff'd, 85 N.Y.2d 1024 (1994).

§ 220.18. Criminal possession of a controlled substance in the second degree.

A person is guilty of criminal possession of a controlled substance in the second degree when he or she knowingly and unlawfully possesses:

1. one or more preparations, compounds, mixtures or substances containing a narcotic drug and said preparations, compounds, mixtures or substances are of an aggregate weight of four ounces or more; or

2. one or more preparations, compounds, mixtures or substances containing methamphetamine, its salts, isomers or salts of isomers and said preparations, compounds, mixtures or substances are of an aggregate weight of two ounces or more; or

3. a stimulant and said stimulant weighs ten grams or more; or

4. lysergic acid diethylamide and said lysergic acid diethylamide weighs twenty-five milligrams or more; or

5. a hallucinogen and said hallucinogen weighs six hundred twenty-five milligrams or more; or

6. a hallucinogenic substance and said hallucinogenic substance weighs twenty-five grams or more; or

7. methadone and said methadone weighs two thousand eight hundred eighty milligrams or more.

Criminal possession of a controlled substance in the second degree is a class A-II felony.

Added by L. 1973, Ch. 276; **Amended** by L. 1973, Ch. 1051; L. 1975, Ch. 785; L. 1979, Ch. 410; L. 1995, Ch. 75, § 4, eff. June 10, 1995, and amendment applies only to offenses committed on or after that date, pursuant to L. 1995, Ch. 75, § 20; L. 2004, Ch. 738, § 21, eff. Dec. 14, 2004, amending opening para. and subd. 1.

ANNOTATIONS

Possession is necessary element.—The People must prove that the defendant possessed the controlled substance, even though the possession may be constructive or actual, and that such possession was knowing. People v. Sierra, 45 N.Y.2d 56, 407 N.Y.S.2d 669, 379 N.E.2d 196 (1978).

—Even brief possession may be criminal. People v. Sierra, 45 N.Y.2d 56, 407 N.Y.S.2d 669, 379 N.E.2d 196 (1978); but see People v. Marshall, 72 A.D.2d 922, 422 N.Y.S.2d 187 (4th Dept. 1979) (defendant only briefly possessed drugs when co-defendant, in car with defendant and an undercover officer, asked defendant to hand them over to the putative buyer).

—People did not have to prove that defendant knew his possession was unlawful, but only that he knowingly possessed the controlled substance. People v. Georgens, 107 A.D.2d 820, 484 N.Y.S.2d 657 (2d Dept. 1985).

Knowing possession.—Defendant's knowledge that he possesses a controlled substance may be proved directly as well as circumstantially; guilt may be inferred from evasive conduct or contradictory statements. People v. Reisman, 29 N.Y.2d 278, 327 N.Y.S.2d 342, 277 N.E.2d 396 (1971), cert. denied, 405 U.S. 1041 (1972).

—Although defendant's theory was one of his mere presence, and that he did not have knowing possession when he removed package containing drugs from garbage, evidence established that defendant had been given package, and the inconsistencies in his witness's testimony supported the inference of defendant's knowing possession. People v. Elizondo, 168 A.D.2d 295, 562 N.Y.S.2d 516 (1st Dept. 1990).

—Defendant, denying knowledge of drugs found in his vehicle, had participated in similar recent drug transactions; evidence admissible on issue of knowledge. People v. Sbraccia, 92 A.D.2d 628, 459 N.Y.S.2d 921 (3d Dept. 1983).

—Defendant went to mailbox, extracted envelope, and, holding it up, said "it's here," thus supporting inference of knowledge that the envelope contained LSD. People v. Morrison, 181 A.D.2d 1027, 581 N.Y.S.2d 512 (4th Dept. 1992).

Constructive possession.—Defendant did not constructively possess controlled substance recovered from a car which he had driven on a prior occasion, but had not been seen driving the car when the drugs were recovered, possessed the registration and insurance card for the car, but did not own the car and did not possess the parking ticket for the lot in which the car was recovered; defendant was arrested as he walked toward the passenger seat, after a long meeting, and a third party was seated in driver's seat. People v. Francis, 79 N.Y.2d 925, 582 N.Y.S.2d 982, 591 N.E.2d 1168 (1992).

—When a van was driven by co-defendants, but defendant had followed the van closely in his car, and stopped with the van in a parking area for several minutes during the trip, defendant constructively possessed the cocaine seized shortly thereafter from the van. People v. Manini, 79 N.Y.2d 561, 584 N.Y.S.2d 282, 594 N.E.2d 563 (1992).

—The mere fact that a co-conspirator still owed defendant money for the sale of cocaine, in that defendant sold the cocaine on credit, was not a valid basis to impute constructive possession to defendant. People v. Manini, 79 N.Y.2d 561, 584 N.Y.S.2d 282, 594 N.E.2d 563 (1992).

—Defendant was found in same apartment where drugs were recovered, which was an apartment associated with drug dealing activity; but there was no further evidence that he had dominion and control over the premises; not constructive possession. People v. Headley, 74 N.Y.2d 858, 547 N.Y.S.2d 827, 547 N.E.2d 82 (1989); accord People v. Williams, 135 A.D.2d 763, 522 N.Y.S.2d 667 (2d Dept. 1987) (defendant was not a resident of the apartment, nor was he the tenant, but had only slept on the porch on occasion; mere presence in room where drugs were recovered was insufficient to establish dominion and control).

—Even though bag containing vials of crack was found in a part of a park removed from defendant, defendant had been acting in concert with co-defendant in connection with a vale count, and bag had been in proximity to co-defendant; defendant was deemed to exercise dominion and control over the bag. People v. Cann, 191 A.D.2d 290, 595 N.Y.S.2d 27 (1st Dept. 1993).

—When defendant was in custody, and handcuffed, and police had not found drugs during a patdown, drugs found on seat of patrol car were constructively possessed by defendant. People v. Turner, 173 A.D.2d 381, 570 N.Y.S.2d 11 (1st Dept. 1991)

—In order to prove constructive possession, the People need only prove that the drugs were within defendant's immediate reach and control. People v. Francis, 172 A.D.2d 342, 569 N.Y.S.2d 403 (1st Dept.), rev'd on other grounds, 79 N.Y.2d 925, 582 N.Y.S.2d 982, 591 N.E.2d 1168 (1991).

—Defendant's possession of stolen car, which he was driving, gave him dominion and control over vials of crack found in the glove compartment. People v. Parks, 199 A.D.2d 426, 605 N.Y.S.2d 347 (2d Dept. 1993).

—Defendant arrested in hotel lobby had key to hotel room where additional drugs were recovered; when asked if he could get his shoes, he went to that room; defendant had asked hotel to transfer calls from that room to another room; conviction for second degree possession affirmed on a theory of constructive possession. People v. Ennis, 186 A.D.2d 145, 587 N.Y.S.2d 722 (2d Dept. 1992).

—Defendant's presence in the apartment a few feet outside room where two ounces of cocaine and a triple beam scale, empty vials and glassine packets were recovered, was sufficient to affirm conviction for possession in the second degree on a constructive possession theory. People v. Andrews, 182 A.D.2d 768, 582 N.Y.S.2d 495 (2d Dept. 1992).

—During police raid, defendant had been standing in an entrance hallway next to the kitchen; from that location, police could see a scale, large amount of marijuana and glassine envelopes on the kitchen table; police then recovered the glassine bags of cocaine from on top of refrigerator; conviction for possession in the second degree affirmed on constructive possession theory. People v Riddick, 159 A.D.2d 596, 552 N.Y.S.2d 455 (2d Dept. 1990).

—Defendant was standing in the kitchen with a bag containing 17 vials of cocaine between her feet; she constructively possessed the cocaine. People v. Dawkins, 136 A.D.2d 726, 524 N.Y.S.2d 64 (2d Dept. 1988).

—Where defendant was not a resident of the apartment, nor was he the tenant, but had only slept on the porch on occasion, his mere presence in room where drugs were recovered was insufficient to establish dominion and control. People v. Williams, 135 A.D.2d 763, 522 N.Y.S.2d 667 (2d Dept. 1987).

—When defendant directed co-defendant to give cocaine to the undercover officer, defendant constructively possessed cocaine extracted by co-defendant from a nearby hole in a wall. People v. Diaz, 112 A.D.2d 311, 491 N.Y.S.2d 758 (2d Dept. 1985).

—Defendant was sitting, intoxicated, in a car in which cocaine was recovered, constituting his constructive possession. People v. Jenkins, 216 A.D.2d 193, 628 N.Y.S.2d 669 (3d Dept. 1995).

—Testimony by an accomplice established that the suitcase in which the cocaine was found belonged to defendant, the suitcase contained defendant's identification documents and personal effects, and additional evidence established that defendant had occupied the room prior to his arrest, provided basis for defendant's constructive possession of the cocaine; conviction for criminal possession in the second degree sustained. People v. Williams, 195 A.D.2d 889, 600 N.Y.S.2d 836 (3d Dept. 1993).

—Although defendant charged on a theory of constructive possession in connection with crack recovered from an apartment had a key giving him access to common areas of the building, police entry had destroyed the lock to the apartment itself, so that the key could not be tested against the lock, defendant was not a registered tenant and other occupants testified that defendant had not been present prior to the police raid; although he was found in possession of vials which were similar to vials recovered from the apartment, these vials also were connected to several other drug arrests; conviction for possession in the second degree reversed. People v. Brown, 188 A.D.2d 930, 592 N.Y.S.2d 90 (3d Dept. 1992).

—Defendant constructively possessed the drugs which were recovered from a bedroom which he shared with co-defendant; theory of possession not defeated by opportunity for other persons, also present, to have placed the drugs in that location. People v. Rosenholm, 181 A.D.2d 943, 581 N.Y.S.2d 466 (3d Dept. 1992).

—Defendant's conviction of possession of a controlled substance in the second degree, based on evidence that he was the front seat passenger in a car driven by co-defendant and a grocery bag filled with 178 baggies of cocaine was located at defendant's feet, was supported by sufficient evidence. People v. Kinchen, 278 A.D.2d 874, 717 N.Y.S.2d 435 (4th Dept. 2000).

—Defendant constructively possessed cocaine recovered from a bedroom which contained many of his personal effects and identification, even if he was not present at the time of the search. People v. Nevins, 203 A.D.2d 936, 611 N.Y.S.2d 69 (4th Dept. 1994).

—Defendant's presence in bedroom where cocaine, a ledger, and a bundle of cash was located, about fifteen feet away, was constructive possession. People v. Westbrook, 177 A.D.2d 1039, 578 N.Y.S.2d 52 (4th Dept. 1991); accord People v. Shuron W., 185 A.D.2d 852, 587 N.Y.S.2d 357 (2d Dept. 1992).

—Even though drugs were found on co-defendant, co-defendant had purchased defendant's airline ticket, they sat next to each other on the plane and exited the plane together, then went to the same address, although by separate cabs, so that there was a basis to charge defendant with possession in the second degree on a constructive possession theory. People v. Nunez-Mezon, 168 A.D.2d 991, 564 N.Y.S.2d 934 (4th Dept. 1990).

—Drugs found in filing cabinet in a garage while defendant was present, when only defendant had the keys to the cabinet, were constructively possessed by defendant. People v. Rowell, 163 A.D.2d 833, 558 N.Y.S.2d 367 (4th Dept. 1990).

Knowledge of weight.—When drugs were contained in vials, knowledge of weight could be inferred. People v. Sanchez, 86 N.Y.2d 27, 629 N.Y.S.2d 179, 652 N.E.2d 925 (1995).

—Failure to prove defendant's knowledge of weight for aggregate weight count does not preclude reduction to criminal possession in the seventh degree, which lacks a weight element. People v. Gordan, 86 N.Y.2d 10, 629 N.Y.S.2d 173, 652 N.E.2d 919, rev'g 204 A.D.2d 22, 618 N.Y.S.2d 261 (1st Dept. 1994); accord People v. Lawrence, 204 A.D.2d 969, 614 N.Y.S.2d 84 (4th Dept. 1994).

—When defendant is tried on a theory that he possessed in excess of a statutory weight requirement, the People must prove beyond a reasonable doubt that defendant knew the weight which he possessed; knowledge, though, can be proved by inference. People v. Ryan, 82 N.Y.2d 497, 605 N.Y.S.2d 235, 626 N.E.2d 51 (1993).

—When aggregate weight is charged, defendant's handling of the controlled substance may support an inference of knowledge of the weight. People v. Ryan, 82 N.Y.2d 497, 605 N.Y.S.2d

235, 626 N.E.2d 51 (1993); *accord* People v. Sanchez, 86 N.Y.2d 27, 629 N.Y.S.2d 179, 652 N.E.2d 925 (1995).

—Negotiations by defendant concerning price, quantity or quality could support an inference that he knew the weight which he sold possessed with intent to sell.People v. Ryan, 82 N.Y.2d 497, 605 N.Y.S.2d 235, 626 N.E.2d 51 (1993); *accord* People v. Hill, 85 N.Y.2d 256, 624 N.Y.S.2d 79, 648 N.E.2d 455 (1995).

—Defendant "handled" contraband when he threw it out of window; weight of four ounces permitted inference that defendant knew that its weight exceeded two ounces; defendant's possession of the contraband while in the car would have triggered presumption that he knew weight under PL § 220.25; conviction for criminal possession in the second degree affirmed. People v. Dillon, 207 A.D.2d 793, 616 N.Y.S.2d 625 (2d Dept. 1994).

—Indictment reinstated where defendant was the only person in the livery cab where the contraband was discovered, and the packages each contained an amount just under the weight specified in the statute charged, permitting the inference that defendant was aware that the aggregate weight exceeded the statutory specification. People v. Olivo, 230 A.D.2d 653, 646 N.Y.S.2d 506 (1st Dept. 1996).

—Element that defendant possesses 625 mgs. of a hallucinogen refers to the chemical weight; hence, when defendant was charged with criminal possession in the second degree arising from his possession of psilocybin mushrooms, the weight of the psilocybin, not the weight of the mushrooms, had to exceed the statutory weight. People v. Ryan, 184 A.D.2d 24, 591 N.Y.S.2d 218 (3d Dept. 1992), *rev'd on other grounds,* 82 N.Y.2d 497, 605 N.Y.S.2d 235, 626 N.E.2d 51 (1993).

Testing methods for weight.—In an aggregate weight case, it was irrelevant whether testing by police chemists had reduced the weight of the cocaine by extracting water. People v. Francis, 172 A.D.2d 342, 569 N.Y.S.2d 403 (1st Dept.), *rev'd on other grounds,* 79 N.Y.2d 925, 582 N.Y.S.2d 982, 591 N.E.2d 1168 (1991).

—When defendant was charged with possession of in excess of 1/8 ounce of cocaine, the fact that his chemist's testing determined a lesser weight was not dispositive; the police chemists had used a different testing method, which satisfactorily established the requisite weight. People v. Nelson, 190 A.D.2d 823, 593 N.Y.S.2d 836 (2d Dept. 1993).

Decided under former PL § 220.23

Sufficiency of evidence.—The trier of fact could reasonably infer defendant's knowledge of and participation in a drug transaction where the people showed that a co-defendant came into possession of the drugs during a ride in defendant's car, that defendant was carrying a loaded gun, and that defendant waited for a co-defendant in a hotel lobby while the sale of drugs to an undercover officer took place. People v. Dordal, 55 N.Y.2d 954, 449 N.Y.S.2d 179, 434 N.E.2d 248 (1982).

—Evidence that defendant obtained the drug percodan from various drug stores by using false names and addresses on prescriptions in which the doctor's signature had been forged, testimony by six pharmacists that they filled defendant's forged prescriptions, descriptions of seven such transactions, and evidence of the doctor's signature on his application for a medical license, was sufficient to support defendant's conviction for criminal possession of a controlled substance in the first degree. People v. Tagliamonte, 78 A.D.2d 566, 431 N.Y.S.2d 738 (3d Dept. 1980).

Tapes of sale cases; inadmissible.—It was reversible error to admit in evidence tape recordings that related to prior sale counts of which the defendant had been acquitted, at his subsequent trial for possession of a controlled substance in the first degree, since the tapes did not relate to the possession charge being tried. People v. Hyman, 78 A.D.2d 701, 432 N.Y.S.2d 510 (2d Dept. 1980).

"Knowledge" and "possession."—PL § 220.18 requires that knowledge and possession occur at the same time, and the separate element of "knowledge" cannot occur before "possession" occurs. People v. Cullen, 50 N.Y.2d 168, 428 N.Y.S.2d 456, 405 N.E.2d 1021 (1980).

§ 220.21. Criminal possession of a controlled substance in the first degree.

A person is guilty of criminal possession of a controlled substance in the first degree when he or she knowingly and unlawfully possesses:

1. one or more preparations, compounds, mixtures or substances containing a narcotic drug and said preparations, compounds, mixtures or substances are of an aggregate weight of eight ounces or more; or

2. methadone and said methadone weighs five thousand seven hundred sixty milligrams or more.

Criminal possession of a controlled substance in the first degree is a class A-I felony.

Added by L. 1973, Ch. 276; **Amended** by L. 1973, Ch. 1051; L. 1975, Ch. 785; L. 1979, Ch. 410; L. 1995, Ch. 75, § 5, eff. June 10, 1995, and offenses committed prior to that date will be governed by laws in effect at the time the offenses were committed, pursuant to L. 1995, Ch. 75, § 20; L. 2004, Ch. 738, § 22, eff. Dec. 14, 2004, amending opening para. and subd. 1.

ANNOTATIONS

Constructive possession.—Defendant was a livery driver who carried package, containing cocaine, from taxi to delivery location; however, the police informant indicated that he had never met defendant, or that defendant had been present at any time when contents of package would have been revealed. People v. Acosta, 174 A.D.2d 181, 579 N.Y.S.2d 947 (1st Dept. 1992).

—When defendant was seen standing a few feet from a table containing four ounces of cocaine, in plain view, and cocaine paraphernalia were found in same room, defendant could be charged with constructive possession in the first degree. People v. Claggett, 182 A.D.2d 694, 582 N.Y.S.2d 282 (2d Dept. 1992).

—Constructive possession could be predicated on defendant's presence in room near coffee grinder containing cocaine residue, large box of aluminum foil, large sum of cash, and a telephone pager; large amount of cocaine, cocaine paraphernalia and cash were found in bedroom; defendant's coat was on bedroom door, and defendant's passport and other personal documents were located in bedroom; defendant's conviction for criminal possession in the first degree affirmed. People v. Vega, 175 A.D.2d 932, 573 N.Y.S.2d 767 (2d Dept. 1991).

—Cocaine discovered during vehicle search in car, on the person of another occupant, coupled with inculpatory statement of co-defendant, provided basis to impute constructive possession to defendant as basis to charge her with criminal possession in the first degree. People v. Brinson, 200 A.D.2d 784, 606 N.Y.S.2d 451 (3d Dept. 1994).

—In view of lack of evidence that defendant had seen cocaine in apartment or even knew of co-tenant's possession, mere fact that cocaine was recovered from apartment shared with co-defendant was an insufficient basis on which to predicate constructive possession by defendant. People v. Orta, 184 A.D.2d 1052, 585 N.Y.S.2d 265 (4th Dept. 1992).

Buyers liable for possession offense.—Evidence that the defendant was acting solely as an agent of the buyer is properly employed to determine whether he is guilty of possession instead of sale, the fact that the defendant was acting as a buyer is no defense to a possession charge when the Legislature has made buyers liable for the offense. People v. Lam Lek Chong, 45 N.Y.2d 64, 407 N.Y.S.2d 674, 379 N.E.2d 200 (1978), *cert. denied,* 439 U.S. 935.

Defendant must knowingly possess.—A conviction of criminal possession of a controlled substance, first degree, requires proof that the accused knowingly possessed the illicit substance; where defendant stored a package of cocaine but no evidence was adduced regarding his involvement in the sale, nor his knowledge of the contents of the package, the conviction was reversed and the indictment was dismissed. People v. Scott, 64 A.D.2d 525, 406 N.Y.S.2d 799 (1st Dept. 1978).

Knowledge of weight.—Indictment reinstated where defendant was the only person in the livery cab where the contraband was discovered, and the packages each contained an amount just under the weight specified in the statute charged, permitting the inference that defendant was aware that the aggregate weight exceeded the statutory specification. People v. Olivo, 230 A.D.2d 653, 646 N.Y.S.2d 506 (1st Dept. 1996).

—Evidence adduced at trial revealed that defendant did not know that aggregate weight of cocaine in his possession was four or more ounces; however, since evidence did prove that defendant knew weight of cocaine was two or more ounces, conviction was reduced to lesser included offense of criminal possession of a controlled substance in the second degree. People v. Wilson, 245 A.D.2d 402, 667 N.Y.S.2d 377 (2d Dept. 1997).

—Trial court erred in refusing to instruct jury that defendant must know the weight of the controlled substance as an element of the crime. People v. Warren, 232 A.D.2d 589, 648 N.Y.S.2d 670 (2d Dept. 1996).

Defense of agency.—The conviction of defendant for criminal possession of a controlled substance, first degree, must stand since agency would not be a defense where the evidence established that defendant, however transitorily, was knowingly in possession of heroin. People v. Roche, 45 N.Y.2d 78, 407 N.Y.S.2d 682, 379 N.E.2d 208 (1978), cert. denied, 439 U.S. 958.

Sufficiency of evidence; agreement to purchase.—An agreement to purchase eight ounces of cocaine for a specified price and in specified packaging is insufficient to support a charge of attempted criminal possession of a controlled substance. People v. Warren, 103 A.D.2d 1009, 478 N.Y.S.2d 388 (4th Dept. 1984).

Lesser included offense.—A conviction for criminal possession of a controlled substance in the third degree based upon possession of ½ ounce of a controlled substance containing cocaine was reversed and dismissed where the conviction was an inclusory concurrent offense to criminal possession of a controlled substance in the first degree based on possession of more than four ounces of a substance containing cocaine. People v. Reyes, 264 A.D.2d 531, 696 N.Y.S.2d 462 (2d Dept. 1999).

§ 220.25. Criminal possession of a controlled substance; presumption.

1. The presence of a controlled substance in an automobile, other than a public omnibus, is presumptive evidence of knowing possession thereof by each and every person in the automobile at the time such controlled substance was found; except that such presumption does not apply (a) to a duly licensed operator of an automobile who is at the time operating it for hire in the lawful and proper pursuit of his trade, or (b) to any person in the automobile if one of them, having obtained the controlled substance and not being under duress, is authorized to possess it and such controlled substance is in the same container as when he received possession thereof, or (c) when the controlled substance is concealed upon the person of one of the occupants.

2. The presence of a narcotic drug, narcotic preparation, marihuana or phencyclidine in open view in a room, other than a public place, under circumstances evincing an intent to unlawfully mix, compound, package or otherwise prepare for sale such controlled substance is presumptive evidence of knowing possession thereof by each and every person in close proximity to such controlled substance at the time such controlled substance was found; except that such presumption does not apply to any such persons if (a) one of them, having obtained such controlled substance and not being under duress, is authorized to possess it and such controlled substance is in the same container as when he received possession thereof, or (b) one of them has such controlled substance upon his person.

Amended by L. 1973, Chs. 276, 278; L. 1978; L. 1985, Ch. 341.

ANNOTATIONS

Chauffeur; presumption does not apply.—The presumption of possession does not apply to a licensed chauffeur acting in that capacity even though at the time of his arrest his license had been temporarily suspended. People v. Allison, 117 Misc. 2d 463, 458 N.Y.S.2d 496 (Sup. Ct. N.Y. Co. 1983).

Generally.—Presumption pursuant to PL § 220.25(2) is rebuttable. People v. Claggett, 182 A.D.2d 694, 582 N.Y.S.2d 282 (2d Dept. 1992).

—PL § 220.25 does not require a large or a particular amount of a controlled substance to be in open view. People v. Hathaway, 159 A.D.2d 748, 551 N.Y.S.2d 975 (3d Dept. 1990).

In open view in a room.—Evidence was sufficient to establish that defendant was inside apartment and in close proximity to crack cocaine being packaged for sale in open view; drug factory presumption permitted the jury to conclude that defendant knowingly possessed those drugs People v. Jiminez, 292 A.D.2d 196, 738 N.Y.S.2d 344 (1st Dept. 2002).

—Court properly charged "room presumption" where drugs and paraphernalia were in open view, defendant was in close proximity to them and it was a very small apartment. People v. Collado, 267 A.D.2d 122, 700 N.Y.S.2d 148 (1st Dept. 1999).

—A plastic packet containing cocaine seen on the outside of a paneless window, behind the bottom wooden frame of the window itself, and hidden from ordinary sight until it was seen from a distance of about two feet away could not be held to be "in open view" or "in a room." People v. Diaz, 108 Misc. 2d 213, 437 N.Y.S.2d 253 (Sup. Ct. N.Y. Co. 1981).

Presumption of possession.—Evidence clearly establishing defendant's presence in apartment containing large amounts of drugs, money, and weapons in plain view supported presumption of possession. People v. Bundy, 90 N.Y.2d 918, 663 N.Y.S.2d 837, 686 N.E.2d 496 (1997).

—The defendant's conviction was reversed where the people failed to offer any fact or circumstance beyond his presence in the room, where the drugs were located, to show a knowing and unlawful possession of the contraband. People v. Lopez, 85 A.D.2d 568, 445 N.Y.S.2d 702 (1st Dept. 1981).

—Presence of over four pounds of cocaine in the trunk of the car in which defendants were passengers entitled People to rely upon statutory presumption to establish possession in order to present a prima facie case. People v. Gonzalez, 235 A.D.2d 493, 653 N.Y.S.2d 929 (2d Dept. 1997).

—Court properly instructed jury that it could "presume or infer" possession: charge was sufficient to inform jurors that the law permits, but does not require, them to presume or infer knowing possession in some circumstances. (Rejecting defendant's contention that court erred in refusing to charge jury that presumption of possession is only "an inference of fact.") People v. Lowery, 232 A.D.2d 581, 648 N.Y.S.2d 985 (2d Dept. 1996).

—Absent evidence that defendant was "in close proximity" to the cocaine or that defendant exercised dominion and control over the premises, the Grand Jury proof did not sufficiently establish that defendant possessed the cocaine or drug paraphernalia. People v. Scott, 75 A.D.2d 858, 427 N.Y.S.2d 840 (2d Dept. 1980).

—Presumption of possession is applicable to defendant indicted and subsequently convicted of possession of a controlled substance in the second degree, where defendant was the front seat passenger in a car driven by co-defendant and a grocery bag filled with 178 baggies of cocaine was located at defendant's feet. People v. Kinchen, 278 A.D.2d 874, 717 N.Y.S.2d 435 (4th Dept. 2000).

—Defendant's position as the sole passenger in the back seat of a car where the contraband was hidden was legally sufficient evidence to convict defendant of possession in light of presumption of possession. People v. Mallory, 238 A.D.2d 933, 661 N.Y.S.2d 554 (4th Dept. 1997).

Presumption relating to presence of drug in automobile; evidence sufficient to overcome presumption.—Statutory presumption of possession of a controlled substance was properly charged where the cocaine was discovered in a vehicle driven by the defendant who had bloodshot and watery eyes and who was sniffling quite frequently; the presumption applies notwithstanding fact that defendant had borrowed the car from an individual who already was a bailer of the vehicle. People v. Hunt, 116 A.D.2d 812, 497 N.Y.S.2d 194 (3d Dept. 1986).

§ 220.31. Criminal sale of a controlled substance in the fifth degree.

A person is guilty of criminal sale of a controlled substance in the fifth degree when he knowingly and unlawfully sells a controlled substance.

Criminal sale of a controlled substance in the fifth degree is a class D felony.

Added by L. 1973, Ch. 276; **Amended** by L. 1979, Ch. 410.

ANNOTATION

Decided under former PL § 220.30

Elements.—The identity of the person to whom the defendant sold drugs is not a material element of the offense of criminal sale of a controlled substance. People v. Brown, 196 A.D.2d 428, 601 N.Y.S.2d 282 (1st Dept. 1993).

§ 220.34. Criminal sale of a controlled substance in the fourth degree.

A person is guilty of criminal sale of a controlled substance in the fourth degree when he knowingly and unlawfully sells:

1. a narcotic preparation; or

2. a dangerous depressant or a depressant and the dangerous depressant weighs ten ounces or more, or the depressant weighs two pounds or more; or

3. concentrated cannabis as defined in paragraph (a) of subdivision four of section thirty-three hundred two of the public health law; or

4. phencyclidine and the phencyclidine weighs fifty milligrams or more; or

5. methadone; or

6. any amount of phencyclidine and has previously been convicted of an offense defined in this article or the attempt or conspiracy to commit any such offense; or

6-a. ketamine and said ketamine weighs four thousand milligrams or more;

7. a controlled substance in violation of section 220.31 of this article, when such sale takes place upon school grounds; or

8. a controlled substance in violation of section 220.31 of this article, when such sale takes place upon the grounds of a child day care or educational facility under circumstances evincing knowledge by the defendant that such sale is taking place upon such grounds. As used in this subdivision, the phrase "the grounds of a child day care or educational facility" shall have the same meaning as provided for in subdivision five of section 220.44 of this article. For the purposes of this subdivision, a rebuttable presumption shall be established that a person has knowledge that they are within the grounds of a child day care or educational facility when notice is conspicuously posted of the presence or proximity of such facility; or

9. one or more preparations, compounds, mixtures or substances containing gamma hydroxybutyric acid, as defined in paragraph four of subdivision (e) of schedule I of section thirty-three hundred six of the public health law, and said preparations, compounds, mixtures or substances are of an aggregate weight of twenty-eight grams or more.

Criminal sale of a controlled substance in the fourth degree is a class C felony.

Added by L. 1979, Ch. 410; **Amended** by L. 1985, Ch. 34; L. 1986, Ch. 280; L. 1994, Ch. 292, § 2, eff. Nov. 1, 1994, amending subd. 7; L. 1995, Ch. 75, § 6, amending subds. 2 and 4, eff. June 10, 1995, and offenses committed prior to that date will be governed by laws in effect at the time the offenses were committed; L. 1997, Ch. 635, eff. Jan. 22, 1998, adding subd. 6-a; L. 1998, Ch. 537, § 16, eff. Nov. 1, 1998, and Ch. 289, § 1, eff. Sept. 1, 1998; L. 2003, Ch. 264, § 27, eff. Nov. 1, 2003, amending subd. 8 and adding subd. 9.

ANNOTATIONS

Charge.—The Court must charge that evidence of uncharged sales to others is admissible only to show the method of operation when the evidence comes in and again in its charge at the end of the case, where the defendant is indicted for the sale of a controlled substance to a particular individual. People v. Williams, 50 N.Y.S.2d 996, 431 N.Y.S.2d 477, 409 N.E.2d 949 (1980).

Punishment.—The retroactive application of the 1975 Penal Law provisions, in sentencing for offenses committed prior to its effective date, does not appear to be an unconstitutional application, since PL § 220.34 does not increase the maximum punishment to be imposed for the unlawful sale of methadone and in fact is designed to ameliorate the prior strict sentencing structure. People v. Morales, 87 Misc. 2d 675, 386 N.Y.S.2d 737 (Sup. Ct. N.Y. Co. 1976).

Mental state of defendant.—The culpable mental state for criminal sale of a controlled substance is knowledge; the People do not have to prove that the defendant acted with the specific intent to sell drugs. People v. Hill, 199 A.D.2d 111, 605 N.Y.S.2d 734 (1st Dept. 1993).

§ 220.39. Criminal sale of a controlled substance in the third degree.

A person is guilty of criminal sale of a controlled substance in the third degree when he knowingly and unlawfully sells:

1. a narcotic drug; or

2. a stimulant, hallucinogen, hallucinogenic substance, or lysergic acid diethylamide and has previously been convicted of an offense defined in article two hundred twenty or the attempt or conspiracy to commit any such offense;

3. a stimulant and the stimulant weighs one gram or more; or

4. lysergic acid diethylamide and the lysergic acid diethylamide weighs one milligram or more; or

5. a hallucinogen and the hallucinogen weighs twenty-five milligrams or more; or

6. a hallucinogenic substance and the hallucinogenic substance weighs one gram or more; or

7. one or more preparations, compounds, mixtures or substances containing methamphetamine, its salts, isomers or salts of isomers and the preparations, compounds, mixtures or substances are of an aggregate weight of one-eighth ounce or more; or

8. phencyclidine and the phencyclidine weighs two hundred fifty milligrams or more; or

9. a narcotic preparation to a person less than twenty-one years old.

Criminal sale of a controlled substance in the third degree is a class B felony.

Added by L. 1973, Ch. 276; **Amended** by L. 1973, Chs. 278, 1051; L. 1979, Ch. 410; L. 1985, Ch. 341; L. 1995, Ch. 75, § 7, amending subds. 3 through 8, eff. June 10, 1995, and offenses committed before that date will be governed by laws in effect at the time the offenses were committed.

ANNOTATIONS

Agency.—When a defendant charged with selling drugs to an undercover officer has purchased a portion of the drugs for his own use and the balance as an agent for the officer, he may nevertheless be entitled to an agency defense as to the balance. People v. Andujas, 79 N.Y.2d 113, 580 N.Y.S.2d 719, 588 N.E.2d 754 (1992).

—A defendant is entitled to an agency charge only where there is some view of the evidence upon which a trier of the facts could find that the defendant, in selling the controlled substance, was acting only as an agent for the buyer without any independent desire or inclination to promote the transaction; the test is whether there is a pattern emerging from the evidence as a whole from which agency can be inferred. People v. Simpson, 85 A.D.2d 306, 448 N.Y.S.2d 170 (1st Dept. 1982).

—Where none of the testimony at trial supported an inference that the defendant was acting as an instrumentality of the undercover officer, no agency charge was required. People v. Perry, 159 A.D.2d 593, 552 N.Y.S.2d 451 (2d Dept. 1990).

—The receipt of a $1 "tip" by the defendant did not, in and of itself, necessarily negate the agency defense. People v. Kirk, 143 A.D.2d 683, 532 N.Y.S.2d 925 (2d Dept. 1988).

—Agency defense was properly rejected where the defendant set the price, touted the cocaine's quality and at all times acted as an owner of the substance. People v. Wolf, 141 A.D.2d 972, 531 N.Y.S.2d 35 (3d Dept. 1988).

"Buy" money.—There is no requirement that the buy money used in a direct undercover sale be introduced into evidence in order to convict the defendant of criminal sale of a controlled substance, especially where the People introduced into evidence photocopies of the money in question. People v. Benton, 115 A.D.2d 170, 495 N.Y.S.2d 239 (3d Dept. 1985).

Conviction for sale of controlled substance not inconsistent with acquittal on charge of possession.—Defendant's conviction on count of criminal sale of a controlled substance, third degree, was not inconsistent with his acquittal on charges of criminal possession of a controlled substance, third and seventh degrees, where the evidence revealed that defendant negotiated with and accepted money from two undercover agents in exchange for a small quantity of heroin, although defendant never actually had the drugs in his possession and physical delivery to the agents was made by a third person.

People v. Dilan, 58 A.D.2d 655, 396 N.Y.S.2d 65 (2d Dept. 1977).

Disclosure of informant's identity.—It was proper for the trial court to deny defendant's request for disclosure of the informant's identity where the primary and overwhelming evidence against the defendant was supplied by a detective and testimony to corroborate the evidence was provided by members of the "back up team" assigned to the operation, thus, any testimony the informant would give would be cumulative as to the question of identification or whether a transaction took place. People v. Lucks, 83 A.D.2d 516, 441 N.Y.S.2d 265 (1st Dept. 1981).

Evidence.—"[I]n order to support a conviction under an offering for sale theory, there must be evidence of a bona fide offer to sell, *i.e.,* that defendant had both the intent and the ability to proceed with the sale"; however, "direct evidence in the form of contraband or other physical evidence is not the only adequate proof and, where the People depend on circumstantial evidence, such evidence may take many forms and need not specifically include proof of previous transactions involving the same defendants." People v. Samuels, 99 N.Y.2d 20, 750 N.Y.S.2d 828, 780 N.E.2d 513 (2002).

—In prosecution for criminal sale of a controlled substance, court erred in admitting into evidence testimony by detective concerning aborted sale of 3,000 vials of crack. People v. Ortiz, 142 A.D.2d 248, 535 N.Y.S.2d 604 (1st Dept. 1988).

—Crack is a concentrated, smokeable form of cocaine and is a "narcotic drug," as defined by PL § 220.00 (7) and Public Health Law § 3306, schedule II(b)(4), sale of crack is prohibited under criminal sale of a controlled substance in the third degree. People v. Monday, 309 A.D.2d 977, 765 N.Y.S.2d 705 (3d Dept. 2003)

—Defendant cannot be convicted of criminal sale of a controlled substance, or attempted criminal sale of a controlled substance, when the item sold was not a controlled substance, even if he mistakenly believed it was. People v. Alameen, 264 A.D.2d 937, 697 N.Y.S.2d 173 (3d Dept. 1999).

Evidence concerning uncharged crime.—Defendant's conviction was affirmed and the admission into evidence of testimony from a police officer that he believed he observed defendant trafficking in cocaine was not prejudicial where the defense raised a general denial of guilt, as the prosecution had to prove every element of the crime, including intent. People v. Rose, 84 A.D.2d 645, 444 N.Y.S.2d 302 (3d Dept. 1981), *aff'd,* 57 N.Y.2d 837, 455 N.Y.S.2d 760, 442 N.E.2d 57 (1982).

Inconsistent verdicts.—Defendant who was charged with criminal sale of a controlled substance in the third degree and criminal possession of a controlled substance in the third degree could not properly be found guilty of criminal sale and not guilty of criminal possession since the only basis for the jury's not guilty verdict on the charge of criminal possession could have been acceptance of the defendant's agency and/or entrapment defenses. People v. Brown, 81 A.D.2d 619, 437 N.Y.S.2d 701 (2d Dept. 1981).

Informant, disclosure of identity.—Defendant was entitled to disclosure of the identity of an informant who was present at the alleged sale of cocaine by defendant to an undercover policeman where defendant's testimony denied the event, the prosecution had little success in discrediting his testimony, there were several very close factual issues and the prosecution made no attempt to show that the informant was in any danger or could not be located. People v. Lamar, 86 A.D.2d 749, 447 N.Y.S.2d 773 (4th Dept. 1982).

Penalties not unconstitutional.—PL § 70.00 (2)(a); (3)(a)(ii)(iii) imposing a mandatory maximum sentence of life imprisonment and minimums from one to six years to eight and one-third years are constitutional. People v. Broadie, 37 N.Y.2d 100, 371 N.Y.S.2d 471, 332 N.E.2d 338 (1975).

Proof of intent necessary.—The people must prove that the defendant intended to sell the heroin to the undercover officer and the mere fact that the transaction between the defendant and another person took place within the undercover officers sight was insufficient to support an inference that defendant knew the other party intended to give the heroin to anyone else. People v. Maner, 92 A.D.2d 554, 459 N.Y.S.2d 126 (2d Dept. 1983).

Quantity.—PL § 220.39(1) contains no requirement that the People prove that the defendant sold any particular quantity of a narcotic in order to establish the elements of the crime;

"residue" is sufficient to establish the crime. People v. Rencher, 141 A.D.2d 676, 529 N.Y.S.2d 803 (2d. Dept. 1988).

Sale; possession of dangerous drug.—Only concurrent sentences could be imposed after the defendant's conviction of the non-inclusory concurrent counts of criminal sale of a controlled substance in the third degree (PL § 220.39) and criminal possession of a controlled substance with intent to sell (PL § 220.16). People v. Gaul, 63 A.D.2d 563, 404 N.Y.S.2d 603 (1st Dept. 1978).

—Since the offenses of criminal possession of a controlled substance, third degree, (PL § 220.16) and criminal sale of a controlled substance, third degree (PL § 220.39) are both class A-III felonies subject to the same penal sanctions, the former cannot be a lesser inclusory concurrent count with respect to the latter within the meaning of CPL § 300.40(3) (b). People v. Weathersby, 44 N.Y.2d 686, 405 N.Y.S.2d 436, 376 N.E.2d 908 (1978).

—Criminal sale of dangerous drugs in the third degree, criminal possession in the fourth degree, and criminal possession in the sixth degree were all inclusory concurrent counts, and a verdict of guilty on the sale charge must be deemed a dismissal of the possession charges. People v. Droz, 46 A.D.2d 751, 360 N.Y.S.2d 681 (1st Dept. 1974).

Scienter.—Where defendant, indicted for criminal sale of a controlled substance in the third degree, had in fact sold common wheat flour to the undercover officers, it was error for the trial court to deny defendant's motion to dismiss the sale charge; to support the sale charge, evidence of a knowing sale of a substance containing a narcotic drug is required. People v. Trent, 71 A.D.2d 866, 419 N.Y.S.2d 195 (2d Dept. 1979).

—The scienter requirement of PL § 220.39 must be read to extend to knowledge of the content or nature of the substance sold, and thus it was reversible error for the court to instruct the jury that it was of no consequence if the defendant, charged with criminal sale of LSD, thought he was selling mescaline when in fact it was LSD; the jury had to find beyond a reasonable doubt that defendant knew that the substance which he sold was LSD. People v. Carelock, 58 A.D.2d 996, 396 N.Y.S.2d 941 (4th Dept. 1977).

Testimony.—No error was committed when the court permitted the prosecution witness to testify to statements made by the defendant at the time of the drug transaction. People v. Bowden, 48 A.D.2d 962, 369 N.Y.S.2d 558 (3d Dept. 1975).

§ 220.41. Criminal sale of a controlled substance in the second degree.

A person is guilty of criminal sale of controlled substance in the second degree when he knowingly and unlawfully sells:

1. one or more preparations, compounds, mixtures or substances containing a narcotic drug and the preparations, compounds, mixtures or substances are of an aggregate weight of one-half ounce or more; or

2. one or more preparations, compounds, mixtures or substances containing methamphetamine, its salts, isomers or salts of isomers and the preparations, compounds, mixtures or substances are of an aggregate weight of one-half ounce or more; or

3. a stimulant and the stimulant weighs five grams or more; or

4. lysergic acid diethylamide and the lysergic acid diethylamide weighs five milligrams or more; or

5. a hallucinogen and the hallucinogen weighs one hundred twenty-five milligrams or more; or

6. a hallucinogenic substance and the hallucinogenic substance weighs five grams or more; or

7. methadone and the methadone weighs three hundred sixty milligrams or more.

Criminal sale of a controlled substance in the second degree is a class A-II felony.

Added by L. 1973, Ch. 276; **Amended** by L. 1973, Ch. 1051; L. 1975, Ch. 785; L. 1979, Ch. 410; L. 1995, Ch. 75, § 8, amending subds. 1 through 7, eff. June 10, 1995, and offenses committed before that date will be governed by laws in effect at the time the offenses were committed, pursuant to L. 1995, Ch. 75, § 20.

ANNOTATION

Submission of counts to jury.—Submission of the sale count only to the jury was proper where the proof to support any criminal conviction of the defendants came only from the testimony of the undercover officer, cross-examination was indiscriminately ineffective and defendants denied both the sale and possession counts of the indictment with equal persistence since there would be no rational explanation for accepting the officer's testimony as to possession but disbelieving that with respect to sale. People v. Scarborough, 49 N.Y.2d 364, 426 N.Y.S.2d 234, 402 N.E.2d 1127 (1980).

§ 220.43. Criminal sale of a controlled substance in the first degree.

A person is guilty of criminal sale of a controlled substance in the first degree when he knowingly and unlawfully sells:

1. one or more preparations, compounds, mixtures or substances containing a narcotic drug and the preparations, compounds, mixtures or substances are of an aggregate weight of two ounces or more; or

2. methadone and the methadone weighs two thousand eight hundred eighty milligrams or more.

Criminal sale of a controlled substance in the first degree is a class A-I felony.

Added by L. 1973, Ch. 276; **Amended** by L. 1975, Ch. 785; L. 1979, Ch. 410; L. 1995, Ch. 75, § 9, amending subds. 1 and 2, eff. June 10, 1995, and offenses committed before that date will be governed by laws in effect at the time the offenses were committed, pursuant to L. 1995, Ch. 75, § 20.

ANNOTATIONS

Agent.—Where defendant admitted at trial that he had arranged a large drug sale and hoped to receive a substantial benefit in the form of business loans from the grateful buyers, the jury could not find that defendant was merely an agent. People v. Lam Lek Chong, 45 N.Y.2d 64, 407 N.Y.S.2d 674, 379 N.E.2d 200 (1978), *cert. denied*, 439 U.S. 935.

Elements.—In prosecution for first degree sale of a controlled substance, a defendant can be held liable as an accomplice without proof that he acted with the specific intent to sell a controlled substance. People v. Kaplan, 76 N.Y.2d 140, 556 N.Y.S.2d 976, 556 N.E.2d 415 (1990).

Lesser included offenses.—Since expert testimony showed that several tests performed on the contents of each of four separately wrapped packets found them to be the same and that the substance tested contained morphine, and nothing developed in detailed cross-examination of the chemist or in other testimony suggesting that the substance in any one package differed in any respect from that in the others, there was no "identifiable rational basis" upon which jury could have concluded that one or more of the packets contained morphine and that the substance in the others did not, and thus there was no reason for the judge to charge the jury on lesser included offenses. People v. Gupta, 87 A.D.2d 990, 450 N.Y.S.2d 123 (4th Dept. 1982).

Mention of name and weight; not a violation.—The designation of a substance by a generic street name and of a specific weight thereof for possible future delivery is insufficient legally to constitute a violation. People v. Boscia, 83 Misc. 2d 501, 373 N.Y.S.2d 309 (Sup. Ct. Bronx Co. 1975).

§ 220.44. Criminal sale of a controlled substance in or near school grounds.

A person is guilty of criminal sale of a controlled substance in or near school grounds when he knowingly and unlawfully sells:

1. a controlled substance in violation of any one of subdivisions one through six-a of section 220.34 of this article, when such sale takes place upon school grounds; or

2. a controlled substance in violation of any one of subdivisions one through eight of section 220.39 of this article, when such sale takes place upon school grounds; or

3. a controlled substance in violation of any one of subdivisions one through six-a of section 220.34 of this article, when such sale takes place upon the grounds of a child day care or educational facility under circumstances evincing knowledge by the defendant that such sale is taking place upon such grounds; or

4. a controlled substance in violation of any one of subdivisions one through eight of section 220.39 of this article, when such sale takes place upon the grounds of a child day care or educational facility under circumstances evincing knowledge by the defendant that such sale is taking place upon such grounds.

5. For purposes of subdivisions three and four of this section, "the grounds of a child day care or educational facility" means (a) in or on or within any building, structure, athletic playing field, a playground or land contained within the real property boundary line of a public or private child day care center as such term is defined in paragraph (c) of subdivision one of section three hundred ninety of the social services law, or nursery, pre-kindergarten or kindergarten, or (b) any area accessible to the public located within one thousand feet of the real property boundary line comprising any such facility or any parked automobile or other parked vehicle located within one thousand feet of the real property boundary line comprising any such facility. For the purposes of this section an "area accessible to the public" shall mean sidewalks, streets, parking lots, parks, playgrounds, stores and restaurants.

6. For the purposes of this section, a rebuttable presumption shall be established that a person has knowledge that they are within the grounds of a child day care or educational facility when notice is conspicuously posted of the presence or proximity of such facility.

Criminal sale of a controlled substance in or near school grounds is a class B felony.

Added by L. 1986, Ch. 280; **Amended** L. 1994, Ch. 292, § 3, eff. Nov. 1, 1994, amending subds. 1 and 2; L. 1997, Ch. 635, eff. Jan. 22, 1998; L. 1998, Ch. 289, § 2, eff. Sept. 1, 1998.

ANNOTATIONS

Defendant's knowledge.—People were not required to prove that defendant knew that the sale of the controlled substance was on or near school grounds. People v. Gonzales, 240 A.D.2d 255, 653 N.Y.S.2d 929 (1st Dept. 1997).

Evidence.—"[T]he proper way to determine whether a sale was 1000 feet or less from a school is by a straight-line or 'as the crow flies' method, and not as measured along the route a pedestrian would be required to travel, including detours around obstructions. The statute provides for a 1000-foot radius without regard to whether the geographic area is occupied by any obstructions to pedestrian traffic." People v. Robbins, 10 A.D.3d 570, 782 N.Y.S.2d 80 (1st Dept.), *appeal granted*, 4 N.Y.3d 747, 790 N.Y.S.2d 660, 824 N.E.2d 61 (2004), *motion granted*, 4 N.Y.3d 774, 792 N.Y.S.2d 893, 825 N.E.2d 1088 (2005).

—Evidence that defendant and another were approached by an undercover officer on the stoop of a building 139 feet from a school and negotiated a purchase of cocaine was sufficient to sustain a conviction under this section. People v. Perez, 277 A.D.2d 1, 715 N.Y.S.2d 402 (1st Dept. 2000).

—Evidence was legally sufficient to support indictment for criminal sale of controlled substance in or near school grounds where the police officer testified that the sale took place within 1000 feet of school property and "about a block away" from two schools. People v. Zelaya, 232 A.D.2d 261, 648 N.Y.S.2d 93 (1st Dept. 1996).

Expert testimony.—Expert testimony was permissible to assist the jury in understanding the specialized terminology and techniques used in narcotics street sales; testimony may be helpful to the jury in understanding the evidence presented and in resolving material factual issues, such as why no drugs or buy money were found on defendant. People v. Brown, 97 N.Y.2d 500, 743 N.Y.S.2d 374, 769 N.E.2d 1266 (2002).

§ 220.45. Criminally possessing a hypodermic instrument.

A person is guilty of criminally possessing a hypodermic instrument when he knowingly and unlawfully possesses or sells a hypodermic syringe or hypodermic needle.

Criminally possessing a hypodermic instrument is a class A misdemeanor.

ANNOTATIONS

Defense of medical necessity.—Defendants demonstrated medical necessity in connection with their giving out free, clean hypodermic needles as a means to help users avoid spread of HIV infection and AIDS, in view of their offer of proof that an insufficient number of needle exchange programs existed for addicts but medical evidence demonstrated that such needle exchange programs reduced spread of infection; defendants also proved a defense of medical necessity in that, by giving out needles, they were not seeking to thwart the statute, and harm sought to be avoided was greater than harm caused by statutory violation. People v. Bordowitz, 155 Misc. 2d 128, 588 N.Y.S.2d 507 (N.Y.C. Crim. Ct. 1991).

Constructive possession.—Hypodermic needle found on top of dresser, but defendant was not registered tenant, stayed in apartment only on a transient basis, and had been out of apartment for about three hours, returning in close proximity to police raid; not constructive possession. People v. Crespo, 198 A.D.2d 85, 603 N.Y.S.2d 838 (1st Dept. 1993).

—Hypodermic needle recovered from stolen car in which defendant was passenger; however, constructive possession could not be proved absent proof that defendant knew of presence of needle; similarly, charge alleging criminal possession of stolen property had to be dismissed absent proof of scienter. People v. Williams, 97 A.D.2d 491, 468 N.Y.S.2d 12 (2d Dept. 1983).

Burden of proof.—The defendant has the burden of establishing by a preponderance of the evidence that his "possession" of the hypodermic syringe and needle were for a lawful purpose. The People must prove beyond a reasonable doubt that the hypodermic syringe and needle are "adapted for the administering of narcotic drugs." The jury may itself determine whether the devices are adapted for this purpose. People v. Strong, 47 A.D.2d 798, 365 N.Y.S.2d 310 (4th Dept. 1975).

Criminal possession of a hypodermic instrument.—Pursuant to PL § 220.45 and aside from the question of unlawful and knowing possession, the jury must determine whether the item unlawfully possessed was, in fact, a hypodermic needle or syringe but need not determine whether the hypodermic instrument is functional. People v. Strong, 42 N.Y.2d 868, 397 N.Y.S.2d 779, 366 N.E.2d 867 (1977).

—In the Court of Appeals it was held that the evidence was insufficient to show defendant's constructive possession of a hypodermic needle found in an apartment rented by defendant's girl friend whom he visited at the apartment several nights a week. The court stated that the proof offered in support of an inference of defendant's possession or control of the apartment was not beyond a reasonable doubt and fell far short of the standard necessary to establish his constructive possession of the narcotics paraphernalia found there. People v. Siplin, 29 N.Y.2d 841, 327 N.Y.S.2d 854, 277 N.E.2d 786 (1971).

—Proof that hypodermic instrument was "functional" is not required for conviction. People v. Lewin, 49 A.D.2d 1006, 374 N.Y.S.2d 97 (4th Dept. 1975).

§ 220.46. Criminal injection of a narcotic drug.

A person is guilty of criminal injection of a narcotic drug when he knowingly and unlawfully possesses a narcotic drug and he intentionally injects by means of a hypodermic syringe or hypodermic needle all or any portion of that drug into the body of another person with the latter's consent.

Criminal injection of a narcotic drug is a class E felony.

Added by L. 1971, Ch. 896.

ANNOTATION

Consent to injection.—Even if the person injected consents to the injection, if he or she dies as a result of the injection, the injector may be charged with homicide. People v. Cruciani, 36 N.Y.2d 304, 367 N.Y.S.2d 758, 327 N.E.2d 803 (1975).

§ 220.50. Criminally using drug paraphernalia in the second degree.

A person is guilty of criminally using drug paraphernalia in the second degree when he knowingly possesses or sells:

1. Diluents, dilutants or adulterants, including but not limited to, any of the following: quinine hydrochloride, mannitol, mannite, lactose or dextrose, adapted for the dilution of narcotic drugs or stimulants under circumstances evincing an intent to use, or under circumstances evincing knowledge that some person intends to use, the same for purposes of unlawfully mixing, compounding, or otherwise preparing any narcotic drug or stimulant; or

2. Gelatin capsules, glassine envelopes, vials, capsules or any other material suitable for the packaging of individual quantities of narcotic drugs or stimulants under circumstances evincing an intent to use, or under circumstances evincing knowledge that some person intends to use, the same for the purpose of unlawfully manufacturing, packaging or dispensing of any narcotic drug or stimulant; or

3. Scales and balances used or designed for the purpose of weighing or measuring controlled substances, under circumstances evincing an intent to use, or under circumstances evincing knowledge that some person intends to use, the same for purpose of unlawfully manufacturing, packaging or dispensing of any narcotic drug or stimulant.

Criminally using drug paraphernalia in the second degree is a class A misdemeanor.

Amended by L. 1973, Ch. 276; L. 1990, Ch. 627.

ANNOTATIONS

Drug factory.—This offense is available when police raid a "drug factory" and drugs are not recovered, but paraphernalia is recovered. People v. Tirado, 38 N.Y.2d 955, 384 N.Y.S.2d 151, 348 N.E.2d 608 (1976).

Constructive possession.—When defendant and co-defendant were observed fleeing from apartment where drug paraphernalia was recovered, they had exercised sufficient dominion and control over the apartment to have constructively possessed the contraband therein. People v. Santos, 210 A.D.2d 129, 620 N.Y.S.2d 62 (1st Dept. 1994).

Evidence of use.—Defendant's possession of a scale, strainers, pestle for grinding, a calculator and playing cards, which were implements for using, packaging and selling drugs, supported inference that he used these as drug paraphernalia. People v. Vega, 209 A.D.2d 220, 618 N.Y.S.2d 309 (1st Dept. 1994).

Generally.—An intent to use drug paraphernalia and sell narcotics may be inferred from the fact that a large quantity of drug paraphernalia was found. People v. Downs, 195 A.D.2d 477, 599 N.Y.S.2d 865 (2d Dept. 1993).

—The plain and clear language of Penal Law 220.50 does not require that the paraphernalia be part of a drug factory nor does it exclude from the parameters of the statute manufacturing, packaging, mixing, compounding, or preparing narcotic drugs for personal use. People v. Rodriguez, 159 Misc. 2d 670, 606 N.Y.S.2d 536, 541-542 (Crim. Ct. N.Y. Co. 1994).

Knowledge of age; sale to person under 18 years of age.—When the term "knowingly" appears in a section in which the age of a child is an element, knowledge of such age is not an element of the offense and the defendant may not assert a lack thereof as a defense. (PL § 15.20(3)). People v. Wenzel, 77 A.D.2d 715, 430 N.Y.S.2d 431 (3d Dept. 1980).

Indictment; failure to name person; criminally using drug paraphernalia; constitutionality.—A defendant should be allowed to withdraw his negotiated plea of guilty to assault in the first and third degree where the court incorrectly advised defendant during plea negotiations as to minimum amount of time he would have to serve and it was obvious that the inducement for defendant's guilty plea centered on the length of his sentence. People v Moore, 78 A.D.2d 997, 433 N.Y.S.2d 689 (4th Dept. 1980).

—Common sense meaning of "sell" implies that sale is to person and failure to name purchaser is of no consequence in stating essential element of prohibited conduct implicit in crime of selling dangerous drug. However, defendant is entitled to name of buyer in bill of particulars and grand jury minutes to assure that crime described is same. Although burden of proving that conduct violates statute may be heavy, such fact cannot declare statute unconstitutional when it is definite, precise and reasonable under modern social conditions concerning drug problem. People v. Taylor, 70 Misc. 2d 970, 335 N.Y.S.2d 324 (Dutchess Co. Ct. 1972).

§ 220.55. Criminally using drug paraphernalia in the first degree.

A person is guilty of criminally using drug paraphernalia in the first degree when he commits the crime of criminally using drug paraphernalia in the second degree and he has previously been convicted of criminally using drug paraphernalia in the second degree.

Criminally using drug paraphernalia in the first degree is a class D felony.

Added by L. 1971, Ch. 970.

§ 220.60. Criminal possession of precursors of controlled substances.

A person is guilty of criminal possession of precursors of controlled substances when, with intent to manufacture a controlled substance unlawfully, he possesses at the same time:

(a) carbamide (urea) and propanedioc and malonic acid or its derivatives; or

(b) ergot or an ergot derivative and diethylamine or dimethylformamide or diethylamide; or

(c) phenylacetone (1-phenyl-2 propanone) and hydroxylamine or ammonia or formamide or benzaldehyde or nitroethane or methylamine; or

(d) pentazocine and methyliodide; or

(e) phenylacetonitrile and dichlorodiethyl methylamine or dichlorodiethyl benzylamine; or

(f) diephenylacetonitrile* and dimethylaminoisopropyl chloride; or

(g) piperidine and cyclohexanone and bromobenzene and lithium or magnesium; or

(h) 2, 5-dimethoxy benzaldehyde and nitroethane and a reducing agent.

Criminal procession* of precursors of controlled substances is a class E felony.

* As originally enacted.

Amended by L. 1973, Ch. 276; L. 1974, Ch. 394.

§ 220.65. Criminal sale of a prescription for a controlled substance.

A person is guilty of criminal sale of a prescription for a controlled substance when, being a practitioner, as that term is defined in section thirty-three hundred two of the public health law, he knowingly and unlawfully sells a prescription for a controlled substance. For the purpose of this section, a person sells a prescription for a controlled substance unlawfully when he does so other than in good faith in the course of his professional practice.

Criminal sale of a prescription is a class C felony.

Added by L. 1986, Ch. 118.

ANNOTATION

Sufficiency of evidence.—Defendant psychiatrist and his office manager sold prescriptions for valium to undercover officers; undercover officers acted as addicts, indicated to defendants that they had past drug use, which should have alerted a psychiatrist that valium ought not be prescribed; interviews of undercover officers were perfunctory; dosages were unduly high for standard treatment of anxiety; and psychiatrist bargained with putative addicts to sell increased quantities for higher payments; evidence sufficient. People v. Dias, 197 A.D.2d 387, 602 N.Y.S.2d 353 (1st Dept. 1993).

§ 220.70. Criminal possession of methamphetamine manufacturing material in the second degree.

A person is guilty of criminal possession of methamphetamine manufacturing material in the second degree when he or she possesses a precursor, a chemical reagent or a solvent with the intent to use or knowing another intends to use such precursor, chemical reagent, or solvent to unlawfully produce, prepare or manufacture methamphetamine.

Criminal possession of methamphetamine manufacturing material in the second degree is a class A misdemeanor.

Added by L. 2005, Ch. 394, § 4, eff. Oct. 1, 2005.

§ 220.71. Criminal possession of methamphetamine manufacturing material in the first degree.

A person is guilty of criminal possession of methamphetamine manufacturing material in the first degree when he or she commits the offense of criminal possession of methamphetamine manufacturing material in the second degree, as defined in section 220.70 of this article, and has previously been convicted within the preceding five years of criminal possession of methamphetamine manufacturing material in the second degree, as defined in section 220.70 of this article, or a violation of this section.

Criminal possession of methamphetamine manufacturing material in the first degree is a class E felony.

Added by L. 2005, Ch. 394, § 4, eff. Oct. 1, 2005.

§ 220.72. Criminal possession of precursors of methamphetamine.

A person is guilty of criminal possession of precursors of methamphetamine when he or she possesses at the same time a precursor and a solvent or chemical reagent, with intent to use or knowing that another intends to use each such precursor, solvent or chemical reagent to unlawfully manufacture methamphetamine.

Criminal possession of precursors of methamphetamine is a class E felony.

Added by L. 2005, Ch. 394, § 4, eff. Oct. 1, 2005.

§ 220.73. Unlawful manufacture of methamphetamine in the third degree.

A person is guilty of unlawful manufacture of methamphetamine in the third degree when he or she possesses at the same time and location, with intent to use, or knowing that another intends to use each such product to unlawfully manufacture, prepare or produce methamphetamine:

1. Two or more items of laboratory equipment and two or more precursors, chemical reagents or solvents in any combination; or

2. One item of laboratory equipment and three or more precursors, chemical reagents or solvents in any combination; or

3. A precursor:

(a) mixed together with a chemical reagent or solvent; or

(b) with two or more chemical reagents and/or solvents mixed together.

Unlawful manufacture of methamphetamine in the third degree is a class D felony.

Added by L. 2005, Ch. 394, § 4, eff. Oct. 1, 2005.

§ 220.74. Unlawful manufacture of methamphetamine in the second degree.

A person is guilty of unlawful manufacture of methamphetamine in the second degree when he or she:

1. Commits the offense of unlawful manufacture of methamphetamine in the third degree as defined in section 220.73 of this article in the presence of another person under the age of sixteen, provided, however, that the actor is at least five years older than such other person under the age of sixteen; or

2. Commits the crime of unlawful manufacture of methamphetamine in the third degree as defined in section 220.73 of this article and has previously been convicted within the preceding five years of the offense of criminal possession of precursors of methamphetamine as defined in section 220.72 of this article, criminal possession of methamphetamine manufacturing material in the first degree as defined in section 220.71 of

this article, unlawful disposal of methamphetamine laboratory material as defined in section 220.76 of this article, unlawful manufacture of methamphetamine in the third degree as defined in section 220.73 of this article, unlawful manufacture of methamphetamine in the second degree as defined in this section, or unlawful manufacture of methamphetamine in the first degree as defined in section 220.75 of this article.

Unlawful manufacture of methamphetamine in the second degree is a class C felony.

Added by L. 2005, Ch. 394, § 4, eff. Oct. 1, 2005.

§ 220.75. Unlawful manufacture of methamphetamine in the first degree.

A person is guilty of unlawful manufacture of methamphetamine in the first degree when such person commits the crime of unlawful manufacture of methamphetamine in the second degree, as defined in subdivision one of section 220.74 of this article, after having previously been convicted within the preceding five years of unlawful manufacture of methamphetamine in the third degree, as defined in section 220.73, unlawful manufacture of methamphetamine in the second degree, as defined in section 220.74 of this article, or unlawful manufacture of methamphetamine in the first degree, as defined in this section.

Unlawful manufacturer of methamphetamine in the first degree is a class B felony.

Added by L. 2005, Ch. 394, § 4, eff. Oct. 1, 2005.

§ 220.76. Unlawful disposal of methamphetamine laboratory material.

A person is guilty of unlawful disposal of methamphetamine laboratory material when, knowing that such actions are in furtherance of a methamphetamine operation, he or she knowingly disposes of, or possesses with intent to dispose of, hazardous or dangerous material under circumstances that create a substantial risk to human health or safety or a substantial danger to the environment.

Unlawful disposal of methamphetamine laboratory material is a class E felony.

Added by L. 2005, Ch. 394, § 4, eff. Oct. 1, 2005.

ARTICLE 221—OFFENSES INVOLVING MARIHUANA

Editor's Note: L. 2004, Ch. 738, § 30, as amended, provides:

"1. Notwithstanding any contrary provision of law, any person convicted of a felony defined in article 220 or 221 of the penal law, other than a class A-I felony offense defined in article 220 of the penal law, which was committed prior to the effective date of this section [Jan. 13, 2005], and sentenced thereon to an indeterminate term of imprisonment pursuant to provisions of the law in effect prior to the effective date of this section and who meets the eligibility requirements of paragraph (d) of subdivision 1 of section 803 of the correction law as it existed on the effective date of this section, may receive an additional merit time allowance not to exceed one-sixth of the minimum term or period imposed by the court provided the inmate either: (i) successfully participates or has participated in two or more of the four program objectives set forth in paragraph (d) of subdivision 1 of section 803 of the correction law, or (ii) successfully participates in one of the program objectives set forth in paragraph (d) of subdivision 1 of section 803 of the correction law and successfully maintains employment while in a work release program or any other continuous temporary release program for a period of not less than three months.

"2. Such allowance shall be withheld for any serious disciplinary infraction or upon a judicial determination that the person, while an inmate, commenced or continued a civil action, proceeding or claim that was found to be frivolous as defined in subdivision (c) of section 8303-a of the civil practice law and rules, or an order of a federal court pursuant to Rule 11 of the federal rules of civil procedure imposing sanctions in an action commenced by a person, while an inmate, against a state agency, officer or employee."

LexisNexis Cross Reference

See generally Defense of Narcotics Cases.

§ 221.00. Marihuana; definitions.

Unless the context in which they are used clearly otherwise requires, the terms occurring in this article shall have the same meaning ascribed to them in article two hundred twenty of this chapter.

ANNOTATIONS

Effective date.—Penal Law, Article 221 applies to offenses committed on and after July 29, 1977. People v. Prator, 93 Misc. 2d 303, 402 N.Y.S.2d 739 (Dist. Ct. Nassau Co. 1978).

Constitutionality.—Marihuana Reform Act of 1977 is constitutional. People v. Fillhart, 93 Misc. 2d 911, 403 N.Y.S.2d 642 (Jefferson Co. Ct. 1978).

§ 221.05. Unlawful possession of marihuana.

A person is guilty of unlawful possession of marihuana when he knowingly and unlawfully possesses marihuana.

Unlawful possession of marihuana is a violation punishable only by a fine of not more than one hundred dollars. However, where the defendant has previously been convicted of an offense defined in this article or article 220 of this chapter, committed within the three years immediately preceding such violation, it shall be punishable (a) only by a fine of not more than two hundred dollars, if the defendant was previously convicted of one such offense committed during such period, and (b) by a fine of not more than two hundred fifty dollars or a term of imprisonment not in excess of fifteen days or both, if the defendant was previously convicted of two such offenses committed during such period.

ANNOTATIONS

Compassionate purpose of possessing marijuana is not a basis to dismiss in the interest of justice.—Defendant, not a doctor, but a sufferer from chronic fatigue syndrome and a founder of a "Medical Marijuana Buyer's club," distributed marijuana at cost to AIDS sufferers, in belief that it had beneficial effects, and possessed it for his own use in belief that its consumption ameliorated some of his medical conditions; despite claim that defendant acted out of a "mission of mercy," which was essentially uncontradicted, court denied motion to dismiss in the interest of justice. People v. Moore, 167 Misc. 2d 994, 637 N.Y.S.2d 652 (Crim. Ct. N.Y. Co. 1996).

Inference of knowledge.—A police officer's observation of a marijuana cigarette as well as cocaine in car seat, when defendant had been in driver's seat but companion in passenger seat fled at approach of police, accompanied by defendant's claim that only the marijuana was his, was a sufficient basis to infer defendant's knowledge. People v. Carpenter, 187 A.D.2d 519, 589 N.Y.S.2d 912 (2d Dept. 1992).

Inference of dominion and control.—Although significant quantities of marijuana were recovered from apartment in which defendant was sole occupant at time of police raid, there was no evidence that he resided there, frequented the apartment, or exercised dominion and control over the living room where the marijuana was found, when defendant was in the kitchen. People v. Dawkins, 136 A.D.2d 726, 524 N.Y.S.2d 64 (3d Dept. 1988).

Inference of possession.—Although the marijuana was recovered from a lady's handbag which was lying a few feet away from the defendant, a man, and defendant claimed that the marijuana belonged to the female apartment occupant, People's evidence established that a female regularly delivered quantities of marijuana to defendant in a handbag, and had done so on the day of his arrest. People v. Civitello, 152 A.D.2d 812, 543 N.Y.S.2d 1003 (3d Dept. 1989).

Illegal seizure of marijuana does not bar administrative disciplinary proceeding.—Charges dismissed against law enforcement officer in connection with recovery of marijuana from his vehicle; however, this did not bar department from discharging him after a hearing. Boyd v. Constantine, 81 N.Y.2d 189, 597 N.Y.S.2d 605, 613 N.E.2d 511 (1993), rev'g 180 A.D.2d 186, 586 N.Y.S.2d 439 (4th Dept. 1992).

Packaging of marijuana.—When police stopped a car in which defendant was driving, and observed a small manilla envelope on the floor, which upon being opened, was seen to contain plant-like material, despite the fact that the envelope was in plain view, there was no indicia of criminality in plain view, since the envelope, by itself, was innocuous; court did not find probable cause supported by officer's testimony that he often had seen marijuana carried in such envelopes. People v. Grovner, 172 A.D.2d 1035, 569 N.Y.S.2d 544 (4th Dept. 1991).

Possession incorporates growing marijuana.—Evidence that apartment, leased by defendant's brother, contained marijuana growing operation as well as a rolling machine, pipes and other paraphernalia, was sufficient to impute possession to defendant, who was present at time of police seizure. People v. Nelson, 165 A.D.2d 899, 560 N.Y.S.2d 364 (3d Dept. 1990).

—The offense of criminal possession of marijuana also prohibits growing marijuana which, if possession or dominion and control can be proved, would constitute possession. People v. Reynolds, 124 A.D.2d 356, 507 N.Y.S.2d 295 (3d Dept. 1986), aff'd, 71 N.Y.2d 552, 528 N.Y.S.2d 15, 523 N.E.2d 291 (1986).

—Growing of marijuana in an "open field" constituted a waiver of any privacy which anyone might expect to be constitutionally guaranteed by the Fourth Amendment; to do so, is to invite confiscation without a warrant. People v. Fillhart, 93 Misc. 2d 911, 403 N.Y.S.2d 642 (Jefferson Co. Ct. 1978).

§ 221.10. Criminal possession of marihuana in the fifth degree.

A person is guilty of criminal possession of marihuana in the fifth degree when he knowingly and unlawfully possesses:

1. marihuana in a public place, as defined in section 240.00 of this chapter, and such marihuana is burning or open to public view; or

2. one or more preparations, compounds, mixtures or substances containing marihuana and the preparations, compounds, mixtures or substances are of an aggregate weight of more than twenty-five grams.

Criminal possession of marihuana in the fifth degree is a class B misdemeanor.

Added by L. 1977, Ch. 360; **Amended** by L. 1979, Ch. 265; L. 1995, Ch. 75, § 10, amending subd. 2, eff. June 10, 1995.

Possession of "blunt."—The officer was entitled to take child into custody under Family Court Act § 305.2(2) on basis that he had probable cause to believe that she had committed a misdemeanor; officer observed a "blunt," which he knew was used to smoke marijuana, in her possession in plain view, in a public place, which supported the inference that she possessed marijuana. In re Camille H., 215 A.D.2d 143, 626 N.Y.S.2d 120 (1st Dept. 1995).

—Police observation of defendant standing with a group of men in a parking lot, discard an object, later identified as a "blunt," which he had by his mouth moments before throwing it on the ground, along with the "blunt" which was recovered, was sufficient to support the charge of criminal possession. People v. Robinson, 265 A.D.2d 812, 695 N.Y.S.2d 848 (4th Dept. 1999).

Public place.—The inside of a parked car on a Manhattan street may constitute a public place where the interior of the car was intentionally visible to members of the public to facilitate drug transactions. People v. Butler, 195 Misc. 2d 228, 757 N.Y.S.2d 674 (Crim. Ct. N.Y. Co. 2003).

§ 221.15. Criminal possession of marihuana in the fourth degree.

A person is guilty of criminal possession of marihuana in the fourth degree when he knowingly and unlawfully possesses one or more preparations, compounds, mixtures or substances containing marihuana and the preparations, compounds, mixtures or substances are of an aggregate weight of more than two ounces.

Criminal possession of marihuana in the fourth degree is a class A misdemeanor.

Added by L. 1977, Ch. 360; **Amended** by L. 1979, Ch. 265; L. 1995, Ch. 75, § 11, eff. June 10, 1995.

§ 221.20. Criminal possession of marihuana in the third degree.

A person is guilty of criminal possession of marihuana in the third degree when he knowingly and unlawfully possesses one or more preparations, compounds, mixtures or substances containing marihuana and the preparations, compounds, mixtures or substances are of an aggregate weight of more than eight ounces.

Criminal possession of marihuana in the third degree is a class E felony.

Added by L. 1977, Ch. 360; **Amended** by L. 1979, Ch. 265; L. 1995, Ch. 75, § 12, eff. June 10, 1995.

Conviction is basis for attorney discipline.—Attorney, possessing over eight ounces of marijuana plants, consisting of 110 plants, which he grew on farm land which he owned, was convicted of the federal offense of growing marijuana; he could have been convicted of possessory offense under state law; basis for suspension from practice of law. In re Proyect, 192 A.D.2d 868, 597 N.Y.S.2d 175 (3d Dept. 1993).

§ 221.25. Criminal possession of marihuana in the second degree.

A person is guilty of criminal possession of marihuana in the second degree when he knowingly and unlawfully possesses one or more preparations, compounds, mixtures or substances containing marihuana and the preparations, compounds, mixtures or substances are of an aggregate weight of more than sixteen ounces.

Criminal possession of marihuana in the second degree is a class D felony.

Added by L. 1977, Ch. 360; **Amended** by L. 1979, Ch. 265; L. 1995, Ch. 75, § 13, eff. June 10, 1995.

ANNOTATIONS

Constructive possession.—Proof that police observed co-defendant's apartment over a four month period on suspicion that drug trafficking occurred therein, from which defendant was seen to exit on two occasions, once in co-defendant's company, after which police entered the apartment, was insufficient proof of defendant's constructive possession of contraband recovered from the apartment; conviction for criminal possession of marijuana in the second degree and other charges reversed. People v. Hill, 182 A.D.2d 1087, 583 N.Y.S.2d 74 (4th Dept. 1992).

Aggregate weight: marijuana plants.—The requisite aggregate weight for conviction of criminal possession of marijuana in the second degree could be established by aggregate weight of marijuana plants, after dirt was removed from roots; the People did not have to prove pure weight. People v. Nelson, 144 A.D.2d 714, 535 N.Y.S.2d 132 (3d Dept. 1988).

—Aggregate weight of marijuana seized in various locations in the house had to be reduced by the weight of those portions over which defendant had not exercised dominion and control, effectively reducing amount for which defendant could be charged from over 16 ounces to in excess of eight ounces; conviction modified to criminal possession in the third. People v. Cicero, 106 A.D.2d 901, 483 N.Y.S.2d 545 (4th Dept. 1984), *cert. denied,* 472 U.S. 1003.

§ 221.30. Criminal possession of marihuana in the first degree.

A person is guilty of criminal possession of marihuana in the first degree when he knowingly and unlawfully possesses one or more preparations, compounds, mixtures or substances containing marihuana and the preparations, compounds, mixtures or substances are of an aggregate weight of more than ten pounds.

Criminal possession of marihuana in the first degree is a class C felony.

Added by L. 1977, Ch. 360; **Amended** by L. 1979, Ch. 265; L. 1995, Ch. 75, § 14, eff. June 10, 1995.

ANNOTATIONS

Inference of knowledge.—When police officer, disguised as U.P.S. delivery man, delivered package containing marijuana to defendant's house, and defendant accepted delivery, the People established inference that he knew what he took possession of; however, defendant met "slight burden" of rebutting the inference of knowledge on basis of his testimony that he noticed that the name of the addressee was spelled differently from his name, he wrote "turn to sender" on package, the package was not opened, and claimed that he was about to call U.P.S. to pick up the package when he was momentarily distracted by his wife and a friend. and a few minutes later police broke down his door and arrested him; conviction of criminal possession of marijuana in the first degree reversed and charge dismissed. People v. Walzer, 227 A.D.2d 945, 643 N.Y.S.2d 838 (4th Dept. 1996).

Large quantity of marijuana does not defeat exigency in support of no knock/all hours warrant.—The court rejected defendant's contention that a no knock, all hours warrant, should have been invalidated insofar as his possession of thirteen pounds of mrijuana and eight ounces of hashish could not be easily destroyed or removed. People v. Roxby, 224 A.D.2d 864, 638 N.Y.S.2d 215 (3d Dept. 1996).

Possession.—Conviction under PL § 221.30 was affirmed,

even though defendant never physically possessed the package containing marihuana addressed to him sent via UPS; defendant's attempts to retrieve package personally and his accompanying another who did actually receive package from UPS constituted constructive possession, in that defendant's actions established "satisfactory evidence that defendant exercised dominion and control over . . . the person who actually possessed the drugs" in order to support his conviction under statute. People v. Moore, 17 A.D.3d 786, 792 N.Y.S.2d 721 (3d Dept. 2005).

—While access to a vehicle by others does not necessarily foreclose a finding of constructive possession, the lack of any direct evidence linking defendant to marihuana in trunk placed a "heavy burden" on People to establish essential element; evidence of defendant's mere presence in vehicle where drugs are found is not sufficient evidence of constructive possession. People v. Burns, 17 A.D.3d 709, 792 N.Y.S.2d 700 (3d Dept. 2005).

§ 221.35. Criminal sale of marihuana in the fifth degree.

A person is guilty of criminal sale of marihuana in the fifth degree when he knowingly and unlawfully sells, without consideration, one or more preparations, compounds, mixtures or substances containing marihuana and the preparations, compounds, mixtures or substances are of an aggregate weight of two grams or less; or one cigarette containing marihuana.

Criminal sale of marihuana in the fifth degree is a class B misdemeanor.

Added by L. 1977, Ch. 360; **Amended** by L. 1979, Ch. 265; L. 1995, Ch. 75, § 15, eff. June 10, 1995, offenses committed before that date will be governed by laws in effect at the time the offenses were committed pursuant to L. 1995, Ch. 75, § 20.

§ 221.40. Criminal sale of marihuana in the fourth degree.

A person is guilty of criminal sale of marihuana in the fourth degree when he knowingly and unlawfully sells marihuana except as provided in section 221.35 of this article.

Criminal sale of marihuana in the fourth degree is a class A misdemeanor.

ANNOTATION

Medicinal use of marijuana.—Defendant, not a doctor, but a sufferer from chronic fatigue syndrome and a founder of a "Medical Marijuana Buyer's club," distributed marijuana at cost to AIDS sufferers, in belief that it had beneficial effects, and possessed it for his own use in belief that its consumption ameliorated some of his medical conditions; despite claim that defendant acted out of a "mission of mercy," which was essentially uncontradicted, court denied motion to dismiss in the interest of justice. People v. Moore, 167 Misc. 2d 994, 637 N.Y.S.2d 652 (N.Y.C. Crim. Ct. N.Y. Co. 1996).

§ 221.45. Criminal sale of marihuana in the third degree.

A person is guilty of criminal sale of marihuana in the third degree when he knowingly and unlawfully sells one or more preparations, compounds, mixtures or substances containing marihuana and the preparations, compounds, mixtures or substances are of an aggregate weight of more than twenty-five grams.

Criminal sale of marihuana in the third degree is a class E felony.

Added by L. 1977, Ch. 360; **Amended** by L. 1979, Ch. 265; L. 1995, Ch. 75, § 16, eff. June 10, 1995.

ANNOTATION

Agency defense unavailable.—Informant had smoked marijuana with defendant, which supported inference that defendant was representing the quality of the "crop," and informant indicated interest in purchasing some; a week later, informant telephoned defendant and arranged for a sale the following day; sale was undertaken without informant having to advance cash, which supported inference that defendant acted as entrepreneur rather than as informant's agent; defendant did not make subsequent sales, but defense of agency as to the single sale was defeated. People v. Rotundo, 194 A.D.2d 943, 599 N.Y.S.2d 322 (3d Dept. 1993).

§ 221.50. Criminal sale of marihuana in the second degree.

A person is guilty of criminal sale of marihuana in the second degree when he knowingly and unlawfully sells one or more preparations, compounds, mixtures or substances containing marihuana and the preparations, compounds, mixtures or substances are of an aggregate weight of more than four ounces, or knowingly and unlawfully sells one or more preparations, compounds, mixtures or substances containing marihuana to a person less than eighteen years of age.

Criminal sale of marihuana in the second degree is a class D felony.

Added by L. 1977, Ch. 360; **Amended** by L. 1979, Ch. 265; L. 1995, Ch. 75, § 17, eff. June 10, 1995.

ANNOTATION

Knowledge element relates to weight, rather than age.— Although the People must prove that defendant sold the requisite weight of marijuana to someone less than eighteen years of age, the element of knowledge relates to the weight; there is no element that defendant must know of the buyer's age; hence, it was not error to decline to instruct the jury that the People had to prove defendant's knowledge of age. People v. Wenzel, 77 A.D.2d 715, 430 N.Y.S.2d 431 (3d Dept. 1980).

§ 221.55. Criminal sale of marihuana in the first degree.

A person is guilty of criminal sale of marihuana in the first degree when he knowingly and unlawfully sells one or more preparations, compounds, mixtures or substances containing marihuana and the preparations, compounds, mixtures or substances are of an aggregate weight of more than sixteen ounces.

Criminal sale of marihuana in the first degree is a class C felony.

Added by L. 1977, Ch. 360; **Amended** by L. 1979, Ch. 265; L. 1995, Ch. 75, § 18, eff. June 10, 1995.

ARTICLE 225—GAMBLING OFFENSES

LexisNexis Cross Reference

New York Criminal Practice (2d ed.), Vol. 7, Ch. 76, Gambling Related Offenses.

§ 225.00. Gambling offenses; definitions of terms.

The following definitions are applicable to this article:

1. "Contest of chance" means any contest, game, gaming scheme or gaming device in which the outcome depends in a material degree upon an element of chance, notwithstanding that skill of the contestants may also be a factor therein.

2. "Gambling." A person engages in gambling when he stakes or risks something of value upon the outcome of a contest of chance or a future contingent event not under his control or influence, upon an agreement or understanding that he will receive something of value in the event of a certain outcome.

3. "Player" means a person who engages in any form of gambling solely as a contestant or bettor, without receiving or becoming entitled to receive any profit therefrom other than personal gambling winnings, and without otherwise rendering any material assistance to the establishment, conduct or operation of the particular gambling activity. A person who gambles at a social game of chance on equal terms with the other participants therein does not otherwise render material assistance to the establishment, conduct or operation thereof by performing, without fee or remuneration, acts directed toward the arrangement or facilitation of the game, such as inviting persons to play, permitting the use of premises therefor and supplying cards or other equipment used therein. A person who engages in "bookmaking", as defined in this section is not a "player."

4. "Advance gambling activity." A person "advances gambling activity" when, acting other than as a player, he engages in conduct which materially aids any form of gambling activity. Such conduct includes but is not limited to conduct directed towards the creation or establishment of the particular game, contest, scheme, device or activity involved, toward the acquisition or maintenance of premises, paraphernalia, equipment or apparatus therefor, toward the solicitation or inducement of persons to participate therein, toward the actual conduct of the playing phases thereof, toward the arrangement of any of its financial or recording phases, or toward any other phase of its operation. One advances gambling activity when, having substantial proprietary or other authoritative control over premises being used with his knowledge for purposes of gambling activity, he permits such to occur or continue or makes no effort to prevent its occurrence or continuation.

5. "Profit from gambling activity." A person "profits from gambling activity" when, other than as a player, he accepts or receives money or other property pursuant to an agreement or understanding with any person whereby he participates or is to participate in the proceeds of gambling activity.

6. "Something of value" means any money or property, any token, object or article exchangeable for money or property, or any form of credit or promise directly or indirectly contemplating transfer of money or property or of any interest therein, or involving extension of a service, entertainment or a privilege of playing at a game or scheme without charge.

7. "Gambling device" means any device, machine, paraphernalia or equipment which is used or usable in the playing phases of any gambling activity, whether such activity consists of gambling between persons or gambling by a person involving the playing of a machine. Notwithstanding the foregoing, lottery tickets, policy slips and other items used in the playing phases of lottery and policy schemes are not gambling devices.

7-a. A "coin operated gambling device" means a gambling device which operates as a result of the insertion of something of value. A device designed, constructed or readily adaptable or convertible for such use is a coin operated gambling device notwithstanding the fact that it may require adjustment, manipulation or repair in order to operate as such.

8. "Slot machine" means a gambling device which, as a result of the insertion of a coin or other object, operates, either completely automatically or with the aid of some physical act by the player, in such manner that, depending upon elements of chance, it may eject something of value. A device so constructed, or readily adaptable or convertible to such use, is no less a slot machine because it is not in working order or because some mechanical act of manipulation or repair is required to accomplish its adaptation, conversion or workability. Nor is it any less a slot machine because, apart from its use or adaptability as such, it may also sell or deliver something of value on a basis other than chance. A machine which sells items of merchandise which are of equivalent value, is not a slot machine merely because such items differ from each other in composition, size, shape or color. A machine which awards free or extended play is not a slot machine merely because such free or extended play may constitute something of value provided that the outcome depends in a material degree upon the skill of the player and not in a material degree upon an element of chance.

9. "Bookmaking" means advancing gambling activity by unlawfully accepting bets from members of the public as a business, rather than in a casual or personal fashion, upon the outcomes of future contingent events.

10. "Lottery" means an unlawful gambling scheme in which (a) the players pay or agree to pay something of value for chances, represented and differentiated by numbers or by combinations of numbers or by some other media, one or more of which chances are to be designated the winning ones; and (b) the winning chances are to be determined by a drawing or by some other method based upon the element of chance; and (c) the holders of the winning chances are to receive something of value provided, however, that in no event shall the provisions of this subdivision be construed to include a raffle as such term is defined in subdivision three-b of section one hundred eighty-six of the general municipal law.

11. "Policy" or "the numbers game" means a form of lottery in which the winning chances or plays are not determined upon the basis of a drawing or other act on the part of persons conducting or connected with the scheme, but upon the basis of the outcome or outcomes of a future contingent event or events otherwise unrelated to the particular scheme.

12. "Unlawful" means not specifically authorized by law.

Amended by L. 1967, Ch. 791; L. 1987, Ch. 632; L. 1994, Ch. 550, § 1, eff. Jan. 22, 1995, amending subd. 10.

ANNOTATIONS

Lottery.—Game known as "Quick Draw" had all essential elements of a lottery: player tenders money for a numerical selection, winning numbers are randomly drawn, and if numbers match, player wins prize; official sponsorship of the game was within Article I, § 9(1) of the N.Y. Constitution. Trump v. Perlee, 228 A.D.2d 367, 644 N.Y.S.2d 270 (1st Dept. 1996).

Shell game.—A shell game, in which the defendant was seen manipulating bottle tops on top of a box with his hands and encouraging passersby to place five dollar bets, is a game of chance rather than a game of skill; the dealer, rather than the player, controls the game with consummate skill at creating an illusion, but the dealer's skill, while it may influence the player's decisions, cannot predict the player's selection. People v. Turner, 165 Misc. 2d 222, 629 N.Y.S.2d 661 (Crim. Ct. N.Y. Co. 1995); but see People v. Hunt, 162 Misc. 2d 70, 616 N.Y.S.2d 168 (Crim. Ct. N.Y. Co. 1994) (three card monte, absent trickery or deception, is game of skill rather than game of chance).

Out-of-state lottery.—The sale of out-of-state lottery tickets in New York, even if the lottery is legal where conducted, is not authorized under New York Constitution, and is basis for violation of New York gambling laws. People v. Kim, 154 Misc. 2d 346, 585 N.Y.S.2d 310 (Crim. Ct. Bronx Co. 1992).

Gambling device.—"Joker poker" machine, a video game with which player can play poker, the outcome of which depends in material degree on chance, and win credits, which have no intrinsic value but can be exchanged with the proprietor for cash, is a gambling device. Plato's Cave Corp. v. State Liquor Auth., 68 N.Y.2d 791, 506 N.Y.S.2d 856, 498 N.E.2d 420 (1986).

—Joker poker machine, when winning player would fill out receipt indicating number of credits won, for which he would be given a certain amount of money per credit, would be a gambling device. People v. Herman, 133 A.D.2d 377, 519 N.Y.S.2d 550 (2d Dept. 1987).

—Since a machine which only provides receipts for lottery bets, which is not a lottery ticket vending machine, is not itself the instrumentality of the gambling, it is not a gambling device. People v. Kim, 154 Misc. 2d 346, 585 N.Y.S.2d 310 (Crim. Ct. Bronx Co. 1992).

—Monte cards constitute gambling device. People v. Brown, 112 Misc. 2d 471, 447 N.Y.S.2d 129 (Crim. Ct. N.Y. Co. 1982).

§ 225.05. Promoting gambling in the second degree.

A person is guilty of promoting gambling in the second degree when he knowingly advances or profits from unlawful gambling activity.

Promoting gambling in the second degree is a class A misdemeanor.

ANNOTATIONS

Advances gambling activity.—"Knowingly advances" is an alternative element to "knowingly profits". People v. Giordano, 87 N.Y.2d 441, 640 N.Y.S.2d 432, 663 N.E.2d 588 (1995).

—Evidence that defendant directed a gambling patron to co-defendant's gambling enterprise, and acted as a "sheet writer" for that patron, accepting the patron's bets from which defendant received a commission, established that defendant shared co-defendant's criminal intent as an accessory. People v. Tomasello, 189 A.D.2d 903, 593 N.Y.S.2d 65 (2d Dept. 1993).

—Tavern owner who maintained "joker poker" machine, and who paid cash to winner of game in proportion to the number of credits he achieved, was promoting gambling in the second degree. People v. Herman, 133 A.D.2d 377, 519 N.Y.S.2d 550 (2d Dept. 1987).

—Where defendant was sitting in close proximity to slips which police officer recognized to be mutuel horse racing policy slips, and accepted a one dollar bet, defendant acted other than as a player and evidence clearly indicated that, considering his conduct and proximity to policy slips, defendant was rendering material assistance to the conduct or operation of a gambling enterprise. People v. Hernandez, 145 Misc. 2d 962, 548 N.Y.S.2d 853 (Crim. Ct. N.Y. Co. 1989); *cf.* People v. Cea, 141 Misc. 2d 234, 533 N.Y.S.2d 239 (Crim. Ct. N.Y. Co. 1988) (bare allegation that defendant exercised dominion and control over area containing slot machine and gambling records was insufficient to support charge).

—Defendant acted in concert to promote gambling in the second degree by aiding monte players by acting as lookout, even though he did not possess the cards or hold the money. People v. Brown, 112 Misc. 2d 471, 447 N.Y.S.2d 129 (Crim. Ct. N.Y. Co. 1982).

Gambling records recovered from third party which implicate defendant.—Gambling records recovered from co-defendant which implicated defendant as a "sheet writer" were hearsay; however, error was harmless in view of overwhelming independent evidence. People v. Tomasello, 189 A.D.2d 903, 593 N.Y.S.2d 65 (2d Dept. 1993).

Defendant as gambler.—Defendant's arrest and subsequent frisk, which revealed the weapon in this weapons possession case, could not be upheld on the basis of evidence which failed to establish that defendant acted other than a mere player in dice game, and did not even establish that he had possessed the dice, so that he was not guilty of a crime related to gambling; arrest and frisk upheld on other bases. People v. King, 102 A.D.2d 710, 476 N.Y.S.2d 847 (1st Dept. 1984), *aff'd,* 65 N.Y.2d 702, 492 N.Y.S.2d 1, 481 N.E.2d 541 (1985).

—Evidence which indicated that defendant placed his own wagers was legally insufficient to support defendant's conviction of promoting gambling in the second degree; an individual placing his own bet is not proscribed; rather, offense is an individual advancing gambling or profiting therefrom by placing bets for other persons. People v. Tomasello, 189 A.D.2d 903, 593 N.Y.S.2d 65 (2d Dept. 1993).

Sale of out-of-state lottery tickets in New York.—The sale of out-of-state lottery tickets in New York, even if the lottery is legal where conducted, is not authorized under New York Constitution, and therefore is an illegal promotion of gambling. People v. Kim, 154 Misc. 2d 346, 585 N.Y.S.2d 310 (Crim. Ct. Bronx Co. 1992).

Gambling activities on Native American reservation.—Federal law does not preempt state's criminal law with respect to gambling activities on reservations; unless gambling activities are explicitly authorized by state law, on reservation they are illegal. People v. Snyder, 141 Misc. 2d 444, 532 N.Y.S.2d 827 (Co. Ct. Erie Co. 1988).

Conviction as basis for attorney discipline.—An attorney's conviction for promoting gambling in the second degree is a basis for suspension from practice. *In re* Bayer, 135 A.D.2d 338, 526 N.Y.S.2d 15 (2d Dept. 1988).

Lookout; three card monte.—A lookout who yelled "police" to three card monte players who fled with the cards and money was criminally liable as a principal in promoting gambling. People v. Brown, 112 Misc. 2d 471, 447 N.Y.S.2d 129 (Crim. Ct. N.Y. Co. 1982).

Repugnant verdict.—Where the jury found that defendant had not knowingly maintained financial records of a bookmaking scheme or enterprise (PL § 225.05), it was repugnant to find defendant guilty of knowingly possessing "writings, papers, instruments or articles of a kind commonly used in the operation or promotion of a bookmaking scheme or enterprise, representing more than five bets totaling more than $5,000" (PL § 225.20(1)), since a person who does not knowingly maintain gambling records, cannot be found to have knowingly intended to possess the same. People v. Kramer, 70 A.D.2d 888, 417 N.Y.S.2d 97 (2d Dept. 1979).

§ 225.10. Promoting gambling in the first degree.

A person is guilty of promoting gambling in the first degree when he knowingly advances or profits from unlawful gambling activity by:

1. Engaging in bookmaking to the extent that he receives or accepts in any one day more than

five bets totaling more than five thousand dollars; or

2. Receiving, in connection with a lottery or policy scheme or enterprise, (a) money or written records from a person other than a player whose chances or plays are represented by such money or records, or (b) more than five hundred dollars in any one day of money played in such scheme or enterprise.

Promoting gambling in the first degree is a class E felony.

ANNOTATIONS

Defendant is "sheet writer."—Evidence was replete with instances of defendant's participation in a gambling operation, including audiotaped phone calls, and gambling records, indicating that defendant was a "sheet writer" who steered bettors to the operation and profited from their losses. People v. Brady, 189 A.D.2d 884, 592 N.Y.S.2d 763 (2d Dept. 1993).

Dismissal of charges does not require return of property.—Even though charge of promoting gambling in the first degree and possession of gambling records in the first degree, was dismissed, the police department would not be compelled to return to the defendant money, gambling records, and a tape recorder, telephone and computer equipment used in connection with gambling activities, which had been seized from defendant's residence. Property Clerk, New York City Police Department v. Hurd, 130 Misc. 2d 358, 496 N.Y.S.2d 197 (Sup. Ct. N.Y. Co. 1985).

Geographic jurisdiction in county.—When bookmaking operation was located in New York County, and only contact with Nassau County was that defendants would occasionally "hedge" their bets placed in New York County, by telephone from New York County to Nassau County, Nassau County had geographic jurisdiction on basis that gambling activity was advanced in Nassau County; aggravating element was a separate element and was not required for purposes of geographic jurisdiction. People v. Giordano, 87 N.Y.2d 441, 640 N.Y.S.2d 432, 663 N.E.2d 588 (1995).

—Conviction for promoting gambling in first degree affirmed on basis that county had geographic jurisdiction on basis of inter-county phone conversation; wire room operation was conducted in Queens County, but defendant supervised operation by telephone from his home in Nassau County; although Queens County wire room accepted in excess of five bets totalling more than $5,000 daily, surveillance evidence did not indicate that defendant, in Nassau County, had participated in more than five bets totalling more than $5,000 daily, the threshold elements of promoting gambling in the first degree; however, under PL § 20.40, defendant could have been prosecuted for the complete crime in Nassau County, inasmuch as at least one element of the offense (knowingly advancing gambling activity) occurred in Nassau County, notwithstanding that aggravating element enhancing degree of the offense occurred elsewhere. People v. Botta, 100 A.D.2d 311, 474 N.Y.S.2d 72 (2d Dept. 1984).

Attachment of assets of gambling operation.—Upon defendant's conviction for promoting gambling in the first degree and related offenses, District Attorney had basis to seek attachment of some $15 million in assets relating to the gambling operation; the order of attachment did not place defendant, who already had been convicted and sentenced, in double jeopardy. District Attorney v. Iadarola, 164 Misc. 2d 204, 623 N.Y.S.2d 999 (Sup. Ct. Kings Co.), *aff'd,* 634 N.Y.S.2d 738 (2d Dept. 1995), *cert. denied,* 517 U.S. 1209 (1996).

Conviction as basis for attorney discipline.—An attorney's conviction of attempted promotion of gambling in the first degree was a basis to censure the attorney. *In re* Constantino, 89 A.D.2d 248, 455 N.Y.S.2d 93 (2d Dept. 1982).

Four-year concurrent sentences for gambling are excessive.—Sentencing a defendant convicted after trial of promoting gambling and possession of gambling records to concurrent indeterminate terms of four years on such felony counts is excessive. Sentence reduced to concurrent indeterminate terms of three years in State Prison. People v. DiPaolo, 37 Misc. 2d 823, 325 N.Y.S.2d 190 (1st Dept. 1971).

Written records.—The evidence was sufficient to show that defendant received written records "from a person other than a player" when it was shown that at least one of the slips handed to him was a "collector's slip" (one made by an individual who receives and records bets from players). People v. Paranzino, 40 N.Y.2d 1005, 391 N.Y.S.2d 391, 359 N.E.2d 981 (1976).

§ 225.15. Possession of gambling records in the second degree.

A person is guilty of possession of gambling records in the second degree when, with knowledge of the contents or nature thereof, he possesses any writing, paper, instrument or article:

1. Of a kind commonly used in the operation or promotion of a bookmaking scheme or enterprise; or

2. Of a kind commonly used in the operation, promotion or playing of a lottery or policy scheme or enterprise; except that in any prosecution under this subdivision, it is a defense that the writing, paper, instrument or article possessed by the defendant constituted, reflected or represented plays, bets or chances of the defendant himself in a number not exceeding ten.

3. Of any paper or paper product in sheet form chemically converted to nitrocellulose having explosive characteristics.

4. Of any water soluble paper or paper derivative in sheet form.

Possession of gambling records in the second degree is a class A misdemeanor.

Amended by L. 1969, Ch. 974.

ANNOTATIONS

Receipts for out-of-state lottery.—Since selling lottery tickets in New York in connection with an out-of-state lottery is an illegal promotion of gambling under New York law, even if the lottery is legal where conducted, the possession of receipts related to that lottery is illegal possession of gambling records. People v. Kim, 154 Misc. 2d 346, 585 N.Y.S.2d 310 (Crim. Ct. Bronx Co. 1992).

Intercepted conversations as basis for warrant.—When police intercepted conversations including defendant pursuant to an eavesdropping warrant predicated on defendant's narcotics activity, and conversations also alluded to defendant's gambling activities, which had not been specified in the warrant application, the evidence was validly received in prosecution for promoting gambling in the second degree, and no retroactive amendment of the warrant was required. People v. Mastrodonato, 75 N.Y.2d 18, 550 N.Y.S.2d 580, 549 N.Y.S.2d 1151 (1989).

Dominion and control.—When defendant was sitting alone, behind a glass counter, within arm's length of 21 slips of paper which the undercover officer recognized to be mutuel horse racing policy slips, and then accepted a one dollar bet from the undercover officer, he exercised sufficient dominion and control over the location of the slips to constitute possession of gambling records in the second degree. People v. Hernandez, 145 Misc. 2d 962, 548 N.Y.S.2d 853 (Crim. Ct. N.Y. Co. 1989). *Compare with* People v. Cea, 141 Misc. 2d 234, 533 N.Y.S.2d 239 (Crim. Ct. N.Y. Co. 1988) (bare allegation that defendant exercised dominion and control over area containing slot machine and gambling records was insufficient to support charge).

Attachment of assets of gambling operation.—Upon defendant's conviction for promoting gambling in the first degree and related offenses, District Attorney had basis to seek attachment of some $15 million in assets relating to the gambling operation; the order of attachment did not place defendant, who already had been convicted and sentenced, in double jeopardy.

District Attorney v. Iadarola, 164 Misc. 2d 204, 623 N.Y.S.2d 999 (S. Ct. Kings Co. 1995), *aff'd*, 634 N.Y.S.2d 738 (2d Dept. 1995), *cert. denied*, 517 U.S. 1209 (1996).

Conviction as basis for professional discipline.—Licensed practical nurse could be suspended on basis of conviction for possession of gambling records in the second degree, notwithstanding issuance of certificate of relief from disabilities in the interim. Pietranico v. Ambach, 82 A.D.2d 625, 442 N.Y.S.2d 827 (3d Dept. 1981), *aff'd*, 55 N.Y.2d 861, 447 N.Y.S.2d 924, 432 N.E.2d 796 (1982).

§ 225.20. Possession of gambling records in the first degree.

A person is guilty of possession of gambling records in the first degree when, with knowledge of the contents thereof, he possesses any writing, paper, instrument or article:

1. Of a kind commonly used in the operation or promotion of a bookmaking scheme or enterprise, and constituting, reflecting or representing more than five bets totaling more than five thousand dollars; or

2. Of a kind commonly used in the operation, promotion or playing of a lottery or policy scheme or enterprise, and constituting, reflecting or representing more than five hundred plays or chances therein.

Possession of gambling records in the first degree is a class E felony.

ANNOTATIONS

Gambling records.—Records recovered from defendant's home documenting in excess of $6000 in bets were of a kind commonly used in gambling; jury could infer that defendant intended to use the records in the operation of a bookmaking scheme. People v. Brady, 189 A.D.2d 884, 592 N.Y.S.2d 763 (2d Dept. 1993).

Dominion and control.—Defendant's constructive possession was proved by evidence that defendant headed a numbers operation, and that the co-defendant found in possession of the gambling records worked under and in concert with him, and received the seized evidence on defendant's behalf. People v. Passero, 83 A.D.2d 769, 443 N.Y.S.2d 481 (4th Dept. 1981).

Compelled disclosure of hand writing exemplars in connection with gambling records.—CPL § 240.40(2)(b)(vi) provides for non-testimonial disclosure of hand writing exemplars, in this case to connect defendants with gambling records; however, prosecutor had filed only a felony complaint charging defendants with possession of gambling records in first degree, which essentially is of a hearsay nature, and is not one of the accusatory instruments enumerated in § 240, which is strictly construed; court lacked jurisdiction to consider application until there was a pending indictment or information. People v. Hunce, 141 Misc. 2d 401, 533 N.Y.S.2d 204 (Crim. Ct. Bronx Co. 1988).

Dismissal of charges does not require return of property.—Even though charge of promoting gambling in the first degree and possession of gambling records in the first degree, was dismissed, the police department would not be compelled to return to the defendant money, gambling records, and a tape recorder, telephone and computer equipment used in connection with gambling activities, which had been seized from defendant's residence. Property Clerk, New York City Police Department v. Hurd, 130 Misc. 2d 358, 496 N.Y.S.2d 197 (Sup. Ct. N.Y. Co. 1985).

Attachment of assets of gambling operation.—Upon defendant's conviction for promoting gambling in the first degree and related offenses, District Attorney had basis to seek attachment of some $15 million in assets relating to the gambling operation; the order of attachment did not place defendant, who already had been convicted and sentenced, in double jeopardy. District Attorney v. Iadarola, 164 Misc. 2d 204, 623 N.Y.S.2d

999 (Sup. Ct. Kings Co.), *aff'd,* 634 N.Y.S.2d 738 (2d Dept.), *lv. denied,* 87 N.Y.2d 903 (1995), *cert. denied,* 116 S. Ct. 1825 (1996).

Indictment.—Indictment, charging defendant with possession of gambling records in the first degree (PL § 225.20(1)) was jurisdictionally defective where it lacked an allegation that he possessed the alleged gambling records "with knowledge of the contents thereof"; the fact that the indictment recited that it charged a violation of PL § 225.20(1) did not cure the defect. People v. Colloca, 57 A.D.2d 1039, 395 N.Y.S.2d 811 (4th Dept. 1977).

Possession—It was reversible error for the court to charge that possession under PL § 10.00(8) "can also mean that the items are so situated that the defendant can readily seize it or can otherwise exercise dominion or control over such property even when he does not have it in his physical possession;" "Possess" means to have physical possession or otherwise to exercise dominion or control over tangible property. People v. Lowrance, 65 A.D.2d 531, 409 N.Y.S.2d 227 (1st Dept. 1978).

—Defendant's conviction was sustained where the testimony of three accomplices corroborated by the physical evidence and the testimony of three police officers, one of whom qualified as an expert on illegal gambling established that he had constructive possession of the numbers records. People v. Passero, 83 A.D.2d 769, 443 N.Y.S.2d 481 (4th Dept. 1981).

Repugnant verdict.—Where the jury found that defendant had not knowingly maintained financial records of a bookmaking scheme or enterprise (PL § 225.05), it was repugnant to find defendant guilty of knowingly possessing "writings, papers, instruments or articles of a kind commonly used in the operation or promotion of a bookmaking scheme or enterprise, representing more than five bets totaling more than $5,000" (PL § 225.20(1)), since a person who does not knowingly maintain gambling records, cannot be found to have knowingly intended to possess the same. People v. Kramer, 70 A.D.2d 888, 417 N.Y.S.2d 97 (2d Dept. 1979).

§ 225.25. Possession of gambling records; defense.

In any prosecution for possession of gambling records, it is a defense that the writing, paper, instrument or article possessed by the defendant was neither used nor intended to be used in the operation or promotion of a bookmaking scheme or enterprise, or in the operation, promotion or playing of a lottery or policy scheme or enterprise.

ANNOTATION

Failure to give jury instruction.—When defendant was charged with possession of gambling records in the first degree, and promoting gambling in the second degree, on a constructive possession theory, the trial court erred in failing to charge the statutory defense upon defendant's request. People v. Sztuk, 126 A.D.2d 950, 511 N.Y.S.2d 720 (4th Dept.), *lv. denied,* 69 N.Y.2d 887 (1987).

§ 225.30. Possession of a gambling device.

a. A person is guilty of possession of a gambling device when, with knowledge of the character thereof, he or she manufactures, sells, transports, places or possesses, or conducts or negotiates any transaction affecting or designed to affect ownership, custody or use of:

1. A slot machine, unless such possession is permitted pursuant to article nine-A of the general municipal law; or

2. Any other gambling device, believing that the same is to be used in the advancement of unlawful gambling activity; or

3. A coin operated gambling device with intent

to use such device in the advancement of unlawful gambling activity.

b. Possession of a slot machine shall not be unlawful where such possession and use is pursuant to a gaming compact, duly executed by the governor and an Indian tribe or Nation, under the Indian Gaming Regulatory Act, as codified at 25 U.S.C. §§ 2701–2721 and 18 U.S.C. §§ 1166–1168, where the use of such slot machine or machines is consistent with such gaming compact and where the state receives a negotiated percentage of the net drop (defined as gross money wagered after payout, but before expenses) from any such slot machine or machines.

c. Transportation and possession of a slot machine shall not be unlawful where such transportation and possession is necessary to facilitate the training of persons in the repair and reconditioning of such machines as are used or are to be used for operations in those casinos authorized pursuant to a tribal-state compact as provided for pursuant to section eleven hundred seventy-two of title fifteen of the United States Code in the state of New York.

Possession of a gambling device is a class A misdemeanor.

Amended by L. 1987, Ch. 632; L. 2001, Ch. 383, Part B, § 4, eff. Oct. 29, 2001; L. 2003, Ch. 498, § 1, eff. Oct. 9, 2003, adding subd. c.

ANNOTATIONS

Machine which provides receipts.—Since a machine which only provides receipts for lottery bets, which is not a lottery ticket vending machine, is not itself the instrumentality of the gambling, it is not a gambling device. People v. Kim, 154 Misc. 2d 346, 585 N.Y.S.2d 831 (N.Y.C. Crim. Ct. Bronx Co. 1992).

Conviction as basis for attorney discipline.—An attorney's conviction for possession of a gambling device is a basis for suspension from practice. *In re* Bayer, 135 A.D.2d 338, 526 N.Y.S.2d 15 (2d Dept. 1988).

Joker poker machine.—When tavern owner maintained a joker poker machine on the premises, he possessed a gambling device. People v. Herman, 133 A.D.2d 377, 519 N.Y.S.2d 550 (2d Dept.), *lv. denied,* 70 N.Y.2d 932 (1987).

Lookout for monte game.—Even though defendant did not possess the monte cards, and acted only as lookout, nevertheless, he was guilty of acting in concert to possess a gambling device. People v. Brown, 112 Misc. 2d 471, 447 N.Y.S.2d 129 (N.Y.C. Crim. Ct. N.Y. Co. 1982).

Search warrant; probable cause.—Without regard to information obtained by a "pen register" used without judicial authorization, there was adequate evidence to establish probable cause for the defendant's arrest and for the seizure of his briefcase during a search of his two apartments. People v. Magaril, 31 N.Y.2d 802, 339 N.Y.S.2d 458, 291 N.E.2d 583 (1972).

§ 225.32. Possession of a gambling device; defenses.

1. In any prosecution for possession of a gambling device specified in subdivision one of section 225.30 of this chapter, it is an affirmative defense that: (a) the slot machine possessed by the defendant was neither used nor intended to be used in the operation or promotion of unlawful gambling activity or enterprise and that such slot machine is an antique; for purposes of this section

proof that a slot machine was manufactured prior to nineteen hundred forty-one shall be conclusive proof that such a machine is an antique; (b) the slot machine possessed by the defendant was manufactured or assembled by the defendant for the sole purpose of transporting such slot machine in a sealed container to a jurisdiction outside this state for purposes which are lawful in such outside jurisdiction; (c) the slot machine possessed by the defendant was neither used nor intended to be used in the operation or promotion of unlawful gambling activity or enterprise, is more than thirty years old, and such possession takes place in the defendant's home; or (d) the slot machine was transported into this state in a sealed container for the purpose of product development, research, or additional manufacture or assembly, and such slot machine will be or has been transported in a sealed container to a jurisdiction outside of this state for purposes which are lawful in such outside jurisdiction.

2. Where a defendant raises an affirmative defense provided by subdivision one hereof, any slot machine seized from the defendant shall not be destroyed, or otherwise altered until a final court determination is rendered. In a final determination rendered in favor of said defendant, such slot machine shall be returned, forthwith, to said defendant, notwithstanding any provisions of law to the contrary.

Added by L. 1979, Ch. 526; **Amended** by L. 1983, Ch. 676; L. 1997, Ch. 619, eff. Nov. 1, 1997; L. 1998, Ch. 346, § 1, eff. Nov. 1, 1998.

§ 225.35. Gambling offenses; presumptions.

1. Proof of possession of any gambling device or of any gambling record specified in sections 225.15 and 225.20, is presumptive evidence of possession thereof with knowledge of its character or contents.

2. In any prosecution under this article in which it is necessary to prove the occurrence of a sporting event, a published report of its occurrence in any daily newspaper, magazine or other periodically printed publication of general circulation shall be admissible in evidence and shall constitute presumptive proof of the occurrence of such event.

3. Possession of three or more coin operated gambling devices or possession of a coin operated gambling device in a public place shall be presumptive evidence of intent to use in the advancement of unlawful gambling activity.

Amended by L. 1987, Ch. 632.

ANNOTATIONS

Presumptions.—Recovery of gambling records from defendant's home, documenting bets in excess of $6000, was presumptive evidence that defendant possessed them with knowledge of their character. People v. Brady, 189 A.D.2d 884, 592 N.Y.S.2d 763 (2d Dept.), *lv. denied,* 81 N.Y.2d 882 (1993).

Constructive knowledge.—The trial court found defendant guilty of promoting gambling, second degree, and possession of gambling records, first degree, based on the statutory provision that possession of gambling records is presumptive evidence of knowledge of their contents (PL § 225.35), and the fact that defendant was in exclusive dominion of the apartment in her bedroom (PL § 225.20) where the trial evidence revealed that on a single day one or two bets were placed over the telephone in her apartment with a co-defendant who was acquitted for lack of proof. People v. Hodson, 50 A.D.2d 871, 377 N.Y.S.2d 145 (2d Dept. 1975).

Gambling records; possession; presumption.—The jury could well conclude that the defendant was fully aware of what the envelope contained in view of the fact that the defendant was seen in actual possession of the envelope containing the seized gambling slips; that he had been observed frequently entering and leaving the apartment used to conduct a gambling business but did not reside there; and that racing forms and other items generally associated with gambling were found therein. People v. Paranzino, 40 N.Y.2d 1005, 391 N.Y.S.2d 391, 359 N.E.2d 981 (1976).

—Presumption that person possessing gambling records has knowledge of their character and contents is merely permissive, and it was reversible error where court's charge implied that such presumption was conclusive. People v. Couvertier, 52 A.D.2d 772, 383 N.Y.S.2d 1 (1st Dept. 1976).

§ 225.40. Lottery offenses; no defense.

Any offense defined in this article which consists of the commission of acts relating to a lottery is no less criminal because the lottery itself is drawn or conducted without the state and is not violative of the laws of the jurisdiction in which it was so drawn or conducted.

ARTICLE 230—PROSTITUTION OFFENSES

LexisNexis Cross Reference

New York Criminal Practice (2d ed.), Vol. 7. Ch. 77, Prostitution and Offenses Against Public Sensibilities.

§ 230.00. Prostitution.

A person is guilty of prostitution when such person engages or agrees or offers to engage in sexual conduct with another person in return for a fee.

Prostitution is a class B Misdemeanor. [*]

[*] As originally enacted.

Amended by L. 1969, Ch. 169.

ANNOTATIONS

Entrapment.—Although a defendant may assert the affirmative defense of entrapment, the defense does not vary on the basis that the defendant is charged with patronizing a prostitute, and he still must prove the affirmative defense by a preponderance of the evidence; where the defendant denied having agreed to pay money to the undercover officer in exchange for sex, there was no reasonable view of the evidence establishing entrapment. People v. Brown, 82 N.Y.2d 869, 609 N.Y.S.2d 164, 631 N.E.2d 106 (1993).

Jury trial.—Prostitution related misdemeanors punishable by not more than six months incarceration are not "serious crimes" within the meaning of the Sixth Amendment, so that New York City policy of requiring a non-jury trial was not unconstitutional. Morgenthau v. Erlbaum, 59 N.Y.2d 143, 464 N.Y.S.2d 392, 451 N.E.2d 150, cert. denied, 464 US 993 (1983).

Communicating acceptance of an offer.—When an undercover officer discussed fee arrangements with a third party, and defendant nodded in agreement, defendant entered the van with the undercover officer; when the officer indicated that he did not want to get "shortchanged," the defendant responded, "no problem, you'll have a good time," effectively communicating that sex would be exchanged for the fee. In re Marco, 158 A.D.2d 342, 551 N.Y.S.2d 204 (1st Dept. 1990).

Fee negotiated by third party.—When a third party made the offer to the undercover officer, but defendant nodded his head in agreement, and the defendant was to provide the sex, defendant was guilty of prostitution. In re Marco, 158 A.D.2d 342, 551 N.Y.S.2d 204 (1st Dept. 1990).

Constitutionality.—Declaratory judgment action challenging constitutionality of prostitution offenses on basis that the Penal Law therein interfered with private commercial relations between consenting adults, dismissed for lack of plaintiffs' standing; female plaintiff was a prostitute, but she could demonstrate no commercial injury; male plaintiff patronized prostitutes, but he could show no aggrievement in the sense that the existence of the law had not stopped him from patronizing prostitutes; neither plaintiff had been arrested. Cherry v. Koch, 126 A.D.2d 346, 514 N.Y.S.2d 30 (2d Dept. 1987), lv. denied, 70 N.Y.2d 603.

—There is no constitutional right of privacy to use public places to agree to engage in sexual acts in exchange for a fee. In re Dora P., 68 A.D.2d 719, 418 N.Y.S.2d 597 (3d Dept. 1979).

—Even though PL Article 230 does not define the term "sexual conduct," it has commonly understood definition, so that statutory utilization of the term was not unconstitutionally vague. People v. Costello, 90 Misc. 2d 431, 395 N.Y.S.2d 139 (1977).

—New York definition of prostitution is not unconstitutionally vague. United States v. Herrera, 584 F.2d 1137 (2d Cir. 1978)

Accomplice testimony.—When five of the trial witnesses were prostitutes who had performed as prostitutes in various of the establishments which defendant illegally maintained for prostitution, which formed the basis of the charges of promoting prostitution, they were accomplices under CPL § 60.22 and the testimony had to be corroborated on that basis; however, such accomplice testimony was held to same "tending to connect" standard of corroboration as any other accomplice testimony; no more rigorous standard was required. People v. Griffin, 83 A.D.2d 180, 443 N.Y.S.2d 935 (4th Dept. 1981).

Filmed sexual activity.—When sexual acts are performed on film in exchange for a fee, the actor, as well as the party paying the actor, would be guilty of prostitution. People v. Kovner, 96 Misc. 2d 414, 409 N.Y.S.2d 349 (Sup. Ct. N.Y. Co. 1978).

Facial sufficiency of accusatory instrument.—Accusatory instrument charging defendant with prostitution without specifying how defendant expressed her assent was not conclusory and was not insufficient on its face; "[t]he specific manner in which the defendant manifested her assent is a matter for trial." People v. Polianskaia, 189 Misc. 2d 237, 730 N.Y.S.2d 685 (Crim. Ct. N.Y. Co. 2001).

—Accusatory instrument to be sufficient must state the evidentiary facts of the prostitution which provide reasonable cause to believe that the defendant committed the offense of patronizing a prostitute, by non-hearsay allegations which establish, if true, every element of the offense and defendant's commission thereof; i.e. that the defendant offered an undercover officer money in exchange for sexual intercourse. People v. Kenrick, 162 Misc. 2d 75, 615 N.Y.S.2d 859 (Crim. Ct. N.Y. Co. 1994).

—Complaint based solely on hearsay allegations of an unidentified undercover officer render accusatory instrument facially insufficient; even though the deponent's name need not be revealed, there must be some means of establishing that the person executing the supporting deposition is in fact the person named as the informant in the complaint; a badge number as the identifying insignia is a recognized means, if it is listed in the complaint as well as in the deposition; charge of prostitution dismissed. People v. Drucker, 159 Misc. 2d 205, 603 N.Y.S.2d 651 (Crim. Ct. N.Y. Co. 1993).

Verification of the accusatory instrument.—In view of apparent discrepancies in signatures on supporting depositions, purportedly by the same undercover officer, relating to several prostitution arrests on the same day, a question of fact was presented whether the identified officer had actually verified the allegations set forth therein; hearing required. People v. Kenrick, 162 Misc. 2d 75, 615 N.Y.S.2d 859 (Crim. Ct. N.Y. Co. 1994).

Proscribed conduct.—The term "sexual conduct," not defined in PL Article 230, includes masturbation, homosexual acts, sexual intercourse, and physical contact between genitals, whether clothed or unclothed, or with a woman's breast; the term was not intended by legislature to include non-genital sadomasochistic acts such as foot licking, spanking, domination and submission, even if done for money. People v. Georgia A., 163 Misc. 2d 634, 621 N.Y.S.2d 779 (Crim. Ct. Kings Co. 1994).

Relation with loitering for purposes of prostitution.—A prior conviction of prostitution or patronizing a prostitute in the second degree is a basis to enhance the offense of loitering for the purpose of engaging in a prostitution offense (PL § 240.37) from a violation to a misdemeanor. People v. Denise L., 159 Misc. 2d 1080, 608 N.Y.S.2d 40 (Crim. Ct. Queens Co. 1994).

Definition "with another person."—PL § 230.00 can not be construed to include agreements which do not involve physical touching between the parties. People v. Greene, 110 Misc. 2d 40, 441 N.Y.S.2d 636 (Crim. Ct. N.Y. Co. 1981).

Prostitution; no corroboration needed.—The crime of prostitution is by itself prohibited by law, and requires no reciprocity. Thus, police officer to whom offer was allegedly made could not be considered an accomplice of the prostitute, and his testimony required no corroboration. People v. Thomas, 74 Misc. 2d 6, 343 N.Y.S.2d 1010 (Rochester City Ct. 1973).

§ 230.02. Patronizing a prostitute; definitions.

1. A person patronizes a prostitute when:

(a) Pursuant to a prior understanding, he pays a fee to another person as compensation for such person or a third person having engaged in sexual conduct with him; or

(b) He pays or agrees to pay a fee to another person pursuant to an understanding that in return therefor such person or a third person will engage in sexual conduct with him; or

(c) He solicits or requests another person to engage in sexual conduct with him in return for a fee.

2. As used in this article, "person who is patronized" means the person with whom the defendant engaged in sexual conduct or was to have engaged in sexual conduct pursuant to the understanding, or the person who was solicited or requested by the defendant to engage in sexual conduct.

Amended by L. 1978, Ch. 627.

ANNOTATIONS

Role of police officer.—It is not a defense that the police officer, in fact, was not acting as "another person." People v. Bailey, and People v. Reid, 108 Misc. 2d 1075, 442 N.Y.S.2d 701 (App. T. Second and Eleventh Districts 1981); accord People v. Sharif, 141 Misc. 2d 80, 532 N.Y.S.2d 709 (New York City Crim. Ct. N.Y. Co. 1988).

Civil forfeiture proceeding does not bar subsequent criminal action on double jeopardy grounds.—When the defendant was charged with patronizing a prostitute, in which his car was used, the car was seized as an instrumentality of the crime; defendant agreed to pay $1000 to the property clerk for the return of the vehicle, then contended that the payment of the settlement amount constituted an excessive fine, which was actual punishment barring subsequent criminal action would impose additional punishment; however, court contended that criminal court judge had no jurisdiction to intervene in civil proceeding, so that the proceedings were jurisdictionally distinct, and the amount of the fine in the civil proceeding was irrelevant to the outcome of the criminal proceeding. People v. Milone, 158 Misc. 2d 316, 600 N.Y.S.2d 1010 (New York City Crim. Ct. 1993).

Solicitation of police decoy.—PL § 230.05 is violated when one person solicits another person to engage in sexual conduct with him in return for a fee, and it is immaterial whether the person solicited is or is not a prostitute. People v. Bronski, 76 Misc. 2d 341, 351 N.Y.S.2d 73 (Crim. Ct. N.Y.C. 1973).

§ 230.03. Patronizing a prostitute in the fourth degree.

A person is guilty of patronizing a prostitute in the fourth degree when he patronizes a prostitute.

Patronizing a prostitute in the fourth degree is a class B misdemeanor.

Added by L. 1978, Ch. 627.

ANNOTATION

Refusal to allow to plea.—Where all those arrested for the same offense are being treated in the same manner, no discriminatory practices are being exerted against any individual and, thus, a district attorney's policy of not allowing any defendants charged with the offense of patronizing a prostitute to take a plea cannot be considered as anything more than an exercise of prosecutorial discretion. People v. Iszak, 99 Misc. 2d 543, 416 N.Y.S.2d 1004 (N.Y.C. Crim. Ct. N.Y. Co. 1979).

Sufficiency of accusatory instrument.—Accusatory instrument was facially sufficient where People specified sexual conduct, here sexual intercourse, which forms basis of agreement. People v. Bah, 180 Misc. 2d 39, 688 N.Y.S.2d 397 (Crim. Ct. N.Y. Co. 1999)

§ 230.04. Patronizing a prostitute in the third degree.

A person is guilty of patronizing a prostitute in the third degree when, being over twenty-one years of age, he patronizes a prostitute and the person patronized is less than seventeen years of age.

Patronizing a prostitute in the third degree is a class A misdemeanor.

Added by L. 1978, Ch. 627.

ANNOTATIONS

Age of undercover decoy may render crime impossible.—Police officer, by virtue of membership on the force, was more than seventeen years of age; rendered accusatory instrument facially insufficient; defendant's subjective belief in the decoy's age did not cure the defect. However, defendant could be charged with patronizing a prostitute in the fourth degree in superseding information. People v. Kevin Doe, 135 Misc. 2d 578, 515 N.Y.S.2d 982 (N.Y.C. Crim. Ct. N.Y. Co. 1987).

Age of undercover decoy not relevant to attempt crime.—It was no defense to charge of attempting to patronize a prostitute in the third degree, requiring that the person patronized be less than seventeen years of age, that decoy officer was over seventeen years of age; she had told defendant that she was sixteen years old; since the offense was an attempt crime, impossibility of commission on this basis was not a defense. People v. Sharif, 141 Misc. 2d 80, 532 N.Y.S.2d 709 (N.Y.C. Crim. Ct. N.Y. Co. 1988).

Role of police officer.—It is not a defense that the police officer, in fact, was not acting as a prostitute. People v. Sharif, 141 Misc. 2d 80, 532 N.Y.S.2d 709 (N.Y.C. Crim. Ct. N.Y. Co. 1988).

§ 230.05. Patronizing a prostitute in the second degree.

A person is guilty of patronizing a prostitute in the second degree when, being over eighteen years of age, he patronizes a prostitute and the person patronized is less than fourteen years of age.

Patronizing a prostitute in the second degree is a class E felony.

Added by L. 1978, Ch. 627.

§ 230.06. Patronizing a prostitute in the first degree.

A person is guilty of patronizing a prostitute in the first degree when he patronizes a prostitute and the person patronized is less than eleven years of age.

Patronizing a prostitute in the first degree is a class D felony.

Added by L. 1978, Ch. 627.

§ 230.07. Patronizing a prostitute; defense.

In any prosecution for patronizing a prostitute in the first, second or third degrees, it is a defense that the defendant did not have reasonable grounds to believe that the person was less than the age specified.

Added by L. 1978, Ch. 627, eff. Sept. 1, 1978.

§ 230.10. Prostitution and patronizing a prostitute; no defense.

In any prosecution for prostitution or patronizing a prostitute, the sex of the two parties or prospective parties to the sexual conduct engaged in, contemplated or solicited is immaterial, and it is no defense that:

1. Such persons were of the same sex; or

2. The person who received, agreed to receive or solicited a fee was a male and the person who paid or agreed or offered to pay such fee was a female.

§ 230.15. Promoting prostitution; definitions of terms.

The following definitions are applicable to this article:

1. "Advance prostitution." A person "advances prostitution" when, acting other than as a prostitute or as a patron thereof, he knowingly causes or aids a person to commit or engage in prostitution, procures or solicits patrons for prostitution, provides persons or premises for prostitution purposes, operates or assists in the operation of a house of prostitution or a prostitution enterprise, or engages in any other conduct designed to institute, aid or facilitate an act or enterprise of prostitution.

2. "Profit from prostitution." A person "profits from prostitution" when, acting other than as a prostitute receiving compensation for personally rendered prostitution services, he accepts or receives money or other property pursuant to an agreement or understanding with any person whereby he participates or is to participate in the proceeds of prostitution activity.

ANNOTATIONS

Evidence that defendant tried to induce person to act as prostitute.—Evidence that defendant would approach females in public places, ask them if they were interested in modeling, invite them to his place of business, ostensibly a modeling agency, encourage the girls to become escorts, drive them to "dates," and then retain half of the proceeds paid to the girls by their patrons, established that defendant was advancing prostitution. People v. Pasini, 112 A.D.2d 1013, 492 N.Y.S.2d 819 (2d Dept. 1985), *lv. denied,* 67 N.Y.2d 655 (1986).

—Defendant's conduct of trying to persuade young girls to act as prostitutes encompassed conduct "designed to institute, aid or facilitate an act or enterprise of prostitution" so that he was guilty of advancing prostitution. People v. Simone-Taylor III, 148 A.D.2d 933, 539 N.Y.S.2d 171 (4th Dept.), *lv. denied,* 74 N.Y.2d 669 (1989).

Evidence that defendant controlled two prostitutes.—Defendant was advancing prostitution when he arranged for one girl to meet patrons in a motel room, which defendant rented, and defendant received financial benefit from acts of prostitution committed there, and arranged for another girl to meet patrons in a bar, with payment delivered from prostitute to bar owner and from bar owner to defendant. People v. Carey, 109 A.D.2d 982, 486 N.Y.S.2d 797 (3d Dept. 1985).

Advancing prostitution: impossibility of commission when "prostitute" and "patron" are both police decoys.—Unlike a single decoy case, in which there can be an agreement, at least on the part of one of the parties, to engage in prostitution, when the putative prostitute as well as the putative patron are both police decoys, there is no potential prostitution being advanced, so that offense of promoting prostitution was impossible of commission; however, attempt to promote prostitution could be proved on these facts. People v. Behncke, 141 Misc. 2d 630, 534 N.Y.S.2d 79 (N.Y.C. Crim. Ct. N.Y. Co. 1988).

Dismissal of criminal charges; commencement of civil action for malicious prosecution.—Civil plaintiff, after a stag party in his honor, provided a van where acts of prostitution took place; this was the premises wherein plaintiff could have been charged with advancing prostitution; fact that charge of promoting prostitution in the second degree was dismissed would not have precluded charging plaintiff under a lesser degree of promoting prostitution; civil judgment for plaintiff reversed and new trial ordered. Antonucci v. Town of Irondequoit, 81 A.D.2d 743, 438 N.Y.S.2d 417 (4th Dept. 1981).

§ 230.20. Promoting prostitution in the fourth degree.

A person is guilty of promoting prostitution in the fourth degree when he knowingly advances or profits from prostitution.

Promoting prostitution in the fourth degree is a class A misdemeanor.

Amended by L. 1978, Ch. 607. changing third degree to fourth degree.

ANNOTATIONS

Impossibility of commission.—When the defendant hotel proprietor rented a room to an undercover male and undercover female who had indicated that they wanted to rent the room for a tryst, the substantive offense was impossible of commission; however, this was no defense to a charge of attempting to promote prostitution in the fourth degree, in that defendant had attempted to knowingly advance prostitution while not acting as a prostitute or a patron himself. People v. Behncke, 141 Misc. 2d 630, 534 N.Y.S.2d 79 (N.Y.C. Crim. Ct. N.Y. Co. 1988).

Defense of entrapment.—When the officers, acting as businessmen who were interested in the services of prostitutes, did not actively induce or encourage the defendant prostitute, but merely afforded her an opportunity to commit the offense of promoting prostitution in the fourth degree, court did not err by declining to submit entrapment instruction. People v. Rollova, 124 A.D.2d 886, 508 N.Y.S.2d 653 (3d Dept.), lv. denied, 69 N.Y.2d 716 (1986).

Corroboration; testimony of prostitute.—Prostitutes are the accomplices of the promotor and their testimony must be corroborated and one prostitute cannot corroborate the testimony of another. People v. Griffin, 83 A.D.2d 180, 443 N.Y.S.2d 935 (4th Dept. 1981).

§ 230.25. Promoting prostitution in the third degree.

A person is guilty of promoting prostitution in the third degree when he knowingly:

1. Advances or profits from prostitution by managing, supervising, controlling or owning, either alone or in association with others, a house of prostitution or a prostitution business or enterprise involving prostitution activity by two or more prostitutes; or

2. Advances or profits from prostitution of a person less than nineteen years old.

Promoting prostitution in the third degree is a class D felony.

Amended by L. 1978, Ch. 627.

ANNOTATIONS

Solicitation provides sufficient evidence.—Defendant's solicitation of two 17-year-old girls to act as prostitutes for him was legally sufficient evidence, even though the girls refused. People v. Simone-Taylor III, 148 A.D.2d 933, 539 N.Y.S.2d 171 (4th Dept.), lv. denied, 74 N.Y.2d 669 (1989).

Defendant's offer of the services of two prostitutes.—When the defendant offered the services of two prostitutes to the undercover officers for a stated price, the evidence was sufficient to convict him of promoting prostitution in the third degree on the theory that he advanced or profited from prostitution by managing, supervising, or controlling a prostitution enterprise involving prostitution activity by two prostitutes. People v. Williams, 126 A.D.2d 975, 511 N.Y.S.2d 749 (4th Dept.), lv. denied, 69 N.Y.2d 888 (1987).

Prostitutes under nineteen years of age.—Defendant controlled two separate prostitutes, one in a motel room which

defendant rented and from which he received a financial benefit, and the other in a bar, from which defendant also received a benefit, both of whom were under nineteen years of age; evidence legally sufficient. People v. Carey, 109 A.D.2d 982, 486 N.Y.S.2d 797 (3d Dept. 1985).

Commercial nature of the operation, rather than the number of occurrences, distinguishes third from fourth degree of the offense.—The court rejected defendant's theory that her premises were only used once for prostitution purposes which warranted reduction to misdemeanor; rather, court noted that the commercial nature of the enterprise of running a house of prostitution was the means by which the legislature had distinguished felony from misdemeanor degrees of the offense of promoting prostitution. People v. Freaney, 108 A.D.2d 228, 488 N.Y.S.2d 759 (2d Dept. 1985).

Evidence sufficient to establish that defendant ran a house of prostitution.—Evidence from an undercover officer who had become a member of defendant's social club established that the club was monitored by a doorman who would screen admitees and collect an admission fee; club contained a "love shower" in which dancers would bath for the customers' entertainment; club advertised by sign on wall that it catered to bachelor parties and undercover officer had seen bachelor parties utilize the premises, undercover officer made arrangements to run a bachelor party; and he was offered the services of women in exchange for specified fees and, in fact, women had started removing clothes of undercover when backup team arrived, was sufficient to establish that the defendant managed a house of prostitution. People v. Freaney, 108 A.D.2d 228, 488 N.Y.S.2d 759 (2d Dept. 1985).

Mere steering activity insufficient to demonstrate control over prostitution operation.—Defendant merely steered patrons to a prostitute, and on one occasion requested a financial benefit; evidence insufficient to demonstrate that defendant managed, supervised, controlled or owned a house of prostitution; conviction reduced to promoting prostitution in the fourth degree. People v. Davilla, 110 A.D.2d 545, 488 N.Y.S.2d 2 (1st Dept. 1985).

Lesser included offense: defendant claimed to act merely as doorman.—When defendant was convicted of promoting prostitution in the third degree, but claimed that he was only the doorman, and there was no evidence that he negotiated prices, or owned or leased the premises, and no indication that keys or money were recovered from the defendant, he should have been entitled to submission of lesser included offense of promoting prostitution in the fourth degree, on theory that he merely advanced prostitution without the aggravating factors which enhanced conduct to a felony. People v. Rodriguez, 104 A.D.2d 547, 480 N.Y.S.2d 214 (1st Dept. 1984).

Actors and actresses.—PL § 230.25(1) was obviously designed to prevent organized prostitution activity and was inapplicable where the evidence pointed toward a single stag party. People v. Gallucci, 62 A.D.2d 1129, 404 N.Y.S.2d 768 (4th Dept. 1978).

—The hiring of actors and actresses for the purpose of engaging in filmed sexual conduct constitutes prostitution. People v. Kovner, 96 Misc. 2d 414, 409 N.Y.S.2d 349 (Sup. Ct. N.Y. Co. 1978).

§ 230.30. Promoting prostitution in the second degree.

A person is guilty of promoting prostitution in the second degree when he knowingly:

1. Advances prostitution by compelling a person by force or intimidation to engage in prostitution, or profits from such coercive conduct by another; or

2. Advances or profits from prostitution of a person less than sixteen years old.

Promoting prostitution in the second degree is a class C felony.

Amended by L. 1978, Ch. 627.

ANNOTATIONS

Decoy is less than 16 years of age.—Strict liability attaches to age of victim for promoting prostitution in the second degree, which is the aggravating circumstance which makes the offense a felony, rather than to proscribed result, so that the result that the defendant is mistaken as to the target's age does not render evidence legally insufficient. People v. Coleman, 74 N.Y.2d 381, 547 N.Y.S.2d 814, 547 N.E.2d 69 (1989).

—When the defendant was charged with attempted promotion of a prostitute in the second degree when he endeavored to persuade a female who claimed to be less than 16 years old to be a prostitute, and there was evidence that he believed her representation, but she was a police decoy who was older than sixteen years old, the defendant could not invoke defense of impossibility of commission on basis that ostensible target was less than the statutory age. People v. Liggins, 156 A.D.2d 125, 548 N.Y.S.2d 28 (1st Dept. 1989), *lv. denied,* 75 N.Y.2d 921 (1990); *accord* People v. Coleman, 143 A.D.2d 552, 532 N.Y.S.2d 862 (1st Dept. 1988), *aff'd,* 74 N.Y.2d 381, 547 N.Y.S.2d 814, 547 N.E.2d 69 (1989).

Legal sufficiency.—Evidence at trial proved that defendant, acting in concert with another, participated in and orchestrated coercion against complainant who was kept under guard at defendant's apartment and forced to engage in acts of prostitution over an extended period of time. People v. Shao Ying Pan, 245 A.D.2d 149, 666 N.Y.S.2d 154 (1st Dept. 1997).

—Evidence was legally sufficient to sustain charge of promoting prostitution in the second degree where defendant arranged for a 16-year-old girl to meet patrons in a motel room, and he received a financial benefit from such acts of prostitution. People v. Carey, 109 A.D.2d 982, 486 N.Y.S.2d 797 (3d Dept. 1985).

Corroboration of complaining witness.—Testimony by witness who was 15 years old at the time her prostitution that defendant held himself out as her pimp, arranged for her to rent a motel room for purposes of meeting and servicing patrons, and arranged for himself to benefit financially from her acts of prostitution, did not require corroboration, insofar as the witnesses was not and accomplice as a matter of law with respect to a charge of promoting prostitution in the second degree; a 17-year-old girl who also acted as a prostitute for defendant, for which he was charged with promoting prostitution in the third degree, also did not require corroboration, by virtue of her age. People v. Carey, 109 A.D.2d 982, 486 N.Y.S.2d 797 (3d Dept. 1985).

—Since the complainant was not an accomplice to the crime of promoting prostitution in the second degree, when defendant was charged under provision which has an element of force (PL § 230.30(1), her testimony did not have to be corroborated under CPL § 60.22. People v. Bennett, 144 A.D.2d 942, 534 N.Y.S.2d 609 (4th Dept. 1988), *lv. denied,* 74 N.Y.2d 736 (1989).

Venue.—Venue for offense of promoting prostitution in the second degree is proper in the county where an element of the offense, such as the acts of prostitution, occurred. People v. Sanders, 112 A.D.2d 648, 491 N.Y.S.2d (3d Dept.), *lv. denied,* 66 N.Y.2d 618 (1985).

§ 230.32. Promoting prostitution in the first degree.

A person is guilty of promoting prostitution in the first degree when he knowingly advances or profits from prostitution of a person less than eleven years old.

Promoting prostitution in the first degree is a class B felony.

Added by L. 1978, Ch. 627.

§ 230.33. Compelling prostitution.

A person is guilty of compelling prostitution when, being twenty-one years of age or older, he or she knowingly advances prostitution by compelling a person less than sixteen years old, by force or intimidation, to engage in prostitution.

Compelling prostitution is a class B felony.

Added by L. 2005, Ch. 450, § 1, eff. Nov. 1, 2005.

§ 230.35. Promoting or compelling prostitution; accomplice.

In a prosecution for promoting or compelling prostitution, a person less than seventeen years of age from whose prostitution activity another person is alleged to have advanced or attempted to advance or profited or attempted to profit shall not be deemed to be an accomplice.

Added by L. 1978, Ch. 627; **Amended** by L. 2005, Ch. 450, § 2, eff. Nov. 1, 2005.

ANNOTATIONS

Witnesses less than 17 years of age.—When the five young women who were part of defendant's prostitution operation were less than 17 years of age when they participated in the operation, they were not accomplices as a matter of law. People v. Pasini, 112 A.D.2d 1013, 492 N.Y.S.2d 819 (2d Dept. 1985).

—Testimony by witnesses who were 15 years old and 17 years old at the time of their prostitution that defendant held himself out as their pimp, arranged for them to rent a motel room, or to be available in a bar, for purposes of meeting and servicing patrons, and arranged for himself to benefit financially from their acts of prostitution, did not require corroboration, insofar as these witnesses were not accomplices as a matter of law with respect to charges of promoting prostitution in the second and third degree, by virtue of their ages. People v. Carey, 109 A.D.2d 982, 486 N.Y.S.2d 797 (3d Dept. 1985).

Witnesses older than 17 years of age.—Absent evidence that prostitutes, willingly engaging in prostitution, are less than seventeen years of age pursuant to PL § 230.35, they are accomplices of the promoter and their testimony against the promoter must be corroborated under CPL § 60.22. People v. Griffin, 83 A.D.2d 180, 443 N.Y.S.2d 935 (4th Dept. 1981).

Complainant whose prostitution is coerced is not an accomplice.—In kidnapping case, where there was no evidence that the complainant had willingly participated in promotion of prostitution, she was not an accomplice, and the fact that she was not under seventeen years of age was irrelevant. People v. Valero, 120 Misc. 2d 539, 466 N.Y.S.2d 600 (Suffolk Co. Ct. 1983).

Charge to jury on corroboration.—It was error for court's instruction to allow jury to use testimony by one prostitute accomplice to corroborate testimony of another prostitute accomplice. People v. Griffin, 83 A.D.2d 180, 443 N.Y.S.2d 935 (4th Dept. 1981).

§ 230.40. Permitting prostitution.

A person is guilty of permitting prostitution when, having possession or control of premises which he knows are being used for prostitution purposes, he fails to make reasonable effort to halt or abate such use.

Permitting prostitution is a class B misdemeanor.

ANNOTATIONS

Use of premises.—The prostitute and patron need not actually enter the room which they have rented in order to charge the hotel proprietor who had rented them the room with permitting prostitution on theory that he knew premises were being used for prostitution and he failed to make a reasonable effort to halt such use. People v. Behncke, 141 Misc. 2d 630, 534 N.Y.S.2d 79 (N.Y.C. Crim. Ct. N.Y. Co. 1988).

Impossibility of commission when "prostitute" and "patron" are both police decoys.—Unlike a single decoy case, in which there can be an agreement, at least on the part of one of the parties, to engage in prostitution, when the putative prostitute as well as the putative patron are both police decoys, the offense of prostitution was impossible of commission, so that the use of premises for prostitution purposes is impossible of commission. People v. Behncke, 141 Misc. 2d 630, 534 N.Y.S.2d 79 (N.Y.C. Crim. Ct. N.Y. Co. 1988).

Inference of knowledge.—Defendant, although subsequently claiming not to know the prostitute, allowed the prostitute, who was not a tenant, and a decoy officer into his building where prostitution was to occur; when prostitute was arrested, police warned defendant that his premises were being used for prostitution which could subject him to arrest; on a second occasion, defendant again allowed a prostitute, who was not a tenant, into the building with a decoy officer; prostitute had indicated to officer that part of her fee paid rent for the temporary use of the room; despite fact that defendant had not verbalized consent for use of premises for purposes of prostitution, his conduct evinced his knowledge that premises were being used for prostitution, and he failed to take reasonable steps to halt such use. People v. Taliaferrow, 121 Misc. 2d 307, 467 N.Y.S.2d 522 (N.Y.C. Crim. Ct. Kings Co. 1983).

Constitutionality.—Requirement that defendant make "reasonable" efforts to halt use of his premises for prostitution is not unconstitutionally vague. People v. Gilmore, 120 Misc. 2d 741, 468 N.Y.S.2d 965 (City Ct. Mount Vernon 1983).

ARTICLE 235—OBSCENITY AND RELATED OFFENSES

LexisNexis Cross References

Criminal Law Advocacy, Vol. 1, Ch. 20, Preparation of an Obscenity Case; *New York Criminal Practice (2d ed.),* Vol. 7, Ch. 78, Indecent Materials to Minors; *Criminal Defense Techniques,* Vol. 3, Ch. 54, Defense of an Obscenity Case; *Prosecution and Defense of Sex Crimes,* Ch. 8, Obscenity and Pornography.

§ 235.00. Obscenity; definitions of terms.

The following definitions are applicable to sections 235.05, 235.10 and 235.15:

1. "Obscene." Any material or performance is "obscene" if (a) the average person, applying contemporary community standards, would find that considered as a whole, its predominant appeal is to the prurient interest in sex, and (b) it depicts or describes in a patently offensive manner, actual or simulated: sexual intercourse, criminal sexual act, sexual bestiality, masturbation, sadism, masochism, excretion or lewd exhibition of the genitals, and (c) considered as a whole, it lacks serious literary, artistic, political, and scientific value. Predominant appeal shall be judged with reference to ordinary adults unless it appears from the character of the material or the circumstances of its dissemination to be designed for children or other specially susceptible audience.

2. "Material" means anything tangible which is capable of being used or adapted to arouse interest, whether through the medium of reading, observation, sound or in any other manner.

3. "Performance" means any play, motion picture, dance or other exhibition performed before an audience.

4. "Promote" means to manufacture, issue, sell, give, provide, lend, mail, deliver, transfer, transmute, publish, distribute, circulate, disseminate, present, exhibit or advertise, or to offer or agree to do the same.

5. "Wholesale promote" means to manufacture, issue, sell, provide, mail, deliver, transfer, transmute, publish, distribute, circulate, dissemi-nate or to offer or agree to do the same for purposes of resale.

6. "Simulated" means the explicit depiction or description of any of the types of conduct set forth in clause (b) of subdivision one of this section, which creates the appearance of such conduct.

7. "Criminal sexual act" means any of the types of sexual conduct defined in subdivision two of section 130.00 provided, however, that in any prosecution under this article the marital status of the persons engaged in such conduct shall be irrelevant and shall not be considered.

Amended by L. 1967, Ch. 791; L. 1969, Ch. 583; L. 1974, Ch. 989; L. 2003, Ch. 264, § 28, eff. Nov. 1, 2003, amending subds. 1 and 7.

ANNOTATIONS

Constitutionality.—New York standards defining the border between free expression and obscenity are consistent with federal standards. People v. Hollman, 68 N.Y.2d 202, 204, n.2, 507 N.Y.S.2d 977, 500 N.E.2d 297 (1986).

—New York State Constitution imposes more exacting standard than federal constitution for issuance of search warrant authoriz-ing seizure of allegedly obscene material; under state law, magistrate must make independent finding of probable cause that materials to be seized are obscene, rather than relying on police affidavits alleging that they are obscene. People v. P.J. Video, Inc., 68 N.Y.2d 296, 508 N.Y.S.2d 907, 501 N.E.2d 556 (1986), *on remand from* New York v. P.J. Video, Inc., 475 U.S. 868, 106 S. Ct. 1610, 89 L. Ed. 2d 871 (1986), *cert. denied,* 479 U.S. 1091 (1987).

—Even the sale of non-obscene materials, if they depict child sexual performances, may be constitutionally restricted without infringing on right of free expression. People v. Ferber, 57 N.Y.2d 256, 455 N.Y.S.2d 582, 441 N.E.2d 1100 (1982), *on remand from* New York v. Ferber, 458 U.S. 747, 102 S. Ct. 3348, 73 L. Ed. 2d 1113 (1982).

—Definition of obscenity in Article 235, which parallels federal definition, which has been found constitutional, is not unconsti-tutionally vague, but clearly proscribes hard core pornography; the state constitution does not afford broader rights to free expression with respect to obscenity than federal constitution, so penal law definition also is constitutional under N.Y. Constitution, Article I § 8. People v. North Street Book Shoppe, Inc., 139 A.D.2d 18, 530 N.Y.S.2d 869 (3d Dept.), *lv. denied,* 72 N.Y.2d 1048 (1988).

—Local ordinance which permitted revocation or suspension of theater license on basis of past conduct of showing an obscene film was an unconstitutional prior restraint on free speech. Colonie Theater v. City of Schenectady, 89 A.D.2d 631, 453 N.Y.S.2d 94 (3d Dept. 1982).

—Local ordinance which required owners and operators of motion picture theaters to file a certificate of registration stating their names and addresses, was a reasonable exercise of local police power, providing information in event of a violation of law, and did not violate right against self-incrimination. Doe v. City of Buffalo, 84 A.D.2d 920, 446 N.Y.S.2d 652 (4th Dept. 1981).

—Injunction under CPLR § 6630 which would prevent future sale or distribution of material which had not yet been determined to be obscene would be unreasonable prior restraint in violation of first amendment. Cosgrove, District Attorney of Erie Co. v. Cloud Books, Inc., 83 A.D.2d 789, 443 N.Y.S.2d 450 (4th Dept. 1981).

Preemption of local laws.—The Penal Law totally occupies the field of obscenity and disseminating indecent material to minors; hence, local law prohibiting sale or distribution of obscene material to minors was preempted; however, local community still could control means of distribution by zoning, or by recourse to CPLR § 6630 for civil relief. Penny Lane/East Hampton, Inc., 191 A.D.2d 19, 598 N.Y.S.2d 806 (2d Dept. 1993).

Contract to produce illegal film void.—Even if the contract contemplates that an obscene film will be distributed legally in another jurisdiction, if the obscene film was produced in New York, it violated state law, and the contract is unenforceable in all respects; plaintiffs, who loaned money to defendant to produce the film, could not recover on the debt. Braunstein v. Jason Tarantella, Inc., 87 A.D.2d 203, 450 N.Y.S.2d 862 (2d Dept. 1982).

Nature of "performance."—Even though defendant, who masturbated in direction of three young girls, had an "audience," this conduct does not fit within the statutory definition; implicitly, the audience must be willing to see the performance. People v. Laracuente, 186 A.D.2d 97, 588 N.Y.S.2d 30 (1st Dept. 1992).

Prurient.—Prosecutor did not impermissible expand statutory definition of "prurient" by describing it in terms of being "erotic." People v. Allies Boulevard Book Store, Inc., 125 A.D.2d 910, 510 N.Y.S.2d 271 (3d Dept. 1986), *lv. denied,* 69 N.Y.2d 876 (1987).

Community standards to be applied.—Standards for constitutional purposes are set by state law; under New York law, national standards are not applicable; rather, standard is that of the average New Yorker. People v. P.J. Video, Inc., 68 N.Y.2d 296, 508 N.Y.S.2d 907, 501 N.E.2d 556 (1986), *on remand from* New York v. P.J. Video, Inc., 475 U.S. 868, 106 S. Ct. 1610, 89 L. Ed. 2d 871 (1986), *cert. denied,* 479 U.S. 1091 (1987).

—Court declined to reconsider People v. Heller, 33 N.Y.2d 314 (1973), retaining constitutional construction that state community standard, rather than local community standard, is to be employed in determining issues of obscenity. People v. Calbud, Inc., 49 N.Y.2d 389, 426 N.Y.S.2d 238, 402 N.E.2d 1140 (1980).

Instructions to the grand jury; community standards.—When the district attorney, in instructing the grand jury by reciting the statutory definition of obscenity, but neglected to further instruct them that the grand jury should utilize state community standards, error did not render the indictment defective; while this information would be essential for a petit jury to consider, it was not essential for the grand jury; order dismissing indictment reversed and indictment re-instated. People v. Calbud, Inc., 49 N.Y.2d 389, 426 N.Y.S.2d 238, 402 N.E.2d 1140 (1980).

Instructions to grand jury; affirmative defense.—Prosecutor was not obliged to instruct the grand jury on the affirmative defense to obscenity. People v. Allies Boulevard Book Store, Inc., 125 A.D.2d 910, 510 N.Y.S.2d 271 (3d Dept. 1986), *lv. denied,* 69 N.Y.2d 876 (1987).

Indictment; relation between items sold and number of

counts.—Although the defendant sold two obscene magazines to an undercover officer, which resulted in two separate counts, the sales should have been combined into a single count. People v. North Street Book Shoppe, Inc., 139 A.D.2d 18, 53 N.Y.S.2d 869 (3d Dept.), *lv. denied,* 72 N.Y.2d 1048 (1988).

Depictions not sexually arousing.—In landlord tenant case, tenant's sale of merchandise, which depicted male genitalia, which was not sexually arousing, was not obscene and not a violation of the lease; depictions of genitalia are not in and of themselves obscene. Philex Enterprises, Inc. v. Lanzer, 131 A.D.2d 452, 515 N.Y.S.2d 874 (2d Dept. 1987).

Constitutionality of section.—Court upheld constitutionality of PL § 235.00 (1); it rejected the claim it is unduly vague. People v. North Street Book Shoppe Inc., 139 A.D.2d 118, 530 N.Y.S.2d 869 (3d Dept. 1988).

Prior version of statute.—Traffic in obscene materials is beyond the limits of First Amendment protection; in determining whether any material is patently offensive or obscene, the community standard to be applied is a "state" standard. Thus, former PL § 235.00(1) (Laws 1965) was directed against hard core pornography and sufficiently described the conduct it sought to be proscribed so as to be constitutional. People v. Heller, 33 N.Y.2d 314, 352 N.Y.S.2d 601, 307 N.E.2d 805 (1973).

Obscenity; legal test.—Material will be considered "obscene" if the dominant theme of the material taken as a whole appeals to prurient interests in sex, is patently offensive because it conflicts with contemporary community standards relating to the description or representation of sexual matters, and is utterly without redeeming social value. People v. Mature Enterprises, Inc., 73 Misc. 2d 749, 343 N.Y.S.2d 911 (Crim. Ct. N.Y. Co. 1973), *aff'd,* 352 N.Y.S.2d 346, 76 Misc. 2d 660 (App. Term 1st Dept. 1974), *modified,* 35 N.Y.2d 520, 364 N.Y.S.2d 170, 323 N.E.2d 704 (1974).

Obscenity; standard of measurement.—Where a movie was almost totally devoid of plot, and depicted various acts of actual deviate sexual intercourse for practically the entire length of the film, and where the camera angle emphasized "a maximum exposure in detail of the genitalia," the movie could be deemed obscene by any standard legal measurement. People v. Mature Enterprises, Inc., 73 Misc. 2d 749, 343 N.Y.S.2d 911 (Crim. Ct. N.Y. Co. 1973), *aff'd,* 76 Misc. 2d 660, 352 N.Y.S.2d 346 (App. Term. 1st Dept. 1974), *modified,* 35 N.Y.2d 520, 364 N.Y.S.2d 170, 323 N.E.2d 704 (1974).

Standards to be applied.—The contemporary standards of communities throughout the State are the proper measure of what is "obscene" within the meaning of the Penal Law. People v. Calbud, Inc., 49 N.Y.2d 389, 426 N.Y.S.2d 238, 402 N.E.2d 1140 (1980).

Prior judicial scrutiny.—Prior judicial scrutiny is required where evidence is seized as obscene and arrests are based on the same. Judge may attend theater and his conclusion regarding film may then be based on "prior judicial scrutiny." Adversary hearing is not required. People v. Heller, 29 N.Y.2d 319, 327 N.Y.S.2d 628, 277 N.E.2d 651 (1971).

§ 235.05. Obscenity in the third degree.

A person is guilty of obscenity in the third degree when, knowing its content and character, he:

1. Promotes, or possesses with intent to promote, any obscene material; or

2. Produces, presents or directs an obscene performance or participates in a portion thereof which is obscene or which contributes to its obscenity.

Obscenity in the third degree is a class A misdemeanor.

Amended by L. 1969, Ch. 583; L. 1982, Ch. 649.

ANNOTATIONS

Produces, presents, directs.—When defendant broke into a residence and masturbated in front of young girls, he did not produce, present, or direct a performance within the meaning of Article 235; conviction for obscenity in the third degree was reversed. People v. Laracuente, 186 A.D.2d 97, 588 N.Y.S.2d 30 (1st Dept. 1992).

Jury charge.—Defendant, charged with obscenity in the third degree, was entitled to have final charge direct jury only to those elements set forth in § 235.05; when court charged jury with respect to entire definition of obscenity included in § 235.00, which included acts not alleged in the indictment, but which were nevertheless were elicited by proof at trial, the error could not be considered harmless; and conviction for obscenity in the third degree was reversed. People v. AJS Advertising, Inc., 162 A.D.2d 990, 559 N.Y.S.2d 52 (4th Dept. 1990).

Community standards; effect of acquittal of seller of comparable literature.—The fact that a defendant claims that a local jury had acquitted another seller of comparable magazines does not establish a baseline for community standards; the acquittal only means that in that case the prosecution did not prove every element of the offense charged. People v. North Street Book Shoppe, Inc., 139 A.D.2d 18, 530 N.Y.S.2d 869 (3d Dept.), *lv. denied,* 72 N.Y.2d 1048 (1988).

Indictment; relation between items sold and number of counts.—Although the defendant sold two obscene magazines to an undercover officer, which resulted in two separate counts, the sales should have been combined into a single count. People v. North Street Book Shoppe, Inc., 139 A.D.2d 18, 530 N.Y.S.2d 869 (3d Dept.), *lv. denied,* 72 N.Y.2d 1048 (1988).

Adversary hearing.—It was not an unconstitutional act for the court to issue a warrant for the seizure of film to be used as evidence in a prosecution against the exhibition without first conducting an adversary hearing on the issue of obscenity; the number of films authorized to be seized was limited to six and was reasonably dictated by prosecutorial requirements and the seizure was not designed to place a prior restraint on defendant's distribution of such films. People v. Durocher, 85 Misc. 2d 78, 378 N.Y.S.2d 960 (Crim. Ct. N.Y.C. 1976).

Cartoons depicting exaggerated and perverted sexual organs activity.—A comic book depicting acts of bestiality, incest, masturbation and other forms of sexual behavior, together with exaggerated drawings of sex organs, among others, accompanied by use of four letter words, was deemed obscene. People v. Kirpatrick, 316 N.Y.S.2d 37 (N.Y.C. Crim. Ct. 1970), *aff'd,* 69 Misc. 2d 212, 329 N.Y.S.2d 769 (App. Term 1st Dept. 1971), *aff'd,* 32 N.Y.2d 17, 343 N.Y.S.2d 70, 295 N.E.2d 753, *dismissed,* 414 U.S. 948, 94 S. Ct. 283, 38 L. Ed. 2d 204 (1973).

Need for prosecution to introduce experts on issue of obscenity.—The need for an expert witness for the prosecution does not obtain in every case. Where the material is patently offensive, expert testimony is not required. People v. Kirpatrick, 64 Misc. 2d 1055, 316 N.Y.S.2d 37 (N.Y.C. Crim. Ct. 1970), *aff'd,* 329 N.Y.S.2d 769 (App Term 1st Dept. 1971), *aff'd,* 69 Misc. 2d 212, 32 N.Y.2d 17, 343 N.Y.S.2d 70, 295 N.E.2d 753, *dismissed,* 414 U.S. 948, 94 S. Ct. 283, 38 L. Ed. 2d 204 (1973).

Motion to suppress; necessity for warrant.—Defendant was arrested and charged with possession of obscene matter, and moved to suppress the evidence based on the absence of a search warrant. The police contended that no new warrant was needed, since a magazine with the same title had previously been found obscene by another judge in the same court. However, since the previous warrant related to a totally different person and place, and there is a need for a fresh warrant in conjunction with every seizure, the motion to suppress was granted. People v. Gomez, 73 Misc. 2d 623, 342 N.Y.S.2d 903 (Crim. Ct. N.Y. Co. 1973).

No prior judicial scrutiny to arrest. The arrest, without prior judicial scrutiny, of topless female dancers, for participating in an obscene performance and of male defendants for promoting said performance was upheld where the movements which were the basis of the officer's arrest were innovative and spontaneous and would not necessarily be the same as yesterday's or tomorrow's. People v. Morgan, 86 Misc. 2d 377, 382 N.Y.S.2d 666 (Crim. Ct. N.Y.C. 1976).

Obscenity; owners' knowledge of contents of store.—Where defendants were in possession of obscene material which was for sale in their bookshop, it was a permissible inference that they knew the contraband nature of the material. Furthermore, it was held that the statutory presumption that a seller of contraband material knows the contents of that material is valid. People v. Kirkpatrick, 32 N.Y.2d 17, 343 N.Y.S.2d 70,

295 N.E.2d 753 (1973), *dismissed* 414 U.S. 948, 94 S. Ct. 283, 38 L. Ed. 2d 204 (1973).

Promotion or possession of more than one item.—In a prosecution for promoting obscenity, the promotion or possession of more than one item at the same time and on the same date constitutes one crime, and cannot be split into as many crimes as there are items. Braunstein v. Frawley, 64 A.D.2d 772, 407 N.Y.S.2d 250 (3d Dept. 1978).

Proof of knowledge of contents; failure to read offending material.—The evidence in a prosecution against sellers of allegedly obscene material was sufficient to indicate knowledge of the material's nature and contents although the defendants might never have read it. People v. Kirkpatrick, 64 Misc. 2d 1055, 316 N.Y.S.2d 37 (Crim. Ct. 1970), *aff'd,* 69 Misc. 2d 212, 329 N.Y.S.2d 769 (App. Term 1st Dept. 1971), *aff'd,* 32 N.Y.2d 17, 343 N.Y.S.2d 70, 295 N.E.2d 753 (1973), *dismissed,* 414 U.S. 948, 94 S. Ct. 283, 38 L. Ed. 2d 204 (1973).

§ 235.06. Obscenity in the second degree.

A person is guilty of obscenity in the second degree when he commits the crime of obscenity in the third degree as defined in subdivisions one and two of section 235.05 of this chapter and has been previously convicted of obscenity in the third degree.

Obscenity in the second degree is a class E felony.

Added by L. 1982, Ch. 649.

ANNOTATION

Community standards: instructions to the grand jury.—When the district attorney, in instructing the grand jury by reciting the statutory definition of obscenity in the second degree, but neglected to further instruct them that the grand jury should utilize state community standards, error did not render the indictment defective; while this information would be essential for a petit jury to consider, it was not essential for the grand jury; order dismissing indictment reversed and indictment re-instated. People v. Calbud, Inc., 49 N.Y.2d 389, 426 N.Y.S.2d 238, 402 N.E.2d 1140 (1980).

§ 235.07. Obscenity in the first degree.

A person is guilty of obscenity in the first degree when, knowing its content and character, he wholesale promotes or possesses with intent to wholesale promote, any obscene material.

Obscenity in the first degree is a class D felony.

Added by L. 1969, Ch. 583; **Amended** by L. 1982, Ch. 649.

ANNOTATIONS

Photographs of nude females; sexual activity not depicted—Magazines containing pictures of nude females in various poses and stages of nudity which do not show sexual activity of any kind are protected under the First Amendment to the United States Constitution and, therefore, as a matter of law are not obscene. People v. Stabile, 58 Misc. 2d 905, 296 N.Y.S.2d 815 (N.Y.C. Crim. Ct. 1969).

Photographs of nudes; no prior judicial declaration of obscenity—A police officer may not seize photographs of nude females on the ground that the photographs are obscene where there has been no prior determination by a judicial officer that the photographs are obscene. People v. Kozak, 56 Misc. 2d 337, 288 N.Y.S.2d 692 (N.Y.C. Crim. Ct. 1968).

§ 235.10. Obscenity; presumptions.

1. A person who promotes or wholesale promotes obscene material, or possesses the same with intent to promote or wholesale promote it, in the course of his business is presumed to do so with knowledge of its content and character.

2. A person who possesses six or more identical or similar obscene articles is presumed to possess them with intent to promote the same.

The provisions of this section shall not apply to public libraries or association libraries as defined in subdivision two of section two hundred fifty-three of the education law, or trustees or employees of such public libraries or association libraries when acting in the course and scope of their duties or employment

Amended by L. 1969, Ch. 583; L. 1980, Ch. 267; L. 1982, Ch. 110.

ANNOTATIONS

Knowledge established.—Defendant's management and frequent presence in the theater which was the subject of the indictment, when coupled with the presumption contained in § 235.10, established defendant's knowledge of the content and character of the film involved. People v. Young, 89 A.D.2d 915, 453 N.Y.S.2d 603 (2d Dept. 1982).

Presumption not rebutted.—"[P]roof of scienter requires focusing on the *particular* material in question and not solely on the many other unoffending titles on the shelves" of a bookstore. Therefore, the presumption under Penal Law § 235.10, was not rebutted by evidence that a store contains "thousands of volumes on many subjects" and that magazines like the allegedly obscene material in question constitutes less than one percent of the gross yearly sales. People v. Kirkpatrick, 64 Misc. 2d 1055, 316 N.Y.S.2d 37 (N.Y.C. Crim. Ct. 1970), aff'd, 69 Misc. 2d 212, 329 N.Y.S.2d 769 (App. T. 1st Dept. 1971), aff'd, 32 N.Y.2d 17, 343 N.Y.S.2d 70, 295 N.E.2d 753, dismissed, 414 U.S. 948, 94 S. Ct. 283, 38 L. Ed. 2d 204 (1973).

§ 235.15. Obscenity or disseminating indecent material to minors in the second degree; defense.

1. In any prosecution for obscenity, or disseminating indecent material to minors in the second degree in violation of subdivision three of section 235.21 of this article, it is an affirmative defense that the persons to whom allegedly obscene or indecent material was disseminated, or the audience to an allegedly obscene performance, consisted of persons or institutions having scientific, educational, governmental or other similar justification for possessing, disseminating or viewing the same.

2. In any prosecution for obscenity, it is an affirmative defense that the person so charged was a motion picture projectionist, stage employee or spotlight operator, cashier, doorman, usher, candy stand attendant, porter or in any other non-managerial or non-supervisory capacity in a motion picture theatre; provided he has no financial interest, other than his employment, which employment does not encompass compensation based upon any proportion of the gross receipts, in the promotion of obscene material for sale, rental or exhibition or in the promotion, presentation or direction of any obscene performance, or is in any way responsible for acquiring obscene material for sale, rental or exhibition.

Amended by L. 1971, Ch. 1031; L. 1996, Ch. 600, § 1, amending section heading and subd. 1, eff. Nov. 1, 1996.

ANNOTATIONS

Instructions to grand jury; affirmative defense.— Prosecutor was not obliged to instruct the grand jury on the affirmative defense to obscenity. People v. Allies Boulevard Book Store, Inc., 125 A.D.2d 910, 510 N.Y.S.2d 271 (3d Dept. 1986), lv. denied, 69 N.Y.2d 876 (1987).

Criminal investigation is not a "government purpose."— Defendant book store could not avail itself of affirmative defense, claiming that it sold obscene book to government agent, when the book was sold to an undercover investigator. People v. Allies Boulevard Book Store, Inc., 125 A.D.2d 910, 510 N.Y.S.2d 271 (3d Dept. 1986), lv. denied, 69 N.Y.2d 876 (1987).

Signage restricting classes of patrons.—Mere fact that bookstore had sign indicating that it sold only to persons having scientific, educational, governmental or similar justification, did not qualify book store for affirmative defense, especially since undercover officer told book clerk that he was buying obscene material as a gag gift. People v. Allies Boulevard Book Store, Inc., 125 A.D.2d 910, 510 N.Y.S.2d 271 (3d Dept. 1986), lv. denied, 69 N.Y.2d 876 (1987).

Affirmative defense.—It remains the People's obligation to initially prove beyond a reasonable doubt every element of the crime charged including the obscene character of the performance which places it beyond the protection of the First Amendment; the defendants' successful establishment of either of the affirmative defenses will serve only to negate their criminal responsibility. People v. Martin, 100 Misc. 2d 774, 420 N.Y.S.2d 318 (N.Y.C. Crim. Ct. 1979).

Bookstore cashier.—The mere fact that PL § 235.15 exempts a motion picture projectionist from prosecution from obscenity but does not extend the defense to cashiers in bookstores, does not discriminate and violate the constitutional right to equal protection as guaranteed by the Fourteenth Amendment. People v. Victoria, 96 Misc. 2d 926, 409 N.Y.S.2d 937 (Crim. Ct. N.Y.C. 1978).

Constitutionality.—PL § 235.15(1) does not violate the due process clause and is constitutional; PL § 235.15(2) does not violate the equal protection clause and is constitutional. People v. Illardo, 97 Misc. 2d 294, 411 N.Y.S.2d 142 (Erie Co. Ct. 1978), aff'd, 48 N.Y.2d 408, 423 N.Y.S.2d 470, 399 N.E.2d 59 (1979).

Limited availability of scientific justification defense.— Application of the scientific justification defense contained in PL § 235.15 is expressly limited to the offenses stated in the statute and is not available as a defense to PL § 263.16, possessing a sexual performance by a child. People v. Fraser, 96 N.Y.2d 318, 728 N.Y.S.2d 115, 752 N.E.2d 244 (2001), cert. denied, 533 U.S. 951 (2001).

§ 235.20. Disseminating indecent material to minors; definitions of terms.

The following definitions are applicable to sections 235.21, 235.22, 235.23 and 235.24 of this article:

1. "Minor" means any person less than seventeen years old.

2. "Nudity" means the showing of the human male or female genitals, pubic area or buttocks with less than a full opaque covering, or the showing of the female breast with less than a fully opaque covering of any portion thereof below the top of the nipple, or the depiction of covered male genitals in a discernably [sic] turgid state.

3. "Sexual conduct" means acts of masturbation, homosexuality, sexual intercourse, or physical contact with a person's clothed or unclothed genitals, pubic area, buttocks or, if such person be a female, breast.

4. "Sexual excitement" means the condition of human male or female genitals when in a state of sexual stimulation or arousal.

5. "Sado-masochistic abuse" means flagellation or torture by or upon a person clad in undergarments, a mask or bizarre costume, or the condition of being fettered, bound or otherwise physically restrained on the part of one so clothed.

6. "Harmful to minors" means that quality of any description or representation, in whatever form, of nudity, sexual conduct, sexual excitement, or sado-masochistic abuse, when it:

(a) Considered as a whole, appeals to the prurient interest in sex of minors; and

(b) Is patently offensive to prevailing standards in the adult community as a whole with respect to what is suitable material for minors; and

(c) Considered as a whole, lacks serious literary, artistic, political, and scientific value for minors.

7. The term "access software" means software (including client or server software) or enabling tools that do not create or provide the content of the communication but that allow a user to do any one or more of the following:

(a) filter, screen, allow or disallow content;

(b) pick, choose, analyze or digest content; or

(c) transmit, receive, display, forward, cache, search, subset, organize, reorganize or translate content.

Added by L. 1967, Ch. 791; **Amended** by L. 1974, Ch. 989; L. 1996, Ch. 600, § 2, amending opening para. of section, eff. Nov. 1, 1996; L. 1996, Ch. 600, § 3, adding subd. 7, eff. Nov. 1, 1996.

ANNOTATIONS

Constitutionality.—Statute which prohibits a defendant from disseminating indecent material over the Internet for the purpose of luring a minor into sexual conduct does not suffer from the same constitutional infirmity of a statute which only seeks to regulate Internet transmissions. Statute is not vague or overly broad. People v. Barrows, 174 Misc. 2d 367, 664 N.Y.S.2d 410 (Sup. Ct. Kings Co. 1997).

Preemption of local laws.—The Penal Law totally occupies the field of obscenity and disseminating indecent material to minors; hence, local law prohibiting sale or distribution of obscene material to minors was preempted; however, local community still could control means of distribution by zoning, or by recourse to CPLR § 6630 for civil relief. Penny Lane/East Hampton, Inc., 191 A.D.2d 19, 598 N.Y.S.2d 806 (2d Dept. 1993).

§ 235.21. Disseminating indecent material to minors in the second degree.

A person is guilty of disseminating indecent material to minors in the second degree when:

1. With knowledge of its character and content, he sells or loans to a minor for monetary consideration:

(a) Any picture, photograph, drawing, sculpture, motion picture film, or similar visual representation or image of a person or portion of the human body which depicts nudity, sexual conduct or sado-masochistic abuse and which is harmful to minors; or

(b) Any book, pamphlet, magazine, printed matter however reproduced, or sound recording which contains any matter enumerated in paragraph (a) hereof, or explicit and detailed verbal descriptions or narrative accounts of sexual excitement, sexual conduct or sado-masochistic abuse and which, taken as a whole, is harmful to minors; or

2. Knowing the character and content of a motion picture, show or other presentation which, in whole or in part, depicts nudity, sexual conduct or sado-masochistic abuse, and which is harmful to minors, he:

(a) Exhibits such motion picture, show or other presentation to a minor for a monetary consideration; or

(b) Sells to a minor an admission ticket or pass to premises whereon there is exhibited or to be exhibited such motion picture, show or other presentation; or

(c) Admits a minor for a monetary consideration to premises whereon there is exhibited or to be exhibited such motion picture show or other presentation; or

3. Knowing the character and content of the communication which, in whole or in part, depicts actual or simulated nudity, sexual conduct or sado-masochistic abuse, and which is harmful to minors, he intentionally uses any computer communication system allowing the input, output, examination or transfer, of computer data or computer programs from one computer to another, to initiate or engage in such communication with a person who is a minor.

Disseminating indecent material to minors in the second degree is a class E felony.

Added by L. 1967, Ch. 791; **Amended** by L. 1969, Ch. 582; L. 1996, Ch. 600, § 4, amending section heading, opening and closing paras., and subd. 2(c), eff. Nov. 1, 1996; L. 1996, Ch. 600, § 5, adding subd. 3, eff. Nov. 1, 1996.

ANNOTATION

Constitutionality.—Penal Law § 235.21(3) violates the Commerce Clause of the U.S. Constitution. American Library Ass'n v. Pataki, 969 F. Supp. 160 (S.D.N.Y. 1997). *See also* Reno v. American Civil Liberties Union, 521 U.S. 844, 117 S. Ct. 2329, 138 L. Ed. 2d 874 (1997).

§ 235.22. Disseminating indecent material to minors in the first degree.

A person is guilty of disseminating indecent material to minors in the first degree when:

1. Knowing the character and content of the communication which, in whole or in part, depicts

actual or simulated nudity, sexual conduct or sado-masochistic abuse, and which is harmful to minors, he intentionally uses any computer communication system allowing the input, output, examination or transfer, of computer data or computer programs from one computer to another, to initiate or engage in such communication with a person who is a minor; and

2. by means of such communication he importunes, invites or induces a minor to engage in sexual intercourse, oral sexual conduct or anal sexual conduct, or sexual contact with him, or to engage in a sexual performance, obscene sexual performance, or sexual conduct for his benefit.

Disseminating indecent material to minors in the first degree is a class D felony.

Added by L. 1996, Ch. 600, § 6, eff. Nov. 1, 1996; L. 2003, Ch. 264, § 29, eff. Nov. 1, 2003, amending subd. 2.

ANNOTATIONS

Constitutionality.—The speech-conduct targeted and prohibited by statute (i.e., the endangerment of children through the dissemination of sexually explicit and graphic material over the Internet) does not merit First Amendment protection; furthermore, the statute is not a total ban on dissemination, but only a limitation. People v. Foley, 94 N.Y.2d 668, 708 N.Y.S.2d 349, 729 N.E.2d 1148 (2000).

—Penal Law § 235.22, taken in its entirety, is not unconstitutionally vague or overbroad. People v. Barrows, 174 Misc. 2d 367, 664 N.Y.S.2d 410 (Sup. Ct. Kings Co. 1997).

§ 235.23. Disseminating indecent material to minors; presumption and defenses.

1. A person who engages in the conduct proscribed by section 235.21 is presumed to do so with knowledge of the character and content of the material sold or loaned, or the motion picture, show or presentation exhibited or to be exhibited.

2. In any prosecution for disseminating indecent material to minors in the second degree pursuant to subdivision one or two of section 235.21 of this article, it is an affirmative defense that:

(a) The defendant had reasonable cause to believe that the minor involved was seventeen years old or more; and

(b) Such minor exhibited to the defendant a draft card, driver's license, birth certificate or other official or apparently official document purporting to establish that such minor was seventeen years old or more.

3. In any prosecution for disseminating indecent material to minors in the second degree pursuant to subdivision three of section 235.21 of this article or disseminating indecent material to minors in the first degree pursuant to section 235.22 of this article, it shall be a defense that:

(a) the defendant made a reasonable effort to ascertain the true age of the minor and was unable to do so as a result of actions taken by the minor; or

(b) the defendant has taken, in good faith, reasonable, effective and appropriate actions under the circumstances to restrict or prevent access by minors to materials specified in such subdivision, which may involve any appropriate measures to restrict minors from access to such communications, including any method which is feasible under available technology; or

(c) the defendant has restricted access to such materials by requiring use of a verified credit card, debit account, adult access code or adult personal identification number; or

(d) the defendant has in good faith established a mechanism such that the labelling, segregation or other mechanism enables such material to be automatically blocked or screened by software or other capabilities reasonably available to responsible adults wishing to effect such blocking or screening and the defendant has not otherwise solicited minors not subject to such screening or blocking capabilities to access that material or to circumvent any such screening or blocking.

Added by L. 1967, Ch. 791; Renumbered by L. 1996, Ch. 600, § 6, eff. Nov. 1, 1996; Amended by L. 1996, Ch. 600, § 7, eff. Nov. 1, 1996.

§ 235.24. Disseminating indecent material to minors; limitations.

In any prosecution for disseminating indecent material to minors in the second degree pursuant to subdivision three of section 235.21 of this article or disseminating indecent material to minors in the first degree pursuant to section 235.22 of this article:

1. No person shall be held to have violated such provisions solely for providing access or connection to or from a facility, system, or network not under that person's control, including transmission, downloading, intermediate storage, access software, or other related capabilities that are incidental to providing such access or connection that do not include the creation of the content of the communication.

(a) the limitations provided by this subdivision shall not be applicable to a person who is a conspirator with an entity actively involved in the creation or knowing distribution of communications that violate such provisions, or who knowingly advertises the availability of such communications.

(b) the limitations provided by this subdivision shall not be applicable to a person who provides access or connection to a facility, system, or network engaged in the violation of such provisions that is owned or controlled by such person.

2. No employer shall be held liable under such provisions for the actions of an employee or agent unless the employee's or agent's conduct is within the scope of his employment or agency and the employer having knowledge of such conduct,

authorizes or ratifies such conduct, or recklessly
disregards such conduct.

Added by L. 1996, Ch. 600, § 8, eff. Nov. 1, 1996.

TITLE N—OFFENSES AGAINST PUBLIC ORDER, PUBLIC SENSIBILITIES AND THE RIGHT TO PRIVACY

ARTICLE 240—OFFENSES AGAINST PUBLIC ORDER

LexisNexis Cross References

New York Criminal Practice (2d ed.), Vol. 7, Ch. 80, Offenses Against Public Order.

§ 240.00. Offenses against public order; definitions of terms.

The following definitions are applicable to this article:

1. "Public place" means a place to which the public or a substantial group of persons has access, and includes, but is not limited to, highways, transportation facilities, schools, places of amusement, parks, playgrounds, and hallways, lobbies and other portions of apartment houses and hotels not constituting rooms or apartments designed for actual residence.

2. "Transportation facility" means any conveyance, premises or place used for or in connection with public passenger transportation, whether by air, railroad, motor vehicle or any other method. It includes aircraft, watercraft, railroad cars, buses, school buses as defined in section one hundred forty-two of the vehicle and traffic law, and air, boat, railroad and bus terminals and stations and all appurtenances thereto.

3. "School grounds" means in or on or within any building, structure, school bus as defined in section one hundred forty-two of the vehicle and traffic law, athletic playing field, playground or

land contained within the real property boundary line of a public or private elementary, parochial, intermediate, junior high, vocational or high school.

4. "Hazardous substance" shall mean any physical, chemical, microbiological or radiological substance or matter which, because of its quantity, concentration, or physical, chemical or infectious characteristics, may cause or significantly contribute to an increase in mortality or an increase in serious irreversible or incapacitating reversible illness, or pose a substantial present or potential hazard to human health.

5. "Age" means sixty years old or more.

6. "Disability" means a physical or mental impairment that substantially limits a major life activity.

Amended by L. 1999, Ch. 561, § 1, eff. Dec. 1, 1999, adding subd. 4; L. 2000, Ch. 107, § 5, eff. Oct. 8, 2000, adding subds. 5 and 6; L. 2001, Ch. 395, § 1, eff. Nov. 1, 2001, amending subd. 2.

ANNOTATIONS

Public place.—Defendant's intent is irrelevant in determining what is a public place. People v. McNamara, 78 N.Y.2d 626, 578 N.Y.S.2d 476, 585 N.E.2d 788 (1991).

—Definition of public place under Article 240 does not define public place under Penal Law Article 245, proscribing public lewdness. The former Article addresses itself to public order, while the latter statute addresses itself to public sensibilities. People v. McNamara, 78 N.Y.2d 626, 578 N.Y.S.2d 476, 585 N.E.2d 788 (1991).

—Corridor of a single room occupancy hotel is not part of a person's dwelling, but is a public place under P.L. § 240.00, for purposes of justification defense. People v. Mickens, 219 A.D.2d 543, 631 N.Y.S.2d 687 (1st Dept.), lv. denied, 87 N.Y.2d 904 (1995).

—A parking lot is a public place within the meaning of section 240.00. People v. Robinson, 265 A.D.2d 812, 695 N.Y.S.2d 848 (4th Dept. 1999).

§ 240.05. Riot in the second degree.

A person is guilty of riot in the second degree when, simultaneously with four or more other persons, he engages in tumultuous and violent conduct and thereby intentionally or recklessly causes or creates a grave risk of causing public alarm.

Riot in the second degree is a class A misdemeanor.

Amended by L. 1967, Ch. 791.

ANNOTATIONS

Evidence.—Evidence established that appellant committed acts that, if committed by an adult, would constitute the crimes of riot in the second degree and unlawful assembly; while acting in concert with at least four other people, defendant, wearing the colors associated with one gang, was punching and kicking another individual wearing red clothing, which was associated with a rival gang. In re Donovan B., 278 A.D.2d 95, 717 N.Y.S.2d 180 (1st Dept. 2000), appeal denied, 96 N.Y.2d 709 (2001).

Lesser included offense.—Disorderly conduct is a lesser included offense of riot in the second degree; error for court to deny request for charge. People v. Bollander, 156 A.D.2d 456, 549 N.Y.S.2d 27 (2d Dept.), lv. denied, 75 N.Y.2d 867 (1990).

Public place.—Defendant's intent is irrelevant in

determining what is a public place. People v. McNamara, 78 N.Y.2d 626, 578 N.Y.S.2d 476, 585 N.E.2d 788 (1991).

—Definition of public place under Article 240 does not define public place under Penal Law Article 245, proscribing public lewdness. The former Article addresses itself to public order, while the latter statute addresses itself to public sensibilities. People v. McNamara, 78 N.Y.2d 626, 578 N.Y.S.2d 476, 585 N.E.2d 788 (1991).

—Corridor of a single room occupancy hotel is not part of a person's dwelling, but is a public place under P.L. § 240.00, for purposes of justification defense. People v. Mickens, 219 A.D.2d 543, 631 N.Y.S.2d 687 (1st Dept.), lv. denied, 87 N.Y.2d 904 (1995).

§ 240.06. Riot in the first degree.

A person is guilty of riot in the first degree when he:

1. Simultaneously with ten or more other persons, engages in tumultuous and violent conduct and thereby intentionally or recklessly causes or creates a grave risk of causing public alarm, and in the course of and as a result of such conduct, a person other than one of the participants suffers physical injury or substantial property damage occurs; or

2. While in a correctional facility, as that term is defined in subdivision four of section two of the correction law, simultaneously with ten or more other persons, engages in tumultuous and violent conduct and thereby intentionally or recklessly causes or creates a grave risk of causing alarm within such correctional facility and in the course of and as a result of such conduct, a person other than one of the participants suffers physical injury or substantial property damage occurs.

Riot in the first degree is a class E felony.

Added by L. 1967, Ch. 791; Amended by L. 2005, Ch. 294, § 1, eff. Nov. 1, 2005.

ANNOTATIONS

Evidence.—People were not required to prove that defendant was present at, or participating in, the riot when victim was injured, "riot statute permits a riot participant to be held criminally liable for the acts of other participants, in the course of the same continuing riot, even after his or her own participation may have terminated." People v. Ortiz, 8 A.D.3d 55, 777 N.Y.S.2d 640 (1st Dept. 2004).

Public alarm.—Evidence that defendant was part of a mob that descended on job site, not to request jobs, but to terrorize an insufficiently compliant contractor by presence in force and by crude weaponry, in full public view and with obviously intended public consequences, was ample to prove public alarm. People v. Graham, 228 A.D.2d 299, 644 N.Y.S.2d 203 (1st Dept. 1996).

Lesser included offense.—When evidence indicated that defendant and ten to twenty others were waving weapons in a threatening and terrifying manner, which went beyond mere noise making, and there was no reasonable view of the evidence that defendant had been joined by less than ten others, the court properly denied defendant's request to submit riot in the second degree as a lesser included offense. People v. Oliveras, 204 A.D.2d 226, 612 N.Y.S.2d 41 (1st Dept.), lv. denied, 84 N.Y.2d 830 (1994).

§ 240.08. Inciting to riot.

A person is guilty of inciting to riot when he urges ten or more persons to engage in tumultuous and violent conduct of a kind likely to create public alarm.

Inciting to riot is a class A misdemeanor.

Added by L. 1967, Ch. 791.

ANNOTATIONS

Inciting.—When police tried clearing public park after a concert, defendant tried inciting about 100 other persons to resist, pointing at police and shouting "the pigs are here to try to shut off the power and if you want the party to continue, you better let them know it...they are trying to shut us down. what are we going to do? We are going to resist" and police testified that they thought they heard defendant use the term "riot"; defendant waved the crowd toward the stage, about 100 people surged forward, and Parks Department employees were subjected to body blocks when they tried to ascend steps to the stage; as police responded, defendant and others started to swing at the officers, a bottle was thrown and shattered, and defendant was arrested; verdict convicting him of incitement to riot was valid. People v. Tolia, 214 A.D.2d 57, 631 N.Y.S.2d 632 (1st Dept. 1995).

Mental state.—The statute contains no mental state element; court rejected defendant's contention that, implicitly, defendant must be proved to have intended to incite violence; however, for purposes of First Amendment, in order to uphold statute, defendant must intend to present a clear and present danger, which was proved under circumstances where defendant relentlessly urged a crowd of 100 people to attack police and resist attempts to terminate a concert in a public park. People v. Tolia, 214 A.D.2d 57, 631 N.Y.S.2d 632 (1st Dept. 1995).

"Urges."—Court's utilization of terms "provoked" and "stimulated" to define "urges" adequately conveyed the correct meaning of the statutory phrase to the jury. People v. Tolia, 214 A.D.2d 57, 631 N.Y.S.2d 632 (1st Dept. 1995).

Evidence sufficient to sustain conviction.—The evidence was sufficient to sustain defendant's conviction for inciting to riot when the arresting officer testified that: the defendant was in a crowd attempting to gain entrance to a concert hall to free one of their number who was held inside by security guards; that the defendant and his group were asked by the arresting officer to leave three times but defendant instead of leaving urged the crowd on by shouting; "You have no right to keep us out of here. We have all the right to stay in here, we paid our fare" and "These cops can't get away with what they are doing. I will move when I'm ready;" that the defendant upon seeing the police arrest one of the crowd called out; "They can't get away with that. If we had guns we would break it up. They wouldn't do that if we had guns"; and that the police asked defendant to move on to which defendant replied; "We ain't going no place" and the defendant urged the crowd not to leave shouting "Stay right here. They can't make us move." People v. Winston, 64 Misc. 2d 150, 314 N.Y.S.2d 489 (Co. Ct. 1970).

§ 240.10. Unlawful assembly.

A person is guilty of unlawful assembly when he assembles with four or more other persons for the purpose of engaging or preparing to engage with them in tumultuous and violent conduct likely to cause public alarm, or when, being present at an assembly which either has or develops such purpose, he remains there with intent to advance that purpose.

Unlawful assembly is a class B misdemeanor.

Amended by L. 1967, Ch. 791.

ANNOTATIONS

Evidence.—Defendant's act of joining with a group of youths advancing upon a group of police officers in a subway station with the purpose of engaging in "tumultuous and violent conduct likely to cause public harm" supported a conviction under this section. *In re* Danielle V., 293 A.D.2d 373, 740 N.Y.S.2d 212 (1st Dept. 2002).

—Evidence established that appellant committed acts that, if committed by an adult, would constitute the crimes of riot in the second degree and unlawful assembly; while acting in concert with at least four other people, defendant, wearing the colors associated with one gang, was punching and kicking another individual wearing red clothing, which was associated with a rival gang. *In re* Donovan B., 278 A.D.2d 95, 717 N.Y.S.2d 180 (1st Dept. 2000), *appeal denied,* 96 N.Y.2d 709 (2001).

Charge of unlawful assembly; failure to allege facts describing tumultuous and violent conduct.—An information charging defendant with unlawful assembly was defective because it failed to set forth facts describing the tumultuous and violent conduct allegedly engaged in by defendant. People v. Garfield, 63 Misc. 2d 79, 312 N.Y.S.2d 830 (Oneida City Ct. 1970).

§ 240.15. Criminal anarchy.

A person is guilty of criminal anarchy when (a) he advocates the overthrow of the existing form of government of this state by violence, or (b) with knowledge of its contents, he publishes, sells or distributes any document which advocates such violent overthrow, or (c) with knowledge of its purpose, he becomes a member of any organization which advocates such violent overthrow.

Criminal anarchy is a class E felony.

§ 240.20. Disorderly conduct.

A person is guilty of disorderly conduct when, with intent to cause public inconvenience, annoyance or alarm, or recklessly creating a risk thereof:

1. He engages in fighting or in violent, tumultuous or threatening behavior; or

2. He makes unreasonable noise; or

3. In a public place, he uses abusive or obscene language, or makes an obscene gesture; or

4. Without lawful authority, he disturbs any lawful assembly or meeting of persons; or

5. He obstructs vehicular or pedestrian traffic; or

6. He congregates with other persons in a public place and refuses to comply with a lawful order of the police to disperse; or

7. He creates a hazardous or physically offensive condition by any act which serves no legitimate purpose.

Disorderly conduct is a violation.

ANNOTATIONS

Constitutionality.—Prohibition of unreasonable noise with intent to cause public inconvenience, annoyance or harm, is not unconstitutionally vague or overbroad. People v. Bakolas, 59 N.Y.2d 51, 462 N.Y.S.2d 844, 449 N.E.2d 738 (1983).

—Since statute only addresses words in public places that are intended to cause a breach of the peace and are likely to do so, the statute does not on its face violate First Amendment's guarantee of free speech. People v. O'Leary, 153 Misc. 2d 641, 583 N.Y.S.2d 881 (City Ct. of Oswego, Oswego Co. 1992); *accord* People v. Stephen, 153 Misc. 2d 382, 581 N.Y.S.2d 981 (N.Y.C. Crim. Ct. N.Y. Co. 1992).

—Penal Law § 240.20(3) is not overbroad and facially unconstitutional under the First and Fourteenth Amendments of the United States Constitution. People v. Zongone, 102 Misc. 2d 265, 423 N.Y.S.2d 400 (Westchester Co. Ct. 1979).

—Penal Law § 240.20(2) and (3) are constitutional. People v. Grandy, 96 Misc. 2d 494, 409 N.Y.S.2d 77 (Long Beach City Ct. 1978).

Standard to apply.—If abusive words are the gravamen of the disorderly conduct charge, the court should look at the context in which the abusive words are spoken, and whether the words have a public rather than merely private impact, employing the standard of the reasonable man in the same position as the complainant and evaluating defendant's intent as to the meaning of the words and their effect. People v. O'Leary, 153 Misc. 2d 641, 583 N.Y.S.2d 881 (City Ct. of Oswego, Oswego Co. 1992).

Failure to respond to police intervention in dispute.—Defendant, stopped for a traffic violation, became abusive to officer, refused to turn off vehicle, but stood in roadway forcing oncoming traffic to swerve away; refused officer's order to move out of the roadway; arrested for disorderly conduct. People v. Bakolas, 59 N.Y.2d 51, 462 N.Y.S.2d 844, 449 N.E.2d 738 (1983).

—Defendant was among group of youths obstructing pedestrian traffic; police asked him to move on; defendant responded with vulgarities, followed by a second request, which was responded to with a second refusal; arrested for disorderly conduct. In re James T., 189 A.D.2d 580, 592 N.Y.S.2d 36 (1st Dept. 1993); compare with People v. Stephen, 153 Misc. 2d 382, 581 N.Y.S.2d 981 (N.Y.C. Crim. Ct. N.Y. Co. 1992) (People proceeded on theory that defendant's threats to female police officer and vulgar language, constituted violent, tumultuous or threatening behavior under PL § 240.20(1); the threats were not seriously capable of realization, and did not threaten to breach the peace, even if members of a gathering crowd repeated the comments).

—When defendant, who had been arguing on a public street with a woman, whom he slapped, was directed by police, who had intervened, to disperse, defendant failed to cooperate; after initially walking away yelling and cursing, defendant stopped in the middle of the street, slowing traffic almost to a halt; convicted under PL § 240.20(5)relating to disruption of pedestrian or vehicular traffic; defendant claimed that the disruption of traffic was temporary, and he had not intended to cause a public inconvenience, and that his anger was directed at police rather than motorists; defendant's motion to set aside the verdict denied. People v. Carter, 163 Misc. 2d 643, 621 N.Y.S.2d 797 (N.Y.C. Crim. Ct. N.Y. Co. 1994).

Public behavior.—The disruptive behavior which is the basis of a charge of disorderly conduct must be of a public rather than an individual nature. People v. Munafo, 50 N.Y.2d 326, 331, 428 N.Y.S.2d 924, 406 N.E.2d 780 (1980).

—A protestor who blocks pedestrian traffic by refusing to comply with police directive to step behind a police barrier, is within the statute. People v. Munafo, 50 N.Y.2d 326, 331, 428 N.Y.S.2d 924, 406 N.E.2d 780 (1980).

—Defendant, in an area known for prostitution, stopped three vehicles in a twenty minute period to talk to male drivers, thereby obstructing traffic, was charged with disorderly conduct. People v. Denise L., 159 Misc. 2d 1080, 608 N.Y.S.2d 40 (N.Y.C. Crim. Ct. Queens Co. 1994).

—Conduct of defendant in swerving in front of wife's vehicle, apparently trying to drive her off of the road, was of a private, rather than public, nature, and did not constitute disorderly conduct. Seymour v. Seymour, 56 Misc. 2d 546, 289 N.Y.S.2d 515 (Fam. Ct. Tioga Co. 1968).

Refusal to pay fare.—In civil suit alleging unlawful arrest, court concluded that civil plaintiff's conduct in refusing to pay train fare and refusing to leave train, threatened a breach of the peace and validly supported arrest for disorderly conduct. Goldstein v. Metro-North Commuter Railroad Co., 207 A.D.2d 723, 616 N.Y.S.2d 595 (1st Dept. 1994).

Abusive or obscene language in public place.—Defendant, confronted by police in a public theater, made obscene gestures and remarks, in front of about 100 people, constituting the statutory requirements. People v. Perkins, 150 Misc. 2d 543, 576 N.Y.S.2d 750 (App. Term Ninth and Tenth Jud. Dist.'s), lv. denied, 78 N.Y.2d 1129 (1991); compare with People v. Stephens, 153 Misc. 2d 382, 581 N.Y.S.2d 981 (N.Y.C. Crim. Ct. N.Y. Co. 1992) (People proceeded on theory that defendant's threats to female police officer and vulgar language, constituted violent, tumultuous or threatening behavior under PL § 240.20(1); the threats were not seriously capable of realization, and did not threaten to breach the peace, even if members of a gathering crowd repeated the comments).

Physically offensive condition.—Public urination is a physically offensive condition within the statute. People v. Cooke,

152 Misc. 2d 311, 578 N.Y.S.2d 76 (J. Ct. Village of South Nyack, Rockland Co. 1991).

Unreasonable noise.—Defendant's conduct, when stopped for traffic infraction, of yelling at police officer, was basis for charge on theory, inter alia, that defendant created an unreasonable noise; term unreasonable noise, evaluated on an objective basis, was not vague or overbroad. People v. Bakolas, 59 N.Y.2d 51, 462 N.Y.S.2d 844, 449 N.E.2d 738 (1983).

—Disturbs lawful assembly: Protestors who entered cathedral during mass to protest church policies, wherein they created a significant disturbance and interrupted services, were arrested on theory, inter alia, that they disturbed a lawful assembly. People v. King, 148 Misc. 2d 859, 561 N.Y.S.2d 395 (N.Y.C. Crim. Ct. N.Y. Co. 1990).

Order of protection.—Showing that respondent committed acts constituting harassment and disorderly conduct warranted issuance of order of protection by family court. In re Pesce, 223 A.D.2d 647, 637 N.Y.S.2d 18 (2d Dept. 1996).

—When step-father sought order of protection against steps-son, family court had jurisdiction; dispositive consideration is not blood kinship, or whether they shared the same residence, but whether they may be considered to be members of the same family. Nadeau v. Sullivan, 204 A.D.2d 913, 612 N.Y.S.2d 501 (3d Dept. 1994).

—Step-son's conduct of throwing firecrackers from a window above step-father's head, when step-father was only person on the floor at the time, despite extant order of protection in favor of step-father against step-son, constituted disorderly conduct in violation of the order of protection. Nadeau v. Sullivan, 204 A.D.2d 913, 612 N.Y.S.2d 501 (3d Dept. 1994).

Evidence seized pursuant to arrest.—Defendant, stopped by police on suspicion of connection with a crime, agreed to accompany officer to precinct; defendant carried pouch; officer could not open the pouch, but could remove it from defendant during trip to ensure his own safety, provided the pouch was returned unopened upon arrival at precinct; however, defendant physically resisted removal of the pouch, which was the basis for the charge of disorderly conduct, which then authorized officer to seize the pouch pursuant to arrest. People v. Brewer, 200 A.D.2d 579, 606 N.Y.S.2d 292 (2d Dept.), lv. denied, 83 N.Y.2d 869, 635 N.E.2d 299, 613 N.Y.S.2d 130 (1994), cert. denied sub. nom. Brewer v. New York, 115 S. Ct. 148 (1994).

City ordinance.—City ordinance which proscribed disorderly conduct in private premises was held unconstitutional in that such activity is not prohibited under PL § 240.20 which pre-empts varying local laws under the "home rule" provision of the State Constitution, Article 9, Section 2(c) (ii) (c) (10). People v. O'Neal, 93 Misc. 2d 953, 404 N.Y.S.2d 250 (1978).

Conduct.—Conduct did not rise to the level required by the statute where the disturbance complained of was not public, but private in nature, and only the occupants of two apartments complained of the noise. People v. Canner, 88 Misc. 2d 85, 388 N.Y.S.2d 812 (App. Term 2-11 Jud. Dist. 1975), aff'd, 40 N.Y.2d 886, 389 N.Y.S.2d 361, 357 N.E.2d 1016 (1975).

Disorderly conduct; guilty intent; free speech and assembly.—Defendant who dressed as turkey with another dressed as Santa Claus, distributing politically critical handbills was convicted for disorderly conduct for recklessly disregarding the risk of public inconvenience or annoyance and disobeying a police order to disperse aimed solely at maintaining order and avoiding obstruction to vehicular and pedestrian traffic, not arbitrarily issued to silence defendant's unpopular view or opinions and thus not violative of constitutional rights. People v. Pettigrew, 69 Misc. 2d 985, 332 N.Y.S.2d 33 (Dist. Ct. Suffolk Co. 1972).

Protest actions.—Actions taken by defendant as a protest to the appropriation of right-of-way over his farm by the State Power Authority, by positioning himself in the right-of-way, did not make out a case of disorderly conduct, where the actions were undertaken in broad daylight on a secluded stretch of his own property far removed from any public thoroughfare or business or residential area and where not a single bypasser was attracted to the scene. People v. Munafo, 50 N.Y.2d 326, 428 N.Y.S.2d 924, 406 N.E.2d 780 (1980)

Refusal to obey officer's direction to move on.—A reply using obscene language to a police officer's direction to move on, under the circumstance of the case, coupled with a refusal to move, was sufficient to sustain a conviction for disorderly conduct. People v. Todaro, 26 N.Y.2d 325, 310 N.Y.S.2d 258 N.E.2d 711 (1970).

—There was no probable cause to arrest defendant, when after officer observed a group of people drinking wine and blocking sidewalk and dispersed them, he then ordered defendant on the side of street, neither drinking wine nor disturbing passing pedestrians, to leave and arrested him when he failed to comply with the order. People v. McDougall, 48 A.D.2d 802, 369 N.Y.S.2d 443 (1st Dept. 1975).

Fight between teenagers; no evidence of disruptive intent.—Defendant was not guilty of disorderly conduct where evidence showed that fight between him and another boy was a "purely personal clash and momentary teenage flareup" and that, although crowd gathered, there was no disruptive intent on defendant's part or any recklessness which could engender a risk of disruption or disorder. People v. Pritchard, 27 N.Y.2d 245, 317 N.Y.S.2d 4, 265 N.E.2d 532 (1970).

§ 240.21. Disruption, or disturbance of religious service.

A person is guilty of aggravated disorderly conduct, who makes unreasonable noise or disturbance while at a lawfully assembled religious service or within one hundred feet thereof, with intent to cause annoyance or alarm or recklessly creating a risk thereof.

Aggravated disorderly conduct is a class A misdemeanor.

Added by L. 1967, Ch. 614.

ANNOTATIONS

Constitutionality.—Defendant and several others ascended to the altar, spoke loudly in an effort to drown out the liturgy, and approached and crowded parishioners in protest of what defendant anticipated would be a service honoring gay pride. To the extent that the misdemeanor classification of Penal Law §240.21 affords greater protection to those attending worship services than is generally available to those attending secular meetings, the statute does not impermissibly advance religion over nonreligion. People v. McDaniel, 172 Misc. 2d 854, 661 N.Y.S.2d 904 (Sup. Ct. App. T. 1st Dept. 1997).

—Fact that disruption of religious service is a misdemeanor, but disruption of a non-religious assembly, constituting disorderly conduct, is only a violation, does not offend the establishment clause; statute serves legitimate government interest of protecting freedom to worship. People v. Morrisey, 161 Misc. 2d 295, 614 N.Y.S.2d 686 (N.Y.C. Crim. Ct. N.Y. Co. 1994).

—Court rejected claim that defendants were restricted in their own worship; although protestors were reciting rosary at time of their arrest, they did so in a manner calculated to interfere with the orderly progress of the service, and they grabbed microphone from persons conducting readings and tried to pull them from the pulpit; first amendment does not guarantee the absolute right to worship at any time, in any place and in any manner. People v. Morrisey, 161 Misc. 2d 295, 614 N.Y.S.2d 686 (N.Y.C. Crim. Ct. N.Y. Co. 1994).

—Statute applied so as to prohibit protestors from interfering with Catholic mass was not intended to punish protestors for their exercise of religion, but to protect the rights of others to exercise their own religious beliefs without impermissible interference. People v. Morrisey, 161 Misc. 2d 295, 614 N.Y.S.2d 686 (N.Y.C. Crim. Ct. N.Y. Co. 1994).

—Statute is not overly broad. People v. Morrisey, 161 Misc. 2d 295, 614 N.Y.S.2d 686 (N.Y.C. Crim. Ct. N.Y. Co. 1994).

Conduct within.—Conduct must consist of standing within one hundred feet of a religious assembly, with intent to disrupt the service; there is no element that the defendant must, in fact, disturb the service. People v. Morrisey, 161 Misc. 2d 295, 614 N.Y.S.2d 686 (N.Y.C. Crim. Ct. N.Y. Co. 1994).

—Defendants disrupted Catholic mass at St. Patrick's Cathedral in protest to church policies, by entering during mass, handcuffing themselves to pews, shouting slogans, thereby making an unreasonable noise, and refusing to leave, requiring that the defendants be carried out by police. People v. King, 148 Misc. 2d 859, 561 N.Y.S.2d 395 (N.Y.C. Crim. Ct. N.Y. Co. 1990).

Celebrant is not a necessary witness.—Defendants, charged

with disrupting a religious service and disorderly conduct arising out of their protest actions at St. Patrick's Cathedral, subpoenaed the Cardinal, who had been the celebrant; in quashing subpoena, court noted that the issue was not whether the Cardinal had been interrupted, which was not directly relevant to trial issues, but whether defendants' action caused a disturbance which interfered with the ability to celebrate mass of those gathered for that purpose. People v. King, 148 Misc. 2d 859, 561 N.Y.S.2d 395 (N.Y.C. Crim. Ct. N.Y. Co. 1990).

Court forbidden to interpret and weigh church doctrine.—Seven nuns and one laywoman were charged with lying in the center aisle of St. Patrick's Cathedral during a high mass thereby causing a disturbance of the religious service without permission or authority. The defendants contended these acts were proper and within established Catholic tradition and ritual, citing the Constitution on the Sacred Liturgy, and moved to dismiss the complaint. The court, granting the motion, held these are internal matters to be decided within the Church. To reach the question raised by the defendants would require the court to engage in the forbidden process of interpreting and weighing church doctrine. People v. Steele, 70 Misc. 2d 351, 333 N.Y.S.2d 959 (N.Y.C. Crim. Ct. 1972).

§ 240.25. Harassment in the first degree.

A person is guilty of harassment in the first degree when he or she intentionally and repeatedly harasses another person by following such person in or about a public place or places or by engaging in a course of conduct or by repeatedly committing acts which places such person in reasonable fear of physical injury. This section shall not apply to activities regulated by the national labor relations act, as amended, the railway labor act, as amended, or the federal employment labor management act, as amended.

Harassment in the first degree is a class B misdemeanor.

Added by L. 1992, Ch. 345, eff. Nov. 1, 1992; **Amended** by L. 1994, Ch. 109.

ANNOTATIONS

Constitutionality.—Former § 240.25(2) was unconstitutional on its face. People v. Dietz, 75 N.Y.2d 47, 550 N.Y.S.2d 595, 549 N.E.2d 1166 (1989).

Threats must be serious.—Defendant's threat that he would "beat the crap out of" the victim some day under circumstances of the case was not intended to be serious or to be taken seriously, and intent to do so was not confirmed by additional evidence. People v. Dietz, 75 N.Y.2d 47, 550 N.Y.S.2d 595, 549 N.E.2d 1166 (1989).

Right to jury trial.—Since harassment in the first degree is a petty offense, authorizing imprisonment for six months or less, so that there is no sixth amendment right to a jury trial. People v. Foy, 166 Misc. 2d 358, 636 N.Y.S.2d 559 (1st Dept.), lv. granted, 87 N.Y.2d 901 (1995).

—There was no basis, either in constitutional law or in public policy, to add together potential sentences for several misdemeanor offenses to reach a potential cumulative sentence in excess of six months so as to invoke right to a jury trial. People v. Foy, 166 Misc. 2d 358, 636 N.Y.S.2d 559 (1st Dept.), lv. granted, 87 N.Y.2d 901 (1995).

Intent.—In civil proceeding in which plaintiff challenged basis of his arrest, court took notice that allegations that plaintiff, upon being stopped upon entering a street sealed off by police, engaged in a verbal altercation with the officer, shoved the officer, accused the officer of a crime, shoved his finger into the officer's chest, and grabbed the officer's badge, would have supported the inference that defendant intended to place the officer in fear for his safety. Kellermueller v. Port Auth. of New York and New Jersey, 201 A.D.2d 427, 607 N.Y.S.2d 942 (1st Dept. 1994).

Relation with Family Court proceedings.—Harassment as defined in the penal law is a family offense within the meaning of F.C.A. 812. Boyd v. Boyd, 193 A.D.2d 1039, 598 N.Y.S.2d 380 (3d Dept. 1993).

Relation with Civil Rights Law.—Harassment in connection with a person's race, creed, color, national origin, sex, marital status or disability may also be basis for violation of Civil Rights Law 40-d. People v. Fuller, 155 Misc. 2d 812, 590 N.Y.S.2d 159 (N.Y.C. Crim. Ct. Kings Co. 1992).

—Although the Attorney General must be given notice in the event of the commencement of a civil rights action, such notice is not a condition precedent to the commencement of the criminal prosecution. People v. Fuller, 155 Misc. 2d 812, 590 N.Y.S.2d 159 (N.Y.C. Crim. Ct. Kings Co. 1992).

Sufficiency of evidence.—Where defendant, almost daily for a two-month period, stood approximately 25 feet from the front of complainant's store window and stared at complainant, acted erratically, and then left the area as soon as the complainant acknowledged him, conviction under this section could stand, even though complainant never feared for his safety. People v. Corichi, 195 Misc. 2d 518, 759 N.Y.S.2d 286 (Sup. Ct. App. T. 2003).

§ 240.26. Harassment in the second degree.

A person is guilty of harassment in the second degree when, with intent to harass, annoy or alarm another person:

1. He or she strikes, shoves, kicks or otherwise subjects such other person to physical contact, or attempts or threatens to do the same; or

2. He or she follows a person in or about a public place or places; or

3. He or she engages in a course of conduct or repeatedly commits acts which alarm or seriously annoy such other person and which serve no legitimate purpose.

Subdivisions two and three of this section shall not apply to activities regulated by the national labor relations act, as amended, the railway labor act, as amended, or the federal employment labor management act, as amended.

Harassment in the second degree is a violation.

Amended by L. 1967, Ch. 791; L. 1988, Ch. 86; L. 1992, Ch. 345, eff. Nov. 1, 1992, L. 1994 Ch. 109.

ANNOTATIONS

Relation with Family Court proceedings.—Harassment in the second degree is a family offense within the meaning of FCA § 812(1) (see also CPL § 530.11(1)), which vests jurisdiction in Family Court. Eileen W. v. Mario A., 169 Misc. 2d 484, 644 N.Y.S.2d 452 (Fam. Ct. N.Y. Co. 1996).

—The fact that the harassment occurred in another state would not deprive Family Court of jurisdiction; legislature did not evince an intention to limit Family Court jurisdiction in the event that an act occurs out of the state, as contrasted with CPL Article 20, which applies to criminal, rather than Family Court, proceedings. Eileen W. v. Mario A., 169 Misc. 2d 484, 644 N.Y.S.2d 452 (Fam. Ct. N.Y. Co. 1996).

Arrest.—Only a person in whose presence the offenses of harassment was committed is authorized to make the arrest. People v. Giorgetti, 103 Misc. 2d 118, 425 N.Y.S.2d 502 (Suffolk Co. Ct. 1980).

Disorderly conduct not a lesser included offense of harassment.—People v. Alvarez, 66 Misc. 2d 205, 319 N.Y.S.2d 1017 (1st Dept. 1971).

Harassment not lesser included offense of assault for purposes of conviction after verdict.—Harassment requires an intent to harass, annoy or alarm, which is not included in or required by the language of Penal Law § 120.00, which defines assault. Therefore, harassment is not a lesser included offense of assault for purposes of conviction after verdict. People v. Moyer, 27 N.Y.2d 252, 317 N.Y.S.2d 9 (1970).

Harassment; derisive and offensive name calling.—Use of the words "stupid bastard" and "son of a bitch" to police officers were disorderly remarks constituting harassment within meaning of statute under standard of what offends common intelligence of the average person. People v. Cuomo, 70 Misc. 2d 757, 335 N.Y.S.2d 219 (N.Y.C. Crim. Ct. N.Y. Co. 1972).

Harassment; racial slur.—Defendant could not be convicted of harassment when he stated to a friend that "there was a nigger on the door," referring to a black police officer, which remark was overheard by another police officer. Penal Law § 240.25 requires an affirmative showing that a person was annoyed or harassed and the addressee of the remark indicated that he did not care nor was he upset by what defendant said. Further, this statement is not as a matter of law abusive or obscene. People v. DiFeo, 69 Misc. 2d 1036, 331 N.Y.S.2d 554 (Onondaga Co. Ct. 1972).

Information; insufficient.—Where the information failed to specify an essential element of the crime that the acts be done with intent to harass, annoy or alarm it was jurisdictionally defective. People v. Hall, 48 N.Y.2d 927, 425 N.Y.S.2d 56, 401 N.E.2d 179 (1979).

Lesser included offense.—Harassment in the second degree is not a lesser included offense of menacing in the second degree. People v. Bartkow, 96 N.Y.2d 770, 725 N.Y.S.2d 589, 749 N.E.2d 158 (2001).

Juvenile offender.—A youth cannot be adjudged a juvenile delinquent based on the charges of harassment, since harassment is a violation and not a crime. In re Smith, 108 Misc. 2d 1063, 439 N.Y.S.2d 272 (Fam. Ct. Rensselaer Co. 1981).

Factors amounting to harassment of police officer.—Defendant was guilty of harassment of a police officer where he: (1) accused the officer of a crime in a public place; (2) placed his finger on the officer's chest; and (3) attempted to search the officer's person. People v. Hare, 66 Misc. 2d 207, 319 N.Y.S.2d 890 (App. Term 1st Dept. 1971).

Charge of harassment based on threat to get arresting officer.—A statement made to a police officer by a defendant arrested for disorderly conduct that "I'll get you for this" is not harassment. People v. Todaro, 26 N.Y.2d 325, 310 N.Y.S.2d 303, 258 N.E.2d 711 (1970).

Conduct proscribed by section.—If the defendant committed any acts which indicated he harassed or tampered with the complainant as a witness, then any similar events or acts committed by his accomplices and relatives in concert with and in furtherance of his criminal activity, as related by complainant or her employer, could be found by the jury to have been circumstantially tied to the defendant. People v. Plumber, 36 N.Y.2d 161, 365 N.Y.S.2d 842, 325 N.E.2d 161 (1975).

—Conviction for harassment in the second degree was supported by a preponderance of evidence in the record which established that despite the existence of an order of protection, defendant continued to threaten the victim and continued in a menacing and threatening manner even after others had intervened. McGuffog v. Ginsberg, 266 A.D.2d 136, 699 N.Y.S.2d 26 (1st Dept. 1999).

—Allegations that defendant made more than one threatening phone call to complainant daily over a period of two months, standing alone, provides a "reasonable basis to infer that defendant intended to communicate with complainant in a manner likely to cause annoyance or alarm." People v. Tiffany, 186 Misc. 2d 917, 721 N.Y.S.2d 741 (Crim. Ct. N.Y. Co. 2001).

—Motion to dismiss granted where complainant alleged that he was threatened by defendant, who operated a garage and auto repair shop to the annoyance of the neighborhood, since such an act did not rise to the level of the crime of harassment (PL § 240.25). People v. Markovitz, 102 Misc. 2d 575, 423 N.Y.S.2d 996 (Crim. Ct. N.Y. Co. 1979).

—Allegations that defendant tavern owner made excessive noise, littered adjoining property, and used obscene and abusive language fell within purview of harassment statute which is not unconstitutional or too vague to be enforced. People v. Lamb, 86 Misc. 2d 1023, 384 N.Y.S.2d 929 (Rochester City Ct. 1976).

—Since PL § 240.25(5) provides that a person is guilty of harassment if he "engages in a course of conduct or repeatedly commits acts," the use of the disjunctive "or" indicates that the language is to be construed in the alternative sense and it is unnecessary for the defendant to repeatedly commit acts in order for a pattern of behavior to constitute a "course of conduct."

People v. Tralli, 88 Misc. 2d 117, 387 N.Y.S.2d 37 (Sup. Ct. App. Term 9-10 Jud. Dist. 1976).

—Penal Law § 240.25(2) should be construed as proscribing obscene words and/or gestures which "substantially annoy a person to a degree that there would be a direct tendency that the person addressed would react by an act of violence or a breach of the public peace." Therefore, a defendant who made a fleeting obscene remark, accompanied by an obscene gesture, directed at a police officer, could not be guilty under penal Law § 240.25(2). In a prosecution for harassment part of the circumstances considered must include the addressee, what his role is or should be, or into what class he falls. People v. Benders, 63 Misc. 2d 572, 312 N.Y.S.2d 603 (City Ct. 1970).

Defendant indicted for assault second; judge not required to charge jury as to harassment.—Harassment is a violation, not a crime. Therefore, the court need not charge the jury concerning harassment where a defendant is charged with assault second. CCP § 445 requires a charge only as to lesser degrees or included *crimes*. People v. McDowell, 35 A.D.2d 611, 312 N.Y.S.2d 477 (3d Dept. 1970), *modified on other grounds,* 28 N.Y.2d 373, 321 N.Y.S.2d 894, 270 N.E.2d 716 (1971).

Information; amendment.—Where information accused defendant of disorderly conduct and was never amended, and thereafter defendant was found guilty of harassment, it was error not to amend charge and advise defendant of change. People v. Gingello, 69 Misc. 2d 845, 330 N.Y.S.2d 921 (Monroe Co. Ct. 1972).

Intent to harass, annoy or harm.—Mother who barred the door to nine-year-old son's bedroom with her body, informed police they could not go in, and struggled with police after they seized her, was not guilty of harassment where People failed to prove she intended to harass, annoy or alarm the officers. People v. Schmidt, 76 Misc. 2d 976, 352 N.Y.S.2d 399 (Crim. Ct. Bronx Co. 1974).

Private residence not public place.—Where defendant was charged with using obscene and abusive language toward another person in a public place and with following that person in a public place with the intent to harass, annoy or alarm that person, the court dismissed the information on the ground that the acts complained of took place in a private residence and it was irrelevant that the language was overheard by people outside the residence. A private residence does not become a public place within Penal Law § 240.00 unless there are special circumstances shown, and such circumstances are alleged in the information charging the harassment. People v. Paradiso, 58 Misc. 2d 370, 295 N.Y.S.2d 561 (Ct. Spec. Sess. 1968).

Obscene and abusive language.—Defendant's statements in the midst of a heated discussion to complainant, "The first chance I get to f---you, I'm going to f---you big time. It might not be on the job, but I'm going to f---you." were more than just "abusive or vulgar." The words were "classic fighting words" which are capable of conveying a threat of harm to a reasonable person. The exact meaning of the defendant's words is a question of fact for the jury. People v. Barbara, 173 Misc. 2d 669, 662 N.Y.S.2d 211 (1st Dist. Nassau Co. 1997).

—A prosecution for harassment based on the use of directed abusive and obscene language may lie only where the words are uttered as a deliberate challenge to a breach of the peace, in order to pass the constitutional muster the gravamen of the offense cannot be solely in the repugnancy of the words alleged or even that they were intended to be offensive but rather that the offending words were calculated to provoke a reasonable man into an immediate and violent breach of the peace and had no other purpose. People v. Cerbone, 113 Misc. 2d 740, 449 N.Y.S.2d 903 (Town Ct. Harrison, 1982).

Offense; crime; inquiry.—Harassment, one of the lesser offenses designated a "violation," falls within the generic term "offense," and conviction for harassment was therefore a proper subject of inquiry during trial. If the legislature had intended a different result, it merely had to use the word "crime." People v. Gray, 41 A.D.2d 125, 341 N.Y.S.2d 485 (3d Dept. 1973), *aff'd,* 34 N.Y.2d 903, 359 N.Y.S.2d 286, 316 N.E.2d 719, *cert. denied,* 419 U.S. 1055 (1974).

Resisting arrest; basis of lawful arrest; self defense; harassment as lesser offense of assault; failure to object.—Where defendant was obstructing traffic and was uncooperative with policeman who placed him under arrest to which he answered "No, for what." he evidenced verbal conduct clearly showing requisite intent for resisting properly authorized arrest

and subsequent physical conduct was not self defense against excessive physical force. Thus, refusal of court to answer jury's question as to difference between resisting arrest and self defense was proper, and defendant failure to object that harassment was not lesser included crime of assault, was waiver of that claim. People v. Stevenson, 31 N.Y.2d 108, 335 N.Y.S.2d 52, 286 N.E.2d 445 (1972).

Transfer; jurisdiction.—Stepfather was charged with assault in the second degree of his stepson. Charges were later reduced to assault in the third degree and harassment. In response to defendant's motion to transfer the action to the Family Court, the Crim. Ct. held that a stepson is not a member of the same family or household, as the terms are used in the Family Court Act, so as to vest exclusive jurisdiction of the controversy in the Family Court, and therefore a transfer from the Crim. Ct. to the Family Court was not necessary. People v. Weisman, 72 Misc. 2d 465, 339 N.Y.S.2d 482 (Crim. Ct. N.Y. Co. 1973).

§ 240.30. Aggravated harassment in the second degree.

A person is guilty of aggravated harassment in the second degree when, with intent to harass, annoy, threaten or alarm another person, he or she:

1. Either

(a) communicates with a person, anonymously or otherwise, by telephone, or by telegraph, mail or any other form of written communication, in a manner likely to cause annoyance or alarm; or

(b) causes a communication to be initiated by mechanical or electronic means or otherwise with a person, anonymously or otherwise, by telephone, or by telegraph, mail or any other form of written communication, in a manner likely to cause annoyance or alarm; or

2. Makes a telephone call, whether or not a conversation ensues, with no purpose of legitimate communication; or

3. Strikes, shoves, kicks, or otherwise subjects another person to physical contact, or attempts or threatens to do the same because of a belief or perception regarding such person's race, color, national origin, ancestry, gender, religion, religious practice, age, disability or sexual orientation, regardless of whether the belief or perception is correct; or

4. Commits the crime of harassment in the first degree and has previously been convicted of the crime of harassment in the first degree as defined by section 240.25 of this article within the preceding ten years.

Aggravated harassment in the second degree is a class A misdemeanor.

Amended by L. 1969, Ch. 290; L. 1982, Ch. 191; L. 1992, Ch. 345, eff. Nov. 1, 1992, adding subd. 4; L. 2000, Ch. 107, eff. Oct. 8, 2000, amending subd. 3; L. 2001, Ch. 385, eff. Nov. 1, 2001, amending subd. 1.

ANNOTATIONS

Constitutionality.—Statute defining aggravated harassment in the second degree did not impermissibly restrict freedom of expression, was not facially unconstitutional, was not overbroad, and did not violate due process. People v. Shack, 86 N.Y.S.2d 529, 634 N.Y.S.2d 660, 658 N.E.2d 706 (1995).

—The defendant's right to free speech is subordinated to the complainant's substantial privacy rights. People v. Shack, 86 N.Y.2d 529, 634 N.Y.S.2d 660, 658 N.E.2d 706 (1995).

—Since phone calls must have no legitimate purpose in order to invoke the statute's prohibitions, the statute would not criminalize all phone calls, during which anger is vented, to psychologists of other persons providing a service, and hence statute is not overbroad. People v. Shack, 86 N.Y.2d 529, 634 N.Y.S.2d 660, 658 N.E.2d 706 (1995).

Relation to Civil Rights Law.—Harassment in connection with a person's race, creed, color, national origin, sex, marital status or disability may also be basis for violation of Civil Rights Law § 40-d. People v. Fuller, 155 Misc. 2d 812, 590 N.Y.S.2d 159 (N.Y.C. Crim. Ct. Kings Co. 1992).

—Although the Attorney General must be given notice in the event of the commencement of a civil rights action, such notice is not a condition precedent to the commencement of the criminal prosecution. People v. Fuller, 155 Misc. 2d 812, 590 N.Y.S.2d 159 (N.Y.C. Crim. Ct. Kings Co. 1992); *accord* People v. Mulqueen, 155 Misc. 2d 632, 589 N.Y.S.2d 246 (Dist. Ct. Nassau Co. 1992).

—Even though defendant was acquitted of two counts charging him with aggravated harassment arising out of his phone calls on basis of complainant's race, creed or national origin, verdict convicting him of violation of Civil Rights Law § 40-c was valid; Civil Rights Law violation addressed, not the defendant's speech, but his conduct. People v. Mulqueen, 155 Misc. 2d 632, 589 N.Y.S.2d 246 (Dist. Ct. Nassau Co. 1992).

Harassing telephone calls.—Defendant's messages, which "were crude and offensive but made in the context of complaining about government actions, on a telephone answering machine set up for the purpose (among others) of receiving complaints from the public," did not fall within any of the proscribed class of speech or conduct under the statute. People v. Mangano, 100 N.Y.2d 569, 764 N.Y.S.2d 379, 796 N.E.2d 470 (2003).

—Defendant, who was mentally ill, but had stopped taking his medication, called his cousin, a psychologist, who, however, had no professional relationship with him, hundreds of times after she had told him not to call her until he resumed taking his medication; these calls became threatening, dozens were made on the day she underwent surgery, for the apparent purpose of annoying her, and the calls had no legitimate purpose. People v. Shack, 86 N.Y.2d 529, 634 N.Y.S.2d 660, 658 N.E.2d 706 (1995).

—Evidence that defendant placed two threatening telephone calls to his wife in violation of an order of protection, was sufficient to support his convictions for harassment and criminal contempt even though she did not actually answer the phone and speak to defendant, it was enough that the answering machine recorded defendant's message. People v. Ruey Dei, 2 A.D.3d 1459, 769 N.Y.S.2d 772 (4th Dept. 2003).

—Defendant committed aggravated harassment by making a series of offensive and disparaging phone calls to the complainant. People v. Miguez, 153 Misc. 2d 442, 590 N.Y.S.2d 156 (App. Term 1st Dept. 1992).

—Allegations that defendant made more than one threatening phone call to complainant daily over a period of two months, which included the threat, "If you try to keep me away from my son I'm going to put a bullet through your head," constituted a genuine threat and was facially sufficient to support the charges. People v. Tiffany, 186 Misc. 2d 917, 721 N.Y.S.2d 741 (Crim. Ct. N.Y. Co. 2001).

—Court dismissed count of indictment charging a violation of this section where defendant did not place the telephone call or initiate the contact with complainant; however, court did not preclude possibility that section could be violated in situations where although complainant placed call to defendant, defendant precipitated call for purpose of communicating threats or abuse. People v. Monroe, 183 Misc. 2d 374, 703 N.Y.S.2d 690 (Crim. Ct. N.Y. Co. 2000).

—A single telephone call containing threats and intimidating statements is facially sufficient to withstand a motion to dismiss. People v. Liberato, 180 Misc. 2d 199, 689 N.Y.S.2d 363 (Crim. Ct. N.Y. Co. 1999).

Threatening mail.—Petitioner's conduct of mailing a death threat to the Governor, but signing it in the name of a person who was involved in a traffic accident with petitioner, constituted aggravated harassment in the second degree, and was proper basis to terminate employment of police officer. Mahabir v. Kelly, 215 A.D.2d 280, 627 N.Y.S.2d 346 (1st Dept. 1995).

—Harassing and threatening messages sent via the Internet are encompassed within the prohibitions of this section. People v. Munn, 179 Misc. 2d 903, 688 N.Y.S.2d 384 (Crim Ct. Queens Co. 1999).

Prior uncharged crimes.—Evidence that defendant, who was charged with making a series of harassing and disparaging phone calls to complainant, had made similar calls on prior occasions, and had followed him in a car, was admissible as being probative of defendant's intent and was inextricably intertwined with evidence relevant to identity. People v. Miguez, 153 Misc. 2d 442, 590 N.Y.S.2d 156 (App. Term 1st Dept. 1992).

Continuing crime.—Aggravated harassment can be committed by a single act, or it may be committed by a pattern or sequence of acts, and hence may be a continuing crime; accusatory instrument which charged defendant in a single count alleging numerous phone calls over a six month period sufficiently put defendant on notice of the charge. People v. Shack, 86 N.Y.2d 529, 634 N.Y.S.2d 660, 658 N.E.2d 706 (1995).

Prosecutor's summation.—When defendant was charged with aggravated harassment in the second degree arising out of harassment on basis of race, creed, national origin, prosecutor's reference in summation to defendant being a bigot was fair comment on the evidence and was germane to a trial issue (bias motivated attacks) and was within bounds of fair advocacy. People v. Fratta, 190 A.D.2d 1089, 593 N.Y.S.2d 707 (4th Dept. 1993).

Citizens' band radios.—Upon examination of the statutory language and legislative intent, PL § 240.30(1) cannot be construed in its present form to cover communication by citizens' band radio. People v. Viau, 50 N.Y.2d 1052, 431 N.Y.S.2d 702, 409 N.E.2d 1376 (1980).

Proper conviction.—Defendant was properly convicted of violating PL § 240.30 when he called the Police Department 27 times in 3 hours and 20 minutes after they had informed him that a previous investigation disclosed that the matter was civil rather than criminal in nature. People v. Smith, 89 Misc. 2d 789, 392 N.Y.S.2d 968 (App. Term 9-10 Jud. Dist. 1977), *cert. denied,* 434 U.S. 920.

Racially motivated.—Court properly allowed jury to consider pictures of defendant's tattoos as well as testimony from an expert certified in bias and hate crimes as to the customary meaning of letters, symbols and images represented in those tattoos, evidence was not compelled testimony in violation of Fifth Amendment privilege against self-incrimination. People v. Slavin, 1 N.Y.3d 392, 775 N.Y.S.2d 210, 807 N.E.2d 259, *cert. denied,* — U.S. —, 125 S. Ct. 64 (2004).

—Jury was entitled to conclude that defendant's actions were racially motivated where evidence was presented that defendants used racial epithets during the assault. People v. Pirozzi, 237 A.D.2d 628, 656 N.Y.S.2d 42 (2d Dept. 1997).

§ 240.31. Aggravated harassment in the first degree.

A person is guilty of aggravated harassment in the first degree when with intent to harass, annoy, threaten or alarm another person, because of a belief or perception regarding such person's race, color, national origin, ancestry, gender, religion, religious practice, age, disability or sexual orientation, regardless of whether the belief or perception is correct, he or she:

1. Damages premises primarily used for religious purposes, or acquired pursuant to section six of the religious corporation law and maintained for purposes of religious instruction, and the damage to the premises exceeds fifty dollars; or

2. Commits the crime of aggravated harassment in the second degree in the manner proscribed by the provisions of subdivision three of

section 240.30 of this article and has been previously convicted of the crime of aggravated harassment in the second degree for the commission of conduct proscribed by the provisions of subdivision three of section 240.30 or he has been previously convicted of the crime of aggravated harassment in the first degree within the preceding ten years.

Aggravated harassment in the first degree is a class E felony.

Added by L. 1982, Ch. 191; **Amended** by L. 1983, Ch. 958; L. 2000 Ch. 107, § 4, eff. Oct. 8, 2000, amending opening paragraph.

§ 240.32. Aggravated harassment of an employee by an inmate.

An inmate or respondent is guilty of aggravated harassment of an employee by an inmate when, with intent to harass, annoy, threaten or alarm a person in a facility whom he knows or reasonably should know to be an employee of such facility or the division of parole or the office of mental health, or a probation department, bureau or unit, or a police officer, he causes or attempts to cause such employee to come into contact with blood, seminal fluid, urine or feces, by throwing, tossing or expelling such fluid or material.

For purposes of this section, "inmate" means an inmate or detainee in a correctional facility, local correctional facility or a hospital, as such term is defined in subdivision two of section four hundred of the correction law. For purposes of this section, "respondent" means a juvenile in a secure facility operated and maintained by the office of children and family services who is placed with or committed to the office of children and family services. For purposes of this section, "facility" means a correctional facility or local correctional facility, hospital, as such term is defined in subdivision two of section four hundred of the correction law, or a secure facility operated and maintained by the office of children and family services.

Aggravated harassment of an employee by an inmate is a class E felony.

Added by L. 1996, Ch. 92, eff. June 5, 1996. **Amended** by L. 2000, Ch. 422, § 1, and Ch. 441, § 1, eff. Nov. 1, 2000.

ANNOTATIONS

Sufficiency of evidence.—Testimony that defendant threw a cup containing feces and urine at two corrections officers supported defendant's conviction for aggravated harassment of an employee by an inmate. People v. Agaro, 303 A.D.2d 518, 756 N.Y.S.2d 444 (2d Dept. 2003).

—Evidence that the liquid defendant threw at and struck the correction officer with smelled of urine, together with the other evidence submitted by the People, was legally sufficient to support a conviction under this section. People v. Ortiz, 305 A.D.2d 979, 758 N.Y.S.2d 566 (4th Dept. 2003).

§ 240.35. Loitering.

A person is guilty of loitering when he:

1. Loiters, remains or wanders about in a public place for the purpose of begging; or

2. Loiters or remains in a public place for the purpose of gambling with cards, dice or other gambling paraphernalia; or

3. Loiters or remains in a public place for the purpose of engaging, or soliciting another person to engage, in oral sexual conduct, anal sexual conduct or other sexual behavior of a deviate nature; or

4. Being masked or in any manner disguised by unusual or unnatural attire or facial alteration, loiters, remains or congregates in a public place with other persons so masked or disguised, or knowingly permits or aids persons so masked or disguised to congregate in a public place; except that such conduct is not unlawful when it occurs in connection with a masquerade party or like entertainment if, when such entertainment is held in a city which has promulgated regulations in connection with such affairs, permission is first obtained from the police or other appropriate authorities; or

5. Loiters or remains in or about school grounds, a college or university building or grounds or a children's overnight camp as defined in section one thousand three hundred ninety-two of the public health law or a summer day camp as defined in section one thousand three hundred ninety-two of the public health law, or loiters, remains in or enters a school bus as defined in section one hundred forty-two of the vehicle and traffic law, not having any reason or relationship involving custody of or responsibility for a pupil or student, or any other specific, legitimate reason for being there, and not having written permission from anyone authorized to grant the same or loiters or remains in or about such children's overnight camp or summer day camp in violation of conspicuously posted rules or regulations governing entry and use thereof; or

6. Loiters or remains in any transportation facility, unless specifically authorized to do so, for the purpose of soliciting or engaging in any business, trade or commercial transactions involving the sale of merchandise or services, or for the purpose of entertaining persons by singing, dancing or playing any musical instrument; or

7. Loiters or remains in any transportation facility, or is found sleeping therein, and is unable to give a satisfactory explanation of his presence.

Loitering is a violation.

Amended by L. 1967, Ch. 791; L. 1968, Ch. 668; L. 1978, Ch. 446; L. 1979, Ch. 698; L. 2000, Ch. 533, § 2, eff. Oct. 4, 2000; L. 2001, Ch. 350, eff. Sept. 19, 2001, and Ch. 395, eff. Nov. 1, 2001, amending subds. 5 and 7; L. 2003, Ch. 264, § 30, eff. Nov. 1, 2003, amending subd. 3.

ANNOTATIONS

Constitutionality.—To the extent that a loitering statute which prohibits loitering for a specific illegal purpose, or loitering in a specific place of restricted public access, it would not fail for vagueness; PL § 240.35 (7) held unconstitutionality vague and unconstitutional on the ground that it required a citizen to relinquish his constitutional right against compulsory self-incrimination in order to avoid arrest. People v. Bright, 71 N.Y.2d 376, 526 N.Y.S.2d 66, 520 N.E.2d 1355 (1988).

—PL § 240.35(7), regarding loitering in transportation facilities, is unconstitutional; requiring defendant to give a "satisfactory explanation" of his presence is unconstitutionally vague, in that it does not provide sufficient notice as to what explanation would be satisfactory, despite the fact that the provision limited these requirements to transportation facilities, and by not including objective criteria, it allows for arbitrary interpretation by the responding police officer; the same phrasing violates the defendant's Fifth Amendment right to remain silent when approached by police. People v. Bright, 71 N.Y.2d 376, 526 N.Y.S.2d 66, 520 N.E.2d 1355 (1988) (necessarily overruling People v. Goodwin, 136 Misc. 2d 657, 519 N.Y.S.2d 189 (Dist. Ct. Nassau Co. 1987), finding provision to be constitutional as applied).

—PL § 240.35(3) is unconstitutional as there is no requirement that the conduct prescribed be in any way offensive or annoying to other. People v. Uplinger, 58 N.Y.2d 936, 460 N.Y.S.2d 514 (1983), *dismissed,* 464 U.S. 812 (1984).

—PL § 240.35(6) is unconstitutional. People v. Berk, 32 N.Y.2d 567, 347 N.Y.S.2d 33, 300 N.E.2d 411, *cert. denied,* 414 U.S. 1093.

—Anti-mask provision of loitering statute restrains conduct, not speech, and defendants failed to show that their bandanas were a necessary corollary of their First Amendment rights of association. People v. Aboaf, 187 Misc. 2d 173, 721 N.Y.S.2d 725 (Crim. Ct. N.Y. Co. 2001).

—PL § 240.35(1), prohibiting loitering in a public place for the purpose of begging, is constitutional. People v. Schrader, 162 Misc. 2d 789, 617 N.Y.S.2d 429 (N.Y.C. Crim. Ct. 1994).

—PL § 240.35(2) likely is unconstitutional, though the court did not have to reach the issue; court noted that gambling per se is not criminal activity, insofar as the Penal Law prohibits only the promotion of gambling and possession of gambling records or a gambling device; if the activity for which the defendant loiters, to gamble, is not illegal, then the loitering itself cannot be criminalized. People v. Melton, 152 Misc. 2d 649, 578 N.Y.S.2d 377 (Sup. Ct. Monroe Co. 1991).

Public place.—A transportation facility is a public place, and by its nature actually invites conduct which could be construed to be loitering. People v. Bright, 71 N.Y.2d 376, 526 N.Y.S.2d 66, 520 N.E.2d 1355 (1988); *but see* People v. Schrader, 162 Misc. 2d 789, 617 N.Y.S.2d 429 (N.Y.C. Crim. Ct. 1994) (transit system is a nonpublic forum).

Begging.—Begging is constitutionally protected speech. Loper v New York City Police Dept., 802 F. Supp. 1029 (S.D.N.Y.), *aff'd,* 999 F.2d 699 (2d Cir. 1993).

—Although begging is constitutionally protected, a ban on begging in the transit system is a reasonable limitation on speech in a non-public forum, being a safety precaution and not a restriction of the content of the speech. People v. Schrader, 162 Misc. 2d 789, 617 N.Y.S.2d 429 (N.Y.C. Crim. Ct. 1994) (transit system is a nonpublic forum).

Search and seizure pursuant to loitering.—When officer observed defendant and others apparently gambling, with cash and dice in plain view, he had probable cause to arrest; however, the legality of the arrest depended on the constitutionality of this provision of the loitering statute; he did not then arrest defendant, though, but asked, and received consent, to frisk defendant for weapons, upon which drugs were found in defendant's pocket; as such, whether or not PL § 240.35(2) is constitutional, did not invalidate the arrest. People v. Melton, 152 Misc. 2d 649, 578 N.Y.S.2d 377 (Sup. Ct. Monroe Co. 1991).

Failure to present proof that defendant loitered for an appreciable period.—Where there was no proof of loitering by defendant for any appreciable period of time, the conjunctive elements of Penal Law § 240.35(6) are not sufficiently established. People v. Beltrand, 67 Misc. 2d 324, 324 N.Y.S.2d 477 (App. Term 1st Dept. 1971).

Guilty plea.—Defendant by pleading guilty to loitering charge waived his claim that no probable cause existed for the arrest. People v. Smith, 34 N.Y.2d 758, 358 N.Y.S.2d 135, 314 N.E.2d 875 (1974).

Narcotics; use in private home.—Smoking marijuana in a private home does not taint owner of home as violator of statute unless the maintenance of the premises for that purpose is continuing and available for users with some degree of regularity so as to constitute a public nuisance. People v. Fiedler, 31 N.Y.2d 176, 335 N.Y.S.2d 377, 286 N.E.2d 878 (1972).

Loitering; no probable cause for arrest.—Where defendant and friend were standing in plain view in unlocked lobby of apartment house at approximately 10:30 P.M., and had engaged in conversation with a third person for about ten minutes when confronted by a policeman, and neither was acting in a furtive or strange manner or sought to avoid the encounter with the policeman, there was no probable cause to arrest the defendant for loitering. Furthermore, defendant's refusal to identify himself or explain his presence did not justify arrest or conviction. People v. Stokes, 32 N.Y.2d 202, 344 N.Y.S.2d 859, 298 N.E.2d 49 (1973).

Search and seizure; standing to test constitutionality.—It was of no consequence that the defendant, absent from his apartment when a search was made, failed to claim a proprietary interest in the premises at the hearing on his motion to suppress evidence seized. Charged with possessory crimes, he had standing conferred on him on the simple showing that the People sought to use the contraband evidence against him. However, the court held that defendant's arrest for loitering, on the day of the search of his apartment, did not constitute an illegal pretext for conducting a search of his person. People v. Gonzalez, 31 N.Y.2d 787, 339 N.Y.S.2d 112, 291 N.E.2d 391 (1972), *cert. denied,* 410 U.S. 988 (1973).

§ 240.36. Loitering in the first degree.

A person is guilty of loitering in the first degree when he loiters or remains in any place with one or more persons for the purpose of unlawfully using or possessing a controlled substance, as defined in section 220.00 of this chapter.

Loitering in the first degree is a class B misdemeanor.

Amended by L. 1973, Ch. 276.

ANNOTATIONS

Mere presence.—After a buy and bust operation for a street corner drug sale, defendant, who neither bought nor sold the drugs, was arrested and charged with loitering in the first degree on the basis of his presence at the scene; however, mere presence is an insufficient basis to support a charge of loitering, absent additional evidence that he was present for the purpose of using or possessing drugs. People v. Reynolds, 136 Misc. 2d 307, 518 N.Y.S.2d 551 (N.Y.C. Crim. Ct. Bronx Co. 1987).

Participation in drug sale.—When defendant acted as a steerer in a drug transaction, pursuant to which he asked for drugs as an ostensible agent for the buyer, he was present in the apartment where the transaction occurred for the purpose of possessing drugs. People v. Duprey, 98 A.D.2d 110, 469 N.Y.S.2d 702 (1st Dept. 1983).

Evidence insufficient to establish loitering for purpose of using or possessing dangerous drugs.—Defendant was not guilty of violating Penal Law § 240.36, on the ground he was found with others in his backyard at a table on which there was a pipe containing hashish, where purpose of defendant and others being in yard was to listen to music and police responded to complaint that music was too loud. People v. L, 66 Misc. 2d 191, 320 N.Y.S.2d 456 (Dist. Ct. 1971).

Loitering for purpose of using dangerous drug; definition of "place."—The loitering statutes may apply to public places, semi-public buildings or areas, and to the common ways of private buildings but are not applicable to loitering in a private apartment. People v. Nowak, 46 A.D.2d 469, 363 N.Y.S.2d 142 (4th Dept. 1975).

§ 240.37. Loitering for the purpose of engaging in a prostitution offense.

1. For the purposes of this section, "public place" means any street, sidewalk, bridge, alley or alleyway, plaza, park, driveway, parking lot

or transportation facility or the doorways and entrance ways to any building which fronts on any of the aforesaid places, or a motor vehicle in or on any such place.

2. Any person who remains or wanders about in a public place and repeatedly beckons to, or repeatedly stops, or repeatedly attempts to stop, or repeatedly attempts to engage passers-by in conversation, or repeatedly stops or attempts to stop motor vehicles, or repeatedly interferes with the free passage of other persons, for the purpose of prostitution, or of patronizing a prostitute as those terms are defined in article two hundred thirty of the penal law, shall be guilty of a violation and is guilty of a class B misdemeanor if such person has previously been convicted of a violation of this section or of sections 230.00 or 230.05 of the penal law.

3. Any person who remains or wanders about in a public place and repeatedly beckons to, or repeatedly stops, or repeatedly attempts to stop, or repeatedly attempts to engage passers-by in conversation, or repeatedly stops or attempts to stop motor vehicles, or repeatedly interferes with the free passage of other persons, for the purpose of promoting prostitution as defined in article two hundred thirty of the penal law is guilty of a class A misdemeanor.

Added by L. 1976, Ch. 344.

ANNOTATIONS

Constitutionality.—PL § 240.37 is constitutional; statute does not allow arrest based merely on loitering, or even loitering by a known prostitute, but requires loitering plus additional objective conduct evincing that loitering is for purposes of prostitution; experienced police officer should be able to distinguish between soliciting prostitutes or patrons, manifested by a series of acts, and mere casual street encounters. People v. Smith, 44 N.Y.2d 613, 407 N.Y.S.2d 462, 378 N.E.2d 1032 (1978).

Prior conviction.—If the classification of the offense is to be enhanced under PL § 240.37(2) from a violation to a B misdemeanor on the basis of a prior conviction under this section, or a conviction for prostitution or patronizing a prostitute in the second degree, since these factors then become an element of the crime, the prosecutor must file a special information detailing the prior conviction; mere reliance on a reference to the defendant's criminal record is insufficient; the statute, though, is silent on this requirement, which was construed by the court by analogy with CPL § 200.60; the exception would be if the defendant admits the prior conviction. People v. Denise L., 159 Misc. 2d 1080, 608 N.Y.S.2d 40 (N.Y.C. Crim. Ct. Queens Co. 1994).

Experience of arresting officer.—In order for a prima facie case to be established in the information, the officer should submit an affidavit or supporting deposition indicating his experience as the basis for his cognizance that the defendant was loitering for purposes of prostitution rather than merely engaging in innocent street encounters. People v. Denise L., 159 Misc. 2d 1080, 608 N.Y.S.2d 40 (N.Y.C. Crim. Ct. Queens Co. 1994).

Inference that defendant was not present to use transportation facilities or commercial premises.—Evidence that there were no commercial or transportation facilities open at that location when the defendant was observed doing the acts alleged supported the inference of illegality. People v. Koss, 153 Misc. 2d 68, 580 N.Y.S.2d 629 (N.Y.C. Crim. Ct. N.Y. Co. 1992).

Conduct suggesting prostitution.—Information was legally sufficient when it was alleged that female defendants stopped a number of male motorists but no female motorists, that the area was known for prostitution activity, that defendants were standing in the middle of the street, and, for one defendant, it was relevant that she wore a two piece black leopard bathing suit and high heels. People v. Koss, 153 Misc. 2d 68, 580 N.Y.S.2d 629 (N.Y.C. Crim. Ct. N.Y. Co. 1992).

—Information was legally insufficient when officer alleged only that he saw defendant loiter in an area known for prostitution for a fifteen minute period, during which she stopped three male motorists or passersby, but no females, she was in the middle of the street, and there were no open stores or restaurants nearby at that time. People v. Byrd, 149 Misc. 2d 350, 565 N.Y.S.2d 414 (N.Y.C. Crim. Ct. 1991).

—Information was legally sufficient where officer stated that defendant was a known prostitution, standing near other known prostitutes, in front of a hotel which was patronized by prostitutes, she stopped three males, but no females, in a short time period, and entered the hotel with one of the males. People v. Smith, 89 Misc. 2d 754, 393 N.Y.S.2d 239 (App. Term 1st Dept. 1977), aff'd, People v. Smith, 44 N.Y.2d 613, 407 N.Y.S.2d 462, 378 N.E.2d 1032 (1978).

Family court jurisdiction.—Family court has jurisdiction over juvenile delinquency proceeding under FCA § 301.2(1) only if juvenile was charged with an act which, if committed by an adult, would constitute a crime; Family court, then, would have jurisdiction if the juvenile could have been charged under PL § 240.37 as a violation; the 13-year-old juvenile, charged with loitering for purposes of prostitution, having a lengthy conviction record under PL § 240.37, would be charged with a misdemeanor, divesting Family court of jurisdiction. In re C.S., 155 Misc. 2d 1014, 591 N.Y.S.2d 691 (Fam. Ct. N.Y. Co. 1992).

§ 240.40. Appearance in public under the influence of narcotics or a drug other than alcohol.

A person is guilty of appearance in public under the influence of narcotics or a drug other than alcohol when he appears in a public place under the influence of narcotics or a drug other than alcohol to the degree that he may endanger himself or other persons or property, or annoy persons in his vicinity.

Appearance in public under the influence of narcotics or a drug other than alcohol is a violation.

Amended by L. 1974, Ch. 1068.

ANNOTATIONS

Public intoxication; narcotics; constitutionality; probable cause.—Where defendant was walking erratically, holding his sides and staggering, was unresponsive to police inquiries and had running eyes, police were justified in concluding that he was under influence of narcotics and a danger to himself, arrest and search him. Statute met constitutional standard of advancing a legitimate public health and safety purpose so that arrest was with probable cause and fruits of search were admissible to prove possession of drug, hypodermic and attempted sale. People v. Myers, 39 A.D.2d 122, 332 N.Y.S.2d 242 (2d Dept. 1972).

—The intoxication of a person in a public place, as alleged in an information, is not sufficient to charge public intoxication in the absence of allegations that the defendant was endangering himself, other persons or property, or was annoying persons in the vicinity. People v. Jensen, 54 Misc. 2d 807, 283 N.Y.S.2d 530 (Suffolk Co. Dist. Ct. 1967).

§ 240.45. Criminal nuisance in the second degree.

A person is guilty of criminal nuisance in the second degree when:

1. By conduct either unlawful in itself or

unreasonable under all the circumstances, he knowingly or recklessly creates or maintains a condition which endangers the safety or health of a considerable number of persons; or

2. He knowingly conducts or maintains any premises, place or resort where persons gather for purposes of engaging in unlawful conduct.

Criminal nuisance in the second degree is a class B misdemeanor.

Amended by L. 1989, Ch. 585.

ANNOTATIONS

Legislative intent of scope of statute.—The drafters of the legislation contemplated that in most instances criminal nuisance would pertain to manufacturing and industrial plants which emit noxious fumes, or entertainment resorts or establishments, which are responsible for excessive noise. People v. Daguiar, 166 Misc. 2d 123, 631 N.Y.S.2d 801 (N.Y.C. Crim. Ct. N.Y. Co. 1995).

Relationship with disorderly conduct.—Disorderly conduct typically addresses isolated incidents of temporary duration, while criminal nuisance addresses continuing conditions. People v. Daguiar, 166 Misc. 2d 123, 631 N.Y.S.2d 801 (N.Y.C. Crim. Ct. N.Y. Co. 1995).

Sufficiency of accusatory instrument.—Information, alleging in conclusory terms that the defendant operated a social club which where persons gathered for purposes of engaging in unlawful conduct, which was alleged to constitute criminal nuisance in the second degree, without specifying the nature of the unlawful conduct in which the engaged or intended to engage, was facially insufficient. People v. Rodriguez, 140 Misc. 2d 1, 529 N.Y.S.2d 688 (N.Y.C. Crim. Ct. N.Y. Co. 1988).

—Information which alleged in conclusory terms that the social club operated by defendant sold alcoholic beverages without having a license, which was alleged to constitute criminal nuisance in the second degree, without support of factual allegations indicating the basis of the arresting officers knowledge or belief that the premises were unlicensed, was facially defective. People v. Rodriguez, 140 Misc. 2d 1, 529 N.Y.S.2d 688 (N.Y.C. Crim. Ct. N.Y. Co. 1988).

Civil action to abate nuisance.—When a criminal nuisance is established under P.L. § 240.45, this is deemed to be a public nuisance authorizing injunctive relief under N.Y.C. Admin. Code (7-706 et.seq.); code provision authorized in rem jurisdiction for court. City of New York v. 924 Columbus Assocs., L.P., 219 A.D.2d 19, 640 N.Y.S.2d 497 (1st Dept. 1996).

—When landlords had notice that premises of commercial tenant were being used for illegal drug activity, city had basis to seek court order closing the building. City of New York v. 924 Columbus Assocs., L.P., 219 A.D.2d 19, 640 N.Y.S.2d 497 (1st Dept. 1996).

—City had basis to conclude that operation of a bathhouse which was a notorious forum for unsafe sexual practices, in the midst of the AIDS epidemic, constituted a knowing and reckless condition which endangered the health or safety of a large number of persons, in violation of PL § 240.45(1); city had basis for civil injunctive relief including closure. City of New York v. The New Saint Marks Baths, 130 Misc. 2d 911, 497 N.Y.S.2d 979 (Sup. Ct. N.Y. Co. 1986), aff'd, 122 A.D.2d 747, 505 N.Y.S.2d 1015 (1st Dept. 1986), app. dism'd, 70 N.Y.2d 693, 512 N.E.2d 555, 518 N.Y.S.2d 1029 (1987), app. denied, 78 N.Y.2d 854 (1991).

—Closure of bathhouse notorious as a forum for unsafe sexual practices, did not infringe on First Amendment right of association. City of New York v. The New Saint Marks Baths, 130 Misc. 2d 911, 497 N.Y.S.2d 979 (Sup. Ct. N.Y. Co. 1986), aff'd, 122 A.D.2d 747, 505 N.Y.S.2d 1015 (1st Dept. 1986), app. dism'd, 70 N.Y.2d 693, 512 N.E.2d 555, 518 N.Y.S.2d 1029 (1987), app. denied, 78 N.Y.2d 854 (1991).

No preemption of local regulation of noise nuisances.—PL § 240.45 does not by its terms manifest a legislative intent to preempt local authority regulating and criminalizing excessive noise. People v. New York Trap Rock Corp., 57 N.Y.2d 371, 456 N.Y.S.2d 711, 442 N.E.2d 1222 (1982) (in this case,

though, the local noise ordinance, imposing criminal liability on violators, was unconstitutionally vague).

Condition which endangers health or safety of a large number of persons.—The operation of a bathhouse which was a notorious forum for unsafe sexual practices, in the midst of the AIDS epidemic, constituted a knowing and reckless condition which endangered the health or safety of a large number of persons, in violation of PL § 240.45(1). City of New York v. The New Saint Marks Baths, 130 Misc. 2d 911, 497 N.Y.S.2d 979 (Sup. Ct. N.Y. Co. 1986), aff'd, 122 A.D.2d 747, 505 N.Y.S.2d 1015 (1st Dept. 1986), app. dism'd, 70 N.Y.2d 693, 512 N.E.2d 555, 518 N.Y.S.2d 1029 (1987), app. denied, 78 N.Y.2d 854 (1991).

Building code violations.—Although the defendant's failure to comply with court ordered repairs to his multiple dwelling theoretically could constitute criminal nuisance, information was dismissed insofar as there was no showing that the failure to repair dangerous conditions endangered the public. People v. Kotler, 141 Misc. 2d 675, 533 N.Y.S.2d 841 (N.Y.C. Crim. Ct. Kings Co. 1989).

Blocking traffic.—Criminal nuisance does not criminalize temporarily blocking traffic by double parking a vehicle, although that conduct might constitute disorderly conduct, when accompanied by additional factors, such as motorist refusing to respond to police request for identification. People v. Daguiar, 166 Misc. 2d 123, 631 N.Y.S.2d 801 (N.Y.C. Crim. Ct. N.Y. Co. 1995).

Narcotics; use in private home.—Smoking marijuana in a private home does not taint owner of home as violation of statute unless the maintenance of the premises for that purpose is continuing and available for users with some degree of regularity so as to constitute a public nuisance. People v. Fiedler, 31 N.Y.2d 176, 335 N.Y.S.2d 377, 286 N.E.2d 878 (1972).

Proof of acquiescence with knowledge sufficient to sustain conviction.—Proof that defendant acquiesced in the use of his apartment as a gathering place for the smoking of marijuana along with proof that defendant knew that marijuana was being smoked there was enough to sustain a conviction for criminal nuisance. People v. Schriber, 34 A.D.2d 852, N.Y.S.2d 551 (3d Dept. 1970), aff'd, 29 N.Y.2d 80, 327 N.Y.S.2d 68, 277 N.E.2d 187 (1971).

§ 240.46. Criminal nuisance in the first degree.

A person is guilty of criminal nuisance in the first degree when he knowingly conducts or maintains any premises, place or resort where persons come or gather for purposes of engaging in the unlawful sale of controlled substances in violation of section 220.39, 220.41, or 220.43 of this chapter, and thereby derives the benefit from such unlawful conduct.

Criminal nuisance in the first degree is a class E felony.

Added by L. 1989, Ch. 585.

ANNOTATIONS

Evidence.—Conviction under this section affirmed, defendant's admission to police that drugs had been distributed out of her trailer for a couple of months satisfied the accomplice corroboration requirement, co-defendants' statements that they had regularly purchased cocaine out of defendant's trailer, and that there was a lot of drug traffic in and out of the trailer demonstrated that defendant knowingly acquiesced in the trailer's use for the unlawful sale of controlled substances, defendant's further admission they received cocaine for their personal use satisfied the benefit element of the crime. People v. Monday, 309 A.D.2d 977, 765 N.Y.S.2d 705 (3d Dept. 2003).

§ 240.48. Disseminating a false registered sex offender notice.

A person is guilty of disseminating a false

registered sex offender notice when, knowing the information he or she disseminates or causes to be disseminated to be false or baseless, such person disseminates or causes to be disseminated any notice which purports to be an official notice from a government agency or a law enforcement agency and such notice asserts that an individual is a registered sex offender.

Disseminating a false registered sex offender notice is a class A misdemeanor.

Added by L. 2004, Ch. 106, § 2, eff. June 8, 2004.

§ 240.50. Falsely reporting an incident in the third degree.

A person is guilty of falsely reporting an incident in the third degree when, knowing the information reported, conveyed or circulated to be false or baseless, he:

1. Initiates or circulates a false report or warning of an alleged occurrence or impending occurrence of a crime, catastrophe or emergency under circumstances in which it is not unlikely that public alarm or inconvenience will result; or

2. Reports, by word or action, to an official or quasi-official agency or organization having the function of dealing with emergencies involving danger to life or property, an alleged occurrence or impending occurrence of a catastrophe or emergency which did not in fact occur or does not in fact exist; or

3. Gratuitously reports to a law enforcement officer or agency (a) the alleged occurrence of an offense or incident which did not in fact occur; or (b) an allegedly impending occurrence of an offense or incident which in fact is not about to occur; or (c) false information relating to an actual offense or incident or to the alleged implication of some person therein; or

4. Reports, by word or action, to the statewide central register of child abuse and maltreatment, as defined in title six of article six of the social services law, an alleged occurrence or condition of child abuse or maltreatment which did not in fact occur or exist.

Falsely reporting an incident in the third degree is a class A misdemeanor.

Amended by L. 1971, Ch. 357; L. 1973, Ch. 276; L. 1976, Ch. 185; L. 1979, Ch. 146; L. 2001, Ch. 301, § 1, amending the closing paragraph, and Ch. 302, § 1, amending subd. 3 and adding subd. 4, eff. Sept. 17, 2001.

ANNOTATIONS

Validity of information from citizen informants.—Courts recognize the presumptive validity of information provided by citizen informants which establishes probable cause insofar as the knowing fabrication of such information subjects the informant to prosecution for falsely reporting an incident in the third degree. *See, e.g.*, People v. Jean-Charles, 226 A.D.2d 395, 640 N.Y.S.2d 266 (2d Dept. 1996).

Good faith report of false information.—When a citizen informant provides information which supports probable cause for an arrest, if the information is false, it may subject the information to prosecution under PL § 240.50; however, the required mental state is scienter; if the informant does not knowingly supply false information, there is no criminal liability. *Cf.* People v. Cruz, 149 Misc. 2d 151, 545 N.Y.S.2d 561 (1st Dept. 1989).

False report of burglary to conceal criminal conduct.—Defendant, after an altercation with the complainant, fired a shot from a concealed location at the complainant's residence; police recovered the weapon, which could be connected to defendant; defendant, though, reported that his residence had been burglarized and the gun stolen, which constituted falsely reporting an incident in the third degree. People v. McCarthy, 126 A.D.2d 935, 511 N.Y.S.2d 708 (4th Dept. 1987).

No private cause of action.—Plaintiff failed to demonstrate that a private right of action to recover damages may be implied from Penal Law § 240.50. Kwasnik v. City of New York, 298 A.D.2d 502, 748 N.Y.S.2d 510 (2d Dept. 2002).

§ 240.55. Falsely reporting an incident in the second degree.

A person is guilty of falsely reporting an incident in the second degree when, knowing the information reported, conveyed or circulated to be false or baseless, he or she:

1. Initiates or circulates a false report or warning of an alleged occurrence or impending occurrence of a fire, explosion, or the release of a hazardous substance under circumstances in which it is not unlikely that public alarm or inconvenience will result;

2. Reports, by word or action, to any official or quasi-official agency or organization having the function of dealing with emergencies involving danger to life or property, an alleged occurrence or impending occurrence of a fire, explosion, or the release of a hazardous substance which did not in fact occur or does not in fact exist; or

3. Knowing the information reported, conveyed or circulated to be false or baseless and under circumstances in which it is likely public alarm or inconvenience will result, he or she initiates or circulates a report or warning of an alleged occurrence or an impending occurrence of a fire, an explosion, or the release of a hazardous substance upon any private premises.

Falsely reporting an incident in the second degree is a class E felony.

Added by L. 1973, Ch. 276; **Amended** by L. 1979, Ch. 146; L. 1989, Ch. 477; L. 1999, Ch. 561, § 2, eff. Dec. 1, 1999, amending subds. 1 and 2; L. 2001, Ch. 3001, §§ 2 and 3, redesignating subd. 4 and amending closing paragraph, eff. Sept. 17, 2001.

ANNOTATIONS

Generally.—Defendant, upon being informed by sheriff's office that a fire on adjacent property was a controlled burn, and that the local fire department was present, nevertheless telephoned a neighboring fire department to report a fire; although it was true that there was a fire, defendant had been informed that there was no threat to him from the fire, which constituted the falsity of the report. People v. Bayes, 78 N.Y.2d 546, 577 N.Y.S.2d 585, 584 N.E.2d 643 (1991).

In camera inspection.—In order to investigate allegation that defendant gave false report of child abuse to Department of Social Services, the court allowed an in camera inspection of otherwise confidential records in order to allow the District Attorney's office to proceed with the criminal proceeding.

People v. Berliner, 179 Misc. 2d 844, 686 N.Y.S.2d 673 (City Ct. New Rochelle 1999).

§ 240.60. Falsely reporting an incident in the first degree.

A person is guilty of falsely reporting an incident in the first degree when he:

1. commits the crime of falsely reporting an incident in the second degree as defined in section 240.55 of this article, and has previously been convicted of that crime; or

2. commits the crime of falsely reporting an incident in the third degree as defined in subdivisions one and two of section 240.50 of this article or falsely reporting an incident in the second degree as defined in subdivisions one and two of section 240.55 of this article and another person who is an employee or member of any official or quasi-official agency having the function of dealing with emergencies involving danger to life or property; or who is a volunteer firefighter with a fire department, fire company, or any unit thereof as defined in the volunteer firefighters' benefit law; or who is a volunteer ambulance worker with a volunteer ambulance corporation or any unit thereof as defined in the volunteer ambulance workers' benefit law suffers serious physical injury or is killed in the performance of his or her official duties in traveling to or working at or returning to a firehouse, police station, quarters or other base facility from the location identified in such report; or

3. commits the crime of falsely reporting an incident in the third degree as defined in subdivisions one and two of section 240.50 of this article or falsely reporting an incident in the second degree as defined in subdivisions one and two of section 240.55 of this article and another person suffers serious physical injury or is killed as a result of any vehicular or other accident involving any emergency vehicle which is responding to, operating at, or returning from the location identified in such report.

4. An emergency vehicle as referred to in subdivision three of this section shall include any vehicle operated by any employee or member of any official or quasi-official agency having the function of dealing with emergencies involving danger to life or property and shall include, but not necessarily be limited to, an emergency vehicle which is operated by a volunteer firefighter with a fire department, fire company, or any unit thereof as defined in the volunteer firefighters' benefit law; or by a volunteer ambulance worker with a volunteer ambulance corporation, or any unit thereof as defined in the volunteer ambulance workers' benefit law.

5. Knowing the information reported, conveyed or circulated to be false or baseless and under circumstances in which it is likely public alarm or inconvenience will result, he or she initiates or circulates a report or warning of an alleged occurrence or an impending occurrence of a fire, an explosion, or the release of a hazardous substance upon school grounds and it is likely that persons are present on said grounds.

6. Knowing the information reported, conveyed or circulated to be false or baseless and under circumstances in which it is likely public alarm or inconvenience will result, he or she initiates or circulates a report or warning of an alleged occurrence or impending occurrence of a fire, explosion or the release of a hazardous substance in or upon a sports stadium or arena, mass transportation facility, enclosed shopping mall, any public building or any public place, and it is likely that persons are present. For purposes of this subdivision, the terms "sports stadium or arena, mass transportation facility or enclosed shopping mall" shall have their natural meaning and the term "public building" shall have the meaning set forth in section four hundred one of the executive law.

Falsely reporting an incident in the first degree is a class D felony.

Added by L. 1977, Ch. 485; **Amended** by L. 1990, Ch. 576; L. 1995, Ch. 528, amending subd. 2 and adding subds. 3 and 4, eff. Nov. 1, 1995; L. 1999, Ch. 561, § 3, eff. Dec. 1, 1999, adding subd. 5; L. 2001, Ch. 244, § 1, adding subd. 6, and Ch. 301, § 4, amending subd. 6 and closing paragraph, eff. Nov. 1, 2001.

§ 240.61. Placing a false bomb or hazardous substance in the second degree.

A person is guilty of placing a false bomb or hazardous substance in the second degree when he or she places, or causes to be placed, any device or object that by its design, construction, content or characteristics appears to be or to contain, a bomb, destructive device, explosive or hazardous substance, but is, in fact, an inoperative facsimile or imitation of such a bomb, destructive device, explosive or hazardous substance and which he or she knows, intends or reasonably believes will appear to be a bomb, destructive device, explosive or hazardous substance under circumstances in which it is likely to cause public alarm or inconvenience.

Placing a false bomb or hazardous substance in the second degree is a class E felony.

Added by L. 1996, Ch. 355, eff. Nov. 1, 1996; **Amended** by L. 1999, Ch. 561, § 4, eff. Dec. 1, 1999, redesignating offense as second degree; L. 2001, Ch. 301, § 5, amending closing paragraph, eff. Sept. 17, 2001; L. 2004, Ch. 1, § 14 (Part A), eff. July 23, 2004.

§ 240.62. Placing a false bomb or hazardous substance in the first degree.

A person is guilty of placing a false bomb or hazardous substance in the first degree when he or she places, or causes to be placed, in or upon school grounds, a public building, or a public place any device or object that by its design, construction, content or characteristics appears to be or to contain, a bomb, destructive device, explosive or hazardous substance, but is, in fact, an inoperative facsimile or imitation of such a bomb, destructive device, explosive or hazardous substance and which he or she knows, intends or reasonably believes will appear to be a bomb, destructive device, explosive or hazardous substance under circumstances in which it is likely to cause public alarm or inconvenience. For purposes of this section the term "public building" shall have the meaning set forth in section four hundred one of the executive law.

Placing a false bomb or hazardous substance in the first degree is a class D felony.

Added by L. 1999, Ch. 561, § 5, eff. Dec. 1, 1999; Amended by L. 2001, Ch. 301, § 6, eff. Sept. 17, 2001; L. 2004, Ch. 1, § 15 (Part A), eff. July 23, 2004.

§ 240.63. Placing a false bomb or hazardous substance in a sports stadium or arena, mass transportation facility or enclosed shopping mall.

A person is guilty of placing a false bomb or hazardous substance in a sports stadium or arena, mass transportation facility or enclosed shopping mall when he or she places, or causes to be placed, in a sports stadium or arena, mass transportation facility or enclosed shopping mall, in which it is likely that persons are present, any device or object that by its design, construction, content or characteristics appears to be or to contain a bomb, destructive device, explosive or hazardous substance, but is, in fact, an inoperative facsimile or imitation of such a bomb, destructive device, explosive or hazardous substance and which he or she knows, intends or reasonably believes will appear to be a bomb, destructive device, explosive or hazardous substance under circumstances in which it is likely to cause public alarm or inconvenience. For purposes of this section, "sports stadium or arena, mass transportation facility or enclosed shopping mall" shall have its natural meaning.

Placing a false bomb or hazardous substance in a sports stadium or arena, mass transportation facility or enclosed shopping mall is a class D felony.

Added by L. 2001, Ch. 244, § 2, eff. Nov. 1, 2001; Amended by L. 2001, Ch. 301, § 7, eff. Nov. 1, 2001; L. 2004, Ch. 1, § 16 (Part A), eff. July 23, 2004.

§ 240.65. Unlawful prevention of public access to records.

A person is guilty of unlawful prevention of public access to records when, with intent to prevent the public inspection of a record pursuant to article six of the public officers law, he willfully conceals or destroys any such record.

Unlawful prevention of public access to records is a violation.

Added by L. 1989, Ch. 705.

§ 240.70. Criminal interference with health care services or religious worship in the second degree.

1. A person is guilty of criminal interference with health services or religious worship in the second degree when:

(a) by force or threat of force or by physical obstruction, he or she intentionally injures, intimidates or interferes with, or attempts to injure, intimidate or interfere with, another person because such other person was or is obtaining or providing reproductive health services; or

(b) by force or threat of force or by physical obstruction, he or she intentionally injures, intimidates or interferes with, or attempts to injure, intimidate or interfere with, another person in order to discourage such other person or any other person or persons from obtaining or providing reproductive health services; or

(c) by force or threat of force or by physical obstruction, he or she intentionally injures, intimidates or interferes with, or attempts to injure, intimidate or interfere with, another person because such person was or is seeking to exercise the right of religious freedom at a place of religious worship; or

(d) he or she intentionally damages the property of a health care facility, or attempts to do so, because such facility provides reproductive health services, or intentionally damages the property of a place of religious worship.

2. A parent or legal guardian of a minor shall not be subject to prosecution for conduct otherwise prohibited by paragraph (a) or (b) of subdivision one of this section which is directed exclusively at such minor.

3. For purposes of this section:

(a) the term "health care facility" means a hospital, clinic, physician's office or other facility that provides reproductive health services, and includes the building or structure in which the facility is located;

(b) the term "interferes with" means to restrict a person's freedom of movement;

(c) the term "intimidates" means to place a person in reasonable apprehension of physical injury to himself or herself or to another person;

(d) the term "physical obstruction" means rendering impassable ingress to or egress from a facility that provides reproductive health services or to or from a place of religious worship, or rendering passage to or from such a facility or place of religious worship unreasonably difficult or hazardous; and

(e) the term "reproductive health services" means health care services provided in a hospital, clinic, physician's office or other facility and includes medical, surgical, counseling or referral services relating to the human reproductive system, including services relating to pregnancy or the termination of a pregnancy.

Criminal interference with health care services or religious worship in the second degree is a class A misdemeanor.

Added by L. 1999, Ch. 635, § 14, eff. Dec. 1, 1999.

§ 240.71. Criminal interference with health care services or religious worship in the first degree.

A person is guilty of criminal interference with health care services or religious worship in the first degree when he or she commits the crime of criminal interference with health care services or religious worship in the second degree and has been previously convicted of the crime of criminal interference with health care services or religious worship in the first or second degree.

Criminal interference with health care services or religious worship in the first degree is a class E felony.

Added by L. 1999, Ch. 635, § 14, eff. Dec. 1, 1999.

PL

ARTICLE 241—HARASSMENT OF RENT REGULATED TENANTS

241.00   Harassment of a rent regulated tenant; definition of terms.

241.05   Harassment of a rent regulated tenant.

§ 241.00. Harassment of a rent regulated tenant; definition of terms.

[*Effective until June 15, 2011.*]

As used in this article:

1. "Rent regulated tenant" shall mean a person occupying a housing accommodation which is subject to the regulations and control of residential rents and evictions pursuant to the emergency housing rent control law, the local emergency housing rent control act, the emergency tenant protection act of nineteen seventy-four, the New York city rent and rehabilitation law or the New York city rent stabilization law of nineteen hundred sixty-nine, and such person is either a party to a lease or rental agreement for such housing accommodation, a statutory tenant or a person who lawfully occupies such housing accommodation with such party to a lease or rental agreement or with such statutory tenant. The definition of "rent regulated tenant" as used in this subdivision shall be applicable only to the provisions of this article and shall not be applicable to any other provision of law.

2. "Housing accommodations" shall mean housing accommodations which are subject to the regulations and control of residential rents and evictions pursuant to the emergency housing rent control law, the local emergency housing rent control act, the emergency tenant protection act of nineteen seventy-four, the New York city rent and rehabilitation law or the New York city rent stabilization law of nineteen hundred sixty-nine.

3. "Owner" shall mean an owner, lessor, sublessor, assignee, net lessee, or a proprietary lessee of a housing accommodation in a structure or premises owned by a cooperative corporation or association, or an owner of a condominium unit or the sponsor of such cooperative corporation or association or condominium development, or any other person or entity receiving or entitled to receive rent for the use or occupation of any housing accommodation, or an agent of or any person acting on behalf of any of the foregoing.

Added by L. 1997, Ch. 116, § 28, eff. July 19, 1997 and applicable to acts or offenses committed on or after July 19, 1997; L. 2003, Chs. 70–73, 82, extending expiration date to June 15, 2011.

§ 241.05. Harassment of a rent regulated tenant. [*Effective until June 15, 2011.*]

An owner is guilty of harassment of a rent regulated tenant when with intent to cause a rent regulated tenant to vacate a housing accommodation, such owner:

1. With intent to cause physical injury to such tenant, causes such injury to such tenant or to a third person; or

2. Recklessly causes physical injury to such tenant or to a third person.

Harassment of a rent regulated tenant is a class E felony.

Added by L. 1997, Ch. 116, § 28, eff. July 19, 1997 and applicable to acts or offenses committed on or after July 19, 1997; L. 2003, Chs. 70–73, 82, extending expiration date to June 15, 2011.

ARTICLE 245—OFFENSES AGAINST PUBLIC SENSIBILITIES

Section

§ 245.00. Public lewdness.

A person is guilty of public lewdness when he intentionally exposes the private or intimate parts of his body in a lewd manner or commits any other lewd act (a) in a public place, or (b) in private premises under circumstances in which he may readily be observed from either a public place or from other private premises, and with intent that he be so observed.

Public lewdness is a class B misdemeanor.

Amended by L. 1968, Ch. 748.

ANNOTATIONS

Public place.—Term "public place" has no "cut and dried meaning" and is not governed either by Article 240 or by Fourth Amendment conventions; must be interpreted to comport with statute's purpose to prevent open flouting of societal conventions, rather than to proscribe conduct by persons who intend their conduct to be private and take reasonable precautions to ensure privacy; parked car in which sexual activity occurs is a public place only if the objective circumstances establish that lewd acts committed there can, and likely will, be seen by the casual passerby. People v. McNamara, 78 N.Y.2d 626, 578 N.Y.S.2d 476, 585 N.E.2d 788 (1991).

—Defendant, by grabbing his exposed penis and shouting epithets at the female bystanders, went beyond mere public nudity to commit public lewdness. In re Jeffrey V., 185 A.D.2d 241, 586 N.Y.S.2d 18 (2d Dept. 1992).

—Where evidence revealed that defendant broke into homes with the intent to expose himself to the person or people inside, intended conduct did not occur within a public place as required by statute. People v. Pangburn, 298 A.D.2d 989, 747 N.Y.S.2d 672 (4th Dept. 2002).

—Defendant masturbating in public restroom in front of persons using the restroom, who was not in a stall or otherwise shielded from public view, could not avail himself of "McNamara" doctrine. People v. Davis, 164 Misc. 2d 89, 624 N.Y.S.2d 353 (N.Y.C. Crim. Ct. N.Y. Co. 1994).

—Lewdness statute was intended to proscribe exhibitionist behavior, and not punish conduct where participants try to be clandestine; couple engaged in sexual conduct in parked car on a street which was not a major thoroughfare on a dark night, away from street lights, were not in "public place." People v. Anonymous Female, 143 Misc. 2d 197, 539 N.Y.S.2d 868 (City Ct. of Buffalo, Erie Co. 1989).

—When defendant tried to be clandestine in sexual encounter with another man in a national park, which occurred off of a bicycle park in shrubbery, and defendant, when arrested, was fully clothed, the evidence did not establish public lewdness. United States v. Doe, 884 F. Supp. 78 (E.D.N.Y. 1995).

Private premises seen from public place.—Testimony that defendant was seen masturbating and making obscene remarks to bystander in front of a window in his residence in full public view satisfied statutory requirement. In re Paul R., 131 A.D.2d 764, 516 N.Y.S.2d 790 (2d Dept. 1987).

Lewdness; "erotic dance" performance.—Where lewdness statute was intended to prohibit indecent public exposure directed toward unsuspecting and unwilling viewers, "erotic dance" performance inside building before audience of paying, consenting adults, did not violate statute. People v. Conrad, 70 Misc. 2d 408, 334 N.Y.S.2d 180 (Buffalo City Ct. 1972).

Nude sunbathing.—Where evidence only showed that defendant was sunbathing in the nude with other persons on a public beach, absent any proof showing that she intentionally exposed her private parts in a public place in a lewd manner, conviction warranted reversal. People v. Hardy, 77 Misc. 2d 1092, 357 N.Y.S.2d 970 (App. Term 2d Dept. 1974).

Lesser included offenses.—A defendant may be found guilty of a lesser offense as an alternative to being found guilty, on the evidence, of the greater offense. The proper test to be applied is: Does the lesser offense require proof of an element which is not required to establish the greater offense? People v. Gilbert, 72 Misc. 2d 795, 339 N.Y.S.2d 743 (Crim. Ct. N.Y. Co. 1973).

Review; on appeal.—In the absence of a statutory requirement of corroboration the scope of review should be limited to ascertaining whether or not the evidence against the accused is otherwise satisfactory under legal standards. People v. Nisoff, 36 N.Y.2d 560, 369 N.Y.S.2d 686, 330 N.E.2d 638 (1975).

§ 245.01. Exposure of a person.

A person is guilty of exposure if he appears in a public place in such a manner that the private or intimate parts of his body are unclothed or exposed. For purposes of this section, the private or intimate parts of a female person shall include that portion of the breast which is below the top of the areola. This section shall not apply to the breastfeeding of infants or to any person entertaining or performing in a play, exhibition, show or entertainment.

Exposure of a person is a violation.

Nothing in this section shall prevent the adoption by a city, town or village of a local law prohibiting exposure of a person as herein defined in a public place, at any time, whether or not such person is entertaining or performing in a play, exhibition, show or entertainment.

Added by L. 1983, Ch. 216; Amended by L. 1984, Ch. 633.

ANNOTATIONS

Exposure of female breast in noncommercial manner.—Underlying principle of People v. Price is still followed, that purpose of statute was to discourage topless waitressing rather than non-commercial display of breasts. Hence, PL § 245.01 would not be applicable to conduct by females displaying their breasts in public park; concurring opinion would have reached equal protection argument, that persons were treated differently on the basis of gender, and would have invalidated the statute on constitutional grounds. People v. Santorelli, 80 N.Y.2d 875, 587 N.Y.S.2d 601, 600 N.E.2d 232 (1992).

—Statute prohibiting women, but not men, from exposing their breasts, violates equal protection guarantees of the constitution. People v. David, 152 Misc. 2d 66, 585 N.Y.S.2d 149 (Monroe Co. Ct. 1991); compare with People v. Craft, 149 Misc. 2d 223, 564 N.Y.S.2d 695 (Monroe Co. Ct. 1991) (prohibition as it applies to women is substantially related to achievement of important governmental interest of protecting public from invasion of its sensibilities), rev'd by People v. Santorelli, 80 N.Y.2d 875, 600 N.E.2d 232, 587 N.Y.S.2d 601 (1992) (declining to address equal protection argument).

—Mere display of female breasts at a public beach did not constitute exposure of a private or intimate part of a person's body, if statute was to be construed in a gender-neutral manner. People v. David, 152 Misc. 2d 66, 585 N.Y.S.2d 149 (Monroe Co. Ct. 1991).

Exposure of male anatomy.—The defendant's exposure of his penis on a subway to a female passenger, observed by a police officer, was the very sort of conduct which the statute was intended to proscribe. People v. Harris, 129 Misc. 2d 577, 493 N.Y.S.2d 733 (N.Y.C. Crim. Ct. N.Y. Co. 1985).

Acts which do not constitute exposure.—Public lewdness statute is not limited to acts of exposure, but also prohibited a defendant from publicly stroking a covered erect penis and rubbing it against the buttocks of three females. People v. Darryl M., 123 Misc. 2d 723, 475 N.Y.S.2d 704 (N.Y.C. Crim. Ct. 1984).

—If act is committed in public place, as contrasted with a private premises which can be observed from a public place, there is no element that defendant intends that his act be observed. People v. Darryl M., 123 Misc. 2d 723, 475 N.Y.S.2d 704 (N.Y.C. Crim. Ct. 1984)

Nude sunbathing.—To the extent that statute proscribed nude sunbathing on a public beach, it did not infringe on defendant's First Amendment right of free expression. People v. Hollman, 68 N.Y.2d 202, 507 N.Y.S.2d 977, 500 N.E.2d 297 (1986).

Constitutional Overbreadth.—Statute was not unconstitutionally broad to the extent that it was construed to prohibit nude sunbathing on a public beach. People v. Hollman, 68 N.Y.2d 202, 507 N.Y.S.2d 977, 500 N.E.2d 297 (1986).

Intent of statute.—PL § 245.01 was aimed at discouraging "topless" waitresses and their promoters and it should not be applied to noncommercial, perhaps accidental, and certainly not lewd, exposure. People v. Price, 33 N.Y.2d 831, 351 N.Y.S.2d 973, 307 N.E.2d 46 (1973).

Statute constitutional.—There is the presumption that a statute is constitutional until proven otherwise beyond a reasonable doubt. Women, or particular classes of women, may be singled out for special treatment in the exercise of the State's protective power without violation of the Fourteenth Amendment, and classification may be based on differences either in their physical characteristics or in the social conditions which surround their employment. People v. Gilbert, 72 Misc. 2d 795, 339 N.Y.S.2d 743 (Crim. Ct. N.Y. Co. 1973).

Topless dancers; prohibition by local law; police powers; free speech.—Town, as political subdivision of state, could be delegated legislative power to prohibit topless dancing as exercise of police power governing public morals, and even though it prohibited that which state law permitted, topless entertainment, it was not an unconstitutional abridgement of free speech or equal protection of the laws. People v. Moreira, 70 Misc. 2d 68, 333 N.Y.S.2d 215 (Dist. Ct. Suffolk Co. 1972).

—A state or local governing body acting through the charter of its government, cannot totally restrict topless dancing under all circumstances and an ordinance that is overbroad in its scope is a violation of the constitution. People v. Wehnke, 107 Misc. 2d 881, 436 N.Y.S.2d 137 (Rome City Ct. 1981).

Violation of law.—Exposure of a person is a violation, not a crime, and therefore could not support defendant's convictions for first or second degree burglary where defendant's plea allocution revealed that his intent in breaking into each home was to expose himself to a person or people inside. People v. Pangburn, 298 A.D.2d 989, 747 N.Y.S.2d 672 (4th Dept. 2002).

§ 245.02. Promoting the exposure of a person.

A person is guilty of promoting the exposure of a person when he knowingly conducts, maintains, owns, manages, operates or furnishes any public premise or place where a person in a public place appears in such a manner that the private or intimate parts of his body are unclothed or exposed. For purposes of this section, the private or intimate parts of a female person shall include that portion of the breast which is below the top

of the areola. This section shall not apply to the breastfeeding of infants or to any person entertaining or performing in a play, exhibition, show or entertainment.

Promoting the exposure of a person is a violation.

Nothing is this section shall prevent the adoption by a city, town or village of a local law prohibiting the exposure of a person substantially as herein defined in a public place, at any time, whether or not such person is entertaining or performing in a play, exhibition, show or entertainment.

Added by L. 1983, Ch. 216; **Amended** by L. 1984, Ch. 633.

ANNOTATIONS

Exposure of female in public place; constitutionality; equal protection; indictment.—Defendant who made nude female available at his premises for photographing by police undercover agent did not violate statute prohibiting the promotion of exposure of a female in a public place, which excluded entertainers, because statute was arbitrary, caused unreasonable interference with legitimate business and denied defendant the equal protection of the laws. People v. Wilhelm, 69 Misc. 2d 523, 330 N.Y.S.2d 279 (Buffalo City Ct. 1972).

Promoting exposure of a female; topless entertainment in cabarets.—Regulation 20(a) of the New York City Department of Consumer Affairs could not bar defendant from permitting topless entertainment in his cabaret in view of PL § 245.02 which permits such performances in the absence of a local law adopted by a city, town or village to the contrary. The court stated that if topless entertainment in cabarets is to be banned in New York City, it must be by some act of the City Council, not by virtue of the instant regulation. People v. Soto, 68 Misc. 2d 801, 327 N.Y.S.2d 992 (N.Y.C. Crim. Ct. 1971).

§ 245.05. Offensive exhibition.

A person is guilty of offensive exhibition when he knowingly produces, operates, manages or furnishes premises for, or in any way promotes or participates in, an exhibition in the nature of public entertainment or amusement in which:

1. A person competes continuously without respite for a period of more than eight consecutive hours in a dance contest, bicycle race or other contest involving physical endurance; or

2. A person is held up to ridicule or contempt by voluntarily submitting to indignities such as the throwing of balls or other articles at his head or body; or

3. A firearm is discharged or a knife, arrow or other sharp or dangerous instrument is thrown or propelled at or toward a person.

Offensive exhibition is a violation.

Amended by L. 1968, Ch. 680.

§ 245.10. Public display of offensive sexual material; definitions of terms.

The following definitions are applicable to section 245.11:

1. "Nudity" means the showing of the human male or female genitals, pubic area or buttocks

with less than a full opaque covering, or the showing of the female breast with less than a fully opaque covering of any portion thereof below the top of the nipple, or the depiction of covered male genitals in a discernibly turgid state.

2. "Sexual conduct" means an act of masturbation, homosexuality, sexual intercourse, or physical contact with a person's clothed or unclothed genitals, pubic area, buttocks or, if such person be a female, breast.

3. "Sado-masochistic abuse" means flagellation or torture by or upon a person clad in undergarments, a mask or bizarre costume, or the condition of being fettered, bound or otherwise physically restrained on the part of one so clothed.

4. "Transportation facility" means any conveyance, premises or place used for or in connection with public passenger transportation, whether by air, railroad, motor vehicle or any other method. It includes aircraft, watercraft, railroad cars, buses, and air, boat, railroad and bus terminals and stations and all appurtenances thereto.

Added by L. 1971, Ch. 962.

ANNOTATIONS

Cards in store.—Display of cards in a stationery store depicting bare buttocks was not sexually offensive material as a matter of law; by contrast, photo of man fondling bare buttocks of a woman depicted a highly suggestive erotic act, and did not evade the statute's definition. People v. Oshry, 131 Misc. 2d 888, 502 N.Y.S.2d 590 (Just. Ct. Town of Clarkstown, Rockland Co. 1986).

Offensive sexual material; public display.—A two-inch patch depicting allegedly offensive sexual activity displayed in a store showroom window three feet deep and six feet wide among a variety of non offensive, youth-oriented items of merchandise did not violate statute intended to protect unwilling audiences from indiscriminate thrust of offensive sexual material. People v. Isaac, 69 Misc. 2d 758, 331 N.Y.S.2d 322 (Crim. Ct. Bronx Co. 1972).

Prostitution; constitutionality of statute; degree of corroboration.—Convictions of defendant in profiting from prostitution arising out of operation of massage parlor and employment of girls under 19 years of age upheld as statutory terms of "sexual conduct" and "fee" were not impermissibly vague and there was corroborative proof on every material element of crime to support testimony of prostitutes. People v. Block, 71 Misc. 2d 714, 337 N.Y.S.2d 153 (Nassau Co. Ct. 1972).

§ 245.11. Public display of offensive sexual material.

A person is guilty of public display of offensive sexual material when, with knowledge of its character and content, he displays or permits to be displayed in or on any window, showcase, newsstand, display rack, wall, door, billboard, display board, viewing screen, moving picture screen, marquee or similar place, in such manner that the display is easily visible from or in any: public street, sidewalk or thoroughfare; transportation facility; or any place accessible to members of the public without fee or other limit or condition of admission such as a minimum age requirement and including but not limited to schools, places of amusement, parks and playgrounds but excluding rooms or apartments designed for actual residence; any pictorial, three-dimensional or other visual representation of a person or a portion of the human body that predominantly appeals to prurient interest in sex, and that:

(a) depicts nudity, or actual or simulated sexual conduct or sado-masochistic abuse; or

(b) depicts or appears to depict nudity, or actual or simulated sexual conduct or sado-masochistic abuse, with the area of the male or female subject's unclothed or apparently unclothed genitals, pubic area or buttocks, or of the female subject's unclothed or apparently unclothed breast, obscured by a covering or mark placed or printed on or in front of the material displayed, or obscured or altered in any other manner.

Public display of offensive sexual material is a Class* A misdemeanor.

* As originally enacted.

Added by L. 1971, Ch. 962; **Amended** by L. 1972, Ch. 814; L. 1985, Ch. 231.

ANNOTATIONS

Constitutionality.—PL § 245.11 is constitutional. People v. Low Bern Broadway, Inc., 68 Misc. 2d 112, 325 N.Y.S.2d 806 (N.Y.C. Crim. Ct. 1971).

Offensive sexual material; public display.—A two-inch patch depicting allegedly offensive sexual activity displayed in a store showroom window three feet deep and six feet wide among a variety of non offensive, youth-oriented items of merchandise did not violate statute intended to protect unwilling audiences from indiscriminate thrust of offensive sexual material. People v. Isaac, 69 Misc. 2d 758, 331 N.Y.S.2d 322 (Cr. Ct. Bronx Co. 1972).

PL

ARTICLE 250—OFFENSES AGAINST THE RIGHT TO PRIVACY

LexisNexis Cross Reference

New York Criminal Practice (2d ed.), Vol. 7, Ch. 79, Offenses Against Right to Privacy.

§ 250.00. Eavesdropping; definitions of terms.

The following definitions are applicable to this article:

1. "Wiretapping" means the intentional overhearing or recording of a telephonic or telegraphic communication by a person other than a sender or receiver thereof, without the consent of either the sender or receiver, by means of any instrument, device or equipment. The normal operation of a telephone or telegraph corporation and the normal use of the services and facilities furnished by such corporation pursuant to its tariffs or necessary to protect the rights or property of said corporation shall not be deemed "wiretapping."

2. "Mechanical overhearing of a conversation" means the intentional overhearing or recording of a conversation or discussion, without the consent of at least one party thereto, by a person not present thereat, by means of any instrument, device or equipment.

3. "Telephonic communication" means any aural transfer made in whole or in part through the use of facilities for the transmission of communications by the aid of wire, cable or other like connection between the point of origin and the point of reception (including the use of such connection in a switching station) furnished or operated by any person engaged in providing or operating such facilities for the transmission of communications and such term includes any electronic storage of such communications.

4. "Aural transfer" means a transfer containing the human voice at any point between and including the point of origin and the point of reception.

5. "Electronic communication" means any transfer of signs, signals, writing, images, sounds, data, or intelligence of any nature transmitted in whole or in part by a wire, radio, electromagnetic, photoelectronic or photo-optical system, but does not include:

(a) any telephonic or telegraphic communication; or

(b) any communication made through a tone only paging device; or

(c) any communication made through a tracking device consisting of an electronic or mechanical device which permits the tracking of the movement of a person or object; or

(d) any communication that is disseminated by the sender through a method of transmission that is configured so that such communication is readily accessible to the general public.

6. "Intercepting or accessing of an electronic communication" and "intentionally intercepted or accessed" mean the intentional acquiring, receiving, collecting, overhearing, or recording of an electronic communication, without the consent of the sender or intended receiver thereof, by means of any instrument, device or equipment, except when used by a telephone company in the ordinary course of its business or when necessary to protect the rights or property of such company.

7. "Electronic communication service" means any service which provides to users thereof the ability to send or receive wire or electronic communications.

8. "Unlawfully" means not specifically authorized pursuant to article seven hundred or seven

hundred five of the criminal procedure law for the purposes of this section and sections 250.05, 250.10, 250.15, 250.20, 250.25, 250.30 and 250.35 of this article.

Amended by L. 1988, Ch. 744; L. 2003, Ch. 69, § 2, eff. Aug. 11, 2003, amending subd. 8

ANNOTATIONS

Behavior not within statute.—When the witness at defendant's perjury trial overheard through a crack in the floor the conversations between defendant and her husband which formed the basis of criminal charges against the husband, and tape recorded the conversations, which formed the basis of the perjury charges against the defendant, since no additional means had to be taken to hear and record the conversations, and the witness was not a law enforcement official, no violation of PL § 250.20 occurred. People v. Kirsh, 176 A.D.2d 652, 575 N.Y.S.2d 306 (1st Dept. 1991), *lv. denied,* 79 N.Y.2d 949 (1992).

Informant's consent.—When the informant, in exchange for lenient treatment on an outstanding charge, consented to wearing a body wire, which recorded conversations during his ostensible drug purchase from defendant, since at least one person to the conversation consented to the mechanical recording of the conversation pursuant to PL § 250.00(2), an eavesdropping warrant was not required pursuant to CPL § 700.05(3)(b). People v. Dieppa, 176 A.D.2d 1076, 575 N.Y.S.2d 384 (3d Dept. 1991), *lv. denied,* 79 N.Y.2d 855, 588 N.E.2d 762, 580 N.Y.S.2d 727 (1992); *accord* People v. Hills, 176 A.D.2d 375, 574 N.Y.S.2d 82 (3d Dept. 1991).

—Where fourteen-year-old female complainant, in presence of her parents, consented in writing to the mechanical recording of a conversation with the defendant, charged with several sex offenses as well as endangering the welfare of a child, since this constituted the consent of one of the parties in the conversation, there was no violation of PL §§ 250.00(1) and 250.05. People v. Bastian, 125 A.D.2d 909, 510 N.Y.S.2d 269 (3d Dept. 1986), *lv. denied,* 69 N.Y.2d 824 (1987).

Participant's consent.—Although both the defendant and other party to the taped conversation denied recording the conversation or giving consent to having it recorded, evidence that the tape was made in a car and that the only occupants of the car were defendant and the other party, coupled with testimony at the *Huntley* hearing that the two had in the past "routinely" taped their conversations, supported court's determination that tape was made with consent of at least one of the parties. People v. Wood, 299 A.D.2d 739, 751 N.Y.S.2d 106 (3d Dept. 2002).

—Where the father recorded his own conversations with his children, since he consented to his own conversations being recorded, pursuant to P.L. 250.00(2), there was no violation of the eavesdropping statute, and recording could not on this basis be precluded from subsequent family court visitation proceeding. Harry R. v. Esther R., 134 Misc. 2d 404, 510 N.Y.S.2d 792 (Fam. Ct. Bronx Co. 1986).

Consent of nonparticipant.—In order for consent to be effective, it must be provided by a participant to the conversation; consent by the owner of the telephone when the owner is not participating in the overheard conversation would be ineffective. Pica v. Pica, 70 A.D.2d 931, 417 N.Y.S.2d 528 (2d Dept. 1979).

Eavesdropping prohibited by other rule or regulation.—Even though the complainant, a postal employee, was prohibited from eavesdropping by the rules of her employment, this did not render illegal under PL § 250.00 and 250.05 her recording of defendant's harassing phone calls from another postal employee; since she was one of the parties to the conversation, there was no violation of the eavesdropping statute on this basis. People v. Lasher, 58 N.Y.2d 962, 460 N.Y.S.2d 522, 447 N.E.2d 70 (1983).

—Upon a showing that the recording in issue had been obtained through unlawful eavesdropping, the court properly precluded defendant from making use of a transcript of the recorded phone conversation. People v. Sanjuan, 6 A.D.3d 247, 774 N.Y.S.2d 338 (1st Dept. 2004).

Cordless telephonic conversations.—Cordless telephone conversations, despite being transmitted over the public airways

and easily intercepted, are protected from electronic surveillance by PL § 250.00 and 250.05, even if the protection would not be afforded under federal law; even if cordless telephones do not specifically fall within the statutory prohibition, contrary result would subject private conversations in the privacy of one's home to unrestricted surveillance. People v. Fata, 159 A.D.2d 180, 559 N.Y.S.2d 348 (2d Dept.), *lv. denied,* 76 N.Y.2d 985 (1990); *accord* Sharon v. Sharon, 147 Misc. 2d 665, 558 N.Y.S.2d 468 (Sup. Ct. Nassau Co. 1990) (son, listening to a program on his short wave radio, heard telephonic conversation from his mother's cordless telephone which accidentally was picked up by the radio; the son tape recorded the conversation, which the father subsequently tried to use in a subsequent matrimonial action; suppressed as the product of a felonious recording).

Application to video images.—PL Article 250 applies to aural communications or electronic communications; it does not apply to the recording of images, such as when law enforcement authorities placed camera in dentist's office to record images during visits by patients whom he sexually abused. People v. Teicher, 52 N.Y.2d 638, 439 N.Y.S.2d 846, 422 N.E.2d 506 (1981) (Editorial Note: ruling preceded 1988 amendments which added proscription with respect to electronic communications, but amendments do not specifically address visual images recorded by camera).

Motion to suppress; eavesdropping; probable cause.—There was sufficient probable cause for issuance of search warrant after defendant's telephone conversation was inadvertently overheard by an overseas telephone operator who then called the police and gave information (which later proved to be reliable and accurate) concerning a shipment of narcotics to New York. People v. Sierra, 74 Misc. 2d 332, 343 N.Y.S.2d 196 (Sup. Ct. N.Y. Co. 1973).

§ 250.05. Eavesdropping.

A person is guilty of eavesdropping when he unlawfully engages in wiretapping, mechanical overhearing of a conversation, or intercepting or accessing of an electronic communication.

Eavesdropping is a class E felony.

Amended L. 1988, Ch. 744.

ANNOTATION

Husband; wife.—It is a violation of PL § 250.05 for a husband, without his wife's consent, to tap the phone in the marital residence and record her conversations with other men for the purpose of obtaining evidence against her in a divorce action; the evidence derived from these recordings can be excluded in a divorce proceeding. Connin v. Connin, 89 Misc. 2d 548, 392 N.Y.S.2d 530 (Sup. Ct. Monroe Co. 1976).

§ 250.10. Possession of eavesdropping devices.

A person is guilty of possession of eavesdropping devices when, under circumstances evincing an intent to use or to permit the same to be used in violation of section 250.05, he possesses any instrument, device or equipment designed for, adapted to or commonly used in wiretapping or mechanical overhearing of a conversation.

Possession of eavesdropping devices is a class A misdemeanor.

§ 250.15. Failure to report wiretapping.

A telephone or telegraph corporation is guilty of failure to report wiretapping when, having knowledge of the occurrence of unlawful wiretapping, it does not report such matter to an appropriate law enforcement officer or agency.

Failure to report wiretapping is a class B misdemeanor.

§ 250.20. Divulging an eavesdropping warrant.

A person is guilty of divulging an eavesdropping warrant when, possessing information concerning the existence or content of an eavesdropping warrant issued pursuant to article seven hundred of the criminal procedure law, or concerning any circumstance attending an application for such a warrant, he discloses such information to another person; except that such disclosure is not criminal or unlawful when permitted by section 700.65 of the criminal procedure law or when made to a state or federal agency specifically authorized by law to receive reports concerning eavesdropping warrants, or when made in a legal proceeding, or to a law enforcement officer or agency connected with the application for such warrant, or to a legislative committee or temporary state commission, or to the telephone or telegraph corporation whose facilities are involved, or to any entity operating an electronic communications service whose facilities are involved.

Divulging an eavesdropping warrant is a class A misdemeanor.

Amended L. 1988, Ch. 744.

ANNOTATIONS

Constitutionality.—PL § 250.20 is not facially overbroad, nor overbroad as applied to defendant who discloses the existence of a wiretap to the target of a criminal investigation, nor does it unduly restrict the constitutional protection of free expression. People v. Tansey and Smith, 156 Misc. 2d 233, 593 N.Y.S.2d 426 (Sup. Ct. N.Y. Co. 1992).

—Defendant's disclosure of the existence of an eavesdropping device to the target of an ongoing investigation into criminal activity at the Jacob Javits Center violated PL § 250.20. People v. Tansey, 156 Misc. 2d 233, 593 N.Y.S.2d 426 (Sup. Ct. N.Y. Co. 1992).

Corroboration of accomplice testimony.—When the defendant, a police officer, divulged to a person who subsequently became an informant that his telephone was wiretapped, in exchange for cash which constituted the offense of bribery, that person became an accomplice to the bribery as well as to the offense of divulging an eavesdropping warrant, so that his testimony establishing the offense required corroboration under CPL § 60.22. People v. Dennison, 83 A.D.2d 754, 443 N.Y.S.2d 516 (1981).

§ 250.25. Tampering with private communications.

A person is guilty of tampering with private communications when:

1. Knowing that he does not have the consent of the sender or receiver, he opens or reads a sealed letter or other sealed private communication; or

2. Knowing that a sealed letter or other sealed private communication has been opened or read in violation of subdivision one of this section, he divulges without the consent of the sender or receiver, the contents of such letter or communication, in whole or in part, or a resume of any portion of the contents thereof; or

3. Knowing that he does not have the consent of the sender or receiver, he obtains or attempts to obtain from an employee, officer or representative of a telephone or telegraph corporation, by connivance, deception, intimidation or in any other manner, information with respect to the contents or nature thereof of a telephonic or telegraphic communication; except that the provisions of this subdivision do not apply to a law enforcement officer who obtains information from a telephone or telegraph corporation pursuant to section 250.35; or

4. Knowing that he does not have the consent of the sender or receiver, and being an employee, officer or representative of a telephone or telegraph corporation, he knowingly divulges to another person the contents or nature thereof of a telephonic or telegraphic communication; except that the provisions of this subdivision do not apply to such person when he acts pursuant to section 250.35.

Tampering with private communications is a class B misdemeanor.

ANNOTATIONS

Public letters.—PL § 250.25(1) is not intended to protect private communications, addressed to municipal employees and sent in care of the municipality. People v. Freedman, 87 Misc. 2d 585, 386 N.Y.S.2d 306 (City Ct. of Rochester, Monroe Co. 1976).

Public policy.—Birnbaum v. United States, 436 F. Supp. 967 (E.D.N.Y. 1977), aff'd in part, rev'd inn part, 588 F.2d 319 (2d Cir. 1978).

§ 250.30. Unlawfully obtaining communications information.

A person is guilty of unlawfully obtaining communications information when, knowing that he does not have the authorization of a telephone or telegraph corporation, he obtains or attempts to obtain, by deception, stealth or in any other manner, from such corporation or from any employee, officer or representative thereof:

1. Information concerning identification or location of any wires, cables, lines, terminals or other apparatus used in furnishing telephone or telegraph service; or

2. Information concerning a record of any communication passing over telephone or telegraph lines of any such corporation.

Unlawfully obtaining communications information is a class B misdemeanor.

§ 250.35. Failing to report criminal communications.

1. It shall be the duty of a telephone or telegraph corporation, or an entity operating an electronic communications service, and of any

employee, officer or representative thereof having knowledge that the facilities of such corporation or entity are being used to conduct any criminal business, traffic or transaction, to furnish or attempt to furnish to an appropriate law enforcement officer or agency all pertinent information within his possession relating to such matter, and to cooperate fully with any law enforcement officer or agency investigating such matter.

2. A person is guilty of failing to report criminal communications when he knowingly violates any duty prescribed in subdivision one of this section.

Failing to report criminal communications is a class B misdemeanor.

Amended L. 1988, Ch. 744.

§ 250.40. Unlawful surveillance; definitions.

The following definitions shall apply to sections 250.45, 250.50, 250.55 and 250.60 of this article:

1. "Place and time when a person has a reasonable expectation of privacy" means a place and time when a reasonable person would believe that he or she could fully disrobe in privacy.

2. "Imaging device" means any mechanical, digital or electronic viewing device, camera or any other instrument capable of recording, storing or transmitting visual images that can be utilized to observe a person.

3. "Sexual or other intimate parts" means the human male or female genitals, pubic area or buttocks, or the female breast below the top of the nipple, and shall include such part or parts which are covered only by an undergarment.

4. "Broadcast" means electronically transmitting a visual image with the intent that it be viewed by a person.

5. "Disseminate" means to give, provide, lend, deliver, mail, send, forward, transfer or transmit, electronically or otherwise to another person.

6. "Publish" means to (a) disseminate, as defined in subdivision five of this section, with the intent that such image or images be disseminated to ten or more persons; or (b) disseminate with the intent that such images be sold by another person; or (c) post, present, display, exhibit, circulate, advertise or allows access, electronically or otherwise, so as to make an image or images available to the public; or (d) disseminate with the intent that an image or images be posted, presented, displayed, exhibited, circulated, advertised or made accessible, electronically or otherwise and to make such image or images available to the public.

7. "Sell" means to disseminate to another person, as defined in subdivision five of this section, or to publish, as defined in subdivision

six of this section, in exchange for something of value.

Added by L. 2003, Ch. 69, § 3, eff. Aug. 11, 2003.

§ 250.45. Unlawful surveillance in the second degree.

A person is guilty of unlawful surveillance in the second degree when:

1. For his or her own, or another person's amusement, entertainment, or profit, or for the purpose of degrading or abusing a person, he or she intentionally uses or installs, or permits the utilization or installation of an imaging device to surreptitiously view, broadcast or record a person dressing or undressing or the sexual or other intimate parts of such person at a place and time when such person has a reasonable expectation of privacy, without such person's knowledge or consent; or

2. For his or her own, or another person's sexual arousal or sexual gratification, he or she intentionally uses or installs, or permits the utilization or installation of an imaging device to surreptitiously view, broadcast or record a person dressing or undressing or the sexual or other intimate parts of such person at a place and time when such person has a reasonable expectation of privacy, without such person's knowledge or consent; or

3. (a) For no legitimate purpose, he or she intentionally uses or installs, or permits the utilization or installation of an imaging device to surreptitiously view, broadcast or record a person in a bedroom, changing room, fitting room, restroom, toilet, bathroom, washroom, shower or any room assigned to guests or patrons in a motel, hotel or inn, without such person's knowledge or consent.

(b) For the purposes of this subdivision, when a person uses or installs, or permits the utilization or installation of an imaging device in a bedroom, changing room, fitting room, restroom, toilet, bathroom, washroom, shower or any room assigned to guests or patrons in a hotel, motel or inn, there is a rebuttable presumption that such person did so for no legitimate purpose; or

4. Without the knowledge or consent of a person, he or she intentionally uses or installs, or permits the utilization or installation of an imaging device to surreptitiously view, broadcast or record, under the clothing being worn by such person, the sexual or other intimate parts of such person.

Unlawful surveillance in the second degree is a class E felony.

Added by L. 2003, Ch. 69, § 3, eff. Aug. 11, 2003; **Amended** by L. 2003, Ch. 157, § 1, eff. Aug. 11, 2003, amending subds. 1–3.

§ 250.50. Unlawful surveillance in the first degree.

A person is guilty of unlawful surveillance in the first degree when he or she commits the crime of unlawful surveillance in the second degree and has been previously convicted within the past ten years of unlawful surveillance in the first or second degree.

Unlawful surveillance in the first degree is a class D felony.

Added by L. 2003, Ch. 69, § 3, eff. Aug. 11, 2003.

§ 250.55. Dissemination of an unlawful surveillance image in the second degree.

A person is guilty of dissemination of an unlawful surveillance image in the second degree when he or she, with knowledge of the unlawful conduct by which an image or images of the sexual or other intimate parts of another person or persons were obtained and such unlawful conduct would satisfy the essential elements of the crime of unlawful surveillance in the first or second degree, intentionally disseminates such image or images.

Dissemination of an unlawful surveillance image in the second degree is a class A misdemeanor.

Added by L. 2003, Ch. 69, § 3, eff. Aug. 11, 2003.

§ 250.60. Dissemination of an unlawful surveillance image in the first degree.

A person is guilty of dissemination of an unlawful surveillance image in the first degree when:

1. He or she, with knowledge of the unlawful conduct by which an image or images of the sexual or other intimate parts of another person or persons were obtained and such unlawful conduct would satisfy the essential elements of the crime of unlawful surveillance in the first or second degree, sells or publishes such image or images; or

2. Having created a surveillance image in violation of section 250.45 or 250.50 of this article, or in violation of the law in any other jurisdiction which includes all of the essential elements of either such crime, or having acted as an accomplice to such crime, or acting as an agent to the person who committed such crime, he or she intentionally disseminates such unlawfully created image; or

3. He or she commits the crime of dissemination of an unlawful surveillance image in the second degree and has been previously convicted within the past ten years of dissemination of an unlawful surveillance image in the first or second degree.

Dissemination of an unlawful surveillance image in the first degree is a class E felony.

Added by L. 2003, Ch. 69, § 3, eff. Aug. 11, 2003; **Amended** by L. 2003, Ch. 157, § 2, eff. Aug. 11, 2003, amending subds. 1 and 2.

§ 250.65. Additional provisions.

1. The provisions of sections 250.45, 250.50, 250.55 and 250.60 of this article do not apply with respect to any: (a) law enforcement personnel engaged in the conduct of their authorized duties; (b) security system wherein a written notice is conspicuously posted on the premises stating that a video surveillance system has been installed for the purpose of security; or (c) video surveillance devices installed in such a manner that their presence is clearly and immediately obvious.

2. With respect to sections 250.55 and 250.60 of this article, the provisions of subdivision two of section 235.15 and subdivisions one and two of section 235.24 of this chapter shall apply.

Added by L. 2003, Ch. 69, § 3, eff. Aug. 11, 2003.

TITLE O—OFFENSES AGAINST MARRIAGE, THE FAMILY, AND THE WELFARE OF CHILDREN AND INCOMPETENTS

ARTICLE 255—OFFENSES AFFECTING THE MARITAL RELATIONSHIP

LexisNexis Cross Reference

Prosecution and Defense of Sex Crimes, Ch. 12, Prosecution and Defense of Spouse Abuse and Marital Rape.

§ 255.00. Unlawfully solemnizing a marriage.

A person is guilty of unlawfully solemnizing a marriage when:

1. Knowing that he is not authorized by the laws of this state to do so, he performs a marriage ceremony or presumes to solemnize a marriage; or

2. Being authorized by the laws of this state to perform marriage ceremonies and to solemnize marriages, he performs a marriage ceremony or solemnizes a marriage knowing that a legal impediment to such marriage exists.

Unlawfully solemnizing a marriage is a class A misdemeanor.

§ 255.05. Unlawfully issuing a dissolution decree.

A person is guilty of unlawfully issuing a dissolution decree when, not being a judicial officer authorized to issue decrees of divorce or annulment, he issues a written instrument reciting or certifying that he or some other purportedly but not actually authorized person has issued a valid decree of civil divorce, annulment or other dissolution of a marriage.

Unlawfully issuing a dissolution decree is a class A misdemeanor.

§ 255.10. Unlawfully procuring a marriage license.

A person is guilty of unlawfully procuring a marriage license when he procures a license to marry another person at a time when he has a living spouse, or the other person has a living spouse.

Unlawfully procuring a marriage license is a class A misdemeanor.

§ 255.15. Bigamy.

A person is guilty of bigamy when he contracts or purports to contract a marriage with another person at a time when he has a living spouse, or the other person has a living spouse.

Bigamy is a class E felony.

ANNOTATION

Rape charge.—Regardless of claim that victim of charge of rape was claimed to be his second wife under Nigerian law, it was a bigamous marriage under New York law, absolutely void as against public policy; as such, the claimed marriage is irrelevant as a factual defense to the charge of rape. People v. Ezeonu, 155 Misc. 2d 344, 588 N.Y.S.2d 116 (Sup. Ct. Bronx Co. 1992).

§ 255.17. Adultery.

A person is guilty of adultery when he engages in sexual intercourse with another person at a time when he has a living spouse, or the other person has a living spouse.

Adultery is a class B misdemeanor.

Added by L. 1965, Ch. 1037.

ANNOTATIONS

Contracts contemplating adultery.—Agreements which have as an element of consideration that the parties cohabit, implying sexual relations, while one of the parties is still married, are unenforceable; plaintiff, who was still married although separated, entered contract with defendant for payment of annual salary on consideration that she cohabit with defendant, as well as perform other services. Donnell v. Stogel, 139 Misc. 2d 72, 526 N.Y.S.2d 744 (Sup. Ct. Queens Co. 1988), *rev'd,* 161 A.D.2d 93, 560 N.Y.S.2d 200 (2d Dept. 1990), on basis that divorce had been finalized by time of the agreement, and contract did not specifically contemplate adultery.

Adultery and child custody.—Even though adultery is a crime, it does not brand a person to be unfit as a parent, per se, and would not bar woman from maintaining paternity proceedings to have a man other than her husband declared the father of the child. LaCroix v. Deyo, 108 Misc. 2d 382, 437 N.Y.S.2d 517 (Fam. Ct. Ulster Co. 1981).

§ 255.20. Unlawfully procuring a marriage license, bigamy, adultery: defense.

In any prosecution for unlawfully procuring a marriage license, bigamy, or adultery, it is an affirmative defense that the defendant acted under a reasonable belief that both he and the other person to the marriage or prospective marriage or to the sexual intercourse, as the case may be, were unmarried.

Amended by L. 1965, Ch. 1037.

§ 255.25. Incest.

A person is guilty of incest when he or she marries or engages in sexual intercourse, oral sexual conduct or anal sexual conduct with a person whom he or she knows to be related to him or her, either legitimately or out of wedlock, as an ancestor, descendant, brother or sister of either the whole or the half blood, uncle, aunt, nephew or niece.

Incest is a class E felony.

Amended by L. 1984, Ch. 649; L. 2003, Ch. 264, § 31, eff. Nov. 1, 2003.

ANNOTATIONS

Incest not classed as a sex offense.—Incest is classified as an offense against marriage, rather than as a sex offense, which distinguishes the analysis of the legislation, such as regarding corroboration, from sex offenses. People v. Facey, 115 A.D.2d 11, 499 N.Y.S.2d 517 (4th Dept. 1986).

Work release not available.—Persons convicted of incest under PL § 255.25 are not eligible for work release under Corr. Law § 851(2). Diggins v. Recore, 163 Misc. 2d 607, 621 N.Y.S.2d 447 (Sup. Ct. Albany Co. 1995).

Victim not accomplice.—Where the victim was not an accomplice to the incest, corroboration under CPL § 60.22 was not required. People v. Thomas, 210 A.D.2d 992, 620 N.Y.S.2d 693 (4th Dept. 1994); *accord* People v. Jones, 133 A.D.2d 972, 521 N.Y.S.2d 123 (3d Dept. 1987), *lv. denied*, 70 N.Y.2d 956 (1988).

—As a general rule, insofar as a child under the age of seventeen cannot, as a matter of law, consent to sex, the child cannot commit incest, and cannot be an accomplice to incest; by contrast, a person over seventeen who voluntarily engages in an incestuous relationship also commits incest and testimony from such person is subject to the rules governing corroboration of the testimony of an accomplice. People v. Facey, 115 A.D.2d 11, 499 N.Y.S.2d 517 (4th Dept. 1986).

—Issue of whether adult daughter of defendant consented to incest was an issue of fact; court erred by instructing jury that "victim" of incest is not an accomplice as a matter of law. People v. Facey, 115 A.D.2d 11, 499 N.Y.S.2d 517 (4th Dept. 1986).

Victim is accomplice.—Accepting for sake of argument that victim of incest might have been an accomplice, her testimony was adequately corroborated by medical evidence establishing that she had had sexual intercourse, that seminal fluid was found in her vagina, but no sperm was found, which was consistent with evidence that defendant had had a vasectomy; defendant's claim of impotence was medically disproved; social worker testified that victim's behavior conformed to profile of a sexually abused child. People v. Bosilkofski, 134 A.D.2d 869, 521 N.Y.S.2d 601 (4th Dept. 1987).

Family Court proceedings; collateral estoppel.—Evidence adduced in family court civil proceeding relevant to issue of whether child should be removed from parental home as a result of sexual abuse in connection with incest did not collaterally estop criminal prosecution of incest charges. People v. Bosilkofski, 134 A.D.2d 869, 521 N.Y.S.2d 601 (4th Dept. 1987).

Request for pretrial hearing to determine whether complainant had been subjected to suggestive interviewing techniques.—The statute does not provide for a hearing, but in appropriate circumstances, the trial court has inherent authority to conduct a hearing to determine if the physician treating the child had engaged in a suggestive interview procedure. People v. Michael M., 162 Misc. 2d 803, 618 N.Y.S.2d 171 (Sup. Ct. Kings Co. 1994).

Evidence of victim's other sexual encounters.—Since the victim's other sexual experiences is only relevant if defendant submits a defense of consensual relations with the victim, and since consent is not a defense to incest, the court did not err in precluding cross-examination of victim in this regard, when defendant tried to demonstrate that victim had fabricated claims. People v. Perryman, 178 A.D.2d 916, 578 N.Y.S.2d 785 (4th Dept. 1991), *lv. denied*, 79 N.Y.2d 1005 (1992), *error coram nobis denied*, 207 A.D.2d 1043, 617 N.Y.S.2d 701 (4th Dept. 1994).

Legal sufficiency.—*See* People v. Ali, 178 A.D.2d 418, 576 N.Y.S.2d 807 (2d Dept. 1991).

—Evidence which established that defendant had sexual intercourse with his 14-year-old daughter, who he knew to be his child, satisfied the charge of incest. People v. Chapin, 265 A.D.2d 738, 697 N.Y.S.2d 713 (3d Dept. 1999), *appeal denied*, 94 N.Y.2d 917 (2000).

—Section 255.25 requires independent corroboration of nature of relationship between the complainant and defendant. People v. Braithwaite, 176 Misc. 2d 79, 670 N.Y.S.2d 970 (Sup. Ct. Queens Co. 1998).

Evidence of prior acts of incest.—Incest requires no special intent, but only a general intention to perform the incestuous act; whether victim consented or defendant was predisposed to have amorous relations with the victim is irrelevant; evidence of prior acts of incest between defendant and the particular victim is not justified under the theories of admissibility, and did not clear up any ambiguities, when victim established that defendant was her father, and defendant admitted having sexual encounters with victim, so that its introduction required reversal. People v. Lewis, 69 N.Y.2d 321, 514 N.Y.S.2d 205, 506 N.E.2d 915 (1987).

§ 255.30. Adultery and incest; corroboration.

1. A person shall not be convicted of adultery or of an attempt to commit adultery solely upon the testimony of the other party to the adulterous act or attempted act, unsupported by other evidence tending to establish that the defendant attempted to engage with the other party in sexual intercourse, and that the defendant or the other party had a living spouse at the time of the adulterous act or attempted act.

2. A person shall not be convicted of incest or of an attempt to commit incest solely upon the testimony of the other party unsupported by other evidence tending to establish that the defendant married the other party, or that the defendant was a relative of the other party of a kind specified in section 255.25.

Amended by L. 1972, Ch. 373; L. 1982, Ch. 659.

ANNOTATIONS

Proof of kinship.—Corroboration which is required for incest prosecution is proof tending to establish kinship; evidence was properly received from the victim's mother that the defendant was the victim's father, and from the aunt to establish that acts of sexual intercourse had occurred between defendant and the victim. People v. Lewis, 69 N.Y.2d 321, 514 N.Y.S.2d 205, 506 N.E.2d 915 (1987).

Corroboration of the sex act for incest prosecution.—1982 amendment to statute deleted requirement that the victim's testimony had to be corroborated to the extent of requiring additional proof tending to establish that the defendant had sex with the victim; although the amendment recognized that many incest cases involved children, the ameliorative effect of the amendment was not limited to child victims. People v. Facey, 115 A.D.2d 11, 499 N.Y.S.2d 517 (4th Dept. 1986).

ARTICLE 260—OFFENSES RELATING TO CHILDREN, DISABLED PERSONS AND VULNERABLE ELDERLY PERSONS

LexisNexis Cross References

Criminal Defense Techniques, Vol. 1B, Ch. 42A, Litigating on Behalf of Children in Institutions; Vol. 4, Ch. 78A, Examination of the Child Witness; *New York Criminal Practice (2d ed.),* Vol. 7, Ch. 81, Offenses Specifically Relating to Children and Incompetents; *Prosecution and Defense of Sex Crimes,* Ch. 9, The Prosecution and Defense of Child Sexual Assault; Ch. 11, The Prosecution and Defense of Child Abuse.

§ 260.00. Abandonment of a child.

A person is guilty of abandonment of a child when, being a parent, guardian or other person legally charged with the care or custody of a child less than fourteen years old, he deserts such child in any place with intent to wholly abandon it.

Abandonment of a child is a class E felony.

§ 260.03. Abandonment of a child; defense.

In any prosecution for abandonment of a child, pursuant to section 260.00 of this article, based upon an alleged desertion of a child not more than five days old with an intent to wholly abandon such child, it is an affirmative defense that, with the intent that the child be safe from physical injury and cared for in an appropriate manner, the defendant left the child with an appropriate person or in a suitable location and promptly notified an appropriate person of the child's location.

Added by L. 2000, Ch. 156, § 3, eff. July 18, 2000.

§ 260.05. Non-support of a child in the second degree.

A person is guilty of non-support of a child when, being a parent, guardian or other person legally charged with the care or custody of a child less than sixteen years old, he fails or refuses without lawful excuse to provide support for such child when he is able to do so, or becomes unable to do so, when, though employable, he voluntarily terminates his employment, voluntarily reduces his earning capacity or fails to diligently seek employment.

Non-support of a child in the second degree is a class A misdemeanor.

Amended by L. 1972, Ch. 687; L. 1997, Ch. 397, § 1, eff. Sept. 1, 1997.

ANNOTATIONS

A putative father is a "parent" within meaning of PL § 260.05 and he is legally charged with the care of a child. —People v. Little, 105 Misc. 2d 899, 430 N.Y.S.2d 534 (Onondaga Co. Ct. 1980).

Non-support of child.—A person is guilty of non-support of a child not only when he is able to provide support and fails to do so but also when he becomes unable to do so by voluntarily terminating his employment, voluntarily reducing his earning capacity or failing to diligently seek employment. People v. Hinton, 40 N.Y.2d 345, 386 N.Y.S.2d 703, 353 N.E.2d 617 (1976).

Grounds for extradition.—Extradition order was valid where there was a prima facie showing that petitioner would have violated § 265.05 if consequences of his actions affected New York: petitioner is the parent of the infant at issue; voluntarily entered into a separation agreement and consent judgment of divorce providing for child support; actually paid child support for a period of two years and admitted that he failed to pay support upon the mistaken premise and sole ground that he had no legal obligation to provide child support because his former wife did not in fact establish a New York residence. Fabri v. Pataki, 169 Misc. 1026, 648 N.Y.S.2d 219 (Sup. Ct. Westchester Co. 1996), *aff'd,* 237 A.D.2d 520, 655 N.Y.S.2d 586 (2d Dept. 1997).

§ 260.06. Non-support of a child in the first degree.

A person is guilty of non-support of a child in the first degree when:

1. Being a parent, guardian or other person legally charged with the care or custody of a child less than sixteen years old, he or she fails or refuses without lawful excuse to provide support for such child when he or she is able to do so; and

2. He or she has previously been convicted in the preceding five years of the crime defined in section 260.05 of this article.

Non-support of a child in the first degree is a class E felony.

Added by L. 1997, Ch. 397, § 2, eff. Sept. 1, 1997.

§ 260.10. Endangering the welfare of a child.

A person is guilty of endangering the welfare of a child when:

1. He knowingly acts in a manner likely to be injurious to the physical, mental or moral welfare of a child less than seventeen years old or directs or authorizes such child to engage in an occupation involving a substantial risk of danger to his life or health; or

2. Being a parent, guardian or other person legally charged with the care or custody of a child less than eighteen years old, he fails or refuses to exercise reasonable diligence in the control of such child to prevent him from becoming an "abused child," a "neglected child," a "juvenile delinquent" or a "person in need of supervision," as those terms are defined in articles ten, three and seven of the family court act.

Endangering the welfare of a child is a class A misdemeanor.

Amended by L. 1967, Ch. 791; L. 1970, Chs. 389, 962; L. 1982, Ch. 920; L. 1990, Ch. 476.

ANNOTATIONS

Constitutionality.—Penal Law § 260.10 is not unconstitutionally vague. People v. Padmore, 221 A.D.2d 663, 634 N.Y.S.2d 215 (2d Dept. 1995), *lv. denied,* 87 N.Y.2d 1023 (1996), *overruling* People v. Villacis, 143 Misc. 2d 568, 541 N.Y.S.2d 178.

—Application of statute to prohibit defendant from contacting children over computer bulletin board and conducting sexually explicit conversations with them was not an unconstitutional infringement of the right to free expression; protection of children is a compelling state interest.. People v. Poplaski, 162 Misc. 2d 209, 616 N.Y.S.2d 434 (Dist. Ct. Nassau Co. 1994).

—The statute sufficiently gives notice that a person may not use a computer bulletin board to solicit sexually explicit conversations with children. People v. Poplaski, 162 Misc. 2d 209, 616 N.Y.S.2d 434 (Dist. Ct. Nassau Co. 1994).

—Statute is not intended to prohibit only acts but not speech.

People v. Poplaski, 162 Misc. 2d 209, 616 N.Y.S.2d 434 (Dist. Ct. Nassau Co. 1994).

—Statute was not unconstitutionally vague, insofar as it clearly put father on notice that he was required to not allow his child to be abused by his unstable wife. People v. Scully, 134 Misc. 2d 906, 513 N.Y.S.2d 625 (N.Y.C. Crim. Ct. Kings Co. 1987).

Civil proceeding does not collaterally bar criminal proceeding.—Family court proceeding resulting in determination that defendant had neglected his daughter did not collaterally estop criminal proceeding in which defendant was charged, inter alia, with endangering the welfare of a child, arising out of same acts as family court proceeding; family court proceeding determined defendant's ability to adequately care for his child, rather than his culpability; similarly, prosecution could use evidence adduced in family court proceeding without violating bar against double jeopardy. People v. Roselle, 84 N.Y.2d 350, 618 N.Y.S.2d 753, 643 N.E.2d 72 (1994).

Military prosecution bars state prosecution for similar offense arising out of same conduct.—General court martial by military tribunal under military law is equivalent of conviction by court; military charges arose out of defendant's rape of defendant's 13-year-old niece while he was off duty; statutory double jeopardy prohibition of CPL Article 40 barred state prosecution for rape and endangering the welfare arising from the same conduct. Booth v. Clary, 83 N.Y.2d 675, 613 N.Y.S.2d 110, 635 N.E.2d 279 (1994).

Parent's neglect.—Father's conduct of placing child in very hot bath water, scalding her foot and buttocks, resulting in severe burning, was sufficient evidence that defendant failed to exercise reasonable diligence in care of the child. People v. Roselle, 84 N.Y.2d 350, 618 N.Y.S.2d 753, 643 N.E.2d 72 (1994).

—Failure to seek medical help for a distressed child, such as when another guardian abuses the child, can support a charge of endangering the welfare of a child against the "passive" guardian. People v. Wong, 81 N.Y.2d 600, 601 N.Y.S.2d 440, 619 N.E.2d 377 (1993).

—In New York, parents have a non-delegable affirmative duty to provide adequate medical care to their children, the omission of which responsibility can subject parents to criminal charges. People v. Steinberg, 170 A.D.2d 50, 573 N.Y.S.2d 965 (1st Dept. 1991), *aff'd,* 79 N.Y.2d 673.

—Mother's failure to keep medical appointments for baby, keeping baby in filthy bassinet, where he died, keeping baby in urine soaked diapers, keeping baby in garbage filled apartment with constant exposure to cat feces and fruit flies, and mother's refusal to accept assistance from public health nurse, were omissions of a nondelegable duty which constituted endangering the welfare of a child. People v. Manon, 226 A.D.2d 774, 640 N.Y.S.2d 318 (3d Dept. 1996).

—Parents' conduct of supplying at least twenty-five ounces of 80 proof alcohol to their fifteen-year-old child over a short period of time, resulting in blood alcohol count of .41 and his death, was sufficient evidence that defendants knew that this conduct posed a substantial risk to the child's health; indictment reinstated. People v. Garbarino, 152 A.D.2d 254, 549 N.Y.S.2d 527 (3d Dept. 1989), *lv. denied,* 75 N.Y.2d 919 (1990).

—Father's failure to keep his child away from his wife, the child's mother, who was an abusive drug addict, after he had removed the child temporarily on one occasion out of a concern for the wife's abuse, constituted endangering the welfare of a child. People v. Scully, 134 Misc. 2d 906, 513 N.Y.S.2d 625 (N.Y.C. Crim. Ct. Kings Co. 1987).

Inappropriate conduct which is not legally sufficient.—Defendant's conduct of often kissing the daughter of his girlfriend, with whom he resided, on the cheek, occasionally acquiescing in her requests to stop, and on a single occasion kissing her on the back while she was in bed, but clothed, was not sufficient to constitute endangering the welfare of a child. People v. Camacho, 209 A.D.2d 534, 618 N.Y.S.2d 842 (2d Dept. 1994); *compare with* People v. Dunavin (173 A.D.2d 1032, 570 N.Y.S.2d 369 (3d Dept.), *lv. denied,* 78 N.Y.2d 965 (1991)), in which the defendant showed the young girl a sexually explicit movie, pinched her buttocks, and a photo depicted the young girl sitting in defendant's trailer, clothed, but without underwear.

Acts of discipline.—Defendant's conduct of repeatedly slapping the five-year-old child, hitting him with a dowel and a piece of plastic molding, causing those instruments to break, resulting in his death, was endangering the welfare of a child. People v. Ross, 117 A.D.2d 684, 498 N.Y.S.2d 424 (2d Dept. 1986).

—Conduct of foster parent, twisting child's arms and pulling ears, resulting in injuries, endangered the child's welfare. People v. Caccese, 211 A.D.2d 976, 621 N.Y.S.2d 735 (3d Dept.), *lv. denied,* 86 N.Y.2d 780 (1995).

—Evidence at trial that defendant ordered her five-year-old son to drink household bleach as a punishment for failing to clean his room was sufficient to support a conviction under this section; "it is well settled that a defendant's intent to cause physical injury to the victim may be inferred from defendant's conduct and the surrounding circumstances." People v. Synder, 306 A.D.2d 949, 761 N.Y.S.2d 921 (4th Dept. 2003).

—In civil proceeding plaintiff teacher, claiming false arrest, had responded to ten-year-old girl's misbehavior in class by placing her on floor, straddling her and spanking her twelve times; this was not endangering the welfare of a child. Malte v. State of New York, 125 A.D.2d 958, 510 N.Y.S.2d 353 (4th Dept. 1986), *lv. denied,* 69 N.Y.2d 607 (1987).

Shaken baby syndrome.—Shaken baby syndrome, in which father lost temper with baby who would not sleep and shook baby hard, without supporting head, resulting in baby's death, constitutes endangering the welfare of a child. *Cf.* People v. Van Norstrand, 85 N.Y.2d 131, 623 N.Y.S.2d 767, 647 N.E.2d 1275 (1995) (assault conviction reversed on other grounds).

—When one parent or guardian does the shaking, and the other "passive" parent or guardian refrains, the "passive" parent or guardian may still be guilty on a theory of neglect. People v. Wong, 81 N.Y.2d 600, 601 N.Y.S.2d 440, 619 N.E.2d 377 (1993).

—Mere presence in the apartment by the "passive" parent or guardian, while the "active" parent or guardian injures the child, is an insufficient basis on which to predicate culpability; where People's evidence failed to establish which guardian shook the baby, let alone that the "passive" guardian was actually aware that shaking had occurred and that such conduct created a risk of danger, and there was no sound evidence upon which to base an inference of knowledge, convictions against both defendants were reversed and indictment dismissed. People v. Wong, 81 N.Y.2d 600, 601 N.Y.S.2d 440, 619 N.E.2d 377 (1993).

Other criminal conduct constituting endangering the welfare of a child.—Father's use of cocaine and marijuana in the presence of his daughter constituted endangering the welfare of a child. People v. Hetrick, 80 N.Y.2d 344, 590 N.Y.S.2d 183, 604 N.E.2d 732 (1992).

—Defendant was a passenger in the van, and at some point drove the van, in which the complainant and her infant child were held against complainant's will, and which also contained a machete used to intimidate complainant; evidence legally sufficient to convict defendant of endangering the welfare of the child. People v. Vasquez, 191 A.D.2d 659, 595 N.Y.S.2d 223 (2d Dept. 1993).

Knowing conduct.—When defendant forcibly sodomized victim, her five-year-old son entered room; despite her pleas that he stop, defendant refused to stop, although he did try to cover the child's eyes; evidence sufficient to establish defendant's knowledge with respect to the effect on the child. People v. Parr, 155 A.D.2d 945, 548 N.Y.S.2d 121 (4th Dept. 1989), *lv. denied,* 75 N.Y.2d 870 (1990).

Child victim's testimonial capacity.—Requirement regarding receipt of sworn testimony from child did not validity a child's hearsay statements used as a predicate for probable cause in support of a warrant. People v. Hetrick, 80 N.Y.2d 344, 590 N.Y.S.2d 183, 604 N.E.2d 732 (1992).

—Although it was error to permit six-year-old child to testify under oath concerning sexual abuse which formed basis of endangering the welfare charge, child's testimony was corroborated and error was harmless. People v. Lynch, 216 A.D.2d 929, 629 N.Y.S.2d 136 (4th Dept.), *lv. denied,* 87 N.Y.2d 904 (1995).

Opinion testimony.—Nurse was qualified to offer lay opinion testimony that she was familiar with calamine lotion, and that she observed that it covered marks and bruises on child victim's hand. People v. Caccese, 211 A.D.2d 976, 621 N.Y.S.2d 735 (3d Dept.), *lv. denied,* 86 N.Y.2d 780 (1995).

Evidence of prior instances involving same defendant.— Evidence that guardians, who were hired to care for infant child of working couple, who died in their care as a consequence of shaking baby syndrome, had had two prior instances in which children in their care had to be hospitalized, was admissible. People v. Wong, 182 A.D.2d 98, 588 N.Y.S.2d 119 (1st Dept. 1992), *rev'd on other grounds,* 81 N.Y.2d 600, 601 N.Y.S.2d 440, 619 N.E.2d 377 (1993).

—People could introduce medical records indicating that defendant, a foster parent, had two prior foster children who also had suffered injuries similar to the injuries suffered by present two child victims which formed basis of endangering the welfare charge. People v. Caccese, 211 A.D.2d 976, 621 N.Y.S.2d 735 (3d Dept.), *lv. denied,* 86 N.Y.2d 780 (1995).

—Trial court properly admitted evidence of defendant's prior conviction of endangering the welfare of a child involving his son in the instant proceeding where defendant was accused of assault in the first degree and endangering the welfare of a child regarding the injuries sustained by his two-month-old daughter; evidence established the "absence of accident or mistake." People v. Brewer, 295 A.D.2d 1013, 743 N.Y.S.2d 920 (4th Dept. 2002).

—Evidence of a prior conviction for defendant's endangering the welfare of a child was admissible as relevant to defendant's credibility, in case where defendant was convicted of sexually abusing his daughter's 12-year-old girlfriend while threatening her with a knife. People v. Limpert, 186 A.D.2d 1005, 588 N.Y.S.2d 461 (4th Dept.), *lv. denied,* 81 N.Y.2d 764 (1992).

Victim is unborn child.—Offense of endangering the welfare of a child does not pertain to conduct which threatens harm to a fetus; mother ingested cocaine; when legislature intends statute addressing children to apply also to unborn children, it specifies so. People v. Morabito, 151 Misc. 2d 259, 580 N.Y.S.2d 843 (City Ct. of Geneva, Ontario Co. 1992).

Continuing offense.—Endangering the welfare of a child readily permits characterization as a continuing offense over a period of time. People v. Keindl, 68 N.Y.2d 410, 421, 509 N.Y.S.2d 790, 502 N.E.2d 577, *reh'g denied,* 69 N.Y.2d 823; *accord* People v. Dunavin, 173 A.D.2d 1032, 570 N.Y.S.2d 369 (3d Dept.), *lv. denied,* 78 N.Y.2d 965 (1991).

—Endangering the welfare of a child is a continuing offense, which may consist of one act, or of numerous acts or omissions which collectively causes the danger; mother's conduct of missing pediatric appointments, keeping baby in filthy conditions, and refusing medical assistance for the baby's welfare, collectively constituted the offense. People v. Manon, 226 A.D.2d 774, 640 N.Y.S.2d 318 (3d Dept. 1996).

—Since endangering the welfare of a child is a continuing offense, the commencement of the statute of limitations would be dated from the last charged act constituting the offense. People v. DeLong, 206 A.D.2d 914, 615 N.Y.S.2d 168 (4th Dept. 1994).

Lack of specificity as to dates of offenses.—The claim that the indictment and bill of particulars failed to sufficiently specify the exact dates when acts occurred, must be preserved; defendant's acknowledgment that the prosecutor tried to comply in good faith with court's directive to better particularize the dates, coupled with the failure to raise the specificity issue again until appeal, waived the challenge. People v. Stabley, 192 A.D.2d 1056, 596 N.Y.S.2d 247 (4th Dept.), *lv. denied,* 81 N.Y.2d 1080 (1993).

Charge to jury: mens rea.—Required mental state is that defendant actually knew that conduct is likely to be injurious to child; reversible error to charge jury that defendant knew or should have known that conduct was likely to be injurious to child. People v. Simmons, 221 A.D.2d 994, 635 N.Y.S.2d 373 (4th Dept. 1995), *lv. denied,* 88 N.Y.2d 885 (1996).

Severance.—Court did not err, in case charging defendant with multiple counts of sodomy and endangering the welfare of a child, by denying defendant's motion to sever cases of four child victims; all of the cases, arising out of defendant showing the boys pornographic films, masturbating in front of them, and convincing two to engage in sodomy with him, were the same or similar in law, each victim testified about separate sexual encounters with the defendant, the proof was not confusing and the court gave an adequate instruction to the jury directing them to evaluate each event separately. People v. Halm, 180 A.D.2d 841, 579 N.Y.S.2d 765 (3d Dept. 1992), *aff'd,* 81 N.Y.2d 819, 595 N.Y.S.2d 380, 611 N.E.2d 281 (1993).

—In case charging defendant with sexual offenses in connection with a child as well as an adult complainant, and endangering the welfare of a child in connection with only the child complainant, court properly denied severance of the indictments;

evidence of the incident with the child, which occurred immediately prior to the incident with the adult, was relevant to disproving defendant's alibi and thus was relevant and admissible on the trial of the other counts of the indictment and was probative of defendant's intent in connection with the latter incident. People v. Tardbania, 130 A.D.2d 954, 515 N.Y.S.2d 936 (4th Dept. 1987), aff'd, 72 N.Y.2d 852, 532 N.Y.S.2d 354, 528 N.E.2d 507 (1988).

Repugnant verdicts.—Defendant's acquittal of sodomy "did not negate any essential element" of either sexual abuse in the first degree or endangering the welfare of a child. People v. Lewis, 5 A.D.3d 1073, 773 N.Y.S.2d 694 (4th Dept. 2004).

—Defendant's acquittal of two counts of sexual abuse in the second degree did not require acquittal of endangering the welfare of a child conviction; disposition of the sexual abuse counts was not conclusive as to all elements of the latter charge. People v. Gross, 184 A.D.2d 1051, 584 N.Y.S.2d 705 (4th Dept.), lv. denied, 80 N.Y.2d 904 (1992).

Duplicitous verdicts.—Defendant's conviction of sodomy in the first degree was based on elements distinct from elements of endangering the welfare of a child, so that a conviction on the former charge did not bar conviction of the latter charge, albeit based on the same acts. People v. Bacchus, 175 A.D.2d 248, 572 N.Y.S.2d 368 (2d Dept.), lv. denied, 79 N.Y.2d 824 (1991).

Appropriate sentence.—Mother's sentence of six months incarceration for neglect which resulted in death of her baby was not harsh or excessive. People v. Manon, 226 A.D.2d 774, 640 N.Y.S.2d 318 (3d Dept. 1996).

Aid to runaway; information dismissed.—Information alleging that defendant, a 17-year-old youth, assisted a 15-year-old female to run away from home and found her lodging, so that she would not be placed in an institution for girls, should be dismissed as insufficient as a matter of law. People v. Adamo, 94 Misc. 2d 686, 405 N.Y.S.2d 566 (Dist. Ct. Suffolk Co. 1978).

General.—The offense of endangering the welfare of a child may be committed by multiple acts and may be a continuing offense committed over a period of time. People v. Conte, 159 A.D.2d 993, 552 N.Y.S.2d 743, 744 (4th Dept. 1990).

—Endangering the welfare of a child is a continuing offense, therefore, the Statute of Limitations does not commence until after the last act of abuse occurs. People v. DeLong, 206 A.D.2d 914, 615 N.Y.S.2d 168, 169-170 (4th Dept. 1994).

Corroboration; unlawful imprisonment; endangering welfare of child; crimes independent of rape.—Information charging unlawful imprisonment and endangering welfare of child recited independent crimes from rape and did not require corroboration where 10-year-old girl's complaint was that defendant blindfolded her in street, led her to his apartment, raped her, then brought her to a vacant apartment leaving her locked therein. People v. Goldberg, 39 A.D.2d 948, 332 N.Y.S.2d 903 (2d Dept. 1972).

Sufficiency of evidence.—Evidence was legally sufficient to support conviction under this section where defendant kept 23 firearms and failed to lock them away; 14-year-old son of defendant's fiancee took one of five handguns located in an open tool tray in a doorless second floor room and loaded it, then took the gun outside, where it fired and caused injury. People v. Hitchcock, 98 N.Y.2d 586, 750 N.Y.S.2d 580, 780 N.E.2d 181 (2002).

—In order to support a conviction under this section, it is not required that defendant's acts be directed against the children. Thus, here, evidence was sufficient where the defendant attacked the mother of the children on the street, overturning the baby carriage in which one of the children was sitting, and continued his verbal and physical abuse against the mother into their apartment where the attack continued. Defendant threatened to kill the children's mother in their presence, and for over ten hours they hid in their bedroom, listening to defendant's yelling and cursing, their mother's screams, and the sounds of breaking glass. People v. Johnson, 95 N.Y.2d 368, 718 N.Y.S.2d 1, 740 N.E.2d 1075 (2000).

—Actual harm to child need not be established in order to support conviction of endangering the welfare of a child; it is enough that harm is likely to result to child. Defendant's acts of repeatedly making mocking and vulgar remarks to 23-month-old child for almost a six-week period, during a critical time of her intellectual and social development, was sufficient to

establish criminal liability under this section. People v. Simmons, 92 N.Y.2d 829, 677 N.Y.S.2d 58, 699 N.E.2d 417 (1998).

—Credible testimony from disinterested bystanders, along with medical evidence, established that defendant forcefully kicked a five-year-old child, causing him to fall against a wall, conduct that created the type of risk to a child contemplated by the statute. People v Zeifman, 11 A.D.3d 288, 782 N.Y.S.2d 461 (1st Dept. 2004).

—Where defendant engaged in deviant sexual intercourse, by forcible compulsion, with a person less than 11 years of age, this conduct endangered the welfare of that victim and his young companion. People v. Maurice C., 168 A.D.2d 506, 562 N.Y.S.2d 747 (2d Dept. 1990).

—Conviction affirmed where defendant admitted sexual abuse of seven-year-old stepdaughter over a period of one and one-half years. People v. Munroe, 307 A.D.2d 588, 763 N.Y.S.2d 691 (3d Dept. 2003).

—Overt acts such as striking a child are covered under subdivision one, which addresses "knowing acts," whereas acts of omission are covered by subdivision two, which also includes one parent's failure to protect a child from the acts of another. People v. Phelps, 268 A.D.2d 692, 701 N.Y.S.2d 494 (3d Dept. 2000).

—Jury's decision to infer that defendant was aware that his conduct in ordering his daughter to leave his home and in failing to provide her with food or shelter "created a likelihood of harm" to his daughter was sufficient to support conviction. People v. Scutt, 19 A.D.3d 1131, 796 N.Y.S.2d 816 (4th Dept. 2005).

—Conviction for endangering the welfare of a child was affirmed where evidence at trial established that defendant beat his 22-month-old daughter and she died from the injuries she sustained. People v. Weeks, 15 A.D.3d 845, 789 N.Y.S.2d 373 (4th Dept. 2005).

—Evidence that defendant beat mother of his two children in their presence and in the presence of the mother's other child, all under the age of 10, was sufficient to support a conviction for endangering the welfare of a child. People v. Spickerman, 307 A.D.2d 774, 762 N.Y.S.2d 470 (4th Dept. 2003).

—Evidence did not support a conviction under this section where defendant had hidden gun by wrapping it in rags and placing it in back of speaker in his bedroom, and where the gun was later found by his brother after he secretly peeked through the keyhole of the door and saw defendant cleaning a gun; "criminal liability for endangering the welfare of a child is imposed when a defendant engages in conduct knowing it will present a 'likelihood' of harm to a child"; People "must establish that harm was likely to occur, and not merely possible." People v. Duenas, 190 Misc. 2d 801, 742 N.Y.S.2d 468 (Sup. Ct. Richmond Co. 2002), aff'd sub nom. People v. Hitchcock, 98 N.Y.2d 586, 750 N.Y.S.2d 580, 780 N.E.2d 181 (2002).

—A challenge to the information on the basis of legal sufficiency was rejected where it charged defendant, who was responsible to transport child to and from school, with a violation of this section for dropping a seven-year-old child at home unattended and the child remained in the home alone and scared in a locked apartment for two and one half hours. People v. Watson, 182 Misc. 2d 644, 700 N.Y.S.2d 651 (Crim. Ct. Bronx Co. 1999).

—Jury had the authority to find defendant's act of leaving her two children, ages ten and three, alone in a parked car on the street in New York City for a period of two to three hours sufficient to support a conviction for endangering the welfare of a child. People v. Cenat, 176 Misc. 2d 39, 671 N.Y.S.2d 578 (Crim. Ct. Kings Co. 1998).

—The allegations that the defendant pointed a gun at and threatened the complainant while her 11-year-old daughter was standing next to her were sufficient to establish a prima facie charge of Endangering the Welfare of a Child. People v. Alexander, 149 Misc. 2d 361, 565 N.Y.S.2d 681 (Crim. Ct. Kings Co. 1990).

PL § 260.10(1) is constitutional.—People v. Prainito, 97 Misc. 2d 66, 410 N.Y.S.2d 772 (Sup. Ct. Bronx Co. 1978).

§ 260.11. Endangering the welfare of a child; corroboration.

A person shall not be convicted of endangering

the welfare of a child, or of an attempt to commit the same, upon the testimony of a victim who is incapable of consent because of mental defect or mental incapacity as to conduct that constitutes an offense or an attempt to commit an offense referred to in section 130.16, without additional evidence sufficient pursuant to section 130.16 to sustain a conviction of an offense referred to in section 130.16, or of an attempt to commit the same.

Added by L. 1972, Ch. 373; **Amended** by L. 1974, Ch. 14; L. 1984, Ch. 89.

ANNOTATIONS

Defendant's statement.—Defendant, charged with endangering the welfare of a child and sexual abuse arising out of his conduct of having his young daughter masturbate him, gave statement which indicated that her hands had been on his genitals and that they moved up and down; this was sufficient corroboration. People v. Morey, 224 A.D.2d 730, 637 N.Y.S.2d 500 (3d Dept.), *lv. denied,* 87 N.Y.2d 1022 (1996).

Sufficiency of evidence.—Evidence that defendant lived with an 11-year-old child and her mother in defendant's one-bedroom apartment, and that the child had not gone out of the apartment for months, although the mother left the apartment daily and at times left defendant alone with the child, was sufficient to support the charges against defendant. People v. Sheffield, 265 A.D.2d 258, 697 N.Y.S.2d 269 (1st Dept. 1999).

Child victims corroborating each other.—Although corroboration rules might be applied to each child victim, the testimony of each child could corroborate the testimony of the other child. People v. Dunavin, 173 A.D.2d 1032, 570 N.Y.S.2d 369 (3d Dept.), *lv. denied,* 78 N.Y.2d 965 (1991).

§ 260.15. Endangering the welfare of a child; defense.

In any prosecution for endangering the welfare of a child, pursuant to section 260.10:

1. based upon an alleged failure or refusal to provide proper medical care or treatment to an ill child, it is an affirmative defense that the defendant (a) is a parent, guardian or other person legally charged with the care or custody of such child; and (b) is a member or adherent of an organized church or religious group the tenets of which prescribe prayer as the principal treatment for illness; and (c) treated or caused such ill child to be treated in accordance with such tenets; or

2. based upon an alleged desertion of a child not more than five days old, it is an affirmative defense that, with the intent that the child be safe from physical injury and cared for in an appropriate manner, the defendant left the child with an appropriate person or in a suitable location and promptly notified an appropriate person of the child's location.

Amended by L. 1967, Ch. 791; L. 2000, Ch. 156, § 4, eff. July 18, 2000, amending subd. 1 and adding subd. 2.

§ 260.20. Unlawfully dealing with a child in the first degree.

A person is guilty of unlawfully dealing with a child in the first degree when:

1. He knowingly permits a child less than eighteen years old to enter or remain in or upon a place, premises or establishment where sexual activity as defined by article one hundred thirty, two hundred thirty or two hundred sixty-three of this chapter or activity involving controlled substances as defined by article two hundred twenty of this chapter or involving marihuana as defined by article two hundred twenty-one of this chapter is maintained or conducted, and he knows or has reason to know that such activity is being maintained or conducted; or

2. He gives or sells or causes to be given or sold any alcoholic beverage, as defined by section three of the alcoholic beverage control law, to a person less than twenty-one years old; except that this subdivision does not apply to the parent or guardian of such a person or to a person who gives or causes to be given any such alcoholic beverage to a person under the age of twenty-one years, who is a student in a curriculum licensed or registered by the state education department, where the tasting or imbibing of alcoholic beverages is required in courses that are part of the required curriculum, provided such alcoholic beverages are given only for instructional purposes during classes conducted pursuant to such curriculum.

It is no defense to a prosecution pursuant to subdivision two of this section that the child acted as the agent or representative of another person or that the defendant dealt with the child as such.

Unlawfully dealing with a child in the first degree is a class A misdemeanor.

Amended by L. 1982, Ch. 159; L. 1985, Ch. 274; L. 1986, Chs. 107, 210; L. 1992, Ch. 362, eff. Nov. 1, 1992.

ANNOTATIONS

Age no defense.—Sixteen-year-old defendant was properly convicted of giving alcohol to 15-year-old victim; court specifically rejected defendant's defense that statute excluded minors from criminal culpability. People v. Houis, 196 Misc. 2d 754, 766 N.Y.S.2d 754 (City Ct. of N.Y. 2003).

Culpability. —The purchase of beer by defendant, of legal age, for underage drinkers, with their money and at their request, constituted the offense. People v. Wing, 77 N.Y.2d 851, 568 N.Y.S.2d 8, 569 N.E.2d 867 (1991).

—Evidence that defendant gave marijuana to minor was sufficient to sustain a conviction under this section. People v. Littebrant, 307 A.D.2d 772, 762 N.Y.S.2d 857 (3d Dept. 2003).

—Prohibition against selling alcohol to minors applies to the serving of alcohol to a minor by a person who is not the representative of the parent or guardian. People v. Himmel, 252 A.D.2d 273, 686 N.Y.S.2d 504 (3d Dept. 1999).

—Defendant's admission that he gave alcohol to 17-year-old victim supported his conviction under this section. People v. Remington, 305 A.D.2d 1021, 758 N.Y.S.2d 588 (4th Dept. 2003).

—Evidence that defendant touched genitals of 11-year-old male and that same male child touched his genitals supported conviction of endangering the welfare of a minor. People v. Morin, 196 Misc. 2d 114, 763 N.Y.S.2d 705 (Sup. Ct. App. T. 2003).

—When the 20-year-old defendant gave a glass of beer to another 20-year-old person, even though the defendant, also, was in the class of persons sought to be protected by the statute, this did not negate his culpability. People v. Kaufman, 132 Misc. 2d 530, 504 N.Y.S.2d 361 (City Ct. of Oswego Co. 1986); *compare with* People v. Jackson, 127 Misc. 2d 754, 487 N.Y.S.2d 270 (Chautauqua Co. Ct. 1985) (eighteen-year-old girl gave beer to another 18-year-old girl; since the defendant was, by definition, an "infant" under New York law, and was a member of the class to be protected by the statute, she could not be charged with the offense).

Not a continuing crime.—For purposes of testimonial capacity, underage drinkers, for whom the legal aged defendant purchased beer, could not be accomplices, insofar as they were the class of persons which the statute was intended to protect, and the receipt of their testimony was not restricted by the accomplice-corroboration rule of CPL § 60.22. People v. Wing, 77 N.Y.2d 851, 568 N.Y.S.2d 8, 569 N.E.2d 867 (1991).

—Unlike endangering the welfare of a child, the offense of unlawfully dealing with a child, specifically by providing alcoholic beverages, contemplates a single act or, at most, a series of acts at one time and place; counts of indictment indicating separate acts at separate places would be duplicitous. People v. Conte, 159 A.D.2d 993, 552 N.Y.S.2d 743 (4th Dept. 1990), *lv. denied*, 76 N.Y.2d 733 (1990).

§ 260.21. Unlawfully dealing with a child in the second degree.

A person is guilty of unlawfully dealing with a child in the second degree when:

1. Being an owner, lessee, manager or employee of a place where alcoholic beverages are sold or given away, he permits a child less than sixteen years old to enter or remain in such place unless:

(a) The child is accompanied by his parent, guardian or an adult authorized by a parent or guardian; or

(b) The entertainment or activity is being conducted for the benefit or under the auspices of a non-profit school, church or other educational or religious institution; or

(c) Otherwise permitted by law to do so; or

(d) The establishment is closed to the public for a specified period of time to conduct an activity or entertainment, during which the child is in or remains in such establishment, and no alcoholic beverages are served, given away or consumed at such establishment during such period. The state liquor authority shall be notified in writing by the licensee of such establishment, of the intended closing of such establishment, to conduct any such activity or entertainment, not less than ten days prior to any such closing; or

2. He marks the body of a child less than eighteen years old with indelible ink or pigments by means of tattooing; or

3. He sells or causes to be sold tobacco in any form to a child less than eighteen years old.

It is no defense to a prosecution pursuant to subdivision three of this section that the child acted as the agent or representative of another person or that the defendant dealt with the child as such.

Unlawfully dealing with a child in the second degree is a class B misdemeanor.

Added by L. 1992, Ch. 362, eff. Nov. 1, 1992. **Amended** by L. 1996, Ch. 478, § 1, amending subd. 1, eff. Nov. 1, 1996.

§ 260.25. Endangering the welfare of an incompetent or physically disabled person.

A person is guilty of endangering the welfare of an incompetent or physically disabled person when he knowingly acts in a manner likely to be injurious to the physical, mental or moral welfare of a person who is unable to care for himself or herself because of physical disability, mental disease or defect.

Endangering the welfare of an incompetent or physically disabled person is a class A misdemeanor.

Amended by L. 1998, Ch. 381, § 2, eff. Nov. 1, 1998.

ANNOTATIONS

Corroboration.—There was ample corroboration of the testimony of the 19-year-old mentally retarded complainant in connection with her allegation that defendant had raped her, consisting of the presence of sperm on her clothing, testimony by a passenger that she had seen defendant and the complainant alone in the van, testimony by the complainant's mother about the complainant's physical appearance when she arrived home, and evidence of the complainant's immediate outcry. People v. Novak, 212 A.D.2d 740, 622 N.Y.S.2d 783 (2d Dept.), *lv. denied*, 85 N.Y.2d 941 (1995), *pet. for writ of coram nobis denied*, 636 N.Y.S.2d 1015 (1996).

Evidence.—The evidence was sufficient to support the indictment where it revealed that defendant, a nurse's aid, on two occasions placed human waste into the mouth of an 80-year-old nursing home patient who was severely retarded. People v. Mravlja, 67 A.D.2d 768, 412 N.Y.S.2d 444 (3d Dept. 1979).

—Conviction affirmed where defendant admitted sexual abuse of seven-year-old stepdaughter over a period of one and one-half years. People v. Munroe, 307 A.D.2d 588, 763 N.Y.S.2d 691 (3d Dept. 2003).

—Defendant's conduct of offering money to a 29-year-old mentally disabled person to do push-ups and sit-ups in a well traveled urban street, during which the victim was hit by a car, constituted legally sufficient evidence. People v. Rolston, 190 A.D.2d 1000, 593 N.Y.S.2d 383 (4th Dept.), *lv. denied*, 81 N.Y.2d 1019 (1993).

§ 260.30. Vulnerable elderly persons; definitions. [*Another version of § 260.30 follows.*]*

For the purpose of sections 260.32 and 260.34 of this article, the following definitions shall apply:

1. "Caregiver" means a person who (i) assumes responsibility for the care of a vulnerable elderly person pursuant to a court order; or (ii) receives monetary or other valuable consideration for providing care for a vulnerable elderly person.

2. "Sexual contact" means any touching of the sexual or other intimate parts of a person not married to the actor for the purpose of gratifying sexual desire of either party. It includes the touching of the actor by the victim, as well as the touching of the victim by the actor, whether directly or through clothing.

3. "Vulnerable elderly person" means a person sixty years of age or older who is suffering from a disease or infirmity associated with advanced age and manifested by demonstrable physical,

mental or emotional dysfunction to the extent that the person is incapable of adequately providing for his or her own health or personal care.

   *** Editor's Note:** In 1998, the Legislature enacted two versions of § 260.30. It is assumed that the Legislature intended to number the sections consecutively rather than identically.

   Added by L. 1998, Ch. 381, § 3, eff. Nov. 1, 1998.

§ 260.30. Misrepresentation by a child day care provider. [*Another version of § 260.30 is set forth above.*] *

   A person is guilty of misrepresentation by a child day care provider when, being a child day care provider or holding himself or herself out as such, he or she makes any willful and intentional misrepresentation, by act or omission, to a parent or guardian of a child in the care of such provider (or a child whose prospective placement in such care is being considered by such parent or guardian) to any state or local official having jurisdiction over child day care providers, or to any police officer or peace officer as to the facts pertaining to such child day care provider, including, but not limited to: (i) the number of children in the facility or home where such number is in violation of the provisions of section three hundred ninety of the social services law, (ii) the area of the facility, home, or center used for child day care, or (iii) the credentials or qualifications of any child day care provider, assistant, employee, or volunteer. A misrepresentation subject to the provisions of this section must substantially place at risk the health or safety of a child in the care of a child day care provider.

   Misrepresentation by a child day care provider is a class A misdemeanor.

   *** Editor's Note:** In 1998, the Legislature enacted two versions of § 260.30. It is assumed that the Legislature intended to number the sections consecutively rather than identically.

   Added by L. 1998, Ch. 600, § 2, eff. Nov. 1, 1998.

§ 260.32. Endangering the welfare of a vulnerable elderly person in the second degree.

   A person is guilty of endangering the welfare of a vulnerable elderly person in the second degree when, being a caregiver for a vulnerable elderly person:

   1. with intent to cause physical injury to such person, he or she causes such injury to such person; or

   2. he or she recklessly causes physical injury to such person; or

   3. with criminal negligence, he or she causes physical injury to such person by means of a deadly weapon or a dangerous instrument; or

   4. he or she subjects such person to sexual contact without the latter's consent. Lack of consent under this subdivision results from forcible compulsion or incapacity to consent, as those terms are defined in article one hundred thirty of this chapter, or any other circumstances in which the vulnerable elderly person does not expressly or impliedly acquiesce in the caregiver's conduct. In any prosecution under this subdivision in which the victim's alleged lack of consent results solely from incapacity to consent because of the victim's mental disability or mental incapacity, the provisions of section 130.16 of this chapter shall apply. In addition, in any prosecution under this subdivision in which the victim's lack of consent is based solely upon his or her incapacity to consent because he or she was mentally disabled, mentally incapacitated or physically helpless, it is an affirmative defense that the defendant, at the time he or she engaged in the conduct constituting the offense, did not know of the facts or conditions responsible for such incapacity to consent.

   Endangering the welfare of a vulnerable elderly person in the second degree is a class E felony.

   Added by L. 1998, Ch. 381, § 4, eff. Nov. 1, 1998; **Amended** by L. 2000, Ch. 1, eff. Feb. 1, 2001.

§ 260.34. Endangering the welfare of a vulnerable elderly person in the first degree.

   A person is guilty of endangering the welfare of a vulnerable elderly person in the first degree when, being a caregiver for a vulnerable elderly person:

   1. with intent to cause physical injury to such person, he or she causes serious physical injury to such person; or

   2. he or she recklessly causes serious physical injury to such person.

   Endangering the welfare of a vulnerable elderly person in the first degree is a class D felony.

   Added by L. 1998, Ch. 381, § 5, eff. Nov. 1, 1998.

ARTICLE 263—SEXUAL PERFORMANCE BY A CHILD

LexisNexis Cross References

Prosecution and Defense of Sex Crimes, Ch. 8, Obscenity and Pornography; Ch. 9, The Prosecution and Defense of Child Sexual Assault; Ch. 11, The Prosecution and Defense of Child Abuse.

§ 263.00. Definitions.

As used in this article the following definitions shall apply:

1. "Sexual performance" means any performance or part thereof which, for purposes of section 263.16 of this article, includes sexual conduct by a child less than sixteen years of age or, for purposes of section 263.05 or 263.15 of this article, includes sexual conduct by a child less than seventeen years of age.

2. "Obscene sexual performance" means any performance which, for purposes of section 263.11 of this article, includes sexual conduct by a child less than sixteen years of age or, for purposes of section 263.10 of this article, includes sexual conduct by a child less than seventeen years of age, in any material which is obscene, as such term is defined in section 235.00 of this chapter.

3. "Sexual conduct" means actual or simulated sexual intercourse, oral sexual conduct, anal sexual conduct, sexual bestiality, masturbation, ado-masochistic abuse, or lewd exhibition of the genitals.

4. "Performance" means any play, motion picture, photograph or dance. Performance also means any other visual representation exhibited before an audience.

5. "Promote" means to procure, manufacture, issue, sell, give, provide, lend, mail, deliver, transfer, transmute, publish, distribute, circulate, disseminate, present, exhibit or advertise, or to offer or agree to do the same.

6. "Simulated" means the explicit depiction of any of the conduct set forth in subdivision three of this section which creates the appearance of such conduct and which exhibits any uncovered portion of the breasts, genitals or buttocks.

7. "Oral sexual conduct" and "anal sexual conduct" mean the conduct defined by subdivision two of section 130.00 of this chapter.

8. "Sado-masochistic abuse" means the conduct defined in subdivision five of section 235.20 of this chapter.

Amended by L. 2000, Ch. 1, eff. Feb. 1, 2001; L. 2003, Ch. 264, § 32, eff. Nov. 1, 2003, amending subds. 3 and 7.

ANNOTATIONS

First amendment and non-obscene sexual depictions of children.—The state is not precluded from enacting laws prohibiting live performances or visual displays of children in sexual contexts, despite the absence of obscenity. New York v. Ferber, 458 U.S. 747, 102 S. Ct. 3348, 73 L. Ed. 2d 1113 (1982).

—When defendant knowingly sold films whose main subject was sexual conduct by young boys, prosecuting the defendant for the crime of promoting a sexual performance by a child did not unduly restrict the First Amendment's protection of free expression. People v. Ferber, 57 N.Y.2d 256, 455 N.Y.S.2d 582, 441 N.E.2d 1100 (1982), *on remand from* New York v. Ferber, 458 U.S. 747, 102 S. Ct. 3348, 73 L. Ed. 2d 1113 (1982).

—There was no dissemination of ideas protected by First amendment arising from defendant's conduct of soliciting juveniles to have sex with other juveniles for pay, or asking juveniles to undress and displaying sexually provocative photographs. People v. Folk, 109 Misc. 2d 738, 440 N.Y.S.2d 984 (Sup. Ct. N.Y. Co. 1981) (decided prior to *Ferber*).

"Lewd exhibition of genitals."—Dismissal of counts predicated on photographs of six-year-old girl's buttocks and bare chest as not constituting a lewd exhibition of the genitals was not error. People v. Pinkoski, 300 A.D.2d 834, 752 N.Y.S.2d 421 (3d Dept. 2002).

Double jeopardy.—When defendant, a member of the military, was tried and convicted under military law for offenses which were the equivalent of use of a child in a sexual performance, subsequent prosecution for the violation of state law, based on the same acts for which defendant was prosecuted under military law, was barred by the prohibition against double jeopardy; Article 78 petition seeking prohibition was granted. Northrup v. Relin, 197 A.D.2d 228, 613 N.Y.S.2d 506 (4th Dept.), *lv. denied,* 84 N.Y.2d 803 (1994).

Performance.—Although PL § 263.00(4) contemplates that an audience might exist for the performance, the public or commercial nature of the performance is not a pre-condition to prosecution under Article 263; the taking of photographs for personal purposes satisfies the statutory proscription of "performace." People v. Gaito, 199 A.D.2d 615, 604 N.Y.S.2d 992 (3d Dept. 1993), *lv. denied,* 83 N.Y.2d 805 (1994).

Specification of proscribed acts.—When the defendant is charged with offenses under Article 263 involving the sexual conduct of children, the defendant is entitled to a bill of particulars setting forth the nature of the charged conduct and the number of sexual performances which occurred. People v. Capitello, 139 Misc. 2d 618, 528 N.Y.S.2d 262 (Co. Ct. Suffolk Co. 1988).

Simulated sexual conduct.—Over the course of a videotape prepared by defendant of he and a thirteen year old, the teen, on several occasions, fleetingly pretended to masturbate while fully clothed, defendant also parodied momentary acts of sexual intercourse, and deviate sexual intercourse with the teen while both are fully clothed, as well as instances where either defendant or the teen exhibits uncovered portions of his genitals or buttocks, however, none of the depictions of simulated sexual conduct actually involves any nakedness, therefore these acts do not meet statutory definition of simulated sexual conduct nor constitute sexual conduct. People v. Gibeault, 5 A.D.3d 952, 773 751 (3d Dept. 2004).

§ 263.05. Use of a child in a sexual performance.

A person is guilty of the use of a child in a sexual performance if knowing the character and content thereof he employs, authorizes or induces a child less than seventeen years of age to engage in a sexual performance or being a parent, legal guardian or custodian of such child, he consents to the participation by such child in a sexual performance.

Use of a child in a sexual performance is a class C felony.

Amended by L. 2000, Ch. 1, eff. Feb. 1, 2001.

ANNOTATIONS

Performance.—Defendant conducted sexually explicit photography sessions using two girls, twelve and thirteen years old; defendant's putative defense that the photographs would not be distributed commercially, and there was no public audience, was rejected, insofar as statutory term "performance" was not self limiting to commercial exploitation of children, but also covered private displays. People v. Gaito, 199 A.D.2d 615, 604 N.Y.S.2d 992 (3d Dept. 1993), *lv. denied,* 83 N.Y.2d 805 (1994).

—Father's photograph of four-year-old son lying on a couch naked with an erection constituted the use of a child in a sexual performance. *In re* Glenn G., 154 Misc. 2d 677, 587 N.Y.S.2d 464 (Fam. Ct. 1992), *aff'd sub nom. In re* Josephine G., 218 A.D.2d 656, 630 N.Y.S.2d 348 (2d Dept. 1995), *lv. denied, In re* Josephine G., 87 N.Y.2d 803, 662 N.E.2d 791, 639 N.Y.S.2d 310 (1995).

Right of privacy.—To the extent that PL § 263.05 prohibits acts which occur entirely within one's own home, there is no violation of the constitutional right to privacy, nor is the statute unconstitutionally overbroad. People v. Duboy, 150 A.D.2d 882, 540 N.Y.S.2d 905 (3d Dept.), *lv. denied,* 74 N.Y.2d 846 (1989); *accord* People v. Levitz, 137 Misc. 2d 591, 521 N.Y.S.2d 977 (Co. Ct. Nassau Co. 1987).

—There is no distinction between commercial pornography and pornography which occurs within one's home for purposes of the statute. People v. Duboy, 150 A.D.2d 882, 540 N.Y.S.2d 905 (3d Dept.), *lv. denied,* 74 N.Y.2d 846 (1989); *accord* People v. Levitz, 137 Misc. 2d 591, 521 N.Y.S.2d 977 (Co. Ct. Nassau Co. 1987).

—The defendant's photography of a seven-year-old boy, containing "lewd exhibitions of his genitals" clearly satisfied definition of performance; term "performance" was not unconstitutionally vague. People v. Capitello, 139 Misc. 2d 618, 528 N.Y.S.2d 262 (Co. Ct. Suffolk Co. 1988).

Constitutionality.—Defendant's guilty plea to PL § 263.05 was constitutional where he solicited juveniles to have sex with other juveniles for pay; asking them to undress; and showing them sexually explicit photographs; as this is an area within the police power of the state to punish and defendant's first amendment rights may be constitutionally sacrificed to protect the psychological development of children. People v. Folk, 109 Misc. 2d 738, 440 N.Y.S.2d 984 (Sup. Ct. N.Y. Co. 1981).

Nude photographs of child.—The taking of photographs of defendant's 12-year-old niece in various degrees of undress and in various postures was a "performance" and thus punishable under PL § 263.05. People v. McIntyre, 77 A.D.2d 810, 430 N.Y.S.2d 761 (4th Dept. 1980).

Sufficiency of evidence.—Evidence that defendant showed his 14-year-old grand-nephew naked picture of boys he printed off the internet and asked him to pose naked for photographs as well, although preparatory, did not make out an actionable attempt under this section. People v. Horner, 300 A.D.2d 841, 752 N.Y.S.2d 147 (3d Dept. 2002).

§ 263.10. Promoting an obscene sexual performance by a child.

A person is guilty of promoting an obscene sexual performance by a child when, knowing the character and content thereof, he produces, directs or promotes any obscene performance which includes sexual conduct by a child less than seventeen years of age.

Promoting an obscene sexual performance by a child is a class D felony.

Amended by L. 2000, Ch. 1, eff. Feb. 1, 2001.

ANNOTATIONS

Private display.—The defendant's intention to only privately display obscene magazines including children as subjects seized in a hotel room did not bar prosecution for "promotion" under PL § 263.10. People v. Godek, 113 Misc. 2d 599, 499 N.Y.S.2d 428 (Sup. Ct. Nassau Co. 1982), *cert. denied,* 464 U.S. 1047 (1984).

Constitutionality.—PL § 263.10 is constitutional on its face and as applied in case in which defendant displayed pornographic magazines with child subjects. People v. Godek, 112 Misc. 2d 512, 447 N.Y.S.2d 214 (S. Ct. Nassau Co. 1982), *cert. denied,* 464 U.S. 1047 (1984).

Enhancement of punishment when pornography involves children.—Legislature could enhance penalties for promotion of obscene materials when children are involved, contrasting PL § 235.05 and PL § 263.10, without violating federal constitution. People v. Godek, 112 Misc. 2d 512, 447 N.Y.S.2d 214 (Sup. Ct. Nassau Co. 1982), *cert. denied,* 464 U.S. 1047 (1984).

§ 263.11. Possessing an obscene sexual performance by a child.

A person is guilty of possessing an obscene sexual performance by a child when, knowing the character and content thereof, he knowingly has in his possession or control any obscene performance which includes sexual conduct by a child less than sixteen years of age.

Possessing an obscene sexual performance by a child is a class E felony.

Added by L. 1996, Ch. 11, eff. Nov. 1, 1996.

§ 263.15. Promoting a sexual performance by a child.

A person is guilty of promoting a sexual performance by a child when, knowing the character and content thereof, he produces, directs or promotes any performance which includes sexual conduct by a child less than seventeen years of age.

Promoting a sexual performance by a child is a class D felony.

Amended by L. 2000, Ch. 1, eff. Feb. 1, 2001.

ANNOTATIONS

No protection afforded by First Amendment.—When defendant knowingly sold films whose main subject was sexual conduct by young boys, prosecuting the defendant for the crime of promoting a sexual performance by a child did not unduly restrict the First Amendment's protection of free expression. People v. Ferber, 57 N.Y.2d 256, 455 N.Y.S.2d 582, 441 N.E.2d 1100 (1982), *on remand from* New York v. Ferber, 458 U.S. 747, 102 S. Ct. 3348, 73 L. Ed. 2d 1113 (1982).

Procurement for private use is promotion.—By procuring child pornography through the mail, and procuring child pornography in his own home from an undercover officer when defendant knew the contents of the material, defendant "promoted" the child's sexual performance; fact that the procurement was intended for private use did not remove the conduct from the ambit of the statute. People v. Keyes, 75 N.Y.2d 343, 553 N.Y.S.2d 81, 552 N.E.2d 617 (1990), *appeal after remand*, People v. Keyes, 193 A.D.2d 936, 597 N.Y.S.2d 785 (3d Dept.), *lv. denied*, 82 N.Y.2d 756 (1993).

Constitutionality.—Constitutional challenge to statute as overly broad dismissed; statute's legitimate purpose in battling harm to victims of child pornography outweighs any overbreadth which may exist. People v. Foley, 94 N.Y.2d 668, 708 N.Y.S.2d 349, 729 N.E.2d 1148 (2000).

—PL § 263.15 is constitutional and does not violate the right of freedom of expression guaranteed by the state constitution. People v. Ferber, 57 N.Y.2d 256, 455 N.Y.S.2d 582, 441 N.E.2d 1100 (1982).

§ 263.16. Possessing a sexual performance by a child.

A person is guilty of possessing a sexual performance by a child when, knowing the character and content thereof, he knowingly has in his possession or control any performance which includes sexual conduct by a child less than sixteen years of age.

Possessing a sexual performance by a child is a class E felony.

Added by L. 1996, Ch. 11, eff. Nov. 1, 1996.

ANNOTATION

Available defenses.—Application of the scientific justification defense contained in PL § 235.15 is expressly limited to the offenses stated in the statute and is not available as a defense to PL § 263.16. People v. Fraser, 96 N.Y.2d 318, 728 N.Y.S.2d 115, 752 N.E.2d 244 (2001), *cert denied*, 533 U.S. 951 (2001).

Sufficiency of evidence.—Possession of over 100 of photographs of boys under age of 16 printed off Internet, including "a series of 'crotch shots' of young boys, some clothed and some nude," supported a finding of a prohibited exhibition of the genitalia; "both the exhibition of nude genitalia and activity of a prurient nature are not required to make out a violation under this section. People v. Horner, 300 A.D.2d 841, 752 N.Y.S.2d 147 (3d Dept. 2002).

—Conviction for attempted possession of a sexual performance by a child was supported by nude photographs defendant took of his two daughters, age five and seven; jury found defendant, with knowledge of their character and content, attempted to possess photographs depicting a lewd exhibition of a child's genitals. People v. Bimonte, 195 Misc. 2d 587, 759 N.Y.S.2d 839 (Sup. Ct. Queens Co. 2003).

§ 263.20. Sexual performance by a child; affirmative defenses.

1. Under this article, it shall be an affirmative defense that the defendant in good faith reasonably believed the person appearing in the performance was, for purposes of section 263.11 or 263.16 of this article, sixteen years of age or over or, for purposes of section 263.05, 263.10 or 263.15 of this article, seventeen years of age or over.

2. In any prosecution for any offense pursuant to this article, it is an affirmative defense that the person so charged was a librarian engaged in the normal course of his employment, a motion picture projectionist, stage employee or spotlight operator, cashier, doorman, usher, candy stand attendant, porter or in any other non-managerial or non-supervisory capacity in a motion picture theatre; provided he has no financial interest, other than his employment, which employment does not encompass compensation based upon any proportion of the gross receipts, in the promotion of a sexual performance for sale, rental or exhibition or in the promotion, presentation or direction of any sexual performance, or is in any way responsible for acquiring such material for sale, rental or exhibition.

Amended by L. 2000, Ch. 1, eff. Feb. 1, 2001.

ANNOTATION

Evidence.—Defendant failed to establish his affirmative defense by a preponderance of the evidence, specifically, that he had a good faith basis to believe that the person appearing in the performance was 16 years of age or older. People v. Manngard, 275 A.D.2d 378, 712 N.Y.S.2d 582 (2d Dept. 2000), *appeal denied*, 95 N.Y.2d 966 (2000).

§ 263.25. Proof of age of child.

Whenever it becomes necessary for the purposes of this article to determine whether a child who participated in a sexual performance was under an age specified in this article, the court or jury may make such determination by any of the following: personal inspection of the child; inspection of a photograph or motion picture which constituted the sexual performance; oral testimony by a witness to the sexual performance as to the age of the child based upon the child's appearance; expert medical testimony based upon the appearance of the child in the sexual performance; and any other method authorized by any applicable provision of law or by the rules of evidence at common law.

Added by L. 1977, Ch. 910; Amended by L. 2000, Ch. 1, eff. Feb. 1, 2001.

TITLE P—OFFENSES AGAINST PUBLIC SAFETY

ARTICLE 265—FIREARMS AND OTHER DANGEROUS WEAPONS

LexisNexis Cross Reference

New York Criminal Practice (2d ed.), Vol. 7, Ch. 82, Firearms and Other Dangerous Weapons Offenses.

§ 265.00. Definitions.

As used in this article and in article four hundred, the following terms shall mean and include:

1. "Machine-gun" means a weapon of any description, irrespective of size, by whatever name known, loaded or unloaded, from which a number of shots or bullets may be rapidly or automatically discharged from a magazine with one continuous pull of the trigger and includes a sub-machine gun.

2. "Firearm silencer" means any instrument, attachment, weapon or appliance for causing the firing of any gun, revolver, pistol or other firearms to be silent, or intended to lessen or muffle the noise of the firing of any gun, revolver, pistol or other firearms.

3. "Firearm" means (a) any pistol or revolver; or (b) a shotgun having one or more barrels less than eighteen inches in length; or (c) a rifle having one or more barrels less than sixteen inches in length; or (d) any weapon made from a shotgun or rifle whether by alteration, modification, or otherwise if such weapon as altered, modified, or otherwise has an overall length of less than twenty-six inches; or (e) an assault weapon. For the purpose of this subdivision the length of the barrel on a shotgun or rifle shall be determined by measuring the distance between the muzzle and the face of the bolt, breech, or breechlock when closed and when the shotgun or rifle is cocked; the overall length of a weapon made from a shotgun or rifle is the distance between the extreme ends of the weapon measured along a line parallel to the center line of the bore. Firearm does not include an antique firearm.

4. "Switchblade knife" means any knife which has a blade which opens automatically by hand pressure applied to a button, spring or other device in the handle of the knife.

5. "Gravity knife" means any knife which has

a blade which is released from the handle or sheath thereof by the force of gravity or the application of centrifugal force which, when released, is locked in place by means of a button, spring, lever or other device.

5-a. "Pilum ballistic knife" means any knife which has a blade which can be projected from the handle by hand pressure applied to a button, lever, spring or other device in the handle of the knife.

5-b. "Metal knuckle knife" means a weapon that, when closed, cannot function as a set of metal knuckles, nor as a knife and when open, can function as both a set of metal knuckles as well as a knife.

6. "Dispose of" means to dispose of, give, give away, lease, loan, keep for sale, offer, offer for sale, sell, transfer and otherwise dispose of.

7. "Deface" means to remove, deface, cover, alter or destroy the manufacturer's serial number or any other distinguishing number or identification mark.

8. "Gunsmith" means any person, firm, partnership, corporation or company who engages in the business of repairing, altering, assembling, manufacturing, cleaning, polishing, engraving or trueing, or who performs any mechanical operation on, any firearm, large capacity ammunition feeding device or machine-gun.

9. "Dealer in firearms" means any person, firm, partnership, corporation or company who engages in the business of purchasing, selling, keeping for sale, loaning, leasing, or in any manner disposing of, any assault weapon, large capacity ammunition feeding device, pistol or revolver.

10. "Licensing officer" means in the city of New York the police commissioner of that city; in the county of Nassau the commissioner of police of that county; in the county of Suffolk the sheriff of that county except in the towns of Babylon, Brookhaven, Huntington, Islip and Smithtown, the commissioner of police of that county; for the purposes of section 400.01 of this chapter the superintendent of state police; and elsewhere in the state a judge or justice of a court of record having his office in the county of issuance.

11. "Rifle" means a weapon designed or redesigned, made or remade, and intended to be fired from the shoulder and designed or redesigned and made or remade to use the energy of the explosive in a fixed metallic cartridge to fire only a single projectile through a rifled bore for each single pull of the trigger.

12. "Shotgun" means a weapon designed or redesigned, made or remade, and intended to be fired from the shoulder and designed or redesigned and made or remade to use the energy of the explosive in a fixed shotgun shell to fire through a smooth bore either a number of ball shot or a single projectile for each single pull of the trigger.

13. "Cane Sword" means a cane or swagger stick having concealed within it a blade that may be used as a sword or stilletto.

14. [See also subd. 14 below.] "Chuka stick" means any device designed primarily as a weapon, consisting of two or more lengths of a rigid material joined together by a thong, rope or chain in such a manner as to allow free movement of a portion of the device while held in the hand and capable of being rotated in such a manner as to inflict serious injury upon a person by striking or choking. These devices are also known as nunchakus and centrifugal force sticks.

14. [See also subd. 14 above.] "Antique firearm" means:

Any unloaded muzzle loading pistol or revolver with a matchlock, flintlock, percussion cap, or similar type of ignition system, or a pistol or revolver which uses fixed cartridges which are no longer available in the ordinary channels of commercial trade.

15. "Loaded firearm" means any firearm loaded with ammunition or any firearm which is possessed by one who, at the same time, possesses a quantity of ammunition which may be used to discharge such firearm.

15-a. "Electronic dart gun" means any device designed primarily as a weapon, the purpose of which is to momentarily stun, knock out or paralyze a person by passing an electrical shock to such person by means of a dart or projectile.

15-b. "Kung Fu star" means a disc-like object with sharpened points on the circumference thereof and is designed for use primarily as a weapon to be thrown.

15-c. "Electronic stun gun" means any device designed primarily as a weapon, the purpose of which is to stun, cause mental disorientation, knock out or paralyze a person by passing a high voltage electrical shock to such person.

16. "Certified not suitable to possess a self-defense spray device, a rifle or shotgun" means that the director or physician in charge of any hospital or institution for mental illness, public or private, has certified to the superintendent of state police or to any organized police department of a county, city, town or village of this state, that a person who has been judicially adjudicated incompetent, or who has been confined to such institution for mental illness pursuant to judicial authority, is not suitable to possess a self-defense spray device, as defined in section 265.20 of this article, or a rifle or shotgun.

17. "Serious offense" means (a) any of the following offenses defined in the former penal law as in force and effect immediately prior to September first, nineteen hundred sixty-seven:

illegally using, carrying or possessing a pistol or other dangerous weapon; making or possessing burglar's instruments; buying or receiving stolen property; unlawful entry of a building; aiding escape from prison; that kind of disorderly conduct defined in subdivisions six and eight of section seven hundred twenty-two of such former penal law; violations of sections four hundred eighty-three, four hundred eighty-three-b, four hundred eighty-four-h and article one hundred six of such former penal law; that kind of criminal sexual act or rape which was designated as a misdemeanor; violation of section seventeen hundred forty-seven-d and seventeen hundred forty-seven-e of such former penal law; any violation of any provision of article thirty-three of the public health law relating to narcotic drugs which was defined as a misdemeanor by section seventeen hundred fifty-one-a of such former penal law, and any violation of any provision of article thirty-three-A of the public health law relating to depressant and stimulant drugs which was defined as a misdemeanor by section seventeen hundred forty-seven-b of such former penal law.

(b) any of the following offenses defined in the penal law: illegally using, carrying or possessing a pistol or other dangerous weapon; possession of burglar's tools; criminal possession of stolen property in the third degree; escape in the third degree; jostling; fraudulent accosting; that kind of loitering defined in subdivision three of section 240.35; endangering the welfare of a child; the offenses defined in article two hundred thirty-five; issuing abortional articles; permitting prostitution; promoting prostitution in the third degree; stalking in the third degree; stalking in the fourth degree; the offenses defined in article one hundred thirty; the offenses defined in article two hundred twenty.

18. "Armor piercing ammunition" means any ammunition capable of being used in pistols or revolvers containing a projectile or projectile core, or a projectile or projectile core for use in such ammunition, that is constructed entirely (excluding the presence of traces of other substances) from one or a combination of any of the following: tungsten alloys, steel, iron, brass, bronze, beryllium copper, or uranium.

19. "Duly authorized instructor" means (a) a duly commissioned officer of the United States Army, Navy, Marine Corps or Coast Guard, or of the National Guard of the State of New York; or (b) a duly qualified adult citizen of the United States who has been granted a certificate as an instructor in small arms practice issued by the United States army, navy or marine corps, or by the adjutant general of this state, or by the National Rifle Association of America, a not-for-profit corporation duly organized under the laws of this state; or (c) by a person duly qualified and designated by the Department of Environmental Conservation under paragraph d of subdivision six of section 11-0713 of the Environmental Conservation Law as its agent in the giving of instruction and the making of certifications of qualification in responsible hunting practices.

20. "Disguised gun" means any weapon or device capable of being concealed on the person from which a shot can be discharged through the energy of an explosive and is designed and intended to appear to be something other than a gun.

21. "Semiautomatic" means any repeating rifle, shotgun or pistol, regardless of barrel or overall length, which utilizes a portion of the energy of a firing cartridge or shell to extract the fired cartridge case or spent shell and chamber the next round, and which requires a separate pull of the trigger to fire each cartridge or shell.

22. "Assault weapon" means

(a) a semiautomatic rifle that has an ability to accept a detachable magazine and has at least two of the following characteristics:

(i) a folding or telescoping stock;

(ii) a pistol grip that protrudes conspicuously beneath the action of the weapon;

(iii) a bayonet mount;

(iv) a flash suppressor or threaded barrel designed to accommodate a flash suppressor;

(v) a grenade launcher; or

(b) a semiautomatic shotgun that has at least two of the following characteristics:

(i) a folding or telescoping stock;

(ii) a pistol grip that protrudes conspicuously beneath the action of the weapon;

(iii) a fixed magazine capacity in excess of five rounds;

(iv) an ability to accept a detachable magazine; or

(c) a semiautomatic pistol that has an ability to accept a detachable magazine and has at least two of the following characteristics:

(i) an ammunition magazine that attaches to the pistol outside of the pistol grip;

(ii) a threaded barrel capable of accepting a barrel extender, flash suppressor, forward handgrip, or silencer;

(iii) a shroud that is attached to, or partially or completely encircles, the barrel and that permits the shooter to hold the firearm with the nontrigger hand without being burned;

(iv) a manufactured weight of fifty ounces or more when the pistol is unloaded;

(v) a semiautomatic version of an automatic rifle, shotgun or firearm; or

(d) any of the weapons, or functioning frames or receivers of such weapons, or copies or duplicates of such weapons, in any caliber, known as:

(i) Norinco, Mitchell, and Poly Technologies Avtomat Kalashnikovs (all models);

(ii) Action Arms Israeli Military Industries UZI and Galil;

(iii) Beretta Ar70 (SC-70);

(iv) Colt AR-15;

(v) Fabrique National FN/FAL, FN/LAR, and FNC;

(vi) SWD M-10, M-11, M-11/9, and M-12;

(vii) Steyr AUG;

(viii) INTRATEC TEC-9, TEC-DC9 and TEC-22; and

(ix) revolving cylinder shotguns, such as (or similar to) the Street Sweeper and Striker 12;

(e) provided, however, that such term does not include: (i) any rifle, shotgun or pistol that (A) is manually operated by bolt, pump, lever or slide action; (B) has been rendered permanently inoperable; or (C) is an antique firearm as defined in 18 U.S.C. 921(a)(16);

(ii) a semiautomatic rifle that cannot accept a detachable magazine that holds more than five rounds of ammunition;

(iii) a semiautomatic shotgun that cannot hold more than five rounds of ammunition in a fixed or detachable magazine;

(iv) a rifle, shotgun or pistol, or a replica or a duplicate thereof, specified in appendix A to section 922 of 18 U.S.C. as such weapon was manufactured on October first, nineteen hundred ninety-three. The mere fact that a weapon is not listed in appendix a shall not be construed to mean that such weapon is an assault weapon; or

(v) a semiautomatic rifle, a semiautomatic shotgun or a semiautomatic pistol or any of the weapons defined in paragraph (d) of this subdivision lawfully possessed prior to September fourteenth, nineteen hundred ninety-four.

23. "Large capacity ammunition feeding device" means a magazine, belt, drum, feed strip, or similar device, manufactured after September thirteenth, nineteen hundred ninety-four, that has a capacity of, or that can be readily restored or converted to accept, more than ten rounds of ammunition; provided, however, that such term does not include an attached tubular device designed to accept, and capable of operating only with,.22 caliber rimfire ammunition.

Amended by L. 1967, Ch. 791; L. 1969, Ch. 123; L. 1972, Chs. 588, 605; L. 1974, Chs. 179, 462, 986, 1041; L. 1976, Ch. 217; L. 1982, Ch. 492; L. 1985, Ch. 61; L. 1986, Chs. 328, 646; L. 1988, Ch. 264; L. 1990, Ch. 264; L. 1995, Ch. 219, § 2, adding subd. 5-b, eff. Nov. 1, 1995; L. 1996, Ch. 354, § 2, amending subd. 16, eff. Nov. 1, 1996; L. 1997, Ch. 446, § 2, eff. Aug. 25, 1997 and applicable to licenses issued on or after Aug. 25, 1997; L. 1998, Ch. 378, § 1, eff. Nov. 1, 1998; L. 1999, Ch. 210, eff. Nov. 1, 1999, amending subd. 10; L. 1999, Ch. 635, §§ 11 and 15, amending subd. 17(b), eff. Dec. 1, 1999; L. 2000, Ch. 189, §§ 8–10, eff. Nov. 1, 2000, amending subds. 3, 8, and 9, and adding subds. 21–23. This act shall take effect immediately, provided, that the amendments to subdivision 3 of section 265.00 of the penal law made by section eight of this act shall apply to offenses committed in violation of article 265 of the penal law on or after the first day of November next succeeding the date on which this act shall have become a law [Nov. 1, 2000]; L. 2003, Ch. 264, § 33, eff. Nov. 1, 2003, amending subd. 17(a).

ANNOTATIONS

Constitutionality.—Court upholds constitutionality of PL § 265.00 and rejects claim that it is unconstitutionally vague. People v. Crivillaro, 142 Misc. 2d 527, 538 N.Y.S.2d 152, 155 (Sup. Ct. Bronx Co. 1989).

Defenses.—Criminal prosecution for possession of a weapon may not be avoided by the claim that the weapon was possessed merely for protection. People v. Abdul-Hakeem 172 A.D.2d 177, 567 N.Y.S.2d 710, 711 (1st Dept. 1991).

Subd. 3

Sawed-off shotgun.—Since there is no indication that the Legislature intended the statute to apply retroactively, the defendant, who possessed a 26-inch-long sawed-off shotgun, which trial court had ruled was a concealable firearm, will not receive the benefit of a subsequent amendment to the statute defining a firearm as a sawed-off shotgun less than 26 inches long. People v. Ahern, 65 N.Y.2d 802, 493 N.Y.S.2d 117 (1985).

—Where ballistic expert's testimony did not conclusively establish the actual length of the barrel of the sawed-off shotgun, and the record contained no further information regarding the length of the barrel, defendant was entitled to a charge defining "firearm" that contained the requirement that the jury must find the barrel of the gun was shorter than 18 inches; court's refusal to include such a charge was reversible error. People v. Jennings, 279 A.D.2d 284, 720 N.Y.S.2d 4 (1st Dept.), *appeal denied*, 96 N.Y.2d 830 (2001).

—Evidence was sufficient to support a finding that the defendant possessed a sawed-off shotgun even though the gun was never found and there was nothing in the record to indicate the length of the gun. People v. Purpera, 81 A.D.2d 1007, 440 N.Y.S.2d 102 (4th Dept. 1981).

—Sawed-off shotgun with an overall size of 27 inches in length and a padded stock or butt measuring 12 inches in circumference was not a concealable weapon as defined in PL § 265.00(3). People v. Eldridge, 53 A.D.2d 1037, 385 N.Y.S.2d 912 (4th Dept. 1976).

—A 22-inch sawed-off shotgun is a firearm capable of concealment where the defendant actually and factually concealed the weapon on his person. People v Davis, 107 Misc. 2d 1, 433 N.Y.S.2d 56 (Crim. Ct. Queens Co. 1980).

Whether the sawed-off shotgun in defendant's possession was of a size which may be concealed upon the person presented a triable issue of fact. People v. Roberts, 79 Misc. 2d 243, 360 N.Y.S.2d 151 (Sup. Ct. App. Term 1974); *See also* People v. Ahern, 104 Misc. 2d 13, 427 N.Y.S.2d 549 (Sup. Ct. N.Y. Co. 1980).

Subd. 5

Gravity knife.—At trial, the People established the operability of the gravity knife, the basis of the conviction of criminal possession of a weapon in the third degree, the fact that during one of the several demonstrations of the knife for the jury in open court the knife malfunctioned and did not operate, did not defeat the proof of operability. People v. Smith, 309 A.D.2d 608, 765 N.Y.S.2d 777 (1st Dept. 2003).

—Information was sufficient without a statement that a "gravity knife" fulfilled the definition in the statute or that it was operational. People v. William, 191 Misc. 2d 293, 742 N.Y.S.2d 772 (App. T. 2d Dept. 2002).

Subd. 8

Possession of a defaced weapon; definition.—Criminal possession of a weapon in the second degree requires proof of actual or constructive possession of a weapon; if constructive, the proof must establish that defendant exercised dominion and control over the weapon or the area in which it was found. People v. Kirby, 280 A.D.2d 775, 721 N.Y.S.2d 130 (3d Dept. 2001).

—The court reversed defendant's conviction for possession of a weapon defaced for the purpose of concealing a crime, holding that since the statute prohibiting such possession defines defacing as "to remove, deface, cover, alter or destroy the manufacturer's serial number or any other distinguishing number or identification mark," it was not intended to prohibit possession of a weapon that has merely been shortened. People v. Foster, 42 A.D.2d 1046, 348 N.Y.S.2d 639 (4th Dept. 1973).

Subd. 10

Judge's discretion.—Judge's reliance upon a "conclusion" of the investigative agency without supportive evidence was insufficient to sustain his denial of pistol license to applicant. Guida v. Dier, 54 A.D.2d 86, 387 N.Y.S.2d 720 (3d Dept. 1976).

Subd. 14

Muzzle loaders.—If it should be established at the trial that a certain class of revolvers were historically and are now commonly known as "muzzle loaders"", the exemption in § 265.00 (14) must be held to extend to such a class. Long Island Antique Gun Collectors Association, Inc. v. Frank, 53 A.D.2d 644, 384 N.Y.S.2d 500 (2d Dept. 1976).

Subd. 15

Automatic standing.—Where the possession of the property seized at the time of the contested search and seizure is an essential element of the offense charge, the defendant has "automatic standing" to contest the seizure. People v. Buckley, 74 A.D.2d 757, 425 N.Y.S.2d 806 (1st Dept. 1980).

Loaded firearm.—"[B]y failing to test-fire the ammunition found at the scene before presenting the case to the grand jury, the People failed to prove that weapon was indeed a loaded firearm within the meaning of" PL § 265.00(15). People v. Colon, 15 A.D.3d 777, 790 N.Y.S.2d 288 (3d Dept. 2005).

§ 265.01. Criminal possession of a weapon in the fourth degree.

A person is guilty of criminal possession of a weapon in the fourth degree when:

(1) He possesses any firearm, electronic dart gun, electronic stun gun, gravity knife, switchblade knife, pilum ballistic knife, metal knuckle knife, cane sword, billy, blackjack, bludgeon, metal knuckles, chuka stick, sand bag, sandclub, wrist-brace type slingshot or slung-shot, shirken or "Kung Fu star"; or

(2) He possesses any dagger, dangerous knife, dirk, razor, stiletto, imitation pistol or any other dangerous or deadly instrument or weapon with intent to use the same unlawfully against another; or

(3) He knowingly has in his possession a rifle, shotgun or firearm in or upon a building or grounds, used for educational purposes, of any school, college or university, except the forestry lands, wherever located, owned and maintained by the State University of New York college of environmental science and forestry, without the written authorization of such educational institution; or

(4) He possesses a rifle or shotgun and has been convicted of a felony or serious offense; or

(5) He possesses any dangerous or deadly weapon and is not a citizen of the United States; or

(6) He is a person who has been certified not suitable to possess a rifle or shotgun, as defined in subdivision sixteen of section 265.00, and refuses to yield possession of such rifle or shotgun upon the demand of a police officer. Whenever a person is certified not suitable to possess a rifle or shotgun, a member of the police department to which such certification is made, or of the state police, shall forthwith seize any rifle or shotgun possessed by such person. A rifle or shotgun seized as herein provided shall not be destroyed, but shall be delivered to the headquarters of such police department, or state police, and there retained until the aforesaid certificate has been rescinded by the director or physician in charge, or other disposition of such rifle or shotgun has been ordered or authorized by a court of competent jurisdiction.

(7) He knowingly possesses a bullet containing an explosive substance designed to detonate upon impact.

(8) He possesses any armor piercing ammunition with intent to use the same unlawfully against another.

Criminal possession of a weapon in the fourth degree is a class A misdemeanor.

Added by L. 1974, Ch. 1041; **Amended** by L. 1976, Ch. 217; L. 1981, Ch. 807; L. 1982, Ch. 840; L. 1983, Ch. 621; L. 1985, Ch. 61; L. 1986, Chs. 328, 646; L. 1988, Ch. 220; L. 1990, Ch. 264; L. 1995, Ch. 219, § 3, amending subd. 1, eff. Nov. 1, 1995.

ANNOTATIONS

Insufficient evidence.—Allegation that juvenile had produced a "straight blade knife with an orange handle" was legally insufficient to establish that knife was a dangerous knife under PL § 265.01(2). In re Edward K., 641 N.Y.S.2d 933 (4th Dept. 1996).

Blackjack.—The flexibility of the handle is an essential physical property requisite to the classification of a device as a blackjack. People v. Guevara, 86 Misc. 2d 1044, 384 N.Y.S.2d 681 (Crim. Ct. N.Y.C. 1976).

Bludgeon.—A "spring whip" is not a "bludgeon" within the meaning of PL § 265.01. People v. Braunhut, 101 Misc. 2d 684, 421 N.Y.S.2d 763 (N.Y.C. Crim Ct. 1979).

Criminal liability; intent.—Scienter, guilty knowledge or intent is not a necessary element of the crime of possessing a concealed weapon. People v. Davis, 112 Misc. 2d 138, 446 N.Y.S.2d 159 (Crim. Ct. Bronx Co. 1981).

Knife.—Although possession of a dangerous knife is presumptive evidence of intent to use the instrument unlawfully, the presumption was insufficient to maintain a conviction since the jury could have found that the defendant used the knife in self defense against the complainant who was in possession of a baseball bat. People v. Hunter, 61 A.D.2d 990, 402 N.Y.S.2d 604 (2d Dept. 1978).

Gravity knife.—Trial court denied defendant's motion to dismiss information that alleged defendant possessed a "gravity knife, which opens and locks open when flipped"; information was facially sufficient, and mistaken identification of weapon as a gravity knife in the information, discovered only after motion decided, was a latent defect properly addressed at trial. People v. Pestana, 195 Misc.2d 833, 762 N.Y.S.2d 786 (N.Y.C. Crim. Ct. 2003).

Inclusory concurrent count of weapons possession.—Where the defendant could not have committed the robbery without committing grand larceny and possession a weapon, a verdict of guilty on the robbery count is deemed a dismissal of the grand larceny and gun possession counts. People v. Blake, 58 A.D.2d 757, 396 N.Y.S.2d 235 (1st Dept. 1977).

Negligence.—Section 265.01 defines "criminal possession of a weapon in the fourth degree," but does not impose or suggest a standard of care from which an allegation of negligence can arise. McDonald v. Cook, 252 A.D.2d 302, 681 N.Y.S.2d 900 (3d Dept. 1998).

Lesser included offense.—Criminal possession of a weapon in the fourth degree is not a lesser included offense of criminal possession of a weapon in the second degree. People v. Van Billard, 277 A.D.2d 958, 716 N.Y.S.2d 546 (4th Dept. 2000), *appeal denied,* 96 N.Y.2d 788 (2001).

Operability of gun.—Proof of operability is an essential element of the crime of criminal possession of a weapon and the jury must be so instructed. People v. Hechavarria, 158 A.D.2d 423, 551 N.Y.S.2d 922 924 (1st Dept. 1990).

—Reversal of defendant's conviction for criminal possession of a weapon in the fourth degree was mandated where the People presented no evidence that the gun found in defendant's glove compartment was operable, thereby failing to prove that defendant possessed a "firearm" under the Penal Law. People v. Actie, 99 A.D.2d 815, 472 N.Y.S.2d 147 (2d Dept. 1984).

—It was error for trial court to decline defendant's request to charge of operability requirement of rifle possession that was the subject of the charge. "It is well settled that 'all the elements of an indicted crime which are not conceded by defendant or defendant's counsel must be charged.' . . . Operability is a required element of the crime of criminal possession of a handgun, rifle or shotgun." People v. Rowland, 14 A.D.3d 886, 787 N.Y.S.2d 741 (3d Dept. 2005).

Overlapping of elements with criminal possession of a weapon in the second degree.—Although the elements of criminal possession of a weapon in the second and fourth degrees are identical in those circumstances where the culpable act is possession of a loaded firearm, the overlapping of elements does not render the statutes unconstitutional. People v. Vaccaro, 44 N.Y.2d 885, 407 N.Y.S.2d 631, 379 N.E.2d 159 (1978).

Pepper spray.—Conviction for attempted robbery in the first degree and criminal possession of a weapon in the fourth degree vacated; insufficient evidence to establish pepper spray was "dangerous instrument." People v. Sinatra, 302 A.D.2d 615, 755 N.Y.S.2d 312 (2d Dept. 2003).

Possession of gun; circumstantial evidence; constructive possession.—Where police officer entered defendant's apartment and upon opening his half closed bedroom door observed him lying alone in bed and a gun on the dresser, and defendant, who appeared intoxicated, arose to state the apartment was his home, such circumstantial evidence was sufficient to prove constructive possession of the gun. People v. Mebane, 44 A.D.2d 607, 353 N.Y.S.2d 529 (2d Dept. 1974).

Inoperable pistol; not an imitation pistol.—PL § 265.01(2) is neither at odds with nor exclusive of Administrative Code § 436.50(g). People v. Judiz, 38 N.Y.2d 529, 381 N.Y.S.2d 467, 344 N.E.2d 399 (1976).

—Since the pistol was incapable of firing a bullet it was not a firearm and the charge under PL § 265.01 was dismissed; however, defendant was held for trial for violating Administrative Code § 436.50(g) which prohibits possession of a toy or imitation pistol. People v. Pearson, 85 Misc. 2d 1029, 381 N.Y.S.2d 401 (N.Y.C. Crim. Ct. 1976).

—An inoperable real pistol or revolver cannot be considered an imitation pistol under the Administrative Code § 436-5.0(g). People v. Rivers, 76 Misc. 2d 972, 351 N.Y.S.2d 622 (Crim. Ct. N.Y. Co. 1974).

Possession of partly exposed knife.—Officer who observed long handle of a knife protruding from a case attached to defendant's belt with the blade concealed inside his trousers did not have probable cause to arrest him. People v. Diamond, 77 Misc. 2d 412, 353 N.Y.S.2d 688 (N.Y.C. Crim. Ct. Bronx C. 1974).

Possession of a pistol with a target permit.—A defendant could not be charged with violating PL § 265.01 where he had a target permit and was in possession of the starters pistol when he was neither at nor in transit to or from a range. People v. Ocasio, 108 Misc. 2d 349, 441 N.Y.S.2d 148 (Sup. Ct. App. Term 1981).

Straight razor.—Parolee, arrested for possession of a straight razor could not be charged with violation of a parole where it was not proven he possessed it "with intent to use the same unlawfully against another.", mere possession does not lead to the inference of unlawful intent to use. People *ex rel.*

Pena v. New York State Div. of Parole, 83 A.D.2d 887, 442 N.Y.S.2d 99 (2d Dept. 1981).

Temporary innocent possession of a weapon.—Charge on temporary, innocent possession as a defense should have been given even in the absence of a request to charge, where there was a factual issue for jury as to whether defendant's possession of weapon was innocent and temporary, despite defendant's claim that he never had sufficient control over gun to fire it. People v. Pendergraft, 50 A.D.2d 531, 374, N.Y.S.2d 669 (1st Dept. 1975).

—Where defendant shot deceased twice, he was not entitled to instruction on temporary innocent possession of the weapon. People v. DePass, 130 A.D.2d 586, 515 N.Y.S.2d 521 (2d Dept. 1987).

—Reversible error to deny a requested defense charge that temporary innocent possession of a weapon is not criminally proscribed. People v. Reagan, 49 A.D.2d 913, 374 N.Y.S.2d 33 (2d Dept. 1975).

—Although defendant may not have done anything unlawful to possess the weapon, which he claims was brought into his home by a guest several weeks earlier, those facts alone will not warrant charge to jury of the defense of temporary and lawful possession of a weapon. People v. Myers, 265 A.D.2d 598, 697 N.Y.S.2d 178 (3d Dept. 1999).

§ 265.02. Criminal possession of a weapon in the third degree.

A person is guilty of criminal possession of a weapon in the third degree when:

(1) He commits the crime of criminal possession of a weapon in the fourth degree as defined in subdivision one, two, three or five of section 265.01, and has been previously convicted of any crime; or

(2) He possesses any explosive or incendiary bomb, bombshell, firearm silencer, machine-gun or any other firearm or weapon simulating a machine-gun and which is adaptable for such use; or

(3) He knowingly has in his possession a machine-gun, firearm, rifle or shotgun which has been defaced for the purpose of concealment or prevention of the detection of a crime or misrepresenting the identity of such machine-gun, firearm, rifle or shotgun; or

(4) Such person possesses any loaded firearm. Such possession shall not, except as provided in subdivision one or seven, constitute a violation of this section if such possession takes place in such person's home or place of business; or

(5) (i) Such person possesses twenty or more firearms; or (ii) such person possesses a firearm and has been previously convicted of a felony or a class a misdemeanor defined in this chapter within the five years immediately preceding the commission of the offense and such possession did not take place in the person's home or place of business; or

(6) Such person knowingly possesses any disguised gun; or

(7) Such person possesses an assault weapon; or

(8) Such person possesses a large capacity ammunition feeding device.

Criminal possession of a weapon in the third degree is a class D felony.

Added by L. 1974, Ch. 1041; **Amended** by L. 1980, Ch. 233; L. 1981, Ch. 175; L. 1987, Ch. 695; L. 1998, Ch. 378, § 3, eff. Nov. 1, 1998; L. 2000, Ch. 189, § 11, eff. Nov..1, 2000, amending subds. 4 through 6 and adding subds. 7 and 8.

ANNOTATIONS

Operability of weapon.—At trial, the People established the operability of the gravity knife, the basis of the conviction of criminal possession of a weapon in the third degree, the fact that during one of the several demonstrations of the knife for the jury in open court the knife malfunctioned and did not operate, did not defeat the proof of operability. People v. Smith, 309 A.D.2d 608, 765 N.Y.S.2d 777 (1st Dept. 2003).

—Because certified copy of ballistics test which contained the result of the test establishing that the gun was operable satisfied the operability requirements of Penal Law § 265.02, indictment was sufficient. People v. Rodriguez, 235 A.D.2d 504, 653 N.Y.S.2d 358 (2d Dept. 1997).

—The proof was entirely adequate when the trial evidence established that the gun was operable and that the cartridges in the chambers were capable of being chambered in the gun and that they were live rounds. People v. Samarati, 53 A.D.2d 999, 385 N.Y.S.2d 952 (3d Dept. 1976).

—Since there was testimony that, although the cylinder head and stop were not operating on the gun, the cylinder could be rotated and aligned manually to operate and discharge the weapon three times, the jury could properly find that the gun qualified as a deadly weapon. People v. Howard, 37 A.D.2d 178, 323 N.Y.S.2d 119 (3d Dept. 1971).

—A pistol incapable of being fired is not a pistol, revolver or other firearm within the statute. A pistol incapable of discharging a bullet is not a firearm but may still qualify as a dangerous weapon if "with reasonable preparation it can still be made effective and fit for the use . . . what constitutes a reasonable preparation depends of course upon the time required, the changes that have to be made in the weapon, the parts which have to be inserted and all other attendant factors." *In re* B., 66 Misc. 2d 279, 320 N.Y.S.2d 813 (Fam. Ct. 1971).

Predicate felony.—Court found no legal or policy-based reason to exclude third degree criminal possession of a weapon under PL § 265.02(4) as a valid predicate felony offense sufficient to support criminal liability under PL § 270.20, charging unlawfully wearing a body vest. People v. Heath, 86 N.Y.2d 723, 631 N.Y.S.2d 117, 655 N.E.2d 158 (1995).

Standing; automatic standing rule.—Defendant, a passenger in the vehicle, failed to establish a reasonable expectation of privacy in the car and thus lacks standing to challenge the search. Further, defendant was charged with constructive possession of a weapon under PL § 265.02(4), but not with possession in 265.15(3), so the automatic standing rule does not apply. People v. Reynolds, 216 A.D.2d 883, 629 N.Y.S.2d 355 (4th Dept. 1995).

Accessorial conduct.—If the jury believed that the defendant did not know the co-defendant's possession of the weapon was unlawful but merely believed it probable that such was the case, and further found that instead of intentionally aiding the co-defendant to commit the crime, the defendant indifferently provided him with the means to commit the crime, it could convict him of facilitation but he could not be found guilty as an accessory. People v. Howard, 75 A.D.2d 1007, 429 N.Y.S.2d 131 (4th Dept. 1980).

"Any crime."—The phrase "any crime" in CPL § 265.02(1) means any crime no matter where, when or how committed, and needs no judicial interpretation. People v. Cornish, 104 Misc. 2d 72, 427 N.Y.S.2d 564 (Sup. Ct. Kings Co. 1980).

Arrest; seizure of pistol.—The seizure and arrest were sustained where pistol protruded from defendant's outside breast pocket so that the handle and slide were visible to the arresting officer, who was familiar with this kind of weapon. People v. Chamerlain, 46 A.D.2d 981, 362 N.Y.S.2d 265 (3d Dept. 1974).

Basis for resentencing.—Although the six-month sentence imposed for criminal possession of a weapon in the third degree was not excessive, resentencing was required in view of the probation report and the fact that defendant had been on bail for two years after the sentence and had been in no trouble.

People v. Miller, 90 A.D.2d 705, 455 N.Y.S.2d 370 (1st Dept. 1982).

Chain of custody.—A gap in the chain of custody of a gun did not preclude its admission into evidence where police officer had marked it with his initials at the time of its recovery and testified at trial that it was the same gun; a deficiency in the chain of custody goes to the weight of the evidence, not its admissibility. People v. Capers, 105 A.D.2d 842, 482 N.Y.S.2d 37 (2d Dept. 1984).

Circumstantial evidence.—Circumstantial evidence supported conclusion that defendant possessed firearm that was loaded and operational, even though no witness testified that defendant was in possession of firearm. People v. Jackson, 302 A.D.2d 748, 757 N.Y.S.2d 114 (3d Dept. 2003).

Constitutional right to bear arms not violated.—Defendant's constitutional right to bear arms and the right to travel was not violated or infringed when he was convicted of criminal possession of a weapon in the third degree while in New York on a trip from Arizona to Florida. People v. Morrill, 101 A.D.2d 927, 475 N.Y.S.2d 648 (3d Dept. 1984).

Constructive possession.—Defendant was properly convicted of constructive possession of a weapon. People v. Lind, 173 A.D.2d 179, 569 N.Y.S.2d 416, 420 (1st Dept. 1991).

—Defendant was properly found to be in constructive possession of weapons where, although he did not reside in the apartment, he occasionally spent the night there and was frequently on the premises, and he kept a change of clothes and some personal effects in the apartment. People v. Charnock 172 A.D.2d 1009, 569 N.Y.S.2d 534 (4th Dept. 1991).

Criminal liability; intent.—Although mens rea is not an element of the crime of possession of a weapon as a felony, if possession is incidental to disarming a wrongful possessor or in self-defense the offer of such explanation must be allowed by the Court and the jury must be instructed as to the parameters of the defense being offered. People v. Messado, 49 A.D.2d 560, 370 N.Y.S.2d 616 (1st Dept. 1975).

—Although intent is not a statutory element of the crime of criminal possession of a weapon in the third degree, where there is evidence in the record that defendant's possession of the weapon might have been innocent, the jury should be instructed that it might find such possession to be innocent. People v. Duncan, 75 A.D.2d 826, 427 N.Y.S.2d 471 (2d Dept. 1980).

—Possession of a weapon must be voluntary in order to be culpable. People v. Valentine, 54 A.D.2d 568, 387 N.Y.S.2d 25 (2d Dept. 1976).

—Although intent is not by statute a necessary ingredient of the crime charged, case law indicates that, where there is evidence in the record that defendant's possession of the weapon might have been innocent, the jury should be instructed that it might find that such possession was innocent. People v. Trucchio, 47 A.D.2d 934, 367 N.Y.S.2d 76 (2d Dept. 1975).

Conviction for dangerous weapons reversed; introduction of report prejudicial to defendant.—It was prejudicial error and grounds for reversal where prosecution induced defense counsel to introduce into evidence secret investigatory reports unrelated to the case at bar, since this may have created the impression that the charge against the defendant was related to his involvement with organized crime. People v. Donnelley, 42 A.D.2d 595, 344 N.Y.S.2d 726 (2d Dept. 1973).

Defacing of firearm.—A motion to dismiss a count of an indictment charging defendant with "defacing" a firearm was granted, where the firearm was a .22 caliber rifle with its stock cut down and its barrel sawed off to a length of 7 inches, and defendant did not remove or obliterate the manufacturer's serial or identification number inasmuch as the firearm did not have such a number. People v. Keating, 68 Misc. 2d 811, 327 N.Y.S.2d 906 (Monroe Co. Ct. 1972).

Defective indictment; missing element.—An indictment which omitted the allegation that defendant's possession of a weapon was outside of his home or business where he was accused of Criminal possession of a weapon in the third degree, was jurisdictionally defective and could not be waived. People v. Newell, 95 A.D.2d 815, 463 N.Y.S.2d 538 (2d Dept. 1983).

Equal protection.—PL § 265.02(1) does not violate the Equal Protection Clause of the U.S. Constitution. People v. Robinson, 86 Misc. 2d 992, 385 N.Y.S.2d 697 (Sup. Ct. N.Y. Co. 1975).

Explosive substance; bottle of kerosene with wick.—Indictment charging defendant with possession of explosive substance must be dismissed since kerosene is exempted from such definition by various statutes, although it could be construed as an incendiary bomb under PL 265.05(1), with which defendant was not charged. People v. Sullivan, 39 A.D.2d 631, 331 N.Y.S.2d 298 (4th Dept. 1972).

Explosive substance; bottle of gasoline with wick.—Failure of indictment to indicate degree of crime or where possession took place cannot support a felony conviction but is sufficient for misdemeanor conviction.People v. Meyer, 46 A.D.2d 904, 362 N.Y.S.2d 190 (2d Dept. 1974).

—Defendant's possession of a bottle containing 200 millilitres of gasoline with a twisted piece of paper serving as a wick constituted possession of an "incendiary bomb" within the meaning of this statute. People v. Valentin, 93 Misc. 2d 1123, 404 N.Y.S.2d 66 (Sup. Ct. Bronx Co. 1978).

Failure to prove prior convictions.—Defendant's act of sneaking up behind victim and stabbing him in the back was a deliberate act of retaliation for an earlier altercation between the two, but evidence of this alone could not support a conviction under PL § 265.02 without evidence of a prior conviction. People v. Parker, 293 A.D.2d 278, 740 N.Y.S.2d 49 (1st Dept. 2002).

—Conviction after trial of criminal possession of a weapon in the third degree, a felony, was reduced to the class A misdemeanor of criminal possession of a weapon in the fourth degree because of the failure of the People to introduce evidence at the trial of defendant's previous convictions. People v. Minnis, 101 A.D.2d 739, 475 N.Y.S.2d 56 (1st Dept. 1984).

Felonious possession of a weapon.—Felonious possession of a weapon is a crime in and of itself and capable of standing independently. People v. Edge, 76 Misc. 2d 802, 351 N.Y.S.2d 502 (Sup. Ct. Bronx Co. 1973).

Hatchet; not violent felony.—Criminal possession of a weapon in the third degree is not a violent felony offense when the weapon involved is a hatchet; such offense is a violent felony only where it involves a firearm. People v. Dembo, 114 A.D.2d 317, 494 N.Y.S.2d 112 (1st Dept. 1985).

"Home."—The lobby of a shelter for men that is open to the public is not a "home." People v. Powell, 54 N.Y.2d 524, 446 N.Y.S.2d 232, 430 N.E.2d 1285 (1981).

—Defendant's possession of a loaded gun in the console of his car parked in the fenced driveway of his home is not covered within the exception of P.L. § 265.02(4). People v. Tolbert, 253 A.D.2d 832, 680 N.Y.S.2d 832 (2d Dept. 1998).

—Defendant's possession of loaded firearm in girlfriend's apartment did not satisfy the requirements of "home," where defendant's girlfriend testified that he only visited once or twice a week and did not have a key and, further, defendant admitted he lived with his mother. People v. Trinidad, 237 A.D.2d 635, 655 N.Y.S.2d 640 (2d Dept. 1997).

—T-shaped hallway, in a wing of a single-residency hotel, which contained two bathrooms and a kitchen and was for the communal use of occupants of the seven individual rooms in the wing was part of the "home" of the occupants of the seven rooms. People v. Bargeman, 92 Misc. 2d 173, 399 N.Y.S.2d 393 (Sup. Ct. N.Y. Co. 1977).

—Firearm was possessed in his "home" where defendant was arrested while lying with half of his body on the stoop and half in the inner hallway of a two family house in which he resided on the first floor. People v. Taylor, 92 Misc. 2d 29, 399 N.Y.S.2d 575 (Crim. Ct. N.Y.C. 1977).

—Abode where loaded gun was found was defendant's "home"; he had a strong social connection with the lady at that address and spent at least as much time there as at his other abode; defendant therefore was guilty of violation of weapons possession as misdemeanor, not felony. People v. Douglas, 82 Misc. 2d 971, 372 N.Y.S.2d 459 (Sup. Ct. Kings Co. 1975).

—Did not extend to a garbage can standing outside the house occupied by defendant charged with possession of loaded revolver found in the garbage can. People v. Lemelle, 81 Misc. 2d 674, 366 N.Y.S.2d 837 (Crim. Ct. N.Y.C. 1975).

Fireworks.—Section 265.02 does not cover fireworks. People v. Santorelli, 95 Misc. 2d 886, 408 N.Y.S.2d 893 (Sup. Ct. Kings Co. 1978).

Illegal seizure of evidence.—Since the first gun was observed to be in the passenger's possession before he placed it under the seat, no presumption of possession was chargeable to the driver. As for the second gun, once the arrested men were outside the car and handcuffed, there was no reasonable basis for any apprehension on the part of the arresting officers of any danger to themselves or of any threat of destruction of any contraband (both or either of which would have justified a search of the car). While it may be that these apprehensions arose when the arrested men were placed back into the driver's car, their availability as bases for the search was attributable to the unnecessary action taken by the police in commandeering the car. Accordingly, they could not be utilized to justify the seizure of the second gun. People v. Garcia, 41 A.D.2d 560, 340 N.Y.S.2d 35 (2d Dept. 1973).

Imitation pistol.—A starter's pistol, altered to accept live cartridges and actually loaded with live rounds of ammunition but inoperable is an imitation pistol and its possession is a misdemeanor under Admin. Code § 436-5.0(g); in order to be a copy or imitation some intentional shaping or altering must take place and here sufficiently extensive alterations transformed a starter's pistol into an imitation 22 caliber pistol. People v. Williams, 113 Misc. 2d 595, 449 N.Y.S.2d 846 (Crim Ct. N.Y. Co. 1982).

Inoperable pistol not prosecutable under penal law or administrative code.—A starter's pistol designed to fire blanks and be used as a signaling device is an imitation pistol under N.Y.C. Admin. Code § 436-5.0(g); however a .25 caliber pistol loaded with four rounds, but inoperable because of a faulty firing pin, is neither prosecutable under Article 265 of the Penal Law as an operable firearm, nor as a "toy or imitation pistol or revolver," within the meaning and intent of the Administrative Code. See People v. Ross, 61 N.Y.2d 316, 473 N.Y.S.2d 783, 461 N.E.2d 1270 (1984).

Intoxication charge to jury.—Where evidence of intoxication was not limited to negating only the element of intent, but relevant to defendant's knowing possession of a firearm and that the firearm was loaded, jury should have received a charge on issue of intoxication. People v. Ressler, 302 A.D.2d 921, 754 N.Y.S.2d 485 (4th Dept. 2003).

Insufficiency of evidence.—Defendant's conviction was reversed where nothing in the record established ready access to the handgun on the date he was charged with its possession and constructive possession requires ready access. People v. Lucas, 84 A.D.2d 582, 443 N.Y.S.2d 422 (2d Dept. 1981).

—Since it was not shown that .22 caliber shell found in the defendant's possession was capable of discharging the gun found in his possession, conviction was modified from felony possession to misdemeanor possession. People v. McCoy, 50 A.D.2d 747, 376 N.Y.S.2d 523 (1st Dept. 1975). See also People v. Thomas, 70 A.D.2d 571, 417 N.Y.S.2d 67 (1st Dept. 1979).

Legal seizure of evidence; weapon in automobile.—The police may lawfully conduct an inventory search of an illegally parked motor vehicle after it has been towed away. People v. D'Abate, 37 N.Y.2d 922, 378 N.Y.S.2d 390 340 N.E.2d 750 (1975).

Unlawful possession of weapon; comment by judge not prejudicial.—The judge's statement that defendant would be guilty regardless of how he came into possession of a gun, was wrong in view of the defense that defendant had just disarmed someone and was taking the gun to the police. The error was not prejudicial, however, because the defense was so intrinsically inconsistent and contradictory to the rest of the testimony as to be totally incredible. People v. Arthurs, 24 N.Y.2d 688, 301 N.Y.S.2d 614, 249 N.E.2d 462 (1969).

New trial; extrajudicial statements of co-defendants.—Appellants charged with riot and possession of dangerous weapons, were entitled to a new trial where oral and written extrajudicial statements of their co-defendants were admitted into evidence despite their incrimination of appellants. The judge's charge attempting to limit the jury's consideration of the statements could not overcome the prejudice caused by their admission. People v. Cassidy, 30 A.D.2d 795, 291 N.Y.S.2d 822 (1st Dept. 1968).

Possession of unlicensed pistol by Department of Mental Hygiene officer.—A safety officer who was designated a special policeman by the director of a state hospital and who possessed an unlicensed pistol violated PL § 265.05, where at the time he was arrested for unlawful possession of the pistol he was not performing any duties in or arising out of his employment. (See MHL § 34). People v. Kortright, 62 Misc. 2d 141, 307 N.Y.S.2d 359 (N.Y.C. Crim. Ct. 1970).

Place of business.—Defendant's conviction for criminal

possession of a weapon affirmed; place of business exception of P.L. § 265.02(4) did not include street corner near cab for purpose of waiting to escort customer to cab. People v. Solomon, 253 A.D.2d 692, 679 N.Y.S.2d 97 (1st Dept. 1998).

—Place of business exception did not include postal employee arrested for carrying a revolver on his post office job. People v. Francis, 45 A.D.2d 431, 358 N.Y.S.2d 148 (2d Dept. 1974).

—Place of business exception which would make possession of weapon a misdemeanor was inapplicable where defendant shot and killed a co-worker at their place of employment because he believed the victim was trying to have him fired; the legislature provided a lesser offense for persons protecting themselves or their property either in their home or place of business. People v. Fearon, 58 A.D.2d 1041, 397 N.Y.S.2d 294 (4th Dept. 1977), cert. denied, 434 U.S. 1036.

—Court did not allow defendant's possession of loaded gun at his place of employment to be indicted as felony; the place of business exception of the possession statute limited the offense to a misdemeanor. People v. Buckmire, 167 Misc. 2d 581, 638 N.Y.S.2d 883 (Sup. Ct. N.Y. Co. 1995).

—Place of business exception did not apply to an employee of a corporation who possessed the gun without authorization from his corporate employer. People v. Rondon, Misc. 2d 439 N.Y.S.2d 803 (Sup. Ct. N.Y. Co. 1981).

—Criminal Possession of a Loaded Firearm in one's place of business (PL § 265.01) is a lesser included offense of Criminal Possession of a Loaded Firearm in the Third Degree (PL § 165.02(4)). People v. La Paz, 95 Misc. 2d 756, 408 N.Y.S.2d 288 (Sup. Ct. Kings Co. 1978).

Possession of licensed weapon in place other than permitted in premises license.—Where all that is asserted is that the weapon for which defendant held a license "to have and possess in his place of business by a merchant or storekeeper" was possessed in a place other than that specified in the license, defendant could not be prosecuted for criminal possession of a weapon in the third degree, a class D feony, pursuant to CPL § 265.02, in view of PL § 400.00(15) which makes such a violation a class A misdemeanor. People v. Serrano, 71 A.D.2d 258, 422 N.Y.S.2d 672 (1st Dept. 1979).

Possession of contraband weapons; intent.—Defendants, who were acquitted of conspiracy to murder, rob and burglarize and were convicted for possession of weapons and testimony of 2 undercover agent witnesses, were guilty of convicted crimes even though rifle was unloaded and contemplated use was not immediate and where one supplied ashcan fire crackers as ingredient for home-made bomb he was guilty as accessory to unlawful possession of bomb by others. People v. Lay, 39 A.D.2d 904, 334 N.Y.S.2d 398 (1st Dept. 1972).

—The possession of the weapon must be voluntary in order to be culpable. People v. Trisvan, 49 A.D.2d 913, 373 N.Y.S.2d 405 (2d Dept. 1975).

—In order to convict defendant of criminal possession of a weapon in the third degree the jury must find that he had knowing possession of the weapon. People v. Cohen, 57 A.D.2d 790, 394 N.Y.S.2d 683 (1st Dept. 1977).

—Defendant's conviction for criminal possession of a weapon, third degree, was proper where the contraband was found on premises under defendant's control since it could be inferred that he had both knowledge and control of it. People v. Sacco, 64 A.D.2d 324, 409 N.Y.S.2d 909 (4th Dept. 1978).

Possession of weapon as incident of robbery.—Where possession of a gun was merely incidental to and part of robbery, separate crime of possession of weapon before or following robbery was not shown. People v. Graham, 48 A.D.2d 646, 368 N.Y.S.2d 518 (1st Dept. 1975), aff'd, 39 N.Y.2d 775, 385 N.Y.S.2d 31, 350 N.E.2d 408 (1976).

Possession of weapon; transfer of charge to Family Court.—The court denied a motion to transfer a charge of possession of a pistol to the Family Court. The possession was disclosed as a result of a phone call from defendant's wife after an argument between her and defendant. However, the wrongful possession did not depend on an intent to use the pistol on the wife. The act of possession was "prosecutable" without any evidence of intent to use the weapon against her. People v. Mancuso, 59 Misc. 2d 941, 300 N.Y.S.2d 1003 (Dist. Ct. 1969).

Previous conviction of a crime.—It was error for the court to charge jury on crime of possession of a weapon as a felony by reason of prior conviction where defendant was indicted only

for possession of a loaded revolver. People v. Davis, 43 A.D.2d 926, 352 N.Y.S.2d 476 (1st Dept. 1974).

—Since Legislature did not impose a limit as to the remoteness of the prior conviction which could be used pursuant to PL § 265.02, court did not err in admitting at the trial a certificate of conviction which indicated that defendant had been convicted of a misdemeanor in 1963. People v. Kittell, 135 A.D.2d 1021, 522 N.Y.S.2d 962, 964 (3d Dept. 1987).

—All of the evidence of the previous conviction must be submitted, in accordance with CPL 200.60(2), (3)(a)(b), before the close of the People's case. People v. Ireland, 47 A.D.2d 580, 363 N.Y.S.2d 177 (4th Dept. 1975).

Proof of intent to use weapon necessary.—Count of indictment charging criminal possession of a weapon in the third degree was dismissed as fatally defective where it did not allege that the defendant intended to use the weapon, a knife, unlawfully. People v. Bahamundi, 99 A.D.2d 534, 471 N.Y.S.2d 322 (2d Dept. 1984).

Family Court jurisdiction; assault of wife plus related offenses.—Defendant was charged with attempted assault of his wife, burglary, and felonious possession of a dangerous weapon. Since the Family Court has jurisdiction over assault offenses between spouses, and since the assault and nonassault charges were so inextricably related, the transaction lay in the first instance within the jurisdiction of the Family Court. People v. Williams, 24 N.Y.2d 274, 300 N.Y.S.2d 89, 248 N.E.2d 8 (1969).

Repugnant verdict.—Since an essential element of first degree robbery under PL § 160.15(2) is identical with that of third degree criminal possession of a weapon under PL § 265.02(4), namely actual physical possession of or control or dominion over a weapon, including a firearm, a verdict of not guilty of robbery under PL § 160.15(2) is repugnant to a simultaneous verdict of guilty of criminal possession under PL § 265.02(4). People v. Tucker, 96 Misc. 2d 67, 409 N.Y.S.2d 105 (Monroe Co. Sup. Ct. 1978).

Statutory exemptions from charge of possession of dangerous weapon.—Although not within the obvious intent of the legislature, under statutory law a police officer has immunity from prosecution for possession of weapons (including firearms), for unauthorized manufacture of such weapons, for defacing of weapons, and for possession and use of unauthorized weapons. People v. Desthers, 73 Misc. 2d 1085, 343 N.Y.S.2d 887 (Crim. Ct. N.Y. Co. 1973).

Temporary innocent possession of a weapon.—Failure to grant defendant's request to charge the jury on innocent possession of a firearm in prosecution for criminal possession of a weapon in the third degree was not reversible error where evidence was utterly at odds with any claim of innocent possession; upon discovering the weapon, defendant moved the weapon and concealed it in the new hiding place, removing it as he pleased and handling it in a reckless manner. People v. Williams, 50 N.Y.2d 1043, 431 N.Y.S.2d 698, 409 N.E.2d 1372 (1980).

—Defendant's request was properly denied as duplicative or cumulative where defendant requested a charge that he must be found not guilty of criminal possession of a weapon in the third degree (PL § 265.02) if the jury found "that defendant picked up the gun from the ground and then was arrested immediately" after the court had twice charged that "fleeting or momentary possession" was not sufficient to support a conviction on the possession counts. People v. Coonan, 48 N.Y.2d 772, 423 N.Y.S.2d 914, 399 N.E.2d 944 (1979).

—At trial for felonious possession of a weapon, it was reversible error for the court to charge the jury in answer to their inquiries that if the police saw defendant with a gun in hand, there was no necessity to have it tested for fingerprints, and that powder traces on defendant's hands were not an element because the count charged possession of a gun since in both instances, the jury should have been instructed as to a temporary, lawful possession of the gun by defendant. People v. Davis, 61 A.D.2d 760, 402 N.Y.S.2d 9 (1st Dept. 1978).

—If the jury believed that defendant found the gun and gave it to the police, his properly explained temporary possession would not have been unlawful. People v. Richardson, 55 A.D.2d 514, 389 N.Y.S.2d 14 (1st Dept. 1976).

—Where there was a factual issue for jury as to whether defendant's possession of weapon was innocent and temporary, despite defendant's claim that he never had sufficient control over gun to fire it. Charge on temporary, innocent possession as a defense should have been given even in the absence of a request to charge. People v. Pendergraft, 50 A.D.2d 531, 374 N.Y.S.2d 669 (1st Dept. 1975).

—Reversal was required where there were sufficient facts for the jury to conclude that defendant's possession of the gun was temporary and resulted from a struggle and the trial court failed to charge, as defense counsel requested, that temporary possession of a weapon, properly explained, did not constitute a crime. People v. Monger, 71 A.D.2d 641, 418 N.Y.S.2d 471 (2d Dept. 1979).

—Reversible error to deny a requested defense charge that temporary innocent possession of a weapon is not criminally proscribed. People v. Reagan, 49 A.D.2d 913, 374 N.Y.S.2d 33 (2d Dept. 1975).

Testimony; contradiction of flagrant character.—Where defendant was convicted of possession of dangerous weapon upon testimony of police officer who at trial said he could see the handle of the gun above the belt and no arrest was made until after the gun was seen which was in basic contradiction to his testimony at a suppression hearing, new trial was required in the interests of justice. People v. McCormick, 39 A.D.2d 590, 331 N.Y.S.2d 840 (2d Dept. 1972).

Weapon used and possessed by co-defendant.—Where defendant and two others assaulted a police officer, the three being charged with the assault, and one of the other two shot the officer with the officer's own revolver, and then carried the revolver away, it was error for the court to submit to the jury an additional count against the defendant of possession of weapons and dangerous instruments where such count arose from the co-defendant's use and possession of the police officer's revolver. People v. Quick, 30 A.D.2d 561, 291 N.Y.S.2d 132 (2d Dept. 1968), aff'd, 26 N.Y.2d 773, 309 N.Y.S.2d 208, 257 N.E.2d 655 (1970).

Criminal liability; intent.—Intent is not an element of the crime of possessing, without a license, a loaded pistol or revolver which might be concealed on the person of an accused. Guilty knowledge, or scienter, is not an element of the crime of unlawful possession of a firearm. People v. Newton., 72 Misc. 2d 646, 340 N.Y.S.2d 77 (Sup. Ct. Queens Co. 1973).

Illegal possession of firearm; outside premises.—Defendant who fired an illegally possessed gun while outside his store was properly convicted of felonious possession of a firearm. People v. Ali, 44 A.D.2d 232, 354 N.Y.S.2d 426 (1st Dept. 1974), aff'd, 36 N.Y.2d 880, 372 N.Y.S.2d 212, 334 N.E.2d 11 (1975).

Possession.—Police officers executing outstanding warrants on a probation violation properly seized a .9 millimeter luger which was under the defendant's thigh while sitting andwhich was partially visible to officers when they ordered him to put his hands in plain view, although defendant denied owning the handgun, which was loaded with 14 rounds of ammunition, evidence was sufficient to support his conviction of criminal possession of a weapon in the third degree. People v. Wheeler, 2 N.Y.3d 370, 779 N.Y.S.2d 164, 811 N.E.2d 531 (2004).

—Testimony from the arresting officer that he observed defendant reach into his vest pocket, saw defendant pull a metal object from that pocket, and drop it to the ground and immediately walk away, coupled with the officer's testimony that the object recovered was a loaded and fully operable firearm, supported defendant's conviction under Penal Law § 265.02(4). People v. Rodriguez, 238 A.D.2d 447, 657 N.Y.S.2d 344 (2d Dept. 1997).

Possession of dangerous weapon; taxicab is "place of business."—Illegal possession of a firearm by driver of a fleet-owned, privately-owned, medallion or gypsy taxi, whether weapon is kept in cash box or on the driver's person constitutes possession in "such person's place of business." People v. Santana, 77 Misc. 2d 414, 354 N.Y.S.2d 387 (Crim. Ct. Queens Co. 1974).

—Although the evidence warranted holding the matter for trial, charge of possession of firearm found in defendant's cab could be reduced to a misdemeanor, since the cab constituted a "place of business" and was therefore an exception to the statute concerning possession of weapons. People v. Anderson, 74 Misc. 2d 415, 344 N.Y.S.2d 15 (Crim. Ct. Bronx Co. 1973).

Possession of a firearm; taxi is "place of business."—Where defendant was arrested after being found in possession of a gun (which was in a cigar box used to hold his receipts

from driving a taxi), a motion to dismiss the indictment was properly granted, since a taxicab is a "place of business" within the meaning of Section 265.05(2) of the Penal Law. People v. Santiago, 74 Misc. 2d 10, 343 N.Y.S.2d 805 (Sup. Ct. N.Y. Co. 1971).

Possession of dangerous weapon; sawed-off shotgun.—Sawed-off shotgun with an overall size of 27 inches in length and a padded stock or butt measuring 12 inches in circumference was not a concealable weapon as defined in PL § 265.00(3). People v. Eldridge, 53 A.D.2d 1037, 385 N.Y.S.2d 912 (4th Dept. 1976).

—Where defendant was charged with possession of a dangerous weapon, there was insufficient evidence to find the defendant guilty, since the firearm was too large to be concealed upon the person and the legislative intent of the statute was directed at a type of weapon which could be concealed rather than at a particular weapon. People v. Roberts, 73 Misc. 2d 500, 342 N.Y.S.2d 757 (Dist. Ct. Suffolk Co. 1973), dismissed 79 Misc. 2d 243, 360 N.Y.S.2d 151 (Sup Ct, App. Term 9th & 10th Jud. Dists. 1974).

Possession of a defaced weapon; definition.—The court reversed defendant's conviction for possession of a weapon defaced for the purpose of concealing a crime, holding that since the statute prohibiting such possession defines defacing as "to remove, deface, cover, alter or destroy the manufacturer's serial number or any other distinguishing number or identification mark," it was not intended to prohibit possession of a weapon that has merely been shortened. People v. Foster, 42 A.D.2d 1046, 348 N.Y.S.2d 639 (4th Dept. 1973).

Test required to ascertain whether bullets are "live."—The decision in People v. Daniels, 77 A.D.2d 745, 430 N.Y.S.2d 881 that in a prosecution involving a loaded firearm the people must establish beyond a reasonable doubt that the ammunition possessed by the defendant had been test fired to establish that it was live is to be applied prospectively and not retroactively. People v. Little, 88 A.D.2d 671, 451 N.Y.S.2d 257 (3d Dept. 1982).

—Reversal was required for a conviction on one count of criminal possession of a weapon in the third degree based upon defendant's alleged possession of a loaded firearm since, although an expert witness testified that nothing indicated to him that the bullets confiscated would not fire if detonated within the weapon defendant allegedly possessed, the bullets were never test-fired to determine if the ammunition was live and therefore the prosecution failed to establish beyond a reasonable doubt that the ammunition was live. People v. Daniels, 77 A.D.2d 745, 430 N.Y.S.2d 881 (3d Dept. 1980).

§ 265.03. Criminal possession of a weapon in the second degree.

A person is guilty of criminal possession of a weapon in the second degree when, with intent to use the same unlawfully against another:

(1) He possesses a machine-gun; or

(2) He possesses a loaded firearm; or

(3) He possesses a disguised gun.

Criminal possession of a weapon in the second degree is a class C felony.

Added by L. 1974, Ch. 1041; L. 1998, Ch. 378, § 4, eff. Nov. 1, 1998.

ANNOTATIONS

Continuing crime.—Continuous possession of a weapon throughout the duration of defendant's criminal acts does not, in and of itself, determine whether the resulting sentences for convictions for criminal acts committed during that time will run consecutively or concurrently; here, defendant's act of possession of a weapon was separate and apart from the murder, and consecutive sentences were properly imposed. People v. Salcedo, 92 N.Y.2d 1019, 684 N.Y.S.2d 480, 707 N.E.2d 435 (1998).

—Criminal possession of a weapon in the second degree can be a continuing offense which supports a single count in an indictment. People v. Rivera, 157 A.D.2d 540, 549 N.Y.S.2d 728, 729 (1st Dept. 1990).

Defense of justification; repugnant verdict.—In prosecution charging attempted murder, assault, and criminal possession of a weapon, second degree, where defendant relied on the defense of justification claiming that he was attacked and came into possession of the weapon during that attack, acquittal on the attempted murder and assault counts and conviction on the weapon possession count did not constitute a repugnant verdict. People v. Curinaj, 65 A.D.2d 705, 410 N.Y.S.2d 87 (1st Dept. 1978).

Failure to establish intent to use weapon unlawfully.— Court reduced conviction of criminal possession of a weapon in the second degree to criminal possession of a weapon in the third degree on the ground that the evidence did not establish beyond a reasonable doubt that defendant intended to use the pistol unlawfully against another. People v. Tejada, 101 A.D.2d 757, 475 N.Y.S.2d 400 (1st Dept. 1984).

Inferred intent.—The jury could infer the intent necessary for criminal possession of a weapon in the second degree from the circumstances of the case, which included reliable information as to a "contract" to kill an individual and the defendant's suspicious behavior on the street where such individual resided. People v. Evans, 106 A.D.2d 527, 483 N.Y.S.2d 339 (1st Dept. 1984).

—Evidence that defendant's authorization to possess a weapon was terminated by the New York City Department of Corrections more than two years before incident at issue was probative of defendant's unlawful possession of a weapon and was properly admitted into evidence. People v. Glen, 278 A.D.2d 243, 716 N.Y.S.2d 908 (2d Dept. 2000), *appeal denied,* 96 N.Y.2d 829 (2001).

Lesser included offense.—Criminal possession of a weapon in the fourth degree is not a lesser included offense of criminal possession of a weapon in the second degree. People v. Van Billard, 277 A.D.2d 958, 716 N.Y.S.2d 546 (4th Dept. 2000), *appeal denied,* 96 N.Y.2d 788 (2001).

Possession of weapon imputed to defendant.—Although defendant did not personally have control over the gun, it could reasonably be found that he aided accomplice in the unlawful use of the gun against murder victim since defendant and accomplice assaulted victim, fled, then returned to the crime scene where accomplice shot victim while defendant looked on. People v. Bosque, 78 A.D.2d 986, 433 N.Y.S.2d 658 (4th Dept. 1980), *cert. denied,* 451 U.S. 992 (1981).

Repugnant verdict.—Jury's verdict convicting defendant of two counts of assault in the second degree and acquitting him of criminal possession of a weapon in the second degree was repugnant, since it necessarily meant that the jury found that defendant intended to cause injury by means of a handgun, but found he did not intend to use the handgun unlawfully against another. People v. Williams, 87 A.D.2d 876, 449 N.Y.S.2d 319 (2d Dept. 1982).

—A reversal of the murder conviction requires the reversal of the conviction for possession of a weapon in the second degree when the weapon charge is factually related to the murder charge. People v. Cohen, 77 A.D.2d 627, 430 N.Y.S.2d 640 (2d Dept. 1980), *aff'd,* 58 N.Y.2d 840, 460 N.Y.S.2d 18, 446 N.E.2d 774 (1983), *cert. denied,* 461 U.S. 930 (1983).

—Conviction for criminal possession of a weapon in the second degree, which contemplates possession of a loaded firearm with the intent to use it unlawfully against another, was not inconsistent with acquittal on charges of assault in the first degree; a person can possess a loaded firearm with the intent to use it against another person, but not intend to inflict serious physical injury on that person. People v. Hart, 698 N.Y.S.2d 72, 266 A.D.2d 584 (3d Dept. 1999), *appeal denied,* 94 N.Y.2d 903 (2000).

Sufficiency of Evidence.—Evidence was legally insufficient to support conviction for criminal possession of a weapon in the second degree; there was no evidence that defendant possessed a weapon at time of crime, was aware of robbery plan, shared intent of the co-defendants, or aided them in any way. People Eldridge, 302 A.D.2d 934, 755 N.Y.S.2d 193 (4th Dept. 2003).

Temporary innocent possession of a weapon.—Where there was a factual issue for jury as to whether defendant's possession of weapon was innocent and temporary, despite defendant's claim that he never had sufficient control over gun

to fire it. Charge on temporary, innocent possession as a defense should have been given even in the absence of a request to charge, People v. Pendergraft, 50 A.D.2d 531, 374 N.Y.S.2d 669 (1st Dept. 1975).

—Reversible error to deny a requested defense charge that temporary innocent possession of a weapon is not criminally proscribed. People v. Reagan, 49 A.D.2d 931, 374 N.Y.S.2d 33 (2d Dept. 1975).

Verdict of guilty of assault in the second degree.—Verdict of guilty of assault, second degree, (PL § 125.05) was not repugnant to a verdict of acquittal of criminal possession of a weapon, second degree, (PL § 165.03) since the elements of the crimes are not identical and the jury may have concluded that the defendant possessed the weapon initially without any intent to use it unlawfully but, in the course of the altercation, decided to and did use weapon offensively, that is, beyond the lawful bounds of self-defense. People v. Garcia, 72 A.D.2d 356, 424 N.Y.S.2d 697 (1st Dept. 1980), *aff'd,* 52 N.Y.2d 716, 436 N.Y.S.2d 273, 417 N.E.2d 567 (1980).

§ 265.04. Criminal possession of a dangerous weapon in the first degree.

A person is guilty of criminal possession of a dangerous weapon in the first degree when he possesses any explosive substance with intent to use the same unlawfully against the person or property of another.

Criminal possession of a weapon in the first degree is a class B felony.

Added by L. 1974, Ch. 1041.

ANNOTATIONS

Explosive substance.—Shotgun shells do not qualify as an explosive substance under this section. People v. Crute, 236 A.D.2d 208, 653 N.Y.S.2d 549 (1st Dept. 1997).

—A "molotov cocktail" is an incendiary device designed to start a fire without the instantaneous lethal percussion aspects of an explosive. People v. McCrawford, 47 A.D.2d 318, 366 N.Y.S.2d 424 (1st Dept. 1975).

Lesser included offense.—Criminal possession of a dangerous weapon in the first degree is not a lesser included offense of first degree robbery and, as such, a plea cannot be entered to criminal possession of a dangerous weapon to satisfy a charge of robbery in the first degree. People v. Crute, 236 A.D.2d 208, 653 N.Y.S.2d 549 (1st Dept. 1997).

Temporary innocent possession of a weapon.—Where there was a factual issue for jury as to whether defendant's possession of weapon was innocent and temporary, despite defendant's claim that he never had sufficient control over gun to fire it. Charge on temporary, innocent possession as a defense should have been given even in the absence of a request to charge, People v. Pendergraft, 50 A.D.2d 531, 374 N.Y.S.2d 669 (1st Dept. 1975).

—Reversible error to deny a requested defense charge that temporary innocent possession of a weapon is not criminally proscribed. People v. Reagan, 49 A.D.2d 931, 374 N.Y.S.2d 33 (2d Dept. 1975).

§ 265.05. Unlawful possession of weapons by persons under sixteen.

It shall be unlawful for any person under the age of sixteen to possess any air-gun, spring-gun or other instrument or weapon in which the propelling force is a spring or air, or any gun or any instrument or weapon in or upon which any loaded or blank cartridges may be used, or any loaded or blank cartridges or ammunition therefor, or any dangerous knife; provided that the possession of rifle or shotgun or ammunition therefor by the holder of a hunting license or permit issued pursuant to article eleven of the environmental conservation law and used in accordance with said law shall not be governed by this section.

A person who violates the provisions of this section shall be adjudged a juvenile delinquent.

Added by L. 1974, Ch. 1041; **Amended** by L. 1985, Ch. 56.

ANNOTATIONS

Constitutionality.—PL § 265.05 is unconstitutional because "dangerous knife" is not sufficiently defined and therefore vague and the statute does not require unlawful intent. *In re* Alicia P., 112 Misc. 2d 326, 446 N.Y.S.2d 1009 (Fam. Ct. N.Y. Co. 1982). *In re* Thomas A. F., 85 Misc. 2d 791, 381 N.Y.S.2d 392 (Fam. Ct. Dutchess Co.).

Dangerous instrument.—Where defendant and co-defendant were convicted of robbery in the first degree based upon the display of a dangerous instrument, a knife, by the co-defendant, defendant could also be convicted for criminal use of a firearm in the first degree based upon the toy pistol he displayed during the robbery. People v. Leiva, 63 N.Y.2d 288, 481 N.Y.S.2d 664, 471 N.E.2d 436 (1984).

Evidence.—A straight razor/box-cutter is a dangerous knife within the meaning of section 265.05, and evidence that defendant possessed a box-cutter on school premises was sufficient to support a violation of this section. *In re* Gilberto A., 237 A.D.2d 285, 654 N.Y.S.2d 400 (2d Dept. 1997).

§ 265.06. Unlawful possession of a weapon upon school grounds.

It shall be unlawful for any person age sixteen or older to knowingly possess any air-gun, spring-gun or other instrument or weapon in which the propelling force is a spring, air, piston or CO_2 cartridge in or upon a building or grounds, used for educational purposes, of any school, college or university, without the written authorization of such educational institution. Unlawful possession of a weapon upon school grounds is a violation.

Added by L. 1994, Ch. 268, § 1, eff. Sept. 1, 1994.

§ 265.08. Criminal use of a firearm in the second degree.

A person is guilty of criminal use of a firearm in the second degree when he commits any class C violent felony offense as defined in paragraph (b) of subdivision one of section 70.02 and he either:

(1) possesses a deadly weapon, if the weapon is a loaded weapon from which a shot, readily capable of producing death or other serious injury may be discharged; or

(2) displays what appears to be a pistol, revolver, rifle, shotgun, machine gun or other firearm.

Criminal use of a firearm in the second degree is a class C felony.

Added by L. 1980, Ch. 233.

§ 265.09. Criminal use of a firearm in the first degree.

(1) A person is guilty of criminal use of a firearm in the first degree when he commits any class B violent felony offense as defined in paragraph (a) of subdivision one of section 70.02 and he either:

(a) possesses a deadly weapon, if the weapon is a loaded weapon from which a shot, readily capable of producing death or other serious injury may be discharged; or

(b) displays what appears to be a pistol, revolver, rifle, shotgun, machine gun or other firearm.

Criminal use of a firearm in the first degree is a class B felony.

(2) Sentencing. Notwithstanding any other provision of law to the contrary, when a person is convicted of criminal use of a firearm in the first degree as defined in subdivision one of this section, the court shall impose an additional consecutive sentence of five years to the minimum term of an indeterminate sentence imposed on the underlying class B violent felony offense where the person convicted of such crime displays a loaded weapon from which a shot, readily capable of producing death or other serious injury may be discharged, in furtherance of the commission of such crime, provided, however, that such additional sentence shall not be imposed if the court, having regard to the nature and circumstances of the crime and to the history and character of the defendant, finds on the record that such additional consecutive sentence would be unduly harsh and that not imposing such sentence would be consistent with the public safety and would not deprecate the seriousness of the crime. Notwithstanding any other provision of law to the contrary, the aggregate of the five year consecutive term imposed pursuant to this subdivision and the minimum term of the indeterminate sentence imposed on the underlying class b violent felony shall constitute the new aggregate minimum term of imprisonment, and a person subject to such term shall be required to serve the entire aggregate minimum term and shall not be eligible for release on parole or conditional release during such term. This subdivision shall not apply where the defendant's criminal liability for displaying a loaded weapon from which a shot, readily capable of producing death or other serious injury may be discharged, in furtherance of the commission of crime is based on the conduct of another pursuant to section 20.00 of the penal law.

Added by L. 1980, Ch. 233; **Amended** by L. 1996, Ch. 650, § 1, eff. Nov. 1, 1996.

ANNOTATION

Toy pistol.—Where defendant and co-defendant were convicted of robbery in the first degree based upon the display of a dangerous instrument, a knife, by the co-defendant, defendant could also be convicted for criminal use of a firearm in the first degree based upon the toy pistol he displayed during the robbery. People v. Leiva, 63 N.Y.2d 288, 481 N.Y.S.2d 664, 471 N.E.2d 436 (1984).

§ 265.10. Manufacture, transport, disposition and defacement of weapons and dangerous instruments and appliances.

1. Any person who manufactures or causes to be manufactured any machine-gun, assault weapon, large capacity ammunition feeding device or disguised gun is guilty of a class D felony. Any person who manufactures or causes to be manufactured any switchblade knife, gravity knife, pilum ballistic knife, metal knuckle knife, billy, blackjack, bludgeon, metal knuckles, Kung Fu star, chuka stick, sandbag, sandclub or slungshot is guilty of a class A misdemeanor.

2. Any person who transports or ships any machine-gun, firearm silencer, assault weapon or large capacity ammunition feeding device or disguised gun, or who transports or ships as merchandise five or more firearms, is guilty of a class D felony. Any person who transports or ships as merchandise any firearm, other than an assault weapon, switchblade knife, gravity knife, pilum ballistic knife, billy, blackjack, bludgeon, metal knuckles, Kung Fu star, chuka stick, sandbag or slungshot is guilty of a class A misdemeanor.

3. Any person who disposes of any machine-gun, assault weapon, large capacity ammunition feeding device or firearm silencer is guilty of a class D felony. Any person who knowingly buys, receives, disposes of, or conceals a machine-gun, firearm, large capacity ammunition feeding device, rifle or shotgun which has been defaced for the purpose of concealment or prevention of the detection of a crime or misrepresenting the identity of such machine-gun, firearm, large capacity ammunition feeding device, rifle or shotgun is guilty of a class D felony.

4. Any person who disposes of any of the weapons, instruments or appliances specified in subdivision one of section 265.01, except a firearm, is guilty of a class A misdemeanor, and he is guilty of a class D felony if he has previously been convicted of any crime.

5. Any person who disposes of any of the weapons, instruments, appliances or substances specified in section 265.05 to any other person under the age of sixteen years is guilty of a class A misdemeanor.

6. Any person who wilfully defaces any machine-gun, large capacity ammunition feeding device or firearm is guilty of a class D felony.

7. Any person, other than a wholesale dealer, or gunsmith or dealer in firearms duly licensed pursuant to section 400.00, lawfully in possession of a firearm, who disposes of the same without first notifying in writing the licensing officer in the city of New York and counties of Nassau and Suffolk and elsewhere in the state the executive department, division of state police, Albany, is guilty of a class A misdemeanor.

Amended by L. 1974, Chs. 179, 1041; L. 1978, Ch. 3; L. 1980, Ch. 233; L. 1985, Ch. 61; L. 1986, Ch. 328; L. 1987, Ch. 695; L. 1991, Ch. 174, amending subd. (2), eff. Nov. 1, 1991; L. 1995, Ch. 219, § 4, amending subd. (1), eff. Nov. 1, 1995; L. 1998, Ch. 378, § 5, eff. Nov. 1, 1998; L. 2000, Ch. 189, § 12, eff. Nov. 1, 2000.

ANNOTATIONS

Constitutionality; allegation of vagueness.—Penal Law §§ 1897(4) and 1898(5) were not unconstitutional on the grounds of vagueness. They contained a clear expression of the Legislature's intent and must be interpreted to effect that intent. People v. Nieke, 56 Misc. 2d 363, 289 N.Y.S.2d 448 (App. Term 2d Dept. 1967).

Defacing firearm; insufficiency of evidence.—Where defendant was charged with defacing a firearm, the court had insufficient reason to hold the defendant on this charge, since there was no evidence that he had defaced the manufacturer's serial number. People v. Caffrey, 73 Misc. 2d 504, 342 N.Y.S.2d 754 (Crim. Ct. N.Y. Co. 1973).

Inclusory counts.—Defendant's conviction for criminal possession of a weapon in the fourth degree had to be reversed where it was an inclusory concurrent count of PL § 265.10. People v. Richburg, 81 A.D.2d 926, 439 N.Y.S.2d 178 (2d Dept. 1981).

Possession of dangerous weapon; taxicab is "place of business."—Although the evidence warranted holding the matter for trial, charge of possession of firearm found in defendant's cab could be reduced to a misdemeanor, since the cab constituted a "place of business" and was therefore an exception to the statute concerning possession of weapons. People v. Anderson, 74 Misc. 2d 415, 344 N.Y.S.2d 15 (Crim. Ct. Bronx Co. 1973).

Statutory exemptions from charge of possession of dangerous weapon.—Although not within the obvious intent of the legislature, under statutory law a police officer has immunity from prosecution for possession of weapons (including firearms), for unauthorized manufacture of such weapons, for defacing of weapons, and for possession and use of unauthorized weapons. People v. Desthers, 73 Misc. 2d 1085, 343 N.Y.S.2d 887 (Crim. Ct. N.Y. Co. 1973).

Sufficiency of the evidence.—Where defendant directed the informant and undercover officers to the residence of a third party who handed over a brown paper bag containing four handguns, and, upon returning to defendant's residence, the officers at defendant's direction put the money on a table and the informant handed it to the defendant, there was sufficient evidence for the jury to find that defendant was guilty beyond a reasonable doubt of unlawfully disposing of the weapons. People v. Pray, 71 A.D.2d 763, 419 N.Y.S.2d 333 (3d Dept. 1979).

§ 265.11. Criminal sale of a firearm in the third degree.

A person is guilty of criminal sale of a firearm in the third degree when he is not authorized pursuant to law to possess a firearm and he unlawfully either:

(1) sells, exchanges, gives or disposes of a firearm or large capacity ammunition feeding device to another person; or

(2) possesses a firearm with the intent to sell it.

Criminal sale of a firearm in the third degree is a class D felony.

Added by L. 1980, Ch. 233; Amended by L. 1991, Ch. 496, amending section to "third" degree, eff. Nov. 1, 1991; L. 1995, Ch. 310, § 1, eff. Nov. 1, 1995; L. 1998, Ch. 654, eff. Nov. 1, 1999, changing felony designation from E to D; L. 2000, Ch. 189, § 13, eff. Nov. 1, 2000, amending subd. 1.

§ 265.12. Criminal sale of a firearm in the second degree.

A person is guilty of criminal sale of a firearm in the second degree when he unlawfully sells, exchanges, gives or disposes of to another ten or more firearms.

Criminal sale of a firearm in the second degree is a class C felony.

Added by L. 1980, Ch. 233; **Amended** by L. 1991, Ch. 496, eff. Nov. 1, 1991, amending section to read "second" degree; L. 1998, Ch. 654, eff. Nov. 1, 1999, changing felony designation from D to C.

ANNOTATIONS

Sufficiency of evidence.—Aggregation of different sales to same buyer are not permitted to meet statutory thresholds of "20 or more firearms" (Penal Law § 265.13) or "10 or more firearms" (Penal Law § 265.12). People v. Brown, 99 N.Y.2d 488, 758 N.Y.S.2d 602, 788 N.E.2d 1030 (2003).

§ 265.13. Criminal sale of a firearm in the first degree.

A person is guilty of a criminal sale of a firearm in the first degree when he unlawfully sells, exchanges, gives or disposes of to another twenty or more firearms.

Criminal sale of a firearm in the first degree is a class B felony.

Added by L. 1991, Ch 496, eff. Nov. 1, 1991; **Amended** by L. 1998, Ch. 654, eff. Nov. 1, 1999, changing felony designation from C to B.

ANNOTATION

Sufficiency of evidence.—Aggregation of different sales to same buyer are not permitted to meet statutory thresholds of "20 or more firearms" (Penal Law § 265.13) or "10 or more firearms" (Penal Law § 265.12). People v. Brown, 99 N.Y.2d 488, 758 N.Y.S.2d 602, 788 N.E.2d 1030 (2003).

§ 265.14. Criminal sale of a firearm with the aid of a minor.

A person over the age of eighteen years of age is guilty of criminal sale of a weapon with the aid of a minor when a person under sixteen years of age knowingly and unlawfully sells, exchanges, gives or disposes of a firearm in violation of this article, and such person over the age of eighteen years of age, acting with the mental culpability required for the commission thereof, solicits, requests, commands, importunes or intentionally aids such person under sixteen years of age to engage in such conduct.

Criminal sale of a firearm with the aid of a minor is a class C felony.

Added by L. 1991, Ch. 175, eff. Nov. 1, 1991; **Amended** by L. 1998, Ch. 654, eff. Nov. 1, 1999, changing felony designation from D to C.

§ 265.15. Presumptions of possession, unlawful intent and defacement.

1. The presence in any room, dwelling, structure or vehicle of any machine-gun is presumptive evidence of its unlawful possession by all persons occupying the place where such machine-gun is found.

2. The presence in any stolen vehicle of any weapon, instrument, appliance or substance specified in sections 265.01, 265.02, 265.03, 265.04 and 265.05 is presumptive evidence of its possession by all persons occupying such vehicle at the time such weapon, instrument, appliance or substance is found.

3. The presence in an automobile, other than a stolen one or a public omnibus, of any firearm, large capacity ammunition feeding device, defaced firearm, defaced rifle or shotgun, defaced large capacity ammunition feeding device, firearm silencer, explosive or incendiary bomb, bombshell, gravity knife, switchblade knife, pilum ballistic knife, metal knuckle knife, dagger, dirk, stiletto, billy, blackjack, metal knuckles, chuka stick, sandbag, sandclub or slungshot is presumptive evidence of its possession by all persons occupying such automobile at the time such weapon, instrument or appliance is found, except under the following circumstances: (a) if such weapon, instrument or appliance is found upon the person of one of the occupants therein; (b) if such weapon, instrument or appliance is found in an automobile which is being operated for hire by a duly licensed driver in the due, lawful and proper pursuit of his or her trade, then such presumption shall not apply to the driver; or (c) if the weapon so found is a pistol or revolver and one of the occupants, not present under duress, has in his or her possession a valid license to have and carry concealed the same.

4. The possession by any person of the substance as specified in section 265.04 is presumptive evidence of possessing such substance with intent to use the same unlawfully against the person or property of another if such person is not licensed or otherwise authorized to possess such substance. The possession by any person of any dagger, dirk, stiletto, dangerous knife or any other weapon, instrument, appliance or substance designed, made or adapted for use primarily as a weapon, is presumptive evidence of intent to use the same unlawfully against another.

5. The possession by any person of a defaced machine-gun, firearm, rifle or shotgun is presumptive evidence that such person defaced the same.

6. The possession of five or more firearms by any person is presumptive evidence that such person possessed the firearms with the intent to sell same.

Amended by L. 1970, Chs. 1012, 1022; L. 1974, Chs. 179, 1041; L. 1980, Ch. 233; L. 1986, Ch. 328; L. 1987 Ch. 695; L. 1995, Ch. 219, § 5, amending subd. 3, eff. Nov. 1, 1995; L. 2000, Ch. 189, § 14, amending subd. 3, eff. Nov. 1, 2000.

ANNOTATIONS

Proof; intent inferable.—Defendant's guilt of criminal possession of a weapon in the second and third degrees was proven beyond a reasonable doubt. Under PL § 265.15(4), defendant's possession of the gun was presumptive evidence of his intent to use it "unlawfully against another"; the requisite intent was inferable from the evidence that defendant removed the gun from his car, pulled back the slide which would chamber a round, and pointed it at someone in the crowd. People were not required to prove that the gun was loaded. People v. Toribio, 216 A.D.2d 189, 629 N.Y.S.2d 210 (1st Dept. 1995).

—Evidence of defendant's possession of an unlicensed loaded firearm entitled jury to presume that defendant intended to use it unlawfully. People v. Topsy, 265 A.D.2d 353, 696 N.Y.S.2d 47 (2d Dept. 1999).

Actual possession; effect on operation of presumption.— Presumption contained in subd. 3 was improperly charged where undisputed evidence showed weapon in question was observed in the *actual* possession of a person other than defendant just prior to defendant's apprehension. People v. Scott, 53 A.D.2d 703, 384 N.Y.S.2d 878 (2d Dept. 1976).

Charge.—It was reversible error for the judge to charge the jury that possession of a weapon, was presumptive evidence of intent to use the weapon and the judge failed to inform the jury that it could reject the presumption even if no defense evidence was presented. People v. Knox, 87 A.D.2d 504, 447 N.Y.S.2d 477 (1st Dept. 1982).

—Reversal was required when the court instructed the jury that the defendant "must come forward and give an explanation that satisfies the jury" since the charge improperly shifted the burden of proof to the defendant. People v. Jones, 57 A.D.2d 595, 393 N.Y.S.2d 606 (2d Dept. 1977).

Charge; stolen vehicle.—Trial court's charge on presumption of possession by all persons occupying a stolen vehicle may have been misleading because it failed to include instructions that such presumption was rebuttable, after defense counsel has asked the court to explain "presumptive evidence," and accordingly convictions for weapon possession were reversed and counts dismissed. People v. Baldwin, 53 A.D.2d 646, 384 N.Y.S.2d 847 (2d Dept. 1976).

—Reversal was required when the trial court's charge to the jury on the presumption of possession by all persons occupying a stolen vehicle of any weapon found therein failed to include instructions that the presumption was rebuttable, despite defense counsel's request to explain the meaning of "presumptive evidence." People v. Jackson, 52 A.D.2d 630, 382 N.Y.S.2d 358.

Chauffeur; presumption does not apply.—The presumption of possession does not apply to a licensed chauffeur acting in that capacity even though at the time of his arrest his license had been temporarily suspended. People v. Allison, 117 Misc. 2d 463, 458 N.Y.S.2d 496 (Sup. Ct. N.Y. Co. 1983).

Defacing firearm; insufficiency of evidence.—Where defendant was charged with defacing a firearm, since there was no evidence that he had defaced the manufacturer's serial number, the court had insufficient reason to hold defendant on this charge. People v. Caffrey, 73 Misc. 2d 504, 342 N.Y.S.2d 754 (Crim. Ct. N.Y. Co. 1973).

Illegal seizure of evidence.—Since the first gun was observed to be in the passenger's possession before he placed it under the seat, no presumption of possession was chargeable to the driver. As for the second gun, once the arrested men were outside the car and handcuffed, there was no reasonable basis for any apprehension on the part of the arresting officers of any danger to themselves or of any threat of destruction of any contraband (both or either of which would have justified a search of the car). While it may be that these apprehensions arose when the arrested men were placed back into the driver's car, their availability as bases for the search was attributable to the unnecessary action taken by the police in commandeering the car. Accordingly, they could not be utilized to justify the seizure of the second gun. People v. Garcia, 41 A.D.2d 560, 340 N.Y.S.2d 35 (2d Dept. 1973).

Instructions.—Defendant's motion to dismiss the Grand Jury proceeding as defective was granted where the District Attorney had failed to instruct the Grand Jury concerning the permissible nature of the presumption from the presence of a weapon in an automobile to possession by all occupants. People v. Garcia, 103 Misc. 2d 915, 427 N.Y.S.2d 360 (Sup. Ct. Bronx Co. 1980).

Possession of rifle and shotgun; erroneous jury instruction.—Where defendant was charged with possession of a shotgun and rifle found in his dwelling house, and the evidence clearly showed the weapons belonged to his wife and son, and

there was no evidence that the defendant ever possessed or handled them, it was improper for the court to instruct the jury that if they found that "the defendant had immediate control and reach of the weapons . . . which were within his immediate reach and control . . . and that the weapons were available to the defendant . . . your verdict should be guilty." People v. Law, 31 A.D.2d 554, 294 N.Y.S.2d 394 (3d Dept. 1968).

Presumption.—Possession of an unlicensed firearm is presumptive evidence of intent to use it unlawfully against another; requisite intent was inferred from evidence defendant who waved gun and pointed it at complainant. People v. Gibbs, 254 A.D.2d 209, 681 N.Y.S.2d 10 (1st Dept. 1998).

—Court properly charged statutory automobile presumption where defendant was the only passenger in a taxicab, seated in the rear next to a shopping bag where the gun was located, and defendant's holster and ammunition were in plain view when police stopped cab for traffic violation. People v. Hwi Jin An, 253 A.D.2d 657, 679 N.Y.S.2d 94 (1st Dept. 1998).

—Statutory presumption contained in P.L. § 256.15(4) entitled jury to infer from defendant's possession of a loaded firearm in his waistband that it was his intent to unlawfully use firearm against another person. Although this presumption is rebuttable, it was not negated by the evidence in this case. People v. Walcott, 235 A.D.2d 368, 653 N.Y.S.2d 323 (1st Dept. 1997).

—The presumption created by PL § 265.15(3), with reference to the presence in an automobile of a firearm, is presumptive evidence of its possession by all persons occupying the automobile and is clearly a rebuttable one and the jury has the right to treat each defendant separately and to weigh the evidence concerning each defendant in order to determine the guilt or innocence of each. People v. Jenkins, 47 A.D.2d 735, 365 N.Y.S.2d 540 (1st Dept. 1975).

—It was error for court to have found defendant guilty of attempted possession of a weapon in the third degree based upon the presumptions found in Penal Law § 265.15(3). People v. Thompson, 239 A.D.2d 529, 658 N.Y.S.2d 350 (2d Dept. 1997).

Presumption inapplicable where chain of occupancy broken.—The statutory presumption in PL § 265.15 operates only against a person occupying an automobile *at the time the weapon is found;* therefore, where the suspect automobile was left unlocked and unattended after defendant was taken to the station house until police, having procured a computer printout, discovered the gun while checking the vehicle identification number, the chain of occupancy was broken and the presumption was held not to apply. People v. Astor, 98 Misc. 2d 1084, 415 N.Y.S.2d 354 (Sup. Ct. Bronx Co. 1979).

Rebuttable presumption; jury instruction must not override presumption of innocence.—Jury was instructed that a weapon found in the stolen vehicle with defendant was presumptive evidence that it was in the possession of all the occupants of the vehicle, and the court failed to explain that the presumption is permissive and may be disregarded by the jury. The improper instruction required a reversal of conviction because the jury may have incorrectly assumed that the presumption was conclusive and that it overrode the presumption of defendant's innocence. People v. Williams, 94 A.D.2d 255, 464 N.Y.S.2d 525 (2d Dept. 1983).

Statutory exemptions from charge of possession of dangerous weapon.—Although not within the obvious intent of the legislature, under statutory law a police officer has immunity from prosecution for possession of weapons (including firearms), for unauthorized manufacture of such weapons, for defacing of weapons, and for possession and use of unauthorized weapons. People v. Desthers, 73 Misc. 2d 1085, 343 N.Y.S.2d 887 (Crim. Ct. N.Y. Co. 1973).

Weapon found in area occupied by several people; access.—If the driver would testify that he was at all times the owner and in possession of the revolver, such testimony would serve to rebut the presumption that defendant and the other occupants of the car likewise possessed the weapon found in the automobile. People v. Kitt, 50 A.D.2d 757, 376 N.Y.S.2d 530 (1st Dept. 1975).

—Defendant's knowledge of the gun's whereabouts and his willingness to direct the police to its location did not constitute dominion and control since they merely indicated access; access was not sufficient for a finding of guilt in view of the evidence that other adults were present in the house, many of whom could have possessed the same knowledge but none of whom were asked. People v. Vastola, 70 A.D.2d 918, 417 N.Y.S.2d 287 (2d Dept. 1979).

—The statutory presumption could not be invoked where the undisputed evidence indicated that another person in the car had personally possessed the weapon and had concealed it below the rear seat moments before the arrest of the occupants of the vehicle by the police officer. People v. Lester, 61 A.D.2d 844, 402 N.Y.S.2d 220 (2d Dept. 1978).

Weapon in auto; presumption valid.—The presumption was valid against all the occupants of the car even though the gun was found in a woman's purse and there was only one woman in the car with three males. People v. Lemmons, 40 N.Y.2d 505, 387 N.Y.S.2d 97, 354 N.E.2d 836 (1976). *See also* People v. Williams, 93 Misc. 2d 93, 402 N.Y.S.2d 289 (Sup. Ct. N.Y. Co. 1978); People v. Joseph, 93 Misc. 2d 267, 402 N.Y.S.2d 751 (Sup. Ct. N.Y. Co. 1978).

—Since the defendant did not present clear-cut evidence that the passenger in the rear was in exclusive possession of the shotgun, the court correctly charged the automobile presumption. People v. Williams, 171 A.D.2d 551, 567 N.Y.S.2d 263 (1st Dept. 1991).

—Statute providing for presumption that persons riding in a vehicle are possessors of an illegal weapon found therein is not unconstitutional. People v. Rodriguez, 75 A.D.2d 730, 427 N.Y.S.2d 418 (1st Dept. 1980).

—The presumption was valid against defendant, a passenger, where he was observed fleeing from the car and where a gun was found in the car immediately afterward; before any person who had not been an occupant of the car could have placed it there. People v. Hunter, 82 A.D.2d 893, 440 N.Y.S.2d 287 (2d Dept. 1981), *aff'd,* 55 N.Y.2d 930, 449 N.Y.S.2d 191, 434 N.E.2d 260 (1981).

—Although the court erred in charging the jury as to the presumption of possession, it was harmless error where the evidence of guilt was overwhelming. People v. Mace, 91 A.D.2d 864, 458 N.Y.S.2d 379 (4th Dept. 1982).

Statutory presumption of possession not applicable to bread knife and starter's pistol.—Trial court erred in charging jury that defendant was presumed to have had possession of bread knife and a starter's pistol which were found in the automobile in which he was an occupant; defendant's actual possession of the bread knife and starter's pistol was not proved and they are not within the category of weapons to which the statutory presumption applies. People v. Brown, 37 A.D.2d 623, 323 N.E.2d 537 (2d Dept. 1971).

§ 265.16. Criminal sale of firearm to a minor.

A person is guilty of criminal sale of a firearm to a minor when he is not authorized pursuant to law to possess a firearm and he unlawfully sells, exchanges, gives or disposes of a firearm to another person who is or reasonably appears to be less than nineteen years of age who is not licensed pursuant to law to possess a firearm.

Criminal sale of a firearm to a minor is a class C felony.

Amended by L. 1998, Ch. 654, eff. Nov. 1, 1999, changing felony designation from D to C.

§ 265.17. Criminal purchase of a weapon.

A person is guilty of criminal purchase of a weapon when:

1. Knowing that he or she is prohibited by law from possessing a firearm, rifle or shotgun because of a prior conviction or because of some other disability which would render him or her ineligible to lawfully possess a firearm, rifle or shotgun in this state, such person attempts to purchase a firearm, rifle or shotgun from another person; or

2. Knowing that it would be unlawful for another person to possess a firearm, rifle or shotgun, he or she purchases a firearm, rifle or shotgun for, on behalf of, or for the use of such other person.

Criminal purchase of a weapon is a class A misdemeanor.

Added by L. 2000, Ch. 189, § 14-a, eff. Nov. 1, 2000.

§ 265.20. Exemptions.

a. Sections 265.01, 265.02, 265.03, 265.04, 265.05, 265.10, 265.11, 265.12, 265.13, 265.15 and 270.05 shall not apply to:

1. Possession of any of the weapons, instruments, appliances or substances specified in sections 265.01, 265.02, 265.03, 265.04, 265.05 and 270.05 by the following:

(a) Persons in the military service of the state of New York when duly authorized by regulations issued by the adjutant general to possess the same.

(b) Police officers as defined in subdivision thirty-four of section 1.20 of the criminal procedure law.

(c) Peace officers as defined by section 2.10 of the criminal procedure law.

(d) Persons in the military or other service of the United States, in pursuit of official duty or when duly authorized by federal law, regulation or order to possess the same.

(e) Persons employed in fulfilling defense contracts with the government of the United States or agencies thereof when possession of the same is necessary for manufacture, transport, installation and testing under the requirements of such contract.

(f) A person voluntarily surrendering such weapon, instrument, appliance or substance, provided that such surrender shall be made to the superintendent of the division of state police or a member thereof designated by such superintendent, or to the sheriff of the county in which such person resides, or in the county of Nassau or in the towns of Babylon, Brookhaven, Huntington, Islip and Smithtown in the county of Suffolk to the commissioner of police or a member of the police department thereof designated by such commissioner, or if such person resides in a city, town other than one named in this subparagraph, or village to the police commissioner or head of the police force or department thereof or to a member of the force or department designated by such commissioner or head; and provided, further, that the same shall be surrendered by such person in accordance with such terms and conditions as may be established by such superintendent, sheriff, police force or department. Nothing in this paragraph shall be construed as granting immunity from prosecution for any crime or offense except that of unlawful possession of such weapons, instruments, appliances or substances surrendered as herein provided. A person who possesses any such weapon, instrument, appliance or substance as an executor or administrator or any other lawful possessor of such property of a decedent may continue to possess such property for a period not over fifteen days. If such property is not lawfully disposed of within such period the possessor shall deliver it to an appropriate official described in this paragraph or such property may be delivered to the superintendent of state police. Such officer shall hold it and shall thereafter deliver it on the written request of such executor, administrator or other lawful possessor of such property to a named person, provided such named person is licensed to or is otherwise lawfully permitted to possess the same. If no request to deliver the property is received by such official within two years of the delivery of such property, such official shall dispose of it in accordance with the provisions of section 400.05 of this chapter.

2. Possession of a machine-gun, large capacity ammunition feeding device, firearm, switchblade knife, gravity knife, pilum ballistic knife, billy or blackjack by a warden, superintendent, headkeeper or deputy of a state prison, penitentiary, workhouse, county jail or other institution for the detention of persons convicted or accused of crime or detained as witnesses in criminal cases, in pursuit of official duty or when duly authorized by regulation or order to possess the same.

3. Possession of a pistol or revolver by a person to whom a license therefor has been issued as provided under section 400.00 or 400.01 of this chapter; provided, that such a license shall not preclude a conviction for the offense defined in subdivision three of section 265.01 of this article.

4. Possession of a rifle, shotgun or longbow for use while hunting, trapping or fishing, by a person, not a citizen of the United States, carrying a valid license issued pursuant to Section 11-0713 of the environmental conservation law.

5. Possession of a rifle or shotgun by a person who has been convicted as specified in subdivision four of Section 265.01 to whom a certificate of good conduct has been issued pursuant to section seven hundred three-b of the correction law.

6. Possession of a switchblade or gravity knife for use while hunting, trapping or fishing by a person carrying a valid license issued to him pursuant to Section 11-0713 of the environmental conservation law.

7. Possession, at an indoor or outdoor shooting range for the purpose of loading and firing, of a rifle or shotgun, the propelling force of which is gunpowder by a person under sixteen years of age but not under twelve, under the immediate supervision, guidance and instruction of (a) a duly commissioned officer of the United States army, navy, air force, marine corps or coast guard, or of the national guard of the state of New York; or (b) a duly qualified adult citizen of the United States who has been granted a certificate as an instructor in small arms practice issued by the United States army, navy, air force or marine corps, or by the adjutant general of this state, or by the national rifle association of America, a not-for-profit corporation duly organized under the laws of this state; or (c) a parent, guardian, or a person over the age of eighteen designated in writing by such parent or guardian who shall have a certificate of qualification in responsible hunting, including safety, ethics, and landowner relations-hunter relations, issued or honored by the department of environmental conservation; or (d) an agent of the department of environmental conservation appointed to conduct courses in responsible hunting practices pursuant to article eleven of the environmental conservation law.

7-a. Possession and use, at an indoor or outdoor pistol range located in or on premises owned or occupied by a duly incorporated organization organized for conservation purposes or to foster proficiency in small arms or at a target pistol shooting competition under the auspices of or approved by the national rifle association for the purpose of loading and firing the same, by a person duly licensed to possess a pistol or revolver pursuant to section 400.00 or 400.01 of this chapter of a pistol or revolver duly so licensed to another person who is present at the time.

7-b. Possession and use, at an indoor or outdoor pistol range located in or on premises owned or occupied by a duly incorporated organization organized for conservation purposes or to foster proficiency in small arms or at a target pistol shooting competition under the auspices of or approved by the national rifle association for the purpose of loading and firing the same, by a person who has applied for a license to possess a pistol or revolver and pre-license possession of same pursuant to section 400.00 or 400.01 of this chapter, who has not been previously denied a license, been previously convicted of a felony or serious offense, and who does not appear to be, or pose a threat to be, a danger to himself or to others, and who has been approved for possession and use herein in accordance with section 400.00 or 400.01 of this chapter; provided however, that such possession shall be of a pistol or revolver duly licensed to and shall be used under the supervision, guidance and instruction of, a person specified in paragraph seven of this subdivision and provided further that such possession and use be within the jurisdiction of the licensing officer with whom the person has made application therefor or within the jurisdiction of the superintendent of state police in the case of a retired sworn member of the division of state police who has made an application pursuant to section 400.01 of this chapter.

7-c. Possession for the purpose of loading and firing, of a rifle, pistol or shotgun, the propelling force of which may be either air, compressed gas or springs, by a person under sixteen years of age but not under twelve, under the immediate supervision, guidance and instruc-tion of (a) a duly commissioned officer of the united states army, navy, marine corps or coast guard, or of the national guard of the State of New York; or (b) a duly qualified adult citizen of the United States who has been granted a certificate as an instructor in small arms practice issued by the United States army, navy or marine corps, or by the adjutant general of this state, or by the national rifle association of America, a not-for-profit corporation duly organized under the laws of this state; or (c) a parent, guardian, or a person over the age of eighteen designated in writing by such parent or guardian who shall have a certificate of qualification in responsible hunting, including safety, ethics, and landowner relations-hunter relations, issued or honored by the department of environmental conservation.

7-d. Possession, at an indoor or outdoor shooting range for the purpose of loading and firing, of a rifle, pistol or shotgun, the propelling force of which may be either air, compressed gas or springs, by a person under twelve years of age, under the immediate supervision, guidance and instruction of (a) a duly commissioned officer of the United States army, navy, marine corps or coast guard, or of the national guard of the State of New York; or (b) a duly qualified adult citizen of the united states who has been granted a certificate as an instructor in small arms practice issued by the United States army, navy or marine corps, or by the adjutant general of this state, or by the national rifle association of America, a not-for-profit corporation duly organized under the laws of this state; or (c) a parent, guardian, or a person over the age of eighteen designated in writing by such parent or guardian who shall have a certificate of qualification in responsible hunting, including safety, ethics, and landowner relations-hunter relations, issued or honored by the department of environmental conservation.

7-e. Possession and use of a pistol or revolver, at an indoor or outdoor pistol range located in or on premises owned or occupied by a duly incorporated organization organized for conservation purposes or to foster proficiency in small arms or at a target pistol shooting competition under the auspices of or approved by an association or organization described in paragraph 7-a of this subdivision for the purpose of loading and firing the same by a person at least eighteen years of age but under the age of twenty-one who has not been previously convicted of a felony or serious offense, and who does not appear to be, or pose a threat to be, a danger to himself or to others; provided however, that such possession shall be of a pistol or revolver duly licensed to and shall be used under the immediate supervision, guidance and instruction of, a person specified in paragraph seven of this subdivision.

8. The manufacturer of machine-guns, assault weapons, large capacity ammunition feeding devices, disguised guns, pilum ballistic knives, switchblade or gravity knives, billies or blackjacks as merchandise and the disposal and shipment thereof direct to a regularly constituted or appointed state or municipal police department, sheriff, policeman or other peace officer, or to a state prison, penitentiary, workhouse, county jail or other institution for the detention of persons convicted or accused of crime or held as witnesses in criminal cases, or to the military service of this state or of the United States.

9. The regular and ordinary transport of firearms as merchandise, provided that the person transporting such firearms, where he knows or has reasonable means of ascertaining what he is transporting, notifies in writing the police commissioner, police chief or other law enforcement officer performing such functions at the place of delivery, of the name and address of the consignee and the place of delivery, and withholds delivery to the consignee for such reasonable period of time designated in writing by such police commissioner, police chief or other law enforcement officer as such official may deem necessary for investigation as to whether the consignee may lawfully receive and possess such firearms.

9-a.   a. Except as provided in subdivision b hereof, the regular and ordinary transport of pistols or revolvers by a manufacturer of firearms to whom a license as a dealer in firearms has been issued pursuant to section 400.00 of this chapter, or by an agent or employee of such manufacturer of firearms who is otherwise duly licensed to carry a pistol or revolver and who is duly authorized in writing by such manufacturer of firearms to transport pistols or revolvers on the date or dates specified, directly between places where the manufacturer of firearms regularly conducts business provided such pistols or revolvers are transported unloaded, in a locked opaque container. For purposes of this subdivision, places where the manufacturer of firearms regularly conducts business includes, but is not limited to places where the manufacturer of firearms regularly or customarily conducts development or design of pistols or revolvers, or regularly or customarily conducts tests on pistols or revolvers, or regularly or customarily participates in the exposition of firearms to the public.

b. The transportation of such pistols or revolvers into, out of or within the city of New York may be done only with the consent of the police commissioner of the city of New York. To obtain such consent, the manufacturer must notify the police commissioner in writing of the name and address of the transporting manufacturer, or agent or employee of the manufacturer who is authorized in writing by such manufacturer to transport pistols or revolvers, the number, make and model number of the firearms to be transported and the place where the manufacturer regularly conducts business within the city of New York and such other information as the commissioner may deem necessary. The manufacturer must not transport such pistols and revolvers between the designated places of business for such reasonable period of time designated in writing by the police commissioner as such official may deem necessary for investigation and to give consent. The police commissioner may not unreasonably withhold his consent.

10. Engaging in the business of gunsmith or dealer in firearms by a person to whom a valid license therefor has been issued pursuant to section 400.00.

11. Possession of a firearm or large capacity ammunition feeding device by a police officer or sworn peace officer of another state while conducting official business within the state of New York.

12. Possession of a pistol or revolver by a person who is a member or coach of an accredited college or university target pistol team while transporting the pistol or revolver into or through New York state to participate in a collegiate, Olympic or target pistol shooting competition under the auspices of or approved by the national rifle association, provided such pistol or revolver is unloaded and carried in a locked carrying case and the ammunition therefor is carried in a separate locked container.

13. Possession of pistols and revolvers by a person who is a nonresident of this state while attending or traveling to or from, an organized competitive pistol match or league competition under auspices of, or approved by, the National Rifle Association and in which he is a competitor, within forty-eight hours of such event or by a person who is a non-resident of the state while attending or traveling to or from an organized match sanctioned by the International Handgun Metallic Silhouette Association and in which he is a competitor, within forty-eight hours of such event, provided that he has not been previously convicted of a felony or a crime which, if committed in New York, would constitute a felony, and further provided that the pistols or revolvers are transported unloaded in a locked opaque container together with a copy of the match program, match schedule or match registration card. Such documentation shall constitute prima facie evidence of exemption, providing that such person also has in his possession a pistol license or firearms registration card issued in accordance with the laws of his place of residence. For purposes of this subdivision, a person licensed in a jurisdiction which does not authorize such license by a person who has been previously convicted of a felony shall be presumed to have no prior conviction. The superintendent of state police shall annually review the laws of jurisdictions within the United States and Canada with respect to the applicable requirements for licensing or registration of firearms and shall publish a list of those jurisdictions which prohibit possession of a firearm by a person previously convicted of a felony or crimes which if committed in New York state would constitute a felony.

13-a. Except in cities not wholly contained within a single county of the state, possession of pistols and revolvers by a person who is a nonresident of this state while attending or traveling to or from, an organized convention or exhibition for the display of or education about firearms, which is conducted under auspices of, or approved by, the National Rifle Association and in which he is a registered participant, within forty-eight hours of such event, provided that he has not been previously convicted of a felony or a crime which, if committed in New York, would constitute a felony, and further provided that the pistols or revolvers are transported unloaded in a locked opaque container together with a copy of the convention or exhibition program, convention or exhibition schedule or convention or exhibition registration card. Such documentation shall constitute prima facie evidence of exemption, providing that such person also has in his possession a pistol license or firearms registration card issued in accordance with the laws of his place of residence. For purposes of this paragraph, a person licensed in a jurisdiction which does not authorize such license by a person who has been previously convicted of a felony shall be presumed to have no prior conviction. The superintendent of state police shall annually review the laws of jurisdictions within the United States and Canada with respect to the applicable requirements for licensing or registration of firearms and shall publish a list of those jurisdictions which prohibit possession of a firearm by a person previously convicted of a felony or crimes which if committed in New York state would constitute a felony.

14. Possession in accordance with the provisions of this paragraph of a self-defense spray device as defined herein for the protection of a person or property and use of such self-defense spray device under circumstances which would justify the use of physical force pursuant to article thirty-five of this chapter.

(a) As used in this section "self-defense spray device" shall mean a pocket sized spray device which contains and releases a chemical or organic substance which is intended to produce temporary physical discomfort or disability through being vaporized or otherwise dispensed in the air or any like device containing tear gas, pepper or similar disabling agent.

(b) The exemption under this paragraph shall not apply to a person who:

(i) is less than eighteen years of age; or

(ii) has been previously convicted in this state of a felony or any assault; or

(iii) has been convicted of a crime outside the

State of New York which if committed in new york would constitute a felony or any assault crime.

(c) The department of health, with the cooperation of the division of criminal justice services and the superintendent of state police, shall develop standards and promulgate regulations regarding the type of self-defense spray device which may lawfully be purchased, possessed and used pursuant to this paragraph. The regulations shall include a requirement that every self-defense spray device which may be lawfully purchased, possessed or used pursuant to this paragraph have a label which states: "WARNING: The use of this substance or device for any purpose other than self-defense is a criminal offense under the law. The contents are dangerous – use with care. This device shall not be sold by anyone other than a licensed or authorized dealer. Possession of this device by any person under the age of eighteen or by anyone who has been convicted of a felony or assault is illegal. Violators may be prosecuted under the law."

15. Possession and sale of a self-defense spray device as defined in paragraph fourteen of this subdivision by a dealer in firearms licensed pursuant to section 400.00 of this chapter, a pharmacist licensed pursuant to article one hundred thirty-seven of the education law or by such other vendor as may be authorized and approved by the superintendent of state police.

(a) Every self-defense spray device shall be accompanied by an insert or inserts which include directions for use, first aid information, safety and storage information and which shall also contain a toll free telephone number for the purpose of allowing any purchaser to call and receive additional information regarding the availability of local courses in self-defense training and safety in the use of a self-defense spray device.

(b) Before delivering a self-defense spray device to any person, the licensed or authorized dealer shall require proof of age and a sworn statement on a form approved by the superintendent of state police that such person has not been convicted of a felony or any crime involving an assault. Such forms shall be forwarded to the division of state police at such intervals as directed by the superintendent of state police. Absent any such direction the forms shall be maintained on the premises of the vendor and shall be open at all reasonable hours for inspection by any peace officer or police officer, acting pursuant to his or her special duties. No more than two self-defense spray devices may be sold at any one time to a single purchaser.

16. The terms "rifle," "shotgun," "pistol," "revolver," and "firearm" as used in paragraphs three, four, five, seven, seven-a, seven-b, nine, nine-a, ten, twelve, thirteen and thirteen-a of this subdivision shall not include a disguised gun or an assault weapon.

b. Section 265.01 shall not apply to possession of that type of billy commonly known as a "police baton" which is twenty-four to twenty-six inches in length and no more than one and one-quarter inches in thickness by members of an auxiliary police force of a city with a population in excess of one million persons or the county of Suffolk when duly authorized by regulation or order issued by the police commissioner of such city or such county respectively. Such regulations shall require training in the use of the police baton including but not limited to the defensive use of the baton and instruction in the legal use of deadly physical force pursuant to article thirty-five of this chapter. Notwithstanding the provisions of this section or any other provision of law, possession of such baton shall not be authorized when used intentionally to strike another person except in those situations when the use of deadly physical force is authorized by such article thirty-five.

c. Sections 265.01, 265.10 and 265.15 shall not apply to possession of billies or blackjacks by persons:

1. while employed in fulfilling contracts with New York state, its agencies or political subdivisions for the purchase of billies or blackjacks; or

2. while employed in fulfilling contracts with sister states, their agencies or political subdivisions for the purchase of billies or blackjacks; or

3. while employed in fulfilling contracts with foreign countries, their agencies or political subdivisions for the purchase of billies or blackjacks as permitted under federal law.

Amended by L. 1967, Ch. 791; L. 1969, Chs. 341, 425, 674; L. 1970, Chs. 13, 233, 475; L. 1971, Chs. 435, 1097; L. 1974, Ch. 1041; L. 1976, Ch. 498; L. 1978, Ch. 10; L. 1979, Chs. 90, 667; L. 1980, Chs. 233, 843; L. 1981, Ch. 469; L. 1982, Ch. 733; L. 1983, Ch. 75; L. 1984, Chs. 262, 608; L. 1985, Chs. 189, 778; L. 1986, Chs. 328, 370; L. 1988, Chs. 141, 150, 442; L. 1991, Ch. 496, eff. Nov. 1, 1991; L. 1995, Ch. 376, § 1 amending subd. (a)(1)(f), eff. Aug. 2, 1995; L. 1995, Ch. 376, § 2, repealing subd. (b) and relettering (c) to (b), eff. Aug. 2, 1995; L. 1996, Ch. 354, § 3, adding subds. (a)14 and 15, eff. Nov. 1, 1996; L. 1996, Ch. 651, § 1, amending subd. (a)7, eff. Nov. 1, 1996; L. 1996, Ch. 651, § 2, adding subds. 7-c and 7-d, eff. Nov. 1, 1996; L. 1998, Ch. 180, § 1, eff. Jan. 1, 1999, and Ch. 378, §§ 6 and 7, eff. Nov. 1, 1998; L. 1999, Ch. 210, eff. Nov. 1, 1999, amending subds. a(3), a(7-a), and a(7-b); L. 2000, Ch.189, §§ 15–17, eff. Nov. 1, 2000, amending subds. a(2), a(8), a(11), and a(16), and adding a(7-e); L. 2003, Ch. 172, § 1, eff. July 22, 2003, adding subd. c.

ANNOTATIONS

Claim of statutory exemption not available.—Police Officer, who sold firearms to an undercover Police Officer, believing such undercover's possession to be illegal, was estopped from pleading the undercover's statutory exemption as a defense and was criminally liable for the undercover's possession on the theory of accessorial liability. People v. Coleman, 104 A.D.2d 780, 480 N.Y.S.2d 889 (1st Dept. 1984).

Informant's tip; lower standard of probable cause required.—Where police receive an informant's tip, the standard of reasonable suspicion for stopping a person is lower than the standard of probable cause for an arrest, if it has been determined that the informant's tip has sufficient indicia of reliability to justify stopping and searching the person. People v. Moore, 32 N.Y.2d 67, 343 N.Y.S.2d 107, 295 N.E.2d 780 (1973), cert. denied, 414 U.S. 1011 (1973).

Part-time deputy sheriff.—PL § 265.20(a)(1)(b) provides

persons in the service of the United States immunity from prosecution for weapon possession when that possession is duty-related or duly authorized by federal law, regulation or rule. People v. Marrero, 71 A.D.2d 376, 422 N.Y.S.2d 384 (1st Dept. 1979).

—A part-time deputy sheriff is not a peace office and is not exempt from prosecution under PL § 265.20. People v. Smith, 105 Misc. 2d 586, 432 N.Y.S.2d 612 (Sup. Ct. N.Y. Co. 1980).

—PL § 265.20(a)(11) exemption applies only to police officers or sworn peace officers of other States "while conducting official business within the State of New York." People v. Basile, 100 Misc. 2d 693, 420 N.Y.S.2d 143 (N.Y.C. Crim. Ct. 1979).

Peace officers; license to carry firearms.—Special Officers of the Department of Social Services appointed pursuant to the Administrative Code of New York City, section 434a-7.0(e), are not peace officers exempt from the requirement of obtaining a license to carry firearms. Velez v. Sugarman, 75 Misc. 2d 746, 349 N.Y.S.2d 53 (Sup. Ct. N.Y. Co. 1973).

Police officers; possession of a dangerous weapon.—Police officer who is suspended is not exempt under Penal Law § 265.20(a)(1)(b), which exempts police officers. People v. Epperson, 82 N.Y.2d 697, 601 N.Y.S.2d 471 (1993).

—A police officer may not carry a weapon for an unlawful purpose which would be outside the scope of his employment. People v. DiDominick, 94 Misc. 2d 392, 406 N.Y.S.2d 420 (Sup. Ct. Kings Co. 1978).

—Police officers were charged with a multi-count indictment, including a charge of possession of a dangerous weapon, a blackjack. In accordance with the statutory wording, they were entitled to have this count dismissed, since city police officers are statutorily exempt from prosecution for possession of a weapon with intent to use same unlawfully. People v. Desthers, 73 Misc. 2d 1085, 343 N.Y.S.2d 887 (Crim. Ct. N.Y. Co. 1973).

—Possession of unlicensed pistol by Department of Mental Hygiene Officer—A safety officer who was designated a special policeman by the director of a state hospital and who possessed an unlicensed pistol violated Penal Law § 265.05, where at the time he was arrested for unlawful possession of the pistol he was not performing any duties in or arising out of his employment. (See MHL § 34). People v. Kortright, 62 Misc. 2d 141, 307 N.Y.S.2d 359 (N.Y.C Crim. Ct. 1970).

Stop and frisk; reasonable cause; dangerous weapon.—After police had investigated the altercation between plaintiff-husband and defendant wife (and had found that she had threatened her husband with a knife), the husband informed police that defendant was "sick" and had a gun. A warrantless search of defendant and her handbag at the police station produced the gun. The search was held valid, based on reasonable cause, even though police officer did not allege that he had any fear for his own safety or the safety of others at the time of the search. People v. Moore, 32 N.Y.S.2d 67, 343 N.Y.S.2d 107, 295 N.E.2d 780 (1973).

Statutory exemptions from charge of possession of dangerous weapon.—The evidence before the Grand Jury was not legally sufficient to establish the commission by the defendant of unlawful possession of a gun or any lesser included offense, where it indicated that defendant was arrested after he had approached an airline worker on his stop-over in New York on a flight from Spain to Chicago, informed him that the pilot had held his gun on the flight from Spain to New York and inquired if he could give it to the pilot on the New York to Chicago leg of the journey. People v. Martorelli, 87 Misc. 2d 1035, 387 N.Y.S.2d 42 (Sup. Ct. Queens Co. 1976).

—Although not within the obvious intent of the legislature, under statutory law a police officer has immunity from prosecution for possession of weapons (including firearms), for unauthorized manufacture of such weapons, for defacing of weapons, and for possession and use of unauthorized weapons. People v. Desthers, 73 Misc. 2d 1085, 343 N.Y.S.2d 887 (Crim. Ct. N.Y. Co. 1973).

Weapon in automobile; statute unconstitutional as applied.—The court held that trial of defendant solely on the presumption created in PL § 265.15(3) was unconstitutional where there was no evidence that defendant, a passenger in an automobile, had access to a gun found therein within his immediate control or reach, nor that the gun was available for his use if he so desired, nor that he could have possessed it according to the definition of "possess" under PL § 10.00(8),

nor that the gun was in plain view or that defendant could have known about its presence. People v. Alston, 94 Misc. 2d 89, 404 N.Y.S.2d 277 (1978).

Voluntary delivery of weapon; not accomplished by defendant's declaration of suitcase contents.—Defendant's declaration that he had two handguns in his suitbag when he was brought to an airport security checkpoint was not a "voluntary delivery" of the weapons, as he did not offer them to the police and he intended to bring the weapons, along with the rest of his luggage, in the cargo hold of the plane, and regain possession of them at the end of the trip; the circumstances show that defendant, late for a flight, felt compelled to announce the presence of the weapons, under circumstances that were suspicious. People v. Estenson, 88 A.D.2d 776, 451 N.Y.S.2d 514 (4th Dept. 1982).

§ 265.25. Certain wounds to be reported.

Every case of a bullet wound, gunshot wound, powder burn or any other injury arising from or caused by the discharge of a gun or firearm, and every case of a wound which is likely to or may result in death and is actually or apparently inflicted by a knife, ice pick or other sharp or pointed instrument, shall be reported at once to the police authorities of the city, town or village where the person reporting is located by: (a) the physician attending or treating the case; or (b) the manager, superintendent or other person in charge, whenever such case is treated in a hospital, sanitarium or other institution. Failure to make such report is a class A misdemeanor. This subdivision shall not apply to such wounds, burns or injuries received by a member of the armed forces of the United States or the state of New York while engaged in the actual performance of duty.

ANNOTATION

Exception to physician-patient privilege.—Penal Law § 265.26 requires hospitals and medical professionals to report to law enforcement authorities certain cases of serious burns and is an exception to the physician-patient priviledge. In re New York County, 98 N.Y.2d 525, 749 N.Y.S.2d 462, 779 N.E.2d 173 (2002).

§ 265.26. Burn injury and wounds to be reported.

Every case of a burn injury or wound, where the victim sustained second or third degree burns to five percent or more of the body and/or any burns to the upper respiratory tract or laryngeal edema due to the inhalation of super-heated air, and every case of a burn injury or wound which is likely to or may result in death, shall be reported at once to the office of fire prevention and control. The state fire administrator shall accept the report and notify the proper investigatory agency. A written report shall also be provided to the office of fire prevention and control within seventy-two hours. The report shall be made by (a) the physician attending or treating the case; or (b) the manager, superintendent or other person in charge, whenever such case is treated in a hospital, sanitarium, institution or other medical facility.

The intentional failure to make such report is a class A misdemeanor.

Added L. 1985, Ch. 201.

§ 265.30. Certain convictions to be reported.

Every conviction under this article or section 400.00, of a person who is not a citizen of the United States, shall be certified to the proper officer of the United States government by the district attorney of the county in which such conviction was had.

§ 265.35. Prohibited use of weapons.

1. Any person hunting with a dangerous weapon in any county wholly embraced within the territorial limits of a city is guilty of a class A misdemeanor.

2. Any person who wilfully discharges a loaded firearm or any other gun, the propelling force of which is gunpowder, at an aircraft while such aircraft is in motion in the air or in motion or stationary upon the ground, or at any railway or street railroad train as defined by the public service law, or at a locomotive, car, bus or vehicle standing or moving upon such railway, railroad or public highway, is guilty of a class D felony if thereby the safety of any person is endangered, and in every other case, of a class E felony.

3. Any person who, otherwise than in self defense or in the discharge of official duty, (a) wilfully discharges any species of firearms, airgun or other weapon, or throws any other deadly missile, either in a public place, or in any place where there is any person to be endangered thereby, or, in Putnam county, within one-quarter mile of any occupied school building other than under supervised instruction by properly authorized instructors although no injury to any person ensues; (b) intentionally, without malice, points or aims any firearm or any other gun, the propelling force of which is gunpowder, at or toward any other person; (c) discharges, without injury to any other person, firearms or any other guns, the propelling force of which is gunpowder, while intentionally without malice, aimed at or toward any person; or (d) maims or injures any other person by the discharge of any firearm or any other gun, the propelling force of which is gunpowder, pointed or aimed intentionally, but without malice, at any such person, is guilty of a class A misdemeanor.

Amended by L. 1974, Ch. 1041.

ANNOTATION

Felonious possession of a weapon.—Felonious possession of a weapon is a crime in and of itself and capable of standing independently. People v. Edge, 76 Misc. 2d 802, 351 N.Y.S.2d 502 (Sup. Ct. Bronx Co. 1973).

§ 265.40. Purchase of rifles and/or shotguns in contiguous states.

Definitions. As used in this act:

1. "Contiguous state" shall mean any state having any portion of its border in common with a portion of the border of the state of New York;

2. All other terms herein shall be given the meaning prescribed in Public Law 90-618 known as the "Gun Control Act of 1968" (18 U.S.C. 921).

It shall be lawful for a person or persons residing in this state, to purchase or otherwise obtain a rifle and/or shotgun in a contiguous state, and to receive or transport such rifle and/or shotgun into this state; provided, however, such person is otherwise eligible to possess a rifle and/or shotgun under the laws of this state.

Amended by L. 1971, Ch. 900.

ARTICLE 270—OTHER OFFENSES RELATING TO PUBLIC SAFETY

LexisNexis Cross Reference

New York Criminal Practice (2d ed.), Vol. 7, Ch. 83, Fireworks and Other Offenses Relating to Public Safety.

§ 270.00. Unlawfully dealing with fireworks and dangerous fireworks.

1. Definition of "fireworks" and "dangerous fireworks". The term "fireworks," as used in this section, is defined and declared to be and to include any blank cartridge, blank cartridge pistol, or toy cannon in which explosives are used, firecrackers, sparklers or other combustible or explosive of like construction, or any preparation containing any explosive or inflammable compound or any tablets or other device commonly used and sold as fireworks containing nitrates, chlorates, oxalates, sulphides of lead, barium, antimony, arsenic, mercury, nitroglycerine, phosphorus or any compound containing any of the same or other explosives, or any substance or combination of substances, or article prepared for the purpose of producing a visible or an audible effect by combustion, explosion, deflagration or detonation, or other device containing any explosive substance and the term "dangerous fireworks" means any fireworks capable of causing serious physical injury and which are: firecrackers containing more than fifty milligrams of any explosive substance, torpedoes, skyrockets and rockets including all devices which employ any combustible or explosive substance and which rise in the air during discharge, roman candles, bombs, sparklers more than ten inches in length or one-fourth of one inch in diameter, or chasers including all devices which dart or travel about the surface of the ground during discharge. "Fireworks" and "dangerous fireworks" shall not be deemed to include (1) flares of the type used by railroads or any warning lights commonly known as red flares, or marine distress signals of a type approved by the United States coast guard or (2) toy pistols, toy canes, toy guns or other devices in which paper caps containing twenty-five hundredths grains or less of explosive compound are used, providing they are so constructed that the hand cannot come in contact with the cap when in place for use, and toy pistol paper caps which contain less than twenty-hundredths grains of explosive mixture, the sale and use of which shall be permitted at all times, or (3) bank security devices which contain not more than fifty grams of any compound or substance or any combination thereof, together with an igniter not exceeding 0.2 gram, capable of producing a lachrymating and/or visible or audible effect, where such device is stored or used only by banks, national banking associations, trust companies, savings banks, savings and loan associations, industrial banks, or credit unions, or by any manufacturer, wholesaler, dealer, jobber or common carrier for such devices and where the total storage on any one premises does not exceed one hundred devices.

2. Offense. (a) Except as herein otherwise provided, or except where a permit is obtained pursuant to section 405.00;

(i) any person who shall offer or expose for sale, sell or furnish, any fireworks or dangerous fireworks is guilty of a class B misdemeanor;

(ii) any person who shall offer or expose for sale, sell or furnish any fireworks or dangerous fireworks valued at five hundred dollars or more shall be guilty of a class A misdemeanor;

(b) (i) Except as herein otherwise stated, or except where a permit is obtained pursuant to section 405.00, any person who shall possess, use, explode or cause to explode any fireworks or dangerous fireworks is guilty of a violation.

(ii) A person who shall offer or expose for sale, sell or furnish, any dangerous fireworks to any person who is under the age of eighteen is guilty of a class A misdemeanor.

(iii) A person who has previously been convicted of a violation of subparagraph (ii) of this paragraph within the preceding five years and who shall offer or expose for sale, sell or furnish, any dangerous fireworks to any person who is under the age of eighteen, shall be guilty of a class E felony.

(c) Possession of fireworks or dangerous fireworks valued at fifty dollars or more shall be a presumption that such fireworks were intended to be offered or exposed for sale.

3. The provisions of this section shall not apply to articles of the kind and nature herein mentioned, while in possession of railroads and transportation agencies for the purpose of transportation to points without the state, the shipment of which is not prohibited by the interstate commerce commission regulations as formulated and published from time to time, unless the same be held voluntarily by such railroads or transportation companies as warehousemen for delivery to points within the state; provided, that none of the provisions of this section shall apply to signaling devices used by railroad companies or motor vehicles referred to in subdivision seventeen of section three hundred seventyfive of the vehicle and traffic law, or to high explosives for blasting or similar purposes; provided that none of the provisions of this section shall apply to fireworks or dangerous fireworks and the use thereof by the army and navy departments of the state and federal government; nor shall anything in this act contained be construed to prohibit any manufacturer, wholesaler, dealer or jobber from manufacturing, possessing or selling at wholesale such fireworks or dangerous fireworks to municipalities, religious or civic organizations, fair associations, amusement parks, or other organizations or groups of individuals authorized to possess and use fireworks or dangerous fireworks under this act, or the sale or use of blank cartridges for a show or theatre, or for signal purposes in athletic sports, or for dog trials or dog training, or the use, or the storage, transportation or sale for use of fireworks or dangerous fireworks in the preparation for or in connection with television broadcasts; nor shall anything in this act contained be construed to prohibit the manufacture of fireworks or dangerous fireworks, nor the sale of any kind of fireworks or dangerous fireworks, provided the same are to be shipped directly out of the state.

4. Sales of ammunition not prohibited. Nothing contained in this section shall be construed to prevent, or interfere in any way with, the sale of ammunition for revolvers or pistols of any kind, or for rifles, shot guns, or other arms, belonging or which may belong to any persons whether as sporting or hunting weapons or for the purpose of protection to them in their homes, or, as they may go abroad; and manufacturers are authorized to continue to manufacture, and wholesalers and dealers to continue to deal in and freely to sell ammunition to all such persons for such purposes.

5. Notwithstanding the provisions of subdivision four of this section, it shall be unlawful for any dealer in firearms to sell any ammunition designed exclusively for use in a pistol or revolver to any person, not authorized to possess a pistol or revolver. The violation of this section shall constitute a class B misdemeanor.

Amended by L. 1967, Ch. 791; L. 1969, Ch. 709; L. 1975,

Ch. 840; L. 1978, Ch. 286; L. 1986, Ch. 166; L. 1997, Ch. 180, § 1, eff. Nov. 1, 1997.

ANNOTATIONS

Classification of seized fireworks.—PL § 270.00 definition of fireworks is very specific; where defendant was charged on basis of possession of "class C" fireworks, People had burden of defining this category, which is not specified in Penal Law; failure of supporting deposition to define classification required dismissal. People v. Christopher, 167 Misc. 2d 468, 634 N.Y.S.2d 948 (New York City Crim. Ct. Bronx Co. 1995).

Destruction of seized fireworks: without court order.—People's failure to comply with provisions of PL § 405.05, thereby depriving defendant of an opportunity to inspect evidence against him, required dismissal. People v. Christopher, 167 Misc. 2d 468, 634 N.Y.S.2d 948 (New York City Crim. Ct. Bronx Co. 1995).

Predicate for stop.—During routine traffic stop, officer observed fireworks in plain view on front seat of car; defendant admitted that he had no permit to possess fireworks; this admission coupled with plain view observation established probable cause justifying warrantless arrest. People v. Miller, 177 A.D.2d 989, 578 N.Y.S.2d 10 (4th Dept. 1991).

Constructive possession.—Manager of grocery store in which fireworks were found exercised sufficient dominion and control over the premises to be deemed to constructively possess the fireworks; employee next to whom the fireworks were found, in an area of the store to which customers did not have access, also could be deemed to constructively possess the fireworks. People v. Whitehead and Smallwood, 159 A.D.2d 741, 552 N.Y.S.2d 685 (2d Dept. 1990).

Civil compensation barred to injured plaintiff when injuries arose from plaintiff's possession of explosive device.—The 19-year-old plaintiff was carrying a homemade pipebomb, which exploded causing injuries to plaintiff, which he had constructed using gun powder from fireworks purchased from the civil defendant; plaintiff's own conduct barred him from seeking compensation. Barker v. Kallash, 63 N.Y.2d 19, 479 N.Y.S.2d 201, 468 N.E.2d 39 (1984).

Blank cartridge pistol.—The mere possession of a blank cartridge pistol constitutes the violation, for criminal intent is not required. People v. Johnson, 77 Misc. 2d 228, 354 N.Y.S.2d 85 (Crim. Ct. Queens Co. 1974).

Model rockets are not fireworks.—Model rocket engines containing sulphur, carbon and sodium of potassium nitrate, the common components of black powder are not "fireworks" within the meaning of this section People v. Bochter, 63 Misc. 2d 249, 311 N.Y.S.2d 186 (Dist. Ct. 1970).

Statute held constitutional.—People v. Jackson, 76 Misc. 2d 872, 352 N.Y.S.2d 376 (Erie Co. Ct. 1974), aff'd, 36 N.Y.2d 726, 367 N.Y.S.2d 975, 328 N.E.2d 487 (1975).

§ 270.05. Unlawfully possessing or selling noxious material.

1. As used in this section, "noxious material" means any container which contains any drug or other substance capable of generating offensive, noxious or suffocating fumes, gases or vapours, or capable of immobilizing a person.

2. A person is guilty of unlawfully possessing noxious material when he possesses such material under circumstances evincing an intent to use it or to cause it to be used to inflict physical injury upon or to cause annoyance to a person, or to damage property of another, or to disturb the public peace.

3. Possession of noxious materials is presumptive evidence of intent to use it or cause it to be used in violation of this section.

4. Bank security devices not prohibited. Notwithstanding the provisions of subdivision one of

this section, it shall not be unlawful for any bank, national banking association, trust company, savings bank, savings and loan association, industrial bank, or credit union to store, possess, transport, use or cause to discharge any bank security device as described in subdivision one of section 270.00 of this chapter; nor shall it be unlawful for any manufacturer, wholesaler, dealer, jobber or common carrier to manufacture, store, possess, transport, or sell such a device to banks, national banking associations, trust companies, savings banks, savings and loan associations, industrial banks or credit unions.

5. Self-defense spray devices not prohibited. Notwithstanding the provisions of subdivisions two and three of this section, it shall not be unlawful for a person eighteen years of age or older to possess a self-defense spray device as defined in paragraph fourteen of subdivision a of section 265.20 of this chapter in accordance with the provisions set forth therein.

6. A person is guilty of unlawfully selling a noxious material when he or she sells a self-defense spray device as defined in paragraph fourteen of subdivision a of section 265.20 of this chapter and such sale was not authorized in accordance with the provisions of paragraph fifteen of subdivision a of section 265.20 of this chapter.

Unlawfully possessing or selling noxious material is a class B misdemeanor.

Amended by L. 1969, Ch. 452; L. 1978, Ch. 286; L. 1996, Ch. 354, § 4, amending the heading and closing paragraph, and adding subds. 5 and 6, eff. Nov. 1, 1996.

ANNOTATIONS

Constitutionality.—PL § 270.05 does not violate due process by reason of its being overly broad. People v. Hertz, 85 Misc. 1036, 381 N.Y.S.2d 586 (Sup. Ct. App. Term 9th & 10th Jud. Dists. 1976).

Corporation.—Where the evidence clearly and unequivocally established that the corporation of which defendant was president, was a wholesaler of the noxious material, the inference can only be that there was no intent to use or cause it to be used in violation of PL § 270.05(2) and the statutory presumption contained in PL § 270.05(3) cannot be inferred. People v. Duskin, 85 Misc. 2d 839, 380 N.Y.S.2d 895 (Dist. Ct. Nassau Co. 1976).

Substances included.—Possession of a canister of tear gas would satisfy the statute. People v. Snead, 160 Misc. 2d 466, 609 N.Y.S.2d 520 (Dist. Ct. Nassau Co. 1994).

Supporting evidence.—When defendant was arrested ostensibly in possession of a canister of tear gas, the People's failure to support accusatory instrument with lab report establishing the existence of tear gas in the canister. People v. Gunatilaka, 156 Misc. 2d 958, 595 N.Y.S.2d 664 (New York City Crim. Ct. 1993).

—Since the contents of the canister, rather than the canister's operability, is the subject matter of the statute, the People's failure to document the canister's operability in support of the accusatory instrument was not relevant to its facial validity. People v. Gunatilaka, 156 Misc. 2d 958, 595 N.Y.S.2d 664 (New York City Crim. Ct. 1993).

Warrantless search of automobile.—Because of the mobility of automobiles, search of defendant's car without a warrant was reasonable where based on probable cause. People v. Caputo, 41 A.D.2d 165, 341 N.Y.S.2d 920 (3d Dept. 1973), cert. denied sub nom. Caputo v. New York, 414 U.S. 1135 (1974).

§ 270.10. Creating a hazard.

A person is guilty of creating a hazard when:

1. Having discarded in any place where it might attract children, a container which has a compartment of more than one and one-half cubic feet capacity and a door or lid which locks or fastens automatically when closed and which cannot easily be opened from the inside, he fails to remove the door, lid, locking or fastening device; or

2. Being the owner or otherwise having possession of property upon which an abandoned well or cesspool is located, he fails to cover the same with suitable protective construction.

Creating a hazard is a class B misdemeanor.

§ 270.15. Unlawfully refusing to yield a party line.

1. As used in this section:

(a) "Party line" means a subscriber's line telephone circuit, consisting of two or more main telephone stations connected therewith, each station with a distinctive ring or telephone number.

(b) "Emergency call" means a telephone call to a police or fire department, or for medical aid or ambulance service, necessitated by a situation in which human life or property is in jeopardy and prompt summoning of aid is essential.

2. A person is guilty of unlawfully refusing to yield a party line when, being informed that a party line is needed for an emergency call, he refuses immediately to relinquish such line.

Unlawfully refusing to yield a party line is a class B misdemeanor.

§ 270.20. Unlawful wearing of a body vest.

1. A person is guilty of the unlawful wearing of a body vest when acting either alone or with one or more other persons he commits any violent felony offense defined in section 70.02 while possessing a firearm, rifle or shotgun and in the course of and in furtherance of such crime he wears a body vest.

2. For the purposes of this section a "body vest" means a bullet-resistant soft body armor providing, as a minimum standard, the level of protection known as threat level I which shall mean at least seven layers of bullet-resistant material providing protection from three shots of one hundred fifty-eight grain lead ammunition fired from a .38 calibre handgun at a velocity of eight hundred fifty feet per second.

The unlawful wearing of a body vest is a class E felony.

Added by L. 1984, Ch. 56; Amended by L. 2001, Ch. 317, § 1, eff. Nov. 1, 2001, amending subd. 1.

ANNOTATIONS

Predicate offenses.—Criminal possession of a weapon in the third degree qualifies as a violent felony offense as a predicate to unlawfully wearing a body vest; even though PL § 270.20 also requires that defendant possess a firearm while wearing the vest, insofar as this statutory element does not require that the firearm must be loaded, there is no duplicitousness between the criminal possession of a weapon offense, requiring that the firearm be loaded, and this element of unlawfully wearing a body vest. People v. Heath, 86 N.Y.2d 723, 631 N.Y.S.2d 117, 655 N.E.2d 158 (1995). *See also* People v. Nikac, 155 Misc. 2d 304, 588 N.Y.S.2d 998 (Sup. Ct. Bronx Co. 1992), *app. withdrawn* 188 A.D.2d 1092, 592 N.Y.S.2d 244 (1st Dept. 1992), in which the court also concluded that criminal possession of a weapon in the third degree was a valid predicate felony, but dismissed the charge on the basis that the mere passive possession of a firearm could not satisfy the possession of a firearm element of the offense; *Heath, supra,* would seem to reject *Nikac sub silencio.*

Firearm.—For purposes of PL § 270.20, statutory requirement that defendant must possess a firearm does not require that the firearm must be loaded. People v. Heath, 86 N.Y.2d 723, 631 N.Y.S.2d 117, 655 N.E.2d 158 (1995).

Specifications of the vest.—Specifications of vest, specifically, velocity of ammunition used in testing body vest, were properly supported by testimony of firearms expert. People v. Charlotte, 236 A.D.2d 284, 654 N.Y.S.2d 303 (1st Dept. 1997).

—PL § 270.20(2) sets forth minimum specifications defining the type of body vest which is proscribed by the statute; the People's failure to affirmatively prove that the body vest seized from defendant complied with these specifications rendered the evidence legally insufficient. People v. Garcia, 202 A.D.2d 189, 608 N.Y.S.2d 425 (1st Dept.), *lv. denied,* 83 N.Y.2d 1003 (1994).

ARTICLE 275—OFFENSES RELATING TO UNAUTHORIZED RECORDING

§ 275.00. Definitions.

The following definitions are applicable to this article:

1. "Person" means any individual, firm, partnership, corporation or association.

2. "Owner" means (a) the person who owns, or has the exclusive license in the United States to reproduce or the exclusive license in the United States to distribute to the public copies of the sounds fixed in a master phonograph record, master disc, master tape, master film or any other device used for reproducing sounds on phonograph records, discs, tapes, films, videocassettes, or any other articles upon which sound is recorded, and from which the transferred recorded sounds are directly derived; or (b) the person who owns the rights to record or authorize the recording of a live performance.

3. "Fixed" means embodied in a recording by or under the authority of the author, so that the matter embodied is sufficiently permanent or stable to permit it to be perceived, reproduced, or otherwise communicated for a period of more than transitory duration.

4. "Performer" means the person or persons appearing in a performance.

5. "Performance" means, whether live before an audience or transmitted by wire or through the air by radio or television, a recitation, rendering, or playing of a series of images, musical, spoken, or other sounds, or a combination of images and sounds, in an audible sequence.

6. "Recording" means an original phonograph record, disc, tape, audio or video cassette, wire, film, or any other medium on such sounds, images, or both sounds and images are or can be recorded or otherwise stored, or a copy or reproduction that duplicates in whole or in part the original.

Added by L. 1990, Ch. 460; L. 1995, Ch. 419, § 1, amending subd. 2, eff. Nov. 1, 1995.

§ 275.05. Manufacture of unauthorized recordings in the second degree.

A person is guilty of the manufacture of unauthorized recordings in the second degree when such person:

1. knowingly, and without the consent of the owner, transfers or causes to be transferred any sound recording, with the intent to rent or sell, or cause to be rented or sold for profit, or used to promote the sale of any product, such article to which such recording was transferred, or

2. transports within this state, for commercial advantage or private financial gain, a recording, knowing that the sounds have been reproduced or transferred without the consent of the owner; provided, however, that this section shall only apply to sound recordings initially fixed prior to February fifteenth, nineteen hundred seventy-two.

Manufacture of unauthorized recordings in the second degree is a class A misdemeanor.

Added by L. 1990, Ch. 460; L. 1995, Ch. 419, § 2, amending subd. 2, eff. Nov. 1, 1995.

§ 275.10. Manufacture of unauthorized recordings in the first degree.

A person is guilty of manufacture of unauthorized recordings in the first degree when he commits the crime of manufacture of unauthorized recordings in the second degree as defined in section 275.05 of this article and either:

1. has previously been convicted of that crime within the past five years; or

2. commits that crime by the manufacture of one thousand unauthorized sound recordings; provided, however, that this section shall only apply to sound recordings initially fixed prior to February fifteenth, nineteen hundred seventy-two.

Manufacture of unauthorized recordings in the first degree is a class E felony.

Added by L. 1990, Ch. 460; L. 1995, Ch. 419, § 3, amending subd. 2, eff. Nov. 1, 1995.

§ 275.15. Manufacture or sale of an unauthorized recording of a performance in the second degree.

A person commits the crime of manufacture or sale of an unauthorized recording of a performance in the second degree when he knowingly, and without the consent of the performer, records or fixes or causes to be recorded or fixed on a recording a performance, with the intent to sell or rent or cause to be sold or rented such recording, or with the intent to use such recording to promote the sale of any product; or when he knowingly possesses, transports or advertises, for purposes of sale, resale or rental or sells, resells, rents or offers for rental, sale or resale, any recording that the person knows has been produced in violation of this section.

Manufacture or sale of an unauthorized recording of a performance in the second degree is a class a misdemeanor.

Added by L. 1990, Ch. 460; L. 1995, Ch. 419, § 4, eff. Nov. 1, 1995.

§ 275.20. Manufacture or sale of an unauthorized recording of a performance in the first degree.

A person commits the crime of unauthorized recording of a performance in the first degree when he commits the crime of manufacture or sale of an unauthorized recording of a performance in the second degree as defined in section 275.15 of this article and either:

1. such person has previously been convicted of that crime within the past five years; or

2. commission of that crime involves at least one thousand unauthorized sound recordings or at least one hundred unauthorized audiovisual recordings.

Manufacture or sale of an unauthorized recording of a performance in the first degree is a class E felony.

Added by L. 1990, Ch. 460; L. 1995, Ch. 419, § 5, eff. Nov. 1, 1995.

§ 275.25. Advertisement or sale of unauthorized recordings in the second degree.

A person is guilty of the advertisement or sale of unauthorized recordings in the second degree when such person knowingly advertises, offers for sale, resale, or rental, or sells, resells, rents, distributes or possesses for any such purposes, any recording that has been produced or transferred without the consent of the owner; provided, however, that this section shall only apply to sound recordings initially fixed prior to February fifteenth, nineteen hundred seventy-two.

Advertisement or sale of unauthorized recordings in the second degree is a class A misdemeanor.

Added by L. 1990, Ch. 460; L. 1995, Ch. 419, § 6, eff. Nov. 1, 1995.

ANNOTATION

Preemption.—Application of statute to indict owner of video store for renting unauthorized recording of a videocassette was preempted by federal Copyright Revision Act (17 USC § 301), insofar as state as well as federal statute proscribe sale, resale and rental of videocassettes. People v. Borriello, 155 Misc. 2d 261, 588 N.Y.S.2d 991 (Sup. Ct. Kings Co. 1992).

§ 275.30. Advertisement or sale of unauthorized recordings in the first degree.

A person is guilty of the advertisement or sale of unauthorized recordings in the first degree when such person commits the crime of advertisement or sale of unauthorized recordings in the second degree as defined in section 275.25 of this article and either:

1. such person has previously been convicted of that crime within the past five years; or

2. commission of that crime involves at least one thousand unauthorized sound recordings or at least one hundred unauthorized audiovisual recordings.

Advertisement and sale of unauthorized recordings in the first degree is a class E felony.

Added by L. 1990, Ch. 460.

§ 275.32. Unauthorized operation of a recording device in a motion picture theater.

1. A person is guilty of unauthorized operation of a recording device in a motion picture theater when without written authority or permission from the operator of a motion picture theater, the person operates a recording device in such theater.

2. As used in this section "recording device" means a photographic or video camera, or any audio video recorder used for recording the sound or picture of a motion picture, and "motion picture theater" means a theater or other auditorium in which a motion picture is exhibited.

Unauthorized operation of a recording device in a motion picture theater is a violation.

Added L. 1994, Ch. 374, § 2, eff. Nov. 1, 1994.

§ 275.35. Failure to disclose the origin of a recording in the second degree.

A person is guilty of failure to disclose the origin of a recording in the second degree when, for commercial advantage or private financial gain, he knowingly advertises or offers for sale, resale, or rental, or sells, resells, or rents, or possesses for such purposes, a recording the cover, box, jacket or label does not clearly and conspicuously disclose the actual name and address of the manufacturer or the name of the performer or principal artist.

The omission of the actual name and address of the manufacturer, or the omission of the name of the performer or principal artist, or the omission of both, shall constitute the failure to disclose the origin of a recording.

Failure to disclose the origin of a recording in the second degree is a class A misdemeanor.

Added by L. 1990, Ch. 460; L. 1995, Ch. 419, § 7. eff. Nov. 1, 1995.

ANNOTATION

Preemption; infringement—State provision, addressing labeling and packaging of videocassettes, as applied in this case, did not address infringement of the rights of owners of the copyright, which was the substantive concern of the federal statute, so that the state statute was not preempted. People v. Borriello, 155 Misc. 2d 261, 588 N.Y.S.2d 991 (Sup. Ct. Kings Co. 1992).

§ 275.40. Failure to disclose the origin of a recording in the first degree.

A person is guilty of failure to disclose the origin of a recording in the first degree when such person commits the crime of failure to disclose the origin of a recording in the second degree as defined in section 275.35 of this article and commission of that crime involves at least one thousand unauthorized sound recordings or at least one hundred unauthorized audiovisual recordings.

Failure to disclose the origin of a recording in the first degree is a class E felony.

Added by L. 1990, Ch. 460.

§ 275.45. Limitations of application.

1. This article does not apply to:

(a) any broadcaster who, in connection with or as part of a radio, television, or cable broadcast transmission, or for the purpose of archival preservation, transfers any such recorded sounds or images; or

(b) any person who transfers such sounds or images for personal use, and without profit for such transfer.

2. This article shall neither enlarge nor diminish the rights of parties in civil litigation.

Added by L. 1990, Ch. 460.

PART FOUR—ADMINISTRATIVE PROVISIONS

TITLE W—PROVISIONS RELATING TO FIREARMS, FIREWORKS, PORNOGRAPHY EQUIPMENT AND VEHICLES USED IN THE TRANSPORTATION OF GAMBLING RECORDS

ARTICLE 400—LICENSING AND OTHER PROVISIONS RELATING TO FIREARMS

Section

LexisNexis Cross Reference

Forensic Sciences, Vol. 4, Ch. 38, Firearm Injuries.

§ 400.00. Licenses to carry, possess, repair and dispose of firearms.

1. Eligibility. No license shall be issued or renewed pursuant to this section except by the licensing officer, and then only after investigation and finding that all statements in a proper application for a license are true. No license shall be issued or renewed except for an applicant (a) twenty-one years of age or older, provided, however, that where such applicant has been honorably discharged from the United States army, navy, marine corps, air force or coast guard, or the national guard of the state of New York, no such age restriction shall apply; (b) of good moral character; (c) who has not been convicted anywhere of a felony or a serious offense; (d) who has stated whether he or she has ever suffered any mental illness or been confined to any hospital or institution, public or private, for mental illness; (e) who has not had a license revoked or who is not under a suspension or ineligibility order issued pursuant to the provisions of section 530.14 of the criminal procedure law or section eight hundred forty-two-a of the family court act; (f) in the county of Westchester, who has successfully completed a firearms safety course and test as evidenced by a certificate of completion issued in his or her name and endorsed and affirmed under the penalties of perjury by a duly authorized instructor, except that: (i) persons who are honorably discharged from the United States army, navy, marine corps or coast guard, or of the national guard of the state of New York, and produce evidence of official qualification in firearms during the term of service are not required to have completed those hours of a firearms safety course pertaining to the safe use, carrying, possession, maintenance and storage of a firearm; and (ii) persons who were licensed to possess a pistol

or revolver prior to the effective date of this paragraph are not required to have completed a firearms safety course and test; and (g) concerning whom no good cause exists for the denial of the license. No person shall engage in the business of gunsmith or dealer in firearms unless licensed pursuant to this section. An applicant to engage in such business shall also be a citizen of the United States, more than twenty-one years of age and maintain a place of business in the city or county where the license is issued. For such business, if the applicant is a firm or partnership, each member thereof shall comply with all of the requirements set forth in this subdivision and if the applicant is a corporation, each officer thereof shall so comply.

2. Types of licenses. A license for gunsmith or dealer in firearms shall be issued to engage in such business. A license for a pistol or revolver, other than an assault weapon or a disguised gun, shall be issued to (a) have and possess in his dwelling by a householder; (b) have and possess in his place of business by a merchant or storekeeper; (c) have and carry concealed while so employed by a messenger employed by a banking institution or express company; (d) have and carry concealed by a justice of the supreme court in the first or second judicial departments, or by a judge of the New York city civil court or the New York city criminal court; (e) have and carry concealed while so employed by a regular employee of an institution of the state, or of any county, city, town or village, under control of a commissioner of correction of the city or any warden, superintendent or head keeper of any state prison, penitentiary, workhouse, county jail or other institution for the detention of persons convicted or accused of crime or held as witnesses in criminal cases, provided that application is made therefor by such

commissioner, warden, superintendent or head keeper; (f) have and carry concealed, without regard to employment or place of possession, by any person when proper cause exists for the issuance thereof; and (g) have, possess, collect and carry antique pistols which are defined as follows: (i) any single shot, muzzle loading pistol with a matchlock, flintlock, percussion cap, or similar type of ignition system manufactured in or before 1898, which is not designed for using rimfire or conventional centerfire fixed ammunition; and (ii) any replica of any pistol described in clause (i) hereof if such replica—

(1) is not designed or redesigned for using rimfire or conventional centerfire fixed ammunition, or

(2) uses rimfire or conventional centerfire fixed ammunition which is no longer manufactured in the United States and which is not readily available in the ordinary channels of commercial trade.

3. Applications. (a) Applications shall be made and renewed, in the case of a license to carry or possess a pistol or revolver, to the licensing officer in the city or county, as the case may be, where the applicant resides, is principally employed or has his principal place of business as merchant or storekeeper; and, in the case of a license as gunsmith or dealer in firearms, to the licensing officer where such place of business is located. Blank applications shall, except in the city of New York, be approved as to form by the superintendent of state police. An application shall state the full name, date of birth, residence, present occupation of each person or individual signing the same, whether or not he is a citizen of the United States, whether or not he complies with each requirement for eligibility specified in subdivision one of this section and such other facts as may be required to show the good character, competency and integrity of each person or individual signing the application. An application shall be signed and verified by the applicant. Each individual signing an application shall submit one photograph of himself and a duplicate for each required copy of the application. Such photographs shall have been taken within thirty days prior to the filing of the application. In case of a license as gunsmith or dealer in firearms, the photographs submitted shall be two inches square, and the application shall also state the previous occupation of each individual signing the same and the location of the place of such business, or of the bureau, agency, subagency, office or branch office for which the license is sought, specifying the name of the city, town or village, indicating the street and number and otherwise giving such apt description as to point out reasonably the location thereof. In such case, if the applicant is a firm, partnership or corporation, its name, date and place of formation, and principal place of business shall be stated. For such firm or partnership, the application shall be signed and verified by each individual composing or intending to compose the same, and for such corporation, by each officer thereof.

(b) Application for an exemption under paragraph seven-b of subdivision a of section 265.20 of this chapter. Each applicant desiring to obtain the exemption set forth in paragraph seven-b of subdivision a of section 265.20 of this chapter shall make such request in writing of the licensing officer with whom his application for a license is filed, at the time of filing such application. Such request shall include a signed and verified statement by the person authorized to instruct and supervise the applicant, that has met with the applicant and that he has determined that, in his judgment, said applicant does not appear to be or poses a threat to be, a danger to himself or to others. He shall include a copy of his certificate as an instructor in small arms, if he is required to be certified, and state his address and telephone number. He shall specify the exact location by name, address and telephone number where such instruction will take place. Such licensing officer shall, no later than ten business days after such filing, request the duly constituted police authorities of the locality where such application is made to investigate and ascertain any previous criminal record of the applicant pursuant to subdivision four of this section. Upon completion of this investigation, the police authority shall report the results to the licensing officer without unnecessary delay. The licensing officer shall no later than ten business days after the receipt of such investigation, determine if the applicant has been previously denied a license, been convicted of a felony, or been convicted of a serious offense, and either approve or disapprove the applicant for exemption purposes based upon such determinations. If the applicant is approved for the exemption, the licensing officer shall notify the appropriate duly constituted police authorities and the applicant. Such exemption shall terminate if the application for the license is denied, or at any earlier time based upon any information obtained by the licensing officer or the appropriate police authorities which would cause the license to be denied. The applicant and appropriate police authorities shall be notified of any such terminations.

4. Investigations. Before a license is issued or renewed, there shall be an investigation of all statements required in the application by the duly constituted police authorities of the locality where such application is made. For that purpose, the records of the appropriate office of the department of mental hygiene concerning previous or present mental illness of the applicant shall be available for inspection by the investigating officer of the police authority. In order to ascertain any previous criminal record, the investigating officer shall take the fingerprints and physical descriptive data in quadruplicate of each individual by whom application is signed and verified. Two copies of

such fingerprints shall be taken on standard fingerprint cards eight inches square, and one copy may be taken on a card supplied for that purpose by the federal bureau of investigation; provided, however, that in the case of a corporate applicant that has already been issued a dealer in firearms license and seeks to operate a firearm dealership at a second or subsequent location, the original fingerprints on file may be used to ascertain any criminal record in the second or subsequent application unless any of the corporate officers have changed since the prior application, in which case the new corporate officer shall comply with procedures governing the initial application for such license. When completed, one standard card shall be forwarded to and retained by the division of criminal justice services in the executive department, at Albany. A search of the files of such division and written notification of the results of the search to the investigating officer shall be made without unnecessary delay. Thereafter, such division shall notify the licensing officer and the executive department, division of state police, Albany, of any criminal record of the applicant filed therein subsequent to the search of its files. A second standard card, or the one supplied by the federal bureau of investigation, as the case may be, shall be forwarded to that bureau at Washington with a request that the files of the bureau be searched and notification of the results of the search be made to the investigating police authority. The failure or refusal of the federal bureau of investigation to make the fingerprint check provided for in this section shall not constitute the sole basis for refusal to issue a permit pursuant to the provisions of this section. Of the remaining two fingerprint cards, one shall be filed with the executive department, division of state police, Albany, within ten days after issuance of the license, and other remain on file with the investigating police authority. No such fingerprints may be inspected by any person other than a peace officer, except on order of a judge or justice of a court of record either upon notice to the licensee or without notice, as the judge or justice may deem appropriate. Upon completion of the investigation, the police authority shall report the results to the licensing officer without unnecessary delay.

4-a. Processing of license applications. Applications for licenses shall be accepted for processing by the licensing officer at the time of presentment. Except upon written notice to the applicant specifically stating the reasons for any delay, in each case the licensing officer shall act upon any application for a license pursuant to this section within six months of the date of presentment of such an application to the appropriate authority. Such delay may only be for good cause and with respect to the applicant. In acting upon an application, the licensing officer shall either deny the application for reasons specifically and concisely stated in writing or grant the application and issue the license applied for.

4-b. Westchester County firearms safety course certificate. In the county of Westchester, at the time of application, the licensing officer to which the license application is made shall provide a copy of the safety course booklet to each license applicant. Before such license is issued, such licensing officer shall require that the applicant submit a certificate of successful completion of a firearms safety course and test issued in his or her name and endorsed and affirmed under the penalties of perjury by a duly authorized instructor.

5. Filing of approved applications. The application for any license, if granted, shall be filed by the licensing officer with the clerk of the county of issuance, except that in the city of New York and, in the counties of Nassau and Suffolk, the licensing officer shall designate the place of filing in the appropriate division, bureau or unit of the police department thereof, and in the county of Suffolk the county clerk is hereby authorized to transfer all records or applications relating to firearms to the licensing authority of that county. The name and address of any person to whom an application for any license has been granted shall be a public record. Upon application by a licensee who has changed his place of residence such records or applications shall be transferred to the appropriate officer at the licensee's new place of residence. A duplicate copy of such application shall be filed by the licensing officer in the executive department, division of state police, Albany, within ten days after issuance of the license. Nothing in this subdivision shall be construed to change the expiration date or term of such licenses if otherwise provided for in law.

6. License: validity. Any license issued pursuant to this section shall be valid notwithstanding the provisions of any local law or ordinance. No license shall be transferable to any other person or premises. A license to carry or possess a pistol or revolver, not otherwise limited as to place or time of possession, shall be effective throughout the state, except that the same shall not be valid within the city of New York unless a special permit granting validity is issued by the police commissioner of that city. Such license to carry or possess shall be valid within the city of New York in the absence of a permit issued by the police commissioner of that city, provided that (a) the firearms covered by such license have been purchased from a licensed dealer within the city of New York and are being transported out of said city forthwith and immediately from said dealer by the licensee in a locked container during a continuous and uninterrupted trip; or provided that (b) the firearms covered by such license are being transported by the licensee in a locked container and the trip through the city of New York is continuous and uninterrupted; or provided that (c) the firearms covered by such license are

carried by armored car security guards transporting money or other valuables, in, to, or from motor vehicles commonly known as armored cars, during the course of their employment; or provided that (d) the licensee is a retired police officer as police officer is defined **pursu**ant to subdivision thirty-four of section 1.20 of the criminal procedure law or a retired federal law enforcement officer, as defined in section 2.15 of the criminal procedure law, who has been issued a license by an authorized licensing officer as defined in subdivision ten of section 265.00 of this chapter; provided, further, however, that if such license was not issued in the city of New York it must be marked "Retired Police Officer" or "Retired Federal Law Enforcement Officer", as the case may be, and, in the case of a retired officer the license shall be deemed to permit only police or federal law enforcement regulations weapons; or provided that (e) the licensee is a peace officer described in subdivision four of section 2.10 of the criminal procedure law and the license, if issued by other than the city of New York, is marked "New York State Tax Department Peace Officer" and in such case the exemption shall apply only to the firearm issued to such licensee by the department of taxation and finance. A license as gunsmith or dealer in firearms shall not be valid outside the city or county, as the case may be, where issued.

7. License: form. Any license issued pursuant to this section shall, except in the city of New York, be approved as to form by the superintendent of state police. A license to carry or possess a pistol or revolver shall have attached the licensee's photograph, and a coupon which shall be removed and retained by any person disposing of a firearm to the licensee. Such license shall specify the weapon covered by calibre, make, model, manufacturer's name and serial number, or if none, by any other distinguishing number or identification mark, and shall indicate whether issued to carry on the person or possess on the premises and if on the premises, shall also specify the place where the licensee shall possess the same. If such license is issued to an alien, or to a person not a citizen of and usually a resident in the state, the licensing officer shall state in the license the particular reason for the issuance and the names of the persons certifying to the good character of the applicant. Any license as gunsmith or dealer in firearms shall mention and describe the premises for which it is issued and shall be valid only for such premises.

8. License: exhibition and display. Every licensee while carrying a pistol or revolver shall have on his or her person a license to carry the same. Every person licensed to possess a pistol or revolver on particular premises shall have the license for the same on such premises. Upon demand, the license shall be exhibited for inspection to any peace officer, who is acting pursuant to his or her special duties, or police officer. A license as gunsmith or dealer in firearms shall be prominently displayed on the licensed premises. A gunsmith or dealer of firearms may conduct business temporarily at a location other than the location specified on the license if such temporary location is the location for a gun show or event sponsored by any national, state, or local organization, or any affiliate of any such organization devoted to the collection, competitive use or other sporting use of firearms. Any sale or transfer at a gun show must also comply with the provisions of article thirty-nine-DD of the general business law. Records of receipt and disposition of firearms transactions conducted at such temporary location shall include the location of the sale or other disposition and shall be entered in the permanent records of the gunsmith or dealer of firearms and retained on the location specified on the license. Nothing in this section shall authorize any licensee to conduct business from any motorized or towed vehicle. A separate fee shall not be required of a licensee with respect to business conducted under this subdivision. Any inspection or examination of inventory or records under this section at such temporary location shall be limited to inventory consisting of, or records related to, firearms held or disposed at such temporary locations. Failure of any licensee to so exhibit or display his or her license, as the case may be, shall be presumptive evidence that he or she is not duly licensed.

9. License: amendment. Elsewhere than in the city of New York, a person licensed to carry or possess a pistol or revolver may apply at any time to his licensing officer for amendment of his license to include one or more such weapons or to cancel weapons held under license. If granted, a record of the amendment describing the weapons involved shall be filed by the licensing officer in the executive department, division of state police, Albany. Notification of any change of residence shall be made in writing by any licensee within ten days after such change occurs, and a record of such change shall be inscribed by such licensee on the reverse side of his license. Elsewhere than in the city of New York, and in the counties of Nassau and Suffolk, such notification shall be made to the executive department, division of state police, Albany, and in the city of New York to the police commissioner of that city, and in the county of Nassau to the police commissioner of that county, and in the county of Suffolk to the licensing officer of that county, who shall, within ten days after such notification shall be received by him, give notice in writing of such change to the executive department, division of state police, at Albany.

10. License: expiration, certification and renewal. Any license for gunsmith or dealer in firearms and, in the city of New York, any license to carry or possess a pistol or revolver, issued at any time pursuant to this section or prior to the first day of July, nineteen hundred sixty-three and

not limited to expire on an earlier date fixed in the license, shall expire not more than three years after the date of issuance. In the counties of Nassau, Suffolk and Westchester, any license to carry or possess a pistol or revolver, issued at any time pursuant to this section or prior to the first day of July, nineteen hundred sixty-three and not limited to expire on an earlier date fixed in the license, shall expire not more than five years after the date of issuance; however, in the county of Westchester, any such license shall be certified prior to the first day of April, two thousand, in accordance with a schedule to be contained in regulations promulgated by the commissioner of the division of criminal justice services, and every such license shall be recertified every five years thereafter. For purposes of this section certification shall mean that the licensee shall provide to the licensing officer the following information only: current name, date of birth, current address, and the make, model, caliber and serial number of all firearms currently possessed. Such certification information shall be filed by the licensing officer in the same manner as an amendment. Elsewhere than in the city of New York and the counties of Nassau, Suffolk and Westchester, any license to carry or possess a pistol or revolver, issued at any time pursuant to this section or prior to the first day of July, nineteen hundred sixty-three and not previously revoked or cancelled, shall be in force and effect until revoked as herein provided. Any license not previously cancelled or revoked shall remain in full force and effect for thirty days beyond the stated expiration date on such license. Any application to renew a license that has not previously expired, been revoked or cancelled shall thereby extend the term of the license until disposition of the application by the licensing officer. In the case of a license for gunsmith or dealer in firearms, in counties having a population of less than two hundred thousand inhabitants, photographs and fingerprints shall be submitted on original applications and upon renewal thereafter only at six year intervals. Upon satisfactory proof that a currently valid original license has been despoiled, lost or otherwise removed from the possession of the licensee and upon application containing an additional photograph of the licensee, the licensing officer shall issue a duplicate license.

11. License: revocation and suspension. The conviction of a licensee anywhere of a felony or serious offense shall operate as a revocation of the license. A license may be revoked or suspended as provided for in section 530.14 of the criminal procedure law or section eight hundred forty-two-a of the family court act. Except for a license issued pursuant to section 400.01 of this article, a license may be revoked and cancelled at any time in the city of New York, and in the counties of Nassau and Suffolk, by the licensing officer, and elsewhere than in the city of New York by any judge or justice of a court of record; a license issued pursuant to section 400.01 of this article may be revoked and cancelled at any time by the licensing officer or any judge or justice of a court of record. The official revoking a license shall give written notice thereof without unnecessary delay to the executive department, division of state police, Albany, and shall also notify immediately the duly constituted police authorities of the locality.

12. Records required of gunsmiths and dealers in firearms. Any person licensed as gunsmith or dealer in firearms shall keep a record book approved as to form, except in the city of New York, by the superintendent of state police. In the record book shall be entered at the time of every transaction involving a firearm the date, name, age, occupation and residence of any person from whom a firearm is received or to whom a firearm is delivered, and the calibre, make, model, manufacturer's name and serial number, or if none, any other distinguishing number or identification mark on such firearm. Before delivering a firearm to any person, the licensee shall require him to produce either a license valid under this section to carry or possess the same, or proof of lawful authority as an exempt person pursuant to section 265.20. In addition, before delivering a firearm to a peace officer, the licensee shall verify that person's status as a peace officer with the division of state police. After completing the foregoing, the licensee shall remove and retain the attached coupon and enter in the record book the date of such license, number, if any, and name of the licensing officer, in the case of the holder of a license to carry or possess, or the shield or other number, if any, assignment and department, unit or agency, in the case of an exempt person. The original transaction report shall be forwarded to the division of state police within ten days of delivering a firearm to any person, and a duplicate copy shall be kept by the licensee. The record book shall be maintained on the premises mentioned and described in the license and shall be open at all reasonable hours for inspection by any peace officer, acting pursuant to his special duties, or police officer. In the event of cancellation or revocation of the license for gunsmith or dealer in firearms, or discontinuance of business by a licensee, such record book shall be immediately surrendered to the licensing officer in the city of New York, and in the counties of Nassau and Suffolk, and elsewhere in the state to the executive department, division of state police.

12-a. State police regulations applicable to licensed gunsmiths engaged in the business of assembling or manufacturing firearms. The superintendent of state police is hereby authorized to issue such rules and regulations as he deems reasonably necessary to prevent the manufacture and assembly of unsafe firearms in the state. Such rules and regulations shall establish safety standards in regard to the manufacture and assembly of firearms in the state, including specifications as to materials and parts used, the proper storage and shipment of firearms, and minimum standards of quality control. Regulations issued by the state police pursuant to this subdivision shall apply to any person licensed as a gunsmith under this section engaged in the business of manufacturing or assembling firearms, and any violation thereof shall subject the licensee to revocation of license pursuant to subdivision eleven of this section.

12-c. * Firearms records. (a) Every employee of a state or local agency, unit of local government, state or local commission, or public or private organization who possesses a firearm or machine-gun under an exemption to the licensing requirements under this chapter, shall promptly report in writing to his employer the make, model, calibre and serial number of each such firearm or machine-gun. Thereafter, within ten days of the acquisition or disposition of any such weapon, he shall furnish such information to his employer, including the name and address of the person from whom the weapon was acquired or to whom it was disposed.

(b) Every head of a state or local agency, unit of local government, state or local commission, public authority or public or private organization to whom an employee has submitted a report pursuant to paragraph (a) of this subdivision shall promptly forward such report to the superintendent of state police.

(c) Every head of a state or local agency, unit of local government, state or local commission, public authority, or any other agency, firm or corporation that employs persons who may lawfully possess firearms or machine-guns without the requirement of a license therefor, or that employs persons licensed to possess firearms or machine-guns, shall promptly report to the superintendent of state police, in the manner prescribed by him, the make, model, calibre and serial number of every firearm or machine-gun possessed by it on the effective date of this act for the use of such employees or for any other use. Thereafter, within ten days of the acquisition or disposition of any such weapon, such head shall report such information to the superintendent of the state police, including the name and address of the person from whom the weapon was acquired or to whom it was disposed.

13. Expenses. The expense of providing a licensing officer with blank applications, licenses and record books for carrying out the provisions of this section shall be a charge against the county, and in the city of New York against the city.

14. Fees. In the city of New York and the county of Nassau, the annual license fee shall be twenty-five dollars for gunsmiths and fifty dollars for dealers in firearms. In such city, the city council and in the county of Nassau the Board of Supervisors shall fix the fee to be charged for a license to carry or possess a pistol or revolver and provide for the disposition of such fees.

Elsewhere in the state, the licensing officer shall collect and pay into the county treasury the following fees: for each license to carry or possess a pistol or revolver, not less than three dollars nor more than ten dollars as may be determined by the legislative body of the county; for each amendment thereto, three dollars, and five dollars in the county of Suffolk; and for each license issued to a gunsmith or dealer in firearms, ten dollars. The fee for a duplicate license shall be five dollars. The fee for processing a license transfer between counties shall be five dollars. The fee for processing a license or renewal thereof for a qualified retired police officer as defined under subdivision thirty-four of section 1.20 of the criminal procedure law, or a qualified retired sheriff, undersheriff, or deputy sheriff of the city of New York as defined under subdivision two of section 2.10 of the criminal procedure law, or a qualified retired bridge and tunnel officer, sergeant or lieutenant of the triborough bridge and tunnel authority as defined under subdivision twenty of section 2.10 of the criminal procedure law, or a qualified retired uniformed court officer in the unified court system, or a qualified retired court clerk in the unified court system in the first and second judicial departments, as defined in paragraphs a and b of subdivision twenty-one of section 2.10 of the criminal procedure law or a retired correction officer as defined in subdivision twenty-five of section 2.10 of the criminal procedure law shall be waived in all counties throughout the state.

15. Any violation by any person of any provision of this section is a class A misdemeanor.

16. Unlawful disposal. No person shall except as otherwise authorized pursuant to law dispose of any firearm unless he is licensed as gunsmith or dealer in firearms.

17. Applicability of section. The provisions of article two hundred sixty-five of this chapter relating to illegal possession of a firearm, shall not apply to an offense which also constitutes a violation of this section by a person holding an otherwise valid license under the provisions of this section and such offense shall only be punishable as a class A misdemeanor pursuant to this section. In addition, the provisions of such article two hundred sixty-five of this chapter shall not apply to the possession of a firearm in a place not authorized by law, by a person who holds an otherwise valid license or possession of a firearm by a person within a one year period after the stated expiration date of an otherwise valid license which has not been previously cancelled or revoked shall only be punishable as a class A misdemeanor pursuant to this section.

Amended by L. 1967, Ch. 791; L. 1971, Chs. 796, 1097; L. 1973, Chs. 172, 546, 593; L. 1974, Chs. 1041, 1042; L. 1976, Ch. 584; L. 1977, Ch. 480; L. 1980, Chs. 233, 843; L. 1981, Ch. 175; L. 1982, Ch. 71; L. 1984, Ch. 739; L. 1985, Ch. 778; L. 1986, Ch. 539; L. 1988, Ch. 437; L. 1990, Ch. 707; L. 1991, Ch. 414, eff. July 19, 1991; L. 1992, Ch. 320, amending subd. (8), eff. Nov. 1, 1992; L. 1993, Chs. 448, 449, 498; L. 1994,

Ch. 332, § 1, amending subd. 5, eff. Nov. 1, 1994; L. 1994, Chs. 636, 637, amending subd. 14, eff. Aug. 2, 1994; L. 1995, Ch. 236, § 1, amending subd. 10, eff. July 26, 1995; L. 1995, Ch. 370, § 1, amending subd. 10, eff. Aug. 2, 1995; L. 1996, Ch. 644, § 5, amending subd. 1, eff. Nov. 1, 1996; L. 1996, Ch. 644, § 6, amending subd. 11, eff. Nov. 1, 1996; L. 1997, Ch. 446, §§ 3–6, eff. Aug. 25, 1997 and applicable to licenses issued on or after Aug. 25, 1997, and Ch. 447, § 2. eff. Aug. 25, 1997, the same date as a chapter of the laws of 1997, amending the penal law enacting the Westchester county handgun record-keeping and accountability act, as proposed in legislative bills numbers S. 5498-A and A. 8311-A, takes effect, and nothing contained in such chapter shall be construed as abridging the five year period applicable within Suffolk county with respect to the expiration of licenses to carry or possess a revolver; L. 1998, Ch. 378, § 8, eff. Nov. 1, 1998; L. 1999, Ch. 210, eff. Nov. 1, 1999, amending subds. 11 and 17; L. 2000, Ch. 189, §§ 18 and 19, amending subd. § 20, eff. Aug. 8, 2000, amending subds. 1, 2, and 8, respectively; L. 2002, Ch. 318, § 5, eff. Aug. 6, 2002, amending subd. 6; L. 2005, Ch. 331, § 1, amending subd. 4, eff. July 26, 2005; L. 2005, Ch. 195, § 1, amending subd. 14, eff. July 12, 2005.

ANNOTATIONS

Generally.—Penal Law § 400.00 is the exclusive statutory mechanism for the licensing of firearms in New York State. O'Connor v. Scarpino, 83 N.Y.2d 919, 615 N.Y.S.2d 305, 638 N.E.2d 950 (1994).

—Respondent's denial of petitioner's application for a pistol permit was properly based upon respondent's recent rejection of petitioner's application to become a police officer for psychological reasons, coupled with petitioner's numerous summonses for moving violations and irregularities in the addresses provided on the permit. Guttierrez v. Safir, 280 A.D.2d 263, 721 N.Y.S.2d 7 (1st Dept. 2001).

—Possession of a handgun license is a privilege and not a right. Tartaglia v. Kelly, 215 A.D.2d 166, 626 N.Y.S.2d 156 (1st Dept. 1995).

Abuse of discretion.—The police commissioner abused his discretion in revoking petitioner's pistol license where (1) petitioner's arrest related solely to his operation of a motor vehicle and none of the circumstances surrounding the arrest dealt with use or misuse of a handgun (2) no abuse of the pistol license or the obligations inherent therein was ever claimed (3) petitioner's business need for a gun was undisputed and (4) the arrest was the single transgression on the record of petitioner whose voluntary public service as an auxiliary police inspector had in the past merited awards and citations from the city. Klein v. Police Com'r of City of New York, 99 Misc. 2d 186, 415 N.Y.S.2d 735 (Sup. Ct. N.Y. Co. 1979).

Additional pistol authorization.—Where petitioner had obtained, pursuant to PL § 400.00, a license to possess a pistol in his dwelling, he had satisfied the four requirements of the statute for the issuance of an additional pistol purchase authorization coupon. Archibald v. Codd, 59 A.D.2d 867, 399 N.Y.S.2d 235 (1st Dept. 1977).

—Police commissioner was not empowered to deny the holder of an on-premises pistol license the right to acquire an additional pistol on the basis of "insufficient need" pursuant to PL § 400.00. Archibald v. Codd, 90 Misc. 2d 455, 395 N.Y.S.2d 336 (Sup. Ct. N.Y. Co. 1977), aff'd, 59 A.D.2d 867, 399 N.Y.S.2d 235 (1st Dept. 1977).

Age of licensee.—The denial of a target pistol permit to petitioner on the basis of a blanket rule forbidding issuance to anyone under the age of 21 without any further inquiry was erroneous as a matter of law and was arbitrary and capricious and an abuse of discretion (CPLR 7803(3)). Kreshesky v. Codd, 89 Misc. 2d 439, 391 N.Y.S.2d 792 (Sup. Ct. N.Y. Co. 1976).

Defense.—To establish a defense under PL § 400.00 it is incumbent upon the defendant, in the first instance, to go forward with evidence that he possesses an appropriate firearms license. People v. Psilakis, 148 A.D.2d 475, 538 N.Y.S.2d 623 (2d Dept. 1989).

Impermissible exercise of discretion.—It was an impermissible exercise of the issuing officer's discretion to disapprove the application where the petitioner indicated that if granted a pistol license she would engage in practice and competitive pistol shooting sponsored by organizations affiliated with the National Rifle Association of which she was a member. Davis v. Clyne, 58 A.D.2d 947, 397 N.Y.S.2d 186 (3d Dept. 1977).

No standard of care.—Section 400.00 governs issuance of firearms but does not impose standard of care upon defendants and, therefore, does not form basis of allegation of negligence. McDonald v. Cook, 252 A.D.2d 302, 681 N.Y.S.2d 900 (3d Dept. 1998).

Validity of licenses.—In Labor Law case in which security guards challenged the termination of their employment on basis that they refused to carry firearms on belief that the license was invalid in Suffolk County, court noted that licenses are valid throughout the state, regardless of whether the licensee had moved its operations between counties. Hughes v. Gibson Courier Servs. Corp., 218 A.D.2d 684, 630 N.Y.S.2d 552 (2d Dept. 1995).

Subd. 1

Proper cause.—The fact that a licensing officer did not conduct a "proper cause" inquiry during two applications to amend the unrestricted license did not preclude another officer from conducting a "proper cause" inquiry in connection with a third such application, upon which the formerly valid unrestricted license was modified to include restrictions. O'Brien v. Keegan, 87 N.Y.2d 436, 639 N.Y.S.2d 1004, 663 N.E.2d 316 (1996).

—"Proper cause" denotes a legitimate reason, a circumstance or combination of circumstances justifying the granting of a privilege; a generalized desire to carry a concealed weapon for protection does not constitute proper cause. In re O'Connor, 154 Misc. 2d 694, 585 N.Y.S.2d 1000 (Sup. Ct. Westchester Co. 1992), aff'd, 195 A.D.2d 1009, 600 N.Y.S.2d 574 (2d Dept. 1993), aff'd, 83 N.Y.2d 919, 638 N.E.2d 950, 615 N.Y.S.2d 305 (1994).

—A sincere intention to engage in target shooting and hunting can constitute proper cause. However, the license could be restricted to such use. In re O'Connor, 154 Misc. 2d 694, 585 N.Y.S.2d 1000 (Sup. Ct. Westchester Co. 1992), aff'd, 195 A.D.2d 1009, 600 N.Y.S.2d 574 (2d Dept. 1993), aff'd, 83 N.Y.2d 919, 638 N.E.2d 950, 615 N.Y.S.2d 305 (1994).

Serious crime.—Although ordinarily a person who has been convicted of a felony is automatically barred from obtaining a pistol permit, the grant of a certificate of relief from disabilities removed that automatic bar from petitioner, who had been convicted of a felony 16 years earlier. Hecht v. Bivona, 306 A.D.2d 410, 761 N.Y.S.2d 485 (2d Dept. 2003).

—Although the charge which was the basis for the revocation of the licensee's permit was dismissed, reinstatement had to be denied on basis of prior, previously undisclosed, conviction of a "serious crime"; the initial granting of the application had been erroneous. Silinovich v. Vogt, 194 A.D.2d 1030, 599 N.Y.S.2d 694 (3d Dept. 1993).

Inaccurate application.—Inaccuracies in the application constitute a basis to deny the application for a handgun license. Tartaglia v. Kelly, 215 A.D.2d 166, 626 N.Y.S.2d 156 (1st Dept. 1995).

—The application for a "carry business" permit could be denied on basis of applicant's false statement on application that he had never been arrested. Conciatori v. Brown, 201 A.D.2d 323, 607 N.Y.S.2d 46 (1st Dept. 1994).

—An applicant's failure to list a 1976 arrest in connection with a 1991 application for a pistol permit was a sufficient basis to deny the application. Hanna v. Police Dept. of the County of Nassau, 205 A.D.2d 689, 613 N.Y.S.2d 668 (2d Dept. 1994).

—An applicant's failure to report in his application a prior arrest for driving while intoxicated would be a valid basis to deny the application. The licensing officer may reject the applicant's claim that he had not known that his appearance ticket constituted an arrest. Di Monda v. Bristol, 219 A.D.2d 830, 631 N.Y.S.2d 968 (4th Dept. 1995).

Good cause to deny application.—Although ordinarily a person who has been convicted of a felony is automatically barred from obtaining a pistol permit, the grant of a certificate of relief from disabilities removed that automatic bar from petitioner, who had been convicted of a felony 16 years earlier. Hecht v. Bivona, 306 A.D.2d 410, 761 N.Y.S.2d 485 (2d Dept. 2003).

—The applicant's use of a false name on a prior occasion, when he was stopped for speeding, was the basis for an arrest; this arrest was not disclosed on the application; good cause to deny application. Westfall v. Lange, 175 A.D.2d 290, 572 N.Y.S.2d 739 (2d Dept. 1991).

Good cause to deny reinstatement.—When suspension resulted from wife filing criminal charges against licensee, which were dropped, licensee applied for reinstatement of the gun permit; at that time, the parties were still embroiled in an acrimonious divorce; wife had expressed concerns for her personal safety; valid basis to maintain suspension until divorce was finalized. Fromson v. Nelson, 178 A.D.2d 479, 577 N.Y.S.2d 417 (2d Dept. 1991).

Firearms permit; mental illness.—PL § 400.00(1) (c) renders ineligible for a firearms permit anyone who has ever suffered any mental illness, and mental capacity at a subsequent time is irrelevant. In re David H., 96 Misc. 2d 117, 408 N.Y.S.2d 759 (Ontario Co. Ct. 1978).

Good moral character.—Revocation of pistol permit upheld based on evidence that petitioner assaulted his girlfriend in violation of a criminal restraining order, coupled with evidence of petitioner's poor judgment and inability to control anger. Robertson v. Kerik, 300 A.D.2d 90, 751 N.Y.S.2d 469 (1st Dept. 2002).

—Revocation of pistol permit on grounds petitioner lacked good moral character was affirmed where evidence established that petitioner was a member of the Hell's Angels Motorcycle Gang and an officer of the corporation which sold the group's merchandise, coupled with evidence that other members had been convicted of crimes and that the group was linked to criminal activities, even though there was no evidence that petitioner was directly involved. Biganini v. Gallagher, 293 A.D.2d 603, 742 N.Y.S.2d 73 (2d Dept. 2002).

—Even though conviction of a misdemeanor might not be a "serious crime" within the disability set forth in § 400.00(11), it could constitute a lack of good character, upon which basis the application could be denied under § 400.00(1). Davi v. Cosgrove, 211 A.D.2d 788, 621 N.Y.S.2d 386 (2d Dept. 1995).

—Determination denying petitioner's application for a pistol license was annulled where petitioner was not informed of the reason for disapproval until he received the licensing officer's verified answer in a subsequent Article 78 proceeding which stated that the sole reason for withholding such license was a 1965 juvenile delinquency adjudication in Delaware which was subsequently expunged by that state's family court; the court ordered a new determination allowing petitioner reasonable opportunity to respond to the moral character objection and to submit proof in support thereof. Bobrick v. Liggett, 71 A.D.2d 869, 419 N.Y.S.2d 667 (2d Dept. 1979).

—Prior convictions for forgery-related offenses in several jurisdictions including New York would be a valid basis to deny license application for lack of good character, despite a Certificate of Good Conduct from the Division of Parole and despite a Certificate of Relief from Disabilities from the New York conviction. Hines v. Kelly, 635 N.Y.S.2d 31 (1st Dept. 1995), lv denied, 87 N.Y.2d 810 (1996); accord Unger v. Rozzi, 206 A.D.2d 974, 615 N.Y.S.2d 147 (4th Dept. 1994).

Subd. 2

Proper cause to grant permit.—The fact that a licensing officer did not conduct a "proper cause" inquiry during two applications to amend the unrestricted license did not preclude another officer from conducting a "proper cause" inquiry in connection with a third such application, upon which the formerly valid unrestricted license was modified to include restrictions. O'Brien v. Keegan, 87 N.Y.2d 436, 639 N.Y.S.2d 1004, 663 N.E.2d 316 (1996).

—Applicant's inability to explain to licensing officer why he needed to carry up to five concealed weapons at any one time, except that it "made (him) feel better," failed to establish proper cause under PL § 400.00(2)(f). O'Brien v. Keegan, 87 N.Y.2d 436, 639 N.Y.S.2d 1004, 663 N.E.2d 316 (1996).

—Licensing officer's power to determine the existence of proper cause for the issuance of a license necessarily and inherently includes the power to restrict the use of the license to the extent that the applicant has justified the issuance of the license in the first place. O'Brien v. Keegan, 87 N.Y.2d 436, 639 N.Y.S.2d 1004, 663 N.E.2d 316 (1996); accord O'Connor v. Scarpino, 83 N.Y.2d 919, 615 N.Y.S.2d 305, 638 N.E.2d 950 (1994).

—The types of licenses set forth in PL § 400.00(2) usually are

restricted, so that proper cause must be demonstrated in connection with each restricted category; it is consistent with this statutory underpinning to allow a licensing officer to further restrict a "carry permit" under § 400.00(2)(f) even if the applicant believes that proper cause has been shown for a mere carry permit. O'Connor v. Scarpino, 83 N.Y.2d 919, 615 N.Y.S.2d 305, 638 N.E.2d 950 (1994).

—The claim that the applicant made weekly cash deposits in connection with business, and that he undertook elevator repair work in crime prone area, did not sufficiently distinguish applicant from general population to suffice as proper cause. Milo v Kelly, 211 A.D.2d 488, 621 N.Y.S.2d 322 (1st Dept. 1995).

—"Proper cause" denotes a legitimate reason, a circumstance or combination of circumstances justifying the granting of a privilege; a generalized desire to carry a concealed weapon for protection does not constitute proper cause. In re O'Connor, 154 Misc. 2d 694, 585 N.Y.S.2d 1000 (Sup. Ct. Westchester Co. 1992), aff'd, 195 A.D.2d 1009, 600 N.Y.S.2d 574 (2d Dept. 1993), aff'd, 83 N.Y.2d 919, 638 N.E.2d 950, 615 N.Y.S.2d 305 (1994).

—A sincere intention to engage in target shooting and hunting can constitute proper cause. However, the license could be restricted to such use. In re O'Connor, 154 Misc. 2d 694, 585 N.Y.S.2d 1000 (Sup. Ct. Westchester Co. 1992), aff'd, 195 A.D.2d 1009, 600 N.Y.S.2d 574 (2d Dept. 1993), aff'd, 83 N.Y.2d 919, 638 N.E.2d 950, 615 N.Y.S.2d 305 (1994).

Target pistol license.—When the licensee failed to carry his loaded target pistol in a locked container, and was not en route between his residence and the target range, there was a basis to revoke the license. Bocchiano v. New York City Police Dept., 213 A.D.2d 264, 624 N.Y.S.2d 21 (1st Dept. 1995).

—A target pistol license is not merely a possess license, but is a carry license, insofar as it contemplates that the gun will be carried to and from target practice; the geographic range of carrying the handgun for the restricted purpose is not limited in the statute. People v Keung Li Lap, 150 Misc. 2d 724, 570 N.Y.S.2d 28 (N.Y.C. Crim. 1991).

Carry pistol permit.—Attorney, with an artificial leg, who engaged in practice of matrimonial and criminal law and who received cash and checks (not in unusually high amounts) in the ordinary course of business and who had, also, received threats from dissatisfied clients did not show uncommon occurrences sufficient to distinguish petitioner from other attorneys engaged in similar practice and was not entitled to a carry pistol license. Klenosky v. New York City Police Dept., 75 A.D.2d 793, 428 N.Y.S.2d 256 (1st Dept. 1980), aff'd, 53 N.Y.2d 685, 439 N.Y.S.2d 108, 421 N.E.2d 503; see also Bernstein v. Police Dept. of the City of New York, 85 A.D.2d 574, 445 N.Y.S.2d 716 (1st Dept. 1981).

Subd. 3

Residency.—Although statute does not explicitly have a residency requirement, the requirement in § 400.00(3) that the application be filed in the city or county where the applicant principally resides implies a residency requirement; court construed residency to equate with domicile; fact that the applicant, a New Jersey domiciliary, owned land at the New York location specified in the application was not the equivalent of residency; purpose of specifying domicile is to allow for appropriate investigation into good character. Mahoney v. Lewis, 199 A.D.2d 734, 605 N.Y.S.2d 168 (3d Dept. 1993).

Subd. 4

No right to a hearing.—The denial of the application for the reasons stated in writing, if the applicant is given an opportunity to respond, does not confer on the applicant a due process right to a hearing. Savitch v. Lange, 114 A.D.2d 372, 493 N.Y.S.2d 889 (2d Dept. 1985); accord Di Monda v. Bristol, 219 A.D.2d 830, 631 N.Y.S.2d 968 (4th Dept. 1995).

Denial with explanation must be in writing.—The failure to state in writing the reason for denial of the application for a pistol permit violates § 400.00(4-a), which requires that the determination be annulled. Deyo v. County Court Judge, 215 A.D.2d 758, 627 N.Y.S.2d 962 (2d Dept. 1995).

—Before the application can be denied, the applicant must have an opportunity to respond to the reason for the denial; if applicant had opportunity to respond, fact that he had not informed his character witness about his prior conviction for driving while intoxicated would be good cause to deny application. Novick v. Hillery, 183 A.D.2d 1007, 583 N.Y.S.2d 589 (3d Dept. 1992).

—Upon remittur, the applicant must be given the specific reasons for denial of the application, and the applicant must be provided an opportunity to submit evidence in response. Anderson v. Mulroy, 186 A.D.2d 1045, 590 N.Y.S.2d 777 (4th Dept. 1992).

Subd. 5

Public record.—Even though applications for pistol or revolver licenses are public records under PL § 400.00(5), in order for a not-for-profit organization to obtain addresses along with names pursuant to a FOIL request, it must demonstrate that the request is not exempt under the state Public Officers Law, § 87; FOIL requests are to be liberally construed and exemptions therefrom are to be narrowly construed; even so, the request of a licensee list for fund raising purposes by a not-for-profit gun organization was inconsistent with the privacy exemption (§ 87(2)(b)) and was not a valid basis for the FOIL request. Federation of New York State Rifle and Pistol Clubs, Inc. v. New York City Police Dept., 73 N.Y.2d 92, 538 N.Y.S.2d 226, 535 N.E.2d 279 (1989).

—Although PL § 400.00(3) specifies the inclusion of certain information in connection with applications for licenses, nothing in the statute precludes the expansion of the information to be supplied by the submission of additional or supplemental information; the public record aspect of the license application is not limited to the information supplied pursuant to § 400.00(3) and does not preclude FOIL disclosure of personal information supplied in § 400.00(5). Kwitney v. McGuire (in book), *aff'd,* 53 N.Y.2d 968, 441 N.Y.S.2d 659 (1981).

Change of residence.—The fact that the licensee changes his residence to another county within the state does not render the license invalid, nor need the licensee secure a duplicate license; the licensee need only apply to transfer the license and records to the county of his new residence. Mulligan v. Williams, 169 A.D.2d 280, 572 N.Y.S.2d 471 (3d Dept. 1991).

Subd. 9

Application.—The application for an amendment of the license does not restrict the reviewing licensing officer to the actual amendment nor does it preclude the licensing officer from modifying the initial license when denying the specific amendment sought. O'Brien v. Keegan, 87 N.Y.2d 436, 639 N.Y.S.2d 1004, 663 N.E.2d 316 (1996).

—The applicant's failure to provide a timely notification of a change of residence was a valid basis to deny a request for reinstatement of a pistol license. Dixie v. Mulroy, 216 A.D.2d 947, 629 N.Y.S.2d 349 (4th Dept. 1995).

Subd. 6

Denial of validation; absence of rational basis; reversed and remanded.—Supreme Court decision upholding the determination of the Police Department of the City of New York, which denied appellant's application for a special permit to carry a pistol in the city, was reversed and the matter remanded to the police department for further consideration where appellant, who was licensed to carry a pistol in Suffolk County and had a background indicating substantial experience in the use of a pistol, had a job in Suffolk County which required him to carry large sums of money to the bank after closing hours and where an electronic alarm system prevented him from returning the pistol to the store before going back to his home, five blocks within New York City limits. Babernitz v. Police Dept. of City of New York, 65 A.D.2d 320, 411 N.Y.S.2d 309 (1st Dept. 1978).

Subd. 10

Change of residence.—A change of residence is not a valid basis to issue a duplicate license; upon the licensee's arrangements to transfer license and record to new county of residence, duplicate license for new county is to be voided, insofar as original license was still in effect. Mulligan v. Williams, 169 A.D.2d 280, 572 N.Y.S.2d 471 (3d Dept. 1991).

Non-statutory limits on duration.—The licensing officer may not limit the license to a term not authorized by the statute. Bitondo v. State of New York, 151 Misc. 2d 182, 573 N.Y.S.2d

127 (Sup. Ct. Cortland Co. 1991), *modified* 182 A.D.2d 948, 582 N.Y.S.2d 819 (3d Dept. 1992).

Authorization to purchase "antique firearms" is not required. —Livingston v. Codd, 93 Misc. 2d 908, 403 N.Y.S.2d 662 (Sup. Ct. N.Y. Co. 1978).

On-premises license; requirements.—Although a premises license under §400.00(2)(a) limits possession to that licensee's dwelling, court did not view respondent's expansion of that right to allow transport of such arms to authorized target ranges and hunting areas for proficiency enhancement and recreation, as supplanting the statute, but merely supplementing it. De Illy v. Kelly, 6 A.D.3d 217, 775 N.Y.S.2d 256 (1st Dept. 2004).

—If applicant meets the four requirements delineated in PL § 400.00(1), he is entitled to issuance of an "on-premises" license. "Proper cause exists for issuance thereof" is only a requirement when applicant seeks a "carry" permit without regard to employment or place of possession. Shapiro v. Cawley, 46 A.D.2d 633, 360 N.Y.S.2d 7 (1st Dept. 1974).

—There was no justification for the withholding of a pistol purchase authorization from petitioner on the ground of "no showing of need," since proof of "need" was not a requisite for the granting of an on-premises pistol, as distinguished from an application to carry a concealed weapon. Livingston v. Codd, 93 Misc. 2d 908, 403 N.Y.S.2d 662 (Sup. Ct. N.Y. Co. 1978).

—With regard to the issuance of an on-premises pistol license a finding of need was not essential; applicant only had to show compliance with the four eligibility provisions of PL 400.00(1). Turner v. Codd, 85 Misc. 2d 483, 378 N.Y.S.2d 888 (Sup. Ct. N.Y. Co. 1975).

Subd. 11

License revocation.—The power to revoke a license under PL § 400.00(11) confers on the licensing officer the power to amend an existing unrestricted license to add restrictions. O'Brien v. Keegan, 87 N.Y.2d 436, 639 N.Y.S.2d 1004, 663 N.E.2d 316 (1996).

—Conviction of a licensee for a felony upon his guilty plea has as a "collateral consequence" of such plea the automatic revocation of the right to possess firearms, concerning which the defendant-licensee need not specifically be advised by the court. People v Ford, 86 N.Y.2d 397, 633 N.Y.S.2d 270, 657 N.E.2d 265 (1995).

Automatic revocation for felony conviction.—The licensee's conviction of a felony automatically revokes his handgun license; since it is revoked, despite the absence of any formalities of revocation, his continued possession of the handgun subjects him to a subsequent prosecution and conviction for criminal possession of a weapon. People v. Condello, 210 A.D.2d 921, 621 N.Y.S.2d 262 (4th Dept. 1994), *lv. denied,* 86 N.Y.2d 733 (1995).

No hearing required for revocation.—Since the license is only a privilege rather than a right, there is no requirement for a quasi-judicial or adversarial hearing prior to revocation. Shapiro v. New York City Police Department (License Division), 157 Misc. 2d 28, 595 N.Y.S.2d 864 (Sup. Ct. N.Y. Co. 1993), *aff'd,* 201 A.D.2d 333, 607 N.Y.S.2d 320 (1st Dept. 1994).

—Even if the officer relied on a faulty tape recording of her prior testimony injected potential bias into the proceeding, and counsel for the applicant should have been given access to the tape, nevertheless, there was no violation of the applicant's administrative due process rights, insofar as the license could have been revoked even in the absence of a hearing. Shapiro v. New York City Police Dept. (License Division), 157 Misc. 2d 28, 595 N.Y.S.2d 864 (Sup. Ct. N.Y. Co. 1993), *aff'd,* 201 A.D.2d 333, 607 N.Y.S.2d 320 (1st Dept. 1994).

Meaningful opportunity to respond.—The licensee must have an opportunity to respond to the reasons given for revocation; requesting licensee to appear in connection with a "review," without notifying licensee that the interview was in connection with revocation, did not give the licensee a meaningful opportunity to respond. Demchik v. Hannigan, 182 A.D.2d 1133, 583 N.Y.S.2d 334 (4th Dept. 1992).

Good cause for revocation.—Revocation was supported by substantial evidence indicating lack of moral character and fitness to possess a firearm including an arrest on theft and fencing charges in New Jersey, resolution of those charges by restitution to the victim, failure to notify the License Division of the arrest for more than a year, and failure to promptly notify the License Division of a robbery at petitioner's business. Cerciello v. Kelly, 8 A.D.3d 128, 779 N.Y.S.2d 46 (1st Dept. 2004).

—When the licensee failed to carry his loaded target pistol in a locked container, and was not en route between his residence and the target range, there was good cause to revoke the license. Bocchiano v. New York City Police Dept., 213 A.D.2d 264, 624 N.Y.S.2d 21 (1st Dept. 1995).

—The arrests of the licensee for assaulting his wife followed by the wife's obtaining of an order of protection was good cause to revoke a target pistol permit. Waskiewicz, 211 A.D.2d 603, 622 N.Y.S.2d 240 (1st Dept. 1995); *accord* Iacono v. Police Dept. of the City of New York, 204 A.D.2d 225, 612 N.Y.S.2d 140 (1st Dept. 1994), *lv. dism'd in part, denied in part,* 85 N.Y.2d 848, 624 N.Y.S.2d 366, 648 N.E.2d 786 (1995).

—The belief by an FBI special agent, based upon information supplied by a formerly reliable informant, that the licensee, a former police officer carrying a handgun under a retired Member of Service permit, was involved in jury tampering, was good cause for revocation; the lower court overstepped its authority under CPLR article 78 in rejecting the reliability of the information. Sewell v. City of New York, 182 A.D.2d 469, 583 N.Y.S.2d 255 (1st Dept. 1992), *lv. denied,* 80 N.Y.2d 756 (1992).

—Suspension of defendant's pistol permit upheld, defendant displayed and threatened to use his handgun to shoot the engine of an all-terrain vehicle used by two 14-year-old girls he spotted in the distance on his property without permission, after they failed to respond to his yells to leave, he fired a warning shot, threatened to shoot out their engine and told them they were under arrest. Manne v. Main, 8 A.D.3d 790, 778 N.Y.S.2d 210 (3d Dept. 2004).

Dismissal of criminal proceedings not a bar.—The dismissal of the criminal proceedings against petitioner did not operate as a bar to subsequent administrative proceedings or the determination to revoke petitioner's pistol license based upon circumstances underlying the criminal charges. St. Oharra v. Colucci, 67 A.D.2d 1104, 415 N.Y.S.2d 142 (4th Dept. 1979).

Review of revocation order.—While the issuance or denial or revocation of a license to carry a pistol is within the discretion of the licensing officer, the exercise thereof is not beyond review; an Article 78 proceeding may be brought. Charbonneau v. Brown, 69 A.D.2d 925, 415 N.Y.S.2d 126 (3d Dept. 1979).

Subd. 15

Possession of licensed weapon in place other than permitted in premises license.—Where all that is asserted is that the weapon for which defendant held a license "to have and possess in his place of business by a merchant or storekeeper" was possessed in a place other than that specified in the license, defendant could not be prosecuted for criminal possession of a weapon in the third degree, a class D felony, pursuant to CPL § 265.02, in view of CPL § 400.00(15) which makes such a violation a class A misdemeanor. People v. Serrano, 71 A.D.2d 258, 422 N.Y.S.2d 672 (1st Dept. 1979), *aff'd,* 52 N.Y.2d 936, 437 N.Y.S.2d 669, 419 N.E.2d 347 (1981).

§ 400.01. License to carry and possess firearms for retired sworn members of the division of state police.

1. A license to carry or possess a firearm for a retired sworn member of the division of state police shall be granted in the same manner and upon the same terms and conditions as licenses issued under section 400.00 of this article provided, however, that applications for such license shall be made to, and the licensing officer shall be, the superintendent of state police.

2. For purposes of this section, a "retired sworn member of the division of state police" shall mean a former sworn member of the division

of state police, who upon separation from the division of state police was immediately entitled to receive retirement benefits under the provisions of the retirement and social security law.

3. The provisions of this section shall only apply to license applications made or renewals which must be made on or after the effective date of this section. A license to carry or possess a pistol or revolver issued pursuant to the provisions of section 400.00 of this article to a person covered by the provisions of this section shall be valid until such license would have expired pursuant to the provisions of section 400.00 of this article; provided that, on or after the effective date of this section, an application or renewal of such license shall be made pursuant to the provisions of this section.

4. Except for the designation of the superintendent of state police as the licensing officer for retired sworn members of the division of state police, all of the provisions and requirements of section 400.00 of this article and any other provision of law shall be applicable to individuals licensed pursuant to this section. In addition all provisions of section 400.00 of this article, except for the designation of the superintendent of state police as licensing officer are hereby deemed applicable to individuals licensed pursuant to this section.

Added by L. 1999, Ch. 210, § 7, eff. Nov. 1, 1999.

§ 400.05. Disposition of weapons and dangerous instruments, appliances and substances.

1. Any weapon, instrument, appliance or substance specified in article two hundred sixty-five, when unlawfully possessed, manufactured, transported or disposed of, or when utilized in the commission of an offense, is hereby declared a nuisance. When the same shall come into the possession of any police officer or peace officer, it shall be surrendered immediately to the official mentioned in paragraph (f) of subdivision one of section 265.20, except that such weapon, instrument, appliance or substance coming into the possession of the state police shall be surrendered to the superintendent of state police.

2. The official to whom the weapon, instrument, appliance or substance which has subsequently been declared a nuisance pursuant to subdivision one of this section is so surrendered shall, at any time but at least once each year, destroy the same or cause it to be destroyed, or render the same or cause it to be rendered ineffective and useless for its intended purpose and harmless to human life.

3. Notwithstanding subdivision two of this section, the official to whom the weapon, instrument, appliance or substance is so surrendered shall not destroy or deliver the same if (a) a judge or justice of a court of record, or a district

attorney, shall file with the official a certificate that the non-destruction thereof is necessary or proper to serve the ends of justice; or (b) the official directs that the same be retained in any laboratory conducted by any police or sheriff's department for the purpose of research, comparison, identification or other endeavor toward the prevention and detection of crime.

4. In the case of any machine-gun firearm taken from the possession of any person, the official to whom such weapon is surrendered pursuant to subdivision one of this section shall immediately notify the executive department, division of state police, Albany, giving the calibre, make, model, manufacturer's name and serial number, or if none, any other distinguishing number or identification mark. A search of the files of such division and notification of the results of the search to such official shall immediately be made.

5. Before any machine-gun or firearm is destroyed pursuant to subdivision two of this section, (a) the official to whom the same has been surrendered shall forward to the executive department, division of state police, Albany, a notice of intent to destroy and the calibre, make, model, manufacturer's name and serial number, or if none, any other distinguishing number or identification mark of the machine-gun or firearm; (b) such division shall make and keep a record of such description together with the name and address of the official reporting the same and the date such notice was received; and (c) a search of the files of such division and notification of the results of the search to such official shall be made without unnecessary delay.

6. A firearm which is surrendered or voluntarily delivered pursuant to section 265.20 of this chapter and which has not been declared a nuisance pursuant to subdivision one of this section, shall be retained by the official to whom it was delivered for a period not to exceed one year. Prior to the expiration of such time period, the person who surrendered such firearm or firearms, shall have the right to arrange for the sale, or transfer, of such weapons to a dealer in firearms licensed in accordance with this chapter or for the transfer of such weapons to himself provided that a license therefor has been issued in accordance

with this chapter. If no such disposition is made within the time provided, the weapon, or weapons concerned shall be declared a nuisance and shall be disposed of in accordance with the provisions of this section.

Amended by L. 1980, Ch. 843; L. 1982, Ch. 179; L. 1986, Ch. 350; L. 1991, Ch. 166; L. 2001, Ch. 95, § 16, eff. July 13, 2001, the amendments to subdivisions 2 and 3 of section 400.05 of the penal law made by sections three hundred seventy-seven and three hundred seventy-eight of this act shall expire on July 1, 1992 and upon such date the provisions of such subdivisions shall revert and shall be read as if the provisions of this act had not been enacted.

§ 400.10. Report of theft or loss of a firearm, rifle or shotgun.

1. (a) Any owner or other person lawfully in possession of a firearm, rifle or shotgun who suffers the loss or theft of said weapon shall within twenty-four hours of the discovery of the loss or theft report the facts and circumstances of the loss or theft to a police department or sheriff's office.

(b) Whenever a person reports the theft or loss of a firearm, rifle or shotgun to any police department or sheriff's office, the officer or department receiving such report shall forward notice of such theft or loss to the division of state police via the New York Statewide Police Information Network. The notice shall contain information in compliance with the New York Statewide Police Information Network Operating Manual, including the caliber, make, model, manufacturer's name and serial number, if any, and any other distinguishing number or identification mark on the weapon.

2. The division of state police shall receive, collect and file the information referred to in subdivision one of this section. The division shall cooperate, and undertake to furnish or make available to law enforcement agencies this information, for the purpose of coordinating law enforcement efforts to locate such weapons.

3. Notwithstanding any other provision of law, a violation of paragraph (a) of subdivision one of this section shall be punishable only by a fine not to exceed one hundred dollars.

Added by L. 1984, Ch. 531; Amended by L. 2000, Ch. 189, §§ 23 and 24, eff. Nov. 1, 2000, amending subd. 1 and adding subd 3, respectively.

ARTICLE 405—LICENSING AND OTHER PROVISIONS RELATING TO FIREWORKS

LexisNexis Cross Reference

Forensic Sciences, Vol. 4, Ch. 38B, Investigation of Explosions.

§ 405.00. Permits for public displays of fireworks.

1. Definition of "permit authority." The term "permit authority," as used in this section, means and includes the agency authorized to grant and issue the permits provided in this section, which agency in the territory within a state park shall be the state agency having custody and control thereof, in the territory within a county park shall be the county park commission, or such other agency having jurisdiction, control and/or operation of the parks or parkways within which any fireworks are to be displayed, in a city shall be the duly constituted licensing agency thereof and, in the absence of such agency, shall be an officer designated for the purpose by the legislative body thereof, in a village shall be an officer designated for the purpose by the board of trustees thereof and in the territory of a town outside of villages shall be an officer designated for the purpose by the town board thereof.

2. Permits for public displays. Notwithstanding the provisions of section 270.00, the permit authority of a state park, county park, city, village or town may upon application in writing, grant a permit for the public display of fireworks by municipalities, fair associations, amusement parks or organizations of individuals. The application for such permit shall set forth:

(a) The name of the body sponsoring the display and the names of the persons actually to be in charge of the firing of the display.

(b) The date and time of day at which the display is to be held.

(c) The exact location planned for the display.

(d) The age, experience and physical characteristics of the persons who are to do the actual discharging of the fireworks.

(e) The number and kind of fireworks to be discharged.

(f) The manner and place of storage of such fireworks prior to the display.

(g) A diagram of the grounds on which the display is to be held showing the point at which the fireworks are to be discharged, the location of all buildings, highways and other lines of communication, the lines behind which the audience will be restrained and the location of all nearby trees, telegraph or telephone lines or other overhead obstructions.

(h) Such other information as the permit authority may deem necessary to protect persons or property.

3. Applications for permits. All applications for permits for the public display of fireworks shall be made at least five days in advance of the date of the display and the permit shall contain provisions that the actual point at which the fireworks are to be fired shall be at least two hundred feet from the nearest permanent building, public highway or railroad or other means of travel and at least fifty feet from the nearest above ground telephone or telegraph line, tree or other overhead obstruction, that the audience at such display shall be restrained behind lines at least one hundred and fifty feet from the point at which the fireworks are discharged and only persons in active charge of the display shall be allowed inside these lines, that all fireworks that fire a projectile shall be so set up that the projectile will go into the air as nearby as possible in a vertical direction, unless such fireworks are to be fired form the shore of a lake or other large body of water, when they may be directed in such manner that the falling residue from the deflagration will fall into such lake or body of water, that any fireworks that remain unfired after the display is concluded shall be immediately disposed of in a way safe for the particular type of fireworks remaining, that no fireworks display shall be held during any wind storm in which the wind reaches a velocity of more than thirty miles per hour, that all the persons in actual charge of firing the

fireworks shall be over the age of eighteen years, competent and physically fit for the task, that there shall be at least two such operators constantly on duty during the discharge and at least two sodaacid * or other approved type fire extinguishers of at least two and one-half gallons capacity each shall be kept at as widely separated points as possible within the actual area of the display. The legislative body of a state park, county park, city, village or town may provide for approval of such permit by the head of the police or fire department or both where there are such departments. No permit granted and issued hereunder shall be transferable. After such permit shall have been granted, sales, possession, use and distribution of fireworks for such display shall be lawful solely therefor.

3-a. Notwithstanding the provisions of subdivision three of this section, no permit may be issued to conduct a public display of fireworks upon any property where the boundary line of such property is less than five hundred yards from the boundary line of any property which is owned, leased or operated by any breeder as defined in subdivision four of section two hundred forty-four of the racing, pari-mutuel wagering and breeding law.

4. Bonds. Before granting and issuing a permit for a public display of fireworks as herein provided, the permit authority shall require an adequate bond from the applicant therefor, unless it is a state park, county park, city, village or town, or from the person to whom a contract for such display shall be awarded, in a sum to be fixed by the permit authority, which, however, shall not be less than five thousand dollars, conditioned for the payment of all damages, which may be caused to a person or persons or to property, by reason of the display so permitted and arising from any acts of the permittee, his agents, employees, contractors or subcontractors. Such bond shall run to the state park, county park, city, village or town in which the permit is granted and issued and shall be for the use and benefit of any person or persons or any owner or owners of any property so injured or damaged, and such person or persons or such owner or owners are hereby authorized to maintain an action thereon, which right of action also shall accrue to the heirs, executors, administrators, successors or assigns of such person or persons or such owner or owners. The permit authority may accept, in lieu of such bond, an indemnity insurance policy with liability coverage and indemnity protection equivalent to the terms and conditions upon which such bond is predicated and for the purposes herein provided.

5. Local ordinances superseded. All local ordinances regulating or prohibiting the display of fireworks are hereby superseded by the provisions of this section. Every city, town or village shall have the power to enact ordinances or local laws regulating or prohibiting the use, or the storage, transportation or sale for use of fireworks in the preparation for or in connection with television broadcasts.

* As originally enacted.

Amended by L. 1972, Ch. 661; L. 2002, Ch. 151, § 1, eff. Oct. 21, 2002, adding subd. 3-a.

L. 1985, Ch. 230, eff. June 18, 1985, provides:

Notwithstanding the provisions of subdivision three of section 405.00 of the penal law or any other statute, local law, rule or regulation, the fire department of the city of New York may grant permits from time to time for public displays of fireworks fired from the roof of the structure located at 45 River Avenue in the borough of the Bronx (Block 2490 Lot 1) provided that a permit shall be obtained for each such display. Such permit shall set forth such limitations, terms and conditions as the fire department of the city of New York shall deem necessary to protect the health, safety and well-being of persons and property.

§ 405.05. Seizure and destruction of fireworks.

Fireworks possessed unlawfully may be seized by any peace officer, acting pursuant to his special duties, or police officer, who must deliver the same to the magistrate before whom the person arrested is required to be taken. The magistrate must, upon the examination of the defendant, or if such examination is delayed or prevented, without awaiting such examination, determine whether the fireworks had been possessed by the defendant in violation of the provisions of section 270.00; and if he finds that the fireworks had been so possessed by the defendant, he must cause such fireworks to be destroyed, in a way safe for the particular type of such fireworks, or to be delivered to the district attorney of the county in which the defendant is liable to indictment or trial, as the interests of justice and public safety may, in his opinion, require. Upon the conviction of the defendant, the district attorney must cause to be destroyed, in a way safe for the particular type of such fireworks, the fireworks in respect whereof the defendant stands convicted, and which remain in the possession or under the control of the district attorney.

Amended by L. 1980, Ch. 843

ANNOTATIONS

Destruction of fireworks.—The destruction of seized fireworks without a magistrate's order violates PL § 405.05. Only the magistrate, and not law enforcement authorities, has the authority to determine that speedy destruction is warranted for health and safety reasons. People v. Christopher, 167 Misc. 2d 468, 634 N.Y.S.2d 948 (N.Y.C. Crim. Ct. Bronx Co. 1995).

Standing to challenge destruction of fireworks.—Although only the owner of seized fireworks has sufficient proprietary interest to seek compensation, standing to challenge the improper destruction of the fireworks as evidence extends to any person arrested in connection with the fireworks, such as the transporting party. People v. Christopher, 167 Misc. 2d 468, 634 N.Y.S.2d 948 (N.Y.C. Crim. Ct. Bronx Co. 1995).

Remedy for violation of statute.—The statute is silent as to remedy to be imposed when law enforcement authorities destroy fireworks in violation of PL § 405.05; although court must consider degree of prosecutorial culpability, overriding concern must be prejudice to defendant; dismissal is not warranted if lesser sanctions will suffice. People v. Christopher, 167 Misc. 2d 468, 634 N.Y.S.2d 948 (N.Y.C. Crim. Ct. Bronx Co. 1995).

PL

—Where prosecution repeatedly ignored defense requests for preservation, prosecutor disregarded statutory requirement that only magistrate may order destruction, and destruction of fireworks was intentional rather than inadvertent, but defendant never claimed that he was requesting preservation in order to arrange for an inspection by an independent expert, defendant never denied that the seized property was fireworks, and defendant never specified how the wrongful destruction of the fireworks would impair his defense, an adverse inference instruction was the appropriate remedy. People v. Christopher, 167 Misc. 2d 468, 634 N.Y.S.2d 948 (N.Y.C. Crim. Ct. Bronx Co. 1995).

§ 405.10. Permits for indoor pyrotechnics.

1. Definitions. For the purposes of this section, the following terms have the following meanings:

a. Airburst. A pyrotechnic device that is suspended in the air to simulate outdoor aerial fireworks shells without producing hazardous debris.

b. Areas of public assembly. All buildings or portions of buildings used for gathering together fifty or more persons for amusement, athletic, civic, dining, educational, entertainment, patriotic, political, recreational, religious, social, or similar purposes, the entire fire area of which they are a part, and the means of egress therefrom.

c. Assistant. A person who works under the supervision of the pyrotechnic operator.

d. Audience. Spectators whose primary purpose is to view a performance.

e. Building. A combination of any materials, whether portable or fixed, having a roof, to form a structure affording shelter for persons, animals, or property. The word "building" shall be construed for the purposes of this section as though followed by the words "or part or parts thereof", unless the context clearly requires a different meaning.

f. Concussion mortar. A device specifically designed and constructed to produce a loud noise and a violent jarring shock for dramatic effect without producing any damage.

g. Fallout area. The area in which any hazardous debris falls after a pyrotechnic device is fired. The fallout area is defined as a circle that, in turn, is defined by the fallout radius.

h. Fallout radius. A line that defines the fallout area of a pyrotechnic device. The line is defined by two points. The first point is at the center of a pyrotechnic device. The second point is the point most distant from the center of the pyrotechnic device at which any hazardous debris from the device can fall.

i. Fire area. The floor area of a story of a building within exterior walls, party walls, fire walls, or any combination thereof.

j. Hazardous debris. Any debris, produced or expelled by the functioning of a pyrotechnic device, that is capable of causing personal injury or unpredicted property damage. This includes, but is not limited to, hot sparks, heavy casing fragments, and unignited components. Materials such as confetti, lightweight foam pieces, feathers, or novelties are not to be construed as hazardous debris.

k. Owner. Any person, agent, firm, association, limited liability company, partnership, or corporation having a legal or equitable interest in the property.

l. Performance. The enactment of a musical, dramatic, operatic, or other entertainment production. The enactment may begin and progress to its end according to a script, plan, or other preconceived list of events, or deviate therefrom. A performance includes any encores.

m. Performer. Any person active in a performance during which pyrotechnics are used and who is not part of the audience or support personnel. Among others, performers include, but are not limited to, actors, singers, musicians, and acrobats.

n. Permit authority. The agency authorized to grant and issue the permits provided for in this section, which agency in the territory within a state park shall be the state agency having custody and control thereof, in the territory within a county park shall be the county park commission, or such other agency having jurisdiction, control, and/or operation of the parks or parkways within which any pyrotechnics are to be used, in a city shall be the duly constituted licensing agency thereof and, in the absence of such agency, shall be an officer designated for the purpose by the legislative body thereof, in a village shall be an officer designated for the purpose by the board of trustees thereof, and, in the territory of a town outside of villages, shall be an officer designated for the purpose by the town board thereof.

o. Permittee. (1) The person or persons who are responsible, as provided in subparagraph two of this paragraph, for obtaining the necessary permit or permits for the use of indoor pyrotechnics in areas of public assembly or for a production, or who are responsible for obtaining such permit or permits under an applicable local law or ordinance authorized pursuant to subdivision five of this section.

(2) The owner of a place of public assembly or building in which pyrotechnics are to be used shall be responsible for obtaining such permit or permits; provided, however, that such owner, in writing, by agreement or lease, may require or otherwise authorize a lessee, licensee, pyrotechnic operator, or other party to be responsible for obtaining such permit or permits, in which case such other party or parties shall be deemed responsible for obtaining such permit or permits and shall be the permittee for purposes of this article; provided further that the structure is

otherwise appropriate for such use under the New York state fire prevention and building code or other such applicable code.

p. Producer. An individual who has overall responsibility for the operation and management of the performance where the pyrotechnics are to be used. Generally, the producer is an employee of the promotion company, entertainment company, festival, theme park, or other entertainment group.

q. Production. All the performances of a musical, dramatic, operatic, or other show or series of shows.

r. Pyrotechnic device. Any device containing pyrotechnic materials and capable of producing a special effect as defined in this subdivision.

s. Pyrotechnic material (Pyrotechnic special effects material). A chemical mixture used in the entertainment industry to produce visible or audible effects by combustion, deflagration, or detonation. Such a chemical mixture consists predominantly of solids capable of producing a controlled, self-sustaining, and self-contained exothermic chemical reaction that results in heat, gas, sound, light, or a combination of these effects. The chemical reaction functions without external oxygen.

t. Pyrotechnic operator (Special effects operator). An individual who has responsibility for pyrotechnic safety and who controls, initiates, or otherwise creates special effects.

u. Pyrotechnic special effect. A special effect created through the use of pyrotechnic materials and devices.

v. Pyrotechnics. Controlled exothermic chemical reactions that are timed to create the effects of heat, gas, sound, dispersion of aerosols, emission of visible electromagnetic radiation, or a combination of these effects to provide the maximum effect from the least volume.

w. Rocket. A pyrotechnic device that moves by the ejection of matter produced by the internal combustion of propellants.

x. Special effect. A visual or audible effect used for entertainment purposes, often produced to create an illusion. For example, smoke might be produced to create the impression of fog being present, or a puff of smoke, a flash of light, and a loud sound might be produced to create the impression that a cannon has been fired.

y. Support personnel. Any individual who is not a performer or member of the audience. Among others, support personnel include the road crew of any production, stage hands, property masters, security guards, fire watch officers, janitors, or any other employee.

z. Venue manager. An individual who has overall responsibility for the operation and management of the facility where pyrotechnics are to be used in a performance.

2. Permit requirements. a. All uses of all pyrotechnics in areas of public assembly shall be approved by the permit authority. The permit authority shall determine that appropriate measures are established to provided acceptable crowd management, security, fire protection, (including sprinklers), and other emergency services. All planning and use of pyrotechnics shall be coordinated with the venue manager and producer.

b. Before the performance of any production, the permittee shall submit a plan for the use of pyrotechnics to the permit authority. After a permit has been granted, the permittee shall keep the plan available at the site for safety inspectors or other designated agents of the permit authority. Any addition of pyrotechnics to a performance or any significant change in the presentation of pyrotechnics shall require approval by the permit authority, except that reducing the number or size of pyrotechnics to be used in a performance shall not be considered to be a significant change in the presentation.

c. (1) The plan for the use of pyrotechnics shall be made in writing or such other form as is required or approved by the permit authority.

(2) The plan shall provide the following:

(a) Name of the person, group, organization, or other entity sponsoring the production.

(b) Date and time of day of the production.

(c) Exact location of the production.

(d) Name of the person actually in charge of firing the pyrotechnics (i.e., the pyrotechnic operator).

(e) Number, names, and ages of all assistants who are to be present.

(f) Qualifications of the pyrotechnic operator.

(g) Pyrotechnic experience of the operator.

(h) Confirmation of any applicable local, state, and federal licenses held by the operator or assistant.

(i) Evidence of the permittee's insurance carrier or financial responsibility.

(j) Number and types of pyrotechnic devices and materials to be used, the operator's experience with those devices and effects, and a definition of the general responsibilities of assistants.

(k) Diagram of the grounds or facilities where the production is to be held. This diagram shall show the point at which the pyrotechnic devices are to be fired, the fallout radius for each pyrotechnic device used in the performance, the lines behind which the audience shall be restrained, and the placement of sprinkler systems.

(l) Point of on-site assembly of pyrotechnic devices.

(m) Manner and place of storage of the pyrotechnic materials and devices.

(n) Material safety data sheet (MSDS) for the pyrotechnic materials to be used.

(o) Certification that the set, scenery, and rigging materials are inherently flame-retardant or have been treated to achieve flame retardancy.

(p) Certification that all materials worn by performers in the fallout area during use of pyrotechnic effects shall be inherently flame-retardant or have been treated to achieve flame retardancy.

(3) All plans shall be submitted as soon as is possible so that the permit authority has time to be present and to notify other interested parties. In no event shall such advance notice be less than five business days.

d. A walk-through and a representative demonstration of the pyrotechnics shall be approved by the permit authority before a permit is approved. The permit authority may waive this requirement based on past history, prior knowledge, and other factors; provided that the authority is confident that the discharge of pyrotechnics can be conducted safely. The demonstration shall be scheduled with sufficient time allowed to reset/reload the pyrotechnics before the arrival of the audience.

e. All pyrotechnic operators shall be at least twenty-one years old and licensed or approved by the permit authority in accordance with all applicable laws, if any. All assistants shall be at least eighteen years old.

3. Conduct of pyrotechnic performances.

a. Two or more fire extinguishers of the proper classification and size as approved by the permit authority shall be readily accessible while the pyrotechnics are being loaded, prepared for firing, or fired. In all cases, at least two pressurized water or pump extinguishers shall be available. Additional fire extinguishing equipment shall be provided as required by the permit authority. Personnel who have a working knowledge of the use of the applicable fire extinguishers shall be present while the pyrotechnics are being handled, used, or removed. No personnel shall use or handle pyrotechnic materials or devices while under the influence of intoxicating beverages, narcotics, controlled substances, and prescription or nonprescription drugs that can impair judgment. Fire detection and life safety systems shall not be interrupted during the operation of pyrotechnic effects.

b. (1) All pyrotechnic devices shall be mounted in a secure manner to maintain their proper positions and orientations so that, when they are fired, the pyrotechnic effects described in the plan submitted by the permittee are produced. Pyrotechnic devices shall be mounted so that no fallout from the device endangers human lives, results in personal injury, or damages property. Pyrotechnic materials shall be fired only from equipment specifically constructed for the purpose of firing pyrotechnic materials. The pyrotechnic operator shall be responsible for selecting equipment and materials that are compatible.

(2) Where rockets are launched before an audience, performers, or support personnel, the rockets shall be attached securely to a guide wire or cable with both ends securely attached and placed on an impact-resistant surface located at the terminal end of the guide. This guide wire or cable shall be of sufficient strength and flame resistance to withstand the exhaust from the rocket. An effective arrangement to stop the rocket shall be provided.

(3) Pyrotechnics shall be: (a) placed so that any hazardous debris falls into a safe, flame-resistant area; (b) fired so that the trajectory of their pyrotechnic material is not carried over the audience; and (c) placed for firing so that no flammable materials are within their fallout area.

(4) Pyrotechnic devices and materials used indoors shall be specifically manufactured and marked for indoor use by the manufacturer.

(5) Airbursts shall be permitted to be fired above the assembled audience, subject to the following conditions:

(a) The airburst shall be suspended by a minimum 30-gauge metal wire that is attached securely to a secure support acceptable to the authority having jurisdiction.

(b) The airburst shall occur at a minimum height of three times the diameter of the effect.

(c) Where the effect is demonstrated, there shall be no burning or glowing particles below the fifteen-foot level above the floor.

c. Each pyrotechnic device fired during a performance shall be separated from the audience by at least fifteen feet but not by less than twice the fallout radius of the device. Concussion mortars shall be separated from the audience by a minimum of twenty-five feet. There shall be no glowing or flaming particles within ten feet of the audience.

d. (1) The facility where pyrotechnic materials and devices are handled and used shall be maintained in a neat and orderly condition and shall be kept free of any conditions that can create a fire hazard.

(2) Smoking shall not be permitted within twenty-five feet of the area where pyrotechnics are being handled or fired; provided that smoking by performers as part of the performance shall be permitted as blocked in rehearsals and if expressly approved by the pyrotechnic operator and the permit authority.

e. (1) The pyrotechnic effect operator shall advise all performers and support personnel that they are exposed to a potentially hazardous situation when performing or otherwise carrying out their responsibilities in the vicinity of a pyrotechnic effect. Performers and support personnel familiar and experienced with the pyrotechnic effects being used shall be permitted to be in the area of a pyrotechnic effect, but only voluntarily and in the performance of their duties.

(2) No part, projectile, or debris from the pyrotechnic material or device shall be propelled so that it damages overhead properties, overhead equipment, or the ceiling and walls of the facility.

(3) Immediately before any performance, the pyrotechnic operator shall make a final check of wiring, positions, hook-ups, and pyrotechnic devices to ensure that they are in proper working order. The pyrotechnic operator also shall verify safety distances.

(4) The placement and wiring of all pyrotechnic devices shall be designed to minimize the possibility of performers and support personnel disturbing the devices during a performance.

(5) The pyrotechnic operator shall exercise extreme care throughout the performance to ensure that the pyrotechnic devices function correctly and that the performers, support personnel, and audience are clear of the devices.

(6) When pyrotechnics are fired, the quantity of smoke developed shall be controlled so as not to obscure the visibility of exit signs or paths of egress.

4. Bonds. Before granting and issuing a permit for a use of pyrotechnics as provided in this section, the permit authority shall require an adequate bond from the applicant therefor, unless such applicant is a state park, county park, city, village, or town, or from the person to whom a contract for such use shall be awarded, in a sum to be fixed by the permit authority, which, however, shall not be less than five hundred thousand dollars, conditioned for the payment of all damages which may be caused to a person or persons or to property by reason of the use so permitted and arising from any acts of the permittee, his or her agents, employees, contractors, or subcontractors. Such bond shall run to the owner of the facility for which the permit is granted and issued and shall be for the use and benefit of any person or persons or any owner or owners of any property so injured or damaged, and such person or persons or such owner or owners are hereby authorized to maintain an action thereon, which right of action also shall accrue to the heirs, executors, administrators, successors, or assigns of such person or persons or such owner or owners. The permit authority may accept, in lieu of such bond, an indemnity insurance policy with liability coverage and indemnity protection equivalent to the terms and conditions upon which such bond is predicated and for the purposes herein provided.

5. Local laws or ordinances superseded. All local laws or ordinances regulating the use of pyrotechnics within the contemplation of this section are hereby superseded by the provisions of this section, with the exception of:

a. all laws or ordinances enacted by a city of one million or more; and

b. other local laws or ordinances that prohibit the use of indoor pyrotechnics.

Added by L. 2003, Ch. 584, eff. Nov. 1, 2003, "provided that any state agency and any political subdivision of the state are authorized to promulgate any and all rules and regulations and take any other measures necessary to implement this act on its effective date on or before such date."

§ 405.12. Unpermitted use of indoor pyrotechnics in the second degree.

A person is guilty of unpermitted use of indoor pyrotechnics in the second degree when he or she is responsible for obtaining a necessary permit to use indoor pyrotechnics, as required by paragraph o of subdivision one of section 405.10 of this article, and, without obtaining such permit or knowing that he or she is not in compliance with the terms of a permit, he or she intentionally ignites or detonates pyrotechnics for which such permit is required, or knowingly permits another to ignite or detonate such pyrotechnics, in a building, as defined in paragraph e of subdivision one of section 405.10 of this article.

Unpermitted use of indoor pyrotechnics in the second degree is a class A misdemeanor.

Added by L. 2003, Ch. 584, eff. Nov. 1, 2003, "provided that any state agency and any political subdivision of the state are authorized to promulgate any and all rules and regulations and take any other measures necessary to implement this act on its effective date on or before such date."

§ 405.14. Unpermitted use of indoor pyrotechnics in the first degree.

A person is guilty of unpermitted use of indoor pyrotechnics in the first degree when he or she commits the crime of unpermitted use of indoor pyrotechnics in the second degree, as defined in section 405.12 of this article, and, within the previous five year period, he or she has been convicted one or more times of the crime of unpermitted use of indoor pyrotechnics in the second degree, as defined in section 405.12 of this article, or unpermitted use of indoor pyrotechnics in the first degree, as defined in this section.

Unpermitted use of indoor pyrotechnics in the first degree is a class E felony.

Added by L. 2003, Ch. 584, eff. Nov. 1, 2003, "provided that any state agency and any political subdivision of the state are authorized to promulgate any and all rules and regulations and take any other measures necessary to implement this act on its effective date on or before such date."

§ 405.16. Aggravated unpermitted use of indoor pyrotechnics in the second degree.

A person is guilty of aggravated unpermitted

use of indoor pyrotechnics in the second degree
when he or she commits the crime of unpermitted
use of indoor pyrotechnics in the second degree,
as defined in section 405.12 of this article, and,
by means of igniting or detonating such indoor
pyrotechnics, he or she recklessly: (1) causes
physical injury to another person; or (2) damages
the property of another person in an amount that
exceeds two hundred fifty dollars.

Aggravated unpermitted use of indoor pyrotechnics in the second degree is a class E felony.

Added by L. 2003, Ch. 584, eff. Nov. 1, 2003, "provided
that any state agency and any political subdivision of the state
are authorized to promulgate any and all rules and regulations
and take any other measures necessary to implement this act
on its effective date on or before such date."

§ 405.18. Aggravated unpermitted use of indoor pyrotechnics in the first degree.

A person is guilty of aggravated unpermitted
use of indoor pyrotechnics in the first degree
when he or she commits the crime of unpermitted
use of indoor pyrotechnics in the second degree,
as defined in section 405.12 of this article, and,
by means of igniting or detonating such indoor
pyrotechnics, he or she recklessly causes serious
physical injury or death to another person.

Aggravated unpermitted use of indoor pyrotechnics in the first degree is a class D felony.

Added by L. 2003, Ch. 584, eff. Nov. 1, 2003, "provided
that any state agency and any political subdivision of the state
are authorized to promulgate any and all rules and regulations
and take any other measures necessary to implement this act
on its effective date on or before such date."

ARTICLE 410—SEIZURE AND FORFEITURE OF EQUIPMENT USED IN PROMOTING PORNOGRAPHY

Section

410.00 Seizure and forfeiture of equipment used in photographing, filming, producing, manufacturing, projecting or distributing pornographic still or motion pictures.

LexisNexis Cross Reference

Prosecution and Defense of Forfeiture Cases, Vol. 2, Part II, Criminal Forfeiture.

§ 410.00. Seizure and forfeiture of equipment used in photographing, filming, producing, manufacturing, projecting or distributing pornographic still or motion pictures.

1. Any peace officer, acting pursuant to his special duties, or police officer of this state may seize any equipment used in the photographing, filming, printing, producing, manufacturing or projecting of pornographic still or motion pictures and may seize any vehicle or other means of transportation, other than a vehicle or other means of transportation used by any person as a common carrier in the transaction of business as such common carrier, used in the distribution of such obscene prints and articles and such equipment or vehicle or other means of transportation shall be subject to forfeiture as hereinafter in this section provided.

2. The seized property shall be delivered by the police officer or peace officer having made the seizure to the custody of the district attorney of the county wherein the seizure was made, except that in the cities of New York, Yonkers and Buffalo, the seized property shall be delivered to the custody of the police department of such cities, together with a report of all the facts and circumstances of the seizure.

3. It shall be the duty of the district attorney of the county wherein the seizure was made, if elsewhere than in the cities of New York or Buffalo, and where the seizure is made in either such city it shall be the duty of the corporation counsel of the city, to inquire into the facts of the seizure so reported to him and if it appears probable that a forfeiture has been incurred, for the determination of which the institution of proceedings in the supreme court is necessary, to cause the proper proceedings to be commenced and prosecuted, at any time after thirty days from the date of seizure, to declare such forfeiture, unless, upon inquiry and examination such district attorney or corporation counsel decides that such proceedings can not probably be sustained or that the ends of public justice do not require that they should be instituted or prosecuted, in which case, the district attorney or corporation counsel shall cause such seized property to be returned to the owner thereof.

4. Notice of the institution of the forfeiture proceeding shall be served either (a) personally on the owners of the seized property or (b) by registered mail to the owners' last known address and by publication of the notice once a week for two successive weeks in a newspaper published or circulated in the county wherein the seizure was made.

5. Forfeiture shall not be adjudged where the owners established by preponderance of the evidence that (a) the use of such seized property was not intentional on the part of any owner, or (b) said seized property was used by any person other than an owner thereof, while such seized property was unlawfully in the possession of a person who acquired possession thereof in violation of the criminal laws of the United States, or of any state.

6. The district attorney or the police department having custody of the seized property, after such judicial determination of forfeiture, shall, by a public notice of at least five days, sell such forfeited property at public sale. The net proceeds of any such sale, after deduction of the lawful expenses incurred, shall be paid into the general fund of the county wherein the seizure was made except that the net proceeds of the sale of property seized in the cities of New York and Buffalo shall be paid into the respective general funds of such cities.

7. Whenever any person interested in any property which is seized and declared forfeited under the provisions of this section files with a justice of the supreme court a petition for the recovery of such forfeited property, the justice of the supreme court may restore said forfeited property upon such terms and conditions as he deems reasonable and just, if the petitioner establishes either of the affirmative defenses set forth in subdivision five of this section and that the petitioner was without personal or actual knowledge of the forfeiture proceedings. If the petition be filed after the sale of the forfeited property, any judgment in favor of the petitioner shall be limited to the net proceeds of such sale, after deduction of the lawful expenses and costs incurred by the district attorney, police department or corporation counsel.

8. No suit or action under this section for wrongful seizure shall be instituted unless such suit or action is commenced within two years after the time when the property was seized.

9. For the purposes of this section only, a pornographic still or motion picture,* is defined as a still or motion picture showing acts of sexual intercourse or acts of sexual perversion. This section shall not be construed as applying to bona fide medical photographs or films.

* Punctuation as originally enacted.

Amended by L. 1980, Ch. 843; L. 1983, Ch. 608.

ANNOTATIONS

Constitutionality.—PL § 410.00 is unconstitutional because it permits peace officers to seize films and equipment which are used to show films which depict "acts of sexual intercourse or sexual perversion" without conforming to the definition of obscenity established by the United States Supreme Court in *Miller v. California*, 413 U.S. 15, 93 S. Ct. 2607, 37 L. Ed. 2d 419 (1973); in addition, the provisions in PL § 410.00 which permit seizure of motion picture equipment without a prior or subsequent adversary hearing violates the owner's First and Fourteenth Amendment rights. Plaza Redevelopment Corp. v. Vogt, 52 A.D.2d 396, 384 N.Y.S.2d 67 (3d Dept. 1976). *See also* Circle Cinema, Inc. v. Town of Colonie, 82 Misc. 2d 527, 371 N.Y.S.2d 344 (Sup. Ct. Albany Co. 1975).

—The procedure outlined in PL § 410.00 and followed by the police, without any inquiry by judicial authority into the factual basis for the officer's conclusion, is a procedure which falls short of the constitutional requirements demanding necessary sensitivity to freedom of expression and the police officers acted in an unconstitutional manner. Circle Cinema, Inc. v. Town of Colonie, 82 Misc. 2d 527, 371 N.Y.S.2d 344 (Sup. Ct. Albany Co. 1975).

Forfeiture.—The criminal court is not empowered to adjudge a forfeiture as an incident to conviction. Accordingly, the corporate defendant's right to a jury trial did not come into play in a prosecution under PL § 235.05 for showing the film "Deep Throat" since the criminal proceedings were not "tantamount to forfeiture proceedings." People v. Mature Enterprises, Inc., 35 N.Y.2d 520, 364 N.Y.S.2d 170, 323 N.E.2d 704 (1974).

ARTICLE 415—SEIZURE AND FORFEITURE OF—VEHICLES, VESSELS AND AIRCRAFT USED TO TRANSPORT OR CONCEAL GAMBLING RECORDS

Section

415.00 Seizure and forfeiture of vehicles, vessels and aircraft used to transport or conceal gambling records.

LexisNexis Cross References

Prosecution and Defense of Forfeiture Cases, Vol. 2, Part II, Criminal Forfeiture; *see generally New York Suppression Manual.*

§ 415.00. Seizure and forfeiture of vehicles, vessels and aircraft used to transport or conceal gambling records.

1. It shall be unlawful to transport, carry, convey or conceal in, upon or by means of any vehicle, vessel or aircraft, with knowledge of the contents thereof, any writing, paper, instrument or article:

(a) Of a kind commonly used in the operation or promotion of a bookmaking scheme or enterprise, and constituting, reflecting or representing more than five bets totaling more than five thousand dollars; or

(b) Of a kind commonly used in the operation, promotion or playing of a lottery or policy scheme or enterprise, and constituting, reflecting or representing more than five hundred plays or chances therein.

2. Any vehicle, vessel or aircraft which has been or is being used in violation of subdivision one by a person other than a bettor, player or shareholder whose bets, plays or shares are represented by all such writings, papers, instruments or articles, shall be seized by any peace officer, who is acting pursuant to his special duties, or police officer, and forfeited as provided in this section. However, such forfeiture and seizure provisions shall not apply to any vehicle, vessel or aircraft used by any person as a common carrier in the transaction of business as such common carrier.

3. The seized property shall be delivered by the police officer or peace officer having made the seizure to the custody of the district attorney of the county wherein the seizure was made, except that in the cities of New York, Yonkers and Buffalo, the seized property shall be delivered to the custody of the police department of such cities, together with a report of all the facts and circumstances of the seizure.

4. It shall be the duty of the district attorney of the county wherein the seizure is made, if elsewhere than in the cities of New York, Yonkers or Buffalo, and where the seizure is made in either such city it shall be the duty of the corporation counsel of the city, to inquire into the facts of the seizure so reported to him and if it appears probable that a forfeiture has been incurred by reason of a violation of this section, for the determination of which the institution of proceedings in the supreme court is necessary, to cause the proper proceedings to be commenced and prosecuted, at any time after thirty days from the date of seizure, to declare such forfeiture, unless, upon inquiry and examination, such district attorney or corporation counsel decides that such proceedings can not probably be sustained or that the ends of public justice do not require that they should be instituted or prosecuted, in which case, the district attorney or corporation counsel shall cause such seized property to be returned to the owner thereof.

5. Notice of the institution of the forfeiture proceeding shall be served either (a) personally on the owners of the seized property, or (b) by registered mail to the owners' last known address and by publication of the notice once a week for two successive weeks in a newspaper published or circulated in the county wherein the seizure was made.

6. Forfeiture shall not be adjudged where the owners establish by preponderance of the evidence that (a) the use of such seized property, in violation of subdivision one of this section, was not intentional on the part of any owner, or (b) said seized property was used in violation of subdivision one of this section by any person other than an owner thereof, while such seized property was unlawfully in the possession of a person who acquired possession thereof in violation of the criminal laws of the United States, or of any state.

7. The district attorney or the police department having custody of the seized property, after such judicial determination of forfeiture, shall, at their discretion, either retain such seized property for the official use of their office or department, or, by a public notice of at least five days, sell such forfeited property at public sale. The net proceeds of any such sale, after deduction of the lawful expenses incurred, shall be paid into the

general fund of the county wherein the seizure was made except that the net proceeds of the sale of property seized in the cities of New York, Yonkers and Buffalo shall be paid into the respective general funds of such cities.

8. Whenever any person interested in any property which is seized and declared forfeited under the provisions of this section files with a justice of the supreme court a petition for the recovery of such forfeited property, the justice of the supreme court may restore said forfeited property upon such terms and conditions as he deems reasonable and just, if the petitioner establishes either of the affirmative defenses set forth in subdivision six of this section and that the petitioner was without personal or actual knowledge of the forfeiture proceeding. If the petition be filed after the sale of the forfeited property, any judgment in favor of the petitioner shall be limited to the net proceeds of such sale after deduction of the lawful expenses and costs incurred by the district attorney, police department or corporation counsel.

9. No suit or action under this section for wrongful seizure shall be instituted unless such suit or action is commenced within two years after the time when the property was seized.

Added by L. 1969, Ch. 920; **Amended** by L. 1980, Ch. 843; L. 1983, Ch. 608.

ANNOTATION

Conditional bill of sale.—Where GMAC had a security interest by way of a conditional bill of sale in vehicle seized under PL § 415.00 the court directed the district attorney to pay the balance due on the contract to GMAC if he elected to retain the seized vehicle, or if he elected to sell it, then said sale was subject to the GMAC lien and any excess from the sale was to be paid into the general funds of the County of Nassau pursuant to PL § 415.00(7). Dillon v. Reese, 93 Misc. 2d 464, 402 N.Y.S.2d 713 (Sup. Ct. Nassau Co. 1977).

ARTICLE 420—SEIZURE AND DESTRUCTION OF UNAUTHORIZED RECORDINGS OF SOUND AND FORFEITURE OF EQUIPMENT USED IN THE PRODUCTION THEREOF

LexisNexis Cross References

Prosecution and Defense of Forfeiture Cases, Vol. 2, Part II, Criminal Forfeiture; *see generally New York Suppression Manual.*

§ 420.00. Seizure and destruction of unauthorized recordings.

Any article produced in violation of article two hundred seventy-five of this chapter may be seized by any police officer upon the arrest of any individual in possession of same. Upon final determination of the charges, the court shall, upon proper notice by the district attorney or representative of the crime victim or victims, after prior notice to the district attorney and custodian of the seized property, enter an order preserving any goods manufactured, sold, offered for sale, distributed or produced in violation of this article, as evidence for use in other cases, including a civil action. This notice must be received within thirty days of final determination of the charges. The cost of storage, security, and destruction of goods so ordered for preservation and use as evidence in a civil action, other than a civil action under article thirteen-A of the civil practice law and rules initiated by the district attorney, shall be paid by the party seeking preservation of the evidence for a civil action. If no such order is entered within the thirty day period, the district attorney or custodian of the seized property must cause such articles to be destroyed. Destruction shall not include auction, sale, or distribution of the items in their original form.

Amended by L. 1990, Ch. 460; L. 2001, Ch. 542, eff. Mar. 12, 2002; L. 2002, Ch. 149, § 1, eff. Mar. 12, 2002.

§ 420.05. Seizure and forfeiture of equipment used in the production of unauthorized recordings.

1. Any police officer of this state may seize any equipment, or components, used in the manufacture or production of unauthorized recordings of sound and may seize any vehicle or other means of transportation, other than a vehicle or means of transportation used by any person as a common carrier in the transaction of business as such common carrier, used in the distribution of such unauthorized recordings of sound and such equipment or vehicle or other means of transportation shall be subject to forfeiture as provided in this section.

2. The seized property shall be delivered by the police officer having made the seizure to the custody of the district attorney of the county wherein the seizure was made, except that in the cities of New York, Yonkers and Buffalo, the seized property shall be delivered to the custody of the police department of such cities, together with a report of all the facts and circumstances of the seizure.

3. It shall be the duty of the district attorney of the county wherein the seizure was made, if elsewhere than in the city of New York, Yonkers or Buffalo, and where the seizure is made in either such city, it shall be the duty of the corporation counsel of the city, to inquire into the facts of the seizure so reported to him and if it appears probable that a forfeiture has been incurred for the determination of which the institution of proceedings in the supreme court is necessary, to cause the proper proceedings to be commenced and prosecuted, at any time after thirty days from the date of seizure, to declare such forfeiture, unless, upon inquiry and examination such district attorney or corporation counsel decides that such proceedings cannot probably be sustained or that the ends of public justice do not require that they should be instituted or prosecuted, in which case, the district attorney or corporation counsel shall cause such seized property to be returned to the owner thereof.

4. Notice of the institution of the forfeiture proceeding shall be served either:

(a) personally on the owners of the seized property; or

(b) by registered mail to the owners' last known address and by publication of the notice once a week for two successive weeks in a newspaper published or circulated in the county wherein the seizure was made.

5. Forfeiture shall not be adjudged where the owners established by preponderance of the evidence that:

(a) the use of such seized property was not intentional on the part of any owner; or

(b) said seized property was used by any person other than an owner thereof, while such seized property was unlawfully in the possession of a person who acquired possession thereof in violation of the criminal laws of the United States, or of any state.

6. The district attorney or the police department having custody of the seized property, after such judicial determination of forfeiture, shall, by a public notice of at least five days, sell such forfeited property at public sale. The net proceeds of any such sale, after deduction of the lawful expenses incurred, shall be paid into the general fund of the county wherein the seizure was made except that the net proceeds of the sale of property seized in the cities of New York, Yonkers and Buffalo shall be paid into the respective general funds of such cities.

7. Whenever any person interested in any property which is seized and declared forfeited under the provisions of this section files with a justice of the supreme court a petition for the recovery of such forfeited property, the justice of the supreme court may restore said forfeited property upon such terms and conditions as he deems reasonable and just, if the petitioner establishes either of the affirmative defenses set forth in subdivision five of this section and that the petitioner was without personal or actual knowledge of the forfeiture proceeding. If the petition be filed after the sale of the forfeited property, any judgment in favor of the petitioner shall be limited to the net proceeds of such sale, after deduction of the lawful expenses and costs incurred by the district attorney, police department or corporation counsel.

8. No suit or action under this section for wrongful seizure shall be instituted unless such suit or action is commenced within two years after the time when the property was seized.

Amended by L. 1983, Ch. 608; 1990, Ch. 460.

ARTICLE 450—DISPOSAL OF STOLEN PROPERTY

Section

450.10 Disposal of stolen property.

§ 450.10. Disposal of stolen property.

1. When property, other than contraband including but not limited to those items subject to the provisions of sections 410.00, 415.00, 420.00 and 420.05 of this chapter, alleged to have been stolen is in the custody of a police officer, a peace officer or a district attorney and a request for its release is made prior to or during the criminal proceeding, it may not be released except as provided in subdivisions two, three and four of this section. When a request is made for the return of stolen property under this section, the police officer, peace officer or district attorney in possession of such property must provide written notice to the defendant or his counsel of such request as soon as practicable. Such notice shall advise the defendant or his counsel of the date on which the property will be released and the name and address of a person with whom arrangements can be made for the examination, testing, photographing, photocopying or other reproduction of said property.

2. Both the defendant's counsel and the prosecutor thereafter shall make a diligent effort to examine, test and photograph, photocopy or otherwise reproduce the property. Either party may apply to the court for an extension of any period allowed for examination, testing, photographing, photocopying or otherwise reproducing the property. For good cause shown the court may order retention of the property for use as evidence by either party. Unless extended by a court order sought by either party on notice to the other, the property shall be released no later than the time periods for retention set forth in subdivisions three and four of this section to the person making such request after satisfactory proof of such person's entitlement to the possession thereof. Unless a court, upon applicaton * of either party with notice to the other, orders otherwise, the release of property in accordance with the provisions of this section shall be unconditional.

3. Except as provided in subdivision four of this section, when a request is made for the release of property described in subdivision one of this section, the property shall be retained until either the expiration of a fifteen day period from receipt by the defendant or his counsel of the notice of the request, or the examination ** testing and photographing, photocopying or other reproduction of such property, by the parties, whichever event occurs first. The fifteen day period may be extended by up to five additional days by agreement between the parties.

4. (a) Except as provided in paragraphs (b) and (c) of this subdivision and in subdivision eleven of this section, when a request is made for the release of property described in subdivision one of this section, and the property shall consist of perishables, fungible retail items, motor vehicles or any other property release of which is necessary for either the operation of a business or the health or welfare of any person, the property shall be retained until either the expiration of a forty-eight hour period from the receipt by the defendant's counsel of the notice of the request, or the examination, testing and photocopying, photographing or other reproduction of such property, by the parties whichever event occurs first. The forty-eight hour period may be extended by up to twenty-four additional hours by agreement between the parties. For the purposes of this section, perishables shall mean any property likely to spoil or decay or diminish significantly in value within twenty days of the initial retention of the property.

(b) If, upon oral or written application by the district attorney with notice to the defendant or his counsel, a court determines that immediate release of property described in paragraph (a) of this subdivision is required under the attendant circumstances, the court shall issue an order releasing the property and, if requested by either party, setting, as a part of such order, any condition appropriate in the furtherance of justice.

(c) A motor vehicle alleged to have been stolen but not alleged to have been used in connection with any crime or criminal transaction other than the theft or unlawful use of said motor vehicle, which is in the custody of a police officer, a peace officer or a district attorney, may be released expeditiously to its registered owner or the owner's representative without prior notice to the defendant. Before such release, evidentiary photographs shall be taken of such motor vehicle. Such photographs shall include the vehicle identification number, registration on windshield, license plates, each side of the vehicle, including vent windows, door locks and handles, the front and back of the vehicle, the interior of the vehicle, including ignition lock, seat to floor clearance, center console, radio receptacle and dashboard area, the motor, and other interior or exterior surfaces showing any and all damage to the vehicle. Notice of such release, and the photographs taken of said vehicle, shall be furnished to the defendant within fifteen days after arraignment or after counsel initially appears on behalf of the defendant or respondent, whichever occurs later.

5. If stolen property comes into the custody of a court, it must, unless temporary retention be deemed necessary in furtherance of justice, be delivered to the owner, on satisfactory proof of his title, and on his paying the necessary expenses

incurred in its preservation, to be certified by the court.

6. If stolen property has not been delivered to the owner, the court before which a trial is had for stealing it, may, on proof of his title, order it to be restored to the owner.

7. If stolen property is not claimed by the owner, before the expiration of six months from the conviction of a person for stealing it, the court or other officer having it in custody must, on payment of the necessary expenses incurred in its preservation, deliver it to the county commissioner of social services, or in the city of New York, to the commissioner of social services, to be applied for the benefit of the poor of the county or city, as the case may be.

8. Except in the city of New York, when money or other property is taken from a defendant, arrested upon a charge of an offense, the officer taking it must, at the time, give duplicate receipts therefor, specifying particularly the amount of property taken, one of which receipts he must deliver to the defendant, and the other of which he must forthwith file with the court in which the criminal action is pending.

9. The commissioners of police of the city of New York may designate some person to take charge of all property alleged to be stolen, and which may be brought into the police office, and all property taken from the person of a prisoner, and may prescribe regulations in regard to the duties of the clerk or clerks so designated, and to require and take security for the faithful performance of the duties imposed by this subdivision, and it shall be the duty of every officer into whose possession such property may come, to deliver the same forthwith to the person so designated.

10. Where there has been a failure to comply with the provisions of this section, and where the district attorney does not demonstrate to the satisfaction of the court that such failure has not caused the defendant prejudice, the court shall instruct the jury that it may consider such failure in determining the weight to be given such evidence and may also impose any other sanction set forth in subdivision one of section 240.70 of the criminal procedure law; provided, however, that unless the defendant has convinced the court that such failure has caused him undue prejudice, the court shall not preclude the district attorney from introducing into evidence the property, photographs, photocopies, or other reproductions of the property or, where appropriate, testimony concerning its value and condition, where such evidence is otherwise properly authenticated and admissible under the rules of evidence. Failure to comply with any one or more of the provisions of this section shall not for that reason alone be grounds for dismissal of the accusatory instrument.

11. When a request for the release of stolen property is made pursuant to paragraph (a) of subdivision four of this section and the defendant is not represented by counsel the notice required pursuant to subdivision one of this section shall be personally delivered to the defendant and release of said property shall not occur for a period less than five days: from (a) the delivery of such notice; or (b) in the case of delivery to such person in custody, from the first appearance before the court, whichever is later.

* As originally enacted.

** Comma absent in original legislation.

Amended by L. 1980, Ch. 843; L. 1981, Ch. 567; L. 1982, Ch. 892); L. 1984, Ch. 795; L. 1992, Ch. 421, eff. Nov. 1, 1992, amending subd. (4)(a) and adding subd. (4)(c).

ANNOTATIONS

Appropriate standard.—When discoverable property in the custody of the prosecutor or police is lost, the People have the heavy burden of establishing that diligent, good faith efforts were taken to preserve the property. People v. Kelly, 62 N.Y.2d 516, 478 N.Y.S.2d 834, 467 N.E.2d 498 (1984).

Failure to comply: considerations.—When the People inexcusably fail to preserve property and dispose of it without securing a court order pursuant to PL § 450.10, the court should consider the degree of prosecutorial fault, but the overriding concern is to eliminate prejudice to the defendant while at the same time protecting the interests of society. People v. Kelly, 62 N.Y.2d 516, 478 N.Y.S.2d 834, 467 N.E.2d 498 (1984).

—Where People's noncompliance did not cause undue prejudice, and there was no proof presented that the violation was intentional or in bad faith, court will not reverse. People v. Watkins, 239 A.D.2d 448, 658 N.Y.S.2d 39 (2d Dept. 1997).

Failure to comply: remedy.—When police had returned decoy wallet and cash ostensibly stolen by defendants to undercover officer, defendant claimed that failure to preserve property precluded assertion of entrapment defense and restricted impeachment of the decoy officer; criminal court dismissed charges as a sanction; Court of Appeals, in reinstating charges, concluded that there were less drastic sanctions available, and remitted to trial court to impose a lesser sanction. People v. Kelly, 62 N.Y.2d 516, 478 N.Y.S.2d 834, 467 N.E.2d 498 (1984); *accord* People v. Perry, 161 A.D.2d 1156, 555 N.Y.S.2d 515 (4th Dept.), *lv. denied,* 76 N.Y.2d 863 (1990).

—Insofar as police, who released stolen car to owner without giving notice to defendant, had photographed the car, and the photographs were available to the defense, and there was no evidence of bad faith by the People, the trial court did not improvidently exercise its discretion in denying motion to dismiss the indictment. People v. Whiten, 156 A.D.2d 606, 549 N.Y.S.2d 112 (2d Dept. 1989), *lv. denied,* 75 N.Y.2d 926 (1990).

Failure to comply: lack of prejudice.—When the car was promptly photographed at time of arrest, depicting the car's condition, and defendant's expert could offer opinion on basis of photograph, no prejudice accrued to defendant when he did not examine the car. People v. Thomas, 211 A.D.2d 506, 621 N.Y.S.2d 558 (1st Dept. 1995).

—Since defendant, who had tried to unlawfully jump-start a car, was allowed an opportunity to inspect the car which was the subject of the attempted grand larceny, the court ordered disclosure of photos of the car taken after the incident, and defendant had ample opportunity to cross-examine witnesses in connection with their observations of damage to the car, there was no prejudice arising from the owner's retention of the car. People v. Trotty, 188 A.D.2d 353, 591 N.Y.S.2d 171 (1st Dept. 1992), *lv. denied,* 81 N.Y.2d 848 (1993).

—It was disingenuous for defendant to claim prejudice arising from the failure of police to impound the car which he attempted to steal: defendant was provided an opportunity at arraignment on the day of the theft to inspect the car, but failed to do so; defense counsel consented to admissibility of testimony by police officers concerning their observations of the condition of the car, including the broken steering column; and defense counsel stipulated to a valuation of the car which was in excess of $10,000. People v. Burwell, 172 A.D.2d 412, 568 N.Y.S.2d 933 (1st Dept.1), *lv. denied,* 78 N.Y.2d 963 (1991).

—Absent a showing of prejudice or bad faith, the People's failure to provide defendant with notice pursuant to this section, that the complainant's stolen telephone card, which was recovered from the defendant when he was arrested, was returned prior to trial, did not warrant reversal. People v. McDowell,, 696 N.Y.S.2d 465 (2d Dept. 1999).

—Court will not impose sanctions against People for failure to comply with procedures in section 450.10 where defendant failed to prove undue prejudice from People's release of property to complainant. People v. Woodberry, 239 A.D.2d 448, 658 N.Y.S.2d 40 (2d Dept. 1997).

—When police, who failed to provide notice to defendant that they would be returning the stolen car to its owner, did not act in bad faith and defendant failed to show prejudice, the trial court did not err in denying preclusion and in not giving an adverse inference instruction. People v. Dent, 183 A.D.2d 723, 583 N.Y.S.2d 301 (2d Dept.), *lv. denied,* 80 N.Y.2d 928 (1992).

—When police, who had released the stolen car from custody without giving statutory notice, nevertheless had photographed the car's exterior, defendant did not suffer prejudice from the failure of police to also photograph the car's interior. People v. Whiten, 156 A.D.2d 606, 549 N.Y.S.2d 112 (4th Dept. 1989), *lv. denied,* 75 N.Y.2d 926 (1990).

Property not in police custody.—When the complainant was a police officer whose car defendant had attempted to steal, the theft was not completed, with the result that the defendant was charged only with attempted grand larceny, and the complainant retained his own car, there was no police custody within the meaning of PL § 450.10. People v. Thomas, 211 A.D.2d 506, 621 N.Y.S.2d 558 (1st Dept. 1995).

—The requirements of PL § 450.10 were not triggered, and the court did not err in denying motion to preclude evidence, when victim of pickpocketing immediately retrieved wallet from defendant, and establishment's private security guard only looked at wallet momentarily; police never had custody of the wallet. People v. Faucette, 201 A.D.2d 252, 607 N.Y.S.2d 268 (1st Dept. 1994).

—Since the police never impounded the car which the defendant had attempted to illegally jump-start in order to steal it, PL § 450.10 did not apply, and the court properly denied dismissal and, alternatively, preclusion. People v. Trotty, 188 A.D.2d 353, 591 N.Y.S.2d 171 (1st Dept. 1992), *lv. denied,* 81 N.Y.2d 848 (1993).

—When the victim of a pickpocketing retrieved the wallet from the defendant, and only momentarily handed it to police officer before retrieving it, the wallet was not in police custody within the meaning of PL § 450.10. Morgenthau v. Marks, 177 A.D.2d 131, 581 N.Y.S.2d 296 (1st Dept. 1992).

Effect of using previously stolen property as decoy.—Defendant, who was a fence who had purchased property from an undercover officer who was an ostensible burglar, could assert defense that the charge of his criminal possession of stolen property was impossible of commission; the decoy property had previously been stolen and when the rightful owners were not located, the property remained in police custody; once police had custody of the property, it was no longer "stolen," insofar as police acted as agents for the owners; hence, PL § 450.10 did not apply. People v. Zaborski, 59 N.Y.2d 863, 465 N.Y.S.2d 927, 452 N.E.2d 1255 (1983).

Defendant receiving notice not represented by counsel.—The fact that a defendant is not represented by counsel when notice is given, does not invalidate the notice, insofar as PL § 450.10(11) explicitly contemplates an unrepresented recipient of notice; the validity of the notice is not impaired even if the defendant is a juvenile. *In re* James C., 179 A.D.2d 639, 578 N.Y.S.2d 589 (2d Dept. 1992); *accord In re* Nicomedes F., 177 A.D.2d 316, 575 N.Y.S.2d 873 (1st Dept. 1991) (reversing Family Court's order of preclusion). *But see In re* Marpole, 145 Misc. 2d 549, 547 N.Y.S.2d 1007 (Family Ct. N.Y. Co. 1989), decided before Nicomedes, but within the geographic jurisdiction of the First Department, in which Family Court concluded that juvenile had to be represented by counsel or waive right to notice before putative § 450.10 notice could be effective.

Diligence by defendant.—When the car was available for defendant's inspection up to time of trial, but he had not made diligent efforts to examine it, his request during trial for a continuance so that he could examine the car was properly

denied. People v. Thomas, 211 A.D.2d 506, 621 N.Y.S.2d 558 (1st Dept. 1995).

—If defendant has properly been placed on notice, he is obliged to examine and inspect the property in a diligent manner; if defendant failed to avail himself of opportunity to inspect, it would be error for trial court to preclude evidence concerning the property. *In re* Nicomedes F., 177 A.D.2d 316, 575 N.Y.S.2d 873 (1st Dept. 1991).

Form of notice.—The People complied with the notice requirements of PL § 450.10 by providing defendant with written notice of the intended release of the victim's purse. People v. Mellette, 176 A.D.2d 480, 574 N.Y.S.2d 559 (1st Dept. 1991), *lv. denied,* 79 N.Y.2d 861 (1992).

Time to make motion.—An oral motion to suppress physical evidence consisting of jewelry, allegedly stolen by defendant from department store, on basis that it had been returned to stock without defendant receiving § 450.10 notice, was untimely. People v. Mitchell, 106 A.D.2d 478, 482 N.Y.S.2d 574 (2d Dept. 1984).

Department store property returned to stock.—When jewelry allegedly stolen by defendant was inadvertently returned to stock, but, upon discovery of the § 450.10 violation by the prosecutor, the same jewelry was retrieved from stock, after which defendant had ample opportunity to request inspection, any violation of PL § 450.10 was cured. People v. Mitchell, 106 A.D.2d 478, 482 N.Y.S.2d 574 (2d Dept. 1984).

Department store property returned to stock.—Where police failed to follow procedures set forth in PL § 450.10 prior to returning recovered money to complainant, proper sanction would be to preclude the People from introducing on its direct case any evidence relating to the recovery of money from the defendant upon his arrest. People v. Johnson, 114 A.D.2d 515, 494 N.Y.S.2d 733 (2d Dept. 1985).

—Although the district attorney is precluded from adducing any evidence at trial with respect to the theft or possession of property from a department store which was not kept in the officer's custody but was returned to stock, the district attorney is free to prosecute the defendant for trespass. People v. Foye, 113 Misc. 2d 934, 448 N.Y.S.2d 919 (Crim Ct. N.Y. 1981).

Failure to comply; effect thereof.—Notwithstanding the Penal Law Section 450.10 violation, defendant's request for sanctions was properly denied where defendant was offered an opportunity to inspect the property in question and declined. People v. Burwell, 172 A.D.2d 412, 568 N.Y.S.2d 933 (1st Dept. 1991).

—PL § 450.10 applies to juvenile delinquency adjudications. *In re* James County, 179 A.D.2d 639, 578 N.Y.S.2d 589, 590 (2d Dept. 1992).

—Defendant was not prejudiced by the auctioning off of the car involved in the crime since it was available for inspection by the defendant for almost six months before it was auctioned off. People v. Scott, 140 A.D.2d 557, 528 N.Y.S.2d 423 (2d Dept. 1988).

—Court properly denied defense motion for a mistrial despite the improper release of allegedly stolen property where it was able to resort to the less severe remedies of striking testimony and submitting a lesser charge to the jury. People v. Martin, 131 A.D.2d 884, 517 N.Y.S.2d 241 (2d Dept. 1987).

—The purpose of PL § 450.10 is to provide the defendant with an opportunity to examine stolen property and determine its value in preparation for trial. People v. Griffin, 132 A.D.2d 670, 518 N.Y.S.2d 40 (2d Dept. 1987).

—Dismissal of the indictment or modification of the judgment was not warranted where People's failure to comply with CPL § 450.10 was not in bad faith and did not prejudice the defendant. People v. Bowman, 122 A.D.2d 65, 504 N.Y.S.2d 219 (2d Dept. 1986).

—Failure of the State Police to follow the notice requirements of PL § 450.10 prior to releasing stolen car to its owner did not require reversal where the defendant made no effort to request an examination of the vehicle. People v. Welsh, 124 A.D.2d 301, 508 N.Y.S.2d 278 (3d Dept. 1986).

—Court did not abuse discretion in failing to impose sanction on People for failing to follow notice procedures to inform defendant prior to the return of property to the owner/victim; no showing of prejudice to defendant or bad faith by police. People v. Fair, 254 A.D.2d 768, 678 N.Y.S.2d 759 (4th Dept. 1998).

PL

—Court properly refused to grant defense an adverse inference charge for failure to notify defendant prior to releasing property to owners where defendant did not seek to test gun or ammunition prior to trial and defendant failed to show prejudice from police action and did not produce evidence that police acted in bad faith. People v. Lathigee, 254 A.D.2d 687, 679 N.Y.S.2d 483 (4th Dept. 1998).

—Noncompliance with PL § 450.10(1) alone is not sufficient to require reversal particularly where defendant did not request permission to examine the property prior to trial. People v. Borders, 163 A.D.2d 852, 558 N.Y.S.2d 767 (4th Dept. 1990).

—Even though key, registration and insurance identification were returned to owner in violation of PL § 450.10, the court refused to impose a sanction in the absence of prejudice to the defendant. People v. Blyden, 160 Misc. 2d 355, 608 N.Y.S.2d 1003, 1007 (Sup. Ct. Kings Co. 1994).

Notice.—Where police notify defendant prior to releasing car to registered owner, provisions of section 450.10(4)(c) do not apply. People v. Marro, 241 A.D.2d 972, 661 N.Y.S.2d 389 (4th Dept. 1997).

—Prosecutor's statutory obligation to furnish notice of impending release of stolen property was satisfied when it handed the notice to defense counsel at arraignment; defendant did not have to be personally served with notice nor did the attorney, who was assigned after arraignment, have to be given notice. People v. Passas, 130 Misc. 2d 748, 497 N.Y.S.2d 301 (Sup. Ct. Queens Co. 1986).

TITLE X—ORGANIZED CRIME CONTROL ACT

ARTICLE 460—ENTERPRISE CORRUPTION

LexisNexis Cross References

Criminal Defense Techniques, Vol. 3A, Ch. 62A, "RICO" Racketeer Influenced and Corrupt Organizations Act; *New York Criminal Practice (2d ed.),* Vol. 6, Ch. 56, Attempt, Solicitation, Conspiracy and Facilitation; Vol. 7, Ch. 84, Enterprise Corruption, Money Laundering, Insurance Fraud and Martin Act; *see generally Prosecution and Defense of Criminal Conspiracy Cases*; *Complex Criminal Litigation: Prosecuting Drug Enterprises and Organized Crime.*

§ 460.00. Legislative findings.

The legislature finds and determines as follows:

Organized crime in New York state involves highly sophisticated, complex and widespread forms of criminal activity. The diversified illegal conduct engaged in by organized crime, rooted in the illegal use of force, fraud, and corruption, constitutes a major drain upon the state's economy, costs citizens and businesses of the state billions of dollars each year, and threatens the peace, security and general welfare of the people of the state.

Organized crime continues to expand its corrosive influence in the state through illegal enterprises engaged in such criminal endeavors as the theft and fencing of property, the importation and distribution of narcotics and other dangerous drugs, arson for profit, hijacking, labor racketeering, loansharking, extortion and bribery, the illegal disposal of hazardous wastes, syndicated gambling, trafficking in stolen securities, insurance and investment frauds, and other forms of economic and social exploitation.

The money and power derived by organized crime through its illegal enterprises and endeavors is increasingly being used to infiltrate and corrupt businesses, unions and other legitimate enterprises and to corrupt our democratic processes. This infiltration takes several forms with legitimate enterprises being employed as instrumentalities, injured as victims, or taken as prizes. Through such infiltration the power of an enterprise can be diverted to criminal ends, its resources looted, or it can be taken over entirely, either on paper or de facto. Thus, for purposes of making both criminal and civil remedies available to deal with the corruption of such enterprises, the concept of criminal enterprise should not be limited to traditional criminal syndicates or crime families, and may include persons who join together in a criminal enterprise, as defined by subdivision three of section 460.10 of this article, for the purpose of corrupting such legitimate enterprises or infiltrating and illicitly influencing industries.

One major cause of the continuing growth of organized criminal activities within the state is the inadequacy and limited nature of sanctions and remedies available to state and local law enforcement officials to deal with this intricate and varied criminal conduct. Existing penal law provisions are primarily concerned with the commission of specific and limited criminal acts without regard to the relationships of particular criminal acts or the illegal profits derived therefrom, to legitimate or illicit enterprises operated or controlled by organized crime. Further, traditional penal law provisions only provide for the imposition of conventional criminal penalties, including imprisonment, fines and probation, for entrenched organized crime enterprises. Such penalties are not adequate to enable the state to effectively fight organized crime. Instead, new penal prohibitions and enhanced sanctions, and new civil and criminal remedies are necessary to deal with the unlawful activities of persons and enterprises engaged in organized crime. Comprehensive statutes enacted at the federal level and in a number of other states with significant organized crime problems, have provided law enforcement agencies with an effective tool to fight organized crime. Such laws permit law enforcement authorities (i) to charge and prove patterns of criminal activity and their connection to ongoing enterprises, legitimate or illegal, that are controlled or operated by organized crime, and (ii) to apply criminal and civil penalties designed to prevent and eliminate organized crime's involvement with such enterprises. The organized crime control act is a statute of comparable purpose but tempered by reasonable limitations on its applicability, and by due regard for the rights of innocent persons. Because of its more rigorous definitions, this act will not apply to some situations encompassed within comparable statutes in other jurisdictions. This act is vital to the peace, security and general welfare of the state.

In part because of its highly diverse nature, it is impossible to precisely define what organized crime is. This article, however, does attempt to define and criminalize what organized crime does. This article focuses upon criminal enterprises because their sophistication and organization make them more effective at their criminal purposes and because their structure and insulation protect their leadership from detection and prosecution.

At the same time, this article is not intended to be employed to prosecute relatively minor or isolated acts of criminality which, while related to an enterprise and arguably part of a pattern as defined in this article, can be adequately and more fairly prosecuted as separate offenses. Similarly, particular defendants may play so minor a role in a criminal enterprise that their culpability would be unfairly distorted by prosecution and punishment for participation in the enterprise.

The balance intended to be struck by this act cannot readily be codified in the form of restrictive definitions or a categorical list of exceptions. General, yet carefully drawn definitions of the terms "pattern of criminal activity" and "criminal enterprise" have been employed. Notwithstanding the provisions of section 5.00 of this chapter these definitions should be given their plain meaning, and should not be construed either liberally or strictly, but in the context of the legislative purposes set forth in these findings. Within the confines of these and other applicable definitions, discretion ought still be exercised. Once the letter of the law is complied with, including the essential showing that there is a pattern of conduct which is criminal under existing statutes, the question whether to prosecute under those statutes or for the pattern itself is essentially one of fairness. The answer will depend on the particular situation, and is best addressed by those institutions of government which have traditionally exercised that function: the grand jury, the public prosecutor, and an independent judiciary.

ANNOTATIONS

Constitutionality.—The OCCA is not unconstitutionally vague as applied here, where both defendants were convicted of at least three criminal acts. People v. Association of Trade Waste Removers, 267 A.D.2d 137, 701 N.Y.S.2d 12 (1st Dept. 1999), *appeal denied sub nom.* People v. Francolino, 94 N.Y.2d 919, *cert. denied,* 531 U.S. 918 (2000).

Minor or isolated criminal acts.—When a defendant committed insurance fraud by delivering his car to a salvage yard and then reporting it stolen, although this was a criminal enterprise, prosecution of defendant for enterprise corruption was inconsistent with legislative findings that the Act was not intended to be used to prosecute relatively minor or isolated criminal acts in which the particular defendant played a minor role. People v. Scarantino, 167 Misc. 2d 388, 640 N.Y.S.2d 726 (Sup. Ct. Queens Co. 1996).

Double jeopardy.—The defendant moved to dismiss the state's indictment on double jeopardy grounds, where the defendant had been acquitted of charges under RICO. The court held that OCCA permits the subsequent state prosecution of a crime specifically included in the pattern of racketeering activity in a prior federal prosecution. People v. Cooper, 143 Misc. 2d 654, 541 N.Y.S.2d 713 (Sup. Ct. Bronx Co. 1989).

§ 460.10. Definitions.

The following definitions are applicable to this article.

1. "Criminal act" means conduct constituting any of the following crimes, or conspiracy or attempt to commit any of the following felonies:

(a) Any of the felonies set forth in this chapter: sections 120.05, 120.10 and 120.11 relating to assault; sections 125.10 to 125.27 relating to homicide; sections 130.25, 130.30 and 130.35 relating to rape; sections 135.20 and 135.25 relating to kidnapping; section 135.65 relating to coercion; sections 140.20, 140.25 and 140.30 relating to burglary; sections 145.05, 145.10 and 145.12 relating to criminal mischief; article one hundred fifty relating to arson; sections 155.30, 155.35, 155.40 and 155.42 relating to grand larceny; article one hundred sixty relating to robbery; sections 165.45, 165.50, 165.52 and 165.54 relating to criminal possession of stolen property; sections 170.10, 170.15, 170.25, 170.30, 170.40, 170.65 and 170.70 relating to forgery; sections 175.10, 175.25, 175.35, 175.40 and 210.40 relating to false statements; sections 176.15, 176.20, 176.25 and 176.30 relating to insurance fraud; sections 178.20 and 178.25 relating to criminal diversion of prescription medications and prescriptions; sections 180.03, 180.08, 180.15, 180.25, 180.40, 180.45, 200.00, 200.03, 200.04, 200.10, 200.11, 200.12, 200.20, 200.22, 200.25, 200.27, 215.00, 215.05 and 215.19 relating to bribery; sections 190.40 and 190.42 relating to criminal usury; section 190.65 relating to schemes to defraud; sections 205.60 and 205.65 relating to hindering prosecution; sections 210.10, 210.15, and 215.51 relating to perjury and contempt; section 215.40 relating to tampering with physical evidence; sections 220.06, 220.09, 220.16, 220.18, 220.21, 220.31, 220.34, 220.39,

220.41, 220.43, 220.46, 220.55 and 220.60 relating to controlled substances; sections 225.10 and 225.20 relating to gambling; sections 230.25, 230.30, and 230.32 relating to promoting prostitution; sections 235.06, 235.07 and 235.21 relating to obscenity; section 263.10 relating to promoting an obscene performance by a child; sections 265.02, 265.03, 265.04, 265.11, 265.12, 265.13 and the provisions of section 265.10 which constitute a felony relating to firearms and other dangerous weapons; and sections 265.14 and 265.16 relating to criminal sale of a firearm; and section 275.10, 275.20, 275.30, or 275.40 relating to unauthorized recordings; and sections 470.05, 470.10, 470.15 and 470.20 relating to money laundering; or

(b) Any felony set forth elsewhere in the laws of this state and defined by the tax law relating to alcoholic beverage, cigarette, gasoline and similar motor fuel taxes; title * seventy-one of the environmental conservation law relating to water pollution, hazardous waste or substances hazardous or acutely hazardous to public health or safety of the environment; article twenty-three-a of the general business law relating to prohibited acts concerning stocks, bonds and other securities or article twenty-two of the general business law concerning monopolies.

2. "Enterprise" means either an enterprise as defined in subdivision one of section 175.00 of this chapter or criminal enterprise as defined in subdivision three of this section.

3. "Criminal enterprise" means a group of persons sharing a common purpose of engaging in criminal conduct, associated in an ascertainable structure distinct from a pattern of criminal activity, and with a continuity of existence, structure and criminal purpose beyond the scope of individual criminal incidents.

4. "Pattern of criminal activity" means conduct engaged in by persons charged in an enterprise corruption count constituting three or more criminal acts that:

(a) were committed within ten years of the commencement of the criminal action;

(b) are neither isolated incidents, nor so closely related and connected in point of time or circumstance of commission as to constitute a criminal offense or criminal transaction, as those terms are defined in section 40.10 of the criminal procedure law; and

(c) are either: (i) related to one another through a common scheme or plan or (ii) were committed, solicited, requested, importuned or intentionally aided by persons acting with the mental culpability required for the commission thereof and associated with or in the criminal enterprise.

* As originally enacted. Should probably be "article."

Amended by L. 1995, Ch. 401, § 1, amending subd. 1(a), eff. Aug. 2, 1995; L. 1995, Ch. 419, § 8, amending subd. 1(a),

eff. Nov. 1, 1995; L. 1996, Ch. 102, § 1, amending subd. 1(a), eff. Nov. 1, 1996; L. 1996, Ch. 371, § 1, amending subd. 1(a), eff. Nov. 1, 1996; L. 1998, Ch. 369, § 1, eff. Nov. 1, 1998, and Ch. 2, § 39, eff. Nov. 1, 1998; L. 2000, Ch. 489, § 2-a, eff. Nov. 1, 2000, amending subd. 1(a).

ANNOTATIONS

Constitutionality.—An ordinarily intelligent person would understand from the statutory elements that his participation in a criminal scheme which benefited organized crime was the prohibited conduct, so that the enterprise corruption statute was not unconstitutionally vague. People v. Barone, 221 A.D.2d 553, 635 N.Y.S.2d 35 (2d Dept.), *lv. denied,* 87 N.Y.2d 897 (1995); People v. Cantarella, 160 Misc. 2d 8, 606 N.Y.S.2d 942 (Sup. Ct. N.Y. Co. 1993).

—Terms "enterprise," "pattern of criminal activity" are neither vague nor overbroad. People v. Capaldo, 151 Misc. 2d 114, 572 N.Y.S.2d 989 (Sup. Ct. N.Y. Co. 1991).

—New York's statute was designed to target criminal enterprises that were more precisely defined than RICO. People v. Moscatiello, 149 Misc. 2d 752, 566 N.Y.S.2d 823 (Sup. Ct. N.Y. Co. 1990).

Comparison with federal offense.—The federal offense of enterprise corruption is not the equivalent of the state offense. *In re* Weinig, 220 A.D.2d 184, 642 N.Y.S.2d 654 (1st Dept. 1996).

—Federal conviction of participation in a racketeering enterprise was essentially similar to state felony of enterprise corruption to warrant automatic disbarment of an attorney. *In re* Christiansen, 220 A.D.2d 98, 642 N.Y.S.2d 24 (1st Dept. 1996).

—Even if same organization is conducting fraudulent sale of tax shelters, if acquittal on federal charges relates to transactions which were different from transactions at basis of state indictment, double jeopardy does not attach except as to substantive offenses which could have been, albeit were not, charged as overt acts in federal conspiracy prosecution. Mason v. Rothwax, 152 A.D.2d 272, 548 N.Y.S.2d 926 (1st Dept. 1989), *lv. denied,* 75 N.Y.2d 705 (1990).

—The legislature intended to define the scope of the state offense more rigorously than the federal offense. People v. Cantarella, 160 Misc. 2d 8, 606 N.Y.S.2d 942 (Sup. Ct. N.Y. Co. 1993); People v. Moscatiello, 149 Misc. 2d 752, 566 N.Y.S.2d 823 (Sup. Ct. N.Y. Co. 1990).

—State offense is narrower than federal offense, and federal offense has withstood federal constitutional challenge. People v. Capaldo, 151 Misc. 2d 114, 572 N.Y.S.2d 989 (Sup. Ct. N.Y. Co. 1991).

—Federal RICO conviction predicated on murder of victim in furtherance of the a criminal enterprise, the "Westies," barred state prosecution for enterprise corruption arising from the same offense; not a case of separate prosecutions for separate offenses which merely have a common event. People v. Bokun, 145 Misc. 2d 860, 548 N.Y.S.2d 604 (Sup. Ct. N.Y. Co. 1989).

Constitutionality of statute upheld.—The defendants moved to dismiss the enterprise corruption counts on three grounds: 1) that OCCA's enterprise corruption sections were unconstitutionally vague; 2) that in the interest of justice the count should be dismissed because it is inconsistent with the intention of the Legislature, and 3) that the indictment failed to allege a criminal enterprise as defined in Penal Law § 460.10(3). The court upheld the constitutionality of the statute. People v. Wakefield Financial Corp., 155 Misc. 2d 775, 590 N.Y.S.2d 382 (Sup. Ct. N.Y. Co. 1992).

—Court dismissed the defendant's motions to dismiss the indictment on two grounds. First, the court held that OCCA was not unconstitutionally vague. Second, the court ruled that the rights of a union official to the position he or she holds is "property" for purposes of the larceny statute. People v. Capaldo, 151 Misc. 2d 114, 572 N.Y.S.2d 989 (Sup. Ct. N.Y. Co. 1991).

Criminal enterprise.—The court held the 41-count indictment, which included charges of enterprise corruption, bribing a labor official, and bribe receiving by a labor official, failed to show a criminal enterprise. The court found that the defendants were not associated in an ascertainable structure distinct from a pattern of criminal activity and with a scope of existence, structure, and criminal purpose beyond the scope of individual criminal incidents. People v. Moscatiello, 149 Misc. 2d 752, 566 N.Y.S.2d 823 (Sup. Ct. N.Y. Co. 1990).

§ 460.20. Enterprise corruption.

1. A person is guilty of enterprise corruption when, having knowledge of the existence of a criminal enterprise and the nature of its activities, and being employed by or associated with such enterprise, he:

(a) intentionally conducts or participates in the affairs of an enterprise by participating in a pattern of criminal activity; or

(b) intentionally acquires or maintains any interest in or control of an enterprise by participating in a pattern of criminal activity; or

(c) participates in a pattern of criminal activity and knowingly invests any proceeds derived from that conduct, or any proceeds derived from the investment or use of those proceeds, in an enterprise.

2. For purposes of this section, a person participates in a pattern of criminal activity when, with intent to participate in or advance the affairs of the criminal enterprise, he engages in conduct constituting, or, is criminally liable for pursuant to section 20.00 of this chapter, at least three of the criminal acts included in the pattern, provided that:

(a) Two of his acts are felonies other than conspiracy;

(b) Two of his acts, one of which is a felony, occurred within five years of the commencement of the criminal action; and

(c) Each of his acts occurred within three years of a prior act.

3. For purposes of this section, the enterprise corrupted in violation of subdivision one of this section need not be the criminal enterprise by which the person is employed or with which he is associated, and may be a legitimate enterprise.

Enterprise corruption is a class B felony.

ANNOTATIONS

Pattern of criminal activity.—Where the defendant falsely reported stolen his car which he actually had sold to a chop shop, although he was validly charged with three separate substantive offenses relating to insurance fraud, falsifying business records and grand larceny, this was still a single transaction rather than a pattern of criminal activity. People v. Scarantino, 167 Misc. 2d 388, 640 N.Y.S.2d 726 (Sup. Ct. Queens Co. 1996).

—The pattern of criminal activity is an element separate from the element of enterprise corruption, and must be separately proved. People v. Cantarella, 160 Misc. 2d 8, 606 N.Y.S.2d 942 (Sup. Ct. N.Y. Co. 1993).

—Three criminal acts constitute a criminal pattern only when they evince the elements of continuity and relatedness. The acts must be relatively close in time, must evince continuous and not sporadic criminality, but not be so close in time and circumstance as to constitute a single offense or single criminal transaction. People v. Cantarella, 160 Misc. 2d 8, 606 N.Y.S.2d 942 (Sup. Ct. N.Y. Co. 1993).

Criminal enterprise.—When defendant delivered his car to a co-defendant's salvage yard, then reported it stolen, upon which he received partial payment, there was sufficient evidence of a criminal enterprise. People v. Scarantino, 167 Misc. 2d 388, 640 N.Y.S.2d 726 (Sup. Ct. Queens Co. 1996).

—Criminal enterprise is threshold element; must demonstrate the existence of a group of people sharing a common purpose of engaging in criminal conduct, in the context of an ascertainable structure to the group, which exists beyond the individual identity of its members. People v. Cantarella, 160 Misc. 2d 8, 606 N.Y.S.2d 942 (Sup. Ct. N.Y. Co. 1993).

—The fact that there is a pattern of criminal activity does not, per se, require the conclusion that there is a criminal enterprise. The enterprise must have a continuous existence which supersedes the time period of a particular crime or criminal pattern. People v. Cantarella, 160 Misc. 2d 8, 606 N.Y.S.2d 942 (Sup. Ct. N.Y. Co. 1993).

—The criminal enterprise need not be static; members may leave and new members may enter without vitiating the underlying continuity of the enterprise. People v. Wakefield Financial Corp., 155 Misc. 2d 775, 590 N.Y.S.2d 382 (Sup. Ct. N.Y. Co. 1992).

—Fact that otherwise independent securities brokers acted together to control the prices and supplies of particular securities on an ongoing basis, with some brokers entering price quotes into the NASDAQ system at the behest of other brokers, sufficiently established the requisite structure as the statutory foundation for a criminal enterprise. The fact that within the structure, parties changed roles, and there was no proven or lasting hierarchy, did not defeat proof that the structure existed distinct from the mere pattern of criminal activity. People v. Wakefield Financial Corp., 155 Misc. 2d 775, 590 N.Y.S.2d 382 (Sup. Ct. N.Y. Co. 1992).

—Bribe giving and receiving among three union officials and contractors established only a pattern of criminal activity, which did not have a continuous existence beyond those criminal acts, and the participants were not demonstrated to be part of any criminal structure; the fact that the three participants played different roles did not impart the requisite structure to their criminal activities. People v. Moscatiello, 149 Misc. 2d 752, 566 N.Y.S.2d 823 (Sup. Ct. N.Y. Co. 1990).

Descriptive terms relating to criminal enterprise.—When the specified criminal enterprise had notoriety, the court denied motion to preclude reference to that particular enterprise: the existence of the enterprise thus identified was a material fact to be proved at trial. People v. Ciauri, 162 Misc. 2d 394, 617 N.Y.S.2d 287 (Sup. Ct. N.Y. Co. 1994).

—When the defendant's activities are alleged to have advanced the interests of a particular mafia family, the terms "mafia," "la cosa nostra" and "family" became relevant for purposes of proving the existence of the criminal enterprise, despite potential prejudice to individual defendants. People v. Ciauri, 162 Misc. 2d 394, 617 N.Y.S.2d 287 (Sup. Ct. N.Y. Co. 1994).

Nature of the criminal acts.—The three acts required by the statute must be demonstrably related to the criminal enterprise, either as part of a single conspiracy or, if parts of separate conspiracies, engaged in by persons connected to the criminal enterprise, thus including in charge of enterprise corruption multiple transactions by virtue of the fact that they are undertaken by the same criminal organization People v. Cantarella, 160 Misc. 2d 8, 606 N.Y.S.2d 942 (Sup. Ct. N.Y. Co. 1993).

—People need not prove that a particular defendant in a multiple defendant case participated in each of the three criminal acts required by statute to prove enterprise corruption; People need only prove that the defendant knew of the existence of the criminal enterprise, was associated with the criminal enterprise, intended to participate in the criminal enterprise's activities, and commits one of the three acts included within the charged pattern of criminal activity. People v. Cantarella, 160 Misc. 2d 8, 606 N.Y.S.2d 942 (Sup. Ct. N.Y. Co. 1993).

—Since petit larceny is not among one of the criminal acts designated in PL 460.10(1). People v. Cantarella, 160 Misc. 2d 8, 606 N.Y.S.2d 942 (Sup. Ct. N.Y. Co. 1993).

Pattern of criminal activity.—Federal conviction for conspiring to launder money did not establish "pattern of criminal activity" under Penal Law Article 460. In re Weinig, 220 A.D.2d 184, 642 N.Y.S.2d 654 (1st Dept. 1996).

Corroboration and testimony of accomplices establishing criminal acts.—"[T]he testimony of the accomplices need not be corroborated for each pattern act but [are] sufficiently corroborated if the jury determined that some independent evidence tended to connect defendants to the offense of enterprise corruption." People v. Besser, 96 N.Y.2d 136, 726 N.Y.S.2d 48, 749 N.E.2d 727 (2001).

—A finding that a defendant committed a "criminal act" which forms basis of enterprise corruption charge is not a "conviction," but only establishes an element of the offense of enterprise corruption; hence, if evidence of the "criminal act" is provided by an accomplice, the accomplice corroboration rule set forth in CPL § 60.22 is not invoked as to that element. People v. Ciauri, 166 Misc. 2d 615, 632 N.Y.S.2d 404 (Sup. Ct. N.Y. Co. 1995).

§ 460.25. Enterprise corruption; limitations.

1. For purposes of subdivision one of section 460.20 of this article, a person does not acquire or maintain an interest in an enterprise by participating in a pattern of criminal activity when he invests proceeds derived from a pattern of criminal activity in such enterprise.

2. For purposes of subdivision one of section 460.20 of this article, it shall not be unlawful to:

(a) purchase securities on the open market with intent to make an investment, and without the intent of controlling or participating in the control of the issuer, or of assisting another to do so, if the securities of the issuer held by the purchaser, the members of his immediate family, and his or their accomplices in any pattern of criminal activity do not amount in the aggregate to five percent of the outstanding securities of any one class and do not confer, either in the law or in fact, the power to elect one or more directors of the issuer;

(b) make a deposit in an account maintained in a savings and loan association, or a deposit in any other such financial institution, that creates an ownership interest in that association or institution;

(c) purchase shares in co-operatively owned residential or commercial property;

(d) purchase non-voting shares in a limited partnership, with intent to make an investment, and without the intent of controlling or participating in the control of the partnership.

§ 460.30. Enterprise corruption; forfeiture.

1. Any person convicted of enterprise corruption may be required pursuant to this section to criminally forfeit to the state:

(a) any interest in, security of, claim against or property or contractual right of any kind affording a source of influence over any enterprise whose affairs he has controlled or in which he has participated in violation of subdivision one of section 460.20 of this article and for which he was convicted and the use of which interest, security, claim or right by him contributed directly and materially to the crime for which he was convicted unless such forfeiture is disproportionate to the defendant's gain from his association or employment with the enterprise, in which event the jury may recommend forfeiture of a portion thereof;

(b) any interest, including proceeds, he has acquired or maintained in an enterprise in violation of subdivision one of section 460.20 of this article and for which he was convicted unless such forfeiture is disproportionate to the conduct he engaged in and on which the forfeiture is based, in which event the jury may recommend forfeiture of a portion thereof; or

(c) any interest, including proceeds he has derived from an investment of proceeds in an enterprise in violation of subdivision one of section 460.20 of this article and for which he was convicted unless such forfeiture is disproportionate to the conduct he engaged in and on which the forfeiture is based, in which event the jury may recommend forfeiture of a portion thereof.

2. (a) Forfeiture may be ordered when the grand jury returning an indictment charging a person with enterprise corruption has received evidence legally sufficient to establish, and providing reasonable cause to believe, that the property or other interest is subject to forfeiture under this section. In that event, the grand jury shall file a special information, not to be disclosed to the jury in the criminal action prior to verdict on the criminal charges, specifying the property or other interest for which forfeiture is sought and containing a plain and concise factual statement which sets forth the basis for the forfeiture. Alternatively, where the defendant has waived indictment and consented to be prosecuted by superior court information pursuant to article one hundred ninety-five of the criminal procedure law, the prosecutor may file, in addition to the superior court information charging enterprise corruption, a special information specifying the property or other interest for which forfeiture is sought and containing a plain and concise factual statement which sets forth the basis for the forfeiture.

(b) After returning a verdict of guilty on an enterprise corruption count or counts, the jury shall be given the special information and hear any additional evidence which is relevant and legally admissible upon the forfeiture count or counts of the special information. After hearing such evidence, the jury shall then deliberate upon the forfeiture count or counts and, based upon all the evidence received in connection with the indictment or superior court information and the special information, may, if satisfied by proof beyond a reasonable doubt that the property or other interest, or a portion thereof, is subject to forfeiture under this section return a verdict determining such property or other interest, or portion thereof, is subject to forfeiture, provided, however, where a defendant has waived a jury trial pursuant to article three hundred twenty of the criminal procedure law, the court may hear and receive all of the evidence upon the indictment or superior court information and the special information and render a verdict upon the enterprise corruption count or counts and the forfeiture count or counts.

(c) After the verdict of forfeiture, the court shall hear arguments and may receive additional evidence upon a motion of the defendant that the verdict of forfeiture (i) is against the weight of the evidence, or (ii) is, with respect to a forfeiture pursuant to paragraph (a) of subdivision one of this section, disproportionate to the defendant's gain from his association or employment with the enterprise, or, with respect to a forfeiture pursuant to paragraph (b) or (c) of subdivision one of this section, disproportionate to the conduct he engaged in on which the forfeiture is based. Upon such a finding the court may in the interests of justice set aside, modify, limit or otherwise condition an order of forfeiture.

3. (a) An order of criminal forfeiture shall authorize the prosecutor to seize all property or other interest declared forfeited under this section upon such terms and conditions as the court shall deem proper. If a property right or other interest is not exercisable or transferable for value by the prosecutor, it shall expire and shall not revert to the convicted person. The court ordering any forfeiture may remit such forfeiture or any portion thereof.

(b) No person shall forfeit any right, title or interest in any property or enterprise under this article who has not been convicted of a violation of section 460.20 of this article. Any person other than the convicted person claiming an interest in forfeited property or other interest may bring a special proceeding to determine that claim, before or after trial, pursuant to section thirteen hundred twenty-seven of the civil practice law and rules, provided, however, that if such an action is brought before trial, it may, upon motion of the prosecutor, and in the court's discretion, be postponed by the court until completion of the trial. In addition, any person claiming an interest in property subject to forfeiture may petition for remission as provided in subdivision seven of section thirteen hundred eleven of such law and rules.

4. All property and other interests which are criminally forfeited following the commencement of an action under this article, whether by plea, verdict or other agreement, shall be disposed of in accordance with the provisions of section thirteen hundred forty-nine of the civil practice law and rules. In any case where one or more of the counts upon which a person is convicted specifically includes as a criminal act a violation of any offense defined in article two hundred twenty of this chapter, the court shall determine what portion of that property or interest derives from or relates to such criminal act, and direct that distribution of that portion be conducted in the manner prescribed for actions grounded upon offenses in violation of article two hundred twenty.

5. Any person convicted of a violation of section 460.20 of this article through which he derived pecuniary value, or by which he caused personal injury or property damage or other loss, may be sentenced to pay a fine not in excess of three times the gross value he gained or three times the gross loss he caused, whichever is greater. Moneys so collected shall be paid as restitution to victims of the crime for medical expenses actually incurred, loss of earnings or property loss or damage caused thereby. Any excess after restitution shall be paid to the state treasury. In any case where one or more of the counts upon which a person is convicted specifically includes as a criminal act a violation of any offense defined in article two hundred twenty of this chapter, the court shall determine what proportion of the entire pattern such criminal acts constitute and distribute such portion in the manner prescribed by section three hundred forty-nine of the civil practice law and rules for forfeiture actions grounded upon offenses in violation of article two hundred twenty. When the court imposes a fine pursuant to this subdivision, the court shall make a finding as to the amount of the gross value gained or the gross loss caused. If the record does not contain sufficient evidence to support such a finding the court may conduct a hearing upon the issue. In imposing a fine, the court shall consider the seriousness of the conduct, whether the amount of the fine is disproportionate to the conduct in which he engaged, its impact on victims and the enterprise corrupted by that conduct, as well as the economic circumstances of the convicted person, including the effect of the imposition of such a fine upon his immediate family.

6. The imposition of an order of criminal forfeiture pursuant to subdivision one of this section, a judgment of civil forfeiture pursuant to article thirteen-A of the civil practice law and rules, or a fine pursuant to subdivision five of this section or paragraph (b) of subdivision one of section 80.00 of this chapter, shall preclude the imposition of any other such order or judgment of forfeiture or fine based upon the same criminal conduct, provided however that where an order of criminal forfeiture is imposed pursuant to subdivision one of this section, an action pursuant to article thirteen-A of the civil practice law and rules may nonetheless be brought, and an order imposed in that action, for forfeiture of the proceeds of a crime or the substituted proceeds of a crime where such proceeds are not subject to criminal forfeiture pursuant to subdivision one of this section. The imposition of a fine pursuant to subdivision five of this section or paragraph (b) of subdivision one of section 80.00 of this chapter, shall preclude the imposition of any other fine pursuant to any other provision of this chapter.

7. Other than as provided in subdivision six, the imposition of a criminal penalty, forfeiture or fine under this section shall not preclude the application of any other criminal penalty or civil

remedy under this article or under any other provision of law.

8. Any payment made as restitution to victims pursuant to this section shall not limit, preclude or impair any liability for damages in any civil action or proceeding for an amount in excess of such payment.

ANNOTATIONS

Contrast with other forfeiture statutes.—Penal Law § 460.30 provides for special information voted by grand jury which precedes trial, although petit jury would vote on forfeiture after conviction; CPLR Article 13-A provides for a separate and distinct forfeiture proceeding which occurs after conviction. District Attorney of Kings County v. Iadarola, 164 Misc. 2d 204, 623 N.Y.S.2d 999 (Sup. Ct. Kings Co.), *aff'd,* 222 A.D.2d 454, 634 N.Y.S.2d 738 (2d Dept.), *lv. denied,* 87 N.Y.2d 903 (1995), *cert. denied,* 517 U.S. 1209 (1996).

—Items forfeitable under PL § 460.30 differ from items forfeitable under CPLR Article 13-A. District Attorney of Kings County v. Iadarola, 164 Misc. 2d 204, 623 N.Y.S.2d 999 (Sup. Ct. Kings Co.), *aff'd,* 222 A.D.2d 454, 634 N.Y.S.2d 738 (2d Dept.), *lv. denied,* 87 N.Y.2d 903 (1995), *cert. denied,* 517 U.S. 1209 (1996).

—Forfeiture under PL § 460.30 is limited; it does not include cash removed from the criminal enterprise, nor substitute proceeds of a crime, nor a money judgment equivalent to the proceeds of a crime. District Attorney of Kings County v. Iadarola, 164 Misc. 2d 204, 623 N.Y.S.2d 999 (Sup. Ct. Kings Co.), *aff'd,* 222 A.D.2d 454, 634 N.Y.S.2d 738 (2d Dept.), *lv. denied,* 87 N.Y.2d 903 (1995), *and cert. denied,* 517 U.S. 1209 (1996).

§ 460.40. Enterprise corruption; jurisdiction.

A person may be prosecuted for enterprise corruption:

1. in any county in which the principal place of business, if any, of the enterprise was located at the time of the offense, and, if the enterprise had a principal place or business located in more than one county, then in any such county in which any conduct occurred constituting or requisite to the completion of the offense of enterprise corruption; or

2. in any county in which any act included in the pattern of criminal activity could have been prosecuted pursuant to article twenty of the criminal procedure law; provided, however, that such person may not be prosecuted for enterprise corruption in such county based on this subdivision if the jurisdiction of such county is based solely on section 20.60 of the criminal procedure law; or

3. in any county in which he:

(a) conducts or participates in the affairs of the enterprise in violation of subdivision one of section 460.20 of this article,

(b) acquires or maintains an interest in or control of the enterprise in violation of subdivision one of section 460.20 of this article,

(c) invests proceeds in an enterprise in violation of subdivision one of section 460.20 of this article; or

4. in any county in which the conduct of the actor had or was likely to have a particular effect upon such county or a political subdivision or part thereof, and was performed with intent that it would, or with knowledge that it was likely to, have such particular effect therein.

§ 460.50. Enterprise corruption; prosecution.

1. Subject to the provisions of section 460.60 of this article, a charge of enterprise corruption may be prosecuted by: (a) the district attorney of any county with jurisdiction over the offense pursuant to section 460.40 of this article; (b) the deputy attorney general in charge of the statewide organized crime task force when authorized by subdivision seven of section seventy-a of the executive law; or (c) the attorney general when he is otherwise authorized by law to prosecute each of the criminal acts specifically included in the pattern of criminal activity alleged in the enterprise corruption charge.

2. For purposes of paragraph (c) of subdivision one of this section, a criminal act or an offense is specifically included in a pattern of criminal activity when the count of the accusatory instrument charging a person with enterprise corruption alleges a pattern of criminal activity and the act is alleged to be a criminal act within the pattern of criminal activity.

§ 460.60. Enterprise corruption; consent to prosecute.

1. For purposes of this section, when a grand jury proceeding concerns a possible charge of enterprise corruption, or when an accusatory instrument includes a count charging a person with enterprise corruption, the affected district attorneys are the district attorneys otherwise empowered to prosecute any of the underlying acts of criminal activity in a county with jurisdiction over the offense of enterprise corruption pursuant to section 460.40 of this article, in which:

(a) there has been substantial and significant activity by the particular enterprise; or

(b) conduct occurred constituting a criminal act specifically included in the pattern of criminal activity charged in the accusatory instrument and not previously prosecuted; or

(c) the particular enterprise has its principal place of business.

2. A grand jury proceeding concerning a possible charge of enterprise corruption may be instituted only with the consent of the affected district attorneys. Should the possibility of such a charge develop after a grand jury proceeding has been instituted, the consent of the affected district attorneys shall be sought as soon as is practical, and an indictment charging a person with

enterprise corruption may not be voted upon by the grand jury without such consent.

3. A person may be charged in an accusatory instrument with enterprise corruption only with the consent of the affected district attorneys. When it is impractical to obtain the consent specified in subdivision two of this section prior to the filing of the accusatory instrument, then that consent must be secured within twenty days thereafter.

4. When the prosecutor is the deputy attorney general in charge of the statewide organized crime task force, the consent required by subdivisions two and three of this section shall be in addition to that required by subdivision seven of section seventy-a of the executive law.

5. Within fifteen days after the arraignment of any person on an indictment charging a person with the crime of enterprise corruption the prosecutor shall provide a copy of the indictment to those district attorneys whose consent was required pursuant to subdivision three of this section, and shall notify the court and defendant of those district attorneys whose consent the prosecutor has secured. The court shall then review the indictment and the grand jury minutes, notify any district attorney whose consent under subdivision one of this section should have been but was not obtained, direct that the prosecutor provide that district attorney with the portion of the indictment and grand jury minutes that are relevant to a determination whether that district attorney is an "affected district attorney" within the meaning of subdivision one of this section.

6. The failure to obtain from any district attorney the consent required by subdivision two or three of this section shall not be grounds for dismissal of the accusatory instrument or for any other relief upon motion of a defendant in the criminal action.

Upon motion of a district attorney whose consent, pursuant to subdivision three of this section, the court determines was required but not obtained, the court may not dismiss the accusatory instrument or any count thereof but may grant any appropriate relief. Such relief may include, but is not limited to:

(a) ordering that any money forfeited by a defendant in the criminal action, or the proceeds from the sale of any other property forfeited in the criminal action by a defendant, which would have been paid to the county of that district attorney pursuant to section thirteen hundred forty-nine of the civil practice law and rules had the forfeiture action been prosecuted in the county of that district attorney, be paid in whole or in part to the county of that district attorney; or

(b) upon consent of the defendant, ordering the transfer of the prosecution, or any part thereof, to that district attorney or to any other prosecutor with jurisdiction over the prosecution, of the part thereof to be transferred. However, prior to ordering any transfer of the prosecution, the court shall provide to those district attorneys who have previously consented to the prosecution an opportunity to intervene and be heard concerning such transfer.

7. A district attorney whose consent, pursuant to subdivision three of this section, the court determines was required but not obtained may seek the relief described in subdivision six of this section exclusively by a pre-trial motion in the criminal action based on the indictment charging the crime of enterprise corruption. Such relief must be sought within forty-five days of the receipt of notice from the court pursuant to subdivision five of this section.

§ 460.70. Provisional remedies.

1. The provisional remedies authorized by article thirteen-A of the civil practice law and rules shall be available in all criminal actions in which criminal forfeiture or a fine pursuant to section 460.60 is sought to the extent and under the same terms and conditions as provided in article thirteen-A of such law and rules.

2. Upon the filing of an indictment and special information seeking criminal forfeiture under this article all further proceedings with respect to provisional remedies shall be heard by the judge or justice in the criminal part to which the indictment and special information are assigned.

3. For purposes of this section, the indictment and special information seeking criminal forfeiture shall constitute the summons and complaint referred to in article thirteen-A of the civil practice law and rules.

§ 460.80. Court ordered disclosure.

Notwithstanding the provisions of article two hundred forty of the criminal procedure law, when forfeiture is sought pursuant to section 460.30 of this chapter, the court may order discovery of any property not otherwise disclosed which is material and reasonably necessary for preparation by the defendant with respect to the forfeiture proceeding pursuant to such section. The court may issue a protective order denying, limiting, conditioning, delaying or regulating such discovery where a danger to the integrity of physical evidence or a substantial risk of physical harm, intimidation, economic reprisal, bribery or unjustified annoyance or embarrassment to any person or an adverse effect upon the legitimate needs of law enforcement, including the protection of the confidentiality of informants, or any other factor or set of factors outweighs the usefulness of the discovery.

ARTICLE 470—MONEY LAUNDERING

LexisNexis Cross Reference

New York Criminal Practice (2d ed.), Vol. 7, Ch. 84, Enterprise Corruption, Money Laundering, Insurance Fraud and Martin Act; *see generally Complex Criminal Litigation: Prosecuting Drug Enterprises and Organized Crime.*

§ 470.00. Definitions.

The following definitions are applicable to this article.

1. "Monetary instrument" means coin and currency of the United States or of any other country; personal checks; bank checks; traveler's checks; money orders; and investment securities and negotiable instruments, in bearer form or otherwise, in such form that title thereto passes on delivery, except that "monetary instrument" shall not include payments to attorneys for legal services.

2. "Conducts" includes initiating, concluding or participating in initiating or concluding a transaction.

3. "Transaction" includes a payment, purchase, sale, loan, pledge, gift, transfer, or delivery, and with respect to a financial institution includes a deposit, withdrawal, transfer between accounts, exchange of currency, loan, extension of credit, purchase or sale of any stock, bond, certificate of deposit, or other monetary instrument, use of a safe deposit box, or any other payment, transfer, or delivery by, through, or to a financial institution, by whatever means effected, except that "transaction" shall not include payments to attorneys for legal services.

4. "Criminal conduct" means conduct which is a crime under the laws of this state or conduct committed in any other jurisdiction which is or would be a crime under the laws of this state.

5. "Specified criminal conduct" means criminal conduct committed in this state constituting a criminal act, as the term criminal act is defined in section 460.10 of this chapter, or constituting the crime of enterprise corruption, as defined in section 460.20 of this chapter, or conduct committed in any other jurisdiction which is or would be specified criminal conduct if committed in this state.

6. "Financial institution" means:

(a) an insured bank, as defined in section 3(b) of the Federal Deposit Insurance Act, 12 U.S.C. 1813(h);

(b) a commercial bank or trust company;

(c) a private banker;

(d) an agency or branch of a foreign bank in the United States;

(e) a credit union;

(f) a thrift institution;

(g) a broker or dealer registered with the Securities and Exchange Commission under the Securities and Exchange Act of 1934, U.S.C. 78a et seq.;

(h) a broker or dealer in securities or commodities;

(i) an investment banker or investment company;

(j) a currency exchange;

(k) an issuer, redeemer, or cashier of travelers' checks, checks, money orders, or similar instruments;

(l) an operator of a credit card system;

(m) an insurance company;

(n) a dealer in precious metals, stones, or jewels;

(o) a pawnbroker;

(p) a loan or finance company;

(q) a travel agency;

(r) a person licensed to engage in the business of receiving money for transmission or transmitting the same by whatever means, or any other person engaged in such business as an agent of a licensee or engaged in such business without a license;

(s) a telegraph company;

(t) a business engaged in vehicle sales, including automobile, airplane and boat sales;

(u) persons involved in real estate closings and settlements;

(v) the United States Postal Service;

(w) an agency of the United States government or of a state or local government carrying out a duty or power of a business described in this subdivision;

(x) a casino, gambling casino, or gaming establishment with an annual gaming revenue of more than a million dollars which:

(i) is licensed as a casino, gambling casino or gaming establishment under the laws of any state or any political subdivision of any state; or

(ii) is an Indian gaming operation conducted under or pursuant to the Indian gaming regulatory act other than an operation which is limited to class 1 gaming as defined in subdivision six of section four of such act; or

(y) any business or agency engaged in any activity which the superintendent of banks or the United States Secretary of the Treasury determines, by regulation, to be an activity which is similar to, related to, or a substitute for activity which any business as described in this subdivision is authorized to engage.

7. "Financial transaction" means a transaction involving:

(a) the movement of funds by wire or other means; or

(b) one or more monetary instruments; or

(c) the transfer of title to any real property, vehicle, vessel or aircraft; or

(d) the use of a financial institution.

8. "Represented" means any representation made by a law enforcement officer, or by another person at the direction of, or with the approval of, such law enforcement officer.

9. "Law enforcement officer" means any public servant, federal or state, who is authorized to conduct an investigation, prosecute or make an arrest for a criminal offense.

10. For the purpose of this article, each of the five counties in the city of New York shall be considered as a separate county.

Amended by L. 1990, Ch. 543; L. 2000, Ch. 489, § 3, eff. Nov. 1, 2000.

ANNOTATIONS

Monetary instruments.—Currency and bank checks are monetary instruments. People v. Capparelli, 158 Misc. 2d 996, 603 N.Y.S.2d 99 (Sup. Ct. N.Y. Co. 1993).

Specified criminal conduct.—Grand larceny, predicated on a theory of larceny by extortion, is a specified criminal conduct under PL § 470.00(4). The defendant, a racketeer, coerced the corporate victim to accept large sums of cash, initially paid by the victim to the defendant as part of an extortion scheme, to deposit the cash in the company's account and to issue a company check drawn to the defendant or to the defendant's wife. People v. Capparelli, 158 Misc. 2d 996, 603 N.Y.S.2d 99 (Sup. Ct. N.Y. Co. 1993).

Proceeds of a crime.—When racketeer extorted from the victim large sums of cash, in specific denominations, in a defined time period, then at the end of the time period coerced victim to deposit in the victim's bank account $400,000 in cash in same denominations, which approximated the amount extorted, the inference could be drawn that the proceeds of the extortion constituted the funds which were being deposited, against which a company check would be drawn, establishing the specified criminal conduct. People v. Capparelli, 158 Misc. 2d 996, 603 N.Y.S.2d 99 (Sup. Ct. N.Y. Co. 1993).

Equivalent property.—The purchase of a house with the proceeds of extortion is not itself money laundering, since real estate is not equivalent property under PL § 470.00(2). People v. Capparelli, 158 Misc. 2d 996, 603 N.Y.S.2d 99 (Sup. Ct. N.Y. Co. 1993).

—Credit in an account of a financial institution is a form of "equivalent property" under P.L. § 470.00(2). People v. Capparelli, 158 Misc. 2d 996, 603 N.Y.S.2d 99 (Sup. Ct. N.Y. Co. 1993).

Financial transaction.—A deposit of money into a bank account is a "financial transaction" within the meaning of PL § 470.00(3). People v. Capparelli, 158 Misc. 2d 996, 603 N.Y.S.2d 99 (Sup. Ct. N.Y. Co. 1993).

—Not every transaction involving the proceeds of specified criminal conduct is money laundering; under PL § 470.00(3), the "transaction" must result in an exchange of the criminal proceeds for financial instruments or equivalent property. When the defendant's attempt to consummate the exchange is prevented, as when he cannot withdraw the proceeds from the bank, the resulting crime is attempted money laundering. People v. Capparelli, 158 Misc. 2d 996, 603 N.Y.S.2d 99 (Sup. Ct. N.Y. Co. 1993).

—Arranging for the exchange of the monetary instrument to be paid to a third party, rather than to the defendant directly, does not defeat the element of "transaction" under PL § 470.00(3). People v. Capparelli, 158 Misc. 2d 996, 603 N.Y.S.2d 99 (Sup. Ct. N.Y. Co. 1993).

§ 470.03. Money laundering: aggregation of value; other matters.

1. For purposes of subdivisions one and three of sections 470.05, 470.10, 470.15, 470.21, 470.22 and 470.23, and for purposes of subdivisions one and two of sections 470.20 and 470.24 of this article, financial transactions may be considered together and the value of the property involved may be aggregated, provided that the transactions are all part of a single "criminal transaction" as defined in subdivision two of section 40.10 of the criminal procedure law.

2. For purposes of subdivision two of sections 470.05, 470.10, 470.15, 470.21, 470.22 and 470.23 of this article, separate occasions involving the transport, transmittal or transfer of monetary instruments may be considered together and the value of the monetary instruments involved

may be aggregated, provided that the occasions are all part of a single "criminal transaction" as defined in subdivision two of section 40.10 of the criminal procedure law.

3. Nothing in sections 470.05, 470.21, 470.22, 470.23 and 470.24; paragraph (b) of subdivision one, paragraph (b) of subdivision two and paragraph (b) of subdivision three of section 470.10; paragraph (b) of subdivision one, paragraph (b) of subdivision two and paragraph (b) of subdivision three of section 470.15; or paragraph (b) of subdivision one and paragraph (b) of subdivision two of section 470.20 of this article shall make it unlawful to return funds held in escrow:

(a) as a portion of a purchase price for real property pursuant to a contract of sale; or

(b) to satisfy the tax or other lawful obligations arising out of an administrative or judicial proceeding concerning the person who provided the escrow funds.

Added by L. 2000, Ch. 489, § 4, eff. Nov. 1, 2000; Amended by L. 2004, Ch. 1, § 17 (Part A), eff. July 23, 2004.

§ 470.05. Money laundering in the fourth degree.

A person is guilty of money laundering in the fourth degree when:

1. Knowing that the property involved in one or more financial transactions represents the proceeds of criminal conduct:

(a) he or she conducts one or more such financial transactions which in fact involve the proceeds of specified criminal conduct:

(i) With intent to:

(A) promote the carrying on of criminal conduct; or

(B) engage in conduct constituting a felony as set forth in section eighteen hundred two, eighteen hundred three, eighteen hundred four, eighteen hundred five, eighteen hundred seven or eighteen hundred eight of the tax law; or

(ii) Knowing that the transaction or transactions in whole or in part are designed to:

(A) conceal or disguise the nature, the location, the source, the ownership or the control of the proceeds of criminal conduct; or

(B) avoid any transaction reporting requirement imposed by law; and

(b) The total value of the property involved in such financial transaction or transactions exceeds five thousand dollars; or

2. Knowing that one or more monetary instruments represents the proceeds of criminal conduct:

(a) he or she transports, transmits, or transfers on one or more occasions, monetary instruments which in fact represent the proceeds of specified criminal conduct:

(i) With intent to promote the carrying on of criminal conduct; or

(ii) Knowing that such transportation, transmittal, or transfer is designed in whole or in part to:

(A) conceal or disguise the nature, the location, the source, the ownership, or the control of the proceeds of criminal conduct; or

(B) avoid any transaction reporting requirement imposed by law; and

(b) The total value of such monetary instrument or instruments exceeds ten thousand dollars; or

3. He or she conducts one or more financial transactions:

(a) involving property represented to be the proceeds of specified criminal conduct, or represented to be property used to conduct or facilitate specified criminal conduct, with intent to:

(i) promote the carrying on of specified criminal conduct; or

(ii) conceal or disguise the nature, the location, the source, the ownership or the control of property believed to be the proceeds of specified criminal conduct; or

(iii) avoid any transaction reporting requirement imposed by law; and

(b) the total value of the property involved in such financial transaction or transactions exceeds ten thousand dollars.

Money laundering in the fourth degree is a class E felony.

Former section **Repealed** and new section **Added** by L. 2000, Ch. 489, § 5, eff. Nov. 1, 2000.

ANNOTATIONS

Attempt to conceal and disguise the nature and source of the funds.—The defendant, who was a construction subcontractor for the corporate victim, having extorted cash from the victim over a period of time, coerced the victim to deposit the cash in the victim's own bank account and endorse to defendant a company check, in an attempt to make the expenditure appear to be legitimate. The evidence was sufficient to establish the element of defendant's intent to conceal and disguise the nature and source of the funds as the product of extortion, under § 470.05(1). People v. Capparelli, 158 Misc. 2d 996, 603 N.Y.S.2d 99 (Sup. Ct. N.Y. Co. 1993).

Benefit.—The defendant, having coerced the corporate victim to deposit in the defendant's account the proceeds of the extortion in exchange for a corporate check in the same amount which had the appearance of legitimacy, when defendant used the proceeds of the check to purchase a house, the defendant acted to benefit himself pursuant to PL § 470.05(2). People v. Capparelli, 158 Misc. 2d 996, 603 N.Y.S.2d 99 (Sup. Ct. N.Y. Co. 1993).

—The fact that the defendant intends that the laundered monetary instrument be paid to his wife, rather than himself, does not defeat the element of "benefit" under PL § 470.05(2). People v. Capparelli, 158 Misc. 2d 996, 603 N.Y.S.2d 99 (Sup. Ct. N.Y. Co. 1993).

§ 470.10. Money laundering in the third degree.

A person is guilty of money laundering in the third degree when:

1. Knowing that the property involved in one or more financial transactions represents:

(a) the proceeds of the criminal sale of a controlled substance, he or she conducts one or more such financial transactions which in fact involve the proceeds of the criminal sale of a controlled substance:

(i) With intent to:

(A) promote the carrying on of specified criminal conduct; or

(B) engage in conduct constituting a felony as set forth in section eighteen hundred two, eighteen hundred three, eighteen hundred four, eighteen hundred five, eighteen hundred seven or eighteen hundred eight of the tax law; or

(ii) Knowing that the transaction or transactions in whole or in part are designed to:

(A) conceal or disguise the nature, the location, the source, the ownership or the control of the proceeds of specified criminal conduct; or

(B) avoid any transaction reporting requirement imposed by law; and

(iii) The total value of the property involved in such financial transaction or transactions exceeds ten thousand dollars; or

(b) the proceeds of criminal conduct, he or she conducts one or more such financial transactions which in fact involve the proceeds of specified criminal conduct:

(i) With intent to:

(A) promote the carrying on of criminal conduct; or

(B) engage in conduct constituting a felony as set forth in section eighteen hundred two, eighteen hundred three, eighteen hundred four, eighteen hundred five, eighteen hundred seven or eighteen hundred eight of the tax law; or

(ii) knowing that the transaction or transactions in whole or in part are designed to:

(A) conceal or disguise the nature, the location, the source, the ownership or the control of the proceeds of criminal conduct; or

(B) avoid any transaction reporting requirement imposed by law; and

(iii) The total value of the property involved in such financial transaction or transactions exceeds fifty thousand dollars; or

2. Knowing that one or more monetary instruments represent:

(a) the proceeds of the criminal sale of a controlled substance, he or she transports, transmits, or transfers or attempts to transport, transmit or transfer, on one or more occasions, monetary instruments which in fact represent the proceeds of the criminal sale of a controlled substance from a place in any county in this state to or through a place outside that county or to a place in any county in this state from or through a place outside that county:

(i) With intent to promote the carrying on of specified criminal conduct; or

(ii) Knowing that such transportation, transmittal or transfer is designed in whole or in part to:

(A) conceal or disguise the nature, the location, the source, the ownership or the control of the proceeds of specified criminal conduct; or

(B) avoid any transaction reporting requirement imposed by law; and

(iii) The total value of such monetary instrument or instruments exceeds ten thousand dollars; or

(b) the proceeds of criminal conduct, he or she transports, transmits, or transfers or attempts to transport, transmit or transfer, on one or more occasions monetary instruments which in fact represent the proceeds of specified criminal conduct from a place in any county in this state to or through a place outside that county or to a place in any county in this state from or through a place outside that county:

(i) With intent to promote the carrying on of criminal conduct; or

(ii) Knowing that such transportation, transmittal or transfer is designed in whole or in part to:

(A) conceal or disguise the nature, the location, the source, the ownership, or the control of the proceeds of criminal conduct; or

(B) avoid any transaction reporting requirement imposed by law; and

(iii) The total value of such monetary instrument or instruments exceeds fifty thousand dollars; or

3. He or she conducts one or more financial transactions involving property represented to be:

(a) the proceeds of the criminal sale of a controlled substance, or represented to be property used to conduct or facilitate the criminal sale of a controlled substance:

(i) With intent to:

(A) promote the carrying on of specified criminal conduct; or

(B) conceal or disguise the nature, the location, the source, the ownership or the control of property believed to be the proceeds of specified criminal conduct; or

(C) avoid any transaction reporting requirement imposed by law; and

(ii) The total value of the property involved in such financial transaction or transactions exceeds ten thousand dollars; or

(b) the proceeds of specified criminal conduct, or represented to be property used to conduct or facilitate specified criminal conduct:

(i) With intent to:

(A) promote the carrying on of specified criminal conduct; or

(B) conceal or disguise the nature, the location, the source, the ownership or the control of property believed to be the proceeds of specified criminal conduct; or

(C) avoid any transaction reporting requirement imposed by law; and

(ii) The total value of the property involved in such financial transaction or transactions exceeds fifty thousand dollars.

Money laundering in the third degree is a class D felony.

Former section **Repealed** and new section **Added** by L. 2000, Ch. 489, § 5, eff. Nov. 1, 2000.

ANNOTATIONS

Attempt to conceal and disguise the nature and source of the funds.—The defendant, who was a construction subcontractor for the corporate victim, having extorted cash from the victim over a period of time, coerced the victim to deposit the cash in the victim's own bank account and endorse to defendant a company check, in an attempt to make the expenditure appear to be legitimate. The evidence was sufficient to establish the element of defendant's intent to conceal and disguise the nature and source of the funds as the product of extortion, under § 470.10(1). People v. Capparelli, 158 Misc. 2d 996, 603 N.Y.S.2d 99 (Sup. Ct. N.Y. Co. 1993).

Benefit.—The defendant, having coerced the corporate victim to deposit in the defendant's account the proceeds of the extortion in exchange for a corporate check in the same amount which had the appearance of legitimacy, when defendant used the proceeds of the check to purchase a house, the defendant acted to benefit himself pursuant to PL § 470.10(2). People v. Capparelli, 158 Misc. 2d 996, 603 N.Y.S.2d 99 (Sup. Ct. N.Y. Co. 1993).

—The fact that the defendant intends that the laundered monetary instrument be paid to his wife, rather than himself, does not defeat the element of "benefit" under PL § 470.10(2). People v. Capparelli, 158 Misc. 2d 996, 603 N.Y.S.2d 99 (Sup. Ct. N.Y. Co. 1993).

Comparison with federal offense.—The elements of the federal money laundering statute are not equivalent to those of PL § 470.10. The state offense requires greater culpability and has a different mens rea. *In re* Weinig, 220 A.D.2d 184, 642 N.Y.S.2d 654 (1st Dept. 1996); *In re* Stern, 205 A.D.2d 162, 619 N.Y.S.2d 1 (1st Dept. 1994).

—A conviction of money laundering would lead to automatic disbarment of an attorney licensed to practice in New York; however, a conviction for the federal offense of money laundering would not result in automatic disbarment, entitling the attorney to a disciplinary hearing. *In re* Weinig, 220 A.D.2d 184, 642 N.Y.S.2d 654 (1st Dept. 1996); *In re* Stern, 205 A.D.2d 162, 619 N.Y.S.2d 1 (1st Dept. 1994).

§ 470.15. Money laundering in the second degree.

A person is guilty of money laundering in the second degree when:

1. Knowing that the property involved in one or more financial transactions represents:

(a) the proceeds of the criminal sale of a controlled substance, he or she conducts one or more such financial transactions which in fact involve the proceeds of the criminal sale of a controlled substance:

(i) With intent to:

(A) promote the carrying on of specified criminal conduct; or

(B) engage in conduct constituting a felony as set forth in section eighteen hundred two, eighteen hundred three, eighteen hundred four, eighteen hundred five, eighteen hundred seven or eighteen hundred eight of the tax law; or

(ii) Knowing that the transaction or transactions in whole or in part are designed to:

(A) conceal or disguise the nature, the location, the source, the ownership or the control of the proceeds of specified criminal conduct; or

(B) avoid any transaction reporting requirement imposed by law; and

(iii) the total value of the property involved in such financial transaction or transactions exceeds fifty thousand dollars; or

(b) the proceeds of specified criminal conduct, he or she conducts one or more such financial transactions which in fact involve the proceeds of specified criminal conduct:

(i) With intent to:

(A) promote the carrying on of specified criminal conduct; or

(B) engage in conduct constituting a felony as set forth in section eighteen hundred two, eighteen hundred three, eighteen hundred four, eighteen hundred five, eighteen hundred seven or eighteen hundred eight of the tax law; or

(ii) Knowing that the transaction or transactions in whole or in part are designed to:

(A) conceal or disguise the nature, the location, the source, the ownership or the control of the proceeds of specified criminal conduct; or

(B) avoid any transaction reporting requirement imposed by law; and

(iii) The total value of the property involved in such financial transaction or transactions exceeds one hundred thousand dollars; or

2. Knowing that one or more monetary instruments represent:

(a) the proceeds of the criminal sale of a controlled substance, he or she transports, transmits, or transfers or attempts to transport, transmit or transfer, on one or more occasions, monetary instruments which in fact represent the proceeds of the criminal sale of a controlled substance from a place in any county in this state to or through a place outside that county or to a place in any county in this state from or through a place outside that county:

(i) With intent to promote the carrying on of specified criminal conduct; or

(ii) Knowing that such transportation, transmittal or transfer is designed in whole or in part to:

(A) conceal or disguise the nature, the location, the source, the ownership or the control of the proceeds of specified criminal conduct; or

(B) avoid any transaction reporting requirement imposed by law; and

(iii) The total value of such monetary instrument or instruments exceeds fifty thousand dollars; or

(b) the proceeds of specified criminal conduct, he or she transports, transmits, or transfers or attempts to transport, transmit or transfer, on one or more occasions, monetary instruments which in fact represent the proceeds of specified criminal conduct from a place in any county in this state to or through a place outside that county or to a place in any county in this state from or through a place outside that county:

(i) With intent to promote the carrying on of specified criminal conduct; or

(ii) Knowing that such transportation, transmittal or transfer is designed in whole or in part to:

(A) conceal or disguise the nature, the location, the source, the ownership or the control of the proceeds of specified criminal conduct; or

(B) avoid any transaction reporting requirement imposed by law; and

(iii) The total value of such monetary instrument or instruments exceeds one hundred thousand dollars; or

3. He or she conducts one or more financial transactions involving property represented to be:

(a) the proceeds of the criminal sale of a controlled substance, or represented to be property used to conduct or facilitate the criminal sale of a controlled substance:

(i) With intent to:

(A) promote the carrying on of specified criminal conduct; or

(B) conceal or disguise the nature, the location, the source, the ownership or the control of property believed to be the proceeds of specified criminal conduct; or

(C) avoid any transaction reporting requirement imposed by law; and

(ii) The total represented value of the property involved in such financial transaction or transactions exceeds fifty thousand dollars; or

(b) the proceeds of specified criminal conduct, or represented to be property used to conduct or facilitate specified criminal conduct:

(i) With intent to:

(A) promote the carrying on of specified criminal conduct;

(B) conceal or disguise the nature, the location, the source, the ownership or the control of property believed to be the proceeds of specified criminal conduct; or

(C) avoid any transaction reporting requirement imposed by law; and

(ii) The total represented value of the property involved in such financial transaction or transactions exceeds one hundred thousand dollars.

Money laundering in the second degree is a class C felony.

Former section **Repealed** and new section **Added** by L. 2000, Ch. 489, § 5, eff. Nov. 1, 2000.

ANNOTATIONS

Attempt to conceal and disguise the nature and source of the funds.—The defendant, who was a construction subcontractor for the corporate victim, having extorted cash from the victim over a period of time, coerced the victim to deposit $400,000 in the victim's own bank account and endorse to defendant a company check, in an attempt to make the expenditure appear to be legitimate. The evidence was sufficient to establish the element of defendant's intent to conceal and disguise the nature and source of the funds as the product of extortion, under § 470.15(1). People v. Capparelli, 158 Misc. 2d 996, 603 N.Y.S.2d 99 (Sup. Ct. N.Y. Co. 1993).

Benefit.—The defendant, having coerced the corporate victim to deposit in the defendant's account the proceeds of the extortion in exchange for a corporate check in the amount of $400,000 which had the appearance of legitimacy, when defendant used the proceeds of the check to purchase a house, the defendant acted to benefit himself pursuant to PL § 470.15(2). People v. Capparelli, 158 Misc. 2d 996, 603 N.Y.S.2d 99 (Sup. Ct. N.Y. Co. 1993).

—The fact that the defendant intends that the laundered monetary instrument worth $50,000 to be paid to his wife, rather than himself, does not defeat the element of "benefit" under PL § 470.15(2). People v. Capparelli, 158 Misc. 2d 996, 603 N.Y.S.2d 99 (Sup. Ct. N.Y. Co. 1993).

§ 470.20. Money laundering in the first degree.

A person is guilty of money laundering in the first degree when:

1. Knowing that the property involved in one or more financial transactions represents:

(a) the proceeds of the criminal sale of a controlled substance, he or she conducts one or more such financial transactions which in fact involve the proceeds of the criminal sale of a controlled substance:

(i) With intent to:

(A) promote the carrying on of specified criminal conduct; or

(B) engage in conduct constituting a felony as set forth in section eighteen hundred two, eighteen hundred three, eighteen hundred four, eighteen hundred five, eighteen hundred seven or eighteen hundred eight of the tax law; or

(ii) Knowing that the transaction or transactions in whole or in part are designed to:

(A) conceal or disguise the nature, the location, the source, the ownership or the control of the proceeds of specified criminal conduct; or

(B) avoid any transaction reporting requirement imposed by law; and

(iii) the total value of the property involved in such financial transaction or transactions exceeds five hundred thousand dollars; or

(b) the proceeds of a class A, B or C felony, or of a crime in any other jurisdiction that is or would be a class A, B or C felony under the laws of this state, he or she conducts one or more such financial transactions which in fact involve the proceeds of any such felony:

(i) With intent to:

(A) promote the carrying on of specified criminal conduct; or

(B) engage in conduct constituting a felony as set forth in section eighteen hundred two, eighteen hundred three, eighteen hundred four, eighteen hundred five, eighteen hundred seven or eighteen hundred eight of the tax law; or

(ii) Knowing that the transaction or transactions in whole or in part are designed to:

(A) conceal or disguise the nature, the location, the source, the ownership or the control of the proceeds of specified criminal conduct; or

(B) avoid any transaction reporting requirement imposed by law; and

(iii) the total value of the property involved in such financial transaction or transactions exceeds one million dollars.

2. He or she conducts one or more financial transactions involving property represented to be:

(a) the proceeds of the criminal sale of a controlled substance, or represented to be property used to conduct or facilitate the criminal sale of a controlled substance:

(i) With intent to:

(A) promote the carrying on of specified criminal conduct; or

(B) conceal or disguise the nature, the location, the source, the ownership or the control of property believed to be the proceeds of specified criminal conduct; or

(C) avoid any transaction reporting requirement imposed by law; and

(ii) The total represented value of the property involved in such financial transaction or transactions exceeds five hundred thousand dollars; or

(b) the proceeds of a class A, B or C felony

or of a crime in any other jurisdiction that is or would be a class A, B or C felony under the laws of this state, or represented to be property used to conduct or facilitate such crimes:

(i) With intent to:

(A) promote the carrying on of specified criminal conduct; or

(B) conceal or disguise the nature, the location, the source, the ownership or the control of property believed to be the proceeds of specified criminal conduct; or

(C) avoid any transaction reporting requirement imposed by law; and

(ii) The total represented value of the property involved in such financial transaction or transactions exceeds one million dollars.

Money laundering in the first degree is a class B felony.

Former section **Renumbered** to § 470.25 and new section **Added** by L. 2000, Ch. 489, § 5, eff. Nov. 1, 2000.

§ 470.21. Money laundering in support of terrorism in the fourth degree.

A person is guilty of money laundering in support of terrorism in the fourth degree when:

1. Knowing that the property involved in one or more financial transactions represents either the proceeds of an act of terrorism as defined in subdivision one of section 490.05 of this part, or a monetary instrument given, received or intended to be used to support a violation of article four hundred ninety of this part:

(a) he or she conducts one or more such financial transactions which in fact involve either the proceeds of an act of terrorism as defined in subdivision one of section 490.05 of this part, or a monetary instrument given, received or intended to be used to support a violation of article four hundred ninety of this part:

(i) With intent to:

(A) promote the carrying on of criminal conduct; or

(B) engage in conduct constituting a felony as set forth in section eighteen hundred two, eighteen hundred three, eighteen hundred four, eighteen hundred five, eighteen hundred seven or eighteen hundred eight of the tax law; or

(ii) Knowing that the transaction or transactions in whole or in part are designed to:

(A) conceal or disguise the nature, the location, the source, the ownership or the control of either the proceeds of an act of terrorism as defined in subdivision one of section 490.05 of this part, or a monetary instrument given, received or intended to be used to support a violation of article four hundred ninety of this part; or

(B) avoid any transaction reporting require-ment imposed by law; and

(b) the total value of the property involved in such financial transaction or transactions exceeds one thousand dollars; or

2. Knowing that one or more monetary instru-ments represents either the proceeds of an act of terrorism as defined in subdivision one of section 490.05 of this part, or a monetary instrument given, received or intended to be used to support a violation of article four hundred ninety of this part:

(a) he or she transports, transmits, or transfers on one or more occasions, monetary instruments which in fact represent either the proceeds of an act of terrorism as defined in subdivision one of section 490.05 of this part, or a monetary instru-ment given, received or intended to be used to support a violation of article four hundred ninety of this part:

(i) With intent to promote the carrying on of criminal conduct; or

(ii) Knowing that such transportation, trans-mittal, or transfer is designed in whole or in part to:

(A) conceal or disguise the nature, the loca-tion, the source, the ownership, or the control of either the proceeds of an act of terrorism as defined in subdivision one of section 490.05 of this part, or a monetary instrument given, received or intended to be used to support a violation of article four hundred ninety of this part; or

(B) avoid any transaction reporting require-ment imposed by law; and

(b) the total value of such monetary instrument or instruments exceeds two thousand dollars; or

3. He or she conducts one or more financial transactions:

(a) involving property represented to be either the proceeds of an act of terrorism as defined in subdivision one of section 490.05 of this part, or a monetary instrument given, received or intended to be used to support a violation of article four hundred ninety of this part, with intent to:

(i) promote the carrying on of specified crimi-nal conduct; or

(ii) conceal or disguise the nature, the location, the source, the ownership or the control of prop-erty believed to be either the proceeds of an act of terrorism as defined in subdivision one of section 490.05 of this part, or a monetary instru-ment given, received or intended to be used to support a violation of article four hundred ninety of this part; or

(iii) avoid any transaction reporting require-ment imposed by law; and

(b) the total value of the property involved in

such financial transaction or transactions exceeds two thousand dollars.

Money laundering in support of terrorism in the fourth degree is a class E felony.

Added by L. 2004, Ch. 1, § 18 (Part A), eff. July 23, 2004.

§ 470.22. Money laundering in support of terrorism in the third degree.

A person is guilty of money laundering in support of terrorism in the third degree when:

1. Knowing that the property involved in one or more financial transactions represents either the proceeds of an act of terrorism as defined in subdivision one of section 490.05 of this part, or a monetary instrument given, received or intended to be used to support a violation of article four hundred ninety of this part:

(a) he or she conducts one or more such financial transactions which in fact involve either the proceeds of an act of terrorism as defined in subdivision one of section 490.05 of this part, or a monetary instrument given, received or intended to be used to support a violation of article four hundred ninety of this part:

(i) With intent to:

(A) promote the carrying on of specified crim-inal conduct; or

(B) engage in conduct constituting a felony as set forth in section eighteen hundred two, eighteen hundred three, eighteen hundred four, eighteen hundred five, eighteen hundred seven or eighteen hundred eight of the tax law; or

(ii) Knowing that the transaction or transac-tions in whole or in part are designed to:

(A) conceal or disguise the nature, the loca-tion, the source, the ownership or the control of either the proceeds of an act of terrorism as defined in subdivision one of section 490.05 of this part, or a monetary instrument given, received or intended to be used to support a violation of article four hundred ninety of this part; or

(B) avoid any transaction reporting require-ment imposed by law; and

(b) the total value of the property involved in such financial transaction or transactions exceeds five thousand dollars; or

2. Knowing that one or more monetary instru-ments represent either the proceeds of an act of terrorism as defined in subdivision one of section 490.05 of this part, or a monetary instrument given, received or intended to be used to support a violation of article four hundred ninety of this part:

(a) he or she transports, transmits, or transfers or attempts to transport, transmit or transfer, on one or more occasions, monetary instruments which in fact represent either the proceeds of an act of terrorism as defined in subdivision one of section 490.05 of this part, or a monetary instrument given, received or intended to be used to support a violation of article four hundred ninety of this part from a place in any county in this state to or through a place outside that county or to a place in any county in this state from or through a place outside that county:

(i) With intent to promote the carrying on of specified criminal conduct; or

(ii) Knowing that such transportation, transmittal or transfer is designed in whole or in part to:

(A) conceal or disguise the nature, the location, the source, the ownership or the control of either the proceeds of an act of terrorism as defined in subdivision one of section 490.05 of this part, or a monetary instrument given, received or intended to be used to support a violation of article four hundred ninety of this part; or

(B) avoid any transaction reporting requirement imposed by law; and

(b) The total value of such monetary instrument or instruments exceeds five thousand dollars; or

3. He or she conducts one or more financial transactions involving property represented to be either the proceeds of an act of terrorism as defined in subdivision one of section 490.05 of this part, or a monetary instrument given, received or intended to be used to support a violation of article four hundred ninety of this part:

(a) With intent to:

(i) promote the carrying on of specified criminal conduct; or

(ii) conceal or disguise the nature, the location, the source, the ownership or the control of property believed to be either the proceeds of an act of terrorism as defined in subdivision one of section 490.05 of this part, or a monetary instrument given, received or intended to be used to support a violation of article four hundred ninety of this part; or

(iii) avoid any transaction reporting requirement imposed by law; and

(b) The total value of the property involved in such financial transaction or transactions exceeds five thousand dollars.

Money laundering in support of terrorism in the third degree is a class D felony.

Added by L. 2004, Ch. 1, § 18 (Part A), eff. July 23, 2004.

§ 470.23. Money laundering in support of terrorism in the second degree.

A person is guilty of money laundering in support of terrorism in the second degree when:

1. Knowing that the property involved in one or more financial transactions represents either the proceeds of an act of terrorism as defined in subdivision one of section 490.05 of this part, or a monetary instrument given, received or intended to be used to support a violation of article four hundred ninety of this part:

(a) he or she conducts one or more such financial transactions which in fact involve either the proceeds of an act of terrorism as defined in subdivision one of section 490.05 of this part, or a monetary instrument given, received or intended to be used to support a violation of article four hundred ninety of this part:

(i) With intent to:

(A) promote the carrying on of specified criminal conduct; or

(B) engage in conduct constituting a felony as set forth in section eighteen hundred two, eighteen hundred three, eighteen hundred four, eighteen hundred five, eighteen hundred seven or eighteen hundred eight of the tax law; or

(ii) Knowing that the transaction or transactions in whole or in part are designed to:

(A) conceal or disguise the nature, the location, the source, the ownership or the control of either the proceeds of an act of terrorism as defined in subdivision one of section 490.05 of this part, or a monetary instrument given, received or intended to be used to support a violation of article four hundred ninety of this part; or

(B) avoid any transaction reporting requirement imposed by law; and

(b) the total value of the property involved in such financial transaction or transactions exceeds twenty-five thousand dollars; or

2. Knowing that one or more monetary instruments represent either the proceeds of an act of terrorism as defined in subdivision one of section 490.05 of this part, or a monetary instrument given, received or intended to be used to support a violation of article four hundred ninety of this part:

(a) he or she transports, transmits, or transfers or attempts to transport, transmit or transfer, on one or more occasions, monetary instruments which in fact represent either the proceeds of an act of terrorism as defined in subdivision one of section 490.05 of this part, or a monetary instrument given, received or intended to be used to support a violation of article four hundred ninety of this part from a place in any county in this state to or through a place outside that county or to a place in any county in this state from or through a place outside that county:

(i) With intent to promote the carrying on of specified criminal conduct; or

(ii) Knowing that such transportation, transmittal or transfer is designed in whole or in part to:

(A) conceal or disguise the nature, the location, the source, the ownership or the control of either the proceeds of an act of terrorism as defined in subdivision one of section 490.05 of this part, or a monetary instrument given, received or intended to be used to support a violation of article four hundred ninety of this part; or

(B) avoid any transaction reporting requirement imposed by law; and

(b) the total value of such monetary instrument or instruments exceeds twenty-five thousand dollars; or

3. He or she conducts one or more financial transactions involving property represented to be either the proceeds of an act of terrorism as defined in subdivision one of section 490.05 of this part, or a monetary instrument given, received or intended to be used to support a violation of article four hundred ninety of this part:

(a) With intent to:

(i) promote the carrying on of specified criminal conduct; or

(ii) conceal or disguise the nature, the location, the source, the ownership or the control of property believed to be either the proceeds of an act of terrorism as defined in subdivision one of section 490.05 of this part, or a monetary instrument given, received or intended to be used to support a violation of article four hundred ninety of this part; or

(iii) avoid any transaction reporting requirement imposed by law; and

(b) The total value of the property involved in such financial transaction or transactions exceeds twenty-five thousand dollars.

Money laundering in support of terrorism in the second degree is a class C felony.

Added by L. 2004, Ch. 1, § 18 (Part A), eff. July 23, 2004.

§ 470.24. Money laundering in support of terrorism in the first degree.

A person is guilty of money laundering in support of terrorism in the first degree when:

1. Knowing that the property involved in one or more financial transactions represents either the proceeds of an act of terrorism as defined in subdivision one of section 490.05 of this part, or a monetary instrument given, received or intended to be used to support a violation of article four hundred ninety of this part:

(a) he or she conducts one or more financial transactions which in fact involve either the proceeds of an act of terrorism as defined in subdivision one of section 490.05 of this part, or a monetary instrument given, received or intended to be used to support a violation of article four hundred ninety of this part:

(i) With intent to:

(A) promote the carrying on of specified criminal conduct; or

(B) engage in conduct constituting a felony as set forth in section eighteen hundred two, eighteen hundred three, eighteen hundred four, eighteen hundred five, eighteen hundred seven or eighteen hundred eight of the tax law; or

(ii) Knowing that the transaction or transactions in whole or in part are designed to:

(A) conceal or disguise the nature, the location, the source, the ownership or the control of the proceeds of either the proceeds of an act of terrorism as defined in subdivision one of section 490.05 of this part, or a monetary instrument given, received or intended to be used to support a violation of article four hundred ninety of this part; or

(B) avoid any transaction reporting requirement imposed by law; and

(iii) The total value of the property involved in such financial transaction or transactions exceeds seventy-five thousand dollars.

2. He or she conducts one or more financial transactions involving property represented to be either the proceeds of an act of terrorism as defined in subdivision one of section 490.05 of this part, or a monetary instrument given, received or intended to be used to support a violation of article four hundred ninety of this part:

(a) With intent to:

(i) promote the carrying on of specified criminal conduct; or

(ii) conceal or disguise the nature, the location, the source, the ownership or the control of property believed to be either the proceeds of an act of terrorism as defined in subdivision one of section 490.05 of this part, or a monetary instrument given, received or intended to be used to support a violation of article four hundred ninety of this part; or

(iii) avoid any transaction reporting requirement imposed by law; and

(b) The total represented value of the property involved in such financial transaction or transactions exceeds one hundred twenty-five thousand dollars.

Money laundering in support of terrorism in the first degree is a class B felony.

Added by L. 2004, Ch. 1, § 18 (Part A), eff. July 23, 2004.

§ 470.25. Money laundering; fines.

1. Any person convicted of a violation of section 470.05, 470.10, 470.15, or 470.20 of this article may be sentenced to pay a fine not in excess of two times the value of the monetary instruments which are the proceeds of specified criminal activity. When a fine is imposed pursuant to this subdivision, the court shall make a finding

as to the value of such monetary instrument or instruments. If the record does not contain sufficient evidence to support such a finding the court may conduct a hearing upon the issue. In imposing a fine, the court shall consider the seriousness of the conduct, whether the amount of the fine is disproportionate to the conduct in which he engaged, its impact on victims, as well as the economic circumstances of the convicted person, including the effect of the imposition of such a fine upon his immediate family.

2. The imposition of a fine pursuant to subdivision one of this section or paragraph b of subdivision one of section 80.00 of this chapter, shall preclude the imposition of any other order or judgment of forfeiture or fine based upon the same criminal conduct.

Former section **Renumbered** from § 470.20 and newly designated section **Amended** by L. 2000, Ch. 489, § 6, eff. Nov. 1, 2000.

PL

ARTICLE 480—CRIMINAL FORFEITURE—
FELONY CONTROLLED SUBSTANCE OFFENSES

Section
480.00 Definitions.
480.05 Felony controlled substance offenses; forfeiture.
480.10 Procedure.
480.20 Disposal of property.
480.25 Election of remedies.
480.30 Provisional remedies.
480.35 Rebuttable presumption.

LexisNexis Cross References

Prosecution and Defense of Forfeiture Cases, Part II, Criminal Forfeiture; *Defense of Narcotics Cases,* Vol. 2, Ch. 4B, Forfeiture Proceedings; *Criminal Defense Techniques,* Vol. 3A, Ch. 62B, Defense of Forfeiture Cases.

§ 480.00. Definitions.

The following definitions are applicable to this article.

1. "Felony offense" means only a felony defined in article two hundred twenty of this chapter, or an attempt or conspiracy to commit any such felony, provided such attempt or conspiracy is punishable as a felony, or solicitation of any such felony provided such solicitation is punishable as a felony.

2. "Property" means real property, personal property, money, negotiable instruments, securities, or anything of value or an interest in a thing of value.

3. "Proceeds" means any property obtained by a defendant through the commission of a felony controlled substance offense, and includes any appreciation in value of such property.

4. "Substituted proceeds" means any property obtained by a defendant by the sale or exchange of proceeds of a felony controlled substance offense, and any gain realized by such sale or exchange.

5. "Instrumentality of a felony controlled substance offense" means any property, other than real property and any buildings, fixtures, appurtenances, and improvements thereon, whose use contributes directly and materially to the commission of a felony controlled substance offense.

6. "Real property instrumentality of a crime" means an interest in real property the use of which contributes directly and materially to the commission of a specified felony offense.

7. "Specified felony offense" means:

(a) a conviction of a person for a violation of section 220.18, 220.21, 220.41, or 220.43 of this chapter, or where the accusatory instrument charges one or more of such offenses, conviction upon a plea of guilty to any of the felonies for which such plea is otherwise authorized by law or a conviction of a person for conspiracy to commit a violation of section 220.18, 220.21, 220.41, or 220.43 of the penal law, where the controlled substances which are the object of the conspiracy are located in the real property which is the subject of the forfeiture action; or

(b) three or more violations of any of the felonies defined in section 220.09, 220.16, 220.18, 220.21, 220.31, 220.34, 220.39, 220.41, 220.43, or 221.55 of this chapter, which violations do not constitute a single criminal offense as defined in subdivision one of section 40.10 of the criminal procedure law, or a single criminal transaction, as defined in paragraph (a) of subdivision two of section 40.10 of the criminal procedure law, and at least one of which resulted in a conviction of such offense, or where the accusatory instrument charges one or more of such felonies, conviction upon a plea of guilty to a felony for which such plea is otherwise authorized by law; or

(c) a conviction of a person for a violation of section 220.09, 220.16, 220.34, 220.39, or 221.30 of this chapter, or where the accusatory instrument charges any such felony, conviction upon a plea of guilty to a felony for which the plea is otherwise authorized by law, together with evidence which: (i) provides substantial indicia that the defendant used the real property to engage in a continual, ongoing course of conduct involving the unlawful mixing, compounding, manufacturing, warehousing, or packaging of controlled substances or where the conviction is for a violation of section 221.30 of this chapter, marijuana as part of an illegal trade or business for gain; and (ii) establishes, where the conviction is for possession of a controlled substance or where the conviction is for a violation of section 221.30 of this chapter, marijuana, that such possession was with the intent to sell it.

ANNOTATIONS

Constitutional restrictions on civil forfeiture.—Civil forfeiture seizures in drug cases are still subject to the Fourth Amendment's protections against unreasonable searches and seizures. United States v. Lasanta, 978 F.2d 1300 (2d Cir. 1992).

—In view of New York's broad recognition under state constitution to a defendant's right to counsel of choice, court is empowered to require prosecutor to provide for payment of counsel out of forfeited assets. However, the fee for representation should be taken only from assets seized in New York, rather than federal, forfeiture proceeding. People v. Martinez, 151 Misc. 2d 641, 574 N.Y.S.2d 467 (Sup. Ct. N.Y. Co. 1991).

Right to jury trial of forfeiture proceedings.—Under former law, state forfeiture proceedings, even if technically civil in nature, which provided for forfeiture of a defendant's property upon conviction, entitled defendant to a jury trial. People v. Witherill, 29 N.Y.2d 446, 328 N.Y.S.2d 668 (1972).

Simultaneous criminal trial and forfeiture proceeding.—The District Attorney may prosecute the defendant for the underlying felony and at the same time conduct forfeiture proceedings under Article 480 in connection with such felony. In re Harnischfeger; In re Markert, 158 Misc. 2d 299, 600 N.Y.S.2d 894 (Sup. Ct. Monroe Co. 1993); compare with CPLR § 1311, in which civil forfeiture proceeding is stayed pending outcome of criminal proceeding.

Forfeit authorities constrained by in personam jurisdiction.—Penal Law Article 480 is in personam in nature and is limited to same jurisdictional limitations as CPLR Article 13-A. People v. Martinez, 151 Misc. 2d 641, 574 N.Y.S.2d 467 (Sup. Ct. N.Y. Co. 1991).

—New York law enforcement authorities have no jurisdiction solely by virtue of forfeiture provisions of Article 480 over funds located outside of New York borders, in this case defendant's bank account in Puerto Rico People v. Martinez, 151 Misc. 2d 641, 574 N.Y.S.2d 467 (Sup. Ct. N.Y. Co. 1991).

—New York forfeiture laws are largely ineffective in securing a defendant's out-of-state assets prior to conviction. People v. Martinez, 151 Misc. 2d 641, 574 N.Y.S.2d 467 (Sup. Ct. N.Y. Co. 1991).

—New York prosecutors may rely on federal forfeiture provisions under U.S.C. Title 21 to seize out-of-state assets when a jurisdictional bar exists under New York law. People v. Martinez, 151 Misc. 2d 641, 574 N.Y.S.2d 467 (Sup. Ct. N.Y. Co. 1991).

—New York courts may issue an order enjoining a defendant from encumbering or removing out-of-state property, but, absent a jurisdictional predicate allowing for forfeiture under Article 480, the sole remedy for violation of the order is a contempt proceeding. People v. Martinez, 151 Misc. 2d 641, 574 N.Y.S.2d 467 (Sup. Ct. N.Y. Co. 1991).

Forfeit of non-criminal's assets.—Article 480 forfeiture is not a vehicle to seize the assets of a non-criminal defendant in a CPLR Article 13-A proceeding. People v. Martinez, 151 Misc. 2d 641, 574 N.Y.S.2d 467 (Sup. Ct. N.Y. Co. 1991). See also Morgenthau v. Citysource, Inc., 68 N.Y.2d 211, 508 N.Y.S.2d 152, 500 N.E.2d 850 (1986) (prohibiting civil forfeiture of assets of non-criminal defendant, except for proceeds of the crime, the substituted proceeds of the crime or an instrumentality of a crime, in CPLR Article 13-A proceeding).

Automobile as instrumentality of drug sale.—When a car is used to carry out a drug sale, it is subject to forfeiture as the instrumentality of a felony. In re Harnischfeger; In re Markert, 158 Misc. 2d 299, 600 N.Y.S.2d 894 (Sup. Ct. Monroe Co. 1993).

Probable cause as predicate for seizure.—Police should apply for seizure warrant on showing of probable cause that the property to be seized was used as the instrumentality of a felony. In re Harnischfeger; In re Markert, 158 Misc. 2d 299, 600 N.Y.S.2d 894 (Sup. Ct. Monroe Co. 1993).

Property purchased with proceeds of a felony.—The mere fact that the proceeds of a drug sale were demonstrably used to purchase four automobiles was not a basis under Article 480 to seize those automobiles on the basis that they were used to facilitate the commission of a felony, nor on the basis that the automobiles were the proceeds of a felony. In re Harnischfeger; In re Markert, 158 Misc. 2d 299, 600 N.Y.S.2d 894 (Sup. Ct. Monroe Co. 1993).

—Automobiles purchased with the proceeds of a felony drug sale constituted "substituted proceeds" within the meaning of § 480.00(4). In re Harnischfeger; In re Markert, 158 Misc. 2d 299, 600 N.Y.S.2d 894 (Sup. Ct. Monroe Co. 1993).

§ 480.05. Felony controlled substance offenses; forfeiture.

1. When any person is convicted of a felony offense, the following property is subject to forfeiture pursuant to this article:

(a) Any property constituting the proceeds or substituted proceeds of such offense, unless the forfeiture is disproportionate to the defendant's gain from or participation in the offense, in which event the trier of fact may direct forfeiture of a portion thereof; and

(b) Any property constituting an instrumentality of such offense, other than a real property instrumentality of a crime, unless such forfeiture is disproportionate to the defendant's gain from or participation in the offense, in which event the trier of fact may direct forfeiture of a portion thereof.

2. When any person is convicted of a specified offense, the real property instrumentality of such specified offense is subject to forfeiture pursuant to this article, unless such forfeiture is disproportionate to the defendant's gain from or participation in the offense, in which event the trier of fact may direct forfeiture of a portion thereof.

3. Property acquired in good faith by an attorney as payment for the reasonable and bona fide fees of legal services or reimbursement of reasonable and bona fide expenses related to the representation of a defendant in connection with a civil or criminal forfeiture proceeding or a related criminal matter, shall be exempt from a judgment of forfeiture. For purposes of this subdivision, "bona fide" means that the attorney who acquired such property had no reasonable basis to believe that the fee transaction was a fraudulent or sham transaction designed to shield property from forfeiture, hide its existence from governmental investigative agencies, or was conducted for any purpose other than legitimate.

ANNOTATIONS

"Substituted proceeds."—Automobiles purchased with the proceeds of a felony drug sale constituted "substituted proceeds" within the meaning of § 480.00(4). In re Harnischfeger; In re Markert, 158 Misc. 2d 299, 600 N.Y.S.2d 894 (Sup. Ct. Monroe Co. 1993).

Automobile as instrumentality of drug sale.—When a car is used to carry out a drug sale, it is subject to forfeiture as the instrumentality of a felony. In re Harnischfeger; In re Markert, 158 Misc. 2d 299, 600 N.Y.S.2d 894 (Sup. Ct. Monroe Co. 1993).

§ 480.05 may be invoked only upon conviction.—Article 480 forfeiture is not a vehicle to seize the assets of a non-criminal defendant in a CPLR Article 13-A proceeding. People v. Martinez, 151 Misc. 2d 641, 574 N.Y.S.2d 467 (Sup. Ct. N.Y. Co. 1991). See also Morgenthau v. Citysource, Inc., 68 N.Y.2d 211, 508 N.Y.S.2d 152, 500 N.E.2d 850 (1986) (prohibiting civil forfeiture of assets of non-criminal defendant, except for proceeds of the crime, the substituted proceeds of the crime or an instrumentality of a crime, in CPLR Article 13-A proceeding).

Payment of legal fees.—In view of New York's broad recognition under state constitution to a defendant's right to counsel of choice, court is empowered to require prosecutor to provide for payment of counsel out of forfeited assets. However, the fee for representation should be taken only from assets seized in New York, rather than federal, forfeiture proceeding. People v. Martinez, 151 Misc. 2d 641, 574 N.Y.S.2d 467 (Sup. Ct. N.Y. Co. 1991).

Generally.—Even unusable cocaine residue found in defendant's possession is sufficient to support a charge of possession of a controlled substance in the seventh degree and evidence thereof is sufficient to subject automobile to forfeiture. *See* New York City Police Dept. v. Larouche, 187 A.D.2d 289, 589 N.Y.S.2d 459 (1st Dept. 1992).

§ 480.10. Procedure.

1. After the grand jury votes to file an indictment charging a person with a felony offense as that term is defined in section 480.00 of this article, it may subsequently receive evidence that property is subject to forfeiture under this article. If such evidence is legally sufficient and provides reasonable cause to believe that such property is subject to forfeiture under this article, the grand jury shall file together with the indictment a special forfeiture information specifying the property for which forfeiture is sought and containing a plain and concise factual statement which sets forth the basis for the forfeiture. Alternatively, where the defendant has waived indictment and has consented to be prosecuted for a felony offense by superior court information pursuant to article one hundred ninety-five of the criminal procedure law, the prosecutor may, in addition to the superior court information, file a special forfeiture information specifying the property for which the forfeiture is sought and containing a plain and concise factual statement which sets forth the basis for the forfeiture.

2. At any time before entry of a plea of guilty to an indictment or commencement of a trial thereof, the prosecutor may file a superseding special forfeiture information in the same court in accordance with the provisions of subdivision one of this section. Upon the filing of such a superseding forfeiture information the court must, upon application of the defendant, order any adjournment of the proceedings which may, by reason of such superseding special forfeiture information, be necessary to accord the defendant adequate opportunity to prepare his defense of the forfeiture action.

3. A motion to inspect and reduce made pursuant to section 210.20 of the criminal procedure law may seek modification of a special forfeiture information dismissing a claim with respect to any property interest therein where the court finds the evidence before the grand jury was legally insufficient to support a claim against such interest.

4. The prosecutor shall promptly file a copy of the special forfeiture information, including the terms thereof, with the state division of criminal justice services and with the local agency responsible for criminal justice planning. Failure to file

such information shall not be grounds for any relief under this chapter.

5. In addition to information required to be disclosed pursuant to article two hundred forty of the criminal procedure law, when forfeiture is sought pursuant to this article, and following the defendant's arraignment on the special forfeiture information, the court shall order discovery of any information not otherwise disclosed which is material and reasonably necessary for preparation by the defendant with respect to a forfeiture proceeding brought pursuant to this article. Such material shall include those portions of the grand jury minutes and such other information which pertain solely to the special forfeiture information and shall not include information which pertains to the criminal charges. Upon application of the prosecutor, the court may issue a protective order pursuant to section 240.40 of the criminal procedure law with respect to any information required to be disclosed pursuant to this subdivision.

6. (a) Trial of forfeiture counts by jury or by the court. Evidence which relates solely to the issue of forfeiture shall not be presented during the trial on the underlying felony offense or specified felony offense, and the defendant shall not be required to present such evidence prior to the verdict on such offense. A defendant who does not present evidence in his defense with respect to the trial of the underlying offense is not precluded on account thereof from presenting evidence during the trial of the forfeiture count or counts.

(b) Trial of forfeiture counts by the jury. After returning a verdict of guilty of a felony offense or specified felony offense, or where the defendant has pled guilty to a felony offense or a specified felony offense and has not waived a jury trial of the forfeiture count or counts pursuant to article three hundred twenty of the criminal procedure law, the jury shall be given the forfeiture information and shall hear any additional evidence which is relevant and legally admissible upon the forfeiture count or counts. After hearing such evidence, the jury shall then deliberate upon the forfeiture count or counts, and based upon all the evidence admitted in connection with the indictment or superior court information and the forfeiture information, may, if satisfied by proof beyond a reasonable doubt that the property, or a portion thereof, is subject to forfeiture pursuant to this article, return a verdict directing that such property, or portion thereof, is subject to forfeiture.

(c) Trial of forfeiture counts by the court. Where a defendant has waived a jury trial of the forfeiture count or counts pursuant to article three hundred twenty of the criminal procedure law, the court shall hear all evidence upon the forfeiture information and may, if satisfied by proof beyond a reasonable doubt that the property, or a portion thereof, is subject to forfeiture under this article, render a verdict determining that such property, or a portion thereof, is subject to forfeiture under this article.

(d) After the verdict of forfeiture, the court shall hear arguments and may receive additional evidence upon a motion of the defendant that the verdict of forfeiture (i) is against the weight of the evidence, or (ii) is, with respect to a forfeiture pursuant to this article, disproportionate to the defendant's gain from the offense, or the defendant's interest in the property, or the defendant's participation in the conduct upon which the forfeiture is based. Upon such a finding, the court may in the interest of justice set aside, modify, limit or otherwise condition the verdict of forfeiture.

7. A final judgment or order of forfeiture issued pursuant to this article shall authorize the prosecutor to seize all property directed to be forfeited under this article upon such terms and conditions as the court deems proper. If a property right is not exercisable or transferable for value by the prosecutor, it shall expire and shall not revert to the convicted person.

8. Where the forfeited property consists of real property, the court may at any time prior to a verdict of forfeiture, enter an order pursuant to subdivision four-a of section thirteen hundred eleven of the civil practice law and rules.

9. No person shall forfeit any right, title, or interest in any property under this article who has not been convicted of a felony offense or specified felony offense, as the case may be. Any person claiming an interest in property subject to forfeiture may institute a special proceeding to determine that claim, before or after the trial, pursuant to section thirteen hundred twenty-seven of the civil practice law and rules; provided, however, that if such special proceeding is initiated before trial on the forfeiture count or counts, it may, upon written motion of the prosecutor, and in the court's discretion, be postponed by the court until completion of the trial. In addition, any person claiming an interest in property subject to forfeiture may petition for remission as provided for in subdivision seven of section thirteen hundred eleven of the civil practice law and rules.

10. Testimony of the defendant or evidence derived therefrom introduced in the trial of the forfeiture count may not be used by the prosecution in any post-trial motion proceedings, appeals, or retrials relating to the defendant's criminal liability for the underlying criminal offense unless the defendant has previously referred to such evidence in such post-trial proceeding, appeal, or retrial relating to the underlying offense and the evidence is presented by the prosecutor in response thereto. Upon vacatur or reversal on appeal of a judgment of conviction upon which a verdict of forfeiture is based, any verdict of forfeiture which is based upon such conviction shall also be vacated or reversed.

ANNOTATION

Simultaneous criminal trial and forfeiture proceeding.— The District Attorney may prosecute the defendant for the underlying felony and at the same time conduct forfeiture proceedings under Article 480 in connection with such felony. *In re* Harnischfeger; *In re* Markert, 158 Misc. 2d 299, 600 N.Y.S.2d 894 (Sup. Ct. Monroe Co. 1993); *compare with* CPLR § 1311, in which civil forfeiture proceeding is stayed pending outcome of criminal proceeding.

Waiver of appeal—Defendant's voluntary forfeiture of funds seized at the time of his arrest pursuant to a negotiated plea agreement was upheld despite failure of court and prosecutor to abide by procedural guidelines of Penal Law § 480.10 or CPLR Article 13-A; "no public policy precludes a defendant from waiving his right to appeal as a condition of a plea and agreed upon sentence." People v. Sczepankowski, 293 A.D.2d 212, 746 N.Y.S.2d 46 (3d Dept. 2002).

§ 480.20. Disposal of property.

All property which is forfeited pursuant to this article shall be disposed of in accordance with the provisions of section thirteen hundred forty-nine of the civil practice law and rules. All reports required to be filed pursuant to article thirteen-A of such law and rules by a claiming authority shall be filed by the prosecutor in a forfeiture action brought pursuant to this article.

ANNOTATIONS

Payment of legal fees from seized assets.—Article 13-A of CPLR, and by direct reference to Article 13-A, PL § 480.20, does not violate right to counsel under state constitutional law; forfeit authorities must prove that the need for forfeiture of the assets outweighs hardship on defendant. Morgenthau v. Citysource, Inc., 68 N.Y.2d 211, 508 N.Y.S.2d 152, 500 N.E.2d 850 (1986).

—Court is empowered to order forfeit authority to provide for defendant's legal expenses for counsel of choice, under state constitution, from assets to be disposed of. People v. Martinez, 151 Misc. 2d 641, 574 N.Y.S.2d 467 (Sup. Ct. N.Y. Co. 1991).

§ 480.25. Election of remedies.

The imposition of a judgment or order of forfeiture pursuant to this article with respect to a defendant's interest in property shall preclude the imposition of a judgment or order of forfeiture with respect to such interest in property pursuant to the provisions of any other state or local law based upon the same criminal conduct.

§ 480.30. Provisional remedies.

1. The provisional remedies authorized by article thirteen-a of the civil practice law and rules shall be available in an action for criminal forfeiture pursuant to this article to the extent and under the same terms, conditions and limitations as provided in article thirteen-a of such law and rules, except as specifically provided herein.

2. Upon the filing of an indictment and special forfeiture information, or a superior court information and special forfeiture information, seeking forfeiture pursuant to this article, all further proceedings with respect to provisional remedies shall be heard by the judge or justice in the criminal part to which the criminal action is assigned.

3. For purposes of this section, the indictment

and special forfeiture information or superior court information and special forfeiture information seeking criminal forfeiture shall constitute the summons with notice or summons and verified complaint referred to in article thirteen-A of the civil practice law and rules.

ANNOTATIONS

Jurisdictional remedies.—Penal Law Article 480 is limited to same jurisdictional limitations as CPLR Article 13-A. People v. Martinez, 151 Misc. 2d 641, 574 N.Y.S.2d 467 (Sup. Ct. N.Y. Co. 1991).

Simultaneous criminal trial and forfeiture proceeding.—Minimum due process satisfied by provisions of CPLR Article 13-A. Morgenthau v. Citysource, Inc., 68 N.Y.2d 211, 508 N.Y.S.2d 152, 500 N.E.2d 850 (1986).

—The District Attorney may prosecute the defendant for the underlying felony and at the same time conduct forfeiture proceedings under Article 480 in connection with such felony. *In re* Harnischfeger; *In re* Markert, 158 Misc. 2d 299, 600 N.Y.S.2d 894 (Sup. Ct. Monroe Co. 1993). *Compare with* CPLR § 1311, in which civil forfeiture proceeding is stayed pending outcome of criminal proceeding.

§ 480.35. Rebuttable presumption.

1. In a criminal forfeiture proceeding commenced pursuant to this article, the following rebuttable presumption shall apply: all currency or negotiable instruments payable to the bearer shall be presumed to be the proceeds of a felony offense when such currency or negotiable instruments are (i) found in close proximity to a controlled substance unlawfully possessed by the defendant in an amount sufficient to constitute a violation of section 220.18 or 220.21 of the penal law, or (ii) found in close proximity to any quantity of a controlled substance or marihuana unlawfully possessed by such defendant in a room, other than a public place, under circumstances evincing an intent to unlawfully mix, compound, package, distribute or otherwise prepare for sale such controlled substance or marihuana.

2. The presumption established by this section shall be rebutted by credible and reliable evidence which tends to show that such currency or negotiable instruments payable to the bearer is not the proceeds of a felony offense. In an action tried before a jury, the jury shall be so instructed. Any sworn testimony of a defendant offered to rebut the presumption and any other evidence which is obtained as a result of such testimony, shall be inadmissible in any subsequent proceeding relating to the forfeiture action, or in any other civil or criminal action, except in a prosecution for a violation of article two hundred ten of this chapter. In an action tried before a jury, at the commencement of the trial, or at such other time as the court reasonably directs, the prosecutor shall provide notice to the court and to the defendant of its intent to request that the court charge such presumption.

ANNOTATIONS

Sufficiency of evidence to support presumption.—Court rejected challenge of forfeiture by defendant charged with criminal sale of controlled substances who pleaded guilty to that charge in an agreement which also included voluntary forfeiture of funds seized from his person at the time of his arrest; even without valid plea agreement, funds seized would have been forfeited under these circumstances pursuant to rebuttable presumption. People v. Sczepankowski, 293 A.D.2d 212, 746 N.Y.S.2d 46 (3d Dept. 2002).

TITLE Y—HATE CRIMES ACT OF 2000

ARTICLE 485—HATE CRIMES

Section

§ 485.00. Legislative findings.

The legislature finds and determines as follows: criminal acts involving violence, intimidation and destruction of property based upon bias and prejudice have become more prevalent in New York state in recent years. The intolerable truth is that in these crimes, commonly and justly referred to as "hate crimes", victims are intentionally selected, in whole or in part, because of their race, color, national origin, ancestry, gender, religion, religious practice, age, disability or sexual orientation. Hate crimes do more than threaten the safety and welfare of all citizens. They inflict on victims incalculable physical and emotional damage and tear at the very fabric of free society. Crimes motivated by invidious hatred toward particular groups not only harm individual victims but send a powerful message of intolerance and discrimination to all members of the group to which the victim belongs. Hate crimes can and do intimidate and disrupt entire communities and vitiate the civility that is essential to healthy democratic processes. In a democratic society, citizens cannot be required to approve of the beliefs and practices of others, but must never commit criminal acts on account of them. Current law does not adequately recognize the harm to public order and individual safety that hate crimes cause. Therefore, our laws must be strengthened to provide clear recognition of the gravity of hate crimes and the compelling importance of preventing their recurrence.

Accordingly, the legislature finds and declares that hate crimes should be prosecuted and punished with appropriate severity.

Added by L. 2000, Ch. 107, § 2, eff. Oct. 8, 2000.

§ 485.05. Hate crimes.

1. A person commits a hate crime when he or she commits a specified offense and either:

(a) intentionally selects the person against whom the offense is committed or intended to be committed in whole or in substantial part because of a belief or perception regarding the race, color, national origin, ancestry, gender, religion, religious practice, age, disability or sexual orientation of a person, regardless of whether the belief or perception is correct, or

(b) intentionally commits the act or acts constituting the offense in whole or in substantial part because of a belief or perception regarding the race, color, national origin, ancestry, gender, religion, religious practice, age, disability or sexual orientation of a person, regardless of whether the belief or perception is correct.

2. Proof of race, color, national origin, ancestry, gender, religion, religious practice, age, disability or sexual orientation of the defendant, the victim or of both the defendant and the victim does not, by itself, constitute legally sufficient evidence satisfying the people's burden under paragraph (a) or (b) of subdivision one of this section.

3. A "specified offense" is an offense defined by any of the following provisions of this chapter: section 120.00 (assault in the third degree); section 120.05 (assault in the second degree); section 120.10 (assault in the first degree); section 120.12 (aggravated assault upon a person less than eleven years old); section 120.13 (menacing in the first degree); section 120.14 (menacing in the second degree); section 120.15 (menacing in the third degree); section 120.20 (reckless endangerment in the second degree); section 120.25 (reckless endangerment in the first degree); subdivision one of section 125.15 (manslaughter in the second degree); subdivision one, two or four of section 125.20 (manslaughter in the first degree); section 125.25 (murder in the second degree); section 120.45 (stalking in the fourth degree); section 120.50 (stalking in the third degree); section 120.55 (stalking in the second degree); section 120.60 (stalking in the first degree); subdivision one of section 130.35 (rape in the first degree); subdivision one of section 130.50 (criminal sexual act in the first degree); subdivision one of section 130.65 (sexual abuse in the first degree); paragraph (a) of subdivision one of section 130.67 (aggravated sexual abuse in the second degree); paragraph (a) of subdivision one of section 130.70 (aggravated sexual abuse in the first degree); section 135.05 (unlawful imprisonment in the second degree); section 135.10 (unlawful imprisonment in the first degree); section 135.20 (kidnapping in the second degree); section 135.25 (kidnapping in the first degree); section 135.60 (coercion in the second degree); section 135.65 (coercion in the first degree); section 140.10 (criminal trespass in the third degree); section 140.15 (criminal trespass in the second degree); section 140.17 (criminal trespass in the first degree); section 140.20 (burglary in the third degree); section 140.25 (burglary in the second degree); section 140.30 (burglary in the first degree); section 145.00 (criminal mischief in the

fourth degree); section 145.05 (criminal mischief in the third degree); section 145.10 (criminal mischief in the second degree); section 145.12 (criminal mischief in the first degree); section 150.05 (arson in the fourth degree); section 150.10 (arson in the third degree); section 150.15 (arson in the second degree); section 150.20 (arson in the first degree); section 155.25 (petit larceny); section 155.30 (grand larceny in the fourth degree); section 155.35 (grand larceny in the third degree); section 155.40 (grand larceny in the second degree); section 155.42 (grand larceny in the first degree); section 160.05 (robbery in the third degree); section 160.10 (robbery in the second degree); section 160.15 (robbery in the first degree); section 240.25 (harassment in the first degree); subdivision one, two or four of section 240.30 (aggravated harassment in the second degree); or any attempt or conspiracy to commit any of the foregoing offenses.

4. For purposes of this section:

(a) the term "age" means sixty years old or more;

(b) the term "disability" means a physical or mental impairment that substantially limits a major life activity.

Added by L. 2000, Ch. 107, § 2, eff. Oct. 8, 2000; **Amended** by L. 2003, Ch. 264, § 34, eff. Nov. 1, 2003, amending subd. 3.

§ 485.10. Sentencing.

1. When a person is convicted of a hate crime pursuant to this article, and the specified offense is a violent felony offense, as defined in section 70.02 of this chapter, the hate crime shall be deemed a violent felony offense.

2. When a person is convicted of a hate crime pursuant to this article and the specified offense is a misdemeanor or a class C, D or E felony, the hate crime shall be deemed to be one category higher than the specified offense the defendant committed, or one category higher than the offense level applicable to the defendant's conviction for an attempt or conspiracy to commit a specified offense, whichever is applicable.

3. Notwithstanding any other provision of law, when a person is convicted of a hate crime pursuant to this article and the specified offense is a class B felony:

(a) the maximum term of the indeterminate sentence must be at least six years if the defendant is sentenced pursuant to section 70.00 of this chapter;

(b) the term of the determinate sentence must be at least eight years if the defendant is sentenced pursuant to section 70.02 of this chapter;

(c) the term of the determinate sentence must be at least twelve years if the defendant is sentenced pursuant to section 70.04 of this chapter;

(d) the maximum term of the indeterminate sentence must be at least four years if the defendant is sentenced pursuant to section 70.05 of this chapter; and

(e) the maximum term of the indeterminate sentence or the term of the determinate sentence must be at least ten years if the defendant is sentenced pursuant to section 70.06 of this chapter.

4. Notwithstanding any other provision of law, when a person is convicted of a hate crime pursuant to this article and the specified offense is a class A-1 felony, the minimum period of the indeterminate sentence shall be not less than twenty years.

Added by L. 2000, Ch. 107, § 2, eff. Oct. 8, 2000.

TITLE Y-1—TERRORISM

ARTICLE 490—TERRORISM

§ 490.00. Legislative findings.

The devastating consequences of the recent barbaric attack on the World Trade Center and the Pentagon underscore the compelling need for legislation that is specifically designed to combat the evils of terrorism. Indeed, the bombings of American embassies in Kenya and Tanzania in 1998, the federal building in Oklahoma City in 1995, Pan Am Flight number 103 in Lockerbie in 1988, the 1997 shooting atop the Empire State Building, the 1994 murder of Ari Halberstam on the Brooklyn Bridge and the 1993 bombing of the World Trade Center, will forever serve to remind us that terrorism is a serious and deadly problem that disrupts public order and threatens individual safety both at home and around the world. Terrorism is inconsistent with civilized society and cannot be tolerated.

Although certain federal laws seek to curb the incidence of terrorism, there are no corresponding state laws that facilitate the prosecution and punishment of terrorists in state courts. Inexplicably, there is also no criminal penalty in this state for a person who solicits or raises funds for, or provides other material support or resources to, those who commit or encourage the commission of horrific and cowardly acts of terrorism. Nor do our criminal laws proscribe the making of terrorist threats or punish with appropriate severity those who hinder the prosecution of terrorists. Finally, our death penalty statute must be strengthened so that the cold-blooded execution of an individual for terrorist purposes is a capital offense.

A comprehensive state law is urgently needed to complement federal laws in the fight against terrorism and to better protect all citizens against terrorist acts. Accordingly, the legislature finds that our laws must be strengthened to ensure that terrorists, as well as those who solicit or provide financial and other support to terrorists, are prosecuted and punished in state courts with appropriate severity.

Added by L. 2001, Ch. 300, § 4, eff. Sept. 17. 2001.

§ 490.05. Definitions.

As used in this article, the following terms shall mean and include:

1. "Act of terrorism":

(a) for purposes of this article means an act or acts constituting a specified offense as defined in subdivision three of this section for which a person may be convicted in the criminal courts of this state pursuant to article twenty of the criminal procedure law, or an act or acts constituting an offense in any other jurisdiction within or outside the territorial boundaries of the United States which contains all of the essential elements of a specified offense, that is intended to:

(i) intimidate or coerce a civilian population;

(ii) influence the policy of a unit of government by intimidation or coercion; or

(iii) affect the conduct of a unit of government by murder, assassination or kidnapping; or

(b) for purposes of subparagraph (xiii) of paragraph (a) of subdivision one of section 125.27 of this chapter means activities that involve a violent act or acts dangerous to human life that are in violation of the criminal laws of this state and are intended to:

(i) intimidate or coerce a civilian population;

(ii) influence the policy of a unit of government by intimidation or coercion; or

(iii) affect the conduct of a unit of government by murder, assassination or kidnapping.

2. "Material support or resources" means currency or other financial securities, financial services, lodging, training, safehouses, false documentation or identification, communications equipment, facilities, weapons, lethal substances, explosives, personnel, transportation, and other physical assets, except medicine or religious materials.

3. (a) "Specified offense" for purposes of this article means a class A felony offense other than an offense as defined in article two hundred twenty, a violent felony offense as defined in section 70.02, manslaughter in the second degree as defined in section 125.15, criminal tampering in the first degree as defined in section 145.20, identity theft in the second degree as defined in section 190.79, identity theft in the first degree as defined in section 190.80, unlawful possession of personal identification information in the second degree as defined in section 190.82, unlawful possession of personal identification information in the first degree as defined in section 190.83, money laundering in support of terrorism in the fourth degree as defined in section 470.21, money laundering in support of terrorism in the third degree as defined in section 470.22, money laundering in support of terrorism in the second degree as defined in section 470.23, money laundering in support of terrorism in the first degree as defined in section 470.24 of this chapter, and includes an attempt or conspiracy to commit any such offense.

(b) Notwithstanding the provisions of paragraph (a) of this subdivision, a specified offense shall not mean an offense defined in sections 490.37, 490.40, 490.45, 490.47, 490.50, and 490.55 of this article, nor shall a specified offense mean an attempt to commit any such offense.

4. "Renders criminal assistance" for purposes of sections 490.30 and 490.35 of this article shall have the same meaning as in section 205.50 of this chapter.

5. "Biological agent" means any microorganism, virus, infectious substance, or biological product that may be engineered as a result of biotechnology, or any naturally occurring or bioengineered component of any such microorganism, virus, infectious substance, or biological product, capable of causing:

(a) death, disease, or other biological malfunction in a human, an animal, a plant, or another living organism;

(b) deterioration of food, water, equipment, supplies, or material of any kind; or

(c) deleterious alteration of the environment.

6. "Toxin" means the toxic material of plants, animals, microorganisms, viruses, fungi, or infectious substances, or a recombinant molecule, whatever its origin or method of production, including:

(a) any poisonous substance or biological product that may be engineered as a result of biotechnology produced by a living organism; or

(b) any poisonous isomer or biological product, homolog, or derivative of such a substance.

6. "Toxin" means the toxic material of plants, animals, micro-organisms, viruses, fungi, or infectious substances, or a recombinant molecule, whatever its origin or method of production, including:

(a) any poisonous substance or biological product that may be engineered as a result of biotechnology produced by a living organism; or

(b) any poisonous isomer or biological product, homolog, or derivative of such a substance.

7. "Delivery system" means:

(a) any apparatus, equipment, device, or means of delivery specifically designed to deliver or disseminate a biological agent, toxin, or vector; or

(b) any vector.

8. "Vector" means a living organism, or molecule, including a recombinant molecule, or biological product that may be engineered as a result of biotechnology, capable of carrying a biological agent or toxin to a host.

9. "Biological weapon" means any biological agent, toxin, vector, or delivery system or combination thereof.

10. "Chemical weapon" means the following, together or separately:

(a) a toxic chemical or its precursors;

(b) a munition or device specifically designed to cause death or other harm through the toxic properties of a toxic chemical or its precursors, which would be released as a result of the employment of such munition or device;

(c) any equipment specifically designed for use directly in connection with the employment of munitions or devices; or

(d) any device that is designed to release radiation or radioactivity at a level dangerous to human life.

11. "Precursor" means any chemical reactant that takes part at any stage in the production by whatever method of a toxic chemical, including any key component of a binary or multicomponent chemical system, and includes precursors which have been identified for application of verification measures under article VI of the convention in schedules contained in the annex on chemicals of the chemical weapons convention.

12. "Key component of a binary or multicomponent chemical system" means the precursor

which plays the most important role in determining the toxic properties of the final product and reacts rapidly with other chemicals in the binary or multicomponent system.

13. "Toxic chemical" means any chemical which through its chemical action on life processes can cause death, serious physical injury or permanent harm to humans or animals, including all such chemicals, regardless of their origin or of their method of production, and regardless of whether they are produced in facilities, in munitions or elsewhere, and includes toxic chemicals which have been identified by the commissioner of health and included on the list of toxic chemicals pursuant to subdivision twenty of section two hundred six of the public health law.

14. "The terms "biological agent", "toxin", and "toxic chemical" do not include any biological agent, toxin or toxic chemical that is in its naturally occurring environment, if the biological agent, toxin or toxic chemical has not been cultivated, collected, or otherwise extracted from its natural source.

15. "Select chemical agent" shall mean a chemical weapon which has been identified in regulations promulgated pursuant to subdivision twenty of section two hundred six of the public health law.

16. "Select biological agent" shall mean a biological weapon which has been identified in regulations promulgated pursuant to subdivision twenty-one of section two hundred six of the public health law.

17. "Chemical weapons convention" and "convention" mean the convention on the prohibition of the development, production, stockpiling and use of chemical weapons and on their destruction, opened for signature on January thirteenth, nineteen hundred ninety-three.

Added by L. 2001, Ch. 300, § 4, eff. Sept. 17, 2001; **Amended** by L. 2002, Ch. 619, § 4, amending subd. 3, eff. Nov. 1, 2002; L. 2004, Ch. 1, §§ 7 & 8 (Part A), eff. July 23, 2004, amending subd. 3 and adding subds 5–17.

§ 490.10. Soliciting or providing support for an act of terrorism in the second degree.

A person commits soliciting or providing support for an act of terrorism in the second degree when, with intent that material support or resources will be used, in whole or in part, to plan, prepare, carry out or aid in either an act of terrorism or the concealment of, or an escape from, an act of terrorism, he or she raises, solicits, collects or provides material support or resources.

Soliciting or providing support for an act of terrorism in the second degree is a class D felony.

§ 490.15. Soliciting or providing support for an act of terrorism in the first degree.

A person commits soliciting or providing support for an act of terrorism in the first degree when he or she commits the crime of soliciting or providing support for an act of terrorism in the second degree and the total value of material support or resources exceeds one thousand dollars.

Soliciting or providing support for an act of terrorism in the first degree is a class C felony.

Added by L. 2001, Ch. 300, § 4, eff. Sept. 17. 2001.

§ 490.20. Making a terroristic threat.

1. A person is guilty of making a terroristic threat when with intent to intimidate or coerce a civilian population, influence the policy of a unit of government by intimidation or coercion, or affect the conduct of a unit of government by murder, assassination or kidnapping, he or she threatens to commit or cause to be committed a specified offense and thereby causes a reasonable expectation or fear of the imminent commission of such offense.

2. It shall be no defense to a prosecution pursuant to this section that the defendant did not have the intent or capability of committing the specified offense or that the threat was not made to a person who was a subject thereof.

Making a terroristic threat is a class D felony.

Added by L. 2001, Ch. 300, § 4, eff. Sept. 17. 2001.

§ 490.25. Crime of terrorism.

1. A person is guilty of a crime of terrorism when, with intent to intimidate or coerce a civilian population, influence the policy of a unit of government by intimidation or coercion, or affect the conduct of a unit of government by murder, assassination or kidnapping, he or she commits a specified offense.

2. Sentencing.

(a) When a person is convicted of a crime of terrorism pursuant to this section, and the specified offense is a class B, C, D or E felony offense, the crime of terrorism shall be deemed a violent felony offense.

(b) When a person is convicted of a crime of terrorism pursuant to this section, and the specified offense is a class C, D or E felony offense, the crime of terrorism shall be deemed to be one category higher than the specified offense the defendant committed, or one category higher than the offense level applicable to the defendant's conviction for an attempt or conspiracy to commit the offense, whichever is applicable.

(c) When a person is convicted of a crime of terrorism pursuant to this section, and the specified offense is a class B felony offense, the crime of terrorism shall be deemed a class A-I felony offense and the sentence imposed upon conviction of such offense shall be in accordance with section 70.00 of this chapter.

(d) Notwithstanding any other provision of law, when a person is convicted of a crime of terrorism pursuant to this section, and the specified offense is a class A-I felony offense, the sentence upon conviction of such offense shall be life imprisonment without parole; provided, however, that nothing herein shall preclude or prevent a sentence of death when the specified offense is murder in the first degree as defined in section 125.27 of this chapter.

Added by L. 2001, Ch. 300, § 4, eff. Sept. 17. 2001.

§ 490.30. Hindering prosecution of terrorism in the second degree.

A person is guilty of hindering prosecution of terrorism in the second degree when he or she renders criminal assistance to a person who has committed an act of terrorism, knowing or believing that such person engaged in conduct constituting an act of terrorism.

Hindering prosecution of terrorism in the second degree is a class C felony.

Added by L. 2001, Ch. 300, § 4, eff. Sept. 17. 2001.

§ 490.35. Hindering prosecution of terrorism in the first degree.

A person is guilty of hindering prosecution of terrorism in the first degree when he or she renders criminal assistance to a person who has committed an act of terrorism that resulted in the death of a person other than one of the participants, knowing or believing that such person engaged in conduct constituting an act of terrorism.

Hindering prosecution of terrorism in the first degree is a class B felony.

Added by L. 2001, Ch. 300, § 4, eff. Sept. 17. 2001.

§ 490.37. Criminal possession of a chemical weapon or biological weapon in the third degree.

A person is guilty of criminal possession of a chemical weapon or biological weapon in the third degree when he or she possesses any select chemical agent or select biological agent under circumstances evincing an intent by the defendant to use such weapon to cause serious physical injury or death to another person.

Criminal possession of a chemical weapon or biological weapon in the third degree is a class C felony.

Added by L. 2004, Ch. 1, § 9, eff. July 23, 2004.

§ 490.40. Criminal possession of a chemical weapon or biological weapon in the second degree.

A person is guilty of criminal possession of a chemical weapon or biological weapon in the second degree when he or she possesses any chemical weapon or biological weapon with intent to use such weapon to:

1. (a) cause serious physical injury to, or the death of, another person; and

(b) (i) intimidate or coerce a civilian population;

(ii) influence the policy of a unit of government by intimidation or coercion; or

(iii) affect the conduct of a unit of government by murder, assassination, or kidnapping.

2. cause serious physical injury to, or the death of, more than two persons.

Criminal possession of a chemical weapon or biological weapon in the second degree is a class B felony.

Added by L. 2004, Ch. 1, § 9, eff. July 23, 2004.

§ 490.45. Criminal possession of a chemical weapon or biological weapon in the first degree.

A person is guilty of criminal possession of a chemical weapon or biological weapon in the first degree when he or she possesses:

1. any select chemical agent, with intent to use such agent to:

(a) cause serious physical injury to, or the death of, another person; and

(b) (i) intimidate or coerce a civilian population;

(ii) influence the policy of a unit of government by intimidation or coercion; or

(iii) affect the conduct of a unit of government by murder, assassination, or kidnapping.

2. any select chemical agent, with intent to use such agent to cause serious physical injury to, or the death of, more than two other persons; or

3. any select biological agent, with intent to use such agent to cause serious physical injury to, or the death of, another person.

Criminal possession of a chemical weapon or biological weapon in the first degree is a class A-I felony.

Added by L. 2004, Ch. 1, § 9, eff. July 23, 2004.

§ 490.47. Criminal use of a chemical weapon or biological weapon in the third degree.

A person is guilty of criminal use of a chemical

weapon or biological weapon in the third degree when, under circumstances evincing a depraved indifference to human life, he or she uses, deploys, releases, or causes to be used, deployed, or released any select chemical agent or select biological agent, and thereby creates a grave risk of death or serious physical injury to another person not a participant in the crime.

Criminal use of a chemical weapon or biological weapon in the third degree is a class B felony.

Added by L. 2004, Ch. 1, § 9, eff. July 23, 2004.

§ 490.50. Criminal use of a chemical weapon or biological weapon in the second degree.

A person is guilty of criminal use of a chemical weapon or biological weapon in the second degree when he or she uses, deploys, releases, or causes to be used, deployed, or released, any chemical weapon or biological weapon, with intent to:

1. cause serious physical injury to, or the death of, another person; and

2. (a) intimidate or coerce a civilian population;

(b) influence the policy of a unit of government by intimidation or coercion; or

(c) to affect the conduct of a unit of government by murder, assassination, or kidnapping.

Criminal use of a chemical weapon or biological weapon in the second degree is a class A-II felony.

Added by L. 2004, Ch. 1, § 9, eff. July 23, 2004.

§ 490.55. Criminal use of a chemical weapon or biological weapon in the first degree.

A person is guilty of criminal use of a chemical weapon or biological weapon in the first degree when:

1. with intent to:

(a) cause serious physical injury to, or the death of, another person; and

(b) (i) intimidate or coerce a civilian population;

(ii) influence the policy of a unit of government by intimidation or coercion; or

(iii) affect the conduct of a unit of government by murder, assassination, or kidnapping;

he or she uses, deploys, releases, or causes to be used, deployed, or released any select chemical agent and thereby causes serious physical injury to, or the death of, another person who is not a participant in the crime.

2. with intent to cause serious physical injury to, or the death of, more than two persons, he or she uses, deploys, releases, or causes to be used, deployed, or released any select chemical agent and thereby causes serious physical injury to, or the death of, more than two persons who are not participants in the crime; or

3. with intent to cause serious physical injury to, or the death of, another person, he or she uses, deploys, releases, or causes to be used, deployed, or released any select biological agent and thereby causes serious physical injury to, or the death of, another person who is not a participant in the crime.

Criminal use of a chemical weapon or biological weapon in the first degree is a class A-I felony.

Added by L. 2004, Ch. 1, § 9, eff. July 23, 2004.

§ 490.70. Limitations.

1. The provisions of sections 490.37, 490.40, 490.45, 490.47, 490.50, and 490.55 of this article shall not apply where the defendant possessed or used:

(a) any household product generally available for sale to consumers in this state in the quantity and concentration available for such sale;

(b) a self-defense spray device in accordance with the provisions of paragraph fourteen of subdivision a of section 265.20 of this chapter;

(c) a chemical weapon solely for a purpose not prohibited under this chapter, as long as the type and quantity is consistent with such a purpose; or

(d) a biological agent, toxin, or delivery system solely for prophylactic, protective, bona fide research, or other peaceful purposes.

2. For the purposes of this section, the phrase "purposes not prohibited by this chapter" means the following:

(a) any peaceful purpose related to an industrial, agricultural, research, medical, or pharmaceutical activity or other peaceful activity;

(b) any purpose directly related to protection against toxic chemicals and to protection against chemical weapons;

(c) any military purpose of the United States that is not connected with the use of a chemical weapon or that is not dependent on the use of the toxic or poisonous properties of the chemical weapon to cause death or other harm; and

(d) any law enforcement purpose, including any domestic riot control purpose and including imposition of capital punishment.

Added by L. 2004, Ch. 1, § 9, eff. July 23, 2004.

TITLE Z—LAWS REPEALED; TIME OF TAKING EFFECT

ARTICLE 500—LAWS REPEALED; TIME OF TAKING EFFECT

Section

500.05 Laws repealed.
500.10 Time of taking effect.

§ 500.05. Laws repealed.

Chapter eighty-eight of the laws of nineteen hundred nine, entitled "An act providing for the punishment of crime, constituting chapter forty of the consolidated laws," and all acts amendatory thereof and supplemental thereto, constituting the penal law as heretofore in force, are hereby repealed.

ANNOTATION

Sentence under Correction Law Article 7-A.—A defendant who pleaded guilty to a misdemeanor committed prior to September 1, 1967, the effective date of the new Penal Law, and who was sentenced to the New York City Penitentiary pursuant to Article 7-A of the Correction Law, received an improper sentence where the sentence was imposed subsequent to the effective date of Article 7-A's repeal. The defendant should have been sentenced pursuant to the Penal Law of 1909 which applied to offenses committed prior to September 1, 1967. People v. Monteleone, 30 A.D.2d 158, 290 N.Y.S.2d 823 (2d Dept. 1968).

§ 500.10. Time of taking effect.

This act shall take effect September first, nineteen hundred sixty-seven.

CORRECTION LAW

AN ACT in relation to the correction and detention of persons in state correctional institutions, constituting chapter forty-three of the consolidated laws.

CHAPTER 43 OF THE CONSOLIDATED LAWS

CORRECTION LAW
SYNOPSIS OF ARTICLES

ARTICLE 1—SHORT TITLE; DEFINITIONS

Derivation—Prison L. article 1, amended by L. 1929, Ch. 43 § 3, in effect Apr. 2, adding "Definitions" to article 1 and section 2.

§ 1. Short title.

This chapter shall be known as the "Correction Law."

Added by L. 1929, Ch. 243.

ANNOTATIONS

Determinations of timeliness.—Reckoning provisions of General Construction Law are applicable to determinations of timeliness made under General Correction Law. Persing v. Coughlin, 632 N.Y.S.2d 366 (4th Dept. 1995).

Parole revocation; right to counsel.—A parole revocation hearing is in the nature of an administrative proceeding. It is not to be equated with criminal prosecution in any sense. There is no constitutional or statutory provision or case law entitling in alleged parole violator to assistance of counsel at a preliminary hearing, and a person who has been denied assistance of counsel at the preliminary stages of an administrative proceeding is not denied due process of law if he has assistance of counsel in subsequent proceedings resulting in the final administrative order. People *ex rel.* Calloway v. Skinner, 41 A.D.2d 06, 341 N.Y.S.2d 775 (4th Dept. 1973).

Preliminary hearing; basis.—There is no provision in the Correction Law for the holding of a preliminary hearing to determine whether probable cause or reasonable grounds exist to believe that a parolee has violated his parole conditions. People *ex rel.* Calloway v. Skinner, 41 A.D.2d 106, 341 N.Y.S.2d 775 (4th Dept. 1973).

§ 2. Definitions.

When used in this chapter, unless otherwise expressly stated or the context or subject matter otherwise requires, the following terms have the following meanings:

1. "Department" means the state department of correctional services;

2. "Commissioner" means the state commissioner of correctional services;

3. "Commission" means the state commission of correction;

4. (a) "Correctional facility." Any place operated by the department and designated by the commissioner as a place for the confinement of persons under sentence of imprisonment or persons committed for failure to pay a fine. Except as provided in paragraph (b) of this subdivision, whenever reference has been or hereafter will be made in any statute, judgment, sentence, commitment, court order or otherwise to a state prison, state reformatory, reception center, diagnostic center or other institution or facility in the department, such reference shall be deemed to mean correctional facility."

(b) The term "correctional facility" shall not, however, be deemed to mean or to include any place operated by the department for the care and confinement of persons who have been found to be mentally defective or mentally ill by a court and who are confined in such place pursuant to an order of a court based upon such finding.

(c) Whenever the term "institution" is used in this chapter or elsewhere in such context as to mean an institution in the department, such term shall be deemed to include correctional facilities and any other place operated by the department as a place for the confinement of persons.

5. "Reception center." A correctional facility for reception, classification and program-planning for purposes of confinement, treatment and transfer.

6. "Residential treatment facility." A correctional facility consisting of a community based residence in or near a community where employment, educational and training opportunities are readily available for persons who are on parole or conditional release and for persons who are or who will soon be eligible for release on parole who intend to reside in or near that community when released.

7. "Detention center." A correctional facility for the temporary detention of persons taken into custody upon violation of parole or upon violation of a condition of release, or of persons being transferred from other correctional facilities, or of persons who are assigned to other correctional facilities for confinement but whose presence is required in court or for some other purpose at a location that is distant from the institution of confinement.

8. "Correctional Camp." A correctional facility consisting of a camp maintained for the purpose of including conservation work in the program of inmates.

9. "Diagnostic and treatment center." A correctional facility operated for the purpose of providing intensive physical, mental and sociological diagnostic and treatment services including pre-parole diagnostic evaluation, where

requested by the board of parole, and scientific study of the social and mental aspects of the causes of crime.

10. "General confinement facility." A correctional facility for confinement and treatment of persons under institutional programs oriented to education, vocational training and industry.

11. "Work release facility." A facility designated by the commissioner as an institutional that may conduct a work release program.

12. "Superintendent." The chief administrative officer of a correctional facility. Whenever the term "warden" appears in this chapter in such context as to mean an officer of a state correctional facility, such reference shall be deemed to mean "superintendent."

13. "Infant" or "minor" means a person who has not attained the age of eighteen years.

14. [*Expires Sept. 1, 2007.*] "Community treatment facility." A residential chemical dependence facility approved As provided in section 32.01 of the mental hygiene law or pursuant to section 32.31 of such law used exclusively to provide substance abuse treatment services to persons eligible pursuant to section seventy-two-a of this chapter and who are otherwise eligible for temporary release pursuant to subdivision two of section eight hundred fifty-one of this chapter. These facilities shall be separate and distinct so as not to replace existing substance abuse treatment services.

15. "Shock incarceration correctional facility." A correctional facility designated by the commissioner as an institution that may conduct a shock incarceration program.

16. (a) "Local correctional facility." Any place operated by a county or the city of New York as a place for the confinement of persons duly committed to secure their attendance as witnesses in any criminal case, charged with crime and committed for trial or examination, awaiting the availability of a court, duly committed for any contempt or upon civil process, convicted of any offense and sentenced to imprisonment therein or awaiting transportation under sentence to imprisonment in a correctional facility, or pursuant to any other applicable provisions of law.

(b) Whenever the term "jail," "penitentiary" or "workhouse" is used in this chapter, such term shall be deemed to mean local correctional facility.

(c) Whenever the term "sheriff" is used in this chapter, such term shall be deemed to include the warden, superintendent, or other person in charge of a local correctional facility.

17. "Alcohol and substance abuse treatment facility." A correctional facility designed to house medium security inmates as defined by department rules and regulations and operated for the purpose of providing intensive alcohol and substance abuse treatment services. Such services shall ensure comprehensive treatment for alcoholism and substance abuse to inmates who have been identified by the commissioner or his or her designee as having had or presently having a history of alcoholism or substance abuse. Such services shall be provided in the facility in accordance with minimum standards promulgated by the department after consultation with the division of alcoholism and alcohol abuse and the division of substance abuse services.

18. [*Effective until Sept. 1, 2007.*] "Alcohol and substance abuse treatment correctional annex." A medium security correctional facility consisting of one or more residential dormitories which provide intensive alcohol and substance abuse treatment services to inmates who: (i) are otherwise eligible for temporary release, or (ii) stand convicted of a felony defined in article two hundred twenty or two hundred twenty-one of the penal law, and are within six months of being an eligible inmate as that term is defined in subdivision two of section eight hundred fifty-one of this chapter including such inmates who are participating in such program pursuant to subdivision six of section 60.04 of the penal law. Notwithstanding the foregoing provisions of this subdivision, any inmate to be enrolled in this program pursuant to subdivision six of section 60.04 of the penal law shall be governed by the same rules and regulations promulgated by the department, including without limitation those rules and regulations establishing requirements for completion and those rules and regulations governing discipline and removal from the program. No such period of court ordered corrections based drug abuse treatment pursuant to this subdivision shall be required to extend beyond the defendant's conditional release date. Such treatment services may be provided by one or more outside service providers pursuant to contractual agreements with both the department and the division of parole, provided, however, that any such provider shall be required to continue to provide, either directly or through formal or informal agreement with other providers, alcohol and substance abuse treatment services to inmates who have successfully participated in such provider's incarcerative treatment services and who have been paroled or conditionally released under the supervision of the division of parole and who are, as a condition of their parole or conditional release, required to participate in alcohol or substance abuse treatment. Such incarcerative services shall be provided in the facility in accordance with minimum standards promulgated by the department after consultation with the office of alcoholism and substance abuse services. Such services to parolees shall be provided in accordance with standards promulgated by the division of parole after consultation with the office of alcoholism and substance abuse services. Notwithstanding any other provision of law, any person who has

successfully completed no less than six months of intensive alcohol and substance abuse treatment services in one of the department's eight designated alcohol and substance abuse treatment correctional annexes having a combined total capacity of two thousand five hundred fifty beds may be transferred to a program operated by or at a residential treatment facility, provided however, that a person under a determinate sentence as a second felony drug offender for a class B felony offense defined in article two hundred twenty of the penal law, who was sentenced pursuant to section 70.70 of such law, shall not be eligible to be transferred to a program operated at a residential treatment facility until the time served under imprisonment for his or her determinate sentence, including any jail time credited pursuant to the provisions of article seventy of the penal law, shall be at least eighteen months. The commissioner shall report annually to the temporary president of the senate and the speaker of the assembly commencing January first, nineteen hundred ninety-two as to the efficacy of such programs including but not limited to a comparative analysis of state-operated and private sector provision of treatment services and recidivism. Such report shall also include the number of inmates received by the department during the reporting period who are subject to a sentence which includes enrollment in substance abuse treatment in accordance with subdivision six of section 60.04 of the penal law, the number of such inmates who are not placed in such treatment program and the reasons for such occurrences.

18. [*Effective Sept. 1, 2007.*] "Alcohol and substance abuse treatment correctional annex." A medium security correctional facility consisting of one or more residential dormitories which provide intensive alcohol and substance abuse treatment services to inmates who: (i) are otherwise eligible for temporary release, or (ii) stand convicted of a felony defined in article two hundred twenty or two hundred twenty-one of the penal law, and are within six months of being an eligible inmate as that term is defined in subdivision two of section eight hundred fifty-one of this chapter including such inmates who are participating in such program pursuant to subdivision six of section 60.04 of the penal law. Notwithstanding the foregoing provisions of this subdivision, any inmate to be enrolled in this program pursuant to subdivision six of section 60.04 of the penal law shall be governed by the same rules and regulations promulgated by the department, including without limitation those rules and regulations establishing requirements for completion and those rules and regulations governing discipline and removal from the program. No such period of court ordered corrections based drug abuse treatment pursuant to this subdivision shall be required to extend beyond the defendant's conditional release date. Such treatment services may be provided by one or more outside service providers pursuant to contractual agreements with both the department and the division of parole, provided, however, that any such provider shall be required to continue to provide, either directly or through formal or informal agreement with other providers, alcohol and substance abuse treatment services to inmates who have successfully participated in such provider's incarcerative treatment services and who have been paroled or conditionally released under the supervision of the division of parole and who are, as a condition of their parole or conditional release, required to participate in alcohol or substance abuse treatment. Such incarcerative services shall be provided in the facility in accordance with minimum standards promulgated by the department after consultation with the office of alcoholism and substance abuse services. Such services to parolees shall be provided in accordance with standards promulgated by the division of parole after consultation with the office of alcoholism and substance abuse services. The commissioner shall report annually to the majority leader of the senate and the speaker of the assembly commencing January first, nineteen hundred ninety-two as to the efficacy of such programs including but not limited to a comparative analysis of state-operated and private sector provision of treatment services and recidivism. Such report shall also include the number of inmates received by the department during the reporting period who are subject to a sentence which includes enrollment in substance abuse treatment in accordance with subdivision six of section 60.04 of the penal law, the number of such inmates who are not placed in such treatment program and the reasons for such occurrences.

19. * "Vocational and skills training facility" means a correctional facility designated by the commissioner to provide a vocational and skills training program ("VAST") to inmates who need such service before they participate in a work release program. The VAST facility shall provide intensive assessment, counseling, job search assistance and where appropriate academic and vocational instruction to program participants. Such assistance may include an assessment of any inmate's education attainment level and skills aptitudes; career counseling and exploration; the development of a comprehensive instructional plan including identification of educational and training needs that may extend beyond the date of entry into work release; instructional programs including GED preparation or post-secondary instruction as appropriate; occupational skills training; life skills training; employment readiness including workplace behavior; and job search assistance. The department and the department of labor shall jointly develop activities providing career counseling, job search assistance, and job placement services for participants. Nothing contained in this section shall be deemed to modify the eligibility requirements provided by law applicable to inmates participating in a work release program.

20. "Drug treatment campus" means a facility operated by the department to provide a program of intensive drug treatment services for individuals sentenced to parole supervision sentences pursuant to section 410.91 of the criminal procedure law or for certain parole violators. Such institution may also be used for certain offenders confined by the department who have been granted early parole release pursuant to a chapter of the laws of nineteen hundred ninety-five which added this subdivision and who, in the judgment of a member or members of the board of parole, warrant such placement. All such treatment services shall be provided by, or with the approval of and pursuant to a plan developed in conjunction with, the office of alcoholism and substance abuse services, and which plan shall include but not be limited to provision for an appropriate continuum of care that includes a needs assessment and treatment services for individuals while at this facility and upon discharge from such facility, including an enhanced aftercare program.

* Subdivision 19 was added to Correct. Law § 2 by L. 1994, Ch. 63, § 130, which amended L. 1994, Ch. 60, § 44—the legislation that originally added the subdivision to the Correction Law—by shifting the subdivision from Correct. Law § 24(4) to section 2(19). Under L. 1994, Ch. 63, § 133, section 130 of Ch. 63 "shall be deemed to expire on the same date as chapter 60." As Ch. 60 shall, with certain exceptions, expire on Mar. 31, 1995, L. 1994, Ch. 60, § 46, it would appear that the shift of the subdivision would expire on that date and the subdivision would revert to section 24(4). The intent of the Legislature, however, was probably to apply to section 2(19) the exception to the Mar. 31, 1995, expiration date contained in Ch. 60, § 46(d)—that the new subdivision of the Correct.

Law does not expire on Mar. 31, 1995—and not to have the subdivision revert to section 24(4).

Added by L. 1929, Ch. 243; **Amended** by L. 1970, Chs. 475, 476; L. 1972, Ch. 567; L. 1974, Ch. 921; L. 1983, Ch. 418, eff. July 8, 1983; L. 1986, Ch. 554, eff. July 24, 1986, adding subd. 14, and shall remain in effect until September 30, 1989; L. 1987, Chs. 261, 604; L. 1989, Ch. 338, eff. July 10, 1989; L. 1989, Ch. 338, eff. July 10, 1989; L. 1990, Ch. 681, eff. Nov. 1, 1990; L. 1992, Ch. 55, § 322, eff. Apr. 10, 1992, extending expiration date of subd. 14 to Sept. 30, 1995; L. 1992, Ch. 55, eff. Apr. 10, 1992 and shall remain in effect until Apr. 30, 1993 and be applicable to all persons entering the program on or before Mar. 31, 1993; L. 1994, Ch. 60, eff. Apr. 1, 1994, and shall expire Sept. 1, 1995, and Ch. 63, L. 1995, Ch. 3, § 21, adding subd. 20, eff. June 10, 1995; L. 1997, Ch. 435, § 52, extending expiration date of subd. 14 to Sept. 1, 1999, eff. Aug. 20, 1997, and §§ 49 and 51, extending expiration date of amendments to subd. 18 to Sept. 1, 1999, eff. Aug. 20, 1997; L. 1999, Ch. 452, § 6, extending expiration date of subd. 14 to Sept. 1, 2001, eff. Sept. 1, 1999, and §§ 3 and 5, extending expiration date of amendments to subd. 18 to Sept. 1, 2001, eff. Sept. 1, 1999, and Ch. 558, § 26, eff. Oct. 5, 1999, amending subd. 14; L. 2001, Ch. 95, eff. July 13, 2001, extending expiration date of amendments to subd. 18 to Sept. 1, 2003; L. 2003, Ch. 16, §§ 5, 7, 8, eff. March 31, 2003, extending expiration date of amendments to subd. 14 and subd. 18 to Sept. 1, 2005; L. 2004, Ch. 738, §§ 1 and 2, eff. Dec. 14, 2004, amending subd. 18; L. 2005, Ch. 56, Part D, §§ 5, 8, eff. Apr. 1, 2005, extending effective and expiration dates to Sept. 1, 2007.

ANNOTATION

Prison now deemed correctional facilities.—Prisoners objections to being transferred to a "correctional facility" because he was sentenced to a designated "place of imprisonment," were without merit, since Correction Law § 2 deems every institution formerly known as a state prison, to now be a "correctional facility." People *ex rel.* Rabinowitz v. Smith, 51 A.D.2d 632, 378 N.Y.S.2d 207 (4th Dept. 1976).

ARTICLE 2—DEPARTMENT OF CORRECTIONAL SERVICES; STATE BOARD OF PAROLE

§ 5. Department of correctional services; commissioner.

1. There shall be in the state government a department of correctional services. The head of the department shall be the commissioner of correctional services, who shall be appointed by the governor, by and with the advice and consent of the senate, and hold office at the pleasure of the governor by whom he was appointed and until his successor is appointed and has qualified.

2. The commissioner of correctional services shall be the chief executive officer of the department.

3. The principal office of the department of correctional services shall be in the county of Albany.

4. The commissioner is hereby authorized and empowered to convert the sentence of a person serving an indeterminate sentence of imprisonment, except a person serving a sentence with a maximum term of life imprisonment, to a determinate sentence of imprisonment equal to two-thirds of the maximum or aggregate maximum term imposed where such conversion is necessary to make such person eligible for transfer either to federal custody or to foreign countries under treaties that provide for the voluntary transfer of such persons on the execution of penal sentences entered into by the government of the united states with foreign countries.

5. The commissioner upon request, may in his or her discretion, authorize the purchase and presentation of a flag of the state of New York to the person designated to dispose of the remains of a deceased correction officer.

Amended by L. 1961, Ch. 358; L. 1970, Ch. 475; L. 1995, Ch. 547, § 1, adding subd. 4, eff. Aug. 2, 1995; L. 2000, Ch. 448, § 1, adding subd. 5, eff. Sept. 20, 2000.

§ 7. Organization of department of correctional services officers and employees; delegation by commissioner.

1. The commissioner of correctional services may, from time to time, create, abolish, transfer, and consolidate divisions, bureaus and other units within the department not expressly established by law as he may determine necessary for the efficient operation of the department, subject to the approval of the director of the budget.

2. The commissioner of correctional services may appoint such deputies, directors, assistants and other officers and employees as may be needed for the performance of his duties and may prescribe their powers and duties and fix their compensation within the amounts appropriated therefor.

3. The commissioner may by order filed in the department of correctional services delegate any of his powers to or direct any of his duties to be performed by a deputy commissioner or a head of a division or bureau of such department.

4. The commissioner shall not appoint any person as a correction officer unless such person has attained his twenty-first birthday.

Added by L. 1970, Ch. 475; **Amended** by L. 1980, Ch. 519; L. 1984, Ch. 35.

§ 8. Testing of certain applicants for employment. [*Effective until September 1, 2007, pursuant to L. 1983, Ch. 887, § 2, as amended.*]

1. Any applicant for employment with the department as a correction officer at a facility of the department, shall be tested in accordance with the requirements of this section.

2. The department is hereby authorized to conduct, or to enter into agreements necessary for conducting tests for psychological screening of applicants covered by this section. Any such tests shall consist of at least three independent psychological instruments and shall meet the level of the art for psychological instruments to be used in a validation study developed for selection of such applicants. Such psychological instruments shall be used in testing and selection of applicants for positions referred to in subdivision one of this section. Persons who have been determined by a psychologist licensed under the laws of this state as suffering from psychotic disorders, serious character disorders, or other disorders which could hinder performance on the job may be deemed ineligible for appointment; provided, however, that other components of the employee selection process may be taken into consideration in reaching the determination as to whether a candidate is deemed eligible or ineligible for certification to a list of eligible candidates. The department's testing program shall include a component consisting of criteria related validity studies or other validity studies acceptable under relevant federal law governing equal employment.

3. The commissioner or his designee shall advise those candidates who have been deemed ineligible for appointment through psychological screening and shall notify such persons of their right to appeal their disqualification. A person so deemed may apply to the commissioner for a review of the findings within thirty days of the date of notification. The commissioner shall refer the matter to an independent advisory board to review any recommendation. A copy of the advisory board's recommendations shall be promptly forwarded to the parties and to the commissioner. If the advisory board's recommendation is rejected by the commissioner, wholly or in part, the commissioner shall state his reasons for such rejection in writing.

4. The advisory board shall consist of three members who shall be selected by the president of the civil service commission. The membership of the board shall consist of: A psychologist, and a psychiatrist, both of whom shall be licensed under the laws of this state, and a third member who shall be a representative of the department of civil service. The department of civil service shall maintain a list of alternate board members comprised of psychologists and psychiatrists, licensed under the laws of this state, and representatives nominated by the president of the civil service commission, who shall sit on the advisory board in the event a designated member is unable to serve, provided however at all times the advisory board must be comprised of a psychiatrist, a psychologist and a representative of the department of civil service. Each of the members of the advisory board and their alternates so selected shall serve at the pleasure of the president of the civil service commission. Each of the members and alternates so selected shall be reimbursed for services and actual costs at a per diem rate not to exceed nine hundred dollars for the psychiatrist, seven hundred dollars for the psychologist and six hundred dollars for the representative of the civil service department; provided, however, that if any member of or alternate to the advisory board is an employee of the state of New York, then such representative shall only receive reimbursement for actual costs incurred.

5. The commissioner or his designee shall advise the department of civil service of those persons who have been determined under this section as being eligible for appointment from any list of eligible candidates.

6. Notwithstanding any other provision of law, the results of the tests administered pursuant to this section shall be used solely for the qualification of a candidate for correction officer and the validation of the psychological instruments utilized. For all other purposes, the results of the examination shall be confidential and the records sealed by the department of correctional services, and not be available to any other agency or person except by authorization, of the applicant or, upon written notice by order of from a court of this state or the United States.

7. Prior to March first of each year, the commissioner of the department of correctional services will report to the governor, president of the senate and speaker of the assembly on the conduct of the psychological testing program and the results of such program in improving the quality of correction officer candidates.

Added by L. 1983, Ch. 887; **Amended** by L. 1984, Ch. 338; L. 1986, Ch. 354, eff. July 17, 1986, amending subds. 3, 4, 6, and providing that this act remain in effect until Apr. 1, 1989; L. 1989, Ch. 15, § 1, eff. Mar. 31, 1989, extending expiration date; L. 1992, Ch. 55, § 319, eff. Apr. 10, 1992, extending expiration date until Apr. 1, 1994; L. 1994, Ch. 47, § 2, eff. Apr. 11, 1994, extending expiration date until Apr. 1, 1996; L. 1996, Ch. 37, § 1, eff. Apr. 2, 1996, extending expiration date until Apr. 1, 1998; L. 1998, Ch. 32, § 1, eff. Mar. 31, 1998, extending expiration date until Apr. 1, 2000; L. 2000, Ch. 15, § 1, eff. Mar. 30, 2000, extending expiration date until Sept. 1, 2001; L. 2001, Ch. 95 § 7, extending expiration date to Sept. 1, 2003, eff. July 13, 2001; L. 2002, Ch. 205, § 1, eff. July 30, 2002, amending subd. 4; L. 2003, Ch. 16, § 1, extending expiration date to Sept. 1, 2005, eff. Mar. 31, 2003.

§ 15-b. Education.

The present director of vocational education shall be the director of education with the powers and duties of the director of education and hereafter shall be appointed by the commissioner. The director of education, at any time appointed, shall be a person whose education, training and experience shall cover fields of penology and of professional education. The educational qualifications shall include the satisfactory completion of three years of graduate work in education, penology, and allied fields. The head of the division of education shall have the direct supervision of all educational work in the department of correction and shall have full authority to visit and inspect all institutions of the department to observe, study, organize, and develop the educational activities of such institutions in harmony with the general educational program of the department. He shall be responsible to the commissioner and deputy commissioner of correction.

§ 15-c. The commissioner, with the approval of the governor, may accept as agent of the state any grant, including federal grants, or any gift for any of the purposes of this article.

Any moneys so received may be expended by the department to develop and promote programs for the study and treatment of crime and delinquency, education and training of inmates, staff improvement, research and evaluation, improvement of facilities, or any other lawful purpose, subject to the same limitations as to approval of expenditures and audit as are prescribed for state moneys appropriated for the purpose of this article.

Added by L. 1996, Ch. 647.

§ 16. Expense of autopsy; state charge.

The reasonable expense of any inquiry, autopsy, examination or report prepared thereon conducted by a coroner, coroner's physician or medical examiner as required by law with respect to any death occurring to an inmate of an institution operated by the department shall, to the extent not otherwise reimbursed by the state, be a state charge. Reimbursement of such expense shall be made on vouchers submitted annually and certified by the chief fiscal officer of the county or city as the case may be on the audit and warrant of the comptroller.

Added by L. 1980, Ch. 109, eff. May 6, 1980.

§ 18. Superintendents of correctional facilities.

1. Each correctional facility shall have a superintendent who shall be appointed by the commissioner of correctional services. Each such superintendent shall be in the non-competitive-confidential class but shall be appointed from employees of the department who have at least three years of experience in correctional work in the department and (i) who have a permanent civil service appointment of salary grade twenty-seven or higher or who have a salary equivalent to a salary grade of twenty-seven or higher for correctional facilities with an inmate population capacity of four hundred or more inmates, or (ii) who have a permanent civil service appointment of salary grade twenty-three or higher or who have a salary equivalent to a salary grade of twenty-three or higher for correctional facilities with an inmate population capacity of fewer than four hundred inmates; provided that for correctional facilities of either capacity, the employee shall be appointed superintendent at the hiring rate set forth in section nineteen of this article or such other rate as may be appropriate, subject to the approval of the director of the budget; provided that in no event shall the salary upon appointment exceed the job rate. Such superintendents shall serve at the pleasure of the commissioner and shall have such other qualifications as may be prescribed by the commissioner of correctional services, based on differences in duties, levels of responsibility, size and character of the correctional facility, knowledge, skills and abilities required, and other factors affecting the position.

2. Subject to the rules and statutory powers of the commissioner of correctional services, or rules approved by him, the superintendent of a correctional facility shall have the supervision and management thereof.

3. Subject to the direction of the commissioner of correctional services, and of the deputy and assistant commissioners in their respective fields of supervision, the superintendent of a correctional facility shall direct the work and define the duties of all officers and subordinates of the facility.

Amended by L. 1960, Ch. 54; L. 1970, Ch. 476; L. 1975, Ch. 829, L. 1984, ch. 708, eff. Aug. 3, 1984; L. 1985, ch. 306, eff. Apr. 1, 1985.

ANNOTATIONS

Library.—The inmates were not deprived of "access to the courts" by library use regulations that called for the library to be open between 10:00 A.M. and 3:50 P.M. with some restrictions concerning its use during recreation periods, inclement weather or by an inmate who had lost some privilege, since respondent allowed inmates to assist other inmates in the preparation of court papers and the inmates had representation by the Prisoners Assistance Project and the assistance of counsel assigned by the court. Ford v. LaVallee, 55 A.D.2d 799, 390 N.Y.S.2d 269 (3d Dept. 1976).

Restriction of visitation privileges where inmates not confined to segregation unit.—It was a violation of regulations to restrict the visitation privileges of inmates not confined in a segregation unit to less than those available to the inmates in the general population for the purpose of punishment or discipline, since it was not shown that the contraband found in the possession of the inmates was obtained through contact visitation, limitation of his visitation privileges to the restricted visitation area was arbitrary, capricious and illegal. Chambers v. Coughlin, 76 A.D.2d 980, 429 N.Y.S.2d 74 (3d Dept. 1980).

Superintendent's right to foster order and security.— There is no deprivation of an inmate's constitutional rights arising from Superintendent's denial of his request to correspond with an inmate at another correctional facility; there is a legitimate interest in fostering order and security in a penal institution, and this justifies the imposition of certain restraints on inmates correspondence; such denial is not arbitrary or capricious. Boehme v. Smith, 51 A.D.2d 670, 378 N.Y.S.2d 170 (4th Dept. 1976).

§ 19. Salary and emoluments of superintendents.

1. This section shall apply to each superintendent of a correctional facility appointed on or after August ninth, nineteen hundred seventy-five and any superintendent heretofore appointed who elects to be covered by the provisions thereof by filing such election with the commissioner.

a. The salary schedule for superintendents of a correctional facility with an inmate population capacity of four hundred or more inmates shall be as follows:

Effective April first, two thousand four:

Hiring Rate	Job Rate
$93,576	$127,974

Effective April first, two thousand five:

Hiring Rate	Job Rate
$96,149	$131,493

Effective April first, two thousand six:

Hiring Rate	Job Rate
$99,033	$135,438

Effective April first, two thousand seven:

Hiring Rate	Job Rate
$99,833	$136,238

b. The salary schedule for superintendents of correctional facilities with an inmate population capacity of fewer than four hundred inmates shall be as follows:

Effective April first, two thousand four:

Hiring Rate	Job Rate
$72,600	$91,944

Effective April first, two thousand five:

Hiring Rate	Job Rate
$74,597	$94,472

Effective April first, two thousand six:

Hiring Rate	Job Rate
$76,835	$97,306

Effective April first, two thousand seven:

Hiring Rate	Job Rate
$77,635	$98,106

2. Employees to whom the provisions of this section apply whose basic annual salary is less than the job rate herein specified may receive periodic performance advancement payments based on periodic evaluations of work performance in accordance with rules and regulations promulgated by the director of the budget; provided, however, that in no event may such a payment result in a basic annual salary in excess of the job rate of such grade. Such payments shall be part of the employee's basic annual salary. Payments pursuant to this subdivision shall commence no earlier than July first, nineteen hundred seventy-nine.

3. Employees to whom the provisions of this section apply whose basic annual salary at the time of the performance award evaluation equals or exceeds the job rate of the salary schedule of their positions may receive performance award payments in accordance with rules and regulations promulgated by the director of the budget. Such payments shall be lump sum payments and shall be in addition to and shall not be part of the employee's basic annual salary; provided, however, that any amounts payable pursuant to this subdivision shall be included as compensation for retirement purposes.

4. The salary herein provided shall be in lieu of all other compensation or emolument, benefit of entitlement of office of the office of superintendent except as may be necessarily incidental to the discharge of the duties of such office or provided by law.

Added by L. 1979, Ch. 307; L. 1985, Ch. 306, L. 1982, Ch. 460; L. 1984, Ch. 708; L. 1985, Ch. 732; L. 1992, Ch. 497; L. 1995, Ch. 314, § 2, repealing subd. 1 and adding a new one, eff. Oct. 2, 1997 for officers and employees on the administrative payroll and Sept. 25, 1997 for officers on the institutional payroll, pursuant to L. 1995, Ch. 314, § 13; L. 2000, Ch. 68 Part B, § 2, eff. June 20, 2000, deemed eff. Apr. 1, 1999, amending subd. 1; L. 2004, Ch. 103, § 2 (Part B), repealing subd. 1 and adding a new one, eff. June 4, 2004.

§ 20. Library.

A library shall be provided in the department of correction containing the leading books on parole, probation and other correctional activities, together with reports and other documents on correlated topics, criminology and social work.

§ 21. Acquisition of real property by purchase and acquisition.

1. The commissioner, when an appropriation therefor has been made by the legislature, may acquire any real property which he may deem necessary for the purposes of the department by purchase or pursuant to the eminent domain procedure law. Title to any such real property shall be taken in the name of and be vested in the people of the state of New York; provided, however, that no real property shall be so acquired

CORR. L.

by purchase unless the title thereto shall be approved by the attorney general.

2. Whenever title to real property is to be acquired pursuant to the eminent domain procedure law the commissioner shall cause to be made by the state department of transportation an accurate acquisition map as so provided in said law.

3. On the approval of such map by the commissioner, the original tracing of such map shall, pursuant to the eminent domain procedure law, be filed in the main office of the department.

4. If the commissioner shall determine, prior to the filing of such map in the office of the clerk or register of the county, that changes, alterations or modifications of such map as filed in the main office of the department should be made, he or she shall, subject to the provisions of article two of the eminent domain procedure law, if applicable, direct the preparation by the department of transportation of an amended map. On the approval of such amended map by the commissioner, it shall be filed in the main office of the department and the amended map shall thereupon in all respects and for all purposes supersede the map previously filed.

5. If the commissioner shall determine, prior to the filing of a copy of such acquisition map in the office of the county clerk or register as provided in section four hundred two of the eminent domain procedure law, that such map should be withdrawn, he or she may file a certificate of withdrawal in the offices of the department and of the department of law. Upon the filing of such certificate of withdrawal, the map to which it refers shall be cancelled and all rights thereunder shall cease and determine.

6. The commissioner shall deliver to the attorney general a copy of such acquisition map, whereupon it shall be the duty of the attorney general to advise and certify to the commissioner the names of the owners of the property, easements, interests or rights described in the said acquisition map, including the owners of any right, title or interest therein, pursuant to the requirements of section four hundred three of the eminent domain procedure law.

7. If, at or after the vesting of title to such property in the people of the state of New York, as provided for in the eminent domain procedure law, the commissioner shall deem it necessary to cause the removal of an owner or occupant from any real property so acquired, he may cause such owner or occupant to be removed therefrom by proceeding in accordance with section four hundred five of the eminent domain procedure law. The proceeding shall be brought in the name of the commissioner as agent of the state and the attorney general shall represent the petitioner in the proceedings. No execution shall issue for costs, if any, awarded against the state or the commissioner, but they shall be part of the costs of the acquisition of the real property and be paid in like manner. Proceedings may be brought separately against one or more of the owners or occupants of any such property, or one proceeding may be brought against all or several of the owners or occupants of any or all such property within the territorial jurisdiction of the same court, justice or judge; judgment shall be given for immediate removal of persons defaulting in appearance or in answering, or withdrawing their answers, if any, without awaiting the trial or decision of issues raised by contestants, if any.

8. Upon making any agreement provided for in section three hundred four of the eminent domain procedure law, the commissioner shall deliver to the comptroller such agreement and a certificate stating the amount due such owner or owners thereunder on account of such appropriation of his or their property and the amounts so fixed shall be paid out of the state treasury after audit by the comptroller from moneys appropriated for the acquisition of such real property, but not until there shall have been filed with the comptroller a certificate of the attorney general showing the person or persons claiming the amount so agreed upon to be legally entitled thereto.

9. Application for reimbursement of incidental expenses as provided in section seven hundred two of the eminent domain procedure law shall be made to the commissioner upon forms prescribed by him and shall be accompanied by such information and evidence as the commissioner may require. Upon approval of such application, the commissioner shall deliver a copy thereof to the comptroller together with a certificate stating the amount due thereof, and the amount so fixed shall be paid out of the state treasury after audit by the comptroller from moneys appropriated for the obtaining of title to property under this section.

10. The commissioner, with the approval of the director of the budget, shall establish and may from time to time amend rules and regulations authorizing the payment of actual reasonable and necessary moving expenses of occupants of property acquired pursuant to this section; of actual direct losses of tangible personal property as a result of moving or discontinuing a business or farm operation, but not exceeding an amount equal to the reasonable expenses that would have been required to relocate such property, as determined by the commissioner; and actual reasonable expenses in searching for a replacement business or farm; or in hardship cases for the advance payment of such expenses and losses. For the purposes of making payment of such expenses and losses only the term "business" means any lawful activity conducted primarily for assisting in the purchase, sale, resale, manufacture, processing or marketing of products, commodities, personal property or services by the erection and

maintenance of an outdoor advertising display or displays, whether or not such display or displays are located on the premises on which any of the above activities are conducted. Such rules and regulations may further define the terms used in this subdivision. In lieu of such actual reasonable and necessary moving expenses, any such displaced owner or tenant of residential property may elect to accept a moving expense allowance, plus a dislocation allowance, determined in accordance with a schedule prepared by the commissioner and made a part of such rules and regulations. In lieu of such actual, reasonable and necessary moving expenses, any such displaced owner or tenant of commercial property who relocates or discontinues his business or farm operation may elect to accept a fixed relocation payment in an amount equal to the average annual net earnings of the business or farm operation, except that such payment shall be not less than two thousand five hundred dollars nor more than ten thousand dollars. In the case of a business, no such fixed relocation payment shall be made unless the commissioner finds and determines that the business cannot be relocated without a substantial loss of its existing patronage, and that the business is not part of a commercial enterprise having at least one other establishment, which is not being acquired by the state or the United States, which is engaged in the same or similar business. In the case of a business which is to be discontinued but for which the findings and determinations set forth above cannot be made, the commissioner may prepare an estimate of what the actual reasonable and necessary moving expenses, exclusive of any storage charges, would be if the business were to be relocated and enter into an agreed settlement with the owner of such business for an amount not to exceed such estimate in lieu of such actual reasonable and necessary moving expenses. Application for payment under this subdivision shall be made to the commissioner upon forms prescribed by him and shall be accompanied by such information and evidence as the commissioner may require. Upon approval of such application, the commissioner shall deliver a copy thereof to the comptroller together with a certificate stating the amount due thereunder, and the comptroller from moneys appropriated for the acquisition of property under this section. As used in this subdivision the term "commercial property" shall include property owned by an individual, family, partnership, corporation, association or a nonprofit organization and includes a farm operation. As used in this subdivision the term "business" means any lawful activity, except a farm operation, conducted primarily for the purchase, sale, lease and rental of personal and real property, and for the manufacture, processing, or marketing of products, commodities, or any other personal property; for the sale of services to the public; or by a nonprofit organization.

11. Authorization is hereby given to the commissioner to make supplemental relocation payments, separately computed and stated, to displaced owners and tenants of residential property acquired pursuant to this section who are entitled thereto, as determined by him. The commissioner, with the approval of the director of the budget, may establish and from time to time amend rules and regulations providing for such supplemental relocation payments. Such rules and regulations may further define the terms used in this subdivision. In the case of property acquired pursuant to this section which is improved by a dwelling actually owned and occupied by the displaced owner for not less than one hundred eighty days immediately prior to initiation of negotiations for the acquisition of such property, such payment to such owner shall not exceed fifteen thousand dollars. Such payment shall be the amount, if any, which, when added to the acquisition payment equals the average price, established by the commissioner on a class, group or individual basis, required to obtain a comparable replacement dwelling that is decent, safe and sanitary to accommodate the displaced owner, reasonably accessible to public services and places of employment and available on the private market, but in no event shall such payment exceed the difference between acquisition payment and the actual purchase price of the replacement dwelling. Such payment shall include an amount which will compensate such displaced owner for any increased interest costs which such person is required to pay for financing the acquisition of any such comparable replacement dwelling. Such amount shall be paid only if the dwelling acquired pursuant to this section was encumbered by a bona fide mortgage which was a valid lien on such dwelling for not less than one hundred eighty days prior to the initiation of negotiations for the acquisition of such dwelling. Such amount shall be equal to the excess in the aggregate interest and other debt service costs of that amount of the principal of the mortgage on the replacement dwelling which is equal to the unpaid balance of the mortgage on the acquired dwelling, over the remainder term of the mortgage on the acquired dwelling, reduced to discounted present value. The discount rate shall be the prevailing interest rate paid on savings deposits by commercial banks in the general area in which the replacement dwelling is located. Any such mortgage interest differential payment shall, notwithstanding the provisions of section twenty-six-b of the general construction law, be in lieu of and in full satisfaction of the requirements of such section. Such payment shall include reasonable expenses incurred by such displaced owner for evidence of title, recording fees and other closing costs incident to the purchase of the replacement dwelling, but not including prepaid expenses. Such payment shall be made only to a displaced owner who purchases and occupies a replacement dwelling which is decent, safe and sanitary within one year subsequent to the date on which he is required

to move from the dwelling acquired pursuant to this section or the date on which he receives from the state final payment of all costs of the acquired dwelling, whichever occurs later, except advance payment of such amount may be made in hardship cases. In the case of property acquired pursuant to this section from which an individual or family, not otherwise eligible to receive a payment pursuant to the above provisions of this subdivision, is displaced from any dwelling thereon which has been actually and lawfully occupied by such individual or family for not less than ninety days immediately prior to the initiation of negotiations for the acquisition of such property, such payment to such individual or family shall not exceed four thousand dollars. Such payment shall be the amount which is necessary to enable such individual or family to lease or rent for a period not to exceed four years, a decent, safe, and sanitary dwelling of standards adequate to accommodate such individual or family in areas not generally less desirable in regard to public utilities and public and commercial facilities and reasonably accessible to his place of employment, but shall not exceed four thousand dollars, or to make the down payment, including reasonable expenses incurred by such individual or family for evidence of title, recording fees, and other closing costs incident to the purchase of the replacement dwelling, but not including prepaid expenses, on the purchase of, a decent, safe and sanitary dwelling of standards adequate to accommodate such individual or family in areas not generally less desirable in regard to public utilities and public and commercial facilities, but shall not exceed four thousand dollars, except if such amount exceeds two thousand dollars, such person must equally match any such amount in excess of two thousand dollars, in making the down payment. Such payments may be made in installments as determined by the commissioner. Application for payment under this subdivision shall be made to the commissioner upon forms prescribed by him and shall be accompanied by such information and evidence as the commissioner may require. Upon approval of such application, the commissioner shall deliver a copy thereof to the comptroller, together with a certificate stating the amount due thereunder, and the amount so fixed shall be paid out of the state treasury after audit by the comptroller from moneys appropriated for the acquisition of property under this section.

12. The owner of any real property so acquired may present to the court of claims pursuant to section five hundred three of the eminent domain procedure law a claim for the value of such property acquired and for legal damages caused by such appropriation, as provided by law for the filing of claims with the court of claims. Awards and judgments of the court of claims shall be paid in the same manner as awards and judgments of that court for the acquisition of lands generally and shall be paid out of the state treasury after audit by the comptroller from moneys appropriated for the acquisition of such real property.

13. If the commissioner shall determine subsequent to the acquisition of a temporary easement in any real property that the purposes for which such easement right was acquired have been accomplished and that the exercise of such easement is no longer necessary, he shall make his certificate that the exercise of such easement is no longer necessary and that such easement right is therefore terminated, released and extinguished. The commissioner shall cause such certificate to be filed in the office of the department of state and upon such filing all rights acquired by the state in such property shall cease and determine. The commissioner shall cause a certified copy of such certificate as so filed in the office of the department of state to be mailed to the owner of the property affected, as certified by the attorney general, if the place of residence of such owner is known or can be ascertained by a reasonable effort and such commissioner shall cause a further certified copy of such certificate to be filed in the office of the recording officer of each county in which the property affected or any part thereof is situated. On the filing of such certified copy of such certificate with such recording officer, it shall be his duty to record the same in his office in the books used for recording deeds and to index the same against the name of the people of the state of New York as grantor.

Repealed former § 21 and Added new § 21 by L. 1977, Ch. 840; **Amended** by L. 1996, Ch. 394, § 7, effective July 30, 1996.

§ 22. Institution officers not to be interested in institution contracts.

A commissioner of correction, superintendent or other officer or employee, employed at any of the institutions in the department who:

1. Shall be directly or indirectly interested in any contract, purchase or sale, for, by, or on account of such institution; or,

2. Accepts a present from a contractor or contractor's agent, directly or indirectly, or employes the labor of an inmate or another person employed in such institution on any work for the private benefit of such commissioner, superintendent, officer or employee, is guilty of a misdemeanor.

Amended by L. 1970, Ch. 476; L. 1975, Ch. 829.

§ 22-a. Qualification for employment as a correction officer.

No person, on or after the effective date of this section, may be appointed to the position of a correction officer in any institution in the department who has been convicted of a felony or of any offense in any other jurisdiction which if committed in this state would constitute a felony. The commissioner may in his discretion, bar the appointment of a person, on or after the effective date of this section, to the position of correction officer in any institution in the department, who has been convicted of a misdemeanor or of any offense in any other jurisdiction which if committed in this state would constitute a misdemeanor where he has determined that the employment of such person is not in the best interest of the department. Notwithstanding the foregoing provisions of this section, no person shall be disqualified pursuant to this section unless he shall have first been furnished a written statement of the reasons for such disqualification and afforded an opportunity by the commissioner, or his designee, to make an explanation and to submit facts in opposition thereto.

Added by L. 1984, Ch. 134, eff. June 22, 1984.

§ 23. Transfer of inmates from one correctional facility to another; treatment in outside hospitals.

1. The commissioner of correction shall have the power to transfer inmates from one correctional facility to another. Whenever the transfer of inmates from one correctional facility to another shall be ordered by the commissioner of correction, the superintendent of the facility from which the inmates are transferred shall take immediate steps to make the transfer. The transfer shall be in accordance with rules and regulations promulgated by the department for the safe delivery of such inmates to the designated facility.

2. The commissioner of correction, in his discretion, may be written order permit inmates to receive medical diagnosis and treatment in outside hospitals, upon the recommendation of the superintendent or director that such outside treatment or diagnosis is necessary by reason of inadequate facilities within the institution. Such inmates shall remain under the jurisdiction and in the custody of the department while in said outside hospital and said superintendent or director shall enforce proper measures in each case to safely maintain such jurisdiction and custody.

3. The cost of transporting inmates between facilities and to outside hospitals shall be paid from funds appropriated to the department of correction for such purpose.

Amended by L. 1970, Chs. 475, 476.

ANNOTATIONS

Commissioner of Corrections; power to transfer inmates.—Inmate's argument that transferring him from Sing Sing prison to Attica correctional facility, was a modification of his sentence was without basis, since Correction Law § 23 gives Commissioner of Corrections the power to transfer inmates from one correctional facility to another. People ex rel. Rabinowitz v. Smith, 51 A.D.2d 682, 378 N.Y.S.2d 207 (4th Dept. 1976).

—The Commissioner of Correction has the power to determine the correctional facility where a prisoner is to be confined, as well as the power to transfer a prisoner from one facility to another; he also has the power to determine what degree of supervision is required, whether for the protection of the prisoner or of the public. Ramirez v. Ward, 64 A.D.2d 995, 408 N.Y.S.2d 833 (3d Dept. 1978).

—Under ordinary circumstances the transfer of inmates is purely an administrative matter about which the prisoner has no standing to complain. Scott v. Smith, 77 A.D.2d 681, 429 N.Y.S.2d 804 (3d Dept. 1980).

New York City Commissioner of Corrections; authority to transfer on waiver only.—Since neither state law nor the New York City Administrative Code authorizes the New York City Commissioner of Corrections to transfer inmates from one correctional facility to another, the court ruled that the sole authority for the transfers challenged by relators was the waivers signed by them. Thus, the court ordered retransfer to the reformatory if any of the relators should notify the appropriate authority of a revocation of his waiver. People ex rel. Cromwell v. Warden, 74 Misc. 2d 642, 345 N.Y.S.2d 381 (Sup. Ct. Bronx Co. 1973).

Representative to prison's Inmate Grievance Resolution Committee (IGRC); transfer.—Correction Law § 139 imposes a limitation upon the exercise of the Commissioners discretion to transfer an inmate who is a member of the IGRC in that he may not be transferred without a prior hearing, the rules of which must embrace the protection provided for in Wolff v. McDonnell, 418 U.S. 539, 94 S. Ct. 2963, 41 L. Ed. 2d 935, unless the member's presence or conduct at the institution or facility creates an emergency and transfer is immediately necessary to protect the facility or its personnel in which event the hearing on his transfer shall be held as soon as practicable at the receiving facility. Johnson v. Ward, 64 A.D.2d 186, 409 N.Y.S.2d 670 (3d Dept. 1978).

Transfer from reformatory to prison; power of Correction Commission; due process and equal protection of the laws.—The new statute authorized the Correction Commission to transfer inmates without limitation and there is no denial of due process when he complies with the statute and the reformatory sentence remains unaltered entitling the inmate to reformatory type treatment in a prison, or other institution, or release if none is available. Evidence was that rehabilitation facilities in Green Haven were equal to or better than at Elmira. People ex rel. Batista v. Zelker, 39 A.D.2d 343, 334 N.Y.S.2d 207 (2d Dept. 1972).

§ 24. Civil actions against department personnel.

1. No civil action shall be brought in any court of the state, except by the attorney general on behalf of the state, against any officer or employee of the department, in his personal capacity, for damages arising out of any act done or the failure to perform any act within the scope of the employment and in the discharge of the duties by such officer or employee.

2. Any claim for damages arising out of any act done or the failure to perform any act within the scope of the employment and in the discharge of the duties of any officer or employee of the department shall be brought and maintained in the court of claims as a claim against the state.

3. This section shall apply with respect to claims arising on or after the effective date of this section.

Editor's Note: L. 1994, Ch. 60, § 44, added a subdivision four to section 24 relating to the definition of "vocational and skills training facility." Pursuant to L. 1994, Ch. 63, § 130, the provisions of Ch. 60, § 44, were amended to change the placement of the subdivision from section 24(4) to Correct. Law § 2(19). See section 2(19) and the footnote to that subdivision.

Added by L. 1972, Ch. 283; **Amended** by L. 1974, Ch. 537; L. 1978, Ch. 466, eff. Sept. 5, 1978, repealing subds. 3, 4, 5, and 6 and amended and renumbered subd. 7 to subd. 3.

Suing a corrections employee in an individual capacity.— When determining if a Department of Correctional Services employee can be sued in an individual capacity, conduct that occurs during the course of employment will not be considered to have occurred within the scope of employment if the conduct departs substantially from normal methods of performing duties. Gore v. Kulhman, 217 A.D.2d 890, 630 N.Y.S.2d 141 (3d Dept. 1995).

§ 24-a. Actions against persons rendering health care services at the request of the department; defense and indemnification.

The provisions of section seventeen of the public officers law shall apply to any person holding a license to practice a profession pursuant to article one hundred thirty-one, one hundred thirty-one-B, one hundred thirty-two, one hundred thirty-three, one hundred thirty-six, one hundred thirty-seven, one hundred thirty-nine, one hundred forty-one, one hundred forty-three, one hundred fifty-six or one hundred fifty-nine of the education law, who is rendering or has rendered professional services authorized under such license while acting at the request of the department or a facility of the department in providing health care and treatment or professional consultation to inmates of state correctional facilities, or to the infant children of inmates while such infants are cared for in facility nurseries pursuant to section six hundred eleven of this chapter, without regard to whether such health care and treatment or professional consultation is provided within or without a correctional facility.

Repealed former § 24-a and **Added** new § 24-a by L. 1978, Ch. 466, eff. Sept. 5, 1978; **Amended** by L. 1991, Ch. 351, eff. July 15, 1991; L. 1992, Ch. 481, eff. July 17, 1992.

§ 25. Mutual assistance by institutional and local fire fighting facilities.

In cooperation with the development and operation of plans for mutual aid in cases of fire and other public emergencies, the warden or superintendent of any state institution in the department, with the approval of the commissioner, may authorize the fire department of the institution to furnish aid to such territory surrounding the institution as may be practical in cases of fire and such emergencies, having due regard to the safety of the inmates and property of the institution and to engage in practice and training programs in connection with the development and operation of such mutual aid plans. Any lawfully organized fire-fighting forces or firemen from such surrounding territory may enter upon the grounds of the institution to furnish aid in cases of fire and such emergencies.

Amended by L. 1970, Ch. 475.

§ 26. Establishment of commissaries or canteens in correctional institutions.

The commissioner may authorize the head of any institution in the department to establish a commissary or a canteen in such institution for the use and benefit of inmates. The moneys received by the head of the institution as profits from the sales of the commissary or canteen shall be deposited in a special fund to be known as the commissary or canteen fund and such funds shall be used for the general purposes of the institution subject to the provisions of section fifty-three of the state finance law. *

* Section 53 of the State Finance Law in effect at the time of the enactment of this section was repealed in 1981.

Amended by L. 1970, Ch. 475; L. 1994, Ch. 487, § 1, eff. July 26, 1994.

§ 29. Department statistics.

1. The department shall continue to collect, maintain, and analyze statistical and other information and data with respect to persons subject to the jurisdiction of the department, including but not limited to: (a) the number of such persons: placed in the custody of the department, assigned to a specific department program, accorded temporary release, paroled or conditionally released, paroled or conditionally released and declared delinquent, recommitted to a state correctional institution upon revocation of parole or conditional release, or discharge upon maximum expiration of sentence; (b) the criminal history of such persons; (c) the social, educational, and vocational circumstances of any such persons; and, (d) the institutional, parole and conditional release programs and behavior of such persons. Provided, however, in the event any statistical information on the ethnic background of the inmate population of a correctional facility or facility is collected by the department, such statistical information shall contain, but not be limited to, the following ethnic categories: (i) Caucasian; (ii) Asian; (iii) American Indian; (iv) Afro-American/Black: and (v) Spanish speaking/Hispanic which category shall include, but not be limited to, the following subcategories consisting of: (1) Puerto Ricans; (2) Cubans; (3) Dominicans; and (4) other Hispanic nationalities.

2. The commissioner of correctional services shall make rules as to the privacy of records, statistics and other information collected, obtained and maintained by the department, its institutions or the board of parole and information obtained in an official capacity by officers, employees or members thereof.

3. The commissioner of correctional services shall have access to records and criminal statistics collected by the division of criminal justice services and the commissioner of criminal justice services shall have access to records and criminal

statistics collected by the department of correctional services, as the commissioners of correctional services and criminal justice services shall mutually determine.

4. The commissioner of the department of correctional services shall provide an annual report to the legislature on the staffing of correction officers and correction sergeants in state correctional facilities. Such report shall include, but not be limited to the following factors: the number of security posts on the current plot plan for each facility that have been closed on a daily basis, by correctional facility security classification (minimum, medium and maximum); the number of security positions eliminated by correctional facility since two thousand compared to the number of inmates incarcerated in each such facility; a breakdown by correctional facility security classification (minimum, medium, and maximum) of the staff hours of overtime worked, by year since two thousand and the annual aggregate costs related to this overtime. In addition, such report shall be delineated by correctional facility security classification, the annual number of security positions eliminated, the number of closed posts and amount of staff hours of overtime accrued as well as the overall overtime expenditures that resulted. Such report shall be provided to the chairs of the senate finance, assembly ways and means, senate crime and corrections and assembly correction committees by December thirty-first.

Added by L. 1974, Ch. 654; **Amended** by L. 1989, Ch. 411, eff. Aug. 15, 1989; L. 1990, Ch. 598, eff. July 18, 1990, amending subd. 1 and shall be deemed to have been in full force and effect on and after August 15, 1989; L. 2003, Ch. 62, Part H, § 1, adding subd. 4, eff. May 15, 2003; L. 2004, Ch. 56, § 1 (Part N), eff. Aug. 20, 2004; L. 2005, Ch. 56, Part R, § 1, amending subd. 4, eff. Apr. 1, 2005.

ANNOTATION

Parole Board meeting minutes.—Minutes of Parole Board meetings are not specifically exempted by either Corr. Law § 29 or § 221. Zuckerman v. New York State Bd. of Parole, 53 A.D.2d 405, 385 N.Y.S.2d 811 (3d Dept. 1976).

ARTICLE 3—STATE COMMISSION OF CORRECTION

§ 40. Definitions.

As used in this article the following terms have the following meanings:

1. "Commission" means the state commission of correction.

2. "Local correctional facility" means any county jail, county penitentiary, county lockup, city jail, police station jail, town or village jail or lockup, court detention pen or hospital prison ward.

3. "Correctional facility" means any institution operated by the state department of correctional services, any local correctional facility, or any place used, pursuant to a contract with the state or a municipality, for the detention of persons charged with or convicted of a crime, or, for the purpose of this article only, a secure facility operated by the state division for youth.

4. "Municipal official" means (a) the sheriff or, where a local correctional facility is under the jurisdiction of a county department, the head of such department, and clerk of the board of supervisors, in the case of a county jail; (b) the sheriff or other officer having custody or administrative jurisdiction and the clerk of the board of supervisors, in the case of a county penitentiary; (c) the clerk of the board of supervisors in the case of a county lockup; (d) the mayor and the city clerk, in the case of a city jail or police station jail; (e) the supervisor and town clerk, in the case of a town jail or lockup; (f) the mayor and village clerk, in the case of a village jail or lockup; (g) the clerk of the board of supervisors of the county wherein located and the officer having custody or control, in the case of a court detention pen or a hospital prison ward.

5. "Board" means the correction medical review board.

6. "Council" means the citizen's policy and complaint review council.

Amended by L. 1996, Ch. 309, § 55, amending subd. 3, effective July 13, 1996.

§ 41. State commission of correction; organization.

1. There shall be within the executive department a state commission of correction. It shall consist of three persons to be appointed by the governor, by and with the advice and consent of the senate. The governor shall designate one of the appointed members as chairman to serve as such at the pleasure of the governor. The members shall devote full time to their duties and shall hold no other salaried public position.

2. The members shall hold office for terms of five years; provided that of the three members first appointed, one shall serve for a term of two years, one shall serve for a term of three years and one shall serve for a term of five years from January first next succeeding their appointment. No member shall serve for more than ten years. Any member of the commission may be removed by the governor for cause after an opportunity to be heard in his defense.

3. Any member chosen to fill a vacancy created other than by expiration of term shall be appointed for the unexpired term of the member whom he is to succeed. Vacancies caused by expiration of term or otherwise shall be filled in the same manner as original appointments.

§ 42. Citizen's policy and complaint review council; organization; functions, powers and duties.

(a) 1. There shall be within the commission a citizen's policy and complaint review council. It shall consist of nine persons to be appointed by the governor, by and with the advice and consent of the senate. One person so appointed shall have served in the armed forces of the United States in Indochina at any time from the first day of January, nineteen hundred sixty-three, to an including the seventh day of May, nineteen hundred seventy-five who was discharged therefrom under other than dishonorable conditions, or shall be a duly licensed mental health professional who has professional experience or training with regard to post-traumatic stress syndrome. One person so appointed shall be an attorney admitted to practice in this state. One person so appointed shall be a former inmate of a correctional facility. One person so appointed shall be a former correction officer. One person so appointed shall be a former resident of a division for youth secure center. One person so appointed shall be a former employee of the division for youth who has directly supervised youth in a secure residential center operated by the division. In addition, the governor shall designate one of the full-time members other than the chairman of the commission as chairman of the council to serve as such at the pleasure of the governor.

2. The nine appointed members of the council shall hold office for five years; provided that of the seven members first appointed, two shall be appointed for a term of one year, two shall be appointed for a term of two years, one shall be appointed for a term of three years, one shall be appointed for a term of four years, and one shall be appointed for a term of five years from January first next succeeding their appointment. Any appointed member of the council may be removed by the governor for cause after an opportunity to be heard in his defense.

3. Any member chosen to fill in a vacancy created other than by expiration of term shall be appointed for the unexpired term of the member whom he is to succeed. Vacancies caused by the expiration of term or otherwise shall be filled in the same manner as original appointments.

4. The members of the council other than the chairman shall receive no compensation for their services but each member other than the chairman shall be entitled to receive his or her actual and necessary expenses incurred in the performance of his or her duties.

5. No appointed member of the council shall qualify or enter upon the duties of his office, or remain therein, while he is an officer or employee of the department of correctional services or any correctional facility or is in a position where he exercise administrative supervision over any correctional facility. The council shall have such staff as shall be necessary to assist it in the performance of its duties within the amount of the appropriation therefor as determined by the chairman of the commission.

(b) The council and each member thereof shall have the following functions, powers and duties:

1. To investigate, review or take such other action as shall be deemed necessary or proper with respect to complaints or grievances regarding any local correctional facility or part thereof as shall be called to its attention in writing.

2. To have access, at any and all times, to any local correctional facility or part thereof and to all books, records, and data pertaining to any local correctional facility which are deemed necessary

for carrying out the council's functions, powers and duties.

3. To obtain from administrators, officers or employees of any local correctional facility any information deemed necessary for the purpose of carrying out its functions, powers and duties.

4. To request and receive temporary office space in any local correctional facility for the purpose of carrying out its functions, powers and duties.

5. To report periodically to the commission and, where appropriate, to make such recommendations as are necessary to fulfill the purposes of this article to the commission and to the administrator of any local correctional facility.

(c) In addition to the functions, powers and duties prescribed by subdivision (b) of this section, the council shall

1. Advise and assist the commission in developing policies, plans and programs for improving the commission's performance of its duties and for coordinating the efforts of the commission and of correctional officials to improve conditions of care, treatment, safety, supervision, rehabilitation, recreation, training and education in correctional facilities.

2. Foster and promote research and study in areas of correctional policy and program development deemed necessary or desirable by the commission or the council.

3. Meet at least once per calendar month at a time and place designated by the chairman of the council.

Amended by L. 1987, Ch. 131, eff. June 15, 1987; L. 1992, Ch. 55, eff. Apr. 10, 1992, amending subd. a(4); L. 1994, Ch. 86, § 1, amending subd. a(1); L. 1996, Ch. 309, § 56, amending subd. a(1) and (2), eff. July 13, 1996.

§ 43. Correction medical review board; organization.

1. There shall be within the commission a correction medical review board. It shall consist of six persons to be appointed by the governor by and with the advice and consent of the senate. In addition, the governor shall designate one of the full-time members other than the chairman of the commission and the chairman of the council as chairman of the board to serve as such at the pleasure of the governor. Of the appointed members of the board one shall be a physician duly licensed to practice in this state; one shall be a physician duly licensed to practice in this state and shall be a board certified forensic pathologist; one shall be a physician duly licensed to practice in this state and shall be a board certified forensic psychiatrist; one shall be an attorney admitted to practice in this state; two shall be members appointed at large.

2. The six appointed members of the board shall hold office for five years; provided that of

the two members first appointed; after December thirty-first, nineteen hundred eighty-seven who are not appointed to succeed any other member of the board, one shall be appointed for a term of four years and one shall be appointed for a term of five years from January first next succeeding their appointment. Any appointed member of the board may be removed by the governor for cause after an opportunity to be heard in his defense.

3. Any member chosen to fill a vacancy created other than by expiration of term shall be appointed for the unexpired term of the member whom he is to succeed. Vacancies caused by expiration of term or otherwise shall be filled in the same manner as original appointments.

4. The members of the board shall receive no compensation for their services but each member shall be entitled to receive his actual and necessary expenses incurred in the performance of his duties.

Amended by L. 1988, Ch. 379, eff. July 29, 1988, amending subds. 1 and 2.

ANNOTATION

Board certified.—The term "board certified" means certification by a medical specialty board, it is a term of art understood to refer to approval by a designated group of professionals, especially in context of describing physicians; Legislature has also used the term "board certified" to refer to a medical specialty board as in § 43(1). Belmonte v. Snashall, 2 N.Y.3d 560, 780 N.Y.S.2d 541, 813 N.E.2d 621 (2004).

§ 44. Chairman of commission.

1. The chairman shall be the executive officer of the commission, the board and the council.

2. The chairman may appoint such assistants, officers and employees, committees and consultants for the board and the council as he may determine necessary, prescribe their powers and duties, fix their compensation and provide for reimbursement of their expenses within amounts appropriated therefor.

3. The chairman may, from time to time, create, abolish, transfer and consolidate bureaus and other units within the commission, the board and the council not expressly established by law as he may determine necessary for the efficient operation of the commission, the board and the council, subject to the approval of the director of the budget.

4. The chairman may request and receive from any department, division, board, bureau, commission or other agency of the state or any political subdivision thereof or any public authority such assistance, information and data as will enable the commission, the board and the council properly to carry out its functions, powers and duties.

§ 45. Functions, powers and duties of the commission.

The commission shall have the following functions, powers and duties:

1. Advise and assist the governor in developing policies, plans and programs for improving the administration of correctional facilities and the delivery of services therein.

2. Make recommendations to administrators of correctional facilities for improving the administration of such correctional facilities and the delivery of services therein.

3. Visit, inspect and appraise the management of correctional facilities with specific attention to matters such as safety, security, health of inmates, sanitary conditions, rehabilitative programs, disturbance and fire prevention and control preparedness, and adherence to laws and regulations governing the rights of inmates.

4. Establish procedures to assure effective investigation of grievances of, and conditions affecting, inmates of local correctional facilities. Such procedures shall include but not be limited to receipt of written complaints, interviews of persons, and on-site monitoring of conditions. In addition, the commission shall establish procedures for the speedy and impartial review of grievances referred to it by the commissioner of the department of correctional services.

5. Ascertain and recommend such system of employing inmates of correctional facilities as may, in the opinion of said commission, be for the best interest of the public and of said inmates and not in conflict with the provisions of the constitution or laws of the state relating to the employment of inmates.

6. Promulgate rules and regulations establishing minimum standards for the care, custody, correction, treatment, supervision, discipline, and other correctional programs for all persons confined in correctional facilities. Such rules and regulations shall be forwarded to the governor, the temporary president of the senate and the speaker of the assembly no later than January first, nineteen hundred seventy-six and annually thereafter.

6-a. Promulgate rules and regulations to assure that persons in custody in local correctional facilities, including persons awaiting arraignment, are furnished or have access to the type of food required by their religious dietary rules or medically prescribed diets, if any.

6-b. Promulgate rules and regulations, in consultation with the division for youth, establishing minimum standards for the care, custody, rehabilitation, treatment, supervision, discipline and other programs for correctional facilities operated by the division for youth.

7. Place such members of its staff as it deems appropriate as monitors in any local correctional facility which, in the judgment of the commission, presents an imminent danger to the health, safety or security of the inmates or employees of such correctional facility or of the public.

8. (a) Close any correctional facility which is unsafe, unsanitary or inadequate to provide for the separation and classification of prisoners required by law or which has not adhered to or complied with the rules or regulations promulgated with respect to any such facility by the commission pursuant to the provisions of subdivision six of this section; provided, however, that before such facility may be closed due to conditions which are unsafe, unsanitary or inadequate to provide for the separation and classification of prisoners, the commission shall cause a citation to be mailed to the appropriate municipal or other official at least ten days before the return day thereof directing the responsible authorities designated to appear before such commission at the time and place set forth in the citation, and show cause why such correctional facility should not be closed. After a hearing thereon or upon the failure to appear, such commission is empowered to order such facility designated in the citation closed within twenty days, during which time the respondent authority may review such order in the manner provided in article seventy-eight of the civil practice law and rules, in the supreme court. Fifteen days after the order to close has been served by a registered letter upon the appropriate official if no court review has been taken, and fifteen days after the order of such commission has been confirmed by the court, in case of court review, such facility designated in the order shall be closed, and it shall be unlawful to confine or detain any person therein and any officer confining or detaining any person therein shall be guilty of a class A misdemeanor.

(b) Before a correctional facility as defined in subdivision four of section two of this chapter, correctional facility annex, or any special housing unit established to confine inmates in accordance with the provisions of subdivision six of section one hundred thirty-seven of this chapter, may be closed for a reason other than those set forth in paragraph (a) of this subdivision, the provisions of section seventy-nine-a of this chapter shall be adhered to.

9. For the purpose of providing for adequate care, custody, correction, treatment, supervision, discipline and other correctional programs for all persons confined in correctional facilities, the commission shall establish, maintain and operate a correctional training program for such personnel employed by correctional facilities as the commission shall deem necessary. Such program shall be satisfactorily completed by such personnel prior to their undertaking their duties or within one year following the date of their appointment or at such times as the commission may prescribe; provided, however, the commission may exempt from such requirement (i) personnel employed by any correctional facility which, in the opinion of the commission, maintains and operates a basic correctional training program of a standard equal to or higher than that established, maintained and operated by the commission, and (ii) such personnel employed by any correctional institution as of the effective date of this section who, in the opinion of the commission, possess sufficient qualifications for the care, custody, correction, treatment, supervision and discipline of persons confined in correctional facilities. The cost of such program shall be borne by the commission within the amount available therefor by appropriation; provided, however, that the salary and actual expenses of personnel engaged in such program shall be borne by the correctional facility employing them.

9-a. For the purpose of providing for adequate care, custody, correction, treatment, supervision, discipline and other correctional programs for all persons confined in local correctional facilities, the commission shall promulgate rules and regulations for the certification of part-time local correctional officers employed by local correctional facilities who have satisfactorily completed an in-service correctional training program sponsored by the local correctional facility. The program shall include the same instruction which is given to local correctional officers who attend training sessions which are sponsored by the commission.

10. Approve or reject plans and specifications for the construction or improvement of correctional facilities.

11. Collect and disseminate statistical and other information and undertake research, studies and analyses, through the personnel of the commission or in cooperation with any public or private agency in respect to the administration, programs, effectiveness and coordination of correctional facilities.

12. Make an annual report to the governor and legislature concerning its work and the work of the board and the council during the preceding year, and such further interim reports to the governor, or to the governor and legislature, as it shall deem advisable, or as shall be required by the governor.

13. Accept, with the approval of the governor, as agent of the state any grant, including federal grants, or any gift for any of the purposes of this article. Any moneys so received may be expended by the commission to effectuate any purpose of this article, subject to the same limitations as to approval of expenditures and audit as are prescribed for state moneys appropriated for the purposes of this article.

14. Enter into contracts with any person, firm, corporation, municipality, or governmental agency.

15. Adopt, amend or rescind such rules and regulations as may be necessary or convenient to the performance of the functions, powers and duties of the commission.

16. Do all other things necessary or convenient

to carry out its functions, powers and duties expressly set forth in this article.

Amended by L. 1979, Ch. 577, eff. Sept. 8, 1979; L. 1981, Ch. 752, added subd. 9-a; L. 1982, Ch. 85, eff. Sept. 1, 1982, amending subd. 9; L. 1996, Ch. 309, § 57, adding subd. 6-b, eff. July 13, 1996; L. 2005, Ch. 57, Part S, § 1, amending subd. 8, eff. Apr. 12, 2005; L. 2005, Ch. 63, Part D, § 2, amending subd. 8, eff. Apr. 12, 2005.

ANNOTATION

Sheriff's rule making power.—The rule making power conferred upon the Sheriffs as jail keeper by Correction Law § 500-c is curtailed or diminished by Correction Law § 45(6). McNulty v. Chinlund, 62 A.D.2d 682, 406 N.Y.S.2d 558 (3d Dept. 1978).

§ 46. Additional functions, powers and duties of the commission.

1. The commission, any member or any employee designated by the commission must be granted access at any and all times to any correctional facility or part thereof and to all books, records, and data pertaining to any correctional facility deemed necessary for carrying out the commission's functions, powers and duties. The commission, any member or any employee designated by the chairman may require from the officers or employees of a correctional facility any information deemed necessary for the purpose of carrying out the commission's functions, powers and duties.

2. In the exercise of its functions, powers and duties, the commission and any member is authorized to issue and enforce a subpoena and a subpoena duces tecum, administer oaths and examine persons under oath, in accordance with and pursuant to civil practice law and rules. A person examined under oath pursuant to this subdivision shall have the right to be accompanied by counsel who shall advise the person of their rights subject to reasonable limitations to prevent obstruction of, or interference with, the orderly conduct of the examination.

3. In any case where a person in charge or control of a correctional facility or an officer or employee thereof shall fail to comply with the provisions of subdivision one, the commission may apply to the supreme court for an order directed to such person requiring compliance therewith. Upon such application the court may issue such order as may be just and a failure to comply with the order of the court shall be a contempt of court and punishable as such.

4. In any case where any rule or regulation promulgated by the commission pursuant to subdivision six of section forty-five or the laws relating to the construction, management and affairs of any correctional facility or the care, treatment and discipline of its inmates, are being or are about to be violated, the commission shall notify the person in charge or control of the facility of such violation, recommend remedial action, and direct such person to comply with the rule, regulation or law, as the case may be. Upon the failure of such person to comply with the rule, regulation or law the commission may apply to the supreme court for an order directed to such person requiring compliance with such rule, regulation or law. Upon such application the court may issue such order as may be just and a failure to comply with the order of the court shall be a contempt of court and punishable as such.

Amended by L. 1994, Ch. 536, § 1, eff. July 26, 1994, amending subd. 2.

§ 47. Functions, powers and duties of the board.

1. The board shall have the following functions, powers and duties:

(a) Investigate and review the cause and circumstances surrounding the death of any inmate of a correctional facility.

(b) Visit and inspect any correctional facility wherein an inmate has died.

(c) Cause the body of the deceased to undergo such examinations, including an autopsy, as in the opinion of the board, are necessary to determine the cause of death, irrespective of whether any such examination or autopsy shall have previously been performed.

(d) Upon review of the cause of death and circumstances surrounding the death of any inmate, the board shall submit its report thereon to the commission and, where appropriate, make recommendations to prevent the recurrence of such deaths to the commission and the administrator of the appropriate correctional facility.

(e) Investigate and report to the commission on the condition of systems for the delivery of medical care to inmates of correctional facilities and where appropriate recommend such changes as it shall deem necessary and proper to improve the quality and availability of such medical care.

2. Every administrator of a correctional facility shall immediately report to the board the death of an inmate of any such facility in such manner and form as the board shall prescribe, together with an autopsy report.

Amended by L. 1987, Ch. 491, eff. July 30, 1987.

§ 48. Preference.

Any action or proceeding commenced by the commission pursuant to this article shall have a preference over all other cases, except habeas corpus proceedings, pending before the court.

ARTICLE 4—ESTABLISHMENT OF CORRECTIONAL FACILITIES, COMMITMENTS TO DEPARTMENT AND CUSTODY OF INMATES

CORR. L.

§ 70. Establishment, use and designation of correctional facilities.

1. (a) Except as provided in paragraphs (b) and (c) of this subdivision, every institution operated by the department for the confinement of persons under sentence of imprisonment, or for the confinement of persons committed for failure to pay a fine, shall be a correctional facility.

(b) An institution operated by the department for the care and confinement of persons who have been found to be mentally defective or mentally ill by a court and who are confined in such place pursuant to an order of a court based upon such finding shall not be deemed to be a correctional facility.

(c) An institution operated by the department as a drug treatment campus, as defined in subdivision twenty of section two of this chapter and used to provide intensive drug treatment services for parolees and certain parole violators, shall not be deemed to be a correctional facility.

2. Correctional facilities shall be used for the purpose of providing places of confinement and programs of treatment for persons in the custody of the department. Such use shall be suited, to the greatest extent practicable, to the objective of assisting sentenced persons to live as law abiding citizens. In furtherance of this objective the department may establish and maintain any type of institution or program of treatment, not inconsistent with other provisions of law, but with due regard to:

(a) The safety and security of the community;

(b) The right of every person in the custody of the department to receive humane treatment; and

(c) The health and safety of every person in the custody of the department.

3. (a) The commissioner may continue to maintain, as a correctional facility, any institution operated by the department prior to May eighth, nineteen hundred seventy, and may add to or close any such place, and may establish and maintain new correctional facilities, in accordance with the needs of the department and provided expenditures for such purposes are within amounts made available therefor by appropriation; provided, however, that before the closure of any correctional facility, correctional facility annex, or any special housing unit established to confine inmates in accordance with the provisions of subdivision six of section one hundred thirty-seven of this chapter, for reasons other than those set forth in paragraph (a) of subdivision eight of section forty-five of this chapter, the provisions of section seventy-nine-a of this article shall be adhered to.

(b) A correctional camp or a shock incarceration correctional facility may be established by the department (i) upon land controlled and designated by the commissioner of correctional services, or (ii) on land controlled and designated by the commissioner of parks, recreation and historic preservation or, in the sixth park region, by the commissioner of environmental conservation.

4. Two or more correctional facilities may be maintained or established in the same building or on the same premises so long as the inmates of each are at all times kept separate and apart from each other except that the inmates of one may be permitted to have contact with inmates of the other in order to perform duties, receive therapeutic treatment, attend religious services and engage in like activities as specifically provided in the rules and regulations of the department.

5. Each correctional facility must be designated in the rules and regulations of the department and no correctional facility can be used by the department for confinement of persons unless the rules and regulations of the department specify at least the following:

(a) The name and location of the facility;

(b) Whether the facility is to be used for the

confinement of males or for the confinement of females;

(c) The age range of the persons who may be confined in the facility; and

(d) The classification of the facility.

6. Correctional facilities shall be classified by the commissioner in accordance with the following types of classifications:

(a) Each facility shall be classified with respect to the type of security maintained as either a maximum, medium or minimum security facility.

(b) Each facility shall be classified with respect to the function served in accordance with one or more of the following categories: (i) reception center; (ii) residential treatment facility; (iii) detention center; (iv) correctional camp; (v) diagnostic and treatment center; (vi) general confinement facility; (vii) work release facility; (viii) shock incarceration correctional facility; (ix) alcohol and substance abuse treatment facility; (x) alcohol and substance abuse treatment correctional annex.

7. The commissioner of correction shall have the authority to enter into leases within the amount appropriated therefor, for the purpose of maintaining or establishing any correctional facility or any adjunct thereto.

8. The commissioner of correction is authorized to enter into contracts, within the amount appropriated therefor, with any university, social agency or qualified person to render professional services to any correctional facility.

Added by L. 1970, Ch. 476; **Amended** by L. 1972, Chs. 567, 661; L. 1974, Chs. 141, 239, 660; L. 1975, Ch. 667; L. 1980, Ch. 471 repealed subd. 9; L. 1987; ch. 261 amending subds. 3(b) and 6(b), eff. July 13, 1987; L. 1989, Ch. 338, amending subd. 6(b), eff. July 10, 1989; L. 1995, Ch. 3, § 23, adding subd. 1(c), eff. June 10, 1995; L. 2005, Ch. 57, Part S, § 2, amending subd. 3(a), eff. Apr. 12, 2005; L. 2005, Ch. 63, Part D, § 2, amending subd. 3(a), eff. Apr. 12, 2005.

ANNOTATION

Placement facility not a correctional facility.—Court-ordered placement in a drug treatment campus program as part of conditions of parole does not constitute incarceration and, therefore, placement in such a facility cannot be the basis of a motion for a writ of habeas corpus. Morejon v. Parole Board, 183 Misc. 2d 435, 706 N.Y.S.2d 566 (Sup. Ct. Bronx Co. 1999).

§ 71. Persons received into the custody of the department.

1. [*Effective until Sept. 1, 2009.*] Persons committed to the custody of the department under an indeterminate or determinate sentence of imprisonment shall be delivered to correctional facilities designated as reception centers in the rules and regulations of the department. The commissioner may designate any correctional facility as a reception center subject, however, to the following criteria:

[*Effective Sept. 1, 2009.*] Persons committed to the custody of the department under an indeterminate or a reformatory sentence of imprisonment shall be delivered to correctional facilities designated as reception centers in the rules and regulations of the department. The commissioner may designate any correctional facility as a reception center subject, however, to the following criteria:

(a) Males and females shall not be received at the same correctional facility;

(b) Males under the age of twenty one at the time sentence is imposed shall not be received at the same correctional facility as males who are twenty one or over at the time sentence is imposed.

1-a. The commissioner shall ensure that each general confinement facility law library has information on international offender transfers sufficient to inform those persons who are citizens of a treaty nation of the existence of such treaties and of the means by which such persons may initiate a request for return to the person's country of citizenship for service of the sentence imposed. Such law libraries shall also contain the most recent annual Amnesty International report published by Amnesty international describing the conditions of prisons in each treaty nation and, to the extent practicable, other materials describing such prison conditions published by the United Nations, United States Department of State or human rights organizations. In addition, to the extent practicable, such law libraries shall contain information either listing each foreign country's provisions for the reduction of the terms of confinement for penal sentences as well as the availability of inmate programs or, shall contain a list of officials in the United States Department of Justice or the embassy of the foreign country to whom an inmate may write for information. To the extent practicable, newly received inmates who are identified as foreign nationals of treaty Nations shall, as part of the reception process, be advised of the existence of such treaties and the possibility of the initiation of a transfer request.

1-b. The commissioner shall promulgate rules and regulations setting forth the procedures by which an inmate may apply to be considered for transfer to a foreign nation. The commissioner, or his designee, shall retain sole and absolute authority to approve or disapprove an inmate's application for transfer. Nothing herein shall be construed to confer upon an inmate a right to be a transferred to a foreign nation. Notwithstanding any other law, rule or regulation to the contrary, no inmate application for transfer shall be processed unless the inmate has first indicated his willingness and desire in writing, on a form prescribed by the commissioner, to be considered for transfer to the foreign nation. Such form shall also contain a copy of the inmate's most recent legal date computation printout indicating the term or aggregate term of the sentence originally imposed and the release dates resulting therefrom.

If a request for transfer is approved by the commissioner or his designee, facility staff shall assist in the preparation and submission of all materials and forms necessary to effectuate the person's request for transfer to the United States Department of Justice for purposes of finalization of the transfer process, including verification proceedings before a United States district court judge, United States magistrate or other appointed United States official to assure and document the inmate's voluntary request for transfer.

1-c. For purposes of this section, the term "treaty nation" means a foreign country under treaty that provides for the voluntary transfer of persons on the execution of penal sentences entered into by the government of the United States with foreign countries.

2. Persons returned to the custody of the department as parole or conditional release violators shall be delivered to institutions designated in the rules and regulations of the department.

3. Persons who are committed, transferred, certified to or placed in the care or custody of the department as mental defectives shall be delivered to a special institution maintained for the care, treatment, training and custody of mental defectives in accordance with article seventeen of this chapter.

4. Persons who are committed, transferred, certified to or placed in the care or custody of the department while mentally ill shall be delivered to a special institution maintained for the care, treatment and custody of the mentally ill in accordance with article sixteen of this chapter.

5. The commissioner of correction shall file copies of written orders with the clerk of each court having jurisdiction to commit persons to the custody of the department designating the institutions to which persons committed by such court shall be delivered. Such orders may be amended or superseded by the commissioner from time to time and any change shall become effective immediately upon receipt by the clerk of the court.

6. A commitment to a specified institution in the department, rather than to the custody of the department, which is valid in all other respects shall not be void for such reason but shall be deemed a commitment to the custody of the department and the person so commitment shall be conveyed to the proper institution as prescribed by this section.

7. Whenever the department receives information that a person committed to the department is a social services recipient and a certificate of conviction and the term of the sentence imposed has not previously been delivered by the sentencing court to the local commissioner of social services pursuant to section 380.80 of the criminal procedure law, the department shall deliver the certificate of conviction and provide notification

of the sentence imposed to the commissioner of social services. Such commissioner shall deliver the certificate of conviction and the term of sentence imposed to the appropriate local commissioner of social services.

Added by L. 1974, Ch. 62; L. 1995, Ch. 3, § 24, amending subd. 1, eff. Oct. 1, 1995, and amendment repealed on Sept. 30, 2005 pursuant to L. 1995, Ch. 3, § 74(d); L. 1995, Ch. 547, § 2, adding subds. 1-a through 1-c, eff. Aug. 2, 1995; L. 1996, Ch. 700, eff. Jan. 7, 1997, adding subd. 7; L. 2005, Ch. 56, Part D, § 20, eff. Apr. 1, 2005, extending expiration and effective date of subd. 1 introductory language to Sept. 1, 2009.

§ 72. Confinement of persons by the department.

1. Except as otherwise provided in this section, all persons committed, transferred, certified to or placed in the care or custody of the department shall be confined in institutions maintained by the department until paroled, conditionally released, transferred to the care of another agency or released or discharged in accordance with the law.

2. The commissioner, or the superintendent or director of an institution in which an inmate is confined, may permit an inmate to be taken, under guard, to any place or for any purpose authorized by law, and the commissioner must provide for delivery of an inmate, under guard, to any place where his presence is required pursuant to an order of a court that has authority to require his presence.

2-a. The commissioner, superintendent, or director of an institution in which an inmate is confined, may permit an inmate, wishing to do so, to leave the institution under guard for the purpose of performing volunteer labor or services when in the public interest upon the threat or occurrence of a natural disaster, including but not limited to flood, earthquake, hurricane, landslide or fire.

2-b. The commissioner, or his designee as authorized by the commissioner, may permit an inmate to be taken under guard to any place to participate in an industrial training program.

3. The superintendent or director of an institution may permit inmates to leave the institution for the purpose of performing maintenance work or farm work, or any other work necessary or appropriate for the upkeep, operations or business of the institution or the department.

4. Any inmate who is confined in a correctional facility and who is eligible for parole or who will become eligible for parole within two years or who has one year or less remaining to be served under his sentence may be transferred by the commissioner to a correctional camp and may be permitted, by the superintendent, to leave the camp to engage in conservation or forestry work or for any purpose permitted under subdivisions two and three of this section.

5. [*Effective until Sept. 1, 2007.*] An inmate

may be permitted to leave the institution to participate in a temporary release program in accordance with the provisions of article twenty-six of this chapter.

5. [*Effective Sept. 1, 2007.*] An inmate of a work release facility may be permitted to leave the facility to participate in a work release program in accordance with the provisions of article twenty-six of this chapter.

6. An inmate of a residential treatment facility may be permitted to leave such facility in accordance with the provisions of section seventy-three of this article.

7. An inmate of a shock incarceration correctional facility may be permitted to leave the facility to participate in programs in accordance with the provisions of article twenty-six-A of this chapter.

8. In any case where the decision to permit an inmate to leave an institution is made by a person other than the commissioner or a deputy commissioner of correction such action and the manner in which it is carried out shall be in strict accordance with the rules and regulations of the department. Such rules and regulations may restrict or limit the authority of the superintendent or director in any manner deemed advisable by the commissioner.

9. The provisions of this section shall not be construed in such manner as to be in conflict with any provision of law that specifically provides for circumstances under which inmates may be permitted to leave institutions.

Added by L. 1970, Ch. 476; **Amended** by L. 1972, Chs. 339, 567; L. 1973, Ch. 268; L. 1974, Chs. 536, 966; L. 1976, Ch. 471; L. 1977, Ch. 691; L. 1978, Ch. 691; L. 1979, Ch. 485; L. 1980, Ch. 296; L. 1981, Ch. 495; L. 1982, Ch. 137; L. 1983; Ch. 519; L. 1984, Ch. 983; L. 1985, Ch. 573, eff. Sept. 1, 1985; L. Ch. 395, eff. Sept. 1, 1986, extending the expiration date of subd. 5 to September 1, 1987; L. 1987, Ch. 261, eff. July 13, 1987, renumbered subds. 7 and 8 to subds. 8 and 9 and added subd. 7 and extended the expiration date of subd. 5 to September 1, 1991; L. 1991, Ch. 511, § 5, eff. July 19, 1991, extending expiration date of subd. 5 to Sept. 1, 1994; L. 1992, Ch. 55, § 321; L. 1994, Ch. 61, § 8, eff. Apr. 1, 1994, extending expiration date of subd. 5 to Sept. 1, 1995; L. 1995, Ch. 3, § 50, eff. June 10, 1995, extending expiration date of subd. 5 to Sept. 1, 1997; L. 1997, Ch. 435, § 50, extending expiration date of subd. 5 to Sept. 1, 1999; L. 1999, Ch. 452, § 4, extending expiration date of subd. 5 to Sept. 1, 2001; L. 2001, Ch, 95, § 6, extending expiration date to Sept. 1, 2003; L. 2003, Ch. 16, § 6, extending expiration date to Sept. 1, 2005, eff. Mar. 31, 2003.

§ 72-a. Community treatment facilities.
[*Effective until Sept. 1, 2007, pursuant to L. 1986, Ch. 554, § 5, as amended.*]

1. Transfer of eligible inmate. Notwithstanding the provisions of section seventy-two of this chapter, any inmate confined in a correctional facility who is an "eligible inmate" as defined by subdivision two of section eight hundred fifty-one of this chapter and has been certified by the division of substance abuse services as being in need of substance abuse treatment and rehabilitation may be transferred by the commissioner to a community treatment facility.

2. Designation of facilities. A community treatment facility shall be designated by the director of the division of substance abuse services and the commissioner. Such facility shall be operated by a provider or sponsoring agency that has provided approved residential substance abuse treatment services for at least two years duration.

3. Operating standards. The commissioner, after consultation with the director of the division of substance abuse services, shall promulgate rules and regulations which provide for minimum standards of operation, including but not limited to the following:

(a) provision for adequate security and protection of the surrounding community;

(b) adequate physical plant standards;

(c) provisions for adequate program services, staffing, and record keeping; and

(d) provision for the general welfare of the inmates.

4. Parole supervision. The department shall contract with the division of parole for the provision of parole supervision services. Pursuant to such contract, all inmates residing in a community treatment facility shall be assigned to parole officers for supervision. Such parole officers shall be responsible to the division of parole for the purpose of providing such supervision. As part of its supervisory functions the division shall be required to provide reports to the department every two months on each inmate under its supervision. Such reports shall include, but not be limited to:

(a) an evaluation of the inmate's participation in such program; and

(b) a statement of any problems relative to an inmate's participation in such program and the manner in which such problems were resolved; and

(c) a recommendation with respect to the inmate's continued participation in the program.

5. Reports. The department and the division of substance abuse services shall jointly issue quarterly reports including a description of those facilities which have been designated as community treatment facilities, the number of inmates confined in each facility, a description of the programs within each facility, and the number of absconders, if any, as well as the nature and number of re-arrests, if any, during the individuals' parole period. Copies of such reports, as well as copies of any inspection report issued by the department or the commission on correction shall be sent to the director of the budget, the chairman

of the senate finance committee, the chairman of the senate crime and correction committee, the chairman of the assembly ways and means committee and the chairman of the assembly committee on codes.

6. Reimbursement. (a) The commissioner, in consultation with the director of the division of substance abuse services, shall enter into an agreement with the division of substance abuse services whereby the division of substance abuse services will contract with community treatment facilities for provision of services pursuant to this section within amounts made available by the department. Each contract shall provide for frequent visitation, inspection of the facility, and enforcement of the minimum standards and shall authorize the supervision of inmates residing in a community treatment facility by parole officers.

(b) The commissioner shall promulgate rules and regulations specifying those costs related to the general operation of community treatment facilities which shall be eligible for reimbursement. Such eligible costs shall not include debt service, whether principal or interest, or costs for which state or federal aid or reimbursement is otherwise available. Such rules and regulations shall be subject to the approval of the director of the budget.

(c) The division shall not contract for provisions of services to more than fifty inmates at any one facility.

(d) At least thirty days prior to final approval of any such contract, a copy of the proposed contract shall be sent to the director of the budget, the chairman of the senate finance committee, the chairman of the senate crime and correction committee, the chairman of the assembly ways and means committee, and the chairman of the assembly committee on codes.

Added by L. 1986, Ch. 554, eff. July 24, 1986 and shall remain in effect until Sept. 30, 1989; L. 1989, Ch. 338, eff. July 10, 1989; L. 1992, Ch. 55, § 322, eff. Apr. 10, 1992 extending expiration date to Sept. 30, 1995; L. 1995, Ch. 3, § 53, eff. June 10, 1995, extending expiration date to Sept. 30, 1997; L. 1997, Ch. 435, § 52, eff. Aug. 20, 1997 extending expiration date to Sept. 1, 1999; L. 1999, Ch. 452, § 6, extending expiration date to Sept. 1, 2001; L. 2001, Ch. 95, § 8, extending expiration date to Sept. 1, 2003; L. 2003, Ch. 16, § 8, eff. Mar. 31, 2003, extending expiration date to Sept. 1, 2005.

§ 72-b. Discharge of inmates to adult care facilities.

1. An inmate about to be discharged to an adult home, enriched housing program or residence for adults, as defined in section two of the social services law, shall be referred only to such home, program or residence that is consistent with that person's needs and that operates pursuant to section four hundred sixty of the social services law. No inmate shall be directly referred to any facility that is required to be certified as an adult care facility under the provisions of article seven of the social services law, unless it has been determined that such facility has a valid operating certificate.

2. No inmate about to be paroled, conditionally released, transferred, released or discharged shall be referred to any adult home, enriched housing program or residence for adults, as defined in section two of the social services law, where the department of correctional services or state division of parole has received written notice that the facility has been placed on the "do not refer list" pursuant to subdivision fifteen of section four hundred sixty-d of the social services law.

Added by L. 2004, Ch. 58, Part B, § 48, eff. Aug. 20, 2004.

Editor's Note: L. 2004, Ch. 58, Part B, § 56(7)–(12), eff. Aug. 20, 2004, provides:

"7. Provided, however, that any rules or regulations necessary to implement the provisions of this act may be promulgated and any procedures, forms, or instructions necessary for such implementation may be adopted and issued on or after the date this act shall have become law;

"8. This act shall not be construed to alter, change, affect, impair or defeat any rights, obligations, duties or interests accrued, incurred or conferred prior to the enactment of this act;

"9. The commissioner of health and the superintendent of insurance and any appropriate council may take any steps necessary to implement this act prior to its effective dates;

"10. Notwithstanding any inconsistent provision of the state administrative procedure act or any other provision of law, rule or regulation, the commissioner of health and the superintendent of insurance and any appropriate council is authorized to adopt or amend or promulgate on an emergency basis any regulation he or she or such council determines necessary to implement any provision of this act on its effective date;

"11. The provisions of this act shall be effective notwithstanding the failure of the commissioner of health or the superintendent of insurance or any council to adopt or amend or promulgate regulations implementing this act;

"12. Nothing contained in this act shall be deemed to affect the application, qualification, expiration, reversion or repeal of any provision of law amended by any section of this act and the provisions of this act shall be applied or qualified or shall expire or revert or be deemed repealed in the same manner, to the same extent and on the same date as the case may be as otherwise provided by law."

§ 72-c. Notice to local social services districts.

Prior to the release, discharge, parole or release to post-release supervision of an inmate designated a level two or three sex offender pursuant to the sex offender registration act, the department shall provide notification to the local social services district in the county in which the inmate expects to reside, when information available to the department pursuant to section one hundred sixty-eight-e of this chapter or any other prerelease procedures indicates that such person is likely to seek to access local social services for homeless persons. The department shall provide such notice, when practicable, thirty days or more before such person's release, but in any event, in advance of such person's arrival in the jurisdiction of such local social services district.

Added by L. 2005, Ch. 410, § 1, eff. Oct. 1, 2005. Section 2 of L. 2005, Ch. 410 provides: "This act shall take effect on the sixtieth day after it shall have become a law; provided that effective immediately the department of correctional services may begin to collect information and provide the notice required by section 72-c of the correction law, as added by section one of this act, regarding inmates scheduled to be released prior to such effective date in order to comply with the provisions of such section."

§ 73. Residential treatment facilities.

1. The commissioner may transfer any inmate of a correctional facility who is eligible for parole or who will become eligible for parole within six months after the date of transfer or who has one year or less remaining to be served under his sentence to a residential treatment facility and such person may be allowed to go outside the facility during reasonable and necessary hours to engage in any activity reasonably related to his rehabilitation and in accordance with the program established for him. While outside the facility he shall be at all times in the custody of the department of correction and under the supervision of the state division of parole.

2. The division of parole shall be responsible for securing appropriate education, on-the-job training and employment for inmates transferred to residential treatment facilities. The division also shall supervise such inmates during their participation in activities outside any such facility and at all times while they are outside any such facility.

3. Programs directed toward the rehabilitation and total reintegration into the community of persons transferred to a residential treatment facility shall be established jointly by the department of correction and the division of parole. Each inmate shall be assigned a specific program by the superintendent of the facility and a written memorandum of such program shall be delivered to him.

4. If at any time the superintendent of a residential treatment facility is of the opinion that any aspect of the program assigned to an individual is inconsistent with the welfare or safety of the community or of the facility or its inmates, the superintendent may suspend such program or any part thereof and restrict the inmate's activities in any manner that is necessary and appropriate. Upon taking such action the superintendent shall promptly notify the commissioner of correction and pending decision by the commissioner the superintendent may keep such inmate under such security as may be necessary.

5. The commissioner may at any time and for any reason transfer an inmate from a residential treatment facility to another correctional facility. The chairman of the state board of parole may request the commissioner of correction to transfer a person out of a residential treatment facility if at any time the chairman is of the opinion that such person should no longer be allowed to follow a program that permits him to engage in activities in the community. Upon receipt of any such request, the commissioner shall forthwith transfer the inmate to a correctional facility other than a residential treatment facility.

6. Where a person who is an inmate of a residential treatment facility absconds, or fails to return thereto as specified in the program approved for him, he may be arrested and returned by an officer or employee of the department of correction or the division of parole or by any peace officer, acting pursuant to his special duties, or police officer without a warrant; or a member of the board of parole or an officer of the division of parole designated by such board may issue a warrant for the retaking of such person. A warrant issued pursuant to this subdivision shall have the same force and effect, and shall be executed in the same manner, as a warrant issued for violation of parole.

7. The provisions of this chapter relating to good behavior allowances and conditional release shall apply to behavior of inmates while assigned to a residential treatment facility for behavior on the premises and outside the premises of such facility and good behavior allowances may be granted, withheld, forfeited or cancelled in whole or in part for behavior outside the premises of the facility to the same extent and in the same manner as is provided in inmates within the premises of any facility.

8. The board of parole may grant parole to any inmate of a residential treatment facility at any time after he becomes eligible therefor. Such parole shall be in accordance with provisions of law that would apply if the person were still confined in the facility from which he was transferred, except that any personal appearance before the board may be at any place designated by the board.

9. The earnings of any inmate of a residential treatment facility shall be dealt with in accordance with the procedure set forth in section eight hundred fifty-seven of this chapter.

10. The commissioner of correction and the chairman of the board of parole are authorized to enter into an agreement for the use of any residential treatment facility as a residence for persons who are on parole or conditional release, and persons under supervision of the board of parole who reside in such facility shall be subject to conditions of parole or release imposed by the board.

Added by L. 1970, Ch. 476; **Amended** by L. 1980, Ch. 843, eff. Sept. 1, 1980.

ANNOTATIONS

Custody of department of corrections.—Participation in Day Reporting Program, which entitles certain inmates incarcerated in state correctional facility to reside outside the correctional facility in an approved residence with certain restrictions, does not render inmate beyond the reach of the temporary release program rules or the custody of the department of correction; violation of temporary release rules and restrictions properly resulted in revocation of temporary release status. Hall v. ZenZen, 20 A.D.3d 840, 798 N.Y.S.2d 801 (3d Dept. 2005).

§ 74. Discharge on holidays, Saturdays and Sundays.

Where the date of release on parole or conditional release, or where the date of discharge from the care or custody of the department, falls on Saturday or Sunday, it shall be deemed to fall on the preceding Friday. Where the date of such release or discharge falls on a legal holiday it shall be deemed to fall on the preceding day, except that when such legal holiday falls on a Monday the date of release shall be deemed to fall on the preceding Friday.

Added by L. 1970, Ch. 476.

§ 79. Leasing of state institutions to cities or counties for the confinement of prisoners.

The commissioner is hereby authorized and empowered to lease to any city or county, upon such terms and conditions as he may deem appropriate, all or any part of any state correctional institution or facility under his jurisdiction, to be used as an adjunct to a jail, penitentiary or correctional institution of such city or county, for the confinement of persons sentenced to such jail, penitentiary, or correctional institution. Such lease may provide for the commissioner to have the superintendence, management and control of the state correctional institution or facility, or part thereof, which is the subject of such lease. Such lease shall provide for such city or county to pay to the state the actual per capita daily cost, as certified to the appropriate local official by the commissioner, for the care of such persons for each day of confinement, but, in any case, the reimbursement rate shall not exceed five dollars per day per capita.

Added by L. 1966, Ch. 651; Amended by L. 1968, Ch. 1080; L. 1970, Ch. 475; L. 1973, Ch. 1054.

§ 79-a. Closure of correctional facilities; notice.

Before the closure of any correctional facility, which for purposes of this section shall include a correctional facility annex, or any special housing unit established to confine inmates in accordance with the provisions of subdivision six of section one hundred thirty-seven of this chapter,

for reasons other than those set forth in paragraph (a) of subdivision eight of section forty-five of this chapter, the commissioner shall take the following actions:

1. confer with the department of civil service, the governor's office of employee relations and any other appropriate state agencies to develop strategies which attempt to minimize the impact of the closure on the state work force;

2. consult with the department of economic development and any other appropriate state agencies to develop strategies which attempt to minimize the impact of such closures on the local and regional economies; and

3. provide notice by certified mail to (i) all local governments of any political subdivision in which the correctional facility is located, (ii) all employee labor organizations operating within, or representing employees of, the correctional facility, and (iii) managerial and confidential employees employed within the correctional facility at least twelve months prior to any such closure.

Added by L. 2005, Ch. 57, Part S, § 3, eff. Apr. 12, 2005; Amended by L. 2005, Ch. 63, Part D, § 2, eff. Apr. 12, 2005.

§ 79-b. Adaptive reuse plan for consideration prior to prison closure.

Not later than six months prior to the effective date of closure of a correctional facility, the commissioner shall, in consultation with the commissioners of economic development, civil service and the division of criminal justice services and the director of the governor's office of employee relations, provide a report for an adaptive reuse plan for any facility slated for closure which will evaluate the community impact of the proposed closure including but not limited to the following factors: the potential to utilize the property for another state government purpose, including for a new purpose as part of the state criminal justice system; potential for the sale or transfer of the property to a local government or other governmental entity; potential for the sale of the property to a private entity for development into a business, residential or other purpose; community input for local development; and the condition of the facility and the investments required to keep the structure in good repair, or to make it viable for reuse.

Added by L. 2005, Ch. 57, Part S, § 3, eff. Apr. 12, 2005; Amended by L. 2005, Ch. 63, Part D, § 2, eff. Apr. 12, 2005.

CORR. L.

ARTICLE 4-B—ALTERNATE CORRECTIONAL FACILITIES FOR THE CITY OF NEW YORK

§ 86. Purpose of alternate correctional facilities.

The purpose of this article is to provide an extraordinary method for relieving existing emergency space pressures in New York city local correctional facilities.

§ 87. Definitions.

As used in this article, the following terms shall have the following meanings:

1. "Alternate correctional facility" shall mean a correctional facility designed to house medium security inmates as defined by department rules and regulations, which is owned by the city of New York, operated by the department pursuant to the rules and regulations promulgated by the commissioner and in accordance with the operation agreement as defined in subdivision five of this section, and used for the confinement of eligible inmates, as defined by subdivision four of this section.

2. "Panel" shall mean the alternate correctional facility review panel established pursuant to section eighty-nine-e of this article.

3. "Construction agreement" shall mean an agreement entered into pursuant to section eighty-eight of this article by the commissioner and the city of New York which governs the construction of two alternate correctional facilities of approximately seven hundred beds each, one at Ogdensburg and one at Cape Vincent, New York.

4. "Eligible inmates" shall mean male inmates of a New York city correctional facility who are at least nineteen years of age, who are serving a definite, but not an intermittent, sentence of imprisonment, and who do not have criminal charges pending against them.

5. "Operation agreement" shall mean an agreement entered into pursuant to section eighty-eight of this article by the commissioner and the city of New York which governs the operation of one or both alternate correctional facilities and addresses all related issues, including, but not limited to, general staffing levels and nature of staffing positions; composition of medical staff; availability of outside medical services; procedures and criteria for selecting eligible inmates; availability and frequency of transportation of inmates and visitors of inmates to such facility; availability, content and frequency of programming for inmates; mechanisms to establish, monitor and review operating and capital expenditures; and legal representation of both inmates and employees of such facilities.

§ 88. Authorization for alternate correctional facilities.

1. As hereinafter provided in this article, the department is authorized and empowered to establish, operate and maintain under its jurisdiction no more than two alternate correctional facilities.

2. In carrying out the purposes of this article, the department may acquire land for and construct the alternate correctional facilities authorized pursuant to this section.

3. Any acquisition of land for or construction of an alternate correctional facility shall be governed by section twenty-one of this chapter, section one hundred twenty-seven of the state finance law and any other provisions of law applicable to the acquisition of land for and construction of state correctional facilities. The department, if it elects, shall be the lead agency for all purposes under article eight of the environmental conservation law with respect to alternate correctional facilities.

4. For each alternate correctional facility, the commissioner is hereby authorized and empowered to enter into a construction agreement, an operation agreement, and any other agreements or leases with the city of New York which are deemed by the commissioner to be necessary or convenient for the establishment, operation and maintenance of an alternate correctional facility. An operation agreement shall govern the operation of an alternate correctional facility for up to ten years after the commencement of housing of eligible inmates at such facility. The commissioner shall not operate an alternate correctional facility except pursuant to an executed operation agreement.

5. All agreements entered into by the commissioner and the city of New York pursuant to this section shall be approved by the director of the budget and filed with the chairman of the senate finance committee, the chairman of the assembly ways and means committee, the chairman of the senate crime and corrections committee and the chairman of the assembly committee on correction.

§ 88-a. Authorization for the city of New York to acquire and utilize alternate correctional facilities.

As set forth in this article, the city of New York, acting by and through its mayor, is authorized and empowered:

1. To enter into a construction agreement as defined in this article and pursuant to such agreement to advance payment for the construction of and to acquire from the state two alternate correctional facilities, one in Ogdensburg and one in Cape Vincent, and to finance such construction and acquisition in the manner provided by law under which the city of New York is authorized to finance property acquired or constructed for public purposes regardless of the period of any operation agreement relating to such facilities.

2. To enter into an operation agreement or agreements as defined in this article and pursuant to any such agreements to utilize alternate correctional facilities for the housing of certain inmates of New York city correctional facilities.

3. To pay to the state the costs, both capital and operating, which may be required of the city of New York by the state in accordance with a

construction agreement or an operation agreement in the manner set forth in any such agreement, including payment in advance of receipt of services.

4. To sell, subject to the provisions of section eighty-nine-k of this article, facilities which were originally acquired from the state as alternate correctional facilities. Upon sale for cash by the city of New York of any facility originally acquired pursuant to a construction agreement as defined in this article, an amount equal to the principal amount of any bonds then outstanding used to finance such acquisition shall be utilized by the city of New York for its general capital purposes.

5. To make provision for indemnification in any construction or operation agreement to conform with the requirements set forth in section eighty-nine-l of this article.

6. From time to time, to authorize, issue and sell obligations, pursuant to the local finance law, to pay the costs of acquiring property, of constructing, alternate correctional facilities, of constructing, reconstructing or otherwise providing other public improvements and appurtenances, including in each case architectural and engineering fees, and of purchasing original furnishings, equipment, machinery and apparatus therefor pursuant to this section. The acquisition of such property, the construction of such correctional facilities, the construction, reconstruction or other provision of other public improvements and appurtenances and the purchase of such original furnishings, equipment, machinery and apparatus are hereby declared city purposes.

§ 89. Establishment of alternate correctional facilities.

An alternate correctional facility shall be deemed to have been established when the commissioner has filed with the secretary of state a designation of such facility which sets forth, at a minimum, the name and location of the facility, a copy of the department's rules and regulations for the operation of that facility, and a copy of all applicable agreements, including a construction agreement and an operation agreement.

§ 89-a. Management of alternate correctional facilities.

1. Superintendence, management and control of alternate correctional facilities and the eligible inmates housed therein shall be as directed by the commissioner consistent with the following: an alternate correctional facility shall be operated pursuant to rules and regulations promulgated for such facilities by the commissioner in consultation with the state commission of correction and the provisions of the operation agreement. The commissioner shall operate such facility insofar as practicable in the same manner as a general

confinement facility which houses medium security state inmates. Nothing herein, however, shall preclude the commissioner from enhancing staffing or programming to accommodate the particular needs of eligible inmates pursuant to the operation agreement. No inmate shall be housed in any alternate correctional facility until such facility has been established in accordance with the provisions of section eighty-nine of this article. The population in an alternate correctional facility shall not exceed its design capacity of approximately seven hundred eligible inmates except pursuant to variances permitted by law, rule or regulation or court order.

2. Notwithstanding any other provisions of law, no variance authorizing an alternate correctional facility to exceed its design capacity shall be granted after March fifteenth, nineteen hundred ninety-two unless the mayor of the city of New York submits, together with the variance request, a certificate of emergency demonstrating the need for such variance and that reasonable alternatives to the granting of the variance do not exist, and containing a detailed summary of measures that will be taken to restore compliance with such design capacity. The chairman of the state commission of correction shall transmit, in a timely manner, notice of such request to the chairman of the senate crime and correction committee and the assembly correction committee.

Amended by L. 1991, Ch. 409, eff. Apr. 1, 1991.

§ 89-b. Good behavior time allowances against definite sentences served in alternate correctional facilities.

Notwithstanding any other provision of law, the commissioner shall be authorized to grant, withhold, cause to be forfeited, or cancel time allowances as provided in and in compliance with section eight hundred four of the correction law.

§ 89-c. Use of alternate correctional facilities.

1. Alternate correctional facilities shall serve only to supplement local correctional facilities within the city of New York. In considering whether to assign an eligible inmate to an alternate correctional facility or to transfer such inmate from such facility, preference shall be given to available space suitable for housing sentenced inmates at local correctional facilities within the city of New York.

2. Consistent with the provisions of this article and subject to the applicable rules and regulations for operation of alternate correctional facilities and the provisions of the operation agreement, assignment of inmates to alternate correctional facilities shall be made jointly by the commissioner and the commissioner of the New York city

department of correction. In making such assignments, consideration shall be given to inmates who have a greater period of time remaining to be served on their sentences, taking into account any applicable jail time and good behavior time. No inmate who is eligible for educational services pursuant to subdivision seven of section three thousand two hundred two of the education law and who chooses to avail himself of such services shall be assigned to an alternate correctional facility.

3. Inmates assigned to alternate correctional facilities shall be returned to a local correctional facility within the city of New York at any such time as the commissioner determines:

(a) that the assignment was not in accordance with this article, or

(b) that the confinement of an inmate in an alternate correctional facility is no longer suitable because it potentially endangers the safety, security or order of the facility.

4. Any inmate who is eligible for educational services pursuant to subdivision seven of section three thousand two hundred two of the education law shall also be returned to a New York city local correctional facility if he chooses to avail himself of such services.

5. Inmates assigned to alternate correctional facilities shall be returned to a New York city correctional facility within the city of New York no later than seven days prior to their scheduled release or discharge from incarceration.

6. Notwithstanding any other provisions of law, no inmates from jurisdictions other than the city of New York shall be housed at any time in an alternate correctional facility.

§ 89-d. Transportation.

The state of New York shall have no responsibility, financial or otherwise, for transporting inmates between a New York city local correctional facility and an alternate correctional facility, regardless of the reason for such transfer. The city of New York shall be responsible for all such costs, as well as the actual transportation and supervision of inmates during transport.

§ 89-e. Alternate correctional facility review panel.

1. The alternate correctional facility review panel is hereby established and shall consist of the commissioner, the chairman of the state commission of correction, the chairman of the board of parole, the director of the division of probation and correctional alternatives, the commissioner of correction of the city of New York, the president of the New York State Sheriffs' Association Institute, Inc., and the president of the Correctional Association of New York or their

designees. The governor shall appoint a chairman and vice-chairman from among the members.

2. The panel shall be authorized to enter and inspect at any and all times each alternate correctional facility or any part thereof and shall have access to all books, records and data pertaining to any such facility within the possession of the department relating to subdivision three of this section.

3. The panel shall examine whether alternate correctional facilities should continue to be utilized, whether all steps practicable have been taken by the city of New York toward finding alternatives to housing eligible inmates in alternate correctional facilities, including the construction of correctional facilities within the city of New York and the development of alternatives to incarceration, and whether there has been compliance with all applicable laws, rules and regulations and the operation agreement.

4. The panel shall prepare an annual report which shall be filed with the governor, the mayor of the city of New York, the chairman of the senate crime and correction committee, and the chairman of the assembly committee, on correction no later than the first day of March of each year.

§ 89-f. Oversight.

The state commission of correction shall exercise the same powers and duties concerning each alternate correctional facility as the commission is required to exercise concerning a New York state correctional facility. The commission shall prepare an annual report on each alternate correctional facility which shall evaluate and assess the department's compliance with all rules and regulations applicable to that facility and the operation agreement and which shall include an analysis of the frequency and severity of all unusual incidents and assaults occurring in that facility. The annual reports shall be filed with the governor, the mayor of the city of New York, the chairman of the senate crime and correction committee, and the chairman of the assembly committee on correction no later than the first day of June of each year.

§ 89-g. Costs for establishing, operating and maintaining alternate correctional facilities.

1. When the city of New York has entered into the agreements as set forth in section eighty-eight of this article, it shall be obligated, to pay, in accordance with such agreements and at such times and in such amounts as may be determined by the commissioner and approved by the director of the budget, all direct and indirect costs associated with the acquisition, construction, establishment, capital repairs and improvements, operation

and maintenance of the alternate correctional facility.

2. Upon completion of the acquisition, construction and establishment of an alternate correctional facility, the commissioner shall make a final determination of the cost of such project and shall certify such cost to the comptroller and to the city of New York. Notwithstanding any other provision of law to the contrary, upon receipt of such certification of the commissioner, the comptroller shall forthwith refund any amounts received from the city of New York in excess of the costs so certified to the city of New York, including interest accrued thereon.

3. On or before October fifteenth of each year, the comptroller shall certify to the commissioner the actual operation and maintenance costs of each alternate correctional facility for the preceding state fiscal year and the amounts paid by the city of New York for such operation and maintenance costs. To the extent that the amounts so paid by the city of New York are less than the operation and maintenance costs for such state fiscal year, the commissioner shall include the amount of such underpayment in the next payment required to be received from the city of New York, or if operation by the state has terminated, the commissioner shall bill the city of New York for the amounts due and such amounts shall be paid by the city within thirty days of receipt of such a bill. To the extent that the amounts so paid by the city of New York are more than the operation and maintenance costs for such state fiscal year, the commissioner shall reduce the next scheduled payment to be received from the city of New York by the amount of the overpayment or if operation by the state has terminated, the commissioner shall refund the overpayment within sixty days of the determination of overpayment.

§ 89-h. Alternate correctional facilities operating fund.

1. There is hereby established in the joint custody of the state comptroller and the commissioner of taxation and finance a special revenue fund to be known as the alternate correctional facilities operating fund.

2. Such fund shall consist of all moneys received by the commissioner pursuant to the operation agreement and all monies received pursuant to section eighty-nine-1 of this article. Any interest accruing on amounts deposited in this fund shall be credited to this fund by the state comptroller and shall reduce the amounts the city of New York would otherwise be obligated to pay pursuant to this article. Upon termination of the operation agreement, any balance in the fund less any amount due from the city of New York hereunder shall be paid to the city of New York within sixty days.

3. In the event that any amounts owed by the

city of New York pursuant to section eighty-nine-g of this article are not paid to the commissioner within thirty days of the time such payment is due, the commissioner shall certify the unpaid amount to the state comptroller and the comptroller shall, to the extent not otherwise prohibited by law and subject to any other provision of law providing for withholding of payments to the city of New York which shall take precedence over this subdivision, withhold any such unpaid amount from the next succeeding payments of state aid or local assistance otherwise payable to the city of New York. The amounts so withheld by the comptroller shall be deposited by the comptroller to the fund established by this section.

4. All payments from this account shall be made on the audit of the comptroller on vouchers certified or approved by the commissioner or an employee of the department designated by the commissioner.

§ 89-i. Local taxes.

Alternate correctional facilities shall be exempt from all local property taxes while fee title to such facilities is vested in the city of New York.

§ 89-j. Title to facilities.

Upon payment by the city of New York of the costs of acquisition and construction, the state of New York shall transfer title in fee simple absolute to the city of New York without additional consideration. Notwithstanding the foregoing, as long as an operation agreement entered into pursuant to this article is in effect, the department shall have sole and exclusive authority to operate, manage and maintain such facility including but not limited to the authority to authorize or make without obtaining approval from the city of New York any capital repairs or improvements deemed necessary.

§ 89-k. Termination of operation agreement.

At the termination of the operation agreement as to either or both alternate correctional facilities, the department shall have an exclusive option to purchase, from the city of New York, the facility or facilities for which the operation agreement has terminated, at a fair market value price or prices which shall be negotiated by the state office of general services and the city of New York. The duration of the state's option to purchase shall commence on the date notice is received from the city of New York of its intent to terminate such agreement and shall continue for a period of six months or until the next succeeding April first, whichever is longer. Such option to purchase shall be deemed exercised upon execution of an agreement to purchase. Notwithstanding any other provision of law, these facilities shall not be operated as correctional facilities except by the department.

§ 89-l. Indemnification.

The city of New York shall indemnify and hold harmless the state of New York in any action or proceeding arising out of the construction, maintenance or operation of an alternate correctional facility which is constructed, maintained or operated in accordance with the provisions of this article. The obligation to indemnify and hold harmless imposed herein shall include reasonable attorney's fees, court costs, and costs of litigation including witness fees, incurred by the state of New York in connection with the defense of any such action or proceeding. Such obligation shall extend to any expenses incurred by the state of New York pursuant to section seventeen of the public officers law for the defense and indemnification of state officers and employees in any action or proceeding arising out of the construction, maintenance or operation of any such facility constructed, maintained and operated in accordance with the provisions of this article and the operating agreement or agreements. The city of New York's obligation to indemnify and hold harmless the state of New York shall in no way be construed as relieving the state of its obligation to comply with any and all orders or injunctions issued by any court of competent jurisdiction.

ARTICLE 5—COORDINATED USE OF STATE AND LOCAL CORRECTIONAL INSTITUTIONS

Section
90.   Purposes of article.
91.   Agreements for custody of definite sentence inmates.
92.   Effect of agreement for custody of definite sentence inmates.
93.   Temporary custody of sentenced inmates in emergencies.
94.   Use of local government institutions for residential treatment of persons under the custody of the state department of correction.
95.   Use of local government institutions for confinement of persons under custody with or awaiting transfer to the department.

§ 90. Purposes of article.

The purposes of the provisions of this article are:

1. To provide correctional programs for persons who receive sentences of imprisonment with terms of one year or less and who otherwise would be confined in institutions in counties that do not have a sufficient number of inmates to justify construction of an adequate correctional institution or operation of a modern correctional program;

2. To provide a method of relieving space pressure in correctional institutions operated by local government; and

3. To expand the use of programs designed to bridge the gap between incarceration and activities in the community, through the use of institutions operated by local government as facilities for residential treatment of persons in the custody of the state department of correction.

Added by L. 1970, Ch. 478.

§ 91. Agreements for custody of definite sentence inmates.

1. The state commissioner of correction may enter into an agreement with any county or with the city of New York to provide for custody by the state department of correction of persons who received definite sentences of imprisonment with terms in excess of ninety days who otherwise would serve such sentences in the jail, workhouse, penitentiary or other local correctional institution maintained by such locality.

2. Any such agreement, except one that is made with the city of New York, may be made with the sheriff, warden, superintendent, local commissioner of correction or other person in charge of such county institution and shall be subject to the approval of the chief executive officer of the county. An agreement made with the city of New York may be made with the commissioner of correction of that city and shall be subject to the approval of the mayor.

3. An agreement made under this section shall not require the locality to pay the cost of treatment, maintenance and custody furnished by the state department of correction and shall contain at least the following provisions:

(a) A provision specifying the minimum length of the term of imprisonment of persons who may be received by the state department of correction under the agreement, which may be any term in excess of ninety days agreed to by the parties and which need not be the same in each agreement;

(b) A provision that no charge will be made to the state or to the state department of correction or to any of its institutions during the pendency of such agreement for delivery of inmates to the state department of correction by officers of the locality, and that the provisions of section six hundred two of this chapter or of any similar law shall not apply for delivery of inmates during such time;

(c) A provision that no charge shall be made to or shall be payable by the state during the pendency of such agreement for the expense of maintaining parole violators pursuant to section two hundred sixteen of this chapter, for the expense of maintaining coram nobis prisoners pursuant to section six hundred one-b of this chapter, or for the expense of maintaining felony prisoners pursuant to section six hundred one-c of this chapter, or for the expense of maintaining alternative local reformatory inmates pursuant to section eight hundred thirty-five in institutions maintained by the locality;

(d) A provision, approved by the state comptroller, for reimbursement of the state department of correction by the locality for expenses incurred under subdivision two or three of section one hundred twenty-five of this chapter relating to clothing, money and transportation furnished upon release or discharge of inmates delivered to the state department of correction pursuant to the agreement;

(e) Designation of the correctional facility or facilities to which persons under sentences covered by the agreement are to be delivered;

(f) Any other provision the state commissioner

CORR. L.

of correction may deem necessary or appropriate; and

(g) A provision giving either party the right to cancel the agreement by giving the other party notice in writing, with cancellation to become effective on such date as may be specified in such notice.

4. A copy of such agreement shall be filed with the secretary of state and with the clerk of each court having jurisdiction to impose sentences covered by the agreement in the county or city to which it applies.

Added by L. 1970, Ch. 478.

§ 92. Effect of agreement for custody of definite sentence inmates.

1. After a copy of an agreement made under section ninety-one of this article is filed with the secretary of state, all commitments under sentences covered by the agreement by courts in the county or city to which it applies shall be deemed to be to the custody of the state department of correction and shall be so construed and interpreted irrespective of the institution or agency to which the commitments are made.

2. Any inmate who is serving a term of imprisonment covered by the agreement imposed prior to the filing of such agreement, and any inmate who is under consecutive definite sentences of imprisonment with an aggregate term of the length covered by the agreement, irrespective of whether one or more of such sentences was imposed prior to the filing of the agreement, may be transferred to the care of the state department of correction upon request of the head of the county or city institution and approval of the state commissioner of correction.

3. Inmates who are deemed committed to the custody of the state department of correction under subdivision one of this section, or who may be transferred to the care of the state department of correction under subdivision two of this section, shall be dealt with in all respects in the same manner as inmates committed to the custody of the state department of correction.

4. In the event any such agreement is cancelled, inmates delivered to the state department of correction prior to the date of cancellation shall continue to serve their sentences in the custody of such department and the provisions of such agreement shall continue to apply with respect to such inmates. A copy of the notice of cancellation shall be filed with the secretary of state and with the clerks of courts in the manner provided in subdivision four of section ninety-one of this article, and no inmates shall be delivered to the custody of the state department of correction under such agreement after the date on which such cancellation becomes effective.

Added by L. 1970, Ch. 478.

§ 93. Temporary custody of sentenced inmates in emergencies.

1. Whenever a state of emergency shall be declared by the chief executive officer of a local government pursuant to section two hundred nine-m of the general municipal law, the chief executive officer of the county in which such state of emergency is declared, or where a county or counties are wholly within a city the mayor of such city, may request the governor to remove all or any number of sentenced inmates from institutions maintained by such county or city. Upon receipt of such request, if the governor is satisfied that the public interest so requires, the governor may, in his discretion, authorize and direct the state commissioner of correction to remove such inmates.

2. Upon receipt of any such direction the state commissioner of correction shall transport such inmates to any correctional facility in the department and such inmates shall be retained in the custody of the department, subject to all laws and rules and regulations pertaining to inmates in the custody of the department, until returned to the institution from which they were removed or discharged or released in accordance with the law.

3. In the event that the state department of correction does not have space in its correctional facilities to accommodate all or any number of the inmates so removed from a local institution, the commissioner of correction shall have the power to lodge any number of such inmates in any county jail, workhouse or penitentiary within the state that has room to receive them and such institution shall be required to receive such inmates. Inmates so lodged shall be subject to all rules and regulations pertaining to inmates committed to such institution until returned to the institution from which they were removed, or removed to a state correctional facility, or discharged or released in accordance with the law; provided, however, that inmates discharged or released from any such local institution shall be entitled to receive clothing, money and transportation from the state department of correction to the same extent as inmates discharged or released from a state correctional facility.

4. When sentenced inmates have been removed from a penitentiary pursuant to this section, such penitentiary may be used for the purpose of detention of prisoners awaiting trial or for any other purpose to which a county jail may be put.

5. The original order of commitment and any other case record pertaining to inmates removed pursuant to this section shall be delivered to the head of any institution in which he may be lodged and shall be returned to the institution from which he was removed at the time of his return to such institution or upon his release or discharge in accordance with the law.

6. Inmates removed from a local institution pursuant to a request made under subdivision one of this section may be returned to such institution by the state commissioner of correction, subject to the approval of the governor, at any time such commissioner is satisfied that the return of such inmates is not inconsistent with the public interest.

7. The county or city maintaining the institution from which inmates are removed pursuant to subdivision one of this section shall be liable for all damages arising out of any act performed pursuant to this section and for reimbursement for the following items:

(a) The cost of clothing, money and transportation furnished to any inmate who is released or discharged prior to the return of such inmate to the institution from which he is removed shall be paid to the state department of correction; and

(b) The cost of maintaining any inmate in a county jail, workhouse or penitentiary shall be paid to the local government that maintains such institution. Such cost shall be the actual per capita daily cost, as certified to the state commissioner of correction.

Added by L. 1970, Ch. 478.

§ 94. Use of local government institutions for residential treatment of persons under the custody of the state department of correction.

1. The state commissioner of correction is hereby authorized to transfer any inmate under the care or custody of the department who is eligible to be transferred to a residential treatment facility under section seventy-three of this chapter to any county jail, workhouse or penitentiary for the purpose of having such inmate engage in a residential treatment facility program; provided, however, that:

(a) Such inmate has resided or was employed or has dependents or parents who reside in the county or in a county that is contiguous to the county, in which the institution to which he would be transferred is located;

(b) Arrangements have been made for the education, on-the-job training, employment or for some other rehabilitative treatment of such inmate in the county, or in a county that is contiguous to the county, in which the institution to which he would be transferred is located; and

(c) The sheriff, warden, superintendent, local commissioner of correction or other person in charge of the institution to which the inmate would be transferred consents to such transfer.

2. An inmate so transferred shall continue to be in the custody of the state department of correction but shall, during the period of such transfer, be in the care of the head of the institution to which he is transferred. The provisions of section seventy-three of this chapter shall apply in the case of any such transfer as fully and completely as if the inmate were transferred to a residential treatment facility, and the head of the institution to which the inmate is transferred and the officers and employees thereof shall have and may exercise all of the powers of the superintendent of a residential treatment facility with respect to the care or custody of such inmate.

In any case where an inmate is employed, however, the provisions of subdivision nine of such section seventy-three shall not apply and the wages or salary of such inmate shall be dealt with under the provisions applicable to a work release program in the type of institution to which he is transferred as provided in sections one hundred fifty-four, eight hundred seventy-two or eight hundred ninety-three as the case may be; and in the event such inmate is returned to a state correctional facility, any balance remaining in the trust fund account shall be paid over to the superintendent of such facility and shall be deposited by him as inmates' funds pursuant to section one hundred sixteen of this chapter.

3. If at any time the head of a local institution to which an inmate is transferred under this section is of the opinion that continued care of such inmate in such institution is inconsistent with the welfare or safety of the community or of the institution or its inmates, he may request the state commissioner to return such inmate to a state correctional facility and, upon the receipt of any such request, the commissioner shall cause such inmate to be so returned promptly and at the expense of the state department of correction.

4. The expenses of any such transfer shall be paid by the state department of correction and the commissioner is hereby authorized to reimburse the local institution for a sum determined by the head of such institution and agreed to in advance by the state commissioner of correction to be the cost of food, lodging and clothing within the institution, and the actual and necessary food, travel and other expenses required for a program outside the institution, incurred or advanced by the institution; provided, however, that:

(a) In any case where the state commissioner of correction has a pending agreement with a locality under section ninety-one of this article, the commissioner of correction shall not reimburse the local institution for any costs incurred for food, lodging and clothing within the institution; and

(b) The wages or salary, if any, of such inmate shall be used for such reimbursement and shall be applied to defray any costs authorized to be paid under this section before any amount shall be paid by the commissioner of correction hereunder, and any such wages or salary may be so applied irrespective of the provisions of paragraph (a) of this subdivision.

Added by L. 1970, Ch. 478, eff. July 1, 1970.

§ 95. Use of local government institutions for confinement of persons under custody with or awaiting transfer to the department.

1. Notwithstanding any other provision of law, the commissioner is hereby authorized to contract with any county or the city of New York for the use of a local correctional facility to provide for the care and custody of any person convicted of an offense and sentenced to a determinate or to an indeterminate sentence of imprisonment who is awaiting transfer to or has been transferred to the custody of the department as required by section 430.20 of the criminal procedure law; provided, however, that any such contract under this section shall not include persons charged with or found to be in violation of parole or conditional release pursuant to subdivision three of section two hundred fifty-nine-i of the executive law.

2. Any such inmate shall be deemed to be in the custody of and subject to the jurisdiction of the department but shall, during the period of his or her local confinement, be under the care of the head of the local correctional facility in which he or she resides.

3. If at any time the head of the local correctional facility is of the opinion that the continued care of such inmate in the local correctional facility is inconsistent with the welfare or safety of the inmate, the community, the facility or other inmates, he may demand that such inmate be transferred forthwith to the custody of the department. Thereafter, the department shall be obligated to receive into its custody such inmate in the manner prescribed for the acceptance of newly sentenced inmates required by section 430.20 of the criminal procedure law unless the contract specifies an alternative method of transfer. Notwithstanding the foregoing, in any case where the inmate in the care of the local correctional facility pursuant to a contract as provided for in this section is convicted of a class A-1 felony offense or a class B violent felony offense or a class C violent felony offense, the head of the local correctional facility may demand that such inmate be transferred forthwith to the custody of the department. Thereafter, the department shall be obligated to receive into its custody such inmate within forty-eight hours of receipt of such demand from the head of the local correctional facility.

4. The commissioner is hereby authorized to reimburse the contracting county or the city of New York for a sum equivalent to the actual per day per capita cost, as certified by the appropriate local official, or one hundred dollars per day per capita, whichever is less.

5. No inmate shall be housed in a local correctional facility or series of local correctional facilities pursuant to a contract under subdivision one of this section for a period exceeding six months.

Added by L. 1995, Ch. 3, § 59, eff. June 10, 1995; **Amended** by L. 1997, Ch. 435, § 46, eff. Aug. 20, 1997; L. 1999, Ch. 518, § 1, eff. Sept. 28, 1999.

ARTICLE 5-A—INTERSTATE CORRECTIONS COMPACT

Section

§ 100. Compact.

The interstate corrections compact as set forth in this article is hereby adopted and entered into with all jurisdictions joining therein.

§ 101. Short title; purpose.

This article shall be known and may be cited as the "interstate corrections compact." The party states, desiring common action to fully utilize and improve their institutional facilities and provide adequate programs for the confinement, treatment and rehabilitation of various types of offenders, declare that it is the policy of each of the party states to provide such facilities and programs on a basis of cooperation with one another, thereby serving the best interests of such offenders and of society and effecting economies in capital expenditures and operational costs. The purpose of this compact is to provide for the mutual development and execution of such programs of cooperation for the confinement, treatment and rehabilitation of offenders with the most economical use of human and material resources.

§ 102. Definitions.

As used in this compact, unless the context clearly requires otherwise:

(a) "State" means a state of the United States; the United States of America; a territory or possession of the United States; the District of Columbia; the Commonwealth of Puerto Rico.

(b) "Sending state" means a state party to this compact in which conviction or court commitment was had.

(c) "Receiving state" means a state party to this compact to which an inmate is sent for confinement other than a state in which conviction or court commitment was had.

(d) "Inmate" means a male or female offender who is committed, under sentence to or confined in a penal or correctional institution.

(e) "Institution" means any penal or correctional facility, including but not limited to a facility for the mentally ill or mentally defective, in which inmates as defined in subdivision (d) hereof may lawfully be confined.

§ 103. Contracts.

(a) Each party state may make one or more contracts with any one or more of the other party states for the confinement of inmates on behalf of a sending state in institutions situated within receiving states. Any such contract shall provide for:

1. Its duration.

2. Payments to be made to the receiving state by the sending state for inmate maintenance, extraordinary medical and dental expenses, and any participation in or receipt by inmates of rehabilitative or correctional services, facilities, programs or treatment not reasonably included as part of normal maintenance.

3. Participation in programs of inmate employment, if any; the disposition or crediting of any payments received by inmates on account thereof; and the crediting of proceeds from or disposal of any products resulting therefrom.

4. Delivery and retaking of inmates.

5. Such other matters as may be necessary and appropriate to fix the obligations, responsibilities and rights of the sending and receiving states.

(b) The terms and provisions of this compact shall be a part of any contract entered into by the authority of or pursuant thereto, and nothing in any such contract shall be inconsistent therewith.

§ 104. Procedures and rights.

(a) Whenever the duly constituted authorities in a state party to this compact, and which has entered into a contract pursuant to section one hundred three of this article, shall decide that confinement in, or transfer of an inmate to, an institution within the territory of another party state is necessary or desirable in order to provide adequate quarters and care or an appropriate program of rehabilitation or treatment, said officials may direct that the confinement be within an institution within the territory of said other party state, the receiving state to act in that regard solely as agent for the sending state.

(b) The appropriate officials of any state party to this compact shall have access, at all reasonable times, to any institution in which it has a contractual right to confine inmates for the purpose of inspecting the facilities thereof and visiting such of its inmates as may be confined in the institution.

(c) Inmates confined in an institution pursuant to the terms of this compact shall at all times be subject to the jurisdiction of the sending state and may at any time be removed therefrom for transfer to a prison or other institution within the sending state, for transfer to another institution in which the sending state may have a contractual or other right to confine inmates, for release on probation or parole, for discharge, or for any other purpose permitted by the laws of the sending state; provide that the sending state shall continue to be obligated to such payments as may be required pursuant to the terms of any contract entered into under the terms contained in section one hundred three of this article.

(d) Each receiving state shall provide regular reports to each sending state on the inmates of that sending state in institutions pursuant to this compact including a conduct record of each inmate and certify said record to the official designated by the sending state, in order that each inmate may have official review of his or her record in determining and altering the disposition of said inmate in accordance with the law which may obtain in the sending state and in order that the same may be a source of information for the sending state.

(e) All inmates who may be confined in an institution pursuant to the provisions of this compact shall be treated in a reasonable and humane manner and shall be treated equally with such similar inmates of the receiving state as may be confined in the same institution. The fact of confinement in a receiving state shall not deprive any inmate so confined of any legal rights which said inmate would have had if confined in an appropriate institution of the sending state.

(f) Any hearing or hearings to which an inmate confined pursuant to this compact may be entitled by the laws of the sending state may be had before the appropriate authorities of the sending state, or of the receiving state if authorized by the sending state. The receiving state shall provide adequate facilities for such hearings as may be conducted by the appropriate officials of a sending state. In the event such hearing or hearings are had before officials of the receiving state, the governing law shall be that of the sending state and a record of the hearing or hearings as prescribed by the sending state shall be made. Said record together with any recommendations of the hearing officials shall be transmitted forthwith to the official or officials before whom the hearing would have been had if it had taken place in the sending state. In any and all proceedings had pursuant to the provisions of this subdivision, the officials of the receiving state shall act solely as agents of the sending state and no final determination shall be made in any matter except by the appropriate officials of the sending state.

(g) Any inmate confined pursuant to this compact shall be released within the territory of the sending state unless the inmate, and the sending and receiving states, shall agree upon release in some other place. The sending state shall bear the cost of such return to its territory.

(h) Any inmate confined pursuant to the terms of this compact shall have any and all rights to participate in and derive any benefits or incur or be relieved of any obligations or have such obligations modified or his status changed on account of any action or proceeding in which he could have participated if confined in any appropriate institution of the sending state located within such state.

(i) The parent, guardian, trustee, or other person or persons entitled under the laws of the sending state to act for, advise, or otherwise function with respect to any inmate shall not be deprived of or restricted in his exercise of any power in respect to any inmate confined pursuant to the terms of this compact.

§ 105. Acts not reviewable in receiving state; extradition.

(a) Any decision of the sending state in respect to any matter over which it retains jurisdiction pursuant to this compact shall be conclusive upon and not reviewable within the receiving state, but if at the time the sending state seeks to remove an inmate from an institution in the receiving state there is pending against the inmate within such state any criminal charge or if the inmate is formally accused of having committed within such state a criminal offense, the inmate shall not be returned without the consent of the receiving state until discharged from prosecution or other form of proceeding, imprisonment or detention for such offense. The duly accredited officers of the sending state shall be permitted to transport inmates pursuant to this compact through any and all states party to this compact without interference.

(b) Any inmate who escapes from an institution in which he is confined pursuant to this compact shall be deemed a fugitive from the sending state and from the state in which the institution is situated. In the case of any escape to a jurisdiction other that the sending or receiving state, the responsibility for institution of extradition or rendition proceedings shall be that of the sending state, but nothing contained herein shall be construed to prevent or affect the activities of officers and agencies of any jurisdiction directed toward the apprehension and return of the escapee.

§ 106. Federal aid.

Any state party to this compact may accept federal aid for use in connection with any institution or program, the use of which is or may be affected by this compact or any contract pursuant hereto and any inmate in a receiving state pursuant to this compact may participate in any such federally aided program or activity for which the sending and receiving states have made contractual provision, provided that if such program or activity is not part of the customary correctional regimen, the express consent of the appropriate official of the sending state shall be required therefor.

§ 107. Entry into force.

This compact shall enter into force and become effective and binding upon the states so acting when it has been enacted into law by any two states. Thereafter, this compact shall enter into force and become effective and binding as to any other of said states upon similar action by such state.

§ 108. Withdrawal and termination.

This compact shall continue in force and remain binding upon a party state until it shall have enacted a statute repealing the same and providing for the sending of formal written notice of withdrawal from the compact to the appropriate officials of all other party states. An actual withdrawal shall not take effect until one year after the notices provided in said statute have been sent. Such withdrawal shall not relieve the withdrawing state from its obligations assumed hereunder prior to the effective date of withdrawal. Before the effective date of withdrawal, a withdrawing state shall remove to its territory, at its own expense, such inmates as it may have confined pursuant to the provisions of this compact.

§ 109. Construction and severability.

(a) Nothing contained in this compact shall be construed to abrogate or impair any agreement or other arrangement which a party state may have with a nonparty state for the confinement, rehabilitation or treatment of inmates nor to repeal any other laws of a party state authorizing the making of cooperative institutional arrangements.

(b) The provisions of this compact shall be liberally construed and shall be severable. If any phrase, clause, sentence or provision of this compact is declared to be contrary to the constitution of any participating state or of the United States or the applicability thereof to any government, agency, person or circumstance is held invalid, the validity of the remainder of this compact and the applicability thereof to any government, agency, person or circumstance shall not be affected thereby. If this compact shall be held contrary to the constitution of any state participating therein, the compact shall remain in full force and effect as to the remaining states and in full force and effect as to the state affected as to all severable matters.

Added by L. 1984, Ch. 400, eff. July 19, 1984.

CORR. L.

ARTICLE 6—MANAGEMENT OF CORRECTIONAL FACILITIES

§ 112. Powers and duties of commissioner of correction relating to correctional facilities.

1. The commissioner of correction shall have the superintendence, management and control of the correctional facilities in the department and of the inmates confined therein, and of all matters relating to the government, discipline, policing, contracts and fiscal concerns thereof. He shall have the power and it shall his duty to inquire into all matters connected with said correctional facilities. He shall make such rules and regulations, not in conflict with the statutes of this state, for the government of the officers and other employees of the department assigned to said facilities, and in regard to the duties to be performed by them, and for the government and discipline of each correctional facility, as he may deem proper, and shall cause such rules and regulations to be recorded by the superintendent of the facility, and a copy thereof to be furnished to each employee assigned to the facility. He shall also prescribe a system of accounts and records to be kept at each correctional facility, which system shall be uniform at all of said facilities, and he shall also make rules and regulations for a record of photographs and other means of identifying each inmate received into said facilities. He shall appoint and remove, subject to the civil service law and rules, subordinate officers and other employees of the department who are signed to correctional facilities.

2. The commissioner of correction may require reports from the superintendent or any other officer or employee of the department assigned to any correctional facility in relation to his conduct as such officer or employee, and shall have the power to inquire into any improper conduct which may be alleged to have been committed by any person at any correctional facility, and for that purpose to issue subpoenas to compel the attendance of witnesses, and the production before him of books, writings and papers. A subpoena issued under this section shall be regulated by the civil practice law and rules. The commissioner of correction is authorized and empowered to lease the railroad, constructed

under and by the authority of the laws of eighteen hundred and seventy-eight, chapter one hundred and forty-eight, for such term of years and upon such terms and conditions as shall be approved of in writing, by the governor and comptroller of this state.

Amended by L. 1960, Ch. 54L. 1962, Ch. 310. L. 1970. Ch. 476; L. 1971 Ch. 1097; L. 1995, Ch. 1, § 33, repealing subd. 3, eff. Sept. 1, 1995.

ANNOTATIONS

Constitutionality.—Directive which required newly committed inmates to submit to a haircut and shave upon commencing their sentence was unconstitutional as applied to defendant, an avowed Rastafarian. People v. Lewis, 115 A.D.2d 597, 496 N.Y.S.2d 258 (2d Dept. 1985).

—Because it has been held that assessment of mandatory penalty surcharge does not violate inmate's due process rights, court rejected petitioner's claim that imposition of surcharge was unconstitutional; Correction Law §§ 112 and 137 vest Commissioner of Correctional Services with discretion to impose such a surcharge. Doggett v. Goord, 252 A.D.2d 867, 675 A.D.2d 714 (3d Dept. 1998).

§ 113. Absence of inmate for funeral and deathbed visits or to report at an induction center for preinduction examination authorized.

The commissioner of correctional services may permit any inmate confined by the department except one awaiting the sentence of death to attend the funeral of his or her father, mother, guardian or former guardian, child, brother, sister, husband, wife, grandparent, grandchild, ancestral uncle or ancestral aunt within the state, or to visit such individual during his or her illness if death be imminent or to report to an induction center for the purpose of being examined for possible induction into the armed forces of the United States; but the exercise of such power shall be subject to such rules and regulations as the commissioner of correctional services shall prescribe, respecting the granting of such permission, duration of absence from the institution, custody, transportation and care of the inmate, and guarding against escape. Any expense incurred under the provisions of this section, with respect to any inmate permitted to attend a funeral or visit a relative during last illness, shall be deemed an expense of maintenance of the institution and be paid from moneys available therefor; but the superintendent, if the rules and regulations of the commissioner of correctional services shall so provide, may allow the inmate or anyone in his behalf to reimburse the state for such expense. Any expense of custodial officers incurred in delivering and returning inmates to and from an induction center shall be deemed an expense of the institution and be paid from moneys available therefor but expenses of such inmates shall not be defrayed by the institution or department of the state.

Amended by L. 1973, Ch. 269 L. 1979, Ch. 145, eff. May 29, 1979.

ANNOTATION

Constitutionality.—Because it has been held that assessment of mandatory penalty surcharge does not violate inmate's due process rights, court rejected petitioner's claim that imposition of surcharge was unconstitutional; Correction Law §§ 112 and 137 vest Commissioner of Correctional Services with discretion to impose such a surcharge. Doggett v. Goord, 252 A.D.2d 867, 675 A.D.2d 714 (3d Dept. 1998).

§ 115. Fiscal accounts and records.

1. The superintendent of each correctional facility shall maintain books of entry and such other records as may be deemed necessary by the commissioner of correction in order to fully account for cash receipts from all sources and all cash disbursements from accounts established in the name of the facility or the superintendent. Such books and records shall be in a form prescribed by the commissioner of correction and shall be open at all times to the commissioner and the comptroller and their authorized representatives.

2. The superintendent of each correctional facility shall also cause to be prepared an annual inventory of the equipment and furnishings received by the facility and to maintain same for the purpose of audit or examination by the commissioner, the comptroller or their authorized representatives.

3. All purchases for the use of any correctional facility shall be made in conformance with the rules and regulations in effect or established by the commissioner of correction, the comptroller and the Commissioner of the office of general service. The superintendent of each correctional, facility shall cause to be maintained a record of all bills and receipts for expenditures made for goods or services for the facility for the purpose of audit or examination by the commissioner, the comptroller or their designated representatives.

Repealed former § 115 and Added new § 115 by L. 1970. Ch. 476.

§ 116. Inmates' funds.

The warden or superintendent of each of the institutions within the jurisdiction of the department of correction shall deposit at least once in each week to his credit as such warden, or superintendent, in such bank or banks as may be designated by the comptroller, all the moneys received by him as such warden, or superintendent, as inmates' funds, and send to the comptroller and also to the commissioner of correction monthly, a statement showing the amount so received and deposited. Such statement of deposits shall be certified by the proper officer of the bank receiving such deposit or deposits. The warden, or superintendent, shall also verify by his affidavit that the sum so deposited is all the money received by him as inmates' funds during the month. Any bank in which such deposits shall be made shall, before receiving any such deposits, file a bond with the comptroller of the state, subject to his approval, for such sum as he shall deem necessary. Upon a certificate of approval issued by the director of the budget, pursuant to the provisions of section fifty-three of the state finance law, the amount of interest, if any, heretofore accrued and hereafter to accrue on moneys so deposited, heretofore and hereafter credited to the warden, or superintendent, by the bank from time to time, shall be available for expenditure by the warden, or superintendent, subject to the direction of the commissioner, for welfare work among the inmates in his custody. The withdrawal of moneys so deposited by such warden, or superintendent, as inmates' funds, including any interest so credited, shall be subject to his check. Each warden, or superintendent, shall each month provide the comptroller and also the commissioner with a record of all withdrawals from inmates' funds. As used in this section, the term "inmates' funds" means the funds in the possession of the inmate at the time of his admission into the institution, funds earned by him as provided in section one hundred eighty-seven of this chapter and any other funds received by him or on his behalf and deposited with such warden or superintendent in accordance with the rules and regulations of the commissioner. Whenever the total unencumbered value of funds in an inmate's account exceeds ten thousand dollars, the superintendent shall give written notice to the state crime victims board.

Amended by L. 2001, Ch. 62, §5, eff. June 25, 2001, and shall apply to: (i) all judgments originally entered prior to such effective date, regardless whether such judgment is subsequently amended or satisfied on or after such effective date; and (ii) all judgments, obligations or agreements to pay profits from a crime or funds of a convicted person entered, incurred or entered into on or after the effective date of this act.

§ 117. Estimates of expenses.

The superintendent of each correctional facility shall cause to be prepared, at the direction of the commissioner, periodic estimates of expenditures in such form and detail and for such periods as the commissioner may deem appropriate.

Repealed former § 117 and Added new § 117 by L. 1970, Ch. 476.

§ 118. Custody and supervision of persons in Westchester County correctional facilities.

1. The duty of maintaining the custody and supervision of persons detained or confined in a local correctional facility as defined in subdivision sixteen of section two of this chapter and such facility is located in the county of Westchester shall be performed solely by correction officers of the Westchester County correction department. This duty, in whole or in part, shall not be delegated, transferred or assigned.

2. As used in this section, "correction officer" of the Westchester County correction department means a correction officer, correction officer-sergeant, correction officer-captain, assistant warden, associate warden or warden.

Added by L. 1997, Ch. 583, § 1, eff. Sept. 17, 1997.

§ 119. Daily report concerning inmates.

The superintendent of each correctional facility shall make a daily report to the commissioner of correction, stating the names of all inmates received into the facility during the preceding day, the counties in which they were tried, the crimes of which they were convicted, the nature and duration of their sentences, their former trade, employment or occupation, their habits, color, age, place of nativity degree of instruction, and a description of their persons, and also stating whether any such inmates have ever been confined in any state or county correctional institution, and if so, stating the offence for which they were confined, and the duration of their punishment, and also stating in such report the names of all the inmates transferred or released to the community or delivered to other governmental authority on the preceding day, and all other particulars required to be stated in relation to the inmates received in the facility.

Amended by L. 1970, Ch. 476.

§ 122. Control of fiscal transactions and recovery of debts.

All the fiscal transactions and dealings on accounts of each correctional facility shall be conducted by and in the name of the superintendent thereof, who shall have control over all matters of finance relating to such facility, subject to the direction and supervision of the commissioner of correction. Such superintendent shall be capable in law of suing in all courts and places, and in all matters concerning the facility, by his name of office, and by that name shall be authorized to sue for and recover all sums of money due from any person to any former agent, gent and superintendent or superintendent of the facility, or to the people of this state on account of such facility. But it shall not be lawful in any such suit or action for any defendant to plead or give in evidence any offset or matter by way of recoupment or counterclaim except for payments made, and not credited to such defendant, or to recover any judgment against such superintendent in such suit or action other than for the costs and disbursements therein. Each superintendent shall enforce the payment of all debts due to the facility under his charge with as little delay as possible, but subject to the approbation of the commissioner of correction, he may accept any security from any debtor on granting him time, that he may deem, conducive to the interests of the state. The commissioner of correction or any person authorized in the rules and regulations of the department may at any time exercise the powers granted to a superintendent hereunder.

Amended by L. 1970, Ch. 476.

§ 125. Inmates' money, clothing and other property; what to be furnished them on their release.

1. The superintendent, or an employee covered by bond who is designated by the superintendent, of each correctional facility shall take charge of all moneys and other articles which may be brought to the facility by the inmates, and shall cause the same, immediately upon the receipt thereof, to be entered among the receipts of the facility; which money and other articles whenever the inmate from whom the same was received shall be discharged from the custody of the department, or the same shall be otherwise legally entitled to the same, and vouchers shall be taken therefor. The commissioner shall promulgate rules and regulations concerning the custody and transfer of such money and other articles in cases where inmates are transferred from one facility to another.

2. The superintendent of each of said facilities shall furnish to each inmate who shall be discharged or released from said facility by pardon, parole, conditional release or otherwise, except such inmates as are released for return for resentence or new trial or upon a certificate of reasonable doubt, and except such inmates who are released to participate in a program outside the facility who are required to return to the facility, suitable clothing adapted to the season in which he is discharged not to exceed sixty-five dollars in value and transportation to the county of his conviction or to such other place as the commissioner of correctional services may designate. In addition, the commissioner shall take such steps as are necessary to ensure that inmates have at least forty dollars available upon release.

3. In any case where an inmate is not entitled to receive clothing and transportation under subdivision two of this section the superintendent, in his discretion, but subject to the rules of the department, may furnish an inmate who is released from a facility with clothing or transportation not in excess of the value for each item specified in subdivision two of this section.

Amended by L. 1973, Ch. 462; L. 1992, Ch. 55, eff. Apr. 10, 1992, amending subds. 2 and 3.

ANNOTATION

Generally.—Prison officials have the right to control the property and possessions within the prison under their supervision. Marcelin v. Coughlin, 193 A.D.2d 981, 598 N.Y.S.2d 354 (3d Dept. 1993).

§ 126. Punishment of superintendent for neglect of duty.

If the superintendent of a correctional facility shall wilfully neglect or refuse to make any weekly or monthly return, estimate or statement, or to transmit any statement and certificate of such deposits to the comptroller, as hereby directed, it shall be the duty of the comptroller to notify the commissioner of correction of such omissions, and it shall be the duty of the commissioner of correction to order the superintendent to be prosecuted for the recovery of any moneys which may be in his hands belonging to the state. The superintendent of a correctional facility shall be liable to indictment and punishment for any wilful neglect of duty, or for any malpractice in the discharge of the duties of his office.

Amended by L. 1970, Ch. 476: L. 1971, Ch. 460.

§ 130. Custody of inmate sentenced to death and commuted by governor.

The commissioner shall designate appropriate correctional facilities to receive, on the order of the governor, any person convicted of any crime punishable by death, or who shall be pardoned, on condition of being confined either for life or a term of years in a correctional facility, and such person shall be confined according to the terms of such condition.

Amended by L. 1970, Ch. 476.

§ 132. Retaking of an escaped inmate.

If an inmate escapes from a correctional facility, he may be arrested and returned by the superintendent or by an officer or employee of the department or by any peace officer, acting pursuant to his special duties, or police officer without a warrant; or a magistrate may cause such escaped inmate to be arrested and held in custody until he can be removed to a correctional facility, as in the case of a commitment. Rewards for the taking of such escaped inmates may be provided for by the rules of the department.

Repealed former § 132 and Added new § 132 by L. 1970, Ch. 476; Amended by L. 1980. Ch, 843 eff. Sept. 1, 1980.

§ 133. Superintendent to report concerning inmate believed mentally ill when crime was committed.

Whenever the superintendent of a correctional facility shall have reason to believe that any inmate in the facility was mentally ill at the time he committed the offense for which he was sentenced, such superintendent shall communicate in writing to the commissioner of correction his reason for such opinion and shall refer the commissioner of correction to all the source of information with which he may be acquainted in relation to the mental illness of such inmate. The commissioner of correction shall then transmit such opinion and information to the governor with his recommendations thereon.

Amended by L. 1970, Ch. 476, L. 1978 550. eff. July 24, 1978.

§ 136. Correctional education.

The objective of correctional education in its broadest sense should be the socialization of the inmates through varied impressional and expressional activities, with emphasis on individual inmate needs. The objective of this program shall be the return of these inmates to society with a more wholesome attitude toward living, with a desire to conduct themselves as good citizens and with the skill and knowledge which will give them a reasonable chance to maintain themselves and their dependents through hones labor. To this end each inmate shall be given a program of education which, on the basis of available data, seems most likely to further the process of socialization and rehabilitation. The time daily devoted to such education shall be such as is required for meeting the above objectives. The director of education, subject to the direction of the commissioner of correction and after consultation by such commissioner with the state commissioner of education, shall develop the curricula and the education programs that are required to meet the special needs of each correctional facility in the department. The state commissioner of education, in cooperation with the commissioner of correction and the director of education, shall set up the educational requirements for the certification of teachers in all such correctional facilities. Such educational requirements shall be sufficiently broad and comprehensive to include training in penology, sociology, psychology, philosophy, in the special subjects to be taught, and in any other professional courses as may be deemed necessary by the responsible officers. No certificates for teaching service in the state institutions shall be issued unless minimum of our years of training beyond the high school has been secured, or an acceptable equivalent. Existing requirements for the certification of teachers in the institutions shall continue in force until changed pursuant to the provisions of this section.

Amended by L. 1970, Ch. 476.

§ 137. Program of treatment, control, discipline at correctional facilities.

1. The commissioner shall establish program and classification procedures designed to assures the complete study of the background and condition of each inmate in the care of custody of the department and the assignment of such inmate to a program that is most likely to be useful in assisting him to refrain from future violations of the law. Such procedures shall be incorporated into the rules and regulations of the department and shall require among other things: consideration of the physical, mental and emotional condition of the inmate; consideration of his education and vocational needs; consideration of the danger he presents to the community or to other inmates' the recording of continuous case histories including notations as to apparent success or failure of treatment employed; and periodic review of case histories and treatment methods used.

2. The commissioner shall provide for such measures as he may deem necessary or appropriate for the safety, security and control of correctional facilities and the maintenance of order therein.

3. Each inmate shall be entitled to clothing suited to the season and weather conditions and to a sufficient quantity of wholesome and nutritious food. To the extent practicable, the clothing and bedding of inmates shall be manufactured and laundered in institutions in the department.

4. Whenever there shall be a sufficient number of cells or rooms in a correctional facility, each inmate shall be given sleeping accommodations in a separate cell or room, provided, however, that nothing herein contained shall be construed so as to limit the right of the department to utilize dormitory-type accommodations where necessary or where appropriate to a program of treatment.

5. No inmate in the care or custody of the department shall be subjected to degrading treatment, and no officer or other employee of the department shall inflict any blows whatever upon any inmate, unless in self defense, or to suppress a revolt or insurrection. When any inmate, or group of inmates, shall offer violence to any person, or do or attempt to do any injury to property, or attempt to escape, or resist or disobey any lawful direction, the officers and employees shall use all suitable means to defend themselves, to maintain order, to enforce observation of discipline, to secure the persons of the offenders and to prevent any such attempts or escape.

6. The superintendent of a correctional facility may keep any inmate confined in a cell or room, apart from the accommodations provided for inmates who are participating in programs of the facility, for such period as may be necessary for maintenance or order or discipline, but in any such case the following conditions shall be observed:

(a) The inmate shall be supplied with a sufficient quantity of wholesome and nutritious food, provided, however, that such food need not be the same as the food supplied to inmates who are participating in programs of the facility;

(b) Adequate sanitary and other conditions required for the health of the inmate shall be maintained;

(c) Where such confinement is for a period in excess of twenty-four hours, the superintendent shall arrange for the facility health services director or a registered nurse of physician's associate approved by the facility health services director, to visit such inmate at the expiration of twenty-four hours and at least once in every twenty-four hour period thereafter, during the period of such confinement, to examine into the state of health of the inmate, and the superintendent shall give full consideration to any recommendation that may be made by the facility health services director for measures with respect to dietary needs or conditions of confinement of such inmate required to maintain the health of such inmate; and

(d) The superintendent shall make a full report to the commissioner at least once a week concerning the condition of such inmate and shall forth with report to the commissioner any recommendation relative to health maintenance or health care delivery made by the facility health services director that is not endorsed or carried out, as the case may be, by the superintendent.

Repealed former § 137 and **Added** new § 137 by L. 1970, Ch 476; **Amended** by L. 1974, Ch. 490.

ANNOTATIONS

Chain of custody.—In order to annual a determination upon an alleged chain of custody defect, a petition must point to evidence adduced at the hearing indicating that the specimen could have been confused with similar samples or that there was no evidence to substantiate the chain of custody. Price v. Coughlin, 116 A.D.2d 898, 498 N.Y.S.2d 209 (3d Dept. 1986).

Counseling and rehabilitative program.—An adjournment before trial, in order for the defendant to participate in a counseling and rehabilitative program (operation Midway) was not an abuse of discretion, notwithstanding the fact that the prosecutor had not consented, People v. Fusco, 85 Misc. 2d 147, 378 N.Y.S.2d 902 (Nassau Co. Ct. 1975).

Censorship of mail.—Censorship of direct personal correspondence of prison inmates is justified if such overview of correspondence is in furtherance of a government interest to preserve internal order and discipline and to maintain institutional security against escape or unauthorized entry. Montgomery v. Jones, 88 A.D.2d 1003, 451 N.Y.S.2d 897 (3d Dept. 1982).

Disciplinary proceeding; evidence.—Written misbehavior report prepared by a corrections officer who witnessed the incident, supported by a taped interview with that officer constituted substantial evidence in disciplinary proceeding. Johnson v. Smith, 115 A. D. 2d 284, 496 N.Y.S.2d 153 (4th Dept. 1985).

Hearing.—Since there is no right to confrontation or cross examination, and consequently no requirement that the disciplinary authority call any adverse witnesses to testify at the hearing, the failure of the hearing officer to call three inmate officers (which was done for their protection) did not violate any constitutional right of petitioner. Smith v. Lefeure, 116 A.D.2d 782, 497 N.Y.S.2d 174 (3d Dept. 1986).

Knowledge of disciplinary rules.—Actual not merely constructive knowledge of facility rules by inmate is prerequisite to discipline of inmate for violation of a rule. Barnes v. Smith, 115 A.D.2d 221, 496 N.Y.S.2d 124 (4th Dept. 1985).

Proof.—An inmate charged with a violation of prison rules is entitled to a hearing and any finding of misbehavior must be supported by substantial evidence contained in the hearing record. Harris v. Coughlin, 116 A.D.2d 896, 498 N.Y.S.2d 276 (3d Dept. 1986).

Security risk.—Arbitration award which reinstated correctional officer who was dismissed for flying a Nazi flag from his house, although in violation of a "well-defined and explicit public policy" of the State, was affirmed; pursuant to the grievance procedure, it was properly the subject of arbitration and within the power of the arbitrator to decide; § 137(2) & (5), which would bar an officer's reinstatement for security reasons, may not be used to override reinstatement in light of the arbitrator's findings that officer posed no such security risk. New York State Corrections Officers & Police Ben. Ass'n v. New York, 94 N.Y.2d 321, 704 N.Y.S.2d 914, 726 N.E.2d 462 (1999).

Unauthorized possession of medication.—Petitioner's admission that he possessed ampicillin which he obtained from a source other than the prison pharmacy constituted substantial evidence to support charge of unauthorized possession of medication. Sanchez v. Hoke, 116 A.D.2d 965, 498 N.Y.S.2d 535 (3d Dept. 1986)

Waiver at hearing.—Petitioner's failure to request Spanish translations of urinalysis forms at the hearing at a time when the issue could have been addressed and, if necessary, cured effectively waived that objection. Sanchez v. Hoke, 116 A.D.2d 871, 498 N.Y.S.2d 191 (3d Dept. 1986).

§ 138. Institutional rules and regulations for inmates at all correctional facilities.

1. All institutional rules and regulations defining and prohibiting inmates misconduct shall be published and posted in prominent locations within the institution and set forth in both the English and Spanish language.

2. All inmates shall be provided with written copies of these rules and regulations upon admission to the institution and all inmates presently incarcerated with written copies of these rules and regulations.

3. Facility rules shall be specified and precise giving all inmates actual notice of the conduct prohibited. Facility rules shall state the range of disciplinary sanctions which can be imposed for violation of each rule.

4. Inmates shall not be disciplined for making written or oral statements, demands, or requests involving a change a institutional conditions, policies, rules, regulations, or laws affecting an institution.

5. No inmate shall be disciplined except for a violation of a published and posted written rule or regulation, a copy of which has been provided the inmate.

6. All rules and regulations pertaining to inmates established by the department of correctional services and all rules and regulations pertaining to inmates established by any institutional staff at any state correctional facility shall be reviewed annually by the commissioner of the department of correctional services.

Added by L. 1975, Ch. 231.

ANNOTATIONS

Acquittal of criminal charges.—The fact that petitioner was acquitted of the criminal charges that resulted from the incident did not require a finding that he did not violate certain prison disciplinary rules given the different standards of proud involved Rogers v. Mitchell, 194 A.D.2d 1059, 599 N.Y.S.2d 646 (3d Dept. 1993).

Appeal.—Where a prisoner challenge the constitutionality of a rule regulating administrative appeals from disciplinary hearings, the issue can be advanced for the first time in a judicial proceeding. Zaro v. Coughlin, 195 A.D.2d 1003, 601, N.Y.S.2d 744, 745 (4th Dept. 1993).

Basis for finding.—The hearing officer erred in failing to notify petitioner before issuing a determination that confidential information would be considered and in failing to articulate a reason for keeping that information confidential; however, the error was harmless. Lee v. Coughlin, 195 A.D.2d 997, 600 N.Y.S.2d 559 (4th Dept. 1993).

—The positive EMIT test provided substantial evidence to support the finding that petitioner had used as illegal drug. *In re* Coughlin, 193 A.D.2d 989, N.Y.S.2d 370, 371 (3d Dept. 1993).

—Failure to disclose memorandum did not require annulment where hearing officer did not rely on the memorandum in making his determination. Boyce v. Coughlin, 191 A.D.2d 936, 595 N.Y.S.2d 140 (3d Dept. 1993)

Bias—Petitioner waived his argument that the hearing officer was not impartial because of his involvement in the matter at issue by failing to raise it at the tier III hearing. Cowart v. Coughlin, 193 A.D.2d 887, 597 N.Y.S.2d 821 (3d Dept. 1993).

—The mere fact that the hearing officer spoke brusquely with petitioner in attempting to control him did not evidence bias. Firzgerald v. Coughlin, 191 A.D.2d 941, 595 N.Y.S.2d 253 (3d Dept. 1993).

—The mere fact that hearing officer ruled against petitioner was insufficient to established bias. Martinez v. Scully, 194 A.d.2d 679 599 N.Y.S.2d 104 (2d Dept. 1993).

Constitutionality of disciplinary rules.—The disciplinary rules prohibiting fighting (DR 100.13) and violent conduct (DR 104.11) both comply with CL § 138 and are not unconstitutionally vague; rules are sufficiently particular to provide a person of ordinary intelligence with notice that engaging in a physical altercation with another inmate is proscribed conduct. Brown v. Selsky, 5 A.D.3d 905, 772 N.Y.S.2d 757 (3d Dept. 2004).

Corr. Law § 138 held not to cover Penal Law offenses.—Defendant inmate, charged with promoting prison contraband and possessing a controlled substance, was not entitled to the protection of Section 138 of the Correction Law which concerns discipline for violation of an institutional rule or regulation and does not apply were a defendant inmate is indicted for conduct proscribed by the Penal Law. People v. Quintana, 71 A.D.2d 764, 419 N.Y.S.2d 325 (3d Dept. 1979).

Credibility.—It was well within the hearing officer's province to disregard petitioner's version of events as incredible. Madlock v. Rossi, 195 A.D.2d 646, 600 N.Y.S.2d 283, 284 (3d Dept. 1993).

Misbehavior report.—The misbehavior report by itself can constitute substantial evidence of an inmate's misconduct. Vega v. Coughlin, 195 A.D.2d 1076, 1077 (4th Dept. 1993).

—Petitioner waived receipt of a Spanish translation of the misbehavior report by affirmatively requesting that the hearing proceed without immediate production of the report. Polanco v. Coughlin, 193 A.D.2d 918, 597 N.Y.S.2d 810 (3d Dept. 1993).

—The focus of the inquiry is not on whether the misbehavior report is based on hearsay information, but rather on whether the report has sufficient relevance and probative value to constitute substantial evidence. Gallagher v. Coughlin 193 A.D.2d 847, 597 N.Y.S.2d 495 (3d Dept. 1993).

Right to be present.—There was no error in the hearing officer's ejection of petitioner from the sharing after he refused to follow orderly procedure. Garcia v. Coughlin, 194 A.D.2d 896, 599 N.Y.S.2d 147 (3d Dept. 1993).

Rights.—Petitioner had no right to counsel at a disciplinary hearing; an inmate's right to call witnesses is limited and may be abridged where it would be unduly hazardous to institutional safety or correction goals. Arner v. Warne, 54 A.D.2d 1075, 600 N.Y.S.2d 539, 540 (4th Dept. 1993).

Statements; subd. 4.—Correction Law § 38(4) does not allow inmates to make statements that constitute violations of prison rules. Mays v. Goord, 245 A.D.2d 610, 664 N.Y.S.2d 854 (3d Dept. 1997).

Waiver.—Where petitioner did not request that hearing officer make a personal inquiry into the reason for a witness's failure to testify, he waived his right to object that such an inquiry was not conducted. Cowart v. Coughlin, 194 A.D.2d 1036, 599 N.Y.S.2d 677, 678 (3d Dept. 1993).

—Petitioner waived any argument that written statements of correction officer/complainant has to be produced, by failing to raise the issue on administrative appeal. Nina C. Coughlin, 191 A.d.2d 942, 595 N.Y.S.2d 833 (3d Dept. 1993).

Witnesses.—There existed a rational basis for the hearing officer's determination that the informant, as well as the alleged co-conspirators, could not be called as witness for security reasons. *In re* Giakoumelos, 192, A.D.2d 998, 597 N.Y.S.2d 232 233 (3d Dept. 1993).

—Hearing officer did not err in denying petitioner's requests to produce documentary evidence and to call witnesses, because the documents and testimony was irrelevant or redundant. Mabry v. Coughlin 196 A.D.2d 931, 601 N.Y.S.2d 975 (3d Dept. 1993).

—Although petitioner was not provided with a written reason for the exclusion of one of the witnesses, there was no resulting prejudice, because the reasons for the denial were fully set forth at the hearing. Murray v. Mann, 193 A.D.2d 1038, 598 N.Y.S.2d 373, 374 (3d Dept. 1993).

§ 139. Grievance procedures.

1. The commissioner shall establish, in each correctional institution under his jurisdiction, grievance resolution committees to resolve grievances of persons within such correctional institution. Such grievance resolution committees shall consist of five persons four of whom shall be entitled to vote, two of whom shall be inmates of such correctional institution, and a non-voting chairman.

2. The commissioner shall promulgate rules and regulations establishing such procedures for the fair, simple and expeditious resolution of grievances as shall be deemed appropriate, having due regard for the constitutions and laws of the United States and of the state of New York. Such procedures shall include but not be limited to setting time limitations for the filing of complaints and replies thereto and for each stage of the grievance resolution process.

3. A person aggrieved by the decision of a grievance resolution committee may apply to the commissioner for review of the decision. The commissioner or his deputy may take such action as he deems appropriate to fairly and expeditiously resolve the grievance to the satisfaction of all parties.

4. The commission shall annually evaluate and assess the grievance procedures in correctional facilities, and make any recommendations with respect to the proper operation or improvement of the grievance procedures and provide such report to the commissioner and the chairman of the senate codes and crime and corrections and assembly codes and correction committees.

5. The commissioner shall semi-annually report to the chairman of the senate codes and crime and corrections committees and the assembly codes and correction committees on the nature and type of inmate grievances and unusual incidents, by facility.

6. The commissioner shall, upon request, provide the commission with any information or data necessary for the commission to carry out the mandates of this section.

Added by L. 1975, Ch. 866; **Amended** by L. 1975, Ch. 867; L. 1990, Ch. 373, eff. July 7, 1990, amending subd. 3 and adding subds. 4, 5, and 6.

ANNOTATION

Representative to prison's Inmate Grievance Resolution Committee (IGRC); transfer.—Correction Law § 139 imposes a limitation upon the exercise of the Commissioners discretion to transfer an inmate who is a member of the IGRC in that he may not be transferred without a prior hearing, the rules of which must embrace the protection provided for in *Wolff v. McDonnell,* 418 U.S. 539, 94 S. Ct. 2963, 41 L. Ed. 2d 935, unless the member's presence or conduct at the institution or facility creates an emergency and transfer is immediately necessary to protect the facility or its personnel in which event the hearing on his transfer shall be held as soon as practicable at the receiving facility. *Johnson v. Ward,* 64 A.D.2d 186, 409 N.Y.S.2d 670 (3d Dept. 1978).

§ 140. Provision for routine medical, dental and mental health services and treatment.

1. Where an inmate who is not yet eighteen years of age has been committed or transferred to the custody of the department and no medical consent has been obtained prior to commitment or transfer, the commitment order shall be deemed to grant to the minor the capacity to consent to routine medical, dental and mental health services and treatment to such an individual.

2. Subject to the regulations of the department of health, routine medical, dental and mental health services and treatment is defined for the purposes of this section to mean any routine diagnosis or treatment, including without limitation the administration of medications or nutrition, the extraction of bodily fluids for analysis, and dental care performed with a local anesthetic. Routine mental health treatment shall not include psychiatric administration of medication unless it is part of an ongoing mental health plan or unless it is otherwise authorized by law.

3. (a) At any time prior to the date the inmate becomes eighteen years of age, the inmate's parent or legal guardian may institute legal proceedings pursuant to section 70.20 of the penal law objecting to the provision of routine medical, dental or mental health services and treatment being provided to the inmate.

(b) Such notice of motion shall be served on the inmate, the facility and the department not less than seven days prior to the return date of the motion. The persons on whom the notice of motion is served shall answer the motion not less than two days before the return date. On examining the motion and answer and, in its discretion, after hearing argument, the court shall enter an order, granting or denying the motion.

4. Nothing in this section shall preclude an inmate from consenting on his or her own behalf to any medical, dental or mental health service and treatment where otherwise authorized by law to do so.

Added by L. 1995, Ch. 516, § 1, eff. Aug. 2, 1995.

§ 141. Contagious disease in facility.

In case any pestilence or contagious disease shall break out among the inmates in any of the correctional facilities, or in the vicinity of such facilities, the commissioner of correction may cause the inmates confined in such facility, or any of them, to be removed to some suitable place of security, where such of them as may be sick shall receive all necessary care and medical assistance; such inmates shall be returned as soon as may be feasible to the facility from which they were taken, to be confined therein according to their respective sentences.

Amended by L. 1970, Ch. 476.

§ 142. Fire in facility.

Whenever by reason of any correctional facility, or any building contiguous to such facility, being on fire, there shall be reason to apprehend that the inmates may be injured or endangered by such fire, or may escape, it shall be the duty of the superintendent of such facility to remove such inmates to some safe and convenient place and there confine them until the necessity of such removal shall have ceased.

Amended by L. 1970, Ch. 476.

§ 143. Custody of persons convicted of crimes against the United States.

The commissioner is authorized to enter into agreements for the care and custody of persons convicted and sentenced to imprisonment by the United States courts in this state. Persons may be confined in correctional facilities pursuant to any such agreement and all provisions of law applicable to the care and custody of inmates sentenced by courts of this state, except provisions governing the duration of sentence and other related incidents of the sentence provided by federal law, shall apply to the care and custody of such persons.

Repealed former § 143 and **Added** new § 143 by L. 1970, Ch. 476.

§ 146. Persons authorized to visit correctional facilities.

1. The following persons shall be authorized to visit at pleasure all correctional facilities: The governor and lieutenant-governor, commissioner of general services, secretary of state, comptroller and attorney-general, members of the commission of correction, members of the legislature, judges of the court of appeals, supreme court and county judges, district attorneys and every minister of the gospel having charge of a congregation in the town wherein any such facility is situated. No other person not otherwise authorized by law shall be permitted to enter a correctional facility except by authority of the commissioner of correction under such regulations as the commissioner shall prescribe. The provisions of this section shall not apply to such portion of a correctional facility in which inmates under sentence of death are confined.

2. Notwithstanding any other provision of law to the contrary, on each September thirteenth

anniversary date of the nineteen hundred seventy-one retaking of Attica correctional facility, in the absence of an emergency situation or other exigent circumstance, the commissioner shall ensure that any surviving state employees who were held as hostages and any immediate family members, as that term is defined in subdivision four of section 120.40 of the penal law, of any of the state employees who were held hostage for any period by rioting inmates during the period from September ninth through September thirteenth, nineteen hundred seventy-one, shall be afforded access to the outside grounds of Attica correctional facility to conduct a private commemorative ceremony in front of the Attica monument upon which are inscribed the names of employees who died as a result of the uprising and subsequent retaking.

Amended by L. 1962, Ch. 37; L. 1970, Ch. 476; L. 2005, Ch. 56, Part E, § 3, eff. Apr. 1, 2005.

§ 147. Alien inmates of correctional facilities.

The commissioner shall within three months after admission of an alien inmate to a correctional facility cause an investigation to be made of the record and past history of such alien and shall upon the termination of such investigation cause the record of such alien, together with all facts disclosed by such investigation, and his recommendations as to deportation, to be forwarded to the United States immigration authorities having such matters in charge.

Amended by L. 1970, Ch. 476.

§ 148. Psychiatric and diagnostic clinics.

The commissioner of correction and the chairman of the board of parole are hereby authorized and directed to assist and cooperate with the commissioner of mental hygiene in the establishment and conduct of such psychiatric and diagnostic clinics in the institutions and facilities under their jurisdiction as such commissioners and chairman may deem necessary within the amount appropriated therefor. The persons conducting the work of such clinics shall determine the physical and mental condition of all inmates serving an indeterminate term, having a minimum of one day and a maximum of natural life, and of such other inmates whose criminal record, behavior or other factors indicate to those in charge of such clinics the need of study and treatment. The work of the clinics shall include scientific study and psychiatric evaluation of each such inmate, including his career and life history, investigation of the cause of the crime and recommendations for the care, training and employment of such inmates with a view to their reformation and to the protection of society. Each of the different phases of the work of the clinics shall be so coordinated with all the other phases of clinic work as to be a part of a unified and comprehensive scheme in the study and treatment of such inmates. After classification in the clinics the inmate sentenced to state prison shall be certified to the warden and recommendation made to the commissioner of correction as to their disposition.

Amended by L. 1964, Ch. 81.

§ 149. Released inmates; notification to sheriff, police, and district attorney.

In the case of any inmate convicted two or more times of a felony, it shall be the duty of the department at least forty-eight hours prior to the release of any such inmate from a correctional facility to notify the chief of police both of the city, town or village in which such inmate proposes to reside and of the city, town or village in which such inmate resided at the time of his or her conviction and the district attorney of the county where the offense for which the inmate is incarcerated was prosecuted, of the contemplated release of such inmate, informing such chief of police and the district attorney of the name and aliases of the inmate, the address at which he or she proposes to reside, the amount of time remaining to be served, if any, on the full term for which he or she was sentenced, and the nature of the crime for which he or she was sentenced, transmitting at the same time to the chief of police a copy of such inmate's fingerprints and photograph and a summary of his or her criminal record. Where such inmate proposes to reside outside of a city, such notification shall be sent to the sheriff of the county in which such inmate proposes to reside.

Amended by L. 1970, Ch. 476; L. 2005, Ch. 186, § 4, eff. Sept. 1, 2005.

§ 149-a. Released inmates; notification to victims and family members. [Repealed.]

Repealed by L. 1998, Ch. 43, eff. Aug. 6, 1998.

Editor's Note: L. 1998, Ch. 1, § 42 provides:

"Notwithstanding any other provision of law, by January 1, 1999, the department of correctional services shall establish an automated telephone system that a victim, family member of a victim, a witness or any member of the general public may call to obtain information relating to the crime and sentence of an inmate who is serving a determinate or indeterminate sentence of imprisonment. The department of correctional services, in consultation with the department of motor vehicles, shall also develop a public awareness campaign and disseminate information regarding the availability of the automated telephone system in conjunction with licensing and motor vehicle registration, application and renewal procedures of the department of motor vehicles. In addition, by April 1, 1999, the division of parole, in cooperation with the department of correctional services, shall implement a program to provide a victim, family member of a victim, a witness, or any member of the general public with access to information concerning the community of residence of a person who has been paroled, conditionally released or released to post-release supervision and the address and telephone number of the regional parole office to which such person has been assigned."

ARTICLE 6-A—WORK RELEASE PROGRAM IN NEW YORK CITY CORRECTIONAL INSTITUTIONS

§ 150. Definitions.

As used in this article:

1. "City" means the City of New York.

2. "Commissioner" means the commissioner of correction of the city provided, however, that if there be established by law a correctional administration in the city, "commissioner" shall mean the correctional administrator of the City.

3. "Department" means the department of correction of the city provided, however, that if there shall be established by law a correctional administration in the city, "department" shall mean such administration.

4. "Work release program" means a program in which the limits of place of confinement are extended for the purpose of seeking or engaging in employment or self-employment, attending an educational institution, participating in a training program or obtaining medical treatment not otherwise available, caring for the prisoner's household and family or for some other compelling reason consistent with the public interest.

Added by L. 1968, Ch. 788; Amended by L. 1971, Ch. 625; L. 1976, Ch. 71.

§ 151. Work release program.

The department shall establish work release programs for prisoners sentenced to New York City correctional institutions. The commissioner may extend the limits of the place of confinement of a prisoner as to whom there is reasonable cause to believe he will honor his trust by authorizing him to participate in a work release program in the community on a voluntary basis while continuing as a prisoner of the institution or facility in which he is confined. An extension of limits shall be under such prescribed conditions and for such reasonable hours or reasonable periods of time as the commissioner deems necessary. Such extension of limits may be withdrawn at any time.

Added by L. 1968, Ch. 788.

§ 152. Employment.

The department shall endeavor to secure employment for a prisoner deemed eligible to participate in a work release program and assist him in contacting prospective employers. In carrying out this function, the department shall coordinate its efforts with other departments or agencies furnishing employment placement services.

Added by L. 1968, Ch. 788.

§ 153. Conditions of employment.

1. A prisoner shall be permitted to be employed only if:

(a) The rates of pay and other conditions of employment will not be less than those paid or provided for work of similar nature in the locality in which the work is to be performed.

(b) The commissioner finds, after consultation with representatives of local union central bodies or similar labor union organizations, that such employment will not result in the displacement of employed workers, impair existing contracts for services, or be applied, except where a prisoner is to be hired by an employer for whom he worked prior to his conviction, in skills, crafts, or trades in which there is a surplus of available gainful labor in the locality.

2. The State Department of Labor shall exercise the same supervision over conditions of employment for prisoners participating in work release programs as such department does over conditions of employment for free persons.

3. In no event shall a prisoner be employed in an establishment which has a labor dispute.

Added by L. 1968, Ch. 788.

§ 154. Disposition of earnings.

The earnings of a prisoner participating in a work release program, less any payroll deductions required or authorized by law, shall be deposited with the department in a trust fund account. Such earnings shall not be subject to attachment or garnishment in the hands of the department. The commissioner is authorized to provide for disbursements from the trust fund account for any or all of the following purposes:

1. Such costs incident to the prisoner's confinement as the commissioner deems appropriate and reasonable.

2. Such costs related to the prisoner's work release program as the commissioner deems appropriate and reasonable.

3. Support of the prisoner's dependents.

4. Payment of court fines, mandatory surcharge, sex offender registration fee, DNA databank fee, restitution or reparation, or forfeitures.

The balance of such earnings, if any, after disbursements for any of the foregoing purposes shall be paid to the prisoner upon termination of his imprisonment.

Added by L. 1968, Ch. 788; Amended by L. 1988, Ch. 661, eff. Oct. 1, 1988; L. 2003, Ch. 62, Part F, § 3, eff. May 15, 2003, amending subd. 4.

§ 156. Liability for a prisoner on work release.

No prisoner participating in a work release program or whose place of confinement is extended pursuant to this article shall be deemed an agent, employee or involuntary servant of the department or the city while employed or going to and from such employment or released from confinement pursuant to this article; provided, however, that where a prisoner is employed and paid by the city, his relationship to the city arising out of such employment shall be determined in the same manner as if he were a free person so employed.

Added by L. 1968, Ch. 788.

§ 157. Rules and regulations.

The commissioner may make such rules and regulations as he shall deem necessary and appropriate to carry out the purposes of this article.

Added by L. 1968, Ch. 788.

§ 158. Designation of place of confinement.

The commissioner may designate as a place of confinement of a prisoner any available, suitable and appropriate correctional institution or facility whether maintained by the city, state or federal government and may at any time transfer a prisoner from one place of confinement to another. Where such designation or transfer is to either a state or federal correctional institution or facility, it shall be subject to the prior approval of the appropriate person or agency having jurisdiction and control over such facility and upon such terms and conditions as such person or agency deems appropriate.

Added by L. 1968, Ch. 788.

§ 159. Eligibility for other programs.

The participation of any prisoner in a work release program established pursuant to this article shall in no way prejudice his eligibility for conditional release, parole or discretionary reduction of sentence.

Added by L. 1968, Ch. 788.

§ 160. Annual report of commissioner.

The commissioner shall annually prepare a report of the work release program which shall be transmitted to the legislature on or before the first day of March in each year. Such annual report shall include a summary of the operations and activities of the program for the preceding year and such recommendations for the improvement of the program as the commissioner shall deem necessary and proper.

Added by L. 1968, Ch. 788.

ARTICLE 6-C—SEX OFFENDER REGISTRATION ACT

[Added by L. 1995, Ch. 192, eff. Jan. 21, 1996.]

LexisNexis Cross References

Prosecution and Defense of Sex Crimes, Ch. 18, Sex Offender Registration and Community Notification; *New York Criminal Practice (2d ed.),* Vol. 6, Ch. 59, Sex Offenses and Offenses Against Marriage.

§ 168. Short title.

This article shall be known and may be cited as the "Sex Offender Registration Act".

ANNOTATIONS

Constitutionality.—The Sex Offender Registration Act is constitutional as applied to persons convicted of sex crimes prior to the effective date of the Act, *i.e.,* January 21, 1996, and retroactive application of Corr. Law § 168 et seq. does not violate the Ex Post Facto Clause of the U.S. Constitution. Parolee S.V. v. Calabrese, 246 A.D.2d 655, 668 N.Y.S.2d 53 (2d Dept.), *app. denied,* 91 N.Y.2d 814, 676 N.Y.S.2d 127, 698 N.E.2d 956 (1998).

—The Act is not an impermissible ex post facto law; however, order reversed and remitted, as county court should have set forth findings of fact and conclusions of law on the record. People v. Lee, 292 A.D.2d 639, 738 N.Y.S.2d 903 (3d Dept. 2002).

—The retroactive application of SORA to sex offenders convicted prior to the act's effective date does not violate the constitutional prohibition against ex post facto laws. People v. Langdon, 258 A.D.2d 937, 685 N.Y.S.2d 877 (4th Dept. 1999).

Constitutionality; procedure for challenging.—The proper manner for challenging the constitutionality of SORA is to commence a declaratory judgment action in Supreme Court.

People v. Davis, 17 A.D.3d 1155, 794 N.Y.S.2d 554 (4th Dept. 2005).

Conviction requiring registration.—Defendant's federal conviction under 18 U.S.C. § 2252A(a)(2) and (b)(1) (attempt to knowingly receive or distribute child pornography or material containing child pornography) is not a felony conviction requiring registration under SORA, since the analogous New York offense is attempted possession of a sexual performance by a child, a class A misdemeanor. People v. Millan, 295 A.D.2d 267, 743 N.Y.S.2d 872 (1st Dept. 2002).

—Defendant's conviction for unlawful imprisonment under PL § 135.05, involving a victim over the age of 17, was not a conviction of a "sex offense" within the meaning of the Act and did not require defendant to register under the section. People v. Lewis, 294 A.D.2d 847, 741 N.Y.S.2d 760 (4th Dept. 2002).

—County court properly determined that defendant, convicted in 1977 of first degree sodomy, and then sentenced for manslaughter, which defendant committed while on parole, is subject to sex offender registration requirements where sentences were to be served consecutively. "Defendant is subject to both sentences until he reaches the maximum expiration date, which extends beyond the effective date of SORA Accordingly, . . . defendant is subject to the requirements of SORA." People v. Curley, 285 A.D.2d 274, 730 N.Y.S.2d 625 (4th Dept. 2001).

Due process.—Court rejected defendant's assertion that SORA violates his right to substantive due process by failing to include a "no risk" category that exempts purportedly non-dangerous offenders from having to register; SORA requires defendant to register based on his conviction of an enumerated sex offense, not because of his level of dangerousness. SORA also does not deny the defendant equal protection under the law. Although it treats sex offenders differently by imposing registration requirements, this is rationally based on the high danger of recidivism among sex offenders and the need to prevent repeat offenses. People v. Hood, 16 A.D.3d 778, 790 N.Y.S.2d 757 (3d Dept. 2005).

§ 168-a. Definitions.

As used in this article, the following definitions Apply:

1. "Sex offender" includes any person who is convicted of any of the offenses set forth in subdivision two or three of this section. Convictions that result from or are connected with the same act, or result from offenses committed at the same time, shall be counted for the purpose of this article as one conviction. Any conviction set aside pursuant to law is not a conviction for purposes of this article.

2. "Sex offense" means:

(a) (i) a conviction of or a conviction for an attempt to commit any of the provisions of sections 130.20, 130.25, 130.30, 130.40, 130.45, 130.60, 250.50 and 255.25 or article two hundred sixty-three of the penal law, or section 135.05, 135.10, 135.20 or 135.25 of such law relating to kidnapping offenses, provided the victim of such kidnapping or related offense is less than seventeen years old and the offender is not the parent of the victim, or sections 230.04, where the person patronized is in fact less than seventeen years of age, 230.05 or 230.06 or subdivision two of section 230.30, section 230.32 of the penal law, or (ii) a conviction of or a conviction for an attempt to commit any of the provisions of section 235.22 of the penal law, or (iii) a conviction of or a conviction for an attempt to commit any provisions of the foregoing sections committed or attempted as a hate crime defined in section 485.05 of the penal law or as a crime of terrorism defined in section 490.25 of such law; or

(b) a conviction of or a conviction for an attempt to commit any of the provisions of section 130.52 or 130.55 of the penal law, provided the victim of such offense is less than eighteen years of age; or

(c) a conviction of or a conviction for an attempt to commit any of the provisions of section 130.52 or 130.55 of the penal law regardless of the age of the victim and the offender has previously been convicted of: (i) a sex offense defined in this article, (ii) a sexually violent offense defined in this article, or (iii) any of the provisions of section 130.52 or 130.55 of the penal law, or an attempt thereof; or

(d) a conviction of (i) an offense in any other jurisdiction which includes all of the essential elements of any such crime provided for in paragraph (a), (b), or (c) of this subdivision or

(ii) a felony in any other jurisdiction for which the offender is required to register as a sex offender in the jurisdiction in which the conviction occurred or, (iii) any of the provisions of 18 U.S.C. 2251, 18 U.S.C. 2251A, 18 U.S.C. 2252, 18 U.S.C. 2252A, or 18 U.S.C. 2260, provided that the elements of such crime of conviction are substantially the same as those which are a part of such offense as of the date on which this subparagraph takes effect. *

(e) a conviction of any of the provisions of subdivision two, three or four of section 250.45 of the penal law, unless upon motion by the defendant, the trial court, having regard to the nature and circumstances of the crime and to the history and character of the defendant, is of the opinion that registration would be unduly harsh and inappropriate.

3. "Sexually violent offense" means:

(a) (i) a conviction of or a conviction for an attempt to commit any of the provisions of sections 130.35, 130.50, 130.65, 130.66, 130.67, 130.70, 130.75 and 130.80 of the penal law, or (ii) a conviction of or a conviction for an attempt to commit any of the provisions of sections 130.53, 130.65-a and 130.90 of the penal law, or (iii) a conviction of or a conviction for an attempt to commit any provisions of the foregoing sections committed or attempted as a hate crime defined in section 485.05 of the penal law or as a crime of terrorism defined in section 490.25 of such law; or

(b) a conviction of an offense in any other jurisdiction which includes all of the essential elements of any such felony provided for in paragraph (a) of this subdivision or conviction of a felony in any other jurisdiction for which the offender is required to register as a sex offender in the jurisdiction in which the conviction occurred.

4. "Law enforcement agency having jurisdiction" means: (a) (i) the chief law enforcement officer in the village, town or city in which the offender expects to reside upon his or her discharge, probation, parole, release to post-release supervision or upon any form of state or local conditional release; or (ii) if there be no chief law enforcement officer in such village, town or city, the chief law enforcement officer of the county in which the offender expects to reside; or (iii) if there be no chief enforcement officer in such village, town, city or county, the division of state police and (b) in the case of a sex offender who is or expects to be employed by, enrolled in, attending or employed, whether for compensation or not, at an institution of higher education, (i) the chief law enforcement officer in the village, town or city in which such institution is located; or (ii) if there be no chief law enforcement officer in such village, town or city, the chief law enforcement officer of the county in which such institution is located; or (iii) if there be no chief

law enforcement officer in such village, town, city or county, the division of state police; and (iv) if such institution operates or employs a campus law enforcement or security agency, the chief of such agency.

5. "Division" means the division of criminal justice services as defined by section eight hundred thirty-seven of the executive law.

6. "Hospital" means a hospital as defined in subdivision two of section four hundred of this chapter and applies to persons committed to such hospital by order of commitment made pursuant to article sixteen of this chapter.

7. (a) "Sexual predator" means a sex offender who has been convicted of a sexually violent offense defined in subdivision three of this section and who suffers from a mental abnormality or personality disorder that makes him or her likely to engage in predatory sexually violent offenses.

(b) "Sexually violent offender" means a sex offender who has been convicted of a sexually violent offense defined in subdivision three of this section.

(c) "Predicate sex offender" means a sex offender who has been convicted of an offense set forth in subdivision two or three of this section when the offender has been previously convicted of an offense set forth in subdivision two or three of this section.

8. "Mental abnormality" means a congenital or acquired condition of a person that affects the emotional or volitional capacity of the person in a manner that predisposes that person to the commission of criminal sexual acts to a degree that makes the person a menace to the health and safety of other persons.

9. "Predatory" means an act directed at a stranger, or a person with whom a relationship has been established or promoted for the primary purpose of victimization.

10. "Board" means the "board of examiners of sex offenders" established pursuant to section one hundred sixty-eight-1 of this article.

11. "Local correctional facility" means a local correctional facility as that term is defined in subdivision sixteen of section two of this chapter.

12. Probation means a sentence of probation imposed pursuant to article sixty-five of the penal law and shall include a sentence of imprisonment imposed in conjunction with a sentence of probation.

13. "Institution of higher education" means an institution in the state providing higher education as such term is defined in subdivision eight of section two of the education law.

14. "Nonresident worker" means any person required to register as a sex offender in another jurisdiction who is employed or carries on a vocation in this state, on either a full-time or a part-time basis, with or without compensation, for more than fourteen consecutive days, or for an aggregate period exceeding thirty days in a calendar year.

15. "Nonresident student" means a person required to register as a sex offender in another jurisdiction who is enrolled on a full-time or part-time basis in any public or private educational institution in this state including any secondary school, trade or professional institution or institution of higher education.

* Punctuated as enacted.

Added by L. 1995, Ch. 192, eff. Jan. 21, 1996; **Amended** by L. 1999, Ch. 453, eff. Jan. 1, 2000, amending subds. 2 and 3, which amendments shall apply to persons convicted of an offense committed prior to Jan. 1, 2000, who, on such date, have not completed service of the sentence imposed thereon; also amending subd. 4 and adding subd. 12; L. 2002, Ch. 11, eff. Mar. 11, 2002; L. 2003, Ch. 69, § 4, eff. Aug. 11, 2003, amending subd. 2(a) and adding subd. 2(e); L. 2004, Ch. 146, § 1, eff. July 13, 2004, amending subd. 2(d)(i).

Pursuant to L. 2002, Ch. 11, § 24, the amendments to subds. 2 and 3 of this section shall apply to offenses committed on or after such effective date, except that:

(i) the provisions of subparagraphs (ii) and (iii) of paragraph (a) of subdivision 2 of section 168-a of the correction law as added by section shall apply to persons convicted of such an offense prior to the effective date of this act who, on such effective date, have not completed service of the sentence imposed thereon;

(ii) the provisions of subparagraph (iii) of paragraph (d) of subdivision 2 of section 168-a of the correction law as added by section one of this act shall apply to persons convicted of such an offense prior to the effective date of this act who, on such effective date, have not completed service of the sentence imposed thereon;

(iii) the provisions of subparagraphs (ii) and (iii) of paragraph (a) of subdivision 3 of section 168-a of the correction law as added by section two of this act shall apply to persons convicted of such an offense prior to the effective date of this act who, on such effective date, have not completed service of the sentence imposed thereon.

The amendments to subd. 7 of this section "shall apply to sex offenders for whom an initial risk level determination has not been made prior to such effective date or who, on the effective date of this act, are not members of the plaintiff class in the U.S. District Court, Southern District of New York case entitled Doe v. Pataki, Index Number 96CIV1657 (DC)."

ANNOTATIONS

Court martial.—The phrase "any other jurisdiction," as used in Corr. Law § 168-a(2)(d)(ii), includes a military court-martial for purposes of determining whether defendant committed a sex offense under the statute. People v. Kennedy, 20 A.D.3d 137, 797 N.Y.S.2d 219 (4th Dept. 2005).

Sexually violent offender.—Court determined that defendant is a sexually violent offender pursuant to Corr. Law § 168-a(7)(b) because defendant was convicted of a prior offense (a Maryland felony), which the defendant was required to register as a sex offender and was convicted of an offense in another jurisdiction which includes all the essential elements of Penal Law § 130.65. People v. Johnson, 2 Misc. 3d 777, 770 N.Y.S.2d 844 (Dist. Ct. Nassau Co. 2003).

Subd. (2); sex offense.—Conviction by summary court martial to indecent assault and sodomy by force without consent is a sex offense within the present statute requiring defendant to register as a sex offender, but defendant was not subject to terms of the amended statute because his conviction pre-dates the effective date of the act. Coram v. Board of Examiners Sex Offender Registry, 195 Misc. 2d 392, 758 N.Y.S.2d 235 (Sup. Ct. Kings Co. 2003).

§ 168-b. Duties of the division; registration information.

1. The division shall establish and maintain a file of individuals required to register pursuant to the provisions of this article which shall include the following information of each registrant:

(a) The sex offender's name, all aliases used, date of birth, sex, race, height, weight, eye color, driver's license number, home address and/or expected place of domicile, any internet accounts belonging to such offender and any internet screen names used by such offender.

(b) [*Effective until Apr. 12, 2006.*] A photograph and set of fingerprints.

(b) [*Effective Apr. 12, 2006.*] A photograph and set of fingerprints. For a sex offender given a level three designation, the division shall, during the period of registration, update such photograph once each year. For a sex offender given a level one or level two designation, the division shall, during the period of registration, update such photograph once every three years. The division shall notify the sex offender by mail of the duty to appear and be photographed at the specified law enforcement agency having jurisdiction. Such notification shall be mailed at least thirty days and not more than sixty days before the photograph is required to be taken pursuant to subdivision two of section one hundred sixty-eight-f of this article.

(c) A description of the offense for which the sex offender was convicted, the date of conviction and the sentence imposed.

(d) The name and address of any institution of higher education at which the sex offender is or expects to be enrolled, attending or employed, whether for compensation or not, and whether such offender resides in or will reside in a facility owned or operated by such institution.

(e) If the sex offender has been given a level three designation, such offender's employment address and/or expected place of employment.

(f) Any other information deemed pertinent by the division.

2. The division is authorized to make the registry available to any regional or national registry of sex offenders for the purpose of sharing information. The division shall accept files from any regional or national registry of sex offenders and shall make such files available when requested pursuant to the provisions of this article. The division shall require that no information included in the registry shall be made available except in the furtherance of the provisions of this article.

3. The division shall develop a standardized registration form to be made available to the appropriate authorities and promulgate rules and regulations to implement the provisions of this section. Such form shall be written in clear and concise language and shall advise the sex offender of his or her duties and obligations under this article.

4. The division shall mail a nonforwardable verification form to the last reported address of the person for annual verification requirements.

5. The division shall also establish and operate a telephone number as provided for in section one hundred sixty-eight-p of this article.

6. The division shall also establish a sexually violent predator subdirectory pursuant to section one hundred sixty-eight-q of this article.

7. The division shall also establish a public awareness campaign to advise the public of the provisions of this article.

8. The division shall charge a fee of ten dollars each time a sex offender registers any change of address or any change of his or her status of enrollment, attendance, employment or residence at any institution of higher education as required by subdivision four of section one hundred sixty-eight-f of this article. The fee shall be paid to the division by the sex offender. The state comptroller is hereby authorized to deposit such fees into the general fund.

9. The division shall, upon the request of any children's camp operator, release to such person any information in the registry relating to a prospective employee of any such person or entity in accordance with the provisions of this article. The division shall promulgate rules and regulations relating to procedures for the release of information in the registry to such persons.

Added by L. 1995, Ch. 192, eff. Jan. 21, 1996; **Amended** by L. 2000, Ch. 1, eff. Feb. 1, 2001; L. 2002, Ch. 11, eff. Mar. 11, 2002, amending subds. 1 and 3; L. 2002, Ch. 694, eff. Jan. 30, 2003, adding subd. 1(e); L. 2003, Ch. 10, §§ 1, 2, eff. Mar. 7, 2003, amending subd. e and designating former subd. e as current subd. f; Ch. 62, Part F, § 4, eff. May 15, 2003, adding subd. 8; L. 2004, Ch. 361, § 2, eff. Sept. 9, 2004, amending subd. 5; L. 2005, Ch. 56, Part O, § 1, amending subd. 1(b), eff. Apr. 12, 2006; L. 2005, Ch. 260, § 5, adding subd. 9, eff. Aug. 18, 2005.

Editor's Note: L. 2003, Ch. 10, § 8 provides: "This act shall take effect immediately; provided that sections one, two, three, four, five and six of this act shall take effect on the same date and in the same manner as [L. 2002, Ch. 694] takes effect."

ANNOTATION

Sex offender risk level determination.—"The sex offender risk level determination is regulatory, rather than criminal, in nature. and is not intended to effect punishment. Since the publication of the directory is merely a proper exercise of the state's police power to regulate present and ongoing conduct and to protect the community, the defendant has no due process right to appear and be heard regarding the impact of this regulatory issue upon him." People v. Mitchell, 300 A.D.2d 377,751 N.Y.S.2d 530 (2d Dept. 2002).

§ 168-c. Sex offender; relocation; notification.

1. In the case of any sex offender, it shall be the duty of the department, hospital or local correctional facility at least ten calendar days prior to the release or discharge of any sex

offender from a correctional facility, hospital or local correctional facility to notify the division of the contemplated release or discharge of such sex offender, informing the division in writing on a form provided by the division indicating the address at which he or she proposes to reside and the name and address of any institution of higher education at which he or she expects to be enrolled, attending or employed, whether for compensation or not, and whether he or she resides in or will reside in a facility owned or operated by such institution. If such sex offender changes his or her place of residence while on parole, such notification of the change of residence shall be sent by the sex offender's parole officer within forty-eight hours to the division on a form provided by the division. If such sex offender changes the status of his or her enrollment, attendance, employment or residence at any institution of higher education while on parole, such notification of the change of status shall be sent by the sex offender's parole officer within forty-eight hours to the division on a form provided by the division.

2. In the case of any sex offender on probation, it shall be the duty of the sex offender's probation officer to notify the division within forty-eight hours of the new place of residence on a form provided by the division. If such sex offender changes the status of his or her enrollment, attendance, employment or residence at any institution of higher education while on probation, such notification of the change of status shall be sent by the sex offender's probation officer within forty-eight hours to the division on a form provided by the division.

3. In the case in which any sex offender escapes from a state or local correctional facility or hospital, the designated official of the facility or hospital where the person was confined shall notify within twenty-four hours the law enforcement agency having had jurisdiction at the time of his or her conviction, informing such law enforcement agency of the name and aliases of the person, and the address at which he or she resided at the time of his or her conviction, the amount of time remaining to be served, if any, on the full term for which he or she was sentenced, and the nature of the crime for which he or she was sentenced, transmitting at the same time a copy of such sex offender's fingerprints and photograph and a summary of his or her criminal record.

4. The division shall provide general information, in registration materials and annual correspondence, to registrants concerning notification and registration procedures that may apply if the registrant is authorized to relocate and relocates to another state or United States possession, or commences employment or attendance at an education institution in another state or United States possession. Such information shall include addresses and telephone numbers for relevant agencies from which additional information may be obtained.

Added by L. 1995, Ch. 192, eff. Jan. 21, 1996; L. 2002, Ch. 11, eff. Mar. 11, 2002; L. 2004, Ch. 410, § 1, adding subd. 4, eff. Nov. 15, 2004.

ANNOTATIONS

Address change; failure to notify.—Absent a certified document from DCJS or an affidavit from a DCJS employee with personal knowledge, the conclusory hearsay allegations that the defendant failed to register under SORA that he had a change of address within 10 days was defective. Court denied motion to dismiss and granted the People leave to move to amend or otherwise cure the hearsay pleading. People v. Cobb, 2 Misc. 3d 237, 768 N.Y.S.2d 295 (Crim. Ct. Queens Co. 2003).

§ 168-d. Duties of the court.

1. (a) Except as provided in paragraphs (b) and (c) of this subdivision, upon conviction of any of the offenses set forth in subdivision two or three of section one hundred sixty-eight-a of this article the court shall certify that the person is a sex offender and shall include the certification in the order of commitment, if any, and judgment of conviction, except as provided in paragraph (e) of subdivision two of section one hundred sixty-eight-a of this article. The court shall also advise the sex offender of his or her duties under this article. Failure to include the certification in the order of commitment or the judgment of conviction shall not relieve a sex offender of the obligations imposed by this article.

(b) Where a defendant stands convicted of an offense defined in paragraph (b) of subdivision two of section one hundred sixty-eight-a of this article and the defendant controverts an allegation that the victim of such offense was less than eighteen years of age, the court, without a jury, shall, prior to sentencing, conduct a hearing, and the people may prove by clear and convincing evidence that the victim was less than eighteen years of age by any evidence admissible under the rules applicable to a trial of the issue of guilt. The court in addition to such admissible evidence may also consider reliable hearsay evidence submitted by either party provided that it is relevant to the determination of the age of the victim. Facts concerning the age of the victim proven at trial or ascertained at the time of entry of a plea of guilty shall be deemed established by clear and convincing evidence and shall not be relitigated. At the conclusion of the hearing, or if the defendant does not controvert an allegation that the victim of the offense was less than eighteen years of age, the court must make a finding and enter an order setting forth the age of the victim. If the court finds that the victim of such offense was under eighteen years of age, the court shall certify the defendant as a sex offender, the provisions of paragraph (a) of this subdivision shall apply and the defendant shall register with the division in accordance with the provisions of this article.

(c) Where a defendant stands convicted of an offense defined in paragraph (c) of subdivision two of section one hundred sixty-eight-a of this article and the defendant controverts an allegation that the defendant was previously convicted of a sex offense or a sexually violent offense defined in this article or has previously been convicted of or convicted for an attempt to commit any of the provisions of section 130.52 or 130.55 of the penal law, the court, without a jury, shall, prior to sentencing, conduct a hearing, and the people may prove by clear and convincing evidence that the defendant was previously convicted of a sex offense or a sexually violent offense defined in this article or has previously been convicted of or convicted for an attempt to commit any of the provisions of section 130.52 or 130.55 of the penal law, by any evidence admissible under the rules applicable to a trial of the issue of guilt. The court in addition to such admissible evidence may also consider reliable hearsay evidence submitted by either party provided that it is relevant to the determination of whether the defendant was previously convicted of a sex offense or a sexually violent offense defined in this article or has previously been convicted of or convicted for an attempt to commit any of the provisions of section 130.52 or 130.55 of the penal law. At the conclusion of the hearing, or if the defendant does not controvert an allegation that the defendant was previously convicted of a sex offense or a sexually violent offense defined in this article or has previously been convicted of or convicted for an attempt to commit any of the provisions of section 130.52 or 130.55 of the penal law, the court must make a finding and enter an order determining whether the defendant was previously convicted of a sex offense or a sexually violent offense defined in this article or has previously been convicted of or convicted for an attempt to commit any of the provisions of section 130.52 or 130.55 of the penal law. If the court finds that the defendant has such a previous conviction, the court shall certify the defendant as a sex offender, the provisions of paragraph (a) of this subdivision shall apply and the defendant shall register with the division in accordance with the provisions of this article.

2. Any sex offender, who is released on probation or discharged upon payment of a fine, conditional discharge or unconditional discharge shall, prior to such release or discharge, be informed of his or her duty to register under this article by the court in which he or she was convicted. At the time sentence is imposed, such sex offender shall register with the division on a form prepared by the division. The court shall require the sex offender to read and sign such form and to complete the registration portion of such form. The court shall on such form obtain the address where the sex offender expects to reside upon his or her release, and the name and address of any institution of higher education he or she expects to be employed by, enrolled in, attending or employed, whether for compensation or not, and whether he or she expects to reside in a facility owned or operated by such an institution, and shall report such information to the division. The court shall give one copy of the form to the sex offender and shall send two copies to the division which shall forward the information to the law enforcement agencies having jurisdiction. The court shall also notify the district attorney and the sex offender of the date of the determination proceeding to be held pursuant to subdivision three of this section, which shall be held at least forty-five days after such notice is given. The court shall also advise the sex offender that he or she has a right to a hearing prior to the court's determination, that he or she has the right to be represented by counsel at the hearing and that counsel will be appointed if he or she is financially unable to retain counsel. If the sex offender applies for assignment of counsel to represent him or her at the hearing and counsel was not previously assigned to represent the sex offender in the underlying criminal action, the court shall determine whether the offender is financially unable to retain counsel. If such a finding is made, the court shall assign counsel to represent the sex offender pursuant to article eighteen-B of the county law. Where the court orders a sex offender released on probation, such order must include a provision requiring that he or she comply with the requirements of this article. Where such sex offender violates such provision, probation may be immediately revoked in the manner provided by article four hundred ten of the criminal procedure law.

3. For sex offenders released on probation or discharged upon payment of a fine, conditional discharge or unconditional discharge, it shall be the duty of the court applying the guidelines established in subdivision five of section one hundred sixty-eight-l of this article to determine the level of notification pursuant to subdivision six of section one hundred sixty-eight-l of this article and whether such sex offender shall be designated a sexual predator, sexually violent offender, or predicate sex offender as defined in subdivision seven of section one hundred sixty-eight-a of this article. At least fifteen days prior to the determination proceeding, the district attorney shall provide to the court and the sex offender a written statement setting forth the determinations sought by the district attorney together with the reasons for seeking such determinations. The court shall allow the sex offender to appear and be heard. The state shall appear by the district attorney, or his or her designee, who shall bear the burden of proving the facts supporting the determinations sought by clear and convincing evidence. Where there is a dispute between the parties concerning the determinations, the court shall adjourn the hearing as necessary to permit the sex offender or the district attorney to obtain materials relevant to the determinations from any state or local facility, hospital, institution, office, agency, department or division. Such materials may be obtained by subpoena if not voluntarily

provided to the requesting party. In making the determinations, the court shall review any victim's statement and any relevant materials and evidence submitted by the sex offender and the district attorney and the court may consider reliable hearsay evidence submitted by either party provided that it is relevant to the determinations. Facts previously proven at trial or elicited at the time of entry of a plea of guilty shall be deemed established by clear and convincing evidence and shall not be relitigated. The court shall render an order setting forth its determinations and the findings of fact and conclusions of law on which the determinations are based. A copy of the order shall be submitted by the court to the division. Upon application of either party, the court shall seal any portion of the court file or record which contains material that is confidential under any state or federal statute. Either party may appeal as of right from the order pursuant to the provisions of articles fifty-five, fifty-six and fifty-seven of the civil practice law and rules. Where counsel has been assigned to represent the sex offender upon the ground that the sex offender is financially unable to retain counsel, that assignment shall be continued throughout the pendency of the appeal, and the person may appeal as a poor person pursuant to article eighteen-B of the county law.

Added by L. 1995, Ch. 192, eff. Jan. 21, 1996; Amended by L. 1999, Ch. 453, eff. Jan. 1, 2000; L. 2002, Ch. 11, eff. Mar. 11, 2002; L. 2003, Ch. 69, § 5, eff. Aug, 11, 2003, amending subd. 1(a).

Pursuant to L. 2002, Ch. 11, § 24, the amendments to subd. 1 of this section shall apply to offenses committed on or after such effective date, and the amendments to subd. 3 "shall apply to sex offenders for whom an initial risk level determination has not been made prior to such effective date or who, on the effective date of this act, are not members of the plaintiff class in the U.S. District Court, Southern District of New York case entitled Doe v. Pataki, Index Number 96CIV1657 (DC)."

ANNOTATIONS

Appealability of court's actions.—Legislature mandated that SORA certification occur "upon conviction" and contemplated that determination would be part of final adjudication of criminal proceedings against defendant. People v. Nieves, 2 N.Y.3d 310, 778 N.Y.S.2d 75, 811 N.E.2d 13 (2004).

—Certification of defendant as a sex offender was part of court's final adjudication with respect to defendant's crimes and formed an integral part of conviction and sentencing; it is subject to appellate review. People v. Hernandez, 93 N.Y.2d 261, 689 N.Y.S.2d 695, 711 N.E.2d 972 (1999).

—The certification of defendant as a sex offender, the risk level designation, and the court's direction that defendant subject himself to the notification requirements of Sex Offender Registration Act, are not part of the judgment of conviction and cannot be challenged on direct appeal. People v. Grice, 254 A.D.2d 710, 679 N.Y.S.2d 771 (4th Dept. 1999).

Board of Examiners of Sex Offenders; no right to sue.—Board of Examiners of Sex Offenders lacks the capacity to sue to challenge the determination of a sentencing court with respect to sex offender risk level; the Sex Offender Registration Act does not authorize the Board to sue or be sued. New York State Bd. of Examiners of Sex Offenders v. Ransom, 249 A.D.2d 891, 672 N.Y.S.2d 185 (4th Dept. 1998).

Classification of sex offenders.—County court properly evaluated defendant's score by ten points, increasing his sex offender risk status to level III, given the three-year-old victim's complaint of pain and obvious physical helplessness against the sexual assault of an adult male, coupled with the undisputed

facts in defendant's case summary demonstrating defendant's long history of mental health and emotional problems. People v. Moon, 3 A.D.3d 600, 771 N.Y.S.2d 223 (3d Dept. 2004).

—Presumptively defendant's risk level under the Sex Offender Registration Act was a level one category; however, for purposes of duration and extent to register as a sex offender and the amount of information that could be given to the public, the court could classify defendant as a level two offender because defendant had engaged in sexual misconduct on two separate occasions with two very young victims over a period of several months. People v. Lombardo, 167 Misc. 2d 942, 640 N.Y.S.2d 995 (County Court Nassau Co. 1996).

Constitutionality.—Section 169-d did not violate Ex Post Facto Clause, even though defendant committed the underlying offenses of attempted rape and sexual abuse in February 1995 and SORA was not effective until January 1996. People v. Hernandez, 264 A.D.2d 783, 695 N.Y.S.2d 126 (2d Dept.), *appeal denied,* 94 N.Y.2d 863 (1999).

—Because defendant failed at his sentencing to raise claim that the Sex Offender Registration Act violates the Ex Post Facto Clause as applied to him, he failed to preserve the claim for appellate review. People v. Lyday, 241 A.D.2d 950, 661 N.Y.S.2d 325 (4th Dept. 1997).

Defendant's admission of guilt.—Defendant claimed that court had improperly found that he admitted the element of forcible compulsion. Although defendant did not admit his guilt as part of the *Alford* plea, the evidence was elicited at the time of the entry of the plea of guilty, and it was thus deemed established for purposes of SORA classification. People v. Jones, 15 A.D.3d 929, 789 N.Y.S.2d 382 (4th Dept. 2005).

Due process requirements.—Prosecution's right to be heard was waived by its failure to provide the court and defendant with sufficient prior notice of the assessment sought; the one day's notice was insufficient to provide defendant with a meaningful opportunity to respond. People v. MacNeil, 283 A.D.2d 835, 727 N.Y.S.2d 485 (3d Dept. 2001).

—SORA requires that the offender be afforded a prior written statement of the assessment sought by the prosecution and the reasons for seeking it. Here, the prosecution's right to be heard was waived by its failure to provide the court with prior notice of the assessment sought, in violation of defendant's due process rights. People v. Neish, 281 A.D.2d 817, 722 N.Y.S.2d 815 (3d Dept. 2001).

—The minimal due process requirements for risk level classification proceedings for an offender receiving probation, pursuant to Correction Law § 168-d, can best be protected by the following procedures: (1) offender must be given oral or written notice by the court that the court intends to assign a specific risk level based on the risk factors considered by the court; (2) court should inform offender of his right to have counsel present at the proceeding; (3) offender should be allowed to submit materials to the court and make oral arguments; (4) in preparation for the proceeding, the offender should be allowed to review the presentence report, clinical assessments attached to it, and any other written material provided to the People or reviewed by the court; (5) once the offender controverts any information relied on by the court, the People have the burden to prove, by a preponderance of the evidence, that the information is reliable and accurate; and (6) the court has the discretion to conduct a summary hearing on any controverted fact that is substantial and calls into question the reliability and accuracy of the information presented to the court which provides the basis for the court's decision. People v. Roe, 177 Misc. 2d 960, 677 N.Y.S.2d 895 (Nassau Co. Ct. 1998).

Failure to inform.—Defendant unsuccessfully moved to withdraw pleas on charges of attempted first degree sexual abuse and first degree criminal attempt, and for violating an order of protection regarding this same victim, based on failure of court and defense counsel to inform the defendant that his plea to these counts brought him within the purview of the Sex Offender Registration Act; since the consequences to the plea were collateral, neither the court nor counsel had to inform defendant that certification was a required effect of his plea. People v. Clark, 261 A.D.2d 97, 704 N.Y.S.2d 149 (3d Dept.), *appeal denied,* 95 N.Y.2d 833 (2000).

Voluntariness of plea.—Defendant challenged the voluntariness of his plea on the ground that the court and counsel failed to advise him that by pleading guilty he would fall within the purview of SORA. The Appellate Division found that since the purpose of certification is administrative and ministerial rather than punitive, the consequences are collateral, which obviated the need for the court or counsel to have informed defendant that certification was a necessary outcome of his plea. People v. Clark, 261 A.D.2d 97, 704 N.Y.S.2d 149 (3d Dept. 2000).

§ 168-e. Discharge of sex offender from correctional facility; duties of official in charge.

1. Any sex offender, to be discharged, paroled, released to post-release supervision or released from any state or local correctional facility, hospital or institution where he or she was confined or committed, shall at least fifteen calendar days prior to discharge, parole or release, be informed of his or her duty to register under this article, by the facility in which he or she was confined or committed. The facility shall require the sex offender to read and sign such form as may be required by the division stating the duty to register and the procedure for registration has been explained to him or her and to complete the registration portion of such form. The facility shall obtain on such form the address where the sex offender expects to reside upon his or her discharge, parole or release and the name and address of any institution of higher education he or she expects to be employed by, enrolled in, attending or employed, whether for compensation or not, and whether he or she expects to reside in a facility owned or operated by such an institution, and shall report such information to the division. The facility shall give one copy of the form to the sex offender, retain one copy and shall send one copy to the division which shall provide the information to the law enforcement agencies having jurisdiction. The facility shall give the sex offender a form prepared by the division, to register with the division at least fifteen calendar days prior to release and such form shall be completed, signed by the sex offender and sent to the division by the facility at least ten days prior to the sex offender's release or discharge.

2. The division shall also immediately transmit the conviction data and fingerprints to the Federal Bureau of Investigation if not already obtained.

Added by L. 1995, Ch. 192, eff. Jan. 21, 1996; **Amended** by L. 1999, Ch. 453, eff. Jan. 1, 2000, amending subd. 1; L. 2002, Ch. 11, eff. July 1, 2002, amending subd. 1.

§ 168-f. Duty to register and to verify.

1. Any sex offender shall, (a) at least ten calendar days prior to discharge, parole, release to post-release supervision or release from any state or local correctional facility, hospital or institution where he or she was confined or committed, or, (b) at the time sentence is imposed for any sex offender released on probation or discharged upon payment of a fine, conditional discharge or unconditional discharge, register with the division on a form prepared by the division.

2. For a sex offender required to register under this article on each anniversary of the sex offender's initial registration date during the period in which he is required to register under this section the following applies:

(a) the sex offender shall mail the verification form to the division within ten calendar days after receipt of the form.

(b) the verification form shall be signed by the sex offender, and state that he still resides at the address last reported to the division.

(b-1) If the sex offender has been given a level three designation, such offender shall sign the verification form, and state that he or she still is employed at the address last reported to the division.

(b-2) [*Effective Apr. 12, 2006.*] If the sex offender has been given a level three designation, he or she shall personally appear at the law enforcement agency having jurisdiction within twenty days of the first anniversary of the sex offender's initial registration and every year thereafter during the period of registration for the purpose of providing a current photograph of such offender. The law enforcement agency having jurisdiction shall photograph the sex offender and shall promptly forward a copy of such photograph to the division. For purposes of this paragraph, if such sex offender is confined in a state or local correctional facility, the local law enforcement agency having jurisdiction shall be the warden, superintendent, sheriff or other person in charge of the state or local correctional facility.

(b-3) [*Effective Apr. 12, 2006.*] If the sex offender has been given a level one or level two designation, he or she shall personally appear at the law enforcement agency having jurisdiction within twenty days of the third anniversary of the sex offender's initial registration and every three years thereafter during the period of registration for the purpose of providing a current photograph of such offender. The law enforcement agency having jurisdiction shall photograph the sex offender and shall promptly forward a copy of such photograph to the division. For purposes of this paragraph, if such sex offender is confined in a state or local correctional facility, the local law enforcement agency having jurisdiction shall be the warden, superintendent, sheriff or other person in charge of the state or local correctional facility.

(c) If the sex offender fails to mail the signed verification form to the division within ten calendar days after receipt of the form, he or she shall be in violation of this section unless he proves that he or she has not changed his or her residence address.

(c-1) [*Effective Apr. 12, 2006.*] If the sex offender, to whom a notice has been mailed at the last reported address pursuant to paragraph b of subdivision one of section one hundred sixty-eight-b of this article, fails to personally appear at the law enforcement agency having jurisdiction, as provided in paragraph (b-2) or (b-3) of this subdivision, within twenty days of the anniversary of the sex offender's initial registration, or an alternate later date scheduled by the law enforcement agency having jurisdiction, he or she shall be in violation of this section. The duty to personally appear for such updated photograph shall be temporarily suspended during any period in which the sex offender is confined in any hospital or institution, and such sex offender shall personally appear for such updated photograph no later than ninety days after release from such hospital or institution, or an alternate later date scheduled by the law enforcement agency having jurisdiction.

3. The provisions of subdivision two of this section shall be applied to a sex offender required to register under this article except that such sex offender designated as a sexual predator or having been given a level three designation must personally verify his or her address with the local law enforcement agency every ninety calendar days after the date of release or commencement of parole or post-release supervision, or probation, or release on payment of a fine, conditional discharge or unconditional discharge. The duty to personally verify shall be temporarily suspended during any period in which the sex offender is confined to any state or local correctional facility, hospital or institution and shall immediately recommence on the date of the sex offender's release.

4. Any sex offender shall register with the division no later than ten calendar days after any change of address or any change of his or her status of enrollment, attendance, employment or residence at any institution of higher education. A fee of ten dollars, as authorized by subdivision eight of section one hundred sixty-eight-b of this article, shall be submitted by the sex offender each time such offender registers any change of address or any change of his or her status of enrollment, attendance, employment or residence at any institution of higher education. Any failure or omission to submit the required fee shall not affect the acceptance by the division of the change of address or change of status.

5. The duty to register under the provisions of this article shall not be applicable to any sex offender whose conviction was reversed upon appeal or who was pardoned by the governor.

6. Any nonresident worker or nonresident student, as defined in subdivisions fourteen and fifteen of section one hundred sixty-eight-a of this article, shall register his or her current address and the address of his or her place of employment or educational institution attended with the division within ten calendar days after such nonresident worker or nonresident student commences employment or attendance at an educational institution in the state. Any nonresident worker or nonresident student shall notify the division of any change of residence, employment or educational institution address no later than ten days after such change. The division shall notify the law enforcement agency where the nonresident worker is employed or the educational institution is located that a nonresident worker or nonresident student is present in that agency's jurisdiction.

Added by L. 1995, Ch. 192, eff. Jan. 21, 1996; **Amended** by L. 1999, Ch. 453, eff. Jan. 1, 2000, amending the heading and subds. 1, 2(c), and 3; L. 2002, Ch. 11, amending subd. 3, eff. Mar. 11, 2002, and amending subd. 4 and adding subd. 6, eff. July 1, 2002; L. 2002, Ch. 694, § 2, eff. Jan. 30, 2003, adding subd. 2(b-1); L. 2003, Ch. 10, § 3, eff. Mar. 7, 2003, amending subd. 2(b-1); L. 2003, Ch. 62, Part F, § 5, eff. May 15, 2003, amending subd. 4; L. 2005, Ch. 56, Part O, § 2, adding subd. 2(b-2), 2(b-3), and 2(c-1), eff. Apr. 12, 2006.

Editor's Note: L. 2003, Ch. 10, § 8 provides: "This act shall take effect immediately; provided that sections one, two, three, four, five and six of this act shall take effect on the same date and in the same manner as [L. 2002, Ch. 694] takes effect."

ANNOTATIONS

Generally.—A misdemeanor complaint charging defendant, a level II convicted sex offender, with violating the SORA by failing to report an address change with within the requisite 10-day period is facially defective and must be dismissed in the absence of any allegation setting forth the date defendant purportedly changed his address. People v. Armfield, 189 Misc. 2d 556, 734 N.Y.S.2d 817 (Crim. Ct. Richmond Co. 2001).

Duty to comply with registration requirements.—Each state has enacted statutes designed to protect its communities from sex offenders, and the statutes include a registration component. States have the power to choose the administrative manner for exercising the registration requirements; these requirements are not governed by the procedures in effect in the state where the offender previously resided. Thus, a convicted sex offender who moves into New York must comply with New York's registration requirements, rather than the requirements of the state where he previously resided. People v. Arotin, 19 A.D.3d 845, 796 N.Y.S.2d 743 (3d Dept. 2005).

Duty to report address.—Defendant, on parole for his conviction of sex abuse in the first degree, was required to register annually with the Division of Criminal Justice Services for 10 years, notify them of any address change, and verify his residence with local authorities every 90 days. Defendant misrepresented his address and failed to list properly his residence on five separate filings with the sheriff; accordingly, defendant was convicted of offering a false instrument for filing. People v. Willette, 290 A.D.2d 576, 735 N.Y.S.2d 645 (3d Dept. 2002).

SORA registration; no plea bargaining of requirement.—Court stated it was disturbed that defendant was permitted to bargain away potential eligibility for registration as a sex offender pursuant to SORA, which was enacted for the benefit of the public, and its protections should not be bargained away merely to avoid the time and expense of a trial. People v. Guerrero, 307 A.D.2d 935, 762 N.Y.S.2d 888 (2d Dept. 2003).

§ 168-g. Prior convictions; duty to inform and register.

1. The division of parole or department of probation and correctional alternatives in accordance with risk factors pursuant to section one hundred sixty-eight-l of this article shall determine the duration of registration and notification for every sex offender who on the effective date of this article is then on parole or probation for an offense provided for in subdivision two or

three of section one hundred sixty-eight-a of this article.

2. Every sex offender who on the effective date of this article is then on parole or probation for an offense provided for in subdivision two or three of section one hundred sixty-eight-a of this article shall within ten calendar days of such determination register with his parole or probation officer. On each anniversary of the sex offender's initial registration date thereafter, the provisions of section one hundred sixty-eight-f of this article shall apply. Any sex offender who fails or refuses to so comply shall be subject to the same penalties as otherwise provided for in this article which would be imposed upon a sex offender who fails or refuses to so comply with the provisions of this article on or after such effective date.

3. It shall be the duty of the parole or probation officer to inform and register such sex offender according to the requirements imposed by this article. A parole or probation officer shall give one copy of the form to the sex offender and shall, within three calendar days, send two copies electronically or otherwise to the division which shall forward one copy electronically or otherwise to the law enforcement agency having jurisdiction where the sex offender resides upon his parole, probation, or upon any form of state or local conditional release.

4. A petition for relief from this section is permitted to any sex offender required to register while released on parole or probation pursuant to section one hundred sixty-eight-o of this article.

Added by L. 1995, Ch. 192, eff. Jan. 21, 1996.

ANNOTATIONS

Constitutional challenge.—"Procedural due process requires that this defendant on probation when SORA went into effect, should have received notice and an opportunity to be heard before his SORA risk level determination was made." People v. David W., 95 N.Y.2d 130, 711 N.Y.S.2d 134, 733 N.E.2d 206 (2000).

DPCA determination.—The Sex Offender Registry Unit of the New York State Division of Probation and Correction Alternatives (DPCA) properly determined that defendant was assessed points for forcible compulsion rape, even though he was not indicted for such, based on the victim's statement that the defendant forced her legs apart and held her down; furthermore, defendant did not object during a taped conversation with the victim, in which she stated, "You took advantage of me by giving me that vodka to drink, and then forced yourself on me." Youngs v. Division of Probation and Corr. Alternatives, 175 Misc. 2d 51, 667 N.Y.S.2d 1021 (Co. Ct. Yates Co. 1997).

Numerical risk methodology not arbitrary.—Defendant was indeed a subject of the New York's Sex Offender Registration Act. The numerical risk methodology is not an arbitrary and capricious procedure for calculating risk assessment under the act. The guidelines do not try to predict an offender's future conduct, but recognize that certain factors are relevant, such as the crime itself, whether violence was involved, the relationship between the offender and the victim, behavior while in prison, and participation in treatment programs. People v. Nieves, 172 Misc. 2d 346, 659 N.Y.S.2d 972 (Sup. Ct. Bronx Co. 1997).

Risk level three for pedophilia.—A presumptive risk assessment of level three automatically results when one of four specified "overriding factors" is present, one of which includes a diagnosis of suffering from a chronic inability to control impulsive sexual behavior such as petitioner's pedophilia.

O'Brien v. New York Division of Probation and Correctional Servs., 263 A.D.2d 804, 693 N.Y.S.2d 735 (3d Dept. 1999).

Upward departure proper.—It was not irrational, arbitrary, or capricious for respondent to make an upward departure from presumptive risk level in light of fact that petitioner's prior conviction for endangering welfare of a child was not otherwise taken into consideration on the Risk Assessment Instrument. O'Brien v. New York Division of Probation and Correctional Services, 263 A.D.2d 804, 693 N.Y.S.2d 735 (3d Dept. 1999).

Youthful offender adjudication.—Court disagreed with defendant that consideration by the Board of a youthful offender adjudication for sexual abuse in the third degree was improper. The risk assessment guidelines expressly provide that youthful offender adjudications are to be treated as crimes for purposes of assessing the defendant's likelihood of re-offending and danger to public safety. People v. Moore, 1 A.D.3d 421, 766 N.Y.S.2d 700 (2d Dept. 2003).

—A youthful offender adjudication may be considered a prior crime or prior offense for purposes of assessing a risk level under SORA. People v. Vite-Acosta, 184 Misc. 2d 206, 708 N.Y.S.2d 583 (Sup. Ct. Bronx Co. 2000).

§ 168-h. Duration of registration and verification.

1. The duration of registration and verification for a sex offender who has not been designated a sexual predator, or a sexually violent offender, or a predicate sex offender, or who, as of March eleventh, two thousand two, was classified as a level one or level two risk, shall be annually for a period of ten years from the initial date of registration.

2. The duration of registration and verification for a sex offender who, on or after March eleventh, two thousand two, is designated a sexual predator, or a sexually violent offender, or a predicate sex offender, or who is, as of March eleventh, two thousand two, classified as a level three risk, shall be annually for life. Notwithstanding the foregoing, a sex offender who, as of March eleventh, two thousand two, was classified as a level three risk, may be relieved of the duty to register and verify as provided by subdivision one of section one hundred sixty-eight-o of this article.

3. Any sex offender having been designated a level three risk or a sexual predator shall also personally verify his or her address every ninety calendar days with the local law enforcement agency having jurisdiction where the offender resides.

Added by L. 1995, Ch. 192, eff. Jan. 21, 1996; **Amended** by L. 1999, Ch. 453, eff. Jan. 1, 2000; L. 2002, Ch. 11, eff. Mar. 11, 2002.

§ 168-i. Registration and verification requirements.

Registration and verification as required by this article shall consist of a statement in writing signed by the sex offender giving the information that is required by the division and the division shall enter the information into an appropriate electronic data base or file.

Added by L. 1995, Ch. 192, eff. Jan. 21, 1996; **Amended** by L. 1999, Ch. 453, eff. Jan. 1, 2000.

§ 168-j. Notification of local law enforcement agencies of change of address.

1. Upon receipt of a change of address by a sex offender required to register under this article, the division shall notify the local law enforcement agency having jurisdiction of the new place of residence and the local law enforcement agency where the sex offender last resided of the new place of residence.

2. Upon receipt of change of address information, the local law enforcement agency having jurisdiction of the new place of residence shall adhere to the notification provisions set forth in subdivision six of section one hundred sixty-eight-l of this article.

3. The division shall, if the sex offender changes residence to another state, notify the appropriate agency within that state of the new place of residence.

4. Upon receipt of a change in the status of the enrollment, attendance, employment or residence at an institution of higher education by a sex offender required to register under this article, the division shall notify each law enforcement agency having jurisdiction which is affected by such change.

5. Upon receipt of change in the status of the enrollment, attendance, employment or residence at an institution of higher education by a sex offender required to register under this article, each law enforcement agency having jurisdiction shall adhere to the notification provisions set forth in subdivision six of section one hundred sixty-eight-l of this article.

Added by L. 1995, Ch. 192, eff. Jan. 21, 1996; **Amended** by L. 1999, Ch. 453, eff. Jan. 1, 2000; L. 2002, Ch. 11, amending subds. 1 and 2, and adding subd. 3, eff. Mar. 11, 2002, and adding subds. 4 and 5, eff. July 1, 2002.

§ 168-k. Registration for change of address from another state.

1. A sex offender who has been convicted of an offense which requires registration under paragraph (d) of subdivision two or paragraph (b) of subdivision three of section one hundred sixty-eight-a of this article shall notify the division of the new address no later than ten calendar days after such sex offender establishes residence in this state.

2. The division shall advise the board that the sex offender has established residence in this state. The board shall determine whether the sex offender is required to register with the division. If it is determined that the sex offender is required to register, the division shall notify the sex offender of his or her duty to register under this article and shall require the sex offender to sign a form as may be required by the division acknowledging that the duty to register and the procedure for registration has been explained to the sex offender. The division shall obtain on such form the address where the sex offender expects to reside within the state and the sex offender shall retain one copy of the form and send two copies to the division which shall provide the information to the law enforcement agency having jurisdiction where the sex offender expects to reside within this state. No later than thirty days prior to the board making a recommendation, the sex offender shall be notified that his or her case is under review and that he or she is permitted to submit to the board any information relevant to the review. After reviewing any information obtained, and applying the guidelines established in subdivision five of section one hundred sixty-eight-l of this article, the board shall within sixty calendar days make a recommendation regarding the level of notification pursuant to subdivision six of section one hundred sixty-eight-l of this article and whether such sex offender shall be designated a sexual predator, sexually violent offender, or predicate sex offender as defined in subdivision seven of section one hundred sixty-eight-a of this article. This recommendation shall be confidential and shall not be available for public inspection. It shall be submitted by the board to the county court or supreme court and to the district attorney in the county of residence of the sex offender and to the sex offender. It shall be the duty of the county court or supreme court in the county of residence of the sex offender, applying the guidelines established in subdivision five of section one hundred sixty-eight-l of this article, to determine the level of notification pursuant to subdivision six of section one hundred sixty-eight-l of this article and whether such sex offender shall be designated a sexual predator, sexually violent offender, or predicate sex offender as defined in subdivision seven of section one hundred sixty-eight-a of this article. At least thirty days prior to the determination proceeding, such court shall notify the district attorney and the sex offender, in writing, of the date of the determination proceeding and the court shall also provide the district attorney and sex offender with a copy of the recommendation received from the board and any statement of the reasons for the recommendation received from the board. The court shall also advise the sex offender that he or she has a right to a hearing prior to the court's determination, that he or she has the right to be represented by counsel at the hearing and that counsel will be appointed if he or she is financially unable to retain counsel. A returnable form shall be enclosed in the court's notice to the sex offender on which the sex offender may apply for assignment of counsel. If the sex offender applies for assignment of counsel and the court finds that the offender is financially unable to retain counsel, the court shall assign counsel to represent the sex offender pursuant to article eighteen-B of the county law. If the district attorney seeks a determination that differs from the recommendation

submitted by the board, at least ten days prior to the determination proceeding the district attorney shall provide to the court and the sex offender a statement setting forth the determinations sought by the district attorney together with the reasons for seeking such determinations. The court shall allow the sex offender to appear and be heard. The state shall appear by the district attorney, or his or her designee, who shall bear the burden of proving the facts supporting the determinations sought by clear and convincing evidence. It shall be the duty of the court applying the guidelines established in subdivision five of section one hundred sixty-eight-l of this article to determine the level of notification pursuant to subdivision six of section one hundred sixty-eight-l of this article and whether such sex offender shall be designated a sexual predator, sexually violent offender, or predicate sex offender as defined in subdivision seven of section one hundred sixty-eight-a of this article. Where there is a dispute between the parties concerning the determinations, the court shall adjourn the hearing as necessary to permit the sex offender or the district attorney to obtain materials relevant to the determinations from the state board of examiners of sex offenders or any state or local facility, hospital, institution, office, agency, department or division. Such materials may be obtained by subpoena if not voluntarily provided to the requesting party. In making the determinations the court shall review any victim's statement and any relevant materials and evidence submitted by the sex offender and the district attorney and the recommendation and any material submitted by the board, and may consider reliable hearsay evidence submitted by either party, provided that it is relevant to the determinations. If available, facts proven at trial or elicited at the time of a plea of guilty shall be deemed established by clear and convincing evidence and shall not be relitigated. The court shall render an order setting forth its determinations and the findings of fact and conclusions of law on which the determinations are based. A copy of the order shall be submitted by the court to the division. Upon application of either party, the court shall seal any portion of the court file or record which contains material that is confidential under any state or federal statute. Either party may appeal as of right from the order pursuant to the provisions of articles fifty-five, fifty-six and fifty-seven of the civil practice law and rules. Where counsel has been assigned to represent the sex offender upon the ground that the sex offender is financially unable to retain counsel, that assignment shall be continued throughout the pendency of the appeal, and the person may appeal as a poor person pursuant to article eighteen-B of the county law.

3. The division shall undertake an information campaign designed to provide information to officials and appropriate individuals in other states and United States possessions concerning the notification procedures required by this article. Such information campaign shall be ongoing, and shall include, but not be limited to, letters, notice forms and similar materials providing relevant information about this article and the specific procedures required to effect notification. Such materials shall include an address and telephone number which such officials and individuals in other states and United States possessions may use to obtain additional information.

Added by L. 1995, Ch. 192, eff. Jan. 21, 1996; **Amended** by L. 1999, Ch. 453, eff. Jan. 1, 2000; L. 2002, Ch. 11, eff. Mar. 11, 2002; L. 2004, Ch. 146, § 2, eff. July 13, 2004, amending subd. 1; L. 2004, Ch. 410, § 2, adding subd. 3, eff. Nov. 15, 2004.

ANNOTATIONS

Appeal of determination.—Following his conviction in Florida of lewd or lascivious exhibition (a felony for which defendant was required to register as a sex offender in Florida), defendant moved to New York. The New York Board of Examiners of Sex Offenders determined that defendant was required to register as a sex offender in New York, and defendant challenged this on the ground that for committing the underlying acts in New York, he would not have had to register. The trial court lacked subject matter jurisdiction to vacate the determination of the State Board of Examiners of Sex Offenders requiring him to register as a sex offender. The proper procedure is an Article 78 proceeding. People v. Caraballo, 309 A.D.2d 1227, 765 N.Y.S.2d 724 (4th Dept. 2003).

—Where a defendant convicted under a federal statute of knowingly possessing child pornography challenged the decision of the New York State Board of Examiners of Sex Offenders which informed him, upon taking up residence in New York, that he was required to register as a sex offender and notified him that a hearing to determine a risk level was required to be held, the proper vehicle to challenge that Board determination was an Article 78 proceeding. *In re* Mandel, 184 Misc. 2d 897, 711 N.Y.S.2d 313 (Cty. Ct. Nassau Co. 2000).

§ 168-l. Board of examiners of sex offenders.

1. There shall be a board of examiners of sex offenders which shall possess the powers and duties hereinafter specified. Such board shall consist of five members appointed by the governor. Three members who shall be experts in the field of the behavior and treatment of sex offenders shall be employees of the division of parole and the remaining two members shall be from the department. The term of office of each member of such board shall be for six years; provided, however, that any member chosen to fill a vacancy occurring otherwise than by expiration of term shall be appointed for the remainder of the unexpired term of the member whom he is to succeed. In the event of the inability to act of any member, the governor may appoint some competent informed person to act in his stead during the continuance of such disability.

2. The governor shall designate one of the members of the board as chairman to serve in such capacity at the pleasure of the governor or until the member's term of office expires and a successor is designated in accordance with law, whichever first occurs.

3. Any member of the board may be removed

by the governor for cause after an opportunity to be heard.

4. Except as otherwise provided by law, a majority of the board shall constitute a quorum for the transaction of all business of the board.

5. The board shall develop guidelines and procedures to assess the risk of a repeat offense by such sex offender and the threat posed to the public safety. Such guidelines shall be based upon, but not limited to, the following:

(a) criminal history factors indicative of high risk of repeat offense, including:

(i) whether the sex offender has a mental abnormality or personality disorder that makes him or her likely to engage in predatory sexually violent offenses;

(ii) whether the sex offender's conduct was found to be characterized by repetitive and compulsive behavior, associated with drugs or alcohol;

(iii) whether the sex offender served the maximum term;

(iv) whether the sex offender committed the felony sex offense against a child;

(v) the age of the sex offender at the time of the commission of the first sex offense;

(b) other criminal history factors to be considered in determining risk, including:

(i) the relationship between such sex offender and the victim;

(ii) whether the offense involved the use of a weapon, violence or infliction of serious bodily injury;

(iii) the number, date and nature of prior offenses;

(c) conditions of release that minimize risk or re-offense, including but not limited to whether the sex offender is under supervision; receiving counseling, therapy or treatment; or residing in a home situation that provides guidance and supervision;

(d) physical conditions that minimize risk of re-offense, including but not limited to advanced age or debilitating illness;

(e) whether psychological or psychiatric profiles indicate a risk of recidivism;

(f) the sex offender's response to treatment;

(g) recent behavior, including behavior while confined;

(h) recent threats or gestures against persons or expressions of intent to commit additional offenses; and

(i) review of any victim impact statement.

6. Applying these guidelines, the board shall within sixty calendar days prior to the discharge, parole, release to post-release supervision or release of a sex offender make a recommendation which shall be confidential and shall not be available for public inspection, to the sentencing court as to whether such sex offender warrants the designation of sexual predator, sexually violent offender, or predicate sex offender as defined in subdivision seven of section one hundred sixty-eight-a of this article. In addition, the guidelines shall be applied by the board to make a recommendation to the sentencing court which shall be confidential and shall not be available for public inspection, providing for one of the following three levels of notification depending upon the degree of the risk of re-offense by the sex offender.

(a) If the risk of repeat offense is low, a level one designation shall be given to such offender. In such case the law enforcement agency or agencies having jurisdiction and the law enforcement agency or agencies having had jurisdiction at the time of his or her conviction shall be notified pursuant to this article.

(b) If the risk of repeat offense is moderate, a level two designation shall be given to such sex offender. In such case the law enforcement agency or agencies having jurisdiction and the law enforcement agency or agencies having had jurisdiction at the time of his or her conviction shall be notified and may disseminate relevant information which shall include a photograph and description of the offender and which may include the exact name and any aliases used by the sex offender, approximate address based on sex offender's zip code, background information including the offender's crime of conviction, modus of operation, type of victim targeted, the name and address of any institution of higher education at which the sex offender is enrolled, attends, is employed or resides and the description of special conditions imposed on the offender to any entity with vulnerable populations related to the nature of the offense committed by such sex offender. Any entity receiving information on a sex offender may disclose or further disseminate such information at its discretion.

(c) If the risk of repeat offense is high and there exists a threat to the public safety a level three designation shall be given to such sex offender. In such case, the law enforcement agency or agencies having jurisdiction and the law enforcement agency or agencies having had jurisdiction at the time of his or her conviction shall be notified and may disseminate relevant information which shall include a photograph and description of the offender and which may include the sex offender's exact name and any aliases used by the offender, exact address, address of the offender's place of employment, background information including the offender's crime of conviction, modus of operation, type of victim targeted, the name and address of any institution of higher education at which the sex offender is enrolled, attends, is employed or resides and the description of special conditions imposed on the offender to any entity with vulnerable populations related to the nature of the offense committed by such sex offender. Any entity receiving information on a sex offender may disclose or further disseminate such information at its discretion. In addition, in such case, the information described herein shall also be provided in the subdirectory established in this article and notwithstanding any other provision of law, such information shall, upon request, be made available to the public.

7. Upon request by the court, pursuant to section one hundred sixty-eight-o of this article, the board shall provide an updated report pertaining to the sex offender petitioning for relief of the duty to register or for a modification of his or her level of notification.

8. A failure by a state or local agency or the board to act or by a court to render a determination within the time period specified in this article shall not affect the obligation of the sex offender to register or verify under this article nor shall such failure prevent a court from making a determination regarding the sex offender's level of notification and whether such offender is required by law to be registered for a period of ten years or for life. Where a court is unable to make a determination prior to the date scheduled for a sex offender's discharge, parole, release to post-release supervision or release, it shall adjourn the hearing until after the offender is discharged, paroled, released to post-release supervision or released, and shall then expeditiously complete the hearing and issue its determination.

Added by L. 1995, Ch. 192, eff. Jan. 21, 1996; **Amended** by L. 1999, Ch. 453, eff. Jan. 1, 2000, amending subd. 6 and adding subd. 8; L. 2002, Ch. 11, §§ 16–19, amending subds. 5(a)(i), 6, 7, and 8, eff. Mar. 11, 2002, amending subds. 1 and 3; L. 2002, Ch. 694, § 3, eff. Jan. 30, 2003, amending subd. 6(c); L. 2003, Ch. 10, § 4, eff. Mar. 7, 2003, amending subd. 6(c); L. 2003, Ch. 316, § 1, eff. Nov. 1, 2003, amending subd. 6(b) and (c); L. 2003, Ch. 10, § 6, eff May 30, 2003, repealed L. 2002, Ch. 694, § 3, which amended subd. 6(c) of this section; L. 2005, Ch. 318, § 1, amending subd. 6(b) and (c), eff. Oct. 24, 2005.

Editor's Notes: Pursuant to L. 2002, Ch. 11, § 24, the amendments to the opening paragraph of subd. 6 and subd. 8 of this section "shall apply to sex offenders for whom an initial risk level determination has not been made prior to such effective date or who, on the effective date of this act, are not members of the plaintiff class in the U.S. District Court, Southern District of New York case entitled Doe v. Pataki, Index Number 96CIV1657 (DC)."

Editor's Note: L. 2003, Ch. 10, § 8 provides: "This act shall take effect immediately; provided that sections one, two, three, four, five and six of this act shall take effect on the same date and in the same manner as [L. 2002, Ch. 694] takes effect."

ANNOTATIONS

Challenging classification; procedure.—Absent an Article 78 proceeding, the court lacks the authority to review the board's registration determination. *In re* Mandel, 293 A.D.2d 750, 742 N.Y.S.2d 321 (2d Dept. 2002).

—The proper procedure for challenging a classification under the Sex Offender Registration Act is a proceeding pursuant to CPLR article 78. People v. Cash, 242 A.D.2d 976, 664 N.Y.S.2d 696 (4th Dept. 1997).

—Board may consider information outside of defendant's conviction in determining recommendation of risk level to sentencing court, including, but not limited to, the case file, the offender's admissions, statement of the victim, evaluative reports of the supervising parole or probation officer, or any other reliable source. People v. Saleemi, 186 Misc. 2d 177, 718 N.Y.S.2d 139 (Sup. Ct. Queens Co. 2000).

—Where a defendant convicted under a federal statute of knowingly possessing child pornography challenged the decision of the New York State Board of Examiners of Sex Offenders which informed him, upon taking up residence in New York, that he was required to register as a sex offender and notified him that a hearing to determine a risk level was required to be held, the proper vehicle to challenge that Board determination was an Article 78 proceeding. *In re* Mandel, 184 Misc. 2d 897, 711 N.Y.S.2d 313 (Cty. Ct. Nassau Co. 2000).

Continuous course of sexual contact.—Under the risk assessment guidelines, multiple acts of sexual contact within a 24-hour period could not be considered a continuous course of sexual contact; reversal required because trial court misapplied guidelines. People v. Madlin, 302 A.D.2d 751, 755 N.Y.S.2d 121 (3d Dept. 2003).

Effect of amendments to Correction Law.—Defendant contends he was denied due process because of an amendment to Correction Law 168-l(6)(c), which was amended subsequent to his risk assessment level hearing. Because the sex offender risk level determination is regulatory rather than criminal in nature and it is not intended to effect punishment, and since the publication of the directory of sexually violent predators is merely a proper expense of the state's police power; the defendant has no due process right to appear and be heard regarding the impact of this regulatory issue upon him. People v. Mitchell, 300 A.D.2d 377, 751 N.Y.S.2d 530 (2d Dept. 2002).

Failing to accept responsibility.—Defendant's denial of guilt during interview by Department of Corrections justified the assessment of points for failing to accept responsibility for the crime of conviction. People v. Vite-Acosta, 184 Misc. 2d 206, 708 N.Y.S.2d 583 (Sup. Ct. Bronx Co. 2000).

—The hearing court properly relied on its recollection of the plea proceeding, presentence report and case summary of the Board of Examiners of Sex Offenders rather than upon defendant's statements to the contrary in finding that defendant failed to accept responsibility for the crime and refused treatment. People v. Mitchell, 300 A.D.2d 377, 751 N.Y.S.2d 530 (2d Dept. 2002).

Familial relationship.—Where the relationship between the defendant and victim was familial in nature, defendant did not initiate or establish the relationship with her for the primary purpose of victimization, and thus, could not be assessed points in this category. People v. Terdeman, 175 Misc. 2d 379, 669 N.Y.S.2d 136 (Crim. Ct. Queens Co. 1997).

Misapplication of Guidelines allows appellate review.— Under the Risk Assessment Guidelines, multiple acts of sexual contact within one 24 hour period can not be considered "continuous course of sexual contact," nor does the subcategory for "sexual intercourse, deviate intercourse or aggravated sexual abuse," include attempted commissions, only completed acts; court; court may deviate from Guidelines under limited circumstances but can not misapply them. People v. Madlin, 302 A.D.2d 751, 755 N.Y.S.2d 121 (3d Dept. 2003).

No appellate review of risk assessment.—Trial court's assessment that defendant was a sexually violent predator under SORA was not independently appealable from the criminal judgment of conviction. People v. Kearns, 95 N.Y.2d 816, 712 N.Y.S.2d 431,734 N.E.2d 743 (2000).

—Offender's classification in the "sexually violent predator" category is neither an amendment to a conviction nor a resentencing, and the registration and notification requirements do not trigger the direct criminal appellate review that these classified offenders seek; neither Megan's Law nor the CPL allows for criminal appeal from the risk level determination. People v. Stevens, 91 N.Y.2d 270, 669 N.Y.S.2d 962, 692 N.E.2d 985 (1998).

—In the absence of a legislative provision, the Appellate Division lacks jurisdiction to review a sex offender's risk assessment under the Sex Offender Registration Act. People v. Rodriguez, 240 A.D.2d 351, 660 N.Y.S.2d 714 (1st Dept. 1997), *app. denied, mot. dismissed,* 91 N.Y.2d 912, 669 N.Y.S.2d 256, 692 N.E.2d 125 (1998).

—A sentencing court's assessment of the defendant as a "sexually violent predator" under the Sex Offender Registration Act is not reviewable. People v. Kearns, 253 A.D.2d 768, 677 N.Y.S.2d 497 (2d Dept. 1998) (*see also* concurring opinion, in which Justice Friedmann criticizes the fact that there is no system of review of SORA classifications).

—The absence of any right to appeal the determination of risk level under the Sex Offender Registration Act does not compel the conclusion that relief is available by way of application for a writ of prohibition; to hold otherwise would convert this "extraordinary" writ into routine in sex-crime cases. Raphael S. v. Leventhal, 246 A.D.2d 659, 668 N.Y.S.2d 50 (2d Dept. 1998).

—Defendant has no right to appeal the propriety of the risk level designation assigned to him by County Court. People v. Campbell, 279 A.D.2d 715, 719 N.Y.S.2d 191 (3d Dept. 2001).

—Because defendant failed to include in the record the risk assessment instrument and any of the other documents on which the court relied in classifying the defendant, the Appellate Division was unable to review the defendant's contention that the court abused its discretion in classifying him as a level three sex offender. People v. Davis, 17 A.D.3d 1155, 794 N.Y.S.2d 554 (4th Dept. 2005).

—Defendant attempted to appeal from an order of County Court determining that he is a level three sex offender under the Sex Offender Registration Act; except when the issue is raised on appeal from a judgment of conviction, a classification determination pursuant to SORA may not be challenged on appeal. People v. Cash, 242 A.D.2d 976, 664 N.Y.S.2d 696 (4th Dept. 1997); *see also* People v. Fitzgerald, 249 A.D.2d 630, 671 N.Y.S.2d 766 (3d Dept. 1998).

—The advisory power of a criminal court ends with the imposition of sentence, which marks the termination of the criminal action; the classification of a sex offender is neither an amendment to the judgment of conviction nor a resentencing. Therefore, there is no authority in the CPL or Megan's Law for review by the sentencing court of risk level classifications by the Department of Probation. People v. Doyle, 177 Misc. 2d 74, 675 N.Y.S.2d 854 (Sup. Ct. Suffolk Co. 1998).

—A Megan's Law determination and any hearing held in connection with such a determination is civil in nature, therefore, there is no right to appeal from an adverse determination pursuant to the provisions of the CPL. People v. Sumpter, 177 Misc. 2d 492, 676 N.Y.S.2d 825 (Crim. Ct. Queens Co. 1998); *see also* People v. Harris, 178 Misc. 2d 858, 682 N.Y.S.2d 808 (Crim. Ct. Queens Co. 1998).

Presumptive level three assessment.—Consideration of defendant's criminal history was clearly permitted by the Act; the Board's presumptive assessment of a level III risk for a defendant who is already a repeat felony sex offender is clearly consistent with SORA's provisions. People v. Scott, 288 A.D.2d 763, 733 N.Y.S.2d 744 (3d Dept. 2001).

—Defendant's risk factor constitutes an override and a presumptive level three assessment, based on the fact that he caused the death of a person while he was on parole from a conviction for sodomy of a child. People v. Curley, 184 Misc. 2d 692, 710 N.Y.S.2d 517 (Sup. Ct. Monroe Co. 2000).

—Defendant argued that the presumptive override of Correction Law 168-l, allowing for classification of risk level III recommendation where the crime involved "the infliction of serious physical injury or the causing of death," is essentially a mandatory presumption and such presumption could not be used to prove a material element of a crime beyond a reasonable doubt. The court found that the grand jury minutes, victim's medical records, plea minutes, defendant's hearing testimony and other evidence presented by defendant warranted the court's determination of defendant's risk level. The determination was properly based on clear and convincing evidence related to statutory factors. People v. Brown, 302 A.D.2d 919, 755 N.Y.S.2d 183 (4th Dept. 2003).

Risk of repeat offense.—If risk of repeat offense is high and there is a threat to public safety, a level three designation is appropriate; in order to assess the risk of a repeat offense by a sex offender and the threat posed to public safety, criminal history factors should be considered—those that reflect a high risk of repeat offense, including, but not limited to, whether the sex offender committed the felony sex offense against a child and the age of the sex offender at the time of the commission of the first sex offense. People v. Heichel, 20 A.D.3d 934, 798 N.Y.S.2d 633 (4th Dept. 2005).

—Defendant, who served two consecutive sentences for his conviction in the "Central Park Jogger Case," challenged the recommendation by the Board of Examiners of Sex Offenders that he be assessed at the highest level of notification; court found that the risk of repeat offense was high, there existed a threat to public safety, and the risk level three was correct. People v. Salaam, 174 Misc. 2d 726, 666 N.Y.S.2d 881 (Sup. Ct. N.Y. Co. 1997).

Split sentence.—A split sentence must be considered an incarceratory sentence for purposes of the Sex Offender Registration Act, and the Board of Sex Examiners must submit its recommendation to the sentencing court. People v. Brown, 174 Misc. 2d 941, 666 N.Y.S.2d 908 (Sup. Ct. Bronx Co. 1997).

§ 168-m. Review.

Notwithstanding any other provision of law to the contrary, any state or local correctional facility, hospital or institution, district attorney, law enforcement agency, probation department, division of parole, court or child protective agency shall forward relevant information pertaining to a sex offender to be discharged, paroled, released to post-release supervision or released to the board for review no later than one hundred twenty days prior to the release or discharge and the board shall make recommendations as provided in subdivision six of section one hundred sixty-eight-l of this article within sixty days of receipt of the information. Information may include but may not be limited to all or a portion of the arrest file, prosecutor's file, probation or parole file, child protective file, court file, commitment file, medical file and treatment file pertaining to such person. Such person shall be permitted to submit to the board any information relevant to the review. Upon application of the sex offender or the district attorney, the court shall seal any portion of the board's file pertaining to the sex offender which contains material that is confidential under any state or federal law; provided, however, that in any subsequent proceedings in which the sex offender who is the subject of the sealed record is a party and which requires the board to provide a recommendation to the court pursuant to this article, such sealed record shall be available to the sex offender, the district attorney, the court and the attorney general where the attorney general is a party, or represents a party, in the proceeding.

Added by L. 1995, Ch. 192, eff. Jan. 21, 1996; **Amended** by L. 1999, Ch. 453, eff. Jan. 1, 2000.

§ 168-n. Judicial determination.

1. A determination that an offender is a sexual predator, sexually violent offender, or predicate sex offender as defined in subdivision seven of section one hundred sixty-eight-a of this article shall be made prior to the discharge, parole, release to post-release supervision or release of such offender by the sentencing court applying the guidelines established in subdivision five of section one hundred sixty-eight-l of this article after receiving a recommendation from the board pursuant to section one hundred sixty-eight-l of this article.

2. In addition, applying the guidelines established in subdivision five of section one hundred sixty-eight-l of this article, the sentencing court shall also make a determination with respect to the level of notification, after receiving a recommendation from the board pursuant to section one hundred sixty-eight-l of this article. Both determinations of the sentencing court shall be made thirty calendar days prior to discharge, parole or release.

3. No later than thirty days prior to the board's recommendation, the sex offender shall be notified that his or her case is under review and that he or she is permitted to submit to the board any information relevant to the review. Upon receipt of the board's recommendation, the sentencing court shall determine whether the sex offender was previously found to be eligible for assigned counsel in the underlying case. Where such a finding was previously made, the court shall assign counsel to represent the offender, pursuant to article eighteen-B of the county law. At least twenty days prior to the determination proceeding, the sentencing court shall notify the district attorney, the sex offender and the sex offender's counsel, in writing, of the date of the determination proceeding and shall also provide the district attorney, the sex offender and the sex offender's counsel with a copy of the recommendation received from the board and any statement of the reasons for the recommendation received from the board. The written notice to the sex offender shall also advise the offender that he or she has a right to a hearing prior to the court's determination, and that he or she has the right to be represented by counsel at the hearing. If counsel has been assigned to represent the offender at the determination proceeding, the notice shall also provide the name, address and telephone number of the assigned counsel. Where counsel has not been assigned, the notice shall advise the sex offender that counsel will be appointed if he or she is financially unable to retain counsel, and a returnable form shall be enclosed in the court's notice to the sex offender on which the sex offender may apply for assignment of counsel. If the sex offender applies for assignment of counsel and the court finds that the offender is financially unable to retain counsel, the court shall assign counsel to represent the sex offender pursuant to article eighteen-B of the county law. If the district attorney seeks a determination that differs from the recommendation submitted by the board, at least ten days prior to the determination proceeding the district attorney shall provide to the court and the sex offender a statement setting forth the determinations sought by the district attorney together with the reasons for seeking such determinations. The court shall allow the sex offender to appear and be heard. The state shall appear by the district attorney, or his or her designee, who shall bear the burden of proving the facts supporting the determinations sought by clear and convincing evidence. Where there is a dispute between the parties concerning the determinations, the court shall adjourn the hearing as necessary to permit the sex offender or the district attorney to obtain materials relevant to the determinations from the state board of examiners of sex offenders or any state or local facility, hospital, institution, office, agency, department or division. Such materials may be obtained by subpoena if not voluntarily provided to the requesting party. In making the determinations the court shall review any victim's statement and any relevant materials and evidence submitted by the sex offender and the district attorney and the recommendation and any materials submitted by the board, and may consider reliable hearsay evidence submitted by either party, provided that it is relevant to the determinations. Facts previously proven at trial or elicited at the time of entry of a plea of guilty shall be deemed established by clear and convincing evidence and shall not be relitigated. The court shall render an order setting forth its determinations and the findings of fact and conclusions of law on which the determinations are based. A copy of the order shall be submitted by the court to the division. Upon application of either party, the court shall seal any portion of the court file or record which contains material that is confidential under any state or federal statute. Either party may appeal as of right from the order pursuant to the provisions of articles fifty-five, fifty-six and fifty-seven of the civil practice law and rules. Where counsel has been assigned to represent the sex offender upon the ground that the sex offender is financially unable to retain counsel, that assignment shall be continued throughout the pendency of the appeal, and the person may appeal as a poor person pursuant to article eighteen-B of the county law.

4. Upon determination that the risk of repeat offense and threat to public safety is high, the sentencing court shall also notify the division of such fact for the purposes of section one hundred sixty-eight-l of this article.

5. Upon the reversal of a conviction of a sexual offense defined in paragraphs (a) and (b) of subdivision two or three of section one hundred sixty-eight-a of this article, the appellate court shall remand the case to the lower court for entry of an order directing the expungement of any records required to be kept herein.

Added by L. 1995, Ch. 192, eff. Jan. 21, 1996; **Amended** by L. 1999, Ch. 453, eff. Jan. 1, 2000, amending subds. 1, 2, 3, and 5; L. 2002, Ch. 11, eff. Mar. 11, 2002.

Pursuant to L. 2002, Ch. 11, § 24, the amendments to subds. 1 and 3 of this section "shall apply to sex offenders for whom an initial risk level determination has not been made prior to such effective date or who, on the effective date of this act, are not members of the plaintiff class in the U.S. District Court, Southern District of New York case entitled Doe v. Pataki, Index Number 96CIV1657 (DC)."

ANNOTATIONS

Classification of sex offenders.—Although within court's discretion to depart from presumptive risk level based upon facts in record, utilization of Risk Assessment Instrument will generally "result in the proper classification in most cases so that departures will be the exception not the rule." People v. Guaman, 8 A.D.3d 545, 778 N.Y.S.2d 704 (2d Dept. 2004).

—Defendant was improperly classified as risk level III sex offender based solely on existence of a presumptive override factor—a 1988 conviction of attempted sodomy in the first degree; however SORA does not mandate automatic risk level III designation in the presence of an override factor, but instead requires that the risk be assessed in light of all pertinent factors; failure to do so was not harmless error. People v. Sanchez, 20 A.D.3d 693, 798 N.Y.S.2d 258 (3d Dept. 2005).

—Presumptively defendant's risk level under the Sex Offender Registration Act was a level one category; however, for purposes of duration and extent to register as a sex offender and the amount of information that could be given to the public, the court could classify defendant as a level two offender because defendant had engaged in sexual misconduct on two separate occasions with two very young victims over a period of several months. People v. Lombardo, 167 Misc. 2d 942, 640 N.Y.S.2d 995 (Co. Ct. Nassau Co. 1996).

Clear and convincing evidence.—Defendant's plea allocution, as well as the case summary prepared by the Board of Examiners, clearly established that, under the principles of accomplice liability, the defendant used a dangerous instrument in commission of the crime because he forced the victim to submit to a sex offense by taking advantage of his unapprehended accomplice's threatened use of a box cutter. The court properly assessed the defendant a level three sex offender. People v. Jack, 15 A.D.3d 270, 789 N.Y.S.2d 492 (1st Dept. 2005).

—Single instance of appellant's receipt of marijuana from a visitor while in prison did not prove by clear and convincing evidence that at the time of his classification as a sex offender, he had a history of drug or alcohol abuse, or that there was use of any drug, order reversed, appellant reclassified as level two offender. People v. Collazo, 7 A.D.3d 595, 775 N.Y.S.2d 887 (2d Dept. 2004).

—Risk assessment instrument, case summary prepared by Board of Examiners of Sex Offenders, and defendant's presentence report constituted clear and convincing evidence sufficient to support an increase to level three offender status. People v. Burgess, 6 A.D.3d 686, 775 N.Y.S.2d 534 (2d Dept. 2004).

—Court's risk level III classification was supported by clear and convincing evidence, including the case summary, presentence investigation, and other proof in the record. The court considered all appropriate statutory factors. People v. Hunt, 17 A.D.3d 713, 792 N.Y.S.2d 698 (3d Dept. 2005).

—Court's risk assessment and classification was supported by clear and convincing evidence, and the fact that the defendant attempted to withdraw his guilty plea prior to sentencing and consistently maintained his innocence since then supported court's determination that defendant had not sincerely accepted responsibility for his actions. People v. Walker, 15 A.D.3d 692, 788 N.Y.S.2d 723 (3d Dept. 2005).

—Although case summaries alone have been held to provide necessary clear and convincing evidence supporting sex offender classifications under SORA, a case summary prepared almost entirely on information derived from reports prepared by out-of-state authorities, which was not a probation report and contained hearsay without any attempt at verification that was presented over defendant's continuing objection that it was unreliable hearsay, did not provide clear and convincing proof to support County Court's sex offender classification. People v. Brown, 7 A.D.3d 831, 776 N.Y.S.2d 366 (3d Dept.), *on remand*, 5 Misc. 3d 440, 785 N.Y.S.2d 277 (Co. Ct. Warren Co. 2004).

—Clear and convincing proof establishing defendant's presumptive classification as a risk level III sex offender was presented in the form of the case summary, together with the presentence investigation report and information presented at the hearing. People v. Tucker, 20 A.D.3d 938, 797 N.Y.S.2d 339 (4th Dept. 2005).

—Clear and convincing evidence supported level two classification of defendant even though defendant claimed he accepted responsibility for his actions; defendant's own statements to police and sex offender examiner indicate that defendant perceived his sexual abuse of incapacitated victim as a consensual relationship. People v. Warwick, 5 A.D.3d 1050, 773 N.Y.S.2d 686 (4th Dept. 2004).

—There is clear and convincing evidence, as required by 168-n(3), that defendant established his relationships with the victims for the purpose of victimizing them. He volunteered in many youth-oriented activities, which is how he met his victims. People v. Carlton, 307 A.D.2d 763, 762 N.Y.S.2d 560 (4th Dept. 2003).

—Where there is clear and convincing evidence that appellant established relationships with young boys for the sole purpose of later victimizing them, the risk assessment of the Board will not be disturbed. People v. Carlton, 307 A.D.2d 763, 762 N.Y.S.2d 560 (4th Dept. 2003).

—Appellant's risk level III will not be disturbed where People established by clear and convincing evidence that appellant did not accept responsibility for his sexual abuse of his four-year-old daughter until after he realized that he would be subject to a higher risk assessment if he did not accept responsibility. People v. Tilley, 305 A.D.2d 1041, 758 N.Y.S.2d 891 (4th Dept. 2003).

Counsel's presence at hearing.—Where defendant was not notified of his right to have counsel present at the hearing as required by Correction Law § 168-n(3), and defendant did not waive this right, this requirement must be complied with on remittal. People v. Hoppe, 1 A.D.3d 712, 766 N.Y.S.2d 639 (3d Dept. 2003).

Court determines risk level.—Defendant was properly classified as a level II sex offender by board of review based on his use of violence, drug and alcohol abuse, and release environment category; although factors resulted in a score of 65, a level I offender, the board has discretion to increase the level based on defendant's history of mental illness and circumstances underlying the crime. People v. Roland, 292 A.D.2d 271, 739 N.Y.S.2d 694 (1st Dept. 2002).

—Determination by Board of Examiners of Sex Offenders is merely a recommendation; the sentencing court is charged with making the actual determination and may depart from that recommendation and determine the sex offender's risk level based on the facts and circumstances that appear in the record. People v. Douglas, 18 A.D.3d 967, 794 N.Y.S.2d 730 (3d Dept. 2005).

—Court is not bound by recommendation of Board and may depart from that recommendation and determine the sex offender's risk level based on facts and circumstances that appear in the record. People v. Dorato, 291 A.D.2d 580, 738 N.Y.S.2d 400 (3d Dept. 2002).

—County court must include in record findings of fact and conclusions of law upon which determination of risk level is based. People v. Lee, 292 A.D.2d 639, 738 N.Y.S.2d 903 (3d Dept. 2002).

—Although risk assessment instrument resulted in presumptive classification of defendant as level one offender, and Board determined that departure from that presumptive risk level was not warranted, court's determination that level two designation was proper under facts and circumstances in record was proper exercise of its discretion. People v. Girup, 9 A.D.3d 913, 780 N.Y.S.2d 698 (4th Dept. 2004).

—The Board of Examiners of Sex Offenders (Board) can recommend upward departure from risk assessment instrument (RAI) classification based upon factors not adequately taken into account by the RAI, the County Court has discretion to agree with Board that upward departure from presumptive risk level classification was warranted. People v. Skellen, 4 A.D.3d 863, 771 N.Y.S.2d 482 (4th Dept. 2004).

—Sentencing court has ultimate decision as to risk level after receiving recommendation from the Board. People v. Saleemi, 186 Misc. 2d 177, 718 N.Y.S.2d 139 (Sup. Ct. Queens Co. 2000).

—The court retains the ultimate responsibility for determining the offender's risk level after receiving the board's recommendation. People v. Salaam, 174 Misc. 2d 726, 666 N.Y.S.2d 881 (Sup. Ct. N.Y. Co. 1997).

Court can reconsider its determination.—County court had statutory and inherent authority to reconsider or correct its determination of risk level under SORA based on further argument by the People and/or additional information from the People. People v. Wroten, 286 A.D.2d 189, 732 N.Y.S.2d 513 (4th Dept. 2001).

Court's consideration of defendant's statement.—In classifying defendant as a risk level III sex offender, court properly considered defendant's statement that he was misled as to the

CORR. L.

ages of the victims, which reflected his failure to fully accept responsibility for his conduct. People v. Ashley, 19 A.D.3d 882, 797 N.Y.S.2d 623 (3d Dept. 2005).

Court's findings of fact.—Trial court failed to set forth its findings of fact and conclusions of law in support of its determination that defendant was a level III sex offender. Because the record contained no information about if and when the defendant was required to complete sex offender counseling and whether the court considered the defendant's assertion that he had remained drug-free for years, Appellate Division remitted the case to the trial court for a hearing on these facts, after which it must render a new determination. People v. Villane, 17 A.D.3d 336, 793 N.Y.S.2d 90 (2d Dept. 2005).

—If the defendant concedes the accuracy of the factual assertions set forth in the case summary of the Board of Examiners of Sex Offenders, the evidence is sufficient to support a classification in an appropriate case. In this case, defendant disputed the central allegation about the sexual abuse, and the court failed to comply with the mandate of the statute to render an order setting forth its determinations and the findings of fact and conclusions of law on which the determinations are based. People v. Hill, 17 A.D.3d 715, 792 N.Y.S.2d 695 (3d Dept. 2005).

—County court's determination, consisting only of a standardized form indicating it was adopting the Board's recommendations without explanation, does not satisfy the statutory requirement that it "render an order setting forth its determinations and the findings of fact and conclusions of law on which the determinations are based." People v. Marr, 20 A.D.3d 692, 798 N.Y.S.2d 260 (3d Dept. 2005).

—Where county court failed to set forth findings of fact and conclusions of law upon which its determination was based, the matter must be remitted; once the findings of fact and conclusions of law are stated, then appellate review can occur. People v. Sturdivant, 307 A.D.2d 382, 762 N.Y.S.2d 443 (3d Dept. 2003).

—Remittal required where court which classified defendant as a risk level III sex offender failed to set forth its findings of fact and conclusions of law, which prevented the Appellate Division from assessing the propriety of that decision. People v. Sturdivant, 307 A.D.2d 382, 762 N.Y.S.2d 443 (3d Dept. 2003).

—Where County Court failed to set forth the findings of fact and conclusions of law supporting its decision to classify defendant as a risk level III sex offender, order must be reversed and matter remitted for compliance with the statute. People v. Hoppe, 1 A.D.3d 712, 766 N.Y.S.2d 639 (3d Dept. 2003).

Defendant's presence at hearing.—The same waiver-forfeiture analysis applies to a SORA hearing as a criminal action when the court determines if the action may proceed in the defendant's absence. Because due process protections required for a risk level classification proceeding are not as extensive as those required in a plenary criminal or civil trial, and a defendant's presence at a SORA hearing is entirely voluntary, court properly determined that defendant forfeited his right to be present. People v. Brooks, 308 A.D.2d 99, 763 N.Y.S.2d 86 (2d Dept. 2003).

Downward departure warranted.—Clear and convincing evidence of a special circumstance supported downward departure from a level III to a level II risk; underlying rape conviction of defendant, then 21, was for sexual intercourse with a person less than 17; however, victim was a willing participant and a few months shy of 17, and failure to complete sex offender treatment was due to discharge from prison. People v. Santiago, 20 A.D.3d 885, 798 N.Y.S.2d 612 (4th Dept. 2005).

—An upward or downward departure from the presumptive risk level is warranted where there is clear and convincing evidence of the existence of an aggravating or mitigating factor of a kind, or to a degree, not otherwise adequately taken into account by the guidelines; here, the court found special circumstances warranting an upward departure from the Board's recommendation. People v. Marinconz, 178 Misc. 2d 30, 679 N.Y.S.2d 244 (Sup. Ct. Bronx Co. 1998).

—Court found that downward departure from presumptive risk level was warranted, because he had no prior criminal history, admitted his crime, and participated in a six-week sex offender program. Defendant's crime was egregious, but it was a crime of opportunity and defendant neither sought victim out nor was he a stranger to her. In addition, defendant suffers from poor eyesight and a heart condition, and he appears to pose little risk of re-offense in the community at large. People v. Jimenez, 178 Misc. 2d 319, 679 N.Y.S.2d 510 (Sup. Ct. Kings Co. 1998).

Upward departure.—An upward departure from the presumptive risk level is warranted when, after considering the indicated factors, there exists an aggravating or mitigating factor of a kind or to a degree not otherwise adequately taken into account by the guidelines. The determination to make an upward departure must be supported by clear and convincing evidence in the record. People v. Mount, 17 A.D.3d 714, 792 N.Y.S.2d 697 (3d Dept. 2005).

—Record did not support county court's upward departure from classification recommended by the Board where there was no evidence that defendant attempted to deny or downplay his commission of the acts underlying his plea, and he clearly acknowledged his conduct, the impact of it on his victim, and his expression of remorse. People v. Mallory, 293 A.D.2d 881, 740 N.Y.S.2d 530 (3d Dept. 2002).

—An upward departure from the presumptive risk level is warranted where it is supported by clear and convincing evidence in the record; the upward departure was justified here, where defendant had a 1991 conviction for sex abuse in the second degree involving his 11-year-old stepdaughter, after which he underwent one and a half years of sex offender counseling which was unsuccessful because he subsequently committed the instant offense and he continued to fantasize about children and place himself in situations where he would be alone with children. People v. Bottisti, 285 A.D.2d 841, 727 N.Y.S.2d 787 (3d Dept. 2001).

—Although defendant's point total on the Board's Risk Assessment Instrument was 75, resulting in a level two risk assignment, the court's decision to assign appellant level three risk was proper where the Board's risk assessment score did not fully take into account the number and nature of defendant's prior misdemeanor sex offenses and a prior violent felony conviction. People v. Thomas, 307 A.D.2d 759, 762 N.Y.S.2d 548 (4th Dept. 2003).

No automatic right to witnesses at hearing.—Defendant has no automatic right to call civilian witnesses at a hearing granted to give the defendant an opportunity to challenge the risk assessment recommended by the Board of Examiners of Sex Offenders. People v. Tucker, 177 Misc. 2d 418, 676 N.Y.S.2d 841 (Nassau Co. Ct. 1998).

Presumptive override to classification.—There is a presumptive override to a level III classification by reason of inflicting serious physical injury. The presumptive override cannot defeat the defendant's statutory right to appear and be heard at the SORA hearing. People v. Barnes, 6 Misc. 3d 469, 789 N.Y.S.2d 843 (Sup. Ct. Monroe Co. 2004).

Relevant material or information.—The increase of appellant's risk assessment to level three had sufficient evidentiary support, three-year old victim's "pain and obvious 'physical helplessness' against the sexual assault of an adult male," coupled with uncontested facts in defendant's case summary including a lengthy history of mental health issues and emotional problems. People v. Moon, 3 A.D.3d 600, 771 N.Y.S.2d 223 (3d Dept. 2004).

—Court properly considered complainant's affidavit indicating that defendant had used a knife in the commission of underlying crime, as well as his two prior drug convictions and admitted history of extensive marihuana use; defendant failed to take responsibility for his acts and denied using weapon; increase to level three affirmed as proper exercise of discretion. People v. Carswell, 8 A.D.3d 1073, 778 N.Y.S.2d 646 (4th Dept. 2004).

—An upward departure must be supported by factors adequately reflected in Risk Assessment Instrument, and failure of court to support departure will result in reversal of order and restoration of original assessment. People v. Barnwell, 6 A.D.3d 1146, 775 N.Y.S.2d 658 (4th Dept. 2004)

—Court properly considered additional information not taken into account by RAI, in support of its increased of defendant to a level three offender, including number and nature of defendant's prior crimes or the fact that defendant acknowledged that he had made acquaintance of another 14-year-old girl on the "chat line," met her in person, and had conversations with her of a sexual nature, including telling her of his sexual activity with victim in this case. People v. Stevens, 4 A.D.3d 786, 771 N.Y.S.2d 459 (4th Dept. 2004)

—The provisions of SORA require a court to review "any

relevant materials and evidence" submitted either by defendant or district attorney; a conviction on a prior sex offense was properly considered by court in determining proper risk level after defendant's conviction on second sex offense. People v. Case, 298 A.D.2d 929, 748 N.Y.S.2d 90 (4th Dept. 2002).

Reliable hearsay evidence.—Defendant's testimony along with his admissions to prison drug treatment providers properly considered by court in classifying him as level two sex offender; §168-n(3) specifically authorizes a hearing court to utilize reliable hearsay evidence in reaching its determination. People v. Brown, 7 A.D.3d 595, 775 N.Y.,S.2d 885 (2d Dept. 2004)

—Reliable hearsay, consisting in this case of the hearing judge's trial notes from the appellant's trial on the original charges, recollection from trial and the case summary of the Board of Examiners of Sex Offenders, was proper to support determination that defendant was a level two sex offender based upon criminal record and use of dangerous instruments during commission of crimes. People v. Meyers, 306 A.D.2d 334, 760 N.Y.S.2d 681 (2d Dept. 2003).

—SORA permits consideration of reliable hearsay evidence. People v. Ashley, 19 A.D.3d 882, 797 N.Y.S.2d 623 (3d Dept. 2005).

—If either the People or the sex offender disagree with the recommendation of the Board of Examiners of Sex Offenders in the sentencing court, the parties shall be afforded a hearing, at which the sentencing court has wide discretion regarding the conduct and admission of testimony and evidence. Formal rules of evidence are inapplicable to this type of proceeding, and reliable hearsay may be used to support the court's final determination. People v. Hernandez, 7 Misc. 3d 151, 794 N.Y.S.2d 797 (Sup. Ct. Bronx Co. 2005).

—The sentencing court may consider testimony presented in the grand jury proceedings as "reliable hearsay evidence" in determining the appropriate risk level. People v. Victor R., 186 Misc. 2d 28, 715 N.Y.S.2d 283 (Sup. Ct. Bronx Co. 2000).

Sexual predator, sexually violent offender, or predicate sex offender.—Pursuant to 2002 amendments to SORA, County Court was required not only to determine risk level classification of defendant, who was convicted upon a plea of sexual abuse in the first degree, but also to determine whether defendant is a sexual predator, sexually violent offender, or predicate sex offender as defined by Correction Law 168-a(7). People v. Lockwood, 308 A.D.2d 640, 764 N.Y.S.2d 290 (3d Dept. 2003).

§ 168-o. Petition for relief or modification.

1. Any sex offender who, as of March eleventh, two thousand two, was classified as a level three risk required to register or verify pursuant to this article who has been registered for a minimum period of thirteen years may be relieved of any further duty to register upon the granting of a petition for relief by the sentencing court or by the court which made the determination regarding duration of registration and level of notification. The sex offender shall bear the burden of proving by clear and convincing evidence that his or her risk of repeat offense and threat to public safety is such that registration or verification is no longer necessary. Such petition, if granted, shall not relieve the petitioner of the duty to register pursuant to this article upon conviction of any offense requiring registration in the future. Such a petition shall not be considered more than annually. In the event that the sex offender's petition for relief is granted, the district attorney may appeal as of right from the order pursuant to the provisions of articles fifty-five, fifty-six and fifty-seven of the civil practice law and rules. Where counsel has been assigned to represent the sex offender upon the ground that the sex offender is financially unable to retain counsel, that assignment shall be continued throughout the pendency of the appeal, and the person may appeal as a poor person pursuant to article eighteen-B of the county law.

2. Any sex offender required to register or verify pursuant to this article may petition the sentencing court or the court which made the determination regarding the level of notification for an order modifying the level of notification. The petition shall set forth the level of notification sought, together with the reasons for seeking such determination. The sex offender shall bear the burden of proving the facts supporting the requested modification by clear and convincing evidence. Such a petition shall not be considered more than annually. In the event that the sex offender's petition to modify the level of notification is granted, the district attorney may appeal as of right from the order pursuant to the provisions of articles fifty-five, fifty-six and fifty-seven of the civil practice law and rules. Where counsel has been assigned to represent the sex offender upon the ground that the sex offender is financially unable to retain counsel, that assignment shall be continued throughout the pendency of the appeal, and the person may appeal as a poor person pursuant to article eighteen-B of the county law.

3. The district attorney may file a petition to modify the level of notification for a sex offender with the sentencing court or with the court which made the determination regarding the level of notification, where the sex offender (a) has been convicted of a new crime, or there has been a determination after a proceeding pursuant to section 410.70 of the criminal procedure law or section two hundred fifty-nine-i of the executive law that the sex offender has violated one or more conditions imposed as part of a sentence of a conditional discharge, probation, parole or post-release supervision for a designated crime, and (b) the conduct underlying the new crime or the violation is of a nature that indicates an increased risk of a repeat sex offense. The petition shall set forth the level of notification sought, together with the reasons for seeking such determination. The district attorney shall bear the burden of proving the facts supporting the requested modification, by clear and convincing evidence. In the event that the district attorney's petition is granted, the sex offender may appeal as of right from the order, pursuant to the provisions of articles fifty-five, fifty-six and fifty-seven of the civil practice law and rules. Where counsel has been assigned to represent the offender upon the ground that he or she is financially unable to retain counsel, that assignment shall be continued throughout the pendency of the appeal, and the person may proceed as a poor person, pursuant to article eighteen-B of the county law.

4. Upon receipt of a petition submitted pursuant to subdivision one, two or three of this section,

the court shall forward a copy of the petition to the board and request an updated recommendation pertaining to the sex offender and shall provide a copy of the petition to the other party. The court shall also advise the sex offender that he or she has the right to be represented by counsel at the hearing and counsel will be appointed if he or she is financially unable to retain counsel. A returnable form shall be enclosed in the court's notice to the sex offender on which the sex offender may apply for assignment of counsel. If the sex offender applies for assignment of counsel and the court finds that the offender is financially unable to retain counsel, the court shall assign counsel to represent the offender, pursuant to article eighteen-B of the county law. Where the petition was filed by a district attorney, at least thirty days prior to making an updated recommendation the board shall notify the sex offender and his or her counsel that the offender's case is under review and he or she is permitted to submit to the board any information relevant to the review. The board's updated recommendation on the sex offender shall be confidential and shall not be available for public inspection. After receiving an updated recommendation from the board concerning a sex offender, the court shall, at least thirty days prior to ruling upon the petition, provide a copy of the updated recommendation to the sex offender, the sex offender's counsel and the district attorney and notify them, in writing, of the date set by the court for a hearing on the petition. After reviewing the recommendation received from the board and any relevant materials and evidence submitted by the sex offender and the district attorney, the court may grant or deny the petition. The court may also consult with the victim prior to making a determination on the petition. The court shall render an order setting forth its determination, and the findings of fact and conclusions of law on which the determination is based. If the petition is granted, it shall be the obligation of the court to submit a copy of its order to the division. Upon application of either party, the court shall seal any portion of the court file or record which contains material that is confidential under any state or federal statute.

Added by L. 1995, Ch. 192, eff. Jan. 21, 1996; Amended by L. 1999, Ch. 453, eff. Jan. 1, 2000; L. 2002, Ch. 11, eff. Mar. 11, 2002, amending subds. 1, 2, and 3.

§ 168-p. Special telephone number.

1. Pursuant to section one hundred sixty-eight-b of this article, the division shall also operate a telephone number that members of the public may call free of charge and inquire whether a named individual required to register pursuant to this article is listed. The division shall ascertain whether a named person reasonably appears to be a person so listed and provide the caller with the relevant information according to risk as described in subdivision six of section one hundred sixty-eight-l of this article. The division shall

decide whether the named person reasonably appears to be a person listed, based upon information from the caller providing information that shall include (a) an exact street address, including apartment number, driver's license number or birth date, along with additional information that may include social security number, hair color, eye color, height, weight, distinctive markings, ethnicity; or (b) any combination of the above listed characteristics if an exact birth date or address is not available. If three of the characteristics provided include ethnicity, hair color, and eye color, other identifying characteristics shall be provided. Any information identifying the victim by name, birth date, address or relation to the person listed by the division shall be excluded by the division.

2. When the telephone number is called, a preamble shall be played which shall provide the following information:

(a) notice that the caller's telephone number will be recorded;

(b) that there is no charge for use of the telephone number;

(c) notice that the caller is required to identify himself or herself to the operator and provide current address and shall be maintained in a written record;

(d) notice that the caller is required to be eighteen years of age or older;

(e) a warning that it is illegal to use information obtained through the telephone number to commit a crime against any person listed or to engage in illegal discrimination or harassment against such person;

(f) notice that the caller is required to have the birth date, driver's license or identification number, or address or other identifying information regarding the person about whom information is sought in order to achieve a positive identification of that person;

(g) a statement that the number is not a crime hotline and that any suspected criminal activity should be reported to local authorities;

(h) a statement that an information package which will include a description of the law and sex abuse and abduction prevention materials is available upon request from the division. Such information package shall include questions and answers regarding the most commonly asked questions about the sex offender registration act, and current sex abuse and abduction prevention material.

2-a. (a) The division shall establish a program allowing non-profit and not-for-profit youth services organizations to pre-register with the division for use of the telephone number. Pre-registration shall include the identification of up to two officials of the organization who may call the telephone number and obtain information on behalf of the organization. A pre-registered certificate issued under this subdivision shall be valid for two years, unless earlier revoked by the division for good cause shown. No fee shall be charged to an applicant for the issuance of a pre-registered certificate pursuant to this subdivision.

(b) An organization granted a pre-registered certificate pursuant to this subdivision may, upon calling the telephone number, inquire whether multiple named individuals are listed on the sex offender registry. Notwithstanding any per call limitation the division may place on calls by private individuals, the division shall allow such pre-registered organizations to inquire about up to twenty prospective coaches, leaders or volunteers in each call to the telephone number.

(c) For purposes of this subdivision, "youth services organization" shall mean a formalized program operated by a corporation pursuant to subparagraph five of paragraph (a) of section one hundred two of the not-for-profit corporation law that functions primarily to: (a) provide children the opportunity to participate in adult-supervised sporting activities; or (b) match children or groups of children with adult volunteers for the purpose of providing children with positive role models to enhance their development.

3. Whenever there is reasonable cause to believe that any person or group of persons is engaged in a pattern or practice of misuse of the telephone number, the attorney general, any district attorney or any person aggrieved by the misuse of the number is authorized to bring a civil action in the appropriate court requesting preventive relief, including an application for a permanent or temporary injunction, restraining order or other order against the person or group of persons responsible for the pattern or practice of misuse. The foregoing remedies shall be independent of any other remedies or procedures that may be available to an aggrieved party under other provisions of law. Such person or group of persons shall be subject to a fine of not less than five hundred dollars and not more than one thousand dollars.

4. The division shall submit to the legislature an annual report on the operation of the telephone number. The annual report shall include, but not be limited to, all of the following:

(a) number of calls received;

(b) a detailed outline of the amount of money expended and the manner in which it was expended for purposes of this section;

(c) number of calls that resulted in an affirmative response and the number of calls that resulted in a negative response with regard to whether a named individual was listed;

(d) number of persons listed; and

(e) a summary of the success of the telephone number program based upon selected factors.

Added by L. 1995, Ch. 192, eff. Jan. 21, 1996; **Amended** by L. 2000, Ch. 1, eff. Feb. 1, 2001, amendments to subd. 2 expire on Sept. 1, 2001 and addition of subd. 2-a expires and repealed on September 1, 2001; L. 2000, Ch. 608, eff. Apr. 28, 2001; L. 2001, Ch. 95, eff. July 13, 2001, repealing the changes made to subd. 2(b) by L. 2000, Ch. 608 and extending expiration date to Sept. 1, 2003; L. 2004, 361, § 1, eff. Sept. 9, 2004, amending section and section heading.

§ 168-q. Subdirectory of level three sex offenders.

1. The division shall maintain a subdirectory of level three sex offenders. The subdirectory shall include the exact address, address of the offender's place of employment and photograph of the sex offender along with the following information, if available: name, physical description, age and distinctive markings. Background information including the sex offender's crime of conviction, modus of operation, type of victim targeted, the name and address of any institution of higher education at which the sex offender is enrolled, attends, is employed or resides and a description of special conditions imposed on the sex offender shall also be included. The subdirectory shall have sex offender listings categorized by county and zip code. A copy of the subdirectory shall annually be distributed to the offices of local village, town, city, county or state law enforcement agencies for purposes of public access. The division shall distribute monthly updates to the offices of local village, town, city, county or state law enforcement agencies for purposes of public access. Such departments shall require that a person in writing provide their name and address prior to viewing the subdirectory. Any information identifying the victim by name, birth date, address or relation to the sex offender shall be excluded from the subdirectory distributed for purposes of public access. The subdirectory provided for herein shall be updated monthly to maintain its efficiency and usefulness and shall be computer accessible. Such subdirectory shall be made available at all times on the internet via the division homepage.

2. Any person who uses information disclosed pursuant to this section in violation of the law shall in addition to any other penalty or fine imposed, be subject to a fine of not less than five hundred dollars and not more than one thousand dollars. Unauthorized removal or duplication of the subdirectory from the offices of local, village or city police department shall be punishable by a fine not to exceed one thousand dollars. In addition, the attorney general, any district attorney, or any person aggrieved is authorized to bring a civil action in the appropriate court requesting preventive relief, including an application for a permanent or temporary injunction, restraining order, or other order against the person or group of persons responsible for such action. The foregoing remedies shall be independent of any other remedies or procedures that may be available to an aggrieved party under other provisions of law.

Added by L. 1995, Ch. 192, eff. Jan. 21, 1996; **Amended** by L. 1999, Ch. 113, eff. Sept. 20, 1999, and Chs. 453, eff. Jan. 1, 2000, amending heading and subd. 1; L. 2000, Ch. 490, eff. Jan. 1, 2001; L. 2002, Ch. 11, amending section heading and subd. 1, eff. July 1, 2002; L. 2002, Ch. 694, § 4, eff. Jan. 30, 2003, amending subd. 1; L. 2003, Ch. 10, § 5, eff. Mar. 7, 2003, amending subd. 1.

Editor's Notes: L. 2003, Ch. 10, § 8 provides: "This act shall take effect immediately; provided that sections one, two, three, four, five and six of this act shall take effect on the same date and in the same manner as [L. 2002, Ch. 694] takes effect."

L. 2003, Ch. 10, § 6, eff. May 30, 2003, repealed L. 2002, Ch. 694, § 4, which amended subd. 1 of this section.

§ 168-r. Immunity from liability.

1. No official, employee or agency, whether public or private, shall be subject to any civil or criminal liability for damages for any discretionary decision to release relevant and necessary information pursuant to this section, unless it is shown that such official, employee or agency acted with gross negligence or in bad faith. The immunity provided under this section applies to the release of relevant information to other employees or officials or to the general public.

2. Nothing in this section shall be deemed to impose any civil or criminal liability upon or to give rise to a cause of action against any official, employee or agency, whether public or private, for failing to release information as authorized in this section unless it is shown that such official, employee or agency acted with gross negligence or in bad faith.

Added by L. 1995, Ch. 192, eff. Jan. 21, 1996.

§ 168-s. Annual report.

The division shall on or before February first in each year file a report with the governor, and the legislature detailing the program, compliance with provisions of this article and effectiveness of the provisions of this article, together with any recommendations to further enhance the intent of this article.

Added by L. 1995, Ch. 192, eff. Jan. 21, 1996.

§ 168-t. Failure to register or verify; penalty.

Any sex offender required to register or to verify pursuant to the provisions of this article who fails to register or verify in the manner and within the time periods provided for herein shall be guilty of a class A misdemeanor upon conviction for the first offense, and upon conviction for a second or subsequent offense shall be guilty of a class D felony. Any such failure to register or verify may also be the basis for revocation of parole pursuant to section two hundred fifty-nine-i of the executive law or the basis for revocation of probation pursuant to article four hundred ten of the criminal procedure law.

Added by L. 1995, Ch. 192, eff. Jan. 21, 1996; **Amended** by L. 1999, Ch. 453, eff. Jan. 1, 2000.

ANNOTATIONS

Generally.—Section 168-t imposes strict liability upon a sex offender who fails to register as required; the People need not prove the failure to register was intentional in order to prove a violation of this section. People v. Patterson, 185 Misc. 2d 519, 708 N.Y.S.2d 815 (Crim. Ct. Bronx Co. 2000).

Jurisdiction.—Defendant may be prosecuted in Bronx County where his original sex crime was committed and where he still lives, even though the Sex Offender Monitoring Unit where defendant failed to register was in New York County. Bronx County has jurisdiction over this case pursuant to the injured forum statute, CPL § 20.40(2)(c), because defendant's failure to register affects the Bronx in that the police and the community in the Bronx will not receive appropriate SORA notifications about defendant. People v. Patterson, 185 Misc. 2d 519, 708 N.Y.S.2d 815 (N.Y.C. Crim. Ct. 2000).

—The materially harmful impact to Bronx County caused by defendant's alleged failure to register with a Sex Offender Monitoring Unit in New York County furnished grounds, pursuant to CPL § 20.40(2)(c), for the court to properly exercise jurisdiction over the prosecution. People v. Olivera, 184 Misc. 2d 327, 708 N.Y.S.2d 586 (Crim. Ct. Bronx Co. 2000).

No violation of registration requirement.—Where defendant was charged with violation of § 168-t, for failing to register with local law enforcement agency as a sexually violent predator within 90 days after his initial release or commencement of probation, court found that accusatory instrument was facially insufficient because it did not identify the day on which the 90-day registration period began to run, and the People themselves were unable to accurately identify the date or event from which the 90-day period began to run. People v. Manson, 173 Misc. 2d 806, 661 N.Y.S.2d 773 (N.Y.C. Crim. Ct. 1997).

§ 168-u. Unauthorized release of information.

The unauthorized release of any information required by this article shall be a class B misdemeanor.

Added by L. 1995, Ch. 192, eff. Jan. 21, 1996.

§ 168-v. Separability.

If any section of this article, or part thereof shall be adjudged by a court of competent jurisdiction to be invalid, such judgment shall not affect, impair or invalidate the remainder or any other section or part thereof.

Added by L. 1995, Ch. 192, eff. Jan. 21, 1996; L. 2003, Ch. 200, § 1, eff. Nov. 1, 2003, redesignating Section 168-v as Section 168-w; L. 2004, Ch. 106, § 1, eff. Aug. 7, 2004, repealing former Section 168-v and redesignating Section 168-w as Section 168-v.

ARTICLE 7—LABOR IN CORRECTIONAL INSTITUTIONS

§ 170. Contracts prohibited.

1. The commissioner of correctional services shall not, nor shall any other authority whatsoever, make any contract by which the labor or time of any inmate in any state or local correctional facility in this state, or the product or profit of his work, shall be contracted, let, farmed out, given or sold to any person, firm, association or corporation; except that the inmates in said correctional institutions may work for, and the products of their labor may be disposed of to, the state or any political subdivision thereof, any public institution owned or managed and controlled by the state, or any political subdivision thereof.

2. Notwithstanding any other provision of law, it shall be lawful for an inmate of the department to work in an institution of the department in the manufacture and production of goods, including out not limited to, license plates, identification plates and insignia for vehicles, and for the department to sell or otherwise dispose of for profit such goods to the government of the United States or to any state of the United States, or political subdivision thereof, or any public corporation or eleemosynary association or corporation funded in whole or in part by any federal, state or local funds.

Added by L. 1974, Ch. 491; **Amended** by L. 1988, Ch. 269, eff. Aug. 18, 1988 amending subd. 2; L. 1991, Ch. 166, eff. June 12, 1991, amending subds. 1 and 2; L. 1999, Ch. 113, eff. Sept. 20, 1999, amending subd. 1.

§ 171. Inmates to be employed; products of labor of inmates.

1. The commissioner of correctional services and the superintendents and officials of all penitentiaries in the state may cause inmates in the state correctional facilities and such penitentiaries who are physically capable thereof to be employed for not to exceed eight hours of each day other than Sundays and public holidays. Notwithstanding any other provisions of this section, however, the commissioner and superintendents of state correctional facilities may employ inmates on a volunteer basis on Sundays and public holidays in specialized areas of the facility, including kitchen areas, vehicular garages, rubbish pickup and grounds maintenance, providing, however, that inmates so employed shall be allowed an alternative free day within the normal work week.

2. Such labor shall be either for the purpose of the production of supplies for said institutions, or for the state, or any political subdivision thereof, or for any public institution owned or managed and controlled by the state, or any political subdivision thereof; or for the purpose of industrial training and instruction, or partly for one, and partly for the other of such purposes.

Amended by L. 1983, Ch. 364.

ANNOTATION

Mandating hard labor.—A sentence for murder and weapon possession that mandates serving hard labor is illegal. People v. Johnson, 216 A.D.2d 583, 629 N.Y.S.2d 55 (2d Dept. 1995).

§ 177. Labor of inmates in state and local correctional facilities.

1. The labor of inmates in the state correctional facilities, after the necessary labor for and manufacture of all needed supplies for said institutions, shall be primarily devoted to the state, the public buildings and institutions thereof, and the manufacture of supplies for the state, and public institutions thereof, and secondly to the political subdivisions of the state, and public institutions thereof;

2. The labor of inmates in local correctional facilities after the necessary labor for and manufacture of all needed supplies for the same, shall

be primarily devoted to the counties, respectively, in which said local correctional facilities are located, and the towns, cities and villages therein, and to the manufacture of supplies for the public institutions of the counties, or the political subdivisions thereof, and secondly to the state and the public institutions thereof;

3. However, for the purpose of distributing, marketing or sale of the whole or any part of the product of any correctional facility in the state, other than by said state correctional facilities, to the state or to any political subdivisions thereof or to any public institutions owned or managed and controlled by the state, or by any political subdivisions thereof, or to any public corporation, authority, or eleemosynary [sic] association funded in whole or in part by any federal, state or local funds, the sheriff of any such local correctional facility and the commissioner of correctional services may enter into a contract or contracts which may determine the kinds and qualities of articles to be produced by such institution and the method of distribution and sale thereof by the commissioner of correctional services or under his direction, either in separate lots or in combination with the products of other such institutions and with the products produced by inmates in state correctional facilities. Such contracts may fix and determine any and all terms and conditions for the disposition of such products and the disposition of proceeds of sale thereof and any and all other terms and conditions as may be agreed upon, not inconsistent with the constitution. However, no such contract shall be for a period of more than one year and any prices fixed by such contract shall be the prices established pursuant to section one hundred eighty-six of this article for like articles or shall be approved by the department of correctional services and the director of the budget on presentation to them of a copy of such contract or proposed contract, and provided further that any distribution or diversification of industries provided for by such contract shall be in accordance with the rules and regulations established by the department of correctional services or shall be approved by such department on presentation to it of a copy of such contract or proposed contract.

4. No product manufactured in whole or in part by inmates in any correctional facility of the state or of a political subdivision thereof, shall be sold, or otherwise disposed of for profit, by any officer, or administrative body, of such institution, or by any officer, or administrative body of the state, or of a political subdivision thereof, except to the state itself or to a political subdivision thereof, the government of the United States or to any state of the United States, or to an officer or administrative body of the state, or of a political subdivision thereof, or to or for a public institution owned or managed and controlled by the state or by any political subdivision thereof, or to a public corporation, authority, or eleemosynary association funded in whole or in part by federal, state or local funds. In no case shall said products be purchased for the purpose of resale or for their disposition for profit in a manner not herein provided for in the first instance.

5. A violation of any of the foregoing provisions shall constitute sufficient cause for the removal of such officer or board of administration by the duly constituted authority having jurisdiction.

Amended by L. 1962, Ch. 37; L. 1972, Ch. 337; L. 1980, Ch. 413, eff. Sept. 21, 1980; L. 1991, Ch. 166, eff. June 12, 1991.

§ 178. Participation in work release and other community activities.

Nothing contained in this article shall be construed or applied so as to prohibit private employment of inmates in the community under a work release program, or a residential treatment facility program formulated pursuant to any provision of this chapter.

Repealed former § 178 and **Added** new § 178 by L. 1970, Ch. 476.

§ 183. Classification of industries; report concerning industries.

1. It shall be the duty of the commissioner of correctional services to distribute, among the correctional institutions under his jurisdiction, the labor and industries assigned to said institutions, due regard being had to the location and convenience of the prisons, and of the other institutions to be supplied, the machinery now therein and the number of prisoners, in order to secure the best service and distribution of the labor, and to employ the prisoners, so far as practicable, in occupations in which they will be most likely to obtain employment after their discharge from imprisonment. The commissioner of correctional services shall change or dispose of the present plants and machinery in said institutions now used in industries which shall be discontinued, and which can not be used in the industries hereafter to be carried on in said prisons, due effort to be made by full notice to probable purchasers, in case of sales of industries or machinery, to obtain the best price possible for the property sold, and good will of the business to be discontinued.

2. The commissioner shall submit reports, quarterly, to the senate finance committee, the assembly ways and means committee, and the director of the budget, regarding industries under his jurisdiction. Such reports shall include, but not be limited to, the following:

(a) all materials, machinery or other property procured, and the cost thereof;

(b) all other expenditures and the nature thereof;

(c) all receipts and the nature thereof;

(d) all inventory on hand at the opening and closing of the quarter;

(e) recommendations regarding the continuance of the program.

Amended by L. 1981, Ch. 464 eff. July 7, 1981.

§ 184. Articles manufactured to be furnished to the state or subdivisions thereof.

1. The commissioner of correctional services is authorized and directed to cause to be manufactured or prepared by the inmates in the state correctional facilities, such articles as are needed and used therein, and also, such articles as are required by the state or political subdivisions thereof, and in the buildings, offices and public institutions owned or managed and controlled by the state, including articles and materials to be used in the erection of the buildings, and including material for the construction, improvement or repair of highways, streets and roads.

2. All such articles manufactured or prepared in the state correctional facilities, or by inmates, and not required for use therein, shall be of the styles, patterns, designs and qualities fixed by the department of correctional services, except where the same have been or may be fixed by the office of general services in the executive department. Such articles may be furnished to the state, or to any political subdivision thereof, or for or to any public institution owned or managed and controlled by the state, or any political subdivision thereof, government of the United States or to any state of the United States or subdivision thereof or to any public corporation, authority, or eleemosynary association funded in whole or in part by any federal, state of local funds, at and for such prices as shall be fixed and determined as hereinafter provided, upon the requisitions of the proper officials thereof. No article so manufactured or prepared shall be purchased from any other source, for the state or public institutions of the state, or the political subdivisions thereof, or public benefit corporations, authorities or commissions, unless the commissioner of correctional services shall certify that the same can not be furnished upon such requisition, and no claim therefor shall be audited or paid without such certificate.

Amended by L. 1962, Ch. 37; L. 1991, Ch. 166, eff. June 12, 1991.

§ 185. Estimates of articles required to be furnished.

On or before July first in each year, the proper officials of the state, and the political subdivisions thereof, and of the institutions of the state, or political subdivisions thereof, shall report to the department of correctional services estimates for the ensuing year of the amount of supplies of different kinds required to be purchased by them that can be furnished by the correctional facilities in the state. The commissioner of correctional services is authorized to make regulations for said reports, to provide for the manner in which requisitions shall be made for supplies, and to provide for the proper diversification of the industries in the correctional facilities.

Amended by L. 1991, Ch. 266, eff. June 12, 1991.

§ 186. Prices of labor performed and articles manufactured in correctional facilities.

1. The commissioner of correctional services shall establish the prices at which all services performed, and all articles manufactured in the correctional facilities in this state, and furnished to the state, or the political subdivisions thereof, or to the public institutions thereof, or to public benefit corporation, authorities or commissions. However, prices for goods or services furnished by the local correctional facilities to or for the county in which they are located, or the political subdivisions thereof, shall be fixed by the board of supervisors of such counties, except the counties located within New York city, in which the prices shall be fixed by the commissioner of correction. It shall also be the duty of such boards, respectively, to classify the buildings, offices and institutions owned or managed and controlled by the state, and the political subdivisions thereof, and to fix and determine the styles, patterns, designs and qualities of the articles to be manufactured for such buildings, offices and public institutions, except where the same have been fixed or their specifications approved by the office of general services in the executive department. So far as practicable, all supplies used in such buildings, offices and public institutions shall be uniform for each class, and of the styles, patterns, designs and qualities can be manufactured in the correctional facilities in this state.

2. The prices established by the commissioner shall be based upon costs as determined pursuant to this subdivision, but shall not exceed a reasonable fair market price determined at or within ninety days before the time of sale. Fair market price as used herein means the price at which a vendor of the same or similar product or service who is regularly engaged in the business of selling such product or service offers to sell such a product or service under similar terms in the same market. However, the price established by the commissioner for license plates sold to the New York state department of motor vehicles shall in no event exceed an amount approved by the director of the budget.

First instance appropriations to the department of correctional services for correctional industries shall be reimbursed pursuant to an agreement with the director of the budget. In the absence of a first instance appropriation, costs shall be determined in accordance with an agreement between the commissioner of correctional services and the director of the budget. Any such agreement shall include, among other provisions deemed necessary by the budget director for the purposes of enabling programmatic overview and fiscal controls, one or more methodologies for the determination of costs attributable to correctional industries or to any product manufactured in the institutions of the department or distributed, marketed or sold by the commissioner pursuant to this section, section one hundred seventy-seven of this article or section one hundred seventy-five of the state finance law.

3. A purchaser of any such product or services may, at any time prior to or within thirty days of the time of sale, appeal the purchase price on the basis that it unreasonably exceeds fair market price. Such appeal shall be raised in a form to be provided for by the commissioner pursuant to rule and shall include a verified statement setting forth the basis of an alternative fair market price determined according to the standards for establishing prices set forth in subdivision two of this section.

An appeal brought by such a purchaser as to the reasonableness of the fair market price established pursuant to subdivision two of this section shall be decided by majority vote of a three-member price review board consisting of the director of the budget, the commissioner of correctional services and the commissioner of the office of general services or their representatives.

All hearings before such price review board shall be governed by the rules to be adopted and prescribed by such board. The hearings of such board may, in the discretion of a majority of its members, be open to the public, but shall not be bound by the technical rules of evidence. The price review board shall permit the parties to such an appeal to present such evidence, in person or through their attorneys, as the board may deem necessary for its determination. A stenographic record shall be kept of any proceeding before such board and the decision of the board shall be in writing and state the reasons for such decision.

The decision of such board as to the reasonableness of the price established by the commissioner shall be conclusive on all parties. If the board finds that a price unreasonably exceeds the fair market price, it may adjust the sales price with respect to such purchaser. Prices so adjusted shall otherwise apply prospectively to purchases made subsequent to such adjustment until such time as new prices are established pursuant to subdivision two of this section. In the event that payment has been made, upon such adjustment of price, any excess paid to the state shall be refunded to such purchaser on a voucher signed by the commissioner within amounts available therefor or at the option of the purchaser, the commissioner may credit such excess amount toward any future purchase.

4. The state or the political subdivisions thereof, or public institutions thereof, or public benefit corporations, authorities or commission shall purchase the products manufactured in correctional institutions in this state in accordance with their needs and at prices established pursuant to this section.

Amended by L. 1962, Ch. 37; L. 1980, Ch. 413, eff. Sept. 21, 1980; L. 1991, Ch. 166, eff. June 12, 1991; L. 1995, Ch. 83, § 36, amending subd. 3, taking full force and eff Apr. 1, 1995.

§ 187. Earnings of inmates.

1. Every inmate confined in a state correctional facility, subject to the rules and regulations of the department of correctional services, and every inmate confined in a local correctional facility, in the discretion of the sheriff thereof, may receive compensation for work performed during his or her imprisonment. Such compensation shall be graded by the department of correctional services with regard to inmates employed in prison industries, based upon the work performed by such prisoners for prisoners confined in state correctional facilities, and by the sheriffs in all local correctional facilities for inmates confined therein.

2. The department of correctional services shall adopt rules, subject to the approval of the director of the budget, for establishing in all of the state correctional facilities a system of compensation for the inmates confined therein. Such rules shall provide for the payment of compensation to each inmate, who shall meet the requirements established by the department of correctional services, based upon the work performed by such inmates.

3. The department shall prepare graded wage schedules for inmates, which schedule shall be based upon classifications according to the value of work performed by each. Such schedules need not be uniform in all institutions. The rules of the department shall also provide for the establishment of a credit system for each inmate and the manner in which such earnings shall be paid to the inmate or his dependents or held in trust for him until his release.

4. Any compensation paid to an inmate under this article shall be based on the work performed by such inmate. Compensation may be paid from moneys appropriated to the department and available to facilities for nonpersonal service.

Amended by L. 1953, Ch. 342; L. 1946, Ch. 389; L. 1942, Ch. 738; L. 1972, Ch. 338; L. 1974, Ch. 240; L. 1991, Ch. 166, eff. June 12, 1991.

§ 189. Disposition of moneys paid to prisoner for his labor. [*Effective until Sept. 1, 2007, pursuant to L. 1995, Ch. 3, § 74(h), as amended.*]

1. The amount of such compensation to the

credit of any prisoner may be drawn by the prisoner during his imprisonment, only upon approval of the commissioner to aid dependent relatives of such prisoner, or for such other purposes as the commissioner may approve. Such disbursement to aid a dependent relative of a prisoner may be made without the consent of such prisoner upon the certificate of the commissioner of social services, or other officer performing the duties of a commissioner of welfare, of the community in which such dependent is located. Any balance to the credit of any prisoner at the time of his conditional release as provided by this chapter shall be subject to the draft of the prisoner in such amounts and at such times as the commissioner shall approve; provided, however, that at the date of absolute discharge of any prisoner the balance as aforesaid shall be paid to such prisoner.

2. The commissioner may collect from the compensation paid to a prisoner for work performed while housed in a general confinement facility an incarceration fee, not to exceed one dollar per week, for each week of confinement to help defray the costs of incarceration. The commissioner shall waive the collection of such fee where it is determined that the payment of the fee would work an unreasonable hardship on the prisoner or his or her immediate family.

§ 189. Disposition of moneys paid to prisoner for his labor. [*Effective Sept. 1, 2007.*]

The amount of such compensation to the credit of any prisoner may be drawn by the prisoner during his imprisonment, only upon approval of the commissioner to aid dependent relatives of such prisoner, or for such other purposes as the commissioner may approve. Such disbursement to aid a dependent relative of a prisoner may be made without the consent of such prisoner upon the certificate of the commissioner of welfare, or other officer performing the duties of a commissioner of welfare, of the community in which such dependent is located. Any balance to the credit of any prisoner at the time of his conditional release as provided by this chapter shall be subject to the draft of the prisoner in such amounts and at such times as the commissioner shall approve; provided, however, that at the date of absolute discharge of any prisoner the balance as aforesaid shall be paid to such prisoner.

Amended by L. 1942, Ch. 738; L. 1995, Ch. 3, § 55, eff. June 10, 1995, amendment expires Sept. 1, 1997; L. 1997, Ch 435, § 53, eff. Aug. 20, 1997, extending expiration date; L. 1999, Ch 453, § 7, eff. Sept. 1, 1999, extending expiration date; L. 2001, Ch. 95, § 9, extending expiration date; L. 2003, Ch. 16, § 9, eff. Mar. 31, 2003, extending expiration date to Sept. 1, 2005; L. 2005, Ch. 56, part D, § 9, eff. Apr. 1, 2005, extending expiration date to Sept. 1, 2007.

§ 190. Monthly statement of receipts and expenditures for industries.

The warden of each of the state prisons shall,

on the first of each month, make a full detailed statement of all materials, machinery or other property procured, and of the cost thereof, and of the expenditures made during the last preceding month for manufacturing purposes, together with a statement of all materials then on hand to be manufactured, or in process of manufacture, or manufactured, and of machinery, fixtures or other appurtenances for the purpose of carrying on the labor of the prisoners, and the amount and kinds of work done, and the earnings realized, and the total amount of moneys coming into his hands as such warden during such last preceding month as the proceeds of the labor of the prisoners at such prison, which statement shall be verified by the oath of such warden to be just and true, and shall be by him forwarded to the department of correction.

§ 193. Disposition of machinery on discontinuance of industry.

Whenever any trade or industry is discontinued at any state correctional institution and it appears to the satisfaction of the commissioner, that such trade or industry will not again be put in operation in any state correctional institution, he must report that fact to the comptroller, and at the same time furnish the comptroller with a schedule of the machinery, tools, apparatus and other appurtenances belonging to such trade or industry or used in connection therewith, and an estimate of the value of same, and also the quantity and value of the stock and manufactured product of such trade or industry then on hand, and the commissioner shall, with the approval of the comptroller, sell and dispose of all such unused and unnecessary machinery, tools, apparatus, stock and manufactured product. Said property shall be sold as provided in section one hundred seventy-eight of the state finance law. Any moneys received from such sale as aforesaid, after deducting all necessary and actual expenses, shall be deposited in the treasury to the credit of the correctional industry fund.

Amended by L. 1942, Ch. 738.

§ 196. Violations of institutional labor regulations.

Any contract made by the commissioner of correction or warden of any prison, or by any officer or any other authority whatsoever, of any prison, reformatory, penitentiary or other correctional institution of this state, in violation of, or contrary to, the provisions of this article, shall be null and void. It shall be the duty of any such officer or authorities to furnish to the attorney-general, upon demand therefor, a true copy, if in writing, and if not, in substance, of any contract made by such officer or authorities, relating in any way to the system of labor adopted, or to the employment of prisoners in any of said prisons, reformatories, penitentiaries or other correctional institutions. Whenever the attorney-general shall be satisfied that any contract made as aforesaid is contrary to or in violation of this article, or that any of the officers or authorities aforesaid have entered into or are engaged in any contract or arrangement for the labor of prisoners, or relating to the system adopted or continued in said institutions, which contract or arrangement is contrary to or in violation of law as aforesaid, if he shall be of the opinion that the facts require such action, he is hereby authorized to bring an action in the supreme court in the name of the people of the state of New York, in any county which he may select, for the purpose of testing the validity of any contract or arrangement made by any of the officers herein named relating in any way to the system of labor adopted, or the employment of prisoners in any of said prisons, reformatories, penitentiaries or other correctional institutions, or to determine the validity of any act or thing done by any officer herein mentioned, which act or thing shall be alleged to have been in violation of this article. Any party to such contract, agreement or arrangement as aforesaid, or interested in the determination of such action, shall be made defendant, and pending the trial or hearing of the facts alleged, or of any issue made as aforesaid, the court shall, upon notice of the attorney-general, and upon a petition duly verified showing the making of any contract or arrangement in violation of the provisions of this article, or the doing of any act or thing by any of the parties defendant, in violation of this article, grant an injunction order, restraining the parties named in said order from the further prosecution of the business complained of, or from the further performance of the contract or arrangement claimed to have been entered into as aforesaid, and to restrain and enjoin such officer from the further continuance of any act alleged to be in violation of this article. And any disobedience of such injunction order shall be punishable as provided by article nineteen of the judiciary law. And upon any trial had, judgment shall follow the findings of fact made by the court or jury, as in other cases, and with costs, in the discretion of the court.

§ 197. Occupational therapy.

Nothing in this article contained shall be deemed to apply to occupational therapy in any penal or correctional institution, or to prohibit the sale of the products resulting therefrom. Such sale and the disposition of the proceeds thereof shall be governed by rules and regulations of the head of the department or other like governmental authority having jurisdiction. For the purpose of this section, occupational therapy is defined as any activity in the nature of individual art or handicraft, prescribed, guided or supervised for the purpose of contributing to the welfare or rehabilitation of any inmate or inmates of such institutions.

§ 198. Inmate occupational therapy fund.

1. The commissioner of correctional services may authorize the superintendent or director of any correctional institution to establish an inmate occupational therapy fund for the receipt of proceeds from a product sold, as authorized by section one hundred ninety-seven, by one or more inmates as incident to an avocational or vocational project approved by the commissioner, including but not limited to, art, music, drama, handicraft, or sports.

2. Pursuant to rules, regulations or directions of the commissioner, moneys of the fund may: (a) be made available to the superintendent or director to be used for the general benefit of the inmates of the correctional institution wherein the product was produced, including but not limited to, furnishing materials and supplies to an inmate or inmates for an avocational or vocational project and the transporting of a product thereof for sale, display or otherwise and for recreational activities; or (b) be disbursed as follows: (i) an amount equal to the proceeds from the sale of a product produced by one inmate may be deposited to the account of such inmate pursuant to section one hundred sixteen of the correction law; or (ii) an amount equal to the proceeds from the sale of a product produced by two or more inmates may be divided equally among such inmates and deposited to their respective accounts pursuant to section one hundred sixteen of the correction law.

3. In determining the amount of the proceeds from a sale of a product that may be deposited to the account of an inmate, the commissioner of correctional services may provide for the deduction from the sum of the proceeds the reasonable expenses of the department of correctional services incident to the sale, including but not limited to, the value of materials and supplies for the production of the product supplied without financial charge to the inmate and the expenses of transporting the product for sale or display or otherwise.

Added by L. 1974, Ch. 240.

§ 200. Department programs and incentive allowances.

1. For the purpose of this section the term "incentive allowance" means monies allowed an inmate of a state correctional institution for the efficient and willing performance of duties assigned or progress and achievement in educational, career and industrial training programs.

2. In lieu of the system of labor in correctional institutions established by this article, the commissioner may, in order to facilitate an inmate's eventual reintegration into society, establish for the inmates in one or more state correctional institutions a system of educational, career and industrial training programs, and of incentive allowances for each such program.

3. For each institution wherein such system is established the commissioner shall prepare, and may at times revise, graded incentive allowance schedules for the inmates within each such program based upon the levels of performance and achievement by an inmate in a program to which he has been assigned. Upon the approval of the director of the budget such schedules or revisions thereof may be promulgated.

4. The commissioner shall also provide for the establishment of a credit system for each inmate and the manner in which incentive allowances shall be paid to the inmate or his dependents or held in trust for him until his release. The amount of incentive allowed to the credit of any inmate shall be disposed of as provided by section one hundred eighty-nine.

5. Incentive allowances may be paid from monies provided to the department and available to the facilities for non-personal services or from the correctional industry training and career education fund.

6. Except as otherwise provided by this section, those provisions of law dealing with labor in state correctional institutions shall apply to industrial training in state correctional institutions including the disposition of services rendered and products produced incidental to such industrial training.

Added by L. 1974, Ch. 536; **Amended** by L. 1996, Ch. 301, § 46, amending subds. 1, 2, and 5, effective July 10, 1996.

CORR. L.

ARTICLE 11—EXECUTIVE CLEMENCY

§ 261. Subpoena on application for executive clemency.

The governor shall have the power in any matter pertaining to an application for clemency, to issue a subpoena to compel the attendance of a person before him at a time and place designated in said subpoena; and he shall also have the power to compel the production of any book, paper or writing by a subpoena duces tecum, directed to a person in whose custody either may be, at a time and place designated in said subpoena. But the provisions of this article shall not apply to any book, paper or writing filed in any office of record in any civil division of this state.

§ 262. Appointment of person to hear application.

The governor may appoint a person to conduct a hearing in a matter pertaining to an application for clemency, and his compensation shall not exceed ten dollars for each day's actual service. Such person, upon the conclusion of such hearing, shall forward to the governor without delay, the testimony taken before him. The governor may direct that a person subpoenaed by him, in conformity to the provisions of the preceding section, appear before a person designated by him to conduct a hearing as provided by this section; and a person so subpoenaed shall produce any book, paper or writing before said person so designated by the governor, in conformity with the provisions of the preceding section of this article.

§ 263. Oath of witnesses.

The governor or a person designated by him to conduct a hearing in a matter pertaining to an application for clemency, shall have power to administer an oath to a person brought before him.

§ 264. Form and service of subpoena; witness fees.

A subpoena, or subpoena duces tecum, issued in conformity with the provisions of this article, shall be signed by the governor's secretary, and be attested by the privy seal of the state. A subpoena issued under this section shall be regulated by the civil practice law and rules.

Amended by L. 1962, Ch. 310.

§ 265. Penalty for failure of witness to appear.

A person subpoenaed who fails to appear, refuses to answer, or produce a book, paper or writing as provided in this article, shall upon conviction be adjudged guilty of a criminal contempt. And in addition thereto a person so subpoenaed shall be subject to all the provisions of law which now or may hereafter exist, relating to witnesses in civil or criminal actions at law; and the governor shall possess all the powers in relation to said provisions which are possessed by any court or judge, but he shall be limited to the matters arising under the provisions of this article.

§ 266. Disbursements.

Any disbursements necessary to be made for any of the purposes mentioned in this article shall be paid from the treasury upon the approval of the governor's secretary, on the audit and warrant of the comptroller, out of any moneys in the treasury not otherwise appropriated.

ARTICLE 12—LOCAL CONDITIONAL RELEASE COMMISSION

[Expires and repealed Sept. 1, 2005.]

§ 270. **Definitions.**
§ 271. **Local conditional release commission; organization.**
§ 272. **Local conditional release commission; function, powers and duties.**
§ 273. **Conditional release; procedures for application and determinations.**
§ 274. **Conditional release; procedures for violation, delinquency, warrants and revocation.**
§ 275. **Transfer of custody and supervision of conditional releasee.**

§ 270. Definitions. [*Expires and repealed September 1, 2005.*]

As used in this article, the following terms have the following meanings:

1. "Commission" means the local conditional release commission.

2. "County" means each county in the state, except a county within the city of New York, and the city of New York.

3. "County executive" means the county commissioner, county manager, county director, mayor or county president.

4. "Division" means the division of probation and correctional alternatives.

Added by L. 1989, Ch. 79; **Amended** by L. 1990, Ch. 117, § 1, extending expiration date; L. 1991, Ch. 83, § 1, extending expiration date; L. 1992, Ch. 55, § 323, extending expiration date; L. 1993, Ch. 39, § 1, extending expiration date; L. 1994, Ch. 61, § 6, extending expiration date; L. 1997, Ch. 86, § 1, effective May 30, 1997, amending subsection (2), Chs. 57, 117, 145, 162, 194, 211, 264, and 435 § 54, effective Aug. 20, 1997, extending expiration date; any provision of law which expired prior to Aug. 20, 1997 shall be revived and shall be deemed to have been in full force and effect from and after the date of the applicable expiration; L. 1999, Ch. 453, eff. Sept. 1, 1999, extending effective date; L. 2001, Ch. 95, § 12, eff. July 13, 2001, extending effective date; L. 2003, Ch. 16, § 10, extending expiration date to Sept. 1, 2005, eff. Mar. 31, 2003.

§ 271. Local conditional release commission; organization. [*Expires and repealed September 1, 2005.*]

1. There shall be in every county a commission appointed by the county executive. Each commission shall consist of at least three members. Each member of the commission shall have graduated from an accredited four year college or university and shall have had at least five years of experience in the field of criminology, administration of criminal justice, law enforcement, probation, parole, law, social work, social science, psychology, psychiatry or corrections.

2. The term of office of each member of such commission shall be for four years; provided, however, that any member chosen to fill a vacancy occurring otherwise than by expiration of term shall be appointed for the remainder of the unexpired term of the member whom the person is to succeed. Vacancies caused by expiration of term or otherwise shall be filled in the same manner as original appointments.

3. No member of the commission shall serve as a representative of any political party on an executive committee or other governing body thereof, as an executive officer or employee of any political committee, organization or association, nor be a judge or justice, a sheriff or district attorney.

4. Any member may be removed by the county executive for cause, after notice and an opportunity to be heard.

Added by L. 1989, Ch. 79; **Amended** by L. 1990, Ch. 117, § 1, extending expiration date; L. 1991, Ch. 83, § 1, extending expiration date; L. 1992, Ch. 55, § 323, extending expiration date; L. 1993, Ch. 39, § 1, extending expiration date; L. 1994, Ch. 61, § 6, extending expiration date; L. 1997, Chs. 57, 117, 145, 162, 194, 211, 264, and 435 § 54, effective Aug. 20, 1997, extending expiration date; any provision of law which expired prior to Aug. 20, 1997 shall be revived and shall be deemed to have been in full force and effect from and after the date of the applicable expiration; L. 1999, Ch. 453, eff. Sept. 1, 1999, extending effective date; L. 2001, Ch. 95, § 12, eff. July 13, 2001, extending effective date; L. 2003, Ch. 16, § 10, extending expiration date to Sept. 1, 2005, eff. Mar. 31, 2003.

§ 272. Local conditional release commission; function, powers and duties. [*Expires and repealed September 1, 2005.*]

The commission shall:

1. Have the power and duty of determining which persons sentenced within the county and serving a definite sentence of imprisonment and eligible for conditional release pursuant to subdivision two of section 70.40 of the penal law may be released on conditional release and when and under what conditions in accordance with section two hundred seventy-three of this article;

2. Determine, as each inmate applies for conditional release, the need for supplemental investigation of the background of such inmate and cause such investigation as may be necessary to be made as soon as practicable. The commission may require that the probation department located in the jurisdiction of the commission conduct such supplemental investigation. The results of such investigation together with all other information compiled by the local correctional facility and the complete criminal record and family court record

of such inmate shall be readily available when the conditional release of such inmate is being considered. Such information shall include a complete statement of the crime for which the inmate has been sentenced, the circumstances of such crime, all presentence memoranda, the nature of the sentence, the court in which such inmate was sentenced, the name of the judge and district attorney and copies of such probation reports as may have been made as well as reports as to the inmate's social, physical, mental and psychiatric condition and history;

3. Have the legal custody of persons conditionally released and placed under the supervision of the local probation department until the expiration of the maximum term or period of sentence or return to the custody of the local correction facility located in the jurisdiction of the commission, as the case may be;

4. Have the power to revoke the conditional release of any person in the legal custody of the commission and to issue declarations of delinquency and authorize the issuance of a warrant for the retaking of such person, as provided for in section two hundred seventy-four of this article;

5. For the purpose of any investigation necessary in the performance of its duties, have the power to issue subpoenas, to compel the attendance of witnesses and the production of books, papers, and other documents pertinent to the subject of its inquiry;

6. Have the power to authorize any members thereof to administer oaths and take the testimony of persons under oath;

7. Notify in writing the appropriate local probation department prior to release of a conditionally released person of such department's responsibilities to supervise such person;

Such notice shall include the name and residence of the person, the date of release, the conditions of release, and all necessary records maintained on such person to aid the local probation department in the performance of its responsibilities pursuant to subdivision six of section two hundred fifty-six of the executive law; and

8. have the power to transfer the legal custody of persons conditionally released in accordance with the provisions of section two hundred seventy-five of this article;

9. notwithstanding any other provision of law to the contrary, where a person serving a definite sentence for an offense defined in article one hundred thirty, two hundred thirty-five or two hundred sixty-three of the penal law or section 255.25 of the penal law and the victim of such offense was under the age of eighteen at the time of such offense, is conditionally released pursuant to section 70.40 of the penal law, the local conditional release commission shall require, as a mandatory condition of such release, that such

sentenced offender shall refrain from knowingly entering into or upon any school grounds, as that term is defined in paragraph (a) of subdivision fourteen of section 220.00 of the penal law or any other facility or institution primarily used for the care or treatment of persons under the age of eighteen while one or more of such persons under the age of eighteen are present, provided however, that when such sentenced offender is a registered student or participant or an employee of such facility or institution or entity contracting therewith or has a family member enrolled in such facility or institution, such sentenced offender may, with the written authorization of his or her probation officer and the superintendent or chief administrator of such facility, institution or grounds, enter such facility, institution or upon such grounds for the limited purposes authorized by the probation officer and superintendent or chief officer. Nothing in this subdivision shall be construed as restricting any lawful condition of supervision that may be imposed on such sentenced offender.

Added by L. 1989, Ch. 79; **Amended** by L. 1990, Ch. 117, § 1, extending expiration date; L. 1991, Ch. 83, § 1, extending expiration date; L. 1992, Ch. 55, § 323, extending expiration date; L. 1993, Ch. 39, § 1, extending expiration date; L. 1994, Ch. 61, § 6, extending expiration date; L. 1997, Chs. 57, 117, 145, 162, 194, 211, 264, and 435 § 54, effective Aug. 20, 1997, extending expiration date; any provision of law which expired prior to Aug. 20, 1997 shall be revived and shall be deemed to have been in full force and effect from and after the date of the applicable expiration; L. 1999, Ch. 453, eff. Sept. 1, 1999, extending effective date; L. 2000, Ch. 1, adding subd. 9, eff. Feb. 1, 2001; L. 2001, Ch. 95, § 12, eff. July 13, 2001, extending effective date; L. 2003, Ch. 16, § 10, extending expiration date to Sept. 1, 2005, eff. Mar. 31, 2003.

§ 273. Conditional release; procedures for application and determinations. [*Expires and repealed September 1, 2005.*]

1. Any inmate who is eligible for conditional release by a commission pursuant to subdivision two of section 70.40 of the penal law and who has served a minimum period of thirty days in a local correctional facility may apply for conditional release. Application shall be made in writing, on forms prescribed by the division, to the commission in the county where the sentence was imposed.

2. The commission shall review and make a determination on each application within thirty days of receipt of such application. No determination granting or denying such application shall be valid unless made by a majority vote of at least three commission members present.

3. If conditional release is granted, the commission shall set the conditions for release of the person in accordance with rules and regulations promulgated by the division. Such person shall be given a copy of the conditions of release. Such conditions shall, where appropriate, include a requirement that the person comply with any

restitution order previously imposed by a court of competent jurisdiction that applies to the person.

4. No person who has been granted conditional release shall be released until such person has served a minimum period of incarceration of sixty days, in accordance with subdivision two of section 70.40 of the penal law, and unless such person has agreed in writing to the conditions set by the commission. Such agreement shall state in plain, easily understandable language the consequences of a violation of one or more of the conditions of release.

5. Persons who have been granted conditional release shall, while on conditional release, be in the legal custody of the commission until the expiration of the maximum term or period of sentence, or return to the custody of the local correctional facility located in the jurisdiction of the commission, as the case may be. The probation department located in the jurisdiction of the commission has the duty of supervising the person during the period of such conditional release.

6. If conditional release is not granted, the commission shall inform the person in writing of the factors and reasons for such denial of conditional release within fifteen days of the decision. Such reasons shall be given in detail and not in conclusory terms. Inmates denied conditional release are eligible to reapply sixty days after the date of submission of the denied application.

Added by L. 1989, Ch. 79; **Amended** by L. 1990, Ch. 117, § 1, extending expiration date; L. 1991, Ch. 83, § 1, extending expiration date; L. 1992, Ch. 55, § 323, extending expiration date; L. 1993, Ch. 39, § 1, extending expiration date; L. 1994, Ch. 61, § 6, extending expiration date; L. 1997, Chs. 57, 117, 145, 162, 194, 211, 264, and 435 § 54, effective Aug. 20, 1997, extending expiration date; any provision of law which expired prior to Aug. 20, 1997 shall be revived and shall be deemed to have been in full force and effect from and after the date of the applicable expiration; L. 1999, Ch. 453, eff. Sept. 1, 1999, extending effective date; L. 2001, Ch. 95, § 12, eff. July 13, 2001, extending effective date; L. 2003, Ch. 16, § 10, extending expiration date to Sept. 1, 2005, eff. Mar. 31, 2003.

ANNOTATIONS

Timeliness of application.—Under statute, application that has been denied cannot be resubmitted until "[60] days after the date of submission of the denied application," since Respondent's submission was made within less than 60 days, it was improper for, Commission to consider it. Winn v. Rensselaer County Conditional Release Comm'n,, 6 A.D.3d 929, 775 N.Y.S.2d 412 (3d Dept. 2004)

§ 274. Conditional release; procedures for violation, delinquency, warrants and revocation. [*Expires and repealed September 1, 2005.*]

1. If at any time during the period of conditional release, the commission, or any member thereof, has reasonable cause to believe that a person who has been conditionally released has lapsed into criminal ways or company, or has violated one or more conditions of conditional release, the commission or such member may declare such person delinquent and issue a written declaration of delinquency. Upon such declaration, such commission or such member may issue a warrant for the retaking and temporary detention of such person.

2. A warrant issued pursuant to this section shall constitute sufficient authority to the chief administrative officer of any local correctional facility to whom it is delivered to hold in temporary detention the person named therein.

3. A warrant issued pursuant to this section may be executed by any probation officer or any officer authorized to serve criminal process or any peace officer, who is acting pursuant to his or her special duties, or any police officer. Any such officer to whom such warrant shall be delivered is authorized and required to execute such warrant by taking such person and having him or her detained as provided for in this section.

4. The alleged violator shall, within three days of the execution of the warrant, be given written notice of the time, place and purpose of the hearing. The notice shall state what conditions of conditional release are alleged to have been violated and in what manner and shall inform the alleged violator of his or her right to counsel as provided for in subdivision seven of this section.

5. The alleged conditional release violator shall appear before the commission, or any member thereof, within fifteen days of the execution of the warrant. At the time of such appearance the commission or such member shall ask the alleged violator whether he or she wishes to make any statement with respect to the violation. If the alleged violator makes a statement, the commission or such member may accept it and base a decision thereon. If the commission or such member does not accept it, or if the alleged violator does not make a statement, the commission or such member shall proceed with the hearing.

6. The commission, or any member thereof, may receive any relevant evidence. The alleged violator may cross examine witnesses and may present evidence on his or her own behalf.

7. The alleged violator is entitled to counsel at all stages of any proceeding under this section and the commission, or any member thereof, shall advise him or her of such right upon delivering to the alleged violator written notice, required pursuant to subdivision four of this section.

8. At the conclusion of the hearing, the commission, or any member thereof, shall issue a finding. If the commission or such member is not satisfied that there is a preponderance of evidence in support of the violation, the commission or such member shall dismiss the violation, cancel delinquency and restore the person to supervision. If the commission or such member is satisfied that there is a preponderance of evidence that the alleged violator violated one or more conditions

CORR. L.

of conditional release in an important respect, the commission or such member shall so find.

9. Upon a finding in support of the violation, the commission, or any member thereof, may revoke the conditional release, or continue or modify the conditions of such conditional release. Where the commission or such member revokes a person's conditional release, such person shall be committed to the custody of the chief administrative officer of the local correctional facility to serve the time remaining on his or her sentence, in accordance with subdivision three of section 70.40 of the penal law. Where the commission or such member modifies the conditions of the conditional release, the commission or such member shall inform the person, in writing, of such modified conditions.

10. Any actions by the commission, or any member thereof, pursuant to this article shall be deemed a judicial function and shall not be reviewable if done in accordance with law.

Added by L. 1989, Ch. 79; Amended by L. 1990, Ch. 117, § 1, extending expiration date; L. 1991, Ch. 83, § 1, extending expiration date; L. 1992, Ch. 55, § 323, extending expiration date; L. 1993, Ch. 39, § 1, extending expiration date; L. 1994, Ch. 61, § 6, extending expiration date; L. 1997, Chs. 57, 117, 145, 162, 194, 211, 264, and 435 § 54, effective Aug. 20, 1997, extending expiration date; any provision of law which expired prior to Aug. 20, 1997 shall be revived and shall be deemed to have been in full force and effect from and after the date of the applicable expiration; L. 1999, Ch. 453, eff. Sept. 1, 1999, extending effective date; L. 2001, Ch. 95, § 12, eff. July 13, 2001, extending effective date; L. 2003, Ch. 16, § 10, extending expiration date to Sept. 1, 2005, eff. Mar. 31, 2003.

§ 275. Transfer of custody and supervision of conditional releasee. [*Expires and repealed September 1, 2005.*]

1. Authority to transfer. If a person who has been granted conditional release pursuant to this article resides or desires to reside in a place other than the one located within the jurisdiction of the commission which has legal custody of such person, such commission, or any member thereof, may designate any other commission to assume custody of such person and may so transfer custody.

2. Where custody of a person who has been granted conditional release pursuant to this article is transferred pursuant to subdivision one of this section, upon designation and prior to transfer, the commission making the designation shall notify the commission which has been designated to receive custody of such transfer. The commission making the designation shall immediately forward its entire case record regarding such person to the receiving commission. The commission to which legal custody has been transferred shall assume the same powers and duties exercised by the designating commission and shall have the sole custody of such person.

3. The commission making the designation shall, upon designation and prior to transfer, notify the local probation department located in the jurisdiction of the receiving commission of the duties of supervision and conditions of release of such person. Upon such notification, such probation department shall assume responsibilities of supervision. The commission making the designation shall immediately forward its entire case record regarding such person to such probation department.

Added by L. 1989, Ch. 79. Amended by L. 1990, Ch. 117, § 1, extending expiration date; L. 1991, Ch. 83, § 1, extending expiration date; L. 1992, Ch. 55, § 323, extending expiration date; L. 1993, Ch. 39, § 1, extending expiration date; L. 1994, Ch. 61, § 6, extending expiration date; L. 1997, Chs. 57, 117, 145, 162, 194, 211, 264, and 435 § 54, effective Aug. 20, 1997, extending expiration date; any provision of law which expired prior to Aug. 20, 1997 shall be revived and shall be deemed to have been in full force and effect from and after the date of the applicable expiration; L. 1999, Ch. 453, eff. Sept. 1, 1999, extending effective date; L. 2001, Ch. 95, § 12, eff. July 13, 2001, extending effective date; L. 2003, Ch. 16, § 10, extending expiration date to Sept. 1, 2005, eff. Mar. 31, 2003.

ARTICLE 12-B—RESIDENT PAROLE FACILITY FOR YOUTH

Section
315.   **Resident parole facility.**

§ 315. Resident parole facility.

There shall be in the division of parole a short-term state parole facility to be known as the resident parole facility consisting of such camps or residences as the board of parole shall from time to time establish for the care, treatment, and rehabilitation of males and females who were between the ages of sixteen and twenty-one years at the time of the commission of the act for which they were adjudged youthful offenders, wayward minors of convicted of a crime or offense and who are under the supervision of the board of parole. The division shall have the custody of such parolees in accordance with the terms and conditions established by the board of parole for such parolees.

Added by L. 1960, Ch. 883.

CORR. L.

ARTICLE 13—CARE OF PROPERTY OF PERSON CONFINED FOR LIFE

§ 320. Who may apply for appointment of committee.

Whenever any person has been convicted and sentenced to imprisonment in this states for life, the husband, wife, relatives or next of kin or any creditor of such person may apply to the supreme court, at a special term thereof in the judicial district in which said person resided at the time of his conviction for the appointment of a committee of such person's estate, both real and personal.

§ 321. Application for appointment of committee.

Such application shall be made upon personal notice of not less than twenty days to such convicted person and to the district attorney of the county where the conviction was had, and upon notice to such other persons and upon notice to such other persons as would be entitled to notice of application for the probate of the will of such convicted person if he were then dead leaving a will of real and personal property, to be given in like manner as notice of application for such probate. The application shall, among other things, set forth the amount of the property of such person, and the names and residences of his heirs-at-law and next of kin, as near as the same are known or can be ascertained by the applicant. Upon such application and due proof of the service of the notice herein required, the court may, in its discretion, appoint a committee of the estate of such convicted person. The person or persons so appointed as such committee shall file a bond in the county clerk's office of such county, and in such amount and with such sureties as the said court shall direct. A copy of the order appointing such committee certified by the clerk of the county in which the order is filed, shall be filed in every county in which any real estate of such convicted person is situated.

§ 322. Payment of debts and application of property.

The court shall direct the payment of the debts of such convicted person from said property, and may also in its discretion direct the application of the income, and if need be, of the principal of such property, to the support, education and maintenance of such persons as the said convicted person would be legally liable to support if he had not been so convicted. Or. the court may direct the care and preservation of the income and principal of such estate until the natural death of the person so convicted.

§ 323. Sale of property.

The court in the judicial district in which a person is sentenced to life imprisonment may empower, authorize and direct a committee of such person to sell any of the real or personal property of such person, and to do whatever may be deemed necessary in the management of any of such person's property in the manner prescribed for a committee of an incompetent. The court may from time to time, in the manner prescribed upon the sale of the property of an infant, if it deems it necessary, or that the estate will be benefited thereby, direct the sale of any of the real or personal property by said committee, and the investment of the proceeds of such sale. The court shall control such committees in the performance of their duties; and may from time to time modify and alter its direction or orders in any matter pertaining to an estate.

Amended by L. 1962, Ch. 310.

§ 324. Report of committee; compensation.

The committee so appointed shall annually render an account to the court of his management and of his receipts and disbursements, and transmit a copy thereof to the person so convicted. The court may grant such compensation to the committee as it deems proper, not exceeding, however, the amount that may be allowed to an administrator.

§ 325. Proceedings on pardon or commutation of sentence.

Should said convicted person be pardoned, or his sentence be commuted, the court shall direct the committee to transfer to him, after his discharge from prison, all of said property remaining in his hands not lawfully applied or used as herein provided for, and upon the death of such convicted person not pardoned or commuted as aforesaid, the court shall direct the distribution

of such property as upon the natural death of a
person not convicted.

ARTICLE 14—CARE OF PROPERTY OF PERSON CONFINED FOR LESS THAN LIFE

§ 350. When and to what court application to be made.

Where a person is imprisoned in a state prison, for a term less than for life or in a penitentiary or county jail, for a criminal offense, for a longer term than one year; one or more trustees, to take charge of his property of the county, or the supreme court may be appointed, as prescribed in this article, by the county court in the judicial district, where he resided at the time of his imprisonment, or if he was not then a resident of the state, where he is imprisoned.

§ 351. Who may apply.

A petition for such an appointment may be presented by either of the following persons:

1. A creditor of the prisoner.

2. The prisoner's husband, wife, or child.

3. One or more of his next of kin, or, where he owns real property, of his heirs presumptive.

4. A relative whom he is bound to support.

5. Any relative or other person, in behalf of his infant child or children.

§ 352. Creditor must relinquish security.

A creditor of the prisoner, who has a judgment, mortgage, or other security, specified in section fifty-nine of the debtor and creditor law, can not apply for such an appointment, with respect to the debt so secured, unless he appends to or includes in his petition, the declaration, required by that section from a consenting creditor; which declaration has the same effect as the declaration of a consenting creditor, as therein specified.

§ 353. Contents of petition.

The petition must be in writing, and verified by the affidavit of the petitioner, to the effect, that the matters of fact therein stated are true, to the best of the petitioner's knowledge and belief. It must set forth the facts, showing that the applicant is entitled to make the application, and that the application is made to the proper court; the name and residence of each person, who is entitled to make such an application, as prescribed in the last section but one, except the fifth subdivision thereof; and a brief description of the property, real and personal, of the prisoner, and the value thereof. If the applicant is a creditor, and not a resident of the state, he must annex to his petition, the papers specified in section sixty-two of the debtor and creditor law. If any of the facts, herein required to be set forth can not be ascertained by the petitioner, after the exercise of due diligence, that fact must be stated; and the court may, in its discretion, issue a subpoena, requiring any person to attend and testify, respecting any matter, which, in its opinion, ought to be more fully and certainly set forth.

§ 354. Copy of sentence and affidavit to be presented.

The petition must be accompanied with a copy of the sentence of conviction of the prisoner, duly certified by the clerk of the court by which he was sentenced, under the seal thereof; together with an affidavit of the applicant, stating that the person so convicted is actually imprisoned thereunder.

§ 355. Proceedings upon presentation of the papers.

Upon the presentation of the papers, the court may, in its discretion, make an order, either appointing one or more fit persons trustees of the property of the prisoner, or requiring all creditors of the prisoner, and all persons interested in his estate, to show cause, at a time and place specified therein, why such an appointment should not be made. In the latter case, the order must direct the manner of service thereof, by publication or otherwise.

§ 356. Proceedings on return of order to show cause.

Upon the return of an order to show cause, made as prescribed in the last section, proof of the service thereof, as required thereby, must first be made; whereupon the court must hear the allegations and proofs of the creditors, and other persons interested in the estate, who appear. Where the prisoner is indebted to any person, the court must appoint one or more trustees, unless the persons interested in the prisoner's property pay the debt, or give such security, as the court prescribes, for the payment thereof, either absolutely, or contingently upon a recovery in an action; in which case or where the prisoner is not indebted, the court may grant or deny the prayer of the petition, as justice requires.

§ 357. Effect of order appointing trustee.

The entry of the order, appointing one or more trustees, and the filing of the papers upon which it was granted, vests in the trustee or trustees all the right, title and interest of the prisoner, in and to any property, real or personal. Where the prisoner owns real property, an exemplified copy of the order must be recorded, in the proper office for recording deeds, in each county where the real property is situated.

§ 358. Removal of trustee; appointment of new trustee.

Upon the application of any person, entitled to apply for an order, appointing trustees of the prisoner's property, and upon such a notice as the court prescribes, to the petitioner, and to such other persons interested, as the court thinks proper to designate, the court, by which the order was granted, may, in its discretion, remove any trustee, and appoint another in his place; or may appoint one or more additional trustees. The new trustee or trustees, so appointed, have the same power and authority, are vested with the same right, title, and interest, and are subject to the same duties and liabilities, as if he or they have been appointed by the original order.

§ 359. Prisoner's property; how applied.

After deducting their commissions and expenses, allowed by law, and paying the prisoner debts, the trustees may, from time to time, under the direction of the court by which they were appointed, apply the surplus of any money in their hands, to the support of the prisoner's spouse and children, and of such other relatives as the prisoner is bound to support, and to the education of such prisoner's children.

§ 360. Prisoner's property to be delivered to him on his discharge.

When the prisoner dies, or is lawfully discharged from imprisonment, the trustee or trustee must deliver over to him, or to his legal representatives, all his property, remaining in their hands after deducting therefrom their lawful expense and commissions.

§ 361. Application of this article to persons heretofore sentenced.

This article applies to a prisoner who has been sentenced before this chapter takes effect, and to his property; except where one or more trustee of his property have been theretofore appointed by proceedings taken in pursuance of a statute then in force.

ARTICLE 16—PROVISIONS RELATING TO MENTALLY ILL INMATES

§ 400. Definitions.

As used in this article the following terms:

(1) "Examining physician" means a physician licensed to practice medicine in the state of New York, but who is not on the staff of the facility where the inmate is confined.

(2) "Hospital" means a hospital in the department of mental hygiene which is designated as such by the commissioner of mental hygiene for the care and treatment of mentally ill inmates.

(3) "In immediate need of care and treatment" means that the inmate is apparently mentally ill and is not able to be properly cared for at the place where he is confined and is in need of immediate care and treatment in a hospital.

(4) "In need of care and treatment" means that a person has a mental illness for which in-patient care and treatment in a hospital is necessary.

(5) "Inmate" means a person committed to the custody of the department of correctional services, or a person convicted of a crime and committed to the custody of the sheriff, the county jail, or a local department of correction.

(6) "Mental illness" means an affliction with a mental disease or mental condition which is manifested by a disorder or disturbance in behavior, feeling, thinking, or judgment to such an extent that the person afflicted requires care and treatment.

(7) "Superintendent" means a superintendent of a state correctional facility or the person in charge of a local correctional facility by whatever title he may be known.

§ 401. Establishment of programs inside correctional facilities.

The commissioner, in cooperation with the commissioner of mental hygiene, shall establish programs in such correctional facilities as he may deem appropriate for the treatment of mentally ill inmates confined in state correctional facilities who are in need of psychiatric services but who do not require hospitalization for the treatment of mental illness. The administration and operation of programs established pursuant to this section shall be the responsibility of the commissioner of mental hygiene. The professional health care personnel for such programs shall be employees of the department of mental hygiene. All other personnel shall be employees of the department.

§ 402. Commitment of mentally ill inmates.

1. Whenever the physician of any correctional facility, any county penitentiary, county jail or workhouse, any reformatory for women, or of any other correctional institution, shall report in writing to the superintendent that any person undergoing a sentence of imprisonment or adjudicated to be a youthful offender or juvenile delinquent confined therein is, in his opinion, mentally ill, such superintendent shall apply to a judge of the county court or justice of the supreme court in the county to cause an examination to be made of such person by two examining physicians. Such physicians shall be designated by the judge to whom the application is made. Each such physician, if satisfied, after a personal examination, that such inmate is mentally ill and in need of care and treatment, shall make a certificate to such effect. Before making such certificate, however, he shall consider alternative forms of care and treatment available during confinement in such correctional facility, penitentiary, jail, reformatory or correctional institution that might be adequate to provide for such inmate's needs without requiring hospitalization. If the examining physician knows that the person he is examining has been under prior treatment, he shall, insofar as possible, consult with the physician or psychologist furnishing such prior treatment prior to making his certificate.

2. In the city of New York, if the physician of a workhouse, city prison, jail, penitentiary or reformatory reports in writing to the superintendent of such institution that a prisoner confined therein, serving a sentence of imprisonment, is in his opinion mentally ill, the superintendent of said institution shall either transfer said prisoner to Bellevue or Kings county hospital for observation as to his mental condition by two examining physicians or shall secure two examining physicians to make such examination in his institution. Each such physician, if satisfied after a personal examination and observation that the prisoner is mentally ill and in need of care and treatment,

shall make a certificate to such effect. Before making such certificate, however, he shall consider alternative forms of care and treatment available during confinement in such correctional facility, penitentiary, jail, reformatory or correctional institution that might be adequate to provide for such inmate's needs without requiring hospitalization. If the examining physician knows that the person he is examining has been under prior treatment, he shall, insofar as possible, consult with the physician or psychologist furnishing such prior treatment prior to making his certificate.

3. Upon such certificates of the examining physicians being so made, it shall be delivered to the superintendent who shall thereupon apply by petition forthwith to a judge of the county court or justice of the supreme court in the county, annexing such certificate to his petition, for an order committing such inmate to a hospital for the mentally ill. Upon every such application for such an order of commitment, notice thereof in writing, of at least five days, together with a copy of the petition, shall be served personally upon the alleged mentally ill person, and in addition thereto such notice and a copy of the petition shall be served upon either the wife, the husband, the father or mother or other nearest relative of such alleged mentally ill person, if there be any such known relative within the state; and if not, such notice shall be served upon any known friend of such alleged mentally ill person within the state. If there be no such known relative or friend within the state, the giving of such notice shall be dispensed with, but in such case the petition for the commitment shall recite the reasons why service of such notice on a relative or friend of the alleged mentally ill person was dispensed with and, in such case, the order for commitment shall recite why service of such a notice on a relative or friend of the alleged mentally ill person was dispensed with. Copies of the notice, the petition and the certificates of the examining physicians shall also be given the mental hygiene legal service. The mental hygiene legal service shall inform the inmate and, in proper cases, others interested in the inmate's welfare, of the procedures for placement in a hospital and of the inmate's right to have a hearing, to have judicial review with a right to a jury trial, to be represented by counsel and to seek an independent medical opinion. The mental hygiene legal service shall have personal access to such inmate for such purposes.

4. The judge to whom such application for the commitment of the alleged mentally ill person is made may, if no demand is made for a hearing on behalf of the alleged mentally ill person, proceed forthwith on the return day of such notice to determine the question of mental illness and, if satisfied that the alleged mentally ill person is mentally ill and in need of care and treatment, may immediately issue an order for the commitment of such alleged mentally ill person to a hospital for a period not to exceed six months from the date of the order.

5. Upon the demand for a hearing by any relative or near friend on behalf of such alleged mentally ill person, the judge shall, or he may upon his own motion where there is no demand for a hearing, issue an order directing the hearing of such application before him at a time not more than five days from the date of such order, which shall be served upon the parties interested in the application and upon such other persons as the judge, in his discretion, may name. Upon such day or upon such other day to which the proceedings shall be regularly adjourned, he shall hear the testimony introduced by the parties and shall examine the alleged mentally ill person, if deemed advisable in or out of court, and render a decision in writing as to such person's mental illness and need for care and treatment. If such judge cannot hear the application, he may, in his order directing the hearing, name some referee who shall hear the testimony and report the same forthwith, with his opinion thereon, to such judge, who shall, if satisfied with such report, render his decision accordingly. If it be determined that such person is mentally ill and in need of care and treatment, the judge shall forthwith issue his order committing him to a hospital for a period not to exceed six months from the date of the order. Such superintendent shall thereupon cause such mentally ill person to be delivered to the director of the appropriate hospital as designated by the commissioner of mental hygiene and such mentally ill person shall be received into such hospital and retained there until he is determined to be no longer in need of care and treatment by the director of such hospital or legally discharged or for the period specified in the order of commitment or in any subsequent order authorizing continued retention of such person in said hospital. Such superintendent, before delivering said mentally ill person, shall see that he is bodily clean. If such judge shall refuse to issue an order of commitment, he shall certify in writing his reasons for such refusal.

6. When an order of commitment is made, such order and all papers in the proceeding shall be presented to the director of the appropriate hospital at the time when the mentally ill person is delivered to such institution and a copy of the order and of each such paper shall be filed with the department of mental hygiene and also in the office of the county clerk of the county wherein the court is located which made the order of commitment. The judge shall order all such papers so filed in the county clerk's office to be sealed and exhibited only to parties to the proceedings, or someone properly interested, upon order of the court.

7. The costs necessarily incurred in determining the question of mental illness, including the fees of the medical examiners, shall be a charge upon the state or the municipality, as the case may

CORR. L.

be, at whose expense the institution is maintained, which has custody of the alleged mentally ill person at the time of the application for his commitment to the hospital under the provisions of this section.

8. During the pendency of such proceeding the judge may forthwith commit such alleged mentally ill person to a hospital for the mentally ill upon petition and the affidavit of two examining physicians that the superintendent is not able to properly care for such person at the institution where he is confined and that such person is in immediate need of care and treatment. Any person so committed shall be delivered to the director of the appropriate hospital as designated in the rules and regulations of the department of mental hygiene.

9. Except as provided in subdivision two pertaining to prisoners confined in the city of New York, an inmate of a correctional facility or a county jail may be admitted on an emergency basis to the Central New York Psychiatric Center upon the certification by two examining physicians, including physicians employed by the office of mental health and associated with the correctional facility in which such inmate is confined, that the inmate suffers from a mental illness which is likely to result in serious harm to himself or others as defined in subdivision (a) of section 9.39 of the mental hygiene law. Any person so committed shall be delivered by the superintendent within a twenty-four hour period, to the director of the appropriate hospital as designated in the rules and regulations of the office of mental health. Upon delivery of such person to a hospital operated by the office of mental health, a proceeding under this section shall immediately be commenced.

10. If the director of a hospital for the mentally ill shall deem that the condition of such mentally ill person requires his further retention in a hospital he shall, during the period of retention authorized by the last order of the court, apply to the supreme court or county court in the county where such hospital is located, for an order authorizing continued retention of such mentally ill person. The procedures for obtaining any order pursuant to this subdivision shall be in accordance with the provisions of the mental hygiene law for the retention of involuntary patients.

11. If a mentally ill person whose commitment, retention or continued retention has been authorized pursuant to this section, or any relative or friend in his behalf, be dissatisfied with any such order, he may, within thirty days after the making of any such order, obtain a rehearing and a review of the proceedings already had and of such order, upon a petition to a justice of the supreme court other than the judge or justice presiding over the court making such order. Such justice shall cause a jury to be summoned and shall try the question of the mental illness and

the need for care and treatment of the person so committed or so authorized to be retained. Any such mentally ill person or the person applying on his behalf for such review may waive the trial of the fact by a jury and consent in writing to trial of such fact by the court. No such petition for the hearing and review shall be made by anyone other than the person so committed or authorized to be retained or the father, mother, husband, wife or child of such person, unless the petitioner shall have first obtained the leave of the court upon good cause shown. If the verdict of the jury, or the decision of the court when jury trial has been waived, be that such person is not mentally ill, the justice shall order the removal of such person from the hospital and such person shall forthwith be transferred to a state correctional facility, or returned to the superintendent of the institution from which he was received if such institution was not a state correctional facility. Where the verdict of the jury, or the decision of the court where a jury trial has been waived, be that such person is mentally ill, the justice shall certify that fact and make an order authorizing continued retention under the original order. Proceedings under the order shall not be stayed pending an appeal therefrom, except upon an order of a justice of the supreme court, and made upon notice and after hearing, with provision made therein for such temporary care and confinement of the alleged mentally ill person as may be deemed necessary.

12. The notice provided for herein shall be served by the sheriff of the counties of the state of New York, in which case the charges of such sheriff shall be a disbursement in such proceeding, or by registered mail on all person required to be served, except that the superintendent of a correctional facility or the director of a hospital for the mentally ill, or their designees, shall be authorized to personally serve notice upon an alleged mentally ill person or a mentally ill person, as provided in this section.

Amended by L. 1978, Ch. 551, eff. July 24, 1978; L 1985, Ch. 789; L. 1986, Ch. 164, eff. June 16, 1986, amending subds. 9 and 12.

ANNOTATIONS

Constitutionality.—Correction Law § 402(9) is not unconstitutional. *In re* Linder, 71 A.D.2d 829, 419 N.Y.S.2d 375 (4th Dept. 1979).

—Correction Law 402(9) is constitutional and adequately protective of prisoner's due process rights. State of New York, on Relation of Overton v. Director, Central New York Psychiatric Center, 99 Misc. 2d 1116, 418 N.Y.S.2d 254 (Sup. Ct. Oneida Co. 1979).

§ 403. Department or superintendent to provide certain records.

The department or superintendent shall furnish to the department of mental hygiene a copy of the health and psychiatric records and a sentence calculation for each inmate placed in a hospital. The sentence calculation shall include the maximum expiration date and tentative conditional release date and the parole eligibility or release consideration hearing date. Such records shall be furnished to the director of the hospital upon delivery of the inmate.

§ 404. Disposition of mentally ill inmates upon release to parole, conditional release, or expiration of sentence.

1. Whenever an inmate committed to a hospital in the department of mental hygiene shall continue to be mentally ill and in need of care and treatment at the time of his conditional release, release to parole supervision, or when his sentence to a term of imprisonment expires, the director of the hospital may apply for the person's admission to a hospital for the care and treatment of the mentally ill in the department of mental hygiene as provided in the mental hygiene law.

2. The director may discharge any inmate at the expiration of the term for which he was sentenced who is still mentally ill, but who, in the opinion of the director, is reasonably safe to be at large. Such discharged inmate shall be entitled to suitable clothing adapted to the season in which he is discharged, and if it cannot be otherwise obtained, the business officer, or other officer having like duties shall, upon the order of the director, or of the commissioner of mental hygiene, as the case may be, furnish the same,

and money in an amount to be fixed by such commissioner with the approval of the director of the budget, to defray his expenses until he can reach his relatives or friends, or find employment to earn a subsistence.

ANNOTATION

Determination of mental competency; not a precondition to parole violation proceedings.—Mental illness does not render a petitioner incompetent to participate in his parole revocation proceedings; a determination of mental competency was not a precondition to parole violation proceeding nor a denial of due process; rather a parolee's mental illness was one factor that might mitigate or excuse parole violations. Newcomb v. New York State Board of Parole, 88 A.D.2d 1098, 452 N.Y.S.2d 912 (3d Dept. 1982).

§ 405. Duty of the department to the director of a hospital.

The department shall notify the director of a hospital in advance of hearings to be held at such hospital as may be necessary to carry out the duties of the board of parole or the department. The department shall assist the department of mental hygiene in establishing or continuing the operation of grievance procedures at such hospital. Where the subject matter of the grievance primarily involves a policy or practice of the department of mental hygiene, the commissioner shall transfer the review of the grievance to the commissioner of mental hygiene for resolution pursuant to subdivision three of section one hundred thirty-nine of the correction law.

CORR. L.

ARTICLE 17—INSTITUTIONS FOR THE RETARDED IN THE DEPARTMENT OF CORRECTION

§ 430. Establishment and purpose of state institutions for the retarded in the department of correction.

1. The department of correction may maintain one or more institutions to be used for the purpose of the care, treatment, training and custody of persons over sixteen years of age who are found to be mental defectives and who are committed thereto or placed therein as provided in this article.

2. The commissioner of correction may continue to maintain, as an institution for such purpose, any institution operated by the department pursuant to former articles sixteen-A, seventeen and seventeen-A of this chapter as authorized and required prior to the effective date of this act, and may add to or close any such institution, and may establish and maintain one or more new institutions for such purpose, in accordance with the needs of the department, provided any such action, other than the continuance of such formerly authorized institution, is approved by the commissioner of mental hygiene, and provided that expenditures are within amounts made available therefor by appropriation.

3. The commissioner of correction shall promulgate rules and regulations designating the name and location of each institution to be used for such purpose and the sex, age range and other factors relevant to the classifications of persons who may be received therein. A copy of such rules and regulations shall be transmitted to the clerk of each court having jurisdiction to make a commitment under this article, and persons committed, placed or transferred as provided in this article shall be delivered to the proper institution as designated in such rules and regulations.

4. Wherever reference has been or hereafter will be made in any statute, judgment, sentence, commitment, court order or otherwise to the Beacon state institution, Eastern correctional institution, the institution for male defective delinquents at Napanoch, or to Albion state training school or the institution for mentally defective women at Albion, or to an institution for the retarded in the department of correction, such reference shall be deemed to be to and to include any institution designated in the rules and regulations of the department pursuant to this section.

5. The commissioner of correction shall have power to transfer inmates from one such institution to another and the provisions of law applicable to transfers between correctional facilities shall apply to any transfer between institutions

for the retarded that may be ordered by the commissioner.

6. Any institution to be continued or to be established pursuant to this section shall be subject to the visitation and inspection of the state commission of correction and the head of the department of mental hygiene and their authorized representatives.

7. An institution for the retarded may be maintained or established in the same building or on the same premises as any other institution in the department and the commissioner of correction may provide by regulation for the use of any part of such other institution in the department by person confined in an institution for the retarded continued or established pursuant to this section, but such persons shall at all times be kept separate and apart from the inmates of such other institution.

Repealed former § 430 and **Added** new § 430 by L. 1970, Ch. 476.

§ 431. Certain powers and duties of commissioner with respect to such institution.

The commissioner of correction shall:

1. See that the purposes of such institution are carried into effect, and to that end have all necessary powers not inconsistent with law.

2. Establish rules and regulations for its internal government, discipline and management; but the commissioner may prescribe matters as to which rules and regulations, subject to revocation or suspension by him, may be adopted by the superintendent of the institution.

3. If lands are required for the use of the institution, acquire the same by purchase or condemnation, subject to the approval of and within appropriations therefor granted by the legislature.

§ 432. Superintendent.

Where an institution continued or established pursuant to section four hundred thirty of this article is located on the grounds of any other institution in the department, the superintendent or director of such other institution may be the chief executive officer of both institutions. In such case the term superintendent as used in this article shall be deemed to mean such person, irrespective of the title by which he may be known. In any other case a superintendent shall be appointed to be the head of each institution established pursuant to section four hundred thirty, or the head of any institution continued under such section shall continue in office, in accordance with and subject to the provisions of section eighteen of this chapter.

Repealed former § 432 and **Added** new § 432 by L. 1970, Ch. 476.

§ 433. General powers and duties of superintendent.

The superintendent shall be the chief executive officer of such institution. Subject to the statutory powers of the commissioner of correction, and rules and regulations established by him, the superintendent shall have the management of such institution. The superintendent shall cause to be kept full and fair accounts and records of all his doings and of the entire business and operation of the institution. The superintendent shall be the treasurer of the institution.

Amended by L. 1960, Ch. 54.

§ 434. General powers and duties of treasurer.

The superintendent as treasurer shall give an undertaking to the people of the state, with such sureties and in such amount as the commissioner of correction shall require, subject to the approval of the comptroller, to the effect that he will faithfully perform his duties as treasurer of such institution. Such undertaking shall be filed in the office of the attorney-general. The treasurer shall have the custody of all moneys received from the comptroller or otherwise for the use of the institution, except the proceeds of the labor of prisoners. He shall keep a full and accurate account of all receipts and disbursements, and perform such other duties, relative to the finances of the institution, as may be required by the rules and regulations, not inconsistent with law.

Amended by L. 1942, Ch. 738.

§ 435. Steward.

The steward, if there be one, and otherwise an officer or employee designated to exercise and perform the functions of steward, shall make the necessary purchases for the institution, when such purchases are authorized by the commissioner of correction and the commissioner of general services, pursuant to the state finance law, and issue the orders for material, equipment and supplies, purchased or contracted for by the commissioner of general services, and covered by requisitions approved by such commissioner or authorized by him, as the same shall be needed. He shall keep full and accurate accounts of the purchases made and orders issued by him. He shall also perform such duties relative to the care of material and supplies and the preparation of pay-rolls and other matters, as the superintendent of the institution shall direct.

Amended by L. 1962, Ch. 37.

§ 438. Persons who may be confined in an institution for the retarded.

1. No person shall hereafter be committed or transferred or certified to or placed in an institution for the retarded in the department of correction except as provided in this section.

2. Any person under the care or custody of the state department of correction who is found to be a mental defective may be committed to and confined in an institution for the retarded in the department of correction in accordance with the procedure set forth in section four hundred thirty-nine of this article.

3. Any person confined in a county jail or workhouse or in a penitentiary under a sentence of imprisonment with a term that has more than ninety days to run, after deduction of all credits other than the credit for good behavior time, or any person confined in a local reformatory under an alternative local reformatory sentence of imprisonment, who is found to be a mental defective may be committed to and confined in an institution for the retarded in the department of correction in accordance with the procedure set forth in section four hundred thirty-nine of this article.

Amended by L. 1973, Ch. 195; L. 1974, Ch. 629.

§ 439. Commitment to an institution for the retarded in the department of correction.

1. A proceeding for commitment of an inmate who may be committed to an institution for the retarded in the department of correction, as authorized by subdivision two or three of section four hundred thirty-eight, may be commenced and shall be carried out as herein provided on application of the superintendent or other officer in charge of the institution in which such inmate is confined, provided, however, that in the case of any inmate covered by subdivision two of section four hundred thirty-eight, no such proceeding shall be commenced without permission of the commissioner of correction.

2. Such superintendent or other officer in charge of the institution shall apply to a judge of a court of record to cause an examination to be made of such inmate by two examining physicians or by an examining physician and a certified phychologist * other than one connected with the institution in which such inmate is confined. The physicians or the physician and phychologist* shall be designated by the judge to whom the application is made and shall possess the qualifications prescribed by the provisions of section 1.05 ** of the mental hygiene law. If the persons so designated are satisfied after a personal examination that such inmate is mentally retarded, as defined in section 1.05 of the mental hygiene law, they shall make a certificate to such effect.

3. Upon such certificate being so made, it shall be delivered to the superintendent or other officer in charge, who may thereupon apply by petition to a judge of a court of record, annexing such certificate to his petition, for an order committing such inmate to an institution for the retarded in the department. Except as hereinafter provided, upon every such application for such an order of

commitment, notice thereof in writing of at least five days, together with a copy of the petition, shall be served upon the alleged mentally defective person, and in addition thereto such notice and copy of the petition shall be served by registered mail upon either the wife, the father or mother or other nearest relative of such alleged mentally defective person, if there be any such known relative with the state; and if not, such notice shall be served upon any known friend of such alleged mentally defective person within the state. If there be no such known relative or friend within the state, the giving of such notice shall be dispensed with, but in such case the petition for the commitment shall recite the reasons why service of such notice on a relative or friend of the alleged mentally defective person was dispensed with and in such case the order for commitment shall recite why service of such notice on a relative or friend of the alleged mentally defective person was dispensed with. Notwithstanding the foregoing provisions, if the judge to whom such application is made be satisfied from any statement made in the papers or proceedings, or from inquiry, that personal service of the notice on the alleged mentally defective person would be ineffective or detrimental to such person, he may in his discretion dispense therewith, and he shall dispense therewith if the examining physicians or the examining physician and certified psychologist state in writing that personal service upon the alleged mentally defective person would in their opinion be detrimental to such person. Copies of the notice, the petition and the certificate or certificates of the examining physicians shall also be given the mental health hygiene legal service.

4. The judge to whom such application for the commitment of the alleged mentally defective person is made may, if no demand is made for a hearing in behalf of the alleged mentally defective person, proceed forthwith on the return day of such notice to determine the question of mental condition and if satisfied that the alleged mentally defective person is mentally retarded, as defined in section 1.05 ** of the mental hygiene law, may immediately issue an order for the commitment of such alleged mentally defective person to an institution for the retarded in the department of correction for a period not to exceed sixty days for the purpose of observation and treatment.

5. Upon the demand for a hearing by the inmate, any relative or near friend on behalf of such alleged mentally defective person, the judge shall, or he may upon his own motion where there is no demand for a hearing, issue an order directing the hearing of such application before him at a time not more than five days from the date of such order which shall be served upon the parties interested in the application and upon such other persons as the judge, in his discretion, may name. Upon such day or upon such other day to which the proceedings shall be regularly adjourned, he

shall hear the testimony introduced by the parties and shall examine the alleged mentally defective person, if deemed advisable in or out of court, and render a decision in writing as to such person's mental defect. If such judge cannot hear the application, he may, in his order directing the hearing, name some referee who shall hear the testimony and report the same forthwith, with his opinion thereon, to such judge, who shall, if satisfied with such report, render his decision accordingly. If it be determined that such person is a mental defective, the judge shall forthwith issue his order committing him to an institution for the retarded in the department of correction for a period not to exceed sixty days for the purpose of observation and treatment. Such superintendent or other officer in charge shall thereupon cause such mentally defective person to be delivered to the superintendent of the appropriate institution for the retarded in the department of correction as designated in the rules and regulations of that department and such mental defective shall be received therein and retained in such an institution until transferred or discharged or otherwise released in accordance with the law, for the period specified in the order of commitment or in any subsequent order authorizing continued retention of such person in such institution. Such superintendent or other person in charge before delivering said mentally defective person shall see that he is bodily clean. At the time of such transfer there shall be submitted to the superintendent of the institution for the retarded the original certificate or conviction. If such judge shall refuse to issue an order of commitment, he shall certify in writing his reasons for such refusal.

6. When an order of commitment is made, such order and all papers in the proceeding shall be presented to the superintendent of the institution for the retarded at the time when the mentally defective person is delivered to such institution and a copy of the order and of each such paper shall be filed with the department of mental hygiene and also in the office of the county clerk of the county wherein the court is located which made the order of commitment. The judge shall order all such papers so filed in the county clerk's office to be sealed and exhibited only to parties to the proceedings, or someone properly interested, upon order of the court.

7. At any time prior to the expiration of sixty days from the date a mentally defective person is delivered to the superintendent of an institution for the retarded in the department of correction pursuant to this section, if a physician designated by the commissioner of correction finds that such person is in need of continued care and treatment therein, the superintendent of the institution may file with the court that made the commitment an application for continued retention of such person accompanied by a certificate of the physician setting forth his findings as to the condition of the inmate and the need for the continued care

and treatment of such inmate in such an institution. If the court is satisfied that continued retention of such person in such an institution is warranted, the court shall approve the application and the papers shall be filed in accordance with subdivision six of this section. Upon the filing thereof the order theretofore made by the court shall become a final order and such person shall be retained in such an institution until transferred or discharged or otherwise released in accordance with the law. If the court is not satisfied that such continued retention is warranted, the court shall vacate the commitment and certify in writing his reasons for such action. Pending such decision of the court, the inmate shall be retained in such an institution. Where the commitment is vacated, or where an application is not made pursuant to the subdivision the inmate shall forthwith be transferred to a state correctional facility, or returned to the warden or other officer in charge of the institution from which he was received if such institution was not a state correctional facility.

8. If a mental defective whose commitment has been authorized pursuant to this section, or any relative or friend in his behalf, be dissatisfied with the commitment or the final order, he may, within thirty days after the making of any such order obtain a rehearing and a review of the proceeding already had and of such order, upon a petition to a justice of the supreme court other than the judge or justice presiding over the court making such order, who shall cause a jury to be summoned as in the case of proceedings for the appointment of a committee for a mentally ill person where the question of fact arising upon the competency of the person is tried by a jury, and shall try the question of the mental defect of the person so committed or so authorized to be retained, in the same manner as provided in said proceedings. Any such mentally defective person or the person applying on his behalf for such review may waive the trial of the fact by a jury and consent in writing to trial of such fact by the court. If such petition for the hearing and review be made by any other than the person so committed or authorized to be retained or the father, mother, husband, wife or child of such person, before such hearing or review shall be had, the petitioner shall make a deposit or give a bond, to be approved by a justice of the supreme court, for the payment of the costs and expenses of such rehearing or review and determination of the question of mental defect by a jury as aforesaid, if the order of commitment or authorizing continued retention is sustained. If the verdict of the jury, or the decision of the court when jury trial has been waived, be that such person is not mentally defective, the justice shall order the removal of such person from an institution for the retarded in the department of correction and such person shall forthwith be transferred to a state correctional facility, or returned to the warden or other officer in charge of the institution from which he was received if such institution was not

a state correctional facility. Where the verdict of the jury, or the decision of the court where a jury trial has been waived, be that such person is mentally defective, the justice shall certify that fact and make an order authorizing continued intention under the original order. Proceedings under the order shall not be stayed pending an appeal therefrom, except upon an order of a justice of the supreme court, and made upon notice and after hearing, with provision made therein for such temporary care and confinement of the alleged mentally defective person as may be deemed necessary.

9. The costs necessarily incurred in determining the question of mental condition including the nerves of the physicians and psychologists who serve as examiners, shall be a charge upon the state or the municipality, as the case may be, at those expense the institution is maintained, which has custody of the alleged mentally defective person at the time of the application for his commitment under provisions of this section.

10. During the pendency of such proceeding, the judge may forthwith commit such allegedly mentally defective person to an institution for the retarded in the department of correction upon petition and the affidavit of two examining physicians or an examining physician and a certified psychologist that the warden or other officer in charge is not able to properly care for such person of the institution where he is confined, and that such person is in need of immediate treatment.

11. The notice provided for herein shall be served by the sheriff of the counties of the state of New York, in which case the charges of such sheriff shall be a disbursement in such proceeding, or by registered mail on all persons required to be served other than the alleged mentally defective person.

* As enacted.
** Now covered by Mental Hygiene Law § 1.03.

Amended by L. 1973, Ch. 195; L. 1985, Ch. 789, eff. Apr. 1986 amended subd. 3 by deleting reference to "mental health formation service" and inserting "mental hygiene legal service."

§ 439-a. Transfers to certain institutions under the jurisdiction of the department of mental hygiene.

1. Any person less than twenty-one years of age who is confined in an institution for the retarded in the department of correction, may be transferred to a state school under the jurisdiction of the department of mental hygiene whenever it appears to the satisfaction of the commissioner of correction that such person will substantially benefit from care and treatment in such a state school and that the interests of the state will be best served thereby. Such a transfer may be made only upon written order of the commissioner of correction certifying the reasons therefor and upon the written consent and approval of the

commissioner of mental hygiene and the commissioner of social service. Where any such transfer is ordered and approved as herein provided prior to the time such person is delivered to an institution for the retarded in the department of correction, the transfer shall be made directly from the institution in which the inmate is confined.

2. Each state institution to which a person is transferred as in this section provided shall, and it is hereby authorized to, receive, treat and otherwise care for such person in the same manner as other persons certified to such institution.

3. A person so transferred shall continue to be under the general care and supervision of the department of correction, except that he shall be temporarily cared for and treated in the institution to which the transfer is made. While in such latter institution he shall be subject to the laws and rules appertaining thereto, except that his parole and discharge shall continue to be governed by the laws and rules appertaining to the institution from which he was transferred.

4. The term of detention or confinement of a person transferred in accordance with the provisions of this section shall not be extended or increased by reason of any such transfer.

5. Whenever it is found that the confinement of any person in an institution to which he shall have been transferred as hereinbefore in this section provided is no longer suitable, for any reason, and the commissioner of mental hygiene shall so certify to the commissioner of correction, such person so transferred shall be forthwith returned by the director or other official in charge of the institution in which he is confined to the institution from which he was transferred.

6. All expenses incident to a transfer under this section shall be borne by the department from which the transfer is made.

Amended by L. 1954, Ch. 803; L. 1970, Ch. 476.

§ 439-c. Transfers of mental defectives to certain institutions under the jurisdiction of the department of mental hygiene.

1. Any person over twenty-one years of age who is confined in an institution for the retarded in the department of correction and who has been so confined for five years or longer, may be transferred to a state school under the jurisdiction of the department of mental hygiene whenever it appears to the satisfaction of the commissioner of correction that such person will substantially benefit from care and treatment in such a state school and that the interest of the state will be best served thereby. Such a transfer may be made only upon written order of the commissioner of correction certifying the reasons therefor and upon the written consent and approval of the commissioner of mental hygiene.

2. Each state institution to which a person is transferred pursuant to this section shall receive, treat and otherwise care for such person in the same manner as other persons certified or admitted to such institution in accordance with the provisions of the mental hygiene law.

3. A person transferred pursuant to this section shall be subject to the rules and regulations of the department of mental hygiene and of the institution to which he is transferred, including rules and regulations governing convalescent status and release. Upon certification by the commissioner of mental hygiene and upon approval by the commissioner of correction, any such person may be finally discharged from confinement or from convalescent care.

4. Whenever it is determined that a person confined in an institution to which he has been transferred pursuant to this section is no longer suitable for treatment in such institution and the commissioner of mental hygiene so certifies to the commissioner of correction, such person shall be forthwith returned by the director or other official in charge of the mental hygiene institution to the institution from which he was transferred and such person shall thereafter again be subject to the rules and regulations of the institution from which he was originally transferred.

5. In the event that a person transferred pursuant to this section is under an indeterminate or determinate sentence of imprisonment, the provisions of subdivisions three, four and five of section four hundred thirty-nine-a of this article shall apply to such transfer in lieu of the provisions of subdivisions three and four of this section.

6. All expenses incident to a transfer under this section shall be borne by the department from which the transfer is originally made.

Added by L. 1962, Ch. 463; Amended by L. 1967, Ch. 477; L. 1970, Ch. 476; L. 2004, Ch. 738, § 4, eff. Dec. 14, 2004, amending subd. 5.

§ 440. Transfer of mentally ill inmates.

The provisions of section four hundred eight* of this chapter shall apply to an inmate of an institution for the retarded in the department of correction to the same extent as a person who is confined in a correctional facility. A state hospital in the department may receive any such person committed thereto, and such person shall be dealt with in accordance with the provisions of article sixteen of this chapter.

* Now covered by Corr. Law § 402.

Added by L. 1970, Ch. 476.

§ 441. Disposition of mentally defective inmates at expiration of terms.

Every person confined in an institution under the jurisdiction of the state department of correction for the care, treatment, training and custody of mental defectives, under a definite, indeterminate or determinate sentence of imprisonment, whose sentence has expired shall be dealt with as hereinafter provided. Whenever any such person shall continue to be mentally defective and in need of institutional care the director of such institution may apply for his admission to a state school under the jurisdiction of the department of mental hygiene for the care and treatment of mental defectives as provided in the mental hygiene law. The director of the correctional institution may, if it is his opinion that any such person is so dangerously mentally defective that his presence in a state school in the department of mental hygiene would be dangerous to the safety of the other patients therein, the officers or employees thereof, or the community, make application to the court as provided in section 29.13 of the mental hygiene law and the provisions of such section shall govern such proceedings before such court. The director of the correctional institution may discharge any such person at the expiration of his sentence who is still mentally defective, but who, in the opinion of the director, is reasonably safe to be at large. Such discharged person shall be entitled to such allowances as are granted to prisoners, on their discharge, by the provisions of this chapter.

Repealed former § 441 and Added new § 441 by L. 1967, Ch. 477; Amended by L. 1973, Ch. 195; L. 1995, Ch. 3, § 25, amendment applies to offenses committed on or after Oct. 1, 1995, and amendment is repealed Sept. 1, 2009.

§ 441-a. Discharge of other inmates.

Subject to the provisions of article seven hundred thirty of the criminal procedure law where applicable, the superintendent of an institution for the retarded in the department of correction, with the approval of the commissioner of correction, may discharge any inmate thereof, committed thereto without sentence or under an indefinite sentence, if it be found that his further confinement therein is unsuitable.

Added by L. 1958, Ch. 197; Amended by L. 1970, Ch. 476; L. 1971, Ch. 1097.

§ 442. Return of inmates to other institutions.

If, before the expiration of the term for which an inmate, received from another institution, was sentenced, it be found that his confinement in an institution for the retarded in the department of correction is unsuitable, for any reason, and the commissioner of correction shall so certify in writing to the officer in charge of the institution from which such person was received, such person shall be forthwith returned to the institution from which he came, by the superintendent of the institution for the retarded; provided, however, that if he was received from a correctional facility, he shall be transferred to and received by such correctional facility as the commissioner shall direct. Upon any such return or transfer all credits earned against the sentence of the inmate in the institution for the retarded shall be deemed to have been earned in the institution to which he is returned or transferred.

Amended by L. 1950, Ch. 160; L. 1958, Ch. 197; L. 1970, Ch. 476.

§ 443. Certificate of conviction to be delivered and copy filed.

Whenever a prisoner is transferred to such institution at Napanoch, the warden or superintendent in charge of the prison, penitentiary or reformatory from which such prisoner is transferred shall cause a copy of the original certificate of conviction of such prisoner to be filed in the office of such warden or superintendent, and shall deliver the original certificate to the superintendent of such institution at Napanoch; and whenever any such prisoner shall be transferred to any correctional institution from such institution at Napanoch, the superintendent shall deliver to the warden or superintendent in charge of such correctional institution such original certificate which shall be filed in the clerk's office of the same.

§ 445. Paroles.

The state board of parole in the executive department shall exercise its parole jurisdiction and supervise inmates of the Eastern correctional institution committed thereto under section four hundred thirty-eight of the correction law, who have been convicted of a criminal offense and not been recommitted after expiration of sentence, and those inmates transferred thereto under sections four hundred thirty-eight-a, * four hundred thirty-eight-b, * and four hundred thirty-nine * of the correction law and the Albion state training school. An inmate paroled from the institution for defective delinquents located at Napanoch or the Albion state training school shall remain in the legal custody of the superintendent of such institution but shall be under the direct supervision of the division of parole. At any time during the parole period the inmate shall be accessible to the parole officers or other duly authorized representatives of the state board of parole. If a member of the state board of parole shall determine that such a paroled person has violated his parole or that the behavior of such paroled person makes him a menace to himself or the members of his family or the community, such member of the board of parole may order such parolee returned to the institution from which he was released on parole. The superintendent of the institution shall accept the paroled or conditionally released violator and the state board of parole shall determine what action is to be taken in the case of a person so returned.

The institution and the state board of parole and the division of parole in the executive department shall not be liable in any manner whatsoever for such person while on parole. Such liability shall devolve upon the parent, legal guardian, relative, or persons to whose care the inmate is paroled or the proper welfare official of the municipality in which he may have found domicile. An inmate shall not be paroled before he might have been paroled from another institution, if any, to which he was originally committed or before he would have been paroled if he had been committed to a reformatory or correctional institution under a similar charge.

* Repealed.

Amended by L. 1964, Ch. 240.

§ 445-a. Discharge of mental defectives on parole.

An inmate paroled pursuant to the foregoing provisions of section four hundred forty-five of this chapter, who is on parole, may be discharged from custody and parole by state board of parole.

Added by L. 1951, Ch. 297; **Amended** by L. 1964, Ch. 240.

§ 445-b. Parole and conditional release of persons committed under sentence of imprisonment imposed after September first, nineteen hundred sixty-seven.

The provisions of sections four hundred forty-five and four hundred forty-five-a shall not apply to any person sentenced on or after September first, nineteen hundred sixty-seven. In the case of any such person, his parole and conditional release and his discharge from parole or conditional release shall be governed by the laws and rules appertaining to the sentence imposed by the court without regard to the fact that he is or has been confined in a correctional institution for mental defectives.

Added by L. 1967, Ch. 477.

§ 446. Habeas corpus.

At the hearing on the return of a writ of habeas corpus, if any, lawfully granted, under which the delivery from custody of an inmate of such institution is sought, and where the fact of his mental defectiveness is material to the inquiry, the history of the inmate as it appears in the case records may be given in evidence, and the superintendent of the institution, or any other proper person, may be sworn touching the mental condition of such person. Where a second or subsequent application is made for the delivery from custody of such inmate, any party to the proceeding may introduce in evidence any testimony in relation to the mental condition of such inmate received upon any former hearing or trial, together with all the exhibits introduced in evidence upon such hearing or trial in connection with such testimony without calling the witnesses who gave such testimony; such evidence to have the same force and effect as if such witnesses had been called.

§ 447. Estimates and financial statements.

Estimates of expenditures for such institution, the revision thereof and drafts to meet such expenditures, for purposes mentioned in the estimates as revised and approved, shall be made at the times and in the manner provided in section one hundred and seventeen of this chapter. Verified statements of receipts and expenditures shall be made and such statements and accompanying vouchers transmitted to the comptroller in the manner provided in section one hundred and eighteen * of this chapter. Such sections shall apply to such institution and in applying them the superintendent shall have the duties of a warden.

* Repealed.

§ 449. State to pay expenses of transportation for certain inmates.

Notwithstanding any other provision of law, general, special or local, on and after the effective date of this section, any transportation of inmates to or from the institution at Napanoch or transportation of inmates to or from the Albion state training school, the sheriff or other person delivering or in charge of transportation of any such inmate shall be paid from the treasury after audit by and on the warrant of the comptroller in the manner provided by law.

The sheriff or other person shall be reimbursed for the amount of expenses actually and necessarily incurred by him for railroad fare or cost of other transportation and for cost of maintenance of himself and each inmate in going to Napanoch or Albion, and for his railroad fare or other cost of transportation in returning home, and cost of maintenance while so returning.

CORR. L.

ARTICLE 18—RETIREMENT OF EMPLOYEES OF THE DEPARTMENT OF CORRECTION AND OF STATE CORRECTIONAL INSTITUTIONS

Section

§ 470. When guards and other employees may be retired.

A guard or other employee in a state prison or reformatory, or an employee in the department of correction, who shall have served a term of employment of twenty-five years, which employment, in the case of a guard or employee in a state prison or reformatory, was either wholly in such prison or reformatory or partly therein and partly an another prison or reformatory or in a state hospital or penitentiary, or which employment, in the case of an employee of the department of correction, was either wholly in such department of the former prison department, or partly therein and partly as a guard or other employee in a prison, reformatory, hospital or penitentiary, or on one or more of them, and which, in the case of any such guard or employee in a state prison or reformatory or employee in the department of correction, was either in one consecutive term or on two or more terms which shall together amount to a total period of employment of twenty-five years, may if unable to perform his regular duties in a manner satisfactory to the commissioner of correction be retired as hereinafter provided at one-half his annual salary for the year immediately preceding such retirement. An employee who retires on or after April first, nineteen hundred seventy, shall receive an additional pension of two percentum of his average annual salary earned during the three years immediately preceding retirement for each year of service in excess of twenty-five; provided, however, that the total pension provided by the state pursuant to this section shall not exceed seventy-five percentum of the average annual salary earned during the three years immediately preceding retirement. Any such guard or employee who is physically or mentally incapacitated for the performance of duty after a total period of employment of twenty years shall be retired and paid annually a pension of forty per cent of his annual salary for the year immediately preceding such retirement plus an additional two per cent for each year of service after twenty years; provided, however, that such pension shall not exceed one-half his annual salary for the year immediately preceding such retirement. Such pension shall be paid annually as long as such disability continues, upon certification of a board consisting of the commissioner of correction, the attorney general and the comptroller. Any such guard or employee who shall have reached the age of seventy years, who shall have served a term of employment of not less than fifteen years, may if unable to perform his regular duties in a manner satisfactory to the commissioner of correction be retired as hereinafter provided, and be paid such proportion of one-half of his annual salary for the year immediately preceding such retirement, as the number of years served bears to the full term of twenty-five years. Prison or reformatory service shall include the service in time of war of honorably discharged officers, soldiers, sailors, marines, and army nurses who were actual residents of the state at the time of their entry into the military service of the United States, and the service of members of the national guard in the military service of the United States pursuant to call of the president for Mexican border service. Such payment shall be payable out of moneys appropriated therefor, and shall not be revoked, diminished or subject to the claims of creditors. Such guard or employee may be retired when such action shall be in the interest of the state in the following manner; A guard or employee of the department of correction shall be retired upon approval of the commissioner of correction at the expiration of twenty-five years of service, upon application for such retirement to the commissioner of correction. Within the meaning of this section, an employee of the department of correction means any person employed under the commissioner of correction.

Amended by L. 1938, Ch. 692; L. 1963, Ch. 145; L. 1970, Ch. 457.

§ 470-a. Salary basis for computing retirement benefits; temporary.

If a guard or other employee in a state prison or reformatory or an employee of the department of correction shall retire pursuant to section four hundred and seventy of this chapter, the reduction of his salary, during all or as to any part of the year immediately preceding his retirement, made in accordance with a scale of percentage reductions prescribed by a law or laws enacted by the legislature at its annual sessions of the years nineteen hundred thirty-three and nineteen hundred thirty-four, shall not operate to reduce his retirement compensation or pension. The basis for computing his retirement compensation or pension of one-half or a proportion of one-half, as the case may be, of the salary paid to him for the year immediately preceding his retirement shall be his full salary on which the percentage reduction so prescribed is computed, according to the several pay-rolls, and which he would have been paid had such percentage reductions not been made or required.

Added by L. 1933, Ch. 345.

§ 470-b. Options.

1. A guard or employee, entitled to a retirement pension under section four hundred seventy of this article, or if he is an incompetent, his spouse or the committee of his property, or if he is a conservative, his spouse or the conservator of his property, may if he shall have completed thirty-five years of service allowable under such section, elect to receive the actuarial equivalent of his pension at the time of his retirement, in the form of a smaller pension payable to him for life and one of the following optional settlements:

Option One. If he dies before he has received payments equal to the present value of his pension, as it was at the time of his retirement, the balance thereof shall be paid to his estate or to the beneficiary so designated.

Option Two. Upon his death, the pension in an amount equal to that paid to him shall be paid for life to the beneficiary so designated.

Option Three. Upon his death, a pension of one-half the amount paid to him shall be paid for life to the beneficiary so designated.

Option Four. Such other optional benefit or benefits as the commissioner of correction, with the approval of the comptroller, shall approve and which shall be the actuarial equivalent of his pension at the time of his retirement.

2. All elections under this section shall be made on blanks prepared by the commissioner of correction for that purpose. Any such election may be made at any time, but not less than thirty days prior to the effective date of the retirement of such guard or employee.

An optional election shall not become effective if the guard or employee dies before the effective date of his retirement, or within thirty days after the filing in the office of the commissioner of correction of the application for his retirement. An election of an option may be withdrawn or a new option may be chosen within the period provided in this subdivision two for the making of such an election. In all cases where an optional election is not made or does not become effective, retirement shall be without option.

3. A person having an insurable interest in the life of a guard or employee may be designated by such guard or employee, or by the person authorized by this section to make an election in his behalf, as his beneficiary under any of the options herein provided. Each such designation shall be:

a. Made in writing on a blank provided by the commissioner of correction for such purpose, and

b. Ineffective until it is filed in the commissioner's office, and

c. Revocable to the extent that:

(1) 1 new beneficiary under Option One may be designated at any time during the life of the guard or employee.

(2) A new beneficiary under any other option may be designated at any time within the period provided for the making of an election pursuant to this section.

Added by L. 1954, Ch. 807; **Amended** by L. 1981, Ch. 115, eff. May 18, 1981.

§ 471. Retirement subject to revocation of governor.

The retirement of a guard or employee, pursuant to this article, shall be subject at any time to revocation by the governor, who shall serve to notice of such revocation on the commissioner of correction, and thereupon such retirement and all payments on account thereof shall cease. Upon such revocation such guard or employee shall be entitled to reassume his duties in the state prison or reformatory, or department, from which he was retired at the salary or compensation received by him at the time of retirement.

§ 472. Death or disability benefits.

The following benefits shall be paid by the state on account of the death or disability of guard or other employee in a state prison of reformatory, or an employee in the former prison department or present department of correction who is not a member of the state retirement system.

1. To the widow, until she be married again or the dependent minor children or the dependent mother of a guard or other employee in a state prison or reformatory, or of an employee in the department of correction or former prison department who is not a member of the state retirement system, whose death has heretofore been cause or shall hereafter be caused by an injury or actual disability incurred while in the performance on duty at some definite time and place and upon proof that such death or disability was not the result of wilful negligence on his part, there shall be paid annually as long as such dependence continues upon certification of a board consisting of the commissioner of correction, the attorney general and the state comptroller, one-half the salary including maintenance allowance received by him at the time of his death.

2. If the widow dies or remarries before any

child of such deceased employee shall have attained the age of eighteen years, such payment shall be then made to his child or children under such age, divided in such manner as the commissioner of correction in his discretion shall determine, to continue until every such child dies or attains said age.

3. To a guard or other employee in a state prison or reformatory or an employee in the department of correction or former prison department who is physically or mentally incapacitated for the performance of duty as a natural and approximate result of an accident or injury sustained while in the actual performance of duty, upon proof that such disability was not the result of wilful negligence, there shall be paid annually as long as such disability continues, upon certification of a board consisting of the commissioner of correction, the attorney-general and the comptroller, or their designees, a pension of three-quarters of the annual salary and maintenance allowance received by such guard or employee at the time of the termination of his service for the state in case he continues in such service after such accident or injury.

4. Before a benefit shall be awarded under this section on account of the disability or death of a person who also is covered by the provisions of the workmen's compensation law, there shall be an adjudication of his case under the provisions of such law by the state industrial board, except that if the maximum payment under the workmen's compensation law would, in any event, be less than the full benefit under this section, the comptroller may authorize payment of all or part of such excess pending such adjudication by the state industrial board. Any amounts paid or payable under the provisions of the workmen's compensation law to such person or to the dependents of such person on account of any disability or death shall be offset against and payable in lieu of any benefits payable under the provisions of his article on account of such person because of such disability or death, except that the cost of medical treatment and care of injured employees provided under section thirteen of the workmen's compensation law shall not be deducted from any benefits under the provisions of this article.

Amended by L. 1956, Ch. 267.

§ 472-a. Compulsory separation from service of members of the correction department.

1. Any member of the correction department who elects to contribute in accordance with the provisions of section eighty-eight [*] of the retirement and social security law, and (a) who prior to the effective date of this act has attained sixty-three years of age or who shall attain such age on or before March thirty-first, nineteen hundred sixty-six and (b) who on or after January first, nineteen hundred sixty-six and on or before March thirty-first, nineteen hundred sixty-six shall complete twenty-five years of total service as a member of the correction department shall be separated from such service on March thirty-first, nineteen hundred sixty-six.

2. Any member who shall complete twenty-five years of such total service on or after April first, nineteen hundred sixty-six but who has not attained sixty-three years of age at the time of completion of such period of service, shall be separated from such service upon attaining such age.

3. Any member who shall attain sixty-three years of age on or after April first, nineteen hundred sixty-six, but who has not completed twenty-five years of such total service at the time of attaining such age, shall be separated from such service upon completing such period of service.

4. Any member appointed on or after April first, nineteen hundred sixty-five shall be separated from such service upon attaining sixty-three years of age.

5. The foregoing provisions of this section shall not apply to any member who on the effective date of this act has completed twenty-five years of such total service as a member of the correction department, regardless of age.

6. For the purpose of this section, in computing twenty-five years of total service full credit shall be given for the time that a member was on military leave from service as a member of the correction department.

[*] Now § 89.

Added by L. 1965, Ch. 890.

§ 473. Application of article.

The provisions of this article shall not apply to guards or other employees in a state prison or reformatory or an employee in the department of correction who shall have entered or re-entered service in such prisons, reformatory or department or the former prison department on or after April eleventh, nineteen hundred and twenty-five, or hereafter shall enter or re-enter such service.

ARTICLE 20—LOCAL CORRECTIONAL FACILITIES

§ 500. Application of article.

The provisions of this article shall apply to all local correctional facilities as defined by subdivision fifteen of section two of this chapter.

Added by L. 1987, Ch. 604, eff. Sept. 2, 1987. Former § 500 renumbered § 500-n.

§ 500-a. Use of jails.

1. Each county jail shall be used:

(a) For the detention of persons duly committed to secure their attendance as witnesses in any criminal case;

(b) For the detention of persons charged with crime, and committed for trial or examination;

(c) For the detention of persons awaiting the availability of a court, pursuant to the provisions of section 210.10 or subdivision two of section 530.70 or subdivision two of section 410.40 of the criminal procedure law;

(d) For the confinement of persons duly committed for any contempt, or upon civil process;

(e) For the confinement of persons convicted of any offense and sentenced to imprisonment therein, or awaiting transportation under sentence to imprisonment in another county.

2. The Onondaga county jail may also be used for the detention of persons under arrest beings held for arraignment.

2-a. Notwithstanding any other provision of law, the city council of the city of Elmira may enter into an agreement with the county of Chemung by which the county, through its facilities at the Chemung county jail, shall undertake to provide services pertaining to the confinement of individuals arrested or detained by police officers or other law enforcement officers within the city of Elmira who have been detained and are awaiting arraignment or initial court appearances.

2-b. The Erie county holding center and the Erie county correctional facility may also be used for the detention of persons under arrest being held for arraignment.

2-c. * [*Added by L. 2003, Ch. 135.*] The Yates county jail may also be used for the detention of persons under arrest being held for arraignment in any court located in the county of Yates.

2-c. * [*Added by L. 2003, Ch. 171.*] Notwithstanding any other law, rule or regulation to the contrary, the Cortland county jail may also be used for the detention of persons under arrest and being held for arraignment in any court located in the county of Cortland.

2-c. * [*Added by L. 2003, Ch. 189.*] Notwithstanding any other provision of law, the city of Rochester may enter into an agreement with the county of Monroe by which the county, through its facilities at the Monroe county jail, shall undertake to provide services pertaining to the confinement of individuals arrested or detained by police officers or other law enforcement officers within the city of Rochester who have been detained and are awaiting arraignment or initial court appearances.

   * [In 2003, the Legislature enacted three subds. 2-c.]

2-d. [*Added by L. 2003, Ch. 171.*] Notwithstanding any other law, rule or regulation to the contrary, the Cortland county jail may also be used for the detention of persons under arrest and being held for arraignment in any court located in the county of Cortland.

2-d. [*Added by L. 2004, Ch. 559.*] The Putnam county jail may also be used for the detention of persons under arrest being held for arraignment in any court located in the county of Putnam.

[In 2004, the Legislature enacted two subds. 2-d.]

2-e. Notwithstanding any other provision of law, the city of Rochester may enter into an agreement with the county of Monroe by which the county, through its facilities at the Monroe county jail, shall undertake to provide services pertaining to the confinement of individuals arrested or detained by police officers or other law enforcement officers within the city of Rochester who have been detained and are awaiting arraignment or initial court appearances.

2-f. The Warren county jail may also be used for the detention of persons under arrest being held for arraignment in any court located in the county of Warren.

2-g. [*Added by L. 2005, Ch. 84.*] The Niagara county jail may also be used for the detention of persons under arrest being held for arraignment in any court located in the county of Niagara.

2-g. [*Added by L. 2005, Ch. 258.*] The Genesee county jail may also be used for the detention of persons under arrest being held for arraignment in any court located in the county of Genesee.

[In 2005, the Legislature enacted two subds. 2-g.]

2-h. The Allegany county correctional facility may also be used for the detention of persons under arrest being held for arraignment in any court located in the county of Allegany.

3. The buildings, now used as jails of the counties of the state, shall continue to be the jails of those counties respectively, until other buildings have been designated or erected for that purpose, according to law.

Added by L. 1950, Ch. 695; **Amended** by L. 1968, Ch. 226; L. 1990, Ch. 681, eff. Nov. 1, 1990, renumbered subds. 3, 4, 5 to subds. 4, 5, 6 and added a new subd. 3; L. 1994, Ch. 541, § 1, eff. July 26, 1994, renumbering the opening paragraph and subds. 1 through 5 as subd. 1(a) through (e), adding new subd. 2, and renumbering subd. 6 as subd. 3; L. 1997, Ch. 633, eff. Sept. 24, 1997, adding subd. 2-a; L. 2002, Ch. 413, § 1, eff. Aug. 13, 2002, adding subd. 2-b; L. 2003, Chs. 135, 171, and 189, each eff. July 22, 2003, and each adding subd. 2-c; L. 2004, Ch. 555, §§ 1-3, renumbering versions of subd. 2-c to 2-d and 2-e and adding subd. 2-f, eff. Oct. 5, 2004; L. 2004, Ch. 559, § 1, adding version of subd. 2-d, eff. Oct. 5, 2004; L. 2005, Ch. 84, § 1, adding subd. 2-g, eff. June 7, 2005; L. 2005, Ch. 258, § 1, adding subd. 2-g, eff. July 19, 2005; L. 2005, Ch. 311, § 1, adding subd. 2-h, eff. July 26, 2005.

ANNOTATIONS

Treatment of prisoners.—Official regulation of correspondence by convicted prisoners and by pretrial detainees is permissible where justified. People v. Van Diezelski, 78 Misc. 2d 69, 355 N.Y.S.2d 556 (Nassau Co. Ct. 1974).

—Pretrial detainees and convicted prisoners can be housed separately within the same building. People v. Von Diezelski, 78 Misc. 2d 69, 355 N.Y.S.2d 556 (Nassau Co. Ct. 1974).

§ 500-b. Housing of prisoners and other persons in custody. [*Effective until Sept. 1, 2007, pursuant to L. 1984, Ch. 907, § 12, as amended. Another § 500-b follows.*]

1. As used in this section, the term "chief administrative officer" shall mean the person responsible pursuant to section five hundred-c of this article for receiving and safely keeping persons committed to a county jail.

2. In any case in which the chief administrative officer has more than one jail under his jurisdiction, he may confine a civil or criminal prisoner in any such jail and may remove the prisoner from one jail to another, within the county, whenever he deems it necessary for his safekeeping, or for the prisoner's appearance at court.

3. No female confined in a county jail shall be assigned to or housed in a facility housing unit with a male; and if detained on civil process, or for contempt, or as a witness, she shall not be put or kept in the same room with a man, except her husband.

4. No person under nineteen years of age shall be placed or kept or allowed to be at any time with any prisoner or prisoners nineteen years of age or older, in any room, dormitory, cell or tier of the buildings of such institution unless separately grouped to prevent access to persons under nineteen years of age by prisoners nineteen years of age or older.

5. [*Repealed.*]

6. The commission shall promulgate rules and regulations in accordance with subdivisions seven and eight of this section to assure that persons

in custody in local correctional facilities will be afforded appropriate precautions for their personal safety and welfare in assignment to housing.

7. (a) Consistent with the commission's rules and regulations regarding the assignment of inmates to housing units, the chief administrative officer shall exercise good judgment and discretion and shall take all reasonable steps to ensure that the assignment of persons to facility housing units:

(1) fosters the safety, security and good order of the jail; and

(2) affords appropriate precautions for the personal safety and welfare of persons in custody with particular attention to those who are known to be vulnerable to assault or any physical or mental abuse.

(b) The chief administrative officer shall consider the following in complying with this subdivision:

(1) prior victimization in jail or prison;

(2) prior history of mental illness;

(3) prior history of sex offenses;

(4) prior history of a hostile relationship with another inmate;

(5) prior attempts at self-injury or suicide;

(6) prior attempted escapes;

(7) any mental or physical handicapping condition; and

(8) any other information concerning the safety or welfare of the inmate.

(c) In considering the above information, the chief administrative officer shall examine the following:

(1) records made available to such officer at the time of the commitment by the court or law enforcement agency;

(2) determinations made upon an interview with an inmate at the time of classification;

(3) records, to the extent relevant and known to the chief administrative officer, maintained by the department of correctional services and/or any local correctional facility in this state and which are accessible and available to the chief administrative officer; and

(4) any other relevant information brought to the attention of the chief administrative officer by any person with knowledge of the conditions of the defendant.

8. Where the commission finds substantial noncompliance with commission rules and regulations with regard to (a) minimum staffing requirements; or (b) maximum jail capacity and security requirements; or (c) where it is determined that the county does not have an approved service plan in effect pursuant to article thirteen-A

of the executive law or is found to be in noncompliance therewith, as provided in section two hundred sixty-three of such law, it shall prohibit the commingling of any of the following categories of inmates;

(1) persons in custody on civil process, or committed for contempt, or detained as witnesses with persons detained for trial or examination upon a criminal charge with convicts under sentence;

(2) persons detained for trial or examination upon a criminal charge with convicts under sentence;

(3) persons under nineteen years of age with persons nineteen years of age or older; or

(4) a woman detained in any county jail or penitentiary upon a criminal charge or as a convict under sentence with a man; and if detained on civil process, or for contempt, or as a witness in a room in which there are no other prisoners with a man, except her husband.

Such prohibition shall continue until such time as the commission finds that the county is no longer in substantial noncompliance with paragraphs (a), (b) and (c) of this subdivision.

Notwithstanding the provisions of this subdivision to the contrary, classification as authorized pursuant to this section may occur without compliance with paragraphs (b) and (c) of this subdivision for a period not to exceed six months immediately following the submission of a plan to the division pursuant to section two hundred sixty-two of the executive law. During such six month period the commission shall undertake to review, observe and assess the classification of inmates in local correctional facilities as authorized under this section to thereby ascertain safeguards which should be incorporated in its rules and regulations. Further, during such six month period in which such classification shall be permitted pursuant to this subdivision, the commission shall evaluate whether a local correctional facility is in substantial noncompliance with rules and regulations regarding the requirements specified in paragraphs (a), (b) and (c) of this subdivision and shall determine at the end of such six month period whether substantial noncompliance exists. At the expiration of the six month period if the commission finds a local facility in substantial noncompliance, the commission shall order that the prohibition set forth in this subdivision immediately take effect. The commissioner shall advise the chief administrative officer of such facility of the specific nature of the noncompliance and the specific measures which should be undertaken to remedy the noncompliance. When such measures have been implemented, the chief administrative officer shall certify same to the commissioner and upon the verification thereof by the commissioner, shall permit the chief administrative officer to classify inmates as provided under this section. In the event substantial noncompliance is not found at the expiration of the six month period, then the local correctional facility may continue to classify inmates as authorized in this section.

9. The chief administrative officer shall forward to the commission a quarterly report relative to the housing of inmates. The report shall include, but not be limited to:

(a) all unusual incidents or assaults occurring in a housing unit;

(b) staffing;

(c) daily prisoner population counts;

(d) verification that the locality is maintaining security and supervision records as mandated pursuant to the commission's rules and regulations;

(e) court orders which have been issued and which relate to staffing, jail capacity or security requirements; and

(f) any other information requested by the commission and available to the chief administrative officer with respect to this section.

10. The commission shall conduct on-site inspections and review reports required by this section to monitor the assignment of persons to facility housing units as governed by this section.

11. The commission shall submit to the governor, the temporary president of the senate, the speaker of the assembly, the chairman of the senate crime and correction committee and the chairman of the assembly committee on codes, by March first of each year, its evaluation and assessment of housing in county jails, together with any recommendations with respect to the proper operation or improvement of housing in county jails.

12. The provisions of this section shall govern only the assignment of persons to facility housing units and shall not be construed to prohibit the commingling of persons during their participation in any facility program or activity, including meals and visitations.

13. Where in the opinion of the chief administrative officer an emergency overcrowding condition exists in a local correctional facility caused in part by the prohibition against the commingling of persons under nineteen years of age with persons nineteen years of age or older or the commingling of persons nineteen years of age or older with persons under nineteen years of age, the chief administrative officer may apply to the commission for permission to commingle the aforementioned categories of inmates for a period not to exceed thirty days as provided herein. The commission shall acknowledge to the chief administrative officer the receipt of such application upon its receipt. The chief administrative officer shall be permitted to commingle such inmates upon acknowledgment of receipt of the application by the commission. The commission shall

assess the application within seven days of receipt. The commission shall deny any such application and shall prohibit the continued commingling of such inmates where it has found that the local correctional facility does not meet the criteria set forth in this subdivision and further is in substantial noncompliance with minimum staffing requirements as provided in commission rules and regulations. In addition, the commission shall determine whether the commingling of such inmates presents a danger to the health, safety or welfare of any such inmate. If no such danger exists the chief administrative officer may continue the commingling until the expiration of the aforementioned thirty day period or until such time as he determines that the overcrowding which necessitated the commingling no longer exists, whichever occurs first. In the event the commission determines that such danger exists, it shall immediately notify the chief administrative officer, and the commingling of such inmates shall cease. Such notification shall include specific measures which should be undertaken by the chief administrative officer, to correct such dangers. The chief administrative officer may correct such dangers and reapply to the commission for permission to commingle; however, no commingling may take place until such time as the commission certifies that the facility is now in compliance with the measures set forth in the notification under this subdivision. When such certification has been received by the chief administrative officer, the commingling may continue for thirty days, less any time during which the chief administrative officer commingled such inmates following his application to the commission, or until such time as he determines that the overcrowding which necessitated the commingling no longer exists, whichever occurs first. The chief administrative officer may apply for permission to commingle such inmates for up to two additional thirty day periods, in conformity with the provisions and the requirements of this subdivision, in a given calendar year. For the period ending December thirtieth, nineteen hundred eighty-four, a locality may not apply for more than one thirty day commingling period.

Added by L. 1984, Chs. 907 and 908, eff. Aug. 6, 1984, and expires Sept. 30, 1987; L. 1987, Ch. 754, eff. Aug. 5, 1987, extended the expiration date to Sept. 30, 1988 and repealed subds. 5 and 14; L. 1988, Ch. 421; L. 1989, Chs. 338, 339; L. 1990, Ch. 193, eff. Apr. 1, 1990, extending the expiration date to Sept. 30, 1991; L. 1991, Ch. 511, eff. July 19, 1991; L. 1992, Ch. 55, eff. Apr. 10, 1992; L. 1993, Ch. 60, eff. Apr. 15, 1993, extending expiration date to September 30, 1994; L. 1994, Ch. 61, § 7, extending expiration date to Sept. 30, 1997. **Amended** by L. 1985, Ch. 574, eff. July 26, 1985, changing "chief corrections officer" to "chief administrative officer"; L. 1997, Ch. 435, § 57, extending effective date to Sept. 1, 1999, eff. Aug. 20, 1997; L. 1999, Ch. 452, § 11, eff. Sept. 1, 1999, extending effective date to Sept. 1, 2001; L. 2001, Ch. 95, § 15, eff. July 13, 2001, extending effective date to Sept. 1, 2003; L. 2003, Ch. 16, § 13, extending effective date to Sept. 1, 2005; L. 2005, Ch. 56, Part D, § 12, eff. Apr. 1, 2005, extending effective date to Sept. 1, 2007.

§ 500-b. Rooms for segregation of prisoners. [*Suspended until Sept. 1, 2007, pursuant to L. 1984, Ch. 907, § 12, as amended.*]

Each county jail shall contain:

1. A sufficient number of rooms for the confinement of persons committed on criminal process, or detained for trial, or examination as witness in a criminal case, separately from prisoners under sentence;

2. A sufficient number of rooms for the separate confinement of persons committed on civil process, or for contempt;

3. A sufficient number of rooms for the solitary confinement of prisoners under sentence.

Added by L. 1950, Ch. 695; **Amended** by L. 1984, Chs. 907 and 908, eff. Aug. 6, 1984, which provide that the effectiveness of this section be suspended until Sept. 30, 1987 during which period the following new section is to be in full force and effect; L. 1987; Ch. 754; L. 1988, Ch. 421, L. 1989, Chs. 338, 339; L. 1990, Ch. 193, eff. Apr. 1, 1990, extended the suspension date to Sept. 30, 1991; L. 1991, Ch. 511, eff. July 19, 1991; L. 1992, Ch. 55, eff. Apr. 10, 1992; L. 1993, Ch. 60, eff. Apr. 15, 1993, extending suspension date to September 30, 1994; L. 1994, Ch. 61, § 7, extending suspension date to Sept. 30, 1997; L. 1997, Ch. 435, § 57, extending suspension date to Sept. 1, 1999, eff. Aug. 20, 1997; L. 1999, Ch. 452, § 11, eff. Sept. 1, 1999, extending suspension date to Sept. 1, 2001; Ch. 95, § 15, eff. July 13, 2001, extending suspension date to Sept. 1, 2003; L. 2003, Ch. 16, 13, extending suspension date to Sept. 1, 2005; L. 2005, Ch. 56, Part D, § 12, eff. Apr. 1, 2005, extending suspension date to Sept. 1, 2007.

§ 500-c. Custody and control of prisoners. [*Effective until Sept. 1, 2007, pursuant to L. 1984, Ch. 907, § 12, as amended. Another § 500-c follows.*]

1. Except as provided in subdivision two of this section, the sheriff of each county shall have custody of the county jail of such county.

2. In the counties within the city of New York, the city commissioner of correction shall have custody of the correctional facilities within the jurisdiction of the New York city department of correction. In the county of Westchester, the county commissioner of correction shall have custody of all county correctional facilities.

3. Whenever a person is committed to the custody of the sheriff, such commitment shall be deemed to be to the custody of the person designated in subdivisions one and two of this section hereinafter referred to as the chief administrative officer.

4. The chief administrative officer shall receive and safely keep in the county jail of his county each person lawfully committed to his custody pursuant to the provisions of sections five hundred-a and five hundred four of this article and any other applicable provisions of law. Such officer shall not be held personally liable for receiving or detaining any person under and in accordance with a commitment issued by a judicial officer; nor shall he, without lawful authority, let any such person out of jail.

5. All persons confined in a county jail or penitentiary shall, as far as practicable, be allowed to converse with their counsel, or religious advisor, under such reasonable regulations and restrictions as the chief administrative officer may fix. The chief administrative officer may prevent all other conversation by any prisoner in the jail when he shall deem it necessary and proper.

6. Notwithstanding any other provision of law, in the county of Onondaga all of the provisions of this section shall equally apply in any case where the sheriff is holding a person under arrest, for arraignment, prior to commitment, as if such person had been judicially committed to the custody of the sheriff and such person may be held in the Onondaga county jail.

7. A sheriff, the New York city commissioner of correction, or the Westchester county commissioner of correction, as the case may be, shall maintain an institutional fund account on behalf of every lawfully sentenced inmate or prisoner in his custody and shall for the benefit of the person make deposits into said accounts of any prisoner funds. As used in this section, the term "prisoner funds" means (i) funds in the possession of the prisoner at the time of admission into the institution; (ii) funds earned by a prisoner as provided in section one hundred eighty-seven of this chapter; and (iii) any other funds received by or on behalf of the prisoner and deposited with such sheriff or municipal official in accordance with the written procedures established by the commission. Whenever the total value of unencumbered funds in a prisoner's account exceeds ten thousand dollars, such sheriff or official shall give written notice to the state crime victims board.

8. A sheriff, the New York city commissioner of correction, or the Westchester county commissioner of correction, as the case may be, shall provide written notice to all inmates serving a definite sentence for a specified crime defined in paragraph (e) of subdivision one of section six hundred thirty-two-a of the executive law who may be subject to any requirement to report to the crime victims board any funds of a convicted person as defined in section six hundred thirty-two-a of the executive law, the procedures for such reporting and any potential penalty for a failure to comply.

9. Notwithstanding any other provision of law, in the county of Erie all of the provisions of this section shall equally apply in any case where the sheriff is holding a person under arrest for arraignment, prior to commitment, as if such person had been judicially committed to the custody of the sheriff and such person may be held in the

Erie county holding center or the Erie county correctional facility.

10. Notwithstanding any other provision of law, in the county of Yates all of the provisions of this section shall equally apply in any case where the sheriff is holding a person under arrest for arraignment, prior to commitment, as if such person had been judicially committed to the custody of the sheriff and such person may be held in the Yates county jail.

11. * [Added by L. 2003, Ch. 171. Effective until Sept. 1, 2005.] Notwithstanding any other provision of law, in the county of Cortland, all of the provisions of this section shall equally apply in any case where the sheriff is holding a person under arrest for arraignment, prior to commitment, as if such person had been judicially committed to the custody of the sheriff.

11. * [Added by L. 2003, Ch. 559. Effective until Sept. 1, 2005.] Notwithstanding any other provision of law, in the county of Putnam, all of the provisions of this section shall equally apply in any case where the sheriff is holding a person under arrest for arraignment, prior to commitment, as if such person had been judicially committed to the custody of the sheriff and such person may be held in the Putnam county jail.

12. [Effective until Sept. 1, 2005.] Notwithstanding any other provision of law, in the county of Warren all the provisions of this section shall equally apply in any case where the sheriff is holding a person under arrest for arraignment prior to commitment, as if such person had been judicially committed to the custody of the sheriff and such person may be held in the Warren county jail.

* [In 2004, the Legislature enacted two subds. 11.]

13. [Added by L. 2005, Ch. 84.] Notwithstanding any other provision of law, in the county of Niagara, all of the provisions of this section shall equally apply in any case where the sheriff is holding a person under arrest for arraignment, prior to commitment, as if such person had been judicially committed to the custody of the sheriff and such person may be held in the Niagara county jail.

13. [Added by L. 2005, Ch. 258.] Notwithstanding any other provision of law, in the county of Genesee all the provisions of this section shall equally apply in any case where the sheriff is holding a person under arrest for arraignment prior to commitment, as if such person had been judicially committed to the custody of the sheriff and such person may be held in the Genesee county jail.

[In 2005, the Legislature enacted two subds. 13.]

14. Notwithstanding any other provision of law, in the county of Allegany all the provisions of this section shall equally apply in any case where the sheriff is holding a person under arrest for arraignment prior to commitment, as if such person had been judicially committed to the custody of the sheriff and such person may be held in the Allegany county correctional facility.

Amended by L. 1961, Ch. 407; L. 1968, Ch. 251; L. 1970, Ch. 70; L. 1974, Ch. 921; L. 1976, Ch. 24; L. 1977, Ch. 189; L. 1980, Ch. 400; L. 1981, Ch. 790, eff. July 27, 1981; L. 1991, Ch. 508, eff. Sept. 1, 1991; L. 1980, Ch. 400, provides in part that the provisions of Ch. 400 shall not become operative unless and until an amendment to the Monroe county charter contained in a local law entitled "A Local Law Amending the Monroe County Charter in Relation to Creating a Monroe County Department of Community Corrections" shall have become effective; L. 1984, Chs. 907 and 908, eff. Aug. 6, 1984, which provide that the effectiveness of this section be suspended until Sept. 30, 1987 during which period the following new section below is to be in full force and effect; L. 1987, Ch. 754, eff. Aug. 5, 1987; L. 1988, Ch. 421; L. 1989, Chs. 338, 339, eff. July 10, 1989, extending effective date to Sept. 30, 1990; L. 1991, Ch. 511, eff. July 19, 1991; L. 1992, Ch. 55, eff. Apr. 10, 1992; L. 1993, Ch. 60, eff. Apr. 15, 1993, extending effective date to September 30, 1994; L. 1994, Ch. 61, § 7, extending effective date to Sept. 30, 1997; L. 1997, Ch. 435, § 57, extending effective date to Sept. 1, 1999, eff. Aug. 20, 1997; L. 1999, Ch. 452, § 11, eff. Sept. 1, 1999, extending effective date to Sept. 1, 2001; L. 2001, Ch. 62, §§ 6, 7, eff. June 25, 2001; Ch. 95, § 15, eff. July 13, 2001, extending effective date to Sept. 1, 2003; L. 2002, Ch. 413, § 2, eff. Aug. 13, 2002, adding subd. 9; L. 2003, Ch. 16, 13, extending effective date, and Chs. 135 and 171, each eff. July 22, 2003, and each adding subd. 10; L. 2004, Ch. 555, §§ 4 & 5, renumbering subd. 10 to subd. 11 and adding subd. 12, eff. Oct. 5, 2004; L. 2004, Ch. 559, § 2, adding subd. 11, eff. Oct. 5, 2004; L. 2005, Ch. 56, Part D, § 12, eff. Apr. 1, 2005, extending expiration date to Sept. 1, 2007; L. 2005, Ch. 84, § 2, eff. June 7, 2005, adding subd. 13; L. 2005, Ch. 258, § 2, eff. July 19, 2005, adding subd. 13; L. 2005, Ch. 311, § 2, eff. July 26, 2005, adding subd. 14.

Editor's Note: L. 2001, Ch. 62, § 18 provides:

"This act shall take effect immediately and, notwithstanding the expiration of any other statute of limitations, shall apply to: (i) all judgments originally entered prior to such effective date, regardless whether such judgment is subsequently amended or satisfied on or after such effective date; and (ii) all judgments, obligations or agreements to pay profits from a crime or funds of a convicted person entered, incurred or entered into on or after the effective date of this act. Provided, however, that the amendment to section 500-c of the correction law made by section six of this act shall take effect upon the reversion of such section as provided for in chapter 907 of the laws of 1984, as amended, and upon such date section seven of this act, amending section 500-c of the correction law, shall be deemed expired and repealed therewith."

§ 500-c. Custody and control of prisoners. [Suspended until Sept. 1, 2007, pursuant to L. 1984, Ch. 907, § 12, as amended.]

Each sheriff, except the sheriff of the city of New York, and the sheriff of the county of Westchester, shall have custody of the county jails and shall receive and safely keep, in the county jail of his county, every person lawfully committed to his custody for safekeeping, examination or trial, or as a witness, or committed or sentenced to imprisonment therein, or committed for contempt. In the counties within the city of New York, the city commissioner of correction, and in the county of Westchester, the county sheriff, shall have custody of civil jails and shall safely keep every person lawfully committed to his custody. A sheriff, the New York city commissioner of correction, or the Westchester county commissioner of correction, as the case may be, shall not be held personally liable for receiving and/or detaining any person under and in accordance with a commitment issued by a judicial officer; nor shall he, without lawful authority, let any such person out of jail. Persons in custody on civil process, or committed for contempt, or detained as witnesses shall not be put or kept in the same room with persons detained for trial or examination upon a criminal charge, or with convicts under sentence. Persons detained for trial or examination upon a criminal charge shall not be put or kept in the same room with convicts under sentence. Persons under the age of twenty-one years shall not be put or kept in the same room with prisoners twenty-one years of age or older. The foregoing requirements for the segregation of persons, including persons under the age of twenty-one years, committed to the custody of a sheriff, the New York city commissioner of correction, or the Westchester county commissioner of correction may be waived, in the discretion of such sheriff, New York city commissioner of correction, or the Westchester county commissioner of correction, for the sole purpose of enabling such persons to participate in educational, vocational, divine worship and with the consent of said person, recreational programs conducted within the jail. A woman detained in any county jail or penitentiary upon a criminal charge, or as a convict under sentence, shall not be kept in the same room with a man; and if detained on civil process, or for contempt, or as a witness, she shall not be put or kept in the same room with a man, except with her husband, in a room in which there are no other prisoners. In the conduct of educational, vocational or divine worship programs, the strict separation of sexes need not be followed. If a woman committed to or confined in any county jail or penitentiary is then pregnant or is the mother of a nursing child in her care, under one year of age, or is the mother of and has exclusive care of a child more than one year of age, such mother and her child or children shall be subject to the provisions of section six hundred eleven of this chapter. All persons confined in a county jail or penitentiary shall, as far as practicable, be kept separate from each other, and shall be allowed to converse with their counsel, or religious adviser, under such reasonable regulations and restrictions as the keeper of the jail may fix. Convicts under sentence shall not be allowed to converse with any other person, except in the presence of a keeper. The keeper may prevent all other conversations by any other prisoner in the jail when he shall deem it necessary and proper.

[No subds. 1-6 were enacted.]

7. A sheriff, the New York city commissioner of correction, or the Westchester county commissioner of correction, as the case may be, shall maintain an institutional fund account on behalf of every lawfully sentenced inmate or prisoner in his custody and shall for the benefit of the person make deposits into said accounts of any prisoner funds. As used in this section, the term "prisoner funds" means (i) funds in the possession of the prisoner at the time of admission into the institution; (ii) funds earned by a prisoner as provided in section one hundred eighty-seven of this chapter; and (iii) any other funds received by or on behalf of the prisoner and deposited with such sheriff or municipal official in accordance with the written procedures established by the commission. Whenever the total value of unencumbered funds in a prisoner's account exceeds ten thousand dollars, such sheriff or official shall give written notice to the state crime victims board.

8. A sheriff, the New York city commissioner of correction, or the Westchester county commissioner of correction, as the case may be, shall provide written notice to all inmates serving a definite sentence for a specified crime defined in paragraph (e) of subdivision one of section six hundred thirty-two-a of the executive law who may be subject to any requirement to report to the crime victims board any funds of a convicted person as defined in section six hundred thirty-two-a of the executive law, the procedures for such reporting and any potential penalty for a failure to comply.

Amended by L. 1961, Ch. 407; L. 1968, Ch. 251; L. 1970, Ch. 70; L. 1974, Ch. 921; L. 1976, Ch. 24; L. 1977, Ch. 189; L. 1980, Ch. 400; L. 1981, Ch. 790, eff. July 27, 1981; L. 1991, Ch. 508, eff. Sept. 1, 1991; L. 1980, Ch. 400, provides in part that the provisions of Ch. 400 shall not become operative unless and until an amendment to the Monroe county charter contained in a local law entitled "A Local Law Amending the Monroe County Charter in Relation to Creating a Monroe County Department of Community Corrections" shall have become effective; L. 1984, Chs. 907 and 908, eff. Aug. 6, 1984, which provide that the effectiveness of this section be suspended until Sept. 30, 1987 during which period the following new section below is to be in full force and effect; L. 1987, Ch. 754, eff. Aug. 5, 1987; L. 1988, Ch. 421; L. 1989, Chs. 338, 339, eff. July 10, 1989, extended the suspension date to Sept. 30, 1990; L. 1991, Ch. 511, eff. July 19, 1991; L. 1992, Ch. 55, eff. Apr. 10, 1992; L. 1993, Ch. 60, eff. Apr. 15, 1993, extending suspension date to September 30, 1994; L. 1994, Ch. 61, § 7, extending suspension date to Sept. 30, 1997; L. 1997, Ch. 435, § 57, extending suspension date to Sept. 1, 1999, eff. Aug. 20, 1997; L. 1999, Ch. 452, § 11, eff. Sept. 1, 1999, extending suspension date to Sept. 1, 2001; L. 2001, Ch. 62, §§ 6, 7, eff. June 25, 2001; Ch. 95, § 15, eff. July 13, 2001, extending suspension date to Sept. 1, 2003; L. 2003, Ch. 16, 13, extending suspension date; L. 2005, Ch. 56, Part D, § 12, eff. Apr. 1, 2005, extending suspension date to Sept. 1, 2007.

Editor's Note: L. 2001, Ch. 62, § 18 provides:

"This act shall take effect immediately and, notwithstanding the expiration of any other statute of limitations, shall apply to: (i) all judgments originally entered prior to such effective date, regardless whether such judgment is subsequently amended or satisfied on or after such effective date; and (ii) all judgments, obligations or agreements to pay profits from a crime or funds of a convicted person entered, incurred or entered into on or after the effective date of this act. Provided, however, that the amendment to section 500-c of the correction law made by section six of this act shall take effect upon the reversion of such section as provided for in chapter 907 of the laws of 1984, as amended, and upon such date section seven of this act, amending section 500-c of the correction law, shall be deemed expired and repealed therewith."

Court's discretion.—A county, through the office of the Sheriff, is charged by statute (County Law § 650, Judiciary Law § 403, and Correction Law § 500-c) with the responsibility for maintaining security in the courtroom, and whether the degree of restraint employed by the sheriff in carrying out his duty goes beyond that which is necessary for the defendant's detention to answer the charge is ultimately a decision for the trial judge to make. People v. Morgan, 178 Misc. 2d 615, 682 N.Y.S.2d 512 (Fulton Co. Ct. 1998).

Duty to protect.—County could not be held liable to petitioner where wet floor conditions which led to injury inducing fall by petitioner were created by sheriff's deputies. Dugan v. County of Rensselaer, 115 A.D.2d 806, 495 N.Y.S.2d 753 (3d Dept. 1985).

—Corrections officers have a duty to provide inmates with reasonable protection against foreseeable risks of attack by other prisoners. Kemp v. Waldron, 115 A.D.2d 869, 497 N.Y.S.2d 158 (3d Dept. 1985).

Sheriff's rule making power.—The rule making power conferred upon the Sheriffs as jail keeper by Correction Law § 500-c is curtailed or diminished by Correction Law § 45(6). McNulty v. Chinlund, 62 A.D.2d 682, 406 N.Y.S.2d 558 (3d Dept. 1978).

§ 500-d. Food and labor.

Prisoners detained for trial, and those under sentence, shall be provided with a sufficient quantity of plain but wholesome food, at the expense of the county; such foods shall be purchased in the manner and subject to the regulations provided in section four hundred eight of the county law; but prisoners detained for trial may, at their own expense, and under the direction of the keeper, be supplied with any other proper articles of food. Such keeper shall cause each prisoner committed to his jail for imprisonment under sentence, to be constantly employed at hard labor when practicable, during every day, except Sunday, but the Sunday exception shall not apply where a prisoner under sentence of intermittent imprisonment serves less than the five preceding days in the jail and the keeper has adopted an employment program designed especially for intermittent imprisonment, and the board of supervisors of the county, or judge of the county, may prescribe the kind of labor at which such prisoner shall be employed; and the keeper shall account, at least annually, with the board of supervisors of the county, for the proceeds of such labor. Such keeper may, with the consent of the board of supervisors of the county, or the county judge, from time to time, cause such of the convicts under his charge as are capable of hard labor, to be employed outside of the jail in the same, or in an adjoining county, upon such terms as may be agreed upon between the keepers and the officers, or persons, under whose direction such convicts shall be placed, subject to such regulations as the board or judge may prescribe; and the board of supervisors of the several counties are authorized to employ convicts under sentence to confinement in the county jails, in building and repairing penal institutions of the county and in building and repairing the highways in their respective counties or in preparing the materials for such highways for sale to and for the use of the state, counties, towns, villages or cities, and in cutting wood and performing other work which is commonly carried on at a prison camp, and to make rules and regulations for their employment; and the said board of supervisors are hereby authorized to cause money to be raised by taxation for the purpose of furnishing materials and carrying this provision into effect; and the courts of this state are hereby authorized to sentence convicts committed to detention in the county jails to such hard labor as may be provided for them by the boards of supervisors. This section as amended shall not affect a county wholly included within a city.

Added by L. 1950, Ch. 695; Amended by L. 1951, Ch. 487; L. 1986, Ch. 403, eff. July 21, 1986.

Mandating hard labor.—A sentence for murder and weapon possession that mandates serving hard labor is illegal. People v. Johnson, 261 A.D.2d 583, 629 N.Y.S.2d 55 (2d Dept. 1995).

§ 500-e. Reading matter; divine service.

Each keeper shall provide a bible to be kept in each room of the jail in his charge, and he shall permit the pardons therein confined to be supplied with other suitable and proper books and papers, and if practicable, he shall cause divine service to be conducted for the benefit of the prisoners, at least once each Sunday, if there shall be room in the prison that may be safely used for that purpose.

Added by L. 1950, Ch. 695, eff. Jan. 1, 1951.

§ 500-f. Record of commitments and discharges.

Each keeper shall keep a daily record to be provided at the expense of the county, of the commitments and discharges of all prisoners delivered to his charge which shall contain the date of entrance, name, offense, term of sentence, fine, age, sex, place of birth, color, social relations, education, secular and religious, for what and by whom committed, how and when discharged, trade or occupation, whether so employed when arrested, number of previous convictions. The daily record shall be a public record, and shall be kept permanently in the office of the keeper.

Amended by L. 1968, Ch. 251; L. 1985, Ch. 413, eff. July 19, 1995.

§ 500-g. Commitment by United States courts. [Effective until Sept. 1, 2007, pursuant to L. 1984, Ch. 907, § 12, as amended. Another § 500-g follows.]

The chief administrative officer shall receive and keep in his jail every person duly committed thereto, for any offense against the United States, by any court or officer of the United States, until he shall be duly discharged, the United States supporting such person during his confinement; provided such official shall not violate any of the provisions of section five hundred-b of this article in receiving or detaining such persons; and the provisions of this article relative to the mode of confining prisoners shall apply to all persons so committed by any court or officer of the United States.

Added by L. 1950, Ch. 695; Amended by L. 1951, Ch. 487; L. 1984, Ch. 907, eff. Aug. 6, 1984; L. 1987, Ch. 754, eff. Aug. 5, 1987; L. 1988, Ch. 421; L. 1989, Chs. 338, 339; L. 1990, Ch. 193, eff. Apr. 1, 1990; L. 1991, Ch. 511, eff. July 19, 1991; L. 1992, Ch. 55, eff. Apr. 10, 1992; L. 1993, Ch. 60, eff. Apr. 15, 1993, extending expiration date to September 30, 1994; L. 1994, Ch. 61, § 7, extending expiration date. L. 1985, Ch. 574, eff. July 26, 1985, changing "chief corrections officer" to "chief administrative officer"; L. 1997, Ch. 435, § 57, extending expiration date to Sept. 1, 1999, eff. Aug. 20, 1997; L. 1999, Ch. 452, § 11, extending expiration date to Sept. 1, 2001, eff. Sept. 1, 1999; Ch. 95, § 15, eff. July 13, 2001, extending expiration date to Sept. 1, 2003; L. 2003, Ch. 16, § 13, extending expiration date to Sept. 1, 2005; L. 2005, Ch. 56, Part D, § 12, eff. Apr. 1, 2005, extending expiration date to Sept. 1, 2007.

§ 500-g. Commitment by United States courts. [Suspended until Sept. 1, 2007, pursuant to L. 1984, Ch. 907, § 12, as amended.]

Such keeper shall receive and keep in his jail every person duly committed thereto, for any offense against the United States, by any court or officer of the United States, until he shall be duly discharged; the United States supporting such person during his confinement; provided such official shall not violate any of the provisions of section five hundred-c of this article in receiving or detaining such persons; and the provisions of this article relative to the mode of confining prisoners and convicts, shall apply to all persons so committed by any court or officer of the United States.

Added by L. 1950, Ch. 695; Amended by L. 1951, Ch. 487; L. 1984, Ch. 907; L. 1987, Ch. 754; L. 1988, Ch. 421; L. 1989, Chs. 338, 339; L. 1990, Ch. 193; L. 1991, Ch. 511; L. 1992, Ch. 55; L. 1993, Ch. 60, eff. Apr. 15, 1993, extending suspension date to September 30, 1994; L. 1994, Ch. 61, § 7, extending suspension date to Sept. 30, 1997; L. 1997, Ch. 435, § 57, extending suspension date to Sept. 1, 1999, eff. Aug. 20, 1997; L. 1999, Ch. 452, § 11, extending suspension date to Sept. 1, 2001, eff. Sept. 1, 1999; Ch. 95, § 15, eff. July 13, 2001, extending suspension date to Sept. 1, 2003; L. 2003, Ch. 16, § 13, extending suspension date to Sept.1, 2005; L. 2005, Ch. 56, Part D, § 12, eff. Apr. 1, 2005, extending suspension date to Sept. 1, 2007.

§ 500-h. Payment of costs for medical and dental services.

1. Diagnoses, tests, studies or analyses for the diagnosis of a disease or disability, and care and treatment by a hospital, as defined in article twenty-eight of the public health law, or by a physician, or by a dentist to inmates of a local correctional facility which are provided by a county or the city of New York shall be available without cost or charge to the inmates receiving such examinations, care or treatment.

2. Notwithstanding the provisions of subdivision one of this section, any county or the city of New York may, by local law, provide that such entity may be reimbursed for costs paid pursuant to subdivision one of this section from any third party coverage or indemnification carried by an inmate. Such third party coverage or indemnification shall first be applied against the total cost to the hospital or other provider as established in accordance with the provisions of section twenty-eight hundred seven of the public health law relating to rates of payment of an individual's care and treatment, as provided herein.

Added by L. 1991, Ch. 481, eff. July 19, 1991.

§ 500-i. County workhouses.

The board of supervisors of any county may establish and maintain a workhouse for the confinement of persons convicted within the county of crimes and criminal offenses, the punishment for which is imprisonment in the county jail, and may provide for the imprisonment and employment therein of all persons sentenced thereto, and any court or judicial officer may sentence such person to such workhouse instead of to the county jail.

Added by L. 1950 Ch. 695.

§ 500-j. Who may visit jails and workhouses.

The following persons may visit at pleasure all county jails and workhouses: The governor and lieutenant-governor, secretary of state, comptroller and attorney-general, members of the legislature, judges of the court of appeals, justices of the supreme court and county judges, district attorneys and every minister of the gospel having charge of a congregation in the town in which such jail or workhouse is located. No other person not otherwise authorized by law shall be permitted to enter the rooms of a county jail or workhouse in which convicts are confined, unless under such regulations as the sheriff of the county, or in counties within the city of New York, the commissioner of correction of such city, or in the county of Westchester, the commissioner of correction of such county shall prescribe.

Amended by L. 1991, Ch. 508, eff. July 19, 1991.

§ 500-k. Treatment of inmates.

Subdivisions five and six of section one hundred thirty-seven of this chapter relating to the treatment of inmates in state correctional facilities are applicable to inmates confined in county jails; except that the report required by paragraph (d) of subdivision six of such section shall be made to a person designated to receive such report in the rules and regulations of the state commission of correction, or in any county or city where there is a department of correction, to the head of such department.

Added by L. 1968, Ch. 226; **Amended** by L. 1970, Ch. 476.

§ 500-l. Release on holidays, Saturdays and Sundays.

When the date of release from imprisonment in any county jail or jail farm, any city prison or workhouse, falls on Saturday or Sunday, it shall be deemed to fall on the preceding Friday. When the date of such release falls on a legal holiday it shall be deemed to fall on the preceding day, except that when such legal holiday falls on a Monday the date of release shall be deemed to fall on the preceding Friday. This section shall also apply to civil prisoners confined in any jail or prison. This section shall not apply to a sentence of intermittent imprisonment imposed pursuant to article eighty-five or paragraph (d) of subdivision two of section 60.01 of the penal law.

Amended by L. 1987, Ch. 304, eff. Sept. 18, 1987.

§ 500-m. Special provision relating to city of New York.

Unless specifically provided by law to the contrary, within the city of New York or the counties constituting such city the term sheriff shall be deemed to mean the commissioner of correction of such city.

Added by L. 1977, Ch. 189.

§ 500-n. Prisoners; unlawful fees prohibited. [*Effective until Sept. 1, 2007, pursuant to L. 1984, Ch. 907, § 3 and Ch. 908 § 2, as amended. Another § 500-n follows.*]

1. Except as otherwise provided by law, a sheriff or other person in charge of a correctional facility or any person employed at such facility shall not charge a prisoner or other person in custody with any sum of money, or demand or receive from him money, or any valuable thing for any drink, food or other thing, furnished or provided for such prisoner or person at any correctional facility.

2. A sheriff or other public officer or employee shall not demand or receive from a prisoner or other person, while in his custody, a gratuity or reward, upon any pretense or for any purpose.

3. A sheriff, or other public officer or employee, shall not demand or receive from a prisoner or other person in custody, money or any valuable thing for rent in a jail or any fee, compensation, or reward for the commitment, detaining in custody, release, or discharge of a prisoner, other than the fees expressly allowed therefor by law.

Amended [formerly § 500] by L. 1984, Chs. 907 and 908, eff. Aug. 6, 1984; L. 1987, Ch. 604, renumbered from § 500; L. 1988, Ch. 421; L. 1989, Ch. 338, eff. July 10, 1989; L. 1990,

Ch. 193, eff. Apr. 1, 1990; L. 1991, Ch. 511; L. 1992, Ch. 55; L. 1993, Ch. 60; L. 1994, Ch. 61; L. 1999, Ch. 452, § 11, extending effective date to Sept. 1, 2001; Ch. 95, § 15, eff. July 13, 2001, extending effective date to Sept. 1, 2003; L. 2003, Ch. 16, § 13, extending effective date to Sept. 1, 2005; L. 2005, Ch. 56, Part D, § 12, eff. Apr. 1, 2005, extending expiration date to Sept. 1, 2007.

§ 500-n. Civil prisoners. [*Suspended until Sept. 1, 2007, pursuant to L. 1984, Ch. 907, § 3 and Ch. 908, § 2, as amended.*]

1. A sheriff or other officer shall not charge a civil prisoner with any sum of money, or demand or receive from him money, or any valuable thing, for any drink, victuals or other thing, furnished or provided for the officer or for the prisoner, at any public house.

2. A sheriff or other officer shall not demand or receive from a civil prisoner, while in his custody, a gratuity or reward, upon any pretense or for any purpose.

3. If a person arrested in a civil cause is kept in a house, other than the jail of the county, the officer arresting him, or the person in whose custody he is, shall not demand or receive from him any greater sum, for lodging, drink, victuals, or any other thing, than has been theretofore prescribed by the court of sessions or county court of the county; or, if no rate has been prescribed by the court of sessions or county court, than is allowed by a justice of the peace of the same town or city, upon proof that the lodging or other thing was actually furnished, at the request of the prisoner.

4. A civil prisoner arrested and kept in a house, other than the jail of the county, may send for and have drink and necessary food, and such bedding, linen and other necessary things, as he thinks fit, from whom he pleases, without detention of the same or any part thereof by, or paying for the same, or any part thereof to, the officer arresting him, or the person in whose custody he is.

5. A sheriff, jailer, or other officer, shall not demand or receive money, or any valuable thing, for chamber rent in a jail; or any fee, compensation, or reward, for the commitment, detaining in custody, release, or discharge of a civil prisoner, other than the fees expressly allowed therefor by law.

6. A prisoner, arrested in a civil cause, must not be kept in a room, in which any prisoner, detained on a criminal charge or conviction, is confined.

7. Male and female civil prisoners must not be put in the same room; except that a husband and his wife may be put or kept together, in a room wherein there are no other prisoners.

8. The sheriff of a county, in which there is more than one jail, or in the county of Westchester

the commissioner of correction of such county in the case of a criminal prisoner and the sheriff in the case of a civil prisoner, may confine a civil or criminal prisoner in either or any of such county jails; and may remove him from one jail to another, within the county, whenever he deems it necessary for his safe-keeping, or for his appearance at court.

Amended by L. 1968, Ch. 251.; L. 1984, Chs. 907 and 908, eff. Aug. 6, 1984 which provide that the effectiveness of this section be suspended until Sept. 30, 1987 during which period the following new section is to be in full force and effect; L. 1987, Ch. 754, eff. Aug. 5, 1987; L. 1988, Ch. 421; L. 1989, Ch. 338, eff. July 10, 1989; L. 1990, Ch. 193, eff. Apr. 1, 1990; L. 1991, Ch. 511; L. 1992, Ch. 55; L. 1993, Ch. 60, postponed the effective date until Sept. 30, 1994; L. 1994, Ch. 61, § 7, extending suspension date to Sept. 30, 1997; L. 1999, Ch. 452, § 11, extending suspension date to Sept. 1, 2001; Ch. 95, § 15, eff. July 13, 2001, extending suspension date to Sept. 1, 2003; L. 2003, Ch. 16, § 13, extending suspension date to Sept. 1, 2005; L. 2005, Ch. 56, Part D, § 12, eff. Apr. 1, 2005, extending expiration date to Sept. 1, 2007.

§ 501. Jail physician.

The board of supervisors of each county, except New York, must appoint some reputable physician, duly authorized to practice medicine, as the physician to the jail of the county. If there is more than one jail they must appoint a physician to each. The physician to a jail holds his office at the pleasure of the board which appointed him, except in the county of Kings. In that county, the term of his office is three years.

§ 502. Use of liquor in jails.

Spirituous, fermented or other liquor shall not be brought into a jail for the use of a person confined therein, except as authorized by federal statute and then only upon a written permit by the physician to the jail, which must be delivered to and kept by the keeper thereof, specifying the quantity and kind of liquor which may be furnished, the name of the civil prisoner for whom, and the time during which the same may be furnished.

§ 503. Permit to bring liquor into jail.

A permit by a jail physician as specified in the last section shall not be granted, unless the physician is satisfied, that the liquor allowed to be furnished is necessary for the health of the civil prisoner, for whose use it is permitted and that fact must be stated in the permit.

§ 504. Designation of substitute jail.

1. If there is no jail in a county, or the jail becomes unfit or unsafe for the confinement of some or all of the inmates, civil or criminal, or is destroyed by fire or otherwise, or if a pestilential disease breaks out in the jail or in the vicinity of the jail and the physician to the jail certifies that it is likely to endanger the health of any or all of the inmates in the jail, the state commission of correction, upon application, must, by an instrument in writing, filed with the clerk of the county, designate another suitable place within the county, or the jail of any other county, for the confinement of some or all of the inmates, as the case requires. The place so designated thereupon becomes, to all intents and purposes, except as otherwise prescribed in this article, the jail of the county for which it has been so designated, and the purposes expressed in the instrument designating the same. The designation may be amended, modified or revoked by the state commission of correction by a subsequent instrument in writing filed with the clerk of the county.

2. Where the jail in a county becomes unfit or unsafe for the confinement of some or all of the inmates due to an inmate disturbance or a natural disaster including but not limited to flood, earthquake, hurricane, landslide or fire, or other extraordinary circumstances upon the request of the municipal official as defined in subdivision four of section forty of this chapter and no other suitable place within the county nor the jail of any other county is immediately available to house some or all of the inmates, the commissioner of correctional services is hereby authorized and empowered to make available, upon such terms and conditions as he may deem appropriate, all or any part of a state correctional institution for the confinement of some or all of such inmates as an adjunct to the county jail for a period not to exceed thirty days. However, if the county jail remains unfit or unsafe for the confinement of some or all of such inmates beyond thirty days, the state commission of correction, with the consent of the commissioner of correctional services, may extend the availability of a state correctional institution for one or more additional thirty day periods. The state commission of correction shall promulgate rules and regulations governing the temporary transfer of inmates to state correctional institutions from county jails including but not limited to provisions for confinement of such inmates in the nearest correctional facility, to the maximum extent practicable, taking into account necessary security. The county shall reimburse the state for the actual costs of confinement as approved by the director of the division of the budget. On or before the expiration of each thirty day period, the state commission of correction must make an appropriate designation pursuant to subdivision one if the county jails remains unfit or unsafe for the confinement of some or all of the inmates and consent to the continued availability of a state correctional institution as required for herein. The superintendence, management and control of a state correctional institution or part thereof made available pursuant hereto and the inmates housed therein shall be as directed by the commissioner of correctional services.

3. The county clerk must serve a copy of the designation, duly certified by him, under his official seal, on the sheriff and keeper of the jail

of the county designated. The sheriff of that county must, upon the delivery of the sheriff of the county for which the designation is made, receive into his jail, and there safely keep, all persons who may be lawfully confined therein, pursuant to this article; and he is responsible for their safekeeping, as if he was sheriff of the county for which the designation is made.

4. In any county where a jail is under the jurisdiction of a commissioner of correction the term sheriff as set forth in this section shall be deemed to mean the commissioner of correction of such county.

Amended by L. 1968, Ch. 251; L. 1974, Ch. 799, amending § 504 and renumbering subds. 1 and 2 of former § 506 to subds. 3 and 4 of § 504; L. 1982, Ch. 506, eff. July 13, 1982 repealed subd. 2 and added new subd. 2.

ANNOTATION

Designation mandatory.—Difficulties arising from unavailability of county jail due to overcrowding must be addressed through section 504; the statute makes no provision for confining an accused in detention cell of court. Howell v. McGinity, 129 A.D.2d 60, 516 N.Y.S.2d 694 (2d Dept. 1987).

§ 507. Removal of prisoners in case of fire.

If, by reason of a jail, or a building near a jail, being on fire, there is reason to apprehend that some or all of the prisoners confined in the jail, may be injured, or may escape, the sheriff or keeper of the jail may, in his discretion, remove them to some safe and convenient place, and there confine them, until they can be safely returned to the jail or, if the jail is destroyed, or so injured, that it is unfit or unsafe for the confinement of the prisoners, until a designation is made, as prescribed in section five hundred and four of this article.

§ 508. Removal of sick prisoners from jail.

1. If the physician to a jail, or, in case of a vacancy, a physician acting as such, and the warden or jailer, certify in writing, that a prisoner confined in the jail, either in a civil cause or upon a criminal charge, is in such a state of bodily health that he requires immediate medical or surgical treatment and that in their opinion he should be removed to a hospital for treatment, the county judge, or one of the justices of the supreme court, must, upon application, make an order, directing the removal of a prisoner to a hospital within the county designated by the judge; or, if there is none, to such nearest hospital as the judge directs; provided, however, that in an emergency the sheriff of the county may order a prisoner's removal to a hospital, pending the issuance of a court order; that the prisoner be kept in the custody of the officials in charge of the jail to which he is committed until he has sufficiently recovered from his illness, to be safely returned to the jail; that the chief officer of the hospital then notify the sheriff, warden or jailer, that the latter thereupon return the prisoner to the jail to which he is committed: provided, however, that when a city or county maintains and operates a public general hospital containing a prison ward approved by the state department of correction the sheriff may make such removal and return of the prisoner without such order.

2. A sheriff, in his discretion, may be written order permit inmates confined in a local correctional facility upon a sentence of imprisonment to receive medical diagnosis and treatment in outside hospitals, upon the determination that such outside treatment and diagnosis is necessary by reason of inadequate facilities within the local correctional facility. Such inmates shall remain under the jurisdiction and in the custody of said sheriff while in a hospital and said sheriff shall enforce proper measures in each case to safely maintain such jurisdiction and custody.

3. a. If a physician to a jail or in case of a vacancy a physician acting as such and the warden or jailer certify in writing that a prisoner confined in a jail either in a civil cause or upon a criminal charge is in such a state of mental health that he is in need of involuntary care and treatment and in their opinion should be removed to a psychiatric hospital for treatment, the warden or jailer shall immediately notify the director who shall have the responsibility for providing treatment for such prisoner. If such director after examination of the prisoner by an examining physician designated by him shall determine that such prisoner is in need of involuntary care and treatment, the director shall file an application for the involuntary hospitalization of such prisoner pursuant to article nine of the mental hygiene law in a hospital operated by the department of mental hygiene or in the case of a prisoner confined in a jail in a city or county which maintains or operates a general hospital containing a psychiatric prison ward approved by the department of mental hygiene to such prison ward for care and treatment or to any other psychiatric hospital if such prison ward is filled to capacity. Such application shall be supported by the certificate of two physicians in accordance with the requirements of section 9.27 of the mental hygiene law and thereupon such prisoner shall be admitted forthwith to the hospital in which such application is filed, and the procedures of the mental hygiene law governing the hospitalization of such prisoner. The jailer or warden having custody of the prisoner shall deliver the prisoner to the hospital with which the director has filed the application. If such jailer or warden shall certify that such prisoner has a mental illness which is likely to result in serious harm to himself or others and for which care in a psychiatric hospital is appropriate such jailer or warden shall effect the admission of such prisoner to a hospital forthwith in accordance with the provisions of section 9.37 or 9.39 of the mental hygiene law and the hospital

shall admit such prisoner. Upon admission of the prisoner, pursuant to section 9.37 or 9.39 of the mental hygiene law, the jailer or warden shall notify the director, the prisoner's attorney, and his family, where information about the family is available. While the prisoner is in the hospital he shall remain in the custody under sufficient guard of the jailer or warden in charge of the jail from which he came. A prisoner admitted to a psychiatric hospital pursuant to section 9.27, 9.37 or 9.39 of the mental hygiene law may be retained at the hospital pursuant to the provisions of the mental hygiene law until he has improved sufficiently in his mental illness so that hospitalization is no longer necessary or until ordered by the court to be returned to the jail whichever comes first and in either event, the prisoner shall thereupon be returned to jail. The cost of the care and treatment of such prisoners in the hospital shall be defrayed in accordance with the provisions of the mental hygiene law in such cases provided.

From the time of admission of a prisoner to a hospital under this section the retention of such prisoner for care and treatment shall be subject to the provisions for notice, hearing, review and judicial approval of continued retention or transfer and continued retention provided by article nine of the mental hygiene law for the admission and retention of involuntary patients.

b. As used in this section, the following terms shall have the following meanings:

(i) "Director" means (a) the director of a state hospital operated by the department of mental hygiene, or (b) the director of a hospital operated by any local government of the state that has been certified by the commissioner of mental hygiene as having adequate facilities to treat a mentally ill person or (c) the director of community mental health services or the designees of any of the foregoing. The appropriate director to whom a jailer or warden shall certify the need for involuntary care and treatment and who shall have the responsibility for such care and treatment shall be determined in accordance with rules jointly adopted by the judicial conference and the commissioner of mental hygiene.

(ii) "Mental illness" shall mean an affliction with a mental disease or mental condition which is manifested by a disorder or a disturbance in behavior, feeling, thinking, or judgment to such an extent that the person afflicted requires care and treatment.

(iii) "In need of involuntary care and treatment" shall mean that a person has a mental illness for which care and treatment as a patient in a hospital is essential to such person's welfare and whose judgement is so impaired that he is unable to understand the need for such care and treatment.

(iv) "Likelihood to result in serious harm" shall mean (1) substantial risk of physical harm to himself as manifested by threats of or attempts at suicide or serious bodily harm or other conduct demonstrating that he is dangerous to himself or (2) a substantial risk of physical harm to other persons as manifested by homicidal or other violent behavior by which others are placed in reasonable fear or serious physical harm.

c. If at any time the hospital in which a prisoner is hospitalized pursuant to this subdivision determines that the prisoner is not in such state of mental health to be in need of involuntary care and treatment the prisoner shall be returned to the jail forthwith.

d. If at any time the director of a hospital in which a prisoner is hospitalized pursuant to this subdivision has reason to believe that the prisoner may be an incapacitated defendant as defined in article seven hundred thirty of the criminal procedure law he shall so notify the court in which the criminal charges are pending and such court shall thereupon issue an examination order pursuant to the provisions of article seven hundred thirty of the criminal procedure law.

e. Nothing in this subdivision shall prevent the release of the prisoner from custody where appropriate by recognizance, bail, or otherwise as the court may direct.

* As originally enacted. Probably should be "jailer."

Amended by L. 1946, Ch. 700; L. 1961, Ch. 151; L. 1962, Ch. 536; L. 1968, Ch. 251; L. 1974, Ch. 656; L. 1988, Ch. 240, eff. July 8, 1988, repealed subd. 2 and added new subd. 2; L. 2002, Ch. 283, § 1, eff. Aug. 6, 2002, amending subd. 3(a).

§ 509. Absence of inmate for funeral and deathbed visits.

The sheriff of a local correctional facility or his designee may permit any inmate confined in his local correctional facility to attend the funeral of his or her father, mother, guardian or former guardian, child, brother, sister, husband, wife, grandparent, grandchild, ancestral uncle or ancestral aunt within the state, or to visit such individual during his or her illness if death be imminent; but the exercise of such power shall be subject to such rules and regulations as the commission shall prescribe, respecting the granting of such permission, duration of absence from the institution, custody, transportation and care of the inmate, and guarding against escape.

Added by L. 1987, Ch. 229, eff. Nov. 4, 1987; **Amended** by L. 1989, Ch. 419, eff. Aug. 15, 1989.

§ 514. Confinement of civil prisoner.

A civil prisoner, committed to jail upon process for contempt, or committed for misconduct in a case prescribed by law, must be actually confined and detained within the jail, until he is discharged by due course of law, or is removed to another jail or place of confinement, in a case prescribed by law. A sheriff or keeper of a jail, who suffers such a prisoner to go or be at large out of his jail; except by virtue of a writ of habeas corpus, or by the special direction of the court committing him, or in a case specially prescribed by law; is liable to the party aggrieved, for his damages sustained thereby, and is guilty of a misdemeanor. If the commitment was for the non-payment of a sum of money, the amount thereof, with interest, is the measure of damages.

§ 523. Revocation of designation of jail.

When a jail is erected for the county, for whose use the designation pursuant to section five hundred and four of this chapter was made, or its jail is rendered fit and safe for the confinement of prisoners, or the reason for the designation of another jail or place has otherwise ceased to be operative, the designation must be revoked, as prescribed in this article and section five hundred and five of this chapter.

§ 524. Manner and effect of revocation.

The county clerk must immediately serve a copy of the revocation, duly certified by him under his official seal, upon the sheriff of the same county; who must remove the civil and criminal prisoners belonging to his custody, and confined without his county, to his proper jail. If a prisoner has been admitted to the jail liberties in the other county, he must also be removed; and he is entitled to the liberties of the jail of the county, to which he is removed, without a new bond, as if he had been originally admitted to the jail liberties in that county; and the bond given by him applies accordingly to those liberties.

§ 529. Term of imprisonment of a recaptured prisoner.

A prisoner arrested or committed in a civil action or proceeding, who escapes from custody, upon his voluntary return or recapture, shall be imprisoned for a term equal to that portion of his original term of imprisonment which remains unexpired at the time of his escape.

Amended by L. 1943, Ch. 143.

ARTICLE 22—MISCELLANEOUS PROVISIONS

§ 600. Certain correctional officers to administer oaths.

The commissioner of correction and the deputy and assistant commissioners of correction may administer oaths and take affidavits in all matters relating to the affairs of the state prisons. The warden, principal keeper, chief clerk, of each prison are authorized and required to take affidavits, in all matters of accounts against their respective prisons, and also in relation to fees of sheriffs in bringing prisoners to any of said prisons.

Amended by L. 1942, Ch. 126.

§ 600-a. Jail time records and certificates.

A record shall be kept by the sheriff, or in counties within the city of New York by the commissioner of correction of such city, of all jail time to which the defendant is entitled under subdivision three of section 70.30 of the penal law. In any case where the sheriff or the commissioner of correction of the city of New York has the duty of delivering a defendant to an institution not under his jurisdiction pursuant to sentence and commitment, such person shall deliver a certified transcript of such record to the person to whom the defendant is to be delivered.

Added by L. 1971, Ch. 545.

ANNOTATIONS

Calculation of jail time credit.—Pursuant to section 600-a, the City Commissioner is required to keep a record of the jail time to which a prisoner is entitled pursuant to PL § 70.30, and this calculation of jail time credit involves "a continuing, nondiscretionary, ministerial obligation." A motion brought pursuant to Article 78 for a recalculation of jail time credit is properly commenced within four months "after the respondent's refusal, upon the demand of the petitioner . . ., to perform its duty." (CPLR 217[1]). Bottom v. Goord, 96 N.Y.2d 870, 730 N.Y.S.2d 767, 756 N.E.2d 55 (2001).

Erroneous transcript.—A later judicial determination that the Sheriff's certification of jail time credit was erroneous and that the defendant had been incarcerated beyond his appropriate release date did not impose liability upon the State since it was acting under a warrant of commitment valid on its face and it cannot be held responsible for any possible dereliction of duty on the part of the Sheriff or other local officers or employees. Middleton v. State of New York, 54 A.D.2d 450, 389 N.Y.S.2d 159 (3d Dept. 1976).

§ 601. Delivery of commitment with inmate; payment of fees for transportation.

(a) [*Effective until Sept. 1, 2009.*] Whenever an inmate shall be delivered to the superintendent of a state correctional facility pursuant to an indeterminate or determinate sentence, the officer so delivering such inmate shall deliver to such superintendent, a certified copy of the sentence and a certificate of conviction pursuant to section 380.70 of the criminal procedure law received by such officer from the clerk of the court by which such inmate shall have been sentenced, a copy

CORR. L.

of the report of the probation officer's investigation and report or a detailed statement covering the facts relative to the crime and previous history certified by the district attorney, a copy of the inmate's fingerprint records, a detailed summary of available medical records, psychiatric records and reports relating to assaults, or other violent acts, attempts at suicide or escape by the inmate while in the custody of the local correctional facility; any such medical or psychiatric records in the possession of a health care provider other than the local correctional facility shall be summarized in detail and forwarded by such health care provider to the medical director of the appropriate state correctional facility upon request; the superintendent shall present to such officer a certificate of the delivery of such inmate, and the fees of such officer for transporting such inmate shall be paid from the treasury upon the audit and warrant of the comptroller. Whenever an inmate of the state is delivered to a local facility, the superintendent shall forward summaries of such records to the local facility with the inmate.

(a) [*Effective Sept. 1, 2009.*] Whenever an inmate shall be delivered to the superintendent of a state correctional facility pursuant to an indeterminate or determinate sentence, the officer so delivering such inmate shall deliver to such superintendent, a certified copy of the sentence received by such officer from the clerk of the court by which such inmate shall have been sentenced, a copy of the report of the probation officer's investigation and report or a detailed statement covering the facts relative to the crime and previous history certified by the district attorney, a copy of the inmate's fingerprint records, a detailed summary of available medical records, psychiatric records and reports relating to assaults, or other violent acts, attempts at suicide or escape by the inmate while in the custody of the local correctional facility; any such medical or psychiatric records in the possession of a health care provider other than the local correctional facility shall be summarized in detail and forwarded by such health care provider to the medical director of the appropriate state correctional facility upon request; the superintendent shall present to such officer a certificate of the delivery of such inmate, and the fees of such officer for transporting such inmate shall be paid from the treasury upon the audit and warrant of the comptroller. Whenever an inmate of the state is delivered to a local facility, the superintendent shall forward summaries of such records to the local facility with the inmate.

(b) [*Effective until Sept. 1, 2009.*] Whenever an inmate is sentenced by a court of this state to an indeterminate sentence, but the inmate is immediately returned to a correctional facility under the jurisdiction of the United States or of a sister state, the clerk of the court shall immediately send to the commissioner of the department a certified copy of the sentence, a copy of the probation report and a copy of the fingerprint records of the inmate.

(b) [*Effective Sept. 1, 2009.*] Whenever an inmate is sentenced by a court of this state to an indeterminate or determinate sentence, but the inmate is immediately returned to a correctional facility under the jurisdiction of the United States or of a sister state, the clerk of the court shall immediately send to the commissioner of the department a certified copy of the sentence, a copy of the probation report and a copy of the fingerprint records of the inmate.

(c) In order to comply with section five hundred-b of this chapter, to afford appropriate precautions for the personal safety and welfare of persons in custody, and to foster the safety, security and good order of the local correctional facility, a sheriff upon the lawful commitment of a person to his custody may request, and a sheriff to whom such request is made shall deliver, such information in his possession or summaries thereof as specified in subdivision (a) of this section with the exception of medical and psychiatric records which would be forwarded pursuant to subdivision (d) of this section.

(d) Any medical or psychiatric records in the possession of a health care provider shall be summarized in detail and forwarded by such health care provider to the medical director of the receiving local correctional facility upon the request of such sheriff or medical director. Requests for such information shall be made when the information is necessary for the timely and effective medical evaluation or treatment.

(e) Information, however received, pursuant to subdivisions (c) and (d) of this section which is confidential as required by law shall be kept confidential by the party receiving such information and any limitation on the release of such information imposed by law upon the party furnishing the information shall also apply to the party receiving such information. Any disclosure of confidential material made pursuant to this section shall be limited to that information which is necessary in light of the reason for disclosure.

(f) The state commission of correction shall promulgate a rule and regulation which prescribes the manner in which confidential material shall be transmitted between local correctional facilities.

Amended by L. 1977, Ch. 39; L. 1981, Ch. 227 eff. Sept. 13, 1981; L. 1988, Ch. 640, eff. Dec. 30, 1988, adding subds. c, d, e, and f; L. 1995, Ch. 3, § 26, eff. Oct. 1, 1995, and amendment repealed Sept. 1, 2009 (as amended); L. 2004, Ch. 738, §§ 5 & 6, amending subds. a & b.

§ 601-a. Return of persons erroneously sentenced for the purpose of resentence.

Whenever it shall appear to the satisfaction of

the warden of any state prison based on facts submitted on behalf of a person sentenced and confined in a state prison, that any such person has been erroneously sentenced as a second, third or fourth offender, it shall become his duty to communicate with the district attorney of the county in which such person was convicted. If upon investigation, such district attorney believes that the person has been so erroneously sentenced, he shall notify the warden of the state prison wherein such person is confined. The warden thereupon shall notify the sheriff of the county, or in counties within the city of New York or the county of Westchester, the commissioner of correction of such city or county from which such person was committed, who shall remove such person from such prison and cause him to be taken before the court in which he was sentenced for the purpose of resentence. The cost and expense of the return of such person necessarily incurred shall be a charge against the county from which he was committed.

Amended by L. 1968, Ch. 251, L. 1980, Ch. 400, eff. Jan. 1, 1981; L. 1991, Ch. 508, eff. July 19, 1991.

§ 601-b. Coram nobis prisoners; reimbursement for costs.

Whenever a prisoner is transferred from a state penal institution to a county jail or penitentiary, or a city prison operated by a city having a population of one million or more inhabitants, to await judicial review of his trial, the state shall pay to the city or county operating such facility the actual per day per capita cost, certified to the commissioner by the appropriate local official, for the care of such prisoner but, in any case, the reimbursement rate shall not exceed twenty dollars per day per capita.

Added by L. 1965, Ch. 1031; Amended by L. 1978, Ch. 499, eff. Apr. 1, 1979; L. 1985, Ch. 494, eff. July 1, 1985.

§ 601-c. Felony prisoners; reimbursement for costs.

1. The expense of maintaining persons convicted of a felony who shall be sentenced to imprisonment in a local correctional facility prior to April first, nineteen hundred ninety-nine shall be paid by the state at the actual per day per capita cost, as certified to the commissioner by the appropriate local official, for the care of such prisoner but, in any case, the reimbursement rate shall not exceed twenty dollars per day per capita to the county or city operating such facility.

2. Notwithstanding the provisions of subdivision one of this section, the expense of maintaining a persons convicted of a felony whose sentence has been pronounced and which requires that he be committed to the custody of the commissioner, and who has not been accepted for custody by the commissioner within five days of receipt of written notification by the department from the appropriate local official that he is prepared to transport such person to the facility designated by the department, provided that there has been compliance with subdivision (a) of section six hundred one of this article, shall be paid by the state at the actual per day per capita cost, as certified by the appropriate local official, or thirty dollars per day per capita and, effective on and after the first day of April, nineteen hundred eighty-eight, forty dollars per day per capita, whichever is less, beginning with the first day of receipt of written notification by the department. Nothing contained herein shall be construed to affect, impair, modify, restrict, define or expand any other provision of law with regard to any obligation to deliver or receive any such inmates by any state or local official or any requirement of timely compliance therewith.

Added by L. 1967, Ch. 680; Amended by L. 1978, Ch. 499, eff. Apr. 1, 1979; L. 1985, Ch. 494, eff. July 1, 1985 amending subd. 1 and adding subd. 2; L. 1987, Chs. 261 and 262, eff. July 13, 1987, amending subd. 2; L. 1999, Ch. 412, Part C, eff. Aug. 9, 1999, deemed in full force and effect Apr. 1, 1999, amending subd. 1.

§ 602. Expenses of sheriff for transporting prisoners.

For conveying a prisoner or prisoners to a state prison from the county prison, the sheriff or person having charge of the same shall be reimbursed for the amount of expenses actually and necessarily incurred by him for railroad fare or cost of other transportation and for cost of maintenance of himself and each prisoner in going to the prison, and for his railroad fare or other cost of transportation in returning home, and cost of his maintenance while so returning. The county shall be reimbursed for a portion of the salary of such sheriff or person for the period, not to exceed thirty-six hours, from the commencement of transportation from the county prison to the return of such sheriff or person to the county prison, the amount of such reimbursement to be computed by adding to the amount of such salary the total amount of the aforesaid expenses incurred for transportation and maintenance and reducing the resulting aggregate amount, first, by fifty per centum of such aggregate amount and, second, by the total amount of the aforesaid expenses incurred for transportation and maintenance.

Amended by L. 1962, Ch. 891.

§ 603. Rendering accounts for conveying of prisoners.

On the conveying of any such prisoners to the warden of such prison and upon returning home, the sheriff or other person having charge of the same, shall make and render to the warden of the prison, an account showing the distance and route traveled, the method of transportation and the items of expenditure paid or incurred, allowable under section six hundred and two; which account shall then be subscribed and affirmed by him as true under the penalties of perjury to which shall be added the certificate of the warden of such prison, setting forth the number of prisoners so conveyed, and the distance from such prison to the place of their conviction.

Amended by L. 1965, Ch. 845.

§ 604. Payment of accounts for transporting prisoners.

The account, certified and attested as provided in the preceding section, shall be subject to audit by the comptroller, and be paid out of the treasury, unless otherwise provided.

§ 605. Prisoners sentenced at one session of court to be transported at same time.

All the prisoners who shall be sentenced to imprisonment in the same state prison, at one session of a criminal court, shall be transported at the same time, unless said court shall expressly direct otherwise.

§ 605-a. Transportation of female inmates.

Whenever any female inmate is conveyed to an institution in the state department of correction pursuant to sentence or commitment, such female inmate shall be accompanied by at least one female officer.

Added by L. 1970, Ch. 476.

§ 606. Payment of costs for prosecution of inmates.

1. When an inmate of an institution of the department is alleged to have committed an offense while an inmate of such institution, the state shall pay all reasonable costs for the prosecution of such offense, including but not limited to, costs for: a grand jury impaneled to hear and examine evidence of such offense, petit jurors, witnesses, the defense of any inmate financially unable to obtain counsel in accordance with the provisions of the county law, the district attorney, the costs of the sheriff and the appointment of additional court attendants, officers, or other judicial personnel.

2. It shall be the duty of the board of supervisors of any county wherein such prosecution occurs to cause a sworn statement of all costs to be forwarded to the department. Upon certification by the department that such costs as authorized by this statute have been incurred, the department shall forward the proper vouchers to the state comptroller. It shall be the duty of the comptroller to examine such statement and to correct same by striking therefrom any and all items which are not authorized pursuant to the provisions of this section and after correcting such statement, the comptroller shall draw his warrant

for the amount of any such costs in favor of the appropriate county treasurer, which sum shall be paid to said county treasurer out of any moneys appropriated therefor.

3. The department shall, after consultation with the director of the budget promulgate rules and regulations to carry out the provisions of this section.

Added by L. 1985, Ch. 824, eff. Sept. 1, 1985.

§ 610. Freedom of worship.

1. All persons who may have been or may hereafter be committed to or taken charge of by any of the institutions mentioned in this section, are hereby declared to be and entitled to the free exercise and enjoyment of religious profession and worship, without discrimination or preference.

2. This section shall be deemed to apply to every incorporated or unincorporated society for the reformation of its inmates, as well as houses of refuge, penitentiaries, protectories, reformatories or other correctional institutions, continuing to receive for its use, either public moneys, or a per capita sum from any municipality for the support of inmates.

3. The rules and regulations established for the government of the institutions mentioned in this section shall recognize the right of the inmates to the free exercise of their religious belief, and to worship God according to the dictates of their consciences, including baptism by immersion, in accordance with the provisions of the constitution; and shall allow religious services on Sunday and for private ministration to the inmates in such manner as may best carry into effect the spirit and intent of this section and be consistent with the proper discipline and management of the institution; and the inmates of such institutions shall be allowed such religious services and spiritual advice and spiritual ministration from some recognized clergyman of the denomination or church which said inmates may respectively prefer to which they may have belonged prior to their being confined in such institutions; but if any of such inmates shall be minors under the age of sixteen years, then such services, advice and spiritual ministration shall be allowed in accordance with the methods and rites of the particular denomination or church which the parents or guardians of such minors may select; such services to be held and such advice and ministration to be given within the buildings or grounds, whenever possible, where the inmates are required by law to be confined, in such manner and at such hours as will be in harmony, as aforesaid, with the discipline and the rules and regulations of the institution and secure to such inmates free exercise of their religious beliefs in accordance with the provisions of this section. In case of a violation of any of the provisions of this section any person feeling himself aggrieved thereby may institute

proceedings in the supreme court of the district where such institution is situated, which is hereby authorized and empowered to enforce the provisions of this section.

Amended by L. 1969, Ch. 268.

ANNOTATIONS

Generally.—Denial of petitioner's grievance charging religious discrimination was arbitrary and capricious, and "although religious freedom within a prison cannot be unfettered," petitioner established that he was not permitted to practice his Shi'a Muslim faith and that the only services provided and available to him were administered by the Sunni Muslim chaplain whose teaching were inconsistent with and antagonistic to the Shi'a Muslim faith. Cancel v. Goord, 278 A.D.2d 321, 717 N.Y.S.2d 610 (2d Dept. 2000), *appeal denied,* 96 N.Y.2d 707 (2001).

Constitutional restrictions on observer of Hasidic Judaism.—Court agreed with hospital's assessment that the defendant, an observer of Hasidic Judaism who had previously escaped, was still an escape risk, was diagnosed with a dangerous mental disorder, posed a danger to himself and others, and should be kept in the secure facility. Accordingly, court found that restrictions on defendant's ability to practice his religion were not unconstitutional. People *ex rel.* Abraham J. v. Sarkis, 175 Misc. 2d 433, 668 N.Y.S.2d 435 (Sup. Ct. Kings Co. 1997).

Requiring religious celebrations to be practiced in cell; permitting non-Muslims to use mosque.—Prison policies requiring Muslim inmates to practice the Salat in their cells and permitting non-Muslim inmates and employees to use the mosque at the correctional facility did not violate the Muslim inmates' right to religious freedom under the New York Constitution. Allen v. Coombe, 225 A.D.2d 1084, 639 N.Y.S.2d 197 (4th Dept. 1996).

Nude shower; constitutional.—A requirement that inmates shower in the nude is valid for hygienic reasons and does not violate the inmate's freedom to worship even though he was a Sunni Moslem which religion requires that the genitals be covered when in a communal bath. Shahid v. Coughlin, 83 A.D.2d 25, 444 N.Y.S.2d 264 (3d Dept. 1981).

§ 611. Births to inmates of correctional institutions and care of children of inmates of correctional institutions.

1. If a woman confined in any institution under the control of the state department of correction, or in any penitentiary or jail be pregnant and about to give birth to a child, the officer in charge of such institution, a reasonable time before the anticipated birth of such child, shall cause such woman to be removed from such institution and provided with comfortable accommodations, maintenance and medical care elsewhere, under such supervision and safeguards to prevent her escape from custody as he may determine, and subject to her return to such institution as soon after the birth of her child as the state of her health will permit. If such woman is confined in a penitentiary or jail, the expense of such accommodation, maintenance and medical care shall be paid by such woman or her relatives or from any available funds of the penitentiary or jail and if not available from such sources, shall be a charge upon the county, city or town in which is located the court from which such inmate was committed to such penitentiary or jail. If such woman is confined in any institution under the control of the state department of correction, the expense of

such accommodation, maintenance and medical care shall be paid by such woman or her relatives and if not available from such sources, such maintenance and medical care shall be paid by the state. In cases where payment of such accommodations, maintenance and medical care is assumed by the county, city or town from which such inmate was committed the pay or shall make payment by issuing payment instrument in favor of the agency or individual that provided such accommodations and services, after certification has been made by the head of the institution to which the inmate was legally confined, that the charges for such accommodations, maintenance and medical care were necessary and are just, and that the institution has no available funds for such purpose.

2. A child so born may be returned with its mother to the correctional institution in which the mother is confined unless the chief medical officer of the correctional institution shall certify that the mother is physically unfit to care for the child, in which case the statement of the said medical officer shall be final. A child may remain in the correctional institution with its mother for such period as seems desirable for the welfare of such child, but not after it is one year of age, provided, however, if the mother is in a state reformatory and is to be paroled shortly after the child becomes one year of age, such child may remain at the state reformatory until its mother is paroled, but in no case after the child is eighteen months old. The officer in charge of such institution may cause a child cared for therein with its mother to be removed from the institution at any time before the child is one year of age. He shall make provision for a child removed from the institution without its mother or a child born to a woman inmate who is not returned to the institution with its mother as hereinafter provided. He may, upon proof being furnished by the father or other relatives of their ability to properly care for and maintain such child, give the child into the care and custody of such father or other relatives, who shall thereafter maintain the same at their own expense. If it shall appear that such father or other relatives are unable to properly care for and maintain such child, such officer shall place the child in the care of the commissioner of public welfare or other officer or board exercising in relation to children the power of a commissioner of public welfare of the county from which such inmate was committed as a charge upon such county. The officer in charge of the correctional institution shall send to such commissioner, officer or board a report of all information available in regard to the mother and the child. Such commissioner of public welfare or other officer or board shall care for or place out such child as provided by law in the case of a child becoming dependent upon the county.

3. If any woman, committed to any such correctional institution at the time of such commitment is the mother of a nursing child in her care

under one year of age, such child may accompany her to such institution if she is physically fit to have the care of such child, subject to the provisions of subdivision two of this section. If any woman committed to any such institution at the time of such commitment is the mother of and has under her exclusive care a child more than one year of age the justice or magistrate committing such woman shall refer such child to the commissioner of public welfare or other officer or board exercising in relation to children the power of a commissioner of public welfare of the county from which the woman is committed to be cared for as provided by law in the case of a child becoming dependent upon the county.

Amended by L. 1954, Ch. 222; L. 1963, Ch. 168; L. 1968, Ch. 758.

ANNOTATION

Incarceration of mother and infant.—An incarcerated mother is entitled to take her child under one-year-old to live in jail with her until the child attains one year, provided that the mother is physically able to care for the child. If the chief medical officer has determined that the mother is physically capable of caring for the child, the sheriff only has discretion to remove the child if the incarceration endangers its welfare. Apgar v. Beauter, 75 Misc. 2d 439, 347 N.Y.S.2d 872 (Sup. Ct. Tioga Co. 1973).

§ 611-a. Commitments to county or regional correctional institutions.

1. Any commitment to a county or regional correctional institution pursuant to subdivision two of section 70.20 of the penal law shall be deemed a commitment to the county jail, workhouse or penitentiary, or to a penitentiary outside the county in the case of an agreement pursuant to section four hundred eighty of this chapter, as the case may be, and the order of commitment shall specify the institution in which the sentence is to be served.

2. Nothing in this section shall affect or limit any other provision of law with respect to transfers of persons so committed.

Renumbered former § 802 as § 611-a by L. 1970, Ch. 476.

§ 612. United States prisoners.

A sheriff must receive into his jail and keep a prisoner, committed to the same, by virtue of civil process issued by a court of record, instituted under the authority of the United States, until he is discharged by the due course of the laws of the United States, in the same manner as if he was committed by virtue of a mandate in a civil action, issued from a court of the state. A sheriff or jailer, to whose jail a civil prisoner is committed, as prescribed herein, is answerable for his safe keeping in the courts of the United States, according to the laws thereof.

§ 613. Conveyance of prisoner after arrest.

A sheriff or other officer, who has lawfully arrested a civil prisoner, may convey his prisoner through one or more other counties, in the ordinary route of travel, from the place where the prisoner was arrested, to the place where he is to be delivered or confined.

§ 614. Care and support of civil prisoner.

A person arrested, by virtue of an order of arrest, in an action or special proceeding brought in a court of record; or of an execution issued upon a judgment rendered in a court of record; or surrendered in exoneration of his bail; must be safely kept in custody, in the manner prescribed by law, and, except as herein otherwise provided, at his own expense, until he satisfies the judgment rendered against him, or is discharged according to law. In any county, if a prisoner, actually confined in jail, makes oath before the sheriff, jailer, or deputy-jailer, that he is unable to support himself during his imprisonment, his support is a county charge.

Amended by L. 1952, Ch. 596.

§ 618. Duties of state correctional institutions, penitentiaries, county jails and reformatories.

1. It shall also be the duty of the commissioner to continue to make or have impressions made of the finger and thumbprints of all inmates in any of the institutions under the jurisdiction of the department; in his discretion, to cause said inmates to be measured and described; and to cause to be obtained and recorded, so far as possible, modus operandi statements of said inmates. The commissioner shall cause such impressions and measurements of persons confined in state correctional institutions to be made by a person or persons in the official service of the state in conformity with the system now in use in the division of criminal justice services, and shall prescribe rules and regulations for obtaining and recording such modus operandi statements, and for keeping accurate records of such impressions, measurements and statements, in the offices of such institutions.

2. It is hereby made the duty of the officials having charge of all the penitentiaries and county jails in the state to cause inmates confined therein under sentence for any crime to be measured and described and the fingerprint impressions of such inmates to be made according to the rules and methods prescribed by the commissioner of criminal justice services. It shall also be the duty of such officials in charge of such institutions to procure so far as possible modus operandi statements from all such prisoners. And it shall be the duty of such officials to cause duplicate records

of such measurements, impressions and statements to be made, two copies to be transmitted to the division of criminal justice services within twenty-four hours following the time of the reception of such inmates in said institutions.

3. There shall continue to be maintained in the various state prisons, penitentiaries, reformatories and other penal institutions of the state during the time that prisoners are therein confined complete individual case histories of each prisoner so confined.

Amended by L. 1973, Ch. 108; L. 1974, Ch. 654; L. 1993, Ch. 413.

§ 619. Cooperation with authorized agencies of the department of social services.

It shall be the duty of an official of any institution under the jurisdiction of the commissioner of correctional services to cooperate with an authorized agency of the department of social services in making suitable arrangements for an inmate confined therein to visit with his or her child pursuant to subdivision seven of section three hundred eighty-four-b of the social services law.

Added by L. 1983, Ch. 911.

§ 620. Service of papers in civil judicial proceedings upon a prisoner.

An officer to whom a paper in a civil judicial proceeding is delivered, in compliance with the requirements for service of the paper upon a prisoner in his custody, shall note thereon the date and time of its receipt and forthwith deliver it to the prisoner. The officer is liable to the prisoner for any damages resulting from a violation of this section.

Added by L. 1962, Ch. 310.

ANNOTATION

Alternative method of service.—Section 620 merely authorizes alternative method of service on a prisoner; thus, service of process was effective when copy of summons and complaint was delivered to defendant's daughter, despite the fact that defendant was in prison at the time of such service. Defendant listed daughter's address on defendant's driver's license and kept belongings there. Montes v. Seda, 208 A.D.2d 388, 626 N.Y.S.2d 61 (1st Dept. 1995).

§ 621. Interstate cooperation with law enforcement officers and agencies of other states and the federal government.

1. All law enforcement officers and agencies of this state and its subdivisions, including the division of criminal justice services, are hereby authorized to cooperate with agencies of other states and of the United States, having similar powers, to develop and carry on a complete interstate, national and international system of criminal identification and investigation, and to obtain and furnish, or to assist in obtaining and furnishing, any information from and to a law enforcement officer or agency of another jurisdiction to assist in the conduct of an investigation into any criminal matter or for use in a criminal prosecution.

2. Nothing in this section shall be construed to authorize or empower any law enforcement officer or agency to engage in any activity or type of work for which he or it does not otherwise have authority in conducting investigations or prosecutions in connection with crimes alleged to have been committed within this state, but the obtaining and furnishing of information pursuant to this section shall be deemed a part of the regular functions of the officer or agency obtaining and furnishing the same.

Added by L. 1963, Ch. 577; **Amended** by L. 1992, Ch. 232, eff. June 30, 1992, amending subd. 1.

CORR. L.

ARTICLE 22-A—PRISONER FURLOUGHS

[Article 22-A shall expire and be deemed repealed on Sept. 1, 2007, pursuant to L. 1997, Ch. 435, § 47, as amended.]

Section

§ 630. Applicability. [*Effective until Sept. 1, 2007.*]

This article shall be applicable only to prisoners sentenced to institutions operated by a department of correction in cities having a population of one million or more or by a county which elects to have this article apply thereto.

Added by L. 1972, Ch. 886; **Amended** by L. 1973, Ch. 622; L. 1974, Ch. 299; L. 1976, Ch. 473; L. 1977, Ch. 691; L. 1978, Ch. 691; L. 1979, Ch. 485; L. 1980, Ch. 296; L. 1981, Ch. 495; L. 1982, Ch. 137, eff. Sept. 1, 1982; L. 1983, Ch. 519; L. 1984, Ch. 983; L. 1985, Ch. 573; L. 1986, Ch. 395, eff. Sept. 1, 1986; L. 1987, Ch. 261, effective July 13, 1987; L. 1992, Ch. 55, eff, Apr. 10, 1992, extending the expiration due to Sept.1, 1994; L. 1994, Ch. 61, § 9, extending expiration date to Sept. 1, 1995; L. 1995, Ch. 3 § 47, extending expiration date to Sept. 1, 1997; L. 1997, Ch. 435, § 47, extending expiration date to Sept. 1, 1999; L. 1999, Ch. 452, § 1, extending expiration date to Sept. 1, 2001, eff. Sept. 1, 1999; L. 2001, Ch. 95, §3, eff. July 13, 2001, extending expiration date to Sept. 1, 2003; L. 2003, Ch. 16, § 3, eff. Mar. 31, 2003, extending expiration date to Sept. 1, 2005; L. 2005, Ch. 56, Part D, § 3, eff. Apr. 1, 2005, extending expiration date to Sept. 1, 2007.

§ 631. Definitions. [*Effective until Sept. 1, 2007.*]

As used in this article the following terms shall have the following meanings:

1. "Institution" means any institution under the jurisdiction of the commissioner of correction in any city having a population of one million or more or of a county which elects to have this article apply thereto.

2. "Eligible inmate" means a person confined in a city prison or reformatory in a city having a population of one million or more or in a county jail and penitentiaries of a county which elects to have this article apply thereto where a furlough program has been established who is sentenced to a definite period of six months or more or to a reformatory sentence of imprisonment and has served a minimum of six months of any such sentence.

3. "Furlough program" means a program under which eligible inmates may be granted the privilege of leaving the premises of a prison for a period not exceeding seventy-two hours for the purpose of seeking employment, maintaining family ties, solving family problems, to undergo surgery or to receive medical treatment or dental treatment not available in the correctional institution, or for any matter necessary to the furtherance of any such purposes.

4. "Extended bounds of confinement" means the area in which an inmate participating in a furlough program may travel, the routes he is permitted to use, the places he is authorized to visit, and the hours, days, or specially defined period during which he is permitted to be absent from the premises of the institution. An extension of limits shall be under such prescribed conditions as the commissioner deems necessary. Such extension of limits may be withdrawn at any time.

5. "Furlough committee" means the body of persons which may include members of the public, appointed pursuant to regulations promulgated by the commissioner for the purposes of formulating, modifying and revoking furlough programs at an institution.

6. "Warden" means the person in charge of an institution by whatever title he may be known.

7. "Commissioner" means the commissioner of correction in a city having a population of one million or more or that official having similar duties in any county which elects to have this article apply thereto, by whatever title he may be known.

8. "Department" means the applicable department of correction or, where no such department exists, the office of the commissioner.

Added by L. 1972, Ch. 886; **Amended** by L. 1973, Chs. 411, 622; L. 1974, Ch. 299; L. 1976, Ch. 473; L. 1977, Ch. 691; L. 1978, Ch. 691; L. 1979, Ch. 485; L. 1980, Ch. 296; L. 1981, Ch. 495; L. 1982, Ch. 137; L. 1983, Ch. 519; L. 1984, Ch. 983; L. 1985, Ch. 573; L. 1986, Ch. 395, eff. Sept. 1, 1986; L. 1987. Ch. 261, effective July 13, 1987; L. 1992, Ch. 55, eff. Apr. 10, 1992, extending the expiration date to Sept. 1, 1994; L. 1994, Ch. 61, § 9, extending expiration date to Sept. 1, 1995; L. 1995, Ch. 3, § 47, extending expiration date to Sept. 1, 1997; L. 1997, Ch. 435, § 47, extending expiration date to Sept. 1, 1999; L. 1999, Ch. 452, § 1, extending expiration date to Sept. 1, 2001, eff. Sept. 1, 1999; L. 2001, Ch. 95, §3, eff. July 13, 2001, extending expiration date to Sept. 1, 2003; L. 2003, Ch. 16, § 3, eff. Mar. 31, 2003, extending the expiration date to Sept. 1, 2005; L. 2005, Ch. 56, Part D, § 3, eff. Apr. 1, 2005, extending expiration date to Sept. 1, 2007.

ANNOTATIONS

Eligibility.—Application for a furlough made two months after prisoner commenced serving his sentence was premature and properly denied. People *ex rel.* Dioguardi v. Warden, 80 Misc. 2d 972, 365 N.Y.S.2d 446 (Sup. Ct. Bronx Co. 1975).

Refusal.—A refusal to release a prisoner on furlough is not judicially reviewable absent a violation of a positive statutory requirement, or a denial or any constitutional rights. Rosati v. Grenis, 50 A.D.2d 818, 376 N.Y.S.2d 570 (2d Dept. 1975).

§ 632. Establishment of a furlough program. [*Effective until Sept. 1, 2007.*]

1. The commissioner shall designate, in the rules and regulations of the department, appropriate employees or an appropriate unit of the department, to be responsible for (a) securing education, on-the-job training and employment opportunities for inmates who are eligible to participate in a furlough program and (b) supervising inmates during their participation in a furlough program outside the premises of the institution.

Added by L. 1972, Ch. 886; **Amended** by L. 1974, Ch. 299; L. 1976, Ch. 473; L. 1977, Ch. 691; L. 1978, Ch. 691; L. 1979, Ch. 485; L. 1980, Ch. 296; L. 1981, Ch. 495; L. 1982, Ch. 137; L. 1983, Ch. 519; L. 1984, Ch. 983; L. 1985, Ch. 573; L. 1986, Ch. 395, eff. Sept. 1, 1986; L. 1987, Ch. 261, effective July 13, 1987; L. 1992, Ch. 55, eff. Apr. 10, 1992, extending expiration date to September 1, 1994; L. 1994, Ch. 61, § 9, extending expiration date to Sept. 1, 1995; L. 1995, Ch. 3, § 47, extending expiration date to Sept. 1, 1997; L. 1997, Ch. 435, § 47, extending expiration date to Sept. 1, 1999; L. 1999, Ch. 452, § 1, extending expiration date to Sept. 1, 2001, eff. Sept. 1, 1999; L. 2001, Ch. 95, §3, eff. July 13, 2001, extending expiration date to Sept. 1, 2003; L. 2003, Ch. 16, § 3, eff. Mar. 31, 2003, extending expiration date to Sept. 1, 2005; L. 2005, Ch. 56, Part D, § 3, eff. Apr. 1, 2005, extending expiration date to Sept. 1, 2007.

§ 633. Procedure for furlough release of eligible inmates. [*Effective until Sept. 1, 2007.*]

1. A person confined in a city prison or a county jail and penitentiaries of a county which elects to have this article apply thereto who is, or who within thirty days will become, an eligible inmate, may make application to the furlough release committee of the institution for permission to participate in a furlough program.

2. Any eligible inmate may make application to the furlough committee for leave of absence provided, however, that in exigent circumstances such application may be made directly to the warden of the institution and the warden may exercise all of the powers of the furlough committee subject, however, to any limitations or requirements set forth in the rules and regulations of the department and subject further to the discretion of the commissioner.

3. If the furlough committee determines that a furlough program for the applicant is consistent with the safety of the community, is in the best interests of rehabilitation of the applicant, and is consistent with the rules and regulations of the department, the committee, with the assistance of the employees designated by the commissioner pursuant to section six hundred thirty-two of this chapter, shall develop a suitable furlough program for the applicant.

4. The committee shall then prepare a memorandum setting forth the details of the furlough program including the extended bounds of confinement and any other matter required by the rules and regulations of the department. Such memorandum shall be transmitted to the warden who may approve or reject the program. If the warden approves the program, he shall indicate such approval in writing by signing the memorandum. If the warden rejects the program, such decision shall be reviewed by the commissioner.

5. In order for the applicant to accept the furlough program, he shall agree to be bound by all the terms and conditions thereof and shall indicate such agreement by signing the memorandum of the program immediately below a statement reading as follows:

"I accept the foregoing program and agree to be bound by the terms and conditions thereof. I understand I will be under the supervision of the department while I am away from the premises of the institution and I agree to comply with the instructions of any employee of the department assigned to supervise me. I will carry a copy of this memorandum on my person at all times while I am away from the premises of the institution and I will exhibit it to any peace officer or police officer upon his request. I understand that my participation in the program is a privilege which may be revoked at any time, and that if I violate any provision of the program I may be taken into custody by any peace officer or police officer and I will be subject to disciplinary procedures. I further understand that if I intentionally fail to return to the institution at or before the time specified in the memorandum I may be found guilty of a misdemeanor."

6. After approving the program of furlough, the warden may then permit an eligible inmate who has accepted such program to go outside the premises of the institution within the limits of the extended bounds of confinement described in the memorandum; provided, however, that no such permission shall become effective in the case of a furlough program prior to the time at which the person to be released becomes an eligible inmate.

7. Participation in a furlough release program shall be a privilege. Nothing contained in this article may be construed to confer upon any inmate the right to participate, or to continue to participate in a furlough program. The warden of the institution may at any time, and upon recommendation of the furlough committee or of the commissioner, revoke any inmate's privilege to participate in a program of furlough.

Added by L. 1972, Ch. 886; **Amended** by L. 1974, Ch. 299; L. 1976, Ch. 473; L. 1977, Ch. 691; L. 1978, Ch. 691; L. 1979, Ch. 485; L. 1980, Ch. 296; L. 1981, Ch. 495; L. 1982, Ch. 137; L. 1983, Ch. 519; L. 1984, Ch. 983; L. 1985, Ch. 573, eff. Sept. 1, 1985; L. 1986, Ch. 395, eff. Sept. 1, 1986; L. 1987, Ch. 261, effective July 13, 1987; L. 1992, Ch. 55, eff. Apr. 10, 1992, extending expiration date; L. 1994, Ch. 61, § 9, extending expiration date; L. 1995, Ch. 3, § 47, extending expiration date; L. 1997, Ch. 435, § 47, extending expiration date; L. 1999, Ch. 452, § 1, extending expiration date, eff. Sept. 1, 1999; L. 2001, Ch. 95, § 3, extending expiration date, eff. July 13, 2001; L. 2003, Ch. 16, eff. March 31, 2003, extending expiration date to Sept. 1, 2005; L. 2005, Ch. 56, Part D, § 3, eff. Apr. 1, 2005, extending expiration date to Sept. 1, 2007.

§ 634. Conduct of inmates participating in furlough program. [*Effective until Sept. 1, 2007.*]

1. An inmate who is permitted to leave the premises of an institution to participate in a furlough program shall have on his person a copy of the memorandum of that program as signed by the warden of the institution and shall exhibit such copy to any peace officer or police officer upon request of such officer.

2. If the inmate violates any provision of the program, or any rule, or regulation promulgated by the commissioner for conduct of inmates participating in furlough programs, he shall be subject to disciplinary measures to the same extent as if he violated a rule or regulation of the commissioner for conduct of inmates within the premises of the institution.

3. The provisions of this section relating to good behavior of inmates while participating in furlough programs outside the premises of institutions, and such allowances may be granted, withheld, forfeited or cancelled in whole or part for behavior outside the premises of an institution to the same extent and in the same manner as is provided for behavior of inmates within the premises of the institutions.

4. An inmate who is in violation of the provisions of his furlough program may be taken into custody by any peace officer or police officer and, in such event the inmate shall be returned forthwith to the institution that released him. In any case where the institution is in a county other than the one in which the inmate is apprehended, the officer may deliver the inmate to the nearest institution, jail or lockup and it shall be the duty of the person in charge of said facility to hold such inmate securely until such time as he is delivered into the custody of an officer of the institution from which he was released. Upon delivering the inmate to an institution, jail or lockup, other than the one from which he was released, the officer who apprehended the inmate shall forthwith notify the warden of the institution from which the inmate was released and it shall be the duty of the warden to effect the expeditious return of the inmate to the institution.

Added by L. 1972, Ch. 886; **Amended** by L. 1973, Ch. 622; L. 1974, Ch. 299; L. 1976, Ch. 473; L. 1977, Ch. 691; L. 1978, Ch. 691; L. 1979, Ch. 485; L. 1980, Chs. 296, 843; L. 1981, Ch. 495; L. 1982, Ch. 137, eff. Sept. 1, 1982; L. 1983, Ch. 519; L. 1984, Ch. 983; L. 1985, Ch. 573; L. 1986, Ch. 395, eff. Sept. 1, 1986; L. 1987, Ch. 261, effectively July 13, 1987; L. 1992, Ch. 55, eff. Apr. 10, 1992, extending the expiration date to Sept. 1, 1994; L. 1994, Ch. 61, § 9, extending expiration date to Sept. 1, 1995; L. 1995, Ch. 3, § 47, extending expiration date to Sept. 1, 1997; L. 1997, Ch. 435, § 47, extending expiration date to Sept. 1, 1999; L. 1999, Ch. 452, § 1, extending expiration date to Sept. 1, 2001, eff. Sept. 1, 1999; L. 2001, Ch. 95, §3, eff. July 13, 2001, extending expiration date to Sept. 1, 2003; L. 2003, Ch. 16, § 3, eff. Mar. 31, 2003, extending expiration date to Sept. 1, 2005; L. 2005, Ch. 56, Part D, § 3, eff. Apr. 1, 2005, extending expiration date to Sept. 1, 2007.

ARTICLE 22-B—THE DEATH PENALTY

[L. 1995, Ch. 1, § 32, repealed former Art. 22-B in its entirety, eff. Sept. 1, 1995, and added the following new version of Art. 22-B, also eff. Sept. 1, 1995.]

§ 650. Warrant for execution of death sentence.

1. When a person is sentenced to the punishment of death, the justice or judge who presided at the sentencing proceeding, or if that justice or judge is unavailable for any reason, then any justice of the supreme court of the department in which the defendant was sentenced, must, within seven days, make out, sign and deliver to the sheriff of the county, a warrant directed to the commissioner or to the superintendent of an institution in the department designated by the commissioner. Such warrant shall state the conviction and sentence, appoint a week on which the sentence shall be executed, and command the commissioner to execute the sentence within that week. In counties within the city of New York, or in the county of Westchester, such warrant shall be made out as aforesaid, signed and delivered to the commissioner of correction of such city or county.

2. If the execution of the sentence shall be delayed while the conviction or sentence is being appealed, a justice or judge authorized to act pursuant to subdivision one of this section, at the conclusion of the state appellate process, if the conviction or sentence is not set aside, must, within seven days, make out, sign and deliver another warrant as provided in subdivision one of this section. If the execution of the sentence on the date appointed is delayed by any other cause, the justice or judge shall, as soon as such cause ceases to exist, make out, sign and deliver another warrant.

Added by L. 1995, Ch. 1, § 32, eff. Sept. 1, 1995.

§ 651. Time of execution.

The week of execution appointed in the warrant shall be not less than thirty days and not more than sixty days after the issuance of the warrant. The date of execution within said week shall be left to the discretion of the commissioner, but the date and hour of the execution shall be announced publicly no later than seven days prior to said execution.

Added by L. 1995, Ch. 1, § 32, eff. Sept. 1, 1995.

§ 652. Delivery of warrant and confinement.

1. Within ten days after the issuance of a warrant as provided in section six hundred fifty of this article, the sheriff or the commissioner of correction, if within the city of New York or county of Westchester, must deliver the warrant and the person sentenced, if that person is not already in the custody of the department, to the department or to the superintendent of the state institution designated by the commissioner. Upon the issuance of the warrant the court shall cause a copy to be personally delivered to the convicted person and shall send a copy of the warrant to the convicted person's last attorney of record.

2. From the time of the delivery of the warrant and until the imposition of the punishment of death upon the convicted person, unless discharged from the sentence, such person may, in the commissioner's discretion, either be kept isolated from the general prison population in a designated institution or confined as otherwise provided by law. The commissioner, in his discretion, may determine that the safety and security of the facility, or of the inmate population, or of the staff, or of the inmate, would not be jeopardized by the inmate's confinement within the general prison population.

3. The commissioner may promulgate rules

and regulations concerning visitation of inmates sentenced to death. Such rules and regulations may provide that inmates sentenced to death are subject to different visitation policies and procedures than inmates who are not sentenced to death.

Added by L. 1995, Ch. 1, § 32, eff. Sept. 1, 1995.

§ 653. Transmittal of record to the governor.

Within a reasonable time following the issuance of the warrant as provided in section six hundred fifty of this article, the clerk of the court in the county in which the person was sentenced to death shall transmit to the governor a statement of conviction and sentence, and the transcripts of both the trial and the sentencing proceedings, including, to the extent practicable, any exhibits introduced therein.

Added by L. 1995, Ch. 1, § 32, eff. Sept. 1, 1995.

§ 654. Governor may consult.

The governor is authorized to request the opinion of the attorney general, the district attorney, and the convicted person's counsel, or any of them, as to whether the execution of the person should be reprieved or suspended.

Added by L. 1995, Ch. 1, § 32, eff. Sept. 1, 1995.

§ 655. Governor only to reprieve.

No judge, court, or officer, other than the governor, can reprieve the execution of a person sentenced to death. This section does not apply to a stay authorized by law.

Added by L. 1995, Ch. 1, § 32, eff. Sept. 1, 1995.

§ 656. Proceeding when person under sentence of death may be incompetent.

1. The state may not execute an inmate who is incompetent. An inmate is "incompetent" when, as a result of mental disease or defect, he lacks the mental capacity to understand the nature and effect of the death penalty and why it is to be carried out.

2. Upon the filing of a petition in the supreme court in either the county in which an inmate sentenced to death is confined or in the county in which the inmate was prosecuted alleging that the inmate is incompetent, the court shall issue an order staying the execution if and to the extent a stay is necessary to permit determination of the petition. Upon application of either the inmate's counsel or the district attorney the petition may be transferred to the court in which the inmate was convicted unless such transfer would be unduly burdensome or impracticable. Promptly upon filing the petition, the court shall appoint a commission of three psychiatric examiners,

hereinafter referred to as "the psychiatric commissioners," to inquire into the inmate's competence. The psychiatric commissioners shall be impartial and must be qualified psychiatrists or certified psychologists. Before commencing an inquiry, the psychiatric commissioners must take the oath prescribed in rule forty-three hundred fifteen of the civil practice law and rules to be taken by referees. The petition may be filed by the inmate, the inmate's counsel, an employee of the department, the inmate's legal guardian, a member of such inmate's immediate family or, in the event that the inmate does not have regular contact with a member of his or her immediate family, a bona fide friend who has maintained regular contact with the inmate. The petition must be accompanied by an affidavit of at least one qualified psychiatrist or certified psychologist who, based at least in part on personal examination, attests that in the psychiatrist's or psychologist's professional opinion the inmate is incompetent and lists the pertinent facts therefor. For purposes of this section the terms "qualified psychiatrist" and "certified psychologist" have the meaning set forth in section 730.10 of the criminal procedure law.

3. The petition shall be served upon either the district attorney who prosecuted the inmate or upon the district attorney for the county in which the inmate is confined. If the petition is served upon the district attorney for the county in which the inmate is confined, the court shall promptly notify the district attorney who prosecuted the inmate. Immediately upon appointing the psychiatric commissioners, the court shall direct that an examination of the convicted person promptly take place with all three of the psychiatric commissioners present at the same time. The court shall also direct, upon application of the inmate or the district attorney, that the inmate be examined by a qualified psychiatrist or certified psychologist designated by the inmate or the district attorney. Counsel for the inmate and the district attorney shall have the right to be present at each such examination. Upon the filing of a petition pursuant to subdivision two of this section, if the inmate does not have counsel and is financially unable to obtain counsel the court shall appoint competent counsel experienced in the trial of criminal matters to represent the inmate.

4. The psychiatric commissioners must receive and consider evidence offered by the inmate's counsel and the district attorney, including written submissions, testimony and expert psychiatric evidence. The proceeding before the psychiatric commissioners shall be conducted on the record but need not be conducted in accordance with the rules governing the admission of evidence at trial, but counsel for the people and the inmate shall have the right to cross-examine witnesses.

5. When the proceeding before the psychiatric commissioners has been concluded, they must

forthwith provide a transcript of the proceeding, together with their findings of fact, to the court with their opinion thereon. Unless impracticable, the psychiatric commissioners shall so act within sixty days from the filing of the petition. When an inmate shall be found incompetent by a majority of the psychiatric commissioners, the court shall accept such finding unless clearly erroneous, and promptly enter an order finding the inmate to be incompetent, staying the execution of the inmate and directing that the inmate be committed to a secure facility under the jurisdiction of the office of mental health if the inmate's incompetency is the result of mental illness. In all other cases, the inmate shall remain in the custody of the department. When an inmate is found competent by a majority of the psychiatric commissioners, the court shall accept such finding unless clearly erroneous, promptly enter an order finding the inmate to be competent and vacating any stay previously issued, and the court shall promptly inform the judge or justice who issued the warrant for the execution of the inmate of the court's finding. Upon being so informed, the judge or justice shall promptly issue a new warrant in accordance with subdivision two of section six hundred fifty of this article. Any other provision of law notwithstanding, no other review, judicial or otherwise, shall be available with respect to an order finding the inmate to be incompetent or competent. If the court rejects the finding of a majority of the psychiatric commissioners on the ground that it is clearly erroneous, the court shall appoint another commission to proceed as provided in this section.

6. When an inmate has been committed to a secure facility pursuant to this section, the inmate shall remain there until the facility administrator determines that the inmate may be competent. Upon so determining, the facility administrator shall promptly notify the court that entered the order finding the inmate to be incompetent, and the court shall promptly notify counsel and the district attorneys and appoint another commission to proceed as provided in this section.

7. The court shall allow reasonable fees to the psychiatric commissioners. The court shall allow reasonable fees for time spent in court and for time reasonably expended out of court to counsel appointed pursuant to this section. The court shall allow all reasonably necessary costs, including without limitation the costs attendant to fees for the examination of the inmate by a qualified psychiatrist or certified psychologist, incurred by the inmate and the district attorney in connection with a petition pursuant to this section. Each claim for compensation and reimbursement shall be supported by a sworn statement specifying the time expended, services rendered, expenses incurred and reimbursement or compensation applied for or received in the same case from any other source. All such fees and costs shall be a state charge payable on vouchers approved by the court after audit by and on the warrant of the comptroller.

8. When a petition has previously been filed and determined pursuant to this section, the court in which a subsequent petition is filed or to which a subsequent petition is transferred, shall not issue an order staying the execution of the inmate unless the court finds, after notice to the district attorney who prosecuted the inmate and after affording the district attorney a reasonable opportunity to be heard in writing, that there is reasonable cause to believe that the inmate is incompetent; provided, however, that the court may issue an order staying the execution of the inmate, to the extent a stay is necessary to afford the district attorney an opportunity to be heard and such reasonable cause determination to be made.

Added by L. 1995, Ch. 1, § 32, eff. Sept. 1, 1995.

§ 657. Proceeding when person under sentence of death is pregnant.

1. A sentence of death may not be carried out upon a woman while she is pregnant.

2. When the superintendent of the correctional facility where the inmate is confined is informed that reasonable grounds exist that a convicted person under sentence of death may be pregnant, the superintendent shall appoint a qualified physician to examine the convicted person and determine if she is pregnant.

3. Upon being informed by the superintendent that such convicted person is pregnant, the governor shall stay execution of the warrant to the extent necessary.

Added by L. 1995, Ch. 1, § 32, eff. Sept. 1, 1995.

§ 658. Death penalty inflicted by lethal injection.

The punishment of death shall be inflicted by lethal injection; that is, by the intravenous injection of a substance or substances in a lethal quantity into the body of a person convicted until such person is dead.

Added by L. 1995, Ch. 1, § 32, eff. Sept. 1, 1995.

§ 659. Facility.

The commissioner shall provide and maintain a suitable and efficient facility, enclosed from public view, within the confines of a designated correctional institution for the imposition of the punishment of death. That facility shall contain the apparatus and equipment necessary for the carrying out of executions by lethal injection.

Added by L. 1995, Ch. 1, § 32, eff. Sept. 1, 1995.

§ 660. Persons authorized to be present at execution.

1. The commissioner, any persons designated

CORR. L.

by the commissioner to act as execution technicians or otherwise to assist in the execution, including correction officers, and a licensed physician or physicians may be present at the execution. The commissioner shall also select and invite the presence, by at least three days' prior notice, of a justice of the supreme court, the counsel for the convicted person, the district attorney and the sheriff of the county where the conviction was had, together with six adult citizens. The names of the execution technician or technicians shall never be disclosed, notwithstanding any other provision of law to the contrary, including article six of the public officers law. The names of the six adult citizens who witnessed the execution shall not be disclosed until after the execution.

2. The commissioner shall, at the request of the person sentenced to death, authorize and permit two clergymen to be present at the execution.

3. The inmate sentenced to death may name four relatives or bona fide friends to witness the execution, and the commissioner shall authorize said named relatives or friends of the inmate to witness the execution unless the commissioner determines that the presence of any named relative or friend at the execution would pose a threat to the safety or security of the designated correctional institution. No person under eighteen years of age shall be permitted to witness any execution.

Added by L. 1995, Ch. 1, § 32, eff. Sept. 1, 1995.

§ 661. Examination of convicted person's body and certificate.

1. Immediately after the execution an examination of the body of the convicted person shall be made by the licenced physicians present at the execution and their report in writing stating the nature of the examination and occurrence of death, so made by them, shall be annexed to the certificate provided for in subdivision two of this section and filed therewith.

2. The commissioner shall prepare and sign a certificate setting forth the time and place of the execution and stating that the execution was conducted in conformity to the sentence of the court and the provisions of this article. The commissioner shall cause the certificate to be filed, within ten days after the execution, with the office of clerk of the court in which the conviction was had.

3. The commissioner may appoint a deputy with the department to execute the warrant of execution and to perform all other duties imposed upon the commissioner under this article.

Added by L. 1995, Ch. 1, § 32, eff. Sept. 1, 1995.

§ 662. Disposition of body.

1. Prior to the execution, the convicted person shall be given the opportunity to decide in writing to whom his or her body shall be delivered after the execution. The commissioner or his or her designee shall sign and authorize the convicted person's request if the request is not contrary to law. If the convicted person does not indicate to whom such person's body shall be delivered, or if the person's request is contrary to law, the commissioner may deliver the convicted person's body to a relative by blood or marriage or a bona fide friend. If the body is not claimed by a relative or bona fide friend within seven days after execution, the body shall be delivered to a duly authorized and incorporated pathological and anatomical association in the state, if requested by an authorized association.

2. If the body of the convicted person is not claimed by a relative, bona fide friend, or a duly authorized and incorporated pathological and anatomical association, the commissioner shall cause the body to be disposed of in the same manner as are bodies of prisoners dying in the institution. Notwithstanding any other provision of law, no autopsy shall be required for the body of an inmate upon whom a sentence of death has been carried out.

Added by L. 1995, Ch. 1, § 32, eff. Sept. 1, 1995.

ARTICLE 23—DISCRETIONARY RELIEF FROM FORFEITURES AND DISABILITIES AUTOMATICALLY IMPOSED BY LAW

§ 700. Definitions and rules of construction.

1. As used in this article the following terms have the following meanings:

(a) Eligible offender" shall mean a person who has been convicted of a crime or of an offense, but who has not been convicted more than once of a felony.

(b) "Felony" means a conviction of a felony in this state, or of an offense in any other jurisdiction for which a sentence to a term of imprisonment in excess of one year, or a sentence of death, was authorized.

(c) "Revocable sentence" means a suspended sentence or a sentence upon which execution was suspended pursuant to the penal law in effect prior to September first, nineteen hundred sixty-seven; or a sentence of probation or of conditional discharge imposed pursuant to the penal law in effect after September first, nineteen hundred sixty-seven.

2. For the purposes of this article the following rules of construction shall apply:

(a) Two or more convictions of felonies charged in separate counts of one indictment or information shall be deemed to be one conviction;

(b) Two or more convictions of felonies charged in two or more indictments or informations, filed in the same court prior to entry of judgment under any of them, shall be deemed to be one conviction; and

(c) A plea or a verdict of guilty upon which sentence or the execution of sentence has been suspended or upon which a sentence of probation, conditional discharge, or unconditional discharge has been imposed shall be deemed to be a conviction.

Amended by L. 1972, Ch. 342.

§ 701. Certificate of relief from disabilities.

1. A certificate of relief from disabilities may be granted as provided in this article to relieve an eligible offender of any forfeiture or disability, or to remove any bar to his employment, automatically imposed by law by reason of his conviction of the crime or of the offense specified therein. Such certificate may be limited to one or more enumerated forfeitures, disabilities or bars, or may relieve the eligible offender of all forfeitures, disabilities and bars. Provided, however, that no such certificate shall apply, or be construed so as to apply, to the right of such person to retain or to be eligible for public office.

2. [*Effective until Oct. 1, 2007, pursuant to L. 1993, Ch. 533, § 9, as amended.*] Notwithstanding any other provision of law, except subdivision five of section twenty-eight hundred six of the public health law or paragraph (b) of subdivision two of section eleven hundred ninety-three of the vehicle and traffic law, a conviction of a crime or of an offense specified in a certificate of relief from disabilities shall not cause automatic forfeiture of any license, permit, employment or franchise, including the right to register for or vote at an election, or automatic forfeiture of any other right or privilege, held by the eligible offender and covered by the certificate. Nor shall such conviction be deemed to be a conviction within the meaning of any provision of law that imposes, by reason of a conviction, a bar to any employment, a disability to exercise any right or a disability to apply for or to receive any license, permit or other authority or privilege, covered by the certificate; provided, however, a conviction for a second or subsequent violation of any subdivision of section eleven hundred ninety-two of the vehicle and traffic law committed within the preceding ten years shall impose a disability to apply for or receive an operator's license during the period provided in such law. A certificate of relief from a disability imposed pursuant to subparagraph (v) of paragraph b of subdivision two and paragraphs i and j of subdivision six of section five hundred ten of the vehicle and traffic law may only be issued upon a determination that compelling circumstances warrant such relief.

2. [*Effective Oct. 1, 2007, pursuant to L. 1993,*

Ch. 533, § 9, as amended.] Notwithstanding any other provision of law, except subdivision five of section twenty-eight hundred six of the public health law or paragraph (b) of subdivision two of section eleven hundred ninety-three of the vehicle and traffic law, a conviction of a crime or of an offense specified in a certificate of relief from disabilities shall not cause automatic forfeiture of any license, permit, employment or franchise, including the right to register for or vote at an election, or automatic forfeiture of any other right or privilege, held by the eligible offender and covered by the certificate. Nor shall such conviction be deemed to be a conviction within the meaning of any provision of law that imposes, by reason of a conviction, a bar to any employment, a disability to exercise any right or a disability to apply for or to receive any license, permit or other authority or privilege, covered by the certificate; provided, however, a conviction for a second or subsequent violation of any subdivision of section eleven hundred ninety-two of the vehicle and traffic law committed within the preceding ten years shall impose a disability to apply for or receive an operator's license during the period provided in such law.

3. A certificate of relief from disabilities shall not, however, in any way prevent any judicial, administrative, licensing or other body, board or authority from relying upon the conviction specified therein as the basis for the exercise of its discretionary power to suspend, revoke, refuse to issue or refuse to renew any license, permit or other authority or privilege.

Amended by L. 1972, Ch. 342; L. 1983, Ch. 584; L. 1985, Ch. 718, eff. Nov. 1, 1985, amended subd. 2 and applies to suspensions and revocations mandated to begin on and after Nov. 1, 1985; L. 1988, Ch. 47, eff. Nov. 1988, amended subd. 2; L. 1993, Ch. 533, adding the last sentence of subd. 2, is in effect until October 1, 1994; L. 1994, Ch. 286, § 1, eff. July 13, 1994, extending the expiration date to Oct. 1, 1995, of subd. 2; L. 1996, Ch. 309, § 78, extending expiration date of amendments to subd. 2 to Oct. 1, 1997; L. 1996, Ch. 400, § 1, extending effective date of amendments to subd. 2 to Oct. 1, 1997; L. 1997, Ch. 382, § 1, extending effective date of amendments to subd. 2 to Oct. 1, 1997; L. 1998, Ch. 58, Part E § 27, extending effective date of amendments to subd. 2 to Oct. 1, 1999, eff. Apr. 28, 1998, deemed in full force and effect Apr. 1, 1998; L. 1999, Ch. 512, extending effective date of amendments to subd. 2 to Oct. 1, 2000, eff. Sept. 28, 1998; L. 2000, Ch. 447, extending effective date of amendments to subd. 2 to Oct. 1, 2001, eff. Sept. 20, 2000; L. 2001, Ch. 242, § 1, extending effective date of amendments to subd. 2 to Oct. 1, 2002, eff. Sept. 4, 2001; L. 2002, Ch. 84, Part A, § 1, eff. May 29, 2002, extending effective date of amendments to subd. 2 to Oct. 1, 2003; L. 2003, Ch. 487, § 1, eff. Sept. 9, 2003, extending effective date of amendments to subd. 2 to Oct. 1, 2005; L. 2005, Ch. 60, Part D, § 1, eff. Apr. 1, 2005, extending effective date of amendments to subd. 2 to Oct. 1, 2007.

ANNOTATIONS

Effect on felony convictions on gun ownership.— Certificate of relief from all civil disabilities granted to two ex-convicts did not erase their felony convictions or remove the statutory bar to applying for or receiving a state pistol permit; however, they were allowed to possess guns that did not require a state permit like guns legally allowed for hunting and they could also take gun safety classes and apply for a hunting license. *In re* M. Alarie, 168 Misc. 2d 329, 643 N.Y.S.2d 926 (Monroe County Court 1996).

Requirement to disclose conviction to prospective employer.—Although unemployment compensation claimant received a certificate of relief from disabilities following her felony conviction, she still had to disclose the conviction to a prospective employer on an application; and the failure to disclose could result in the Unemployment Insurance Appeals Board disqualifying her from receiving benefits for misconduct based on the failure to disclose. Ghorab v. Sweeney, 219 A.D.2d 793, 631 N.Y.S.2d 786 (3d Dept. 1995).

Effect.—The fact that the petitioner received a certificate of relief from disabilities did not prevent the Public Health Council from exercising its power to revoke, limit or annual her license to establish a nursing home since the certificate does not eradicate or expunge the underlying conviction. Sturman v. Public Health Council, 58 A.D.2d 389, 397 N.Y.S.2d 168 (3d Dept. 1977).

—Issuance of a certificate of relief from disabilities does not preclude a licensing agency from exercising its discretion to revoke a license over which it has authority; it only precludes the automatic revocation of the license—in this case, petitioner's license to sell real estate. Plantone v. New York Dept. of State, 251 A.D.2d 1049, 674 N.Y.S.2d 560 (4th Dept. 1998).

—Certificate of Relief from Disabilities and Forfeitures did not preclude Commissioner of Health, State of New York, from acting to revoke plaintiff's certificate to own and operate nursing homes. Springer v. Whalen, 92 Misc. 2d 922, 402 N.Y.S.2d 131 (Sup. Ct. Albany Co. 1978), *aff'd*, 415 N.Y.S.2d 106.

Notary public.—The court did not have the discretion to order the deletion of "the right to retain or to be eligible for public office" from the certificate, issued to the defendant, in order that he could obtain the public office of Notary Public from the Secretary of State to work in the courts as a court reporter. People v. Olensky, 91 Misc. 2d 225, 397 N.Y.S.2d 565 (Sup. Ct. Queens Co. 1977).

Ability of licensing board to deny license for prior convictions.—Denying defendant's application for a target pistol license because defendant had prior convictions for false pretenses, criminal possession of a forged instrument, and conspiracy to defraud the United States by dealing in counterfeit securities was not arbitrary and capricious even though defendant had a certificate of relief from forged instrument conviction, a certificate of good conduct from the parole division, and a letter from the Department of Treasury restoring firearms privileges. Hines v. Kelly, 222 A.D.2d 277, 635 N.Y.S.2d 31 (1st Dept. 1995).

§ 702. Certificates of relief from disabilities issued by courts.

1. Any court of this state may, in its discretion, issue a certificate of relief from disabilities to an eligible offender for a conviction that occured* in such court, if the court either (a) imposed a revokable sentence or (b) imposed a sentence other than one executed by commitment to an institution under the jurisdiction of the state department of correctional services. Such certificate may be issued (i) at the time sentence is pronounced, in which case it may grant relief from forfeitures as well as from disabilities, or (ii) at any time thereafter, in which case it shall apply only to disabilities.

2. Such certificate shall not be issued by the court unless the court is satisfied that:

(a) The person to whom it is to be granted is an eligible offender, as defined in section seven hundred;

(b) The relief to be granted by the certificate is consistent with the rehabilitation of the eligible offender; and

(c) The relief to be granted by the certificate is consistent with the public interest.

3. Where a certificate of relief from disabilities is not issued at the time sentence is pronounced it shall only be issued thereafter upon verified application to the court. The court may, for the purpose of determining whether such certificate shall be issued, request its probation service to conduct an investigation of the applicant, or if the court has no probation service it may request the probation service of the county court for the county in which the court is located to conduct such investigation, or if there be no such probation service the court may request the state director of probation and correctional alternatives to arrange for such investigation. Any probation officer requested to make an investigation pursuant to this section shall prepare and submit to the court a written report in accordance with such request.

4. Where the court has imposed a revocable sentence and the certificate of relief from disabilities is issued prior to the expiration or termination of the time which the court may revoke such sentence, the certificate shall be deemed to be a temporary certificate until such time as the court's authority to revoke the sentence has expired or its terminated. While temporary, such certificate (a) may be revoked by the court for violation of the conditions of the sentence, and (b) shall be revoked by the court if it revokes the sentence and commits the person to an institution under the jurisdiction of the state department of correctional services. Any such revocation shall be upon notice and after an opportunity to be heard. If the certificate is not so revoked, it shall become a permanent certificate upon expiration or termination of the court's authority to revoke the sentence.

5. Any court that has issued a certificate of relief from disabilities may at any time issue a new certificate to enlarge the relief previously granted, provided, however, that the provisions of subdivision one through four of this section shall apply to the issuance of any such new certificate.

6. Any written report submitted to the court pursuant to this section is confidential and may not be made available to any person or public or private agency except where specifically required or permitted by statute or upon specific authorization of the court. However, it shall be made available by the court for examination by the applicant's attorney, or the applicant himself, if he has no attorney. In its discretion, the court may except from disclosure a part or parts of the report which are not relevant to the granting of a certificate, or sources of information which have been obtained on a promise of confidentiality, or any other portion thereof, disclosure of which would not be in the interest of justice. The action of the court excepting information from disclosure shall

be subject to appellate review. The court, in its discretion, may hold a conference in open court or in chambers to afford an applicant an opportunity to controvert or to comment upon any portions of the report. The court may also conduct a summary hearing at the conference on any matter relevant to the granting of the application and may take testimony under oath.

[*] As enacted.

Added by L. 1971, Ch. 748; L. 1972, Ch. 342; L. 1976, Ch. 931; **Amended** by L. 1982, Ch. 121, eff. May 24, 1982, added subd. 6; L. 1985, Ch. 134, eff. Apr. 1, 1985.

ANNOTATIONS

Certificate of relief from disabilities; discretion.— Defendant's application to amend his Certificate of Relief from Disabilities is granted, where more than 21 years have elapsed since he was discharged from his jail sentence for sexual abuse in the first degree, he has had no criminal history in the interim, and his prior conviction will have no bearing on his ability or fitness to operate a bus transporting persons under the age of 21 or persons of any age who are mentally or physically disabled. People v. Martin, 196 Misc. 2d 583, 764 N.Y.S.2d 546 (Co. Ct. Yates Co. 2003).

—The relief provided under section 702 is discretionary and should not be granted to individuals convicted of a crime, unless certain standards and requirements are met. However, while it is unquestioned that the state may differentiate between the rights granted to one group of citizens and those granted to another, such differentiation must be based upon some rational basis or compelling state interest. Da Grossa v. Goodman, 72 Misc. 2d 806, 339 N.Y.S.2d 502 (Sup. Ct. N.Y. Co. 1972).

Certificate of relief from disabilities; effect.—A certificate of relief from disabilities prevents the mandatory forfeiture of any license, permit, employment, or franchise, including the right to register for, or vote at, an election. Da Grossa v. Goodman, 72 Misc. 2d 806, 339 N.Y.S.2d 502 (Sup. Ct. N.Y. Co. 1972).

Certificate of relief from disabilities; unconstitutionality of prohibition.—It is violative of Article 1, section 11, of the New York State Constitution to prohibit one convicted in a federal court from filing in state court for a certificate of relief. Da Grossa v. Goodman, 72 Misc. 2d 806, 339 N.Y.S.2d 502 (Sup. Ct. N.Y. Co. 1972).

§ 703. Certificates of relief from disabilities issued by the board of parole.

1. The state board of parole shall have the power to issue a certificate of relief from disabilities to:

(a) any eligible offender who has been committed to an institution under the jurisdiction of the state department of correctional services. Such certificate may be issued by the board at the time the offender is released from such institution under the board's supervision or otherwise or at any time thereafter;

(b) any eligible offender who resides within this state and whose judgment of conviction was rendered by a court in any other jurisdiction.

2. Where the board of parole has issued a certificate of relief from disabilities, the board may at any time issue a new certificate enlarging the relief previously granted.

3. The board of parole shall not issue any certificate of relief from disabilities pursuant to

subdivisions one or two, unless the board is satisfied that:

(a) The person to whom it is to be granted is an eligible offender, as defined in section seven hundred;

(b) the relief to be granted by the certificate is consistent with the rehabilitation of the eligible offender; and

(c) the relief to be granted by the certificate is consistent with the public interest.

4. Any certificate of relief from disabilities issued by the board of parole to an eligible offender who at time of the issuance of the certificate is under the board's supervision, shall be deemed to be a temporary certificate until such time as the eligible offender is discharged from the board's supervision, and, while temporary, such certificate may be revoked by the board for violation of the conditions of parole or release. Revocation shall be upon notice to the parolee, who shall be accorded an opportunity to explain the violation prior to decision thereon. If the certificate is not so revoked, it shall become a permanent certificate upon expiration or termination of the board's jurisdiction over the offender.

5. In granting or revoking a certificate of relief from disabilities the action of the board of parole shall be by unanimous vote of the members authorized to grant or revoke parole. Such action shall be deemed a judicial function and shall not be reviewable if done according to law.

6. For the purpose of determining whether such certificate shall be issued, the board may conduct an investigation of the applicant.

Amended by L. 1971, Ch. 748; L. 1972, Ch. 342; L. 1974, Ch. 475; L. 1976, Ch. 931; L. 1988, Ch. 378, eff. July 29, 1988, adding subd. 6.

ANNOTATIONS

Certificate of relief from disabilities; effect.—Issuance to disbarred attorney of certificate of relief from disabilities by the New York State Board of Parole pursuant to Correction Law § 703 did not effect the previous order striking his name from the roll of attorneys and counsellors-at-law. In re Sugarman, 51 A.D.2d 170, 380 N.Y.S.2d 12 (1st Dept. 1976).

Parole board must be petitioned.—Application made to Supreme Court for relief from civil disabilities incurred as a consequence of convictions was premature; because petitioner was convicted of various felonies, she was required to make her application to the state parole board. In re Application of Helmsley, 152 Misc. 2d 215, 575 N.Y.S.2d 1009 (Sup. Ct. N.Y. Co. 1991).

§ 703-a. Certificate of good conduct.

1. A certificate of good conduct may be granted as provided in this section to relieve an individual of any disability, or to remove any bar to his employment, automatically imposed by law by reason of his conviction of the crime or of the offense specified therein. Such certificate may be limited to one or more enumerated disabilities or bars, or may relieve the individual of all disabilities and bars.

2. Notwithstanding any other provision of law, a conviction of a crime or of an offense specified in a certificate of good conduct shall not be deemed to be a conviction within the meaning of any provision of law that imposes, by reason of a conviction, a bar to any employment, a disability to exercise any right or a disability to apply for or to receive any license, permit or other authority or privilege, covered by the certificate.

3. A certificate of good conduct shall not, however, in any way prevent any judicial administrative, licensing or other body, board or authority from considering the conviction specified therein in accordance with the provisions of article twenty-three-a of this chapter.

Added by L. 1976, Ch. 931.

§ 703-b. Issuance of certificate of good conduct.

1. The state board of parole, or any three members thereof by unanimous vote, shall have the power to issue a certificate of good conduct to any person previously convicted of a crime in this state when the board is satisfied that:

(a) The applicant has conducted himself in a manner warranting such issuance for a minimum period in accordance with the provisions of subdivision three of this section;

(b) The relief to be granted by the certificate is consistent with the rehabilitation of the applicant; and

(c) The relief to be granted is consistent with the public interest.

2. The state board of parole, or any three members thereof by unanimous vote, shall have the power to issue a certificate of good conduct to any person previously convicted of a crime in any other jurisdiction, when the board is satisfied that:

(a) The applicant has demonstrated that there exist specific facts and circumstances, and specific sections of New York state law that have an adverse impact on the applicant and warrant the application for relief to be made in New York; and

(b) The provisions of paragraphs (a), (b) and (c) of subdivision one of this section have been met.

3. The minimum period of good conduct by the individual referred to in paragraph (a) of subdivision one of this section, shall be as follows: where the most serious crime of which the individual was convicted is a misdemeanor, the minimum period of good conduct shall be one year; where the most serious crime of which the individual was convicted is a class C, D or E felony, the minimum period of good conduct shall be three years; and, where the most serious crime of which the individual was convicted is a class

B or A felony, the minimum period of good conduct shall be five years. Criminal acts committed outside the state shall be classified as acts committed within the state based on the maximum sentence that could have been imposed based on such conviction pursuant to the laws of such foreign jurisdiction. Such minimum period of good conduct by the individual shall be measured either from the date of the payment of any fine imposed upon him or the suspension of sentence, or from the date of his unrevoked release from custody by parole, commutation or termination of his sentence. The board shall have power and it shall be its duty to investigate all persons when such application is made and to grant or deny the same within a reasonable time after the making of the application.

4. Where the board of parole has issued a certificate of good conduct, the board may at any time issue a new certificate enlarging the relief previously granted.

5. Any certificate of good conduct by the board of parole to an individual who at time of the issuance of the certificate is under the board's supervision, shall be deemed to be a temporary certificate until such time as the individual is discharged from the board's supervision, and, while temporary, such certificate may be revoked by the board for violation of the conditions of parole or release. Revocation shall be upon notice to the parolee, who shall be accorded an opportunity to explain the violation prior to decision thereon. If the certificate is not so revoked, it shall become a permanent certificate upon expiration or termination of the board's jurisdiction over the individual.

Added by L. 1976, Ch. 931; **Amended** by L. 1985, Ch. 386, eff. July 18, 1985, amended subd. 1, renumbered subd. 2, 3, and 4 to 3, 4, and 5, added new subd. 2 and amended renumbered subd. 3.

§ 704. Effect of revocation; use of revoked certificate.

1. Where a certificate of relief from disabilities is deemed to be temporary and such certificate is revoked, disabilities and forfeitures thereby relieved shall be reinstated as of the date upon which the person to whom the certificate was issued receives written notice of such revocation. Any such person shall upon receipt of such notice surrender the certificate to the issuing court or board.

2. A person who knowingly uses or attempts to use, a revoked certificate of relief from disabilities in order to obtain or to exercise any right or privilege that he would not be entitled to obtain or to exercise without a valid certificate shall be guilty of a misdemeanor.

§ 705. Forms and filing.

1. All applications, certificates and orders of revocation necessary for the purposes of this article shall be upon forms prescribed pursuant to agreement among the state commissioner of correctional services, the chairman of the state board of parole and the administrator of the state judicial conference. Such forms relating to certificates of relief from disabilities shall be distributed by the director of the state division of probation and correctional alternatives and forms relating to certificates of good conduct shall be distributed by the chairman of the board of parole.

2. Any court or board issuing or revoking any certificate pursuant to this article shall immediately file a copy of the certificate, or of the order of revocation, with the New York state identification and intelligence system.

Amended by L. 1971, Ch. 748; L. 1985, Ch. 134, eff. Apr. 1, 1985; L. 1991, Ch. 193, eff. July 21, 1991, amending subd. 1.

§ 706. Certificate not to be deemed to be a pardon.

Nothing contained in this article shall be deemed to alter or limit or affect the manner of applying for pardons to the governor, and no certificate issued hereunder shall be deemed or construed to be a pardon.

CORR. L.

ARTICLE 23-A—LICENSURE AND EMPLOYMENT OF PERSONS PREVIOUSLY CONVICTED OF ONE OR MORE CRIMINAL OFFENSES

Section

§ 750. Definitions.

For the purposes of this article, the following terms shall have the following meanings:

(1) "Public agency" means the state or any local subdivision thereof, or any state or local department, agency, board or commission.

(2) "Private employer" means any person, company, corporation, labor organization or association which employs ten or more persons.

(3) "Direct relationship" means that the nature of criminal conduct for which the person was convicted has a direct bearing on his fitness or ability to perform one or more of the duties or responsibilities necessarily related to the license or employment sought.

(4) "License" means any certificate, license, permit or grant of permission required by the laws of this state, its political subdivisions or instrumentalities as a condition for the lawful practice of any occupation, employment, trade, vocation, business, or profession. Provided, however, that "license" shall not, for the purposes of this article, include any license or permit to own, possess, carry, or fire any explosive, pistol, handgun, rifle, shotgun, or other firearm.

(5) "Employment" means any occupation, vocation or employment, or any form of vocational or educational training. Provided, however, that "employment" shall not, for the purposes of this article, include membership in any law enforcement agency.

§ 751. Applicability.

The provisions of this article shall apply to any application by any person who has previously been convicted of one or more criminal offenses, in this state or in any other jurisdiction, to any public agency or private employer for a license or employment, except where a mandatory forfeiture, disability or bar to employment is imposed by law, and has not been removed by an executive pardon, certificate of relief from disabilities or certificate of good conduct.

ANNOTATION

Lawyer disbarred because of felony conviction.—A certificate of relief from disability is not an executive pardon and does not reinstate a former member of the bar who was convicted of a felony. *In re* Glucksman, 57 A.D.2d 205, 394 N.Y.S.2d 191 (1st Dept. 1977).

§ 752. Unfair discrimination against persons previously convicted of one or more criminal offenses prohibited.

No application for any license or employment, to which the provisions of this article are applicable, shall be denied by reason of the applicant's having been previously convicted of one or more criminal offenses, or by reason of a finding of lack of "good moral character" when such finding is based upon the fact that the applicant has previously been convicted of one or more criminal offenses, unless:

(1) there is a direct relationship between one or more of the previous criminal offenses and the specific license or employment sought; or

(2) the issuance of the license or the granting of the employment would involve an unreasonable risk to property or to the safety or welfare of specific individuals or the general public.

ANNOTATIONS

Direct relationship.—The Commissioner of the New York State Department of Environmental Conservation did not violate the provisions of this section when he denied petitioner's application for a permit to expand a municipal solid waste disposal facility based on substantial evidence, including petitioner's criminal history, which had a direct relationship to the operation of this business. Al Turi Landfill Inc. v. N.Y.S. Dept. of Envtl. Conservation, 98 N.Y.2d 758, 751 N.Y.S.2d 827, 781 N.E.2d 892 (2002).

Discrimination in terminating employment.—The same public policy that prohibits discrimination in hiring on the basis of a criminal record also prohibits discrimination in terminating someone's employment on the basis of a criminal record; thus, Housing Authority was not liable for its failure to terminate an employee after learning of his undisclosed convictions. Givens v. New York City Hous. Auth., 249 A.D.2d 133, 671 N.Y.S.2d 479 (1st Dept. 1998).

—"The decision of an administrative agency to deny a license 'cannot be disturbed unless it is arbitrary and capricious.' However, '[a] decision of an administrative agency which neither adheres to its own prior precedent nor indicates its reason for reaching a different result on essentially the same facts is arbitrary and capricious.'" Klein v. Levin, 305 A.D.2d 316, 760 N.Y.S.2d 462 (1st Dept. 2003).

Unreasonable risk to public.—Denial of renewal of petitioner's application to renew his license as a real estate salesperson and denial of his application for a real estate broker's license were proper given that the issuance of the licenses would involve an unreasonable risk to the safety or welfare of the general public. Fogel v. Department of State, 209 A.D.2d 615, 619 N.Y.S.2d 104 (2d Dept. 1994).

§ 753. Factors to be considered concerning a previous criminal conviction; presumption.

1. In making a determination pursuant to section seven hundred fifty-two of this chapter, the public agency or private employer shall consider the following factors:

(a) The public policy of this state, as expressed in this act, to encourage the licensure and employment of persons previously convicted of one or more criminal offenses.

(b) The specific duties and responsibilities necessarily related to the license or employment sought.

(c) The bearing, if any, the criminal offense or offenses for which the person was previously convicted will have on his fitness or ability to perform one or more such duties or responsibilities.

(d) The time which has elapsed since the occurrence of the criminal offense or offenses.

(e) The age of the person at the time of occurrence of the criminal offense or offenses.

(f) The seriousness of the offense or offenses.

(g) Any information produced by the person, or produced on his behalf, in regard to his rehabilitation and good conduct.

(h) The legitimate interest of the public agency or private employer in protecting property, and the safety and welfare of specific individuals or the general public.

2. In making a determination pursuant to section seven hundred fifty-two of this chapter, the public agency or private employer shall also give

consideration to a certificate of relief from disabilities or a certificate of good conduct issued to the applicant, which certificate shall create a presumption of rehabilitation in regard to the offense or offenses specified therein.

ANNOTATIONS

Certificate of relief from disabilities.—In denying teaching license to petitioner, Board did not have to rebut presumption of rehabilitation created by the issuance of a certificate of relief from disabilities petitioner received for felony cocaine sale ten years prior to his application for a teaching license. The Board to review the factors set forth in § 753 in its determination that the seriousness and nature of petitioner's conviction made him unfit to be a teacher. Matter of Arrocha v. Board of Education, 93 N.Y.2d 361, 690 N.Y.S.2d 503, 712 N.E.2d 699 (1999).

Discrimination in terminating employment.—The same public policy that prohibits discrimination in hiring on the basis of a criminal record also prohibits discrimination in terminating someone's employment on the basis of a criminal record; thus, Housing Authority was not liable for its failure to terminate an employee after learning of his undisclosed convictions. Givens v. New York City Hous. Auth., 249 A.D.2d 133, 671 N.Y.S.2d 479 (1st Dept. 1998).

§ 754. Written statement upon denial of license or employment.

At the request of any person previously convicted of one or more criminal offenses who has been denied a license or employment, a public agency or private employer shall provide, within thirty days of a request, a written statement setting forth the reasons for such denial.

§ 755. Enforcement.

1. In relation to actions by public agencies, the provisions of this article shall be enforceable by a proceeding brought pursuant to article seventy-eight of the civil practice law and rules.

2. In relation to actions by private employers, the provisions of this article shall be enforceable by the division of human rights pursuant to the powers and procedures set forth in article fifteen of the executive law, and, concurrently, by the New York city commission on human rights.

ARTICLE 24—PROVISIONS APPLICABLE TO SENTENCES IMPOSED UNDER THE REVISED PENAL PLAN

§ 800. Applicability.

The provisions of this article shall apply, to the exclusion of all other provisions of this chapter relating to good behavior allowances, where sentence has been imposed pursuant to the provisions of the penal law as enacted by chapter ten hundred thirty of the laws of nineteen hundred sixty-five, as amended, or where the sentence is a reformatory sentence of imprisonment. Matters not expressly covered herein or covered in such penal law shall be governed by such other provisions of law as may be applicable.

Amended by L. 1970, Ch. 476; L. 1974, Ch. 653.

ANNOTATION

Confinement; good behavior allowance; equal protection.—Defendant, a "mentally ill" prisoner, was entitled to a hearing on the issue of his competency to determine whether he could elect good behavior allowances and obligations provided by statute for all prisoners. People *ex rel.* Bram v. Herold, 29 N.Y.2d 939, 329 N.Y.S.2d 574 (1972).

§ 803. Good behavior allowances against indeterminate and determinate sentences.

[The following version of § 803 is effective Oct. 1, 1995, pursuant to L. 1995, Ch. 3, § 74, paragraph (e), and repealed Sept. 1, 2009, pursuant to L. 1995, Ch. 3, § 74, paragraph (d). This version applies to offenses committed on or after Oct. 1, 1995, and offenses committed before Oct. 1, 1995 will be governed by the provisions of law in effect at the time the offense was committed, pursuant to L. 1995, Ch. 3, § 74, paragraph (e).]

1. (a) Every person confined in an institution of the department or a facility in the department of mental hygiene serving an indeterminate or determinate sentence of imprisonment, except a person serving a sentence with a maximum term of life imprisonment, may receive time allowance against the term or maximum term of his sentence imposed by the court. Such allowances may be granted for good behavior and efficient and willing performance of duties assigned or progress and achievement in an assigned treatment program, and may be withheld, forfeited or canceled in whole or in part for bad behavior, violation of institutional rules or failure to perform properly in the duties or program assigned.

(b) A person serving an indeterminate sentence of imprisonment may receive time allowance against the maximum term of his sentence not to exceed one-third of the maximum term imposed by the court.

(c) A person serving a determinate sentence of imprisonment may receive time allowance against the term of his sentence not to exceed one-seventh of the term imposed by the court.

(d) *[Expires and repealed Sept. 1, 2009.]*

(i) Except as provided in subparagraph (ii) of this paragraph, every person under the custody of the department or confined in a facility in the department of mental hygiene serving an indeterminate sentence of imprisonment with a minimum period of one year or more or a determinate sentence of imprisonment of one year or more imposed pursuant to section 70.70 or 70.71 of the penal law, may earn a merit time allowance.

(ii) Such merit time allowance shall not be available to any person serving an indeterminate sentence authorized for an A-I felony offense, other than an A-I felony offense defined in article two hundred twenty of the penal law, or any sentence imposed for a violent felony offense as defined in section 70.02 of the penal law, manslaughter in the second degree, vehicular manslaughter in the second degree, vehicular manslaughter in the first degree, criminally negligent homicide, an offense defined in article one hundred thirty of the penal law, incest, or an offense defined in article two hundred sixty-three of the penal law, or aggravated harassment of an employee by an inmate.

(iii) The merit time allowance credit against the minimum period of the indeterminate sentence shall be one-sixth of the minimum period imposed by the court except that such credit shall be one-third of the minimum period imposed by the court for an A-I felony offense defined in article two hundred twenty of the penal law. In the case of such a determinate sentence, in addition to the time allowance credit authorized by paragraph (c) of this subdivision, the merit time allowance credited against the term of the determinate sentence pursuant to this paragraph shall be one-seventh of the term imposed by the court.

(iv) Such merit time allowance may be granted

when an inmate successfully participates in the work and treatment program assigned pursuant to section eight hundred five of this article and when such inmate obtains a general equivalency diploma, an alcohol and substance abuse treatment certificate, a vocational trade certificate following at least six months of vocational programming or performs at least four hundred hours of service as part of a community work crew.

Such allowance shall be withheld for any serious disciplinary infraction or upon a judicial determination that the person, while an inmate, commenced or continued a civil action, proceeding or claim that was found to be frivolous as defined in subdivision (c) of section eight thousand three hundred three-a of the civil practice law and rules, or an order of a federal court pursuant to rule 11 of the federal rules of civil procedure imposing sanctions in an action commenced by a person, while an inmate, against a state agency, officer or employee.

(v) The provisions of this paragraph shall apply to persons in custody serving an indeterminate sentence on the effective date of this paragraph as well as to persons sentenced to an indeterminate sentence on and after the effective date of this paragraph and prior to September first, two thousand five and to persons sentenced to a determinate sentence prior to September first, two thousand eleven for a felony as defined in article two hundred twenty or two hundred twenty-one of the penal law.

2. If a person is serving more than one sentence, the authorized allowances may be granted separately against the term or maximum term of each sentence or, where consecutive sentences are involved, against the aggregate maximum term. Such allowances shall be calculated as follows:

(a) A person serving two or more indeterminate sentences which run concurrently may receive time allowance not to exceed one-third of the indeterminate sentence which has the longest unexpired time to run.

(b) A person serving two or more indeterminate sentences which run consecutively may receive time allowance not to exceed one-third of the aggregate maximum term.

(c) A person serving two or more determinate sentences which run concurrently may receive time allowance not to exceed one-seventh of the determinate sentence which has the longest unexpired time to run.

(d) A person serving two or more determinate sentences which run consecutively may receive time allowance not to exceed one-seventh of the aggregate maximum term.

(e) A person serving one or more indeterminate sentence and one or more determinate sentence which run concurrently may receive time allowance not to exceed one-third of the indeterminate sentence which has the longest unexpired

term to run or one-seventh of the determinate sentence which has the longest unexpired time to run, whichever allowance is greater.

(f) A person serving one or more indeterminate sentence and one or more determinate sentence which run consecutively may receive time allowance not to exceed the sum of one-third of the maximum or aggregate maximum of the indeterminate sentence or sentences and one-seventh of the term or aggregate maximum of the determinate sentence or sentences.

2-a. [*Expires and repealed Sept. 1, 2009.*] If a person is serving more than one sentence, the authorized merit time allowances may be granted against the period or aggregate minimum period of the indeterminate sentence or sentences, or against the term or aggregate term of the determinate sentence or sentences, or where consecutive determinate and indeterminate sentences are involved, against the aggregate minimum period as calculated pursuant to subparagraph (iv) of paragraph (a) of subdivision one of section 70.40 of the penal law. Such allowances shall be calculated as follows:

(a) A person serving two or more indeterminate sentences which run concurrently may receive a merit time allowance not to exceed one-sixth of the minimum period of the indeterminate sentence imposed for an offense other than an A-I felony offense defined in article two hundred twenty of the penal law, or one-third of the minimum period of the indeterminate sentence imposed for an A-I felony offense defined in article two hundred twenty of the penal law, whichever allowance results in the longest unexpired time to run.

(b) A person serving two or more indeterminate sentences which run consecutively may receive a merit time allowance not to exceed the amount of one-third of the minimum or aggregate minimum period of the sentences imposed for an A-I felony offense defined in article two hundred twenty of the penal law, plus one-sixth of the minimum or aggregate minimum period of the sentences imposed for an offense other than such A-I felony offense.

(c) A person serving two or more determinate sentences for an offense defined in article two hundred twenty or two hundred twenty-one of the penal law which run concurrently may receive a merit time allowance not to exceed one-seventh of the term of the determinate sentence which has the longest unexpired time to run.

(d) A person serving two or more determinate sentences for an offense defined in article two hundred twenty or two hundred twenty-one of the penal law which run consecutively may receive a merit time allowance not to exceed one-seventh of the aggregate term of such determinate sentences.

(e) A person serving one or more indeterminate sentences and one or more determinate sentences for an offense defined in article two hundred twenty or two hundred twenty-one of the penal law which run concurrently may receive a merit time allowance not to exceed one-sixth of the minimum period of the indeterminate sentence imposed for an offense other than an A-I felony offense defined in article two hundred twenty of the penal law, one-third of the minimum period of the indeterminate sentence imposed for an A-I felony offense defined in article two hundred twenty of the penal law, or one-seventh of the term of the determinate sentence, whichever allowance results in the largest unexpired time to run.

(f) A person serving one or more indeterminate sentences and one or more determinate sentences which run consecutively may receive a merit time allowance not to exceed the sum of one-sixth of the minimum or aggregate minimum period of the indeterminate sentence or sentences imposed for an offense other than an A-I felony offense defined in article two hundred twenty of the penal law, one-third of the minimum or aggregate minimum period of the indeterminate sentence or sentences imposed for an A-I felony offense defined in article two hundred twenty of the penal law and one-seventh of the term or aggregate term of the determinate sentence or sentences.

(g) The provisions of this subdivision shall apply to persons in custody serving an indeterminate sentence on the effective date of this subdivision as well as to persons sentenced to an indeterminate sentence on and after the effective date of this subdivision and prior to September first, two thousand five and to persons sentenced to a determinate sentence prior to September first, two thousand eleven for a felony as defined in article two hundred twenty or two hundred twenty-one of the penal law.

2-b. [*Expires and repealed Sept. 1, 2007.*] Notwithstanding the foregoing, if a person is serving more than one indeterminate sentence, at least one of which is imposed for a class A-I felony offense defined in article two hundred twenty of the penal law, the authorized merit time allowance granted pursuant to paragraph (d) of subdivision one of this section shall be calculated as follows:

(a) In the event a person is serving two or more indeterminate sentences with different minimum periods which run concurrently, the merit time allowance shall be based upon the sentence with the longest unexpired minimum period. If the sentence with the longest unexpired minimum period was imposed for a class A-I felony, the merit time credit shall be one-third of such sentence's minimum period; if such sentence was imposed for an offense other than a class A-I felony, such merit time credit shall be one-sixth of such sentence's minimum period. Provided,

however, that where the minimum period of any other concurrent indeterminate sentence is greater than such reduced minimum period, the minimum period of such other concurrent indeterminate sentence shall also be reduced but only to the extent that the minimum period of such other concurrent sentence, as so reduced, is equal to the reduced minimum period of such sentence with the longest unexpired minimum period to run.

(b) A person serving two or more indeterminate sentences with the same minimum periods which run concurrently, and no concurrent indeterminate sentence with any greater minimum period, shall have the minimum period of each such sentence reduced in the amount of one-third of such minimum period if all such sentences were imposed for a class A-I felony.

(c) A person serving two or more indeterminate sentences that run consecutively shall have the aggregate minimum period of such sentences reduced in the amount of one-third of such aggregate minimum period of the sentences imposed for a class A-I felony, plus one-sixth of such aggregate minimum period of the sentences imposed for an offense other than a class A-I felony.

3. The commissioner of correctional services shall promulgate rules and regulations for the granting, withholding, forfeiture, cancellation and restoration of allowances authorized by this section in accordance with the criteria herein specified. Such rules and regulations shall include provisions designating the person or committee in each correctional institution delegated to make discretionary determinations with respect to the allowances, the books and records to be kept, and a procedure for review of the institutional determinations by the commissioner.

4. No person shall have the right to demand or require the allowances authorized by this section. The decision of the commissioner of correctional services as to the granting, withholding, forfeiture, cancellation or restoration of such allowances shall be final and shall not be reviewable if made in accordance with law.

5. Time allowances granted prior to any release on parole or prior to any conditional release shall be forfeited and shall not be restored if the paroled or conditionally released person is returned to an institution under the jurisdiction of the state department of correctional services for violation of parole, violation of the conditions of release or by reason of a conviction for a crime committed while on parole or conditional release. A person who is so returned may, however, subsequently receive time allowances against the remaining portion of his term, maximum term or aggregate maximum term pursuant to this section and provided such remaining portion of his term, maximum term, or aggregate maximum term is more than one year.

6. Upon commencement of an indeterminate

or a determinate sentence the provisions of this section shall be furnished to the person serving the sentence and the meaning of same shall be fully explained to him by a person designated by the commissioner to perform such duty.

Amended by L. 1969, Ch. 270; L. 1974, Ch. 653; L. 1975, Ch. 148; L. 1976, Ch. 766; L. 1987, Ch. 126, eff. June 15, 1987; L. 1995, Ch. 3, § 74 and repealed Sept. 30, 2005; L. 1997, Ch. 435, §§ 43 and 44, eff. Aug. 20, 1997, to be repealed Sept. 1, 2002; L. 2002, Ch. 81, Part D § 1, eff. May 29, 2002, extending effective dates of subd. 1(d) and 2 to Sept. 1, 2003; L. 2003, Ch. 16, § 19, extending effective dates to Sept. 1, 2005; L. 2003, Ch. 62, Part E, §§ 1–3, eff. May 15, 2003 and shall be deemed effective Apr. 1, 2003, amending subds. 1(d), 2-a and adding 2-b, and subd. 2-b to be repealed on the same date as L. 1997, Ch. 435, § 76, subd. 6; L. 2004, Ch. 553, § 1, amending subd. 1(d), eff. Oct. 5, 2004; L. 2004, Ch. 738, §§ 7 & 9, repealing and replacing subds. 1(d) and 2-a, eff. Dec. 14, 2004; L. 2005, Ch. 56, Part D, §§ 4, 17, 20, extending effective dates.

Editor's Note: L. 2004, Ch. 738, § 41(c-1) provides: "[T]he provisions of sections seven, eight, nine, ten and ten-a of this act, and subdivision 2-a of section 803 of the correction law, as added by section eleven of this act shall apply to persons in custody serving an indeterminate sentence on the effective date of such provisions as well as to persons sentenced to an indeterminate sentence on and after the effective date of such provisions and prior to September 1, 2005 and to persons sentenced to a determinate sentence prior to September 1, 2011 for a felony as defined in article 220 or 221 of the penal law."

ANNOTATIONS

Considerations.—An inmate's failure to participate in recommended therapeutic programs provides a rational basis for withholding a good time allowance. Benjamin v. N.Y.S. Dept. of Corr. Servs., 19 A.D.3d 832, 796 N.Y.S.2d 747 (3d Dept. 2005).

—Committee's decision to withhold all of petitioner's good time allowance, totaling six years and eight months, due to petitioner's failure to participate in a recommended residential substance abuse treatment program was affirmed on appeal where record reflected that drugs played role in crimes for which he was incarcerated and "good behavior allowances are in the nature of a privilege . . . and no inmate has the right to demand or to require that any good behavior allowance be granted." McPherson v. Goord, 17 A.D.3d 750, 793 N.Y.S.2d 230 (3d Dept. 2005).

—Granting or withholding of merit time is a discretionary determination; no abuse of discretion was found where petitioner was denied eligibility for a merit time allowance because his disciplinary record included 213 days of keeplock confinement. LaRocco v. Goord, 15 A.D.3d 809, 790 N.Y.S.2d 265 (3d Dept. 2005).

—Two separate disciplinary rule violations involving lewd and sexual conduct toward female correction officers which resulted in a total recommended loss of 15 months were properly considered in withholding good time allowance along with petitioner's performance of assigned duties, participation in various programs and positive adjustments while incarcerated. Worthy v. Selsky, 6 A.D.3d 840, 773 N.Y.S.2d 914 (3d Dept. 2004).

—Inmate's refusal to participate in "recommended" as opposed to "assigned" programs may be considered in the Time Allowance Committee's determination. Ferry v. Goord, 268 A.D.2d 720, 704 N.Y.S.2d 315 (3d Dept. 2000).

Constitutionality.—Correction Law § 803(5) does not violate the equal protection guarantee by limiting good time eligibility to a person returned whose remaining maximum or aggregate maximum term or period is more than one year. Foster v. Smith, 52 A.D.2d 1088, 384 N.Y.S.2d 591 (4th Dept. 1976).

Denial of parole.—Parole denial does not entitle one to release until the unserved portion of the maximum sentence equals his total jail time and good behavior allowance. People ex rel. Hayward v. O'Mara, 55 A.D.2d 979, 390 N.Y.S.2d 677 (3d Dept. 1977).

Forfeiture of good time credit.—Where defendant forfeited

five years of good time as a result of penalties imposed at disciplinary hearings, the determinations of which he did not challenge, those years were properly subtracted from the jail time credit he received in determining his actual good time credit. Porter v. Senkowski, 245 A.D.2d 919, 666 N.Y.S.2d 853 (3d Dept. 1997).

Good behavior allowance.—The granting or withholding of merit time is a discretionary determination. La Rocco v. Goord, 15 A.D.3d 809, 790 N.Y.S.2d 265 (3d Dept. 2005).

—Petitioner's article 78 petition challenging denial of merit time consideration under this section because he was convicted of an A-1 felony offense could not lie; granting or withholding of merit time is a discretionary determination. Coleman v. Goord, 307 A.D.2d 462, 761 N.Y.S.2d 556 (3d Dept. 2003).

—Petitioner's record of repeated acts of violent misconduct and extended periods of disciplinary confinement, which contributed to his failure to participate in rehabilitative programs while serving an indeterminate term of 4½ years to 13½ years for robbery in the first degree, supported determination to deny petitioner good time allowance. Rivera v. Goord, 297 A.D.2d 844, 746 N.Y.S.2d 850 (3d Dept. 2002)

—Good behavior allowances are a privilege and are not granted as of right; as long as the decision is made in accordance with the law and based on a review of the inmate's entire institutional record, that discretionary decision is not subject to judicial review; board properly considered petitioner's refusal to participate in programs for sex offenders because he pleaded guilty only to burglary charges, although presentence report and allocution revealed sex counts were not contested. Bolster v. Goord, 300 A.D.2d 711, 752 N.Y.S.2d 403 (3d Dept. 2002).

—Since good time is not a matter of right, a prisoner remains lawfully imprisoned and habeas corpus is not a proper vehicle to challenge a determination of the time allowance board. Miranda v. Kuhlman, 127 A.D.2d 924, 511 N.Y.S.2d 981 (3d Dept. 1987).

—Petitioner serving a sentence on a prior conviction with a maximum term of life imprisonment is not eligible for good behavior allowances. Emm v. Hollins, 299 A.D.2d 850, 750 N.Y.S.2d 251 (4th Dept. 2002).

Good behavior allowance; ineligibility.—Because petitioner is serving a sentence on a prior conviction with a maximum term of life imprisonment, he is not eligible for good behavior allowances. People v. ex rel. Emm v. Hollins, 299 A.D.2d 850, 750 N.Y.S.2d 251 (4th Dept. 2002).

Hearing.—A full scale hearing is not required before a decision is reached on a prisoner's good time allowance. Amato v. Ward, 41 N.Y.S.2d 469, 393 N.Y.S.2d 934, 362 N.E.2d 566 (1977).

Prisoner; loss of good time; denial of hearing.—Defendant was entitled to a hearing on the issue of whether the deprivation of 90 days good time for alleged participation in a disturbance was made in violation of lawful procedure. Salinas v. Henderson. 40 A.D.2d 939, 337 N.Y.S.2d 583 (4th Dept. 1972).

—The Time Allowance Committee does not adjudicate specific disciplinary violations, nor does it exact punishment; its function is to evaluate the entire disciplinary record of an inmate and to make a recommendation of the amount of good behavior time to be granted (7 NYCRR 260.3[b], 261.3[d]); such action does not require the procedures of an adversary proceeding Amato v. Ward, 52 A.D.2d 945, 383 N.Y.S.2d 891 (2d Dept. 1976), aff'd, 41 N.Y.2d 469, 393 N.Y.S.2d 934, 362 N.E.2d 566 (1977).

—Prisoner was not entitled to a time allowance hearing when a review of the file disclosed that he was afforded the total amount of good time authorized by statute (Correction Law § 803(1)), reduced only by the period lost for disciplinary violations in superintendent's hearings. People ex rel. Moore v. Jones, 77 A.D.2d 679, 430 N.Y.S.2d 16 (3d Dept. 1980).

Reformatory sentences; grant of good behavior time.— Where relators challenged the constitutionality of reformatory sentences, claiming that they were denied equal protection of the law since inmates sentenced to reformatory terms were not entitled to the benefit of the good behavior time awarded inmates sentenced to indefinite terms, the court determined that recent practices and amendment to the law had undermined the rational basis that might have existed to justify the disparity in treatment, and, accordingly, it ordered the New York City Commissioner of Correction to examine the institutional records of relators to determine whether their past infractions and violations warranted the forfeiture of good behavior time. People *ex rel.* Cromwell v. Warden, 74 Misc. 2d 642, 345 N.Y.S.2d 381 (Sup. Ct. Bronx Co. 1973).

Retroactivity of forfeiture provision.—The forfeiture provision of Correction Law § 803 subdivision 5 is not retroactive. The law in effect at the time of a parolee's release and the declaration of his delinquency should control the consequences of his parole violation. People *ex rel.* Richardson v. Deegan, 34 A.D.2d 835, 312 N.Y.S.2d 666 (2d Dept. 1970).

§ 804. Good behavior allowances against definite sentences.

1. Every person confined in an institution serving a definite sentence of imprisonment may receive time allowances as discretionary reductions of the term of his sentence not to exceed in the aggregate one-third of the term imposed by the court. Such allowances may be granted for good behavior and efficient and willing performance of duties assigned or progress and achievement in an assigned treatment program, and may be withheld, forfeited or cancelled in whole or in part for bad behavior, violation of institutional rules or failure to perform properly in the duties or program assigned.

2. If a person is serving more than one sentence, the authorized allowances may be granted separately against the term of each sentence or, where consecutive sentences are involved, against the aggregate term. Allowances based upon sentences of less than one month may be granted, and in such case the maximum allowance shall be one day for every three days of the sentence. In no case, however, shall the total of all allowances granted to any such person exceed one-third of the time he would be required to serve, computed without regard to this section.

3. No person shall have the right to demand or require the allowances authorized by this section. The decision of the sheriff, superintendent, warden or other person in charge of the institution, or where such institution is under the jurisdiction of a county or city department the decision of the head of such department, as to the granting, withholding, forfeiture, cancellation or restoration of such allowances shall be final and shall not be reviewable if made in accordance with law.

4. A person who has earned a reduction of sentence pursuant to this section and who has been conditionally released under subdivision two of section 70.40 of the penal law shall not forfeit such reduction by reason of conduct causing his return to the institution. Provided, nevertheless, that such reduction may be forfeited by reason of subsequent conduct while serving the remainder of his term.

5. The state commission of correction shall promulgate record keeping rules and regulations for the granting, withholding, forfeiture, cancellation and restoration of allowances authorized by this section.

6. Notwithstanding anything to the contrary in this section, in any case where a person is serving a definite sentence in an institution under the jurisdiction of the state department of correction, subdivisions three and four of section eight hundred three of this chapter shall apply.

7. Upon commencement of any definite sentence the provisions of this section shall be furnished to the person serving the sentence and the meaning of same shall be fully explained to him by an officer designated in the regulation to perform such duty.

Amended by L. 1976, Ch. 145.

ANNOTATIONS

Conditional civil orders of commitment.—A conditional civil order of commitment need not explicitly state that the imposed condition is one determined to be within the committed person's "power to perform" before such person can be denied consideration for good time behavior pursuant to section 804(a). McLeod v. Stancari, 150 Misc. 2d 115, 568 N.Y.S.2d 519 (Sup. Ct. Westchester Co. 1991).

"Good time" allowance; intermittent sentence.—"Good time" allowances are unavailable to one serving an intermittent sentence under Penal Law Article 85, which allowances, under Corr. Law § 804, are restricted to definite sentences. People *ex rel.* Turano v. Cunningham, 57 A.D.2d 801, 395 N.Y.S.2d 4 (1st Dept. 1977).

Hearing.—Prior to a determination to grant a merit time allowance by the Commissioner or his designee, petitioner remains ineligible for parole until his parole eligibility date. Erdheim v. Dillard, 290 A.D.2d 642, 736 N.Y.S.2d 142 (3d Dept. 2002).

Habeas corpus proceeding; double jeopardy no defense.—Where petitioner was in a work-release program and failed to return on time, it was proper to take away credit for good time along with adding on time lost while he was at large. Furthermore, defendant's conviction for the crime of escape was proper, and it was not double jeopardy to the defendant, since the crime of escape was separate and apart from any administrative proceeding which revoked good time. State *ex rel.* Mitchell v. Warden, 74 Misc. 2d 152, 343 N.Y.S.2d 545 (Sup. Ct. N.Y. Co. 1973).

Habeas corpus; loss of good time; rights of defendant.—Since an inmate must earn good time by positive effort and obedience to institutional rules, it can be cancelled in whole or in part for violations of the Penal Law or institutional rules, and the Department of Correction has sole jurisdiction. Such rules must be promulgated and made readily available to inmates, but there is no need to promulgate the Penal Law as every inmate is presumed to know it. Also, the inmate must be informed of the infraction charged in writing at least 24 hours before the hearing and he has the right to testify, produce documents and call witnesses, but he has no right to counsel, confrontation or cross-examination. If any of such rights are violated the remedy is either habeas corpus or an Article 78 proceeding, which can only be brought a reasonable time before the inmate's release date. People *ex rel.* Bright v. Warden New York City Correctional Institution for Men, 79 Misc. 2d 959, 361 N.Y.S.2d 809 (Sup. Ct. Bronx Co. 1974).

Prisoner; loss of good time; denial of hearing.—Defendant was entitled to a hearing on the issue of whether the deprivation of 90 days good time for alleged participation in a disturbance was made in violation of lawful procedure. Salinas v. Henderson, 40 A.D.2d 939, 337 N.Y.S.2d 583 (4th Dept. 1972).

Reformatory sentences; grant of good behavior time.—Where relators challenged the constitutionality of reformatory sentences, claiming that they were denied equal protection of the law since inmates sentenced to reformatory terms were not entitled to the benefit of the good behavior time awarded inmates sentenced to indefinite terms, the court determined that recent practices and amendment to the law had undermined the rational basis that might have existed to justify the disparity in treatment, and, accordingly, it ordered the New York City Commissioner of Correction to examine the institutional records of relators to comparison whether their past infractions and violations warranted the forfeiture of good behavior time. People *ex rel.* Cromwell v. Warden, 74 Misc. 2d 642, 345 N.Y.S.2d 381 (Sup. Ct. Bronx Co. 1973).

Sentence; release date.—If Department of Correction improperly extended defendant's maximum release date it cannot be raised on appeal from judgment of conviction but by Article 78 proceeding. People v. Blake, 39 A.D.2d 587, 331 N.Y.S.2d 851 (2d Dept. 1972).

§ 804-a. Good behavior allowances for certain civil commitments.

1. Every person confined in an institution serving a civil commitment for a fixed period of time, whose release is not conditional upon any act within his power to perform, may receive time allowances as discretionary reductions of the term of his commitment not to exceed, in the aggregate, one-third of the term imposed by the court. Such allowances may be granted for good behavior and efficient and willing performance of duties assigned or progress and achievement in an assigned treatment program, and may be withheld, forfeited or cancelled in whole or in part for bad behavior, violation of institutional rules or failure to perform properly in the duties or program assigned.

2. Allowances based upon commitments of less than one month may be granted, and in such case the maximum allowances shall be one day for every three days of the commitment. In no case, however, shall the total of all allowances granted to any such person exceed one-third of the time he would be required to serve, computed without regard to this section.

3. No person shall have the right to demand or require the allowances authorized by this section. The decision of the sheriff, superintendent, warden or other person in charge of the institution, or where such institution is under the jurisdiction of a county or city department the decision of the head of such department, as to the granting, withholding, forfeiture, cancellation, or restoration of such allowances shall be final and shall not be reviewable if made in accordance with law.

4. The state commission of correction shall promulgate record keeping rules and regulations for the granting, withholding, forfeiture, cancellation and restoration of allowances authorized by this section.

5. Upon commencement of any civil commitment as described in subdivision one of this section, the provisions of this section shall be furnished to the person serving the commitment and the meaning of same shall be fully explained to him by an officer designated in the regulation to perform such duty.

Added by L. 1987, Ch. 220, eff. Sept. 5, 1987.

§ 805. Earned eligibility program. [*Effective until Sept. 1, 2007.*]

[*The following version of § 805 became effective Oct. 1, 1995, pursuant to L. 1995, Ch. 3, § 74, paragraph (e), and will be repealed Sept. 1, 2009, pursuant to L. 1995, Ch. 3, § 74, para. (d), as amended. This version applies to offenses committed on or after Oct. 1, 1995. Offenses committed before Oct. 1, 1995 will be governed by the provisions of law in effect at the time the offense was committed, pursuant to L. 1995, Ch. 3, § 74, para. (e).*]

Persons committed to the custody of the department under an indeterminate or determinate sentence of imprisonment shall be assigned a work and treatment program as soon as practicable. No earlier than two months prior to the inmate's eligibility to be paroled pursuant to subdivision one of section 70.40 of the penal law, the commissioner shall review the inmate's institutional record to determine whether he has complied with the assigned program. If the commissioner determines that the inmate has successfully participated in the program he may issue the inmate a certificate of earned eligibility. Notwithstanding any other provision of law, an inmate who is serving a sentence with a minimum term of not more than eight years and who has been issued a certificate of earned eligibility, shall be granted parole release at the expiration of his minimum term or as authorized by subdivision four of section eight hundred sixty-seven of this chapter unless the board of parole determines that there is a reasonable probability that, if such inmate is released, he will not live and remain at liberty without violating the law and that his release is not compatible with the welfare of society. Any action by the commissioner pursuant to this section shall be deemed a judicial function and shall not be reviewable if done in accordance with law.

Added by L. 1987, Ch. 261, eff. July 13, 1987; **Amended** by L. 1987, Ch. 262, eff. July 13, 1987; L. 1991, Ch. 511, eff. July 19, 1991; L. 1992, Ch. 55, eff. Apr. 10, 1992, and expires on Sept. 1, 1994; L. 1995, Ch. 3, § 28, eff. Oct. 1, 1995, repealed Sept. 30, 2005, and offenses committed before Oct. 1, 1995 will be governed by laws in effect at the time the offenses were committed; L. 1997, Ch. 435, § 48, eff. Aug. 20, 1997, extending expiration date of 1987 amendments to Sept. 1, 1999; L. 1999, Ch. 452, § 2, eff. Sept. 1, 1999, extending expiration date of 1987 amendments to Sept. 1, 2001, and shall not apply to persons committed to the custody of the department after such expiration date; L. 2001, Ch. 95, § 4, extending expiration date to Sept. 1, 2003; L. 2003, Ch. 16, § 4, extending expiration date to Sept. 1, 2005; L. 2003, Ch. 16, § 4, eff. Mar. 31, 2003; L. 2003, Ch. 62, Part E, § 4, eff. May 15, 2003 and deemed eff. Apr. 1, 2003; L. 2005, Ch. 56, Part D, §§ 4, 20, extending expiration and repeal dates.

ANNOTATIONS

Certificate of earned eligibility.—Although a certificate of earned eligibility creates a "rebuttable presumption favoring release," it is one of many factors considered by Parole Board in determination whether to grant parole; in this case, Parole Board's determination that reasonable probability existed that petitioner would not remain at liberty without violating the law and that release was incompatible with welfare of community was not irrational. Wallman v. Travis, 18 A.D.3d 304, 794 N.Y.S.2d 381 (1st Dept. 2005).

—Where the previous determination found that Parole Board's determination was irrational bordering on impropriety, Parole Board's denial of petitioner's release for same reason without new or additional information was irrational, and petitioner should have been released. Marino v. Travis, 13 A.D.3d 453, 787 N.Y.S.2d 54 (2d Dept. 2004).

—Denial of a certificate of earned eligibility is an interlocutory determination that may be considered by the Board of Parole in making its determination as to whether or not to grant parole; here, based on a number of factors, including petitioner's failure to secure a certificate of earned eligibility due to poor attendance, the petitioner was denied parole. *In re* Jarvis v. Comm'r of N.Y.S. Dept. of Corrections, 277 A.D.2d 556, 714 N.Y.S.2d 825 (3d Dept. 2000).

—"An inmate's participation in a temporary release program is a privilege," and the review of a determination denying participation in that program is limited to whether or not that decision violated any statutory provision, denied a constitutional right, or was "affected by irrationality bordering on impropriety." Dixon v. Recore, 271 A.D.2d 778, 707 N.Y.S.2d 254 (3d Dept. 2000).

—Certificate of earned eligibility does not guarantee parole; the Board can deny parole if it finds that there is a "reasonable probability" that the inmate would violate the law if released or the inmate's release would not be compatible with the welfare of the community as a whole. Nieves v. New York State Div. of Parole, 251 A.D.2d 836, 675 N.Y.S.2d 158 (3d Dept. 1998).

§ 806. Presumptive release program for nonviolent inmates. [*Repealed Sept. 1, 2007, pursuant to L. 2003, Ch. 62, Part E, § 15, para. (d).*]

1. Notwithstanding any other provision of law to the contrary and except as provided in subdivision two of this section, an inmate who has been awarded a certificate of earned eligibility by the commissioner as set forth in section eight hundred five of this article may be entitled to presumptive release at the expiration of the minimum or aggregate minimum period of his or her indeterminate term of imprisonment, provided that:

i. the inmate has not been convicted previously of, nor is presently serving a sentence imposed for a class A-I felony, a violent felony offense as defined in section 70.02 of the penal law, manslaughter in the second degree, vehicular manslaughter in the second degree, vehicular manslaughter in the first degree, criminally negligent homicide, an offense defined in article one hundred thirty of the penal law, incest, or an offense defined in article two hundred sixty-three of the penal law,

ii. the inmate has not committed any serious disciplinary infraction, and

iii. there has been no judicial determination that the person while an inmate commenced or continued a civil action, proceeding or claim that was found to be frivolous as defined in subdivision (c) of section eight thousand three hundred three-a of the civil practice law and rules, or an order has not been issued by a federal court pursuant to rule 11 of the federal rules of civil procedure imposing sanctions in an action commenced by the inmate against a state agency, officer or employee.

2. In the case of an inmate who meets the criteria set forth in subdivision one of this section and who also meets the criteria for merit time as provided for in paragraph (d) of subdivision one of section eight hundred three of this article, such inmate may be entitled to presumptive release, as provided in this section, at the expiration of five-sixths of the minimum or aggregate minimum period of his or her indeterminate term of imprisonment.

3. Any inmate eligible for presumptive release pursuant to this section shall be required to apply for such release pursuant to section two hundred fifty-nine-g of the executive law. Upon release from the department of correctional services, such person shall be in the legal custody of the division of parole as provided in subdivisions two, three, four, five, six and seven of section two hundred fifty-nine-i of the executive law.

4. The commissioner shall promulgate rules and regulations for the granting, withholding, cancellation and recission* of presumptive release authorized by this section in accordance with law.

5. No person shall have the right to demand or require presumptive release authorized by this section. The commissioner may revoke at any time an inmate's scheduled presumptive release pursuant to this section for any disciplinary infraction committed by the inmate or for any failure to continue to participate successfully in any assigned work and treatment program after the certificate of earned eligibility has been awarded. The commissioner may deny presumptive release to any inmate whenever the commissioner determines that such release may not be consistent with the safety of the community or the welfare of the inmate. Any action by the commissioner pursuant to this section shall be deemed a judicial function and shall not be reviewable if done in accordance with law.

6. Any eligible inmate who is not released pursuant to subdivision one or two of this section shall be considered for discretionary release on parole pursuant to the provisions of section eight hundred five of this article or section two hundred fifty-nine-i of the executive law, whichever is applicable.

7. Any reference to parole and conditional release in this chapter shall also be deemed to include presumptive release.

* As enacted.

Added by L. 2003, Ch. 62, deemed eff. Apr. 1, 2003, and to expire and be deemed repealed on the same date as L. 1997, Ch. 435, § 76, subd. 6; **Amended** by L. 2005, Ch. 56, Part D, § 17, extending expiration date to Sept. 1, 2007.

ARTICLE 26—TEMPORARY RELEASE PROGRAMS FOR STATE CORRECTIONAL INSTITUTIONS

§ 851. Definitions. [*Expires Sept. 1, 2007.*]

As used in this article the following terms have the following meanings:

1. [*Effective until Sept. 1, 2007.*] "Institution" means any institution under the jurisdiction of or designated by the commissioner of the state department of correctional services or an institution designated by the commissioner pursuant to section seventy-two-a of this chapter.

1. [*Effective Sept. 1, 2007.*] "Institution" means any institution under the jurisdiction of the state department of correctional services.

1. [*Effective only upon expiration of L. 1972, Ch. 339, § 10 and L. 1986, Ch. 554, § 3.*] "Institution" means any institution under the jurisdiction of the state department of correction.

2. [*Effective until Sept 1, 2007.*] "Eligible inmate" means: a person confined in an institution who is eligible for release on parole or who will become eligible for release on parole or conditional release within two years. Provided, however, that a person under sentence for an offense defined in paragraphs (a) and (b) of subdivision one of section 70.02 of the penal law, where such offense involved the use or threatened use of a deadly weapon or dangerous instrument shall not be eligible to participate in a work release program until he or she is eligible for release on parole or who will be eligible for release on parole or conditional release within eighteen months. Provided, further, however, that a person under a determinate sentence as a second felony drug offender for a class B felony offense defined in article two hundred twenty of the penal law, who was sentenced pursuant to section 70.70 of such law, shall not be eligible to participate in a temporary release program until the time served under imprisonment for his or her determinate sentence, including any jail time credited pursuant to the provisions of article seventy of the penal law, shall be at least eighteen months. In the case of a person serving an indeterminate sentence of

imprisonment imposed pursuant to the penal law in effect after September one, nineteen hundred sixty-seven, for the purposes of this article parole eligibility shall be upon the expiration of the minimum period of imprisonment fixed by the court or where the court has not fixed any period, after service of the minimum period fixed by the state board of parole. If an inmate is denied release on parole, such inmate shall not be deemed an eligible inmate until he or she is within two years of his or her next scheduled appearance before the state parole board. In any case where an inmate is denied release on parole while participating in a temporary release program, the department shall review the status of the inmate to determine if continued placement in the program is appropriate. No person convicted of any escape or absconding offense defined in article two hundred five of the penal law shall be eligible for temporary release. Further, no person under sentence for aggravated harassment of an employee by an inmate as defined in section 240.32 of the penal law for, any homicide offense defined in article one hundred twenty-five of the penal law, for any sex offense defined in article one hundred thirty of the penal law, or for an offense defined in section 255.25 of the penal law shall be eligible to participate in a work release program as defined in subdivision three of this section. Nor shall any person under sentence for any sex offense defined in article one hundred thirty of the penal law be eligible to participate in a community services program as defined in subdivision five of this section. Notwithstanding the foregoing, no person who is an otherwise eligible inmate who is under sentence for a crime involving: (a) infliction of serious physical injury upon another as defined in the penal law or (b) any other offense involving the use or threatened use of a deadly weapon may participate in a temporary release program without the written approval of the commissioner. The commissioner shall promulgate regulations giving direction to the temporary release committee at each institution in order to aid such committees in carrying out this mandate.

The governor, by executive order, may exclude or limit the participation of any class of otherwise eligible inmates from participation in a temporary release program. Nothing in this paragraph shall be construed to affect either the validity of any executive order previously issued limiting the participation of otherwise eligible inmates in such program or the authority of the commissioner of the department of correctional services to impose appropriate regulations limiting such participation.

2. [*Effective Sept. 1, 2007.*] "Eligible inmate" means: a person confined in an institution who is eligible for release on parole or who will become eligible for release on parole or conditional release within two years. Provided, that a person under a determinate sentence as a second felony drug offender for a class B felony offense defined in article two hundred twenty of the penal law, who was sentenced pursuant to section 70.70 of such law, shall not be eligible to participate in a temporary release program until the time served under imprisonment for his or her determinate sentence, including any jail time credited pursuant to the provisions of article seventy of the penal law, shall be at least eighteen months. In the case of a person serving an indeterminate sentence of imprisonment imposed pursuant to the penal law in effect after September one, nineteen hundred sixty-seven, for the purposes of this article parole eligibility shall be upon the expiration of the minimum period of imprisonment fixed by the court or where the court has not fixed any period, after service of the minimum period fixed by the state board of parole. If an inmate is denied release on parole, such inmate shall not be deemed an eligible inmate until he or she is within two years of his or her next scheduled appearance before the state parole board. In any case where an inmate is denied release on parole while participating in a temporary release program, the department shall review the status of the inmate to determine if continued placement in the program is appropriate. No person convicted of any escape or absconding offense defined in article two hundred five of the penal law shall be eligible for temporary release. Nor shall any person under sentence for any sex offense defined in article one hundred thirty of the penal law be eligible to participate in a community services program as defined in subdivision five of this section. Notwithstanding the foregoing, no person who is an otherwise eligible inmate who is under sentence for a crime involving: (a) infliction of serious physical injury upon another as defined in the penal law, (b) a sex offense involving forcible compulsion, or (c) any other offense involving the use or threatened use of a deadly weapon may participate in a temporary release program without the written approval of the commissioner. The commissioner shall

promulgate regulations giving direction to the temporary release committee at each institution in order to aid such committees in carrying out this mandate.

The governor, by executive order, may exclude or limit the participation of any class of otherwise eligible inmates from participation in a temporary release program. Nothing in this paragraph shall be construed to affect either the validity of any executive order previously issued limiting the participation of otherwise eligible inmates in such program or the authority of the commissioner of the department of correctional services to impose appropriate regulations limiting such participation.

2. [*Effective only upon expiration of L. 1972, Ch. 339, § 10 and L. 1994, Ch. 60, § 42.*] "Eligible inmate" means a person confined in an institution where a work release program has been established who is eligible for release on parole or who will become eligible for release on parole within one year.

2-a. Notwithstanding subdivision two of this section, the term "eligible inmate" shall also include a person confined in an institution who is eligible for release on parole or who will become eligible for release on parole or conditional release within two years, and who was convicted of a homicide offense as defined in article one hundred twenty-five of the penal law or an assault offense defined in article one hundred twenty of the penal law, and who can demonstrate to the commissioner that: (a) the victim of such homicide or assault was a member of the inmate's immediate family as that term is defined in section 120.40 of the penal law or had a child in common with the inmate; (b) the inmate was subjected to substantial physical, sexual or psychological abuse committed by the victim of such homicide or assault; and (c) such abuse was a substantial factor in causing the inmate to commit such homicide or assault. With respect to an inmate's claim that he or she was subjected to substantial physical, sexual or psychological abuse committed by the victim, such demonstration shall include corroborative material that may include, but is not limited to, witness statements, social services records, hospital records, law enforcement records and a showing based in part on documentation prepared at or near the time of the commission of the offense or the prosecution thereof tending to support the inmate's claim. Prior to making a determination under this subdivision, the commissioner is required to request and take into consideration the opinion of the district attorney who prosecuted the underlying homicide or assault offense and the opinion of the sentencing court. If such opinions are received within forty-five days of the request, the commissioner shall take them into consideration. If such opinions are not so received, the commissioner may proceed with the determination. Any action by the commissioner pursuant to this subdivision shall be deemed a judicial function and shall not be reviewable in any court.

2-b. When calculating in advance the date on which a person is or will be eligible for release on parole or conditional release, for purposes of determining eligibility for temporary release or for placement at an alcohol and substance abuse treatment correctional annex, the commissioner shall consider and include credit for all potential credits and reductions including but not limited to merit time and good behavior allowances. Nothing in this subdivision shall be interpreted as precluding the consideration and inclusion of credit for all potential credits and reductions including, but not limited to, merit time and good behavior allowances when calculating in advance for any other purpose the date on which a person is or will be eligible for release on parole or conditional release.

3. "Work release program" means a program under which eligible inmates may be granted the privilege of leaving the premises of an institution for a period not exceeding fourteen hours in any day for the purpose of on-the-job training or employment, or for any matter necessary to the furtherance of any such purposes. No person shall be released into a work release program unless prior to release such person has a reasonable assurance of a job training program or employment. If after release, such person ceases to be employed or ceases to participate in the training program, the inmate's privilege to participate in such work release program may be revoked in accordance with rules and regulations promulgated by the commissioner.

4. "Furlough program" means a program under which eligible inmates may be granted the privilege of leaving the premises of an institution for a period not exceeding seven days for the purpose of seeking employment, maintaining family ties, solving family problems, seeking post-release housing, attending a short-term educational or vocational training course, or for any matter necessary to the furtherance of any such purposes.

5. "Community services program" means a program under which eligible inmates may be granted the privilege of leaving the premises of an institution for a period not exceeding fourteen hours in any day for the purpose of participation in religious services, volunteer work, or athletic events, or for any matter necessary to the furtherance of any such purposes.

6. "Leave of absence" means a privilege granted to an inmate, who need not be an "eligible inmate," to leave the premises of an institution for the period of time necessary:

(a) to visit his or her spouse, child, brother, sister, grandchild, parent, grandparent or ancestral aunt or uncle during his or her last illness if death appears to be imminent;

(b) to attend the funeral of such individual;

(c) to undergo surgery or to receive medical or dental treatment not available in the correctional institution only if deemed absolutely necessary to the health and well-being of the inmate and whose approval is granted by the commissioner or his designated representative.

7. "Educational leave" means a privilege granted to an eligible inmate to leave the premises of an institution for a period not exceeding fourteen hours in any day for the purpose of education or vocational training, or for any matter necessary to the furtherance of any such purposes.

8. "Industrial training leave" means a privilege granted to an eligible inmate to leave the premises of an institution for a period not exceeding fourteen hours in any day for the purpose of participating in an industrial training program, or for any matter necessary to the furtherance of any such purpose.

9. "Temporary release program" means a "work release program," a "furlough program," a "community services program," and "industrial training leave," an "educational leave," or a "leave of absence."

10. "Extended bounds of confinement" means the area in which an inmate participating in a temporary release program may travel, the routes he or she is permitted to use, the places he or she is authorized to visit, and the hours, days, or specially defined period during which he or she is permitted to be absent from the premises of the institution.

11. "Temporary release committee" means the body of persons, which may include members of the public, appointed pursuant to regulations promulgated by the commissioner to serve at the pleasure of the commissioner for the purpose of formulating, modifying and revoking temporary release programs at an institution.

12. "Superintendent" means the person in charge of an institution, by whatever title he or she may be known.

Added by L. 1969, Ch. 472; **Amended** by L. 1972, Ch. 339; L. 1973, Ch. 269; L. 1974, Ch. 966; L. 1976, Ch. 471; L. 1977, Ch. 691; L. 1978, Ch. 691; L. 1979, Ch. 485; L. 1980, Ch. 296; L. 1981, Ch. 495; L. 1982, Ch. 137, eff. Sept. 1, 1982, extending the expiration date of the 1972 amendment to Sept. 1, 1983; Ch. 519, L. 1983 eff. Sept. 1, 1983 extended the expiration date of the 1972 amendment to Sept. 1, 1984; Ch. 983, L. 1984; L. 1985, Ch. 573; L. 1986, Ch. 395, eff. Sept. 1, 1986, extending expiration date to Sept. 1, 1987; L. 1986, Ch. 554, eff. July 24, 1986, amending subd. 1 to include "an institution designated by the commissioner pursuant to § 72-a of this chapter," and shall remain in effect until Sept. 30, 1989; L. 1989, Ch. 338, eff. July 10, 1989, extending expiration date to Sept. 30, 1992; L. 1987, Ch. 261, eff. July 13, 1987, amending subd. 2 and extending expiration date to Sept. 1, 1991; L. 1991, Ch. 447, eff. July 19, 1991, amending subd. 2; L. 1991, Ch. 511, eff. July 19, 1991; L. 1992, Ch. 55, eff. Apr. 10, 1992, extending expiration date to Sept. 1, 1994; L. 1994, Ch. 60, § 42, eff. Apr. 1, 1994, expiring Sept. 1, 1995, and Ch. 60, § 43, eff. Oct. 1, 1995; L. 1995, Ch. 3, § 29, adding closing paragraph to subd. 2, eff. June 10, 1995; L. 1996, Ch. 92, § 4, amending subd. 2, effective June 5, 1996, and amendment expires September

1, 1997; L. 1997, Ch. 435, § 50, extending expiration date of § 851 to Sept. 1, 1999, and §§ 51 and 52, eff. Aug. 20, 1997, extending expiration date of subds. 1 and 2 to Sept. 1, 1999; L. 1999, Ch. 452, § 4, eff. Sept. 1, 1999, extending expiration date of § 851 to Sept. 1, 2001, and §§ 5 and 6, eff. Sept. 1, 1999, extending expiration date of subds. 1 and 2 to Sept. 1, 2001; L. 2001, Ch. 95, §§ 6–8, eff. July 13, 2001, extending expiration date to Sept. 1, 2003; L. 2002, Ch. 251, § 1, eff. July 30, 2002, adding subd. 2-a; L. 2003, Ch. 16, §§ 6–8, extending expiration date to Sept. 1, 2005; L. 2004, Ch. 738, § 3, adding subd. 2-b, eff. Dec. 14, 2004, § 12, amending first setout of subd. 2, eff. Jan. 13, 2005, and § 13, amending second setout of subd. 2; L. 2005, Ch. 252, §§ 1–2, eff. July 19, 2005, amending subd. 2; L. 2005, Ch. 56, Part D, §§ 6–7, extending expiration date to Sept. 1, 2007.

ANNOTATIONS

Governor's executive order concerning temporary release; separation of powers.—When the governor issued an executive order directing the Commissioner of the Department of Correctional Services to change the requirements for the temporary release program by eliminating inmates convicted of violent felonies from future participation, the order was unconstitutional because it violated the separation of powers by imposing restrictions that were inconsistent with the eligibility requirements the legislature set forth; additionally, the statutory amendment authorizing the Governor to exclude or limit participation did not retroactively validate the order as the amendment operated prospectively. Dorst v. Pataki, 167 Misc. 2d 329, 633 N.Y.S.2d 730 (Sup. Ct. Albany Co. 1995), aff'd, 90 N.Y.2d 696, 665 N.Y.S.2d 65, 687 N.E.2d 1348 (1997).

Commissioner's authority.—Commissioner did not exceed his authority in promulgating regulations which extended the statutory provision barring inmates convicted of homicide and certain sex crimes from participating in work release programs. Quartaro v. New York State Dept. of Correctional Servs., 222 A.D.2d 758, 634 N.Y.S.2d 824 (Albany Co. 1995).

Ex post facto doctrine.—Participation in temporary work release program is a privilege, not a right; thus, Governor's executive order eliminating defendant's eligibility for temporary release consideration did not violate Ex Post Facto Clause. People v. Fioravantes, 229 A.D.2d 784, 646 N.Y.S.2d 893 (3d Dept. 1996).

—Ex post facto doctrine does not apply to inmate temporary release programs. Waters v. Coombe, 224 A.D.2d 852, 638 N.Y.S.2d 362 (3d Dept. 1996).

—Defendant contended that a statutory amendment precluding inmates convicted of manslaughter from participating in a work release program which was enacted after defendant was ex post facto; such a contention was improperly raised on direct appeal from conviction because the amendment did not affect the propriety of defendant's sentence. People v. Fornal, 221 A.D.2d 361, 633 N.Y.S.2d 372 (2d Dept. 1995).

—An amendment which makes an inmate statutorily ineligible for a temporary work release program was not an ex post facto law because participating in a temporary work release program is a privilege and because the amendment applied to all inmates who had not entered the program as of April 1, 1994. Jandelli v. Coughlin, 217 A.D.2d 733, 629 N.Y.S.2d 303 (3d Dept. 1995).

Approval for work release; denial of parole.—Where, petitioner, in October 1977, had been approved to participate in the work release program but before he began participation he was denied parole and his next appearance before the parole board was set for July 1979, more than a year hence, the petitioner had a cognizable expectation that, upon reapplication when he was again within one year of parole consideration, he would automatically be restored to the work release program. Horton v. Hongisto, 70 A.D.2d 1040, 417 N.Y.S.2d 565 (4th Dept. 1979).

Denial of temporary release.—Since petitioner's request for temporary release was denied for valid reasons relating to the violent nature of his past acts, the petitioner was not entitled to challenge the grounds upon which he was also found to be mentally unstable, since that finding was irrelevant to the denial of his application. Maisonet v. Wilson, 87 A.D.2d 925, 450 N.Y.S.2d 68 (3d Dept. 1982).

—An inmate's participation in a temporary release program is a privilege. Here, the determination denying petitioner's application for temporary release was neither arbitrary nor capricious because respondent considered both petitioner's criminal history and his acts of recidivism after being given the privileges of temporary work release and parole release as well as petitioner's positive custodial adjustment and program involvement. Dixon v. Recore, 271 A.D.2d 778, 707 N.Y.S.2d 254 (3d Dept. 2000).

—To the extent that determination denying petitioner's application for industrial training leave was based on 1994 amendment limiting "work release program" eligibility of those sentenced for certain homicide and sex offenses, decision was irrational: "industrial training leave" is not the same as a "work release program," and the legislature specifically limited the eligibility exclusion to the work release program as defined in subdivision 3 of section 851. Diggins v. Recore, 163 Misc. 2d 607, 621 N.Y.S.2d 447 (Sup. Ct. Albany Co. 1995).

Work release; termination.—Prior to termination of prisoner's participation in work release program, he is entitled to the procedural due process safeguards noted in Wolff v. McDonald, 418 U.S. 539, 94 S. Ct. 2963, 41 L. Ed. 2d 935. Roman v. Ternullo, 81 Misc. 2d 1023, 367 N.Y.S.2d 197 (Sup. Ct. Dutchess Co. 1975).

—Inmates on an Education and Work Release Program pursuant to Correction Law § 851 et seq. are not given substantially the same degree of freedom in open society as are parolees, and therefore, are not entitled to the same degree of procedural due process for revocation of their privileges. Morales v. Ward, 89 Misc. 2d 651, 392 N.Y.S.2d 197 (Sup. Ct. Albany Co. 1977).

Subd. 2

Commissioner need only address approved requests for release.—Petitioner's argument that the Commissioner was required to pass upon the merits of his request for furlough regardless of whether petitioner was recommended for participation was rejected; the Commissioner must only rule upon applications of inmates falling within the parameters of section 851(2) if release of such inmate is first approved by the Temporary Release Committee, the Superintendent, and the central office. DiGioia v. Turner, 215 A.D.2d 815, 626 N.Y.S.2d 572 (3d Dept. 1995).

Constitutionality; separation of powers.—The legislature's amendment to Corr. Law § 851(2) did not unconstitutionally delegate the law-making power of the Legislature to the Governor, who, as Chief Executive Officer, manages the divisions of the executive branch, including the Department of Correctional Services; Governor could properly make decisions regarding inmates eligible for temporary release. Dorst v. Pataki, 90 N.Y.2d 696, 665 N.Y.S.2d 65, 687 N.E.2d 1348 (1997).

Due process and temporary release programs.—Due process mandates a hearing and review process for inmates who are approved for a temporary release program but are then denied participation because of a change in eligibility. Dorst v. Pataki, 167 Misc. 2d 329, 633 N.Y.S.2d 730 (Sup. Ct. Albany Co. 1995).

§ 852. Establishment of temporary release. [Expires Sept. 1, 2007.]

1. The commissioner, guided by consideration for the safety of the community and the welfare of the inmate, shall review and evaluate all existing rules, regulations and directives relating to current temporary release programs and consistent with the provisions of this article for the administration of temporary release programs shall by January first, nineteen hundred seventy-eight promulgate new rules and regulations for the various forms of temporary release. Such rules and regulations shall reflect the purposes of the different programs and shall include but not be limited to selection criteria, supervision and procedures for the disposition of each application.

2. The commissioner shall appoint or cause to be appointed a temporary release committee for each institution which shall meet on a regularly

scheduled basis to review all applications for temporary release.

3. Work release programs may be established only at institutions classified by the commissioner as work release facilities. Educational release programs may be established only at those educational institutions which shall maintain attendance records for participating inmates.

4. The commissioner shall designate in the rules and regulations of the department appropriate employees or an appropriate unit of the department to be responsible for (a) securing education, on-the-job training and employment opportunities for inmates who are eligible to participate in a work release program, and (b) assisting such inmates in such other manner as necessary or desirable to assure the success of the program.

5. All inmates participating in temporary release programs shall be assigned to parole officers for supervision. Such parole officers shall be responsible to the division of parole for the purpose of providing such supervision. The division shall provide to the department supervision in accordance with the contract required by subdivision six of this section. As part of its supervisory functions the division shall be required to provide reports to the department every two months on each inmate under its supervision. Such reports shall include but not be limited to:

(a) an evaluation of the individual's participation in such programs;

(b) a statement of any problems and the manner in which such problems were resolved relative to an individual's participation in such programs; and

(c) a recommendation with respect to the individual's continued participation in the program.

6. The department shall contract with the division of parole for the provision of parole supervision services set forth in subdivision five of this section.

Added by L. 1969, Ch. 472; **Amended** by L. 1972, Ch. 339; L. 1977, Ch. 691; L. 1981, Ch. 495; L. 1987, Ch. 261, effective July 13, 1987 extending the expiration date to September 1, 1991; L. 1991, Ch. 447, eff. July 19, 1991; L. 1992, Ch. 55, eff. Apr. 10, 1992, extending expiration date to September 1, 1994; L. 1997, Ch. 435, § 50, extending expiration date of § 852 to Sept. 1, 1999; L. 1999, Ch. 452, § 4, extending expiration date of § 852 to Sept. 1, 2001, eff. Sept. 1, 1999; L. 2001, Ch. 95, §6, eff. July 13, 2001; L. 2003, Ch. 16, § 6 extending expiration date to Sept. 1, 2005, eff. Mar. 31, 2003; L. 2005, Ch. 56, Part D, § 6, extending expiration date to Sept. 1, 2007.

ANNOTATIONS

Establishing temporary release programs; separation of powers.—The Governor did not usurp the legislature's ability to create and/or change law when he issued an order requiring the Commissioner of the Department of Correctional Services to prevent transfer to a temporary release program of anyone sentenced as a violent felony offender convicted of crime involving inflicting serious physical injury, using or threatening to use a dangerous instrument or deadly weapon. Day v. Pataki,

166 Misc. 2d 432, 633 N.Y.S.2d 747 (Sup. Ct. Albany Co. 1995).

Responsibility for temporary release programs.—The Commissioner of the Department of Correctional Services is responsible for forming and administering a temporary release program for inmates. Day v. Pataki, 166 Misc. 2d 432, 633 N.Y.S.2d 747 (Sup. Ct. Albany Co. 1995).

Restrictions upon release.—Prisoner's participation in temporary work release program combining work release days with furlough, and thereby permitting him to spend five nights at home and two nights at prison, violated the Corrections Law and 7 NYCRR § 1903.2(3)(6)(iv), which prohibits an inmate's presence in the community for more than 14 hours in any given day. McNamara v. Coughlin, 165 Misc. 2d 397, 627 N.Y.S.2d 278 (Sup. Ct. N.Y. Co. 1995), aff'd, 644 N.Y.S.2d 507 (1st Dept. 1996).

§ 853. Reporting and information.

To ensure the accurate maintenance and availability of statistics and records with respect to participation in temporary release programs, the department shall maintain the following information relative to the operation of temporary release programs:

(a) number of inmate participants in each temporary release program;

(b) number of inmates participating in temporary release for whom written approval of the commissioner was required pursuant to subdivision two of section eight hundred fifty-one of this chapter;

(c) number and type of individual programs approved for each participant;

(d) approved participating employers and educational institutions;

(e) number of inmates arrested;

(f) inmates involuntarily returned for violations by institution;

(g) absconders still at large;

(h) number of disciplinary proceedings initiated and the results thereof;

(i) number of temporary release committee decisions appealed and the results thereof by institution;

(j) reports or information made available to the department with respect to the participation of individuals in such programs, including any incidents of absconding or re-arrest.

The department shall also forward to the state commission of correction quarterly reports including, but not limited to, the information identified in subdivisions (a), (b), (d), (e), (f) and (g) of this section and such other information requested by the commission or available to the department with respect to such programs.

Renumbered former § 853 to § 855 and **Added** new § 853 by L. 1977, Ch. 691; **Amended** by L. 1981, Ch. 757 eff. July 27, 1981; L. 1997, Ch. 435, § 50, extending expiration date of § 853 to Sept. 1, 1999; L. 1999, Ch. 452, § 4, extending expiration date of § 853 to Sept. 1, 2001, eff. Sept. 1, 1999.

ANNOTATION

Memorandum; parole and conditional release.—The

prohibition on leaving the State imposed on parolees and those on conditional release (7 NYCRR 1915.10) is to be set forth by means of a written agreement, to be signed by the inmate, in which the inmate to be paroled or conditionally released states: "I will not leave the state of New York." Molese v. Bayer, 57 A.D.2d 962, 395 N.Y.S.2d 64 (2d Dept. 1977).

§ 854. Evaluation and recommendation.

In recognition of the need for an independent evaluation of, and recommendations with respect to, temporary release, the commission of correction shall evaluate and assess the administration and operation of all temporary release programs conducted pursuant to this article and shall submit to the governor and the legislature by March first, nineteen hundred seventy-eight, its findings together with any recommendations with respect to the proper operation or the improvement of such temporary release programs.

Renumbered former § 854 to § 856 and **Added** new § 854 by L. 1977, Ch. 691; **Amended** by L. 1997, Ch. 435, § 50, extending expiration date of § 854 to Sept. 1, 1999; L. 1999, Ch. 452, § 4, extending expiration date of § 854 to Sept. 1, 2001, eff. Sept. 1, 1999.

§ 855. Procedure for temporary release of inmates. [*Expires September 1, 2007.*]

1. A person confined in an institution designated for the conduct of work release programs who is an eligible inmate, may make application to the temporary release committee of the institution for permission to participate in a work release program.

2. Any eligible inmate may make application to the temporary release committee for participation in a furlough program or community services program, or for an industrial training leave or educational leave.

3. Any inmate may make application to the temporary release committee for a leave of absence provided, however, that in exigent circumstances such application may be made directly to the superintendent of the institution and the superintendent may exercise all of the powers of the temporary release committee subject, however, to any limitation or requirement set forth in the rules and regulations of the department and subject further to the discretion of the commissioner. All leave of absences provided in exigent circumstances shall state the reasons for approval or disapproval of the application and shall be included in the inmate's institutional parole file.

4. If the temporary release committee determines that a temporary release program for the applicant is consistent with the safety of the community and the welfare of the applicant, and is consistent with rules and regulations of the department, the committee, with the assistance of the employees or unit designated by the commissioner pursuant to subdivision four of section eight hundred fifty-two of this article, shall develop a suitable program of temporary release for the applicant. Consistent with these provisions, any educational leave program shall consider the scheduling of classes to insure a reduction of release time not spent in educational pursuits.

5. The committee shall then prepare a memorandum setting forth the details of the temporary release program including the extended bounds of confinement and any other matter required by rules or regulations of the department. Such memorandum shall be transmitted to the superintendent who may approve or reject the program, subject to rules and regulations promulgated by the commissioner. If the superintendent approves the program, he shall indicate such approval in writing by signing the memorandum. If the superintendent rejects the program, he shall state his reasons in writing and a copy of his statement shall be given to the inmate and to the commissioner and such decision shall be reviewed by the commissioner. If the commissioner rejects the program, he shall state his reasons in writing. A copy of such statement shall be filed in the inmate's institutional file.

6. In order for an applicant to accept a program of temporary release, such inmate shall agree to be bound by all the terms and conditions thereof and shall indicate such agreement by signing the memorandum of the program immediately below a statement reading as follows: "I accept the foregoing program and agree to be bound by the terms and conditions thereof. I understand that I will be under the supervision of the state department of correctional services while I am away from the premises of the institution and I agree to comply with the instructions of any parole officer or other employee of the department assigned to supervise me. I understand that my participation in the program is a privilege which may be revoked at any time, and that if I violate any provision of the program I may be taken into custody by any peace officer or police officer and I will be subject to disciplinary procedures. I further understand that if I intentionally fail to return to the institution at or before the time specified in the memorandum I may be found guilty of a felony." Such agreement shall be placed on file at the institution from which such temporary release is granted.

7. After approving the program of temporary release, the superintendent may then permit an inmate who has accepted such program to go outside the premises of the institution within the limits of the extended bounds of confinement described in the memorandum; provided, however, that no such permission shall become effective in the case of a work release or furlough program prior to the time at which the person to be released becomes an eligible inmate.

8. At least three days before releasing an inmate on a temporary release program, the superintendent shall notify in writing the sheriff or chief of police of the community into which the inmate is to be released.

9. Participation in a temporary release program shall be privilege. Nothing contained in this article may be construed to confer upon any inmate the right to participate, or to continue to participate, in a temporary release program. The superintendent of the institution may at any time, and upon recommendation of the temporary release committee or of the commissioner or of the chairman of the state board of parole or his designee shall, revoke any inmate's privilege to participate in a program of temporary release in accordance with regulations promulgated by the commissioner.

Added by L. 1969, Ch. 472 as § 853; Amended by L. 1972, Ch. 339; L. 1974, Ch. 966; L. 1977, Ch. 691 renumbered to § 855; L. 2001, Ch. 95, §6, eff. July 13, 2001; L. 2003, Ch. 16, § 6, extending expiration date to Sept. 1, 2005, eff. Mar. 31, 2003; L. 2005, Ch. 56, Part D, § 6, extending expiration date to Sept. 1, 2007.

ANNOTATIONS

Appellate review.—Appellate Division's review of a determination denying an inmate participation in a temporary release program is limited to whether the determination "violated any positive statutory requirement or denied a constitutional right of the inmate and whether [it] is affected by irrationality bordering on impropriety." Here, court could not conclude that respondent's determination was irrational. Peana v. Recore, 257 A.D.2d 862, 685 N.Y.S.2d 120 (3d Dept. 1999).

No automatic entitlement to temporary release.—The fact that petitioner is an eligible inmate for participation in a temporary release program does not make him automatically entitled to a temporary release, because it must first be determined that temporary release is consistent with the safety of the community and the welfare of the applicant. Romer v. Goord, 242 A.D.2d 574, 662 N.Y.S.2d 132 (2d Dept. 1997).

Subd. 4

Commissioner's discretion.—7 NYCRR § 1900.4(c)(ii)(a), which provides that, if an inmate is committed to a local New York state jurisdiction for a definite sentence, his participation in a temporary release program is barred unless the sentencing judge states in writing that the court has no objection, is a valid exercise of the Commissioner's authority to administer the temporary release program in a manner consistent with the "safety of the community and the welfare of the applicant." Risher v. Coughlin, 146 Misc. 2d 451, 550 N.Y.S.2d 1014 (Sup. Ct. Dutchess Co. 1990).

Denial of release.—The Temporary Release Committee should enunciate the controlling bases and conclusions upon which a prisoner is denied temporary release in accordance with Correct. Law § 853(4). White v. Vincent, 88 Misc. 2d 914, 390 N.Y.S.2d 499 (Sup. Ct. Dutchess Co. 1975).

Denial of parole and denial of early parole release under special programs; when reasons must be furnished.—Written report by parole board after parole release hearing informing petitioner that petition for parole was denied because of seriousness of crime and his unwillingness to appreciate conduct for which he was convicted, was sufficient to meet minimal requirements for disclosure of reasons for denial; no statement of reasons is required where hearing held is not parole release hearing, but rather a hearing to determine eligibility for early parole release under a special program. Strafford v. New York State Bd. of Parole, 90 Misc. 2d 948, 396 N.Y.S.2d 564 (Sup. Ct. Dutchess Co. 1977).

Temporary release; statement of reasons for denial required.—Temporary Release Committee violated statutory requirement in not specifying reasons for refusal of request for furlough rationally related to standards, provided in Corr. L. § 853(4) (presently Corr. L § 855(4)). Friedman v. Hassan, 90 Misc. 2d 55, 396 N.Y.S.2d 567 (Sup. Ct. Queens Co. 1977).

Subd. 9

Participation.—Since participation in temporary release is a privilege, the scope of judicial review of a determination denying participation is limited to whether respondents have violated any positive statutory requirement or denied a constitutional right of the inmate, and whether respondents' determination is affected by irrationality bordering on impropriety. Grant v. Temporary Release Committee, 209 A.D.2d 617, 619 N.Y.S.2d 106 (2d Dept. 1994).

—Given that petitioner was convicted of three counts of sodomy involving forcible compulsion, no basis existed for disturbing the denial of temporary release predicated upon the seriousness of petitioner's crime. DiGioia v. Turner, 215 A.D.2d 815, 626 N.Y.S.2d 572 (3d Dept. 1995).

—Participation in the temporary work release program is a privilege, not a right, making the ex post facto doctrine inapplicable; the 1994 amendment to the Correction Law restricting eligibility in the work release program was applicable to petitioner, who unsuccessfully applied to the program in 1993. McCormack v. Posillico, 213 A.D.2d 913, 624 N.y.S.2d 304 (3d Dept. 1995).

§ 856. Conduct of inmates participating in a temporary release program.
[Expires September 1, 2007.]

1. An inmate who is permitted to leave the premises of an institution to participate in a temporary release program shall have on his or her person a card identifying him or her as a participant in a temporary release program as signed by the superintendent of the institution at all times while outside the premises of the institution and shall exhibit such card to any peace officer or police officer upon request of such officer. The commissioner may, by regulation, require such information, including effective dates, to be included in such card as he shall deem necessary and proper.

2. If the inmate violates any provision of the program, or any rule or regulation promulgated by the commissioner for conduct of inmates participating in temporary release programs, such inmate shall be subject to disciplinary measures to the same extent as if he or she violated a rule or regulation of the commissioner for conduct of inmates within the premises of the institution. The failure of an inmate to voluntarily return to the institution of his confinement more than ten hours after his prescribed time of return shall create a rebuttable presumption that the failure to return was intentional. Any inmate who is found to have intentionally failed to return pursuant to this subdivision shall be an absconder in violation of his temporary release program and will not be an eligible inmate as defined in subdivision two of section eight hundred fifty-one of this chapter. The creation of such rebuttable presumption shall not be admissible in any court of law as evidence of the commission of any crime defined in the penal law. A full report of any such violation, a summary of the facts and findings of the disciplinary hearing and disciplinary measures taken, shall be made available to the board for the inmate's next scheduled appearance before the state board of parole including any defense or explanation offered by the inmate in response at such hearing.

3. The provisions of this chapter relating to good behavior allowances shall apply to behavior

of inmates while participating in temporary release programs outside the premises of institutions, and such allowances may be granted, withheld, forfeited or cancelled in whole or in part for behavior outside the premises of an institution to the same extent and in the same manner as is provided for behavior of inmates within the premises of institutions.

4. An inmate who is in violation of the provisions of his or her temporary release program may be taken into custody by any peace officer or police officer and, in such event, the inmate shall be returned forthwith to either the institution that released him or her, or to the nearest secure facility where greater security is indicated. In any case where the institution is in a county other than the one in which the inmate is apprehended, the officer may deliver the inmate to the nearest institution, jail or lock up and it shall be the duty of the person in charge of said facility to hold such inmate securely until such time as he or she is delivered into the custody of an officer of the institution from which he or she was released. Upon delivering the inmate to an institution, jail or lockup, other than the one from which the inmate was released, the officer who apprehended the inmate shall forthwith notify the superintendent of the institution from which the inmate was released and it shall be the duty of the superintendent to effect the expeditious return of the inmate to the institution.

5. Upon the conclusion or termination of a temporary release program, a full report of the inmate's performance in such program shall be prepared in accordance with regulations of the commissioner. Such report shall include but not be limited to: adjustment to release, supervision contacts, statement of any violations of the terms and conditions of release and of any disciplinary actions taken, and an assessment of the inmate's suitability for parole. Such report shall be made available to the state board of parole for the inmate's next scheduled appearance before such board.

Added by L. 1969, Ch. 472 as § 854; Amended by L. 1972, Ch. 339; L. 1977, Ch. 691 renumbered to § 856; L. 2001, Ch. 95, §6, eff. July 13, 2001; L. 2003, Ch. 16, § 6, extending expiration date to Sept. 1, 2005, eff. Mar. 31, 2003; L. 2005, Ch. 56, Part D, § 6, extending expiration date to Sept. 1, 2007.

ANNOTATIONS

Procedure for securing return of inmate in violation of program.—"Authorization for Detention and Return" issued pursuant to section 856(4) does not have the benefit of judicial review and does not empower an investigator in the absconder and escape unit of the Department of Correctional Services to enter a third person's home to search for escaped prisoner constituted a warrantless entry. People v. Jimenez, 163 Misc. 2d 30, 619 N.Y.S.2d 519 (Crim. Ct. N.Y. Co. 1994).

Removal from temporary release program; due process.—Petitioner's removal from Temporary Release Program constitutes a grievous loss of a liberty interest sufficient to invoke due process considerations; it is reasonable for the defendant to assume that once he is granted temporary release that the will remain in the program absent any misbehavior on

his part. Ketwig v. Ward, 93 Misc. 2d 103, 402 N.Y.S.2d 149 (Sup. Ct. Orleans Co. 1978).

Revocation of temporary release.—The superintendent's proceeding relating to revocation of temporary release provided the petitioner with procedural protections which far exceeded the basic due process requirements, where it provided for written notice of the formal charge more than 24 hours prior to the commencement of the proceeding, the opportunity to be assisted in the defense thereof by a prison employee, notice that any statement he made could not be used in a criminal action or proceeding, the right to make a statement in his behalf and a written disposition which included a statement of the evidence relied upon. People ex rel. Cunningham v. Metz, 61 A.D.2d 590, 403 N.Y.S.2d 330 (3d Dept. 1978).

§ 857. Complaint and abuse review

Any person may submit to the commission of correction any complaint he or she may have concerning programmatic abuses. The commission of correction shall evaluate such complaints and, where indicated, conduct any needed investigation. If the commission concludes that a complaint is valid, the commission shall make recommendations to the department for corrective action. Where the commission believes sufficient evidence exists to support a criminal charge, the commission shall report such evidence to the appropriate law enforcement agencies.

Renumbered former § 857 to § 860 and new § 857 **added** by L. 1977, Ch. 691.

§ 858. Application of labor laws.

The laws of the state and its political subdivisions with respect to employment conditions shall apply to inmates participating in work release programs.

Added by L. 1969, Ch. 472; **Renumbered** § 855 to § 858 by L. 1977, Ch. 691.

§ 859. When employment prohibited.

No employment under a work release program may be approved or continued if (a) such employment results in the displacement of employed workers, or is applied in skills, crafts or trades in which there is a surplus of available labor in the locality, or (b) the rates of pay and other conditions of employment are not at least equal to those paid or provided for work of similar nature in the locality in which the work is to be performed, or (c) there is any labor strike or lockout in the establishment in which the inmate is employed.

Added by L. 1969, Ch. 472; **Renumbered** § 856 to § 859 by L. 1977, Ch. 691.

ANNOTATION

Participation is privilege.—Inmate's participation in a temporary release program is a privilege and not a right and, accordingly, court's review of denial of inmate's application to participate in a temporary release program was limited to determining whether the denial of the privilege violated any positive statutory requirement or denied a constitutional right of the inmate and whether it was affected by irrationality bordering on impropriety. In re Williams, 251 A.D.2d 833, 675 N.Y.S.2d 383 (3d Dept. 1998).

§ 860. Disposition of earnings.

The earnings of an inmate participating in a

work release program, less any payroll deductions required or authorized by law, shall be turned over to the warden who shall deposit such receipts as inmates' funds pursuant to section one hundred sixteen of this chapter. Such receipts shall not be subject to attachment or garnishment in the hands of the warden. The commissioner of correction may authorize the warden to make disbursements of such receipts, and such receipts may be disbursed, for any or all of the following purposes:

1. Appropriate and reasonable costs related to the inmate's participation in the work release program;

2. Support of the inmate's dependents;

3. Payment of fines imposed by any court;

4. Payment of any court ordered restitution or reparation to the victim of the inmate's crime.

5. Purchases by the inmate from the commissary of the institution.

The balance of such receipts, if any, after disbursements for the foregoing purposes shall be paid to the inmate upon termination of his imprisonment.

Added by L. 1969, Ch. 472; **Amended** by L. 1974, Ch. 966; **Renumbered** § 857 to § 860 by L. 1977, Ch. 691; L. 1985, Ch. 233, eff. Nov. 1, 1985, renumbered subd. 4 to 5 and added new subd. 4.

§ 861. Inmate not agent of state.

An inmate participating in a work release program shall not, merely by reason of such participation, be deemed an agent, employee or servant of the state while outside the premises of an institution pursuant to the terms of a work release program.

Added by L. 1969, Ch. 472; **Amended** by L. 1974, Ch. 966; **Renumbered** § 858 to § 861 by L. 1977, Ch. 691.

CORR. L.

ARTICLE 26-A—SHOCK INCARCERATION PROGRAM FOR STATE CORRECTIONAL INMATES

Section

§ 865. Definitions.

As used in this article, the following terms mean:

1. "Eligible inmate" means a person sentenced to an indeterminate term of imprisonment who will become eligible for release on parole within three years or sentenced to a determinate term of imprisonment who will become eligible for conditional release within three years, who has not reached the age of forty years, who has not previously been convicted of a felony upon which an indeterminate or determinate term of imprisonment was imposed and who was between the ages of sixteen and forty years at the time of commission of the crime upon which his or her present sentence was based except, however, an eligible inmate shall not include a person sentenced to a determinate sentence of three and one-half years or more as a second felony drug offender pursuant to subdivision three of section 70.70 of the penal law for a conviction of a class B felony offense defined in article two hundred twenty of the penal law. Notwithstanding the foregoing, no person who is convicted of any of the following crimes shall be deemed eligible to participate in this program: (a) a violent felony offense as defined in article seventy of the penal law, (b) an A-I felony offense, (c) manslaughter in the second degree, vehicular manslaughter in the second degree, vehicular manslaughter in the first degree, and criminally negligent homicide as defined in article one hundred twenty-five of the penal law, (d) rape in the second degree, rape in the third degree, criminal sexual act in the second degree, criminal sexual act in the third degree, attempted sexual abuse in the first degree, attempted rape in the second degree and attempted criminal sexual act in the second degree as defined in articles one hundred ten and one hundred thirty of the penal law and (e) any escape or absconding offense as defined in article two hundred five of the penal law.

2. "Shock incarceration program" means a program pursuant to which eligible inmates are selected directly at reception centers to participate in the program and serve a period of six months in a shock incarceration facility, which shall provide rigorous physical activity, intensive regimentation and discipline and rehabilitation therapy and programming.

Amended by L. 1987, Ch. 262, eff. July 13, 1987; L. 1988, Ch. 636, eff. Sept. 1, 1988, amending subd. 1; L. 1988, Ch. 59, eff. Apr. 24, 1988; L. 1989, Ch. 338, eff. July 10, 1989;

L. 1992, Ch. 55, eff. Apr. 10, 1992, amending subd. 1; L. 1999, Ch. 412, Part B, eff. Aug. 9, 1999, amending subd. 1; L. 2003, Ch. 264, § 52, eff. Nov. 1, 2003, amending subd. 1; L. 2004, Ch. 738, § 14, eff. Jan. 13, 2005, amending subd. 1.

§ 866. Establishment of shock incarceration program.

1. The commissioner, guided by consideration for the safety of the community and the welfare of the inmate, shall promulgate rules and regulations for the shock incarceration program. Such rules and regulations shall reflect the purpose of the program and shall include, but not be limited to, selection criteria, inmate discipline, programming and supervision, and program structure and administration.

2. For each reception center the commissioner shall appoint or cause to be appointed a shock incarceration selection committee, which shall meet on a regularly scheduled basis to review all applications for the shock incarceration program.

3. Shock incarceration programs may be established only at institutions classified by the commissioner as shock incarceration facilities.

4. The department may contract with the division of substance abuse services for the provision of such services as may be required to assure the success of the program.

5. The department shall conduct an ongoing evaluation of the program to ensure that the programmatic objectives are met. The department shall undertake studies and prepare reports periodically on the impact of the program.

§ 867. Procedure for selection of participants in shock incarceration program.

1. An eligible inmate may make an application to the shock incarceration screening committee for permission to participate in the shock incarceration program.

2. If the shock incarceration screening committee determines that an inmate's participation in the shock incarceration program is consistent with the safety of the community, the welfare of the applicant and the rules and regulations of the department, the committee shall forward the application to the commissioner or his designee for approval or disapproval.

3. Applicants cannot participate in the shock

incarceration program unless they agree to be bound by all the terms and conditions thereof and indicate such agreement by signing the memorandum of the program immediately below a statement reading as follows:

"I accept the foregoing program and agree to be bound by the terms and conditions thereof. I understand that my participation in the program is a privilege that may be revoked at any time at the sole discretion of the commissioner. I understand that I must successfully complete the entire program to obtain a certificate of earned eligibility upon the completion of said program, and in the event that I do not successfully complete said program, for any reason, I will be transferred to a nonshock incarceration correctional facility to continue service of my sentence."

4. An inmate who has successfully completed a shock incarceration program shall be eligible to receive such a certificate of earned eligibility pursuant to section eight hundred five of this chapter. Notwithstanding any other provision of law, an inmate sentenced to a determinate sentence of imprisonment who has successfully completed a shock incarceration program shall be eligible to receive such a certificate of earned eligibility and shall be immediately eligible to be conditionally released.

5. Participation in the shock incarceration program shall be a privilege. Nothing contained in this article may be construed to confer upon any inmate the right to participate or continue to participate therein.

Amended by L. 1989, Ch. 338, eff. July 10, 1989; L. 1992, Ch. 55, eff. Apr. 10, 1992, amending subds. 1 and 4; L. 2004, Ch. 738, § 15, amending subd. 4, eff. Jan. 13, 2005.

CORR. L.

ARTICLE 27—WORK RELEASE PROGRAM FOR COUNTY JAILS

Section

§ 870. Establishment of program.

The sheriff, upon approval of the legislative body of the county, may establish a work release program pursuant to which prisoners, sentenced to and confined in any county jail under his jurisdiction, may be granted the privilege of leaving confinement for the purpose of working at gainful employment, participating in a privately or publicly sponsored program of vocational training, with or without compensation, or attending an educational institution. The work release program may also include the release from confinement during necessary and reasonable hours for the purpose of caring for the prisoner's family.

Amended by L. 1976, Ch. 71.

§ 871. Procedures.

(a) Any prisoner sentenced to and confined in any jail for which the sheriff has established a work release program may apply to the sheriff for permission to participate in such program. Pursuant to rules and regulations promulgated by the sheriff and approved by the state commission of correction, the sheriff may approve or disapprove the application. In the event of approval, the sheriff shall prepare a specific, written work release plan for the prisoner which shall contain such terms and conditions as shall be deemed reasonably proper and necessary. The prisoner shall signify in writing his agreement to the terms of the work release plan in such form as the sheriff shall specify and a copy of the work release plan shall be delivered to the prisoner prior to his participation therein. The work release plan may be revoked, suspended or modified by the sheriff at any time for good cause, with or without notice to the prisoner. Any disapproval, revocation, suspension or modification of a work release application or plan shall be reviewable by the state commission of correction upon written request of the prisoner which shall be forwarded immediately to the commission by the sheriff. The decision of the commission shall be final and not be subject to judicial review.

(b) The sheriff shall appoint a committee, to be known as the work release committee, composed of at least one member of the county department of probation and of such members of the staff of the jail of confinement as he shall deem proper. The work release committee may also include such other persons whom the sheriff may deem proper, and such persons shall be selected upon the basis of their knowledge and experience in the field of penology, law, medicine, labor, commerce, theology or social services. The committee shall advise and assist the sheriff in administering the work release program provided, however, that any determination to approve, disapprove, revoke, suspend or modify any work release application or plan shall rest solely in the discretion of the sheriff subject to review by the commission of correction as se forth in subdivision (a) of this section.

(c) The sheriff and work release committee may assist prisoners seeking admission to the work release program in securing gainful employment or participation in a publicly or privately sponsored program of vocational training.

(d) A work release plan may include employment within a county other than that in which the jail of confinement is located. The sheriff may arrange with the sheriff or the superintendent or other person in charge of a jail or penitentiary or any other county which has adopted a work release program to maintain custody of any prisoner employed in such other county during the period of employment or until his discharge from confinement, whichever shall occur first. In such event, the sheriff or superintendent of the jail or penitentiary having such custody of the prisoner shall dispose of the earnings of the prisoner pursuant to section eight hundred seventy-two of this article.

ANNOTATIONS

Application resubmitted; new evaluation called for.—The committee acted improperly by blindly adhering to the initial decision of 19 months earlier in a case where an inmate resubmitted his application for a temporary release program as the committee should have considered the possibility of progress toward rehabilitation. Ortiz v. Wilson, 113 Misc. 2d 226, 448 N.Y.S.2d 918 (Sup. Ct. Albany Co. 1981).

State Division of Human Rights is without jurisdiction to

determine prisoner grievances about work release program.—State Div. of Human Rights v. County of Monroe, 65 A.D.2d 947, 410 N.Y.S.2d 734 (4th Dept. 1978).

§ 872. Disposition of earnings.

(a) The wages or salary of a prisoner participating in the work release program, less payroll deductions required by law, shall be deposited with the sheriff in a trust fund account, which and shall not be subject to garnishment or attachment. The sheriff shall keep a ledger of the account of each prisoner and he may disburse from the said trust fund account:

(1) such sum as the prisoner may be legally obligated to pay for the support of his dependents as recommended by the department of social services of the county in which such dependents side, provided, however, that the prisoner may authorize that a sum greater than that so recommended be disbursed for this purpose;

(2) a sum determined by the sheriff to be the cost to the county of providing food, lodging and clothing for such prisoner subject, however, to approval by the state commission of correction;

(3) a sum determined by the sheriff to be the cost to the county of the actual and necessary food, travel and other expenses of such prisoner when released from confinement for the purpose of participating in the work release program;

(4) such sums as may be necessary to satisfy any fines outstanding against the prisoner;

(5) such sums as may be necessary to satisfy any outstanding legal obligations of the prisoner, acknowledged by him in writing and filed with the sheriff in such from as the sheriff shall specify.

(b) Any balance remaining in the trust fund account after such disbursements shall be paid to the prisoner upon his discharge from confinement.

(c) On or before the thirty-first day of January of each year, the sheriff shall prepare a summary of receipts and disbursements of all accounts kept during the previous year and shall forward the summary to the chief executive officer of the county. The summary shall be a public record.

Amended by L. 1984, Ch. 236, eff. June 19, 1984, adding subd. c.

§ 873. Separate housing.

The sheriff may designate separate facilities within the jail for the quartering of prisoners participating in the work release program.

§ 874. When employment prohibited.

(a) No employment under the work release program for any prisoner shall be approved if:

(1) it is ascertained by the sheriff that such employment will result in the displacement of employed workers, or be applied in skills, crafts

or trades in which there is a surplus of available labor in the locality, except in the case of a prisoner who is to be employed by an employer for whom he was employed as a free person prior to the commencement of his sentence, and;

(2) the rates of pay and other conditions of employment are not at least equal to those paid or provided for work of a similar nature in the locality in which the work is to be performed.

(b) The state department of labor shall exercise the same supervision over conditions of employment for prisoners participating in the work release program as such department does over conditions of employment for free persons.

(c) In no event shall any work release program be permitted when there is any labor strike or lock-out in the establishment in which the prisoner is, or is to be, employed.

§ 875. [*Repealed.*]

§ 876. Eligibility for reduction of sentence, parole or conditional release.

Nothing in this article shall be construed to prejudice the eligibility of any prisoner participating in a work release program for the purposes of discretionary reduction of sentence, parole or conditional release except absconding from work release as defined by section 205.16 of the penal law provided, however, that the participation of any prisoner in such program may be considered favorably for such purposes if such participation has assisted in the rehabilitation of such prisoner.

Amended by L. 1969, Ch. 678.

§ 877. Prisoner not an agent of county.

No prisoner participating in a work release program shall be deemed an agent, employee or involuntary servant of the county while released from the jail of confinement pursuant to the terms of any work release plan; provided, however, that when a prisoner is employed by the state or a local municipality, his relationship to the state or local municipality arising out of such employment shall be determined in the same manner as if he were a free person so employed.

§ 878. Annual report.

The sheriff shall annually prepare a report of the work release program which shall be transmitted to the legislature on or before the first day of March in each year. Such annual report shall include a summary of the operations and activities of the program for the preceding year and such recommendations for the improvement of the program as the sheriff shall deem necessary and proper.

§ 879. Application of article.

This article shall not apply to any sheriff in the city of New York or to the commissioner of correction in the city of New York.

PART 2

RELATED MISCELLANEOUS CRIMINAL PROVISIONS

CIVIL PRACTICE LAW AND RULES

(ARTS. 13-A, 13-B, 45, 70, 78)

ARTICLE 13-A

PROCEEDS OF CRIME—FORFEITURE

(L. 1984, Ch. 669, eff. August 1, 1984, repealed former Article 13-A and added new Article 13-A, which applies to crimes committed on and after August 1, 1984.)

LexisNexis Cross References

See generally Prosecution and Defense of Forfeiture Cases; The Law of Asset Forfeiture.

§ 1310. Definitions.

In this article:

1. "Property" means and includes: real property, personal property, money, negotiable instruments, securities, or any thing of value or any interest in a thing of value.

2. "Proceeds of a crime" means any property obtained through the commission of a felony crime defined in subdivisions five and six hereof, and includes any appreciation in value of such property.

3. "Substituted proceeds of a crime" means any property obtained by the sale or exchange of proceeds of a crime, and any gain realized by such sale or exchange.

4. "Instrumentality of a crime" means any property, other than real property and any buildings, fixtures, appurtenances, and improvements thereon, whose use contributes directly and materially to the commission of a crime defined in subdivisions five and six hereof.

4-a. "Real property instrumentality of a crime" means an interest in real property the use of which contributes directly and materially to the commission of a specified felony offense.

4-b. "Specified felony offense" means:

(a) A conviction of a person for a violation of section 220.18, 220.21, 220.41, or 220.43 of the penal law, or where the accusatory instrument charges one or more of such offenses, conviction upon a plea of guilty to any of the felonies for which such plea is otherwise authorized by law or a conviction of a person for conspiracy to commit a violation of section 220.18, 220.21, 220.41, or 220.43 of the penal law, where the controlled substances which are the object of the conspiracy are located in the real property which is the subject of the forfeiture action; or

(b) On three or more occasions, engaging in conduct constituting a violation of any of the felonies defined in section 220.09, 220.16, 220.18, 220.21, 220.31, 220.34, 220.39, 220.41, 220.43 or 221.55 of the penal law, which violations do not constitute a single criminal offense as defined in subdivision one of section 40.10 of the criminal procedure law, or a single criminal transaction, as defined in paragraph (a) of subdivision two of section 40.10 of the criminal procedure law, and at least one of which resulted in a conviction of such offense, or where the accusatory instrument charges one or more of such felonies, conviction upon a plea of guilty to a felony for which such plea is otherwise authorized by law; or

(c) A conviction of a person for a violation of section 220.09, 220.16, 220.34 or 220.39 of the penal law, or a conviction of a criminal defendant for a violation of section 221.30 of the penal law, or where the accusatory instrument charges any such felony, conviction upon a plea of guilty to a felony for which the plea is otherwise authorized by law, together with evidence which: (i) provides substantial indicia that the defendant used the real property to engage in a continual, ongoing course of conduct involving the unlawful mixing, compounding, manufacturing, warehousing, or packaging of controlled substances or where the conviction is for a violation of section 221.30 of the penal law, marijuana, as part of an illegal trade or business for gain; and (ii) establishes, where the conviction is for possession of a controlled substance or where the conviction is for a violation of section 221.30 of the penal law, marijuana, that such possession was with the intent to sell it.

5. "Post-conviction forfeiture crime" means any felony defined in the penal law or any other chapter of the consolidated laws of the state.

6. "Pre-conviction forfeiture crime" means only a felony defined in article two hundred twenty or section 221.30 or 221.55 of the penal law.

7. "Court" means a superior court.

8. "Defendant" means a person against whom a forfeiture action is commenced and includes a

"criminal defendant" and a "non-criminal defendant."

9. "Criminal defendant" means a person who has a criminal liability for a crime defined in subdivisions five and six hereof. For purposes of this article, a person has criminal liability when (a) he has been convicted of a post-conviction forfeiture crime, or (b) the claiming authority proves by clear and convincing evidence that such person has committed an act in violation of article two hundred twenty or section 221.30 or 221.55 of the penal law.

10. "Non-criminal defendant" means a person, other than a criminal defendant, who possesses an interest in the proceeds of a crime, substituted proceeds of a crime or in an instrumentality of a crime.

11. "Claiming authority" means the district attorney having jurisdiction over the offense or the attorney general for purpose of those crimes for which the attorney general has criminal jurisdiction in a case where the underlying criminal charge has been, is being or is about to be brought by the attorney general, or the appropriate corporation counsel or county attorney, provided that the corporation counsel or county attorney may act as a claiming authority only with the consent of the district attorney or the attorney general, as appropriate.

12. "Claiming agent" means and shall include all persons described in subdivision thirty-four of section 1.20 of the criminal procedure law, and sheriffs, undersheriffs and deputy sheriffs of counties within the city of New York.

13. "Fair consideration" means fair consideration is given for property, or obligation, (a) when in exchange for such property, or obligation, as a fair equivalent therefor, and in good faith, property is conveyed or an antecedent debt is satisfied, or (b) when such property, or obligation is received in good faith to secure a present advance of antecedent debt in amount not disproportionately small as compared with the value of the property, or obligation obtained.

Amended by L. 1986, Ch. 174, eff. Nov. 1, 1986, amending subd. 12; L. 1990, Ch. 655, Nov. 1, 1990, adding subds. 4-a, 4-b, and amending subd. 11.

ANNOTATION

Proceeds.—Forfeiture is available for crime proceeds or substituted proceeds. Morgenthau v. Clifford, 157 Misc. 2d 331, 597 N.Y.S.2d 843, 850 (Sup. Ct. N.Y. Co. 1993).

§ 1311. Forfeiture actions.

1. A civil action may be commenced by the appropriate claiming authority against a criminal defendant to recover the property which constitutes the proceeds of a crime, the substituted proceeds of a crime, an instrumentality of a crime or the real property instrumentality of a crime or to recover a money judgment in an amount equivalent in value to the property which constitutes the proceeds of a crime, the substituted proceeds of a crime, an instrumentality of a crime or the real property instrumentality of a crime. A civil action may be commenced against a non-criminal defendant to recover the property which constitutes the proceeds of a crime, the substituted proceeds of a crime, an instrumentality of a crime, or the real property instrumentality of a crime provided, however, that a judgment of forfeiture predicated upon clause (A) of subparagraph (iv) of paragraph (b) of subdivision three hereof shall be limited to the amount of the proceeds of the crime. Any action under this article must be commenced within five years of the commission of the crime and shall be civil, remedial, and in personam in nature and shall not be deemed to be a penalty or criminal forfeiture for any purpose. Except as otherwise specially provided by statute, the proceedings under this article shall be governed by this chapter. An action under this article is not a criminal proceeding and may not be deemed to be a previous prosecution under article forty of the criminal procedure law.

(a) Actions relating to post-conviction forfeiture crimes. An action relating to a post-conviction forfeiture crime must be grounded upon a conviction of a felony defined in subdivision five of section one thousand three hundred ten of this article, or upon criminal activity arising from a common scheme or plan of which such a conviction is a part, or upon a count of an indictment or information alleging a felony which was dismissed at the time of a plea of guilty to a felony in satisfaction of such count. A court may not grant forfeiture until such conviction has occurred. However, an action may be commenced, and a court may grant a provisional remedy provided under this article, prior to such conviction having occurred. An action under this paragraph must be dismissed at any time after sixty days of the commencement of the action unless the conviction upon which the action is grounded has occurred, or an indictment or information upon which the asserted conviction is to be based is pending in a superior court. An action under this paragraph shall be stayed during the pendency of a criminal action which is related to it; provided, however, that such stay shall not prevent the granting or continuance of any provisional remedy provided under this article or any other provisions of law.

(b) Actions relating to pre-conviction forfeiture crimes. An action relating to a pre-conviction forfeiture crime need not be grounded upon conviction of a pre-conviction forfeiture crime, provided, however, that if the action is not grounded upon such a conviction, it shall be necessary in the action for the claiming authority to prove the commission of a pre-conviction forfeiture crime by clear and convincing evidence. An action under this paragraph shall be stayed during the pendency of a criminal action which is related to it; provided, that upon motion of a defendant in the forfeiture action or the claiming authority, a court may, in the interest of justice and for good cause, and with the consent of all parties, order that the forfeiture action proceed despite the pending criminal action; and provided that such stay shall not prevent the granting or continuance of any provisional remedy provided under this article or any other provision of law.

2. All defendants in a forfeiture action brought pursuant to this article shall have the right to trial by jury on any issue of fact.

3. In a forfeiture action pursuant to this article the following burdens of proof shall apply:

(a) In a forfeiture action commenced by a claiming authority against a criminal defendant, except for those facts referred to in paragraph (b) of subdivision nine of section one thousand three hundred ten and paragraph (b) of subdivision one of this section which must be proven by clear and convincing evidence, the burden shall be upon the claiming authority to prove by a preponderance of the evidence the facts necessary to establish a claim for forfeiture.

(b) In a forfeiture action commenced by a claiming authority against a non-criminal defendant:

(i) in an action relating to a pre-conviction forfeiture crime, the burden shall be upon the claiming authority to prove by clear and convincing evidence the commission of the crime by a person, provided, however, that it shall not be necessary to prove the identity of such person.

(ii) if the action relates to the proceeds of a crime, except as provided in subparagraph (i) hereof, the burden shall be upon the claiming authority to prove by a preponderance of the evidence the facts necessary to establish a claim for forfeiture and that the non-criminal defendant either (A) knew or should have known that the proceeds were obtained through the commission of a crime, or (B) fraudulently obtained his or her interest in the proceeds to avoid forfeiture.

(iii) if the action relates to the substituted proceeds of a crime, except as provided in subparagraph (i) hereof, the burden shall be upon the claiming authority to prove by a preponderance of the evidence the facts necessary to establish a claim for forfeiture and that the non-criminal defendant either (A) knew that the property sold or exchanged to obtain an interest in the substituted proceeds was obtained through the commission of a crime, or (B) fraudulently obtained his or her interest in the substituted proceeds to avoid forfeiture.

(iv) if the action relates to an instrumentality of a crime, except as provided for in subparagraph (i) hereof, the burden shall be upon the claiming authority to prove by a preponderance of the evidence the facts necessary to establish a claim for forfeiture and that the non-criminal defendant either (A) knew that the instrumentality was or would be used in the commission of a crime or (B) knowingly obtained his or her interest in the instrumentality to avoid forfeiture.

(c) In a forfeiture action commenced by a claiming authority against a non-criminal defendant the following rebuttable presumptions shall apply:

(i) a non-criminal defendant who did not pay fair consideration for the proceeds of a crime, the substituted proceeds of a crime or the instrumentality of a crime, shall be presumed to know that such property was the proceeds of a crime, the substituted proceeds of a crime, or an instrumentality of a crime.

(ii) a non-criminal defendant who obtains an interest in the proceeds of a crime, substituted proceeds of a crime or an instrumentality of a crime with knowledge of an order of provisional remedy relating to said property issued pursuant to this article, shall be presumed to know that such property was the proceeds of a crime, substituted proceeds of a crime, or an instrumentality of a crime.

(iii) in an action relating to a post-conviction forfeiture crime, a non-criminal defendant who the claiming authority proves by clear and convincing evidence has criminal liability under section 20.00 of the penal law for the crime of conviction or for criminal activity arising from a common scheme or plan of which such crime is a part and who possesses an interest in the proceeds, the substituted proceeds, or an instrumentality of such criminal activity is presumed to know that such property was the proceeds of a crime, the substituted proceeds of a crime, or an instrumentality of a crime.

(iv) a non-criminal defendant who participated in or was aware of a scheme to conceal or disguise the manner in which said non-criminal obtained his or her interest in the proceeds of a crime, substituted proceeds of a crime, or an instrumentality of a crime is presumed to know that such property was the proceeds of a crime, the substituted proceeds of a crime, or an instrumentality of a crime.

(v) if the action relates to a real property instrumentality of a crime, the burden shall be upon the claiming authority to prove those facts referred to in subdivision four-b of section thirteen hundred ten of this article by clear and convincing evidence. The claiming authority shall also prove by a clear and convincing evidence that the non-criminal defendant knew that such property was or would be used for the commission of specified felony offenses, and either (a) knowingly and unlawfully benefitted from such conduct or (b) voluntarily agreed to the use of such property for the commission of such offenses by consent freely given. For purposes of this subparagraph, a non-criminal defendant knowingly and unlawfully benefits from the commission of a specified felony offense when he derives in exchange for permitting the use or occupancy of such real property by a person or persons committing such specified offense a substantial benefit that would otherwise not accrue as a result of the lawful use or occupancy of such real property. "Benefit" means benefit as defined in subdivision seventeen of section 10.00 of the penal law.

(d) In a forfeiture action commenced by a claiming authority against a defendant, the following rebuttable presumption shall apply: all currency or negotiable instruments payable to the bearer shall be presumed to be the proceeds of a pre-conviction forfeiture crime when such currency or negotiable instruments are (i) found in close proximity to a controlled substance unlawfully possessed by the defendant in an amount sufficient to constitute a violation of section 220.18 or 220.21 of the penal law, or (ii) found in close proximity to any quantity of a controlled substance or marihuana unlawfully possessed by such defendant in a room, other than a public place, under circumstances evincing an intent to unlawfully mix, compound, distribute, package or otherwise prepare for sale such controlled substance or marihuana.

(e) The presumption set forth pursuant to paragraph (d) of this subdivision shall be rebutted by credible and reliable evidence which tends to show that such currency or negotiable instrument payable to the bearer is not the proceeds of a preconviction forfeiture crime. In an action tried before a jury, the jury shall be so instructed. Any sworn testimony of a defendant offered to rebut the presumption and any other evidence which is obtained as a result of such testimony, shall be inadmissible in any subsequent proceeding relating to the forfeiture action, or in any other civil or criminal action, except in a prosecution for a violation of article two hundred ten of the penal law. In an action tried before a jury, at the commencement of the trial, or at such other time as the court reasonably directs, the claiming authority shall provide notice to the court and to the defendant of its intent to request that the court charge such presumption.

3-a. Conviction of a person in a criminal action upon an accusatory instrument which includes one or more of the felonies specified in subdivision four-b of section thirteen hundred ten of this article, of any felony other than such felonies, shall not preclude a defendant, in any subsequent proceeding under this article where that conviction is at issue, from adducing evidence that the conduct underlying the conviction would not establish the elements of any of the felonies specified in such subdivision other than the one to which the criminal defendant pled guilty. If the defendant does adduce such evidence, the burden shall be upon the claiming authority to prove, by clear and convincing evidence, that the conduct underlying the criminal

conviction would establish the elements of the felony specified in such subdivision. Nothing contained in this subdivision shall affect the validity of a settlement of any forfeiture action negotiated between the claiming authority and a criminal defendant contemporaneously with the taking of a plea of guilty in a criminal action to any felony defined in article two hundred twenty or section 221.30 or 221.55 of the penal law, or to a felony conspiracy to commit the same.

4. The court in which a forfeiture action is pending may dismiss said action in the interests of justice upon its own motion or upon an application as provided for herein.

(a) At any time during the pendency of a forfeiture action, the claiming authority who instituted the action, or a defendant may (i) apply for an order dismissing the complaint and terminating the forfeiture action in the interest of justice, or (ii) may apply for an order limiting the forfeiture to an amount equivalent in value to the value of property constituting the proceeds or substituted proceeds of a crime in the interest of justice.

(b) Such application for the relief provided in paragraph (a) hereof must be made in writing and upon notice to all parties. The court may, in its discretion, direct that notice be given to any other person having an interest in the property.

(c) An application for the relief provided for in paragraph (a) hereof must be brought exclusively in the superior court in which the forfeiture action is pending.

(d) The court may grant the relief provided in paragraph (a) hereof if it finds that such relief is warranted by the existence of some compelling factor, consideration or circumstance demonstrating that forfeiture of the property of** any part thereof, would not serve the ends of justice. Among the factors, considerations and circumstances the court may consider, among others, are:

(i) the seriousness and circumstances of the crime to which the property is connected relative to the impact of forfeiture of property upon the person who committed the crime; or

(ii) the adverse impact of a forfeiture of property upon innocent persons; or

(iii) the appropriateness of a judgment of forfeiture in an action relating to pre-conviction forfeiture crime where the criminal proceeding based on the crime to which the property is allegedly connected results in an acquittal of the criminal defendant or a dismissal of the accusatory instrument on the merits; or

(iv) in the case of an action relating to an instrumentality, whether the value of the instrumentality substantially exceeds the value of the property constituting the proceeds or substituted proceeds of a crime.

(e) The court must issue a written decision

stating the basis for an order issued pursuant to this subdivision.

4-a.   (a) the court in which a forfeiture action relating to real property is pending may, upon its own motion or upon the motion of the claiming authority which instituted the action, the defendant, or any other person who has a lawful property interest in such property, enter an order:

(i) Appointing an administrator pursuant to section seven hundred seventy-eight of the real property actions and proceedings law when the owner of a dwelling is a defendant in such action, and when persons who are not defendants in such action lawfully occupy one or more units within such dwelling, in order to maintain and preserve the property on behalf of such persons or any other person or entity who has a lawful property interest in such property, or in order to remedy any other condition which is dangerous to life, health or safety; or

(ii) otherwise limiting, modifying or dismissing the forfeiture action in order to preserve or protect the lawful property interest of any non-criminal defendant or any other person who is not a criminal defendant, or the lawful property interest of a defendant which is not subject to forfeiture; or

(iii) where such action involves interest in a residential leasehold or a statutory tenancy, directing that upon entry of a judgment of forfeiture, the lease or statutory tenancy will be modified as a matter of law to terminate only the interest of the defendant or defendants, and to continue the occupancy or tenancy of any other person or persons who lawfully reside in such demised premises, with such rights as such parties would otherwise have had if the defendant's interest had not been forfeited pursuant to this article.

(b) For purposes of this subdivision the term "owner" has the same meaning as prescribed for that term in section seven hundred eighty-one of the real property actions and proceedings law and the term "dwelling" shall mean any building or structure or portion thereof which is principally occupied in whole or part as the home, residence or sleeping place of one or more human beings.

5. An action for forfeiture shall be commenced by service pursuant to this chapter of a summons with notice or summons and verified complaint. No person shall forfeit any right, title, or interest in any property who is not a defendant in the action.

The claiming authority shall also file a copy of such papers with the state division of criminal justice services; provided, however, failure to file such papers shall not be grounds for any relief by a defendant in this section.

6. On the motion of any party to the forfeiture action, and for good cause shown, a court may seal any papers, including those pertaining to any provisional remedy, which relate to the forfeiture action until such time as the property which is the subject of the forfeiture action has been levied upon. A motion to seal such papers may be made *ex parte* and in camera.

7. Remission. In addition to any other relief provided under this chapter, at any time within one year after the entry of a judgment of forfeiture, any person, claiming an interest in the property subject to forfeiture who did not receive actual notice of the forfeiture action may petition the judge before whom the forfeiture action was held for a remission or mitigation of the forfeiture and restoration of the property or the proceeds of any sale resulting from the forfeiture, or such part thereof, as may be claimed by him. The court may restore said property upon such terms and conditions as it deems reasonable and just if (i) the petitioner establishes that he or she was without actual knowledge of the forfeiture action or any related proceeding for a provisional remedy and did not or should not have known that the forfeited property was connected to a crime or fraudulently conveyed and (ii) the court determines that restoration of the property would serve the ends of justice.

8. The total amount that may be recovered by the claiming authority against all criminal defendants in a forfeiture action or actions involving the same crime shall not exceed the value of the proceeds of the crime or substituted proceeds of the crime, whichever amount is greater, and, in addition, the value of any forfeited instrumentality used in the crime. Any such recovery against criminal defendants for the value of the proceeds of the crime or substituted proceeds of the crime shall be reduced by an amount which equals the value of the same proceeds of the same crime or the same substituted proceeds of the same crime recovered against all non-criminal defendants. Any such recovery for the value of an instrumentality of a crime shall be reduced by an amount which equals the value of the same instrumentality recovered against any non-criminal defendant.

The total amount that may be recovered against all non-criminal defendants in a forfeiture action or actions involving the same crime shall not exceed the value of the proceeds of the crime or the substituted proceeds of the crime, whichever amount is greater, and, in addition, the value of any forfeited instrumentality used in the crime. Any such recovery against non-criminal defendants for the value of the proceeds of the crime or substituted proceeds of the crime shall be reduced by an amount which equals the value of the proceeds of the crime or substituted proceeds of the crime recovered against all criminal defendants. A judgment against a non-criminal defendant pursuant to clause A of subparagraph (iv) of paragraph (b) of subdivision three of this section shall be limited to the amount of the proceeds of the crime. Any recovery for the value of an instrumentality of the crime shall be reduced by an amount equal to the value of the same instrumentality recovered against any criminal defendant.

9. Any defendant in a forfeiture action who knowingly and intentionally conceals, destroys, dissipates, alters, removes from the jurisdiction, or otherwise disposes of, property specified in a provisional remedy ordered by the court or in a judgment of forfeiture in knowing contempt of said order or judgment shall be subject to criminal liability and sanctions under sections 80.05 and 215.80 of the penal law.

10. The proper venue for trial of an action for forfeiture is:

(a) In the case of an action for post-conviction forfeiture commenced after conviction, the county where the conviction occurred.

(b) In all other cases, the county where a criminal prosecution could be commenced under article twenty of the criminal procedure law, or, in the case of an action commenced by the office of prosecution, special narcotics courts of the city of New York, under section one hundred seventy-seven-b of the judiciary law.

11. (a) any stipulation or settlement agreement between the parties to a forfeiture action shall be filed with the clerk of the court in which the forfeiture action is pending. No stipulation or settlement agreement shall be accepted for filing unless it is accompanied by an affidavit from the claiming authority that written notice of the stipulation or settlement agreement, including the terms of such, has been given to the state crime victims board, the state division of criminal justice services, and in the case of a forfeiture based on a felony defined in article two hundred twenty or section 221.30 or 221.55 of the penal law, to the state division of substance abuse services.

(b) No judgment or order of forfeiture shall be accepted for filing unless it is accompanied by an affidavit from the claiming authority that written notice of judgment or order, including the terms of such, has been given to the state crime victims board, the state division of criminal justice services, and in the case of a forfeiture based on a felony defined in article two hundred twenty or section 221.30 or 221.55 of the penal law, to the state division of substance abuse services.

(c) Any claiming authority or claiming agent which receives any property pursuant to chapter thirteen of the food and drug laws (21 U.S.C. § 801 *et seq.*) of the United States and/or chapter four of the customs duties laws (19 U.S.C. § 1301 *et seq.*) of the United States and/or chapter 96 of the crimes and criminal procedure laws (18 U.S.C. § 1961 *et seq.*) of the united states shall provide an affidavit to the commissioner of the division of criminal justice services stating the estimated present value of the property received.

12. Property acquired in good faith by an attorney as payment for the reasonable and bona fide fees of legal services or reimbursement of reasonable and bona fide expenses related to the representation of a defendant in connection with a civil or criminal forfeiture proceeding or a related criminal matter, shall be exempt from a judgment of forfeiture. For purposes of this subdivision and subdivision four of section one thousand three hundred twelve of this article, "bona fide" means that the attorney who acquired such property had no reasonable basis to believe that the fee transaction was a fraudulent or sham transaction designed to shield property from forfeiture, hide its existence from governmental investigative agencies, or was conducted for any purpose other than for legitimate legal representation.

* So in original.

** So in original. Probably should read "or," connected relative to the impact of forfeiture of property upon the person who committed the crime.

Amended by L. 1985, Ch. 379, eff. November 1, 1985; L. 1990, Ch. 655, eff. Nov. 1, 1990.

ANNOTATIONS

Burden of proof.—State forfeiture statute applicable to felonies requires claiming authority to prove by a preponderance of the evidence that an owner, who is not a criminal defendant, either "knew that the instrumentality was or would be used in the commission of a crime or. . .knowingly obtained his or her interest in the instrumentality to avoid forfeiture, "however, Nassau County forfeiture statute that authorized police to seize property for almost any infraction under the VTL, including minor offenses was unconstitutional, a punitive forfeiture of an instrumentality of a crime violates Excessive Fines Clause. County of Nassau v. Canavan, 1 N.Y.3d 134, 770 N.Y.S.2d 277, 802 N.E.2d 616 (2003).

—Because forfeiture is a civil proceeding, the Property Clerk need only prove by a preponderance of the evidence that seized property is subject to forfeiture. Property Clerk v. Milone, 185 A.D.2d 151, 586 N.Y.S.2d 7 (1st Dept. 1992).

—Upon a search by the police, defendant was discovered to have on him a quantity of white powder which appeared to be heroin to experienced police officers and which a subsequent laboratory report, admitted as record maintained in the ordinary course of business, confirmed was heroin; the Supreme Court was incorrect in requiring the testimony of a chemist. Property Clerk v. McDermott, 185 A.D.2d 134, 585 N.Y.S.2d 746 (1st Dept. 1992).

—Defendant's unverified answer, prepared by his attorney and founded upon information and belief, was insufficient to controvert petitioner's evidence and therefore defendant did not sustain his burden of presenting evidentiary facts sufficient to show that the seizure and possession of his vehicle was unlawful and improper. Property Clerk v. Fanning, 162 A.D.2d 282, 556 N.Y.S.2d 874 (1st Dept. 1990).

—Since the evidence by the petitioner tended to establish that the property was contraband and subject to forfeiture, it was incumbent upon respondent to then come forward and offer some explanation and proof to the contrary; respondent relied exclusively on the conclusory allegation of his attorney, who did not possess any personal knowledge of the arrest and attendant search and seizure, and such an affirmation by counsel had no evidentiary value. Property Clerk v. Batista, 111 A.D.2d 135, 489 N.Y.S.2d 739 (1st Dept. 1985).

—Defendant failed to rebut plaintiff's allegations of trafficking with sworn affidavits, as required, and put forth only an attorney's affidavit having no probative value; defendant's counsel merely suggested that the money could have come from any one of a number of legitimate sources. Vergari v. Lockhart, 144 Misc. 2d 860, 545 N.Y.S.2d 223 (Sup. Ct. Westchester Co. 1989).

Generally.—A claim of innocence will not defeat forfeiture.

Property Clerk v. Molomo, 81 N.Y.2d 936, 597 N.Y.S.2d 661, 613 N.E.2d 567 (1993).

—The statute authorizes the commencement of a forfeiture action against putative "criminal defendants" who have been indicted but not convicted, although it is equally clear that the court may not grant a forfeiture of the seized assets unless there is a subsequent conviction in the underlying felony prosecution. Morgenthau v. Citisource Inc., 68 N.Y.2d 211, 508 N.Y.S.2d 152, 500 N.E.2d 850 (1986).

—The dismissal of criminal charges is not determinative of the issues to be resolved in a civil forfeiture proceeding. Property Clerk v. Hurlston, 104 A.D.2d 312, 478 N.Y.S.2d 906 (1st Dept. 1984).

—The Criminal Court does not have the authority to intervene in a civil matter regarding civil forfeiture proceedings pursuant to the Administrative Code. People v. Milone, 158 Misc. 2d 316, 600 N.Y.S.2d 1010, 1012 (Crim. Ct. Bronx Co. 1993).

—Because a forfeiture action is in personam, the court possesses the power in the forfeiture order to direct a defendant to dispose of property outside the state in order to satisfy the judgment. District Attorney of Queens County v. McAuliffe, 129 Misc. 2d 416, 493 N.Y.S.2d 406 (Sup. Ct. Queens Co. 1985).

Plea bargain.—Prosecutor did not possess the authority to promise the defendant in a narcotics case that the vehicle seized would be returned to him pursuant to the plea agreement. Property Clerk v. Ferris, 77 N.Y.2d 428, 568 N.Y.S.2d 428, 570 N.E.2d 225 (1991).

Relief.—Provisional relief, including attachment, is available in post-conviction forfeiture actions predicated upon any felony defined in the penal law or any other chapter of the consolidated laws of the state. Dillon v. Kim, 158 Misc. 2d 711, 601 N.Y.S.2d 405, 406 (Sup. Ct. Nassau Co. 1993).

§ 1311-a. Subpoena duces tecum.

1. At any time before an action pursuant to this article is commenced, the claiming authority may, pursuant to the provisions of subdivision two of this section, apply without notice for the issuance of a subpoena duces tecum.

2. An application for a subpoena duces tecum pursuant to this section:

(a) Shall be made in the judicial district in which the claiming authority may commence an action pursuant to this article, and shall be made in writing to a justice of the supreme court, or a judge of the county court; and

(b) Shall be supported by an affidavit, and such other written documentation as may be submitted which: (i) sets forth the identity of the claiming authority and certifies that the applicant is authorized to make the application on the claiming authority's behalf; (ii) demonstrates reasonable grounds to believe that the execution of the subpoena would be reasonably likely to lead to information about the nature and location of any debt or property against which a forfeiture judgment may be enforced; (iii) states whether any other such subpoena or provisional remedy has been previously sought or obtained with respect to the subject matter of the subpoena or the matter to which it relates; (iv) contains a factual statement which sets forth the basis for the issuance of the subpoena, including a particular description of the nature of the information sought to be obtained; (v) states whether the issuance of the subpoena is sought without notice to any interested party; and (vi) where the application seeks the issuance of the subpoena without

notice to any interested party, contains a statement setting forth the factual basis for the claiming authority's belief that providing notice of the application for the issuance of the subpoena may result in any property being destroyed, removed from the jurisdiction of the court, or otherwise being unavailable for forfeiture or to satisfy a money judgment that may be entered in the forfeiture action, and may interfere with law enforcement investigations or judicial proceedings.

3. An application made pursuant to this section may be granted, in the court's discretion, upon a determination that the application meets the requirements set forth in subdivision two of this section; provided, however, that no such subpoena may be issued or directed to an attorney with regard to privileged records or documents or attorney work-product relating to a client. When a subpoena has been issued pursuant to this section, the claiming authority shall have the right to possession of the subpoenaed material. The possession shall be for a period of time, and on such reasonable terms and conditions, as the court may direct. The reasonableness of such possession, time, terms and conditions shall be determined with consideration for, among other things, (a) the good cause shown by the party issuing the subpoena or in whose behalf the subpoena is issued, (b) the rights and legitimate needs of the person subpoenaed and (c) the feasibility and appropriateness of making copies of the subpoenaed material. Where the application seeks a subpoena to compel the production of an original record or document, the court in its discretion may order the production of a certified transcript or certified copy thereof.

4. Upon a determination pursuant to subdivision three of this section that the subpoena should be granted, the court shall issue the subpoena, seal all papers relating thereto, and direct that the recipient shall not, except as otherwise ordered by the court, disclose the fact of issuance or the subject of the subpoena to any person or entity; provided, however, that the court may require that notice be given to any interested party prior to the issuance of the subpoena, or at any time thereafter, when: (a) an order granting a provisional remedy pursuant to this article with respect to the subject matter of the subpoena or the matter to which it relates has been served upon the defendant whose books and records are the subject matter of the subpoena, whether such books and records are in the possession of the defendant or a third party; or (b) the court determines that providing notice of the application (i) will not result in any property being destroyed, removed from the jurisdiction of the court, or otherwise being unavailable for forfeiture or to satisfy a money judgment that may be entered in the forfeiture action and (ii) will not interfere with law enforcement investigations or judicial proceedings. For purposes of this section, "interested

party" means any person whom the court determines might have an interest in the property subject to the forfeiture action brought pursuant to this article.

5. Notwithstanding the provisions of subdivision four of this section, where a subpoena duces tecum has been issued pursuant to this section without notice to any interested party, the claiming authority shall serve written notice of the fact and date of the issuance of the subpoena duces tecum, and of the fact that information was obtained thereby, upon any interested party not later than ninety days after the date of compliance with such subpoena, or upon commencement of a forfeiture action, whichever occurs first; provided, however, where the action has not been commenced and upon a showing of good cause, service of the notice required herein may be postponed by order of the court for a reasonable period of time. The court, upon the filing of a motion by any interested party served with such notice, may, in its discretion, make available to such party or the party's counsel for inspection such portions of the information obtained pursuant to the subpoena as the court directs.

6. Nothing contained in this section shall be construed to diminish or impair any right of subpoena or discovery that may otherwise be provided for by law to the claiming authority or to a defendant in a forfeiture action.

Added by L. 1990, Ch. 655, Nov. 1, 1990.

§ 1312. Provisional remedies; generally.

1. The provisional remedies of attachment, injunction, receivership and notice of pendency provided for herein, shall be available in all actions to recover property or for a money judgment under this article.

2. On a motion for a provisional remedy, the claiming authority shall state whether any other provisional remedy has previously been sought in the same action against the same defendant. The court may require the claiming authority to elect between those remedies to which it would otherwise be entitled.

3. A court may grant an application for a provisional remedy when it determines that: (a) there is a substantial probability that the claiming authority will prevail on the issue of forfeiture and that failure to enter the order may result in the property being destroyed, removed from the jurisdiction of the court, or otherwise be unavailable for forfeiture; (b) the need to preserve the availability of the property through the entry of the requested order outweighs the hardship on any party against whom the order may operate; and (c) in an action relating to real property, that entry of the requested order will not substantially diminish, impair, or terminate the lawful property interest in such real property of any person or persons other than the defendant or defendants.

4. Upon motion of any party against whom a provisional remedy granted pursuant to this article is in effect, the court may issue an order modifying or vacating such provisional remedy if necessary to permit the moving party to obtain funds for the payment of reasonable living expenses, other costs or expenses related to the maintenance, operation, or preservation of property which is the subject of any such provisional remedy or reasonable and bona fide attorneys' fees and expenses for the representation of the defendant in the forfeiture proceeding or in a related criminal matter relating thereto, payment for which is not otherwise available from assets of the defendant which are not subject to such provisional remedy. Any such motion shall be supported by an affidavit establishing the unavailability of other assets of the moving party which are not the subject of such provisional remedy for payment of such expenses or fees.

Amended by L. 1990, Ch. 655, eff. Nov. 1, 1990, amending subd. 3 and adding subd. 4.

ANNOTATIONS

Generally.—The hearing court properly found that there was a substantial probability that the plaintiff claiming authority would prevail on the issue of forfeiture, that without an order of attachment, the assets seized from the defendant's drug-filled apartment would probably be dissipated, and that the need to attach the assets outweighed any potential hardship to the defendant. Dillon v. Woolnough, 203 A.D.2d 235, 609 N.Y.S.2d 657 (2d Dept. 1994).

—The provisional remedy relief granted by the court serves the substantial governmental need of preventing the judicial process from being frustrated by the dissipation of assets; the governmental need to preserve available assets is particularly appropriate where the profits of the criminal defendants' alleged crimes are misappropriated public funds which can potentially be restored to the taxpayers. Kuriansky v. Bed-Stuy Health Care Corp., 135 A.D.2d 160, 525 N.Y.S.2d 225 (2d Dept. 1988).

—Where relevant party is an estate, it too is entitled to obtain the release of funds for "the reasonable payment of reasonable living expenses," which the court interpreted to "include reasonable expense for the administration of the estate." Dillon v. Marelli, 185 Misc. 2d 461, 713 N.Y.S.2d 449 (Co. Ct. Nassau Co. 2000).

Hearing.—The court had the discretion to order an evidentiary hearing on the issue of forfeiture. Morgenthau v. Young, 204 A.D.2d 118, 611 N.Y.S.2d 855 (1st Dept. 1994).

§ 1313. Debt or property subject to attachment; proper garnishee.

Any debt or property against which a forfeiture judgment may be enforced as provided under this article is subject to attachment. The proper garnishee of any such property or debt is the person designated as a proper garnishee for purposes of enforcing money judgments in section five thousand two hundred one of this chapter. For the purpose of applying the provisions to attachment, references to a "judgment debtor" in section five thousand two hundred one and in subdivision (i) of section one hundred five of this chapter shall be construed to mean "defendant."

§ 1314. Attaching creditor's rights in personal property.

Where the claiming authority has delivered an

order of attachment to a claiming agent, the claiming authority's rights in a debt owned to a defendant or in an interest of a defendant in personal property against which debt or property a judgment may be enforced, are superior to the extent of the amount of the attachment to the rights of any transferee of the debt or property, except:

1. A transferee who acquired the debt or property before it was levied upon for fair consideration and without knowledge of the order of attachment; or

2. A transferee who acquired the debt or property for fair consideration after is was levied upon without knowledge of the levy while it was not in the possession of the claiming agent.

§ 1315. Discharge of garnishee's obligation.

A person who, pursuant to an order of attachment, pays or delivers to the claiming agent money or other personal property in which a defendant has or will have an interest, or so pays a debt he or she owes the defendant, is discharged from his or her obligation to the defendant to the extent of the payment or delivery.

§ 1316. Order of attachment on notice; temporary restraining order; contents.

Upon a motion on notice for an order of attachment, the court may, without notice to the defendant, grant a temporary restraining order prohibiting the transfer of assets by a garnishee as provided in subdivision two of section one thousand three hundred twenty of this article. The contents of the order of attachment granted pursuant to this section shall be as provided in subdivision one of section one thousand three hundred seventeen of this article.

§ 1317. Order of attachment without notice.

1. When granted; contents. An order of attachment may be granted without notice, before or after service of summons and at any time prior to judgment. It shall specify the amount to be secured by the order of attachment including any interest, costs and any claiming agent's fees and expenses, be endorsed with the name and address of the claiming authority and shall be directed to a claiming agent in any county or in the city of New York where any property in which the defendant has an interest is located or where a garnishee may be served. The order shall direct the claiming agent to levy within his or her jurisdiction, at any time before final judgment, upon such property in which the defendant has an interest and upon such debts owing to the defendant as will satisfy the amount specified in the order of attachment.

2. Confirmation of order. An order of attachment granted without notice shall provide that within a period not to exceed five days after levy, the claiming authority shall move, on such notice as the court shall direct to the defendant, the garnishee, if any, and the claiming agent, for an order confirming the order of attachment. If the claiming authority fails to make such motion within the required period, the order of attachment and levy thereunder shall have no further effect and shall be vacated upon motion. Upon the motion to confirm, the provisions of subdivision two of section one thousand three hundred twenty-nine of this article shall apply. An order of attachment granted without notice may provide that the claiming agent refrain from taking any property levied upon into his actual custody, pending further order of the court.

§ 1318. Motion papers; filing; demand; damages.

1. Affidavit; other papers. On a motion for an order of attachment, or for an order to confirm an order of attachment, the claiming authority shall show, by affidavit and such other written evidence as may be submitted, that there is a cause of action and showing grounds for relief as required by section one thousand three hundred twelve of this article.

2. Filing. Within ten days after the granting of an order of attachment, the claiming authority shall file it and the affidavit and other papers upon which it was based and the summons and complaint or proposed complaint in the action. A court for good cause shown may extend the time for such filing upon application of the claiming authority. Unless the time for filing has been extended, the order shall be invalid if not so filed, except that a person upon whom it is served shall not be liable for acting upon it as if it were valid without knowledge of the invalidity.

3. Demand for papers. At any time after property has been levied upon, the defendant may serve upon the claiming authority a written demand that the papers upon which the order of attachment was granted and the levy made be served upon him or her. As soon as practicable after service of the demand, the claiming authority shall cause the papers demanded to be served by mailing the same to the address specified in the demand. A demand under this subdivision shall not of itself constitute an appearance in the action.

4. Damages. The claiming authority shall be liable to the defendant for all costs and damages, including reasonable attorney's fees, which may be sustained by reason of the attachment if the defendant recovers judgment, or if it is finally decided that the claiming authority was not entitled to an attachment of the defendant's property. In order to establish the claiming authority's liability, the defendant must prove by a preponderance of the evidence that in obtaining the order

of attachment the claiming authority acted without reasonable cause, and not in good faith.

§ 1319. Service of summons.

An order of attachment granted before service is made on the defendant against whom the attachment is granted is valid only if, within sixty days after the order is granted, a summons is served upon the defendant or first publication of the summons against the defendant is made pursuant to an order and publication is subsequently completed, except that a person upon whom the order of attachment is served shall not be liable for acting upon it as if it were valid without knowledge of the invalidity. If the defendant dies within sixty days after the order is granted and before the summons is served upon him or her or publication is completed, the order is valid only if the summons is served upon his or her executor or administrator within sixty days after letters are issued. Upon such terms as may be just and upon good cause shown the court may extend the time, not exceeding sixty days, within which the summons must be served or publication commenced pursuant to this section, provided that the application for extension is made before the expiration of the time fixed.

Amended by L. 1992, Ch. 216, eff. July 1, 1992. Until January 1, 1993, an action shall be deemed validly commenced if the action is commenced as provided in this act or if, such action is commenced in accordance with the law including section 306-a of the civil practice law and rules as added by L. 1991, Ch. 166, in effect immediately prior to the enactment of this act.

§ 1320. Levy upon personal property by service of order.

1. Method of levy. The claiming agent shall levy upon any interest of the defendant in personal property, or upon any debt owed to the defendant, by serving a copy of the order of attachment upon the garnishee, or upon the defendant if property to be levied upon is in the defendant's possession or custody, in the same manner as a summons except that such service shall not be made by delivery of a copy to a person authorized to receive service of summons solely by a designation filed pursuant to a provision of law other than rule three hundred eighteen of this chapter.

2. Effect of levy; prohibition of transfer. A levy by service of an order of attachment upon a person other than the defendant is effective only if, at the time of service, such person owes a debt to the defendant or such person is in the possession or custody of property in which such person knows or has reason to believe the defendant has an interest, or if the claiming authority has stated in a notice which shall be served with the order that a specified debt is owed by the person served to the defendant or that the defendant has an interest in specified property in the possession or custody of the person served. All property in which the defendant is known or believed to have an interest then in and thereafter coming into the possession or custody of such a person, including any specified in the notice, and all debts of such person, including any specified in the notice, then due and thereafter coming due to the defendant, shall be subject to the levy. Unless the court orders otherwise, the person served with the order shall forthwith transfer or deliver all such property, and pay all such debts upon maturity, up to the amount specified in order of attachment, to the claiming agent and execute any document necessary to effect the payment, transfer or delivery. After such payment, transfer or delivery, property coming into the possession or custody of the garnishee, or debt incurred by him or her, shall not be subject to the levy. Until such payment, transfer or delivery is made, or until the expiration of ninety days after the service of the order of attachment upon him or her, or of such further time as is provided by any subsequent order of the court served upon him or her, whichever event first occurs, the garnishee is prohibited to make or suffer any sale, assignment or transfer of, or any interference with any such property, or pay over or otherwise dispose of any such debt, to any person other than the claiming agent except upon direction of the claiming agent or pursuant to an order of the court. A garnishee, however, may collect or redeem an instrument received by him or her for such purpose and he or she may sell or transfer in good faith property held as collateral or otherwise pursuant to pledge thereof or at the direction of any person other than the defendant authorized to direct sale or transfer, provided that the proceeds in which the defendant has an interest be retained subject to the levy. A claiming authority who has specified personal property or debt to be levied upon in a notice served with an order of attachment shall be liable to the owner of the property or the person to whom the debt is owed, if other than the defendant, for any damages sustained by reason of the levy. In order to establish the claiming authority's liability, the owner of the property of * the person to whom the debt is owed must prove by a preponderance of the evidence that, in causing the levy to occur, the claiming authority acted without reasonable cause and not in good faith.

3. Seizure by claiming agent; notice of satisfaction. Where property or debts have been levied upon by service of an order of attachment, the claiming agent shall take into his or her actual custody all such property capable of delivery and shall collect and receive all such debts. When the claiming agent has taken into his or her actual custody property or debts having value sufficient to satisfy the amount specified in the order of attachment, the claiming agent shall notify the defendant and each person upon whom the order of attachment was served that the order of attachment has been fully executed.

4. Proceeding to compel payment or delivery.

Where property or debts have been levied upon by service of an order of attachment, the claiming authority may commence a special proceeding against the garnishee served with the order to compel the payment, delivery or transfer to the claiming agent of such property or debts, or to secure a judgment against the garnishee. Notice of petition shall also be served upon the parties to the action and the claiming agent. A garnishee may assert any defense or counterclaim which he or she may have asserted against the defendant. The court may permit any adverse claimant to intervene in the proceeding and may determine his or her rights in accordance with section one thousand three hundred twenty-seven of this article.

5. Failure to proceed. At the expiration of ninety days after a levy is made by service of the order of attachment, or of such further time as the court, upon motion of the claiming authority on notice to the parties to the action, has provided, the levy shall be void except as to property or debts which the claiming agent has taken into his or her actual custody, collected or received or as to which a proceeding under subdivision four hereof has been commenced.

* Should be "or."

§ 1321. Levy upon personal property by seizure.

If the claiming authority shall so direct the collecting agent, as an alternative to the method prescribed by section one thousand three hundred twenty of this article, shall levy upon property capable of delivery by taking the property into his actual custody. In cases in which the collecting agent is a sheriff, the sheriff may require that the claiming authority furnish indemnity that is either satisfactory to the sheriff or is fixed by the court. The collecting agent shall within four days serve a copy of the order of attachment in the manner prescribed by subdivision one of section one thousand three hundred twenty of this article upon the person from whose possession or custody the property was taken.

§ 1322. Levy upon real property.

The claiming agent shall levy upon any interest of the defendant in real property by filing with the clerk of the county in which the property is located a notice of attachment endorsed with the name and address of the claiming authority and stating the names of the parties to the action, the amount specified in the order of attachment and a description of the property levied upon. The clerk shall record and index the notice in the same books, in the same manner and with the same effect, as a notice of the pendency of an action.

§ 1323. Additional undertaking to carrier garnishee.

A garnishee who is a common carrier may transport or deliver property actually loaded on a conveyance, notwithstanding the service upon him or her of an order of attachment, if it was loaded without reason to believe that an order of attachment affecting the property had been granted, unless the claiming authority gives an undertaking in an amount fixed by the court, that the claiming authority shall pay any such carrier all expenses and damages which may be incurred for unloading the property and for detention of the conveyance necessary for that purpose.

§ 1324. Claiming agent's duties after levy.

1. Retention of property. The claiming agent shall hold and safely keep all property or debts paid, delivered, transferred or assigned to him or her or taken into his or her custody to answer any judgment that may be obtained against the defendant in the action, unless otherwise directed by the court or the claiming authority, subject to the payment of the claiming agent's fees and expenses, if any. Any money shall be held for the benefit of the parties to the action in an interest-bearing trust account at a national or state bank or trust company. If the urgency of the case requires, the court may direct sale or other disposition of property, specifying the manner and terms thereof, with notice to the parties to the action and the garnishee who has possession of such property.

2. Inventory. Within fifteen days after service of an order of attachment or forthwith after such order has been vacated or annulled, the claiming agent shall file an inventory of property seized, a description of real property levied upon, the names and addresses of all persons served with the order of attachment, and an estimate of the value of all property levied upon.

§ 1325. Garnishee's statement.

Within ten days after service upon a garnishee of an order of attachment, or within such shorter time as the court may direct, the garnishee shall serve upon the claiming agent a statement specifying all debts of the garnishee to the defendant, when the debts are due, all property in the possession or custody of the garnishee in which the defendant has an interest, and the amounts and value of the debts and property specified. If the garnishee has money belonging to, or is indebted to, the defendant in at least the amount of the attachment, he or she may limit his or her statement to that fact.

§ 1326. Disclosure.

Upon motion of any interested person, at any time after the granting of an order of attachment and prior to final judgment in the action, upon such notice as the court may direct, the court may order disclosure by any person of information regarding any property in which the defendant has or may have interest, or any debts owed or which may be owed to the defendant.

§ 1327. Proceedings to determine adverse claims.

Prior to the application of property or debt to the satisfaction of a judgment, any person, other than a party to the action, who has an interest in the property subject to forfeiture may commence a special proceeding against the claiming authority to determine the rights of adverse claimants to the property or debt, and in such proceeding shall serve a notice of petition upon the claiming agent and upon each party in the same manner as a notice of motion. The proceeding may be commenced in the county where the property was levied upon, or in the county where the order of attachment is filed. The court may vacate or discharge the attachment, void the levy, direct the disposition of the property or debt, direct that undertakings be provided or released, or direct that damages be awarded. Where there appear to be disputed questions of fact, the court shall order a separate trial, indicating the person who shall have possession of the property pending a decision and the undertaking, if any, which such person shall give. If the court determines that the adverse claim was fraudulent or made without any reasonable basis whatsoever, it may require the claimant to pay the claiming authority the reasonable expenses incurred in the proceeding, including reasonable attorney's fees, and any other damages suffered by reason of the claim. The commencement of the proceeding shall not of itself subject the adverse claimant to personal jurisdiction with respect to any matter other than the claim asserted in the proceeding.

Amended by L. 1994, Ch. 563, § 4, eff. July 26, 1994.

§ 1328. Discharge of attachment.

1. A defendant whose property or debt has been levied upon may move, upon notice to the claiming authority and the claiming agent, for any* order discharging the attachment as to all or part of the property or debt upon payment of the claiming agent's fees and expenses, if any. On such a motion, the defendant shall give an undertaking, in an amount equal to the value of the property or debt sought to be discharged, that the defendant will pay to the claiming authority the amount of any judgment which may be recovered in the action against him or her, not exceeding the amount of the undertaking. Making a motion or giving an undertaking under this section shall not of itself constitute an appearance in the action.

2. When a motion to discharge is made in the case of property levied upon pursuant to a claimed violation of the tax law, the amount of the undertaking required shall be an amount equal to the lesser of:

(a) The amount specified in subdivision one of this section; or

(b) The aggregate amount of all unpaid tax and civil penalties for such violation.

* Should be "an."

Amended by L. 1985, Ch. 65, eff. Apr. 17, 1985, adding subd. 2.

§ 1329. Vacating or modifying attachment.

1. Motion to vacate or modify. Prior to the application of property or debt to the satisfaction of a judgment, the defendant, the garnishee or any person having an interest in the property or debt may move, on notice to each party and the claiming agent, for an order vacating or modifying the order of attachment. Upon the motion, the court may give the claiming authority a reasonable opportunity to correct any defect. If, after the defendant has appeared in the action, the court determines that the attachment is unnecessary to the security of the claiming authority, it shall vacate the order of attachment. Such a motion shall not of itself constitute an appearance in the action.

2. Burden of proof. Upon a motion to vacate or modify an order of attachment the claiming authority shall have the burden of establishing the grounds for the attachment, the need for continuing the levy and the probability that he or she will succeed on the merits.

§ 1330. Annulment of attachment.

An order of attachment is annulled when the action in which it was granted abates or is discontinued or a judgment entered therein in favor of the claiming authority is fully satisfied, or a judgment is entered therein in favor of the defendant. In the last specified case a stay of proceedings suspends the effect of the annulment, and a reversal or vacating of the judgment revives the order of attachment.

§ 1331. Return of property; directions to clerk and claiming agent.

Upon motion of any interested person, on notice to the claiming agent and each party, the court may direct the clerk of any county to cancel a notice of attachment and may direct the claiming agent to dispose of, account for, assign, return or release any property or debt, or the proceeds thereof, or any undertaking, or to file additional inventories or returns, subject to the payment of the claiming agent's fees, and expenses, if any. The court shall direct that notice of the motion be given to the claiming authority and plaintiffs in other orders of attachment, if any, and to the judgment creditors of executions, if any, affecting any property or debt, or the proceeds thereof, sought to be returned or released.

MISC. LAWS

ANNOTATION

Jurisdiction.—As the court in which the delinquency case was tried, Family Court possessed, at least under certain circumstances, the requisite jurisdiction to order the police property clerk to return the property taken from a juvenile at the time of his arrest. *In re* Charles W., 125 Misc. 2d 545, 479 N.Y.S.2d 657 (Fam. Ct. Monroe Co. 1984).

§ 1332. Disposition of attachment property after execution issued; priority of orders of attachment.

Where an execution is issued upon a judgment entered against the defendant, the claiming agent's duty with respect to custody and disposition of property or debt levied upon pursuant to an order of attachment is the same as if he or she had levied upon it pursuant to the execution. The priority among two or more orders of attachment against the same defendant shall be in the order in which they were delivered to the officer who levied upon the property or debt. The priority between an order of attachment and an execution, or a payment, delivery or receivership order, is set forth in section five thousand two hundred thirty-four of this chapter.

§ 1333. Grounds for preliminary injunction and temporary restraining order.

A preliminary injunction may be granted in any action under this article, whether for money damages or otherwise, where it appears that the defendant threatens or is about to do, or is doing or procuring or suffering to be done, an act in violation of the claiming authority's rights respecting the subject of the action, and thereby tending to render a resulting judgment ineffectual. A temporary restraining order may be granted pending a hearing for a preliminary injunction where it appears that immediate and irreparable injury, loss or damage will result unless the defendant is restrained before the hearing can be had. A preliminary injunction may be granted only upon notice to the defendant. Notice of the motion may be served with the summons or at any time thereafter and prior to judgment.

§ 1334. Motion papers.

Affidavit; other papers. On a motion for a preliminary injunction the claiming authority shall show, by affidavit and such other written evidence as may be submitted, that there is a cause of action and showing grounds for relief as required by section one thousand three hundred twelve of this article.

§ 1335. Temporary restraining order.

1. Generally. If, on a motion for a preliminary injunction, the claiming authority shall show that immediate and irreparable injury, loss or damages may result unless the defendant is restrained before a hearing can be had, a temporary restraining order may be granted without notice. Upon granting a temporary restraining order, the court shall set the hearing for the preliminary injunction at the earliest possible time.

2. Service. Unless the court orders otherwise, a temporary restraining order together with the papers upon which it was based, and a notice of hearing for the preliminary injunction, shall be personally served in the same manner as a summons.

§ 1336. Vacating or modifying preliminary injunction or temporary restraining order.

A defendant enjoined by a preliminary injunction may move at any time, on notice to the claiming authority, to vacate or modify it. On motion, without notice, made by a defendant enjoined by a temporary restraining order, the judge who granted it, or in his or her absence or disability, another judge, may vacate or modify the order. An order granted without notice and vacating or modifying a temporary restraining order shall be effective when, together with the papers upon which it is based, it is filed with the clerk and served upon the claiming authority. As a condition to granting an order vacating or modifying a preliminary injunction or a temporary restraining order, a court may require the defendant to give an undertaking, in an amount to be fixed by the court, that the defendant shall pay to the claiming authority any loss sustained by reason of the vacating or modifying order.

§ 1337. Ascertaining damages sustained by reason of preliminary injunction or temporary restraining order.

The damages sustained by reason of a preliminary injunction or temporary restraining order may be ascertained upon motion on such notice to all interested persons as the court shall direct. Where the defendant enjoined was an officer of a corporation or joint-stock association or a representative of another person, the damages sustained by such corporation, association or person represented, to the amount of such excess, may also be ascertained. The amount of damages so ascertained is conclusive upon all persons who were served with notice of the motion and such amount may be recovered by the person entitled thereto in a separate action. In order to establish the claiming authority's liability for damages, the person seeking such damages must prove by a preponderance of the evidence that, in causing the temporary restraining order or preliminary injunction to be granted, the claiming authority acted without reasonable cause and not in good faith.

§ 1338. Appointment and powers of temporary receiver.

1. Appointment of temporary receiver; joinder of moving party. Upon motion of the claiming authority on* any other person having an apparent interest in property which is the subject of an action pursuant to this article, a temporary receiver of the property may be appointed, before or after service of summons and at any time prior to judgment, or during the pendency of an appeal, where there is danger that the property will be removed from the state, or lost, materially injured or destroyed. A motion made by a person not already a party to the action constitutes an appearance in the action and the person shall be joined as a party.

2. Powers of temporary receiver. The court appointing a receiver may authorize him or her to take and hold real and personal property, and sue for, collect and sell debts or claims, upon such conditions and for such purposes as the court shall direct. A receiver shall have no power to employ counsel unless expressly so authorized by order of the court. Upon motion of the receiver or a party, powers granted to a temporary receiver may be extended or limited or the receivership may be extended to another action involving the property.

3. Duration of temporary receivership. A temporary receivership shall not continue after final judgment unless otherwise directed by the court.

* Should be "or."

§ 1339. Oath.

A temporary receiver, before entering upon his or her duties, shall be sworn faithfully and fairly to discharge the trust committed to him or her. The oath may be administered by any person authorized to take acknowledgments of deeds by the real property law. The oath may be waived upon consent of all parties.

§ 1340. Undertaking.

A temporary receiver shall give an undertaking in an amount to be fixed by the court making the appointment, that he or she will faithfully discharge his or her duties.

§ 1341. Accounts.

A temporary receiver shall keep written accounts itemizing receipts and expenditures, and describing the property and naming the depository of receivership funds, which shall be open to inspection by any person having an apparent interest in the property. [Upon motion of the receiver or of any person having an apparent interest in the property,]* the court may require the keeping of particular records or direct or limit inspection or require presentation of a temporary receiver's accounts. Notice of a motion for the presentation of a temporary receiver's accounts shall be served upon the sureties on his or her undertaking as well as upon each party.

* **Editor's Note:** Bracketed material apparently was omitted due to an oversight.

§ 1342. Removal.

Upon motion of any party or upon its own initiative, the court which appointed a receiver may remove him or her at any time.

§ 1343. Notice of pendency; constructive notice.

A notice of pendency may be filed in any action brought pursuant to this article in which the judgment demanded would affect the title to, or the possession, use or enjoyment of, real property. The pendency of such an action is constructive notice, from the time of filing of the notice only, to a purchaser from, or incumbrancer against, any defendant named in a notice of pendency indexed in a block index against a block in which property affected is situated or any defendant against whose name a notice of pendency is indexed. A person whose conveyance or incumbrance is recorded after the filing of the notice is bound by all proceedings taken in the action after such filing to the same extent as in her or she were a party.

§ 1344. Filing, content and indexing of notice of pendency.

1. Filing. In a case specified in section one thousand three hundred forty-three of this article the notice of pendency shall be filed in the office of the clerk of any county where property affected is situated, before or after service of a summons and at any time prior to judgment. Unless it has already been filed in that county, the complaint shall be filed with the notice of pendency.

2. Content, designation of index. A notice of pendency shall state the names of the parties to the action, that the action is for forfeiture pursuant to this article and a description of the property affected. A notice of pendency filed with a clerk who maintains a block index shall contain a designation of the number of each block on the land map of a county which is affected by the notice. A notice of pendency filed with a clerk who does not maintain a block index shall contain a designation of the names of each defendant against whom the notice is directed to be indexed.

3. Indexing. Each county clerk with whom a notice of pendency is filed shall immediately record and index it against the blocks or names designated. A county clerk who does not maintain a block index shall index a notice of pendency of an action for partition against the names of each claiming authority and each defendant not designated as wholly fictitious.

§ 1345. Service of summons.

A notice of pendency filed before an action is commenced is effective only if, within thirty days after filing, a summons is served upon the defendant or first publication of the summons against the defendant is made pursuant to an order and publication is subsequently completed. If the defendant dies within thirty days after filing and before the summons served upon him or her or publication is completed, the notice is effective only if the summons is served upon his or her executor or administrator within sixty days after letters are issued.

§ 1346. Duration of notice of pendency.

A notice of pendency shall be effective for a period of three years from the date of filing. Before expiration of a period or extended period, the court, upon motion of the claiming authority and upon such notice as it may require, for good cause shown, may grant an extension for a like additional period. An extension order shall be filed, recorded and indexed before expiration of the prior period.

§ 1347. Motion for cancellation of notice of pendency.

1. Mandatory cancellation. The court, upon motion of any person aggrieved and upon such notice as it may require, shall direct any county clerk to cancel a notice of pendency, if service of a summons has not been completed within the time limited by section one thousand three hundred forty-five of this article; or if the action has been settled, discontinued or abated; or if the time to appeal from a final judgment against the claiming authority has expired.

2. Discretionary cancellation. The court, upon a motion of any person aggrieved and upon such notice as it may require, may direct any county clerk to cancel a notice of pendency, if the claiming authority has not commenced or prosecuted the action in good faith.

3. Costs and expenses. The court, in an order canceling a notice of pendency under this section, may direct the claiming authority to pay any costs and expenses occasioned by the filing and cancellation, in addition to any costs of the action. In order to establish the claiming authority's liability for such costs and expenses, the person seeking such costs and expenses must prove by a preponderance of the evidence that, in causing the notice to pendency to be filed, the claiming authority acted without reasonable cause and not in good faith.

4. Cancellation by stipulation. At any time prior to entry of judgment, a notice of pendency shall be cancelled by the county clerk without an order, on the filing with him or her of:

(a) An affidavit by the claiming authority showing which defendants have been served with process, which defendants are in default in appearing or answering, and which defendants have appeared or answered and by whom; and

(b) A stipulation consenting to the cancellation, signed by the claiming authority and by the attorneys for all the defendants who have appeared or answered including those who have waived all notices, and executed and acknowledged, in the form required to entitle a deed to be recorded, by the defendants who have been served with process and have not appeared but whose time to do so has not expired, and by any defendants who have appeared in person.

5. Cancellation by a claiming authority. At any time prior to the entry of a judgment a notice of pendency of action shall be cancelled by the county clerk without an order on the filing with him or her of an affidavit by the claiming authority showing that there have been no appearances and that the time to appear has expired for all parties.

§ 1348. Undertaking for cancellation of notice of pendency.

The court, upon motion of any person aggrieved and upon such notice of pendency as it may require, may direct any county clerk to cancel a notice of pendency, upon such terms as are just, whether or not the judgment demanded would affect specific real property, if the moving party shall give an undertaking in an amount to be fixed by the court, and if the court finds that adequate relief can be secured to the claiming authority by the giving of such an undertaking.

§ 1349. Disposal of property.

1. Any judgment or order of forfeiture issued pursuant to this article shall include provisions for the disposal of the property found to have been forfeited.

2. If any other provision of law expressly governs the manner of disposition of property subject to the judgment or order of forfeiture, that provision of law shall be controlling. Upon application by a claiming agent for reimbursement of moneys directly expended by a claiming agent in the underlying criminal investigation for the purchase of contraband which were converted into a non-monetary form or which have not been otherwise recovered, the court shall direct such reimbursement from money forfeited pursuant to this article. Upon application of the claiming agent, the court may direct that any vehicles, vessels or aircraft forfeited pursuant to this article be retained by the claiming agent for law enforcement purposes, unless the court determines that such property is subject to a perfected lien, in which case the court may not direct that the property be retained unless all such liens on the property to be retained have been satisfied or

pursuant to the court's order will be satisfied. In the absence of an application by the claiming agent, the claiming authority may apply to the court to retain such property for law enforcement purposes. Upon such application, the court may direct that such property be retained by the claiming authority for law enforcement purposes, unless the court determines that such property is subject to a perfected lien. If not so retained, the judgment or order shall direct the claiming authority to sell the property in accordance with article fifty-one of this chapter, and that the proceeds of such sale and any other moneys realized as a consequence of any forfeiture pursuant to this article shall be apportioned and paid in the following descending order of priority:

(a) Amounts ordered to be paid by the court in satisfaction of any lien or claim against property forfeited. A fine imposed pursuant to the penal law shall not be deemed to constitute a lien or claim for purposes of this section;

(b) Amounts ordered to be paid by the defendant in any other action or proceeding as restitution, reparations or damages to a victim of the crime, which crime constitutes the basis upon which forfeiture was effected under this article, to the extent such amounts remain unpaid;

(c) Amounts ordered to be paid by the defendant in any other action or proceeding as restitution, reparations or damages to a victim of any crime committed by the defendant even though such crime did not constitute the basis for forfeiture under this article, to the extent that such amounts remain unpaid;

(d) Amounts actually expended by a claiming authority or claiming agent, which amounts are substantiated by vouchers or other evidence, for the:

(i) Maintenance and operation of real property attached pursuant to this article. Expenditures authorized by this subparagraph are limited to mortgage, tax and other financial obligations imposed by law and those other payments necessary to provide essential services and repairs to real property whose occupants are innocent of the criminal conduct which led to the attachment or forfeiture; and

(ii) proper storage, cleanup and disposal of hazardous substances or other materials, the disposal of which is governed by the environmental conservation law, when such storage, cleanup or disposal is required by circumstances attendant to either the commission of the crime or the forfeiture action, or any order entered pursuant thereto;

(e) In addition to amounts, if any, distributed pursuant to paragraph (d) of this subdivision, fifteen percent of all moneys realized through forfeiture to the claiming authority in satisfaction of actual costs and expenses incurred in the investigation, preparation and litigation of the forfeiture action, including that proportion of the salaries of the attorneys, clerical and investigative personnel devoted thereto, plus all costs and disbursements taxable under the provisions of this chapter;

(f) In addition to amounts, if any, distributed pursuant to paragraph (d) of this subdivision, five percent of all moneys realized through forfeiture to the claiming agent in satisfaction of actual costs incurred for protecting, maintaining and forfeiting the property including that proportion of the salaries of attorneys, clerical and investigative personnel devoted thereto;

(g) Forty percent of all moneys realized through forfeiture which are remaining after distributions pursuant to paragraphs (a) through (f) of this subdivision, to the chemical dependence service fund established pursuant to section ninety-seven-w of the state finance law;

(h) All moneys remaining after distributions pursuant to paragraphs (a) through (g) of this subdivision shall be distributed as follows:

(i) Seventy-five percent of such moneys shall be deposited to a law enforcement purposes subaccount of the general fund of the state where the claiming agent is an agency of the state or the political subdivision or public authority of which the claiming agent is a part, to be used for law enforcement use in the investigation of penal law offenses;

(ii) the remaining twenty-five percent of such moneys shall be deposited to a prosecution services subaccount of the general fund of the state where the claiming authority is the attorney general or the political subdivision of which the claiming authority is a part, to be used for the prosecution of penal law offenses.

Where multiple claiming agents participated in the forfeiture action, funds available pursuant to subparagraph (i) of this paragraph shall be disbursed to the appropriate law enforcement purposes subaccounts in accordance with the terms of a written agreement reflecting the participation of each claiming agent entered into by the participating claiming agents.

3. All moneys distributed to the claiming agent and the claiming authority pursuant to paragraph (h) of subdivision two of this section shall be used to enhance law enforcement efforts and not in supplantation of ordinary budgetary costs including salaries of personnel, and expenses of the claiming authority or claiming agent during the fiscal year in which this section takes effect.

4. The claiming authority shall report the disposal of property and collection of assets pursuant to this section to the state crime victims board, the state division of criminal justice services and the state division of substance abuse services.

Amended by L. 1986, Ch. 231, eff. July 1, 1986; **Repealed**

L. 1990, Ch. 655, eff. Nov. 1, 1990, and new section **added** eff. Nov. 1, 1990. **Amended** by L. 2004, Ch. 398, § 2, eff. Aug. 17, 2004, amending subd. 2(g).

§ 1350. Rules of procedure; in general.

The civil practice law and rules shall govern the procedure in proceedings and actions commenced under this article, except where the procedure is regulated by any inconsistent provisions herein.

§ 1351. Application of article.

If any provision of this article or the application thereof to any person or circumstances shall be adjudged by any court of competent jurisdiction to be invalid or unconstitutional, such judgment shall not affect, impair or invalidate provision, or (ii) in its application to the person or circumstance directly involved in the controversy in which such judgment shall have been rendered.

§ 1352. Preservation of other rights and remedies.

The remedies provided for in this article are not intended to substitute for or limit or supercede * the lawful authority of any public officer or agency or other person to enforce any other right or remedy provided for by law.

* So in original.

ARTICLE 13-B

CIVIL REMEDIES: ENTERPRISE CORRUPTION

[Added by L. 1986, Ch. 516, eff. Nov. 1, 1986, and permits the commencement of a criminal or civil action against a person based upon his participation in a pattern of criminal activity beginning before the effective date of this act only if his participation in the pattern also specifically includes at least one criminal act which was a felony and which was committed on or after such dates.]

Section
  1353.   **Civil remedies.**
  1354.   **Joinder of a party.**
  1355.   **Civil actions notice.**

LexisNexis Cross References

Prosecution and Defense of Forfeiture Cases, Vol. 1, Part I, Civil Forfeiture; *New York Criminal Practice (2d ed.),* Vol. 6, Ch. 56, Attempt, Solicitation, Conspiracy and Facilitation; *see generally Prosecution and Defense of Criminal Conspiracy Cases, Criminal Defense Techniques,* Vol. 3A, Ch. 62A, "RICO" Racketeer Influenced and Corrupt Organizations Act.

§ 1353. Civil remedies.

1. Upon or after conviction of a person of any subdivision of section 460.20 of the penal law, the court may, after making due provision for the rights of innocent persons, enjoin future activity by the person so convicted or an enterprise he controls or in whose control he participates upon a showing that injunctive action is necessary to prevent further violation of that section. In such case the court may:

(a) order the defendant to divest himself of any interest in a specified enterprise;

(b) impose reasonable restrictions upon the future activities or investments of the defendant, including prohibiting the defendant from engaging in the same type of endeavor as the enterprise in which he was engaged in violation of section 460.20 of the penal law;

(c) order the dissolution of any enterprise he controls or the reorganization of any enterprise he controls or of which he participates in the control;

(d) order the suspension or revocation of a license, permit or prior approval granted by any agency of the state or any political subdivision thereof to the defendant or to any enterprise controlled by him or in whose control he participates, provided however, that when the court orders such license, permit or approval revoked or suspended for a period of more than two years, the court shall set a period of time within two years of the date of such revocation or suspension after which the defendant or enterprise may petition the court to permit the defendant or enterprise to request restoration or renewal of such license, permit or approval, by the agency or board empowered to grant it, after notice to and hearing of the party who brought the action in which the revocation or suspension was ordered;

(e) order the revocation of the certificate of incorporation of a corporation organized under the laws of the state in which the defendant has a controlling interest or the revocation of authorization for a conduct business within the state upon a finding that the board of directors or a high managerial agent acting on behalf of the corporation, in conducting the affairs of the corporation, has authorized or engaged in activity made unlawful by section 460.20 of the penal law and that such action is necessary for the prevention of future criminal activity made unlawful by section 460.20 of the penal law.

2. The attorney general, the deputy attorney general in charge of the statewide organized crime task force, or any district attorney may institute civil proceedings in the supreme court under this section. Any action brought under this article shall constitute a special proceeding. In any action brought under this article, the supreme court shall proceed as soon as practicable to the hearing and determination thereof. Pending final determination, the supreme court may, at any time, enter such injunctions, prohibitions, or restraining orders or take such actions, including the acceptance of satisfactory performance bonds, ordering of disclosure under article thirty-one of this chapter, or other action as the court may deem proper.

§ 1354. Joinder of a party.

A person or enterprise not convicted of the

crime of enterprise corruption may be made a party to a civil action under this article, whenever joinder of such person or enterprise is necessary pursuant to section 1001 of this chapter.

§ 1355. Civil actions notice.

Within fifteen days of commencing a civil proceeding pursuant to this article, the prosecutor bringing such action must notify those district attorneys who were affected district attorneys within the meaning of section 460.60 of the penal law in the prior criminal proceeding.

ARTICLE 45

EVIDENCE

MISC. LAWS

LexisNexis Cross References

See generally Bender's New York Evidence—CPLR; Criminal Law Advocacy, Vol. 3, Ch. 3, Evidentiary Implications of Opening Statement and Final Argument; Vol. 3, Ch. 4, Real and Demonstrative Evidence; Vol. 3, Ch. 5, Scientific Evidence: Presentation and Attack; Vol. 3, Ch. 6, Evidence and the Witness Examination Process; Vol. 3, Ch. 7, Privileges; Vol. 3, Ch. 8, Hearsay; *New York Criminal Practice (2d ed.),* Vol. 3, Ch. 33, Evidence; Vol. 3, Ch. 34, Privileged Communications; Vol. 3, Ch. 35, Implications of Co-Conspirators Exception of Hearsay Rule; Vol. 3, Ch. 36, Testimony; *Sexual Assault Trials (2d ed.),* Vol. 1, Ch. 1, Pretrial Issues, Discovery, and Motions; *Criminal Evidentiary Foundations,* Ch. 3, The Competency of Witnesses; Ch. 4, Authentication; Ch. 5, Rule 403 and Legal Relevance Limitations on Credibility Evidence; Ch. 7, Privileges and Similar Doctrines.

§ 4501. Self-incrimination.

A competent witness shall not be excused from answering a relevant question, on the ground only that the answer may tend to establish that he owes a debt or is otherwise subject to a civil suit. This section does not require a witness to give an answer which will tend to accuse himself of a crime or to expose him to a penalty or forfeiture, nor does it vary any other rule respecting the examination of a witness.

ANNOTATION

Privilege arising from marital relationship waived by failure to object; waiver continues through all stages of proceeding.—Defendant-husband's attempt to invoke marital privilege at conclusion of hearing, after complainant-wife had previously extensively testified, was not timely; objection must be made before the confidential matter is disclosed, and waiver of the privilege at one state of a criminal proceeding is a general waiver and continues through all subsequent stages. People v. Santiago, 68 Misc. 2d 85, 326 N.Y.S.2d 332 (Crim. Ct. N.Y. Co. 1971).

§ 4502. Spouse.

(a) Incompetency where issue adultery. A husband or wife is not competent to testify against the other in an action founded upon adultery, except to prove the marriage, disprove the adultery, or disprove a defense after evidence has been introduced tending to prove such defense.

(b) Confidential communication privileged. A husband or wife shall not be required, or, without consent of the other if living, allowed to disclose a confidential communication made by one to the other during marriage.

ANNOTATIONS

Scope of marital privilege.—Communications or threats made during course of physical abuse are not entitled to protections of privilege because maker of statement is not

"relying upon any confidential relationship to preserve the secrecy of his acts and words," Defendant's inculpatory statement that he was so mad that he could kill her "just like he did with that kid," made to wife while he was choking and threatening her, was properly admitted. People v. Mills, 1 N.Y.3d 269, 772 N.Y.S.2d 228, 804 N.E.2d 392 (2003).

—The privilege does not protect all the daily and ordinary exchanges between the spouses, but merely those which would not have been made but for the absolute confidence in, and induced by, the marital relationship. People v. Wilson, 64 N.Y.2d 634, 485 N.Y.S.2d 40, 474 N.E.2d 248 (1984).

—A statement by a spouse that he has committed a crime is privileged. People v. Daghita, 299 N.Y. 194, 86 N.E.2d 172 (1949).

—Discussions between spouses about ordinary business matters are not privileged. Parkhurst v. Berdell, 110 N.Y. 386, 18 N.E. 123 (1878).

—Communications between spouses made in the known presence of third parties are not privileged. People v. Gorman, 150 A.D.2d 797, 542 N.Y.S.2d 225 (2d Dept. 1989).

—The privilege between spouses does not extend to communications between spouses in which they are jointly advancing a criminal conspiracy or aiding each other in the commission of an on-going crime. People v. Watkins, 63 A.D.2d 1033, 406 N.Y.S.2d 343 (2d Dept.), *cert. denied,* 439 U.S. 984 (1978).

—"Where criminal activity is aimed at a spouse, the [marital] privilege is extinguished." People v. Govan, 268 A.D.2d 689, 701 N.Y.S.2d 474 (3d Dept. 2000).

—The husband-wife privilege was not applicable to a statement of the husband to his wife evincing his intent to have intercourse with his children prior to the first such incident. People v. St. John, 74 A.D.2d 85, 426 N.Y.S.2d 863 (3d Dept. 1980).

Communications may include acts of a spouse.—Court erred in allowing defendant's wife to testify that she showed her weapon on a prior occasion. "One spouse may not, without consent, disclose a confidential communication made by the other during marriage. . . . Acts as well as words may be the subject of communications." People v. Marinaccio, 15 A.D.3d 932, 788 N.Y.S.2d 784 (4th Dept. 2005).

"Husband" and "wife" strictly defined.—Spousal privilege is limited to communications between husband and wife and does not extend to "homosexuals in a spousal relationship." Greenwald v. H&P 29th St. Assoc., 241 A.D.2d 307, 659 N.Y.S.2d 473 (1st Dept. 1997).

Claim of privilege not properly made in motion to suppress.—The grounds enumerated in CPL § 710.20 on which a motion to suppress may be made do not include evidence that is claimed to be privileged. People v. Easter, 71 A.D.2d 762, 419 N.Y.S.2d 327 (3d Dept. 1979).

Nonresident wife; non-confidential communications.—A wife who is a New Jersey resident must honor a New York county grand jury subpoena to testify about non-confidential communications with her husband who was a suspect in three murders in New York, and New Jersey Rules of Evidence, Rule 23(2) does not apply as she was separated from her husband. People v. Doe, 105 Misc. 2d 84, 431 N.Y.S.2d 879 (Sup. Ct. N.Y. Co. 1980).

Policy.—One underlying legislative motivation for the creation of the spousal privilege was to encourage husband and wife to share confidences by assuring that they would not be divulged in legal proceedings. People v. Poppe, 3 N.Y.2d 312, 165 N.Y.S.2d 99 (1957).

Presence of a third party.—Spousal privilege for confidential communications falls "when the substance of a communication . . . is revealed to third parties"; where substance of communication between defendant and his wife was revealed to his wife's sister by both defendant and his wife, communication was properly permitted. People v. Weeks, 15 A.D.3d 845, 789 N.Y.S.2d 373 (4th Dept. 2005).

—Communications between husband and wife made in the known presence of a third person are not confidential and hence, are not privileged. People v. Allen, 104 Misc. 2d 136, 427 N.Y.S.2d 698 (Sup. Ct. Westchester Co. 1980).

Suppression hearing.—It was error for the hearing court to suppress the marijuana and drug equipment displayed to police by the wife in the defendant's home since the court failed to perceive that the husband-wife privilege was testimonial, obtaining full import at the trial, not at a suppression hearing, and that by suppressing the evidence, the court deprived the People of the opportunity to demonstrate defendant's ownership of the drug equipment and the marijuana by proof independent of the testimony by the wife. People v. Kemp, 59 A.D.2d 414, 399 N.Y.S.2d 879 (1st Dept. 1977).

Telephone.—The privilege extends to intercepted telephone communications, however, the privilege does not exist as to conversations between married persons that advance a criminal activity. People v. Watkins, 89 Misc. 2d 870, 393 N.Y.S.2d 283 (Sup. Ct. Suffolk Co. 1977), *aff'd*, 63 A.D.2d 1033, 406 N.Y.S.2d 343 (2d Dept.), *cert. denied*, 439 U.S. 984 (1978).

§ 4503. Attorney.

(a) 1. Confidential communication privileged. Unless the client waives the privilege, an attorney or his or her employee, or any person who obtains without the knowledge of the client evidence of a confidential communication made between the attorney or his or her employee and the client in the course of professional employment, shall not disclose, or be allowed to disclose such communication, nor shall the client be compelled to disclose such communication, in any action, disciplinary trial or hearing, or administrative action, proceeding or hearing conducted by or on behalf of any state, municipal or local governmental agency or by the legislature or any committee or body thereof. Evidence of any such communication obtained by any such person, and evidence resulting therefrom, shall not be disclosed by any state, municipal or local governmental agency or by the legislature or any committee or body thereof. The relationship of an attorney and client shall exist between a professional service corporation organized under article fifteen of the business corporation law to practice as an attorney and counselor-at-law and the clients to whom it renders legal services.

2. Personal representatives. (A) For purposes of the attorney-client privilege, if the client is a personal representative and the attorney represents the personal representative in that capacity, in the absence of an agreement between the attorney and the personal representative to the contrary:

(i) No beneficiary of the estate is, or shall be treated as, the client of the attorney solely by reason of his or her status as beneficiary; and

(ii) The existence of a fiduciary relationship between the personal representative and a beneficiary of the estate does not by itself constitute or give rise to any waiver of the privilege for confidential communications made in the course of professional employment between the attorney or his or her employee and the personal representative who is the client.

(B) For purposes of this paragraph, "personal representative" shall mean (i) the administrator, administrator c.t.a., ancillary administrator, executor, preliminary executor, temporary administrator or trustee to whom letters have been issued within the meaning of subdivision thirty-four of section one hundred three of the surrogate's court procedure act, and (ii) the guardian of an incapacitated communicant if and to the extent that the order appointing such guardian under subdivision (c) of section 81.16 of the mental hygiene law or any subsequent order of any court expressly provides that the guardian is to be the personal representative of the incapacitated communicant for purposes of this section; "beneficiary" shall have the meaning set forth in subdivision eight of section one hundred three of the surrogate's court procedure act and "estate" shall have the meaning set forth in subdivision nineteen of section one hundred three of the surrogate's court procedure act.

(b) Wills. In any action involving the probate, validity or construction of a will, an attorney or his employee shall be required to disclose information as to the preparation, execution or revocation of any will or other relevant instrument, but he shall not be allowed to disclose any communication privileged under subdivision (a) which would tend to disgrace the memory of the decedent.

Amended by L. 1977, Ch. 418; L. 2002, Ch. 430, § 1, eff. Aug. 20, 2002, amending subd. a.

ANNOTATIONS

Burden of proof.—The burden of proving each element of the privilege rests on the party asserting it; the defendant failed to meet his burden of establishing that when he spoke to unknown women in a common reception area, his statements were intended to be confidential and made to an employee of his attorney for the purpose of obtaining legal advice. People v. Mitchell, 58 N.Y.2d 368, 461 N.Y.S.2d 267, 448 N.E.2d 121 (1983).

No constitutional guarantee.—The attorney-client privilege is a statutory provision and is not constitutionally guaranteed. People v. O'Connor, 85 A.D.2d 92, 447 N.Y.S.2d 553 (4th Dept. 1982).

Death of client.—"[J]ust as the attorney-client privilege itself survives the death of the client for whose benefit the privilege exists, the right to waive that privilege in the interest of the deceased client's estate also survives and may be exercised by the decedent's personal representative." Mayorga v. Tate, 302 A.D.2d 11, 752 N.Y.S.2d 353 (2d Dept. 2002) (citations omitted).

—The attorney-client privilege can be waived by the executor, particularly where assertion of privilege works to detriment of estate. In re Estate of Johnson, 7 A.D.3d 959, 777 N.Y.S.2d 212 (3d Dept. 2004).

Non-judicial proceedings.—In a grand jury investigation of a client accused of illegally removing her child from state and therefore committing the felony of custodial interference, attorney cannot be compelled to disclose whereabouts of client. In re Grand Jury Investigation, 175 Misc. 2d 398, 669 N.Y.S.2d 179 (Fam. Ct. Onondaga Co. 1998).

Polygraphist retained by attorney.—Where defendant's attorney retained a polygraphist to administer a lie detector test to the defendant, communications given by the defendant to the polygraphist, while he was acting within the scope of his assignment came within CPLR 4503. People v. George, 104 Misc. 2d 630, 428 N.Y.S.2d 825 (Sup. Ct. Bronx Co. 1980).

Privilege; generally.—The attorney-client privilege enables one seeking legal advice to communicate with counsel for this purpose secure in the knowledge that the contents of the exchange will not later be revealed against the client's wishes; the privilege belongs to the client and attaches to information disclosed in confidence to the attorney for the purpose of obtaining legal advice or services. People v. Osorio, 75 N.Y.2d 80, 550 N.Y.S.2d 612, 549 N.E.2d 1183 (1989).

—The attorney-client privilege is not absolute, it may yield to strong public policy considerations, and can not be used as a shield to protect client communications that may have been in furtherance of fraudulent scheme, an alleged breach of fiduciary duty or an accusation of some other wrongful conduct. Ulico Cas. Co. v. Wilson, Elser, Moskowitz, Edelman & Dicker, 1 A.D.3d 2, 767 N.Y.S.2d 228 (1st Dept. 2003).

—Motion to quash subpoena duces tecum should have been granted since materials requested are privileged communications made between an attorney and his client, request was fishing expedition based on speculation that some unspecified information would be found to impeach complaining witness in underlying criminal prosecution. Ferro, Kuba, Bloom, Mangano, Gacovino & Lake, P.C. v. Guerrero, 8 A.D.3d 563, 778 N.Y.S.2d 723 (2d Dept. 2004).

—State agencies have an attorney-client relationship with Attorney General's office, as that office is obligated to prosecute, defend and control all legal business of state agencies; title reports, handwritten notes and diagrams prepared by Attorney General's office were all work product which was privileged and exempt from disclosure, communications between the Attorney General's Real Property Bureau and respondent's employees, made for purpose of facilitating the rendering and obtaining of legal advice or services, were properly withheld as privileged materials. Morgan v. N.Y. State Dept. of Envtl. Conservation, 9 A.D.3d 586, 779 N.Y.S.2d 643 (3d Dept. 2004).

—An attorney must protect his client's interest, but he also must observe basic human standards of decency, having due regard to the need that the legal system accord justice to the interests of society and its individual members. People v. Belge, 50 A.D.2d 1088, 376 N.Y.S.2d 771 (4th Dept. 1975), aff'd, 41 N.Y.2d 60, 390 N.Y.S.2d 867, 359 N.E.2d 377 (1976).

—A subpoena directed to legal fees does not implicate the attorney-client privilege because a lawyer's fee arrangement is not protected by the attorney-client privilege. In re Stolar, 196 Misc. 2d 175, 763 N.Y.S.2d 896 (Sup. Ct. N.Y. Co. 2003).

—The attorney-client privilege survives the death of the client. People v. Vespucci, 192 Misc. 2d 685, 745 N.Y.S.2d 391 (Co. Ct. Nassau Co. 2002).

Scope.—Communications regarding "the identity of a client and information about fees paid by the client" are not generally protected under the privilege, nor are communications regarding "the payment of legal fees by a third person." In re Nassau County Grand Jury (Doe Law Firm), 4 N.Y.3d 665, 797 N.Y.S.2d 790, 830 N.E.2d 1118 (2005).

—The fee arrangements between attorney and client do not ordinarily constitute a confidential communication and are not privileged, nor does the payment of legal fees by a third party create an attorney-client relationship sufficient to sustain a claim of privilege. Priest v. Hennessy, 51 N.Y.2d 62, 431 N.Y.S.2d 511, 409 N.E.2d 983 (1980).

—There is nothing in the law governing attorney-client privilege that precludes the privilege from attaching to client communications made in response to oral requests, as opposed to written requests, from attorneys. New York Times v. Lehrer McGovern Bovis, Inc, 300 A.D.2d 169, 752 N.Y.S.2d 642 (1st Dept. 2002).

—Since defendant did not testify as to the contents of prior conversations with his attorney or the investigator, it was error for the court to compel defense counsel to turn over, for cross-examination of the defendant, the notes counsel or his investigator has made during conversations with the defendant. People v. Marsh, 59 A.D.2d 623, 398 N.Y.S.2d 166 (2d Dept. 1977).

—As long as the communication is primarily of a legal character, the privilege is not lost merely by inclusion or reference to certain non-legal matters. In re Seelig, 302 A.D.2d 721, 756 N.Y.S.2d 305 (3d Dept. 2003).

—Medical records subpoenaed in an anti-fraud investigation from an administrative and managerial corporation that is not a medical corporation licensed under Public Health Law Article 28 are not protected from disclosure by the physician-patient privilege. Comprehensive Habilitation Servs. v. Attorney General, 278 A.D.2d 557, 717 N.Y.S.2d 680 (3d Dept. 2000), appeal denied, 96 N.Y.2d 706 (2001).

—Analyses prepared solely for purpose of providing legal advice to management were protected from disclosure by attorney-client privilege. Di Mascio v. General Elec. Co., 307 A.D.2d 600, 762 N.Y.S.2d 696 (4th Dept. 2003).

—The testimony was admissible since the defendant could not reasonably have expected that statements made to two secretaries and a paralegal in the common waiting room of two attorneys were confidential nor could the communication have been for the purpose of securing legal advice or assistance. People v. Mitchell, 86 A.D.2d 976, 448 N.Y.S.2d 332 (4th Dept. 1982).

—The privilege applies only if (1) the asserted holder of the privilege is or sought to become a client; (2) the person to whom the communication was made (a) is a member of the bar of a court, or his subordinate and (b) in connection with this communication is acting as a lawyer; (3) the communication relates to a fact of which the attorney was informed (a) by his client (b) without the presence of strangers (c) for the purpose of securing primarily either (i) an opinion or law or (ii) legal services or (iii) assistance in some legal proceeding, and not (d) for the purpose of committing a crime or tort; and (4) the privilege has been (a) claimed and (b) not waived by the client. People v. Belge, 59 A.D.2d 307, 399 N.Y.S.2d 539 (4th Dept. 1977).

—The privilege may be overcome where disclosure is required to determine the validity of the claim and to prevent the defendant from being deprived of vital information. In the case at bar, the negligence of the plaintiff's former attorney could only be revealed by the communications between the plaintiff and current counsel regarding whether former counsel had knowledge of the hole in the floor of the worksite where plaintiff was injured. Bennett v. Oot & Assocs., 162 Misc. 2d 160, 616 N.Y.S.2d 163 (Sup. Ct. Tompkins Co. 1994).

Waiver.—Attorney-client privilege, which attached to an internal report coauthored by plaintiff's in-house counsel, was not waived when it was inadvertently produced in a prior related action, nor was it waived by placing the subject matter of the report at issue in this action. L.I. Lighting Co. v. Allianz Underwriters Ins. Co., 301 A.D.2d 23, 749 N.Y.S.2d 488 (1st Dept. 2002).

—Although memo in question was labeled as a "Privileged and Confidential Attorney-Client Communication" and was initially limited in its distribution, defendant waived privilege by failing to exercise due diligence; although defendant knew memo was in possession of third parties who could have copied it and disseminated information contained in it, he took no action to retrieve it. AFA Protective Sys., Inc. v. City of New York, 13 A.D.3d 564, 788 N.Y.S.2d 128 (2d Dept. 2004).

Weapon; attorney-client privilege.—The delivery of ammunition and a clip to an attorney falls within the ambit of the attorney-client privilege but public policy prevents the application of the privilege where there are reasonable grounds to believe this property may be involved in a crime and the property should be turned over to the district attorney without the necessity of the attorney's personally appearing before the grand jury. People v. Investigation into a Certain Weapon, 113 Misc. 2d 348, 448 N.Y.S.2d 950 (Sup Ct. Kings Co. 1982).

Whereabouts of defendant.—Attorney was required to answer questions by grand jury as to defendant's whereabouts where defendant as part of her plea bargain had agreed to undergo psychiatric care and after such treatment return to court for sentencing, and defendant had violated the agreement by leaving the hospital with intent to frustrate the court mandate, and thereafter had contacted her attorney. *In re* Doe, 101 Misc. 2d 388, 420 N.Y.S.2d 996 (N.Y. Co. 1979).

Withdrawal of attorney.—Attorney was permitted to withdraw as counsel for the defendant when it was shown that a conflict of interest had evolved by reason of the fact that counsel had previously represented the informer who would be called as a defense witness in the event the People declined to avail themselves of his testimony. People v. Ayala, 86 Misc. 2d 99, 381 N.Y.S.2d 655 (Suffolk Co. Ct. 1976).

Witness; no implied waiver of attorney-client privilege.— Where statement was prepared as work product of attorney in separate civil suit by defendant, defendant's mention of prior existence of statement in subsequent criminal prosecution for assault in the second degree and for reckless endangerment in the second degree did not constitute a waiver of the attorney-client privilege by implication, and the prosecutor's demand for the statement's production was error. People v. Moore, 42 A.D.2d 268, 346 N.Y.S.2d 363 (2d Dept. 1973).

Work product.—The work product doctrine affords protection only to facts and observations disclosed by attorney to a psychiatrist in order to obtain advice concerning the efficacy of an insanity plea or any trial strategy; it does not operate to insulate other disclosed information from public exposure. People v. Edney, 39 N.Y.2d 620, 385 N.Y.S.2d 23, 350 N.E.2d 400 (1976).

§ 4504. Physician, dentist, podiatrist, chiropractor and nurse.

(a) Confidential information privileged. Unless the patient waives the privilege, a person authorized to practice medicine, registered professional nursing, licensed practical nursing, dentistry, podiatry, or chiropractics shall not be allowed to disclose any information which he acquired in attending a patient in a professional capacity, and which was necessary to enable him to act in that capacity. The relationship of a physician and patient shall exist between a medical corporation, as defined in article forty-four of the public health law, a professional service corporation organized under article fifteen of the business corporation law to practice medicine, a university faculty practice corporation organized under section fourteen hundred twelve of the not-for-profit corporation law to practice medicine or dentistry, and the patients to whom they respectively render professional medical services.

A patient who, for the purpose of obtaining insurance benefits, authorizes the disclosure of any such privileged communication to any person shall not be deemed to have waived the privilege created by this subdivision. For purposes of this subdivision:

1. "person" shall mean any individual, insurer or agent thereof, peer review committee, public or private corporation, political subdivision, government agency, department or bureau of the state, municipality, industry, co-partnership, association, firm, trust, estate or any other legal entity whatsoever; and

2. "insurance benefits" shall include payments under a self-insured plan.

(b) Identification by dentist; crime committed against patient under sixteen. A dentist shall be required to disclose information necessary for identification of a patient. A physician, dentist, podiatrist, chiropractor or nurse shall be required to disclose information indicating that a patient who is under the age of sixteen years has been the victim of a crime.

(c) Mental or physical condition of deceased patient. A physician or nurse shall be required to disclose any information as to the mental or physical condition of a deceased patient privileged under subdivision (a), except information which would tend to disgrace the memory of the decedent, either in the absence of an objection by a party to the litigation or when the privilege has been waived:

1. by the personal representative, or the surviving spouse, or the next of kin of the decedent; or

2. in any litigation where the interests of the personal representative are deemed by the trial judge to be adverse to those of the estate of the decedent, by any party in interest; or

3. if the validity of the will of the decedent is in question, by the executor named in the will, or the surviving spouse or any heir-at-law or any of the next of kin or any other party in interest.

(d) Proof of negligence; unauthorized practice of medicine. In any action for damages for personal injuries or death against a person not authorized to practice medicine under article 131, of the education law for any act or acts constituting the practice of medicine, when such act or acts were a competent producing proximate or contributing cause of such injuries or death, the fact that such person practiced medicine without being so authorized shall be deemed prima facie evidence of negligence.

Amended by L. 1984, Ch. 913, eff. Oct. 5, 1984; L. 1990, Ch. 800, eff. July 25, 1990, adding chiropractor; L. 1991, Ch. 457; L. 1993, Ch. 555.

ANNOTATIONS

Purpose.—The privilege is created for the purposes of protecting people consulting physicians from disclosure of secrets; to protect the relationship between doctor and patient; and to prevent doctors from disclosing information which might result in humiliation, embarrassment, or disgrace to the patient. Grand Jury v. Kuriansky, 69 N.Y.2d 232, 513 N.Y.S.2d 359, 505 N.E.2d 925 (1987).

Scope.—Where compliance with subpoenas would violate physician-patient privilege because "assessment of the nature and causes of the injuries triggering production of the relevant documents involves an inherently medical evaluation," CPLR bars compliance with subpoena, even when released portions would only include notes of injuries readily observable to layperson and patients' contact information. *In re* New York County, 98 N.Y.2d 525, 749 N.Y.S.2d 462, 779 N.E.2d 173 (2002).

—A grand jury subpoena commanding a hospital to supply names and addresses of all persons treated for knife wounds was properly quashed because disclosure would include information concerning diagnosis and treatment. Matter of a Grand Jury Investigation of Onondaga County, 59 N.Y.2d 130, 463 N.Y.S.2d 758, 450 N.E.2d 678 (1983).

MISC. LAWS

—Medical practitioners may not assert the privilege to protect themselves with respect to a crime committed against a patient, but may assert it for the protection of their patients. *In re* Application to Quash, 56 N.Y.2d 348, 452 N.Y.S.2d 361, 437 N.E.2d 1118 (1982).

—Although confidential communications are subject to statutory protections, facts and incidents of a person's medical history are not. Fact of treatment and dates of treatment are all subject to disclosure, but information about nature of treatment rendered and diagnosis made is privileged. Laura Inger M., v. Hillside Children's Ctr., 17 A.D.3d 293,794 N.Y.S.2d 36 (1st Dept. 2005).

—Doctor/patient privilege did not bar admission of hospital records reflecting incidents and admission of insured's past substance abuse and tobacco use, admissible under CPLR 4518(a) as relevant to diagnosis and treatment. Mullen v. Independence Sav. Bank, 267 A.D.2d 169, 700 N.Y.S.2d 447 (1st Dept. 1999).

—Not all hospital records are privileged, records generated at request of quality assurance committee for quality assurance purposes, including compilations, studies or comparisons derived from multiple records, should be privileged, whereas records simply duplicated by committee are not necessarily privileged. Marte v. Brooklyn Hosp. Ctr., — A.D.3d —, 779 N.Y.S.2d 82 (2d Dept. 2004).

—Although plaintiff's request to discover names of other patients who may have witnessed accident was not a request to discover their medical information per se, since disclosure of patients' names would reveal that they were undergoing treatment for cardiac-related conditions, such discovery was prohibited. Gunn v. Sound Shore Med. Ctr., 5 A.D.3d 435, 772 N.Y.S.2d 714 (2d Dept. 2004).

—Motion for protective order properly granted where plaintiff sought to obtain medical records of another patient. Coven v. Lutheran Med. Ctr., 2 A.D.3d 767, 769 N.Y.S.2d 412 (2d Dept. 2003).

—In civil suit for medical malpractice and wrongful death, hospital produced a copy of operating room log for January 30, 1995, redacted only as to names, room numbers, and account numbers of nonparty patients, plaintiff was not entitled to obtain any additional information regarding diagnoses, treatments, and medical and surgical procedures listed on operating room log for nonparty patients. Brandes v. N. Shore Univ. Hosp., 1 A.D.3d 551, 767 N.Y.S.2d 648 (2d Dept. 2003).

—Where the observations made by a physician could have been made by a lay person and did not depend upon any confidential communications by the defendant, the privilege does not apply. People v. Hedges, 98 A.D.2d 950, 470 N.Y.S.2d 577 (2d Dept. 1983).

—Medical records subpoenaed in an anti-fraud investigation from an administrative and managerial corporation that is not a medical corporation licensed under Public Health Law Article 28 are not protected from disclosure by the physician-patient privilege. Comprehensive Habilitation Servs. v. Attorney General, 278 A.D.2d 557, 717 N.Y.S.2d 680 (3d Dept. 2000), *appeal denied,* 96 N.Y.2d 706 (2001).

—Legal duty to maintain physician/patient confidentiality with regard to information obtained in the course of rendering professional services extends to employees of health maintenance organizations, including clerical employees. Doe v. Community Health Plan, 268 A.D.2d 183, 709 N.Y.S.2d 215 (3d Dept. 2000).

—Doctor/patient privilege is testimonial and will not act as a bar to prevent admission of the results of blood-alcohol tests obtained by the prosecution through a valid search warrant. The blood was not drawn as a necessary part of defendant's medical treatment, but was drawn by a person authorized to do so by statute for the sole purpose of testing for alcohol content. People v. Bolson, 183 Misc. 2d 155, 701 N.Y.S.2d 828 (Sup. Ct. Queens Co. 1999).

—Insurance companies cannot claim privilege under 4504(a) and refuse to answer interrogatories; the privilege only extends to actual providers of care. Hudson Med. P.C., v. Allstate Ins. Co., 183 Misc. 2d 749, 704 N.Y.S.2d 437 (Sup. Ct. App. Term 2d Dept. 1999).

Physician-patient.—Communications between defendant and his physicians in furtherance of his treatment were obtained in violation of defendant's physician-patient privilege and should not have been admitted at trial. People v. Sinski, 88 N.Y.2d 487, 646 N.Y.S.2d 651, 669 N.E.2d 809 (1996).

—In a personal injury action brought as a result of a motor vehicle accident where respondent was one of the drivers, once appellant was able to establish that respondent's physical or mental condition was in controversy, the burden shifted back to respondent to show information requested was privileged; here name of treating psychiatrist was not privileged but the specific condition from which she suffers is and cannot be disclosed absent a waiver. Neferis v. DeStefano, 265 A.D.2d 464, 697 N.Y.S.2d 108 (2d Dept. 1999).

—Plaintiff met the threshold burden of demonstrating that the defendant's physical condition was "in controversy" at the time of the accident because she had consumed four beers. However, this did not automatically mean that the discovery of her blood alcohol test results should be permitted. This discovery should have been precluded because under CPLR 4504, this information was protected by the physician-patient privilege. Williams v. McGinty, 205 A.D.2d 617, 613 N.Y.S.2d 218 (2d Dept. 1994).

—A medical examiner's report on victim's blood toxicology that clearly contained exculpatory evidence may not be withheld from a defendant charged with attempted murder on the ground of physician-patient privilege. People v. Davis, 168 Misc. 2d 26, 637 N.Y.S.2d 297 (Nassau Co. Ct. 1995).

Waiver.—A defendant can waive doctor-patient privilege when he or she affirmatively places his or her mental or physical condition in issue, however, to effect a waiver, a defendant must do more than simply deny allegations in complaint; defendant must affirmatively assert condition "either by way of counterclaim or to excuse the conduct complained of by the plaintiff." Bongiorno v. Livingston, 20 A.D.3d 379, 799 N.Y.S.2d 98 (2d Dept. 2005).

—Where appellant neither waived privilege nor affirmatively asserted her mental condition at trial, court improperly allowed testimony from appellant's former physician regarding his treatment of her in violation of doctor-patient privilege. *In re* Rosa B.-S., 1 A.D.3d 355, 767 N.Y.S.2d 33 (2d Dept. 2003).

—Where a defendant in a manslaughter prosecution argued that his condition at the scene of the accident was due to injuries and not to intoxication, blood alcohol tests showing that the defendant was intoxicated at the time of the crash were admissible. People v. Feldman, 110 A.D.2d 906, 488 N.Y.S.2d 455 (2d Dept. 1985).

—In a sexual abuse case where credibility of complainant was critical, court erred when it refused to allow defense counsel to inquire of complainant's mother and psychologist as to past abuse complaints based on privilege under CPLR §§ 4504 and 4507; policy interest underlying statutory privilege must yield to defendant's constitutional right of confrontation; convictions were reversed. People v. Bridgeland, 19 A.D.3d 1122, 796 N.Y.S.2d 768 (4th Dept. 2005).

—Where a mother sues in a representative capacity as parent and natural guardian of an infant, her own medical history is not placed in issue nor does she waive her doctor-patient privilege; only in those instances where there is an issue regarding the time the infant was in utero are the mother's medical records discoverable on the grounds that severance is impossible. Schaner v. Mercy Hosp. of Buffalo, 15 A.D.3d 997, 789 N.Y.S.2d 561 (4th Dept. 2005).

—Defendant waived physician-patient privilege when he placed his medical condition in issue during cross-examination of a police officer; defendant attempted to show that defendant's appearance was due to the car accident and not due to intoxication. People v. Gonzales, 239 A.D.2d 931, 659 N.Y.S.2d 591 (4th Dept. 1997).

—A patient may waive the privilege by expressly testifying as to an injury or illness, by voluntary disclosure of condition or by conduct impliedly waiving the privilege. People v. Lowe, 96 Misc. 2d 33, 408 N.Y.S.2d 873 (Crim. Ct. Bronx Co. 1978).

§ 4505. Confidential communication to clergy privileged.

Unless the person confessing or confiding waives the privilege, a clergyman, or other minister of any religion or duly accredited Christian

Science practitioner, shall not be allowed to disclose a confession or confidence made to him in his professional character as spiritual advisor.

ANNOTATIONS

Disclosure to priest.—The CPLR 4505 privilege protects only the confidential communication or confession made by the penitent to the clergyman; there is no privilege that invests a clergyman's ministry with an immunity against disclosure. Keenan v. Gigante, 64 A.D.2d 585, 407 N.Y.S.2d 163 (1st Dept. 1978), aff'd, 47 N.Y.2d 160, 417 N.Y.S.2d 226, 390 N.E.2d 1151 (1979).

Extent of privilege.—The priest-penitent privilege does not arise solely because the statements are made to clergyman; there must be reason to believe that the information sought required the disclosure of information acquired under the cloak of the confessional or was in any way confidential; absent such a showing defendant, though a clergyman is, like all citizens, obligated to respond to the Grand Jury's questions. Keenan v. Gigante, 47 N.Y.2d 160, 417 N.Y.S.2d 226, 390 N.E.2d 1151 (1979).

—CPLR 4505 is to be interpreted broadly. People v. Shapiro, 308 N.Y. 453, 126 N.E.2d 559 (1955).

No civil liability for breach.—CPLR 4505 does not impose a fiduciary duty of confidentiality upon members of the clergy that subjects them to civil liability for the disclosure of confidential communications. Lightman v. Flaum, 97 N.Y.2d 128, 736 N.Y.S.2d 300, 761 N.E.2d 1027 (2001), cert. denied, 535 U.S. 1096, 122 S. Ct. 2292 (2002).

§ 4506. Eavesdropping evidence; admissibility; motion to suppress in certain cases.

1. The contents of any overheard or recorded communication, conversation or discussion, or evidence derived therefrom, which has been obtained by conduct constituting the crime of eavesdropping, as defined by section 250.05 of the penal law, may not be received in evidence in any trial, hearing or proceeding before any court or grand jury, or before any legislative committee, department, officer, agency, regulatory body, or other authority of the state, or a political subdivision thereof; provided, however, that such communication, conversation, discussion or evidence, shall be admissible in any civil or criminal trial, hearing or proceeding against a person who has, or is alleged to have, committed such crime of eavesdropping.

2. As used in this section, the term "aggrieved person" means:

(a) A person who was a sender or receiver of a telephonic or telegraphic communication which was intentionally overheard or recorded by a person other than the sender or receiver thereof, without the consent of the sender or receiver, by means of any instrument, device or equipment; or

(b) A party to a conversation or discussion which was intentionally overheard or recorded, without the consent of at least one party thereto, by a person not present thereat, by means of any instrument, devise or equipment; or

(c) A person against whom the overhearing or recording described in paragraphs (a) and (b) was directed.

3. An aggrieved person who is a party in any civil trial, hearing or proceeding before any court, or before any department, officer, agency, regulatory body, or other authority of the state, or a political subdivision thereof, may move to suppress the contents of any overheard or recorded communication, conversation or discussion or evidence derived therefrom on the ground that:

(a) The communication, conversation or discussion was unlawfully overheard or recorded; or

(b) The eavesdropping warrant under which it was overheard or recorded insufficient on its face; or

(c) The eavesdropping was not done in conformity with the eavesdropping warrant.

4. The motion prescribed in subdivision three of this section must be made before the judge or justice who issued the eavesdropping warrant. If no eavesdropping warrant was issued, such motion must be made before a justice of the supreme court of the judicial district in which the trial, hearing or proceeding is pending. The aggrieved person must allege in his motion papers that an overheard or recorded communication, conversation or discussion, or evidence derived therefrom, is subject to suppression under subdivision three of this section, and that such communication, conversation or discussion, or evidence, may be used against him in the civil trial hearing or proceeding in which he is a party. The motion must be made prior to the commencement of such trial, hearing or proceeding, unless there was no opportunity to make such motion or the aggrieved person was not aware of the grounds of the motion. If the motion is granted, the contents of the overheard or recorded communication, conversation or discussion or evidence derived therefrom may not be received in evidence in any trial, hearing or proceeding.

ANNOTATIONS

Evidence; wiretap.—CPLR 4506(2) does not include a person called before the Grand Jury within the definition of an aggrieved person entitled to make a motion to suppress evidence obtained through illegal electronic surveillance. People v. McGrath, 46 N.Y.2d 12, 412 N.Y.S.2d 801, 385 N.E.2d 541 (1978), cert. denied, 440 U.S. 972 (1979).

—Defendant properly precluded from using transcript of a recorded telephone conversation, People established a sufficient uncontested basis upon which court could conclude that recording had been obtained through unlawful eavesdropping. People v. Sanjuan, 6 A.D.3d 247, 774 N.Y.S.2d 338 (1st Dept. 2004)

Standing.—Although § 4506(2) does not explicitly recognize type of digital electronic communication captured by a pen register, the definition of "aggrieved person" encompasses those individuals who become identifiable targets of an investigation by virtue of the information gathered by a pen register. People v. Kramer, 92 N.Y.2d 529, 683 N.Y.S.2d 743, 706 N.E.2d 731 (1998).

—The proscriptions of this section apply to civil as well as criminal proceedings; just as illegally obtained wiretap evidence obtained by law enforcement officers will be excluded from court proceedings, so will illegally obtained wiretap evidence obtained by private individuals; the People have standing to move for such exclusion in a criminal case. People v. Qike, 182 Misc. 2d 737, 700 N.Y.S.2d 640 (Sup. Ct. Kings Co. 1999).

§ 4507. Psychologist.

The confidential relations and communications between a psychologist registered under the provisions of article one hundred fifty-three of the education law and his client are placed on the same basis as those provided by law between attorney and client, and nothing in such article shall be construed to require any such privileged communications to be disclosed.

A client who, for the purpose of obtaining insurance benefits, authorizes the disclosure of any such privileged communication to any person shall not be deemed to have waived the privilege created by this section. For purposes of this section:

1. "person" shall mean any individual, insurer or agent thereof, peer review committee, public or private corporation, political subdivision, government agency, department or bureau of the state, municipality, industry, co-partnership, association, firm, trust, estate or any other legal entity whatsoever; and

2. "insurance benefits" shall include payments under a self-insured plan.

Amended by L. 1984, Ch. 913, eff. Oct 5, 1984.

ANNOTATIONS

Scope.—The psychologist-patient privilege is broader than the doctor-patient privilege. People v. Wilkins, 65 N.Y.2d 1172, 490 N.Y.S.2d 759, 480 N.E.2d 373 (1985).

Psychiatric records; Medicaid fraud investigation.—Since the strong state interest in preventing Medicaid fraud outweighs the interest of Medicaid patients in keeping their records a private matter between themselves and their psychologists, the attorney general was entitled to records sought in subpoena duces tecum that reflected the extent and date of his treatment of seven named Medicaid patients. Doe v. Hynes, 104 Misc. 2d 398, 428 N.Y.S.2d 810 (Monroe Co. 1980).

Waiver.—Where insanity is asserted as an affirmative defense and the defendant offers evidence to show insanity, the privilege is waived and the prosecution may call as witnesses psychologists or psychiatrists who have examined the defendant. People v. Edney, 39 N.Y.2d 620, 385 N.Y.S.2d 23, 350 N.E.2d 400 (1976).

—Psychologist-patient privilege was waived by petitioner-patient who actively contested custody action of children; court did not err by allowing psychologist to testify. Sheppard v. Roll, 278 A.D.2d 755, 717 N.Y.S.2d 783 (3d Dept. 2000).

—In a sexual abuse case where credibility of complainant was critical, court erred when it refused to allow defense counsel to inquire of complainant's mother and psychologist as to past abuse complaints based on privilege under CPLR §§ 4504 and 4507; policy interest underlying statutory privilege must yield to defendant's constitutional right of confrontation; convictions were reversed. People v. Bridgeland, 19 A.D.3d 1122, 796 N.Y.S.2d 768 (4th Dept. 2005).

—Mere notice of the intent to present a psychological defense prior to actually interposing such a defense at trial does not constitute a waiver which would allow the State to have access to all of the defendant's medical records prior to trial. People v. Gorman, 123 Misc. 2d 370, 473 N.Y.S.2d 753 (Tompkins Co. Ct. 1984).

§ 4508. Social worker.

(a) Confidential information privileged. A person licensed as a licensed master social worker or a licensed clinical social worker under the provisions of article one hundred fifty-four of the education law shall not be required to disclose a communication made by a client, or his or her advice given thereon, in the course of his or her professional employment, nor shall any clerk, stenographer or other person working for the same employer as such social worker or for such social worker be allowed to disclose any such communication or advice given thereon; except

1. that such social worker may disclose such information as the client may authorize;

2. that such social worker shall not be required to treat as confidential a communication by a client which reveals the contemplation of a crime or harmful act;

3. where the client is a child under the age of sixteen and the information acquired by such social worker indicates that the client has been the victim or subject of a crime, the social worker may be required to testify fully in relation thereto upon any examination, trial or other proceeding in which the commission of such crime is a subject of inquiry;

4. where the client waives the privilege by bringing charges against such social worker and such charges involve confidential communications between the client and the social worker.

(b) Limitations on waiver. A client who, for the purpose of obtaining insurance benefits, authorizes the disclosure of any such privileged communication to any person shall not be deemed to have waived the privilege created by this section. For purposes of this subdivision:

1. "person" shall mean any individual, insurer or agent thereof, peer review committee, public or private corporation, political subdivision, government agency, department or bureau of the state, municipality, industry, co-partnership, association, firm, trust, estate or any other legal entity whatsoever; and

2. "insurance benefits" shall include payments under a self-insured plan.

Amended by L. 1985, Ch. 96, eff. July 20, 1985; L. 2004, Ch. 230, § 1, eff. July 27, 2004, amending subd. a.

ANNOTATIONS

Subd. 2

Admissibility; non-certified social worker.—Non-certified social worker's notes of counseling sessions are not privileged and should have been discoverable to petitioner in family court action. In re Shane MM., 280 A.D.2d 699, 720 N.Y.S.2d 219 (3d Dept. 2001).

—Statements to a non-certified social worker are not inadmissible, pursuant to CPLR 4508, and where there was no evidence that defendant was a client of the social worker, the mere fact that the interview took place in a hospital did not give rise to a physician-patient privilege; defendant was under no misapprehension as to confidentiality where he was specifically informed that no confidentiality would attach to statements concerning a capital offense. People v. Lipsky, 102 Misc. 2d 19, 423 N.Y.S.2d 599 (Monroe Co. 1979).

—CPLR 4508(2) does not prohibit the introduction of evidence that might show that the defendant was perpetrating a fraud upon the Department of Social Services. People v. O'Gorman,

Jr., 91 Misc. 2d 539, 398 N.Y.S.2d 336 (Sup. Ct. Suffolk Co. 1977).

Health and welfare of infant.—The statements made or information given by the father to the social worker bearing adversely upon the health, safety and welfare of the infant were not privileged within the contemplation of the statute and were subject to compulsory disclosure. Perry v. Fiumano, 61 A.D.2d 512, 403 N.Y.S.2d 382 (4th Dept. 1978).

Scope.—In prosecution involving sex crime of a child under the age of 16, testimony by social worker concerning communications by victim to him did not serve to breach confidentiality of records of such communications as provided for by statute. People v. Tissois, 131 A.D.2d 612, 516 N.Y.S.2d 314 (2d Dept. 1987).

—Legal duty to maintain confidentiality of privileged communications between social workers and clients with regard to information obtained in the course of rendering professional services extends to employees of health maintenance organizations, including clerical employees. Doe v. Community Health Plan, 268 A.D.2d 183, 709 N.Y.S.2d 215 (3d Dept. 2000).

Subd. 3

Grand jury.—It was proper for the pediatric social worker to testify to the grand jury that she received a report of suspected child abuse from a doctor and thereafter contacted the father and mother and set up an interview to discuss the case and that during the subsequent interview the father admitted to her that he had "hit" or "harmed" his three-month-old son. People v. Easter, 90 Misc. 2d 713, 395 N.Y.S.2d 926 (Albany Co. Ct. 1977).

§ 4509. Library circulation records.

Records related to the circulation of library materials which contain names or other personally identifying details regarding the users of public, free association, school, college and university libraries and library systems of this state shall be confidential and shall not be disclosed except that such records may be disclosed to the extent necessary for the proper operation of such library and shall be disclosed upon request or consent of the user or pursuant to subpoena, court order or where otherwise required by statute.

ANNOTATION

Library records; generally.—CPLR § 4509 does not grant an absolute privilege prohibiting the disclosure of library records but, rather, limits disclosure pursuant to court order. Petitioner's request to obtain library records in order to ascertain the identity of employees who had allegedly misused its computer system and misappropriated its property in order to initiate civil proceedings only, is not a proper basis for release of the library system's records. Matter of Quad/ Graphics, Inc., v. Southern Adirondack Lib. Sys., 174 Misc. 2d 291, 294, 664 N.Y.S.2d 225 (Sup. Ct. Saratoga Co. 1997).

§ 4510. Rape crisis counselor.

(a) Definitions. When used in this section, the following terms shall have the following meanings:

1. "Rape crisis program" means any office, institution or center which has been approved pursuant to subdivision fifteen of section two hundred six of the public health law, offering counseling and assistance to clients concerning sexual offenses, sexual abuses or incest.

2. "Rape crisis counselor" means any person who has been certified by an approved rape crisis program as having satisfied the training standards specified in subdivision fifteen of section two hundred six of the public health law, and who, regardless of compensation, is acting under the direction and supervision of an approved rape crisis program.

3. "Client" means any person who is seeking or receiving the services of a rape crisis counselor for the purpose of securing counseling or assistance concerning any sexual offenses, sexual abuse, incest or attempts to commit sexual offenses, sexual abuse, or incest, as defined in the penal law.

(b) Confidential information privileged. A rape crisis counselor shall not be required to disclose a communication made by his or her client to him or her, or advice given thereon, in the course of his or her services nor shall any clerk, stenographer or other person working for the same program as the rape crisis counselor or for the rape crisis counselor be allowed to disclose any such communication or advice given thereon nor shall any records made in the course of the services given to the client or recording of any communications made by or to a client be required to be disclosed, nor shall the client be compelled to disclose such communication or records, except:

1. that a rape crisis counselor may disclose such otherwise confidential communication to the extent authorized by the client;

2. that a rape crisis counselor shall not be required to treat as confidential a communication by a client which reveals the intent to commit a crime or harmful act;

3. in a case in which the client waives the privilege by instituting charges against the rape crisis counselor or the rape crisis program and such action or proceeding involves confidential communications between the client and the rape crisis counselor.

(c) Who may waive the privilege. The privilege may only be waived by the client, the personal representative of a deceased client, or, in the case of a client who has been adjudicated incompetent or for whom a conservator has been appointed, the committee or conservator.

(d) Limitation on waiver. A client who, for the purposes of obtaining compensation under article twenty-two of the executive law or insurance benefits, authorizes the disclosure of any privileged communication to an employee of the crime victims board or an insurance representative shall not be deemed to have waived the privilege created by this section.

Added by L. 1993, Ch. 432, eff. Jan. 22, 1994.

§ 4511. Judicial notice of law.

(a) When judicial notice shall be taken without request. Every court shall take judicial notice without request of the common law, constitutions and public statutes of the United States

MISC. LAWS

and of every state, territory and jurisdiction of the United States and of the official compilation of codes, rules and regulations of the state except those that relate solely to the organization or internal management of an agency of the state and of all local laws and county acts.

(b) When judicial notice may be taken without request: when it shall be taken on request. Every court may take judicial notice without request of private acts and resolutions of the congress of the United States and of the legislature of the state; ordinances and regulations of officers, agencies or governmental subdivisions of the state or of the United States; and the laws of foreign countries or their political subdivisions. Judicial notice shall be taken of matters specified in this subdivision if a party requests it, furnishes the court sufficient information to enable it to comply with the request, and has given each adverse party notice of his intention to request it. Notice shall be given in the pleadings or prior to the presentation of any evidence at the trial, but a court may require or permit other notice.

(c) Determination by court; review as matter of law. Whether a matter is judicially noticed or proof is taken, every matter specified in this section shall be determined by the judge or referee, and included in his findings or charged to the jury. Such findings or charge shall be subject to review on appeal as a finding or charge on a matter of law.

(d) Evidence to be received on matter to be judicially noticed. In considering whether a matter of law should be judicially noticed and in determining the matter of law to be judicially noticed, the court may consider any testimony, document, information or argument on the subject, whether offered by a party or discovered through its own research. Whether or not judicial notice is taken, a printed copy of a statute or other written law or a proclamation, edict, decree or ordinance by an executive contained in a book or publication, purporting to have been published by a government or commonly admitted as evidence of the existing law in the judicial tribunals of the jurisdiction where it is in force, is prima facie evidence of such law and the unwritten or common law of a jurisdiction may be proved by witnesses or printed reports of cases of the courts of the jurisdiction.

ANNOTATIONS

Administrative hearing; official notice of agency regulations.—In an administrative hearing, the hearing officer may take official notice of State agency regulations that appear in the Official Compilation of Codes, Rules, and Regulations. Gae Farms, Inc. v. Diamond, 40 A.D.2d 785, 337 N.Y.S.2d 865 (3d Dept. 1972).

Advanced notice; when required.—"[C]ourt has discretion to apply the law of a foreign country notwithstanding the absence of advanced notice or request to do so (citations omitted)." Burns v. Young, 239 A.D.2d 727, 728, 657 N.Y.S.2d 502 (3d Dept. 1997).

Hearing officer; official notice of agency rules permitted.—A hearing officer may take official notice of duly promulgated regulations of agencies of this state; and the court may take judicial notice of the official compilation of Codes, Rules, and Regulations of the state. Wilco Properties Corp. v. Department of Envtl. Conservation, 39 A.D.2d 6, 330 N.Y.S.2d 819 (3d Dept. 1972).

Improper admission.—Harmless error for trial court to have taken judicial notice of affidavit and admit it into evidence on the basis of that notice; judicial notice is appropriate only where facts rest upon knowledge or sources that are so widely accepted and unimpeachable that it does not need an evidentiary basis for admission. Ptasnik v. Schultz, 247 A.D.2d 197, 679 N.Y.S.2d 665 (2d Dept. 1998).

Judicial notice.—In a summary judgment motion converting a foreign judgment to a judgment for execution against a corporate defendant for assets located in New York, court had the discretion to take judicial notice of the laws of Mexico, which are based on a code system, not common law, the construction of which was appropriate for the resolution pursuant to summary judgment. Harris SA De C.V. v. Grupo Sistemas Integrales De Communicacion SA De C.V., 279 A.D.2d 263, 719 N.Y.S.2d 25 (1st Dept.), *appeal denied,* 96 N.Y.2d 709 (2001).

—"It is axiomatic that this court may take judicial notice of its own orders in related actions." Bergstol v. Town of Monroe, 305 A.D.2d 348, 759 N.Y.S.2d 88 (2d Dept. 2003).

—Family court has power to take judicial notice of its own prior proceedings. In re Terrane L., 276 A.D.2d 699, 715 N.Y.S.2d 357 (2d Dept. 2000), *cert. denied,* 533 U.S. 918 (2001).

—Although dicta in past cases has suggested the vicious nature of certain animals, "there is no persuasive authority for the proposition that a court should take judicial notice of the ferocity of any particular type or breed of domestic animal." Roupp v. Conrad, 287 A.D.2d 937; 731 N.Y.S.2d 545 (3d Dept. 2001).

—Court has power to take judicial notice of its own prior proceedings, here a prior PINS adjudication involving oldest child. In re A.R., 309 A.D.2d 1153, 764 N.Y.S.2d 746 (4th Dept. 2003)

—Court may take judicial notice of the common law, Constitution, and statutes of the United States, as well as individual states sua sponte; however, it may not, without request, take judicial notice that an action is time barred by the statute of limitations. Mendez v. Steen Trucking, 254 A.D.2d 715, 680 N.Y.S.2d 134 (4th Dept. 1998).

—Court may take judicial notice of the detrimental effect of environmental tobacco smoke has on health of child. Johnita M.D. v. David D.D., 191 Misc. 2d 301, 740 N.Y.S.2d 811 (Sup. Ct. Oneida Co. 2002).

—Where the general acceptance of a scientific theory is "apparent, open and notorious," courts may take judicial notice of the theory; in the alternative, acceptance of the theory may be established by legal writings and opinions. Zafran v. Zafran, 191 Misc. 2d 60, 740 N.Y.S.2d 596 (Sup. Ct. Nassau Co. 2002).

Court may take judicial notice of prior judicial decisions. In re Thomas, 189 Misc. 2d 487, 733 N.Y.S.2d 591 (Sup. Ct. Crim. T. Kings Co. 2001).

—A trial court may properly take judicial notice of the Official Compilation of Codes, Rules, and Regulations of the State of New York and the absence therein of a Department of Transportation regulation establishing a higher speed limit for a particular road in a particular town; and the court may do so without a request by the People. People v. Leatherbarrow, 69 Misc. 2d 563, 330 N.Y.S.2d 676 (Erie Co. Ct. 1972).

§ 4512. Competency of interested witness or spouse.

Except as otherwise expressly prescribed, a person shall not be excluded or excused from being a witness, by reason of his interest in the event or because he is a party or the spouse of a party.

ANNOTATION

Privilege arising from marital relationship waived by failure to object.—In a criminal action on complaint of defendant's wife, defendant-husband's objection to wife being permitted to testify was denied, as the privilege was waived for his failure to object when she testified earlier. People v. Santiago, 68 Misc. 2d 85 326 N.Y.S.2d 332 (Crim. Ct. N.Y. Co. 1971).

§ 4513. Competency of person convicted of crime.

A person who has been convicted of a crime is a competent witness; but the conviction may be proved, for the purpose of affecting the weight of his testimony, either by cross-examination, upon which he shall be required to answer any relevant question, or by the record. The party cross-examining is not concluded by such person's answer.

§ 4514. Impeachment of witness by prior inconsistent statement.

In addition to impeachment in the manner permitted by common law, any party may introduce proof that any witness has made a prior statement inconsistent with his testimony if the statement was made in a writing subscribed by him or was made under oath.

ANNOTATIONS

Trial minutes; availability to defense counsel.—Where minutes of prior trial were in court room, were requested by defense counsel as aid to cross examination, and refused by District Attorney and Trial Judge declined to direct that they be made available, there was no error since there was no showing of defendant's indigency or inability to obtain copy. However, ordinary professional courtesy suggests that minutes be made available in such a case. People v. Zanotti, 30 N.Y.2d 926, 335 N.Y.S.2d 682, 287 N.E.2d 376 (1972).

Use of statement.—Prosecution properly impeached defendant on cross-examination, eliciting fact that defendant testified differently and inconsistently at his "previous trial" and a motive for doing so. People v. Richardson, 9 A.D.3d 783, 781 N.Y.S.2d 381 (3d Dept. 2004).

—CPLR 4514 does not limit use of prior statement of minor child to impeachment purposes only. STA of Freedonia v. State Liquor Auth., 267 A.D.2d 1037, 700 N.Y.S.2d 782 (4th Dept. 1999).

§ 4515. Form of expert opinion.

Unless the court orders otherwise, questions calling for the opinion of an expert witness need not be hypothetical in form, and the witness may state his opinion and reasons without first specifying the data upon which it is based. Upon cross-examination, he may be required to specify the data and other criteria supporting the opinion.

ANNOTATIONS

Admissibility; generally.—Expert testimony is admissible if the analysis involved is beyond the ken of the typical juror and the results would be relevant to an issue in the case. People v. Allweiss, 48 N.Y.2d 40, 421 N.Y.S.2d 341, 396 N.E.2d 735 (1979).

Discretion.—The trial judge is accorded broad discretion in the admission of expert testimony; it is for the trial judge to determine when jurors are able to draw conclusions from the evidence based on their day-to-day experience, their common observation and their knowledge, and when they would benefit from the specialized knowledge of an expert witness. People v. Cronin, 60 N.Y.2d 430, 470 N.Y.S.2d 110, 458 N.E.2d 351 (1983).

Firearm expert.—An officer qualified as an expert witness in firearms can testify to his opinion without specifying the data upon which the opinion is based. People v. Simmons, 55 A.D.2d 879, 390 N.Y.S.2d 423 (1st Dept. 1977), aff'd, 43 N.Y.2d 806, 402 N.Y.S.2d 391, 373 N.E.2d 285.

—The fact that the People did not prove conclusively that there was no change in the condition of the gun from the time it was fired did not render the expert's testimony inadmissible. People v. Coleman, 55 A.D.2d 981, 390 N.Y.S.2d 680 (3d Dept. 1977).

Form.—Expert opinions need not be asserted with certainty, so long as the witness demonstrates a degree of confidence in his conclusions sufficient to satisfy accepted standards of reliability. People v. Brown, 67 N.Y.2d 555, 505 N.Y.S.2d 574, 496 N.E.2d 663 (1986).

—Expert opinions which are speculative or merely possible lack probative force and are inadmissible; the proposed expert opinion should reflect an acceptable degree of certainty. People v. Miller, 116 A.D.2d 595 (2d Dept. 1986).

Foundation.—Authorized use of facts from outside the evidentiary record does not alter the basic principle that an expert's opinion not based on facts is worthless. People v. Jones, 73 N.Y.2d 427, 541 N.Y.S.2d 340, 539 N.E.2d 96 (1989).

—It is incumbent upon the proponent of expert testimony to lay a proper foundation establishing that the processes and methods employed by the expert in formulating his or her opinions adhere to accepted standards of reliability within the field. People v. Wilson, 133 A.D.2d 179, 518 N.Y.S.2d 690 (2d Dept. 1987).

Hypotheticals.—It is not proper to pose hypothetical questions to an expert which assume facts not in evidence or not established by reliable evidence or not within the witness' field of expertise. People v. Bellini, 162 A.D.2d 693, 557 N.Y.S.2d 407 (2d Dept. 1990).

—Court did not abuse discretion by allowing People's expert witness to render an opinion in hypothetical form, as the question directly mirrored defendant's account of the incident as told the police. People v. Hood, 279 A.D.2d 699, 719 N.Y.S.2d 327 (3d Dept. 2001).

Medical expert.—It was error to permit the prosecution in its direct case to have a medical expert testify to the effects of heroin on the human body and whether it would alter the user's perception, where the purpose was to have the medical expert bolster the identification testimony of two drug addict identification witnesses. People v. Lebron, 46 A.D.2d 776, 360 N.Y.S.2d 468 (2d Dept. 1974).

—Defendant's medical expert could rely on the People's laboratory reports concerning rape victim, even if they were not admitted into evidence, as the basis of his expert opinion with the People having every right to inquire into the sources of his information on cross-examination. People v. Mack, 86 Misc. 2d 364, 382 N.Y.S.2d 424 (Sup. Ct. Westchester Co. 1976).

Standard; admissibility of scientific instrument.— Although perfection in test results is not a prerequisite to the admissibility of evidence obtainable by the use of scientific instruments, the rule has been to grant judicial recognition only after the instrument has been sufficiently established to have gained general acceptance in its particular field. People v. Aeston, 79 Misc. 2d 1077, 362 N.Y.S.2d 356 (Sup. Ct. Bronx Co. 1974).

Trial Judge; explanation of testimony.—The trial judge did not usurp jury's function when he summarized the testimony of medical expert in simpler terms and informed the jury that he was only reviewing the medical testimony for their benefit and that if they disagreed with the review it was their recollection of the medical testimony that was to control. People v. Russo, 46 A.D.2d 904, 362 N.Y.S.2d 191 (2d Dept. 1974).

Ultimate issues in case.—A fire marshal should not be permitted to testify that a fire was incendiary in nature since it states a conclusion as to the ultimate issues in the case, that is, whether or not a fire was intentionally set. People v. Maxwell, 116 A.D.2d 667 (2d Dept. 1987).

§ 4516. Proof of age of child.

Whenever it becomes necessary to determine the age of a child, he may be produced and exhibited to enable the court or jury to determine his age by a personal inspection.

Evidence.—Victim's testimony regarding her age was corroborated; it was readily apparent from her appearance at trial that she was less than 11 years old. People v. Petrie, 3 A.D.3d 665, 771 N.Y.S.2d 242 (3d Dept. 2004).

§ 4517. Prior testimony in a civil action.

(a) **Impeachment of witnesses; parties; unavailable witness.** In a civil action, at the trial or upon the hearing of a motion or an interlocutory proceeding, all or any part of the testimony of a witness that was taken at a prior trial in the same action or at a prior trial involving the same parties or their representatives and arising from the same subject matter, so far as admissible under the rules of evidence, may be used in accordance with any of the following provisions:

1. any such testimony may be used by any party for the purpose of contradicting or impeaching the testimony of the same witness;

2. the prior trial testimony of a party or of any person who was a party when the testimony was given or of any person who at the time the testimony was given was an officer, director, member, employee, or managing or authorized agent of a party, may be used for any purpose by any party who is adversely interested when the prior testimony is offered in evidence;

3. the prior trial testimony of any person may be used by any party for any purpose against any other party, provided the court finds:

   (i) that the witness is dead; or

   (ii) that the witness is at a greater distance than one hundred miles from the place of trial or is out of the state, unless it appears that the absence of the witness was procured by the party offering the testimony; or

   (iii) that the witness is unable to attend or testify because of age, sickness, infirmity, or imprisonment; or

   (iv) that the party offering the testimony has been unable to procure the attendance of the witness by diligent efforts; or

   (v) upon motion on notice, that such exceptional circumstances exist as to make its use desirable, in the interest of justice and with due regard to the importance of presenting the testimony of witnesses orally in open court;

4. the prior trial testimony of a person authorized to practice medicine may be used by any party without the necessity of showing unavailability or special circumstances subject to the right of any party to move for preclusion upon the ground that admission of the prior testimony would be prejudicial under the circumstances.

(b) **Use of part of the prior trial testimony of a witness.** If only part of the prior trial testimony of a witness is read at the trial by a party, any other party may read any other part of the prior testimony of that witness that ought in fairness to be considered in connection with the part read.

(c) **Substitution of parties; prior actions.** Substitution of parties does not affect the right to use testimony previously taken at trial.

Former section **Repealed** and new section **Added** by L. 2000, Ch. 268, § 1, eff. Jan. 1, 2001, and shall apply to actions in which trial commences on or after such date.

Requirements of § 4517.—Usually deposition testimony of a party is admissible upon a showing that the party is not available to testify; however, where plaintiff's counsel made no showing that incarcerated plaintiff was unavailable, in light of court's offer to assist in his production, and where no efforts were made to produce him, the court properly limited admissibility of deposition testimony. Marte v. Speaker, 273 A.D.2d 37, 708 N.Y.S.2d 398 (1st Dept. 2000).

—The requirements of § 4517 must be satisfied when attempting to admit an entire trial transcript for the truth of the matters contained within it. However, under § 4517, the testimony of the parties and conceivably other witnesses may be admissible upon a proper foundation and absence of sustainable objections. Alva v. Hurley, Fox, Selig, Caprari & Kelleher, 162 Misc. 2d 402, 617 N.Y.S.2d 114 (Sup. Ct. Rockland Co. 1994).

—Prior testimony of an unavailable witness is admissible in a civil proceeding under 4514 although the parties to the actions are different; however, to ensure the credibility of the testimony offered those parties must have had the "same opportunity, motive and interest to cross-examine." Morales v. New York, 183 Misc. 2d 839, 705 N.Y.S.2d 176 (Ct. of Claims 2000).

§ 4518. Business records.

(a) **Generally.** Any writing or record, whether in the form of an entry in a book or otherwise, made as a memorandum or record of any act, transaction, occurrence or event, shall be admissible in evidence in proof of that act, transaction, occurrence or event, if the judge finds that it was made in the regular course of any business and that it was the regular course of such business to make it, at the time of the act, transaction, occurrence or event, or within a reasonable time thereafter. An electronic record, as defined in section one hundred two of the state technology law, used or stored as such a memorandum or record, shall be admissible in a tangible exhibit that is a true and accurate representation of such electronic record. The court may consider the method or manner by which the electronic record was stored, maintained or retrieved in determining whether the exhibit is a true and accurate representation of such electronic record. All other circumstances of the making of the memorandum or record, including lack of personal knowledge by the maker, may be proved to affect its weight, but they shall not affect its admissibility. The term business includes a business, profession, occupation and calling of every kind.

(b) **Hospital bills.** A hospital bill is admissible in evidence under this rule and is prima facie evidence of the facts contained, provided it bears a certification by the head of the hospital or by a responsible employee in the controller's or accounting office that the bill is correct, that each of the items was necessarily supplied and that the amount charged is reasonable. This subdivision shall not apply to any proceeding in a surrogate's court nor in any action instituted by or on behalf of a hospital to recover payment for accommodations or supplies furnished or for services rendered by or in such hospital, except that in a proceeding pursuant to section one hundred eighty-nine of the lien law to determine the validity and extent of the lien of a hospital, such certified hospital bills are prima facie evidence of the fact of services and of the reasonableness of any charges which do not exceed the comparable charges made by the hospital in the care of workmen's compensation patients.

(c) Other records. All records, writings and other things referred to in sections 2306 and 2307 are admissible in evidence under this rule and are prima facie evidence of the facts contained, provided they bear a certification or authentication by the head of the hospital, laboratory, library, department or bureau of a municipal corporation or of the state, or by an employee delegated for that purpose or by a qualified physician. Where a hospital record is in the custody of a warehouse, or "warehouseman" as that term is defined by paragraph (h) of subdivision one of section 7-102 of the uniform commercial code, pursuant to a plan approved in writing by the state commissioner of health, admissibility under this subdivision may be established by a certification made by the manager of the warehouse that sets forth (i) the authority by which the record is held, including but not limited to a court order, order of the commissioner, or order or resolution of the governing board or official of the hospital, and (ii) that the record has been in the exclusive custody of such warehouse or warehousemen since its receipt from the hospital or, if another has had access to it, the name and address of such person and the date on which and the circumstances under which such access was had. Any warehouseman providing a certification as required by this subdivision shall have no liability for acts or omissions relating thereto, except for intentional misconduct, and the warehouseman is authorized to assess and collect a reasonable charge for providing the certification described in this subdivision.

(d) Any records or reports relating to the administration and analysis of a genetic marker or DNA test, including records or reports of the costs of such tests, administered pursuant to sections four hundred eighteen and five hundred thirty-two of the family court act or section one hundred eleven-k of the social services law are admissible in evidence under this rule and are prima facie evidence of the facts contained therein provided they bear a certification or authentication by the head of the hospital, laboratory, department or bureau of a municipal corporation or the state or by an employee delegated for that purpose, or by a qualified physician. If such

record or report relating to the administration and analysis of a genetic marker test or DNA test or tests administered pursuant to sections four hundred eighteen and five hundred thirty-two of the family court act or section one hundred eleven-k of the social services law indicates at least a ninety-five percent probability of paternity, the admission of such record or report shall create a rebuttable presumption of paternity, and shall, if unrebutted, establish the paternity of and liability for the support of a child pursuant to articles four and five of the family court act.

(e) Notwithstanding any other provision of law, a record or report relating to the administration and analysis of a genetic marker test or DNA test certified in accordance with subdivision (d) of this rule and administered pursuant to sections four hundred eighteen and five hundred thirty-two of the family court act or section one hundred eleven-k of the social services law is admissible in evidence under this rule without the need for foundation testimony or further proof of authenticity or accuracy unless objections to the record or report are made in writing no later than twenty days before a hearing at which the record or report may be introduced into evidence or thirty days after receipt of the test results, whichever is earlier.

(f) Notwithstanding any other provision of law, records or reports of support payments and disbursements maintained pursuant to title six-A of article three of the social services law by the Department of Social Services or the fiscal agent under contract to the Department for the provision of centralized collection and disbursement functions are admissible in evidence under this rule, provided that they bear a certification by an official of a social services district attesting to the accuracy of the content of the record or report of support payments and that in attesting to the accuracy of the record or report such official has received confirmation from the Department of Social Services or the fiscal agent under contract to the Department for the provision of centralized collection and disbursement functions pursuant to section one hundred eleven-h of the social services law that the record or report of support payments reflects the processing of all support payments in the possession of the Department or the fiscal agent as of a specified date, and that the document is a record or report of support payments maintained pursuant to title six-A of article three of the social services law. If so certified, such record or report shall be admitted into evidence under this rule without the need for additional foundation testimony. Such records shall be the basis for a permissive inference of the facts contained therein unless the trier of fact finds good cause not to draw such inference.

(g) Pregnancy and childbirth costs. Any hospital bills or records relating to the costs of pregnancy or birth of a child for whom proceedings to establish paternity, pursuant to sections four hundred eighteen and five hundred thirty-two of the family court act or section one hundred eleven-k of the social services law have been or are being undertaken, are admissible in evidence under this rule and are prima facie evidence of the facts contained therein, provided they bear a certification or authentication by the head of the hospital, laboratory, department or bureau of a municipal corporation or the state or by an employee designated for that purpose, or by a qualified physician.

Amended by L. 1983, Ch. 311; L. 1984, Ch. 792, eff. Aug. 5, 1984 amending subd. c; L. 1992, Ch. 381, eff. July 17, 1992, amending subd. c; L. 1994, Ch. 170, eff. June 15, 1994; L. 1995, Ch. 81, § 236, adding subd. f, eff. July 1, 1995; L. 1997, Ch. 398, §§ 87–89, amending subds. d and e and adding subd. g, eff. Nov. 11, 1997; L. 2002, Ch. 136, § 1, eff. July 23, 2002, amending subd. a.

ANNOTATIONS

Admissibility; generally.—For a document to be within the business record exception, not only must there be a business duty to record the event, but the person providing the information must be under a contemporaneous business duty to report the occurrence to the one making the entry; each participant in the chain producing the record must be acting within the course of regular business conduct or the declaration recorded must meet the test of some other hearsay exception. *In re* Leon RR, 48 N.Y.2d 117, 421 N.Y.S.2d 863, 397 N.Y.S.2d 374 (1979).

—Laboratory report that tested drugs found in defendant's possession was properly admitted into evidence after a complete foundation was established; defendant's right to cross-examine witness was not affected by admission. People v. Atkins, 273 A.D.2d 11, 709 N.Y.S.2d 39 (1st Dept. 2000).

—Police Department property vouchers describing vehicles seized were properly introduced as business records without the author being called as a witness at trial. These business records contained " 'objective factual material compiled under circumstances indicating it to be inherently reliable' (People ex rel. McGee v. Walters, 62 N.Y.2d 317, 322)." People v. Badia, 232 A.D.2d 241, 242, 649 N.Y.S.2d 2 (1st Dept. 1996).

—The entire file of the child protective agency was properly admissible as a business record, as it contained entries of case workers who were under a business duty to timely record all matters relating to the welfare of the subject children. *In re* R. Children, 264 A.D.2d 423, 694 N.Y.S.2d 126 (2d Dept. 1999).

—"Computer printouts are admissible as business records if the data was stored in the normal course of business. . . ." *In re* Thomma, 232 A.D.2d 422, 422, 648 N.Y.S.2d 453 (2d Dept. 1996).

—In order to admit a photocopy of a business record into evidence, the witness with personal knowledge of record-keeping procedures must testify that the document sought to be admitted was made in the regular course of business, pursuant to regular procedures of the business, at or near the time the information was obtained or the act occurred. People v. Rosa, 156 A.D.2d 733, 549 N.Y.S.2d 487 (2d Dept. 1989).

—Support Collection Unit records documenting respondent's child support arrears must be certified as required by CPLR 4518(f) in order to be properly admitted in family court proceeding. France v. Buck, 299 A.D.2d 716, 749 N.Y.S.2d 746 (3d Dept. 2002).

—Neither caseworker's testimony about nor her written summary of social services hotline reports alerting the state to allegations of abuse and neglect against the petitioner were admissible as business records exception to the hearsay rule. *In re* "Nicole VV," 296 A.D.2d 608, 746 N.Y.S.2d 53 (3d Dept. 2002).

—Admission of county Red Cross file pursuant to business records exception was error since the file contained statements from persons who were under no business duty to report the information to the Red Cross. Shane MM. v. Family and Children Servs., 280 A.D.2d 699, 720 N.Y.S.2d 219 (3d Dept. 2001).

—Letter, which was not produced as a result of day-to-day operations of defendant's business but instead generated as a result of a specific inquiry connected with this litigation, did not qualify for admission under the business record exception. Puznowski v. Spirax Sarco, Inc., 275 A.D.2d 506, 712 N.Y.S.2d 216 (3d Dept. 2000).

—Record of telephone call was improperly admitted into evidence where there was no foundation testimony indicating bookkeeping record procedures that would enable witness to testify that the record was made and kept in the regular course of business, that it was the regular course of business to make the record, and that it was made contemporaneously with the call. People v. Surdis, 275 A.D.2d 553, 711 N.Y.S.2d 875 (3d Dept.), *appeal denied*, 95 N.Y.2d 908 (2000).

—Statements, not germane to doctor's treatment or diagnosis, contained in victim's hospital records, whose source was unknown, were properly excluded from evidence under the business exception. People v. Townsley, 240 A.D.2d 955, 659 N.Y.S.2d 906 (3d Dept. 1997).

—Unusual incident log book of Clinton Correctional Facility was properly excluded from evidence since petitioner failed to show how the instant incident was similar to prior incidents contained in the log. The business record exception to hearsay rule does not over come any other exclusionary rule which might be invoked, petitioner failed to show relevancy or materiality of log. Bostic v. New York, 232 A.D.2d 837, 649 N.Y.S.2d 200 (3d Dept. 1996).

—Drawings were properly excluded from evidence because defendants failed to establish sufficient foundation for their admission as business records. Hess v. Murnane Bldg. Contractors, Inc., 306 A.D.2d 824, 762 N.Y.S.2d 212 (4th Dept. 2003).

—Although police report prepared by investigator may have qualified as a business record, court properly excluded report since a proper foundation for its admission was not established. People v. Pitts, 231 A.D.2d 901, 648 N.Y.S.2d 406 (4th Dept. 1996).

—New York Electronic Signatures and Records Act, N.Y. Tech. Law § 101–109, "in conjunction with CPLR 4518, permits the court to consider a second printout as proof of the original computer record due to the manner in which the document was stored and retrieved." People v. McFarlan, 191 Misc. 2d 531, 744 N.Y.S.2d 287 (Sup. Ct. N.Y. Co. 2001).

Breathalyzer test results.—The admission of certificates to authenticate the reliability of the breathalyzer equipment used, which were offered as a foundation for the introduction of the results of the breathalyzer tests, did not satisfy the business entry exception to the rule against hearsay, since they were not records made in the regular course of the business of the public agency or the private corporation submitting them. People v. Gower, 42 N.Y.2d 117, 397 N.Y.S.2d 368, 366 N.E.2d 69 (1977).

—Before results of a breath test may be admitted in evidence, People are required to lay a proper foundation under "to establish that the particular instrument used to test a defendant's [blood alcohol content]. . .had been tested within a reasonable period in relation to defendant's test and found to be properly calibrated and in working order." People v. Alves, 1 A.D.3d 938, 767 N.Y.S.2d 754 (4th Dept. 2003).

—Certified record of analysis of breathalyzer ampoules were admissible in evidence pursuant to CPLR 4518(a); defendant's attack on accuracy of information contained in record goes to weight rather than admissibility of record. People v. Dailey, 260 A.D.81, 700 N.Y.S.2d 307 (4th Dept. 1999).

Business records.—The trial court correctly admitted as business records certificates that showed analysis of a breathalyzer ampule as they were prepared in the ordinary course of police laboratory business and listed the date of analysis, the individual who conducted the test, material analyzed, and the results. People v. Farrell, 58 N.Y.2d 637, 458 N.Y.S.2d 514, 444 N.E.2d 978 (1982).

—Hearsay statements of defendant's field supervisor were properly admitted as admissions by defendant on issue of its knowledge of existence and extent of danger presented by parapet wall, some of these admissions, which were to effect that wall was in danger of collapsing, were independently recollected by witness, while others were contained in notes made by witness that were properly admitted as business records. Browne v. Prime Contr. Design Corp., 308 A.D.2d 372, 764 N.Y.S.2d 269 (1st Dept. 2003).

—Plaintiff's personnel file was properly admitted into evidence after foundation testimony established that personnel records of company were kept in regular course of business by an officer of company, now deceased, and it was his duty to make a contemporaneous record of complaints or inquiries concerning employees. Kupferle v. Deidra Trans, Inc., 300 A.D.2d 192, 750 N.Y.S.2d 867 (1st Dept. 2002).

—In establishing a proper foundation for admission of various bank records and checks, authenticating witness need not be custodian of records. People v. Crispino, 298 A.D.2d 220, 748 N.Y.S.2d 718 (1st Dept. 2002).

—Objection to improper foundation for evidence submitted under business record exception to hearsay rule must be made to preserve the issue for appellate review. People v. Caldwell, 254 A.D.2d 64, 678 N.Y.S.2d 490 (1st Dept. 1998).

—Court committed error by admitting redacted engineering report into evidence and two other engineering reports read by plaintiff's counsel which were not in admitted, which related to studies conducted by independent engineering firms in connection with a project to rehabilitate bridge, were hearsay, introduced to prove the truth of their contents, plaintiff failed to lay an adequate foundation for their admission as business records. Kane v. Triborough Bridge & Tunnel Auth., 8 A.D.3d 239, 778 N.Y.S.2d 52 (2d Dept. 2004).

—Court improperly allowed plaintiff to submit "LIRR Engineer Department's Bridge Reference Manual" abstract as proof that defendant owned 'site of' 'accident, this evidence was not in admissible form as a business record. Peppas v. City of New York, 6 A.D.3d 596 774 N.Y.S.2d 798 (2d Dept. 2004).

—In medical malpractice action, trial court properly admitted testimony of two drug company representatives that, after searching their own records and causing other persons with business duty to accurately report to them to search their records, they could find no record of defendant receiving samples of two prescription medications, drug companies were not parties to action and were disinterested as to its outcome. Chiu-Caranese v. DeMeo, 2 A.D.3d 766, 769 N.Y.S.2d 729 (2d Dept. 2003).

—Unavailability of declarant is not a prerequisite to the admission of business records. People v. Driscoll, 251 A.D.2d 759, 675 N.Y.S.2d 151 (3d Dept. 1998), *appeal denied,* 92 N.Y.2d 896 (1998).

Chain of custody.—Records establishing the chain of custody for vials of cocaine used to convict defendant were admissible under CPLR 4518(c). Under this section, records that have been produced voluntarily rather than by subpoena may be properly certified and authenticated. People v. Montgomery, 195 A.D.2d 886, 600 N.Y.S.2d 814 (3d Dept. 1993).

Defendant's use of laboratory reports.—Defendant would be permitted to introduce the medical reports he had obtained from the People which had been prepared by the doctor hired by the County to examine the rape victim without laying a foundation, since they were properly authenticated records of a municipal department (CPLR 4518(c); 2307(a)). People v. Mack, 86 Misc. 2d 364, 382 N.Y.S.2d 424 (Sup. Ct. Westchester Co. 1976).

DMV records.—Department of Motor Vehicle records, including a computer-generated printout of defendant's driving record; a "license summary and display," also known as a "driving abstract"; and an "all ticket display" and "expanded ticket display" were properly admitted into evidence after foundation elements required by CPLR 4518 were established. People v. Wray, 183 Misc. 2d 444, 704 N.Y.S.2d 787 (Sup. Ct. Kings Co. 2000).

—DMV records are an exception to the well settled rule that "the mere filing of papers received from other entities, even if they are retained in the regular course of business, is insufficient to qualify the documents as business records." People v. Etienne, 192 Misc. 2d 90, 745 N.Y.S.2d 867 (1st Dist. Nassau Co. 2002).

Genetic marker or DNA tests.—"Where a blood genetic marker test indicates at least a 95% probability of paternity, the admission of the test result creates a rebuttable presumption that the tested individual is the father of the child." Commissioner of Social Servs. of City of N.Y. v. Corey A., 239 A.D.2d 286, 287, 658 N.Y.S.2d 20 (1st Dept. 1997).

—Portion of DNA report that was based on testing supervised by an expert in forensic biology employed by Medical Examiner's Office of the City of New York was properly admitted

under business records exception to hearsay rule. People v. Bones, 17 A.D.3d 689, 793 N.Y.S.2d 545 (2d Dept. 2005).

—Admission of blood genetic marker test results revealing at least a 95% probability of paternity, creates a rebuttable presumption of paternity. Niagara County Dept. of Social Servs. (Bridgette C.O.) v. Wendell R., 233 A.D.2d 949, 649 N.Y.S.2d 263 (4th Dept. 1996).

—Where DNA test is not court-ordered, the director's certification is not valid for automatic admissibility of the test results under CPLR 4518(d) and (e), even though the laboratory was one of a limited number approved for DNA testing. Admissibility must be determined from an analysis of methods used to acquire and analyze samples. Barbara Ann W. v. Wy., 183 Misc. 2d 228, 701 N.Y.S.2d 845 (Fam. Ct. Suffolk Co. 1999).

Hospital records.—Redacted hospital records of complainant properly admitted in trial for assault in first degree, defendant interposed justification defense, no error for court to redact records to strike doctor's notations that complainant was too drunk to grant consent for surgery where other evidence of complainant's intoxication, including toxicology report, available to defense. People v. Andrew, 1 N.Y.3d 546, 772 N.Y.S.2d 235, 804 N.E.2d 399 (2003).

—Statements made by mother and reflected in hospital record that infant/plaintiff was struck by a thrown rock were inadmissible as part of hospital records where mother had no first-hand knowledge of incident, statements were based on information told to mother by third parties, and statements were not germane to plaintiff's treatment or diagnosis. Rivera v. City of New York, 293 A.D.2d 383, 741 N.Y.S.2d 30 (1st Dept. 2002).

—Hospital records reflecting incidents and admissions of insured's past substance abuse and tobacco use were admissible as relevant to diagnosis and treatment in suit by insurance company alleging misrepresentations by insured about substance abuse and tobacco use. Mullen v. Independence Sav. Bank, 267 A.D.2d 169, 700 N.Y.S.2d 447 (1st Dept. 1999).

—Statement in hospital records that complainant "turned while man tried to stab him in the back," was properly admitted pursuant to business records exception to hearsay rule because it was relevant to diagnosis and treatment of complainant's injuries. People v. Dagoberto, 16 A.D.3d 595, 792 N.Y.S.2d 143 (2d Dept. 2005).

—Uncertified hospital records and unsworn medical reports admitted into evidence over defendant's objection to establish plaintiff's damages was not harmless error. Abbas v. Cole, 7 A.D.3d 649, 776 N.Y.S.2d 846 (2d Dept. 2004).

—"Hospital records are admissible as business records to the extent that entries therein are germane to the diagnosis and treatment of the patient's ailments." Rodriguez v. Piccone, 5 A.D.3d 757, 774 N.Y.S.2d 185 (2d Dept. 2004).

—Office records of treating physicians, including medical opinions contained in those records, are admissible as evidence at trial to the extent they are germane to diagnosis and treatment, as long as a proper foundation is established. Bruce-Bishop v. Jafar, 302 A.D.2d 345, 753 N.Y.S.2d 890 (2d Dept. 2003).

—Complainant's statement to treating physician contained in hospital record that she had been "kicked, slapped, pulled by her hair and had a knife to her neck" was properly admitted pursuant to business records exception to the hearsay rule as relevant to diagnosis and treatment of complainant's injuries. People v. Baltimore, 301 A.D.2d 610, 754 N.Y.S.2d 650 (2d Dept. 2003).

—Statements concerning the details of the assault made by victim to nurse who completed the police information questionnaire contained in the New York State Sexual Assault Evidence Collection Kit should not have been admitted as a business record; admission of statements was harmless error. People v. Thomas, 288 A.D.2d 405, 733 N.Y.S.2d 231 (2d Dept. 2001).

—Blood alcohol test result, as contained in a certified medical record, was prima facie evidence of blood alcohol level pursuant to this section. Rodriguez v. Triborough Bridge & Tunnel Auth., 276 A.D.2d 769, 716 N.Y.S.2d 24 (2d Dept. 2000).

—Victim's hospital records and sexual assault information sheet, properly admitted into evidence, statements made by, victim to medical personnel although hearsay, are admissible under, business records exception as long as they are germane to,patient's subsequent medical treatment and diagnosis, and information sheet had,dual purpose of investigation and treatment of,victim's potential physical and psychological injuries, both germane to treatment. People v. Rogers, 8 A.D.3d 888, 780 N.Y.S.2d 393 (3d Dept. 2004).

—Hospital records with the appropriate certification of authenticity are admissible and are prima facie evidence of the facts contained therein. People v. Howard, 79 A.D.2d 1064, 435 N.Y.S.2d 399 (3d Dept. 1981).

—Medical record, an operative report of a surgeon who performed subsequent surgery on plaintiff, which constituted out-of-court material "of a kind accepted in the profession as reliable in forming a professional opinion," was properly admitted into evidence, court erred by preventing plaintiff's expert to testify about. basis for. opinion, which arose from information in report. Shahram v. Horwitz, 5 A.D.3d 1034 773 N.Y.S.2d 642 (4th Dept. 2004).

Litigation.—If the document is produced in preparation for litigation, it does not qualify as a business record and is not admissible; however, where it is in the regular course of business of a governmental agency to maintain records for business reasons, the fact that such a record may be subsequently used in litigation, which was not the sole purpose when the record was made, does not prohibit its use at trial. People v. D'Agostino, 120 Misc. 2d 437, 465 N.Y.S.2d 834 (Monroe Co. Ct. 1983).

Police laboratory report.—Photocopies of forensic laboratory log book and laboratory submission receipts were properly admitted into evidence after foundation had been established. People v. Gentle, 245 A.D.2d 463, 666 N.Y.S.2d 455 (2d Dept. 1997), *appeal denied,* 91 N.Y.2d 973 (1998).

—Ballistics report of the Police Department is admissible under the business records exception to the hearsay rule and the person who prepared the report need not testify. *In re* Ronald B., 61 A.D.2d 204, 401 N.Y.S.2d 544 (2d Dept. 1978).

—In Family Court delinquency proceeding, the Police Laboratory chemist's certified report is admissible without his testimony under the general "business record" exception to the rule against hearsay [CPLR 4518(a)], as well as the exception for a record certified by an employee of a department or bureau of a municipal corporation [CPLR 4518(c) and 2307(a)], and the exception for a certificate of a public officer [CPLR 4520]. *In re* Kevin G., 80 Misc. 2d 517, 363 N.Y.S.2d 999 (Fam. Ct. N.Y. Co. 1975).

Police reports.—As a general rule, police reports and 911 reports do not fall within the business records exception on the ground that the person who made the statements in the report was not under a duty to impart that information. People v. Torres, 165 A.D.2d 801, 564 N.Y.S.2d 61 (1st Dept. 1990).

—The tape recording of the contents of an anonymous 911 call did not qualify as a business record. People v. Smith, 162 A.D.2d 736, 557 N.Y.S.2d 424 (2d Dept. 1990).

—Court improperly allowed plaintiff/decedent to submit the safety check report prepared by police eight days after fatal motorcycle crash, report was not admissible and plaintiff failed to offer an acceptable excuse for her failure to obtain requisite certification or authentication to render report admissible. Green v. Mazurski, 2 A.D.3d 1370, 768 N.Y.S.2d 869 (4th Dept. 2003).

Question of law.—While business records, once admitted, have no more probative force than any other evidence admitted pursuant to a hearsay exception, the threshold determination that they are business records satisfying the requirements of the statute is one of law. People v. Kennedy, 68 N.Y.2d 569, 510 N.Y.S.2d 853, 503 N.E.2d 501 (1986).

Subsequent death of person making entry.—When chemist, who performed the intoxication test and subsequently died prior to trial, and his son worked in same laboratory, business records of deceased were properly admitted into evidence at the trial where son testified that his father had performed many such tests and always, immediately thereafter, entered them in log, and identified log handwriting as that of his father. People v. Porter, 46 A.D.2d 307, 362 N.Y.S.2d 249 (3d Dept. 1974).

§ 4519. Personal transaction or communication between witness and decedent or mentally ill person.

Upon the trial of an action or the hearing upon the merits of a special proceeding, a party or a person interested in the event, or a person from, through or under whom such a party or interested person derives his interest or title by assignment or otherwise, shall not be examined as a witness in his own behalf or interest, or in behalf of the party succeeding to his title or interest against the executor, administrator or survivor of a deceased person or the committee of a mentally ill, person or a person deriving his title or interest from through or under a deceased person or mentally ill person, by assignment or otherwise, concerning a personal transaction or communication between the witness and the deceased person or mentally ill person except where the executor, administrator, survivor, committee or person so deriving title or interest is examined in his own behalf, or the testimony of a mentally ill person or deceased person is given in evidence, concerning the same transaction or communication. A person shall not be deemed interested for the purposes of this section by reason of being a stockholder or officer of any banking corporation which is a party to the action or proceeding, or interested in the event thereof. No party or person interested in the event, who is otherwise competent to testify, shall be disqualified from testifying by the possible imposition of costs against him or the award of costs to him. A party or person interested in the event or a person from, through or under whom such a party or interested person derives his interest or title by assignment or otherwise, shall not be qualified for the purposes of this section, to testify in his own behalf or interest, or in behalf of the party succeeding to his title or interest, to personal transactions or communications with the donee of a power of appointment in an action or proceeding for the probate of a will, which exercises or attempts to exercise a power of appointment granted by the will of a donor of such power, or in an action or proceeding involving the construction of the will of the donee after its admission to probate.

Nothing contained in this section, however, shall render a person incompetent to testify as to the facts of an accident or the results therefrom where the proceeding, hearing, defense or cause of action involves a claim of negligence or contributory negligence in an action wherein one or more parties is the representative of a deceased or incompetent person based upon, or by reason of, the operation or ownership of a motor vehicle being operated upon the highways of the state, or the operation or ownership of aircraft being operated in the air space over the state, or the operation or ownership of a vessel on any of the lakes, rivers, streams, canals or other waters of this state, but this provision shall not be construed as permitting testimony as to conversations with the deceased.

Amended by L. 1978, Ch. 550.

ANNOTATIONS

Dead man's statute; generally.—Trial court committed reversible error by allowing defendant, a home health care aid charged with conversion by fraud, to testify about alleged arrangement he had with 80-year-old mentally failing decedent in his care, whereby decedent allegedly allowed defendant to deposit ten mortgage checks made out to the decedent in defendant's bank account. Sepulveda v. Aviles, 308 A.D.2d 1, 762 N.Y.S.2d 358 (1st Dept. 2003).

—Where decedent was both officer and majority owner of (1000 our of 1100 shares), corporate defendant may invoke Dead Man's Statute, defendants did not waive that statute by consenting to joint introduction of portions of decedent's deposition testimony at trial because portions that were admitted had nothing to do with the topic on which plaintiff wished to testify, exception applies only when deposition testimony concerns "the same transaction or communication" about which the survivor wants to testify. Herrmann v. Sklover Group, Inc., 2 A.D.3d 307 768 N.Y.S.2d 600 (1st Dept. 2003).

—" 'Since the purpose of CPLR 4519 is adversarial balance,' deposition testimony should be held inadmissible under the Dead Man's Statute where, as here, the deceased never had his own deposition taken on the relevant matter." Wall St. Assocs. v. Brodsky, 295 A.D.2d 262, 744 N.Y.S.2d 378 (1st Dept. 2002).

—Dead man's statute does not prevent introduction into evidence of receipt acknowledging the installation of a smoke detector purportedly signed by the decedent, especially where the signature is not disputed and other evidence authenticates the document. Acevedo v. Audubon Mgmt., 280 A.D.2d 91, 721 N.Y.S.2d 332 (1st Dept. 2001).

—Petitioner waived the protection of CPLR 4519 when he opened the door and elicited testimony from the proponent of the will regarding otherwise-protected transactions involving the decedent. In re Pennino, 289 A.D.2d 248, 734 N.Y.S.2d 477 (2d Dept. 2001).

—Section 4519 prohibits a party interested in event from testifying as a witness in his or her own behalf, against executor, as to a personal transaction or communication with decedent, purpose of statute is to protect estate, however, that petitioner may benefit from increased commissions as executor of estate does not make him a person interested in a personal transaction with decedent, as against executor. In re Estate of Johnson, 7 A.D.3d 959, 777 N.Y.S.2d 212 (3d Dept. 2004).

—Affidavit containing decedent's statement was not barred by dead man's statute when it was offered not as testimony but in opposition to plaintiff's claim. Duger v. Estate of Carey, 307 A.D.2d 675, 763 N.Y.S.2d 172 (3d Dept. 2003).

—Decedent's next of kin were not precluded under dead man's statute from submitting testimony of disinterested third parties on the question of how decedent wanted to be laid to rest after his death. Booth v. Huff, 273 A.D.2d 576, 708 N.Y.S.2d 757 (3d Dept. 2000).

Transactions with agent; statute inapplicable.—Transactions with an agent do not suffer the bar of the dead man's statute (CPLR 4519); an interested party may testify to transactions with an agent, even if both the principal and agent are dead at time of trial. International Packaging Corp. v. Marshall, 68 Misc. 2d 575, 326 N.Y.S.2d 462 (Civ. Ct. N.Y. Co. 1971).

Interested party incompetent to testify.—Dead man's statute precludes admission of statements of an interested party; therefore, even if the signature on the disputed document is authenticated, beneficiary is incompetent to offer testimony regarding the document as a matter of law. This is to protect the estate against "perjurious claims and . . . post-death fabrications." Glatter v. Borten, 233 A.D.2d 166, 168-169, 649 N.Y.S.2d 677 (1st Dept. 1996).

—Defendant was properly precluded from testifying regarding a gratuitous bailment transaction with decedent. French v. O'Donohue, 239 A.D.2d 903, 659 N.Y.S.2d 655 (4th Dept. 1997).

—Interested party was not only incompetent to testify at trial but also was incompetent to offer affidavit in support of motion for summary judgment. In re Naber, 231 A.D.2d 849, 647 N.Y.S.2d 611 (4th Dept. 1996).

Summary judgment.—Evidence excludable by CPLR 4519 may be considered to defeat a motion for summary judgment. In re Cavallo, 6 A.D.3d 434, 774 N.Y.S.2d 371 (2d Dept. 2004).

—Defendant, decedent's attorney-in-fact, could not rely upon his conversations with decedent in order to support a transfer to himself of decedent's property where power of attorney did not specifically authorize such a transfer, those conversations

were excludable at trial as a violation of the Dead Man's Statute, however they could be used to defeat a motion for summary judgment, even though such statements can not be sole proof in support of opposing party's claim. Marszal v. Anderson, 9 A.D.3d 711, 780 N.Y.S.2d 432 (3d Dept. 2004).

—Evidence generally barred by the dead man's statute may still be used to defeat a claim of summary judgment; however, if it is the only evidence, it will be insufficient to support the claim. Mantella v. Mantella, 268 A.D.2d 852, 701 N.Y.S.2d 715 (3d Dept. 2000).

Waiver—In case of divorced parents of decedent seeking allocation of proceeds of wrongful death action, father did not waive protections of Dead Man's statute when conversations with decedent son were elicited by mother's counsel on cross-examination. In re Estate of Ellers, 309 A.D.2d 1055, 765 N.Y.S.2d 910 (3d Dept. 2003).

—Petitioner who introduces deposition testimony in which respondent testified that she received money from decedent following a withdrawal from decedent's savings account, waived protection of the Dead Man's Statute and opened door to otherwise incompetent testimony of respondent at the hearing. In re Estate of Lamparelli, 6 A.D.3d 1218, 776 N.Y.S.2d 665 (4th Dept. 2004).

—Where plaintiff waives protection of Dead Man's statute, court properly allowed testimony regarding transactions with decedents. Cowles v. Minicucci, 1 A.D.3d 1060, 767 N.Y.S.2d 746 (4th Dept. 2003).

§ 4520. Certificate or affidavit of public officer.

Where a public officer is required or authorized, by special provision of law, to make a certificate or an affidavit to a fact ascertained, or an act performed, by him in the course of his official duty, and to file or deposit it in a public office of the state, the certificate or affidavit so filed or deposited is prima facie evidence of the facts stated.

ANNOTATIONS

DMV abstract.—Department of Motor Vehicles abstract, a written declaration that the licensee's privilege to drive has been suspended by the Commissioner as a result of a failure to answer a summons or pay a fine, is a business record admissible pursuant to CPLR § 4520 and must be authenticated. It is also admissible as a common law public document exception to the hearsay rule. People v. Michaels, 174 Misc. 2d 982, 667 N.Y.S.2d 646 (Crim. Ct. Richmond Co. 1997).

Mimeographed letter from mission to United Nations.—Mimeographed letter from the United States Mission to the United Nations, stating that a vehicle bearing diplomatic license plates, which had repeatedly been found in violation of no parking restrictions, was registered to a member of a permanent mission to the United Nations and "was used on official business when violations occurred," is insufficient to establish that acts complained of are protected by diplomatic immunity not only because it does not comply with CPLR 4520 but also because there is no showing that it is a public document entitled to the common law exception to the hearsay rule. People v. Doe, 101 Misc. 2d 789, 421 N.Y.S.2d 1015 (Greenburgh Just. Ct., Westchester Co. 1979).

Police laboratory report; narcotics.—In Family Court delinquency proceeding, the Police Laboratory chemist's certified report is admissible without his testimony under the general "business record" exception to the rule against hearsay [CPLR 4518(a)], as well as the exception for a record certified by an employee of a department or bureau of a municipal corporation [CPLR 4518(c) and 2307(a)], and the exception for a certificate of a public officer [CPLR 4520]. In re Kevin G., 80 Misc. 2d 517, 363 N.Y.S.2d 999 (Fam. Ct. N.Y. Co. 1975).

Public Safety Laboratory test results; breathalyzer.—A document which is inadmissible under CPLR 4520 may be admissible under the common-law exception when a public officer is authorized by the nature of his official duty to keep records of transactions occurring in the course of his duty since the record so made by him or under his supervision is admissible in evidence. People v. Hoats, 102 Misc. 2d 1004, 425 N.Y.S.2d 497 (Monroe Co. Ct. 1980).

§ 4521. Lack of record.

A statement signed by an officer or a deputy of an officer having legal custody of specified official records of the United States or of any state, territory or jurisdiction of the United States, or of any court thereof, or kept in any public office thereof, that he has made diligent search of the records and has found no record or entry of a specified nature, is prima facie evidence that the records contain no such record or entry, provided that the statement is accompanied by a certificate that legal custody of the specified official records belongs to such person, which certificate shall be made by a person described in rule 4540.

§ 4522. Ancient filed maps, surveys and records affecting real property.

All maps, surveys and official records affecting real property, which have been on file in the state in the office of the register of any county, any county clerk, any court of record or any department of the city of New York for more than ten years, are prima facie evidence of their contents.

ANNOTATIONS

Evidence.—Plaintiffs properly relied on subdivision map allegedly filed with County Clerk in 1990, to establish prima facie evidence of contents, however failure to attach that map to motion papers was fatal to their summary judgment motion. McFarland v. Michel, 2 A.D.3d 1297 770 N.Y.S.2d 544 (4th Dept. 2003).

§ 4523. Search by title insurance or abstract company.

A search affecting real property, when made and certified to by a title insurance, abstract or searching company, organized under the laws of this state, may be used in place of, and with the same legal effect as, an official search.

§ 4524. Conveyance of real property without the state.

A record of a conveyance of real property situated within another state, territory or jurisdiction of the United States, recorded therein pursuant to its laws, is prima facie evidence of conveyance and of due execution.

§ 4525. Copies of statements under article nine of the uniform commercial code.

A copy of a statement which is noted or certified by a filing officer pursuant to section 9–523 of the uniform commercial code and which states that the copy is a true copy is prima facie evidence of the facts stated in the notation or certification and that the copy is a true copy of a statement filed in the office of the filing officer.

Amended by L. 2001, Ch. 84, eff. July 1, 2001.

§ 4526. Marriage certificate.

An original certificate of a marriage made by the person by whom it was solemnized within the state, or the original entry thereof made pursuant to law in the office of the clerk of a city or a town within the state, is prima facie evidence of the marriage.

§ 4527. Death or other status of missing person.

(a) **Presumed death.** A written finding of presumed death, made by any person authorized to make such findings by the federal missing persons act is prima facie evidence of the death, and the date, circumstances and place of disappearance. In the case of a merchant seaman, a written finding of presumed death, made by the maritime war emergency board or by the war shipping administration or the successors or assigns of such board or administration in connection with war risk insurance is prima facie evidence of the death, and the date, circumstances and place of disappearance.

(b) **Death, internment, capture and other status.** An official written report or record that a person is missing, missing in action, interned in a neutral country, or beleaguered, besieged [sic] or captured by an enemy, or is dead, or is alive, made by an officer or employee of the United States authorized by law of the United States to make it is prima facie evidence of such fact.

§ 4528. Weather conditions.

Any record of the observations of the weather, taken under the direction of the United States weather bureau, is prima facie evidence of the facts stated.

§ 4529. Inspection certificate issued by United States department of agriculture.

An inspection certificate issued by the authorized agents of the United States department of agriculture on file with the United States secretary of agriculture is prima facie evidence of the facts stated.

§ 4530. Certificate of population.

(a) **Prima facie evidence.** A certificate of the officer in charge of the census of the United States, attested by the United States secretary of commerce, giving the result of the census is, except as hereinafter provided, prima facie evidence of such result.

(b) Conclusive evidence. Where the population of the state or a subdivision, or a portion of a subdivision of the state is required to be determined according to the federal or state census or enumeration last preceding a particular time, a certificate of the officer in charge of the census of the United States, attested by the United States secretary of commerce, as to such population as shown by such federal census, or a certificate of the secretary of state as to such population as shown by such state enumeration, is conclusive evidence of such population.

§ 4531. Affidavit of service or posting notice by person unavailable at trial.

An affidavit by a person who served, posted or affixed a notice, showing such service, posting or affixing is prima facie evidence of the service, posting or affixing if the affiant is dead, mentally ill or cannot be compelled with due diligence to attend at the trial.

Amended by L. 1978, Ch. 550.

§ 4532. Self-authentication of newspapers and periodicals of general circulation.

Extrinsic evidence of authenticity as a condition precedent to admissibility is not required with respect to printed materials purporting to be newspapers or periodicals of general circulation; provided however, nothing herein shall be deemed to preclude or limit the right of a party to challenge the authenticity of such printed material, by extrinsic evidence or otherwise, prior to admission by the court or to raise the issue of authenticity as an issue of fact.

Added by L. 1986, Ch. 89, eff. May 23, 1986, which also **repealed** former section.

§ 4532-a. Admissibility of graphic, numerical, symbolic or pictorial representations of medical or diagnostic tests.

A graphic, numerical, symbolic or pictorial representation of the results of a medical or diagnostic procedure or test is admissible in evidence provided:

(1) the name of the injured party, the date when the information constituting the graphic, numerical, symbolic or pictorial representation was taken, and such additional identifying information as is customarily inscribed by the medical practitioner or medical facility is inserted on such graphic, numerical, symbolic or pictorial representation; and

(2) (a) the representation has been previously received or examined by the party or parties against whom it is being offered; or (b)(i) at least ten days before the date of trial of the action, the party intending to offer such graphic, numerical, symbolic or pictorial representation as a proposed exhibit serves upon the party or parties against whom said proposed exhibit is to be offered, a notice of intention to offer such proposed exhibit in evidence during the trial and that the same is available for inspection; and (ii) the notice aforesaid is accompanied by an affidavit or affirmation of such physician identifying such graphic, numerical, symbolic or pictorial representation and attesting to the identifying information inscribed thereon, attesting that the identifying information inscribed thereon is the same as is customarily inscribed by the medical practitioner or facility, and further attesting that, if called as a witness in the action, he or she would so testify.

Nothing contained in this rule, however, shall prohibit the admissibility of a graphic, numerical, symbolic or pictorial representation in evidence where otherwise admissible.

Amended by L. 1979, Ch. 124; L. 1993, Ch. 482; L. 2001, Ch. 392, eff. Jan. 1, 2002; L. 2004, Ch. 375, § 1, eff. Jan. 1, 2005.

ANNOTATIONS

Admissibility; generally.—MRI films not yet in evidence were not admissible pursuant to CPLR 4532-a, providing for self-authentication of diagnostic tests, plaintiff failed to meet section's requirements, or show that MRI films were admissible pursuant to business records exception to hearsay rule. Kovacev v. Ferreira Bros. Contr., Inc., 9 A.D.3d 253, 779 N.Y.S.2d 204 (1st Dept. 2004).

—It was a proper exercise of court's discretion to preclude admission of MRI (magnetic resonance imaging) films in light of plaintiff's failure to comply with CPLR 4532-a's requirements. Wierzbicki v. Mathew, 8 A.D.3d 476, 778 N.Y.S.2d 302 (2d Dept. 2004).

—Properly authenticated computerized axial tomography scan films were properly admitted into evidence. McDade v. Wright, 268 A.D.2d 570, 702 N.Y.S.2d 845 (2d Dept. 2000).

§ 4533. Market reports.

A report of a regularly organized stock or commodity market published in a newspaper or periodical of general circulation or in an official publication or trade journal is admissible in evidence to prove the market price or value of any article regularly sold or dealt in on such market. The circumstances of the preparation of such a report may be shown to affect its weight, but they shall not affect its admissibility.

§ 4533-a. Prima facie proof of damages.

An itemized bill or invoice, receipted or marked paid, for services or repairs of an amount not in excess of two thousand dollars is admissible in evidence and is prima facie evidence of the reasonable value and necessity of such services or repairs itemized therein in any civil action provided it bears a certification by the person, firm or corporation, or an authorized agent or employee thereof, rendering such services or making such repairs and charging for the same, and contains a verified statement that no part of the payment therefor will be refunded to the debtor, and that the amounts itemized therein are the usual and customary rates charged for such services or repairs by the affiant or his employer; and provided that a true copy of such itemized bill or invoice together with a notice of intention to introduce such bill or invoice into evidence pursuant to this rule is served upon each party at least ten days before the trial. No more than one bill or invoice from the same person, firm or corporation to the same debtor shall be admissible in evidence under this rule in the same action.

Amended by L. 1975, Ch. 103; L. 1981, Ch. 355; L. 1988, Ch. 249, eff. July 8, 1988, increased amount to "two thousand dollars."

ANNOTATION

Dental expenses; issues of necessity and reasonableness matter of expert opinion and not properly sought by notice to admit; use of § 4533-a suggested.—In a support proceeding, the evidentiary problem encountered as to the necessity and reasonable value of most of the medical and dental expenses for which the claim was made might have been avoided by the use of CPLR 4533-a, which became available in all civil actions as of September 1, 1970; notice to admit sought the husband's admission of the necessity and reasonableness of certain dental treatment, but these issues were matters of expert opinion, not of fact, and were at the heart of the dispute between the parties; accordingly, they were not a proper part of a request for admission under CPLR 3123, Haroche v. Haroche, 38 A.D.2d 957, 331 N.Y.S.2d 466 (2d Dept. 1972).

§ 4533-b. Proof of payment by joint tort-feasor.

In an action for personal injury, injury to property or for wrongful death, any proof as to payment by or settlement with another joint tortfeasor, or one claimed to be a joint tort-feasor, offered by a defendant in mitigation of damages, shall be taken out of the hearing of the jury. The court shall deduct the proper amount, as determined pursuant to section 15-108 of the general obligations law, from the award made by the jury.

Amended by L. 1974, Ch. 742.

§ 4534. Standard of measurement used by surveyor.

An official certificate of any state, county, city, village, or town sealer elected or appointed pursuant to the laws of the state, or the statement under oath of a surveyor, that the chain or measure used by him conformed to the state standard at the time a survey was made is prima facie evidence of conformity, and an official certificate made by any sealer that the implement used in measuring such chain or other measure was the one provided the sealer pursuant to the provisions of the laws of the state is prima facie evidence of that fact.

§ 4536. Proof of writing by comparison of handwriting.

Comparison of a disputed writing with any writing proved to the satisfaction of the court to be the handwriting of the person claimed to have made the disputed writing shall be permitted.

ANNOTATIONS

Court order.—Order, directing petitioners, who were not the subjects of a pending criminal proceeding, to appear in the District Attorney's office and to supply handwriting exemplars did not violate the Fourth and Fourteenth Amendments to the Federal Constitution and section 12 of article 1 of the state constitution. District Attorney of Kings County v. Angelo G. 48 A.D.2d 576, 371 N.Y.S.2d 127 (2d Dept. 1975).

Handwriting comparison.—CPLR 4536 provides the comparison of a disputed writing with a satisfactory standard is permissible, and the jury in its deliberation may make such comparison whether or not an expert offers an opinion. People v. Hunter, 34 N.Y.2d 432, 358 N.Y.S.2d 360, 315 N.E.2d 436 (1974).

—In breach of contract action, court did not abuse its discretion in precluding opinion testimony of defendant's purported handwriting expert, however it did err in refusing to admit in evidence, as irrelevant, handwriting exemplars of defendant's president for purpose of comparison to his purported signature on contract in issue. Am. Linen Supply Co. v. M.W.S. Enters., 6 A.D.3d 1079, 776 N.Y.S.2d 387(4th Dept. 2004).

§ 4537. Proof of writing subscribed by witness.

Unless a writing requires a subscribing witness for its validity, it may be proved as if there was no subscribing witness.

§ 4538. Acknowledged, proved or certified writing; conveyance of real property without the state.

Certification of the acknowledgment or proof of a writing, except a will, in the manner prescribed by law for taking and certifying the acknowledgment or proof of a conveyance of real property within the state is prima facie evidence that it was executed by the person who purported to do so. A conveyance of real property, situated within another state, territory or jurisdiction of the United States, which has been duly authenticated, according to the laws of the state, territory or jurisdiction, so as to be read in evidence in the courts thereof, is admissible in evidence in the state.

ANNOTATION

Acknowledgment *prima facie* proof of signature's authenticity, but subject to rebuttal.—A certification of acknowledgment is *prima facie* proof of the authenticity of a signature (CPLR 4538); in an action to foreclose a mortgage, while such proof is not conclusive (RPAPL 301(1)), it is sufficient to send the case to the jury; the *prima facie* proof of the authenticity of a signature may, however, be rebutted by proof which is credible to the trier of fact. Dart Assocs. v. Rosal Meat Market, Inc., 39 A.D.2d 564, 331 N.Y.S.2d 853 (2d Dept. 1972).

§ 4539. Reproductions of original.

(a) If any business, institution, or member of a profession or calling, in the regular course of business or activity has made, kept or recorded any writing, entry, print or representation and in the regular course of business has recorded, copied, or reproduced it by any process, including reproduction, which accurately reproduces or forms a durable medium for reproducing the original, such reproduction, when satisfactorily identified, is as admissible in evidence as the original, whether the original is in existence or not, and an enlargement or facsimile of such reproduction is admissible in evidence if the original reproduction is in existence and available for inspection under direction of the court. The introduction of a reproduction does not preclude admission of the original.

(b) A reproduction created by any process which stores an image of any writing, entry, print or representation and which does not permit additions, deletions, or changes without leaving a record of such additions, deletions, or changes, when authenticated by competent testimony or affidavit which shall include the manner or method by which tampering or degradation of the reproduction is prevented, shall be as admissible in evidence as the original.

Amended by L. 1996, Ch. 27, eff. Nov. 1, 1996.

§ 4540. Authentication of official record of court or government office in the United States.

(a) Copies permitted. An official publication, or a copy attested as correct by an officer or a deputy of an officer having legal custody of an official record of the United States or of any state, territory or jurisdiction of the United States, or of any of its courts, legislature, offices, public bodies or boards is prima facie evidence of such record.

(b) Certificate of officer of the state. Where the copy is attested by an officer of the state, it shall be accompanied by a certificate signed by, or with a facsimile of the signature of, the clerk of a court having legal custody of the record, and, except where the copy is used in the same court or before one of its officers, with the seal of the court affixed; or signed by, or with a facsimile of the signature of, the officer having legal custody of the original, or his deputy or clerk, with his official seal affixed; or signed by, or with a facsimile of the signature of, the presiding officer, secretary or clerk of the public body or board and, except where it is certified by the clerk or secretary of either house of the legislature, with the seal of the body or board affixed. If the certificate is made by a county clerk, the county seal shall be affixed.

(c) Certificate of officer of another jurisdiction. Where the copy is attested by an officer of another jurisdiction, it shall be accompanied by a certificate that such officer has legal custody of the record, and that his signature is believed to be genuine, which certificate shall be made by a judge of a court of record of the district or political subdivision in which the record is kept, with the seal of the court affixed; or by any public officer having a seal of office and having official duties that in district or political subdivision with respect to the subject matter of the record, with the seal of his office affixed.

(d) Printed tariff or classification subject to public service commission, commissioner of transportation or interstate commerce commission. A printed copy of a tariff or classification which shows a public service commission or commissioner of transportation number of this state and an effective date, or a printed copy of a tariff or classification which shows an interstate commerce commission number and an effective date, is admissible in evidence, without certification, and is prima facie evidence of the filed original tariff or classification.

ANNOTATIONS

Generally.—Use of a copy of a document is permitted when there is no dispute as to the authenticity or ownership of the document in question, here a bank note. Banco Nacional de Mexico, SZ v. Ecoban Fin. Ltd, 276 A.D.2d 284, 713 N.Y.S.2d 869 (1st Dept. 2000).

Abstract of driving record.—Defendant's conviction of aggravated unlicensed operation of a motor vehicle in the first degree, which requires proof that defendant operated a vehicle with 10 or more license suspensions in effect, was reduced where the abstract of defendant's driving record was not properly certified as required and no other evidence of the suspensions was contained in the record. People v. Sikorski, 280 A.D.2d 414, 721 N.Y.S.2d 48 (1st Dept. 2001).

Breathalyzer ampule analysis; photocopy.—A photocopy of breathalyzer ampule analysis result signed by the senior chemist of the Police Public Safety Laboratory, accompanied by an original certification signed by the acting director and containing a declaration that the test was made in the regular course of business, with state seals on both, satisfied CPLR 4540. People v. Hoats, 102 Misc. 2d 1004, 425 N.Y.S.2d 497 (Monroe Co. Ct. 1980).

Certificate of conviction.—It was error to receive unauthenticated documentation of defendant's purported conviction of a drug violation in Puerto Rico where the certificates of conviction, while attested to, lacked the certificate, under seal, that the attestor was the legal custodian of the records and that his signature was genuine. People v. Gonzalez, 64 A.D.2d 534, 406 N.Y.S.2d 488 (1st Dept. 1978).

Prior conviction in Puerto Rico.—Once documents evidencing defendant's prior conviction in Puerto Rico had been received in evidence without objection, it was discretionary with the court whether to permit the defendant to withdraw his waiver of objection or to strike the documents. People v. Parsons, 84 A.D.2d 510, 443 N.Y.S.2d 159 (1st Dept. 1981).

§ 4541. Proof of proceedings before justice of the peace.

(a) Of the state. A transcript from the docket-book of a justice of the peace of the state, subscribed by him, and authenticated by a certificate signed by the clerk of the county in which the justice resides, with the county seal affixed, to the effect that the person subscribing the transcript is a justice of the peace of that county, is prima facie evidence of any matter stated in the transcript which is required by law to be entered by the justice in his docket-book.

(b) Of another state. A transcript from the docket-book of a justice of the peace of another state, of his minutes of the proceedings in a cause, of a judgment rendered by him, of an execution, when subscribed by him, and authenticated as prescribed in this subdivision is prima facie evidence of his jurisdiction in the cause and of the matters shown by the transcript. The transcript shall be authenticated by a certificate of the justice to the effect that it is in all respects correct and that he had jurisdiction of the cause; and also by a certificate of the clerk or prothonotary of the county in which the justice resides, with his official seal affixed, to the effect that the person subscribing the certificate attached to the transcript is a justice of the peace of that county.

ANNOTATION

Certificates of conviction.—Photocopy of attorney's certification that defendant had been convicted of misdemeanors was insufficient to prove that defendant had been convicted; this document was a copy and had to be attested to as correct to be received into evidence. However, the certificates of conviction accompanied by signatures of the county clerk were original documents that required no attestation and were properly admitted. People v. Sykes, 167 Misc. 2d 588, 638 N.Y.S.2d 1010 (Sup. Ct. Monroe Co. 1995), aff'd, 223 A.D.2d 1093, 639 N.Y.S.2d 188 (4th Dept. 1996).

Out of state records. —Requirement for certificate of attestation is applicable only when a copy is used instead of original official publication, reasonable interpretation of requirement that clerk certify copy "as correct" is that it is satisfied by an assertion that it is a true copy of original. Sparaco v. Sparaco, 309 A.D.2d 1029, 765 N.Y.S.2d 683 (3d Dept. 2003).

—Court improperly determined defendant was a second felony offender based upon a contested Florida accusatory instrument in evidence without certification required by CPLR § 4541(c). People v. James, 4 A.D.3d 774, 772 N.Y.S.2d 151 (4th Dept. 2004).

§ 4542. Proof of foreign records and documents.

(a) Foreign record. A foreign official record, or an entry therein, when admissible for any purpose, may be evidenced by an official publication thereof; or a copy thereof, attested by a person authorized to make the attestation, and accompanied by a final certification as to the genuineness of the signature and official position

    1. of the attesting person, or

    2. of any foreign official whose certificate of genuineness of signature and official position

    (i) relates to the attestation, or

    (ii) is in a chain of certificates of genuineness of signature and official position relating to the attestation.

(b) Final certification. A final certification may be made by a secretary of an embassy or legation, consul general, consul, vice consul, or consular agent of the United States, or a diplomatic or consular official of the foreign country assigned or accredited to the United States. If reasonable opportunity has been given to all parties to investigate the authenticity and accuracy of the documents, the court may, for good cause shown, admit an attested copy without final certification, or permit the foreign official record to be evidenced by an attested summary with or without a final certification.

(c) Lack of record. A written statement that after diligent search no record or entry of a specified tenor was found to exist in the foreign records designated by the statement, authenticated

in compliance with the requirements set forth in subdivisions (a) and (b) for a copy of a foreign record is admissible as evidence that the records contain no such record or entry.

ANNOTATIONS

Proof of foreign records and documents; generally.— English translations of Russian documents, not properly authenticated, were properly excluded. American Minority Petroleum v. Valfai, 237 A.D.2d 105, 655 N.Y.S.2d 344 (1st Dept. 1997).

Requisites for admission of foreign document; if met, contentions as to reliability of document go to weight, not admissibility.—For a copy of a foreign record to be admitted in evidence, the requirements set forth in CPLR 4542 are attestation and the genuineness of the signature of the attesting person; since these requirements were met in the instant case, respondent's contentions as to the reliability of the documents went to the weight, not the admissibility, of the documents. In re Barabash, 31 N.Y.2d 76, 334 N.Y.S.2d 890, 286 N.E.2d 268 (1972).

§ 4543. Proof of facts or writing by methods other than those authorized in this article.

Nothing in this article prevents the proof of a fact or a writing by any method authorized by any applicable statute or by the rules of evidence at common law.

ANNOTATIONS

Generally.—Production of a securing order is not necessary to establish the offense of escape where testimony of a court clerk and investigator present at defendant's arraignment established that defendant was in custody pursuant to a court order. People v. Richardson, 88 N.Y.2d 1049, 650 N.Y.S.2d 633, 673 N.E.2d 918 (1996).

Print size less than eight point proper as affirmative defense.—Appellant's affirmative defense against plaintiff reinstated since it appeared to court that print in lease was less than the eight points in size in contravention of statute. General Elec. Capital Auto Lease v. D'Ngnese, 239 A.D.2d 462, 658 N.Y.S.2d 55 (2d Dept. 1997).

"Rules of evidence at common law."—The common law recognizes a copy sworn to as accurate by a witness who compared it and a copy certified by a public officer. People v. Hoats, 102 Misc. 2d 1004, 425 N.Y.S.2d 497 (Monroe Co. Ct. 1980).

§ 4544. Contracts in small print.

The portion of any printed contract or agreement involving a consumer transaction or a lease for space to be occupied for residential purposes where the print is not clear and legible or is less than eight points in depth or five and one-half points in depth for upper case type may not be received in evidence in any trial, hearing or proceeding on behalf of the party who printed or prepared such contract or agreement, or who caused said agreement or contract to be printed or prepared. As used in the immediately preceding sentence, the term "consumer transaction" means a transaction wherein the money, property or service which is the subject of the transaction is primarily for personal, family or household purposes. No provision of any contract or agreement waiving the provisions of this section shall be effective. The provisions of this section shall not apply to agreements or contracts entered into prior to the effective date of this section.

Amended by L. 1975, ch. 370; L. 1979, Ch. 474, eff. Sept. 1, 1979.

§ 4545. Admissibility of collateral source of payment.

(a) Action for medical, dental or podiatric malpractice. In any action for medical, or podiatric malpractice where the plaintiff seeks to recover for the cost of medical care, dental care, podiatric care, custodial care or rehabilitation services, loss of earnings, or other economic loss, evidence shall be admissible for consideration by the court to establish that any such past or future cost or expense was or will, with reasonable certainty, be replaced or indemnified, in whole or in part, from any collateral source such as insurance (except for life insurance), social security (except those benefits provided under title XVIII of the social security act), workers' compensation or employee benefit programs (except such collateral sources entitled by law to liens against any recovery of the plaintiff). If the court finds that any such cost or expense was or will, with reasonable certainty, be replaced or indemnified from any collateral source, it shall reduce the amount of the award by such finding, minus an amount equal to the premiums paid by the plaintiff for such benefits for the two-year period immediately preceding the accrual of such action and minus an amount equal to the projected future cost to the plaintiff of maintaining such benefits. In order to find that any future cost or expense will, with reasonable certainty, be replaced or indemnified by the collateral source, the court must find that the plaintiff is legally entitled to the continued receipt of such collateral source, pursuant to a contract or otherwise enforceable agreement, subject only to the continued payment of a premium and such other financial obligations as may be required by such agreement.

(b) Certain actions against a public employer for personal injury and wrongful death. 1. In any action against a public employer or a public employee who is subject to indemnification by a public employer with respect to such action or both for personal injury or wrongful death arising out of an injury sustained by a public employee while acting within the scope of his public employment or duties, where the plaintiff seeks to recover for the cost of medical care, custodial care or rehabilitation services, loss of earnings or other economic loss, evidence shall be admissible for consideration by the court to establish that any such cost or expense was replaced or indemnified, in whole or in part, from a collateral source provided or paid for, in whole or in part, by the public employer, including but not limited to paid sick leave, medical benefits, death benefits, dependent benefits, a disability retirement allowance and social security (except those benefits provided under title XVIII of the social security act) but shall not include those collateral sources entitled by law to liens against

any recovery of the plaintiff. If the court finds that any such cost or expense was replaced or indemnified from any such collateral source, it shall reduce the amount of the award by such finding. minus an amount equal to the contributions of the injured public employee for such benefit.

2. As used in this subdivision, the term "public employer" means the state of New York, a county, city, town, village or any other political subdivision of the state, any public authority operating a rapid transit, commuter railroad, omnibus, marine, airport or aviation facility, a school district or any governmental entity operating a public school, college or university and any municipal housing authority. The term "public employee" means any person holding a position by election, appointment or employment in the service of a public employer, while acting within the scope of his public employment or duties, whether or not compensated, or a volunteer expressly authorized to participate in a volunteer program sponsored by a public employer but does not include an independent contractor. The term public employee includes a former employee, his estate or judicially appointed personal representative.

3. For the purposes of this subdivision a certified report of the actuary of the appropriate public employee retirement system shall be admissible evidence of the present value of any death benefit, dependent benefit or disability retirement allowance.

4. The provisions of this subdivision shall not be construed to affect, alter or amend any provisions of the workers' compensation law or to apply to any claims under such law.

(c) Actions for personal injury, injury to property or wrongful death. In any action brought to recover damages for personal injury, injury to property or wrongful death, where the plaintiff seeks to recover for the cost of medical care, dental care, custodial care or rehabilitation services, loss of earnings or other economic loss, evidence shall be admissible for consideration by the court to establish that any such past or future cost or expense was or will, with reasonable certainty, be replaced or indemnified, in whole or in part, from any collateral source such as insurance (except for life insurance), social security (except those benefits provided under title XVIII of the social security act), workers' compensation or employee benefit programs (except such collateral sources entitled by law to liens against any recovery of the plaintiff). If the court finds that any such cost or expense was or will, with reasonable certainty, be replaced or indemnified from any collateral source, it shall reduce the amount of the award by such finding, minus an amount equal to the premiums paid by the plaintiff for such benefits for the two-year period immediately preceding the accrual of such action and minus an amount equal to the projected future cost to the plaintiff of maintaining such benefits. In order to find that any future cost or expense will, with reasonable certainty, be replaced or indemnified by the collateral source, the court must find that the plaintiff is legally entitled to the continued receipt of such collateral source, pursuant to a contract or otherwise enforceable agreement, subject only to the continued payment of a premium and such other financial obligations as may be required by such agreement.

(d) **Voluntary charitable contributions excluded as a collateral source of payment.** Voluntary charitable contributions received by an injured party shall not be considered to be a collateral source of payment that is admissible in evidence to reduce the amount of any award, judgment or settlement.

Added by L. 1984, Ch. 701, eff. Oct. 1, 1984, and applicable to actions commenced on and after that date; **Amended** by L. 1985, Ch. 294, eff. July 1, 1985 amending subd. a and applicable to any action for dental or medical malpractice commenced on or after that date; L. 1985, Ch. 760, eff. July 1, 1985, amended subd. a without including changes made by L. 1985, Ch. 294, and applies to any action occurring on or after July 1, 1985; L. 1986, Ch. 220, eff. June 28, 1986, added subd. c, which applies to any action or proceeding commenced on or after June 28, 1986, Ch. 221 amending Ch. 220 to except an action commenced pursuant to sections four and five of chapter of the laws of 1986, as proposed in legislative bill number S. 9391-A; L. 1986, Ch. 485, eff. July 21, 1986, amending subd. a and applies to any acts, omissions or failures occurring on and after July 21, 1986; L. 2002, Ch. 672, eff. Dec. 9, 2002.

ANNOTATIONS

Offsetting; when authorized.—In recovery for physical disability to plaintiff employee for which defendant was liable, court properly declined to charge jury that plaintiff was required to seek vocational rehabilitation to mitigate his damages, defendant-general contractor had not carried its burden to show that plaintiff employee's "future cost or expense" from lost earnings "was or will, with reasonable certainty, be replaced or indemnified, in whole or in part, from any collateral source." Williams v. Turner Constr. Inc., 2 A.D.3d 217, 768 N.Y.S.2d 314 (1st Dept. 2003).

—In action for legal malpractice and breach of contract brought after plaintiff got food poisoning at Club Med resort, court erred when it dismissed defendants' affirmative defense asserting collateral source rule, measure of plaintiffs' damages, if any, will be value of their lost claims as against resort, defendants are entitled to mitigate such damages, if any, by offering evidence that such damages would have been reduced by collateral source rule. Stein v. Levine, 8 A.D.3d 652, 779 N.Y.S.2d 556 (2d Dept. 2004).

—CPLR 4545 provides for a reduction in an award of damages after a trial based on reimbursement from collateral sources, purpose of rule is to prevent multiple recoveries for same loss by an injured party, that purpose would not be served by its application to subrogation claims. Kaczmarski v. Suddaby, 9 A.D.3d 847, 779 N.Y.S.2d 394 (4th Dept. 2004).

—Although section 4545 prevents plaintiff's from receiving "windfalls and double recoveries for the same loss" a defendant still may be held responsible in subrogation to plaintiff's health care insurer, Omiatek v. Marine Midland Bank, N.A., 9 A.D.3d 831, 781 N.Y.S.2d 389 (4th Dept. 2004).

—Offsetting under this section is "authorized only when the collateral source payment represents reimbursement for a particular loss that duplicates or corresponds to the category of loss for which damages were awarded"; plaintiff was awarded damages for loss of future "earning and benefits," but defendant failed to establish what portion of that was for lost pension benefits which could have been offset by the amount of disability pension benefits. Boshnakov v. Board of Educ. of Town of Eden, 277 A.D.2d 996, 716 N.Y.S.2d 520 (4th Dept. 2000), *appeal denied,* 96 N.Y.2d 703 (2001).

—Proceeds of insurance policy properly offset damage award to widow of public employee in wrongful death action where public employer provided or paid for that insurance policy. Rodd v. Luxfer USA, Ltd., 187 Misc. 2d 341, 723 N.Y.S.2d 308 (Sup. Ct. Suffolk Co. 2000).

§ 4546. Loss of earnings and impairment of earning ability in actions for medical, dental or podiatric malpractice.

1. In any action for medical, dental or podiatric malpractice where the plaintiff seeks to recover damages for loss of earnings or impairment of earning ability, evidence shall be admissible for consideration by the court, outside of the presence of the jury, to establish the federal, state and local personal income taxes which the plaintiff would have been obligated by law to pay.

2. In any such action, the court shall instruct the jury not to deduct federal, state and local personal income taxes in determining the award, if any, for loss of earnings and impairment of earning ability. The court shall further instruct the jury that any reduction for such taxes from any award shall, if warranted, be made by the court.

3. In any such action, the court shall, if warranted by the evidence, reduce any award for loss of earnings or impairment of earning ability by the amount of federal, state and local personal income taxes which the court finds, with reasonable certainty, that the plaintiff would have been obligated by law to pay.

Added by L. 1986, Chs. 266, 267, eff. July 8, 1986; **Amended** by L. 1987, Ch. 507, eff. July 30, 1987, and shall apply to any acts, omissions or failures occurring on and after such date.

§ 4547. Compromise and offers to compromise.

Evidence of (a) furnishing, or offering or promising to furnish, or (b) accepting, or offering or promising to accept, any valuable consideration in compromising or attempting to compromise a claim which is disputed as to either validity or amount of damages, shall be inadmissible as proof of liability for or invalidity of the claim or the amount of damages. Evidence of any conduct or statement made during compromise negotiations shall also be inadmissible. The provisions of this section shall not require the exclusion of any evidence, which is otherwise discoverable, solely because such evidence was presented during the course of compromise negotiations. Furthermore, the exclusion established by this section shall not limit the admissibility of such evidence when it is offered for another purpose, such as proving bias or prejudice of a witness, negating a contention of undue delay or proof of an effort to obstruct a criminal investigation or prosecution.

Added by L. 1998, Ch. 317, § 1, eff. July 14, 1998.

§ 4548. Privileged communications; electronic communication thereof.

No communication privileged under this article shall lose its privileged character for the sole reason that it is communicated by electronic means or because persons necessary for the delivery or facilitation of such electronic communication may have access to the content of the communication.

Added by L. 1998, Ch. 156, § 1, eff. July 7, 1998; L. 1999, Ch. 56, eff. May 25, 1999, renumbered from § 4547.

ARTICLE 70

HABEAS CORPUS

Section

§ 7001. Application of article; special proceeding.

Except as otherwise prescribed by statute, the provisions of this article are applicable to common law or statutory writs of habeas corpus and common law writs of certiorari to inquire into detention. A proceeding under this article is a special proceeding.

ANNOTATIONS

Availability of other relief.—Dismissal of defendant's prior appeal for want of prosecution acted as an adjudication on the merits of all claims that could have been litigated had the appeal been timely argued or submitted. People v. Corley, 67 N.Y.2d 105, 500 N.Y.S.2d 633, 491 N.E.2d 1090 (1986).

—A writ of habeas corpus did not lie where the petitioner neither moved to dismiss the indictment on the grounds now asserted nor raised the issue on a prior appeal. People ex rel. Lester v. Scully, 191 A.D.2d 664, 595 N.Y.S.2d 227, 228 (2d Dept. 1993).

—Post-judgment collateral relief by way of a petition for a writ of habeas corpus is not available to review issues that could and should have been raised on an earlier appeal. People v. Bantum, 123 A.D.2d 800, 507 N.Y.S.2d 275 (2d Dept. 1986).

—Parolee was not required to resort to a futile administrative remedy before seeking judicial relief. People ex rel. Alexander v. Lefeure, 116 A.D.2d 869, 498 N.Y.S.2d 485 (3d Dept. 1986).

—A writ of habeas corpus is inappropriate to review issues which could have been raised on appeal or through a motion to dismiss the indictment but were not. People ex rel. Goss v. Smith, 116 A.D.2d 968, 498 N.Y.S.2d 594 (4th Dept. 1986).

—Where the defendant asserts that he was deprived of his right to appear before the grand jury, the issue should be raised on appeal from the judgment of conviction; a writ of habeas corpus could not be utilized to review this error. People ex rel. Stephens v. Smith, 64 A.D.2d 1008, 409 N.Y.S.2d 287 (4th Dept. 1978).

Burden of proof.—Where petitioner claimed that the warrant of arrest was improper, the burden of proof as to the petitioner's allegation that she was not in Connecticut at the time crime was committed or that she was not a resident of the State was on the petitioner on the return date of the habeas corpus writ. People ex rel. Pray v. Allen, 63 A.D.2d 1056, 405 N.Y.S.2d 822 (3d Dept. 1978).

—Defendant was granted an immediate hearing on the merits of his habeas corpus petition without regard to the pending appeal where defendant's appeal from his judgment of conviction had been pending for more than four years and had not been perfected. People ex rel. Lee v. Montanye, 58 A.D.2d 987, 397 N.Y.S.2d 266 (4th Dept. 1977).

Double jeopardy.—Habeas corpus is the proper remedy to raise the question of double jeopardy and it is of no consequence that relator has other alternatives available by way of appeal. People ex rel. Pendleton v. Smith, 54 A.D.2d 195, 388 N.Y.S.2d 426 (4th Dept. 1976).

Generally.—Since petitioner would not be entitled to immediate release from custody, but rather only a new trial or appeal, he was not entitled to habeas corpus release. People ex rel. Kaplan v. Commissioner of Correction of the City of New York, 60 N.Y.2d 648, 467 N.Y.S.2d 566, 454 N.E.2d 1309 (1983).

—Having escaped from custody, petitioner no longer had his liberty restrained so as to entitle him to the relief of a writ of habeas corpus. People ex rel. Barrett v. New York State Board of Parole, 58 N.Y.2d 729, 458 N.Y.S.2d 912, 444 N.E.2d 1331 (1982).

—Petitioner, on parole, and no longer restrained in his liberty was not entitled to habeas corpus relief. People ex rel. Brooks v. New York State Bd. of Parole, 65 A.D.2d 763, 410 N.Y.S.2d 4 (2d Dept. 1978).

—A writ of habeas corpus requires that a detained person be brought before the court solely in order to determine the legality of the detention. Wilna v. Prowda, 158 Misc. 2d 579, 601 N.Y.S.2d 518, 519 (Sup. Ct. N.Y. Co. 1993).

Habeas corpus; bail.—A prisoner may bring a writ of habeas corpus to claim that his or her incarceration is illegal due to the fixing of excessive bail or the improper denial of bail. People v. Fredericks, 157 Misc. 2d 822, 598 N.Y.S.2d 682 (Sup. Ct. Bronx Co. 1993).

Parole denial.—An Article 78 proceeding, not a habeas corpus proceeding, is the proper procedure to question whether the Parole Board's denial of parole was given in a meaningful and adequate manner. People v. New York State Dept. of Parole, 54 A.D.2d 1088, 388 N.Y.S.2d 746 (4th Dept. 1976).

—The remedy, when the Board of Parole fails to inform the prisoner of the facts and reasons for the denial of parole, is not habeas corpus leading to release of the prisoner, but an Article 78 proceeding. People ex rel. Ward v. Smith, 52 A.D.2d 755, 382 N.Y.S.2d 415 (4th Dept. 1976).

—Habeas corpus is an appropriate remedy for review of parole revocation proceedings where petitioner did not allege procedural violations. People ex rel. Spann v. Rodriguez, 130 Misc. 2d 1077, 498 N.Y.S.2d 957 (Sup. Ct. Dutchess Co. 1986).

—Habeas Corpus is a proper proceeding through which to test the legality of the denial of due process at a parole revocation hearing. Godfrey v. Preiser, 80 Misc. 2d 361, 363 N.Y.S.2d 463 (Sup. Ct. Erie Co. 1975).

Pro se petition.—Where plaintiff, confined and awaiting trial, sued out two separate writs of habeas corpus concerning the conditions obtaining at the prison, but not at all in derogation of his commitment, the fact that counsel assigned to defend him on the criminal charge did not participate in the habeas corpus proceedings did not prevent the defendant from conducting the proceedings *pro se*. People *ex rel*. Cender v. Warden, Bronx House of Detention for Men, 63 A.D.2d 632, 405 N.Y.S.2d 97 (1st Dept. 1978).

Speedy trial.—When the action is brought to trial, habeas corpus brought on the ground of denial of the right to a speedy trial generally should be denied, without necessarily reaching the merits, but such denial does not preclude raising the issue again provided it has been preserved by proper objection, motion or otherwise. People v. Harrison, 38 N.Y.2d 1025, 384 N.Y.S.2d 450, 348 N.E.2d 926 (1976).

—Once a trial has commenced, a petition for a writ of habeas corpus brought on the ground of denial of the right to a speedy trial should generally be denied since the speedy trial claim may be raised on the direct appeal. Kassebaum v. al-Rahman, 212 A.D.2d 482, 624 N.Y.S.2d 573 (1st Dept. 1995).

§ 7002. Petition.

(a) **By whom made.** A person illegally imprisoned or otherwise restrained in his liberty within the state, or one acting on his behalf, or a party in a child abuse proceeding subsequent to an order of the family court may petition without notice for a writ of habeas corpus to inquire into the cause of such detention and for deliverance. A judge authorized to issue writs of habeas corpus having evidence, in a judicial proceeding before him, that any person is so detained shall, on his own initiative, issue a writ of habeas corpus for the relief of that person.

(b) **To whom made.** Except as provided in paragraph five of this subdivision, a petition for the writ shall be made to:

1. the supreme court, in the judicial district in which the person is detained or

2. the appellate division in the department in which the person is detained; or

3. any justice of the supreme court; or

4. a county judge being or residing within the county in which the person is detained; where there is no judge within the county capable of issuing the writ, or if all within the county capable of doing so have refused, the petition may be made to a county judge being or residing within an adjoining county.

5. in a city having a population of one million or more inhabitants, a person held as a trial inmate in a city detention institution shall petition for writ to the supreme court in the county in which the charge for which the inmate is being detained is pending. Such inmate may also petition for a writ to the appellate division in the department in which he is detained or to any justice of the supreme court provided that the writ shall be made returnable before a justice of the supreme court held in the county in which the charge for which the inmate is being detained is pending.

(c) **Content.** The petition shall be verified and shall state, or shall be accompanied by an affidavit which shall state,

1. that the person in whose behalf the petition is made is detained, naming the person by whom he is detained and the place of detention if they are known, or describing them if they are not

known; where the detention is by virtue of a mandate, a copy of it shall be annexed to the petition, or sufficient reason why a copy could not be obtained shall be stated;

2. the cause or pretense of the detention, according to the best knowledge and belief of the petitioner;

3. that a court or judge of the United States does not have exclusive jurisdiction to order him released;

4. if the writ is sought because of an illegal detention, the nature of the illegality;

5. whether any appeal has been taken from any order by virtue of which the person is detained and, if so, the result;

6. the date, and the court or judge to whom made, or every previous application for the writ, the disposition of each such application and of any appeal taken, and the new facts, if any, presented in the petition that were not presented in any previous application; and

7. if the petition is made to a county outside the county in which the person is detained, the facts which authorize such judge to act.

Amended by L. 1986, Ch. 355, eff. July 17, 1986, amending subds. b(1) and (5).

ANNOTATIONS

Petition; contents.—Although it is well settled that a writ of habeas corpus may not be used to review questions that could have been raised on direct appeal; where appellant claimed that he was improperly jailed on contempt charges and assessed a fine without a hearing, that fundamental statutory claim presented and the circumstances of the case were an exception to the general rule. Kuby v. Warden, 305 A.D.2d 339, 757 N.Y.S.2d 889 (2d Dept. 2003).

—Court properly denied appellant's habeas motion based upon the nature of the issues raised in the application, namely, that he was arrested pursuant to a defective warrant and that the grand jury lacked jurisdiction to indict him; these were the proper subject of a direct appeal or could have been raised in his CPL § 440 motion. Walsh v. Sabourin, 305 A.D.2d 759, 757 N.Y.S.2d 913 (3d Dept. 2003).

—Petition must be denied where on its face it fails to allege facts showing that the petitioner was illegally detained. People *ex rel*. Batsford v. State Div. of Parole, 91 A.D.2d 1112, 458 N.Y.S.2d 365 (3d Dept. 1983).

—Allegations in unverified petition that relator was deprived of legal and writing material were inadequate to establish restraint in excess of constitutional guarantees. People *ex rel*. La Rocca v. Conboy, 40 A.D.2d 936, 336 N.Y.S.2d 724 (3d Dept. 1972).

—In a habeas corpus attack on the probable cause determination in a parole revocation preliminary hearing, the petition must be accompanied by a copy of the hearing minutes, if such is available to the relator, or, at the very least, by a copy of the hearing officer's written report (Board of Parole form 9013-Decision and Summary); an Article 78 proceeding is available to compel the hearing officer to furnish parolee with a written report of the hearing should he fail to do. People *ex rel*. Ayers v. Lombard, 87 Misc. 2d 355, 385 N.Y.S.2d 242 (Monroe Co. Ct. 1976), *aff'd*, 55 A.D.2d 1051, 391 N.Y.S.2d 242 (4th Dept.).

Second petition.—Application for writ of habeas corpus pursuant to CPLR 7002(b)(2) seeking admission to bail was denied where the petition presented no ground not presented in a prior application for habeas corpus relief made to and denied by the Supreme Court, Westchester County. People *ex rel*. Madden v. Mayone, 50 A.D.2d 1010, 377 N.Y.S.2d 255 (3d Dept. 1975).

—Habeas corpus was not a proper vehicle for prison inmate to attack indictment for alleged assault upon correction officer, since the relief requested would not result in his discharge from prison and the grounds for relief asserted had all been previously considered and rejected either in pretrial motions or in a similar application for a writ which was earlier denied. People *ex rel.* Alim v. Smith, 57 A.D.2d 728, 396 N.Y.S.2d 116 (4th Dept. 1977).

To whom made; generally.—Court of Appeals lacks jurisdiction to entertain habeas corpus application. People *ex rel.* Downs v. Amicucci, 90 N.Y.2d 931, 664 N.Y.S.2d 264, 686 N.E.2d 1360 (1998).

—Court of Appeals has jurisdiction to review determination of Commissioner of Correctional Services which found petitioner guilty of violating disciplinary rules relating to possession of controlled substances. People *ex rel.* Fisher v. Stinton, 648 N.Y.S.2d 48, 232 A.D.2d 697 (3d Dept. 1996).

§ 7003. When the writ shall be issued.

(a) **Generally.** The court to whom the petition is made shall issue the writ without delay on any day, or, where the petitioner does not demand production of the person detained or it is clear that there is no disputable issue of fact, order the respondent to show cause why the person detained should not be released. If it appears from the petition or the documents annexed thereto that the person is not illegally detained or that a court or judge of the United States has exclusive jurisdiction to order him released, the petition shall be denied.

(b) **Successive petitions for writ.** A court is not required to issue a writ of habeas corpus if the legality of the detention has been determined by a court of the state on a prior proceeding for a writ of habeas corpus and the petition presents no ground not theretofore presented and determined and the court is satisfied that the ends of justice will not be served by granting it.

(c) **Penalty for violation.** For a violation of this section in refusing to issue the writ, a judge, or, if the petition was made to a court, each member of the court who assents to the violation, forfeits to the person detained one thousand dollars, to be recovered by an action in his name or in the name of the petitioner to his use.

ANNOTATIONS

Res judicata.—Res judicata is theoretically inapplicable to habeas corpus, and a court is always competent to issue a new habeas corpus writ on the same grounds as those of a prior dismissed writ. However, the court will normally dismiss a writ containing nothing new. People *ex rel.* Anderson v. Warden, 68 Misc. 2d 463, 325 N.Y.S.2d 829 (Sup. Ct. Bronx Co. 1971).

Successive petitions.—Where court entertained habeas corpus application for bail pending sentence, after another justice had remanded the applicant without bail pending sentence, it was required to examine bail application anew and it was error to view examination of the merits as a form of appellate review of a justice of coordinate jurisdiction. People *ex rel.* Holtzman v. Malcolm, 50 A.D.2d 746, 376 N.Y.S.2d 4 (1st Dept. 1975).

§ 7004. Content of writ.

(a) **For whom issued.** The writ shall be issued on behalf of the state, and where issued upon the petition of a private person, it shall show that it was issued upon his relation.

(b) **To whom directed.** The writ shall be

directed to, and the respondent shall be, the person having custody of the person detained.

(c) **Before whom returnable.** A writ to secure the discharge of a person from a state institution shall be made returnable before a justice of the supreme court of a county judge being or residing within the county in which the person is detained; if there is no such judge it shall be made returnable before the nearest accessible supreme court justice or county judge. In all other cases, the writ shall be made returnable in the county where it was issued, except that where the petition was made to the supreme court or to a supreme court justice outside the county in which the person is detained, such court or justice may make the writ returnable before any judge authorized to issue it in the county of detention.

(d) **When returnable.** The writ may be made returnable forthwith or on any day or time certain, as the case requires.

(e) **Expenses; undertaking.** A court issuing a writ directed to any person other than a public officer may require the petitioner to pay the charges of bringing up the person detained and to deliver an undertaking to the person having him in custody, in an amount fixed by the court, to pay the charges for taking back the person detained if he should be remanded. Service of the writ shall not be complete until such charge is paid or tendered and such undertaking is delivered.

ANNOTATIONS

Habeas corpus petition; where returnable.—Supreme Court can properly entertain merits of habeas corpus application. People *ex rel.* Backus v. Broome County Dept. of Social Servs., 240 A.D.2d 786, 658 N.Y.S.2d 709 (3d Dept. 1997).

—The failure to make a timely objection to venue constitutes a waiver. People v. Stewart, 83 A.D.2d 713, 442 N.Y.S.2d 643 (3d Dept. 1981).

—Where a writ of habeas corpus is directed to a warden of a state prison, it must be made returnable in the county of detention. The purpose of this rule is to relieve the warden of having to transport the inmate to a county other than the county of detention and of having to incur the resultant travel expenses to distant court houses. People *ex rel.* Cordero v. Thomas, 69 Misc. 2d 28, 329 N.Y.S.2d 131 (Sup. Ct. Kings Co. 1972), *citing* Hogan v. Culkin, 18 N.Y.2d 330, 274 N.Y.S.2d 881 (1966).

§ 7005. Service of the writ.

A writ of habeas corpus may be served on any day. Service shall be made by delivering the writ and a copy of the petition to the person to whom it is directed. If he cannot with due diligence be found, the writ may be served by leaving it and a copy of the petition with any person who has custody of the person detained at the time. Where the person to whom the writ is directed conceals himself or refuses admittance, the writ may be served by affixing it and a copy of the petition in a conspicuous place on the outside either of his dwelling or of the place where the person is detained and mailing a copy of the writ and the petition to him at such dwelling or place, unless the court which issues the writ determines, for good cause shown, that such mailing shall be dispensed with, or directs service in some other manner which it finds reasonably calculated to give notice to such person of the proceeding. If the person detained is in the custody of a person other than the one to whom the writ is directed, a copy of the writ may be served upon the person having such custody with the same effect as if the writ had been directed to him.

§ 7006. Obedience to the writ.

(a) Generally; defects in form. A person upon whom the writ or a copy thereof is served, whether it is directed to him or not, shall make a return to it and, if required by it, produce the body of the person detained at the time and place specified, unless the person detained is too sick or infirm to make the required trip. A writ of habeas corpus shall not be disobeyed for defect of form so long as the identity of the person detained may be derived from its contents.

(b) Compelling obedience. If the person upon whom the writ or a copy thereof is served refuses or neglects fully to obey it, without showing sufficient cause, the court before whom the writ is returnable, upon proof of its service, shall forthwith issue a warrant of attachment against him directed to the sheriff in any county in which such person may be found requiring him to be brought before the court issuing the warrant; he may be ordered committed in close custody to the county jail until he complies with the order of the court. Where such person is a sheriff, the warrant shall be directed to any coroner of the county or to a person specifically designated to execute it. Such coroner or other person shall have power to call to his aid the same assistance as the sheriff in executing the warrant; a sheriff shall be committed to a jail in a county other than his own.

(c) Precept to bring up person detained. A court issuing a warrant of attachment as prescribed in subdivision (b) may at the same time or thereafter, issue a precept to the person to whom the warrant is directed ordering him immediately to bring before the court the person detained.

§ 7007. Warrant preceding or accompanying writ.

A court authorized to issue a writ of habeas corpus, upon satisfactory proof that a person is wrongfully detained and will be removed from the state or suffer irreparable injury before he can be relieved by habeas corpus, shall issue a warrant of attachment directed to an appropriate officer requiring him immediately to bring the person detained before the court. A writ of habeas corpus directed to the person having custody of the person detained shall also be issued. Where it appears that the detention constitutes a criminal offense, the warrant may order the apprehension of the person responsible for the detention, who shall then be brought before the court issuing the warrant and examined as in a criminal case.

§ 7008. Return.

(a) When filed and served. The return shall consist of an affidavit to be served in the same manner as an answer in a special proceeding and filed at the time and place specified in the writ, or, where the writ is returnable forthwith, within twenty-four hours after its service.

(b) Content. The affidavit shall fully and explicitly state whether the person detained is or has been in the custody of the person to whom the writ is directed, the authority and cause of the detention, whether custody has been transferred to another, and the facts of and authority for any such transfer. A copy of any mandate by virtue of which the person is detained shall be annexed to the affidavit, and the original mandate shall be produced at the hearing; where the mandate has been delivered to the person to whom the person detained was transferred, or a copy of it cannot be obtained, the reason for failure to produce it and the substance of the mandate shall be stated in the affidavit.

ANNOTATIONS

Generally.—Special Term did not err in granting respondent an extension of time in which to serve answering papers where respondent stated that the closing of the Attorney-General's office in Sullivan County necessitated the extension, and petitioner failed to show any prejudice. People ex rel. Vanderburgh v. Coombe, 102 A.D.2d 951, 477 N.Y.S.2d 797 (3d Dept. 1984).

Technical irregularities.—Technical irregularities in respondent's return were promptly cured in accordance with court's directive and did not constitute factual issues that would entitle petitioner to an evidentiary hearing. People ex. rel. Jackson v. New York State Dept. of Correctional Servs., 253 A.D.2d 919, 678 N.Y.S.2d 304 (3d Dept. 1998).

§ 7009. Hearing.

(a) Notice before hearing. Where the detention is by virtue of a mandate, the court shall not adjudicate the issues in the proceeding until written notice of the time and place of the hearing has been served either personally eight days prior to the hearing, or in any other manner or time as the court may order,

1. where the mandate was issued in a civil cause, upon the person interested in continuing the detention or upon his attorney; or,

2. where a person is detained by order of the family court, or by order of any court while a proceeding affecting him is pending in the said family court, upon the judge who made the order. In all such proceedings the court shall be represented by the corporation counsel of the city of New York, or outside the city of New York, by the county attorney; or

3. in any other case, upon the district attorney of the county in which the person was detained when the writ was served and upon the district

attorney of the county from which he was committed.

(b) Reply to return. The petitioner or the person detained may deny under oath, orally or in writing, any material allegation of the answering affidavits or allege any fact showing that the person detained is entitled to be discharged.

(c) Hearing to be summary. The court shall proceed in a summary manner to hear the evidence produced in support of and against the detention and to dispose of the proceeding as justice requires.

(d) Sickness or infirmity of person detained. Where it is proved to the satisfaction of the court that the person detained is too sick or infirm to be brought to the appointed place, the hearing may be held without his presence, may be adjourned, or may be held at the place where the prisoner is detained.

(e) Custody during proceeding. Pending final disposition, the court may place the person detained in custody or parole him or admit him to bail as justice requires.

ANNOTATION

Hearing.—Petitioner's application for writ of habeas corpus can be denied without a hearing if documentary proof negates defendant's contention of an unauthorized delegation of authority. People ex rel. Dudley v. West, 87 Misc. 2d 967, 386 N.Y.S.2d 555 (Sup. Ct. Kings Co. 1976).

§ 7010. Determination of proceeding.

(a) Discharge. If the person is illegally detained a final judgment shall be directed discharging him forthwith. No person detained shall be discharged for a defect in the form of the commitment, or because the person detaining him is not entitled to do so if another person is so entitled. A final judgment to discharge a person may be enforced by the court issuing the order by attachment in the manner prescribed in subdivision (b) of section 7006.

(b) Bail. If the person detained has been admitted to bail but the amount fixed is so excessive as to constitute an abuse of discretion, and he is not ordered discharged, the court shall direct a final judgment reducing bail to a proper amount. If the person detained has been denied bail, and he is not ordered discharged, the court shall direct a final judgment admitting him to bail forthwith, if he is entitled to be admitted to bail as a matter of right, or if it appears that the denial of bail constituted an abuse of discretion. Such judgment must fix the amount of bail, specify the time and place at which the person detained is required to appear, and order his release upon bail being given in accordance with the criminal procedure law.

(c) Remand. If the person detained is not ordered discharged and not admitted to bail, a final judgment shall be directed dismissing the proceeding, and, if he was actually produced in court, remanding him to the detention from which he was taken, unless the person then detaining him was not entitled to do so, in which case he shall be remanded to proper detention.

ANNOTATIONS

Bail.—Where the record supports the denial of bail, it is an exercise of discretion resting on a rational basis and thus beyond correction in habeas corpus; in the case, the denial of bail was based upon the determination that defendant, if released on bail, would be likely to flee the jurisdiction. People ex rel. Parker v. Hasenauer, 62 N.Y.2d 777, 477 N.Y.S.2d 320, 465 N.E.2d 1256 (1984).

—When reviewing a bail determination, the habeas corpus court is limited to the record that was before the nisi prius court, and evidence of a change in circumstances which may affect a bail determination must be submitted to the bail setting court for reconsideration; the decision of that court on the renewal of the bail application would then be subject to review by writ of habeas corpus. People ex rel. Taylor v. Meloni, 96 A.D.2d 1149, 468 N.Y.S.2d 94 (4th Dept. 1983).

—In a habeas corpus proceeding seeking to review the denial of bail, the scope of the inquiry is only as to the legality of the denial of bail, as to whether or not the denying Court has abused its discretion by denying bail without reason or for reasons insufficient in law. People ex rel. Gugino v. Braun, 58 A.D.2d 738, 395 N.Y.S.2d 861 (4th Dept. 1977).

Habeas corpus; hearing.—The evidentiary hearing concerning the legality of a detention is to be before the habeas court rather than the detaining agency. People ex rel. Robertson v. New York State Division of Parole, 67 N.Y.2d 197, 501 N.Y.S.2d 634, 492 N.E.2d 762 (1986).

—Absent extraordinary circumstances, the evidence to be considered by a court on the return of a writ of habeas corpus is limited to that adduced before the bail-setting court because the function of the former is limited to collateral review of the exercise of discretion by the latter. People ex rel. Mordkofsky v. Stancari, 93 A.D.2d 826, 460 N.Y.S.2d 830 (2d Dept. 1983).

Jurisdiction.—Habeas corpus is not an appropriate remedy to collaterally attack a judgment of conviction upon constitutional grounds, nor can it be used as a substitute to review alleged errors which were raised on direct appeal from the judgment of conviction or those which could have been raised but were not. People ex rel. Schauer v. Fogg, 92 A.D.2d 647, 460 N.Y.S.2d 144 (3d Dept. 1983).

§ 7011. Appeal.

An appeal may be taken from a judgment refusing to grant a writ of habeas corpus or refusing an order to show cause issued under subdivision (a) of section 7003, or from a judgment made upon the return of such a writ or order to show cause. A person to whom notice is given pursuant to subdivision (a) of section 7009 is a party for purposes of appeal. The attorney-general may appeal in the name of the state in any case where a district attorney might do so. Where an appeal from a judgment admitting a person to bail is taken by the state, his release shall not be stayed thereby.

ANNOTATIONS

Appeals; generally.—No appeal lies from an order entered upon consent, nor from an intermediate order in a habeas corpus proceeding. People ex rel. Falaq v. Dalsheim, 122 A.D.2d 93, 504 N.Y.S.2d 236 (2d Dept. 1986).

—Intermediate order in habeas corpus proceeding is not appealable. Theodore LL v. Phelan, 254 A.D.2d 605, 678 N.Y.S.2d 921 (3d Dept. 1998).

—An order fixing bail is non-appealable, and thus, not reviewable on a direct appeal from the judgment of conviction; such an order may properly be reviewed in a habeas corpus proceeding. People v. Wolcott, 111 A.D.2d 943, 490 N.Y.S.2d 40 (3d Dept. 1985).

Appeal dismissed as moot.—Defendant's appeal was dismissed as moot since he had completed serving the sentence upon which he was paroled. People *ex rel.* Moore v. Dalsheim, 81 A.D.2d 844, 438 N.Y.S.2d 851 (2d Dept. 1981).

—Given that the specific relief requested by petitioner was release on reduced bail or on his own recognizance, his subsequent guilty plea rendered his appeal moot. People *ex rel.* Ferguson v. Campbell, 186 A.D.2d 319, 587 N.Y.S.2d 798 (3d Dept. 1992).

Determination.—The grant of the writ of habeas corpus discharging the defendant from custody was improper since relator only attacked the validity of his incarceration under the day to life term and not the validity of his conviction. People *ex rel.* Hutchings v. Smith, 50 A.D.2d 1097, 377 N.Y.S.2d 336 (4th Dept. 1975).

§ 7012. Redetention after discharge.

A person discharged upon the return of a writ of habeas corpus shall not be detained for the same cause, except by virtue of a subsequent lawful mandate.

MISC. LAWS

ARTICLE 78

PROCEEDING AGAINST BODY OR OFFICER

Section

§ 7801. Nature of proceeding.

Relief previously obtained by writs of certiorari to review, mandamus or prohibition shall be obtained in a proceeding under this article. Wherever in any statute reference is made to a writ or order of certiorari, mandamus or prohibition, such reference shall, so far as applicable, be deemed to refer to the proceeding authorized by this article. Except where otherwise provided by law, a proceeding under this article shall not be used to challenge a determination:

1. which is not final or can be adequately reviewed by appeal to a court or to some other body or officer or where the body or officer making the determination is expressly authorized by statute to rehear the matter upon the petitioner's application unless the determination to be reviewed was made upon a rehearing, or a rehearing has been denied, or the time within which the petitioner can procure a rehearing has elapsed; or

2. which was made in a civil action or criminal matter unless it is an order summarily punishing a contempt committed in the presence of the court.

ANNOTATIONS

Availability of alternative remedies.—It was error for the Appellate Division to have entertained the application for Article 78 relief in the nature of prohibition where the issue could be raised on direct appeal. Wilcox v. Dwyer, 48 N.Y.2d 1003, 425 N.Y.S.2d 550, 401 N.E.2d 908 (1980).

—The extraordinary remedy of prohibition was properly denied because petitioners can institute proceedings in the event of an adverse administrative determination. Beecher v. Brown, 192 A.D.2d 495, 597 N.Y.S.2d 36, 37 (1st Dept. 1993).

—Advisory opinion of the Town of Huntington Ethics Board and Financial Disclosure was not final and is not subject to review in an Article 78 proceeding. Scarparti-Reilly v. Town of Huntington, 300 A.D.2d 404, 751 N.Y.S.2d 753 (2d Dept. 2002).

—Article 78 petition was properly dismissed where appellant failed to exhaust all administrative remedies, completely bypassing the inmate grievance program; there was no final administrative determination to be the subject of review of this Article 78 proceeding. Boddie v. Goord, 307 A.D.2d 555, 762 N.Y.S.2d 295 (3d Dept. 2003).

—The extraordinary remedy of mandamus does not lie since the trial Judge's denial of defendants application to appoint a psychiatrist was reviewable on appeal. DeJesus v. Armer, 74 A.D.2d 736, 425 N.Y.S.2d 705 (4th Dept. 1980).

Discovery issues.—In prohibition proceeding brought to prevent disclosure of grand jury minutes due to lack of jurisdiction, Court of Appeals held that a trial court's preliminary assessment of the sufficiency of the grand jury minutes to support the indictment does not preclude a later disclosure direction. Attorney General v. Firetog, 94 N.Y.2d 477, 706 N.Y.S.2d 666, 727 N.E.2d 1220 (2000).

—Prohibition was properly granted to review an order of the Supreme Court permitting removal of petitioner's hair for use as evidence against him in a criminal charge, in light of the gravity of the possible harm to the individual, the length of time an appeal from a conviction would endure, and the fact that the compulsion may indeed implicate a serious invasion of the individual's constitutional rights if not corrected at once. Barber v. Rubin, 72 A.D.2d 347, 424 N.Y.S.2d 453 (2d Dept. 1980).

—An Article 78 proceeding was an appropriate vehicle for the prosecution to contest an order requiring disclosure of operating and training manuals for breathalyzer machine with the threat of preclusion for non-compliance. Shay v. Mullen, 215 A.D.2d 935, 626 N.Y.S.2d 580 (3d Dept. 1995).

Double jeopardy.—A writ of prohibition is a proper remedy where the defendant was acquitted of the crime of conspiracy to commit murder and he has been indicted in New York for the murder, which constituted double jeopardy and the indictment must be dismissed. Wiley v. Altman, 76 A.D.2d 701, 431 N.Y.S.2d 826 (1st Dept. 1980).

—An Article 78 proceeding lies to prevent double jeopardy in a pending criminal action. Troy v. Jones, 61 A.D.2d 802, 402 N.Y.S.2d 26 (2d Dept. 1978).

—An article 78 proceeding in the nature of prohibition is an appropriate vehicle by which to raise the bar of double jeopardy against further criminal prosecution; petitioner's conviction in a military court did not render the bar of double jeopardy inapplicable. Northrup v. Relin, 197 A.D.2d 228, 613 N.Y.S.2d 506 (4th Dept. 1994).

Generally.—Article 78 proceeding brought by petitioner, a Suffolk County police officer challenging county's refusal to defend him in a civil action arising out of long-running dispute with neighbor, petition dismissed, dispute was not within scope of employment. Salino v. Cimino, 1 N.Y.3d 166, 770 N.Y.S.2d 702, 802 N.E.2d 1100 (2003).

—An interim order of administrative law judge, converting petitioner's motion to dismiss to a motion for summary judgment and then denying it, was not a final determination within meaning of CPLR 7801(1). Bettina Equities Co., LLC v. State, 9 A.D.3d 296, 780 N.Y.S.2d 130 (1st Dept. 2004).

—Article 78 proceeding was converted to a declaratory judgment action because petitioners alleged constitutional violations and a cause of action under CPLR Article 30. Brown v. Wing, 170 Misc. 2d 554, 649 N.Y.S.2d 988 (Sup. Ct. Monroe Co. 1996).

Remedy of prohibition; when available.—Writ of prohibition that alleged trial court exceeded its authority was proper vehicle for the People to challenge the trial court's sua sponte ruling setting aside a jury verdict pursuant to Judiciary Law § 2-b. People v. Dunn, 4 N.Y.3d 495, 796 N.Y.S.2d 331, 829 N.E.2d 295 (2005).

—Remedy of prohibition, although unavailable to review an error of law, is available where a court exceeds its authority or where petitioner challenges the court's subject matter jurisdiction. Pirro v. Angiolillo, 89 N.Y.2d 351, 653 N.Y.S.2d 237, 675 N.E.2d 1189 (1996).

—Prohibition is not available to correct mere errors of law, procedural or substantive in litigation, rather, it is the means to prevent an arrogation of power in violation of a person's rights, particularly constitutional rights. Nicholson v. State Comm. on Judicial Conduct, 50 N.Y.2d 597, 431 N.Y.S.2d 340, 409 N.E.2d 848 (1980).

—In a special proceeding seeking relief by way of a writ of prohibition, it is incumbent on the applicant to demonstrate that a public officer is proceeding in excess of his or her authority. Cain v. Fernandez, 191 A.D.2d 322, 595 N.Y.S.2d 181, 183 (1st Dept. 1993).

—Writ of prohibition can be used to prohibit prosecution of a criminal case when the prosecution "intrudes on the prerogatives of another branch of the government" or it is alleged that the underlying prosecution is placed in the "wrong venue, known as geographical jurisdiction" (CPL Article 20). Norman v. Hynes, 20 A.D.3d 125, 799 N.Y.S.2d 222 (2d Dept. 2005).

—The extraordinary remedy of prohibition is available only where there is a clear legal right and, in cases where judicial authority is questioned, only when the court acts or threatens to act without jurisdiction or in excess of its authorized powers. Mahl v. Donovan, 191 A.D.2d 565, 595 N.Y.S.2d 107, 108 (2d Dept. 1993).

—Although prohibition is an appropriate remedy for a challenge to the geographic jurisdiction of a district attorney to indict and prosecute a defendant and may be used to prevent the re-indictment of a defendant, "a writ of prohibition does not issue as of right but, rather, is a discretionary remedy." McLaughlin v. Eidens, 292 A.D.2d 712, 740 N.Y.S.2d 147 (3d Dept. 2002).

—Even when appropriate, the writ of prohibition may be denied in the court's discretion. Carney v. Feldstein, 193 A.D.2d 1016, 597 N.Y.S.2d 982, 984 (3d Dept. 1993).

—Where the foundation of petitioner's challenge to a warrant of arrest and order of extradition is that the Governor exceeded his jurisdiction and power by overruling a prior Family Court decision and by failing to follow the mandates set out in CPL § 570.16, and where petitioner was released on bail, petitioner was entitled to an Article 78 proceeding. Fabbri v. Pataki, 169 Misc. 2d 1026, 648 N.Y.S.2d 219 (Sup. Ct. Westchester Co. 1996).

Grand jury issues.—Whether the Trial Justice shall inspect the grand jury minutes is within the sound discretion of the Trial Justice and is not reviewable by an appellate court either on direct appeal or in the guise of an Article 78 proceeding. Ruiz v. Sullivan, 58 A.D.2d 754, 395 N.Y.S.2d 1017 (1st Dept. 1977).

—The matter of presentation of evidence of an offense to a Grand Jury is a matter of prosecutorial discretion and the question of the existence of reasonable cause to hold defendants for Grand Jury action is a matter of judicial discretion; mandamus therefore will not issue to compel the performance of these discretionary acts. Coppola v. People, 87 Misc. 2d 801, 386 N.Y.S.2d 279 (Sup. Ct. Ulster Co. 1976).

Jurisdiction.—Prohibition was proper to challenge the geographical jurisdiction of Kings County to indict and prosecute defendants; challenge to geographical jurisdiction may be properly made prior to trial. Steingut v. Gold, 42 N.Y.2d 311, 397 N.Y.S.2d 765, 366 N.E.2d 854 (1977).

—The law is well settled where, determination is unambiguous and its effect certain, statutory period to institute an Article 78 proceeding commences as soon as aggrieved party is notified. Pirrone v. Town of Wallkill, 6 A.D.3d 447, 774 N.Y.S.2d 361 (2d Dept. 2004).

—An administrative determination, specifically a determination of the New York City Transit Authority, issued by respondent after a hearing which demoted petitioner from his position as Manager/Superintendent of Division of Security, cannot be disturbed unless it is arbitrary and capricious. Kreisler v. N.Y. City Transit Auth., 2 A.D.3d 856, 770 N.Y.S.2d 402 (2d Dept. 2003), aff'd, 2 N.Y.3d 775, 780 N.Y.S.2d 302, 812 N.E.2d 1250 (2004).

—The procedure for challenging a retirement system service credit determination is to request a hearing and redetermination, if a party is not satisfied with final determination, next step would be to commence an article 78 proceeding. Cole-Hatchard v. McCall, 4 A.D.3d 715, 772 N.Y.S.2d 415 (3d Dept. 2004).

Mandamus to compel.—Newspaper reporter seeking disclosure of 911 tapes and transcripts from September 11, 2001, successfully brought article 78 proceeding to compel disclosure of those taped communications from the Fire Department after FOIL request had been denied. N.Y. Times Co. v. City of New York Fire Dept., 4 N.Y.3d 477, 796 N.Y.S.2d 302, 829 N.E.2d 266 (2005).

—Where a person seeks to compel the performance of a purely ministerial act, such as a motion to compel the recalculation of jail time credit, such relief may be sought through a petition in the nature of mandamus to compel. Bottom v. Goord, 96 N.Y.2d 870, 730 N.Y.S.2d 767, 756 N.E.2d 55 (2001).

—Writ of mandamus was proper vehicle for a criminal appellant to have employed to pursue the return of property seized pursuant to a search warrant. People v. Reynolds, (In re Search Warrant), 19 A.D.3d 107, 795 N.Y.S.2d 450 (1st Dept. 2005).

—Petitioner's article 78 petition challenging denial of merit time consideration under this section because he was convicted of an A-1 felony offense could not lie; granting or withholding of merit time is a discretionary determination. Coleman v. Goord, 307 A.D.2d 462, 761 N.Y.S.2d 556 (3d Dept. 2003)

Miscellaneous.—Relief under CPLR article 78 in the nature of mandamus does not lie to compel the removal by a superior court of charges pending in a local criminal court in order to assure a defendant trial before a lawyer-trained Judge. Legal Aid Society of Sullivan County v. Scheinman, 53 N.Y.2d 12, 439 N.Y.S.2d 882, 422 N.E.2d 542 (1981).

—There is a proper case for an application for a writ of prohibition, when the validity of a search warrant will go unchallenged as there is no prosecution, no indication that there ever will be a prosecution, and thus no opportunity for a motion to suppress the evidence. B.T. Productions, Inc. v. Barr, 44 N.Y.2d 226, 405 N.Y.S.2d 9, 376 N.E.2d 171 (1978).

—Where defendant pled guilty to a lesser offense relying on the special prosecutor's representation that his subsequent testimony before a special grand jury would be brought to the attention of the State Liquor Authority, cancellation of defendant's license was successfully challenged in an Article 78 proceeding for failure to give much weight to the special prosecutor's promise and defendant's cooperation. Chaipis v. State Liquor Auth., 44 N.Y.2d 57, 404 N.Y.S.2d 76, 375 N.E.2d 32 (1978).

—Petitioner's argument that the district attorney improperly conditioned consent to an adjournment in contemplation of dismissal, CPL § 170.55, on her waiver of her statutory right to the return of her fingerprints, CPL § 160.50, was not properly raised by an Article 78 proceeding; prohibition lies only where the very jurisdiction and power of the court are at issue. Streisfeld v. Vergari, 69 A.D.2d 864, 415 N.Y.S.2d 440 (2d Dept. 1979).

—Prohibition was granted where District Attorney improperly proceeded by way of ex parte application and obtained orders directing the police department to deliver the internal investigation file to the District Attorney's office where it would be available for inspection by the defense since the District Attorney could have subpoenaed it before the County Court or the Grand Jury. Rochester Police Dept. v. Bergin, 68 A.D.2d 340, 416 N.Y.S.2d 938 (4th Dept. 1979).

Parole issues.—It was improper, pursuant to CPLR Article 78, for the court to accelerate the date of petitioner's next scheduled release hearing where no impropriety on the part of the parole board in the original hearing was found. Ryder v. New York State Bd. of Parole, 87 A.D.2d 891, 449 N.Y.S.2d 529 (2d Dept. 1982).

Plea issues.—Prohibition was granted where the judge exceeded her authority by directing the District Attorney to modify his policy on accepting guilty pleas to reduced charges in driving while intoxicated cases. Cosgrove v. LaMendola, 73 A.D.2d 810, 423 N.Y.S.2d 736 (4th Dept. 1979).

—Prohibition was granted to extent of annulling the court action in vacating, sua sponte, the defendant's pleas of guilty to manslaughter, first degree; instead of vacating defendant's pleas the court should have afforded the defendant the option (1) of withdrawing his pleas in view of possible self-defense, or (2) if the court concluded on the basis of the probation reports that the "promised" sentence was inadequate it should have given defendant the alternative of either withdrawing his pleas and standing trial, or allowing the pleas to remain if he accepted a sentence other than "promised." Fernandez v. Silbowitz, 59 A.D.2d 837, 398 N.Y.S.2d 896 (1st Dept. 1977).

Recusal.—Even if actual bias or prejudice is shown, it would not be grounds for disqualification of the trial judge but would only be reviewable on appeal on a showing that it had unjustly affected the result. Katz v. Denzer, 70 A.D.2d 548, 416 N.Y.S.2d 607 (1st Dept. 1979).

Replevin.—In a proceeding pursuant to Article 78 to recover certain property claimed to be in the possession of the Police Property Clerk, the allegations contained in the petition were more properly cognizable in an action for replevin and not, as pleaded, in the posture of an Article 78 proceeding. Stanley v. Property Clerk of Police Dept. of the Town of Ramapo, 63 A.D.2d 970, 405 N.Y.S.2d 763 (2d Dept. 1978).

Review.—In Article 78 proceeding to review the revocation of petitioner's pistol permit on the grounds that he lacked "good moral character," Commissioner's determination was not arbitrary or capricious and was supported by substantial evidence in the record; although there was no evidence of petitioner's direct involvement in criminal activity, evidence showed that he was a member of the Hell's Angels Motorcycle Gang and an officer of the corporation that sold the group's merchandise, that other members of the group had been convicted of crimes, and that the group was linked to criminal activities. Biganini v. Gallagher, 293 A.D.2d 603, 742 N.Y.S.2d 73 (2d Dept. 2002).

—"[T]he remedy for the return of property allegedly wrongfully withheld by the police after the dismissal of a criminal proceeding is the commencement of an action for replevin or a CPLR article 78 proceeding to review a refusal by municipal officials after a demand." Smith v. Scott, 294 A.D.2d 11, 740 N.Y.S.2d 425 (2d Dept. 2002).

—Absent an Article 78 proceeding, a court lacks the authority to review the board's registration determination under the Sex Offender Registration Act. In re Mandel, 293 A.D.2d 750, 742 N.Y.S.2d 321 (2d Dept. 2002).

—A prisoner's Article 78 proceeding to be transferred back to the original correctional facility will be denied where he fails to show that he was transferred as a disciplinary matter or there were unusual circumstances which would have reasonably established a restriction on the power of the commissioner to transfer the inmate. Sebastiano v. Harris, 76 A.D.2d 1004, 429 N.Y.S.2d 288 (2d Dept. 1980).

—Determination by commissioner of correctional services finding petitioner guilty of violating a disciplinary rule, drug possession, was supported by substantial evidence. Cliff v. Kingsley, 293 A.D.2d 954, 742 N.Y.S.2d 408 (3d Dept. 2002).

—In review of petitioner's tier III disciplinary hearing, court found that "in the absence of any support in the record for the hearing officer's conclusion that the two inmate witnesses could not provide relevant testimony, petitioner was denied the right to call witnesses and, therefore, the determination must be annulled." Dawes v. Selsky, 286 A.D.2d 806, 730 N.Y.S.2d 563 (3d Dept. 2001).

—The remedy, when the Board of Parole fails to inform the prisoner of the facts and reasons for the denial of parole, is not habeas corpus leading to release of the prisoner, but an Article 78 proceeding. People ex rel. Ward v. Smith, 52 A.D.2d 755, 382 N.Y.S.2d 415 (4th Dept. 1976).

Sentencing.—Prohibition is not available to defeat the court's power to impose sentence on an absconding petitioner at the appropriate and designated time. Whitley v. Cioffi, 74 A.D.2d 230, 427 N.Y.S.2d 23 (1st Dept. 1980).

Speedy trial.—The extraordinary remedy of a writ of prohibition does not lie where the claim is a denial of statutory or constitutional speedy trial rights. Cummings v. Koppell, 212 A.D.2d 11, 627 N.Y.S.2d 480 (3d Dept. 1995).

—An Article 78 proceeding for a judgment prohibiting the District Attorney and the Judge of the County Court from proceeding on an indictment will not lie where it is claimed that the defendant has been denied his right to a speedy trial—whether that claim is based on statutory or constitutional grounds. Valenti v. Mark, 59 A.D.2d 651, 398 N.Y.S.2d 390 (4th Dept. 1977).

Statute of limitations.—An administrative determination becomes "final and binding upon the petitioner," so as to trigger the four-month limitations period for Article 78 review, when two requirements are met: (1) the agency must have reached a definitive position on the issue that inflicts actual, concrete injury; and (2) the injury inflicted cannot be prevented or significantly ameliorated by further administrative action or by steps available to the complaining party. In this case, grant of a 60-day grace period did not change the definitiveness of the agency's position and was not included in calculating four-month period. Best Payphones, Inc., v. Dept. of Information

& Tech. of City of New York, 5 N.Y.3d 30, 799 N.Y.S.2d 182, 832 N.E.2d 38 (2005); Stop-the-Barge v. Cahill, 1 N.Y.3d 218, 771 N.Y.S.2d 40, 803 N.E.2d 361 (2003).

—Agency action was final when petitioner was notified that it was required to file a new application for its landfill proposal with the Adirondack Park Agency (APA), since agency gave definitive response that there would be no further administrative action until a new application was filed. Essex v Zagata, 91 N.Y.2d 447, 672 N.Y.S.2d 281, 695 N.E.2d 232 (1998).

—Four-month statute of limitations began to run upon county police departments' refusal to expunge petitioner's arrest record upon his demand. Loren v. Rozzi, 73 A.D.2d 934, 423 N.Y.S.2d 506 (2d Dept. 1980).

—Considering the mandamus nature of petitioner's proceeding, the four-month Statue of Limitations under CPLR 217 commenced to run, not from the date of respondent's denial of parole, but from the date of the Parole Board Chairman's refusal to perform a duty imposed upon him by law. Chamberlain v. Regan, 52 A.D.2d 1039, 384 N.Y.S.2d 578 (4th Dept. 1976).

§ 7802. Parties.

(a) Definition of "body or officer." The expression "body or officer" includes every court, tribunal, board, corporation, officer, or other person, or aggregation of persons, whose action may be affected by a proceeding under this article.

(b) Persons whose terms of office have expired; successors. Whenever necessary to accomplish substantial justice, a proceeding under this article may be maintained against an officer exercising judicial or quasi-judicial functions, or member of a body whose term of office has expired. And any party may join the successor of such officer or member of a body or other person having custody of the record of proceedings under review.

(c) Prohibition in favor of another. Where the proceeding is brought to restrain a body or officer from proceeding without or in excess of jurisdiction in favor of another, the latter shall be joined as a party.

(d) Other interested persons. The court may direct that notice of the proceeding be given to any person. It may allow other interested persons to intervene.

Amended by L. 1981, Ch. 502 eff. July 15, 1981.

ANNOTATIONS

Intervention.—Court in Article 78 proceeding has greater latitude in allowing intervention by virtue of wording contained in statute than in actions brought under CPLR 1013, which requires intervention in an action to involve a "common question of law or fact." Ferguson v. Barrios-Paoli, 279 A.D.2d 396, 720 N.Y.S.2d 43 (1st Dept. 2001).

—Intervention of "interested parties" is permitted by statute (CPLR § 7802) and is more liberal than the intervention permitted under CPLR § 1013. In addition, the decision to allow intervention lies within the discretion of the court. Tennessee Gas Pipeline Co. v. Town of Chatham Bd. of Assessors, 239 A.D.2d 831, 657 N.Y.S.2d 269 (3d Dept. 1997).

Parties.—Article 78 may not be used against executive officials; therefore, Article 78 proceeding against governor was not available avenue to prevent him from signing agreement. Saratoga County Chamber of Commerce Inc. v. Pataki, 100 N.Y.2d 801, 766 N.Y.S.2d 654, 798 N.E.2d 1047 (2003).

—State is not a "body or officer" against whom a CPLR article 78 proceeding may be brought. Capruso v. New York State Police, 300 A.D.2d 27, 751 N.Y.S.2d 179 (1st Dept. 2002).

—The attorney for a defendant in a criminal case is not a proper party petitioner, even nominally, to bring an Article 78 proceeding. Katz v. Denzer, 70 A.D.2d 548, 416 N.Y.S.2d 607 (1st Dept. 1979).

—A special district attorney who is duly appointed has standing to bring an Article 78 proceeding to enforce proper sentencing, in this case, to annul the order of the Rensselaer County Conditional Release Commission granting respondent conditional release from jail when commission exceeded its authority by considering a resubmitted petition within less than sixty days after the initial petition was denied, in violation of CL § 273. Winn v. Rensselaer County Conditional Release Comm'n, 6 A.D.3d 929, 775 N.Y.S.2d 412 (3d Dept. 2004).

§ 7803. Questions raised.

The only questions that may be raised in a proceeding under this article are:

1. whether the body or officer failed to perform a duty enjoined upon it by law; or

2. whether the body or officer proceeded, is proceeding or is about to proceed without or in excess of jurisdiction; or

3. whether a determination was made in violation of lawful procedure, was affected by an error of law or was arbitrary and capricious or an abuse of discretion, including abuse of discretion as to the measure or mode of penalty or discipline imposed; or

4. whether a determination made as a result of a hearing held, and at which evidence was taken, pursuant to direction by law is, on the entire record, supported by substantial evidence.

5. A proceeding to review the final determination or order of the state review officer pursuant to subdivision three of section forty-four hundred four of the education law shall be brought pursuant to article four of this chapter and such subdivision; provided, however, that the provisions of this article shall not apply to any proceeding commenced on or after the effective date of this subdivision.

Amended by L. 2003, Ch. 492, § 2, eff. Sept. 1, 2003, adding subd. 5, and shall apply to proceedings commenced on or after such effective date.

ANNOTATIONS

Affected by error of law.—The New York City Loft Board's determination of abandonment was properly annulled as either a violation of lawful procedure or affected by an error of law since at time landlord applied for abandonment order, it had not registered loft as an interim multiple dwelling or paid annual registration fees, as required by 29 RCNY 2-05(e)(1)(i). Conley v. N.Y. City Loft Bd., 5 A.D.3d 175, 772 N.Y.S.2d 519 (1st Dept. 2004).

—Plaintiff's challenge to housing authority's decision to terminate her tenancy due to plaintiff violating agreement to exclude her son from premises because of his drug-related arrest was appropriately brought as an Article 78 proceeding; proceeding raised the question whether housing authority's determination was "affected by an error of law" and was governed by the statute of limitations contained in CPLR 217. Blackman v. New York City Housing Auth., 280 A.D.2d 324, 720 N.Y.S.2d 141 (1st Dept. 2001).

Judicial review limited.—Judicial review under § 7803(3) is limited to whether an administrative agency's determinations are arbitrary or capricious; New York City Department of Citywide Administrative Services, which has policymaking authority and functional responsibility for civil service matters in city, is afforded discretion; if rational basis for agency's

conclusions are present, determination will not be disturbed. Hughes v. Doherty, 5 N.Y.3d 100, 800 N.Y.S.2d 85, 833 N.E.2d 228 (2005).

—Upon finding that Division of Housing and Community Renewals' (DHCR) decision to deny owners deregulation was arbitrary and capricious, and determination was affected by an error of law, Court of Appeals reversed order and remitted matter to DHCR for further proceedings. Classic Realty, LLC. V. New York State Div. of Hous. & Community Renewal, 2 N.Y.3d 142, 777 N.Y.S.2d 1, 808 N.E.2d 1260 (2004).

—The Appellate Division is subject to the same limited scope of review applicable to the Court of Appeals review of administrative sanctions: "the sanction must be upheld unless it shocks the judicial conscience and, therefore, constitutes an abuse of discretion as a matter of law." Featherstone v. Franco, 95 N.Y.2d 550, 720 N.Y.S.2d 93, 742 N.E.2d 607 (2000).

—Court cannot substitute its judgment for that of an administrative agency unless the agency has acted in a manner that is irrational, arbitrary, capricious, or illegal. Arrocha v. Board of Educ., 93 N.Y.2d 361, 690 N.Y.S.2d 503, 712 N.E.2d 699 (1999).

—Standard of judicial review of.Civil Service Commission's action under Civil Service Law § 50(4) is whether that body's action was arbitrary or capricious, or an abuse of discretion. City of New York v. O'Connor, 9 A.D.3d 328, 780 N.Y.S.2d 590 (1st Dept. 2004).

—"The decision of an administrative agency to deny a license 'cannot be disturbed unless it is arbitrary and capricious.' However, '[a] decision of an administrative agency which neither adheres to its own prior precedent nor indicates its reason for reaching a different result on essentially the same facts is arbitrary and capricious.' " Klein v. Levin, 305 A.D.2d 316, 760 N.Y.S.2d 462 (1st Dept. 2003).

—Denial of an article 78 petition to annul a "certificate of appropriateness" (COA) issued by respondent New York City Landmarks Preservation Commission with regard to proposed plans for the construction of a new building, was proper where the issuance of the COA had a rational basis in the "judgment . . . of the Commission's historians and architects." Citineighbors Coalition of Historic Carnegie Hill v. N.Y.C. Landmarks Preservation Comm'n, 306 A.D.2d 113, 762 N.Y.S.2d 59 (1st Dept. 2003).

—Since determination to terminate petitioner's employment as a probationary teacher as well as her teaching certificate and license was neither arbitrary nor capricious, determination will not be disturbed in Article 78 proceeding. Von Gizycki v. Levy, 3 A.D.3d 572, 771 N.Y.S.2d 174 (2d Dept. 2004).

—Parole Board's determination which complies with applicable statutory requirements, is not subject to judicial review; judicial intervention warranted only upon a "showing of irrationality bordering on impropriety;" Board considered relevant factors, and concluded that there was a reasonable probability that petitioner could not live at liberty without violating law. Erdheim v. Travis, 7 A.D.3d 876, 776 N.Y.S.2d 920 (3d Dept. 2004).

Mandamus to compel.—Motion to compel granted; request pursuant to Freedom of Information Law (FOIL) for documents pertaining to traffic safety, which were not subject to discovery in lawsuits arising out of traffic accidents, was improperly denied, since documents were subject to disclosure pursuant to FOIL. Newsday, Inc., v. State Dept. of Transp., 5 N.Y.3d 84, 800 N.Y.S.2d 67, 833 N.E.2d 210 (2005).

—Where a person seeks to compel the performance of a purely ministerial act, such as a motion to compel the recalculation of jail time credit, such relief may be sought through a petition in the nature of mandamus to compel. Bottom v. Goord, 96 N.Y.2d 870, 730 N.Y.S.2d 767, 756 N.E.2d 55 (2001).

—Court properly refused to compel respondents to pay petitioner upon his retirement for accrued but unused vacation time in excess of 90 days pursuant to Nassau County Ordinance No. 543-1995 § 3.4(b), since decision was not arbitrary, capricious, or an abuse of discretion, respondent Office of the Comptroller for the County of Nassau did not have authority to make payment without a request from respondent Office of the County Executive for the County of Nassau, and County Executive's failure to authorize payment was in turn rational and had a reasonable basis in law. Seckler v. County of Nassau, 7 A.D.3d 720, 778 N.Y.S.2d 41 (2d Dept. 2004).

—"[T]he extraordinary remedy of mandamus will lie only to

compel the performance of a ministerial act and only when there exists a clear legal right to the relief sought." Midgley v. Goldberg, 2 A.D.3d 735, 768 N.Y.S.2d 624 (2d Dept. 2003).

—In order to commence a mandamus to compel proceeding, "it is necessary to make a demand and await refusal. The Statute of Limitations begins to run on the date of the refusal and expires four months thereafter." Vestal Teacher's Ass'n v. Vestal Cent. Sch. Dist., 5 A.D.3d 922, 773 N.Y.S.2d 468 (3d Dept. 2004), aff'd, 4 N.Y.3d 175, 791 N.Y.S.2d 507, 824 N.E.2d 947 (2005).

—"Mandamus to compel is appropriate only where a clear legal right to the relief sought has been shown, the action sought to be compelled is one commanded to be performed by law and no administrative discretion is involved." N.Y. Civ. Liberties Union v. State, 3 A.D.3d 811, 771 N.Y.S.2d 563 (3d Dept. 2004).

—Mandamus to compel is an extraordinary remedy and is available against an administrative officer only to compel the performance of a duty enjoined by law; defendant has no right to be present at the autopsy of the victim conducted at the District Attorney's request. Scheufler v. Bruno, 250 A.D.2d 268, 684 N.Y.S.2d 305 (3d Dept. 1999).

Mandamus to review.—The new premises license, issued pursuant to 38 RCNY § 5-23(a), effective June 2001, permitted, transport of firearms to authorized target ranges and hunting areas, since respondent neither exceeded his jurisdiction nor violated State law in promulgating these new licensing regulations and procedures, petitioner failed to show that the State's enabling statute preempted any and all local regulation in this field, dismissal of petitioner's Article 78 petition affirmed. De Illy v. Kelly, 6 A.D.3d 217, 775 N.Y.S.2d 256 (1st Dept. 2004).

—Grounds for mandamus to review set forth in CPLR § 7803(3) are governed by a four-month statute of limitations. Schulz v. Town Bd., 253 A.D.2d 956, 677 N.Y.S.2d 826 (3d Dept. 1998).

Miscellaneous—Article 78 proceeding was appropriate to annul a determination of Rensselaer County Conditional Release Commission granting respondent conditional release from jail when commission exceeded its authority by considering a resubmitted petition within less than sixty days after the initial petition was denied as required by statute. Winn v. Rensselaer County Conditional Release Comm'n, 6 A.D.3d 929, 775 N.Y.S.2d 412 (3d Dept. 2004).

Parole denial.—Appeals unit decision affirming revocation of parole and penalty is a final and binding determination and "triggers the statute of limitations when the petitioner is aggrieved by the determination"; the proceeding challenging that determination must be commenced within four months. Carter v. New York State, Division of Parole, 95 N.Y.2d 267, 716 N.Y.S.2d 364, 739 N.E.2d 730 (2000).

—Record makes clear that parole board considered factors mandated by Exec. Law § 259-i in making its determination; board's emphasis on the serious nature of the prisoner's crime was permissible and does not, in and of itself, demonstrate that the Board's ultimate decision was vitiated by "irrationality bordering on impropriety." Henderson v. N.Y. State Div. of Parole, 295 A.D.2d 678, 743 N.Y.S.2d 198 (3d Dept. 2002).

—In an Article 78 proceeding challenging the determination of the Parole Board's denial of petitioner's application for release, evidence that Board considered petitioner's earned eligibility credit and institutional record, as well as his lack of insight into the nature and effect of his crime, was sufficient to support the determination. Santos v. New York State Dept. of Parole, 267 A.D.2d 533, 698 N.Y.S.2d 563 (3d Dept. 1999).

Probationary employment.—Superintendent's notice to petitioner that he would recommend the end of petitioner's probationary employment was not a "final determination subject to review in a proceeding subject to CPLR 7803." Perlin v. South Orangetown Central School Dist., 240 A.D.2d 499, 658 N.Y.S.2d 141 (2d Dept. 1997).

Prohibition.—Prohibition was not available to plaintiffs in a suit to prevent governor from signing a contract allowing gambling on Indian lands within the state and an injunction against the state to prevent the use of state funds for the project. Saratoga County Chamber of Commerce Inc., v. Pataki, 100 N.Y.2d 801, 766 N.Y.S.2d 654, 798 N.E.2d 1047 (2003).

—In prohibition proceeding brought to prevent disclosure of grand jury minutes due to lack of jurisdiction, the Court of Appeals held that a trial court's preliminary assessment of the sufficiency of the grand jury minutes to support the indictment does not preclude a later disclosure direction. Attorney General v. Firetog, 94 N.Y.2d 477, 706 N.Y.S.2d 666, 727 N.E.2d 1220 (2000).

—Prohibition was not applicable where the trial court's order compelling the District Attorney to disclose the identity of the informant was not in excess of the court's jurisdiction. In re Santucci, 81 A.D.2d 872, 439 N.Y.S.2d 43 (2d Dept. 1981).

—An Article 78 proceeding was the proper vehicle to test the jurisdiction of the Kings County Grand Jury where all of the misconduct charged in the indictment occurred in New York County. Steingut v. Gold, 54 A.D.2d 481, 388 N.Y.S.2d 622 (2d Dept. 1976), aff'd, 42 N.Y.2d 311, 397 N.Y.S.2d 765, 366 N.E.2d 854.

—Prohibition should only issue where a court commits acts in excess of its jurisdiction so serious as to constitute a gross abuse of power and which requires summary correction. B.T. Productions, Inc. v. Barr, 54 A.D.2d 315, 388 N.Y.S.2d 483 (4th Dept. 1976), aff'd, 44 N.Y.2d 226, 405 N.Y.S.2d 9, 376 N.E.2d 171.

Review of religious discrimination grievance.—Petitioner properly brought Article 78 proceeding to review determination of the Department of Corrections Services Inmate Grievance Program Central Office Review Committee, which denied petitioner's religious discrimination grievance. Cancel v. Goord, 278 A.D.2d 321, 717 N.Y.S.2d 610 (2d Dept. 2000), appeal denied, 96 N.Y.2d 707 (2001).

—Petitioner brought an Article 78 proceeding to ask for a review of the respondent's denial of access to certain documents requested pursuant to the Freedom of Information Act, upon review, court determined that additional documents were not privileged and should have been released. Morgan v. N.Y. State Dept. of Envtl. Conservation, 9 A.D.3d 586, 779 N.Y.S.2d 643 (3d Dept. 2004).

Substantial evidence standard.—In a proceeding pursuant to CPLR 7803, substantial evidence is the standard and hearsay is admissible and can be used alone to support a finding of substantial evidence. BiCounty Brokerage S. Corp. v. State of N.Y. Ins. Dept., 4 A.D.3d 470, 771 N.Y.S.2d 690 (2d Dept. 2004).

—Where proceeding does not raise a substantial evidence question, transfer from Supreme Court to Appellate Division pursuant to CPLR 7804(g) was error. Martinez v. Goord, 6 A.D.3d 1208, 775 N.Y.S.2d 716 (4th Dept. 2004).

—Where determination which found petitioner guilty of seven specifications of incompetence and misconduct following a hearing held pursuant to Civil Service Law § 75 and then dismissed him from his position as director library, was supported by substantial evidence, including petitioner's failure to draft or propose a short-or long-term plan for library, prepare a budget or conduct staff evaluations, determination was not an abuse of discretion and will not be disturbed. Hodosy v. Bd. of Trs., 5 A.D.3d 982, 773 N.Y.S.2d 316 (4th Dept. 2004).

—Substantial evidence standard described in subd. 4 does not apply to the administrative hearing afforded petitioner pursuant to the Alcoholic Beverage Control Law § 54(3) because it is not an "adversarial, quasi-judicial hearing." Capizzi v. New York State Div. of Alcohol Beverage Control, 231 A.D.2d 881, 647 N.Y.S.2d 594 (4th Dept. 1996).

§ 7804. Procedure.

(a) Special proceeding. A proceeding under this article is a special proceeding.

(b) Where proceeding brought. A proceeding under this article shall be brought in the supreme court, in the county specified in subdivision (b) of section 506 except as that subdivision otherwise provides.

(c) Time for service of notice of petition and answer. Unless the court grants an order to show cause to be served in lieu of a notice of petition at a time and in a manner specified therein, a notice of petition, together with the petition and affidavits specified in the notice, shall be served on any adverse party at least twenty days before the time at which the partition is noticed to be heard. An answer and supporting affidavits, if any, shall be served at least five days before such time. A reply, together with supporting affidavits, if any, shall be served at least one day before such time. In the case of a proceeding pursuant to this article against a state body or officers, or against members of a state body or officers whose terms have expired as authorized by subdivision (b) of section 7802 of this chapter, commenced either by order by other to show cause or notice of petition, in addition to the service thereof provided in this section; the order to show cause or notice of petition must be served upon the attorney general by delivery of such order or notice to an assistant attorney general at an office of the attorney general in the county in the county in which venue of the proceeding is designated, or if there is no office of the attorney general within such county, at the office of the attorney general nearest such county. In the case of a proceeding pursuant to this article against members of bodies of governmental subdivisions whose terms have expired as authorized by subdivision (b) of section 7802 of this chapter, the order to show cause or notice of petition must be served upon such governmental subdivision in accordance with section 311 of this chapter.

(d) **Pleadings.** There shall be a verified petition, which may be accompanied by affidavits or other written proof. Where there is an adverse party there shall be a verified answer, which must state pertinent and material facts showing the grounds of the respondent's action complained of. There shall be a reply to a counterclaim denominated as such and there shall be a reply to new matter in the answer or where the accuracy of proceedings annexed to the answer is disputed. The court may permit such other pleadings as are authorized in an action upon such terms as it may specify.

(e) **Answering affidavits; record to be filed; default.** The body or officer shall file with the answer a certified transcript of the record of the proceedings under consideration, unless such a transcript has already been filed with the clerk of the court. The respondent shall also serve and submit with the answer affidavits or other written proof showing such evidentiary facts as shall entitle him to a trial of any issue of fact. The court may order the body or officer to supply any defect or omission in the answer, transcript or an answering affidavit. Statements made in the answer, transcript or an answering affidavit are not conclusive upon the petitioner. Should the body or officer fail either to file and serve an answer or to move to dismiss, the court may either issue a judgment in favor of the petitioner or order that an answer be submitted.

(f) **Objections in point of law.** The respondent may raise an objection in point of law by setting it forth in his answer or by a motion to dismiss the petition, made upon notice within the time allowed for answer. If the motion is denied, the court shall permit the respondent to answer, upon such terms as may be just; and unless the order specifies otherwise, such answer shall be served and filed within five days after service of the order with notice of entry; and the petitioner may re-notice the matter for hearing upon two days' notice, or the respondent may re-notice the matter for hearing upon service of the answer upon seven days' notice. The petitioner may raise an objection in point of law to new matter contained in the answer by setting it forth in his reply or by moving to strike such matter on the day the petition is noticed or re-noticed to be heard.

(g) **Hearing and determination; transfer to appellate division.** Where the substantial evidence issue specified in question four of section 7803 is not raised, the court in which the proceeding is commenced shall itself dispose of the issues in the proceeding. Where such an issue is raised, the court shall first dispose of such other objections as could terminate the proceeding, including but not limited to lack of jurisdiction, statute of limitations and res judicata, without reaching the substantial evidence issue, if the determination of the other objections does not terminate the proceeding, the court shall make an order directing that it be transferred for disposition to a term of the appellate division held within the judicial department embracing the county in which the proceeding was commenced. When the proceeding comes before it, whether by appeal or transfer, the appellate division shall dispose of all issues in the proceeding, or, if the papers are insufficient, it may remit the proceeding.

(h) **Trial.** If a triable issue of fact is raised in a proceeding under this article, it shall be tried forthwith. Where the proceeding was transferred to the appellate division, the issue of fact shall be tried by a referee or by a justice of the supreme court and the verdict, report or decision rendered after the trial shall be returned to, and the order thereon made by, the appellate division.

(i) **Appearance by judicial officer.** Notwithstanding any other provision of law, where a proceeding is brought under this article against a justice, judge or referee appointed by a court and (1) it is brought by a party to a pending action or proceeding, and (2) it is based upon an act or acts performed by the respondent in that pending action or proceeding either granting or denying relief sought by a party thereto, and (3) the respondent is not a named party to the pending action or proceeding, in addition to service on the respondent, the petitioner shall serve a copy of the petition together with copies of all moving papers upon all other parties to the pending action or proceeding. All such parties shall be designated as respondents. Unless ordered by the court upon application of a party the respondent justice, judge or referee need not appear in the proceeding in which case the allegations of the shall not be deemed admitted or denied by him. Upon election

MISC. LAWS

of the justice, judge or referee not to appear, any ruling, order or judgment of the court in such proceeding shall bind said respondent. If such respondent does appear he shall respond to the petition and shall be entitled to be represented by the attorney general. If such respondent does not elect to appear all other parties shall be given notice thereof.

Amended by L. 1981, Ch. 502 eff. July 15, 1981; L. 1981, Ch. 580; L. 1986, Ch. 355, eff. July 17, 1986 amending subds. b and h; L. 1987, Ch. 384, eff. July 23, 1987; L. 1990, Ch. 575, eff. Jan. 1, 1991, amending subd. g; L. 1993, Ch. 202.

ANNOTATIONS

Discovery—With exception of one discovery device not at issue here, a notice to admit, disclosure is available only by leave of court in an Article 78 proceeding(7804(a)), petitioner should not have been granted leave to conduct discovery absent a showing that discovery sought was likely to be material and necessary to prosecution or defense of this proceeding. Stapleton Studios, LLC v. City of New York, 7 A.D.3d 273, 776 N.Y.S.2d 46 (1st Dept. 2004).

Generally.—Article 78 proceeding brought to annul Department of Environmental Conservation's determination denying petitioner's application for permit to expand municipal solid waste disposal facility was dismissed; agency's determination was based on substantial evidence, including petitioner's criminal history which had a direct relationship to the operation of this business. Al Turi Landfill Inc. v. N.Y.S. Dept. of Envtl. Conservation, 98 N.Y.2d 758, 751 N.Y.S.2d 827, 781 N.E.2d 892 (2002).

—Prohibition is a civil remedy, available only via a civil proceeding brought pursuant to CPLR Art. 78, it may not be obtained by motion made in the course of a criminal proceeding. People v. Rosenberg, 45 N.Y.2d 251, 408 N.Y.S.2d 368, 380 N.E.2d 199 (1978).

—County Planning Commission's decision to deny special use permit to petitioner was advisory opinion only and not appealable under CPLR 7804. Headriver, LLC v. Town Bd. of Town of Riverhead, 307 A.D.2d 314, 762 N.Y.S.2d 808 (2d Dept. 2003).

—Proceeding under this article began with an order to show cause issued with stringent service requirements for petitioner, failure of an inmate to satisfy service requirements will require dismissal unless inmate can prove conditions of imprisonment made compliance with service requirements impossible. Grassia v. Tracy, 232 A.D.2d 930, 649 N.Y.S.2d 489 (3d Dept. 1996).

Hearing and transfer to Appellate Division.—A petition which challenges sufficiency of evidence supporting a determination of guilt and raises a question of substantial evidence should have been transferred to appellate division in first instance, in a de novo determination, appellate court found substantial evidence did not support determination of guilt and annulled it to that extent and ordered all references expunged from petitioner's institutional record, remittal for a redetermination of penalty was not necessary as no loss of good time was imposed and petitioner has already served his penalty. Encarnacion v. Goord, 8 A.D.3d 843, 778 N.Y.S.2d 552 (3d Dept. 2004).

—Evidence presented was insufficient to decide issue of continuous service and hearing on this point was required, rather than transferral of the matter to the Appellate Division, since it was not a "substantial evidence" issue. Leland v. Board of Educ., 173 Misc. 2d 545, 662 N.Y.S.2d 160 (Sup. Ct. Albany Co. 1996).

Petition.—Article 78 proceeding to preclude the judge and district attorney from conducting further proceedings against the defendant who had no notice of the grand jury proceeding as required by CPL § 190.50(5) was dismissed for lack of a petition by the aggrieved party; a petition by counsel in lieu of his client does not suffice absent a showing of unusual necessity. Klein v. Hoft, 68 A.D.2d 872, 415 N.Y.S.2d 1 (1st Dept. 1979).

—Article 78 Petition dismissed due to petitioner's lack of standing, petitioner challenging an agency's land use determination failed to demonstrate that he had suffered "direct

harm. . .that is in some way different from that of the public at large" and that the injury "falls within the 'zone of interests,' or concerns, sought to be promoted or protected by the statutory provision under which the agency has acted." Oefelein v. Town of Thompson Planning Bd., 9 A.D.3d 556, 780 N.Y.S.2d 406 (3d Dept. 2004).

—Petitioner's challenge to determination was time barred because petitioner failed to file his verified petition within the relevant four-month statute of limitations period. Chavis v. Goord, 8 A.D.3d 786, 777 N.Y.S.2d 918 (3d Dept. 2004).

—Papers served by pro se petitioner that did not contain a document labeled "petition" as required, but could be liberally construed to sufficiently constitute a petition under this section, was sufficient to confer personal jurisdiction over the respondent. Ali v. Goord, 267 A.D.2d 520, 698 N.Y.S.2d 566 (3d Dept. 1999).

—Wrongfully brought writ may be converted to an article 78 proceeding to decide the validity of an incarcerated petitioner's contention that he is entitled to parole status because of the failure of the Parole Board to carry out a statutory mandate. People ex rel. South v. Hammock, 80 A.D.2d 947, 438 N.Y.S.2d 34 (3d Dept. 1981).

Certified transcript.—Although transcript of hearing filed with respondent's answer was not certified as required by statute, omission was disregarded where no prejudice to the substantial rights of the parties occurred. Cliff v. Kingsley, 293 A.D.2d 954, 742 N.Y.S.2d 408 (3d Dept. 2002).

Substantial evidence.—Where no substantial evidence question was presented, petitioner's request to review contempt finding imposed by Family Court as a result of disorderly and insolent behavior during a court proceeding was improperly before the Appellate Division. Pozefsky v. Jung, 268 A.D.2d 646, 701 N.Y.S.2d 470 (3d Dept. 2000).

—Respondent's petition to transfer proceeding from Supreme Court to Appellate Division due to the substantial evidence question raised was not supported by the record; where the "petition raises issues that can terminate the proceeding without reference to substantial evidence, the Supreme Court must decide the case." Nembhard v. Turner, 183 Misc. 2d 73, 703 N.Y.S.2d 673 (Sup. Ct. N.Y. Co. 1999).

§ 7805. Stay.

On the motion of any party or on its own initiative, the court may stay further proceedings, or the enforcement of any determination under review, upon terms including notice, security and payment of costs, except that the enforcement of an order or judgment granted by the appellate division in a proceeding under this article may be stayed only by order of the appellate division or the court of appeals. Unless otherwise ordered, security given on a stay is effective in favor of a person subsequently joined as a party under section 7802.

ANNOTATIONS

Jurisdiction.—Court properly dismissed proceeding for lack of personal jurisdiction because petitioner failed to serve the writ on respondents. People ex rel. Fields v. Murray, 289 A.D.2d 1089, 735 N.Y.S.2d 466 (4th Dept. 2001).

No likelihood of success on the merits.—Inmates commenced CPLR Art. 78 proceedings for review of a policy banning smoking at the Westchester County Jail. Court found that prisoners do not have a fundamental right to smoke cigarettes, and petitioners failed to show a likelihood of success on the merits. Jarrett v. Westchester County Dept. of Health, 166 Misc. 2d 777, 638 N.Y.S.2d 269 (Sup. Ct. Westchester Co. 1995), dismissed, 646 N.Y.S.2d 223.

§ 7806. Judgment.

The judgment may grant the petitioner the relief to which he is entitled, or may dismiss the proceeding either on the merits or with leave to renew. If the proceeding was brought to review a determination, the judgment may annul or confirm the determination in whole or in part, or modify it, and may direct or prohibit specified action by the respondent. Any restitution or damages granted to the petitioner must be incidental to the primary relief sought by the petitioner, and must be such as he might otherwise recover on the same set of facts in a separate action or proceeding suable in the supreme court against the same body or officer in its or his official capacity.

MISC. LAWS

EXECUTIVE LAW

(ARTS. 12-B, 23, 35, 36, 49-B)

ARTICLE 12-B—STATE DIVISION OF PAROLE

§ 259. Division of parole; organization.

1. There shall be in the executive department of state government a state division of parole. The chairman of the state board of parole shall be the chief executive officer of the division. He shall appoint and shall have the power to remove, in accordance with the provisions of the civil service law, all officers and employees of the division, and shall prescribe their powers and duties and fix their compensation within the amounts appropriated therefor.

2. The chairman shall promulgate such regulations as are necessary and proper for the efficient operation of the division. He shall have the authority to contract with public or private agencies for the performance of such functions as he deems necessary or desirable to promote the efficient operation of the division and the fulfillment of all lawful responsibilities of the division or employees thereof except the functions defined in subdivisions three, four and five of section two hundred fifty-nine-a of this article.

3. The chairman may, from time to time, create, abolish, transfer and consolidate bureaus and other units within the division, not expressly established by law as he may determine necessary for the efficient operation of the division, subject to the approval of the director of the budget.

4. The principal office of the division shall be in the county of Albany.

§ 259-a. Division of parole; functions, powers and duties.

Subject to the authority of the chairman:

1. The division shall cause to be obtained and filed as soon as practicable, information as complete as may be obtainable with regard to each inmate who is received in an institution under the jurisdiction of the state department of correctional services. Such information shall include a complete statement of the crime for which the inmate has been sentenced, the circumstances of such crime, all presentence memoranda, the nature of

MISC. LAWS

the sentence, the court in which he was sentenced, the name of the judge and district attorney and copies of such probation reports as may have been made as well as reports as to the inmate's social, physical, mental and psychiatric condition and history.

2. The division shall cause complete records to be kept of every person on presumptive release, parole, conditional release or post-release supervision. Such records shall contain the aliases and photograph of each such person, and the other information referred to in subdivision one of this section, as well as all reports of parole officers in relation to such persons. Such records shall be maintained by the division and may be made available as deemed appropriate by the chairman for use by the department of correctional services, the division, and the board of parole. Such records shall be organized in accordance with methods of filing and indexing designed to insure the immediate availability of complete information about such persons.

3. The division shall have responsibility for the preparation of reports and other data required by the state board of parole in the exercise of its functions.

4. The division shall supervise all inmates released on parole or conditional release, except that the division may consent to the supervision of a released inmate by the United States parole commission pursuant to the witness security act of nineteen hundred eighty-four.

5. The division shall conduct such investigations as may be necessary in connection with alleged violations of presumptive release, parole, conditional release or post-release supervision.

6. The division shall assist inmates eligible for presumptive release, parole or conditional release and inmates who are on presumptive release, parole, conditional release or post-release supervision to secure employment, educational or vocational training.

6-a. The division shall have the duty to provide written notice to persons who are serving a term of parole, parole supervision, conditional release or post release supervision of any requirement to report to the crime victims board any funds of a convicted person as defined in section six hundred thirty-a of this chapter, the procedure for such reporting and any potential penalty for a failure to comply.

7. The division shall encourage apprenticeship training of such persons through the assistance and cooperation of industrial, commercial and labor organizations.

8. The division may establish a parole transition program which is hereby defined as community-based residential facilities designed to aid presumptive release, parole, conditional release or post-release supervision violators develop an increased capacity for adjustment to community

living. Presumptive releasees, parolees, conditional releasees and those under post-release supervision who have either (i) been found pursuant to section two hundred fifty-nine-i of this article to have violated one or more conditions of release in an important respect, or (ii) who have allegedly violated one or more of such conditions upon a finding of probable cause at a preliminary hearing or upon the waiver thereof may be placed in a parole transition facility. Placement in a parole transition facility upon a finding of probable cause or the waiver thereof shall not preclude the conduct of a revocation hearing, nor, absent a waiver, operate to deny the releasee's right to such revocation hearing.

9. [*Expires Sept. 1, 2007.*]

(a) The division shall collect a fee of thirty dollars per month, from all persons over the age of eighteen who after the effective date of this subdivision are supervised on presumptive release, parole, conditional release or post-release supervision by the division. The division shall waive all or part of such fee where, because of the indigence of the offender, the payment of said fee would work an unreasonable hardship on the person convicted, his or her immediate family, or any 8 other person who is dependent on such person for financial support.

(b) The supervision fee authorized by this subdivision shall not constitute nor be imposed as a condition of parole supervision.

(c) In the event of non-payment of any fees which have not been waived by the division, the division may seek to enforce payment in any manner permitted by law enforcement of a debt owed to the state.

(d) Nothing contained in this subdivision affects or limits the provisions of section two hundred fifty-nine-m of this article, relating to out-of-state parole supervision. Prior to a transfer of parole supervision to another state, the division shall eliminate any supervision fee imposed pursuant to this subdivision. The division may collect a fee, pursuant to this subdivision and regulations promulgated thereunder, from any person whose parole supervision is transferred to this state from another.

(e) The chairman of the division shall submit a report to the governor, temporary president of the senate, speaker of the assembly and the chairperson of the senate crime and correction committee and assembly corrections committee, senate codes committee and the assembly codes committee on or before January first, nineteen hundred ninety-three and January first, nineteen hundred and ninety-four regarding the division's experience with the parole supervision fee. The report shall include, but not be limited to, amounts of fees imposed and collected, rates of payment for different categories of convictions and types of offenders, and remedies utilized and costs incurred for collection in cases of non-payment.

Amended by L. 1983, Ch. 419, eff. July 8, 1983; L. 1984, Ch. 451, eff. Nov. 1, 1984; L. 1985, Ch. 635, eff. July 28, 1985; L. 1990, Ch. 117, extending expiration date of subd. 4; L. 1992, Ch. 55, extending expiration date of subd. 4; L. 1992, Ch. 55, § 381, renumbering subd. 9 as subd. 10 and adding a new subd. 9; L. 1993, Ch. 39, extending expiration date of subd. 4; L. 1994, Ch. 61, § 4, extending expiration date of subd. 9, § 6, extending expiration date of subd. 4; L. 1997, Ch. 57, § 42, Ch. 117, § 41, Ch. 145, § 14, Ch. 162, § 42, Ch. 194, § 35, Ch. 211, § 55, and Ch. 264, § 34, extending expiration date of subd. 4 to Aug. 1, 1997, eff. July 23, 1997, in full force and effect Apr. 1, 1997; L. 1997, Ch. 435, §§ 54 and 55, extending expiration dates of subds. 4 and 9 to Sept. 1, 1999, eff. Aug. 20, 1997; any provision of law which expired prior to Aug. 20, 1997 shall be revived and shall be deemed to have been in full force and effect from and after the date of the applicable expiration; L. 1998, Ch. 1, §§ 16–21, eff. Aug. 6, 1998, and shall apply to offenses committed on or after Sept. 1, 1998. Offenses committed prior to Sept. 1, 1998 shall be governed by the provisions of law in effect at the time the offense was committed; provided, however, that nothing contained herein shall be deemed to affect the application, qualification, expiration, reversion or repeal of any provision of law amended by any section of L. 1998, Ch. 1 and the provisions of L. 1998, Ch. 1 shall be applied or qualified or shall expire or revert or be deemed repealed in the same manner, to the same extent and on the same date as the case may be as otherwise provided by law; L. 1999, Ch. 452, §§ 8 and 9, eff. Sept. 1, 1999; L. 2001, Ch. 62, § 15, eff. June 25, 2001; L. 2003, Ch. 62, Part E, § 6, eff. May 15, 2003, and deemed effective Apr. 1, 2003, amending subds. 2, 4–6, 8 and 9(a); L. 2003, Ch. 16, §§ 10, 11, extending effective dates to Sept. 1, 2005; L. 2005, Ch. 56, Part D, § 10, eff. Apr. 1, 2005, extending expiration date of subd. 9 to Sept. 1, 2007.

ANNOTATION

No right to counsel a preliminary fact finding interview.— Although a parolee has an absolute right to be represented by counsel at a final parole revocation hearing, this right does not extend to a preliminary fact finding interview. People v. Bantum, 113 Misc. 2d 448 N.Y.S.2d 975 (Sup. Ct. Bronx Co. 1982).

§ 259-b. State board of parole; organization.

1. There shall be in the state division of parole a state board of parole which shall possess the powers and duties hereinafter specified. Such board shall consist of not more than nineteen members appointed by the governor with the advice and consent of the senate. The term of office of each member of such board shall be for six years; provided, however, that any member chosen to fill a vacancy occurring otherwise than by expiration of term shall be appointed for the remainder of the unexpired term of the member whom he is to succeed. In the event of the inability to act of any member, the governor may appoint some competent informed person to act in his stead during the continuance of such disability.

2. Each member of the board shall have been awarded a degree from an accredited four-year college or university or a graduate degree from such college or university or accredited graduate school and shall have had at least five years of experience in one or more of the fields of criminology, administration of criminal justice, law enforcement, sociology, law, social work, corrections, psychology, psychiatry or medicine.

3. The governor shall designate one of the members of the board as chairman to serve in such capacity at the pleasure of the governor or until the member's term of office expires and a successor is designated in accordance with law, whichever first occurs.

4. The members of the state board of parole shall not hold any other public office; nor shall they, at any time of their appointment nor during their incumbency, serve as a representative of any political party on an executive committee or other governing body thereof, nor as an executive officer or employee of any political committee, organization or association.

5. Each member of the state board of parole shall receive for his services an annual salary to be fixed by the governor within the amount appropriated therefor. Each member of such board shall also receive his necessary expenses actually incurred in the discharge of his duties.

6. Any member of the state board of parole may be removed by the governor for cause after an opportunity to be heard.

7. Except as otherwise provided by law, a majority of the state board of parole shall constitute a quorum for the transaction of all business of the board.

Amended by L. 1983, Ch. 714, eff. Sept. 1, 1983, amending subds. 1 and 2; L. 1987, Ch. 123, eff. June 15, 1987, amending subd. 1; L. 1989, Ch. 111, eff. May 30, 1989, amending subd. 2.

§ 259-c. State board of parole; functions, powers and duties.

The state board of parole shall:

1. [*Effective until Sept. 1, 2007.*] have the power and duty of determining which inmates serving an indeterminate or determinate sentence of imprisonment may be released on parole, or on medical parole pursuant to section two hundred fifty-nine-r of this article, and when and under what conditions;

1. [*Effective Sept. 1, 2007, until Sept. 1, 2009.*] have the power and duty of determining which inmates serving an indeterminate or a reformatory or determinate sentence of imprisonment may be released on parole and when and under what conditions;

1. [*Effective Sept. 1, 2009.*] have the power and duty of determining which inmates serving an indeterminate or reformatory sentence of imprisonment may be released on parole and when and under what conditions;

2. [*Effective until Sept. 1, 2007.*] have the power and duty of determining the conditions of release of the person who may be presumptively released, conditionally released or subject to a period of post-release supervision under an indeterminate or determinate sentence of imprisonment;

2. [*Effective Sept. 1, 2007, until Sept. 1, 2009.*]

have the power and duty of determining the conditions of release of the person who may be conditionally released or subject to a period of post-release supervision under an indeterminate or determinate sentence of imprisonment and of determining which inmates serving a definite sentence of imprisonment may be conditionally released and when and under what conditions;

2. [*Effective Sept. 1, 2009.*] have the power and duty of determining the conditions of release of the person who may be conditionally released under an indeterminate or reformatory sentence of imprisonment and of determining which inmates serving a definite sentence of imprisonment may be conditionally released and when and under what conditions;

3. determine, as each inmate is received by the department of correctional services, the need for further investigation of the background of such inmate and cause such investigation as may be necessary to be made as soon as practicable, the results of such investigation together with all other information compiled by the division pursuant to subdivision one of section two hundred fifty-nine-a and the complete criminal record and family court record of such inmate to be filed so as to be readily available when the parole of such inmate is being considered;

4. establish written guidelines for its use in making parole decisions as required by law, including the fixing of minimum periods of imprisonment or ranges thereof for different categories of offenders;

5. through its members, officers and employees, study or cause to be studied the inmates confined in institutions over which the board has jurisdiction, so as to determine their ultimate fitness to be paroled;

6. have the power to revoke the presumptive release, parole, conditional release or post-release supervision status of any person and to authorize the issuance of a warrant for the re-taking of such persons;

7. have the power to grant and revoke certificates of relief from disabilities and certificates of good conduct as provided for by law;

8. have the power and perform the duty, when requested by the governor, of reporting to the governor the facts, circumstances, criminal records and social, physical, mental and psychiatric conditions and histories of inmates under consideration by the governor for pardon or commutation of sentence and of applicants for restoration of the rights of citizenship;

9. for the purpose of any investigation in the performance of duties made by it or any member thereof, have the power to issue subpoenas, to compel the attendance of witnesses and the production of books, papers, and other documents pertinent to the subject of its inquiry;

10. have the power to authorize any members thereof and hearing officers to administer oaths and take the testimony of persons under oath;

11. make rules for the conduct of its work, a copy of such rules and of any amendments thereto to be filed by the chairman with the secretary of state;

12. in any case where a person is entitled to jail time credit under the provisions of paragraph (c) of subdivision three of section 70.40 of the penal law, to certify to the person in charge of the institution in which such person's sentence is being served the amount of such credit;

13. transmit a report of the work of the state board of parole for the preceding calendar year to the governor and the legislature annually;

14. notwithstanding any other provision of law to the contrary, where a person serving a sentence for an offense defined in article one hundred thirty, one hundred thirty-five or two hundred sixty-three of the penal law or section 255.25 of the penal law and the victim of such offense was under the age of eighteen at the time of such offense, is released on parole or conditionally released pursuant to subdivision one or two of this section, the board shall require, as a mandatory condition of such release, that such sentenced offender shall refrain from knowingly entering into or upon any school grounds, as that term is defined in paragraph (a) of subdivision fourteen of section 220.00 of the penal law, or any other facility or institution primarily used for the care or treatment of persons under the age of eighteen while one or more of such persons under the age of eighteen are present, provided however, that when such sentenced offender is a registered student or participant or an employee of such facility or institution or entity contracting therewith or has a family member enrolled in such facility or institution, such sentenced offender may, with the written authorization of his or her parole officer and the superintendent or chief administrator of such facility, institution or grounds, enter such facility, institution or upon such grounds for the limited purposes authorized by the parole officer and superintendent or chief officer. Nothing in this subdivision shall be construed as restricting any lawful condition of supervision that may be imposed on such sentenced offender.*

15. have the duty to provide written notice to such inmates prior to release on presumptive release, parole, parole supervision, conditional release or post release supervision or pursuant to subdivision six of section 410.91 of the criminal procedure law of any requirement to report to the crime victims board any funds of a convicted person as defined in section six hundred thirty-two-a of this chapter, the procedure for such reporting and any potential penalty for a failure to comply.

* Punctuation as enacted.

Amended by L. 1990, Ch. 117, extending expiration date of subd. 2; L. 1992, Ch. 55, § 287, amending subd. 1, § 323, extending expiration date of subd. 2; L. 1993, Ch. 39, extending expiration date of subd. 2; L. 1994, Ch. 61, § 3, extending expiration date of subd. 1, § 6, extending expiration date of subd. 2; L. 1995, Ch. 3, § 38, amending subds. 1 and 2, eff. Oct. 1, 1995, amendment repealed Sept. 30, 2005 pursuant to L. 1995, Ch. 3, § 74, paragraph (d); L. 1996, Ch. 48, extending expiration date of subd. 1 to Apr. 10, 1998, eff. Apr. 12, 1996; L. 1997, Ch. 57, § 42, Ch. 117, § 41, Ch. 145, § 14, Ch. 162, § 42, Ch. 194, § 35, Ch. 211, § 55, and Ch. 264, § 34, extending expiration date of subd. 2 to Aug. 1, 1997, eff. July 23, 1997, in full force and effect Apr. 1, 1997; L. 1997, Ch. 435, § 54, extending expiration date of subd. 2 to Sept. 1, 1999, eff. Aug. 20, 1997; any provision of law which expired prior to Aug. 20, 1997 shall be revived and shall be deemed to have been in full force and effect from and after the date of the applicable expiration; L. 1998, Ch. 1, §§ 22 and 23, eff. Aug. 6, 1998, and shall apply to offenses committed on or after Sept. 1, 1998. Offenses committed prior to Sept. 1, 1998 shall be governed by the provisions of law in effect at the time the offense was committed; provided, however, that nothing contained herein shall be deemed to affect the application, qualification, expiration, reversion or repeal of any provision of law amended by any section of L. 1998, Ch. 1 and the provisions of L. 1998, Ch. 1 shall be applied or qualified or shall expire or revert or be deemed repealed in the same manner, to the same extent and on the same case as the case may be as otherwise provided by law; and L. 1998, Ch. 38, § 1, extending expiration date of subd. 1 as amended by L. 1996, Ch. 48, to Apr. 10, 2000; L. 1999, Ch. 452, § 8, eff. Sept. 1, 1999, extending expiration date of subd. 2 as amended by L. 1989, Ch. 79; L. 2000, Ch. 16, § 1, eff. Mar. 30, 2000, extending expiration date of subd. 2 as amended by L. 1992, Ch. 55; L. 2000, Ch. 1, eff. Feb. 1, 2001; L. 2001, Ch. 62, § 14, eff. June 25, 2001; L. 2003, Ch. 62, Part E, § 7, eff. May 15, 2003 and deemed effective Apr. 1, 2003, amending subds. 2, 6 and 15; Ch. 16, §§ 10, 17, extending expiration date to Sept. 1, 2005; L. 2005, Ch. 56, Part D, §§ 15, 20, eff. Apr. 1, 2005, extending effective and expiration dates of subds. 1 and 2.

ANNOTATIONS

Generally.—Article 78 proceeding brought by petitioner that challenged various parole decisions rendered between 1991 and 2003 and named supreme court as sole respondent was dismissed for failure to include Division of Parole as a necessary party to proceeding; Division of Parole, which includes Board of Parole, has exclusive jurisdiction to make decisions with respect to parole; either Division of Parole or one of its agents or employees is a necessary party to proceeding. Bressett v. Supreme Court, 18 A.D.3d 1082, 795 N.Y.S.2d 475 (3d Dept. 2005).

—Exec. Law § 259-c(4) "does not require the establishment of a specific time range for petitioner or any other offender; statute requires that guidelines be established, but specifies neither the form nor the content of the guidelines, leaving the specifics to the Board's expertise and judgment." Douglas v. Travis, 290 A.D.2d 903, 737 N.Y.S.2d 165 (3d Dept. 2002).

Decision denying parole need not be annulled; board can consider crime defendant was not convicted of.—In light of board's knowledge that petitioner had been convicted of first degree robbery, and not of the murder of a state trooper by one of his partners in the robbery, there was still ample justification for the board's denial of parole based upon prisoner's prior criminal history of violent, aggressive behavior and his need for continued and extensive psychotherapy to treat his emotional antisocial characteristics, even though the board erred in placing petitioner's guideline range under section 259-c(4) of the Executive Law in the unspecified range. DiChiaro v. Hammock, 87 A.D.2d 957, 451 N.Y.S.2d 248 (3d Dept. 1982).

Special conditions.—It is within the discretion of the Division of Parole to impose the special condition of securing approved housing to sex offenders and not allow them to be released to a homeless shelter even though the condition must be satisfied before the request of conditional release may be granted. Monroe v. Travis, 280 A.D.2d 675, 721 N.Y.S.2d 377 (2d Dept. 2001).

—Board is authorized to impose special conditions on an inmate's release from prison; imposition of requirement of suitable residence was rational under circumstances where petitioner had a history of violent conduct coupled with sexual assault against his daughter. Billups v. N.Y.S. Div. of Parole, 18 A.D.3d 1085, 795 N.Y.S.2d 408 (3d Dept. 2005).

§ 259-d. Hearing officers.

1. The chairman of the state board of parole shall appoint hearing officers who shall be authorized to conduct parole revocation proceedings. A hearing officer conducting such proceedings shall, when delegated such authority by the board in rules adopted by the board, be required to make a written decision in accordance with standards and rules adopted by the board. Nothing in this article shall be deemed to preclude a member of the state board of parole from exercising all of the functions, powers and duties of a hearing officer upon request of the chairman.

2. The chairman, acting in cooperation with the civil service commission, shall establish standards, preliminary requisites and requisites to govern the selection and appointment of hearing officers. Such standards and requisites shall be designed to assure that persons selected as hearing officers have the ability to conduct parole revocation proceedings fairly and impartially. Such standards shall not require prior experience as a parole officer.

Amended by L. 1991, Ch. 166, eff. June 12, 1991, amending subd. (1).

ANNOTATION

Associate counsel as hearing officer.—The conduct of a parole revocation hearing by an associate counsel for the division of parole appointed by the chairman of the parole board to act as hearing officer is valid. People ex rel. Shippens v. Smith, 91 A.D.2d 868, 458 N.Y.S.2d 371 (4th Dept. 1982).

§ 259-e. Institutional parole services.

The division shall provide institutional parole services. Subject to the authority of the chairman, these shall include preparation of reports and other data required by the state board of parole in the exercise of its functions with respect to release on presumptive release, parole, conditional release or post-release supervision of inmates. Employees of the division who collect data, interview inmates and prepare reports for the state board of parole in institutions under the jurisdiction of the department of correctional services shall not work under the direct or indirect supervision of the head of the institution.

Amended by L. 1985, Ch. 34, eff. Apr. 1, 1985; L. 1998, Ch. 1, § 24, eff. Aug. 6, 1998, and shall apply to offenses committed on or after Sept. 1, 1998. Offenses committed prior to Sept. 1, 1998 shall be governed by the provisions of law in effect at the time the offense was committed; provided, however, that nothing contained herein shall be deemed to affect the application, qualification, expiration, reversion or repeal of any provision of law amended by any section of L. 1998, Ch. 1 and the provisions of L. 1998, Ch. 1 shall be applied or qualified or shall expire or revert or be deemed repealed in the same manner, to the same extent and on the same date as the case may be as otherwise provided by law; L. 2003, Ch. 62, Part E, § 8, eff. May 15, 2003 and deemed effective Apr. 1, 2003.

MISC. LAWS

§ 259-f. Parole officers.

1. Employees in the division who perform the duties of supervising inmates released on presumptive release, parole, conditional release or post-release supervision, and employees who perform professional duties in institutions and who are assigned to provide institutional parole services pursuant to section two hundred fifty-nine-e of this article, shall be parole officers.

2. No person shall be eligible for the position of parole officer who is under twenty-one years of age or who does not possess a baccalaureate degree conferred by a post-secondary institution accredited by an accrediting agency recognized by the United States office of education, or who is not fitted physically, mentally and morally. Parole officers selection shall be based on definite qualifications as to character, ability and training with an emphasis on capacity and ability to provide a balanced approach to influencing human behavior and to use judgment in the enforcement of the rules and regulations of presumptive release, parole and conditional release. Parole officers shall be persons likely to exercise a strong and helpful influence upon persons placed under their supervision while retaining the goal of protecting society.

3. The chairman, acting in cooperation with the civil service commission, shall establish standards, preliminary requisites and requisites to govern the selection and appointment of parole officers.

4. A parole or warrant officer, in performing or in attempting to perform an arrest pursuant to and in conformance with the provisions of article one hundred forty of the criminal procedure law, shall be deemed to have performed such actions, relating to such arrest, in the course of employment in the division for purposes of disability or death from any injuries arising therefrom. The provisions of this subdivision shall apply whether or not such parole or warrant officer was on duty for the division at the time of performing such actions or performed such actions outside of his or her regular or usual duties within the division.

Amended by L. 1981, Ch. 501, eff. July 15, 1981, adding subd. 4; L. 1985, Ch. 34, eff. Apr. 1, 1985, amended subd. 1; L. 1998, Ch. 1, § 25, eff. Aug. 6, 1998, amending subd. 1, and shall apply to offenses committed on or after Sept. 1, 1998. Offenses committed prior to Sept. 1, 1998 shall be governed by the provisions of law in effect at the time the offense was committed; provided, however, that nothing contained herein shall be deemed to affect the application, qualification, expiration, reversion or repeal of any provision of law amended by any section of L. 1998, Ch. 1 and the provisions of L. 1998, Ch. 1 shall be applied or qualified or shall expire or revert or be deemed repealed in the same manner, to the same extent and on the same date as the case may be as otherwise provided by law; L. 2003, Ch. 62, Part E, § 9, eff. May 15, 2003 and deemed effective Apr. 1, 2003, amending subds. 1 and 2.

§ 259-g. Applications for presumptive release or conditional release.

1. All requests for presumptive release or conditional release shall be made in writing on forms prescribed and furnished by the division of parole. Within one month from the date any such application is received, if it appears that the applicant is eligible for presumptive release or conditional release or will be eligible for such release during such month, the conditions of release shall be fixed in accordance with rules prescribed by the board. Such conditions shall be substantially the same as conditions imposed upon parolees.

2. No person shall be presumptively released or conditionally released unless the applicant has agreed in writing to the conditions of release. The agreement shall state in plain, easily understandable language the consequences of a violation of one or more of the conditions of release.

Amended by L. 2003, Ch. 62, Part E, § 10, eff. May 15, 2003 and deemed effective Apr. 1, 2003.

ANNOTATION

Special conditions.—It is within the discretion of the Division to impose the special condition of securing approved housing to sex offenders and not allow them to be released to a homeless shelter even though the condition must be satisfied before the request of conditional release may be granted. Monroe v. Travis, 280 A.D.2d 675, 721 N.Y.S.2d 377 (2d Dept. 2001).

§ 259-h. Parole eligibility for certain inmates sentenced for crimes committed prior to September first, nineteen hundred sixty-seven.

1. The provisions of this subdivision shall apply in any case where a person is under one or more of the following sentences imposed pursuant to the penal law in effect prior to September first, nineteen hundred sixty-seven:

(a) Life imprisonment for the crime of murder in the first degree pursuant to section ten hundred forty-five or ten hundred forty-five-a of such law;

(b) Life imprisonment for the crime of kidnapping pursuant to section twelve hundred fifty of such law; or

(c) Death commuted to life imprisonment for the crime of murder in the first degree or for the crime of kidnapping pursuant to one of the above sections.

Any such person who is not otherwise or who will not sooner become eligible for release on parole under such sentence shall be or become eligible for release on parole after service of a minimum period of imprisonment of twenty years.

2. The provisions of this subdivision shall apply in any case where a person is under one or more of the following sentences imposed pursuant to the penal law in effect prior to September first, nineteen hundred sixty-seven:

(a) A minimum term of twenty years or more

and a maximum of natural life for the crime of murder in the second degree pursuant to section ten hundred forty-eight of such law;

(b) A minimum term of twenty years or more and a maximum of natural life for the crime of kidnapping imposed pursuant to section twelve hundred fifty of such law;

(c) A minimum term of fifteen years or more and a maximum of natural life for a third conviction of a felony under laws relating to narcotic drugs pursuant to section nineteen hundred forty-one of such law; or

(d) A minimum term of fifteen years or more and a maximum of natural life for a fourth conviction of a felony pursuant to section nineteen hundred forty-two of such law.

Any person who is not otherwise or who will not sooner become eligible for release on parole under such sentence shall be or become eligible for release on parole after service of a minimum period of imprisonment of fifteen years.

3. The provisions of this subdivision shall apply in any case where a person is under a sentence imposed pursuant to the penal law in effect prior to September first, nineteen hundred sixty-seven, other than a sentence specified in subdivisions one and two of this section. Any person who is not otherwise or who will not sooner become eligible for release on parole shall be or become eligible for release on parole under such sentence after service of a minimum period of imprisonment of eight years and four months.

Notwithstanding the provisions of subdivisions one and two hereof, inmates convicted of murder, second degree, and sentenced pursuant to the provisions of the penal law in effect prior to September first, nineteen hundred sixty-seven, who are not otherwise or who will not sooner become eligible for release on parole, shall be eligible for release on parole under such sentence after service of a minimum period of imprisonment of eight years and four months.

4. In calculating time required to be served prior to eligibility for parole under the minimum periods of imprisonment established by this section the following rules shall apply:

(a) Service of such time shall be deemed to have commenced on the day the inmate was received in an institution under the jurisdiction of the department pursuant to the sentence;

(b) Where an inmate is under more than one sentence, (i) if the sentences run concurrently, the time served under imprisonment on any of the sentences shall be credited against the minimum periods of all the concurrent sentences, and (ii) if the sentences run consecutively, the minimum periods of imprisonment shall merge in and be satisfied by service of the period that has the longest unexpired time to run;

(c) No credit shall be allowed for "good conduct and efficient and willing performance of duties," under former section two hundred thirty of the correction law, repealed by chapter four hundred seventy-six of the laws of nineteen hundred seventy and continued in effect as to certain inmates, or under any other provision of law;

(d) Calculations with respect to "jail time," "time served under vacated sentence" and interruption for "escape" shall be in accordance with the provisions of the subdivisions three, five and six of section 70.30 of the penal law as enacted by chapter ten hundred thirty of the laws of nineteen hundred sixty-five, as amended.

5. The provisions of this section shall not be construed as diminishing the discretionary authority of the board of parole to determine whether or not an inmate is to be paroled.

§ 259-i. Procedures for the conduct of the work of the state board of parole.

1. Establishment of minimum periods of imprisonment.

(a) In any case where a person is received in an institution under the jurisdiction of the department of correctional services with an indeterminate sentence, and the court has not fixed a minimum period of imprisonment, the board shall cause to be brought before one or more members in accordance with the rules of the board within one hundred twenty days from the date on which such person is received in an institution under the jurisdiction of the department of correctional services pursuant to such sentence or as soon thereafter as practicable, all information with regard to such persons referred to in subdivision three of section two hundred fifty-nine-c of this article. The member or members receiving such information shall study the same and shall personally interview the sentenced person. Upon conclusion of the interview, he shall determine the minimum period of imprisonment to be served prior to parole consideration in accordance with the guidelines adopted pursuant to subdivision four of section two hundred fifty-nine-c of this article. Such guidelines shall include (i) the seriousness of the offense with due consideration to the type of sentence, length of sentence and recommendations of the sentencing court, the district attorney, the attorney for the inmate, the pre-sentence probation report as well as consideration of any mitigating and aggravating factors, and activities following arrest and prior to confinement; and (ii) prior criminal record, including the nature and pattern of offenses, adjustment to any previous probation or parole supervision and institutional confinement. Such determination shall have the same force and effect as a minimum period fixed by a court, except that the board may provide by rule for the making of subsequent determinations reducing such minimum period

MISC. LAWS

which shall not be reduced to less than one year. Notification of such determination and of any subsequent determinations and of the reasons therefor shall be furnished in writing to the sentenced person and to the person in charge of the institution as soon as practicable. Such reasons shall be given in detail and not in conclusory terms.

(b) In any case where the minimum period of imprisonment is fixed independent of the criteria adopted by the board pursuant to subdivision four of section two hundred fifty-nine-c of this article, written reasons shall be given for such determination in detail and not in conclusory terms.

2. Parole. (a) [*Repealed eff. Sept. 1, 2009.*] (i) Except as provided in subparagraph (ii) of this paragraph, at least one month prior to the date on which an inmate may be paroled pursuant to subdivision one of section 70.40 of the penal law, a member or members as determined by the rules of the board shall personally interview such inmate and determine whether he should be paroled in accordance with the guidelines adopted pursuant to subdivision four of section two hundred fifty-nine-c of this article. If parole is not granted upon such review, the inmate shall be informed in writing within two weeks of such appearance of the factors and reasons for such denial of parole. Such reasons shall be given in detail and not in conclusory terms. The board shall specify a date not more than twenty-four months from such determination for reconsideration, and the procedures to be followed upon reconsideration shall be the same. If the inmate is released, he shall be given a copy of the conditions of parole. Such conditions shall where appropriate, include a requirement that the parolee comply with any restitution order, mandatory surcharge, sex offender registration fee and DNA databank fee previously imposed by a court of competent jurisdiction that applies to the parolee. The board of parole shall indicate which restitution collection agency established under subdivision eight of section 420.10 of the criminal procedure law, shall be responsible for collection of restitution, mandatory surcharge, sex offender registration fees and DNA databank fees as provided for in section 60.35 of the penal law and section eighteen hundred nine of the vehicle and traffic law.

(ii) Any inmate who is scheduled for presumptive release pursuant to section eight hundred six of the correction law shall not appear before the parole board as provided in subparagraph (i) of this paragraph unless such inmate's scheduled presumptive release is forfeited, canceled, or rescinded subsequently as provided in such law. In such event, the inmate shall appear before the parole board for release consideration as provided in subparagraph (i) of this paragraph as soon thereafter as is practicable.

(a) [*Effective Sept. 1, 2009.*] At least one month prior to the expiration of the minimum period or periods of imprisonment fixed by the court or board, a member or members as determined by the rules of the board shall personally interview an inmate serving an indeterminate sentence and determine whether he should be paroled at the expiration of the minimum period or periods in accordance with the guidelines adopted pursuant to subdivision four of section two hundred fifty-nine-c. If parole is not granted upon such review, the inmate shall be informed in writing within two weeks of such appearance of the factors and reasons for such denial of parole. Such reasons shall be given in detail and not in conclusory terms. The board shall specify a date not more than twenty-four months from such determination for reconsideration, and the procedures to be followed upon reconsideration shall be the same. If the inmate is released, he shall be given a copy of the conditions of parole. Such conditions shall where appropriate, include a requirement that the parolee comply with any restitution order and mandatory surcharge previously imposed by a court of competent jurisdiction that applies to the parolee. The board of parole shall indicate which restitution collection agency established under subdivision eight of section 420.10 of the criminal procedure law, shall be responsible for collection of restitution and mandatory surcharge as provided for in section 60.35 of the penal law and section eighteen hundred nine of the vehicle and traffic law.

(b) Persons presumptively released, paroled, conditionally released or released to post-release supervision from an institution under the jurisdiction of the department of correctional services or the department of mental hygiene shall, while on presumptive release, parole, conditional release or post-release supervision, be in the legal custody of the division of parole until expiration of the maximum term or period of sentence, or expiration of the period of supervision, including any period of post-release supervision, or return to the custody of the department of correctional services, as the case may be.

(c) (A) Discretionary release on parole shall not be granted merely as a reward for good conduct or efficient performance of duties while confined but after considering if there is a reasonable probability that, if such inmate is released, he will live and remain at liberty without violating the law, and that his release is not incompatible with the welfare of society and will not so deprecate the seriousness of his crime as to undermine respect for law. In making the parole release decision, the guidelines adopted pursuant to subdivision four of section two hundred fifty-nine-c of this article shall require that the following be considered: (i) the institutional record including program goals and accomplishments, academic achievements, vocational education, training or work assignments, therapy and interpersonal relationships with staff and inmates; (ii) performance, if any, as a participant in a temporary release program; (iii) release plans including community resources, employment, education and training and support services available to the inmate; (iv) any deportation order issued by the federal government against the inmate while in the custody of the department of correctional services and any recommendation regarding deportation made by the commissioner of the department of correctional services pursuant to section one hundred forty-seven of the correction law; and (v) any statement made to the board by the crime victim or the victim's representative, where the crime victim is deceased or is mentally or physically incapacitated. The board shall provide toll free telephone access for crime victims. In the case of an oral statement made in accordance with subdivision one of section 440.50 of the criminal procedure law, the parole board member shall present a written report of the statement to the parole board. A crime victim's representative shall mean the crime victim's closest surviving relative, the committee or guardian of such person, or the legal representative of any such person. Such statement submitted by the victim or victim's representative may include information concerning threatening or intimidating conduct toward the victim, the victim's representative, or the victim's family, made by the person sentenced and occurring after the sentencing. Such information may include, but need not be limited to, the threatening or intimidating conduct of any other person who or which is directed by the person sentenced. Notwithstanding the provisions of this section, in making the parole release decision for persons whose minimum period of imprisonment was not fixed pursuant to the provisions of subdivision one of this section, in addition to the factors listed in this paragraph the board shall consider the factors listed in paragraph (a) of subdivision one of this section.

(B) Where a crime victim or victim's representative as defined in subparagraph (A) of this paragraph, or other person submits to the parole board a written statement concerning the release of an inmate, the parole board shall keep that individual's name and address confidential.

(d) (i) Notwithstanding the provisions of paragraphs (a), (b) and (c) of this subdivision, after the inmate has served his minimum period of imprisonment imposed by the court, or at any time after the inmate's period of imprisonment has commenced, provided that the inmate has had a final order of deportation issued against him and provided further that the inmate is not convicted of either an A-I felony offense other than an A-I felony offense as defined in article two hundred twenty of the penal law or a violent felony offense as defined in section 70.02 of the penal law, if the inmate is subject to deportation by the United States Immigration and Naturalization Service, in addition to the criteria set forth in paragraph (c), the board may consider, as a factor warranting

earlier release, the fact that such inmate will be deported, and may grant parole to such inmate conditioned specifically on his prompt deportation. The board may make such conditional grant of early parole only where it has received from the United States Immigration and Naturalization Service assurance (A) that an order of deportation will be executed or that proceedings will promptly be commenced for the purpose of deportation upon release of the inmate from the custody of the department of correctional services, and (B) that the inmate, if granted parole pursuant to this paragraph, will not be released from the custody of the United States Immigration and Naturalization Service, unless such release be as a result of deportation without providing the board a reasonable opportunity to arrange for execution of its warrant for the retaking of such parolee.

(ii) An inmate who has been granted parole pursuant to this paragraph shall be delivered to the custody of the United States Immigration and Naturalization Service along with the board's warrant for his retaking to be executed in the event of his release from such custody other than by deportation. In the event that such person is not deported, the board shall execute the warrant, effect his return to the custody of the department of correctional services and within sixty days after such return, provided that the minimum period of imprisonment has been served, personally interview him to determine whether he should be paroled in accordance with the provisions of paragraphs (a), (b) and (c) of this subdivision. The return of a person granted parole pursuant to this paragraph for the reason set forth herein shall not be deemed to be a parole delinquency and the interruptions specified in subdivision three of section 70.40 of the penal law shall not apply, but the time spent in the custody of the United States Immigration and Naturalization Service shall be credited against the term of the sentence in accordance with the rules specified in paragraph (c) of that subdivision. Notwithstanding any other provision of law, any inmate granted parole pursuant to this paragraph who is subsequently committed to the custody of the Department of Correctional Services for a felony offense committed after release pursuant to this paragraph shall have his parole eligibility date on the sentence for the new felony offense extended by the amount of time between the date on which such inmate was released from the custody of the Department of Correctional Services pursuant to this paragraph and the date on which such inmate would otherwise have completed service of the minimum period of imprisonment on the prior felony offense.

(e) Notwithstanding the requirements of paragraph (a) of this subdivision, the determination to parole an inmate who has successfully completed the shock incarceration program pursuant to section two hundred sixty-seven of the correction law may be made without a personal

MISC. LAWS

interview of the inmate and shall be made in accordance with procedures set forth in the rules of the board. If parole is not granted, the time period for reconsideration shall not exceed the court imposed minimum.

3. Revocation of presumptive release, parole, conditional release and post-release supervision.

(a) (i) [*Expires Sept. 1, 2007.*] If the parole officer having charge of a presumptively released, paroled or conditionally released person or a person released to post-release supervision or a person received under the uniform act for out-of-state parolee supervision shall have reasonable cause to believe that such person has lapsed into criminal ways or company, or has violated one or more conditions of his presumptive release, parole, conditional release or post-release supervision, such parole officer shall report such fact to a member of the board of parole, or to any officer of the division designated by the board, and thereupon a warrant may be issued for the retaking of such person and for his temporary detention in accordance with the rules of the board. The retaking and detention of any such person may be further regulated by rules and regulations of the division not inconsistent with this article. A warrant issued pursuant to this section shall constitute sufficient authority to the superintendent or other person in charge of any jail, penitentiary, lockup or detention pen to whom it is delivered to hold in temporary detention the person named therein; except that a warrant issued with respect to a person who has been released on medical parole pursuant to section two hundred fifty-nine-r of this article and whose parole is being revoked pursuant to paragraph (h) of subdivision four of such section shall constitute authority for the immediate placement of the parolee only into the custody of the department of correctional services to hold in temporary detention. A warrant issued pursuant to this section shall also constitute sufficient authority to the person in charge of a drug treatment campus, as defined in subdivision twenty of section two of the correction law, to hold the person named therein, in accordance with the procedural requirements of this section, for a period of at least ninety days to complete an intensive drug treatment program mandated by the board of parole as an alternative to presumptive release or parole or conditional release revocation, or the revocation of post-release supervision, and shall also constitute sufficient authority for return of the person named therein to local custody to hold in temporary detention for further revocation proceedings in the event said person does not successfully complete the intensive drug treatment program. The board's rules shall provide for cancellation of delinquency and restoration to supervision upon the successful completion of the program.

(i) [*Effective Sept. 1, 2007.*] If the parole officer having charge of a paroled or conditionally released person or a person released to post-release supervision or a person received under the uniform act for out-of-state parolee supervision shall have reasonable cause to believe that such person has lapsed into criminal ways or company, or has violated one or more conditions of his parole, conditional release or post-release supervision, such parole officer shall report such fact to a member of the board of parole, or to any officer of the division designated by the board, and thereupon a warrant may be issued for the retaking of such person and for his temporary detention in accordance with the rules of the board. The retaking and detention of any such person may be further regulated by rules and regulations of the division not inconsistent with this article. A warrant issued pursuant to this section shall constitute sufficient authority to the superintendent or other person in charge of any jail, penitentiary, lockup or detention pen to whom it is delivered to hold in temporary detention the person named therein. A warrant issued pursuant to this section shall also constitute sufficient authority to the person in charge of a drug treatment campus, as defined in subdivision twenty of section two of the correction law, to hold the person named therein, in accordance with the procedural requirements of this section, for a period of at least ninety days to complete an intensive drug treatment program mandated by the board of parole as an alternative to parole or conditional release revocation, or the revocation of post-release supervision, and shall also constitute sufficient authority for return of the person named therein to local custody to hold in temporary detention for further revocation proceedings in the event said person does not successfully complete the intensive drug treatment program. The board's rules shall provide for cancellation of delinquency and restoration to supervision upon the successful completion of the program.

(ii) Whenever a presumptively released, paroled or conditionally released person or a person under post-release supervision or a prisoner received under the uniform act for out-of-state parolee supervision has, pursuant to this paragraph, been placed in any county jail or penitentiary, or a city prison operated by a city having a population of one million or more inhabitants, for any period that such person is not detained pursuant to commitment based on an indictment, an information, a simplified information, a prosecutor's information, a misdemeanor complaint or a felony complaint, an arrest warrant or a bench warrant, or any order by a court of competent jurisdiction, the state shall pay to the city or county operating such facility the actual per day per capita cost as certified to the state commissioner of correctional services by the appropriate local official for the care of such person and as approved by the director of the budget. The reimbursement rate shall not, however, exceed thirty dollars per day per capita and forty dollars per day per capita on and after the first day of April, nineteen hundred eighty-eight.

(iii) A warrant issued for a presumptive release, a parole, a conditional release or a post-release supervision violator may be executed by any parole officer or any officer authorized to serve criminal process or any peace officer, who is acting pursuant to his special duties, or police officer. Any such officer to whom such warrant shall be delivered is authorized and required to execute such warrant by taking such person and having him detained as provided in this paragraph.

(iv) Where the alleged violator is detained in another state pursuant to such warrant and is not under parole supervision pursuant to the uniform act for out-of-state parolee supervision or where an alleged violator under parole supervision pursuant to the uniform act for out-of-state parolee supervision is detained in a state other than the receiving state, the warrant will not be deemed to be executed until the alleged violator is detained exclusively on the basis of such warrant and the division of parole has received notification that the alleged violator (A) has formally waived extradition to this state or (B) has been ordered extradited to this state pursuant to a judicial determination. The alleged violator will not be considered to be within the convenience and practical control of the division of parole until the warrant is deemed to be executed.

(b) A person who shall have been taken into custody pursuant to this subdivision for violation of one or more conditions of presumptive release, parole, conditional release or post-release supervision shall, insofar as practicable, be incarcerated in the county or city in which the arrest occurred.

(c) (i) Within fifteen days after the warrant for retaking and temporary detention has been executed, unless the releasee has been convicted of a new crime committed while under presumptive release, parole, conditional release or post-release supervision, the board of parole shall afford the alleged presumptive release, parole, conditional release or post-release supervision violator a preliminary revocation hearing before a hearing officer designated by the board of parole. Such hearing officer shall not have had any prior supervisory involvement over the alleged violator.

(ii) The preliminary presumptive release, parole, conditional release or post-release supervision revocation hearing shall be conducted at an appropriate correctional facility, or such other place reasonably close to the area in which the alleged violation occurred as the board may designate.

(iii) The alleged violator shall, within three days of the execution of the warrant, be given written notice of the time, place and purpose of the hearing unless he is detained pursuant to the provisions of subparagraph (iv) of paragraph (a) of this subdivision. In those instances, the alleged violator will be given written notice of the time, place and purpose of the hearing within five days of the execution of the warrant. The notice shall state what conditions of presumptive release, parole, conditional release or post-release supervision are alleged to have been violated, and in what manner; that such person shall have the right to appear and speak in his own behalf; that he shall have the right to introduce letters and documents; that he may present witnesses who can give relevant information to the hearing officer; that he has the right to confront the witnesses against him. Adverse witnesses may be compelled to attend the preliminary hearing unless the prisoner has been convicted of a new crime while on supervision or unless the hearing officer finds good cause for their non-attendance.

(iv) The preliminary hearing shall be scheduled to take place no later than fifteen days from the date of execution of the warrant. The standard of proof at the preliminary hearing shall be probable cause to believe that the presumptive releasee, parolee, conditional releasee or person under post-release supervision has violated one or more conditions of his presumptive release, parole, conditional release or post-release supervision in an important respect. Proof of conviction of a crime committed while under supervision shall constitute probable cause for the purposes of this section.

(v) At the preliminary hearing, the hearing officer shall review the violation charges with the alleged violator, direct the presentation of evidence concerning the alleged violation, receive the statements of witnesses and documentary evidence on behalf of the prisoner, and allow cross examination of those witnesses in attendance.

(vi) At the conclusion of the preliminary hearing, the hearing officer shall inform the alleged violator of his decision as to whether there is probable cause to believe that the presumptive releasee, parolee, conditional releasee or person on post-release supervision has violated one or more conditions of his release in an important respect. Based solely on the evidence adduced at the hearing, the hearing officer shall determine whether there is probable cause to believe that such person has violated his presumptive release, parole, conditional release or post-release supervision in an important respect. The hearing officer shall in writing state the reasons for his determination and the evidence relied on. A copy of the written findings shall be sent to both the alleged violator and his counsel.

(vii) If the hearing officer is satisfied that there is no probable cause to believe that such person has violated one or more conditions of release in an important respect, he shall dismiss the notice of violation and direct such person be restored to supervision.

(viii) If the hearing officer is satisfied that there is probable cause to believe that such person has violated one or more conditions of release in an important respect, he shall so find.

(d) [*Repealed eff. Sept. 1, 2009.*] If a finding of probable cause is made pursuant to this subdivision either by a determination at a preliminary hearing or by the waiver thereof, or if the releasee has been convicted of a new crime while under presumptive release, parole, conditional release or post-release supervision, the board's rules shall provide for (i) declaring such person to be delinquent as soon as practicable and shall require reasonable and appropriate action to make a final determination with respect to the alleged violation or (ii) ordering such person to be restored to presumptive release, parole, conditional release or post-release supervision under such circumstances as it may deem appropriate or (iii) when a presumptive releasee, parolee, conditional releasee or person on postrelease supervision has been convicted of a new felony committed while under such supervision and a new indeterminate or determinate sentence has been imposed, the board's rules shall provide for a final declaration of delinquency. The inmate shall then be notified in writing that his release has been revoked on the basis of the new conviction and a copy of the commitment shall accompany said notification. The inmate's next appearance before the board shall be governed by the legal requirements of said new indeterminate or determinate sentence, or shall occur as soon after a final reversal of the conviction as is practicable.

(d) [*Effective Sept. 1, 2009.*] If a finding of probable cause is made pursuant to this subdivision either by determination at a preliminary hearing or by the waiver thereof, or if the releasee has been convicted of a new crime while under his present parole or conditional release supervision, the board's rules shall provide for (i) declaring such person to be delinquent as soon as practicable and shall require reasonable and appropriate action to make a final determination with respect to the alleged violation or (ii) ordering such person to be restored to parole supervision under such circumstances as it may deem appropriate or (iii) when a parolee or conditional releasee has been convicted of a new felony committed while under his present parole or conditional release supervision and a new indeterminate sentence has been imposed, the board's rules shall provide for a final declaration of delinquency. The inmate shall then be notified in writing that his release has been revoked on the basis of the new conviction and a copy of the commitment shall accompany said notification. The inmate's next appearance before the board shall be governed by the legal requirements of said new indeterminate sentence, or shall occur as soon after a final reversal of the conviction as is practicable.

(e) (i) If the alleged violator requests a local revocation hearing, he shall be given a revocation hearing reasonably near the place of the alleged violation or arrest if he has not been convicted of a crime committed while under supervision. However, the board may, on its own motion, designate a case for a local revocation hearing.

(ii) If there are two or more alleged violations, the hearing may be conducted near the place of the violation chiefly relied upon as a basis for the issuance of the warrant as determined by the board.

(iii) If a local revocation hearing is not ordered pursuant to subparagraph one the alleged violator shall be given a revocation hearing upon his return to a state correctional facility.

(f) (i) Revocation hearings shall be scheduled to be held within ninety days of the probable cause determination. However, if an alleged violator requests and receives any postponement of his revocation hearing, or consents to a postponed revocation proceeding initiated by the board, or if an alleged violator, by his actions otherwise precludes the prompt conduct of such proceedings, the time limit may be extended.

(ii) The revocation hearing shall be conducted by a presiding officer who may be a member or a hearing officer designated by the board in accordance with rules of the board.

(iii) Both the alleged violator and an attorney who has filed a notice of appearance on his behalf in accordance with the rules of the board of parole shall be given written notice of the date, place and time of the hearing as soon as possible but at least fourteen days prior to the scheduled date.

(iv) The alleged violator shall be given written notice of the rights enumerated in subparagraph (iii) of paragraph (c) of this subdivision as well as of his right to present mitigating evidence relevant to restoration to presumptive release, parole, conditional release or post-release supervision and his right to counsel.

(v) The alleged violator shall be permitted representation by counsel at the revocation hearing. In any case where such person is financially unable to retain counsel, the criminal court of the city of New York, the county court or district court in the county where the violation is alleged to have occurred or where the hearing is held, shall assign counsel in accordance with the county or city plan for representation placed in operation pursuant to article eighteen-B of the county law. He shall have the right to confront and cross examine adverse witnesses, unless there is good cause for their nonattendance as determined by the presiding officer; present witnesses and documentary evidence in defense of the charges; and present witnesses and documentary evidence relevant to the question whether reincarceration of the alleged violator is appropriate.

(vi) At the revocation hearing, the charges shall be read and the alleged violator shall be permitted to plead not guilty, guilty, guilty with explanation or to stand mute. As to each charge, evidence shall be introduced through witnesses and documents, if any, in support of that charge. At the conclusion of each witness's direct testimony, he shall be made available for cross-examination. If the alleged violator intends to present a defense to the charges or to present evidence of mitigating circumstances, the alleged violator shall do so after presentation of all the evidence in support of a violation of presumptive release, parole, conditional release or post-release supervision.

(vii) All persons giving evidence at the revocation hearing shall be sworn before giving any testimony as provided by law.

(viii) At the conclusion of the hearing the presiding officer may sustain any or all of the violation charges or may dismiss any or all violation charges. He may sustain a violation charge only if the charge is supported by a preponderance of the evidence adduced.

(ix) If the presiding officer is not satisfied that there is a preponderance of evidence in support of the violation, he shall dismiss the violation, cancel the delinquency and restore the person to presumptive release, parole, conditional release or post-release supervision.

(x) If the presiding officer is satisfied that there is a preponderance of evidence that the alleged violator violated one or more conditions of release in an important respect, he or she shall so find. For each violation so found, the presiding officer may (A) direct that the presumptive releasee, parolee, conditional releasee or person serving a period of post-release supervision be restored to supervision; (B) as an alternative to reincarceration, direct the presumptive releasee, parolee, conditional releasee or person serving a period of post-release supervision be placed in a parole transition facility for a period not to exceed one hundred eighty days and subsequent restoration to supervision; (C) in the case of presumptive releasee, parolees or conditional releasees, direct the violator's reincarceration and fix a date for consideration by the board for re-release on presumptive release, or parole or conditional release, as the case may be; or (D) in the case of persons released to a period of post-release supervision, direct the violator's reincarceration for a period of at least six months and up to the balance of the remaining period of post-release supervision, not to exceed five years. Where a date has been fixed for the violator's re-release on presumptive release, parole or conditional release, as the case may be, the board or board member may waive the personal interview between a member or members of the board and the violator to determine the suitability for re-release; provided, however, that the board shall retain the authority to suspend the date fixed for re-release and to require a personal interview

based on the violator's institutional record or on such other basis as is authorized by the rules and regulations of the board. If an interview is required, the board shall notify the violator of the time of such interview in accordance with the rules and regulations of the board. If the violator is placed in a parole transition facility or restored to supervision, the presiding officer may impose such other conditions of presumptive release, parole, conditional release, or post-release supervision as he may deem appropriate, as authorized by rules of the board.

(xi) If the presiding officer sustains any violations, he must prepare a written statement, to be made available to the alleged violator and his counsel, indicating the evidence relied upon and the reasons for revoking presumptive release, parole, conditional release or post-re lease supervision, and for the disposition made.

(g) Revocation of presumptive release, parole, conditional release or post-release supervision shall not prevent re-parole or re-release provided such re-parole or re-release is not inconsistent with any other provisions of law.

(h) If the alleged violation is not sustained and the alleged violator is restored to supervision, the interruptions specified in subdivision three of section 70.40 of the penal law shall not apply, but the time spent in custody in any state or local correctional institution shall be credited against the term of the sentence in accordance with the rules specified in paragraph (c) of such subdivision.

(i) Where there is reasonable cause to believe that a presumptive releasee, parolee, conditional releasee or person under post-release supervision has absconded from supervision the board may declare such person to be delinquent. This paragraph shall not be construed to deny such person a preliminary revocation hearing upon his retaking, nor to relieve the division of parole of any obligation it may have to exercise due diligence to retake the alleged absconder, nor to relieve the parolee or releasee of any obligation he may have to comply with the conditions of his release.

4. Appeals.

(a) Except for determinations made upon preliminary hearings upon allegations of violation of presumptive release, parole, conditional release or post-release supervision, all determinations made pursuant to this section may be appealed in accordance with rules promulgated by the board. Any board member who participated in the decision from which the appeal is taken may not participate in the resolution of that appeal. The rules of the board may specify a time within which any appeal shall be taken and resolved.

(b) Upon an appeal to the board, the inmate may be represented by an attorney. Where the inmate is financially unable to provide for his own attorney, upon request an attorney shall be assigned pursuant to the provisions of subparagraph (v) of paragraph (f) of subdivision three of this section.

5. Actions of the board. Any action by the board or by a hearing officer pursuant to this article shall be deemed a judicial function and shall not be reviewable if done in accordance with law.

6. Record of proceedings. (a) The board shall provide for the making of a verbatim record of each parole release interview, except where a decision is made to release the inmate to parole supervision, and each preliminary and final revocation hearing except when the decision of the presiding officer after such hearings result in a dismissal of all charged violations of parole, conditional release or post release supervision.

(b) The chairman of the board of parole shall maintain records of all parole interviews and hearings for a period of twenty-five years from the date of the parole release interview or until expiration of the maximum term of sentence.

7. Deaf person before the board. Whenever any deaf person participates in an interview, parole release hearing, preliminary hearing or revocation hearing, there shall be appointed a qualified interpreter who is certified by a recognized national or New York state credentialing authority to interpret the proceedings to and the statements or testimony of such deaf person. The board shall determine a reasonable fee for all such interpreting services, the cost of which shall be a charge upon the division of parole.

Amended by L. 1978, Ch. 499; L. 1980, Ch. 76, Ch. 412; L. 1981, Ch. 430; L. 1983, Ch. 417, amending subd. 3(f)(x); L. 1984, Ch. 238, amending subd. 3(d), L. 1984, Ch. 413, amending subds. 3(c)(i) and 3(d); L. 1984, Ch. 435, adding subd. 3(a)(iv); L. 1985, Ch, 78, amending subd. 2(c); L. 1985, Ch. 372, adding subd. 2(d); L. 1985, Ch. 494; L. 1986, Ch. 230, amending subd. 2(b); Ch. 466, adding last sentence which applies to all pending parole proceedings; L. 1987, Chs. 261, 262, amending subd. 3(a)(ii); L. 1987, Ch. 396, amending subd. 2(a) and applies to all pending parole proceedings; L. 1989, Ch. 73, amending subd. 3(f)(x); L. 1989, Ch. 432, amending subd. 3(c)(iii); L. 1991, Ch. 166, amending subds. 3(f)(x), 3(f)(xi) and 5; L. 1991, Ch. 703; L. 1992, Ch. 55, eff. Apr. 10, 1992, added subd. 2(e) and, by § 288, amended subd. 3(a)(i); L. 1994, Ch. 61, § 3, extending expiration date of subd. 3(a)(i); L. 1994, Ch. 559, § 2, eff. Nov. 1, 1994, amending subd. 2(c); L. 1995, Ch. 3, § 39, amending subd. 2(a), eff. Oct. 1, 1995, amendment repealed Sept. 30, 2005 pursuant to L. 1995, Ch. 3, § 74, paragraph (d); L. 1995, Ch. 3, § 40, amending subds. 2(d)(i) and (2)(d)(ii), eff. June 10, 1995; L. 1995, Ch. 3, § 41, amending subd. 3(a)(i); L. 1995, Ch. 3, § 42, amending subd. 3(d), eff. Oct. 1, 1995, repealed Sept. 30, 2005 pursuant to L. 1995, Ch. 3, § 74, paragraph (d); L. 1996, Ch. 48, extending expiration date of subd. 3(a)(i) to Apr. 10, 1998, eff. Apr. 12, 1996; L. 1997, Ch. 581, § 1, eff. Jan. 1, 1998, amending subd. 2(c); L. 1998, Ch. 1, §§ 26–39, eff. Aug. 6, 1998, and shall apply to offenses committed on or after Sept. 1, 1998. Offenses committed prior to Sept. 1, 1998 shall be governed by the provisions of law in effect at the time the offense was committed; provided, however, that nothing contained herein shall be deemed to affect the application, qualification, expiration, reversion or repeal of any provision of law amended by any section of L. 1998, Ch. 1 and the provisions of L. 1998, Ch. 1 shall be applied or qualified or shall expire or revert or be deemed repealed in the same manner, to the same extent and on the same date as the case may be as otherwise provided by

law; and L. 1998, Ch. 38, § 1, eff. Apr. 8, 1998, extending the expiration date of subd. 3(a)(i) as amended by L. 1992, Ch. 55, § 288, to Apr. 10, 2000; L. 1999, Ch. 126, eff. June 29, 1999, amending subd. 2(c), and Ch. 40, eff. May 10, 1999, amending subd. 2(c); L. 2000, Ch. 16, eff. Mar. 30, 2000, extending the expiration date of the amendments made to subd. 3(a)(i) by L. 1992, Ch. 55; L. 2001, Ch. 95, § 18, eff. July 13, 2001, extending the expiration date; L. 2003, Ch. 62, Part E, § 11, eff. May 15, 2003 and deemed effective Apr. 1, 2003, amending subds. 2 and 3; Ch. 62, Part F, § 9, eff. May 15, 2003, amending subd. 2; Ch. 62, Part T, § 1, deemed eff. Apr. 1, 2003, amending subd. 6; Ch. 16, § 17, extending expiration date until Sept. 1, 2005, eff. Mar. 31, 2003; L. 2004, Ch. 56, Part J, § 1, eff. Aug. 20, 2004, amending subd. 3(a)(ii); L. 2005, Ch. 56, Part D, §§ 15, 20, eff. Apr. 1, 2005, extending effective and expiration dates of subds. 2(a)(i), 3(a)(i), and 3(d).

ANNOTATIONS

Adjournments.—Where a parolee requests an adjournment to obtain counsel or to await disposition of pending criminal charges, the rule requiring parole revocation hearings within ninety days of the probable cause determination is extended. People ex rel. Moulier v. Smith, 115 A.D.2d 307, 496 N.Y.S.2d 309 (4th Dept. 1986).

Burden of proof.—The burden rests upon the parole authorities in every instance in which timely hearings have not been held to demonstrate that they were unable to do so because the parolee was not subject to their convenience and practical control. Vasquez v. New York State Bd. of Parole, 58 N.Y.2d 981, 460 N.Y.S.2d 918, 447 N.E.2d 1279 (1983).

—Entrapment is a defense to charge of violation of general parole rule 12. People ex rel. Dowdy v. Smith, 48 N.Y.2d 477, 423 N.Y.S.2d 862, 399 N.E.2d 894 (1979).

—The standard of proof at a preliminary parole violation hearing is "probable cause." People ex rel. Van Fossen v. Dillon, 72 A.D.2d 166, 424 N.Y.S.2d 550 (4th Dept. 1980).

—The standard of proof at the preliminary hearing is only probable cause; however, at the final parole revocation hearing the charges must be proved by a preponderance of the evidence. People ex rel. Wallace v. State, 67 A.D.2d 1093, 415 N.Y.S.2d 157 (4th Dept. 1979).

Collateral estoppel.—Defendant's acquittal based upon the prosecution's failure to meet its burden of proof, does not invoke the doctrine of collateral estoppel to prevent parole authorities from revoking parole when the parolee has been acquitted of criminal charges based upon the same conduct which underlies the alleged violations of parole. People ex rel. Singletary v. Dalsheim, 84 A.D.2d 553, 443 N.Y.S.2d 172 (2d Dept. 1981).

Conditional parole for deportation only.—Initial grant of conditional parole for deportation only (CPDO) to defendant was properly revoked when the presentence report informed parole board that defendant was a direct link to the Cali cartel and was in charge of the cartel operations in the New York metropolitan area. The purpose of the subsequent Parole Board hearing is to correct mistakes made in the initial determination that granted parole to an inmate before release. Although defendant was eligible for release based on the crime for which he was incarcerated, that is but one factor which is considered in the determination to grant CPDO. Ortiz v. New York State Dept. of Parole, 239 A.D.2d 52, 668 N.Y.S.2d 823 (4th Dept. 1998).

De novo hearing.—Following Division of Parole's failure, after three attempts, to provide petitioner with a fair hearing, the proper remedy was to remand for a de novo hearing before a different panel rather than to release petitioner on parole. Quartararo v. New York State Div. of Parole, 224 A.D.2d 266, 637 N.Y.S.2d 721 (1st Dept. 1996).

Delay.—Three-month delay between petitioner's parole violation and the execution of the parole violation warrant was not unreasonable. People ex rel. Crooks v. State Div. of Parole, 195 A.D.2d 297, 600 N.Y.S.2d 9 (1st Dept. 1993).

—Petitioner was restored to parole under the conditions that existed at the time of his original release where 10 months had elapsed following his arrest for alleged parole violation and he had not received a final parole revocation hearing; such delay, where not chargeable to petitioner, was unreasonable and results in a deprivation of due process. People ex rel. Allen v. Dalsheim, 63 A.D.2d 973, 406 N.Y.S.2d 104 (2d Dept. 1978).

—Even if petitioner had been denied his right to appear before the Parole Board, petitioner would not be entitled to immediate release; "parole decisions are discretionary and prisoners have no right to be released prior to the expiration of their sentences." Daniels v. Beaver, 303 A.D.2d 1025, 757 N.Y.S.2d 195 (4th Dept. 2003).

—Although a delay of the hearing beyond the statutory 90-day period is unreasonable *per se,* the time limit may be extended when the alleged violator by his actions, such as failing to appear, otherwise precludes the prompt conduct of such proceedings. People *ex rel.* Sincento v. New York State Bd. of Parole, 78 A.D.2d 574, 432 N.Y.S.2d 418 (4th Dept. 1980).

—Writ of habeas corpus was granted where defendant, although within the convenience and practical control of the parole board, was subjected to a delay of over 90 days, excluding statutory exceptions, between the finding of probable cause of a parole violation and the final revocation hearing; such delay was held to be unreasonable *per se.* People *ex rel.* Goodman v. Smith, 73 A.D.2d 800, 423 N.Y.S.2d 724 (4th Dept. 1979).

Determination of MPI; consideration of crime charged.—Consideration solely of the seriousness of the offense, where defendant, armed with a shotgun, attempted to rob the occupants of an armored truck, constituted a sufficient and meaningful reason for the board's action in fixing the minimum period of imprisonment. Hintze v. New York State Bd. of Parole, 66 A.D.2d 848, 411 N.Y.S.2d 389 (1st Dept. 1978).

—In making decisions concerning the release of an inmate to parole supervision, the Division of Parole may consider the crime for which the inmate was convicted. Gerena v. Rodriguez, 192 A.D.2d 606, 596 N.Y.S.2d 143, 144 (2d Dept. 1993).

—Petitioner's article 78 proceeding was dismissed where the Parole Board exceeded the established time range for his minimum period of imprisonment of 18 to 26 months; since the reasons for the Board's decision were sufficiently detailed, namely, the serious nature of the offense, the victim was a 15-year-old youth and a prior history of alcoholism and sex crimes. Weyant v. Hammock, 84 A.D.2d 901, 445 N.Y.S.2d 42 (3d Dept. 1981).

—The Board determined that, despite his good institutional record, the gravity of the crime for which the petitioner was convicted, murder in the second degree, and the gruesome manner in which it was committed were so egregious that the release of the petitioner on parole would "so deprecate the seriousness of his crime as to undermine respect for the law." Rentz v. Herbert, 206 A.D.2d 944, 615 N.Y.S.2d 178 (4th Dept. 1994).

Determination of MPI; generally.—It was proper for Parole Board to fix the minimum period of incarceration (MPI) in excess of one third of maximum where the court failed to fix a minimum sentence even though the court could not have fixed such a sentence itself; in light of the board's expertise and the fact that responsibility for a difficult and complex function has been committed to it, there would have to be a showing of irrationality bordering on impropriety before intervention would be warranted. Russo v. New York State Bd. of Parole, 50 N.Y.2d 69, 427 N.Y.S.2d 982, 405 N.E.2d 225 (1980).

—It was improper for the Board of Parole to set the petitioner's minimum period of imprisonment at the same length as the maximum term imposed by the sentencing court; such a ruling is contra not only to the legislative intention in enacting Article 12-B of the Executive Law, but also to the reasonable expectation of the sentencing court in imposing an indeterminate sentence with no stated minimum. Russo v. Board of Parole, 69 A.D.2d 520, 419 N.Y.S.2d 166 (2d Dept. 1979).

—Decisions by the Parole Board are discretionary and are not subject to judicial review if made in accordance with the law. Augle v. New York State Parole Bd., 192 A.D.2d 1031, 597 N.Y.S.2d 213 (3d Dept. 1993).

—The parole board in determining the minimum period of imprisonment must take into consideration the recommendations of the trial judge. Jorge v. Hammock, 84 A.D.2d 362, 446 N.Y.S.2d 585 (3d Dept. 1982).

—In the absence of any convincing showing to the contrary, it must be presumed that the board fulfilled its statutory duty and considered the enumerated factors for setting the defendant's minimum period of imprisonment. Friedman v. Hammock, 80 A.D.2d 976, 438 N.Y.S.2d 628 (3d Dept. 1981).

—Where the Board of Parole impermissibly sets a prisoner's MPI or fails to state reasons for the MPI, the remedy is not

habeas corpus leading to release of the prisoner, but an Article 78 proceeding to compel compliance. People *ex rel.* Holmes v. Smith, 61 A.D.2d 1128, 403 N.Y.S.2d 162 (4th Dept. 1978).

Ex-post facto application.—Ex-post facto application of standards of Exec. Law § 259-i is generally not unconstitutional even though petitioner's conviction pre-dated enactment of statute since there is no disadvantage to petitioner. People *ex rel.* Gilmore v. New York State Parole Board, 241 A.D.2d 793, 661 N.Y.S.2d 78 (3d Dept. 1997).

Exclusionary rule.—In revocation of petitioner's parole it was improper for the Board of Parole to consider evidence obtained in violation of petitioner's right against illegal search. People *ex rel.* Piccarillo, 64 A.D.2d 641, 406 N.Y.S.2d 865 (2d Dept. 1978), *aff'd,* 48 N.Y.2d 76, 421 N.Y.S.2d 842, 397 N.E.2d 354 (1979).

—Statements made by the parolee in the absence of counsel may be used in a parole revocation hearing, as a parole revocation hearing is not a stage of a criminal prosecution. Utsey v. New York State Bd. of Parole, 89 A.D.2d 965, 454 N.Y.S.2d 114 (1982).

—The statements were not admissible in the parole revocation hearing since the state failed to sustain its burden of showing that there was sufficient attenuation between the illegal arrest, search and seizure and the admissions made by parolee to his parole officer. People *ex rel.* Jones v. New York State Bd. of Parole, 76 A.D.2d 782, 429 N.Y.S.2d 14 (1st Dept. 1980).

—Although the exclusionary rule has been applied to administrative hearings, it should not be applied to a parole-revocation hearing where the evidence sought to be suppressed (confession) "was not seized by the agents of, or for the purposes of, the agency conducting the administrative proceeding." People *ex rel.* King v. New York State Bd. of Parole, 65 A.D.2d 465, 412 N.Y.S.2d 138 (1st Dept. 1978).

Hearing officers.—The recommendation of the hearing officer at the parole revocation hearing is advisory and not binding on the Board of Parole, which has the authority to establish a higher minimum period of incarceration. People v. Smith, 75 A.D.2d 706, 427 N.Y.S.2d 108 (4th Dept. 1980).

Hearing not afforded on basis of more current information without showing of impropriety.—Executive Law § 259-i does not afford the right to a new hearing "in the interest of justice" to permit an evaluation of parole violator's status on the basis of more current information, without the showing of some impropriety. Kaminsky v. Hammock, 76 A.D.2d 758, 428 N.Y.S.2d 677 (1st Dept. 1980).

Hospital prison ward constructively state correction facility.—The prison wards in a hospital are under the constructive jurisdiction of the Department of Correction for the purposes of computing defendants' jail time. People *ex rel.* Laurence v. New York State Bd. of Parole, 68 A.D.2d 830, 414 N.Y.S.2d 230 (1st Dept. 1979).

"Important respect."—Petitioner's failure to notify parole officer of his unexpected trip out of the county to be with his six-year-old sister for a medical emergency which occurred after hours was sustained by a preponderance of evidence, but was not a violation in an "important respect"; petitioner had been granted permission to visit the family out of county before without a travel pass upon mere notification of parole officer. Here notification was attempted, but not accomplished because of the late hour. Bayham v. Meloni, 182 Misc. 2d 831, 700 N.Y.S.2d 649 (Co. Ct. Monroe Co. 1999).

Notice and discovery.—Exec. L. § 259-i(3)(c)(iii) is not a jurisdictional notice requirement like section 259-i(3)(c)(i); therefore, absent a showing of prejudice, a four-month lapse between the notice and the hearing is not actionable where realtor was represented by counsel, consented to the adjournments, and had ample time to prepare and assert challenges. People *ex rel.* Washington v. New York State Division of Parole, 279 A.D.2d 379, 720 N.Y.S.2d 22 (1st Dept. 2001).

—The three-day period prescribed by statute ended on a Sunday, and was therefore extended, by operation of Gen. Constr. Law § 25-a(1), to the following day. People *ex rel.* Atkinson v. Warden, 201 A.D.2d 271, 607 N.Y.S.2d 256 (1st Dept. 1994).

—When the substantive offense prohibits drug use generally, due process does not require that the parolee be informed of the exact time and place that he allegedly used the illegal drugs. Gonzalez v. New York State Parole Bd., 193 A.D.2d 356, 597 N.Y.S.2d 40 (1st Dept. 1993).

—Board of Parole was not required by either statute or case

law to reveal the name of the member of the Board who had reviewed the findings of the parole hearing officer in connection with the parole revocation hearing. People ex rel. Lambertis v. Board of Parole, 72 A.D.2d 694, 421 N.Y.S.2d 365 (1st Dept. 1979).

—Since the Board of Parole and Department of Correctional Services did not show any "overriding reason to maintain their confidentiality," the petitioner should be afforded access to those portions of his parole file requested, prior to his final revocation hearing. People ex rel. Stern v. New York State Bd. of Parole, 57 A.D.2d 561, 393 N.Y.S.2d 183 (2d Dept. 1977).

—One-day delay in three-day notice requirement of parole violation and preliminary hearing did not require dismissal of parole violation warrant. Petitioner's restoration to parole where the preliminary hearing was conducted timely and there was no claim of prejudice or inadequate notice by delay. People ex rel. Williams v. Walsh, 241 A.D.2d 979, 661 N.Y.S.2d 371 (4th Dept. 1997).

—Motion to quash subpoena for state parole records of complainant was granted where defendant, charged with assault, first degree, and criminal possession of a weapon, fourth degree, claimed that he needed the parole records to establish that complainant was lying about the incident in order to avoid a finding of a parole violation, since any motive to lie arose from the complainant's parole status itself and not from what was contained in the records; the defendant was free to cross examine the complainant with respect to his being on parole. People v. Casanova, 101 Misc. 2d 874, 422 N.Y.S.2d 307 (Sup. Ct. Bronx Co. 1979).

Out of state parole.—Petitioner, although in technical violation of his parole for not residing in his mother's Connecticut home as was authorized in his travel permit, was restored to parole because such travel permit was issued by his parole officer without affording the receiving state an opportunity to investigate the home, and the improper travel permit had a real bearing on the subsequent parole violation since an investigation would have revealed that there was no room at the designated home for the petitioner. People ex rel. Adams v. Vincent, 63 A.D.2d 664, 404 N.Y.S.2d 394 (2d Dept. 1978).

Parole credit granted for Board's misconduct.—Where the Board of Parole refused to provide written reasons for its denial of petitioner's application for release, even after petitioner brought a successful Article 78 proceeding compelling the Board to do so, forcing petitioner to obtain release from custody by means of a writ of habeas corpus, petitioner was awarded parole credit for the entire period from his release through the subsequent protracted litigation on the ground that the Board's conduct could not be condoned and contributed to petitioner's anxiety to clarify his status. Biondo v. Regan, 69 A.D.2d 880, 415 N.Y.S.2d 690 (2d Dept. 1979).

Parole eligibility hearing.—There was no error committed in denying petitioner a new hearing where the parole board considered the inmate's institutional record and met its obligation of informing petitioner in writing of the reasons for denial of parole. Collins v. Hammock, 52 N.Y.2d 798, 436 N.Y.S.2d 704, 417 N.E.2d 1245 (1980).

Parole factors.—Parole board need not enumerate every statutory factor considered in its decision nor give each factor equal weight; hearing transcript contained details of premeditated double murder as well as exemplary prison disciplinary record, positive program accomplishments, and post-release plans; Board can give greater weight to violent nature of crimes in finding that release would present a danger to the community. Mandala v. Dennison, 20 A.D.3d 757, 798 N.Y.S.2d 563 (3d Dept. 2005).

—Where petitioner was serving concurrent 25 years to life sentences for role in a 1976 social club fire that killed 25 people, Board's decision to give greater weight to serious and violent nature of crime over positive prison record which was specifically considered by Board was justified; denial of application did not evince "irrationality bordering on impropriety." Mendez v. N.Y.S. Bd. of Parole, 20 A.D.3d 742, 797 N.Y.S.2d 782 (3d Dept. 2005).

—Board is not required to grant parole merely to reward a petitioner's positive rehabilitative efforts, nor is Board required to assign equal weight to all factors considered; violent nature of beating death and dismemberment of off-duty police officer supported Board's denial of parole. Vasquez v. N.Y.S. Div.of Parole, 19 A.D.3d 960, 797 N.Y.S.2d 655 (3d Dept. 2005).

—Receipt of a certificate of earned eligibility does not guarantee

grant of parole, but is just one of many factors Board considers, and parole can be denied, notwithstanding certificate, where Board determines, based on all factors, that inmate's release is not compatible with the welfare of society or that petitioner cannot live at liberty without violating the law. Morrero v. Dennison, 19 A.D.3d 960, 797 N.Y.S.2d 638 (3d Dept. 2005).

—Judicial intervention is warranted only upon a showing that Parole Board's determination exhibits "irrationality bordering on impropriety"; however, no such showing exists where Board considered factors set forth in this section, placing particular emphasis on violent nature of crime, disregard for human life, as well as prior history of criminal conduct. Board is not obligated to discuss or reveal each factor considered. Henderson v. N.Y.S. Div. of Parole, 7 A.D.3d 898, 775 N.Y.S.2d 920 (3d Dept. 2004).

—Board's consideration of relevant statutory factors, including petitioner's involvement in a robbery and burglary of elderly couple in their home while on parole, his significant criminal record and his numerous prison disciplinary infractions as well as positive program accomplishments and work evaluations, in concluding that his release would pose a threat to safety and welfare of community, did not exhibit "irrationality bordering on impropriety" and was not subject to further judicial review. Moore v. Travis, 8 A.D.3d 717, 777 N.Y.S.2d 778 (3d Dept. 2004).

—Petitioner has no protected liberty interest in parole release once his minimum sentence is served; record of proceeding revealed that in addition to particular emphasis placed on instant offense, all relevant statutory factors were considered, including institutional and educational achievements, and supported Board's decision that petitioner's release would be incompatible with public welfare. Warren v. N.Y.S. Div. of Parole, 307 A.D.2d 493, 761 N.Y.S.2d 883 (3d Dept. 2003).

—Although Board is required to consider each of the factors listed in this section, it is not required to give equal weight to all factors considered. Ek v. N.Y.S. Bd. of Parole, 307 A.D.2d 433, 761 N.Y.S.2d 553 (3d Dept. 2003).

—Petitioner's good conduct while incarcerated standing alone does not guarantee a favorable outcome; in denying petitioner's parole for the fourth time, Board considered, among other things, the serious and violent nature of the crime coupled with fact that petitioner was on parole for a previous felony conviction when this latest crime was committed. Lomonaco v. N.Y.S. Bd. of Parole, 302 A.D.2d 829, 754 N.Y.S.2d 603 (3d Dept. 2003).

—Petitioner's argument that Board's decision denying discretionary release was arbitrary and capricious was rejected notwithstanding his exemplary behavior while in prison, which is just one of several factors Board must consider. Lue-Shing v. Pataki, 301 A.D.2d 827, 754 N.Y.S.2d 96 (3d Dept. 2003).

—As Board is required to consider same statutory factors each time an inmate appears before it, it is expected that in many cases the same issues contained in that inmate's record will repeatedly weigh against grant of parole release. Bridget v. Travis, 300 A.D.2d 776, 750 N.Y.S.2d 795 (3d Dept. 2002)

—DoCS has a "continuing, nondiscretionary, ministerial duty" to make accurate calculations of terms of imprisonment, a duty that requires it to correct known errors regardless of the benefit or detriment to the petitioner. Patterson v. Goord, 299 A.D.2d 769, 750 N.Y.S.2d 362 (3d Dept. 2002).

—Record makes clear that parole board considered factors mandated by Exec. Law § 259-i in making its determination; board's emphasis on the serious nature of the prisoner's crime was permissible and does not, in and of itself, demonstrate that the Board's ultimate decision was vitiated by "irrationality bordering on impropriety." Henderson v. N.Y. State Div. of Parole, 295 A.D.2d 678, 743 N.Y.S.2d 198 (3d Dept. 2002).

—Board considered all statutory factors before concluding that petitioner was not a suitable candidate for release on parole due to the violent nature of his crime and his failure to voice either remorse or insight into the causes of his brutal attack on his wife, which occurred while a valid order of protection from petitioner was in effect. Jones v. Travis, 293 A.D.2d 800, 739 N.Y.S.2d 656 (3d Dept. 2002).

—Although the Board is required to consider each of the parole factors in its determination, it is not required to expressly discuss each one or to give the same weight to each; the Board's focus on the gravity of the crime and the petitioner's failure to take responsibility for the death of his estranged wife which he viewed as accidental even though it was a direct result of his forcible sedation of her with chloroform which caused her death. Ramahlo v. Travis, 290 A.D.2d 911, 737 N.Y.S.2d 160 (3d Dept. 2002).

—Where the Board's decision contained sufficient detail to inform petitioner of the reasons for the denial of his request for release on parole, including that he committed the current offense, armed robbery, while still on parole for an earlier offense, the court concluded that 9 NYCRR 8001.3(c) "does not impose an additional requirement regarding the details to be contained in the Board's decision where the decision involves the denial of a parole release request and not the imposition of a minimum period of imprisonment." Richards v. Travis, 288 A.D.2d 604; 732 N.Y.S.2d 465 (3d Dept. 2001).

—The Board is not required to give the same weight to each and every statutory factor or to discuss each one expressly; as long as they are all considered, the emphasis on one, i.e., the serious nature of petitioner's crime, is permissible. Collado v. N.Y. State Div. of Parole, 287 A.D.2d 921, 731 N.Y.S.2d 680 (3d Dept. 2001).

—In an Article 78 proceeding challenging the determination of the Parole Board denying petitioner's application for release, evidence that Board considered petitioner's earned eligibility credit, and institutional record as well as his lack of insight into the nature and effect of his crime was sufficient to support the determination. Santos v. New York State Dept. of Parole, 267 A.D.2d 533, 698 N.Y.S.2d 563 (3d Dept. 1999).

—Appeal from denial of parole dismissed where Board properly considered appropriate factors, including petitioner's disciplinary record, criminal history, plans for release, and failure to take advantage of drug programs to treat his addiction. Warburton v. Department of Correctional Servs., 254 A.D.2d 659, 680 N.Y.S.2d 26 (3d Dept. 1998).

—Parole Board's denial of petitioner's parole upheld, notwithstanding his receipt of certificate of earned eligibility, where Board found that there was a reasonable probability that petitioner could not remain at liberty without violating the law and that his release was not compatible with the welfare of society; Board's finding was based on petitioner's refusal to take responsibility for his crime of attempted rape and his failure to participate in sex offender therapy program. Hendricks v. New York State Div. of Parole, 253 A.D.2d 965, 678 N.Y.S.2d 313 (3d Dept. 1998).

Personally interviewed.—Parole Board's use of a two-way television in order to conduct petitioner's interview did not violate statute's requirement that he be "personally interviewed" in the absence of a showing of prejudice. Vanier v. Travis, 274 A.D.2d 797, 711 N.Y.S.2d 920 (3d Dept. 2000).

Preliminary hearing.—The statute requires that the preliminary hearing be held within 15 days after the warrant for temporary detention and retaking has been executed and execution of the parole violation takes place when a copy thereof is served upon the alleged parole violator, and he is reduced to the custody of the authorities seeking his arrest. People ex rel. Delrow v. New York State Div. of Parole, 75 A.D.2d 324, 429 N.Y.S.2d 659 (1st Dept. 1980).

—Preliminary hearing is designed to determine if there is probable cause that a parole violation occurred, failure of ALJ to address one of charges does not preclude it from being raised at final revocation hearing, petitioner had notice that all charges could be raised final hearing. Poladian v. Travis, 8 A.D.3d 770, 778 N.Y.S.2d 232 (3d Dept. 2004).

—Full Faith and Credit Clause did not bar New York from treating petitioner's guilty plea as a conviction for purposes of denying a preliminary hearing on a parole violation. People ex rel. Cassarino v. New York State Div. of Parole, 170 Misc. 2d 47, 649 N.Y.S.2d 323 (Sup. Ct. Kings Co. 1996).

Reviewability of board action.—The Parole Board performs a very significant function in determining the length of time which an inmate will spend in prison and it is entitled to exercise substantial discretion within its sphere. King v. New York State Div. of Parole, 190 A.D.2d 423, 598 N.Y.S.2d 245 (1st Dept. 1993).

—Discretionary denial of parole is not subject to judicial review. Almeyda v. N.Y. S. Div. of Parole, 4 A.D.3d 525, 771 N.Y.S.2d 722 (3d Dept. 2004).

—Discretionary decisions of the Board of Parole which take into consideration the criteria set forth in section 259-i(5) are

not judicially reviewable. Secilmic v. Keane, 225 A.D.2d 628, 639 N.Y.S.2d 437 (2d Dept. 1996).

—Since the petitioner did not make a convincing showing that the New York State Division of Parole did not act properly in accordance with the statutory requirements, the determination denying him parole was not subject to judicial review. Heath v. New York State Division of Parole, 201 A.D.2d 732, 608 N.Y.S.2d 308 (2d Dept. 1994).

—Decision of the Parole Board is "deemed a judicial function," and not reviewable if in accordance with law, judicial intervention with a decision of the Board is warranted only when there is a "showing of irrationality bordering on impropriety." Lewis v. Travis, 9 A.D.3d 800, 780 N.Y.S.2d 243 (3d Dept. 2004).

—Parole Board's determination which complies with applicable statutory requirements, is not subject to judicial review; judicial intervention warranted only upon a "showing of irrationality bordering on impropriety;" Board considered relevant factors, and concluded that there was a reasonable probability that petitioner could not live at liberty without violating law. Erdheim v. Travis, 7 A.D.3d 876, 776 N.Y.S.2d 920 (3d Dept. 2004).

—Appellate court is not permitted to substitute its discretion for that of individuals in charge of designing terms of petitioner's parole release, as long as a special condition upon which the release of an inmate is conditioned is made in accordance with law, it is not subject to judicial review. Ahlers v. N.Y.S. Div. of Parole, 1 A.D.3d 849, 767 N.Y.S.2d 289 (3d Dept. 2003).

—Once it has been determined that Board complied with statutory requirements of this section in reaching its decision, further judicial review is precluded. Hakim v. Travis, 302 A.D.2d 82, 754 N.Y.S.2d 600 (3d Dept. 2003).

—Parole Board's decision to revoke petitioner's parole upon his guilty plea for failing to report to parole officer was discretionary act within the Board's authority and not subject to review if made in accordance with the law. Smith v. Travis, 253 A.D.2d 955, 678 N.Y.S.2d 917 (3d Dept. 1998).

—Judicial review of Board's determination is precluded where record reveals Board considered all relevant factors in their determination. Jerrell v. Ibsen, 253 A.D.2d 917, 677 N.Y.S.2d 817 (3d Dept. 1998).

—Denial of application for parole release is a discretionary decision and will not be disturbed unless it can be shown that there has been a deviation from statutory requirements, or the presence of legal error or "irrationality bordering on impropriety." Epps v. Travis, 241 A.D.2d 738, 660 N.Y.S.2d 1016 (3d Dept. 1997).

—There is no requirement that the same members constitute the second panel as were on the first or that the second panel must follow the recommendation of the first. Flores v. New York State Board of Parole, 210 A.D.2d 555, 620 N.Y.S.2d 141 (3d Dept. 1994).

—Judicial review of alleged errors in the parole revocation process is precluded prior to the exhaustion of administrative remedies. People ex rel. Woods v. McGreevy, 191 A.D.2d 938, 594 N.Y.S.2d 906 (3d Dept. 1993).

—Where there was no indication in the record that the administrative law judge acted in bad faith in order to deny relator his right to a timely hearing, the proper remedy is a new hearing rather than restoration to parole supervision. McDaniel v. Travis, 288 A.D.2d 940, 734 N.Y.S.2d 751 (4th Dept. 2001).

—New information provided to the Board was significant in that it revealed that petitioner was a high level manager of the Cali Cartel responsible for importation and distribution of tons of cocaine in the State of New York and constituted substantial evidence to support respondent's determination to rescind petitioner's early release. Rizo v. New York State Bd. of Parole, 251 A.D.2d 997, 674 N.Y.S.2d 180 (4th Dept. 1998).

—Where an adjournment of the parole revocation hearing is made at the request of the alleged parole violator and granted, the matter is usually adjourned to next available date. However, the delay is not chargable to Division of Parole, even if matter is not rescheduled for next available date and especially in light of counsel's failure to request an earlier adjourn date. People ex rel. Lewis v. Meloni, 233 A.D.2d 947, 649 N.Y.S.2d 580 (4th Dept. 1996).

—"In the absence of a convincing demonstration to the contrary, it is presumed that the New York State Division of Parole acted properly in accordance with statutory requirements" (citations omitted). Discretionary decisions will not be reviewed absent a showing of deviation from statutory requirements. Putland v. Herbert, 231 A.D.2d 893, 648 N.Y.S.2d 401 (4th Dept. 1996).

—Actions of Parole Board carry a rebuttable presumption of propriety. Zane v. Travis, 231 A.D.2d 848, 647 N.Y.S.2d 886 (4th Dept. 1996).

—The court can only examine the record to determine if the required procedural rules were followed and if there is any evidence which, if believed, would support the parole board's determination, it may not make its own determinations based on its assessment of the credibility of the witnesses. People ex rel. Walker v. Hammock, 78 A.D.2d 369, 435 N.Y.S.2d 410 (4th Dept. 1981).

—In assessing the credibility of witnesses the County Court exceeded the limited power of review permitted it in parole matters; on finding that there was evidence in the record sufficient to support a finding of probable cause and that the required procedures were followed, the court's power to review was exhausted and it should have dismissed the writ. People ex rel. Wallace v. State, 67 A.D.2d 1093, 415 N.Y.S.2d 157 (4th Dept. 1979).

Revocation hearing.—Pursuant to Exec. L. § 259-i(3)(a)(iv), the Division of Parole has no obligation to hold a parole revocation hearing until the out-of-state petitioner, presently serving a sentence in federal custody, completed serving his federal sentence and was available for extradition. People ex rel. Matthews v. New York State Division of Parole, 95 N.Y.2d 640, 722 N.Y.S.2d 213, 744 N.E.2d 1149 (2001).

—Failure to hold a timely parole revocation hearing required dismissal of parole violation charges, and fact that a parole eligibility hearing was eventually conducted some four years later on the new conviction was not relevant, as a parole eligibility hearing may not serve as a substitute for a final revocation hearing. Lindsay v. New York State Bd. of Parole, 48 N.Y.2d 833, 424 N.Y.S.2d 883, 400 N.E.2d 1335 (1979).

—The fact that the correction authorities failed to notify the division of parole that petitioner was transferred to a prison 400 miles from where the final parole revocation hearing was to be held is not an acceptable excuse for denying petitioner his right to a prompt revocation hearing. People ex. rel. Herrara v. Schager, 93 A.D.2d 847, 461 N.Y.S.2d 75 (2d Dept. 1983).

—The delay was properly charged to the petitioner and his right to a speedy hearing was not violated where a final revocation hearing was scheduled within the prescribed 90-day period but petitioner's attorney requested an adjournment because of a scheduling conflict to a day beyond the 90-day period. People ex rel. Sloan v. New York State Parole Bd., 88 A.D.2d 666, 450 N.Y.S.2d 512 (2d Dept. 1982).

—Delay in the revocation hearing was not justified where the parolee was in custody, but not within the jurisdiction of the parole board, as a prompt final parole revocation hearing is required whenever the parolee is or may be brought within the convenience and practical control of the parole authorities; New Jersey officials would have made petitioner available for New York parole revocation hearing. People ex rel. Order v. Walters, 86 A.D.2d 619, 446 N.Y.S.2d 86 (2d Dept. 1981).

—Defendant's writ of habeas corpus was sustained and he was restored to parole status with the requested treatment conditions where it was determined that a new hearing was not the proper remedy because the time period for a final parole revocation hearing had expired. Schwartz v. Warden, New York State Correctional Facility, 82 A.D.2d 870, 440 N.Y.S.2d 270 (2d Dept. 1981).

—Waiver of right to a preliminary hearing is equivalent to a probable cause determination for purposes of Exec. Law § 259-i(3)(f)(i); therefore when calculating the 90-day time period the date of waiver is excluded and then the clock starts to run. If the ninetieth day is on a Sunday, then the hearing must be held the following Monday to be timely. People ex rel. Gray v. Campbell, 241 A.D.2d 723, 660 N.Y.S.2d 186 (3d Dept. 1997).

—Adjournment of final parole revocation hearing already in progress without the consent of the parolee can be granted in the discretion of the presiding officer, for good cause if the adjournment does not extend the final hearing beyond the 90-day limit. People ex rel. Wentsley v. Dillon, 85 A.D.2d 927, 446 N.Y.S.2d 771 (4th Dept. 1981).

—The Executive Law § 259-i(3)(f)(i) requirement that parole revocation hearings be held within 90 days of the probable cause determination is subject to the limitation that the parolee must be subject to the convenience and practical control of the Parole Board. People v. Smith, 74 A.D.2d 725, 425 N.Y.S.2d 689 (4th Dept. 1980).

—Before parole may be revoked, the Board is required to find after a final hearing that relator violated the terms and conditions of parole by a preponderance of the evidence; the hearing officer need not follow the strict rules of evidence and any evidence offered may be accepted, but there must be a residuum of legal evidence to support the findings. People ex rel. Wallace v. State, 70 A.D.2d 781, 417 N.Y.S.2d 531 (4th Dept. 1979).

—Delay of more than 41 months in granting petitioner his final parole revocation hearing was prejudicial and a denial of his constitutional rights mandating dismissal of the parole detainer warrant with prejudice, and, upon expiration of the sentence imposed for the subsequent crime, he must be released to parole status. Piersma v. Henderson, 60 A.D.2d 1001, 401 N.Y.S.2d 666 (4th Dept. 1978), aff'd, 44 N.Y.2d 982, 408 N.Y.S.2d 332, 380 N.E.2d 164.

Revocation hearing following conviction on new charge.—Petitioner was not entitled to a preliminary parole revocation hearing because he was convicted of new crimes while on parole. People ex rel. Pino v. Amacucci, 300 A.D.2d 607, 752 N.Y.S.2d 548 (2d Dept. 2002).

—A petitioner who is convicted of a felony while on parole release and duly sentenced on that conviction will have his parole revoked by operation of law without the necessity of a parole revocation hearing. Oquendo v. Travis, 300 A.D.2d 773, 750 N.Y.S.2d 801 (3d Dept. 2002).

—Defendant's convictions of new charges stemming from arrest that occurred while on parole release resulted in an automatic revocation of defendant's parole by operation of law. Adams v. New York State Division of Parole, 278 A.D.2d 621, 720 N.Y.S.2d 211 (3d Dept. 2000).

—Petitioner was not denied due process when he received no notice of Board's action that resulted in automatic revocation of his parole by operation of law when petitioner was convicted of new felony charges and given an indeterminate sentence. Bennett v. Kelly, 251 A.D.2d 776, 674 N.Y.S.2d 797 (3d Dept. 1998).

—Parole revocation hearing was not required, petitioner's conviction of a felony committed while under parole supervision revoked his parole by operation of law. Stevenson v. Beaver, 309 A.D.2d 1171, 765 N.Y.S.2d 291 (4th Dept. 2003).

Revocation hearing; due process.—Due process requires "a written statement by the factfinders as to the evidence relied on and the reasons for revoking parole" in order to permit an aggrieved party to challenge the determination and for adequate judicial review. People ex rel. Hacker v. New York State Div. of Parole, 228 A.D.2d 849, 644 N.Y.S.2d 97 (3d Dept. 1996).

Revocation hearing; 90-day period.—The Division of Parole was entitled to await the disposition of the Federal bank robbery charges before lodging the parole violation warrant in this case, and the delay between the date of petitioner's conviction and the date the warrant was lodged did not constitute a denial of due process. People ex rel. Jackson v. New York State Division of Parole, 211 A.D.2d 585, 622 N.Y.S.2d 238 (1st Dept. 1995).

—Generally a parolee is entitled to a final revocation hearing within 90 days of the preliminary hearing; a parolee convicted of committing a new crime while on parole and sentenced to a new definite term, however, need only receive a final revocation hearing. Bagby v. New York State Div. of Parole, 211 A.D.2d 715, 621 N.Y.S.2d 651 (2d Dept. 1995).

—A final parole revocation hearing must be conducted within 90 days after a finding of probable cause unless the parolee requests or consents to an adjournment or otherwise causes or is responsible for extending the time. People ex rel. Bush v. Stenzel, 195 A.D.2d 495, 600 N.Y.S.2d 119 (2d Dept. 1993).

—Fact that decision by the parole board was rendered 33 days after the revocation hearing and 104 days after the determination of probable cause, did not violate the statutory requirement. People ex rel. James Cambareri v. Scully, 80 A.D.2d 625, 436 N.Y.S.2d 69 (2d Dept. 1981).

—Parole revocation must be vacated and parole reinstated where the relator did not receive the required final notice of parole revocation hearing. People ex rel. Sloan v. Warden, 80 A.D.2d 520, 435 N.Y.S.2d 604 (1st Dept. 1981).

—Revocation of the parole is valid even though the parolee's attorney did not receive the notice of the revocation of parole until 50 days after the hearing. People *ex rel.* Knowles v. Smith, 78 A.D.2d 975, 433 N.Y.S.2d 890 (4th Dept. 1980), *aff'd,* 54 N.Y.2d 259, 445 N.Y.S.2d 103, 429 N.E.2d 781 (1981).

Revocation hearing; prejudice.—Petitioner's right to a parole revocation hearing before a "neutral and detached hearing body" was denied by virtue of the fact that the hearing officer had appeared as an attorney for the state at a prior proceeding in which petitioner's underlying conviction had been challenged. People *ex rel.* Pyclik v. Smith, 81 A.D.2d 1016, 440 N.Y.S.2d 145 (4th Dept. 1981).

Reasons; denial of parole.—Parole board has the right to consider the circumstances surrounding defendant's conviction by an *Alford* plea of manslaughter in the first degree for the brutal murder of his wife, for which was sentenced to a term of five to fifteen years, and the fact that after serving five years of that term "he 'lack[ed] remorse and insight' and accepted no responsibility for the 'actions that resulted in the brutal homicide' "; decision of parole board denying parole will not be disturbed. Silmon v. Travis, 95 N.Y.2d 470, 718 N.Y.S.2d 704, 741 N.E.2d 501 (2000).

—Discretionary release to parole supervision is not to be granted to an inmate merely as a reward for good behavior while in prison, but after considering whether "there is a reasonable probability that, if such inmate is released, he will live and remain at liberty without violating the law, and that his release is not incompatible with the welfare of society and will not so deprecate the seriousness of his crime as to undermine respect for law." King v. New York State Division of Parole, 83 N.Y.2d 788, 610 N.Y.S.2d 954, 632 N.E.2d 1277 (1994).

—In denying the petitioner's application for parole, the New York State Division for Parole determined that the petitioner's release was incompatible with the welfare of society, and that the petitioner would not remain at liberty without violating the law; in support of these conclusions, it cited the multiple counts for which the petitioner was imprisoned, the excessive violence and bizarre nature of the offenses, and that the petitioner was a police sergeant who totally disregarded and placed himself above the law. Pike v. New York State Division of Parole, 188 A.D.2d 602, 591 N.Y.S.2d 495 (2d Dept. 1992).

—It is presumed that the board of parole acted properly and the mere failure to discuss each factor with the petitioner at the hearing does not constitute convincing evidence that it did not consider them. Mackall v. New York State Bd. of Parole, 91 A.D.2d 1023, 458 N.Y.S.2d 251 (2d Dept. 1983).

—Discretionary finding of board will not be disturbed absent demonstration that board's actions were "irrational bordering on improper"; board considered all appropriate statutory factors and was not required to expressly comment on each. Felder v. Travis, 278 A.D.2d 570, 717 N.Y.S.2d 683 (3d Dept. 2000).

—Certificate of earned eligibility does not guarantee parole; Board can deny parole if it finds a "reasonable probability" that inmate would violate the law if released or if inmate's release would not be compatible with the welfare of the community as a whole. Nieves v. New York State Div. of Parole, 251 A.D.2d 836, 675 N.Y.S.2d 158 (3d Dept. 1998).

—Defendant's denial of parole was affirmed where the parole board's inquiry into the circumstances surrounding the grand larceny was not tantamount to the board's finding defendant accountable for kidnapping which he was acquitted of; furthermore, the board set forth other reasons for the denial of parole, to wit, conviction of grand larceny and conviction of attempted escape. Lynch v. Division of Parole, 82 A.D.2d 1012, 442 N.Y.S.2d 179 (3d Dept. 1981).

Erroneous computation.—Relator's arrest and subsequent incarceration was without any lawful basis where the board of parole issued an order authorizing the relator's release and that order had not been withdrawn by the board. People *ex rel.* Spinks v. Harris, 53 N.Y.2d 784, 439 N.Y.S.2d 909, 422 N.E.2d 569 (1981).

Right to counsel.—Where the administrative officer presiding at the final parole revocation hearing made no inquiry to determine whether relator understood the advantages of being represented by counsel or the disadvantages, of proceeding *pro se,* there was no basis in the record for a determination that relator's waiver of his right to counsel was knowing, intelligent and voluntary. People *ex rel.* Brown v. Smith, 115 A.D.2d 255, 496 N.Y.S.2d 123 (4th Dept. 1986).

—The rule that a suspect who is known to be represented by counsel may not waive his rights in the absence of counsel does not apply to knowing and intelligent waivers made before hearing officers in parole revocation hearings. People *ex rel.* Racona v. Hammock, 115 A.D.2d 306, 496 N.Y.S.2d 308 (4th Dept. 1986).

Right to call witnesses.—Reversal was required when the record failed to show that petitioner had been advised of his right to call witnesses. Tolden v. Coughlin, 90 A.D.2d 929, 457 N.Y.S.2d 942 (3d Dept. 1983). *See also* Santana v. Coughlin, 90 A.D.2d 947, 457 N.Y.S.2d 944 (3d Dept. 1982).

Right to preliminary parole revocation hearing; waiver.—Petitioner waived his right to a preliminary parole revocation hearing upon his return from another state when he failed to request counsel in New York, and a final revocation hearing was held within the 90-day period prescribed by Section 259-i of the Executive Law. People *ex rel.* Ronald Miller v. Wilson Walters, III, as Warden, 60 N.Y.2d 899, 470 N.Y.S.2d 574 (1983).

Sister state; control.—Imprisonment in a sister state does not necessarily mean that the parolee is not subject to the convenience and control of the New York State Parole authorities and the burden of showing that the parolee is beyond its convenience and control lies with the Parole board. People *ex rel.* Gonzales v. Dalsheim, 52 N.Y.2d 9, 436 N.Y.S.2d 199 (1980).

Statute of limitations.—In an Article 78 proceeding challenging the State Board of Parole's decision on parole status, the four-month Statute of Limitations does not begin to run until petitioner is aggrieved, and he is not aggrieved, as a matter of law, until he is informed and has notice of the appeal board's determination. Biondi v. New York State Bd. of Parole, 60 N.Y.2d 832, 470 N.Y.S.2d 131 (1983).

Termination of temporary release privileges.—In a case where the Parole Board extends the parole eligibility date of an inmate enrolled in a temporary release program at the time of decision beyond one year, thereby rendering the inmate ineligible for participation in the program, as part of its decision the Board shall set forth the reasons for the extension in excess of one year and the Board must consider the inmate's history of participation in the program in its determination to extend parole eligibility of currently enrolled inmates beyond one year; the serious nature of the initial offense, standing alone, is not a sufficient basis for termination of temporary release privileges. People *ex rel.* Silberstein v. Hammock, 113 Misc. 2d 1030, 450 N.Y.S.2d 687 (Sup. Ct. N.Y. Co. 1982).

Waiver of right to attend revocation hearing; proof.—A finding of a voluntary and intelligent waiver of a constitutional right to attend a final parole revocation hearing requires legal proof and may not be founded on hearsay evidence. People *ex rel.* Herrera v. Schager, 88 A.D.2d 983, 451 N.Y.S.2d 786 (2d Dept. 1982).

—A parolee must make a clear, knowing, informed waiver of his right to adequate notice of a parole revocation hearing. People *ex rel.* Howser v. New York State Div. of Parole, 86 A.D.2d 831, 447 N.Y.S.2d 257 (1st Dept. 1982).

Waiver of right to be present at revocation hearing.—Defendant who was given notice of the revocation hearing and failed to attend is deemed to have waived his right to be present, absent an affidavit disputing the giving of written notice. People *ex rel.* Dorian McFadden v. New York State Div. of Parole, 79 A.D.2d 952, 435 N.Y.S.2d 589 (1st Dept. 1981).

Waiver of parole violation.—A hearing was required to determine whether the New York parole authorities had knowledge that the parolee, who had absconded, had been living in Florida for three years; such knowledge, especially if actual rather than constructive, could constitute a waiver of the parole violation. People v. *ex rel.* Stracci v. Warden N.Y.C. House of Detention for Men, 72 A.D.2d 393, 424 N.Y.S.2d 704 (1st Dept. 1980).

§ 259-j. Merit termination of sentence and discharge from presumptive release, parole and conditional release. [*Effective until Sept. 1, 2009.*]

1. The division of parole may grant to any

person a merit termination of sentence from presumptive release, parole or from conditional release prior to the expiration of the full term or maximum term, provided it is determined by the division of parole that such merit termination is in the best interests of society, such person is not required to register as a sex offender pursuant to article six-c of the correction law, and such person is not on presumptive release, parole or conditional release from a term of imprisonment imposed for any of the following offenses, or for an attempt to commit any of the following offenses:

(a) a violent felony offense as defined in section 70.02 of the penal law;

(b) murder in the first degree or murder in the second degree;

(c) an offense defined in article one hundred thirty of the penal law;

(d) unlawful imprisonment in the first degree, kidnapping in the first degree, or kidnapping in the second degree, in which the victim is less than seventeen years old and the offender is not the parent of the victim;

(e) an offense defined in article two hundred thirty of the penal law involving the prostitution of a person less than nineteen years old;

(f) disseminating indecent material to minors in the first degree or disseminating indecent material to minors in the second degree;

(g) incest;

(h) an offense defined in article two hundred sixty-three of the penal law;

(i) a hate crime as defined in section 485.05 of the penal law; or

(j) an offense defined in article four hundred ninety of the penal law.

2. A merit termination granted by the division of parole under this section shall constitute a termination of the sentence with respect to which it was granted. No such merit termination shall be granted unless the division of parole is satisfied that termination of sentence from presumptive release, parole or from conditional release is in the best interest of society, and that the parolee or releasee, otherwise financially able to comply with an order of restitution and the payment of any mandatory surcharge previously imposed by a court of competent jurisdiction, has made a good faith effort to comply therewith.

3. A merit termination of sentence may be granted after two years of presumptive release or parole to a person serving a sentence for a class A felony offense as defined in article two hundred twenty of the penal law. A merit termination of sentence may be granted to all other eligible persons after one year of presumptive release, parole or conditional release.

3-a. The division of parole must grant termination of sentence after three years of unrevoked parole to a person serving an indeterminate sentence for a class A felony offense defined in article two hundred twenty of the penal law, and must grant termination of sentence after two years of unrevoked parole to a person serving an indeterminate sentence for any other felony offense defined in article two hundred twenty or two hundred twenty-one of the penal law.

4. Except where a determinate sentence or a sentence with a maximum term of life imprisonment was imposed for a felony other than a felony defined in article two hundred twenty of the penal law, if the board of parole is satisfied that an absolute discharge from presumptive release, parole or conditional release is in the best interests of society, the board may grant such a discharge prior to the expiration of the full term or maximum term to any person who has been on unrevoked presumptive release, parole or conditional release for at least three consecutive years. A discharge granted under this section shall constitute a termination of the sentence with respect to which it was granted. No such discharge shall be granted unless the board of parole is satisfied that the parolee or releasee, otherwise financially able to comply with an order of restitution and the payment of any mandatory surcharge, sex offender registration fee, or DNA database fee previously imposed by a court of competent jurisdiction, has made a good faith effort to comply therewith.

5. The chairman of the board of parole shall promulgate rules and regulations governing the issuance of merit terminations of sentence and discharges from presumptive release, parole and conditional release to assure that such terminations and discharges are consistent with public safety.

§ 259-j. Discharge from parole and conditional release. [*Effective Sept. 1, 2009.*]

1. Except where a determinate sentence is imposed for a violent felony offense as defined in section 70.02 of the penal law, or a sentence with a maximum term of life imprisonment was imposed for a felony other than a felony defined in article two hundred twenty of the penal law, if the board of parole is satisfied that an absolute discharge from parole or from conditional release is in the best interests of society, the board may grant such a discharge prior to the expiration of the full maximum term to any person who has been on unrevoked parole or conditional release for at least three consecutive years. A discharge granted under this section shall constitute a termination of the sentence with respect to which it was granted. No such discharge shall be granted unless the board of parole is satisfied that the parolee, otherwise financially able to comply with an order of restitution and the payment of any

mandatory surcharge, sex offender registration fee or DNA databank fee previously imposed by a court of competent jurisdiction, has made a good faith effort to comply therewith.

2. The division of parole must grant termination of sentence after three years of unrevoked parole to a person serving an indeterminate sentence for a class A felony offense defined in article two hundred twenty of the penal law, and must grant termination of sentence after two years of unrevoked parole to a person serving an indeterminate sentence for any other felony offense defined in article two hundred twenty or two hundred twenty-one of the penal law.

Amended by L. 1986, Ch. 466, eff. July 21, 1986, adding last sentence which applies to all pending parole proceedings; L. 1987, Ch. 396, eff. July 23, 1987, and amendment applies to all pending parole proceedings; L. 1995, Ch. 3, § 43, by adding the phrase "term or" before "maximum term," eff. Oct. 1, 1995, amendment repealed Sept. 30, 2005, pursuant to L. 1995, Ch. 3, § 74, paragraph (d), and amendment applies only to offenses committed on or after Oct. 1, 1995 pursuant to L. 1995, Ch. 3, § 74, paragraph (e); L. 1998, Ch. 1, § 40, eff. Aug. 6, 1998; L. 2003, Ch. 62, Part F, §§ 10, 11, eff. May 15, 2003; Ch. 62, Part N, § 2, eff. May 15, 2003 and deemed effective on Apr. 1, 2003; L. 2004, Ch. 738, § 37, eff. Feb. 12, 2005, adding subd. 3-a; L. 2004, Ch. 738, § 38, eff. Dec. 14, 2004, amending section and adding subd. 2; L. 2005, Ch. 56, Part D, § 20, eff. Apr. 1, 2005, extending repeal date of amendment to Sept. 1, 2009.

§ 259-k. Access to records and institutions.

1. All case files shall be maintained by the division of parole for use by the division and board of parole. The division and board of parole and authorized officers and employees thereof shall have complete access to such files and the right to make such entries as the division or board of parole shall deem appropriate in accordance with law.

2. The board shall make rules for the purpose of maintaining the confidentiality of records, information contained therein and information obtained in an official capacity by officers, employees or members of the division or board of parole.

3. Members of the board and officers and employees of the division designated by the chairman shall have free access to all inmates confined in institutions under the jurisdiction of the department of correctional services and the department of mental hygiene in order to enable them to perform their functions, provided, however, that the department of mental hygiene may temporarily restrict such access where it determines, for significant clinical reasons, that such access would interfere with its care and treatment of the mentally ill inmate. If under the provisions of this subdivision an inmate is not accessible for release consideration by the board, that inmate shall be scheduled to see the board in the month immediately subsequent to the month within which he was not available.

4. Upon a determination by the division and board of parole that its records regarding an individual presently under the supervision of the division and board are relevant to an investigation of child abuse or maltreatment conducted by a child protective service pursuant to title six of article six of the social services law, the division and board shall provide the records determined to be relevant to the child protective service conducting the investigation. The division, and board shall promulgate rules for the transmission of records required to be provided under this section.

Amended by L. 1986, Ch. 230, eff. July 1, 1986, amending subd. 3; L. 1992, Ch. 707, eff. July 31, 1992, adding subd. 4.

ANNOTATION

Confidentiality of parole records.—Although there is a presumption that records are open to the public, there is a clear legislative intent to exempt parole records and maintain their confidentiality; denial of Freedom of Information Act request for parole records affirmed. Collins v. New York State Div. of Parole, 251 A.D.2d 738, 674 N.Y.S.2d 145 (3d Dept.), *appeal denied,* 92 N.Y.2d 811 (1998).

§ 259-l. Cooperation.

1. It shall be the duty of the commissioner of correctional services to insure that all officers and employees of the department of correctional services shall at all times cooperate with the division of parole and shall furnish to such division, members of the board of parole and officers and employees of the division such information as may be necessary to enable them to perform their functions.

2. The official in charge of each institution wherein any person is confined under a definite sentence of imprisonment, all officers and employees thereof and all other public officials shall at all times cooperate with the board of parole, and shall furnish to such board, its officers and employees such information as may be required by the board to perform its functions hereunder. The members of the board, its officers and employees shall at all times be given free access to all persons confined in any such institution under such sentence and shall be furnished with appropriate working space in such institution for such purpose without charge therefor.

3. It shall be the duty of the clerk of the court, the commissioner of mental hygiene and all probation officers and other appropriate officials to send such information as may be in their possession or under their control to the chairman of the board of parole upon request in order to facilitate the work of the board.

§ 259-m. Compacts with other states for out-of-state parolee supervisions. [*Repealed as stated in 2003 note below.*]

1. The governor is hereby authorized and directed to enter into a compact on behalf of the

state of New York with any state of the United States legally joining therein in the form substantially as follows:

A COMPACT

Entered into by and among the contracting states, signatories hereto, with the consent of the Congress of the United States of America, granted by an act entitled "An act granting the consent of Congress to any two or more states to enter into agreements or compacts for cooperative effort and mutual assistance in the prevention of crime and for other purposes."

The contracting states solemnly agree:

(1) That it shall be competent for the duly constituted judicial and administrative authorities of a state party to this compact (herein called "sending state") to permit any person convicted of an offense within such state and placed on probation or released on parole to reside in any other state party to this compact (herein called "receiving state") while on probation or parole, if

(a) Such person is in fact a resident of or has his family residing within the receiving state and can obtain employment there;

(b) Though not a resident of the receiving state and not having his family residing there, the receiving state consents to such person being sent there.

Before granting such permission, opportunity shall be granted to the receiving state to investigate the home and prospective employment of such person.

A resident of the receiving state, within the meaning of this section, is one who has been an actual inhabitant of such state continuously for more than one year prior to his coming to the sending state and has not resided within the sending state more than six continuous months immediately preceding the commission of the offense for which he has been convicted.

(2) That each receiving state will assume the duties of visitation of and supervision over probationers or parolees of any sending state and in the exercise of those duties will be governed by the same standards that prevail for its own probationers and parolees.

(3) That duly accredited officers of a sending state may at all times enter a receiving state and there apprehend and retake any person on probation or parole. For that purpose no formalities will be required other than establishing the authority of the officer and the identity of the person to be retaken. All legal requirements to obtain extradition of fugitives from justice are hereby expressly waived on the part of states party hereto, as to such persons. The decision of the sending state to retake a person on probation or parole shall

be conclusive upon and not reviewable within the receiving state; provided, however, that if at the time when a state seeks to retake a probationer or parolee there should be pending against him within the receiving state any criminal charge, or he should be suspected of having committed within such state a criminal offense, he shall not be retaken without the consent of the receiving state until discharged from prosecution or from imprisonment for such offense.

(4) That the duly accredited officers of the sending state will be permitted to transport prisoners being retaken through any and all states parties to this compact, without interference.

(5) That the governor of each state may designate an officer who, acting jointly with like officers of other contracting states, if and when appointed, shall promulgate such rules and regulations as may be deemed necessary to more effectively carry out the terms of this compact.

(6) That this compact shall become operative immediately upon its ratification by any state as between it and any other state or states so ratifying. When ratified it shall have the full force and effect of law within such state, the form of ratification to be in accordance with the laws of the ratifying state.

(7) That this compact shall continue in force and remain binding upon each ratifying state until renounced by it. The duties and obligations hereunder of a renouncing state shall continue as to parolees or probationers residing therein at the time of withdrawal until retaken or finally discharged by the sending state. Renunciation of this compact shall be by the same authority which ratified it, by sending six months' notice in writing of its intention to withdraw from the compact to the other states party hereto.

2. The chairman of the board of parole shall have power and shall be charged with the duty of promulgating such rules and regulations as may be deemed necessary to carry out the terms of a compact entered into by the state pursuant to this section.

3. If any section, sentence, subdivision or clause of this section is for any reason held invalid or to be unconstitutional, such decision shall not affect the validity of the remaining portions of this section.

4. This section may be cited as the uniform act for out-of-state parolee supervision.

2003 Note: L. 2003, Ch. 688, § 3, eff. Oct. 21, 2003, as amended by L. 2004, Ch. 368, § 2, eff. Aug. 17, 2004, provides:

"This act shall take effect immediately, except that section one of this act [adding Exec. Law § 259-mm] shall take effect on the first of January next succeeding the date on which it shall have become a law, and shall remain in effect until the first of September, 2007, upon which date this act shall be deemed repealed and have no further force and effect; provided that section one of this act shall only take effect with respect to any compacting state which has enacted an interstate compact entitled 'Interstate compact for adult offender supervision' and having an identical effect to that added by section one of this act and provided further that with respect to any such compacting state, upon the effective date of section one of this act, section 259-m of the executive law is hereby deemed RE-PEALED and section 259-mm of the executive law, as added by section one of this act, shall take effect; and provided further that with respect to any state which has not enacted an interstate compact entitled 'Interstate compact for adult offender supervision' and having an identical effect to that added by section one of this act, section 259-m of the executive law shall take effect and the provisions of section one of this act, with respect to any such state, shall have no force or effect until such time as such state shall adopt an interstate compact entitled 'Interstate compact for adult offender supervision' and having an identical effect to that added by section one of this act in which case, with respect to such state, effective immediately, section 259-m of the executive law is deemed repealed and section 259-mm of the executive law, as added by section one of this act, shall take effect."

ANNOTATION

Generally.—Where a petitioner originally released on parole from one state has his parole supervision transferred to New York and then subsequently violates that parole by being convicted of a crime in New York, New York has no authority to effect a warrant issued by out-of-state agency for violation of parole; the only grounds for an action in New York would lie if the issuing officer was not authorized to issue the warrant or if petitioner's identity was in question. Booker v. Garvin, 280 A.D.2d 799, 720 N.Y.S.2d 36 (3d Dept. 2001).

§ 259-mm. Interstate compact for adult offender supervision. [*Repealed Sept. 1, 2007; see 2003 note below.*].

The interstate compact for adult offender supervision as set forth in this section is hereby adopted, enacted into law and entered into with all other jurisdictions joining therein. The compact shall be as follows:

INTERSTATE COMPACT FOR ADULT OFFENDER SUPERVISION

ARTICLE I
PURPOSE

The compacting states to this interstate compact recognize that each state is responsible for the supervision of adult offenders in the community who are authorized pursuant to the bylaws and rules of this compact to travel across state lines both to and from each compacting state in such a manner as to track the location of offenders, transfer supervision authority in an orderly and efficient manner, and when necessary return offenders to the originating jurisdictions. The compacting states also recognize that Congress, by enacting the Crime Control Act, 4 U.S.C. Section 112 (1965), has authorized and encouraged compacts for cooperative efforts and mutual assistance in the prevention of crime. It is the purpose of this compact and the interstate commission created pursuant to this compact, through means of joint and cooperative action among the compacting states: to provide the framework for the promotion of public safety and protect the rights of victims through the control and regulation of the interstate movement of offenders in the community; to provide for the effective tracking, supervision and rehabilitation of these offenders by the sending and receiving states; and to equitably distribute the costs, benefits and obligations of the compact among the compacting states. In addition, this compact will: create an interstate commission which will establish uniform procedures to manage the movement between states of adults placed under community supervision and released to the community under the jurisdiction of courts, paroling authorities, corrections or other criminal justice agencies which will promulgate rules to achieve the purpose of this compact; ensure an opportunity for input and timely notice to victims and to jurisdictions where defined offenders are authorized to travel or to relocate across state lines; establish a system of uniform data collection, access to information on active cases by authorized criminal justice officials, and regular reporting of compact activities to heads of state councils, state executive, judicial and legislative branches, and criminal justice administrators; monitor compliance with rules governing interstate movement of offenders and initiate interventions to address and correct non-compliance; and coordinate training and education regarding regulations of interstate movement of offenders for officials involved in such activity. The compacting states recognize that there is no "right" of any offender to live in another state and that duly accredited officers of a sending state may at all times enter a receiving state and there apprehend and retake any offender under supervision subject to the provisions of this compact and bylaws and rules promulgated

MISC. LAWS

thereto. It is the policy of the compacting states that the activities conducted by the interstate commission created by this compact are the formation of public policies and are therefore public business.

ARTICLE II
DEFINITIONS

As used in this compact, unless the context clearly requires a different construction:

(a) "Adult" means both individuals legally classified as adults and juveniles treated as adults by court order, statute or operation of law.

(b) "By-laws" means those by-laws established by the interstate commission for its governance, or for directing or controlling the interstate commission's actions or conduct.

(c) "Compact administrator" means the individual in each compacting state appointed pursuant to the terms of this compact responsible for the administration and management of the state's supervision and transfer of offenders subject to the terms of this compact, the rules adopted by the interstate commission and policies adopted by the state council under this compact.

(d) "Compacting state" means any state which has enacted the enabling legislation for this compact.

(e) "Commissioner" means the voting representative of each compacting state appointed pursuant to article III of this compact.

(f) "Interstate commission" means the interstate commission for adult offender supervision established by this compact.

(g) "Member" means the commissioner of a compacting state or designee, who shall be a person officially connected with the commissioner.

(h) "Non-compacting state" means any state which has not enacted the enabling legislation for this compact.

(i) "Offender" means an adult placed under, or subject to, supervision as the result of the commission of a criminal offense and released to the community under the jurisdiction of courts, paroling authorities, corrections or other criminal justice agencies.

(j) "Person" means any individual, corporation, business enterprise or other legal entity, either public or private.

(k) "Rules" means acts of the interstate commission, duly promulgated pursuant to article VIII of this compact, substantially affecting interested parties in addition to the interstate commission, which shall have the force and effect of law in the compacting states.

(l) "State" means a state of the United States, the District of Columbia and any other territorial possessions of the United States.

(m) "State council" means the resident members of the state council for interstate adult offender supervision created by each state under article IV of this compact.

ARTICLE III
THE COMPACT COMMISSION

The compacting states hereby create the "interstate commission for adult offender supervision". The interstate commission shall be a body corporate and joint agency of the compacting states. The interstate commission shall have all the responsibilities, powers and duties set forth in this compact, including the power to sue and be sued, and such additional powers as may be conferred upon it by subsequent action of the respective legislatures of the compacting states in accordance with the terms of this compact.

The interstate commission shall consist of commissioners selected and appointed by resident members of a state council for interstate adult offender supervision for each state. In addition to the commissioners who are the voting representatives of each state, the interstate commission shall include individuals who are not commissioners but who are members of interested organizations; such non-commissioner members must include a member of the national organizations of governors, legislators, state chief justices, attorneys general and crime victims. All non-commissioner members of the interstate commission shall be ex-officio (nonvoting) members. The interstate commission may provide in its by-laws for such additional, ex-officio, non-voting members as it deems necessary.

Each compacting state represented at any meeting of the interstate commission is entitled to one vote. A majority of the compacting states shall constitute a quorum for the transaction of business, unless a larger quorum is required by the by-laws of the interstate commission. The interstate commission shall meet at least once each calendar year. The chairperson may call additional meetings and, upon the request of twenty-seven or more compacting states, shall call additional meetings. Public notice shall be given of all meetings and meetings shall be open to the public.

The interstate commission shall establish an executive committee which shall include commission officers, members and others as shall be determined by the by-laws. The executive committee shall have the power to act on behalf of the interstate commission during periods when the interstate commission is not in session, with the exception of rulemaking and/or amendment to the compact. The executive committee oversees the day-to-day activities managed by the executive director and interstate commission staff; administers enforcement and compliance with the provisions of the compact, its by-laws and as directed by the interstate commission and performs other duties as directed by the commission or set forth in the by-laws.

ARTICLE IV
THE STATE COUNCIL

Each member state shall create a state council for interstate adult offender supervision which shall be responsible for the appointment of the commissioner who shall serve on the interstate commission from that state. Each state council shall appoint as its commissioner the compact administrator from that state to serve on the interstate commission in such capacity under or pursuant to applicable law of the member state. While each member state may determine the membership of its own state council, its membership must include at least one representative from the legislative, judicial and executive branches of government, victims groups and compact administrators. Each compacting state retains the right to determine the qualifications of the compact administrator who shall be appointed by the state council or by the governor in consultation with the legislature and the judiciary. In addition to appointment of its commissioner to the national interstate commission, each state council shall exercise oversight and advocacy concerning its participation in interstate commission activities and other duties as may be determined by each member state including but not limited to, development of policy concerning operations and procedures of the compact within that state. The compact administrator shall be appointed by the governor in consultation with the temporary president of the senate, the speaker of the assembly and the chief judge of the court of appeals. The state council shall appoint the compact administrator to serve on the interstate commission pursuant to this section.

ARTICLE V
POWERS AND DUTIES OF THE INTERSTATE COMMISSION

The interstate commission shall have the following powers:

(a) to adopt a seal and suitable by-laws governing the management and operation of the interstate commission;

(b) to promulgate rules which shall have the force and effect of statutory law and shall be binding in the compacting states to the extent and in the manner provided in this compact;

(c) to oversee, supervise and coordinate the interstate movement of offenders subject to the terms of this compact and any by-laws adopted and rules promulgated by the compact commission;

(d) to enforce compliance with compact provisions, interstate commission rules, and by-laws using all necessary and proper means, including but not limited to, the use of judicial order;

(e) to establish and maintain offices;

(f) to purchase and maintain insurance and bonds;

(g) to borrow, accept or contract for services of personnel, including, but not limited to, members and their staffs;

(h) to establish and appoint committees and hire staff which it deems necessary for the carrying out of its functions including, but not limited to, an executive committee as required by article III of this compact which shall have the power to act on behalf of the interstate commission in carrying out its powers and duties pursuant to this compact;

(i) to elect or appoint such officers, attorneys, employees, agents or consultants, and to fix their compensation, define their duties and determine their qualifications; and to establish the interstate commission's personnel policies and programs relating to, among other things, conflicts of interest, rates of compensation and qualifications of personnel;

(j) to accept any and all donations and grants of money, equipment, supplies, materials and services, and to receive, utilize and dispose of same;

(k) to lease, purchase, accept contributions or donations of, or otherwise to own, hold, improve or use any property, real, personal or mixed;

(l) to sell, convey, mortgage, pledge, lease, exchange, abandon or otherwise dispose of any property, real, personal or mixed;

(m) to establish a budget and make expenditures and levy dues as provided in article X of this compact;

(n) to sue and be sued;

(o) to provide for dispute resolution among compacting states;

(p) to perform such functions as may be necessary or appropriate to achieve the purposes of this compact;

(q) to report annually to the legislatures, governors, judiciary and state councils of the compacting states concerning the activities of the interstate commission during the preceding year. Such reports shall also include any recommendations that may have been adopted by the interstate commission;

(r) to coordinate education, training and public awareness regarding the interstate movement of offenders for officials involved in such activity; and

(s) to establish uniform standards for the reporting, collecting and exchanging of data.

ARTICLE VI
ORGANIZATION AND OPERATION OF THE INTERSTATE COMMISSION

(a) By-laws. The interstate commission shall, by a majority of the members, within twelve months of the first interstate commission meeting, adopt by-laws to govern its conduct as may be necessary or appropriate to carry out the purposes of the compact, including, but not limited to:

1. establishing the fiscal year of the interstate commission;

2. establishing an executive committee and such other committees as may be necessary;

3. providing reasonable standards and procedures:

a. for the establishment of committees, and

b. governing any general or specific delegation of any authority or function of the interstate commission;

4. providing reasonable procedures for calling and conducting meetings of the interstate commission, and ensuring reasonable notice of each such meeting;

5. establishing the titles and responsibilities of the officers of the interstate commission;

6. providing reasonable standards and procedures for the establishment of the personnel policies and programs of the interstate commission. Notwithstanding any civil service or other similar laws of any compacting state, the by-laws shall exclusively govern the personnel policies and programs of the interstate commission;

7. providing a mechanism for winding up the operations of the interstate commission and the equitable return of any surplus funds that may exist upon the termination of the compact after the payment and/or reserving of all of its debts and obligations;

8. providing transition rules for "start up" administration of the compact; and

9. establishing standards and procedures for compliance and technical assistance in carrying out the compact.

(b) Officers and staff. The interstate commission shall, by a majority of the members, elect from among its members a chairperson and a vice chairperson, each of whom shall have such authorities and duties as may be specified in the by-laws. The chairperson or, in his or her absence or disability, the vice chairperson, shall preside at all meetings of the interstate commission. The officers so elected shall serve without compensation or remuneration from the interstate commission; provided that, subject to the availability of budgeted funds, the officers shall be reimbursed for any actual and necessary costs and expenses incurred by them in the performance of their duties and responsibilities as officers of the interstate commission.

The interstate commission shall, through its executive committee, appoint or retain an executive director for such period, upon such terms and conditions and for such compensation as the interstate commission may deem appropriate. The executive director shall serve as secretary to the interstate commission, and hire and supervise such other staff as may be authorized by the interstate commission, but shall not be a member.

(c) Corporate records of the interstate commission. The interstate commission shall maintain its corporate books and records in accordance with the by-laws.

(d) Qualified immunity, defense and indemnification. The members, officers, executive director and employees of the interstate commission shall be immune from suit and liability, either personally or in their official capacity, for any claim for damage to or loss of property or personal injury or other civil liability cause or arising out of any actual or alleged act, error or omission that occurred within the scope of interstate commission employment, duties or responsibilities; provided, that nothing in this subdivision shall be construed to protect any such person from suit and/or liability for any damage, loss, injury or liability caused by the intentional or willful and wanton misconduct of any such person. The interstate commission shall defend the commissioner of a compacting state, or his or her representatives or employees, or the interstate commission's representatives or employees, in any civil action seeking to impose liability, arising out of any actual or alleged act, error or omission that occurred within the scope of interstate commission employment, duties or responsibilities, or that the defendant had a reasonable basis for believing occurred within the scope of interstate commission employment, duties or responsibilities; provided, that the actual or alleged act, error or omission did not result from intentional wrongdoing on the part of such person.

The interstate commission shall indemnify and hold the commissioner of a compacting state, the appointed designee or employees, or the interstate commission's representatives or employees, harmless in the amount of any settlement or judgment obtained against such persons arising out of any actual or alleged act, error or omission that occurred within the scope of interstate commission employment, duties or responsibilities, or that such persons had a reasonable basis for believing occurred within the scope of interstate commission employment, duties or responsibilities, provided, that the actual or alleged act, error or omission did not result from gross negligence or intentional wrongdoing on the part of such person.

ARTICLE VII
ACTIVITIES OF THE
INTERSTATE COMMISSION

The interstate commission shall meet and take such actions as are consistent with the provisions of this compact.

Except as otherwise provided in this compact and unless a greater percentage is required by the by-laws, in order to constitute an act of the interstate commission, such act shall have been taken at a meeting of the interstate commission and shall have received an affirmative vote of a majority of the members present.

Each member of the interstate commission shall have the right and power to cast a vote to which that compacting state is entitled and to participate in the business and affairs of the interstate commission. A member shall vote in person on behalf of the state and shall not delegate a vote to another member state. However, a state council shall appoint another authorized representative, in the absence of the commissioner from that state, to cast a vote on behalf of the member state at a specified meeting. The by-laws may provide for members' participation in meetings by telephone or other means of telecommunication or electronic communication. Any voting conducted by telephone, or other means of telecommunication or electronic communication shall be subject to the same quorum requirements of meetings where members are present in person.

The interstate commission shall meet at least once during each calendar year. The chairperson of the interstate commission may call additional meetings at any time and, upon the request of a majority of the members, shall call additional meetings.

The interstate commission's by-laws shall establish conditions and procedures under which the interstate commission shall make its information and official records available to the public for inspection or copying. The interstate commission may exempt from disclosure any information or official records to the extent they would adversely affect personal privacy rights or proprietary interests. In promulgating such rules, the interstate commission may make available to law enforcement agencies records and information otherwise exempt from disclosure, and may enter into agreements with law enforcement agencies to receive or exchange information or records subject to nondisclosure and confidentiality provisions.

Public notice shall be given of all meetings and all meetings shall be open to the public, except as set forth in the rules or as otherwise provided in the compact. The interstate commission shall promulgate rules consistent with the principles contained in the "Government in Sunshine Act," 5 U.S.C. Section 552(b), as may be amended. The interstate commission and any of its committees may close a meeting to the public where it determines by a two-thirds vote that an open meeting would be likely to:

(a) relate solely to the interstate commission's internal personnel practices and procedures;

(b) disclose matters specifically exempted from disclosure by statute;

(c) disclose trade secrets or commercial or financial information which is privileged or confidential;

(d) involve accusing any person of a crime, or formally censuring any person;

(e) disclose information of a personal nature where disclosure would constitute a clearly unwarranted invasion of personal privacy;

(f) disclose investigatory records compiled for law enforcement purposes;

(g) disclose information contained in or related to examination, operating or condition reports prepared by, or on behalf of or for the use of, the interstate commission with respect to a regulated entity for the purpose of regulation or supervision of such entity;

(h) disclose information, the premature disclosure of which would significantly endanger the life of a person or the stability of a regulated entity; or

(i) specifically relate to the interstate commission's issuance of a subpoena, or its participation in a civil action or proceeding.

For every meeting closed pursuant to this article, the interstate commission's chief legal officer shall publicly certify that, in his or her opinion, the meeting may be closed to the public, and shall reference each relevant exemptive provision. The interstate commission shall keep minutes which shall fully and clearly describe all matters discussed in any meeting and shall provide a full and accurate summary of any actions taken, and the reasons therefor, including a description of each of the views expressed on any item and the record of any rollcall vote (reflected in the vote of each member on the question). All documents considered in connection with any action shall be identified in such minutes.

The interstate commission shall collect standardized data concerning the interstate movement of offenders as directed through its by-laws and rules which shall specify the data to be collected, the means of collection and data exchange and reporting requirements.

ARTICLE VIII
RULEMAKING FUNCTIONS OF
THE INTERSTATE COMMISSION

The interstate commission shall promulgate rules in order to effectively and efficiently achieve the purposes of the compact including transition rules governing administration of the compact during the period in which it is being considered and enacted by the states.

Rulemaking shall occur pursuant to the criteria set forth in this article and the by-laws and rules adopted pursuant thereto. Such rulemaking shall substantially conform to the principles of the federal Administrative Procedure Act, 5 U.S.C.S. section 551 et seq., and the Federal Advisory Committee Act, 5 U.S.C.S. app. 2, section 1 et seq., as may be amended (hereinafter referred to as "APA"). All rules and amendments shall become binding as of the date specified in each rule or amendment.

If a majority of the legislatures of the compacting states rejects a rule, by enactment of a statute or resolution in the same manner used to adopt the compact, then such rule shall have no further force and effect in any compacting state.

When promulgating a rule, the interstate commission shall:

(a) publish the proposed rule stating with particularity the text of the rule which is proposed and the reason for the proposed rule;

(b) allow persons to submit written data, facts, opinions and arguments, which information shall be publicly available;

(c) provide an opportunity for an informal hearing; and

(d) promulgate a final rule and its effective date, if appropriate, based on the rulemaking record.

Not later than sixty days after a rule is promulgated, any interested person may file a petition in the United States District Court for the District of Columbia or in the Federal District Court where the interstate commission principal office is located for judicial review of such rule. If the court finds that the interstate commission's action is not supported by substantial evidence, (as defined in the APA), in the rulemaking record, the court shall hold the rule unlawful and set it aside. Subjects to be addressed within twelve months after the first meeting must at a minimum include:

1. notice to victims and opportunity to be heard;

2. offender registration and compliance;

3. violations/returns;

4. transfer procedures and forms;

5. eligibility for transfer;

6. collection of restitution and fees from offenders;

7. data collection and reporting;

8. the level of supervision to be provided by the receiving state;

9. transition rules governing the operation of the compact and the interstate commission during all or part of the period between the effective date of the compact and the date on which the last eligible state adopts the compact; and

10. mediation, arbitration and dispute resolution.

The existing rules governing the operation of the previous compact superceded by this compact shall be null and void twelve months after the first meeting of the interstate commission created pursuant to this compact.

Upon determination by the interstate commission that an emergency exists, it may promulgate an emergency rule which shall become effective immediately upon adoption, provided that the usual rulemaking procedures provided hereunder shall be retroactively applied to said rule as soon as reasonably possible, in no event later than ninety days after the effective date of the rule.

ARTICLE IX
OVERSIGHT, ENFORCEMENT AND DISPUTE RESOLUTION BY THE INTERSTATE COMMISSION

(a) Oversight. The interstate commission shall oversee the interstate movement of adult offenders in the compacting states and shall monitor such activities being administered in noncompacting states which may significantly affect compacting states.

The courts and executive agencies in each compacting state shall enforce this compact and shall take all actions necessary and appropriate to effectuate the compact's purposes and intent. In any judicial or administrative proceeding in a compacting state pertaining to the subject matter of this compact which may affect the powers, responsibilities or actions of the interstate commission, the interstate commission shall be entitled to receive all service of process in any such proceeding, and shall have standing to intervene in the proceeding for all purposes.

(b) Dispute resolution. The compacting states shall report to the interstate commission on issues or activities of concern to them, and cooperate with and support the interstate commission in the discharge of its duties and responsibilities.

The interstate commission shall attempt to resolve any disputes or other issues which are subject to the compact and which may arise among compacting states and non-compacting states.

The interstate commission shall enact a by-law or promulgate a rule providing for both mediation and binding dispute resolution for disputes among the compacting states.

(c) Enforcement. The interstate commission, in the reasonable exercise of its discretion, shall enforce the provisions of this compact using any or all means set forth in article XII, subdivision (b), of this compact.

ARTICLE X
FINANCE

The interstate commission shall pay or provide

for the payment of the reasonable expenses of its establishment, organization and ongoing activities.

The interstate commission shall levy on and collect an annual assessment from each compacting state to cover the cost of the internal operations and activities of the interstate commission and its staff which must be in a total amount sufficient to cover the interstate commission's annual budget as approved each year. The aggregate annual assessment amount shall be allocated based upon a formula to be determined by the interstate commission, taking into consideration the population of the state and the volume of interstate movement of offenders in each compacting state and shall promulgate a rule binding upon compacting states which governs said assessment.

The interstate commission shall not incur any obligations of any kind prior to securing the funds adequate to meet the same; nor shall the interstate commission pledge the credit of any of the compacting states, except by and with the authority of the compacting state.

The interstate commission shall keep accurate accounts of all receipts and disbursements. The receipts and disbursements of the interstate commission shall be subject to the audit and accounting procedures established under its by-laws. However, all receipts and disbursements of funds handled by the interstate commission shall be audited yearly by a certified or licensed public accountant and the report of the audit shall be included in and become part of the annual report of the interstate commission.

ARTICLE XI
COMPACTING STATES, EFFECTIVE DATE AND AMENDMENT

Any state, as defined in article II of this compact, is eligible to become a compacting state. The compact shall become effective and binding upon legislative enactment of the compact into law by no less than thirty-five of the states. The initial effective date shall be the later of July first, two thousand three, or upon enactment into law by the thirty-fifth jurisdiction. Thereafter it shall become effective and binding, as to any other compacting state and in the state of New York, upon enactment of the compact into law by that state. The governors of non-member states or their designees will be invited to participate in interstate commission activities on a non-voting basis prior to adoption of the compact by all states and territories of the United States.

Amendments to the compact may be proposed by the interstate commission for enactment by the compacting states. No amendment shall become effective and binding upon the interstate commission and the compacting states unless and until it is enacted into law by unanimous consent of the compacting states.

ARTICLE XII
WITHDRAWAL, DEFAULT, TERMINATION AND JUDICIAL ENFORCEMENT

(a) Withdrawal. Once effective, the compact shall continue in force and remain binding upon each and every compacting state; provided, that a compacting state may withdraw from the compact ("withdrawing state") by enacting a statute specifically repealing the statute which enacted the compact into law.

The effective date of withdrawal is the effective date of the repeal.

The withdrawing state shall immediately notify the chairperson of the interstate commission in writing upon the introduction of legislation repealing this compact in the withdrawing state. The interstate commission shall notify the other compacting states of the withdrawing state's intent to withdraw within sixty days of its receipt thereof.

The withdrawing state is responsible for all assessments, obligations and liabilities incurred through the effective date of withdrawal, including any obligations, the performance of which extend beyond the effective date of withdrawal. Reinstatement following withdrawal of any compacting state shall occur upon the withdrawing state reenacting the compact or upon such later date as determined by the interstate commission.

(b) Default. If the interstate commission determines that any compacting state has at any time defaulted ("defaulting state") in the performance of any of its obligations or responsibilities under this compact, the by-laws or any duly promulgated rules the interstate commission may impose any or all of the following penalties:

1. Fines, fees and costs in such amounts as are deemed to be reasonable as fixed by the interstate commission;

2. Remedial training and technical assistance as directed by the interstate commission;

3. Suspension and termination of membership in the compact. Suspension shall be imposed only after all other reasonable means of securing compliance under the by-laws and rules have been exhausted. Immediate notice of suspension shall be given by the interstate commission to the governor, the chief justice or chief judicial officer of the state, the majority and minority leaders of the defaulting state's legislature, and the state council.

The grounds for default include, but are not limited to, failure of a compacting state to perform such obligations or responsibilities imposed upon it by this compact, interstate commission by-laws, or duly promulgated rules. The interstate commission shall immediately notify the defaulting state in writing of the penalty imposed by the interstate commission on the defaulting state pending a cure of the default. The interstate commission shall stipulate the conditions and the time period within which the defaulting state must cure its default. If the defaulting state fails to cure the default within the time period specified by the interstate commission, in addition to any other penalties imposed herein, the defaulting state may be terminated from the compact upon an affirmative vote of a majority of the compacting states and all rights, privileges and benefits conferred by this compact shall be terminated from the effective date of suspension. Within sixty days of the effective date of termination of a defaulting state, the interstate commission shall notify the governor, the chief justice or chief judicial officer, the majority and minority leaders of the defaulting state's legislature, and the state council of such termination.

The defaulting state is responsible for all assessments, obligations and liabilities incurred through the effective date of termination including any obligations, the performance of which extends beyond the effective date of termination.

The interstate commission shall not bear any costs relating to the defaulting state unless otherwise mutually agreed upon between the interstate commission and the defaulting state.

Reinstatement following termination of any compacting state requires both a reenactment of the compact by the defaulting state and the approval of the interstate commission pursuant to the rules.

(c) Judicial enforcement. The interstate commission may, by majority vote of the members, initiate legal action in the United States District Court for the District of Columbia or, at the discretion of the interstate commission, in the federal district where the interstate commission has its offices to enforce compliance with the provisions of the compact, its duly promulgated rules and by-laws, against any compacting state in default. In the event judicial enforcement is necessary the prevailing party shall be awarded all costs of such litigation including reasonable attorneys' fees.

(d) Dissolution of compact. The compact dissolves effective upon the date of the withdrawal or default of the compacting state which reduces membership in the compact to one compacting state.

Upon the dissolution of this compact, the compact becomes null and void and shall be of no further force or effect, and the business and affairs of the interstate commission shall be wound up and any surplus funds shall be distributed in accordance with the by-laws.

ARTICLE XIII
SEVERABILITY AND CONSTRUCTION

The provisions of this compact shall be severable, and if any phrase, clause, sentence or provision is deemed unenforceable, the remaining provisions of the compact shall be enforceable.

The provisions of this compact shall be liberally constructed to effectuate its purposes.

ARTICLE XIV
BINDING EFFECT OF COMPACT AND OTHER LAWS

(a) Other laws. Nothing in this compact prevents the enforcement of any other law of a compacting state that is not inconsistent with this compact.

All compacting states' laws conflicting with this compact are superseded to the extent of the conflict.

(b) Binding effect of the compact. All lawful actions of the interstate commission, including all rules and by-laws promulgated by the interstate commission, are binding upon the compacting states.

All agreements between the interstate commission and the compacting states are binding in accordance with their terms.

Upon the request of a party to a conflict over meaning or interpretation of interstate commission actions, and upon a majority vote of the compacting states, the interstate commission may issue advisory opinions regarding such meaning or interpretation.

In the event any provision of this compact exceeds the constitutional limits imposed on the legislature of any compacting state, the obligations, duties, powers or jurisdiction sought to be conferred by such provision upon the interstate commission shall be ineffective and such obligations, duties, powers or jurisdiction shall remain in the compacting state and shall be exercised by the agency thereof to which such obligations, duties, powers or jurisdiction are delegated by law in effect at the time this compact becomes effective.

Added by L. 2003, Ch. 688, § 1, eff. as stated in 2003 note below; **Amended** by L. 2004, Ch. 368, eff. Aug. 17, 2004, § 1, amending Art. IV, and § 2, providing for Sept. 1, 2007, repeal date.

2003 Note: L. 2003, Ch. 688, § 3, eff. Oct. 21, 2003, as amended by L. 2004, Ch. 368, § 2, eff. Aug. 17, 2004, provides:

"This act shall take effect immediately, except that section one of this act [adding Exec. Law § 259-mm] shall take effect on the first of January next succeeding the date on which it shall have become a law, and shall remain in effect until the first of September, 2007, upon which date this act shall be deemed repealed and have no further force and effect; provided that section one of this act shall only take effect with respect to any compacting state which has enacted an interstate compact entitled 'Interstate compact for adult offender supervision' and having an identical effect to that added by section one of this act and provided further that with respect to any such compacting state, upon the effective date of section one of this act, section 259-m of the executive law is hereby deemed REPEALED and section 259-mm of the executive law, as added by section one of this act, shall take effect; and provided further that with respect to any state which has not enacted an interstate compact entitled 'Interstate compact for adult offender supervision' and having an identical effect to that added by section one of this act, section 259-m of the executive law shall take effect and the provisions of section one of this act, with respect to any such state, shall have no force or effect until such time as such state shall adopt an interstate compact entitled 'Interstate compact for adult offender supervision' and having an identical effect to that added by section one of this act in which case, with respect to such state, effective immediately, section 259-m of the executive law is deemed repealed and section 259-mm of the executive law, as added by section one of this act, shall take effect."

L. 2003, Ch. 688, § 2, as amended by L. 2004, Ch. 368, § 2, eff. Aug. 17, 2004, provides:

"Pursuant to article IV of section 259-mm of the Executive Law there is hereby created within the Division of Parole a state council for interstate adult offender supervision which shall consist of a compact administrator, to be appointed by the governor in consultation with the speaker of the assembly, temporary president of the senate and the chief judge of the court of appeals, two legislative representatives to be appointed by the speaker of the assembly, two legislative representatives to be appointed by the temporary president of the senate, a judicial representative to be appointed by the governor upon recommendation of the chief judge of the court of appeals, the chairperson of the Board of Parole or his or her designee, the Director of Probation and Correctional Alternatives or his or her designee, the chairperson of the Crime Victims Board or his or her designee, the Commissioner of the Division of Criminal Justice Services or his or her designee, and a victims rights representative to be appointed by the governor. The council shall exercise oversight and advocacy concerning its participation in interstate commission activities and other duties as the council may determine, including but not limited to, the development of policy concerning the operations and procedures of the compact within the state. Each appointed member of the council shall serve a term of five years. Any member chosen to fill a vacancy created other than by expiration of term shall be appointed for the unexpired term of the member whom he is to succeed. Vacancies caused by the expiration of term shall be filled in the same manner as original appointments and for a term of five years. The council members shall serve without salary but shall be entitled to receive reimbursement for travel and other related expenses associated with participation in the work of the council."

§ 259-n. [Repealed.]

§ 259-o. Interstate hearings for parole violations.

1. For the purposes of this section, "preliminary violation hearing" means a hearing to determine whether there are reasonable grounds to believe that a person released on parole has violated the conditions of his parole.

2. Whenever there is reasonable cause to believe that a person released on parole in another state but under the parole supervision of this state pursuant to section two hundred fifty-nine-m of this article has violated the conditions thereof, a member or designee of the board of parole, upon request of the sending state, may conduct a preliminary violation hearing unless such hearing is waived by the parolee.

3. Whenever there is reasonable cause to believe that a person released on parole in this state but under the parole supervision of another state pursuant to section two hundred fifty-nine-m of this article has violated the conditions thereof, any person duly authorized in such other state to conduct preliminary violation hearings, upon request of the chairman of the board of parole, may conduct such hearing, unless such hearing is waived by the parolee. The preliminary violation hearing and the determinations made thereat shall have the same force and effect as preliminary violation hearing conducted in this state by the board of parole or a member, hearing officer or panel thereof.

4. Whenever a preliminary violation hearing is conducted in another state pursuant to this section, the alleged violator must be afforded a final hearing within ninety days from the date of his return to this state.

Amended by L. 1984, Ch. 435, eff. Nov. 1, 1984, adding subd. 4; L. 1985, Ch. 211, eff. June 18, 1985.

ANNOTATION

Final revocation hearing; out-of-state incarceration.— Relator, serving a sentence in a foreign state for a crime committed there, could not have been returned to New York before the end of his commitment for a final revocation hearing, since he was not in a "compact institution" under Executive Law § 259-n(1)(d) and section 259-o of the Executive Law does not provide for final revocation hearings. People ex rel. Copeland v. Smith, 78 A.D.2d 1008, 434 N.Y.S.2d 50 (4th Dept. 1980); see also People ex rel. Pyclik v. Smith, 78 A.D.2d 1008, 434 N.Y.S.2d 51 (4th Dept. 1980).

§ 259-p. Deputization of out-of-state officers.

The director of the division of parole is hereby authorized and empowered to deputize any parole officer or peace officer of another state to act as an officer and agent of this state in effecting the return of any person who has violated the terms and conditions of parole or probation as granted by this state.

Any deputization pursuant to this section shall be in writing and any person authorized to act as an agent of this state pursuant hereto shall carry formal evidence of his deputization and shall produce the same upon demand.

The director for the division of parole is hereby authorized, subject to the approval of the comptroller, to enter into contracts with similar officials of any other state or states for the purpose of sharing an equitable portion of the cost of effecting the return of any person who has violated the terms and conditions of parole or probation as granted by this state.

§ 259-q. Civil actions against division personnel.

1. No civil action shall be brought in any court of the state, except by the attorney general on behalf of the state, against any officer or employee of the division, in his personal capacity,

for damages arising out of any act done or the failure to perform any act within the scope of the employment and in the discharge of the duties by such officer or employee.

2. Any claim for damages arising out of any act done or the failure to perform any act within the scope of the employment and in the discharge of the duties of any officer or employee of the division shall be brought and maintained in the court of claims as a claim against the state.

3. The state shall save harmless and indemnify any officer or employee of the division from financial loss resulting from a claim filed in a court of the United States for damages arising out of an act done or the failure to perform any act that was (a) within the scope of the employment and in the discharge of the duties of such officer or employee, and (b) not done or omitted with the intent to violate any rule or regulation of the division or of any statute or governing case law of the state or of the United States at the time the damages were sustained; provided that the officer or employee shall comply with the provisions of subdivision four of section seventeen of the public officers law.

4. (a) The provisions of this section shall supplement, and be available in addition to, the provisions of section seventeen of the public officers law and, insofar as this section is inconsistent with section seventeen of the public officers law, the provisions of this section shall be controlling.

(b) The provisions of this section shall not be construed in any way to impair, modify or abrogate any immunity available to any officer or employee of the division under the statutory or decisional law of the state or the United States.

5. This section shall not in any way impair, limit or modify the rights and obligations of any insurer under any policy of insurance.

6. The benefits of subdivision three hereof shall inure only to officers and employees of the division and shall not enlarge or diminish the rights of any other party.

7. This section shall apply with respect to claims arising on or after the effective date of this section. Claims arising prior thereto shall be governed by section seventeen of the public officers law or section twenty-four of the correction law as the case may be.

Amended by L. 1978, Ch. 466, eff. Sept. 4, 1978, amending subd. 3, repealing subd. 4 and adding new subd. 4.

L. 1978, Ch. 466, § 24 provides: "This act shall not be construed to impair any rights or interests of any state employee accrued or conferred prior to the effective date of this act, including the rights of any employee under an employment contract or a collective bargaining agreement."

§ 259-r. Release on medical parole. [Expires Sept. 1, 2007.]

1. (a) [Repealed eff. Sept. 1, 2009.] The board shall have the power to release on medical parole any inmate serving an indeterminate or determinate sentence of imprisonment who, pursuant to subdivision two of this section, has been certified to be suffering from a terminal condition, disease or syndrome and to be so debilitated or incapacitated as to create a reasonable probability that he or she is physically incapable of presenting any danger to society, provided, however, that no inmate serving a sentence imposed upon a conviction for any of the following offenses shall be eligible for such release: murder in the first degree, murder in the second degree, manslaughter in the first degree, any offense defined in article one hundred thirty of the penal law or an attempt to commit any of these offenses.

(a) [Effective Sept. 1, 2009.] The board shall have the power to release on medical parole any inmate serving an indeterminate sentence of imprisonment who, pursuant to subdivision two of this section, has been certified to be suffering from a termination condition, disease or syndrome and to be so debilitated or incapacitated as to create a reasonable probability that he or she is physically incapable of presenting any danger to society, provided, however, that no inmate serving a sentence imposed upon a conduction for any of the following offenses in the second degree, manslaughter in the first degree, any offense defined in article one hundred thirty of the penal law or an attempt to commit any of these offenses.

(b) Such release shall be granted only after the board considers whether, in light of the inmate's medical condition, there is a reasonable probability that the inmate, if released, will live and remain at liberty without violating the law, and that such release is not incompatible with the welfare of society and will not so deprecate the seriousness of the crime as to undermine respect for the law, and shall be subject to the limits and conditions specified in subdivision four of this section. Such release may be granted at any time during the term of an inmate's sentence, notwithstanding any other provision of law.

(c) The board shall afford notice to the sentencing court, the district attorney and the attorney for the inmate that the inmate is being considered for release pursuant to this section and the parties receiving notice shall have fifteen days to comment on the release of the inmate. Release on medical parole shall not be granted until the expiration of the comment period provided for in this paragraph.

2. (a) The commissioner of correctional services, on the commissioner's own initiative or at the request of an inmate, may, in the exercise of the commissioner's discretion, direct that a diagnosis be made of an inmate who appears to be suffering from a terminal condition, disease or syndrome. Any such medical diagnosis shall be made by a physician licensed to practice medicine in this state pursuant to section sixty-five hundred

twenty-four of the education law. Such physician shall either be employed by the department of correctional services, shall render professional services at the request of the department of correctional services, or shall be employed by a hospital or medical facility used by the department of correctional services for the medical treatment of inmates. The diagnosis shall be reported to the commissioner of correctional services and shall include but shall not be limited to a description of the terminal condition, disease or syndrome suffered by the inmate, a prognosis concerning the likelihood that the inmate will not recover from such terminal condition, disease or syndrome, a description of the inmate's physical incapacity which shall include a prediction respecting the likely duration of the incapacity, and a statement by the physician of whether the inmate is so debilitated or incapacitated as to be severely restricted in his or her ability to self-ambulate and to care for him or herself.

(b) The commissioner, or the commissioner's designee, shall review the diagnosis and may certify that the inmate is suffering from such terminal condition, disease or syndrome and that the inmate is so debilitated or incapacitated as to create a reasonable probability that he or she is physically incapable of presenting any danger to society. If the commissioner does not so certify then the inmate shall not be referred to the board of parole for consideration for release on medical parole. If the commissioner does so certify, then the commissioner shall refer the inmate to the board of parole for consideration for release on medical parole. however, no such referral of an inmate to the board of parole shall be made unless the inmate has been examined by a physician and diagnosed as having a terminal condition, disease or syndrome as previously described herein at some time subsequent to such inmate's admission to a facility operated by the department of correctional services.

(c) When the commissioner refers an inmate to the board, the commissioner shall provide an appropriate medical discharge plan established by the department of correctional services. The board may reject all or part of the discharge plan submitted by the department of correctional services, and may postpone its decision pending submission of a new discharge plan, or may deny release based on inadequacy of the discharge plan. The department of correctional services and the division of parole shall jointly develop standards for the medical discharge plan that are appropriately adapted to the criminal justice setting, based on standards established by the department of health for hospital medical discharge planning.

3. Any certification by the commissioner or the commissioner's designee pursuant to this section shall be deemed a judicial function and shall not be reviewable if done in accordance with law.

4. (a) Medical parole granted pursuant to this section shall be for a period of six months.

(b) The board shall require as a condition of release on medical parole that the releasee agree to remain under the care of a physician while on medical parole and in a hospital established pursuant to article twenty-eight of the public health law, a hospice established pursuant to article forty of the public health law or any other placement that can provide appropriate medical care as specified in the medical discharge plan required by subdivision two of this section. The medical discharge plan shall state that the availability of the placement has been confirmed, and by whom.

(c) The board shall require as a condition of release that medical parolees be supervised on intensive caseloads at reduced supervision ratios similar to the caseloads for parolees released pursuant to the shock incarceration program established by article twenty-six-A of the correction law.

(d) The board shall require as a condition of release on medical parole that the releasee undergo periodic medical examinations and a medical examination at least one month prior to the expiration of the period of medical parole and, for the purposes of making a decision pursuant to paragraph (e) of this subdivision, that the releasee provide the board with a report, prepared by the treating physician, of the results of such examination. Such report shall specifically state whether or not the parolee continues to suffer from a terminal condition, disease, or syndrome, and to be so debilitated or incapacitated as to be severely restricted in his or her ability to self-ambulate and to care for him or herself.

(e) Prior to the expiration of the period of medical parole the board shall review the medical examination report required by paragraph (d) of this subdivision and may again grant medical parole pursuant to this section; provided, however, that the provisions of paragraph (c) of subdivision one and subdivision two of this section shall not apply.

(f) If the updated medical report presented to the board states that a parolee released pursuant to this section is no longer so debilitated or incapacitated as to create a reasonable probability that he or she is physically incapable of presenting any danger to society or if the releasee fails to submit the updated medical report then the board may not make a new grant of medical parole pursuant to paragraph (e) of this subdivision. Where the board has not granted medical parole pursuant to such paragraph (e) the board shall promptly conduct through one of its members, or cause to be conducted by a hearing officer designated by the board, a hearing to determine whether the releasee is suffering from a terminal condition, disease or syndrome and is so debilitated or incapacitated as to create a reasonable probability that he or she is physically incapable of presenting any danger to society and does not present a danger to society. If the board makes such a determination then it may make a new grant of medical parole pursuant to the standards of paragraph (b) of subdivision one of this section. At the hearing, the releasee shall have the right to representation by counsel, including the right, if the releasee is financially unable to retain counsel, to have the appropriate court assign counsel in accordance with the county or city plan for representation placed in operation pursuant to article eighteen-b of the county law.

(g) The hearing and determination provided for by paragraph (f) of this subdivision shall be concluded within the four month period of medical parole. If the board does not renew the grant of medical parole, it shall order that the releasee be returned immediately to the custody of the department of correctional services.

(h) In addition to the procedures set forth in paragraph (f) of this subdivision, medical parole may be revoked at any time upon any of the grounds specified in paragraph (a) of subdivision three of section two hundred fifty-nine-i of this article, and in accordance with the procedures specified in subdivision three of section two hundred fifty-nine-i of this article.

(i) A releasee who is on medical parole and who becomes eligible for parole pursuant to the provisions of subdivision two of section two hundred fifty-nine-i of this article shall be eligible for parole consideration pursuant to such subdivision.

5. A denial of release on medical parole or expiration of medical parole in accordance with the provisions of paragraph (f) of subdivision four of this section shall not preclude the inmate from reapplying for medical parole or otherwise affect an inmate's eligibility for any other form of release provided for by law.

6. To the extent that any provision of this section requires disclosure of medical information for the purpose of processing an application or making a decision, regarding release on medical parole or renewal of medical parole, or for the purpose of appropriately supervising a person released on medical parole, and that such disclosure would otherwise be prohibited by article twenty-seven-F of the public health law, the provisions of this section shall be controlling.

7. The commissioner of correctional services and the chairman of the board of parole shall be authorized to promulgate rules and regulations for their respective agencies to implement the provisions of this section.

8. Any decision made by the board pursuant to this section may be appealed pursuant to subdivision four of section two hundred fifty-nine-i of this article.

9. The chairman shall report annually to the governor, the temporary president of the senate and the speaker of the assembly, the chairpersons of the assembly and senate codes committees, the chairperson of the senate crime and corrections committee, and the chairperson of the assembly corrections committee the number of inmates who have applied for medical parole; the number who have been granted medical parole; the nature of the illness of the applicants, the counties to which they have been released and the nature of the placement pursuant to the medical discharge plan; the categories of reasons for denial for those who have been denied; the number of releasees who have been granted an additional period or periods of medical parole and the number of such grants; the number of releasees on medical parole who have been returned to the custody of the department of correctional services and the reasons for return.

Added by L. 1992, Ch. 55, § 289, eff. Apr. 10, 1992, and scheduled to expire on Apr. 10, 1994; **Amended** by L. 1994, Ch. 61, § 3, extending expiration date; L. 1994, Ch. 503, § 1, eff. July 26, 1994, amending subds. 2 and 3, and L. 1994, Ch. 503, § 2, eff. July 26, 1994, amending subd. 4(a) and (d), neither amendment affecting expiration as provided in L. 1992, Ch. 55, § 427(r); L. 1995, Ch. 3, § 44, amending subd. 1(a) by adding the phrase "or determinate," eff. Oct. 1, 1995, amendment repealed Sept. 30, 2005 pursuant to L. 1995, Ch. 3, § 74, paragraph (d); L. 1996, Ch. 48, extending expiration date of 1995 amendment to Apr. 10, 1998; L. 1998, Ch. 38, § 1, eff. Apr. 8, 1998; L. 2000, Ch. 16, § 1, eff. Mar. 30, 2000, extending expiration date of section to Sept. 1, 2001; L. 2001, Ch. 95, § 18, eff. July 13, 2001, extending expiration date of section to Sept. 1, 2003; L. 2003, Ch. 16, § 17, eff. Mar. 31, 2003, extending expiration date to Sept. 1, 2005; L. 2005, Ch. 56, Part D, §§ 15, 20, eff. Apr. 1, 2005, extending expiration date of section to Sept. 1, 2007, and effective and expiration dates of subd. 1(a) to Sept. 1, 2009.

ARTICLE 23

FAIR TREATMENT STANDARDS FOR CRIME VICTIMS

* **Editor's Note:** Two versions of § 646 have been enacted.

§ 640. Fair treatment standards for crime victims.

1. The commissioner of the division of criminal justice services, in consultation with the chairman of the crime victims board and other appropriate officials, shall promulgate standards for the treatment of the innocent victims of crime by the agencies which comprise the criminal justice system of the state.

2. For the purposes of this article the term "criminal justice" shall include juvenile justice and the objectives and criteria set forth in sections six hundred forty-one and six hundred forty-two of this article shall apply to presentment agencies as defined in subdivision twelve of section 301.2 of the family court act.

Amended by L. 1985, Ch. 414, eff. Sept 17, 1985.

§ 641. Objectives of fair treatment standards.

The object of such fair treatment standards shall be to:

1. Ensure that crime victims routinely receive emergency social and medical services as soon as possible and are given information pursuant to section six hundred twenty-five-a of this chapter on the following:

(a) availability of crime victim compensation;

(b) availability of appropriate public or private programs that provide counseling, treatment or support for crime victims, including but not limited to the following: rape crisis centers, victim/witness assistance programs, elderly victim services, victim assistance hotlines and domestic violence shelters;

(c) the role of the victims in the criminal justice process, including what they can expect from the system as well as what the system expects from them; and

(d) stages in the criminal justice process of significance to a crime victim, and the manner in which information about such stages can be obtained.

2. Ensure routine notification of a victim or witness as to steps that law enforcement officers or district attorneys can take to protect victims and witnesses from intimidation.

3. Ensure notification of victims, witnesses, relatives of those victims and witnesses who are minors, and relatives of homicide victims, if such persons provide the appropriate official with a current address and telephone number, either by phone or by mail, if possible, of judicial proceedings relating to their case, including:

(a) the arrest of an accused;

(b) the initial appearance of an accused before a judicial officer;

(c) the release of an accused pending judicial proceedings; and

(d) proceedings in the prosecution of the accused including entry of a plea of guilty, trial, sentencing, but prior to sentencing specific information shall be provided regarding the right to seek restitution and reparation, and where a term of imprisonment is imposed, specific information shall be provided regarding maximum and minimum terms of such imprisonment.

Amended by L. 1985, Ch. 688, eff. Aug. 1, 1985; L. 1992, Ch. 618, eff. Nov. 1, 1992, amending subd. 3(d).

§ 642. Criteria for fair treatment standards.

Such fair treatment standards shall provide that:

1. The victim of a violent felony offense, a

felony involving physical injury to the victim, a felony involving property loss or damage in excess of two hundred fifty dollars, a felony involving attempted or threatened physical injury or property loss or damage in excess of two hundred fifty dollars or a felony involving larceny against the person shall be consulted by the district attorney in order to obtain the views of the victim regarding disposition of the criminal case by dismissal, plea of guilty or trial. In such a case in which the victim is a minor child, or in the case of a homicide, the district attorney shall consult for such purpose with the family of the victim. In addition, the district attorney shall consult and obtain the views of the victim or family of the victim, as appropriate, concerning the release of the defendant in the victim's case pending judicial proceedings upon an indictment, and concerning the availability of sentencing alternatives such as community supervision and restitution from the defendant. The failure of the district attorney to so obtain the views of the victim or family of the victim shall not be cause for delaying the proceedings against the defendant nor shall it affect the validity of a conviction, judgment or order.

2. The victims and other prosecution witnesses shall, where possible, be provided, when awaiting court appearances, a secure waiting area that is separate from all other witnesses.

2-a. (a) All police departments, as that term is defined in subdivision a of section eight hundred thirty-seven-c of this chapter, district attorneys' offices and presentment agencies, as that term is defined in subdivision twelve of section 301.2 of the family court act, shall provide a private setting for interviewing victims of a crime defined in article one hundred thirty or section 255.25 of the penal law. For purposes of this subdivision, "private setting" shall mean an enclosed room from which the occupants are not visible or otherwise identifiable, and whose conversation cannot be heard, from outside such room. Only (i) those persons directly and immediately related to the interviewing of a particular victim, (ii) the victim, (iii) a social worker, rape crisis counselor, psychologist or other professional providing emotional support to the victim, unless the victim objects to the presence of such person and requests the exclusion of such person from the interview, and (iv) where appropriate, the parent or parents of the victim, if requested by the victim, shall be present during the interview of the victim.

(b) All police departments, as that term is defined in subdivision a of section eight hundred thirty-seven-c of this chapter, shall provide victims of a crime defined in article one hundred thirty of the penal law with the name, address, and telephone of the nearest rape crisis center in writing.

3. Law enforcement agencies and district attorneys shall promptly return property held for evidentiary purposes unless there is a compelling reason for retaining it relating to proof at trial.

4. The victim or witness who so requests shall be assisted by law enforcement agencies and district attorneys in informing employers that the need for victim and witness cooperation in the prosecution of the case may necessitate absence of that victim or witness from work. In addition, a victim or witness who, as a direct result of a crime or of cooperation with law enforcement agencies or the district attorney in the investigation or prosecution of a crime is unable to meet obligations to a creditor, creditors or others should be assisted by such agencies or the district attorney in providing to such creditor, creditors or others accurate information about the circumstances of the crime, including the nature of any loss or injury suffered by the victim, or about the victim's or witness' cooperation, where appropriate.

5. Victim assistance education and training, with special consideration to be given to victims of domestic violence, sex offense victims, elderly victims, child victims, and the families of homicide victims, shall be given to persons taking courses at state law enforcement training facilities and by district attorneys so that victims may be promptly, properly and completely assisted.

Amended by L. 1986, Ch. 642, eff. Aug. 1, 1986; L. 1989, Ch. 45, eff. Apr. 1, 1990; L. 1991, Ch. 301, eff. Apr. 1, 1992, amending subd. 2-a; L. 2005, Ch. 186, § 2, eff. Sept. 1, 2005, amending subd. 1.

§ 642-a. Guidelines for fair treatment of child victims as witnesses.

To the extent permitted by law, criminal justice agencies, crime victim-related agencies, social services agencies and the courts shall comply with the following guidelines in their treatment of child victims:

1. To minimize the number of times a child victim is called upon to recite the events of the case and to foster a feeling of trust and confidence in the child victim, whenever practicable, a multidisciplinary team involving a prosecutor, law enforcement agency personnel, and social services agency personnel should be used for the investigation and prosecution of child abuse cases.

2. Whenever practicable, the same prosecutor should handle all aspects of a case involving an alleged child victim.

3. To minimize the time during which a child victim must endure the stress of his involvement in the proceedings, the court should take appropriate action to ensure a speedy trial in all proceedings involving an alleged child victim. In ruling on any motion or request for a delay or continuance of a proceeding involving an alleged child victim, the court should consider and give weight to any potential adverse impact the delay or

continuance may have on the well-being of the child.

4. The judge presiding should be sensitive to the psychological and emotional stress a child witness may undergo when testifying.

5. In accordance with the provisions of article sixty-five of the criminal procedure law, when appropriate, a child witness as defined in subdivision one of section 65.00 of such law should be permitted to testify via live, two-way closed-circuit television.

6. In accordance with the provisions of section 190.32 of the criminal procedure law, a person supportive of the "child witness" or "special witness" as defined in such section should be permitted to be present and accessible to a child witness at all times during his testimony, although the person supportive of the child witness should not be permitted to influence the child's testimony.

7. A child witness should be permitted in the discretion of the court to use anatomically correct dolls and drawings.

Added by L. 1986, Ch. 263, eff. Jan. 1, 1987.

ANNOTATION

Child witness.—Court did not err in permitting child witness to hold a teddy bear while she testified; statute directs the judge to be sensitive to the psychological and emotional stress a child witness may undergo when testifying. People v. Gutkaiss, 206 A.D.2d 628, 614 N.Y.S.2d 599 (3d Dept. 1994).

§ 643. Fair treatment standards for crime victims; agencies generally.

1. As used in this section, "crime victim-related agency" means any agency of state government which provides services to or deals directly with crime victims, including (a) the department of social services, the office of the aging, the division of veterans affairs, the division of probation, the division of parole, the crime victims board, the department of motor vehicles, the office of vocational rehabilitation, the worker's compensation board, the department of health, the office of mental health, every transportation authority and the division of state police, and (b) any other agency so designated by the governor within ninety days of the effective date of this section.

2. Each crime victim-related agency shall review its practices, procedures, services, regulations and laws to determine the adequacy and appropriateness of its services with respect to crime victims, including victims with special needs, particularly the elderly, disabled or victims of child abuse, domestic violence or sex-related offenses. Such review shall include reasonable opportunity for public comment and consultation with crime victims or their representatives, and may include public hearings.

3. After the review, and not later than one-hundred eighty days after the effective date of this section, each crime victim-related agency shall submit a report to the governor and the legislature, setting forth the findings of the review including a description of the services provided by the agency and recommendations for changes in its practices, procedures, services, regulations and laws to improve its services to crime victims and to establish and implement fair treatment standards for crime victims.

4. Subject to the direction of the governor, and to the extent practicable, each crime victim-related agency shall expeditiously implement the recommendations of its report.

§ 644. Implementation.

The commissioner of the division of criminal justice services and the chairman of the crime victims board shall assist criminal justice agencies in implementing the guidelines promulgated by the commissioner.

§ 645. Fair treatment standards for crime victims in the courts.

The chief administrator of the courts, in consultation with the commissioner of the division of criminal justice services, the chairman of the crime victims board and other appropriate officials, shall promulgate standards for the treatment of the innocent victims of crime by the unified court system. These standards shall conform to and be consistent with the regulations promulgated pursuant to section six hundred forty of this article.

Added by L. 1986, Ch. 893, eff. Aug. 5, 1986. Renumbered former Section 645 to Section 649.

§ 646. Police reports. *

A victim of crime shall be entitled, regardless of physical injury, without charge to a copy of a police report of the crime.

* **Editor's Note:** In 1986, two versions of § 646 were enacted, each without reference to the other. Another version follows.

Added by L. 1986, Ch. 548, eff. Sept. 1, 1986.

§ 646. Objectives. *

The object of these fair treatment standards shall be to:

1. Ensure that crime victims are given information on the following:

(a) the role of the victims in the criminal justice process, including what they can expect from the system as well as what the system expects from them;

(b) stages in the criminal justice process of significance to a crime victim, and the manner in which information about such stages can be obtained; and

(c) how the court can address the needs of the victims, at sentencing.

2. Ensure routine notification of a victim or witness as to steps that the court can take to protect victims and witnesses from intimidation, including the issuance of orders of protection and temporary orders of protection.

3. Ensure notification of victims, witnesses, relatives of those victims and witnesses who are minors, and relatives of homicide victims, if such persons provide the appropriate court official with a current address and telephone number, either by phone or by mail, if possible, of judicial proceedings relating to their case, including:

(a) the initial appearance of an accused before a judicial officer;

(b) the release of an accused pending judicial proceedings;

(c) proceedings in the prosecution of the accused, including entry of a plea of guilty, trial, sentencing, and where a term of imprisonment is imposed, specific information shall be provided regarding maximum and minimum terms of such imprisonment; and

(d) the reversal or modification of the judgment by an appellate court.

  * **Editor's Note:** In 1986, two versions of § 646 were enacted, each without reference to the other. See preceding version.

  Added by L. 1986, Ch. 893, eff. Aug. 5, 1986.

§ 646-a. Information relative to the fair treatment standards; pamphlet.

1. The district attorney shall provide the victim, at the earliest time possible, with an informational pamphlet detailing the rights of crime victims which shall be prepared by the division of criminal justice services in cooperation with the crime victims board.

2. The pamphlet shall summarize provisions of this article. It shall also include specific information with appropriate statutory references on the following:

(a) the rights of crime victims to compensation and services;

(b) the rights of crime victims to routine notification of judicial proceedings relating to their case as provided in section six hundred forty-one of this article, in section 330.20, and section 440.50 of the criminal procedure law and section one hundred forty-nine-a of the correction law;

(c) the rights of crime victims to be protected from intimidation and to have the court, where appropriate, issue protective orders as provided in sections 530.12 and 530.13 of the criminal procedure law and sections 215.15, 215.16 and 215.17 of the penal law;

(d) the rights of crime victims to submit, where appropriate, a victim impact statement for the pre-sentencing report and the parole hearing as provided in section 390.30 of the criminal procedure law and section two hundred fifty-nine-i of this chapter;

(e) the rights of crime victims, where a defendant is being sentenced for a felony, to request the right to make a statement at the time of sentencing as provided in section 380.50 of the criminal procedure law; and

(f) the rights of crime victims to request restitution and have the district attorney present such request to the court and assist the crime victim in the filing and collection of a restitution order in cooperation with the designated agency of the court as provided in section 420.10 of the criminal procedure law and section 60.27 of the penal law.

(g) the rights of crime victims to be aware of the defendant's incarceration status by providing the division of parole's contact information, including the division's toll-free telephone number, as provided for in subdivision two of section two hundred fifty-nine-i of this chapter. Such notice shall advise the crime victim to use the division's toll-free telephone number to update contact information.

3. This pamphlet shall provide space for the insertion of the following information:

(a) The address and phone number of the nearest crime victims board office;

(b) The address and phone numbers of local victim service programs, where appropriate;

(c) The name, phone number and office location of the person in the district attorney's office to whom inquiries concerning the victims case may be directed; and

(d) Any other information the division deems appropriate.

  Added by L. 1994, Ch. 67, eff. Jan. 1, 1995; **Amended** by L. 2005, Ch. 186, § 1, eff. Sept. 1, 2005, adding subd. 2(g).

§ 647. Criteria.

Fair treatment standards for crime victims in the courts shall provide that:

1. The court shall consider the views of the victim of a violent felony offense, a felony involving physical injury to the victim, a felony involving property loss or damage in excess of two hundred fifty dollars, a felony involving attempted or threatened physical injury or property loss or damage in excess of two hundred fifty dollars or a felony involving larceny against the person or of the family of a homicide victim or minor child, regarding discretionary decisions relating to the criminal case, including but not limited to, plea agreements and sentence. In addition, the court shall consider the views of the victim or family of the victim, as appropriate,

concerning the release of the defendant in the victim's case pending judicial proceedings upon an indictment, and concerning the availability of sentencing alternatives such as community supervision and restitution from the defendant. The failure of the court to consider the views of the victim or family of the victim shall not be cause for delaying the proceedings against the defendant nor shall it affect the validity of a conviction, judgment or order.

2. The victims and other prosecution witnesses shall, where possible, be provided, when awaiting court appearances, a secure waiting area that is separate from all other witnesses.

3. the court shall assist in and expedite the return of property held for evidentiary purposes unless there is a compelling reason for retaining it relating to proof at trial.

4. Victim assistance education shall be given to judicial and nonjudicial personnel of the unified court system so that victims may be promptly, properly and completely assisted.

Added by L. 1986, Ch. 893, eff. Aug. 5, 1986.

§ 648. Review; report and implementation.

1. The chief administrator of the unified court system shall review court practices, procedures, services, regulations and laws to determine the adequacy and appropriateness of its services with respect to crime victims, including victims with special needs, particularly the elderly, disabled or victims of child abuse, domestic violence or sex-related offenses. Such review shall include reasonable opportunity for public comment and consultation with crime victims or their representatives, and may include public hearings.

2. After the review, and not later than two hundred seventy days after the effective date of this section, the chief administrator of the unified court system shall submit a report to the governor and the legislature, setting forth the findings of the review, including a description of the services provided by the components of the unified court system and recommendations for changes in its procedures, services, regulations and laws to improve its services to crime victims and to establish and implement fair treatment standards for crime victims.

3. Subject to the direction of the chief administrator, the components of the unified court system shall expeditiously implement the recommendations of its report.

Added by L. 1986, Ch. 893, eff. Aug. 5, 1986.

§ 649. Miscellaneous.

Nothing in this article shall be construed as creating a cause of action for damages or injunctive relief against the state or any of its political subdivisions or officers or any agency thereof.

Renumbered by L. 1986, Ch. 893, formerly § 645.

MISC. LAWS

ARTICLE 35

DIVISION OF CRIMINAL JUSTICE SERVICES

* **Editor's Note:** Two versions of § 837-m have been enacted.

** **Editor's Note:** Two versions of § 846 have been enacted.

§ 835. Definitions.

1. "Division" means the division of criminal justice services.

2. [*Repealed by L. 1992, Ch. 55, § 150, eff. April 10, 1992.*]

3. "Commissioner" means the commissioner of the division of criminal justice services.

4. "Council" means the municipal police training council.

5. "Federal acts" means the federal omnibus

crime control and safe streets act of nineteen hundred sixty-eight, the federal juvenile delinquency prevention and control act of nineteen hundred sixty-eight, and any act or acts amendatory or supplemental thereto.

6. "Municipality" means any county, city, town, park commission, village, or police district in the state.

7. "Police officer" means a member of a police force or other organization of a municipality who is responsible for the prevention and detection of crime and the enforcement of the general criminal laws of the state, but shall not include any person serving as such solely by virtue of his occupying any other office or position, nor shall such term include a sheriff, under-sheriff, commissioner of police, deputy or assistant commissioner of police, chief of police, deputy or assistant chief of police or any person having an equivalent title who is appointed or employed by a municipality to exercise equivalent supervisory authority.

7-a. "Police officer," for the purpose of the central state registry, means a person designated as such in subdivision thirty-four of section 1.20 of the criminal procedure law.

7-b. "Peace officer" means a person designated as such in section 2.10 of the criminal procedure law.

8. "Police agency" means any agency or department of any municipality, commission, authority or other public benefit corporation having responsibility for enforcing the criminal laws of the state.

9. "Qualified agencies" means courts in the unified court system, the administrative board of the judicial conference, probation departments, sheriffs' offices, district attorneys' offices, the state department of correctional services, the state division of probation, the department of correction of any municipality, the insurance frauds bureau of the state department of insurance, the office of professional medical conduct of the state department of health for the purposes of section two hundred thirty of the public health law, the temporary state commission of investigation, the criminal investigations bureau of the banking department, police forces and departments having responsibility for enforcement of the general criminal laws of the state and the Onondaga County Center for Forensic Sciences Laboratory when acting within the scope of its law enforcement duties.

10. "Criminal justice function" means the prevention, detection and investigation of the commission of an offense, the apprehension of a person for the alleged commission of an offense, the detention, release on recognizance or bail of a person charged with an offense prior to disposition of the charge, the prosecution and defense of a program charged with an offense, the detention release on recognizance or bail of a person convicted of an offense prior to sentencing, the sentencing of offenders, probation, incarceration, parole, and proceedings in a court subsequent to a judgment of conviction relating thereto.

Amended by L. 1975, Ch. 839; L. 1977, Ch. 306; L. 1979, Ch. 482, L. 1980, Ch. 843, eff. Sept. 1, 1980; L. 1981, Ch. 720, added subd. 47, eff. Oct 1, 1981, which ceases on Jan. 1, 1984; L. 1983, Ch. 399, extending subd. 47; L. 1985, Ch. 134, eff. Apr. 1, 1985; L. 1987, Chs. 24, 325, eff. Apr. 13, 1987 and July 20, 1987 extends the expiration date of subd. 47 to Jan. 1, 1992; L. 1987, Ch. 711, eff. Nov. 1, 1987, added subds. 11, 12 and 13 and these provisions shall be deemed repealed on Nov. 1, 1990; L. 1990, Ch. 193, eff. Apr. 1, 1990, extended to Nov. 1, 1991; L. 1991, Ch. 371, § 2, extending expiration date of subd. 9; L. 1991, Ch. 511, eff. July 19, 1991; L. 1992, Ch. 55, § 324 eff. Apr. 10, 1992, extended expiration date of subds. 11, 12 & 13 to Nov. 1, 1995; L. 1999, Ch. 610, § 2, amending subd. 9, eff. Nov. 9, 1999; L. 2004, Ch. 175, § 1, eff. July 20, 2004; L. 2004, Ch. 574, § 1, eff. Oct. 5, 2004, amending subd. 9.

§ 836. Division of criminal justice services; commissioner, organization and employees.

1. There shall be in the executive department a division of criminal justice services.

2. The head of the division shall be a commissioner, who shall be appointed by the governor, by and with the advice and consent of the senate, and hold office at the pleasure of the governor by whom he was appointed and until his successor is appointed and qualified. The commissioner shall be the chief executive officer of and in sole charge of the administration of the division. The commissioner shall receive an annual salary to be fixed by the governor within the amount available therefor by appropriation; and he shall be entitled to receive reimbursement for expenses actually and necessarily incurred by him in the performance of his duties.

3. The commissioner may, from time to time, create, abolish, transfer and consolidate bureaus and other units within the division not expressly established by law as he may determine necessary for the efficient operation of the division, subject to the approval of the director of the budget.

4. The commissioner may appoint such deputies, directors, assistants and other officers and employees, committees and consultants as he may deem necessary, prescribe their powers and duties, fix their compensation and provide for reimbursement of their expenses within the amount appropriated therefor.

5. The commissioner may request and receive from any department, division, board, bureau, commission or other agency of the state or any political subdivision thereof or any public authority such assistance, information and data as will enable the division properly to carry out its functions, powers and duties.

6. The principal office of the division shall be in the county of Albany.

MISC. LAWS

§ 837. Functions, powers and duties of division.

The division shall have the following functions, powers and duties:

1. Advise and assist the governor in developing policies, plans and programs for improving the coordination, administration and effectiveness of the criminal justice system;

2. Make recommendations to agencies in the criminal justice system for improving their administration and effectiveness:

3. Act as the official state planning agency pursuant to the federal acts; in accordance therewith, prepare, evaluate and revise statewide crime control and juvenile delinquency prevention and control plans; and receive and disburse funds from the federal government;

4. In cooperation with the state administrator of the unified court system as well as any other public or private agency,

(a) through the central data facility collect, analyze, evaluate and disseminate statistical and other information and data; and

(b) undertake research, studies and analyses and act as a central repository, clearinghouse and disseminator of research studies, in respect to criminal justice functions and any agency responsible for a criminal justice function, with specific attention to: the effectiveness of existing programs and procedures for the efficient and just processing and disposition of criminal cases; the number of persons arrested for the alleged commission of a felony, the particular felony for which the person was arrested and the disposition of the charge, including but not limited to, as the case may be, dismissal, acquittal, the offense to which the defendant pleaded guilty, the offense the defendant was convicted of after trial and the sentence; and

(c) collect and analyze statistical and other information and data with respect to the number of crimes reported or known to police officers or peace officers, the number of persons arrested for the commission of offense, the offense for which the person was arrested, the county within which the arrest was made and the accusatory instrument filed, the disposition of the accusatory instrument including, but not limited to, as the case may be, dismissal, acquittal, the offense to which the defendant pled guilty, the offense the defendant was convicted of after trial, and the sentence; and where a firearm as defined in section 265.00 of the penal law or machine gun, rifle or shotgun comes into the custody of police officers or peace officers in the course of an investigation of such crime or offense, the make, model type, caliber and magazine or cylinder capacity of any such firearm and whether possession of such firearm by the defendant is licensed or unlicensed and if confiscated at arrest, the style and manufacturer of any ammunition; and

(d) Supply data, upon request, to federal bureaus or departments engaged in collecting national criminal statistics; and

(e) Supply data, including confidential and sealed criminal history record information, for bona fide research purposes. Such information shall be disseminated in accordance with procedures established by the division to assure the security and privacy of identification and information data, which shall include the execution of an agreement which protects the confidentiality of the information and reasonably protects against data linkage to individuals; and

(f) Accomplish all of the functions, powers and duties set forth in paragraphs (a), (b), (c) and (d) of this subdivision with respect to the processing and disposition of cases involving violent felony offenses specified in subdivision one of section 70.02 of the penal law.

4-a. In cooperation with the state administrator of the unified court system as well as any other public or private agency, collect and analyze statistical and all other information and data with respect to the number of environmental crimes and offenses in violation of articles twenty-seven, thirty-seven and forty, and titles twenty-seven and thirty-seven of article seventy-one of the environmental conservation law reported or known to the department of environmental conservation, the division of state police, and all other police or peace officers, the number of persons arrested for the commission of said violation, the offense for which the person was arrested, the county within which the arrest was made and the accusatory instrument filed, the disposition of the accusatory instrument filed, including, but not limited to, as the case may be, dismissal, acquittal, the offense to which the defendant pled guilty, the offense the defendant was convicted of after trial, and the sentence or monetary penalty levied, or the civil disposition of the offense if such offense was adjudicated by civil means.

4-b. In cooperation with any public or private agency or entity, collect and analyze statistical data and all other information and data with respect to the number of crimes and offenses committed against employees of the city of New York responsible for enforcing certain regulations in such city, while such employees were enforcing or attempting to enforce such regulations and reported or known to any law enforcement agency, the number of persons arrested for the commission of said offenses, the offense for which the person was arrested, the county within which the arrest was made and the accusatory instrument filed, the disposition of the accusatory instrument filed, including but not limited to, as the case may be, dismissal, acquittal, the offense to which the defendant pled guilty, the offense the defendant was convicted of after trial, and the sentence or other penalty levied. For the purposes of this subdivision, an employee of the city of

New York responsible for enforcing certain regulations in such city shall mean a traffic enforcement agent or an employee of the department of sanitation who is authorized to issue notices of violation, summons or appearance tickets.

4-c. In cooperation with the chief administrator of the courts as well as any other public or private agency, including law enforcement agencies, collect and analyze statistical and all other information and data with respect to the number of hate crimes reported to or investigated by the division of state police, and all other police or peace officers, the number of persons arrested for the commission of such crimes, the offense for which the person was arrested, the county within which the arrest was made and the accusatory instrument filed, the disposition of the accusatory instrument filed, including, but not limited to, as the case may be, dismissal, acquittal, the offense to which the defendant pled guilty, the offense the defendant was convicted of after trial, and the sentence imposed. The division shall include the statistics and other information required by this subdivision in the annual report submitted to the governor and legislature pursuant to subdivision twelve of this section.

5. Conduct studies and analyses of the administration or operations of any criminal justice agency when requested by the head of such agency, and make the results thereof available for the benefit of such agency;

5-a. Undertake to furnish or make available to the district attorney of the state such supportive services and technical assistance as the commissioner and any one or more of the district attorneys shall agree are appropriate to promote the effective performance of his or their prosecutorial functions.

6. Establish, through electronic data processing and related procedures, a central data facility with a communication network serving qualified agencies anywhere in the state, so that they may, upon such terms and conditions as the commissioner, and the appropriate officials of such qualified agencies shall agree, contribute information and, except as provided in subdivision two of section 306.2 of the family court act, have access to information contained in the central data facility, which shall include but not be limited to such information as criminal record, personal appearance data, fingerprints, photographs, and handwriting samples;

7. Receive, process and file fingerprints, photographs and other descriptive data for the purpose of establishing identity and previous criminal record;

7-a. Receive, process and file orders granting a change of name to persons convicted of a felony subject to the provisions of subdivision two of section sixty-one of the civil rights law;

8. Adopt appropriate measures to assure the security and privacy of identification and information data;

8-a. Charge a fee when, pursuant to statute or the regulations of the division, it conducts a search of its criminal history records and returns a report thereon in connection with an application for employment or for a license or permit. The division shall adopt and may, from time to time, amend a schedule of such fees which shall be in amounts determined by the division to be reasonably related to the cost of conducting such searches and returning reports thereon but, in no event, shall any such fee exceed twenty-five dollars and an additional surcharge of fifty dollars. The comptroller is hereby authorized to deposit such fees into the general fund, provided, however, that the monies received by the division of criminal justice services for payment of the additional surcharge shall be deposited in equal amounts to the general fund and to the fingerprint identification and technology account.

8-b. Notwithstanding any other provision of law to the contrary, charge a fee for the provision of agency materials and publications, conferences, criminal history record reviews, legal services, the provision of services to analyze or prepare data that is not prepared in the ordinary course of business, the provision of information in a computerized format, the service and repair of municipal law enforcement agency equipment and collect reimbursement and other moneys. Such fees shall be reasonably related to the actual costs incurred, including the costs of salaries, computer time, shipping and handling, as appropriate. The comptroller is hereby authorized to deposit such fees into the general fund effective August thirty-first, nineteen hundred ninety-six.

8-c. Notwithstanding the provisions of section one hundred three of the general municipal law, section one hundred seventy-four of the state finance law and any other general, special or local law to the contrary, any officer, board or agency of a political subdivision or state agency authorized to make purchases of materials, equipment or supplies, may make such purchases of statewide automated fingerprint identification system-related materials, equipment or supplies, through the agreement executed between the division and North American Morpho Systems, Inc. Notwithstanding any other law to the contrary, the division shall be authorized to enter into voluntary cost-sharing arrangements with local criminal justice agencies for expanded facsimile services and criminal justice information access through the criminal justice data communications network.

9. Accept, agree to accept and contract as agent of the state with the approval of the governor, any grant, including federal grants, or any gift for any of the purposes of this article;

10. Fees: pay (a) a fee of thirty-six dollars for processing of the application, investigation of the

applicant and for the initial biennial registration period. Such fees shall be deposited to the credit of the licensing examinations services account established pursuant to the provisions of section ninety-seven-aa of the state finance law; and (b) a fee pursuant to subdivision eight-a of section eight hundred thirty-seven of the executive law, and amendments thereto, for the cost of the division's full search and retain procedures, which fee shall be remitted by the department to the division for deposit by the comptroller into the general fund effective August thirty-first, nineteen hundred ninety-six; and

11. Enter into contracts with any person, firm, corporation, municipality, or governmental agency;

12. Make an annual report to the governor and legislature concerning its work during the preceding year, and such further interim reports to the governor, or to the governor and legislature, as it shall deem advisable, or as shall be required by the governor;

13. Adopt, amend or rescind such rules and regulations as may be necessary or convenient to the performance of the functions, powers and duties of the division;

14. Do all other things necessary or convenient to carry out the functions, powers and duties expressly set forth in this article.

15. Promulgate, in consultation with the superintendent of state police and the state office for the prevention of domestic violence, a standardized "domestic violence incident report form" for use by state and local law enforcement agencies in the reporting, recording and investigation of all alleged incidents of domestic violence, regardless of whether an arrest is made as a result of such investigation. Such form shall be prepared in multiple parts, one of which shall be immediately provided to the victim, and shall include designated spaces for: the recordation of the results of the investigation by the law enforcement agency and the basis for any action taken; the recordation of a victim's allegations of domestic violence; the age and gender of the victim and the alleged offender or offenders; and immediately thereunder a space on which the victim may sign and verify such victim's allegations. Such form shall also include, but not be limited to spaces to identify:

(a) What other services or agencies, including but not limited to medical, shelter, advocacy and other supportive services are or have previously been involved with the victim; and

(b) Whether the victim has been provided with the written notice described in subdivision five of section eight hundred twelve of the family court act and subdivision six of section 530.11 of the criminal procedure law.

16. Operate a toll-free twenty-four hour telephone number that members of the public may call to obtain information as to resources available to the public to assist in the location and recovery of missing persons. Such toll-free telephone line may be operated by the division as part of the toll-free telephone line established pursuant to section eight hundred thirty-seven-f of this article. Furthermore, all such information relating to the locating and recovery of missing persons may be included on the division homepage established pursuant to section eight hundred forty-three of this article.

Amended by L. 1975, Ch. 831; L. 1976, Ch. 548; L. 1978, Ch. 481; L. 1980, Ch. 843; L. 1987, Ch. 631. L. 1989, Ch. 779, adding subd. 4-b, and L. 1990, Ch. 1, eff. July 1, 1990, amending subd. 4-b; this subdivision shall apply in the case of any proceeding commenced on or after such date to acts which occur on or after such date, provided however, that these provisions shall be effective only to the extent of appropriations specifically made available therefor; L. 1992, Ch. 55, amended subds. 3 and 9; L. 1994, Ch. 169; L. 1994, Ch. 431, amending subd. 4-b; L. 1994, Ch. 222, § 27, eff. Jan. 1, 1995, adding subd. 15; L. 1995, Ch. 512, § 1, amending subd. 4(c); L. 1996, Ch. 309, §§ 67 and 68, amending subds. 8-a and 8-b, respectively, eff. Aug. 31, 1996; L. 1996, Ch. 645, § 5, amending subd. 6, eff. Sept. 13, 1996, and this amendment applies retroactively to a person whose fingerprints were taken pursuant to section 306.1 of the family court act or who was initially fingerprinted as a juvenile offender on or after January 1, 1986, and whose fingerprints are on file with the division of criminal justice services, provided that in the case of a juvenile offender action, the case was subsequently removed to family court, pursuant to L. 1996, Ch. 645, § 6; L. 1997, Ch. 626, eff. Sept. 17, 1997; L. 1999, Ch. 22, § 6, eff. Jan. 1, 2000, adding subd. 16; L. 2000, Ch. 107, § 8, eff. Oct. 8, 2000, adding subd. 4-c; L. 2000, Ch. 549, § 6, as amended, adding subd. 7-a, eff. Jan. 24, 2001, and shall apply to all convictions that are entered on, after or before such date for which a petition is filed on, after or before the effective date of this act [Jan. 24, 2001] and is pending before a court on or after the effective date of this act [Jan. 24, 2001]; L. 2003, Ch. 62, Part G, § 1, eff. May 15, 2003, amending subd. 8-a.

ANNOTATION

Fee for fingerprint searches.—Defendant may lawfully charge plaintiff fees for fingerprint searches to be performed by it with respect to applicants to plaintiff for licenses or registrations. Waterfront Comm'n v. Commissioner of Div. of Criminal Justice Servs., 63 A.D.2d 915, 406 N.Y.S.2d 457 (1st Dept. 1978).

§ 837-a. Additional functions, powers and duties of the division.

In addition to the functions, powers and duties otherwise provided by this article, the division shall:

1. Collect and analyze statistical and other information and data with respect to the number of persons charged with the commission of a felony, including but not limited to, the felony provisions of articles twenty-seven, thirty-seven and forty, and titles twenty-seven and thirty-seven of article seventy-one of the environmental conservation law, article four of the insurance law, sections 176.15, 176.20, 176.25 and 176.30 of the penal law relative to insurance fraud, as such term is defined in section 176.05 of such law, by indictment or the filing of a superior court information, the felony with which the person was charged therein, the county within which the indictment or superior court information was

filed, the disposition thereof including, but not limited to, as the case may be, dismissal, acquittal, the offense to which the defendant pleaded guilty, the offense the defendant was convicted of after trial, and the sentence.

2. The division shall present to the governor, temporary president of the senate, minority leader of the senate, speaker of the assembly and the minority leader of the assembly a quarterly report containing the statistics and other information required by subdivision one hereof. The initial report required by this paragraph shall be for the period beginning September first, nineteen hundred seventy-three and ending December thirty-first, nineteen hundred seventy-three and shall be presented no later than January fifteen, nineteen hundred seventy-four. Thereafter, each quarterly report shall be presented no later than thirty days after the close of each quarter.

3. Present to the governor, temporary president of the senate, minority leader of the senate, speaker of the assembly, and the minority leader of the assembly a semi-annual report analyzing the processing and disposition of cases covered by the provisions of a chapter of the laws of nineteen hundred seventy-eight relating to the imposition of mandatory sentences of imprisonment and plea bargaining restrictions upon violent felony offenders, second violent felony offenders and persistent violent felony offenders. The report shall assess the effect of such law on the ability of the criminal justice system to deal with violent crime, and its impact on the resources of the criminal justice system, and shall make recommendations for any changes in such law which may be necessary to accomplish its objectives. The initial report required by this subdivision shall be for the period beginning September first, nineteen hundred seventy-eight and ending February twenty-eight, nineteen hundred seventy-nine and shall be presented no later than April first, nineteen hundred seventy-nine. Thereafter, each semi-annual report shall be presented no later than thirty days after the close of the six-month period.

4. Collect, analyze and maintain all reports, statements and transcripts forwarded to the division concerning the reasons for imposition of a sentence other than an indeterminate sentence of imprisonment upon an armed felony offender as defined in subdivision forty-one of section 1.20 of the criminal procedure law; the reasons for the removal of an action involving a juvenile offender, as defined in subdivision forty-two of section 1.20 of the criminal procedure law, to the family court; and the reasons for a finding that a youth who has been convicted of an armed felony offense is to be treated as a youthful offender. Such reports, statements and transcripts shall be made available for public inspection except that in the case of a juvenile offender or a youthful offender, those portions which identify the offender shall be deleted. The commissioner may promulgate such rules and regulations with

respect to the form of such reports, statements and transcripts.

5. Make certain that such statistical information relating to the commission of offenses in violation of article twenty-seven, thirty-seven or forty, or title twenty-seven or thirty-seven of article seventy-one of the environmental conservation law article four of the insurance law, sections 176.15, 176.20, 176.25 and 176.30 of the penal law relative to insurance fraud, as such term is defined in section 176.05 of such law, is included and becomes a part of any and all published statistical studies on the occurrence of crime in this state or crime dispositions by the courts of this state or incarcerations in the correctional facilities of this state.

6. Present to the governor, temporary president of the senate, minority leader of the senate, speaker of the assembly and the minority leader of the assembly and annual report analyzing the disposal of property forfeited pursuant to the provisions of article thirteen-A of the civil practice law and rules and article four hundred eighty of the penal law. The initial report required by this subdivision shall be for the period beginning November first, nineteen hundred ninety and ending May thirty-first, nineteen hundred ninety-one and shall be presented no later that July first, nineteen hundred ninety-one. Thereafter, each annual report shall be presented no later that February first. The commissioner may promulgate rules and regulations with respect to the form of such report.

7. Contract with an organization having substantial knowledge and experience in the prosecution of serious criminal matters for the development and provision of continuing legal education, training, advice and assistance for prosecutors in the prosecution of capital cases.

Amended by L. 1975, Ch. 459; L. 1978, Ch. 481; L. 1987, Ch. 631, eff. Nov. 1, 1987; L. 1990, Ch. 655, eff. Nov. 1, 1990, adding subd. 6; L. 1992, Ch. 480, eff. Jan. 13, 1993, amending subds. 1 and 5; L. 1995, Ch. 1, § 35, adding subd. 7, eff. Apr. 1, 1995.

§ 837-b. Duties of courts and peace officers.

1. It is hereby made the duty of the state administrator of the unified court system; and of every sheriff, county or city commissioner of correction and head of every police department, state, county, or local, and also railroad, steamship, park, aqueduct and tunnel police and town constables, of every district attorney, of every probation agency; and of head of every institution or department, state, county and local, dealing with criminals and of every other officer, person or agency, dealing with crimes or criminals or with delinquency or delinquents, to transmit to the commissioner not later than the fifteenth day of each calendar month, or at such times as provided in the rules and regulations adopted by

the commissioner, such information as may be necessary to enable him to comply with subdivision four of section eight hundred thirty-seven. Such reports shall be made upon forms which shall be supplied by the commissioner.

2. Such officers and agencies shall install and maintain records needed for reporting data required by the commissioner and shall give him or his accredited agents access to records for the purpose of inspection.

3. For every neglect to comply with the requirements of this section, the commissioner may apply to the supreme court for an order directed to such person responsible requiring compliance. Upon such application the court may issue such order as may be just, and a failure to comply with the order of the court shall be a contempt of court and punishable as such.

Amended by L. 1975, Ch. 459.

§ 837-c. Processing requests submitted by police departments.

a. As used in this section, the term "police department" means any police department or sheriff's office of this state or any of its political subdivisions.

b. The police department may forward and the division shall receive, process and, subject to subdivision e of this section, retain fingerprints and such descriptive data as the division may require of persons applying for employment with such department.

c. It shall be the duty of the division to forward to the police department any arrest record involving any person described in subdivision b of this section.

d. It shall be the duty of the police department to notify the division if an applicant for employment by the police department has not been hired, or an employee has died, resigned, retired or been dismissed.

e. Upon receiving notification in accordance with subdivision d of this section, the division shall either return to the police department or destroy all documents forwarded to it pursuant to subdivision b of this section.

Amended by L. 1977, Ch. 482.

§ 837-d. Soft body ballistic armor vests for police officers.

1. As used in this section, the following terms have the following meanings:

(a) "Eligible police officer" means a police officer as defined in subdivision thirty-four of section 1.20 of the criminal procedure law whose regular duties are such as the commissioner determines may expose the officer to serious physical injury which may result in death or disability;

(b) "Vest" means a soft body ballistic armor vest;

(c) "Municipal corporation" means a county, city, town, village or police district;

(d) "Public authority" means an independent autonomous public corporation created by special act of the legislature;

(e) "Public benefit corporation" means a corporation organized to construct or operate a public improvement wholly within the state;

(f) "State agency" means a department, board, bureau, commission, agency or other division of state government;

(g) "Applicant" means a state agency, municipal corporation, public authority, public benefit corporation, or the highest official thereof.

2. An application which is authorized to and employs police officers may apply to the commissioner for reimbursement of funds expended for the purchase of vests for eligible police officers.

3. Reimbursement shall be made only for vests which at the time of purchase meet or exceed the minimum standards and specifications in effect on that date as prescribed by rules and regulations promulgated pursuant to subdivisions six and six-a of this section, and shall be limited to the total amount appropriated for such purpose. Reimbursement for any vest shall not exceed an amount which in the judgment of the commissioner would be the cost of a vest conforming to minimum standards and specifications in effect at the time the vest was purchased. Selection of vests shall be a determination to be made by the applicant in accordance with rules and regulations promulgated by the commissioner. Such rules and regulations shall provide that, subject to the provisions of subdivisions six and six-a of this section, the applicant may select from a range of vests including those commonly known or classified as type I, type II-A, type II, or type III-A in such standard classification systems as the national institute of justice standards for ballistic resistance of police body armor.

4. The commissioner shall require any applicant seeking reimbursement for vests to apply for any available federal funds. Any applicant failing to do so shall not be entitled to reimbursement under this section. The commissioner may waive such failure for good cause. The commissioner shall maintain a public record of all such waivers and the reasons therefor. Reimbursement may be withheld pending the determination of an application for federal funds.

4-a. An applicant for reimbursement pursuant to this section shall report the name of each eligible police officer for whom reimbursement is sought. The applicant shall report whether such eligible police officer or officers have, at any time during the ten years immediately preceding the application for reimbursement, been provided with any other vest for which reimbursement pursuant to this section was provided, the date of any such prior reimbursement and any other information that the commissioner may require for accurate record-keeping and accountability and for evaluation of performance, wear and officer use of vests.

5. The amount of any reimbursement authorized to be made pursuant to subdivision three of this section shall be reduced by the amount of any federal funds granted to the applicant for the purpose of purchasing vests, and by the amount of any other funds received directly or indirectly for that purpose by the applicant.

6. The commissioner shall promulgate regulations prescribing standards and specifications for vests and procedures for vest selection by and reimbursement to applicants. In promulgating such regulations, the commissioner shall give due consideration to:

(a) the maximum total weight of a vest which provides adequate protection against ballistic penetration and trauma, and which may be worn in comfort throughout an eight hour tour of duty;

(b) the ballistic specifications which the vest or any part thereof must be capable of defeating which shall include, but not be limited to the ballistic specifications of any firearms considered to be standard issue to eligible police officers;

(c) the testing procedures appropriate to determining the effectiveness of such vests;

(d) the labeling requirements for the vests and component parts thereof; and

(e) the commercial availability of conforming vests.

6-a. In the evaluation of an application for reimbursement, the commissioner shall, at the request of the applicant, give consideration to the ballistic specifications of any firearm or firearms considered by the applicant to be standard issue to its police officers.

7. The contract specifications for bid for the sale of vests shall require that certificate of insurance evidencing that liability insurance providing a minimum coverage of at least five hundred thousand dollars per occurrence for injury or death suffered as a result of a defect in the manufacture shall be and remain in effect for the projected life of any vest purchased.

8. Neither the state nor the applicant or any employee thereof shall be liable to a police officer or officer's heirs, executors, administrators or assigns, for the death of or injury to the officer resulting from any defect or deficiency in a vest for which reimbursement is made pursuant to this section.

9. A police officer who suffers an injury or death as a result of the officer's failure to wear a vest for which reimbursement is made pursuant to this section, and officer's heirs, executors, administrators or assigns shall not suffer any loss or be denied any benefit or right to which they are otherwise entitled; provided, however, that nothing contained herein shall prevent the officer from being subject to a disciplinary proceeding for failure to obey a lawful order of a superior officer requiring the officer to wear a vest.

10. Nothing contained in this section shall be construed to prohibit an applicant from expending its own funds for vests in amounts exceeding the established state reimbursement limitations.

11. The commissioner is authorized to promulgate rules and regulations to provide for the orderly effectuation of the provisions of this section.

12. The commissioner shall establish and maintain a record containing the name of each eligible police officer who receives a vest for which reimbursement has been provided pursuant to this section, the applicant to whom reimbursement for such vest is provided, the date on which such reimbursement was provided and any other information that the commissioner may require for accurate record-keeping and accountability and for evaluation of performance, wear and officer use of vests.

13. Nothing in this section shall be deemed to supersede the provisions of section three of chapter eight hundred seventy-six of the laws of nineteen hundred eighty applicable to members of the division of state police or to alter a valid labor-management agreement covering employees of the state serving in police officer positions in the security services negotiating unit established pursuant to article fourteen of the civil service law which is in effect on the effective date of this section.

Added by L. 1984, Ch. 84, eff. Apr. 1, 1984; **Amended** by L. 1988, Ch. 555, eff. Aug. 11, 1988, amending subds. 3 and 6; repealing subd. 12; and adding subds. 4-a, 6-a, and 12; L. 1991, Ch. 503, eff. July 19, 1991, amending subd. 3.

§ 837-e. Statewide central register for missing children.

1. There is hereby established through electronic data processing and related procedures, a statewide central register for missing children which shall be compatible with the national crime information center register maintained pursuant to the federal missing children act of nineteen hundred eighty-two such missing child hereinafter defined as any person under the age of eighteen years missing from his or her normal and ordinary place of residence and whose whereabouts cannot be determined by a person responsible for the child's care and any child known to have been taken, enticed or concealed from the custody of his or her lawful guardian by a person who has no legal right to do so.

1-a.   (a) Upon the entry of a report of a

missing child born in New York into the register, the division shall notify the commissioner of the state department of health or if the child was born in the city of New York, the commissioner of the New York city department of health, of such entry and shall provide such commissioner with information concerning the identity of the missing child and request that the birth certificate record of such child be flagged in accordance with section four thousand one hundred of the public health law.

(b) If the division has reason to believe that a missing child has at any time been enrolled in a New York school, it shall notify the last known school at which time the school shall flag the missing child's schooling record in accordance with section three thousand two hundred twenty-two of the education law. If the division has reason to believe that a child who is listed as a missing child is currently enrolled in and attending a New York school, it shall notify the school and upon receiving notification, such school shall immediately notify the statewide central register for missing children within the division of criminal justice services.

(c) Upon learning of the recovery of any missing child whose birth certificate record or schooling record has been flagged as the result of notification made pursuant to this subdivision, the division shall so notify the state commissioner of health or if the child was born in the city of New York, the commissioner of the New York city department of health, and the school as appropriate.

2. The following may make inquiries to determine if any entries in the register or in the national crime information center register could match the subject of the inquiry:

(a) a police or criminal justice agency investigating a report of a missing or unidentified child, whether living or deceased; and

(b) the agency licensing, certifying or registering a family day care home, day care or head start program funded pursuant to Title V of the Federal Economic Opportunity Act of nineteen hundred sixty-four as amended, when an operator or director of such program has reasonable cause to believe that a child in attendance at the home, center or program may be a missing person provided, however, that upon notification that such child appears to match a child registered herein such agency shall immediately notify such operator or director to contact an appropriate local criminal justice agency; and

(c) a district attorney or a county medical examiner or coroner upon a showing that information contained in the register may be necessary for the determination of an issue regarding a missing or unidentified child; and

(d) an authorized agency or state official

pursuant to subdivision seven of section three hundred seventy-two of the social services law; and

(e) a superintendent of schools or his authorized representative pursuant to paragraph a of subdivision two of section three thousand two hundred twelve of the education law. No civil or criminal liability shall arise or attach to any school district or employee thereof for any act or omission to act as a result of, or in connection with, the duties or activities authorized or directed by this paragraph.

3. The central register shall contain all available identifying data of any child including, but not limited to, fingerprints, blood types, dental information, and photographs subject to the following conditions:

(a) Except as provided for in paragraph (c) of this subdivision and in section eight hundred thirty-seven-f of this article, the data contained in the register shall be confidential;

(b) Any person who knowingly and intentionally permits the release of any data and information contained in the central register to persons or agencies not permitted by this title shall be guilty of a class A misdemeanor.

(c) Such data may be made available only to:

(i) police or criminal justice agency investigating a report of a missing child or unidentified child, whether living or deceased;

(ii) the public at large, to expedite the finding of a missing child, when the parent or legal guardian of such a child provides written authorization to the investigating police department for the release of such data except when, according to such department, the release of such data would jeopardize the investigation or the safety of the child. When such department deems the release of such data to be appropriate, it shall transmit such written authorization to the division; and

(iii) any qualified person engaged in bona fide research when approved by the commissioner, provided that the researcher in no event disclose information tending to identify the child or his or her family or caregiver.

4. The commissioner shall promulgate rules and regulations:

(a) insuring the timeliness, completeness and confidentiality of the data contained in the register;

(b) prescribing the manner in which entries to the register shall be made and updated as the investigation progresses;

(c) prescribing the form and manner in which entries and inquiries to the register and notice to other agencies and entities shall be made and processed;

(d) insuring that criminal justice agencies and

agencies defined by subdivision seven of section three hundred seventy-two of the social services law making inquiries to the register will be promptly informed if any entries in the statewide central register or in the national crime information center register could match the subject of the inquiry;

(e) insuring the proper disposition of all obsolete register data, provided however that such data for a person who has reached the age of eighteen and remains missing shall be preserved; and

(f) linking the register with the national crime information center register.

5. The division shall not charge a fee for inquiries made pursuant to this section.

6. When a previously reported missing has been found alive and there is no ground for criminal action, the superintendent of state police, sheriff, chief of police, coroner or medical examiner, or other criminal justice agency shall purge and destroy identifying material contained in such records and documents with respect to such person which are made and maintained pursuant to this section and shall report to the division that the person has been found and that the identifying materials contained in such records and documents have been so purged or destroyed. After receiving such a report, the division shall purge identifying material contained in such records with respect to such person and/or destroy any identifying material contained in documents which are maintained pursuant to this section.

Added by L. 1984, Ch. 627, eff. Nov. 24, 1984; **Amended** by. L. 1985, Ch. 749, eff. Aug. 1, 1985, by relettering subd. 2(b) to 2(c) and adding subd. 2(b); L. 1985, Ch. 617; L 1986, Ch. 880, eff. Jan. 1, 1987; L. 1987, Ch. 252, eff. Sept. 1, 1987, amending subds. 1, 2, 3, 4, and 6; L. 1994, Ch. 690, §§ 4, 5, 6, eff. Aug. 18, 1994, amending subd. 1, adding subd. 1-a, and amending subd. 4(c), respectively.

§ 837-f. Missing and exploited children clearinghouse.

There is hereby established within the division a missing and exploited children clearinghouse to provide a comprehensive and coordinated approach to the tragic problems of missing and exploited children. In addition to the activities of the statewide central register for missing children, the commissioner shall be authorized to:

1. Plan and implement programs to ensure the most effective use of federal, state and local resources in the investigation of missing and exploited children;

2. Exchange information and resources with other states, and within New York state, concerning missing and exploited children;

3. Establish a case data base which will include nonidentifying information on reported children and facts developed in the phases of a search, and analyze such data for the purposes of:

assisting law enforcement in their current investigations of missing and exploited children, developing prevention programs and increasing understanding of the nature and extent of the problem; and share the data and analysis on a regular basis with the National Center for Missing and Exploited Children;

4. Disseminate a directory of resources to assist in the locating of missing children;

5. Cooperate with public and private schools and organizations to develop education and prevention programs concerning child safety for communities, parents and children;

6. Provide assistance in returning recovered children who are located out-of-state;

7. By January first, nineteen hundred eighty-seven arrange for the development of a curriculum for the training of law enforcement personnel investigating cases involving missing and exploited children;

8. Assist federal, state and local agencies in the investigation of cases involving missing and exploited children;

9. Utilize available resources to duplicate photographs and posters of children reported as missing by police and with consent of parents, guardians or others legally responsible, disseminate this information throughout the state;

10. Beginning on January first, nineteen hundred eighty-seven, disseminate, on a regular basis, a bulletin containing information on children in the missing children's register to the state education department which shall then forward such bulletin to every public and private school where parents, guardians or others legally responsible for such children have given consent;

10-a. (a) By November first, nineteen hundred ninety-seven prescribe general guidelines to enable the state legislature and state agencies to assist in the location and recovery of missing children. The guidelines shall provide information relating to:

(i) the form and manner in which materials and information pertaining to missing children including but not limited to biographical data and pictures, sketches or other likenesses may be included in stationery, newsletters and other written or electronic printings;

(ii) appropriate sources from which such materials and information may be obtained;

(iii) the procedures by which such materials and information may be obtained; and

(iv) any other matter the clearinghouse considers appropriate.

(b) By January first, nineteen hundred ninety-eight arrange for the transmission of biographical information and pictures, sketches or other likenesses of missing children to state agencies, departments and the legislature to use in printings.

11. Operate a toll-free twenty-four hour hotline for the public to use to relay information concerning missing children;

12. Submit an annual report to the governor and legislature regarding the activities of the clearinghouse including statistical information involving reported cases of missing children pursuant to section eight hundred thirty-seven-m of this article and a summary of the division's efforts with respect to the use of monies from the missing and exploited children clearinghouse fund created pursuant to section ninety-two-w of the state finance law; and

13. Take such other steps as necessary to assist in education, prevention, service provision and investigation of cases involving missing and exploited children.

14. (a) In consultation with the division of state police and other appropriate agencies, develop, and regularly update and distribute, model missing child prompt response and notification plans, which shall be available for use, in their discretion, as appropriate, by local communities and law enforcement personnel. Such plans shall involve a pro-active, coordinated response, planned in advance, that may be promptly triggered by law enforcement personnel upon confirmation by a police officer, peace officer or police agency of a report of a missing child, as defined in subdivision one of section eight hundred thirty-seven-e of this article.

(b) Such plans shall, at a minimum, provide that:

(i) the name of such missing child, a description of the child and other pertinent information may be promptly dispatched over the police communication system, pursuant to subdivision three of section two hundred twenty-one of this chapter;

(ii) such information may be immediately provided orally, electronically or by facsimile transmission to one or more radio stations and other broadcast media outlets serving the community including, but not limited to, those which have voluntarily agreed, in advance, to promptly notify other such radio stations and other broadcast media outlets in like manner;

(iii) such information may be immediately provided by electronic mail message to one or more internet service providers and commercial mobile service providers serving the community including, but not limited to, those which have voluntarily agreed, in advance, to promptly notify other such internet service providers in like manner;

(iv) participating radio stations and other participating broadcast media outlets serving the community may voluntarily agree to promptly broadcast a missing child alert providing pertinent details concerning the child's disappearance,

breaking into regular programming where appropriate;

(v) participating internet service providers and commercial mobile service providers serving the community may voluntarily agree to promptly provide by electronic mail message a missing child alert providing pertinent details concerning the child's disappearance;

(vi) police agencies not connected with the basic police communication system in use in such jurisdiction may transmit such information to the nearest or most convenient electronic entry point, from which point it may be promptly dispatched, in conformity with the orders, rules or regulations governing the system; and

(vii) no dispatch or transmission of a report concerning a missing child shall be required by such plan if the investigating police department advises, in its discretion, that the release of such information may jeopardize the investigation or the safety of the child, or requests forbearance for any reason.

(c) The commissioner shall also designate a unit within the division that shall assist law enforcement agencies and representatives of radio stations, broadcast media outlets, internet service providers and commercial mobile service providers in the design, implementation and improvement of missing child prompt response and notification plans. Such unit shall make ongoing outreach efforts to local government entities and local law enforcement agencies to assist such entities and agencies in the implementation and operation of such plans with the goal of implementing and operating such plans in every jurisdiction in New York state.

(d) The commissioner shall also maintain and make available to appropriate state and local law enforcement agencies up-to-date information concerning technological advances that may assist in facilitating the recovery of missing children. Such information shall include, but not be limited to, technology using computer assisted imaging to "age enhance" photographs of missing children, and technology that may be used to enter such photographs and other pertinent information concerning missing children into a database accessible to appropriate officials and persons.

Added by L. 1986, Ch. 880, eff. Jan. 1, 1987; Amended by L. 1997, Ch. 600, § 2, eff. Sept. 17, 1997, adding subd. 10-a, and Ch. 579, § 4, eff. Nov. 1, 1997, amending subd. 12; L. 2002, Ch. 375, § 2, eff. Dec. 11, 2002, adding subd. 14; L. 2004, Ch. 381, § 1, amending subd. 14, eff. Dec. 15, 2004, except that the division of criminal justice services is immediately authorized and directed to take any and all actions necessary to ensure the implementation of the provisions of this act on or before such effective date; L. 2005, Ch. 348, § 1, eff. July 26, 2005, amending subd. 14(c).

§ 837-g. Livery vehicle safety training program establishment.

There is hereby created within the division a

livery vehicle safety program, * to be administered by the commissioner, to distribute funds to provider agencies for the provision of program services to eligible drivers of livery vehicles.

* So in original. ("safety program" should be "safety training program".)

Added by L. 2000, Ch. 148, § 7, eff. July 12, 2000.

§ 837-h. Livery vehicle safety training program; standards; eligibility; reports.

1. The commissioner, in consultation with the division of state police and the local licensing authority as defined in section six hundred twenty-one of this chapter, shall promulgate rules and regulations necessary for the efficient operation of a livery vehicle safety training program. Such rules and regulations issued, adopted or amended must at a minimum provide:

(a) the development of a training program curriculum which includes instruction on:

(i) methods to maximize personal safety, including information on available equipment and technologies;

(ii) effective passenger management and communications skills;

(iii) vehicular and pedestrian safety, including a review of the applicable provisions of the vehicle and traffic law; and

(iv) any other subject relevant to the public health and safety in the operation of livery vehicles;

(b) the procedure by which the provider agencies make application to receive funding to operate a program and the form of the application;

(c) the procedure by which provider agencies report to the commissioner regarding the provision of program services and the form of the report;

(d) the procedure for periodic monitoring and evaluation of the livery vehicle safety training program.

2. Each provider agency shall prepare a plan, to be approved by the commissioner, for the provision of program services to eligible drivers. Such plan shall include, at a minimum, the nature of the services to be rendered, how the services comply with the developed curriculum, the cost associated with rendering such services and a description of how the services will enhance livery vehicle safety. For the purposes of this section the term "provider agency" shall mean a county, municipal, local unit of government or a college or a university or a law enforcement agency or a not-for-profit entity.

3. Each provider agency shall furnish the commissioner a written report in a format and at a time to be determined by the commissioner,

subject to standards promulgated pursuant to this section which shall, at a minimum contain:

(a) a description of how the assistance provided, in accordance with the program established herein, enhanced livery vehicle services; and

(b) the nature and costs of program services provided.

4. For the purposes of this section the term "livery vehicle" shall have the same meaning as the term "livery", as defined in section six hundred twenty-one of this chapter.

5. Nothing contained in this section shall impose liability upon the division or the state for death, injury or loss incurred by a driver by reason of that driver having participated in the livery vehicle safety training program.

Added by L. 2000, Ch. 148, § 7, eff. July 12, 2000.

§ 837-i. Uniform parking ticket.

1. The commissioner, in cooperation with the commissioner of the department of motor vehicles, and in consultation with the chief executive officers of cities with a population in excess of one hundred thousands persons according to the nineteen hundred eighty United States census shall prescribe the form and content of uniform parking tickets for such cities in all cases involving a parking, standing or stopping violation as defined in accordance with the vehicle and traffic law hereinafter referred to as parking violations, or of any local law, ordinance, rule or regulation adopted pursuant to the vehicle and traffic law relating to parking violations. Upon written application of the chief executive officer of such city, the commissioner, after consultation with the commissioner of the department of motor vehicles, may authorize the use of a parking ticket other than the uniform parking ticket prescribed pursuant to this section if he or she determines that use of such other parking ticket is not inconsistent with, and will not diminish the effectiveness of, the parking violations enforcement and disposition program established pursuant to section eight hundred thirty-seven-j of this chapter, and may also authorize for a specified time period the use of a parking ticket which was used by such city on or before the effective date of this section.

2. The commissioner in consultation with the chief executive officers of cities with a population in excess of one hundred thousand persons according to the nineteen hundred eighty United States census shall establish a system to record and monitor the issuance and disposition of parking tickets, to monitor the collection of the mandatory surcharge required by section eighteen hundred nine-a of the vehicle and traffic law and to receive information from cities for this purpose. Each such city shall report on such parking violations on a monthly basis in the form and manner prescribed by the commissioner including, but not limited to, the parking tickets issued,

the dispositions of such tickets and the amount of fines, penalties and mandatory surcharges collected. The commissioner shall collect, process and analyze such information and present periodic reports on the parking violations enforcement and disposition program.

3. The commissioner shall have the power from time to time to adopt such rules and regulations as may be necessary to accomplish the purposes of this section.

Added by L. 1991, Ch. 166, eff. June 12, 1991.

§ 837-j. Parking violations enforcement and disposition program. [Repealed Sept. 1, 2007.]

1. The commissioner and the commissioner of the department of motor vehicles may enter into an agreement to effect the enhanced collection of the mandatory surcharges imposed pursuant to section eighteen hundred nine-a of the vehicle and traffic law. The terms of such agreement shall authorize the exchange between the division and the department of motor vehicles of information concerning outstanding fines, penalties and unpaid mandatory surcharges and identification information concerning persons with adjudicated parking violations subject to the imposition of such fines, penalties, and mandatory surcharges.

2. The commissioner and the commissioner of the department of motor vehicles shall enter into any necessary joint enforcement agreements, which agreements shall be consistent with any agreement authorized by subdivision one of this section.

3. The commissioner of the department of motor vehicles shall be authorized to cooperate with traffic and law enforcement agencies of other states and of the United States, to obtain and furnish any assistance or information necessary for the enforcement and collection of fines, penalties and mandatory surcharges for parking violations.

4. The commissioner, in consultation with the commissioner of the department of motor vehicles, shall promulgate such rules and regulations as may be necessary to effect the purposes of this section.

Added by L. 1991, Ch. 166, eff. June 12, 1991; **Amended** by L. 1994, Ch. 61, § 11, extending expiration date to Nov. 1, 1997; L. 1997, Ch. 435, § 64, eff. Aug. 20, 1997, extending expiration date to Nov. 1, 1999; L. 1999, Ch. 452, § 12, eff. Sept. 1, 1999, deemed in full force and effect Apr. 1, 1999, extending expiration date to Nov. 1, 2001; L. 2001, Ch. 95, § 16, eff. July 13, 2001, extending expiration date to Nov. 1, 2003; L. 2003, Ch. 16, § 14, eff. Mar. 31, 2003, extending expiration date until Sept. 1, 2005; L. 2005, Ch. 56, Part D, § 13, eff. Apr. 1, 2005, extending expiration date to Sept. 1, 2007.

§ 837-k. Safe house for children.

1. Within one hundred twenty days after the effective date of this section, the division shall design and adopt an official symbol and sign which may use McGruff as created by the national crime prevention council if practicable, to be used to designate homes and businesses where a child may seek temporary help when he or she is traveling, without adult supervision or protection, in neighborhoods having such homes or businesses.

2. (a) Law enforcement agencies:

(i) may voluntarily provide symbols to persons who apply for them;

(ii) may require that persons receiving symbols apply in writing and agree in writing to specific terms and conditions in order to participate in the program;

(iii) shall develop community based selection procedures to assure the suitability of the persons and location which are the subjects of an application prior to issuing symbols after conducting a background check, including, but not limited to, information available in its jurisdiction, and inquiry of the department of social services register of child abuse and maltreatment regarding the applicant and any persons residing at the location. Until such procedures are developed and implemented, law enforcement agencies may access records of the division maintained pursuant to section eight hundred thirty-seven of this article;

(iv) shall maintain a register of locations using the official, sign or symbol and any other known locations using other symbols for similar purposes pursuant to subdivision five of this section;

(v) shall make efforts, themselves or through arrangements with school districts, not-for-profits, or other organizations, to educate children to recognize the correct symbol and the program.

(b) For purposes of this subdivision:

(i) the term "law enforcement agency" shall mean any agency or department of any municipality or any police district employing a police officer or police officers as that term is defined in paragraphs (b) and (d) of subdivision thirty-four of section 1.20 of the criminal procedure law; and

(ii) the symbols provided by law enforcement agencies for purposes of this program are the property of said agency.

3. Persons who are issued a symbol by a law enforcement agency shall:

(a) display it or any related or similar symbol or sign that is visible from the outside of their building only upon such terms and conditions as may be specified by the law enforcement agency; and

(b) return said symbol to the law enforcement agency immediately upon demand therefor by said agency.

4. (a) Any person who possesses, uses, or duplicates the symbol or sign created pursuant to

subdivision one of this section, or any symbol authorized for use pursuant to subdivision two of this section, without complying with the provisions of this section shall be liable for a civil fine of fifty dollars.

(b) Possession, use or duplication of the symbol or sign created pursuant to subdivision one of this section, or any symbol authorized for use pursuant to subdivision two of this section, with the intent to attract children into the location for any purpose other than protecting them when they are threatened is a misdemeanor.

(c) No symbol except the symbol authorized in subdivisions one or five of this section shall be used to designate a safe house.

5. Children's safe haven/safe home programs existing on the effective date of this section may continue to use the same symbol on existing or new locations and expand service areas using symbols in use on such date.

Added by L. 1993, Ch. 203.

§ 837-l. Capital prosecution extraordinary assistance program.

There is hereby created within the division a capital prosecution extraordinary assistance program to be administered by the commissioner, to distribute funds to district attorneys for the prosecution of capital cases. Such funds shall be distributed where the commissioner determines, on the basis of a written certification by the applicant district attorney, that due to the nature or number of capital cases being prosecuted by the district attorney a significant financial burden has resulted and financial assistance is necessary in order to fulfill such district attorney's responsibilities; provided, however, that such funds shall not be used to supplant existing resources. Such funds may also be distributed to a district attorney who, upon the request of another district attorney, has provided assistance in the prosecution of a capital case.

Added by L. 1995, Ch. 1, § 36, eff. Apr. 1, 1995.

§ 837-m. Reporting duties of law enforcement departments with respect to missing children.
[*Another version of § 837-m follows.*] *

The chief of every police department, each county sheriff and the superintendent of state police shall report, at least semi-annually, to the division with respect to specified cases of missing children that are closed. Such reports shall be in the form and manner prescribed by the division and shall contain such information as the division deems necessary including, but not limited to, information regarding recovered children who were arrested, children who were the victims of criminal activity or exploitation and children who were found deceased and information regarding the alleged abductor or killer of such children.

* **Editor's Note:** In 1997, the Legislature enacted two versions of § 837-m, each without reference to the other. A second § 837-m follows.

Added by L. 1997, Ch. 579, § 1, eff. Nov. 1, 1997.

§ 837-m. Criminal history records search for certain employment, appointments, licenses or permits in the city of New York. *

1. As used in this section:

(a) "Department" shall mean the New York City Department of Investigation.

(b) "Applicant" shall mean a person applying for:

(1) employment with the city of New York in a position providing child day care services, as such term is defined in subdivision one of section three hundred ninety of the social services law, or providing such services through an entity pursuant to a contract between such entity and the city of New York to provide such services or providing such child day care services through an entity required to have a permit for such services issued by the Health Department of the City of New York; or

(2) employment with the department, or appointment to a senior position in an office of an elected official or agency of the city of New York or of a public authority, board, committee, commission, or public benefit corporation, where such person is to be the subject of a background investigation pursuant to subdivisions (a) and (b) of section seven of executive order number sixteen of the mayor of the city of New York dated July twenty-sixth, nineteen hundred seventy-eight, as amended by section one of executive order seventy-two of the mayor of the city of New York dated April twenty-third, nineteen hundred eighty-four; or

(3) mayoral appointment as a judge of the New York City Criminal Court or the New York City Civil Court or the Family Court of the State of New York Within the City of New York; or

(4) a license, certificate of approval, class a photo identification card or employment, pursuant to the following provisions of the administrative code of the city of New York which require the submission of fingerprints:

A. Title 16-a: New York City Trade Waste Commission section 16-508(b);

B. Title 22: Fulton Fish Market distribution area and other seafood distribution areas, section 22-216(a)(1); and

C. Title 20: regulation of shipboard gambling, section 20-954(b)(1), as added to the administrative code of the city of New York by a nineteen ninety-seven local law of the city of New York.

2. As a condition of eligibility for such licenses, certificate of approval, class a photo identification card, contract to provide services, or employment, the department, appointing or issuing agency shall obtain the applicant's fingerprints and submit such fingerprints to the division for purposes of determining the criminal history of the applicant. The department may submit two sets of fingerprints to the division.

3. The first set of fingerprints received by the division shall be used to identify the individual and to conduct a criminal history records search of the division's New York state files to determine whether such individual has been convicted of a criminal offense in this state. The division shall forward the second set of such individual's fingerprints to the Federal Bureau of Investigation for the purpose of a nationwide criminal history record check to determine whether such applicant has been convicted of a criminal offense in any state or federal jurisdiction.

4. The division shall promptly transmit the reports of these New York state and nationwide criminal records searches to the requesting department, appointing or issuing agency. Such reports, when received by the requesting department, appointing or issuing agency, shall be marked confidential and securely stored, and shall not be disclosed to any person other than the applicant, although the contents of the report may be disclosed to the agency or agencies whose consideration of such applicant prompted the ordering of such reports.

5. (a) Each applicant shall sign a release authorizing the department, appointing or issuing agency to submit such applicant's fingerprints to the division and to receive the results of such criminal history record searches supplied by the division and the Federal Bureau of Investigation. Such release, a copy of which shall be supplied to the applicant, shall also advise the applicant that a criminal history record search will be conducted concerning the applicant and that he or she may obtain a copy of his or her criminal history record and seek correction of any information contained in such record pursuant to regulations promulgated by the division.

(b) each such applicant shall, in advance, make payment to the division of any reasonable fee required by law which is reasonably related to the cost of conducting the searches authorized by this section. All fingerprints supplied by the applicant shall be returned to the applicant upon termination or denial of the license, certificate of approval, class A photo identification card, contract to provide services, or employment in connection with which such fingerprints were obtained.

*Editor's Note:** In 1997, the Legislature enacted two versions of § 837-m, each without reference to the other. See preceding version.

Added by L. 1997, Ch. 584, § 1, eff. Nov. 16, 1997.

§ 837-n. Criminal history information of caregivers; requirements.

1. Definitions. For the purposes of this section:

(a) "Caregiver" shall mean a person employed to provide fifteen or more hours of care per week to a child or children in the home of such a child or children.

(b) "Criminal history information" shall mean a record of all convictions of crimes and any pending criminal charges maintained on an individual by the division of criminal justice services.

2. (a) Upon request, a caregiver may provide a prospective employer with a set of fingerprints, or two such sets of fingerprints if the prospective employer also seeks to obtain a criminal history report from the Federal Bureau of Investigation, in such form and manner as shall be specified by the division of criminal justice services, but in any event, no less than two digit imprints. The prospective employer shall submit the fingerprints to the division of criminal justice services for screening, together with the prescribed processing fee, as set forth in subdivision eight-a of section eight hundred thirty-seven of this article and any fees associated with obtaining fingerprints under this subdivision, provided, however, that the commissioner shall develop a reduced fee based upon the prospective employer's ability to pay. If the prospective employer also seeks to obtain a criminal history report from the FBI, the required fee for such report shall also be included.

(b) Every set of fingerprints taken pursuant to this subdivision shall be promptly submitted to the division of criminal justice services. The division of criminal justice services shall compare such fingerprints against the records of such division and upon request of the prospective employer shall forward a set of such fingerprints to the Federal Bureau of Investigation at Washington with a request that the files of the bureau be searched and notification of the results of such search and a report thereon shall be made. The division of criminal justice services shall formulate a standard criminal history information report and the standard form for such reporting. The division of criminal justice services shall forward such criminal history information report to the prospective employer in a timely manner. All such reports processed and sent to such prospective employer pursuant to this paragraph shall not be published or in any way disclosed or redisclosed to persons other than the prospective employer, or the prospective caregiver. Any person who discloses or rediscloses such reports in violation of this section shall be guilty of a class A misdemeanor.

(c) The office of children and family services shall prepare and disseminate information to advise the public of the right to obtain the criminal history information of a prospective caregiver.

Such information shall also include, but not be limited to, the following:

(i) the voluntary nature of the criminal history information check;

(ii) the steps necessary to use the criminal history information check, including information on form availability, fingerprinting and fees;

(iii) applicable confidentiality requirements; and

(iv) other information that is available to prospective employers upon the consent of a prospective caregiver including but not limited to department of motor vehicles records, educational records and credit records, including, where relevant and available, phone numbers, addresses and a description of the content and potential uses of such records.

(d) The commissioner of the division of criminal justice services shall promulgate all rules and regulations necessary to implement the provisions of this section.

Added by L. 1998, Ch. 3, § 3, eff. Oct. 27, 1998.

§ 837-o. Search for arson conviction records of volunteer firefighter applicants.

1. Any person who applies for membership in a fire company, as such term is defined in section three of the volunteer firefighters' benefit law, or who seeks to transfer as a member to another fire company, shall be required to authorize the submission of his or her name and other authorized identifying information to the division which shall search its files for records indicating whether the person stands convicted of the crime of arson. The chief of the fire company to which application is made shall provide written notice to the applicant that a search will be conducted, and if the applicant desires to proceed, he or she shall complete a search request on the form provided for this purpose by the division of criminal justice services.

2. Within ten business days of receipt from the applicant, the chief of the fire company shall send the completed search request form to either (i) the sheriff's department of the county in which the fire company is located, or (ii) the department of state, office of fire prevention and control, as follows:

(a) the sheriff's department of the county in which the fire company is located shall be responsible for receiving the search requests and processing the search requests with the division within ten business days of receipt from the chief of the fire company, unless the county legislative body adopts and files with the secretary of state pursuant to the municipal home rule law a local law providing that the sheriff's department shall not have such responsibility;

(b) in all other instances where a county legislative body has adopted a local law pursuant to paragraph (a) of this subdivision, the department of state, office of fire prevention and control shall be responsible for receiving search requests and forwarding the search requests to the division. The department of state, office of fire prevention and control is hereby authorized to establish a communication network with the division for the purpose of forwarding search requests and receiving search results pursuant to paragraph (b) of this subdivision.

The department of state, office of fire prevention and control is hereby authorized to establish a communication network with the division for the purpose of forwarding search requests and receiving search results pursuant to paragraph (b) of this subdivision.

3. (a) All searches concerning the application for membership in a fire company shall be conducted under the provisions of subdivision six of section eight hundred thirty-seven of this article without the assessment of any fee to the applicant or fire company and shall pertain solely to ascertaining whether the applicant stands convicted of arson.

(b) The results of the search shall be communicated in writing, within ten business days of receipt from the division, to the chief of the fire company from which the search request originated by either the sheriff's department or the department of state, office of fire prevention and control, and shall be kept confidential by the chief, except as provided in paragraph (c) of this subdivision. The results of the search shall only state either that: (i) the applicant stands convicted of arson, or (ii) the applicant has no record of conviction for arson. The results of the search shall not divulge any other information relating to the criminal history of the applicant.

(c) At the time an applicant is advised that he or she is ineligible for membership due to a record of conviction for arson, he or she shall also be advised of the rights to challenge and appeal the information contained in the record of conviction as provided in the rules and regulations of the division. The applicant shall continue to be barred from membership until all administrative and judicial challenges to the accuracy of such information or appeals therefrom, are ultimately resolved in his or her favor, or if such a determination is unchallenged.

Added by L. 1999, Ch. 423, eff. Apr. 1, 2000; **Amended** by L. 2002, Ch. 689, eff. Feb. 18, 2003, amending subds. 2 and 3.

§ 837-p. Criminal history records search for certain licenses and registrations in the county of Westchester.

1. As used in this section:

(A) "commission" shall mean the Westchester county solid waste commission.

(B) "applicant" shall mean a person applying for a license or registration pursuant to chapter eight hundred twenty-six-a of the laws of Westchester county which requires the submission of fingerprints.

2. As a condition of eligibility for such licenses and/or registrations, the commission shall obtain two sets of the applicant's fingerprints and submit such fingerprints to the division for purposes of determining the criminal history of the applicant.

3. The first set of fingerprints received by the division shall be used to identify the applicant and to conduct a criminal history records search of the division's New York state files to determine whether or not such applicant has a criminal history in this state. The division shall forward the second set of such applicant's fingerprints to the federal bureau of investigation for the purpose of a nationwide criminal history record check to determine whether such applicant has a criminal history in any state or federal jurisdiction.

4. The division shall promptly transmit the reports of the New York state criminal record search to the executive director of the commission. The federal bureau of investigation reports of nationwide criminal records searches shall be transmitted to the executive director of the commission by the most direct means authorized by federal law, rules and regulations. All such reports, when received by the commission, shall be marked confidential and securely stored, and shall not be disclosed to any person other than the applicant, although the contents of the report may be disclosed to the members of the commission.

5. (a) Each applicant shall sign a release authorizing the commission to submit such applicant's fingerprints to the division and the federal bureau of investigation, and for the executive director of the commission to receive the results of such criminal history record searches supplied by the division and the federal bureau of investigation. Such release shall also advise the applicant that a criminal history record search will be conducted concerning the applicant and that he or she may obtain a copy of his or her criminal history record and seek correction of any information contained in such record pursuant to regulations promulgated by the division.

(b) Each such applicant shall, in advance, make payment to the commission of the fee required pursuant to subdivision eight-a of section eight hundred thirty-seven of this article and any fee imposed by the federal bureau of investigation.

Added by L. 2000, Ch. 525, eff. Oct. 4, 2000.

§ 837-q. Payments to Westchester county for policing special parkways.

The commissioner of the division of criminal justice services is hereby authorized and directed, pursuant to annual appropriations, to make payments to Westchester county for costs associated with policing special parkways as defined in subdivision two of section seventy of the transportation law.

Added by L. 2003, Ch. 62, Part K, § 1, eff. May 15, 2003.

§ 838. Identification of unknown dead and missing persons.

1. Every county medical examiner and coroner shall furnish the division promptly with copies of fingerprints on standardized eight inch by eight inch fingerprint cards, personal descriptions and other identifying data, including date and place of death, of all deceased persons whose deaths are in a classification requiring inquiry by the coroner where the deceased is not identified or the medical examiner or coroner is not satisfied with the decedent's identification.

2. In any case where it is not physically possible to furnish prints of the ten fingers of the deceased, prints or partial prints of any fingers with other identifying data shall be forwarded by the county medical examiner or coroner to the division.

3. In addition to the foregoing provisions of this section, the county medical examiner or coroner shall cause a dentist authorized to practice pursuant to article one hundred thirty-three of the education law to carry out a dental examination of the deceased. The medical examiner or coroner shall forward the dental examination records to the division on a form supplied by the division for that purpose.

4. The division shall compare the fingerprints received from the county medical examiners or coroners to fingerprints on file with the division for purposes of attempting to determine the identity of the deceased. Other descriptive data supplied with the fingerprints shall also be compared to records maintained by the division concerning missing persons. The division shall submit the results of the comparisons to the appropriate medical examiner or coroner and if a tentative or positive identification is made, to the law enforcement authority which submitted the report of the missing person.

5. (a) (i) When any person makes a report of a missing person to a law enforcement authority, the authority shall request a member of the family or next of kin of the missing person to authorize the release to the division of the dental records of the person reported missing. The release shall be on a form supplied by the division. If the person reported missing is still missing thirty days after the report is made, the law

enforcement authority shall deliver the release to the dentist or dentists of the missing person, and request the dentist or dentists to deliver such records, including dental x-rays, to the division within ten days. The form of such request shall also include means by which the law enforcement authority shall be notified of the delivery of such records.

(ii) When the person reported missing has not been found within thirty days and no family or next of kin exists or can be located, the law enforcement authority may execute a written declaration, stating that an active investigation seeking the location of the missing person is being conducted, and that the dental records are necessary for the exclusive purpose of furthering the investigation. Such written declaration, signed by a peace officer, is sufficient authority for the dentist or dentists to release the missing person's dental records, including dental x-rays, to the division.

(b) Upon receipt of a properly executed release and request or declaration, the dentist or dentists shall forward the dental records, including dental x-rays, to the division, where a file shall be maintained concerning persons reported to it as missing and who have not been reported to it as found. The file shall contain dental records and such other information as the division finds to be relevant to assisting in the location of a missing person. The law enforcement authority shall be notified of the delivery of such records.

6. The division shall compare the dental records received from the county medical examiners or coroners to dental records of missing persons on file with the division. The division shall submit the results of the comparison to the appropriate medical examiner or coroner and if a tentative or positive identification is made, to the law enforcement authority which submitted the report of the missing person.

7. When a person previously reported missing has been found, the superintendent of state police, sheriff, chief of police, coroner or medical examiner, or other law enforcement authority shall erase all records with respect to such person and/or destroy any documents which are maintained pursuant to this section and shall report to the division that the person has been found and that the records and documents have been so erased or destroyed. After receiving such a report, the division shall erase all records with respect to such person and/or destroy any documents which are maintained pursuant to this section.

8. The information contained in the division's missing person files shall be made available by it to law enforcement agencies attempting to locate missing persons.

9. Notwithstanding any other provision of law, no criminal justice agency shall establish or maintain any policy which requires the observance of a waiting period before accepting and

investigating a missing child report. Upon receipt of a report of a missing child, criminal justice agencies shall make entries of such report to the register in the manner provided by section eight hundred thirty-seven-e of this article.

Amended by L. 1987, Ch. 652, eff. Sept. 1, 1987, amending subd. a.

§ 839. Municipal police training council.

1. There is hereby created within the division a municipal police training council composed of eight members, who shall be selected as follows:

(a) three shall be appointed by the governor:

(b) two shall be appointed by the governor from a list of at least six nominees submitted by the New York state sheriffs' association, who shall be incumbent sheriffs in the state having at least two years of service on the law enforcement training committee of such association or having other specialized experience in connection with police training which, in the opinion of the man of such law enforcement training committee, provides the sheriff with at least an equivalent background in the field of police training; and

(c) two shall be appointed by the governor from a list of at least six nominees submitted by the New York state association of chiefs of police, who shall be incumbent chiefs of police or commissioners of police of a municipality in the state having at least two years of service on the police training committee of such association or having other specialized experience in connection with police training which, in the opinion of the chairman of such training committee, provides the chief of police or commissioner of police with at least an equivalent background in the field of police training, and

(d) one shall be the commissioner of police of the city of New York or a member of his department, designated by such commissioner and approved by the governor.

2. The governor shall designate from among the members of the council a chairman who shall serve during the pleasure of the governor.

3. All members of the council appointed by the governor shall be appointed for terms of two years, such terms to commence on April first, and expire on March thirty-first. Any member chosen to fill a vacancy created otherwise than by expiration of term shall be appointed for the unexpired term of the member whom he is to succeed. Vacancies caused by expiration of a term or otherwise shall be filled in the same manner as original appointments. Any member may be reappointed for additional terms.

4. Any member of the council appointed pursuant to paragraphs (b) or (c) of subdivision one of this section as an incumbent sheriff, chief of police or commissioner of police, as the case may be, shall immediately upon the termination of his

holding of said office or employment, cease to be a member of the council.

5. The council shall meet at least four times in each year. Special meetings may be called by the chairman and shall be called by him at the request of the governor or upon the written request of five members of the council. The council may establish its own requirements as to quorum and its own procedures with respect to the conduct of its meetings and other affairs; provided, however, that all recommendations made by the council to the governor pursuant to subdivision one of section eight hundred forty of this chapter shall require the affirmative vote of five members of the council;

6. Membership on the council shall not constitute the holding of an office, and members of the council shall not be required to take and file oaths of office before serving on the council. The council shall not have the right to exercise any portion of the sovereign power of the state.

7. The members of the council shall receive no compensation for their services but shall be allowed their actual and necessary expenses incurred in the performance of their functions hereunder.

8. No member of the council shall be disqualified from holding any public office or employment, nor shall he forfeit any such office or employment, by reason of his appointment hereunder, notwithstanding the provisions of any general, special or local law, ordinance or city charter.

§ 840. Functions, powers and duties of council.

1. The council may recommend to the governor rules and regulations with respect to:

(a) The approval, or revocation thereof, of police training schools administered by municipalities;

(b) Minimum courses of study, attendance requirements, and equipment and facilities to be required at approved municipal police training schools;

(c) Minimum qualifications for instructors at approved police training schools;

(d) The requirements of minimum basic training which police officers appointed to probationary terms shall complete before being eligible for permanent appointment, and the time within which such basic training must be completed following such appointment to a probationary term;

(e) The requirements of minimum basic training which police officers not appointed for probationary terms but appointed on other than a permanent basis shall complete in order to be eligible for continued employment or permanent appointment, and the time within which such basic training must be completed following such appointment on a non-permanent basis;

(f) The requirements of minimum basic training which peace officers must complete before being eligible for certification as peace officers pursuant to section 2.30 of the criminal procedure law;

(g) Categories or classifications of advanced in-service training programs and minimum courses of study and attendance requirements with respect to such categories or classifications; and

(h) Exemptions from particular provisions of this article in the case of any city having a population of one million or more, or in the case of the state department of correctional services if in its opinion the standards of police officer or peace officer training established and maintained by such city or department are higher than those established pursuant to this article; or revocation in whole or in part of such exemption, if in its opinion the standards of police officer or peace officer training established and maintained by such city or department are lower than those established pursuant to this article.

(i) The establishment, in cooperation with the division of state police, of a formalized consumer product tampering training program for all law enforcement personnel.

(j) (1) Development, maintenance and dissemination of written policies and procedures pursuant to title six of article six of the social services law and applicable provisions of article ten of the family court act, regarding the mandatory reporting of child abuse or neglect, reporting procedures and obligations of persons required to report, provisions for taking a child into protective custody, mandatory reporting of deaths, immunity from liability, penalties for failure to report and obligations for the provision of services and procedures necessary to safeguard the life or health of the child; and

(2) establishment and implementation on an ongoing basis, of a training program for all current and new police officers regarding the policies and procedures establishment pursuant to this paragraph; and (3) establishment of a training program for police officers whose main responsibilities are juveniles and the laws pertaining thereto, which training program shall be successfully completed before such officers are accredited pursuant to section eight hundred forty-six-h of this chapter.

[There is no subd. (k); see amendment history.]

(l) Exemptions from particular provisions of this article in the case of peace officers appointed by the superintendent of state police if in its opinion the standards of peace officer training provided by the division of state police exceed those established pursuant to this article.

2. The council shall promulgate, and may from time to time amend, such rules and regulations prescribing height, weight and physical fitness requirements for eligibility of persons for provisional or permanent appointment in the competitive class of the civil service as police officers of any county, city, town, village or police district as it deems necessary and proper for the efficient performance of police duties.

3. The council may, in addition:

(a) Consult with, advise and make recommendations to the commissioner with respect to the exercise of his functions, powers and duties as set forth in section eight hundred forty-one;

(b) Recommend studies, surveys and reports to be made by the commissioner regarding the carrying out of the objectives and purposes of this section;

(c) Visit and inspect any police training school approved by the commissioner or for which application for such approval has been made;

(d) Make recommendations, from time to time, to the commissioner, the governor and the legislature, regarding the carrying out of the purposes of this section; and

(e) Perform such other acts as may be necessary or appropriate to carry out the functions of the council.

(f) Develop, maintain and disseminate, in consultation with the state office for the prevention of domestic violence, written policies and procedures consistent with article eight of the family court act and applicable provisions of the criminal procedure and domestic relations laws, regarding the investigation of and intervention by new and veteran police officers in incidents of family offenses. Such policies and procedures shall make provisions for education and training in the interpretation and enforcement of New York's family offense laws, including but not limited to:

(1) intake and recording of victim statements, on a standardized "domestic violence incident report form" promulgated by the division of criminal justice services in consultation with the superintendent of state police, representatives of local police forces and the state office for the prevention of domestic violence, and the investigation thereof so as to ascertain whether a crime has been committed against the victim by a member of the victim's family or household as such terms are defined in section eight hundred twelve of the family court act and section 530.11 of the criminal procedure law; and

(2) the need for immediate intervention in family offenses including the arrest and detention of alleged offenders, pursuant to subdivision four of section 140.10 of the criminal procedure law, and notifying victims of their rights, including but not limited to immediately providing the victim with the written notice required in subdivision six of section 530.11 of the criminal procedure law and subdivision five of section eight hundred twelve of the family court act.

Amended by L. 1980, Ch. 843, eff. Sept. 1, 1980; L. 1987, Ch. 324, eff. Nov. 1, 1987, adding subd. 1(i); L. 1988, Ch. 504, eff. Apr. 1, 1989; L. 1990, Ch. 617, eff. Nov. 15, 1990, provided, however, that the municipal police training council shall recommend to the governor, and the governor shall promulgate, rules and regulations necessary to effectuate the provisions of this act prior to such effective date; L. 1991, Ch. 166, eff. June 12, 1991, adding subd. 1(k); L. 1994, Ch. 222, § 28, eff. Jan. 1, 1995, relettering subd. 1(k) as 1(l) and adding a new 1(k), but not relettering the new subd. 1(l) back to 1(k); L. 1994, Ch. 224, § 4, eff. Jan. 1, 1995, repealing the new subd. 1(k); L. 1994, Ch. 224, § 5, eff. Jan. 1, 1995, adding subd. 3(f).

ANNOTATIONS

Generally.—By adopting regulations as to height requirements "as it deems necessary and proper," the respondent conformed to its obligation under subdivision 2 of section 840 of the Executive Law. Police Conference of New York, Inc. v. Municipal Police Training Council, 51 N.Y.2d 810, 433 N.Y.S.2d 95, 412 N.E.2d 1321 (1980).

—Executive Law § 840(2) grants MPTC broad discretion to promulgate and amend rules and regulations prescribing height, weight and physical fitness standards for police officers; that discretion may not be disturbed unless it is arbitrary or illegal. Rice v. Schuyler County Civil Serv. Comm'n, 183 A.D.2d 974, 583 N.Y.S.2d 583 (3d Dept. 1992).

§ 841. Functions, powers and duties of the commissioner with respect to the council.

In addition to the functions, powers and duties otherwise provided by this article, the commissioner shall, with the general advice of the council, and, in the case of subdivisions one, two and three, only in accordance with rules and regulations promulgated by the governor pursuant to section eight hundred forty-two;

1. Approve police training schools administered by municipalities and issue certificates of approval to such schools, and revoke such approval or certificate;

2. Certify, as qualified, instructors at approved police training schools and issue appropriate certificates to such instructors;

3. Certify police officers and peace officers who have satisfactorily completed basic training programs and issue certificates to such police officers and peace officers, including the issuance of equivalency certificates for basic training certificates issued to peace officers, where such officers received a certificate for successful completion of a basic training for police officers program or an approved course for state university of New York public safety officers during a period in which such peace officer was not employed as a police officer, upon demonstration of adequate equivalent training, the completion of supervised field training, requisite job-related law enforcement experience as determined by the commissioner, and if deemed necessary, the successful completion of relevant police officer training courses pursuant to section two hundred nine-q of the general municipal law;

4. Cause studies and surveys to be made relating to the establishment, operation and approval of municipal police training schools;

5. Consult with and cooperate with municipal police training schools for the development of advanced in-service training programs for police officers and peace officers and issue appropriate certificates to police officers and peace officers, attesting to their satisfactory completion of such advanced training programs;

6. Consult with and cooperate with universities, colleges and institutes in the state for the development of specialized courses of study for police officers and peace officers in police science and police administration;

7. Consult with and cooperate with other departments and agencies of the state concerned with police officer and peace officer training;

8. Report to the council at each regular meeting of the council and at such other times as may be appropriate.

9. Prepare, update and distribute to appropriate law enforcement officials the form and content of the written notice required to be given to victims of family offenses pursuant to subdivision five of section eight hundred twelve of the family court act and subdivision six of section 530.11 of the criminal procedure law.

Amended by L. 1980, Ch. 843; 1986, Ch. 847, eff. Nov. 1, 1986, adding subd. 9; L. 1998, Ch. 421, § 1, eff. Nov. 1, 1998, amending subd. 3; L. 2001, Ch. 551, eff. Mar. 12, 2002, amending subd. 3, provided, however, the commissioner of the division of criminal justice services may take any steps necessary, including promulgation of rules and regulations, if necessary, to implement the provisions of this act prior to its effective date.

§ 841-a. Security guard advisory council.

1. There is hereby created within the division a security guard advisory council composed of seventeen members who are knowledgeable about the security guard industry. In addition, the council shall include as ex-officio non-voting members, the secretary of state and the commissioner of the division of criminal justice services, or their respective designees. All members shall be residents of the state and shall be selected as follows:

(a) Eight shall be appointed by the governor, one of whom shall be a representative of a contractual security company, one of whom shall be a representative of a proprietary security company, one of whom shall be a person actively employed as a security guard for a contractual security company and one of whom shall be a person actively employed as a security guard for a proprietary security company;

(b) Three shall be appointed by the governor on the recommendation of the temporary president of the senate;

(c) One shall be appointed by the governor on the recommendation of the minority leader of the senate;

(d) Three shall be appointed by the governor on the recommendation of the speaker of the assembly;

(e) One shall be appointed by the governor on the recommendation of the minority leader of the assembly;

(f) One shall be appointed by the governor who shall be a full-time faculty member of a college or university who teaches and whose area of expertise is in the field of security.

2. The governor shall designate from among the members of the council a chairperson and a vice-chairperson who shall each serve at the pleasure of the governor.

3. All members of the council appointed by the governor shall be appointed for terms of three years, such terms to commence on January first, and expire on December thirty-first; provided, however, that of the members first appointed, four shall be appointed for one year terms and four shall be appointed for two year terms. Any member chosen to fill a vacancy created otherwise than by expiration of term shall be appointed for the unexpired term of the member whom he is to succeed. vacancies caused by expiration of a term or otherwise shall be filled in the same manner as original appointments. Any member may be reappointed for additional terms.

4. The council shall meet as frequently as it deems necessary but in no event less than one time in each year. Special meetings may be called by the chairperson and shall be called by him or her at the request of the governor or upon the written request of nine members of the council. The council may establish its own requirements as to quorum and its own procedures with respect to the conduct of its meetings and other affairs; provided, however, that all recommendations made by the council to the governor pursuant to section eight hundred forty-one-b of this article shall require the affirmative vote of a majority of the council.

5. Membership on the council shall not constitute the holding of an office, and members of the council shall not be required to take and file oaths of office before serving on the council. The council shall not have the right to exercise any portion of the sovereign powers of the state.

6. The members of the council shall receive no compensation for their services but shall be allowed their actual and necessary expenses incurred in the performance of their functions hereunder.

7. No member of the council shall be disqualified from holding any public office or employment, nor shall he or she forfeit any such office or employment, by reason of his or her appointment hereunder, notwithstanding the provisions of any general, special or local law, ordinance or city charter.

Added by L. 1992, Ch. 336, eff. July 12, 1993; **Amended** by L. 1994, Ch. 634, § 18, eff. Aug. 2, 1994, amending subds. 1 and 4.

§ 841-b. Functions, powers and duties of council.

1. The council shall recommend to the commissioner rules and regulations with respect to:

(a) The approval, or revocation thereof, of security guard training schools and training programs;

(b) Minimum courses of study duration, attendance requirements, and equipment and facilities to be required at approved security guard training schools and training programs, taking into account subject matter, the hours each subject is to be taught and special requirements unique to particular assignments, employers and work sites;

(c) Minimum qualifications for instructors at approved security guard training schools and training programs; and

(d) The subject matter of all training requirements which security guards and security guard applicants must complete before being registered as unarmed and armed security guards.

2. The council may, in addition:

(a) Consult with, advise and make recommendations to the commissioner with respect to the exercise of his or her functions, powers and duties as set forth in this section;

(b) Recommend studies, surveys and reports to be made by the commissioner regarding the carrying out of the objectives and purposes of this section;

(c) Visit and inspect any security guard training school approved by the commissioner or for which application for such approval has been made;

(d) Make recommendations, from time to time, to the commissioner, the governor, the legislature and the secretary of state, with regard to implementation of the purposes of this section and of article seven-a of the general business law; and

(e) Perform such other acts as may be necessary or appropriate to carry out the functions of the council.

Added by L. 1992, Ch. 336, eff. July 12, 1993.

§ 841-c. Functions, powers and duties of the commissioner with respect to the council.

In addition to the functions, powers and duties otherwise provided by this section and article seven-A of the general business law, the commissioner shall, upon the recommendation and with the general advice of the council:

1. Prescribe minimum requirements for the eight hours of preassignment training; the on-the-job training program to be completed within ninety working days following employment as a security guard; the forty-seven hours of firearms training for a special armed guard registration card; the eight hour annual in-service training course; and the eight hour in-service training course for armed security guards;

2. Approve and certify security guard training schools, programs and courses which meet or exceed the minimum requirements prescribed pursuant to subdivision one of this section and issue certificates of approval to such schools, and revoke such approval or certificate provided, however, that the commissioner may permit any such school, program or course in existence on the effective date of this section, to remain in effect for a period of one year following the effective date;

3. Certify, as qualified, instructors of security guards and issue appropriate certificates to such instructors;

4. Certify security guards or applicants who have satisfactorily completed basic training programs and issue appropriate certificates to such security guards or applicants;

5. Cause studies and surveys to be made relating to the establishment, operation and approval of security guard training schools and training programs;

6. Consult with and cooperate with approved security guard training schools and programs for the development of advanced in-service training programs for security guards and issue appropriate certificates to security guards, attesting to their satisfactory completion of such advanced training programs;

7. Consult with and cooperate with universities, colleges and institutes in the state for the development of specialized courses of study for security guards;

8. Consult with and cooperate with other departments and agencies of the state concerned with security guard training;

9. Consult with, cooperate with and provide technical assistance to the council and to the department of state on matters concerning security guards;

10. Report to the council at each regular meeting of the council and at other such times as may be appropriate;

11. Waive the training requirements as specified in article seven-A of the general business law with respect to applicants employed by a security guard company, if the security guard applicant provides appropriate documentation to demonstrate that he or she was or is subject to training requirements which meet or exceed the requirements established pursuant to such article;

12. Waive the training requirements as specified in article seven-A of the general business law with respect to applicants employed by a security guard company on a proprietary basis for its own use when such company presents adequate documentation that such training is not directly relevant to the applicant's job responsibilities and such applicant does not, in the course of their employment duties:

(a) wear a uniform or other readily apparent indicia of authority; or

(b) as a requisite of employment, carry a gun, and

(c) have interactions with the public or expend a majority of the time spent in their employment duties in contract* with the public; and

13. In consultation with the council, adopt and promulgate any rules and regulations necessary to implement the provisions of this section and sections eight hundred forty-one-a and eight hundred forty-one-b of this article and of article seven-a of the general business law.

* So in original.

Added by L. 1992, Ch. 336, eff. July 12, 1993; Amended by L. 1994, Ch. 634, § 19, eff. Aug. 2, 1994, renumbering old subd. 11 as subd. 13 and adding new subds. 11 and 12.

§ 841-d. Saving clause.

In case it be judicially determined that any phrase, clause, part, paragraph or section of any of the provisions of section eight hundred forty-one-a, eight hundred forty-one-b, or eight hundred forty-one-c of this article is unconstitutional or otherwise invalid, such determination shall not affect the validity or effect of the remaining provisions of the aforementioned sections.

Added by L. 1992, Ch. 336, eff. July 12, 1993.

§ 842. Council rules and regulations promulgated by the governor.

The governor, in his discretion, may adopt and promulgate any or all of the rules and regulations recommended by the council to the governor pursuant to subdivision one of section eight hundred forty. When the governor promulgates any rule or regulation recommended by the council, he shall transmit a certified copy thereof to the secretary of state, in accordance with the requirements of subdivision one of section one hundred two, including a statement as to the effective date of such rules or regulations.

§ 843. Division homepage on the internet.

1. Definitions. For the purposes of this section the following terms shall have the following meanings:

(a) "Internet" shall mean an international computer network of both federal and non-federal interoperable packet switched data networks which users may access through a service provider.

(b) "Homepage" shall mean an individual site or address of a document or file where particular information can be located.

2. The commissioner shall construct, operate and maintain a homepage on the internet for the purpose of providing a mechanism for the wide dissemination of information relating to criminal justice issues.

3. The homepage directed to be created by this section shall include pictures and such other information as the commissioner deems necessary pertaining to missing children who resided in New York at the time of their disappearance or whose parent, parents or legal guardian currently reside in New York state.

4. Such homepage shall also contain pictures and information regarding the ten most wanted criminals in New York state as determined by the superintendent of state police.

5. Such homepage shall also contain the subdirectory of high risk sex offenders maintained pursuant to section one hundred sixty-eight-q of the correction law.

6. The commissioner shall promulgate rules and regulations necessary to carry out the provisions of this section. Such rules and regulations shall include procedures for determining whether issues of confidentiality or constitutionality exist with regard to any information proposed to be included on the homepage created by the division. Where there is a question as to whether the dissemination of certain information by the state would be a violation of confidentiality or of an individual's constitutional rights, such information shall not be included on the division's homepage.

Added by L. 1996, Ch. 674, eff. Sept. 25, 1996; L. 2000, Ch. 490, renumbering subd. 5 to 6 and adding a new subd. 5, eff. Jan. 21, 2001.

§ 844. [Repealed.]

§ 844-a. The New York statewide law enforcement telecommunications committee.

There shall be established a committee within the division which shall be known as the New York statewide law enforcement telecommunications committee [NYSLETC] which shall establish standards and guidelines for the use and management of law enforcement radio frequencies which have been assigned by the federal communications commission for statewide use for all law enforcement agencies within the state. The committee shall be comprised of four representatives of the division of state police, four representatives of the New York state association of chiefs of police, four representatives of the New York state sheriffs association, two local frequency advisors of the associated public safety communication, inc. representing federal communications commission mandated frequency coordination for the northern and southern regions of the state, one representative of the New York city police department and two representatives of the division who shall serve in an advisory capacity to the committee. All members of the committee shall serve without compensation for their services as such. The division may appear as the representative of the committee in any application or proceeding before the federal communications commission relating to statewide law enforcement radio frequencies which have been assigned for statewide use by law enforcement agencies. The committee may recommend to the division for promulgation such rules and regulations as may be necessary to carry out the purposes of this section.

Added by L. 1991, Ch. 505, eff. Nov. 1, 1991.

§ 844-b. New York state committee for the coordination of police services to elderly persons.

1. Establishment of the committee. There is hereby established within the division the "New York state committee for the coordination of police services to elderly persons", hereinafter the "committee".

2. Membership of committee.

(a) The committee shall consist of a representative of the commissioner, representative of the superintendent of the New York state police, two representatives of the New York state sheriffs association, two representatives of the New York state association of chiefs of police, two representatives of the New York state district attorneys' association, a representative of the attorney general, a representative of the chairperson of the crime victims board, a representative of the director of the state office for the aging, a representative of the commissioner of social services, a representative of the commissioner of the New York city police department, a representative of the New York state crime prevention coalition and two elderly representatives one to be appointed by the temporary president of the senate and the other by the speaker of the assembly. The commissioner shall make appointments to the committee in accordance with nominations submitted by the relevant agencies or organizations. Each member of the committee shall be appointed by the commissioner to serve a two year term. Any member appointed by the commissioner may be reappointed for additional terms. Any vacancies shall be filled in the same manner as the original appointment and vacancies created otherwise than by expiration of term shall be filled for the remainder of that unexpired term.

(b) In the performance of its functions, the committee shall, to the extent possible, solicit the participation and involvement of retired law enforcement personnel.

(c) The representative of the commissioner and the superintendent of the state police shall serve as co-chairpersons of the committee.

(d) Membership of the committee shall not constitute the holding of a public office, and members of the committee shall not be required to take and file oaths of office before serving on the committee.

(e) The members of the committee shall receive no compensation for their services as members.

(f) No member of the committee shall be disqualified from holding any public office or employment, nor shall any member forfeit any employment or office by reason of his or her membership on the committee.

(g) The committee shall meet as often as deemed necessary, but in no event less than two times per year.

3. Duties and responsibilities. The committee shall advise the division, the state police, county sheriffs and other local law enforcement agencies, and senior advocates chosen in consultation with the state office for the aging, in the study and evaluation of "Triad Programs" as an effective response to the problems of crime against elderly persons. The committee may also consult with experts, service providers and representative organizations engaged in the protection of the elderly and may recommend the development of "Triad Programs" in the state of New York to assist the elderly to avoid criminal victimization through the coordinated efforts of state and local law enforcement agencies and organizations which provide services for the elderly. The committee may also recommend policies and programs to assist law enforcement agencies to implement "Triad Programs", including training and prevention standards and technical assistance. Such recommendations may include the following:

(a) the establishment of statewide and central clearinghouse for information and education materials;

(b) the development of innovative community police programs for the elderly;

(c) providing assistance to the municipal police training council in the development and delivery of training to law enforcement professionals involved in the "Triad Programs" including, but not limited to, the subjects of:

(i) crimes against the elderly and the protection of elderly persons;

(ii) police sensitivity to the needs of elderly persons as victims and witnesses;

(iii) social and human services;

(d) providing assistance to state and local law

MISC. LAWS

enforcement officials and to not-for-profit corporations, organizations with respect to effective policies and responses to crimes against elderly persons;

(e) promoting and facilitating cooperation among state agencies and local units of government;

(f) effective advocacy of services to protect elderly persons and elderly victims of crime;

(g) evaluating the relationship between crimes against elderly persons and other problems confronting elderly persons, and making recommendations for effective policy response;

(h) the collection of statistical data and research; and

(i) rules and regulations as may be necessary to carry out the purposes of this section.

3-a. Reports. On or before March first, nineteen hundred ninety-eight and annually thereafter the committee shall report to the temporary president of the senate, the speaker of the assembly, the chair of the assembly committee on aging and the chair of the senate committee on aging, on the incidence of reports of abuse of elderly persons. Such report shall consist of information from reports forwarded to the committee by local law enforcement agencies pursuant to section 140.10 of the criminal procedure law including number of reported incidents, ages of victims and alleged offenders, circumstances of the incident whether arrests were made and the sentence, if any, of the offenders. Such report shall also recommend policies and programs to aid law enforcement agencies, the courts and the New York state crime victims board in efforts to assist elder victims of domestic violence. The report shall also include recommendations designed to assist law enforcement agencies in implementing "Triad Programs".

4. Definition. As used in this section, the term "Triad Program" shall mean the triad cooperative model developed by the American Association of retired* Persons, the National Sheriffs' Association and the International Association of Chiefs of Police which calls for the participation of the sheriff, at least one police chief, and a representative of at least one senior citizens' organization within a county and may include participation by general service coalitions of law enforcement, victim service, and senior citizen advocate organizations.

If there is not both a sheriff and a police chief in a county or if the sheriff or a police chief do not participate, a Triad may include in the place of the sheriff or police chief another key law enforcement official in the county such as a district attorney.

* So in original.

Added by L. 1993, Ch. 111, § 2, eff. Apr. 1, 1994; **Amended** by L. 1993, Ch. 427, § 1, eff. Apr. 1, 1994; L. 1995, Ch. 393, § 1, eff. Aug 2, 1995, amending subd. 2(a); L. 1997, Ch. 626,

§ 2, eff. Sept 17, 1997, adding subd. 3-a; **Repealed** by L. 2004, Ch. 642, § 3, eff. Oct. 26, 2004; **Reinstated** by L. 2005, Ch. 87, § 2, eff. June 7, 2005, deemed eff. on and after Oct. 26, 2004.

§ 845. Central state registry of police officers.

1. The division shall collect information to maintain, on a current basis, a registry of all police officers in the state. Such registry shall contain, with respect to each police officer, his name, date of birth, social security number, rank or title, department, and whether he is employed full-time or part-time.

2. Each head of a state or local agency, unit of local government, state or local commission, or public authority which employs police officers shall transmit to the division, no later than the fifteenth day of January, nineteen hundred eighty, a list containing the name of every police officer employed by his agency, government, commission, authority or organization on the first day of January, nineteen hundred eighty, indicating with respect to each police officer his date of birth, social security number, rank or title, department, whether he is employed full-time or part-time. Each such head shall thereafter, no later than the tenth day of each January and July, transmit to the division a list of those police officers who have been appointed, have had a change of rank, or have ceased to serve in the preceding six calendar months and, in the instance of new appointees, shall include all the information required to be furnished in the initial listing.

3. Each such head shall have the option to enter into an agreement with the division whereby the required semi-annual updating of registry information may be regularly done on a more frequent basis.

Amended by L. 1979, Ch. 482.

§ 845-a. Central state registry of peace officers.

1. The division shall collect information to maintain on a current basis a registry of all peace officers in the state. Such registry shall contain with respect to each peace officer, his name, date of birth, rank or title, official station and whether he is employed full-time or part-time.

2. Each head of a state or local agency, unit or local government, state or local commission, or public authority, or public or private organization which employs peace officers shall transmit to the division no later than the fifteenth day of January in the year next succeeding the year in which the provisions of this section become effective, a list containing the name of every peace officer employed by his agency, government, commission, authority or organization on the fifteenth day of such month of January indicating with respect to each peace officer his name,

date of birth, rank or title, official station and whether he is employed full-time or part-time. Each such head shall thereafter, no later than the fifteenth day of each January and July, transmit to the division a list of those peace officers who have been appointed or have ceased to serve in the preceding calendar month and, in the instance of new appointees, shall include all the information required to be furnished in the initial listing.

3. Each such head shall have the option to enter into an agreement with the division whereby the required semi-annual updating of registry information may be regularly done on a more frequent basis.

4. The division shall establish rules and regulations to provide for a permanent system of identification for each peace officer.

5. Upon the failure or refusal to comply with the requirements of subdivision two of this section, the commissioner shall apply to the supreme court for an order directed to the person responsible requiring compliance. Upon such application the court may issue such order as may be just, and a failure to comply with the order of the court shall be a contempt of court and punishable as such.

6. The division shall cooperate with the division of state police in making the information in the central peace officer registry available for the purpose of verifying transactions involving firearms.

Added by L. 1980, Ch. 843, eff. Sept. 1, 1980.

ANNOTATION

Generally.—Sections 845 and 845-a of the Executive Law created a central Registry of Peace Officers, which provided that DCJS must maintain a current listing of peace officers within the state, such information to be reported to the DCJS by the heads of certain organizations as defined in § 845-a(2); nothing is mentioned in the statute that empowers the DCJS to determine who is or is not a peace officer. People v. Ferrera, 128 Misc. 2d 687, 490 N.Y.S.2d 462 (Sup. Ct. Richmond Co. 1985).

§ 845-b. Requests for criminal history information.

1. Definitions. As used in this section:

(a) "Authorized agency" means a state agency authorized to check criminal history information pursuant to subdivision two of this section.

(b) "Authorized person" means the one individual designated by a provider who is authorized to request, receive and review criminal history information pursuant to this section, except that where the number of applications received by a provider is so great that one person cannot reasonably perform the functions of the authorized person, a provider may designate one or more additional persons to serve as authorized persons pursuant to this section.

(c) "Criminal history information" means a record of pending criminal charges, criminal convictions which are not vacated or reversed, and certificates filed pursuant to subdivision two of section seven hundred five of the correction law, and which the division is authorized to maintain pursuant to subdivision six of section eight hundred thirty-seven of this article.

(d) "Subject individual" means a person for whom a provider is authorized to request a check of criminal history information pursuant to subdivision two of this section.

(e) "Provider" means a person or entity authorized to request a check of criminal history information pursuant to subdivision two of this section.

2. Where a provider is authorized or required to request a check of criminal history information by an authorized agency pursuant to section 16.33 or 31.35 of the mental hygiene law, such provider shall proceed pursuant to the provisions of this section and in a manner consistent with the provisions of article twenty-three-A of the correction law, subdivisions fifteen and sixteen of section two hundred ninety-six of this chapter and all other applicable laws.

3. Procedures for criminal history information check requests by providers. (a) A provider authorized to request a check of criminal history information pursuant to subdivision two of this section shall designate one authorized person who shall request a check of criminal history information on behalf of such provider pursuant to this section and review the results of such check. Only such authorized person or his or her designee and the subject individual to whom such criminal history information relates shall have access to such information; provided, however, that criminal history information received by a provider may be disclosed to other persons who are directly participating in any decision in regard to such subject individual; and provided, further, that such other persons shall also be subject to the confidentiality requirements and all other provisions of this section. Each provider shall specifically identify to the authorized agency in writing, in advance of disclosure, the authorized person and each other such agent or employee of the provider who is authorized to have access to the results of a check of criminal history information pursuant to this section. Any person who willfully permits the release of any confidential criminal history information contained in the report to persons not permitted by this section to receive such information shall be guilty of a misdemeanor.

(b) A provider requesting a check of criminal history information pursuant to this section shall do so by completing a form established for such purpose by the authorized agency in consultation with the division. Such form shall include a sworn statement of the authorized person certifying that:

(i) the person for whose criminal history information a check is requested is a subject individual for whom criminal history information is available by law;

(ii) the specific duties which qualify the provider to request a check of criminal history information;

(iii) the results of such criminal history information check will be used by the provider solely for purposes authorized by law; and

(iv) the provider and its agents and employees are aware of and will abide by the confidentiality requirements and all other provisions of this article.

(c) A provider authorized to request a criminal history information check pursuant to this section may inquire of a subject individual in the manner authorized by subdivision sixteen of section two hundred ninety-six of this chapter. Prior to requesting such information, a provider shall:

(i) inform the subject individual in writing that the provider is authorized or, where applicable, required to request a check of his or her criminal history information and review the results of such check pursuant to this section;

(ii) inform the subject individual that he or she has the right to obtain, review and seek correction of his or her criminal history information under regulations and procedures established by the division;

(iii) obtain the signed, informed consent of the subject individual on a form supplied by the authorized agency which indicates that such person has:

A. been informed of the right and procedures necessary to obtain, review and seek correction of his or her criminal history information;

B. been informed of the reason for the request for his or her criminal history information;

C. consented to such request for a report; and

D. supplied on the form a current mailing or home address. Upon receiving such written consent, the provider shall receive or obtain the fingerprints of such subject individual pursuant to such regulations as may be necessary to be established by the authorized agency in consultation with the division, and promptly transmit them to the authorized agency.

(d) A subject individual may withdraw his or her application for employment pursuant to this section, without prejudice, at any time before employment is offered or declined, regardless of whether the subject individual or provider has reviewed such subject individual's criminal history information.

4. Procedures for criminal history information checks by authorized agencies. (a) The authorized agency shall pay the processing fee imposed pursuant to subdivision eight-a of section eight hundred thirty-seven of this article and shall promptly submit the fingerprints and the processing fee to the division for its full search and retain processing. The authorized agency may charge a provider a fee in amount no greater than the fee established pursuant to law by the division for processing such a criminal history information check, in such amounts as may be established by the authorized agency and approved by the director of the division of the budget. Nothing in this section shall prohibit the authorized agency or provider from claiming the cost of such fees and related costs, including administrative costs, as a reimbursable cost under the medical assistance program, Medicare or other payor, to the extent permitted by federal law.

(b) The division shall promptly provide requested criminal history information to the authorized agency after the receipt of a request pursuant to this section if such request is:

(i) made pursuant to a request by an authorized person on behalf of a provider authorized to make such a request pursuant to subdivision two of this section;

(ii) accompanied by the completed form described in this section; and

(iii) accompanied by fingerprints of the subject individual obtained pursuant to this section.

(c) Criminal history information provided by the division pursuant to this section shall be furnished only by mail or other method of secure and confidential delivery, addressed to the authorized agency. Such information and the envelope in which it is enclosed, if any, shall be prominently marked "confidential", and shall at all times be maintained by the authorized agency in a secure place.

5. After reviewing any criminal history information provided by the division concerning a subject individual, the authorized agency shall take the following actions:

(a) Where the criminal history information concerning a subject individual reveals a felony conviction at any time for a sex offense, a felony conviction within the past ten years involving violence, or a conviction for endangering the welfare of an incompetent or physically disabled person pursuant to section 260.25 of the penal law, the authorized agency shall deny the application for or renewal of the operating certificate, contract, approval, employment of the subject individual or other authorization to provide services, or direct the provider to deny employment, as applicable, unless the authorized agency determines, in its discretion, that approval of the application or renewal or employment will not in any way jeopardize the health, safety or welfare of the beneficiaries of such services.

(b) Where the criminal history information concerning a subject individual reveals a conviction for a crime other than one set forth in paragraph (a) of this subdivision, the authorized agency may deny the application or renewal, or direct the provider to deny employment of the subject individual, consistent with article twenty-three-A of the correction law.

(c) Where the criminal history information concerning a subject individual reveals a charge for any felony, the authorized agency shall, and for any misdemeanor, the authorized agency may hold the application, renewal or employment in abeyance until the charge is finally resolved.

(d) Prior to making a determination to deny an application or renewal, or directing an employer to deny employment, the authorized agency shall afford the subject individual an opportunity to explain, in writing, why the application should not be denied.

(e) Upon receipt of criminal history information from the division, the authorized agency may request, and is entitled to receive, information pertaining to any crime identified in such criminal history information from any state or local law enforcement agency, district attorney, parole officer, probation officer or court for the purposes of determining whether any ground relating to such crime exists for denying an application, renewal, or employment.

(f) The authorized agency shall thereafter promptly notify the provider concerning whether its check has revealed any criminal history information, and if so, what actions shall or may be taken by the authorized agency and the provider.

(g) Where the authorized agency denies the application for or renewal of an operating certificate, contract, approval or other authorization to provide services, or directs a provider to deny employment of the subject individual on account of the subject individual's criminal history information, the notification by the authorized agency shall include a summary of the criminal history information provided by the division.

(h) Where the authorized agency directs a provider to deny employment based on criminal history information, the provider must notify the subject individual that such information is the basis of the denial.

6. Upon request from an employee who has already been cleared for employment by an authorized agency and who subsequently leaves a particular employer and applies for employment with another, the authorizing agency shall adhere to its previous authorization when the criminal history information is unchanged and the circumstances of employment are substantially similar for the purposes of this section.

7. Any criminal history information provided by the division, and any summary of the criminal history information provided by the authorized agency to an employer pursuant to this section is confidential and shall not be available for public inspection; provided, however, nothing in this subdivision shall prevent an authorized agency or provider from disclosing criminal history information at any administrative or judicial proceeding relating to the denial or revocation of an application, employment, license or registration. Where the authorized agency denies the application for or renewal of an operating certificate, contract, approval or other authorization to provide services, or directs a provider to deny employment of the subject individual, the subject of the criminal history information check conducted pursuant to this section shall be entitled to receive, upon written request, a copy of the summary of the criminal history information provided by the authorized agency to the provider.

8. A provider shall advise the authorized agency when a subject individual is no longer subject to such check. The authorized agency shall inform the division when a subject individual is no longer subject to such check so that the division may terminate its retain processing with regard to such individual. At least once a year, the authorized agency shall be required to conduct a validation of the records maintained by the division.

9. Provided that an authorized agency or a provider reasonably and in good faith complies with the provisions of this section, there shall be no criminal or civil liability on the part of and no cause of action for damages shall accrue against any authorized agency, provider or employee thereof on account of, arising out of or relating to criminal history information pursuant to this section, or any act or omission relating to criminal history information pursuant to this section.

10. Fingerprints received by the division pursuant to this section shall be used only to assist the division in providing criminal history information to authorized agencies under this section.

11. An authorized agency or provider authorized to request criminal history information pursuant to this section may temporarily approve an applicant while the results of the criminal history information check are pending, so long as such person does not have unsupervised physical contact with clients, as shall be defined by the authorized agency pursuant to regulation. Such regulation shall recognize the differences in the staffing patterns of various service models and the supervision required to ensure the safety of clients.

12. The authorized agency in consultation with the commissioner shall promulgate any rules and regulations necessary to implement the provisions of this section, which shall include convenient procedures for persons to promptly verify the accuracy of their criminal history information and, to the extent authorized by law, to have access to relevant documents related thereto.

Added by L. 2003, Ch. 643, § 3, eff. Oct. 7, 2003; **Amended** by L. 2004, Ch. 575, § 3, amending section and section heading, eff. Apr. 1, 2005.

MISC. LAWS

§ 846. Programs for the aging. [*Another version of § 846 follows.*] *

To provide that the interests of the elderly are sufficiently represented in the considerations of the local criminal justice coordinating councils, as may be formed pursuant to the federal omnibus crime control and safe streets act of nineteen hundred sixty-eight, as amended, such councils shall include at least one member who is a representative of persons aged sixty and over.

   * **Editor's Note:** There are two versions of § 846. A second § 846 follows.

§ 846. Programs for the aging. *

1. The division, in consultation with the state office for the aging, shall take all necessary and appropriate measures to develop, plan, provide, and implement programs for the protection of persons aged sixty and over, hereafter referred to in this section as elderly persons, from situations and criminal acts which threaten their safety, security, and property, within the resources available to such agencies for such purposes.

2. Pursuant to the requirements of subdivision one of this section, the division, in consultation with the municipal police training council and the New York state committee for the coordination of police services for the elderly, shall develop an in-service training program, designed to address the problems associated with the investigation of crimes against elderly persons, and to reduce the criminal victimization of the elderly and issue an appropriate certificate to such officers attesting to their satisfactory completion of such special training program.

   * **Editor's Note:** There are two versions of § 846. See preceding version.

Former section **repealed** and new section **added** by L. 1998, Ch. 83, § 1, eff. June 2, 1998; **Repealed** by L. 2004, Ch. 642, § 3, eff. Oct. 26, 2004; **Reinstated** by L. 2005, Ch. 87, § 2, eff. June 7, 2005, deemed eff. on and after Oct. 26, 2004.

ARTICLE 36

NEIGHBORHOOD PRESERVATION CRIME PREVENTION ACT

(Selected section)

Section

846-h.   Law enforcement agency accreditation council; membership; organization and procedure.

* * *

§ 846-h. Law enforcement agency accreditation council; membership; organization and procedure.

1. (a) There shall be, within the division, a law enforcement agency accreditation council.

(b) The council shall develop model standards for law enforcement agencies. Such standards shall be designed:

(i) To increase the effectiveness and efficiency of law enforcement agencies in the delivery of law enforcement services utilizing existing personnel, equipment and facilities to the extent possible;

(ii) To promote increased cooperation and coordination among law enforcement agencies and other agencies of the criminal justice system;

(iii) To ensure the appropriate training of law enforcement personnel, not inconsistent with other provisions of law; and

(iv) To promote public confidence in law enforcement agencies.

(c) The council shall recommend rules and regulations establishing an accreditation process that encourages and provides law enforcement agencies with a voluntary opportunity to demonstrate that they meet the model standards developed by the council. The accreditation process shall provide that applications for accreditation shall be submitted by the chief law enforcement officer of the agency so applying only upon the approval of the chief elected officer, or if there is no chief elected officer, by the local governing body. Such model standards and rules and regulations shall be transmitted to the temporary president of the senate, the speaker of the assembly, every law enforcement agency, mayor and appropriate town and county official in the state on or before April first, nineteen hundred eighty-nine. The rules and regulations in final form shall be transmitted to the governor on or after June first, nineteen hundred eighty-nine and shall be effective following their approval by the governor.

2. (a) The law enforcement agency accreditation council shall consist of:

(i) Three incumbent sheriffs of the state;

(ii) Three incumbent chiefs of police;

(iii) One incumbent deputy sheriff;

(iv) One incumbent police officer;

(v) The superintendent of state police;

(vi) The commissioner of police of the city of New York;

(vii) One incumbent chief executive officer of a county of the state;

(viii) One incumbent mayor of a city or village of the state;

(ix) One incumbent chief executive officer of a town of the state;

(x) One member of a statewide labor organization representing police officers as that term is defined in subdivision thirty-four of section 1.20 of the criminal procedure law;

(xi) One full-time faculty member of a college or university who teaches in the area of criminal justice or police science; and

(xii) Two members appointed pursuant to subparagraph (ix) of paragraph (c) of this subdivision.

(b) With the exception of the superintendent of state police and the commissioner of police of the city of New York, each member of the council shall be appointed by the governor to serve a two year term. Any member appointed by the governor may be reappointed for additional terms.

(c) The governor shall make appointments to the council as follows:

(i) Each member who is an incumbent sheriff of the state shall be chosen from a list of two eligible persons submitted by the New York state sheriffs' association;

(ii) Each member who is an incumbent chief of police shall be chosen from a list of two eligible persons submitted by the New York state association of chiefs of police;

(iii) The member who is an incumbent deputy sheriff shall be chosen from a list of two eligible persons submitted jointly by the New York state sheriffs' association and the New York state deputy sheriffs' association, inc.;

(iv) The member who is an incumbent police officer shall be chosen from a list of two eligible persons submitted jointly by the New York state association of chiefs of police and a statewide labor organization representing police officers as that term is defined in subdivision thirty-four of section 1.20 of the criminal procedure law;

(v) The member who is an incumbent chief executive officer of a county of the state shall be chosen from a list of two eligible persons submitted by the New York state association of counties;

(vi) The member who is an incumbent mayor of a city or village of the state shall be chosen from a list of two eligible persons submitted by the New York state conference of mayors;

(vii) The member who is an incumbent chief executive officer of a town of the state shall be chosen from a list of two eligible persons submitted by the association of towns of the state of New York;

(viii) The governor may appoint any eligible person to be a member who is an active member of a statewide labor organization representing police officers; and

(ix) The temporary president of the senate and the speaker of the assembly shall each nominate one member as provided in subparagraph (xii) of paragraph (a) of this subdivision.

(d) In making such appointments, the governor shall select individuals from municipalities that are representative, to the extent possible, of the varying sizes of communities and law enforcement agencies in the state.

(e) Any member chosen to fill a vacancy, including a vacancy in the chairperson, created otherwise than by expiration of term shall be appointed by the governor for the unexpired term of the member he is to succeed. Any such vacancy shall be filled in the same manner as the original appointment.

(f) Any member who shall cease to hold the position which qualified him for such appointment shall cease to be a member of the council.

3. Each member of the council shall have one vote, which shall not be transferrable; provided, however, that the superintendent of state police may designate a deputy superintendent to attend meetings as his representative and cast his vote and the commissioner of police of the city of New York may designate his first deputy commissioner, chief of department or one of the five bureau chiefs to attend meetings as his representative and cast his vote.

4. The governor shall designate from among the members of the council a chairperson who shall serve at the pleasure of the governor.

5. The law enforcement agency accreditation council shall meet at least four times in a year. Special meetings may be called by the chairperson and shall be called by him at the request of the governor or upon the written request of nine members of the council. The council may establish its own rules and procedures with respect to the conduct of its meetings and other affairs not inconsistent with law.

6. Membership on the law enforcement agency accreditation council shall not constitute the holding of a public office, and members of the council shall not be required to take and file oaths of office before serving on the council.

7. The members of the law enforcement agency accreditation council shall receive no compensation for their services but shall be allowed their actual and necessary expenses incurred in the performance of their functions hereunder.

8. No member of the law enforcement agency accreditation council shall be disqualified from holding any public office or employment, nor shall he forfeit any such office or employment, by reason of his appointment hereunder.

9. For the purposes of this section, the following terms shall have the following meanings:

(a) The term "law enforcement agency" shall mean any agency or department of any municipality, any police district, or any agency, department, commission, authority or public benefit corporation of the state of New York employing a police officer or police officers as that term is defined in paragraphs (a), (b), (c), (d), (e), (f), (j), (k), (l), (o), (p), and (s) of subdivision thirty-four of section 1.20 of the criminal procedure law.

(b) The term "chief of police" shall mean a chief of police, commissioner of police, or other official having equivalent cognizance, jurisdiction, supervision and control of a police department of a municipality of the state.

(c) The term "deputy sheriff" shall mean a deputy sheriff employed by the sheriff's department of any county outside the city of New York who has police officer status as defined in subdivision thirty-four of section 1.20 of the criminal procedure law.

(d) The term "police officer" shall mean a police officer as defined in subdivision thirty-four of section 1.20 of the criminal procedure law.

10. On or before January first, nineteen hundred ninety, and on or before January first of each succeeding year, the commissioner shall report to the governor, temporary president of the senate and speaker of the assembly on the operation and results of the accreditation program. Such report shall identify these law enforcement agencies making application for accreditation, the agencies so accredited, and the fiscal impact on law enforcement agencies that have been accredited.

Added by L. 1988, Ch. 521, eff. Sept. 1, 1988; **Amended** by. L. 2005, Ch. 625, § 1, eff. Aug. 30, 2005, amending subd. 9(a).

L. 1988, Ch. 521, § 3 provides:

"Notwithstanding the provisions of section eight hundred forty-six-h of the executive law, as added by section one of this act, the members of the law enforcement agency accreditation council first appointed by the governor shall be appointed as follows: The three members who are incumbent sheriffs of the state shall be chosen from a list of five nominees submitted by the New York state sheriffs' association, and the three members who are chiefs of police shall be chosen from a list of five nominees submitted by the New York state association of chiefs of police. The remaining members shall be appointed in the manner provided for in section eight hundred forty-six-h of the executive law, as added by section one of this act.

"Of the members first appointed by the governor, two chosen from the list of nominees submitted by the New York state sheriffs' association, two chosen from the list submitted by the New York state association of chiefs of police, and one chosen from the lists submitted by the New York state association of counties, New York state conference of mayors, and the association of towns of the state of New York, at the governor's designation, and the member representing a statewide labor organization shall have three year terms."

ARTICLE 49-B

COMMISSION ON FORENSIC SCIENCE AND ESTABLISHMENT OF DNA IDENTIFICATION INDEX

[Added by L. 1994, Ch. 737, § 1, eff. Aug. 2, 1994, except as indicated.]

LexisNexis Cross References

See generally Forensic Sciences; Police Investigation Handbook; Criminal Law Advocacy, Vol. 3, Ch. 5, Scientific Evidence: Presentation and Attack.

§ 995. Definitions.

When used in this article, the following words and terms shall have the meanings ascribed to them in this section:

1. For purposes of general forensic analysis the term "forensic laboratory" shall mean any laboratory operated by the state or unit of local government that performs forensic testing on evidence in a criminal investigation or proceeding or for purposes of identification provided, however, that the examination of latent fingerprints by a police agency shall not be subject to the provisions of this article.

2. For purposes of forensic DNA analysis, the term "forensic DNA laboratory" shall mean any forensic laboratory operated by the state or unit of local government, that performs forensic DNA testing on crime scenes or materials derived from the human body for use as evidence in a criminal proceeding or for purposes of identification and the term "Forensic DNA testing" shall mean any test that employs techniques to examine deoxyribonucleic acid (DNA) derived from the human body for the purpose of providing information to resolve issues of identification. Regulations pursuant to this article shall not include DNA testing on materials derived from the human body pursuant to title five of article five of the public health law for the purpose of determining a person's genetic disease or medical condition and shall not include a laboratory operated by the federal government.

3. "DNA testing methodology" means methods and procedures used to extract and analyze DNA material, as well as the methods, procedures, assumptions, and studies used to draw statistical inferences from the test results.

4. "Blind external proficiency testing" means a test sample that is presented to a forensic laboratory for forensic DNA testing through a second agency, and which appears to the analysts to involve routine evidence submitted for forensic DNA testing.

5. "DNA" means deoxyribonucleic acid.

6. "State DNA identification index" means the DNA identification record system for New York state established pursuant to this article.

7. "Designated offender" means a person convicted of and sentenced for any one or more of the following provisions of the penal law:

(a) sections 120.05, 120.10, and 120.11, relating to assault; sections 125.15 through 125.27 relating to homicide; sections 130.25, 130.30, 130.35, 130.40, 130.45, 130.50, 130.67 and 130.70, relating to sex offenses; sections 205.10, 205.15, 205.17 and 205.19, relating to escape and other offenses, where the offender has been convicted within the previous five years of one of the other felonies specified in this subdivision; or section 255.25, relating to incest, a violent felony offense as defined in subdivision one of section 70.02 of the penal law, attempted murder in the first degree, as defined in section 110.00 and section 125.27 of the penal law, kidnapping in the first degree, as defined in section 135.25 of the penal law, arson in the first degree, as defined in section 150.20 of the penal law, burglary in the third degree, as defined in section 140.20 of the penal law, attempted burglary in the third degree, as defined in section 110.00 and section 140.20 of the penal law, a felony defined in article four hundred ninety of the penal law relating to terrorism or any attempt to commit an offense defined in such article relating to terrorism which is a felony; or

(b) criminal possession of a controlled substance in the first degree, as defined in section 220.21 of the penal law; criminal possession of a controlled substance in the second degree, as defined in section 220.18 of the penal law; criminal sale of a controlled substance, as defined in article 220 of the penal law; or grand larceny in the fourth degree, as defined in subdivision five of section 155.30 of the penal law; or

(c) any misdemeanor or felony defined as a sex offense or sexually violent offense pursuant to paragraph (a), (b) or (c) of subdivision two or paragraph (a) of subdivision three of section one hundred sixty-eight-a of the correction law; or

(d) any of the following felonies, or an attempt thereof where such attempt is a felony offense: aggravated assault upon a person less than eleven years old, as defined in section 120.12 of the penal law; menacing in the first degree, as defined in section 120.13 of the penal law; reckless endangerment in the first degree, as defined in section 120.25 of the penal law; stalking in the second degree, as defined in section 120.55 of the penal law; criminally negligent homicide, as defined in section 125.10 of the penal law; vehicular manslaughter in the second degree, as defined in section 125.12 of the penal law; vehicular manslaughter in the first degree, as defined in section 125.13 of the penal law; persistent sexual abuse, as defined in section 130.53 of the penal law; aggravated sexual abuse in the fourth degree, as defined in section 130.65-a of the penal law; female genital mutilation, as defined in section 130.85 of the penal law; facilitating a sex offense with a controlled substance, as defined in section 130.90 of the penal law; unlawful imprisonment in the first degree, as defined in section 135.10 of the penal law; custodial interference in the first degree, as defined in section 135.50 of the penal law; criminal trespass in the first degree, as defined in section 140.17 of the penal law; criminal tampering in the first degree, as defined in section 145.20 of the penal law; tampering with a consumer product in the first degree, as defined in section 145.45 of the penal law; robbery in the third degree as defined in section 160.05 of the penal law; identity theft in the second degree, as defined in section 190.79 of the penal law; identity theft in the first degree, as defined in section 190.80 of the penal law; promoting prison contraband in the first degree, as defined in section 205.25 of the penal law; tampering with a witness in the third degree, as defined in section 215.11 of the penal law; tampering with a witness in the second degree, as defined in section 215.12 of the penal law; tampering with a witness in the first degree, as defined in section 215.13 of the penal law; criminal contempt in the first degree, as defined in subdivisions (b), (c) and (d) of section 215.51 of the penal law; aggravated criminal contempt, as defined in section 215.52 of the penal law; bail jumping in the second degree, as defined in section 215.56 of the penal law; bail jumping in the first degree, as defined in section 215.57 of the penal law; patronizing a prostitute in the second degree, as defined in section 230.05 of the penal law; patronizing a prostitute in the first degree, as defined in section 230.06 of the penal law; promoting prostitution in the second degree, as defined in section 230.30 of the penal law; promoting prostitution in the first degree, as defined in section 230.32 of the penal law; disseminating indecent materials to minors in the second degree, as defined in section 235.21 of the penal law; disseminating indecent materials to minors in the first degree, as defined in section 235.22 of the penal law; riot in the first degree, as defined in section 240.06 of the penal law; criminal anarchy, as defined in section 240.15 of the penal law; aggravated harassment of an employee by an inmate, as defined in section 240.32 of the penal law; unlawful surveillance in the second degree, as defined in section 250.45 of the penal law; unlawful surveillance in the first degree, as defined in section 250.50 of the penal law; endangering the welfare of a vulnerable elderly person in the second degree, as defined in section 260.32 of the penal law; endangering the welfare of a vulnerable elderly person in the first degree, as defined in section 260.34 of the penal law; use of a child in a sexual performance, as defined in section 263.05 of the penal law; promoting an obscene sexual performance by a child, as defined in section 263.10 of the penal law; possessing an obscene sexual performance by a child, as defined in section 263.11 of the penal law; promoting a sexual performance by a child, as defined in section 263.15 of the penal law; possessing a sexual performance by a child, as defined in section 263.16 of the penal law; criminal possession of a weapon in the third degree, as defined in section 265.02 of the penal law; criminal sale of a firearm in the third degree, as defined in section 265.11 of the penal law; criminal sale of a firearm to a minor, as defined in section 265.16 of the penal law; unlawful wearing of a body vest, as defined in section 270.20 of the penal law; hate crimes, as defined in section 485.05 of the penal law; and crime of terrorism, as defined in section 490.25 of the penal law.

8. "DNA record" means DNA identification information prepared by a forensic DNA laboratory and stored in the state DNA identification index for purposes of establishing identification in connection with law enforcement investigations or supporting statistical interpretation of the results of DNA analysis. A DNA record is the objective form of the results of a DNA analysis sample.

9. "DNA subcommittee" shall mean the subcommittee on forensic DNA laboratories and forensic DNA testing established pursuant to subdivision thirteen of section nine hundred ninety-five-b of this article.

10. "Commission" shall mean the commission on forensic science established pursuant to section nine hundred ninety-five-a of this article.

Amended by L. 1999, Ch. 560, eff. Dec. 1, 1999, amending subd. 7; L. 2000, Ch. 8, eff. Mar. 6, 2000, deemed eff. Dec. 1, 1999, amending subd. 7(b), shall take effect and apply only to designated offenders convicted on or after the effective date of this act; L. 2004, Ch. 1, § 13 (Part A), eff. July 23, 2004, amending subd. 7(a); L. 2004, Ch. 138, § 1, eff. July 6, 2004, amending subd. 7; L. 2004, Ch. 576, § 1, eff. July 6, 2004, amending subd. 7, and such amendments shall apply to designated offenses committed on or after this effective date, as well as to designated offenses committed prior to this effective date where service of the sentence imposed upon conviction of the designated offense has not been completed prior to the effective date of this act.

L. 2004, Ch. 138, § 3 provides: "This act shall take effect immediately; provided, however, that paragraphs (c) and (d) of subdivision 7 of section 995 of the executive law, as added by section one of this act, shall apply to designated offenses committed on or after the effective date of this act, as well as to designated offenses committed prior to the effective date of this act where service of the sentence imposed upon conviction of the designated offense has not been completed prior to the effective date of this act."

L. 1999, Ch. 560, § 9 provides: "[P]aragraph (a) of subdivision seven of section 995 of the executive law, as amended by section one of this act shall apply to designated offenses committed on or after the effective date of this act, as well as to designated offenses committed prior to the effective date of this act where service of the sentence imposed upon conviction of the designated offense has not been completed prior to the effective date of this act, provided further, . . . paragraph (b) of subdivision seven of section 995 of the executive law, as amended by section one of this act, shall take effect and apply only to designated offenders convicted on or after the effective date of this act; and provided further that an appeal pursuant to subdivision 5 of section 450.10 of the criminal procedure law as added by section seven of this act or subdivision 11 of section 450.20 of the criminal procedure law, as added by section eight of this act, shall apply to motions pursuant to subdivision 1-a of section 440.30 of the criminal procedure law determined prior to, or on or after, such effective date of this act."

§ 995-a. Commission on forensic science.

1. There is hereby created in the executive department, the commission on forensic science, which shall consist of the following fourteen members: (a) the commissioner of the division of criminal justice services who shall be chair of the commission and the commissioner of the department of health or his or her designee, who shall serve as an ex-officio member of the commission;

(b) twelve members appointed by the governor.

2. Of the members appointed by the governor,

(a) one member shall be the chair of the New York state crime laboratory advisory committee;

(b) one member shall be the director of a forensic laboratory located in New York state;

(c) one member shall be the director of the office of forensic services within the division of criminal justice services;

(d) two members shall be a scientist having experience in the areas of laboratory standards or quality assurance regulation and monitoring and shall be appointed upon the recommendation of the commissioner of health;

(e) one member shall be a representative of a law enforcement agency and shall be appointed upon the recommendation of the commissioner of criminal justice services;

(f) one member shall be a representative of prosecution services who shall be appointed upon the recommendation of the commissioner of criminal justice services;

(g) one member shall be a representative of the public criminal defense bar who shall be appointed upon the recommendation of an organization representing public defense services;

(h) one member shall be a representative of the private criminal defense bar who shall be appointed upon the recommendation of an organization of such bar;

(i) two members shall be members-at-large, one of whom shall be appointed upon the recommendation of the temporary president of the senate, and one of whom shall be appointed upon the recommendation of the speaker of the assembly; and

(j) one member, who shall be an attorney or judge with a background in privacy issues and biomedical ethics, shall be appointed upon the recommendation of the chief judge of the court of appeals.

3. Of the members appointed by the governor, each member shall be appointed to serve a three year term. Any member appointed by the governor may be reappointed for additional three year terms.

4. Any member chosen to fill a vacancy created otherwise than by expiration of term shall be appointed by the governor for the unexpired term of the member he or she is to succeed. Any such vacancy shall be filled in the same manner as the original appointment.

5. The commission shall meet at least four times each year and may establish its own rules and procedures concerning the conduct of its meetings and other affairs not inconsistent with law.

6. No member of the commission on forensic science shall be disqualified from holding any public office or employment, nor shall he or she forfeit any such office or employment, by reason of his or her appointment hereunder, and members of the commission shall not be required to take and file oaths of office before serving on the commission.

7. Members of the commission shall receive no compensation for their services but shall be allowed their actual and necessary expenses incurred in the performance of their functions hereunder.

§ 995-b. Powers and duties of the commission.

1. The commission shall develop minimum standards and a program of accreditation for all forensic laboratories in New York state, including establishing minimum qualifications for forensic laboratory directors and such other personnel as the commission may determine to be necessary and appropriate, and approval of forensic laboratories for the performance of specific forensic methodologies. Nothing in this article shall be deemed to preclude forensic laboratories from performing research and validation studies on new methodologies and technologies which may not yet be approved by the commission at that time.

In designing a system of accreditation pursuant to this article, the commission shall evaluate other systems of accreditation.

2. The minimum standards and program of accreditation shall be designed to accomplish the following objectives:

(a) increase and maintain the effectiveness, efficiency, reliability, and accuracy of forensic laboratories, including forensic DNA laboratories;

(b) ensure that forensic analyses, including forensic DNA testing, are performed in accordance with the highest scientific standards practicable;

(c) promote increased cooperation and coordination among forensic laboratories and other agencies in the criminal justice system;

(d) ensure compatibility, to the extent consistent with the provisions of this article and any other applicable provision of law pertaining to privacy or restricting disclosure or redisclosure of information, with other state and federal forensic laboratories to the extent necessary to share and exchange information, data and results of forensic analyses and tests; and

(e) Set forth minimum requirements for the quality and maintenance of equipment.

2-a. Any program of forensic laboratory accreditation with respect to a DNA laboratory pursuant to this section shall be under the direction of the DNA subcommittee established pursuant to subdivision thirteen of this section. Such subcommittee shall have the sole authority to grant, deny, review or modify a DNA forensic laboratory accreditation pursuant to this article, provided that such authority shall be effectuated through binding recommendations made by the DNA subcommittee to the commission. In the event the commission disagrees with any of the binding recommendations of the DNA subcommittee made pursuant to this article, the commission may so notify such subcommittee and request such subcommittee to reasonably review such

binding recommendations. The DNA subcommittee shall conduct such review and either forward revised binding recommendations to the commission or indicate, with the reasons therefor, that following such review such subcommittee has determined that such binding recommendations shall not be revised.

3. The program of forensic laboratory accreditation shall include, at a minimum, the following requirements:

(a) an initial laboratory inspection, and routine inspections, as necessary, to ensure compliance with accreditation requirements;

(b) routine internal and external proficiency testing of all laboratory personnel involved in forensic analysis, including blind external proficiency testing if the commission, or the DNA subcommittee as the case may be, determines such a blind proficiency testing program to be practicable and appropriate. In determining whether a blind proficiency testing program is practicable and appropriate, the commission, or the DNA subcommittee as the case may be, shall consider such factors as accuracy and reliability of laboratory results, cost-effectiveness, time, allocation of resources, and availability;

(c) quality control and quality assurance protocols, a method validation procedure and a corrective action and remedial program;

(d) annual certification to the commission by the forensic laboratories of their continued compliance with the requirements of the accreditation program which certification, in the case of a forensic DNA laboratory, shall be forwarded to the DNA subcommittee;

(e) the accreditation of a forensic laboratory may be revoked, suspended or otherwise limited, upon a determination by the commission or, in the case of a forensic DNA laboratory, upon the binding recommendation of the DNA subcommittee, that the laboratory or one or more persons in its employ:

(i) is guilty of misrepresentation in obtaining a forensic laboratory accreditation;

(ii) rendered a report on laboratory work actually performed in another forensic laboratory without disclosing the fact that the examination or procedure was performed by such other forensic laboratory;

(iii) showed a pattern of excessive errors in the performance of forensic laboratory examination procedures;

(iv) failed to file any report required to be submitted pursuant to this article or the rules and regulations promulgated pursuant thereto; or

(v) violated in a material respect any provision of this article or the rules and regulations promulgated pursuant thereto; and

(f) No forensic laboratory accreditation shall

be revoked, suspended, or otherwise limited without a hearing. The commission shall serve written notice of the alleged violation, together with written notice of the time and place of the hearing, which notice shall be mailed by certified mail to the holder of the forensic laboratory accreditation at the address of such holder at least twenty-one days prior to the date fixed for such hearing. An accredited laboratory may file a written answer to the charges with the commission, not less than five days prior to the hearing.

4. A laboratory director who knowingly operates a laboratory without obtaining the accreditation required by this article, or who, with the intent to mislead or deceive, misrepresents a material fact to the commission or DNA subcommittee, shall be subject to a civil penalty not to exceed seventy-five hundred dollars and such other penalties as are prescribed by the law.

5. The commission and the DNA subcommittee established pursuant to subdivision thirteen of this section may require and receive from any agency of the state or any political subdivision thereof such assistance and data as may be necessary to enable the commission or DNA subcommittee to administer the provisions of this article. The commission or DNA subcommittee may enter into such cooperative arrangements with the division of criminal justice services, the department of health, and any other state agency, each of which is authorized to enter into such cooperative arrangements as shall be necessary or appropriate. Upon request of the commission or DNA subcommittee, any state agency may transfer to the commission such officers and employees as the commission or DNA subcommittee may deem necessary from time to time to assist the commission or DNA subcommittee in carrying out its functions and duties. Officers and employees so transferred shall not lose their civil service status or rights, and shall remain in the negotiating unit, if any, established prior to such transfer.

6. All of the commission's records, reports, assessments, and evaluation with respect to accreditation, implementation of quality assurance standards (including proficiency testing) and monitoring thereof, shall be archived by the commission.

7. The commission and DNA subcommittee may establish, appoint, and set terms of members to as many advisory councils as it deems necessary to provide specialized expertise to the commission with respect to new forensic technologies including DNA testing methodologies.

8. The commission or DNA subcommittee shall designate one or more entities for the performance of proficiency tests required pursuant to the provisions of this article.

9. After reviewing recommendations from the division of criminal justice services, the commission, in consultation with the DNA subcommittee,

shall promulgate a policy for the establishment and operation of a DNA identification index consistent with the operational requirements and capabilities of the division of criminal justice services. Such policy shall address the following issues:

(a) the forensic DNA methodology or methodologies to be utilized in compiling the index;

(b) procedures for assuring that the state DNA identification index contains the following safeguards:

(i) That any records maintained as part of such an index are accurate and complete;

(ii) that effective software and hardware designs are instituted with security features to prevent unauthorized access to such records;

(iii) that periodic audits will be conducted to ensure that no illegal disclosures of such records have taken place;

(iv) that access to record information system facilities, systems operating environments, data file contents whether while in use or when stored in a media library is restricted to authorized personnel only;

(v) that operation programs are used that will prohibit inquiry, record updates, or destruction of records from any source other than an authorized source of inquiry, update, or destruction of records;

(vi) that operational programs are used to detect and store for the output of authorized employees only all unauthorized attempts to penetrate the state DNA identification index;

(vii) that adequate and timely procedures exist to insure that any subject of the state DNA identification index has the right of access to and review of records relating to such individual contained in such index for the purpose of ascertaining their accuracy and completeness, including procedures for review of information maintained about such individuals and administrative review (including procedures for administrative appeal) and the necessary documentation to demonstrate that the information is inaccurate or incomplete;

(viii) that access to the index will be granted to an agency authorized by this article to have such access only pursuant to a written use and dissemination agreement, a copy of which is filed with the commission, which agreement sets forth the specific procedures by which such agency shall implement the provisions of subparagraphs (i) through (vii) of this paragraph, as applicable, and which agreement specifically prohibits the redisclosure by such agency of any information obtained from the DNA identification index; and

(ix) such policy shall provide for the mutual exchange, use and storage of DNA records with the system of DNA identification utilized by the

Federal Bureau of Investigation provided that the commission determines that such exchange, use and storage are consistent with the provisions of this article and applicable provisions of law.

10. Review, and if necessary, recommend modifications to, a plan for implementation of the DNA identification index submitted by the commissioner of criminal justice services pursuant to section nine hundred ninety-five-c of this article.

11. Upon the recommendation of the DNA subcommittee established pursuant to subdivision thirteen of this section, the commission shall designate one or more approved methodologies for the performance of forensic DNA testing, and shall review and act upon applications by forensic DNA laboratories for approval to perform forensic DNA testing.

12. Promulgate standards for a determination of a match between the DNA records contained in the state DNA identification index and a DNA record of a person submitted for comparison therewith.

13. (a) The commission shall establish a subcommittee on forensic DNA laboratories and forensic DNA testing. The chair of the subcommittee shall be appointed by the chair of the commission. The chair of the subcommittee shall appoint six other members to the subcommittee, one of whom shall represent the discipline of molecular biology and be appointed upon the recommendation of the commissioner of the department of health, one of whom shall represent the discipline of population genetics and be appointed upon the recommendation of the commissioner of the department of health, one of whom shall be representative of the discipline of laboratory standards and quality assurance regulation and monitoring and be appointed upon the recommendation of the commissioner of health, one of whom shall be a forensic scientist and be appointed by the commissioner of health, one of whom shall be representative of the discipline of population genetics and be appointed upon the recommendation of the commissioner of criminal justice services and one of whom shall be representative of the discipline of forensic science and be appointed upon the recommendation of the commissioner of criminal justice services. Members of the DNA subcommittee shall serve for three year terms and be subject to the conditions of service specified in section nine hundred ninety-five-a of this article.

(b) The DNA subcommittee shall assess and evaluate all DNA methodologies proposed to be used for forensic analysis, and make reports and recommendations to the commission as it deems necessary. The DNA subcommittee shall make binding recommendations for adoption by the commission addressing minimum scientific standards to be utilized in conducting forensic DNA analysis including, but not limited to, examination of specimens, population studies and methods

employed to determine probabilities and interpret test results. The DNA subcommittee may require a demonstration by an independent laboratory of any proposed forensic DNA testing methodology proposed to be used by a forensic laboratory.

(c) The DNA subcommittee shall make binding recommendations for adoption by the commission with regard to an accreditation program for laboratories performing forensic DNA testing in accordance with the provisions of the state administrative procedure act. Such recommendations shall include the adoption and implementation of internal and external proficiency testing programs, including, if possible, a blind external proficiency testing program for forensic laboratories performing forensic DNA testing. The DNA subcommittee shall also provide the commission with a list of accepted proficiency testers.

(d) The DNA subcommittee shall be authorized to advise the commission on any other matters regarding the implementation of scientific controls and quality assurance procedures for the performance of forensic DNA testing, or on any other matters referred to it by the commission.

Amended by L. 1999, Ch. 560, § 2, amending subd. 13(a), eff. Dec. 1, 1999.

§ 995-c. State DNA identification index.

1. Following the promulgation of a policy by the commission pursuant to subdivision nine of section nine hundred ninety-five-b of this article, the commissioner of criminal justice services is authorized to promulgate a plan for the establishment of a computerized state DNA identification index within the division of criminal justice services.

2. Following the review and approval of the plan by the DNA subcommittee and the commission and the filing of such plan with the speaker of the assembly and the temporary president of the senate, the commissioner of criminal justice services is hereby authorized to establish a computerized state DNA identification index pursuant to the provisions of this article.

3. Any designated offender subsequent to conviction and sentencing for a crime specified in subdivision seven of section nine hundred ninety-five of this article, shall be required to provide a sample appropriate for DNA testing to determine identification characteristics specific to such person and to be included in a state DNA identification index pursuant to this article.

4. The commissioner of the division of criminal justice services, in consultation with the commission, the commissioner of health, the divisions of parole and of probation and correctional alternatives and the department of correctional services, shall promulgate rules and regulations governing the procedures for notifying designated offenders of the requirements of this section.

MISC. LAWS

5. The sample shall be collected, stored and forwarded to any forensic DNA laboratory which has been authorized by the commission to perform forensic DNA testing and analysis for inclusion in the state DNA identification index. Such laboratory shall promptly perform the requisite testing and analysis, and forward the resulting DNA record only to the state DNA identification index in accordance with the regulations of the division of criminal justice services. Such laboratory shall perform DNA analysis only for those markers having value for law enforcement identification purposes. For the purposes of this article, the term "marker" shall have the meaning generally ascribed to it by members of the scientific community experienced in the use of DNA technology.

6. DNA records contained in the state DNA identification index shall be released only for the following purposes:

(a) to a federal law enforcement agency, or to a state or local law enforcement agency or district attorney's office for law enforcement identification purposes upon submission of a DNA record in connection with the investigation of the commission of one or more crimes or to assist in the recovery or identification of specified human remains, including identification of missing persons, provided that there exists between the division and such agency a written agreement governing the use and dissemination of such DNA records in accordance with the provisions of this article;

(b) for criminal defense purposes, to a defendant or his or her representative, who shall also have access to samples and analyses performed in connection with the case in which such defendant is charged;

(c) after personally identifiable information has been removed by the division, to an entity authorized by the division for the purpose of creating or maintaining a population statistics database or for identification research and protocol development for forensic DNA analysis or quality control purposes.

7. Requests for DNA records must be in writing, or in a form prescribed by the division authorized by the requesting party, and, other than a request pursuant to paragraph (b) of subdivision six of this section, maintained on file at the state DNA identification index in accordance with rules and regulations promulgated by the commissioner of the division of criminal justice services.

8. The defendant, including the representative of a defendant, in a criminal action or proceeding shall have access to information in the state DNA identification index relating to the number of requests previously made for a comparison search and the name and identity of any requesting party.

9.   (a) Upon receipt of notification of a reversal or a vacatur of a conviction, or of the granting of a pardon pursuant to article two-A of this chapter, of an individual whose DNA record has been stored in the state DNA identification index in accordance with this article by the division of criminal justice services, the DNA record shall be expunged from the state DNA identification index, and such individual may apply to the court in which the judgment of conviction was originally entered for an order directing the expungement of any DNA record and any samples, analyses, or other documents relating to the DNA testing of such individual in connection with the investigation or prosecution of the crime which resulted in the conviction that was reversed or vacated or for which the pardon was granted. A copy of such application shall be served on the district attorney and an order directing expungement may be granted if the court finds that all appeals relating to the conviction have been concluded; that such individual will not be retried, or, if a retrial has occurred, the trier of fact has rendered a verdict of complete acquittal, and that expungement will not adversely affect the investigation or prosecution of some other person or persons for the crime. The division shall, by rule or regulation, prescribe procedures to ensure that the DNA record in the state DNA identification index, and any samples, analyses, or other documents relating to such record, whether in the possession of the division, or any law enforcement or police agency, or any forensic DNA laboratory, including any duplicates or copies thereof, at the discretion of the possessor thereof, are either destroyed or returned to such individual, or to the attorney who represented him or her at the time such reversal, vacatur or pardon, was granted. The commissioner shall also adopt by rule and regulation a procedure for the expungement in other appropriate circumstances of DNA records contained in the index.

(b) As prescribed in this paragraph, if an individual, either voluntarily or pursuant to a warrant or order of a court, has provided a sample for DNA testing in connection with the investigation or prosecution of a crime and (i) no criminal action against the individual relating to such crime was commenced within the period specified by section 30.10 of the criminal procedure law, or (ii) a criminal action was commenced against the individual relating to such crime which resulted in a complete acquittal, or (iii) a criminal action against the individual relating to such crime resulted in a conviction that was subsequently reversed or vacated, or for which the individual was granted a pardon pursuant to article two-A of this chapter, such individual may apply to the supreme court or the court in which the judgment of conviction was originally entered for an order directing the expungement of any DNA record and any samples, analyses, or other documents relating to the DNA testing of such individual in connection with the investigation or prosecution of such crime. A copy of such application shall be served on the district attorney and an order directing expungement may be granted if the court finds that the individual has satisfied the conditions of one of the subparagraphs of this paragraph; that if a judgment of conviction was reversed or vacated, all appeals relating thereto have been concluded and the individual will not be retried, or, if a retrial has occurred, the trier of fact has rendered a verdict of complete acquittal, and that expungement will not adversely affect the investigation or prosecution of some other person or persons for the crime. If an order directing the expungement of any DNA record and any samples, analyses or other documents relating to the DNA testing of such individual is issued, such record and any samples, analyses, or other documents shall, at the discretion of the possessor thereof, be destroyed or returned to such individual or to the attorney who represented him or her in connection with the application for the order of expungement.

Added by L. 1994, Ch. 737, § 1, eff. Jan. 1, 1996, and shall apply to any designated offenders who are convicted on or after that date, pursuant to L. 1994, Ch. 737, § 3; **Amended** by L. 1999, Ch. 560, §§ 3 and 4, amending subds. 3 and 5, eff. Dec. 1, 1999; L. 2002, Ch. 524, § 1, amending subd. 9, eff. Sept. 17, 2002; L. 2004, Ch. 576, § 2, eff. July 6, 2004, amending subd. 3.

ANNOTATIONS

Expungement of records.—Petitioner unsuccessfully moved pursuant to Article 78 proceeding in nature of mandamus to expunge all records pertaining to petitioner's DNA sample pursuant to this section, court determined that petitioner failed to demonstrate clear right to relief. Midgley v. Goldberg, 2 A.D.3d 735, 768 N.Y.S.2d 624 (2d Dept. 2003).

Probable cause required for subsequent blood tests.— People established probable cause for order authorizing another blood sample from defendant after blood sample for DNA testing, obtained from defendant after a conviction for an unrelated crime pursuant to § 995-c, resulted in a "potential investigative lead" when entered into DNA profile—a match between defendant's DNA profile and semen sample taken from victim. People v. Afrika, 13 A.D.3d 1218, 787 N.Y.S.2d 774 (4th Dept. 2004).

Retroactive application of amendments upheld.—Since DNA information index is to be used in future investigations to assist investigators and not to punish, the retroactive application of amendment comports with the Ex Post Facto Clause. Kellogg v. Travis, 100 N.Y.2d 407, 764 N.Y.S.2d 376, 796 N.E.2d 467 (2003).

§ 995-d. Confidentiality.

1. All records, findings, reports, and results of DNA testing performed on any person shall be confidential and may not be disclosed or redisclosed without the consent of the subject of such DNA testing. Such records, findings, reports and results shall not be released to insurance companies, employers or potential employers, health providers, employment screening or personnel companies, agencies, or services, private investigation services, and may not be disclosed in response to a subpoena or other compulsory legal process or warrant, or upon request or order of any agency, authority, division, office, corporation, partnership, or any other private or public entity or person, except that nothing contained herein shall prohibit disclosure in response to a subpoena issued on behalf of the subject of such DNA record or on behalf of a party in a civil proceeding where the subject of such DNA record has put such record in issue.

2. Notwithstanding the provisions of subdivision one of this section, records, findings, reports, and results of DNA testing, other than a DNA record maintained in the state DNA identification index, may be disclosed in a criminal proceeding to the court, the prosecution, and the defense pursuant to a written request on a form prescribed by the commissioner of the division of criminal justice services. Notwithstanding the provisions of subdivision one of this section, a DNA record maintained in the state DNA identification index may be disclosed pursuant to section nine hundred ninety-five-c of this article.

Amended by L. 1999, Ch. 560, § 5, amending subd. 2, eff. Dec. 1, 1999.

§ 995-e. Applicability.

This article shall not apply to a forensic DNA laboratory operated by any agency of the federal government, or to any forensic DNA test performed by any such federal laboratory.

§ 995-f. Penalties.

Any person who (a) intentionally discloses a DNA record, or the results of a forensic DNA test or analysis, to an individual or agency other than one authorized to have access to such records pursuant to this article or (b) intentionally uses or receives DNA records, or the results of a forensic DNA test or analysis, for purposes other than those authorized pursuant to this article or (c) any person who knowingly tampers or attempts to tamper with any DNA sample or the collection container without lawful authority shall be guilty of a class E felony.

Amended by L. 1999, Ch. 560, § 6, eff. Dec. 1, 1999.

MISC. LAWS

FAMILY COURT ACT

(ARTS. 3, 7, 8, 10)

(Uniform Rules for the New York State Trial Courts—PART 205—Uniform Rules for the Family Court—are set forth in Part 3, Miscellaneous Court Rules, *infra*.)

ARTICLE 3

JUVENILE DELINQUENCY

Summary of Article

Part 1. Jurisdiction and preliminary procedures

§ 301.1. Purpose.

The purpose of this article is to establish procedures in accordance with due process of law (a) to determine whether a person is a juvenile delinquent and (b) to issue an appropriate order of disposition for any person who is adjudged a juvenile delinquent. In any proceeding under this article, the court shall consider the needs and best interests of the respondent as well as the need for protection of the community.

ANNOTATION

Construction.—Family Court is not precluded from reference to either case law interpretations of the CPL or the CPL itself in construing the Family Court Act speedy trial provisions. *In re* Rodney M., 130 Misc. 2d 928, 498 N.Y.S.2d 272 (Fam. Ct. Richmond Co. 1986).

§ 301.2. Definitions.

As used in this article, the following terms shall have the following meanings:

1. "Juvenile delinquent" means a person over seven and less than sixteen years of age, who, having committed an act that would constitute a crime if committed by an adult, (a) is not criminally responsible for such conduct by reason of infancy, or (b) is the defendant in an action ordered removed from a criminal court to the family court pursuant to article seven hundred twenty-five of the criminal procedure law.

2. "Respondent" means the person against whom a juvenile delinquency petition is filed pursuant to section 310.1. Provided, however, that any act of the respondent required or authorized under this article may be performed by his attorney or law guardian unless expressly provided otherwise.

3. "Detention" means the temporary care and maintenance of children away from their own homes as defined in section five hundred two of the executive law. Detention of a person alleged to be or adjudicated as a juvenile delinquent shall be authorized only in a facility certified by the division for youth as a detention facility pursuant to section five hundred three of the executive law.

4. "Secure detention facility" means a facility characterized by physically restricting construction, hardware and procedures.

5. "Non-secure detention facility" means a facility characterized by the absence of physically restricting construction, hardware and procedures.

6. "Fact-finding hearing" means a hearing to determine whether the respondent or respondents committed the crime or crimes alleged in the petition or petitions.

7. "Dispositional hearing" means a hearing to determine whether the respondent requires supervision, treatment or confinement.

8. "Designated felony act" means an act which, if done by an adult, would be a crime: (i) defined in sections 125.27 (murder in the first degree); 125.25 (murder in the second degree); 135.25 (kidnapping in the first degree); or 150.20 (arson in the first degree) of the penal law committed by a person thirteen, fourteen or fifteen years of age; (ii) defined in sections 120.10 (assault in the first degree); 125.20 (manslaughter in the first degree); 130.35 (rape in the first degree); 130.50 (criminal sexual act in the first degree); 130.70 (aggravated sexual abuse in the first degree); 135.20 (kidnapping in the second degree) but only where the abduction involved the use or threat of use of deadly physical force; 150.15 (arson in the second degree) or 160.15 (robbery in the first degree) of the penal law committed by a person thirteen, fourteen or fifteen years of age; (iii) defined in the penal law as an attempt to commit murder in the first or second degree or kidnapping in the first degree committed by a person thirteen, fourteen or fifteen years of age; (iv) defined in section 140.30 (burglary in the first degree); subdivision one of section 140.25 (burglary in the second degree); subdivision two of section 160.10 (robbery in the second degree) of the penal law; subdivision four of section 265.02 of the penal law, where such firearm is possessed on school grounds, as that phrase is defined in subdivision fourteen of section 220.00 of the penal law; or section 265.03 of the penal law, where such machine gun or such firearm is possessed on school grounds, as that phrase is defined in subdivision fourteen of section 220.00 of the penal law committed by a person fourteen or fifteen years of age; (v) defined in section 120.05 (assault in the second degree) or 160.10 (robbery in the second degree) of the penal law committed by a person fourteen or fifteen years of age but only where there has been a prior finding by a court that such person has

previously committed an act which, if committed by an adult, would be the crime of assault in the second degree, robbery in the second degree or any designated felony act specified in paragraph (i), (ii), or (iii) of this subdivision regardless of the age of such person at the time of the commission of the prior act; or (vi) other than a misdemeanor committed by a person at least seven but less than sixteen years of age, but only where there has been two prior findings by the court that such person has committed a prior felony.

9. "Designated class A felony act" means a designated felony act defined in paragraph (i) of subdivision eight.

10. "Secure facility" means a residential facility in which the respondent may be placed under this article, which is characterized by physically restricting construction, hardware and procedures, and is designated as a secure facility by the division for youth.

11. "Restrictive placement" means a placement pursuant to section 353.5.

12. "Presentment agency" means the agency or authority which pursuant to section two hundred fifty-four or two hundred fifty-four-a is responsible for presenting a juvenile delinquency petition.

13. "Incapacitated person" means a respondent who, as a result of mental illness, mental retardation or developmental disability as defined in subdivisions twenty, twenty-one and twenty-two of section 1.03 of the mental hygiene law, lacks capacity to understand the proceedings against him or to assist in his own defense.

14. Any reference in this article to the commission of a crime includes any act which, if done by an adult, would constitute a crime.

15. "Aggravated circumstances" shall have the same meaning as the definition of such term in subdivision (j) of section one thousand twelve of this act.

16. "Permanency hearing" means an initial hearing or subsequent hearing held in accordance with the provisions of this article for the purpose of reviewing the foster care status of the respondent and the appropriateness of the permanency plan developed by the commissioner of social services or the office of children and family services.

17. "Designated educational official" shall mean (a) an employee or representative of a school district who is designated by the school district or (b) an employee or representative of a charter school or private elementary or secondary school who is designated by such school to receive records pursuant to this article and to coordinate the student's participation in programs which may exist in the school district or community, including: non-violent conflict resolution programs, peer mediation programs and youth

courts, extended day programs and other school violence prevention and intervention programs which may exist in the school district or community. Such notification shall be kept separate and apart from such student's school records and shall be accessible only by the designated educational official. Such notification shall not be part of such student's permanent school record and shall not be appended to or included in any documentation regarding such student and shall be destroyed at such time as such student is no longer enrolled in the school district. At no time shall such notification be used for any purpose other than those specified in this subdivision.

Amended by L. 1983, Ch. 398, eff. July 1, 1983; L. 1985, Ch. 663, eff. Aug. 27, 1985; L. 1987, Ch. 419, eff. Sept. 1, 1987; L. 1992, Ch. 465, eff. Jan. 14, 1992, amending subd. 3, and shall apply to all persons placed in or committed to the custody of the division of youth on or after such date; L. 1998, Ch. 435, § 8, eff. Nov. 1, 1998, amending subd. 8; L. 1999, Ch. 7, eff. Feb. 11, 1999, adding subds. 15 and 16; L. 2000, Ch. 8, § 17, eff. Nov. 1, 2000, adding subd. 17; L. 2001, Ch. 380, § 8, eff. Oct. 23, 2001, and deemed in full force and effect on and after Nov. 1, 2000, amending subd. 17; L. 2003, Ch. 264, § 59, eff. Nov. 1, 2003, amending subd. 8(ii); L. 2005, Ch. 3, Part B, § 1, eff. Nov. 21, 2005, amending subd. 15.

ANNOTATIONS

Designated felony act.—The plain language of FCA § 301.2(8) requires only "two prior findings" of prior felonies, and the existence of dispositional orders is irrelevant. It was therefore irrelevant that two prior findings of felonies were combined into a single order of disposition. In re Manuel R., 227 A.D.2d 355, 642 N.Y.S.2d 902 (1st Dept. 1996), aff'd, 89 N.Y.2d 1043, 659 N.Y.S.2d 825, 681 N.E.2d 1271 (1997).

"Designated felony act"; jurisdiction.—The Family Court and the criminal justice system have concurrent original jurisdiction over the overlapping crimes defined in CPL § 1.20(42), PL § 10.00(18), PL § 30.00(2), and FCA § 301.2(8), and the district attorney's decision not to prosecute the matter did not bar the designated felony petition from being presented in Family Court. In re Meleick H., 170 Misc. 2d 230, 647 N.Y.S.2d 669 (Fam. Ct. Kings Co. 1996).

Policy underlying adjudication of juvenile delinquents.—Individual is adjudged a juvenile delinquent because he or she "committed an act that would constitute a crime if committed by an adult"; State may not be held liable in negligence for injuries inflicted by the adjudicated juvenile delinquent who escaped from the Division for Youth facility. Sebastian v. State, 93 N.Y.2d 790, 698 N.Y.S.2d 601, 720 N.E.2d 878 (1999).

—Juvenile delinquency proceeding must be predicated on conduct that would constitute a crime, not merely a violation. In re Elizabeth G., 280 A.D.2d 478, 721 N.Y.S.2d 65 (2d Dept. 2001).

§ 301.3. Applicability of article to actions and matters occurring before and after effective date.

1. The provisions of this article apply exclusively to:

(a) all juvenile delinquency actions and proceedings commenced upon or after the effective date thereof and all appeals and other post-judgment proceedings relating or attaching thereto; and

(b) all matters of juvenile delinquency procedure prescribed in this article which do not constitute a part of any particular action or case occurring upon or after such effective date.

MISC. LAWS

2. The provisions of this article apply to:

(a) all juvenile delinquency actions and proceedings commenced prior to the effective date thereof but still pending on such date; and

(b) all appeals and other post-judgment proceedings commenced upon or after such effective date which relate or attach to juvenile delinquency actions and proceedings commenced or concluded prior to such effective date provided that, if application of such provisions in any particular case would not be feasible or would work injustice, the provisions of article seven pertaining to juvenile delinquency actions apply thereto, as such article seven read immediately prior to the effective date of this article.

3. The provisions of this article do not impair or render ineffectual any proceedings or procedural matters which occurred prior to the effective date thereof.

Amended by L. 1983, Ch. 398, eff. July 1, 1983.

§ 301.4. Separability clause.

If any clause, sentence, paragraph, section or part of this article shall be adjudged by any court of competent jurisdiction to be invalid, such judgment shall not affect, impair, or invalidate the remainder thereof, but shall be confined in its operation to the clause, sentence, paragraph, section or part thereof directly involved in the controversy in which such judgment shall have been rendered.

§ 302.1. Jurisdiction.

1. The family court has exclusive original jurisdiction over any proceeding to determine whether a person is a juvenile delinquent.

2. In determining the jurisdiction of the court the age of such person at the time the delinquent act allegedly was committed is controlling.

ANNOTATION

Jurisdiction; generally.—Family Court lacks jurisdiction over counts in a juvenile delinquency petition that charged respondent with acts which, if committed by an adult, would constitute the crime of first degree assault, where respondent was not first charged in New York City Criminal Court as a juvenile offender and then removed to Family Court. *In re* Elizabeth R., 169 Misc. 2d 58, 646 N.Y.S.2d 240 (Fam. Ct. New York Co. 1996).

§ 302.2. Statute of limitations.

A juvenile delinquency proceeding must be commenced within the period of limitation prescribed in section 30.10 of the criminal procedure law or, unless the alleged act is a designated felony as defined in subdivision eight of section 301.2, commenced before the respondent's eighteenth birthday, whichever occurs earlier. When the alleged act constitutes a designated felony as defined in subdivision eight of section 301.2 such proceeding must be commenced within such period of limitation or before the respondent's twentieth birthday, whichever occurs earlier.

§ 302.3. Venue.

1. Juvenile delinquency proceedings shall be originated in the county in which the act or acts referred to in the petition allegedly occurred. For purposes of determining venue, article twenty of the criminal procedure law shall apply.

2. Upon motion of the respondent or the appropriate presentment agency the family court in which the proceedings have been originated may order, for good cause shown, that the proceeding be transferred to another county. If the order is issued after motion by the presentment agency, the court may impose such conditions as it deems equitable and appropriate to ensure that the transfer does not subject the respondent to an unreasonable burden in making his defense.

3. Any motion made pursuant to subdivision two by the respondent shall be made within the time prescribed by section 332.2. Any such motion by a presentment agency must be based upon papers stating the ground therefor and must be made within thirty days from the date that the action was originated unless such time is extended for good cause shown.

4. Except for designated felony act petitions, after entering a finding pursuant to subdivision one of section 345.1, and prior to the commencement of the dispositional hearing the court may, in its discretion and for good cause shown, order that the proceeding be transferred to the county in which the respondent resides. The court shall not order such a transfer, however, unless it grants the respondent and the presentment agency an opportunity to state on the record whether each approves or disapproves of such a transfer and the reasons therefor. The court shall take into consideration the provisions of subdivisions two and three of section 340.2 in determining such transfer.

Amended by L. 1999, Ch. 173, eff. Oct. 4, 1999, amending subd. 4.

§ 303.1. Criminal procedure law.

1. The provisions of the criminal procedure law shall not apply to proceedings under this article unless the applicability of such provisions are specifically prescribed by this act.

2. A court may, however, consider judicial interpretations of appropriate provisions of the criminal procedure law to the extent that such interpretations may assist the court in interpreting similar provisions of this article.

§ 303.2. Double jeopardy.

The provisions of article forty of the criminal procedure law concerning double jeopardy shall apply to juvenile delinquency proceedings.

§ 303.3. Defenses.

The provisions of articles twenty-five, thirty-five and forty and section 30.05 of the penal law shall be applicable to juvenile delinquency proceedings.

§ 304.1. Detention.

1. A facility certified by the state division for youth as a juvenile facility must be operated in conformity with the regulations of the state division for youth and shall be subject to the visitation and inspection of the state board of social welfare.

2. No child to whom the provisions of this article may apply shall be detained in any prison, jail, lockup, or other place used for adults convicted of crime or under arrest and charged with crime without the approval of the state division for youth in the case of each child and the statement of its reasons therefor. The state division for youth shall promulgate and publish the rules which it shall apply in determining whether approval should be granted pursuant to this subdivision.

3. The detention of a child under ten years of age in a secure detention facility shall not be directed under any of the provisions of this article.

4. A detention facility which receives a child under subdivision four of section 305.2. shall immediately notify the child's parent or other person legally responsible for his care or, if such legally responsible person is unavailable, the person with whom the child resides, that he has been placed in detention.

Amended by L. 1982, Ch. 926, eff. July 1, 1983; L. 1983, eff. July 1, 1983; L. 1987, Ch. 419, eff. Sept. 1, 1987.

§ 304.2. Temporary order of protection.

(1) Upon application by the presentment agency, the court may issue a temporary order of protection against a respondent for good cause shown, *ex parte* or upon notice, at any time after a juvenile is taken into custody, pursuant to section 305.1 or 305.2 or upon the issuance of an appearance ticket pursuant to section 307.1 or upon the filing of a petition pursuant to section 310.1.

(2) A temporary order of protection may contain any of the provisions authorized on the making of an order of protection under section 352.3.

(3) A temporary order of protection is not a finding of wrongdoing.

(4) A temporary order of protection may remain in effect until an order of disposition is entered.

Amended by L. 1984, Ch. 683, eff. Aug. 31, 1984.

§ 305.1. Custody by a private person.

1. A private person may take a child under the age of sixteen into custody in cases in which he may arrest an adult for a crime under section 140.30 of the criminal procedure law.

2. Before taking such child under the age of sixteen into custody, a private person must inform the child of the cause thereof and require him to submit, except when he is taken into custody on pursuit immediately after the commission of a crime.

3. After taking such child into custody, a private person must take the child, without unnecessary delay, to the child's home, to a family court, or to a police officer or peace officer.

Amended by L. 1983, Ch. 398, eff. July 1, 1983.

§ 305.2. Custody by a peace officer or a police officer without a warrant.

1. For purposes of this section, the word "officer" means a peace officer or a police officer.

2. An officer may take a child under the age of sixteen into custody without a warrant in cases in which he may arrest a person for a crime under article one hundred forty of the criminal procedure law.

3. If an officer takes such child into custody or if a child is delivered to him under section 305.1, he shall immediately notify the parent or other person legally responsible for the child's care, or if such legally responsible person is unavailable the person with whom the child resides, that the child has been taken into custody.

4. After making every reasonable effort to give notice under subdivision three, the officer shall:

(a) release the child to the custody of his parents or other person legally responsible for his care upon the issuance in accordance with section 307.1 of a family court appearance ticket to the child and the person to whose custody the child is released; or

(b) forthwith and with all reasonable speed take the child directly, and without his first being taken to the police station house, to the family court located in the county in which the act occasioning the taking into custody allegedly was committed, unless the officer determines that it is necessary to question the child, in which case he may take the child to a facility designated by the chief administrator of the courts as a suitable place for the questioning of children or, upon the consent of a parent or other person legally responsible for the care of the child, to the child's residence and there question him for a reasonable period of time; or

(c) take the child to a place certified by the state division for youth as a juvenile detention facility for the reception of children.

5. If such child has allegedly committed a

MISC. LAWS

designated felony act as defined in subdivision eight of section 301.2, and the family court in the county is in session, the officer shall forthwith take the child directly to such family court unless the officer takes the child to a facility for questioning in accordance with paragraph (b) of subdivision four. If such child has not allegedly committed a designated felony act and such family court is in session, the officer shall either forthwith take the child directly to such family court unless the officer takes the child to a facility for questioning in accordance with paragraph (b) of subdivision four or release the child in accordance with paragraph (a) of subdivision four.

6. In all other cases, and in the absence of special circumstances, the officer shall release the child in accordance with paragraph (a) of subdivision four.

7. A child shall not be questioned pursuant to this section unless he and a person required to be notified pursuant to subdivision three if present, have been advised:

(a) of the child's right to remain silent;

(b) that the statements made by the child may be used in a court of law;

(c) of the child's right to have an attorney present at such questioning; and

(d) of the child's right to have an attorney provided for him without charge if he is indigent.

8. In determining the suitability of questioning and determining the reasonable period of time for questioning such a child, the child's age, the presence or absence of his parents or other persons legally responsible for his care and notification pursuant to subdivision three shall be included among relevant considerations.

Amended by L. 1983, Ch. 398, eff. July 1, 1983; L. 1985, Ch. 663, eff. Aug. 27, 1985; L. 1987, Ch. 492, eff. July 30, 1987.

ANNOTATIONS

Proper detention.—An officer's reasonable suspicion justifies detention of a juvenile if it is supported by probable cause to believe that the juvenile may be a runaway. *In re* Marrhonda G., 81 N.Y.2d 942, 597 N.Y.S.2d 662, 663, 613 N.E.2d 568 (1993).

Refusal of parent to respond.—Repeated refusal of petitioner's mother to go to police precinct upon notification of her son's detention pursuant to FCA § 305.2(c) removed police officer's duty to advise her of her son's rights over the phone prior to advising her son of those rights. *In re* Johnnie A., 253 A.D.2d 579, 679 N.Y.S.2d 1 (1st Dept. 1998).

§ 306.1. Fingerprinting of certain alleged juvenile delinquents.

1. Following the arrest of a child alleged to be a juvenile delinquent, or the filing of a delinquency petition involving a child who has not been arrested, the arresting officer or other appropriate police officer or agency shall take or cause to be taken fingerprints of such child if:

(a) the child is eleven years of age or older

and the crime which is the subject of the arrest or which is charged in the petition constitutes a class A or B felony; or

(b) the child is thirteen years of age or older and the crime which is the subject of the arrest or which is charged in the petition constitutes a class C, D or E felony.

2. Whenever fingerprints are required to be taken pursuant to subdivision one, the photograph and palmprints of the arrested child may also be taken.

3. The taking of fingerprints, palmprints, photographs, and related information concerning the child and the facts and circumstances of the acts charged in the juvenile delinquency proceeding shall be in accordance with standards established by the commissioner of the division of criminal justice services and by applicable provisions of this article.

4. Upon the taking of fingerprints pursuant to subdivision one the appropriate officer or agency shall, without unnecessary delay, forward such fingerprints to the division of criminal justice services and shall not retain such fingerprints or any copy thereof. Copies of photographs and palmprints taken pursuant to this section shall be kept confidential and only in the exclusive possession of such law enforcement agency, separate and apart from files of adults.

Amended by L. 1996, Ch. 645, § 1, amending subd. 1, eff. Sept. 13, 1996, and applying retroactively to a person whose fingerprints were taken pursuant to section 306.1 of the family court act or who was initially fingerprinted as a juvenile offender on or after January 1, 1986 and whose fingerprints are on file with the division of criminal justice services, provided that in the case of a juvenile offender action the case was subsequently removed to family court, pursuant to L. 1996, Ch. 645, § 6.

ANNOTATION

When required.—In the case of the adoption of a minor child who had previously been placed in the same home for foster case, the court was permitted to waive the fingerprinting of the prospective mother's 16-year-old son, who had no criminal record and who objected to the fingerprinting, which is neither required by the Social Services Law nor Family Court Act § 306.1, as that section only authorizes the fingerprinting of juveniles over the age of 11 who have committed a felony. *In re* Paul Y., 182 Misc. 2d 65, 696 N.Y.S.2d 796 (Fam. Ct. Queens Co. 1999).

§ 306.2. Fingerprinting; duties of the division of criminal justice services.

1. Upon receipt of fingerprints taken pursuant to section 306.1. the division of criminal justice services shall retain such fingerprints distinctly identifiable from adult criminal records except as provided in section 354.1 and shall not release such fingerprints to a federal depository or to any person except as authorized by this act. The division shall promulgate regulations to protect the confidentiality of such fingerprints and related information and to prevent access thereto, by, and

the distribution thereof to, persons not authorized by law.

2. Upon receipt of such fingerprints, the division of criminal justice services shall classify them and search its records for information concerning an adjudication or pending matter involving the person arrested. The division shall promptly transmit to such forwarding officer or agency a report containing any information on file with respect to such person's previous adjudications and pending matters or a report stating that the person arrested has no previous record according to its files. Notwithstanding the foregoing, where the division has not received disposition information within two years of an arrest, the division shall, until such information or up-to-date status information is received, withhold the record of that arrest and any related activity in disseminating criminal history information.

3. Upon receipt of a report of the division of criminal justice services pursuant to this section, the recipient office or agency must promptly transmit two copies of such report to the family court in which the proceeding may be originated and two copies thereof to the presentment agency who shall furnish a copy thereof to counsel for the respondent or to the respondent's law guardian.

Amended by L. 1983, Ch. 398, eff. July 1, 1983; L. 1996, Ch. 645, § 2, amending subd. 2, eff. Sept. 13, 1996, and applying retroactively to a person whose fingerprints were taken pursuant to section 306.1 of the family court act or who was initially fingerprinted as a juvenile offender on or after January 1, 1986 and whose fingerprints are on file with the division of criminal justice services, provided that in the case of a juvenile offender action the case was subsequently removed to family court, pursuant to L. 1996, Ch. 645, § 6.

§ 307.1. Family court appearance ticket.

1. A family court appearance ticket is a written notice issued and subscribed by a peace officer or police officer, a probation service director or his designee or the administrator responsible for operating a detention facility or his designee, directing a child and his parent or other person legally responsible for his care to appear, without security, at a designated probation service on a specified return date in connection with the child's alleged commission of the crime or crimes specified on such appearance ticket. The form of a family court appearance ticket shall be prescribed by rules of the chief administrator of the courts.

2. If the crime alleged to have been committed by the child is a designated felony as defined by subdivision eight of section 301.2. the return date shall be no later than seventy-two hours excluding Saturdays, Sundays and public holidays after issuance of such family court appearance ticket. If the crime alleged to have been committed by such child is not a designated felony, the return date shall be no later than fourteen days after the issuance of such appearance ticket.

3. A copy of the family court appearance ticket shall be forwarded by the issuing person or agency to the complainant, respondent, respondent's parent, and appropriate probation service within twenty-four hours after its issuance.

Amended by L. 1983, Ch. 398, eff. July 1, 1983.

§ 307.2. Appearance ticket procedures.

1. If a child fails to appear on the return date specified on a family court appearance ticket, the probation service may refer the matter forthwith to the appropriate presentment agency or may, in its discretion, attempt to secure the attendance of the child. Upon exercise of its discretion, probation services shall take appropriate action under law including, but not limited to, written notification to the child and parent or other person legally responsible for his care or telephone communications with the child and parent or other person legally responsible for his care. Efforts to secure the attendance of the child shall not extend beyond seven days subsequent to such return date and the probation service must refer the matter to the appropriate presentment agency within such period. Upon referral, the presentment agency may take whatever action it deems appropriate, including the filing of a petition pursuant to section 311.1.

2. If the complainant fails to appear on the return date specified on such appearance ticket, the probation service may in its discretion, attempt to secure his voluntary attendance. Upon exercise of its discretion, probation services may take appropriate action under law including, but not limited to, written notification to the complainant or telephone communications with the complainant. Efforts to secure the voluntary attendance of such person shall not extend beyond seven days subsequent to such return date and the probation service shall refer the matter to the appropriate presentment agency within such period. Upon referral, the presentment agency may take whatever action it deems appropriate, including the issuance of a subpoena or the filing of a petition pursuant to section 311.1.

3. If a petition is filed subsequent to the issuance of an appearance ticket the appearance ticket shall be made part of the probation service file.

Amended by L. 1983, Ch. 398, eff. July 1, 1983; L. 1985, Ch. 586, eff. July 28, 1985.

§ 307.3. Rules of court authorizing release before filing of petition.

1. The agency responsible for operating a detention facility pursuant to section two hundred eighteen-a of the county law, five hundred ten-a of the executive law or other applicable provisions of law, shall release a child in custody before the filing of a petition to the custody of his parents or other person legally responsible for

MISC. LAWS

his care, or if such legally responsible person is unavailable, to a person with whom he resides, when the events occasioning the taking into custody do not appear to involve allegations that the child committed a delinquent act.

2. When practicable such agency may release a child before the filing of a petition to the custody of his parents or other person legally responsible for his care, or if such legally responsible person is unavailable, to a person with whom he resides, when the events occasioning the taking into custody appear to involve allegations that the child committed a delinquent act.

3. If a child is released under this section, the child and the person legally responsible for his care shall be issued a family court appearance ticket in accordance with section 307.1.

4. If the agency for any reason does not release a child under this section, such child shall be brought before the appropriate family court within seventy-two hours or the next day the court is in session, whichever is sooner. Such agency shall thereupon file an application for an order pursuant to section 307.4 and shall forthwith serve a copy of the application upon the appropriate present-ment agency. Nothing in this subdivision shall preclude the adjustment of suitable cases pursuant to section 308.1.

Amended by L. 1987, Ch. 419, eff. Sept. 1, 1987.

§ 307.4. Hearing following detention.

1. If a child in custody is brought before a judge of the family court before a petition is filed upon a written application pursuant to subdivision four of section 307.3, the judge shall hold a hearing for the purpose of making a preliminary determination of whether the court appears to have jurisdiction over the child.

2. At such hearing the court must appoint a law guardian to represent the child pursuant to the provisions of section two hundred forty-nine if independent legal representation is not available to such child.

3. The provisions of sections 320.3 and 341.2 shall apply at such hearing.

4. After such hearing, the judge shall order the release of the child to the custody of his parent or other person legally responsible for his care if:

(a) the court does not appear to have jurisdic-tion, or

(b) the events occasioning the taking into custody do not appear to involve allegations that the child committed a delinquent act, or

(c) the events occasioning the taking into custody appear to involve acts which constitute juvenile delinquency, unless the court finds and states facts and reasons which would support a detention order pursuant to section 320.5.

5. Such hearing shall be held within seventy-two hours of the time detention commenced or the next day the court is in session, whichever is sooner.

6. The appropriate presentment agency shall present the application at a hearing pursuant to this section.

7. A petition shall be filed and a probable-cause hearing held under section 325.1 within four days of the conclusion of a hearing under this section. If a petition is not filed within four days the child shall be released.

8. Upon a finding of facts and reasons which support a detention order pursuant to section 320.5 of this chapter, the court shall also deter-mine and state in any order directing detention:

(a) whether the continuation of the child in the child's home would be contrary to the best inter-ests of the child based upon, and limited to, the facts and circumstances available to the court at the time of the hearing held in accordance with this section; and

(b) where appropriate and consistent with the need for protection of the community, whether reasonable efforts were made prior to the date of the court hearing that resulted in the detention order issued in accordance with this section to prevent or eliminate the need for removal of the child from his or her home or, if the child had been removed from his or her home prior to the initial appearance, where appropriate and consis-tent with the need for protection of the commu-nity, whether reasonable efforts were made to make it possible for the child to safely return home.

Amended by L. 1987, Ch. 419, eff. Sept. 1, 1987; L. 2000, Ch. 145, eff. July 1, 2000.

ANNOTATION

Purpose of hearing.—Pre-petition detention application filed by detention facility requires that a juvenile be afforded a hearing within four days or the juvenile must be released; purpose of the hearing is to evaluate the reasons for the continuation of detention prior to the filing of the petition to adjudicate youth a juvenile delinquent. *In re* Benjamin L., 92 N.Y.2d 660, 685 N.Y.S.2d 400, 708 N.E.2d 156 (1998).

§ 308.1. Rules of court for preliminary procedure.

1. Rules of court shall authorize and determine the circumstances under which the probation service may confer with any person seeking to have a juvenile delinquency petition filed, the potential respondent and other interested persons concerning the advisability of requesting that a petition be filed.

2. Except as provided in subdivisions three and four, the probation service may, in accor-dance with rules of court, adjust suitable cases before a petition is filed. The inability of the respondent or his or her family to make restitution shall not be a factor in a decision to adjust a case

or in a recommendation to the presentment agency pursuant to subdivision six of this section. Nothing in this section shall prohibit the probation service or the court from directing a respondent to obtain employment and to make restitution from the earnings from such employment.

3. The probation service shall not adjust a case in which the child has allegedly committed a designated felony act unless it has received the written approval of the court.

4. The probation service shall not adjust a case in which the child has allegedly committed a delinquent act which would be a crime defined in section 120.25, (reckless endangerment in the first degree), subdivision one of section 125.15, (manslaughter in the second degree), subdivision one of section 130.25, (rape in the third degree), subdivision one of section 130.40, (criminal sexual act in the third degree), subdivision one or two of section 130.65, (sexual abuse in the first degree), section 135.65, (coercion in the first degree), section 140.20, (burglary in the third degree), section 150.10, (arson in the third degree), section 160.05, (robbery in the third degree), subdivision two, three or four of section 265.02, (criminal possession of a weapon in the third degree), section 265.03, (criminal possession of a weapon in the second degree), or section 265.04, (criminal possession of a dangerous weapon in the first degree) of the penal law where the child has previously had one or more adjustments of a case in which such child allegedly committed an act which would be a crime specified in this subdivision unless it has received written approval from the court and the appropriate presentment agency.

5. The fact that a child is detained prior to the filing of a petition shall not preclude the probation service from adjusting a case; upon adjusting such a case the probation service shall notify the detention facility to release the child.

6. The probation service shall not transmit or otherwise communicate to the presentment agency any statement made by the child to a probation officer. However, the probation service may make a recommendation regarding adjustment of the case to the presentment agency and provide such information, including any report made by the arresting officer and record of previous adjustments and arrests, as it shall deem relevant.

7. No statement made to the probation service prior to the filing of a petition may be admitted into evidence at a fact-finding hearing or, if the proceeding is transferred to a criminal court, at any time prior to a conviction.

8. The probation service may not prevent any person who wishes to request that a petition be filed from having access to the appropriate presentment agency for that purpose.

9. Efforts at adjustment pursuant to rules of court under this section may not extend for a period of more than two months without leave of the court, which may extend the period for an additional two months.

10. If a case is not adjusted by the probation service, such service shall notify the appropriate presentment agency of that fact within forty-eight hours or the next court day, whichever occurs later.

11. The probation service may not be authorized under this section to compel any person to appear at any conference, produce any papers, or visit any place.

12. The probation service shall certify to the division of criminal justice services and to the appropriate police department or law enforcement agency whenever it adjusts a case in which the potential respondent's fingerprints were taken pursuant to section 306.1 in any manner other than the filing of a petition for juvenile delinquency for an act which, if committed by an adult, would constitute a felony, provided, however, in the case of a child eleven or twelve years of age, such certification shall be made only if the act would constitute a class A or B felony.

13. The provisions of this section shall not apply where the petition is an order of removal to the family court pursuant to article seven hundred twenty-five of the criminal procedure law.

Amended by L. 2003, Ch. 264, § 60, eff. Nov. 1, 2003, amending subd. 4.

§ 310.1. Originating a juvenile delinquency proceeding.

1. A proceeding to adjudicate a person a juvenile delinquent is originated by the filing of a petition.

2. Only a presentment agency may originate a juvenile delinquency proceeding.

3. If the appropriate agency does not originate a proceeding within thirty days of receipt of notice from the probation service pursuant to subdivision ten of section 308.1, it shall notify in writing the complainant of that fact.

Amended by L. 1982, Ch. 926, eff. July 1, 1983; L. 1983, Ch. 398, eff. July 1, 1983; L. 2003, Ch. 264, § 60, eff. Nov. 1, 2003, amending subd. 4.

§ 310.2. Speedy trial.

After a petition has been filed, or upon the signing of an order of removal pursuant to section 725.05 of the criminal procedure law, the respondent is entitled to a speedy fact-finding hearing.

Amended by L. 1990, Ch. 223, eff. June 13, 1990.

ANNOTATIONS

Generally.—The statutory time limits for juvenile delinquency proceedings are to be rigorously enforced, with dismissal the appropriate remedy for noncompliance; this rule

MISC. LAWS

applies to the time limits regarding fact-finding hearings as well as dispositional hearings. *In re* Lakiesha Y, 195 A.D.2d 821, 600 N.Y.S.2d 361, 362 (3d Dept. 1993).

Speedy trial.—Although juveniles have a right to a speedy trial, there is no per se rule regarding speedy trial violations; the court must balance the factors enumerated in *People v. Taranovich*, 37 N.Y.2d 442, in determining the merits of a speedy trial claim. *In re* Benjamin L., 92 N.Y.2d 660, 685 N.Y.S.2d 400, 708 N.E.2d 156 (1998).

§ 311.1. The petition; definition and contents.

1. A petition originating a juvenile delinquency proceeding is a written accusation by an authorized presentment agency.

2. A petition shall charge at least one crime and may, in addition, charge in separate counts one or more other crimes, provided that all such crimes are joinable in accord with section 311.6.

3. A petition must contain:

(a) the name of the family court in which it is filed;

(b) the title of the action;

(c) the fact that the respondent is a person under sixteen years of age at the time of the alleged act or acts;

(d) a separate accusation or count addressed to each crime charged, if there be more than one;

(e) the precise crime or crimes charged;

(f) a statement in each count that the crime charged was committed in a designated county;

(g) a statement in each count that the crime charged therein was committed on, or on or about, a designated date, or during a designated period of time;

(h) a plain and concise factual statement in each count which, without allegations of an evidentiary nature, asserts facts supporting every element of the crime charged and the respondent's commission thereof with sufficient precision to clearly apprise the respondent of the conduct which is the subject of the accusation;

(i) the name or names, if known, of other persons who are charged as co-respondents in the family court or as adults in a criminal court proceeding in the commission of the crime or crimes charged;

(j) a statement that the respondent requires supervision, treatment or confinement; and

(k) the signature of the appropriate presentment attorney.

4. A petition shall be verified in accordance with the civil practice law and rules and shall conform to the provisions of section 311.2.

5. If the petition alleges that the respondent committed a designated felony act, if shall so state, and the term "designated felony act petition" shall be prominently marked thereon. Certified copies of prior delinquency findings shall constitute sufficient proof of such findings for the purpose of filing a designated felony petition. If all the allegations of a designated felony act are dismissed or withdrawn or the respondent is found to have committed crimes which are not designated felony acts, the term "designated felony act petition" shall be stricken from the petition.

6. The form of petition shall be prescribed by the chief administrator of the courts. A petition shall be entitled "In the Matter of," followed by the name of the respondent.

7. When an order of removal pursuant to article seven hundred twenty-five of the criminal procedure law is filed with the clerk of the court, such order and those pleadings and proceedings, other than the minutes of any hearing inquiry or trial, grand jury proceeding, or of any plea accepted or entered, held in this action that has not yet been transcribed shall be transferred with it and shall be deemed to be a petition filed pursuant to subdivision one of section 310.1 containing all of the allegations required by this section notwithstanding that such allegations may not be set forth in the manner therein prescribed. Where the order or the grand jury request annexed to the order specified an act that is a designated felony act, the clerk shall annex to the order a sufficient statement and marking to make it a designated felony act petition. The date such order is filed with the clerk of the court shall be deemed the date a petition was filed under this article. For purposes of service in accord with section 312.1, however, only the order of removal shall be deemed the petition. All minutes of any hearing inquiry or trial held in this action, the minutes of any grand jury proceeding and the minutes of any plea accepted and entered shall be transferred to the family court within thirty days.

Amended by L. 1982, Ch. 926, eff. July 1, 1983; L. 1983, Ch. 398, eff. July 1, 1983.

ANNOTATIONS

Amendment of petition.—Amended petition must meet the same requirements as original petition and any defect is non-waivable. If amended petition is facially deficient containing hearsay allegations to support crimes charged, it is jurisdictionally defective and must be dismissed. *In re* Michael C., 238 A.D.2d 680, 656 N.Y.S.2d 412 (3d Dept. 1997).

Defective petition.—Photocopied petition served on appellant did not bear required marking of "Designated Felony" as required; failure to notify appellant adequately of outstanding charges after removal rendered petition jurisdictionally defective and precluded Family Court from rendering a finding. *In re* Jose M., 245 A.D.2d 173, 666 N.Y.S.2d 177 (1st Dept. 1997).

Fair notice.—Juvenile delinquency petitions must satisfy fair notice requirements contained in the state and federal constitutions, thereby stating the precise crime or crimes charged; charging nuisance but then attempting to prove loitering for the purpose of prostitution violates fair notice requirements. *In re* Elizabeth G., 280 A.D.2d 478, 721 N.Y.S.2d 65 (2d Dept. 2001).

Removal orders.—Although § 311.1(7) exempts removal orders from compliance with general requirements for contents of a petition under § 311.1, it does not waive the nonhearsay requirements of § 311.2; removal orders "must be supported by nonhearsay factual allegations to establish every element of the crimes charged and the juvenile's commission of these crimes." *In re* Michael M., 3 N.Y.3d 441, 788 N.Y.S.2d 299, 821 N.E.2d 537 (2004).

Verification.—The Family Court Act does not require that the delinquency petition be verified by the complainant. *In re* Henry M., 194 A.D.2d 606, 599 N.Y.S.2d 291, 292 (2d Dept. 1993).

§ 311.2. Sufficiency of petition.

A petition, or a count thereof, is sufficient on its face when:

1. it substantially conforms to the requirements prescribed in section 311.1; and

2. the allegations of the factual part of the petition, together with those of any supporting depositions which may accompany it, provide reasonable cause to believe that the respondent committed the crime or crimes charged; and

3. non-hearsay allegations of the factual part of the petition or of any supporting depositions establish, if true, every element of each crime charged and the respondent's commission thereof.

ANNOTATIONS

Sufficiency.—Jurisdictional requirements for filing in Family Court are not met when an order of removal and accompanying pleadings and proceedings contain only hearsay allegations; § 311.2 requires "non-hearsay allegations [to] establish, if true, every element of each crime charged and the respondent's commission thereof," and this jurisdictional deficiency is not waivable. *In re* Michael M., 3 N.Y.3d 441, 788 N.Y.S.2d 299, 821 N.E.2d 537 (2004).

—Neither petition nor allocution was defective for failure to specify crime appellant intended to commit when he unlawfully entered victim's premises, as with an adult, People are not required to plead or prove a specific crime was intended, same result with juvenile delinquency proceedings. *In re* Collie W., 309 A.D.2d 611, 765 N.Y.S.2d 611 (1st Dept. 2003).

—Non-hearsay allegations contained in petition, when read together with the supporting deposition, identify that the respondent was the perpetrator and establish every element of the crime charged, petition is sufficient. *In re* Errol D., 241 A.D.2d 732, 660 N.Y.S.2d 185 (3d Dept. 1997).

—Failure of petition to state affirmatively that witness under 12 years old has been judicially determined competent to swear to supporting deposition does not render petition facially insufficient and require dismissal. *In re* Nelson R., 90 N.Y.2d 359, 660 N.Y.S.2d 707, 683 N.E.2d 329 (1997).

—The petition and supporting depositions, taken together, must contain non-hearsay allegations which, if believed, would support a finding beyond a reasonable doubt that respondent had committed the crime charged. Because the petition did not contain any factual allegation establishing that the car in question had a monetary value exceeding $100, the count was properly dismissed. *In re* Basille N., 228 A.D.2d 323, 644 N.Y.S.2d 233 (1st Dept. 1996).

—The validity of a petition must be ascertained from its facial sufficiency. *In re* Rodney J., 194 A.D.2d 342, 598 N.Y.S.2d 487, 489 (1st Dept. 1993).

—Juvenile delinquency petition and supporting deposition contained sufficient nonhearsay allegations to establish appellant's commission of acts constituting a crime, officer approached appellant requesting that he get into truancy van to be arrested, then testified appellant shouted obscenities at officer, was belligerent, and bumped officer. *In re* Darnell C., 305 A.D.2d 405, 759 N.Y.S.2d 739 (2d Dept. 2003).

—In order for a petition to be legally sufficient it must set forth a prima facie case, *i.e.,* evidence sufficient to warrant a conviction if unexplained or uncontradicted. *In re* Shannon G., 195 A.D.2d 556, 600 N.Y.S.2d 478 (2d Dept. 1993).

—The Board is not required to give the same weight to each and every statutory factor or to discuss each one expressly; as long as they are all considered, the emphasis on one, i.e., the

serious nature of petitioner's crime, is permissible. Collado v. N.Y. State Div. of Parole, 287 A.D.2d 921, 731 N.Y.S.2d 680 (3d Dept. 2001).

—Petition to adjudicate respondent a juvenile delinquent was facially defective where the petition and the supporting documents failed to make out a prima facie case and the non-hearsay allegations were not sworn to. *In re* Charles BB., 277 A.D.2d 756, 716 N.Y.S.2d 165 (3d Dept. 2000).

—Juvenile delinquency petition must contain non-hearsay allegations establishing every element of the crime (here, menacing in the second degree); however, defendant's telephone conversation with a third party in which he stated he intended to harm two classmates, without evidence that those threats were ever communicated to the intended victims, and thus did not put them in "reasonable fear of physical injury," did not support the charges. *In re* Kyle L., 268 A.D.2d 836, 701 N.Y.S.2d 525 (3d Dept. 2000).

—Petition that contained factual allegations establishing that victim sustained a physical injury as a result of a long and severe beating by defendant was sufficient to sustain determination that "physical injury" had been established. *In re* Shane "E," 255 A.D.2d 674, 679 N.Y.S.2d 209 (3d Dept. 1998).

—Petition was sufficient on its face where it was accompanied by supporting deposition of respondent's mother in which she averred that respondent communicated to her through nonverbal communications that he started the fire. *In re* Terrance W., 251 A.D.2d 1004, 674 N.Y.S.2d 529 (4th Dept.), *appeal denied,* 92 N.Y.2d 810 (1998).

—Petition was held sufficient where it incorporated respondent's statement to the police and complainant's properly verified supporting deposition. *In re* Joseph H., 224 A.D.2d 1037, 637 N.Y.S.2d 574 (4th Dept. 1996).

— No merit to claim petition is facially deficient because the supporting depositions are not attached to it, § 311.2 determines sufficiency of a petition by sum of its two parts: verified petition and any supporting depositions filed with e petition, as they were here. *In re* Bobby Jo F., 2 A.D.3d 1472 770 N.Y.S.2d 522 (4th Dept. 2003).

Verification of supporting deposition.—Although verification statement in supporting deposition did not contain exact wording found in CPL § 100.30(1)(d), the statement comported with the section's substantive requirements by acknowledging that making a false statement is a crime. *In re* Dominic CC., 222 A.D.2d 999, 636 N.Y.S.2d 142 (3d Dept. 1995).

§ 311.3. Petition; fact-finding hearings.

1. When two or more respondents are charged in separate petitions with the same crime or crimes the court shall conduct a single or consolidated fact-finding hearing. The court, however, upon motion of a respondent or the presentment agency, may, in its discretion and for good cause shown, order that any respondent be granted a fact-finding hearing separate from the other respondents. Such motion must be made within the period prescribed in section 332.2.

2. If such petitions, in addition to charging the same crime or crimes against the different respondents, charge other crimes not common to all, the court may nevertheless conduct a single fact-finding hearing for the crime or crimes common to all.

§ 311.4. Substitution of petition or finding.

1. At any time in the proceedings the court, upon motion or a respondent or its own motion, may, with the consent of the presentment agency and with the consent of the respondent, substitute a petition alleging that the respondent is in need

of supervision for a petition alleging that the respondent is a juvenile delinquent.

2. At the conclusion of the dispositional hearing the court, upon motion of the respondent or its own motion, may in its discretion and with the consent of the respondent, substitute a finding that the respondent is a person in need of supervision for a finding that the respondent is a juvenile delinquent.

Amended by L. 1983, Ch. 1983, Ch. 398, eff. July 1, 1983.

ANNOTATIONS

Substitution; generally.—Court abused its discretion when it adjudicated appellant, an eight-year-old boy, a juvenile delinquent instead of a person in need of supervision upon a determination that he had committed acts which if committed by an adult would have constituted sodomy in the first degree. *In re* Devon R., 278 A.D.2d 15, 717 N.Y.S.2d 145 (1st Dept. 2000), *appeal denied*, 96 N.Y.2d 707 (2001).

—Although generally there must be more than one incident to support a determination that a child is in need of supervision, where respondent consents to the substitution and admits to the incident, this rule is inapplicable. *In re* Theresa C., 222 A.D.2d 1107, 636 N.Y.S.2d 249 (4th Dept. 1995).

§ 311.5. Amendment of the petition.

1. At any time before or during the fact-finding hearing, the court may, upon application of the presentment agency and with notice to the respondent and an opportunity to be heard, order the amendment of a petition with respect to defects, errors or variances from the proof relating to matters of form, time, place, names of persons and the like, when such amendment does not tend to prejudice the respondent on the merits. Upon permitting such an amendment, the court must, upon application of the respondent, order any adjournment which may be necessary to accord the respondent an adequate opportunity to prepare his defense.

2. A petition may not be amended for the purpose of curing:

(a) a failure to charge or state a crime; or

(b) legal insufficiency of the factual allegations; or

(c) a misjoinder of crimes.

§ 311.6. Joinder, severance and consolidation.

1. Two crimes are joinable and may be included as separate counts in the same petition when:

(a) they are based upon the same act or upon the same criminal transaction, as that term is defined in subdivision two; or

(b) even though based upon different criminal transactions, such crimes, or the criminal transactions underlying them, are of such nature that either proof of the first crime would be material and admissible as evidence in chief upon a fact-finding hearing of the second, or proof of the

second would be material and admissible as evidence in chief upon a fact-finding hearing of the first; or

(c) even though based upon different criminal transactions, and even though not joinable pursuant to paragraph (b), such crimes are defined by the same or similar statutory provisions and consequently are the same or similar in law.

2. "Criminal transaction" means conduct which establishes at least one crime, and which is comprised of two or more or a group of acts either:

(a) so closely related and connected in point of time and circumstance of commission as to constitute a single criminal incident; or

(b) so closely related in criminal purpose or objective as to constitute elements or integral parts of a single criminal venture.

3. In any case where two or more crimes or groups of crimes charged in a petition are based upon different criminal transactions, and where their joinability rests solely upon the fact that such crimes, or as the case may be at least one offense of each group, are the same or similar in law, as prescribed in paragraph (c) of subdivision one, the court, in the interest of justice and for good cause shown, may upon application of either the respondent or the presentment agency order that any one of such crimes or groups of crimes be tried separately from the other or others, or that two or more thereof be tried together but separately from two or more others thereof. Such application must be made within the period prescribed in section 332.2.

4. When two or more petitions against the same respondent charge different crimes of a kind that are joinable in a single petition pursuant to subdivision one, the court may, upon application of either the presentment agency or respondent order that such petitions be consolidated and treated as a single petition for trial purposes. Such application must be made within the period prescribed in section 332.2. If the respondent requests consolidation with respect to crimes which are, pursuant to paragraph (a) of subdivision one, of a kind that are joinable in a single petition by reason of being based upon the same act or criminal transaction, the court must order such consolidation unless good cause to the contrary be shown.

Amended by L. 1983, Ch. 398, eff. July 1, 1983.

ANNOTATIONS

Amendment; generally.—FCA § 311.5 is applicable to a petition originating a juvenile delinquency proceeding, however, it does not apply to a petition alleging a violation of probation since it is not part of the adjudicative process in the juvenile delinquency proceedings but is dispositional in nature. *In re* Vincent B., 239 A.D.2d 925, 659 N.Y.S.2d 594 (4th Dept. 1997).

Extent of amendment.—The overall intent of this section is to allow the correction of minor errors "while precluding the rectification of major deficiencies, such as a failure to state a crime"; where the amendment to the petition allowed a "substitution of charges which altered the essential legal elements necessary to the establishment of a prima facie case" without the benefit of an adjournment to prepare, the resulting prejudice required reversal. *In re* Anthony "Y," 293 A.D.2d 792, 740 N.Y.S.2d 487 (3d Dept. 2002).

§ 312.1. Issuance and service of summons.

1. After a petition has been filed, the court may cause a copy thereof and a summons to be issued, requiring the respondent personally and his parent or other person legally responsible for his care, or, if such legally responsible person is not available, a person with whom he resides, to appear for the initial appearance as defined by section 320.1 at a time and place named. The summons shall be signed by a judge or by the clerk of the court.

2. Service of a summons and petition shall be made by delivery of a true copy thereof to the person summoned at least twenty-four hours before the time stated therein for appearance.

3. If after reasonable effort, personal service as provided in subdivision two is not made, the court may at any stage in the proceedings make an order providing for service in any manner the court directs.

§ 312.2. Issuance of a warrant.

1. The court may issue a warrant, directing that the respondent personally or other person legally responsible for his or her care or, if such legally responsible person is not available, a person with whom he or she resides, be brought before the court, when a petition has been filed and it appears that:

(a) a summons cannot be served; or

(b) such person has refused to obey a summons or family court appearance ticket; or

(c) the respondent or other person is likely to leave the jurisdiction; or

(d) a summons, in the court's opinion, would be ineffectual; or

(e) a respondent has failed to appear.

2. Upon issuance of a warrant due to the respondent's failure to appear for a scheduled court date, the court shall adjourn the matter to a date certain within thirty days for a report on the efforts made to secure the respondent's appearance in court. The court may order that the person legally responsible for the respondent's care or, if such legally responsible person is not available, a person with whom the respondent resides, appear on the adjourned date. Upon receiving the report, for good cause, the court may order further reports and may require further appearances of the person legally responsible for the respondent's care or, if such person legally responsible is not available, a person with whom

the respondent resides. Upon receiving the initial or any subsequent report, the court shall set forth in writing its findings of fact as to the efforts, if any, made up to that date to secure the respondent's appearance in court.

Amended by L. 1994, Ch. 501, § 1, eff. July 26, 1994, amending the existing text, numbering it as subd. 1, and adding subd. 2.

§ 315.1. Motion to dismiss; defective petition.

1. A petition or a count thereof is defective when:

(a) it does not substantially conform to the requirements stated in sections 311.1 and 311.2; provided that a petition may not be dismissed as defective, but must instead be amended when the defect or irregularity is of a kind that may be cured by amendment pursuant to section 311.5, and where the presentment agency moves to so amend; or

(b) the allegations demonstrate that the court does not have jurisdiction of the crime charged; or

(c) the statute defining the crime charged is unconstitutional or otherwise invalid.

2. An order dismissing a petition as defective may be issued upon motion of the respondent or of the court itself.

3. A motion to dismiss under this section must be made within the time provided for in section 332.2.

Amended by L. 1985, Ch. 663, eff. Aug. 27, 1985.

§ 315.2. Motion to dismiss in furtherance of justice.

1. A petition or any part or count thereof may at any time be dismissed in furtherance of justice when, even though there may be no basis for dismissal as a matter of law, such dismissal is required as a matter of judicial discretion by the existence of some compelling further consideration or circumstances clearly demonstrating that a finding of delinquency or continued proceedings would constitute or result in injustice. In determining whether such compelling further consideration or circumstances exist, the court shall, to the extent applicable, examine and consider, individually and collectively, the following:

(a) the seriousness and circumstances of the crime;

(b) the extent of harm caused by the crime;

(c) any exceptionally serious misconduct of law enforcement personnel in the investigation and arrest of the respondent or in the presentment of the petition;

(d) the history, character and condition of the respondent;

MISC. LAWS

(e) the needs and best interest of the respondent;

(f) the need for protection of the community; and

(g) any other relevant fact indicating that a finding would serve no useful purpose.

2. An order dismissing a petition in the interest of justice may be issued upon motion of the presentment agency, the court itself or of the respondent. Upon issuing such an order, the court must set forth its reasons therefor upon the record.

3. Such a motion brought by the presentment agency or the respondent must be in writing and may be filed at any time subsequent to the filing of the petition. Notice of the motion shall be served upon the opposing party not less than eight days prior to the return date of the motion. Answering affidavits shall be served at least two days prior to the return date of such motion.

Amended by L. 1982, Ch. 926, eff. July 1, 1983.

§ 315.3. Adjournment in contemplation of dismissal.

1. Except where the petition alleges that the respondent has committed a designated felony act, the court may at any time prior to the entering of a finding under section 352.1 and with the consent of the respondent order that the proceeding be "adjourned in contemplation of dismissal." An adjournment in contemplation of dismissal is an adjournment of the proceeding, for a period not to exceed six months, with a view to ultimate dismissal of the petition in furtherance of justice. Upon issuing such an order, providing such terms and conditions as the court deems appropriate, the court must release the respondent. The court may,

as a condition of an adjournment in contemplation of dismissal order, in cases where the record indicates that the consumption of alcohol may have been a contributing factor, require the respondent to attend and complete an alcohol awareness program established pursuant to paragraph six-a of subdivision (a) of section 19.07 of the mental hygiene law. Upon *ex parte* motion by the presentment agency, or upon the court's own motion, made at the time the order is issued or at any time during its duration, the court may restore the matter to the calendar. If the proceeding is not restored, the petition is, at the expiration of the order, deemed to have been dismissed by the court in furtherance of justice.

2. Rules of court shall define the permissible terms and conditions which may be included in an order that the proceeding be adjourned in contemplation of dismissal; such permissible terms and conditions may include supervision by the probation service, a requirement that the respondent cooperate with a mental health, social services or other appropriate community facility or agency to which the respondent may be referred and a requirement that the respondent comply with such other reasonable conditions as the court shall determine to be necessary or appropriate to ameliorate the conduct which gave rise to the filing of the petition or to prevent placement with the commissioner of social services or the division for youth.

3. An order adjourning a petition in contemplation of dismissal may be issued upon motion of the presentment agency, the court itself, or the respondent. Upon issuing such an order, the court must set forth its reasons therefor upon the record.

Amended by L. 1985, Ch. 880; L. 1987, Ch. 101; L. 1989, Ch. 161; L. 1991, Ch. 198, eff. June 28, 1991; L. 1991, Ch. 237, eff. July 31, 1991, amending subd. (1).

Part 2. Initial appearance and probable cause hearing

§ 320.1. The initial appearance; definition.

When used in this article "initial appearance" means the proceeding on the date the respondent first appears before the court after a petition has been filed and any adjournments thereof, for the purposes specified in section 320.4.

§ 320.2. The initial appearance; timing; adjournment and appointment of counsel.

1. If the respondent is detained, the initial appearance shall be held no later than seventy-two hours after a petition is filed or the next day the court is in session, whichever is sooner. If the respondent is not detained, the initial appearance shall be held as soon as practicable, and, absent good cause shown, within ten days after a petition is filed. If a warrant for the respondent's arrest has been issued pursuant to section 312.2 of this article due to the respondent's failure to appear for an initial appearance of which he or she had notice, computation of the time within which the initial appearance must be held shall exclude the period extending from the date the court issues the warrant to the date the respondent is returned pursuant to the warrant or appears voluntarily; provided, however, no period of time may be excluded hereunder unless the respondent's location cannot be determined by the exercise of due diligence or, if the respondent's location is known, his or her presence in court cannot be obtained by the exercise of due diligence. In determining whether due diligence has been exercised, the court shall consider, among other factors, the report presented to the court pursuant to subdivision two of section 312.2 of this article.

2. At the initial appearance the court must appoint a law guardian to represent the respondent pursuant to the provisions of section two hundred forty-nine if independent legal representation is not available to such respondent.

3. The initial appearance may be adjourned for no longer than seventy-two hours or until the next court day, whichever is sooner, to enable an appointed law guardian or other counsel to appear before the court.

4. The clerk of the court shall notify the presentment agency and any appointed law guardian of the initial appearance date.

Amended by L. 1985, Ch. 663, eff. Aug. 27, 1985; L. 1994, Ch. 501, § 2, eff. July 26, 1994, amending subd. 1.

ANNOTATIONS

Counsel.—The court properly denied the request by juvenile's third counsel to withdraw, as such right is not absolute. *In re* Jamieko A., 193 A.D.2d 409, 597 N.Y.S.2d 72 (1st Dept. 1993).

Dismissal of petition pursuant to Section 320.2.—Refiling of a juvenile delinquency petition must be accomplished within the 60-day speedy trial period required by section 340.1. Here the petition was initially dismissed due a violation of section 320.2, specifically, respondent's non-appearance within ten days and the presentment agency's failure to demonstrate due diligence in securing respondent's appearance. Second petition should not have been dismissed where the original 60-day speedy trial time had not yet run. *In re* Steven S., 238 A.D.2d 226, 657 N.Y.S.2d 10 (1st Dept. 1997).

Speedy trial.—Although juveniles have a right to a speedy trial, there is no per se rule regarding speedy trial violations; court must balance the factors enumerated in *People v. Taranovich,* 37 N.Y.2d 442, in determining the merits of a speedy trial claim. *In re* Benjamin L., 92 N.Y.2d 660, 685 N.Y.S.2d 400, 708 N.E.2d 156 (1998).

§ 320.3. Notice of rights.

At the time the respondent first appears before the court, the respondent and his parent or other person legally responsible for his care shall be advised of the respondent's right to remain silent and of his right to be represented by counsel chosen by him or by a law guardian assigned by the court. Provided, however, that in the event of the failure of the respondent's parent or other person legally responsible for his care to appear, after reasonable and substantial effort has been made to notify such parent or responsible person of the commencement of the proceeding and such initial appearance, the court shall appoint a law guardian.

§ 320.4. The initial appearance; procedures.

1. At the initial appearance the court must inform the respondent, or cause him to be informed in its presence, of the charge or charges contained in the petition, and the presentment agency must cause the respondent and his counsel or law guardian to be furnished with a copy of the petition.

2. At the initial appearance the court shall determine:

(a) whether detention is necessary pursuant to section 320.5; and

(b) whether the case should be referred to the probation service pursuant to section 320.6; and

(c) if the child is detained, the date of the probable-cause hearing pursuant to section 325.1 unless such hearing has already been held; and

(d) the date of the fact-finding hearing; and

(e) such other issues as may be properly before it.

§ 320.5. The initial appearance; release or detention.

1. At the initial appearance, the court in its discretion may release the respondent or direct his detention.

2. Rules of court shall define permissible terms and conditions of release. The court may in its discretion release the respondent upon such terms and conditions as it deems appropriate. The respondent shall be given a written copy of any such terms and conditions. The court may modify or enlarge such terms and conditions at any time prior to the expiration of the respondent's release.

3. The court shall not direct detention unless it finds and states the facts and reasons for so finding that unless the respondent is detained:

(a) there is a substantial probability that he will not appear in court on the return date; or

(b) there is a serious risk that he may before the return date commit an act which if committed by an adult would constitute a crime.

4. At the initial appearance the presentment agency may introduce the respondent's previous delinquency findings entered by a family court. If the respondent has been fingerprinted for the current charge pursuant to section 306.1, the presentment agency may also introduce the fingerprint records maintained by the division of criminal justice services. The clerk of court and the probation service shall cooperate with the presentment agency in making available the appropriate records. At the conclusion of the initial appearance such fingerprint records shall be returned to the presentment agency and shall not be made a part of the court record.

5. Upon a finding of facts and reasons which support a detention order pursuant to subdivision three of this section, the court shall also determine and state in any order directing detention:

(a) whether the continuation of the respondent in the respondent's home would be contrary to the best interests of the respondent based upon, and limited to, the facts and circumstances available to the court at the time of the initial appearance; and

(b) where appropriate and consistent with the need for protection of the community, whether reasonable efforts were made prior to the date of the court appearance that resulted in the detention order issued in accordance with this section to prevent or eliminate the need for removal of the respondent from his or her home or, if the respondent had been removed from his or her home prior to the initial appearance, where appropriate and consistent with the need for protection of the community, whether reasonable efforts were made to make it possible for the respondent to safely return home.

Amended by L. 1982, Ch. 926, eff. July 1, 1983; L. 1985, Ch. 319, eff. July 11, 1985; L. 2000, Ch. 145, eff. July 1, 2000.

§ 320.6. The initial appearance; referral to the probation service.

1. If the petition alleges the commission of the designated felony act or the commission of a crime enumerated in subdivision four of section 308.1. the probation service shall make a recommendation to the court at the initial appearance regarding the suitability of adjusting the case pursuant to section 308.1.

2. At the initial appearance the court may, with the consent of the victim or complainant and the respondent, refer a case to the probation service for adjustment services. In the case of a designated felony petition the consent of the presentment agency shall also be required to refer a case to probation services for adjustment services.

3. If the court refers a case to the probation service pursuant to this section and the probation service adjusts the case, the petition shall be dismissed.

4. If such case is referred to the probation service, the provisions of section 308.1, except subdivision thirteen thereof, shall apply.

Amended by L. 1982, Ch. 926, eff. July 1, 1983; L. 1983, Ch. 398, eff. July 1, 1983.

ANNOTATION

Purpose.—The very existence of the adjustment machinery

at Intake demonstrates a recognition that potential delinquency matters should be diverted from the Court where appropriate; while adjustment service at Intake has long been a distinguishing feature of pre-petition juvenile delinquency procedure, the Legislature has specifically authorized the use of such services even after the filing of the petition, and to allow a complainant to veto an otherwise appropriate disposition by his or her mere absence from Court would work a manifest injustice to the respondent while encumbering an already overburdened Court system with a case that is more suited to resolution in a nonjudicial forum. *In re* Vincent F., 121 Misc. 2d 992, 469 N.Y.S.2d 563 (Fam. Ct. Richmond Co. 1983).

§ 321.1. Entry of an admission or a denial.

1. At the initial appearance the respondent shall admit or deny each charge contained in the petition unless the petition is dismissed or the proceeding otherwise terminated.

2. If the respondent refuses to admit or deny each such charge or remains mute, the court must enter a denial in his behalf as to any charge neither admitted nor denied.

§ 321.2. Admissions to part of a petition; admissions concerning other petitions.

1. A respondent may as a matter of right enter an admission to those allegations in the petition which are determinable at the fact-finding hearing.

2. Where the petition charges but one crime, a respondent may, with the consent of the court and the appropriate presentment agency, enter an admission of a lesser included crime as defined in section 1.20 of the criminal procedure law.

3. Where the petition charges more than one crime in separate counts a respondent may, with the consent of the court and the appropriate presentment agency, enter an admission to part of the petition or a lesser included crime upon the condition that such admission constitutes a complete disposition of these allegations in the petition which are determinable at the fact-finding hearing.

Amended by L. 1982, Ch. 926, eff. July 1, 1983; L. 1983, Ch. 980, eff. Aug. 8, 1983.

§ 321.3. Acceptance of an admission.

1. The court shall not consent to the entry of an admission unless it has advised the respondent of his right to a fact-finding hearing. The court shall also ascertain through allocation of the respondent and his parent or other person legally responsible for his care, if present, that

(a) he committed the act or acts to which he is entering an admission,

(b) he is voluntarily waiving his right to a fact-finding hearing, and

(c) he is aware of the possible specific dispositional orders. The provisions of this subdivision shall not be waived.

2. Upon consenting to the entry of an admission pursuant to this section, the court must state the reasons for granting such consent.

3. Upon the entry of an admission pursuant to this section the court shall enter an appropriate order pursuant to section 345.1 and schedule a dispositional hearing pursuant to section 350.1.

ANNOTATIONS

Generally.—FCA § 321.3 does not require that respondent signify his or her agreement before the court may consent to the entry of an admission; respondent was fully advised of his rights, and he knowingly agreed to accept the plea agreement. *In re* Brian K.J., 223 A.D.2d 643, 636 N.Y.S.2d 417 (2d Dept. 1996).

Allocution.

—Failure of court to obtain allocution of juvenile's mother as to her understanding of the consequences of juvenile's admission resulted in reversal; court must also determine that juvenile was aware of "possible specific dispositional alternatives." *In re* Anthony S., 302 A.D.2d 531, 755 N.Y.S.2d 294 (2d Dept. 2003).

—Family Court failed to ascertain at the time of appellant's admission whether he was aware of the "possible specific dispositional orders" that the court might issue, failed to advise appellant of his right to a fact-finding hearing, and failed to obtain proper allocution from appellant's mother, who was present in court. *In re* James D.H., 254 A.D.2d 290, 678 N.Y.S.2d 125 (2d Dept. 1998).

—Inadequacies in allocution, specifically failure of court to apprise appellant of consequences of waiving his rights, including all dispositional alternatives, required reversal. *In re* Harrison C., 239 A.D.2d 341, 657 N.Y.S.2d 988 (2d Dept. 1997).

—Family Court's failure to ascertain whether respondent was voluntarily waiving his right to a fact-finding hearing and whether respondent was aware of the possible specific dispositional orders that could be imposed warranted reversal. *In re* Timothy M., 225 A.D.2d 915, 639 N.Y.S.2d 182 (3d Dept. 1996).

—Court's acceptance of entry of respondent's admission was error because court failed to conduct allocution of respondent and his mother as required by statute; order reversed. *In re* Brian H., 239 A.D.2d 925, 661 N.Y.S.2d 575 (4th Dept. 1997).

Parent or person legally responsible for care.—Admission of guilt must be vacated because respondent's mother, who was present in court, was not advised by the court of the consequences of the respondent's admissions. *In re* Perry O., 232 A.D.2d 225, 647 N.Y.S.2d 785 (1st Dept. 1996).

§ 321.4. Withdrawal of an admission or denial.

1. A respondent who has entered a denial of a petition may as a matter of right withdraw such denial at any time before the conclusion of the fact-finding hearing and enter an admission to the entire petition.

2. At any time prior to the entry of a finding under section 352.1 the court in its discretion may permit a respondent who has entered an admission to the entire petition or to part of the petition to withdraw such admission, and in such event the entire petition as it existed at the time of the admission shall be restored.

Amended by L. 1983, Ch. 398, eff. July 1, 1983.

§ 322.1. Incapacitated person; examination reports.

1. At any proceeding under this article, the

court must issue an order that the respondent be examined as provided herein when it is of the opinion that the respondent may be an incapacitated person. Notwithstanding the provisions of this or any other law, the court may direct that the examination be conducted on an outpatient basis when the respondent is not in custody at the time the court issues an order of examination. The court shall order that two qualified psychiatric examiners as defined in subdivision seven of section 730.10 of the criminal procedure law examine the respondent to determine if he is mentally ill, mentally retarded or developmentally disabled.

2. If an order of examination has been issued pursuant to subdivision one, the proceedings shall be adjourned until the examination reports have been filed with the court. Every such report shall be filed within ten days after entry of such order. Upon a showing of special circumstances and a finding that a longer period is necessary to complete the examination and report, the court may extend the time for filing the examination report.

3. Each report shall state the examiner's opinion as to whether the respondent is or is not an incapacitated person, the nature and extent of his examination and, if he finds the respondent is an incapacitated person, his diagnosis and prognosis and a detailed statement of the reasons for his opinion by making particular reference to those aspects of the proceedings wherein the respondent lacks capacity to understand or to assist in his own defense. The chief administrator of the courts shall prescribe the form for the examination report.

Amended by L. 1994, Ch. 566, § 2, eff. July 26, 1994, amending subd. 1.

§ 322.2. Proceedings to determine capacity.

1. Upon the receipt of examination reports ordered under section 322.1, the court shall conduct a hearing to determine whether the respondent is an incapacitated person. The respondent, the counsel or law guardian for the respondent, the presentment agency and the commissioner of mental health or the commissioner of mental retardation and developmental disabilities, as appropriate, shall be notified of such hearing at least five days prior to the date thereof and afforded an opportunity to be heard.

2. If the court finds that the respondent is not an incapacitated person, it shall continue the delinquency proceedings.

3. If the court finds that the respondent is an incapacitated person, the court shall schedule a hearing to determine whether there is probable cause to believe that the respondent committed a crime. The order of proceeding at such hearing shall conform to section 325.2.

4. If the court finds that there is probable cause

to believe that the respondent committed a misdemeanor, the respondent shall be committed to the custody of the appropriate commissioner for a reasonable period not to exceed ninety days. The court shall dismiss the petition on the issuance of the order of commitment.

5. (a) If the court finds that there is probable cause to believe that the respondent committed a felony, it shall order the respondent committed to the custody of the commissioner of mental health or the commissioner of mental retardation and developmental disabilities for an initial period not to exceed one year from the date of such order. Such period may be extended annually upon further application to the court by the commissioner having custody or his designee. Such application must be made not more than sixty days prior to the expiration of such period of forms that have been prescribed by the chief administrator of the courts. At that time, the commissioner must give written notice of the application to the respondent, the counsel or law guardian representing the respondent and the mental hygiene legal service if the respondent is at a residential facility. Upon receipt of such application, the court must conduct a hearing to determine the issue of capacity. If, at the conclusion of a hearing conducted pursuant to this subdivision, the court finds that the respondent is no longer incapacitated, he shall be returned to the family court for further proceedings pursuant to this article. If the court is satisfied that the respondent continues to be incapacitated, the court shall authorize continued custody of the respondent by the commissioner for a period not to exceed one year. Such extensions shall not continue beyond a reasonable period of time necessary to determine whether the respondent will attain the capacity to proceed to a fact finding hearing in the foreseeable future but in no event shall continue beyond the respondent's eighteenth birthday.

(b) If a respondent is in the custody of the commissioner upon the respondent's eighteenth birthday, the commissioner shall notify the clerk of the court that the respondent was in his custody on such date and the court shall dismiss the petition.

(c) If the court finds that there is probable cause to believe that the respondent has committed a designated felony act, the court shall require that treatment be provided in a residential facility within the appropriate office of the department of mental hygiene.

(d) The commissioner shall review the condition of the respondent within forty-five days after the respondent is committed to the custody of the commissioner. He shall make a second review within ninety days after the respondent is committed to his custody. Thereafter, he shall review the condition of the respondent every ninety days. The respondent and the counsel or law guardian for the respondent, shall be notified of any such review and afforded an opportunity to be heard. The commissioner having custody shall apply to the court for an order dismissing the petition whenever he determines that there is a substantial probability that the respondent will continue to be incapacitated for the foreseeable future. At the time of such application the commissioner must give written notice of application to the respondent, the presentment agency and the mental hygiene legal service if the respondent is at a residential facility. Upon receipt of such application, the court may on its own motion conduct a hearing to determine whether there is substantial probability that the respondent will continue to be incapacitated for the foreseeable future and it must conduct such hearing if a demand therefor is made by the respondent or the mental hygiene legal service within ten days from the date that notice of application was given to them. The respondent may apply to the court for an order of dismissal on the same ground.

6. Any order pursuant to this section dismissing a petition shall not preclude an application for voluntary or involuntary care and treatment in a facility of the appropriate office of the department of mental hygiene pursuant to the provisions of the mental hygiene law. Unless the respondent is admitted pursuant to such an application he shall be released.

7. If the commissioner having custody of a child committed to a residential facility determines at any time that such child may be more appropriately treated in a non-residential facility, he may petition the family court for a hearing. If the court finds after a hearing that treatment in a non-residential facility would be more appropriate for such child, the court shall modify its order of commitment to authorize transfer of such child to a non-residential facility. Application for such a hearing may be made by the respondent.

8. If the commissioner having custody of the child determines at any time that such child is not an incapacitated person, he shall petition the court for a hearing. The respondent and the presentment agency shall be notified of such hearing within twenty-four hours of the scheduling of such hearing and afforded an opportunity to be heard. Application for such a hearing may be made by the respondent. If the court finds after the hearing that the child is no longer incapacitated, he shall be returned to the family court for further proceedings pursuant to this article.

9. Time spent by the respondent in the custody of a commissioner of an office within the department of mental hygiene or in a local hospital or detention facility pending transfer to the custody of the commissioner after a finding of incapacity, shall be credited and applied towards the period of placement specified in a disposition order on the original petition.

Amended by L. 1985, Ch. 789, eff. Apr. 1, 1986.

ANNOTATION

Hearing.—Notwithstanding statute's requirement for a hearing, no hearing is warranted where the presentment agency concedes that respondent is incapacitated and respondent raises no factual issues to warrant a hearing. *In re* Terrance W., 251 A.D.2d 1004, 674 N.Y.S.2d 529 (4th Dept. 1998).

§ 325.1. The probable-cause hearing; time.

1. At the initial appearance, if the respondent denies a charge contained in the petition and the court determines that he shall be detained for more than three days pending a fact-finding hearing, the court shall schedule a probable-cause hearing to determine the issues specified in section 325.3.

2. Such probable-cause hearing shall be held within three days following the initial appearance or within four days following the filing of a petition, whichever occurs sooner.

3. For good cause shown, the court may adjourn the hearing for no more than an additional three court days.

4. The respondent may waive the probable-cause hearing, but the fact that the respondent is not ready for a fact-finding hearing shall not be deemed such a waiver.

5. Where the petition consists of an order of removal pursuant to article seven hundred twenty-five of the criminal procedure law, unless the removal was pursuant to subdivision three of section 725.05 of such law and the respondent was not afforded a probable cause hearing pursuant to subdivision three of section 180.75 of such law for a reason other than his waiver thereof pursuant to subdivision two of section 180.75 of such law, the petition shall be deemed to be based upon a determination that probable cause exists to believe the respondent is a juvenile delinquent and the respondent shall not be entitled to any further inquiry on the subject of whether probable cause exists. After the filing of any such petition the court must, however, exercise independent, de novo discretion with respect to release or detention as set forth in section 320.5.

Amended by L. 1983, Ch. 398, eff. July 1, 1983.

§ 325.2. The probable-cause hearing; order of proceeding.

1. The order of a probable-cause hearing held pursuant to section 325.1 or 322.2 shall be as follows:

(a) the presentment agency must call and examine witnesses and offer evidence in support of the charge;

(b) the respondent may, as a matter of right, testify in his own behalf; if the respondent so testifies, his testimony may not be introduced against him in any future proceeding, except to impeach his testimony at such future proceeding as inconsistent prior testimony;

(c) upon request of the respondent, the court shall, except for good cause shown, permit him to call and examine other witnesses or to produce other evidence in his behalf.

2. Each witness, whether called by the presentment agency or by the respondent, must, unless he would be authorized to give unsworn evidence at a fact-finding hearing, testify under oath. Each witness, including any respondent testifying in his own behalf, may be cross-examined.

3. Only non-hearsay evidence shall be admissible to demonstrate reasonable cause to believe that the respondent committed a crime; except that reports of experts and technicians in professional and scientific fields and sworn statements of the kinds admissible at a hearing upon a felony complaint in a criminal court may be admitted, unless the court determines, upon application of the respondent, that such hearsay evidence is, under the particular circumstances of the case, not sufficiently reliable, in which case the court shall require that the witness testify in person and be subject to cross-examination.

4. Such hearing should be completed at one session. In the interest of justice however, it may be adjourned by the court, but no such adjournment may be for more than one court day.

§ 325.3. The probable-cause hearing; determination.

1. At the conclusion of a probable-cause hearing held pursuant to section 325.1 the court shall determine in accordance with the evidentiary standards applicable to a hearing on a felony complaint in a criminal court:

(a) whether it is reasonable to believe that a crime was committed; and

(b) whether it is reasonable to believe that the respondent committed such crime.

2. The court shall state on the record the section or sections of the penal law or other law which it is reasonable to believe the respondent violated.

3. If the court finds that there is reasonable cause pursuant to subdivision one, it shall further determine whether continued detention is necessary pursuant to section 320.5.

4. If the court does not find that there is reasonable cause to believe that a crime was committed and that the respondent committed it, the case shall be adjourned and the respondent released from detention. If the court or the presentment agency cannot hold a probable cause hearing within the limits of subdivision two of section 325.1, the court may dismiss the petition without prejudice or for good cause shown adjourn the hearing and release the respondent pursuant to section 320.5.

Amended by L. 1982, Ch. 926, eff. July 1, 1983.

ANNOTATIONS

Quantum of evidence.—Where the record revealed that defendant voluntarily, knowingly, and intelligently, and with the assistance of counsel, admitted to committing acts that constitute assault in the third degree, there was probable cause to detain him at the conclusion of the probable cause hearing. *In re* Raymond "WW," 291 A.D.2d 682, 737 N.Y.S.2d 562 (3d Dept. 2002).

—At the probable cause hearing, the presentment agency must present evidence not from the hearing to demonstrate reasonable cause to believe that the respondent committed a crime. *In re* Christopher R., 192 A.D.2d 180, 600 N.Y.S.2d 531, 533 (4th Dept. 1993).

Part 3. Discovery

LexisNexis Cross Reference

Sexual Assault Trials (2d ed.), Vol. 1, Ch. 1, Pretrial Issues, Discovery, and Motions.

§ 330.1. Bill of particulars.

1. Definitions.

(a) "Bill of particulars" is a written statement by the presentment agency specifying, as required by this section, items of factual information which are not recited in the petition and which pertain to the offense charged and including the substance of each respondent's conduct encompassed by the charge which the presentment agency intends to prove at a fact-finding hearing on its direct case, and whether the presentment agency intends to prove that the respondent acted as principal or accomplice or both. However, the presentment agency shall not be required to include in the bill of particulars matters of evidence relating to how the presentment agency intends to prove the elements of the offense charged or how the presentment agency intends to prove any item of factual information included in the bill of particulars.

(b) "Request for a bill of particulars" is a written request served by respondent upon the presentment agency, without leave of the court, requesting a bill of particulars, specifying the items of factual information desired, and alleging that respondent cannot adequately prepare or conduct his defense without the information requested.

2. Bill of particulars upon request. Upon a timely request for a bill of particulars by a respondent against whom a petition is pending, the presentment agency shall within fifteen days of the service of the request or as soon thereafter as is practicable, serve upon the respondent or his attorney or law guardian and file with the court, the bill of particulars, except to the extent the presentment agency shall have refused to comply

with the request pursuant to subdivision four of this section. If the respondent is detained, the court shall direct the filing of the bill of particulars on an expedited basis and prior to the commencement of the fact-finding hearing.

3. Timeliness of request. A request for a bill of particulars shall be timely if made within thirty days after the conclusion of the initial appearance and before commencement of the fact-finding hearing. If the respondent is not represented by counsel or a law guardian, and has requested an adjournment to retain counsel or to have a law guardian appointed, the thirty-day period shall commence, for the purposes of a request for a bill or particulars by the respondent, on the date counsel or a law guardian initially appeared on respondent's behalf. However, the court may direct compliance with a request for a bill of particulars that, for good cause shown, could not have been made within the time specified.

4. Request refused. The presentment agency may refuse to comply with the request for a bill of particulars or any portion of the request for a bill of particulars to the extent it reasonably believes that the item of factual information requested is not authorized to be included in a bill of particulars, or that such information is not necessary to enable the respondent adequately to prepare or conduct his defense, or that a protective order would be warranted or that the demand is untimely. Such refusal shall be made in writing, which shall set forth the grounds of such belief as fully as possible, consistent with the reason for the refusal. Within fifteen days of the request or as soon thereafter as practicable, the refusal shall be served upon the respondent and a copy shall be filed with the court.

5. Court ordered bill of particulars. Where a

presentment agency has timely served a written refusal pursuant to subdivision four of this section and upon motion, made in writing, of a respondent, who has made a request for a bill of particulars and whose request has not been complied with in whole or in part, the court must, to the extent a protective order is not warranted, order the presentment agency to comply with the request if it is satisfied that the items of factual information requested are authorized to be included in a bill of particulars, and that such information is necessary to enable the respondent adequately to prepare or conduct his defense and, if the request was untimely, a finding of good cause for the delay. Where a presentment agency has not timely served a written refusal pursuant to subdivision four of this section the court must, unless it is satisfied that the presentment agency has shown good cause why such an order should not be issued, issue an order requiring the presentment agency to comply or providing for any other order authorized by subdivision one of section 331.6.

6. Motion procedure. A motion for a bill of particulars shall be made as prescribed in section 332.1. Upon an order granting a motion pursuant to this section, the presentment agency must file with the court a bill of particulars, reciting every item of information designated in the order, and serve a copy thereof upon the respondent. Pending such filing and service, the fact-finding hearing is stayed.

7. Protective order.

(a) The court may, upon motion of the presentment agency, or of any affected person, or upon determination of a motion of respondent for a court-ordered bill of particulars, or upon its own initiative, issue a protective order denying, limiting, conditioning, delaying or regulating the bill or particulars for good cause, including constitutional limitations, danger to the integrity of physical evidence or a substantial risk of physical harm, intimidation, economic reprisal, bribery or unjustified annoyance or embarrassment to any person or an adverse effect upon the legitimate needs of law enforcement, including the protection of the confidentiality of informants, or any other factor or set of factors which outweighs the need for the bill of particulars.

(b) An order limiting, conditioning, delaying or regulating the bill of particulars may, among other things, require that any material copied or derived therefrom be maintained in the exclusive possession of the attorney or law guardian for the respondent and be used for the exclusive purpose of preparing for the defense of the juvenile delinquency proceeding.

8. Amendment. At any time before commencement of the fact-finding hearing, the presentment agency may, without leave of the court, serve upon respondent and file with the court an amended bill of particulars. At any time during the fact-finding hearing, upon application of the presentment agency and with notice to the respondent and an opportunity for him to be heard, the court must, upon finding that no undue prejudice will accrue to respondent and that the presentment agency has acted in good faith, permit the presentment agency to amend the bill of particulars. Upon any amendment of the bill of particulars, the court must, upon application of respondent, order an adjournment of the fact-finding hearing or any other action it deems appropriate which may, by reason of the amendment, be necessary to accord the respondent an adequate opportunity to defend.

Added by L. 1983, Ch. 398, eff. July 1, 1983.

§ 330.2. Suppression of evidence.

1. A respondent in a juvenile delinquency proceeding may make a motion to suppress evidence in accordance with sections 710.20 and 710.60 of the criminal procedure law.

2. Whenever the presentment agency intends to offer at a fact-finding hearing evidence described in section 710.20 or subdivision one of section 710.30 of the criminal procedure law, such agency must serve upon respondent notice of such intention. Such notice must be served within fifteen days after the conclusion of the initial appearance or before the fact-finding hearing, whichever occurs first, unless the court, for good cause shown, permits later service and accords the respondent a reasonable opportunity to make a suppression motion thereafter. If the respondent is detained, the court shall direct that such notice be served on an expedited basis.

3. When a motion to suppress evidence is made before the commencement of the fact-finding hearing, the fact-finding hearing shall not be held until the determination of the motion.

4. After the pre-trial determination and denial of the motion, if the court is satisfied, upon a showing by the respondent, that additional pertinent facts have been discovered by the respondent which could not have been discovered by the respondent with reasonable diligence before determination of the motion, it may permit him to renew. Such motion to renew shall be made prior to the commencement of the fact-finding hearing, unless the additional pertinent facts were discovered during the fact-finding hearing.

5. Upon granting a motion to suppress evidence, the court must order that the evidence in question be excluded. When the order excludes tangible property unlawfully taken from the respondent's possession, and when such property is not otherwise subject to lawful retention, the court may, upon request of the respondent, further order that such property be restored to him.

6. An order finally denying a motion to suppress evidence may be reviewed upon an appeal

from an ensuing finding of delinquency, notwithstanding the fact that such finding is entered upon an admission made by the respondent, unless the respondent, upon an admission, expressly waives his right to appeal.

7. A motion to suppress evidence is the exclusive method of challenging the admissibility of evidence upon the grounds specified in this section, and a respondent who does not make such a motion waives his right to judicial determination of any such contention.

8. In the absence of service of notice upon a respondent as prescribed in this section, no evidence of a kind specified in subdivision two may be received against him at the fact-finding hearing unless he has, despite the lack of such notice, moved to suppress such evidence and such motion has been denied.

9. An order granting a motion to suppress evidence shall be deemed an order of disposition appealable under section eleven hundred twelve. In taking such an appeal the presentment agency must file, in addition to a notice of appeal, a statement alleging that the deprivation of the use of the evidence ordered suppressed has rendered the sum of the proof available to the presentment agency either:

(a) insufficient as a matter of law, or

(b) so weak in its entirety that any reasonable possibility of proving the allegations contained in the petition has been effectively destroyed. If the respondent is in detention he shall be released pending such appeal unless the court, upon conducting a hearing, enters an order continuing detention. An order continuing detention under this subdivision may be stayed by the appropriate appellate division.

10. The taking of an appeal by the presentment agency pursuant to subdivision nine constitutes a bar to the presentment of the petition involving the evidence ordered suppressed, unless and until such suppression is reversed upon appeal and vacated.

Amended by L. 1985, Ch. 663, eff. Aug. 27, 1985.

ANNOTATION

Good cause.—Where no consent to continuance of suppression hearing is obtained, speedy trial clock continues to runs; speedy trial right is not automatically waived by pretrial motion practice, although suppression hearing is good cause for adjournment of hearing. *In re* George T., 99 N.Y.2d 307, 756 N.Y.S.2d 103, 786 N.E.2d 2 (2002).

§ 331.1. Discovery; definition of terms.

The following definitions are applicable to this section and sections 331.2 through 331.7.

1. "Demand to produce" means a written notice served by and on a party, without leave of the court, demanding to inspect property pursuant to section 331.2 or 331.3 and giving reasonable notice of the time at which the demanding party wishes to inspect the property designated.

2. "Attorneys' work product" means property to the extent that it contains the opinions, theories or conclusions of the presentment agency, law guardian, counsel for the respondent or members of their staffs.

3. "Property" means any existing tangible personal or real property, including but not limited to, books, records, reports, memoranda, papers, photographs, tapes or other electronic recordings, articles of clothing, fingerprints, blood samples, fingernail scrapings or handwriting specimens, but excluding attorneys' work product.

4. "Co-respondent" means a person whose name appears in the petition pursuant to paragraph (1) of subdivision three of section 311.1.

Amended by L. 1983, Ch. 398, eff. July 1, 1983.

ANNOTATION

Subpoena.—A subpoena duces tecum may not be used to expand the discovery available under existing law; juvenile's subpoena directing assistant principal to produce in court "the names, addresses and telephone numbers of students" who may have witnessed incident in question was properly quashed. *In re* Terry D., 81 N.Y.2d 1042, 601 N.Y.S.2d 452, 453, 619 N.E.2d 389 (1993).

§ 331.2. Discovery; upon demand of a party.

1. Except to the extent protected by court order, upon a demand to produce by a respondent, the presentment agency shall disclose to the respondent and make available for inspection, photography, copying or testing, the following property:

(a) any written, recorded or oral statement of the respondent, or by a co-respondent, made, other than in the course of the criminal transaction, to a public servant engaged in law enforcement activity or to a person then acting under his direction or in cooperation with him;

(b) any transcript of testimony relating to the proceeding pending against the respondent, given by the respondent, or by a co-respondent, before any grand jury;

(c) any written report or document, or portion thereof, concerning a physical or mental examination, or scientific test or experiment, relating to the proceeding which was made by, or at the request or direction of a public servant engaged in law enforcement activity or which was made by a person whom the presentment agency intends to call as a witness at a hearing, or which the presentment agency intends to introduce at a hearing;

(d) any photograph or drawing relating to the proceeding which was made or completed by a public servant engaged in law enforcement activity, or which was made by a person whom the presentment agency intends to call as a witness at a hearing, or which the presentment agency intends to introduce at a hearing;

(e) any other property obtained from the respondent or a co-respondent;

(f) any tapes or other electronic recordings which the presentment agency intends to introduce at the fact-finding hearing, irrespective of whether such recording was made during the course of the criminal transaction;

(g) anything required to be disclosed, prior to the fact-finding hearing, to the respondent by the presentment agency, pursuant to the constitution of this state or of the United States; and

(h) the approximate date, time and place of the offense charged and of respondent's arrest.

2. (a) The presentment agency shall make a diligent, good faith effort to ascertain the existence of property demanded pursuant to subdivision one and to cause such property to be made available for discovery where it exists but is not within the presentment agency's possession, custody or control; provided, that the presentment agency shall not be required to obtain by subpoena duces tecum demanded material which the respondent may thereby obtain.

(b) In any case in which the property includes grand jury testimony, the presentment agency shall forthwith request that the district attorney provide a transcript of such testimony; upon receiving such a request, the district attorney shall promptly apply to the appropriate criminal court, with written notice to the presentment agency and the respondent, for a written order pursuant to section three hundred-twenty-five of the judiciary law releasing a transcript of testimony to the presentment agency.

3. Except to the extent protected by court order, upon demand to produce by the presentment agency, the respondent shall disclose and make available for inspection, photography, copying or testing, subject to constitutional limitations.

(a) any written report or document, or portion thereof, concerning a physical examination, or scientific test, experiment, or comparison, made by or at the request or direction of, the respondent, if the respondent intends to introduce such report or document at a hearing or if the respondent has filed a notice of defense of mental disease or defect pursuant to section 335.1 and such report or document relates thereto, or if such report or document was made by a person, other than respondent, whom respondent intends to call as a witness at a hearing; and

(b) any photograph, drawing, tape or other electronic recording which the respondent intends to introduce at a hearing.

4. Except to the extent protected by court order, upon demand to produce by the presentment agency, a respondent who has served a written notice, under section 335.1 of intention to rely upon the defense of mental disease or defect shall disclose and make available for

inspection, photography, copying or testing, subject to constitutional limitations, any written report or document, or portion thereof, concerning a mental examination made by or at the request or direction of the respondent.

5. The respondent shall make a diligent good faith effort to make such property available for discovery pursuant to subdivisions three and four where it exists but the property is not within his possession, custody or control, provided that the respondent shall not be required to obtain by subpoena duces tecum demanded material that the presentment agency may thereby obtain.

6. Notwithstanding the provisions of subdivisions one through five, the presentment agency or the respondent, as the case may be, may refuse to disclose any information which he reasonably believes is not discoverable by a demand to produce, or for which he reasonably believes a protective order pursuant to section 331.5 would be warranted. Such refusal shall be made in writing, which shall set forth the grounds of such belief as fully as possible, consistent with the objective of the refusal. The writing shall be served upon the demanding party and a copy shall be filed with the court.

Amended by L. 1983, Ch. 398, eff. July 1, 1983.

§ 331.3. Discovery; upon court order.

1. Upon motion of respondent the court, (a) must order discovery as to any material not disclosed upon a demand pursuant to section 331.2, if it finds that the presentment agency's refusal to disclose such material is not justified; (b) must, unless it is satisfied that the presentment agency has shown good cause why such an order should not be issued, order discovery or any other order authorized by subdivision one of section 331.6 as to any material not disclosed upon demand pursuant to section 331.2 where the presentment agency has failed to serve a timely written refusal pursuant to subdivision six of section 331.2; and (c) may order discovery with respect to any other property which the presentment agency intends to introduce at the fact-finding hearing, upon a showing by the respondent that discovery with respect to such property is material to the preparation of his defense, and that the request is reasonable. Upon granting the motion pursuant to paragraph (c) hereof, the court shall, upon motion of the presentment agency showing such to be material to the preparation of its case and that the request is reasonable, condition its order of discovery by further directing discovery by the presentment agency of property, of the same kind or character as that authorized to be inspected by the respondent which he intends to introduce at the fact-finding hearing.

2. Upon motion of the presentment agency, and subject to constitutional limitation, the court:

(a) must order discovery as to any property not

disclosed upon a demand pursuant to section 331.2, if it finds that the respondent's refusal to disclose such material is not justified; and

(b) may order the respondent to provide non-testimonial evidence. Such order may, among other things, require the respondent to:

(i) appear in a line-up;

(ii) speak for identification by witness or potential witness;

(iii) be fingerprinted, provided that the respondent is subject to fingerprinting pursuant to this article;

(iv) pose for photographs not involving reenactment of an event, provided the respondent is subject to fingerprinting pursuant to this article;

(v) permit the taking of samples of blood, hair or other materials from his body in a manner not involving an unreasonable intrusion thereof or a risk of serious physical injury thereto;

(vi) provide specimens of his handwriting; and

(vii) submit to a reasonable physical or medical inspection of his body.

This subdivision shall not be construed to limit, expand or otherwise affect the issuance of a similar court order, as may be authorized by law, before the filing of a petition consistent with such rights as the respondent may derive from this article, the constitution of this state or of the United States.

3. An order pursuant to this section may be denied, limited or conditioned as provided in section 331.5.

Amended by L. 1983, Ch. 398, eff. July 1, 1983.

§ 331.4. Discovery; of prior statements and history of witnesses.

1. At the commencement of the fact-finding hearing, the presentment agency shall, subject to a protective order, make available to the respondent:

(a) any written or recorded statement, including any testimony before a grand jury and any examination videotaped pursuant to section 190.32 of the criminal procedure law, made by a person whom the presentment agency intends to call as a witness at the fact-finding hearing, and which relates to the subject matter of the witness's testimony. When such a statement includes grand jury testimony, the presentment agency shall request that the district attorney provide a transcript of testimony prior to the commencement of the fact-finding hearing; upon receiving such a request, the district attorney shall promptly apply to the appropriate criminal court, with written notice to the presentment agency and the respondent, for a written order pursuant to section three hundred twenty-five of the judiciary law releasing a transcript of testimony to the presentment agency;

(b) a record of judgment of conviction of a witness the presentment agency intends to call at the fact-finding hearing if such record is known by the presentment agency to exist;

(c) the existence of any pending criminal action against a witness the presentment agency intends to call at the fact-finding hearing, if the pending criminal action is known by the presentment agency to exist.

The provisions of paragraphs (b) and (c) shall not be construed to require the presentment agency to fingerprint a witness or otherwise cause the division of criminal justice services or other law enforcement agency or court to issue a report concerning a witness.

2. At the conclusion of the presentment agency's direct case and before the commencement of the respondent's direct case, the respondent shall, subject to a protective order, make available to the presentment agency

(a) any written or recorded statement made by a person other than the respondent whom the respondent intends to call as a witness at the fact-finding hearing and which relates to the subject matter of the witness's testimony;

(b) a record of judgment of conviction of a witness, other than the respondent, the respondent intends to call at a hearing if the record of conviction is known by the respondent to exist; and

(c) the existence of any pending criminal action against a witness other than the respondent, the respondent intends to call at a hearing, if the pending criminal action is known by the respondent to exist.

3. Subject to a protective order, at a pre-fact-finding hearing held upon a motion pursuant to section 330.2, at which a witness is called to testify, each party at the conclusion of the direct examination of each of its witnesses, shall, upon request of the other party, make available to that party to the extent not previously disclosed:

(a) any written or recorded statement, including any testimony before a grand jury, made by such witness other than the respondent, which relates to the subject-matter of the witness's testimony. When such a statement includes grand jury testimony, the presentment agency shall request that the district attorney provide a transcript of testimony prior to the commencement of the pre-fact-finding hearing; upon receiving such a request, the district attorney shall promptly apply to the appropriate criminal court, with written notice to the presentment agency and the respondent, for a written order pursuant to section three hundred twenty-five of the judiciary law releasing a transcript of testimony to the presentment agency;

(b) a record of a judgment of conviction of such witness other than the respondent if the record of conviction is known by the presentment agency or respondent, as the case may be, to exist; and

(c) the existence of any pending criminal action against such witness other than the respondent, if the pending criminal action is known by the presentment agency or respondent, as the case may be, to exist.

Amended by L. 1983, Ch. 398, eff. July 1, 1983; L. 1985, Ch. 584, eff. July 28, 1985.

ANNOTATIONS

Statements of witnesses.—Appellant's assertion that presentment agency had failed to turn over witness's statements as required by *Rosario* was unsupported by the record. *In re* Robert H., 240 A.D.2d 409, 658 N.Y.S.2d 1009 (2d Dept. 1997).

—Generally, a juvenile is entitled to the prior statements of a prosecution witness and the failure to provide such statements for use during cross-examination is reversible error. *In re* Ronnell J., 116 A.D.2d 577, 497 N.Y.S.2d 434 (2d Dept. 1986).

§ 331.5. Discovery; protective orders, continuing duty to disclose.

1. The court may, upon motion of either party, or of any affected person, or upon determination of a motion of either party for an order of discovery, or upon its own initiative, issue a protective order denying, limiting, conditioning, delaying or regulating discovery for good cause, including constitutional limitations, danger to the integrity of physical evidence or a substantial risk or physical harm, intimidation, economic reprisal, bribery or unjustified annoyance or embarrassment to any person or an adverse effect upon the legitimate needs of law enforcement, including the protection of the confidentiality of informants, or any other factor or set of factors which outweighs the usefulness of the discovery.

2. An order limiting, conditioning, delaying or regulating discovery may, among other things, require that any material copied or derived therefrom be maintained in the exclusive possession of the attorney for the discovering party and be used for the exclusive purpose of preparing for the defense or presentment of the action.

3. A motion for a protective order shall suspend discovery of the particular matter in dispute.

4. If, after complying with the provisions of sections 331. 2 through 331.7 or an order pursuant thereto, a party finds, either before or during the fact-finding hearing, additional material subject to discovery or covered by such order, he shall promptly comply with the demand or order, refuse to comply with the demand where refusal is authorized, or apply for a protective order pursuant to this section.

§ 331.6. Discovery; sanctions.

1. If, during the course of discovery proceedings, the court finds that a party has failed to comply with any of the provisions of sections 331.2 through 331.7, the court may order such party to permit discovery of the property not previously disclosed, grant a continuance, issue a protective order, prohibit the introduction of certain evidence or the calling of certain witnesses or take any other appropriate action.

2. The failure of the presentment agency to call as a witness a person specified in subdivision one of section 331.2 or any party to introduce disclosed material at the fact-finding hearing shall not, by itself constitute grounds for any sanction or for adverse comment thereupon by any party.

§ 331.7. Discovery; demand and motion procedure.

1. If the respondent is in detention:

(a) a demand to produce shall be made within seven days after the conclusion of the initial appearance or prior to the commencement of the fact-finding hearing, whichever occurs sooner, unless the court grants an extension for good cause shown;

(b) a refusal to comply with a demand to produce shall be made within five days of the service of the demand to produce, but for good cause may be made thereafter;

(c) absent a refusal to comply with a demand to produce, compliance with such demand shall be made within seven days of the service of the demand or as soon thereafter as practicable. The court, however, may order compliance within a shorter period of time.

2. If the respondent is not in detention:

(a) a demand to produce shall be made within fifteen days after the conclusion of the initial appearance unless extended for good cause shown, but in no event later than the commencement of the fact-finding hearing;

(b) a refusal to comply with a demand to produce shall be made within fifteen days of the service of the demand to produce, but for good cause may be made thereafter;

(c) absent a refusal to comply with a demand to produce, compliance with such demand shall be made within fifteen days of the service of the demand or as soon thereafter as practicable.

3. If the respondent is not in detention, a motion by the presentment agency for discovery shall be made within thirty days after the conclusion of the initial appearance, but for good cause shown may be made at any time before commencement of the fact-finding hearing. If the respondent is in detention such motion shall be made within fourteen days after the conclusion of the initial appearance or prior to the commencement of the fact-finding hearing, whichever occurs sooner.

4. A motion by a respondent for discovery shall be made as prescribed in section 332.2.

5. Where the interests of justice so require, the court may permit a party to a motion for an order of discovery or a protective order, or other affected person, to submit papers or to testify *ex parte* or in camera. Any such papers and transcripts of such testimony shall be sealed, but shall constitute a part of the record on appeal. If practical, a judge who receives papers or testimony in camera shall refer the case to a different judge of the same court to preside at the fact-finding hearing.

§ 332.1. Pre-trial motions; definition.

"Pre-trial motion" as used in this article means any motion by a respondent which seeks an order of the court:

1. transferring a proceeding pursuant to section 302.3; or

2. granting a separate fact-finding hearing pursuant to section 311.3; or

3. granting separate fact-finding hearings or consolidating petitions pursuant to section 311.6; or

4. dismissing a petition pursuant to section 315.1; or

5. granting a bill of particulars pursuant to section 330.1; or

6. granting discovery pursuant to section 331.3; or

7. suppressing the use at the fact-finding hearing of any evidence pursuant to section 330.2; or

8. dismissing a petition, or any count thereof, on the ground that the respondent has been denied a speedy fact-finding hearing contrary to section 310.2; or

9. dismissing a petition, or any count thereof, on the ground that the proceeding is untimely, pursuant to section 302.2; or

10. dismissing a petition, or any count thereof, on the ground that the proceeding is barred in accordance with the laws applicable pursuant to section 303.2.

Amended by L. 1983, Ch. 398, eff. July 1, 1983.

§ 332.2. Pre-trial motions; procedure.

1. Except as otherwise expressly provided in this article, all pretrial motions shall be filed within thirty days after the conclusion of the initial appearance and before commencement of the fact-finding hearing, or within such additional times as the court may fix upon application of the respondent made prior to entering a finding pursuant to section 345.1. If the respondent is not represented by counsel or a law guardian and has requested an adjournment to retain counsel or to have a law guardian appointed, such thirty-day

period shall commence on the date counsel or a law guardian initially appears on the respondent's behalf. A motion made pursuant to subdivision eight of section 332.1 must be made prior to the commencement of a fact-finding hearing or the entry of an admission.

2. All pre-trial motions with supporting affidavits, exhibits and memoranda of law, if any, shall be included within the same set of motion papers wherever practicable, and shall be made returnable on the same date, unless the respondent shows that it would be prejudicial to the defense were a single judge to consider all such motions. Where one motion seeks to provide the basis for making another motion, it shall be deemed impracticable to include both motions in the same set of motion papers.

3. Notwithstanding the provisions of subdivisions one and two, the court must entertain and decide on its merits, at any time before the conclusion of the fact-finding hearing, any appropriate motion based upon grounds of which the respondent could not, with due diligence, have been previously aware, or which, for other good cause, could not reasonably have raised within the period specified in subdivision one. Any other pre-trial motions made after such thirty day period may be summarily denied, but the court, in the interest of justice and for good cause shown may, in its discretion, at any time before a finding is entered, entertain and dispose of the motion on the merits.

4. If the respondent is detained, the court shall hear and determine pre-trial motions on an expedited basis.

Amended by L. 1983, Ch. 398, eff. July 1, 1983.

ANNOTATION

Suppression hearing.—Although suppression motion must be decided before fact-finding hearing begins, speedy trial right is not automatically waived by pretrial motion practice; where there was no consent to 47-day continuance of suppression hearing to allow witness to testify, speedy trial clock continued to run, and speedy trial violation resulted. *In re* George T., 99 N.Y.2d 307, 756 N.Y.S.2d 103, 786 N.E.2d 2 (2002).

§ 335.1. Notice of defense of mental disease or defect.

Evidence of mental disease or defect of the respondent excluding his responsibility under this article is not admissible at the fact-finding hearing unless the respondent serves upon the presentment agency and files with the court a written notice of intention to rely upon such defense. Such notice must be served and filed before the fact-finding hearing and not more than thirty days after the conclusion of the initial appearance, whichever is sooner. In the interest of justice and for good cause shown, however, the court may permit such service and filing to be made at any later time prior to the conclusion of the fact-finding hearing.

MISC. LAWS

§ 335.2. Notice of alibi.

1. At any time not more than fifteen days after the conclusion of the initial appearance and before the fact-finding hearing the presentment agency may serve upon the respondent and file a copy thereof with the court, a demand that if the respondent intends to offer a defense that at the time of the commission of the crime charged he was at some place or places other than the scene of the crime, and to call witnesses in support of such defense, he must within ten days of service of such demand, serve upon such agency, and file a copy thereof with the court, a "notice of alibi," reciting;

(a) the place or places where the respondent claims to have been at the time in question, and

(b) the names, the residential addresses, the places of employment and the addresses thereof of every such alibi witness upon whom he intends to rely. For good cause shown, the court may extend the period for service of the notice.

2. Within a reasonable time after receipt of the respondent's witness list but not later than ten days before the fact-finding hearing, the presentment agency must serve upon the respondent and file a copy thereof with the court, a list of witnesses such agency proposes to offer in rebuttal to discredit the respondent's alibi at the trial together with the residential addresses, the places of employment and the addresses thereof of any such rebuttal witnesses. A witness who will testify that the respondent was at the scene of the crime is not such an alibi rebuttal witness. For good cause shown, the court may extend the period for service.

3. If at the trial the respondent calls such an alibi witness without having served the demanded notice of alibi, or if having served such a notice he calls a witness not specified therein, the court may exclude any testimony of such witness relating to the alibi defense. The court may in its discretion receive such testimony, but before doing so, it must, upon application of the presentment agency, grant a reasonable adjournment.

4. Similarly, if the presentment agency fails to serve and file a list of any rebuttal witnesses, the provisions of subdivision three shall reciprocally apply.

5. Both the respondent and the presentment agency shall be under a continuing duty to promptly disclose the names and addresses of additional witnesses which come to the attention of either party subsequent to filing his witness list as provided in this section.

Part 4. The fact-finding hearing

MISC. LAWS

§ 340.1. Time of fact-finding hearing.

1. If the respondent is in detention and the highest count in the petition charges the commission of a class A, B, or C felony, the fact-finding hearing shall commence not more than fourteen days after the conclusion of the initial appearance except as provided in subdivision four. If the respondent is in detention and the highest count in such petition is less than a class C felony the fact-finding hearing shall commence no more than three days after the conclusion of the initial appearance except as provided in subdivision four.

2. If the respondent is not in detention the fact-finding hearing shall commence not more than sixty days after the conclusion of the initial appearance except as provided in subdivision four.

3. For the purposes of this section, in any case where a proceeding has been removed to the family court pursuant to an order issued pursuant to section 725.05 of the criminal procedure law, the date specified in such order for the defendant's appearance in the family court shall constitute the date of initial appearance.

4. The court may adjourn a fact-finding hearing:

(a) on its own motion or on motion of the presentment agency for good cause shown for not more than three days if the respondent is in detention and not more than thirty days if the respondent is not in detention; provided, however,

that if there is probable cause to believe the respondent committed a homicide or a crime which resulted in a person being incapacitated from attending court, the court may adjourn the hearing for a reasonable length of time; or

(b) on motion by the respondent for good cause shown for not more than thirty days; or

(c) on its own motion for not more than six months if the proceeding has been adjourned in contemplation of dismissal pursuant to section 315.3.

5. The court shall state on the record the reason for any adjournment of the fact-finding hearing.

6. Successive motions to adjourn a fact-finding hearing shall not be granted in the absence of showing, on the record, of special circumstances; such circumstances shall not include calendar congestion or the status of the court's docket or backlog.

7. For purposes of this section, if a warrant for the respondent's arrest has been issued pursuant to section 312.2 of this article due to the respondent's failure to appear for a scheduled fact-finding hearing, computation of the time within which such hearing must take place shall exclude the period extending from the date of issuance of the bench warrant for respondent's arrest because of his or her failure to appear to the date the respondent subsequently appears in court pursuant to a bench warrant or appears voluntarily; provided, however, no period of time

may be excluded hereunder unless the respondent's location cannot be determined by the exercise of due diligence or, if the respondent's location is known, his or her presence in court cannot be obtained by the exercise of due diligence. In determining whether due diligence has been exercised, the court shall consider, among other factors, the report presented to the court pursuant to subdivision two of section 312.2 of this article.

Amended by laws 1985, Ch. 663, eff, Aug. 27, 1985; L. 1990, Ch. 223, eff. June 13, 1990, amending subds. (1), (2), adding new subd. (3), and renumbering subds. (3), (4), (5) to (4), (5), (6); L. 1994, Ch. 501, § 3, eff. July 26, 1994.

ANNOTATIONS

Adjournment; homicide.—Where there was probable cause to believe that respondent had committed a homicide, and where adjournments were granted for purpose of completing hearings on respondent's own motion to suppress and motion to dismiss, and where adjournments did not exceed more than a few days, timing of fact-finding hearing met statute's goal of prompt adjudication. In addition, subdivision (6), precluding successive motions to adjourn, is not applicable in homicide cases. *In re* Neron C., 223 A.D.2d 409, 636 N.Y.S.2d 773 (1st Dept. 1996).

Arrest warrant.—Failure of presentment agency to exercise due diligence in enforcement of arrent warrant will result in 27 of the 35 days respondent was absent not to be excludable for the purposes of speedy trial computations. *In re* Crumb, 175 Misc. 2d 466, 668 N.Y.S.2d 1016 (Fam. Ct. N.Y. Co. 1998).

Good cause.—Presentment agency established "good cause" to adjourn fact-finding hearing one day beyond the statutory 14-day period where co-respondent filed papers that required response to determine need for suppression hearing and severance of cases would have been a waste of judicial resources. *In re* Jesus M., 255 A.D.2d 220, 680 N.Y.S.2d 234 (1st Dept. 1998).

—Request for an adjournment could not be viewed as dilatory in view of amendment of the juvenile delinquency petition and since statutory law provides for an adjournment of up to 30 days for good cause shown. *In re* John C., 117 A.D.2d 567, 498 N.Y.S.2d 838 (1st Dept. 1986).

—Petition dismissed for speedy trial violations since no "good cause" existed for adjournment to conduct *Wade* hearing when witness was available and present in court. Court erred in not commencing hearing on that date even if hearing could not be completed on same day. Statute only sets time limitation upon start of fact finding hearing not on completion. *In re* Malik Y., 231 A.D.2d 731, 732, 647 N.Y.S.2d 859 (2d Dept. 1996).

Special circumstances.—Adjournment of the fact-finding hearing beyond the 14-day limit set by FCA § 340.1, due to complaining witness' failure to appear without demonstration of special circumstances justifying further adjournments, properly resulted in the dismissal of the petition. *In re* Martin R., 268 A.D.2d 277, 700 N.Y.S.2d 712 (1st Dept. 2000).

—Finding of special circumstances to justify successive adjournments is subject to more stringent criteria than "good cause" and is decided on a case by case basis with a strict eye toward stated goal of prompt adjudication; special circumstances caused by severe winter coupled with appellant's detention in distant facility and his refusal to be housed closer satisfied stringent test of special circumstances that could not have been planned or anticipated. *In re* David W., 241 A.D.2d 388, 660 N.Y.S.2d 419 (1st Dept. 1997).

—Special circumstances consist of those for which presentment agency could not have anticipated or planned, i.e., grandmother/guardian's decision to send respondent to school on date of hearing because she had to respond to jury summons and school would not release respondent without adult and no adult was available. *In re* Jamel C., 302 A.D.2d 457, 755 N.Y.S.2d 97 (2d Dept. 2003).

Speedy trial.—Although suppression motion must be decided before fact-finding hearing begins, and suppression hearing is good cause for adjournment of hearing, speedy trial right is not automatically waived by pretrial motion practice; where there was no consent to 47-day continuance of suppression

hearing to allow witness to testify, speedy trial clock continued to run, and speedy trial violation resulted. *In re* George T., 99 N.Y.2d 307, 756 N.Y.S.2d 103, 786 N.E.2d 2 (2002).

—Although juveniles have a right to a speedy trial, there is no per se rule regarding speedy trial violations; court must balance the factors enumerated in *People v. Taranovich*, 37 N.Y.2d 442, in determining the merits of a speedy trial claim. *In re* Benjamin L., 92 N.Y.2d 660, 685 N.Y.S.2d 400, 708 N.E.2d 156 (1998).

—"By its plain language and structure, § 340.1 applies only to adjournments of the commencement of the fact-finding hearing, not to adjournments after the fact-finding hearing has started." *In re* David R., 3 A.D.3d 348, 769 N.Y.S.2d 893 (1st Dept. 2004).

—A petitioner who consents to an adjournment of the hearing past the 60-day speedy trial time period waives his right to claim a violation of speedy trial provisions. *In re* Christopher Scott F., 264 A.D.2d 395, 693 N.Y.S.2d 227 (2d Dept. 1999).

—There is nothing within terms of Family Court Act that requires a fact-finding hearing to commence with the taking of sworn testimony; it may commence with an opening statement, if one is offered, or with the presentation of evidence. *In re* Richard S., 195 Misc. 2d 752, 761 N.Y.S.2d 779 (Fam. Ct. Queens Co. 2003).

Time to commence hearing.—Family court acted in conformity with speedy trial provisions when, acknowledging that speedy trial rights of detained juveniles could not be met because the fact finding hearings were not going to commence within the required time limit, it denied the motion to dismiss and released them. The court then scheduled the hearings within the time limits allowed for non-detained juveniles. *In re* Bernard T., 92 N.Y.2d 738, 686 N.Y.S.2d 338, 709 N.E.2d 79 (1999).

—The 60-day period for commencing a fact-finding hearing begins with the initial appearance on the first petition when the petition is refiled due to dismissal of the first petition. *In re* Willie E., 88 N.Y.2d 205, 644 N.Y.S.2d 130, 666 N.E.2d 1043 (1996).

—References to adjournments contained in § 340.1 pertain to adjournments of the commencement of a fact-finding hearing and not to delays in completing the hearing, which are addressed to the court's sound discretion. *In re* Nathaniel F., 1 A.D.3d 203,767 N.Y.S.2d 217 (1st Dept. 2003).

—Hearing commenced on 56th day was timely where juvenile was not detained, since presenting agency had 60 days within which to commence hearing. *In re* Jose H., 254 A.D.2d 20, 677 N.Y.S.2d 786 (1st Dept. 1998).

—Since respondent was not in detention but released after his initial appearance, the 60-day time period of section 340.1(2) was applicable rather than the 3-day time period imposed by section 340.1(1). *In re* Jamal H., 235 A.D.2d 270, 652 N.Y.S.2d 36 (1st Dept. 1997).

—On day 43 after respondent's first appearance, respondent consented to an almost two-month adjournment that waived any "speedy trial" objection during that time; respondent's waiver operated to toll the statutory 60-day period within which the fact-finding hearing must be commenced; court erred when it dismissed the petition on the next adjourn date prior to the 60-day expiration period. *In re* Curnelle T., 17 A.D.3d 472, 792 N.Y.S.2d 344 (2d Dept. 2005).

—When a petition charges multiple youths with an offense that was committed by acting in concert, the time within which a single or consolidated hearing must be held is measured from the first appearance of each individual defendant, not the first defendant of the group, unless it is established that by staggering the appearances, the presentment agency has engaged in a deliberate attempt to prolong the period of time within which the hearing must be held. *In re* Andre P., 11 A.D.3d 617, 783 N.Y.S.2d 639 (2d Dept. 2004).

—There is "no blanket exception for administrative delay"; presentment agency's failure to exercise due diligence in securing respondent's presence, specifically when they knew of respondent's propensity to spend the evenings at his mother's house and never checked there, properly resulted in dismissal. *In re* Yusef B., 268 A.D.2d 429, 702 N.Y.S.2d 314 (2d Dept. 2000).

—FCA § 340.1 only establishes a time limit for the commencement of the fact-finding hearing, not the completion, and there is no requirement that all witnesses must be available to testify at the commencement of the hearing. *In re* Stephen H., 251 A.D.2d 664, 676 N.Y.S.2d 187 (2d Dept. 1998).

—Petition dismissed where court failed to conduct fact-finding hearing on detained respondent within three-day period specified by statute; record indicated no good cause for delay, and holiday weekend, in and of itself, is insufficient reason for the delay. *In re* Kerry V. M., 267 A.D.2d 1035, 701 N.Y.S.2d 584 (4th Dept. 1999).

§ 340.2. Presiding judge.

1. The judge who presides at the commencement of the fact-finding hearing shall continue to preside until such hearing is concluded and an order entered pursuant to section 345.1 unless a mistrial is declared.

2. The judge who presides at the fact-finding hearing or accepts an admission pursuant to section 321.3 shall preside at any other subsequent hearing in the proceeding, including but not limited to the dispositional hearing.

3. Notwithstanding the provisions of subdivision two, the rules of the family court shall provide for the assignment of the proceeding to another judge of the court when the appropriate judge cannot preside:

(a) by reason of illness, disability, vacation or no longer being a judge of the court in that county; or

(b) by reason of removal from the proceeding due to bias, prejudice or similar grounds; or

(c) Because it is not practicable for the judge to preside.

4. The provisions of this section shall not be waived.

Amended by L. 1999, Ch. 173, § 2, eff. Oct. 4, 1999, amending subd. 3.

ANNOTATIONS

Ministerial violations.—Ministerial violations of this section that do not interfere with the general rule of judicial continuity established by the section do not invalidate written order of the judge after fact-finding hearing. *In re* Marvin R., 253 A.D.2d 679, 677 N.Y.S.2d 470 (1st Dept. 1998).

Presiding judge.—Extension of placement petition need not be heard by same judge who heard original placement petition since it is a separate entity requiring a new hearing and new dispositional order. *In re* Rudolph M., 174 Misc. 2d 273, 664 N.Y.S.2d 399 (Fam. Ct. Kings Co. 1997).

§ 341.1. Exclusion of general public.

The general public may be excluded from any proceeding under this article and only such persons and the representatives of authorized agencies as have a direct interest in the case shall be admitted thereto.

§ 341.2. Presence of respondent and his parent.

1. The respondent and his counsel or law guardian shall be personally present at any hearing under this article and at the initial appearance.

2. If a respondent conducts himself in so disorderly and disruptive a manner that the hearing cannot be carried on with him in the courtroom, the court may order a recess for the purpose of enabling his parent or other person responsible for his care and his law guardian or counsel to exercise full efforts to assist the respondent to conduct himself so as to permit the proceedings to resume in an orderly manner. If such efforts fail, the respondent may be removed from the courtroom if, after he is warned by the court that he will be removed, he continues such disorderly and disruptive conduct. Such time shall not extend beyond the minimum period necessary to restore order.

3. The respondent's parent or other person responsible for his care shall be present at any hearing under this article and at the initial appearance. However, the court shall not be prevented from proceeding by the absence of such parent or person if reasonable and substantial effort has been made to notify such parent or other person and if the respondent and his law guardian or counsel are present.

ANNOTATIONS

Presence of parent.—Absence of respondent's parents from the hearing, despite their presence in the hall outside the courtroom, is not a basis for reversal in the absence of a request from them that they attend the hearing. *In re* Willie E., 88 N.Y.2d 205, 644 N.Y.S.2d 130, 666 N.E.2d 1043 (1996).

—The court failed, prior to taking guilty plea, to make "reasonable and substantial efforts" to secure the presence of the appellant's mother in court during the proceedings or at least to inquire into the efforts made to obtain her presence or notify her of the proceedings against her son. *In re* Delfin A., 123 A.D.2d 318, 506 N.Y.S.2d 215 (2d Dept. 1986).

§ 342.1. The fact-finding hearing; order of procedure.

The order of the fact-finding hearing shall be as follows:

1. The court shall permit the parties to deliver opening addresses. If both parties deliver opening addresses, the presentment agency's address shall be delivered first.

2. The presentment agency must offer evidence in support of the petition.

3. The respondent may offer evidence in his defense.

4. The presentment agency may offer evidence in rebuttal of the respondent's evidence, and the respondent may then offer evidence in rebuttal of the presentment agency's evidence. The court may in its discretion permit the parties to offer further rebuttal or surrebuttal evidence in this pattern. In the interest of justice, the court may permit either party to offer evidence upon rebuttal which is not technically of a rebuttal nature but more properly a part of the offering party's original case.

5. At the conclusion of the evidence, the respondent shall have the right to deliver a summation.

6. The presentment agency shall then have the right to deliver a summation.

7. The court must then consider the case and enter a finding.

ANNOTATIONS

Adjournment.—Rather than dismissing petition, court should have granted the short adjournment requested by the presentment agency to secure the presence of the complaining witness, whose absence was due to a misunderstanding. *In re* Bryant J., 195 A.D.2d 463, 600 N.Y.S.2d 128, 129 (2d Dept. 1993).

Continuance.—Court did not abuse its discretion in denying respondent's application for a continuance to produce a witness in view of respondent's unsubstantiated assertion regarding the witness's availability. *In re* Peter R., 191 A.D.2d 214, 594 N.Y.S.2d 203, 204 (1st Dept. 1993).

Cross-examination.—Court did not err when it permitted the presentment agency to cross-examine the appellant as to whether he committed certain specific criminal acts, as the agency had a good faith basis for the questions. *In re* Carlos U., 192 A.D.2d 661, 597 N.Y.S.2d 85 (2d Dept. 1993).

§ 342.2. Evidence in fact-finding hearings; required quantum.

1. Only evidence that is competent, material and relevant may be admitted at a fact-finding hearing.

2. Any determination at the conclusion of a fact-finding hearing that a respondent committed an act or acts which if committed by an adult would be a crime must be based on proof beyond a reasonable doubt.

3. An order of removal pursuant to a direction authorized by sections 220.10, 310.85 and 330.25 of the criminal procedure law constitutes proof beyond a reasonable doubt and a determination that the respondent did the act or acts specified therein in accordance with section 725.05 of the criminal procedure law.

ANNOTATIONS

Burden of proof.—It is the burden of the party presenting the petition in a Family Court juvenile delinquency proceeding to prove beyond a reasonable doubt that a person committed an act or acts which, if committed by an adult, would be a crime. *In re* Jerry XX., 115 A.D.2d 797, 495 N.Y.S.2d 736 (3d Dept. 1985).

Credibility and weight of evidence.—Testimony of arresting officer, who identified contraband, and chemist, who gave "reasonable assurance" that the crack cocaine received in evidence was the same cocaine recovered from the appellant and that it was in the same condition but for the chemical testing, helped to establish the chain of custody of the contraband; deficiencies in the vouchering procedure went to the weight rather than the admissibility of the evidence. *In re* Kassan D., 287 A.D.2d 564, 731 N.Y.S.2d 487 (2d Dept. 2001).

—Family court judge serves as the trier of fact and his resolution of disputed facts is to be accorded the same weight as that given to a jury verdict; where the findings of fact are resolved against a respondent, the party bringing the petition is entitled to the most favorable view of the evidence. *In re* Michael D., 109 A.D.2d 633, 634, 486 N.Y.S.2d 213 (2d Dept. 1985).

—Finding of delinquency can be based on uncorroborated testimony of witness; court has broad discretion in determining that a child may give sworn testimony so long as it can be sufficiently established "that the child understood the difference between the truth and a lie, understood her obligation to tell the truth in the court setting and understood that the court could impose punishment upon her if she failed to tell the truth." *In re* Jordan E., 305 A.D.2d 778, 759 N.Y.S.2d 807 (3d Dept. 2003).

§ 343.1. Rules of evidence; testimony given by children.

1. Any person may be a witness in a delinquency proceeding unless the court finds that, by reason of infancy or mental disease or defect, he does not possess sufficient intelligence or capacity to justify reception of his evidence.

2. Every witness more than nine years old may testify only under oath unless the court is satisfied that such witness cannot, as a result of mental disease or defect, understand the nature of an oath. A witness less than nine years old may not testify under oath unless the court is satisfied that he or she understands the nature of an oath. If under either of the above provisions, a witness is deemed to be ineligible to testify under oath, the witness may nevertheless be permitted to give unsworn evidence if the court is satisfied that the witness possesses sufficient intelligence and capacity to justify the reception thereof.

3. A respondent may not be found to be delinquent solely upon the unsworn evidence given pursuant to subdivision two.

4. A child witness may give testimony in accordance with the provisions of article sixty-five of the criminal procedure law, provided such child is declared vulnerable in accordance with subdivision one of section 65.10 of such law. A child witness means a person fourteen years old or less who is or will be called to testify in any proceeding concerning an act defined in article one hundred thirty of the penal law or section 255.25 of such law, which act would constitute a crime if committed by an adult. The provisions of this subdivision shall expire and be deemed repealed on the same date as article sixty-five of the criminal procedure law expires and is deemed repealed pursuant to section five of chapter five hundred five of the laws of nineteen hundred eighty-five, as from time to time, amended.

Amended by L. 1988, Ch. 331, § 1, eff. Nov. 1, 1988, adding subd. 4; L. 2003, Ch. 264, § 61, eff. Nov. 1, 2003, amending subd. 2; L. 2004, Ch. 362, § 1, eff. Nov. 1, 2004, amending subd. 4.

ANNOTATIONS

Witness less than 12 years old.—Petition's failure to state affirmatively that witness less than 12 years old had been adjudged competent to swear to supporting deposition is not fatal as long as affidavit is facially valid and is sworn to before a notary public. Any defect in petition relating to capacity of affiant was latent; dismissal of petition at onset was not required. *In re* Nelson R., 90 N.Y.2d 359, 660 N.Y.S.2d 707, 683 N.E.2d 329 (1997).

—Court may allow unsworn testimony of witness under age of 12 if court determines that witness does not understand significance of oath but is satisfied that witness possesses sufficient intelligence and capacity to justify reception of unsworn testimony. *In re* Richard S., 195 Misc.2d 752, 761 N.Y.S.2d 779 (Fam. Ct. Queens Co. 2003).

§ 343.2. Rules of evidence; corroboration of accomplice testimony.

1. A respondent may not be found to be

delinquent upon the testimony of an accomplice unsupported by corroborative evidence tending to connect the respondent with the commission of the crime or crimes charged in the petition.

2. An "accomplice" means a witness in a juvenile delinquency proceeding who, according to evidence adduced in such proceeding, may reasonably be considered to have participated in:

(a) the crime charged; or

(b) a crime based on the same or some of the same facts or conduct which constitutes the crime charged in the petition.

3. A witness who is an accomplice as defined in subdivision two is no less such because a proceeding, conviction or finding of delinquency against him would be barred or precluded by some defense or exemption such as infancy, immunity or previous prosecution amounting to a collateral impediment to such proceeding, conviction or finding, not affecting the conclusion that such witness engaged in the conduct constituting the crime with the mental state required for the commission thereof.

ANNOTATION

Uncorroborated accomplice testimony insufficient.— Uncorroborated testimony of respondent's accomplice is insufficient as a matter of law to sustain a petition for a finding of juvenile delinquency. *In re* Luz B., 235 A.D.2d 256, 652 N.Y.S.2d 511 (1st Dept. 1997).

§ 343.3. Rules of evidence; identification by means of previous recognition in absence of present identification.

1. In any juvenile delinquency proceeding in which the respondent's commission of a crime is in issue, testimony as provided in subdivision two may be given by a witness when:

(a) such witness testifies that:

(i) he observed the person claimed by the presentment agency to be the respondent either at the time and place of the commission of the crime or upon some other occasion relevant to the case; and

(ii) on a subsequent occasion he observed, under circumstances consistent with such rights as an accused person may derive under the constitution of this state or of the United States, a person whom he recognized as the same person whom he had observed on the first incriminating occasion; and

(iii) he is unable at the proceeding to state, on the basis of present recollection, whether or not the respondent is the person in question; and

(b) it is established that the respondent is in fact the person whom the witness observed and recognized on the second occasion. Such fact may be established by testimony of another person or

persons to whom the witness promptly declared his recognition on such occasion.

2. Under circumstances prescribed in subdivision one, such witness may testify at the proceeding that the person whom he observed and recognized on the second occasion is the same person whom he observed on the first or incriminating occasion. Such testimony, together with the evidence that the respondent is in fact the person whom the witness observed and recognized on the second occasion, constitutes evidence in chief.

§ 343.4. Rules of evidence; identification by means of previous recognition, in addition to present identification.

In any juvenile delinquency proceeding in which the respondent's commission of a crime is in issue, a witness who testifies that;

(a) he observed the person claimed by the presentment agency to be the respondent either at the time and place of the commission of the crime or upon some other occasion relevant to the case, and

(b) on the basis of present recollection, the respondent is the person in question, and

(c) on a subsequent occasion he observed the respondent, under circumstances consistent with such rights as an accused person may derive under the constitution of this state or of the United States, and then also recognized him as the same person whom he had observed on the first or incriminating occasion, may, in addition to making an identification of the respondent at the delinquency proceeding on the basis of present recollection as the person whom he observed on the first or incriminating occasion, also describe his previous recognition of the respondent and testify that the person whom he observed on such second occasion is the same person whom he had observed on the first or incriminating occasion. Such testimony constitutes evidence in chief.

§ 343.5. Rules of evidence; impeachment of own witness by proof of prior contradictory statement.

1. When, upon examination by the party who called him, a witness in a delinquency proceeding gives testimony upon a material issue of the case which tends to disprove the position of such party, such party may introduce evidence that such witness has previously made either a written statement signed by him or an oral statement under oath contradictory to such testimony.

2. Evidence concerning a prior contradictory statement introduced pursuant to subdivision one may be received only for the purpose of impeaching the credibility of the witness with respect to his testimony upon the subject, and does not constitute evidence in chief.

MISC. LAWS

3. When a witness has made a prior signed or sworn statement contradictory to his testimony in a delinquency proceeding upon a material issue of the case, but his testimony does not tend to disprove the position of the party who called him and elicited such testimony, evidence that the witness made such prior statement is not admissible, and such party may not use such prior statement for the purpose of refreshing the recollection of the witness in a manner that discloses its contents to the court.

§ 344.1. Rules of evidence; proof of previous conviction or delinquency finding.

1. If in the course of a juvenile delinquency proceeding, any witness, including a respondent, is properly asked whether he was previously convicted of a specified offense and answers in the negative or in an equivocal manner, the party adverse to the one who called him may independently prove such conviction. If in response to proper inquiry whether he has ever been convicted of any offense the witness answers in the negative or in an equivocal manner, the adverse party may independently prove any previous conviction.

2. If a respondent in a juvenile delinquency proceeding, through the testimony of a witness other than respondent called by him, offers evidence of his good character, the presentment agency may independently prove any previous finding of delinquency of the respondent for a crime the commission of which would tend to negate any character trait or quality attributed to the respondent in such witness' testimony.

§ 344.2. Rules of evidence; statements of respondent; corroboration.

1. Evidence of a written or oral confession, admission, or other statement made by a respondent with respect to his participation or lack of participation in the crime charged, may not be received in evidence against him in a juvenile delinquency proceeding if such statement was involuntarily made.

2. A confession, admission or other statement is "involuntarily made" by a respondent when it is obtained from him:

(a) by any person by the use or threatened use of physical force upon the respondent or another person, or by means of any other improper conduct or undue pressure which impaired the respondent's physical or mental condition to the extent of undermining his ability to make a choice whether or not to make a statement; or

(b) by a public servant engaged in law enforcement activity or by a person then acting under his direction or in cooperation with him;

(i) by means of any promise or statement of fact, which promise or statement creates a substantial risk that the respondent might falsely incriminate himself; or

(ii) in violation of such rights as the respondent may derive from the constitution of this state or of the United States; or

(iii) in violation of section 305.2.

3. A child may not be found to be delinquent based on the commission of any crime solely upon evidence of a confession or admission made by him without additional proof that the crime charged has been committed.

§ 344.3. Rules of evidence; psychiatric testimony in certain cases.

When, in connection with a defense of mental disease or defect, a psychiatrist or licensed psychologist who has examined the respondent testifies at the fact-finding hearing concerning the respondent's mental condition at the time of the conduct charged to constitute a crime, he must be permitted to make a statement as to the nature of the examination, the diagnosis of the mental condition of the respondent and his opinion as to the extent, if any, to which the capacity of the respondent to know or appreciate the nature and consequences of such conduct, or its wrongfulness, was impaired as a result of mental disease or defect at that time. The psychiatrist must be permitted to make any explanation reasonably serving to clarify his diagnosis and opinion, and may be cross-examined as to any matter bearing on his competency or credibility or the validity of his diagnosis or opinion.

§ 344.4. Rules of evidence; admissibility of evidence of victim's sexual conduct in sex offense cases.

Evidence of a victim's sexual conduct shall not be admissible in a juvenile delinquency proceeding for a crime or an attempt to commit a crime defined in article one hundred thirty of the penal law unless such evidence:

1. proves or tends to prove specific instances of the victim's prior sexual conduct with the accused; or

2. proves or tends to prove that the victim has been convicted of an offense under section 230.00 of the penal law within three years prior to the sex offense which is the subject of the juvenile delinquency proceeding; or

3. rebuts evidence introduced by the presentment agency of the victim's failure to engage in sexual intercourse, oral sexual conduct, anal sexual conduct or sexual contact during a given period of time; or

4. rebuts evidence introduced by the presentment agency which proves or tends to prove that the accused is the cause of pregnancy or disease

of the victim, or the source of semen found in the victim; or

5. is determined by the court after an offer of proof by the accused, or such hearing as the court may require, and a statement by the court of its findings of fact essential to its determination, to be relevant and admissible in the interests of justice.

Added by L. 1987, Ch. 761, eff. Nov. 1, 1987; L. 2003, Ch. 264, § 62, eff. Nov. 1, 2003, amending subd. 3.

§ 345.1. Orders.

1. If the allegations of a petition or specific counts of a petition concerning the commission of a crime or crimes are established, the court shall enter an appropriate order and schedule a dispositional hearing pursuant to section 350.1. The order shall specify the count or counts of the petition upon which such order is based and the section or sections of the penal law or other law under which the act or acts so stated would constitute a crime if committed by an adult. If the respondent or respondents are found to have committed a designated felony act, the order shall so state.

2. If the allegations of a petition or specific counts of a petition under this article are not established, the court shall enter an order dismissing the petition or specific counts therein.

ANNOTATIONS

Generally.—In attempted rape prosecution, the fact that the Family Court did not sustain the attempted rape charge as to the co-respondent did not render the court's finding repugnant, as accomplice liability may be imposed notwithstanding the co-respondent's "acquittal" on the attempted rape. *In re* Khaliek W., 193 A.D.2d 683, 598 N.Y.S.2d 29 (2d Dept. 1993).

Physical injury.—The complainant's testimony that he experienced persistent headaches and dizziness after being struck by defendant was sufficient to show substantial pain within the meaning of Penal Law §§ 10.00(9) and 120.00(1). *In re* Robert M., 194 A.D.2d 377, 598 N.Y.S.2d 500 (1st Dept. 1993).

§ 346.1. Fact-finding hearing; removal.

1. Where the proceeding was commenced by the filing of an order of removal pursuant to a direction authorized by section 220.10, 310.85 or 330.25 of the criminal procedure law, the requirements of a fact-finding hearing shall be deemed to have been satisfied upon the filing of the order and no further fact-finding hearing need be held; provided, however, that where any specification required by subdivision five of section 725.05 of the criminal procedure law is not clear, the court may examine such records or hold such hearing as it deems necessary to clarify said specification.

§ 347.1. Required testing of the respondent in certain proceedings.

1. (a) In any proceeding where the respondent is found pursuant to section 345.1 or 346.1 of this article, to have committed a felony offense enumerated in any section of article one hundred thirty of the penal law, or any subdivision of section 130.20 of such law, for which an act of "sexual intercourse", "oral sexual conduct" or "anal sexual conduct", as those terms are defined in section 130.00 of the penal law, is required as an essential element for the commission thereof, the court must, upon a request of the victim, order that the respondent submit to human immunodeficiency (HIV) related testing. The testing is to be conducted by a state, county, or local public health officer designated by the order. Test results, which shall not be disclosed to the court, shall be communicated to the respondent and the victim named in the order in accordance with the provisions of section twenty-seven hundred eighty-five-a of the public health law.

(b) For the purposes of this section, the term "victim" means the person with whom the respondent engaged in an act of "sexual intercourse", "oral sexual conduct" or "anal sexual conduct", as those terms are defined in section 130.00 of the penal law, where such conduct with such victim was the basis for the court's finding that the respondent committed acts constituting one or more of the offenses specified in paragraph (a) of this subdivision.

2. Any request made by the victim pursuant to this section must be in writing, filed with the court and provided by the court to the defendant and his or her counsel. The request must be filed with the court prior to or within ten days after the filing of an order in accordance with section 345.1 or 346.1 of this article, provided that, for good cause shown, the court may permit such request to be filed at any time prior to the entry of an order of disposition.

3. Any requests, related papers and orders made or filed pursuant to this section, together with any papers or proceedings related thereto, shall be sealed by the court and not made available for any purpose, except as may be necessary for the conduct of judicial proceedings directly related to the provisions of this section. All proceedings on such requests shall be held in camera.

4. The application for an order to compel a respondent to undergo an HIV related test may be made by the victim but, if the victim is an infant or incompetent person, the application may also be made by a representative as defined in section twelve hundred one of the civil practice law and rules. The application must state that (a) the applicant was the victim of the offense, enumerated in paragraph (a) of subdivision one of this section, which the court found the defendant to have committed; and (b) the applicant has been offered counseling by a public health officer and been advised of (i) the limitations on the information to be obtained through an HIV test on the proposed subject; (ii) current scientific assessments of the risk of transmission of HIV from the exposure he or she may have experienced; and (iii) the need for the applicant to

undergo HIV related testing to definitively determine his or her HIV status.

5. The court shall conduct a hearing only if necessary to determine if the applicant is the victim of the offense the respondent was found to have committed. The court ordered test must be performed within fifteen days of the date on which the court ordered the test, provided however that whenever the respondent is not tested within the period prescribed by the court, the court must again order that the respondent undergo an HIV related test.

6. (a) Test results shall be disclosed subject to the following limitations, which shall be specified in any order issued pursuant to this section: (i) disclosure of confidential HIV related information shall be limited to that information which is necessary to fulfill the purpose for which the order is granted; (ii) disclosure of confidential HIV related information shall be limited to the person making the application; redisclosure shall be permitted only to the victim, the victim's immediate family, guardian, physicians, attorneys, medical or mental health providers and to his or her past and future contacts to whom there was or is a reasonable risk of HIV transmission and shall not be permitted to any other person or the court.

(b) Unless inconsistent with this section, the court's order shall direct compliance with and conform to the provisions of article twenty seven-f of the public health law. Such order shall include measures to protect against disclosure to others of the identity and HIV status of the applicant and of the person tested and may include such other measures as the court deems necessary to protect confidential information.

7. Any failure to comply with the provisions of this section or section twenty-seven hundred eighty-five-a of the public health law shall not impair the validity of any order of disposition entered by the court.

8. No information obtained as a result of a consent, hearing or court order for testing issued pursuant to this section nor any information derived therefrom may be used as evidence in any criminal or civil proceeding against the respondent which relates to events that were the basis for the respondent's conviction, provided however that nothing herein shall prevent prosecution of a witness testifying in any court hearing held pursuant to this section for perjury pursuant to article two hundred ten of the penal law.

Added by L. 1995, Ch. 76, § 2, eff. Aug. 1, 1995; **Amended** by L. 2003, Ch. 264, § 63, eff. Nov. 1, 2003, amending subd. 1(a) and (b).

Part 5. The dispositional hearing

§ 350.1. Time of dispositional hearing.

1. If the respondent is detained and has not been found to have committed a designated felony act the dispositional hearing shall commence not more than ten days after the entry of an order pursuant to subdivision one of section 345.1. except as provided in subdivision three.

2. In all other cases, the dispositional hearing shall commence not more than fifty days after entry of an order pursuant to subdivision one of section 345.1, except as provided in subdivision three.

3. The court may adjourn the dispositional hearing:

(a) on its own motion or on motion of the presentment agency for good cause shown for not more than ten days; or

(b) on motion by the respondent for good cause shown for not more than thirty days.

4. The court shall state on the record the reason for any adjournment of the dispositional hearing.

5. Successive motions to adjourn a dispositional hearing beyond the limits enumerated in subdivision one or two shall not be granted in the absence of a showing, on the record, of special circumstances; special circumstances shall not include calendar congestion or the status of the court's docket or backlog.

Amended by L. 1982, Ch. 926, eff. July 1, 1983; L. 1983, Ch. 398, eff. July 1, 1983.

ANNOTATIONS

Adjournments.—Findings on the record are a mandatory condition for adjourning a dispositional hearing beyond the statutorily prescribed time limitations. *In re* Leon H., 196 A.D.2d 539, 601 N.Y.S.2d 158 (2d Dept. 1993).

Special circumstances.—Court's need to obtain a probation report after an investigation as well as a mental health evaluation in order to properly evaluate the needs of the juvenile and fashion an appropriate placement which best served the juvenile and protected the community constituted "special circumstances." *In re* Douglas L., 232 A.D. 489, 648 N.Y.S.2d 165 (2d Dept. 1996).

Speedy disposition; no per se rule.—There is no per se rule of dismissal for "speedy disposition lapses." *In re* Jose R., 83 N.Y.2d 388, 610 N.Y.S.2d 937, 632 N.E.2d 1260 (1994).

—Respondent's second and intervening arrest which eliminated the possibility of parole as a resolution of the first matter and sent the issue of appropriate placement back to the Probation Department could not be viewed as dilatory tactic on the part of the Probation Department; no violation of respondent's "speedy disposition" rights occurred. *In re* Perry O., 232 A.D. 225, 226, 647 N.Y.S.2d 785 (1st Dept. 1996).

—Appellant's motion to dismiss on the ground that more than 80 days had elapsed from the date of the fact-finding order was properly denied, as appellant's counsel had requested the adjournment in order to procure a report from appellant's mental health counselor. *In re* John McC., 223 A.D.2d 709, 637 N.Y.S.2d 427 (2d Dept. 1996).

Waiver.—Respondent's right to a timely dispositional hearing was waived where the Law Guardian did not move to dismiss the petition on that ground. *In re* Harry J., 191 A.D.2d 1016, 594 N.Y.S.2d 946 (4th Dept. 1993).

§ 350.2. Order of removal.

1. Where the proceeding has been commenced by the filing of an order of removal pursuant to

a direction authorized by sections 220.10, 310.85 and 330.25 of the criminal procedure law, the date of filing in the family court shall be deemed for purposes of section 350.1 to be the date of the entry of an order pursuant to subdivision one of section 345.1.

2. The clerk of court shall calendar an appearance to be held within seven days from the date the order of removal was filed. At such appearance the court shall schedule a dispositional hearing in accordance with section 350.1 and determine such other issues as may properly be before it.

§ 350.3. Dispositional hearings; evidence and required quantum of proof—appearance of presentment agency.

1. Only evidence that is material and relevant may be admitted during a dispositional hearing.

2. An adjudication at the conclusion of a dispositional hearing must be based on a preponderance of the evidence.

3. The presentment agency shall appear at the dispositional hearing.

ANNOTATION

Sufficiency of evidence.—In juvenile delinquency proceeding, family court's determination that appellant's need for supervision, treatment, and placement was clearly based on a preponderance of material evidence produced at the dispositional hearing. *In re* Tanisha B. (Anonymous), 296 A.D.2d 494, 745 N.Y.S.2d 473 (2d Dept. 2002).

§ 350.4. Order of procedure.

The order of the dispositional hearing shall be as follows:

1. The court, with the consent of the parties, may direct the probation service to summarize its investigation report if one has been prepared and, in its discretion, deliver any further statement concerning the advisability of specific dispositional alternatives.

2. The court may in its discretion call witnesses, including the preparer of probation reports or diagnostic studies, to offer evidence concerning the advisability of specific dispositional alternatives. Such witnesses may be cross-examined by the presentment agency and the respondent.

3. The presentment agency may call witnesses to offer such evidence including the preparer of a probation report or a diagnostic study.

4. The respondent may call witnesses, to offer such evidence, including the preparer of a probation report or a diagnostic study.

5. The court may permit the presentment agency or respondent to offer such rebuttal or surrebuttal evidence as it may deem appropriate.

6. The presentment agency may deliver a statement concerning the advisability of specific dispositional alternatives.

7. The respondent may deliver such a statement.

8. The court shall then permit rebuttal statements by both the presentment agency and the respondent.

9. The court shall then consider the case and enter a dispositional order.

Amended by L. 1982, Ch. 926, eff. July 1, 1983, Ch. 398, eff. July 1, 1983.

§ 351.1. Probation, investigation and diagnostic assessment.

1. Following a determination that a respondent has committed a designated felony act and prior to the dispositional hearing, the judge shall order a probation investigation and a diagnostic assessment. For the purposes of this article, the probation investigation shall include, but not be limited to, the history of the juvenile including previous conduct, the family situation, any previous psychological and psychiatric reports, school adjustment, previous social assistance provided by voluntary or public agencies and the response of the juvenile to such assistance. For the purposes of this article, the diagnostic assessment shall include, but not be limited to, psychological tests and psychiatric interviews to determine mental capacity and achievement, emotional stability and mental disabilities. It shall include a clinical assessment of the situational factors that may have contributed to the act or acts. When feasible, expert opinion shall be rendered as to the risk presented by the juvenile to others or himself, with a recommendation as to the need for a restrictive placement.

2. Following a determination that a respondent committed a crime and prior to the dispositional hearing, the court shall order a probation investigation and may order a diagnostic assessment.

3. A child shall not be placed in accord with section 353.3 unless the court has ordered a probation investigation prior to the dispositional hearing; a child shall not be placed in accord with section 353.4 unless the court has ordered a diagnostic assessment prior to such hearing.

4. When it appears that such information would be relevant to the findings of the court or the order of disposition, each investigation report prepared pursuant to this section shall contain a victim impact statement which shall include an analysis of the victim's version of the offense, the extent of injury or economic loss or damage to the victim, including the amount of unreimbursed medical expenses, if any, and the views of the victim relating to disposition including the amount of restitution sought by the victim, subject to availability of such information. In the case of a homicide or where the victim is unable to assist

in the preparation of the victim impact statement, the information may be acquired from the victim's family. Nothing contained in this section shall be interpreted to require that a victim or his or her family supply information for the preparation of an investigation report or that the dispositional hearing should be delayed in order to obtain such information.

5.   (a) All diagnostic assessments and probation investigation reports shall be submitted to the court and made available by the court for inspection and copying by the presentment agency and the respondent at least five court days prior to the commencement of the dispositional hearing. All such reports shall be made available by the court for inspection and copying by the presentment agency and the respondent in connection with any appeal in the case.

(b) The victim impact statement shall be made available to the victim or the victim's family by the presentment agency prior to sentencing.

6. All reports or memoranda prepared or obtained by the probation service for the purpose of a dispositional hearing shall be deemed confidential information furnished to the court and shall be subject to disclosure solely in accordance with this section or as otherwise provided for by law. Except as provided under section 320.5 such reports or memoranda shall not be furnished to the court prior to the entry of an order pursuant to section 345.1.

7. The probation services which prepare the investigation reports shall be responsible for the collection and transmission to the state division of probation and correctional alternatives, of data on the number of victim impact statements prepared, pursuant to regulations of the division. Such information shall be transmitted to the crime victims board and included in the board's annual report pursuant to subdivision twenty of section six hundred twenty-three of the executive law.

Amended by L. 1983, Ch. 398, eff. July 1, 1983; L. 1985, Ch. 585, eff. July 28, 1985; L. 1985, Ch. 880; L. 1987, Ch. 101; L. 1989, Ch. 161, eff. June 17, 1989; L. 1991, Ch. 198, eff. June 28, 1991; L. 1986, Ch. 418, eff. Nov. 1, 1986; L. 2004, Ch. 317, § 1, eff. Nov. 8, 2004, amending subd. 4.

ANNOTATIONS

History of juvenile.—The history of a juvenile in a probation investigation report mandated by subsection (1) may include prior petitions seeking to adjudicate the juvenile as a person in need of supervision (PINS) as well as prior delinquency petitions with no reported disposition. *In re* Mi-Kell V., 226 A.D.2d 810, 640 N.Y.S.2d 626 (3d Dept. 1996).

Investigation and diagnostic assessment.—Dispositional hearing in which respondent's probation officer testified and an extensive mental health study of respondent was admitted in to evidence satisfied requirements of section 351.1 despite absence of written investigation and report ordered by court. *In re* Christopher R., 235 A.D.2d 299, 652 N.Y.S.2d 612 (1st Dept. 1997).

Notice not required.—Placement agency was not required to provide family court with notice of intent to seek restrictive placement; where juvenile was found to have committed designated felony, restrictive placement was mandated. *In re* Dorrion S., 302 A.D.2d 598, 757 N.Y.S.2d 49 (2d Dept. 2003).

§ 352.1. Findings.

1. If, upon the conclusion of the dispositional hearing, the court determines that the respondent requires supervision, treatment or confinement, the court shall enter a finding that such respondent is a juvenile delinquent and order an appropriate disposition pursuant to section 352.2.

2. If, upon the conclusion of the dispositional hearing, the court determines that the respondent does not require supervision, treatment or confinement, the petition shall be dismissed.

ANNOTATIONS

Generally.—In juvenile delinquency proceeding, family court's determination that appellant's need for supervision, treatment, and placement was clearly based on a preponderance of material evidence produced at the dispositional hearing. *In re* Tanisha B. (Anonymous), 296 A.D.2d 494, 745 N.Y.S.2d 473 (2d Dept. 2002).

—In determining the least restrictive available alternative, Family Court is to be guided not only by the needs and the best interest of the juvenile, but also by the need to protect the community. *In re* Shawn T., 195 A.D.2d 796, 600 N.Y.S.2d 393 (3d Dept. 1993).

§ 352.2. Order of disposition.

1. Upon the conclusion of the dispositional hearing, the court shall enter an order of disposition:

(a) conditionally discharging the respondent in accord with section 353.1; or

(b) putting the respondent on probation in accord with section 353.2; or

(c) continuing the proceeding and placing the respondent in accord with section 353.3; or

(d) placing the respondent in accord with section 353.4; or

(e) continuing the proceeding and placing the respondent under a restrictive placement in accord with section 353.5.

2.   (a) In determining an appropriate order the court shall consider the needs and best interests of the respondent as well as the need for protection of the community. If the respondent has committed a designated felony act the court shall determine the appropriate disposition in accord with section 353.5. In all other cases the court shall order the least restrictive available alternative enumerated in subdivision one which is consistent with the needs and best interests of the respondent and the need for protection of the community.

(b) In an order of disposition entered pursuant to section 353.3 or 353.4 of this chapter, or where the court has determined pursuant to section 353.5 of this chapter that restrictive placement is not required, which order places the respondent with the commissioner of social services or with the office of children and family services for placement with an authorized agency or class of authorized agencies or in such facilities designated by the office of children and family services as are eligible for federal reimbursement pursuant to title IV-E of the social security act, the court in its order shall determine (i) that continuation in the respondent's home would be contrary to the best interests of the respondent; or in the case of a respondent for whom the court has determined that continuation in his or her home would not be contrary to the best interests of the respondent, that continuation in the respondent's home would be contrary to the need for protection of the community; (ii) that where appropriate, and where consistent with the need for protection of the community, reasonable efforts were made prior to the date of the dispositional hearing to prevent or eliminate the need for removal of the respondent from his or her home, or if the child was removed from his or her home prior to the dispositional hearing, where appropriate and where consistent with the need for safety of the community, whether reasonable efforts were made to make it possible for the child to safely return home. If the court determines that reasonable efforts to prevent or eliminate the need for removal of the child from the home were not made but that the lack of such efforts was appropriate under the circumstances, or consistent with the need for protection of the community, or both, the court order shall include such a finding; and (iii) in the case of a child who has attained the age of sixteen, the services needed, if any, to assist the child to make the transition from foster care to independent living.

(c) For the purpose of this section, when an order is entered pursuant to section 353.3 or 353.4 of this article, reasonable efforts to prevent or eliminate the need for removing the respondent from the home of the respondent or to make it possible for the respondent to return safely to the home of the respondent shall not be required where the court determines that:

(1) the parent of such respondent has subjected the respondent to aggravated circumstances, as defined in subdivision fifteen of section 301.2 of this article;

(2) the parent of such child has been convicted of (i) murder in the first degree as defined in section 125.27 or murder in the second degree as defined in section 125.25 of the penal law and the victim was another child of the parent; or (ii) manslaughter in the first degree as defined in section 125.20 or manslaughter in the second degree as defined in section 125.15 of the penal law and the victim was another child of the parent, provided, however, that the parent must have acted voluntarily in committing such crime;

(3) the parent of such child has been convicted of an attempt to commit any of the foregoing crimes, and the victim or intended victim was the child or another child of the parent; or has been convicted of criminal solicitation as defined in article one hundred, conspiracy as defined in article one hundred five or criminal facilitation

as defined in article one hundred fifteen of the penal law for conspiring, soliciting or facilitating any of the foregoing crimes, and the victim or intended victim was the child or another child of the parent;

(4) the parent of such respondent has been convicted of assault in the second degree as defined in section 120.05, assault in the first degree as defined in section 120.10 or aggravated assault upon a person less than eleven years old as defined in section 120.12 of the penal law, and the commission of one of the foregoing crimes resulted in serious physical injury to the respondent or another child of the parent;

(5) the parent of such respondent has been convicted in any other jurisdiction of an offense which includes all of the essential elements of any crime specified in subparagraph two, three or four of this paragraph, and the victim of such offense was the respondent or another child of the parent; or

(6) the parental rights of the parent to a sibling of such respondent have been involuntarily terminated;

unless the court determines that providing reasonable efforts would be in the best interests of the child, not contrary to the health and safety of the child, and would likely result in the reunification of the parent and the child in the foreseeable future. The court shall state such findings in its order.

If the court determines that reasonable efforts are not required because of one of the grounds set forth above, a permanency hearing shall be held pursuant to section 355.5 of this article within thirty days of the finding of the court that such efforts are not required. The social services official or the office of children and family services, where the respondent was placed with such office, shall subsequent to the permanency hearing make reasonable efforts to place the respondent in a timely manner and to complete whatever steps are necessary to finalize the permanent placement of the respondent as set forth in the permanency plan approved by the court. If reasonable efforts are determined by the court not to be required because of one of the grounds set forth in this paragraph, the social services official may file a petition for termination of parental rights in accordance with section three hundred eighty-four-b of the social services law.

(d) For the purposes of this section, in determining reasonable efforts to be made with respect to the respondent, and in making such reasonable efforts, the respondent's health and safety shall be the paramount concern.

(e) For the purpose of this section, a sibling shall include a half-sibling.

3. The order shall state the court's reasons for the particular disposition, including, in the case of a restrictive placement pursuant to section

353.5, the specific findings of fact required in such section.

Amended by L. 1985, Ch. 880; L. 1987, Ch. 101; L. 1989, eff. June 17, 1989; L. 1988, Ch. 478, § 1, eff. Nov. 1, 1988, but not affecting the expiration of this provision as otherwise provided by law; L. 1991, Ch. 198, eff. June 28, 1991, but not effect the expiration of such section; L. 1992, Ch. 465, eff. Jan. 14, 1992, amending subd. (2)(b), and shall apply to all persons placed in or committed to the custody of the division of youth on or after such date; L. 1999, Ch. 7, § 29, eff. Feb. 11, 1999, adding subd. 2(c) through 2(e); L. 2000, Ch. 145, §§ 9, 10, eff. July 1, 2000.

ANNOTATIONS

Discretion.—Placement of appellant in non-secure facility was supported by findings in the record of insufficient supervision at home, subsequent arrest while on probation, and increased incidents of antisocial and disruptive behavior. *In re* Derek B., 267 A.D.2d 45, 700 N.Y.S.2d 114 (1st Dept. 1999).

—Proper exercise of discretion where Family Court placed appellant with Berkshire Farms for a period of 18 months, also where court determined that giving appellant credit for time served would not serve his best interests, nor adequately protect community, especially in light of felony committed by appellant during pendency of instant disposition. *In re* Jamal J., 8 A.D.3d 382, 777 N.Y.S.2d 744 (2d Dept. 2004).

—"The least restrictive alternative test does not require the court to actually try the lowest form of intervention, have it fail, and then try each succeeding level of intervention before ordering . . . placement"; court did not abuse its discretion by ordering placement where psychologist and probation officer testified as to appellant's aggressive, violent, and abuse behavior. *In re* Naiquan T, 265 A.D.2d 331, 696 N.Y.S.2d 79 (2d Dept. 1999).

—Decision to order placement in a title III facility rests within the discretion of the Family Court. *In re* Garfield M., 128 A.D.2d 876, 513 N.Y.S.2d 798 (2d Dept. 1987).

—Although the family court is directed by statute to order the least restrictive alternative, the least alternative "need not be actually tried and fail before more restrictive alternatives can be imposed"; where the record is replete with evidence demonstrating respondent's drug and alcohol dependence and the alcohol dependence of his father, placement of respondent in the custody of social services was not an abuse of discretion. *In re* Jonathan "D," 297 A.D.2d 400, 746 N.Y.S.2d 206 (3d Dept. 2002).

—Respondent's history as a PIN as well as a juvenile delinquent coupled with failure to successfully attend school and refrain from assaultive behavior when previously returned to community satisfied appellate court that no abuse of discretion in placement of respondent with Division of Youth v. Errol D., 241 A.D.2d 732, 660 N.Y.S.2d 185 (3d Dept. 1997).

—Appellant's placement in a limited secure facility was the least restrictive placement where established problems of drug use and assaultive behavior required psychiatric counseling and a structured environment. *In re* Vidal W., 267 A.D.2d 1104, 701 N.Y.S.2d 225 (4th Dept. 1999).

—Revocation of probation and placement of respondent with Division of Youth for one year is authorized by statute after court held a dispositional hearing and determined respondent had violated terms and conditions of probation, no abuse of discretion. *In re* Vincent B., 239 A.D.2d 925, 659 N.Y.S.2d 594 (4th Dept. 1997).

—Respondent's persistent failure to attend school, obey his mother, and abstain from drug use or gang activity, supported court's decision to revoke respondent's probation and recommend a more restrictive placement. *In re* Quentin L., 647 N.Y.S.2d 593, 231 A.D.2d 890 (4th Dept. 1996).

Factors.—Seriousness of appellant's conduct and need for continued counseling supported family court's disposition, which was the least restrictive alternative consistent with appellant's needs. *In re* Sambit M., 277 A.D.2d 29, 718 N.Y.S.2d 814 (1st Dept. 2000).

—Merely because a respondent is already in placement is an insufficient basis upon which to preclude a presentment agency from going forward on its petition. *In re* Kevin B., 128 A.D.2d 63, 514 N.Y.S.2d 971 (1st Dept. 1987).

—Although the court considered the appellant's past success

in a nonrestrictive setting, it concluded that his present needs and his best interest, as well as that of the community, required his placement in a restrictive setting. *In re* William J., 120 A.D.2d 529, 502 N.Y.S.2d 39 (2d Dept. 1986).

—Due to the inadequacy of parental supervision, foster care was the least restrictive alternative commensurate with the best interest of the respondent and the community's protection; while respondent had no previous court record, the predisposition investigative report recounted a series of incidents involving the appellant's use of alcohol and reflected a poor school attendance record. *In re* Jennifer M., 125 A.D.2d 830, 509 N.Y.S.2d 935 (3d Dept. 1986).

—It was improper to modify the stipulated disposition which placed respondent, a juvenile delinquent, in a Title II facility to permit placement in a secure detention under Title III solely because of alleged lack of space in a Title II facility. *In re* Jason M., 109 A.D.2d 1092, 487 N.Y.S.2d 232 (4th Dept. 1985).

Right to counsel.—A respondent's attorney, in a juvenile delinquency proceeding, after a fact-finding, and prior to the dispositional hearing, need not be present and permitted to participate in the diagnostic mental health study of the respondent. *In re* Steven E.H., 124 Misc. 2d 385, 477 N.Y.S.2d 563 (Fam. Ct. Kings Co. 1984).

Standard.—Services to prevent placement are to be provided only where reasonable and appropriate under the circumstances of each case; if the community requires protection and or the respondent needs services that he cannot receive in his home, then placement is appropriate. *In re* Selvin M., 134 Misc. 2d 432, 511 N.Y.S.2d 506 (Fam. Ct. Kings Co. 1987).

Written report.—Court is not required to state findings in open court; the statute requires only a written report. *In re* Brandon J., 302 A.D.2d 755 N.Y.S.2d 534 (4th Dept. 2003).

§ 352.3. Order of protection.

(1) Upon the issuance of an order pursuant to section 315.3 or the entry of an order of disposition pursuant to section 352.2, a court may enter an order of protection against any respondent for good cause shown. The order may require that the respondent: (a) stay away from the home, school, business or place of employment of the victims of the alleged offense; or (b) refrain from harassing, intimidating, threatening or otherwise interfering with the victim or victims of the alleged offense and such members of the family or household of such victim or victims as shall be specifically named by the court in such order.

(2) An order of protection shall remain in effect for the period specified by the court, but shall not exceed the period of time specified in any order of disposition or order adjourning a proceeding in contemplation of dismissal.

Added by L. 1984, Ch. 683, eff. Aug. 31, 1984.

§ 353.1. Conditional discharge.

1. The court may conditionally discharge the respondent if the court, having regard for the nature and circumstances of the crime and for the history, character and condition of the respondent, is of the opinion that consistent with subdivision two of section 352.2, neither the public interest nor the ends of justice would be served by a placement and that probation supervision is not appropriate.

2. When the court orders a conditional discharge the respondent shall be released with respect to the finding upon which such order is based without placement or probation supervision

but subject, during the period of conditional discharge, to such conditions enumerated in subdivision two of section 353.2, as the court may determine. The court shall order the period of conditional discharge authorized by subdivision three and shall specify the conditions to be complied with. The court may modify or enlarge the conditions at any time prior to the expiration or termination of the period of conditional discharge. Such action may not, however, be taken unless the respondent is personally present, except that the respondent need not be present if the modification consists solely of the elimination or relaxation of one or more conditions.

3. The maximum period of a conditional discharge shall not exceed one year.

4. The respondent must be given a written copy of the conditions at the time a conditional discharge is ordered or modified, provided, however, that whenever the respondent has not been personally present at the time of a modification, the court shall notify the respondent in writing within twenty days after such modification, specifying the nature of the elimination or relaxation of any condition and the effective date thereof. A copy of such conditions must be filed with and become part of the record of the case.

5. A finding that the respondent committed an additional crime after the conditional discharge has been ordered and prior to expiration and termination of the period of such order constitutes a ground for revocation of such order irrespective of whether such fact is specified as a condition of the order.

Amended by L. 1983, Ch. 398, eff. July 1, 1983.

§ 353.2. Probation.

1. The court may order a period of probation if the court, having regard for the nature and circumstances of the crime and the history, character and condition of the respondent, is of the opinion that:

(a) placement of respondent is not or may not be necessary;

(b) the respondent is in need of guidance, training or other assistance which can be effectively administered through probation; and

(c) such disposition is consistent with the provisions of subdivision two of section 352.2.

2. When ordering a period of probation or a conditional discharge pursuant to section 353.1, the court may, as a condition of such order require that the respondent;

(a) attend school regularly and obey all rules and regulations of the school;

(b) obey all reasonable commands of the parent or other person legally responsible for the respondent's care;

(c) abstain from visiting designated places or associating with named individuals;

(d) avoid injurious or vicious activities;

(e) co-operate with a mental health, social services or other appropriate community facility or agency to which the respondent is referred;

(f) make restitution or perform services for the public good pursuant to section 353.6 provided the respondent is over ten years of age;

(g) Except when the respondent has been assigned to a facility in accordance with subdivision four of section five hundred four of the executive law, in cases wherein the record indicates that the consumption of alcohol by the respondent may have been a contributing factor, attend and complete an alcohol awareness program established pursuant to section 19.25 of the mental hygiene law; and

(h) comply with such other reasonable conditions as the court shall determine to be necessary or appropriate to ameliorate the conduct which gave rise to the filing of the petition or to prevent placement with the commissioner of social services or the division for youth.

3. When ordering a period of probation, the court may, as a condition of such order, further require that the respondent:

(a) meet with a probation officer when directed to do so by that officer and permit the officer to visit the respondent at home or elsewhere;

(b) permit the probation officer to obtain information from any person or agency from whom respondent is receiving or was directed to receive diagnosis, treatment or counseling;

(c) permit the probation officer to obtain information from the respondent's school;

(d) co-operate with the probation officer in seeking to obtain and in accepting employment, and supply records and reports of earnings to the officer when requested to do so;

(e) obtain permission from the probation officer for any absence from respondent's residence in excess of two weeks; and

(f) with the consent of the division for youth, spend a specified portion of the probation period, not exceeding one year, in a non-secure facility provided by the division for youth pursuant to article nineteen-g of the executive law.

4. A finding that the respondent committed an additional crime after probation supervision has been ordered and prior to expiration or termination of the period of such order constitutes a ground for revocation of such order irrespective of whether such fact is specified as a condition of such order.

5. The respondent must be given a written copy of the conditions at the time probation

supervision is ordered. A copy of such conditions must be filed with and become part of the record of the case.

6. The maximum period of probation shall not exceed two years. If the court finds at the conclusion of the original period and after a hearing that exceptional circumstances require an additional year of probation, the court may continue the probation for an additional year.

Amended by L. 1983, Ch. 398, eff. July 1, 1983; L. 1985 Ch. 880; L. 1987, Ch. 101; L. 1989, Ch. 161; L. 1991, Ch. 198, eff. June 28, 1991; L. 1992, Ch. 465, eff. Jan. 14, 1992, amending subd. (3)(f), and shall apply to all persons placed in or committed to the custody of the division of youth on or after such date; L. 1993, Ch. 124.

ANNOTATIONS

Generally.—Where the report prepared by the Probation Department revealed that respondent was not doing well in school and that he was on academic probation, and was having behavioral problems, it was not error for Family Court to conclude that respondent required supervision to monitor his attendance and school behavior as well as to encourage his academic work. *In re* Jessie GG, 190 A.D.2d 916, 593 N.Y.S.2d 375 (3d Dept. 1993).

Notice.—Where it could not be determined from the record whether appellant was ever informed, either orally or in writing, of the specific terms of his probation, the matter was remitted to the Family Court to first determine whether he was so informed, and, if not, then to dismiss the charge of violating probation. *In re* Donald B., 90 A.D.2d 848, 456 N.Y.S.2d 97 (2d Dept. 1982).

§ 353.3. Placement.

1. In accordance with section 352.2, the court may place the respondent in his own home or in the custody of a suitable relative or other suitable private person or the commissioner of social services or the division for youth pursuant to article nineteen-G of the executive law, subject to the orders of the court.

2. Where the respondent is placed with the commissioner of social services, the court may direct the commissioner to place him with an authorized agency or class of authorized agencies. Unless the dispositional order provides otherwise, the court so directing shall include one of the following alternatives to apply in the event that the commissioner is unable to so place the respondent;

(a) the commissioner shall apply to the court for an order to stay, modify, set aside, or vacate such directive pursuant to the provisions of section 355.1; or

(b) the commissioner shall return the respondent to the family court for a new dispositional hearing and order.

3. Where the respondent is placed with the division for youth, the court shall, unless it directs the division to place him with an authorized agency or class of authorized agencies pursuant to subdivision four authorize the division to do one of the following:

(a) place the respondent in a secure facility without a further hearing at any time or from time to time during the first sixty days of residency in division for youth facilities. Notwithstanding the discretion of the division to place the respondent in a secure facility at any time during the first sixty days of residency in a division for youth facility, the respondent may be placed in a non-secure facility. In the event that the division desires to transfer a respondent to a secure facility at any time after the first sixty days of residency in division facilities, a hearing shall be held pursuant to subdivision three of section five hundred four-a of the executive law; or

(b) place the respondent in a limited secure facility. The respondent may be transferred by the division to a secure facility after a hearing is held pursuant to section five hundred four-a of the executive law; provided, however that during the first twenty days of residency in division facilities, the respondent shall not be transferred to a secure facility unless the respondent has committed an act or acts which are exceptionally dangerous to the respondent or to others; or

(c) place the respondent in a non-secure facility. No respondent placed pursuant to this paragraph may be transferred by the division for youth to a secure facility.

4. Where the respondent is placed with the division for youth, the court may direct the division to place the respondent with an authorized agency or class of authorized agencies and, in the event the division is unable to so place the respondent or, discontinues the placement with the authorized agency, the respondent shall be deemed to have been placed with the division pursuant to paragraph (b) or (c) of subdivision three of this section. In such cases, the division shall notify the court, presentment agency, law guardian and parent or other person responsible for the respondent's care, of the reason for discontinuing the placement with the authorized agency and the level and location of the youth's placement.

5. If the respondent has committed a felony the initial period of placement shall not exceed eighteen months. If the respondent has committed a misdemeanor such initial period of placement shall not exceed twelve months. If the respondent has been in detention pending disposition, the initial period of placement ordered under this section shall be credited with and diminished by the amount of time spent by the respondent in detention prior to the commencement of the placement unless the court finds that all or part of such credit would not serve the needs and best interests of the respondent or the need for protection of the community.

6. The court may at any time conduct a hearing in accordance with section 355.1 concerning the need for continuing a placement.

7. The place in which or the person with whom the respondent has been placed under this section

MISC. LAWS

shall submit a report to the court, law guardian or attorney of record, and presentment agency at the conclusion of the placement period, except as provided in paragraphs (a) and (b) of this subdivision. Such report shall include recommendations and such supporting data as is appropriate. The court may extend a placement pursuant to section 355.3 of this article.

(a) Where the respondent is placed pursuant to subdivision two or three of this section and where the agency is not seeking an extension of the placement pursuant to section 355.3 of this article, such report shall be submitted not later than thirty days prior to the conclusion of the placement.

(b) Where the respondent is placed pursuant to subdivision two or three of this section and where the agency is seeking an extension of the placement pursuant to section 355.3 of this article and a permanency hearing pursuant to section 355.5 of this article, such report shall be submitted not later than sixty days prior to the date on which the permanency hearing must be held and shall be annexed to the petition for a permanency hearing and extension of placement.

(c) Where the respondent is placed pursuant to subdivision two or three of this section, such report shall contain a plan for the release, or conditional release (pursuant to section five hundred ten-a of the executive law), of the respondent to the custody of his or her parent or other person legally responsible, to independent living or to another permanency alternative as provided in paragraph (d) of subdivision seven of section 355.5 of this article. If the respondent is subject to article sixty-five of the education law or elects to participate in an educational program leading to a high school diploma, such plan shall include, but not be limited to, the steps that the agency with which the respondent is placed has taken and will be taking to facilitate the enrollment of the respondent in a school or educational program leading to a high school diploma following release, or, if such release occurs during the summer recess, upon the commencement of the next school term. If the respondent is not subject to article sixty-five of the education law and does not elect to participate in an educational program leading to a high school diploma, such plan shall include, but not be limited to, the steps that the agency with which the respondent is placed has taken and will be taking to assist the respondent to become gainfully employed or enrolled in a vocational program following release.

8. In its discretion, the court may recommend restitution or require services for the public good pursuant to section 353.6 in conjunction with an order of placement.

9. If the court places a respondent with the division for youth pursuant to this section after finding that such child committed a felony the court may, in its discretion, further order that such

respondent shall be confined in a residential facility for a minimum period set by the order, not to exceed six months.

10. A placement pursuant to this section with the commissioner of social services shall not be directed in any detention facility, but the court may direct detention pending transfer to a placement authorized and ordered under this section for no more than thirty days after the order of placement is made or in a city of one million or more, for no more than fifteen days after such order of placement is made. Such direction shall be subject to extension pursuant to subdivision three of section three hundred ninety-eight of the social services law.

Amended by L. 1987, Ch. 419, eff. Sept. 1, 1987; L. 1992, Ch. 465, eff. Jan. 14, 1992, amending subd. (3), (4), and shall apply to all persons placed in or committed to the custody of the division of youth on or after such date; L. 2000, Ch. 181, § 19, eff. Jan. 1, 2001, amending subd. 7.

ANNOTATIONS

Credit.—Where there was no finding by the court that crediting respondent for time spent in detention prior to commencement of placement would not serve needs or best interests of respondent or need to protect community, respondent was entitled to credit for that time. *In re* Maurice P., 302 A.D.2d 319, 754 N.Y.S.2d 875 (1st Dept. 2003).

—The intent of the statute is to credit automatically the juvenile's period of placement with pre-order-of-disposition detention time; absent a specific finding that such credit would not serve the interests of the juvenile or the community, the credit for such time in predisposition detention automatically accrues. *In re* Wayne S., 193 A.D.2d 371, 596 N.Y.S.2d 819 (1st Dept. 1993).

—The Family Court properly determined that an award of predetention credit would result in a period of placement of insufficient duration to serve the best interests of the appellant or to adequately protect the community. *In re* Mack M., 175 A.D.2d 869, 573 N.Y.S.2d 714 (2d Dept. 1991).

Discretion.—The Family Court has broad discretion in ordering placement. *In re* Douglas R.S., 123 A.D.2d 868, 507 N.Y.S.2d 648 (2d Dept. 1986).

—It was not an abuse of discretion for the court to place defendant who had a history of violent and unlawful behavior into a secure facility even though his law guardian recommended a nonsecure facility and defendant was accepted into that facility; "the least restrictive alternative test does not require the court to actually try the lowest form of intervention, have it fail, and then try each succeeding level of intervention before ordering . . . placement." *In re* Stacy S., 17 A.D.3d 1146, 793 N.Y.S.2d 842 (4th Dept. 2005).

Factors.—The latitude for treatment accorded a juvenile sent to a secure facility pursuant to Family Court Act §§ 353.3(3a) and 353.3(5) is broader than that for one placed in restrictive placement for three years pursuant to Family Court Act section 353.5; restrictive placement is for those youths who are considered incorrigible and too dangerous to remain in the community. *In re* Michael W., 111 A.D.2d 36, 489 N.Y.S.2d 68 (1st Dept. 1985).

—Respondent's persistent failure to attend school, obey his mother, and abstain from drug use or gang activity, supported court's decision to revoke respondent's probation and recommend a more restrictive placement. *In re* Quentin L., 647 N.Y.S.2d 593, 231 A.D.2d 890 (4th Dept. 1996).

Mootness.—Respondent's challenge to his placement in a restrictive facility became moot as a result of the expiration of the one-year placement period that was directed in the dispositional order. *In re* Demetrius O., 193 A.D.2d 977, 598 N.Y.S.2d 103, 104 (3d Dept. 1993).

Placement.—This section of the Family Court Act requires the family court to specify one of the enumerated settings when placing the respondent within the Division of Youth. *In re* Dowayne, 278 A.D.2d 706, 718 N.Y.S.2d 112 (3d Dept. 2000).

§ 353.4. Transfer of certain juvenile delinquents.

1. If at the conclusion of the dispositional hearing and in accordance with section 352.2 the court finds that the respondent has a mental illness, mental retardation or developmental disability, as defined in section 1.03 of the mental hygiene law, which is likely to result in serious harm to himself or others, the court may issue an order placing such respondent with the division for youth or, with the consent of the local commissioner, with a local commissioner of social services. Any such order shall direct the temporary transfer for admission of the respondent to the custody of either the commissioner of mental health or the commissioner of mental retardation and developmental disabilities who shall arrange the admission of the respondent to the appropriate facility of the department of mental hygiene. The director of a hospital operated by the office of mental health may, subject to the provisions of section 9.51 of the mental hygiene law, transfer a person admitted to the hospital pursuant to this subdivision to a residential treatment facility for children and youth, as that term is defined in section 1.03 of the mental hygiene law, if care and treatment in such a facility would more appropriately meet the needs of the respondent. Persons temporarily transferred to such custody under this provision may be retained for care and treatment for a period of up to one year and whenever appropriate shall be transferred back to the division for youth pursuant to the provisions of section five hundred nine of the executive law or transferred back to the local commissioner of social services. Within thirty days of such transfer back, application shall be made by the division for youth or the local commissioner of social services to the placing court to conduct a further dispositional hearing at which the court may make any order authorized under section 352.2. except that the period of any further order of disposition shall take into account the period of placement hereunder. Likelihood to result in serious harm shall mean (a) substantial risk of physical harm to himself as manifested by threats or attempts at suicide or serious bodily harm or other conduct demonstrating he is dangerous to himself or (b) a substantial risk of physical harm to other persons as manifested by homicidal or other violent behavior by which others are placed in reasonable fear of serious bodily harm.

2. (a) Where the order of disposition is for a restrictive placement under section 353.5 if the court at the dispositional hearing finds that the respondent has a mental illness, mental retardation or developmental disability, as defined in section 1.03 of the mental hygiene law, which is likely to result in serious harm to himself or others, the court may, as part of the order of disposition, direct the temporary transfer, for a period of up to one year, of the respondent to the custody of the commissioner of mental health or of mental retardation and developmental disabilities who shall arrange for the admission of the respondent to an appropriate facility under his jurisdiction within thirty days of such order. The director of the facility so designated by the commissioner shall accept such respondent for admission.

(b) Persons transferred to the office of mental health or of mental retardation and developmental disabilities, pursuant to this subdivision, shall be retained by such office for care and treatment for the period designated by the court. At any time prior to the expiration of such period, if the director of the facility determines that the child is no longer mentally ill or no longer in need of active treatment, the responsible office shall make application to the family court for an order transferring the child back to the division for youth. Not more than thirty days before the expiration of such period, there shall be a hearing, at which time the court may:

(i) extend the temporary transfer of the respondent for an additional period of up to one year to the custody of the commissioner of mental health or the commissioner of mental retardation and developmental disabilities pursuant to this subdivision; or

(ii) continue the restrictive placement of the respondent in the custody of the division for youth.

(c) During such temporary transfer, the respondent shall continue to be under restrictive placement with the division for youth. Whenever the respondent is transferred back to the division the conditions of the placement as set forth in section 353.5 shall apply. Time spent by the respondent in the custody of the commissioner of mental health or the commissioner of mental retardation and developmental disabilities shall be credited and applied towards the period of placement.

3. No dispositional hearing at which proof of a mental disability as defined in section 1.03 of the mental hygiene law is to be offered shall be completed until the commissioner of mental health or commissioner of mental retardation and developmental disabilities, as appropriate, have been notified and afforded an opportunity to be heard at such dispositional hearing.

4. No order of disposition placing the respondent in accordance with this section shall be entered except upon clear and convincing evidence which shall include the testimony of two examining physicians as provided in section two hundred fifty one.

5. If the respondent has been in detention pending disposition, the initial period of placement ordered under this section shall be credited with and diminished by the amount of time spent by the respondent in detention prior to the commencement of the placement unless the court

finds that all or part of such credit would not serve the needs and best interests of the respondent or the need for protection of the community.

Amended by L. 1987, Ch. 419, eff. Sept. 1, 1987; L. 1992, Ch. 465, eff. Jan. 14, 1992, amending subds. (1) and (2)(c), and shall apply to all persons placed in or committed to the custody of the division of youth on or after such date.

§ 353.5. Designated felony acts; restrictive placement.

1. Where the respondent is found to have committed a designated felony act, the order of disposition shall be made within twenty days of the conclusion of the dispositional hearing and shall include a finding based on a preponderance of the evidence as to whether, for the purposes of this article, the respondent does or does not require a restrictive placement under this section, in connection with which the court shall make specific written findings of fact as to each of the elements set forth in paragraphs (a) through (e) in subdivision two as related to the particular respondent. If the court finds that a restrictive placement under this section is not required, the court shall enter any other order of disposition provided in section 352.2. If the court finds that a restrictive placement is required, it shall continue the proceeding and enter an order of disposition for a restrictive placement. Every order under this section shall be a dispositional order, shall be made after a dispositional hearing and shall state the grounds for the order.

2. In determining whether a restrictive placement is required, the court shall consider:

(a) the needs and best interests of the respondent:

(b) the record and background of the respondent, including but not limited to information disclosed in the probation investigation and diagnostic assessment:

(c) the nature and circumstances of the offense, including whether any injury was inflicted by the respondent or another participant;

(d) the need for protection of the community; and

(e) the age and physical condition of the victim.

3. Notwithstanding the provisions of subdivision two, the court shall order a restrictive placement in any case where the respondent is found to have committed a designated felony act in which the respondent inflicted serious physical injury, as that term is defined in subdivision ten of section 10.00 of the penal law, upon another person who is sixty two years of age or more.

4. When the order is for a restrictive placement in the case of a youth found to have committed a designated class A felony act.

(a) the order shall provide that:

(i) the respondent shall be placed with the division for youth for an initial period of five years. If the respondent has been in detention pending disposition, the initial period of placement ordered under this section shall be credited with and diminished by the amount of time spent by the respondent in detention prior to the commencement of the placement unless the court finds that all or part of such credit would not serve the needs and best interests of the respondent or the need for protection of the community.

(ii) the respondent shall initially be confined in a secure facility for a period set by the order, to be not less than twelve nor more than eighteen months provided however, where the order of the court is made in compliance with subdivision five the respondent shall initially be confined in a secure facility for eighteen months.

(iii) after the period set under clause (ii), the respondent shall be placed in a residential facility for a period of twelve months.

(iv) the respondent may not be released from a secure facility or transferred to a facility other than a secure facility during the period provided in clause (ii) of this paragraph, nor may the respondent be released from a residential facility during the period provided in clause (iii). No home visits shall be permitted during the period of secure confinement set by the court order or one year, whichever is less, except for emergency visits for medical treatment or severe illness or death in the family. All home visits must be accompanied home visits: (A) while a youth is confined in a secure facility, whether such confinement is pursuant to a court order or otherwise; (B) while a youth is confined in a residential facility other than a secure facility within six months after confinement in a secure facility; and (C) while a youth is confined in a residential facility other than a secure facility in excess of six months after confinement in a secure facility unless two accompanied home visits have already occurred. An "accompanied home visit" shall mean a home visit during which the youth shall be accompanied at all times while outside the secure or residential facility by appropriate personnel of the division for youth designated pursuant to regulations of the director of the division.

(b) Notwithstanding any other provision of law, during the first twelve months of the respondent's placement, no motion, hearing or order may be made, held or granted pursuant to section 355.1 provided however, that during such period a motion to vacate the order may be made pursuant to 355.1, but only upon grounds set forth in section 440.10 of the criminal procedure law.

(c) During the placement or any extension thereof:

(i) after the expiration of the period provided in clause (iii) of paragraph (a), the respondent shall not be released from a residential facility without the written approval of the director of the division for youth or his designated deputy director.

(ii) the respondent shall be subject to intensive supervision whenever not in a secure or residential facility.

(iii) the respondent shall not be discharged from the custody of the division for youth, unless a motion therefor under section 355.1 is granted by the court, which motion shall not be made prior to the expiration of three years of the placement.

(iv) unless otherwise specified in the order, the division shall report in writing to the court not less than once every six months during the placement on the status, adjustment and progress of the respondent.

(d) Upon the expiration of the initial period of placement, or any extension thereof, the placement may be extended in accordance with section 355.3 on a petition of any party or the division for youth after a dispositional hearing, for an additional period not to exceed twelve months, but no initial placement or extension of placement under this section may continue beyond the respondent's twenty first birthday.

(e) The court may also make an order pursuant to subdivision two of section 353.4.

5. When the order is for a restrictive placement in the case of a youth found to have committed a designated felony act, other than a designated class A felony act,

(a) the order shall provide that:

(i) the respondent shall be placed with the division for youth for an initial period of three years. If the respondent has been in detention pending disposition, the initial period of placement ordered under this section shall be credited with and diminished by the amount of time spent by the respondent in detention prior to the commencement of the placement unless the court finds that all or part of such credit would not serve the needs and best interests of the respondent or the need for protection of the community.

(ii) the respondent shall initially be confined in a secure facility for a period set by the order, to be not less than six nor more than twelve months.

(iii) after the period set under clause (ii), the respondent shall be placed in a residential facility for a period set by the order, to be not less than six nor more than twelve months.

(iv) the respondent may not be released from a secure facility or transferred to a facility during other than a secure facility the period provided by the court pursuant to clause (ii) nor may the respondent be released from a residential facility during the period provided by the court pursuant to clause (iii) No home visits shall be permitted during the period of secure confinement set by

the court order or one year, whichever is less, except for emergency visits for medical treatment or severe illness or death in the family. All home visits must be accompanied home visits: (A) while a youth is confined in a secure facility, whether such confinement is pursuant to a court order or otherwise; (B) while a youth is confined in a residential facility other than a secure facility within of six months after confinement in a secure facility; and (C) while a youth is confined in a residential facility other than a secure facility in excess of six months after confinement in a secure facility unless two accompanied home visits have already occurred. An "accompanied home visit" shall mean a home visit during which the youth shall be accompanied at all times while outside the secure or residential facility by appropriate personnel of the division for youth designated pursuant to regulations of the director of the division.

(b) Notwithstanding any other provisions of law, during the first six months of the respondent's placement, no motion, hearing or order may be made, held or granted pursuant to section 355.1; provided, however, that during such period a motion to vacate the order may be made pursuant to such section, but only upon grounds set forth in section 440.10 of the criminal procedure law.

(c) During the placement or any extension thereof:

(i) after the expiration of the period provided in clause (iii) of paragraph (a), the respondent shall not be released from a residential facility without the written approval of the director of the division for youth or his designated deputy director.

(ii) the respondent shall be subject to intensive supervision whenever not in a secure or residential facility.

(iii) the respondent shall not be discharged from the custody of his division for youth.

(iv) unless otherwise specified in the order, the division shall report in writing to the court not less than once every six months during the placement on the status, adjustment and progress of the respondent.

(d) Upon the expiration of the initial period of placement or any extension thereof, the placement may be extended in accordance with section 355.3 upon petition of any party or the division for youth, after a dispositional hearing, for an additional period not to exceed twelve months, but no initial placement or extension of placement under this section may continue beyond the respondent's twenty-first birthday.

(e) The court may also make an order pursuant to subdivision two of section 353.4.

6. When the order is for a restrictive placement in the case of a youth found to have committed

any designated felony act and such youth has been found by a court to have committed a designated felony act on a prior occasion, regardless of the age of such youth at the time of commission of such prior act, the order of the court shall be made pursuant to subdivision four.

7. If the dispositional hearing has been adjourned on a finding of specific circumstances pursuant to subdivision six of section 350.1 while the respondent is in detention, where a restrictive placement is subsequently ordered, time spent by the respondent in detention during such additional adjournment shall be credited and applied against any term of secure confinement ordered by the court pursuant to subdivision four or five.

8. The division for youth shall retain the power to continue the confinement of the youth in a secure or other residential facility beyond the periods specified by the court, within the term of the placement.

Amended by L. 1983, Ch. 398, eff. July 1, 1983; by L. 1987, Ch. 419, eff. Sept. 1, 1987; L. 1993, Ch. 687, eff. 120 days after Aug. 4, 1993, amending subds. 4(a)(iv) and 5(a)(iv).

ANNOTATIONS

Extensions.—Consent provision contained in FCA § 355.3(6) does not apply to successive placement of a child under section 353.5(5)(d); therefore, extension of placement of a child over 18 years old under section 353.5(5)(d), where appropriate, will be upheld. *In re* Mickie PP., 279 A.D.2d 943, 720 N.Y.S.2d 571 (3d Dept. 2001).

—The consent of an 18-year-old juvenile delinquent restrictively placed pursuant to section 353.5(4) is not required in order to extend the period of restrictive placement once the initial placement period has expired. *In re* Luis V., 169 Misc. 2d 865, 646 N.Y.S.2d 756 (Fam. Ct. Bronx Co. 1996).

Placement.—"A juvenile delinquent who has committed a designated felony cannot be placed–either initially or pursuant to an extension–for term beyond the age of 21 (FCA § 353.5,) a limitation which dovetails with the language in EL 507-a restricting the authority of OCFS to custody of individuals under the age of 21 in any circumstance," however, Family Court is authorized to order an initial placement that extends beyond a youth's 18th birthday. *In re* Robert J., 2 N.Y.3d 339, 778 N.Y.S.2d 763, 811 N.E.2d 25 (2004).

—Court properly exercised its discretion in placing respondent in Title III facility where the court-retained psychiatrist testified that due to respondent's volatile temper, other psychological problems and past acts of violence, her interests would be best served in the most structured environment available; other evidence indicated that respondent had fled from other nonsecure settings and none of the four less secure facilities for which respondent was eligible would accept her. *In re* Katherine W., 62 N.Y.2d 947, 479 N.Y.S.2d 190, 468 N.E.2d 28 (1984).

—In determining that restrictive placement of respondent was warranted, court properly included specific findings of fact, including fact respondent was adjudicated a juvenile delinquent based on criminal drug activity and other appropriate considerations balancing "needs of appellant and safety of community." *In re* Noel M., 240 A.D.2d 231, 659 N.Y.S.2d 733 (1st Dept. 1997).

—Court did not abuse discretion in placing respondent in a Title II facility where evidence at the hearing included rejections from alternative programs, a history of the defendant's disruptive behavior at various schools, and recommendations that the defendant be placed in strict supervision. *In re* William J., 176 A.D.2d 133, 574 N.Y.S.2d 19 (1st Dept. 1991).

—Where juvenile was found to have committed a designated felony, restrictive placement was mandated, and placement agency was not required to provide family court with notice of intent to seek restrictive placement. *In re* Dorrion S., 302 A.D.2d 598, 757 N.Y.S.2d 49 (2d Dept. 2003).

—Placement in a restrictive setting is a drastic course of action used only as a last resort. In this case, evidence overwhelmingly established that respondent's needs and best interests required that he be placed in a restrictive setting. *In re* Gregory M., 224 A.D.2d 428, 638 N.Y.S.2d 104 (2d Dept. 1996).

—Family Court's imposition of restrictive placement for the maximum period and determination that an award of predisposition credit of some 10 months out of the initial 18-month placement in a secure facility would not serve the needs and best interests of respondent were supported by the numerous recommendations of restrictive placement and the conclusion of a psychologist that respondent "needs a significant period of time" for treatment of various psychological problems. *In re* Kristi L.M., 197 A.D.2d 903, 602 N.Y.S.2d 454 (4th Dept. 1993).

§ 353.6. Restitution.

1. At the conclusion of the dispositional hearing in cases involving respondents over ten years of age the court may:

(a) recommend as a condition of placement, or order as a condition of probation or conditional discharge, restitution in an amount representing a fair and reasonable cost to replace the property, repair the damage caused by the respondent or provide the victim with compensation for unreimbursed medical expenses, not, however, to exceed one thousand five hundred dollars. In the case of a placement, the court may recommend that the respondent pay out of his or her own funds or earnings the amount of replacement, damage or unreimbursed medical expenses, either in a lump sum or in periodic payments in amounts set by the agency with which he or she is placed, and in the case of probation or conditional discharge, the court may require that the respondent pay out of his or her own funds or earnings the amount of replacement, damage or unreimbursed medical expenses, either in a lump sum or in periodic payments in amounts set by the court; and/or

(b) order as a condition of placement, probation or conditional discharge, services for the public good, taking into consideration the age and physical condition of the respondent.

2. If the court recommends restitution or requires services for the public good in conjunction with an order of placement pursuant to section 353.3 or 353.5 the placement shall be made only to an authorized agency, including the division for youth, which has adopted rules and regulations for the supervision of such a program, which rules and regulations, except in the case of the division for youth, shall be subject to the approval of the state department of social services. Such rules and regulations shall include, but not be limited to provisions: (i) assuring that the conditions of work, including wages, meet the standards therefor prescribed pursuant to the labor law; (ii) affording coverage to the respondent under the workers' compensation law as an employee of such agency, department, division or institution; (iii) assuring that the entity receiving such services shall not utilize the same to replace its regular employees; and (iv) providing for reports to the court not less frequently then every six months.

3. If the court requires restitutions or services for the public good as a condition of probation or conditional discharge, it shall provide that an agency or person supervise the restitution or services and that such agency or person report to the court not less frequently than every six months. Upon the written notice submitted by a school district to the court and the appropriate probation department or agency which submits probation recommendations or reports to the court, the court may provide that such school district shall supervise the performance of services for the public good.

4. The court, upon receipt of the reports provided for in subdivisions two and three may, on its own motion or the motion of the agency, probation service or the presentment agency, hold a hearing pursuant to section 355.1 to determine whether the dispositional order should be modified.

Amended by L. 1983, Ch. 877, eff. Aug. 8, 1983; L. 2004, Ch. 317, § 2, eff. Nov. 8, 2004, amending subd. 1(a).

ANNOTATIONS

Court determination.—The determination to impose the maximum amount of restitution rests within the discretion of the court. *In re* James A., 205 A.D.2d 621, 613 N.Y.S.2d 255 (2d Dept. 1994).

—The court erred in delegating to the Probation Department the authority to fix the amount of restitution. *In re* Kim D., 120 A.D.2d 968, 502 N.Y.S.2d 863 (4th Dept. 1986).

Generally.—The statute specifically limits restitution to payments for property damage and does not entitle a victim to receive restitution for other damages. *In re* Keith Z., 195 A.D.2d 729, 600 N.Y.S.2d 302 (3d Dept. 1993).

§ 354.1. Retention and destruction of fingerprints of persons alleged to be juvenile delinquents.

1. If a person whose fingerprints, palmprints or photographs were taken pursuant to section 306.1 or was initially fingerprinted as a juvenile offender and the action is subsequently removed to family court pursuant to article seven hundred twenty five of the criminal procedure law is adjudicated to be a juvenile delinquent for a felony, the family court shall forward or cause to be forwarded to the division of criminal justice services notification of such adjudication and such related information as may be required by such division, provided, however, in the case of a person eleven or twelve years of age such notification shall be provided only if the act upon which the adjudication is based would constitute a class A or B felony.

2. If a person whose fingerprints, palmprints or photographs were taken pursuant to section 306.1 or was initially fingerprinted as a juvenile offender and the action is subsequently removed to family court pursuant to article seven hundred twenty-five of the criminal procedure law has had all petitions disposed of by the family court in any manner other than an adjudication of juvenile delinquency for a felony, but in the case of acts committed when such person was eleven or twelve years of age which would constitute a class A or B felony only, all such fingerprints, palmprints, photographs, and copies thereof, and all information relating to such allegations obtained by the division of criminal justice services pursuant to section 306.1 shall be destroyed forthwith. The clerk of the court shall notify the commissioner of the division of criminal justice services and the heads of all police departments and law enforcement agencies having copies of such records, who shall destroy such records without unnecessary delay.

3. If the appropriate presentment agency does not originate a proceeding under section 310.1 for a case in which the potential respondent's fingerprints were taken pursuant to section 306.1, the presentment agency shall serve a certification of such action upon the division of criminal justice services, and upon the appropriate police department or law enforcement agency.

4. If, following the taking into custody of a person alleged to be a juvenile delinquent and the taking and forwarding to the division of criminal justice services of such person's fingerprints but prior to referral to the probation department or to the family court, an officer or agency, elects not to proceed further, such officer or agency shall serve a certification of such election upon the division of criminal justice services.

5. Upon certification pursuant to subdivision twelve of section 308.1 or subdivision three or four of this section, the department or agency shall destroy forthwith all fingerprints, palmprints, photographs, and copies thereof, and all other information obtained in the case pursuant to section 306.1. Upon receipt of such certification, the division of criminal justice services and all police departments and law enforcement agencies having copies of such records shall destroy them.

6. If a person fingerprinted pursuant to section 306.1 and subsequently adjudicated a juvenile delinquent for a felony, but in the case of acts committed when such a person was eleven or twelve years of age which would constitute a class A or B felony only, is subsequently convicted of a crime, all fingerprints and related information obtained by the division of criminal justice services pursuant to such section and not destroyed pursuant to subdivisions two, five and seven or subdivision twelve of section 308.1 shall become part of such division's permanent adult criminal record for that person, notwithstanding section 381.2 or 381.3.

7. When a person fingerprinted pursuant to section 306.1 and subsequently adjudicated a juvenile delinquent for a felony, but in the case of acts committed when such person was eleven or twelve years of age which would constitute a class A or B felony only, reaches the age of

MISC. LAWS

twenty-one, or has been discharged from placement under this act for at least three years, whichever occurs later, and has no criminal convictions or pending criminal actions which ultimately terminate in a criminal conviction, all fingerprints, palmprints, photographs, and related information and copies thereof obtained pursuant to section 306.1 in the possession of the division of criminal justice services, any police department, law enforcement agency or any other agency shall be destroyed forthwith. The division of criminal justice services shall notify the agency or agencies which forwarded fingerprints to such division pursuant to section 306.1 of their obligation to destroy those records in their possession. In the case of a pending criminal action which does not terminate in a criminal conviction, such records shall be destroyed forthwith upon such determination.

Amended by L. 1983, Ch. 398, eff. July 1, 1983; L. 1996, Ch. 645, amending subds. 2, 6, and 7, eff. Sept. 13, 1996, and applying retroactively to a person whose fingerprints were taken pursuant to section 306.1 of the family court act or who was initially fingerprinted as a juvenile offender on or after January 1, 1986 and whose fingerprints are on file with the division of criminal justice services, provided that in the case of a juvenile offender action the case was subsequently removed to family court, pursuant to L. 1996, Ch. 645, § 6.

ANNOTATIONS

Generally.—A dismissal of a juvenile delinquency petition on the ground that the allegations on which it was based were not established is a finding which is consistent with innocence. *In re* Bryant W., 114 A.D.2d 962, 495 N.Y.S.2d 227 (2d Dept. 1985).

—The power to seal records has been utilized by the Family Court to insure confidentiality of an adjudication that ended favorably to a respondent; the court also has the power to expunge records independent of the statutory grant, however, this power should not be indiscriminately employed particularly where the adjudication which terminates the arrest is for reasons not consistent with complete innocence. *In re* Clueso, 146 Misc. 2d 861, 552 N.Y.S.2d 822 (Fam. Ct. N.Y. Co. 1990).

§ 354.2. Duties of counsel or law guardian.

1. If the court has entered a dispositional order pursuant to section 352.2, it shall be the duty of the respondent's counsel or law guardian to promptly advise such respondent and his parent or other person responsible for his care in writing of his right to appeal to the appropriate appellate division of the supreme court, the time limitations involved, the manner of instituting an appeal and obtaining a transcript of the testimony and the right to apply for leave to appeal as a poor person if he is unable to pay the cost of an appeal. It shall be the further duty of such counsel or law guardian to explain to the respondent and his parent or person responsible for his care the procedures for instituting an appeal, the possible reasons upon which an appeal may be based and the nature and possible consequences of the appellate process.

2. It shall also be the duty of such counsel or law guardian to ascertain whether the respondent

wishes to appeal and, if so, to serve and file the necessary notice of appeal.

3. If the respondent has been permitted to waive the appointment of a law guardian pursuant to section two hundred forty-nine-a, it shall be the duty of the court to provide the notice and explanation pursuant to subdivision one and, if the respondent indicates that he wishes to appeal, the clerk of the court shall file and serve the notice of appeal.

§ 355.1. New hearing; staying, modifying or terminating an order.

1. Upon a showing of a substantial change of circumstances, the court may on its own motion or on motion of the respondent or his parent or person responsible for his care:

(a) grant a new fact finding or dispositional hearing; or

(b) stay execution of, set aside, modify, terminate or vacate any order issued in the course of a proceeding under this article.

2. An order issued under section 353.3, may, upon a showing of a substantial change of circumstances, be set aside, modified, vacated or terminated upon motion of the commissioner of social services or the division for youth with whom the respondent has been placed.

3. If the court issues a new order of disposition under this section the date such order expires shall not be later than the expiration date of the original order.

Amended by L. 1983, Ch. 398, eff. July 1, 1983.

ANNOTATION

Generally.—Section 355.1 is not intended to be the only remedy available to juvenile delinquents; courts possess the inherent power to vacate their orders in the interest of justice. *In re* Carmen R., 123 Misc. 2d 238, 473 N.Y.S.2d 312 (Fam. Ct. St. Lawrence Co. 1984).

§ 355.2. Motion procedures.

A motion for relief pursuant to section 355.1 must be in writing and must state the specific relief requested. If the motion is based upon the existence or occurence* of facts the motion papers must contain sworn allegations thereof; such sworn allegations may be based upon personal knowledge of the affiant or upon information and belief provided that in the latter event the affidavit must state the sources of such information and the grounds of such belief.

2. Notice of such motion, including the court's own motion, shall be served upon the respondent, the presentment agency and the commissioner of social services or the division for youth having custody of the respondent. Motions shall be noticed in accordance with the civil practice law and rules.

3. Each party to the motion shall have the right

to oral argument and the court shall conduct a hearing to resolve any material question of fact.

4. Regardless of whether a hearing is conducted, the court, upon determining the motion, must set forth on the record its findings of fact, its conclusions of law and the reasons for its determination.

5. If the motion is denied, a motion requesting the same or similar relief cannot be filed for a period of ninety days after such denial, unless the order of denial permits renewal at an earlier time.

* Spelled as such in original. Should be "occurrence."

ANNOTATION

Adjournments.—Family Court properly denied respondent's motion to dismiss the petition where he consented to the first adjournment of the dispositional hearing and the presentment agency established special circumstances for the successive one-day adjournment based upon a clerical error in calendaring the wrong date for respondent's production. *In re* Christopher W., 200 A.D.2d 539, 606 N.Y.S.2d 702 (1st Dept. 1994).

§ 355.3. Extension of placement.

1. In any case in which the respondent has been placed pursuant to section 353.3 the respondent, the person with whom the respondent has been placed, the commissioner of social services, or the division for youth may petition the court to extend such placement. Such petition shall be filed at least sixty days prior to the expiration of the period of placement, except for good cause shown but in no event shall such petition be filed after the original expiration date.

2. The court shall conduct a hearing concerning the need for continuing the placement. The respondent, the presentment agency and the agency with whom the respondent has been placed shall be notified of such hearing and shall have the opportunity to be heard thereat. If the petition is filed within sixty days prior to the expiration of the period of placement, the court shall first determine at such hearing whether good cause has been shown. If good cause is not shown, the court shall dismiss the petition.

3. The provisions of sections 350.3 and 350.4 shall apply at such hearing.

4. At the conclusion of the hearing the court may, in its discretion, order an extension of the placement for not more than one year. The court must consider and determine in its order: (i) that where appropriate, and where consistent with the need for the protection of the community, reasonable efforts were made to make it possible for the respondent to safely return to his or her home; (ii) in the case of a respondent who has attained the age of sixteen, the services needed, if any, to assist the child to make the transition from foster care to independent living; and (iii) in the case of a child placed outside New York state, whether the out-of-state placement continues to be appropriate and in the best interests of the child.

5. Pending final determination of a petition to extend such placement filed in accordance with the provisions of this section, the court may, on its own motion or at the request of the petitioner or respondent, enter one or more temporary orders extending a period of placement for a period not to exceed thirty days upon satisfactory proof showing probable cause for continuing such placement and that each temporary order is necessary. The court may order additional temporary extensions, not to exceed a total of fifteen days, if the court is unable to conclude the hearing within the first thirty day temporary extension period. In no event shall the aggregate number of days in extensions granted or ordered under this subdivision total more than forty-five days. The petition shall be dismissed if a decision is not rendered within the period of placement or any temporary extension thereof.

6. Successive extensions of placement under this section may be granted, but no placement may be made or continued beyond the respondent's eighteenth birthday without the child's consent and in no event past the child's twenty first birthday.

Amended by L. 1983, Ch. 398, eff. July 1, 1983; L. 1985, Ch. 663, eff. Aug. 27, 1985; L. 1991, Ch. 198, eff. June 28, 1991, amending subd. 4; L. 1992, Ch. 363, eff. July 17, 1992, amending subd. (5); L. 1993, Ch. 687, eff. 120 days after Aug. 4, 1993, amending subd. 5; L. 1995, Ch. 454, § 1, amending subd. 4, eff. Oct. 1, 1995; L. 2000, Ch. 145, § 11, eff. July 1, 2000.

ANNOTATIONS

Age of juvenile delinquent.—"A juvenile delinquent who has committed a designated felony cannot be placed–either initially or pursuant to an extension–for a term beyond the age of 21 (FCA § 353.5,) a limitation which dovetails with the language in EL 507-a restricting the authority of OCFS to custody of individuals under the age of 21 in any circumstance," however, Family Court is authorized to order an initial placement that extends beyond a youth's 18th birthday. *In re* Robert J., 2 N.Y.3d 339, 778 N.Y.S.2d 763, 811 N.E.2d 25 (2004).

—FCA § 355.3(6) does not bar the initial involuntary or voluntary placement of juvenile delinquent in the custody of the Office of Children and Family Services after that juvenile has reached the age of 18 during the pendency of a delinquency proceeding. *In re* Jude F. (Anonymous), 291 A.D.2d 165, 740 N.Y.S.2d 80 (2d Dept. 2001).

Consent.—Consent provision contained in section 355.3(6) does not apply to successive placement of a child under section 353.5(5)(d); therefore, extension of placement of a child over 18 years old under section 353.5(5)(d), where appropriate, will be upheld. *In re* Mickie PP., 279 A.D.2d 943, 720 N.Y.S.2d 571 (3d Dept. 2001).

Extensions; generally.—The family court may not peremptorily bar the Office of Children and Family Services from applying for an extension of placement for a juvenile delinquent. *In re* Dewayne B., 289 A.D.2d 571, 735 N.Y.S.2d 209 (2d Dept. 2001).

—A placement expires at the end of the term unless an extension of placement is timely sought by a person authorized by statute. *In re* Salvatore A., 154 A.D.2d 930, 547 N.Y.S.2d 165 (4th Dept. 1989).

—An extension of the placement was not required or possible since respondent's unauthorized leave interrupted the running of the placement and lengthened it by that amount of time. *In re* Richard B., 148 Misc. 2d 162, 559 N.Y.S.2d 938 (Fam. Ct. Monroe Co. 1990).

Good cause.—Late filing of petition for extension of placement was supported by good cause where delay was caused by OCFS's decision to await final determination of appellant's criminal proceeding. *In re* Francis H., 253 A.D.2d 691, 677 N.Y.S.2d 474 (1st Dept. 1998).

—Administrative neglect committed by the appellant's counselor did not constitute good cause for the failure to timely file the petition for extension of placement. *In re* Scott B.H., 198 A.D.2d 278, 603 N.Y.S.2d 540 (2d Dept. 1993).

—Good cause established where the acknowledged reason for the delay in processing by the clerk's office was staff shortages due to vacancies and vacations, items admittedly beyond petitioner's control. *In re* Aaron XX., 199 A.D.2d 938, 605 N.Y.S.2d 566 (3d Dept. 1993).

Need not be heard by same judge.—Petition for extension of placement does not have to be heard by same judge who presided over original placement hearing, extension petition is a new proceeding requiring a new hearing and new dispositional order. *In re* Rudolph M., 174 Misc. 2d 273, 664 N.Y.S.2d 399 (Fam. Ct. Kings Co. 1997).

§ 355.4. Provisions for routine medical, dental and mental health services and treatment.

1. At the conclusion of the dispositional hearing pursuant to this article, where the respondent is to be placed with the division for youth, the court shall inquire as to whether the parents or legal guardian of the youth, if present, will consent for the division to provide routine medical, dental and mental health services and treatment.

2. Notwithstanding subdivision one of this section, where the court places a youth with the division pursuant to this article and no medical consent has been obtained prior to an order of disposition, the placement order shall be deemed to grant consent for the division for youth to provide for routine medical, dental and mental health services and treatment to such youth so placed.

3. Subject to regulations of the department of health, routine medical, dental and mental health services and treatment is defined for the purposes of this section to mean any routine diagnosis or treatment, including without limitation the administration of medications or nutrition, the extraction of bodily fluids for analysis, and dental care performed with a local anesthetic. Routine mental health treatment shall not include psychiatric administration of medication unless it is part of an ongoing mental health plan or unless it is otherwise authorized by law.

4. (a) at any time during placement or at an extension of placement hearing, a parent or legal guardian may make a motion objecting to routine medical, dental or mental health services and treatment being provided to such youth as authorized under the provisions of subdivision one of this section.

(b) Such notice of motion shall be served on the youth, the presentment agency and the division not less than seven days prior to the return date of the motion. The persons on whom the notice of motion is served shall answer the motion not less than two days before the return date. On examining the motion and answer and, in its discretion, after hearing argument, the court shall enter an order, granting or denying the motion.

5. Nothing in this section shall preclude a youth from consenting on his or her own behalf to any medical, dental or mental health service and treatment where otherwise authorized by law to do so, or the division for youth from petitioning the court pursuant to section two hundred thirty-three of this act, as appropriate.

Added by L. 1992, Ch. 479, eff. July 17, 1992.

§ 355.5. Permanency hearing.

1. For the purposes of this section the term "non-secure facility" means a facility operated by an authorized agency in accordance with an operating certificate issued pursuant to the social services law or a facility, not including a secure or limited secure facility, with a capacity of twenty-five beds or less operated by the office of children and family services in accordance with section five hundred four of the executive law.

2. Where a respondent is placed with a commissioner of social services or the office of children and family services pursuant to section 353.3 of this article for a period of twelve or fewer months and resides in a foster home or non-secure facility;

(a) The initial permanency hearing shall be held no later than twelve months after the respondent who was placed with a commissioner of social services or the office of children and family services entered foster care and such permanency hearing shall be held in conjunction with an extension of placement hearing held pursuant to section 355.3 of this article.

(b) Subsequent permanency hearings shall be held no later than every twelve months following the respondent's initial permanency hearing and shall be held in conjunction with an extension of placement hearing held pursuant to section 355.3 of this article.

3. Where a respondent is placed with a commissioner of social services or the office of children and family services pursuant to section 353.3 of this article for a period in excess of twelve months and resides in a foster home or in a non-secure facility;

(a) the initial permanency hearing shall be held no later than twelve months after the respondent who was placed with a commissioner of social services or the office of children and family services entered foster care.

(b) subsequent permanency hearings shall be held no later than every twelve months following the respondent's initial twelve months in placement; provided, however, that they shall be held in conjunction with an extension of placement hearing held pursuant to section 355.3 of this article.

4. For the purposes of this section, the

respondent shall be considered to have entered foster care sixty days after the respondent was removed from his or her home pursuant to this article.

5. A petition for an initial or subsequent permanency hearing shall be filed by the office of children and family services or by the commissioner of social services with whom the respondent was placed. Such petition shall be filed no later than sixty days prior to the end of the month in which an initial or subsequent permanency hearing must be held, as directed in subdivision two of this section.

6. The foster parent caring for the respondent or any pre-adoptive parent or relative providing care for the respondent shall be provided with notice of any permanency hearing held pursuant to this section by the office of children and family services or the commissioner of social services with whom the respondent was placed. Such foster parent, pre-adoptive parent and relative shall be afforded an opportunity to be heard at any such hearing; provided, however, no such foster parent, pre-adoptive parent or relative shall be construed to be a party to the hearing solely on the basis of such notice and opportunity to be heard. The failure of the foster parent, pre-adoptive parent, or relative caring for the child to appear at a permanency hearing shall constitute a waiver of the opportunity to be heard and such failure to appear shall not cause a delay of the permanency hearing nor shall such failure to appear be a ground for the invalidation of any order issued by the court pursuant to this section.

7. At the permanency hearing, the court must consider and determine in its order:

(a) where appropriate, that reasonable efforts were made to make it possible for the respondent to return safely to his or her home, or if the permanency plan for the respondent is adoption, guardianship or some other permanent living arrangement other than reunification with the parent or parents of the respondent, that reasonable efforts were made to make and finalize such alternate permanent placement;

(b) in the case of a respondent who has attained the age of sixteen, the services needed, if any, to assist the respondent to make the transition from foster care to independent living;

(c) In the case of a respondent placed outside of this state, whether the out-of-state placement continues to be appropriate and in the best interests of the respondent;

(d) With regard to the completion of placement ordered by the court pursuant to section 353.3 or 355.3 of this article: whether and when the respondent: (i) will be returned to the parent; (ii) should be placed for adoption with the local commissioner of social services filing a petition for termination of parental rights; (iii) should be referred for legal guardianship; (iv) should be placed permanently with a fit and willing relative; or (v) should be placed in another planned permanent living arrangement if the office of children and family services or the local commissioner of social services has documented to the court a compelling reason for determining that it would not be in the best interest of the respondent to return home, be referred for termination of parental rights and placed for adoption, placed with a fit and willing relative, or placed with a legal guardian; and

(e) With regard to the completion or extension of placement ordered by the court pursuant to section 353.3 or 355.3 of this article, the steps that must be taken by the agency with which the respondent is placed to implement the plan for release or conditional release submitted pursuant to paragraph (c) of subdivision seven of section 353.3 of this article, the adequacy of such plan and any modifications that should be made to such plan.

8. The court shall not reduce or terminate the placement of the respondent prior to the completion of the period of placement ordered by the court pursuant to section 353.3 or 355.3 of this article.

Added by L. 1999, Ch. 7, § 30, eff. Feb. 11, 1999; **Amended** by L. 2000, Ch. 181, § 20, eff. Jan. 1, 2001, amending subd. 7(c) and 7(d) and adding subd. 7(e); L. 2000, Ch. 145, § 12, eff. July 1, 2000.

MISC. LAWS

Part 6. Post-dispositional procedures

§ 360.1. Jurisdiction and supervision of respondent placed on probation.

1. A respondent who is placed on probation shall remain under the legal jurisdiction of the court pending expiration or termination of the period of the order of probation.

2. The probation service shall supervise the respondent during the period of such legal jurisdiction.

3. If at any time during the period of probation the court has reasonable cause to believe that the respondent has violated a condition of the probation order, it may issue a search order. A search order is an order directed to a probation officer authorizing such officer to search the person of the respondent or any personal property which he owns or which is in his possession.

4. In executing a search order pursuant to this section, a probation officer may be assisted by a police officer.

ANNOTATION

Generally.—While due process considerations apply to juvenile proceedings, the argument that juvenile conditional release revocation proceedings should mirror adult parole revocation proceedings neglects the reality that the State's relationship to and responsibilities concerning adult prisoners are markedly disparate from its position and duty with respect to delinquent children, and that child on conditional release remains the responsibility of the State for the period of the order of placement. People ex rel. Scherz v. Dennison, 209 A.D.2d 200, 618 N.Y.S.2d 289 (1st Dept. 1994).

§ 360.2. Petition of violation.

1. If at any time during the period of an order of probation or conditional discharge the probation service has reasonable cause to believe that the respondent has violated a condition thereof, it may file a petition of violation.

2. The petition must be verified and subscribed by the probation service or the appropriate presentment agency. Such petition must stipulate the condition or conditions of the order violated and a reasonable description of the time, place, and manner in which the violation occurred. Nonhearsay allegations of the factual part of the petition or of any supporting depositions must establish, if true, every violation charged.

3. The court must promptly take reasonable and appropriate action to cause the respondent to appear before it for the purpose of enabling the court to make a determination with respect to the alleged violation. Such action may include the issuance of a summons under section 312.1 or the issuance of a warrant under section 312.2.

4. If a petition is filed under subdivision one, the period of probation as prescribed by section 353.2 shall be interrupted as of the date of the filing of the petition. Such interruption shall continue until a final determination as to the petition has been made by the court pursuant to a hearing held in accordance with section 360.3 or until such time as the respondent reaches the maximum age of acceptance into a division for youth facility.

5. If the court determines there was no violation of probation by the respondent the period of interruption shall be credited to the period of probation.

ANNOTATIONS

Sufficiency of petition.—Petition must contain reasonable description of time, place, and manner in which violation occurred; petition was insufficient where the presentment agency simply stated that upon information and belief appellant had been discharged from "Project Outreach" and had violated probation. In re Jessica N., 264 A.D.2d 778, 695 N.Y.S.2d 379 (2d Dept. 1999).

—Petition for PINS adjudication upon the ground that respondent was illegally absent from school 22 times between September 20, 2000 and October 24, 2000 was legally defective based on the absence of the attendance forms and a note written by respondent, which were referred to in the petition and formed the basis for its allegations. In re Jodi "W," 295 A.D.2d 659, 743 N.Y.S.2d 195 (3d Dept. 2002).

—A petition that contains only hearsay and is not supported by non-hearsay evidence in the form of a supporting deposition is jurisdictionally defective and must be dismissed; petitioner's admission to the charges contained therein does not cure the defect. In re Todd "D," 288 A.D.2d 740, 732 N.Y.S.2d 488 (3d Dept. 2001).

Tolling period.—Tolling period for probation which occurs when a petition is filed pursuant to section 360.2(1) of the Family Court Act applies to conditional discharges as well. In re Donald MM., 647 N.Y.S.2d 312, 231 A.D.2d 810 (3d Dept. 1996).

§ 360.3. Hearing on violation.

1. The court may not revoke an order of probation or conditional discharge unless: (a) the court has found that the respondent has violated a condition of such order; and (b) the respondent has had an opportunity to be heard. The respondent is entitled to a hearing in accordance with this section promptly after a petition of violation has been filed.

2. At the time of his first appearance following the filing of a petition of violation the court must: (a) advise the respondent of the contents of the petition and furnish him with a copy thereof; (b) determine whether the respondent should be released or detained pursuant to section 320.5; and (c) ask the respondent whether he wishes to make any statement with respect to the violation. If the respondent makes a statement, the court may accept it and base its decision thereon; the provisions of subdivision two of section 321.3 shall apply in determining whether a statement should be accepted. If the court does not accept such statement or if the respondent does not make a statement, the court shall proceed with the hearing. Upon request, the court shall grant a reasonable adjournment to the respondent to enable him to prepare for the hearing.

3. At such hearing, the court may receive any relevant, competent and material evidence. The respondent may cross-examine witnesses and may present evidence on his own behalf.

4. The respondent is entitled to counsel at all stages of a proceeding under this section and the court shall advise him of such right at the outset of the proceeding.

5. The presentment agency shall present the petition in all stages of this part.

6. At the conclusion of the hearing the court may revoke, continue or modify the order of probation or conditional discharge. If the court revokes the order, it shall order a different disposition pursuant to section 352.2. If the court continues the order of probation or conditional discharge, it shall dismiss the petition of violation.

Amended by L. 1982, Ch. 926, eff. July 1, 1983.

ANNOTATIONS

Hearing on violation.—A new violation of probation hearing which contains violations not contained in the first violation starts its own clock running. While it is uncontroverted that a hearing should be promptly held, the standard is not as stringent as those time limits imposed upon fact-finding and dispositional hearings. *In re* Carlos MM., 238 A.D.2d 707, 656 N.Y.S.2d 418 (3d Dept. 1997).

Dispositional hearing.—No new dispositional hearing was required upon finding that juvenile delinquent violated conditions of probation. In re Brandon J., 302 A.D.2d 755 N.Y.S.2d 534 (4th Dept. 2003).

§ 365.1. Appeal; authorized as of right.

1. An appeal to the appropriate appellate division may be taken as of right by the respondent from any order of disposition under this article in accordance with article eleven.

2. An appeal to the appropriate appellate division may be taken as of right by the presentment agency from the following orders of the family court:

(a) an order dismissing a petition prior to the commencement of a fact finding hearing; or

(b) an order of disposition, but only upon the

ground that such order was invalid as a matter of law; or

(c) an order suppressing evidence entered before the commencement of the fact finding hearing pursuant to section 330.2, provided that such presentment agency files a statement pursuant to subdivision nine of section 330.2.

Amended by L. 1985, Ch. 663, eff. Aug. 27, 1985.

ANNOTATIONS

Absent appellant.—Where appellant absconded from her placement with the Division for Youth and a warrant was issued for her arrest, she was unavailable to obey the mandate of the court and the appeal was dismissed. *In re* Magdalene N., 180 A.D.2d 799, 580 N.Y.S.2d 435 (2d Dept. 1992).

Appeal; when authorized.—Presentment agency did not have appeal as of right from order dismissing petition since the order, although finally deciding the proceeding, did not constitute an "order of disposition." *In re* Leon H., 83 N.Y.2d 834, 611 N.Y.S.2d 498, 611 N.E.2d 498 (1994).

—Although the statute does not expressly cover appeals to the Court of Appeals by either a respondent or a presentment agency, the Legislature intended to leave operative earlier decisions treating orders of the Appellate Division as appealable in juvenile delinquency cases appealable pursuant to the provisions of CPLR Article 56. *In re* Jose R., 83 N.Y.2d 388, 610 N.Y.S.2d 937, 632 N.E.2d 1260 (1994).

—Where Family Court denies a suppression motion following a hearing and then reopens it *sua sponte* subsequent to the fact-finding hearing, the presentment agency may pursue an appeal. *In re* Devon H., 225 A.D.2d 135, 650 N.Y.S.2d 120 (1st Dept. 1996).

—Family Court authorizes the petitioner to appeal as of right the dismissal of less than all counts of a petition. *In re* Lee M., 126 A.D.2d 645, 511 N.Y.S.2d 79 (2d Dept. 1987).

Double jeopardy.—An appeal by a presentment agency from a dispositional order, for the purpose of increasing its severity, violates the prohibition against double jeopardy. *In re* Lavar C., 185 A.D.2d 36, 592 N.Y.S.2d 535 (4th Dept. 1992).

§ 365.2. Appeal by permission.

An Appeal may be taken by the respondent in the discretion of the appropriate appellate division, from any other order under this article.

§ 365.3. Notice of appeal.

1. An appeal shall be taken by filing a written notice of appeal, in duplicate, with the clerk of the family court in which the order was entered.

2. If the respondent is the appellant, he must also serve a copy of such notice of appeal upon the appropriate presentment agency.

3. If the presentment agency is the appellant, it must serve a copy of such notice of appeal upon the respondent and upon the attorney or law guardian who last appeared for him in the family court.

4. Following the filing with him of the notice of appeal in duplicate, the clerk of the family court must endorse upon such instruments the filing date and must transmit the duplicate notice of appeal to the clerk of the appropriate appellate division of the supreme court.

ANNOTATION

Notice of appeal.—Family Court Act § 365.3 requires notice of appeal to be served on respondent as well as respondent's law guardian, although failure to do so is not fatal and does not deprive court of jurisdiction to hear appeal or grant petitioner leave to serve respondent and remedy the omission. *In re* Delila M., 238 A.D.2d 342, 656 N.Y.S.2d 306 (2d Dept. 1997).

Part 7. Securing testimony and records

§ 370.1. Securing the attendance of witnesses: securing certain testimony.

1. The provisions of article six hundred twenty of the criminal procedure law concerning the securing of attendance of witnesses by material witness order shall apply to proceedings under this article.

2. Article six hundred sixty, six hundred seventy and six hundred eighty of the criminal procedure law concerning the securing of testimony for use in a subsequent proceeding, the use of testimony given in a previous proceeding and the examination of witness by commission shall apply to proceedings under this article.

3. The provisions of the uniform act to secure attendance of witnesses from without the state in criminal cases, as incorporated in article six hundred forty of the criminal procedure law, shall apply to proceedings under this article.

§ 375.1. Order upon termination of a delinquency action in favor of the respondent.

1. Upon termination of a delinquency proceeding against a respondent in favor of such respondent, unless the presentment agency upon written motion with not less than eight days notice to such respondent demonstrates to the satisfaction of the court that the interests of justice require otherwise or the court on its own motion with not less than eight days notice to such respondent determines that the interest of justice require otherwise and states the reason for such determination on the record, the clerk of the court shall immediately notify the law guardian or counsel for the child, the director of the appropriate presentment agency, and the heads of the appropriate probation department and police department or other law enforcement agency, that the proceeding has terminated in favor of the respondent and, unless the court has directed otherwise, that the records of such action or proceeding, other than those destroyed pursuant to section 354.1 of this act, shall be sealed. Upon receipt of such notification all official records and papers, including judgments and orders of the court, but not including public court decisions or opinions or records and briefs on appeal, relating to the arrest, the prosecution and the probation service proceedings, including all duplicates or copies thereof, on file with the court, police agency, probation service and presentment agency shall be sealed and not made available to any person or public or private agency. Such records shall remain sealed during the pendency of any motion made pursuant to this subdivision.

2. For the purposes of subdivision one, a delinquency proceeding shall be considered terminated in favor of a respondent where:

(a) the petition is withdrawn; or

(b) the petition is dismissed under section 315.1 or 315.2 and the presentment agency has not appealed from such order or the determination of an appeal or appeals from such order has been against the presentment agency; or

(c) the petition has been deemed to have been dismissed under section 315.3 and the presentment agency has not appealed from such order or the determination of an appeal or appeals from such order has been against the presentment agency; or

(d) the petition is dismissed without prejudice under subdivision four of section 325.3 and the presentment agency has not appealed from such order or the determination of an appeal or appeals from such order has been against the presentment agency; or

(e) the entire petition has been dismissed under subdivision two of section 345.1; or

(f) the petition is dismissed under subdivision two of section 352.1; or

(g) prior to the filing of a petition the probation department has adjusted the case or terminated the case without adjustment; or

(h) prior to the filing of a petition the presentment agency chooses not to proceed to petition; or

(i) the petition is dismissed pursuant to a motion made in accordance with subdivision eight, nine or ten of section 332.1.

3. Records sealed pursuant to subdivision one shall be made available to the respondent or his designated agent and the records and papers of a probation service shall be available to any probation service for the purpose of complying with subdivision four of section 308.1.

4. If prior to the filing of a petition the presentment agency elects not to commence a delinquency action it shall serve a certification of such disposition upon the appropriate probation service and the appropriate police department or law

MISC. LAWS

enforcement agency, which, upon receipt thereto, shall comply with the provision of subdivision one in the same manner as is required with respect to an order of the court.

5. If the probation service adjusts a delinquency case it shall serve a certification of such disposition upon the appropriate police department or law enforcement agency which, upon receipt thereof, shall comply with the provisions of subdivision one in the same manner as is required thereunder with respect to an order of a court.

6. A respondent in whose favor a delinquency proceeding was terminated prior to the effective date of this section may upon motion apply to the court, upon not less than twenty days notice to the presentment agency, for an order granting him the relief set forth in subdivision one, and such order shall be granted unless the presentment agency demonstrates to the satisfaction of the court that the interests of justice require otherwise. A respondent in whose favor a delinquency action or proceeding was terminated as defined by subdivisions four and five prior to the effective date of this section, may apply to the appropriate presentment agency or probation service for a certification as described in such subdivisions granting him the relief set forth therein and such certification shall be granted by such presentment agency or probation service.

Amended by L. 1983, Ch. 398, eff. July 1, 1983; L. 1987, Ch. 105, eff. June 8, 1987, Ch. 423, eff. Aug. 27, 1987; L. 1996, Ch. 645, amending subd. 1, eff. Sept. 13, 1996, and applying retroactively to a person whose fingerprints were taken pursuant to section 306.1 of the family court act or who was initially fingerprinted as a juvenile offender on or after January 1, 1986 and whose fingerprints are on file with the division of criminal justice services, provided that in the case of a juvenile offender action the case was subsequently removed to family court, pursuant to L. 1996, Ch. 645, § 6.

ANNOTATIONS

Burden of proof.—The Legislature has placed the burden upon the presentment agency to show that the records should not be sealed and has required the court to apply its discretion in determining whether or not that burden has been satisfied. *In re* Steven R., 121 Misc. 2d 245, 467 N.Y.S.2d 545 (Fam. Ct. Bronx Co. 1983).

Generally.—While the Legislature has granted juvenile respondents the right to have their records sealed if the proceeding against them has been terminated in their favor, it specifically allows the Department of Probation access to those records for the purpose of determining whether or not a future case may be adjusted if the initial proceeding and the future allegations are crimes specified in F.C.A. § 308.1(4). *In re* David H., 124 Misc. 2d 190, 476 N.Y.S.2d 962 (Fam. Ct. Bronx Co. 1984).

Sealing; when authorized.—While sealing is mandatory when a delinquency action has been terminated in favor of a respondent (unless the presentment agency moves to prevent sealing) the mere granting of an ACD is not a termination of the proceeding in respondent's favor. *In re* Theresa W., 142 Misc. 2d 201, 536 N.Y.S.2d 668 (Fam. Ct. Monroe Co. 1988).

—Sealing should be directed where a case has been dismissed in favor of an accused despite the pendency of another proceeding involving the same defendant or respondent. *In re* Robert S., 123 Misc. 2d 225, 473 N.Y.S.2d 112 (Fam. Ct. Kings Co. 1984).

§ 375.2. Motion to seal after a finding.

1. If an action has resulted in a finding of delinquency pursuant to subdivision one of section 352.1 other than a finding that the respondent committed a designated felony act, the court may, in the interest of justice and upon motion of the respondent, order the sealing of appropriate records pursuant to subdivision one of section 375.1.

2. such motion must be in writing and may be filed at any time subsequent to the entering of such finding. Notice of such motion shall be served upon the presentment agency not less than eight days prior to the return date of the motion. Answering affidavits shall be served at least two days before such time.

3. The court shall state on the record its reasons for granting or denying the motion.

4. If such motion is denied, it may not be renewed for a period of one year, unless the order of denial permits renewal at an earlier time.

5. The court shall not order the sealing of any record except as prescribed by this section or section 375.1.

6. Such a motion cannot be filed until the respondent's sixteenth birthday.

Amended by L. 1982, Ch. 926, eff. July 1, 1983; L. 1983, Ch. 398, eff. July 1, 1983.

ANNOTATION

Sealing; when authorized.—Court's denial of request to seal records of appellant's prior adjudication as a juvenile delinquent affirmed; the interests of justice would not be served by sealing due to the serious nature of the underlying charge and the relevance of that charge to the parole board in their consideration of appellant's current application for parole in a subsequent murder conviction. *In re* Carlton B., 268 A.D.2d 368, 702 N.Y.S.2d 270 (1st Dept. 2000).

§ 375.3. Expungement of court records.

Nothing contained in this article shall preclude the court's use of its inherent power to order the expungement of court records.

Added by L. 1983, Ch. 398, eff. July 1.

Part 8. General provisions

§ 380.1. Nature and effect of adjudication.

1. No adjudication under this article may be denominated a conviction and no person adjudicated a juvenile delinquent shall be denominated a criminal by reason of such adjudication.

2. No adjudication under this article shall operate as a forfeiture of any right or privilege or disqualify any person from holding any public office or receiving any license granted by public authority. Such adjudication shall not operate as a disqualification of any person to pursue or engage in any lawful activity, occupation, profession, or calling.

3. Except where specifically required by statute, no person shall be required to divulge information pertaining to the arrest of the respondent or any subsequent proceeding under this article; provided, however, whenever a person adjudicated a juvenile delinquent has been placed with the office of children and family services pursuant to section 353.3 of this article, and is thereafter enrolled as a student in a public or private elementary or secondary school, the court that has adjudicated such person shall provide notification of such adjudication to the designated educational official of the school in which such person is enrolled as a student. Such notification shall be used by the designated educational official only for purposes related to the execution of the student's educational plan, where applicable, successful school adjustment and reentry into the community. Such notification shall be kept separate and apart from such student's school records and shall be accessible only by the designated educational official. Such notification shall not be part of such student's permanent school record and shall not be appended to or included in any documentation regarding such student and shall be destroyed at such time as such student is no longer enrolled in the school district. At no time shall such notification be used for any purpose other than those specified in this subdivision.

Amended by L. 2000, Ch. 181, § 18, amending subd. 3, eff. Nov. 1, 2000.

ANNOTATION

Not a criminal conviction.—A delinquency adjudication cannot constitute a criminal conviction, and a juvenile delinquent cannot be denominated a criminal. Green v. Montgomery, 95 N.Y.2d 693, 723 N.Y.S.2d 744, 736 N.E.2d 1306 (2001).

§ 381.1. Transfer of records and information to institutions and agencies.

Whenever a person is placed in an institution suitable for placement of a person adjudicated a juvenile delinquent maintained by the state or any subdivision thereof or to an authorized agency including the division for youth, the family court placing such person shall forthwith transmit a copy of the orders of the family court pursuant to sections 352.1 and 352.2 and of the probation report and all other relevant evaluative records in the possession of the family court and probation department related to such person, including but not limited to any diagnostic, educational, medical, psychological, and psychiatric records with respect to such person to such institution or agency notwithstanding any contrary provision of law.

§ 381.2. Use of records in other courts.

1. Neither the fact that a person was before the family court under this article for a hearing nor any confession, admission, or statement made by him to the court or to any officer thereof in any stage of the proceeding is admissible as evidence against him or his interests in any other court.

2. Notwithstanding the provisions of subdivision one, another court, in imposing sentence upon an adult after conviction may receive and consider the records and information on file with the family court unless such records and information have been sealed pursuant to section 375.1

Amended by L. 1982, Ch. 926, eff. July 1, 1983.

ANNOTATION

Use in other courts prohibited.—"Juvenile delinquency adjudication cannot be used against the juvenile in any other court for any other purpose." Green v. Montgomery, 95 N.Y.2d 693, 723 N.Y.S.2d 744, 736 N.E.2d 1306 (2001).

§ 381.3. Use of police records.

1. All police records relating to the arrest and disposition of any person under this article shall be kept in files separate and apart from the arrests of adults and shall be withheld from public inspection.

2. Notwithstanding the provisions of subdivision one, the family court in the county in which

the petition was adjudicated may, upon motion and for good cause shown, order such records open:

(a) to the respondent or his parent or person responsible for his care; or

(b) if the respondent is subsequently convicted of a crime, to a judge of the court in which he was convicted, unless such record has been sealed pursuant to section 375.1.

3. An order issued under subdivision two must be in writing.

Amended by L. 1982, Ch. 926, eff. July 1, 1983.

§ 385.1. Reports.

1. In addition to reports filed pursuant to section two hundred thirteen, the chief administrator of the courts shall include in its annual report to the legislature and the governor information, by county, showing the total number of delinquency cases filed under this article, the precise crime or crimes charged in such petitions by penal law section, the number of respondents included in such petitions, the number of cases heard in the designated felony parts, the age of the alleged victim by crime, the length of time and number of adjournments between the filing of a petition and the conclusion of the fact finding process, the number of cases dismissed by the court, the number withdrawn, the number admitted to in whole or in part, the number of contested fact finding hearings and their result, the precise crime, if any, found to have been committed, the length of time and number of adjournments between the fact finding hearing and the conclusion of the dispositional hearing and the final precise disposition of such cases. Designated felony cases shall be separately reported by each event or fact enumerated in this section. Cases removed from criminal courts shall also be separately reported by each event and fact enumerated in this section.

2. The division of probation and correctional alternatives shall include in its annual report to the legislature and the governor information, by county, showing the total number of delinquency cases adjusted prior to filing.

Amended by L. 1985, Ch. 134, eff. Apr. 1, 1985.

§ 385.2. Consolidation of records within a city having a population of one million or more.

Notwithstanding any other provision of law, in a city having a population of one million or more, an index of the records of the local probation departments located in the counties comprising such city for proceedings under article three shall be consolidated and filed in a central office for use by the family court and local probation service in each such county. After consultation with the state administrative judge, the state director of probation and correctional alternatives shall specify the information to be contained in such index and the organization of such consolidated file.

Amended by L. 1985, Ch. 134, eff. Apr. 1, 1985.

ARTICLE 7

PROCEEDINGS CONCERNING WHETHER A PERSON IS IN NEED OF SUPERVISION

SUMMARY OF ARTICLE

Part 1. Jurisdiction

MISC. LAWS

§ 711. Purpose.

The purpose of this article is to provide a due process of law (a) for considering a claim that a person is in need of supervision and (b) for devising an appropriate order of disposition for any person adjudged in need of supervision.

Amended by L. 1976, Ch. 878, eff. July 26, 1976, adding last sentence; L. 1982, Ch. 920, eff. July 1, 1983.

ANNOTATIONS

Adult system distinguished.—The separation of the juvenile from the adult criminal court system is well established in law: a clear distinction is the rehabilitative goal set by the juvenile system, while the criminal system, conversely, demands retribution and mandates punishment to achieve deterrence. People v. Young, 99 Misc. 2d 328, 416 N.Y.S.2d 171 (Fam. Ct. Monroe Co. 1979).

Bail; juvenile respondents.—The Family Court is without power to fix bail for juvenile respondents. People ex rel. Wayburn v. Schupf, 47 A.D.2d 79, 365 N.Y.S.2d 235 (2d Dept. 1975).

Commitment to State Training School held gross abuse of discretion.—Commitment of juvenile to State Training School was held abuse of discretion where the record indicated that the commitment was made solely because the juvenile's heart condition made him unacceptable to Lincoln Hall, a private residential treatment center where his placement was otherwise appropriate, and the Probation Department and the Family Court could not readily locate another suitable philanthropic institution; the use of the State Training School for this purpose was unwarranted and abusive of the court's power. In re S., 37 A.D.2d 977, 328 N.Y.S.2d 235 (2d Dept. 1971).

—CPL Article 30 does not apply to juvenile proceedings; whether there has been an unreasonable delay in a particular case should be determined upon the facts therein and whether actual prejudice has, in fact, occurred. In re Walters, 91 Misc. 2d 728, 398 N.Y.S.2d 806 (Fam. Ct. Suffolk Co. 1977).

Delinquency proceeding; juvenile entitled to voir dire examination.—Appellant, who had been adjudicated a delinquent, was entitled to a voir dire examination to test the lawfulness of the seizure of glassine envelopes by police officer, so he might be in a position to challenge the admissibility of any evidence about them. Moreover, it was improper for the laboratory report to have been destroyed; records such as this should be preserved pending disposition of any appeal. In re P., 40 A.D.2d 638, 336 N.Y.S.2d 212 (1st Dept. 1972).

Disposition; insufficient record.—Judge should have adjourned juvenile delinquency proceeding with a direction to the probation officer to conduct a further investigation where respondent, who had a record of absconding from six prior placements, was clearly in need of therapeutic psychotherapy on a one-to-one basis, and the probation officer's report, which recommended placement in a secure facility, was made without considering the feasibility of placing respondent in a facility which would provide both a secure setting and therapeutic treatment. In re Andre L., 64 A.D.2d 479, 410 N.Y.S.2d 96 (1st Dept. 1978).

Due process; juvenile proceedings.—Due process is preserved in a juvenile proceeding by requiring notice, counsel, and a fact finding hearing before a judge. People v. Young, 99 Misc. 2d 328, 416 N.Y.S.2d 171 (Fam. Ct. Monroe Co. 1979).

Jury trial.—A juvenile should not be granted a jury trial in a juvenile proceeding in Family Court; the rationale is that in exchange for rehabilitation, a juvenile gives up certain constitutional safeguards. People v. Young, 99 Misc. 2d 328, 416 N.Y.S.2d 171 (Fam. Ct. Monroe Co. 1979).

—FCA § 711 does not mandate a jury trial. William v. Harold B., 90 Misc. 2d 173, 393 N.Y.S.2d 535 (Fam. Ct. Kings Co. 1977).

Jurisdiction; delinquency.—Family Court may, even prior to fact-finding, refuse to exercise delinquency jurisdiction over a juvenile respondent when, upon sufficient facts, it is determined that all that must be done is being done. In re Rudy S.,

100 Misc. 2d 1112, 420 N.Y.S.2d 549 (Fam. Ct. Richmond Co. 1979).

Juvenile delinquency proceedings; applicability of CPL provisions.—The pretrial discovery procedures outlined in the CPL apply to juvenile delinquency proceedings in the Family Court. In re Terry T., 90 Misc. 2d 1015, 397 N.Y.S.2d 548 (Fam. Ct. N.Y. Co. 1977).

—Except as to constitutional due process provisions, the procedures of the Family Court, as they affect juvenile delinquency proceedings, are not criminal in nature and the CPL does not apply. In re Parks, 78 Misc. 2d 281, 356 N.Y.S.2d 440 (Fam. Ct. Dutchess Co. 1974).

Juvenile entitled to pretrial suppression hearing.—In Family Court, a juvenile respondent in a designated felony case, is entitled to the same procedural right to a pretrial hearing afforded his adult and juvenile offender counterparts in criminal court; the same judge who will preside over fact finding can preside over the pretrial hearing. In re James A., 102 Misc. 2d 670, 424 N.Y.S.2d 334 (Fam. Ct. Bronx Co. 1980).

Need for protection of the community.—Court denied motion to dismiss the petition or in the alternative that the court accept an admission to the charge and place child on probation since FCA § 711 now requires the court to also consider "the need for the protection of the community" and this additional factor can only be weighed after there has been a finding of fact (FCA § 752) and after a second hearing on disposition (FCA §§ 743, 753). In re Elizabeth J., 98 Misc. 2d 362, 413 N.Y.S.2d 867 (Fam. Ct. N.Y. Co. 1979).

Requirements at hearings.—Order reversed and proceedings remitted where no testimony had been obtained as to whether training school satisfied requirements governing commitment of children held to be in need of supervision as opposed to children found to be delinquent. In re G., 45 A.D.2d 876, 358 N.Y.S.2d 9 (2d Dept. 1974).

Standard of conduct; determination of whether juvenile is sui juris; both civil and criminal law considered.—Family Court juvenile delinquency proceedings are quasi-criminal in nature; therefore, in determining the standard of conduct applicable to a ten-year-old child to render him sui juris, the court looks to both the civil and criminal law. The boy in question here injured petitioner's daughter, age 12, when he shot a bobby pin from a rubber band and struck the girl's eye; the court held that evidence failed to establish criminal intent. In re Riffin, 69 Misc. 2d 761, 330 N.Y.S.2d 850 (Fam. Ct. N.Y. Co. 1972).

§ 712. Definitions.

As used in this article, the following terms shall have the following meanings.

(a) "Person in need of supervision". A person less than eighteen years of age who does not attend school in accordance with the provisions of part one of article sixty-five of the education law or who is incorrigible, ungovernable or habitually disobedient and beyond the lawful control of A parent or other person legally responsible for such child's care, or other lawful authority, or who violates the provisions of section 221.05 of the penal law.

(b) "Detention". The temporary care and maintenance of children away from their own homes as defined in section five hundred two of the executive law.

(c) "Secure detention facility". A facility characterized by physically restricting construction, hardware and procedures.

(d) "Non-secure detention facility". A facility characterized by the absence of physically restricting construction, hardware and procedures.

(e) "Fact-finding hearing". A hearing to determine whether the respondent did the acts alleged to show that he violated a law or is incorrigible, ungovernable or habitually disobedient and beyond the control of his parents, guardian or legal custodian.

(f) "Dispositional hearing". A hearing to determine whether the respondent requires supervision or treatment.

(g) "Aggravated circumstances". Aggravated circumstances shall have the same meaning as the definition of such term in subdivision (j) of section one thousand twelve of this act.

(h) "Permanency hearing". A hearing held in accordance with paragraph (b) of subdivision two of section seven hundred fifty-four or section seven hundred fifty-six-a of this article for the purpose of reviewing the foster care status of the respondent and the appropriateness of the permanency plan developed by the social services official on behalf of such respondent.

(i) "Diversion services". Services provided to children and families pursuant to section seven hundred thirty-five of this article for the purpose of avoiding the need to file a petition or direct the detention of the child. Diversion services shall include: efforts to adjust cases pursuant to this article before a petition is filed, or by order of the court, after the petition is filed but before fact-finding is commenced; and preventive services provided in accordance with section four hundred nine-a of the social services law to avert the placement of the child into foster care, including crisis intervention and respite services.

Amended by L. 1970, Ch. 906; L. 1976, Ch. 878, eff. Feb. 1, 1977, adding subds. (c)-(k); L. 1977, Ch. 283; Ch. 360; L. 1978, Ch. 478, Ch. 481; L. 1979, Ch. 411, eff. Aug. 5, 1979, Ch. 531, eff. Sept. 10, 1979, adding subd. (l); L. 1981, Ch. 335, adding "aggravated sexual abuse" to subd. (h); L. 1982, Ch. 920, eff. July 1, 1983; L. 1987, Ch. 419, eff. Sept. 1, 1987; L. 1992, Ch. 465, eff. Jan. 14, 1992, amending subd. (b), and shall apply to all persons placed in or committed to the custody of the division of youth on or after such date; L. 1999, Ch. 7, § 31, eff. Feb. 11, 1999, adding subds. (g) and (h); L. 2000, Ch. 596, § 2, eff. Nov. 1, 2001; L. 2005, Ch. 3, Part B, § 2, eff. Nov. 21, 2005, amending subd. (g); L. 2005, Ch. 57, Part E, § 1, eff. Apr. 1, 2005, adding subd. (i).

ANNOTATIONS

Age.—In a PINS proceeding, jurisdiction of the court is determined based upon the individual's age at the time he or she was first determined to need supervision but a court has no jurisdiction over an individual as a PINS after the individual turns 18; thus, if an individual is found to be a PINS prior to when she turns 16 years of age, the court may hold supervision proceedings until the individual is 18 years of age. In re Wendy C., 133 A.D.2d 904, 520 N.Y.S.2d 277 (3d Dept. 1987).

Application for order expunging police and court records after reversal of adjudication.—Defendant, after the adjudication that he was a person in need of supervision was reversed, applied to the Family Court for an order expunging all court and police records relating to his arrest. Defendant's application was denied and he appealed. The denial is affirmed as there is no statutory authority for such an order but the order affirming the denial is without prejudice to a new application addressed to the discretion of the Family Court for an order sealing court records pursuant to the Family Court's inherent power to seal records under Family Court Act § 166. Richard S. v. City of New York, 32 N.Y.2d 592, 347 N.Y.S.2d 54 (1973).

Burden of proof.—Article 7 of the FCA makes no provision for a finding with regard to a youth who commits a single illegal act, unless the offense would constitute a misdemeanor or felony if committed by an adult. *In re* O., 31 N.Y.2d 730, 338 N.Y.S.2d 105 (1972).

—It is well settled that there must be more than an isolated incident to support a determination that a juvenile is in need of supervision. *In re* Denise M.W., 122 A.D.2d 556, 505 N.Y.S.2d 18 (4th Dept. 1986).

—A PINS finding must be established by proof beyond a reasonable doubt. *In re* Ian D., 109 Misc. 2d 18, 439 N.Y.S.2d 613 (Fam. Ct. Richmond Co. 1981); *In re* Leifz, 105 Misc. 2d 973, 431 N.Y.S.2d 290 (Fam. Ct. Richmond Co. 1980).

Constitutionality.—Age differentiation between males and females held unconstitutional. Differentiation in FCA § 712(b) between males less than 16 years of age and females less than 18 years of age held to be an unconstitutional discrimination against females. Patricia A. v. City of New York, 31 N.Y.2d 83, 335 N.Y.S.2d 33, 286 N.E.2d 432 (1972).

—FCA § 712(h)(v) does not violate the prohibition against ex post facto laws and is constitutional. *In re* Luis R., 98 Misc. 2d 994, 414 N.Y.S.2d 997 (Fam. Ct. N.Y. Co. 1979).

"Designated felony act."—Even though, in certain cases, it will alert the fact-finding judge to the fact that the juvenile has previously committed a felonious act or acts of an unspecified nature when a designed felony act is alleged, the petition must be so marked and in counties where an appropriate agreement has been entered into, the district attorney rather than the corporation counsel, must present the petition. People v. Samuel P., 77 A.D.2d 879, 430 N.Y.S.2d 669 (2d Dept. 1980).

—Where juvenile's act was transformed into a designated felony by virtue of a prior finding of juvenile delinquency (FCA § 712(h)), all references to the act as a designated felony were ordered stricken from the petition, corporation counsel was substituted for the district attorney to present the petition, and the hearing was placed in the regular, all purpose hearing part so as not to alert the judge at fact finding that the respondent had a prior finding. *In re* Samuel P., 102 Misc. 2d 875, 424 N.Y.S.2d 837 (Fam. Ct. Kings Co. 1980).

—The court construed FCA 731(2) in accordance with the overriding legislative intent of FCA § 750, and directed that the term "designated felony act petition" be prominently marked on petitions alleging designated felony acts in accordance with FCA § 712(h)(v) only after a fact finding hearing establishes that the respondent committed the alleged felony act; the court further requested that the corporation counsel present the case and that the respondent's attorney and the Probation Department be furnished with petition marked designated felony prior to the fact finding so that notice of the charges are known to the law guardian and petition. *In re* Luis R., 98 Misc. 2d 994, 414 N.Y.S.2d 997 (Fam. Ct. N.Y. Co. 1979).

Disposition.—The court should not preconceive the disposition but should conduct an inquiry into the surroundings, conditions and capacities of the juvenile and determine whether the juvenile requires supervision, treatment or confinement. *In re* Warren W., 72 A.D.2d 585, 420 N.Y.S.2d 931 (2d Dept. 1979).

Illegal sentence; confinement of person in need of supervision to institution for juvenile delinquents.—Defendant had been adjudged a person in need of supervision and later, upon recommendation of the Probation Department, was confined in an institution for juvenile delinquents by order of the Family Court. Defendant must be released from the institution as the Family Court Act provides for "confinement" as a possible treatment only for persons adjudged to be juvenile delinquents and not for persons in need of supervision. The purpose of the Family Court Act: to enhance the welfare of the children within its jurisdiction, would be defeated by confining persons in need of supervision to institutions for juvenile delinquents. Ellery C. v. Norman Redlich, 32 N.Y.2d 588, 347 N.Y.S.2d 51, 300 N.E.2d 424 (1973).

Insufficient evidence.—Juvenile's delinquency petition was dismissed where guilt was not proven beyond a reasonable doubt in that he was arrested 100 feet away from where a robbery had taken place 5 minutes before and the sole means of identification, by the complainant, was his having worn the "same" blue jacket and maroon pants as the robber but he did not see his face. *In re* Charles B., 83 A.D.2d 575, 441 N.Y.S.2d 132 (2d Dept. 1981).

Juvenile entitled to minutes of codefendants hearing.— Reversible error was committed when the Family Court failed to provide the juvenile with a copy of the minutes of the codefendants fact finding hearing thereby denying him the full benefit of the witness' statement for impeachment purposes. *In re* John G., 91 A.D.2d 685, 457 N.Y.S.2d 330 (2d Dept. 1982).

Mistrial.—Jeopardy attached against the petitioner when a witness was sworn and testified in the fact-finding hearing and judge should not have declared a mistrial, in view of the law guardian's objections, since there was no "manifest necessity" for doing so, nor would the "ends of public justice have been defeated" had he not done so. People *ex rel.* Thomas v. Judges of Family Ct., 85 Misc. 2d 569, 379 N.Y.S.2d 656 (Sup. Ct. Kings Co. 1976).

PINS dispositional hearing; exclusion of parents and attorney.—Child's parents and their counsel were excluded from the courtroom at the child's PINS dispositional hearing where the court determined, based on reports from psychiatrists and psychologists, that this would be in the child's best interests; the parents were permitted to submit to the Probation Department any recommendation or information they wished the Court to consider on the issue of suitable placement. *In re* Kenneth J., 102 Misc. 2d 415, 423 N.Y.S.2d 821 (Fam. Ct. Richmond Co. 1980).

Suppression motions.—Family Court should follow the procedures set forth in CPL §§ 710.30 and 710.40, which afford the defendant an opportunity to challenge any and all pretrial statements and identification if the People intend to use such evidence against him at trial; by following this procedure the suppression hearing can be held prior to the commencement of the fact finding hearing; if the suppression motion is denied, the hearing can commence immediately following the requisite findings of fact and conclusions of law; if the motion to suppress is granted, the trial can proceed immediately following the requisite findings of fact and conclusions of law, unless the petitioner (ADA or ACC) seek an interlocutory appeal. *In re* Rubin M., 93 Misc. 2d 97, 403 N.Y.S.2d 627 (Fam. Ct. N.Y. Co. 1978).

§ 713. Jurisdiction.

The family court has exclusive original jurisdiction over any proceeding involving a person alleged to be a person in need of supervision.

Amended by L. 1982, Ch. 920, eff. July 1, 1983.

ANNOTATIONS

Burden of proof; age.—In a juvenile delinquency proceeding, age is a jurisdictional fact and the burden of alleging and proving the age of the respondent is upon the prosecution; failure to prove the age of the respondent may result in a dismissal for lack of jurisdiction. *In re* Kalvin, 99 Misc. 2d 996, 417 N.Y.S.2d 826 (Fam. Ct. Onondaga Co. 1979).

Extension of placement nunc pro tunc.—An extension of placement nunc pro tunc may be sought and granted where the original placement was pursuant to Family Court Act, Art. 10 in neglect proceedings, but is not available under Art. 7 in delinquency or PINS proceedings. *In re* Morris W, 79 Misc. 2d 567, 360 N.Y.S.2d 586 (Fam. Ct. Kings Co. 1974).

Transfer; jurisdiction.—A transfer from the Family Court to the Crim. Ct. must be challenged by a defendant in the Family Court see also CPL 440.10(1)(a). People v. Isaacs, 43 A.D.2d 656, 349 N.Y.S.2d 844 (3d Dept. 1973).

§ 714. Determination of age.

(a) In determining the jurisdiction of the court under section seven hundred thirteen the age of the respondent at the time the need for supervision allegedly arose is controlling.

(b) If the respondent is within the jurisdiction of the court, but the proceedings were initiated after the respondent's eighteenth birthday, the family court shall dismiss a petition to determine whether a person is in need of supervision.

Amended by L. 1982, Ch. 920, eff. July 1, 1983.

MISC. LAWS

ANNOTATIONS

Majority; necessary dismissal of delinquency proceeding.—Due to the lack of a legislated alternative, dismissal of a juvenile delinquency proceeding under FCA § 714(b)(ii) was necessary where respondent was 15 years old at the time he allegedly committed the acts in question but was 19 at the time of the hearing in Family Court. *In re* Thomas F., 94 Misc. 2d 154, 404 N.Y.S.2d 210 (1977), *aff'd*, 47 N.Y.2d 1002, 420 N.Y.S.2d 217, 394 N.E.2d 286 (1979).

Person; 7 to 16 years.—The Common law defense of lack of capacity owing to immaturity of persons 7 to 16 years old is available as a defense if proven factually in Juvenile Delinquency proceedings. *In re* Andrew M., 91 Misc. 2d 813, 398 N.Y.S.2d 824 (Fam. Ct. Kings Co. 1977).

Proof of age.—A birth certificate can be offered to establish the age of the respondent in a juvenile proceeding in which age constitutes the basis of the court's jurisdiction, or, at the least, testimony can be offered as to the age the child appeared to be; only averring the age of the respondent in the petition leaves the prosecution subject to dismissal. *In re* Kalvin, 99 Misc. 2d 996, 417 N.Y.S.2d 826 (Fam. Ct. Onondaga Co. 1979).

§ 716. Substitution of petition.

On its own motion and at any time in the proceedings, the court may substitute a neglect petition under article ten for a petition to determine whether a person is in need of supervision.

Amended by L. 1982, Ch. 920, eff. July 1, 1983; L. 1983, Ch. 398, eff. July 1, 1983.

ANNOTATIONS

Abuse and neglect.—Court rejected claim that the acts which were the subject of the PINS proceeding were the result of his parents' abuse and neglect, and therefore, that Family Court erred in failing to exercise its discretion to substitute a Family Court Act article 10 neglect petition for the PINS petition, where the abuse of siblings to which respondent was exposed had not occurred for approximately two and one-half years, that petitioner was actively committed to receiving counseling services to deal with her inability to discipline the children and that, at the time of the acts which were the subject of the proceeding, respondent had been out of foster care and back in the home for three months without incident. *In re* Matthew FF., 179 A.D.2d 928, 579 N.Y.S.2d 178 (3d Dept. 1992).

Failure of mother to appear.—It was an abuse of the court's discretion to fail to substitute a neglect petition in light of the mother's failure to voluntarily appear in court and shelter appellant, and her insistence that he be sent away. *In re* Richard G., 55 A.D.2d 939, 391 N.Y.S.2d 448 (2d Dept. 1977).

Juvenile Justice Reform Act of 1976.—FCA § 716(b) calling for conversion of a delinquency proceeding to one framed in neglect on the court's own motion also extends to the designated felony provisions of Article 7 of the Act. Harold F. v. Helen R., 90 Misc. 2d 122, 393 N.Y.S.2d 887 (Sup. Ct. Kings Co. 1977).

§ 717. Venue.

Proceedings under this article are originated in the county in which the act or acts referred to in the petition allegedly occurred. On motion made on behalf of the respondent or by his parent or other person legally responsible for his care or on the court's motion and for good cause shown, the court may transfer the proceedings to another county.

Amended by L. 1963, Ch. 409, eff. Apr. 16, 1963.

ANNOTATION

Transfer of proceeding.—Once a fact-finding hearing is commenced, the proceeding may not be transferred to another county for good cause shown pursuant to FCA § 717 unless one of the exceptions provided in FCA § 742(1)(i), (ii) is found

to exist. *In re* John Edward B., 70 A.D.2d 1004, 418 N.Y.S.2d 186 (3d Dept. 1979).

§ 718. Return of runaway.

(a) A peace officer, acting pursuant to such peace officer's special duties, or a police officer may return to a parent or other person legally responsible for such child's care any child under the age of eighteen who has run away from home without just cause or who, in the reasonable conclusion of the officer, appears to have run away from home without just cause. For purposes of this action, a police officer or peace officer may reasonably conclude that a child has run away from home when the child refuses to give his or her name or the name and address of a parent or other person legally responsible for such child's care or when the officer has reason to doubt that the name or address given are the actual name and address of the parent or other person legally responsible for the child's care.

(b) A peace officer, acting pursuant to the peace officer's special duties, or a police officer is authorized to take a youth who has run away from home or who, in the reasonable opinion of the officer, appears to have run away from home, to a facility certified or approved for such purpose by the office of children and family services, if the peace officer or police officer is unable, or if it is unsafe, to return the youth to his or her home or to the custody of his or her parent or other person legally responsible for his or her care. Any such facility receiving a youth shall inform a parent or other person responsible for such youth's care.

(c) If a child placed pursuant to this article in the custody of a commissioner of social services or an authorized agency shall run-away from the custody of such commissioner or authorized agency, any peace officer, acting pursuant to his special duties, or a police officer may apprehend, restrain, and return such child to such location as such commissioner shall direct or to such authorized agency and it shall be the duty of any such officer to assist any representative of the commissioner or agency to take into custody any such child upon the request of such representative.

Amended by L. 1963, Chs. 809, 811; L. 1971, Ch. 888; L. 1976, Ch. 607, Ch. 880; L. 1980, Ch. 843, eff. Sept. 1, 1980; L. 1987, Ch. 419, § 17, eff. Sept. 1, 1987; L. 2000, Ch. 596, § 3, eff. Nov. 1, 2001; L. 2005, Ch. 57, Part E, § 2, eff. Apr. 1, 2005, amending subd. (b).

ANNOTATIONS

Standards.—An officer's reasonable opinion justifies detention of a juvenile under Section 718 if it is supported by probable cause to believe that the juvenile may be a runaway. *In re* Marrhonda G., 81 N.Y.2d 942, 597 N.Y.S.2d 662, 613 N.E.2d 568 (1993).

—Police reasonably concluded appellant was a runaway where they received conflicting stories about how he and his companion were related and their planned destination, coupled with the fact appellant had no identification. *In re* Shamel C., 254 A.D.2d 87, 678 N.Y.S.2d 619 (1st Dept. 1998).

—In denying motion to suppress respondent's incriminating

statement that he had "some weed," court found officers were authorized to ask questions of respondent, a minor, in order to secure their safety before bringing respondent to the nearest certified runaway center after finding him at the Port Authority Bus Terminal at 10:30 at night on a school night unaccompanied by an adult. *In re* Michael J., 233 A.D.2d 198, 650 N.Y.S.2d 6 (1st Dept. 1996).

—Officers were authorized to stop and question respondent in light of his youthful appearance, confusion about where he was headed, and presence alone in Port Authority Bus Terminal; officers also were authorized to question respondent further, in absence of *Miranda* warnings, in light of his equivocal response when asked whether he possessed any weapons. *In re* James J., 228 A.D.2d 167, 644 N.Y.S.2d 171 (1st Dept. 1996).

—In denying motion to suppress, court resolved issue of whether a juvenile lawfully detained by the police under the authority of Section 718 may legally be subjected to a "pat-down" search. *In re* Terrence G., 109 A.D.2d 440, 492 N.Y.S.2d 365 (1st Dept. 1985).

MISC. LAWS

Part 2. Custody and detention

Section

§ 720. Detention.

1. No child to whom the provisions of this article may apply, shall be detained in any prison, jail, lockup, or other place used for adults convicted of crime or under arrest and charged with a crime.

2. The detention of a child in a secure detention facility shall not be directed under any of the provisions of this article.

3. Detention of a person alleged to be or adjudicated as a person in need of supervision shall be authorized only in a detention facility certified by the division for youth except as provided in subdivision four of this section.

4. Whenever detention is authorized and ordered pursuant to this article, for a person alleged to be or adjudicated as a person in need of supervision, a family court in a city having a population of one million or more shall, notwithstanding any other provision of law, direct detention in a foster care facility established and maintained pursuant to the social services law. In all other respects, the detention of such a person in a foster care facility shall be subject to the identical terms and conditions for detention as are set forth in this article and in section two hundred thirty-five of this act.

5. (a) The court shall not order or direct detention under this article, unless the court determines that there is no substantial likelihood that the youth and his or her family will continue to benefit from diversion services and that all available alternatives to detention have been exhausted; and

(b) Where the youth is sixteen years of age or older, the court shall not order or direct detention under this article, unless the court determines and states in its order that special circumstances exist to warrant such detention.

Added by L. 1973, Ch. 1037; L. 1976, Ch. 880, eff. Nov. 29, 1976, Ch. 878, eff. Feb. 1, 1977, repealing subd. (a) and renumbering subds. (b) and (c) as 1 and 2; Amended by L. 1978, Ch. 548, eff. Jan. 1, 1979; L. 1978 Ch. 555, eff. July 24, 1978; L. 1987, Ch. 419, eff. Sept. 1, 1987; L. 2001, Ch. 383, Part V, § 3, adding subd. 5, eff. July 1, 2002; L. 2005, Ch. 57, Part E, § 3, eff. Apr. 1, 2005, amending subd. 5.

ANNOTATION

Constitutionality.—Section 720 of the Family Court Act is unconstitutional because it improperly infringes upon the court's power to secure in detention a person in need of supervision who had violated a valid court order and because the statute was not in the child's best interests. *In re* Jennifer G., 196 Misc. 2d 692, 764 N.Y.S.2d 503 (Fam. Ct. Queens Co. 2003).

Power to direct the type of detention facility.—The power to direct the type of detention facility for a remanded child belongs to the state family court and not to the N.Y.C. Commissioner of Juvenile Justice. *In re* Anthony N., 106 Misc. 2d 213, 430 N.Y.S.2d 1012 (Fam. Ct. Richmond Co. 1980).

§ 723. Duties of private person before and after taking into custody.

(a) Before taking into custody, a private person must inform the person to be taken into custody of the cause thereof and require him to submit.

(b) After taking into custody, a private person must take the person, without unnecessary delay, to his home, to a family court judge or deliver him to a peace officer, who is acting pursuant to his special duties, or a police officer.

Amended by L. 1980, Ch. 843, eff. Sept. 1, 1980; L. 1982, Ch. 920, eff. July 1, 1983.

§ 724. Duties of police officer or peace officer after taking into custody or on delivery by private person.

(a) If a peace officer or a police officer takes into custody or if a person is delivered to him under section seven hundred twenty-three, the officer shall immediately notify the parent or other person legally responsible for his care, or the person with whom he is domiciled, that he has been taken into custody.

(b) After making every reasonable effort to give notice under paragraph (a), the officer shall

(i) release the youth to the custody of his or her parent or other person legally responsible for his or her care upon the written promise, without security, of the person to whose custody the youth is released that he or she will produce the youth before the lead agency designated pursuant to section seven hundred thirty-five of this article in that county at a time and place specified in writing; or

(ii) forthwith and with all reasonable speed

take the youth directly, and without first being taken to the police station house, to the designated lead agency located in the county in which the act occasioning the taking into custody allegedly was done, unless the officer determines that it is necessary to question the youth, in which case he or she may take the youth to a facility designated by the chief administrator of the courts as a suitable place for the questioning of youth or, upon the consent of a parent or other person legally responsible for the care of the youth, to the youth's residence and there question him or her for a reasonable period of time; or

(iii) take a youth in need of crisis intervention or respite services to an approved runaway program or other approved respite or crisis program; or

(iv) take the youth directly to the family court located in the county in which the act occasioning the taking into custody was allegedly done, provided that the officer affirms on the record that he or she attempted to exercise the options identified in paragraphs (i), (ii) and (iii) of this subdivision, was unable to exercise these options, and the reasons therefor.

(c) In the absence of special circumstances, the officer shall release the child in accord with paragraph (b) (i).

(d) In determining what is a "reasonable period of time" for questioning a child, the child's age and the presence or absence of his parents or other person legally responsible for his care shall be included among the relevant considerations.

Amended by L. 1963, Ch. 809; L. 1970, Ch. 669; L. of 1972, Ch. 166; L. 1973, Ch. 1037; L. 1976, Ch. 880; L. 1980, Ch. 843, eff. Sept. 1, 1980; L. 1982, Ch. 920, eff. July 1, 1983; L. 1984, Ch. 629, eff. July 27, 1984; L. 1987, Ch. 492, eff. July 30, 1987; L. 2005, Ch. 57, Part E, § 4, eff. Apr. 1, 2005, amending subds. (b)(i), (ii), and (iii) and adding subd. (b)(iv).

ANNOTATIONS

Age of Youth—Protections of FCA § 724 extend only to those youth who were less than sixteen years old at the time of police questioning, appellant was over sixteen at time questioned, an adult under proscribed protocol and not entitled to § 724 protections, even though questioned about events which occurred prior to sixteenth birthday. *In re* Manuel B., 4 Misc. 3d 722, 781 N.Y.S.2d 595 (Fam. Ct. Queens Co. 2004).

Communication with guardian is privileged.—A conversation between a child and his guardian who appears pursuant to the provisions of FCA § 724(a) is privileged. Michelet P. v. Gold, 70 A.D.2d 68, 419 N.Y.S.2d 704 (2d Dept. 1979).

Degree of compliance.—There was substantial compliance with the statute concerning arrest and questioning of juveniles when the parent was notified of the child's arrest after he arrived at the station house, no place had yet been designated by the appropriate Appellate Division for questioning children, and the child was not taken directly to Family Court because the police officer determined that the child should be questioned. Emilio M. v. City of New York, 37 N.Y.2d 173, 371 N.Y.S.2d 697, 332 N.E.2d 874 (1975).

—FCA § 724 merely requires that the peace officer make "every reasonable effort to give notice" and where juvenile refuses to give his name or identify himself it is impossible for the officer to notify the mother and statements made are admissible. *In re* James B., 78 A.D.2d 793, 433 N.Y.S.2d 21 (1st Dept. 1980).

—Juvenile's statement must be suppressed where, although officer stated that no interrogation as to the crime was contemplated, *Miranda* warnings were given and some questioning relative to pedigree and related information ensued in an area not designated for questioning of juveniles, and juvenile was unrepresented and without parent or guardian; strict compliance with FCA § 724 is mandated. *In re* Anthony E., 72 A.D.2d 699, 421 N.Y.S.2d 566 (1st Dept. 1979).

Unavailability of facility designated for questioning.— Since the juvenile's statement was taken in a facility not designated by the Appellate Division, it was not admissible in evidence. *In re* Matthew F., 87 Misc. 2d 644, 386 N.Y.S.2d 534 (Fam. Ct. Monroe Co. 1976).

Juvenile; admissibility of confession; waiver of appointment of law guardian.—A juvenile subject to custodial interrogation is "a subject" of a juvenile delinquency proceeding for the purposes of FCA § 249-a, and thus the presumption that he lacks the requisite knowledge and maturity to waive the appointment of a law guardian cannot be addressed until the law guardian is appointed. *In re* Schaefer, 97 Misc. 2d 487, 411 N.Y.S.2d 977 (Fam. Ct. Onondaga Co. 1978).

Non-compliance; effect on subsequent admissions by juvenile.—Where FCA § 724 is not complied with, the issue of whether the juvenile in a constitutional sense knowingly and voluntarily waived his *Miranda* rights becomes academic; the failure to comply with the statute makes any statement involuntary and inadmissible per se. Michelet P. v. Gold, 70 A.D.2d 68, 419 N.Y.S.2d 704 (2d Dept. 1979).

Notification of party legally responsible for juvenile.—The requirement that a party legally responsible for the juvenile be notified is strict. Michelet P. v. Gold, 70 A.D.2d 68, 419 N.Y.S.2d 704 (2d Dept. 1979).

—Police substantially complied with the requirements of statute where juvenile's statement to police was made in the presence of his uncle prior to the arrival of his mother where the juvenile had a close relationship with his uncle, and lived with him at times, and did not reside with his mother. *In re* Lawrence W., 77 A.D.2d 570, 429 N.Y.S.2d 731 (2d Dept. 1980).

—Statement given to police officers by juvenile defendant should have been suppressed at the hearing where no notification was given to the suspect's parents and they were not present when the statement was made even though suspect's uncle accompanied him to police station and was present when the statement was given. *In re* Brian P.T., 58 A.D.2d 868, 396 N.Y.S.2d 873 (2d Dept. 1977).

—Since FCA § 724(b)(ii) allows questioning of juveniles after every reasonable effort to notify their parents has been made, it was proper for the police to question the juvenile after messages were left and the police waited two and one-half hours for the mother to appear and she later admitted that she delayed going to the police station for about two hours after she learned of her son's arrest. *In re* Raphael, 53 A.D.2d 592, 385 N.Y.S.2d 288 (1st Dept. 1976).

—Section 724 applies where a police officer has taken a juvenile into custody and requires the police officer to immediately notify a parent that the juvenile has been taken into custody, or at least make a reasonable effort to notify the parent or parents before questioning, however this does not preclude investigative inquiry addressed to an individual whom the police have reasonable suspicion to believe has committed a crime. *In re* Mario Y., 75 A.D.2d 954, 428 N.Y.S.2d 71 (3d Dept. 1980).

—The police violated FCA § 724 when they arrested the youth without probable cause and placed him in a show-up without any effort to contact his parents; the standards of probable cause that apply to adults also apply to juveniles. *In re* Martin S., 104 Misc. 2d 1009, 429 N.Y.S.2d 1009 (Fam. Ct. Richmond Co. 1980).

Statements, admission, confession.—Respondent's adjudication as a juvenile delinquent reversed and remanded for a new fact-finding hearing on the ground that the statement, handwritten by the detective and signed by the respondent, should not have been admitted where the detective gave respondent, who, at 15, had a third grade reading level, his *Miranda* warnings in English only, failing to translate them into Spanish for his mother who was present at the questioning but could not understand English. *In re* Rafael M., 57 A.D.2d 816, 395 N.Y.S.2d 170 (1st Dept. 1977).

—A juvenile knowingly and intelligently waived his privilege against self incrimination and his statement was voluntarily given where he and his guardian voluntarily appeared at the precinct; both were taken to a room designated for questioning of juveniles; the juvenile was advised of his rights in the presence of his guardian and had the opportunity to and did converse with his guardian as each of his rights was given to him and then made the statement. *In re* Eduardo M., 80 Misc. 2d 371, 363 N.Y.S.2d 254 (Fam. Ct. N.Y. Co. 1975).

§ 725. Summons or warrant on failure to appear.

The family court before which a person failed to produce a child pursuant to a written promise given under section seven hundred twenty-four may issue a summons requiring the child and the person who failed to produce him to appear at the court at a time and place specified in the summons or may issue a warrant for either or both of them, directing that either or both be brought to the court at a time and place specified in the warrant.

§ 727. Rules of court authorizing release before filing of petition.

(a) The agency responsible for operating a detention facility or in a city of one million or more, the agency responsible for operating a foster care facility, may release a child in custody before the filing of a petition to the custody of his parents or other relative, guardian or legal custodian when the events occasioning the taking into custody appear to involve a petition to determine whether a person is in need of supervision rather than a petition to determine whether a person is a juvenile delinquent.

(b) When a release is made under this section such release may, but need not, be conditioned upon the giving of a recognizance in accord with section seven hundred twenty-four (b)(i).

(c) If the probation service for any reason does not release a child under this section, the child shall promptly be brought before a judge of the court, if practicable, and section seven hundred twenty-eight shall apply.

Amended by L. 1970, Ch. 978, eff. May 19, 1970; L. 1982, Ch. 920, eff. July 1, 1983; L. 1987, Ch. 419, eff. Sept. 1, 1987.

ANNOTATION

No constitutional right to counsel at initial intake conference.—The initial intake conference in juvenile delinquency cases is not a "critical stage" in the proceedings within the meaning of the constitutional guarantee of the right to counsel, in light of the protection afforded the juvenile under the exclusionary rule of FCA 735 as well as the right to have the court or judge determine whether or not any petition will issue against him if a petitioner does not wish an adjustment at intake level and insists upon a petition being drawn. *In re* H., 71 Misc. 2d 1042, 337 N.Y.S.2d 118 (Fam. Ct. Richmond Co. 1972).

§ 728. Discharge, release or detention by judge after hearing and before filing of petition in custody cases.

(a) If a child in custody is brought before a judge of the family court before a petition is filed,

the judge shall hold a hearing for the purpose of making a preliminary determination of whether the court appears to have jurisdiction over the child. At the commencement of the hearing, the judge shall advise the child of his right to remain silent, his right to be represented by counsel of his own choosing, and of his right to have a law guardian assigned in accord with part four of article two of this act. He must also allow the child a reasonable time to send for his parents or other person legally responsible for his care, and for counsel, and adjourn the hearing for that purpose.

(b) After hearing, the judge shall order the release of the child to the custody of his parent or other person legally responsible for his care if the court does not appear to have jurisdiction.

(c) An order of release under this section may, but need not, be conditioned upon the giving of a recognizance in accord with sections seven hundred twenty-four (b)(i).

(d) Upon a finding of facts and reasons which support a detention order pursuant to this section, the court shall also determine and state in any order directing detention:

(i) that there is no substantial likelihood that the youth and his or her family will continue to benefit from diversion services and that all available alternatives to detention have been exhausted; and

(ii) whether continuation of the child in the child's home would be contrary to the best interests of the child based upon, and limited to, the facts and circumstances available to the court at the time of the hearing held in accordance with this section; and

(iii) where appropriate, whether reasonable efforts were made prior to the date of the court hearing that resulted in the detention order, to prevent or eliminate the need for removal of the child from his or her home or, if the child had been removed from his or her home prior to the court appearance pursuant to this section, where appropriate, whether reasonable efforts were made to make it possible for the child to safely return home.

Amended by L. 1982, Ch. 920, eff. July 1, 1983; L. 1987, Ch. 419, eff. Sept. 1, 1987; L. 2000, Ch. 145, eff. July 1, 2000; L. 2005, Ch. 57, Part E, § 5, eff. Apr. 1, 2005, relettering subds. (d)(i) and (ii) as (d)(ii) and (iii) and adding new subd. (d)(i).

ANNOTATIONS

Fact-finding hearing; unreasonably long detention.—Absent special and compelling circumstances, a fact-finding hearing must be conducted within three days once a juvenile is detained. Where the relator had been detained for more than two months because of adjournments of the fact-finding hearing, the Court of Appeals held that the delay violated the time limit prescribed for detention of adults in felony proceedings (CPL § 180.80); it ruled that the restrictive language of FCA sections 747 and 748 is designed to mandate speedier fact-finding hearings, and that it would take a distorted view to believe that adult felony proceedings are designed to be more scrupulous about the rights of detained adults than the Family Court procedures with respect to juveniles. However, because the juvenile had been released on parole, and because the Administrative Judge of the New York City Family Court had adopted an internal regulation in order to avoid such protracted adjournments, the court dismissed the writ solely on the ground of mootness. People *ex rel.* Guggenheim v. Mucci, 32 N.Y.2d 307, 344 N.Y.S.2d 944 (1973).

Preliminary hearing; Family Court.—Complete prohibition of cross-examination at hearing in Family Court was an improvident exercise of discretion and deprived juvenile of benefit of hearing. People *ex rel.* (1) Lauring v. Mucci, 44 A.D.2d 479, 355 N.Y.S.2d 786 (1st Dept. 1974).

§ 729. Duration of detention before filing of petition or hearing.

No person may be detained under this article for more than seventy-two hours or the next day the court is in session, whichever is sooner, without a hearing under section seven hundred twenty-eight.

Amended by L. 1964, Ch. 96, eff. Mar. 16, 1964.

MISC. LAWS

Part 3. Preliminary procedure

Section

§ 732. Originating proceeding to adjudicate need for supervision.

A proceeding to adjudicate a person to be in need of supervision is originated by the filing of a petition, alleging:

(a) the respondent is an habitual truant or is incorrigible, ungovernable, or habitually disobedient and beyond the lawful control of his or her parents, guardian or lawful custodian, and specifying the acts on which the allegations are based and the time and place they allegedly occurred. Where habitual truancy is alleged or the petitioner is a school district or local educational agency, the petition shall also include the steps taken by the responsible school district or local educational agency to improve the school attendance and/or conduct of the respondent;

(b) the respondent was under eighteen years of age at the time of the specified acts;

(c) the respondent requires supervision or treatment; and

(d) the petitioner has complied with the provisions of section seven hundred thirty-five of this article.

Amended by L. 2000, Ch. 596, eff. Nov. 1, 2001; L. 2005, Ch. 57, Part E, § 6, eff. Apr. 1, 2005, amending subds. (a), (b), and (c) and adding subd. (d).

ANNOTATIONS

Sufficiency of petition.—A petition based on hearsay allegations is constitutionally permissible in a proceeding under Family Court Act article 7 to adjudge a person in need of supervision even though a juvenile delinquency petition under Family Court article 3 must be based on non-hearsay allegations. *In re* Keith H., 188 A.D.2d 81, 594 N.Y.S.2d 268 (2d Dept. 1993).

—There is no statutory requirement in Family Court article 7 that a PINS petition contain non-hearsay allegations. *In re* Jodel KK., 189 A.D.2d 63, 595 N.Y.S.2d 835 (3d Dept. 1993).

§ 733. Persons who may originate proceedings.

The following persons may originate a proceeding under this article:

(a) a peace officer, acting pursuant to his special duties, or a police officer;

(b) the parent or other person legally responsible for his care;

(c) any person who has suffered injury as a result of the alleged activity of a person alleged to be in need of supervision, or a witness to such activity;

(d) the recognized agents of any duly authorized agency, association, society or institution; or

(e) the presentment agency that consented to substitute a petition alleging the person is in need of supervision for a petition alleging that the person is a juvenile delinquent pursuant to section 311.4.

Amended by L. 1978, Ch. 481; L. 1980, Ch. 843, eff. Sept. 1, 1980; L. 1982, Ch. 920, eff. July 1, 1983; L. 1983, Ch. 398, eff. July 1, 1983.

ANNOTATIONS

Children's services center; agent of Department of Social Services; standing to institute proceeding.—Children's services institution, with whom respondent had been placed under contract with the Department of Social Services, had standing to initiate a PINS petition where such institution had been given authority to act as agent for the Department of Social Services. *In re* Keelin E., 65 A.D.2d 736, 410 N.Y.S.2d 615 (1st Dept. 1978).

De facto custody of child sufficient under Section 733.—FCA § 733(b) contains no requirement that a petitioner have legal custody of the child in question; therefore, where mother, who had legal custody of child, transferred the child to the father's care, this transfer was sufficient to confer on the father the right to act as a petitioner in a PINS proceeding. *In re* S., 70 Misc.2d 406, 333 N.Y.S.2d 649 (Fam. Ct. N.Y. Co. 1972).

§ 734. Rules of court for preliminary procedure.

[*Repealed pursuant to L. 2005, Ch. 57, Part E, § 6-a, eff. Apr. 1, 2005.*]

§ 735. Preliminary procedure; diversion services.

(a) Each county and any city having a population of one million or more shall offer diversion services as defined in section seven hundred twelve of this article to youth who are at risk of being the subject of a person in need of supervision petition. Such services shall be designed to provide an immediate response to families in crisis, to identify and utilize appropriate alternatives to detention and to divert youth from being the subject of a petition in family court. Each county and such city shall designate either the local social services district or the probation department as lead agency for the purposes of providing diversion services.

(b) The designated lead agency shall:

(i) confer with any person seeking to file a petition, the youth who may be a potential respondent, his or her family, and other interested persons, concerning the provision of diversion services before any petition may be filed; and

(ii) diligently attempt to prevent the filing of a petition under this article or, after the petition is filed, to prevent the placement of the youth into foster care; and

(iii) assess whether the youth would benefit from residential respite services; and

(iv) determine whether alternatives to detention are appropriate to avoid remand of the youth to detention.

(c) Any person or agency seeking to file a petition pursuant to this article which does not have attached thereto the documentation required by subdivision (g) of this section shall be referred by the clerk of the court to the designated lead agency which shall schedule and hold, on reasonable notice to the potential petitioner, the youth and his or her parent or other person legally responsible for his or her care, at least one conference in order to determine the factual circumstances and determine whether the youth and his or her family should receive diversion services pursuant to this section. Diversion services shall include clearly documented diligent attempts to provide appropriate services to the youth and his or her family unless it is determined that there is no substantial likelihood that the youth and his or her family will benefit from further diversion attempts. Notwithstanding the provisions of section two hundred sixteen-c of this act, the clerk shall not accept for filing under this part any petition that does not have attached thereto the documentation required by subdivision (g) of this section.

(d) Diversion services shall include documented diligent attempts to engage the youth and his or her family in appropriately targeted community-based services, but shall not be limited to:

(i) providing, at the first contact, information on the availability of or a referral to services in the geographic area where the youth and his or her family are located that may be of benefit in avoiding the need to file a petition under this article; including the availability, for up to twenty-one days, of a residential respite program, if the youth and his or her parent or other person legally responsible for his or her care agree, and the availability of other non-residential crisis intervention programs such as family crisis counseling or alternative dispute resolution programs.

(ii) scheduling and holding at least one conference with the youth and his or her family and the person or representatives of the entity seeking to file a petition under this article concerning alternatives to filing a petition and services that are available. Diversion services shall include clearly documented diligent attempts to provide appropriate services to the youth and his or her family before it may be determined that there is no substantial likelihood that the youth and his or her family will benefit from further attempts.

(iii) where the entity seeking to file a petition is a school district or local educational agency, the designated lead agency shall review the steps taken by the school district or local educational agency to improve the youth's attendance and/or conduct in school and attempt to engage the school district or local educational agency in further diversion attempts, if it appears from review that such attempts will be beneficial to the youth.

(e) The designated lead agency shall maintain a written record with respect to each youth and his or her family for whom it considers providing or provides diversion services pursuant to this section. The record shall be made available to the court at or prior to the initial appearance of the youth in any proceeding initiated pursuant to this article.

(f) Efforts to prevent the filing of a petition pursuant to this section may extend until the designated lead agency determines that there is no substantial likelihood that the youth and his or her family will benefit from further attempts. Efforts at diversion pursuant to this section may continue after the filing of a petition where the designated lead agency determines that the youth and his or her family will benefit from further attempts to prevent the youth from entering foster care.

(g) (i) The designated lead agency shall promptly give written notice to the potential petitioner whenever attempts to prevent the filing of a petition have terminated, and shall indicate in such notice whether efforts were successful. The notice shall also detail the diligent attempts made to divert the case if a determination has been made that there is no substantial likelihood that the youth will benefit from further attempts. No persons in need of supervision petition may be filed pursuant to this article during the period the designated lead agency is providing diversion services. A finding by the designated lead agency that the case has been successfully diverted shall constitute presumptive evidence that the underlying allegations have been successfully resolved in any petition based upon the same factual allegations. No petition may be filed pursuant to this article by the parent or other person legally responsible for the youth where diversion services have been terminated because of the failure of the parent or other person legally responsible for the youth to consent to or actively participate.

(ii) The clerk of the court shall accept a petition for filing only if it has attached thereto the following:

(A) if the potential petitioner is the parent or other person legally responsible for the youth, a notice from the designated lead agency indicating there is no bar to the filing of the petition as the potential petitioner consented to and actively participated in diversion services; and

(B) a notice from the designated lead agency stating that it has terminated diversion services because it has determined that there is no substantial likelihood that the youth and his or her family will benefit from further attempts, and that the case has not been successfully diverted.

(h) No statement made to the designated lead agency or to any agency or organization to which the potential respondent, prior to the filing of the petition, or if the petition has been filed, prior to the time the respondent has been notified that attempts at diversion will not be made or have been terminated, or prior to the commencement of a fact-finding hearing if attempts at diversion have not terminated previously, may be admitted into evidence at a fact-finding hearing or, if the proceeding is transferred to a criminal court, at any time prior to a conviction.

Added by L. 1985, Ch. 813, eff. Aug. 2, 1985; **Amended** by L. 1988, Ch. 290, § 1, eff. July 25, 1988; Former section **repealed** and new section added by L. 2005, Ch. 57, Part E, § 7, eff. Apr. 1, 2005.

ANNOTATIONS

No constitutional right to counsel at initial intake conference.—In a case decided under previous version of FCA § 735, the court decided that the initial intake conference in juvenile delinquency cases is not a "critical stage" in the proceedings within the meaning of the constitutional guarantee of the right to counsel, in light of the protection afforded the juvenile under the exclusionary rule of FCA § 735 as well as the right to have the court or judge determine whether or not any petition will issue against the juvenile if the juvenile does not wish an adjustment at intake level and insists on a petition being drawn. In re H., 71 Misc. 2d 1042, 337 N.Y.S.2d 118 (Fam. Ct. Richmond Co. 1972); see also In re David J., 70 A.D.2d 276, 421 N.Y.S.2d 411 (3d Dept. 1979).

Limits of FCA § 735 exclusionary rule.—In a case decided under previous version of FCA § 735, the court decided that the exclusionary rule embodied in the statute does not apply where probation intake records are not being sought for the purpose of admitting them in evidence at a fact finding hearing or for use against the juvenile in any proceeding whatsoever; probation intake records gathered in preliminary proceedings for the Family Court are deemed confidential information furnished to the court and are not open to indiscriminate public inspection, but are subject to disclosure as provided for by law or court order, and the Legislature has implicitly given the court discretion in any case to permit inspection of any papers or records, under FCA §§ 166 and 750. People v. Price, 100 Misc. 2d 372, 419 N.Y.S.2d 415 (Sup. Ct. Bronx Co. 1979).

Privilege overcome by right of confrontation.—In a case decided under previous version of FCA § 735, where defendant charged with robbery obtained a judicial subpoena duces tecum ordering the production of the probation intake records of a third party juvenile whom complainant originally identified as her attacker, the Department of Probation's motion to quash the subpoena was denied on the ground that the defendant's Sixth Amendment rights to confrontation and compulsory process outweigh the confidentiality of probation intake records; however, in order to protect matters contained in such reports that might be irrelevant or inadmissible from unwarranted disclosure, the court ordered the production of the subpoenaed records for in camera inspection and redaction. People v. Price, 100 Misc. 2d 372, 419 N.Y.S.2d 415 (Sup. Ct. Bronx Co. 1979).

§ 736. Issuance of summons.

(1) On the filing of a petition under this article, the court may cause a copy of the petition and a summons to be issued, requiring the respondent and his parent or other person legally responsible for his care, or with whom he is domiciled, to appear at the court at a time and place named to answer the petition. The summons shall be signed by the court or by the clerk or deputy clerk of the court. If those on whom a summons must be served are before the court at the time of the filing of a petition, the provisions of part four of this article shall be followed.

(2) In proceedings originated pursuant to subdivision (b) of section seven hundred thirty-three of this article, the court shall cause a copy of the petition and notice of the time and place to be heard to be served upon any parent of the respondent or other person legally responsible for the respondent's care who has not signed the petition, provided that the address of such parent or other person legally responsible is known to the court or is ascertainable by the court. Such petition shall include a notice that, upon placement of the child in the care and custody of the department of social services or any other agency, said parent may be named as a respondent in a child support proceeding brought pursuant to article four of this act. Service shall be made by the clerk of the court by mailing such notice and petition by ordinary first class mail to such parent or other person legally responsible at such person's last known residence.

(3) In proceedings originated pursuant to subdivision (a), (c), (d) or (e) of section seven hundred thirty-three of this article, the court shall cause a copy of the petition and notice of the time and place to be heard to be served upon each parent of the respondent or other person legally responsible for the respondent's care, provided that the address of such parent or other person legally responsible is known to the court or is ascertainable by the court. Service shall be made by the clerk of the court by mailing such notice and petition by ordinary first class mail to such parent or other person legally responsible at such person's last known residence.

Amended by L. 1989, Ch. 474, eff. Aug. 15, 1989; L. 1995, Ch. 652, § 1, amending subd. 2, eff. Aug. 8, 1995.

§ 737. Service of summons.

(a) Service of a summons and petition shall be made by delivery of a true copy thereof to the person summoned at least twenty-four hours before the time stated therein for appearance. If so requested by one acting on behalf of the respondent or by a parent or other person legally responsible for his care, the court shall not proceed with the hearing or proceeding earlier than three days after such service.

(b) If after reasonable effort, personal service is not made, the court may at any stage in the proceedings make an order providing for substituted service in the manner provided for substituted service in civil process in courts of record.

§ 738. Issuance of warrant for respondent or other person legally responsible for care.

The court may issue a warrant, directing that the respondent or other person legally responsible for his care or with whom he is domiciled be brought before the court, when a petition is filed with the court under this article and it appears that

(a) the summons cannot be served; or

(b) the respondent or other person has refused to obey the summons; or

(c) the respondent or other person is likely to leave the jurisdiction; or

(d) a summons, in the court's opinion, would be ineffectual; or

(e) a respondent on bail or on parole has failed to appear.

A warrant issued for a respondent under this section shall expire at the end of six months from the date of its issuance, unless extended for an additional period of not more than six months upon application by the petitioner for good cause shown.

Amended by L. 1986, Ch. 459, eff. Aug. 20, 1986; and shall not apply to warrants issued prior to Aug. 20, 1986.

§ 739. Release or detention after filing of petition and prior to order of disposition.

(a) After the filing of a petition under section seven hundred thirty-two of this article, the court in its discretion may release the respondent or direct his or her detention. However, the court shall not direct detention unless it finds and states the facts and reasons for so finding that unless the respondent is detained there is a substantial probability that the respondent will not appear in court on the return date and all available alternatives to detention have been exhausted.

(b) Unless the respondent waives a determination that probable cause exists to believe that he is a person in need of supervision, no detention under this section may last more than three days (i) unless the court finds, pursuant to the evidentiary standards applicable to a hearing on a felony complaint in a criminal court, that such probable cause exists, or (ii) unless special circumstances

exist, in which cases such detention may be extended not more than an additional three days exclusive of Saturdays, Sundays and public holidays.

(c) Upon a finding of facts and reasons which support a detention order pursuant to subdivision (a) of this section, the court shall also determine and state in any order directing detention:

(i) whether continuation of the respondent in the respondent's home would be contrary to the best interests of the respondent based upon, and limited to, the facts and circumstance available to the court at the time of the court's determination in accordance with this section; and

(ii) where appropriate, whether reasonable efforts were made prior to the date of the court order directing detention in accordance with this section, to prevent or eliminate the need for removal of the respondent from his or her home or, if the respondent had been removed from his or her home prior to the court appearance pursuant to this section, where appropriate, whether reasonable efforts were made to make it possible for the respondent to safely return home.

Amended by L. 1975, Ch. 837; L. 1976, Ch. 880; L. 1978, Ch. 481, eff. Sept. 1, 1978, adding subd. (c); L. 1979, Ch. 411, eff. Aug. 5, 1979; L. 1982, Ch. 920, eff. July 1, 1983; L. 2000, Ch. 145, eff. July 1, 2000; L. 2005, Ch. 57, Part E, § 8, eff. Apr. 1, 2005, amending subd. (a).

ANNOTATIONS

Bail.—FCA § 739 grants the Family Court power to fix bail on juvenile respondents. *In re* Ronald D., 96 Misc. 2d 870, 410 N.Y.S.2d 36 (Fam. Ct. Richmond Co. 1978).

—Detention of respondent over the age of sixteen under FCA § 739(a)(i) without the opportunity to post bail violates his right to equal protection of the law; also since preventive detention is not available in the criminal courts, it is not available to Family Court when the respondent has reached his sixteenth birthday. *In re* Wilson, 89 Misc. 2d 1046, 393 N.Y.S.2d 275 (Fam. Ct. Onondaga Co. 1977).

Initial remand period; duration.—Saturdays, Sundays and public holidays should be included in the remand which precedes the probable cause hearing under FCA § 739(b). *In re* Kenneth D., 102 Misc. 2d 363, 423 N.Y.S.2d 423 (Fam. Ct. Kings Co. 1979).

Pretrial detention.—FCA § 739(a)(ii), authorizing pretrial detention of a youth charged as a juvenile delinquent when there is a serious risk that he may commit a criminal act before the return date of the petition, does not violate the equal protection or due process provisions of our Federal or State Constitution. People *ex rel.* Wayburn v. Schupf, 39 N.Y.2d 682, 385 N.Y.S.2d 518, 350 N.E.2d 906 (1976).

Probable cause hearing.—Juvenile defendant was deprived of his statutory right to a probable cause hearing and his constitutional right to effective assistance of counsel where defendant's attorney informed the court that he had been appointed four days earlier, that he was not prepared to proceed with a fact finding hearing and that he was ready to proceed with a probable cause hearing but the court denied the request for such a hearing and required him to proceed with the fact finding hearing. *In re* Milton D., 72 A.D.2d 812, 421 N.Y.S.2d 909 (2d Dept. 1979).

—It was clearly improper for the Family Court to remand juvenile, previously detained for four days, without a finding of probable cause. People *ex rel.* Kaufmann v. Davis, 57 A.D.2d 597, 393 N.Y.S.2d 746 (2d Dept. 1977).

—Where, at arraignment upon motion of the District Attorney, the criminal court issued an Order of Removal to Family Court without holding a probable cause hearing and respondent did not waive a hearing, he was entitled to a probable cause hearing in Family Court. *In re* Lester, 96 Misc. 2d 1077, 410 N.Y.S.2d 515 (Fam. Ct. Bronx Co. 1978).

§ 740. Temporary order of protection.

(a) Upon the filing of a petition under this article, the court for good cause shown may issue a temporary order of protection which may contain any of the provisions authorized on the making of an order of protection under section seven hundred fifty-nine.

(b) A temporary order of protection is not a finding of wrongdoing.

(c) The court may issue or extend a temporary order of protection *ex parte* or on notice simultaneously with the issuance of a warrant directing that the respondent be arrested and brought before the court pursuant to section seven hundred thirty-eight of this part.

Added by L. 1964, Ch. 566, eff. Apr. 16, 1964; **Amended** by L. 1981, Ch. 416, eff. Aug. 6, 1981, added subds. (b) and (c).

Part 4. Hearings

§ 741. Notice of rights; general provision.

(a) At the initial appearance of a respondent in a proceeding and at the commencement of any hearing under this article, the respondent and his parent or other person legally responsible for his care shall be advised of the respondent's right to remain silent and of his right to be represented by counsel chosen by him or his parent or other person legally responsible for his care, or by a law guardian assigned by the court under part four of article two. Provided, however, that in the event of the failure of the respondent's parent or other person legally responsible for his care to appear, after reasonable and substantial effort has been made to notify such parent or responsible person of the commencement of the proceeding and such initial appearance, the court shall appoint a law guardian and shall, unless inappropriate also appoint a guardian ad litem for such respondent, and in such event, shall inform the respondent of such rights in the presence of such law guardian and any guardian ad litem.

(b) The general public may be excluded from any hearing under this article and only such persons and the representatives of authorized agencies admitted thereto as have a direct interest in the case.

(c) At any hearing under this article, the court shall not be prevented from proceeding by the absence of the respondent's parent or other person responsible for his care if reasonable and substantial effort has been made to notify such parent or responsible person of the occurrence of the hearing and if the respondent and his law guardian are present. The court shall, unless inappropriate, also appoint a guardian ad litem who shall be present at such hearing and any subsequent hearing.

Amended by L. 1975, Ch. 837; L. 1979, Ch. 531, eff. Sept. 10, 1979, adding subd. (d); L. 1981, Ch. 331, eff. Aug. 28, 1981; L. 1982, Ch. 920, eff. July 1, 1983.

ANNOTATIONS

Closure.—Given the special need for confidentiality of juvenile proceedings, exclusion of press and public from a juvenile delinquency proceeding is constitutional. *In re* Robert M., 109 Misc. 2d 427, 439 N.Y.S.2d 986 (Fam. Ct. N.Y. Co. 1981).

Competency.—When a juvenile is found to be incompetent to proceed to an adjudication hearing, and the court finds that the youth is a threat to society as well as to himself, the Family Court can consider the request by the Law Guardian for an examination pursuant to CPL Article 730 to establish whether the youth is competent to proceed as an application sufficient to satisfy Mental Hygiene Law § 33.27(b) and (c) and proceed accordingly. People *ex rel.* Thorpe v. Clark, 62 A.D.2d 216, 403 N.Y.S.2d 910 (2d Dept. 1978).

Fact-finding hearing.—Another fact-finding hearing was required since the court did not engage in sufficiently rigorous allocution before accepting 15-year-old appellant's admission of guilt at hearing where the juvenile was in court without her mother or other familiar person to give her support and without a valid explanation appearing for the absence of such person and was merely confronted by the court's recitation of the charge stated in the petition with no attempt to explain the charge in non-legal terms or to inquire as to whether or not appellant understood the charge or the consequences of her admission. *In re* Myacutta A., 75 A.D.2d 774, 428 N.Y.S.2d 231 (1st Dept. 1980).

—A new fact-finding hearing was required where the judge at the fact-finding hearing, which adjudicated juvenile as a juvenile delinquent, failed to apprise him or his mother of his various constitutional rights or the consequences flowing from a waiver of these rights. *In re* Steven W., 75 A.D.2d 756, 427 N.Y.S.2d 813 (1st Dept. 1980). *See also In re* Theodore F., 47 A.D.2d 945, 367 N.Y.S.2d 103 (2d Dept. 1975).

Appointment of guardian ad litem.—The appointment of a court officer, a stranger to the juvenile, as her guardian ad litem was improper and the impropriety was not nullified by the presence of the law guardian on the juvenile's behalf. *In re* Myacutta A., 75 A.D.2d 774, 428 N.Y.S.2d 231 (1st Dept. 1980); *In re* Donna H., 70 A.D.2d 521, 416 N.Y.S.2d 15 (1st Dept. 1979).

Miranda.—Those parts of the *Miranda* doctrine that invoke fundamental precepts of our constitutional system such as the right to counsel and the privilege against self-incrimination can hardly be deemed inapplicable to a juvenile. *In re* Robert O., 109 Misc. 2d 238, 439 N.Y.S.2d 994 (Fam. Ct. Kings Co. 1981).

Responsibility of court.—Admissions to allegations contained in the PINS petition were insufficient where there was no colloquy between the court and the respondent "whereby the court could assure itself of the integrity of the process or that the admissions were knowing, intelligent or accurate." *In re* Chad H., 278 A.D.2d 601, 717 N.Y.S.2d 725 (3d Dept. 2000).

—In conflict with the Appellate Division, Fourth Department, the Third Department declined to extend the requirements of Family Court Act Section 321.3, pertaining to juvenile delinquency proceedings under Article 7, to PINS proceedings under Article 7. *In re* Jason O., 197 A.D.2d 784, 602 N.Y.S.2d 952 (3d Dept. 1993).

Right to counsel; joint representation.—The propriety of the fact finding hearing was rendered suspect where the court appointed a single law guardian to represent three juveniles who may well have had different participatory roles in the alleged incident; while joint representation is not *per se* a denial of effective assistance of counsel, the court should recognize that a juvenile may not perceive the existence of a conflict of interest and should be satisfied that the juvenile's decision to proceed with joint representation is an informed one. *In re* Jeffrey M., 62 A.D.2d 858, 406 N.Y.S.2d 71 (1st Dept. 1978).

Right to remain silent.—Order of disposition reversed where sparse record did not disclose that appellant had been advised of his right to remain silent at the commencement of the fact finding hearing (FCA § 741) or that he was questioned by the trial court as to any of the facts alleged in the petition. *In re* Felix A., 58 A.D.2d 562, 396 N.Y.S.2d 25 (1st Dept. 1977). *See also In re* Lee G., 46 A.D.2d 910, 363 N.Y.S.2d 9 (2d Dept. 1974); *In re* Martin James A., 60 A.D.2d 997, 401 N.Y.S.2d 658 (4th Dept. 1978).

—A new fact-finding hearing on the delinquency petitions was directed where neither the juvenile nor his mother was advised of his right to remain silent at the fact-finding hearing or of the consequences of his admission to any of the facts. The admission of an involuntary statement by a juvenile at an adjudicatory hearing violates due process. *In re* James K., 47 A.D.2d 946, 367 N.Y.S.2d 312 (2d Dept. 1975).

—Court's admonishment to juvenile that she had the right, but was not required, to testify at a fact-finding hearing, was not equivalent to advising youth of right to remain silent; failure constituted reversible error and resulted in appellate court vacating resulting order of disposition. *In re* Jessica G.G., 19 A.D.3d 765, 797 N.Y.S.2d 574 (3d Dept. 2005).

—PINS order was vacated where no warning was issued by the court at the initial appearance on the petition or at the adjournment advising respondent and respondent's parent or other person legally responsible for his or her care of the right to remain silent; warning was not issued until after juvenile had made admission. *In re* Jodi "W," 295 A.D.2d 659, 743 N.Y.S.2d 195 (3d Dept. 2002).

—Respondent was properly advised of her right to remain silent at the beginning of the fact-finding hearing, prior to the time she made her admission, in addition, although not required, the court also informed respondent that she had a right to the fact finding hearing and informed her of the various dispositional alternatives that could occur. *In re* Libby G., 278 A.D.2d 761, 718 N.Y.S.2d 655 (3d Dept. 2000).

—Article 7 has no specific procedure for accepting a PINS admission of guilt; however, where the petitioner, in the presence of his mother, was advised by the law guardian of his right to remain silent and the possible consequences of his admissions if he decided to give up that right, the petitioner was not prejudiced by the court's failure to put those warnings on the record. *In re* Mark J., 259 A.D.2d 40, 696 N.Y.S.2d 583 (3d Dept. 1999).

—Reversible error where court failed to re-inform juvenile of right to remain silent on day of fact-finding hearing during which court accepted her admission. *In re* Melanie U.U., 254 A.D.2d 632, 679 N.Y.S.2d 185 (3d Dept. 1998).

—Where record reflects respondent was represented by counsel and fully informed of the panoply of rights available to her prior to her admission at each court appearance, and the record was void of objection regarding her representation, it was not error for the court to fail to give respondent her rights again regarding her choice of counsel and the right to remain silent at the dispositional hearing. *In re* Nicole EE., 233 A.D.2d 744, 650 N.Y.S.2d 1010 (3d Dept. 1996).

—Court's admonishment that respondent had right to remain silent was properly administered, and court was not required to advise her of all possible dispositions it could impose in order for her partial admission to petition to be valid. *In re* Crystal A., 11 A.D.3d 897, 782 N.Y.S.2d 474 (4th Dept. 2004).

—Procedural safeguards applicable to juvenile delinquency proceedings pursuant to Article 3 do not apply in proceedings held under Article 7; as petitioner was informed of her right to remain silent as well as the right to be represented by counsel, there was no violation of her procedural rights. *In re* Samantha T., 296 A.D.2d 869, 744 N.Y.S.2d 626 (4th Dept. 2002).

—Family court's failure to advise respondent of his right to remain silent prior to accepting his admissions resulted in reversal of the order adjudicating him a person in need of supervision. *In re* Kevin B., 277 A.D.2d 936, 715 N.Y.S.2d 358 (4th Dept. 2000).

—Because the sentence of probation was predicated upon an invalid admission, due to the court's failure to advise the respondent of his right to remain silent, the order of placement was a nullity and was vacated. *In re* Mark S., 144 A.D.2d 1010, 534 N.Y.S.2d 53 (4th Dept. 1988).

Speedy trial.—CPL § 30.30 does not apply to juvenile delinquency proceedings but to 18-month delay in bringing juvenile delinquency petition, absent justification, deprived juvenile of his constitutional right to a speedy trial. *In re* Anthony P., 104 Misc. 2d 1024, 430 N.Y.S.2d 479 (Fam. Ct. N.Y. Co. 1980).

Waiver of constitutional rights.—Where an alleged juvenile delinquent waives his constitutional rights and pleads guilty, painstaking efforts should be made by the court to make sure that such juvenile and his parent or parents understand the consequences of the waiver and the plea, and that the accused committed an act which constituted the alleged offense and which furnished a basis for the plea. *In re* John R., 71 A.D.2d 896, 419 N.Y.S.2d 625 (2d Dept. 1979).

§ 741-a. Notice and opportunity to be heard.

The foster parent caring for the child or any pre-adoptive parent or relative providing care for the respondent shall be provided with notice of any permanency hearing held pursuant to this article by the social services official. Such foster parent, pre-adoptive parent or relative shall be afforded an opportunity to be heard at any such hearing; provided, however, no such foster parent, pre-adoptive parent or relative shall be construed to be a party to the hearing solely on the basis of such notice and opportunity to be heard. The failure of the foster parent, pre-adoptive parent, or relative caring for the child to appear at a permanency hearing shall constitute a waiver of the opportunity to be heard and such failure to appear shall not cause a delay of the permanency hearing nor shall such failure to appear be a ground for the invalidation of any order issued by the court pursuant to this section.

Added by L. 1999, Ch. 7, § 32, eff. Feb. 11, 1999.

§ 742. Diversion attempts.

(a) Whenever a petition is filed pursuant to this article, the lead agency designated pursuant to section seven hundred thirty-five of this article shall file a written report with the court indicating any previous actions it has taken with respect to the case.

(b) At the initial appearance of the respondent, the court shall review any termination of diversion services pursuant to such section, and the documentation of diligent attempts to provide appropriate services and determine whether such efforts or services provided are sufficient and may, subject to the provisions of section seven hundred forty-eight of this article, order that additional diversion attempts be undertaken by the designated lead agency. The court may order the youth and the parent or other person legally responsible for the youth to participate in diversion services. If the designated lead agency thereafter determines that the case has been successfully resolved, it shall so notify the court, and the court shall dismiss the petition.

Added by L. 1985, Ch. 813, eff. Aug. 2, 1985; **Amended** by L. 2005, Ch. 57, Part E, § 9, eff. Apr. 1, 2005.

§ 744. Evidence in fact-finding hearings; required quantum.

(a) Only evidence that is competent, material and relevant may be admitted in a fact-finding hearing.

(b) Any determination at the conclusion of a fact-finding hearing that a respondent did an act or acts must be based on proof beyond a reasonable doubt. For this purpose, an uncorroborated confession made out of court by a respondent is not sufficient.

Amended by L. 1963, Ch. 529; L. 1976, Ch. 191, eff. May 25, 1976; L. 1978, Ch. 481, eff. Sept. 1, 1978; L. 1982, Ch. 920, eff. July 1, 1983.

ANNOTATIONS

Applicability of CPL.—CPL §§ 60.45 (Confession, statements of defendant), 60.50 (Corroboration of defendant's statement), 60.22 (Corroboration of accomplice testimony), 60.22 (Corroboration of accomplice testimony) apply to Family Court proceedings. *In re* S., 77 Misc. 2d 108, 351 N.Y.S.2d 827 (Fam. Ct. Richmond Co. 1973).

Confession.—When the juvenile requested a voir dire examination in order to test the lawfulness of his confession he was entitled to take the stand and testify as to the circumstances of the confession without generally waiving his privilege against self incrimination and subjecting himself to broad cross examination. *In re* Victor B., 54 A.D.2d 733, 387 N.Y.S.2d 673 (2d Dept. 1976).

CPL §§ 670.10 and 670.20 apply to juvenile delinquency fact finding hearings.—*In re* Barry M., 94 Misc. 2d 925, 405 N.Y.S.2d 949 (Fam. Ct. Queens Co. 1978).

Delinquency hearing; reversible error; failure to permit inspection of grand jury minutes.—Where evidence at fact-finding hearing consisted primarily of testimony of victims, it was reversible error to deny law guardian's timely request to inspect grand jury minutes of their testimony. Also, in the interests of justice, the new hearing should be before a different judge. *In re* David T., 45 A.D.2d 690, 357 N.Y.S.2d 66 (1st Dept. 1974).

Required evidence.—FCA § 744(b) requiring that delinquency "must be based on a preponderance of the evidence" is unconstitutional, guilt must be established "beyond a reasonable doubt." *In re* Tony H., 52 A.D.2d 583, 382 N.Y.S.2d 523 (2d Dept. 1976).

—Family Court may accept an *Alford* plea (North Carolina v. Alford, 400 U.S. 25, 91 S. Ct. 160, 27 L. Ed. 2d 162 (1970)) in lieu of fact finding hearing, in appropriate case. *In re* Tracey B., 94 Misc. 2d 827, 405 N.Y.S.2d 609 (Fam. Ct. N.Y.C. 1978).

Hearing.—At the hearing, it was error to admit as evidence a composite sketch drawn by a police artist from information furnished by the rape victim and permit evidence that the victim had identified the appellant extrajudicially from a photograph. *In re* Brian P.T., 58 A.D.2d 868, 396 N.Y.S.2d 873 (2d Dept. 1977).

—Family Court committed reversible error when it played the role of the county attorney, who was absent, and called and examined witnesses against the respondent at the fact-finding hearing. *In re* Cynthia H., 105 A.D.2d 1149, 482 N.Y.S.2d 394 (4th Dept. 1984).

Juvenile's presence at fact-finding hearing.—Neither the presence of an aberrant juvenile's parent or assigned counsel at the hearing constitutes a knowing waiver of the juvenile's right to be present at his own trial and to be confronted by his accuser. *In re* B., 43 A.D.2d 688, 350 N.Y.S.2d 426 (1st Dept. 1973).

Laboratory report; controlled substance.—Where the weight of the controlled substance was established solely through the admission into evidence of a laboratory report, a new fact finding hearing was necessary since no proper foundation had been laid with respect to the receipt in evidence of the laboratory report which resulted in adjudicating appellant a juvenile delinquent. *In re* Samuel A., 63 A.D.2d 585, 404 N.Y.S.2d 616 (1st Dept. 1978).

Miranda **warnings; pre-custodial interrogation.**—Respondent's oral statement to dean of students was admissible despite lack of *Miranda* warnings; interrogation was not custodial, and school officials are not subject to *Miranda* when not acting as agents of police. *In re* Brendan H., 82 Misc. 2d 1077, 372 N.Y.S.2d 473 (Fam. Ct. Schenectady Co. 1975).

Notification of parent; violation of juvenile's rights.—Statement given to police officers by juvenile defendant should have been suppressed at the hearing where no notification was given to the suspect's parents and they were not present when the statement was made even though suspect's uncle accompanied him to police station and was present when the statement was given. *In re* Brian P.T., 58 A.D.2d 868, 396 N.Y.S.2d 873 (2d Dept. 1977).

Personal records of arresting officer.—Where respondent made a sufficient showing of facts, the court granted his motion, pursuant to Civil Rights Law § 50-a, and directed the Transit Authority to produce the officer's personnel records for an *in camera* review; whether or not any information will be released to the respondent's attorney is a matter resting wholly within the court's discretion. *In re* Cleve C., 101 Misc. 2d 608, 421 N.Y.S.2d 814 (Fam. Ct. N.Y. Co. 1979).

Proof beyond a reasonable doubt.—Statements made by juvenile at fact finding hearing suppressed where there was failure to prove beyond a reasonable doubt that the statements were made knowingly and voluntarily and without violation of his constitutional rights. *In re* Earl M., 57 A.D.2d 960, 395 N.Y.S.2d 61 (2d Dept. 1977).

—The standard of proof required before a minor can be adjudicated a PINS is proof beyond a reasonable doubt. *In re* Kristopher I., 289 A.D.2d 685, 733 N.Y.S.2d 539 (3d Dept. 2001).

§ 745. Evidence in dispositional hearings; required quantum of proof.

(a) Only evidence that is material and relevant may be admitted during a dispositional hearing.

(b) An adjudication at the conclusion of a dispositional hearing must be based on a preponderance of the evidence.

ANNOTATIONS

Evidence standard.—Adjudication at the conclusion of a dispositional hearing must be based on a preponderance of the evidence. Terry U. v. Broome County Dept. of Social Servs., 52 A.D.2d 683, 382 N.Y.S.2d 373 (3d Dept. 1976).

Commencement and conduct of hearing.—Family Court erred in commencing dispositional hearing in the absence of the law guardian who had been appointed to represent juvenile in the proceeding, and in overruling the law guardian's request to cross-examine the psychologist concerning her testimony as to the need for treatment, supervision or confinement. *In re* P., 45 A.D.2d 1010, 358 N.Y.S.2d 78 (2d Dept. 1974).

Disposition hearing.—It was improper to place youth with the Division of Youth, Title III, after disposition hearing where neither his examination by Bureau of Mental Health Services had been completed nor exploration of placement made. *In re* W., 45 A.D.2d 842, 358 N.Y.S.2d 451 (2d Dept. 1974).

—Family court has discretion in admitting confession of juvenile into evidence where he admitted crimes independent of those charged in the petition at a dispositional hearing and considering it at the time of sentence since evidence at a dispositional hearing need not be "competent" only "relevant" and "material." *In re* Kevin J. 108 Misc. 2d 1023, 438 N.Y.S.2d 681 (Fam. Ct. N.Y. Co. 1981).

"Material and relevant."—Evidence at a dispositional hearing need be only "material and relevant," it need not be competent. *In re* Nathan N., 56 A.D.2d 554, 391 N.Y.S.2d 599 (1st Dept. 1977).

Hearing.—A six-year-old victim's prompt disclosure to his mother should not be considered on the issue of corroboration; timely complaint bears only on credibility. *In re* Julius D., 70 A.D.2d 819, 417 N.Y.S.2d 470 (1st Dept. 1979).

Requirement.—FCA § 745 mandates that before a child can be adjudged a delinquent, there must be a need for court intervention—the child must be found to be in need of supervision, treatment or confinement. *In re* Charles C., 83 Misc. 2d 388, 371 N.Y.S.2d 582 (Fam. Ct. N.Y.C 1975).

§ 746. Sequence of hearings.

Upon completion of the fact-finding hearing the dispositional hearing may commence immediately after the required findings are made.

Amended by L. 1963, Ch. 529; L. 1976, Ch. 878, repealing former subd. (b); L. 1978, Ch. 481, eff. Sept. 1, 1978, adding new subd. (b); L. 1982, Ch. 920, eff. July 1, 1983.

ANNOTATIONS

Narcotics arrest and search; lack of probable cause.—The arrest and search of defendant lacked probable cause, and narcotics seized were inadmissible into evidence in a juvenile delinquency proceeding, when, upon being addressed by the police, he ran from the front of a building the police were directed to investigate for narcotics violations. *In re* M., 43 A.D.2d 92, 349 N.Y.S.2d 728 (1st Dept. 1973).

Report; availability to court.—The evidence on the record was convincing in establishing the delinquent conduct of appellant; and, for that reason, the action of the probation officer, in releasing his report too early to the court, could not be considered reversible error. It is the clear policy of the law that the probation service should not communicate reports to the court concerning the alleged delinquent until the fact-finding hearing is completed. Even though the court may not in fact be influenced by what it hears, it is the appearance of prejudice against which the policy is directed, and violation of the statute, albeit inadvertent, should therefore be avoided. *In re* James H., 41 A.D.2d 667, 341 N.Y.S.2d 92 (2d Dept. 1973).

§ 747. Time of fact-finding hearing.

A fact-finding hearing shall commence not more than three days after the filing of a petition under this article if the respondent is in detention.

Amended by L. 1963, Ch. 529, eff. Apr. 23, 1963; L. 1975, Ch. 837, eff. Sept. 1, 1975; L. 1982, Ch. 920, eff. July 1, 1983.

ANNOTATIONS

Application.—CPL §§ 670.10 and 670.20 apply to juvenile delinquency fact finding hearings. *In re* Barry M., 93 Misc. 2d 882, 403 N.Y.S.2d 979 (Fam. Ct. Queens Co. 1978).

Fact-finding hearing; unreasonably long detention.— Absent special and compelling circumstances, a fact-finding hearing must be conducted within three days once a juvenile is detained. Where the relator had been detained for more than two months because of adjournments of the fact-finding hearing, the Court of Appeals held that the delay violated the time limit prescribed for detention of adults in felony proceedings (CPL § 180.80); it ruled that the restrictive language of FCA sections 747 and 748 is designed to mandate speedier fact-finding hearings, and that it would take a distorted view to believe that adult felony proceedings are designed to be more scrupulous about the rights of detained adults than the Family Court procedures with respect to juveniles. However, because the juvenile had been released on parole, and because the Administrative Judge of the New York City Family Court had adopted an internal regulation in order to avoid such protracted adjournments, the court dismissed the writ solely on the ground of mootness. People *ex rel.* Guggenheim v. Mucci, 32 N.Y.2d 307, 344 N.Y.S.2d 944 (1973).

Witness immunity.—Family Court is empowered to grant a witness immunity at a fact-finding hearing in accordance with CPL § 50.30. *In re* Barry M., 93 Misc. 2d 882, 403 N.Y.S.2d 979 (Fam. Ct. Queens Co. 1978).

§ 748. Adjournment of fact-finding hearing.

(a) If the respondent is in detention, the court may adjourn a fact-finding hearing

(i) on its own motion or on motion of the petitioner for good cause shown for not more than three days;

(ii) on motion on behalf of the respondent or by his parent or other person legally responsible for his care for good cause shown, for a reasonable period of time.

(b) Successive motions to adjourn a fact-finding hearing may be granted only under special circumstances.

(c) The court shall state on the record the reason for any adjournment of the fact-finding hearing.

Amended by L. 1963, Ch. 529; L. 1965, Ch. 284; L. 1976, Ch. 878, eff. Feb. 1, 1977; L. 1977, Ch. 283, eff. Aug. 20,. 1977; L. 1982, Ch. 920, eff. July 1, 1983.

ANNOTATIONS

Application.—CPL § 255.20 is applicable to Family Court juvenile delinquency proceedings. *In re* Archer, 89 Misc. 2d 526, 392 N.Y.S.2d 362 (Fam. Ct. Queens Co. 1977).

Adjournment.—Family Court abused its discretion when it refused to grant an adjournment in order to enable the Corporation Counsel to produce the minutes of the complaining witness' preliminary hearing testimony in Criminal Court, where the law guardian had no knowledge, until the cross-examination of the complaining witness at the fact-finding hearing, that the witness had testified at a preliminary hearing in the Crim. Ct. regarding the incident. *In re* Bertha K., 58 A.D.2d 811, 396 N.Y.S.2d 666 (2d Dept. 1977).

—Court erred in granting a total of eight adjournments before and during the dispositional hearing; because respondent was detained, the court was not authorized to adjourn the proceedings for a period of more than 10 days or to grant more than two such adjournments in the absence of special circumstances. *In re* Richard G., 187 A.D.2d 1039, 590 N.Y.S.2d 609 (4th Dept. 1992).

Fact-finding hearing; unreasonably long detention.— Absent special and compelling circumstances, a fact-finding hearing must be conducted within three days once a juvenile is detained. Where the relator had been detained for more than two months because of adjournments of the fact-finding hearing, the Court of Appeals held that the delay violated the time limit prescribed for detention of adults in felony proceedings (CPL § 180.80); it ruled that the restrictive language of CPA sections 747 and 748 is designed to mandate speedier fact-finding hearings, and that it would take a distorted view to believe that adult felony proceedings are designed to be more scrupulous about the rights of detained adults than the Family Court procedures with respect to juveniles. However, because the juvenile had been released on parole, and because the Administrative Judge of the New York City Family Court had adopted an internal regulation in order to avoid such protracted adjournments, the court dismissed the writ solely on the ground of mootness. People *ex rel.* Guggenheim v. Mucci, 32 N.Y.2d 307, 344 N.Y.S.2d 944 (1973).

§ 749. Adjournment after fact-finding hearing or during dispositional hearing.

(a) Upon or after a fact-finding hearing, the court may, upon its own motion or upon a motion of a party to the proceeding, order that the proceeding be "adjourned in contemplation of dismissal." An adjournment in contemplation of dismissal is an adjournment of the proceeding, for a period not to exceed six months with a view to ultimate dismissal of the petition in furtherance of justice. Upon issuing such an order, upon such permissible terms and conditions as the rules of court shall define, the court must release the individual. The court may, as a condition of an adjournment in contemplation of dismissal order, in cases where the record indicates that the consumption of alcohol may have been a contributing factor, require the respondent to attend and complete an alcohol awareness program established pursuant to paragraph six-a of subdivision (a) of section 19.07 of the mental hygiene law. Upon application of the petitioner, or upon the court's own motion, made at any time during the duration of the order, the court may restore the matter to the calendar. If the proceeding is not so restored, the petition is at the expiration of the order, deemed to have been dismissed by the court in furtherance of justice.

(b) On its own motion, the court may adjourn the proceedings on conclusion of a fact finding hearing or during a dispositional hearing to enable it to make inquiry into the surroundings, conditions and capacities of the respondent. An adjournment on the court's motion may not be for a period of more than ten days if the respondent is detained, in which case not more than a total of two such adjournments may be granted in the absence of special circumstances. If the respondent is not detained, an adjournment may be for a reasonable time, but the total number of adjourned days may not exceed two months.

(c) On motion on behalf of the respondent or by his parent or other person legally responsible for his care, the court may adjourn the proceedings on conclusion of a fact-finding hearing or during a dispositional hearing for a reasonable period of time.

Amended by L. 1991, Ch. 237, eff. July 31, 1991, amending subd. (a).

ANNOTATIONS

Adjournment in contemplation of dismissal.—In a juvenile delinquency proceeding, which was transferred to the Family Court of New York County following a fact finding hearing in which appellant was adjudged a juvenile delinquent, the court had authority to exercise its discretion in the interests of justice by invoking an adjournment in contemplation of dismissal, but only for the maximum statutory period of six months. *In re* Jeffrey M., 62 A.D.2d 858, 406 N.Y.S.2d 71 (1st Dept. 1978).

No per se dismissal rule.—There is no per se dismissal rule for failure to provide a speedy dispositional hearing of PINS petitions because such a rule would be inconsistent with the objective of dispositional hearing. *In re* Wayne H., 233 A.D.2d 941, 649 N.Y.S.2d 576 (4th Dept. 1996).

§ 750. Probation reports; probation investigation and diagnostic assessment.

1. All reports or memoranda prepared or obtained by the probation service shall be deemed confidential information furnished to the court and shall be subject to disclosure solely in accordance with this section or as otherwise provided for by law. Except as provided in section seven hundred thirty-five of this article, such reports or memoranda shall not be furnished to the court prior to the completion of the fact-finding hearing and the making of the required findings.

2. After the completion of the fact-finding hearing and the making of the required findings and prior to the dispositional hearing, the reports or memoranda prepared or obtained by the probation service and furnished to the court shall be made available by the court for examination and copying by the child's law guardian or counsel or by the respondent if he is not represented by a law guardian or other counsel. All diagnostic assessments and probation investigation reports shall be submitted to the court at least five court days prior to the commencement of the dispositional hearing. In its discretion the court may except from disclosure a part or parts of the reports or memoranda which are not relevant to a proper disposition, or sources of information which have been obtained on a promise of confidentiality, or any other portion thereof, disclosure of which would not be in the interest of justice. In all cases where a part or parts of the reports or memoranda are not disclosed, the court shall state for the record that a part or parts of the reports or memoranda have been excepted and the reasons for its action. The action of the court excepting information from disclosure shall be subject to review on any appeal from the order of disposition. If such reports or memoranda are made available to respondent or his law guardian or counsel, they shall also be made available to the counsel presenting the petition pursuant to section two hundred fifty-four and, in the court's discretion, to any other attorney representing the petitioner.

Added by L. 1976, Ch. 878, eff. Feb. 1, 1977; Amended by L. 1977, Ch. 204, eff. June 1, 1977; L. 1978, Ch. 478, § 5, eff. Sept. 1, 1978; L. 1985, Ch. 813, eff. Aug. 2, 1985; L. 1986, Ch. 121, eff. July 2, 1986; L. 1987, Ch. 106, eff. July 8, 1987.

ANNOTATIONS

Contempt not available.—Family court does not have the authority to hold a juvenile adjudicated a PINS in contempt for violation of an order of protection. *In re* Edwin G., 296 A.D.2d 7, 742 N.Y.S.2d 53 (1st Dept. 2002). *See also In re* Asia H., 289 A.D.2d 404, 734 N.Y.S.2d 230 (2d Dept. 2001).

—Family court may not "bootstrap" a PINS proceeding into a juvenile delinquency proceeding through the employment of its contempt power to punish the appellant for her failure to comply with one of its orders. *In re* Victoria S. (Anonymous), 297 A.D.2d 323, 746 N.Y.S.2d 264 (2d Dept. 2002).

Diagnostic assessment.—The family court should have ordered a neurological examination and encephalogram, before placing juvenile with the New York State Division for Youth under restrictive placement, in order to help determine whether there was brain damage in this case. *In re* Jose Luis Q., 64 A.D.2d 600, 408 N.Y.S.2d 510 (1st Dept. 1978), *aff'd*, 45 N.Y.2d 811, 409 N.Y.S.2d 131, 381 N.E.2d 338.

Family Court records.—It was an abuse of discretion for the Family Court Judge to deny appellant's motion to have her name expunged from all Family Court and Probation Department records, notwithstanding the history of a sibling and parent having "a problem," where the delinquency petition was originally filed by a neighbor who was feuding with appellant's mother, and was subsequently withdrawn. *In re* Dorothy D., 62 A.D.2d 473, 404 N.Y.S.2d 876 (2d Dept. 1978), *aff'd*, Dorothy D. v New York City Probation Dept., 49 N.Y.2d 212, 424 N.Y.S.2d 890 (1979).

MISC. LAWS

Reports.—FCA § 750(4) which requires that "where the respondent is found to have committed a designated felony act, all diagnostic assessments and probation investigation reports shall be made available to the court and to counsel presenting the petition and for the respondent at least five court days prior to the commencement of the dispositional hearing" applies only to probation reports and assessments; it does not enlarge the court's power to condition an order which permits examination by an expert to require that a copy be given to the Corporation Counsel, the court and the Probation Department. *In re* Norman K., 62 A.D.2d 1038, 404 N.Y.S.2d 39 (2d Dept. 1978).

Part 5. Orders

§ 751. Order dismissing petition.

If the allegations of a petition under this article are not established, the court shall dismiss the petition. The court may in its discretion dismiss a petition under this article, in the interests of justice where attempts have been made to adjust the case as provided for in sections seven hundred thirty-five and seven hundred forty-two of this article and the probation service has exhausted its efforts to successfully adjust such case as a result of the petition's failure to provide reasonable assistance to the probation service.

Amended by L. 1993, Ch. 100.

§ 752. Findings.

If the allegations of a petition under this article are established in accord with part three, the court shall enter an order finding that the respondent is a person in need of supervision. The order shall state the grounds for the finding and the facts upon which it is based.

Amended by L. 1976, Ch. 878, eff. Feb. 1, 1977; L. 1982, Ch. 920, eff. July 1, 1990.

ANNOTATIONS

Lack of treatment facility.—When there is a finding of a need for treatment but such treatment facility does not exist the juvenile cannot be adjudicated a juvenile delinquent or a PINS and petition must be dismissed. *In re* Anthony J., 87 Misc. 2d 34, 383 N.Y.S.2d 851 (Fam. Ct. Onondaga Co. 1976).

Lesser included crime.—Under appropriate circumstances, the court in a juvenile delinquency proceeding may find that a respondent has committed a lesser crime included within the crime charged, and determine the respondent to be a juvenile delinquent based upon the lesser included crime. *In re* Derrick M., 63 A.D.2d 932, 406 N.Y.S.2d 88 (1st Dept. 1978).

Order.—Court erred in issuing dispositional orders adjudicating respondent as a person in need of supervision and placing her on probation for one year but failing to articulate reasons underlying court's determination, matter remitted for further proceedings. *In re* Nicole EE., 233 A.D.2d 744, 650 N.Y.S.2d 1010 (3d Dept. 1996).

§ 754. Disposition on adjudication of person in need of supervision.

1. Upon an adjudication of person in need of supervision, the court shall enter an order of disposition:

(a) Discharging the respondent with warning;

(b) Suspending judgment in accord with section seven hundred fifty-five;

(c) Continuing the proceeding and placing the respondent in accord with section seven hundred fifty-six; provided, however, that the court shall not place the respondent in accord with section seven hundred fifty-six where the respondent is sixteen years of age or older, unless the court determines and states in its order that special circumstances exist to warrant such placement; or

(d) Putting the respondent on probation in accord with section seven hundred fifty-seven.

2. (a) The order shall state the court's reasons for the particular disposition. If the court places the child in accordance with section seven hundred fifty-six of this part, the court in its order shall determine: (i) whether continuation in the child's home would be contrary to the best interest of the child and where appropriate, that reasonable efforts were made prior to the date of the dispositional hearing held pursuant to this article to prevent or eliminate the need for removal of the child from his or her home and, if the child was removed from his or her home prior to the date of such hearing, that such removal was in the child's best interest and, where appropriate, reasonable efforts were made to make it possible for the child to return safely home. If the court determines that reasonable efforts to prevent or eliminate the need for removal of the child from the home were not made but that the lack of such efforts was appropriate under the circumstances, the court order shall include such a finding; and (ii) in the case of a child who has attained the age of sixteen, the services needed, if any, to assist the child to make the transition from foster care to independent living. Nothing in this subdivision shall be construed to modify the standards for directing detention set forth in section seven hundred thirty-nine of this article.

(b) For the purpose of this section, reasonable efforts to prevent or eliminate the need for removing the child from the home of the child or to make it possible for the child to return safely to the home of the child shall not be required where the court determines that:

(i) the parent of such child has subjected the child to aggravated circumstances, as defined in subdivision (g) of section seven hundred twelve of this article;

(ii) the parent of such child has been convicted of (A) murder in the first degree as defined in section 125.27 or murder in the second degree as defined in section 125.25 of the penal law and the victim was another child of the parent; or (B) manslaughter in the first degree as defined in section 125.20 or manslaughter in the second degree as defined in section 125.15 of the penal law and the victim was another child of the parent, provided, however, that the parent must have acted voluntarily in committing such crime;

(iii) the parent of such child has been convicted of an attempt to commit any of the crimes set forth in subparagraphs (i) and (ii) of this paragraph, and the victim or intended victim was the child or another child of the parent; or has been convicted of criminal solicitation as defined in article one hundred, conspiracy as defined in article one hundred five or criminal facilitation as defined in article one hundred fifteen of the penal law for conspiring, soliciting or facilitating any of the foregoing crimes, and the victim or intended victim was the child or another child of the parent;

(iv) the parent of such child has been convicted of assault in the second degree as defined in section 120.05, assault in the first degree as defined in section 120.10 or aggravated assault upon a person less than eleven years old as defined in section 120.12 of the penal law, and the commission of one of the foregoing crimes resulted in serious physical injury to the child or another child of the parent;

(v) the parent of such child has been convicted in any other jurisdiction of an offense which includes all of the essential elements of any crime specified in subparagraph (ii), (iii) or (iv) of this paragraph, and the victim of such offense was the child or another child of the parent; or

(vi) the parental rights of the parent to a sibling of such child have been involuntarily terminated;

unless the court determines that providing reasonable efforts would be in the best interests of the child, not contrary to the health and safety of the child, and would likely result in the reunification of the parent and the child in the foreseeable future. The court shall state such findings in its order.

If the court determines that reasonable efforts are not required because of one of the grounds set forth above, a permanency hearing shall be held within thirty days of the finding of the court

that such efforts are not required. At the permanency hearing, the court shall determine the appropriateness of the permanency plan prepared by the social services official which shall include whether and when the child: (A) will be returned to the parent; (B) should be placed for adoption with the social services official filing a petition for termination of parental rights; (C) should be referred for legal guardianship; (D) should be placed permanently with a fit and willing relative; or (E) should be placed in another planned permanent living arrangement if the social services official has documented to the court a compelling reason for determining that it would not be in the best interest of the child to return home, be referred for termination of parental rights and placed for adoption, placed with a fit and willing relative, or placed with a legal guardian. The social services official shall thereafter make reasonable efforts to place the child in a timely manner and to complete whatever steps are necessary to finalize the permanent placement of the child as set forth in the permanency plan approved by the court. If reasonable efforts are determined by the court not to be required because of one of the grounds set forth in this paragraph, the social services official may file a petition for termination of parental rights in accordance with section three hundred eighty-four-b of the social services law.

(c) For the purpose of this section, in determining reasonable efforts to be made with respect to a child, and in making such reasonable efforts, the child's health and safety shall be the paramount concern.

(d) For the purpose of this section, a sibling shall include a half-sibling.

Amended by L. 1976, Ch. 878, eff. Feb. 1. 1977, adding subd. 2; L. 1985, Ch. 813, eff. Aug. 2, 1985; L. 1987, Ch. 419, eff. Sept. 1, 1987; L. 1988, Ch. 478, § 2, eff. Nov. 1, 1988; L. 1991, Ch. 198, eff. June 28, 1991, amending subd. 2; L. 1999, Ch. 7, § 33, eff. Feb. 11, 1999, amending subd. 2; L. 2001, Ch. 383, Part V, § 4, eff. July 1, 2002, amending subd. 1(c).

ANNOTATIONS

Appeal.—Court need not engage in "least restrictive analysis" in PINS proceeding, but only to "consider the needs and best interest of respondent as well as the need for protection of the community"; record "supports family court's determination that respondent was a threat to himself and the community and in need of treatment and supervision which would best occur in an appropriate residential placement." *In re* Justin H., 278 A.D.2d 555, 717 N.Y.S.2d 406 (3d Dept. 2000).

—Dispositional orders issued adjudicating respondent as a person in need of supervision and placing her on probation for one year failed to articulate reasons underlying court's determination. *In re* Nicole EE., 233 A.D.2d 744, 650 N.Y.S.2d 1010 (3d Dept. 1996).

—Where the Family Court failed to state in its order the reasons for its disposition, the matter was remitted for the purpose of allowing the lower court to amend its order to comply with the statutory mandate. *In re* Eric O., 199 A.D.2d 780, 605 N.Y.S.2d 502 (3d Dept. 1993).

—Where order of disposition complied with statutory requirements setting forth reasons for the particular disposition and why juvenile's continued stay in home was not in best interest of the child, court's determination that placement outside home is in best interest of child is supported by record. *In re* Latoya S., 231 A.D.2d 844, 648 N.Y.S.2d 395 (4th Dept.1996).

Executive law superseded.—FCA § 754 mandates certain dispositions in a PINS situation and therefore supersedes § 502(4) of the Executive Law, which provides that the Division of Youth may in its discretion refuse to admit any youth if such admission would not be in the best interest of the youth. *In re* Felix Louis R., 96 Misc. 2d 221, 409 N.Y.S.2d 79 (Fam. Ct. Kings Co. 1978).

Illegal sentence; confinement of person in need of supervision to institution for juvenile delinquents.—Defendant had been adjudged a person in need of supervision and later, upon recommendation of the Probation Department, was confined in an institution for juvenile delinquents by order of the Family Court. Defendant must be released from the institution as the Family Court Act provides for "confinement" as a possible treatment only for persons adjudged to be juvenile delinquents and not for persons in need of supervision. The purpose of the Family Court Act: to enhance the welfare of the children within its jurisdiction, would be defeated by confining persons in need of supervision to institutions for juvenile delinquents. Ellery C. v. Norman Redlich, 32 N.Y.2d 588, 347 N.Y.S.2d 51 (1973).

Lack of treatment facility.—When there is a finding of a need for treatment but such treatment facility does not exist, the juvenile cannot be adjudicated a juvenile delinquent or a PINS and petition must be dismissed. *In re* Anthony J., 87 Misc. 2d 34, 383 N.Y.S.2d 851 (Fam. Ct. Onondaga Co. 1976).

PINS adjudication and probation.—The "or" between paragraphs (c) and (d) of FCA 754(1) means that the court has the option of either paragraph and cannot use both at the same time. *In re* Leser N.N., 76 A.D.2d 687, 432 N.Y.S.2d 258 (3d Dept. 1980).

Requirement of specific findings.—Where record contained a finding of "extraordinary circumstances" to support the court's placement of the PINS in an unsupervised private placement, the placement will not be disturbed. Gordon "L" v. Michelle "M," 296 A.D.2d 628, 745 N.Y.S.2d 105 (3d Dept. 2002).

—Determination to revoke probation was withheld where the order of disposition adjudicating respondent a person in need of supervision did not contain reason for the disposition or contain the specific findings required for placement pursuant to § 756. *In re* Nathaniel JJ., 265 A.D.2d 660, 696 N.Y.S.2d 293 (3d Dept. 1999), *remitted*, 270 A.D.2d 783, 705 N.Y.S.2d 135 (3d Dept. 2000) (while family court's amended order failed to comply with requirements of FCA § 754(2)(a)(ii) and required case to be remitted again, the omission did not entitle respondent to order of immediate release from placement).

—Dispositional order was not legally deficient simply because the court used a "form" order; order was based on enumerated documents and testimony from the dispositional hearing, and court found by a preponderance of the evidence that petitioner needed supervision and placement outside the home since "continued placement at home would be contrary to respondent's best interests." *In re* Samantha T., 296 A.D.2d 869, 744 N.Y.S.2d 626 (4th Dept. 2002).

§ 755. Suspended judgment.

(a) Rules of court shall define permissible terms and conditions of a suspended judgment. The court may order as a condition of a suspended judgment restitution or services for public good pursuant to section seven hundred fifty-eight-a, and, except when the respondent has been assigned to a facility in accordance with subdivision four of section five hundred four of the executive law, in cases wherein the record indicates that the consumption of alcohol by the respondent may have been a contributing factor, the court may order attendance at and completion of an alcohol awareness program established pursuant to section 19.25 of the mental hygiene law.

(b) The maximum duration of any term or condition of a suspended judgment is one year, unless the court finds at the conclusion of that period that exceptional circumstances require an additional period of one year.

Amended by L. 1976, Ch. 882, eff. Apr. 1, 1977; L. 1993, Ch. 124.

§ 756. Placement.

(a) (i) For purposes of section seven hundred fifty-four, the court may place the child in its own home or in the custody of a suitable relative or other suitable private person or a commissioner of social services, subject to the orders of the court.

(ii) Where the child is placed with the commissioner of social services, the court may direct the commissioner to place the child with an authorized agency or class of authorized agencies. Unless the dispositional order provides otherwise, the court so directing shall include one of the following alternatives to apply in the event that the commissioner is unable to so place the child:

(1) the commissioner shall apply to the court for an order to stay, modify, set aside, or vacate such directive pursuant to the provisions of section seven hundred sixty-two or seven hundred sixty-three; or

(2) the commissioner shall return the child to the family court for a new dispositional hearing and order.

(b) Placements under this section may be for an initial period of twelve months. The court may extend a placement pursuant to section seven hundred fifty-six-a. In its discretion, the court may recommend restitution or require services for public good pursuant to section seven hundred fifty-eight-a in conjunction with an order of placement. For the purposes of calculating the initial period of placement, such placement shall be deemed to have commenced sixty days after the date the child was removed from his or her home in accordance with the provisions of this article. If the respondent has been in detention pending disposition, the initial period of placement ordered under this section shall be credited with and diminished by the amount of time spent by the respondent in detention prior to the commencement of the placement unless the court finds that all or part of such credit would not serve the best interests of the respondent.

(c) A placement pursuant to this section with the commissioner of social services shall not be directed in any detention facility, but the court may direct detention pending transfer to a placement authorized and ordered under this section for no more than than [*] fifteen days after such order of placement is made. Such direction shall be subject to extension pursuant to subdivision three of section three hundred ninety-eight of the social services law, upon written documentation to the office of children and family services that the youth is in need of specialized treatment or placement and the diligent efforts by the commissioner of social services to locate an appropriate placement.

[*] So in original.

Added by L. 1962, Ch. 700, eff. Sept. 1, 1962; **Amended** by L. 1963, Chs. 477, 809, 811, 831; L. 1964, Ch. 333; L. 1965, Ch. 126; L. 1966, Ch. 705; L. 1968, Ch. 874, eff. July 1, 1968; L. 1971, Ch. 947; L. 1974, Ch. 937; L. 1976, Ch. 514, eff. Aug. 1, 1976; repealed subd. (a), as amended L. 1963, Ch. 831, by L. 1976, Ch. 112, eff. Apr. 6, 1976, thereby retaining subd. (a), as amended by L. 1971, Ch. 947; L. 1976, Ch. 882, eff. Apr. 1, 1977; L. 1978, Ch. 478, §§ 9, 10 and 11, eff. Sept. 1, 1978; L. 1986, Ch. 604, eff. Sept. 22, 1986; subd. (c) repealed by L. 1986, Ch. 604, eff. Sept. 22, 1986; L. 1987, Ch. 419, eff. Sept. 1, 1987; L. 1992, Ch. 465, eff. Jan. 14, 1992, amending subd. (a)(iii), (iv), and shall apply to all persons placed in or committed to the custody of the division of youth on or after such date; L. 1996, Ch. 309, § 28, amending subd. (a)(i), eff. July 13, 1996; L. 1996, Ch. 309, § 29, repealing subds. (a)(iii) and (iv), eff. July 13, 1996; pursuant to L. 1996, Ch. 309, § 469, persons in need of supervision in the custody of the division of youth prior to the effective date of the 1996 amendments contained in Ch. 309, §§ 23 through 37 will be governed by laws in effect at the time of their placement; L. 1999, Ch. 7, eff. Feb. 11, 1999, amending subd. (b); L. 2005, Ch. 57, Part E, § 10, eff. Apr. 1, 2005, amending subd. (c).

ANNOTATIONS

Dispositional hearing.—Where all interested parties at the dispositional hearing agreed that the best placement would be in an out-of-state school, approval for which required a showing that no New York State agency would accept placement of the delinquent youth, and transfer to the Division for Youth for such evaluation was prevented by a dispute between the parole officer and law guardian over whether the evaluation should be in a secure or non-secure facility and as a result the out-of-state placement was abandoned and the youth ordered placed in a secure facility, the case was remanded for a further dispositional hearing on the ground that the beneficial ends sought to be achieved should not be frustrated by such a dispute. *In re* Donna H., 70 A.D.2d 521, 416 N.Y.S.2d 15 (1st Dept. 1979).

Executive Law superseded.—FCA § 756 is the more recent statute, and overrides the provisions of Executive Law § 502(4), which permits the Division of Youth to refuse to admit any youth in its discretion when such admission would not be in the best interests of the youth. *In re* Felix Louis R., 96 Misc. 2d 221, 409 N.Y.S.2d 79 (Fam. Ct. Kings Co. 1978).

Extension hearing.—Whether an extension hearing takes place or not or whether the extension is of an interim nature or not, due process requires that a valid opportunity for a hearing before the original placement expires must be given to the child or his guardian by notice duly served or acknowledge. *In re* Bennett, 81 Misc. 2d 200, 366 N.Y.S.2d 289 (Fam. Ct. N.Y. Co. 1975).

Failure to consider rehabilitative needs of juvenile.— Although the court at the dispositional hearing gave proper consideration to the seriousness of the offense committed by the juvenile, his history of absconding from his various residences and his tendency toward compulsive behavior, the court failed to give adequate consideration to the rehabilitative needs of the juvenile when it ordered him placed in a Title III facility and therefore a new dispositional hearing was required. *In re* Michael R., 70 A.D.2d 521, 416 N.Y.S.2d 19 (1st Dept. 1979).

Failure of judge to direct ultimate placement.—Failure of the Family Court Judge to direct the ultimate placement of the juvenile who had committed acts, which, if done by an adult would constitute the crime of robbery, second degree, in a particular agency or class of agencies required a new dispositional hearing. *In re* Kyle S., 64 A.D.2d 666, 407 N.Y.S.2d 512 (2d Dept. 1978).

Placement; generally.—Where record contained a finding of "extraordinary circumstances" to support the court's placement of the PINS in an unsupervised private placement, one of the authorized placements under Article 7, the placement will not be disturbed. Gordon "L" v. Michelle "M," 296 A.D.2d 628, 745 N.Y.S.2d 105 (3d Dept. 2002).

—Court need not engage in "least restrictive analysis" in PINS proceeding, but only to "consider the needs and best interest of respondent as well as the need for protection of the community"; record "supports family court's determination that respondent was a threat to himself and the community and in need of treatment and supervision which would best occur in an appropriate residential placement." *In re* Justin H., 278 A.D.2d 555, 717 N.Y.S.2d 406 (3d Dept. 2000).

—Where the court found the respondent was ineffectually controlled by her mother, that she is a school truant and that she is ungovernable (all of which she admitted) and that placement was necessary to motivate her to attend school regularly and to assist in her self-discipline to complete preparation for high school, then placement was the appropriate alternative. *In re* April FF., 195 A.D.2d 860, 600 N.Y.S.2d 777 (3d Dept. 1993).

—Respondent, a person in need of supervision, was on probation which included certain terms and conditions; after a hearing, court found it was "undisputed that respondent failed to comply with any of those terms and conditions," and Family Court properly placed respondent with authorized agency pursuant to this section. *In re* Crystal A., 11 A.D.3d 897, 782 N.Y.S.2d 474 (4th Dept. 2004).

Placement in State Training School held to be excessively severe punishment.—In a proceeding under Article 7 of the Family Court Act, the Family Court adjudged a 14-year-old girl to be a person in need of supervision and directed that she be placed in the New York State Training School. On appeal, the Appellate Division reversed and remitted the proceeding to the Family Court for the purpose of placing appellant in a more suitable environment. The Appellate Division stated that although it recognized the difficulties facing the Family Court in finding a suitable environment for the appellant, it had to reject the view that children in need of supervision should be confined as quasi criminals because there are allegedly no alternatives, since the Family Court is authorized to seek the cooperation of all children's aid societies and organizations (FCA 255). *In re* H., 38 A.D.2d 570, 328 N.Y.S.2d 251 (2d Dept. 1971).

Placement with Division for Youth after expulsion from facility; hearing required.—Where the order of disposition rely placed the respondent in the custody of the Commissioner of Social Services without restriction as to a particular agency or class of agencies and the agency receiving the placement subsequently sought to expel the respondent for incorrigibility, he could not be placed with the Division for Youth without a hearing to determine that the Commissioner was unable to place the child with any other suitable authorized agency. *In re* D.J., 102 Misc. 2d 701, 424 N.Y.S.2d 102 (Fam. Ct. Ontario Co. 1980).

Time spent in custody prior to commencement of sentence.—Defendant, who was adjudicated a juvenile delinquent and ordered to be placed with the New York State Division for Youth for a period of 18 months, was not entitled to credit for the time he spent in secure detention prior to his placement with the Division of Youth. *In re* John Edward B., 70 A.D.2d 1004, 418 N.Y.S.2d 186 (3d Dept. 1979).

§ 756-a. Extension of placement.

(a) In any case in which the child has been placed pursuant to section seven hundred fifty-six, the child, the person with whom the child has been placed or the commissioner of social services may petition the court to extend such placement. Such petition shall be filed at least sixty days prior to the expiration of the period of placement, except for good cause shown, but in no event shall such petition be filed after the original expiration date.

(b) The court shall conduct a permanency hearing concerning the need for continuing the placement. The child, the person with whom the child has been placed and the commissioner of social services shall be notified of such hearing and shall have the opportunity to be heard thereat.

(c) The provisions of section seven hundred forty-five shall apply at such permanency hearing. If the petition is filed within sixty days prior to the expiration of the period of placement, the court shall first determine at such permanency hearing whether good cause has been shown. If good cause is not shown, the court shall dismiss the petition.

(d) At the conclusion of the permanency hearing the court may, in its discretion, order an extension of the placement for not more than one year. The court must consider and determine in its order:

(i) where appropriate, that reasonable efforts were made to make it possible for the child to safely return to his or her home, or if the permanency plan for the child is adoption, guardianship or some other permanent living arrangement other than reunification with the parent or parents of the child, reasonable efforts are being made to make and finalize such alternate permanent placement;

(ii) in the case of a child who has attained the age of sixteen, the services needed, if any, to assist the child to make the transition from foster care to independent living;

(iii) in the case of a child placed outside New York state, whether the out-of-state placement continues to be appropriate and in the best interests of the child; and

(iv) whether and when the child: (A) will be returned to the parent; (B) should be placed for adoption with the social services official filing a petition for termination of parental rights; (C) should be referred for legal guardianship; (D) should be placed permanently with a fit and willing relative; or (E) should be placed in another planned permanent living arrangement if the social services official has documented to the court a compelling reason for determining that it would not be in the best interest of the child to return home, be referred for termination of parental rights and placed for adoption, placed with a fit and willing relative, or placed with a legal guardian.

(e) Pending final determination of a petition to extend such placement filed in accordance with the provisions of this section, the court may, on its own motion or at the request of the petitioner or respondent, enter one or more temporary orders extending a period of placement not to exceed thirty days upon satisfactory proof showing probable cause for continuing such placement and that each temporary order is necessary. The court may order additional temporary extensions, not to exceed a total of fifteen days, if the court is unable to conclude the hearing within the thirty day temporary extension period. In no event shall the aggregate number of days in extensions granted or ordered under this subdivision total more than forty-five days. The petition shall be dismissed if a decision is not rendered within the period of placement or any temporary extension thereof. Notwithstanding any provision of law to the contrary, the initial permanency hearing shall be held within twelve months of the date the child was placed into care pursuant to section seven

hundred fifty-six of this article and no later than every twelve months thereafter. For the purposes of this section, the date the child was placed into care shall be sixty days after the child was removed from his or her home in accordance with the provisions of this section.

(f) Successive extensions of placement under this section may be granted, but no placement may be made or continued beyond the child's eighteenth birthday without his or her consent and in no event past his or her twenty-first birthday.

Amended by L. 1991, Ch. 198, eff. June 28, 1991, amending subd. (d); L. 1992, Ch. 363, amending subd. (5); L. 1993, Ch. 687, amending subd. (e); L. 1995, Ch. 454, § 2; L. 1996, Ch. 309, § 30, amending subds. (a) and (b), eff. July 13, 1996; pursuant to L. 1996, Ch. 309, § 469, persons in need of supervision in the custody of the division for youth prior to the effective date of the 1996 amendments contained in Ch. 309, §§ 23 through 37 will be governed by the provisions of law in effect at the time of their placement; L. 1999, Ch. 7, §§ 35 through 38, eff. Feb. 11, 1999, amending subds. b through e.

ANNOTATIONS

Extensions.—Court rejected claim that petition had to be dismissed due to failure of the Family Court to enter any temporary order of extension, since the temporary orders of extension were necessarily included in the Family Court's adjournments to dates beyond the expiration of the original placement. *In re* Charles B., 209 A.D.2d 895, 619 N.Y.S.2d 205 (3d Dept. 1994).

Good cause; subd. a.—Good cause was established for seven-day delay in filing petition to extend placement where the delay was caused by a family emergency of one of respondent's caseworker and desire to hold conference prior to finalizing plans for respondent's placement. *In re* Kacey H., 223 A.D.2d 876, 636 N.Y.S.2d 214 (3d Dept. 1996).

§ 756-b. Provisions for routine medical, dental and mental health services and treatment.

[Editor's Note: Section 756-b was repealed, pursuant to L. 1996, Ch. 309, § 31, eff. July 13, 1996. Pursuant to L. 1996, Ch. 309, § 469, persons in need of supervision in the custody of the division for youth prior to the effective date of the 1996 amendments contained in Ch. 309, §§ 23 through 37 will be governed by the provisions of law in effect at the time of their placements.]

§ 757. Probation.

(a) Rules of court shall define permissible terms and conditions of probation.

(b) The maximum period of probation shall not exceed one year. If the court finds at the conclusion of the original period that exceptional circumstances require an additional year of probation, the court may continue probation for an additional year.

(c) The court may order as a condition of probation restitution or services for public good pursuant to section seven hundred fifty-eight-a.

(d) In cases wherein the record indicates that the consumption of alcohol by the respondent may have been a contributing factor, the court may order as a condition of probation attendance at and completion of an alcohol awareness program established pursuant to section 19.25 of the mental hygiene law.

Amended by L. 1970, Ch. 993; L. 1976, Ch. 882, eff. Apr. 1, 1977; L. 1982, Ch. 920, eff. July 1, 1983; L. 1993, Ch. 124; L. 1996, Ch. 309, § 32, amending subd. (d), eff. July 13, 1996; pursuant to L. 1996, Ch. 309, § 469, persons in need of supervision in the custody of the division for youth prior to the effective date of the 1996 amendments contained in Ch. 309, §§ 23 through 37 will be governed by the provisions of law in effect at the time of their placement.

§ 758-a. Restitution.

1. In cases involving acts of infants over ten and less than sixteen years of age, the court may

(a) recommend as a condition of placement, or order as a condition of probation or suspended judgement, restitution in an amount representing a fair and reasonable cost to replace the property or repair the damage caused by the infant, not, however, to exceed one thousand dollars. In the case of a placement, the court may recommend that the infant pay out of his or her own funds or earnings the amount of replacement or damage, either in a lump sum or in periodic payments in amounts set by the agency with which he is placed, and in the case of probation or suspended judgement, the court may require that the infant pay out of his or her own funds or earnings the amount of replacement or damage, either in a lump sum or in periodic payments in amounts set by the court; and/or

(b) Order as a condition of placement, probation or suspended judgement, services for the public good, taking into consideration the age and physical condition of the infant.

2. If the court recommends restitution or requires services for the public good in conjunction with an order of placement pursuant to section seven hundred fifty-six, the placement shall be made only to an authorized agency which has adopted rules and regulations for the supervision of such a program, which rules and regulations shall be subject to the approval of the state department of social services. Such rules and regulations shall include, but not be limited to provisions (i) assuring that the conditions of work, including wages, meet the standards therefor prescribed pursuant to the labor law; (ii) affording coverage to the child under the workers' compensation law as an employee of such agency, department or institution; (iii) assuring that the entity receiving such services shall not utilize the same to replace its regular employees; and (iv) providing for reports to the court not less frequently than every six months, unless the order provides otherwise.

3. If the court requires restitution or services for the public good as a condition of probation or suspended judgement, it shall provide that an agency or person supervise the restitution or services and that such agency or person report to

the court not less frequently than every six months, unless the order provides otherwise. Upon the written notice sent by a school district to the court and the appropriate probation department or agency which submits probation recommendations or reports to the court, the court may provide that such school district shall supervise the performance of services for the public good.

4. The court, upon receipt of the reports provided for in subdivision two or three of this section may, on its own motion or the motion of any party or the agency, hold a hearing to determine whether the placement should be altered or modified.

Added by L. 1976, Ch. 882, eff. Apr. 1, 1977; Amended by L. 1977, Ch. 283, eff. Apr. 1, 1977; L. 1979, Ch. 568, eff. July 10, 1979, Ch. 73, eff. July 30, 1979; L. 1982, Ch. 920, eff. July 1, 1983; L. 1987, Ch. 4, 31, eff. Mar. 24, 1987; L. 1996, Ch. 309, § 33, amending subd. (2), eff. July 13, 1996; pursuant to L. 1996, Ch. 309, § 469, persons in need of supervision in the custody of the division for youth prior to the effective date of the 1996 amendments contained in Ch. 309, §§ 23 through 37 will be governed by the provisions of law in effect at the time of their placement.

§ 759. Order of protection.

The court may make an order of protection in assistance or as a condition of any order issued under this article. The order of protection may set forth reasonable conditions of behavior to be observed for a specified time by a person who is before the court and is a parent or other person legally responsible for the child's care or the spouse of the parent or other person legally responsible for the child's care, or respondent or both. Such an order may require any such person

(a) to stay away from the home, school, business or place of employment of any other party, the other spouse, the other parent or the child, and to stay away from any other specific location designated by the court;

(b) to permit a parent, or a person entitled to visitation by a court order or a separation agreement, to visit the child at stated periods;

(c) to refrain from committing a family offense, as defined in subdivision one of section eight hundred twelve of this act, or any criminal offense against the child or against the other parent or against any person to whom custody of the child is awarded, or from harassing, intimidating or threatening such persons;

(d) to permit a designated party to enter the residence during a specified period of time in order to remove personal belongings not in issue in this proceeding or in any other proceeding or action under this act or the domestic relations law;

(e) to refrain from acts of commission or omission that create an unreasonable risk to the health, safety or welfare of a child;

(f) to participate in family counseling or other professional counseling activities, or other services, including alternative dispute resolution services conducted by an authorized person or an authorized agency to which the youth has been referred or placed, deemed necessary for the rehabilitation of the youth, provided that such family counseling, other counseling activity or other necessary services are not contrary to such person's religious beliefs;

(g) to provide, either directly or by means of medical and health insurance, for expenses incurred for medical care and treatment arising from the incident or incidents forming the basis for the issuance of the order.

The court may also award custody of the child, during the term of the order of protection to either parent, or to an appropriate relative within the second degree. Nothing in this section gives the court power to place or board out any child to an institution or agency. In making orders of protection, the court shall so act as to insure that in the care, protection, discipline and guardianship of the child his religious faith shall be preserved and protected.

Notwithstanding the foregoing provisions, an order of protection, or temporary order of protection where applicable, may be entered against a former spouse and persons who have a child in common, regardless whether such persons have been married or have lived together at any time.

(h) to observe such other conditions as are necessary to further the purposes of protection.

Amended by L. 1976, Ch. 606, eff Sept. 1, 1976, adding subd. (f); L. 1977, Ch. 283; L. 1981, Ch. 965; L. 1984, Ch. 948; L. 1995, Ch. 483, § 9, amending subds. (a)-(e); L. 1995, Ch. 483, § 10, adding subd. (h); L. 1996, Ch. 309, § 34, eff. July 13, 1996, amending subd. (f); pursuant to L. 1996, Ch. 309, § 469, persons in need of supervision in the custody of the division for youth prior to the effective date of the 1996 amendments contained in Ch. 309, §§ 23 through 37 will be governed by the provisions of law in effect at the time of their placement; L. 2005, Ch. 57, Part E, § 11, eff. Apr. 1, 2005, amending subd. (f).

§ 760. Duties of counsel or law guardian.

1. If the court has entered a dispositional order pursuant to section seven hundred fifty-four it shall be the duty of the respondent's counsel or law guardian to promptly advise such respondent and if his parent or other person responsible for his care is not the petitioner, such parent or other person responsible for his care, in writing of his right to appeal to the appropriate appellate division of the supreme court, the time limitations involved, the manner of instituting an appeal and obtaining a transcript of the testimony and the right to apply for leave to appeal as a poor person if he is unable to pay the cost of an appeal. It shall be the further duty of such counsel or law guardian to explain to the respondent and if his parent or other person responsible for his care is not the petitioner, such parent or person responsible for his care, the procedures for instituting an appeal, the possible reasons upon which an appeal may be based and the nature and possible consequences of the appellate process.

2. It shall also be the duty of such counsel or law guardian to ascertain whether the respondent wishes to appeal and, if so, to serve and file the necessary notice of appeal.

3. If the respondent has been permitted to waive the appointment of a law guardian pursuant to section two hundred forty-nine-a, it shall be the duty of the court to provide the notice and explanation pursuant to subdivision one and, if the respondent indicates that he wishes to appeal, the clerk of the court shall file and serve the notice of appeal.

Added by L. 1989, Ch. 9, eff. Nov. 1, 1989.

Part 6. New hearing and reconsideration of orders

§ 761. New hearing.

On its own motion or on motion of any interested person acting on behalf of the respondent, the court may for good cause grant a new fact-finding or dispositional hearing under this article.

Amended by L. 1963, Ch. 529, eff. Apr. 23, 1963; L. 1972, Ch. 721, eff. May 30, 1972.

§ 762. Staying, modifying, setting aside or vacating order.

For good cause, the court on its own motion or on motion of any interested person acting on behalf of the respondent may stay execution of, arrest, set aside, modify or vacate any order issued in the course of a proceeding under this article.

§ 763. Notice of motion.

Notice of motion under section seven hundred sixty-one of seven hundred sixty-two, including the court's own motion, shall be served upon parties and any agency or institution having custody of the child not less than seven days prior to the return date of the motion. The persons on whom the notice of motions is served shall answer the motion not less than two days before the return date. On examining the motion and answer and, in its discretion, after hearing argument, the court shall enter an order, granting or denying the motion.

Amended by L. 1963, Ch. 409, eff. Apr. 16, 1963.

§ 764. Petition to terminate placement.

Any parent or guardian or duly authorized agency or next friend of a person placed under section seven hundred fifty-six may petition to the court for an order terminating the placement. The petition must be verified and must show:

(a) that an application for release of the respondent was made to the duly authorized agency with which the child was placed;

(b) that the application was denied or was not granted within thirty days from the day application was made; and

(c) the grounds for the petition.

Amended by L. 1976, Ch. 878, eff. Feb. 1, 1977; L. 1977, Ch. 283, eff. June 21, 1977; L. 1982, Ch. 920, eff. July 1, 1983.

ANNOTATIONS

Petition, generally.—Request for order terminating respondent's placement Department of Social Services' custody after being adjudged a person in need of supervision was properly petitioned under this section. *In re* Brian J.M., 227 A.D.2d 910, 643 N.Y.S.2d 269 (4th Dept. 1996).

Modify; vacate an order of disposition.—Petitioner, father, did not have the right to summarily discontinue the placement of his son; a hearing on a motion to modify or vacate the order of disposition was required. *In re* Robert H., 87 Misc. 2d 26, 383 N.Y.S.2d 813 (Fam. Ct. Onondaga Co. 1976).

§ 765. Service of petition; answer.

A copy of a petition under section seven hundred sixty-four shall be served promptly upon the duly authorized agency or the institution having custody of the person, whose duty it is to file an answer to the petition within five days from the day of service.

§ 766. Examination of petition and answer; hearing.

The court shall promptly examine the petition and answer. If the court concludes that a hearing should be had, it may proceed upon due notice to all concerned to hear the facts and determine whether continued placement serves the purposes of this article. If the court concludes that a hearing need not be had, it shall enter an order granting or denying the petition.

Amended by L. 1977, Ch. 283, eff. June 21, 1977.

§ 767. Orders on hearing.

(a) If the court determines after hearing that continued placement serves the purposes of this article, it shall deny the petition. The court may, on its own motion, reduce the duration of the placement, change the agency in which the child is placed, or direct the agency to make such other arrangements for the person's care and welfare as the facts of the case may require.

(b) If the court determines after hearing that continued placement does not serve the purposes of this article, the court shall discharge the person from the custody of the agency and may place the person on probation or under the supervision of the court.

Amended by L. 1977, Ch. 283, eff. June 21, 1977.

§ 768. Successive petitions.

If a petition under section seven hundred sixty-four is denied, it may not be renewed for a period of ninety days after the denial, unless the order of denial permits renewal at an earlier time.

Part 7. Compliance with orders

§ 771. Discontinuation of treatment by agency or institution.

If an authorized agency in which a person is placed under section seven hundred fifty-six

(a) discontinues or suspends its work; or

(b) is unwilling to continue to care for the person for the reason that support by the state of New York or one of its political subdivisions has been discontinued; or

(c) so fundamentally alters its program that the person can no longer benefit from it, the person shall be returned by the agency to the court which entered the order of placement.

Amended by L. 1977, Ch. 283, eff. June 21, 1977.

§ 772. Action on return from agency or institution.

If a person is returned to the court under section seven hundred seventy-one, the court may make any order that might have been made at the time the order of placement was made, except that the maximum duration authorized for any such order shall be decreased by the time spent in placement.

Amended by L. 1977, Ch. 283, eff. June 21, 1977.

§ 773. Petition for transfer for incorrigibility.

Any institution, society or agency in which a person was placed under section seven hundred fifty-six may petition to the court which made the order of placement for transfer of that person to a society or agency, governed or controlled by persons of the same religious faith or persuasion as that of the child, where practicable, or, if not practicable, to some other suitable institution, or to some other suitable institution on the ground that such person

(a) is incorrigible and that his or her presence is seriously detrimental to the welfare of the applicant institution, society, agency or other person in its care, or

(b) after placement by the court was released on parole or probation from such institution, society or agency and a term or condition of the release was willfully violated. The petition shall be verified by an officer of the applicant institution, society or agency and shall specify the act or acts bringing the person within this section.

Amended by L. 1977, Ch. 283, eff. June 21, 1977; L. 1982, Ch. 920, eff. July 1, 1983.

ANNOTATION

Transfers for incorrigibility.—The Commissioner of Social Services has the burden of proof on a petition for transfer for incorrigibility to prove that the juvenile (1) is incorrigible and (2) that the commissioner is unable to replace the juvenile with any other agency. In re D.J., 102 Misc. 2d 701, 424 N.Y.S.2d 102 (Fam. Ct. Ontario Co. 1980).

§ 774. Action on petition for transfer.

On receiving a petition under section seven hundred seventy-three, the court may proceed under sections seven hundred thirty-seven, seven hundred thirty-eight or seven hundred thirty-nine with respect to the issuance of a summons or warrant and sections seven hundred twenty-seven and seven hundred twenty-nine govern questions of detention and failure to comply with a promise to appear. Due notice of the petition and a copy of the petition shall also be served personally or by mail upon the office of the locality chargeable for the support of the person involved and upon the person involved and his parents and other persons.

§ 775. Order on hearing.

(a) After hearing a petition under section seven hundred seventy-three, the court may:

(i) dismiss the petition;

(ii) grant the petition, making such placement, if the court was authorized to make such placement upon the original adjudication; or

(iii) terminate the prior order of placement and either discharge the respondent or place him on probation.

(b) If the court grants the petition and orders commitment or placement, the respondent shall thereupon be transferred to the custody of the person, agency or institution provided by the court's order.

§ 776. Failure to comply with terms and conditions of suspended judgment.

If a respondent is brought before the court for failure to comply with reasonable terms and conditions of a suspended judgment issued under this article and if, after hearing, the court is satisfied by competent proof that the respondent failed to comply with such terms and conditions, the court may revoke the suspension of judgment and proceed to make any order that might have been made at the time judgment was suspended.

§ 777. Failure to comply with terms of placement at home.

If a person placed in his own home subject to orders of the court leaves home without the court's permission, he may be brought before the court and if, after hearing, the court is satisfied by competent proof that the respondent left home without just cause, the court may revoke the order of placement and proceed to make any order that might have been made at the time the order of placement was made. It may also continue the order of placement and, on due notice and after hearing, enter an order of protection for the duration of the placement.

§ 778. Failure to comply with terms of placement in authorized agency.

If a person is placed in the custody of a suitable institution in accord with section seven hundred fifty-six and leaves the institution without permission of the superintendent or person in charge and without permission of the court, and if, after hearing, the court is satisfied by competent proof that the respondent left the institution without just cause, the court may revoke the order of placement and proceed to make any order that might have been made at the time the order of placement was made or any order authorized under section seven hundred fifty-six.

Amended by L. 1963, Ch. 809, eff. Apr. 26, 1963; L. 1982, Ch. 920, eff. July 1, 1983.

ANNOTATION

Exclusive remedies.—Family court does not have the authority to hold a juvenile adjudicated a PINS in contempt for violation of an order of protection; the exclusive remedies for violation of a PINS order are contained in FCA § 778. *In re* Edwin G., 296 A.D.2d 7, 742 N.Y.S.2d 53 (1st Dept. 2002).

§ 779. Failure to comply with terms of probation.

If a respondent is brought before the court for failure to comply with reasonable terms and conditions of an order of probation issued under this article and if, after hearing, the court is satisfied by competent proof that the respondent without just cause failed to comply with such terms and conditions, the court may revoke the order of probation and proceed to make any order that might have been made at the time the order of probation was entered.

ANNOTATIONS

Abuse of discretion.—Court abused its discretion when it determined sua sponte that respondent was emancipated and dismissed the violation of probation proceeding against respondent, who had previously been adjudicated a PIN. *In re* Tiffany S., 254 A.D.2d 817, 678 N.Y.S.2d 767 (3d Dept. 1998).

—Where the terms of respondent's probation were modified by the court, but the probation department thereafter advised respondent incorrectly as to the terms and conditions of his probation, respondent did not willfully violate the terms of his probation. *In re* Sean T., 302 A.D.2d 991, 755 N.Y.S.2d 153 (4th Dept. 2003).

§ 779-a. Declaration of delinquency concerning juvenile delinquents and persons in need of supervision.

If, at any time during the period of a disposition of probation, the court has reasonable cause to believe the respondent has violated a condition of the disposition, it may declare the respondent delinquent and file a written declaration of delinquency. Upon such filing, the respondent shall be declared delinquent of his disposition of probation and such disposition shall be tolled. The court then must promptly take reasonable and appropriate action to cause the respondent to appear before it for the purpose of enabling the court to make a final determination with respect to the alleged delinquency. The time for prompt court action shall not be construed against the probation service when the respondent has absconded from probation supervision and the respondent's whereabouts are unknown. The court must be notified promptly of the circumstances of any such probationers.

Added by L. 1981, Ch. 775; **Amended** L. 1996, Ch. 309, § 35, eff. July 13, 1996; pursuant to L. 1996, Ch. 309, § 469, persons in need of supervision in the custody of the division for youth prior to the effective date of the 1996 amendments contained in Ch. 309, §§ 23 through 37 will be governed by the provisions of law in effect at the time of their placement.

§ 780. Failure to comply with order of protection.

If any person is brought before the court for failure to comply with the terms and conditions of an order of protection properly issued under this article and applicable to him and if, after hearing, the court is satisfied by competent proof that that person without just cause failed to comply with such terms and conditions, the court may modify or revoke the order of protection, or commit said person, if he willfully violated the order, to jail for a term not to exceed six months,

MISC. LAWS

or both. The court may suspend an order of commitment under this section on condition that the said person comply with the order of protection.

Added by L. 1963, Ch. 809, eff. Apr. 26, 1963.

Part 8. Effect of proceedings

§ 781. Nature of adjudication.

No adjudication under this article may be denominated a conviction, and no person adjudicated a person in need of supervision under this article shall be denominated a criminal by reason of such adjudication.

Amended by L. 1982, Ch. 920, eff. July 1, 1983.

§ 782. Effect of adjudication.

No adjudication under this article shall operate as a forfeiture of any right or privilege or disqualify any person from subsequently holding public office or receiving any license granted by public authority.

§ 782-a. Transfer of records and information to institutions and agencies.

Whenever a person is placed with an institution suitable for the placement of a person adjudicated in need of supervision maintained by the state or any subdivision thereof or to an authorized agency, the family court so placing such person shall forthwith transmit a copy of the orders of the family court pursuant to sections seven hundred fifty-two and seven hundred fifty four, and of the probation report and all other relevant evaluative records in the possession of the family court and probation department related to such child, including but not limited to any diagnostic, educational, medical, psychological and psychiatric records with respect to such person to such institution or agency, notwithstanding any contrary provision of law.

Added by L. 1976, Ch. 878; Amended by L. 1977, Ch. 283; L. 1982, Ch. 920, eff. July 1, 1983; L. 1996, Ch. 309, § 36, eff. July 13, 1996; pursuant to L. 1996, Ch. 309, § 469, persons in need of supervision in the custody of the division for youth prior to the effective date of the 1996 amendments contained in Ch. 309, §§ 23 through 37 will be governed by the provisions of law in effect at the time of their placement.

§ 783. Use of record in other court.

Neither the fact that a person was before the family court under this article for a hearing nor any confession, admission or statement made by him to the court or to any officer thereof in any stage of the proceeding is admissible as evidence against him or his interests in any other court. Another court, in imposing sentence upon an adult after conviction, may receive and consider the records and information on file with the family court concerning such person when he was a child.

ANNOTATIONS

Person in need of supervision; evidence to support determination.—The court reversed the adjudication by the Family Court that appellant was a person in need of supervision, holding that there must be more than a single isolated incident to support such a determination. In re Erik P., 42 A.D.2d 908, 347 N.Y.S.2d 735 (2d Dept. 1973).

Use of record in administrative proceeding.—Although FCA § 783 does not expressly apply to administrative proceedings, it was error to permit testimony concerning Family Court proceedings in a city housing authority hearing to determine whether the petitioner was eligible for continued occupancy of her apartment, however, the hearing officer may permit inquiry into the facts underlying the Family Court charges. Dukes v. New York City Housing Auth., 63 A.D.2d 690, 404 N.Y.S.2d 889 (2d Dept. 1978).

Waiver.—Juvenile waived his privilege under FCA § 783, when he voluntarily appeared as a defense witness and on direct examination testified that the juvenile delinquency proceeding against him, arising from the same incident, had been dismissed but court inspection of the subpoenaed Family Court records revealed he was in error and the district attorney was permitted to use the Family Court records to reveal that the juvenile had admitted to the crime at the fact finding hearing. People v. Johnson, 90 Misc. 2d 777, 395 N.Y.S.2d 885 (Sup. Ct. N.Y. Co. 1977).

§ 783-a. Consolidation of records within a city having a population of one million or more.

Notwithstanding any other provision of law, in a city having a population of one million or more, an index of the records of the local probation departments located in the counties comprising such city for proceedings under article seven shall be consolidated and filed in a central office for use by the family court and local probation service in each such county. After consultation with the state administrative judge, the state director of probation and correctional alternatives shall specify the information to be contained in such index and the organization of such consolidated file.

Added by L. 1976, Ch. 587, eff. July 1, 1977; Amended by L. 1985, Ch. 134, eff. Apr. 1, 1985.

§ 784. Use of police records.

All police records relating to the arrest and disposition of any person under this article shall be kept in files separate and apart from the arrests of adults and shall be withheld from public inspection, but such records shall be open to

MISC. LAWS

inspection upon good cause shown by the parent, guardian, next friend or attorney of that person upon the written order of a judge of the family court in the county in which the order was made or, if the person is subsequently convicted of a crime, of a judge of the court in which he was convicted.

ANNOTATIONS

No power to expunge names from police record; discretionary power to seal own record.—In a proceeding to adjudge appellant a juvenile delinquent, the petition was withdrawn, but the Family Court denied a motion to expunge the names of appellant and others from all court and police records. The Family Court was held to have properly denied the motion; it is not authorized or empowered to expunge police records. However, the court does have inherent power over its own records. The Appellate Division was of the opinion that the sealing of court records is the proper method of ensuring their confidentiality, and it stated that its affirmance of the order denying the motion to expunge the names was without prejudice to a new application addressed to the discretion of the Family Court as to whether or not it should seal its own record. *In re J.*, 37 A.D.2d 717, 325 N.Y.S.2d 235 (2d Dept. 1971).

Police records.—Attorney, representing the estates of two passengers killed in an automobile accident, was permitted inspection and copying of the accident reports after the documents relating to arrest and disposition of cases involving the infants were delivered to the Supreme Court for determination, upon an *in camera* inspection, as to which documents were prohibited from disclosure under Family Court Act § 784. *Barnett v. Police Dept. of County of Nassau*, 47 A.D.2d 655, 364 N.Y.S.2d 186 (2d Dept. 1975).

ARTICLE 8

FAMILY OFFENSES PROCEEDINGS

SUMMARY OF ARTICLE

Part 1. Jurisdiction

§ 812. Procedures for family offense proceedings.

1. The family court and the criminal courts shall have concurrent jurisdiction over any proceeding concerning acts which would constitute disorderly conduct, harassment in the first degree, harassment in the second degree, aggravated harassment in the second degree, stalking in the first degree, stalking in the second degree, stalking in the third degree, stalking in the fourth degree, menacing in the second degree, menacing in the third degree, reckless endangerment, assault in the second degree, assault in the third degree or an attempted assault between spouses or former spouses, or between parent and child or between members of the same family or household except that if the respondent would not be criminally responsible by reason of age pursuant to section 30.00 of the penal law, then the family court shall have exclusive jurisdiction over such proceeding. Notwithstanding a complainant's election to proceed in family court, the criminal court shall not be divested of jurisdiction to hear a family offense proceeding pursuant to this section. For purposes of this article, "disorderly conduct" includes disorderly conduct not in a public place. For purposes of this article, "members of the same family or household" shall mean the following:

(a) persons related by consanguinity or affinity; and

(b) persons legally married to one another;

(c) persons formerly married to one another; and

(d) persons who have a child in common regardless whether such persons have been married or have lived together at any time.

2. Information to petitioner or complainant. The chief administrator of the courts shall designate the appropriate probation officers, warrant officers, sheriffs, police officers or any other law enforcement officials, to inform any petitioner or complainant bringing a proceeding under this article, before such proceeding is commenced, of the procedures available for the institution of family offense proceedings, including but not limited to the following:

(a) That there is concurrent jurisdiction with respect to family offenses in both family court and the criminal courts;

(b) That a family court proceeding is a civil proceeding and is for the purpose of attempting to stop the violence, end the family disruption and obtain protection. Referrals for counseling, or counseling services, are available through probation for this purpose;

(c) That a proceeding in the criminal courts is for the purpose of prosecution of the offender and can result in a criminal conviction of the offender;

(d) That a proceeding or action subject to the provisions of this section is initiated at the time of the filing of an accusatory instrument or family court petition, not at the time of arrest, or request for arrest, if any;

(e) *Repealed by L. 1994, Ch. 222, § 6, eff. Jan. 1, 1995.*

(f) That an arrest may precede the commencement of a family court or a criminal court proceeding, but an arrest is not a requirement for commencing either proceeding; provided, however, that the arrest of an alleged offender shall be made under the circumstances described in subdivision four of section 140.10 of the criminal procedure law;

(g) That notwithstanding a complainant's election to proceed in family court, the criminal court shall not be divested of jurisdiction to hear a family offense proceeding pursuant to this section.

3. Official responsibility. No official or other person designated pursuant to subdivision two of this section shall discourage or prevent any person who wishes to file a petition or sign a complaint from having access to any court for that purpose.

4. Official forms. The chief administrator of the court shall prescribe an appropriate form to implement subdivision two of this section.

5. Notice. Every police officer, peace officer or district attorney investigating a family offense under this article shall advise the victim of the availability of a shelter or other services in the community, and shall immediately give the victim written notice of the legal rights and remedies available to a victim of a family offense under the relevant provisions of the criminal procedure law, the family court act and the domestic relations law. Such notice shall be available in English and Spanish and, if necessary, shall be delivered orally and shall include but not be limited to the following statement:

"If you are the victim of domestic violence, you may request that the officer assist in providing for your safety and that of your children, including providing information on how to obtain a temporary order of protection. You may also request that the officer assist you in obtaining your essential personal effects and locating and taking you, or assist in making arrangement to take you, and your children to a safe place within such officer's jurisdiction, including but not limited to a domestic violence program, a family member's or a friend's residence, or a similar place of safety. When the officer's jurisdiction is more than a single county, you may ask the officer to take you or make arrangements to take you and your children to a place of safety in the county where the incident occurred. If you or your children are in need of medical treatment, you have the right to request that the officer assist you in obtaining such medical treatment. You may request a copy of any incident reports at no cost from the law enforcement agency. You have the right to seek legal counsel of your own choosing and if you proceed in family court and if it is determined that you cannot afford an attorney, one must be appointed to represent you without cost to you.

You may ask the district attorney or a law enforcement officer to file a criminal complaint. You also have the right to file a petition in the family court when a family offense has been committed against you. You have the right to have your petition and request for an order of protection filed on the same day you appear in court, and such request must be heard that same day or the next day court is in session. Either court may issue an order of protection from conduct constituting a family offense which could include, among other provisions, an order for the respondent or defendant to stay away from you and your children. The family court may also order the payment of temporary child support and award temporary custody of your children. If the family court is not in session, you may seek immediate assistance from the criminal court in obtaining an order of protection.

The forms you need to obtain an order of protection are available from the family court and the local criminal court (the addresses and telephone numbers shall be listed). The resources available in this community for information relating to domestic violence, treatment of injuries, and places of safety and shelters can be accessed by calling the following 800 numbers (the statewide English and Spanish language 800 numbers shall be listed and space shall be provided for local domestic violence hotline telephone numbers).

Filing a criminal complaint or a family court petition containing allegations that are knowingly false is a crime."

The division of criminal justice services in consultation with the state office for the prevention of domestic violence shall prepare the form of such written notice consistent with the provisions of this section and distribute copies thereof to the appropriate law enforcement officials pursuant to subdivision nine of section eight hundred forty-one of the executive law. Additionally, copies of such notice shall be provided to the chief administrator of the courts to be distributed to victims of family offenses through the family court at such time as such persons first come before the court and to the state department of health for distribution to all hospitals defined under article twenty-eight of the public health law. No cause of action for damages shall arise in favor of any person by reason of any failure to comply with the provisions of this subdivision except upon a showing of gross negligence or willful misconduct.

Amended by L. 1964, Ch. 156; L. 1969, Ch. 736; L. 1977, Ch. 449; L. 1978, Ch. 628, 629; L. 1980, Ch. 530, eff. June 24, 1980; L. 1981, Ch. 416, eff. Aug. 6, 1981; L. 1983, Ch. 925, eff. Aug. 8, 1983; L. 1984, Ch. 948, eff. Nov. 1, 1984; L. 1986, Ch. 847, eff. Nov. 1, 1986; L. 1990, Ch. 577, eff. Nov. 1, 1990 amending subd. (2)(e); L. 1990, Ch. 667, eff. Nov. 1, 1990, amending subd. (2)(e) but not including changes contained in Ch. 577; L. 1992, Ch. 345, eff. Nov. 1, 1992; L. 1994, Ch. 222, § 6, eff. Jan. 1, 1995, repealing subd. 2(e); L. 1994, Ch. 222, § 7, eff. Jan. 1, 1995, amending subd. 1; L. 1994, Ch. 222, § 8, eff. Jan. 1, 1995, amending subd. 2(f); L. 1994, Ch. 222, § 9, and Ch. 224, § 1, eff. Jan. 1, 1995, amending subd. 5; L. 1995, Ch. 440, § 1, amending opening paragraph to subd. 1, eff. Nov. 1, 1995; L. 1999, Ch. 125, §§ 3 and 4, eff. June 29, 1999, amending opening paragraph to subd. 1, amending subd. 2(f), and adding subd. g, and Ch. 635, § 7, amending opening paragraph of subd. 1, eff. Dec. 1, 1999.

ANNOTATIONS

Assault upon a child.—In dealing with the matter of an assault upon a child by members of the child's family, the term "exclusive original jurisdiction" in FCA § 812(1) does not prevent subsequent removal of these cases from Family Court to the Criminal Courts when the Family Court deems this appropriate, so long as the initial child abuse proceeding is commenced in Family Court. People v. Tatro, 95 Misc. 2d 178, 407 N.Y.S.2d 135 (Albany Co. Ct. 1978).

Attempted murder; Family Court jurisdiction.—Case should have been instituted in the Family Court, since on the same operative facts defendant is charged with both attempted murder and assault, first degree. In People v. Bronson, *supra,* defendant was charged with attempted murder alone. People *ex rel.* Balk v. Warden, Queens House, 46 A.D.2d 224, 362 N.Y.S.2d 180 (2d Dept. 1974).

—Where defendant attempted to run over his wife with a truck following his threats to kill her, indictment for attempted murder was legitimate course and not attempt to circumvent Family Court, which only has original jurisdiction on assault involving members of a family. People v. Bronson, 39 A.D.2d 464, 337 N.Y.S.2d 215 (4th Dept. 1972).

—Attempted murder is not a charge over which the Family Court has jurisdiction, as it is not included within the meaning of assault, and the fact that a hearing was held on an assault charge and a protection order was issued does not confer such jurisdiction. People v. Coady, 79 Misc. 2d 929, 361 N.Y.S.2d 587 (Sup. Ct. Queens Co. 1974).

Concurrent jurisdiction.—Although the defendant could have raised by way of defense at trial the omission, if any, to advise the complainant of her choice of forums, his failure to do so and his subsequent guilty plea caused defendant to waive all non-jurisdictional defects. People v. Mack, 75 A.D.2d 586, 426 N.Y.S.2d 792 (2d Dept. 1980).

—The People's motion to dismiss without prejudice to any remedy available in the Family Court was granted where the mother instituted action in criminal court, pursuant to FCA § 812, for the sole purpose of helping her son, who was under 18 years old. People v. Daniel T., 95 Misc. 2d 639, 408 N.Y.S.2d 214 (Crim. Ct. N.Y.C. 1978).

Criminal Court.—Where the County Court erroneously dismissed the indictment because FCA § 812 provided the Family Court with exclusive jurisdiction, the proper remedy for the People was an appeal (CPL §§ 450.20, 470.15) and not an Article 78 proceeding against the Judge. People v. Thompson, 70 A.D.2d 968, 417 N.Y.S.2d 125 (3d Dept. 1979).

Failure to give statutory admonitions to complainant.—The giving of the statutory admonitions in Family Court Act § 812(2) is a condition precedent to a binding election of remedies; therefore, where complainant wife who alleged her husband had thrown a bottle at her did not receive such information the criminal court dismissed the proceeding against the defendant husband without prejudice, leaving complainant to pursue her remedy in Family Court. People v. Garcia, 98 Misc. 2d 907, 415 N.Y.S.2d 175 (Crim. Ct. N.Y. Co. 1979).

"Family"; "household."—The term "family" and "household" do not countenance relationships unless they are those that are solemnized through marriage or recognized by common law. People v. Dorns, 88 Misc. 2d 1064, 390 N.Y.S.2d 546 (J. Ct. Westchester Co. 1976).

"Family"; jurisdiction.—Family Court had no jurisdiction to grant petitioner an order of protection against her former stepfather since a relation of affinity (i.e., a relation based upon marriage) is destroyed upon divorce. Orellana v. Escalante, 228 A.D.2d 63, 653 N.Y.S.2d 992 (4th Dept. 1997).

Family Court jurisdiction; family offenses.—Evidence that appellant exhibited violent and harassing behavior in presence of petitioner, alone, or while children were present, which constituted an immediate and ongoing danger to them supported finding appellant committed a family offense, warranting issuance of orders of protection. Charlene J. R. v. Walter A. M., 307 A.D.2d 1038,763 N.Y.S.2d 778 (2d Dept. 2003).

—Family court only has jurisdiction over offenses specified by statute, those criminal acts not specifically enumerated are excluded. Hamm-Jones v. Jones, 267 A.D.2d 904, 702 N.Y.S.2d 130 (3d Dept. 1999).

—Family Court does not have exclusive jurisdiction over family offenses; family court shares concurrent jurisdiction with criminal court over family offenses, including any proceeding concerning acts which constitute assault in second degree. People v. Spickerman, 307 A.D.2d 774, 762 N.Y.S.2d 470 (4th Dept. 2003).

—Amendments to Family Court Act § 812 (L. 1977, Ch. 499, eff. Sept. 1, 1977) divesting Family Court of exclusive original jurisdiction of certain acts between spouses which have come to be known as "family offenses" and giving the criminal courts concurrent jurisdiction with the Family Court over such offenses does not contravene the Constitutions of the United States and the State of New York. People v. Revell, 93 Misc. 2d 159, 402 N.Y.S.2d 522 (Dist. Ct. Nassau Co. 1978).

Incest not act within exclusive original jurisdiction of court.—Incest is not an act within the exclusive original jurisdiction of the Family Court conferred by sections 812 and 812. People v. Lewis, 29 N.Y.2d 923, 329 N.Y.S.2d 100 (1972).

Living as husband and wife but never married; Family Court lacks jurisdiction.—Where parties lived together as husband and wife and were parents of a child but had never married, the Family Court lacked jurisdiction to issue order of protection between the parties; the Family Court's jurisdiction applies to disputes arising in relationships only where there is a legal interdependence through either a solemnized marriage or a recognized common-law union. Potter v. Bennett, 40 A.D.2d 546, 334 N.Y.S.2d 511 (2d Dept. 1972).

Plea; waiver.—Plea of guilty waives right to assert that the criminal action was jurisdictionally defective. People v. Mack, 53 N.Y.2d 803, 439 N.Y.S.2d 912 (1981).

Purpose.—Proceedings under Article 8 of the Family Act are civil in nature and have as their purpose "attempting to stop the violence, end the family disruption and obtain protection;" this stated purpose of family offense proceedings must be the measure by which the reasonableness of an order of protection is determined. In re Jane Y., 123 Misc. 2d 771, 474 N.Y.S.2d 681 (Fam. Ct. Richmond Co. 1984).

Sodomy; Family Court lacks jurisdiction over proceeding concerning same.—The crime of sodomy does not come within the jurisdiction of the Family Court under FCA 812, 813. People v. Monsanto, 70 Misc. 2d 996, 335 N.Y.S.2d 451 (Sup. Ct. Bronx Co. 1972); *see also* People v. Webb, 52 A.D.2d 8, 382 N.Y.S.2d 369 (3d Dept. 1976).

§ 813. Transfer to criminal court.

1. At any time prior to a finding on the petition the court may, with the consent of the petitioner and upon reasonable notice to the district attorney, who shall have an opportunity to be heard, order that any matter which is the subject of a proceeding commenced pursuant to this article be prosecuted as a criminal action in an appropriate criminal court if the court determines that the interests of justice so require.

2. The court may simultaneously with the transfer of any matter to the appropriate criminal court, issue or continue a temporary order of protection which, notwithstanding any other provision of law, shall continue in effect, absent action by the appropriate criminal court pursuant to subdivision three of section 530.12 of the criminal procedure law, until the defendant is arraigned upon an accusatory instrument filed pursuant to this section in such criminal court.

3. Nothing herein shall be deemed to limit or restrict a petitioner's rights to proceed directly and without court referral in either criminal or family court, or both, as provided for in section one hundred fifteen of this act and section 100.07 of the criminal procedure law.

Added by L. 1978, Ch. 628; L. 1980, Ch. 530, eff. Aug. 23, 1980; **Amended** by L. 1994, Ch. 222, § 10, eff. Jan. 1, 1995, repealing subd. 3 and adding a new subd. 3.

ANNOTATIONS

Assault; indictment dismissed pending Family Court disposition.—In an assault (shooting of a spouse), the Family Court has exclusive jurisdiction, and an indictment in the County Court to which the matter was transferred should be dismissed on defendant's motion pending disposition in the Family Court. People v. Berger, 40 A.D.2d 192, 338 N.Y.S.2d 762 (3d Dept. 1972).

Double jeopardy.—Contempt provision of Family Court Act, Article 8 is a lesser included offense of first degree criminal contempt; therefore, prosecution and the imposition of additional punishment for the greater offense, criminal contempt, after prosecution under the Family Court Act, is barred by double jeopardy. People v. Wood, 95 N.Y.2d 509, 719 N.Y.S.2d 639, 742 N.E.2d 114 (2000).

Improper transfer.—Notice to defendant of the impending transfer of the material back to the Criminal Term was required since he had the right to challenge the Family Court either by modification (FCA § 816) or directly by appeal (FCA § 1112); determination should not be made when defendant is without counsel. People v. Dupree, 67 A.D.2d 716, 412 N.Y.S.2d 424 (2d Dept. 1979).

—The Family Court abused its discretion in waiving its "exclusive original jurisdiction" merely on the basis of the severity of the assault charged, and since the Family Court's "exclusive original jurisdiction" was improperly waived, the District Court never acquired jurisdiction and thus the defendant's subsequent plea of guilty and the judgment of conviction in that court were nullities. Librizzi v. Chisholm, 55 A.D.2d 954, 391 N.Y.S.2d 154 (2d Dept. 1977).

Transfer to criminal court; assault by husband upon wife.—Family court did not abuse its discretion by transferring the case to criminal court, in view of the seriousness of the assault and the disintegration of the marriage. People v. Brown, 80 A.D.2d 902, 437 N.Y.S.2d 22 (2d Dept. 1981).

Transfer to Family Court; more than 3 days; no bar to prosecution.—Failure to transfer a case until 5 days after criminal complaint is made does not bar prosecution of the defendant since the defendant can move to compel the transfer if the Court fails to do so timely, and thus a delay does not deprive the defendant of due process of law. People v. Coady, 79 Misc. 2d 929, 361 N.Y.S.2d 587 (Sup. Ct. Queens Co. 1974).

§ 814. Rules of court regarding concurrent jurisdiction.

The chief administrator of the courts pursuant to paragraph (e) of subdivision two of section two hundred twelve of the judiciary law shall promulgate rules to facilitate record sharing and other communication between the criminal and family courts, subject to applicable provisions of the criminal procedure law and the family court act pertaining to the confidentiality, expungement and sealing of records, where such courts exercise concurrent jurisdiction over family offense proceedings.

Added L. 1994, Ch. 222, § 11, eff. Jan. 1, 1995.

§ 814-a. Uniform forms.

The chief administrator of the courts, shall promulgate appropriate uniform temporary orders of protection and orders of protection forms, applicable to proceedings under this article, to be used throughout the state. Such forms shall be promulgated and developed in a manner to ensure the compatability * of such forms with the statewide computerized registry established pursuant to section two hundred twenty-one-a of the executive law.

* Spelled as such in original. Should be "compatibility."

Added by L. 1994, Ch. 224, § 15, eff. Jan. 1, 1995.

§ 815. Transcript of family offense proceedings; request by district attorney.

The court shall, upon the written request of a district attorney stating that such transcript is necessary in order to conduct a criminal investigation or prosecution involving the petitioner or respondent, provide a copy of the transcript of any proceedings under this article, to such district attorney. Such transcript shall not be redisclosed except as necessary for such investigation or prosecution.

Added by L. 1994, Ch. 222, § 12, and Ch. 224, § 2, eff. Jan. 1, 1995.

§ 817. Support, paternity and child protection.

On its own motion and at any time in proceedings under this article, the court may direct the filing of a child protective petition under article ten of this chapter, a support petition under article four, or a paternity petition under article five of this act and consolidate the proceedings.

Amended by L. 1964, Ch. 156, eff. Mar. 23, 1964; L. 1978, Ch. 628, eff. July 24, 1978.

§ 818. Venue.

Proceedings under this article may be originated in the county in which the act or acts referred to in the petition allegedly occurred or in which the family or household resides or in which any party resides. For the purposes of this section, residence shall include any residential program for victims of domestic violence, as defined in subdivision four of section four hundred fifty-nine-a of the social services law, or facility which provides shelter to homeless persons or families on an emergency or temporary basis.

Amended by L. 1964, Ch. 156; L. 1981, Ch. 446; L. 1996, Ch. 539, § 3, eff. Aug. 8, 1996; L. 2004, Ch. 391, § 1, eff. Aug. 17, 2004.

Part 2. Preliminary procedure

§ 821. Originating proceedings.

1. A proceeding under this article is originated by the filing of a petition containing the following:

(a) An allegation that the respondent assaulted or attempted to assault his or her spouse, or former spouse, parent, child or other member of the same family or household or engaged in disorderly conduct, harassment, stalking, menacing or reckless endangerment toward any such person; and

(b) The relationship of the alleged offender to the petitioner;

(c) The name of each and every child in the family or household and the relationship of the child, if any, to the petitioner and to the respondent;

(d) A request for an order of protection or the use of the court's conciliation procedures; and

(e) An allegation as to whether any accusatory instrument alleging an act specified in paragraph (a) of this subdivision has been verified with respect to the same act alleged in the petition. Appended to the copy of the petition provided to the petitioner shall be a copy of the notice described in subdivision five of section eight hundred twelve of this article.

2. When family court is not in session, an arrest and initial appearance by the defendant or respondent may be in a criminal court, as provided in sections one hundred fifty-four-d and one hundred fifty-five of this act.

3. [*Repealed by L. 1994, Ch. 222, § 6, eff. Jan. 1, 1995.*]

Amended by L. 1969, Ch. 736, Sept. 1, 1969; **repealed** by L. 1977, Ch. 449, eff. Sept. 1, 1977 and new § 821 **added**; L. 1978, Ch. 628, 629, eff. July 24, 1978; L. 1984, Ch. 948, eff. Nov. 1, 1984; L. 1988, Ch. 271, § 2, eff. Jul. 19, 1988; L. 1990, Ch. 577, eff. Nov. 1, 1990, amending subds. (2) and (3); L. 1994, Ch. 222, § 13, eff. Jan. 1, 1995, amending subd. (1)(e); L. 1994, Ch. 222, § 6, eff. Jan. 1, 1995, repealing subds. (2) and (3); L. 1994, Ch. 222, § 14, eff. Jan. 1, 1995, amending subd. (4); L. 1997, Ch. 186, § 6, eff. July. 8, 1997, subd. (4) renumbered to (2) and amended; L. 1999, Ch. 635, § 8, amending subd. 1(a), eff. Dec. 1, 1999.

§ 821-a. Preliminary procedure.

1. Upon the filing of a petition under this article, the court shall advise the petitioner of the right to retain legal representation or if indigent, the right to have counsel appointed pursuant to section two hundred sixty-two of this act.

2. Upon the filing of a petition under this article, the court may:

(a) Issue a summons pursuant to section eight hundred twenty-six of this part or issue a warrant pursuant to section eight hundred twenty-seven of this part;

(b) Issue a temporary order of protection in favor of the petitioner and, where appropriate, the petitioner's children or any other children residing in the petitioner's household, pursuant to section eight hundred twenty-eight of this part.

3. Where the respondent is brought before the court pursuant to a summons under section eight hundred twenty-six of this part or a warrant issued under section eight hundred twenty-seven of this part, or where a respondent voluntarily appears before the court after such summons or warrant has been issued, the court shall:

(a) advise the parties of the right to retain legal representation or, if indigent, the right to have counsel appointed pursuant to section two hundred sixty-two of this act;

(b) advise the respondent of the allegations contained in the petition before the court; and

(c) provide the respondent with a copy of such petition; and the court may:

(i) order the release of the respondent on his or her own recognizance pending further appearances as required by the court;

(ii) direct that the respondent post bail in a manner authorized pursuant to section one hundred fifty-five-a of this act in an amount set by the court; or

(iii) issue a commitment order directing that the respondent be remanded to the custody of the county sheriff or other appropriate law enforcement official until such time as bail is posted as required by the court.

4. Where the court directs that the respondent post bail or that the respondent be committed to

the custody of a law enforcement official as provided for herein, and the respondent fails to post bail or otherwise remains in custody, a hearing shall be held without unreasonable delay but in no event later than one hundred twenty hours after the arrest of the respondent or in the event that a Saturday, Sunday, or legal holiday occurs during such custody, one hundred forty-four hours after the arrest of the respondent, to determine upon material and relevant evidence whether sufficient cause exists to keep the respondent in custody. If the court determines that sufficient cause does not exist or if no hearing is timely held, the respondent shall immediately be released on the respondent's own recognizance.

5. (a) At such time as the petitioner first appears before the court, the court shall advise the petitioner that the petitioner may: continue with the hearing and disposition of such petition in the family court; or have the allegations contained therein heard in an appropriate criminal court; or proceed concurrently in both family and criminal court.

(b) Where the petitioner seeks to have the petition heard and determined in the family court, the court shall set the matter down for further proceedings pursuant to the provisions of this article. Nothing herein shall be deemed to limit or restrict petitioner's rights to seek to proceed directly in either criminal or family court, or both, as provided for in section one hundred fifteen of this act and section 100.07 of the criminal procedure law.

6. When both parties first appear before the court, the court shall inquire as to the existence of any other orders of protection involving the parties.

Added by L. 1994, Ch. 222, § 15, eff. Jan. 1, 1995.

§ 822. Person who may originate proceedings.

(a) Any person in the relation to the respondent of spouse, or former spouse, parent, child, or member of the same family or household:

(b) A duly authorized agency, association, society, or institution;

(c) A peace officer, acting pursuant to his special duties, or a police officer;

(d) A person on the court's own motion.

Amended by L. 1980, Ch. 843, eff. Sept. 1, 1980; L. 1984, eff. Nov. 1, 1984.

§ 823. Rules of court for preliminary procedure.

(a) Rules of court may authorize the probation service

(i) to confer with any person seeking to file

a petition, the potential petitioner and other interested persons concerning the advisability of filing a petition under this article, and

(ii) to attempt through conciliation and agreement informally to adjust suitable cases before a petition is filed over which the court apparently would have jurisdiction.

(b) The probation service may not prevent any person who wishes to file a petition under this article from having access to the court for that purpose.

(c) Efforts at adjustment pursuant to rules of court under this section may not extend for a period of more than two months without leave of a judge of the court, who may extend the period for an additional sixty days. Two successive extensions may be granted under this section.

(d) The probation service may not be authorized under this section to compel any person to appear at any conference, produce any papers, or visit any place.

(e) If agreement to cease offensive conduct is reached, it must be reduced to writing and submitted to the family court for approval. If the court approves it, the court without further hearing may thereupon enter an order of protection in accordance with the agreement, which shall be binding upon the respondent and shall in all respects be a valid order. The court record shall show that such order was made upon agreement.

Added by L. 1977, Ch. 449, eff. Sept. 1, 1977.

§ 824. Admissibility of statements made during preliminary conference.

No statement made during a preliminary conference may be admitted into evidence at a fact-finding hearing under this act or in a criminal court at any time prior to conviction.

§ 825. Issuance of summons.

On the filing of a petition under this article, the court may cause a copy of the petition and a summons to be issued, requiring the respondent to appear at the court at a time and place to answer the petition.

§ 826. Service of summons.

(a) Unless the court issues a warrant pursuant to section eight hundred twenty-seven of this part, service of a summons and petition shall be made by delivery of a true copy thereof to the person summoned at least twenty-four hours before the time stated therein for appearance. If so requested by the respondent, the court shall not proceed with the hearing or proceeding earlier than three days after such service.

(b) If after reasonable effort, personal service is not made, the court may at any stage in the proceedings make an order providing for substituted service in the manner provided for substituted service in civil process in courts of record.

Amended by L. 1994, Ch. 222, § 16, eff. Jan. 1, 1995, amending subd. (a).

ANNOTATION

Service.—Out-of-state personal service is impermissible in proceedings brought pursuant to Article 8 of the Family Court Act. Jane O.J. v. Peter L.J., 141 Misc. 2d 434, 532 N.Y.S.2d 955 (Fam. Ct. N.Y. Co. 1988).

§ 827. Issuance of warrant; certificate of warrant.

(a) The court may issue a warrant, directing that the respondent be brought before the court, when a petition is presented to the court under section eight hundred twenty-one and it appears that

(i) the summons cannot be served; or

(ii) the respondent has failed to obey the summons; or

(iii) the respondent is likely to leave the jurisdiction; or

(iv) a summons, in the court's opinion, would be ineffectual; or

(v) the safety of the petitioner is endangered; or

(vi) the safety of a child is endangered; or

(vii) aggravating circumstances exist which require the immediate arrest of the respondent. For the purposes of this section aggravating circumstances shall mean physical injury or serious physical injury to the petitioner caused by the respondent, the use of a dangerous instrument against the petitioner by the respondent, a history of repeated violations of prior orders of protection by the respondent, prior convictions for crimes against the petitioner by the respondent or the exposure of any family or household member to physical injury by the respondent and like incidents, behaviors and occurrences which to the court constitute an immediate and ongoing danger to the petitioner, or any member of the petitioner's family or household.

(b) The petitioner may not serve a warrant upon the respondent, unless the court itself grants such permission upon the application of the petitioner. The clerk of the court may issue to the petitioner or to the representative of an incorporated charitable or philanthropic society having a legitimate interest in the family a certificate stating that a warrant for the respondent has been issued by the court. The presentation of such certificate by said petitioner or representative to any peace officer, acting pursuant to his special duties, or a police officer authorizes him to arrest the respondent and take him to court.

(c) A certificate of warrant expires ninety days from the date of issue but may be renewed from time to time by the clerk of the court.

(d) Rules of court shall provide that a record of all unserved warrants be kept and that periodic reports concerning unserved warrants be made.

Amended by L. 1980, Ch. 843, eff. Sept. 1, 1980; L. 1988, Ch. 271, § 1, eff. July 19, 1988; L. 1994, Ch. 222, § 17, eff. Jan. 1, 1995, amending subd. (a)(vi) and adding subd. (a)(vii).

ANNOTATIONS

Aggravating circumstances.—Aggravating circumstances, justifying an order of protection for three years and exclusion of appellant from marital residence was supported by finding appellant committed numerous violent acts against petitioner. Victoria C., v. Higinio C., 1 A.D.3d 173, 766 N.Y.S.2d 563 (1st Dept. 2003).

—Order of protection modified to included extended period of protection that was warranted in the presence of aggravating circumstances, specifically, violent and harassing behavior by husband in presence of wife and infant child, which constituted an immediate and ongoing danger to them. Reilly v. Reilly, 254 A.D.2d 361, 688 N.Y.S.2d 153 (2d Dept. 1998).

Supreme Court jurisdiction.—"Stay" issued by the Supreme Court was a nullity when it sought to prevent the Family Court from holding a plenary hearing after it had issued an *ex parte* order of protection based on wife's testimony that her husband assaulted her. Ardis S. v. Sanford S., 88 Misc. 2d 724, 389 N.Y.S.2d 529 (Fam. Ct. Kings Co. 1976).

§ 828. Temporary order of protection; temporary order for child support.

1.   (a) Upon the filing of a petition or counter-claim under this article, the court for good cause shown may issue a temporary order of protection, which may contain any of the provisions authorized on the making of an order of protection under section eight hundred forty-two, provided that the court shall make a determination, and the court shall state such determination in a written decision or on the record, whether to impose a condition pursuant to this subdivision, provided further, however, that failure to make such a determination shall not affect the validity of such order of protection. In making such determination, the court shall consider, but shall not be limited to consideration of, whether the temporary order of protection is likely to achieve its purpose in the absence of such a condition, conduct subject to prior orders of protection, prior incidents of abuse, extent of past or present injury, threats, drug or alcohol abuse, and access of weapons.

(b) Upon the filing of a petition under this article, or as soon thereafter as the petitioner appears before the court, the court shall advise the petitioner of the right to proceed in both the family and criminal courts, pursuant to the provisions of section one hundred fifteen of this act.

2. A temporary order of protection is not a finding of wrongdoing.

3. The court may issue or extend a temporary order of protection *ex parte* or on notice simultaneously with the issuance of a warrant, directing that the respondent be arrested and brought before

the court, pursuant to section eight hundred twenty-seven of this article.

4. Notwithstanding the provisions of section eight hundred seventeen of this article the court may, together with a temporary order of protection issued pursuant to this section, issue an order for temporary child support, in an amount sufficient to meet the needs of the child, without a showing of immediate or emergency need. The court shall make an order for temporary child support notwithstanding that information with respect to income and assets of the respondent may be unavailable. Where such information is available, the court may make an award for temporary child support pursuant to the formula set forth in subdivision one of section four hundred thirteen of this act. An order making such award shall be deemed to have been issued pursuant to article four of this act. Upon making an order for temporary child support pursuant to this subdivision, the court shall advise the petitioner of the availability of child support enforcement services by the support collection unit of the local department of social services, to enforce the temporary order and to assist in securing continued child support, and shall set the support matter down for further proceedings in accordance with article four of this act.

Where the court determines that the respondent has employer-provided medical insurance, the court may further direct, as part of an order of temporary support under this subdivision, that a medical support execution be issued and served upon the respondent's employer as provided for in section fifty-two hundred forty-one of the civil practice law and rules.

Added by L. 1964, Ch. 156, eff. Mar. 23, 1964; **Amended** by L. 1977, Ch. 449; L. 1980, Ch. 530, eff. June 24, 1980; L. 1988, Ch. 702, § 2, eff. Sept. 2, 1988; L. 1988, Ch. 706, § 7, eff. Sept. 2, 1988; L. 1994, Ch. 222, § 17-a, eff. Jan. 1, 1995, amending the section heading; L. 1994, Ch. 222, § 18, eff. Jan. 1, 1995, amending subd. 1 and adding subd. 1(b); L. 1994, Ch. 222, § 19, eff. Jan. 1, 1995, adding subd. 4.

Part 3. Hearing

Section

§ 832. Definition of "fact-finding hearing."

When used in this article, fact-finding hearing means a hearing to determine whether the allegations of a petition under section eight hundred twenty-one are supported by a fair preponderance of the evidence.

Amended by L. 1963, Ch. 529, eff. Apr. 23, 1963.

§ 833. Definition of "dispositional hearing."

When used in this article, dispositional hearing means in the case of a petition under this article a hearing to determine what order of disposition should be made.

§ 834. Evidence.

Only competent, material and relevant evidence may be admitted in a fact-finding hearing; only material and relevant evidence may be admitted in a dispositional hearing.

Amended by L. 1963, Ch. 529, eff. Apr. 23, 1963.

§ 835. Sequence of hearings.

(a) Upon completion of the fact-finding hearing, the dispositional hearing may commence immediately after the required findings are made.

(b) Reports prepared by the probation service for use by the court at any time prior to the making of an order of disposition shall be deemed confidential information furnished to the court which the court in a proper case may, in its discretion, withhold from or disclose in whole or in part to the law guardian, counsel, party in interest, or other appropriate person. Such reports may not be furnished to the court prior to the completion of a fact-finding hearing, but may be used in a dispositional hearing.

Amended by L. 1963, Ch. 529, eff. Apr. 23, 1963.

ANNOTATION

Report; availability to court.—The evidence on the record was convincing in establishing the delinquent conduct of appellant; and, for that reason, the action of the probation officer, in releasing his report too early to the court, could not be considered reversible error. It is the clear policy of the law that the probation service should not communicate reports to the court concerning the alleged delinquent until the fact-finding hearing is completed. Even though the court may not in fact be influenced by what it hears, it is the appearance of prejudice against which the policy is directed, and violation of the statute, albeit inadvertent, should therefore be avoided. *In re* James H., 41 A.D.2d 667, 341 N.Y.S.2d 92 (2d Dept. 1973).

§ 836. Adjournments.

(a) The court may adjourn a fact-finding hearing or a dispositional hearing for good cause shown on its own motion or on motion of either party.

(b) At the conclusion of a fact-finding hearing and after it has made findings required before a dispositional hearing may commence, the court may adjourn the proceedings to enable it to make inquiry into the surroundings, conditions, and capacities of the persons involved in the proceedings.

Amended by L. 1963, Ch. 529, eff. Apr. 23, 1963.

§ 838. Petitioner and respondent may have friend or relative present.

Unless the court shall find it undesirable, the petitioner shall be entitled to a non-witness friend, relative, counselor or social worker present in the court room. This section does not authorize any such person to take part in the proceedings. However, at any time during the proceeding, the court may call such person as a witness and take his or her testimony. Unless the court shall find it undesirable, the respondent shall be entitled to a non-witness friend, relative, counselor or social worker present in the court room in the event such respondent is not represented by legal counsel. This section does not authorize any such person to take part in the proceedings. However, at any time during the proceeding, the court may call such person as a witness and take his or her testimony.

Added by L. 1963, Ch. 529, eff. Apr. 23, 1963.

MISC. LAWS

Part 4. Orders

§ 841. Orders of disposition.

At the conclusion of a dispositional hearing under this article, the court may enter an order:

(a) dismissing the petition, if the allegations of the petition are not established; or

(b) suspending judgment for a period not in excess of six months; or

(c) placing the respondent on probation for a period not exceeding one year, and requiring respondent to participate in a batterer's education program designed to help end violent behavior, which may include referral to drug and alcohol counseling, and to pay the costs thereof if respondent has the means to do so, provided however that nothing contained herein shall be deemed to require payment of the costs of any such program by the petitioner, the state or any political subdivision thereof; or

(d) making an order of protection in accord with section eight hundred forty-two of this part; or

(e) directing payment of restitution in an amount not to exceed ten thousand dollars. An order of restitution may be made in conjunction with any order of disposition authorized under subdivisions (b), (c), or (d) of this section. In no case shall an order of restitution be issued where the court determines that the respondent has already paid such restitution as part of the disposition or settlement of another proceeding arising from the same act or acts alleged in the petition before the court.

No order of protection may direct any party to observe conditions of behavior unless the party requesting the order of protection has served and filed a petition or counter-claim in accordance with section one hundred fifty-four-b of this act. Nothing in this section shall preclude the issuance of a temporary order of protection ex parte, pursuant to section eight hundred twenty-eight of this article.

Nothing in this section shall preclude the issuance of both an order of probation and an order of protection as part of the order of disposition.

Notwithstanding the foregoing provisions, an order of protection, or temporary order of protection where applicable, may be entered against a former spouse and persons who have a child in common, regardless whether such persons have been married or have lived together at any time.

Amended by L. 1977, Ch. 449; L. 1980, Ch. 531, eff. June 24, 1980; L. 1981, Ch. 416, eff. Aug. 6, 1981; L. 1984, Ch. 948, eff. Nov. 1, 1984; L. 1988, Ch. 706, § 8, eff. Sept. 2, 1988; L. 1994, Ch. 222, § 20, eff. Jan. 1, 1995, amending subd. (c); L. 1994, Ch. 222, § 21, eff. Jan. 1, 1995, amending subd. (d) and adding subd. (e).

ANNOTATION

Aggravating circumstances.—Where temporary order of protection was not in effect on date of assault of husband by former wife, court erred when it found she had violated temporary order of protection, sentence of former wife to a 30-day term of incarceration for assault exceeded court's authority. Shamper v. Shamper, 1 A.D.3d 441, 766 N.Y.S.2d 696 (2d Dept. 2003).

Commencement of divorce action in Supreme Court does not oust Family Court of jurisdiction.—Petitioner commenced a proceeding upon a petition alleging an assault on her committed by respondent, her husband; before the matter was heard, however, petitioner instituted an action for divorce against respondent, in the Supreme Court, alleging cruelty (based on the assault). The Family Court erroneously concluded that the commencement and maintenance of the divorce action had deprived it of jurisdiction; but the Family Court's exclusive original jurisdiction over a "family offense" proceeding between spouses (vested in the Family Court by Article 8 of the Family Court Act) is in no way affected by the subsequent commencement of a divorce action in the Supreme Court. Such a factor may, however, be considered by the Family Court in concluding that its processes are "inappropriate" or that its aid is not required (FCA § § 816, 841). Hrab v. Hrab, 39 A.D.2d 745, 332 N.Y.S.2d 91 (2d Dept. 1972).

§ 842. Order of protection.

An order of protection under section eight hundred forty-one of this part shall set forth reasonable conditions of behavior to be observed for a period not in excess of two years by the petitioner or respondent or for a period not in excess of five years upon (i) a finding by the court on the record of the existence of aggravating circumstances as defined in paragraph (vii) of subdivision (a) of section eight hundred twenty-seven of this article; or (ii) a finding by the court on the record that the conduct alleged in the petition is in violation of a valid order of protection. Any finding of aggravating circumstances pursuant to this section shall be stated on the record and upon the order of protection. Any order of protection issued pursuant to this section shall specify if an order of probation is in effect. Any order of protection issued pursuant to this section may require the petitioner or the respondent:

(a) to stay away from the home, school, business or place of employment of any other party, the other spouse, the other parent, or the child, and to stay away from any other specific location designated by the court, provided that the court shall make a determination, and shall state such determination in a written decision or on the record, whether to impose a condition pursuant to this subdivision, provided further, however, that failure to make such a determination shall not affect the validity of such order of protection. In making such determination, the court shall consider, but shall not be limited to consideration of, whether the order of protection is likely to achieve its purpose in the absence of such a condition, conduct subject to prior orders of protection, prior incidents of abuse, extent of past or present injury, threats, drug or alcohol abuse, and access to weapons;

(b) to permit a parent, or a person entitled to visitation by a court order or a separation agreement, to visit the child at stated periods;

(c) to refrain from committing a family offense, as defined in subdivision one of section eight hundred twelve of this act, or any criminal offense against the child or against the other parent or against any person to whom custody of the child is awarded, or from harassing, intimidating or threatening such persons;

(d) to permit a designated party to enter the residence during a specified period of time in order to remove personal belongings not in issue in this proceeding or in any other proceeding or action under this act or the domestic relations law;

(e) to refrain from acts of commission or omission that create an unreasonable risk to the health, safety or welfare of a child;

(f) to pay the reasonable counsel fees and disbursements involved in obtaining or enforcing the order of the person who is protected by such order if such order is issued or enforced;

(g) to require the respondent to participate in a batterer's education program designed to help end violent behavior, which may include referral to drug and alcohol counselling, and to pay the costs thereof if the person has the means to do so, provided however that nothing contained herein shall be deemed to require payment of the costs of any such program by the petitioner, the state or any political subdivision thereof; and

(h) to provide, either directly or by means of medical and health insurance, for expenses incurred for medical care and treatment arising from the incident or incidents forming the basis for the issuance of the order:

The court may also award custody of the child, during the term of the order of protection to either parent, or to an appropriate relative within the second degree. Nothing in this section gives the court power to place or board out any child or to commit a child to an institution or agency. The court may also upon the showing of special circumstances extend the order of protection for a reasonable period of time.

Notwithstanding the provisions of section eight hundred seventeen of this article, where a temporary order of child support has not already been issued, the court may in addition to the issuance of an order of protection pursuant to this section, issue an order for temporary child support in an amount sufficient to meet the needs of the child, without a showing of immediate or emergency need. The court shall make an order for temporary child support notwithstanding that information with respect to income and assets of the respondent may be unavailable. Where such information is available, the court may make an award for temporary child support pursuant to the formula set forth in subdivision one of section four hundred thirteen of this act. Temporary orders of support issued pursuant to this article shall be deemed to have been issued pursuant to section four hundred thirteen of this act.

Upon making an order for temporary child support pursuant to this subdivision, the court shall advise the petitioner of the availability of child support enforcement services by the support collection unit of the local department of social services, to enforce the temporary order and to assist in securing continued child support, and shall set the support matter down for further proceedings in accordance with article four of this act.

Where the court determines that the respondent has employer-provided medical insurance, the court may further direct, as part of an order of temporary support under this subdivision, that a medical support execution be issued and served upon the respondent's employer as provided for in section fifty-two hundred forty-one of the civil practice law and rules.

Notwithstanding the foregoing provisions, an order of protection, or temporary order of protection where applicable, may be entered against a former spouse and persons who have a child in common, regardless whether such persons have been married or have lived together at any time.

(i) to observe such other conditions as are necessary to further the purposes of protection.

Amended by L. 1972, Ch. 761; L. 1980, Ch. 532, eff. June 24, 1980; L. 1981, Ch. 416, eff. Aug. 6, 1981; L. 1984, Ch. 948, eff. Nov. 1, 1984, L. 1988, Ch. 702, eff. Sept. 2, 1988; L. 1988, Ch. 706, eff. Sept. 2, 1988; L. 1994, Ch. 222, § 22, and Ch. 224, § 3, eff. Jan. 1, 1995; L. 1995, Ch. 483, § 11, amending subds. (a)-(e), eff. Nov. 1, 1995; L. 1995, Ch. 483, § 12, adding subd. (i), eff. Nov. 1, 1995; L. 2003, Ch. 579, § 1, eff. Oct. 22, 2003, amending opening paragraph.

MISC. LAWS

Aggravating circumstances.—Order of protection properly issued where testimony at Family Court hearing established appellant conducted himself in an offensive and frightening manner and committed acts that would constitute offense of harassment in second degree, a violation of PL § 240.26. Dell'Isola v. Dell'Isola, 19 A.D.3d 488, 796 N.Y.S.2d 242 (2d Dept. 2005).

—Order of protection modified from prohibiting appellant from having contact with children until their 18th birthday to "finding aggravating circumstances, the order of protection shall expire on March 10, 2001," since by statute, the order of protection can only be in effect for one year or, in the presence of aggravating circumstances, three years. Rice v. Rice, 280 A.D.2d 677, 720 N.Y.S.2d 845 (2d Dept. 2001).

—Order of protection modified to included extended period of protection that was warranted in the presence of aggravating circumstances, specifically, violent and harassing behavior by husband in presence of wife and infant child, which constituted an immediate and ongoing danger to them. Reilly v. Reilly, 254 A.D.2d 361, 688 N.Y.S.2d 153 (2d Dept. 1998).

—Where neither the record nor the order support a finding of aggravating circumstances, the order of protection, directing appellant to refrain from acts of physical violence against petitioner, cannot be effective for a period of longer than one year. Walsh v. Walsh, 251 A.D.2d 338, 673 N.Y.S.2d 1006 (2d Dept. 1998).

—Where court's findings on the record did not support a finding of aggravating circumstances, the order of protection could not exceed one year in duration. Baker v. Ratoon, 251 A.D.2d 921, 675 N.Y.S.2d 170 (3d Dept. 1998).

Right to counsel.—"[A]n indigent appellant in a proceeding pursuant to Family Court Act article 8 is entitled to the assignment of counsel. Absent a valid waiver of the right to counsel, the determination made following a proceeding at which the indigent appellant's request for counsel was not honored must be reversed." DuBova v. Lekumovich. 302 A.D.2d 459, 754 N.Y.S.2d 583 (2d Dept. 2003).

§ 842-a. Suspension and revocation of a license to carry, possess, repair or dispose of a firearm or firearms pursuant to section 400.00 of the penal law and ineligibility for such a license; order to surrender firearms.

1. Mandatory and permissive suspension of firearms license and ineligibility for such a license upon the issuance of a temporary order of protection. Whenever a temporary order of protection is issued pursuant to section eight hundred twenty-eight of this article:

(a) the court shall suspend any such existing license possessed by the respondent, order the respondent ineligible for such a license, and order the immediate surrender of any or all firearms owned or possessed where the court receives information that gives the court good cause to believe that: (i) the respondent has a prior conviction of any violent felony offense as defined in section 70.02 of the penal law; (ii) the respondent has previously been found to have willfully failed to obey a prior order of protection and such willful failure involved (A) the infliction of serious physical injury, as defined in subdivision ten of section 10.00 of the penal law, (B) the use or threatened use of a deadly weapon or dangerous instrument as those terms are defined in

subdivisions twelve and thirteen of section 10.00 of the penal law, or (C) behavior constituting any violent felony offense as defined in section 70.02 of the penal law; or (iii) the respondent has a prior conviction for stalking in the first degree as defined in section 120.60 of the penal law, stalking in the second degree as defined in section 120.55 of the penal law, stalking in the third degree as defined in section 120.50 of the penal law or stalking in the fourth degree as defined in section 120.45 of such law; and

(b) the court may where the court finds a substantial risk that the respondent may use or threaten to use a firearm unlawfully against the person or persons for whose protection the temporary order of protection is issued, suspend any such existing license possessed by the respondent, order the respondent ineligible for such a license, and order the immediate surrender of any or all firearms owned or possessed.

2. Mandatory and permissive revocation or suspension of firearms license and ineligibility for such a license upon the issuance of an order of protection. Whenever an order of protection is issued pursuant to section eight hundred forty-one of this part:

(a) the court shall revoke any such existing license possessed by the respondent, order the respondent ineligible for such a license, and order the immediate surrender of any or all firearms owned or possessed where the court finds that the conduct which resulted in the issuance of the order of protection involved

(i) the infliction of serious physical injury, as defined in subdivision ten of section 10.00 of the penal law,

(ii) the use or threatened use of a deadly weapon or dangerous instrument as those terms are defined in subdivisions twelve and thirteen of section 10.00 of the penal law, or

(iii) behavior constituting any violent felony offense as defined in section 70.02 of the penal law; and

(b) the court may, where the court finds a substantial risk that the respondent may use or threaten to use a firearm unlawfully against the person or persons for whose protection the order of protection is issued,

(i) revoke any such existing license possessed by the respondent, order the respondent ineligible for such a license and order the immediate surrender of any or all firearms owned or possessed or

(ii) suspend or continue to suspend any such existing license possessed by the respondent, order the respondent ineligible for such a license, and order the immediate surrender of any or all firearms owned or possessed.

3. Mandatory and permissive revocation or suspension of firearms license and ineligibility for such a license upon a finding of a willful failure

to obey an order of protection. Whenever a respondent has been found, pursuant to section eight hundred forty-six-a of this part to have willfully failed to obey an order of protection issued by this court or an order of protection issued by a court of competent jurisdiction in another state, territorial or tribal jurisdiction, in addition to any other remedies available pursuant to section eight hundred forty-six-a of this part:

(a) the court shall revoke any such existing license possessed by the respondent, order the respondent ineligible for such a license, and order the immediate surrender of any or all firearms owned or possessed where the willful failure to obey such order involves

(i) the infliction of serious physical injury, as defined in subdivision ten of section 10.00 of the penal law,

(ii) the use or threatened use of a deadly weapon or dangerous instrument as those terms are defined in subdivisions twelve and thirteen of section 10.00 of the penal law, or

(iii) behavior constituting any violent felony offense as defined in section 70.02 of the penal law; or

(iv) behavior constituting stalking in the first degree as defined in section 120.60 of the penal law, stalking in the second degree as defined in section 120.55 of the penal law, stalking in the third degree as defined in section 120.50 of the penal law or stalking in the fourth degree as defined in section 120.45 of such law; and

(b) the court may where the court finds a substantial risk that the respondent may use or threaten to use a firearm unlawfully against the person or persons for whose protection the order of protection was issued,

(i) revoke any such existing license possessed by the respondent, order the respondent ineligible for such a license, whether or not the respondent possesses such a license, and order the immediate surrender of any or all firearms owned or possessed or

(ii) suspend any such existing license possessed by the respondent, order the respondent ineligible for such a license, and order the immediate surrender of any or all firearms owned or possessed.

4. Suspension. Any suspension order issued pursuant to this section shall remain in effect for the duration of the temporary order of protection or order of protection, unless modified or vacated by the court.

5. Surrender.

(a) where an order to surrender one or more firearms has been issued, the temporary order of protection or order of protection shall specify the place where such firearms shall be surrendered, shall specify a date and time by which the surrender shall be completed and, to the extent possible, shall describe such firearms to be surrendered and shall direct the authority receiving such surrendered firearms to immediately notify the court of such surrender.

(b) the prompt surrender of one or more firearms pursuant to a court order issued pursuant this section shall be considered a voluntary surrender for purposes of subparagraph (f) of paragraph one of subdivision a of section 265.20 of the penal law. The disposition of any such firearms shall be in accordance with the provisions of subdivision six of section 400.05 of the penal law.

(c) the provisions of this section shall not be deemed to limit, restrict or otherwise impair the authority of the court to order and direct the surrender of any or all pistols, revolvers, rifles, shotguns or other firearms owned or possessed by a respondent pursuant to this act.

6. Notice.

(a) where an order of revocation, suspension or ineligibility has been issued pursuant to this section, any temporary order of protection or order of protection issued shall state that such firearm license has been suspended or revoked or that the respondent is ineligible for such license, as the case may be.

(b) the court revoking or suspending the license, ordering the respondent ineligible for such license, or ordering the surrender of any firearm shall immediately notify the statewide registry of orders of protection and the duly constituted police authorities of the locality of such action.

(c) the court revoking or suspending the license or ordering the defendant ineligible for such license shall give written notice thereof without unnecessary delay to the division of state police at its office in the city of Albany.

(d) where an order of revocation, suspension, ineligibility, or surrender is modified or vacated, the court shall immediately notify the statewide registry of orders of protection and the duly constituted police authorities of the locality concerning such action and shall give written notice thereof without unnecessary delay to the division of state police at its office in the city of Albany.

7. Hearing. The respondent shall have the right to a hearing before the court regarding any revocation, suspension, ineligibility or surrender order issued pursuant to this section, provided that nothing in this subdivision shall preclude the court from issuing any such order prior to a hearing. Where the court has issued such an order prior to a hearing, it shall commence such hearing within fourteen days of the date such order was issued.

8. Nothing in this section shall delay or otherwise interfere with the issuance of a temporary order of protection.

Added by L. 1996, Ch. 644, § 4, eff. Nov. 1, 1996; **Amended** by L. 1998, Ch. 597, § 7, eff. Dec. 22, 1998; L. 1999,

Ch. 625, § 9, eff. Dec. 1, 1999; L. 2000, Ch. 434, § 3, eff. Oct. 20, 2000, amending subd. 1(a).

§ 843. Rules of court.

Rules of court shall define permissible terms and conditions of any order issued under section eight hundred forty-one, paragraphs (b), (c) and (d).

§ 844. Reconsideration and modification.

For good cause shown, the family court may after hearing reconsider and modify any order issued under paragraphs (b), (c) and (d) of section eight hundred forty-one.

§ 845. Effect of order of disposition.

[Repealed pursuant to L. 1994, Ch. 222, § 53, eff. Jan 1, 1995.]

§ 846. Petition; violation of court order.

Proceedings under this part shall be originated by the filing of a petition containing an allegation that the respondent has failed to obey a lawful order of this court or an order of protection issued by a court of competent jurisdiction of another state, territorial or tribal jurisdiction.

(a) Persons who may originate proceedings. The original petitioner, or any person who may originate proceedings under section eight hundred twenty-two of this article, may originate a proceeding under this part.

(b) Issuance of summons. (i) Upon the filing of a petition under this part, the court may cause a copy of the petition and summons to be issued requiring the respondent to show cause why respondent should not be dealt with in accordance with section eight hundred forty-six-a of this part. The summons shall include on its face, printed or typewritten in a size equal to at least eight point bold type, a notice warning the respondent that a failure to appear in court may result in immediate arrest, and that, after an appearance in court, a finding that the respondent willfully failed to obey the order may result in commitment to jail for a term not to exceed six months, for contempt of court. The notice shall also advise the respondent of the right to counsel, and the right to assigned counsel, if indigent.

(ii) Upon the filing of a petition under this part alleging a violation of a lawful order of this or any other court, as provided in this section, the court may, on its own motion, or on motion of the petitioner:

(A) hear the violation petition and take such action as is authorized under this article; or

(B) retain jurisdiction to hear and determine whether such violation constitutes contempt of court, and transfer the allegations of criminal conduct constituting such violation to the district attorney for prosecution pursuant to section eight hundred thirteen of this article; or

(C) transfer the entire proceeding to the criminal court pursuant to section eight hundred thirteen of this article.

(c) Service of summons. Upon issuance of a summons, the provisions of section eight hundred twenty-six of this article shall apply, except that no order of commitment may be entered upon default in appearance by the respondent if service has been made pursuant to subdivision (b) of such section.

(d) Issuance of warrant. The court may issue a warrant, directing that the respondent be arrested and brought before the court, pursuant to section eight hundred twenty-seven of this article.

Added by L. 1980, Ch. 530, eff. June 24, 1990; **Amended** by L. 1994, Ch. 222, § 23, eff. Jan. 1, 1995, amending subd. (b); L. 1998, Ch. 597, § 8, eff. Dec. 22, 1998.

ANNOTATIONS

Double jeopardy.—Contempt provision of Family Court Act, Article 8 is a lesser included offense of criminal contempt in the first degree; therefore, prosecution and the imposition of additional punishment for the greater offense, criminal contempt, after prosecution under the Family Court Act, is barred by double jeopardy. People v. Wood, 95 N.Y.2d 509, 719 N.Y.S.2d 639, 742 N.E.2d 114 (2000).

—Section 846(b)(ii) does not permit Family Court to adjudicate crimes under guise of a violation of an order of protection. There can be no adjudication of whether or not a crime has been committed, only a determination of whether there has been a violation of a protective order. Subsequent criminal prosecution for the underlying act(s) which violated the order of protection are not barred by double jeopardy. People v. Arnold, 174 Misc. 2d 585, 664 N.Y.S.2d 1008 (Fam. Ct. Kings Co. 1997).

§ 846-a. Powers on failure to obey order.

If a respondent is brought before the court for failure to obey any lawful order issued under this article or an order of protection issued by a court of competent jurisdiction of another state, territorial or tribal jurisdiction in a proceeding and if, after hearing, the court is satisfied by competent proof that the respondent has willfully failed to obey any such order, the court may modify an existing order to add reasonable conditions of behavior to the existing order of protection, make a new order of protection in accordance with section eight hundred forty-two, may order the forfeiture of bail in a manner consistent with article five hundred forty of the criminal procedure law if bail has been ordered pursuant to this act, may order the respondent to pay the petitioner's reasonable and necessary counsel fees in connection with the violation petition where the court finds that the violation of its order was willful, and may commit the respondent to jail for a term not to exceed six months. Such commitment may be served upon certain specified days or parts of days as the court may direct, and the court may, at any time within the term of such sentence, revoke such suspension and commit the respondent for the remainder of the original sentence, or suspend the remainder of such sentence. If the court determines that the willful failure to obey such order involves violent behavior constituting the crimes of menacing, reckless endangerment, assault or attempted assault and if such a respondent is licensed to carry, possess, repair and dispose of firearms pursuant to section 400.00 of the penal law, the court may also immediately revoke such license and may arrange for the immediate surrender and disposal of any firearm such respondent owns or possesses. If the willful failure to obey such order involves the infliction of serious physical injury as defined in subdivision ten of section 10.00 of the penal law or the use or threatened use of a deadly weapon or dangerous instrument, as those terms are defined in subdivisions twelve and thirteen of section 10.00 of the penal law, such revocation and immediate surrender and disposal of any firearm owned or possessed by respondent shall be mandatory, pursuant to subdivision eleven of section 400.00 of the penal law.

Amended by L. 1981, Ch. 416; L. 1993, Ch. 498; L. 1994, Ch. 222, § 24, eff. Jan. 1, 1994; L. 1998, Ch. 597, § 9, eff. Dec. 22, 1998.

ANNOTATIONS

Contempt; generally.—Stay-away provisions of order of protection were violated when respondent, in close proximity to appellant, verbally abused her when exercising his court-approved visitation with child. Sarmuksnis v. Priest, 21 A.D.3d 381, 800 N.Y.S.2d 28 (2d Dept. 2005).

—Evidence in record clearly established that defendant violated the family court's order of protection by repeatedly telephoning victim with harassing calls, the tapes of which were made part of the record; however, court could not sentence defendant to an intermittent term of 90 weekends because it exceeded the six-month time period permitted. De Ruzzio v. De Ruzzio, 288 A.D.2d 725, 733 N.Y.S.2d 276 (3d Dept. 2001).

—Court properly imposed sentence of 45 days in jail after determining after hearing the respondent willfully violated temporary order of protection by engaging in conduct constituting the family offense of harassment. Lichorowic v. Lichorowic, 241 A.D.2d 624, 663 N.Y.S.2d 1015 (3d Dept. 1997).

—Contempt should not be granted unless the order violated is clear and explicit and unless the act complained of is clearly proscribed. Kuenen v. Kuenen, 122 A.D.2d 616, 504 N.Y.S.2d 937 (4th Dept. 1986).

Lesser included offense.—Defendant's phone calls to ex-wife on five separate occasions, in violation of an order of protection, which resulted in a contempt conviction under FCA § 846-a, was a lesser included offense of criminal contempt in the first degree, PL § 215.51; double jeopardy precluded further prosecution for the same phone calls under that section. People v. Wood, 260 A.D.2d 102, 698 N.Y.S.2d 122 (4th Dept. 1999), aff'd, 95 N.Y.2d 509, 719 N.Y.S.2d 639, 742 N.E.2d 114 (2000).

Jurisdictional defects.—Court rejected claim that the absence of a warning in the summons concerning possible arrest and incarceration, pursuant to Family Court Act § 846(b) constituted a jurisdictional defect; by contesting the contempt application on the merits and failing to object in a timely manner to the omission of the required notice and warning, the appellant waived the protections afforded by the statute. Lewin v. Lewin, 124 A.D.2d 730, 508 N.Y.S.2d 233 (2d Dept. 1986).

§ 847. Procedures for violation of orders of protection; certain cases.

An assault, attempted assault or other family offense as defined in section eight hundred twelve of this article which occurs subsequent to the issuance of an order of protection under this article shall be deemed a new offense for which the petitioner may file a petition alleging a violation of an order of protection or file a new petition alleging a new family offense and may seek to have an accusatory instrument filed in a criminal court, as authorized by section one hundred fifteen of this act.

Added by L. 1978, Ch. 628, eff. July 24, 1978; **Amended** by L. 1994, Ch. 222, § 25, eff. Jan. 1, 1995.

ANNOTATION

Criminal court complaint.—Petitioner in family offense proceeding who claims a violation of a valid temporary order of protection may seek to pursue that violation through a criminal court complaint. Kampa v. Kampa, 268 A.D.2d 432, 703 N.Y.S.2d 486 (2d Dept. 2000).

MISC. LAWS

ARTICLE 10

CHILD PROTECTIVE PROCEEDINGS

(Selected sections)

SUMMARY OF ARTICLE

[*Parts 6 through 8 are not reprinted in this text. For the text of those Parts, please refer to New York Family Law (Yellowbook) (LexisNexis).*]

Part 1. Jurisdiction

§ 1011. Purpose.

This article is designed to establish procedures to help protect children from injury or mistreatment and to help safeguard their physical, mental, and emotional well-being. It is designed to provide a due process of law for determining when the state, through its family court, may intervene against the wishes of a parent on behalf of a child so that his needs are properly met.

ANNOTATIONS

Child abuse; assault.—Whenever the basis of a child's abuse is assault, the proceedings under Article 10 become operative and Article 8, § 813 has no further applicability once a child protective proceeding is first brought in Family Court. The district attorney may simultaneously or thereafter proceed to take the case into criminal court without disturbing the purpose of § 813. People v. Kenyon, 46 A.D.2d 409, 362 N.Y.S.2d 644 (4th Dept. 1975).

Concurrent jurisdiction of Family and Criminal court.—Pursuant to FCA Article 10, the Family Court and Criminal Court have concurrent jurisdiction over proceedings involving child abuse. People v. Easter, 71 A.D.2d 762, 419 N.Y.S.2d 327 (3d Dept. 1979).

Deceased child.—A deceased child may be the subject of an abuse petition. In re Alijah C., 1 N.Y.3d 375, 774 N.Y.S.2d 483, 806 N.E.2d 491 (2004)

Family Court lacks jurisdiction over neglect proceedings

against certain institutions.—Neglect cases under Article 10 of the Family Court Act are limited to natural persons; the statute does not include institutions such as Willowbrook. Accordingly, the Family Court, as constituted, has no jurisdiction over the welfare of institutionalized children at Willowbrook under § 115(a) or § 1012; nor does the court have jurisdiction over mentally retarded or mentally defective children at Willowbrook; such institutions are regulated under the Mental Hygiene Law. In re D., 70 Misc. 2d 953, 335 N.Y.S.2d 638 (Fam. Ct. Richmond Co. 1972).

Purpose of Article 10: Article 8 distinguished.—FCA Article 8 was intended to preserve the family under certain conditions of stress, whereas Article 10 has the two-fold purpose of protecting children from abuse and neglect and to prosecute concurrently those who mistreat their children. People v. Easter, 71 A.D.2d 762, 419 N.Y.S.2d 327 (3d Dept. 1979).

—Article 10 proceedings are civil in nature and are to be clearly distinguished in purpose and intent from criminal actions; they are not designed to punish offenders for acts against their victims, but to protect their victims from further harm. In re Maureen G., 103 Misc. 2d 109, 426 N.Y.S.2d 384 (Fam. Ct. Richmond Co. 1980).

Office of the District Attorney.—The role of the Office of the District Attorney in Family Court is statutorily limited to child abuse cases and designated felony cases; any lesser charge, i.e. neglect or juvenile delinquency, or findings thereon will deprive the Office of the District Attorney from future standing as a party. In re George, 100 Misc. 2d 1003, 420 N.Y.S.2d 478 (Fam. Ct. Monroe Co. 1979).

Surgery and blood transfusion ordered over parent's objection.—Affirming direction of the Family Court that an operation be performed on a 15-year-old child over his mother's religious objections, the Court of Appeals reaffirmed the power of the Family Court and like courts in neglect proceedings to order necessary surgery, and it stressed that the religious objection of a parent to a blood transfusion does not present a bar, at least where the transfusion is necessary to the success of the required surgery. Sampson v. Taylor, 29 N.Y.2d 900, 328 N.Y.S.2d 686 (1972).

§ 1012. Definitions.

When used in this article and unless the specific context indicates otherwise:

(a) "Respondent" includes any parent or other person legally responsible for a child's care who is alleged to have abused or neglected such child;

(b) "Child" means any person or persons alleged to have been abused or neglected, whichever the case may be;

(c) "A case involving abuse" means any proceeding under this article in which there are allegations that one or more of the children of, or the legal responsibility of, the respondent are abused children;

(d) "Drug" means any substance defined as a controlled substance in section thirty-three hundred six of the public health law;

(e) "Abused child" means a child less than eighteen years of age whose parent or other person legally responsible for his care

(i) inflicts or allows to be inflicted upon such child physical injury by other than accidental means which causes or creates a substantial risk of death, or serious or protracted disfigurement, or protracted impairment of physical or emotional health or protracted loss or impairment of the function of any bodily organ, or

(ii) creates or allows to be created a substantial risk of physical injury to such child by other than accidental means which would be likely to cause death or serious or protracted disfigurement, or protracted impairment of physical or emotional health or protracted loss or impairment of the function of any bodily organ, or

(iii) commits, or allows to be committed an offense against such child defined in article one hundred thirty of the penal law; allows, permits or encourages such child to engage in any act described in sections 230.25, 230.30 and 230.32 of the penal law; commits any of the acts described in section 255.25 of the penal law; or allows such child to engage in acts or conduct described in article two hundred sixty-three of the penal law provided, however, that (a) the corroboration requirements contained in the penal law and (b) the age requirement for the application of article two hundred sixty-three of such law shall not apply to proceedings under this article.

(f) "Neglected child" means a child less than eighteen years of age

(i) whose physical, mental or emotional condition has been impaired or is in imminent danger of becoming impaired as a result of the failure of his parent or other person legally responsible for his care to exercise a minimum degree of care

(A) in supplying the child with adequate food, clothing, shelter or education in accordance with the provisions of part one of article sixty-five of the education law, or medical, dental or optometrical or surgical care, though financially able to do so or offered financial or other reasonable means to do so; or

(B) in providing the child with proper supervision or guardianship, by unreasonably inflicting or allowing to be inflicted harm, or a substantial risk thereof, including the infliction of excessive corporal punishment; or by misusing a drug or drugs; or by misusing alcoholic beverages to the extent that he loses self-control of his actions; or by any other acts of a similarly serious nature requiring the aid of the court; provided, however, that where the respondent is voluntarily and regularly participating in a rehabilitative program, evidence that the respondent has repeatedly misused a drug or drugs or alcoholic beverages to the extent that he loses self-control of his actions shall not establish that the child is a neglected child in the absence of evidence establishing that the child's physical, mental or emotional condition has been impaired or is in imminent danger of becoming impaired as set forth in paragraph (i) of this subdivision; or

(ii) who has been abandoned, in accordance with the definition and other criteria set forth in subdivision five of section three hundred eighty-four-b of the social services law, by his parents or other person legally responsible for his care.

(g) "Person legally responsible" includes the child's custodian, guardian, any other person responsible for the child's care at the relevant time. Custodian may include any person continually or at regular intervals found in the same household as the child when the conduct of such person causes or contributes to the abuse or neglect of the child.

(h) "Impairment of emotional health" and "impairment of mental or emotional condition" includes a state of substantially diminished psychological or intellectual functioning in relation to, but not limited to, such factors as failure to thrive, control of aggressive or self-destructive impulses, ability to think and reason, or acting out or misbehavior, including incorrigibility, ungovernability or habitual truancy; provided, however, that such impairment must be clearly attributable to the unwillingness or inability of the respondent to exercise a minimum degree of care toward the child.

(i) "Child protective agency" means any duly authorized society for the prevention of cruelty to children or the child protective service of the appropriate local department of social services or such other agencies with whom the local department has arranged for the provision of child

MISC. LAWS

protective services under the local plan for child protective services or an Indian tribe that has entered into an agreement with the state department of social services pursuant to section thirty-nine of the social services law to provide child protective services.

(j) "Aggravated circumstances" means where a child has been either severely or repeatedly abused, as defined in subdivision eight of section three hundred eighty-four-b of the social services law; or where a child has subsequently been found to be an abused child, as defined in paragraph (i) or (iii) of subdivision (e) of this section, within five years after return home following placement in foster care as a result of being found to be a neglected child, as defined in subdivision (f) of this section, provided that the respondent or respondents in each of the foregoing proceedings was the same; or where the court finds by clear and convincing evidence that the parent of a child in foster care has refused and has failed completely, over a period of at least six months from the date of removal, to engage in services necessary to eliminate the risk of abuse or neglect if returned to the parent, and has failed to secure services on his or her own or otherwise adequately prepare for the return home and, after being informed by the court that such an admission could eliminate the requirement that the local department of social services provide reunification services to the parent, the parent has stated in court under oath that he or she intends to continue to refuse such necessary services and is unwilling to secure such services independently or otherwise prepare for the child's return home; provided, however, that if the court finds that adequate justification exists for the failure to engage in or secure such services, including but not limited to a lack of child care, a lack of transportation, and an inability to attend services that conflict with the parent's work schedule, such failure shall not constitute an aggravated circumstance; or where a court has determined a child five days old or younger was abandoned by a parent with an intent to wholly abandon such child and with the intent that the child be safe from physical injury and cared for in an appropriate manner.

(k) "Permanency hearing" means a hearing held in accordance with section one thousand eighty-nine of this act for the purpose of reviewing the foster care status of the child and the appropriateness of the permanency plan developed by the social services district or agency.

Amended by L. 1971, Ch. 469; L. 1972, Ch. 1015; L. 1973, Chs. 276, 1039; L. 1976, Ch. 666; L. 1977, Ch. 518, "and shall apply to any act of abuse of any child under the age of eighteen which act shall take place on or after the date on which this act shall have become law"; L. 1981, Ch. 984, subd. (f)(i)(B); L. 1984, Ch. 191, subd. (e)(iii); L. 1985, Ch. 676; L. 1996, Ch. 309, § 276, eff. July 13, 1996, amending subd. (i); L. 1999, Ch. 7, §§ 39 and 40, eff. Feb. 11, 1999, amending subd. (e) and adding subds. (j) and (k); L. 2005, Ch. 3, Part B, § 3, eff. Nov. 21, 2005, amending subd. (j), and Part A, § 8, eff. Dec. 21, 2005, amending subd. (k).

ANNOTATIONS

Child abuse.—Although excessive corporal punishment against child can support finding of abuse, single instance of parent striking child with cane which left no mark is not sufficient to support an abuse finding. In re Peter G., 6 A.D.3d 201, 774 N.Y.S.2d 686 (1st Dept. 2004).

—Once petitioner established that a child of this age and physical abilities does not normally sustain burns from which subject child suffered absent abuse, burden of going forward then shifted to respondents to provide a reasonable and acceptable explanation for these injuries which caused child's death, in light of their failure to do this, finding of abuse was affirmed. In re Benjamin L., 9 A.D.3d 153, 780 N.Y.S.2d 8 (2d Dept. 2004).

—Despite lower court's determination of no abuse, appellate court made independent assessment of witnesses and found child abused, evidence established that a 10-month-old infant sustained an injury which ordinarily would not occur in the absence of abuse or neglect, a skull fracture, petitioner's expert witness, who had training and experience in area of child abuse, determined that neither explanations mother offered at hospital were plausible coupled with mother's initial inability to explain injury and then two subsequent versions of events which raised doubt as to the reliability of her account. In re Peter R., 8 A.D.3d 576, 779 N.Y.S.2d 137 (2d Dept. 2004).

—Despite family court finding that father's conduct of failing to carefully test temperature of water before placing child in bath constituted neglect, appellate court reversed, no evidence that father inflicted physical injury upon child by other than accidental means, nor created a substantial risk of death, or serious or protracted disfigurement or that father sufficiently endangered her by creating a substantial risk of serious injury. In re Reannie D., 2 A.D.3d 851, 770 N.Y.S.2d 399 (2d Dept. 2004).

—Evidence established that child was sexually abused by defendant, despite fact that allegations had occurred five years prior to proceedings, where child's account of abuse was consistent with her in camera testimony, caseworker's testimony, and testimony of two experts, and where child's statements and behavior were consistent with those of a sexually abused child. In re Shannon K., 222 A.D.2d 905, 635 N.Y.S.2d 751 (3d Dept. 1995).

Child neglect; proof.—The prerequisite to finding neglect is "proof of actual (or imminent danger of) physical, emotional or mental impairment to the child" in order to ensure that Family Court "will focus on serious harm or potential harm to the child, not just on what might be deemed undesirable parental behavior." Nicholson v. Scoppetta, 3 N.Y.3d 357, 787 N.Y.S.2d 196, 820 N.E.2d 840 (2004).

—Finding of neglect was properly based on evidence that mother inflicted excessive corporal punishment on one child and exposed others to domestic violence. In re Petagaye S., 295 A.D.2d 178, 744 N.Y.S.2d 318 (1st Dept. 2002).

—Evidence child's mother suffered from a severe mental illness which prevented her from taking care of child, coupled with father's inability or unwillingness to recognize danger that mother posed, supported finding that child was neglected. Miyani M. v George T., 4 A.D.3d 430, 771 N.Y.S.2d 354 (2d Dept. 2004).

—Petition supporting determination that child was neglected was supported by testimony from psychiatrist that father suffered from schizophrenia from which he heard voices which directed him to kill people and molest children. In re Soma H., 306 A.D.2d 351, 761 N.Y.S.2d 684 (2d Dept. 2003).

—Evidence that mother and children resided for years in an apartment with unsafe and unsanitary conditions, which were attributable to the mother's neglect rather than the landlord's inattention, supported a finding of neglect. In re Nathifa B., 294 A.D.2d 432, 742 N.Y.S.2d 646 (2d Dept. 2002).

—Evidence that mother exposed the children to acts of domestic violence was sufficient to support a finding of neglect. In re Francis S. (Anonymous), 296 A.D.2d 507, 745 N.Y.S.2d 486 (2d Dept. 2002).

—Neglect was not established where petitioner, Administration for Children's Services, failed to produce evidence that mother knew or should have known that child who fell out of window was not being supervised properly while mother took a nap; however, neglect petitions based on acts of severe domestic violence between parents did provide sufficient evidence for finding of neglect. *In re* Carlos M. (Anonymous), 293 A.D.2d 617, 741 N.Y.S.2d 82 (2d Dept. 2002).

—Finding of neglect was supported by mother's admission that she habitually used crack cocaine. *In re* Sade W. (Anonymous), 286 A.D.2d 770, 730 N.Y.S.2d 721 (2d Dept. 2001).

—Neglect petition was sufficiently supported by evidence of defendant's conviction for murder of estranged wife and mother of his children; although murder of one parent is not *prima facie* evidence of neglect, the behavior was so outrageous that the lack of testimony regarding "actual injury" to the children was not fatal to the department's case. *In re* Scott JJ., 280 A.D.2d 4, 720 N.Y.S.2d 616 (3d Dept. 2001).

—Respondent's actions of fleeing with her children from Connecticut to Canada to avoid legal process instead of addressing legal matters and seeking assistance for her children supported neglect petition. *In re* Trebor UU., 279 A.D.2d 735, 718 N.Y.S.2d 474 (3d Dept. 2001).

—Finding of neglect was established by uncontested proof of respondent's excessive drinking, during and after which the children were subjected to physical harm and domestic violence. *In re* Andrew MM., 279 A.D.2d 654, 719 N.Y.S.2d 317 (3d Dept. 2001).

—A single occurrence of physical abuse can support a finding of neglect. *In re* Mary P., 278 A.D.2d 750, 718 N.Y.S.2d 442 (3d Dept. 2000).

—Although petition supporting the neglect proceeding was properly detailed, there was no proof presented at trial in the form of documentary or medical testimony to support the allegations of neglect, even though this evidence was readily available. *In re* Shawna K., 277 A.D.2d 747, 716 N.Y.S.2d 139 (3d Dept. 2000).

—Proof that a minor is not attending school in the area where the parents reside establishes a prima facie case of educational neglect; where older child missed first three weeks of school, had learning disabilities in math, and younger child was not registered for school until it had been in session for over a month, and where mother told school she had no interest in sending children to school, a finding of educational neglect was supported. *In re* Chad V., 265 A.D.2d 607, 695 N.Y.S.2d 764 (3d Dept. 1999).

—"A finding of neglect must be based upon a preponderance of the evidence." A single instance can constitute neglect, uncontroverted evidence that child sustained rib fractures and burns while under exclusive control of respondents supported finding that child's physical condition had been impaired which raised a rebuttable presumption of neglect. *In re* Jeffrey D., 650 N.Y.S.2d 340, 233 A.D.2d 668 (3d Dept. 1996).

—Neglect petition requires more than a showing that the mother has mild mental retardation; court found no neglect where there was no allegation of actual harm or neglectful acts by the respondent toward the child. *In re* Loraida G, 183 Misc. 2d 126, 701 N.Y.S.2d 822 (Fam. Ct. Schenectady Co. 1999).

—Court rejected claim that child abuse was involved; since the complainant was 18 years old and no longer a "child" within the meaning of § 1012 of the Family Court Act, no proceedings pursuant to Article 10 could be received by the Family Court. People v. Jhon, 150 Misc. 2d 842, 570 N.Y.S.2d 427 (Crim. Ct. Queens Co. 1991).

Deceased child.—A deceased child may be the subject of an abuse petition. *In re* Alijah C., 1 N.Y.3d 375, 774 N.Y.S.2d 483, 806 N.E.2d 491 (2004)

Impairment of emotional health, etc.—"[A] child's frailties, weakness and special needs must be taken into account when they exist"; for a child with such vulnerabilities, the minimum standard of care will of necessity be an "expansive standard," and court will not ignore the threatened impairment of emotional health when deciding placement. *In re* Sayeh R., 91 N.Y.2d 306, 670 N.Y.S.2d 377, 693 N.E.2d 724 (1997).

Injury.—FCA § 1012 requires that alleged injuries be "serious" or "protracted"; father's act of slapping 17-year-old with hand or belt, which inflicted minor injuries at best, did not satisfy requirements of section. People v. Phelps, 268 A.D.2d 692, 701 N.Y.S.2d 494 (3d Dept.), *appeal denied*, 94 N.Y.2d 924 (2000).

Neglect; excessive corporal punishment.—Excessive corporal punishment, which in this case included the step-father striking the child with an electrical cord, rubber hose, and wooden board, is included in the definition of neglect. *In re* Kim HH., 239 A.D.2d 717, 658 N.Y.S.2d 480 (3d Dept. 1997).

Respondent; person legally responsible.—A battered mother cannot be charged with neglect only because she is a victim of domestic violence and her children witnessed the abuse, but she can be charged with neglect because a preponderance of evidence established that the children were actually or imminently harmed by reason of her failure to exercise even minimal care in providing them with proper oversight. Nicholson v. Scoppetta, 3 N.Y.3d 357, 787 N.Y.S.2d 196, 820 N.E.2d 840 (2004)

—Minor sibling was not intended to be target of statute; fourteen year old half-brother of victims was not a "person legally responsible" for his sisters within the meaning of the statute, even though they were the victims of his sexual abuse; he was not their "custodian" nor were the girls left in his care. *In re* Catherine G., 3 N.Y.3d 175, 785 N.Y.S.2d 369, 818 N.E.2d 1110 (2004).

—The record supported the finding that defendant, the uncle of the abused child, was a person legally responsible for the child. *In re* Yolanda D., 88 N.Y.2d 790, 651 N.Y.S.2d 1, 673 N.E.2d 1228 (1996).

—Definition of "person legally responsible" under FCA § 1012(g) extends to 17-year-old defendant accused of sexually abusing his four-year-old sister where he was responsible for caring for her in the absence of their mother; defendant resided in the same household as his sister and baby-sat for her on previous occasions. *In re* Mary Alice V., 222 A.D.2d 594, 635 N.Y.S.2d 278 (2d Dept. 1995).

—Respondent, who over the preceding two years had a relationship with children's mother, regularly cared for children, and had access to their apartment, was properly within the court's jurisdiction as a "person legally responsible." *In re* Nathaniel TT, 265 A.D.2d 611, 696 N.Y.S.2d 274 (3d Dept.), *appeal denied*, 94 N.Y.2d 757 (1999).

—Respondent, step-grandfather of children, acted as functional equivalent of parent, the person responsible for their care, along with his wife when the children came and stayed with them for two to three days at a time, which in this case this was the relevant time period. *In re* Marta B., 650 N.Y.S.2d 371, 233 A.D.2d 667 (3d Dept. 1996).

—Mere fact that respondent, child's grandmother, was a regular member of child's household is insufficient to establish that respondent acted in loco parentis or as the functional equivalent of the parent. *In re* Austin JJ., 232 A.D.2d 736, 648 N.Y.S.2d 727 (3d Dept. 1996).

—Stepfather was a proper respondent under this section. *In re* Kenisha T., 267 A.D.2d 1065, 701 N.Y.S.2d 572 (4th Dept. 1999).

—Supreme Court erred in finding as a matter of law that the infant plaintiff's uncle could not have been a "person legally responsible" as defined in subsection (g) and in dismissing the complaint; court eliminated any factual issue from its consideration concerning whether plaintiff's teacher had reasonable cause to suspect that plaintiff's uncle was responsible for plaintiff's care. Kimberly S.M. v. Bradford Central School, 226 A.D.2d 85, 649 N.Y.S.2d 588 (4th Dept. 1996).

—"Respondent" includes persons acting *in loco parentis*, regardless of whether they are related to the child. *In re* Commissioner of Social Servs. *ex rel.* R./S., 168 Misc. 2d 11, 637 N.Y.S.2d 607 (Fam. Ct. Kings Co. 1995).

§ 1013. Jurisdiction.

(a) The family court has exclusive original jurisdiction over proceedings under this article alleging the abuse or neglect of a child.

(b) For the protection of children, the family court has jurisdiction over proceedings under this article notwithstanding the fact that a criminal court also has or may be exercising jurisdiction over the facts alleged in the petition or complaint.

(c) In determining the jurisdiction of the court under this article, the age of the child at the time the proceedings are initiated is controlling.

MISC. LAWS

(d) In determining the jurisdiction of the court under this article, the child need not be currently in the care or custody of the respondent of the court otherwise has jurisdiction over the matter.

ANNOTATIONS

Article 10 proceedings do not prevent independent action by District Attorney.—After Family Court proceedings were completed, and the Family Court ordered the child placed in foster homes and granted a protective order against defendant (father), the District Attorney presented the matter to the grand jury which indicted defendant for assault; in the County Court, defendant moved for dismissal of the indictment on the grounds that the Family Court never "referred" the matter to the County Court pursuant to FCA § 812 and therefore the County Court lacked jurisdiction. Because there were prior Family Court proceedings under Article 10, the County Court was not required to transfer the matter to the Family Court, and the motion to dismiss the indictment was accordingly denied. People v. Kenyon, 72 Misc. 2d 92, 338 N.Y.S.2d 496 (Monroe Co. Ct. 1972).

Child abuse proceedings; civil law applies.—The civil law applies to child neglect or child abuse proceedings, therefore where the respondent is incompetent and a guardian ad litem had been appointed the trial can proceed. In re Vance A., 105 Misc. 2d 254, 432 N.Y.S.2d 137 (Fam. Ct. N.Y. Co. 1980).

Concurrent civil and criminal trials; constitutional.—FCA § 1013(b) is constitutional and the conclusion of the Family Court child abuse case before the conclusion of the related criminal prosecution does not violate her privilege against self incrimination. In re Vance A., 105 Misc. 2d 254, 432 N.Y.S.2d 137 (Fam. Ct. N.Y. Co. 1980).

Custodial v. non-custodial parents.—Custodial and non-custodial parents have an obligation to care for the welfare of their children. Section 1013 of the Family Court Act is indiscriminate in its use against custodial or non-custodial parents. Where the non-custodial parent, here the father, knew of the danger his son was in as a result of being abandoned by the mother, and was in a position to help but did not, charges of neglect were properly brought under section 1013 against the father. In re James R., 174 Misc. 2d 133, 663 N.Y.S.2d 760 (Fam. Ct. Queens Co. 1997).

Extension of placement nunc pro tunc.—An extension of placement nunc pro tunc may be sought and granted where the original placement was pursuant to Family Court Act, Art. 10 in neglect proceedings, but is not available under Art. 7 in delinquency or PINS proceedings. In re Morris W., 79 Misc. 2d 567, 360 N.Y.S.2d 586 (Fam. Ct. Kings Co. 1974).

Indigent parent in child neglect proceeding; right to be represented by counsel.—An indigent parent faced with the loss of child's society, as well as with the possibility of criminal charges is entitled to the assistance of counsel, and must be so advised; here appellant clearly did not know that an attorney would be provided if she could not afford to retain one—indeed, the trial judge told her that if she desired an attorney she would have to pay out of her own funds; in light of this statement, appellant's negative answer to the question "Do you want an attorney?" could not possibly be deemed an intelligent or understanding waiver of her right to counsel, and, accordingly, the proceeding was remitted to the Family Court for a rehearing at which appellant would have benefit of counsel. In re B., 30 N.Y.2d 352, 334 N.Y.S.2d 133 (1972).

§ 1014. Transfer to and from family court; concurrent proceedings.

(a) The family court may transfer upon a hearing any proceedings originated under this article to an appropriate criminal court or may refer such proceeding to the appropriate district attorney if it concludes, that the processes of the family court are inappropriate or insufficient. The family court may continue the proceeding under this article after such transfer or referral and if the proceeding is continued, the family court may

enter any preliminary order, as authorized by section one thousand twenty-seven, in order to protect the interests of the child pending a final order of disposition.

(b) Any criminal complaint charging facts amounting to abuse or neglect under this article may be transferred by the criminal court in which the complaint was made to the family court in the county in which the criminal court is located, unless the family court has transferred the proceeding to the criminal court. The family court shall then, upon a hearing, determine what further action is appropriate. After the family court makes this determination, any criminal complaint may be transferred back to the criminal court, with or without retention of the proceeding in the family court, or may be retained solely in the family court, or if there appears to be no basis for the complaint, it may be dismissed by the family court. If the family court determines a petition should be filed, proceedings under this act shall be commenced as soon as practicable.

(c) Nothing in this article shall be interpreted to preclude concurrent proceedings in the family court and a criminal court.

(d) In any hearing conducted by the family court under this section, the court may grant the respondent or potential respondent testimonial immunity in any subsequent criminal court proceeding.

Amended by L. 1972, Ch. 1016, eff. June, 8, 1972.

ANNOTATIONS

Finding of probable cause in a felony hearing; motion to transfer to Family Court denied.—Motion to transfer prosecution to family court was denied where there had been a finding in a felony hearing in criminal court of probable cause sufficient to hold defendant for the Grand Jury even in the absence of Grand Jury indictment, such hearing converted the complaint to an information and hence it could qualify as a "complaint" as used in FCA § 1014(b). People v. Edwards, 101 Misc. 2d 747, 422 N.Y.S.2d 324 (N.Y.C. Crim. Ct. 1979).

Hearing requirement.—The requirement of a hearing contained in FCA § 1014(a) was held to have been satisfied where the Family Court stated that it had taken cognizance of the medical report setting forth the child's injuries and certain statements of the social workers together with admissions by the defendant and that it had made examinations and inquiries into the facts and circumstances of the case and into the surroundings, conditions and capacities of the person involved; conformance with the requirements of a criminal trial or an administrative hearing is unnecessary. People v. Easter, 71 A.D.2d 762, 419 N.Y.S.2d 327 (3d Dept. 1979).

§ 1015. Venue.

(a) Proceedings under this article may be originated in the county in which the child resides or is domiciled at the time of the filing of the petition or in the county in which the person having custody of the child resides or is domiciled. For the purposes of this section, residence shall include a dwelling unit or facility which provides shelter to homeless persons or families on an emergency or temporary basis.

(b) If in another proceeding under this act the

court directs the filing of an abuse or neglect petition, the venue provision of the article under which the other proceeding is brought and the provisions of part seven of article one shall apply.

Amended by L. 1987, Ch. 97, eff. June, 8, 1987.

§ 1015-a. Court ordered services.

In any proceeding under this article, the court may order a social services official to provide or arrange for the provision of services or assistance to the child and his or her family to facilitate the protection of the child, the rehabilitation of the family and, as appropriate, the discharge of the child from foster care. Such order shall not include the provision of any service or assistance to the child and his or her family which is not authorized or required to be made available pursuant to the comprehensive annual services program plan then in effect. In any order issued pursuant to this section the court may require a social service official to make periodic progress reports to the court on the implementation of such order. Nothing in such order shall preclude any party from exercising its rights under this article or any other provision of law relating to the return of the care and custody of the child by a social services official to the parent, parents or guardian. Violation of such order shall be subject to punishment pursuant to section seven hundred fifty-three of the judiciary law.

Amended by L. 1987, Ch. 760, eff. Aug. 7, 1987.

§ 1016. Appointment of law guardian.

The court shall appoint a law guardian to represent a child who has been allegedly abused or neglected upon the earliest occurrence of any of the following: (i) the court receiving notice, pursuant to paragraph (iv) of subdivision (b) of section ten hundred twenty-four of this act, of the emergency removal of the child; (ii) an application for an order for removal of the child prior to the filing of a petition, pursuant to section one thousand twenty-two of this act; or (iii) the filing of a petition alleging abuse or neglect pursuant to this article.

Whenever a law guardian has been appointed by the family court pursuant to section two hundred forty-nine of this act to represent a child in a proceeding under this article, such appointment shall continue without further court order or appointment during (i) an order of disposition issued by the court pursuant to section one thousand fifty-two of this article directing supervision, protection or suspending judgment, or any extension thereof; (ii) an adjournment in contemplation of dismissal as provided for in section one thousand thirty-nine of this article or any extension thereof; or (iii) the pendency of the foster care placement ordered pursuant to section one thousand fifty-two of this article. All notices and reports required by law shall be provided to such law guardian. Such appointment shall terminate upon the expiration of such order, unless another appointment of a law guardian has been made by the court or unless such law guardian makes application to the court to be relieved of his or her appointment. Upon approval of such application to be relieved, the court shall immediately appoint another law guardian to whom all notices and reports required by law shall be provided.

A law guardian shall be entitled to compensation pursuant to applicable provisions of law for services rendered up to and including disposition of the petition. The law guardian shall, by separate application, be entitled to compensation for services rendered subsequent to the disposition of the petition.

Nothing in this section shall be construed to limit the authority of the court to remove a law guardian from his or her assignment.

Added by L. 1990, Ch. 319, eff. Jan. 1, 1991; **Amended** by L. 1990, Ch. 560, eff. Jan. 1, 1991, adding last paragraph; L. 1997, Ch. 353, § 1, eff. Nov. 3, 1997, amending second undesignated paragraph; L. 2005, Ch. 3, Part A, § 9, eff. Dec. 21, 2005, amending second undesignated paragraph.

§ 1017. Placement of children.

1. In any proceeding under this article, when the court determines that a child must be removed from his or her home, pursuant to part two of this article, or placed, pursuant to section one thousand fifty-five of this article, the court shall direct the local commissioner of social services to conduct an immediate investigation to locate any non-respondent parent of the child and any relatives of the child, including all of the child's grandparents, and inform them of the pendency of the proceeding and of the opportunity for becoming foster parents or for seeking custody or care of the child, and that the child may be adopted by foster parents if attempts at reunification with the birth parent are not required or are unsuccessful. The local commissioner of social services shall record the results of such investigation, including, but not limited to, the name, last known address, social security number, employer's address and any other identifying information to the extent known regarding any non-respondent parent, in the uniform case record maintained pursuant to section four hundred nine-f of the social services law. For the purpose of this section, "non-respondent parent" shall include a person entitled to notice of the pendency of the proceeding and of the right to intervene as an interested party pursuant to subdivision (d) of section one thousand thirty-five of this article, and a non-custodial parent entitled to notice and the right to enforce visitation rights pursuant to subdivision (e) of section one thousand thirty-five of this article. The court shall determine:

(a) whether there is a suitable non-respondent parent or other person related to the child with whom such child may appropriately reside; and

(b) in the case of a relative, whether such relative seeks approval as a foster parent pursuant to the social services law for the purposes of providing care for such child, or wishes to provide free care and custody for the child during the pendency of any orders pursuant to this article.

2. The court shall, upon receipt of the report of the investigation ordered pursuant to subdivision one of this section:

(a) where the court determines that the child may reside with a suitable non-respondent parent or other relative or other suitable person, either:

(i) place the child in the custody of such non-respondent parent, other relative or other suitable person pursuant to article six of this act and conduct such other and further investigations as the court deems necessary; or

(ii) place the child in the custody of such non-respondent parent, other relative or other suitable person pursuant to this article during the pendency of the proceeding or until further order of the court, whichever is earlier and conduct such other and further investigations as the court deems necessary; or

(iii) remand or place the child, as applicable, with the local commissioner of social services and direct such commissioner to have the child reside with such relative or other suitable person and further direct such commissioner pursuant to regulations of the office of children and family services, to commence an investigation of the home of such relative or other suitable person within twenty-four hours and thereafter approve such relative or other suitable person, if qualified, as a foster parent. If such home is found to be unqualified for approval, the local commissioner shall report such fact to the court forthwith.

(b) where the court determines that a suitable non-respondent parent or other person related to the child cannot be located, remand or place the child with a suitable person, pursuant to subdivision (b) of section one thousand twenty-seven or subdivision (a) of section one thousand fifty-five of this article, or remand or place the child in the custody of the local commissioner of social services pursuant to subdivision (b) of section one thousand twenty-seven or subdivision (a) of section one thousand fifty-five of this article. The court in its discretion may direct that such commissioner have the child reside in a specific certified foster home where the court determines that such placement is in furtherance of the child's best interests.

3. Nothing in this section shall be deemed to limit, impair or restrict the ability of the court to remove a child from his or her home as authorized by law, or the right of a party to a hearing pursuant to section ten hundred twenty-eight of this article.

Added by L. 1989, Ch. 744, § 1, eff. July 24, 1989; **Amended** by L. 2003, Ch. 657, § 1, eff. Jan. 1, 2004, amending subd. 1; L. 2005, Ch. 3, Part A, § 10, eff. Dec. 21, 2005, amending subds. 1 and 2.

Editor's Note: L. 2003, Ch. 657, § 1, eff. Jan. 5, 2004, provides as follows:

"**Legislative intent.** The legislature hereby finds that, with 413,000 children living in grandparent headed households in New York state, grandparents play a special role in the lives of their grandchildren and are increasingly functioning as care givers in their grandchildrens' lives. In recognition of this critical role that many grandparents play in the lives of their grandchildren, the legislature finds it necessary to provide guidance regarding the ability of grandparents to obtain standing in custody proceedings involving their grandchildren. This guidance is in no way intended to limit the state of the law as it relates to the ability of any third party to obtain standing in custody proceedings between such third party and the child's birth parent or parents."

ANNOTATION

Standard.—The standard of least restrictive placement is the standard in an Article 3 proceeding, but it is not the standard for placement orders in Article 10 proceedings. *In re* Virginia S., 158 Misc. 2d 455, 601 N.Y.S.2d 428 (Fam. Ct. Monroe Co. 1993).

Part 2. Temporary removal and preliminary orders

§ 1021. Temporary removal with consent.

A peace officer, acting pursuant to his or her special duties, or a police officer or an agent of a duly authorized agency, association, society or institution may temporarily remove a child from the place where he or she is residing with the written consent of his or her parent or other person legally responsible for his or her care, if the child is suspected to be an abused or neglected child under this article. The officer or agent shall, coincident with consent or removal, give written notice to the parent or other person legally responsible for the child's care of the right to apply to the family court for the return of the child pursuant to section one thousand twenty-eight of this article, and of the right to be represented by counsel and the procedures for those who are indigent to obtain counsel in proceedings brought pursuant to this article. Such notice shall also include the name, title, organization, address and telephone number of the person removing the child; the name, address and telephone number of the authorized agency to which the child will be taken, if available; and the telephone number of the person to be contacted for visits with the child. A copy of the instrument whereby the parent or legally responsible person has given such consent to such removal shall be appended to the petition alleging abuse or neglect of the removed child and made a part of the permanent court record of the proceeding. A copy of such instrument and notice of the telephone number of the child protective agency to contact to ascertain the date, time and place of the filing of the petition and of the hearing that will be held pursuant to section one thousand twenty-seven of this article shall be given to the parent or legally responsible person. Unless the child is returned sooner, a petition shall be filed within three court days from the date of removal. In such a case, a hearing shall be held no later than the next court day after the petition is filed and findings shall be made as required pursuant to section one thousand twenty-seven of this article.

Amended by L. 1980, Ch. 843, eff. Sept. 1, 1980; L. 1990, Ch. 205, eff. Sept. 1, 1990; L. 2005, Ch. 3, Part A, § 12, eff. Dec. 21, 2005.

§ 1022. Preliminary orders of court before petition filed.

(a) (i) The family court may enter an order directing the temporary removal of a child from the place where he or she is residing before the filing of a petition under this article, if

(A) the parent or other person legally responsible for the child's care is absent or, though present, was asked and refused to consent to the temporary removal of the child and was informed of an intent to apply for an order under this section and of the information required by section one thousand twenty-three of this part; and

(B) the child appears so to suffer from the abuse or neglect of his or her parent or other person legally responsible for his or her care that his or her immediate removal is necessary to avoid imminent danger to the child's life or health; and

(C) there is not enough time to file a petition and hold a preliminary hearing under section one thousand twenty-seven of this part.

(ii) When a child protective agency applies to a court for the immediate removal of a child pursuant to this subdivision, the court shall calendar the matter for that day and shall continue the matter on successive subsequent court days, if necessary, until a decision is made by the court.

(iii) In determining whether temporary removal of the child is necessary to avoid imminent risk to the child's life or health, the court shall consider and determine in its order whether continuation in the child's home would be contrary to the best interests of the child and where appropriate, whether reasonable efforts were made prior to the date of application for the order directing such temporary removal to prevent or eliminate the need for removal of the child from the home. If the court determines that reasonable

MISC. LAWS

efforts to prevent or eliminate the need for removal of the child from the home were not made but that the lack of such efforts was appropriate under the circumstances, the court order shall include such a finding.

(iv) If the court determines that reasonable efforts to prevent or eliminate the need for removal of the child from the home were not made but that such efforts were appropriate under the circumstances, the court shall order the child protective agency to provide or arrange for the provision of appropriate services or assistance to the child and the child's family pursuant to section one thousand fifteen-a of this article or subdivision (c) of this section.

(v) The court shall also consider and determine whether imminent risk to the child would be eliminated by the issuance of a temporary order of protection, pursuant to section one thousand twenty-nine of this part, directing the removal of a person or persons from the child's residence.

(vi) Any order directing the temporary removal of a child pursuant to this section shall state the court's findings with respect to the necessity of such removal, whether the respondent was present at the hearing and, if not, what notice the respondent was given of the hearing, whether the respondent was represented by counsel, and, if not, whether the respondent waived his or her right to counsel.

(vii) At the conclusion of a hearing where it has been determined that a child should be removed from his or her parent or other person legally responsible, the court shall set the date certain for an initial permanency hearing pursuant to paragraph two of subdivision (a) of section one thousand eighty-nine of this act. The date certain shall be included in the written order issued pursuant to subdivision (b) of this section and shall set forth the date certain scheduled for the permanency hearing.

(b) Any written order pursuant to this section shall be issued immediately, but in no event later than the next court day following the removal of the child. The order shall specify the facility to which the child is to be brought. Except for good cause shown or unless the child is sooner returned to the place where he or she was residing, a petition shall be filed under this article within three court days of the issuance of the order. The court shall hold a hearing pursuant to section one thousand twenty-seven of this part no later than the next court day following the filing of the petition if the respondent was not present, or was present and unrepresented by counsel, and has not waived his or her right to counsel, for the hearing pursuant to this section.

(c) The family court, before the filing of a petition under this article, may enter an order authorizing the provision of services or assistance, including authorizing a physician or hospital to provide emergency medical or surgical procedures, if

(i) such procedures are necessary to safeguard the life or health of the child; and

(ii) there is not enough time to file a petition and hold a preliminary hearing under section one thousand twenty-seven. Where the court orders a social services official to provide or contract for services or assistance pursuant to this section, such order shall be limited to services or assistance authorized or required to be made available pursuant to the comprehensive annual services program plan then in effect.

(d) The person removing the child shall, coincident with removal, give written notice to the parent or other person legally responsible for the child's care of the right to apply to the family court for the return of the child pursuant to section one thousand twenty-eight of this act, the name, title, organization, address and telephone number of the person removing the child, the name and telephone number of the child care agency to which the child will be taken, if available, the telephone number of the person to be contacted for visits with the child, and the information required by section one thousand twenty-three of this act. Such notice shall be personally served upon the parent or other person at the residence of the child provided, that if such person is not present at the child's residence at the time of removal, a copy of the notice shall be affixed to the door of such residence and a copy shall be mailed to such person at his or her last known place of residence within twenty-four hours after the removal of the child. If the place of removal is not the child's residence, a copy of the notice shall be personally served upon the parent or person legally responsible for the child's care forthwith, or affixed to the door of the child's residence and mailed to the parent or other person legally responsible for the child's care at his or her last known place of residence within twenty-four hours after the removal. The form of the notice shall be prescribed by the chief administrator of the courts.

(e) Nothing in this section shall be deemed to require that the court order the temporary removal of a child as a condition of ordering services or assistance, including emergency medical or surgical procedures pursuant to subdivision (c) of this section.

(f) The court may issue a temporary order of protection pursuant to section ten hundred twenty-nine of this article as an alternative to or in conjunction with any other order or disposition authorized under this section.

Amended by L. 1982, Ch. 379, eff. Sept. 1, 1982; L. 1987, Ch. 776, eff. Aug. 7, 1987; L. 1988, Ch. 478, § 3 eff. Nov. 1, 1988; L. 1988, Ch. 527, § 1 eff. Aug. 11, 1988; L. 1988, Ch. 673, § 1 eff. Sept. 1, 1988; L. 1988, Ch. 727, § 1 eff. Oct. 1, 1989; L. 1990, Ch. 171, eff. Sept. 1, 1990, amending subd.

(a); L. 2005, Ch. 3, Part A, § 13, eff. Dec. 21, 2005, amending subds. (a) and (b).

Child abuse.—Abuse finding based on failure to provide child with proper nutrition, child was hospitalized for malnourishment (at 12 months old she weighed 10 pounds 2.5 ounces), was basis for child's removal from home, placement with cousin and grandmother reversed on appeal since child would still be allowed to reside in home and no evidence that circumstances which caused condition had been remedied. *In re* Toni G., 8 A.D.3d 379, 777 N.Y.S.2d 741 (2d Dept. 2004).

Ex parte removal.—"If the agency believes that there is insufficient time to file a petition [for removal,] the next step on the continuum should not be emergency removal, but ex parte removal by court order [pursuant to § 1022.]" Nicholson v. Scoppetta, 3 N.Y.3d 357, 787 N.Y.S.2d 196, 820 N.E.2d 840 (2004).

§ 1022-a. Preliminary orders; notice and appointment of counsel.

At a hearing held pursuant to section ten hundred twenty-two of this act at which the respondent is present, the court shall advise the respondent of the allegations in the application and shall appoint counsel for the respondent pursuant to section two hundred sixty-two of this act where the respondent is indigent.

Added by L. 1990, Ch. 336, § 2, eff. Sept. 1, 1990.

§ 1023. Procedure for issuance of temporary order.

Any person who may originate a proceeding under this article may apply for, or the court on its own motion may issue, an order of temporary removal under section one thousand twenty-two or one thousand twenty-seven or an order for the provision of services or assistance, including emergency medical or surgical procedures pursuant to subdivision (c) of section one thousand twenty-two, or a temporary order of protection pursuant to section ten hundred twenty-nine. The applicant or, where designated by the court, any other appropriate person, shall make every reasonable effort, with due regard for any necessity for immediate protective action, to inform the parent or other person legally responsible for the child's care of the intent to apply for the order, of the date and the time that the application will be made, the address of the court where the application will be made, of the right of the parent or other person legally responsible for the child's care to be present at the application and at any hearing held thereon and, of the right to be represented by counsel including procedures for obtaining counsel, if indigent.

Amended by L. 1973, Ch. 1029, eff. Sept. 1, 1973; L. 1987, Ch. 776, eff. Aug. 7, 1987; L. 1988, Ch. 527, eff. Aug. 11, 1988; L. 1988, Ch. 673, § 2, eff. Sept. 1, 1988; L. 1990, Ch. 170, eff. Sept. 1, 1990.

§ 1024. Emergency removal without court order.

(a) A peace officer, acting pursuant to his special duties, police officer, or a law enforcement official, or an agent of a duly incorporated society for the prevention of cruelty to children or a designated employee of a city or county department of social services shall take all necessary measures to protect a child's life or health including, when appropriate, taking or keeping a child in protective custody, and any physician shall notify the local department of social services or appropriate police authorities to take custody of any child such physician is treating, without an order under section one thousand twenty-two and without the consent of the parent or other person legally responsible for the child's care, regardless of whether the parent or other person legally responsible for the child's care is absent, if

(i) such person has reasonable cause to believe that the child is in such circumstance or condition that his continuing in said place of residence or in the care and custody of the parent or person legally responsible for the child's care presents an imminent danger to the child's life or health; and

(ii) there is not time enough to apply for an order under section one thousand twenty-two. *

(b) If a person authorized by this section removes or keeps custody of a child, he shall

(i) bring the child immediately to a place approved for such purpose by the local social services department, unless the person is a physician treating the child and the child is or will be presently admitted to a hospital, and

(ii) make every reasonable effort to inform the parent or other person legally responsible for the child's care of the facility to which he has brought the child, and

(iii) give, coincident with removal, written notice to the parent or other person legally responsible for the child's care of the right to apply to the family court for the return of the child pursuant to section one thousand twenty-eight of this act, and of the right to be represented by counsel in proceedings brought pursuant to this article and procedures for obtaining counsel, if indigent. Such notice shall include the name, title, organization, address and telephone number of the person removing the child, the name, address, and telephone number of the authorized agency to which the child will be taken, if available, the telephone number of the person to be contacted for visits with the child, and the information required by section one thousand twenty-three of this act. Such notice shall be personally served upon the parent or other person at the residence of the child provided, that if such person is not present at the child's residence at the time of removal, a copy of the notice shall be affixed to the door of such residence and a copy shall be mailed to such person at his or her last known place of residence within twenty-four hours after the removal of the child. If the place of removal is not the child's residence, a copy of the notice shall be personally served upon the parent or person legally responsible for the child's care forthwith, or affixed to the door of the child's residence and mailed to the parent or other person legally responsible for the child's care at his or her last known place of residence within twenty-four hours after the removal. An affidavit of such service shall be filed with the clerk of the court within twenty-four hours of serving such notice exclusive of weekends and holidays pursuant to the provisions of this section. The form of the notice shall be prescribed by the chief administrator of the courts. Failure to file an affidavit of service as required by this subdivision shall not constitute grounds for return of the child.

(iv) inform the court and make a report pursuant to title six of the social services law, as soon as possible.

(c) Any person or institution acting in good faith in the removal or keeping of a child pursuant to this section shall have immunity from any liability, civil or criminal, that might otherwise be incurred or imposed as a result of such removal or keeping.

(d) Where the physician keeping a child in his custody pending action by the local department of social services or appropriate police authorities does so in his capacity as a member of the staff of a hospital or similar institution, he shall notify the person in charge of the institution, or his designated agent, who shall then become responsible for the further care of such child.

(e) Any physician keeping a child in his custody pursuant to this section shall have the right to keep such child in his custody until such time as the custody of the child has been transferred to the appropriate police authorities or the social services official of the city or county in which the physician maintains his place of business. If the social services official receives custody of a child pursuant to the provisions of this section, he shall promptly inform the parent or other person responsible for such child's care and the family court of his action.

Amended and subds. (d) and (e) added by L. 1973, Ch. 1039; L. 1976, Ch. 880; L. 1980, Ch. 843, eff. Sept. 1, 1980; L. 1982, Ch. 379, eff. Sept. 1, 1982; L. 1987, Ch. 162, eff. Oct. 27, 1987; L. 1989, Ch. 727, § 3, eff. Oct. 1, 1989; L. 1990, Ch. 170, eff. Sept. 1, 1990, amending subd. (b)(iii).

* 1985 Amendments

Amended by L. 1985, Ch. 677, eff. Aug. 1, 1985, amending § 1024(a) and § 1024(d). Ch. 677, § 29, purportedly amended § 1024(b) without formally indicating an amendment. § 1024(b) appears as follows in § 29 of Ch. 677: "(i) bring the child immediately to a place approved for such purpose by the local social services department, unless the person is a physician treating the child and the child is or will be presently admitted to a hospital, and."

ANNOTATION

Requirement of imminent danger.—"[E]mergency removal is appropriate where the danger is so immediate, so urgent that the child's life or safety will be at risk before an ex parte order can be obtained . . . the standard obviously is a stringent one"; whether "imminent danger to life or healthÜ is present is "a fact-intensive determination"; however, injury in the presence of the case worker is not necessary, nor is it necessary that alleged abuser be present at time the child is taken from the home; "persuasive evidence of serious ongoing abuse and, based upon best investigation reasonably possible under the circumstances," can support finding; emotional injury will rarely, if ever, support removal under this section. Nicholson v. Scoppetta, 3 N.Y.3d 357, 787 N.Y.S.2d 196, 820 N.E.2d 840 (2004).

§ 1026. Action by the appropriate person designated by the court and child protective agency upon emergency removal.

(a) The appropriate person designated by the court or a child protective agency when informed that there has been an emergency removal of a child from his or her home without court order shall

(i) make every reasonable effort to communicate immediately with the child's parent or other person legally responsible for his or her care, and

(ii) except in such cases involving abuse, cause a child thus removed to be returned, if it concludes there is not an imminent risk to the child's health in so doing. In cases involving abuse, the child protective agency may recommend to the court that the child be returned or that no petition be filed.

(b) The child protective agency may, but need not, condition the return of a child under this section upon the giving of a written promise, without security, of the parent or other person legally responsible for the child's care that he or she will appear at the family court at a time and place specified in the recognizance and may also require him or her to bring the child with him or her.

(c) If the child protective agency for any reason does not return the child under this section after an emergency removal pursuant to section one thousand twenty-four of this part on the same day that the child is removed, or if the child protective agency concludes it appropriate after an emergency removal pursuant to section one thousand twenty-four of this part, it shall cause a petition to be filed under this part no later than the next court day after the child was removed. The court may order an extension, only upon good cause shown, of up to three court days from the date of such child's removal. A hearing shall be held no later than the next court day after the petition is filed and findings shall be made as required pursuant to section one thousand twenty-seven of this part.

Amended by L. 2005, Ch. 3, Part A, § 14, eff. Dec. 21, 2005, amending subd. (c).

§ 1027. Hearing and preliminary orders after filing of petition.

(a)   (i) In any case where the child has been

removed without court order or where there has been a hearing pursuant to section one thousand twenty-two of this part at which the respondent was not present, or was not represented by counsel and did not waive his or her right to counsel, the family court shall hold a hearing. Such hearing shall be held no later than the next court day after the filing of a petition to determine whether the child's interests require protection, including whether the child should be returned to the parent or other person legally responsible, pending a final order of disposition and shall continue on successive court days, if necessary, until a decision is made by the court.

(ii) In any such case where the child has been removed, any person originating a proceeding under this article shall, or the law guardian may apply for, or the court on its own motion may order, a hearing at any time after the petition is filed to determine whether the child's interests require protection pending a final order of disposition. Such hearing must be scheduled for no later than the next court day after the application for such hearing has been made.

(iii) In any case under this article in which a child has not been removed from his or her parent or other person legally responsible, any person originating a proceeding under this article or the law guardian may apply for, or the court on its own motion may order, a hearing at any time after the petition is filed to determine whether the child's interests require protection, including whether the child should be removed from his or her parent or other person legally responsible, pending a final order of disposition. Such hearing must be scheduled for no later than the next court day after the application for such hearing has been made.

(iv) Notice of a hearing shall be provided pursuant to section one thousand twenty-three of this part.

(b)   (i) Upon such hearing, if the court finds that removal is necessary to avoid imminent risk to the child's life or health, it shall remove or continue the removal of the child and remand him or her to a place approved for such purpose by the social services district or place him or her in the custody of a suitable person other than the respondent. Such order shall state the court's findings which support the necessity of such removal, whether the respondent was present at the hearing and, if not, what notice the respondent was given of the hearing, and, where a pre-petition removal has occurred, whether such removal took place pursuant to section ten hundred twenty-one, ten hundred twenty-two or ten hundred twenty-four of this article. If the parent or other person legally responsible for the child's care is physically present at the time the child is removed, and has not previously been served with the summons and petition, the summons and petition shall be served upon such parent or

person coincident with such removal. If such parent or person is not physically present at the time the child is removed, service of the summons and petition shall be governed by section one thousand thirty-six of this article. In determining whether removal or continuing the removal of a child is necessary to avoid imminent risk to the child's life or health, the court shall consider and determine in its order whether continuation in the child's home would be contrary to the best interests of the child and where appropriate, whether reasonable efforts were made prior to the date of the hearing held under subdivision (a) of this section to prevent or eliminate the need for removal of the child from the home and, if the child was removed from his or her home prior to the date of the hearing held under subdivision (a) of this section, where appropriate, that reasonable efforts were made to make it possible for the child to safely return home.

(ii) If the court determines that reasonable efforts to prevent or eliminate the need for removal of the child from the home were not made but that the lack of such efforts was appropriate under the circumstances, the court order shall include such a finding.

(iii) If the court determines that reasonable efforts to prevent or eliminate the need for removal of the child from the home were not made but that such efforts were appropriate under the circumstances, the court shall order the child protective agency to provide or arrange for the provision of appropriate services or assistance to the child and the child's family pursuant to section one thousand fifteen-a or as enumerated in subdivision (c) of section one thousand twenty-two of this article, notwithstanding the fact that a petition has been filed.

(iv) The court shall also consider and determine whether imminent risk to the child would be eliminated by the issuance of a temporary order of protection, pursuant to section ten hundred twenty-nine of this article, directing the removal of a person or persons from the child's residence.

The court shall also consider and determine whether imminent risk to the child would be eliminated by the issuance of a temporary order of protection, pursuant to section ten hundred twenty-nine of this act, directing the removal of a person or persons from the child's residence.

(c) Upon such hearing, the court may, for good cause shown, issue a preliminary order of protection which may contain any of the provisions authorized on the making of an order of protection under section one thousand fifty-six of this act.

(d) Upon such hearing, the court may, for good cause shown, release the child to the custody of his parent or other person legally responsible for his care, pending a final order of disposition, in accord with section one thousand fifty-four.

(e) Upon such hearing, the court may authorize a physician or hospital to provide medical or surgical procedures if such procedures are necessary to safeguard the child's life or health.

(f) If the court grants or denies a preliminary order requested pursuant to this section, it shall state the grounds for such decision.

(g) In all cases involving abuse the court shall order, and in all cases involving neglect the court may order, an examination of the child pursuant to section two hundred fifty-one of this act or by a physician appointed or designated for the purpose by the court. As part of such examination, the physician shall arrange to have colored photographs taken as soon as practical of the areas of trauma visible on such child and may, if indicated, arrange to have a radiological examination performed on the child. The physician, on the completion of such examination, shall forward the results thereof together with the color photographs to the court ordering such examination. The court may dispense with such examination in those cases which were commenced on the basis of a physical examination by a physician. Unless colored photographs have already been taken or unless there are no areas of visible trauma, the court shall arrange to have colored photographs taken even if the examination is dispensed with.

(h) At the conclusion of a hearing where it has been determined that a child should be removed from his or her parent or other person legally responsible, the court shall set a date certain for an initial permanency hearing pursuant to paragraph two of subdivision (a) of section one thousand eighty-nine of this act. The date certain shall be included in the written order issued pursuant to subdivision (b) of this section and shall set forth the date certain scheduled for the permanency hearing. A copy of such order shall be provided to the parent or other person legally responsible for the child's care.

Amended by L. 1976, Ch. 880, eff. Nov. 29, 1976; L. 1987, Ch. 469, eff. July 27, 1987; L. 1988, Ch. 478, §§ 4, 5, eff. Nov. 1, 1988; L. 1988, Ch. 527, § 4, eff. Aug. 11, 1988; L. 1989, Ch. 727, § 4, eff. Oct. 1989; L. 1990, Ch. 171, eff. Sept. 1, 1990; L. 1991, Ch. 198, eff. June 28, 1991, amending subd. (b); L. 1994, Ch. 36, eff. Apr. 4, 1994, amending subd. (b); L. 2000, Ch. 145, eff. July 1, 2000; L. 2005, Ch. 3, Part A, § 15, eff. Dec. 21, 2005, amending section heading and subd. (a) and adding subd. (h).

ANNOTATIONS

Hearing.—There is no blanket presumption favoring removal; mere identification of existence of a risk of serious harm is not enough to warrant removal; court must balance, on a case by case basis, "whether the imminent risk to the child can be mitigated by reasonable efforts to avoid removal"; court must consider whether imminent risk to the child might be eliminated by other means, such as temporary order of protection or providing services to victim. Nicholson v. Scoppetta, 3 N.Y.3d 357, 787 N.Y.S.2d 196, 820 N.E.2d 840 (2004).

—Family Court was required to hold a hearing within three court days of application, provided petitioner was not present or given opportunity to be represented by counsel at the preliminary hearing pursuant to FCA § 1027, court had no discretion to deny application without a hearing as long as the conditions established by the plain language of the statute were satisfied. *In re* Cory M., 307 A.D.2d 1035, 763 N.Y.S.2d 771 (2d Dept. 2003).

—Modification of temporary order of protection that allowed alleged abuser visitation rights while supervised by his wife was reversed; evidence presented at hearing was of sufficient to raise concern that one child had been sexually abused, and modification of visitation presented an imminent risk to the health and safety of all of the children. *In re* Naomi R. (Anonymous), 296 A.D.2d 503, 745 N.Y.S.2d 485 (2d Dept. 2002).

—Where injuries sustained by female minor were equally consistent with falling off a bicycle (as mother asserted) and sexual abuse, court properly ordered child to remain with mother pending final determination after a full fact-finding hearing. *In re* Erika B., 268 A.D.2d 586, 702 N.Y.S.2d 110 (2d Dept. 2000).

—Although FCA § 1027 requires a hearing to determine whether or not a protection order is in the best interests of the children and to set forth findings for the court's decision, reversal was not warranted where respondents waived their right to the hearing and no hearing was held. *In re* Amanda S., 255 A.D.2d 1009, 679 N.Y.S.2d 774 (4th Dept. 1998).

§ 1027-a. Placement of siblings.

When a social services official removes a child pursuant to this part, such official shall place such child with his or her minor siblings or half siblings who have been or are being remanded to or placed in the care and custody of such official unless, in the judgment of such official, such placement is contrary to the best interests of the children. Placement with siblings or half-siblings shall be presumptively in the child's best interests unless such placement would be contrary to the child's health, safety, or welfare. If such placement is not immediately available at the time of the removal of the child, such official shall provide or arrange for the provision of such placement within thirty days.

Added by L. 1990, Ch. 854, eff. Sept. 1, 1990.

§ 1028. Application to return child temporarily removed.

(a) Upon the application of the parent or other person legally responsible for the care of a child temporarily removed under this part or upon the application of the law guardian for an order returning the child, the court shall hold a hearing to determine whether the child should be returned (i) unless there has been a hearing pursuant to section ten hundred twenty-seven of this article on the removal of the child at which the parent or other person legally responsible was present and had the opportunity to be represented by counsel, or (ii) upon good cause shown. Except for good cause shown, such hearing shall be held within three court days of the application and shall not be adjourned. Upon such hearing, the court shall grant the application, unless it finds that the return presents an imminent risk to the child's life or health. If a parent or other person legally responsible for the care of a child waives his or her right to a hearing under this section, the court shall advise such person at that time that, notwithstanding such waiver, an application under this section may be made at any time during the pendency of the proceedings.

(b) In determining whether temporary removal of the child is necessary to avoid imminent risk to the child's life or health, the court shall consider and determine in its order whether continuation in the child's home would be contrary to the best interests of the child and where appropriate, whether reasonable efforts were made prior to the date of the hearing to prevent or eliminate the need for removal of the child from the home and where appropriate, whether reasonable efforts were made after removal of the child to make it possible for the child to safely return home.

(c) If the court determines that reasonable efforts to prevent or eliminate the need for removal of the child from the home were not made but that the lack of such efforts was appropriate under the circumstances, the court order shall include such a finding.

(d) If the court determines that reasonable efforts to prevent or eliminate the need for removal of the child from the home were not made but that such efforts were appropriate under the circumstances, the court shall order the child protective agency to provide or arrange for the provision of appropriate services or assistance to the child and the child's family pursuant to section one thousand fifteen-a or as enumerated in subdivision (c) of section one thousand twenty-two of this article, notwithstanding the fact that a petition has been filed.

(e) The court may issue a temporary order of protection pursuant to section ten hundred twenty-nine of this article as an alternative to or in conjunction with any other order or disposition authorized under this section.

(f) The court shall also consider and determine whether imminent risk to the child would be eliminated by the issuance of a temporary order of protection, pursuant to section ten hundred twenty-nine of this article, directing the removal of a person or persons from the child's residence.

Amended by L. 1987, Ch. 469; L. 1988, Ch. 478; L. 1988, Ch. 527 (without reference to amendment in Ch. 478); L. 1988, Ch. 673; L. 1989, Ch. 727; L. 1990, Ch. 140; L. 1992, Ch. 697; L. 1994, Ch. 36; L. 2000, Ch. 145, eff. July 1, 2000.

ANNOTATIONS

Hearing.—Balancing test for child's return under § 1028 is same as test for evaluating removal application under § 1022 or § 1027, balancing "imminent risk with the best interests of the child and, where appropriate, the reasonable efforts made to avoid removal or continuing removal"; courts should not use the term "safer course" "to mask a dearth of evidence or as a watered-down, impermissible presumption." Nicholson v. Scoppetta, 3 N.Y.3d 357, 787 N.Y.S.2d 196, 820 N.E.2d 840 (2004).

—Until a fact finding hearing has been held in view of the child's horrible injuries and the lack of any explanation of the cause of those injuries, child cannot be returned to the parents. *In re* Corey T., 81 A.D.2d 785; 439 N.Y.S.2d 18 (1st Dept. 1981).

—Presenting agency failed to establish that returning the child to the grandmother's custody would present an imminent risk of harm to the child; application for return of child granted. *In re* Shevonne C. (Anonymous), 292 A.D.2d 452, 738 N.Y.S.2d 883 (2d Dept. 2002).

—Pursuant to FCA § 1028, a court must hold a hearing prior

to returning to parents a child who was temporarily removed from their custody; where petitioner requested a full evidentiary hearing and no hearing was held or good cause shown, a hearing must be held. *In re* J. Children, 264 A.D.2d 524, 694 N.Y.S.2d 462 (2d Dept. 1999).

—Mother's motion to have child returned to her after being temporarily removed from her custody was properly denied where evidence presented during hearing demonstrated that return of child to mother would present imminent risk of harm to child. Administration for Children's Servs. *ex rel.* Deborah M. v. Kim M., 254 A.D.2d 481, 679 N.Y.S.2d 623 (2d Dept.1998).

—Court's decision to return child to parents pending final determination after hearing was not an abuse of discretion. Petitioner failed to prove that return of child to parents would present an "imminent risk to child." Conditions placed on parents for child's return, specifically, prohibiting mother from bathing and dressing or undressing 10-year-old child, were proper. *In re* Brunello G., 240 A.D.2d 744, 660 N.Y.S.2d 990 (2d Dept. 1997).

—Court reversed order granting return of four-year-old child to mother. Child was autistic and mentally retarded, neither spoke or exhibited an understanding of language, not even his name. Court's decision was based on mother's lack of understanding of child's condition, unexplained cancellation of doctor's appointments and inability to care for child. *In re* Patriciarche O., 650 N.Y.S.2d 279, 233 A.D.2d 448 (2d Dept. 1996).

—FCA § 1028 does not grant the court any discretion to deny a hearing once one has been demanded. *In re* Melissa H., 62 A.D.2d 1045, 404 N.Y.S.2d 49 (2d Dept. 1978).

§ 1029. Temporary order of protection.

(a) The family court, upon the application of any person who may originate a proceeding under this article, for good cause shown, may issue a temporary order of protection, before or after the filing of such petition, which may contain any of the provisions authorized on the making of an order of protection under section ten hundred and fifty-six. If such order is granted before the filing of a petition and a petition is not filed under this section within ten days from the granting of such order, the order shall be vacated. In any case where a petition has been filed and a law guardian appointed, such law guardian may make application for a temporary order of protection pursuant to the provisions of this section.

(b) A temporary order of protection is not a finding of wrongdoing.

(c) The court may issue or extend a temporary order of protection *ex parte* or on notice simultaneously with the issuance of a warrant directing that the respondent be arrested and brought before the court pursuant to section ten hundred thirty-seven of this article.

(d) Nothing in this section shall: (i) limit the power of the court to order removal of a child pursuant to this article where the court finds that there is imminent danger to a child's life or health; or (ii) limit the authority of authorized persons to remove a child without a court order pursuant to section one thousand twenty four of this article; or (iii) be construed to authorize the court to award permanent custody of a child to a parent or relative pursuant to a temporary order of protection.

Added by L. 1975, Ch. 495, eff. July 29, 1975; **Amended** by L. 1981, Ch. 416, eff. Aug. 6, 1981, added subds. (b) and (c); L. 1987, Ch. 67, § 1, eff. May 16, 1987; L. 1988, Ch. 673, § 4, eff. Sept. 1, 1988.

§ 1030. Order of visitation by a respondent.

(a) A respondent shall have the right to reasonable and regularly scheduled visitation with a child in the temporary custody of a social services official pursuant to this part or pursuant to subdivision (d) of section one thousand fifty-one of this article, unless limited by an order of the family court.

(b) A respondent who has not been afforded such visitation may apply to the court for an order requiring the local social services official having temporary custody of the child pursuant to this part or pursuant to subdivision (d) of section one thousand fifty-one of this article, to permit the respondent to visit the child at stated periods. Such application shall be made upon notice to the local social services official and to any law guardian appointed to represent the child, who shall be afforded an opportunity to be heard thereon.

(c) A respondent shall be granted reasonable and regularly scheduled visitation unless the court finds that the child's life or health would be endangered thereby, but the court may order visitation under the supervision of an employee of a local social services department upon a finding that such supervised visitation is in the best interest of the child.

(d) An order made under this section may be modified by the court for good cause shown, upon application by any party or the child's law guardian, and upon notice of such application to all other parties and the child's law guardian, who shall be afforded an opportunity to be heard thereon.

(e) An order made under this section shall terminate upon the entry of an order of disposition pursuant to part five of this article.

Added by L. 1988, Ch. 457, § 4, eff. Nov. 1, 1988.

Part 3. Preliminary procedure

§ 1031. Originating proceeding to determine abuse or neglect.

(a) A proceeding under this article is originated by the filing of a petition in which facts sufficient to establish that a child is an abused or neglected child under this article are alleged.

(b) Allegations of abuse and neglect may be contained in the same petition. Where more than one child is the legal responsibility of the respondent, it may be alleged in the same petition that one or more children are abused children, or that one or more children are neglected children, or both.

(c) On its own motion and at any time in the proceedings, the court may substitute for a petition to determine abuse a petition to determine neglect if the facts established are not sufficient to make a finding of abuse, as defined by this article.

(d) A proceeding under this article may be originated by a child protective agency pursuant to section one thousand thirty-two, notwithstanding that the child is in the care and custody of such agency. In such event, the petition shall allege facts sufficient to establish that the return of the child to the care and custody of his parent or other person legally responsible for his care would place the child in imminent danger of becoming an abused or neglected child.

(e) In any case where a child has been removed prior to the filing of a petition, the petition alleging abuse or neglect of said child shall state the date and time of the removal, the circumstances necessitating such removal, whether the removal occurred pursuant to section ten hundred twenty-one, ten hundred twenty-two or ten hundred twenty-four of this act, and if the removal occurred without court order, the reason there was not sufficient time to obtain a court order pursuant to section ten hundred twenty-two of this act.

(f) A petition alleging abuse shall contain a notice in conspicuous print that a fact-finding that a child is severely or repeatedly abused as defined in subdivision eight of section three hundred eighty-four-b of the social services law, by clear and convincing evidence, could constitute a basis to terminate parental rights in a proceeding pursuant to section three hundred eighty-four-b of the social services law.

Amended by L. 1976, Ch. 666, eff. Jan. 1, 1977; L. 1990, Ch. 171, eff. Sept. 1, 1990, adding subd. (e); L. 1999, Ch. 7, § 41, eff. Feb. 11, 1999, adding subd. f.

§ 1032. Persons who may originate proceedings.

The following may originate a proceeding under this article:

(a) a child protective agency, or

(b) a person on the court's direction.

ANNOTATIONS

District as originator of Family Court proceeding.—FCA § 158 which provides for Family Court protective custody of material witnesses under sixteen includes situations where the pending case is in another court; the District Attorney may be considered a person directed by the court to bring on child protective proceedings under Fam. Ct. Act § 1032. People v. Louise D., 82 Misc. 2d 68, 368 N.Y.S.2d 746 (Fam. Ct. Bronx Co. 1975).

"Person on the court's direction."—Fact that appropriate child protective agency declined to commence proceeding did not preclude court from directing former law guardian to commence action. In re Katelyn E., 241 A.D.2d 494, 661 N.Y.S.2d 522 (2d Dept. 1997).

—Child protective agency cannot be included in class of "persons" covered by FCA § 1032(b). In re Tiffany A., 183 Misc. 2d 391, 703 N.Y.S.2d 381 (Fam. Ct. Queens Co. 2000).

§ 1033. Access to the court for the purpose of filing a petition.

Any person seeking to file a petition at the court's direction, pursuant to subdivision (b) of section one thousand thirty-two shall have access to the court for the purpose of making an *ex parte* application therefor. Nothing in this section, however, is intended to prevent a family court judge from requiring such person to first report to an appropriate child protective agency.

Former section **repealed** and new section **added** by L. 1973, Ch. 1039, eff. Sept. 1, 1973.

§ 1033-a. Initial appearance.

For the purposes of this section, "initial appearance" means the proceeding on the date the respondent first appears before the court after the petition has been filed and any adjournments thereof.

Added by L. 1990, Ch. 336, eff. Sept. 1, 1990.

§ 1033-b. Initial appearance; procedures.

1. (a) At the initial appearance, the court shall appoint a law guardian to represent the interests of any child named in a petition who is alleged to be abused or neglected, unless a law guardian has already been appointed for such child pursuant to section ten hundred sixteen of this act.

(b) At the initial appearance, the court shall advise the respondent of the allegations in the petition and further advise the respondent of the right to an adjournment of the proceeding in order to obtain counsel. The recitation of such rights shall not be waived except that the recitation of the allegations in the petition may be waived upon the consent of counsel for the respondent and such counsel's representation on the record that he or she has explained such allegations to the respondent and has provided the respondent with a copy of the petition and the respondent's acknowledgement* of receipt of the petition and such explanation.

(c) At the initial appearance, the court shall appoint counsel for indigent respondents pursuant to section two hundred sixty-two of this act.

(d) In any case where a child has been removed, the court shall advise the respondent of the right to a hearing, pursuant to section ten hundred twenty-eight of this act, for the return of the child and that such hearing may be requested at any time during the proceeding. The recitation of such rights shall not be waived.

(e) At the initial appearance, the court shall inquire of the child protective agency whether such agency intends to prove that the child is a severely or repeatedly abused child as defined in subdivision eight of section three hundred eighty-four-b of the social services law, by clear and convincing evidence. Where the agency advises the court that it intends to submit such proof, the court shall so advise the respondent.

2. Notice of the initial appearance shall be given to the respondent or the respondent's

attorney if known, the petitioner and the child's law guardian, if already appointed.

* Spelled as such in original. Should be "acknowledgment."

Added by L. 1990, Ch. 336, eff. Sept. 1, 1990; **Amended** by L. 1991, Ch. 69, eff. Apr. 22, 1991, repealing subd. (2); L. 1991, Ch. 75, eff. Apr. 26, 1991, amending subds. (1)(b), (1)(d) and containing subd. (2); L. 1992, Ch. 111, eff. May 21, 1992, amending subd. (l)(b); L. 1999, Ch. 7, § 42, eff. Feb. 11, 1999, adding subd. 1(e).

ANNOTATION

Failure to advise respondent of allegations in petition.— Although court failed to advise respondent of allegations in petition at initial appearance, matter was adjourned, court appointed counsel for respondent, and, at the next appearance, court stated on the record that it had reviewed the petition with respondent; respondent therefore suffered no prejudice, and reversal was not warranted. *In re* Stephanie A., 224 A.D.2d 1027, 637 N.Y.S.2d 904 (4th Dept. 1996).

§ 1034. Power to order investigations.

1. A family court judge may order the child protective service of the appropriate department of social services or request any other appropriate child protective agency to conduct a child protective investigation as described by the social services law and report its findings to the court:

(a) in any proceedings under this article, or

(b) in order to determine whether a proceeding under this article should be initiated.

2. Where there is probable cause to believe that an abused or neglected child may be found on premises, an order under this section may authorize a person conducting the child protective investigation, accompanied by a police officer, to enter the premises to determine whether such a child is present. The standard of proof and procedure for such an authorization shall be the same as for a search warrant under the criminal procedure law.

Former section **repealed** and new section **added** by L. 1973, Ch. 1039, eff. Sept. 1, 1973; **Amended** by L. 1978, Ch. 627, eff. Sept. 1, 1978.

ANNOTATION

Authority of court.—Although Family Court can direct the Administration for Children's Services to initiate an investigation with respect to possible abuse or neglect, that is the extent of its authority, and it cannot control the manner or outcome of that investigation. *In re* Tiffany A., 183 Misc. 2d 391, 703 N.Y.S.2d 381 (Fam. Ct. Queens Co. 2000).

§ 1035. Issuance of summons; notice to certain interested persons and intervention.

(a) On the filing of a petition under this article where the child has been removed from his or her home, unless a warrant is issued pursuant to section one thousand thirty-seven of this part, the court shall cause a copy of the petition and a summons to be issued the same day the petition is filed, clearly marked on the face thereof "Child Abuse Case", as applicable, requiring the parent or other person legally responsible for the child's care or with whom he or she had been residing to appear at the court within three court days to answer the petition, unless a shorter time for a hearing to occur is prescribed in part two of this article.

(b) In a proceeding to determine abuse or neglect, the summons shall contain a statement in conspicuous print informing the respondent that:

(i) the proceeding may lead to the filing of a petition under the social services law for the termination of respondent's parental rights and commitment of guardianship and custody of the child for the purpose of adoption; and

(ii) if the child is placed and remains in foster care for fifteen of the most recent twenty-two months, the agency may be required by law to file a petition for termination of respondent's parental rights and commitment of guardianship and custody of the child for the purposes of adoption.

(c) On the filing of a petition under this article where the child has not been removed from his or her home, the court shall forthwith cause a copy of the petition and a summons to be issued, clearly marked on the face thereof "Child Abuse Case", as applicable, requiring the parent or other person legally responsible for the child's care or with whom the child is residing to appear at the court to answer the petition within seven court days. The court may also require the person thus summoned to produce the child at the time and place named.

(d) Where the respondent is not the child's parent, service of the summons and petition shall also be ordered on both of the child's parents; where only one of the child's parents is the respondent, service of the summons and petition shall also be ordered on the child's other parent. The summons and petition shall be accompanied by a notice of pendency of the child protective proceeding advising the parents or parent of the right to appear and participate in the proceeding as an interested party intervenor for the purpose of seeking temporary and permanent custody of the child, and to participate thereby in all arguments and hearings insofar as they affect temporary custody of the child during fact-finding proceedings, and in all phases of dispositional proceedings. The notice shall also indicate that:

(i) upon good cause, the court may order an investigation pursuant to section one thousand thirty-four of this part to determine whether a petition should be filed naming such parent or parents as respondents;

(ii) if the court determines that the child must be removed from his or her home, the court may order an investigation to determine whether the non-respondent parent or parents would be suitable custodians for the child; and

(iii) if the child is placed and remains in foster care for fifteen of the most recent twenty-two

months, the agency may be required by law to file a petition for termination of the parental rights of the parent or parents and commitment of guardianship and custody of the child for the purposes of adoption, even if the parent or parents were not named as a respondent or as respondents in the child abuse or neglect proceeding.

(e) The summons, petition and notice of pendency of a child protective proceeding served on the child's non-custodial parent in accordance with subdivision (d) of this section shall, if applicable, be served together with a notice that the child was removed from his or her home by a social services official. Such notice shall also include the name and address of the official to whom temporary custody of the child has been transferred, the name and address of the agency or official with whom the child has been temporarily placed, if different, and shall advise such parent of the right to request temporary and permanent custody and to seek enforcement of visitation rights with the child as provided for in part eight of this article.

(f) The child's adult sibling, grandparent, aunt or uncle not named as respondent in the petition, may, upon consent of the child's parent appearing in the proceeding, or where such parent has not appeared then without such consent, move to intervene in the proceeding as an interested party intervenor for the purpose of seeking temporary or permanent custody of the child, and upon the granting of such motion shall be permitted to participate in all arguments and hearings insofar as they affect the temporary custody of the child during the fact-finding proceedings, and in all phases of dispositional proceedings. Such motions for intervention shall be liberally granted.

Amended by L. 1981, Ch. 739, eff. Oct. 26, 1981, changing old subd. (b) to subd. (c) and adding new subd. (b); L. 1986, Ch. 699, eff. Aug. 29, 1986; L. 1987, Ch. 443, eff. July 27, 1987, adding new subd. (d) and (e); L. 1988, Ch. 457, § 5, eff. Nov. 1, 1988, relettering subd. (e) as subd. (f) and adding new subd. (e); L. 2003, Ch. 526, §§ 1–3, eff. Dec. 16, 2003, amending subds. (b), (d), and (e); L. 2005, Ch. 3, Part A, § 16, eff. Dec. 21, 2005, amending subds. (a) and (c).

ANNOTATION

Intervention.—Family Court correctly denied motion of Law Guardian which was to allow the aunt, to intervene in proceedings and to take custody of child, aunt, who is guardian of siblings of subject, repeatedly had told court she could not and would not care for child, aunt waived right to intervene in custody proceeding brought by foster parent by refusing to become involved in case earlier. *In re* David B. 2 A.D.3d 725, 768 N.Y.S.2d 618 (2d Dept. 2003).

§ 1036. Service of summons.

(a) Except as provided in subdivision (c) of this section, in cases involving abuse, the petition and summons shall be served within two court days after their issuance. If they cannot be served within that time, such fact shall be reported to the court with the reasons thereof within three court days after their issuance and the court shall thereafter issue a warrant in accordance with the provisions of section one thousand thirty-seven. The court shall also, unless dispensed with for good cause shown, direct that the child be brought before the court. Issuance of a warrant shall not be required where process is sent without the state as provided for in subdivision (c) of this section.

(b) Service of a summons and petition shall be made by delivery of a true copy thereof to the person summoned at least twenty-four hours before the time stated therein for appearance.

(c) In cases involving either abuse or neglect the court may send process without the state in the same manner and with the same effect as process sent within the state in the exercise of personal jurisdiction over any person subject to the jurisdiction of the court under section three hundred one or three hundred two of the civil practice law and rules, notwithstanding that such person is not a resident or domiciliary of the state, where the allegedly abused or neglected child resides or is domiciled within the state and the alleged abuse or neglect occurred within the state. In cases involving abuse where service of a petition and summons upon a non-resident or non-domiciliary respondent is required, such service shall be made within ten days after its issuance. If such service cannot be effected within ten days, an extension of the period to effect service may be granted by the court for good cause shown upon application of any party or the law guardian. Where service is effected on an out of state respondent and the respondent defaults by failing to appear and answer the petition, the court may on its own motion, or upon application of any party or the law guardian proceed to a fact finding hearing thereon.

(d) If after reasonable effort, personal service is not made, the court may at any stage in the proceedings make an order providing for substituted service in the manner provided for substituted service in civil process in courts of record.

Amended by L. 1990, Ch. 268, eff. Sept. 1, 1990; L. 1991, Ch. 69, eff. Apr. 22, 1991, amending subd. (c).

ANNOTATION

Long arm jurisdiction.—Long arm jurisdiction exists if the child resides or is domiciled in New York and is the subject of abuse or neglect which occurs in the state. However, location of child is not dispositive, perpetration of abuse in New York State provides sufficient "minimum contacts." *In re* Sayeh R., 91 N.Y.2d 306, 670 N.Y.S.2d 377, 693 N.E.2d 724 (1997).

§ 1037. Issuance of warrant and reports to court.

(a) The court may issue a warrant directing the parent, or other person legally responsible for the child's care or with whom he is residing to be brought before the court, when a petition is filed with the court under this article and it appears that

(i) the summons cannot be served; or

(ii) the summoned person has refused to obey the summons; or

(iii) the parent or other person legally responsible for the child's care is likely to leave the jurisdiction; or

(iv) a summons, in the court's opinion, would be ineffectual; or

(v) the safety of the child is endangered; or

(vi) the safety of a parent, person legally responsible for the child's care or with whom he is residing, foster parent or temporary custodian is endangered.

(b) When issuing a warrant under this section, the court may also direct that the child be brought before the court.

(c) In any case involving abuse, the warrant shall be clearly marked on the face thereof Child Abuse Case. If a warrant is not executed within two court days of its issuance, such fact shall be reported to the court within three court days of its issuance. Rules of court shall provide that reports of unexecuted warrants issued under this article shall be periodically made to the court.

(d) In a proceeding to determine abuse, the warrant shall contain a statement clearly marked on the face thereof, that the proceeding could lead to a proceeding under the social services law for the commitment of guardianship and custody of the child and that the rights of the respondent with respect to said child may be terminated in such proceeding under such law.

Amended by L. 1981, Ch. 739, eff. Oct. 26, 1981, adding subd. (d); L. 1988, Ch. 271, § 3, eff. Jul. 19, 1988.

§ 1038. Records and discovery involving abuse and neglect.

(a) Each hospital and any other public or private agency having custody of any records, photographs or other evidence relating to abuse or neglect, upon the subpoena of the court, the corporation counsel, county attorney, district attorney, counsel for the child, or one of the parties to the proceeding, shall be required to send such records, photographs or evidence to the court for use in any proceeding relating to abuse or neglect under this article. Notwithstanding any other provision of law to the contrary, service of any such subpoena on a hospital may be made by certified mail, return receipt requested, to the director of the hospital. The court shall establish procedures for the receipt and safeguarding of such records.

(b) Pursuant to a demand pursuant to section thirty-one hundred twenty of the civil practice law and rules, a petitioner or social services official shall provide to a respondent or the law guardian any records, photographs or other evidence demanded relevant to the proceeding, for inspection and photocopying. The petitioner or social services official may delete the identity of the persons who filed reports pursuant to section four hundred fifteen of the social services law, unless such petitioner or official intends to offer such reports into evidence at a hearing held pursuant to this article. The petitioner or social services official may move for a protective order to withhold records, photographs or evidence which will not be offered into evidence and the disclosure of which is likely to endanger the life or health of the child.

(c) A respondent or the law guardian may move for an order directing that any child who is the subject of a proceeding under this article be made available for examination by a physician, psychologist or social worker selected by such party or law guardian. In determining the motion, the court shall consider the need of the respondent or law guardian for such examination to assist in the preparation of the case and the potential harm to the child from the examination. Nothing in this section shall preclude the parties from agreeing upon a person to conduct such examination without court order.

Any examination or interview, other than a physical examination, of a child who is the subject of a proceeding under this article, for the purposes of offering expert testimony to a court regarding the sexual abuse of the child, as such term is defined by section one thousand twelve of this article, may, in the discretion of the court, be videotaped in its entirety with access to be provided to the court, the law guardian and all parties. In determining whether such examination or interview should be videotaped, the court shall consider the effect of the videotaping on the reliability of the examination, the effect of the videotaping on the child and the needs of the parties, including the law guardian, for the videotape. Prior to admitting a videotape of an examination or interview into evidence, the person conducting such examination or the person operating the video camera shall submit to the court a verified statement confirming that such videotape is a complete and unaltered videographic record of such examination of the child. The proponent of entry of the videotape into evidence must establish that the potential prejudicial effect is substantially outweighed by the probative value of the videotape in assessing the reliability of the validator in court. Nothing in this section shall in any way affect the admissibility of such evidence in any court proceeding. The chief administrator of the courts shall promulgate regulations protecting the confidentiality and security of such tapes, and regulating the access thereto, consistent with the provisions of this section.

(d) Unless otherwise proscribed by this article, the provisions and limitations of article thirty-one of the civil practice law and rules shall apply to proceedings under this article. In determining any motion for a protective order, the court shall consider the need of the party for the discovery to assist in the preparation of the case and any potential harm to the child from the discovery.

The court shall set a schedule for discovery to avoid unnecessary delay.

Amended by L. 1989, Ch. 272, eff. July 7, 1989; L. 1989, Ch. 724, eff. July 24, 1989; L. 1990, Ch. 867, eff. Sept. 1, 1990, adding subd. (d); L. 1991, Ch. 694, eff. Oct. 31, 1991; L. 1992, Ch. 65, eff. July 13, 1992, amending subd. (c).

ANNOTATIONS

Balancing discovery in abuse and neglect cases.—Court properly exercised its discretion by refusing to allow licensed psychologist, hired by child's mother, to testify as an expert concerning evaluations concerning respondent and child, where among other things, evaluations were conducted without approval of law guardian, psychologist was not qualified as an expert in the field of child abuse, and evaluations violated prior order of protection prohibiting contact between child and respondent. *In re* Melissa K., 254 A.D.2d 770, 678 N.Y.S.2d 759 (4th Dept. 1998).

—In balancing state's need for access to victim in order to prepare for case and law guardian's assertion that yet another interview would not be in the best interest of the child, the court declined to grant a third interview to the state; court found the state failed to show a need for another interview and why the specific information requested could not be obtained through the law guardian. *In re* Thea T., 174 Misc. 2d 227, 663 N.Y.S.2d 502 (Fam. Ct. Suffolk Co. 1997).

Deposition of child witness.—Although children who are the subject of child protective matters are not parties to the proceeding and may not be deposed as a party, they may be required to give information as nonparty witnesses where the person seeking discovery establishes a showing of "adequate special circumstances." In addition, the court must balance the movant's need for discovery against the potential harm to the child witness. *In re* Commissioner of Social Servs. *ex rel.* R.J/S., 170 Misc. 2d 126, 647 N.Y.S.2d 361 (Fam. Ct. Kings Co. 1996).

§ 1038-a. Discovery: upon court order.

Upon motion of a petitioner law guardian, the court may order a respondent to provide nontestimonial evidence, only if the court finds probable cause that the evidence is reasonably related to establishing the allegations in a petition filed pursuant to this article. Such order may include, but not be limited to, provision for the taking of samples of blood, urine, hair or other materials from the respondent's body in a manner not involving an unreasonable intrusion or risk of serious physical injury to the respondent.

Added by L. 1987, Ch. 793, eff. Aug. 7, 1987; **Amended** by L. 1991, Ch. 162, eff. June 10, 1991.

§ 1039. Adjournment in contemplation of dismissal.

(a) Prior to or upon a fact-finding hearing, the court may upon a motion by the petitioner with the consent of the respondent and the child's attorney or law guardian or upon its own motion with the consent of the petitioner, the respondent and the child's attorney or law guardian, order that the proceeding be "adjourned in contemplation of dismissal." Under no circumstances shall the court order any party to consent to an order under this section. The court may make such order only after it has apprised the respondent of the provisions of this section, particularly subdivision (e), and it is satisfied that the respondent understands the effect of such provisions.

(b) An adjournment in contemplation of

MISC. LAWS

dismissal is an adjournment of the proceeding for a period not to exceed one year with a view to ultimate dismissal of the petition in furtherance of justice. Upon the consent of the petitioner, the respondent and the child's attorney or law guardian, the court may issue an order extending such period for such time and upon such conditions as may be agreeable to the parties.

(c) In any order issued pursuant to this section, such agency shall be directed to make a progress report to the court, the parties and the child's law guardian on the implementation of such order, no later than ninety days after the issuance of such order, unless the court determines that the facts and circumstances of the case do not require such reports to be made. The child protective agency shall make further reports to the court, the parties and the law guardian in such manner and at such times as the court may direct.

(d) Upon application of the respondent, the petitioner, the child's attorney or law guardian or upon the court's own motion, made at any time during the duration of the order, if the child protective agency has failed substantially to provide the respondent with adequate supervision or to observe the terms and conditions of the order, the court may direct the child protective agency to observe such terms and conditions and provide adequate supervision or may make any order authorized pursuant to section two hundred fifty-five of this act.

(e) Upon application of the petitioner or the child's attorney or law guardian, or upon the court's own motion, made at any time during the duration of the order, the court may restore the matter to the calendar, if the court finds after a hearing that the respondent has failed substantially to observe the terms and conditions of the order or to cooperate with the supervising child protective agency. In such event, unless the parties consent to an order pursuant to section one thousand fifty-one of this act or unless the petition is dismissed upon the consent of the petitioner, the court shall thereupon proceed to a fact-finding hearing under this article no later than sixty days after such application unless such period is extended by the court for good cause shown.

(f) If the proceeding is not so restored to the calendar, the petition is, at the expiration of the adjournment period, deemed to have been dismissed by the court in furtherance of justice unless an application is pending pursuant to subdivision (e) of this section. If such application is granted the petition shall not be dismissed and shall proceed in accordance with the provisions of such subdivision (e).

(g) Notwithstanding the provisions of this section, the court, may, at any time prior to dismissal of the petition pursuant to subdivision (f), issue an order authorized pursuant to section one thousand twenty-seven.

Added by L. 1975, Ch. 707, eff. Aug. 9, 1975; **Amended** by L. 1985, Ch. 601, eff. Nov. 25, 1985; L. 1990, Ch. 323, eff. Sept. 1, 1990, amending subd. (c); L. 1990, Ch. 167, eff. May 21, 1990, amending subd. (d); L. 1990, Ch. 194, eff. Sept. 1, 1990, amending subd. (e).

ANNOTATIONS

ACD order.—A dispositional order directing a parent to take action cannot be issued unless there has been a finding of neglect or abuse after a hearing or on consent. The only exception is when a petition has been adjourned in contemplation of dismissal. *In re* Brandon C., 237 A.D.2d 821, 658 N.Y.S.2d 461 (3d Dept. 1997).

—In the absence of provisions in an ACD order bearing directly upon the care, treatment and well-being of a child alleged to be neglected, proof of violation of an ACD order cannot by itself support a deprivation of custody. *In re* Paul X., 57 A.D.2d 216, 393 N.Y.S.2d 1005 (3d Dept. 1977).

—Family court's order that child be placed in mother's physical custody, and that petition alleging abuse be adjourned in contemplation of dismissal required consent of petitioner as well as the infant's attorney or law guardian. Amlinger v. Amlinger, 73 A.D.2d 1047, 425 N.Y.S.2d 426 (4th Dept. 1980).

—Evidence that a substantial violation of the ACD has occurred will not automatically restore the neglect or abuse case to the calendar. The court has the authority to explore the violation and determine the implication of the violative conduct to the well-being of the children. The court determined that violation of the ACD, the non-custodial parent's relapse to drinking, which was brief and independently addressed by that parent's re-entry into a treatment program, did not warrant restoration of the case to the calendar. *In re* Jonathan W., 174 Misc. 2d 210, 663 N.Y.S.2d 771 (Fam. Ct. Monroe Co. 1997).

Standing.—Non-custodial parent does not have standing to commence a proceeding under FCA § 1039(e) to enforce compliance with a court order. Millard v. Clapper, 254 A.D.2d 640, 679 N.Y.S.2d 434 (3d Dept. 1998).

§ 1039-a. Procedures following adjournment in contemplation of dismissal.

The local child protective service shall notify the child's law guardian of (a) an indicated report of child abuse or maltreatment in which the respondent is the subject of the report or another person named in the report, as such terms are defined in section four hundred twelve of the social services law, while any order issued pursuant to section ten hundred thirty-nine or extension thereof remains in effect.

Added by L. 1990, Ch. 317, eff. Sept. 1, 1990; **Amended** by L. 1991, Ch. 69, eff. Apr. 22, 1991.

ANNOTATION

Unconstitutionality; ACD Order § 1039(e).—The constitution prohibits a court from ordering the removal of a child from his parents without an actual finding of neglect or abuse; thus Section 1039(e) of the Family Court act is unconstitutional. *In re* Baker, 106 Misc. 2d 994, 436 N.Y.S.2d 833 (Fam. Ct. Oneida Co. 1981).

§ 1039-b. Termination of reasonable efforts.

(a) In conjunction with, or at any time subsequent to, the filing of a petition under section ten hundred thirty-one of this chapter, the social services official may file a motion upon notice requesting a finding that reasonable efforts to return the child to his or her home are no longer required.

(b) For the purpose of this section, reasonable efforts to make it possible for the child to return safely to his or her home shall not be required where the court determines that:

(1) the parent of such child has subjected the child to aggravated circumstances, as defined in subdivision (j) of section ten hundred twelve of this article;

(2) the parent of such child has been convicted of (i) murder in the first degree as defined in section 125.27 or murder in the second degree as defined in section 125.25 of the penal law and the victim was another child of the parent; or (ii) manslaughter in the first degree as defined in section 125.20 or manslaughter in the second degree as defined in section 125.15 of the penal law and the victim was another child of the parent, provided, however, that the parent must have acted voluntarily in committing such crime;

(3) the parent of such child has been convicted of an attempt to commit any of the foregoing crimes, and the victim or intended victim was the child or another child of the parent; or has been convicted of criminal solicitation as defined in article one hundred, conspiracy as defined in article one hundred five or criminal facilitation as defined in article one hundred fifteen of the penal law for conspiring, soliciting or facilitating any of the foregoing crimes, and the victim or intended victim was the child or another child of the parent;

(4) the parent of such child has been convicted of assault in the second degree as defined in section 120.05, assault in the first degree as defined in section 120.10 or aggravated assault upon a person less than eleven years old as defined in section 120.12 of the penal law, and the commission of one of the foregoing crimes resulted in serious physical injury to the child or another child of the parent;

(5) the parent of such child has been convicted in any other jurisdiction of an offense which includes all of the essential elements of any crime specified in paragraph two, three or four of this subdivision, and the victim of such offense was the child or another child of the parent; or

(6) The parental rights of the parent to a sibling of such child have been involuntarily terminated;

unless the court determines that providing reasonable efforts would be in the best interests of the child, not contrary to the health and safety of the child, and would likely result in the reunification of the parent and the child in the foreseeable future. The court shall state such findings in its order.

If the court determines that reasonable efforts are not required because of one of the grounds set forth above, a permanency hearing shall be held within thirty days of the finding of the court

that such efforts are not required. At the permanency hearing, the court shall determine the appropriateness of the permanency plan prepared by the social services official which shall include whether or when the child: (i) will be returned to the parent; (ii) should be placed for adoption with the social services official filing a petition for termination of parental rights; (iii) should be referred for legal guardianship; (iv) should be placed permanently with a fit and willing relative; or (v) should be placed in another planned permanent living arrangement if the social services official has documented to the court a compelling reason for determining that it would not be in the best interest of the child to return home, be referred for termination of parental rights and placed for adoption, placed with a fit and willing relative, or placed with a legal guardian. The social services official shall thereafter make reasonable efforts to place the child in a timely manner and to complete whatever steps are necessary to finalize the permanent placement of the child as set forth in the permanency plan approved by the court. If reasonable efforts are determined by the court not to be required because of one of the grounds set forth in this paragraph, social services official may file a petition for termination of parental rights in accordance with section three hundred eighty-four-b of the social services law.

(c) For the purpose of this section, in determining reasonable effort to be made with respect to a child, and in making such reasonable efforts, the child's health and safety shall be the paramount concern; and

(d) for the purpose of this section, a sibling shall include a half-sibling.

Added by L. 1999, Ch. 7, eff. Feb. 11, 1999.

ANNOTATIONS

Diligent efforts.—Where evidence established that respondent-father raped his eight-year-old daughter and caused serious medical injuries, and respondent-mother waited two hours to seek medical assistance for child while devising lies with father to protect him from criminal charges, diligent efforts to reunite this family were not required. *In re* Marino S., 100 N.Y.2d 361, 763 N.Y.S.2d 796, 795 N.E.2d 21 (2003).

Timeliness.—A "no reasonable efforts" motion brought under this section is brought as "part of the procedural and substantive scheme for determining the appropriate permanency plan for a child in foster care"; a motion brought two years after that plan was determined was untimely. *In re* Jordy O., 182 Misc. 2d 42, 696 N.Y.S.2d 654 (Fam. Ct. N.Y. Co. 1999).

§ 1040. Notice and opportunity to be heard.

The foster parent caring for the child or any pre-adoptive parent or relative providing care for the child shall be provided with notice of any permanency hearing held pursuant to this article by the social services official. Such foster parent, pre-adoptive parent or relative shall be afforded an opportunity to be heard at any such hearing; provided, however, no such foster parent, pre-adoptive parent or relative shall be construed to be a party to the hearing solely on the basis of such notice and opportunity to be heard. The failure of the foster parent, pre-adoptive parent, or relative caring for the child to appear at a permanency hearing shall constitute a waiver of the opportunity to be heard and such failure to appear shall not cause a delay of the permanency hearing nor shall such failure to appear be a ground for the invalidation of any order issued by the court pursuant to this section.

Added by L. 1999, Ch. 7, § 44, eff. Feb. 11, 1999.

Part 4. Hearings

§ 1041. Required findings concerning notice.

No factfinding hearing may commence under this article unless the court enters a finding:

(a) that the parent or other person legally responsible for the child's care is present at the hearing and has been served with a copy of the petition; or

(b) if the parent or other person legally responsible for the care of the child is not present, that every reasonable effort has been made to effect service under section ten hundred thirty-six or ten hundred thirty-seven.

Amended by L. 1972, Ch. 1015, eff. Aug. 7, 1972.

§ 1042. Effect of absence of parent or other person responsible for care.

If the parent or other person legally responsible for the child's care is not present, the court may proceed to hear a petition under this article only if the child is represented by counsel, a law guardian, or a guardian ad litem. The parent or other person legally responsible for the child's care shall be served with a copy of the order of disposition with written notice of its entry pursuant to section one thousand thirty-six of this article. Within one year of such service or substituted service pursuant to section one thousand thirty-six of this article, the parent or other person legally responsible for the child's care may move to vacate the order of disposition and schedule a rehearing. Such motion shall be granted on an affidavit showing such relationship or responsibility and a meritorious defense to the petition, unless the court finds that the parent or other person willfully refused to appear at the hearing, in which case the court may deny the motion.

Amended by L. 2005, Ch. 3, Part B, § 4, eff. Nov. 21, 2005.

ANNOTATIONS

Good cause.—Court's actions in proceeding *in absentia* to terminate respondent's parental rights were upheld where the record showed that respondent failed to maintain contact with children or agency for six months, and that respondent was personally served with a summons and notice of hearing date and failed to appear without good cause. *In re* Olen Jackson H., 251 A.D.2d 136, 674 N.Y.S.2d 309 (1st Dept. 1998).

—Mother's submission of a note that she suffered from herpes, accompanied by a doctor's note to that extent, without the submission of affidavit of merit did not constitute good cause for her failure to appear at dispositional hearing. *In re* Baby Boy P. (Anonymous), 287 A.D.2d 458, 730 N.Y.S.2d 879 (2d Dept. 2001).

—Although father willfully failed to appear at fact-finding hearing, father later presented sufficient evidence that court had failed to examine medical records which may have been dispositive on the question of sexual abuse; fact-finding order and disposition order were properly vacated. Commissioner of Social Servs. *ex rel.* Anna B. v. Amine B., 223 A.D.2d 703, 637 N.Y.S.2d 182 (2d Dept. 1996).

—Respondent's contention that she was not awarded a full and fair hearing pursuant to section 1042 was without merit where, although respondent was jailed and unable to personally attend, she was represented by counsel who was present and represented her interests. *In re* Trebor UU., 279 A.D.2d 735, 718 N.Y.S.2d 474 (3d Dept. 2001).

Hearing held in parent's absence.—Although termination of parental rights hearing was held in parent's absence because petitioner was incarcerated out of state, section 1042 is not applicable to a proceeding brought pursuant to Soc. Serv. Law § 384-b. *In re* Jennifer DD., 227 A.D.2d 675, 641 N.Y.S.2d 652 (3d Dept. 1996).

§ 1043. Hearings not open to the public.

The general public may be excluded from any hearing under this article and only such persons and the representatives of authorized agencies admitted thereto as have an interest in the case.

ANNOTATIONS

Exclusion from courtroom.—Where six-year-old child was reluctant to testify concerning his father's sexual abuse of his three-year-old brother in the father's presence, in court, the exclusion of the father from the courtroom was not justified without a showing that the experience of testifying in the father's presence would have a pathological impact on the child resulting in emotional injury to him, which would outweigh the father's right to be present at the fact-finding hearing. *In re* S. Children, 102 Misc. 2d 1015, 424 N.Y.S.2d 1004 (Fam. Ct. Kings Co. 1980).

Indigent parent in child neglect proceeding; right to be represented by counsel.—An indigent parent faced with the loss of child's society, as well as with the possibility of criminal charges, is entitled to the assistance of counsel, and must be so advised; here appellant clearly did not know that an attorney would be provided if she could not afford to retain one—indeed, the trial judge told her that if she desired an attorney, she would have to pay out of her own funds; in light of this statement, appellant's negative answer to the question "Do you want an attorney?" could not possibly be deemed an intelligent or understanding waiver of her right to counsel, and, accordingly, the proceeding was remitted to the Family Court for a rehearing at which appellant would have benefit of counsel. *In re* B., 30 N.Y.S.2d 352, 334 N.Y.S.2d 133 (1972).

Inspection of the record.—The parties and their attorneys are allowed to inspect and have access to the minutes of the neglect hearing in order to prepare for litigation against the doctor who was a witness in the neglect hearing. Department of Social Servs. v. Land, 110 Misc. 2d 665, 443 N.Y.S.2d 351 (Fam. Ct. Nassau Co. 1981).

§ 1044. Definition of "fact-finding hearing."

When used in this article, "fact-finding hearing" means a hearing to determine whether the child is an abused or neglected child as defined by this article.

§ 1045. Definition of "dispositional hearing."

When used in this article, "dispositional hearing" means a hearing to determine what order of disposition should be made.

ANNOTATION

Requirement of hearing.—While fact-finding determination that children were sexually abused was pending, father was convicted on criminal charges arising out of that abuse, court erred when it released children to custody of mother without holding a dispositional hearing. *In re* Joseph B., 6 A.D.3d 609, 774 N.Y.S.2d 822 (2d Dept. 2004).

§ 1046. Evidence.

(a) In any hearing under this article

(i) proof of the abuse or neglect of one child shall be admissible evidence on the issue of the abuse or neglect of any other child of, or the legal responsibility of, the respondent; and

(ii) proof of injuries sustained by a child or of the condition of a child of such a nature as would ordinarily not be sustained or exist except by reason of the acts or omissions of the parent or other person responsible for the care of such child shall be prima facie evidence of child abuse or neglect, as the case may be, of the parent or other person legally responsible; and

(iii) proof that a person repeatedly misuses a drug or drugs or alcoholic beverages, to the extent that it has or would ordinarily have the effect of producing in the user thereof a substantial state of stupor, unconsciousness, intoxication, hallucination, disorientation, or incompetence, or a substantial impairment of judgment, or a substantial manifestation of irrationality, shall be prima facie evidence that a child of or who is the legal responsibility of such person is a neglected child except that such drug or alcoholic beverage misuse shall not be prima facie evidence of neglect when such person is voluntarily and regularly participating in a recognized rehabilitative program; and

(iv) any writing, record or photograph, whether in the form of an entry in a book or otherwise, made as a memorandum or record of any condition, act, transaction, occurrence or event relating to a child in an abuse or neglect proceeding of any hospital or any other public or private agency shall be admissible in evidence in proof of that condition, act, transaction, occurrence or event, if the judge finds that it was made in the regular course of the business of any hospital, or any other public or private agency and that it was in the regular course of such business to make it, at the time of the act, transaction, occurrence or event, or within a reasonable time thereafter. A certification by the head of or by a responsible employee of the hospital or agency that the writing, record or photograph is the full and complete record of said condition, act, transaction, occurrence or event and that it was made in the regular course of the business of the hospital or agency and that it was in the regular course of such business to make it, at the time of the condition, act, transaction, occurrence or event, or within a reasonable time thereafter, shall be prima facie evidence of the facts contained in such certification. A certification by someone other than the head of the hospital or agency shall be accompanied by a photocopy of a delegation of authority signed by both the head of the hospital or agency and by such other employee. All other circumstances of the making of the memorandum, record or photograph, including lack of personal knowledge of the maker, may be proved to affect its weight, but they shall not affect its admissibility; and

(v) any report filed with the statewide central register of child abuse and maltreatment by a person or official required to do so pursuant to section four hundred thirteen of the social services law shall be admissible in evidence; and

(vi) previous statements made by the child relating to any allegations of abuse or neglect shall be admissible in evidence, but if uncorroborated, such statements shall not be sufficient to make a fact-finding of abuse or neglect. Any other evidence tending to support the reliability of the previous statements, including, but not limited to the types of evidence defined in this subdivision shall be sufficient corroboration. The testimony of the child shall not be necessary to make a fact-finding of abuse or neglect; and

(vii) neither the privilege attaching to confidential communications between husband and wife, as set forth in section forty-five hundred two of the civil practice law and rules, nor the physician-patient and related privileges, as set forth in section forty-five hundred four of the civil practice law and rules, nor the psychologist-client privilege, as set forth in section forty-five hundred seven of the civil practice law and rules, nor the social worker-client privilege, as set forth in section forty-five hundred eight of the civil practice law and rules, shall be a ground for excluding evidence which otherwise would be admissible.

(viii) proof of the "impairment of emotional health" or "impairment of mental or emotional condition" as a result of the unwillingness or inability of the respondent to exercise a minimum degree of care toward a child may include competent opinion or expert testimony and may include proof that such impairment lessened during a period when the child was in the care, custody or supervision of a person or agency other than the respondent.

(b) In a fact-finding hearing: (i) any determination that the child is an abused or neglected child must be based on a preponderance of evidence;

(ii) whenever a determination of severe or repeated abuse is based upon clear and convincing evidence, the fact-finding order shall state that such determination is based on clear and convincing evidence; and

(iii) except as otherwise provided by this article, only competent, material and relevant evidence may be admitted.

(c) In a dispositional hearing and during all other stages of a proceeding under this article, except a fact-finding hearing, only material and relevant evidence may be admitted.

Amended by L. 1972, Ch. 1015, eff. Aug. 7, 1972; L. 1979, Ch. 81, eff. Aug. 8, 1979; L. 1981, Ch. 64, eff. Apr. 8, 1981 subd. (a)(v); L. 1981, Ch. 984, eff. July 31, 1981, subd. (a)(iii); L. 1985, Ch. 724, eff. Aug. 1, 1985, subd. (a)(vi); L. 1999, Ch. 7, § 45, eff. Feb. 11, 1999, amending subd. (b).

ANNOTATIONS

Child abuse proceeding; impeachment of respondent on cross examination.—CPLR § 4513 is appropriate in an Article 10 proceeding; the respondent may be impeached on cross-examination by proof of a prior conviction, and the discretion afforded to the trial judge in a criminal proceeding by *Sandoval* is not available to the trial judge in a child abuse proceeding. *In re* Linda O., 95 Misc. 2d 744, 408 N.Y.S.2d 308 (Fam. Ct. Queens Co. 1978).

Child abuse; derivative proof.—Under Family Court Act Article 10, a finding that a deceased child was abused can support a derivative abuse or neglect petition on behalf of another child. *In re* Alijah, C., 1 N.Y.3d 375, 774 N.Y.S.2d 483, 806 N.E.2d 491 (2004).

—Determination that respondents abused their daughter was supported by evidence that their daughter had anal and rectal injuries; in light of the nature and severity of the abuse established with respect to respondents' daughter, the finding of derivative abuse with respect to their son was proper, even absent direct evidence of his actual abuse. *In re* Anthony S., 280 A.D.2d 302, 720 N.Y.S.2d 137 (1st Dept. 2001).

—Once the petitioner established that a child of this age and physical abilities does not normally sustain burns from which subject child suffered absent abuse, burden of going forward then shifted to respondents to provide a reasonable and acceptable explanation for these injuries which caused child's death, in light of their failure to do this, finding of abuse was affirmed, derivative abuse finding for other foster children in house affirmed as well. *In re* Benjamin L., 9 A.D.3d 153, 780 N.Y.S.2d 8 (2d Dept. 2004).

—Despite lower court's determination of no abuse, appellate court made independent assessment of child abuse based on evidence that a 10-month-old infant sustained an skull fracture under circumstances mother could not explain, this injury ordinarily would not occur in the absence of abuse or neglect, derivative finding of abuse for sibling established as well. *In re* Peter R., 8 A.D.3d 576, 779 N.Y.S.2d 137 (2d Dept. 2004).

—FCA § 1046(a)(i) provides for evidence of abuse of neglect or abuse of one sibling to determine whether other children in household were abused or neglected as well, that determination is not mandated, and where evidence indicates that other child or children were appropriately cared for, a derivative abuse or neglect finding is neither required nor warranted. *In re* Jocelyne J., 8 A.D.3d 978, 778 N.Y.S.2d 624 (4th Dept. 2004).

Child neglect; jurisdiction.—The court should exercise its jurisdiction to interfere with parental guardianship reluctantly, and only upon strong and convincing proof of unfitness on the part of the parent, or for material benefit to the child; a petitioner must show that the best interests, welfare, and safety of the child supersede the basic constitutional right of the parents to have their child at home with them. *In re* J., 72 Misc. 2d 683, 340 N.Y.S.2d 306 (Fam. Ct. 1972). *See also In re* Sais, 94 Misc. 2d 40, 404 N.Y.S.2d 507 (Fam. Ct. Suffolk Co. 1978).

Child neglect; proof.—A showing of neglect must be supported by a preponderance of evidence that (1) "a child's physical, mental or emotional condition has been impaired or is in imminent danger of becoming impaired and [(2)] that the actual or threatened harm to the child is a consequence of the failure of the parent or caretaker to exercise a minimum degree of care in providing the child with proper supervision or guardianship"; the drafters were "deeply concerned" that lack of a precise definition of child neglect could result in "unwarranted state intervention into private family life." Nicholson v. Scoppetta, 3 N.Y.3d 357, 787 N.Y.S.2d 196, 820 N.E.2d 840 (2004).

—In hearing for petition of custody and neglect petition, therapists' reports, administration for Children's Services Reports, and colloquy of therapist were all properly received into evidence, even though they were hearsay, following defendant's admission of neglect; the evidence was admissible in the custody proceeding as well because issues in both proceedings were inextricably interwoven. Nilda S. v. Dawn K., 302 A.D.2d 237, 754 N.Y.S.2d 281 (1st Dept. 2003).

—Finding of neglect based on evidence of acts of severe violence between parents in front of both children need not be supported by expert testimony. *In re* Athena M., 253 A.D.2d 669, 678 N.Y.S.2d 11 (1st Dept. 1998).

—Upon proof to establish a prima facie case, the respondent must offer a satisfactory explanation to rebut the evidence of neglect. *In re* Valerie Leonice T., 107 A.D.2d 327, 487 N.Y.S.2d 10 (1st Dept. 1985).

—Evidence that mother knew of father's sexual and verbal abuse of their daughters and failed to protect them from that abuse was sufficient to support a finding of neglect. *In re* Karen B., 296 A.D.2d 403, 745 N.Y.S.2d 440 (2d Dept. 2002).

—Finding of neglect of one child will support a finding of derivative neglect of other children. *In re* Kayla M. (Anonymous), 295 A.D.2d 613, 744 N.Y.S.2d 696 (2d Dept. 2002).

—Finding of child abuse and neglect not supported by record where only evidence of abuse was the child's out-of-court statement describing the abuse and was not corroborated by either medical or forensic evidence. *In re* Kymberlee P., 647 N.Y.S.2d 238, 231 A.D.2d 526 (2d Dept. 1996).

—Petitioner is deemed to have established a prima facie case once the petition has established the existence of injuries sustained by the child which are substantial in character while the child was in the lawful custody of his parents or other person legally responsible for his care; the burden of coming forward with proof then shifts from the petitioner to the respondent who is required to offer a satisfactory explanation concerning these injuries. *In re* Tashyne L., 53 A.D.2d 629, 384 N.Y.S.2d 472 (2d Dept. 1976).

—Neglect was established by evidence that respondent directly involved his daughter in a tumultuous relationship with and harassment of respondent's estranged wife and mother of his daughter, without regard for child's well-being. *In re* Catherine KK., 280 A.D.2d 732, 720 N.Y.S.2d 238 (3d Dept. 2001).

—Proof that a minor is not attending school in the area where the parents reside established a prima facie case of educational neglect, and this evidence is admissible in neglect proceedings involving another child of respondent. *In re* Chad V., 265 A.D.2d 607, 695 N.Y.S.2d 764 (3d Dept. 1999).

—Hearsay testimony relaying child's statements that respondent had hurt her in her vagina area were properly received pursuant to Family Court Act § 1046(a)(iv). Hover v. Shear, 648 N.Y.S.2d 718, 232 A.D. 2d 749 (3d Dept. 1996).

—Proof of neglect was insufficient to support neglect petition where sole evidence of neglect was based on prior neglect petition involving another child issued 10 months earlier and not supplemented with additional information. *In re* Ronald M., 154 A.D.2d 838, 677 N.Y.S.2d 839 (4th Dept. 1998).

Child neglect; burden of proof.—In a child protection proceeding, the petitioner has the burden of establishing abuse or neglect by a preponderance of the evidence. Christopher S. v. Kathleen S., 116 A.D.2d 653, 497 N.Y.S.2d 724 (2d Dept. 1986).

—In a child neglect proceeding, the petitioner must sustain the burden of proof by a preponderance of relevant, competent, and material evidence. A prima facie case of neglect or possible neglect (where the child was in imminent danger of being impaired) must be proved. In re J., 72 Misc. 2d 683, 340 N.Y.S.2d 306 (Fam. Ct. Richmond Co. 1972).

Constitutionality.—FCA § 1046(a)(ii) does not infringe upon respondent's Fifth and Fourteenth Amendment right against self incrimination.—In re Roman, 94 Misc. 2d 796, 405 N.Y.S.2d 899 (Fam. Ct. Onondaga Co. 1978).

—FCA § 1046(a)(ii) and (b)(i) do not offend constitutional standards of due process. In re J. R., 87 Misc. 2d 900, 386 N.Y.S.2d 774 (Fam. Ct. Bronx Co. 1976).

Corroboration.—Children's out of court statements regarding sexual abuse by defendant corroborated each other. Although that was enough to satisfy the statute, the statements were also corroborated by reenactments with anatomically correct dolls, testimony that they had age-inappropriate sexual knowledge, and physician's testimony. In re Victoria H., 255 A.D.2d 442, 680 N.Y.S.2d 577 (2d Dept. 1998).

—Custody/visitation modification proceeding, which is based on allegations of abuse, is governed by corroboration requirements set forth in Family Court Act § 1046(a)(iv). Here the child's out-of-court statements identifying father as abuser, and describing acts committed by him, coupled with re-enactments with anatomically correct dolls and expert's opinion that child had been abused provided sufficient corroboration to support finding of abuse. Linda P. v. Thomas P., 240 A.D.2d 583, 659 N.Y.S.2d 55 (2d Dept. 1997).

—Victim's out of court statements relating to the abuse are admissible and were corroborated by medical expert's testimony; "whether the corroborative evidence offered actually supports the child's out-of-court statement is a matter left to the considerable discretion of the family court." In re Elizabeth M., 277 A.D.2d 522, 715 N.Y.S.2d 99 (3d Dept. 2000).

—Mere repetition of accusation is not corroborative of child's out-of-court-statement. In re Douglas NN., 277 A.D.2d 749, 716 N.Y.S.2d 156 (3d Dept. 2000).

—Child's out-of-court statement relating to alleged abuse is admissible as evidence at fact-finding hearing and where corroboration is sufficient to establish abuse; here corroboration included testimony by teacher that child had no bruises before the defendant removed her from class and the physical bruises on her body were consistent with beating described by child. In re Ashley D., 268 A.D.2d 803, 702 N.Y.S.2d 209 (3d Dept.), appeal denied, 94 N.Y.2d 763 (2000).

—Child victim's out of court statements relating to allegations of abuse are admissible in evidence if they are corroborated by other evidence supporting the reliability of the statement; testimony from validation expert may corroborate those out of court statements and statements of victims may corroborate each other. In re Elizabeth G., 255 A.D.2d 1010, 680 N.Y.S.2d 32 (4th Dept. 1998).

—Corroboration requirement of Family Court Act § 1046 may be satisfied by expert testimony, e.g., testimony based upon the observations of the reactions and sexual "acting out" of the subject child. Dutchess County Dept. of Social Servs. v. Bertha C., 130 Misc. 2d 1043, 498 N.Y.S.2d 960 (Fam. Ct. Dutchess Co. 1986).

Finding of abuse.—Court refused to disturb finding of sexual abuse and neglect when, on day of dispositional hearing, child victim recanted testimony that respondent had abused her; review of record supported finding of abuse. In re Petagaye S., 295 A.D.2d 178, 744 N.Y.S.2d 318 (1st Dept. 2002).

—Court's findings of sexual abuse were based on a preponderance of the evidence; on matters of credibility, factual findings of trial court are granted great deference. In re Bryan S., 286 A.D.2d 685, 729 N.Y.S.2d 911 (2d Dept. 2001).

—Evidence that respondents, who were legally responsible for child's care, either inflicted or allowed to be inflicted burns on her underarm and buttocks area and did not seek medical assistance or adequate care for her burns, supported a finding of abuse. In re Kianna M., 189 Misc. 2d 791, 736 N.Y.S.2d 850 (Fam. Ct. Suffolk Co. 2001).

Function of court in child protection proceedings.—In child protection proceedings, it is the function of the trial court to determine not only whether neglect or abuse exists, but also whether it is likely to exist; the court sits as parens patriae, and cannot be limited to conditions already existing or to activities which occurred in the past, but must of necessity concern itself with events that might occur should certain conditions continue. In re Baby Boy Santos, 71 Misc. 2d 789, 336 N.Y.S.2d 817 (Fam. Ct. N.Y. Co. 1972).

Psychiatric report; court may consider such report without disclosure to respondent's counsel.—In a neglect proceeding, a "secret" psychiatric report (in the nature of a probation report), made by the Family Court Mental Health Clinic's Medical Director, could properly be considered for dispositional purposes without disclosure to appellants or their counsel. In re J., 38 A.D.2d 711, 329 N.Y.S.2d 349 (2d Dept. 1972).

Presumption.—If a child is in the lawful custody of a parent and injuries occur, it is presumed, subject to further explanation, that the parent caused them. In re Maureen G., 103 Misc. 2d 109, 426 N.Y.S.2d 384 (Fam. Ct. Richmond Co. 1980).

Testimony of interpreter.—An interpreter's testimony as to a statement of a six-year-old deaf child, given to him after the filing of a child abuse and neglect petition, was admissible under FCA § 1046(a)(vi). It is the courts' duty to weigh and evaluate such testimony in light of the circumstances under which it was given. In re Marshall R., 73 A.D.2d 988, 423 N.Y.S.2d 564 (3d Dept. 1980).

§ 1047. Sequence of hearings.

(a) Upon completion of the fact-finding hearing, the dispositional hearing may commence immediately after the required findings are made.

(b) Reports prepared by the probation service or a duly authorized association, agency, society or institution for use by the court at any time for the making of an order of disposition shall be deemed confidential information furnished to the court which the court shall make available for inspection and copying by all counsel. The court may, in its discretion, withhold from disclosure a part or parts of the reports which are not relevant to a proper disposition, or sources of information which have been obtained on a promise of confidentiality, or any other portion thereof, disclosure of which would not be in the interests of justice or in the best interests of the child. In all cases where a part or parts of the reports are not disclosed, the court shall state for the record that a part or parts of the reports have been excepted and the reasons for its action. The action of the court excepting information from disclosure shall be subject to review on appeal from the order of disposition. Such reports may not be furnished to the court prior to the completion of a fact-finding hearing, but may be used in a dispositional hearing.

Amended by L. 1988, Ch. 102, § 1, eff. Jun. 3, 1988.

ANNOTATIONS

Psychiatric report; court may consider such report without disclosure to respondent's counsel.—In a neglect proceeding, a "secret" psychiatric report (in the nature of a probation report), made by the Family Court Mental Health Clinic's Medical Director, could properly be considered for dispositional purposes without disclosure to appellants or their counsel. In re J., 38 A.D.2d 711, 329 N.Y.S.2d 349 (2d Dept. 1972).

—The evidence on the record was convincing in establishing the delinquent conduct of appellant; and, for that reason, the action of the probation officer, in releasing his report too early to the court, could not be considered reversible error. It is the clear policy of the law that the probation service should not communicate reports to the court concerning the alleged delinquent until the fact-finding hearing is completed. Even though the court may not in fact be influenced by what it hears, it is the appearance of prejudice against which the policy is directed, and violation of the statute, albeit inadvertent, should therefore be avoided. *In re* James H., 41 A.D.2d 667, 341 N.Y.S.2d 92 (2d Dept. 1973).

§ 1048. Adjournments.

(a) The court may adjourn a fact-finding hearing or a dispositional hearing for good cause shown on its own motion, or on motion of the corporation counsel, county attorney or district attorney, or on motion of the petitioner or on motion of the child or on his behalf or of the parent or other person legally responsible for the care of the child. If so requested by the parent or other person legally responsible for the care of the child, the court shall not proceed with a fact-finding hearing earlier than three days after service of summons and petition, unless emergency medical or surgical procedures are necessary to safeguard the life or health of the child.

(b) At the conclusion of a fact-finding hearing and after the court has made findings required before a dispositional hearing may commence, the court on its own motion or motion of the respondent, the petitioner or the law guardian order a reasonable adjournment of the proceedings, to enable the court to make inquiry into the surroundings, conditions, and capacities of the persons involved in the proceedings.

(c) Whenever a child has been remanded to the care of an agency or institution under section ten hundred fifty-one of this article, notice of any dispositional hearing shall be served upon the agency or institution with whom the child was placed and upon the agency supervising the care of the child on behalf of the agency with whom the child was placed. Service of notice of the adjourned hearing shall be made in such manner and on such notice as the court may, in its discretion, prescribe. Any such agency or institution served with notice pursuant to this subdivision may apply to the court for leave to be heard.

Amended by L. 1978, Ch. 103, eff. Oct. 1, 1978; L. 1990, Ch. 141, eff. Sept. 1, 1990, amending subd. (b).

§ 1049. Special consideration in certain cases.

In scheduling hearings and investigations, the court shall give priority to proceedings under this article involving abuse or in which a child has been removed from home before a final order of disposition. Any adjournment granted in the course of such a proceeding should be for as short a time as is practicable.

MISC. LAWS

Part 5. Orders

§ 1051. Sustaining or dismissing petition.

(a) If facts sufficient to sustain the petition are established in accord with part four of this article, or if all parties and the law guardian consent, the court shall, subject to the provisions of subdivision (c) of this section, enter an order finding that the child is an abused child or a neglected child and shall state the grounds for the finding.

(b) If the proof does not conform to the specific allegations of the petition, the court may amend the allegations to conform to the proof; provided, however, that in such case the respondent shall be given reasonable time to prepare to answer the amended allegations.

(c) If facts sufficient to sustain the petition under this article are not established, or if, in a case of alleged neglect, the court concludes that its aid is not required on the record before it, the court shall dismiss the petition and shall state on the record the grounds for the dismissal.

(d) If the court makes a finding of abuse or neglect, it shall determine, based upon the facts adduced during the fact-finding hearing and any other additional facts presented to it, whether a preliminary order pursuant to section one thousand twenty-seven is required to protect the child's interests pending a final order of disposition. The court shall state the grounds for its determination. In addition, a child found to be abused or neglected may be removed and remanded to a place approved for such purpose by the local social services department or be placed in the custody of a suitable person, pending a final order of disposition, if the court finds that there is a substantial probability that the final order of disposition will be an order of placement under section one thousand fifty-five. In determining whether substantial probability exists, the court shall consider the requirements of subdivision (b) of section one thousand fifty-two.

(e) If the court makes a finding of abuse, it shall specify the paragraph or paragraphs of subdivision (e) of section one thousand twelve of this act which it finds have been established. If the court makes a finding of abuse as defined in paragraph (iii) of subdivision (e) of section one thousand twelve of this act, it shall make a further finding of the specific sex offense as defined in article one hundred thirty of the penal law. In addition to a finding of abuse, the court may enter a finding of severe abuse or repeated abuse, as defined in paragraphs (a) and (b) of subdivision eight of section three hundred eighty-four-b of the social services law, which shall be admissible in a proceeding to terminate parental rights pursuant to paragraph (e) of subdivision four of section three hundred eighty-four-b of the social services law. If the court makes such additional finding of severe abuse or repeated abuse, the court shall state the grounds for its determination, which shall be based upon clear and convincing evidence.

(f) Prior to accepting an admission to an allegation or permitting a respondent to consent to a finding of neglect or abuse, the court shall inform the respondent that such an admission or consent will result in the court making a fact-finding order of neglect or abuse, as the case may be, and shall further inform the respondent of the potential consequences of such order, including but not limited to the following:

(i) that the court will have the power to make an order of disposition, which may include an order placing the subject child or children in foster care until completion of the initial permanency hearing scheduled pursuant to section one thousand eighty-nine of this act and subject to successive extensions of placement at any subsequent permanency hearings;

(ii) that the placement of the children in foster

care may, if the parent fails to maintain contact with or plan for the future of the child, lead to proceedings for the termination of parental rights and to the possibility of adoption of the child if the child remains in foster care for fifteen of the most recent twenty-two months, the agency may be required by law to file a petition to terminate parental rights;

(iii) that the report made to the state central register of child abuse and maltreatment upon which the petition is based will remain on file until ten years after the eighteenth birthday of the youngest child named in such report, that the respondent will be unable to obtain expungement of such report, and that the existence of such report may be made known to employers seeking to screen employee applicants in the field of child care, and to child care agencies if the respondent applies to become a foster parent or adoptive parent.

Any finding upon such an admission or consent made without such notice being given by the court shall be vacated upon motion of any party. In no event shall a person other than the respondent, either in person or in writing, make an admission or consent to a finding of neglect or abuse.

Amended by L. 1970. Ch. 1016; L. 1976, Ch. 880, eff. Nov. 29, 1976; L. 1981, Ch. 739, eff. Oct. 26, 1981, added subd. (e); L. 1987, Ch. 160, eff. June 29, 1987; L. 1988, Ch. 478, § 7, eff. Nov. 1, 1988; L. 1990, Ch. 187, eff. Sept. 1, 1990, amending subd. (c); L. 1994, Ch. 430, § 1, eff. Oct. 18, 1994, adding subd. (f); L. 1999, Ch. 7, eff. Feb. 11, 1999, §§ 46 and 47, amending subds. (e) and (f)(ii); L. 2005, Ch. 3, Part A, § 17, eff. Dec. 21, 2005, amending subd. (f)(i).

ANNOTATIONS

Amendment.—FCA § 1051(b) has been interpreted to grant courts the broad power to amend petitions to cure minor defects; amendment to petitions to cover new charges of neglect or abuse is also permitted as long as a continuance is granted to allow respondent time to answer and eliminate any potential prejudice; "[a]bsent the destruction of exculpating evidence or the unavailability of a crucial witness, a continuance can mitigate almost all late notice prejudice." *In re* Kianna M., 189 Misc. 2d 791, 736 N.Y.S.2d 850 (Fam. Ct. Suffolk Co. 2001).

Admission.—Where respondent did not move to vacate or withdraw her admission of neglect, she is precluded from subsequently challenging it on grounds that court failed to give requisite warnings, when the court accepts that admission and uses it to support a finding of neglect and sustain the petition. *In re* Nasir H., 251 A.D.2d 1010, 674 N.Y.S.2d 179 (4th Dept.), appeal denied, 92 N.Y.2d 809 (1998).

—Order of neglect entered into on consent of all parties is not appealable. There was no merit to contention that consent was obtained illegally because court failed to give requisite warnings. *In re* Andresha G., 251 A.D.2d 1005, 674 N.Y.S.2d 226 (4th Dept. 1998).

Dismissal of petition.—Dismissal of a petition is authorized only where the court determines that there are insufficient facts to sustain the petition or that the court's intervention is unnecessary; in this case, the court's dismissal of the child neglect petition without any fact-finding whatsoever required reversal. *In re* Melissa B., 225 A.D.2d 452, 639 N.Y.S.2d 348 (1st Dept. 1996).

—Where neglect petition was dismissed for lack of evidence, dispositional order issued upon consent of all parties directing parents to abide by certain conditions upon the release of the child back into their custody was improper. There can be no dispositional order issued absent a finding of neglect or abuse after hearing or on consent, except where there has been an ACD issued in the case. Without a finding of abuse or neglect,

the court lacks the jurisdiction to impose conditions upon the parents. *In re* Brandon C., 237 A.D.2d 821, 658 N.Y.S.2d 461 (3d Dept. 1997).

Specification of paragraphs on which finding of abuse is based.—Family Court's failure to specify the subdivision of section 1012(e) under which the abuse fell and its failure to specify the particular sex offense were harmless errors, as respondent admitted to acts constituting the crime of sodomy. *In re* John F., 228 A.D.2d 812, 643 N.Y.S.2d 758 (3d Dept. 1996).

—Based on evidence in the record, reversal was not warranted merely because of court's failure to specify the paragraph of FCA § 1012(e) it found to have been established. *In re* Stephanie A., 224 A.D.2d 1027, 637 N.Y.S.2d 904 (4th Dept. 1996).

Sufficiency of evidence.—Adjudication of a deceased child as an abused child can support a petition for termination of parental rights. *In re* Alijah C., 1 N.Y.3d 375, 774 N.Y.S.2d 483, 806 N.E.2d 491 (2004).

—In furtherance of purpose of article 10, statute requires that after ACS files a neglect petition, a court must conduct a fact-finding hearing, failure to complete that hearing is grounds for reversal. *In re* Jasmine, 1 A.D.3d 257, 768 N.Y.S.2d 194 (1st Dept. 2003).

—Respondent's admission to allegations that the "children's physical condition was in imminent danger of being impaired" due to respondent's lack of skills and patience necessary to meet the children's needs for specialized feeding was sufficient to support a finding of neglect and sustain the petition. *In re* Nasir H., 251 A.D.2d 1010, 674 N.Y.S.2d 179 (4th Dept. 1998).

§ 1052. Disposition on adjudication.

(a) At the conclusion of a dispositional hearing under this article, the court shall enter an order of disposition; (i) suspending judgment in accord with section one thousand fifty-three; or

(ii) releasing the child to the custody of his parents or other person legally responsible in accord with section one thousand fifty-four; or

(iii) placing the child in accord with section one thousand fifty-five; or

(iv) making an order of protection in accord with one thousand fifty-six; or

(v) placing the respondent under supervision in accord with section one thousand fifty-seven.

(b) (i) The order of the court shall state the grounds for any disposition made under this section. If the court places the child in accord with section one thousand fifty-five of this part, the court in its order shall determine:

(A) whether continuation in the child's home would be contrary to the best interests of the child and where appropriate, that reasonable efforts were made prior to the date of the dispositional hearing held pursuant to this article to prevent or eliminate the need for removal of the child from his or her home and if the child was removed from the home prior to the date of such hearing, that such removal was in the child's best interests and, where appropriate, reasonable efforts were made to make it possible for the child to safely return home. If the court determines that reasonable efforts to prevent or eliminate the need for removal of the child from the home were not made but that the lack of such efforts was appropriate under the circumstances, the court order shall include such a finding, or if the permanency plan for the child is adoption, guardianship or some other permanent living arrangement other than reunification with the parent or parents of the child, the court order shall include a finding that reasonable efforts are being made to make and finalize such alternate permanent placement.

For the purpose of this section, reasonable efforts to prevent or eliminate the need for removing the child from the home of the child or to make it possible for the child to return safely to the home of the child shall not be required where, upon motion with notice by the social services official, the court determines that:

(1) the parent of such child has subjected the child to aggravated circumstances, as defined in subdivision (j) of section one thousand twelve of this article;

(2) the parent of such child has been convicted of (i) murder in the first degree as defined in section 125.27 or murder in the second degree as defined in section 125.25 of the penal law and the victim was another child of the parent; or (ii) manslaughter in the first degree as defined in section 125.20 or manslaughter in the second degree as defined in section 125.15 of the penal law and the victim was another child of the parent, provided, however, that the parent must have acted voluntarily in committing such crime;

(3) the parent of such child has been convicted of an attempt to commit any of the foregoing crimes, and the victim or intended victim was the child or another child of the parent; or has been convicted of criminal solicitation as defined in article one hundred, conspiracy as defined in article one hundred five or criminal facilitation as defined in article one hundred fifteen of the penal law for conspiring, soliciting or facilitating any of the foregoing crimes, and the victim or intended victim was the child or another child of the parent;

(4) the parent of such child has been convicted of assault in the second degree as defined in section 120.05, assault in the first degree as defined in section 120.10 or aggravated assault upon a person less than eleven years old as defined in section 120.12 of the penal law, and the commission of one of the foregoing crimes resulted in serious physical injury to the child or another child of the parent;

(5) the parent of such child has been convicted in any other jurisdiction of an offense which includes all of the essential elements of any crime specified in clause two, three or four of this subparagraph, and the victim of such offense was the child or another child of the parent; or

(6) the parental rights of the parent to a sibling of such child have been involuntarily terminated;

unless the court determines that providing reasonable efforts would be in the best interests of the child, not contrary to the health and safety of the child, and would likely result in the reunification of the parent and the child in the foreseeable future. The court shall state such findings in its order.

If the court determines that reasonable efforts are not to be required because of one of the grounds set forth above, a permanency hearing shall be held within thirty days of the finding of the court that such efforts are not required. At the permanency hearing, the court shall determine the appropriateness of the permanency plan prepared by the social services official which shall include whether or when the child: (i) will be returned to the parent; (ii) should be placed for adoption with the social services official filing a petition for termination of parental rights; (iii) should be referred for legal guardianship; (iv) should be placed permanently with a fit and willing relative; or (v) should be placed in another planned permanent living arrangement if the social services official has documented to the court a compelling reason for determining that it would not be in the best interest of the child to return home, be referred for termination of parental rights and placed for adoption, placed with a fit and willing relative, or placed with a legal guardian. The social services official shall thereafter make reasonable efforts to place the child in a timely manner and to complete whatever steps are necessary to finalize the permanent placement of the child as set forth in the permanency plan approved by the court. If reasonable efforts are determined by the court not to be required because of one of the grounds set forth in this paragraph, the social services official may file a petition for termination of parental rights in accordance with section three hundred eighty-four-b of the social services law.

For the purpose of this section, in determining reasonable effort to be made with respect to a child, and in making such reasonable efforts, the child's health and safety shall be the paramount concern.

For the purpose of this section, a sibling shall include a half-sibling; and

(B) if the child has attained the age of sixteen, the services needed, if any, to assist the child to make the transition from foster care to independent living. Where the court finds that the local department of social services has not made reasonable efforts to prevent or eliminate the need for placement, and that such efforts would be appropriate, it shall direct the local department of social services to make such efforts pursuant to section one thousand fifteen-a of this article, and shall adjourn the hearing for a reasonable period of time for such purpose when the court determines that additional time is necessary and appropriate to make such efforts.

(ii) The court shall also consider and determine whether the need for placement of the child would be eliminated by the issuance of an order of protection, as provided for in paragraph (iv) of subdivision (a) of this section, directing the removal of a person or persons from the child's residence. Such determination shall consider the occurrence, if any, of domestic violence in the child's residence.

(c) Prior to granting an order of disposition pursuant to subdivision (a) of this section following an adjudication of child abuse, as defined in paragraph (i) of subdivision (e) of section ten hundred twelve of this act or a finding of a felony sex offense as defined in sections 130.25, 130.30, 130.35, 130.40, 130.45, 130.50, 130.65 and 130.70 of the penal law, the court shall advise the respondent that any subsequent adjudication of child abuse, as defined in paragraph (i) of subdivision (e) of section one thousand twelve of this act or any subsequent finding of a felony sex offense as defined in those sections of the penal law herein enumerated, arising out of acts of the respondent may result in the commitment of the guardianship and custody of the child or another child pursuant to section three hundred eighty-four-b of the social services law. The order in such cases shall contain a statement that any subsequent adjudication of child abuse or finding of a felony sex offense as described herein may result in the commitment of the guardianship and custody of the child, or another child pursuant to section three hundred eighty-four-b of the social services law.

Amended by L. 1973, Ch. 1039, eff. Sept. 1, 1973; L. 1981, Ch. 739, eff. Oct. 26, 1981, added subd. (c); L. 1984, Ch. 872, eff. Oct. 4, 1984; L. 1986, Ch. 161, eff. June 16, 1986; L. 1988, Ch. 478, § 8, eff. Nov. 1, 1988; L. 1989, Ch. 727, § 6, eff. Oct. 1, 1989; L. 1990, Ch. 206, eff. Sept. 1, 1990; L. 1990, Ch. 323, eff. Sept. 1, 1990; L. 1991, Ch. 198, eff. June 28, 1991; L. 1992, Ch. 538, eff. Sept. 1, 1992, amending subd. (b)(i); L. 1999, Ch. 7, §§ 48 and 49, eff. Feb. 11, 1999, amending subds. (b)(i)(A) and (b)(ii).

ANNOTATIONS

Indigent parent in child neglect proceeding; right to be represented by counsel.—An indigent parent faced with the loss of child's society, as well as with the possibility of criminal charges, is entitled to the assistance of counsel, and must be so advised; here appellant clearly did not know that an attorney would be provided if she could not afford to retain one—indeed, the trial judge told her that if she desired an attorney she would have to pay out of her own funds; in light of this statement, appellant's answer to the question "Do you want an attorney?" could not possibly be deemed intelligent or understanding waiver of her right to counsel, and, accordingly, the proceeding was remitted to the Family Court for a rehearing at which appellant would have benefit of counsel. *In re B.*, 30 N.Y.2d 352, 334 N.Y.S.2d 133 (1972).

Necessity of hearing.—While fact-finding determination that children were sexually abused was pending, father was convicted on criminal charges arising out of that abuse, court erred when it released children to custody of mother without holding a dispositional hearing. *In re Joseph B.*, 6 A.D.3d 609, 774 N.Y.S.2d 822 (2d Dept. 2004).

—A dispositional hearing is a "condition precedent" to the entry of a dispositional order; failure to hold a hearing limited the court's ability to make a placement decision based on the best interests of the child. *In re Amanda B.*, 287 A.D.2d 561, 731 N.Y.S.2d 661 (2d Dept. 2001).

Required warnings.—Where court failed to give father required warnings mandated by this section, but father suffered no prejudice as a result of the technical defect, which was corrected by a modification of the order adding the required language, the order of protection need not be dismissed. *In re Jasmine A.* (Anonymous), 295 A.D.2d 504, 744 N.Y.S.2d 850 (2d Dept. 2002).

§ 1052-a. Post-dispositional procedures.

The local child protective service shall notify the child's law guardian of (a) an indicated report of child abuse or maltreatment in which the respondent is a subject of the report or another person named in the report, as such terms are defined in section four hundred twelve of the social services law, while any order issued pursuant to paragraph (i), (iii), (iv) or (v) of subdivision (a) of section ten hundred fifty-two remains in effect against the respondent.

Added by L. 1990, Ch. 317, eff. Sept. 1, 1990; **Amended** by L. 1991, Ch. 69, eff. Apr. 22, 1991.

§ 1052-b. Duties of counsel.

1. If the court has entered a dispositional order pursuant to section one thousand fifty-two it shall be the duty of the respondent's counsel promptly to advise such respondent in writing of his or her right to appeal to the appropriate division of the supreme court, the time limitation involved, the manner of instituting an appeal and obtaining a transcript of the testimony and the right to apply for leave to appeal as a poor person if the respondent is unable to pay the cost of an appeal. It shall be the further duty of such counsel to explain to the respondent the procedures for instituting an appeal, the possible reasons upon which an appeal may be based and the nature and possible consequences of the appellate procedure.

2. It also shall be the duty of such counsel to ascertain whether the respondent wishes to appeal and, if so, to serve and file the necessary notice of appeal.

Added by L. 1991, Ch. 113, eff. Sept. 1, 1991.

§ 1053. Suspended judgment.

(a) Rules of court shall define permissible terms and conditions of a suspended judgment. These terms and conditions shall relate to the acts or omissions of the parent or other person legally responsible for the care of the child.

(b) The maximum duration of any term or condition of a suspended judgment is one year, unless the court finds at the conclusion of that period, upon a hearing, that exceptional circumstances require an extension thereof for an additional year.

(c) Except as provided for herein, in any order issued pursuant to this section, the court may require the child protective agency to make progress reports to the court, the parties, and the child's law guardian on the implementation of such order. Where the order of disposition is issued upon the consent of the parties and the child's law guardian, such agency shall report to the court, the parties and the child's law guardian no later than ninety days after the issuance of the order, unless the court determines that the facts and circumstances of the case do not require such report to be made.

Amended by L. 1990, Ch. 323, eff. Sept. 1, 1990, adding subd. (c).

§ 1054. Release to custody of parent or other person responsible for care; supervision or order of protection.

(a) If the order of disposition releases the child to the custody of his parent or other person legally responsible for his care at the time of the filing of the petition, the court may place the person to whose custody the child is released under supervision of a child protective agency or of a social services official or duly authorized agency, or may enter an order of protection under section ten hundred fifty-six, or both. An order of supervision entered under this section shall set forth the terms and conditions of such supervision that the respondent must meet and the actions that the child protective agency, social services official or duly authorized agency must take to exercise such supervision.

(b) Rules of court shall define permissible terms and conditions of supervision under this section. The duration of any period of supervision shall be for an initial period of no more than one year and the court may at the expiration of that period, upon a hearing and for good cause shown, make successive extensions of such supervision of up to one year each.

Amended by L. 1973, Ch. 1039, eff. Sept. 1, 1973; L. 1989, Ch. 458, § 1, eff. Nov. 1, 1989; L. 1990, Ch. 206, eff. Sept. 1, 1990.

§ 1055. Placement.

(a) For purposes of section one thousand fifty-two of this part the court may place the child in the custody of a relative or other suitable person, or of the local commissioner of social services or of such other officer, board or department as may be authorized to receive children as public charges, or a duly authorized association, agency, society or in an institution suitable for the placement of a child.

(b) (i) Children placed under this section shall be placed until the court completes the initial permanency hearing scheduled pursuant to article ten-A of this act. Should the court determine pursuant to article ten-A of this act that placement shall be extended beyond completion of the scheduled permanency hearing, such extended placement and any such successive extensions of placement shall expire at the completion of the next scheduled permanency hearing, unless the court shall determine, pursuant to article ten-A of this act, to continue to extend such placement.

(ii) Upon placing a child under the age of one, who has been abandoned, with a local commissioner of social services, the court shall, where either of the parents do not appear after due notice, include in its order of disposition pursuant to section one thousand fifty-two of this part, a direction that such commissioner shall promptly commence a diligent search to locate the child's non-appearing parent or parents or other known relatives who are legally responsible for the child, and to commence a proceeding to commit the guardianship and custody of such child to an authorized agency pursuant to section three hundred eighty-four-b of the social services law, six months from the date that care and custody of the child was transferred to the commissioner, unless there has been communication and visitation between such child and such parent or parents or other known relatives or persons legally responsible for the child. In addition to such diligent search the local commissioner of social services shall provide written notice to the child's parent or parents or other known relatives or persons legally responsible as provided for in this paragraph. Such notice shall be served upon such parent or parents or other known relatives or persons legally responsible in the manner required for service of process pursuant to section six hundred seventeen of this act. Information regarding such diligent search, including, but not limited to, the name, last known address, social security number, employer's address and any other identifying information to the extent known regarding the non-appearing parent, shall be recorded in the uniform case record maintained pursuant to section four hundred nine-f of the social services law.

(iii) Notice as required by paragraph (ii) of this subdivision shall state:

(A) that the local commissioner of social services shall initiate a proceeding to commit the guardianship and custody of the subject child to an authorized agency and that such proceeding shall be commenced six months from the date the child was placed in the care and custody of such commissioner with such date to be specified in the notice;

(B) that there has been no visitation and communication between the parent and the child since the child has been placed with the local commissioner of social services and that if no such visitation and communication with the child occurs within six months of the date the child was placed with such commissioner the child will be deemed an abandoned child as defined in section three hundred eighty-four-b of the social services law and a proceeding will be commenced to commit the guardianship and custody of the subject child to an authorized agency;

(C) that it is the legal responsibility of the local commissioner of social services to reunite and reconcile families whenever possible and to offer services and assistance for that purpose;

(D) the name, address and telephone number of the caseworker assigned to the subject child who can provide information, services and assistance with respect to reuniting the family;

(E) that it is the responsibility of the parent,

relative or other person legally responsible for the child to visit and communicate with the child and that such visitation and communication may avoid the necessity of initiating a petition for the transfer of custody and guardianship of the child. Such notice shall be printed in both Spanish and English and contain in conspicuous print and in plain language the information set forth in this paragraph.

(c) No placement may be made or continued under this section beyond the child's eighteenth birthday without his or her consent and in no event past his or her twenty-first birthday.

(d) If a child is placed in the custody of the local commissioner of social services or other officer, board or department authorized to receive children as public charges, such person shall provide for such child as in the case of a destitute child or as otherwise authorized by law.

(e) If the parent or person legally responsible for the care of any such child or with whom such child resides receives public assistance and care, any portion of which is attributable to such child, a copy of the order of the court providing for the placement of such child from his or her home shall be furnished to the appropriate social services official, who shall reduce the public assistance and care furnished such parent or other person by the amount attributable to such child, provided, however, that when the child service plan prepared pursuant to section four hundred nine-e of the social services law includes a goal of discharge of the child to the parent or person legally responsible for the care of the child or other member of the household, such social services official shall not, to the extent that federal reimbursement is available therefor, reduce the portion attributable to such child which is intended to meet the cost of shelter and fuel for heating.

(f) Any order made under this section shall be suspended upon the entry of an order of disposition with respect to a child whose custody and guardianship have been committed pursuant to section three hundred eighty-four-b of the social services law, and shall expire upon the expiration of the time for appeal of such order or upon the final determination of any such appeal and any subsequent appeals authorized by law; provided, however, that where custody and guardianship have been committed pursuant to section three hundred eighty-four-b of the social services law or where the child has been surrendered pursuant to section three hundred eighty-three-c or three hundred eighty-four of the social services law, the child shall nonetheless be deemed to continue in foster care until such time as an adoption or other alternative living arrangement is finalized. A permanency hearing or hearings regarding such child shall be conducted in accordance with article ten-A of this act. Nothing in this subdivision shall cause such order of placement to be suspended or to expire with respect to any parent or other person whose consent is required for an adoption against whom an order of disposition committing guardianship and custody of the child has not been made.

(g) In making an order under this section, the court may direct a local commissioner of social services to place the subject child together with minor siblings or half-siblings who have been placed in the custody of the commissioner, or to provide or arrange for regular visitation and other forms of communication between such child and siblings where the court finds that such placement or visitation and communication is in the child's best interests. Placement or regular visitation and communication with siblings or half-siblings shall be presumptively in the child's best interests unless such placement or visitation and communication would be contrary to the child's health, safety or welfare, or the lack of geographic proximity precludes or prevents visitation.

Amended by L. 1974, Ch. 937, eff. Sept. 1, 1974; L. 1975, Ch. 220, eff. Aug. 16, 1975, which added (b)(ii) and (iii), new (c) and (d), and relettered former (c), (d) and (e) as (e), (f) and (g); L. 1976, Ch. 666, eff. Jan. 1, 1977; L. 1982, Ch. 117, eff. Sept. 1, 1982; L. 1987, Ch. 75, eff. Sept 19, 1987, Ch. 129, eff. July 15, 1987; L. 1988, Ch. 638, eff. Jan. 1, 1989; L. 1989, Ch. 458, § 2, eff. Nov. 1, 1989; L. 1989, Ch. 747, § 1, eff. July 24, 1989; L. 1990, Ch. 283, eff. Sept. 1, 1990, amending subd. (c); L. 1990, Ch. 323, eff. Sept. 1, 1990, amending subd. (b)(v); L. 1990, Ch. 605, eff. Oct. 1, 1990, adding subd. (b)(vi); L. 1990, Ch. 854, eff. Sept. 1, 1990; L. 1992, Ch. 538, eff. Sept. 1, 1992, amending subd. (b)(iii), renumbering subd. (b)(iv), (v), (vi) to (b)(v), (vi), (vii) and adding a new subd. (b)(iv); L. 1997, Ch. 353, § 2, eff. Nov. 3, 1997, amending subd. (b)(iii); L. 1998, Ch. 164, § 1, eff. July 7, 1998, amending subd. (b)(iv)(B); L. 1999, Ch. 7, § 50, eff. Feb. 11, 1999, amending subd. (b)(i)–(vi); L. 2002, Ch. 663, § 3, eff. Dec. 3, 2002, amending subd. (h); L. 2005, Ch. 3, Part A, § 18, eff. Dec. 21, 2005.

ANNOTATIONS

Burden of proof on one seeking continued placement.— Preponderance of admissible evidence supported finding of neglect based on evidence that father neglected children by leaving them unattended and subjecting them to excessive corporal punishment; however, placement of children with grandmother should not have exceeded one year. *In re* Clarice B., 253 A.D.2d 671, 677 N.Y.S.2d 569 (1st Dept. 1998).

—Petition for extension of foster care placement which provides for 12-month extension can be granted at court's discretion upon a showing by a preponderance of the evidence that the parents are presently unable to care for their children and that continuation of foster placement is in the best interests of the child. *In re* Commissioner of Admin. for Children's Servs., 254 A.D.2d 416, 679 N.Y.S.2d 82 (2d Dept. 1998).

—In a dispositional hearing in a neglected child proceeding, the burden in the first instance is upon the one seeking continued placement, to show the mother's present inability to care for the children and that continued placement would be in the best interests of the children; the burden is not upon the mother to show that the children should be returned to her. *In re* G., 39 A.D.2d 709, 331 N.Y.S.2d 788 (2d Dept. 1972).

Extension of placement; hearing.—Respondent's claim that the petitioner has failed to encourage and strengthen child's relationship with her natural family during the course of her foster placement and extension was without merit. Respondent has continued inappropriate behavior during limited supervised visits that have resulted in early termination of these visits and support petitioner's recommendation that continued placement in foster care is in the best interests of child. *In re* Anna H.H., 232 A.D.2d 782, 648 N.Y.S.2d 734 (3d Dept. 1996).

Hearing concerning need for continued placement.— Foster parents are entitled to notice and have the right to request and participate in hearing; matter remitted for hearing. Department of Social Servs. (Jessica L.) v. Sarah L., 236 A.D.2d 396, 653 N.Y.S.2d 633 (2d Dept. 1997).

Indigent parent in child neglect proceeding; to be represented by counsel.—An indigent parent faced with the loss of a child's society, as well as with the possibility of criminal charges, is entitled to the assistance of counsel, and must be so advised; here appellant clearly did not know that an attorney would be provided if she could not afford to retain one—indeed, the trial judge told her that if she desired an attorney she would have to pay out of her own funds; in light of this statement, appellant's negative answer to the question "Do you want an attorney?" could not possibly be deemed an intelligent or understanding waiver of her right to counsel, and, accordingly, the proceeding was remitted to the Family Court for a rehearing at which appellant would have benefit of counsel. In re B., 30 N.Y.2d 352, 334 N.Y.S.2d 133 (1972).

Placement.—Disposition that terminated children's foster care placement with their grandmother and placed the children in the grandmother's custody outright, rather than in the custody of the Department of Social Services, was not authorized by statute. Court also should not have disposed of petitions in absence of law guardian and without a hearing. In re Mekeia F., 222 A.D.2d 325, 636 N.Y.S.2d 277 (1st Dept. 1995).

—Court abused its discretion when it placed a child without first holding a hearing to determine whether placement was in child's best interest. In re Craig B., 289 A.D.2d 327, 734 N.Y.S.2d 493 (2d Dept. 2001).

Standing.—Foster parent lacks standing to seek permanent custody of child placed in temporary foster care where parents object and their rights and custody or guardianship of the child have not been terminated. In re Marylou L., 182 Misc. 2d 457, 698 N.Y.S.2d 827 (Fam. Ct. Kings Co. 1999).

§ 1055-a. Status of children freed for adoption; periodic permanency hearings. [*Repealed eff. Dec. 21, 2005.*]

1. As used in this section, unless otherwise expressly stated or unless the context requires a different interpretation;

(a) "foster care" shall mean care provided a child in a foster family free or boarding home, group home, agency boarding home, child care institution, health care facility or any combination thereof and for the purpose of court review under this section, shall include care for a child who has been freed for adoption as defined in paragraph (c) of this subdivision but for whom an adoption or other planned permanent living arrangement has not yet been finalized;

(b) "child" shall mean a child under the age of eighteen years for whom an authorized agency is providing foster care;

(c) "child freed for adoption" shall mean a child who was originally placed with a commissioner of social services in accordance with section one thousand fifty-five of this article or section three hundred fifty-eight-a of the social services law and whose custody and guardianship has been subsequently committed to an authorized agency pursuant to section three hundred eighty-three-c, section three hundred eighty-four or section three hundred eighty-four-b of the social services law. Such category shall include a child whose parent or parents have died during the period in which the child was in foster care and for whom there is no surviving parent who would

be entitled to notice or consent pursuant to section one hundred eleven or one hundred eleven-a of the domestic relations law;

(d) "petition for adoption" shall mean a petition filed pursuant to title two of article seven of the domestic relations law.

2. With respect to a child freed for adoption as defined in this section, a petition for a permanency hearing to review the foster care status of such child together with a copy, if any, of the placement, commitment or surrender instrument:

(a) shall be filed in the family court by the authorized agency charged with the guardianship and custody of such child;

(b) may be filed by another authorized agency providing care for or providing supervision of such foster child;

(c) may be filed by the foster parent in whose home the child resides or has resided during such period of twelve months.

3. Such petition:

(a) shall be filed in the family court in the county in which the order committing the custody and guardianship of the child was entered;

(b) shall set forth the disposition sought and the grounds therefor;

(c) shall be filed in the appropriate family court as directed by the court immediately following the commitment of guardianship and custody to an authorized agency pursuant to section three hundred eighty-four-b of the social services law or surrender of the child to an authorized agency pursuant to section three hundred eighty-three-c or three hundred eighty-four of the social services law. The permanency hearing pursuant to this section shall be completed immediately following, but in no event later than sixty days after, the earlier of the court's statement of its order on the record or issuance of its written order. Subsequent permanency petitions shall be filed no later than six months after completion of the last permanency hearing, unless the court directs an earlier filing, and each subsequent permanency hearing shall be completed within sixty days of the filing of the petition.

4. Notice of the permanency hearing, including a statement of the dispositional alternatives of the court, and a copy of the petition shall be served upon the following, each of whom shall be a party entitled to participate in the proceeding:

(a) the authorized agency charged with the guardianship and custody of such child, if such authorized agency is not the petitioner;

(b) the authorized agency providing care for or having supervision of such foster child, if such authorized agency is not the petitioner;

(c) the foster parent in whose home the child resides;

(d) the prospective adoptive parent of a child who has been freed for adoption and in whose home such child has been placed;

(e) the child or the child's law guardian who represented the child in the most recent proceeding pursuant to article ten of this act or section three hundred eighty-four-b of the social services law; and

(f) such other person as the court may, in its discretion, direct.

5. Unless otherwise directed under article six of this act or section three hundred eighty-three-c, three hundred eighty-four or three hundred eighty-four-b of the social services law or unless the court grants an order to show cause to be served in lieu of a notice of the hearing, service of notice of the hearing and the petition shall be made at least twenty days before the date of said hearing in such manner and on such notice as the court may, in its discretion prescribe; provided, however, that where the court prescribes service by mail, such service shall be made by registered mail or certified mail, return receipt requested. If service cannot be made in the manner prescribed by the court, the court may prescribe an alternative method of service.

6. In reviewing the foster care status of the child and in determining its order of disposition, the court shall consider, among other things:

(a) the appropriateness of the child's service plan as required by section four hundred nine-e of the social services law, including but not limited to, whether and when the child:

(i) should be placed for adoption by the social services official with custody and guardianship of the child;

(ii) should be referred for legal guardianship;

(iii) should be placed permanently with a fit and willing relative; or

(iv) should be placed in another planned permanent living arrangement if the social services official has documented to the court a compelling reason for determining that it would not be in the best interest of the child to be placed for adoption, placed with a fit and willing relative, or placed with a legal guardian and that reasonable efforts were made to make and finalize such alternate permanent placement;

(b) which services have been provided to ensure and expedite the adoption of such child;

(c) in the case of a child freed for adoption who is over the age of fourteen and who has withheld his or her consent to an adoption, at the review most immediately following the child's fourteenth birthday, examine the report of the law guardian of such child concerning the facts and circumstances with regard to the child's decision to withhold consent and the reasons therefor; and

(d) any further efforts which have been or will be made to promote the best interests of the child.

7. At the conclusion of such hearing, the court shall, upon the proof adduced, in accordance with the best interest of the child, enter an order of disposition:

(a) directing that placement of the child in foster care be extended for a period of up to one year; or

(b) directing that such child be placed for adoption in the foster family home where he or she resides or has resided or with any other person or persons;

(c) [*Repealed June 30, 2007.*] directing the provision of services or assistance to the child and the prospective adoptive parent authorized or required to be made available pursuant to the comprehensive annual services program plan then in effect. Such order shall include, where appropriate, the evaluation of eligibility for adoption subsidy pursuant to title nine of article six of the social services law, but shall not require the provision of such subsidy. Violation of such an order shall be subject to punishment pursuant to section seven hundred fifty-three of the judiciary law; or

(c) [*Effective June 30, 2007.*] directing the provision of services or assistance to the child and the prospective adoptive parent authorized or required to be made available pursuant to the comprehensive annual services program plan then in effect. Such order shall include, where appropriate, the evaluation of eligibility for adoption subsidy pursuant to title nine of article six of the social services law, but shall not require the provision of such subsidy. Violation of such an order shall be subject to punishment pursuant to section seven hundred fifty-three of the judiciary law;

(d) [*Repealed June 30, 2007.*] recommending that the office of children and family services investigate the facts and circumstances concerning the discharge of responsibilities for the care and welfare of such child by a social services district pursuant to section three hundred ninety-five of the social services law.

(d) [*Effective June 30, 2007.*] recommending that the state department of social services conduct a child welfare services utilization review pursuant to section three hundred ninety-eight-b of the social services law. The court shall make available to the department all relevant court records relating to the proceeding or any related proceedings; or

(e) [*Effective June 30, 2007.*] recommending that the state department of social services investigate the facts and circumstances concerning the discharge of responsibilities for the care and welfare of such child by a social services district pursuant to section three hundred ninety-five of the social services law.

8. An order of disposition entered pursuant to this section shall include the court's findings supporting its determinations that such order is in accordance with the best interest of the child and, if the child has attained the age of sixteen, the services needed, if any, to assist the child to make the transition from foster care to independent living and, in the case of a child placed outside New York state, whether the out-of-state placement continues to be appropriate and in the best interests of the child. If the court promulgates separate findings of fact or conclusions of law, or an opinion in lieu thereof, the order of disposition may incorporate such findings and conclusions, or opinions, by reference. No placement may be made or continued under this section beyond the child's eighteenth birthday without his or her consent and in no event past his or her twenty-first birthday.

9. The court in its discretion may make successive extensions of foster care, as provided by subdivision (h) of section one thousand fifty-five of this act, for additional periods of up to one year each; provided, however, that following the first permanency hearing under this section, petitions for subsequent permanency hearings shall be filed no later than six months after completion of the prior permanency hearing, unless the court directs an earlier filing, and each subsequent permanency hearing shall be completed within sixty days of the filing of the petition.

10. The court shall possess continuing jurisdiction in proceedings under this section and, in the case of children whose placements in foster care are extended, shall rehear the matter whenever it deems necessary or desirable, or upon petition by any party entitled to notice in proceedings under this section, or by the law guardian for the child. In case of a substantial failure of a material condition in a surrender executed pursuant to section three hundred eighty-three-c of the social services law prior to finalization of the adoption of the child, the court shall possess continuing jurisdiction in accordance with subdivision six of such section to rehear the matter upon the filing of a petition by the authorized agency, the parent or the law guardian for the child or whenever the court deems necessary. In such case, the authorized agency shall notify the parent, unless such notice is expressly waived by a statement written by the parent and appended to or included in such instrument, the law guardian for the child and the court that approved the surrender within twenty days of any substantial failure to comply with a material condition of the surrender prior to the finalization of the adoption of the child. In such case, the authorized agency shall file a petition on notice to the parent and law guardian in accordance with this section within thirty days of such failure, except for good cause shown, in order for the court to review such failure and, where necessary, to hold a hearing; provided, however, that in the absence of such

filing, the parent and/or law guardian for the child may file such a petition at any time prior to the adoption of the child. Nothing in this section shall limit the rights and remedies, if any, available to the parties and the law guardian with respect to a failure to comply with a material condition of a surrender subsequent to the finalization of the adoption of the child.

11. Where the court has entered an order of disposition concerning a child freed for adoption and not placed in a prospective adoptive home, pursuant to paragraph (b) or (c) of subdivision seven of this section, directing that the child be placed for adoption or directing the provision of services or assistance to the child and the agency charged with the guardianship and custody of the child fails, prior to the rehearing of the proceeding pursuant to subdivision ten of this section, to comply with such order, the court at the time of such rehearing may, in the best interests of the child, enter an order committing the guardianship and custody of the child to another authorized agency or may make any other order authorized pursuant to section two hundred fifty-five of this act.

12. Upon the filing of a petition pursuant to this section with respect to a child for whom a law guardian had been appointed by the family court in a proceeding pursuant to article ten of this act or pursuant to section three hundred eighty-four-b of the social services law, the appointment of the law guardian shall continue without further court order or appointment, unless another appointment of a law guardian has been made by the court. All notices and reports required by law shall be provided to such law guardian. The law guardian may be relieved of his or her representation upon application to the court for termination of the appointment. Upon approval of such application, the court shall immediately appoint another law guardian to whom all notices and reports required by law shall be provided.

§ 1055-a. Substantial failure of a material condition of surrender; enforcement of a contact agreement. [*Effective Dec. 21, 2005.*]

(a) In case of a substantial failure of a material condition in a surrender executed pursuant to section three hundred eighty-three-c of the social services law prior to finalization of the adoption of the child, the court shall possess continuing jurisdiction in accordance with subdivision six of such section to rehear the matter upon the filing of a petition by the authorized agency, the parent or the law guardian for the child or whenever the court deems necessary. In such case, the authorized agency shall notify the parent, unless such notice is expressly waived by a statement written by the parent and appended to or included in such instrument, the law guardian for the child and the court that approved the surrender within twenty days of any substantial failure to comply with a material condition of the surrender prior to the finalization of the adoption of the child. In such case, the authorized agency shall file a petition on notice to the parent unless notice is expressly waived by a statement written by the parent and appended to or included in such instrument and the law guardian in accordance with this section within thirty days of such failure, except for good cause shown, in order for the court to review such failure and, where necessary, to hold a hearing; provided, however, that in the absence of such filing, the parent and/or law guardian for the child may file such a petition at any time up to sixty days after notification of the failure. Such petition filed by a parent or law guardian must be filed prior to the adoption of the child.

(b) If an agreement for continuing contact and communication pursuant to paragraph (b) of subdivision two of section three hundred eighty-three-c of the social services law is approved by the court, and the child who is the subject of the approved agreement has not yet been adopted, any party to the approved agreement may file a petition with the family court in the county where the agreement was approved to enforce such agreement. A copy of the approved agreement shall be annexed to such petition. The court shall enter an order enforcing communication or contact pursuant to the terms and conditions of the agreement unless the court finds that enforcement would not be in the best interests of the child.

(c) Nothing in this section shall limit the rights and remedies available to the parties and the law guardian pursuant to section one hundred twelve-b of the domestic relations law with respect to a failure to comply with a material condition of a surrender subsequent to the finalization of the adoption of the child.

Added by L. 1988, Ch. 638, eff. Jan. 1, 1989; **Amended** by L. 1991, Ch. 48, eff. Apr. 12, 1991, amending subd. (1)(c); L. 1991, Ch. 198, eff. June 28, 1991, amending subd. (8); L. 1995, Ch. 454, § 3, amending subd. 7(a), eff. Oct. 1, 1995; L. 1995, Ch. 454, § 4, amending subd. 8, eff. Oct. 1, 1995; L. 1997, Ch. 353, §§ 3 and 4, amending subds. 4(d), 4(e), and 12, eff. Nov. 3, 1997; L. 1999, Ch. 7, § 51 through 53, eff. Feb. 11, 1999, amending subds. 3(c), 4, and 6(a), and Ch. 534, §§ 1 and 2, eff. Dec. 27, 1999, amending subds. 1(c) and 3(c); L. 2000, Ch. 145, eff. July 1, 2000; L. 2002, Ch. 83, Part C § 24, amending subd. 7(c), (d), and (e); L. 2002, Ch. 76, § 2, eff. Aug. 19, 2002, amending subd. 7 and 10, deemed in full force and effect on Apr. 1, 2002, and such amendments to expire and be deemed repealed on June 30, 2007; L. 2002, Ch. 663, §§ 4–7, eff. Dec. 3, 2002, amending section heading, subds. 1(a), 2 (opening para.), 3(c), and 5; L. 2003, Ch. 588, § 1, eff. Sept. 22, 2003, amending subd. 3(c); Former section **repealed** and new section **added** by L. 2005, Ch. 3, Part A, § 19, eff. Dec. 21, 2005.

§ 1056. Order of protection.

1. The court may make an order of protection in assistance or as a condition of any other order made under this part. Such order of protection shall remain in effect concurrently with, shall expire no later than the expiration date of, and may be extended concurrently with, such other order made under this part, except as provided in subdivision four of this section. The order of protection may set forth reasonable conditions of behavior to be observed for a specified time by a person who is before the court and is a parent or a person legally responsible for the child's care or the spouse of the parent or other person legally responsible for the child's care, or both. Such an order may require any such person

(a) to stay away from the home, school, business or place of employment of the other spouse, parent or person legally responsible for the child's care or the child, and to stay away from any other specific location designated by the court;

(b) to permit a parent, or a person entitled to visitation by a court order or a separation agreement, to visit the child at stated periods;

(c) to refrain from committing a family offense, as defined in subdivision one of section eight hundred twelve of this act, or any criminal offense against the child or against the other parent or against any person to whom custody of the child is awarded, or from harassing, intimidating or threatening such persons;

(d) to permit a designated party to enter the residence during a specified period of time in order to remove personal belongings not in issue in this proceeding or in any other proceeding or action under this act or the domestic relations law;

(e) to refrain from acts of commission or omission that create an unreasonable risk to the health, safety and welfare of a child;

(f) to provide, either directly or by means of medical and health insurance, for expenses incurred for medical care and treatment arising from the incident or incidents forming the basis for the issuance of the order.

(g) to observe such other conditions as are necessary to further the purposes of protection.

2. The court may also award custody of the child, during the term of the order of protection to either parent, or to an appropriate relative within the second degree. Nothing in this section gives the court power to place or board out any child or to commit a child to an institution or agency. In making orders of protection, the court shall so act as to insure that in the care protection, discipline and guardianship of the child his religious faith shall be preserved and protected.

3. Notwithstanding the foregoing provisions, an order of protection, or temporary order of protection where applicable, may be entered against a former spouse and persons who have a child in common, regardless whether such persons have been married or have lived together at any time.

4. The court may enter an order of protection independently of any other order made under this part, against a person who was a member of the

child's household or a person legally responsible as defined in section one thousand twelve of this chapter, and who is no longer a member of such household at the time of the disposition and who is not related by blood or marriage to the child or a member of the child's household. An order of protection entered pursuant to this subdivision may be for any period of time up to the child's eighteenth birthday and upon such conditions as the court deems necessary and proper to protect the health and safety of the child and the child's caretaker.

Amended by L. 1981, Ch. 965, eff. Aug. 6, 1981, added subd. (f); L. 1984, Ch. 948, eff. Nov. 1, 1984; L. 1989, Ch. 220; eff. Oct. 1, 1989; L. 1990, Ch. 622, eff. Sept. 1, 1990, amending subd. 1 and adding subd. 4; L. 1995, Ch. 483, § 13, amending subds. 1(a)-(e), eff. Nov. 1, 1995; L. 1995, Ch. 483, § 14, adding subd. 1(g), eff. Nov. 1, 1995.

ANNOTATIONS

Generally.—An order of protection prohibiting all contact with children was not overly restrictive and was properly issued upon a showing of respondent's past excessive alcohol use during and after which children were subjected to physical harm and domestic violence. *In re* Andrew MM., 279 A.D.2d 654, 719 N.Y.S.2d 317 (3d Dept. 2001).

Family court jurisdiction.—Family court had jurisdiction to issue order of protection made in aid of an order of supervision that was issued pursuant to FCA § 1057 and was later allowed to expire. *In re* William GG., 222 A.D.2d 752, 635 N.Y.S.2d 711 (3d Dept. 1995).

§ 1057. Supervision.

The court may place the respondent under supervision of a child protective agency or of a social services official or duly authorized agency. An order of supervision entered under this section shall set forth the terms and conditions of such supervision that the respondent must meet and the actions that the child protective agency, social services official or duly authorized agency must take to exercise such supervision. Except as provided for herein, in any order issued pursuant to this section, the court may require the child protective agency to make progress reports to the court, the parties, and the child's law guardian on the implementation of such order. Where the order of disposition is issued upon the consent of the parties and the child's law guardian, such agency shall report to the court, the parties and the child's law guardian no later than ninety days after the issuance of the order, unless the court determines that the facts and circumstances of the case do not require such report to be made. Rules

of court shall define permissible terms and conditions of supervision under this section. The duration of any period of supervision shall be for an initial period of no more than one year and the court may at the expiration of that period, upon a hearing and for good cause shown, make successive extensions of such supervision of up to one year each.

Amended by L., 1973, Ch. 1039, eff. Sept. 1, 1973; L. 1989, Ch. 458, § 3, eff. Nov. 1, 1989; L. 1990, Ch. 206, eff. Sept. 1, 1990; L. 1990, Ch. 323, eff. Sept. 1, 1990.

§ 1058. Expiration of orders.

No later than sixty days prior to the expiration of an order issued pursuant to paragraph (i), (ii), (iv), or (v) of subdivision (a) of section one thousand fifty-two of this part or prior to the conclusion of the period of an adjournment in contemplation of dismissal pursuant to section one thousand thirty-nine of this article, where no application has been made seeking extension of such orders or adjournments and, with respect to an adjournment in contemplation of dismissal, no violations of the court's order are before the court, the child protective agency shall, whether or not the child has been or will be returned to the family, report to the court, the parties, including any non-respondent parent and the child's law guardian on the status and circumstances of the child and family and any actions taken or contemplated by such agency with respect to such child and family.

Added by L. 1990, Ch. 318, eff. Sept. 1, 1990; **Amended** by L. 1991, Ch. 75, eff. Apr. 26, 1991; L. 2005, Ch. 3, Part A, § 20, eff. Dec. 21, 2005.

§ 1059. Abandoned child.

If the court finds that a child was abandoned by his parents or by the other person lawfully charged with his care, it may make an order so finding and may discharge the child to the custody of the commissioner of social services who shall provide for such child as in the case of a destitute child or as otherwise authorized by law. In such case the court shall direct the commissioner to institute a proceeding pursuant to section three hundred eighty-four-b of the social services law to legally free such child for adoption.

Amended by L. 1976, Ch. 666, eff. Jan. 1, 1977, redesignating former section 1058 as section 1059.

JUDICIARY LAW

(ARTS. 5-B, 19, 21-A)

ARTICLE 5-B—

SPECIAL NARCOTICS PARTS OF THE SUPREME COURT IN CITIES WITH A POPULATION OF ONE MILLION OR MORE

§ 177-a. Declaration of legislative findings and intent.

The legislature hereby finds and declares that an emergency of grave dimensions exists in narcotics law enforcement in cities having a population of one million or more. The overall law enforcement effort has not been successful in stemming the distribution of narcotic drugs. The legislature finds that the ineffectiveness of official efforts to contain the narcotics traffic is due in significant part to the inability of the overburdened criminal justice system to cope with the enormous volume of narcotics cases.

The legislature further finds that this crisis, which transcends the traditional jurisdictional boundaries of the counties wholly contained within such cities having a population of one million or more, demands coordinated prosecution, centralized direction and the infusion of massive new resources.

The legislature declares that without these new directions and resources, this crisis will intensify and very shortly overwhelm the already strained criminal justice system.

Based upon the above findings the legislature hereby declares that an emergency narcotics court program is required.

It is the intent of the legislature that the emergency narcotics program should be coordinated by the division of criminal justice of the office of planning services in cooperation with the criminal justice coordinating councils of such cities. The program would be implemented by the joint efforts of the district attorneys of the counties within cities having a population of one million or more, the judiciary, and other criminal justice services acting in accordance with a mutually agreed upon plan. The legislature contemplates that the program authorized herein shall consist of the establishment of special narcotics parts in the supreme court in cities having a population of one million or more to hear and determine narcotic cases from within counties wholly contained in a city having a population of one million or more, commencing not later than the September nineteen hundred seventy-two term and continuing thereafter during the duration of the emergency.

The legislature declares that the resources necessary for these special narcotics parts of the supreme court can be made available only through a combination of federal funds from the law enforcement assistance administration of the United States department of justice, and state and local funds, services and facilities. To this end the legislature declares that in order to utilize presently appropriated federal funds, all necessary agreements shall be entered into forthwith.

Amended by L. 1972, Ch. 633.

ANNOTATIONS

Centralized narcotic part; constitutionality; execution of program.—Where legislature declared narcotic addiction problem in cities of over one million to be of emergency and epidemic proportions, the creation of centralized administrative and judicial facilities to cope with the problem are presumed constitutional, absent any factual showing that execution of program will result in more severe penalties or discrimination against those tried in centralized part. People v. Simmons, 71 Misc. 2d 940, 337 N.Y.S.2d 717 (Sup. Ct. N.Y. Co. 1972).

Constitutionality.—Article 5-B of the Judiciary Law is upheld as valid. People v. Abraham, 44 A.D.2d 721, 354 N.Y.S.2d 956 (2d Dept. 1974).

Trial.—Defendant, who was indicted for a narcotic offense in Kings County was properly tried in the New York City Centralized Narcotics Part located in New York County before a jury drawn only from New York County. People v. Taylor, 39 N.Y.2d 649, 385 N.Y.S.2d 270, 350 N.E.2d 600 (1976).

§ 177-b. Special narcotics parts; establishment.

1. There shall be established in cities having a population of one million or more in the supreme court special narcotics parts in such

MISC. LAWS

numbers and at such locations as shall be designated by the administrative board of the judicial conference of the state of New York to effectuate the purposes of this article. Such parts shall hear and determine narcotics indictments assigned thereto from any part of the supreme court in any county within such cities.

As used in this article, "narcotics indictment" means an indictment charging a crime that is prosecutable in any county wholly contained in a city within cities having a population of one million or more involving the sale or possession of a narcotic drug and any other offense properly joined therewith.

2. Notwithstanding any other provision of law, upon or after arraignment on a narcotics indictment filed in the supreme court in any county within such cities and before entry of a plea of guilty or commencement of trial, such supreme court may order that the indictment and action be assigned to a special narcotics part of the supreme court.

3. The trial of an indictment in a special narcotics part shall for all purposes be deemed to be a trial in the county in which the indictment was filed, but the administrative board of the judicial conference may promulgate rules, orders or regulations to be applicable to such parts in place and instead of the rules, orders or regulations applicable to courts in the county where the indictment was filed. The administrative board shall provide by rule, order or regulation for at least the following matters: the procedure of the part; its auxiliary services; the assignment of judicial personnel; the appointment of terms; and transmittal of all papers in the action, including all undertakings for appearances of the defendant and of the witnesses, to the part of the supreme court to which the action has been assigned.

§ 177-c. Special narcotics parts; prosecutorial organization.

The district attorneys of the counties wholly contained in a city having a population of one million or more shall formulate and adopt a plan designed to effect the purposes of this article. The plan shall provide for the following matters:

(i) the appointment of an assistant district attorney to the staff of one of the district attorneys to administer the program established pursuant to the plan;

(ii) the appointment of a staff to operate under the direction and supervision of the assistant district attorney appointed pursuant to paragraph (i);

(iii) the establishment of standards, administrative policies, and procedures to govern the performance of the prosecutorial functions in connection with narcotics cases, including but not limited to guidelines governing applications by the assistant district attorney appointed pursuant

to paragraph (i) for the impaneling of a grand jury; and

(iv) any other matters pertaining to the effective administration of the program and fulfillment of the purposes of this article.

Amended by L. 1972, Ch. 633.

§ 177-d. Special narcotics parts; procedure.

Notwithstanding any other provision of law,

(i) a narcotics indictment returned in any county within such cities may be prosecuted in the special narcotics part to which it is assigned pursuant to section one hundred seventy-seven-b irrespective of the county in which the part is held and in which the crime charged was committed;

(ii) any assistant district attorney appointed pursuant to the plan authorized by section one hundred seventy-seven-c may prosecute all offenses cognizable by any special narcotics part irrespective of the county in which the part is held and in which the crime charged was committed; and

(iii) upon the application of the assistant district attorney in charge of the special narcotics parts appointed pursuant to the plan authorized by section one hundred seventy-seven-c, one or more grand juries may be drawn and impaneled for a special narcotics part upon the order of the justice assigned to such part, which grand jury may exercise all the powers of a grand jury in the county in which it is impaneled and may in addition exercise its powers with respect to the alleged commission of an offense in any county wholly contained in a city having a population of one million or more involving the sale or possession of a narcotic drug and any other offense that could be properly joined therewith in an indictment.

Amended by L. 1972, Ch. 633.

ANNOTATIONS

Jurisdiction.—The Constitution of the State and the NYC-CCA, by creating one city-wide court of criminal jurisdiction, allow for felony complaints to be filed in any county of the City alleging overt criminal conduct wholly occurring in a different county of the City; such a broad interpretation is also consistent with the legislative intent manifested in Judiciary Law article 5-B. People v. Selby, 148 Misc. 2d 447, 561 N.Y.S.2d 447 (Sup. Ct. N.Y. Co. 1990).

—Special Narcotics Grand Jury did not have authority to return an indictment charging a physician with unlawfully prescribing Valium in Kings County. People v. Shukla, 82 Misc. 2d 912, 371 N.Y.S.2d 219 (Sup. Ct. N.Y. Co. 1975).

—Special Narcotics Grand Jury located in New York County had statutory authority to charge the indictable offense of unlawfully prescribing non-narcotic drug within New York County, People v. Manfredi, 82 Misc. 2d 917, 372 N.Y.S.2d 403 (Sup. Ct. N.Y. Co. 1975).

Jury pool.—Although crime was committed in Kings County and the case was to be tried in New York County, it was proper for the jury to be drawn solely from New York County. People v. Taylor, 39 N.Y.2d 649, 385 N.Y.S.2d 270, 350 N.E.2d 600 (1976).

§ 177-e. Special narcotics parts; probation services.

The state director of probation and correctional alternatives is authorized to supplement the probation services available to the supreme court in such cities by directing that probation services for cases in the special narcotics parts be performed by the state division of probation and correctional alternatives. Such services shall be administered in accordance with the provisions of subdivision two of section two hundred forty-seven of the executive law, except that the two-year limitation contained therein shall not apply.

Amended by L. 1985, Ch. 134, eff. Apr. 1, 1985.

ARTICLE 19—CONTEMPTS

§ 750. Power of courts to punish for criminal contempts.

A. A court of record has power to punish for a criminal contempt, a person guilty of any of the following acts, and no others:

1. Disorderly, contemptuous, or insolent behavior, committed during its sitting, in its immediate view and presence, and directly tending to interrupt its proceedings, or to impair the respect due to its authority.

2. Breach of the peace, noise, or other disturbance, directly tending to interrupt its proceedings.

3. Wilful disobedience to its lawful mandate.

4. Resistance wilfully offered to its lawful mandate.

5. Contumacious and unlawful refusal to be sworn as a witness; or, after being sworn, to answer any legal and proper interrogatory.

6. Publication of a false, or grossly inaccurate report of its proceedings. but a court can not punish as a contempt, the publication of a true, full, and fair report of a trial, argument, decision, or other proceeding therein.

7. Wilful failure to obey any mandate, process or notice issued pursuant to articles sixteen, seventeen, eighteen, eighteen-a or eighteen-b of the judiciary law, or to rules adopted pursuant thereto, or to any other statute relating thereto, or refusal to be sworn as provided therein, or subjection of an employee to discharge or penalty on account of his absence from employment by reason of jury or subpoenaed witness service in violation of this chapter or section 215.11 of the penal law. Applications to punish the accused for a contempt specified in this subdivision may be made by notice of motion or by order to show cause, and shall be made returnable at the term of the supreme court at which contested motions are heard, or of the county court if the supreme court is not in session.

B. In addition to the power to punish for a criminal contempt as set forth in subdivision a, the supreme court has power under this section to punish for a criminal contempt any person who unlawfully practices or assumes to practice law; and a proceeding under this subdivision may be instituted on the court's own motion or on the motion of any officer charged with the duty of investigating or prosecuting unlawful practice of law, or by any bar association incorporated under the laws of this state.

C. A court not of record has only such power to punish for a criminal contempt as is specifically granted to it by statute and no other.

Burden of proof.—Criminal contempt must apparently be proved beyond a reasonable doubt; civil contempt requires proof "with reasonable certainty." N.A. Development Co. Ltd. v. Jones, 99 A.D.2d 238, 472 N.Y.S.2d 363 (1st Dept. 1984).

Contempt; generally.— A court has subject matter jurisdiction over any and all motions in underlying civil action before it, as well as any proceeding arising out of said action seeking to hold one of the parties in civil or criminal contempt. Hirschfeld v. Friedman, 307 A.D.2d 856, 763 N.Y.S.2d 580 (1st Dept. 2003).

—Family court does not have the authority to hold a juvenile adjudicated a PINS in contempt for violation of an order of protection; the exclusive remedies for violation of a PINS order are contained in FCA § 778. In re Edwin G., 296 A.D.2d 7, 742 N.Y.S.2d 53 (1st Dept. 2002).

—Disorderly, contemptuous, or insolent behavior, committed in the court's presence, which tends to interrupt its proceedings or to impair the respect for its authority, may be punished as a criminal contempt, as can willful disobedience of or willful resistance offered to the court's lawful mandate; conduct which manifests an intent to defy the dignity and authority of the court may properly be adjudged contemptuous. Scott v. Hughes, 106 A.D.2d 355, 483 N.Y.S.2d 18 (1st Dept. 1984).

—Where petitioner's conduct during trial was not insolent and did not threaten to disrupt or actually disrupt proceedings or undermine dignity of court proceeding, adjudication of summary contempt was not warranted. Greenberg v. Starkey, 20 A.D.3d 419, 797 N.Y.S.2d 307 (2d Dept. 2005).

—Willful failure to obey a lawful mandate of the court constitutes criminal contempt. Papa v. 24 Caryl Ave. Realty Co., 14 A.D.3d 600, 788 N.Y.S.2d 611 (2d Dept. 2005).

—A court of record has power to punish a party for disobedience of a lawful mandate of court, which constitutes an order of a court of competent jurisdiction which is not void on its face, here it involved an order enjoining bank to pay an instrument in issue, bank was afforded a reasonable time to comply, yet disobeyed lawful mandate and paid instrument, and may be held in contempt. Dalessio v. Kressler, 6 A.D.3d 57, 773 N.Y.S.2d 434 (2d Dept. 2004).

—Grievance committee held defendant-attorney in criminal contempt for failure to comply with an order of disbarment that specifically ordered him to refrain from practicing law in any form and from appearing as an attorney in any court; after being personally served the order, defendant filed a notice of appeal as retained counsel in an action and participated in a plea agreement. In re Meyer, 279 A.D.2d 203, 717 N.Y.S.2d 380 (2d Dept. 2000).

—Court erred in holding defendant in contempt pursuant to section 750 for exercising his right against self-incrimination. Also, failure of the Family Court to personally serve defendant with order to show cause upon a finding of contempt was a non-waivable jurisdictional defect. Howard T.P. v. Maria B., 237 A.D.2d 443, 654 N.Y.S.2d 419 (2d Dept. 1997).

—Petitioner's utterance of an obscenity in court's presence following a ruling with which he disagreed provided a basis for a finding of contempt, however, petitioner's failure to sign the release regarding his psychiatric treatment did not support a finding of criminal contempt and under the particular circumstances presented here, it was error for Family Court to resort to contempt statute when other remedies were available. Frierson v. Goldston, 8 A.D.3d 160, 779 N.Y.S.2d 67 (3d Dept. 2004).

—The acts of a suspended attorney in holding oneself out as an attorney and continuing to practice law constitutes criminal contempt of court in violation of this section. In re Ladas, 9 A.D.3d 234, 781 N.Y.S.2d 723 (4th Dept. 2004).

—Conduct which forms the basis of a summary proceeding must occur in the presence of the court and must be held immediately. Delay in the summary contempt adjudication until the end of the proceeding eliminates the need for the hearing since the purpose is to prevent the disruption or threatened disruption of the court proceeding. In re O'Connell v. Taddeo, 174 Misc. 2d 110, 662 N.Y.S.2d 722 (Fam. Ct. Monroe Co. 1997).

§ 751. Punishment for criminal contempts.

1. Except as provided in subdivisions (2), (3) and (4), punishment for a contempt, specified in section seven hundred fifty, may be by fine, not exceeding one thousand dollars, or by imprisonment, not exceeding thirty days, in the jail of the county where the court is sitting, or both, in the discretion of the court. Where the punishment for contempt is based on a violation of an order of protection issued under section 530.12 or 530.13 of the criminal procedure law, imprisonment may be for a term not exceeding three months. Where a person is committed to jail, for the nonpayment of a fine, imposed under this section, he must be discharged at the expiration of thirty days; but where he is also committed for a definite time, the thirty days must be computed from the expiration of the definite time.

Such a contempt, committed in the immediate view and presence of the court, may be punished summarily; when not so committed, the party charged must be notified of the accusation, and have a reasonable time to make a defense.

2. (a) [*Effective until Oct. 1, 2007.*] Where an employee organization, as defined in section two hundred one of the civil service law, wilfully disobeys a lawful mandate of a court of record, or wilfully offers resistance to such lawful mandate, in a case involving or growing out of a strike in violation of subdivision one of section two hundred ten of the civil service law, the punishment for each day that such contempt persists may be by a fine fixed in the discretion of the court. In the case of a government exempt from certain provisions of article fourteen of the civil service law, pursuant to section two hundred twelve of such law, the court may, as an additional punishment for such contempt, order forfeiture of the rights granted pursuant to the provisions of paragraph (b) of subdivision one of section two hundred eight of such law, for such specified period of time, as the court shall determine or, in the discretion of the court, for an indefinite period of time subject to restoration upon application, with notice to all interested parties, supported by proof of good faith compliance with the requirements of subdivision one of section two hundred ten of the civil service law since the date of such violation, such proof to include, for example, the successful negotiation, without a violation of subdivision one of section two hundred ten of the civil service law, of a contract covering the employees in the unit affected by such violation; provided, however, that where a fine imposed pursuant to this subdivision remains wholly or partly unpaid, after the exhaustion of the cash and securities of the employee organization, such forfeiture shall be suspended to the extent necessary for the unpaid portion of such fine to be accumulated by the public employer and transmitted to the court. In fixing the amount

of the fine and/or duration of the forfeiture, the court shall consider all the facts and circumstances directly related to the contempt, including, but not limited to: (i) the extent of the wilful defiance of or a resistance to the court's mandate (ii) the impact of the strike on the public health, safety, and welfare of the community and (iii) the ability of the employee organization to pay the fine imposed; and the court may consider (i) the refusal of the employee organization or the appropriate public employer, as defined in section two hundred one of the civil service law, or the representatives thereof, to submit to the mediation and fact-finding procedures provided in section two hundred nine of the civil service law and (ii) whether, if so alleged by the employee organization, the appropriate public employer or its representatives engaged in such acts of extreme provocation as to detract from the responsibility of the employee organization for the strike. In determining the ability of the employee organization to pay the fine imposed, the court shall consider both the income and the assets of such employee organization.

(a) [*Effective Oct. 1, 2007.*] Where an employee organization, as defined in section two hundred one of the civil service law, wilfully disobeys a lawful mandate of a court of record, or wilfully offers resistance to such lawful mandate, in a case involving or growing out of a strike in violation of subdivision one of section two hundred ten of the civil service law, the punishment for each day that such contempt persists may be by a fine fixed in the discretion of the court. In the case of a government exempt from certain provisions of article fourteen of the civil service law, pursuant to section two hundred twelve of such law, the court may, as an additional punishment for such contempt, order forfeiture of the rights granted pursuant to the provisions of paragraph (b) of subdivision one of section two hundred eight of such law, for such specified period of time, as the court shall determine or, in the discretion of the court, for an indefinite period of time subject to restoration upon application, with notice to all interested parties, supported by proof of good faith compliance with the requirements of subdivision one of section two hundred ten of the civil service law since the date of such violation, such proof to include, for example, the successful negotiation, without a violation of subdivision one of section two hundred ten of the civil service law, of a contract covering the employees in the unit affected by such violation; provided, however, that where a fine imposed pursuant to this subdivision remains wholly or partly unpaid, after the exhaustion of the cash and securities of the employee organization, such forfeiture shall be suspended to the extent necessary for the unpaid portion of such fine to be accumulated by the public employer and transmitted to the court. In fixing the amount of the fine and/or duration of the forfeiture, the court shall consider all the facts and circumstances directly related to the contempt, including, but not limited to: (i) the extent of the wilful defiance of or a resistance to the court's mandate (ii) the impact of the strike on the public health, safety, and welfare of the community and (iii) the ability of the employee organization to pay the fine imposed; and the court may consider (i) the refusal of the employee organization or the appropriate public employer, as defined in section two hundred one of the civil service law, or the representatives thereof, to submit to the mediation and fact-finding procedures provided in section two hundred nine of the civil service law and (ii) whether, if so alleged by the employee organization, the appropriate public employer or its representatives engaged in such acts of extreme provocation as to detract from the responsibility of the employee organization for the strike. In determining the ability of the employee organization to pay the fine imposed, the court shall consider both the income and the assets of such employee organization.

(b) [*Effective until Oct. 1, 2007.*] In the event membership dues are collected by the public employer as provided in paragraph (b) of subdivision one of section two hundred eight of the civil service law, the books and records of such public employer shall be prima facie evidence of the amount so collected.

(b) [*Effective Oct. 1, 2007.*] In the event membership dues are collected by the public employer as provided in paragraph (b) of subdivision one of section two hundred eight of the civil service law, the books and records of such public employer shall be prima facie evidence of the amount so collected.

(c) (i) An employee organization appealing an adjudication and fine for criminal contempt imposed pursuant to subdivision two of this section, shall not be required to pay such fine until such appeal is finally determined.

(ii) The court to which such an appeal is taken shall, on motion of any party thereto, grant a preference in the hearing thereof.

3. (a) Where a union or hospital wilfully disobeys a lawful mandate of a court of record, or wilfully offers resistance to such lawful mandate, in a case involving or growing out of a violation of section seven hundred thirteen of the labor law, the punishment for each day that such contempt persists may be by a fine fixed in the discretion of the court. In fixing the amount of such fine, the court shall consider all the facts and circumstances directly related to the contempt, including, but not limited to: (i) the extent of the wilful defiance of, or resistance to, the court's mandate (ii) the impact of the strike or lockout on the public health, safety and welfare of the community and (iii) the ability of the union or hospital to pay the fine imposed; and the court may consider (i) the refusal of the union or

hospital, or the representatives thereof, to submit to or comply with, the fact-finding and arbitration procedures provided in section seven hundred sixteen of the labor law. In determining the ability of the union or hospital to pay the fine imposed, the court shall consider both the income and the assets of such union or hospital.

(b) A union or hospital appealing an adjudication and fine for criminal contempt imposed pursuant to this subdivision, shall not be required to pay such fine until such appeal is finally determined. The court to which such an appeal is taken shall, on motion of any party thereto, grant a preference in the hearing thereof.

(c) As used in this subdivision, "union" shall mean any labor organization or company union as defined in section seven hundred one of the labor law, and "hospital" shall mean any non-profit-making hospital or residential care center as defined in that section.

4. Where any person wilfully disobeys a lawful mandate of the supreme court issued pursuant to subdivision twelve of section sixty-three of the executive law, the punishment for each day that such contempt persists may be by a fine fixed in the discretion of the court, but not to exceed five thousand dollars per day. In fixing the amount of the fine, the court shall consider all the facts and circumstances directly related to the contempt, including, but not limited to: (i) the extent of the wilful defiance of or resistance to the court's mandate, (ii) the amount of gain obtained by the wilful disobedience of the mandate, and (iii) the effect upon the public of the wilful disobedience.

5. Where any member of the news media as defined in subdivision two of section two hundred eighteen of this chapter, willfully disobeys a lawful mandate of a court issued pursuant to such section, the punishment for each day that such contempt persists may be by a fine fixed in the discretion of the court, but not to exceed five thousand dollars per day or imprisonment, not exceeding thirty days, in the jail of the county where the court is sitting or both, in the discretion of the court. In fixing the amount of the fine, the court shall consider all the facts and circumstances directly related to the contempt, including, but not limited to: (i) the extent of the willful defiance of or resistance to the court's mandate, (ii) the amount of gain obtained by the willful disobedience of the mandate, and (iii) the effect upon the public and the parties to the proceeding of the willful disobedience.

Amended by L. 1993, Ch. 126, § 1, extending expiration date for amended subd. 2(a) and (b) to Oct. 1, 1995. **Amended** by L. 1999, Ch. 502, § 1, extending expiration date for amended subd. 2(a) and (b) to Oct. 1, 2001; L. 2003, Ch. 342, § 1, eff. Aug. 19, 2003, extending expiration date to Oct. 1, 2005; L. 2005, Ch. 31, § 1, eff. May 10, 2005, extending expiration date to Oct. 1, 2007.

ANNOTATIONS

Generally.—An award of over $8,000 in attorney's fees is not a proper sanction for criminal contempt under this section. Clinton Corner H.D.F.C. v. Lavergne, 279 A.D.2d 339, 719 N.Y.S.2d 77 (1st Dept. 2001).

—Respondent was held in contempt for year-long avoidance of an order directing his appearance at a deposition pursuant to a commission issued by a New Jersey court and fined $1,750, along with sanctions for respondent's attorney for frivolous conduct. Borgenicht v. Bloch, 280 A.D.2d 306, 719 N.Y.S.2d 654 (1st Dept. 2001).

—A motion to punish an adverse party for violating a court order where the violation was not committed in the presence of the court may not be the subject matter of a summary contempt proceeding. STV Group, Inc. v. American Continental Props., Inc., 224 A.D.2d 680, 639 N.Y.S.2d 56 (2d Dept. 1996).

—A criminal contempt proceeding is a criminal proceeding to which the basic fundamentals are applicable to the same extent as in any other criminal trial. Ingraham v. Maurer, 39 A.D.2d 258, 334 N.Y.S.2d 19 (3d Dept. 1972).

—Both civil and criminal contempt statutes authorize penalties of a limited fine, a term of imprisonment of up to a year, or both; however, court was without authority under Judiciary Law to impose a sentence including community service and psychiatric treatment for either civil or criminal contempt. Data-Track Account Servs. v. Lee, 17 A.D.3d 1115, 796 N.Y.S.2d 206 (4th Dept. 2005).

Double jeopardy.—Contempt provision of Family Court Act, Article 8 is a lesser included offense of criminal contempt in the first degree; therefore, prosecution and the imposition of additional punishment for the greater offense, criminal contempt, after prosecution under the Family Court Act, is barred by double jeopardy. People v. Wood, 95 N.Y.2d 509, 719 N.Y.S.2d 639, 742 N.E.2d 114 (2000).

§ 752. Requisites of commitment for criminal contempt; review of certain mandates.

Where a person is committed for contempt, as prescribed in section seven hundred fifty-one, the particular circumstances of his offense must be set forth in the mandate of commitment. Such mandate, punishing a person summarily for a contempt committed in the immediate view and presence of the court, is reviewable by a proceeding under article seventy-eight of the civil practice law and rules.

ANNOTATION

Contempt committed in "immediate view and presence."—Violation of a prior court order which requires testimony to establish does not occur within the "immediate view and presence" of the court. Defendant could not be punished in a summary proceeding for his violation of a prior order not to ingest drugs or alcohol before coming to court, where this violation occurred in defendant's house before attending court and required witnesses to establish. O'Connell v. Taddeo, 174 Misc. 2d 110, 662 N.Y.S.2d 722 (Fam. Ct. Monroe Co. 1997).

§ 753. Power of courts to punish for civil contempts.

A. A court of record has power to punish, by fine and imprisonment, or either, a neglect or violation of duty, or other misconduct, by which a right or remedy of a party to a civil action or special proceeding, pending in the court may be defeated, impaired, impeded, or prejudiced, in any of the following cases:

1. An attorney, counsellor, clerk, sheriff, coroner, or other person, in any manner duly selected or appointed to perform a judicial or ministerial

service, for a misbehavior in his office or trust, or for a wilful neglect or violation of duty therein; or for disobedience to a lawful mandate of the court, or of a judge thereof, or of an officer authorized to perform the duties of such a judge.

2. A party to the action or special proceeding, for putting in fictitious bail or a fictitious surety, or for any deceit or abuse of a mandate or proceeding of the court.

3. A party to the action or special proceeding, an attorney, counsellor, or other person, for the non-payment of a sum of money, ordered or adjudged by the court to be paid, in a case where by law execution can not be awarded for the collection of such sum except as otherwise specifically provided by the civil practice law and rules; or for any other disobedience to a lawful mandate of the court.

4. A person, for assuming to be an attorney or counsellor, or other officer of the court, and acting as such without authority; for rescuing any property or person in the custody of an officer, by virtue of a mandate of the court; for unlawfully detaining, or fraudulently and wilfully preventing, or disabling from attending or testifying, a witness, or a party to the action or special proceeding, while going to, remaining at, or returning from, the sitting where it is noticed for trial or hearing; and for any other unlawful interference with the proceedings therein.

5. A person subpoenaed as a witness, for refusing or neglecting to obey the subpoena, or to attend, or to be sworn, or to answer as a witness.

6. A person duly notified to attend as a juror, at a term of the court, for improperly conversing with a party to an action or special proceeding, to be tried at that term, or with any other person, in relation to the merits of that action or special proceeding; or for receiving a communication from any person, in relation to the merits of such an action or special proceeding, without immediately disclosing the same to the court; or a person who attends and acts or attempts to act as a juror in the place and stead of a person who has been duly notified to attend.

7. An inferior magistrate, or a judge or other officer of an inferior court, for proceeding, contrary to law, in a cause or matter, which has been removed from his jurisdiction to the court inflicting the punishment; or for disobedience to a lawful order or other mandate of the latter court.

8. In any other case, where an attachment or any other proceeding to punish for a contempt, has been usually adopted and practiced in a court of record, to enforce a civil remedy of a party to an action or special proceeding in that court, or to protect the right of a party.

B. A court not of record has such power to punish for a civil contempt as is specifically granted to it by statute.

ANNOTATIONS

Contempt committed in "immediate view and presence."—Violation of a prior court order which requires testimony to establish does not occur within the "immediate view and presence" of the court. Defendant could not be punished in a summary proceeding for his violation of a prior order not to ingest drugs or alcohol before coming to court, where this violation occurred in defendant's house before attending court and required witnesses to establish. O'Connell v. Taddeo, 174 Misc. 2d 110, 662 N.Y.S.2d 722 (Fam. Ct. Monroe Co. 1997).

Contempt; elements.—Although the line between civil and criminal contempt may be difficult to draw in a given case, and the same act may be punishable as both a civil and criminal contempt, the element which escalates a contempt to criminal status is the level of willfulness associated with the conduct. McCain v. Dinkins, 84 N.Y.2d 216, 616 N.Y.S.2d 335, 639 N.E.2d 1132 (1994).

—To sustain a finding of either civil or criminal contempt based on an alleged violation of a court order it is necessary to establish that a lawful order of the court clearly expressing an unequivocal mandate was in effect, and it must also appear with reasonable certainty that the order has been disobeyed; additionally, the party charged must have had knowledge of the court's order. Department of Environmental Protection of the City of New York v. Dept. of Environmental Conservation of the State of New York, 70 N.Y.2d 233, 519 N.Y.S.2d 539, 513 N.E.2d 706 (1987).

Contempt; generally.—A court has subject matter jurisdiction over any and all motions in the underlying civil action before it, as well as any proceeding arising out of said action seeking to hold one of the parties in civil or criminal contempt. Hirschfeld v. Friedman, 307 A.D.2d 856, 763 N.Y.S.2d 580 (1st Dept. 2003).

—Court has the ability to punish petitioner for contempt as a result of his violation of a court order where the violation has not occurred in the court's presence. Michael N.G. v. Elsa R., 233 A.D.2d 264, 650 N.Y.S.2d 140 (1st Dept. 1996).

—The purpose of criminal contempt is to vindicate authority of court, no showing of prejudice to rights of a party to litigation is needed "since the right of the private parties to the litigation is not the controlling factor," Civil contempt "has as its aim the vindication of a private party to litigation" and includes as its elements knowledge of the order and prejudice to the rights of a party to the litigation. Dalessio v. Kressler, 6 A.D.3d 57, 773 N.Y.S.2d 434 (2d Dept. 2004).

—Contempt order's failure to contain required language regarding the fact that appellant's conduct was calculated or actually impaired, impeded or prejudiced the rights of the defendant was not fatal to the validity of the order in light of the undisputed nature of the facts; the omission was a mere irregularity. However, evidence did not support damages awarded; damages should be limited to actual out-of-pocket expenses plus a statutory penalty. Barkan v. Barkan, 271 A.D.2d 466, 706 N.Y.S.2d 902 (2d Dept. 2000).

—Defendant/father properly held in custody for contempt of court where he willfully refused to produce the child or tell court of child's whereabouts, where it was shown that he had the ability to comply with court's requests. In re Baby H., 264 A.D.2d 419, 693 N.Y.S.2d 447 (2d Dept. 1999).

—Divorced mother's failure to abide by terms of visitation in order to allow and encourage children to have a meaningful relationship with their father was proper grounds to find her in civil contempt although it was error to change custodial parents as a sanction, sanctions for civil contempt are limited to fine and or imprisonment. Labanowski v. Labanowski, 4 A.D.3d 690, 772 N.Y.S.2d 734 (3d Dept. 2004).

—Where no unequivocally clear order ever existed by which petitioners were entitled to be compensated at a certain salary grade respondents failure to pay petitioners at that grade did not constitute a violation of a clear order to form the basis of a civil contempt. Steen v. Governor's Office of Employee Rels., 1 A.D.3d 644, 766 N.Y.S.2d 607 (3d Dept. 2003).

—Although the degree of willfulness necessary to establish civil contempt is less than that required to prove criminal contempt, here, the court's order was summary in its terms and was not so unequivocal as to support a finding of willful disobedience; respondents' actions were not willfully or intentionally disobedient and did not significantly prejudice petitioner. Hicks v. Russi, 254 A.D.2d 801, 678 N.Y.S.2d 203 (4th Dept. 1998).

—Refusal to obey an information subpoena is punishable as a contempt of a court order. Mailman v. Belvecchio, 195 Misc. 2d 275, 757 N.Y.S.2d 216 (Sup. Ct. Richmond Co. 2002).

—Court found plaintiff to be in criminal contempt pursuant to section 753(A)(2) for misstatements in his net worth affidavit, upon which the court relied in awarding plaintiff's wife *pendente lite* support and maintenance. Kim v. Kim, 170 Misc. 2d 968, 652 N.Y.S.2d 694 (Sup. Ct. Suffolk Co. 1996).

Unequivocal mandate.—Where the record does not indicate that respondent violated an "unequivocal mandate" regarding the right to joint custody, there can be no finding of civil contempt. Petkovsek v. Snyder, 251 A.D.2d 1085, 675 N.Y.S.2d 573 (4th Dept. 1998).

§ 753-a. Contempts in cases involving or growing out of labor disputes.

1. Notwithstanding any inconsistent provision of law, where the alleged contempt is punishable under section seven hundred fifty and/or section seven hundred fifty-three and arises out of any failure or refusal to obey any mandate of a court contained in or incidental to an injunction order granted by such court in any case involving or growing out of a labor dispute, no punishment, prescribed by either of such sections, shall be meted out except after a trial by jury to which the defendant shall be entitled as a matter of right; provided, however, that this section shall not apply to any alleged contempt of such an injunction order committed in the presence of the court.

2. As used in this section and in subdivision three of section 215.50 of the penal law:

(a) A case shall be held to involve or to grow out of a labor dispute when the case involves persons who are engaged in the same industry, trade, craft or occupation; or who are employees of one employer; or who are members of the same or an affiliated organization of employers or employees; whether such dispute is between one or more employers or associations of employers and one or more employees or associations of employees; between one or more employers or associations of employers and one or more employers or associations of employers; or between one or more employees or associations of employees and one or more employees or associations of employees; or when the case involves any conflicting or competing interests in a "labor dispute" (as hereinafter defined) of "persons participating or interested" therein (as hereinafter defined).

(b) The term "labor dispute" includes any controversy concerning terms or conditions of employment, or concerning the association or representation of persons in negotiating, fixing, maintaining, changing or seeking to arrange terms or conditions of employment, or concerning employment relations, or any other controversy arising out of the respective interests of employer and employee, regardless of whether or not the disputants stand in the relation of employer and employee.

(c) A person or association shall be held to be a person participating or interested in a labor dispute if relief is sought against him or it and if he or it is engaged in the industry, trade, craft or occupation in which such dispute occurs, or is a member, officer or agent of any association of employers or employees engaged in such industry, trade, craft or occupation.

§ 754. Special proceeding to punish for contempt punishable civilly.

Sections seven hundred and fifty, seven hundred and fifty-one, and seven hundred and fifty-two, do not extend to a special proceeding to punish a person in a case specified in section seven hundred and fifty-three. In a case specified in section seven hundred and fifty-three, or in any other case where it is specially prescribed by law, that a court of record, or a judge thereof, or a referee appointed by the court, has power to punish, by fine and imprisonment, or either, or generally as a contempt, a neglect or violation of duty, or other misconduct; and a right or remedy of a party to a civil action or special proceeding pending in the court, or before the judge or the referee, may be defeated, impaired, impeded, or prejudiced thereby, the offense must be punished as prescribed in the following sections of this article.

§ 755. When punishment may be summary.

Where the offense is committed in the immediate view and presence of the court, or of the judge or referee, upon a trial or hearing, it may be punished summarily. For that purpose, an order must be made by the court, judge, or referee, stating the facts which constitute the offense and which bring the case within the provisions of this section, and plainly and specifically prescribing the punishment to be inflicted therefor. Such order is reviewable by a proceeding under article seventy-eight of the civil practice law and rules.

ANNOTATIONS

Generally.—The need for preservation of immediate order in the courtroom justifies the summary procedure—the right and need for an evidentiary hearing, counsel, opportunity for adjournment, reference to another judge, and the like, are not allowable because it would entirely frustrate the maintenance of order; such rigorous procedure is justified only by necessity and must then be based on contemptuous conduct committed in the view and presence of the presiding justice. Katz v. Murtagh, 28 N.Y.2d 234, 321 N.Y.S.2d 104 (1971).

—Petitioner's repeated refusals to comply with Family Court directives to limit her answers to questions posed and to refrain from extraneous comments that interrupted the court proceedings were supported by the record and were proper grounds for contempt findings on four occasions and total fine of $700. Pozefsky v. Jung, 268 A.D.2d 646, 701 N.Y.S.2d 470 (3d Dept. 2000).

—Violation of a prior court order which requires testimony to establish does not occur within the "immediate view and presence" of the court. Defendant could not be punished in a summary proceeding for his violation of a prior order not to ingest drugs or alcohol before coming to court, where this violation occurred in defendant's house before attending court and required witnesses to establish. O'Connell v. Taddeo, 174 Misc. 2d 110, 662 N.Y.S.2d 722 (Fam. Ct. Monroe Co. 1997).

Ability to perform act or duty.—Family court abused its discretion by refusing to release intervenor-mother from custody in view of the fact that she could not produce her son as ordered by the court because a California court had awarded permanent guardianship to the grandparents pursuant to its emergency jurisdiction. *In re* David G., 280 A.D.2d 477 720 N.Y.S.2d 179 (2d Dept. 2001).

Lateness.—Summary contempt was justified and proper based upon attorney's historic pattern of lateness in violation of the court's direct order. Marcus v. Bamberger, 180 A.D.2d 533, 580 N.Y.S.2d 256 (1st Dept. 1992).

Violation occurs outside presence of court.—Where the subject violation occurred outside presence of the court, the proceeding cannot be converted into a summary contempt proceeding as a result of the court's failure to give adequate notice. Michael N.G. v. Elsa R., 233 A.D.2d 264, 650 N.Y.S.2d 140 (1st Dept. 1996).

§ 756. Application to punish for contempt; procedure.

An application to punish for a contempt punishable civilly may be commenced by notice of motion returnable before the court or judge authorized to punish for the offense, or by an order of such court or judge requiring the accused to show cause before it, or him, at a time and place therein specified, why the accused should not be punished for the alleged offense. The application shall be noticed, heard and determined in accordance with the procedure for a motion on notice in an action in such court, provided, however, that, except as provided in section fifty-two hundred fifty of the civil practice law and rules or unless otherwise ordered by the court, the moving papers shall be served no less than ten and no more than thirty days before the time at which the application is noticed to be heard. The application shall contain on its face a notice that the purpose of the hearing is to punish the accused for a contempt of court, and that such punishment may consist of fine or imprisonment, or both, according to law together with the following legend printed or type written in a size equal to at least eight point bold type: **WARNING: YOUR FAILURE TO APPEAR IN COURT MAY RESULT IN YOUR IMMEDIATE ARREST AND IMPRISONMENT FOR CONTEMPT OF COURT.**

ANNOTATIONS

Notice.—Failure of court to properly serve petitioner with notice of contempt proceedings will render action null and void since the court lacked jurisdiction to punish petitioner. Michael N.G. v. Elsa R., 233 A.D.2d 264, 650 N.Y.S.2d 140 (1st Dept. 1996).

—Contempt adjudication finding appellant in contempt for failure to pay $34,000 pursuant to a prior court order must be vacated where appellant did not receive prior notice of the proceeding. DeMorris v. DeMorris, 279 A.D.2d 446, 719 N.Y.S.2d 593 (2d Dept. 2001).

—An application to adjudge an individual in contempt pursuant to this section cannot be oral, it must be written, made with at least 10 days notice, and must contain the required statutory warning; failure to follow these procedural safeguards denies the court jurisdiction to punish the defendant for contempt. Cappello v. Cappello, 274 A.D.2d 538, 712 N.Y.S.2d 41 (2d Dept. 2000).

—Failure to include information required by section 756 resulted in denial of motion to hold defendant in contempt of temporary restraining order. Krissler v. King, 265 A.D.2d 381, 696 N.Y.S.2d 842 (2d Dept. 1999).

—Where the motion to hold defendants in civil contempt was made returnable on 3½ hours notice to the defendants, the proceeding was improperly converted to a summary contempt proceeding, and the order of contempt should be reversed. STV Group, Inc. v. American Continental Properties, Inc., 224 A.D.2d 680, 639 N.Y.S.2d 56 (2d Dept. 1996).

—Order to show cause issued under provisions of Judiciary Law which contained adequate notice as well as warning and notice of penalties was sufficient to protect petitioner's due process rights. By appearing and contesting contempt charge on merits, without mention of alleged notice insufficiencies, petitioner waived those rights. People v. Johnson, 232 A.D.2d 914, 649 N.Y.S.2d 502 (3d Dept. 1996).

—Where the motion for contempt failed to contain required legend in at least eight point bold type, motion was defective and the recipient could not be held in contempt; however, failure to place required warning on contempt application may be waived by party against whom contempt is sought if that party contests application on merits, but fails to timely object to omission of notice and warning. Alizio v. Perpignano, 8 Misc. 3d 1021A, 2005 N.Y. Misc. LEXIS 1589 (Sup. Ct. Nassau Co. 2005).

§ 757. Application to punish for contempt committed before referee.

Where the offense is committed upon the trial of an issue referred to a referee appointed by the court, or consists of a witness's non-attendance, or refusal to be sworn or testify, before him, the application prescribed in this section may be made returnable before him or before the court. The application shall contain on its face a notice that the purpose of the hearing is to punish the accused for a contempt of court, and that such punishment may consist of fine or imprisonment, or both, according to law.

§ 758. Notice to delinquent officer to show cause.

Where it is prescribed by law, or by the rules of civil practice, that a notice may be served in behalf of a party, upon a sheriff or other person, requiring him to return a mandate, delivered to him, or to show cause, at a term of a court, why he should not be punished, or why an attachment should not be issued against him, for a contempt of the court; the party, in whose behalf the notice is served, may, at the time specified therein, file with the clerk, proof, by affidavit or other written evidence, of the delivery of the mandate to the accused; of the default or other act, upon the occurrence of which, he was entitled to serve the notice; of the service of the notice; and of the failure to comply therewith. Thereupon the proceedings are the same, as where an order to show cause is made, and it, and a copy of the affidavits upon which it is granted, are served upon the accused.

ANNOTATION

Notice.—Absent the requisite notice and warning set forth by § 756, Special Term was without jurisdiction to punish for contempt; moreover, an order requiring the performance of an act may not include an additional clause stating that in thereof, the party will be guilty of contempt of court. Murrin v. Murrin, 93 A.D.2d 858, 461 N.Y.S.2d 360 (2d Dept. 1983).

§ 760. When application may be made.

An application may be made, either before or after the final judgment in the action, or the final order in the special proceeding.

§ 761. Notice to accused; service.

An application to punish for contempt in a civil contempt proceeding shall be served upon the accused, unless service upon the attorney for the accused be ordered by the court or judge.

§ 767. When habeas corpus may issue.

If the accused is in the custody of a sheriff, or other officer, by virtue of an execution against his person, or by virtue of a mandate for any other contempt or misconduct, or a commitment on a criminal charge the court, upon proof of the facts, may issue a writ of habeas corpus, directed to the officer, requiring him to bring the accused before it, to answer for the offense charged. The officer to whom the writ is directed, or upon whom it is served, must bring him before the court, and detain him at the place where the court is sitting, until the further order of the court.

§ 770. Final order directing punishment; exception.

Upon the return of an application to punish for contempt, or upon a hearing held upon a warrant of commitment issued pursuant to section seven hundred seventy-two or seven hundred seventy-three of this article, the court shall inform the offender that he or she has the right to the assistance of counsel, and when it appears that the offender is financially unable to obtain counsel, the court may in its discretion assign counsel to represent him or her. If it is determined that the accused has committed the offense charged; and that it was calculated to, or actually did, defeat, impair, impede, or prejudice the rights or remedies of a party to an action or special proceeding, brought in the court, or before the judge or referee; the court, judge, or referee must make a final order directing that he or she be punished by fine or imprisonment, or both, as the nature of the case requires. A warrant of commitment must issue accordingly, except as hereinafter provided. Where an application is made under this article and in pursuance of section two hundred forty-five of the domestic relations law or any other section of law for a final order directing punishment for failure to pay alimony, mainenance or counsel fees pursuant to an order of the court or judge in an action for divorce or separation and the defaulting spouse appears and satisfies the court or a judge before whom the application may be pending that he or she has no means or property or income to comply with the terms of the order at the time, the court or judge may in its or his discretion deny the application to punish the defaulting spouse, without prejudice to the applicant's rights and without prejudice to a renewal of the application upon notice and after proof that the financial condition of the defaulting spouse is changed.

Where an application is made to punish an offender for an offense committed with respect to an enforcement procedure under the civil practice law and rules, if the offender appear and comply and satisfy the court or a judge before whom the application shall be pending that he has at the time no means or property or income which could be levied upon pursuant to an execution issued in such an enforcement procedure, the court or judge shall deny the application to punish the offender without prejudice to the applicant's rights and without prejudice to a renewal of the application upon notice and after proof that the financial condition of the offender has changed.

ANNOTATION

Legal representation—Individual teachers who were represented by union counsel who contested contempt motion on their behalf but who were subsequently adjudicated in contempt of restraining order, were not denied legal representation during proceeding. Children's Village v. Greenburgh Eleven Teachers' Union Federation, 232 A.D.2d 357, 648 N.Y.S.2d 616 (2d Dept. 1996), *leave denied,* 89 N.Y.2d 982 (1997).

Mere irregularity.—Where plaintiff clearly demonstrated that appellants took action, in violation of a court order, which was "calculated to or actually did defeat impair, impede, or prejudice" its rights and appellants submitted no evidence to contradict the plaintiff's proof of civil contempt and prejudice in opposition to plaintiff's motion, trial court's omission of recital required by section 770 was a "mere irregularity not affecting the substantial rights of the parties, which this Court has the inherent power to correct." Home Surplus of Brooklyn, Inc. v. Home Surplus, Inc., 3 A.D.3d 472, 769 N.Y.S.2d 904 (2d Dept. 2004).

§ 771. Punishment upon return of habeas corpus.

Where the accused is brought up by virtue of a writ of habeas corpus, he must, after the final order is made, be remanded to the custody of the sheriff, or other officer, to whom the writ was directed. If the final order directs that he be punished by imprisonment, or committed until the payment of a sum of money, he must be so imprisoned or committed, upon his discharge from custody under the mandate, by virtue of which he is held by the sheriff, or other officer.

§ 772. Punishment upon return of application.

Upon the return of an application to punish for contempt, the questions which arise must be determined, as upon any other motion; and, if the determination is to the effect specified in section seven hundred and seventy, the order thereupon must be to the same effect as the final order therein prescribed.

Except as hereinafter provided, the offender may be committed upon a certified copy of the order so made, without further process. Where the commitment is ordered to punish an offense committed with respect to an enforcement procedure under the civil practice law and rules or pursuant to section two hundred forty-five of the domestic relations law, and the defendant has not appeared upon the return of the application, the final order directing punishment and commitment of the offender shall include a provision granting him leave to purge himself of the contempt within ten days after personal service of the order by performance of the act or duty the omission of which constitutes the misconduct for which he is to be punished, and the act or duty to be performed shall be specified in the order. Upon a certified copy of the order, together with proof by affidavit that more than ten days have elapsed since personal service thereof upon the offender, and that the act or duty specified has not been performed, the court may issue without notice a warrant directed to the sheriff or other enforcement officer of any jurisdiction in which the offender may be found. The warrant shall command such officer to arrest the offender forthwith and bring him before the court, or a judge thereof, to be committed or for such further disposition as the court in its discretion shall direct.

§ 773. Amount of fine.

If an actual loss or injury has been caused to a party to an action or special proceeding, by reason of the misconduct proved against the offender, and the case is not one where it is specially prescribed by law, that an action may be maintained to recover damages for the loss or injury, a fine, sufficient to indemnify the aggrieved party, must be imposed upon the offender, and collected, and paid over to the aggrieved party, under the direction of the court. The payment and acceptance of such a fine constitute a bar to an action by the aggrieved party, to recover damages for the loss or injury.

Where it is not shown that such an actual loss or injury has been caused, a fine may be imposed, not exceeding the amount of the complainant's costs and expenses, and two hundred and fifty dollars in addition thereto, and must be collected and paid, in like manner. A corporation may be fined as prescribed in this section.

If a fine is imposed to punish an offense committed with respect to an enforcement procedure under the civil practice law and rules or pursuant to section two hundred forty-five of the domestic relations law, and it has not been shown that such an actual loss or injury has been caused and the defendant has not appeared upon the return of the application, the order imposing fine, if any, shall include a provision granting the offender leave to purge himself of the contempt within ten days after personal service of the order by appearing and satisfying the court that he is unable to pay the fine or, in the discretion of the court, by giving an undertaking in a sum to be fixed by the court conditioned upon payment of the fine plus costs and expenses and his appearance and performance of the act or duty, the omission of which constitutes the misconduct for which he is to be punished. The order may also include a provision committing the offender to prison until the fine plus costs and expenses are paid, or until he is discharged according to law. upon a certified copy of the order imposing fine, together with proof by affidavit that more than ten days have elapsed since personal service thereof upon the offender, and that the fine plus costs and expenses has not been paid, the court may issue without notice a warrant directed to the sheriff or other enforcement officer of any jurisdiction in which the offender may be found. The warrant shall command such officer to arrest the offender forthwith and bring him before the court, or a judge thereof, to be committed or for such other disposition as the court in its discretion shall direct.

ANNOTATIONS

Attorney's fees.—Section 773 does not authorize recovery of attorney's fees where actual damages are established. G&S Quality v. Bank of China, 233 A.D.2d 215, 650 N.Y.S.2d 97 (1st Dept. 1996).

—Legal fees were properly recoverable by plaintiffs in connection with a contempt finding against defendant for failure to comply with a prior unconditional court order to issue privatized stock to plaintiffs. Blutreich v. Amalgamated Dwellings, Inc., 7 A.D.3d 269, 775 N.Y.S.2d 530 (2d Dept. 2004).

Basis of fine.—Where there is actual loss or injury, the statute does not provide for a general $250 fine, single or multiple, rather it calls for an assessment that will indemnify the harmed party. State v. Unique Ideas, Inc., 44 N.Y.2d 345, 405 N.Y.S.2d 656, 376 N.E.2d 1301 (1978).

—Petitioners were not entitled to pre-verdict interest absent express statutory authorization or proof that interest was part of petitioner's actual loss or injury. Meloni v. Goord, 267 A.D.2d 977, 700 N.Y.S.2d 311 (2d Dept. 1999).

—Appellant's participation in an elaborate scheme to defraud husband's creditor's, her refusal to participate in the judicial process, and her contempt of court all caused the plaintiff's losses in the amount of the judgment, which was the basis of the contempt fine. Corpuel v. Galasso, 240 A.D.2d 531, 659 N.Y.S.2d 65 (2d Dept. 1997).

—Unlike fines for criminal contempt where deterrence is the aim and the State is the aggrieved party entitled to the award, civil contempt fines must be remedial in nature and effect. Department of Housing Preservation and Development of City of New York v. Deka Realty Corp., 208 A.D.2d 37, 620 N.Y.S.2d 837 (2d Dept. 1995).

—A fine for civil contempt cannot include punitive damages; moreover, the plaintiff cannot recover legal costs and expenses as part of the fine. Ellenberg v. Brach, 88 A.D.2d 899, 450 N.Y.S.2d 589 (2d Dept. 1982).

—Inasmuch as § 773 authorizes arrest and imprisonment, it should be strictly construed. Field v. Dadon, 117 Misc. 2d 525, 458 N.Y.S.2d 139 (Dist. Ct. Suffolk Co. 1982).

§ 774. Length of imprisonment and periodic review of proceedings.

1. Where the misconduct proved consists of an omission to perform an act or duty, which is yet in the power of the offender to perform, he shall be imprisoned only until he has performed it, and paid the fine imposed, but if he shall perform the act or duty required to be performed, he shall not be imprisoned for the fine imposed more than three months if the fine is less than five hundred dollars, or more than six months if the fine is five hundred dollars or more. In such case, the order, and the warrant of commitment,

if one is issued, must specify the act or duty to be performed, and the sum to be paid. In every other case, where special provision is not otherwise made by law, the offender may be imprisoned for a reasonable time, not exceeding six months, and until the fine, if any, is paid; and the order, and the warrant of commitment, if any, must specify the amount of the fine, and the duration of the imprisonment. If the term of imprisonment is not specified in the order, the offender shall be imprisoned for the fine imposed three months if the fine is less than five hundred dollars, and six months if the fine imposed is five hundred dollars or more. If the offender is required to serve a specified term of imprisonment, and in addition to pay a fine, he shall not be imprisoned for the nonpayment of such fine for more than three months if such fine is less than five hundred dollars or more than six months if the fine imposed is five hundred dollars or more in addition to the specified time of imprisonment.

2. In all instances where any offender shall have been imprisoned pursuant to article nineteen of the judiciary law and where the term of such imprisonment is specified to be an indeterminate period of time or for a term of more than three months, such offender, if not then discharged by law from imprisonment, shall within ninety days after the commencement of such imprisonment be brought, by the sheriff, or other officer, as a matter of course personally before the court imposing such imprisonment and a review of the proceedings shall then be held to determine whether such offender shall be discharged from imprisonment. At periodic intervals of not more than ninety days following such review, the offender, if not then discharged by law from imprisonment, shall be brought, by the sheriff, or other officer, as a matter of course personally before the court imposing such imprisonment and further reviews of the proceedings shall then be held to determine whether such offender shall be discharged from imprisonment. Where such imprisonment shall have arisen out of or during the course of any action or proceeding, the clerk of the court before which such review of the proceedings shall be held, or the judge or justice of such court in case there be no clerk, shall give reasonable notice in writing of the date, time and place of each such review to each party or his attorney who shall have appeared of record in such action or proceeding, at their last known address.

ANNOTATION

Sentence.—Under Jud. Law § 774, a court may impose a prison term and a fine where the offender does not have the power to perform the act or duty required to purge his contempt. Kuby v. Warden, 305 A.D.2d 339, 757 N.Y.S.2d 889 (2d Dept. 2003).

§ 775. When court may release offender.

Where an offender, imprisoned as prescribed in this article, is unable to endure the imprisonment, or to pay the sum, or perform the act or duty, required to be paid or performed, in order to entitle him to be released, the court, judge, or referee may, in its or his discretion, and upon such terms as justice requires, make an order, directing him to be discharged from the imprisonment.

Where the commitment was made to punish a contempt of court committed with respect to an enforcement procedure under the civil practice law and rules, and the offender has purged himself of contempt as provided in section seven hundred seventy-two or seven hundred seventy-three of this article, the court out of which the execution was issued shall make an order directing him to be discharged from the imprisonment.

ANNOTATION

Release.—Jud. Law § 775 directs that where offender does not have power to perform act or duty required to purge his contempt, release is discretionary, and the court may direct offender's discharge upon "such terms as justice requires." Kuby v. Warden, 305 A.D.2d 339, 757 N.Y.S.2d 889 (2d Dept. 2003).

§ 776. Offender liable to indictment.

A person, punished as prescribed in this article, may, notwithstanding, be indicted for the same misconduct, if it is an indictable offense; but the court, before which he is convicted, must, in forming its sentence, take into consideration the previous punishment.

§ 777. Proceedings when accused does not appear.

Where a person has given an undertaking for his appearance, as prescribed in this article and fails to appear, on the return day of the application, the court may either issue a warrant of commitment, or make an order, directing the undertaking to be prosecuted; or both.

§ 778. Prosecution of undertaking by person aggrieved.

The order directing the undertaking to be prosecuted, may, in the discretion of the court, direct the prosecution thereof, by and in the name of any party aggrieved by the misconduct of the accused. In such a case, the plaintiff may recover damages, to the extent of the loss or injury sustained by him, by reason of the misconduct, together with the costs and expenses of prosecuting the special proceeding in which the warrant was issued; not exceeding the sum specified in the undertaking.

§ 779. Prosecution of undertaking by attorney-general or district attorney.

If no party is aggrieved by the misconduct of the accused, the order must, and, in any case where the court thinks proper so to direct, it may, direct the prosecution of the undertaking, by the attorney-general, or by the district attorney of the

MISC. LAWS

county in which it was given, in the name of the people. In an action, brought pursuant to the order, the people are entitled to recover the entire sum, specified in the undertaking. Out of the money collected, the court, which directed the prosecution, must direct that the person, at whose instance the warrant was issued, be paid such a sum as it thinks proper, to satisfy the costs and expenses incurred by him, and to compensate him for any loss or injury sustained by him, by reason of the misconduct. The residue of the money must be paid into the treasury of the state.

§ 780. Sheriff liable for taking insufficient sureties.

After the return of an execution, issued upon a judgment, rendered in an action upon the undertaking, an action, to recover the amount of the judgment, may be maintained against the sheriff, where it appears that, at the time when the undertaking was given, the sureties were insufficient, and the sheriff had reasonable grounds to doubt their sufficiency. Such an action may be maintained by the plaintiff, in whose favor the judgment was recovered. If the people were plaintiffs, the action must be prosecuted by the attorney-general or the district attorney; and any money collected therein must be disposed of, as prescribed in the last section.

§ 781. Punishment of misconduct at trial term.

Where a misconduct, which is punishable by fine or imprisonment, as prescribed in this article, occurs at a trial term, or with respect to a mandate returnable at such term, and was not punished at the term at which it occurred, the supreme court may inquire into and punish the misconduct, as if it had occurred at a special term of the supreme court, held in the same county, or with respect to a mandate returnable at such a special term.

ARTICLE 21-A

COMMUNITY DISPUTE RESOLUTION CENTERS PROGRAM

Section
849-a. Definitions.
849-b. Establishment and administration of centers.
849-c. Application procedures.
849-d. Payment procedures.
849-e. Funding.
849-f. Rules and regulations.
849-g. Reports.

§ 849-a. Definitions.

For the purposes of this article:

1. "Center" means a community dispute center which provides conciliation, mediation, arbitration or other forms and techniques of dispute resolution.

2. "Mediator" means an impartial person who assists in the resolution of a dispute.

3. "Grant recipient" means any nonprofit organization that administers a community dispute resolution center pursuant to this article, and is organized for the resolution of disputes or for religious, charitable or educational purposes.

§ 849-b. Establishment and administration of centers.

1. There is hereby established the community dispute resolution center program, to be administered and supervised under the direction of the chief administrator of the courts, to provide funds pursuant to this article for the establishment and continuance of dispute resolution centers on the basis of need in neighborhoods.

2. Every center shall be operated by a grant recipient.

3. All centers shall be operated pursuant to contract with the chief administrator and shall comply with all provisions of this article. The chief administrator shall promulgate rules and regulations to effectuate the purposes of this article, including provisions for periodic monitoring and evaluation of the program.

4. A center shall not be eligible for funds under this article unless:

(a) it complies with the provisions of this article and the applicable rules and regulations of the chief administrator;

(b) it provides neutral mediators who have received at least twenty-five hours of training in conflict resolution techniques;

(c) it provides dispute resolution without cost to indigents and at nominal or no cost to other participants;

(d) it provides that during or at the conclusion of the dispute resolution process there shall be a written agreement or decision setting forth the settlement of the issues and future responsibilities of each party and that such agreement or decision shall be available to a court which has adjourned a pending action pursuant to section 170.55 of the criminal procedure law;

(e) it does not make monetary awards except upon consent of the parties and such awards do not exceed the monetary jurisdiction of the small claims part of the justice court, except that where an action has been adjourned in contemplation of dismissal pursuant to section 215.10 of the criminal procedure law, a monetary award not in excess of five thousand dollars may be made; and

(f) it does not accept for dispute resolution any defendant who is named in a filed felony complaint, superior court information, or indictment, charging: (i) a class A felony, or (ii) a violent felony offense as defined in section 70.02 of the penal law, or (iii) any drug offense as defined in article two hundred twenty of the penal law, or (iv) a felony upon the conviction of which defendant must be sentenced as a second felony offender, a second violent felony offender, or a persistent violent felony offender pursuant to sections 70.06, 70.04 and 70.08 of the penal law, or a felony upon the conviction of which defendant may be sentenced as a persistent felony offender pursuant to section 70.10 of such law.

5. Parties must be provided in advance of the dispute resolution process with a written statement relating:

(a) their rights and obligations;

(b) the nature of the dispute;

(c) their right to call and examine witnesses;

(d) that a written decision with the reasons therefor will be rendered; and

(e) that the dispute resolution process will be final and binding upon the parties.

6. Except as otherwise expressly provided in this article, all memoranda, work products, or case files of a mediator are confidential and not subject to disclosure in any judicial or administrative

proceeding. Any communication relating to the subject matter of the resolution made during the resolution process by any participant, mediator, or any other person present at the dispute resolution shall be a confidential communication.

Amended by L. 1985, Ch. 91; L. 1986, Ch. 837, eff. Nov. 1, 1986, amending subd. (4)(e) and (f).

ANNOTATIONS

Awards.—If a dispute is submitted to ADR and there is a written agreement consenting to arbitration, the resulting award will be enforceable, that is, the successful party may proceed under CPLR Article 75 to obtain a judgment on the award and the award will be enforced regardless of the nature of the dispute. Wright v. Brockett, 150 Misc. 2d 1031, 571 N.Y.S.2d 660 (Sup. Ct. Bronx Co. 1991).

—An award of a mediator-arbitrator at a community dispute resolution center may be confirmed by the Supreme Court. Rothchild v. Diamond, 132 Misc. 2d 701, 504 N.Y.S.2d 965 (Sup. Ct. N.Y. Co. 1986).

Records.—Prosecutor was not entitled to access to records of community dispute resolution center due to policy of confidentiality. People v. Snyder, 129 Misc. 2d 137, 492 N.Y.S.2d 890 (Sup. Ct. Erie Co. 1985).

§ 849-c. Application procedures.

1. Funds appropriated or available for the purposes of this article may be allocated for programs proposed by eligible centers. Nothing in this article shall preclude existing resolution centers from applying for funds made available under this article provided that they are otherwise in compliance with this article.

2. Centers shall be selected by the chief administrator from applications submitted.

3. The chief administrator shall require that applications submitted for funding include, but need not be limited to the following:

(a) The cost of each of the proposed centers components including the proposed compensation of employees.

(b) A description of the proposed area of service and number of participants who may be served.

(c) A description of available dispute resolution services and facilities within the proposed geographical area.

(d) A description of the applicant's proposed program, including support of civic groups, social services agencies and criminal justice agencies to accept and make referrals; the present availability of resources; and the applicant's administrative capacity.

(e) Such additional information as is determined to be needed pursuant to rules of the chief administrator.

§ 849-d. Payment procedures.

1. Upon the approval of the chief administrator, funds appropriated or available for the purposes of this article shall be used for the costs of operation of approved programs. The methods of payment or reimbursement for dispute resolution costs shall be specified by the chief administrator and may vary among centers. All such arrangements shall conform to the eligibility criteria of this article and the rules and regulations of the chief administrator.

2. The state share of the cost of any center approved under this section shall include a basic grant of up to twenty thousand dollars for each county served by the center and may include an additional amount not exceeding fifty per centum of the difference between the approved estimated cost of the program and the basic grant.

Amended by L. 1987, Ch. 281, eff. Apr. 1, 1987, amending subd. (2).

§ 849-e. Funding.

1. The chief administrator may accept and disburse from any public or private agency or person, any money for the purposes of this article.

2. The chief administrator may also receive and disburse federal funds for purposes of this article, and perform services and acts as may be necessary for the receipt and disbursement of such federal funds.

(a) A grant recipient may accept funds from any public or private agency or person for the purposes of this article.

(b) The state comptroller, the chief administrator and their authorized representatives, shall have the power to inspect, examine and audit the fiscal affairs of the program.

(c) Centers shall, whenever reasonably possible, make use of public facilities at free or nominal costs.

§ 849-f. Rules and regulations.

The chief administrator shall promulgate rules and regulations to effectuate the purposes of this article.

§ 849-g. Reports.

Each resolution center funded pursuant to this article shall annually provide the chief administrator with statistical data regarding the operating budget, the number of referrals, categories or types of cases referred, number of parties serviced, number of disputes resolved, nature of resolution, amount and type of awards, rate of compliance, returnees to the resolution process, duration and estimated costs of hearings and such other information the chief administrator may require and the cost of hearings as the chief administrator requires. The chief administrator shall thereafter report annually to the governor and the temporary president of the senate, speaker of the assembly, and chairpersons of the judiciary and children and families committees regarding the operation and success of the centers funded pursuant to this article. The chief administrator shall include in such report all the information for each center that is required to be in the report from each center to the chief administrator. Such annual report shall also evaluate and make recommendations regarding the operation and success of such center.

Amended by L. 2005, Ch. 524, § 31, eff. Nov. 14, 2005.

Editor's Note: L. 2005, Ch. 524, §§ 1, 2, eff. Nov. 14, 2005, provide:

"Section 1. This act shall be known and may be cited as the 'reporting requirement reform act'.

"Section 2. Legislative findings and intent. The legislature hereby finds that there are deficiencies in the manner in which the reports by agencies are disseminated to the legislature. In an effort to consolidate and simplify reporting requirements and improve government accountability, this act attempts to establish a more consistent dissemination policy for reports distributed to the legislature. This act also seeks to provide mandate relief through the elimination of unneeded reporting requirements and reduced frequency of other reporting requirements, and improve government accountability through strengthened reporting requirements.

"The legislature also recognizes the important role of the legislative library for enhancing the availability of public documents to legislators and their staff. This act improves the legislature's access to the critical information needed for decision-making by reinforcing the role of the legislative library."

MISC. LAWS

PUBLIC HEALTH LAW

ARTICLE 33—CONTROLLED SUBSTANCES

[**Editor's Note:** Article 33, as passed by the Legislature, is set forth in its entirety. Sections within titles are not numbered consecutively in all cases.]

TITLE I—GENERAL PROVISIONS

TITLE II—MANUFACTURE AND DISTRIBUTION OF CONTROLLED SUBSTANCES

TITLE III—RESEARCH, INSTRUCTIONAL ACTIVITIES, AND CHEMICAL ANALYSIS RELATING TO CONTROLLED SUBSTANCES

MISC. LAWS

TITLE IV—DISPENSING TO ULTIMATE USERS

TITLE V—DISPENSING TO ADDICTS AND HABITUAL USERS

TITLE VI—RECORDS AND REPORTS

TITLE VII—OFFENSES, VIOLATIONS AND ENFORCEMENT

ARTICLE 33—CONTROLLED SUBSTANCES

TITLE I—GENERAL PROVISIONS

§ 3300. Short title.

This article shall be known as the New York State Controlled Substances Act.

§ 3300-a. Legislative purposes.

The purposes of this article are:

1. to combat illegal use of and trade in controlled substances; and

2. to allow legitimate use of controlled substances in health care, including palliative care; veterinary care; research and other uses authorized by this article or other law; under appropriate regulation and subject to this article, title eight of the education law, and other applicable law.

Added by L. 1998, Ch. 537, § 2, eff. Nov. 1, 1998.

§ 3301. Applicability of this article to actions and matters occurring or arising before and after the effective date.

Unless otherwise expressly provided, or unless the context otherwise requires:

(a) the provisions of this article shall govern and control the possession, manufacture, dispensing, administering, and distribution of controlled substances with respect to any matter, act or omission, arising or occurring on or after the effective date hereof;

(b) the provisions of this article do not apply to or govern any matter, act, or omission arising or occurring prior to the effective date hereof. Such matters, acts, or omissions must be governed and construed according to provisions of law existing at the time such matter, act or omission arose or occurred in the same manner as if this article has not been enacted.

§ 3302. Definitions of terms of general use in this article.

Except where different meanings are expressly specified in subsequent provisions of this article, the following terms have the following meanings:

1. "Addict" means a person who habitually uses a controlled substance for a non-legitimate or unlawful use, and who by reason of such use is dependent thereon.

2. "Administer" means the direct application of a controlled substance, whether by injection, inhalation, ingestion, or any other means, to the body of a patient or research subject.

3. "Agent" means an authorized person who acts on behalf of or at the direction of a manufacturer, distributor, or dispenser. No person may be authorized to so act if under title VIII of the education law such person would not be permitted to engage in such conduct. It does not include a common or contract carrier, public warehouseman, or employee of the carrier or warehouseman when acting in the usual and lawful course of the carrier's or warehouseman's business.

4. "Concentrated Cannabis" means

(a) the separated resin, whether crude or purified, obtained from a plant of the genus Cannabis; or

(b) a material, preparation, mixture, compound or other substance which contains more than two and one-half percent by weight of delta-9 tetrahydrocannabinol, or its isomer, delta-8 dibenzopyran numbering system, or delta-1 tetrahydrocannabinol or its isomer, delta 1 (6) monoterpene numbering system.

5. "Controlled substance" means a substance or substances listed in section thirty-three hundred six of this chapter.

6. "Commissioner" means commissioner of health of the state of New York.

7. "Deliver" or "delivery" means the actual, constructive or attempted transfer from one person to another of a controlled substance, whether or not there is an agency relationship.

8. "Department" means the department of health of the state of New York.

9. "Dispense" means to deliver a controlled substance to an ultimate user or research subject by lawful means and includes the packaging, labeling, or compounding necessary to prepare the substance for such delivery.

10. "Distribute" means to deliver a controlled substance other than by administering or dispensing.

11. "Distributor" means a person who distributes a controlled substance.

12. "Diversion" means manufacture, possession, delivery or use of a controlled substance by a person or in a manner not specifically authorized by law.

13. "Drug" means

(a) substances recognized as drugs in the official United States Pharmacopoeia, official Homeopathic Pharmacopoeia of the United States, or official National Formulary, or any supplement to any of them;

(b) substances intended for use in the diagnosis, cure, mitigation, treatment, or prevention of disease in man or animals; and

(c) substances (other than food) intended to

affect the structure or a function of the body of man or animal. It does not include devices or their components, parts, or accessories.

14. "Federal agency" means the Drug Enforcement Administration, United States Department of Justice, or its successor agency.

15. "Federal controlled substances act" means the Comprehensive Drug Abuse Prevention and Control Act of 1970, Public Law 91-513, and any act or acts amendatory or supplemental thereto or regulations promulgated thereunder.

16. "Federal registration number" means such number assigned by the Federal agency to any person authorized to manufacture, distribute, sell, dispense or administer controlled substances.

17. "Habitual user" means any person who is, or by reason of repeated use of any controlled substance for non-legitimate or unlawful use is in danger of becoming, dependent upon such substance.

18. "Institutional dispenser" means a hospital, veterinary hospital, clinic, dispensary, maternity home, nursing home, mental hospital or similar facility approved and certified by the department as authorized to obtain controlled substances by distribution and to dispense and administer such substances pursuant to the order of a practitioner.

19. "License" means a written authorization issued by the department or the New York State Department of Education permitting persons to engage in a specified activity with respect to controlled substances.

20. "Manufacture" means the production, preparation, propagation, compounding, cultivation, conversion or processing of a controlled substance, either directly or indirectly or by extraction from substances of natural origin, or independently by means of chemical synthesis, or by a combination of extraction and chemical synthesis, and includes any packaging or repackaging of the substance or labeling or relabeling of its container, except that this term does not include the preparation, compounding, packaging or labeling of a controlled substance:

(a) by a practitioner as an incident to his administering or dispensing of a controlled substance in the course of his professional practice; or

(b) by a practitioner, or by his authorized agent under his supervision, for the purpose of, or as an incident to, research, teaching, or chemical analysis and not for sale; or

(c) by a pharmacist as an incident to his dispensing of a controlled substance in the course of his professional practice.

21. "Marihuana" means all parts of the plant of the genus Cannabis, whether growing or not; the seeds thereof; the resin extracted from any part of the plant; and every compound, manufacture, salt, derivative, mixture, or preparation of the plant, its seeds or resin. It does not include the mature stalks of the plant, fiber produced from the stalks, oil or cake made from the seeds of the plant, any other compound, manufacture, salt, derivative, mixture, or preparation of the mature stalks (except the resin extracted therefrom), fiber, oil, or cake, or the sterilized seed of the plant which is incapable of germination.

22. "Narcotic drug" means any of the following, whether produced directly or indirectly by extraction from substances of vegetable origin, or independently by means of chemical synthesis, or by a combination of extraction and chemical synthesis:

(a) opium and opiate, and any salt, compound, derivative, or preparation of opium or opiate;

(b) any salt, compound, isomer, derivative, or preparation thereof which is chemically equivalent or identical with any of the substances referred to in subdivision (a), but not including the isoquinoline alkaloids of opium;

(c) opium poppy and poppy straw.

23. "Opiate" means any substance having an addiction-forming or addiction-sustaining liability similar to morphine or being capable of conversion into a drug having addiction-forming or addiction-sustaining liability. It does not include, unless specifically designated as controlled under section 3306 of this article, the dextrorotatory isomer of 3-methoxy-n-methylmorphinan and its salts (dextromethorphan). It does include its racemic and levorotatory forms.

24. "Opium poppy" means the plant of the species Papaver somniferum L., except its seeds.

25. "Person" means individual, institution, corporation, government or governmental subdivision or agency, business trust, estate, trust, partnership or association, or any other legal entity.

26. "Pharmacist" means any person licensed by the state department of education to practice pharmacy.

27. "Pharmacy" means any place registered as such by the New York state board of pharmacy and registered with the Federal agency pursuant to the federal controlled substances act.

28. "Poppy straw" means all parts, except the seeds, of the opium poppy, after mowing.

29. "Practitioner" means:

A physician, dentist, podiatrist, veterinarian, scientific investigator, or other person licensed, or otherwise permitted to dispense, administer or conduct research with respect to a controlled substance in the course of a licensed professional practice or research licensed pursuant to this article. Such person shall be deemed a "Practitioner" only as to such substances, or conduct relating to such substances, as is permitted by his license, permit or otherwise permitted by law.

30. "Prescribe" means a direction or authorization, by prescription, permitting an ultimate user lawfully to obtain controlled substances from any person authorized by law to dispense such substances.

31. "Prescription" shall mean an official New York state prescription, an electronic prescription, an oral prescription, an out-of-state prescription, or any one.

32. "Sell" means to sell, exchange, give or dispose of to another, or offer or agree to do the same.

33. "Ultimate user" means a person who lawfully obtains and possesses a controlled substance for his own use by a member of his household or for an animal owned by him or in his custody. It shall also mean and include a person designated, by a practitioner on a prescription, to obtain such substance on behalf of the patient for whom such substance is intended.

Amended by L. 1998, Ch. 537, § 3, eff. Nov. 1, 1998; L. 2004, Ch. 58, § 4 (Part A), eff. Oct. 20, 2004, amending subd. 31.

§ 3304. Prohibited acts. [*Another version of § 3304 follows.*]*

1. It shall be unlawful for any person to manufacture, sell, prescribe, distribute, dispense, administer, possess, have under his control, abandon, or transport a controlled substance except as expressly allowed by this article.

2. It shall be unlawful for any person to possess or have under his control an official New York state prescription form except as expressly allowed by this article.

* **Editor's Note:** Pub. Health Law § 3304 was later amended by L. 1981, Ch. 795, eff. Sept. 1, 1981, which did not reflect the prior amendment; see alternative version that follows.

Amended by L. 1981, Ch. 547, eff. Sept. 1, 1981, adding subdivision designations and the text of subd. (2).

§ 3304. Prohibited acts.*

a. It shall be unlawful for any person to manufacture, sell, prescribe, distribute, dispense, administer, possess, have under his control, abandon, or transport a controlled substance except as expressly allowed by this article.

b. It shall be unlawful for any physician practicing medicine as defined in section sixty-five hundred twenty-one of the education law to prescribe, dispense or administer any amphetamines or sympathomimetic amine drug or compound thereof, designated as a schedule II controlled substance pursuant to section thirty-three hundred six of this article for the exclusive treatment of obesity, weight control or weight loss. A violation of the provisions of this subdivision shall not be grounds for prosecution under article two hundred twenty of the penal law.

* **Editor's Note:** Pub. Health Law § 3304 was previously amended by L. 1981, Ch. 547, eff. Sept. 1, 1981, but this change was not reflected in L. 1981, Ch. 795; see the alternative version preceding this section.

Amended by L. 1981, Ch. 795, eff. Sept. 1, 1981, adding subdivision designations and the text of subd. (b).

ANNOTATION

Evidence.—Defendant, a pharmacist, who took 130 generic Vicodin pills, a controlled substance included in Schedule III (e)(4) of PHL § 3306, without a prescription was properly charged under this section. People v. Czarnwski, 268 A.D.2d 701, 702 N.Y.S.2d 398 (3d Dept. 2000).

§ 3305. Exemptions.

1. The provisions of this article restricting the possession and control of controlled substances and official New York state prescription forms shall not apply:

(a) to common carriers or to warehouseman, while engaged in lawfully transporting or storing such substances, or to any employee of the same acting within the scope of his employment; or

(b) to public officers or their employees in the lawful performance of their official duties requiring possession or control of controlled substances; or

(c) to temporary incidental possession by employees or agents of persons lawfully entitled to possession, or by persons whose possession is for the purpose of aiding public officers in performing their official duties.

(d) to a duly authorized agent of an incorporated society for the prevention of cruelty to animals or a municipal animal control facility for the limited purpose of buying, possessing, and dispensing to registered and certified personnel, ketamine hydrochloride to anesthetize animals and/or sodium pentobarbital to euthanize animals including but not limited to dogs and cats. The department shall, consistent with the public interest, register such duly authorized agent and such agent shall file, on a quarterly basis, a report of purchase, possession, and use of ketamine hydrochloride and/or sodium pentobarbital, which report shall be certified by the society for the prevention of cruelty to animals or municipal animal control facility as to its accuracy and validity. This report shall be in addition to any other record keeping and reporting requirements of state and federal law and regulation. The department shall adopt rules and regulations providing for the registration and certification of any individual who, under the direction of the duly authorized and registered agent of an incorporated society for the prevention of cruelty to animals, or municipal animal control facility, uses ketamine hydrochloride to anesthetize animals and/or sodium pentobarbital to euthanize animals, including but not limited to dogs and cats. The department may also adopt such other rules and regulations as shall provide for the safe and efficient use of ketamine hydrochloride and/or sodium pentobarbital by incorporated societies for the prevention of cruelty to animals and animal

MISC. LAWS

control facilities. Nothing in this paragraph shall be deemed to waive any other requirement imposed on incorporated societies for the prevention of cruelty to animals and animal control facilities by state and federal law and regulation.

2. The commissioner may, by regulation, provide for the exemption from all or part of the requirements of this article the possession of substances in schedule III or IV and use thereof as part of an industrial process or manufacture of substances other than drugs. The commissioner may impose such conditions upon the granting of such exemption as may be necessary to protect against diversion or misuse of the controlled substance.

3. The commissioner is hereby authorized and empowered to make any rules, regulations and determinations permitting the following categories of persons to obtain, dispense and administer controlled substances under such conditions and in such manner as he shall prescribe:

(a) a person in the employ of the United States government or of any state, territory, district, county, municipal, or insular government, obtaining, possessing, dispensing and administering controlled substances by reason of his official duties;

(b) a master of a ship or a person in charge of any aircraft upon which no physician is regularly employed, or to a physician or surgeon duly licensed in any state, territory, or the District of Columbia to practice his profession, or to a retired commissioned medical officer of the United States army, navy, or public service, employed upon such ship or aircraft, for the actual medical needs of persons on board such ship or aircraft when not in port.

(c) a person in a foreign country in compliance with the provisions of this article.

4. The provisions of this article with respect to the payment of fees and costs shall not apply to the state of New York or any political subdivision thereof or any agency or instrumentality of either.

Amended by L. 1981, Ch. 547, eff. Sept. 1, 1981; L. 1987, Ch. 619, eff. Nov. 1, 1987, by adding subd. (1)(d); L. 1991, Ch. 166, § 359, eff. June 12, 1991, amending subd. (3); L. 1993, Ch. 187, § 1, extending expiration date to June 30, 1995; L. 1997, Ch. 635, eff. Jan. 22, 1998, amending subd. 1(d).

ANNOTATIONS

Agent of police officer.—Defendant's arguing that her possession was lawful because she was the agent of a police officer entitled to possession, is untenable since she had no knowledge or information that the police officer was in fact a police officer and therefore could not consent to act as an agent or employee of such officer. People v. Sierra, 45 N.Y.2d 56, 407 N.Y.S.2d 669, 379 N.E.2d 196 (1978).

Employees or agents—The obvious intent of the statute is to exempt from penal sanction those employees or agents of others whose possession is not proscribed such as, for example, pharmacists' assistants or private citizens acting for and under direction of the police. People v. Sierra, 45 N.Y.2d 56, 407 N.Y.S.2d 669, 379 N.E.2d 196 (1978).

—No binding contract of marriage nor formal agreement of any kind was required to constitute defendant as the agent for his "wife" when, at her request, he picked up, preserved, and put into his trousers her single dose of methadone; this action did not violate PL § 220.10. People v. Stone, 80 Misc. 2d 536, 364 N.Y.S.2d 739 (Sup. Ct. Kings Co. 1975).

§ 3306. Schedules of controlled substances.

There are hereby established five schedules of controlled substances, to be known as schedules I, II, III, IV and V respectively. Such schedules shall consist of the following substances by whatever name or chemical designation known:

SCHEDULE I

(a) Schedule I shall consist of the drugs and other substances, by whatever official name, common or usual name, chemical name, or brand name designated, listed in this section.

(b) Opiates. Unless specifically excepted or unless listed in another schedule, any of the following opiates, including their isomers, esters, ethers, salts, and salts of isomers, esters, and ethers, whenever the existence of such isomers, esters, ethers and salts is possible within the specific chemical designation (for purposes of 3-methylfentanyl only, the term isomer includes the optical and geometric isomers):

(1) Acetyl-alpha-methylfentanyl (N-[1-(-methyl-2-phenethyl) -4-piperidinyl]-N-phenylacetamide.

(2) Acetylmethadol.

(3) Allylprodine.

(4) Alphacetylmethadol (except levo-alphacetylmethadol also known as levo-alpha-acetylmethadol, levomethadyl acetate or LAAM).

(5) Alphameprodine.

(6) Alphamethadol.

(7) Alpha-methylfentanyl (N-[1-(alpha-methyl-beta-phenyl) ethyl-4-piperidyl] propionanilide; 1-(1-methyl-2-phenylethyl) -4-(N-propanilido) piperidine).

(8) Alpha-methylthiofentanyl (N-[1-methyl-2) 2-thienyl) ethyl-4-piperidinyl]-N-phenylpropanamide).

(9) Beta-hydroxyfentanyl (N-[1-2 (2-hydroxy-2-phenethyl) -4-piper-idinyl]-N-phenylpropanamide).

(10) Beta-hydroxy-3-methylfentanyl (other-name:N-[1(2-hydroxy-2-phenethyl)-3-methyl -4-piperidinyl]-N -phenylpropanamide).

(11) Benzethidine.

(12) Betacetylmethadol.

(13) Betameprodine.

(14) Betamethadol.

(15) Betaprodine.

(16) Clonitazene.

(17) Dextromoramide.

(18) Diampromide.

(19) Diethylthiambutene.

(20) Difenoxin.

(21) Dimenoxadol.

(22) Dimepheptanol.

(23) Dimethylthiambutene.

(24) Dioxaphetyl butyrate.

(25) Dipipanone.

(26) Ethylmethylthiambutene.

(27) Etonitazene.

(28) Etoxeridine.

(29) Furethidine.

(30) Hydroxypethidine.

(31) Ketobemidone.

(32) Levomoramide.

(33) Levophenacylmorphan.

(34) 3-Methylfentanyl (N-[3-methyl-1-(2-phenylethyl-4-piperidyl]-N-phenylpropanamide).

(35) 3-Methylthiofentanyl (N-[3-methyl-1-(2-thienyl)ethyl-4-piperidinyl]-N-phenylpropanamide).

(36) Morpheridine.

(37) MPPP (1-methyl-4-phenyl-4-propionoxypiperidine).

(38) Noracymethadol.

(39) Norlevorphanol.

(40) Normethadone.

(41) Norpipanone.

(42) Para-fluorofentanyl (N-(4-fluorophenyl)-N-[1-(2-phenethyl)-4-piperidinyl]-propanamide.

(43) PEPAP (1-(-2-phenethyl)-4-phenyl-4-acetoxypiperidine.

(44) Phenadoxone.

(45) Phenampromide.

(46) Phenomorphan.

(47) Phenoperidine.

(48) Piritramide.

(49) Proheptazine.

(50) Properidine.

(51) Propiram.

(52) Racemoramide.

(53) Thiofentanyl (N-phenyl-N-[1-(2-thienyl) ethyl-4-piperidinyl]-propanamide.

(54) Tilidine.

(55) Trimeperidine.

(c) **Opium derivatives.** Unless specifically excepted or unless listed in another schedule, any of the following opium derivatives, its salts, isomers, and salts of isomers whenever the existence of such salts, isomers, and salts of isomers is possible within the specific chemical designation:

(1) Acetorphine.

(2) Acetyldihydrocodeine.

(3) Benzylmorphine.

(4) Codeine methylbromide.

(5) Codeine-N-oxide.

(6) Cyprenorphine.

(7) Desomorphine.

(8) Dihydromorphine.

(9) Drotebanol.

(10) Etorphine (except hydrochloride salt).

(11) Heroin.

(12) Hydromorphinol.

(13) Methyldesorphine.

(14) Methyldihydromorphine.

(15) Morphine methylbromide.

(16) Morphine methylsulfonate.

(17) Morphine-N-oxide.

(18) Myrophine.

(19) Nicocodeine.

(20) Nicomorphine.

(21) Normorphine.

(22) Pholcodine.

(23) Thebacon.

(d) **Hallucinogenic substances.** Unless specifically excepted or unless listed in another schedule, any material, compound, mixture, or preparation, which contains any quantity of the following hallucinogenic substances, or which contains any of its salts, isomers, and salts of isomers whenever the existence of such salts, isomers, and salts of isomers is possible within the specific chemical designation (for purposes of this paragraph only, the term "isomer" includes the optical, position and geometric isomers):

(1) 4-bromo-2, 5-dimethoxy-amphetamine. Some trade or other names: 4-bromo-2, 5-dimethoxy-α-methylphenethylamine; 4-bromo-2, 5-DMA.

(2) 2, 5-dimethoxyamphetamine. Some trade or other names: 2, 5-dimethoxy-α-methylphenethylamine: 2, 5-DMA.

(3) 4-methoxyamphetamine. Some trade or other names: 4-methoxy-a-methylphenethylamine; paramethoxyamphetamine, PMA.

(4) 5-methoxy-3, 4-methylenedioxy-amphetamine.

(5) 4-methyl-2, 5-dimethoxy-amphetamine. Some trade and other names: 4-methyl-2, 5-dimethoxy-α-methylphenethylamine; "DOM"; and "STP."

(6) 3, 4-methylenedioxy amphetamine.

(7) 3, 4, 5-trimethoxy amphetamine.

(8) Bufotenine. Some trade and other names: 3-(β-dimethylaminoethyl)-5 hydroxindole; 3-(2-dimethylaminoethyl)-5-indolol; N, N-dimethylserotonin;-5-hydroxy-N, N-dimethyltryptamine; mappine.

(9) Diethyltryptamine. Some trade and other names: N, N-diethyltryptamine; DET.

(10) Dimethyltryptamine. Some trade or other names: DMT.

(11) Ibogane. Some trade and other names: 7-ethyl-6, 6β, 7, 8, 9, 10, 12, 13-octahydro-2-methoxy-6, 9-methano-5h-pyrido [1', 2': 1, 2] azepino [5, 4-b] indole: tabernanthe iboga.

(12) Lysergic acid diethylamide.

(13) Marihuana.

(14) Mescaline.

(15) Parahexyl. Some trade or other names: 3-Hexyl-1-hydroxy-7, 8, 9, 10-tetra hydro-6, 6, 9-trimethyl-6H-dibenfo[b, d] pyran.

(16) Peyote. Meaning all parts of the plant presently classified botanically as Lophophora williamsii Lemaire, whether growing or not, the seeds thereof, any extract from any part of such plant, and every compound, manufacture, salts, derivative, mixture, or preparation of such plant, its seeds or extracts.

(17) N-ethyl-3-piperidyl benzilate.

(18) N-methyl-3-piperidyl benzilate.

(19) Psilocybin.

(20) Psilocyn.

(21) Tetrahydrocannabinols. Synthetic equivalents of the substances contained in the plant, or in the resinous extractives of cannabis, sp. and/or synthetic substances, derivatives, and their isomers with similar chemical structure and pharmacological activity such as the following:

Δ1 cis or trans tetrahydrocannabinol, and their optical isomers

Δ6 cis or trans tetrahydrocannabinol, and their optical isomers

Δ3, 4 cis or trans tetrahydrocannibinol, and its optical isomers (since nomenclature of these substances is not internationally standardized, compounds of these structures, regardless of numerical designation of atomic positions covered).

(22) Ethylamine analog of phencyclidine. Some trade or other names: N-ethyl-1-phenylcyclohexylamine, (1-phenylclohexyl) ethylamine, N-(1-phenylcyclohexyl) ethylamine cyclohexamine, PCE.

(23) Pyrrolidine analog of phencyclidine. Some trade or other names 1-(1-phenylcyclohexyl)-pyrrolidine; PCPy; PHP.

(24) Thiophene analog of phencyclidine. Some trade or other names: 1-[1-(2-thienyl)-cyclohexyl]-piperidine, 2-thienylanalog of phencyclidine, TPCP, TCP.

(25) 3,4-methylenedioxymethamphetamine (MDMA).

(26) 3,4-methylendioxy-N-ethylamphetamine (also known as N-ethyl-alpha-methyl-3,4 (methylenedioxy) phenethylamine, N-ethyl MDA, MDE, MDEA.

(27) N-hydroxy-3,4-methylenedioxyamphetamine (also known as N-hydroxy-alpha-methyl-3,4 (methylenedioxy) phenethylamine, and N-hydroxy MDA.

(28) 1-[1-(2-thienyl) cyclohexyl] pyrrolidine. Some other names: TCPY.

(29) Alpha-ethyltryptamine. Some trade or other names: etryptamine; Monase; alpha-ethyl-1H-indole-3-ethanamine; 3-(2-aminobutyl) indole; Alpha-ET or AET.

(30) 2,5-Dimethoxy-4-ethylamphetamine. Some trade or other names: DOET.

(e) Depressants. Unless specifically excepted or unless listed in another schedule, any material, compound, mixture, or preparation which contains any quantity of the following substances having a depressant effect on the central nervous system, including its salts, isomers, and salts of isomers whenever the existence of such salts, isomers, and salts of isomers is possible within the specific chemical designation:

(1) Mecloqualone.

(2) Methaqualone.

(3) Phencyclidine.

(4) Gamma hydroxybutyric acid, and salt, hydroxybutyric compound, derivative or preparation of gamma hydroxybutyric acid, including any isomers, esters and ethers and salts of isomers, esters and ethers of gamma hydroxybutyric acid, except gamma-butyrolactone, whenever the existence of such isomers, esters and ethers and salts is possible within the specific chemical.

(5) Gamma-butyrolactone, including butyrolactone; butyrolactone gamma; 4-butyrolactone; 2(3H)-furanone dihydro; dihydro-2(3H)-furanone; tetrahydro-2-furanone; 1,2-butanolide; 1,4-butanolide; 4-butanolide; gamma-hydroxybutyric acid lactone; 3-hydroxybutyric

acid lactone and 4-hydroxy-butanoic acid lactone with Chemical Abstract Service number (96-48-0) when any such substance is intended for human consumption.

(6) 1,4 butanediol, including butanediol; butane-1,4-diol; 1,4-butylene glyco; butylene glycol; 1,4-dihydroxybutane; 1,4-tetramethylene glycol; tetramethylene glycol; tetramethylene Abstract Service number (110-63-4) when any such substance is intended for human consumption.

(f) Stimulants. Unless specifically excepted or unless listed in another schedule, any material, compound, mixture, or preparation which contains any quantity of the following substances having a stimulant effect on the central nervous system, including its salts, isomers, and salts of isomers:

(1) Fenethylline.

(2) N-ethylamphetamine.

(3) (+ -)cis-4-methylaminorex ((+ -)cis-4,5-dihydro-4-methyl-5-phenyl-2-oxazolamine).

(4) N,N-dimethylamphetamine (also known as N,N-alpha-trimethyl-benzeneethanamine; N,N-alpha-trimethylphenethylamine).

(5) Methcathinone (some other names: 2-(methylamino)-propiophenone; Alpha-(methylamino) propiophenone; 2-(methylamino)-1-phenylpropan1-one; alpha-N-methylaminopropiophenone; monomethylpropion; ephadrone, N-methylcathinone, methylcathinone).

(6) Aminorex. Some other names: aminoxaphen; 2-amino-5-phenyl-2-oxazoline; or 4,5-dihydro-5-phenyl-2-oxazolamine.

(7) Cathinone. Some trade or other names: 2-amino-1-phenyl-1-propanone, alpha-aminopropiophenone, 2-aminopropiophenone, and norephedrone.

SCHEDULE II

(a) Schedule II shall consist of the drugs and other substances, by whatever official name, common or usual name, chemical name, or brand name designated, listed in this section.

(b) Substances, vegetable origin or chemical synthesis. Unless specifically excepted or unless listed in another schedule, any of the following substances whether produced directly or indirectly by extraction from substances of vegetable origin, or independently by means of chemical synthesis, or by a combination of extraction and chemical synthesis:

(1) Opium and opiate, and any salt, compound, derivative, or preparation of opium or opiate, excluding apomorphine, dextrorphan, nalbuphine, nalmefene, naloxone, and naltrexone, and their respective salts, but including the following:

1. Raw opium.

2. Opium extracts.

3. Opium fluid extracts.

4. Powered opium.

5. Granulated opium.

6. Tincture of opium.

7. Codeine.

8. Ethylmorphine.

9. Etorphine hydrochloride.

10. Hydrocodone.

11. Hydromorphone.

12. Metopon.

13. Morphine.

14. Oxycodone.

15. Oxymorphone.

16. Thebaine.

(2) Any salt, compound, derivative, or preparation thereof which is chemically equivalent or identical with any of the substances referred to in this section, except that these substances shall not include the isoquinoline alkaloids of opium.

(3) Opium poppy and poppy straw.

(4) Coca leaves and any salt, compound, derivative, or preparation of coca leaves and any salt, compound, derivative, or preparation thereof which is chemically equivalent or identical with any of these substances including cocaine and ecgonine, their salts, isomers, and salts of isomers, except that the substances shall not include decocainized coca leaves or extraction of coca leaves, which extractions do not contain cocaine or ecgonine.

(5) Concentrate of poppy straw (the crude extract of poppy straw in either liquid, solid or powder form which contains the phenanthrene alkaloids of the opium poppy).

(c) Opiates. Unless specifically excepted or unless in another schedule any of the following opiates, including its isomers, esters, ethers, salts and salts of isomers, esters and ethers whenever the existence of such isomers, esters, ethers, and salts is possible within the specific chemical designation, dextrorphan and levopropoxyphene excepted:

(1) Alfentanil.

(2) Alphaprodine.

(3) Anileridine.

(4) Bezitramide.

(5) Bulk dextropropoxyphene (non-dosage forms).

(6) Carfentanil.

(7) Dihydrocodeine.

(8) Diphenoxylate.

(9) Fentanyl.

(10) Isomethadone.

(11) Levo-alphacetylmethadol (also known as levo-alpha-acetylmethadol, levomethadyl acetate or LAAM).

(12) Levomethorphan.

(13) Levorphanol.

(14) Metazocine.

(15) Methadone.

(16) Methadone-intermediate, 4-cyano-2-dimethylamino-4, 4-diphenyl butane.

(17) Moramide-intermediate, 2-methyl-3-morpholino-1, 1-diphenylpropane-carboxylic acid.

(18) Pethidine (meperidine).

(19) Pethidine-intermediate-A, 4-cyano-1-methyl-4-phenylpiperidine.

(20) Pethidine-intermediate-B, ethyl-4-phenylpiperidine-4-carboxylate.

(21) Pethidine-intermediate-C, 1-methyl-4-phenylpiperidine-4carboxylic

(22) Phenazocine.

(23) Piminodine.

(24) Racemethorphan.

(25) Racemorphan.

(26) Sufentanil.

(d) Stimulants. Unless specifically excepted or unless listed in another schedule, any material, compound, mixture, or preparation which contains any quantity of the following substances having a stimulant effect on the central nervous system:

(1) Amphetamine, its salts, optical isomers, and salts of its optical isomers.

(2) Methamphetamine, its salts, isomers, and salts of its isomers.

(3) Phenmetrazine and its salts.

(4) Methylphenidate.

(e) Depressants. Unless specifically excepted or unless listed in another schedule, any material, compound, mixture, or preparation which contains any quantity of the following substances having a depressant effect on the central nervous system, including its salts, isomers, and salts of isomers whenever the existence of such salts, isomers, and salts of isomers is possible within the specific chemical designation:

(1) Amobarbital.

(2) Glutethimide.

(3) Pentobarbital.

(4) Secobarbital.

(f) Hallucinogenic substances. Nabilone: Another name for nabilone: (+ ,-)-trans -3-(1,1-dimethylheptyl)-6, 6a, 7, 8, 10, 10a-hexahydro-1-hydroxy-6, 6-dimethyl-9H-dibenzo {b,d} pyran-9-one.

(g) Immediate precursors. Unless specifically excepted or unless listed in another schedule, any material, compound, mixture or preparation which contains any quantity of the following substances:

(1) Immediate precursor to amphetamine and methamphetamine:

(i) Phenylacetone Some trade or other names: phenyl-2-propanone: P2P: benzyl methyl ketone: methyl benzyl ketone:

(2) Immediate precursors to phencyclidine (PCP):

(i) 1-phenylcyclohexylamine;

(ii) 1-piperidinocyclohexanecarbonitrile (PCC).

(h) Anabolic steroids. Unless specifically excepted or unless listed in another schedule, "anabolic steroid" shall mean any drug or hormonal substance, chemically and pharmacologically related to testosterone (other than estrogens, progestins and corticosteroids) that promotes muscle growth, any drug or hormonal substance that stimulates the endogenous production of steroids in the human body which acts in the same manner, or any material, compound, mixture, or preparation which contains any amount of the following substances:

(1) Boldenone.

(2) Clostebol.

(3) Dehydrochlormethyltestosterone.

(4) Drostanolone.

(5) Ethylestrenol.

(6) Fluoxymesterone.

(7) Formebulone (formebolone).

(8) Mesterolene.

(9) Methandriol.

(10) Methandrostenolone.

(11) Methenolone.

(12) Methyltestosterone.

(13) Mibolerone.

(14) Nandrolone.

(15) Norethandrolone.

(16) Oxandrolone.

(17) Oxymesterone.

(18) Oxymetholone.

(19) Stanolone.

(20) Stanozolol.

(21) Testosterone.

(22) Trenbolone.

(23) Any salt, ester or isomer of a drug or substance described or listed in this subdivision, if such salt, ester or isomer promotes muscle growth.

(i) Subdivision (h) of this section shall not include any substance containing anabolic steroids expressly intended for administration through implants to cattle or other nonhuman species and that are approved by the federal food and drug administration solely for such use. Any individual who knowingly and willfully administers to himself or another person, prescribes, dispenses or distributes such substances for other than implantation to cattle or nonhuman species shall be subject to the same penalties as a practitioner who violates the provisions of this section or any other penalties prescribed by law.

(j) [*Repealed pursuant to L. 2003, Ch. 591, eff. Sept. 22, 2003.*]

SCHEDULE III

(a) Schedule III shall consist of the drugs and other substances, by whatever official name, common or usual name, chemical name, or brand name designated, listed in this section.

(b) Stimulants. Unless specifically excepted or unless listed in another schedule, any material, compound, mixture, or preparation which contains any quantity of the following substances having a stimulant effect on the central nervous system, including its salts, isomers (whether optical, position, or geometric), and salts of such isomers whenever the existence of such salts, isomers, and salts of isomers is possible within the specific chemical designation:

(1) Those compounds, mixtures, or preparations in dosage unit form containing any stimulant substances listed in schedule II which compounds, mixtures, or preparations were listed on August twenty-five, nineteen hundred seventy-one, as excepted compounds under title twenty-one, section 308.32 of the code of federal regulations and any other drug of the quantitative composition shown in that list for those drugs or which is the same except that it contains a lesser quantity of controlled substances.

(2) Benzphetamine.

(3) Chlorphentermine.

(4) Clortermine.

(5) Ketamine.

(6) Phendimetrazine.

(c) Depressants. Unless specifically excepted or unless listed in another schedule, any material, compound, mixture, or preparation which contains any quantity of the following substances having a depressant effect on the central nervous system:

(1) Any compound, mixture or preparation containing:

(i) Amobarbital:

(ii) Secobarbital:

(iii) Pentobarbital:

or any salt thereof and one or more other active medicinal ingredients which are not listed in any schedule.

(2) Any suppository dosage form containing:

(i) Amobarbital:

(ii) Secobarbital:

(iii) Pentobarbital:

or any salt of any of these drugs and approved by the federal food and drug administration for marketing only as a suppository.

(3) Any substance which contains any quantity of a derivative of barbituric acid or any salt thereof.

(4) Chlorhexadol.

(5) Lysergic acid.

(6) Lysergic acid amide.

(7) Methyprylon.

(8) Sulfondiethylmethane.

(9) Sulfonethylmethane.

(10) Sulfonmethane.

(11) Tiletamine and zolazepam or any salt thereof. Some trade or other names for a tiletamine-zolazepam combination product: Telazol. Some trade or other names or other names for tiletamine: 2-(ethylamino)-2-(2-thienyl)-cyclohexanone. Some trade or other names for zolazepam: 4-(2-fluorophenyl) -6,8-dihydro -1, 3, 8i-trimethylpyrazolo-[3,4-e] [1,4]-diazepin-7(1H)-one, flupyrazapon.

(12) Gamma hydroxybutyric acid, and salt, hydroxybutyric compound, derivative or preparation of gamma hydroxybutyric acid, including any isomers, esters and ethers and salts of isomers, esters and ethers of gamma hydroxybutyric acid, contained in a drug product for which an application has been approved under section 505 of the federal food, drug and cosmetic act.

(d) Nalorphine.

(e) Narcotic drugs. Unless specifically excepted or unless listed in another schedule, any material, compound, mixture, or preparation containing any of the following narcotic drugs, or their salts calculated as the free anhydrous base or alkaloid, in limited quantities as set forth below:

(1) Not more than 1.8 grams of codeine per one hundred milliliters or not more than ninety milligrams per dosage unit, with an equal or

greater quantity of an isoquinoline alkaloid of opium.

(2) Not more than 1.8 grams of codeine per one hundred milliliters or not more than ninety milligrams per dosage unit, with one or more active, nonnarcotic ingredients in recognized therapeutic amounts.

(3) Not more than three hundred milligrams of dihydrocodeinone (hydrocodone) per one hundred milliliters or not more than fifteen milligrams per dosage unit, with a fourfold or greater quantity of an isoquinoline alkaloid of opium.

(4) Not more than three hundred milligrams of dihydrocodeinone (hydrocodone) per one hundred milliliters or not more than fifteen milligrams per dosage unit, with one or more active nonnarcotic ingredients in recognized therapeutic amounts.

(5) Not more than 1.8 grams of dihydrocodeine per one hundred milliliters or not more than ninety milligrams per dosage unit, with one or more active nonnarcotic ingredients in recognized therapeutic amounts.

(6) Not more than three hundred milligrams of ethylmorphine per one hundred milliliters or not more than fifteen milligrams per dosage unit, with one or more active, nonnarcotic ingredients in recognized therapeutic amounts.

(7) Not more than five hundred milligrams of opium per one hundred milliliters or per one hundred grams or not more than twenty-five milligrams per dosage unit, with one or more active, nonnarcotic ingredients in recognized therapeutic amounts.

(8) Not more than fifty milligrams of morphine per one hundred milliliters or per one hundred grams, with one or more active, nonnarcotic ingredients in recognized therapeutic amounts.

(f) Dronabinol (synthetic) in sesame oil and encapsulated in a soft gelatin capsule in a U.S. Food and Drug Administration approved drug product. Some other names for dronabinol: (6aR-trans)-6a, 7, 8, 10a-tetrahydro-6, 6, 9-trimethyl-3-pentyl-6H-dibenzo{b,d} pyran-1-o1, or (-) delta-9-(trans) -tetrahydrocannabinol.

(g) Chorionic gonadotrophin. Unless specifically excepted or unless listed in another schedule any material, compound, mixture, or preparation which contains any amount of chorionic gonadotrophin.

SCHEDULE IV

(a) Schedule IV shall consist of the drugs and other substances, by whatever official name, common or usual name, chemical name, or brand name designated, listed in this section.

(b) Narcotic drugs. Unless specifically excepted or unless listed in another schedule, any

material, compound, mixture, or preparation containing any of the following narcotic drugs, or their salts calculated as the free anhydrous base or alkaloid, in limited quantities as set forth below:

(1) Not more than one milligram of difenoxin and not less than twenty-five micrograms of atropine sulfate per dosage unit.

(2) Dextropropoxyphene (alpha-(+)-4-dimethylamino-1. 2-diphenyl-3-methyl-2-propionoxybutane).

(c) Depressants. Unless specifically excepted or unless listed in another schedule, any material, compound, mixture, or preparation which contains any quantity of the following substances, including its salts, isomers, and salts of isomers whenever the existence of such salts, isomers, and salts of isomers is possible within the specific chemical designation:

(1) Alprazolam.

(2) Barbital.

(3) Bromazepam.

(4) Camazepam.

(5) Chloral betaine.

(6) Chloral hydrate.

(7) Chlordiazepoxide.

(8) Clobazam.

(9) Clonazepam.

(10) Clorazepate.

(11) Clotiazepam.

(12) Cloxazolam.

(13) Delorazepam.

(14) Diazepam.

(15) Estazolam.

(16) Ethchlorvynol.

(17) Ethinamate.

(18) Ethyl Loflazepate.

(19) Fludiazepam.

(20) Flunitrazepam.

(21) Flurazepam.

(22) Halazepam.

(23) Haloxazolam.

(24) Ketazolam.

(25) Loprazolam.

(26) Lorazepam.

(27) Lormetazepam.

(28) Mebutamate.

(29) Medazepam.

(30) Meprobamate.

(31) Methohexital.

(32) Methylphenobarbital (mephobarbital).

(33) Nimetazepam.

(34) Nitrazepam.

(35) Nordiazepam.

(36) Oxazepam.

(37) Oxazolam.

(38) Paraldehyde.

(39) Petrichoral.

(40) Phenobarbital.

(41) Pinazepam.

(42) Prazepam.

(43) Temazepam.

(44) Tetrazepam.

(45) Triazolam.

(46) Midazolam.

(47) Quazepam.

(48) Zolpidem tartrate.

(d) [Repealed]

(e) Stimulants. Unless specifically excepted or unless listed in another schedule, any material, compound, mixture, or preparation which contains any quantity of the following substances having a stimulant effect on the central nervous system, including its salts, isomers, and salts of such isomers:

(1) Cathine ((+) -norpseudoephedrine).

(2) Diethylpropion.

(3) Fencamfamin.

(4) Fenproporex.

(5) Mazindol.

(6) Mefenorex.

(7) Pemoline (including organometallic complexes and chelates thereof).

(8) Phentermine.

(9) Pipradrol.

(10) SPA ((-))-1-dimethylamino-1, 2-diphenylethane).

(f) Other substances. Unless specifically excepted or unless listed in another schedule, any material, compound, mixture or preparation which contains any quantity of the following substances, including its salts:

(1) Pentazocine.

SCHEDULE V

(a) Schedule V shall consist of the drugs and other substances, by whatever official name, common or usual name, chemical name, or brand name designated, listed in this section.

(b) Narcotic drugs containing nonnarcotic active medicinal ingredients. Any compound, mixture, or preparation containing any of the following narcotic drugs, or their salts calculated as the free anhydrous base or alkaloid, in limited quantities as set forth below, which shall include one or more nonnarcotic active medicinal ingredients in sufficient proportion to confer upon the compound, mixture, or preparation valuable medicinal qualities other than those possessed by narcotic drugs alone:

(1) Not more than two hundred milligrams of codeine per hundred milliliters or per one hundred grams.

(2) Not more than one hundred milligrams of dihydrocodeine per one hundred milliliters or per one hundred grams.

(3) Not more than one hundred milligrams of ethylmorphine per one hundred milliliters or per one hundred grams.

(4) Not more than 2.5 milligrams of diphenoxylate and not less than twenty-five micrograms of atropine sulfate per dosage unit.

(5) Not more than one hundred milligrams of opium per one hundred milliliters or per one hundred grams.

(6) Not more than 0.5 milligram of difenoxin and not less than twenty-five micrograms of atropine sulfate per dosage unit.

(c) Narcotic drugs. Unless specifically excepted or unless listed in another schedule, any material compound, mixture or preparation containing any of the following narcotic drugs and their salts, as set forth below:

(1) Buprenorphine.

(d) Stimulants. Unless specifically exempted or excluded or unless listed in another schedule, any material, compound, mixture, or preparation which contains any quantity of the following substances having a stimulant effect on the central nervous system, including its salts, isomers and salts of isomers:

(1) Pyrovalerone.

Added by L. 1985, Ch. 664; **Amended** by L. 1986, Ch. 826, eff. Sept. 1, 1986, relettered subd. (f) to subd. (g) in Schedule II and added a new subd. (f) to Schedule II; L. 1987, Ch. 44, eff. Apr. 21, 1987, amending Schedule I by repealing subd. (b)(2) and renumbering subds. (b)(3) through (b)(46) to subds. (b)(2) through (b)(45) and amending Schedule II by renumbering subds. (c)(1) through (c)(23) to subds. (c)(2) through (c)(24) and adding subd. (c)(1); L. 1989, Ch. 418, eff. Jan. 12, 1990; L. 1990, Ch. 640, eff. July 18, 1990, amending Schedule II (h) and adding Schedule II (j) and shall be deemed to have been in full force and effect on and after Jan. 12, 1990; L. 1992, Ch. 115, eff. June 1, 1992 amended Schedule II, subd. (h) (7) and (9); L. 1993, Ch. 473; L. 1995, Ch. 452, § 1, amending Schedule I, subd. (b)(5), eff. Aug. 2, 1995; L. 1995, Ch. 452, § 2, amending Schedule II, subd. (c), eff. Aug. 2, 1995; L. 1996, Ch. 589, eff. Feb. 4, 1997, amending Schedule I, subd. (b), Schedule II, subds. (b)(1), (c), and (f), Schedule III, subd. (e)(3) and (4); and Schedule IV, subds. (c) and (e); L. 1996, Ch. 589, eff. Feb 4, 1997, adding Schedule I, subds. (d)(25) through (30) and (f)(3) through (7), Schedule III, subd. (c)(11), and Schedule V, subd. (d); L. 1996, Ch. 443, § 1, amending Schedule IV, subd. (d), eff. upon conditions being met in § 2; L. 1997, Ch. 619, eff. Nov. 1, 1997, amending Schedule III, subd. (b); L. 2000, Ch. 1, eff. Feb. 1, 2001; L. 2001, Ch. 565, adding Schedule I, subd. (e)(5) and (6), eff. Jan 1, 2002; Ch. 575, repealing Schedule II, subd. (f)(1), amending Schedule II, subd. (f)(2), and adding Schedule III, subd. (f), eff. Dec. 19, 2001; L. 2003, Ch. 264, §§ 56, 57, eff. Nov. 1, 2003, amending Schedule I, subd. (e)(4), and Schedule III, subd. (c)(12); Ch. 591, §§ 1, 2, eff. Sept. 22, 2003, repealing Schedule II, subd. (j), and adding Schedule III, subd. (g).

ANNOTATION

Narcotic Drug. —Crack is a concentrated, smokeable form of cocaine and is a "narcotic drug," as defined by PL § 220.00 (7) and Public Health Law § 3306, schedule II(b)(4), sale of crack is prohibited under criminal sale of a controlled substance in the third degree. People v. Monday, 309 A.D.2d 977, 765 N.Y.S.2d 705 (3d Dept. 2003).

§ 3307. Exception from schedules.

1. The commissioner may, by regulation, except any compound, mixture, or preparation containing any depressant substance in paragraph (a) of schedule III or in schedule IV from the application of all or any part of this article if (1) the compound, mixture, or preparation contains one or more active medicinal ingredients not having a depressant effect on the central nervous system, and (2) such ingredients are included therein in such combinations, quantity, proportion, or concentration as to vitiate the potential for abuse of the substances which do have a depressant effect on the central nervous system.

2. The commissioner may, by regulation, reclassify as a schedule III substance, any compound, mixture or preparation containing any stimulant substance listed in paragraph (c) of schedule II, if

(a) the compound, mixture or preparation contains one or more active medicinal ingredients not having a stimulant effect on the nervous system; and

(b) such ingredients are included therein in such combinations, quantity, proportion or concentration as to vitiate the potential for abuse of the substances which do have a stimulant effect on the central nervous system.

3. The commissioner may, by regulation, except any compound, mixture or preparation containing a narcotic antagonist substance from the application of all or any part of this article if (1) such compound, mixture or preparation has no potential for abuse, and (2) such compound, mixture or preparation has been excepted or exempted from control under the Federal Controlled Substances Act.

4. The commissioner may by regulation exempt or reclassify any compound, mixture or preparation containing any substance listed in subdivision (h) or (i) of Schedule II of section three thousand three hundred six of this article as a Schedule III, IV, or V substance if (a) the compound, mixture or preparation contains one or more active medicinal ingredients not found in subdivision (h) or (j) of Schedule II of section

three thousand three hundred six of this article; and (b) such ingredients are included therein in such combinations, quantity, proportion or concentration as to substantially reduce the potential for abuse.

Amended by L. 1990, Ch. 640, § 3, eff. July 18, 1990, adding subd. (4) and shall be deemed to have been in full force and effect on and after Jan. 12, 1990, and shall remain in effect until June 1, 1992, unless otherwise extended by law, provided, however, that regulations promulgated pursuant to such section may continue in effect beyond such date; L. 1992, Ch. 115, extending expiration date of subd. 4 to June 1, 1994; L. 1994, Ch. 230, § 1, extending expiration date of subd. 4 to June 1, 1996; L. 1996, Ch. 24, § 1, extending expiration date of subd. 4 to June 1, 1996, eff. immediately and shall be deemed to have been in full force and effect on May 31, 1996; L. 1996; Ch. 640, § 3, extending eff. date of subd. 4 to June 1, 1998; L. 1998, Ch. 106, § 1, eff. June 12, 1998, extending eff. date of subd. 4 to June 1, 2000; L. 2000, Ch. 65, § 1, eff. June 6, 2000, extending eff. date of subd. 4 to June 1, 2002; L. 2002, Ch. 89, § 1, eff. June 11, 2002, deleting expiration date of subd. 4.

§ 3308. Powers and duties of the commissioner.

1. The commissioner, and any representative authorized by him, shall have the power to administer oaths, compel the attendance of witnesses and the production of books, papers and records and to take proof and testimony concerning all matters within the jurisdiction of the department.

2. The commissioner is hereby authorized and empowered to make any rules, regulations and determinations which in his judgment may be necessary or proper to supplement the provisions of this article to effectuate the purposes and intent thereof or to clarify its provisions so as to provide the procedure or details to secure effective and proper enforcement of its provisions.

3. No rule or regulation hereunder shall become effective unless, at least twenty-one days prior to the proposed effective date, persons who have conveyed to the department in writing a request to be notified of proposed changes and additions to the department's rules and regulations under this article have been provided with the text of such proposed rules and regulations and have been given an opportunity to comment in writing thereon.

4. The rules, regulations and determinations, when made and promulgated by the commissioner, shall be the rules, regulations and determinations of the department and, until modified or rescinded, shall have the force and effect of law. It shall be the duty of the department, to enforce all of the provisions of this article and all of the rules, regulations and determinations made thereunder.

5. Notwithstanding any inconsistent provision of this article, the commissioner in consultation with the commissioner of education is hereby authorized to promulgate regulations regarding the prescribing, dispensing, use and transmission of electronic prescriptions, which may be

prescribed and dispensed in lieu of an official New York state prescription.

6. The commissioner in consultation with the commissioner of education is hereby authorized to promulgate regulations regarding the dispensing of out-of-state prescriptions.

Amended by L. 2004, Ch. 58, § 5 (Part A), eff. Oct. 20, 2004, adding subds. 5 and 6.

Editor's Note: L. 2004, Ch. 58, Part A, § 18, provides in part:

"[N]otwithstanding the provisions of the state administrative procedure act or sections four, five, six, seven, eight, nine, ten, eleven, twelve, thirteen, fourteen and fifteen of this act the commissioner of health and where specified, in consultation with the commissioner of education, is authorized to adopt, amend or promulgate on an emergency basis any regulation he or she determines necessary to implement the provisions of such sections, including authority to permit prescriptions written in this state to be written without regard to the provisions of section three of this act for a period not to exceed eighteen months after section three of this act takes effect."

TITLE II—MANUFACTURE AND DISTRIBUTION OF CONTROLLED SUBSTANCES

§ 3310. Licenses for manufacture or distribution of controlled substances.

1. No person shall manufacture or distribute a controlled substance in this state without first having obtained a license to do so from the department.

2. A license issued under this section shall be valid for two years from the date of issue, except that in order to facilitate the renewals of such licenses, the commissioner may upon the initial application for a license, issue some licenses which may remain valid for a period of time greater than two years but not exceeding an additional eleven months.

3. The fee for a license under this section shall be one thousand two hundred dollars; provided however, if the license is issued for a period greater than two years the fee shall be increased, pro rata, for each additional month of validity.

4. Licenses issued under this section shall be effective only for and shall specify:

(a) the name and address of the licensee;

(b) the nature of the controlled substances, either by name or schedule, or both, which may be manufactured or distributed;

(c) whether manufacture or distribution or both such activities are permitted by the license.

5. Upon application of a licensee, a license may be amended to allow the licensee to relocate within the state or to add a manufacturing or distributing activity or to add further substances or schedules to the manufacturing or distribution activity permitted thereunder. The fee for such amendment shall be two hundred fifty dollars.

Amended by L. 1981, Ch. 103; L. 1983, Ch. 269, eff. June 10, 1983, amending subd. (5); L. 1989, Ch. 61, eff. Apr. 19, 1989, amended subds. (3) and (5).

§ 3311. Authority to issue initial licenses, amended licenses, and to renew licenses.

1. Subject to the provisions of this article the commissioner is authorized to issue licenses authorizing the manufacture or distribution of controlled substances.

2. An application for a license, amendment of a license, or renewal of a license which, if granted, would authorize the manufacture or distribution of a controlled substance which the applicant is not then authorized to manufacture or distribute shall, with respect to any such additional authorization, be treated as an application for an initial license.

3. An application for a license which, if granted, would authorize a licensee to continue to manufacture or distribute a controlled substance shall, with respect to such continued manufacture or distribution only, be treated as an application for renewal of a license.

4. A late-filed application for the renewal of a license may, in the discretion of the commissioner, be treated as an application for an initial license.

Amended by L. 1973, Ch. 163.

§ 3312. Application for initial license.

1. An applicant for an initial license to manufacture or distribute controlled substances shall furnish to the department such information as it shall require and evidence that the applicant:

(a) and its managing officers are of good moral character;

(b) possesses sufficient land, buildings and equipment to properly carry on the activity described in the application;

(c) is able to maintain effective control against diversion of the controlled substances for which the license is sought;

(d) is able to comply with all applicable state and federal laws and regulations relating to the manufacture or distribution of the controlled substances for which the license is sought.

2. The application shall include the name, residence address and title of each of the officers and directors and the name and residence address of any person having a ten percentum or greater proprietary, beneficial, equitable or credit interest in the applicant. Each such person, if an individual, or lawful representative if a legal entity, shall submit an affidavit with the application setting forth:

(a) any position of management or ownership during the preceding ten years of a ten percentum or greater interest in any other business, located in or outside this state, manufacturing or distributing drugs; and

(b) whether such person or any such business has been convicted, fined, censured or had a license suspended or revoked in any administrative or judicial proceeding relating to or arising out of the manufacture or distribution of drugs; and

(c) such other information as the commissioner may require.

3. The applicant shall be under a continuing duty to report to the department any change in facts or circumstances reflected in the application on any newly discovered or occurring fact or circumstance which is required to be included in the application.

Amended by L. 1973, Ch. 163.

§ 3313. Granting of initial license.

1. The commissioner shall grant an initial license or amendment to a license as to one or more of the substances or activities enumerated in the application if he is satisfied that:

(a) the applicant will be able to maintain effective control against diversion of controlled substances;

(b) the applicant will be able to comply with all applicable state and federal laws;

(c) the applicant and its officers are ready, willing and able to properly carry on the manufacturing or distributing activity for which a license is sought;

(d) the applicant possesses sufficient land, buildings and equipment to properly carry on the activity described in the application;

(e) it is in the public interest that such license be granted; and

(f) the applicant and its managing officers are of good moral character.

2. If the commissioner is not satisfied that the applicant should be issued an initial license, he shall notify the applicant in writing of those factors upon which further evidence is required. Within thirty days of the receipt of such notification, the applicant may submit additional material to the commissioner or demand a hearing or both.

§ 3315. Applications for renewal of licenses to manufacture or distribute controlled substances.

1. An application for the renewal of any license issued pursuant to this title shall be filed with the department not more than six months nor less than four months prior to the expiration thereof.

2. The application for renewal shall include such information prepared in such manner and detail as the commissioner may require, including but not limited to:

(a) any material change in the circumstances or factors listed in section thirty-three hundred twelve of this article;

(b) every known charge or investigation, pending or concluded during the period of the license, by any governmental agency with respect to:

(i) each incident or alleged incident involving the theft, loss, or possible diversion of controlled substances manufactured or distributed by the applicant; and

(ii) compliance by the applicant with the requirements of the federal controlled substances act, or the laws of any state with respect to any substance listed in section thirty-three hundred six of this article.

3. An applicant for renewal shall be under a continuing duty to report to the department any change in facts or circumstances reflected in the application or any newly discovered or occurring fact or circumstance which is required to be included in the application.

4. If the commissioner is not satisfied that the applicant is entitled to a renewal of such license, he shall within forty-five days after the filing of the application serve upon the applicant or his attorney of record in person or by registered or certified mail an order directing the applicant to show cause why his application for renewal should not be denied. Such order shall specify in detail the respects in which the applicant has not satisfied the commissioner that the license should be renewed.

5. Within thirty days of service of such order, the applicant may either submit additional material to the commissioner or demand a hearing or both. If a hearing is demanded the commissioner shall fix a date for hearing not sooner than fifteen days nor later than thirty days after receipt of the demand, unless such time limitation is waived by the applicant.

Amended by L. 1973, Ch. 163.

§ 3316. Granting of renewal of licenses.

1. The commissioner shall renew a license unless he determines and finds that the applicant:

(a) is unlikely to maintain or be able to maintain effective control against diversion; or

(b) is unlikely to comply with all federal and state laws applicable to the manufacture or distribution of the controlled substance or substances for which the license is sought.

2. For purposes of this section, proof that a licensee, during the period of his license, has failed to maintain effective control against diversion or has knowingly or negligently failed to comply with applicable federal or state laws relating to the manufacture or distribution of controlled substances, shall constitute substantial evidence that the applicant will be unlikely to maintain effective control against diversion or be unlikely to comply with the applicable federal or state statutes during the period of proposed renewal.

§ 3318. Identification of controlled substances.

1. No controlled substance may be manufactured or delivered within this state in solid or capsule form unless it has clearly marked or imprinted upon each such capsule or solid:

(a) an individual symbol or number assigned to the person who manufactured the controlled substance in such form, and

(b) a code number or symbol assigned by the

commissioner identifying such substance or combination of substances.

2. No controlled substance contained within a bottle, vial, carton or other container, or in any way affixed or appended to or enclosed within a package of any kind, and designed or intended for delivery in such container or package to an ultimate consumer, shall be manufactured or distributed within this state unless such container or package has clearly and permanently marked or imprinted upon it:

(a) an individual symbol or number assigned to the person who packaged the controlled substance in such form; and

(b) a code number or symbol assigned by the commissioner identifying such substance or combination of substances.

3. The commissioner shall assign a code number or symbol to each controlled substance, and in his discretion for combinations of substances, so as to provide ready identification of such substance. Upon application by a manufacturer of controlled substances, the commissioner shall assign to such manufacturer an identifying number or symbol. Wherever possible and practical, the commissioner shall assign code numbers which conform to the national drug code system.

Amended by L. 1973, Ch. 163.

§ 3319. Distribution of free samples.

It shall be unlawful to distribute free samples of controlled substances, except to persons licensed pursuant to title III of this article.

§ 3320. Authorized distribution.

1. Controlled substances may be lawfully distributed within this state only to licensed distributors or manufacturers, practitioners, pharmacists, pharmacies, institutional dispensers, and laboratory, research or instructional facilities authorized by law to possess the particular substance distributed.

2. A person authorized to obtain a controlled substance by distribution may lawfully receive such substance only from a distributor licensed pursuant to this article.

§ 3321. Exempt distribution.

1. The commissioner by regulation or ruling may exempt from the licensing requirements of this title:

(a) the return of controlled substances to a manufacturer or distributor by a practitioner or pharmacy;

(b) the sale of controlled substances by a pharmacy or practitioner to a pharmacy or practitioner for the immediate needs of the pharmacy or practitioner receiving such substances; and

(c) the disposition of controlled substances by a person in lawful possession thereof who, not in the ordinary course of business, wishes to discontinue such possession.

2. Records of such transactions shall be prepared and maintained and reports filed in such manner as the commissioner shall require.

Amended by L. 1974, Ch. 965.

§ 3322. Reports and records.

1. Persons licensed under this title shall maintain records of all controlled substances manufactured, received, disposed of or distributed by them. The record shall show the date of receipt or delivery, the name and address, and registration number of the person from whom received or to whom distributed, the kind and quantity of substance received and distributed, the kind and quantity of substance produced or removed from the process of manufacture and the date thereof.

2. Any person licensed under this title shall prepare and maintain a biennial report setting forth the current inventory of controlled substances, the quantities of controlled substances manufactured or distributed within the state during the period covered by the report and such other information as the commissioner shall by regulation prescribe. Maintaining for inspection a biennial inventory of controlled substances prepared and maintained in compliance with federal statutes and regulations shall be deemed in compliance with this section.

3. Any person licensed under this title shall forthwith notify the department of any incident involving the theft, loss or possible diversion of controlled substances manufactured or distributed by the licensee.

4. The records and reports required by this section shall be prepared, preserved, or filed in such manner and detail as the commissioner shall by regulation prescribe.

Amended by L. 1975, Ch.108.

TITLE III—RESEARCH, INSTRUCTIONAL ACTIVITIES, AND CHEMICAL ANALYSIS RELATING TO CONTROLLED SUBSTANCES

§ 3324. Licenses to engage in research, instructional activities, and chemical analysis relating to controlled substances.

1. No person within this state shall manufacture, obtain, possess, administer or dispense a controlled substance for purposes of scientific research, instruction or chemical analysis without having first obtained a license to do so from the department.

2. A license issued under this title shall be valid for two years from the date of issue.

3. The fee for a license under this title shall be forty dollars.

4. Licenses issued under this title shall be effective only for and shall specify:

(a) the name and address of the licensee;

(b) the nature of the project or projects permitted by the license;

(c) the nature of the controlled substance or substances to be used in the project, by name if in schedule I, and by name or schedule or both if in any other schedule;

(d) whether dispensing to human subjects is permitted by the license.

5. Upon application of a person licensed pursuant to this title, a license may be amended to add a further activity or to add further substances or schedules to the project permitted thereunder. The fee for such amendment shall be twenty dollars.

Amended by L. 1974, Ch. 965; L. 1981, Ch. 103, eff. June 1, 1981, amending subds. (3) and (5); L. 1989, Ch. 61, eff. Apr. 19, 1989, amended subds. (3) and (5).

ANNOTATION

License.—Failure to demonstrate that the witness possessed a license as supposedly required by Public Health Law § 3324 is of no importance since the regulatory scheme therein set forth does not purport to govern the competency of licensees to analyze controlled substances. People v. Hood, 47 A.D.2d 971, 366 N.Y.S.2d 696 (3d Dept. 1975).

§ 3325. Authority to issue licenses; applications.

1. Subject to the provisions of this title, the commissioner is authorized to license a person to manufacture, obtain and possess, dispense, and administer controlled substances for purposes of scientific research, chemical analysis or instruction.

2. A license or amendment of a license shall be issued by the department unless the applicant therefor has failed to furnish a satisfactory protocol pursuant to subdivision three of this section, or a satisfactory statement pursuant to section 3326, and proof that the applicant:

(a) and its managing officers are of good moral character;

(b) possesses or is capable of acquiring facilities, staff and equipment sufficient to carry on properly the proposed project detailed in the protocol or statement accompanying the application;

(c) is able to maintain effective control against diversion of the controlled substances for which the license is sought;

(d) is able to comply with all applicable state and federal laws and regulations relating to the controlled substances for which the license is sought.

3. An application for a license or for an amendment to a license shall be accompanied by a detailed protocol setting forth:

(a) the nature of the proposed project;

(b) the proposed quantity or quantities of each controlled substance involved;

(c) the qualifications and competence of the applicant to engage in such project;

(d) specific provisions for the safe administration or dispensing of controlled substances to humans, if such is contemplated, and the proposed method of selecting humans;

(e) such other additional information as the commissioner may require.

4. The application for a license pursuant to this title shall include copies of all papers filed with the Bureau, the Federal Food and Drug Administration and any other governmental agency, whether state or federal, in connection with the applicant's proposed project.

§ 3326. Institutional research licenses.

1. Subject to the provisions of this title, the commissioner is authorized to license an institution, which regularly engages in research, to approve specific projects conducted under its immediate auspices.

2. An institution seeking a license pursuant to this section shall make application in the same manner as an applicant for a license pursuant to section 3325. However, such institution shall submit, in lieu of a detailed protocol of a specific project, a statement including:

(a) the qualifications and such other data as the commissioner may require regarding each member of the committee within the institution which will approve specific projects;

(b) a description of the system within the

institution for approving, supervising and evaluating such projects.

3. Upon approval of each specific project, such institution shall forward to the commissioner a description of the project, the names and qualifications of the individuals working thereon and of those individuals designated to supervise the project. If administration or dispensing to human subjects is contemplated, there shall also be included a description of the provisions for safe administration or dispensing.

4. Such institution shall forward to the commissioner periodic progress reports and evaluations of, as well as amendments to each project, in such manner and in such detail as the commissioner may prescribe.

§ 3327. Procedure.

1. A license or amendment to a license shall be issued or refused by the department within ninety days from the date of filing of a completed application.

2. Within thirty days of notification of such refusal, the applicant may either submit additional material to the commissioner or demand a hearing or both. If a hearing is demanded the commissioner shall fix a date for hearing not sooner than fifteen days nor later than thirty days after receipt of the demand, unless such time limitation is waived by the applicant.

§ 3328. Exemptions from title.

The following persons engaging in the following activities shall be exempt from the provisions of this title:

1. A practitioner lawfully administering, dispensing, or prescribing a controlled substance in the course of his professional practice to an ultimate user for a recognized medical purpose;

2. A licensed manufacturer engaged in research upon non-human subjects or chemical analysis conducted on the premises specified in the manufacturer's license;

3. A licensed distributor engaged in quality control analysis at the premises specified in his license.

4. A practitioner or patient participating in a clinical research program on the therapeutic use of marijuana or tetrahydrocannabinols. (a) Each such clinical research program shall have received protocol approval from the United States Food and Drug Administration, shall possess an effective investigational new drug application and shall have been registered by the Drug Enforcement Administration, United States Department of Justice.

Amended by L. 1980, Ch. 810.

§ 3329. Reports and records.

1. Persons licensed under this title shall keep records showing the receipt, administration, dispensing, or destruction of all controlled substances and maintain the records in such manner and detail as the commissioner, by regulation, shall require.

2. Persons licensed under this title shall submit reports to the department summarizing the activity conducted under the license. Included in such report shall be a detailed inventory of controlled substances, and an accounting for all such substances received or disposed of during the period covered by the report and such other information as the commissioner shall, by regulation, require. Such reports shall be filed with the department at such times as the commissioner may require.

TITLE IV—DISPENSING TO ULTIMATE USERS

§ 3330. Schedule I substances.

No prescription may be made or filled for any controlled substance in schedule I nor may such substance be possessed, distributed, dispensed or administered except pursuant to title III of this article.

ANNOTATION

Violations.—Petitioner physician who issued two illegal prescriptions to a patient for cannabis sativa, in violation of PHL § 3330, knew patient's motivation for obtaining prescriptions was to avoid legal consequences of his marihuana use, petitioner also actively deceived that patient's probation officer representing to that individual that prescriptions issued were "official" and that there was a federal law that authorized petitioner to write prescriptions, conduct sufficient to sustain charges of fraudulent practice, moral unfitness and failure to comply with PHL § 3300. Clarke v. N.Y. State Bd. for Prof'l Med. Conduct, 3 A.D.3d 798, 771 N.Y.S.2d 255 (3d Dept. 2004).

§ 3331. Scheduled substances administering and dispensing by practitioners.

1. Except as provided in titles III or V of this article, no substance in schedules II, III, IV, or V may be prescribed for or dispensed or administered to an addict or habitual user.

2. A practitioner, in good faith, and in the course of his or her professional practice only, may prescribe, administer and dispense substances listed in schedules II, III, IV, and V, or he or she may cause the same to be administered by a designated agent under his or her direction and supervision.

3. A veterinarian, in good faith, and in the course of the practice of veterinary medicine only, may prescribe, administer and dispense substances listed in schedules II, III, IV, and V or he may cause them to be administered by a designated agent under his direction and supervision.

4. No such substance may be dispensed unless it is enclosed within a suitable and durable container, and:

(a) Affixed to such container is a label upon which is indelibly typed, printed or otherwise legibly written the following:

(i) the name and address of the ultimate user for whom the substance is intended, or, if intended for use upon an animal, the species of such animal and the name and address of the owner or person in custody of such animal;

(ii) the name, address, and telephone number of the dispensing practitioner;

(iii) specific directions for use, including but not limited to the dosage and frequency of dosage, and the maximum daily dosage;

(iv) the legend, prominently marked or printed in either boldface or upper case lettering: "CONTROLLED SUBSTANCE, DANGEROUS UNLESS USED AS DIRECTED";

(v) the date of dispensing;

(vi) either the name of the substance or such code number assigned by the department for the particular substance pursuant to section thirty-three hundred eighteen of this article;

(b) Such container shall be identified as a controlled substance by either:

(i) an orange label;

(ii) a label of another color over which is superimposed an orange transparent adhesive tape; or

(iii) an auxiliary orange label affixed to the front of such container and bearing the legend, prominently marked or printed "Controlled Substance, Dangerous Unless Used As Directed";

(c) Any label, transparency, or auxiliary label shall be applied in a manner which would inhibit its removal.

5. No more than a thirty day supply or, pursuant to regulations of the commissioner enumerating conditions warranting specified greater supplies, no more than a three month supply of a schedule II, III or IV substance, as determined by the directed dosage and frequency of dosage, may be dispensed by an authorized practitioner at one time.

6. A practitioner dispensing a controlled substance shall file information pursuant to such dispensing with the department by electronic means in such a manner and detail as the commissioner shall, by regulation, require. Such information shall be filed by not later than the fifteenth day of the next month following the month in which the controlled substance was delivered. This requirement shall not apply to the dispensing by a practitioner pursuant to subdivision five of section thirty-three hundred fifty-one of this article.

7. A practitioner may not administer, prescribe, or dispense any substance referred to in subdivision (h) or subdivision (j) of Schedule II of section three thousand three hundred six of this article for other than therapeutic purposes. A practitioner may not administer, prescribe or dispense any such substance to any individual without first obtaining the informed consent of such individual, or where the individual lacks capacity to give such consent, a person legally authorized to consent on his or her behalf.

Amended by L. 1973, Ch. 728; L. 1974, Ch. 965; L. 1981, Ch. 415; L. 1986, Ch. 433, eff. July 21, 1986, amending subd. (6); L. 1989, Ch. 418, eff. Jan. 12, 1990; L. 1990, Ch. 640, eff. July 18, 1990, amending subd. (7) and shall be deemed to have been in full force and effect on and after Jan. 12, 1990; L. 1998, Ch. 537, § 4, eff. Nov. 1, 1998, amending subds. 2 and 6; L. 2004, Ch. 58, § 6 (Part A), eff. Oct. 20, 2004.

Editor's Notes: L. 2004, Ch. 58, Part A, § 18, provides in part:

"[N]otwithstanding the provisions of the state administrative procedure act or sections four, five, six, seven, eight, nine, ten, eleven, twelve, thirteen, fourteen and fifteen of this act the commissioner of health and where specified, in consultation with the commissioner of education, is authorized to adopt, amend or promulgate on an emergency basis any regulation he or she determines necessary to implement the provisions of such sections, including authority to permit prescriptions written in this state to be written without regard to the provisions of section three of this act for a period not to exceed eighteen months after section three of this act takes effect; provided, further, that the amendments to subdivision 6 of section 3331 of the public health law, made by section six of this act and the amendments to subdivision 4 of section 3333 of the public health law, made by section eight of this act, relating to filing prescription information with the department of health by electronic means, shall not be implemented until the commissioner of health and where specified, in consultation with the commissioner of education, has promulgated regulations relating thereto, and the commissioner of health, in consultation with the commissioner of education, shall notify the legislative bill drafting commission upon the promulgation of such regulations in order that such commission may maintain an accurate and timely effective data base of the official text of the laws of the state of New York in furtherance of effecting the provisions of section 44 of the legislative law and section 70-b of the public officers law."

L. 1998, Ch. 537, § 19, provides:

"This act shall take effect November 1, 1998; provided, however, that the amendments to subdivision 6 of section 3331 of the public health law, made by section four of this act, and the amendments to subdivision 4 of section 3333 of the public health law, made by section six of this act, relating to filing prescription information with the department of health by electronic means, shall not be implemented until the commissioner of health has promulgated regulations relating thereto. [Such regulations were promulgated eff. May 1, 2001. See 10 NYCRR Part 80.]."

ANNOTATIONS

Good faith—The fact that defendant, a doctor, did not conduct a physical examination of the undercover officer before he prescribed seconal was not sufficient, in and of itself, to prove an absence of good faith. People v. Pal, 56 A.D.2d 640, 391 N.Y.S.2d 702 (2d Dept. 1977).

—Court rejected petitioner's contention that because the investigator who posed as a patient was not in reality an addict or habitual user, the charges were unsubstantiated; to adopt petitioner's position would require the authorities to send a true addict or habitual user into a doctor's office during an investigation of the doctor's prescribing practices. Koudouris v. Axelrod, 102 A.D.2d 954, 477 N.Y.S.2d 815 (3d Dept. 1984).

—The term "good faith" requires the physician to have acted for a bona fide medical purpose in supplying or prescribing the drugs. People v. Goldberg, 82 Misc. 2d 474, 369 N.Y.S.2d 989 (Sup. Ct. N.Y. Co. 1975).

§ 3332. Making of official New York state prescriptions for scheduled substances.

1. No controlled substance may be prescribed by a practitioner except on an official New York state prescription, and in good faith and in the course of his or her professional practice only.

2. Such prescription shall be prepared on an official New York state prescription form, written with ink, indelible pencil or, apart from the practitioner's signature, typewriter or electronic printer. The original must contain the following:

(a) the name, address, and age of the ultimate user for whom the substance is intended, or, if

the ultimate user is an animal, the species of such animal and the name and address of the owner or person having custody of such animal;

(b) the name, address, Federal registration number, telephone number, and handwritten signature of the prescribing practitioner;

(c) specific directions for use, including but not limited to the dosage and frequency of dosage and the maximum daily dosage;

(d) the date upon which such prescription was actually signed by the prescribing practitioner.

3. No such prescription shall be made for a quantity of controlled substances which would exceed a thirty day supply if the controlled substance were used in accordance with the directions for use specified on the prescription. A practitioner may, however, issue a prescription for up to a three month supply of a controlled substance provided that the controlled substance has been prescribed to treat one of the conditions that have been enumerated by the commissioner pursuant to regulations as warranting the prescribing of greater than a thirty day supply of a controlled substance and that the practitioner specifies the condition on the face of the prescription. No additional prescriptions for a controlled substance may be issued by a practitioner to an ultimate user within thirty days of the date of any prescription previously issued unless and until the ultimate user has exhausted all but a seven day supply of the controlled substance provided by any previously issued prescription. A practitioner may, however, issue a prescription for up to a six month supply of any substance listed in subdivision (h) of Schedule II of section three thousand three hundred six of this article provided that such substance has been prescribed to treat one of the conditions that have been enumerated by the commissioner pursuant to regulations as warranting the prescribing of a six month supply and that the practitioner specifies the condition on the face of the prescription.

4. The practitioner shall deliver the original to the ultimate user.

Amended by L. 1974, Ch. 965; L. 1986, Ch. 118, eff. Nov. 1, 1986; L. 1990, Ch. 640, eff. July 18, 1990, amending subd. (3) and shall be deemed to have been in full force and effect on and after Jan. 12, 1990; L. 1998, Ch. 537, § 5, eff. Nov. 1, 1998, amending subds. 1, 2, and 4; L. 2004, Ch. 58, § 7 (Part A), eff. Oct. 20, 2004, amending subds. 1 & 3.

Editor's Notes: L. 2004, Ch. 58, Part A, § 18, provides in part:

"[N]otwithstanding the provisions of the state administrative procedure act or sections four, five, six, seven, eight, nine, ten, eleven, twelve, thirteen, fourteen and fifteen of this act the commissioner of health and where specified, in consultation with the commissioner of education, is authorized to adopt, amend or promulgate on an emergency basis any regulation he or she determines necessary to implement the provisions of such sections, including authority to permit prescriptions written in this state to be written without regard to the provisions of section three of this act for a period not to exceed eighteen months after section three of this act takes effect."

L. 1998, Ch. 537, § 17 provides:

"Notwithstanding any inconsistent provision of article 33 of the public health law, practitioners and pharmacists may continue to use official New York state prescriptions, printed in triplicate, that were legally obtained under article 33 of the public health law. The commissioner of health shall establish rules and regulations relating to the continued use of such prescriptions."

ANNOTATION

Diverting controlled substance to physician's own use; proper penalty.—Decision of the State Commissioner of Health finding a physician guilty of violations of law and ordering him to pay a $6,000 fine and suspending his privilege to issue official state prescription forms was proper after he found that the physician had not delivered to his in-laws all the dexedrine he had obtained for delivery to them through the issuance of a prescription, stored some of it in a "tetracycline jar" in his office, and personally used some of the dexedrine he prescribed and picked up for his father-in-law. Reid v. Axelrod, 76 A.D.2d 993, 429 N.Y.S.2d 84 (3d Dept. 1980).

§ 3333. Dispensing upon official New York state prescription.

1. A licensed pharmacist may, in good faith and in the course of his or her professional practice, sell and dispense to an ultimate user controlled substances only upon the delivery of an official New York state prescription to such pharmacist, within thirty days of the date such prescription was signed by an authorized practitioner; provided, however, a pharmacist may dispense a part or portion of such prescription in accordance with regulations of the commissioner in consultation with the commissioner of education. No pharmacy or pharmacist may sell or dispense greater than a thirty day supply of a controlled substance to an ultimate user unless and until the ultimate user has exhausted all but a seven day supply of the controlled substance provided pursuant to any previously issued prescription, except that a pharmacy or pharmacist may sell or dispense up to a three month supply of a controlled substance if there appears, on the face of the official New York state prescription, a statement that the controlled substance has been prescribed to treat one of the conditions that have been enumerated by the regulations of the commissioner as warranting the prescribing of greater than a thirty day supply of a controlled substance. A pharmacy or pharmacist may sell or dispense up to a six month supply of any substance listed in subdivision (h) of Schedule II of section three thousand three hundred six of this article if there appears, on the face of the official New York state prescription, a statement that the substance has been prescribed to treat one of the conditions that have been enumerated by the regulations of the commissioner as warranting the prescribing of a specified greater supply.

2. No controlled substance may be so dispensed or sold unless it is enclosed within a suitable container, and:

(a) Affixed to such container is a label upon which is indelibly typed, printed, or otherwise legibly written the following:

(i) the name and address of the ultimate user for whom the substance is intended, or if intended for use upon an animal, the species of such animal and the name and address of the owner or person in custody of such animal;

(ii) the name, address, and telephone number of the pharmacy from which such substance is dispensed;

(iii) specific directions for use as stated on the prescription;

(iv) the name of the prescribing practitioner;

(v) the legend, prominently marked or printed in either boldface or upper case lettering: "CONTROLLED SUBSTANCE, DANGEROUS UNLESS USED AS DIRECTED";

(vi) the number of the prescription under which it is recorded in the pharmacist's prescription file;

(vii) such code number assigned by the department for the particular substance pursuant to section thirty-three hundred eighteen of this article, or when requested by the practitioner, the name of such substance;

(b) Such container shall be identified as a controlled substance by either:

(i) an orange label;

(ii) a label of another color over which is superimposed an orange transparent adhesive tape; or

(iii) an auxiliary orange label affixed to the front of such container and bearing the legend, prominently marked or printed "Controlled Substance, Dangerous Unless Used As Directed";

(c) Any label, transparency, or auxiliary label shall be applied in a manner which would inhibit its removal.

3. The pharmacist filling the controlled substance prescription shall endorse upon the original the date of delivery and his or her signature.

4. The endorsed original prescription shall be retained by the proprietor of the pharmacy for a period of five years. The proprietor of the pharmacy shall file such prescription information with the department by electronic means in such manner and detail as the commissioner in consultation with the commissioner of education shall, by regulation, require. Such prescription information shall be filed by not later than the fifteenth day of the next month following the month in which the substance was delivered.

5. When filing prescription information electronically pursuant to subdivision four of this section, the proprietor of the pharmacy shall dispose of any electronically recorded prescription information in such manner as the commissioner shall by regulation require.

Amended by L. 1981, Ch. 415, eff. Sept. 1, 1981; L. 1986, Ch. 118, eff. Nov. 1, 1986; L. 1990, Ch. 640, eff. July 18, 1990, amending subd. 1 and shall be deemed to have been in full force

MISC. LAWS

and effect on and after Jan. 12, 1990; L. 1998, Ch. 537, § 6, eff. Nov. 1, 1998, amending subds. 1, 3, and 4, and adding subd. 5; L. 2004, Ch. 58, § 8 (Part A), eff. Oct. 20, 2004.

Editor's Notes: L. 2004, Ch. 58, Part A, § 18, provides in part:

"[N]otwithstanding the provisions of the state administrative procedure act or sections four, five, six, seven, eight, nine, ten, eleven, twelve, thirteen, fourteen and fifteen of this act the commissioner of health and where specified, in consultation with the commissioner of education, is authorized to adopt, amend or promulgate on an emergency basis any regulation he or she determines necessary to implement the provisions of such sections, including authority to permit prescriptions written in this state to be written without regard to the provisions of section three of this act for a period not to exceed eighteen months after section three of this act takes effect; provided, further, that the amendments to subdivision 6 of section 3331 of the public health law, made by section six of this act and the amendments to subdivision 4 of section 3333 of the public health law, made by section eight of this act, relating to filing prescription information with the department of health by electronic means, shall not be implemented until the commissioner of health and where specified, in consultation with the commissioner of education, has promulgated regulations relating thereto, and the commissioner of health, in consultation with the commissioner of education, shall notify the legislative bill drafting commission upon the promulgation of such regulations in order that such commission may maintain an accurate and timely effective data base of the official text of the laws of the state of New York in furtherance of effecting the provisions of section 44 of the legislative law and section 70-b of the public officers law."

L. 1998, Ch. 537, § 19, provides:

"This act shall take effect November 1, 1998; provided, however, that the amendments to subdivision 6 of section 3331 of the public health law, made by section four of this act, and the amendments to subdivision 4 of section 3333 of the public health law, made by section six of this act, relating to filing prescription information with the department of health by electronic means, shall not be implemented until the commissioner of health has promulgated regulations relating thereto. [Such regulations were promulgated eff. May 1, 2001. See 10 NYCRR Part 80.]."

§ 3334. Emergency oral prescriptions for schedule II drugs and certain other controlled substances.

1. In an emergency situation, as defined by rule or regulation of the department, a practitioner may orally prescribe and a pharmacist may dispense to an ultimate user controlled substances in schedule II and those schedule III or schedule IV controlled substances as the commissioner may, by regulation, require; provided however the pharmacist shall:

(a) contemporaneously reduce such prescription to writing;

(b) dispense the substance in conformity with the labeling requirements applicable to the type of prescription which would be required but for the emergency; and

(c) make a good faith effort to verify the practitioner's identity, if the practitioner is unknown to the pharmacist.

2. No oral prescription shall be filled for a quantity of controlled substances which would exceed a five day supply if the substance were used in accordance with the directions for use.

3. Within seventy-two hours after authorizing an emergency oral prescription, the prescribing practitioner shall cause to be delivered to the pharmacist the original of an official New York state prescription. Such prescription shall, in addition to the information otherwise required, also have written or typed upon its face the words: "Authorization for emergency dispensing." If the pharmacist fails to receive such prescription he or she shall notify the department in writing within seven days from the date of dispensing the substance.

4. Such official New York state prescription shall be endorsed, retained and filed in the same manner as is otherwise required for such prescriptions.

Amended by L. 1998, Ch. 537, § 7, eff. Nov. 1, 1998, amending subd. 3; L. 2004, Ch. 58, § 9 (Part A), eff. Oct. 20, 2004.

Editor's Note: L. 2004, Ch. 58, Part A, § 18, provides in part:

"[N]otwithstanding the provisions of the state administrative procedure act or sections four, five, six, seven, eight, nine, ten, eleven, twelve, thirteen, fourteen and fifteen of this act the commissioner of health and where specified, in consultation with the commissioner of education, is authorized to adopt, amend or promulgate on an emergency basis any regulation he or she determines necessary to implement the provisions of such sections, including authority to permit prescriptions written in this state to be written without regard to the provisions of section three of this act for a period not to exceed eighteen months after section three of this act takes effect."

§ 3335. [Repealed pursuant to L. 2004, Ch. 58, § 10 (Part A), eff. Oct. 20, 2004.]

§ 3336. [Repealed pursuant to L. 2004, Ch. 58, § 10 (Part A), eff. Oct. 20, 2004.]

§ 3337. Oral prescriptions schedule III, IV and V substances.

1. Except as provided in section thirty-three hundred thirty-four of this article, a practitioner may orally prescribe and a pharmacist may dispense to an ultimate user controlled substances in schedules III, IV or V provided however the pharmacist shall:

(a) contemporaneously reduce such prescription to writing;

(b) dispense the substance in conformity with the labeling requirements applicable to a prescription; and

(c) make a good faith effort to verify the practitioner's identity, if the practitioner is unknown to the pharmacist.

2. No oral prescription shall be filled for a quantity of controlled substances which would exceed a five day supply if the controlled substance were used in accordance with the directions for use, except that with respect to a schedule IV substance such prescription shall not exceed a thirty-day supply or one hundred dosage

units, whichever is less; provided, however, that this provision shall not apply to any schedule IV controlled substance limited to a five day supply by section thirty-three hundred thirty-four of this article.

3. Within seventy-two hours after authorizing such an oral prescription, the prescribing practitioner shall cause to be delivered to the pharmacist an official New York state prescription. If the pharmacist fails to receive such prescription he shall make a record of such fact in such manner and detail as the commissioner in consultation with the commissioner of education, by regulation, shall require.

4. Such official New York state prescription shall be endorsed, retained and filed in the same manner as is otherwise required for such prescriptions.

Amended by L. 1974, Chs. 960, 961, 965; L. 2004, Ch. 58, § 11 (Part A), eff. Oct. 20, 2004.

§ 3338. Official New York state prescription forms.

1. Official New York state prescription forms shall be prepared and issued by the department in the manner and detail as the commissioner in consultation with the commissioner of education may, by regulation, require, and, each form shall be serialized. Such forms shall be furnished to practitioners authorized to write such prescriptions and to institutional dispensers. Such prescription blanks shall not be transferable.

2. Except as expressly authorized by section thirty-three hundred thirty-four or thirty-three hundred thirty-seven of this article, controlled substances may be prescribed or dispensed only upon an official New York state prescription or, pursuant to regulations, an electronic prescription or out-of-state prescription.

3. The commissioner in consultation with the commissioner of education is hereby authorized and empowered to make rules and regulations, not inconsistent with this article, with respect to the retention or filing of such official New York state prescription forms, electronic prescriptions and out-of-state prescriptions, including information required to be filed with the department, the maximum number of official prescription forms which may be issued at any one time, the manner in which such forms shall be issued, the period of time after issuance by the department that such form shall remain valid for use, and the manner in which practitioners associated with institutional dispensers may use such forms, or any other matter of procedure or detail necessary to effectuate or clarify the provisions of this section and to secure proper and effective enforcement of the provisions of this article.

4. Upon a finding by the commissioner that a person has willfully failed to comply with the provisions of this article, the commissioner may revoke, cancel or withhold official New York state prescription forms which have been issued or for which application has been made.

Amended by L. 1981, Ch. 103; L. 1982, Ch. 129, eff. Jan 1, 1983, amending subd. 1; L. 1997, Ch. 433, § 43, eff. Aug. 20, 1997; L. 1998, Ch. 537, § 10, eff. Nov. 1, 1998, amending subds. 1 and 4; L. 2004, Ch. 58, § 12 (Part A), eff. Oct 20, 2004.

§ 3339. Refilling of prescriptions for controlled substances.

1. Prescriptions for a schedule II controlled substance and those schedule III or schedule IV controlled substances which the commissioner may require by regulation may not be refilled.

2. A prescription, except for a schedule II controlled substance or those schedule III or schedule IV controlled substances which the commissioner may require by regulation may be refilled not more than the number of times specifically authorized by the prescriber upon the prescription, provided however no such authorization shall be effective for a period greater than six months from the date the prescription is signed. In the event that the prescription authorizes the dispensing of more than a thirty day supply of schedule III, schedule IV or schedule V substances pursuant to regulations of the commissioner enumerating conditions warranting specified greater supplies, the prescription may be refilled only once.

3. Unless an earlier refilling is authorized by the prescriber, no prescription for a controlled substance may be refilled earlier than seven days prior to the date the previously dispensed supply would be exhausted if used in conformity with the directions for use..

Amended by L. 1974, Ch. 965; L. 2004, Ch. 58, § 13 (Part A), eff. Oct. 20, 2004.

§ 3341. Institutional dispensers certificates of approval.

1. No institutional dispenser as herein before defined, shall receive, possess or cause controlled substances to be administered or dispensed without first having been issued a certificate of approval authorizing such activity by the commissioner.

2. Upon application of an institutional dispenser for a certificate of approval, the commissioner shall issue such certificate if he is satisfied that:

(a) the applicant and its managing officers are of good moral character;

(b) the applicant possesses the necessary land, building, paraphernalia and staff to properly carry on the activities described in the application;

(c) the applicant will be able to maintain effective control against diversion of controlled substances; and

(d) the applicant will be able to comply with all applicable state and federal laws.

3. Institutional dispensers to whom such certificates have been issued shall thereafter register biennially with the department. The fee for such certificate and for each biennial registration shall be one hundred dollars.

4. Certificates and registrations issued under this section shall be effective only for and shall specify:

(a) the name and address of the institutional dispenser;

(b) the nature of the controlled substance, or substances, either by name or schedule, or both, for which the certificate or registration is issued.

Amended by L. 1981, Ch. 103, eff. June 1, 1981, amending subd. (3); L. 1989, Ch. 61, eff. Apr. 19, 1989, amended subd. (3).

§ 3342. Dispensing and administering by institutional dispensers.

1. An institutional dispenser may cause controlled substances to be administered or dispensed for use on its premises or for the immediate care or treatment of a patient lawfully being transferred in an emergency situation, as defined by rule or regulation of the commissioner, to an alternative medical facility only pursuant to a written order by a practitioner for medication. Such orders shall be made and preserved in the manner and form as the commissioner shall, by regulation, prescribe.

2. An institutional dispenser may dispense controlled substances for use off its premises only pursuant to a prescription, prepared and filed in conformity with this title, provided, however, that in an emergency situation as defined by rule or regulation of the department a practitioner in a hospital without a full-time pharmacy may dispense controlled substances to a patient in a hospital emergency room for use off the premises of the institutional dispenser for a period not to exceed twenty-four hours.

3. An institutional dispenser shall maintain records of all controlled substances dispensed and

administered in such manner as the commissioner shall, by regulation, require.

Amended by L. 1974, Ch. 965; L. 1976, Ch. 692.

§ 3343. Reports and records.

1. Prescriptions and copies of prescriptions shall be preserved in the following manner:

(a) dispensing practitioners filing information electronically pursuant to subdivision six of section thirty-three hundred thirty-one of this article, shall dispose of any electronically recorded information in such manner as the commissioner in consultation with the commissioner of education shall by regulation require;

(b) pharmacists dispensing controlled substances upon prescription shall preserve such prescriptions in such manner as the commissioner in consultation with the commissioner of education shall, by regulation, require.

2. Practitioners and pharmacies shall maintain records of all controlled substances received and dispensed in such manner as the commissioner shall, by regulation, require.

Amended by L. 1998, Ch. 537, § 11, eff. Nov. 1, 1998, amending subd. 1(a); L. 2004, Ch. 58, § 14 (Part A), eff. Oct. 20, 2004.

ANNOTATION

Supervisor's responsibility.—While there was no evidence specifically linking petitioner to the violations, he was nonetheless held responsible, because as a supervising pharmacist he had a clear duty to supervise his employees and make sure adequate records were kept. Amber Rock Pharmacy, Inc. v. Axelrod, 111 A.D.2d 848, 490 N.Y.S.2d 783 (2d Dept. 1985).

§ 3345. Possession of controlled substances by ultimate users original container.

Except for the purpose of current use by the person or animal for whom such substance was prescribed or dispensed, it shall be unlawful for an ultimate user of controlled substances to possess such substance outside of the original container in which it was dispensed.

Violation of this provision shall be an offense punishable by a fine of not more than fifty dollars.

TITLE V—DISPENSING TO ADDICTS AND HABITUAL USERS

§ 3350. Dispensing prohibition.

Controlled substances may not be prescribed for, or administered or dispensed to addicts or habitual users of controlled substances, except as provided by this title or title III.

§ 3351. Dispensing for medical use.

1. Controlled substances may be prescribed for, or administered or dispensed to an addict or habitual user:

(a) during emergency medical treatment unrelated to abuse of controlled substances;

(b) who is a bona fide patient suffering from an incurable and fatal disease such as cancer or advanced tuberculosis;

(c) who is aged, infirm, or suffering from serious injury or illness and the withdrawal from controlled substances would endanger the life or impede or inhibit the recovery of such person.

2. Controlled substances may be ordered for use by an addict or habitual user by a practitioner and administered by a practitioner or registered nurse to relieve acute withdrawal symptoms.

3. Methadone, or such other controlled substance designated by the commissioner as appropriate for such use, may be ordered for use of an addict by a practitioner and dispensed or administered by a practitioner or his designated agent as interim treatment for an addict on a waiting list for admission to an authorized maintenance program.

4. Methadone, or such other controlled substance designated by the commissioner as appropriate for such use, may be administered to an addict by a practitioner or by his designated agent acting under the direction and supervision of a practitioner, as part of a regime designed and intended to withdraw a patient from addiction to controlled substances.

5. Methadone, or such other controlled substance designated by the commissioner as appropriate for such use, may be administered to an addict by a practitioner or by his designated agent acting under the direction and supervision of a practitioner, as part of a substance abuse or chemical dependence program approved pursuant to article twenty-three or thirty-two of the mental hygiene law.

Amended by 1986, Ch. 433, eff. July 21, 1986, adding subd. (5); L. 1999, Ch. 558, § 40, amending subd. 5, eff. Oct. 5, 1999.

§ 3352. Reports and records.

1. Persons certified pursuant to article twenty-three or thirty-two of the mental hygiene law to operate methadone maintenance treatment programs shall keep records showing the receipt, administration, dispensing, or destruction of all controlled substances and maintain the records in such manner and detail as the commissioner, by regulation, shall require.

2. By the tenth day of each month, a person certified to conduct a maintenance program shall file with the department a report summarizing its activity in the preceding month. Such report shall include:

(a) an inventory of the quantity of controlled substance on hand at the commencement and at the conclusion of such month's activity;

(b) the total quantity of controlled substance received, the distributor from whom each order was received, and the form or dosage unit in which such substance was received;

(c) the total quantity of controlled substance prescribed, dispensed, and administered during such month;

(d) each incident or alleged incident involving the theft, loss or possible diversion of controlled substances.

Added by L. 1986, Ch. 433, eff. July 21, 1986, which also repealed former § 3352; Amended by L. 1999, Ch. 558, § 41, amending subd. 1, eff. Oct. 5, 1999.

MISC. LAWS

TITLE VI—RECORDS AND REPORTS

§ 3370. Preserving and inspection of records.

1. Any record, including prescriptions, required to be kept or maintained by this article shall be preserved for a period of at least five years following the date of the event or transaction recorded, unless a shorter period of time is specifically provided.

2. Such records shall be made available during business hours for inspection and copying by any officer or employee of the department who is charged with the enforcement of this article and to any officer or employee of this state charged with the duty of regulating or licensing of any person who by virtue of such license is authorized to obtain, distribute, dispense or administer controlled substances.

3.* Every record, including prescriptions, required to be kept under this article shall be maintained at the premises where the licensed activity is conducted.

3.* The department shall cause to be expunged or otherwise destroyed, within five years from the date of receipt thereof, any record of the name of any patient received by it pursuant to the filing requirements of subdivision six of section thirty-three hundred thirty-one, subdivision four of section thirty-three hundred thirty-three, and subdivision four of section thirty-three hundred thirty-four of this article.

* [There are two subds. 3.]

Amended by L. 1974, Ch. 58, which added subd. 3, and Ch. 965, which also added a subd. 3.

ANNOTATION

Records.—While practitioners are required to maintain written patient records with respect to the administration, dispensing and prescription of controlled substances, such records need not necessarily be distinct from the medical records of such patients. Pal v. Axelrod, 172 A.D.2d 325, 568 N.Y.S.2d 609 (1st Dept. 1991).

§ 3371. Confidentiality of certain records, reports, and information.

1. No person, who has knowledge by virtue of his office of the identity of a particular patient or research subject, a manufacturing process, a trade secret or a formula shall disclose such knowledge, or any report or record thereof, except:

(a) to another person employed by the department, for purposes of executing provisions of this article; or

(b) pursuant to judicial subpoena or court order in a criminal investigation or proceeding; or

(c) to an agency, department of government, or official board authorized to regulate, license or otherwise supervise a person who is authorized by this article to deal in controlled substances, or in the course of any investigation or proceeding by or before such agency, department or board.

(d) to a central registry established pursuant to this article.

(e) to a practitioner to inform him or her that a person under his or her treatment with a controlled substance also may be under treatment with a controlled substance by another practitioner.

2. In the course of any proceeding where such information is disclosed, except when necessary to effectuate the rights of a party to the proceeding, the court or presiding officer shall take such action as is necessary to insure that such information, or record or report of such information is not made public.

(e) to a practitioner to inform him or her that a person under his or her treatment with a controlled substance also may be under treatment with a controlled substance by another practitioner.

Amended by L. 1974, Ch. 965; L. 2004, Ch. 58, § 15 (Part A), eff. Oct. 20, 2004.

ANNOTATION

Methadone patient.—When defendant elected to defend his possession of bottle methadone on the basis that it was lawfully possessed by him in connection with his participation in St. Mary's program, he waived the benefit of the statutory right to anonymity. People v. Still, 48 A.D.2d 366, 369 N.Y.S.2d 759 (2d Dept. 1975).

§ 3372. Practitioner patient reporting.

It shall be the duty of every attending practitioner and every consulting practitioner to report promptly to the commissioner, or his duly designated agent, the name and, if possible, the address of, and such other data as may be required by the commissioner with respect to, any person under treatment if he finds that such person is an addict or a habitual user of any narcotic drug. Such report shall be kept confidential and may be utilized only for statistical, epidemiological or research purposes, except that those reports which originate in the course of a criminal proceeding other than under section 81.25 of the mental hygiene law shall be subject only to the confidentiality requirements of section thirty-three hundred seventy-one of this article.

Amended by L. 1973, Ch. 195.

§ 3373. Confidential communications.

For the purposes of duties arising out of this article, no communication made to a practitioner shall be deemed confidential within the meaning of the civil practice law and rules relating to confidential communications between such practitioner and patient.

Construction.—Communications between defendant and his physicians in furtherance of his treatment were obtained in violation of defendant's physician-patient privilege and should not have been admitted at trial. People v. Sinski, 88 N.Y.2d 487, 646 N.Y.S.2d 651, 669 N.E.2d 809 (1996).

—The exception contained in Public Health Law § 3373 is a limited one, and should be strictly construed in accordance with its terms. People v. Saaratu, 143 Misc. 2d 1075, 541 N.Y.S.2d 889 (Sup. Ct. Bronx Co. 1989).

§ 3374. Notification by licensee.

Persons licensed or certified pursuant to this article shall be under a continuing duty to promptly notify the department of:

1. Each incident or alleged incident of theft, loss or possible diversion of controlled substances manufactured, ordered, distributed or possessed by such person;

2. Any charge or proceeding brought in any court or before any governmental agency, state or federal, in which it is alleged that the licensee, its employees, subsidiaries, managing officers, or directors has failed to comply with the provisions of the federal controlled substances act or the laws of any state relating to controlled substances.

MISC. LAWS

TITLE VII—OFFENSES, VIOLATIONS AND ENFORCEMENT

§ 3380. Inhalation of certain toxic vapors or fumes and certain hazardous inhalants; sale of glue and hazardous inhalants in certain cases.

1. (a) As used in this section the phrase "glue containing a solvent having the property of releasing toxic vapors or fumes" shall mean and include any glue, cement, or other adhesive containing one or more of the following chemical compounds: acetone, cellulose acetate, benzene, butyl alcohol, ethyl alcohol, ethylene dichloride, ethylene trichloride, isopropyl alcohol, methyl alcohol, methyl ethyl ketone, pentachlorophenol, petroleum ether, toluene or such other similar material as the commission shall by regulation prescribe.

(b) As used in this section hazardous inhalants shall mean and include any of the preparations of compounds containing one or more of the chemical compounds; amyl nitrite, isoamyl nitrite, butyl nitrite, isobutyl nitrite, pentyl nitrite or any other akyl nitrite compound that is either designed to be used, or commonly used, as an inhalant.

2. No person shall, for the purpose of causing a condition of intoxication, inebriation, excitement, stupefaction, or the dulling of his brain or nervous system, intentionally smell or inhale the fumes from any hazardous inhalants or from any glue containing a solvent having the property of releasing toxic vapors or fumes; provided, that nothing in this section shall be interpreted as applying to the inhalation of any anesthesia or inhalant for medical or dental purposes.

3. No person shall, for the purpose of violating subdivision two, use, or possess for the purpose of so using, any hazardous inhalants or any glue containing a solvent having the property of releasing toxic vapors or fumes.

4. No person shall sell, or offer to sell, to any other person any tube or other container of any hazardous inhalants or glue containing a solvent having the property of releasing toxic vapors or fumes:

(a) if he has knowledge that the product sold, or offered for sale, will be used for the purpose set forth in subdivision two of this section; or

(b) unless there has been added to such glue a sufficient quantity of an additive, approved by the commission, which shall act as a deterrent to inhalation, and not be harmful or toxic to the human body. This provision shall not apply to hazardous inhalants or glue manufactured and sold for industrial use.

5. (a) No person shall use nitrous oxide for purposes of causing intoxication, inebriation, excitement, stupefaction or the dulling of the brain or nervous system of himself or another.

(b) No person shall sell any canister or other container of nitrous oxide, unless granted an exemption pursuant to this subdivision. In no event shall any canister or other container of nitrous oxide be sold to a person under the age of twenty-one years.

(c) This subdivision shall not apply to the use of nitrous oxide in industrial, medical or dental applications, or to specific products which must use nitrous oxide as a propellant provided such products shall in no event be sold at retail to the public, as shall be determined by the commission pursuant to paragraph (d) of this subdivision.

(d) The commissioner is directed to promulgate regulations to exempt specific products which must use nitrous oxide, or a mixture of nitrous oxide with other gases, as a propellant from the provisions of this chapter provided such regulations shall prohibit the sale of such products at retail to the public.

(e) The provisions of this section shall not be deemed to prohibit the sale of food products containing nitrous oxide provided such products comply with the provisions of section sixteen-a of the agriculture and markets law.

(f) The commissioner may, upon the application of a manufacturer or seller of a product containing nitrous oxide and intended for sale at retail, authorize the sale of such product if there is no evidence of substantial misuse of the product as defined by this subdivision and if the manufacturer or seller takes the following steps to:

(i) clearly indicate the legitimate purpose or use of the product on the package;

(ii) display prominently on the package in heavy type print language which warns of health dangers resulting from the misuse of nitrous oxide;

(iii) demonstrate that the product bears a distinctive feature or features enabling it to be clearly distinguished from the nitrous oxide products of other manufacturers;

(iv) educate wholesale and retail businesses which sell the product of the dangers of nitrous oxide and the need to monitor its sale; and

(v) prevent their sale of the product to any person, firm or corporation who or which sells drug-related paraphernalia as such term is defined by subdivision two of section eight hundred fifty of the general business law.

6. (a) Any person who violates any provision of subdivision two or three of this section shall be guilty of an offense and upon conviction thereof shall be punished by a fine of not more than fifty dollars or by imprisonment for not more than five days, or by both such fine and imprisonment.

(b) Any person who violates any provision of

subdivision four or five of this section shall be guilty of a class A misdemeanor.

Amended by L. 1982, Ch. 771, eff. Jan. 1, 1983, amending subd. (5), renumbering subd. (5) as subd. (6) and adding new subd. (5); L. 1985, Ch. 234, eff. Aug. 17, 1985; L. 1989, Ch. 667, eff. Nov. 1, 1989; L. 1990, Ch. 551, eff. July 18, 1990, amending subd. (5)(b) and (f).

§ 3381. Sale and possession of hypodermic syringes and hypodermic needles. [*Effective until Sept. 1, 2007.*]

1. It shall be unlawful for any person to sell or furnish to another person or persons, a hypodermic syringe or hypodermic needle except:

(a) pursuant to a written prescription of a practitioner; or

(b) to persons who have been authorized by the commissioner to obtain and possess such instruments; or

(c) by a pharmacy licensed under article one hundred thirty-seven of the education law, health care facility licensed under article twenty-eight of this chapter or a health care practitioner who is otherwise authorized to prescribe the use of hypodermic needles or syringes within his or her scope of practice; provided, however, that such sale or furnishing: (i) shall only be to a person eighteen years of age or older; (ii) shall be limited to a quantity of ten or less hypodermic needles or syringes; and (iii) shall be in accordance with subdivision six of this section.

2. It shall be unlawful for any person to obtain or possess a hypodermic syringe or hypodermic needle unless such possession has been authorized by the commissioner or is pursuant to a written prescription, or is pursuant to subdivision six of this section.

3. Any person selling or furnishing a hypodermic syringe or hypodermic needle pursuant to a prescription shall record upon the face of the prescription, over his signature, the date of the sale or furnishing of the hypodermic syringe or hypodermic needle. Such prescription shall be retained on file for a period of five years and be readily accessible for inspection by any public officer or employee engaged in the enforcement of this section. Such prescription may be refilled not more than the number of times specifically authorized by the prescriber upon the prescription, provided however no such authorization shall be effective for a period greater than two years from the date the prescription is signed.

4. The commissioner shall, subject to subdivision six of this section, designate persons, or by regulation, classes of persons who may obtain hypodermic syringes and hypodermic needles without prescription and the manner in which such transactions may take place and the records thereof which shall be maintained.

5. (a) The commissioner, in consultation with the commissioner of alcoholism and substance abuse services, the commissioner of the department of correctional services, the commissioner of the division of criminal justice services, the commissioner of the office of general services, the commissioner of the office of mental health, the commissioner of the office of mental retardation and developmental disabilities and the director of the division for youth shall develop a limited number of cooperative pilot projects to test the practicality and effectiveness of the distribution of syringes for human injection which are intended for single use and which are non-reusable. Such pilot projects shall be demonstrated throughout the state in high risk clinical settings of state operated facilities such as prisons, hospitals, youth detention facilities, developmental centers and other state operated facilities as the commissioner, in consultation with the above listed commissioners and directors determine appropriate.

(b) On or before June thirtieth, nineteen hundred ninety-eight, the commissioner and the commissioners and directors listed in paragraph (a) of this subdivision shall evaluate the pilot projects established pursuant to this subdivision, and shall submit a report of his or her evaluation to the governor, the temporary president of the senate, and the speaker of the assembly.

6. (a) A person eighteen years of age or older may obtain and possess a hypodermic syringe or hypodermic needle pursuant to paragraph (c) of subdivision one of this section.

(b) Subject to regulations of the commissioner, a pharmacy licensed under article one hundred thirty-seven of the education law, a health care facility licensed under article twenty-eight of this chapter or a health care practitioner who is otherwise authorized to prescribe the use of hypodermic needles or syringes within his or her scope of practice, may obtain and possess hypodermic needles or syringes for the purpose of selling or furnishing them pursuant to paragraph (c) of subdivision one of this section or for the purpose of disposing of them, provided that such pharmacy, health care facility or health care practitioner has registered with the department.

(c) Sale or furnishing of hypodermic syringes or hypodermic needles to direct consumers pursuant to this subdivision by a pharmacy, health care facility, or health care practitioner shall be accompanied by a safety insert. Such safety insert shall be developed or approved by the commissioner and shall include, but not be limited to, (i) information on the proper use of hypodermic syringes and hypodermic needles; (ii) the risk of blood borne diseases that may result from the use of hypodermic syringes and hypodermic needles; (iii) methods for preventing the transmission or contraction of blood borne diseases; (iv) proper hypodermic syringe and hypodermic needle disposal practices; (v) information on the dangers of injection drug use, and how to access drug treatment; (vi) a toll-free phone number for information on the human immunodeficiency virus; and (vii) information on the safe disposal of hypodermic syringes and hypodermic needles including the relevant provisions of the environmental conservation law relating to the unlawful release of regulated medical waste. The safety insert shall be attached to or included in the hypodermic syringe and hypodermic needle packaging, or shall be given to the purchaser at the point of sale or furnishing in brochure form.

(d) In addition to the requirements of paragraph (c) of subdivision one of this section, a pharmacy licensed under article one hundred thirty-seven of the education law may sell or furnish hypodermic needles or syringes only if such pharmacy: (i) does not advertise to the public the availability for retail sale or furnishing of hypodermic needles or syringes without a prescription; and (ii) at any location where hypodermic needles or syringes are kept for retail sale or furnishing, stores such needles and syringes in a manner that makes them available only to authorized personnel and not openly available to customers.

(e) The commissioner shall promulgate rules and regulations necessary to implement the provisions of this subdivision which shall include a requirement that such pharmacies, health care facilities and health care practicioners * cooperate in a safe disposal of used hypodermic needles or syringes.

(f) The commissioner may, upon the finding of a violation of this section, suspend for a determinate period of time the sale or furnishing of syringes by a specific entity.

7. The provisions of this section shall not apply to farmers engaged in livestock production or to those persons supplying farmers engaged in livestock production, provided that:

(a) Hypodermic syringes and needles shall be stored in a secure, locked storage container.

(b) At any time the department may request a document outlining:

(i) the number of hypodermic needles and syringes purchased over the past calendar year;

(ii) a record of all hypodermic needles used over the past calendar year; and

(iii) a record of all hypodermic needles and syringes destroyed over the past calendar year.

(c) Hypodermic needles and syringes shall be destroyed in a manner consistent with the provisions set forth in section thirty-three hundred eighty-one-a of this article.

* Spelled as such in original. Should be "practitioners."

§ 3381. Sale and possession of hypodermic syringes and hypodermic needles. [*Effective Sept. 1, 2007.*]

1. It shall be unlawful for any person to sell or furnish to another person or persons, a hypodermic syringe or hypodermic needle except:

(a) pursuant to a written prescription of a practitioner; or

(b) to persons who have been authorized by the commissioner to obtain and possess such instruments.

2. It shall be unlawful for any person to obtain or possess a hypodermic syringe or hypodermic needle unless such possession has been authorized by the commissioner or is pursuant to a written prescription.

3. Any person selling or furnishing a hypodermic syringe or hypodermic needle pursuant to prescription, shall record upon the face of the prescription, over his signature, the date of the sale or furnishing of the hypodermic syringe or hypodermic needle. Such prescription shall be retained on file for a period of five years and be readily accessible for inspection by any public officer or employee engaged in the enforcement of this section. Such prescription may be refilled not more than the number of times specifically authorized by the prescriber upon the prescription, provided however no such authorization shall be effective for a period greater than two years from the date the prescription is signed.

4. The commissioner shall designate persons, or by regulation, classes of persons who may obtain hypodermic syringes and hypodermic needles without prescription and the manner in which such transactions may take place and the records thereof which shall be maintained.

5. (a) The commissioner, in consultation with the commissioner of alcoholism and substance abuse services, the commissioner of the department of correctional services, the commissioner of the division of criminal justice services, the commissioner of office of general services, the commissioner of the office of mental health, the commissioner of the office of mental retardation and developmental disabilities and the director of the division for youth shall develop a limited number of cooperative pilot projects to test the practicality and effectiveness of the distribution of syringes for human injection which are intended for single use and which are non-reusable. Such pilot projects shall be demonstrated throughout the state in high risk clinical settings of state operated facilities such as prisons, hospitals, youth detention facilities, developmental centers and other state operated facilities as the commissioner, in consultation with the above listed commissioners and directors determine appropriate.

(b) On or before June thirtieth, nineteen

hundred ninety-eight, the commissioner and the commissioners and directors listed in paragraph (a) of this subdivision shall evaluate the pilot projects established pursuant to this subdivision, and shall submit a report of his or her evaluation to the governor, the temporary president of the senate, and the speaker of the assembly.

Amended by L. 1973, Ch. 163; L. 1996, Ch. 639, § 121, adding subd. 5, eff. Jan. 1, 1997; L. 2000, Ch. 56, Part G, § 1, eff. Jan. 1, 2001, and amendments deemed repealed Mar. 31, 2003; L. 2002, Ch. 668, § 1, eff. Dec. 9, 2002, adding subd. 7, and the provisions of subd. 7 shall not affect the expiration of such section 3381 pursuant to section 5 of part G of chapter 56 of the laws of 2000, as amended, and shall expire and be deemed repealed therewith; L. 2003, Ch. 16, § 15, eff. Mar. 31, 2003, extending expiration date to Sept. 1, 2007.

§ 3381-a. Destruction of hypodermic syringes and needles.

All hypodermic syringes, needles and disposable hypodermic units which are no longer usable or required shall be crushed, broken or otherwise rendered inoperable in the process of disposal. The department may specify procedures for disposal of such hypodermic syringes, needles and disposable units as may be necessary to protect public health including, but not limited to, placement of such syringes, needles and units in a leakproof, puncture resistant container prior to disposal.

Added by L. 1980, Ch. 429, eff. Aug. 22, 1980; Amended by L. 1985, Ch. 220, eff. June 18, 1985; L. 1991, Ch. 18, § 1, extending amendments made by L. 1990, Ch. 861; L. 1992, Ch. 184, § 4, extending amendments made by L. 1990, Ch. 861, to Aug. 1, 1994.

§ 3382. Growing of the plant known as Cannabis by unlicensed persons

A person who, without being licensed so to do under this article, grows the plant of the genus Cannabis or knowingly allows it to grow on his land without destroying the same, shall be guilty of a class A misdemeanor.

§ 3383. Imitation controlled substances.

1. For purposes of this section, the following terms shall have the following meanings:

a. "Manufacture" means the production, preparation, compounding, tableting, processing, encapsulating, packaging, repackaging, labeling or relabeling of an imitation controlled substance.

b. "Markings" means a simulated trademark, trade name, imprinting or other mark, or likeness thereof, of the manufacturer, distributor or dispenser of a controlled substance or a simulated code number or symbol or likeness thereof identifying a controlled substance or combination of such substances.

c. "Imitation controlled substance" means a substance, other than a drug for which a prescription is required pursuant to article one hundred thirty-seven of the education law, that is not a controlled substance, which by dosage unit appearance, including color, shape and size and by a representation is represented to be a controlled substance, as defined in the penal law. Evidence of representations that the substance is a controlled substance may include but is not limited to oral or written representations by the manufacturer or seller, as the case may be, about the substance with regard to:

(i) its price, nature, use or effect as a controlled substance; or

(ii) its packaging in a manner normally used for illicit controlled substances; or

(iii) markings on the substance.

2. It shall be unlawful for any person to manufacture, sell or possess with the intent to sell, an imitation controlled substance.

3. It shall be unlawful for any person to possess or use any punch, die, plate, stone or any other equipment in order to print, imprint, or reproduce the trademark, trade name or other identifying mark, imprint or device of another or any likeness of any of the foregoing upon any substance or container or labeling thereof with intent to manufacture an imitation controlled substance.

4. No liability shall be imposed by virtue of this section on any person licensed pursuant to article one hundred thirty-one of the education law or licensed under this article who manufactures, distributed, sells, prescribes, dispenses or possesses an imitation controlled substance for use as a placebo or for use in clinical research conducted pursuant to the federal food, drug and cosmetic act.

5. Nothing in this section shall apply to a noncontrolled substance that was initially introduced into commerce prior to the initial introduction into commerce of the controlled substance which it is alleged to imitate.

6. In any prosecution under this section it shall be necessary to prove that the imitation controlled substance was represented to be a controlled substance; however, it shall not be a defense to a prosecution under this section that the accused believed the imitation controlled substance to be a controlled substance.

7. A violation of subdivision two or three of this section shall be a class A misdemeanor. A violation of subdivision two or three of this section by a person previously convicted of a violation of this section within the preceding five years shall be a class E felony.

8. If any provision or part of this section or application thereof is held invalid, the invalidity shall not affect other provisions, parts or applications of this section which can be given effect without the invalid provisions or application, and

MISC. LAWS

to this end the provisions of this section are severable.

Added by L. 1982, Ch. 494, eff. Sept. 1, 1982.

ANNOTATION

Imitation controlled substance.—The statute clearly defines, on its face, what is meant by an imitation controlled substance, and that definition most certainly encompasses imitation heroin. People v. Singleton, 151 Misc. 2d 1051, 574 N.Y.S.2d 631 (Crim. Ct. N.Y. Co. 1991).

§ 3385. Enforcement.

1. (a) The department and its representatives shall have access during business hours to all orders, prescriptions or records required to be kept under this article.

(b) Orders, prescriptions and records required to be kept under this article shall be maintained at the premises where the licensed activity is conducted.

2. For the purposes of enforcing the provisions of this article, each employee of the department designated by the commissioner shall possess all of the powers of a peace officer as set forth in section 2.20 of the criminal procedure law.

Amended by L. 1974, Ch. 58; L. 1980, Ch. 843, eff. Sept. 1, 1980, amending subd. 2.

§ 3387. Seizure and forfeiture of controlled substances, imitation controlled substances and official New York State prescription forms; disposition.

1. Any controlled substance or imitation controlled substance which has been manufactured, distributed, dispensed or acquired in violation of this article, or the lawful possession of which cannot be immediately ascertained, and any official New York state prescription form which has been printed, distributed or acquired in violation of this article or the lawful possession of which cannot be immediately ascertained are hereby declared to be public nuisances and may be seized by a peace officer, acting pursuant to his special duties, or a police officer and shall be forfeited, and disposed of as follows:

(a) except as in this section otherwise provided, the commissioner, the court or magistrate having jurisdiction shall order such controlled substance or imitation controlled substance forfeited or destroyed. A record of the quantity and nature of the substance, of the place where said substance was seized, and of the time, place and manner of destruction, shall be kept, and a return under oath, reporting said destruction, shall be made to the person ordering such destruction by the officer who destroys them;

(b) upon written application by the commissioner, the court or magistrate by whom the forfeiture of controlled substances or imitation

controlled substances has been decreed may order the delivery of any of them, except substances listed in schedule I of section thirty-three hundred six, to such commissioner for distribution or destruction, as hereinafter provided;

(c) upon application by any hospital within this state, not operated for private gain, the commissioner may in his discretion deliver any controlled substance or imitation controlled substance that has come into his custody by authority of this section to the applicants for medicinal use;

(d) the commissioner may from time to time deliver excess stocks of controlled substances or imitation controlled substances to the Bureau or shall destroy the same;

(e) controlled substances or imitation controlled substances which are excess or undesired by persons lawfully possessing the same may be disposed of in such manner as the commissioner shall by regulation require;

(f) official New York state prescription forms which have been seized as provided by this section shall be disposed of by express prepaid shipment to the "State Department of Health, Bureau of Prescription Analysis, Albany, New York," or by delivery to an authorized narcotic control representative of the department.

2. The commissioner shall keep a full and complete record of all controlled substances or imitation controlled substances received and of all controlled substances or imitation controlled substances disposed of, showing the exact kinds, quantities and forms of such substances; the persons from whom received and to whom delivered; by whose authority received, delivered and destroyed; and the dates of the receipt, disposal or destruction. This record shall be open to inspection by all federal or state officers charged with the enforcement of federal and state laws relating to controlled substances or imitation controlled substances.

3. Any raw material product, container or equipment of any kind which is used, or intended for use, in manufacturing, distributing, dispensing or administering a controlled substance or imitation controlled substance in violation of this article shall be seized by any peace officer, acting pursuant to his special duties, or police officer and forfeited in the same manner as property subject to seizure and forfeiture pursuant to section thirty-three hundred eighty-eight of this article, except that such property shall not be retained for use by any official.

Amended by L. 1980, Ch. 843; L. 1981, Ch. 547; L. 1982, Ch. 494, eff. Sept. 1, 1982, amending subds. 1, 2, and 3; L. 1998, Ch. 537, § 12, eff. Nov. 1, 1998, amending subd. 1(e).

ANNOTATION

Purpose.—Public Health Law § 3387(3) is a civil forfeiture provision and not a penal statute; it prescribes no fines or penalties, providing only for an administrative hearing, following a demand for return of the merchandise by the owner, to determine whether there should be a forfeiture of the items seized. Stallone v. Abrams, 183 A.D.2d 555, 584 N.Y.S.2d 535 (1st Dept. 1992).

§ 3388. Seizure and forfeiture of vehicles, vessels or aircraft unlawfully used to conceal, convey or transport controlled substances.

1. Except as authorized in this article, it shall be unlawful to:

(a) transport, carry, or convey any controlled substance in, upon, or by means of any vehicle, vessel or aircraft; or

(b) conceal or possess any controlled substance in or upon any vehicle, vessel or aircraft, or upon the person or anyone in or upon any vehicle, vessel or aircraft; or

(c) use any vehicle, vessel or aircraft to facilitate the transportation, carriage, conveyance, concealment, receipt, possession, purchase, or sale of any controlled substance.

2. Any vehicle, vessel or aircraft which has been or is being used in violation of subdivision one, except a vehicle, vessel or aircraft used by any person as a common carrier in the transaction of business as such common carrier shall be seized by any peace officer, acting pursuant to his special duties, or police officer, and forfeited as hereinafter in this section provided. A vehicle, vessel or aircraft is not subject to forfeiture unless used in connection with acts or conduct which would constitute a felony under article 220 of the penal law.

3. The seized property shall be delivered by the officer having made the seizure to the custody of the district attorney of the county wherein the seizure was made, except that in the cities of New York, Yonkers, Rochester and Buffalo the seized property shall be delivered to the custody of the police department of such cities and such property seized by a member or members of the state police shall be delivered to the custody of the superintendent of state police, together with a report of all the facts and circumstances of this seizure.

4. It shall be the duty of the attorney general in seizures by members of the state police, otherwise it shall be the duty of the district attorney of the county wherein the seizure is made, if elsewhere than in the cities of New York, Yonkers, Rochester or Buffalo, and where the seizure is made in such cities it shall be the duty of the corporation counsel of the city, to inquire into the facts of the seizure so reported to him and if it appears probable that a forfeiture has been incurred by reason of a violation of this section, for the determination of which the institution of proceedings in the supreme court is necessary, to cause the proper proceedings to be commenced and prosecuted, not later than twenty days after written demand by a person claiming ownership thereof, to declare such forfeiture, unless, upon inquiry and examination, such district attorney, attorney general or corporation counsel decides that such proceedings cannot probably be sustained or that the ends of public justice do not require that they should be instituted or prosecuted, in which case, the district attorney, the attorney general or corporation counsel shall cause such seized property to be returned to the owner thereof. The procedure for proceedings instituted under this section shall conform as much as possible to the procedure for attachment.

5. Notice of the institution of the forfeiture proceeding shall be served either:

(a) personally on the owners of the seized property; or

(b) by registered mail to the owners' last known address and by publication of the notice once a week for two successive weeks in a newspaper published or circulated in the county wherein the seizure was made.

6. Forfeiture shall not be adjudged where the owners establish by preponderance of the evidence that:

(a) the use of such seized property, in violation of subdivision one of this section, was not intentional on the part of any owner; or

(b) said seized property was used in violation of subdivision one of this section by any person other than an owner thereof, while such seized property was unlawfully in the possession of a person who acquired possession thereof in violation of the criminal laws of the United States, or of any state.

7. The district attorney, the superintendent of state police or the police department having custody of the seized property, after such judicial determination of forfeiture, shall, at their discretion, either retain such seized property for the official use of their office, division or department, or, by a public notice of at least five days, sell such forfeited property at public sale provided, however, that where such property is subject to a perfected lien such property may not be retained for their official use unless all such liens on the property to retained have been or will be satisfied. The net proceeds of any such sale, after deduction of the lawful expenses incurred, shall be paid into the general fund of the county wherein the seizure was made except that the net proceeds of the sale of property seized in the cities of New York, Yonkers, Rochester and Buffalo shall be paid into the respective general funds of such cities, and of the sale of property seized by the state police into the general fund of the state.

8. Whenever any person interested in any property which is seized and declared forfeited under the provisions of this section files with a justice of the supreme court a petition for the recovery of such forfeited property, the justice of

MISC. LAWS

the supreme court may restore said forfeited property upon such terms and conditions as he deems reasonable and just, if the petitioner establishes either of the affirmative defenses set forth in subdivision six of this section and that the petitioner was without personal or actual knowledge of the forfeiture proceeding. If the petition be filed after the sale of the forfeited property, any judgment in favor of the petitioner shall be limited to the net proceeds of such sale, after deduction of the lawful expenses and costs incurred by the district attorney, police department or corporation counsel.

9. No suit or action under this section for wrongful seizure shall be instituted unless such suit or action is commenced within two years after the time when the property was seized.

Amended by L. 1980, Ch. 843, eff. Sept. 1, 1980, amending subds. 2 and 3; L. 1984, Ch. 717, eff. Aug. 3, 1984; L. 1985, Ch. 621; L. 1986, Ch. 419, eff. July 21, 1986; L. 1987, Ch. 527, eff. July 30, 1987; L. 1990, Ch. 655, eff. Nov. 1, 1990, amending subd. (7).

ANNOTATIONS

Conditional vendor; seized automobile.—The conditional vendor of an automobile, seized by federal authorities in connection with a drug arrest, was an "owner" within PHL § 3388(6) and was afforded the protection of this subdivision because it was not responsible for the defendant's alleged illegal use of this motor vehicle. Blaine v. G.M.A.C., 82 Misc. 2d 653, 370 N.Y.S.2d 323 (Monroe Co. Ct. 1975).

Jury trial.—Petitioner was entitled to a jury trial in the civil proceeding commenced pursuant to Public Health Law § 3388, for a judgment declaring a forfeiture of a vehicle. Abrams v. One 1987 Chevrolet Corvette, 161 A.D.2d 1129, 555 N.Y.S.2d 503 (4th Dept. 1990).

Owner.—Court rejected defendant's contention that his wife was an equitable owner of the vehicle since she used it fifty percent of the time to perform her duties as household manager, parent, spouse and working wife, and despite her claim that she had contributed her earnings to the household which thereby made possible the early discharge of a purchase money automobile loan; the vehicle in question was registered to the defendant and not to his wife. Henry v. Castagnaro, 106 Misc. 2d 574, 434 N.Y.S.2d 592 (Sup. Ct. Suffolk Co. 1984).

Purpose.—The purpose of § 3388 is to discourage the use of vehicles in illegal drug trafficking. Chesworth v. Block, 145 A.D.2d 418, 535 N.Y.S.2d 392 (2d Dept. 1988).

—Public Health Law § 3388, rather than Criminal Procedure Law § 690.10, provides authority for forfeiture. *In re* Harnischfeger, 158 Misc. 2d 299, 600 N.Y.S.2d 894 (Sup. Ct. Monroe Co. 1993).

Seizure of vehicle as contraband; denial.—Where police saw passenger holding a marijuana cigarette and stopped vehicle after chase, vehicle was not contraband under statute pertaining to seizure and forfeiture of vehicles. People v. Kreichman, 45 A.D.2d 697, 357 N.Y.S.2d 82 (1st Dept. 1974).

§ 3390. Revocation of licenses and certificates of approval.

Any license or certificate of approval granted pursuant to this article may be revoked by the commissioner in whole or in part upon a finding that the licensee or certificate holder has:

1. falsified any application, report, or record required by this article;

2. wilfully failed to furnish the department with timely reports or information required to be filed with the department;

3. been convicted of an offense in any jurisdiction relating to any substance listed in this article as a controlled substance;

4. wilfully or negligently failed to comply with any of the provisions of the federal controlled substances act, this article, or the regulations promulgated thereunder;

5. failed to maintain effective control against diversion of controlled substances; or

6. wilfully and unreasonably refused to permit an inspection authorized by this article.

ANNOTATIONS

Constitutionality.—Court rejected claim that § 3390 is an unconstitutional invasion of the pharmacist's right to privacy. People v. Curco Drugs, 76 Misc. 2d 222, 350 N.Y.S.2d 74 (Crim. Ct. Kings Co. 1973).

Generally.—Where the patient records sought did not constitute reports or information otherwise required to be filed and therefore did not fall within the ambit of the statute, there was no basis for respondent to find petitioner in violation of subdivision 2 of the statute. Pal v. Axelrod, 172 A.D.2d 325, 568 N.Y.S.2d 609 (1st Dept. 1991).

Search.—There can be no question but that the State has the right to supervise the receipt and sale of drugs; the defendant upon receiving his license agreed to keep the necessary records and have them available for required inspection. People v. Terraciano, 39 A.D.2d 1005, 333 N.Y.S.2d 903 (3d Dept. 1972).

§ 3391. Revocation and suspension of license or certificate of approval procedure.

1. A proceeding to revoke a license or certificate of approval shall be commenced by a notice served personally or by registered or certified mail upon the licensee or holder of a certificate of approval directing him to show cause why his license or certificate should not be revoked. Such notice shall set forth in detail the grounds for the proposed revocation and shall fix a date for hearing not less than fifteen nor more than thirty days from the date of such notice.

2. Simultaneous with the commencement of a proceeding to revoke a license or certificate or during the course of such proceeding, the commissioner may in the case of a clear and imminent danger to the public health or safety forthwith suspend without prior notice any license or certificate theretofore issued.

3. If the commissioner suspends or revokes a license or certificate, all controlled substances owned or possessed by the licensee or holder of a certificate of approval and in the state of New York at the time of the suspension or the effective date of the revocation and which such licensee or holder of a certificate of approval is no longer authorized to possess, shall be seized or placed under seal in the manner provided in this article.

4. In lieu of revocation of a license or certificate, the commissioner may impose a civil penalty not in excess of ten thousand dollars. Such penalty may be imposed in lieu of revocation only if the commissioner is satisfied that the imposition and

payment of such penalty will serve as a sufficient deterrent to future violations.

§ 3393. Formal hearings procedure.

1. The commissioner or any person designated by him for this purpose, shall have the power to administer oaths, compel the attendance of witnesses and the production of books, records and documents and to take proof and testimony concerning all matters within the jurisdiction of the department.

2. Notice of hearing shall be served at least fifteen days prior to the date of the hearing, provided, however, whenever the commissioner has made a preliminary order suspending a license or directing the cessation of any activity pending the hearing, the commissioner shall provide the person affected thereby with an opportunity to be heard within five days.

3. At a hearing any person who is a party thereto may appear personally, shall have the right of counsel, and may cross-examine witnesses and produce evidence and witnesses in his own behalf.

4. Following a hearing, the commissioner shall make appropriate findings of fact and determinations and shall issue an order in accordance therewith.

5. The person conducting the hearing shall not be bound by the rules of evidence but any determination must be founded upon sufficient legal evidence to sustain it.

6. The commissioner may adopt such rules and regulations governing the procedures to be followed with respect to the hearings as may be consistent with the fair and effective administration of this article.

7. Any notice, application, order or other paper required to be served upon any party to a proceeding hereunder may be served in person, by registered mail or by certified mail upon either the party or an attorney who has appeared on his behalf.

ANNOTATION

Right to counsel.—Though, by statute, petitioner was entitled to be represented by counsel, the record revealed that he was advised of this right by the Notice of Hearing, and that the petitioner chose to rely on the advice of a non-lawyer and proceed without counsel. Di Marsico v. Whalen, 68 A.D.2d 971, 414 N.Y.S.2d 785 (3d Dept. 1979).

§ 3394. Judicial review.

1. All orders or determinations hereunder shall be subject to judicial review as provided in article seventy-eight of the civil practice law and rules. In any such proceeding findings of fact made by the commissioner, if supported by substantial evidence, shall be conclusive.

2. Application for such review must be made within sixty days after service of the order or determination upon the person whose license,

certificate, right or privilege is affected thereby or upon the attorney of record for such person.

3. An order, or the enforcement of an order revoking or suspending a license or revoking or cancelling official forms issued by the department, if accompanied by a finding of a clear and imminent danger to the public health or safety, may not be temporarily stayed or restrained prior to a determination on the merits of the application for judicial review.

ANNOTATION

Standard of review.—Appellate court's review is limited to whether the determination is supported by substantial evidence and has a rational basis. S J Pharmacies, Inc. v. Axelrod, 91 A.D.2d 1131, 458 N.Y.S.2d 728 (3d Dept. 1983).

§ 3396. Violations; penalties.

1. In any civil, criminal or administrative action or proceeding brought for the enforcement of any provision of this article, it shall not be necessary to negate or disprove any exception, excuse, proviso or exemption contained in this article, and the burden of proof of any such exception, excuse, proviso, or exemption shall be upon the person claiming its benefit.

2. Violation of any provision of this article for which a penalty is specifically provided herein shall be punishable as provided herein. Violation of any provision of this article for which no penalty is provided herein, shall be punishable as provided in section twelve-b of article one of this chapter or in the penal law.

3. No person shall be prosecuted for a violation of any provision of this article if such person has been acquitted or convicted under the federal controlled substances act, of the same act or omission which, it is alleged, constitutes a violation of this article.

4. Upon the conviction of any person for violating any provision of this article, a copy of the judgment and sentence, and of the opinion of the court or judge, if any opinion be filed, shall be sent by the clerk of the court, or by the judge, to the board or officer, if any, by whom the convicted defendant has been licensed or registered to practice his profession, or to carry on his business.

5. Upon the imposition of any penalty, warning, reprimand or other sanction against any person for violating any provision of this article, a copy of the order, finding or opinion, if any is made or rendered, shall be sent by the person authorized by law to make such determination, to the board or officer by whom the respondent is licensed or registered to practice a profession or to carry on a business.

Amended by L. 1973, Ch. 163; L. 1974, Ch. 965.

ANNOTATIONS

Burden of proof.—A defendant charged under the statute, unlike one charged under the Penal Law, has the burden of demonstrating the existence of a prescription authorizing the sale of a controlled substance. People v. Vargas, 86 Misc. 2d 1018, 384 N.Y.S.2d 643 (Sup. Ct. N.Y. Co. 1976).

Exemptions.—Physicians are exempt from the restrictions regarding the possession of controlled substances and hypodermic instruments if they are used "lawfully" and for a "recognized medical purpose;" if a physician uses a hypodermic syringe and a controlled substance to satisfy a personal craving, such behavior would not fall within the parameters of the exemptions provided by the public health statutes and would be subject to criminal prosecution. People v. Opris, 161 Misc. 2d 415, 613 N.Y.S.2d 839 (Crim. Ct. Kings Co. 1994).

—The existence of Article 33 of the Public Health Law does not in any way bar the District Attorney from enforcing the comparable criminal statute relating to narcotics enforcement. People v. Garthaffner, 115 Misc. 2d 93, 454 N.Y.S.2d 583 (Sup. Ct. App. Term 1982).

§ 3397. Fraud and deceit.

1. No person shall:

(a) obtain or attempt to obtain a controlled substance, a prescription for a controlled substance or an official New York State prescription form,

(i) by fraud, deceit, misrepresentation or subterfuge; or

(ii) by the concealment of a material fact; or

(iii) by the use of a false name or the giving of a false address;

(b) wilfully make a false statement in any prescription, order, application, report or record required by this article;

(c) falsely assume the title of, or represent himself to be a licensed manufacturer, distributor, pharmacy, pharmacist, practitioner, researcher, approved institutional dispenser, or other authorized person, for the purpose of obtaining a controlled substance;

(d) make or utter any false or forged prescription or false or forged written order;

(e) affix any false or forged label to a package or receptacle containing controlled substances; or

(f) imprint on or affix to any controlled substance a false or forged code number or symbol.

2. Possession of a false or forged prescription for a controlled substance by any person other than a pharmacist in the lawful pursuance of his profession shall be presumptive evidence of his intent to use the same for the purpose of illegally obtaining a controlled substance.

3. Possession of a blank official New York state prescription form by any person to whom it was not lawfully issued shall be presumptive evidence of such person's intent to use same for the purpose of illegally obtaining a controlled substance.

4. Any person who, in the course of treatment, is supplied with a controlled substance or a prescription therefor by one practitioner and who, without disclosing the fact, is supplied during such treatment with a controlled substance or a prescription therefor by another practitioner shall be guilty of a violation of this article.

Amended by L. 1981, Ch. 547, eff. Sept. 1, 1981, renumbering subd. (3) as subd. (4) and adding new subd. (3) an amending subd. (4).

VEHICLE AND TRAFFIC LAW

(ARTS. 1, 12, 20, 21, 22, 30, 31, 45)

ARTICLE 1
(Selected Sections)

WORDS AND PHRASES DEFINED

Section
155.   Traffic infraction.

§ 155. Traffic infraction.

The violation of any provision of this chapter, except articles forty-seven and forty-eight, or of any law, ordinance, order, rule or regulation regulating traffic which is not declared by this chapter or other law of this state to be a misdemeanor or a felony. A traffic infraction is not a crime and the punishment imposed therefor shall not be deemed for any purpose a penal or criminal punishment and shall not affect or impair the credibility as a witness or otherwise of any person convicted thereof. This definition shall be retroactive and shall apply to all acts and violations heretofore committed where such acts and violations would, if committed subsequent to the taking effect of this section, be included within the meaning of the term "traffic infraction" as herein defined. Except in those portions of Suffolk county for which a district court has been established, outside of cities having a population in excess of two hundred thousand in which administrative tribunals have heretofore been established, courts and judicial officers heretofore having jurisdiction over such violations shall continue to do so and for such purpose such violations shall be deemed misdemeanors and all provisions of law relating to misdemeanors except as provided in section eighteen hundred five of this chapter and except as herein otherwise expressly provided shall apply except that no jury trial shall be allowed for traffic infractions. In those portions of Suffolk county for which a district court has been established, and in cities having a population in excess of two hundred thousand in which administrative tribunals have heretofore been established, the criminal courts of such cities or portions of Suffolk county in which a district court has been established shall have jurisdiction to hear and determine any complaint alleging a violation constituting a traffic infraction, except that administrative tribunals heretofore established in such cities or portions of Suffolk county in which a district court has been established shall have jurisdiction to hear and determine any charge of an offense which is a traffic infraction, except parking, standing or stopping. In cities having a population in excess of two hundred thousand in which administrative tribunals have heretofore been established, and any such administrative tribunal established by the city of Yonkers, the city of Peekskill, or the city of Syracuse, such tribunals shall have jurisdiction to hear and determine any charge of an offense which is a parking, standing or stopping violation. Any fine imposed by an administrative tribunal shall be a civil penalty. For purposes of arrest without a warrant, pursuant to article one hundred forty of the criminal procedure law, a traffic infraction shall be deemed an offense.

Amended by L. 2002, Ch. 628, eff. Oct. 9, 2002.

ANNOTATIONS

Basis for arrest.—One in the actual perpetration of an offense, and it matters not whether it is a felony, a misdemeanor or the infraction of speeding, is aware of what he is doing and as long as the peace officer apprehends him in its actual commission, he need not state the obvious and tell the offender the reason for the arrest. Squadrito v. Griebsch, 1 N.Y.2d 471, 154 N.Y.S.2d 37, 136 N.E.2d 504 (1956).

Impeachment of credibility.—Court erred in allowing defendant's subsequent speeding conviction to be considered by jury on the issue of defendant's credibility. Iqbal v. Rubin, 238 A.D.2d 378, 657 N.Y.S.2d 329 (2d Dept. 1997).

Jurisdiction of DEP officers.—Officers of the Department of Environmental Protection (DEP), on patrol within watershed district, who witness traffic infractions within that geographical area, are authorized to stop defendants for traffic infractions and to issue simplified traffic informations for those infractions. People v. Van Buren, 4 N.Y.3d 640, 797 N.Y.S.2d 802, 830 N.E.2d 1130 (2005).

ARTICLE 12
(Selected Sections)

OTHER PROVISIONS

§ 392. False statements, alteration of records or substitution in connection with any examination.

Any person knowingly making a false statement in an application for any document issued by the commissioner or in any proof or statement in writing in connection with such an application, or who shall deceive or substitute or cause another to deceive or substitute in connection with any examination hereunder, or who shall wilfully alter a number plate (except for restoration purposes pursuant to schedule G of subdivision seven of section four hundred one of this chapter), or make a material alteration on any document issued pursuant to this chapter, or unlawfully use a validating device on a certificate of registration, license or any other form, shall be guilty of a misdemeanor. A person who operates a motor vehicle upon the public highway displaying or using any document that he or she knows has been obtained in violation of this section, shall be guilty of a misdemeanor. Nothing contained in this section shall prohibit the imposition of a charge of any other offense set forth in this chapter or any other provision of law for any acts arising out of the same incident.

Amended by L. 1994, Ch. 307, § 1, eff. Sept. 18, 1994; L. 2004, Ch. 710, § 1, eff. Nov. 16, 2004.

§ 392-a. Sale or purchase of stolen, false or fraudulent license, identification card, certificate of registration, or number plate. [Effective until June 30, 2007, pursuant to L. 1996, Ch. 309, as amended.]

A person who knowingly sells or offers to sell or buys or offers to buy a false, fraudulent or stolen license, identification card, certificate of registration or number plate, shall be guilty of a misdemeanor as a first offense and a class E felony as a second or subsequent offense committed within ten years of the prior offense.

§ 392-a. Sale of false or fraudulent license, certificate of registration, or number plate. [Effective June 30, 2007.]

A person who sells or offers to sell a false or fraudulent license, certificate of registration or number plate, shall be guilty of a misdemeanor as a first offense and a felony as a second or subsequent offense committed within ten years of the prior offense.

Amended L. 1991, Ch. 319, § 1, extending expiration date to Jan. 31, 1997; L. 1994, Ch. 307, § 2, eff. Sept. 18, 1994; L. 1996, Ch. 309, § 76, extending expiration date to January 31, 2002, eff. July 13, 1996; L. 2002, Ch. 6, eff. Jan. 31, 2002, extending expiration date to June 30, 2007.

§ 397. Equipping motor vehicles with radio receiving sets capable of receiving signals on the frequencies allocated for police use.

A person, not a police officer or peace officer, acting pursuant to his special duties, who equips a motor vehicle with a radio receiving set capable of receiving signals on the frequencies allocated for police use or knowingly uses a motor vehicle so equipped or who in any way knowingly interferes with the transmission of radio messages by the police without having first secured a permit so to do from the person authorized to issue such a permit by the local governing body or board of the city, town or village in which such person resides, or where such person resides outside of a city or village in a county having a county police department by the board of supervisors of such county, is guilty of a misdemeanor, punishable by a fine not exceeding one thousand dollars, or imprisonment not exceeding six months, or both. Nothing in this section contained shall be construed to apply to any person who holds a valid amateur radio operator's license issued by the federal communications commission and who operates a duly licensed portable mobile transmitter and in connection therewith a receiver or receiving set on frequencies exclusively allocated by the federal communications commission to duly licensed radio amateurs.

ANNOTATION

Generally.—Possession of scanner that can be reprogrammed to receive police communication frequencies, but was actually only used to intercept cellular telephone data frequencies, does not rise to the level of an offense under this section. People v. Garcia, 170 Misc. 2d 543, 647 N.Y.S.2d 355 (Westchester Co. Ct. 1996).

§ 397-a. Radar detectors and laser detectors prohibited.

1. No radar detector or laser detector shall be used in any motor vehicle with a gross vehicle weight rating of more than eighteen thousand pounds or in any commercial vehicle with a gross vehicle weight rating of more than ten thousand pounds. The presence in such vehicle of a radar detector or laser detector connected to a power source and in an operable condition is presumptive evidence of its use by any person operating such vehicle. Such presumption shall be rebutted by any credible and reliable evidence which tends to show that such radar detector or laser detector was not in use.

2. The provisions of this section shall not be construed as authorizing the seizure or forfeiture of a radar detector or laser detector, unless otherwise provided by law.

3. A violation of the provisions of this section shall constitute a traffic infraction punishable by a fine of not less than twenty-five nor more than one hundred dollars.

Amended by L. 1996, Ch. 524, changing the name of the section to include laser detectors, and amending subds. 1 and 2, eff. November 1, 1996.

ARTICLE 20

SUSPENSION AND REVOCATION

§ 510. Suspension, revocation and reissuance of licenses and registrations.

1. Who may suspend or revoke. Any magistrate, justice or judge, in a city, in a town, or in a village, any supreme court justice, any county judge, any judge of a district court, the superintendent of state police and the commissioner of motor vehicles or any person deputized by him, shall have power to revoke or suspend the license to drive a motor vehicle or motorcycle of any person, or in the case of an owner, the registration, as provided herein.

A learner's permit, or a license which has expired but is renewable, shall be deemed a license within the meaning of this section.

2. Mandatory revocations and suspensions.

a. Mandatory revocations. Such licenses shall be revoked and such registrations may also be revoked where the holder is convicted:

(i) of homicide or assault arising out of the operation of a motor vehicle or motorcycle or criminal negligence in the operation of a motor vehicle or motorcycle resulting in death, whether the conviction was had in this state or elsewhere;

(ii) pursuant to section twenty-three hundred eighty-five of title eighteen of the United States code, of the crime of advocating the overthrow of government, whether the conviction was had in this state or elsewhere;

(iii) of any violation of subdivision two of section six hundred or section three hundred ninety-two or of a local law or ordinance making it unlawful to leave the scene of an accident without reporting;

(iv) of a third or subsequent violation, committed within a period of eighteen months, of any provision of section eleven hundred eighty of this chapter, any ordinance or regulation limiting the speed of motor vehicles and motorcycles or any provision constituted a misdemeanor by this chapter, not included in subparagraphs (i) or (iii) of this paragraph, except violations of subdivision one of section three hundred seventy-five of this chapter or of subdivision one of section four hundred one of this chapter and similar violations under any local law, ordinance or regulation committed by an employed driver if the offense occurred while operating, in the course of his employment, a vehicle not owned by said driver, whether such three or more violations were repetitions of the same offense or were different offenses;

(v) of a violation for the conviction of which any such license is subject to revocation under subdivision two of section five hundred ten-b;

(vi) of a violation of any provision of section eleven hundred eighty-two of this chapter;

(vii) of a second violation of any provision of section eleven hundred eighty-two committed within a period of three years of a previous violation of the aforesaid section shall result in a license revocation of one year.

(viii)* of a violation of section twelve hundred twenty-four of this chapter, other than a violation adjudicated by the environmental control board of a city having a population of one million or more pursuant to subdivision seven of such section, and fails to pay the fine imposed thereon pursuant to subdivision seven of such section.

(viii)* of a third violation, committed within a period of three years, of any provision of subdivision a of section eleven hundred seventy-four of this chapter.

   * [There are two para. (viii)'s in VTL § 510(2)(a).]

b. Mandatory suspensions. Such licenses shall be suspended, and such registrations may also be suspended:

(i) For a period of sixty days where the holder is convicted of a violation for the conviction of which such license is subject to suspension pursuant to subdivision one of section five hundred ten-b;

(ii) When the holder forfeits bail given upon being charged with any of the offenses mentioned in this subdivision, until the holder submits to the jurisdiction of the court in which he forfeited bail; and

(iii) Such registrations shall be suspended when necessary to comply with subdivision nine of section one hundred forty or subdivision four of section one hundred forty-five of the transportation law. The commissioner shall have the authority to deny a registration or renewal application to any other person for the same vehicle and may deny a registration or renewal application for any other motor vehicle registered in the name of the applicant where it has been determined that such registrant's intent has been to evade the purposes of this subdivision and where the commissioner has reasonable grounds to believe that such registration or renewal will have the effect of defeating the purposes of this subdivision.

(iv) For a period of not less than thirty nor greater than one hundred eighty days where the holder is convicted of the crime of assault in the first, second or third degree as defined in article one hundred twenty of the penal law, where such offense was committed against a traffic enforcement agent employed by the city of New York or the city of Buffalo while such agent was enforcing or attempting to enforce the traffic regulations of such city.

(v) [*Repealed eff. Oct. 1, 2007.*] For a period of six months where the holder is convicted of, or receives a youthful offender or other juvenile adjudication in connection with, any misdemeanor or felony defined in article two hundred twenty or two hundred twenty-one of the penal law, any violation of the federal controlled substances act, any crime in violation of subdivision four of section eleven hundred ninety-two of this chapter or any out-of-state or federal misdemeanor or felony drug-related offense; provided, however, that any time actually served in custody pursuant to a sentence or disposition imposed as a result of such conviction or youthful offender or other juvenile adjudication shall be credited against the period of such suspension and, provided further, that the court shall determine that such suspension need not be imposed where there are compelling circumstances warranting an exception.

(vi) [*Repealed eff. Oct. 1, 2007.*] Pursuant to subparagraph (v) of this paragraph, the magistrate, justice or judge shall order such suspension or render its findings that are compelling circumstances warranting an exception at the time of sentencing. At that time, the judge, justice or magistrate may also issue an order making said license suspension take effect twenty days after the date of sentencing and, if this is done, the license holder shall be given a copy of the order permitting the continuation of driving privileges.

(vii) [*Repealed eff. Oct. 1, 2007.*] In no event shall the commissioner suspend a driver's license pursuant to subparagraph (v) of this paragraph absent a copy of an order by the magistrate, justice or judge as provided in subparagraph (vi) of this paragraph.

(viii) For a period of sixty days where the holder is convicted of a violation of section twelve hundred twenty-b of this chapter within a period of eighteen months of a previous violation of such section.

(ix) For a period of three months where the holder is sentenced to a license suspension pursuant to paragraph (a) of subdivision five of section sixty-five-b of the alcoholic beverage control law, provided however, that, in accordance with such subdivision five, such suspension shall be only a license suspension.

(x) For a period of six months where the holder is sentenced to a license suspension pursuant to paragraph (b) of subdivision five of section sixty-five-b of the alcoholic beverage control law, provided however, that, in accordance with such subdivision five, such suspension shall be only a license suspension.

(xi) For a period of one year or until the holder reaches the age of twenty-one, whichever is the greater period of time, where the holder is sentenced to a license suspension pursuant to paragraph (c) of subdivision five of section sixty-five-b of the alcoholic beverage control law, provided however, that, in accordance with such subdivision five, such suspension shall be only a license suspension.

(xii) For a period of one year where the holder is convicted of, or receives a youthful offender or juvenile delinquency adjudication in connection with a violation of section 240.62 or subdivision five of section 240.60 of the penal law.

(xiii) for a period of sixty days where the holder is convicted of two or more violations of paragraph two of subdivision (d) or subdivision (f) of section eleven hundred eighty of this chapter.

c. Application of mandatory revocations and suspensions to non-residents and to unlicensed persons. Application of mandatory revocations and suspensions to non-residents and to unlicensed persons. Whenever a non-resident or a person who is unlicensed is convicted of any violation or receives a youthful offender or juvenile delinquency adjudication in conjunction with a violation of section 240.62 or subdivision five of section 240.60 of the penal law, which would require the revocation or suspension of a license, pursuant to the provisions of this chapter, if the person so convicted or adjudicated was the holder of a license issued by the commissioner, such non-resident's privilege of operating a motor vehicle in this state or such unlicensed person's privilege of obtaining a license issued by the commissioner shall be revoked or suspended, and such non-resident's privilege of operation within this state of any motor vehicle owned by such person or such unlicensed person's privilege of obtaining a registration issued by the commissioner may be suspended as if such non-resident or unlicensed person was the holder of a license issued by the commissioner. The provisions of subdivisions six and seven of this section shall be applicable to any such suspension or revocation.

d. Mandatory suspensions; vehicles over eighteen thousand pounds. A license or privilege shall be suspended by the commissioner for a period of sixty days, where the holder is convicted of a violation of subdivision (g) of section eleven hundred eighty of this chapter, and (i) the recorded or entered speed upon which the conviction was based exceeded the applicable speed limit by more than twenty miles per hour or (ii) the recorded or entered speed upon which the conviction was based exceeded the applicable speed limit by more than ten miles per hour and the vehicle was either (a) in violation of any rules or regulations involving an out-of-service defect relating to brake systems, steering components and/or coupling devices, or (b) transporting flammable gas, radioactive materials or explosives. Whenever a license is suspended pursuant to this paragraph, the commissioner shall immediately issue a restricted license provided the holder of such license is otherwise eligible to receive such

restricted license, except that no such restricted license shall be valid for the operation of a vehicle with a GVWR of more than eighteen thousand pounds and further provided that issuing a license to such person does not create a substantial traffic safety hazard.

2-a. Mandatory suspension and revocation of a license and registration in certain cases. (a) within seven days after conviction for a violation of any local law which prohibits the knowing operation or offering to operate or permitting the operation for hire of any vehicle as a taxicab, livery, as defined in section one hundred twenty-one-e of this chapter, coach, limousine, van or wheelchair accessible van or tow truck within the state without first having obtained an appropriate license therefor from the appropriate licensing authority and appropriate for-hire insurance from the appropriate insurance agency, the taxi and limousine commission or other local body having jurisdiction over such offenses with respect to such vehicles shall provide notice of such conviction to the commissioner in a manner agreed upon between any such local body and the commissioner. Upon receipt of such notice, the commissioner shall suspend the license of such operator and the registration of such vehicle for a period of sixty days.

(b) Within seven days after conviction for a violation of any local law which prohibits the knowing operation or offering to operate or permitting the operation for hire of any vehicle as a taxicab, livery, as defined in section one hundred twenty-one-e of this chapter, coach, limousine, van or wheelchair accessible van or tow truck within the state without first having obtained an appropriate license therefor from the appropriate licensing authority and appropriate for hire insurance from the appropriate insurance agency where the operator has, within the previous five years, been convicted of any such violation, the taxi and limousine commission or other local body having jurisdiction over such offenses with respect to such vehicles shall provide notice to the commissioner in a manner agreed upon between any such local body and the commissioner. Upon receipt of such notice, the commissioner shall revoke the license of such operator.

(c) Within seven days after conviction for a violation of any local law which prohibits the knowing operation or offering to operate or permitting the operation for hire of any vehicle as a taxicab, livery, as defined in section one hundred twenty-one-e of this chapter, coach, limousine, van or wheelchair accessible van or tow truck within the state without first having obtained an appropriate license therefor from the appropriate licensing authority and appropriate for hire insurance from the appropriate insurance agency where the registrant has, within the previous five years, been convicted of any such violation, the taxi and limousine commission or other local body having jurisdiction over such offenses with respect to such vehicles shall provide notice to the commissioner in a manner agreed upon between any such local body and the commissioner. Upon receipt of such notice, the commissioner shall revoke the registration of such vehicle, and no new registration shall be issued for at least six months, nor thereafter, except in the discretion of the commissioner.

(d) The provisions of this subdivision shall not apply to any taxicab or livery as defined in section one hundred twenty-one-e of this chapter, coach, limousine, van or wheelchair accessible van or tow truck licensed or permitted for such operation by the appropriate local body of any other municipality, the department of transportation, the metropolitan transportation authority or the interstate commerce commission.

3. Permissive suspensions and revocations. Such licenses and registrations and the privilege of a non-resident of operating a motor vehicle in this state and of operation within this state of any motor vehicle owned by him and the privilege of an unlicensed person of obtaining a license issued by the commissioner and of obtaining a registration issued by the commissioner may be suspended or revoked:

a. for any violation of the provisions of this chapter, except section eleven hundred ninety-two, or for any violation of a local ordinance or regulation prohibiting dangerous driving as shall, in the discretion of the officer acting hereunder, justify such revocation or suspension;

b. because of some physical or mental disability of the holder, the court commitment of the holder to an institution under the jurisdiction of the department of mental hygiene or the disability of the holder by reason of intoxication or the use of drugs;

c. because of the conviction of the holder at any time of a felony;

d. for habitual or persistent violation of any of the provisions of this chapter, or of any lawful ordinance, rule or regulation made by local authorities in relation to traffic;

e. for gross negligence in the operation of a motor vehicle or motorcycle or operating a motor vehicle or motorcycle in a manner showing a reckless disregard for life or property of others;

f. for knowingly permitting or suffering any motor vehicle or motorcycle under the direction or control of the holder to be used in aid or furtherance of the commission of any crime;

g. for preventing lawful identification of any motor vehicle or motorcycle under the holder's direction or control, or evading lawful arrest or prosecution while operating such motor vehicle or motorcycle;

h. for wilfully evading lawful prosecution in this state or in another state or jurisdiction for an offense committed therein against the motor vehicle or traffic laws thereof;

i. for habitual or persistent violation of any provisions of this chapter, and/or any lawful ordinance, rule or regulation made by local authorities in relation to traffic, and/or violations committed in a commercial motor vehicle of any law, statute, ordinance, rule or regulation in relation to traffic made by any other state, District of Columbia, Canadian province or local authority of such state, district or province;

j. except as provided in subdivision one herein or section eleven hundred ninety-three of this chapter upon the conviction of a person under eighteen years of age of any crime or in the case of an adjudication of youthful offender under nineteen years of age, such license or registration may be suspended or revoked for a maximum period of one year by the judge or justice sentencing him;

k. for a period of up to ninety days because of the conviction of the holder of the offenses of menacing as defined in section 120.15 of the penal law, where such offense was committed against a traffic enforcement agent employed by the city of New York or the city of Buffalo while such agent was enforcing or attempting to enforce the traffic regulations of such city.

3-a. Opportunity to be heard and temporary suspensions. Where revocation or suspension is permissive, the holder, unless he shall waive such right, shall have an opportunity to be heard except where such revocation or suspension is based solely on a court conviction or convictions or on a court commitment to an institution under the jurisdiction of the department of mental hygiene. A license or registration, or the privilege of a non-resident of operating a motor vehicle in this state or of the operation within this state of any motor vehicle owned by him, may, however, be temporarily suspended without notice, pending any prosecution, investigation or hearing.

4. Administrative action pursuant to interstate compact. a. Such licenses may be suspended where pursuant to any compact or agreement authorized by section five hundred seventeen of this chapter the holder thereof is issued a summons for a moving traffic violation, is not detained or required to furnish bail or collateral and fails to appear in response to such summons. Such suspension shall remain in effect only until such holder submits to the jurisdiction of the court in which such summons is returnable.

b. If notification is received by the commissioner pursuant to any compact or agreement authorized by section five hundred sixteen-b of this article that the holder of a New York license or an unlicensed New York resident has been convicted of an offense set forth in such compact or agreement, such conviction, for the purpose of administrative action which must or may be taken by the commissioner pursuant to the provisions of this section, shall be deemed to be a conviction of an offense committed within this state in accordance with the provisions of such compact or agreement.

4-a. Suspension for failure to answer an appearance ticket or to pay a fine. (a) Upon receipt of a court notification of the failure of a person to appear within sixty days of the return date or new subsequent adjourned date, pursuant to an appearance ticket charging said person with a violation of any of the provisions of this chapter (except one for parking, stopping, or standing), of any violation of the tax law or of the transportation law regulating traffic or of any lawful ordinance or regulation made by a local or public authority, relating to traffic (except one for parking, stopping, or standing) or the failure to pay a fine imposed by a court the commissioner or his or her agent may suspend the driver's license or privileges of such person pending receipt of notice from the court that such person has appeared in response to such appearance ticket or has paid such fine. Such suspension shall take effect no less than thirty days from the day upon which notice thereof is sent by the commissioner to the person whose driver's license or privileges are to be suspended. Any suspension issued pursuant to this paragraph shall be subject to the provisions of paragraph (j-1) of subdivision two of section five hundred three of this chapter.

(b) The provisions of paragraph (a) of this subdivision shall not apply to a registrant who was not operating a vehicle, but who was issued a summons or an appearance ticket for a violation of section three hundred eighty-five, section four hundred one or section five hundred eleven-a of this chapter. Upon the receipt of a court notification of the failure of such person to appear within sixty days of the return date or a new subsequent adjourned date, pursuant to an appearance ticket charging said person with such violation, or the failure of such person to pay a fine imposed by a court, the commissioner or his or her agent may suspend the registration of the vehicle or vehicles involved in such violation or privilege of operation of any motor vehicle owned by the registrant pending receipt of notice from the court that such person has appeared in response to such appearance ticket or has paid such fine. Such suspension shall take effect no less than thirty days from the day upon which notice thereof is sent by the commissioner to the person whose registration or privilege is to be suspended. Any suspension issued pursuant to this paragraph shall be subject to the provisions of paragraph (j-1) of subdivision two of section five hundred three of this chapter.

(c) Upon receipt of notification from a traffic and parking violations agency of the failure of a person to appear within sixty days of the return date or new subsequent adjourned date, pursuant to an appearance ticket charging said person with a violation of:

(i) any of the provisions of this chapter except one for parking, stopping or standing and except those violations described in paragraphs (a), (b), (d), (e) and (f) of subdivision two of section three hundred seventy-one of the general municipal law;

(ii) section five hundred two or subdivision (a) of section eighteen hundred fifteen of the tax law;

(iii) section fourteen-f (except paragraph (b) of subdivision four of section fourteen-f), two hundred eleven or two hundred twelve of the transportation law; or

(iv) any lawful ordinance or regulation made by a local or public authority relating to traffic (except one for parking, stopping or standing) or the failure to pay a fine imposed for such a violation by a traffic and parking violations agency, the commissioner or his or her agent may suspend the driver's license or privileges of such person pending receipt of notice from the agency that such person has appeared in response to such appearance ticket or has paid such fine. Such suspension shall take effect no less than thirty days from the day upon which notice thereof is sent by the commissioner to the person whose driver's license or privileges are to be suspended. Any suspension issued pursuant to this paragraph shall be subject to the provisions of paragraph (j-1) of subdivision two of section five hundred three of this chapter.

4-b. Suspension of registration for failure to answer or to pay fines with respect to certain violations. Upon receipt of certification from a court or administrative tribunal of appropriate jurisdiction that the owner of a motor vehicle or his representative failed to appear on the return date or dates or any subsequent adjourned date or dates or failed to comply with the rules and regulations of an administrative tribunal following entry of a final decision or decisions in response to twenty-five or more summonses or other process, issued within an eighteen month period charging that such motor vehicle is parked, stopped or standing in violation of any of the provisions of this chapter or of any law, ordinance, rule or regulation made by a local authority, the commissioner shall suspend the registration of such motor vehicle. Such suspension shall take effect no less than thirty days from the date on which notice thereof is sent by the commissioner to the person whose registration is to be suspended and shall remain in effect as long as the summons or summonses remain unanswered, or in the case of an administrative tribunal, the registrant fails to comply with the rules and regulations following the entry of a final decision or decisions.

4-c. [*Repealed eff. Sept. 1, 2007.*] Suspension of registration for failure to answer or to pay fines with respect to parking, stopping and standing violations. Upon receipt of certification from a court or administrative tribunal of appropriate jurisdiction in a city with a population in excess of one hundred thousand persons according to the nineteen hundred eighty united states census that the owner of a motor vehicle or his representative following compliance by such city with the notice provisions of subdivision two of section two hundred thirty-five of this chapter, failed to appear on the return date or dates or any subsequent adjourned date or dates or failed to comply with the rules and regulations of an administrative tribunal following entry of a final decision or decisions, in response to five or more summonses or other process, issued within a twelve month period charging that such motor vehicle is parked, stopped or standing in violation of any of the provisions of this chapter or of any law, ordinance, rule or regulation made by a local authority, the commissioner shall suspend the registration of such motor vehicle. Such suspension shall take effect no less than thirty days from the date on which notice thereof is sent by the commissioner to the person whose registration is to be suspended and shall remain in effect as long as the summons or summonses remain unanswered, or in the case of an administrative tribunal, the registrant fails to comply with the rules and regulations following the entry of a final decision or decisions.

4-d. Suspension of registration for failure to answer or pay penalties with respect to certain violations. Upon the receipt of a notification from a court or an administrative tribunal that an owner of a motor vehicle failed to appear on the return date or dates or a new subsequent adjourned date or dates or failed to pay any penalty imposed by a court or failed to comply with the rules and regulations of an administrative tribunal following entry of a final decision or decisions, in response to five or more notices of liability or other process, issued within an eighteen month period charging such owner with a violation of toll collection regulations in accordance with the provisions of section two thousand nine hundred eighty-five of the public authorities law or sections sixteen-a, sixteen-b and sixteen-c of chapter seven hundred seventy-four of the laws of nineteen hundred fifty, the commissioner or his agent shall suspend the registration of the vehicle or vehicles involved in the violation or the privilege of operation of any motor vehicle owned by the registrant. Such suspension shall take effect no less than thirty days from the date on which notice thereof is sent by the commissioner to the person whose registration or privilege is suspended and shall remain in effect until such registrant has appeared in response to such notices of liability or has paid such penalty or in the case of an administrative tribunal, the registrant has complied with the rules and regulations following the entry of a final decision or decisions.

4-e. [*Repealed eff. June 30, 2007.*] Suspension and disqualification for failure to make child support payments.

(1) The commissioner, on behalf of the department, shall enter into a written agreement with the commissioner of social services, on behalf of the department of social services, which shall set forth the procedures for suspending the driving privileges of individuals who have failed to make payments of child support or combined child and spousal support.

(2) Such agreement shall include:

(i) the procedure under which the department of social services shall notify the department of an individual's liability for support arrears;

(ii) the procedure under which the department shall be notified by the department of social services that an individual has satisfied or commenced payment of his or her support arrears or has made satisfactory payment arrangements thereon and shall have the suspension of his or her driving privileges terminated;

(iii) the procedure for reimbursement of the department and its agents by the department of social services for the full additional costs of carrying out the procedures authorized by this section, and may include, subject to the approval of the director of the budget, a procedure for reimbursement of necessary additional costs of collecting social security numbers pursuant to section five hundred two of this chapter;

(iv) provision for the publicizing of sanctions for nonpayment of child support, including the potential for the suspension of delinquent support obligors' driving privileges if they fail to pay child support or combined child and spousal support; and

(v) such other matters as the parties to such agreement shall deem necessary to carry out the provisions of this section.

(3) Upon receipt of notification from the department of social services of a person's failure to satisfy support arrears or to make satisfactory payment arrangements thereon pursuant to paragraph (e) of subdivision twelve of section one hundred eleven-b of the social services law or from a court issuing an order pursuant to section four hundred fifty-eight-a of the family court act or section two hundred forty-four-b of the domestic relations law, the commissioner or his or her agent shall suspend the license of such person to operate a motor vehicle. In the event such person is unlicensed, such person's privilege of obtaining a license shall be suspended. Such suspension shall take effect no later than fifteen days from the date of the notice thereof to the person whose license or privilege of obtaining a license is to be suspended, and shall remain in effect until such time as the commissioner is advised that the person has satisfied the support arrears or has made satisfactory payment arrangements thereon pursuant to paragraph (e) of subdivision twelve of section one hundred eleven-b of the social services law or until such time as the court issues an order to terminate such suspension;

(4) From the time the commissioner is notified by the department of social services of a person's liability for support arrears under this section, the commissioner shall be relieved from all liability to such person which may otherwise arise under this section, and such person shall have no right to commence a court action or proceeding or to any other legal recourse against the commissioner to recover such driving privileges as authorized by this section. In addition, notwithstanding any other provision of law, such person shall have no right to a hearing or appeal pursuant to this chapter with respect to a suspension of driving privileges as authorized by this section. However, nothing herein shall be construed to prohibit such person from proceeding against the support collection unit pursuant to article seventy-eight of the civil practice law and rules.

(5) Any person whose license has been suspended pursuant to subdivision three of this section may apply for the issuance of a restricted use license as provided in section five hundred thirty of this chapter.

5. Restoration. A license or registration may be restored by direction of the commissioner but not otherwise. Reversal on appeal, of any conviction because of which any license or registration has been revoked or suspended, shall entitle the holder to restoration thereof forthwith. The privileges of a non-resident may be restored by direction of the commissioner in his discretion but not otherwise.

6. Restrictions.

a. Where revocation is mandatory hereunder, no new license shall be issued for at least six months or, in certain cases a longer period as specified in this chapter, nor thereafter, except in the discretion of the commissioner of motor vehicles.

b. Except as otherwise provided in paragraph c of this subdivision, where revocation is mandatory pursuant to subparagraph (iii) of paragraph a of subdivision two of this section, no new commercial driver's license shall be issued for at least one year nor thereafter except in the discretion of the commissioner, except that if such person has previously been found to have refused a chemical test pursuant to section eleven hundred ninety-four of this chapter or has a prior conviction of any of the following offenses: any violation of section eleven hundred ninety-two of this chapter; any violation of subdivision one or two of section six hundred of this chapter; or has a prior conviction of any felony involving the use of a motor vehicle pursuant to paragraph (a) of subdivision one of section five hundred ten-a of this article, then such commercial driver's license revocation shall be permanent.

c. Where revocation is mandatory pursuant to subdivision one of section five hundred ten-a of this chapter or subparagraph (iii) of paragraph a of subdivision two of this section and the violation of subdivision two of section six hundred of this chapter was committed while operating a commercial motor vehicle transporting hazardous materials, no new commercial driver's license shall be issued for at least three years nor thereafter except in the discretion of the commissioner, except that if such person has previously been found to have refused a chemical test pursuant to section eleven hundred ninety-four of this chapter or has a prior conviction of any of the following offenses: any violation of section eleven hundred ninety-two of this chapter; any violation of subdivision one or two of section six hundred of this chapter; or has a prior conviction of any felony involving the use of a motor vehicle pursuant to paragraph (a) of subdivision one of section five hundred ten-a of this article, then such commercial driver's license revocation shall be permanent.

d. The permanent commercial driver's license revocation required by paragraphs b and c of this subdivision may be waived by the commissioner after a period of ten years has expired from such sentence provided:

(i) that during such ten year period such person has not been found to have refused a chemical test pursuant to section eleven hundred ninety-four of this chapter and has not been convicted of any one of the following offenses: any violation of section eleven hundred ninety-two of this chapter; any violation of subdivision one or two of section six hundred of this chapter; or has a prior conviction of any felony involving the use of a motor vehicle pursuant to paragraph (a) of subdivision one of section five hundred ten-a of this article;

(ii) if any of the grounds upon which the permanent commercial driver's license revocation is based involved a finding of refusal to submit to a chemical test pursuant to section eleven hundred ninety-four of this chapter or a conviction of a violation of any subdivision of section eleven hundred ninety-two of this chapter, that such person provides acceptable documentation to the commissioner that such person has voluntarily enrolled in and successfully completed an appropriate rehabilitation program; and

(iii) after such documentation, if required, is accepted, that such person is granted a certificate of relief from disabilities as provided for in section seven hundred one of the correction law by the court in which such person was last penalized.

e. Upon a third finding of refusal and/or conviction of any of the offenses which require a permanent commercial driver's license revocation, such permanent revocation may not be waived by the commissioner under any circumstances.

f. Where revocation is mandatory hereunder,

based upon a conviction had outside this state, no new license shall be issued until after sixty days from the date of such revocation, nor thereafter, except in the discretion of the commissioner.

g. Except as provided in paragraph k of this subdivision, where revocation is permissive, no new license or certificate shall be issued by such commissioner to any person until after thirty days from the date of such revocation, nor thereafter, except in the discretion of the commissioner after an investigation or upon a hearing, provided, however, that where the revocation is based upon a failure in a reexamination pursuant to section five hundred six of this chapter, a learner's permit may be issued immediately and provided further, that where revocation is based upon a conviction of a felony, other than a felony relating to the operation of a motor vehicle or motorcycle, a license shall be issued immediately, if the applicant is otherwise qualified and if the application for such license is accompanied by consent in writing issued by the parole or probation authority having jurisdiction over such applicant.

h. The provisions of this subdivision shall not apply to revocations issued pursuant to sections eleven hundred ninety-three and eleven hundred ninety-four of this chapter.

i. [Repealed eff. Oct. 1, 2007.] Where suspension of a driver's license is mandatory hereunder based upon a conviction of, or youthful offender or other juvenile adjudication in connection with, any misdemeanor or felony as defined in article two hundred twenty or two hundred twenty-one of the penal law, any violation of the federal controlled substances act, any crime in violation of subdivision four of section eleven hundred ninety-two of this chapter or any out-of-state or federal misdemeanor or felony drug-related offense, the commissioner may issue a restricted use license pursuant to section five hundred thirty of this chapter.

j. [Repealed eff. Oct. 1, 2007.] Where suspension of a driver's license is mandatory hereunder based upon a conviction of, or youthful offender or other juvenile adjudication in connection with, any misdemeanor or felony as defined in article two hundred twenty or two hundred twenty-one of the penal law, any violation of the federal controlled substances act, any crime in violation of subdivision four of section eleven hundred ninety-two of this chapter or any out-of-state or federal misdemeanor or felony drug-related offense and the individual does not have a driver's license or the individual's driver's license was suspended at the time of conviction or youthful offender or other juvenile adjudication, the commissioner shall not issue a new license nor restore the former license for a period of six months after such individual would otherwise have become eligible to obtain a new license or to have the former license restored; provided, however, that during such delay period the commissioner may

issue a restricted use license pursuant to section five hundred thirty of this chapter to such previously suspended licensee.

k. Where revocation is permissive hereunder, based upon a finding of a violation of section three hundred ninety-two or section three hundred ninety-two-a of this chapter, no new license or certificate shall be issued until after one year from the date of such revocation, nor thereafter, except in the discretion of the commissioner.

7. Miscellaneous provisions. Except as expressly provided, a court conviction shall not be necessary to sustain a revocation or suspension. Revocation or suspension hereunder shall be deemed an administrative act reviewable by the supreme court as such. Notice of revocation or suspension, as well as any required notice of hearing, where the holder is not present, may be given by mailing the same in writing to him at the address contained in his license or certificate of registration, as the case may be. Proof of such mailing by certified mail to the holder shall be presumptive evidence of the holder's receipt and actual knowledge of such notice. Attendance of witnesses may be compelled by subpoena. Failure of the holder or any other person possessing the license card or number plates, to deliver the same to the suspending or revoking officer is a misdemeanor. Suspending or revoking officers shall place such license cards and number plates in the custody of the commissioner except where the commissioner shall otherwise direct. If any person shall fail to deliver a license card or number plates as provided herein, any police officer, bridge and tunnel officer of the Triborough bridge and tunnel authority, or agent of the commissioner having knowledge of such facts shall have the power to secure possession thereof and return the same to the commissioner, and the commissioner may forthwith direct any police officer, bridge and tunnel officer of the Triborough bridge and tunnel authority, acting pursuant to his special duties, or agent of the commissioner to secure possession thereof and to return the same to the commissioner. Failure of the holder or of any person possessing the license card or number plates to deliver to any police officer, bridge and tunnel officer of the Triborough bridge and tunnel authority, or agent of the commissioner who requests the same pursuant to this subdivision shall be a misdemeanor. Notice of revocation or suspension of any license or registration shall be transmitted forthwith by the commissioner of motor vehicles to the chief of police of the city or prosecuting officer of the locality in which the person whose license or registration so revoked or suspended resides. In case any license or registration shall expire before the end of any period for which it has been revoked or suspended, and before it shall have been restored as provided in this chapter, then and in that event any renewal thereof may be withheld until the end of such period of suspension or until restoration, as the case may be.

VTL

The revocation of a learner's permit shall automatically cancel the application for a license of the holder of such permit.

No suspension or revocation of a license or registration shall be made because of a judgment of conviction if the suspending or revoking officer is satisfied that the magistrate who pronounced the judgment failed to comply with subdivision one of section eighteen hundred seven of this chapter. In case a suspension or revocation has been made and the commissioner is satisfied that there was such failure, he shall restore the license or registration or both as the case may be.

8. Cancellation. Upon receipt of a license which has been surrendered to the licensing authority of any other jurisdiction as a prerequisite to the issuance of a license by such other jurisdiction in accordance with the provisions of the driver license compact or any other laws of such jurisdiction, the commissioner shall cancel such license. Provided, however, that such license shall not be cancelled if the licensee is a resident of this state.

9. Railroad vehicle violations. Upon certification by the commissioner of transportation that there has been a violation of section seventy-six-b of the railroad law, the commissioner of motor vehicles may rescind, cancel or suspend the registration of any motor vehicle described in subdivision one of section seventy-six-b of the railroad law and may rescind, cancel, suspend or take possession of the current registration certificate and number plates of any such motor vehicle.

10. Where a youth is determined to be a youthful offender, following a conviction of a violation for which a license suspension or revocation is mandatory or where a youth receives a juvenile delinquency adjudication in conjunction with a violation of section 240.62 or subdivision five of section 240.60 of the penal law, the court shall impose such suspension or revocation as is otherwise required upon conviction and, further, shall notify the commissioner of said suspension or revocation and its finding that said violator is granted youthful offender status as is required pursuant to section five hundred thirteen of this chapter or received a juvenile delinquency adjudication.

11. [*Expires and repealed eff. Oct. 1, 2007.*] Notwithstanding any contrary provision of law, the division of criminal justice services is authorized to share with the commissioner such criminal history information in its possession as may be necessary to effect the provisions of this chapter.

Amended by L. 1994, Ch. 61, § 11, eff. Apr. 1, 1994, extending expiration date for subd. 4-c; L. 1994, Ch. 307, § 5, eff. Sept. 18, 1994, amending subd. 6(g); L. 1994, Ch. 307, § 6, eff. Sept. 18, 1994, adding subd. 6(k); L. 1994, Ch. 313, § 2, eff. Nov. 1, 1994, adding subd. 2(b)(viii); L. 1994, Ch. 429, § 2, eff. July 20, 1994, adding subd. 2-a; L. 1994, Ch. 431, § 3, eff. July 20, 1994, amending subd. 2(b)(iv); L. 1994, Ch. 431, § 4, eff. July 20, 1994, amending subd. 3(k); L. 1994, Ch.

286, § 1, eff. July 13, 1994, extending to Oct. 1, 1995, expiration date for subd. 2(b)(v), (vi), and (vii), subd. 6(i) and (j), subd. 11; L. 1995, Ch. 3, § 72, amending subd. 2(b)(v), eff. Apr. 1, 1995 pursuant to L. 1995, Ch. 3, § 74, paragraph (j); L. 1995, Ch. 3, § 73, eff. Apr. 1, 1995, extending to Oct. 1, 1996, expiration date for subd. 2(b)(v), (vi), (vii), subd. 6(i) and (j), subd. 11; L. 1995, Ch. 81, § 211, adding subd. 4-e, eff. July 1, 1995, repealed June 30, 1998; L. 1996, Ch. 400, § 1, extending to Oct. 1, 1997, eff. date for subds. 2(b)(v)-(vii), 6(i) and (j), and 11, eff. Jul. 30, 1996; L. 1996, Ch. 309, § 78, extending to Oct. 1, 1997, expiration date for subds. 2(b)(v)-(vii), 6(i) and (j), and 11, eff. Jul. 13, 1996; L. 1997, Ch. 382, § 1, extending expiration date for subd. 2(b)(v)-(vii), subd. 6(i) and (j), and subd. 11 to Oct. 1, 1998, eff. Aug. 5, 1997, Ch. 398, § 133, amending subd. 4-e, eff. Jan. 1, 1998, Ch. 505, § 1, amending subparagraph (b) of the first listed version of subd. (4-a), eff. Oct. 3, 1997, and Ch. 435, § 64, eff. Aug. 20, 1997, extending expiration date of subd. 4-c to Nov. 1, 1999; L. 1998, Ch. 58 Part E, § 27, eff. Apr. 28, 1998, deemed in full force and effect Apr. 1, 1998, extending the expiration date of subds. 2(b)(v)-(vii), 6(i), 6(j), and 11 to Oct. 1, 1999; L. 1998, Ch. 383, § 9, eff. Apr. 1, 1999, adding subd. 2(b)(ix)-(xi), eff. Jan. 1, 1999, and paragraphs to expire and be deemed repealed on Jan. 1, 2002, pursuant to § 10; L. 1998, Ch. 214, § 83-a, eff. July 7, 1998, extending the expiration date of amendments to subd. 4-e to June 30, 1999; L. 1998, Ch. 652, § 1, eff. Apr. 1, 1999, amending subd. 2(b)(ix) by changing the period of suspension from 30 days to three months; L. 1999, Ch. 140, deemed eff. June 30, 1999, extending eff. date of subd. 4-e to June 30, 2001, Ch. 412, eff. Sept. 1, 1999, deemed eff. Apr. 1, 1999, amending subd. 7, expiring Sept. 1, 2002, and Ch. 452, eff. Sept. 1, 1999, deemed eff. Apr. 1, 1999, extending the expiration date of subd. 4-c, and Ch. 512, eff. Sept. 28, 1999, extending the expiration dates of subds. 2(b)(v)-(vii), 6(i) and (j), and 11 to Oct. 1, 2000, and Ch. 561, §§ 6, 7, and 8, eff. Dec. 1, 1999, adding subd. 2(b)(xii), and amending subds. 2(c) and 10, respectively; L. 2000, Ch. 447, eff. Sept. 20, 2000, extending the expiration dates of subds. 2(b)(v)-(vii), 6(i) and (j) and 11 to Oct. 1, 2000; L. 2001, Chs. 549, deleting repeal date of subd. 2(b)(ix)-(xi); L. 2001, Chs. 72, 95, 242, and 549, extending expiration dates; L. 2002, Ch. 84, Part A § 1, extending expiration dates of subds. 2(b)(v)-(vii), 6(i) and (j), and 11 to Oct. 1, 2003; L. 2003, Ch. 62, Part J, § 10, eff. Sept. 12, 2003, repealing and replacing subd. 4-a; L. 2003, Ch. 16, § 14, extending expiration date until Sept. 1, 2005, eff. Mar. 31, 2003; L. 2003, Ch. 87, § 1, eff. June 30, 2003, extending expiration date to June 30, 2005; L. 2003, Ch. 487, § 1, eff. Sept. 9, 2003, extending expiration date to Oct. 1, 2005; L. 2005, Ch. 56, Part D, § 13, eff. Apr. 1, 2005, extending expiration date to Sept. 1, 2007; L. 2005, Ch. 60, Part D, § 1, eff. Apr. 1, 2005, extending expiration date to Oct. 1, 2007, Part E, § 12, eff. Sept. 30, 2005, amending subd. 6(b), (c), and (d)(i), and Part E, § 20, eff. Apr. 1, 2005, extending expiration date to June 30, 2007; L. 2005, Ch. 223, § 2, eff. Nov. 1, 2005, adding subd. 2(b)(xiii).

ANNOTATIONS

Out-of state suspension.—New York State court properly suspended defendant's New York driver's license when he was served with a speeding ticket in Pennsylvania and failed to appear before a Pennsylvania court on that ticket. Samoilov v. N.Y.S. Dept. of Motor Vehicles, 300 A.D.2d 40, 751 N.Y.S.2d 523 (2d Dept. 2002).

Purpose.—The purpose of an administrative licensing hearing pursuant to § 510 is not necessarily punitive, but is a procedure provided by the Legislature for the protection of the traveling public; the hearing is an appropriate method for the investigation of the causes of an accident. Pratt v. Melton, 72 A.D.2d 887, 422 N.Y.S.2d 169 (3d Dept. 1979).

Suspension; conviction of drug offense.—Defendant's conviction of conspiring to possess cocaine was a "drug offense" which warranted suspension of his driver's license. People v. Ferraiolo, 223 A.D.2d 556, 636 N.Y.S.2d 378 (2d Dept. 1996).

Suspension not a prosecution.—"The suspension or revocation of a driver's license is a civil sanction. A criminal conviction is not necessary to sustain a revocation or suspension of a driver's license." Brady v. Department of Motor Vehicles, 278 A.D.2d 233, 717 N.Y.S.2d 906 (2d Dept. 2000), aff'd, 98 N.Y.2d 625, 748 N.Y.S.2d 889, 778 N.E.2d 539 (2002).

—Court rejected defendant's constitutional challenge on double jeopardy grounds to his prosecution under § 511-d on the basis that neither the suspension under § 510 nor § 226 is a prosecution; further prosecution under § 511-d was not violative of double jeopardy. People v. Brignoni, 182 Misc. 2d 779, 701 N.Y.S.2d 253 (Crim. Ct. N.Y. Co. 1999).

§ 510-a. Suspension and revocation of commercial driver's licenses.

1. Revocation. A commercial driver's license shall be revoked by the commissioner whenever the holder is convicted within or outside of this state (a) of a felony involving the use of a motor vehicle except a felony as described in paragraph (b) of this subdivision; (b) of a felony involving manufacturing, distributing or dispensing a drug as defined in section one hundred fourteen-a of this chapter or possession of any such drug with intent to manufacture, distribute or dispense such drug in which a motor vehicle was used; (c) of a violation of subdivision one or two of section six hundred of this chapter; (d) of operating a commercial motor vehicle when, as a result of prior violations committed while operating a commercial motor vehicle, the driver's commercial driver's license is revoked, suspended, or canceled, or the driver is disqualified from operating a commercial motor vehicle; (e) or has been convicted of causing a fatality through the negligent operation of a commercial motor vehicle, including but not limited to the crimes of vehicular manslaughter or criminally negligent homicide.

2. Duration of revocation. (a) Except as otherwise provided in paragraph (b) of this subdivision, where revocation of a commercial driver's license is mandatory pursuant to paragraph (a) of subdivision one of this section no new commercial driver's license shall be issued for at least one year nor thereafter except in the discretion of the commissioner, except that if such person has previously been found to have refused a chemical test pursuant to section eleven hundred ninety-four of this chapter or has a prior conviction of any of the following offenses: any violation of section eleven hundred ninety-two of this chapter, any violation of subdivision one or two of section six hundred of this chapter, or any felony involving the use of a motor vehicle pursuant to paragraph (a) of subdivision one of this section, or has been convicted of operating a commercial motor vehicle when, as a result of prior violations committed while operating a commercial motor vehicle, the driver's commercial driver's license is revoked, suspended, or canceled, or the driver is disqualified from operating a commercial motor vehicle, or has been convicted of causing a fatality through the negligent operation of a commercial motor vehicle, including but not limited to the crimes of vehicular manslaughter or criminally negligent homicide, then such commercial driver's license revocation shall be permanent.

(b) Where revocation is mandatory pursuant to paragraph (a) of subdivision one of this section

and the commercial motor vehicle was transporting hazardous materials, no new commercial driver's license shall be issued for at least three years nor thereafter except in the discretion of the commissioner, except that if such person has previously been found to have refused a chemical test pursuant to section eleven hundred ninety-four of this chapter or has a prior conviction of any of the following offenses: any violation of section eleven hundred ninety-two of this chapter, any violation of subdivision one or two of section six hundred of this chapter, or any felony involving the use of a motor vehicle pursuant to paragraph (a) of subdivision one of this section, or been convicted of operating a commercial motor vehicle when, as a result of prior violations committed while operating a commercial motor vehicle the driver's commercial driver's license is revoked, suspended, or canceled, or the driver is disqualified from operating a commercial motor vehicle, or has been convicted of causing a fatality through the negligent operation of a commercial motor vehicle, including but not limited to the crimes of vehicular manslaughter or criminally negligent homicide, then such commercial driver's license revocation shall be permanent.

(c) The permanent commercial driver's license revocation required by paragraphs (a) and (b) of this subdivision may be waived by the commissioner after a period of ten years has expired from such sentence provided:

(i) that during such ten year period such person has not been found to have refused a chemical test pursuant to section eleven hundred ninety-four of this chapter and has not been convicted of any one of the following offenses: any violation of section eleven hundred ninety-two of this chapter, any violation of subdivision one or two of section six hundred of this chapter, or any felony involving the use of a motor vehicle pursuant to paragraph (a) of subdivision one of this section, or has been convicted of operating a commercial motor vehicle when, as a result of prior violations committed while operating a commercial motor vehicle, the driver's commercial driver's license is revoked, suspended, or canceled, or the driver is disqualified from operating a commercial motor vehicle; or has been convicted of causing a fatality through the negligent operation of a commercial motor vehicle, including but not limited to the crimes of vehicular manslaughter or criminally negligent homicide;

(ii) if any of the grounds upon which the permanent commercial driver's license revocation is based involved a finding of refusal to submit to a chemical test pursuant to section eleven hundred ninety-four of this chapter or a conviction of a violation of any subdivision of section eleven hundred ninety-two of this chapter, that such person provides acceptable documentation to the commissioner that such person has enrolled

VTL

in and successfully completed an appropriate rehabilitation program; and

(iii) after such documentation, if required, is accepted, that such person is granted a certificate of relief from disabilities as provided for in section seven hundred one of the correction law by the court in which such person was last penalized.

(d) Upon a third finding of refusal and/or conviction of any of the offenses which require a permanent commercial driver's license revocation, such permanent revocation may not be waived by the commissioner under any circumstances.

(e) Where revocation is mandatory pursuant to paragraph (b) of subdivision one of this section such revocation shall be permanent and may not be waived by the commissioner under any circumstances.

3. Suspension. (a) A commercial driver's license shall be suspended by the commissioner for a period of sixty days where the holder is convicted, during any three year period, of two serious traffic violations as defined in subdivision four of this section, in separate incidents whether such convictions occurred within or outside of this state.

(b) A commercial driver's license shall be suspended by the commissioner for a period of one hundred twenty days where the holder is convicted, during any three year period, of three serious traffic violations as defined in subdivision four of this section, in separate incidents whether such convictions occurred within or outside of this state.

(c) A commercial driver's license shall be suspended by the commissioner for a period of sixty days where the holder is convicted of a violation of subdivision (g) of section eleven hundred eighty of this chapter, and (i) the recorded or entered speed upon which the conviction was based exceeded the applicable speed limit by more than twenty miles per hour or (ii) the recorded or entered speed upon which the conviction was based exceeded the applicable speed limit by more than ten miles per hour and the vehicle was either (a) in violation of any rules or regulations involving an out-of-service defect relating to brake systems, steering components and/or coupling devices, or (b) transporting flammable gas, radioactive materials or explosives.

(d) A commercial driver's license shall be suspended by the commissioner:

(i) for a period of ninety days where the holder was found to have operated a commercial motor vehicle designed or used to transport property as defined in subparagraphs (i) and (ii) of paragraph (a) of subdivision four of section five hundred one-a of this title, in violation of an out-of-service order as provided for in the rules and regulations of the department of transportation whether such

violation was committed within this state or was the same or a similar violation involving an out-of-service order committed outside of this state;

(ii) for a period of one year if, during any ten-year period, the holder is found to have committed two such violations not arising from the same incident whether such violations were committed within or outside of the state;

(iii) for a period of three years if, during any ten-year period, the holder is convicted of three or more such violations not arising from the same incident whether such violations were committed within or outside of the state;

(iv) for a period of one hundred eighty days if the holder is found to have operated a commercial motor vehicle designed or used to transport passengers or property as defined in subparagraphs (iii) and (v) of paragraph (a) of subdivision four of section five hundred one-a of this title, in violation of an out-of-service order, as provided for in the rules and regulations of the department of transportation, while transporting hazardous materials or passengers whether such violation was committed within this state or was the same or a similar violation committed outside of this state;

(v) for a period of three years if, during any ten-year period, the holder is found to have committed two or more violations, not arising from the same incident, of operating a commercial motor vehicle designed or used to transport passengers or property as defined in subparagraphs (iii) and (v) of paragraph (a) of subdivision four of section five hundred one-a of this title, in violation of an out-of-service order, as provided for in the rules and regulations of the department of transportation, while transporting hazardous materials or passengers whether such violation was committed within this state or was the same or a similar violation involving an out-of-service order committed outside of this state.

(e) A commercial driver's license shall be suspended by the commissioner:

(i) for a period of sixty days where the holder is convicted of a violation of section eleven hundred seventy-one or section eleven hundred seventy-six of this chapter whether such violation was committed within this state or was the same or a similar violation involving railroad grade crossings committed outside of this state.

(ii) for a period of one hundred twenty days where the holder is convicted of a second violation of section eleven hundred seventy-one or section eleven hundred seventy-six of this chapter whether such violations were committed within or outside of this state, both of which were committed within a three year period.

(iii) for a period of one year where the holder is convicted of a third violation of section eleven hundred seventy-one or section eleven hundred seventy-six of this chapter whether such violations were committed within or outside of this state, all of which were committed within a three year period.

4. Serious traffic violations. (a) A serious traffic violation shall mean operating a commercial motor vehicle in violation of any provision of this chapter or the laws of any other state, the District of Columbia or any Canadian province which (i) limits the speed of motor vehicles, provided the violation involved fifteen or more miles per hour over the established speed limit; (ii) is defined as reckless driving by state or local law or regulation; (iii) prohibits improper or erratic lane change; (iv) prohibits following too closely; (v) relates to motor vehicle traffic (other than parking, standing or stopping) and which arises in connection with a fatal accident; (vi) operating a commercial motor vehicle without first obtaining a commercial driver's license as required by section five hundred one of this title; (vii) operating a commercial motor vehicle without a commercial driver's license in the driver's possession; or (viii) operating a commercial motor vehicle without the proper class of commercial driver's license and/or endorsement for the specific vehicle being operated or for the passengers or type of cargo being transported.

(b) Whether any specific violation which occurs without this state is a serious violation shall be dependent upon whether the state or province in which the violation occurs, reports such violation to the commissioner as, or deems it to be, a serious traffic violation under the provisions of the federal commercial motor vehicle safety act of nineteen hundred eighty-six, public law 99-570, title XII or the motor carrier safety improvement act of 1999, public law 106-159 and regulations promulgated thereunder.

4-a. Dismissal. The court shall dismiss any charge of operating a commercial motor vehicle without a commercial driver's license in the driver's possession if, between the date the driver is charged with such violation and the appearance date for such violation, the driver supplies the court with proof that he or she held a valid commercial driver's license on the date of such violation. Such driver must also supply such proof to the law enforcement authority that issued the citation, prior to such driver's appearance in court.

5. Limitation of effect of revocation or suspension. Any revocation or suspension of a commercial driver's license issued pursuant to this section shall be applicable only to that portion of the holder's driver's license or privilege which permits the operation of commercial motor vehicles, and the commissioner shall immediately issue a license, other than a commercial driver's license, to such person, provided that such person is otherwise eligible to receive such license and further provided that issuing a license to such

person does not create a substantial traffic safety hazard.

6. Application of section to persons not holding a commercial driver's license. Whenever a person who is not the holder of a commercial driver's license issued by the commissioner is convicted of a violation which would require the mandatory revocation or suspension of a commercial driver's license pursuant to this section, the privilege of such person to operate a commercial motor vehicle and/or to obtain a commercial driver's license issued by the commissioner will be suspended or revoked for the same periods of time and subject to the same conditions provided in this section which would be applicable to the holder of a commercial driver's license and in addition, the driver's license or privilege of operating a motor vehicle by such person shall be suspended or revoked for the same periods of time for which the privilege of operating a commercial motor vehicle or the privilege to obtain a commercial driver's license are suspended or revoked.

7. Other revocation or suspension action not prohibited. The provisions of this section shall not be construed to prevent any person who has the authority to suspend or revoke a license to drive or privilege of operating pursuant to section five hundred ten of this chapter from exercising any such authority based upon a conviction for which suspension or revocation of a commercial driver's license by the commissioner is mandated.

Amended by L. 2001, Ch. 422, adding subd. 3(e), eff. Apr. 29, 2002; L. 2002, Ch. 569, §§ 1, 2, eff. Dec. 23, 2002, amending subd. 3(d) and (e); L. 2005, Ch. 60, Part E, §§ 13, 14, eff. Sept. 30, 2005, amending subds. 1, 2, and 4 and adding new subd. 4-a.

§ 510-b. Suspension and revocation for violations committed during probationary periods.

1. A license, other than a class DJ or class MJ license or a limited class DJ or class MJ license, shall be suspended, for a period of sixty days, (i) upon the first conviction of the licensee of a violation, committed during the probationary period provided for in subdivision four of section five hundred one of this title, of any provision of section eleven hundred twenty-nine of this chapter, section eleven hundred eighty of this chapter or any ordinance or regulation limiting the speed of motor vehicles and motorcycles, section eleven hundred eighty-two of this chapter, or subdivision one of section eleven hundred ninety-two of this chapter or section twelve hundred twelve of this chapter; or (ii) upon the second conviction of the licensee of a violation, committed during the aforesaid probationary period, of any other provision of this chapter or of any other law, ordinance, order, rule or regulation relating to traffic.

2. A license, other than a class DJ or class MJ

license or a limited class DJ or class MJ license, considered probationary pursuant to subdivision three of this section shall be revoked upon the conviction of the licensee of a violation or violations committed within six months following the restoration or issuance of such license, which conviction or convictions would result in the suspension of a probationary license pursuant to subdivision one of this section.

3. Any license, other than a class DJ or class MJ license or a limited class DJ or class MJ license, which is restored or issued to a person who has had his last valid license suspended or revoked pursuant to the provisions of this section shall be considered probationary until the expiration of six months following the date of restoration or issuance thereof.

4. The provisions of subdivisions one, five, six and seven of section five hundred ten of this chapter shall apply to any suspension or revocation under this section. However, the provisions of this section shall not operate to prevent a mandatory revocation or suspension for a greater period of time under subdivision two of section five hundred ten of this chapter or section eleven hundred ninety-three of this chapter; nor shall the provisions of this section prevent revocation or suspension under subdivisions two and three of section five hundred ten based upon two or more violations, including the same violation which was the basis for suspension or revocation under this section.

Amended by L. 2002, Ch. 644, amending subds. 1–3, eff. Sept. 1, 2003.

§ 510-c. Suspension and revocation of certain class DJ or class MJ learner's permits or driver's licenses.

1. (a) A class DJ or class MJ learner's permit shall be suspended for a period of sixty days:

(i) upon a conviction or finding of a serious traffic violation as defined in subdivision four of this section, committed while the holder had a class DJ or class MJ learner's permit; or

(ii) upon the second conviction or finding of such holder of a violation of any other provision of this chapter or any other law, ordinance, order, rule or regulation relating to traffic, committed while such holder had such learner's permit.

(b) A class DJ or class MJ learner's permit shall be revoked for a period of sixty days upon the conviction or finding of the holder of a violation or violations, committed within six months after the restoration of a class DJ or class MJ learner's permit suspended pursuant to paragraph (a) of this subdivision, which convictions or findings would result in the suspension of such permit pursuant to paragraph (a) of this subdivision.

2. (a) A class DJ or class MJ driver's license or limited class DJ or class MJ license shall be suspended, for a period of sixty days:

(i) upon a conviction or finding of a serious traffic violation as defined in subdivision four of this section, committed while the holder had such license; or

(ii) upon the second conviction or finding of the holder of a violation of any other provision of this chapter or any other law, ordinance, order, rule or regulation relating to traffic, committed while such holder had such license.

(b) A class DJ or class MJ driver's license or a limited class DJ or class MJ license shall be revoked for a period of sixty days upon the conviction or finding of the holder of a violation or violations, committed within six months either after the restoration of such driver's license suspended pursuant to paragraph (a) of this subdivision or after the restoration of a learner's permit suspended or revoked pursuant to subdivision one of this section, which convictions or findings would result in the suspension of such license pursuant to paragraph (a) of this subdivision.

3. A driver's license which has been restored following a suspension of a class DJ or class MJ driver's license or a limited class DJ or class MJ license pursuant to subdivision two of this section shall be revoked for a period of sixty days upon the conviction or finding, within six months of such restoration, of any violation or violations which would result in the suspension of a class DJ or class MJ driver's license or a limited class DJ or class MJ license pursuant to paragraph (a) of subdivision two of this section.

4. For purposes of this section, the term "serious traffic violation" shall mean operating a motor vehicle in violation of any of the following provisions of this chapter: articles twenty-five and twenty-six; subdivision one of section six hundred; section six hundred one; sections eleven hundred eleven, eleven hundred seventy, eleven hundred seventy-two and eleven hundred seventy-four; subdivisions (a), (b), (c), (d) and (f) of section eleven hundred eighty, provided that the violation involved ten or more miles per hour over the established limit; section eleven hundred eighty-two; subdivision three-a of section twelve hundred twenty-nine-c for violations involving use of safety belts or seats by a child under the age of sixteen; and section twelve hundred twelve of this chapter.

Added by L. 2002, Ch. 644, eff. Sept. 1, 2003.

§ 511. Operation while license or privilege is suspended or revoked; aggravated unlicensed operation.

1. Aggravated unlicensed operation of a motor vehicle in the third degree. (a) A person is guilty

of the offense of aggravated unlicensed operation of a motor vehicle in the third degree when such person operates a motor vehicle upon a public highway while knowing or having reason to know that such person's license or privilege of operating such motor vehicle in this state or privilege of obtaining a license to operate such motor vehicle issued by the commissioner is suspended, revoked or otherwise withdrawn by the commissioner.

(b) Aggravated unlicensed operation of a motor vehicle in the third degree is a misdemeanor. When a person is convicted of this offense, the sentence of the court must be: (i) a fine of not less than two hundred dollars nor more than five hundred dollars; or (ii) a term of imprisonment of not more than thirty days; or (iii) both such fine and imprisonment.

(c) When a person is convicted of this offense with respect to the operation of a motor vehicle with a gross vehicle weight rating of more than eighteen thousand pounds, the sentence of the court must be: (i) a fine of not less than five hundred dollars nor more than fifteen hundred dollars; or (ii) a term of imprisonment of not more than thirty days; or (iii) both such fine and imprisonment.

2. Aggravated unlicensed operation of a motor vehicle in the second degree. (a) A person is guilty of the offense of aggravated unlicensed operation of a motor vehicle in the second degree when such person commits the offense of aggravated unlicensed operation of a motor vehicle in the third degree as defined in subdivision one of this section; and

(i) has previously been convicted of an offense that consists of or includes the elements comprising the offense committed within the immediately preceding eighteen months; or

(ii) the suspension or revocation is based upon a refusal to submit to a chemical test pursuant to section eleven hundred ninety-four of this chapter, a finding of driving after having consumed alcohol in violation of section eleven hundred ninety-two-a of this chapter or upon a conviction for a violation of any of the provisions of section eleven hundred ninety-two of this chapter; or

(iii) the suspension was a mandatory suspension pending prosecution of a charge of a violation of section eleven hundred ninety-two of this chapter ordered pursuant to paragraph (e) of subdivision two of section eleven hundred ninety-three of this chapter or other similar statute; or

(iv) such person has in effect three or more suspensions, imposed on at least three separate dates, for failure to answer, appear or pay a fine, pursuant to subdivision three of section two hundred twenty-six or subdivision four-a of section five hundred ten of this chapter.

(b) Aggravated unlicensed operation of a motor vehicle in the second degree is a misdemeanor.

When a person is convicted of this crime under subparagraph (i) of paragraph (a) of this subdivision, the sentence of the court must be: (i) a fine of not less than five hundred dollars; and (ii) a term of imprisonment not to exceed one hundred eighty days; or (iii) where appropriate a sentence of probation as provided in subdivision six of this section; or (iv) a term of imprisonment as a condition of a sentence of probation as provided in the penal law and consistent with this section. When a person is convicted of this crime under subparagraph (ii), (iii) or (iv) of paragraph (a) of this subdivision, the sentence of the court must be: (i) a fine of not less than five hundred dollars nor more than one thousand dollars; and (ii) a term of imprisonment of not less than seven days nor more than one hundred eighty days, or (iii) where appropriate a sentence of probation as provided in subdivision six of this section; or (iv) a term of imprisonment as a condition of a sentence of probation as provided in the penal law and consistent with this section.

3. Aggravated unlicensed operation of a motor vehicle in the first degree. (a) A person is guilty of the offense of aggravated unlicensed operation of a motor vehicle in the first degree when such person: (i) commits the offense of aggravated unlicensed operation of a motor vehicle in the second degree as provided in subparagraph (ii), (iii) or (iv) of paragraph (a) of subdivision two of this section and is operating a motor vehicle while under the influence of alcohol or a drug in violation of subdivision one, two, three, four or five of section eleven hundred ninety-two of this chapter; or

(ii) commits the offense of aggravated unlicensed operation of a motor vehicle in the third degree as defined in subdivision one of this section; and is operating a motor vehicle while such person has in effect ten or more suspensions, imposed on at least ten separate dates for failure to answer, appear or pay a fine, pursuant to subdivision three of section two hundred twenty-six of this chapter or subdivision four-a of section five hundred ten of this article.

(b) Aggravated unlicensed operation of a motor vehicle in the first degree is a class E felony. When a person is convicted of this crime, the sentence of the court must be: (i) a fine in an amount not less than five hundred dollars nor more than five thousand dollars; and (ii) a term of imprisonment as provided in the penal law, or (iii) where appropriate and a term of imprisonment is not required by the penal law, a sentence of probation as provided in subdivision six of this section, or (iv) a term of imprisonment as a condition of a sentence of probation as provided in the penal law.

4. Defense. In any prosecution under this section or section five hundred eleven-a of this chapter, it is a defense that the person operating the motor vehicle has at the time of the offense

a license issued by a foreign country, state, territory or federal district, which license is valid for operation in this state in accordance with the provisions of section two hundred fifty of this chapter.

5. Limitation on pleas. Where an accusatory instrument charges a violation of this section, any plea of guilty entered in satisfaction of such charge must include at least a plea of guilty of one of the offenses defined by this section and no other disposition by plea of guilty to any other charge in satisfaction of such charge shall be authorized; provided, however, that if the district attorney upon reviewing the available evidence determines that the charge of a violation of this section is not warranted, he may set forth upon the record the basis for such determination and consent to a disposition by plea of guilty to another charge in satisfaction of such charge, and the court may accept such plea.

6. Sentence of probation. In any case where a sentence of probation is authorized by this section, the court may in its discretion impose such sentence, provided however, if the court is of the opinion that a program of alcohol or drug treatment may be effective in assisting in prevention of future offenses of a similar nature upon imposing such sentence, the court shall require as a condition of the sentence that the defendant participate in such a program.

7. Exceptions. When a person is convicted of a violation of subdivision one of two of this section, and the suspension was issued pursuant to subdivision four-e of section five hundred ten of this article due to a support arrears, the mandatory penalties set forth in subdivision one or two of this section shall not be applicable if, on or before the return date or subsequent adjourned date, such person presents proof that such support arrears have been satisfied as shown by certified check, notice issued by the court ordering the suspension, or notice from a support collection unit. The sentencing court shall take the satisfaction of arrears into account when imposing a sentence for any such conviction.

Amended by L. 1995, Ch. 81, § 212, adding subd. 7, eff. Oct. 1, 1995; L. 1996, Ch. 196, § 6, amending subd. (2)(a)(ii); L. 1996, Ch. 309, § 76, extending to Jan. 31, 2002, expiration date of amendments to subd. 511(2), pursuant to L. 1981, Ch. 569, § 9, eff. Jul. 13, 1996; L. 1996, Ch. 309, § 78, extending to Oct. 1, 1997, expiration of amendments to subd. 516-b(d), pursuant to L. 1993, Ch. 533, § 4, eff. Jul. 13, 1996; L. 2004, Ch. 673, § 1, eff. Nov. 1, 2005, amending subd. 3(a)(ii).

ANNOTATIONS

Accusatory instrument.—A charge of § 511 can be commenced by a simplified traffic information as defined in Criminal Procedure Law § 100.10(2a). People v. Howell, 158 Misc. 2d 653, 601 N.Y.S.2d 778 (Crim. Ct. Kings Co. 1993).

—An accusatory instrument containing an allegation that the arresting officer conducted a computer check of the records of the New York State Department of Motor Vehicles, revealing that the defendant's driver's license was suspended was hearsay and insufficient to allege that the defendant was operating a motor vehicle while his license was suspended or revoked.

People v Pierre, 157 Misc. 2d 812, 599 N.Y.S.2d 412 (Crim. Ct. N.Y. Co. 1993).

Attempt.—Attempted unlicensed operation of a vehicle is not a crime. People v. Prescott, 95 N.Y.2d 655, 722 N.Y.S.2d 778, 745 N.E.2d 1000 (2001).

Constitutionality—VTL § 511 is not an ex post facto law even though it provides for an enhanced penalty as a result of a preexisting condition, a prior revocation of a driver's license. The law gives fair warning of the increased penalty for an alcohol related driving offense during the continued revocation of an individual's driver's license. People v. Guszack, 237 A.D.2d 715, 654 N.Y.S.2d 845 (3d Dept. 1997).

—Court rejected defendant's argument that section 511(3) is unconstitutionally vague because it fails to give notice that it continues the suspension until the termination of suspension fee has been paid. People v. Cleveland, 238 A.D.2d 897, 660 N.Y.S.2d 771 (4th Dept. 1997).

Elements.—In order to establish a violation of § 511, the People need only show that the requisite number of suspensions are in effect and defendant knew or had reason to know that the suspensions existed. People v. Garcia, 163 Misc. 2d 862, 622 N.Y.S.2d 1019 (Crim. Ct. Bronx Co. 1995).

—To satisfy the key element of intent, the People must establish, prima facie, that the defendant received notice of the suspension or revocation. People v. Parson, 143 Misc. 2d 592, 541 N.Y.S.2d 321 (City Ct. Monroe Co. 1989).

Lesser included offense.—Unlicensed operation of a motor vehicle, a violation of VTL § 509(1), is not a lesser included offense of aggravated unlicensed operation in the first degree. People v. Pacer, — A.D.3d —, 796 N.Y.S.2d 787 (4th Dept. 2005).

Predicate felony for felony assault.—Aggravated unlicensed operation of a motor vehicle in the first degree, a class E felony, may not be used for conviction of first degree felony assault under PL § 120.10(4). The legislature did not intend to increase the penalties for offenses under this section beyond an E felony, and such prosecutions would create an anomaly in grading vehicular offenses. People v. Belizaire, 170 Misc. 2d 653, 655 N.Y.S.2d 225 (Sup. Ct. Kings Co. 1996)

Purpose.—Section 511 is a recidivist statute, not unlike the laws which enhance punishment for predicate felons. People v. Cintron, 163 Misc. 2d 881, 622 N.Y.S.2d 662 (Sup. Ct. Kings Co. 1995).

Repugnant verdict.—Verdict was repugnant where defendant was charged with driving while impaired, driving while intoxicated, and aggravated unlicensed operation of a motor vehicle, but was only found guilty of a violation of VTL § 511, aggravated unlicensed operation. Since an element of aggravated unlicensed operation of a motor vehicle is operation of a motor vehicle while under the influence of drugs or alcohol, conviction for VTL § 511 cannot stand. People v. Miner, 261 A.D.2d 420, 689 N.Y.S.2d 233 (2d Dept. 1999).

Sentencing.—Where defendant's driving while under the influence was element of charge of first degree aggravated unlicensed operation, and both offenses to which defendant pleaded guilty occurred at the same time and place, and both served as the basis of revocation of defendant's license, concurrent sentences were mandated. People v. De Maio, 304 A.D.2d 988, 760 N.Y.S.2d 558 (3d Dept. 2003).

—Sentence of 90 days on conviction fir § 511(1)(b) was not authorized by law, aggravated unlicensed operation of a motor vehicle in the third degree is an unclassified misdemeanor for which the sentence must be a fine of not less than $200 nor more than $500, with a maximum term of imprisonment of not more than 30 days. People v. Edenholm, 9 A.D.3d 892, 779 N.Y.S.2d 688 (4th Dept. 2004).

—Court properly sentenced defendant as a persistent felony offender based on his prior convictions for driving while intoxicated. The court imposed an indeterminate term of 15 years to life upon his present conviction for DWI as a felony and aggravated unlicensed operation; however, in the interests of justice, the appellate court vacated the sentence and re-sentenced defendant as a second felony offender to an indeterminate term of two to four years. People v. Donhauser, 255 A.D.2d 933, 683 N.Y.S.2d 357, *reargument granted and order amended,* 1998 N.Y. App. Div. LEXIS 14474 (4th Dept. Dec. 31, 1998).

Sufficiency of plea.—Defendant successfully moved to vacate his plea to a violation of § 511 where, during the allocution, he stated that he had a valid Pennsylvania drivers license and that he thought his New York driving privileges had been restored at the time of the incident; defendant neither knew or had reason to know that his driving privileges had been suspended. People v. Ham, 265 A.D.2d 674, 697 N.Y.S.2d 359 (3d Dept. 1999).

—Defendant's allocution, in which he stated his belief that he had a valid Pennsylvania license at the time of the offense, may have negated an essential element of aggravated unlicensed operation, which requires that defendant knew or had reason to know that his driver's license was suspended or revoked; new appellate counsel assigned. People v. Ham, 256 A.D.2d 727, 682 N.Y.S.2d 259 (3d Dept. 1998).

—Defendant unsuccessfully challenged validity of plea to VTL §§ 1192 and 511, contending that he was suffering from post-acute withdrawal syndrome. During allocution, court inquired as to defendant's mental state, and defendant responded that although he had a drinking problem, he was not under the influence of drugs or alcohol or suffering from any mental disease or defect. Court found defendant's plea knowing and voluntary. People v. Miller, 254 A.D.2d 627, 681 N.Y.S.2d 367 (3d Dept. 1998).

—Since defendant's allocution negated an element of the crime (intoxication), court was required to inquire further before accepting the plea. People v. Root, 267 N.Y.S.2d 227, 701 N.Y.S.2d 227 (4th Dept. 1999).

—Defendant's plea, in which he admitted that he was operating a motor vehicle while intoxicated and knowing that his license was suspended or revoked, was sufficient to support the charges of driving while intoxicated and aggravated unlicensed operation of a motor vehicle. People v. Francis, 254 A.D.2d 779, 678 N.Y.S.2d 758 (4th Dept. 1998).

Sufficient evidence.—Defendant's conviction of aggravated unlicensed operation of a motor vehicle in the first degree which requires proof that defendant operated a vehicle with 10 or more license suspensions in effect was reduced where the abstract of the defendant's driving record was not properly certified as required and no other evidence of the suspensions was contained in the record. People v. Sikorski, 280 A.D.2d 414, 721 N.Y.S.2d 48 (1st Dept. 2001).

—Evidence that defendant was driving with a revoked learner's permit supported a conviction under this section. People v. Buckmon, 293 A.D.2d 623, 742 N.Y.S.2d 69 (2d Dept. 2002).

—Where the Chief Clerk of the Schenectady City Court testified that defendant had signed an acknowledgment of the order of suspension or revocation, and defendant identified his signature on the order and testified that he believed that a stay on his prior conviction permitted him to drive, the evidence permitted a fact-finder to conclude beyond a reasonable doubt that defendant knew that his license was revoked. People v. Crandall, 199 A.D.2d 867, 606 N.Y.S.2d 357 (3d Dept. 1993).

—Submission of affidavit pursuant to VTL § 214 to establish that defendant knew or had reason to know that his New York driving privilege had been revoked, a required element of aggravated unlicensed operation of a motor vehicle, without establishing at trial that non-appearing witness was unavailable to testify or that defendant previously had opportunity to cross-examine her, violated defendant's right to confrontation; conviction reversed. People v. Pacer, — A.D.3d —, 796 N.Y.S.2d 787 (4th Dept. 2005).

—Evidence is legally sufficient to support conviction of aggravated unlicensed operation of a motor vehicle in the first degree and driving while ability impaired because defendant did "operate" the vehicle, grabbing steering wheel and controlling direction of vehicle fall within definition of operation of a motor vehicle, which is broad in scope. People v. Crombleholme, 8 A.D.3d 1068, 778 N.Y.S.2d 256 (4th Dept. 2004).

—Defendant's operation of a lawn tractor on a public highway in early morning hours, en route from a bar to his home, while his license to operate a motor vehicle was revoked and while he was intoxicated, supported a conviction under this section. People v. Canute, 8 A.D.3d 1125, 778 N.Y.S.2d 247 (4th Dept. 2004).

—Defendant's conviction of both driving while ability impaired and aggravated unlicensed operation in the first degree did not violate the constitutional prohibition against double jeopardy; the commission of driving while ability is impaired is an element of aggravated unlicensed operation in the first degree and, therefore, does not require proof of an additional fact which

aggravated unlicensed operation in the first degree does not. People v. Kahn, 291 A.D.2d 898, 737 N.Y.S.2d 738 (4th Dept. 2002).

—Verdict finding defendant guilty of driving while ability impaired and aggravated unlicensed operation was not against the weight of the evidence where record contained evidence of defendant's poor driving, signs of intoxication, inability to perform sobriety test, and refusal to consent to chemical test. People v. Gelster, 256 A.D.2d 1133, 684 N.Y.S.2d 712 (4th Dept. 1999).

—"The elements of aggravated unlicensed operation of a motor vehicle in the second degree require that defendant operated a vehicle while knowing or having reason to know that his license was 'suspended, revoked or otherwise withdrawn.' " People v. Murray, 192 Misc. 2d 336, 746 N.Y.S.2d 226 (Sup. Ct. App. T. 2002).

—VTL § 214 creates a "statutory presumption that the notice of suspension or revocation of the drivers license was mailed to the defendant if an affidavit of an employee of the Department of Motor Vehicles sets forth the procedure for issuance and mailing of the notice and if a copy of the notice and electronically generated record of entry of suspension or revocation are produced in court." Because of defendant's failure to notify the Department of his change of residence, as required by VTL § 505(5), he is estopped from making a claim of improper service and fails to rebut the presumption of proper notice. People v. Kirksey, 186 Misc. 2d 514, 718 N.Y.S.2d 583 (Ithaca City Ct. 2000).

—Defendant's receipt of several tickets advising him that failure to respond would result in license revocation was sufficient to constitute prima facie non-hearsay evidence that he had reason to know that his license had been suspended. People v. Santiago, 168 Misc. 2d 883, 645 N.Y.S.2d 746 (N.Y.C. Crim. Ct. 1996).

§ 511-a. Facilitating aggravated unlicensed operation of a motor vehicle.

1. A person is guilty of the offense of facilitating aggravated unlicensed operation of a motor vehicle in the third degree when such person consents to the operation upon a public highway of a motor vehicle registered in such person's name knowing or having reason to know that the operator of such vehicle is a person whose license or privilege of operating such motor vehicle in this state or privilege of obtaining a license issued to operate such motor vehicle by the commissioner is suspended, revoked or otherwise withdrawn by the commissioner and the vehicle is operated upon a public highway by such person.

2. Facilitating aggravated unlicensed operation of a motor vehicle in the third degree is a traffic infraction. When a person is convicted thereof the sentence of the court must be: (i) a fine of not less than two hundred dollars nor more than five hundred dollars or (ii) a term of imprisonment of not more than fifteen days, or (iii) both.

3. A person is guilty of facilitating aggravated unlicensed operation of a motor vehicle in the second degree when such person:

(a) commits the offense of facilitating aggravated unlicensed operation of a motor vehicle in the third degree as defined in subdivision one of this section after having been convicted of such offense within the preceding eighteen months; or

(b) consents to the operation upon a public highway of a motor vehicle registered in such person's name knowing or having reason to know that the operator of such vehicle is a person who has in effect three or more suspensions, imposed on at least three separate dates, for failure to answer, appear or pay a fine, pursuant to subdivision three of section two hundred twenty-six or subdivision four-a of section five hundred ten of this chapter; or

(c) commits the crime of facilitating aggravated unlicensed operation of a motor vehicle in the third degree after having been convicted of such an offense two or more times within the preceding five years.

For purposes of this subdivision, "motor vehicle" shall mean any vehicle for hire, including a taxicab, livery, as defined in section one hundred twenty-one-e of this chapter, coach, limousine, van or wheelchair accessible van, tow truck, bus or commercial motor vehicle as defined section five hundred nine-a of this chapter.

Facilitating aggravated unlicensed operation of a motor vehicle in the second degree is a misdemeanor. When a person is convicted of this crime pursuant to paragraphs (a) or (b) of this subdivision, the sentence of the court must be: (i) a fine of not less than five hundred dollars, nor more than seven hundred fifty dollars; or (ii) a term of imprisonment not to exceed sixty days; or (iii) both a fine and imprisonment; or (iv) where appropriate, a sentence of probation; or (v) a term of imprisonment as a condition of a sentence of probation as provided in the penal law. When a person is convicted of this crime pursuant to paragraph (c) of this subdivision, the sentence of the court must be: (i) a fine of not less than five hundred, nor more than one thousand dollars; or (ii) a term of imprisonment not to exceed one hundred eighty days; or (iii) both a fine and imprisonment; or (iv) where appropriate, a sentence of probation; or (v) a term of imprisonment as a condition of probation as provided in the penal law.

4. A person is guilty of facilitating aggravated unlicensed operation of a motor vehicle in the first degree when such person consents to the operation upon a public highway of a motor vehicle registered in such person's name knowing or having reason to know that the operator of such vehicle is a person who has in effect ten or more suspensions, imposed on at least ten separate dates, for failure to answer, appear or pay a fine, pursuant to subdivision three of section two hundred twenty-six or subdivision four-a of section five hundred ten of this chapter.

For purposes of this subdivision, "motor vehicle" shall mean any vehicle for hire, including a taxicab, livery, as defined in section one hundred twenty-one-e of this chapter, coach, limousine, van or wheelchair accessible van, tow truck, bus or commercial motor vehicle as defined in section five hundred nine-a of this chapter.

Facilitating aggravated unlicensed operation of

a motor vehicle in the first degree is a class E felony. When a person is convicted of this crime, the sentence of the court must be: (i) a fine in an amount not less than one thousand dollars nor more than five thousand dollars; and (ii) a term of imprisonment as provided in the penal law; or (iii) where appropriate, a sentence of probation; or (iv) a term of imprisonment as a condition of a sentence of probation as provided in the penal law.

5. Upon a conviction of a violation of subdivision three or four of this section the commissioner shall revoke the registration of the motor vehicle for which the defendant's consent is given and shall only be restored pursuant to the provisions of subdivision five of section five hundred ten of this article. If such defendant is a corporation, partnership, association or other group, none of its officers, principals, directors or stockholders owning more than ten percent of the outstanding stock of the corporation shall be eligible to register the motor vehicle.

§ 511-b. Seizure and redemption of unlawfully operated vehicles.

1. Upon making an arrest or upon issuing a summons or an appearance ticket for the crime of aggravated unlicensed operation of a motor vehicle in the first or second degree committed in his presence, an officer shall remove or arrange for the removal of the vehicle to a garage, automobile pound, or other place of safety where it shall remain impounded, subject to the provisions of this section if: (a) the operator is the registered owner of the vehicle or the vehicle is not properly registered; or (b) proof of financial security is not produced; or (c) where a person other than the operator is the registered owner and, such person or another properly licensed and authorized to possess and operate the vehicle is not present. The vehicle shall be entered into the New York statewide police information network as an impounded vehicle and the impounding police department shall promptly notify the owner and the local authority that the vehicle has been impounded.

2. A motor vehicle so impounded shall be in the custody of the local authority and shall not be released unless:

(a) The person who redeems it has furnished satisfactory evidence of registration and financial security;

(b) Payment has been made for the reasonable costs of removal and storage of the motor vehicle. The registered owner of the vehicle shall be responsible for such payment provided, however, that if he was not the operator at the time of the offense he shall have a cause of action against such operator to recover such costs. Payment prior to release of the vehicle shall not be required in cases where the impounded vehicle was stolen or was rented or leased pursuant to a written agreement for a period of thirty days or less, however the operator of such a vehicle shall be liable for the costs of removal and storage of the vehicle to any entity rendering such service.

(c) Where the motor vehicle was operated by a person who at the time of the offense was the owner thereof, (i) satisfactory evidence that the registered owner or other person seeking to redeem the vehicle has a license or privilege to operate a motor vehicle in this state, and (ii) (a) satisfactory evidence that the criminal action founded upon the charge of aggravated unlicensed operation of a motor vehicle has been terminated and that any fine imposed as a result of a conviction thereon has been paid, or (b) a certificate issued by the court in which the criminal action was commenced ordering release of the vehicle prior to the judgment or compliance therewith in the interest of justice, or (c) a certificate issued by the district attorney or other officer authorized to prosecute such charge waiving the requirement that the vehicle be held as security for appearance before and compliance with the judgment of the court.

3. When a vehicle seized and impounded pursuant to this section has been in the custody of the local authority for thirty days, such authority shall make inquiry in the manner prescribed by the commissioner as to the name and address of the owner and any lienholder and upon receipt of such information shall notify the owner and the lienholder, if any, at his last known address by certified mail, return receipt requested, that if the vehicle is not retrieved pursuant to subdivision two of this section within thirty days from the date the notice is given, it will be forfeited. If the vehicle was registered in New York the last known address shall be that address on file with the commissioner. If the vehicle was registered out-of-state or never registered, notification shall be made in the manner prescribed by the commissioner.

4. A motor vehicle that has been seized and not retrieved pursuant to the foregoing provisions of this section shall be forfeited to the local authority upon expiration of the period of the notice set forth in subdivision three of this section provided, however, in computing such period, the period of time during which a criminal prosecution is or was pending against the owner for a violation of this section shall be excluded. A proceeding to decree such forfeiture and to recover towing and storage costs, if any, to the extent such costs exceed the fair market value of the vehicle may be brought by the local authority in the court in which the criminal action for aggravated unlicensed operation of a motor vehicle was commenced by petition for an order decreeing forfeiture of the motor vehicle accompanied by an affidavit attesting to facts showing that forfeiture is warranted. If the identity and address of the owner and/or lienholder is known

to the local authority, ten days notice shall be given to such party, who shall have an opportunity to appear and be heard prior to entry of an order decreeing forfeiture. Where the court is satisfied that forfeiture of a motor vehicle is warranted in accordance with this section, it shall enter an order decreeing forfeiture of such vehicle. provided, however, that the court at any time prior to entry of such an order may authorize release of the vehicle in accordance with subdivision two of this section upon a showing of good cause for failure to retrieve same prior to commencement of the proceeding to decree forfeiture, but if the court orders release of the motor vehicle as herein provided and the vehicle is not redeemed within ten days from the date of such order, the vehicle shall be deemed to have been abandoned and the court upon application of the local authority must enter an order decreeing its forfeiture.

5. A motor vehicle forfeited in accordance with the provisions of this section shall be and become the property of the local authority, subject however to any lien that was recorded prior to the seizure.

6. For the purposes of this section, the term "local authority" means the municipality in which the motor vehicle was seized; except that if the motor vehicle was seized on property of the New York state thruway authority or property under the jurisdiction of the office of parks, recreation and historic preservation, the department of transportation, or a public authority or commission, the term "local authority" means such authority, office, department, or commission. A county may provide by local law that the county may act as the agent for a local authority under this section.

7. When a vehicle has been seized and impounded pursuant to this section, the local authority or any person having custody of the vehicle shall make the vehicle available or grant access to it to any owner or any person designated or authorized by such owner for the purpose of (i) taking possession of any personal property found within the vehicle and (ii) obtaining proof of registration, financial security, title or documentation in support thereof.

ANNOTATION

Generally—Under § 511-b, police are required to impound a car where the driver is arrested for aggravated unlicensed operation of a motor vehicle in the second degree pursuant to § 511(2), however, where the driver is arrested for aggravated unlicensed operation of a motor vehicle in the third degree, there is no concomitant statutory impoundment obligation. People v. Miles, 3 Misc. 3d 566 774 N.Y.S.2d 647 (Rochester City Ct. 2003).

§ 511-c. Seizure and forfeiture of vehicles used in the unlicensed operation of a motor vehicle under certain circumstances.

1. For purposes of this section:

(a) The term "owner" shall mean an owner as

defined in section one hundred twenty-eight and in subdivision three of section three hundred eighty-eight of this chapter.

(b) The term "security interest" shall mean a security interest as defined in subdivision (k) of section two thousand one hundred one of this chapter.

(c) The term "termination of the criminal proceeding" shall mean the earliest of (i) thirty-one days following the imposition of sentence; or (ii) the date of acquittal of a person arrested for an offense; or (iii) where leave to file new charges or to resubmit the case to a new grand jury is required and has not been granted, thirty-one days following the dismissal of the last accusatory instrument filed in the case, or, if applicable, upon expiration of the time granted by the court or permitted by statute for filing new charges or resubmitting the case to a new grand jury; or (iv) where leave to file new charges or to resubmit the case to a new grand jury is not required, thirty-one days following the dismissal of the last accusatory instrument filed in the case, or, if applicable, upon expiration of the time granted by the court or permitted by statute for filing new charges or resubmitting the case to a new grand jury; or (v) six months from the issuance of an "adjournment in contemplation of dismissal" order pursuant to section 170.55 of the criminal procedure law, where the case is not restored to the court's calendar within the applicable six-month period; or (vi) the date when, prior to the filing of an accusatory instrument against a person arrested for an offense, the prosecuting authority elects not to prosecute such person.

2. Any motor vehicle which has been or is being used in violation of paragraph (a) of subdivision three of section five hundred eleven of this article may be seized by any peace officer, acting pursuant to his or her special duties, or police officer, and forfeited as hereinafter provided in this section.

3. A vehicle may be seized upon service of a notice of violation upon the owner or operator of a vehicle. The seized motor vehicle shall be delivered by the officer having made the seizure to the custody of the district attorney of the county wherein the seizure was made, except that in the cities of New York, Yonkers, Rochester and Buffalo the seized motor vehicle shall be delivered to the custody of the police department of such cities and such motor vehicle seized by a member or members of the state police shall be delivered to the custody of the superintendent of state police, together with a report of all the facts and circumstances of the seizure. Within one business day after the seizure, notice of such violation and a copy of the notice of violation shall be mailed to the owner of such vehicle at the address for such owner set forth in the records maintained by the department of motor vehicles or, for vehicles not registered in New York state, such equivalent record in such state of registration.

4. (a) The attorney general in seizures by members of the state police, or the district attorney of the county wherein the seizure is made, if elsewhere than in the cities of New York, Yonkers, Rochester or Buffalo, or where the seizure is made in such cities, the corporation counsel of the city shall inquire into the facts of the seizure so reported to him or her. If it appears that there is a basis for the commencement and prosecution of a forfeiture proceeding pursuant to this section, any such forfeiture proceeding shall be commenced in supreme court not later than twenty days after the date of receipt of a written demand by a person claiming ownership of the motor vehicle accompanied by the documentation required to be presented upon release of the vehicle pursuant to subparagraphs (i), (ii), and (iv) of paragraph (a) of subdivision five of this section.

(b) Where forfeiture proceedings are commenced and prosecuted pursuant to this section, the motor vehicle which is the subject of such proceedings shall remain in the custody of such district attorney, police department or superintendent of state police, as applicable, pending the final determination of such proceedings.

(c) To the extent applicable, the procedures of article thirteen-a of the civil practice law and rules shall govern proceedings and actions under this section.

5. A motor vehicle seized pursuant to this section shall be released when:

(a) (i) Such attorney general, district attorney or corporation counsel has made a determination not to institute forfeiture proceedings pursuant to this section or the time period within which a forfeiture proceeding could have been commenced pursuant to this section has elapsed and no such forfeiture proceeding was commenced or the criminal proceeding has been terminated in favor of the accused, as defined in subdivision three of section 160.50 of the criminal procedure law; and

(ii) The person seeking to claim the motor vehicle has furnished satisfactory evidence of registration and financial security and, if the person was the operator of the vehicle at the time of the violation of paragraph (a) of subdivision three of section five hundred eleven of this article, satisfactory evidence of payment of any fines or penalties imposed in connection therewith; and

(iii) Payment has been made for the reasonable costs of removal and storage of the motor vehicle. The owner of the motor vehicle shall be responsible for such payment provided, however, that if he or she was not the operator at the time of the offense, such person shall have a cause of action against such operator to recover such costs. Payment prior to release of the motor vehicle shall not be required in cases where the seized motor vehicle was stolen or rented or leased pursuant to a written agreement for a period of thirty days or less, however the operator of such a motor vehicle shall be liable for the costs of removal and storage of the motor vehicle to any entity rendering such service; and

(iv) If the motor vehicle is held as evidence, the person seeking to claim the motor vehicle has presented a release from the prosecuting authority providing that the motor vehicle is not needed as evidence.

(b)　(i) Pending completion of forfeiture proceedings which have been commenced, the person seeking to claim the motor vehicle has posted a bond in a form satisfactory to such attorney general, district attorney or corporation counsel in an amount that shall not exceed an amount sufficient to cover the maximum fines or civil penalties which may be imposed for the violation underlying the seizure and all reasonable costs for removal and storage of such vehicle; and

(ii) The persons seeking to claim the motor vehicle has furnished satisfactory evidence of registration and financial security.

6. Where a demand for the return of a motor vehicle is not made within ninety days after the termination of the criminal proceeding founded upon the charge of aggravated unlicensed operation of a motor vehicle in the first degree, such motor vehicle shall be deemed to be abandoned. Such vehicle shall be disposed of by the county, cities of New York, Yonkers, Rochester or buffalo or the state, as applicable, in accordance with section twelve hundred twenty-four of this chapter or as otherwise provided by law.

7. Notice of the institution of the forfeiture proceeding shall be served:

(a) By personal service pursuant to the civil practice law and rules upon all owners of the seized motor vehicle listed in the records maintained by the department, or for vehicles not registered in New York state, in the records maintained by the state of registration; and

(b) By first class mail upon all individuals who have notified such attorney general, district attorney or corporation counsel that they are an owner of the vehicle and upon all persons holding a security interest in such motor vehicle which security interest has been filed with the department pursuant to the provisions of title ten of this chapter, at the address set forth in the records of such department, or for motor vehicles not registered in New York state, all persons holding a security interest in such motor vehicle which security interest has been filed with such state of registration, at the address provided by such state of registration.

8. Any owner who receives notice of the institution of a forfeiture action who claims an interest in the motor vehicle subject to forfeiture shall assert a claim for the recovery of the motor vehicle or satisfaction of the owner's interest in such motor vehicle by intervening in the forfeiture action in accordance with subdivision (a) of section one thousand twelve of the civil practice law and rules. Any person with a security interest in such vehicle who receives notice of the institution of the forfeiture action shall assert a claim for the satisfaction of such person's security interest in such vehicle by intervening in the forfeiture action in accordance with subdivision (a) of section one thousand twelve of the civil practice law and rules. If the action relates to a vehicle in which a person holding a security interest has intervened pursuant to this subdivision, the burden shall be upon the designated official to prove by clear and convincing evidence that such intervenor knew that such vehicle was or would be used for the commission of a violation of subparagraph (ii) of paragraph (a) of subdivision three of section five hundred eleven of the vehicle and traffic law and either (a) knowingly and unlawfully benefitted from such conduct or (b) voluntarily agreed to the use of the vehicle for the commission of such violation by consent freely given. For purposes of this subdivision, such intervenor knowingly and unlawfully benefited from the commission of such violation when he or she derived in exchange for permitting the use of such vehicle by a person or persons committing such specified violation a substantial benefit that would otherwise not have accrued as a result of the lawful use of such vehicle. "Benefit" means benefit as defined in subdivision seventeen of section 10.00 of the penal law.

9. No motor vehicle shall be forfeited under this section to the extent of the interest of a person who claims an interest in the motor vehicle, where such person pleads and proves that:

(a) The use of such motor vehicle for the conduct that was the basis for a seizure occurred without the knowledge of such person, or if such person had knowledge of such use, without the consent of such person, and that such person did not knowingly obtain such interest in the motor vehicle in order to avoid the forfeiture of such vehicle; or

(b) The conduct that was the basis for such seizure was committed by any person other than such person claiming an interest in the motor vehicle, while such motor vehicle was unlawfully in the possession of a person who acquired possession thereof in violation of the criminal laws of the united states or any state.

10. The court in which a forfeiture action is pending may dismiss said action in the interests of justice upon its own motion or upon an application as provided for herein.

(a) At any time during the pendency of a forfeiture action, the designated official who instituted the action, or a defendant may apply for an order dismissing the complaint and terminating the forfeiture action in the interest of justice.

(b) Such application for the relief provided in paragraph (a) of this subdivision must be made in writing and upon notice to all parties. The court may, in its discretion, direct that notice be given to any other person having an interest in the property.

(c) An application for the relief provided for in paragraph (a) of this subdivision must be brought exclusively in the superior court in which the forfeiture action is pending.

(d) The court may grant the relief provided in paragraph (a) of this subdivision if it finds that such relief is warranted by the existence of some compelling factor, consideration or circumstance demonstrating that forfeiture of the property or any part thereof, would not serve the ends of justice. among the factors, considerations and circumstances the court may consider, among others, are:

(i) the seriousness and circumstances of the crime to which the property is connected relative to the impact of forfeiture of property upon the person who committed the crime; or

(ii) the adverse impact of a forfeiture of property upon innocent persons.

(e) The court must issue a written decision stating the basis for an order issued pursuant to this subdivision.

11. The district attorney, police department or superintendent of state police having custody of the seized motor vehicle, after such judicial determination of forfeiture, shall, by a public notice of at least twenty days, sell such forfeited motor vehicle at public sale. The net proceeds of any such sale, after deduction of the lawful expenses incurred, shall be paid into the general fund of the county wherein the seizure was made, provided, however, that the net proceeds of the sale of a motor vehicle seized in the cities of New York, Yonkers, Rochester and Buffalo shall be paid into the respective general funds of such cities, and provided further that the net proceeds of the sale of a motor vehicle seized by the state police shall be paid into the state police seized assets account.

12. In any action commenced pursuant to this section, where the court awards a sum of money to one or more persons in satisfaction of such person's or persons' interest or interests in the forfeited motor vehicle, the total amount awarded to satisfy such interest or interests shall not exceed the amount of the net proceeds of the sale of the forfeited motor vehicle, after deduction of the lawful expenses incurred by the county, cities of New York, Yonkers, Rochester or Buffalo or the state, as applicable, and storage of the motor vehicle between the time of seizure and the date of sale.

13. At any time within two years after the seizure, any person claiming an interest in a motor vehicle which has been forfeited pursuant to this section who was not sent notice of the commencement of the forfeiture action pursuant to subdivision seven of this section, or who did not otherwise receive actual notice of the forfeiture action, may assert in an action commenced before the justice of the supreme court before whom the forfeiture action was held such claim as could have been asserted in the forfeiture action pursuant to this section. The court may grant the relief sought upon such terms and conditions as it deems reasonable and just if the person claiming an interest in the motor vehicle establishes that he or she was not sent notice of the commencement of the forfeiture action and was without actual knowledge of the forfeiture action, and establishes either of the affirmative defenses set forth in subdivision nine of this section.

14. No action under this section for wrongful seizure shall be instituted unless such action is commenced within two years after the time when the motor vehicle was seized.

§ 511-d. Aggravated failure to answer appearance tickets or pay fines imposed.

1. A person is guilty of the offense of aggravated failure to answer appearance tickets or pay fines imposed when such person has in effect twenty or more suspensions, imposed on at least twenty separate dates, for failure to answer, appear or pay a fine pursuant to subdivision three of section two hundred twenty-six or subdivision four-a of section five hundred ten of this chapter.

2. A person may be prosecuted for a violation of this section in any court of competent jurisdiction in any county: (a) in which more than ten tickets which resulted in suspension for failures to answer, appear or pay fines were issued, or (b) in which the twentieth or any subsequent ticket which resulted in a suspension for failure to answer, appear or pay a fine was issued. The provisions of this subdivision shall not apply to any suspension which has been terminated prior to the defendant's being charged with a violation of this section.

3. Aggravated failure to answer appearance tickets or pay fines imposed is a misdemeanor. When a person is convicted of this crime, the sentence of the court must be: (i) a fine of not less than five hundred dollars; or (ii) a term of imprisonment of not more than one hundred eighty days; or (iii) both such fine and imprisonment.

ANNOTATIONS

Constitutionality.—Statute does not violate double jeopardy principles, nor does it constitute an ex post facto law. People v. Brignoni, 182 Misc. 2d 779, 701 N.Y.S.2d 253 (Crim. Ct. N.Y. Co. 1999).

—Section 511-d is not unconstitutional. People v. Griffin, 162 Misc. 2d 764, 617 N.Y.S.2d 440 (Crim. Ct. Kings Co. 1994).

§ 512. Operation while registration or privilege is suspended or revoked.

Any person who operates any motor vehicle upon a public highway while the certificate of registration of such motor vehicle or privilege of operation of such motor vehicle in this state or privilege of obtaining a certificate of registration issued by the commissioner is suspended or revoked shall be guilty of a misdemeanor, and upon conviction shall be subject to a fine of not less than fifty dollars nor more than one hundred dollars or by imprisonment for not exceeding thirty days or by both such fine and imprisonment for conviction of a first offense; by a fine of not less than one hundred dollars nor more than two hundred dollars or by imprisonment for not exceeding ninety days or by both such fine and imprisonment for a conviction of a second offense committed within a period of eighteen months; by a fine of not less than two hundred dollars nor more than five hundred dollars or by imprisonment for not exceeding one hundred eighty days or by both such fine and imprisonment for a conviction of a third or subsequent offense committed within a period of eighteen months.

§ 513. Certificate of magistrate.

(a) Upon the suspension or revocation of any license or certificate of registration for any reason specified in sections five hundred ten and eleven hundred ninety-three of this chapter as a ground for such suspension or revocation, the magistrate or other officer suspending or revoking the same shall, within ninety-six hours, transmit to the commissioner a certificate stating: (a) whether such license or certificate has been suspended or revoked and, if suspended, the period of such suspension; (b) the name and address of the person whose license or certificate has been suspended or revoked; (c) the nature of the offense committed, or other reason for the suspension or revocation; (d) the number and character of the violations of the provisions of this chapter, or of any lawful local ordinance, rule or regulation in relation to motor vehicle or motorcycle speed or traffic, of which such licensee has been convicted, so far as practicable. Such certificate shall be presumptive evidence of the facts recited therein. At such time, said magistrate or officer shall transmit such license, if surrendered at sentencing, to the commissioner.

(b) Where a person has been granted youthful offender status, the certificate required by subdivision (a) of this section shall specify (i) whether such license or certificate has been suspended or revoked, and if suspended, the period of such suspension; if revoked, the time period within which no new license may be issued; (ii) the name

and address of the person whose license or certificate has been revoked; and (iii) such other information as the commissioner may require by regulation.

§ 514. Certifying convictions, forfeitures and nonappearances to the commissioner and recording convictions.

1. (a) Upon a judgment of conviction of any person of (a) homicide or assault arising out of the operation of a motor vehicle, (b) criminally negligent homicide arising out of the operation of a motor vehicle, (c) a felony involving the use of a commercial motor vehicle, (d) a violation of any of the provisions of this chapter (except one relating to parking, stopping or standing) or (e) a violation of any law, ordinance, rule or regulation made by local authorities in relation to traffic (except one relating to parking, stopping or standing) or upon the forfeiture of bail given upon a charge of violating any such provision, law, ordinance, rule or regulation, the court or the clerk thereof shall within fifteen days certify the facts of the case to the commissioner in such form and in such manner as may be prescribed by the commissioner, who shall record the same in his office. Such certificate shall be presumptive evidence of the facts recited therein. If any such conviction shall be reversed upon appeal therefrom, or shall be vacated or set aside, the person whose conviction has been so reversed, vacated or set aside may serve on the commissioner a certified copy of the appropriate order and the commissioner shall thereupon record the same in connection with the record of such conviction.

(b) Notwithstanding the provisions of paragraph (a), upon a judgment of conviction for any offense for which a mandatory suspension or revocation is required to be imposed, or a permissive suspension or revocation is imposed by the court, the court or the clerk thereof shall within ninety-six hours of the imposition of sentence file the certificate required by paragraph (a) along with the license, when surrendered at sentencing.

(c) Notwithstanding the provisions of paragraphs (a) and (b), the commissioner may prescribe time limitations for the reporting of judgments of conviction and transmission of such license that are longer than those prescribed by this section for any courts to which this section is applicable.

2. [Repealed pursuant to L. 2001, Ch. 406, eff. Jan. 29, 2002.]

3. (a) Upon the failure of a person to appear or answer, within sixty days of the return date or any subsequent adjourned date, or the failure to pay a fine imposed by a court, pursuant to a summons charging him or her with a violation of any of the provisions of this chapter (except one for parking, stopping or standing), section

five hundred two or five hundred twelve of the tax law, section fourteen-f, two hundred eleven or two hundred twelve of the transportation law or of any law, ordinance, rule or regulation made by a local authority, relating to traffic (except for parking, stopping or standing), the trial court or the clerk thereof shall within ten days certify that fact to the commissioner, in the manner and form prescribed by the commissioner, who shall record the same in his or her office. Thereafter and upon the appearance of any such person in response to such summons or the receipt of the fine by the court, the trial court or the clerk thereof shall forthwith certify that fact to the commissioner, in the manner and form prescribed by the commissioner; provided, however, no such certification shall be made unless the court has collected the termination of suspension fee required to be paid pursuant to paragraph (j-1) of subdivision two of section five hundred three of this chapter.

(b) Upon the failure of a person to appear or answer, within sixty days of the return date or any subsequent adjourned date, or the failure to pay a fine imposed by a traffic and parking violations agency pursuant to a summons charging him or her with a violation of:

(1) any of the provisions of this chapter except one for parking, stopping or standing and except those violations described in paragraphs (a), (b), (d), (e) and (f) of subdivision two of section three hundred seventy-one of the general municipal law;

(2) section five hundred two or subdivision (a) of section eighteen hundred fifteen of the tax law;

(3) section fourteen-f (except paragraph (b) of subdivision four of section fourteen-f), two hundred eleven or two hundred twelve of the transportation law; or

(4) any lawful ordinance or regulation made by a local or public authority relating to traffic (except one for parking, stopping or standing); the clerk thereof shall within ten days certify that fact to the commissioner, in the manner and form prescribed by the commissioner, who shall record the same in his or her office. Thereafter and upon the appearance of any such person in response to such summons or the receipt of the fine by the agency, the traffic and parking violations agency or the clerk thereof shall forthwith certify that fact to the commissioner, in the manner and form prescribed by the commissioner; provided, however, no such certification shall be made unless the traffic and parking violations agency has collected the termination of suspension fee required to be paid pursuant to paragraph (j-1) of subdivision two of section five hundred three of this chapter.

4. (a) Upon the failure of the owner of a motor vehicle registered in this state or his representative to appear or answer, on the return date or any subsequent adjourned date, or in the case

of an administrative tribunal fails to comply with the rules and regulations of said tribunal following entry of a final decision in response to three or more summonses or other process issued within an eighteen month period, charging that said motor vehicle was parked, stopped or standing in violation of the provisions of this chapter or any law, ordinance, rule or regulation made by a local authority, the trial court or administrative tribunal of appropriate jurisdiction may certify that fact to the commissioner in the manner and form prescribed by the commissioner, who may record the same in his office.

(b) Upon such certification, the trial court, the clerk thereof, or the administrative tribunal shall notify the registrant by certified or registered mail, return receipt requested, that the commissioner shall deny the registration or renewal application until the registrant provides proof from the court wherein the charges were pending that he has answered or appeared, or in the case of an administrative tribunal provides proof that he has complied with the rules and regulations of said tribunal following entry of a final decision. Thereafter and upon the appearance or answer of any such person in response to such summonses the trial court or clerk thereof shall forthwith certify that fact to the registrant, and to the commissioner upon his request, in a manner and form prescribed by the commissioner. In the case of an administrative tribunal such certification shall be made upon compliance with the rules and regulations of such tribunal.

(c) At least sixty days prior to renewal date the commissioner shall notify the registrant that unless he complies with the provisions of this section as set forth above, his registration or renewal thereof, will be denied.

4-a. (a) Upon the failure of the owner of a motor vehicle registered in this state or his representative to appear or answer, on the return date or dates or any subsequent adjourned date or dates, or in the case of an administrative tribunal, fails to comply with the rules and regulations of said tribunal following entry of a final decision or decisions, in response to twenty or more summonses or other process issued within an eighteen month period, charging that said motor vehicle was parked, stopped or standing in violation of the provisions of this chapter or any law, ordinance, rule or regulation made by a local authority, the trial court or administrative tribunal of appropriate jurisdiction may certify that fact to the commissioner in the manner and form prescribed by the commissioner.

(b) Thereafter and upon the appearance or answer of any such person in response to such summonses the trial court or clerk thereof shall forthwith certify that fact to the registrant, and to the commissioner upon his request, in a manner and form prescribed by the commissioner. In the case of an administrative tribunal, such certification shall be made upon compliance with the rules and regulations of such tribunal.

5. Upon the conviction of any person under eighteen years of age who resides within the household of his parent or guardian, the trial court or clerk shall forthwith transmit written notice of such conviction to the parent or guardian of such minor person; provided, however, that transmittal of such notice of conviction shall not be required in any case in which notice of arraignment of such person upon the charge or charges of which convicted is required by, and shall have been previously transmitted as provided in, subdivision two of section eighteen hundred seven of this chapter.

6. Notwithstanding any inconsistent provision of this section, the commissioner may exempt by regulation additional provisions of this chapter or of other laws, ordinances, rules or regulations from the requirements of subdivisions one and two.

7. Any person chargeable with the duty of reporting to the commissioner a conviction, bail forfeiture or the fact that a person failed to appear or answer pursuant to a summons, who wilfully fails or neglects to do so, shall be punishable by a fine of not more than twenty-five dollars for each separate offense.

Amended by L. 2001, Ch. 406, §§ 5 and 6, amending subd. 1 and repealing subd. 2, eff. Jan. 29, 2002; L. 2003, Ch. 62, Part J, § 11, eff. Sept. 12, 2003, amending subd. 3.

§ 514-a. Notification of convictions, suspensions, revocations, cancellations and disqualifications by commercial motor vehicle operators.

1. Each person who operates a commercial motor vehicle for a New York state employer who is convicted of violating within or outside of this state, in any type of motor vehicle, a state or local law relating to motor vehicle traffic control (other than a parking violation), shall notify his/her current employer of such conviction. Any person who holds a commercial driver's license issued by the commissioner who does not operate a commercial motor vehicle for a New York state employer or who operates a commercial motor vehicle while self-employed who is convicted in any other state, the District of Columbia or a Canadian province of violating any law relating to motor vehicle traffic control (other than a parking violation) while operating a commercial motor vehicle shall notify the commissioner of such conviction. such notification must be made within thirty days after the date that the person has been convicted except that if a person is a bus driver as defined in section five hundred nine-a of this chapter, such notification must be made within five days after the date the person has been convicted as required by section five

hundred nine-i of this chapter. The above notification must be made in writing and contain the following information: (a) driver's full name; (b) driver's license number; (c) date of conviction; (d) the specific criminal or other offense(s), serious traffic violation(s) of state or local law relating to motor vehicle traffic control, for which the person was convicted and any suspension, revocation, cancellation of any driving privileges or disqualification from operating a commercial motor vehicle which resulted from such conviction(s); (e) indication whether the violation was in a commercial motor vehicle; (f) location of offense; (g) court or tribunal in which the conviction occurred; and (h) driver's signature.

2. Each person who operates a commercial motor vehicle for a New York state employer who has a driver's license suspended, revoked, or canceled by the commissioner or by the appropriate authorities of any other state, District of Columbia or Canadian province, or who loses the right to operate a commercial motor vehicle in any state or jurisdiction for any period, or who is disqualified from operating a commercial motor vehicle for any period, shall notify his/her current employer of such suspension, revocation, cancellation, lost privilege, or disqualification.

§ 514-b. Certification of convictions, suspensions, revocations and disqualifications.

Whenever the commissioner receives information relating to a conviction or notice of a suspension, revocation, cancellations and disqualifications of a license or disqualification from operating a commercial motor vehicle through direct notification by the appropriate officials of another state, District of Columbia or Canadian province or through an information system established pursuant to the commercial motor vehicle safety act of nineteen hundred eighty-six, public law 99-570, title xii and regulations promulgated thereunder or through an admission made by an applicant for a driver's license, such information shall be presumptive evidence of the facts contained therein, and the commissioner shall take action as may be required and may take action as may be permitted by this chapter based upon such conviction or notice.

§ 515. Alteration of convictions endorsed on licenses.

No person shall wilfully erase or otherwise make illegible, the record of a conviction which has been endorsed on a license pursuant to the provisions of section five hundred fourteen.

§ 516. Driver license compact.

1. The driver license compact is hereby enacted into law and entered into with all other

VTL

jurisdictions joining therein in the form substantially as follows:

DRIVER LICENSE COMPACT

ARTICLE I
FINDINGS AND DECLARATION OF POLICY

(a) The party states find that:

(1) The safety of their streets and highways is materially affected by the degree of compliance with state and local laws and ordinances relating to the operation of motor vehicles.

(2) Violation of such a law or ordinance is evidence that the violator engages in conduct which is likely to endanger the safety of persons and property.

(3) The continuance in force of a license to drive is predicated upon compliance with laws and ordinances relating to the operation of motor vehicles, in whichever jurisdiction the vehicle is operated.

(b) It is the policy of each of the party states to:

(1) Promote compliance with the laws, ordinances, and administrative rules and regulations relating to the operation of motor vehicles by their operators in each of the jurisdictions where such operators drive motor vehicles.

(2) Make the reciprocal recognition of licenses to drive and eligibility therefor more just and equitable by considering the overall compliance with motor vehicle laws, ordinances and administrative rules and regulations as a condition precedent to the continuance or issuance of any license by reason of which the licensee is authorized or permitted to operate a motor vehicle in any of the party states.

ARTICLE II
DEFINITIONS

As used in this compact:

(a) "State" means a state, territory or possession of the United States, the District of Columbia, the commonwealth of Puerto Rico, or a province of Canada.

(b) "Home state" means the state which has issued and has the power to suspend or revoke the use of the license or permit to operate a motor vehicle.

(c) "Conviction" means a conviction of any offense related to the use or operation of a motor vehicle which is prohibited by state law, municipal ordinance or administrative rule or regulation, or a forfeiture of bail, bond or other security deposited to secure appearance by a person charged with having committed any such offense, and which conviction or forfeiture is required to be reported to the licensing authority.

ARTICLE III
REPORTS OF CONVICTION

The licensing authority of a party state shall report each conviction of a person from another party state occurring within its jurisdiction to the licensing authority of the home state of the licensee. Such report shall clearly identify the person convicted; describe the violation specifying the section of the statute, code or ordinance violated; identify the court in which action was taken; indicate whether a plea of guilty or not guilty was entered, or the conviction was a result of the forfeiture of bail, bond or other security; and shall include any special findings made in connection therewith.

ARTICLE IV
EFFECT OF CONVICTION

(a) The licensing authority in the home state, for the purposes of suspension, revocation or limitation of the license to operate a motor vehicle, shall give the same effect to the conduct reported, pursuant to article iii of this compact, as it would if such conduct had occurred in the home state, in the case of convictions for:

(1) Manslaughter or negligent homicide resulting from the operation of a motor vehicle;

(2) Driving a motor vehicle while under the influence of intoxicating liquor or a narcotic drug, or under the influence of any other drug to a degree which renders the driver incapable of safely driving a motor vehicle;

(3) Any felony in the commission of which a motor vehicle is used;

(4) Failure to stop and render aid in the event of a motor vehicle accident resulting in the death or personal injury of another.

(b) If the laws of a party state do not provide for offenses or violations denominated or described in precisely the words employed in subdivision (a) of this article, such party state shall construe the denominations and descriptions appearing in subdivision (a) hereof as being applicable to and identifying those offenses or violations of a substantially similar nature and the laws of such party state shall contain such provisions as may be necessary to ensure that full force and effect is given to this article.

ARTICLE V
APPLICATIONS FOR NEW LICENSES

Upon application for a license to drive, the licensing authority in a party state shall ascertain whether the applicant has ever held, or is the holder of a license to drive issued by any other party state. The licensing authority in the state where application is made shall not issue a license to drive to the applicant if:

(1) The applicant has held such a license, but the same has been suspended by reason, in whole or in part, of a violation and if such suspension period has not terminated.

(2) The applicant has held such a license, but the same has been revoked by reason, in whole or in part, of a violation and if such revocation has not terminated, except that after the expiration of one year from the date the license was revoked, such person may make application for a new license if permitted by law. The licensing authority may refuse to issue a license to any such applicant if, after investigation, the licensing authority determines that it will not be safe to grant to such person the privilege of driving a motor vehicle on the public highways.

(3) The applicant is the holder of a license to drive issued by another party state and currently in force unless the applicant surrenders such license.

ARTICLE VI
APPLICABILITY OF OTHER LAWS

Except as expressly required by provisions of this compact, nothing contained herein shall be construed to affect the right of any party state to apply any of its other laws relating to licenses to drive to any person or circumstance, nor to invalidate or prevent any driver license agreement or other cooperative arrangement between a party state and a non-party state.

ARTICLE VII
COMPACT ADMINISTRATOR AND INTERCHANGE OF INFORMATION

(a) The head of the licensing authority of each party state shall be the administrator of this compact for his state. The administrators, acting jointly, shall have the power to formulate all necessary and proper procedures for the exchange of information under this compact.

(b) The administrator of each party state shall furnish to the administrator of each other party state any information or documents reasonably necessary to facilitate the administration of this compact.

ARTICLE VIII
ENTRY INTO FORCE AND WITHDRAWAL

(a) This compact shall enter into force and become effective as to any state when it has enacted the same into law.

(b) Any party state may withdraw from this compact by enacting a statute repealing the same, but no such withdrawal shall take effect until six months after the executive head of the withdrawing state has given notice of the withdrawal to the executive heads of all other party states. No withdrawal shall affect the validity or applicability by the licensing authorities of states remaining party to the compact of any report of conviction occurring prior to the withdrawal.

ARTICLE IX
CONSTRUCTION AND SEVERABILITY

This compact shall be liberally construed so as to effectuate the purposes thereof. The provisions of this compact shall be severable and if any phrase, clause, sentence or provision of this compact is declared to be contrary to the constitution of any party state or of the united states or the applicability thereof of any government, agency, person or circumstance is held invalid, the validity of the remainder of this compact and the applicability thereof to any government, agency, person or circumstance shall not be affected thereby. If this compact shall be held contrary to the constitution of any state party thereto, the compact shall remain in full force and effect as to the remaining states and in full force and effect as to the state affected as to all severable matters.

(1) As used in the compact, the term "licensing authority" with reference to this state shall mean the department of motor vehicles. Said department shall furnish to the appropriate authorities of any other party state any information or documents reasonably necessary to facilitate the administration of the compact.

(2) The compact administrator provided for in article seven of the compact shall not be entitled to any additional compensation on account of his service as such administrator, but shall be entitled to expenses incurred in connection with his duties and responsibilities as such administrator, in the same manner as for expenses incurred in

VTL

connection with any other duties or responsibilities of his office or employment.

(3) As used in the compact, with reference to this state, the term "executive head" shall mean the governor.

(4) The conduct to which effect shall be given pursuant to article four-a of the compact shall be conduct which, if it had occurred in this state, would have constituted an offense or violation within the meaning of subparagraphs (i) and (iii) of paragraph (a) of subdivision two, paragraph (f) of subdivision three of section five hundred ten and subparagraph seven of paragraph (b) of subdivision two of section eleven hundred ninety-three of the vehicle and traffic law.

(5) In any case where the application of subdivision five of section five hundred ten of the vehicle and traffic law would require or authorize a result different from that required by article five of the compact, said article five shall govern.

§ 516-a. Reciprocal driver license agreements with provinces of Canada.

The commissioner may execute a reciprocal compact or agreement not inconsistent with the provisions of this chapter with the motor vehicle administrator or other authorized official of any province of Canada to effectuate the purposes set forth in subdivision (b) of article one of section five hundred sixteen of this article.

§ 516-b. Reciprocal agreements concerning reporting of traffic offenses and administrative action thereon.

(a) The commissioner may execute a reciprocal compact or agreement not inconsistent with the provisions of this chapter with the motor vehicle administrator or other authorized official of another state concerning the reporting of convictions for traffic offenses occurring in each state by a person licensed in, or a resident of, the other state to such licensing or residence state and the treating of any such reported conviction in the same manner as if the conviction occurred in the licensing or residence state for the purpose of administrative action. Any such compact or agreement shall specify the offenses subject to the compact or agreement, and shall include a determination of comparable offenses in each state if any such offenses are of a substantially similar nature but are not denominated or described in precisely the same words in each party state.

(b) The word "state" when used in this section shall mean any state, territory, a possession of the United States, district of Columbia or any province of Canada.

(c) Traffic offenses which may be subject to a reciprocal compact or agreement entered into pursuant to this section shall be limited to the following types of offenses in this state and equivalent offenses in each party state:

(1) manslaughter, criminally negligent homicide and assault arising from the operation of a motor vehicle;

(2) operating a motor vehicle while under the influence of alcohol or a drug;

(3) any felony in the commission of which a motor vehicle is used;

(4) leaving the scene of a personal injury or fatal incident without reporting;

(5) any speeding offense;

(6) any offense consisting of disobeying any traffic control device;

(7) any offense involving failure to yield the right-of-way;

(8) any offense involving direction of traffic, overtaking or passing;

(9) any offense involving failure to use a safety belt or child restraint device;

(10) reckless driving; and

(11) passing a stopped school bus.

(d) [*Effective until Oct. 1, 2007.*] Nothing in this section shall be construed to prohibit the reporting or recording of convictions or youthful offender or other juvenile adjudications other than those included in a reciprocal compact or agreement executed pursuant to this section when the laws of either state require or permit action to be taken or sanctions to be imposed on the basis of such convictions or youthful offender or other juvenile adjudications.

(d) [*Effective Oct. 1, 2007.*] Nothing in this section shall be construed to prohibit the reporting or recording of convictions other than those included in a reciprocal compact or agreement executed pursuant to this section when the laws of either state require or permit action to be taken or sanctions to be imposed on the basis of such convictions.

Amended by L. 1994, Ch. 286, § 1, eff. July 13, 1994, extending the expiration date of subd. d; L. 1995, Ch. 3, § 73, extending the expiration date of subd. d; L. 1996, Ch. 400, § 1 extending to Oct. 1, 1997, eff. date of subd. d; L. 1997, Ch. 382, § 1, extending the expiration date of subd. (d) to Oct. 1, 1998, eff. Aug. 5, 1997; L. 1998, Ch. 58 Part E, § 27, eff. Apr. 28, 1998, deemed in full force and effect Apr. 1, 1998, extending the expiration date of subd. d to Oct. 1, 1999; L. 1999, Ch. 512, § 1, eff. Sept. 28, 1999, extending the expiration date of subd. d to Oct. 1, 2000; L. 2001, Ch. 447, § 1, eff. Sept. 20, 2000, extending the expiration date of subd. d to Oct. 1, 2001; L. 2001, Ch. 242, eff. Sept. 4, 2001, extending expiration date of subd. d to Oct. 1, 2002; L. 2002, Ch. 84, Part A, § 1, extending expiration date of subd. d to Oct. 1, 2003; L. 2003, Ch. 487, § 1, eff. Sept. 9, 2003, extending expiration date of subd. d to Oct. 1, 2005; L. 2005, Ch. 60, Part D, § 1, eff. Apr. 1, 2005, extending expiration date of subd. d to Oct. 1, 2007.

§ 517. Interstate compact guaranteeing appearance.

a. The commissioner may execute a reciprocal compact or agreement not inconsistent with the provisions of this chapter with the motor vehicle administrator or other authorized official of another state concerning the appearance of a person licensed in one state to answer a summons or an appearance ticket for a moving traffic violation issued by the other state. Such compact shall provide that if a person licensed by either state is issued a summons or an appearance ticket by the other state for a moving traffic violation covered by the compact or agreement, he shall not be detained or required to furnish bail or collateral, and that if he fails to appear in response to such summons or appearance ticket, his license may be suspended by the state that issued the license until he submits to the jurisdiction of the court or administrative tribunal in which such summons or appearance ticket is returnable. Such compact shall also provide such terms and procedures as are necessary and proper to facilitate its administration.

b. Such interstate compacts may also provide that if a registration or renewal of a motor vehicle would be denied pursuant to either subdivision five-a of section four hundred one of this chapter, for failing to answer summonses or other processes issued for parking infractions, or subdivision four of section one hundred forty-five of the transportation law, with respect to the transportation of household goods, returnable in any court or an administrative tribunal of the department of transportation or for failing to comply with the rules and regulations of any administrative tribunal of appropriate jurisdiction following entry of a final determination with respect to such summons or process, the state issuing the registration or renewal shall likewise deny the registration or renewal, until such applicant submits to the jurisdiction of the court or administrative tribunal in which such summonses or other processes are returnable.

c. The word "state" when used in this section shall mean any state, territory or possession of the United States, the district of Columbia or any province of the dominion of Canada.

Amended by L. 2000, Ch. 117, § 1, eff. July 11, 2000, amending subd. b.

VTL

ARTICLE 21

ALCOHOL AND DRUG REHABILITATION PROGRAM

Section
520.   Statement of findings and declaration of purpose.
523.   Reports.
523-a.   Driver improvement clinic programs.
523-b.   Experimental driver safety programs.

§ 520. Statement of findings and declaration of purpose.

The ever-increasing number of accidents, personal injuries and deaths resulting from alcohol or drug-related traffic offenses is a matter of great concern to the legislature. The diminished perception of intoxicated and impaired operators of motor vehicles presents a constant and intolerable threat to the lives and well-being of the citizens of the state. Efforts aimed at alleviating this threat have proven inadequate. The public interest in the cause of highway safety will be well served by the implementation of a permanent program of rehabilitation for those operators convicted of alcohol or drug-related traffic offenses and certain operators who have been adjudicated youthful offenders for alcohol or drug-related traffic offenses. The commissioner of motor vehicles should have the authority to offer to such operators an opportunity for rehabilitation, thereby reducing the threat aimed at themselves and the people of the state.

ANNOTATIONS

Constitutionality.—There is no perceived violation of the petitioner's right to equal protection from the fact the alcohol and drug rehabilitation programs are limited to individuals convicted of a violation of § 1192 of the Vehicle and Traffic Law. Stark v. New York State Dept. of Motor Vehicles, 104 A.D.2d 194, 483 N.Y.S.2d 824 (3d Dept. 1984).

Purpose.—Broad authority was given to the Commissioner of Motor Vehicles under article 21 of the Vehicle and Traffic Law to institute studies and experimental programs designed to determine the most effective methods of improving driver skills and attitudes in order to reduce traffic violations and motor vehicle accidents. Southworth v. State, 62 A.D.2d 731, 405 N.Y.S.2d 548 (4th Dept. 1978).

—It is undisputed that the Department of Motor Vehicles is authorized to adopt procedures requiring certain individuals to obtain additional counseling after the initial driver improvement clinic program. People v. Ogden, 117 Misc. 2d 900, 459 N.Y.S.2d 545 (City Ct. Genesee Co. 1983).

§ 523. Reports.

The commissioner shall report to the governor and to the legislature annually with respect to the status of the alcohol and drug rehabilitation program, including therein, among other things, the scope and results of procedures for screening and referral of program participants exhibiting an early stage, of alcoholism or chronic life problem with alcohol, providing that such report shall not contain the name of or otherwise identify participants in such program.

§ 523-a. Driver improvement clinic programs.

In addition to the driver rehabilitation program authorized by section eleven hundred ninety-six of this chapter, the commissioner may establish, by regulation, guidelines for alcohol and highway safety programs. The purpose of such programs should be to inform participants of the effects of alcohol on driving, to discuss problem drinking and its effects, to provide assistance to individuals with referral to alcoholism treatment agencies and to provide instruction with respect to proper driving techniques and driver attitude. The commissioner shall establish criteria for requiring attendance at such clinics, and may, pending attendance at such clinic, suspend the driver's license or privilege of any person who fails to attend such clinic as required by such regulations. Such criteria may provide for the required attendance at such clinic of any person who, as a result of the conviction for a moving traffic violation, is referred by the trial court for such attendance. The commissioner shall establish a fee to be paid by any person who attends any such program. Such fee shall be used to defray the ongoing expenses of the program. Where the commissioner has approved any driver improvement program conducted by local authorities, any such fee shall be paid to the agency conducting such program.

ANNOTATION

Legislative intent.—It is the legislative intent to delegate authority to set charges or fees to be assessed against those licensed operators who participate in corrective programs. Redfield v. Melton, 57 A.D.2d 491, 395 N.Y.S.2d 725 (3d Dept. 1977).

§ 523-b. Experimental driver safety programs.

The commissioner may study the feasibility of programs to improve driver behavior, attitude, performance or skills in order to reduce motor vehicle accidents and traffic violations, and to promote highway safety. He shall have the authority to establish such programs on a limited, experimental basis in order to assist in such feasibility study provided any such program is funded by any source other than state funds, or if any such program is to be funded with state funds, then he may establish such program only

with the approval of the director of the division
of the budget.

ARTICLE 22
(Selected Sections)

ACCIDENTS AND ACCIDENT REPORTS

Section

§ 600. Leaving scene of an incident without reporting.

1. Property damage. a. Any person operating a motor vehicle who, knowing or having cause to know that damage has been caused to the real property or to the personal property, not including animals, of another, due to an incident involving the motor vehicle operated by such person shall, before leaving the place where the damage occurred, stop, exhibit his or her license and insurance identification card for such vehicle, when such card is required pursuant to articles six and eight of this chapter, and give his or her name, residence, including street and number, insurance carrier and insurance identification information including but not limited to the number and effective dates of said individual's insurance policy, and license number to the party sustaining the damage, or in case the person sustaining the damage is not present at the place where the damage occurred then he or she shall report the same as soon as physically able to the nearest police station, or judicial officer.

b. It shall be the duty of any member of a law enforcement agency who is at the scene of the accident to request the said operator or operators of the motor vehicles, when physically capable of doing so, to exchange the information required hereinabove and such member of a law enforcement agency shall assist such operator or operators in making such exchange of information in a reasonable and harmonious manner.

A violation of the provisions of paragraph a of this subdivision shall constitute a traffic infraction punishable by a fine of up to two hundred fifty dollars or a sentence of imprisonment for up to fifteen days or both such fine and imprisonment.

2. Personal injury. a. Any person operating a motor vehicle who, knowing or having cause to know that personal injury has been caused to another person, due to an incident involving the motor vehicle operated by such person shall, before leaving the place where the said personal injury occurred, stop, exhibit his or her license and insurance identification card for such vehicle, when such card is required pursuant to articles six and eight of this chapter, and give his or her name, residence, including street and street number, insurance carrier and insurance identification

information including but not limited to the number and effective dates of said individual's insurance policy and license number, to the injured party, if practical, and also to a police officer, or in the event that no police officer is in the vicinity of the place of said injury, then, he or she shall report said incident as soon as physically able to the nearest police station or judicial officer.

b. It shall be the duty of any member of a law enforcement agency who is at the scene of the accident to request the said operator or operators of the motor vehicles, when physically capable of doing so, to exchange the information required hereinabove and such member of a law enforcement agency shall assist such operator or operators in making such exchange of information in a reasonable and harmonious manner.

c. A violation of the provisions of paragraph a of this subdivision resulting solely from the failure of an operator to exhibit his or her license and insurance identification card for the vehicle or exchange the information required in such paragraph shall constitute a class B misdemeanor punishable by a fine of not less than two hundred fifty nor more than five hundred dollars in addition to any other penalties provided by law. Any subsequent such violation shall constitute a class A misdemeanor punishable by a fine of not less than five hundred nor more than one thousand dollars in addition to any other penalties provided by law. Any violation of the provisions of paragraph a of this subdivision, other than for the mere failure of an operator to exhibit his or her license and insurance identification card for such vehicle or exchange the information required in such paragraph, shall constitute a class A misdemeanor, punishable by a fine of not less than five hundred dollars nor more than one thousand dollars in addition to any other penalties provided by law. Any such violation committed by a person after such person has previously been convicted of such a violation shall constitute a class E felony punishable by a fine of not less than one thousand nor more than two thousand five hundred dollars in addition to any other penalties provided by law. Any violation of the provisions of paragraph a of this subdivision, other than for the mere failure of an operator to exhibit his or her license and insurance identification card for such vehicle or exchange the information required in such paragraph, where the personal injury involved (i) results in serious physical injury, as defined in section 10.00 of the penal law, shall constitute a class E felony, punishable by a fine of not less than one thousand nor more than five thousand dollars in addition to any other penalties provided by law, or (ii) results in death shall constitute a class D felony punishable by a fine of not less than two thousand nor more than five thousand dollars in addition to any other penalties provided by law.

Amended by L. 2005, Ch. 49, § 1, eff. Nov. 1, 2005.

ANNOTATION

Evidence.—Record established sufficient evidence to support a conviction under this section where car operated by defendant in a parking lot outside a bar hit two individuals who were walking, causing them both serious physical injury, and defendant drove away from the scene without stopping or reporting the incident. People v. Papineau, 19 A.D.3d 1149, 796 N.Y.S.2d 491 (4th Dept. 2005).

Sentencing.—Concurrent sentences for leaving the scene of an accident without reporting and vehicular assault in the second degree were not required. Each crime has one element in common: that victim sustained a serious physical injury. Since one crime is not a material element of the other, the law does not require concurrent sentences. People v. Chambers, 257 A.D.2d 418, 683 N.Y.S.2d 238 (1st Dept. 1999).

§ 601. Leaving scene of injury to certain animals without reporting.

Any person operating a motor vehicle which shall strike and injure any horse, dog, cat or animal classified as cattle shall stop and endeavor to locate the owner or custodian of such animal or a police, peace or judicial officer of the vicinity, and take any other reasonable and appropriate action so that the animal may have necessary attention, and shall also promptly report the matter to such owner, custodian or officer (or if no one of such has been located, then to a police officer of some other nearby community), exhibiting his or her license and insurance identification card for such vehicle, when such card is required

pursuant to articles six and eight of this chapter, giving his or her name and residence, including street and street number, insurance carrier and insurance identification information and license number. Violation of this section shall be punishable by a fine of not more than one hundred dollars for a first offense and by a fine of not less than fifty nor more than one hundred fifty dollars for a second offense and each subsequent offense; provided, however where the animal that has been struck and injured is a guide dog, hearing dog or service dog, as such terms are defined in section forty-seven-b of the civil rights law which is actually engaged in aiding or guiding a person with a disability, a violation of this section shall be publishable by a fine of not less than fifty nor more than one hundred fifty dollars for a first offense and by a fine of not less than one hundred fifty dollars nor more than three hundred dollars for a second offense and each subsequent offense.

Amended by L. 1997, Ch. 508, § 1, eff. Jan. 1, 1998; L. 2004, Ch. 672, § 1, eff. Nov. 1, 2005.

ANNOTATIONS

Purpose.—The statute's purpose is to prevent negligent motorists from attempting to evade any civil or criminal consequences which may result from the accident. People v. Mullady, 149 Misc. 2d 323, 565 N.Y.S.2d 685 (Suffolk Co. Ct. 1991).

Validity.—The statute is valid in that the duties imposed by it are reasonable exercises of the police power by the State to regulate activities directly relevant. People v. Samuel, 29 N.Y.2d 252, 327 N.Y.S.2d 321, 277 N.E.2d 381 (1971).

§ 602. Arrest for violations of sections six hundred and six hundred one.

A peace officer, acting pursuant to his special duties, or a police officer may, without a warrant, arrest a person, in case of violation of section six hundred and section six hundred one, which in fact have been committed, though not in his presence, when he has reasonable cause to believe that the violation was committed by such person.

VTL

ARTICLE 30
(Selected Sections)

SPEED RESTRICTIONS

Section

1180.   **Basic rule and maximum limits.**

1182.   **Speed contests and races.**

§ 1180. Basic rule and maximum limits.

(a) No person shall drive a vehicle at a speed greater than is reasonable and prudent under the conditions and having regard to the actual and potential hazards then existing.

(b) Except as provided in subdivision (g) of this section and except when a special hazard exists that requires lower speed for compliance with subdivision (a) of this section or when maximum speed limits have been established as hereinafter authorized, no person shall drive a vehicle at a speed in excess of fifty-five miles per hour.

(c) Except as provided in subdivision (g) of this section, whenever maximum school speed limits have been established on a highway adjacent to a school as authorized in section sixteen hundred twenty, sixteen hundred twenty-two, sixteen hundred thirty, sixteen hundred forty-three or sixteen hundred sixty-two-a, no person shall drive in excess of such maximum school speed limits during:

(1) school days at times indicated on the school zone speed limit sign, provided, however, that such times shall be between the hours of seven o'clock A.M. and six o'clock P.M. or alternative times within such hours; or

(2) a period when the beacons attached to the school zone speed limit sign are flashing and such sign is equipped with a notice that indicates that the school zone speed limit is in effect when such beacons are flashing, provided, however, that such beacons shall only flash during student activities at the school and up to thirty minutes immediately before and up to thirty minutes immediately after such student activities.

(d) 1. Except as provided in subdivision (g) of this section, whenever maximum speed limits, other than school speed limits, have been established as authorized in sections sixteen hundred twenty, sixteen hundred twenty-two, sixteen hundred twenty-three, sixteen hundred twenty-seven, sixteen hundred thirty, sixteen hundred forty-three, sixteen hundred forty-four, sixteen hundred fifty-two, sixteen hundred sixty-two-a, sixteen hundred sixty-three, and sixteen hundred seventy, no person shall drive in excess of such maximum speed limits at any time.

2. Except as provided in subdivision (g) of this section, whenever maximum speed limits, other than school speed limits, have been established with respect to any restricted highway as authorized in section sixteen hundred twenty-five, no person shall drive in excess of such maximum speed limits at any time.

(e) The driver of every vehicle shall, consistent with the requirements of subdivision (a) of this section, drive at an appropriate reduced speed when approaching and crossing an intersection or railway grade crossing, when approaching and going around a curve, when approaching a hill crest, when approaching and passing by an emergency situation involving any authorized emergency vehicle which is parked, stopped or standing on a highway and which is displaying one or more red or combination red and white lights pursuant to the provisions of paragraph two of subdivision forty-one of section three hundred seventy-five of this chapter, when traveling upon any narrow or winding roadway, and when any special hazard exists with respect to pedestrians, or other traffic by reason of weather or highway conditions, including, but not limited to a highway construction or maintenance work area.

(f) Except as provided in subdivision (g) of this section and except when a special hazard exists that requires lower speed for compliance with subdivision (a) or (e) of this section or when a lower maximum speed limit has been established, no person shall drive a vehicle through a highway construction or maintenance work area at a speed in excess of the posted work area speed limit. The agency having jurisdiction over the affected street or highway may establish work area speed limits which are less than the normally posted speed limits; provided, however, that such normally posted speed limit may exceed the work area speed limit by no more than twenty miles per hour; and provided further that no such work area speed limit may be established at less than twenty-five miles per hour.

(g) (i) No person who uses a radar or laser detector in a vehicle with a gross vehicle weight rating of more than eighteen thousand pounds, or a commercial motor vehicle with a gross vehicle weight rating of more than ten thousand pounds, shall drive at a speed in excess of fifty-five miles per hour or, if a maximum speed limit other than fifty-five miles per hour as hereinbefore authorized has been established, at a speed in excess of such speed limit. The presence in any such vehicle of either: (1) a radar or laser detector connected to a power source and in an operable condition; or (2) a concealed radar or laser detector where a part of such detector is securely affixed to some part of the vehicle outside of the cab, in a manner which renders the detector not readily observable, is presumptive evidence of its use by any person operating such vehicle. Either such presumption shall be rebutted by any credible and reliable evidence which tends to show that such radar or laser detector was not in use.

(ii) The provisions of this section shall not be construed as authorizing the seizure or forfeiture of a radar or laser detector, unless otherwise provided by law.

(h) Upon a conviction for a violation of subdivision (b), (c), (d), (f) or (g) of this section, the court shall record the speed upon which the conviction was based on the certificate required to be filed with the commissioner pursuant to section five hundred fourteen of this chapter, or if the conviction occurs in an administrative tribunal established pursuant to article two-a of this chapter, the speed upon which the conviction was based shall be entered in the department's records.

1. Every person convicted of a violation of subdivision (b) or paragraph one of subdivision (d) of this section shall be punished as follows:

(i) Where the court or tribunal records or enters that the speed upon which the conviction was based exceeded the applicable speed limit by not more than ten miles per hour, by a fine of not less than forty-five nor more than one hundred fifty dollars;

(ii) Where the court or tribunal records or enters that the speed upon which the conviction was based exceeded the applicable speed limit by more than ten miles per hour but not more than thirty miles per hour, by a fine of not less than ninety nor more than three hundred dollars or by imprisonment for not more than fifteen days or by both such fine and imprisonment;

(iii) Where the court or tribunal records or enters that the speed upon which the conviction was based exceeded the applicable speed limit by more than thirty miles per hour, by a fine of not less than one hundred eighty nor more than six hundred dollars, or by imprisonment for not more than thirty days, or by both such fine and imprisonment.

2. Every person convicted of a violation of subdivision (a) or (e) of 9 this section shall be punished by a fine of not less than forty-five nor more than one hundred fifty dollars, or by imprisonment for not more than fifteen days, or by both such fine and imprisonment.

3. Every person convicted of a violation of paragraph two of subdivision (d), subdivision (f) or (g) of this section shall be punished as follows:

(i) Where the court or tribunal records or

enters that the speed upon which the conviction was based exceeded the applicable speed limit by not more than ten miles per hour, by a fine of not less than ninety nor more than one hundred fifty dollars;

(ii) Where the court or tribunal records or enters that the speed upon which the conviction was based exceeded the applicable speed limit by more than ten miles per hour, but not more than thirty miles per hour, by a fine of not less than one hundred eighty nor more than three hundred dollars or by imprisonment for not more than thirty days, or by both such fine and imprisonment, provided, however, that where the vehicle is either (A) in violation of any rules or regulations involving an out-of-service defect relating to brake systems, steering components and/or coupling devices, or (B) transporting flammable gas, radioactive materials or explosives, the fine shall be three hundred dollars or imprisonment for not more than thirty days, or both such fine and imprisonment;

(iii) Where the court or tribunal records or enters that the speed upon which the conviction was based exceeded the applicable speed limit by more than thirty miles per hour, by a fine of not less than three hundred sixty nor more than six hundred dollars or by imprisonment for not more than thirty days or by both such fine and imprisonment, provided, however, that where the vehicle is either (A) in violation of any rules or regulations involving an out-of-service defect relating to brake systems, steering components and/or coupling devices, or (B) transporting flammable gas, radioactive materials or explosives, the fine shall be six hundred dollars or imprisonment for not more than thirty days, or both such fine and imprisonment.

4. Every person convicted of a violation of subdivision (c) of this section when such violation occurs in a school speed zone during a school day between the hours of seven o'clock A.M. and six o'clock P.M., shall be punished as follows:

(i) Where the court or tribunal records or enters that the speed upon which the conviction was based exceeded the applicable speed limit by not more than ten miles per hour, by a fine of not less than ninety nor more than three hundred dollars;

(ii) Where the court or tribunal records or enters that the speed upon which the conviction was based exceeded the applicable speed limit by more than ten miles per hour but not more than thirty miles per hour, by a fine of not less than one hundred eighty nor more than six hundred dollars or by imprisonment for not more than fifteen days or by both such fine and imprisonment;

(iii) Where the court or tribunal records or enters that the speed upon which the conviction was based exceeded the applicable speed limit by

VTL

more than thirty miles per hour, by a fine of not less than three hundred sixty nor more than one thousand two hundred dollars, or by imprisonment for not more than thirty days, or by both such fine and imprisonment.

5. Notwithstanding the foregoing provisions of this subdivision, the maximum fine provided herein for the violation for which the person is sentenced may be increased by an additional one hundred fifty dollars if the conviction is for a second violation of any subdivision of this 1 section where both violations were committed within an eighteen month period, and the maximum fine provided herein for the violation for which the person is sentenced may be increased by an additional three hundred seventy-five dollars if the conviction is for a third or subsequent violation of any subdivision of this section where all such violations were committed within an eighteen month period. Where an additional fine is provided by this paragraph, a sentence of imprisonment for not more than thirty days may be imposed in place of or in addition to any fine imposed.

Amended by L. 1995, Ch. 446, § 2, amending subd. (h)(1), eff. Sept. 1, 1995; L. 1995, Ch. 446, § 3, amending subd. (h)(3), eff. Sept. 1, 1995; L. 1997, Ch. 432, §§ 72–75, eff. Nov. 18, 1997; L. 1999, Ch. 101, eff. Nov. 1, 1999, amending subd. (g), and Ch. 484, eff. Nov. 1, 1999, amending subd. (h)(1) and (4) and adding (h)(5); L. 2002, Ch. 563, § 1, eff. Sept. 24, 2003, amending subd. c; L. 2003, Ch. 62, Part C, §§ 4–8, eff. May 15, 2003, amending subd. (h); L. 2004, Ch. 211, § 1, eff. Nov. 1, 2004, amending subd. (e).

L. 2002, Ch. 563, § 7 provides: "Notwithstanding any inconsistency with sections two, three, four, five and six of this act, any school zone speed limit established prior to the effective date of this act on a highway passing a school building for not more than three hundred feet in either direction from the building line of a school abutting on the highway may be continued."

ANNOTATIONS

Constitutionality.—Court rejected attack on statute as unconstitutionally vague. People v. Nappi, 18 N.Y.2d 136, 272 N.Y.S.2d 347, 219 N.E.2d 176 (1966).

Opinion evidence.—Opinion evidence of the police officer that the petitioner was driving at a speed nearly twice the legal limit need not be corroborated by mechanical devices and is itself sufficient to sustain a speeding conviction. Martin v. Adduci, 138 A.D.2d 599, 526 N.Y.S.2d 181 (2d Dept. 1988).

Statutory obligations. —In an action for damages for personal injuries resulting from automobile accident, court properly charged jury with statutory obligation of § 1180 after paramedic testified that complainant told him his car was traveling 45 miles per hour, even though he saw the speed limit sign reducing the road speed to 20 miles per hour. Evers v. Carroll, 17 A.D.3d 629, 794 N.Y.S.2d 398 (2d Dept. 2005).

Sufficiency of evidence.—The evidence was insufficient as a matter of law to sustain the charge where prior to the accident the defendant was traveling at about 20 to 25 miles per hour, and the uncontradicted testimony is that when he applied his brakes to halt for the traffic signal the car skidded despite his pumping of the brakes; the slight impact which caused no damage or injury was indicative, not of excessive speed, but poor judgment as to when the defendant should have applied his brakes. People v. Davis, 24 N.Y.2d 796, 300 N.Y.S.2d 580, 248 N.E.2d 176 (1969).

—Court properly charged jury on section 1180(a) on the basis of the plaintiff's testimony that the defendant's drove his limousine "very fast" into the back of the vehicle. Djelosaj v. Gaines Serv. Leasing Corp., 237 A.D.2d 223, 655 N.Y.S.2d 936 (1st Dept. 1997).

—Administrative law judge properly relied on testimony of police officer who testified that he had been trained and was able to visually estimate speed of a passing vehicle, and testimony regarding his estimation coupled with reading from calibrated laser device was sufficient to support a conviction under this section. Clarke v. Martinez, 14 A.D.3d 612, 789 N.Y.S.2d 207 (2d Dept. 2004).

—Substantial evidence supported determination of administrative body where officer's testimony established visual estimate of defendant's speed of 76 miles per hour in a 50 miles per hour zone, that testimony was based on officer's training and expertise, and that estimate was also corroborated by radar. Neiman v. Department of Motor Vehicles, 265 A.D.2d 558, 697 N.Y.S.2d 310 (2d Dept. 1999).

§ 1182. Speed contests and races.

1. Except as provided in section eleven hundred eighty-two-a of this article or section sixteen hundred thirty, sixteen hundred forty, sixteen hundred forty-two or sixteen hundred sixty of this chapter, no races, exhibitions or contests of speed shall be held and no person shall engage in or aid or abet in any motor vehicle or other speed contest or exhibition of speed on a highway. Such event, if held, shall be fully and efficiently patrolled for the entire distance over which such race, exhibition or contest for speed is to be held. Participants in a race, exhibition or contest of speed are exempted from compliance with any traffic laws otherwise applicable thereto, but shall exercise reasonable care. A violation of any of the provisions of this section shall constitute a misdemeanor and be punishable by imprisonment of not more than thirty days or a fine of not less than three hundred dollars nor more than five hundred twenty-five dollars, or both such fine and imprisonment.

2. A second conviction within twelve months of a violation of this section shall be punishable by imprisonment of not more than six months or a fine of not less than five hundred twenty five dollars nor more than seven hundred fifty dollars, or both such fine and imprisonment.

Amended by L. 2003, Ch. 62, Part C, § 9, eff. May 15, 2003, amending subds. 1 and 2.

ANNOTATIONS

Sufficiency of evidence.—Evidence of speeding was supported by substantial evidence to sustain conviction, evidence included police officer's testimony regarding his visual estimate of speed of petitioner's car, together with reading from laser device in officer's car. Koenigsberg v. State of N.Y. DMV Appeals Bd., 8 A.D.3d 383, 777 N.Y.S.2d 745 (2d Dept. 2004).

—Testimony that officer had been trained in visually estimating speed and his visual estimate of speed of petitioner's car, along with reading from calibrated speedometer in officer's patrol car were sufficient to sustain petitioner's conviction for speeding. Mataragas v. N.Y.S. DMV, 6 A.D.3d 537, 774 N.Y.S.2d 409 (2d Dept. 2004).

—Testimony of officer who stopped petitioner for speeding as to his expertise in visually assessing vehicle speeds, his observations respecting the speed of petitioner's vehicle and its manner of operation just prior to stop, constituted substantial evidence to support a charge of speeding. Al-Habshi v. DMV, 309 A.D.2d 641, 765 N.Y.S.2d 787 (1st Dept. 2003).

—Evidence that defendant smelled of alcohol, had slurred speech and glassy eyes, failed two field sobriety tests, and had a BAC of 0.10% within two hours of arrest, which, standing alone, was more than sufficient to establish a prima facie violation of this subdivision, coupled with other evidence, was sufficient to sustain a conviction, absent evidence from which the trier of fact could conclude that defendant's BAC at time of vehicle operation was less than 0.10%. People v. Arnold, 2 A.D.3d 975, 768 N.Y.S.2d 244 (3d Dept. 2003).

ARTICLE 31

ALCOHOL AND DRUG-RELATED OFFENSES AND PROCEDURES APPLICABLE THERETO

LexisNexis Cross References

See generally Apprehending and Prosecuting the Drunk Driver; Defense of Drunk Driving Cases; Drunk Driving and Related Vehicular Offenses (3d ed.); Investigation and Prosecution of DWI and Vehicular Homicide; Prior Convictions in DUI Prosecutions.

§ 1192. Operating a motor vehicle while under the influence of alcohol or drugs.

1. Driving while ability impaired. No person shall operate a motor vehicle while the person's ability to operate such motor vehicle is impaired by the consumption of alcohol.

2. Driving while intoxicated; per se. No person shall operate a motor vehicle while such person has .08 of one per centum or more by weight of alcohol in the person's blood as shown by chemical analysis of such person's blood, breath, urine or saliva, made pursuant to the provisions of section eleven hundred ninety-four of this article.

3. Driving while intoxicated. No person shall operate a motor vehicle while in an intoxicated condition.

4. Driving while ability impaired by drugs. No person shall operate a motor vehicle while the person's ability to operate such a motor vehicle is impaired by the use of a drug as defined in this chapter.

5. Commercial motor vehicles: per se – level I. Notwithstanding the provisions of section eleven hundred ninety-five of this article, no person shall operate a commercial motor vehicle while such person has .04 of one per centum or more but not more than .06 of one per centum by weight of alcohol in the person's blood as shown by chemical analysis of such person's blood, breath, urine or saliva, made pursuant to the provisions of section eleven hundred ninety-four of this article; provided, however, nothing contained in this subdivision shall prohibit the imposition of a charge of a violation of subdivision one of this section, or of section eleven hundred ninety-two-a of this article where a person under the age of twenty-one operates a commercial motor vehicle where a chemical analysis of such person's blood, breath, urine, or saliva, made pursuant to the provisions of section eleven hundred ninety-four of this article, indicates that such operator has .02 of one per centum or more but less than .04 of one per centum by weight of alcohol in such operator's blood.

6. Commercial motor vehicles; per se–level II. Notwithstanding the provisions of section eleven hundred ninety-five of this article, no person shall operate a commercial motor vehicle while such person has more than .06 of one per centum but less than .08 of one per centum by weight of alcohol in the person's blood as shown by chemical analysis of such person's blood, breath, urine or saliva, made pursuant to the provisions of section eleven hundred ninety-four of this article; provided, however, nothing contained in this subdivision shall prohibit the imposition of a charge of a violation of subdivision one of this section.

7. Where applicable. The provisions of this section shall apply upon public highways, private roads open to motor vehicle traffic and any other parking lot. For the purposes of this section "parking lot" shall mean any area or areas of private property, including a driveway, near or contiguous to and provided in connection with

premises and used as a means of access to and egress from a public highway to such premises and having a capacity for the parking of four or more motor vehicles. The provisions of this section shall not apply to any area or areas of private property comprising all or part of property on which is situated a one or two family residence.

8. Effect of prior out-of-state conviction. A prior out-of-state conviction for operating a motor vehicle while under the influence of alcohol or drugs shall be deemed to be a prior conviction of a violation of subdivision one of this section for purposes of determining penalties imposed under this section or for purposes of any administrative action required to be taken pursuant to subdivision two of section eleven hundred ninety-three of this article; provided, however, that such conduct, had it occurred in this state, would have constituted a violation of any of the provisions of this section. This subdivision shall only apply to convictions occurring on or after November twenty-ninth, nineteen hundred eighty-five.

8-a. Effect of prior finding of having consumed alcohol. A prior finding that a person under the age of twenty-one has operated a motor vehicle after having consumed alcohol pursuant to section eleven hundred ninety-four-a of this article shall have the same effect as a prior conviction of a violation of subdivision one of this section solely for the purpose of determining the length of any license suspension or revocation required to be imposed under any provision of this article, provided that the subsequent offense is committed prior to the expiration of the retention period for such prior offense or offenses set forth in paragraph (k) of subdivision one of section two hundred one of this chapter.

9. Conviction of a different charge. A driver may be convicted of a violation of subdivision one, two or three of this section, notwithstanding that the charge laid before the court alleged a violation of subdivision two or three of this section, and regardless of whether or not such conviction is based on a plea of guilty.

10. Plea bargain limitations. (a) In any case wherein the charge laid before the court alleges a violation of subdivision two, three or four of this section, any plea of guilty thereafter entered in satisfaction of such charge must include at least a plea of guilty to the violation of the provisions of one of the subdivisions of this section, other than subdivision five or six, and no other disposition by plea of guilty to any other charge in satisfaction of such charge shall be authorized; provided, however, if the district attorney upon reviewing the available evidence determines that the charge of a violation of this section is not warranted, such district attorney may consent, and the court may allow a disposition by plea of guilty to another charge in satisfaction of such charge; provided, however, in all such cases, the court

shall set forth upon the record the basis for such disposition. In any case wherein the charge laid before the court alleges a violation of subdivision one of this section and the operator was under the age of twenty-one at the time of such violation, any plea of guilty thereafter entered in satisfaction of such charge must include at least a plea of guilty to the violation of such subdivision; provided, however, such charge may instead be satisfied as provided in paragraph (c) of this subdivision, and, provided further that, if the district attorney, upon reviewing the available evidence, determines that the charge of a violation of subdivision one of this section is not warranted, such district attorney may consent, and the court may allow a disposition by plea of guilty to another charge in satisfaction of such charge; provided, however, in all such cases, the court shall set forth upon the record the basis for such disposition.

(b) In any case wherein the charge laid before the court alleges a violation of subdivision one or six of this section while operating a commercial motor vehicle, any plea of guilty thereafter entered in satisfaction of such charge must include at least a plea of guilty to the violation of the provisions of one of the subdivisions of this section and no other disposition by plea of guilty to any other charge in satisfaction of such charge shall be authorized; provided, however, if the district attorney upon reviewing the available evidence determines that the charge of a violation of this section is not warranted, he may consent, and the court may allow, a disposition by plea of guilty to another charge is satisfaction of such charge.

(c) Except as provided in paragraph (b) of this subdivision, in any case wherein the charge laid before the court alleges a violation of subdivision one of this section by a person who was under the age of twenty-one at the time of commission of the offense, the court, with the consent of both parties, may allow the satisfaction of such charge by the defendant's agreement to be subject to action by the commissioner pursuant to section eleven hundred ninety-four-a of this article. In any such case, the defendant shall waive the right to a hearing under section eleven hundred ninety-four-a of this article and such waiver shall have the same force and effect as a finding of a violation of section eleven hundred ninety-two-a of this article entered after a hearing conducted pursuant to such section eleven hundred ninety-four-a. The defendant shall execute such waiver in open court, and, if represented by counsel, in the presence of his attorney, on a form to be provided by the commissioner, which shall be forwarded by the court to the commissioner within ninety-six hours. To be valid, such form shall, at a minimum, contain clear and conspicuous language advising the defendant that a duly executed waiver: (i) has the same force and effect as a guilty finding following a hearing pursuant to section eleven hundred ninety-four-a of this article; (ii) shall subject the defendant to the imposition of sanctions pursuant to such section eleven hundred ninety-four-a; and (iii) may subject the defendant to increased sanctions upon a subsequent violation of this section or section eleven hundred ninety-two-a of this article. Upon receipt of a duly executed waiver pursuant to this paragraph, the commissioner shall take such administrative action and impose such sanctions as may be required by section eleven hundred ninety-four-a of this article.

11. No person other than an operator of a commercial motor vehicle may be charged with or convicted of a violation of subdivision five or six of this section.

12. Driving while intoxicated or while ability impaired by drugs—serious physical injury or death. In every case where a person is charged with a violation of subdivision two, three or four of this section, the law enforcement officer alleging such charge shall make a clear notation in the "Description of violation" section of a simplified traffic information if, arising out of the same incident, someone other than the person charged was killed or suffered serious physical injury as defined in section 10.00 of the penal law; such notation shall be in the form of a "D" if someone other than the person charged was killed and such notation shall be in the form of a "S.P.I." if someone other than the person charged suffered serious physical injury; provided, however, that the failure to make such notation shall in no way affect a charge for a violation of subdivision two, three or four of this section.

Amended by L. 1996, Ch. 196, § 7, amending subds. 5 and 6, eff. Nov. 1, 1996; L. 1996, Ch. 196, § 8, adding subd. 8-a, eff. Nov. 1, 1996; L. 1996, Ch. 196, § 9, amending subd. 10(a), eff. Nov. 1, 1996; L. 1996, Ch. 196, § 10, adding subd. 10(c), eff. Nov. 1, 1996; L. 2002, Ch. 3, §§ 1, 2, eff. Nov. 1, 2003, amending subds. 2 and 6; L. 2003, Ch. 236, § 1, eff. July 1, 2003, amending subds. 5 and 6.

Editor's Note: L. 2003, Ch. 62, § 1 (Part B1), amended L. 2003, Ch. 3, § 5, so as to change the effective date from Nov. 1, 2003, to July 1, 2003.

ANNOTATIONS

Appeal.—In order to challenge the sufficiency of evidence presented during trial on appeal, the issue must be preserved for appellate review. People v. Nielsen, 259 A.D.2d 501, 684 N.Y.S.2d 880 (2d Dept.), *review denied*, 93 N.Y.2d 1023 (1999).

Attempt.—Attempted driving while intoxicated is not a crime. People v. Prescott, 95 N.Y.2d 655, 722 N.Y.S.2d 778, 745 N.E.2d 1000 (2001).

Constitutionality.—Sections 1192 (1) and (3) are not unconstitutionally vague. People v. Cruz, 48 N.Y.2d 419, 423 N.Y.S.2d 625, 399 N.E.2d 513 (1979).

—Prosecution of a defendant under both VTL §§ 1192 and 193 for the same act does not violate the constitutional prohibition against multiple punishments for the same offense, since the bar against double jeopardy does not prevent statutes from imposing both criminal and civil sanctions for the same conduct. People v. Haishun, 238 A.D.2d 521, 656 N.Y.S.2d 660 (2d Dept. 1997).

—Section 1192(2) is not void for vagueness and is constitutional. People v. Mascolo, 175 A.D.2d 812, 572 N.Y.S.2d 937 (2d Dept. 1991).

Generally.—Petitioner who had two convictions of VTL § 1192(3) coupled with DMV records which establish a "physical injury," (concussion) within meaning of PL § 10.00 resulted from each offense, DMV had no discretion to reissue petitioner's driver's license. Rosato v. N.Y.S. DMV, 7 A.D.3d 718, 777 N.Y.S.2d 186 (2d Dept. 2004).

—Attorney was properly disbarred upon a plea of guilty to VTL § 1192, a class E felony. *In re* Angrisani, 2 A.D.3d 14, 768 N.Y.S.2d 17 (2d Dept. 2003).

—Testimony of three police officer witnesses that defendant smelled of alcohol, was sweating profusely, had trouble focusing his eyes, his speech was slurred and deliberate, and he was swaying was sufficient to support a finding that defendant was intoxicated. People v. Kane, 240 A.D.2d 516, 658 N.Y.S.2d 434 (2d Dept. 1997), *appeal denied*, 92 N.Y.2d 927 (1998).

—Police officer's testimony that he saw defendant's truck back up into an intersection and move forward into a parking spot and then, when he approached the truck, saw defendant in the driver's seat with the engine running, was sufficient to establish that defendant was operating the vehicle. People v. Scudds, 274 A.D.2d 834, 712 N.Y.S.2d 180 (3d Dept. 2000), *appeal denied*, 95 N.Y.2d 969 (2000).

—Court's inadvertent oversight which resulted in defendant not being sentenced for his conviction under VTL § 1191(1), with his other offenses, did not negate jury's finding that defendant was guilty of that charge. People v. Keller, 252 A.D.2d 817, 675 N.Y.S.2d 441 (3d Dept. 1998).

—Probable cause existed for defendant's arrest for driving while intoxicated based on his slurred speech and bloodshot eyes, the smell of alcohol on his breath, his admission that he had been drinking and his inability to pass sobriety tests. People v. O'Hanlon, 5 A.D.3d 1012, 773 N.Y.S.2d 633 (4th Dept. 2004).

—Police had probable cause to stop defendant's vehicle based on 911 call indicating that a "drunk driver" named "Jeffery" was about to leave in a specifically described car parked at a specific location, police arrived within minutes, observed car as described and pulled car over as being driven away, police did not need to observe any criminal behavior prior to stop. People v. Jeffery, 2 A.D.3d 1271, 769 N.Y.S.2d 675 (4th Dept. 2003).

—Officer's observation of defendant immediately prior to entering Village of Avon, which included him drive off road three times, drive left of center and fail to signal a left-hand turn gave rise to reasonable suspicion that defendant was driving while intoxicated within village, stop of defendant's car was legal. People v. Nesbitt, 1 A.D.3d 889, 767 N.Y.S.2d 187 (4th Dept. 2003).

—Uncontested testimony that defendant was slumped over the steering wheel of a pickup truck with the engine running and was wearing a seat belt when he was awakened by a police officer, coupled with presence of open beer can in cab of truck, strong smell of alcohol emitting from defendant, and defendant's failure of several field sobriety tests, all supported conviction under this section; jury could reject defendant's testimony that he never drove the truck. People v. Panek, 305 A.D.2d 1098, 759 N.Y.S.2d 619 (4th Dept. 2003).

—Evidence that police stopped defendant after observing him speeding through a parking lot and driving without headlights in the dark supported a legal stop; once stopped, probable cause to arrest for driving while intoxicated was established by defendant's slurred speech, bloodshot eyes, admission he was drinking, and inability to pass field sobriety tests. People v. Chelenza, 303 A.D.2d 991, 757 N.Y.S.2d 660 (4th Dept. 2003).

—There is no requirement that breathalyzer must be calibrated every six months in order for test results to be admissible; People need only establish that instrument was in proper working order. People v. Dargento, 302 A.D.2d 924,755 N.Y.S.2d 535 (4th Dept. 2003).

—Defendant's conviction of both driving while ability impaired and aggravated unlicensed operation in the first degree did not violate the constitutional prohibition against double jeopardy; the commission of driving while ability is impaired is an element of aggravated unlicensed operation in the first degree and, therefore, does not require proof of an additional fact which aggravated unlicensed operation in the first degree does not. People v. Kahn, 291 A.D.2d 898, 737 N.Y.S.2d 738 (4th Dept. 2002).

—Arresting officer who applied for a court-ordered blood test under oath reported that upon arriving at the scene, defendant was unconscious behind the steering wheel of his car, had a strong smell of alcohol on him, and at least one of the pedestrian victims struck by defendant's car was seriously injured, all of which supported the officer's belief that the defendant had operated the vehicle in violation of VTL § 1192. People v. Alshoaibi, 273 A.D.2d 871, 711 N.Y.S.2d 646 (4th Dept. 2000).

—Verdict finding defendant guilty of driving while ability impaired and aggravated unlicensed operation was not against the weight of the evidence where record contained evidence of defendant's poor driving, signs of intoxication, inability to perform sobriety test, and refusal to consent to chemical test. People v. Gelster, 256 A.D.2d 1133, 684 N.Y.S.2d 712 (4th Dept. 1999).

—Defendant's convictions for vehicular manslaughter in the second degree and driving while ability impaired by drugs was supported by evidence that defendant was negligent in driving an all terrain vehicle at dusk without a helmet at a speed that was too fast to be safe with a passenger and under the influence of marijuana, when defendant lost control of the vehicle and the passenger, who also did not have a helmet, was killed. People v. Roth, 256 A.D.2d 1206, 683 N.Y.S.2d 358 (4th Dept. 1998).

—A person is intoxicated when that person "has voluntarily consumed alcohol to the extent that he [or she] is incapable of employing the mental or physical abilities that he [or she] is expected to possess in order to operate a vehicle as a reasonable and prudent driver." People v. Gary, 233 A.D.2d 939, 649 N.Y.S.2d 879 (4th Dept. 1996).

—Evidence supporting a charge of driving while intoxicated under this section is facially sufficient when record contains results of breathalyzer test showing .07 of 1% by weight of alcohol, since this creates a rebuttal presumption (VTL § 1195(2)(a)) that the defendant was not intoxicated. The BAL, coupled with the officer's first hand observations, containing all indications of common law intoxication, support the officer's reasonable cause to believe that defendant was intoxicated. People v. Gristina, 186 Misc. 2d 877, 721 N.Y.S.2d 491 (Crim. Ct. N.Y. Co. 2001).

—Defendant, a long distance hauler with an unblemished driving record for 20 years, admittedly was driving while intoxicated. However, he had been drinking at a friend's house with no intention of driving when was ordered to move his truck by a police officer who came to the door. Defendant got into the truck to move it down the block and moments later was arrested by the same officer for driving while intoxicated. Case dismissed in the interest of justice. People v. Asche, 175 Misc. 2d 639, 669 N.Y.S.2d 788 (Dist. Ct. Nassau Co. 1998).

Lesser included offense.—The use of the word "impairment" in both § 1192(1) and § 1192(4) does not make § 1192(1) a lesser included offense of § 1192(4); where facts of case support impairment due to drugs, not impairment due to consumption of alcohol, court will not allow plea to § 1192(1). People v. Lehman, 183 Misc. 2d 97, 702 N.Y.S.2d 551 (Cty. Ct. Watertown 2000).

Operate.—Where there was evidence that defendant's truck was at a 45-degree angle off the paved road in a ditch with the engine still running and lights on and that defendant, with one hand on the steering wheel and his foot on the gas, was unsuccessfully trying to steer the truck out of the ditch, defendant was operating a motor vehicle within the meaning of the statute, even though the truck did not move and no one saw him drive off the road. People v. Beyer, 21 A.D.3d 592, 799 N.Y.S.2d 620 (3d Dept. 2005).

—The term "operate" is broader than the term "drive" and extends to a situation where a motorist begins to engage the motor for the purpose of putting the vehicle into motion. People v. Totman, 208 A.D.2d 970, 617 N.Y.S.2d 234 (3d Dept. 1994).

—The reason for a jury charge on operating the vehicle is to allow the jury to draw a fair inference that the defendant was sitting behind the wheel with the motor running because he had been driving or was about to drive. People v. O'Connor, 159 Misc. 2d 1072, 607 N.Y.S.2d 856 (Dist. Ct. Nassau Co. 1994).

Repugnant verdict.—Verdict was repugnant where defendant was charged with two violations of VTL § 1192, driving while impaired and driving while intoxicated, as well as aggravated unlicensed operation of a motor vehicle, but was only found guilty of a violation of VTL § 511, aggravated unlicensed operation. Since an element of aggravated unlicensed operation of a motor vehicle is operation of motor vehicle while under

the influence of drugs or alcohol, the conviction for VTL § 511 cannot stand. People v. Miner, 261 A.D.2d 420, 689 N.Y.S.2d 233 (2d Dept. 1999).

Scope.—The vehicular manslaughter statute applies to any person causing a death by driving under the influence of alcohol or drugs, regardless of location, even though there could be no separate punishment for such driving under Vehicle and Traffic Law § 1192 where the driving did not occur on public roads or other areas defined in that section. People v. Harris, 81 N.Y.2d 850, 597 N.Y.S.2d 620, 613 N.Y.S.2d 526 (1993).

Sentencing.—Concurrent sentences for leaving the scene of an accident without reporting and vehicular assault in the second degree were not required. Each crime has one element in common: that victim sustained a serious physical injury. Since one crime is not a material element of the other, the law does not require concurrent sentences. People v. Chambers, 257 A.D.2d 418, 683 N.Y.S.2d 238 (1st Dept.).

—Sentence for felony conviction under VTL § 1192 was proper where court imposed a $1,000 fine plus the mandatory surcharge in addition to a 90-day term of incarceration as a condition of a five-year term of probation. People v. Andrews, 245 A.D.2d 493, 679 N.Y.S.2d 839 (2d Dept. 1998).

—Court properly sentenced defendant as a persistent felony offender based on his prior convictions for driving while intoxicated. The court imposed an indeterminate term of 15 years to life upon his present conviction for DWI as a felony and aggravated unlicensed operation; however, in the interests of justice, the appellate court vacated the sentence and re-sentenced defendant as a second felony offender to an indeterminate term of two to four years. People v. Donhauser, 255 A.D.2d 933, 683 N.Y.S.2d 357, *reargument granted and order amended,* 1998 N.Y. App. Div. LEXIS 14474 (4th Dept. Dec. 31, 1998).

Sufficiency of accusatory instrument.—Factual allegations contained in accusatory instrument alleged that arresting officer observed defendant driving without headlights or taillights, and that upon stopping defendant found that defendant smelled of alcohol, had glassy eyes, impaired speech and motor coordination, and failed field sobriety tests; People were entitled to rebut § 1195(2)(c) presumption at trial, and to the extent that *People v. Gingillo,* 181 Misc. 2d 163 (1999), holds to the contrary, it should not be followed. People v. Blair, 98 N.Y.2d 722, 749 N.Y.S.2d 809, 779 N.E.2d 748 (2002).

—An accusatory instrument charging defendant with operating a motor vehicle while under the influence of alcohol under section 1192(2) must be supported by a chemical test analysis certificate verified by the administrator of the test and must indicate the defendant's blood alcohol level; the absence of either of these factors renders the accusatory instrument jurisdictionally defective. People v. Lopez, 170 Misc. 2d 278, 648 N.Y.S.2d 231 (N.Y.C. Crim. Ct. 1996).

Sufficiency of plea.—Defendant need not be advised that he will be subject to an enhanced criminal sanction for a future violation as a result of the plea in the instant case, driving while intoxicated, in order for the plea to be valid. People v. Lancaster, 260 A.D.2d 660, 688 N.Y.S.2d 711 (3d Dept. 1999).

—Defendant unsuccessfully challenged validity of plea to VTL §§ 1192 and 511, contending that he was suffering from post-acute withdrawal syndrome. During allocution, court inquired into defendant's mental state, and defendant responded that although he had a drinking problem, he was not under the influence of drugs or alcohol nor suffering from any mental disease or defect. Court found defendant's plea knowing and voluntary. People v. Miller, 254 A.D.2d 627, 681 N.Y.S.2d 367 (3d Dept. 1998).

—Defendant's allocution, which included an admission that he had operated a motor vehicle in the parking lot of his apartment complex while intoxicated, is sufficient to support a plea of guilty to this section; parking lot falls within the parameters of subdivision seven. People v. DeFrance, 265 A.D.2d 837, 696 N.Y.S.2d 740 (4th Dept.), *appeal denied,* 94 N.Y.2d 861 (1999).

—Defendant's plea, in which he admitted that he was operating a motor vehicle while intoxicated and knowing that his license was suspended or revoked, was sufficient to support the charges of driving while intoxicated and aggravated unlicensed operation of a motor vehicle. People v. Francis, 254 A.D.2d 779, 678 N.Y.S.2d 758 (4th Dept. 1998).

§ 1192-a. Operating a motor vehicle after having consumed alcohol; under the age of twenty-one; per se.

No person under the age of twenty-one shall operate a motor vehicle after having consumed alcohol as defined in this section. For purposes of this section, a person under the age of twenty-one is deemed to have consumed alcohol only if such person has .02 of one per centum or more but not more than .07 of one per centum by weight of alcohol in the person's blood, as shown by chemical analysis of such person's blood, breath, urine or saliva, made pursuant to the provisions of section eleven hundred ninety-four of this article. Any person who operates a motor vehicle in violation of this section, and who is not charged with a violation of any subdivision of section eleven hundred ninety-two of this article arising out of the same incident shall be referred to the department for action in accordance with the provisions of section eleven hundred ninety-four-a of this article. Except as otherwise provided in subdivision five of section eleven hundred ninety-two of this article, this section shall not apply to a person who operates a commercial motor vehicle. Notwithstanding any provision of law to the contrary, a finding that a person under the age of twenty-one operated a motor vehicle after having consumed alcohol in violation of this section is not a judgment of conviction for a crime or any other offense.

Added L. 1996, Ch. 196, § 11, eff. Nov. 1, 1996.

§ 1193. Sanctions.

1. Criminal penalties. (a) Driving while ability impaired. A violation of subdivision one of section eleven hundred ninety-two of this article shall be a traffic infraction and shall be punishable by a fine of not less than three hundred dollars nor more than five hundred dollars or by imprisonment in a penitentiary or county jail for not more than fifteen days, or by both such fine and imprisonment. A person who operates a vehicle in violation of such subdivision after having been convicted of a violation of any subdivision of section eleven hundred ninety-two of this article within the preceding five years shall be punished by a fine of not less than five hundred dollars nor more than seven hundred fifty dollars, or by imprisonment of not more than thirty days in a penitentiary or county jail or by both such fine and imprisonment. A person who operates a vehicle in violation of such subdivision after having been convicted two or more times of a violation of any subdivision of section eleven hundred ninety-two of this article within the preceding ten years shall be guilty of a misdemeanor, and shall be punished by a fine of not less than seven hundred fifty dollars nor more than fifteen hundred dollars, or by imprisonment of not

more than one hundred eighty days in a penitentiary or county jail or by both such fine and imprisonment.

(b) Driving while intoxicated or while ability impaired by drugs; misdemeanor offenses. A violation of subdivision two, three or four of section eleven hundred ninety-two of this article shall be a misdemeanor and shall be punishable by a fine of not less than five hundred dollars nor more than one thousand dollars, or by imprisonment in a penitentiary or county jail for not more than one year, or by both such fine and imprisonment.

(c) Felony offenses. (i) A person who operates a vehicle in violation of subdivision two, three or four of section eleven hundred ninety-two of this article after having been convicted of a violation of subdivision two, three or four of such section or of vehicular assault in the second or first degree, as defined, respectively, in sections 120.03 and 120.04 of the penal law or of vehicular manslaughter in the second or first degree, as defined, respectively, in sections 125.12 and 125.13 of such law, within the preceding ten years, shall be guilty of a class E felony, and shall be punished by a fine of not less than one thousand dollars nor more than five thousand dollars or by a period of imprisonment as provided in the penal law, or by both such fine and imprisonment.

(ii) A person who operates a vehicle in violation of subdivision two, three or four of section eleven hundred ninety-two of this article after having been convicted of a violation of subdivision two, three or four of such section or of vehicular assault in the second or first degree, as defined, respectively, in sections 120.03 and 120.04 of the penal law or of vehicular manslaughter in the second or first degree, as defined, respectively, in sections 125.12 and 125.13 of such law, twice within the preceding ten years, shall be guilty of a class D felony, and shall be punished by a fine of not less than two thousand dollars nor more than ten thousand dollars or by a period of imprisonment as provided in the penal law, or by both such fine and imprisonment.

(d) Alcohol or drug related offenses; special vehicles. (1) Except as provided in subparagraph four of this paragraph, a violation of subdivision one, two, three or four of section eleven hundred ninety-two of this article wherein the violator is operating a taxicab as defined in section one hundred forty-eight-a of this chapter, or livery as defined in section one hundred twenty-one-e of this chapter, and such taxicab or livery is carrying a passenger for compensation, or a truck with a GVWR of more than eighteen thousand pounds but not more than twenty-six thousand pounds and which is not a commercial motor vehicle shall be a misdemeanor punishable by a fine of not less than five hundred dollars nor more than fifteen hundred dollars or by a period of imprisonment as provided in the penal law, or by both such fine and imprisonment.

(1-a) A violation of subdivision one of section eleven hundred ninety-two of this article wherein the violator is operating a school bus as defined in section one hundred forty-two of this chapter and such school bus is carrying at least one student passenger shall be a misdemeanor punishable by a fine of not less than five hundred dollars nor more than fifteen hundred dollars or by a period of imprisonment as provided in the penal law, or by both such fine and imprisonment.

(2) A violation of subdivision five of section eleven hundred ninety-two of this article shall be a traffic infraction punishable as provided in paragraph (a) of this subdivision. Except as provided in subparagraph three or five of this paragraph, a violation of subdivision one, two, three, four or six of section eleven hundred ninety-two of this article wherein the violator is operating a commercial motor vehicle, or any motor vehicle registered or registrable under schedule F of subdivision seven of section four hundred one of this chapter shall be a misdemeanor. A violation of subdivision one, two, three or four of section eleven hundred ninety-two of this article shall be punishable by a fine of not less than five hundred dollars nor more than fifteen hundred dollars or by a period of imprisonment as provided in the penal law, or by both such fine and imprisonment. A violation of subdivision six of section eleven hundred ninety-two of this article shall be punishable by a fine of not less than five hundred dollars nor more than fifteen hundred dollars or by a period of imprisonment not to exceed one hundred eighty days, or by both such fine and imprisonment. A person who operates any such vehicle in violation of such subdivision six after having been convicted of a violation of subdivision one, two, three, four or six of section eleven hundred ninety-two of this article within the preceding five years shall be punishable by a fine of not less than five hundred dollars nor more than fifteen hundred dollars or by a period of imprisonment as provided in the penal law, or by both such fine and imprisonment.

(3) A violation of subdivision one of section eleven hundred ninety-two of this article wherein the violator is operating a motor vehicle with a gross vehicle weight rating of more than eighteen thousand pounds which contains flammable gas, radioactive materials or explosives shall be a misdemeanor punishable by a fine of not less than five hundred dollars nor more than fifteen hundred dollars or by a period of imprisonment as provided in the penal law, or by both such fine and imprisonment.

(4) (i) A person who operates a vehicle in violation of subdivision one, two, three or four of section eleven hundred ninety-two of this article and which is punishable as provided in subparagraph one, one-a, two or three of this paragraph after having been convicted of a violation of any such subdivision of section eleven hundred ninety-two of this article and penalized under subparagraph one, one-a, two or three of this paragraph within the preceding ten years, shall be guilty of a class E felony, which shall be punishable by a fine of not less than one thousand dollars nor more than five thousand dollars, or by a period of imprisonment as provided in the penal law, or by both such fine and imprisonment. A person who operates a vehicle in violation of subdivision six of section eleven hundred ninety-two of this article after having been convicted of two or more violations of subdivisions one, two, three, four or six of section eleven hundred ninety-two of this article within the preceding five years, any one of which was a misdemeanor, shall be guilty of a class E felony, which shall be punishable by a fine of not less than one thousand dollars nor more than five thousand dollars, or by a period of imprisonment as provided in the penal law, or by both such fine and imprisonment. In addition, any person sentenced pursuant to this subparagraph shall be subject to the disqualification provided in subparagraph three of paragraph (e) of subdivision two of this section.

(ii) A person who operates a vehicle in violation of subdivision one, two, three or four of section eleven hundred ninety-two of this article and which is punishable as provided in subparagraph one, one-a, two or three of this paragraph after having been convicted of a violation of any such subdivision of section eleven hundred ninety-two of this article and penalized under subparagraph one, one-a, two or three of this paragraph twice within the preceding ten years, shall be guilty of a class D felony, which shall be punishable by a fine of not less than two thousand dollars nor more than ten thousand dollars, or by a period of imprisonment as provided in the penal law, or by both such fine and imprisonment. A person who operates a vehicle in violation of subdivision six of section eleven hundred ninety-two of this article after having been convicted of three or more violations of subdivisions one, two, three, four or six of section eleven hundred ninety-two of this article within the preceding five years, any one of which was a misdemeanor, shall be guilty of a class D felony, which shall be punishable by a fine of not less than two thousand dollars nor more than ten thousand dollars, or by a period of imprisonment as provided in the penal law, or by both such fine and imprisonment. In addition, any person sentenced pursuant to this subparagraph shall be subject to the disqualification provided in subparagraph three of paragraph (e) of subdivision two of this section.

(4-a) A violation of subdivision two, three or four of section eleven hundred ninety-two of this article wherein the violator is operating a school bus as defined in section one hundred forty-two of this chapter and such school bus is carrying at least one student passenger shall be a class E felony punishable by a fine of not less than one thousand dollars nor more than five thousand dollars, or by a period of imprisonment as provided in the penal law, or by both such fine and imprisonment.

(5) A violation of subdivision two, three or four of section eleven hundred ninety-two of this article wherein the violator is operating a motor vehicle with a gross vehicle weight rating of more than eighteen thousand pounds which contains flammable gas, radioactive materials or explosives, shall be a class E felony punishable by a fine of not less than one thousand dollars and such other penalties as provided for in the penal law; provided, however, that a conviction for such violation shall not be considered a predicate felony pursuant to section 70.06 of such law, or a previous felony conviction pursuant to section 70.10 of such law.

(6) The sentences required to be imposed by subparagraph one, one-a, two, three, four, four-a or five o paragraph shall be imposed notwithstanding any contrary provision of this chapter or the penal law.

(7) Nothing contained in this paragraph shall prohibit the imposition of a charge of any other felony set forth in this or any other provision of law for any acts arising out of the same incident.

(e) Certain sentences prohibited. Notwithstanding any provisions of the penal law, no judge or magistrate shall impose a sentence of unconditional discharge for a violation of any subdivision of section eleven hundred ninety-two of this article nor shall a judge or magistrate impose a sentence of conditional discharge or probation unless such conditional discharge or probation is accompanied by a sentence of a fine as provided in this subdivision.

(f) Where the court imposes a sentence for a violation of section eleven hundred ninety-two of this article, the court may require the defendant, as a part of or as a condition of such sentence, to attend a single session conducted by a victims impact program. For purposes of this section, "victims impact program" means a program operated by a county, a city with a population of one million or more, by a not-for-profit organization authorized by any such county or city, or a combination thereof, in which presentations are made concerning the impact of operating a motor vehicle while under the influence of alcohol or drugs to one or more persons who have been convicted of such offenses. A description of any such program shall be filed with the commissioner and with the coordinator of the special traffic options program for driving while intoxicated established pursuant to section eleven hundred ninety-seven of this article, and shall be made available to the court upon request. Nothing contained herein shall be construed to require any

governmental entity to create such a victim impact program.

1-a. (a) Except as provided for in paragraph (b) of this subdivision, a person who operates a vehicle in violation of subdivision two or three of section eleven hundred ninety-two of this article after having been convicted of a violation of subdivision two or three of such section within the preceding five years shall, in addition to any other penalties which may be imposed pursuant to subdivision one of this section, be sentenced to a term of imprisonment of five days or, as an alternative to such imprisonment, be required to perform thirty days of service for a public or not-for-profit corporation, association, institution or agency as set forth in paragraph (h) of subdivision two of section 65.10 of the penal law as a condition of sentencing for such violation. Notwithstanding the provisions of this paragraph, a sentence of a term of imprisonment of five days or more pursuant to the provisions of subdivision one of this section shall be deemed to be in compliance with this subdivision.

(b) A person who operates a vehicle in violation of subdivision two or three of section eleven hundred ninety-two of this article after having been convicted on two or more occasions of a violation of any of such subdivisions within the preceding five years shall, in addition to any other penalties which may be imposed pursuant to subdivision one of this section, be sentenced to a term of imprisonment of ten days or, as an alternative to such imprisonment, be required to perform sixty days of service for a public or not-for-profit corporation, association, institution or agency as set forth in paragraph (h) of subdivision two of section 65.10 of the penal law as a condition of sentencing for such violation. Notwithstanding the provisions of this paragraph, a sentence of a term of imprisonment of ten days or more pursuant to the provisions of subdivision one of this section shall be deemed to be in compliance with this subdivision.

(c) A court sentencing a person pursuant to paragraph (a) or (b) of this subdivision shall: (i) order the installation of an ignition interlock device approved pursuant to section eleven hundred ninety-eight of this article on each motor vehicle owned by the person so sentenced. Such devices shall remain installed during any period of license revocation required to be imposed pursuant to paragraph (b) of subdivision two of this section, and, upon the termination of such revocation period, for an additional period as determined by the court; and (ii) order that such person receive an assessment of the degree of their alcohol abuse. Where such assessment indicates the need for treatment, such court is authorized to impose treatment as a condition of such sentence.

2. License sanctions.

(a) Suspensions. Except as otherwise provided in this subdivision, a license shall be suspended and a registration may be suspended for the following periods:

(1) Driving while ability impaired. Ninety days, where the holder is convicted of a violation of subdivision one of section eleven hundred ninety-two of this article;

(2) Persons under the age of twenty-one; driving after having consumed alcohol. Six months, where the holder has been found to have operated a motor vehicle after having consumed alcohol in violation of section eleven hundred ninety-two-a of this article where such person was under the age of twenty-one at the time of commission of such violation.

(b) Revocations. A license shall be revoked and a registration may be revoked for the following minimum periods:

(1) Driving while ability impaired; prior offense. Six months, where the holder is convicted of a violation of subdivision one of section eleven hundred ninety-two of this article committed within five years of a conviction for a violation of any subdivision of section eleven hundred ninety-two of this article.

(1-a) Driving while ability impaired; misdemeanor offense. Six months, where the holder is convicted of a violation of subdivision one of section eleven hundred ninety-two of this article committed within ten years of two previous convictions for a violation of any subdivision of section eleven hundred ninety-two of this article.

(2) Driving while intoxicated or while ability impaired by drugs. Six months, where the holder is convicted of a violation of subdivision two, three or four of section eleven hundred ninety-two of this article.

(3) Driving while intoxicated or while ability impaired by drugs; prior offense. One year, where the holder is convicted of a violation of subdivision two, three or four of section eleven hundred ninety-two of this article committed within ten years of a conviction for a violation of subdivision two, three or four of section eleven hundred ninety-two of this article.

(4) Special vehicles other than school buses. One year, where the holder is convicted of a violation of any subdivision of section eleven hundred ninety-two of this article and is sentenced pursuant to subparagraph one of paragraph (d) of subdivision one of this section.

(4-a) School buses. (A) one year, where the holder is convicted of a violation of any subdivision of section eleven hundred ninety-two of this article, such violation was committed while the holder was driving a school bus, and the holder is sentenced pursuant to subparagraph one, one-a or four-a of paragraph (d) of subdivision one of this section.

(B) three years where the holder is convicted of a violation of any subdivision of section eleven hundred ninety-two of this article, such violation was committed while the holder was driving a school bus, and the holder is sentenced pursuant to subparagraph four of paragraph (d) of subdivision one of this section.

(C) notwithstanding the provisions of the opening paragraph of this paragraph (b), the commissioner shall not revoke the registration of a school bus driven in violation of section eleven hundred ninety-two of this article.

(5) Holder of a commercial driver's license. (i) Except as otherwise provided in this subparagraph, one year where the holder of a commercial driver's license is convicted of a violation of any subdivision of section eleven hundred ninety-two of this article and the holder is sentenced pursuant to subparagraph two of paragraph (d) of subdivision one of this section.

(ii) Three years, where the holder is convicted of a violation of any subdivision of section eleven hundred ninety-two of this article, such violation was committed while the holder was operating a commercial motor vehicle transporting hazardous materials and the holder is sentenced pursuant to subparagraph two of paragraph (d) of subdivision one of this section.

(6) Persons under the age of twenty-one. One year, where the holder is convicted of or adjudicated a youthful offender for a violation of any subdivision of section eleven hundred ninety-two of this article, or is convicted of or receives a youthful offender or other juvenile adjudication for an offense consisting of operating a motor vehicle under the influence of intoxicating liquor where the conviction, or youthful offender or other juvenile adjudication was had outside this state, where such person was under the age of twenty-one at the time of commission of such violation.

(7) Persons under the age of twenty-one; prior offense or finding. One year or until the holder reaches the age of twenty-one, whichever is the greater period of time, where the holder has been found to have operated a motor vehicle after having consumed alcohol in violation of section eleven hundred ninety-two-a of this article, or is convicted of, or adjudicated a youthful offender for, a violation of any subdivision of section eleven hundred ninety-two of this article, or is convicted of or receives a youthful offender or juvenile adjudication for an offense consisting of operating a motor vehicle under the influence of intoxicating liquor where the conviction, or youthful offender or other juvenile adjudication was had outside this state, where such person was under the age of twenty-one at the time of commission of such violation and has previously been found to have operated a motor vehicle after having consumed alcohol in violation of section eleven hundred ninety-two-a of this article, or has previously been convicted of, or adjudicated a

youthful offender for, any violation of section eleven hundred ninety-two of this article not arising out of the same incident, or has previously been convicted of or received a youthful offender or juvenile adjudication for an offense consisting of operating a motor vehicle under the influence of intoxicating liquor when the conviction, or youthful offender or other juvenile adjudication was had outside this state and not arising out of the same.

(8) [*Effective until Oct. 1, 2007.*] Out-of-state offenses. Except as provided in subparagraph six or seven of this paragraph: (i) ninety days, where the holder is convicted of an offense consisting of operating a motor vehicle under the influence of intoxicating liquor where the conviction was had outside this state and (ii) six months, where the holder is convicted of, or receives a youthful offender or other juvenile adjudication, which would have been a misdemeanor or felony if committed by an adult, in connection with, an offense consisting of operating a motor vehicle under the influence of or while impaired by the use of drugs where the conviction or youthful offender or other juvenile adjudication was had outside this state.

(8) [*Effective Oct. 1, 2007.*] Out-of-state offenses. Except as provided in subparagraph six or seven of this paragraph, ninety days, where the holder is convicted of an offense consisting of operating a motor vehicle under the influence of intoxicating liquor or drugs where the conviction was had outside this state.

(9) Effect of rehabilitation program. No period of revocation arising out of subparagraph four, five, six or seven of this paragraph may be set aside by the commissioner for the reason that such person was a participant in the alcohol and drug rehabilitation program set forth in section eleven hundred ninety-six of this chapter.

(10) Action required by commissioner. Where a court fails to impose, or incorrectly imposes, a suspension or revocation required by this subdivision, the commissioner shall, upon receipt of a certificate of conviction filed pursuant to section five hundred fourteen of this chapter, impose such mandated suspension or revocation, which shall supersede any such order which the court may have imposed.

(11) Limitation of certain mandatory revocations. Where revocation is mandatory pursuant to subparagraph five of this paragraph for a conviction of a violation of subdivision five of section eleven hundred ninety-two of this article, such revocation shall be issued only by the commissioner and shall be applicable only to that portion of the holder's driver's license or privilege which permits the operation of commercial motor vehicles, and the commissioner shall immediately issue a license, other than a commercial driver's license, to such person provided that such person is otherwise eligible to receive such license and

further provided that issuing a license to such person does not create a substantial traffic safety hazard.

(c) [*Effective until Oct. 1, 2007.*] Reissuance of licenses; restrictions. (1) Except as otherwise provided in this paragraph, where a license is revoked pursuant to paragraph (b) of this subdivision, no new license shall be issued after the expiration of the minimum period specified in such paragraph, except in the discretion of the commissioner.

(2) Where a license is revoked pursuant to subparagraph two, three or eight of paragraph (b) of this subdivision for a violation of subdivision four of section eleven hundred ninety-two of this article, and where the individual does not have a driver's license or the individual's license was suspended at the time of conviction or youthful offender or other juvenile adjudication, the commissioner shall not issue a new license nor restore the former license for a period of six months after such individual would otherwise have become eligible to obtain a new license or to have the former license restored; provided, however, that during such delay period the commissioner may issue a restricted use license pursuant to section five hundred thirty of this chapter.

(3) In no event shall a new license be issued where a person has been twice convicted of a violation of subdivision three or four of section eleven hundred ninety-two of this article or of driving while intoxicated or of driving while ability is impaired by the use of a drug where physical injury, as defined in section 10.00 of the penal law, has resulted from such offense in each instance.

(c) [*Effective Oct. 1, 2007.*] Reissuance of licenses; restrictions. Where a license is revoked pursuant to paragraph (b) of this subdivision, no new license shall be issued after the expiration of the minimum period specified in such paragraph, except in the discretion of the commissioner; provided, however, that in no event shall a new license be issued where a person has been twice convicted of a violation of subdivision three or four of section eleven hundred ninety-two of this article or of driving while intoxicated or of driving while ability is impaired by the use of a drug where physical injury, as defined in section 10.00 of the penal law, has resulted from such offense in each instance.

(d) Suspension or revocation; sentencing. (1) Notwithstanding anything to the contrary contained in a certificate of relief from disabilities issued pursuant to article twenty-three of the correction law, where a suspension or revocation, other than a revocation required to be issued by the commissioner, is mandatory pursuant to paragraph (a) or (b) of this subdivision, the magistrate, justice or judge shall issue an order suspending or revoking such license upon sentencing, and the license holder shall surrender such license to the court. Except as hereinafter provided, such suspension or revocation shall take effect immediately.

(2) Except where the license holder has been charged with a violation of article one hundred twenty or one hundred twenty-five of the penal law arising out of the same incident or convicted of such violation or a violation of any subdivision of section eleven hundred ninety-two of this article within the preceding five years, the judge, justice or magistrate may issue an order making said license suspension or revocation take effect twenty days after the date of sentencing. The license holder shall be given a copy of said order permitting the continuation of driving privileges for twenty days after sentencing, if granted by the court. The court shall forward to the commissioner the certificates required in sections five hundred thirteen and five hundred fourteen of this chapter, along with a copy of any order issued pursuant to this paragraph and the license, within ninety-six hours of sentencing.

(e) Special provisions.

(1) Suspension pending prosecution; procedure.

a. Without notice, pending any prosecution, the court shall suspend such license, where the holder has been charged with a violation of subdivision two, three or four of section eleven hundred ninety-two of this article and either (i) a violation of a felony under article one hundred twenty or one hundred twenty-five of the penal law arising out of the same incident, or (ii) has been convicted of any violation under section eleven hundred ninety-two of this article within the preceding five years.

b. The suspension under the preceding clause shall occur no later than twenty days after the holder's first appearance before the court on the charges or at the conclusion of all proceedings required for the arraignment. in order for the court to impose such suspension it must find that the accusatory instrument conforms to the requirements of section 100.40 of the criminal procedure law and there exists reasonable cause to believe that the holder operated a motor vehicle in violation of subdivision two, three or four of section eleven hundred ninety-two of this article and either (i) the person had been convicted of any violation under such section eleven hundred ninety-two of this article within the preceding five years; or (ii) that the holder committed a violation of a felony under article one hundred twenty or one hundred twenty-five of the penal law. At such time the holder shall be entitled to an opportunity to make a statement regarding the enumerated issues and to present evidence tending to rebut the court's findings. Where such suspension is imposed upon a pending charge of a violation of a felony under article one hundred twenty or one hundred twenty-five of the penal law and the holder has requested a hearing pursuant to article

one hundred eighty of the criminal procedure law, the court shall conduct such hearing. If upon completion of the hearing, the court fails to find that there is reasonable cause to believe that the holder committed a felony under article one hundred twenty or one hundred twenty-five of the penal law and the holder has not been previously convicted of any violation of section eleven hundred ninety-two of this article within the preceding five years the court shall promptly notify the commissioner and direct restoration of such license to the license holder unless such license is suspended or revoked pursuant to any other provision of this chapter.

(2) Bail forfeiture. A license shall be suspended where the holder forfeits bail upon a charge of a violation of any subdivision of section eleven hundred ninety-two of this article. Such suspension shall not be terminated until the holder submits to the jurisdiction of the court in which the bail was forfeited.

(3) Permanent disqualification from operating certain motor vehicles. a. except as otherwise provided herein, in addition to any revocation set forth in subparagraph four or five of paragraph (b) of this subdivision, any person sentenced pursuant to subparagraph three of paragraph (d) of subdivision one of this section shall be permanently disqualified from operating any vehicle set forth in such paragraph. In addition, the commissioner shall not issue such person a license valid for the operation of any vehicle set forth therein by such person. The commissioner may waive such disqualification and prohibition hereinbefore provided after a period of five years has expired from such sentencing provided:

(i) that during such five year period such person has not violated any of the provisions of section eleven hundred ninety-two of this article or any alcohol or drug related traffic offense in this state or in any jurisdiction outside this state;

(ii) that such person provides acceptable documentation to the commissioner that such person is not in need of alcohol or drug treatment or has satisfactorily completed a prescribed course of such treatment; and

(iii) after such documentation is accepted, that such person is granted a certificate of relief from disabilities as provided for in section seven hundred one of the correction law by the court in which such person was last penalized pursuant to paragraph (d) of subdivision one of this section.

b. Any person who holds a commercial driver's license and is convicted of a violation of any subdivision of section eleven hundred ninety-two of this article who has had a prior finding of refusal to submit to a chemical test pursuant to section eleven hundred ninety-four of this article or has had a prior conviction of any of the following offenses: any violation of section eleven hundred ninety-two of this article; any violation of subdivision one or two of section six hundred of this chapter; or has a prior conviction of any felony involving the use of a motor vehicle pursuant to paragraph (a) of subdivision one of section five hundred ten-a of this chapter, shall be permanently disqualified from operating a commercial motor vehicle. The commissioner may waive such disqualification and prohibition hereinbefore provided after a period of ten years has expired from such sentence provided:

(i) that during such ten year period such person has not been found to have refused a chemical test pursuant to section eleven hundred ninety-four of this article while operating a motor vehicle and has not been convicted of any one of the following offenses while operating a motor vehicle: any violation of section eleven hundred ninety-two of this article; any violation of subdivision one or two of section six hundred of this chapter; or has a prior conviction of any felony involving the use of a motor vehicle pursuant to paragraph (a) of subdivision one of section five hundred ten-a of this chapter;

(ii) that such person provides acceptable documentation to the commissioner that such person is not in need of alcohol or drug treatment or has satisfactorily completed a prescribed course of such treatment; and

(iii) after such documentation is accepted, that such person is granted a certificate of relief from disabilities as provided for in section seven hundred one of the correction law by the court in which such person was last penalized pursuant to paragraph (d) of subdivision one of this section.

c. Upon a third finding of refusal and/or conviction of any of the offenses which require a permanent commercial driver's license revocation, such permanent revocation may not be waived by the commissioner under any circumstances.

(4) Youthful offenders. Where a youth is determined to be a youthful offender, following a conviction of a violation of section eleven hundred ninety-two of this article for which a license suspension or revocation is mandatory, the court shall impose such suspension or revocation as is otherwise required upon conviction and, further, shall notify the commissioner of said suspension or revocation and its finding that said violator is granted youthful offender status as is required pursuant to section five hundred thirteen of this chapter.

(5) Probation. When a license to operate a motor vehicle has been revoked pursuant to this chapter, and the holder has been sentenced to a period of probation pursuant to section 65.00 of the penal law for a violation of any provision of this chapter, or any other provision of the laws of this state, and a condition of such probation is that the holder thereof not operate a motor vehicle or not apply for a license to operate a

motor vehicle during the period of such condition of probation, the commissioner may not restore such license until the period of the condition of probation has expired.

(6) Application for new license. Where a license has been revoked pursuant to paragraph (b) of this subdivision, or where the holder is subject to a condition of probation as provided in subparagraph five of this paragraph, application for a new license may be made within forty-five days prior to the expiration of such minimum period of revocation or condition of probation, whichever expires last.

(7) [Expires and repealed Oct. 1, 2007.] Suspension pending prosecution; excessive blood alcohol content. a. Except as provided in clause a-1 of this subparagraph, a court shall suspend a driver's license, pending prosecution, of any person charged with a violation of subdivision two or three of section eleven hundred ninety-two of this article who, at the time of arrest, is alleged to have had .08 of one percent or more by weight of alcohol in such driver's blood as shown by chemical analysis of blood, breath, urine or saliva, made pursuant to subdivision two or three of section eleven hundred ninety-four of this article.

a-1. A court shall suspend a class DJ or MJ learner's permit or a class DJ or MJ driver's license, pending prosecution, of any person who has been charged with a violation of subdivision one, two and/or three of section eleven hundred ninety-two of this article.

b. The suspension occurring under clause a of this subparagraph shall occur no later than at the conclusion of all proceedings required for the arraignment and the suspension occurring under clause a-1 of this subparagraph shall occur immediately after the holder's first appearance before the court on the charge which shall, whenever possible, be the next regularly scheduled session of the court after the arrest or at the conclusion of all proceedings required for the arraignment; provided, however, that if the results of any test administered pursuant to section eleven hundred ninety-four of this article are not available within such time period, the complainant police officer or other public servant shall transmit such results to the court at the time they become available, and the court shall, as soon as practicable following the receipt of such results and in compliance with the requirements of this subparagraph, suspend such license. In order for the court to impose such suspension it must find that the accusatory instrument conforms to the requirements of section 100.40 of the criminal procedure law and there exists reasonable cause to believe either that (a) the holder operated a motor vehicle while such holder had .08 of one percent or more by weight of alcohol in his or her blood as was shown by chemical analysis of such person's blood, breath, urine or saliva, made pursuant to the provisions of section eleven hundred ninety-four of this article or (b) the person was the holder of a class DJ or MJ learner's permit or a class DJ or MJ driver's license and operated a motor vehicle while such holder was in violation of subdivision one, two and/or three of section eleven hundred ninety-two of this article. At the time of such license suspension the holder shall be entitled to an opportunity to make a statement regarding these two issues and to present evidence tending to rebut the court's findings.

c. Nothing contained in this subparagraph shall be construed to prohibit or limit a court from imposing any other suspension pending prosecution required or permitted by law.

d. Notwithstanding any contrary provision of this chapter, if any suspension occurring under this subparagraph has been in effect for a period of thirty days, the holder may be issued a conditional license, in accordance with section eleven hundred ninety-six of this article, provided the holder of such license is otherwise eligible to receive such conditional license. The commissioner shall prescribe by regulation the procedures for the issuance of such conditional license.

e. If the court finds that the suspension imposed pursuant to this subparagraph will result in extreme hardship, the court must issue such suspension, but may grant a hardship privilege, which shall be issued on a form prescribed by the commissioner. For the purposes of this clause, "extreme hardship" shall mean the inability to obtain alternative means of travel to or from the licensee's employment, or to or from necessary medical treatment for the licensee or a member of the licensee's household, or if the licensee is a matriculating student enrolled in an accredited school, college or university travel to or from such licensee's school, college or university if such travel is necessary for the completion of the educational degree or certificate. The burden of proving extreme hardship shall be on the licensee who may present material and relevant evidence. A finding of extreme hardship may not be based solely upon the testimony of the licensee. In no event shall arraignment be adjourned or otherwise delayed more than three business days solely for the purpose of allowing the licensee to present evidence of extreme hardship. The court shall set forth upon the record, or otherwise set forth in writing, the factual basis for such finding. The hardship privilege shall permit the operation of a vehicle only for travel to or from the licensee's employment, or to or from necessary medical treatment for the licensee or a member of the licensee's household, or if the licensee is a matriculating student enrolled in an accredited school, college or university travel to or from such licensee's school, college or university if such travel is necessary for the completion of the educational degree or certificate.

(f) Notice of charges to parent or guardian. Notwithstanding the provisions of subdivision two of section eighteen hundred seven of this chapter, upon the first scheduled appearance of any person under eighteen years of age who resides within the household of his or her parent or guardian upon a charge of a violation of subdivision one, two and/or three of section eleven hundred ninety-two of this article, the local criminal court before which such first appearance is scheduled shall forthwith transmit written notice of such appearance or failure to make such appearance to the parent or guardian of such minor person; provided, however, that if an arraignment and conviction of such person follows such appearance upon the same day, or in case such person waives arraignment and enters a plea of guilty to the offense as charged in accordance with the provisions of section eighteen hundred five of this chapter, transmittal of notice of his or her conviction as provided in section five hundred fourteen of this chapter shall be sufficient and the notice required by this paragraph need not be given; provided further that the failure of a local criminal court to transmit the notice required by this paragraph shall in no manner affect the validity of a conviction subsequently obtained.

Amended by L. 1994, Ch. 75, § 1, eff. Nov. 1, 1994, amending subd. 1(a); L. 1994, Ch. 75, § 2, eff. Nov. 1, 1994, adding subd. 2(b)(1-a); L. 1994, Ch. 312, § 2, eff. Oct. 1, 1994, amending subd. 2(c); L. 1994, Ch. 312, § 3, eff. Nov. 1, 1994, amending subd. 2(e)(1)(a); L. 1994, Ch. 312, § 4, eff. Nov. 1, 1994 and remaining in effect until Nov. 1, 1996, adding subd. 2(e)(7); L. 1994, Ch. 286, § 1, eff. July 13, 1994, extending the expiration date, to Oct. 1, 1995, of subd. 2(b)(8) and (c); L. 1995, Ch. 3, § 73, extending the expiration date of subd. 2(b)(8) and (c); L. 1996, Ch. 26, § 1, amending subd. 1(d), eff. Nov. 1, 1996; L. 1996, Ch. 196, § 12, amending subd. 2(a), eff. Nov. 1, 1996; L. 1996, Ch. 26, § 2, amending subd. 2(b)(4), eff. Nov. 1, 1996; L. 1996, Ch. 196, § 13, amending subd. 2(b)(7), eff. Nov. 1, 1996; L. 1996, Ch. 26, § 2, adding subd. 2(b)(4-a), eff. Nov. 1, 1996; L. 1996, Ch. 400, § 1, extending to Oct. 1, 1997, eff. date of amendments to subd. 2(b)(8), pursuant to L. 1993, Ch. 533, § 5, eff. Jul. 30, 1996; L. 1996, Ch. 309, § 78, extending to Oct. 1, 1997, expiration date of amendments to subd. 2(b)(8), pursuant to L. 1993, Ch. 533, § 5, eff. Jul. 13, 1996; L. 1996, Ch. 400, § 1, extending to Oct. 1, 1997, eff. date of amendments to subd. 2(c), pursuant to L. 1993, Ch. 533, § 6, eff. Jul. 30, 1996; L. 1996, Ch. 309, § 78, extending to Oct. 1, 1997, expiration date of amendments to subd. 2(c), pursuant to L. 1993, Ch. 533, § 6, eff. Jul. 13, 1996; L. 1996, Ch. 229, § 1, extending to Nov. 1, 1997, repeal date of subd. 2(e)(7), eff. Jun. 26, 1996; L. 1997, Ch. 382, § 1, extending repeal date of subd. (2)(b)(8) and (c) to Oct. 1, 1998, eff. Aug. 5, 1997, and Ch. 131, § 1 extending repeal date of subd. 2(e)(7) to Nov. 1, 2000, eff. June 25, 1997; L. 1998, Ch. 58 Part E, § 27, extending repeal date of subd. (2)(b)(8) and (c) to Oct. 1, 1999, eff. Apr. 28, 1998, deemed in full force and effect Apr. 1, 1998; L. 1999, Ch. 512, § 1, extending repeal date of subd. (2)(b)(8) and (c) to Oct. 1, 2000, eff. Sept. 28, 1999; L. 2000, Ch. 287, §§ 1 and 2, amending subd. (2)(b)(6)-(8), eff. Nov. 1, 2000, and Ch. 447, §§ 1 and 2, extending repeal date of subd. (2)(b)(8), (c) and (e)(7) to Oct. 1, 2001, eff. Sept. 20, 2000, and shall apply to out-of-state convictions occurring on or after such effective date; L. 2001, Ch. 242, eff. Sept. 4, 2001, extending repeal date; L. 2002, Ch. 416, § 1, eff. Aug. 13, 2002, extending repeal date to Oct. 1, 2003; L. 2002, Ch. 571, §§ 1-4, eff. Dec. 23, 2002, amending subd. 2(e)(7)(a) and 2(e)(7)(b), and adding subd. 2(e)(7)(a-1) and 2(f); L. 2002, Ch. 84, Part A § 1, extending repeal date of subd. 2(b)(8), 2(c), 2(e)(7) to Oct. 1, 2003; L. 2002, Ch. 3, § 3, eff. Nov. 1, 2003, amending subd. 2(e)(7)(a) and (b); L. 2002, Ch. 691, § 1, eff. Sept. 30, 2003, adding subd. 1-a; L. 2003, Ch. 62, Part B1, § 1, eff. May 15, 2003; L. 2003, Ch. 487, §§ 1, 2, eff. Sept. 9, 2003, extending repeal date to Oct.

1, 2005; L. 2005, Ch. 60, Part D, §§ 1, 2, eff. Apr. 1, 2005, extending expiration and repeal date to Oct. 1, 2007, Part E, §§ 16, 17, eff. Sept. 30, 2005, amending subd. 2(b)(5) and (e)(3)(b).

ANNOTATIONS

Constitutionality.—The prompt suspension law accords with due process requirements. Pringle v. Wolfe, 88 N.Y.2d 426, 646 N.Y.S.2d 82, 668 N.E.2d 1376 (1996).

—Prosecution of a defendant under both VTL §§ 1192 and 1193 for the same act does not violate the constitutional prohibition against multiple punishments for the same offense, since the bar against double jeopardy does not prevent statutes from imposing both criminal and civil sanctions for the same conduct. People v. Haishun, 238 A.D.2d 521, 656 N.Y.S.2d 660 (2d Dept. 1997).

—Section 1193 is upheld as constitutional. Hauptman v. New York State Dept. of Motor Vehicles, 158 A.D.2d 600, 551 N.Y.S.2d 572 (2d Dept. 1990).

—Criminal prosecution following suspension of defendant's license does not subject defendant to multiple punishment in violation of the Double Jeopardy Clause. Smith v. County Court of Essex County, 224 A.D.2d 89, 649 N.Y.S.2d 507 (3d Dept. 1996).

—The suspension of a defendant's license pursuant to the prompt suspension law set forth in section 1193(2)(e) does not constitute punishment within the meaning of the Double Jeopardy Clause and thus does not prohibit prosecution on DWI charges; nor does the section violate defendant's right to due process. People v. Roach, 226 A.D.2d 55, 649 N.Y.S.2d 607 (4th Dept. 1996).

—Criminal prosecution following suspension of defendant's license does not subject defendant to multiple punishment in violation of the Double Jeopardy Clause. People v. Conrad, 169 Misc. 2d 1066, 654 N.Y.S.2d 226 (Sup. Ct. App. Term 1996).

—VTL § 1193(2) violates the Double Jeopardy Clause. People v. McRobbie, 168 Misc. 2d 151, 636 N.Y.S.2d 975 (Just. Ct. of Henriette, Monroe Co. 1995).

Extreme hardship exception.—"Extreme hardship" does not encompass inconvenience to the defendant or any consideration of whether the defendant is required to operate a vehicle as a condition of employment; defendant, a New York City firefighter residing in Staten Island, did not meet his burden of establishing that he would be unable to use an alternative means of transportation to reach his place of employment. People v. Correa, 168 Misc. 2d 309, 643 N.Y.S.2d 310 (N.Y.C. Crim. Ct. 1996).

Lesser included offense.—Defendant was entitled to consideration of the lesser included offense of driving while impaired under a common-law driving while intoxicated count; court's failure to do so constitutes reversible error. People v. Maharaj, 89 N.Y.2d 997, 657 N.Y.S.2d 392, 679 N.E.2d 631 (1997).

—Misdemeanor driving while ability impaired (DWAI), in violation of section 1193(1), is not a lesser included offense of driving while under the influence, since both offenses are unclassified misdemeanors and DWAI requires proof of an element not required by DWI—i.e., the existence of two prior offenses within the preceding ten years. People v. Jamison, 170 Misc. 2d 974, 652 N.Y.S.2d 495 (Rochester City Ct. 1996).

Sentencing.—Sentence for felony conviction under VTL § 1192 was proper where court imposed a $1,000 fine plus the mandatory surcharge in addition to a 90-day term of incarceration as a condition of a five-year term of probation. People v. Andrews, 245 A.D.2d 493, 679 N.Y.S.2d 839 (2d Dept. 1998).

—Court acted within its discretion when it lowered the fine imposed from the statutory maximum of $5,000 to the minimum of $1,000 upon a showing that defendant was indigent with an income below poverty level. People v. Helm, 260 A.D.2d 803, 687 N.Y.S.2d 827 (3d Dept. 1999).

—This section does not mandate imposition of a fine for driving while ability impaired; rather, it gives the sentencing court the discretion to impose a fine, a period of imprisonment, or both. People v. Swan, 277 A.D.2d 1033, 716 N.Y.S.2d 194 (4th Dept. 2000).

—Court properly sentenced defendant as a persistent felony offender based on his prior convictions for driving while intoxicated. The court imposed an indeterminate term of 15 years to life upon his present conviction for DWI as a felony

and aggravated unlicensed operation; however, in the interests of justice, the appellate court vacated the sentence and re-sentenced defendant as a second felony offender to an indeterminate term of two to four years. People v. Donhauser, 255 A.D.2d 933, 683 N.Y.S.2d 357, *reargument granted and decision amended,* 1998 N.Y. App. Div. LEXIS 14474 (4th Dept. Dec. 31, 1998).

—Where defendant's driving while under the influence was an element of the charge of first degree aggravated unlicensed operation, and both offenses to which defendant pleaded guilty occurred at the same date, time and place, and both served as the basis of the revocation of defendant's license, concurrent sentences were mandated. People v. De Maio, 304 A.D.2d 988, 760 N.Y.S.2d 558 (3d Dept. 2003).

—Sentencing court erred when it imposed a $1,000 fine on defendant for a violation of this section, driving while intoxicated as a class D felony "shall be punished by a fine of not less than two thousand dollars nor more than ten thousand dollars or by a period of imprisonment as provided in the penal law, or by both such fine and imprisonment," court was not required to impose a fine, but if it did, required minimum fine was $2,000. People v. Smith, 309 A.D.2d 1282, 764 N.Y.S.2d 732 (4th Dept. 2003), *remanded,* 309 A.D.2d 1283, 765 N.Y.S.2d 812 (4th Dept. 2003).

§ 1194. Arrest and testing.

1. Arrest and field testing. (a) Arrest. Notwithstanding the provisions of section 140.10 of the criminal procedure law, a police officer may, without a warrant, arrest a person, in case of a violation of subdivision one of section eleven hundred ninety-two of this article, if such violation is coupled with an accident or collision in which such person is involved, which in fact has been committed, though not in the police officer's presence, when the officer has reasonable cause to believe that the violation was committed by such person.

(b) Field testing. Every person operating a motor vehicle which has been involved in an accident or which is operated in violation of any of the provisions of this chapter shall, at the request of a police officer, submit to a breath test to be administered by the police officer. If such test indicates that such operator has consumed alcohol, the police officer may request such operator to submit to a chemical test in the manner set forth in subdivision two of this section.

2. Chemical tests. (a) When authorized. Any person who operates a motor vehicle in this state shall be deemed to have given consent to a chemical test of one or more of the following: breath, blood, urine, or saliva, for the purpose of determining the alcoholic and/or drug content of the blood provided that such test is administered by or at the direction of a police officer with respect to a chemical test of breath, urine or saliva or, with respect to a chemical test of blood, at the direction of a police officer:

(1) having reasonable grounds to believe such person to have been operating in violation of any subdivision of section eleven hundred ninety-two of this article and within two hours after such person has been placed under arrest for any such violation; or having reasonable grounds to believe such person to have been operating in violation

of section eleven hundred ninety-two-a of this article and within two hours after the stop of such person for any such violation,

(2) within two hours after a breath test, as provided in paragraph (b) of subdivision one of this section, indicates that alcohol has been consumed by such person and in accordance with the rules and regulations established by the police force of which the officer is a member;

(3) for the purposes of this paragraph, "reasonable grounds' to believe that a person has been operating a motor vehicle after having consumed alcohol in violation of section eleven hundred ninety-two-a of this article shall be determined by viewing the totality of circumstances surrounding the incident which, when taken together, indicate that the operator was driving in violation of such subdivision. Such circumstances may include any visible or behavioral indication of alcohol consumption by the operator, the existence of an open container containing or having contained an alcoholic beverage in or around the vehicle driven by the operator, or any other evidence surrounding the circumstances of the incident which indicates that the operator has been operating a motor vehicle after having consumed alcohol at the time of the incident; or

(4) notwithstanding any other provision of law to the contrary, no person under the age of twenty-one shall be arrested for an alleged violation of section eleven hundred ninety-two-a of this article. However, a person under the age of twenty-one for whom a chemical test is authorized pursuant to this paragraph may be temporarily detained by the police solely for the purpose of requesting or administering such chemical test whenever arrest without a warrant for a petty offense would be authorized in accordance with the provisions of section 140.10 of the criminal procedure law or paragraph (a) of subdivision one of this section.

(b) Report of refusal. (1) If: (A) such person having been placed under arrest; or (B) after a breath test indicates the presence of alcohol in the person's system; or (C) with regard to a person under the age of twenty-one, there are reasonable grounds to believe that such person has been operating a motor vehicle after having consumed alcohol in violation of section eleven hundred ninety-two-a of this article; and having thereafter been requested to submit to such chemical test and having been informed that the person's license or permit to drive and any non-resident operating privilege shall be immediately suspended and subsequently revoked, or, for operators under the age of twenty-one for whom there are reasonable grounds to believe that such operator has been operating a motor vehicle after having consumed alcohol in violation of section eleven hundred ninety-two-a of this article, shall be revoked for refusal to submit to such chemical test or any portion thereof, whether or not the

person is found guilty of the charge for which such person is arrested or detained, refuses to submit to such chemical test or any portion thereof, unless a court order has been granted pursuant to subdivision three of this section, the test shall not be given and a written report of such refusal shall be immediately made by the police officer before whom such refusal was made. Such report may be verified by having the report sworn to, or by affixing to such report a form notice that false statements made therein are punishable as a class A misdemeanor pursuant to section 210.45 of the penal law and such form notice together with the subscription of the deponent shall constitute a verification of the report.

(2) The report of the police officer shall set forth reasonable grounds to believe such arrested person or such detained person under the age of twenty-one had been driving in violation of any subdivision of section eleven hundred ninety-two or eleven hundred ninety-two-a of this article, that said person had refused to submit to such chemical test, and that no chemical test was administered pursuant to the requirements of subdivision three of this section. The report shall be presented to the court upon arraignment of an arrested person, provided, however, in the case of a person under the age of twenty-one, for whom a test was authorized pursuant to the provisions of subparagraph two or three of paragraph (a) of this subdivision, and who has not been placed under arrest for a violation of any of the provisions of section eleven hundred ninety-two of this article, such report shall be forwarded to the commissioner within forty-eight hours in a manner to be prescribed by the commissioner, and all subsequent proceedings with regard to refusal to submit to such chemical test by such person shall be as set forth in subdivision three of section eleven hundred ninety-four-a of this article.

(3) for persons placed under arrest for a violation of any subdivision of section eleven hundred ninety-two of this article, the license or permit to drive and any non-resident operating privilege shall, upon the basis of such written report, be temporarily suspended by the court without notice pending the determination of a hearing as provided in paragraph (c) of this subdivision. Copies of such report must be transmitted by the court to the commissioner and such transmittal may not be waived even with the consent of all the parties. Such report shall be forwarded to the commissioner within forty-eight hours of such arraignment.

(4) The court or the police officer, in the case of a person under the age of twenty-one alleged to be driving after having consumed alcohol, shall provide such person with a scheduled hearing date, a waiver form, and such other information as may be required by the commissioner. If a hearing, as provided for in paragraph (c) of this subdivision, or subdivision three of section eleven hundred ninety-four-a of this article, is waived by

such person, the commissioner shall immediately revoke the license, permit, or non-resident operating privilege, as of the date of receipt of such waiver in accordance with the provisions of paragraph (d) of this subdivision.

(c) Hearings. Any person whose license or permit to drive or any nonresident driving privilege has been suspended pursuant to paragraph (b) of this subdivision is entitled to a hearing in accordance with a hearing schedule to be promulgated by the commissioner. If the department fails to provide for such hearing fifteen days after the date of the arraignment of the arrested person, the license, permit to drive or non-resident operating privilege of such person shall be reinstated pending a hearing pursuant to this section. The hearing shall be limited to the following issues: (1) did the police officer have reasonable grounds to believe that such person had been driving in violation of any subdivision of section eleven hundred ninety-two of this article; (2) did the police officer make a lawful arrest of such person; (3) was such person given sufficient warning, in clear or unequivocal language, prior to such refusal that such refusal to submit to such chemical test or any portion thereof, would result in the immediate suspension and subsequent revocation of such person's license or operating privilege whether or not such person is found guilty of the charge for which the arrest was made; and (4) did such person refuse to submit to such chemical test or any portion thereof. If, after such hearing, the hearing officer, acting on behalf of the commissioner, finds on any one of said issues in the negative, the hearing officer shall immediately terminate any suspension arising from such refusal. If, after such hearing, the hearing officer, acting on behalf of the commissioner finds all of the issues in the affirmative, such officer shall immediately revoke the license or permit to drive or any non-resident operating privilege in accordance with the provisions of paragraph (d) of this subdivision. A person who has had a license or permit to drive or non-resident operating privilege suspended or revoked pursuant to this subdivision may appeal the findings of the hearing officer in accordance with the provisions of article three-A of this chapter. Any person may waive the right to a hearing under this section. Failure by such person to appear for the scheduled hearing shall constitute a waiver of such hearing, provided, however, that such person may petition the commissioner for a new hearing which shall be held as soon as practicable.

(d) Sanctions.

(1) Revocations.

a. Any license which has been revoked pursuant to paragraph (c) of this subdivision shall not be restored for at least six months after such revocation, nor thereafter, except in the discretion of the commissioner. However, no such license shall be restored for at least one year after such revocation, nor thereafter except in the discretion of the commissioner, in any case where the person has had a prior revocation resulting from refusal to submit to a chemical test, or has been convicted of or found to be in violation of any subdivision of section eleven hundred ninety-two or section eleven hundred ninety-two-a of this article not arising out of the same incident, within the five years immediately preceding the date of such revocation; provided, however, a prior finding that a person under the age of twenty-one has refused to submit to a chemical test pursuant to subdivision three of section eleven hundred ninety-four-a of this article shall have the same effect as a prior finding of a refusal pursuant to this subdivision solely for the purpose of determining the length of any license suspension or revocation required to be imposed under any provision of this article, provided that the subsequent offense or refusal is committed or occurred prior to the expiration of the retention period for such prior refusal as set forth in paragraph (k) of subdivision one of section two hundred one of this chapter.

b. Any license which has been revoked pursuant to paragraph (c) of this subdivision or pursuant to subdivision three of section eleven hundred ninety-four-a of this article, where the holder was under the age of twenty-one years at the time of such refusal, shall not be restored for at least one year, nor thereafter, except in the discretion of the commissioner. Where such person under the age of twenty-one years has a prior finding, conviction or youthful offender adjudication resulting from a violation of section eleven hundred ninety-two or section eleven hundred ninety-two-a of this article, not arising from the same incident, such license shall not be restored for at least one year or until such person reaches the age of twenty-one years, whichever is the greater period of time, nor thereafter, except in the discretion of the commissioner.

c. Any commercial driver's license which has been revoked pursuant to paragraph (c) of this subdivision based upon a finding of refusal to submit to a chemical test shall not be restored for at least one year after such revocation, nor thereafter, except in the discretion of the commissioner, but shall not be restored for at least three years after such revocation, nor thereafter, except in the discretion of the commissioner, if the holder of such license was operating a commercial motor vehicle transporting hazardous materials at the time of such refusal. However, such person shall be permanently disqualified from operating a commercial motor vehicle in any case where the holder has a prior finding of refusal to submit to a chemical test pursuant to this section or has a prior conviction of any of the following offenses: any violation of section eleven hundred ninety-two of this article; any violation of subdivision one or two of section six hundred of this chapter; or has a prior conviction of any felony involving the use of a motor vehicle pursuant to paragraph

(a) of subdivision one of section five hundred ten-a of this chapter. Provided that the commissioner may waive such permanent revocation after a period of ten years has expired from such revocation provided:

(i) that during such ten year period such person has not been found to have refused a chemical test pursuant to this section and has not been convicted of any one of the following offenses: any violation of section eleven hundred ninety-two of this article; refusal to submit to a chemical test pursuant to this section; any violation of subdivision one or two of section six hundred of this chapter; or has a prior conviction of any felony involving the use of a motor vehicle pursuant to paragraph (a) of subdivision one of section five hundred ten-a of this chapter;

(ii) that such person provides acceptable documentation to the commissioner that such person is not in need of alcohol or drug treatment or has satisfactorily completed a prescribed course of such treatment; and

(iii) after such documentation is accepted, that such person is granted a certificate of relief from disabilities as provided for in section seven hundred one of the correction law by the court in which such person was last penalized.

d. Upon a third finding of refusal and/or conviction of any of the offenses which require a permanent commercial driver's license revocation, such permanent revocation may not be waived by the commissioner under any circumstances.

(2) Civil penalties. Except as otherwise provided, any person whose license, permit to drive, or any non-resident operating privilege is revoked pursuant to the provisions of this section shall also be liable for a civil penalty in the amount of three hundred dollars except that if such revocation is a second or subsequent revocation pursuant to this section issued within a five year period, or such person has been convicted of a violation of any subdivision of section eleven hundred ninety-two of this article within the past five years not arising out of the same incident, the civil penalty shall be in the amount of seven hundred fifty dollars. Any person whose license is revoked pursuant to the provisions of this section based upon a finding of refusal to submit to a chemical test while operating a commercial motor vehicle shall also be liable for a civil penalty of three hundred fifty dollars except that if such person has previously been found to have refused a chemical test pursuant to this section while operating a commercial motor vehicle or has a prior conviction of any of the following offenses while operating a commercial motor vehicle: any violation of section eleven hundred ninety-two of this article; any violation of subdivision two of section six hundred of this chapter; or has a prior conviction of any felony involving the use of a commercial motor vehicle pursuant to paragraph (a) of subdivision one of

section five hundred ten-a of this chapter, then the civil penalty shall be seven hundred fifty dollars. No new driver's license or permit shall be issued, or non-resident operating privilege restored to such person unless such penalty has been paid. All penalties collected by the department pursuant to the provisions of this section shall be the property of the state and shall be paid into the general fund of the state treasury.

(3) Effect of rehabilitation program. No period of revocation arising out of this section may be set aside by the commissioner for the reason that such person was a participant in the alcohol and drug rehabilitation program set forth in section eleven hundred ninety-six of this article.

(e) Regulations. The commissioner shall promulgate such rules and regulations as may be necessary to effectuate the provisions of subdivisions one and two of this section.

(f) Evidence. Evidence of a refusal to submit to such chemical test or any portion thereof shall be admissible in any trial, proceeding or hearing based upon a violation of the provisions of section eleven hundred ninety-two of this article but only upon a showing that the person was given sufficient warning, in clear and unequivocal language, of the effect of such refusal and that the person persisted in the refusal.

(g) Results. Upon the request of the person who was tested, the results of such test shall be made available to such person.

3. Compulsory chemical tests. (a) Court ordered chemical tests. Notwithstanding the provisions of subdivision two of this section, no person who operates a motor vehicle in this state may refuse to submit to a chemical test of one or more of the following: breath, blood, urine or saliva, for the purpose of determining the alcoholic and/or drug content of the blood when a court order for such chemical test has been issued in accordance with the provisions of this subdivision.

(b) When authorized. Upon refusal by any person to submit to a chemical test or any portion thereof as described above, the test shall not be given unless a police officer or a district attorney, as defined in subdivision thirty-two of section 1.20 of the criminal procedure law, requests and obtains a court order to compel a person to submit to a chemical test to determine the alcoholic or drug content of the person's blood upon a finding of reasonable cause to believe that:

(1) such person was the operator of a motor vehicle and in the course of such operation a person other than the operator was killed or suffered serious physical injury as defined in section 10.00 of the penal law; and

(2) a. either such person operated the vehicle in violation of any subdivision of section eleven hundred ninety-two of this article, or

b. a breath test administered by a police officer in accordance with paragraph (b) of subdivision one of this section indicates that alcohol has been consumed by such person; and

(3) such person has been placed under lawful arrest; and

(4) such person has refused to submit to a chemical test or any portion thereof, requested in accordance with the provisions of paragraph (a) of subdivision two of this section or is unable to give consent to such a test.

(c) Reasonable cause; definition. For the purpose of this subdivision "reasonable cause" shall be determined by viewing the totality of circumstances surrounding the incident which, when taken together, indicate that the operator was driving in violation of section eleven hundred ninety-two of this article. Such circumstances may include, but are not limited to: evidence that the operator was operating a motor vehicle in violation of any provision of this article or any other moving violation at the time of the incident; any visible indication of alcohol or drug consumption or impairment by the operator; the existence of an open container containing an alcoholic beverage in or around the vehicle driven by the operator; any other evidence surrounding the circumstances of the incident which indicates that the operator has been operating a motor vehicle while impaired by the consumption of alcohol or drugs or intoxicated at the time of the incident.

(d) Court order; procedure. (1) An application for a court order to compel submission to a chemical test or any portion thereof, may be made to any supreme court justice, county court judge or district court judge in the judicial district in which the incident occurred, or if the incident occurred in the city of New York before any supreme court justice or judge of the criminal court of the city of New York. Such application may be communicated by telephone, radio or other means of electronic communication, or in person.

(2) The applicant must provide identification by name and title and must state the purpose of the communication. Upon being advised that an application for a court order to compel submission to a chemical test is being made, the court shall place under oath the applicant and any other person providing information in support of the application as provided in subparagraph three of this paragraph. After being sworn the applicant must state that the person from whom the chemical test was requested was the operator of a motor vehicle and in the course of such operation a person, other than the operator, has been killed or seriously injured and, based upon the totality of circumstances, there is reasonable cause to believe that such person was operating a motor vehicle in violation of any subdivision of section eleven hundred ninety-two of this article and,

after being placed under lawful arrest such person refused to submit to a chemical test or any portion thereof, in accordance with the provisions of this section or is unable to give consent to such a test or any portion thereof. The applicant must make specific allegations of fact to support such statement. Any other person properly identified, may present sworn allegations of fact in support of the applicant's statement.

(3) Upon being advised that an oral application for a court order to compel a person to submit to a chemical test is being made, a judge or justice shall place under oath the applicant and any other person providing information in support of the application. Such oath or oaths and all of the remaining communication must be recorded, either by means of a voice recording device or verbatim stenographic or verbatim longhand notes. If a voice recording device is used or a stenographic record made, the judge must have the record transcribed, certify to the accuracy of the transcription and file the original record and transcription with the court within seventy-two hours of the issuance of the court order. If the longhand notes are taken, the judge shall subscribe a copy and file it with the court within twenty-four hours of the issuance of the order.

(4) If the court is satisfied that the requirements for the issuance of a court order pursuant to the provisions of paragraph (b) of this subdivision have been met, it may grant the application and issue an order requiring the accused to submit to a chemical test to determine the alcoholic and/or drug content of his blood and ordering the withdrawal of a blood sample in accordance with the provisions of paragraph (a) of subdivision four of this section. When a judge or justice determines to issue an order to compel submission to a chemical test based on an oral application, the applicant therefor shall prepare the order in accordance with the instructions of the judge or justice. In all cases the order shall include the name of the issuing judge or justice, the name of the applicant, and the date and time it was issued. It must be signed by the judge or justice if issued in person, or by the applicant if issued orally.

(5) Any false statement by an applicant or any other person in support of an application for a court order shall subject such person to the offenses for perjury set forth in article two hundred ten of the penal law.

(6) The chief administrator of the courts shall establish a schedule to provide that a sufficient number of judges or justices will be available in each judicial district to hear oral applications for court orders as permitted by this section.

(e) Administration of compulsory chemical test. An order issued pursuant to the provisions of this subdivision shall require that a chemical test to determine the alcoholic and/or drug content of the operator's blood must be administered. The provisions of paragraphs (a), (b) and (c) of subdivision four of this section shall be applicable to any chemical test administered pursuant to this section.

4. (a) (1) Testing procedures. At the request of a police officer, the following persons may withdraw blood for the purpose of determining the alcoholic or drug content therein: (i) a physician, a registered professional nurse or a registered physician's assistant; or (ii) under the supervision and at the direction of a physician: a medical laboratory technician or medical technologist as classified by civil service; a phlebotomist; an advanced emergency medical technician as certified by the department of health; or a medical laboratory technician or medical technologist employed by a clinical laboratory approved under title five of article five of the public health law. This limitation shall not apply to the taking of a urine, saliva or breath specimen.

(2) No person entitled to withdraw blood pursuant to subparagraph one of this paragraph or hospital employing such person, and no other employer of such person shall be sued or held liable for any act done or omitted in the course of withdrawing blood at the request of a police officer pursuant to this section.

(3) Any person who may have a cause of action arising from the withdrawal of blood as aforesaid, for which no personal liability exists under subparagraph two of this paragraph, may maintain such action against the state if any person entitled to withdraw blood pursuant to paragraph (a) hereof acted at the request of a police officer employed by the state, or against the appropriate political subdivision of the state if such person acted at the request of a police officer employed by a political subdivision of the state. no action shall be maintained pursuant to this subparagraph unless notice of claim is duly filed or served in compliance with law.

(4) Notwithstanding the foregoing provisions of this paragraph an action may be maintained by the state or a political subdivision thereof against a person entitled to withdraw blood pursuant to subparagraph one of this paragraph or hospital employing such person for whose act or omission the state or the political subdivision has been held liable under this paragraph to recover damages, not exceeding the amount awarded to the claimant, that may have been sustained by the state or the political subdivision by reason of gross negligence or bad faith on the part of such person.

(5) The testimony of any person other than a physician, entitled to withdraw blood pursuant to subparagraph one of this paragraph, in respect to any such withdrawal of blood made by such person may be received in evidence with the same weight, force and effect as if such withdrawal of blood were made by a physician.

(6) The provisions of subparagraphs two, three

and four of this paragraph shall also apply with regard to any person employed by a hospital as security personnel for any act done or omitted in the course of withdrawing blood at the request of a police officer pursuant to a court order in accordance with subdivision three of this section.

(b) Right to additional test. The person tested shall be permitted to choose a physician to administer a chemical test in addition to the one administered at the direction of the police officer.

(c) Rules and regulations. The department of health shall issue and file rules and regulations approving satisfactory techniques or methods of conducting chemical analyses of a person's blood, urine, breath or saliva and to ascertain the qualifications and competence of individuals to conduct and supervise chemical analyses of a person's blood, urine, breath or saliva. If the analyses were made by an individual possessing a permit issued by the department of health, this shall be presumptive evidence that the examination was properly given. The provisions of this paragraph do not prohibit the introduction as evidence of an analysis made by an individual other than a person possessing a permit issued by the department of health.

Amended by L. 1994, Ch. 169, § 122, eff. Apr. 1, 1994, amending subd. 2(d)(2); L. 1996, Ch. 196, § 14, amending subd. 2(a) and (b), eff. Nov. 1, 1996; L. 1996, Ch. 196, § 16, amending subd. 2(d)(1)(a), eff. Nov. 1, 1996; L. 1996, Ch. 196, § 15, amending subd. 2(d)(1)(b), eff. Nov. 1, 1996; L. 1996, Ch. 449, § 1, amending subd. 2(d)(2), eff. Nov. 1, 1996; L. 2005, Part E, § 18, eff. Sept. 30, 2005, amending subd. 2(d)(1)(c).

ANNOTATIONS

Application for blood test.—Despite fact that application was defective based on officer's failure to specify whether he personally observed defendant's "general demeanor," what that demeanor was, and the sources of certain hearsay statements, any error was nevertheless harmless based on the overwhelming proof of defendant's impairment. People v. Isaac, 224 A.D.2d 993, 637 N.Y.S.2d 827 (4th Dept. 1996).

Constitutionality.—The distinction drawn between the conscious driver and the unconscious or incapacitated driver does not offend the equal protection clause. People v. Kates, 53 N.Y.2d 591, 444 N.Y.S.2d 446, 428 N.Y.S.2d 852 (1981).

—Section 1194 is constitutional and does not offend the privilege against self-incrimination. People v. Thomas, 46 N.Y.2d 100, 412 N.Y.S.2d 845, 385 N.E.2d 584 (1978).

—Arresting officer who applied for a court-ordered blood test under oath reported that upon arriving at the scene, defendant was unconscious behind the steering wheel of his car, had a strong smell of alcohol on him, and at least one of the pedestrian victims struck by defendant's car was seriously injured, all of which supported the officer's belief that the defendant had operated the vehicle in violation of VTL § 1192. People v. Alshoaibi, 273 A.D.2d 871, 711 N.Y.S.2d 646 (4th Dept. 2000).

Implied consent.—Denial of defendant's motion to suppress affirmed; "although defendant claims that he did not expressly consent, he never testified that he refused the test; by driving on the roads in this state, defendant gave a statutorily implied consent to submit to a chemical test of his blood." People v. Morrisey, 21 A.D.3d 597, 799 N.Y.S.2d 642 (3d Dept. 2005).

Court-ordered blood test.—Officer satisfied the requirements of section 1194(1) by obtaining court authorization for a blood sample because defendant was unconscious after a fatal motor vehicle accident and, under the circumstances, officer was not required to go through the formalities of arrest. People v. Ladd, 89 N.Y.2d 893, 653 N.Y.S.2d 259, 675 N.E.2d 1211 (1996).

Defendant's right to independent test.—The police are not required to arrange for an independent test or to transport defendant to a place where such test may be performed. People v. Finnegan, 85 N.Y.2d 53, 623 N.Y.S.2d 546, 647 N.E.2d 758 (1995), *cert. denied*, 516 U.S. 919 (1996).

—All that is required is that the police assist defendant by affording him or her a telephone call to arrange for an independent test. People v. Crandall, 228 A.D.2d 794, 644 N.Y.S.2d 817 (3d Dept. 1996).

Elements.—Sworn affidavit in which defendant claimed he was not intoxicated when he drove the wrong way down a one-way street, but rather was "disoriented and dizzy" by a "toxic combination" of medically prescribed drugs and a single alcoholic drink, made out all the elements of an offense under § 1194(4). Property Clerk of the N.Y.C. Police Dept. v. Lizziano, 302 A.D.2d 235, 754 N.Y.S.2d 277 (1st Dept. 2003).

—Production of one witness in prosecution of defendant did not render verdict against the weight of evidence; evidence supported the verdict and included testimony of a 19-year veteran police officer who stopped defendant after he was speeding and observed a strong smell of alcohol and defendant's bloodshot eyes and slurred speech, in addition to defendant's failure of two field sobriety tests and his admission that he had been drinking. People v. Gallup, 302 A.D.2d 681, 755 N.Y.S.2d 498 (3d Dept. 2003).

No double jeopardy.—Suspension and subsequent revocation of a petitioner's driver's license for failure to comply with the implied consent provision of VTL § 1194 is a civil sanction and as such does not constitute punishment for driving under the influence of alcohol. Brennan v. Kmiotek, 233 A.D.2d 870, 649 N.Y.S.2d 611 (4th Dept. 1996).

Physician-patient privilege.—The statute authorizes a registered nurse to withdraw blood for the purpose of determining alcohol content; where nurse, who was treating defendant for injuries sustained in motor vehicle accident, withdrew blood after she observed strong odor of alcohol on defendant's breath, blood shot eyes, and slurred speech, the blood was not drawn as a necessary part of defendant's medical treatment, but was drawn for the sole purpose of testing for alcohol content, and is thus not within the principles governing a physician-patient privilege. People v. Bolson, 183 Misc. 2d 155, 701 N.Y.S.2d 828 (Sup. Ct. Queens Co. 1999).

Physician supervision required.—Where People failed to establish that defendant's blood sample was taken in compliance with § 1194;—specifically, they failed to establish that medical technologist who drew defendant's blood was authorized to do so by a physician—results of the blood test were improperly admitted into evidence at trial. People v. Griesbeck, 17 A.D.3d 717, 793 N.Y.S.2d 227 (3d Dept. 2005).

—VTL § 1194 enumerates persons who, at the request of a police officer, may draw blood from a suspect; failure to draw blood in accordance with the statute results in suppression of blood test results even if defendant consented to procedure. People v. Miller, 17 A.D.3d 708, 793 N.Y.S.2d 231 (3d Dept. 2005).

—Blood drawn by a medical technician at the direction of a registered nurse and not a doctor is not substantial compliance with the statute. Although a doctor need not be personally present at the time the blood is taken, the evidence must show that a physician "directed and supervised all activities in the emergency room and that he authorized taking of the sample." People v. Olmstead, 233 A.D.2d 837, 649 N.Y.S.2d 624 (4th Dept. 1996).

Purpose.—Section 1194 was designed to enable the authorities to deal promptly and effectively with the scourge of drunken drivers by immediate revocation of their licenses either upon chemical proof of intoxication or upon refusal to take the blood test. People v. Craft, 28 N.Y.2d 274, 321 N.Y.S.2d 566, 270 N.E.2d 297 (1971).

—VTL§ 1194(4)(b) is not applicable where, as here, defendant expressly and voluntarily consented to administration of the breathalyzer test and there was no claim or hint of coercion, therefore no requirement that police advise defendant of his right to an additional test administered by a physician of his choosing. People v. Casimiro, 308 A.D.2d 456, 764 N.Y.S.2d 198 (2d Dept. 2003).

Refusal.—Evidence of defendant's refusal to submit to sobriety tests is admissible even without *Miranda* warnings. People v. Berg, 239 A.D.2d 97, 670 N.Y.S.2d 57 (3d Dept. 1998), *aff'd*, 92 N.Y.2d 701, 685 N.Y.S.2d 906, 708 N.E.2d 979 (1999).

—Respondent's refusal to submit to a chemical test to determine blood alcohol level, after given required statutory warnings was established by the record, revocation was affirmed. Eyrich v. Jackson, 267 A.D.2d 237, 699 N.Y.S.2d 316 (2d Dept. 1999).

—Evidence of defendant's impaired condition, which included strong smell of alcohol, glassy eyes, slurred speech, and admission that he had been drinking and was drunk, together with his refusal to submit to a chemical test despite the administration of proper warnings, constituted sufficient proof of his intoxication. People v. Beyer, 21 A.D.3d 592, 799 N.Y.S.2d 620 (3d Dept. 2005).

—Before license can be revoked for refusal to submit to a chemical test, statute requires proof that individual was given sufficient warning to the effect of the refusal and evidence of the refusal. Giacone v. Jackson, 267 A.D.2d 673, 699 N.Y.S.2d 587 (3d Dept. 1999).

—Refusal to submit to a chemical test can be evidenced by words or conduct. Petitioner's response of closing his eyes and turning his head away from the officer when asked to consent to a chemical test was properly interpreted as refusal. Stegman v. Jackson, 233 A.D.2d 597, 649 N.Y.S.2d 529 (3d Dept. 1996).

—Substantial evidence supported determination to revoke petitioner's driver's license based on his refusal to submit to chemical test to determine his blood alcohol level after being clearly and unequivocally provided with the warning prescribed by this section. Scaccia v. Martinez, —A.D.3d—, 779 N.Y.S.2d 680 (4th Dept. 2004).

—People's remarks in summation were fair comment on defendant's refusal to submit to breath test, inference of consciousness of guilt may be drawn from one's refusal to submit to test after receiving fair warning. People v. Schuh, 4 A.D.3d 751, 771 N.Y.S.2d 785 (4th Dept. 2004).

—Witness's statement that she had seen defendant in driver's seat of truck which was crashed into stop sign at intersection coupled with police officer's personal observations of damage to truck and stop sign and defendant in intoxicated condition was reasonable cause to believe that defendant had driven in an intoxicated condition. Pomento v. City of Rome, 647 N.Y.S.2d 604, 231 A.D.2d 875 (4th Dept. 1996).

Right to refuse.—The State Trooper had no obligation to inform defendant that he had a right to refuse to take the field sobriety test. People v. Sheridan, 192 A.D.2d 1057, 596 N.Y.S.2d 245 (4th Dept. 1993).

§ 1194-a. Driving after having consumed alcohol; under twenty-one; procedure.

1. Chemical test report and hearing. (a) Whenever a chemical test of the breath, blood, urine or saliva of an operator who is under the age of twenty-one indicates that such person has operated a motor vehicle in violation of section eleven hundred ninety-two-a of this article, and such person is not charged with violating any subdivision of section eleven hundred ninety-two arising out of the same incident, the police officer who administered the test shall forward a report of the results of such test to the department within twenty-four hours of the time when such results are available in a manner prescribed by the commissioner, and the operator shall be given a hearing notice as provided in subdivision one-a of this section, to appear before a hearing officer in the county where the chemical test was administered, or in an adjoining county under such circumstances as prescribed by the commissioner, on a date to be established in accordance with a schedule promulgated by the commissioner. Such hearing shall occur within thirty days of, but not less than forty-eight hours from, the date that the

chemical test was administered, provided, however, where the commissioner determines, based upon the availability of hearing officers and the anticipated volume of hearings at a particular location, that the scheduling of such hearing within thirty days would impair the timely scheduling or conducting of other hearings pursuant to this chapter, such hearing shall be scheduled at the next hearing date for such particular location. When providing the operator with such hearing notice, the police officer shall also give to the operator, and shall, prior to the commencement of the hearing, provide to the department, copies of the following reports, documents and materials: any written report or document, or portion thereof, concerning a physical examination, a scientific test or experiment, including the most recent record of inspection, or calibration or repair of machines or instruments utilized to perform such scientific tests or experiments and the certification certificate, if any, held by the operator of the machine or instrument, which tests or examinations were made by or at the request or direction of a public servant engaged in law enforcement activity. The report of the police officer shall be verified by having the report sworn to, or by affixing to such report a form notice that false statements made therein are punishable as a class A misdemeanor pursuant to section 210.45 of the penal law and such form notice together with the subscription of the deponent shall constitute verification of the report.

(b) Every person under the age of twenty-one who is alleged to have operated a motor vehicle after having consumed alcohol as set forth in section eleven hundred ninety-two-a of this article, and who is not charged with violating any subdivision of section eleven hundred ninety-two of this article arising out of the same incident, is entitled to a hearing before a hearing officer in accordance with the provisions of this section. Unless otherwise provided by law, the license or permit to drive or any non-resident operating privilege of such person shall not be suspended or revoked prior to the scheduled date for such hearing.

(i) The hearing shall be limited to the following issues: (1) did such person operate the motor vehicle; (2) was a valid request to submit to a chemical test made by the police officer in accordance with the provisions of section eleven hundred ninety-four of this article; (3) was such person less than twenty-one years of age at the time of operation of the motor vehicle; (4) was the chemical test properly administered in accordance with the provisions of section eleven hundred ninety-four of this article; (5) did the test find that such person had driven after having consumed alcohol as defined in section eleven hundred ninety-two-a of this article; and (6) did the police officer make a lawful stop of such person. The burden of proof shall be on the police officer to prove each of these issues by clear and convincing evidence.

(ii) Every person who is entitled to a hearing pursuant to this subdivision has the right to be present at the hearing; the right to be represented by attorney, or in the hearing officer's discretion, by any other person the operator chooses; the right to receive and review discovery materials as provided in this subdivision; the right not to testify; the right to present evidence and witnesses in his own behalf, the right to cross examine adverse witnesses, and the right to appeal from an adverse determination in accordance with article three-A of this chapter. Any person representing the operator must conform to the standards of conduct required of attorneys appearing before state courts, and failure to conform to these standards will be grounds for declining to permit his continued appearance in the hearing.

(iii) Hearings conducted pursuant to this subdivision shall be in accordance with this subdivision and with the provisions applicable to the adjudication of traffic infractions pursuant to the following provisions of part 124 of title fifteen of the codes, rules and regulations of the state of New York: paragraph (b) of section 124.1 regarding the opening statement; paragraph (b) of section 124.2 regarding the right to representation and to remain silent and paragraphs (a) through (e) of section 124.4 regarding the conduct of the hearing, procedure and recusal; provided, however, that nothing contained in this subparagraph shall be deemed to preclude a hearing officer from changing the order of a hearing conducted pursuant to this subdivision as justice may require and for good cause shown.

(iv) The rules governing receipt of evidence in a court of law shall not apply in a hearing conducted pursuant to this subdivision except as follows:

(1) on the merits of the charge, and whether or not a party objects, the hearing officer shall exclude from consideration the following: a privileged communication; evidence which, for constitutional reasons, would not be admissible in a court of law; evidence of prior misconduct, incompetency or illness, except where such evidence would be admissible in a court of law; evidence which is irrelevant or immaterial;

(2) no negative inference shall be drawn from the operator's exercising the right not to testify.

(v) If, after such hearing, the hearing officer, acting on behalf of the commissioner, finds all of the issues set forth in this subdivision in the affirmative, the hearing officer shall suspend or revoke the license or permit to drive or non-resident operating privilege of such person in accordance with the time periods set forth in subdivision two of section eleven hundred ninety-three of this article. If, after such hearing, the hearing officer, acting on behalf of the commissioner, finds any of said issues in the negative, the hearing officer must find that the operator did not drive after having consumed alcohol.

(vi) A person who has had a license or permit to drive or non-resident operating privilege suspended or revoked pursuant to the provisions of this section may appeal the finding of the hearing officer in accordance with the provisions of article three-A of this chapter.

(c) Unless an adjournment of the hearing date has been granted, upon the operator's failure to appear for a scheduled hearing, the commissioner shall suspend the license or permit to drive or non-resident operating privilege until the operator petitions the commissioner and a rescheduled hearing is conducted, provided, however, the commissioner shall restore such person's license or permit to drive or non-resident operating privilege if such rescheduled hearing is adjourned at the request of a person other than the operator. Requests for adjournments shall be made and determined in accordance with regulations promulgated by the commissioner. If such a request by the operator for an adjournment is granted, the commissioner shall notify the operator of the rescheduled hearing, which shall be scheduled for the next hearing date. If a second or subsequent request by the operator for an adjournment is granted, the operator's license or permit to drive or non-resident operating privilege may be suspended pending the hearing at the time such adjournment is granted; provided, however, that the records of the department or the evidence already admitted furnishes reasonable grounds to believe such suspension is necessary to prevent continuing violations or a substantial traffic safety hazard; and provided further, that such hearing shall be scheduled for the next hearing date. If a police officer does not appear for a hearing, the hearing officer shall have the authority to dismiss the charge. Any person may waive the right to a hearing under this subdivision, in a form and manner prescribed by the commissioner, and may enter an admission of guilt, in person or by mail, to the charge of operating a motor vehicle in violation of section eleven hundred ninety-two-a of this article. Such admission of guilt shall have the same force and effect as a finding of guilt entered following a hearing conducted pursuant to this subdivision.

1-a. Hearing notice. The hearing notice issued to an operator pursuant to subdivision one of this section shall be in a form as prescribed by the commissioner. In addition to containing information concerning the time, date and location of the hearing, and such other information as the commissioner deems appropriate, such hearing notice shall also contain the following information: the date, time and place of the offense charged; the procedures for requesting an adjournment of a scheduled hearing as provided in this section, the operator's right to a hearing conducted pursuant to this section and the right to waive such hearing and plead guilty, either in person or by mail, to the offense charged.

2. Civil penalty. Unless otherwise provided,

any person whose license, permit to drive, or any non-resident operating privilege is suspended or revoked pursuant to the provisions of this section shall also be liable for a civil penalty in the amount of one hundred twenty-five dollars, which shall be distributed in accordance with the provisions of subdivision nine of section eighteen hundred three of this chapter.

3. Refusal report and hearing. (a) Any person under the age of twenty-one who is suspected of operating a motor vehicle after having consumed alcohol in violation of section eleven hundred ninety-two-a of this chapter, and who is not charged with violating any subdivision of section eleven hundred ninety-two of this article arising out of the same incident, and who has been requested to submit to a chemical test pursuant to paragraph (a) of subdivision two of section eleven hundred ninety-four of this article and after having been informed that his license or permit to drive and any non-resident operating privilege shall be revoked for refusal to submit to such chemical test or any portion thereof, whether or not there is a finding of driving after having consumed alcohol, and such person refuses to submit to such chemical test or any portion thereof, shall be entitled to a hearing in accordance with a schedule promulgated by the commissioner, and such hearing shall occur within thirty days of, but not less than forty-eight hours from, the date of such refusal, provided, however, where the commissioner determines, based upon the availability of hearing officers and the anticipated volume of hearings at a particular location, that the scheduling of such hearing within thirty days would impair the timely scheduling or conducting of other hearings pursuant to this chapter, such hearing shall be scheduled at the next hearing date for such particular location.

(b) Unless an adjournment of the hearing date has been granted, upon the operator's failure to appear for a scheduled hearing, the commissioner shall suspend the license or permit to drive or non-resident operating privilege until the operator petitions the commissioner and a rescheduled hearing is conducted, provided, however, the commissioner shall restore such person's license or permit to drive or non-resident operating privilege if such rescheduled hearing is adjourned at the request of a person other than the operator. Requests for adjournments shall be made and determined in accordance with regulations promulgated by the commissioner. If such a request by the operator for an adjournment is granted, the commissioner shall notify the operator of the rescheduled hearing, which shall be scheduled for the next hearing date. If a second or subsequent request by the operator for an adjournment is granted, the operator's license or permit to drive or non-resident operating privilege may be suspended pending the hearing at the time such adjournment is granted; provided, however, that the records of the department or the evidence already admitted furnishes reasonable grounds to believe such suspension is necessary to prevent continuing violations or a substantial traffic safety hazard; and provided further, that such hearing shall be scheduled for the next hearing date. If a police officer does not appear for a hearing, the hearing officer shall have the authority to dismiss the charge. Any person may waive the right to a hearing under this subdivision.

(c) The hearing on the refusal to submit to a chemical test pursuant to this subdivision shall be limited to the following issues: (1) was a valid request to submit to a chemical test made by the police officer in accordance with the provisions of section eleven hundred ninety-four of this article; (2) was such person given sufficient warning, in clear or unequivocal language, prior to such refusal that such refusal to submit to such chemical test or any portion thereof, would result in the revocation of such person's license or permit to drive or nonresident operating privilege, whether or not such person is found to have operated a motor vehicle after having consumed alcohol; (3) did such person refuse to submit to such chemical test or any portion thereof; (4) did such person operate the motor vehicle; (5) was such person less than twenty-one years of age at the time of operation of the motor vehicle; (6) did the police officer make a lawful stop of such person. If, after such hearing, the hearing officer, acting on behalf of the commissioner, finds on any one said issue in the negative, the hearing officer shall not revoke the operator's license or permit to drive or non-resident operating privilege and shall immediately terminate any outstanding suspension of the operator's license, permit to drive or non-resident operating privilege arising from such refusal. If, after such hearing, the hearing officer, acting on behalf of the commissioner, finds all of the issues in the affirmative, such hearing officer shall immediately revoke the license or permit to drive or any non-resident operating privilege in accordance with the provisions of paragraph (d) of subdivision two of section eleven hundred ninety-four of this article. A person who has had a license or permit to drive or non-resident operating privilege suspended or revoked pursuant to the provisions of this section may appeal the findings of the hearing officer in accordance with the provisions of article three-A of this chapter.

Added L. 1996, Ch. 196, § 17, eff. Nov. 1, 1996.

§ 1195. Chemical test evidence.

1. Admissibility. Upon the trial of any action or proceeding arising out of actions alleged to have been committed by any person arrested for a violation of any subdivision of section eleven hundred ninety-two of this article, the court shall admit evidence of the amount of alcohol or drugs in the defendant's blood as shown by a test administered pursuant to the provisions of section eleven hundred ninety-four of this article.

2. Probative value. The following effect shall be given to evidence of blood-alcohol content, as determined by such tests, of a person arrested for violation of section eleven hundred ninety-two of this article:

(a) Evidence that there was .05 of one per centum or less by weight of alcohol in such person's blood shall be prima facie evidence that the ability of such person to operate a motor vehicle was not impaired by the consumption of alcohol, and that such person was not in an intoxicated condition;

(b) Evidence that there was more than .05 of one per centum but less than .07 of one per centum by weight of alcohol in such person's blood shall be prima facie evidence that such person was not in an intoxicated condition, but such evidence shall be relevant evidence, but shall not be given prima facie effect, in determining whether the ability of such person to operate a motor vehicle was impaired by the consumption of alcohol; and

(c) Evidence that there was .07 of one per centum but less than .08 of one per centum by weight of alcohol in such person's blood shall be prima facie evidence that such person was not in an intoxicated condition, but such evidence shall be given prima facie effect in determining whether the ability of such person to operate a motor vehicle was impaired by the consumption of alcohol.

3. Suppression. A defendant who has been compelled to submit to a chemical test pursuant to the provisions of subdivision three of section eleven hundred ninety-four of this article may move for the suppression of such evidence in accordance with article seven hundred ten of the criminal procedure law on the grounds that the order was obtained and the test administered in violation of the provisions of such subdivision or any other applicable law.

Amended by L. 2002, Ch. 3, § 4, eff. Nov. 1, 2003, amending subd. 2(c); L. 2003, Ch. 153, § 1, eff. July 1, 2003, amending subd. 2(b) and (c).

ANNOTATIONS

Rebuttable presumption.—Evidence supporting a charge of driving while intoxicated is facially sufficient when record contains results of breathalyzer test showing .07 of 1% by weight of alcohol, since this creates a rebuttable presumption (VTL § 1195(2)(a)) that the defendant was not intoxicated. The BAL, coupled with the officer's first hand observations, containing all indications of common law intoxication, support the officer's reasonable cause to believe that defendant was intoxicated. People v. Gristina, 186 Misc. 2d 877, 721 N.Y.S.2d 491 (Crim. Ct. N.Y. Co. 2001).

—Factual allegations contained in accusatory instrument alleged that arresting officer observed defendant driving without headlights or taillights, and that upon stopping defendant found that defendant smelled of alcohol, had glassy eyes, impaired speech and motor coordination, and failed field sobriety tests; People were entitled to rebut § 1195(2)(c) presumption at trial, and to the extent that People v. Gingillo, 181 Misc. 3d 163 (1999), holds to the contrary, it should not be followed. People v. Blair, 98 N.Y.2d 722,749 N.Y.S.2d 809, 779 N.E.2d 748 (2002).

§ 1196. Alcohol and drug rehabilitation program.

1. Program establishment. There is hereby established an alcohol and drug rehabilitation program within the department of motor vehicles. The commissioner shall establish, by regulation, the instructional and rehabilitative aspects of the program. Such program shall consist of at least fifteen hours and include, but need not be limited to, classroom instruction in areas deemed suitable by the commissioner. No person shall be required to attend or participate in such program or any aspect thereof for a period exceeding eight months except upon the recommendation of the department of mental hygiene or appropriate health officials administering the program on behalf of a municipality.

2. Curriculum. The form, content and method of presentation of the various aspects of such program shall be established by the commissioner. In the development of the form, curriculum and content of such program, the commissioner may consult with the commissioner of mental health, the director of the division of alcoholism and alcohol abuse, the director of the division of substance abuse services and any other state department or agency and request and receive assistance from them. The commissioner is also authorized to develop more than one curriculum and course content for such program in order to meet the varying rehabilitative needs of the participants.

3. Where available. A course in such program shall be available in at least every county in the state, except where the commissioner determines that there is not a sufficient number of alcohol or drug-related traffic offenses in a county to mandate the establishment of said course, and that provisions be made for the residents of said county to attend a course in another county where a course exists.

4. Eligibility. Participation in the program shall be limited to those persons convicted of alcohol or drug-related traffic offenses or persons who have been adjudicated youthful offenders for alcohol or drug-related traffic offenses, or persons found to have been operating a motor vehicle after having consumed alcohol in violation of section eleven hundred ninety-two-a of this article, who choose to participate and who satisfy the criteria and meet the requirements for participation as established by this section and the regulations promulgated thereunder; provided, however, in the exercise of discretion, the judge imposing sentence may prohibit the defendant from enrolling in such program. The commissioner or deputy may exercise discretion, to reject any person from participation referred to such program and nothing herein contained shall be construed as creating a right to be included in any course or program established under this section. In addition, no person shall be permitted to take part in such program if, during the five years immediately preceding commission of an alcohol or drug-related traffic offense or a finding of a violation of section eleven hundred ninety-two-a of this article, such person has participated in a program established pursuant to this article or been convicted of a violation of any subdivision of section eleven hundred ninety-two of this article other than a violation committed prior to November first, nineteen hundred eighty-eight, for which such person did not participate in such program. In the exercise of discretion, the commissioner or a deputy shall have the right to expel any participant from the program who fails to satisfy the requirements for participation in such program or who fails to satisfactorily participate in or attend any aspect of such program. Notwithstanding any contrary provisions of this chapter, satisfactory participation in and completion of a course in such program shall result in the termination of any sentence of imprisonment that may have been imposed by reason of a conviction therefor; provided, however, that nothing contained in this section shall delay the commencement of such sentence.

5. Effect of completion. Except as provided in subparagraph nine of paragraph (b) of subdivision two of section eleven hundred ninety-three or in subparagraph three of paragraph (d) of subdivision two of section eleven hundred ninety-four of this article, upon successful completion of a course in such program as certified by its administrator, a participant may apply to the commissioner on a form provided for that purpose, for the termination of the suspension or revocation order issued as a result of the participant's conviction which caused the participation in such course. In the exercise of discretion, upon receipt of such application, and upon payment of any civil penalties for which the applicant may be liable, the commissioner is authorized to terminate such order or orders and return the participant's license or reinstate the privilege of operating a motor vehicle in this state. However, the commissioner shall not issue any new license nor restore any license where said issuance of restoral is prohibited by subdivision two of section eleven hundred ninety-three of this article.

6. Fees. The commissioner shall establish a schedule of fees to be paid by or on behalf of each participant in the program, and may, from time to time, modify same. Such fees shall defray the ongoing expenses of the program. provided, however, that pursuant to an agreement with the department a municipality, department thereof, or other agency may conduct a course in such program with all or part of the expense of such course and program being borne by such municipality, department or agency. In no event shall such fee be refundable, either for reasons of the participant's withdrawal or expulsion from such program or otherwise.

7. Conditional license. (a) Notwithstanding

any inconsistent provision of this chapter, participants in the program, except those penalized under paragraph (d) of subdivision one of section eleven hundred ninety-three of this article for any violation of subdivision two, three, or four of section eleven hundred ninety-two of this article, may, in the commissioner's discretion, be issued a conditional driver's license, or if the holder of a license issued by another jurisdiction valid for operation in this state, a conditional privilege of operating a motor vehicle in this state. Such a conditional license or privilege shall be valid only for use, by the holder thereof, (1) enroute to and from the holder's place of employment, (2) if the holder's employment requires the operation of a motor vehicle then during the hours thereof, (3) enroute to and from a class or an activity which is an authorized part of the alcohol and drug rehabilitation program and at which his attendance is required, (4) enroute to and from a class or course at an accredited school, college or university or at a state approved institution of vocational or technical training, (5) to or from court ordered probation activities, (6) to and from a motor vehicle office for the transaction of business relating to such license or program, (7) for a three hour consecutive daytime period, chosen by the administrators of the program, on a day during which the participant is not engaged in usual employment or vocation, (8) enroute to and from a medical examination or treatment as part of a necessary medical treatment for such participant or member of the participant's household, as evidenced by a written statement to that effect from a licensed medical practitioner, and (9) enroute to and from a place, including a school, at which a child or children of the holder are cared for on a regular basis and which is necessary for the holder to maintain such holder's employment or enrollment at an accredited school, college or university or at a state approved institution of vocational or technical training. Such license or privilege shall remain in effect during the term of the suspension or revocation of the participant's license or privilege unless earlier revoked by the commissioner.

(b) The conditional license or privilege described in paragraph (a) of this subdivision shall be in a form prescribed by the commissioner, and shall have indicated thereon the conditions imposed by such paragraph.

(c) Upon receipt of a conditional license issued pursuant to this section, any order issued by a judge, justice or magistrate pursuant to paragraph (c) of subdivision two of section eleven hundred ninety-three of this article shall be surrendered to the department.

(d) The commissioner shall require applicants for a conditional license to pay a fee of seventy-five dollars for processing costs. Such fees assessed under this subdivision shall be paid to the commissioner for deposit to the general fund and shall be in addition to any fees established by the commissioner pursuant to subdivision six of this section to defray the costs of the alcohol and drug rehabilitation program.

(e) The conditional license or privileges described in this subdivision may be revoked by the commissioner, for sufficient cause including, but not limited to, failure to register in the program, failure to attend or satisfactorily participate in the sessions, conviction of any traffic infraction other than one involving parking, stopping or standing or conviction of any alcohol or drug-related traffic offense, misdemeanor or felony. In addition, the commissioner shall have the right, after a hearing, to revoke the conditional license or privilege upon receiving notification or evidence that the offender is not attempting in good faith to accept rehabilitation. In the event of such revocation, the fee described in subdivision six of this section shall not be refunded.

(f) It shall be a traffic infraction for the holder of a conditional license or privilege to operate a motor vehicle upon a public highway for any use other than those authorized pursuant to paragraph (a) of this subdivision. when a person is convicted of this offense, the sentence of the court must be a fine of not less than two hundred dollars nor more than five hundred dollars or a term of imprisonment of not more than fifteen days or both such fine and imprisonment. Additionally, the conditional license or privileges described in this subdivision shall be revoked by the commissioner upon receiving notification from the court that the holder thereof has been convicted of this offense.

(g) Notwithstanding anything to the contrary contained in a certificate of relief from disabilities issued pursuant to article twenty-three of the correction law, any conditional license or privilege issued to a person convicted of a violation of any subdivision of section eleven hundred ninety-two of this article shall not be valid for the operation of any commercial motor vehicle. In addition, no such conditional license or privilege shall be valid for the operation of a taxicab as defined in this chapter.

(h) Notwithstanding any inconsistent provision of this chapter, the conditional license described in this subdivision may, pursuant to regulations established by the commissioner, be issued to a person whose license has been suspended pending prosecution pursuant to subparagraph seven of paragraph (e) of subdivision two of section eleven hundred ninety-three of this article.

Amended by L. 1994, Ch. 312, § 5, eff. Nov. 1, 1994, adding subd. 7(h); L. 1996, Ch. 196, § 18, amending subd. 4, eff. Nov. 1, 1996; L. 1996, Ch. 196, § 19, amending subd. 5, eff. Nov. 1, 1996; L. 1996, Ch. 309, § 97, amending subd. 7(d), eff. Aug. 31, 1996; L. 2005, Ch. 60, Part E, § 19, eff. Sept. 30, 2005, amending subd. 7(g).

Admissibility.—Evidence obtained pursuant to section 1194 is admissible in Penal Law prosecutions, notwithstanding the absence of a VTL charge. People v. Ladd, 89 N.Y.2d 893, 653 N.Y.S.2d 259, 675 N.E.2d 1211 (1996).

Discretion.—Whether a defendant may enroll in the alcohol and drug rehabilitation program established by § 1196 is a matter to be addressed by the court at sentencing. People v. Sofia, 201 A.D.2d 685, 608 N.Y.S.2d 254 (2d Dept. 1994).

Legislative intent.—The legislative grouping of offenses in article 31, and the use of the term "alcohol or drug-related traffic offenses" in the text of Vehicle and Traffic Law § 1196 mirroring the title of article 31, evidences the legislative intent to particularize and limit the categories of offenders eligible to benefit from the interplay of § 1196. People *ex rel.* Paganini v. Jablonsky, 79 N.Y.2d 586, 584 N.Y.S.2d 415, 594 N.E.2d 909 (1992).

Probative value of blood alcohol level.—Any error in permitting the prosecution's forensic expert to report defendant's blood alcohol level beyond the second decimal point was harmless in light of defendant's conviction for driving while ability impaired. People v. MacDonald, 89 N.Y.2d 908, 653 N.Y.S.2d 267, 675 N.E.2d 1219 (1996).

§ 1197. Special traffic options program for driving while intoxicated.

"The program", as used in this section, shall mean the special traffic options program for driving while intoxicated, a program established pursuant to this section, and approved by the commissioner of motor vehicles.

1. Program establishment. (a) Where a county establishes a special traffic options program for driving while intoxicated, pursuant to this section, it shall receive fines and forfeitures collected by any court, judge, magistrate or other officer within that county, including, where appropriate, a hearing officer acting on behalf of the commissioner,: * (1) imposed for violations of subparagraphs (ii) and (iii) of paragraph (a) of subdivision two or subparagraph (i) of paragraph (a) of subdivision three of section five hundred eleven of this chapter; (2) imposed in accordance with the provisions of section eleven hundred ninety-three and civil penalties imposed pursuant to subdivision two of section eleven hundred ninety-four-a of this article, including, where appropriate, a hearing officer acting on behalf of the commissioner, from violations of sections eleven hundred ninety-two, eleven hundred ninety-two-a and findings made under section eleven hundred ninety-four-a of this article; and (3) imposed upon a conviction for: vehicular assault in the first degree, pursuant to section 120.04 of the penal law; vehicular assault in the second degree, pursuant to section 120.03 of the penal law; vehicular manslaughter in the first degree, pursuant to section 125.13 of the penal law; and vehicular manslaughter in the second degree, pursuant to section 125.12 of the penal law, as provided in section eighteen hundred three of this chapter. Upon receipt of these moneys, the county shall deposit them in a separate account entitled "special traffic options program for driving while intoxicated" and they shall be under the exclusive care, custody and control of the chief fiscal officer of each county participating in the program.

(b) Expenditures from such account shall only be made pursuant to the approval of a county program by the commissioner of motor vehicles. The chief fiscal officer of each participating county shall, on a quarterly basis, forward to the commissioner a written certificate of moneys expended from such account.

2. Program organization. (a) Where a program is established by a county, it shall be organized by a coordinator for the special traffic options program for driving while intoxicated, who shall be designated by the chief executive officer of the county, if there be one, otherwise the chairman of the governing board of the county, or in the city of New York, a person designated by the mayor thereof. Where a coordinator is designated, the coordinator shall receive such salary and expenses as the board of legislators or other governing body of such county may fix and properly account for such expenses and shall serve at the pleasure of such appointing body or officer.

(b) In counties having a county traffic safety board, the chief executive officer, if there be one, otherwise the chairman of the governing board of the county or the mayor of the city of New York, may designate the chairman of the board or a member thereof as coordinator of the program.

3. Purposes. (a) The program shall provide a plan for coordination of county, town, city and village efforts to reduce alcohol-related traffic injuries and fatalities.

(b) The program shall, where approved by the county board or other governing body, provide funding for such activities as the board or other body may approve, for the above-described purposes.

4. Duties of the coordinator; reports. (a) it shall be the duty of the coordinator to:

(1) Render annually or at the request of the county legislature or other governing body of the county, a verified account of all moneys received and expended by the coordinator or under the coordinator's direction and an account of other pertinent matters.

(2) Submit annually or upon request of the chief fiscal officer of each county participating in the program, in such manner as may be required by law, an estimate of the funds required to carry out the purposes of this section.

(3) Make an annual report to the commissioner, which shall be due on or before the first day of April of each year following the implementation of said program, and shall include the following:

a. the progress, problems and other matters related to the administration of said program; and

b. an assessment of the effectiveness of the program within the geographic area of the county participating therein and any and all recommendations for expanding and improving said program.

(b) Any annual report shall also contain the following, in a form prescribed by the commissioner:

(1) Number of arrests for violations of section eleven hundred ninety-two of this article and subdivision two of section five hundred eleven of this chapter;

(2) Number and description of dispositions resulting therefrom;

(3) Number of suspensions issued in the county for alleged refusals to submit to chemical tests;

(4) Total fine moneys returned to the participating county in connection with the program;

(5) Contemplated programs;

(6) Distribution of moneys in connection with program administration;

(7) Any other information required by the commissioner.

5. Functions of the coordinator. In addition to the duties of the coordinator as provided in subdivision four of this section, the coordinator shall perform the following functions:

(a) Formulate a special traffic options program for driving while intoxicated and coordinate efforts of interested parties and agencies engaged in alcohol traffic safety, law enforcement, adjudication, rehabilitation and preventive education.

(b) Receive proposals from county, town, city or village agencies or nongovernmental groups for activities related to alcohol traffic safety and to submit them to the county board of legislators or other such governing body, together with a recommendation for funding of the activity if deemed appropriate.

(c) Cooperate with and assist local officials within the county in the formulation and execution of alcohol traffic safety programs including enforcement, adjudication, rehabilitation and education.

(d) Study alcohol traffic safety problems with the county and recommend to the appropriate legislative bodies, departments or commissions, such changes in rules, orders, regulations and existing law as the coordinator may deem advisable.

(e) Promote alcohol and drug-related traffic safety education for drivers.

(f) Obtain and assemble data on alcohol-related accident arrests, convictions and accidents and to analyze, study, and consolidate such data

for educational, research and informational purposes.

6. County purpose and charge. The provisions of this section and expenditures made hereunder shall be deemed a county purpose and charge.

7. Program approval. The program, including a proposed operational budget, shall be submitted by each county coordinator to the commissioner for approval. The commissioner shall consider the following before approving said program:

(a) The interrelationship of such program with existing drunk driving related programs in areas including, but not limited to, law enforcement, prosecution, adjudication and education.

(b) Avoidance of duplication of existing programs funded or operated by either the state or any municipality including, but not limited to, the alcohol and drug rehabilitation program, established under section eleven hundred ninety-six of this article.

(c) All other factors which the commissioner shall deem necessary.

8. Duties of the commissioner. (a) The commissioner shall compile the reports submitted by the county coordinators and shall issue a comprehensive report on such programs to the governor and to the legislature.

(b) The commissioner shall monitor all programs to ensure satisfactory implementation in conjunction with the established program application goals.

9. Program cessation. When a participating county wishes to cease its program, the coordinator shall notify the commissioner in writing of the date of termination and all money remaining in the fund established by that county pursuant to subdivision one of this section on such date shall be transferred to the general fund of the state treasury. All fines and forfeitures collected pursuant to the provisions of this section on and after the termination date shall be disposed of in accordance with subdivision one of section eighteen hundred three of this chapter.

10. Program audit. The comptroller is authorized to conduct audits of any program established pursuant to this section for the purposes of determining compliance with the provisions of this section and with generally accepted accounting principles.

* As enacted.

Amended by L. 1996, Ch. 196, § 20, amending subd. 1(a), eff. Nov. 1, 1996; L. 1996, Ch. 688, § 1, amending subd. 1(a), eff. Nov. 1, 1996; L. 1998, Ch. 469, § 4, amending subd. 7, eff. July 22, 1998.

§ 1198. Ignition interlock device program. [*Expires and repealed Sept. 1, 2007.*]

1. Scope of program. There is hereby created

in this state an ignition interlock device program. The provisions of this section shall apply only to persons sentenced by a court located in the following counties: Albany, Erie, Nassau, Onondaga, Monroe, Westchester and Suffolk; except that paragraph (b) of subdivision four, subdivisions five, eight and ten of this section shall apply in all parts of the state if a vehicle has been equipped with an ignition interlock device as a condition of probation. This section shall not be construed to preclude other counties not specifically designated therein from implementing an ignition interlock device program or to prevent courts in other jurisdictions from requiring the installation of an ignition interlock device as a condition of probation.

2. Requirements. (a) In addition to any other penalties prescribed by law, the court may require that any person who has been convicted of a violation of subdivision two or three of section eleven hundred ninety-two of this chapter, or any crime defined by this chapter or the penal law of which an alcohol-related violation of any provision of section eleven hundred ninety-two of this chapter is an essential element, and who has been sentenced to a period of probation, install and maintain, as a condition of such probation, a functioning ignition interlock device in accordance with the provisions of this section; provided, however, the court may not authorize the operation of a motor vehicle by any person whose license or privilege to operate a motor vehicle has been revoked except as provided herein.

(b) Nothing contained in this section shall prohibit a court, upon application by a probation department located in any county set forth in subdivision one of this section, from modifying the conditions of probation of any person convicted of any violation set forth in paragraph (a) of this subdivision prior to the effective date of this section, to require the installation and maintenance of a functioning ignition interlock device, and such person shall thereafter be subject to the provisions of this section.

(c) Nothing contained in this section shall authorize a court to sentence any person to a period of probation for the purpose of subjecting such person to the provisions of this section, unless such person would have otherwise been so sentenced to a period of probation.

3. Conditions. (a) Notwithstanding any other provision of law, the commissioner may grant a post-revocation conditional license, as set forth in paragraph (b) of this subdivision, to a person who has been convicted of a violation of subdivision two or three of section eleven hundred ninety-two of this chapter and who has been sentenced to a period of probation, provided the person has satisfied the minimum period of license revocation established by law and the commissioner has been notified that such person may operate only a motor vehicle equipped with a functioning ignition interlock device. No such request shall be made nor shall such a license be granted, however, if such person has been found by a court to have committed a violation of section five hundred eleven of this chapter during the license revocation period or deemed by a court to have violated any condition of probation set forth by the court relating to the operation of a motor vehicle or the consumption of alcohol. In exercising discretion relating to the issuance of a post-revocation conditional license pursuant to this subdivision, the commissioner shall not deny such issuance based solely upon the number of convictions for violations of any subdivision of section eleven hundred ninety-two of this chapter committed by such person within the ten years prior to application for such license. Upon the termination of the period of probation set by the court, the person may apply to the commissioner for restoration of a license or privilege to operate a motor vehicle in accordance with this chapter.

(b) Notwithstanding any inconsistent provision of this chapter, a post-revocation conditional license granted pursuant to paragraph (a) of this subdivision shall be valid only for use by the holder thereof, (1) enroute to and from the holder's place of employment, (2) if the holder's employment requires the operation of a motor vehicle then during the hours thereof, (3) enroute to and from a class or course at an accredited school, college or university or at a state approved institution of vocational or technical training, (4) to and from court ordered probation activities, (5) to and from a motor vehicle office for the transaction of business relating to such license, (6) for a three hour consecutive daytime period, chosen by the administrators of the program, on a day during which the participant is not engaged in usual employment or vocation, (7) enroute to and from a medical examination or treatment as part of a necessary medical treatment for such participant or member of the participant's household, as evidenced by a written statement to that effect from a licensed medical practitioner, (8) enroute to and from a class or an activity which is an authorized part of the alcohol and drug rehabilitation program and at which participant's attendance is required, and (9) enroute to and from a place, including a school, at which a child or children of the participant are cared for on a regular basis and which is necessary for the participant to maintain such participant's employment or enrollment at an accredited school, college or university or at a state approved institution of vocational or technical training.

(c) The post-revocation conditional license described in this subdivision may be revoked by the commissioner for sufficient cause including but not limited to, failure to comply with the terms of the condition of probation set forth by the court, conviction of any traffic offense other than one involving parking, stopping or standing or conviction of any alcohol or drug related offense, misdemeanor or felony.

(d) Nothing contained herein shall prohibit the court from requiring, as a condition of probation, the installation of a functioning ignition interlock device in any vehicle owned or operated on a regular basis by a person sentenced for a violation of section five hundred eleven or section eleven hundred ninety-two of this chapter, or any crime defined by this chapter or the penal law of which a violation of any provision of section eleven hundred ninety-two of this chapter is an essential element, if the court in its discretion, determines that such a condition is necessary to ensure the public safety. Such a condition shall in no way limit the effect of any period of license suspension or revocation set forth by the commissioner or the court.

(e) Nothing contained herein shall prevent the court from applying any other conditions of probation allowed by law, including treatment for alcohol or drug abuse, restitution and community service.

(f) The commissioner shall note on the operator's record of any person restricted pursuant to this section that, in addition to any other restrictions, conditions or limitations, such person may operate only a motor vehicle equipped with an ignition interlock device.

4. Proof of compliance and recording of condition. (a) If the court imposed the use of an ignition interlock device as a condition of probation it shall require the person to provide proof of compliance with this section to the court and the probation officer as set forth in the order of probation. If the person fails to provide for such proof of installation, absent a finding by the court of good cause for that failure which is entered in the record, the court may revoke, modify, or terminate the person's sentence of probation as provided under law.

(b) When a court imposes the condition specified in subdivision one of this section, the court shall notify the commissioner in such manner as the commissioner may prescribe, and the commissioner shall note such condition on the operating record of the person subject to such conditions.

5. Cost, installation and maintenance. (a) The cost of installing and maintaining the ignition interlock device shall be borne by the person subject to such condition. Such cost shall be considered a fine for the purposes of subdivision five of section 420.10 of the criminal procedure law. Such cost shall not replace, but shall instead be in addition to, any fines, surcharges, or other costs imposed pursuant to this chapter or other applicable laws.

(b) The manufacturer of the device shall be responsible for the installation and maintenance of such device and for the reports required in this section.

6. Certification. (a) The commissioner of the department of health shall approve ignition interlock devices for installation pursuant to subdivision one of this section and shall publish a list of approved devices.

(b) After consultation with manufacturers of ignition interlock devices and the national highway traffic safety administration, the commissioner of the department of health, in consultation with the commissioner and the director of the division of probation and correctional alternatives, shall promulgate regulations regarding standards for, and use of, ignition interlock devices. Such standards shall include provisions for setting a minimum and maximum calibration range and shall include, but not be limited to, requirements that the devices:

(1) have features that make circumventing difficult and that do not interfere with the normal or safe operation of the vehicle;

(2) work accurately and reliably in an unsupervised environment;

(3) resist tampering and give evidence if tampering is attempted;

(4) minimize inconvenience to a sober user;

(5) require a proper, deep, lung breath sample or other accurate measure of blood alcohol content equivalence;

(6) operate reliably over the range of automobile environments;

(7) correlate well with permissible levels of alcohol consumption as may be established by the sentencing court or by any provision of law; and

(8) are manufactured by a party covered by product liability insurance.

(c) The commissioner of the department of health may, in his discretion, adopt in whole or relevant part, the guidelines, rules, regulations, studies, or independent laboratory tests performed on and relied upon for the certification or approval of ignition interlock devices by other states, their agencies or commissions.

7. Information and final report. (a) The division of probation and correctional alternatives, in consultation with the department and the office of court administration, shall develop a standard reporting form that will be used by the courts, such division and the department for collecting data relating to the program.

(b) The division of probation and correctional alternatives and the department shall compare the recidivism rate of those persons subject to the provisions of the program to demographically and statistically similar cases where the program was not applied.

(c) The division of probation and correctional alternatives and the department shall jointly prepare an evaluative report as to the effectiveness, reliability and impact of ignition interlock devices as a sentencing and probation option. Such report shall be submitted to the governor, the temporary president of the senate and the speaker of the assembly no later than the first day of May, two thousand and an updated report no later than the first day of May, two thousand two. In addition, such report and report update shall include, but not be limited to the following information:

(1) record of offenders, including the number of prior alcohol or drug-related convictions relating to the operation of a vehicle;

(2) record of any violations of probation;

(3) record of the number of persons convicted of a violation of subdivisions eight and ten of this section;

(4) the type and manufacturer of the ignition interlock device installed and the record of any malfunctions; and

(5) any other information determined necessary and relevant to the implementation of this section by the division of probation and correctional alternatives and the department.

The division and the department may request technical assistance in the preparation of the report from the national highway traffic safety administration.

8. Use of other vehicles. (a) The requirement of subdivision one of this section that a person operate a vehicle only if it is equipped with an ignition interlock device shall apply to every motor vehicle operated by that person including, but not limited to, vehicles that are leased, rented or loaned.

(b) No person shall knowingly rent, lease, or lend a motor vehicle to a person known to have had his driving privilege restricted pursuant to subdivision one of this section, unless the vehicle is equipped with an ignition interlock device. Any person whose driving privilege is restricted pursuant to subdivision one of this section shall notify any other person who rents, leases, or loans a motor vehicle to him of the driving restriction imposed under this section.

(c) A violation of paragraph (a) or (b) of this subdivision shall be a misdemeanor.

9. Employer vehicle. Notwithstanding the provisions of subdivision one of this section, if a person is required to operate a motor vehicle owned by said person's employer in the course and scope of his employment, the person may operate that vehicle without installation of an approved ignition interlock device if the employer has been notified that the person's driving privilege has been restricted under the provisions of this article and the person whose privilege has

been so restricted has acknowledgement * of the employer notification in his or her possession while operating the employer's vehicle for normal business duties. The person shall notify the court and the probation officer of his or her intention to so operate the employer's vehicle. A motor vehicle owned by a business entity which business entity is all or partly owned or controlled by a person otherwise subject to the provisions of this article is not a motor vehicle owned by the employer for purposes of the exemption provided in this subdivision. The provisions of this subdivision shall apply only to the operation of such vehicle in the scope of such employment.

10. Circumvention of interlock device. (a) No person whose driving privilege is restricted pursuant to subdivision one of this section shall request, solicit or allow any other person to blow into an ignition interlock device, or to start a motor vehicle equipped with the device, for the purpose of providing the person so restricted with an operable motor vehicle.

(b) No person shall blow into an ignition interlock device or start a motor vehicle equipped with the device for the purpose of providing an operable motor vehicle to a person whose driving privilege is restricted pursuant to subdivision one of this section.

(c) No person shall tamper with or circumvent an otherwise operable ignition interlock device.

(d) In addition to any other provisions of law, any person convicted of a violation of paragraph (a), (b) or (c) of this subdivision shall be guilty of a misdemeanor.

11. Warning label. The department of health shall design a warning label which the manufacturer shall affix to each ignition interlock device upon installation in the state. The label shall contain a warning that any person tampering, circumventing, or otherwise misusing the device is guilty of a misdemeanor and may be subject to civil liability.

* Spelled as such in original. Should be "acknowledgment."

Amended by L. 1994, Ch. 413, § 1, eff. July 20, 1994, amending subd. 3(b); L. 1994, Ch. 413, § 2, eff. July 20, 1994, amending subd. 7(c); L. 1994, Ch. 413, § 3, extending expiration date of section 1198 to July 1, 1995; L. 1995, Ch. 168, § 4, extending expiration date of section 1198 to July 1, 1997; L. 1995, Ch. 168, § 1, amending subd. 1, eff. July 19, 1995; L. 1995, Ch. 168, § 2, amending subd. 5(a), eff. July 19, 1995; L. 1995, Ch. 168, § 3, amending subd. 7(c), eff. July 19, 1995; L. 1997, Ch. 150, § 1, amending opening paragraph of subd. 7(c), and § 2, extending repeal date of section 1198 to July 1, 1999, eff. June 30, 1997; L. 1998, Ch. 359, § 1, eff. Aug. 13, 1998, amending subd. 1; L. 1999, Ch. 135, § 2, extending expiration date to July 1, 2001, and Ch. 135, § 1, amending subd. 7; L. 2001, Ch. 86, §§ 1, 2, eff. June 29, 2001, extending expiration date to July 1, 2003; L. 2003, Ch. 16, § 18, eff. Mar. 31, 2003, extending expiration date to Sept. 1, 2005; L. 2005, Ch. 56, Part D, § 16, eff. Apr. 1, 2005, extending expiration and repeal date to Sept. 1, 2007.

ARTICLE 45

PENALTIES AND DISPOSITION OF FINES AND FORFEITURES

Section

§ 1800. Penalties for traffic infractions.

(a) It is a traffic infraction for any person to violate any of the provisions of this chapter or of any local law, ordinance, order, rule or regulation adopted pursuant to this chapter, unless such violation is by this chapter or other law of this state declared to be a misdemeanor or a felony.

(b) Every person convicted of a traffic infraction for a violation of any of the provisions of this chapter or of any ordinance, order, rule or regulation adopted pursuant to section sixteen hundred thirty or sixteen hundred thirty-one for which another penalty is not provided shall for a first conviction thereof be punished by a fine of not more than one hundred fifty dollars or by imprisonment for not more than fifteen days or by both such fine and imprisonment; for a conviction of a second violation, both of which were committed within a period of eighteen months, such person shall be punished by a fine of not more than three hundred dollars or by imprisonment for not more than forty-five days or by both such fine and imprisonment; upon a conviction of a third or subsequent violation, all of which were committed within a period of eighteen months, such person shall be punished by a fine of not more than four hundred fifty dollars or by imprisonment for not more than ninety days or by both such fine and imprisonment, except that a person convicted of a traffic infraction for a violation of paragraph one of subdivision (d) of section one thousand one hundred eleven of this chapter outside of a city having a population of one million or more shall, for a first conviction thereof, be punished by a fine of not less than seventy-five dollars nor more than two hundred twenty-five dollars or by imprisonment for not more than fifteen days or by both such fine and imprisonment; for a conviction of a second violation, both of which were committed within a period of eighteen months, such person shall be punished by a fine of not less than one hundred fifty dollars nor more than three hundred seventy-five dollars or by imprisonment for not more than forty-five days or by both such fine and imprisonment; upon a conviction of a third or subsequent violation, all of which were committed within a period of eighteen months, such person shall be punished by a fine of not less than three hundred seventy-five dollars nor more than six hundred seventy-five dollars or by imprisonment for not more than ninety days or by both such fine and imprisonment except that a person convicted for a violation of paragraph one of subdivision (d) of section one thousand one hundred eleven of this chapter shall, for a first conviction thereof, be punished by a fine of not less than one hundred fifty dollars nor more than four hundred fifty dollars or by imprisonment for not more than fifteen days or by both such fine and imprisonment; for a conviction of a second violation, both of which 1 were committed within a period of eighteen months, such person shall be punished by a fine of not less than three hundred dollars nor more than seven hundred fifty dollars or by imprisonment for not more than forty-five days or by both such fine and imprisonment; upon a conviction of a third or subsequent violation, all of which were committed within a period of eighteen months, such person shall be punished by a fine of not less than seven hundred fifty dollars nor more than one thousand five hundred dollars or by imprisonment for not more than ninety days or by both such fine and imprisonment.

(c) Every person convicted of a traffic infraction for a violation of any local law, ordinance, order, rule, regulation or administrative code provision adopted pursuant to this chapter by any local authority or continued in effect by this chapter, except those adopted pursuant to sections sixteen hundred thirty and sixteen hundred thirty-one, shall be punished in the same manner as has heretofore been prescribed by law unless or until otherwise prescribed by local law, ordinance or state statute.

(d) A conviction of violation of any provision of this chapter shall not be a bar to a prosecution for an assault or for a homicide committed by any person in operating a motor vehicle or motorcycle.

(e) Every person convicted of a violation of the provisions of section eleven hundred forty-four of this chapter shall for a first conviction thereof be punished by a fine of not more than two hundred seventy-five dollars or by imprisonment for not more than fifteen days or by both such fine and imprisonment. For a conviction of a second violation, both of which were committed within a period of eighteen months, such person shall be punished by a fine of not more than four hundred fifty dollars or by imprisonment for not more than forty-five days or by both such fine and imprisonment. For a conviction of a third violation and all subsequent violations, all of which were committed within a period of eighteen months, such person shall be punished by a fine of not more than seven hundred fifty dollars or by imprisonment for not more than ninety days or by both such fine and imprisonment.

(f) Every person convicted of operating a truck, tractor or tractor-trailer combination having a total gross weight in excess of ten thousand pounds in violation of a local law, ordinance, rule or regulation enacted by the legislative body of any city with a population in excess of one million pursuant to the provisions of paragraph ten of subdivision (a) of section sixteen hundred forty of this chapter shall, for a first offense thereof, be punished by a fine of not less than two hundred dollars nor more than five hundred dollars or by imprisonment for not more than fifteen days or by both such fine and imprisonment. For a conviction of a second violation, both of which were committed within a period of eighteen months, such person shall be punished by a fine of not less than five hundred dollars nor more than one thousand dollars or by imprisonment for not more than forty-five days or by both such fine and

imprisonment. For a conviction of a third violation and all subsequent violations, all of which were committed within a period of eighteen months, such person shall be punished by a fine of not less than one thousand dollars nor more than two thousand dollars, or by imprisonment for not more than ninety days or by both such fine and imprisonment.

Amended by L. 1995, Ch. 202, § 1, amending subd. (b), eff. Aug. 25, 1995; L. 2003, Ch. 62, Part C, § 1, eff. May 15, 2003, amending subds. (b) and (e); L. 2003, Ch. 203, § 1, eff. Nov. 1, 2003, adding subd. (f).

§ 1801. Penalties for misdemeanors.

1. Every person convicted of a misdemeanor for a violation of any of the provisions of this chapter for which another penalty is not provided shall for a first conviction thereof be punished by a fine of not more than three hundred dollars or by imprisonment for not more than thirty days or by both such fine and imprisonment; for a conviction of a second violation, both of which were committed within a period of eighteen months, such person shall be punished by a fine of not more than five hundred twenty-five dollars or by imprisonment for not more than ninety days or by both such fine and imprisonment; upon a conviction of a third or subsequent violation, all of which were committed within a period of eighteen months, such person shall be punished by a fine of not more than one thousand one hundred twenty-five dollars or by imprisonment for not more than one hundred eighty days or by both such fine and imprisonment, except that any fine imposed upon conviction of a violation of section twelve hundred twelve of this chapter shall be not less than one hundred dollars.

2. Notwithstanding the provisions of subdivision one of this section, every operator or registered owner of a motor vehicle having a registered maximum gross weight of eighteen thousand pounds or more convicted of a misdemeanor for a violation of the provisions of the closing paragraph of subdivision one of section three hundred seventy-five of this chapter with respect to the knowing disconnection of any set of service brakes on such motor vehicle, shall be punished by a fine of not more than two thousand two hundred fifty dollars.

Amended by L. 2003, Ch. 62, Part C, § 2, eff. May 15, 2003, amending subds. (1) and (2).

§ 1802. Receipts for fines or bail.

Upon receipt of the payment of any fine or penalty collected under a sentence or judgment of conviction of a violation of any of the provisions of this chapter or any local law, ordinance, order, rule or regulation made by local authorities in relation to traffic or the deposit of bail of a person charged with a violation of any such provision, local law, ordinance, order, rule or regulation, the officer or employee receiving such payment or deposit shall issue a receipt therefor when the payment or deposit is made in cash. Whenever any such payment or deposit is made by check, money order or in other property, the officer or employee shall issue a receipt therefor upon request; provided, however, no such receipt shall be issued where a fine or penalty is paid by mail unless the name and address of the payee is known to such officer or employee or enclosed with the payment.

§ 1803. Disposition of fines and forfeitures.

1. Except as otherwise provided in subdivision five of section two hundred twenty-seven of this chapter and as provided in section eleven hundred ninety-seven of this chapter, section ninety of the state finance law and sections fourteen-f and one hundred forty of the transportation law, all fines and penalties collected under a sentence or judgment of conviction of a violation of this chapter or of any act relating to the use of highways by motor vehicles or trailers, now in force or hereafter enacted, shall be distributed in the following manner:

a. for a violation which occurs in a city, town or suburban town, any fine or penalty shall be paid to the city, town or suburban town in which the violation occurs, when such violation is of (1) any of the provisions of title seven of this chapter, but including violations of section eleven hundred eighty only when occurring in state parks for which the office of parks, recreation and historic preservation has established maximum speed limits pursuant to section sixteen hundred thirty and the violations could have been charged under either such established maximum speed limits or another section of this chapter, and when involving maximum speed limits established pursuant to section sixteen hundred forty-three, sixteen hundred forty-four, sixteen hundred sixty-two-a, sixteen hundred sixty-three or sixteen hundred seventy, and excluding violations of sections eleven hundred eighty-two, eleven hundred ninety-two and twelve hundred twelve of this chapter, or (2) any ordinance, order, rule or regulation adopted pursuant to article two-E of the transportation law or section sixteen hundred thirty of this chapter by the East Hudson Parkway Authority or by its successor, or the County of Westchester Department of Parks, Recreation and Conservation, or the state office of parks, recreation and historic preservation. For purposes of this paragraph, violations shall be deemed to be violations of any such ordinance, order, rule or regulation when they occur on highways under the jurisdiction of the enumerated entities and the violations could have been charged under either such ordinance, order, rule or regulation or another section of this chapter.

b. for a violation which occurs in a village in which the office of village justice is established, any fine or penalty shall be paid to the village in which the violation occurs, when such violation is of (1) any of the provisions of title seven of this chapter, but including violations of section eleven hundred eighty only when occurring in state parks for which the office of parks, recreation and historic preservation has established maximum speed limits pursuant to section sixteen hundred thirty and the violations could have been charged under either such established maximum speed limits or another section of this chapter, and when involving maximum speed limits established pursuant to section sixteen hundred forty-three, sixteen hundred forty-four or sixteen hundred seventy, and excluding violations of sections eleven hundred eighty-two, eleven hundred ninety-two and twelve hundred twelve of this chapter, or (2) any ordinance, order, rule or regulation adopted pursuant to article two-E of the transportation law or section sixteen hundred thirty of this chapter by the East Hudson Parkway Authority or by its successor, or the County of Westchester Department of Parks, Recreation and Conservation, or the state office of parks, recreation and historic preservation. For purposes of this paragraph, violations shall be deemed to be violations of any such ordinance, order, rule or regulation when they occur on highways under the jurisdiction of the enumerated entities and the violations could have been charged under either such ordinance, order, rule or regulation, or another section of this chapter. Notwithstanding the foregoing provisions of this paragraph, all fines, penalties and forfeitures for violation of a village ordinance, local law or regulation adopted pursuant to the authorization of paragraph six of subdivision (a) of section sixteen hundred forty of this chapter prohibiting, restricting or limiting the stopping, standing or parking of vehicles shall be paid to such village whether or not the village has established the office of village justice.

c. for compliance with or violations of subdivision nineteen of section three hundred eighty-five of this chapter, notwithstanding any inconsistent provision of law, except as provided in section ninety of the state finance law, the fees and fines collected by the state pursuant to sections two hundred twenty-seven, three hundred eighty-five and eighteen hundred three of this chapter and section ninety-nine-a of the state finance law, shall be made available to the state comptroller for deposit in the general fund except that fines collected within a city not wholly included within one county shall be paid to such city in accordance with the procedures set forth in subdivision four of section two hundred twenty-seven of this chapter for deposit into the general fund of such city.

d. for violations of section eleven hundred eighty which are not included in paragraph a or paragraph b of this subdivision, violations of sections eleven hundred eighty-two, eleven hundred ninety-two, except in those counties adopting a special traffic option program for driving while intoxicated pursuant to section eleven hundred ninety-seven of this chapter, and section twelve hundred twelve of this chapter, and violations of this chapter or of any act relating to the use of highways by motor vehicles or trailers, now in force or hereafter enacted, for which no other distribution is prescribed, all fines, penalties and forfeitures shall be paid to the state.

e. for a violation which occurs within a county which has established a traffic and parking violations agency pursuant to section three hundred seventy of the general municipal law, other than parking, standing or stopping violations except for those set forth in section four hundred two of this chapter, and which violation is disposed of by such agency, any fine or penalty shall be paid to the county in which the violation occurs, when such violation is of any of the provisions of title seven of this chapter, but including violations of section eleven hundred eighty of this chapter only when involving maximum speed limits in state parks established by the office of parks, recreation and historic preservation pursuant to section sixteen hundred thirty of this chapter and when involving maximum speed limits established pursuant to section sixteen hundred forty-three, sixteen hundred forty-four, sixteen hundred sixty-two-a, sixteen hundred sixty-three or sixteen hundred seventy of this chapter, and excluding violations of sections eleven hundred eighty-two, eleven hundred ninety-two and twelve hundred twelve of this chapter.

2. Whenever a defendant is arrested and arraigned before a judicial officer authorized to conduct any proceedings in or in connection with any prosecution triable in any local court of inferior jurisdiction of a city or before a town court, or a village court on a charge in which the state is entitled to all fines and penalties under a sentence or judgment of conviction such city, town or village shall be entitled to receive the fees set forth in section ninety-nine-l of the general municipal law and such fees shall be a state charge and paid as provided in section ninety-nine-a of the state finance law.

3. All fines, penalties and forfeitures paid to a city, town or village pursuant to the provisions of paragraph a of subdivision one of this section shall be credited to the general fund of such city, town or village, unless a different disposition is prescribed by charter, special law, local law or ordinance.

4. All fines, penalties and forfeitures collected in a city, upon conviction or upon forfeiture of bail by any person charged with a violation of any local law, ordinance, order, rule, regulation, administrative code provision or sanitary or health code provision adopted or continued pursuant to this chapter, shall be paid to the city and credited to its general fund, unless a different disposition is prescribed by charter, special law, local law or ordinance.

5. All fines, penalties and forfeitures for violations of section eleven hundred eighty of this chapter, which relate to maximum speed limits established by a village pursuant to sections sixteen hundred forty-three and sixteen hundred forty-four or by a suburban town pursuant to section sixteen hundred sixty-two-a of this chapter, and all bail forfeited by the non-appearance of defendants charged with such violations shall be paid over to the state comptroller by the court, justice or other officer collecting the same within the first ten days of the month following the collection, except as otherwise provided by subdivision three of section ninety-nine-a of the state finance law. Whenever such fines, penalties and forfeitures, including bail forfeited, in any year commencing July first shall aggregate in excess of five dollars for each inhabitant of the village or suburban town, as the case may be, according to the last preceding federal census, such excess shall be the property of the state and shall be paid into the general fund of the state treasury.

6. The comptroller from the moneys received pursuant to this section shall, within six years from the receipt thereof, refund any fine received pursuant to this section which was imposed by a judgment of conviction that has been reversed and any fine, penalty or forfeiture received by the comptroller, payment of which was not required by this section. In any action by the state to recover fines, penalties, or forfeitures collected more than six years before the commencement of the action, the defendant shall be entitled to set off a claim for refund of any such item paid to the state during the ten years preceding the commencement of the action.

7. [Repealed by L. 1997, Ch. 432, § 3, eff. Aug. 20, 1997.]

8. All fines, penalties and forfeitures referred to in subdivision one of this section, except fines, penalties and forfeitures paid to the commissioner of taxation and finance as required by section thirty-nine of the judiciary law, and except as otherwise provided in subdivision three of section ninety-nine-a of the state finance law, shall be paid to the state comptroller by the court, judge, magistrate or other officer within the first ten days of the month following collection. Every such payment to the comptroller shall be accompanied by a statement in such form and detail as the comptroller shall prescribe.

9. Where a county establishes a special traffic options program for driving while intoxicated, approved by the commissioner of motor vehicles, pursuant to section eleven hundred ninety-seven of this chapter, all fines, penalties and forfeitures collected from violations of subparagraphs (ii) and (iii) of paragraph (a) of subdivision two or subparagraph (i) of paragraph (a) of subdivision three of section five hundred eleven,;* all fines, penalties and forfeitures imposed in accordance with section eleven hundred ninety-three of this

chapter collected from violations of section eleven hundred ninety-two of this chapter; and any fines or forfeitures collected by any court, judge, magistrate or other officer imposed upon a conviction for: vehicular assault in the first degree, pursuant to section 120.04 of the penal law; vehicular assault in the second degree, pursuant to section 120.03 of the penal law; vehicular manslaughter in the first degree, pursuant to section 125.13 of the penal law; and vehicular manslaughter in the second degree, pursuant to section 125.12 of the penal law and civil penalties imposed pursuant to subdivision two of section eleven hundred ninety-four-a of this chapter, shall be paid to such county.

(a) Any such fine, penalty, or forfeiture collected by any court, judge, magistrate or other officer referred to in subdivision one of section thirty-nine of the judiciary law, establishing a unified court budget, shall be paid to that county within the first ten days of the month following collection.

(b) Any such fine, penalty, or forfeiture collected by any other court, judge, magistrate or other officer, including, where appropriate, a hearing officer acting on behalf of the commissioner, shall be paid to the state comptroller within the first ten days of the month following collection. Every such payment to the comptroller shall be accompanied by a statement in such form and detail as the comptroller shall provide. The comptroller shall pay these funds to the county in which the violation occurs.

(c) Upon receipt of any monies referred to in this section, the county shall deposit them in a separate account entitled "special traffic options program for driving while intoxicated".

[*] As enacted.

Amended by L. 1996, Ch. 196, § 21, amending subd. 9, eff. Nov. 1, 1996; L. 1996, Ch. 688, § 2, amending the opening para. of subd. 9, eff. Nov. 1, 1996; L. 1997, Ch. 432, §§ 70 and 71, eff. Aug. 20, 1997; L. 1998, Ch. 465, §§ 6 and 7, eff. July 22, 1998, amending subds. 5 and 8; L. 1999, Ch. 385, § 1, eff. July 27, 1999, amending subd. 1; L. 2004, Ch. 740, § 1, eff. Dec. 15, 2004, deemed eff. Aug. 20, 2004, amending subd. 1(a) and (b), repealing amendments made by L. 2004, Ch. 56, Part G, § 1, eff. Aug. 20, 2004.

Editor's Note: L. 2004, Ch. 740, § 3, provides:

"Section 3. This act shall take effect immediately: section one of this act shall be deemed to have been in full force and effect on and after August 20, 2004 and section two of this act shall be deemed to have been in full force and effect on and after September 1, 2004; provided that any revenues made payable, and actually paid, to the state pursuant to the provisions of section 1 of part G of chapter 56 of the laws of 2004 shall be refunded to the chief fiscal officer of the municipality whose court entered the conviction resulting in the payment of such funds; and provided further that, upon written application within sixty days after this act shall have become law, in the form satisfactory to the chief fiscal officer of the municipality, any surcharge paid pursuant to the provisions of section 1809-d of the vehicle and traffic law shall be refunded by the chief fiscal officer of the municipality whose court collected such surcharge to the person who paid such surcharge; and provided further that the provisions of paragraphs a and b of subdivision 1 of section 1803 of the vehicle and traffic law shall revert to and be read as they were immediately prior to the amendments made to them by section 1 of part G of chapter 56 of the laws of 2004."

§ 1805. Plea of guilty, how put in.

The provisions of section 170.10 of the criminal procedure law and the provisions of section eighteen hundred seven of this article may be waived, to the extent hereinafter indicated, by a defendant charged with a violation of any provision of the tax law or the transportation law regulating traffic, or a traffic infraction, as defined in this chapter, other than a third or subsequent speeding violation committed within a period of eighteen months, provided that he shall submit to the local criminal court having jurisdiction, in person, by duly authorized agent, by first class mail or by registered or certified mail, return receipt requested, an application setting forth (a) the nature of the charge, (b) the information or instructions required by section eighteen hundred seven of this article to be given defendant upon arraignment, (c) that defendant waives arraignment in open court and the aid of counsel, (d) that he pleads guilty to the offense as charged, (e) that defendant elects and requests that the charge be disposed of and the fine or penalty fixed by the court, pursuant to this section, (f) any statement or explanation that the defendant may desire to make concerning the offense charged and (g) that defendant makes all statements with respect to such application under penalty of perjury. This application shall be in such form as the commissioner shall prescribe and a copy thereof shall be handed to the defendant by the officer charging him with such offense. Thereupon the local criminal court may proceed as though the defendant had been convicted upon a plea of guilty in open court, provided, however, that any imposition of fine or penalty hereunder shall be deemed tentative until such fine or penalty shall have been paid and discharged in full, prior to which time such court, in its discretion, may annul any proceedings hereunder, including such tentative imposition of fine or penalty, and deny the application, in which event the charge shall be disposed of pursuant to the applicable provisions of law, as though no proceedings had been had under this section. If upon receipt of the aforesaid application such court shall deny the same, it shall thereupon inform the defendant of this fact, and that he is required to appear before the said court at a stated time and place to answer the charge which shall thereafter be disposed of pursuant to the applicable provisions of law.

Amended by L. 2001, Ch. 406, eff. Jan. 29, 2002; L. 2004, Ch. 182, § 1, eff. July 20, 2004.

§ 1806. Plea of not guilty by a defendant charged with a traffic infraction.

In addition to appearing personally to enter a plea of not guilty to a violation of any provision of the tax law or the transportation law regulating traffic, or to a traffic infraction for the violation of any of the provisions of the vehicle and traffic law or of any local law, ordinance, order, rule or regulation relating to the operation of motor vehicles or motor cycles, a defendant may enter a plea of not guilty by mailing to the court of appropriate jurisdiction the ticket making the charge and a signed statement indicating such plea. Such plea must be sent: (a) by registered or certified mail, return receipt requested or by first class mail; and (b) within forty-eight hours after receiving such ticket. Upon receipt of such ticket and statement, the court shall advise the violator of the trial date by first class mail but no warrant of arrest for his failure to appear can be issued until the violator is notified of a new trial date by registered or certified mail, return receipt requested, and he fails to appear.

ANNOTATION

Plea of not guilty; traffic infraction.—Section 1806 is one of the two exceptions to the general rule that a defendant must personally appear at arraignment. However, unless the conditions of section 1806 are strictly adhered to, a personal appearance will be required at arraignment. Defendant's plea by regular mail, almost a month after issuance of the ticket, required defendant personally appear for arraignment. People v. Maran, 174 Misc. 2d 327, 666 N.Y.S.2d 870 (App. Term 2d Dept. 1997).

§ 1806-a. Default judgment in cases of failure to answer.

1. In the event a person charged with a traffic infraction does not answer within the time specified, the court having jurisdiction, other than a court in a city over one million population may, in addition to any other action authorized by law, enter a plea of guilty on behalf of the defendant and render a default judgment of a fine determined by the court within the amount authorized by law. Any judgment entered pursuant to default shall be civil in nature, but shall be treated as a conviction for the purposes of this section. However, at least thirty days after the expiration of the original date prescribed for entering a plea and before a plea of guilty and a default judgment may be rendered, the traffic violations bureau or, if there be none, the clerk of the court, shall notify the defendant by certified mail: (a) of the violation charged; (b) of the impending plea of guilty and default judgment; (c) that such judgment will be filed with the county clerk of the county in which the operator or registrant is located, and (d) that a default or plea of guilty may be avoided by entering a plea or making an appearance within thirty days of the sending of such notice. Pleas entered within that period shall be in a manner prescribed in the notice. In no case shall a default judgment and plea of guilty be rendered more than two years after the expiration of the time prescribed for originally entering a plea. When a person has entered a plea of not guilty and has demanded a hearing, no fine or penalty shall be imposed for any reason, prior to the holding of the hearing which shall be scheduled by the court of such city, village or town within thirty days of such demand.

2. The filing of the default judgment with the county clerk shall have the full force and effect of a judgment duly docketed in the office of such clerk and may be enforced in the same manner and with the same effect as that provided by law in respect to executions issued against property upon judgments of a court of record and such judgment shall remain in full force and effect for eight years notwithstanding any other provision of law.

3. Notwithstanding the provisions of subdivision one of this section, a traffic violations bureau or, if there be none, the clerk of the court, shall have two years from the effective date of this act to serve notice upon an operator or owner of a motor vehicle charged with a traffic violation who has not answered within the time specified and prior to the effective date of this act.

4. In the event a person charged with a parking violation does not answer within the time specified, a traffic and parking violations agency may, in addition to any other action authorized by law, enter a plea of guilty on behalf of the defendant and render a default judgment of a fine determined by the judicial hearing officer within the amount authorized by law. Any judgment entered pursuant to default shall be civil in nature, but shall be treated as a conviction for the purposes of this section. However, at least thirty days after the expiration of the original date prescribed for entering a plea and before a plea of guilty and a default judgment may be rendered, the traffic and parking violations agency shall notify the defendant by certified mail: (a) of the violation charged; (b) of the impending plea of guilty and default judgment; (c) that such judgment will be filed with the county clerk of the county in which the operator or registrant is located, and (d) that a default or plea of guilty may be avoided by entering a plea or making an appearance within thirty days of the sending of such notice. Pleas entered within that period shall be in a manner prescribed in the notice. In no case shall a default judgment and plea of guilty be rendered more than two years after the expiration of the time prescribed for originally entering a plea. When a person has entered a plea of not guilty and has demanded a hearing, no fine or penalty shall be imposed for any reason, prior to the holding of the hearing which shall be scheduled by the traffic and parking violations agency within thirty days of such demand.

5. If a motor vehicle which is owned by a rental or leasing company is ticketed for a traffic infraction, the municipality shall not enter a default judgement under this section against the rental or leasing company if, when the municipality sends the notice to the company, the company sends to the municipality within fifteen days a copy of the rental or leasing agreement covering that vehicle on that date with the name and address of the lessee clearly legible. If this information is not sent to the municipality within such

fifteen day time period, the municipality shall proceed under this section to enter a default judgement and the rental or leasing company shall be liable for the traffic infraction.

Amended by L. 1995, Ch. 83, § 199, amending subd. 1, eff. Apr. 1, 1995, and amendment to expire and be deemed repealed on Apr. 1, 1996, pursuant to L. 1995, Ch. 83, § 362, para. 13; L. 1996, Ch. 40, § 18, extending expiration date of subd. 1 amendments to Apr. 30, 1996; L. 1996, Ch. 73, § 2, extending expiration date of subd. 1 amendments to Apr. 1, 1997.

§ 1807. Provisions applicable to arraignments for traffic violations.

1. The local criminal court, upon the arraignment in this state of a resident of this state charged with a violation of the vehicle and traffic law, or other law or ordinance relating to the operation of motor vehicles or motor cycles, and before accepting a plea, or in the case of such a defendant who has previously pleaded not guilty, as provided in section eighteen hundred six of this chapter, and who wishes to change or withdraw such plea, must inform the defendant at the time of his arraignment or appearance for trial in substance as follows:

A plea of guilty to this charge is equivalent to a conviction after trial. if you are convicted, not only will you be liable to a penalty, but in addition your license to drive a motor vehicle or motor cycle, and your certificate of registration, if any, are subject to suspension and revocation as prescribed by law.

The giving of the foregoing instructions by means of a statement printed in a noticeably distinct manner and in bold type in a size equal to at least twelve point type, upon a summons or ticket issued to a person charged with any such offense shall constitute compliance with the requirements of this section.

The foregoing provisions of this section may be waived as provided in section eighteen hundred five of this chapter.

2. Upon the arraignment of any person under eighteen years of age who resides within the household of his parent or guardian upon a charge of a violation of the vehicle and traffic law or other law or ordinance relating to the operation of motor vehicles or motor cycles, except a violation relating to parking, stopping or standing, the local criminal court which arraigns him shall forthwith transmit written notice of such arraignment to the parent or guardian of such minor person; provided, however, that if a conviction of such person follows such arraignment upon the same day, or in case such person waives arraignment and enters a plea of guilty to the offense as charged in accordance with the provisions of section eighteen hundred five of this chapter, transmittal of notice of his conviction as provided in section five hundred fourteen of this chapter shall be sufficient and the notice of arraignment hereunder need not be given; provided further that the failure of a local criminal court to transmit

such notice of arraignment shall in no manner affect the validity of a conviction subsequently obtained.

Amended by L. 1999, Ch. 493, § 1, eff. Nov. 1, 1999, amending subd. 1.

§ 1808. Effect of stay order on appeal from judgment of conviction of • an offense under this chapter.

(a) When an appeal is taken to an intermediate appellate court from a conviction of an offense under this chapter resulting in the suspension or revocation of the defendant's motor vehicle operator's license, and a stay of execution is granted ordering reinstatement of such license during the pendency and until the determination of such appeal, service of a certified copy of such stay order by mail upon the commissioner of motor vehicles shall be binding upon the commissioner; and during a period of ninety days from the date such stay order was granted, or until such appeal is determined, if sooner than ninety days, such commissioner shall be stayed from taking any proceedings under the vehicle and traffic law to suspend or revoke such license on account of such conviction; and such order shall contain appropriate provisions to that effect.

(b) For good cause shown, such stay may be extended by the court, in its discretion, for additional periods not to exceed ninety days each; such extension order or orders, when served upon the commissioner of motor vehicles in the same manner as the original stay order, shall be binding upon him to the same extent as the original stay order for such additional period or periods.

(c) A stay order or orders issued pursuant to section 460.50 of the criminal procedure law which purport to reinstate a license during the pendency of an appeal from a conviction resulting in the suspension or revocation of a license shall, for the purposes of such reinstatement, be deemed to be issued in accordance with the provisions of this section and the ninety day stay period authorized by this section shall apply.

§ 1809. Mandatory surcharge and crime victim assistance fee required in certain cases.

1. [*Effective until Sept. 1, 2007.*] Whenever proceedings in an administrative tribunal or a court of this state result in a conviction for an offense under this chapter or a traffic infraction under this chapter, or a local law, ordinance, rule or regulation adopted pursuant to this chapter, other than a traffic infraction involving standing, stopping, or parking or violations by pedestrians or bicyclists, or other than an adjudication of liability of an owner for a violation of subdivision (d) of section eleven hundred eleven of this chapter in accordance with section eleven hundred eleven-a of this chapter, there shall be levied

a crime victim assistance fee and a mandatory surcharge, in addition to any sentence required or permitted by law, in accordance with the following schedule:

(a) Whenever proceedings in an administrative tribunal or a court of this state result in a conviction for a traffic infraction pursuant to article nine of this chapter, there shall be levied a crime victim assistance fee in the amount of five dollars and a mandatory surcharge, in addition to any sentence required or permitted by law, in the amount of twenty-five dollars.

(b) Whenever proceedings in an administrative tribunal or a court of this state result in a conviction for a misdemeanor or felony pursuant to section eleven hundred ninety-two of this chapter, there shall be levied, in addition to any sentence required or permitted by law, a crime victim assistance fee in the amount of twenty dollars and a mandatory surcharge in accordance with the following schedule:

(i) a person convicted of a felony shall pay a mandatory surcharge of two hundred fifty dollars;

(ii) a person convicted of a misdemeanor shall pay a mandatory surcharge of one hundred forty dollars.

(c) Whenever proceedings in an administrative tribunal or a court of this state result in a conviction for an offense under this chapter other than a crime pursuant to section eleven hundred ninety-two of this chapter, or a traffic infraction under this chapter, or a local law, ordinance, rule or regulation adopted pursuant to this chapter, other than a traffic infraction involving standing, stopping, or parking or violations by pedestrians or bicyclists, or other than an adjudication of liability of an owner for a violation of subdivision (d) of section eleven hundred eleven of this chapter in accordance with section eleven hundred eleven-a of this chapter or other than an infraction pursuant to article nine of this chapter or other than an adjudication of liability of an owner for a violation of toll collection regulations pursuant to section two thousand nine hundred eighty-five of the public authorities law or sections sixteen-a, sixteen-b and sixteen-c of chapter seven hundred seventy-four of the laws of nineteen hundred fifty, there shall be levied a crime victim assistance fee in the amount of five dollars and a mandatory surcharge, in addition to any sentence required or permitted by law, in the amount of forty-five dollars.

1. [*Effective Sept. 1, 2007, and until as stated in 1991 note below.*] Whenever proceedings in an administrative tribunal or a court of this state result in a conviction for a crime under this chapter or a traffic infraction under this chapter, or a local law, ordinance, rule or regulation adopted pursuant to this chapter, other than a traffic infraction involving standing, stopping, or parking or motor vehicle equipment or violations by pedestrians or bicyclists, or other than an adjudication of liability of an owner for a violation of subdivision (d) of section eleven hundred eleven of this chapter in accordance with section eleven hundred eleven-a of this chapter, there shall be levied a mandatory surcharge, in addition to any sentence required or permitted by law, in the amount of twenty-five dollars.

1. [*Effective Dec. 1, 2009.*] Whenever proceedings in an administrative tribunal or a court of this state result in a conviction for a crime under this chapter or a traffic infraction under this chapter, or a local law, ordinance, rule or regulation adopted pursuant to this chapter, other than a traffic infraction involving standing, stopping, parking or motor vehicle equipment or violations by pedestrians or bicyclists, there shall be levied a mandatory surcharge, in addition to any sentence required or permitted by law, in the amount of twenty-five dollars.

2. [*Effective until Sept. 1, 2007.*] Where a person is convicted of two or more such crimes or traffic infractions committed through a single act or omission, or through an act or omission which in itself constituted one of the crimes or traffic infractions and also was a material element of the other, the court or administrative tribunal shall impose a crime victim assistance fee and a mandatory surcharge mandated by subdivision one of this section for each such conviction; provided however, that in no event shall the total amount of such crime victim assistance fees and mandatory surcharges imposed pursuant to paragraph (a) or (c) of subdivision one of this section exceed one hundred dollars.

2. [*Effective Sept. 1, 2007.*] Where a person is convicted of two or more such crimes or traffic infractions committed through a single act or omission, or through an act or omission which in itself constituted one of the crimes or traffic infractions and also was a material element of the other, the court or administrative tribunal shall impose only one mandatory surcharge mandated by subdivision one of this section.

3. The mandatory surcharge provided for in subdivision one of this section shall be paid to the clerk of the court or administrative tribunal that rendered the conviction. Within the first ten days of the month following collection of the mandatory surcharge the collecting authority shall determine the amount of mandatory surcharge collected and, if it is an administrative tribunal or a town or village justice court, it shall pay such money to the state comptroller who shall deposit such money in the state treasury pursuant to section one hundred twenty-one of the state finance law to the credit of the general fund. If such collecting authority is any other court of the unified court system, it shall, within such period, pay such money to the state commissioner of taxation and finance to the credit of the criminal justice improvement account established by section ninety-seven-bb of the state finance law. The

crime victim assistance fee provided for in subdivision one of this section shall be paid to the clerk of the court or administrative tribunal that rendered the conviction. Within the first ten days of the month following collection of the crime victim assistance fee, the collecting authority shall determine the amount of crime victim assistance fee collected and, if it is an administrative tribunal or a town or village justice court, it shall pay such money to the state comptroller who shall deposit such money in the state treasury pursuant to section one hundred twenty-one of the state finance law to the credit of the criminal justice improvement account established by section ninety-seven-bb of the state finance law.

4. Any person who has paid a mandatory surcharge or crime victim assistance fee under the authority of this section which is ultimately determined not to be required by this section shall be entitled to a refund of such mandatory surcharge or crime victim assistance fee upon application to the state comptroller. The state comptroller shall require such proof as it is necessary in order to determine whether a refund is required by law.

5. When a person who is convicted of a crime or traffic infraction and sentenced to a term of imprisonment has failed to pay the mandatory surcharge or crime victim assistance fee required by this section, the clerk of the court or the administrative tribunal that rendered the conviction shall notify the superintendent or the municipal official of the facility where the person is confined. The superintendent or the municipal official shall cause any amount owing to be collected from such person during his term of imprisonment from moneys to the credit of an inmates' fund or such moneys as may be earned by a person in a work release program pursuant to section eight hundred sixty of the correction law. Such moneys shall be paid over to the state comptroller to the credit of the criminal justice improvement account established by section ninety-seven-bb of the state finance law, except that any such moneys collected which are surcharges or crime victim assistance fees levied in relation to convictions obtained in a town or village justice court shall be paid within thirty days after the receipt thereof by the superintendent or municipal official of the facility to the justice of the court in which the conviction was obtained. For the purposes of collecting such mandatory surcharge or crime victim assistance fee, the state shall be legally entitled to the money to the credit of an inmates' fund or money which is earned by an inmate in a work release program. For purposes of this subdivision, the term "inmates' fund" shall mean moneys in the possession of an inmate at the time of his admission into such facility, funds earned by him as provided for in section one hundred eighty-seven of the correction law and any other funds received by him or on his behalf and deposited with such superintendent or municipal official.

5-a. The provisions of subdivision four-a of section five hundred ten, subdivision three of section five hundred fourteen and subdivision three of section two hundred twenty-seven of this chapter governing actions which may be taken for failure to pay a fine or penalty shall be applicable to a mandatory surcharge or crime victim assistance fee imposed pursuant to this section.

6. Notwithstanding any other provision of this section, where a person has made restitution or reparation pursuant to section 60.27 of the penal law, such person shall not be required to pay a mandatory surcharge or crime victim assistance fee.

7. Notwithstanding any other provision of this section, where a mandatory surcharge or crime victim assistance fee is imposed pursuant to the provisions of section 60.35 of the penal law, no mandatory surcharge or crime victim assistance fee shall be imposed pursuant to the provisions of this section.

8. The provisions of this section shall only apply to offenses committed on or before September first, two thousand seven.

9. Notwithstanding the provisions of subdivision one of this section, in the event a proceeding is in a town or village court, the court shall add an additional five dollars to the surcharges imposed by such subdivision one of this section.

10. For the purposes of this section, the term conviction means and includes the conviction of a felony or a misdemeanor for which a youthful offender finding was substituted and upon such a finding there shall be levied a mandatory surcharge and a crime victim assistance fee to the same extent and in the same manner and amount provided by this section for conviction of the felony or misdemeanor, as the case may be, for which such youthful offender finding was substituted.

Amended by L. 1994, Ch. 61, § 10, eff. Apr. 1, 1994, amending subd. 8; L. 1994, Ch. 61, § 11, eff. Apr. 1, 1994, extending expiration date of subds. 1 and 2; L. 1996, Ch. 309, § 70, amending subd. 3, eff. Aug. 31, 1996; L. 1997, Ch. 435, § 64, eff. Aug. 20, 1997, extending the expiration dates of subds. 1 and 2 to Nov. 1, 1999, and Ch. 452, § 3, eff. Jan. 1, 1998, adding subd. 9; L. 1999, Ch. 385, § 5, amending subd. (5), eff. July 27, 1999, and Ch. 452, § 12–14, eff. Sept. 1, 1999, deemed in full force and effect Apr. 1, 1999, amending subds. 8 and 9 and extending the expiration dates of 1991 amendments to subds. 1 and 2 to Nov. 1, 2001, and Ch. 503, § 2, eff. Sept. 28, 1999, extending the expiration date of 1988 amendments to subd. 1 to Dec. 1, 2004; L. 2000, Ch. 57, § 2, amending subd. 1, eff. May 15, 2000, deemed eff. Apr. 1, 2000; L. 2001, Ch. 95, §§ 16, 17, eff. July 13, 2001, extending expiration date of subd. 1 to Nov. 1, 2003; L. 2003, Ch. 62, Part M, §§ 2, 3, eff. Nov. 11, 2003, amending subds. 1 and 2; Ch. 16, § 14, eff. Mar. 31, 2003, extending expiration date to Sept. 1, 2005; L. 2003, Ch. 16, § 16, eff. Mar. 31, 2003, amending subd. 8; L. 2003, Ch. 261, § 4, eff. July 29, 2003, amending subd. 8; L. 2004, Ch. 56, § 3 (Part F), eff. Feb. 16, 2005, adding subd. 10; L. 2004, Ch. 667, § 2, eff. Oct. 26, 2004, extending effective date of subd. 1 to Dec. 1, 2009; L. 2005, Ch. 56, Part D, §§ 13, 14, eff. Apr. 1, 2005, extending expiration date of subds. 1 and 2 to Sept. 1, 2007, and amending subd. 8.

Editor's Note: L. 1991, Ch. 166, § 406(p), eff. June 12, 1991, as amended, provides:

"The amendments to section 1809 of the vehicle and traffic law made by sections three hundred thirty-seven and three hundred thirty-eight of this act shall not apply to any offense committed prior to such effective date; provided, further, that section three hundred forty-one of this act shall take effect immediately and shall expire November 1, 1993 at which time it shall be deemed repealed; sections three hundred forty-five and three hundred forty-six of this act shall take effect July 1, 1991; sections three hundred fifty-five, three hundred fifty-six, three hundred fifty-seven and three hundred fifty-nine of this act shall take effect immediately and shall expire June 30, 1995 and shall revert to and be read as if this act had not been enacted; section three hundred fifty-eight of this act shall take effect immediately and shall expire June 30, 1998 and shall revert to and be read as if this act had not been enacted; section three hundred sixty-four through three hundred sixty-seven of this act shall apply to claims filed on or after such effective date; sections three hundred sixty-nine, three hundred seventy-two, three hundred seventy-three, three hundred seventy-four, three hundred seventy-five and three hundred seventy-six of this act shall remain in effect until September 1, 2007, at which time they shall be deemed repealed; provided, however, that the mandatory surcharge provided in section three hundred seventy-four of this act shall apply to parking violations occurring on or after said effective date; and provided further that the amendments made to section 235 of the vehicle and traffic law by section three hundred seventy-two of this act, the amendments made to section 1809 of the vehicle and traffic law by sections three hundred thirty-seven and three hundred thirty-eight of this act and the amendments made to section 215-a of the labor law by section three hundred seventy-five of this act shall expire on September 1, 2007 and upon such date the provisions of such subdivisions and sections shall revert to and be read as if the provisions of this act had not been enacted; the amendments to subdivisions 2 and 3 of section 400.05 of the penal law made by sections three hundred seventy-seven and three hundred seventy-eight of this act shall expire on July 1, 1992 and upon such date the provisions of such subdivisions shall revert and shall be read as if the provisions of this act had not been enacted; the state board of law examiners shall take such action as is necessary to assure that all applicants for examination for admission to practice as an attorney and counsellor at law shall pay the increased examination fee provided for by the amendment made to section 465 of the judiciary law by section three hundred eighty of this act for any examination given on or after the effective date of this act notwithstanding that an applicant for such examination may have prepaid a lesser fee for such examination as required by the provisions of such section 465 as of the date prior to the effective date of this act; the provisions of section 306-a of the civil practice law and rules as added by section three hundred eighty-one of this act shall apply to all actions pending on or commenced on or after September 1, 1991, provided, however, that for the purposes of this section service of such summons made prior to such date shall be deemed to have been completed on September 1, 1991; the provisions of section three hundred eighty-three of this act shall apply to all money deposited in connection with a cash bail or a partially secured bail bond on or after such effective date; and the provisions of sections three hundred eighty-four and three hundred eighty-five of this act shall apply only to jury service commenced during a judicial term beginning on or after the effective date of this act; provided, however, that nothing contained herein shall be deemed to affect the application, qualification, expiration or repeal of any provision of law amended by any section of this act and such provisions shall be applied or qualified or shall expire or be deemed repealed in the same manner, to the same extent and on the same date as the case may be as otherwise provided by law."

§ 1809-a. Mandatory surcharge required in certain cities for parking, stopping and standing violations. [*Repealed Sept. 1, 2007.*]

1. The provisions of any other general or special law notwithstanding, whenever, in a city having a population of one hundred thousand or more according to the nineteen hundred eighty United States census, proceedings in an administrative tribunal or a court result in a finding of liability, or conviction for the violation of any statute, local law, ordinance or rule involving the parking, stopping or standing of a motor vehicle, there shall be levied a mandatory surcharge in addition to any other sentence, fine or penalty otherwise permitted or required, in the amount of fifteen dollars. Such surcharge shall not be deemed a monetary penalty for the purposes of section two hundred thirty-seven of this chapter or section 19-203 of the administrative code of the city of New York.

2. The mandatory surcharge provided for in subdivision one of this section shall be paid to the clerk of the court or administrative tribunal that made the determination of liability. Within the first ten days of the month next succeeding the collection of such surcharge, the collecting authority shall pay seven dollars and fifty cents of each surcharge to the justice court fund held by the state comptroller pursuant to section ninety-nine-a of the state finance law which monies shall then be deposited to the credit of the general fund. Each such payment shall be accompanied by a true and complete report in such form and detail as the comptroller shall prescribe. The remaining amount of the surcharge shall be paid to the chief fiscal officer of the municipality and used by the municipality from which it originated for its local criminal justice programs and purposes.

3. Any person who has paid a mandatory surcharge under the authority of this section which is ultimately determined not to be required by this section shall be entitled to a refund of such mandatory surcharge upon written application to the collecting authority. The collecting authority shall require such proof as is necessary in order to determine whether a refund is required by law. If the collecting authority shall refund any portion of the surcharge previously paid to the justice court fund pursuant to subdivision two of this section, the collecting authority may offset an equal amount from a subsequent remittance to the justice court fund, provided, however, that the collecting authority shall prepare such reports and provide such information with respect to such refunds as the comptroller shall direct, and provided, further, that the comptroller, upon review of such reports and information, may direct that any appropriate adjustments be made in future payments to the justice court fund pursuant to subdivision two of this section.

4. Notwithstanding any other provision of this section, where a mandatory surcharge is imposed pursuant to the provisions of section 60.35 of the penal law or section eighteen hundred nine or eighteen hundred nine-b of this article, no mandatory surcharge shall be imposed pursuant to the provisions of this section.

Amended by L. 1994, Ch. 61, § 11, eff. Apr. 1, 1994,

extending expiration date of section 1809-a until Nov. 1, 1997; L. 1996, Ch. 309, § 71, amending subd. 2, eff. Aug. 31, 1996; L. 1996, Ch. 690, § 4, amending subd. 3, eff. Dec. 31, 1996; L. 1997, Ch. 435, § 64, eff. Aug. 20, 1997, extending expiration date to Nov. 1, 1999; L. 1999, Ch. 452, § 12, eff. Sept. 1, 1999, extending expiration date to Nov. 1, 2001; L. 1999, Ch. 497, § 2, eff. Apr. 1, 2000; L. 2001, Ch. 95, § 16, eff. July 13, 2001, extending expiration date to Nov. 1, 2003; L. 2003, Ch. 16, § 14, eff. Mar. 31, 2003, extending expiration date to Sept. 1, 2005; L. 2003, Ch. 62, Part J, § 21, eff. Nov. 11, 2003, amending subds. 1 and 2; L. 2005, Ch. 56, Part D, § 13, eff. Apr. 1, 2005, extending repeal date to Sept. 1, 2007.

§ 1809-b. Mandatory surcharge required for certain violations relating to handicapped parking spaces.

1. Notwithstanding any other provision of law, whenever proceedings in an administrative tribunal or a court result in a finding of liability, or conviction for a violation of section twelve hundred three-a, twelve hundred three-b or twelve hundred three-c of this chapter or any other statute, local law, ordinance or rule involving the parking, stopping or standing of motor vehicles registered pursuant to section four hundred four-a of this chapter or those possessing a special vehicle identification parking permit issued in accordance with section one thousand two hundred three-a of this chapter, there shall be levied a mandatory surcharge in addition to any other sentence, fine or penalty otherwise permitted or required, in the amount of thirty dollars. Such surcharge shall not be deemed a monetary penalty for the purposes of section two hundred thirty-seven of this chapter or section 19-203 of the administrative code of the city of New York.

2. The mandatory surcharge provided for in subdivision one of this section shall be paid to the clerk of the court or administrative tribunal that made the determination of liability. Within the first ten days of the month next succeeding the collection of such surcharge, the collecting authority shall pay fifteen dollars of such surcharge to the chief fiscal officer of the county in which such violation occurred or of the city of New York, for deposit to the credit of the handicapped parking education fund of such county or city established pursuant to section twelve hundred three-g of this chapter which shall be used by such county or city solely for a handicapped parking education program pursuant to such section. The remaining amount of the surcharge shall be paid to the chief fiscal officer of the municipality from which it originated and used by such municipality for its local criminal justice programs and purposes; provided, however, that such municipality shall use ten percent of such funds for developing and implementing a disability awareness program for local law enforcement agencies for the purpose of training local law enforcement personnel to recognize and appropriately respond to persons with disabilities with whom such personnel come into contact in the course of their duties.

Added by L. 1999, Ch. 497, § 3, eff. Apr. 1, 2000.

§ 1809-c. Additional surcharge required for certain violations relating to driving while intoxicated and driving while impaired.

1. Notwithstanding any other provision of law, whenever proceedings in a court of this state result in a conviction pursuant to section eleven hundred ninety-two of this chapter, there shall be levied, in addition to any sentence or other surcharge required or permitted by law, an additional surcharge of twenty-five dollars.

2. The additional surcharge provided for in subdivision one of this section shall be paid to the clerk of the court that rendered the conviction. Within the first ten days of the month following collection of the surcharge the collecting authority shall determine the amount of surcharge collected and it shall pay such money to the state comptroller who shall deposit such money in the state treasury pursuant to section one hundred twenty-one of the state finance law to the credit of the general fund.

3. The provisions of subdivision three of section two hundred twenty-seven, subdivision four-a of section five hundred ten, and subdivision three of section five hundred fourteen of this chapter governing actions which may be taken for failure to pay a fine or penalty shall be applicable to the additional surcharge imposed pursuant to this section.

4. For the purposes of this section, the term conviction means and includes the conviction of a felony or a misdemeanor for a violation of section eleven hundred ninety-two of this chapter for which a youthful offender finding was substituted and upon such a finding there shall be levied an additional surcharge, in addition to any sentence or other surcharge required or permitted by law, to the same extent and in the same manner and amount provided by this section for conviction of the felony or misdemeanor, as the case may be, for which such youthful offender finding was substituted.

Added by L. 2003, Ch. 62, Part J, § 37, eff. Nov. 11, 2003; Amended by L. 2004, Ch. 56, § 4 (Part F), eff. Feb. 16, 2005, adding subd. 4.

§ 1809-d. Mandatory surcharge for violation of maximum speed limits in highway construction or maintenance work areas.

1. Notwithstanding any other provision of law, whenever proceedings in an administrative tribunal or court result in a finding of liability or conviction for a violation of paragraph two of subdivision (d) or subdivision (f) of section

VTL

eleven hundred eighty of this chapter or any other statute, local law, ordinance or rule involving the maximum speed limits in highway construction or maintenance work areas, there shall be levied a mandatory surcharge in addition to any other sentence, fine or penalty otherwise permitted or required, in the amount of fifty dollars. Such surcharge shall not be deemed a monetary penalty for the purposes of section two hundred thirty-seven of this chapter or section 19-203 of the administrative code of the city of New York.

2. The mandatory surcharge provided for in subdivision one of this section shall be paid to the clerk of the court or administrative tribunal that made the determination of liability. Within the first ten days of the month next succeeding the collection of such surcharge, the collecting authority shall pay such money to the state comptroller to be deposited in the highway construction and maintenance safety education fund established by section ninety-nine-n of the state finance law.

Former section **added** by L. 2004, Ch. 56, Part G, § 2, eff. Sept. 1, 2004, expired and repealed Sept. 1, 2005; **Repealed** by L. 2004, Ch. 740, § 2, eff. Dec. 15, 2004, deemed eff. Sept. 1, 2004; new section **added** by L. 2005, Ch. 223, § 3, eff. Nov. 1, 2005.

Editor's Note: L. 2004, Ch. 740, § 3 provides in part:

"[A]ny revenues made payable, and actually paid, to the state pursuant to the provisions of section 1 of part G of chapter 56 of the laws of 2004 shall be refunded to the chief fiscal officer of the municipality whose court entered the conviction resulting in the payment of such funds; and provided further that, upon written application within sixty days after this act shall have become law, in the form satisfactory to the chief fiscal officer of the municipality, any surcharge paid pursuant to the provisions of section 1809-d of the vehicle and traffic law shall be refunded by the chief fiscal officer of the municipality whose court collected such surcharge to the person who paid such surcharge; and provided further that the provisions of paragraphs a and b of subdivision 1 of section 1803 of the vehicle and traffic law shall revert to and be read as they were immediately prior to the amendments made to them by section 1 of part G of chapter 56 of the laws of 2004."

L. 2005, Ch. 223, § 1, provides:

"Section 1. Short title. This act shall be known and may be cited as the 'work zone safety act of 2005'."

§ 1810. Compensation of officers shall not depend upon apprehension or arrests.

(a) No city or village shall employ any officer, agent or person whose compensation shall in any way depend upon the apprehension or arrest of any person or persons for violating any ordinance adopted pursuant to section sixteen hundred four of this chapter or for reckless driving as defined in section twelve hundred twelve of this chapter. If any person be apprehended or arrested or haled before a magistrate for a violation of a local ordinance adopted pursuant to section sixteen hundred four or for reckless driving as defined by section twelve hundred twelve of this chapter by any officer, agent or employee of any city or village who is so employed, the fact of such employment at the time shall be a defense to any charge made for violation of such ordinance or for reckless driving.

(b) No county or town shall employ any officer, agent or person, whether such employee be elected or appointed, whose compensation shall in any way depend upon the apprehension or arrest of any person for reckless driving as defined in section twelve hundred twelve of this chapter. If any person be apprehended or arrested or haled before a magistrate for reckless driving as so defined, by any officer, agent or employee of any county or town who is so employed, the fact of such employment at the time shall be a defense to any charge made for reckless driving as defined in section twelve hundred twelve of this chapter.

PART 3

MISCELLANEOUS COURT RULES

MISCELLANEOUS COURT RULES
As amended through October 2005

Rules of the Chief Judge

29.1 *et seq.* (Electronic Recording and Audio-Visual Coverage of Court Proceedings)

32.1 *et seq.* (Videotaping of Conditional Examinations of Witnesses in Criminal Cases)

37.1 (Costs and Sanctions)

Rules of the Chief Administrator of the Courts

103.1 (Administrative Rules and Orders)

105.1 *et seq.* (Expedited Criminal Appeal of an Order Reducing an Indictment or Dismissing an Indictment and Directing the Filing of a Prosecutor's Information)

111.1 *et seq.* (Procedure Under CPL Article 730)

116.1 *et seq.* (Community Dispute Resolution Centers Program)

125.1 (Uniform Rules for the Engagement of Counsel)

129.1 *et seq.* (Fair Treatment Standards for Crime Victims)

131.1 *et seq.* (Audio-Visual Coverage of Judicial Proceedings)

Uniform Rules for the New York State Trial Courts (Selected Sections)

200.1 *et seq.* (Uniform Rules for Courts Exercising Criminal Jurisdiction)

205.1 *et seq.* (Uniform Rules for the Family Court)

218.1 *et seq.* (Uniform Rules for the Trial Courts in Capital Cases)

220.1 *et seq.* (Uniform Rules for Jury Selection and Deliberation)

Court of Appeals

500.1 *et seq.* (Rules of Practice)

510.1 *et seq.* (Capital Cases)

515.1 *et seq.* (Standards for Appellate and State Post-Conviction Counsel in Capital Cases)

540.0 *et seq.* (Uniform Procedures for Appeals from Pretrial Findings of Mental Retardation in Capital Cases)

First Judicial Department—Appellate Division

600.1 *et seq.* (Appeals)

603.1 *et seq.* (Conduct of Attorneys)

604.1 *et seq.* (Court Decorum)

606.1 *et seq.* (Legal and Medical Services; Duties of Counsel Respecting Appeals)

611.1 *et seq.* (Family Court Law Guardian Plan)

612.0 *et seq.* (Rules to Implement a Criminal Courts Panel Plan)

613.1 *et seq.* (Rules to Implement an Indigent Defense Organization Oversight Committee)

635.9 (Joint Administrative Orders)

First Judicial Department—Appellate Term

640.1 *et seq.* (Rules of Practice)

Second Judicial Department—Appellate Division

Second Judicial Department—Appellate Term

Third Judicial Department—Appellate Division

Fourth Judicial Department—Appellate Division

All Departments

RULES OF THE CHIEF JUDGE

PART 29

ELECTRONIC RECORDING AND AUDIO-VISUAL COVERAGE OF COURT PROCEEDINGS

§ 29.1 General.

(a) Taking photographs, films or videotapes, or audiotaping, broadcasting or telecasting, in a courthouse, including any courtroom, office or hallway thereof, at any time or on any occasion, whether or not the court is in session, is forbidden, unless permission of the Chief Administrator of the Courts or a designee of the Chief Administrator is first obtained; provided, however, that the permission of the Chief Judge of the Court of Appeals or the presiding justice of an Appellate Division shall be obtained with respect to the court over which each presides. Such permission may be granted if:

(1) there will be no detraction from the dignity or decorum of the courtroom or courthouse;

(2) there will be no compromise of the safety of persons having business in the courtroom or courthouse;

(3) there will be no disruption of court activities;

(4) there will be no undue burden upon the resources of the courts; and

(5) granting of permission will be consistent with the constitutional and statutory rights of all affected persons and institutions.

Permission may be conditioned upon compliance with any special requirements that may be necessary to ensure that the above conditions are met.

(b) This section shall not apply to:

(1) audio-visual coverage of proceedings in the appellate courts or the trial courts under section 29.2 or 29.3; and

(2) applications made to the appropriate court for photographing, taping or videotaping by or on behalf of the parties to the litigation and not for public dissemination.

§ 29.2 Appellate courts.

In respect to appellate courts, the Chief Judge hereby authorizes electronic photographic recording of proceedings in such courts, subject to the approval of the respective appellate court and subject to the following conditions.

(a) *Equipment and personnel.* (1) Two portable videotape electronic television cameras and two camera operators shall be permitted in any proceeding in any appellate court.

(2) Two photographers to operate two still cameras with not more than two lenses for each camera and related equipment for print purposes shall be permitted in any proceeding in any appellate court.

(3) One audio system for radio broadcast purposes shall be permitted in any proceeding in any appellate court. Audio pickup for all media purposes shall be accomplished from existing audio systems in the court facility. If no technically suitable audio system exists in the court facility, microphones and related wiring essential for media purposes shall be unobtrusive and shall be located in places designated in advance of any proceeding by the presiding judge or justice of the court hearing the appeal.

(4) Notwithstanding the provisions of paragraphs (1)–(3) of this subdivision, the court may increase or decrease within reasonable limits the amount of equipment that will be permitted into the courtroom on finding (i) that there is a need therefor because of special circumstances, and (ii) that it will not impair the dignity of the court or the judicial process.

(5) Notwithstanding the provisions of paragraphs (1)–(3) of this subdivision, the equipment authorized therein shall not be admitted into the courtroom unless interested members of the electronic media and interested print photographers shall have entered into pooling arrangements, for

their respective groups, including the establishment of necessary procedures, cost sharing, access to material, and selection of a pool representative. The court may not be called upon to mediate or resolve any dispute as to such arrangements. In making pool arrangements, consideration shall be given to educational users' needs for full coverage of entire proceedings.

(6) The pool operator covering the proceedings shall retain pool material for one year. The pool operator shall make available a copy of pool material at cost to educational users, to the appellate court and to the Court of Appeals at their request.

(b) *Sound and light criteria.* (1) Only television photographic and audio equipment and still camera equipment which do not produce distracting sound or light shall be employed to cover judicial proceedings. Specifically, television photographic and audio equipment shall produce no greater sound or light than the equipment designated in section 29.4 of this Part annexed to these rules; and still camera equipment shall produce no greater sound or light than a 35mm Leica "M" Series Rangefinder camera.

(2) It shall be the affirmative duty of media personnel desiring to use equipment other than that authorized in these rules or in section 29.4 of this Part to demonstrate to the court adequately in advance of any proceeding that the equipment sought to be utilized meets the sound and light criteria enunciated herein. A failure to obtain advance approval for equipment shall preclude its use in any proceeding.

(c) *Location of equipment and personnel.* Television and still camera equipment and camera personnel shall be positioned in such locations as shall be designated by the court. The areas designated shall provide reasonable access to coverage with the least possible interference with court proceedings. Videotape recording equipment which is not a component part of a television camera shall be located in an area outside the court facility.

(d) *Movement of equipment during proceedings.* Electronic still photographic and audio equipment shall not be placed in, moved about or removed from the court facility, and related personnel shall not move about the courtroom except prior to commencement or after adjournment of proceedings each day, or during a recess. Television film magazines and still camera film or lenses shall be changed only during a recess in the proceeding.

(e) *Courtroom light sources.* With the concurrence of the court, modifications and additions may be made in light sources existing in the facility, provided such modification or additions are installed and maintained at media expense and provided they are not distracting or otherwise offensive.

(f) *Conferences of counsel.* To protect the attorney-client privilege and effective right to counsel, there shall be no audio pickup or audio broadcast of conferences which occur in a court facility between attorneys and their clients, between co-counsel of a client, or between counsel and the presiding judge held at the bench, without the express consent of all participants in the conference. Nor shall any chambers conference be filmed, recorded or broadcast.

(g) *Consent not required.* Electronic media or print photography coverage of appellate arguments shall not be limited by the objection of counsel or parties, except for good cause shown.

(h) *Appellate review.* An order granting or denying the electronic media from access to any proceeding, or affecting other matters arising under these rules and standards, shall not be appealable insofar as it pertains to and arises under these rules and standards except as otherwise provided and authorized by law.

§ 29.3 Trial courts.

Audio-visual coverage of proceedings in the trial courts shall be permitted only in accordance with the provisions of Part 131 of the Rules of the Chief Administrator.

§ 29.4 Videotape cameras and recorders.

VIDEOTAPE ELECTRONIC CAMERAS

1.	Ikegami	HL-77, HL-33, HL-35, HL-34, HL-51
2.	RCA	TK-76
3.	Sony	DXC-1600 Trinicon
3a.	ASACA	ACC-2006
4.	Hitachi	SK-80, SK-90
5.	Hitachi	FP-3030
6.	Phillips	LDK-25
7.	Sony BVP-200	ENG Camera
8.	Fernseh	Video Camera
9.	JVC-8800 u	ENG Camera
10.	AKAI	CVC-150, VTS-150
11.	Panasonic	WV-3085, NV-3085
12.	JVC	GC-4800 u

VIDEOTAPE RECORDERS/used with video cameras

1.	Ikegami	3800
2.	Sony	3800
3.	Sony	BVU-100
4.	Ampex	Video Recorder
5.	Panasonic	1 inch Video Recorder
6.	JVC	4400
7.	Sony	3800H

PART 32

VIDEOTAPING OF CONDITIONAL EXAMINATIONS OF WITNESSES IN CRIMINAL CASES

(Statutory authority: N.Y. Const., art. VI, § 28[c])

Section

32.1   **When permitted.**
32.2   **Application and notice.**
32.3   **Conduct of examination.**
32.4   **Copies.**
32.5   **Custody of recordings.**
32.6   **Use at trial.**
32.7   **Cost.**
32.8   **Appeal.**

§ 32.1 When permitted.

Conditional examinations authorized pursuant to sections 660.40 and 660.50 of the Criminal Procedure Law may be conducted by means of videotape or photographic recording, provided the recording is made in conformity with this Part.

§ 32.2 Application and notice.

An application requesting that a conditional examination be recorded, for audiovisual reproduction and preservation, by videotape or other photographic method, and any order granting that application shall state the name and address of the operator and of his or her employer.

§ 32.3 Conduct of examination.

(a) The examination shall begin by the operator recording:

(1) his or her name and address;

(2) the name and address of his or her employer;

(3) the date, time and place of the examination;

(4) the caption of the case;

(5) the name of the witness; and

(6) the party on whose behalf the examination is being conducted.

The person being examined shall be sworn as a witness. If the examination requires the use of more than one tape or film, the end of each tape or film and the beginning of each succeeding tape or film shall be announced by the operator.

(b) More than one camera may be used, either in sequence or simultaneously.

(c) At the conclusion of the examination, a statement shall be made on the record that the recording is completed. As soon thereafter as practicable, the videotape or other photographic recording shall be shown to the witness for examination, unless such showing and examination are waived by the witness and the parties. Pursuant to section 660.60 of the Criminal Procedure Law, a transcript and any videotape or photographic recording of the examination must be certified and filed with the court which ordered the examination.

§ 32.4 Copies.

The parties may make copies of the examination and thereafter may purchase additional copies.

§ 32.5 Custody of recordings.

When the tape or film is filed with the clerk of the court, the clerk shall give an appropriate receipt, shall provide secure and adequate facilities for the storage of such recordings, and thereafter shall keep appropriate records as to the possession and custody of such recordings.

§ 32.6 Use at trial.

The use of recordings of examinations at the trial shall be governed by the provisions of the Criminal Procedure Law, and all other relevant statutes, court rules and decisional law relating to depositions and to the admissibility of evidence. The proponent of the examination shall have the responsibility of providing whatever equipment and personnel may be necessary for presenting the examination.

§ 32.7 Cost.

The cost of videotaping or photographic recording shall be borne by the applicant.

§ 32.8 Appeal.

On appeal, videotaped or photographically

recorded examinations shall be transcribed in the same manner as other testimony, and transcripts shall be filed in the appellate court. The transcripts shall remain part of the original record in the case and shall be transmitted therewith.

PART 37

COSTS AND SANCTIONS

Section

     37.1   **General.**

§ 37.1 General.

(a) The Chief Administrator of the Courts, with the advice and consent of the Administrative Board of the Courts, shall adopt rules providing for costs and sanctions as follows:

(1) in civil actions and proceedings in any trial or appellate court in the Unified Court System: providing for the award of costs, including reasonable attorney's fees, or the imposition of financial sanctions, or both, for frivolous conduct in litigation by any party or attorney; and

(2) in actions and proceedings in any trial or appellate court in the Unified Court System: providing for the award of costs, including reasonable attorney's fees, or the imposition of financial sanctions, or both, upon an attorney, who, without good cause, fails to appear at a time and date scheduled for an action or proceeding to be heard before a designated court.

(b) The rules shall include:

(1) a definition of frivolous conduct (civil cases);

(2) the factors to be considered in determining whether costs or sanctions should be awarded or imposed;

(3) a provision that the awarding of costs or imposition of financial sanctions by a court may be upon motion or upon the court's own initiative;

(4) a maximum monetary limit on sanctions;

(5) the opportunity to be heard before costs or sanctions are awarded or imposed; and

(6) a requirement that reasons for the award of costs or imposition of sanctions be set forth in writing or on the record.

(c) The rules may provide that, as appropriate, financial sanctions may be made payable to the Lawyers' Fund for Client Protection established pursuant to section 97-t of the State Finance Law or payable to the court.

RULES OF THE CHIEF ADMINISTRATOR OF THE COURTS

PART 103

ADMINISTRATIVE RULES AND ORDERS

(Statutory authority: Constitution, art. VI, §§ 20[b]–[c], 28[b])

Section
103.1 Administrative rules and orders.

§ 103.1 Administrative rules and orders.

All administrative regulations, rules, orders and directives for the efficient and orderly transaction of business in the trial courts or the administrative office for the courts in effect on March 31, 1978, adopted pursuant to authority subsequently transferred to the Chief Administrator of the Courts in accordance with article VI, section 28(b) of the Constitution, including but not limited to calendar practice, establishment of hours, terms and parts of court, assignments of judges and justices to them, and designations of administrative judges, are continued in effect until superseded, repealed or modified. Unless a contrary construction in required, references to the Administrative Board of the Judicial Conference shall be deemed references to the Chief Judge of the Court of Appeals; references to the State Administrator and State Administrative Judge shall be deemed references to the Chief Administrator of the Courts; and references to the Appellate Division or Presiding Justice shall be deemed references to the Chief Administrator of the Courts.

* * * *

PART 105

EXPEDITED CRIMINAL APPEAL OF AN ORDER REDUCING AN INDICTMENT OR DISMISSING AN INDICTMENT AND DIRECTING THE FILING OF A PROSECUTOR'S INFORMATION

Section
105.1 General.
105.2 Request to expedite appeal.
105.3 Procedure.
105.4 Court-assigned counsel to continue representation.

§ 105.1 General.

This Part shall govern the procedure for an expedited appeal to the Appellate Division, pursuant to CPL 210.20(6)(c), 450.20(1-a) and 450.55, of an order by a superior court reducing a count or counts of an indictment or dismissing an indictment and directing the filing of a prosecutor's information.

§ 105.2 Request to expedite appeal.

After the People file and serve a notice of appeal pursuant to CPL 460.10(1), either party may request that the Appellate Division to which the appeal has been taken expedite the appeal. If a request is made, the Appellate Division shall hear the appeal on an expedited basis as set forth in this Part.

§ 105.3 Procedure.

(a) The Appellate Division shall establish an expedited briefing schedule for the appeal. Briefs may be typewritten or reproduced. The People shall file nine copies of a brief and an appendix, which shall include a copy of the indictment and the trial court's decision and order. The respondent shall file nine copies of a brief and, if necessary, an appendix. One copy of the brief and appendix shall be served on opposing counsel.

(b) The appeal may be taken on one original record, which shall include copies of the indictment, the motion papers, the trial court's decision and order, and the notice of appeal.

(c) The People shall file with the Appellate Division, separately from the record, one copy of the grand jury minutes.

(d) The Appellate Division shall give preference to the hearing of an appeal perfected

pursuant to this Part and shall determine the appeal as expeditiously as possible.

§ 105.4 Court-assigned counsel to continue representation.

Unless otherwise ordered by the Appellate Division, if the defendant is represented in a superior court by court-assigned counsel, such counsel shall continue to represent the defendant in any appeal by the People of an order reducing an indictment or dismissing an indictment and directing the filing of a prosecutor's information.

PART 111

PROCEDURE UNDER CPL ARTICLE 730

(Statutory authority: Constitution, art. VI, §§ 20[b]–[c], 28[b])

Section
111.1   Definitions.
111.2   Examination of defendant.
111.3   Examination report.
111.4   Commitment to custody of Commissioner of Mental Health.
111.5   Order of retention for defendant held under orders of commitment.
111.6   Certificate of custody.
111.7   Procedure following termination of custody by commissioner.
111.8   Official forms.

§ 111.1 Definitions.

Whenever in this Part or in the forms promulgated or approved hereunder, the following terms appear, they shall have the following meaning:

(a) *Director of community mental health services* means the person responsible for the administration of community mental health and mental retardation services in a county or city, whether known or referred to as director, commissioner, or otherwise.

(b) *Facility director,* when used in connection with a hospital, institution or other facility, means the person in charge of the facility, whether known or referred to as director, superintendent, or otherwise.

§ 111.2 Examination of defendant.

(a) An order for the examination of a defendant to determine whether he is an incapacitated person under article 730 of the Criminal Procedure Law shall be addressed to the director of community mental health services of the county where the criminal action is pending, except in the City of New York where the order shall be addressed to the director of community mental health services of such city. If there is no such director of community health services, the order shall be addressed to the director of a hospital

operated by local government within such county or city that has been certified as having adequate facilities for such purpose by the Commissioner of Mental Health or, in the absence of such local hospital, to the director of the State hospital operated by the Department of Mental Hygiene serving the county where the criminal action is pending.

(b) The hospital in which a defendant may be confined for examination pursuant to subdivision (2) or (3) of section 730.20 of the Criminal Procedure Law shall be a hospital operated by local government that has been certified by the Commissioner of Mental Health as having adequate facilities to examine a defendant to determine if he is an incapacitated person. If there be no such local governmental hospital serving the county where the criminal proceeding is pending, the defendant may be confined in a general hospital having a psychiatric unit approved by the Commissioner of Mental Health or in a State hospital operated by the Department of Mental Hygiene approved for such purpose if the person in charge thereof shall have given his consent to the confinement of such defendant therein.

§ 111.3 Examination report.

(a) The examination of the defendant by the

psychiatric examiners may be conducted separately or jointly but each examiner shall execute a separate report. Such report shall be made in the form jointly adopted by the Chief Administrator of the Courts and the Commissioner of Mental Health.

(b) The director of community mental health services charged with causing the examination to be made shall furnish six copies of the examination report to the court for filing and necessary distribution. The court shall require that copies be furnished to counsel for the defendant and to the district attorney.

§ 111.4 Commitment to custody of Commissioner of Mental Health.

(a) If the court is satisfied that the defendant is an incapacitated person and the defendant is not in custody, the court shall cause the defendant to appear before it at the time of issuing a final order of observation, temporary order of observation or order of commitment, or other appropriate order, as the case may be.

(b) The court shall forward to the Commissioner of Mental Health the order committing the defendant to his custody together with a copy of the examination reports, a copy of the accusatory instrument and, if available, a copy of the presentence report. Upon receipt thereof, the Commissioner of Mental Health shall designate the institution in which the defendant is to be placed and give notice of such designation to the sheriff or local correction department, as the case may be, who shall deliver the defendant, if in custody, to the person in charge of the designated institution, except that, in the case of final orders of observation, the Department of Mental Hygiene may provide the transportation to the designated institution.

§ 111.5 Order of retention for defendant held under orders of commitment.

(a) The application for an order of retention of a defendant held pursuant to an order of commitment or order of retention shall be made within 60 days prior to the expiration of the order pursuant to which the defendant is being held. It shall be prepared by the director of the institution where the defendant is confined and shall have annexed to it a summary of the defendant's history and condition supporting the application, a copy of the indictment and a copy of each prior order of commitment or retention. Such director shall serve notice of the application on the defendant, on the defendant's attorney if known to the director, on the district attorney of the county where the criminal proceeding is pending, and on the Mental Health Information Service. Such director shall then promptly file the application with the court which issued the initial order of commitment of the defendant.

(b) The application shall not be brought on for determination by the court prior to 10 days from the date upon which notice of the application was served upon the defendant. A request by the defendant or anyone on his behalf for a hearing shall be forwarded to the court, with a copy to the district attorney and the Mental Health Information Service. The clerk of the court shall notify the defendant, the defendant's attorney if any, the district attorney, the director of the institution where the defendant is confined, and the Mental Health Information Service of the time and place of the hearing.

(c) Upon issuance of an order of retention, the court shall forward copies thereof to the district attorney, to the director of the institution where the defendant is confined, to the Commissioner of Mental Health and to the Mental Health Information Service. The director of the institution where the defendant is confined shall serve a copy of such order personally upon the defendant.

§ 111.6 Certificate of custody.

When defendant is in the custody of the Commissioner of Mental Health at the expiration of the period prescribed in a temporary order of observation or at the expiration of the authorized period prescribed in the last order of retention, the director of the institution where the defendant is confined may act as the agent of the Commissioner of Mental Health in certifying to the court that the defendant was in the custody of the Commissioner of Mental Health on such expiration date.

§ 111.7 Procedure following termination of custody by commissioner.

When a defendant is in the custody of the commissioner on the expiration date of a final or temporary order of observation or an order of commitment, or on the expiration date of the last order of retention, or on the date an order dismissing an indictment is served upon the commissioner, the director of the institution in which the defendant is confined may, pursuant to section 730.70 of the Criminal Procedure Law, retain him for care and treatment for a period of 30 days from such date. If the director determines that the defendant is so mentally ill or mentally defective as to require continued care and treatment in an institution, he may retain the defendant beyond such period only pursuant to the admission procedures set forth in the Mental Hygiene Law. If the defendant is sought to be retained on an involuntary basis, the certificates of two physicians or, in the case of retention at a school for the mentally retarded, one physician and one psychiatrist, shall be filed and an application to a court for an order authorizing retention shall be made before the expiration of the said 30-day period.

§ 111.8 Official forms.

Forms promulgated by the Chief Administrator

of the Courts and the Commissioner of Mental Health, or either of them, shall be the official forms for uniform use throughout the State in implementation of article 730 of the Criminal Procedure Law. Variations in these forms will be permitted if approved by the official or officials indicated in the following index as having adopted them.

PART 116

COMMUNITY DISPUTE RESOLUTION CENTERS PROGRAM

§ 116.1 Definitions.

(a) *Center* means a community dispute center which provides conciliation, mediation, arbitration or other forms and techniques of dispute resolution.

(b) *Mediator* means an impartial person who assists in the resolution of a dispute.

(c) *Grant recipient* means any organization that administers a community dispute resolution center receiving funds pursuant to this Part.

(d) *Chief Administrator* means the Chief Administrator of the Courts or his designee.

§ 116.2 Application.

(a) The provisions of this Part shall apply to the funding of community centers organized to expeditiously resolve minor disputes, especially those matters that would otherwise be handled by the criminal justice system.

(b) Funds available for disbursement pursuant to this Part shall include those funds appropriated by the State Legislature for said purposes, and shall also include funds received by the State from any public or private agency or person, including the Federal government, to be used for the purposes of this Part.

§ 116.3 Eligibility.

To be eligible for funding pursuant to this Part, a center must meet the following conditions:

(a) It must be administered by a nonprofit organization organized for the resolution of disputes or for religious, charitable or educational purposes.

(b) It must provide neutral mediators who have received at least 25 hours of training in conflict resolution techniques.

(c) It must provide dispute resolution services without cost to indigents and at nominal or no cost to other participants.

(d) It shall, whenever reasonably possible, make use of public facilities at free or nominal cost.

(e) It must provide, during or at the conclusion of the dispute resolution process, a written agreement or decision, subscribed to by the parties, setting forth the settlement of the issues and future responsibilities of each party, and must make such agreement or decision available to a court which has adjourned a pending action pursuant to section 170.55 of the Criminal Procedure Law.

(f) It may not make monetary awards except upon consent of the parties, and such awards may not exceed $1,500, except that where an action has been adjourned in contemplation of dismissal pursuant to section 215.10 of the Criminal Procedure Law, a monetary award not in excess of $5,000 may be made.

(g) It may not accept for dispute resolution any defendant who is named in a filed felony complaint, superior court information, or indictment, charging:

(1) a class A felony; or

(2) a violent felony offense as defined in section 70.02 of the Penal Law; or

(3) any drug offense as defined in article 220 of the Penal Law; or

(4) a felony upon the conviction of which defendant must be sentenced as a second felony offender, a second violent felony offender, or a persistent violent felony offender pursuant to sections 70.06, 70.04 and 70.08 of the Penal Law, or a felony upon the conviction of which defendant may be sentenced as a persistent felony offender pursuant to section 70.10 of the Penal Law.

(h) It must provide to parties, in advance of

the dispute resolution process, a written statement relating:

(1) their rights and obligations;

(2) the nature of the dispute;

(3) their right to call and examine witnesses;

(4) that a written settlement or a written decision with the reasons therefor will be rendered; and

(5) that the dispute resolution process will be final and binding upon the parties.

(i) It must permit all parties to appear with representatives, including counsel, and to present all relevant evidence relating to the dispute, including calling and examining witnesses.

(j) It must keep confidential all memoranda, work products or case files of a mediator, and must not disclose any communications relating to the subject matter of the resolution made during the resolution process by any participant, mediator or any person present at the dispute resolution.

§ 116.4 Application procedures.

Applications for funding pursuant to this Part shall be submitted to the Chief Administrator, and shall include the following information:

(a) a description of the organization administering the center, including a description of any sponsoring organizations;

(b) an itemized description of the annual cost of operating the proposed center, including the compensation of employees;

(c) a description of the geographic area of service, the service population and the number of participants capable of being served on an annual basis;

(d) a description of the facilities available in which the proposed center is to be operated;

(e) a detailed description of the proposed program for dispute resolution, including the types of disputes to be handled and the cost, if any, to the participants;

(f) a statement of the present availability of resources to fund the center;

(g) a description of the applicant's administrative capacity to operate the center, including the educational, training and employment background of every member of the staff of the center;

(h) a list of civic groups, social services agencies and criminal justice agencies available to accept and make referrals, written statements from these groups and agencies indicating an intent to accept and make referrals, and a description of how the program will be publicized to make potential referring agencies, the courts and the public aware of its availability;

(i) a description of the past history of the operation of the center, including specific information for the past two years concerning the program, area of service, staff, source of funding, expenditures, referring agencies, number and types of disputes handled, and number and types of disputes resolved;

(j) a list of all other available dispute resolution services and facilities within the proposed geographical area;

(k) documentation that the center meets the eligibility requirements set forth in section 114.3 of this Subchapter; and

(l) such other information as may be required by the Chief Administrator.

§ 116.5 Approval.

(a) The Chief Administrator shall select centers for funding pursuant to this Part and shall determine the amount of funds to be disbursed for each center within available appropriations.

(b) No funds provided by the State shall be disbursed for any center in an amount greater than 50 *per centum* of the estimated annual cost of operating the program as determined by the Chief Administrator.

(c) In determining the centers for which funds may be disbursed, the Chief Administrator shall consider:

(1) the need for the program in that geographical area;

(2) the structure and scope of the proposed program;

(3) the cost of operation;

(4) the availability of sources of funding;

(5) the adequacy and cost of facilities;

(6) the ability of the applicant to administer the program;

(7) the qualifications of the personal staffing the center;

(8) the effectiveness of the program; and

(9) any other consideration which may affect the provision of dispute resolution services pursuant to this Part.

(d) A center may be rejected if the Chief Administrator determines that it will be unable to comply with any of the conditions set forth in section 114.3 of this Subchapter.

(e) Nothing herein shall require the Chief Administrator to approve funding for any applicant.

§ 116.6 Payment.

Payment of funds pursuant to this Part shall be made pursuant to contract entered into between the Unified Court System and the grant recipient.

§ 116.7 Program evaluation.

(a) The Chief Administrator shall monitor and evaluate each program receiving funds pursuant to this Part.

(b) Each grant recipient shall provide to the Chief Administrator on a periodic basis as determined by the Chief Administrator the following information concerning its program:

(1) amount of, and purpose for which, all monies were expended;

(2) number of referrals received by category of cases and the source of each referral;

(3) number of parties serviced;

(4) number of disputes resolved;

(5) nature of the resolution of each dispute, including the type of award and amount of money awarded, if any;

(6) number of cases in which the parties complied with the award, including the nature of the dispute and award in each such case;

(7) number of returnees to the resolution process, including the nature of the dispute and award in each such case;

(8) duration of each hearing;

(9) estimated cost of each hearing; and

(10) any other information as required by the Chief Administrator.

(c) The Chief Administrator shall have the power to inspect at any time the operation of any center receiving funds pursuant to this Part to determine whether the center is complying with the provisions of this Part and the terms of its contract, including the examination and auditing of the fiscal affairs of the program.

(d) The Chief Administrator may halt the disbursement of funds pursuant to this Part at any time he determines that the program is not adequately providing services pursuant to this Part or that any of the provisions of this Part are being violated.

§ 116.8 Records retention.

(a) All financial records of the grant recipient and center pertaining to funding received pursuant to this Part, shall be retained for a minimum of four years after the expiration of the contract entered into with the Unified Court System pursuant to this Part.

(b) A copy of the written agreement or decision subscribed to by the parties, setting forth the settlement of the issues and future responsibilities of each party, referred to in section 116.3(e) of this Part, shall be retained for a period of six years after execution.

(c) A fact sheet or summary of each case from which the center may compile the information required for program evaluation pursuant to section 116.7 of this Part, shall be retained for a period of six years after termination of the case.

(d) No other time requirements for records retention shall apply unless otherwise contracted by the parties.

PART 125

UNIFORM RULES FOR THE ENGAGEMENT OF COUNSEL

Section
125.1   **Engagement of counsel.**

(Part 125 became effective Jan. 6, 1986.)

§ 125.1 Engagement of counsel.

(a) Engagement of counsel shall be a ground for adjournment of an action or proceeding in accordance with this rule.

(b) *Engagement of counsel* shall mean actual engagement on trial or in argument before any State or Federal trial or appellate court, or in a proceeding conducted pursuant to rule 3405 of the CPLR and the rules promulgated thereunder.

(c) Subject to the provisions of subdivision (f) of this section where an attorney has conflicting engagements in the same court or different courts, the affected courts shall determine in which matters adjournments shall be granted and in which matters the parties shall proceed. In making such decisions, they shall, to the extent lawful and practicable, give priority to actions and proceedings in the order in which matters are listed below:

(1) child protective proceedings;

(2) criminal proceedings or juvenile delinquency proceedings wherein the defendant or respondent is incarcerated;

(3) proceedings based on acts which constitute felonies;

(4) proceedings based on acts which constitute misdemeanors; and

(5) civil actions and proceedings, including proceedings conducted pursuant to rule 3405 of the CPLR and the rules promulgated thereunder.

(d) Subject to the provisions of subdivisions (c) and (f) herein, where an attorney has conflicting engagements, such attorney must proceed in whichever matter is entitled to a statutory preference or, if there is none and none of his or her engagements involves exceptional circumstances, in the particular matter first scheduled for the date on which the conflict arises. Matters involving exceptional circumstances shall be given priority over all others, except those entitled to statutory preference. A court may find exceptional circumstances where: (1) there are four or more attorneys engaged for a trial, hearing or appellate argument therein; (2) a party of material witness will be available for a trial or hearing therein only on the date on which the conflict arises or on any subsequent date during the period such trial or hearing reasonably can be expected to extent; (3) a party or material witness thereto is afflicted with an illness which, because of its nature, requires that the trial of the action or proceeding be held on the date on which the conflict arises; or (4) a trial therein must be conducted within statutory time limits and, if trial of the matter is not held on the date on which the conflict arises, there is a reasonable probability that the time limit applicable thereto will elapse.

(e) (1) Each engagement shall be proved by affidavit or affirmation, filed with the court together with proof of service on all parties, setting forth:

(i) the title of the action or proceeding in which counsel is engaged;

(ii) its general nature;

(iii) the court and part in which it is scheduled or, if it is a proceeding conducted pursuant to rule 3405 of the CPLR, the court in which the underlying action was commenced;

(iv) the name of the judge or panel chairman who will preside over it;

(v) the date and time the engagement is to commence or did commence, and the date and time of its probable conclusion.

(2) In determining an application for adjournment on the ground of engagement elsewhere, the court shall consider the affidavit of engagement and may make such further inquiry as it deems necessary, including:

(i) the dates on which each of the actions or proceedings involved were scheduled for the date on which they conflict;

(ii) whether or not the actions or proceedings involved were marked peremptorily for trial or were the subject of some other special marking;

(iii) the number of times each of the actions or proceedings involved was previously adjourned, and upon whose application;

(iv) if any of the attorneys representing a party to one of the actions or proceedings involved is a member or associate of a law firm or office employing more than one attorney, the number of members or associates of his or her firm or office also serving as co-counsel or otherwise involved in such action or proceeding, and their respective engagements elsewhere; and

(v) if applicable, the period of time each of the actions or proceedings involved has been on a calendar from which it has been called.

(f) Where a trial already has commenced, and an attorney for one of the parties has an engagement elsewhere, there shall be no adjournment of the ongoing trial except in the sole discretion of the judge presiding thereat; provided that the judge presiding shall grant a reasonable adjournment where the engagement is in an appellate court.

(g) This subdivision shall apply where a date for trial of an action or proceeding is fixed at least two months in advance thereof upon the consent of all attorneys or by the court. In such event, the attorneys previously designated as trial counsel must appear for trial on that date. If any of such attorneys is actually engaged on trial elsewhere, he or she must produce substitute trail counsel. If neither trial counsel nor substitute trial counsel is ready to try the case on the scheduled date, the court may impose any sanctions permitted by law.

PART 129

FAIR TREATMENT STANDARDS FOR CRIME VICTIMS

§ 129.1 Purpose.

The purpose of these standards is to provide objective guidelines for the fair and uniform treatment of crime victims by the Unified Court System in order to encourage increased public cooperation and support of the criminal justice process, improve the overall effectiveness of the criminal justice system as it concerns crime victims and the public in general and help ensure that courts in the Unified Court System treat crime victims and witnesses with dignity and appropriate understanding.

§ 129.2 Definitions.

(a) *Criminal justice agency* includes any agency or department of the Sate or any political subdivision thereof that performs a criminal justice function as defined in 9 NYCRR 6170.2(c) and a presentment agency as defined in subdivision 12 of section 301.2 of the Family Court Act.

(b) *Criminal justice process* shall mean the process by which a crime charged in an accusatory instrument or in a Family Court petition is processed by the Unified Court System from the initial appearance of the accused to disposition.

(c) *Crime victim* shall mean a natural person against whom an act defined as a misdemeanor or felony by the Penal Law or section 1192 of the Vehicle and Traffic Law has been committed or attempted, where such act is charged in an accusatory instrument as defined in section 1.20(1) of the Criminal Procedure Law or is alleged in a petition filed in Family Court. *Crime victim* shall include the immediate family of a homicide victim or the immediate family or guardian of a minor who is a crime victim. Except as otherwise provided in this Part, a victim shall not include a defense witness or an individual reasonably believed to have been involved in the commission of the crime.

(d) *Witness* shall mean a natural person who has evidence or information concerning a crime and who provides such evidence or information to a criminal justice agency. Where the witness is a minor, *witness* shall include an immediate family member or guardian. Except as otherwise provided in this Part, a witness shall not include a defense witness or an individual reasonably believed to have been involved in the commission of the crime.

(e) *Court* shall mean any court in the Unified Court System that has contact with a crime victim or witness.

§ 129.3 Standards.

(a) When a court has contact with a crime victim or witness, the court shall take steps to ensure:

(1) that the victim has been provided with information concerning:

(i) the victim's role in the criminal justice process, including what the victim can expect from the system as well as what the system expects from the victim;

(ii) the stages of the criminal justice process of significance to the victim and the manner in which information about such stages can be obtained; and

(iii) how the court can address the needs of the victim at sentencing or disposition;

(2) that the victim or witness has been notified as to steps the court can take to protect him or her from intimidation, including the issuance of orders of protection and temporary orders of protection;

(3) that a victim or witness who has provided the appropriate court official or criminal justice agency with a current address and telephone number has been notified, if possible, of judicial proceedings relating to his or her case, including:

(i) the initial appearance of an accused before a judicial officer;

(ii) the release of an accused pending further judicial proceedings;

(iii) proceedings in the prosecution of the accused, including entry of a plea of guilty, trial, sentencing or disposition, and, where a term of imprisonment or confinement is imposed, specific information regarding maximum and minimum terms of such imprisonment or confinement; and

(iv) the reversal or modification of the judgment by an appellate court.

(b) The court shall consider the views of victims of the following felonies regarding disposition of the case by dismissal, plea agreement, trial or sentence:

(1) a violent felony offense;

(2) a felony involving physical injury to the victim;

(3) a felony involving property loss or damage in excess of $250;

(4) a felony involving attempted or threatened physical injury or property loss or damage in excess of $250; and

(5) a felony involving larceny against the person.

(c) The court shall consider the views of the victim or family of the victim, as appropriate, concerning the release of the defendant in the victim's case pending judicial proceedings upon an indictment or petition, and concerning the availability of sentencing or dispositional alternatives such as community supervision and restitution from the defendant.

(d) The court shall take steps to ensure that, whenever possible, victims and other prosecution witnesses awaiting court appearances have been provided with a secure waiting area separate from all other witnesses.

(e) The court shall assist in and expedite the return of property held for evidentiary purposes, unless there is a compelling law enforcement reason for retaining it relating to proof at trial.

(f) Any judicial or nonjudicial personnel of the Unified Court System having contact with a crime victim or witness, whether for the prosecution or the defense, shall treat such crime victim or witness with dignity, courtesy and respect.

(g) The court may direct the district attorney or a criminal justice agency to take such steps as may be necessary and appropriate to ensure compliance with these standards.

§ 129.4 Education and training.

Victim assistance education and training shall be given to judicial and nonjudicial personnel of the Unified Court System so that victims may be promptly, properly and completely assisted.

§ 129.5 Liability.

Nothing in this Part shall be construed as creating a cause of action for damages or injunctive relief against the State or any of its political subdivisions or officers or any agency thereof.

PART 131

AUDIO-VISUAL COVERAGE OF JUDICIAL PROCEEDINGS

§ 131.1 Purpose; general provisions.

(a) These rules are promulgated to comport with the legislative finding that an enhanced public understanding of the judicial system is important in maintaining a high level of public confidence in the Judiciary, and with the legislative concern that cameras in the courts be compatible with the fair administration of justice.

(b) These rules shall be effective for any period when audio-visual coverage in the trial courts is authorized by law and shall apply in all counties in the State.

(c) Nothing in these rules is intended to restrict any preexisting right of the news media to appear at and to report on judicial proceedings in accordance with law.

(d) Nothing in these rules is intended to restrict the power and discretion of the presiding trial judge to control the conduct of judicial proceedings.

(e) No judicial proceeding shall be scheduled, delayed, reenacted or continued at the request of, or for the convenience of, the news media.

(f) In addition to their specific responsibilities as provided in these rules, all presiding judges and all administrative judges shall take whatever steps are necessary to insure that audio-visual coverage is conducted without disruption of court activities, without detracting from or interfering with the dignity or decorum of the court, courtrooms and court facilities, without compromise of the safety of persons having business before the court, and without adversely affecting the administration of justice.

§ 131.2 Definitions.

For purposes of this Part:

(a) *Administrative judge* shall mean the administrative judge of each judicial district; the administrative judge of Nassau County or of Suffolk County; the administrative judge of the Civil Court of the City of New York, the Criminal Court of the City of New York or the Family Court of the City of New York; or the presiding judge of the Court of Claims.

(b) *Audio-visual coverage* or *coverage* shall mean the electronic broadcasting or other transmission to the public of radio or television signals from the courtroom, the recording of sound or light in the courtroom for later transmission or reproduction, or the taking of still or motion pictures in the courtroom by the news media.

(c) *News media* shall mean any news-reporting or news-gathering agency and any employee or agent associated with such agency, including television, radio, radio and television networks, news services, newspapers, magazines, trade papers, in-house publications, professional journals, or any other news-reporting or news-gathering agency, the function of which is to inform the public or some segment thereof.

(d) *Presiding trial judge* shall mean the justice or judge presiding over judicial proceedings at which audio–visual coverage is authorized pursuant to this Part.

(e) *Covert or undercover capacity* shall mean law enforcement activity involving criminal investigation by peace officers or police officers who usually and customarily wear no uniform, badge or other official identification in public view.

(f) *Judicial proceedings* shall mean the proceedings of a court or a judge thereof conducted in a courtroom or any other facility being used as a courtroom.

(g) *Child* shall mean a person who has not attained the age of 16 years.

(h) *Arraignment* shall have the same meaning as such term is defined in subdivision nine of section 1.20 of the Criminal Procedure Law.

(i) *Suppression hearing* shall mean a hearing on a motion made pursuant to the provisions of section 710.20 of the Criminal Procedure Law; a hearing on a motion to determine the admissibility of any prior criminal, vicious or immoral acts of a defendant; and any other hearing held to determine the admissibility of evidence.

(j) *Nonparty witness* shall mean any witness in a criminal trial proceeding who is not a party to such proceeding; except an expert or professional witness, a peace or police officer who acted in the course of his or her duties and was not acting in a covert or undercover capacity in connection with the instant court proceedings, or any government official acting in an official capacity, shall not be deemed to be a nonparty witness.

(k) *Visually obscured* shall mean that the face of a participant in a criminal trial proceeding shall either not be shown or shall be rendered visually unrecognizable to the viewer of such proceeding by means of special editing by the news media.

§ 131.3 Application for audiovisual coverage.

(a) Coverage of judicial proceedings shall be permitted only upon order of the presiding trial judge approving an application made by a representative of the news media for permission to conduct such coverage.

(b) (1) Except as provided in paragraph (2) of this subdivision, an application for permission to conduct coverage of a judicial proceeding shall be made to the presiding trial judge not less than seven days before the scheduled commencement of that proceeding. Where circumstances are such that an applicant cannot reasonably apply more than seven days before commencement of the proceeding, the presiding trial judge may shorten the time period. The application shall be in writing and shall specify such proceeding with sufficient particularity to assist the presiding trial judge in considering the application, and shall set forth which of the types of coverage described in section 131.2(b) of this Part is sought, including whether live coverage is sought. Upon receipt of any application, the presiding trial judge shall cause all parties to the proceeding to be notified thereof.

(2) An application for permission to conduct coverage of an arraignment in a criminal case or of any other proceeding after it has commenced may be made to the presiding trial judge at any time and shall be otherwise subject to the provisions of paragraph (1) of this subdivision.

(3) Each application shall relate to one case or proceeding only, unless the presiding trial judge permits otherwise.

(c) Where more than one representative of the news media makes an application for coverage of the same judicial proceeding, such applications shall be consolidated and treated as one.

§ 131.4 Determination of the application.

(a) Upon receipt of an application pursuant to section 131.3 of this Part, the presiding trial judge shall conduct such review as may be appropriate, including:

(1) consultation with the news media applicant;

(2) consultation with counsel to all parties to the proceeding of which coverage is sought, who shall be responsible for identifying any concerns or objections of the parties, prospective witnesses, and victims, if any, with respect to the proposed coverage, and advising the court thereof; and

(3) review of all statements or affidavits presented to the presiding trial judge concerning the proposed coverage.

Where the proceedings of which coverage is sought involve a child, a victim, a prospective witness, or a party, any of whom object to such coverage, and in any other appropriate instance, the presiding trial judge may hold such conferences and conduct any direct inquiry as may be fitting.

(b) (1) Except as otherwise provided in

paragraphs (2) and (3) of this subdivision or section 131.8 of this Part, consent of the parties, prospective witnesses, victims or other participants in judicial proceedings of which coverage is sought is not required for approval of an application for such coverage.

(2) An application for audio-visual coverage of a trial proceeding in which a jury is sitting, made after commencement of such proceeding, shall not be approved unless counsel to all parties to such proceeding consent to such coverage; provided, however, this paragraph shall not apply where coverage is sought only of the verdict or sentencing, or both, in such proceeding.

(3) Counsel to each party in a criminal trial proceeding shall advise each nonparty witness that he or she has the right to request that his or her image be visually obscured during said witness' testimony, and upon such request the presiding trial judge shall order the news media to visually obscure the visual image of the witness in any and all audio-visual coverage of the judicial proceeding.

(c) In determining an application for coverage, the presiding trial judge shall consider all relevant factors, including but not limited to:

(1) the type of case involved;

(2) whether the coverage would cause harm to any participant;

(3) whether the coverage would interfere with the fair administration of justice, the advancement of a fair trial, or the rights of the parties;

(4) whether any order directing the exclusion of witnesses from the courtroom prior to their testimony could be rendered substantially ineffective by allowing audio-visual coverage that could be viewed by such witnesses to the detriment of any party;

(5) whether the coverage would interfere with any law enforcement activity;

(6) whether the proceedings would involve lewd or scandalous matters;

(7) the objections of any of the parties, prospective witnesses, victims or other participants in the proceeding of which coverage is sought;

(8) the physical structure of the courtroom and the likelihood that any equipment required to conduct coverage of proceedings can be installed and operated without disturbance to those proceedings or any other proceedings in the courthouse; and

(9) the extent to which the coverage would be barred by law in the judicial proceeding of which coverage is sought.

The presiding trial judge also shall consider and give great weight to the fact that any party, prospective witness, victim, or other participant in the proceeding is a child.

(d) Following review of an application for coverage of a judicial proceeding, the presiding trial judge, as soon as practicable, shall issue an order, in writing, approving such application, in whole or in part, or denying it. Such order shall contain any restrictions imposed by the judge on the audio-visual coverage and shall contain a statement advising the parties that any violation of the order is punishable by contempt pursuant to article 19 of the Judiciary Law. Such order shall be included in the record of such proceeding and, unless it wholly approves the application and no party, victim or prospective witness objected to coverage, it shall state the basis for its determination.

(e) Before denying an application for coverage, the presiding trial judge shall consider whether such coverage properly could be approved with the imposition of special limitations, including but not limited to:

(1) delayed broadcast of the proceedings subject to coverage; provided, however, where delayed broadcast is directed, it shall be only for the purpose of assisting the news media to comply with the restrictions on coverage provided by law or by the presiding trial judge;

(2) modification or prohibition of audio-visual coverage of individual parties, witnesses or other trial participants, or portions of the proceedings; or

(3) modification or prohibition of video coverage of individual parties, witnesses, or other trial participants, or portions of the proceedings.

§ 131.5 Review.

(a) Any order determining an application for permission to provide coverage, rendered pursuant to section 131.4(d) of this Part, shall be subject to review by the administrative judge in such form, including telephone conference, as he or she may determine, upon the request of a person who is aggrieved thereby and who is either:

(1) a news media applicant; or

(2) a party, victim, or prospective witness who objected to coverage.

(b) Upon review of a presiding trial judge's order determining an application for permission to provide coverage, the administrative judge shall uphold such order unless it is found that the order reflects an abuse of discretion by the presiding trial judge, in which event the administrative judge may direct such modification of the presiding trial judge's order as may be deemed appropriate. Any order directing a modification or overruling a presiding trial judge's order determining an application for coverage shall be in writing.

(c) No judicial proceeding shall be delayed or

continued to allow for review by an administrative judge of an order denying coverage in whole or in part.

(d) This section shall authorize review by the administrative judge only of a presiding trial judge's order pursuant to paragraph 3 (b) of section 218 of the Judiciary Law, determining an application for permission to provide coverage of judicial proceedings and shall not authorize review of any other orders or decisions of the presiding trial judge relating to such coverage.

§ 131.6 Mandatory pretrial conference.

(a) Where a presiding trial judge has approved, in whole or in part, an application for coverage of any judicial proceeding, the judge, before any such coverage is to begin, shall conduct a pretrial conference for the purpose of reviewing, with counsel to all parties to the proceeding and with representatives of the news media who will provide such coverage, any objections to coverage that have been raised, the scope of coverage to be permitted, the nature and extent of the technical equipment and personnel to be deployed, and the restrictions on coverage to be observed. The court may include in the conference any other person whom it deems appropriate, including prospective witnesses and their representatives. In an appropriate case, the presiding trial judge may conduct the pretrial conference concurrently with any consultations or conferences authorized by section 131.4(a) of this Part.

(b) Where two or more representatives of the news media are parties to an approved application for coverage, no such coverage may begin until all such representatives have agreed upon a pooling arrangement for their respective news media prior to the pretrial conference. Such pooling arrangement shall include the designation of pool operators and replacement pool operators for the electronic and motion picture media and for the still photography media, as appropriate. It also shall include procedures for the cost sharing and dissemination of audiovisual material and shall make due provision for educational users' needs for full coverage of entire proceedings. The presiding trial judge shall not be called upon to mediate or resolve any dispute as to such arrangement. Nothing herein shall prohibit a person or organization that was not party to an approved application for coverage from making appropriate arrangements with the pool operator to be given access to the audiovisual material produced by the pool.

(c) In determining the scope of coverage to be permitted, the presiding trial judge shall be guided by a consideration of all relevant factors, including those prescribed in section 131.4(c) of this Part. Wherever necessary or appropriate, the presiding trial judge shall, at any time before or during the proceeding, proscribe coverage or modify, expand, impose or remove special limitations on coverage, such as those prescribed in section 131.4(e) of this Part.

§ 131.7 Use and deployment of equipment and personnel by the news media.

(a) *Limitations upon use of equipment and personnel in the courtroom.* (1) No more than two electronic or motion picture cameras and two camera operators shall be permitted in any proceeding.

(2) No more than one photographer to operate two still cameras, with not more than two lenses for each camera, shall be permitted in any proceeding.

(3) No more than one audio system for broadcast purposes shall be permitted in any proceeding. Audio pickup for all news media purposes shall be effectuated through existing audio systems in the court facility. If no technically suitable audio system is available, microphones and related wiring essential for media purposes shall be supplied by those persons providing coverage. Any microphones and sound wiring shall be unobtrusive and placed where designated by the presiding trial judge.

(4) Notwithstanding the provisions of paragraphs (1)–(3) of this subdivision, the presiding trial judge on a finding of special circumstances may modify any restriction on the amount of equipment or number of operating personnel in the courtroom, compatible with the dignity of the court or the judicial process.

(b) *Sound and light criteria.* (1) Only electronic and motion picture cameras, audio equipment and still camera equipment that do not produce distracting sound or light may be employed to cover judicial proceedings. The equipment designated in section 131.13 of this Part shall be deemed acceptable.

(2) Use of equipment other than that authorized in section 131.13 of this Part may be permitted by the presiding trial judge, provided the judge is satisfied that the equipment sought to be utilized meets the sound and light criteria specified in paragraph (1) of this subdivision. A failure to obtain advance approval shall preclude use of such equipment in the coverage of the judicial proceeding.

(3) No motorized drives, moving lights, flash attachments, or sudden lighting changes shall be permitted during coverage of judicial proceedings.

(4) No light or signal visible or audible to trial participants shall be used on any equipment during coverage to indicate whether it is operating.

(5) With the concurrence of the presiding trial judge and the administrative judge, modifications

COURT RULES

and additions may be made in light sources existing in the court facility, provided such modifications or additions are installed and maintained at media expense and are not distracting or otherwise offensive.

(c) *Location of equipment and personnel.* Electronic and motion picture cameras, still cameras, and camera personnel shall be positioned in such locations as shall be designated by the presiding trial judge. The areas designated shall provide the news media with reasonable access to the persons they wish to cover while causing the least possible interference with court proceedings. Equipment that is not necessary for audiovisual coverage from inside the courtroom shall be located in an area outside the courtroom.

(d) *Movement of equipment and media personnel.* During the proceedings, operating personnel shall not move about, nor shall there be placement, movement or removal of equipment, or the changing of film, film magazines or lenses. All such activities shall take place each day before the proceeding begins, after it ends, or during a recess.

(e) *Identifying insignia.* Identifying marks, call letters, words, and symbols shall be concealed on all equipment. Persons operating such equipment shall not display any identifying insignia on their clothing.

(f) *Other restrictions.* The presiding trial judge may impose any other restriction on the use and deployment of equipment and personnel as may be appropriate.

§ 131.8 Additional restrictions on coverage.

(a) No audio pickup or audio broadcasts of conferences that occur in a court facility between attorneys and their clients, between co-counsel of a client, or between counsel and the presiding trial judge, shall be permitted without the prior express consent of all participants in the conference.

(b) No conference in chambers shall be subject to coverage.

(c) No coverage of the selection of the prospective jury during *voir dire* shall be permitted.

(d) No coverage of the jury, or of any juror or alternate juror, while in the jury box, in the courtroom, in the jury deliberation room, or during recess, or while going to or from the deliberation room at any time, shall be permitted, provided, however, that, upon consent of the foreperson of a jury, the presiding trial judge may, in his or her discretion, permit audio coverage of such foreperson delivering a verdict.

(e) No coverage shall be permitted of a witness, who as a peace officer or police officer acted in a covert or undercover capacity in connection with the proceedings being covered, without the prior written consent of such witness.

(f) No coverage shall be permitted of a witness, who as a peace officer or police officer is currently engaged in a covert or undercover capacity, without the prior written consent of such witness.

(g) No coverage shall be permitted of the victim in a prosecution for rape, sodomy, sexual abuse, or other sex offense under article 130 or section 255.25 of the Penal Law; notwithstanding the initial approval of a request for audio-visual coverage of such a proceeding, the presiding trial judge shall have discretion throughout the proceeding to limit any coverage that would identify the victim, except that said victim can request of the presiding trial judge that audio-visual coverage be permitted of his or her testimony, or in the alternative can request that coverage of his or her testimony be permitted but that his or her image shall be visually obscured by the news media, and the presiding trial judge in his or her discretion shall grant the request of the victim for the coverage specified.

(h) No coverage of any participant shall be permitted if the presiding trial judge finds that such coverage is liable to endanger the safety of any person.

(i) No coverage of any judicial proceedings that are by law closed to the public, or that may be closed to the public and that have been closed by the presiding trial judge, shall be permitted.

(j) No coverage of any arraignment or suppression hearing shall be permitted without the prior consent of all parties to the proceeding; provided, however, where a party is not yet represented by counsel, consent may not be given unless the party has been advised of his or her right to the aid of counsel pursuant to subdivision 4 of section 170.10 or 180.10 of the Criminal Procedure Law and the party has affirmatively elected to proceed without counsel at such proceeding.

(k) No audio-visual coverage shall be permitted which focuses on or features a family member of a victim or a party in the trial of a criminal case, except while such family member is testifying. Audio-visual coverage operators shall make all reasonable efforts to determine the identity of such persons, so that such coverage shall not occur. The restrictions specified in subdivisions (a) through (k) of this section may not be waived or modified except as provided therein.

§ 131.9 Supervision of audio-visual coverage.

(a) Coverage of judicial proceedings shall be subject to the continuing supervision of the presiding trial judge. No coverage shall take place within the courtroom, whether during recesses or at any other time, when the presiding trial judge is not present and presiding.

(b) Notwithstanding the approval of an

application for permission to provide coverage of judicial proceedings, the presiding trial judge shall have discretion throughout such proceedings to revoke such approval or to limit the coverage authorized in any way. In the exercise of this discretion, the presiding trial judge shall be especially sensitive and responsive to the needs and concerns of all parties, victims, witnesses, and other participants in such proceedings, particularly where the proceedings unnecessarily threaten the privacy or sensibilities of victims, or where they involve children or sex offenses or other matters that may be lewd or scandalous. The presiding trial judge shall be under a continuing obligation to order the discontinuation or modification of coverage where necessary to shield the identity or otherwise insure the protection of any such person, party, witness, or victim, or in order to preserve the welfare of a child.

(c) Counsel to each party in a trial proceeding that is subject to coverage shall inquire of each witness that he or she intends to call regarding any concerns or objections such witness might have with respect to coverage. Where counsel thereby is advised that a witness objects to coverage, counsel shall so notify the presiding trial judge.

§ 131.10 Cooperation with committee.

(a)* All officers and employees of the Unified Court System, and all participants in proceedings where audio-visual coverage was permitted, including judges, attorneys and jurors, shall cooperate with the committee to review audio-visual coverage of court proceedings in connection with the committee's review of the impact of audiovisual coverage on such proceedings.

* **Editor's Note:** So in original. There is no subd. (b).

§ 131.11 Appellate courts.

These rules shall not apply to coverage of proceedings in appellate courts or affect the rules governing such coverage contained in Part 29 of the Rules of the Chief Judge (22 NYCRR Part 29).

§ 131.12 Forms.

The Chief Administrator will promulgate and make available forms for applications pursuant to section 131.3 and for judicial orders pursuant to section 131.4 of this Part.

§ 131.13 Acceptable equipment.

The following equipment shall be deemed acceptable for use in audio-visual coverage of trial court proceeding pursuant to this Part:

(a) Video cameras.

Sony:
BVP-3, BVP-3A, BVP-3U, BVP-5, BVP-30, BVP-33Am, BVP-50J, BVP-110, BVP-150, BVP-250, BVP-300, BVU-300, BVV-1, BVV-5, DXC-3000, M-3

Ikegami:
HL-79, HL-79D, HL-79E, HL-83, HL-95, ITC-170, SP-3A, 75-D, 79-E, 95, 730, 730a, 730ap

JVC:
Ky-1900, KY-2000, KY-2700, BY-110

RCA:
TK-76

Thompson:
501, 601

NEC:
SP-3A

Sharp:
XC-800

Panasonic:
X-100 (the recam system in a camera/recorder combination)

Ampex:
Betacam

(b) Still cameras.

Leica:
M

Nikon:
FE, F-3, FM-2, 2000

Canon:
F-1, T-90

(c) Any other audio or video equipment may be used with the permission of the presiding trial judge.

UNIFORM RULES FOR THE NEW YORK STATE TRIAL COURTS

(Selected Sections)

PART 200

UNIFORM RULES FOR COURTS EXERCISING CRIMINAL JURISDICTION

RULES APPLICABLE TO ALL COURTS

RULES APPLICABLE TO SUPERIOR COURTS

RULES APPLICABLE TO LOCAL CRIMINAL COURTS

CRIMINAL APPEALS TO COUNTY COURTS

RULES APPLICABLE TO ALL COURTS

§ 200.1 Application; definitions.

(a) The rules of this Part shall govern procedures in each criminal court of the State.

(b) For purposes of this Part:

(1) *Chief Administrator of the Courts* shall include the designee of the Chief Administrator.

(2) *Clerk* as used in this Part, shall mean the chief clerk or the appropriate clerk of the trial court, unless the context otherwise requires.

(3) Other words or expressions used in this Part shall have the same meanings as they have under provisions of the Criminal Procedure Law.

§ 200.2 Terms and parts of court.

(a) *Terms of court.* A term of court is a four-week session of court, and there shall be 13 terms of court in a year, unless otherwise provided in the annual schedule of terms established by the Chief Administrator of the Courts, which also shall specify the dates of such terms.

(b) *Parts of court.* A part of court is a designated unit of the court in which specified business of the court is to be conducted by a judge or quasi-judicial officer. There shall be such parts of court as may be authorized to be established from time to time by the Chief Administrator of the Courts.

§ 200.3 Papers filed in a criminal court; form.

In addition to complying with the applicable provisions of CPLR 2101, every paper filed in court, other than an exhibit or printed form, shall contain writing on one side only, and if typewritten, shall have at least double space between each line, except for quotations and the names and addresses of attorneys appearing in the action, and shall have at least one-inch margins.

§ 200.4 Submission of papers to judge of a criminal court.

All papers for signature or consideration of the court shall be presented to the clerk of the trial court in the appropriate courtroom or clerk's office, except that where the clerk is unavailable or the judge so directs, papers may be submitted to the judge and a copy filed with the clerk at the first available opportunity. All papers for any judge that are filed in the clerk's office shall be promptly delivered to the judge by the clerk. The papers shall be clearly addressed to the judge for

whom they are intended and prominently show the nature of the papers, the title and the identification number of the accusatory instrument or instruments by which defendant is charged, the name of the assigned judge, if any, the name of the attorney or party submitting them and the return date of any motion to which the papers refer.

§ 200.5 Appearance of counsel in criminal actions.

Each attorney appearing in a criminal action is required to file a written notice of appearance on or before the time of the attorney's first appearance in court or not later than 10 days after appointment or retainer, whichever is sooner. The notice shall contain the attorney's name, office address and telephone number, the name of the person on whose behalf he or she is appearing, and the identification number of the accusatory instrument or instruments by which such person is charged.

§ 200.6 Engagement of counsel.

No adjournment shall be granted on the ground of engagement of counsel except in accordance with Part 125 of the Rules of the Chief Administrator of the Courts (22 NYCRR Part 125).

§ 200.7 Authorization to administer oaths.

(a) All court clerks employed in court parts devoted in whole or in part to the disposition of criminal actions, and such other employees as the judge presiding therein may designate in accordance with section 105 of the Uniform District Court Act, section 105 of the Uniform City Court Act, section 109 of the Uniform Justice Court Act and section 23(1) of the New York City Criminal Court Act, are authorized to administer oaths, take acknowledgments and sign the process of the court under the seal thereof.

(b) Copies of written authorizations to administer oaths required by section 58 of the New York City Criminal Court Act to be filed with the New York City Criminal Court are to be filed with the chief clerk thereof.

§ 200.8 Official forms.

The forms set forth in Chapter VI of Subtitle D of this Title, designated "Forms for use in courts exercising criminal jurisdiction," shall be the official forms of those courts and shall, in

COURT RULES

substantially the same form as set forth, be uniformly used throughout the State.

§ 200.9 Certificate of relief from disabilities; notification of eligibility.

(a) In all criminal causes, whenever a presentence probation report is submitted to the court, such report shall contain information bearing upon the eligibility of the defendant to obtain a certificate of relief from forfeitures and disabilities under article 23 of the Correction Law and shall further contain a recommendation as to the appropriateness of granting such discretionary relief at the time sentence is pronounced. Whenever a defendant has been sentenced to a period of probation, and has not received such discretionary relief, and if such defendant is apparently eligible for consideration of such discretionary relief, the probation officer supervising such

defendant, prior to the termination of the probation period, shall inform the defendant, of his right to make application to the court for a certificate of relief from disabilities, and shall provide such defendant with the required forms in order to enable him or her to make application to the court if he or she should wish to do so.

(b) In all criminal causes, whenever a defendant who is eligible to receive a certificate of relief from disabilities under article 23 of the Correction Law is sentenced, the court, in pronouncing sentence, unless it grants a certificate at that time, shall advise the defendant of his or her eligibility to make application at a later time for such relief.

(c) Failure to comply with the requirements of subdivision (a) or (b) of this section shall not affect the validity of any sentence.

RULES APPLICABLE TO SUPERIOR COURTS

§ 200.10 Applicability of sections 200.10-200.14.

The rules of these sections shall be applicable to each superior court.

§ 200.11 Assignment of criminal actions.

Criminal actions shall be assigned as follows:

(a) *General.* Except as the Chief Administrator of the Courts may otherwise provide, all criminal actions in Supreme Court and in County Court shall be heard and disposed of in accordance with an individual assignment system.

(b) *Arraignment-conference part.* The Chief Administrator of the Courts may authorize the establishment of an arraignment-conference part for any superior court. Where an arraignment-conference part has been established, upon commencement of a criminal action in the superior court, the action shall be assigned to such part. The judge presiding therein shall arraign the defendant and hear and determine any bail application. If no plea of guilty is entered within 14 calendar days of the defendant's arraignment, or if the judge presiding determines that it is unlikely that a plea of guilty will be entered, the action shall be assigned to a judge as provided in subdivision (c) of this section. If a plea of guilty is entered within such time period, the action shall remain in the arraignment-conference part for sentencing and any further proceedings therein.

(c) *Assignment of actions to individual assignment judges.* Except as provided in subdivision (b) of this section, upon commencement of a criminal action in the superior court, the action shall be assigned to a judge by the clerk of the court in which it is pending pursuant to a method of random selection authorized by the Chief Administrator. The judge thereby assigned shall be known as the "assigned judge" with respect

to such action and, except as otherwise provided in subdivision (d) of this section, shall conduct all further proceedings therein.

(d) *Exceptions.* (1) Where the requirements of matters already assigned to a judge are such as to limit the ability of that judge to handle additional cases, the Chief Administrator may authorize that new assignments to that judge be suspended until the judge is able to handle additional cases.

(2) The Chief Administrator may authorize the assignment of one or more special reserve trial judges. Such judges may be assigned matters for trial in exceptional circumstances where the needs of the courts require such assignment.

(3) Matters requiring immediate disposition may be assigned to a judge designated to hear such matters when the assigned judge is not available.

(4) The Chief Administrator may authorize the transfer of any action and any matter relating to an action from one judge to another in accordance with the needs of the court.

§ 200.12 Preliminary conference.

As soon as practicable after the assignment of an action to an individual assignment judge, the assigned judge shall conduct a preliminary conference. The matters to be considered at such conference shall include establishment of a timetable for completion of discovery and filing and hearing of motions, fixing a date for commencement of trial, and consideration of any other matters that the court may deem relevant. At the conclusion of the conference, the directions by the court to the parties and any stipulations by counsel shall be placed on the record or incorporated in a written court order. In the discretion of the court, failure of a party to comply with these directions shall result in the imposition of such sanctions as are authorized by law. The court may direct the holding of additional preliminary conferences as may be needed.

§ 200.13 Impaneling of grand juries.

There shall be a grand jury drawn and impaneled for such terms of a superior court as may be provided on the annual schedule of terms established by the Chief Administrator of the Courts. Whenever the public interest requires, additional grand juries may be drawn and impaneled as authorized by the Chief Administrator.

§ 200.14 Transfer of indictments between superior courts.

Upon authorization by the Chief Administrator:

(a) An indictment pending in the Supreme Court at a term held in a county outside the City of New York may, prior to entry of a plea of guilty thereto or commencement of a trial thereof, be removed to the County Court of such county.

(b) An indictment pending in a County Court may similarly be removed to the Supreme Court at a term held or to be held in the same county.

§ 200.15 Appointment of a special district attorney.

Any party filing with a superior court an application for appointment of a special district attorney, pursuant to section 701 of the County Law, shall make the application to the Chief Administrator of the Courts. The Chief Administrator, in consultation and agreement with the Presiding Justice of the appropriate Appellate Division, then shall designate a superior court judge to consider the application as provided by law.

§ 200.16 to 200.19   Reserved

RULES APPLICABLE TO LOCAL CRIMINAL COURTS

§ 200.20 Applicability of sections 200.20-200.22.

The rules of these sections shall be applicable to each local criminal court.

§ 200.21 Procedure in local criminal courts; local court rules.

Procedure in each local criminal court shall be as provided by the Criminal Procedure Law and such local court rules as may be adopted in compliance with Part 9 of the Rules of the Chief Judge (22 NYCRR Part 9).

§ 200.22 Assignment of criminal actions.

Criminal actions in a criminal term shall be assigned to judges in a manner authorized by the Chief Administrator of the Courts.

§ 200.23 Recordkeeping requirements for town and village courts.

(a) Each town and village court shall maintain:

(1) case files containing all appears filed, orders issued, any minutes or notes made by the court of proceedings or testimony, and a copy of any original documents or papers forwarded to another court or agency;

(2) an index of cases with a unique number assigned to each case when filed; and

(3) a cashbook which shall chronologically itemize all receipts and disbursements.

(b) In each case, except for parking violations, the court shall assign a unique case number for each defendant. In addition to the papers filed and orders issued, the court shall maintain records which shall include the following information:

(1) the defendant's name, address, and date of birth if under the age of 19;

(2) the State law or local ordinance, including section number, of each offense charged;

(3) a brief description of each offense charged and the date of its alleged commission;

(4) the date of arrest;

(5) the name of the arresting agency or officer;

(6) the date of arraignment;

(7) the name and address of the prosecutor and the defendant's attorney;

(8) a record of the arraignment proceedings, including the following entries: whether the charges were read to the defendant; the constitutional and statutory rights of which defendant was advised; whether counsel was assigned; the plea entered by defendant; a summary of other actions taken by the court at arraignment, including the form of release and amount of bail set; and the date of the next scheduled appearance;

(9) the defendant's NYSID number and court control number, where available, for fingerprintable offenses;

(10) a summary of all other actions taken and proceedings conducted before trial;

(11) the names and addresses of all witnesses sworn;

(12) whether the defendant waived a jury;

(13) each disposition after trial, and each disposition other than by trial and the reasons therefor;

(14) whether a pre-sentence report was ordered and made available to the defendant or the defendant's attorney;

(15) any sentence imposed by the court; and

(16) a summary of all post-judgment proceedings.

(c) A model recordkeeping system which complies with the requirements of this Part will be prepared and distributed by the Office of Court Administration.

§ 200.24 Recordkeeping in city courts.

Each city court may, consistent with the provisions of section 2019 of the Uniform City Court Act, maintain records of all criminal actions and proceedings in accordance with section 200.23 of this Part.

§ 200.25 Procedure for Accepting Guilty Pleas by Mail in the New York City Criminal Court.

(a) *Establishment.* The Administrative Judge of the New York City Criminal Court may establish a procedure for accepting guilty pleas by mail whereby a defendant charged in an information with a designated petty offense defined outside of the Penal Law may enter a plea of guilty to such petty offense, and be sentenced by the Court to pay a fine and any applicable surcharge on the resulting conviction, without making a personal appearance in the action. For purposes of this section, the term "petty offense" shall have the same meaning as in subdivision (39) of section 1.20 of the Criminal Procedure Law.

(b) *Applicability.* The procedure established pursuant to subdivision (a) shall apply only where a defendant has been served with an appearance ticket in lieu of an arrest, returnable in the Summons Part of the New York City Criminal Court, for a petty offense defined outside of the Penal Law that has been specifically designated by the Administrative Judge of the New York City Criminal Court as appropriate for disposition under this section.

(c) *Appearance Ticket; Form and Content.*

(1) The appearance ticket shall be in a form prescribed by the Administrative Judge of the New York City Criminal Court, in consultation with appropriate criminal justice agencies, and shall be served upon the defendant by the issuing officer. The appearance ticket shall contain the nature of the charge, the range of applicable penalties if convicted of the charge, a procedure for pleading guilty by mail, and such other information as may be prescribed by the Administrative Judge.

(2) With respect to the procedure for the entry of a plea of guilty by mail, the appearance ticket shall contain the exact amount of the fine and surcharge to be imposed by the Court, and the manner in which and date by which such fine and surcharge must be paid. The appearance ticket

also shall include a provision advising the defendant that, by entering a plea of guilty by mail to the charge, he or she:

(i) waives arraignment in open court, the right to receive a copy of the accusatory instrument and the right to the aid of counsel;

(ii) pleads guilty to the offense as charged;

(iii) understands that a plea of guilty to the charge is equivalent to a conviction after trial;

(iv) agrees that the charge be disposed of by payment of the fine and any applicable surcharge in accordance with the amounts designated in the appearance ticket; and

(v) understands that the Court may refuse to accept the plea of guilty, because of the defendant's prior criminal record or other special circumstance, in which case, if ultimately convicted, he or she may be sentenced to the full range of penalties set forth in the appearance ticket.

(d) *Procedure.* A defendant served with an appearance ticket pursuant to this section charging the defendant with a designated petty offense defined outside of the Penal Law may enter a plea of guilty by mail by indicating, in accordance with the instructions in the appearance ticket, that he or she pleads guilty to the charge, and by signing and mailing the completed ticket, by first class, registered or certified mail, to the Court at the address provided on the ticket, together with payment of the amount of the fine and surcharge set forth on the ticket for the offense charged. Provided an information has been filed charging such offense, the Court then may dispose of the case as though the defendant had been convicted upon a plea of guilty in open court, or, because of the defendant's prior criminal record or other special circumstance, may refuse to accept the plea of guilty. If the plea is so refused, the Court shall inform the defendant in writing that he or she is required to appear before the Court at a stated time and place to answer the charge, which shall thereafter be disposed of pursuant to the applicable provisions of law, and shall return to the defendant any fine or surcharge payment that may have accompanied the defendant's proffered plea of guilty. Where an information charging a designated petty offense is dismissed by the court, any plea of guilty to such offense entered pursuant to this section shall be refused, and the court shall inform the defendant of the fact of the dismissal and shall return to the defendant any fine or surcharge payment that may have accompanied the defendant's proffered plea of guilty. A plea of guilty to a designated petty offense that is refused pursuant to this section shall be deemed a nullity.

§ 200.26 Issuance of certain securing orders in town and village courts; duties of the court, assignment of and notification to counsel; notification to pretrial services agency.

(a) Where, following an arrest, a defendant is brought, pursuant to CPL § 120.90, 140.20 or 140.27, before a town or village court for arraignment on an accusatory instrument filed with such court, counsel for the defendant shall be given an opportunity to be heard before the court issues a securing order fixing bail or committing the defendant to the custody of the sheriff.

(b) If the defendant appears at such time without counsel, the court shall:

(i) permit the defendant to communicate free of charge by telephone for the purposes of obtaining counsel and informing a relative or friend that he or she has been charged with an offense.

(ii) prior to issuing a securing order fixing bail or committing the defendant to the custody of the sheriff, make an initial determination as to the defendant's eligibility for assigned counsel, provided, however, that this paragraph, as well as subdivisions (c) and (d) of this section, shall not apply where the court determines that the defendant has sufficient funds available to him or her to immediately post bail with the court in the amount and form to be fixed by the court, and such bail is so posted with the court.

(c) Where it appears, pursuant to paragraph (ii) of subdivision (b) of this section, that the defendant is financially unable to obtain counsel, the court shall, prior to issuing a securing order fixing bail or committing the defendant to the custody of the sheriff, assign counsel. Such assignment shall be in accordance with the plan for representation adopted by the county pursuant to County Law § 722, and shall, in accordance with such plan:

(i) direct the administrator of the assigned counsel program to, without delay, select and assign to the defendant, subject to the court's approval, an appropriate attorney from the administrator's list of eligible attorneys:

(ii) direct the local public defender office or legal aid society to represent the defendant; or

(iii) designate a named attorney to represent the defendant. Where assigned counsel is not present in court at the time of the assignment, the court may issue such securing order in the absence of counsel, and in such case shall provide the defendant, in writing, with the name, business address and telephone number of such assigned counsel, or of the administrator of the assigned counsel program or director of the local public defender office or legal aid society, as appropriate. Upon issuing such securing order in the

absence of counsel, or, if not practicable, within 24 hours thereafter, but no later than 48 hours thereafter if extraordinary circumstances so require, the court shall notify such counsel, administrator or director, as well as the director of the local pretrial services agency or head of the pretrial services unit of the county probation department, if any, by telephone, and in writing or by written fax, of the court's assignment, and shall include in such notification the defendant's name, the names of any codefendants, the charge or charges contained in the accusatory instrument, the docket or case number, if available, the adjourn date and time, the terms of the securing order and such other information as the court deems appropriate. The court shall include with such written or faxed notification to such counsel, administrator of the assigned counsel program or director of the local public defender office or legal aid society a copy of the accusatory instrument.

(d) Where it appears, pursuant to paragraph (ii) of subdivision (b) of this section, that the defendant is financially able to retain counsel, the court shall inquire whether the defendant intends to retain counsel, and whether there is a particular attorney the defendant intends to retain. If the defendant identifies a particular attorney he or she intends to retain, the court shall, where such information is readily available, provide the defendant, in writing, with the telephone number of such attorney. Where the defendant does not identify a particular attorney, or where the attorney so identified is not present in court at the time the court intends to issue the securing order fixing bail or committing the defendant to the custody of the sheriff, the court may issue such securing order in the absence of counsel. Upon issuing such securing order in the absence of counsel, or, if not practicable, within 24 hours thereafter, but no later than 48 hours thereafter if extraordinary circumstances so require, the court shall notify the director of the local pretrial services agency or head of the pretrial services unit of the county probation department, if any, and the administrator of the assigned counsel program or director of the local public defender office or legal aid society, as appropriate, by telephone, and in writing or by written fax, of the defendant's appearance before the court and of the court's preliminary determination that the defendant appears to be financially able to retain counsel.

Such notification shall also include the defendant's name, the names of any codefendants, the charge or charges contained in the accusatory instrument, the docket or case number, if available, the adjourn date and time, the terms of the securing order and such other information as the court deems appropriate. The court shall include with such written or faxed notification to the administrator of the assigned counsel program or director of the local public defender office or legal aid society a copy of the accusatory instrument.

(e) Each town and village court shall obtain

from the administrator of the assigned counsel program, public defender, legal aid society or other provider of indigent criminal defense legal services in that jurisdiction, and from the director of the local pretrial services agency or head of the pretrial services unit of the county probation department, if any, the names, addresses, telephone numbers and fax numbers required to effectuate the notification provisions of subdivisions (c) and (d) of this section.

(f) Nothing contained in this section shall be deemed to preclude the court from:

(i) terminating an assignment of counsel made pursuant to subdivision (c) of this section in accordance with the provisions of County Law § 722-d; or

(ii) issuing a securing order releasing the defendant on his or her own recognizance in accordance with CPL § 170.70, 180.80 or any other relevant provision of the Criminal Procedure Law; or

(iii) issuing a securing order releasing the defendant on bail or on his or her own recognizance in accordance with CPL § 30.30(2); or

(iv) entertaining an application for recognizance or bail made pursuant to CPL § 510.20.

(g) Nothing contained in this section shall be deemed to relieve the court of any obligation imposed pursuant to CPL §§ 170.10 and 180.10.

(h) Each town and village court shall maintain a record in the case file of any communications and correspondence initiated or received by the court pursuant to this section, and shall make such records available to the defendant's counsel and the prosecutor upon request.

(i) The Office of Court Administration shall prepare and distribute to each town and village court such forms as may be necessary to implement the notification provisions of this section.

§ 200.27 to 200.29   Reserved

CRIMINAL APPEALS TO COUNTY COURTS

§ 200.30 Applicability of sections 200.30-200.40.

The rules of these sections shall govern procedures in appeals to county courts in criminal actions.

§ 200.31 Judges who may stay judgment pending appeal to county court.

Upon an appeal to county court from a judgment of sentence of a local criminal court, an order pursuant to CPL 460.50, staying or suspending execution of the judgment pending termination of the appeal and either releasing defendant on his own recognizance or fixing bail, may be issued by a judge of the county court to which the appeal has been taken or a justice of the supreme court in the judicial district in which the local court is located. In the case of any appeal as of right from a judgment or sentence of a city court, such order also may be issued by a judge of such city court.

§ 200.32 Duration of order staying or suspending execution of judgment.

(a) An order issued pursuant to CPL 460.50 shall contain a statement that, if an appeal has not been perfected within 120 days after the issuance of the order, the operation of such order terminates and the defendant must surrender himself to the criminal court in which the judgment was entered in order that execution of the judgment be commenced or resumed.

(b) No extension of the 120-day period specified in CPL 460.50 shall be granted except by the county court.

§ 200.33 Perfection of criminal appeals.

(a) When a notice of appeal is filed with a local court, a copy shall be filed with the county clerk by the person filing with the local court. After an appeal has been taken pursuant to CPL 460.10(2), and within 10 days after two transcripts of the stenographic minutes of the proceedings shall have been filed with the local criminal court pursuant to CPL 460.70(1), the local criminal court shall file with the clerk of the county court the notice of appeal, a transcript of the proceedings, a copy of the accusatory instrument and any decision on pretrial motions, and shall notify the appellant and the respondent. If the local criminal court does not file the notice of appeal and transcript within the prescribed period, or if the transcript is defective, the county court, upon application of appellant or respondent, shall order the local criminal court to file them or shall order the parties to settle the transcript before the local court in the manner prescribed by CPLR 5525(c) within a designated time which the county court deems reasonable.

(b) Within 20 days after the affidavit of errors and the return of the lower court have been filed with the county court, where an appeal has been taken pursuant to CPL 460.10(3), or within 20 days after the notice of appeal and transcript have been filed with the county court, where an appeal has been taken pursuant to CPL 460.10(2), appellant shall notice the appeal for the next term or special term of county court by filing with the judge of the county court, not less than 14 days prior to the date for which the appeal has been notice, a brief and notice of argument with proof of service of a copy of each upon respondent. If the defendant is the appellant and the district attorney did not appear in the local criminal court, defendant shall also file proof of service of a copy of the brief and notice of argument upon the district attorney. Respondent's brief, or the district attorney's brief, if any, shall be filed with the judge of the county court within 12 days after service of appellant's brief, with proof of service of a copy upon appellant.

(c) If appellant does not comply herewith, the county court may, upon respondent's motion, or upon its own motion, dismiss the appeal.

(d) Upon motion, the county court judge hearing the appeal may, for good cause shown, extend the time to a subsequent term or special term, in which case the appellant must notice the appeal for such subsequent term. Unless otherwise ordered by the court, appeals may be submitted without oral argument. Motions for reargument may be made after decision is rendered, and must be made within 30 days after service upon the moving party of a copy of the order entered on the decision, with written notice of its entry.

§ 200.34 to 200.39   Reserved

§ 200.40 Obligation of the court to advise of right to counsel on People's appeal.

(a) When a criminal court issues an order suppressing evidence, dismissing an accusatory instrument, setting aside a verdict or sentence, vacating a judgment or denying a motion made pursuant to CPL section 440.40, where such order may be appealed as of right by the People pursuant to CPL § 450.20, the court promptly shall advise the defendant, on the record or in writing, (1) that the People have the right to take an appeal; (2) that the defendant has the right to retain counsel to represent him or her on the appeal or to respond to the appeal pro se; (3) if the defendant can show no financial ability to pay for the cost of counsel on appeal, the defendant may make application to the appellate court for assignment of counsel to respond to the appeal; and (4) that the defendant must provide the court and the defendant's trial counsel with an address where he or she can be contacted should the People appeal the order of the criminal court.

(b) In addition to the circumstances set forth in subdivision (a) of this section, where a court imposes a sentence, and where the People have indicated to the sentencing court their belief that the sentence is invalid as a matter of law and may be appealed by them on that ground, the court, upon imposing the sentence, shall advise the defendant of the rights enumerated in subdivision (a).

PART 205

UNIFORM RULES FOR THE FAMILY COURT

COURT RULES

§ 205.1 Application of Part; waiver; additional rules; definitions.

(a) Application. This Part shall be applicable to all proceedings in the Family Court.

(b) Waiver. For good cause shown, and in the interests of justice, the court in a proceeding may waive compliance with any of these rules in this Part, other than sections 205.2 and 205.3, unless prohibited from doing so by statute or by a rule of the Chief Judge.

(c) Additional rules. Local court rules, not inconsistent with law or with these rules, shall comply with Part 9 of the Rules of the Chief Judge (22 NYCRR Part 9).

(d) Statutory applicability. The provisions of this Part shall be construed consistent with the Family Court Act, the Domestic Relations Law and, where applicable, the Social Services Law. Matters not covered by these rules or the foregoing statutes are governed by the Civil Practice Law and Rules.

(e) Definitions. (1) Chief Administrator of the Courts in this Part also includes a designee of the Administrator.

(2) Unless otherwise defined in this Part, or the context otherwise requires, all terms used in this Part shall have the same meaning as they have in the Family Court Act, the Domestic Relations Law, the Social Services Law and the Civil Practice Law and Rules, as applicable.

§ 205.2 Terms and parts of court.

(a) Terms of court. A term of court is a four-week session of court, and there shall be 13 terms of court in a year, unless otherwise provided in the annual schedule of terms established by the Chief Administrator of the Courts, which also shall specify the dates of such terms.

(b) Parts of court. A part of court is a designated unit of the court in which specified business of the court is to be conducted by a judge or quasi-judicial officer. There shall be such parts of court, including those mandated by statute, as may be authorized from time to time by the Chief Administrator of the Courts.

§ 205.3 Individual assignment system; structure.

(a) General. There shall be established for all proceedings heard in the Family Court an individual assignment system which provides for the continuous supervision of each proceeding by a single judge or, where appropriate, a single support magistrate. For the purposes of this Part, the word "judge" shall include a "support magistrate" where appropriate. Except as otherwise may be authorized by the Chief Administrator or by these rules, every proceeding shall be assigned and heard pursuant to the individual assignment system.

(b) Assignments. Proceedings shall be assigned to a judge of the court upon the filing with the court of the first document in the case. Assignments shall be made by the clerk of the court pursuant to a method of random selection authorized by the Chief Administrator. The judge thereby assigned shall be known as the "assigned judge" with respect to that matter and, except as otherwise provided in subdivision (c) or by law, shall conduct all further proceedings therein.

(c) Exceptions. (1) Where the requirements of matters already assigned to a judge are such as to limit the ability of the judge to handle additional cases, the Chief Administrator may authorize that new assignments to the judge be suspended until the judge is able to handle additional cases.

(2) The Chief Administrator may authorize the establishment in any court of special categories of proceedings for assignment to judges specially assigned to hear such proceedings. Where more than one judge is specially assigned to hear a particular category of proceeding, the assignment of such proceedings to the judges so assigned shall be at random.

(3) Matters requiring immediate disposition may be assigned to a judge designated to hear such matters when the assigned judge is not available.

(4) The Chief Administrator may authorize the transfer of any proceeding and any matter relating to a proceeding from one judge to another in accordance with the needs of the court.

(5) Assignment of cases to judges pursuant to this section shall be consistent with section 205.27 of this Part.

(6) Multiple proceedings involving members of the same family shall be assigned to be heard by a single judge to the extent feasible and appropriate, included, but not limited to, child protective, foster care placement, family offense and custody proceedings.

§ 205.4 Access to Family Court proceedings.

(a) The Family Court is open to the public. Members of the public, including the news media, shall have access to all courtrooms, lobbies, public waiting areas and other common areas of the Family Court otherwise open to individuals having business before the court.

(b) The general public or any person may be excluded from a courtroom only if the judge presiding in the courtroom determines, on a case-by-case basis based upon supporting evidence, that such exclusion is warranted in that case. In exercising this inherent and statutory discretion, the judge may consider, among other factors, whether:

(1) the person is causing or is likely to cause a disruption in the proceedings;

(2) the presence of the person is objected to by one of the parties, including the law guardian, for a compelling reason;

(3) the orderly and sound administration of justice, including the nature of the proceeding, the privacy interests of individuals before the court, and the need for protection of the litigants, in particular, children, from harm requires that some or all observers be excluded from the courtroom;

(4) less restrictive alternatives to exclusion are unavailable or inappropriate to the circumstances of the particular case.

Whenever the judge exercises discretion to exclude any person or the general public from a proceeding or part of a proceeding in Family Court, the judge shall make findings prior to ordering exclusion.

(c) When necessary to preserve the decorum of the proceedings, the judge shall instruct representatives of the news media and others regarding the permissible use of the courtroom and other facilities of the court, the assignment of seats to representatives of the news media on an equitable basis, and any other matters that may affect the conduct of the proceedings and the well-being and safety of the litigants therein.

(d) Audio-visual coverage of Family Court facilities and proceedings shall be governed by Part 29 of the Rules of the Chief Judge and Part 131 of the Rules of the Chief Administrator.

(e) Nothing in this section shall limit the responsibility and authority of the Chief Administrator of the Courts, or the administrative judges with the approval of the Chief Administrator of the Courts, to formulate and effectuate such reasonable rules and procedures consistent with this section as may be necessary and proper to ensure that the access by the public, including the press, to proceedings in the Family Court shall comport with the security needs of the courthouse, the safety of persons having business before the court and the proper conduct of court business.

§ 205.5 Privacy of Family Court records.

Subject to limitations and procedures set by statute and case law, the following shall be permitted access to the pleadings, legal papers formally filed in a proceeding, findings, decisions and orders and, subject to the provisions of CPLR 8002, transcribed minutes of any hearing held in the proceeding:

(a) the petitioner, presentment agency and adult respondent in the Family Court proceeding and their attorneys;

(b) when a child is either a party to, or the child's custody may be affected by, the proceedings:

(1) the parents or persons legally responsible for the care of that child and their attorneys;

(2) the guardian, guardian *ad litem* and law guardian or attorney for that child;

(3) an authorized representative of the child protective agency involved in the proceeding or the probation service;

(4) an agency to which custody has been granted by an order of the Family Court and its attorney; and

(c) a representative of the State Commission on Judicial Conduct, upon application to the appropriate Deputy Chief Administrator, or his or her designee, containing an affirmation that the commission is inquiring into a complaint under article 2-A of the Judiciary Law, and that the inquiry is subject to the confidentiality provisions of said article;

(d) in proceedings under Articles 4, 5, 6 and 8 of the Family Court Act in which temporary or final orders of protection have been issued:

(1) where a related criminal action may, but has not yet been commenced, a prosecutor upon affirmation that such records are necessary to conduct an investigation or prosecution; and

(2) where a related criminal action has been commenced, a prosecutor or defense attorney in accordance with procedures set forth in the Criminal Procedure Law provided, however, that prosecutors may request transcripts of Family Court proceedings in accordance with section 815 of the Family Court Act, and provided further that any records or information disclosed pursuant to this subdivision must be retained as confidential and may not be redisclosed except as necessary for such investigation or use in the criminal action.

(e) another court when necessary for a pending proceeding involving one or more parties or children who are or were the parties in, or subjects of, a proceeding in the Family Court pursuant to Article 4, 5, 6, 8 or 10 of the Family Court Act. Only certified copies of pleadings and orders in, as well as information regarding the status of, such Family Court proceeding may be transmitted without court order pursuant to this section. Any information or records disclosed pursuant to this paragraph may not be re-disclosed except as necessary to the pending proceeding.

Where the Family Court has authorized that the address of a party or child be kept confidential in accordance with Family Court Act § 154-b(2), any record or document disclosed pursuant to this section shall have such address redacted or otherwise safeguarded.

§ 205.6 Periodic reports.

Reports on forms to be furnished by the Office

of Court Administration shall be filed with that office by the Family Court in each county, as follows:

(a) On or before the 20th day of each term, a report shall be filed in the Office of Court Administration for each of the following instances in which an order of disposition was entered in the preceding month:

(1) every proceeding instituted under article 10 of the Family Court Act; and

(2) every proceeding instituted under article 7 of the Family Court Act.

(b) No later than five calendar days thereafter, a separate weekly account for the preceding week ending Sunday shall be filed in the Office of Court Administration concerning:

(1) new cases;

(2) assignment of judges;

(3) appearances of counsel; and

(4) judicial activity;

unless the requirement therefor is otherwise specifically suspended, in whole or in part, by the Office of Court Administration.

(c) On or before the 20th day of the first term of each year, an inventory of the cases pending as of the first day of the first term of that year shall be filed in the Office of Court Administration, and an inventory of pending cases shall also be filed at such other times as may be specified by the Office of Court Administration.

§ 205.7 Papers filed in court; docket number; prefix; forms.

(a) The forms set forth in Chapter IV of Subtitle D of this Title, designated "Forms of the Family Court of the State of New York" and "Adoption Forms of the Family Court and Surrogate's Court of the State of New York," respectively, shall be the official forms of the court and shall, in substantially the same form as set forth, be uniformly used throughout the State. Examples of these forms shall be available at the clerk's office of any Family Court.

(b) The prefixes for the docket numbers assigned to Family Court proceedings shall be:

A—Adoption

AS—Adoption Surrender

B—Commitment of guardianship and custody (§§ 384, 384-b, Social Services Law)

C—Conciliation

D—Delinquency (including transfers from criminal courts)

E—Designated felony delinquency (including transfers from criminal courts)

F—Support

G—Guardianship (§ 661, Family Court Act)

K—Foster care review

L—Approval of foster care placement

M—Consent to marry

N—Neglect or child abuse (child protective proceeding)

O—Family offenses

P—Paternity

R—Referred from Supreme Court (except delinquency)

S—Person in need of supervision

U—Uniform Interstate Family Support Law

V—Custody of minors (§ 651, Family Court Act)

W—Material witness

Z—Miscellaneous

(c) Proceedings for extensions of placement shall bear the prefix of the original proceeding in which the placement was made.

(d) The case docket number shall appear on the outside cover and first page to the right of the caption of every paper tendered for filing in the proceeding. Each such cover and first page also shall contain an indication of the county of venue and a brief description of the nature of the paper and, where the case has been assigned to an individual judge, shall contain the name of the assigned judge to the right of the caption. In addition to complying with the provisions of CPLR 2101, every paper filed in court shall have annexed thereto appropriate proof of service on all parties where required, and every paper, other than an exhibit or a printed official form promulgated in accordance with section 214 of the Family Court Act, shall contain writing on one side only and, if typewritten, shall have at least double space between each line, except for quotations and the names and addresses of attorneys appearing in the action, and shall have at least one-inch margins.

§ 205.8 Submission of papers to judge.

All papers for signature or consideration of the court shall be presented to the clerk of the court in the appropriate courtroom or clerk's office, except that when the clerk is unavailable or the judge so directs, papers may be submitted to the judge and a copy filed with the clerk at the first available opportunity. All papers for any judge which are filed in the clerk's office shall be promptly delivered to the judge by the clerk. The papers shall be clearly addressed to the judge for whom they are intended and prominently show the nature of the papers, the title and docket number of the proceeding in which they are filed, the judge's name and the name of the attorney or party submitting them.

§ 205.9 Miscellaneous proceedings.

All proceedings for which the procedure has not been prescribed by provisions of the Family Court Act, the Domestic Relations Law or the Social Services Law, including but not limited to proceedings involving consent to marry, Interstate Compact on Juveniles and material witnesses, shall be commenced by the filing of a petition and shall require the entry of a written order.

§ 205.10 Notice of appearance.

Each attorney appearing in a proceeding is required to file a written notice of appearance on or before the time of the attorney's first appearance in court or no later than 10 days after appointment or retainer, whichever is sooner. The notice shall contain the attorney's name, office address and telephone number, and the name of the person on whose behalf he or she is appearing.

§ 205.11 Service and filing of motion papers.

Where motions are required to be on notice:

(a) The motion shall be made returnable at such hour as the assigned judge directs.

(b) At the time of service of the notice of motion, the moving party shall serve copies of all affidavits and briefs upon all the of the attorneys for the parties or upon the parties appearing *pro se*. The answering party shall serve copies of all affidavits and briefs as required by CPLR 2214. Affidavits shall be for a statement of the relevant facts, and briefs shall be for a statement of the relevant law. Unless otherwise directed by the court, answering and reply affidavits and all papers required to be furnished to the court by the Family Court Act or CPLR 2214(c) must be filed no later than the time of argument or submission of the motion.

(c) The assigned judge may determine that any or all motions in that proceeding shall be orally argued and may direct that moving and responding papers shall be filed with the court prior to the time of argument.

(d) Unless oral argument has been requested by a party and permitted by the court, or directed by the court, motion papers received by the clerk of the court on or before the return date shall be deemed submitted as of the return date. A party requesting oral argument shall set forth such request in its notice of motion or on the first page of the answering papers, as the case may be. A party requesting oral argument on a motion brought on by an order to show cause shall do so as soon as practicable before the time the motion is to be heard.

(e) Hearings on motions shall be held when required by statute or ordered by the assigned judge in the judge's discretion.

§ 205.12 Conference.

(a) In any proceeding, a conference or conferences shall be ordered by the court as required as soon as practicable after the proceeding has been assigned.

(b) The matters which may be considered at such conference may include, among other things:

(1) completion of discovery;

(2) filing of motions;

(3) argument or hearing of motions;

(4) fixing of a date for fact-finding hearing;

(5) simplification and limitation of issues;

(6) amendment of pleadings or bills of particulars;

(7) admissions of fact;

(8) stipulations as to admissibility of documents;

(9) completion or modification of financial disclosure;

(10) possibilities for settlement; and

(11) limitation of number of expert witnesses.

(c) Where parties are represented by counsel, an attorney thoroughly familiar with the action and authorized to act on behalf of the party or accompanied by a person empowered to act on behalf of the party represented shall appear at such conference.

(d) At the conclusion of a conference, the court shall make a written order including its directions to the parties as well as stipulations of counsel. Alternatively, in the court's discretion, all directions of the court and stipulations of counsel shall be formally placed on the record.

§ 205.13 Engagement of counsel.

No adjournment shall be granted on the ground of engagement of counsel except in accordance with Part 125 of the Rules of the Chief Administrator of the Courts (22 NYCRR Part 125).

§ 205.14 Time limitations for proceedings involving custody or visitation.

In any proceeding brought pursuant to sections 467, 651 or 652 of the Family Court Act to determine temporary or permanent custody or visitation, once a hearing or trial is commenced, it shall proceed to conclusion within 90 days.

§ 205.15 Submission of orders for signature.

(a) Proposed orders, with proof of service on all parties, must be submitted for signature unless otherwise directed by the court within 30 days after the signing and filing of the decision directing that the order be settled or submitted.

(b) When settlement of an order is directed by the court:

(1) a copy of the proposed order or judgment with notice of settlement, returnable at the office of the clerk of the part in which the order or judgment was granted, or before the judge of the court if the court has so directed or if the clerk is unavailable, shall be served on all parties either:

(i) by personal service not less than five days before the date of settlement; or

(ii) by mail not less than ten days before the date of settlement;

(2) proposed counter-orders or judgments shall be made returnable on the same date and at the same place, and shall be served on all parties by personal service, not less than two days, or by mail, not less than seven days, before the date of settlement.

§ 205.16 Motion for judicial determination that reasonable efforts are not required for child in foster care.

(a) This section shall govern any motion for a judicial determination, pursuant to section 352.2(2)(c), 754(2)(b), 1039-b or 1052(b) of the Family Court Act or section 358-a(3)(b) or 392(6-a) of the Social Services Law, that reasonable efforts to prevent or eliminate the need for removal of the child from the home or to make it possible to reunify the child with his or her parents are not required.

(b) A motion for such a determination shall be filed in writing on notice to the parties, including the law guardian, on the form officially promulgated by the Chief Administrator of the Courts and set forth in Chapter IV of Subtitle D of this Title and shall contain all information required therein.

§ 205.17 Permanency hearings for child in foster care.

(a) This section shall govern all permanency hearings conducted pursuant to Articles 3, 7 and 10 of the Family Court Act and sections 358-a and 392 of the Social Services Law.

(b) Filing deadlines.

(1) A petition for the initial permanency hearing in a case brought pursuant to Article 3 or 7 of the Family Court Act or section 358-a or 392 of the Social Services Law shall be filed at least 60 days prior to the expiration of one year following the entry of the child into foster care.

(2) A petition for the initial permanency hearing in a case arising under Article 10 of the Family Court Act shall be filed at least 60 days prior to the expiration of one year following the entry of the child into foster care. For purposes of this paragraph, the child shall be deemed to have entered foster care on the earlier of the date of the fact finding of abuse or neglect of the child

pursuant to section 1051 of the Family Court Act or 60 days after the date the child was removed from his or her home.

(3) In a case brought pursuant to section 1055-a of the Family Court Act with respect to a child who has been freed for adoption but not placed in an adoptive home, or who has been freed for adoption and placed in an adoptive home but for whom a petition for adoption has not been filed, a petition for a permanency hearing shall be filed 60 days prior to the earlier of the expiration of one year following the last permanency hearing or six months after the child has been freed for adoption. With respect to a child freed for adoption for whom an adoption petition is pending, a petition for a permanency hearing shall be filed 60 days prior to the expiration of one year following the last permanency hearing.

(4) In any case in which the court has made a determination, pursuant to section 352.2(2)(c), 754(2)(b), 1039-b or 1052(b) of the Family Court Act or section 358-a(3)(b) or 392(6-a) of the Social Services Law, that reasonable efforts to prevent or eliminate the need for removal of the child from the home or make it possible to reunify the child with his or her parents are not required, a permanency hearing must be held within 30 days of such finding. In such a case, a petition for a permanency hearing shall be filed and served on an expedited basis as directed by the court.

(5) Following the initial permanency hearing in a case in which a child remains in foster care, a petition for a subsequent permanency hearing shall be filed at least 60 days prior to the expiration of one year following the date of the preceding permanency hearing, except as provided in paragraph (3) or (4).

(c) Required notice and service. In addition to serving the petition and accompanying papers upon the parties, including the law guardian, the petitioner shall provide notice of the permanency hearing to the foster parent caring for the child and any pre-adoptive parent or relative providing care for the child in accordance with sections 355.5(6), 741-a, 1040 and 1055-a(4) of the Family Court Act and sections 358-a(4)(c) and 392(4)(i) of the Social Services Law. The petitioner shall submit on or before the return date appropriate proof of service upon the parties and documentation of the notice or notices given to any foster parent, pre-adoptive parent or relative.

(d) Required papers to be filed.

(1) A permanency petition shall be filed on the form officially promulgated by the Chief Administrator of the Courts and set forth in Chapter IV of Subtitle D of this Title, and shall contain all information required therein. The petition shall include, but not be limited to, the following: the date by which the permanency hearing must be held; the date by which any subsequent permanency petition be filed; the proposed permanency goal for the child; the reasonable efforts, if any, undertaken to achieve the child's return to his or her parents and other permanency goal; the visitation plan for the child and his or her sibling or siblings and, if parental rights have not been terminated, for his or her parent or parents; and current information regarding the status of services ordered by the court to be provided, as well as other services that have been provided, to the child and his or her parent or parents.

(2) In all cases, the permanency petition shall be accompanied by the most recent Uniform Case Review containing, at minimum: the child's permanency goal and projected timeframe for its achievement; the reasonable efforts that have been undertaken and are planned to achieve the goal; impediments, if any, that have been encountered in achieving the goal; and the service plan for the child and (where parental rights have not been terminated) the child's parent or parents. The permanency petition shall be accompanied by additional reports as directed by the court. A permanency petition filed pursuant to Article 3 of the Family Court Act shall contain or have annexed to it a plan for the release or conditional release of the child, as required by section 353.3(7) of the Family Court Act.

(3) Not later than five days prior to the date of the permanency hearing, the petitioner shall file a report containing updated information with the court and shall provide copies to the parties, the law guardian, the foster parent caring for the child and any pre-adoptive parent or relative providing care for the child. The report shall provide information, including, but not limited to: the current status of the child; changes, if any, in the child's foster care placement, permanency goal or service plan; updated information regarding allegations in the petition and accompanying documents and any further reports directed by the court.

§ 205.18 to 205.19 Reserved

§ 205.20 Designation of a facility for the questioning of children in custody (juvenile delinquency).

(a) The district administrative judge in each judicial district outside the City of New York and the administrative judge for the Family Court within the City of New York, or a designee, shall arrange for the inspection of any facility within the judicial district proposed for designation as suitable for the questioning of children pursuant to section 305.2 of the Family Court Act, and if found suitable, the district administrative judge or the administrative judge for the Family Court within the City of New York, as appropriate, shall recommend its designation to the Chief Administrator of the Courts.

(b) Every recommendation to the Chief Administrator of the Courts shall include:

(1) the room number or identification, the type of facility in which the room is located, the address and the hours of access;

(2) the name of the police or other law enforcement agency, department of probation, Family Court judge or other interested person or agency which proposed the designation of the particular facility;

(3) a signed and dated copy of the report of inspection of the proposed facility, made at the direction of the district administrative judge or the administrative judge for the Family Court within the City of New York; and

(4) the factors upon which the recommendation is based.

(c) Any facility recommended for designation as suitable for the questioning of children shall be separate from areas accessible to the general public and adult detainees.

(d) Insofar as possible, the district administrative judge or the administrative judge for the Family Court within the City of New York, in making a recommendation for designation, shall seek to assure an adequate number and reasonable geographic distribution of designated questioning facilities, and that:

(1) the room is located in a police facility or in a governmental facility not regularly or exclusively used for the education or care of children;

(2) the room presents an office-like, rather than a jail-like, setting;

(3) the room is clean and well maintained;

(4) the room is well-lit and heated;

(5) there are separate toilet facilities for children or, in the alternative, procedures insuring the privacy and safety of the children when in use;

(6) there is a separate entrance for children, or, in the alternative, there are procedures which minimize public exposure and avoid mingling with the adult detainees;

(7) a person will be in attendance with the child whenever the room is in use as a questioning facility, such person to be a policewoman or other qualified female person when the child is a female; and

(8) any other factors relevant to suitability for designation are considered.

(e) The appropriate district administrative judge or the administrative judge for the Family Court within the City of New York, or a designee, when notified of any material physical change in a facility designated for the questioning of children, shall arrange for the reinspection of such facility concerning its continued suitability for designation.

(f) A current list of facilities designated for the questioning of children within each judicial district and within the City of New York shall be maintained by the district administrative judge and the administrative judge for the Family Court within the City of New York, and shall be kept for easy public inspection in each Family Court in that judicial district and within the City of New York. A current statewide list shall be maintained in the office of the Chief Administrator of the Courts. These lists shall be kept available for public inspection.

§ 205.21 Authorization to detention agency for release of a child taken into custody before the filing of a petition (juvenile delinquency).

(a) When a child is brought to a detention facility prior to the filing of a petition, pursuant to section 305.2 of the Family Court Act, the agency responsible for operating the detention facility is authorized to release the child before the filing of a petition when the events that occasioned the taking into custody do not appear to involve allegations that the child committed a delinquent act.

(b) If the events occasioning the taking into custody do appear to involve allegations that the child committed a delinquent act, the agency is authorized to release the child where practicable and issue an appearance ticket in accordance with section 307.1 of the Family Court Act, unless special circumstances exist which require the detention of the child, including whether:

(1) there is a substantial probability that the child will not appear or be produced at the appropriate probation service at a specified time and place; or

(2) there is a serious risk that, before the petition is filed, the child may commit an act which, if committed by an adult, would constitute a crime; or

(3) the alleged conduct by the child involved the use or threatened use of violence; or

(4) there is reason to believe that a proceeding to determine whether the child is a juvenile delinquent or juvenile offender is currently pending.

(c) Any child released pursuant to this rule shall be released to the custody of his or her parent or other person legally responsible for his or her care, or if such legally responsible person is unavailable, to a person with whom he or she resides.

§ 205.22 Preliminary probation conferences and procedures (juvenile delinquency).

(a) The probation service shall conduct preliminary conferences with any person seeking to have a juvenile delinquency petition filed, the potential respondent and other interested persons, including the complainant or victim, on the same day that such persons appear at a probation service pursuant to section 305.2(4)(a), 307.1 or 320.6 of the Family Court Act, concerning the advisability of requesting that a juvenile delinquency petition be filed and in order to gather information needed for a determination of the suitability of the case for adjustment. The probation service shall permit any participant who is represented by a lawyer to be accompanied by the lawyer at any preliminary conference.

(b) During the preliminary probation conferences, the probation service shall ascertain, from the person seeking to have a juvenile delinquency petition filed, a brief statement of the underlying events and, if known to that person, a brief statement of factors that would be of assistance to the court in determining whether the potential respondent should be detained or released in the event that a petition is filed.

(c) In order to determine whether the case is suitable for the adjustment process, the probation service shall consider the following circumstances, among others:

(1) the age of the potential respondent; and

(2) whether the conduct of the potential respondent allegedly involved:

(i) an act or acts causing or threatening to cause death, substantial pain or serious physical injury to another;

(ii) the use or knowing possession of a dangerous instrument or deadly weapon;

(iii) the use or threatened use of violence to compel a person to engage in sexual intercourse, deviant sexual intercourse or sexual contact;

(iv) the use or threatened use of violence to obtain property;

(v) the use or threatened use of deadly physical force with the intent to restrain the liberty of another;

(vi) the intentional starting of a fire or the causing of an explosion which resulted in damage to a building;

(vii) a serious risk to the welfare and safety of the community; or

(viii) an act which seriously endangered the safety of the potential respondent or another person;

(3) whether there is a substantial likelihood that a potential respondent will not appear at scheduled conferences with the probation service or with an agency to which he or she may be referred;

(4) whether there is a substantial likelihood that the potential respondent will not participate in or cooperate with the adjustment process;

(5) whether there is a substantial likelihood that, in order to adjust the case successfully, the potential respondent would require services that could not be administered effectively in less than four months;

(6) whether there is a substantial likelihood that the potential respondent will, during the adjustment process:

(i) commit an act which, if committed by an adult, would be a crime; or

(ii) engage in conduct that endangers the physical or emotional health of the potential respondent or a member of the potential respondent's family or household; or

(iii) harass or menace the complainant, victim or person seeking to have a juvenile delinquency petition filed, or a member of that person's family or household, where demonstrated by prior conduct or threats;

(7) whether there is pending another proceeding to determine whether the potential respondent is a person in need of supervision, a juvenile delinquent or a juvenile offender;

(8) whether there have been prior adjustments or adjournments in contemplation of dismissal in other juvenile delinquency proceedings;

(9) whether there has been a prior adjudication of the potential respondent as a juvenile delinquent or juvenile offender;

(10) whether there is a substantial likelihood that the adjustment process would not be successful unless the potential respondent is temporarily removed from his or her home and that such removal could not be accomplished without invoking the court process; and

(11) whether a proceeding has been or will be instituted against another person for acting jointly with the potential respondent.

(d) At the first appearance at a conference by each of the persons listed in subdivision (a) of this section, the probation service shall inform such person concerning the function and limitations of, and the alternatives to, the adjustment process, and that:

(1) he or she has the right to participate in the adjustment process;

(2) the probation service is not authorized to and cannot compel any person to appear at any conference, produce any papers or visit any place;

(3) the person seeking to have a juvenile delinquency petition filed is entitled to have access to the appropriate presentment agency at any time for the purpose of requesting that a petition be filed under article 3 of the Family Court Act;

(4) the adjustment process may continue for a period of two months and may be extended for

an additional two months upon written application to the court and approval thereof;

(5) statements made to the probation service are subject to the confidentiality provisions contained in sections 308.1(6) and (7) of the Family Court Act; and

(6) if the adjustment process is commenced but is not successfully concluded, the person participating therein may be notified orally or in writing of that fact and that the case will be referred to the appropriate presentment agency; oral notification will be confirmed in writing.

(e) If the adjustment process is not commenced:

(1) the record of the probation service shall contain a statement of the grounds therefor; and

(2) the probation service shall give written notice to the persons listed in subdivision (a) of this section who have appeared that:

(i) the adjustment process will not be commenced;

(ii) the case will be referred to the appropriate presentment agency; and

(iii) they are entitled to have access to the presentment agency for the purpose of requesting that a petition be filed under article 3 of the Family Court Act.

§ 205.23 Duties of the probation service and procedure relating to the adjustment process (juvenile delinquency).

(a) Upon a determination by the probation service that a case is suitable for the adjustment process, it shall include in the process the potential respondent and any other persons listed in section 205.22(a) of this part who wish to participate therein. The probation service shall permit any participant who is represented by a lawyer to be accompanied by the lawyer at any conference.

(b) If an extension of the period of the adjustment process is sought, the probation service shall apply in writing to the court and shall set forth the services rendered to the potential respondent, the date of commencement of those services, the degree of success achieved, the services proposed to be rendered and a statement by the assigned probation officer that, in the judgment of such person, the matter will not be successfully adjusted unless an extension is granted.

(c) The probation service may discontinue the adjustment process if, at any time:

(1) the potential respondent or the person seeking to have a juvenile delinquency petition filed requests that it do so; or

(2) the potential respondent refuses to cooperate with the probation service or any agency to

which the potential respondent or a member of his or her family has been referred.

(d) If the adjustment process is not successfully concluded, the probation service shall notify all the persons who participated therein in writing:

(1) that the adjustment process has not been successfully concluded;

(2) that the appropriate presentment agency will be notified within 48 hours or the next court day, whichever occurs later; and

(3) that access may be had to the presentment agency to request that a petition be filed;

and, in addition to the above, shall notify the potential respondent in writing of the reasons therefor.

(e) The case record of the probation service required to be kept pursuant to section 243 of the Executive Law and the regulations promulgated thereunder shall contain a statement of the grounds upon which:

(1) the adjustment process was commenced but was not successfully concluded; or

(2) the adjustment process was commenced and successfully concluded.

§ 205.24 Terms and conditions of order adjourning a proceeding in contemplation of dismissal in accordance with section 315.3 of the Family Court Act.

(a) An order adjourning a proceeding in contemplation of dismissal pursuant to section 315.3 of the Family Court Act shall be related to the alleged or adjudicated acts or omissions of respondent and shall contain at least one of the following terms and conditions directing the respondent to:

(1) attend school regularly and obey all rules and regulations of the school;

(2) obey all reasonable commands of the parent or other person legally responsible for respondent's care;

(3) avoid injurious or vicious activities;

(4) abstain from associating with named individuals;

(5) abstain from visiting designated places;

(6) abstain from the use of alcoholic beverages, hallucinogenic drugs, habit-forming drugs not lawfully prescribed for the respondent's use, or any other harmful or dangerous substance;

(7) cooperate with a mental health, social services or other appropriate community facility or agency to which the respondent is referred;

(8) restore property taken from the complainant or victim, or replace property taken from the

COURT RULES

complainant or victim, the cost of said replacement not to exceed $1,500;

(9) repair any damage to, or defacement of, the property of the complainant or victim, the cost of said repair not to exceed $1,500;

(10) cooperate in accepting medical or psychiatric diagnosis and treatment, alcoholism or drug abuse treatment or counseling services and permit an agency delivering that service to furnish the court with information concerning the diagnosis, treatment or counseling;

(11) attend and complete an alcohol awareness program established pursuant to section 19.25 of the Mental Hygiene Law;

(12) abstain from disruptive behavior in the home and in the community;

(13) abstain from any act which, if done by an adult, would be an offense; and

(14) comply with such other reasonable terms and conditions as may be permitted by law and as the court shall determine to be necessary or appropriate to ameliorate the conduct which gave rise to the filing of the petition or to prevent placement with the Commissioner of Social Services or the Office of Children and Family Services.

(b) An order adjourning a proceeding in contemplation of dismissal pursuant to section 315.3 of the Family Court Act may direct that the probation service supervise respondent's compliance with the terms and conditions of said order, and may set a time or times at which the probation service shall report to the court, orally or in writing, concerning compliance with the terms and conditions of said order.

(c) A copy of the order setting forth the terms and conditions imposed, and the duration thereof, shall be furnished to the respondent and to the parent or other person legally responsible for the respondent.

§ 205.25 Terms and conditions of order releasing respondent in accordance with section 320.5 of the Family Court Act.

(a) An order releasing a respondent at the initial appearance in accordance with section 320.5 of the Family Court Act may contain one or more of the following terms and conditions, directing the respondent to:

(1) attend school regularly;

(2) abstain from any act which, if done by an adult, would be an offense;

(3) observe a specified curfew which must be reasonable in relation to the ends sought to be achieved and narrowly drawn;

(4) participate in a program duly authorized as an alternative to detention; or

(5) comply with such other reasonable terms and conditions as the court shall determine to be necessary or appropriate.

(b) A copy of the order setting forth terms and conditions imposed, and the duration thereof, shall be furnished at the time of issuance to the respondent and, if present, to the parent or other person legally responsible for the respondent.

§ 205.26 Procedure when remanded child absconds.

(a) When a child absconds from a facility to which he or she was duly remanded, written notice of that fact shall be given within 48 hours, by an authorized representative of the facility, to the clerk of the court from which the remand was made. The notice shall state the name of the child, the docket number of the pending proceeding in which the child was remanded, the date on which the child absconded and the efforts made to locate and secure the return of the child. Every order of remand shall include a direction embodying the requirements of this subdivision.

(b) Upon receipt of the written notice of absconding, the clerk shall cause the proceeding to be placed on the court calendar no later than the next court day for such action as the court may deem appropriate, and shall give notice of such court date to the presentment agency and law guardian or privately retained counsel of the child.

§ 205.27 Procedure for assignment, in accordance with section 340.2(3) of the Family Court Act, of a proceeding to another judge when the appropriate judge cannot preside.

Except for proceedings transferred in accordance with section 302.3(4) of the Family Court Act, when a judge who has presided at the fact-finding hearing, or accepted an admission pursuant to section 321.3 of such act, in a juvenile delinquency proceeding, cannot preside at another subsequent hearing, including the dispositional hearing, for the reasons set forth in section 340.2(3), the assignment of the proceeding to another judge of the court shall be made as authorized by the Chief Administrator of the Courts.

§ 205.28 Procedures for compliance with Adoption and Safe Families Act.

(a) Pre-petition and pretrial detention; required findings. In any case in which detention is ordered by the court pursuant to sections 307.4 or 320.5 of the Family Court Act, the court shall make additional, specific written findings regarding the following issues:

(1) whether the continuation of the respondent in his or her home would be contrary to his or her best interests; and

(2) where appropriate and consistent with the need for protection of the community, whether reasonable efforts were made, prior to the date of the court hearing that resulted in the detention order, to prevent or eliminate the need for removal of the respondent from his or her home, or, if the respondent had been removed from his or her home prior to the initial appearance, where appropriate and consistent with the need for protection of the community, whether reasonable efforts were made to make it possible for the respondent to safely return home. The court may request the presentment agency and the local probation department to provide information to the court to aid in its determinations and may also consider information provided by the law guardian.

(b) Motion for an order that reasonable efforts are not required. A motion for a judicial determination, pursuant to section 352.2(2)(c) of the Family Court Act, that reasonable efforts to prevent or eliminate the need for removal of the respondent from his or her home or to make it possible to reunify the respondent with his or her parents are not required, shall be governed by section 205.16 of this Part.

(c) Placement; required findings. In any case in which the court is considering ordering placement pursuant to section 353.3 or 353.4 of the Family Court Act, the presentment agency, local probation department, local commissioner of social services and New York State Office of Children and Family Services shall provide information to the court to aid in its required determination of the following issues:

(1) whether continuation in the respondent's home would be contrary to the best interests of the respondent, and, in the case of a respondent for whom the court has determined that continuation in his or her home would not be contrary to the best interests of the respondent, whether continuation in the respondent's home would be contrary to the need for protection of the community;

(2) whether, where appropriate and where consistent with the need for protection of the community, reasonable efforts were made, prior to the date of the dispositional hearing, to prevent or eliminate the need for removal of the respondent from his or her home, and, if the respondent was removed from his or her home prior to the dispositional hearing, where appropriate and where consistent with the need for protection of the community, whether reasonable efforts were made to make it possible for the respondent to return home safely. If the court determines that reasonable efforts to prevent or eliminate the need for removal of the respondent from the home were not made, but that the lack of such efforts was appropriate under the circumstances, or consistent

with the need for protection of the community, or both, the court order shall include such a finding;

(3) in the case of a respondent who has attained the age of 16, the services needed, if any, to assist the respondent to make the transition from foster care to independent living; and

(4) in the case of an order of placement specifying a particular authorized agency or foster care provider, the position of the New York State Office of Children and Family Services or local department of social services, as applicable, regarding such placement.

(d) Permanency hearing; extension of placement. A petition for a permanency hearing and, if applicable, an extension of placement, pursuant to sections 355.3 and 355.5 of the Family Court Act, shall be filed at least 60 days prior to the expiration of one year following the respondent's entry into foster care; provided, however, that if the Family Court makes a determination, pursuant to section 352.2(2)(c) of the Family Court Act, that reasonable efforts are not required to prevent or eliminate the need for removal of the respondent from his or her home or to make it possible to reunify the respondent with his or her parents, the permanency hearing shall be held within 30 days of such finding and the petition for the permanency hearing shall be filed and served on an expedited basis as directed by the court. Following the initial permanency hearing in a case in which the respondent remains in placement, a petition for a subsequent permanency hearing and, if applicable, extension of placement, shall be filed at least 60 days prior to the expiration of one year following the date of the preceding permanency hearing. All petitions for permanency hearings shall be governed by section 205.17 of this Part.

§ 205.29 Reserved

§ 205.30 Preliminary probation conferences and procedures (support).

(a) Any person except a commissioner of social services, a social services official or a person who is receiving paternity and support services pursuant to section 111-g of the Social Services Law, seeking to file a petition for support under article 4 of the Family Court Act, may first be referred to the probation service concerning the advisability of filing a petition.

(b) The probation service shall be available to meet and confer concerning the advisability of filing a petition with the person seeking to file a petition for support, the potential respondent and any other interested person no later than the next regularly scheduled court day. The probation service shall permit any participant who is represented by a lawyer to be accompanied at any preliminary conference by the lawyer, who shall be identified by the probation officer to the other party, and shall not discourage any person from seeking to file a petition.

(c) At the first appearance at a conference by each of the persons listed in subdivision (b) of this section, the probation service shall inform such person concerning the function and limitations of, and the alternative to, the adjustment process, and that:

(1) the purpose of the adjustment process is to discover whether it will be possible to arrive at a voluntary agreement for support without filing a petition;

(2) the person seeking to file a petition for support is entitled to request that the probation service confer with him or her, the potential respondent and any other interested person concerning the advisability of filing a petition for support under article 4 of the Family Court Act;

(3) if the assistance of the probation service is not requested or, if requested, is subsequently declined, the person seeking to file a petition for support is entitled to have access to the court at any time for that purpose and may proceed to file a petition for support;

(4) the probation service is not authorized to, and shall not, compel any person, including the person seeking support, to appear at any conference, produce any papers or visit any place;

(5) the adjustment process must commence within 15 days from the date of the request for a conference, may continue for a period of two months from the date of that request, and may be extended for an additional 60 days upon written application to the court containing the consent of the person seeking to file a petition;

(6) if the adjustment process is not successful, the persons participating therein shall be notified in writing of that fact and that the person seeking to file a petition for support is entitled to access to the court for that purpose; and

(7) if the adjustment of the matter results in a voluntary agreement for support of the petitioner and any dependents:

(i) it shall be reduced to writing by the probation service, signed by both parties to it, and submitted to the Family Court for approval;

(ii) if the court approves it, the court may, without further hearing, enter an order for support pursuant to section 425 of the Family Court Act in accordance with the agreement;

(iii) the order when entered shall be binding upon the parties and shall in all respects be a valid order, and the Family Court may entertain a proceeding for enforcement of the order should there not be compliance with the order; and

(iv) unless the agreement is submitted to the Family Court and an order is issued, the Family Court will not entertain a proceeding for the enforcement of the agreement should the agreement not be complied with.

(d) If the adjustment process is not commenced, the probation service shall give written notice to the persons listed in subdivision (b) of this section that:

(1) the adjustment process will not be commenced, and the reasons therefor;

(2) the person seeking to file a petition for support is entitled to access to the court for that purpose; and

(3) if applicable, the adjustment process was not commenced on the ground that the court would not have jurisdiction over the case, and the question of the court's jurisdiction may be tested by filing a petition.

§ 205.31 Duties of the probation service and procedures relating to the adjustment process (support).

(a) If the assistance of the probation service is requested by the person seeking to file a petition for support, and it appears that it may be possible to arrive at a voluntary agreement for support, the adjustment process shall commence within 15 days from the date of request, and shall include the person seeking to file a petition for support, the potential respondent and any other person listed in subdivision (b) of section 205.30 of this Part who wishes to participate therein. The probation service shall permit any participant who is represented by a lawyer to be accompanied at any conference by the lawyer, who shall be identified by the probation officer to the other party, and shall not discourage any person from seeking to file a petition.

(b) If an extension of the period of the adjustment process is sought, the probation service shall apply in writing to the court and shall set forth the services rendered, the date of commencement of those services, the degree of success achieved and the services proposed to be rendered. The application shall set forth the reasons why, in the opinion of the assigned probation officer, additional time is needed to adjust the matter, and shall contain the signed consent of the person seeking to file a petition for support.

(c) The probation service shall discontinue its efforts at adjustment if, at any time:

(1) the person seeking to file a petition for support or the potential respondent requests that it do so; or

(2) it appears to the probation service that there is no reasonable likelihood that a voluntary agreement for support will result.

(d) If the adjustment process is not successfully concluded, the probation service shall notify all the persons who participated therein, in writing:

(1) that the adjustment process has not been successfully concluded and the reasons therefor; and

(2) that the person seeking to file a petition for support is entitled to access to the court for that purpose.

(e) If the adjustment process results in an agreement for the support of the petitioner and any dependents:

(1) it shall be reduced to writing by the probation service, shall be signed by both parties to it, and shall be submitted to the court, together with a petition for approval of the agreement and a proposed order incorporating the agreement; and

(2) if the agreement is approved by the court, a copy of the order shall be furnished by the probation service to the person seeking to file a petition for support and the potential respondent, in person if they are present, and by mail if their presence has been dispensed with by the court.

§ 205.32 Support magistrates.

(a) Qualifications. Support magistrates shall be appointed by the Chief Administrator of the Courts to hear and determine support proceedings in Family Court pursuant to section 439 of the Family Court Act. They shall be attorneys admitted to the practice of law in New York for at least five years and shall be knowledgable with respect to Family Court procedure, family law and federal and state support law and programs.

(b) Term. (1) Support magistrates shall be appointed as nonjudicial employees of the Unified Court System on a full-time basis for a term of three years and, in the discretion of the Chief Administrator, may be reappointed for subsequent five-year terms, provided that if the Chief Administrator determines that the employment of a full-time support magistrate is not required in a particular court, the services of a full-time support magistrate may be shared by one or more counties or a support magistrate may be appointed to serve within one or more counties on a part-time basis.

(2) In the discretion of the Chief Administrator, an acting support magistrate may be appointed to serve during a support magistrate's authorized leave of absence. In making such appointment, the provisions for selection of support magistrates set forth in subdivision (c) of this section may be modified by the Chief Administrator as appropriate to the particular circumstances.

(3) A support magistrate shall be subject to removal or other disciplinary action pursuant to the procedure set forth in section 25.29(b) of the Rules of the Chief Judge (22 NYCRR 25.29).

(c) Selection of support magistrates. (1) The district administrative judge for the judicial district in which the county or counties where the

support magistrate is authorized to serve is located, or the administrative judge for the courts in Nassau County or the administrative judge for the courts in Suffolk County, if the support magistrate is authorized to serve in either of those counties, or the administrative judge for the Family Court within the City of New York, if the support magistrate is to serve in New York City, shall:

(i) publish an announcement in the law journal serving the affected county or counties inviting application from the bar or, if there is no law journal serving such area, in a newspaper of general circulation; and

(ii) communicate directly with bar associations in the affected county or counties to invite applicants to apply.

(2) The announcements and communications shall set forth the qualifications for selection as contained in subdivision (a) of this section, the compensation, the term of appointment and requirements concerning restrictions on the private practice of law.

(3) A committee consisting of an administrative judge, a judge of the Family Court and a designee of the Chief Administrator shall screen each applicant for qualifications, character and ability to handle the support magistrate responsibilities, and shall forward the names of recommended nominees, with a summary of their qualifications, to the Chief Administrator, who shall make the appointment. The appointment order shall indicate the court or courts in which the support magistrate shall serve. The Chief Administrator further may authorize temporary assignments to additional courts.

(d) Training. The Chief Administrator shall authorize such training for support magistrates as appropriate to ensure the effective performance of their duties.

(e) Compensation and expenses. Compensation for support magistrates shall be fixed by the Chief Administrator. Support magistrates shall be entitled to reimbursement of actual and necessary travel expenses in accordance with the rules governing the reimbursement of the travel expenses of nonjudicial court employees of the State of New York.

§ 205.33 Assignment of support magistrates.

The supervising judge of the Family Court in the county in which the support magistrate will serve, or the deputy administrative judge for the Family Court within the City of New York, if the support magistrate is to serve in New York City, shall assign support magistrates as required by the needs of the courts, in conformance with law and in conformance with section 205.3 of this Part.

COURT RULES

§ 205.34 Referrals to support magistrates.

(a) A summons or warrant in support proceedings shall be made returnable by the clerk of the court before a support magistrate in the first instance, unless otherwise provided by the court. A net worth statement form prescribed by the Chief Administrator shall be appended by the clerk to the summons to be served upon the respondent and shall be given to the petitioner upon the filing of the petition.

(b) Whenever the parties are before a judge of the court when support is an issue, the judge shall make an immediate order, either temporary or permanent, with respect to support. If a temporary order is made, the court shall refer the issues of support to a support magistrate.

(c) The above provisions shall apply to initial determinations of support, subsequent modification or violation proceedings, and support proceedings referred to Family Court by the Supreme Court pursuant to Part 6 of article 4 of the Family Court Act.

§ 205.35 Conduct of hearing.

(a) Unless otherwise specified in the order of reference, the support magistrate shall conduct the hearing in the same manner as a court trying an issue without a jury in conformance with the procedures set forth in the Civil Practice Law and Rules and with section 205.3 of this Part.

(b) If a full or partial agreement is reached between the parties during the hearing, it shall be placed on the record and, if approved, shall be incorporated into an order, which shall be duly entered.

(c) The support magistrate shall require the exchange and filing of affidavits of financial disclosure.

§ 205.36 Findings of fact; transmission of findings of fact and other information; quarterly reports.

(a) Findings of fact shall be in writing and shall include, where applicable, the income and expenses of each party, the basis for liability for support and an assessment of the needs of the children. The findings of fact shall be set forth on a form prescribed by the Chief Administrator. A copy of the findings of fact shall accompany the order of support.

(b) At the time of the entry of the order of support, the clerk of the court shall cause a copy of the findings of fact and order of support to be served either in person or by mail upon the parties to the proceeding or their attorneys. When the findings and order are transmitted to a party appearing *pro se,* they shall be accompanied by information about the objection process, including the requirements for a transcript, the time limitations governing the filing of objections and rebuttals, and the necessity for affidavits of service on the opposing party of all papers filed with the court.

(c) Each support magistrate shall file with the Chief Administrator, in such form as may be required, a quarterly report indicating the matters that have been pending undecided before such support magistrate for a period of 30 days after final submission, and the reasons therefor.

§ 205.37 Recording of hearings; objections.

(a) Hearings may be recorded mechanically. Any equipment used for such mechanical recording or for the production of such recording shall have the prior approval of the Chief Administrator of the Courts.

(b) Mechanical recordings shall be appropriately and clearly identified with the name of the case, docket number and date of hearing for storage and retrieval with proper precautions taken for security and preservation of confidentiality. Where hearings are recorded mechanically, the clerk of the court shall provide a means for the making of a duplicate recording or for an alternative method for preparation of a transcript where required by a judge reviewing objections to an order of a support magistrate or when requested by a party.

(c) A transcript of the proceeding before the support magistrate shall be prepared where required by the judge to whom objections have been submitted for review, in which event costs of duplication and of transcript preparation shall be borne by the objecting party. Either party may request a duplicate recording or transcript, in which event costs of duplication of the recording or preparation of the transcript shall be borne by the requesting party. A transcript shall bear the certification of the transcriber that the transcript is a true and accurate transcription of the proceeding. A party who is financially unable to pay the cost of the duplicate recording or the preparation of a transcript may seek leave of the court to proceed as a poor person pursuant to article 11 of the Civil Practice Law and Rules.

(d) Objections to the order of the support magistrate and rebuttals thereto shall be accompanied by an affidavit of service on the opposing party.

§ 205.38 Record and report of unexecuted warrants issued pursuant to section 428 of the Family Court Act.

(a) The clerk of court for the Family Court in each county shall obtain and keep a record of executed warrants issued pursuant to section 428 of the Family Court Act.

(b) At the end of each six-month period, on the first of January and on the first of July in each year, a report concerning all unexecuted warrants issued pursuant to section 428 of the Family Court Act shall be made and filed with the Office of Court Administration, on a form to be supplied by the Office of Court Administration.

§ 205.39 Authority of probation when there is a failure to obey a lawful order of the court (support).

(a) The probation service, at the request of the petitioner, is authorized to confer with the respondent and the petitioner whenever any respondent fails to obey a lawful order of the court made under article 4 of the Family Court Act or an order of support made under article 5 of the Family Court Act concerning the existence of the violation, the reason for it and the likelihood that there will be compliance in the future. The probation service shall permit any participant who is represented by a lawyer to be accompanied at any conference by the lawyer, who shall be identified by the probation officer to the other party, and shall not discourage any person from seeking to file a petition to enforce compliance.

(b) Before holding any conference pursuant to subdivision (a) of this section:

(1) The probation service shall notify the respondent in writing that:

(i) the probation service is willing to confer with the respondent and must hear from the respondent within seven days if a conference is to be held; and

(ii) the petitioner is entitled to petition the court to enforce compliance with the order;

(2) a copy of this notice shall be furnished to the petitioner; and

(3) if the respondent does not communicate with the probation service within seven days, the probation service shall advise the petitioner that he or she may petition the court to enforce compliance with the order.

(c) If, at a conference held pursuant to subdivision (a) of this section, it shall appear to the probation service that the failure to comply with the order was not willful and that there is a substantial likelihood that compliance with the order will result, the probation service is authorized to adjust the matter informally. An existing order may not be modified by informal adjustment without the filing of a petition for such modification and the approval of the court thereof. Efforts at adjustment pursuant to this subdivision shall not extend beyond the conference held pursuant to subdivision (a) of this section.

(d) The probation service is not authorized to, and shall not, discuss with the petitioner or the respondent:

(1) the advisability or likely outcome of filing a petition to enforce compliance with the order; or

(2) the amount of arrears that would be awarded or cancelled by the court if a petition to enforce the order were filed.

§ 205.40 Preliminary probation conferences and procedures upon a referral from Supreme Court (support).

(a) When an application is referred to the Family Court by the Supreme Court pursuant to part 6 of article 4 of the Family Court Act, the parties may first be referred to the probation service, which shall inform them at the first conference concerning the function and limitations of and the alternatives to the adjustment process in accordance with section 205.30(c) of this Part.

(b) The probation service, at the request of either party to the proceeding, shall be available to meet with the parties and other interested persons no later than the next regularly-scheduled court day concerning the willingness of the parties to resolve those issues by voluntary agreement. The probation service shall permit any participant who is represented by a lawyer to be accompanied at any preliminary conference by the lawyer, who shall be identified by the probation officer to the other party, and shall not discourage any person from seeking to file a petition.

§ 205.41 Duties of the probation service and procedures relating to the adjustment process upon referral from Supreme Court (support).

(a) If the assistance of the probation service is requested by either party to the proceeding, efforts at adjustment shall commence within 15 days from the date of the request and may continue for a period of two months from the date of request. The court may extend the adjustment process for an additional 60 days upon written application containing the consent of the person seeking to file a petition.

(b) The probation service shall permit any participant who is represented by a lawyer to be accompanied at any conference by the lawyer, who shall be identified by the probation officer to the other party.

(c) If an extension of the period of the adjustment process is sought, the probation service shall apply in writing to the court and shall set forth the services rendered, the date of commencement of those services, the degree of success achieved and the services proposed to be rendered. The application shall set forth the reasons why, in the opinion of the assigned probation officer, additional time is needed to adjust the matter, and shall contain the signed consent of the parties and a statement by the probation officer that there is a substantial likelihood that a voluntary agreement would be reached if an extension were granted.

(d) The probation service shall discontinue the adjustment process if, at any time:

(1) either party requests that it do so; or

(2) it appears to the probation service that there is no substantial likelihood that a voluntary agreement will result.

(e) If the adjustment process is not successfully concluded, the probation service shall notify the persons who participated therein in writing:

(1) that the adjustment process has not been successfully concluded, and the reasons therefor;

(2) that either party is entitled to access to the court to have the issues which have been referred determined at a fact-finding hearing.

(f) If the adjustment process results in a voluntary agreement on the issues referred:

(1) it shall be reduced to writing by the probation service, shall be signed by both parties to it, and shall be submitted to the court, together with a petition for approval of the agreement and a proposed order incorporating the agreement;

(2) if the agreement is approved by the court, a copy of the order made by the court shall be furnished by the probation service to the parties, in person if they are present, and by mail if their presence has been dispensed with by the court.

§ 205.42 Submission by support collection units of proposed adjusted orders of support.

(a) A submission by a support collection unit pursuant to section 413 of the Family Court Act for adjustment of a child support order shall include the following, which shall be submitted on forms promulgated by the Chief Administrator of the Courts:

(1) an affidavit from the support collection unit, with findings in support of adjustment;

(2) a proposed adjusted order of support; and

(3) a notice to the parties of the proposed adjusted order and of the rights of the parties, including the addresses of the court and the support collection unit.

The documents set forth in this subdivision shall be filed with the clerk of the court within 10 days of mailing to the parties, together with an affidavit of service of these documents upon the parties.

(b) Where a written objection is received by the clerk of the court within 35 days of mailing to the parties of the documents set forth in subdivision (a) of this section, the court shall schedule a hearing upon notice to the support collection unit and the parties.

(c) Where no timely objection is received by the court, the court shall sign the order upon the court's being satisfied that the requirements of sections 111-h of the Social Services Law and 413 of the Family Court Act have been met, and shall transmit copies of the order to the support collection unit for service on the parties. Absent unusual circumstances, the court shall sign the order or dismiss the application within 10 business days after the conclusion of the 35-day objection period.

§ 205.43 Hearings to determine willful non-payment of child support.

(a) A petition that alleges a willful violation or seeks enforcement of an order of support shall be scheduled as soon as possible for a first appearance date in Family Court but in no event more than 30 days of the filing of the violation or enforcement petition.

(b) After service is made, the judge or support magistrate must commence a hearing to determine a willful violation within 30 days of the date noticed in the summons. The hearing must be concluded within 60 days of its commencement.

(c) Neither party shall be permitted more than one adjournment to secure counsel, except for good cause shown.

(d) On the scheduled hearing date on the issue of willfulness, the hearing may not be adjourned except for the following reasons:

(1) actual engagement of counsel pursuant to Part 125 of the Rules of the Chief Administrator;

(2) illness of a party; or

(3) other good cause shown.

No adjournment shall be in excess of 14 days.

(e) If a willfulness hearing has commenced and must be continued, the adjourned date shall be within seven court days.

(f) Upon the conclusion of a willfulness hearing in a case heard by a support magistrate, the support magistrate shall issue written findings of fact within five court days.

(g) In a case heard by a support magistrate, if the support magistrate makes a finding of willfulness, the written findings shall include the following:

(1) the specific facts upon which the finding of willfulness is based;

(2) the specific amount of arrears established and a money judgment for such amount. An

award of attorney's fees may issued with the findings or at a later date after the case is heard by the Family Court judge;

(3) a recommendation regarding the sanctions that should be imposed, including a recommendation whether the sanction of incarceration is recommended;

(4) a recommendation, as appropriate, regarding a specific dollar amount to be paid or a specific plan to repay the arrears.

(h) In a case heard by a support magistrate, if counsel is assigned, the assignment shall continue through the confirmation proceeding before the Family Court judge without further order of the court.

(i) In a case heard by a support magistrate, a Family Court judge may confirm the findings of the support magistrate by adopting his or her findings and recommendations in whole or in part. Alternatively, the Family Court judge may modify or refuse to confirm the findings and recommendations and may refer the matter back to the support magistrate for further proceedings. The court may, if necessary, conduct an evidentiary hearing.

§ 205.44 Testimony by telephone, audio-visual or other electronic means in child support and paternity cases.

(a) This section shall govern applications for testimony to be taken by telephone, audio-visual means or other electronic means in accordance with sections 433, 531-a and 580-316 of the Family Court Act.

(b) A party or witness seeking to testify by telephone, audio-visual means or other electronic means must complete an application on the form officially promulgated by the Chief Administrator of the Courts and set forth in Chapter IV of Subtitle D of this Title and, except for good cause shown, must file such application with the court not less than three days in advance of the hearing date. The applicant shall attempt to arrange to provide such testimony at a designated tribunal or the child support enforcement agency, as defined in the federal Social Security Act (42 U.S.C. Title IV-D) in that party's state, or county if within the state. The court may permit the testimony to be taken at any suitable location acceptable to the court, including but not limited to, the party's or witness' counsel's office, personal residence or place of business.

(c) The applicant must provide all financial documentation ordered to be disclosed by the court pursuant to section 424 or 580-316 of the Family Court Act, as applicable, before he or she will be permitted to testify by telephone, audio-visual means or other electronic means. The financial documentation may be provided by personal delivery, mailing, facsimile, telecopier or any other electronic means that is acceptable to the court.

(d) The court shall transmit a copy of its decision by mail, facsimile, telecopier, or electronic means to the applicant and the parties.

The court shall state its reasons in writing for denying any request to appear by telephone, audio-visual means or other electronic means.

§ 205.45 to 205.49 Reserved

§ 205.50 Terms and conditions of order suspending judgment in accordance with section 633 of the Family Court Act or section 384-b(8)(c) of the Social Services Law.

(a) An order suspending judgment entered pursuant to section 631 of the Family Court Act or section 384-b(8)(c) of the Social Services Law shall be related to the adjudicated acts or omissions of respondent and shall contain at least one of the following terms and conditions requiring respondent to:

(1) sustain communication of a substantial nature with the child by letter or telephone at stated intervals;

(2) maintain consistent contact with the child, including visits or outings at stated intervals;

(3) participate with the authorized agency in developing and effectuating a plan for the future of the child;

(4) cooperate with the authorized agency's court-approved plan for encouraging and strengthening the parental relationship;

(5) contribute toward the cost of maintaining the child if possessed of sufficient means or able to earn such means;

(6) seek to obtain and provide proper housing for the child;

(7) cooperate in seeking to obtain and in accepting medical or psychiatric diagnosis or treatment, alcoholism or drug abuse treatment, employment or family counselling or child guidance, and permit information to be obtained by the court from any person or agency from whom the respondent is receiving or was directed to receive such services; and

(8) satisfy such other reasonable terms and conditions as the court shall determine to be necessary or appropriate to ameliorate the acts or omissions which gave rise to the filing of the petition.

(b) The order shall set forth the duration, terms and conditions of the suspended judgment. A copy of the order, along with a current service plan, shall be furnished to the respondent. The order shall contain a written statement informing the respondent that a failure to obey the order may lead to its revocation and to the issuance of an order for the commitment of the guardianship and custody of a child. Where the child is in foster care, the order shall set forth the visitation plan for the child and the respondent, as well as for the child and his or her sibling or siblings, if any, and shall require the agency to notify the respondent of case conferences. The order shall further contain a determination in accordance with subdivision 12 of section 384-b of the Social Services Law of the existence of any person or persons to whom notice of an adoption would be required pursuant to section 111-b of the Domestic Relations Law and, if so, whether such person or persons were given notice of the termination of parental rights proceeding and whether such person or persons appeared.

(c) The court may set a time or times at which the respondent or the authorized agency caring the child shall report to the court as to whether there is compliance with the terms and conditions of the suspended judgment.

(d) If a respondent fails to comply with the terms and conditions of an order suspending judgment made pursuant to section 631 of the Family Court Act or section 384-b(8)(c) of the Social Services Law:

(1) a petition for the revocation of the order may be filed;

(2) the petition shall contain a concise statement of the acts or omissions alleged to constitute noncompliance with the order;

(3) service of a summons and a copy of the petition shall be made as provided for by section 617 of the Family Court Act; and

(4) if, after a hearing, the court is satisfied that the allegations of the petition have been established, the court may modify, revise or revoke the order of suspended judgment.

(e) The court may at any time, upon notice and opportunity to be heard to the parties, their attorneys and the law guardian, revise, modify or enlarge the terms and conditions of a suspended judgment previously imposed.

§ 205.51 Proceedings involving custody of a Native American child.

In any proceeding in which the custody of a child is to be determined, the petition shall set forth whether the child is a Native American child subject to the Indian Child Welfare Act of 1978 (25 U.S.C. §§ 1901-1963), and the Court shall proceed further, as appropriate, in accordance with the provisions of that act.

§ 205.52 Adoption rules; application.

(a) Sections 205.53 through 205.55 of this Part shall be applicable to all agency and private-placement adoption proceedings in Family Court.

(b) In any agency adoption, a petition may be filed to adopt a child who is the subject of a termination of parental rights proceeding and whose custody and guardianship has not yet been committed to an authorized agency, provided that:

(i) the adoption petition is filed in the same court where the termination of parental rights proceeding is pending; and

(ii) the adoption petition, supporting documents and the fact of their filing shall not be provided to the judge before whom the petition for termination of parental rights is pending until such time as fact-finding is concluded under that petition.

§ 205.53 Papers required in an adoption proceeding.

(a) All papers submitted in an adoption proceeding shall comply with section 205.7 of this part.

(b) (b) In addition to those papers required by the Domestic Relations Law, the following papers, unless otherwise dispensed with by the court, shall be submitted and filed prior to the placement of any adoption proceeding on the calendar:

(1) a certified copy of the birth certificate of the adoptive child;

(2) an affidavit or affidavits by an attorney admitted to practice in the State of New York or, in the discretion of the court, by a person other than an attorney who is known to the court, identifying each of the parties;

(3) a certified marriage certificate, where the adoptive parents are husband and wife or where an individual adoptive parent is the spouse of the natural parent;

(4) a certified copy of a decree or judgment, where an adoptive parent's marriage has been terminated by decree or judgment;

(5) a certified death certificate, where an adoptive or natural parent's marriage has been terminated by death or where it is alleged that consent or notice is not required because of death;

(6) a proposed order of adoption;

(7) a copy of the attorney's affidavit of financial disclosure filed with the Office of Court Administration pursuant to 22 NYCRR 603.23, 691.23, 806.14 or 1022.33 and either an attorney's affirmation that the affidavit has been personally delivered or mailed in accordance with such rules or the dated receipt from the Office of Court Administration; and

(8) an affidavit of financial disclosure from the adoptive parent or parents, and from any person

whose consent to the adoption is required by law, setting forth the following information:

(i) name, address and telephone number of the affiant;

(ii) status of the affiant in the proceeding and relationship, if any, to the adoptive child;

(iii) docket number of the adoption proceeding;

(iv) the date and terms of every agreement, written or otherwise, between the affiant and any attorney pertaining to any fees, compensation or other remuneration paid or to be paid by or on behalf of the adoptive parents or the natural parents, directly or indirectly, including but not limited to retainer fees on account of or incidental to the placement or adoption of the child or assistance in arrangements for such placement or adoption;

(v) the total amount of fees, compensation or other remuneration to be paid to such attorney by the affiant, directly or indirectly, including the date and amounts of each payment already made, if any, on account of or incidental to the placement or adoption of the child or assistance in arrangements for such placement or adoption;

(vi) the name and address of any other person, agency, association, corporation, institution, society or organization who received or will receive any fees, compensation or other remuneration from the affiant, directly or indirectly, on account of or incidental to the birth or care of the adoptive child, the pregnancy or care of the adoptive child's mother or the placement or adoption of the child and on account of or incidental to assistance in arrangements for such placement or proposed adoption; the amount of each such fee, compensation or other remuneration; and the reason for or services rendered, if any, in connection with each such fee, compensation or other remuneration; and

(vii) the name and address of any person, agency, association, corporation, society or organization who has or will pay the affiant any fee, compensation or other remuneration, directly or indirectly, on account of or incidental to the birth or care of the adoptive child, the pregnancy or care of the adoptive child's mother, or the placement or adoption of the child and on account of or incidental to assistance in arrangements for such placement or adoption; the amount of each such fee, compensation or other remuneration; and the reason for or services rendered, if any, in connection with each such fee, compensation or other remuneration.

(9) in the case of an adoption from an authorized agency in accordance with Title 2 of Article 7 of the Domestic Relations Law, a copy of the criminal history summary report made by the New York State Office of Children and Family Services to the authorized agency pursuant to section 378-a of the Social Services Law regarding the criminal record or records of the prospective adoptive parent or parents and any adult over the age of 18 currently residing in the home.

(c) Prior to the signing of an order of adoption, the court may in its discretion require the filing of a supplemental affidavit by the adoptive parent or parents, any person whose consent to the adoption is required, the authorized agency and the attorney for any of the aforementioned, setting forth any additional information pertaining to allegations in the petition or in any affidavit filed in the proceeding.

§ 205.54 Investigation by disinterested person; adoption.

(a) The probation service or an authorized agency or disinterested person is authorized to, and at the request of the court, shall, interview such persons and obtain such data as will aid the court in determining the truth and accuracy of an adoption petition under article 7 of the Domestic Relations Law, including the allegations set forth in the schedule annexed to the petition pursuant to section 112(3) of that law and such other facts as are necessary to a determination of the petition.

(b) The adoptive parent or parents and other persons concerned with the proceeding shall be notified of the date, time and place of any interview by a disinterested person or authorized agency designated by the court in accordance with sections 112 and 116 of the Domestic Relations Law.

(c) The written report of the investigation conducted pursuant to subdivision (a) of this section shall be submitted to the court within 30 days from the date on which it was ordered, or earlier as the court may direct, unless, for good cause, the court shall grant an extension for a reasonable period of time not to exceed an additional 30 days.

§ 205.55 Special applications.

All applications, including applications to dispense with statutorily required personal appearances, the period of residence of a child, or the period of waiting after filing of the adoption petition, shall be made in writing and shall be accompanied by affidavits setting forth the reasons for the application and all facts relevant thereto.

§ 205.56 Investigation by disinterested person; custody; guardianship.

(a) The probation service or an authorized agency or disinterested person is authorized to, and at the request of the court, shall interview such persons and obtain such data as will aid the court in:

(1) determining custody in a proceeding under section 467 or 651 of the Family Court Act;

(2) exercising its power under section 661 of the Family Court Act to appoint a guardian of the person of a minor under the jurisdiction of the court.

(b) The written report of the investigation conducted pursuant to subdivision (a) of this section shall be submitted to the court within 30 days from the date on which it was ordered, or earlier as the court may direct, unless, for good cause, the court shall grant an extension for a reasonable period of time not to exceed an additional 30 days.

§ 205.57 Petition for guardianship by adoptive parent.

(a) When a petition for temporary guardianship has been filed by an adoptive parent or parents pursuant to section 115-c of the Domestic Relations Law, the clerk of the court in which the petition has been filed shall distribute a written notice to the adoptive parents and lawyers who have appeared, and to the Commissioner of Social Services or the Director of the Probation Service, as appropriate, indicating that:

(1) a petition for adoption must be filed in the court in which the application for temporary guardianship has been brought within 45 days from the date of the signing of the consent to the adoption;

(2) any order or decree of temporary guardianship will expire no later than nine months following its issuance or upon the entry of a final order of adoption whichever is sooner, unless, upon application to the court, it is extended for good cause; and

(3) any order or decree of temporary guardianship will terminate upon withdrawal or denial of a petition to adopt the child, unless the court orders a continuation of such order or decree.

(b) In addition to and without regard to the date set for the hearing of the petition, the clerk of the court shall calendar the case for the 45th day from the date of the signing of the consent to the adoption. If no petition for adoption has been filed by the 45th day, the court shall schedule a hearing and shall order the appropriate agency to conduct an investigation forthwith, if one had not been ordered previously.

§ 205.58 Proceedings for certification as a qualified adoptive parent or parents.

(a) Where the petition in a proceeding for certification as a qualified adoptive parent or parents alleges that petitioner or petitioners will cause a preplacement investigation to be undertaken, the petition shall include the name and address of the disinterested person by whom such investigation will be conducted.

(b) The report of the disinterested person conducting the preplacement investigation shall be filed by such person directly with the court, with a copy of such report delivered simultaneously to the applicant or applicants.

(c) The court shall order a report (1) from the statewide central register of child abuse and maltreatment setting forth whether the child or the petitioner is, or petitioners are, the subject of or another person named in an indicated report, as such terms are defined in section 412 of the Social Services Law, filed with such register; and (2) from the New York State Division of Criminal Justice Services setting forth any existing criminal record of such petitioner or petitioners, in accordance with section 115-d(3-a) of the Domestic Relations Law; provided, however, that were the petitioner(s) have been fingerprinted pursuant to section 378-a of the Social Services Law, the authorized agency in possession of a current criminal history summary report from the New York State Office of Children and Family Services may be requested to provide such report to the court in lieu of a report from the New York State Division of Criminal Justice Services.

§ 205.59 Calendaring of proceedings for adoption from an authorized agency.

Proceedings for adoption from an authorized agency shall be calendared as follows:

(a) Within 60 days of the filing of the petition and documents specified in section 112-a of the Domestic Relations Law, the court shall schedule a review of said petition and documents to take place to determine if there is adequate basis for approving the adoption.

(b) If such basis is found, the court shall schedule the appearance of the adoptive parent(s) and child before the court, for approval of the adoption, within 30 days of the date of the review.

(c) If, upon the court's review, the court finds that there is not an adequate basis for approval of the adoption, the court shall direct such further hearings, submissions or appearances as may be required, and the proceeding shall be adjourned as required for such purposes.

§ 205.60 Designation of a facility for the questioning of children in custody (PINS).

Designation of facilities for the questioning of children pursuant to section 724(b)(ii) of the Family Court Act shall be in accordance with section 205.20 of this Part.

§ 205.61 Authorization to release a child taken into custody before the filing of a petition (PINS).

When a child is brought to a detention facility pursuant to section 724(b)(iii) of the Family Court Act, the administrator responsible for operating the detention facility is authorized, before the filing of a petition, to release the child to the custody of a parent or other relative, guardian or legal custodian when the events that occasioned the taking into custody appear to involve a petition to determine whether the child is a person in need of supervision rather than a petition to determine whether the child is a juvenile delinquent.

§ 205.62 Preliminary probation conferences and procedures (PINS).

(Not applicable in jurisdictions that have designated an assessment service pursuant to an approved assessment and services plan as described in section 243-a of the Executive Law; reference should be made to the procedures set forth in section 735 of the Family Court Act.)

(a) Any person seeking to originate a proceeding under article 7 of the Family Court Act to determine whether a child is a person in need of supervision shall first be referred to the probation service.

(b) The probation service shall begin to conduct preliminary conferences with the person seeking to originate the proceeding, the potential respondent and any other interested person, on the same day that such persons are referred to the probation service, concerning the advisability of filing a petition and in order to gather information needed for a determination of the suitability of the case for adjustment. The probation service shall permit any participant who is represented by a lawyer to be accompanied by the lawyer at any preliminary conference.

(c) During the preliminary probation conferences, the probation service shall ascertain, from the person seeking to originate the proceeding, a brief statement of the underlying events and, if known to that person, a brief statement of factors that would be of assistance to the court in determining whether the potential respondent should be detained or released in the event that a petition is filed.

(d) In order to determine whether the case is suitable for the adjustment process, the probation service shall consider the following circumstances, among others:

(1) the age of the potential respondent;

(2) whether the conduct of the potential respondent allegedly involved:

(i) a serious risk to the welfare and safety of the community; or

(ii) an act which seriously endangered the safety of the potential respondent or another person;

(3) whether there is a substantial likelihood that the potential respondent would not appear at scheduled conferences with the probation service or with an agency to which he or she may be referred;

(4) whether there is a substantial likelihood that the potential respondent will not participate in or cooperate with the adjustment process;

(5) whether there is a substantial likelihood that, in order to adjust the case successfully, the potential respondent would require services that could not be administered effectively in less than four months;

(6) whether there is a substantial likelihood that the potential respondent will, during the adjustment process:

(i) engage in conduct that endangers the physical or emotional health of the potential respondent or a member of the potential respondent's family or household; or

(ii) harass or menace the person seeking to originate the proceeding or the complainant or a member of that person's family or household, where demonstrated by prior conduct or threats;

(7) whether there is pending another proceeding to determine whether the potential respondent is a person in need of supervision, a juvenile delinquent or a juvenile offender;

(8) whether there have been prior adjustments or adjournments in contemplation of dismissal under article 3 or 7 of the Family Court Act;

(9) whether there has been a prior adjudication of the potential respondent as a person in need of supervision, a juvenile delinquent or a juvenile offender;

(10) whether there is a substantial likelihood that the adjustment process would not be successful unless the potential respondent is temporarily removed from his or her home and that such removal could not be accomplished without invoking court process; and

(11) whether the potential respondent refuses to return home or refuses to remain at home and the reasons therefor do not justify the filing of a proceeding under article 10 of the Family Court Act.

(e) At the first appearance at a conference by each of the persons listed in subdivision (b) of this section, the probation service shall inform such person concerning the function and limitations of, and the alternatives to, the adjustment process and that:

(1) he or she has the right to participate in the adjustment process;

(2) the probation service is not authorized to

and cannot compel any person to appear at any conference, produce any papers or visit any place;

(3) the person seeking to originate the proceeding is entitled to have access to the court at any time for the purpose of filing a petition under article 7 of the Family Court Act;

(4) the adjustment process may continue for a period of two months and may be extended for an additional 60 days upon written application to the court;

(5) statements made to the probation service are subject to the confidentiality provisions contained in section 735 of the Family Court Act; and

(6) if the adjustment process is commenced but is not successfully concluded, the persons participating therein may be notified orally or in writing of that fact and that the person seeking to originate the proceeding is entitled to access to the court for the purpose of filing a petition; oral notification will be confirmed in writing.

(f) If the adjustment process is not commenced:

(1) the record of the probation service shall contain a statement of the grounds therefor; and

(2) the probation service shall give written notice to the persons listed in subdivision (b) of this section who have appeared:

(i) that the adjustment process will not be commenced;

(ii) that the person seeking to originate the proceeding is entitled to access to the court for the purpose of filing a petition; and

(iii) that, where applicable, the adjustment process was not commenced on the ground that the court would not have jurisdiction over the case and that the person seeking to originate the proceeding may test the question of the court's jurisdiction by filing a petition.

§ 205.63 Duties of the probation service and procedures relating to the adjustment process (PINS).

(Not applicable in jurisdictions that have designated an assessment service pursuant to an approved assessment and services plan as described in section 243-a of the Executive Law; reference should be made to the procedures set forth in section 735 of the Family Court Act.)

(a) Upon a determination by the probation service that a case is suitable for the adjustment process, it shall include in the process the potential respondent and any other persons listed in section 205.62(b) of this Part who wish to participate therein. The probation service shall permit any participant who is represented by a lawyer to be accompanied by the lawyer at any conference.

(b) If an extension of the period of the adjustment process is sought, the probation service shall apply in writing to the court and shall set forth the services rendered to the potential respondent, the date of commencement of those services, the degree of success achieved, the services proposed to be rendered and a statement by the assigned probation officer that, in the judgment of such person, the matter will not be successfully adjusted unless an extension is granted.

(c) The probation service may discontinue the adjustment process if, at any time:

(1) the potential respondent or the person seeking to originate the proceeding requests that it do so;

(2) the potential respondent refuses to cooperate with the probation service or any agency to which the potential respondent or a member of his or her family has been referred.

(d) If the adjustment process is not successfully concluded, the probation service shall notify all the persons who participated therein, in writing:

(1) that the adjustment process has not been successfully concluded; and

(2) that the person seeking to originate the proceeding is entitled to access to the court for the purposes of filing a petition;

and, in addition to the above, shall notify the potential respondent in writing of the reasons therefor.

(e) The case record of the probation service required to be kept pursuant to section 243 of the Executive Law and the regulations promulgated thereunder shall contain a statement of the grounds upon which:

(1) the adjustment process was commenced but was not successfully concluded; or

(2) the adjustment process was commenced and successfully concluded.

§ 205.64 Procedure when remanded child absconds (PINS).

(a) When a child absconds from a facility to which he or she was remanded pursuant to section 739 of the Family Court Act, written notice of that fact shall be given within 48 hours by an authorized representative of the facility to the clerk of the court from which the remand was made. The notice shall state the name of the child, the docket number of the pending proceeding in which the child was remanded, the date on which the child absconded, and the efforts made to secure the return of the child. Every order of remand pursuant to section 739 shall include a direction embodying the requirements of this subdivision.

(b) Upon receipt of the written notice of absconding, the clerk shall cause the proceeding to be placed on the court calendar no later than the next court day for such action as the court may deem appropriate and shall give notice of such court date to the petitioner, presentment agency and law guardian or privately retained counsel of the child.

§ 205.65 Terms and conditions of order adjourning a proceeding in contemplation of dismissal entered in accordance with section 749(a) of the Family Court Act (PINS).

(a) An order adjourning a proceeding in contemplation of dismissal pursuant to section 749(a) of the Family Court Act shall contain at least one of the following terms and conditions directing the respondent to:

(1) attend school regularly and obey all rules and regulations of the school;

(2) obey all reasonable commands of the parent or other person legally responsible for the respondent's care;

(3) avoid injurious or vicious activities;

(4) abstain from associating with named individuals;

(5) abstain from visiting designated places;

(6) abstain from the use of alcoholic beverages, hallucinogenic drugs, habit-forming drugs not lawfully prescribed for the respondent's use, or any other harmful or dangerous substance;

(7) cooperate with a mental health or other appropriate community facility to which the respondent is referred;

(8) restore property taken from the petitioner, complainant or victim, or replace property taken from the petitioner, complainant or victim, the cost of said replacement not to exceed $1,500;

(9) repair any damage to, or defacement of, the property of the petitioner, complainant or victim, the cost of said repair not to exceed $1,500;

(10) cooperate in accepting medical or psychiatric diagnosis and treatment, alcoholism or drug abuse treatment or counseling services, and permit an agency delivering that service to furnish the court with information concerning the diagnosis, treatment or counseling;

(11) attend and complete an alcohol awareness program established pursuant to section 19.25 of the Mental Hygiene Law;

(12) abstain from disruptive behavior in the home and in the community; or

(13) comply with such other reasonable terms and conditions as may be permitted by law and as the court shall determine to be necessary or appropriate to ameliorate the conduct which gave rise to the filing of the petition.

(b) An order adjourning a proceeding in contemplation of dismissal pursuant to section 749(b) of the Family Court Act may set a time or times at which the probation service shall report to the court, orally or in writing, concerning compliance with the terms and conditions of said order.

(c) A copy of the order setting forth the terms and conditions imposed and the duration thereof shall be furnished to the respondent and to the parent or other person legally responsible for the respondent.

§ 205.66 Terms and conditions of order in accordance with section 755 or 757 of the Family Court Act (PINS).

(a) An order suspending judgment entered pursuant to section 754 of the Family Court Act shall be reasonably related to the adjudicated acts or omissions of the respondent and shall contain at least one of the following terms and conditions directing the respondent to:

(1) attend school regularly and obey all rules and regulations of the school;

(2) obey all reasonable commands of the parent or other person legally responsible for the respondent's care;

(3) avoid injurious or vicious activities;

(4) abstain from associating with named individuals;

(5) abstain from visiting designated places;

(6) abstain from the use of alcoholic beverages, hallucinogenic drugs, habit-forming drugs not lawfully prescribed for the respondent's use, or any other harmful or dangerous substance;

(7) cooperate with a mental health or other appropriate community facility to which the respondent is referred;

(8) make restitution or perform services for the public good;

(9) restore property taken from the petitioner, complainant or victim, or replace property taken from the petitioner, complainant or victim, the cost of said replacement not to exceed $1,000;

(10) repair any damage to, or defacement of, the property of the petitioner, complainant or victim, the cost of said repair not to exceed $1,000;

(11) abstain from disruptive behavior in the home and in the community;

(12) cooperate in accepting medical or psychiatric diagnosis and treatment, alcoholism or drug abuse treatment or counseling services, and permit an agency delivering that service to furnish

COURT RULES

the court with information concerning the diagnosis, treatment or counseling;

(13) attend and complete an alcohol awareness program established pursuant to 19.25 of the Mental Hygiene Law;

(14) comply with such other reasonable terms and conditions as the court shall determine to be necessary or appropriate to ameliorate the conduct which gave rise to the filing of the petition.

(b) An order placing the respondent on probation in accordance with section 757 of the Family Court Act shall contain at least one of the following terms and conditions, in addition to any of the terms and conditions set forth in subdivision (a) of this section, directing the respondent to:

(1) meet with the assigned probation officer when directed to do so by that officer;

(2) permit the assigned probation officer to visit the respondent at home or at school;

(3) permit the assigned probation officer to obtain information from any person or agency from whom the respondent is receiving or was directed to receive diagnosis, treatment or counseling;

(4) permit the assigned probation officer to obtain information from the respondent's school;

(5) cooperate with the assigned probation officer in seeking to obtain and in accepting employment and employment counseling services;

(6) submit records and reports of earnings to the assigned probation officer when requested to do so by that officer;

(7) obtain permission from the assigned probation officer for any absence from the county or residence in excess of two weeks;

(8) attend and complete an alcohol awareness program established pursuant to section 19.25 of the Mental Hygiene Law; or

(9) do or refrain from doing any other specified act of omission or commission that, in the opinion of the court, is necessary and appropriate to implement or facilitate the order placing the respondent on probation.

(c) An order entered pursuant to section 754 of the Family Court Act may set a time or times at which the probation service shall report to the court, orally or in writing, concerning compliance with the terms and conditions of said order.

(d) A copy of the order setting forth the terms and conditions imposed and the duration thereof shall be furnished to the respondent and to the parent or other person legally responsible for the respondent.

§ 205.67 to 205.69   Reserved

§ 205.70 Designation of persons to inform complainant of procedures available for the institution of family offense proceedings.

Pursuant to section 812 of the Family Court Act, the following persons are hereby designated to inform any petitioner or complainant seeking to bring a proceeding under article 8 of the Family Court Act of the procedures available for the institution of these proceedings, before such proceeding or action is commenced:

(a) within the City of New York:

(1) the commanding officer of the police precinct wherein the offense is alleged to have occurred; or

(2) any police officer attached to such precinct who is designated by such commanding officer;

(b) outside the City of New York:

(1) the commanding officer of any law enforcement agency providing police service in the county wherein the offense is alleged to have occurred; or

(2) any police officer attached to such law enforcement agency who is designated by such commanding officer;

(c) the district attorney, corporation counsel or county attorney in the county wherein the offense is alleged to have occurred, or any assistant district attorney, assistant corporation counsel or assistant county attorney who is designated by such district attorney, corporation counsel or county attorney;

(d) any probation officer in the employ of the State of New York, or any political subdivision thereof, providing probation service in the criminal court or in the intake unit of the Family Court in the county in which a proceeding may be instituted;

(e) the clerk of the Family Court and the clerk of the criminal court located in the county in which the proceeding may be instituted, or any clerk in that court designated by such clerk of the family or criminal court; and

(f) judges of all local criminal courts outside the City of New York having jurisdiction over the alleged offense.

§ 205.71 Preliminary probation conferences and procedures (family offenses).

(a) Any person seeking to file a family offense petition under article 8 of the Family Court Act may first be referred to the probation service concerning the advisability of filing a petition.

(b) Upon such referral, the probation service shall inform such person:

(1) concerning the procedures available for the institution of family offense proceedings, including the information set forth in subdivision 2 of section 812 of the Family Court Act; and

(2) that the person seeking to file a family offense petition is entitled to request that the probation service confer with him or her, the potential respondent and any other interested person concerning the advisability of filing a petition requesting:

(i) an order of protection;

(ii) a temporary order of protection; or

(iii) the use of the court's conciliation procedure.

(c) The probation service, at the request of the person seeking to file a family offense petition, shall commence conducting preliminary conferences concerning the advisability of filing a petition with that person, the potential respondent and any other interested person no later than the next regularly scheduled court day. The probation service shall permit any participant who is represented by a lawyer to be accompanied at any preliminary conference by the lawyer, who shall be identified by the probation officer to the other party, and shall not discourage any person from seeking to file a petition.

(d) At the first appearance at a conference by each of the persons listed in subdivision (c) of this section, the probation service shall inform such person concerning the function and limitations of, and the alternatives to, the adjustment process, and that:

(1) the purpose of the adjustment process is to attempt through conciliation and agreement to arrive at a cessation of the conduct forming the basis of the family offense complaint without filing a petition in court;

(2) the probation service may confer with the persons listed in subdivision (c) of this section if it shall appear to the probation service that:

(i) there is a reasonable likelihood that the adjustment process will result in a cessation of the conduct forming the basis of the family offense complaint; and

(ii) there is no reasonable likelihood that the potential respondent will, during the period of the adjustment, inflict or threaten to inflict physical injury on the person seeking to obtain relief, or any other member of the same family or household, if the filing of a petition is delayed;

(3) the probation service is not authorized to, and shall not, compel any person, including the person seeking to file a family offense petition, to appear at any conference, produce any papers or visit any place;

(4) the person seeking to file a family offense petition is entitled to request that the probation service confer with him or her, the potential respondent and any other interested person concerning the advisability of filing a family offense petition under article 8 of the Family Court Act;

(5) if the assistance of the probation service is not requested or, if requested, is subsequently declined, the person seeking to file a family offense petition is entitled to have access to the court at any time, even after having consented to an extension of the adjustment period, and may proceed to file a family offense petition;

(6) no statements made during any preliminary conference with the probation service may be admitted into evidence at a fact-finding hearing held in the Family Court or at any proceeding conducted in a criminal court at any time prior to conviction;

(7) the adjustment process must commence within seven days from the date of the request for a conference, may continue for a period of two months from the date of that request and may be twice extended by the court for two periods of up to 60 days each upon written application to the court containing the consent and signature of the person seeking to file a family offense petition;

(8) if a petition is filed, a temporary order of protection may be issued for good cause shown, and unless a petition is filed, the court may not issue any order of protection;

(9) if the adjustment process is not successful, the persons participating therein shall be notified in writing of that fact, and that the person seeking to file a family offense petition is entitled to access to the court for that purpose;

(10) if the matter has been successfully adjusted, the persons participating therein shall be notified in writing of that fact; and

(11) if the adjustment of the matter results in a voluntary agreement concerning the cessation of the offensive conduct forming the basis of the family offense complaint:

(i) it shall be reduced to writing by the probation service, signed by both parties to it and submitted to the Family Court for approval;

(ii) if the court approves it, the court may, without further hearing, enter an order of protection pursuant to section 823 of the Family Court in accordance with the agreement; and

(iii) the order when entered shall be binding on the respondent and shall in all respects be a valid order.

(e) If the adjustment process is not commenced, the probation service shall give written notice to the persons listed in subdivision (c) of this section that:

(1) the adjustment process was not commenced and the reasons therefor;

COURT RULES

(2) the person seeking to file a family offense petition is entitled to access to the court for that purpose; and

(3) if applicable, the adjustment process was not commenced on the ground that the court would not have jurisdiction over the case, and the person seeking to file a family offense petition may test the question of the court's jurisdiction by filing a petition.

§ 205.72 Duties of the probation service and procedures relating to the adjustment process (family offenses).

(a) If the assistance of the probation service is requested by the person seeking to file a family offense petition, the adjustment process shall commence within seven days from the request. The probation service shall permit any participant who is represented by a lawyer to be accompanied at any conference by the lawyer, who shall be identified by the probation officer to the other party, and shall not discourage any person from seeking to file a petition.

(b) If an extension of the period of the adjustment process is sought, the probation service shall, with the written consent of the person seeking to file a family offense petition, apply in writing to the court and shall set forth the services rendered, the date of commencement of those services, the degree of success achieved, the services proposed to be rendered and a statement by the assigned probation officer: that there is no imminent risk that if an extension of the period is granted the potential respondent will, during the extended period of adjustment, endanger the health or safety of the person seeking to file a family offense petition or any other member of the same family or household, and the facts upon which the opinion is based; and that the matter will not be successfully adjusted unless an extension is granted.

(c) The probation service shall discontinue its efforts at adjustment if, at any time:

(1) the person seeking to file a family offense petition or the potential respondent requests that it do so; or

(2) it appears to the probation service that:

(i) there is no reasonable likelihood that a cessation of the conduct forming the basis of the family offense complaint will result; or

(ii) there is an imminent risk that the potential respondent will inflict or threaten to inflict physical injury upon the person seeking to file a family offense petition or upon any other member of the same family or household; or

(iii) the potential respondent has inflicted or threatened to inflict physical injury on the person seeking to file a family offense petition or any

other member of the same family or household since efforts at adjustment began.

(d) If the adjustment process is not successfully concluded, the probation service shall notify in writing all the persons who participated therein:

(1) that the adjustment process has not been successfully concluded and the reasons therefor; and

(2) that the person seeking to file a family offense petition is entitled to access to the court for that purpose.

(e) If the adjustment process results in an agreement for the cessation of the conduct forming the basis of the family offense complaint:

(1) it shall be reduced to writing by the probation service, shall be signed by both parties to it, and shall be submitted to the court, together with a petition for approval of the agreement and a proposed order incorporating the agreement; and

(2) if the agreement is approved by the court, a copy of the order shall be furnished by the probation service to the person seeking to file a family offense petition and the potential respondent, in person if they are present, and by mail if their presence has been dispensed with by the court.

§ 205.73 Record and report of unexecuted warrants issued pursuant to section 827 of the Family Court Act (family offenses).

(a) The clerk of court for the Family Court in each county shall obtain and keep a record of unexecuted warrants issued pursuant to section 827 of the Family Court Act.

(b) At the end of each six-month period, on the first of January and on the first of July in each year, a report concerning all unexecuted warrants issued pursuant to section 827 of the Family Court Act shall be made and filed with the Office of Court Administration on a form to be supplied by the Office of Court Administration.

§ 205.74 Terms and conditions of order in accordance with sections 841(b)–(e), 842 and 843 of the Family Court Act (family offenses).

(a) An order suspending judgment entered pursuant to section 841(b) of the Family Court Act shall contain at least one of the following terms and conditions directing the respondent to:

(1) stay away from the residence of the person against whom the family offense was committed;

(2) stay away from the place of employment or place of education attended by the person against whom the family offense was committed;

(3) abstain from communicating by any means, including, but not limited to, telephone, letter, e-mail or other electronic means with the person against whom the family offense was committed;

(4) abstain from repeating the conduct adjudicated a family offense at the fact-finding hearing;

(5) cooperate in seeking to obtain and in accepting medical or psychiatric diagnosis and treatment, alcoholism or drug abuse treatment, or employment or counseling or child guidance services, or participate in a batterer's educational program designed to help end violent behavior, and permit information to be obtained by the court from any person or agency from whom the respondent is receiving or was directed to receive such services or participate in such program;

(6) allow medical or psychiatric treatment to be furnished to the person against whom the family offense was committed, or any other named family member or household member who is a dependent of the respondent and whose need for medical or psychiatric treatment was occasioned, in whole or in part, by the conduct adjudicated a family offense;

(7) cooperate with the person against whom the family offense was committed, the head of the household or parent, in maintaining the home or household;

(8) pay restitution in an amount not to exceed $10,000; or

(9) comply with such other reasonable terms and conditions as the court shall deem necessary or appropriate to ameliorate the acts or omissions which gave rise to the filing of the petition.

(b) An order placing the respondent on probation in accordance with section 841(c) of the Family Court Act shall contain at least one of the following terms and conditions, directing the respondent to:

(1) observe one or more of the terms and conditions set forth in subdivision (a) of this section;

(2) meet with the assigned probation officer when directed to do so by that officer;

(3) cooperate with the assigned probation officer in arranging for and allowing visitation in the family residence or household;

(4) cooperate in seeking to obtain and in accepting medical treatment, psychiatric diagnosis and treatment, alcoholism or drug abuse treatment, or employment or counseling services, or participate in a batterer's educational program designed to help end violent behavior, and permit the assigned probation officer to obtain information from any person or agency from whom the respondent is receiving or was directed to receive such services or participate in such program.

(c) An order of protection entered in accordance with section 841(d) of the Family Court Act may, in addition to the terms and conditions enumerated in sections 842 and 842-a of the Family Court Act, require the petitioner, respondent or both, or, if before the court, any other member of the household, to:

(1) abstain from communicating by any means, including, but not limited to, telephone, letter, e-mail or other electronic means with the person against whom the family offense was committed;

(2) stay away from the place of employment or place of education attended by the person against whom the family offense was committed, of a child or a parent, or of another member of the same family or household;

(3) refrain from engaging in any conduct which interferes with the custody of a child as set forth in the order;

(4) cooperate in seeking to obtain and in accepting medical treatment, psychiatric diagnosis and treatment, alcoholism or drug abuse treatment, or employment or counseling services, or participate in a batterer's educational program designated to help end violent behavior, and permit information to be obtained by the court from any person or agency from whom the respondent is receiving or was directed to receive such services or participate in such program;

(5) pay restitution in an amount not to exceed $10,000; or

(6) comply with such other reasonable terms and conditions as the court may deem necessary and appropriate to ameliorate the acts or omissions which gave rise to the filing of the petition.

(d) A copy of the order setting forth its duration and the terms and conditions imposed shall be furnished to the respondent and to the person or persons against whom the family offense was committed.

(e) Each order issued pursuant to section 828 or 841(b), (c), (d) or (e) of the Family Court Act shall contain a written statement informing the respondent that a failure to obey the order may result in commitment to jail for a term not to exceed six months. Each order issued pursuant to section 828 or 841(d) shall contain a written statement informing the respondent that a failure to obey the order may result in incarceration up to seven years.

§ 205.75 to 205.79   Reserved

§ 205.80 Procedure when remanded child absconds (child protective proceeding).

(a) When a child absconds from a shelter or holding facility to which the child was remanded pursuant to section 1027(b) or 1051(d) of the

Family Court Act, written notice of that fact, signed by an authorized representative of the facility, shall be sent within 48 hours to the clerk of the court from which the remand was made. The notice shall state the name of the child, the docket number of the pending proceeding in which the child was remanded, the date on which the child absconded, and the efforts made to secure the return of the child. Every order of remand pursuant to sections 1027(b) or 1051(d) shall include a direction embodying the requirement of this subdivision.

(b) Upon receipt of a written notice of absconding, the clerk of the court shall cause the proceeding to be placed on the calendar for the next court day for such action as the court shall deem appropriate, and shall give notice of such court date to the petitioner and law guardian or privately retained counsel of the child.

§ 205.81 Procedures for compliance with Adoption and Safe Families Act.

(a) Temporary removal; required findings. In any case in which removal of the child is ordered by the court pursuant to Part 2 of Article 10 of the Family Court Act, the court shall make additional, specific written findings regarding the following issues:

(1) whether the continuation of the child in his or her home would be contrary to his or her best interests; and

(2) whether reasonable efforts, where appropriate, were made, prior to the date of the court hearing that resulted in the removal order, to prevent or eliminate the need for removal of the child from his or her home, and, if the child had been removed from his or her home prior to such court hearing, whether reasonably efforts, where appropriate, were made to make it possible for the child to safely return home. The petitioner shall provide information to the court to aid in its determinations. The court may also consider information provided by respondents and the law guardian.

(b) Motion for an order that reasonable efforts are not required. A motion for a judicial determination, pursuant to section 1039-b of the Family Court Act, that reasonable efforts to prevent or eliminate the need for removal of the child from his or her home or to make it possible to reunify the child with his or her parents are not required shall be governed by section 205.16 of this Part.

(c) Placement; required findings. In any care in which the court is considering ordering placement pursuant to section 1055 of the Family Court Act, the petitioner shall provide information to the court to aid in its required determination of the following issues:

(1) whether continuation in the child's home

would be contrary to his or her best interests and, if the child was removed from his or her home prior to the date of such hearing, whether such removal was in his or her best interests;

(2) whether reasonably efforts, where appropriate, were made, prior to the date of the dispositional hearing, to prevent or eliminate the need for removal of the child from his or her home and, if the child was removed from his or her home prior to the date of such hearing, whether reasonably efforts, where appropriate, were made to make it possible for the child to return safely home. If the court determines that reasonable efforts to prevent or eliminate the need for removal of the child from his or her home were not made, but that the lack of such efforts was appropriate under the circumstances, the court order shall include such a finding;

(3) in the case of a child for whom the permanency plan is adoption, guardianship or some other permanent living arrangement other than reunification with the parent or parents of the child, whether reasonable efforts have been made to make and finalize such other permanency plan;

(4) in the case of a respondent who has attained the age of 16, the services needed, if any, to assist the respondent to make the transition from foster care to independent living; and

(5) in the case of an order of placement specifying a particular authorized agency or foster care provider, the position of the local commissioner of social services regarding such placement.

(d) Permanency hearing; extension of placement. A petition for a permanency hearing and, if applicable, an extension of placement, pursuant to section 1055 of the Family Court Act, shall be filed at least 60 days prior to the expiration of one year following the child's entry into foster care. For purposes of this section, the child's entry into foster care shall be deemed to have commenced the earlier of the date of the fact finding of abuse or neglect of the child pursuant to section 1051 of the Family Court Act or 60 days after the date the child was removed from his or her home; provided, however, that if the court makes a determination, pursuant to section 1039-b of the Family Court Act, that reasonable efforts are not required to prevent or eliminate the need for removal of the child from his or her home or to make it possible to reunify the child with his or her parents, the permanency hearing shall be held within 30 days of such determination and the petition for the permanency hearing shall be filed and served on an expedited basis as directed by the court. Following the initial permanency hearing in a case in which the child remains in placement, a petition for a subsequent permanency hearing and, if applicable, extension of placement shall be filed at least 60 days prior to the expiration of one year following the date of the preceding permanency hearing. All petitions for permanency hearings shall be governed by section 205.17 of this Part.

§ 205.82 Record and report of unexecuted warrants issued pursuant to article 10 of the Family Court Act (child protective proceeding).

(a) The clerk of court for the Family Court in each county shall obtain and keep a record of unexecuted warrants issued pursuant to article 10 of the Family Court Act.

(b) At the end of each six-month period, on the first of January and on the first of July in each year, a report concerning all unexecuted warrants issued pursuant to article ten of the Family Court Act shall be made and filed with the Office of Court Administration on a form to be supplied by the Office of Court Administration.

§ 205.83 Terms and conditions of order in accordance with sections 1053, 1054 and 1057 of the Family Court Act (child protective proceeding).

(a) An order suspending judgment entered pursuant to section 1052 of the Family Court Act shall, where the child is in foster care, set forth the visitation plan between respondent and the child and between the child and his or her sibling or siblings, if any, and shall require the agency to notify the respondent of case conferences. A copy of the order, along with a current service plan, shall be furnished to the respondent. Any order suspending judgment entered pursuant to section 1052 of the Family Court Act shall contain at least one of the following terms and conditions that relate to the adjudicated acts or omissions of the respondent, directing the respondent to:

(1) refrain from or eliminate specified acts or conditions found at the fact-finding hearing to constitute or to have caused neglect or abuse;

(2) provide adequate and proper food, housing, clothing, medical care, and for the other needs of the child;

(3) provide proper care and supervision to the child and cooperate in obtaining, accepting or allowing medical or psychiatric diagnosis or treatment, alcoholism or drug abuse treatment, counseling or child guidance services for the child;

(4) take proper steps to insure the child's regular attendance at school; and

(5) cooperate in obtaining and accepting medical treatment, psychiatric diagnosis and treatment, alcoholism or drug abuse treatment, employment or counseling services, or child guidance, and

permit a child protective agency to obtain information from any person or agency from whom the respondent or the child is receiving or was directed to receive treatment or counseling.

(b) An order pursuant to section 1054 of the Family Court Act placing the person to whose custody the child is released under the supervision of a child protective agency, social services officer or duly authorized agency, or an order pursuant to section 1057 placing the respondent under the supervision of a child protective agency, social services official or authorized agency, shall contain at least one of the following terms and conditions requiring the respondent to:

(1) observe any of the terms and conditions set forth in subdivision (a) of this section;

(2) cooperate with the supervising agency in remedying specified acts or omissions found at the fact-finding hearing to constitute or to have caused the neglect or abuse;

(3) meet with the supervising agency alone and with the child when directed to do so by that agency;

(4) report to the supervising agency when directed to do so by that agency;

(5) cooperate with the supervising agency in arranging for and allowing visitation in the home or other place;

(6) notify the supervising agency immediately of any change of residence or employment of the respondent or of the child;

(7) do or refrain from doing any other specified act of omission or commission that, in the judgment of the court, is necessary to protect the child from injury or mistreatment and to help safeguard the physical, mental and emotional well-being of the child.

(c) When an order is made pursuant to section 1054 or 1057 of the Family Court Act:

(1) the court shall notify the supervising agency in writing of its designation to act and shall furnish to that agency a copy of the order setting forth the terms and conditions imposed;

(2) the order shall be accompanied by a written statement informing the respondent that a willful failure to obey the terms and conditions imposed may result in commitment to jail for a term not to exceed six months; and

(3) the court may, if it concludes that it is necessary for the protection of the child, direct the supervising agency to furnish a written report to the court at stated intervals not to exceed six months setting forth whether, and to what extent:

(i) there has been any alteration in the respondent's maintenance of the child that is adversely affecting the child's health or well-being;

(ii) there is compliance with the terms and conditions of the order of supervision; and

COURT RULES

(iii) the supervising agency has furnished supporting services to the respondent.

(d) A copy of the order, setting forth its duration and the terms and conditions imposed, shall be furnished to the respondent.

§ 205.84   [*Repealed.*]

§ 205.85 Procedure when a child who has been placed absconds (child protective proceeding).

(a) When a child placed pursuant to section 1055 of the Family Court Act absconds, written notice of that fact shall be sent within 48 hours to the clerk of the court from which the placement was made. The notice shall be signed by the custodial person or by an authorized representative of the place of placement and shall state the name of the child, the docket number of the proceeding in which the child was placed, the date on which the child absconded, and the efforts made to secure the return of the child. Every order of placement pursuant to section 1055 shall include a direction embodying the requirement of this subdivision.

(b) Upon receipt of the written notice of absconding, the clerk of the court shall cause the proceeding to be placed on the calendar no later than the next court day for such action as the court may deem appropriate.

§ 205.86 Videotapes of interviews of children alleged to have been sexually abused.

(a) In any case in which, pursuant to section 1038(c) of the Family Court Act, a videotape is made of an expert's interview with a child alleged to have been sexually abused, the attorney for the party requesting the videotaping, or the party, if unrepresented, shall promptly after the videotaping has been completed:

(1) cause to be prepared a duplicate videotape, certified by the preparer as a complete and unaltered copy of the original videotape;

(2) deposit the original videotape, certified by the preparer as the original, with the Clerk of the Family Court; and

(3) submit for signature to the judge before whom the case is pending a proposed order authorizing the retention of the duplicate videotape by the attorney, (or the party, if unrepresented) and directing that retention be in conformance with this section.

Both the original videotape and the duplicate thereof shall be labelled with the name of the case, the Family Court docket number, the name of the child, the name of the interviewer, the name and address of the technician who prepared the videotape, the date of the interview, and the total elapsed time of the videotape.

(b) Upon receipt, the clerk shall hold the original videotape in a secure place limited to access only by authorized court personnel.

(c) (1) Except as provided in paragraph (2) of this subdivision, the duplicate videotape shall remain in the custody of the attorney for the party who requested it, or the party, if not represented (the "custodian").

(2) The duplicate videotape shall be available for pretrial disclosure pursuant to article 10 of the Family Court Act and any other applicable law. Consistent therewith, the custodian shall permit an attorney for a party, or the party, if not represented by counsel, to borrow the duplicate videotape for a reasonable period of time so that it may be viewed, provided the person to whom it is loaned first certifies, by affidavit filed with the court, that he or she will comply with this subdivision.

(3) A person borrowing the duplicate videotape as provided in paragraph (2) of this subdivision shall not lend it or otherwise surrender custody thereof to any person other than the custodian, and upon returning such videotape to the custodian, such person shall certify, by affidavit filed with the court, that he or she has complied with the provisions of this subdivision.

(4) Subject to court order otherwise, the duplicate videotape may not be viewed by any person other than a party or his or her counsel or prospective expert witnesses. No copy of the duplicate videotape may be made.

(d) Failure to comply with the provisions of this rule shall be punishable by contempt of court.

PART 218

UNIFORM RULES FOR THE TRIAL COURTS IN CAPITAL CASES

218.6   Remittitur.

218.7   Capital case data reports.

218.1 Record transcription and reproduction; settlement.

(a) During the course of capital proceedings before the superior court, and at all times thereafter, the clerk of the superior court shall take all necessary steps to insure the accuracy and completeness of the record of the proceedings.

(b) The court reporter shall take minutes of all capital proceedings occurring in the superior court. Transcription shall proceed in compliance with any relevant superior court order and the Court of Appeals capital appeal management order (22 NYCRR 510.4(c)(4); 510.8(a)). Where a copy of the minutes of any proceedings in the superior court was ordered during the course of the superior court proceedings, defense counsel and the prosecutor shall preserve their respective copies of the transcript. Transcripts shall be settled pursuant to CPLR 5525(c) within such time limits and pursuant to such additional procedures as may be set by Court of Appeals order.

(c) Upon the filing of a notice of appeal, the superior court clerk shall expeditiously assemble, reproduce, and transmit to appellant the record of the proceedings. Appellant shall be responsible for the timely preparation and filing of the record on appeal in accordance with the capital appeal management order issued by the Court of Appeals pursuant to 22 NYCRR 510.4(c)(4) or 510.8(a).

(d) The record on appeal shall comply with 22 NYCRR 510.11(b), and be stipulated to or settled on motion. The parties may stipulate to the correctness of the contents of the record on appeal using the process provided by CPLR 5525(c)(1). Where the parties are unable to agree and stipulate to the contents of the record on appeal, appellant shall move, on notice, to settle the record in the superior court from which the appeal is taken.

218.2 Capital sentencing determination and findings form.

In all criminal actions in which a separate sentencing proceeding is conducted in accordance with the procedures set forth in section 400.27 of the Criminal Procedure Law, the superior court shall provide the jury with a sentencing determination and findings form, as prescribed by the Court of Appeals, on which the jury must record its determination of sentence and its specification of those mitigating and aggravating factors considered and those mitigating factors established by the defendant. The superior court judge shall instruct the jury on how to complete the form and shall ensure that the form is properly completed.

218.3 Notice to the capital defender office.

(a) The clerk of the superior court in whose office a judgment that includes a sentence of death has been entered shall notify the capital defender office by the end of business on the day such determination is handed down.

(b) Notice to the capital defender office required pursuant to subdivision (a) of this section shall consist of telephone, facsimile, electronic mail or other prompt electronic means of communication, which shall be followed by first class mail notification within two business days after rendition of the sentence.

(c) The clerk of the superior court shall retain a written record of the electronic and written notice given pursuant to subdivision (b) of this section.

218.4 Stays of execution: automatic or determined by superior court.

(a) *Upon appeal from a judgment including a sentence of death (CPL 460.40(1)).* The taking of an appeal by a defendant directly to the Court of Appeals from a superior court judgment including a sentence of death stays the execution of such sentence until determination of the appeal.

(b) *Initial CPL article 440 proceedings (CPL 460.40(3)).* Upon motion to the superior court judge or justice who signed the warrant of execution, a defendant sentenced to death shall be granted a stay of execution of a death warrant issued pursuant to Correction Law, article 22-B to allow the defendant an opportunity to prepare and timely file an initial motion in superior court pursuant to CPL 440.10 or 440.20. The order staying execution shall provide that the stay of execution shall continue until (1) the time for taking an appeal to the Court of Appeals from the superior court's denial of such CPL article 440 motion has expired, or (2) if an appeal is taken, until the Court of Appeals determines the appeal.

(c) *Subsequent CPL article 440 proceedings (CPL 460.40(3)).*

(1) In the event a defendant sentenced to death files a motion for postconviction relief pursuant to CPL 440.10 or 440.20 subsequent to the final determination of an initial CPL article 440 motion, the superior court may grant a stay of execution of a death warrant issued pursuant to Correction Law, article 22-B only for good cause shown.

(2) By the end of business on the date a notice of appeal from a superior court order granting or denying a motion for a stay of execution has been filed, the clerk of the superior court, and appellant or appellant's counsel, shall notify the clerk of the Court of Appeals by telephone of such filing. Telephone notice to the Court of Appeals does not relieve the clerk of the superior court of the duties imposed by section 218.5 of this Part.

218.5 Case history.

Within 15 days after the filing of a notice of appeal to the Court of Appeals in a case involving a sentence of death, except in those appeals taken pursuant to CPL 460.40(3) from an order of a superior court granting or denying a motion for a stay of execution, the clerk of the superior court in which the judgment or order being appealed from was rendered shall transmit to the clerk of the Court of Appeals a case history including:

(1) the duplicate notice of appeal;

(2) a chronological list of all proceedings below giving rise to this particular appeal, noting which transcripts have been, or must be, prepared; and

(3) a list of all exhibits introduced in the proceedings below giving rise to this particular appeal.

The clerk of the superior court shall transmit to counsel for the parties copies of paragraphs (2) and (3) of this subsection.

218.6 Remittitur.

The remittitur of the Court of Appeals containing the court's adjudication, together with the return papers filed with the court, shall be sent to the clerk of the court to which the case is remitted, there to be proceeded upon according to law. Any order to effect the adjudication contained in the Court of Appeals' remittitur shall be sought, entered and enforced in the superior court.

218.7 Capital case data reports.

(a) In each criminal action in which the defendant has been indicted for commission of an offense defined in section 125.27 of the Penal Law, except those in which the indictment is dismissed or the defendant is acquitted, the clerk of the superior court, within 45 days after the disposition of the action in such court, shall prepare and send to the Court of Appeals a capital case data report in the form prescribed by the Court of Appeals. Data reports shall be prepared by the clerk of the superior court by reviewing the record and upon consultation with the prosecutor and counsel for the defendant. Such data reports shall not constitute a part of the record in the underlying criminal action. The clerk of the superior court shall retain, in a confidential file kept separate from the record in the underlying criminal action, a copy of each such data report sent to the Court of Appeals, and may disclose a data report, or any part thereof, only upon order of the Court of Appeals for exceptional cause shown.

(b) All capital case data reports received by the Court of Appeals shall be compiled into a uniform capital case data report, which may consist of a computer data base containing the information in each capital case data report. Upon request, the uniform capital case data report shall be made available to the parties on appeal to the Court of Appeals in cases where a sentence of death has been imposed, and otherwise may be available upon order of the Court of Appeals to the extent and in a form and manner prescribed, and for such fee as fixed, by the Court of Appeals.

(c) If the conviction in such criminal action is subsequently reversed or modified, the capital case data report shall be notated to reflect the reversal or modification. If an intermediate appellate court reverses or modifies the conviction, that court shall forward a copy of its remittitur to the Court of Appeals within 10 days after entry. If a new disposition in the action ensues in the superior court, the superior court clerk shall prepare a new capital case data report. Upon completion, the superior court clerk shall send the new capital case data report to the clerk of the Court of Appeals with a notice that the new report should be substituted in the data base for the previous report.

PART 220

UNIFORM RULES FOR JURY SELECTION AND DELIBERATION

SUBPART A. UNIFORM RULES FOR JURY SELECTION

SUBPART B. UNIFORM RULES FOR JUROR DELIBERATION

SUBPART A

UNIFORM RULES FOR JURY SELECTION

§ 220.1 Nondesignated alternate jurors.

(a) *Application.* Upon consent of the parties, a court trying a civil case heard by a jury may adopt the procedure provided for in this section concerning the formation of the trial jury.

(b) *Number of jurors.* The number of jurors selected shall be as permitted by law.

(c) *Designation of jurors.* If more than six jurors are selected, they shall not at that time be designated as trial jurors and alternate jurors. Instead, if at the conclusion of the evidence more than six jurors remain on the jury, at that time the clerk of the court, in the presence of the court and the parties, shall randomly draw the names of six of the remaining jurors, who shall be the jurors who retire to deliberate upon a verdict. Unless otherwise determined by the court, the juror whose name was first drawn shall be designated as the foreperson. After the deliberating jurors have retired to deliberate, the remaining non-deliberating jurors shall be discharged. The court may, in appropriate circumstances, direct the discharged jurors no to discuss the case while the jury deliberates.

(d) *Peremptory challenges.* If the court adopts the procedure set forth in this section, the number of peremptory challenges specified in section 4109 of the Civil Practice Law and Rules shall be increased by one for every two jurors selected beyond the first six selected.

SUBPART B

UNIFORM RULES FOR JUROR DELIBERATION

§ 220.10 Note-taking by jurors.

(a) *Application.* This section shall apply to all cases, both civil and criminal, heard by a jury in any court.

(b) After the jury has been sworn and before any opening statements or addresses, the court shall determine if the jurors may take notes at any stage of the proceedings. In making this determination, the court shall consider the probable length of the trial and the nature and complexity of the evidence likely to be admitted.

(c) If the court authorizes note-taking, it shall direct the jurors that they may make written notes [of the proceedings, except the opening statements or addresses, closing statements or summations and the court's charge to the jury,] if they so desire and that the court will provide materials for that purpose if they so request. The court also shall instruct the jurors in the proper use of any notes taken, and its instructions shall include but not be limited to the following:

(1) jurors should not permit their note-taking to distract them from the proceedings;

(2) any notes taken are only an aid to memory and should not take precedence over a juror's independent recollection;

(3) those jurors who choose not to take notes should rely on their own independent recollection of the evidence and should not be influenced by any notes that another juror may take;

(4) any notes taken are only for the note-taker's own personal use in refreshing his or her recollection of the evidence;

(5) if there is a discrepancy between a juror's recollection of the evidence and the juror's notes,

COURT RULES

the jury should request a readback of the record and the court's transcript prevails over a juror's notes; and

(6) These notes are not a substitute for the official record or for the governing principles of law as enunciated by the trial court.

These instructions shall be repeated at the conclusion of the case as part of the court's charge prior to the commencement of jury deliberations.

(d) The court shall require the jurors to print their names or other identifier on the cover of the binder that contains the notes and shall collect each juror's notes at the end of each trial day until the jury retires to deliberate. The jurors may refer to their notes during the proceedings and deliberations.

(e) Any notes taken are confidential and shall not be available for examination or review by any party or other person. After the jury has rendered its verdict, the court shall ensure that the notes are promptly collected and destroyed.

§ 220.11 Copy of judge's charge to jury.

(a) *Application.* This section shall apply to all civil cases heard by a jury in any court.

(b) Where the court determines that the jury's deliberations may be expedited or assisted by having a copy of the court's instructions available during deliberations, the court, upon its own motion or the motion of a party and after affording the parties an opportunity to be heard, may direct that at least one copy of the instructions be furnished to the jury when it retires to consider its verdict. If the court so directs, it shall state its reasons for doing so on the record. Where the copy thereby furnished is other than a transcript of the minutes of the proceedings, the court shall certify thereon that it is a correct copy of its instructions. Any copy of the instructions provided to the jurors in accordance with this subdivision shall be retrieved from the jury at the close of deliberations, and shall be filed with the clerk of the court.

§ 220.12 Juror notebooks.

(a) *Contents.* At the discretion of the trial court, in cases of appropriate complexity, the court may authorize the distribution to each juror of identical notebooks, which may include copies of:

(1) selected exhibits that have been ruled admissible (or excerpts thereof);

(2) stipulations of the parties;

(3) other material not subject to genuine dispute, which may include:

(i) *curricula vitae* of experts;

(ii) lists or seating charts identifying attorneys and their respective clients;

(iii) lists or indices of admitted exhibits;

(iv) glossaries;

(v) chronologies or timelines; and

(vi) other material approved by the court for inclusion.

(b) *Procedure to determine contents.* (1) The court shall require counsel to confer on the contents of the notebooks before trial begins and at any appropriate time thereafter.

(2) If counsel cannot agree on the contents of the notebooks, each party shall be afforded the opportunity to submit its proposal and to comment upon any proposal submitted by another party. The court shall be the final arbiter of the contents of the notebooks.

(c) *Use of notebooks at trial.* (1) At the time of distribution, the court shall instruct the jurors concerning the purpose and use of the notebooks.

(2) During the course of trial, the court may permit the parties to supplement the materials contained in the notebook with additional documents as these become relevant and after they have been ruled admissible or otherwise approved by the court for inclusion.

(3) The court shall collect the notebooks at the end of each trial day until the jury retires to deliberate. The notebooks shall be available to the jurors during deliberations.

(4) Whenever note-taking is permitted by jurors, the court shall require the jurors to print their names or other identifier on the cover of their notebooks.

RULES OF THE COURT OF APPEALS OF THE STATE OF NEW YORK

PART 500

RULES OF PRACTICE

GENERAL MATTERS

APPEALS

CRIMINAL LEAVE APPLICATIONS

MOTIONS

PRIMARY ELECTION SESSION

Section
　500.26　　Primary election session procedures.

CERTIFIED QUESTIONS

Section
　500.27　　Discretionary proceedings to review certified questions from federal courts and other courts of last resort.

GENERAL MATTERS

§ 500.1 General requirements.

(a) All papers shall comply with applicable statutes and rules, particularly the signing requirement of 22 NYCRR 130 1.1 a.

(b) *Method of reproduction.* All briefs, papers submitted pursuant to sections 500.10 and 500.11 of this Part, motion papers and appendices (hereinafter "papers filed") may be reproduced by any method that produces a permanent, legible, black image on white paper. Reproduction on both sides of the paper is encouraged.

(c) *Necessary information.* Where this Part requires the filing of multiple copies of papers, the parties shall identify on its cover the original document filed. All papers filed by or on behalf of a corporation or other business entity shall list all its parents, subsidiaries and affiliates, or state that no such parents, subsidiaries and affiliates exist (hereinafter "disclosure statement"). Where New York authorities are cited in any submissions, New York Official Law Report citations shall be included, if available. Copies of decisions that are not officially published, or are not otherwise readily available, shall be included in the submission in which such decisions are cited.

(d) *Paper quality, size and binding.* Paper shall be opaque, unglazed, white and eleven by eight and one half inches. Briefs, appendices, records and motion papers shall be bound on the left side in a manner that keeps all pages securely together, without plastic covers or any metal fasteners or similar hard material that protrudes or presents a bulky surface or sharp edge.

(e) *Computer generated papers filed.* Papers filed prepared on a computer shall be printed in either a serifed, proportionally spaced typeface, such as Times Roman, or a serifed monospaced typeface, such as Courier. Narrow or condensed typefaces and condensed font spacing shall not be used. Except in headings, words shall not be in bold type or type consisting of all capital letters.

(1) *Papers filed using a proportionally spaced typeface.* The body of any papers filed using a proportionally spaced typeface shall be printed in 14 point type. Footnotes shall be printed in type of no less than 12 points.

(2) *Papers filed using a monospaced type-face.* The body of any papers filed using a monospaced typeface shall be printed in 12 point type containing no more than 10 and one half characters per inch. Footnotes shall be printed in type of no less than 10 points.

(f) *Typewritten papers filed.* Typewritten papers filed shall be neatly prepared in clear type no smaller than elite and in a pitch of no more than twelve characters per inch. The original, ribbon typescript of any papers filed shall be signed and filed as the original required by this Part. Carbon copies will not be accepted.

(g) *Margins, line spacing and page numbering of computer generated and typewritten papers filed.* Computer generated and typewritten papers filed shall have margins of one inch on all sides of the page. Text shall be double spaced, but quotations more than two lines long may be indented and single spaced. Headings and footnotes may be single spaced. Pages shall be consecutively numbered in the center of the bottom margin of each page.

(h) *Handwritten papers.* Self represented litigants may serve and file handwritten papers. Such papers shall be neatly prepared in cursive script or hand printing in black ink. Pages shall be consecutively numbered in the center of the bottom margin of each page. The filing of handwritten papers is not encouraged. The clerk of the Court may reject illegible papers.

(i) *Filing of Papers.* All papers filed shall be addressed to the clerk of the Court at 20 Eagle Street, Albany, New York 12207 1095, not to a Judge or Judges of the Court, and shall be served on each other party in accordance with the requirements of this Part. Submissions shall not be filed by facsimile transmission or electronic mail, except when requested by the clerk of the Court.

(j) *Acknowledgment of receipt of papers.* A request for an acknowledgment of receipt of papers shall be accompanied by the papers filed and a self addressed, postage pre paid postcard or envelope. Parties proceeding as poor persons or requesting poor person relief shall comply with this requirement if acknowledgment of receipt of papers is desired.

(k) *Nonconforming Papers.* The clerk of the

Court may reject papers that do not conform to the requirements of this Part.

§ 500.2 Companion filings on compact disk, read only memory (CD ROM).

(a) The Court allows the submission of briefs, records or appendices on compact disk, read-only memory (CD ROM) as companions to the requisite number of printed briefs, records and appendices filed and served in accordance with this Part if all parties have consented to the filing of the companion CD ROM brief and record or appendix. The Court, by order on motion of any party or on its own motion, may require such filing by a party or amicus.

(b) The companion CD ROM brief, record or appendix shall comply with the current technical specifications available from the clerk's office.

(c) The companion CD ROM brief, record or appendix shall be identical in content and format (including page numbering) to the printed version, except that each shall also be word searchable and shall provide electronic links (hyperlinks) to the complete text of any authorities cited therein, and to all documents or other material constituting the record on appeal. The disk and container shall be labeled to indicate the title of the case and the documents reproduced on the disk.

(d) Unless the Court requires a greater number, 10 disks or sets of disks shall be filed, with (i) proof of service of at least one disk or set on each other party and (ii) a copy of the parties' stipulation permitting, or the Court's order directing, such filing.

(e) Unless the Court requires otherwise, appellant's filing and respondent's filing, or a joint filing by appellant and respondent, are due 10 days after the final due date for filing appellant's reply brief (see section 500.12(d) of this Part).

§ 500.3 Fees.

(a) Upon the filing of record material in a civil appeal pursuant to section 500.11, 500.12 or 500.26(a) of this Part, appellant shall provide the clerk of the Court the fee in the amount specified in CPLR 8022 in the form of an attorney's check, certified check, cashier's check or money order payable to "State of New York, Court of Appeals" unless:

(1) appellant demonstrates exemption from the fee requirements by statute or other authority;

(2) other payment arrangements have been made with the clerk of the Court;

(3) the appeal is accompanied by a motion requesting poor person relief or a motion requesting relief from payment of the filing fee; or

(4) appellant in the Court of Appeals provides a copy of an order issued by any court in the action or proceeding to which the appeal relates granting that party poor person relief, together with a sworn affidavit that the same financial circumstances exist at the time of filing in the Court of Appeals as when the order granting poor person relief was issued.

(b) Upon the filing of each motion or cross motion in a civil case pursuant to section 500.21 through 500.24 or 500.26(b) of this Part, movant shall provide the clerk of the Court with the fee in the amount specified in CPLR 8022 in the form of an attorney's check, certified check, cashier's check or money order payable to "State of New York, Court of Appeals" unless:

(1) movant demonstrates exemption from the fee requirements by statute or other authority;

(2) other payment arrangements have been made with the clerk of the Court;

(3) the motion or cross motion is accompanied by a motion requesting poor person relief or a motion requesting relief from payment of the filing fee; or

(4) movant in the Court of Appeals provides a copy of an order issued by any court in the action or proceeding to which the motion relates granting that party poor person relief, together with a sworn affidavit that the same financial circumstances exist at the time of filing in the Court of Appeals as when the order granting poor person relief was issued.

(c) Except as provided in subsections (a) or (b) above or where otherwise specifically required by law or by the Court, no fees shall be charged by the clerk of the Court.

§ 500.4 *Pro hac vice* admission.

An attorney or the equivalent who is a member of the bar of another state, territory, district or foreign country may apply to appear *pro hac vice* with respect to a particular matter pending in this Court (*see* 22 NYCRR 520.11(a) [Rules of the Court of Appeals for the Admission of Attorneys and Counselors at Law—Admission *Pro Hac Vice*]). The application shall consist of a letter request to the clerk of the Court, with proof of service on each other party, and shall include current certificates of good standing from each jurisdiction in which the applicant is admitted and any orders of the courts below granting such relief in the matter for which *pro hac vice* status is sought.

§ 500.5 Sealed documents.

(a) Documents under seal are not available for public viewing.

(b) Any papers sealed by a court below or otherwise required by statute to be sealed shall be sealed in the Court of Appeals.

(c) Any party to an appeal or motion may

COURT RULES

request that papers not sealed below be sealed in this Court. Such requests shall be by an original and one copy of a motion pursuant to section 500.21 of this Part, with proof of service of one copy on each other party.

(d) Documents and transcripts ordered sealed by the Court of Appeals or a court below shall be reproduced in separate volumes of the record on appeal. Each such volume shall be clearly identified on the cover as containing sealed material.

§ 500.6 Developments affecting appeals, certified questions, motions and criminal leave applications.

Counsel shall timely inform the clerk's office and each other party by letter of all developments affecting appeals, section 500.27 certified questions, motions and criminal leave applications pending in this Court, including contemplated and actual settlements, circumstances or facts that could render the matter moot and pertinent developments in applicable case law, statutes and regulations. The writing shall contain proof of service on each other party.

§ 500.7 Post briefing, post submission and post argument communications.

Except for communications providing the information required by section 500.6 of this Part or those specifically requested by the Court, post briefing, post submission and post argument written communications to the Court are not favored, and shall be returned to the sender unless accepted by the clerk of the Court following a written request with a copy of the proposed submission and proof of timely service of one copy on each other party.

§ 500.8 Withdrawal of appeal, motion or criminal leave application.

(a) *Appeals.*

(1) Before argument or submission, an appeal shall be marked withdrawn upon receipt by the clerk of the Court of a stipulation of withdrawal signed by counsel for all parties and by all self represented litigants and, in criminal appeals, additionally by defendant.

(2) After argument or submission, a request to withdraw an appeal shall be supported by a stipulation of withdrawal signed by counsel for all parties and by all self represented litigants and, in criminal appeals, additionally by defendant. The request shall be submitted to the Court for determination.

(b) *Motions.*

(1) Before its return date, a motion shall be marked withdrawn upon receipt by the clerk of the Court of a written notice of withdrawal signed by counsel for the moving party, with proof of service of one copy on each other party.

(2) After the return date, a request to withdraw a motion shall be supported by a stipulation of withdrawal signed by counsel for all parties and by all self represented litigants. The request shall be submitted to the Court for determination.

(c) *Criminal leave applications.* A request to withdraw an application shall be in writing and, if made on behalf of a defendant, shall be signed by defendant. The request shall contain an indication of service of one copy upon all parties and, if the request is made by defendant personally, proof of service upon defense counsel, if defendant is represented. The request shall be submitted to the assigned Judge for determination.

APPEALS

§ 500.9 Preliminary appeal statement.

(a) Within 10 days after an appeal is taken by (1) filing a notice of appeal in the place and manner required by CPLR 5515, (2) entry of an order granting a motion for leave to appeal in a civil case, or (3) issuance of a certificate granting leave to appeal in a non capital criminal case, appellant shall file with the clerk of the Court an original and one copy of a preliminary appeal statement on the form prescribed by the Court, with the required attachments and proof of service of one copy on each other party. No fee is required at the time of filing the preliminary appeal statement.

(b) Where a party asserts that a statute is unconstitutional, appellant shall give written notice to the Attorney General before filing the preliminary appeal statement, and a copy of the notification shall be attached to the preliminary appeal statement. The notification and a copy of

the preliminary appeal statement shall be sent to the Solicitor General, Department of Law, The Capitol, Albany, New York 12224.

(c) After review of the Preliminary Appeal Statement, the clerk will notify the parties either that review pursuant to section 500.10 or section 500.11 of this Part shall commence or that the appeal shall proceed in the normal course.

§ 500.10 Examination of subject matter jurisdiction.

On its own motion, the Court may examine its subject matter jurisdiction over an appeal based on the papers submitted in accordance with section 500.9 of this Part. The clerk of the Court shall notify all parties by letter when an appeal has been selected for examination pursuant to this section, stating the jurisdictional concerns identified in reviewing the preliminary appeal statement and setting a due date for filing and service of comments in letter form from all parties. Such examination shall result in dismissal of the appeal by the Court or in notification to the parties that the appeal shall proceed either under the review process described in section 500.11 of this Part or in the normal course, with or without oral argument. This examination of jurisdiction shall not preclude the Court from addressing any jurisdictional concerns at any time.

§ 500.11 Alternative procedure for selected appeals.

(a) On its own motion, the Court may review selected appeals by an alternative procedure. Such appeals shall be determined on the intermediate appellate court record or appendix and briefs, the writings in the courts below and additional letter submissions on the merits. The clerk of the Court shall notify all parties by letter when an appeal has been selected for review pursuant to this section. Appellant may request such review in its preliminary appeal statement. Respondent may request such review by letter to the clerk of the Court, with proof of service of one copy on each other party within five days after the appeal is taken.

(b) Appeals may be selected for alternative review on the basis of:

(1) questions of discretion, mixed questions of law and fact or affirmed findings of fact, which are subject to a limited scope of review;

(2) recent, controlling precedent;

(3) narrow issues of law not of statewide importance;

(4) nonpreserved issues of law;

(5) a party's request for such review; or

(6) other appropriate factors.

(c) *Appellant's filing.* Within 25 days after the date of the clerk of the Court's letter initiating the alternative review procedure, appellant shall:

(1) file three copies of the intermediate appellate court record or appendix and three copies of each brief filed by each party in the intermediate appellate court. Original exhibits to be relied upon which are not in the record or appendix at the intermediate appellate court shall be filed or, if they are on file with the clerk of the trial court, subpoenaed to this Court and the Court so advised by letter. Such exhibits shall be clearly identified and, where appropriate, their authenticity shall be certified or stipulated to;

(2) file an original and two copies of a letter stating its arguments in support of appellant's position on the merits. If appellant objects to review pursuant to this section, the letter shall also explain that position;

(3) file a disclosure statement pursuant to section 500.1(c) of this Part, if necessary;

(4) file proof of service of one copy of its arguments on each other party; and

(5) remit the fee, if any, required by section 500.3(a) of this Part.

(d) *Respondent's filing.* Within 20 days after service of appellant's submission, respondent shall file an original and two copies of a letter stating its arguments in support of its position on the merits. If respondent objects to review pursuant to this section, the letter shall also explain that position. Respondent shall file a disclosure statement pursuant to section 500.1(c) of this Part, if necessary, and proof of service of one copy of its arguments on each other party.

(e) *Abandonment of arguments.* A party shall be deemed to have abandoned any argument made in the intermediate appellate court briefs not addressed or reserved in the written submission to this Court.

(f) *Review of subject matter jurisdiction.* An appeal selected for review pursuant to this section is subject to dismissal on the Court's own motion, should it be determined that the Court is without subject matter jurisdiction.

(g) *Termination of alternative procedure.* If the Court terminates its review of the appeal pursuant to this section before disposition, the clerk of the Court will notify counsel by letter and set a schedule for full briefing of the appeal.

(h) *Amicus curiae relief.* The Attorney General of the State of New York may file, no later than the filing date set for respondent's submission, an original and two copies of an *amicus curiae* submission without leave of the Court, with proof of service of one copy on each party. Any other proposed *amicus curiae* shall request *amicus curiae* relief pursuant to section 500.23(a)(2) of this Part.

§ 500.12 Filing of record material and briefs in normal course appeals.

(a) *Scheduling letter.* Generally, in an appeal tracked for normal course treatment, the clerk of the Court issues a scheduling letter after the filing of the preliminary appeal statement. A scheduling letter also issues upon the termination of an inquiry pursuant to section 500.10 or 500.11 of this Part. The scheduling letter sets the filing dates for record material and briefs.

(b) *Appellant's initial filing.* On or before the date specified in the scheduling letter, appellant shall serve and file record material in compliance with section 500.14 of this Part, and shall remit the fee, if any, required by section 500.3(a) of this Part. Appellant also shall file an original and 24 copies of a brief, with proof of service of three copies on each other party. If no scheduling letter is issued, appellant's papers shall be served and filed within 60 days after appellant took the appeal by (1) filing a notice of appeal in the place and manner required by CPLR 5515, (2) entry of an order granting a motion for leave to appeal in a civil case, or (3) issuance of a certificate granting leave to appeal in a non capital criminal case.

(c) *Respondent's filing.* On or before the date specified in the scheduling letter, respondent shall serve and file an original and 24 copies of a brief and a supplementary appendix, if any, with proof of service of three copies on each other party. If no scheduling letter is issued, respondent's papers shall be filed within 45 days after service of appellant's brief.

(d) *Reply briefs.* A reply brief is not required but may be served and filed by appellant on or before the date specified in the scheduling letter. If no scheduling letter is issued, a reply brief may be served and filed within 15 days after service of respondent's brief. Where cross appeals are filed, the cross appellant may serve and file a reply brief to the main appellant's responsive brief. An original and 24 copies of a reply brief shall be served and filed, with proof of service of three copies on each other party.

(e) *Amicus curiae briefs.* The Attorney General of the State of New York may file, no later than the filing date set for respondent's brief, an original and 24 copies of an *amicus curiae* brief without leave of the Court, with proof of service of three copies on each party. Any other proposed *amicus curiae* shall request amicus curiae relief pursuant to section 500.23(a)(1) of this Part.

(f) *Briefs in response to amicus curiae briefs.* Briefs in response to an *amicus curiae* brief are not required but may be served and filed by a party whose position is adverse to that of the *amicus curiae.* The brief shall be served and filed within 15 days after the date of this Court's order granting a motion for *amicus curiae* relief or within 15 days after the service of an *amicus curiae* brief by the Attorney General of the State of New York. An original and 24 copies shall be filed, with proof of service of three copies on each other party and one copy on each *amicus curiae.*

(g) *Sur reply briefs.* Sur reply briefs are not permitted.

§ 500.13 Content and form of briefs in normal course appeals.

(a) *Content.* All briefs shall conform to the requirements of section 500.1 of this Part and contain a table of contents, a table of cases and authorities and a disclosure statement pursuant to section 500.1(c) of this Part, if necessary. Respondent's brief may have a supplementary appendix attached to it. The original of each brief shall be signed and dated, shall have the affidavit of service affixed to the inside of the back cover and shall be identified on the front cover as the original.

(b) *Brief covers.* Brief covers shall be white and shall contain the caption of the case and name, address, telephone number, and facsimile number of counsel or self represented litigant and the party on whose behalf the brief is submitted, and the date on which the brief was completed. In the upper right corner, the brief cover shall indicate whether the party proposes to submit the brief without oral argument or, if argument time is requested, the amount of time requested and the name of the person who will present oral argument (*see* section 500.18 of this Part). If a time request does not appear on the brief, generally no more than 10 minutes will be assigned. The Court will determine the argument time, if any, to be assigned to each party.

§ 500.14 Records, appendices and exhibits in normal course appeals.

(a) *Record material.* Appellant shall supply the Court with record material in one of the following ways:

(1) Appellant may subpoena the original file to this Court from the clerk of the court of original instance or other custodian, and submit original exhibits to be relied upon, and supplement these with an original and 24 copies of an appendix conforming to subdivision (b) below, with proof of service of three copies of the appendix on each other party. If appellant is represented by assigned counsel, or has established indigency, an oral or written request may be made of the clerk of this Court to obtain the original file.

(2) Appellant may file with the clerk of the Court one copy of the reproduced record used at the court below. This record shall be supplemented by an original and 24 copies of an appendix conforming to subdivision (b) below, with proof of service of three copies of the appendix on each other party.

(3) Appellant may file with the clerk of the Court an original and 24 copies of a new and full record which shall include the record used at the court below, the notice of appeal or order granting leave to appeal to this Court, the decision and order appealed from to this Court, and any other decision and order brought up for review, with proof of service of three copies of the new record on each other party.

(b) *Appendix.* An appendix shall conform to the requirements of CPLR 5528 and 5529, and shall be sufficient by itself to permit the Court to review the issues raised on appeal without resort to the original file (*see* subsection (a)(1) of this section) or reproduced record used at the court below (*see* subsection (a)(2) of this section). The appendix shall include, as relevant to the appeal, the following:

(1) the notice of appeal or order or certificate granting leave to appeal;

(2) the order, judgment or determination appealed from to this Court;

(3) any order, judgment or determination which is the subject of the order appealed from, or which is otherwise brought up for review;

(4) any decision or opinion relating to the orders set forth in subsections (b)(2) and (3) above; and

(5) the testimony, affidavits, and written or photographic exhibits useful to the determination of the questions raised on appeal.

(c) *Respondent's appendix.* A respondent's brief may include a supplementary appendix.

(d) *Inadequate appendix.* When appellant has filed an inadequate appendix, respondent may move to strike the appendix (*see* section 500.21 of this Part) or may submit an original and 24 copies of an appendix containing such additional parts of the record as respondent deems necessary to consider the questions involved, with proof of service of three copies of the appendix on each other party. The Court may direct appellant to supplement the appendix with additional parts of the record it deems necessary to consider the questions involved.

(e) *Correctness of the record.* The correctness of the reproduced record or the appendix and additional papers shall be authenticated pursuant to CPLR 2105 or stipulated to pursuant to CPLR 5532.

§ 500.15 Extensions of time.

The clerk of the Court is authorized to grant, for good cause shown, a reasonable extension of time for filing papers on an appeal. A request for an extension may be by telephone call to the clerk's office, and shall be made no earlier than 20 days before the filing due date set by the clerk's office or otherwise prescribed by this Part. The party requesting an extension shall advise the clerk of the Court of the position of each other party with regard to the request. A party granted an extension shall file a confirmation letter, with proof of service of one copy on each other party, unless the clerk's office has notified all parties in writing of the determination of the request.

§ 500.16 Failure to proceed or file papers.

(a) *Dismissal of appeal.* If appellant has not filed and served the papers required by section 500.11, 500.12 or 500.26(a) of this Part within the time set by the clerk's office or otherwise prescribed by this Part, the clerk of the Court shall enter an order dismissing the appeal.

(b) *Preclusion.* If respondent has not filed and served the papers required by section 500.11, 500.12 or 500.26(a) of this Part within the time set by the clerk's office or otherwise prescribed

by this Part, the clerk of the Court shall enter an order precluding respondent's filing.

(c) *Judicial review.* The Court may review dismissal and preclusion orders entered pursuant to subsections (a) and (b) above by motion on notice in accordance with section 500.21 of this Part.

§ 500.17 Calendar.

(a) *Notification of argument time and date.* When the calendar has been prepared, the clerk of the Court shall advise counsel by letter of the date and time assigned for oral argument.

(b) *Calendar preferences.* A party seeking a preference shall address a letter to the clerk of the Court, with proof of service of one copy on each other party. The letter shall state why a preference is needed, why alternative remedies, such as review pursuant to section 500.11 of this Part or submission without argument, are not appropriate, and opposing counsel's position on the request.

(c) *Notification of unavailability.* Counsel have a continuing obligation to notify the clerk's office of days of known or possible unavailability for oral argument during the Court's scheduled Albany sessions.

(d) *Adjournments.* Requests for adjournment of a calendared appeal are not favored. A party seeking an adjournment shall address a letter to the clerk of the Court, with proof of service of one copy on each other party. The letter shall state why the adjournment is necessary, why submission on the brief filed and having substitute counsel argue are not viable alternatives, and opposing counsel's position on the request.

§ 500.18 Oral argument.

(a) *Argument time.* Maximum argument time is 30 minutes per party, unless otherwise directed or permitted by the Court upon advance request by letter addressed to the clerk of the Court with proof of service of one copy on each other party. In requesting argument time, counsel shall presume the Court's familiarity with the facts, procedural history and legal issues the appeal presents. The Court may assign time for argument that varies from a party's request and may determine that the appeal be submitted by any party or all parties without oral argument (*see* section 500.13(b) of this Part).

(b) *Arguing counsel.* Only one counsel is permitted to argue for a party, unless otherwise directed or permitted by the Court upon advance request by letter addressed to the clerk of the Court with proof of service of one copy on each other party.

(c) *Rebuttal.* Prior to beginning argument, appellant may orally request permission from the Chief Judge to reserve a specific number of minutes for rebuttal. The time reserved shall be subtracted from the total time assigned to appellant. Respondent may not request permission to reserve time for sur rebuttal.

§ 500.19 Remittitur.

(a) The remittitur of the Court, containing the Court's adjudication, together with the return papers filed with the Court, shall be sent to the clerk of the court of original instance or to the clerk of the court to which the case is remitted, there to be proceeded upon according to law.

(b) The court of original instance or the court to which the case is remitted issues any order to effect the adjudication in this Court's remittitur, including an award of costs.

CRIMINAL LEAVE APPLICATIONS

§ 500.20 Criminal leave applications.

(a) *Letter application.* Applications to the Chief Judge for leave to appeal in a criminal case (CPL 460.20) shall be by letter addressed to 20 Eagle Street, Albany, New York 12207 1095, and shall be sent to the clerk of the Court, with proof of service of one copy on the adverse party. The letter shall indicate:

(1) the names of all codefendants in the trial court, if any, and the status of their appeals, if known;

(2) whether an application has been addressed to a justice of the Appellate Division;

(3) whether oral argument in person or by telephone conference call is requested; and

(4) the grounds upon which leave to appeal is sought. Particular written attention shall be given to reviewability and preservation of error, identifying and reproducing the particular portions of the record where the questions sought to be reviewed are raised and preserved.

After the application is assigned to a Judge for review, counsel will be given an opportunity to serve and file additional submissions, if any, and opposing counsel will be given an opportunity to respond.

(b) *Material to be provided with application.*

(1) *Orders of intermediate appellate courts determining appeals to those courts.* An application for leave to appeal from an intermediate appellate court order determining an appeal taken to that court shall include:

(i) one copy of each brief submitted by defendant to the intermediate appellate court;

(ii) one copy of each brief submitted by the People to the intermediate appellate court;

(iii) the order and decision of the intermediate appellate court sought to be appealed from; and

(iv) all relevant opinions or memoranda of the courts below, along with any other papers to be relied on in furtherance of the application.

(2) *Orders of intermediate appellate courts determining applications for writs of error coram nobis.* An application for leave to appeal from an intermediate appellate court order determining an application for *coram nobis* relief shall include:

(i) the order and decision sought to be appealed from;

(ii) the papers in support of and opposing the application filed in the intermediate appellate court; and

(iii) the intermediate appellate court decision and order sought to be vacated, as well as the briefs filed on the underlying appeal, if available.

(c) *Assignment.* The Chief Judge directs the assignment of each application to a Judge of the Court through the clerk of the Court; counsel shall not apply directly to a Judge or request that an application be assigned to a particular Judge. The assigned Judge shall advise the parties if oral argument of the application will be entertained.

(d) *Reargument or reconsideration.* Requests for reargument or reconsideration shall be in letter form addressed to the clerk of the Court, with proof of service on the adverse party, and shall be assigned to the Judge who ruled on the original application. A request for reargument or reconsideration shall not be based on the assertion for the first time of new points, except for extraordinary and compelling reasons. Unless otherwise permitted by the assigned Judge, the reargument or reconsideration request shall be served not later than 30 days after the date of the certificate determining the application of which reargument or reconsideration is sought.

(e) *Counsel.* This Court does not assign counsel for criminal leave applications. One set of motion papers addressed to this Court under section 500.21 of this Part for assignment of counsel on a criminal appeal may be filed, with proof of service of one copy on the adverse party, only after leave to appeal is granted.

(f) *Stay requests.* Whether incorporated in an application for leave to appeal or made separately by letter with proof of service of one copy on the adverse party, a request for a stay (CPL 460.60; 530.50) shall state:

(1) whether the relief sought has been previously requested;

(2) whether defendant is presently incarcerated and the incarceration status, if known, of any co defendants; and,

(3) if the defendant is at liberty,

(i) whether a surrender date has been set; and

(ii) the conditions of release (e.g., on defendant's own recognizance or on a set bail amount).

(g) *Applications for extensions of time to seek leave to appeal.* An application for an extension of time to seek leave to appeal (CPL 460.30) shall be by one set of motion papers in compliance with section 500.21 of this Part, with proof of service of one copy on the adverse party.

MOTIONS

§ 500.21 Motions–general procedures.

(a) *Return date.* Regardless whether the Court is in session, motions shall be returnable on a Monday or, if Monday is a legal holiday, the first business day of the week unless otherwise provided by statute, order to show cause or stipulation so ordered by a Judge of the Court. Motions shall be submitted without oral argument, unless the Court directs otherwise. No adjournments shall be permitted other than in those limited instances provided by statute (CPLR 321(c) and 1022).

(b) *Notice and service.* Movant shall serve a notice of motion and supporting papers on sufficient notice to each other party, as set forth in the CPLR and below. In computing the notice period, the date of service shall not be included.

(1) When movant's papers are personally served, movant shall give at least eight days' notice (CPLR 2214(b)).

(2) When movant's papers are served by regular mail, movant shall give at least 13 days' notice (CPLR 2103(b)(2)).

(3) When movant's papers are served by overnight delivery service, movant shall give at least nine days' notice (CPLR 2103(b)(6)).

(4) When movant's papers are served by facsimile transmission, movant shall comply with CPLR 2103(b)(5), and give at least eight days' notice.

(c) *Filing.* Unless otherwise permitted by the Court or clerk of the Court, movant shall file its papers, with proof of service on each other party of the required number of copies, at Court of Appeals Hall no later than noon on the Friday preceding the return date. On or before the return date of the motion, respondent may file papers in opposition to the motion, with proof of service on each other party of the required number of copies. Submissions shall not be filed by facsimile transmission or electronic mail, except when requested by the clerk of the Court. The Court's motion practice does not permit the filing of reply briefs and memoranda. A request for permission to file papers after the return date of the motion is governed by section 500.7 of this Part.

(d) *Number of required copies.* Except in cases of indigency, where subsection (g) below applies, the number of copies required to be filed is as follows:

(1) *Motions for permission to appeal in civil cases.* Movant shall file an original and six copies of its papers, with proof of service of two copies on each other party. Respondent may file an original and six copies of papers in opposition to the motion, with proof of service of two copies on each other party.

(2) *Motions for reargument of appeals, reargument of motions for permission to appeal and reargument of decisions on certified questions.* Movant shall file an original and six copies of its papers, with proof of service of two copies on each other party. Respondent may file an original and six copies of papers in opposition to the motion, with proof of service of two copies on each other party.

(3) *Other motions.* For motions other than those addressed in subsections (d)(1) and (2) above, movant shall file an original and one copy of its papers, with proof of service of one copy on each other party. Respondent may file an original and one copy of papers in opposition to the motion, with proof of service of one copy on each other party.

(e) *Fee required.* Movant shall remit the fee, if any, required by section 500.3(b) of this Part with each motion and cross motion filed.

(f) *Form of papers.* Movant's papers and opposing papers shall comply in form with section 500.1 of this Part. The papers shall include a disclosure statement pursuant to section 500.1(c) of this Part, if required.

(g) *Proof of indigency.* Any motion may be made on one set of papers, with proof of service of one copy on each other party, where:

(1) the motion requests poor person relief and contains the information required by CPLR 1101(a), or

(2) movant provides a copy of an order, issued by any court in the action or proceeding to which the motion relates, granting that party poor person relief, together with a sworn affidavit that the same financial circumstances exist at the time of filing in the Court of Appeals as when the order granting poor person relief was issued.

§ 500.22 Motions for permission to appeal in civil cases.

(a) *Filing and notice.* Movant shall file an original and six copies of its papers, with proof of service of two copies on each other party. The motion shall be noticed for a return date in compliance with CPLR 5516 and section 500.21(b) of this Part.

(b) *Content.* Movant's papers shall be a single

document, bound on the left, and shall contain in the order here indicated:

(1) A notice of motion (see CPLR 2214).

(2) A statement of the procedural history of the case, including a showing of the timeliness of the motion.

(i) If no prior motion for leave to appeal to the Court of Appeals was filed at the Appellate Division, movant's papers to this Court shall demonstrate timeliness by stating the date movant was served (*see* CPLR 2103(b)) with the order or judgment sought to be appealed from, with notice of entry.

(ii) If a prior motion for leave to appeal to the Court of Appeals was filed at the Appellate Division, movant's papers filed in this Court shall demonstrate that the timeliness chain is intact by stating:

(a) the date movant was served with the order or judgment sought to be appealed from, with notice of entry,

(b) the date movant served the notice of motion addressed to the Appellate Division upon each other party, and

(c) the date movant was served with the Appellate Division order denying leave to appeal with notice of entry.

(3) A showing that this Court has jurisdiction of the motion and of the proposed appeal, including that the order or judgment sought to be appealed from is a final determination or comes within the special class of nonfinal orders appealable by permission of the Court of Appeals (*see* CPLR 5602(a)(2)).

(4) A concise statement of the questions presented for review and why the questions presented merit review by this Court, such as that the issues are novel or of public importance, present a conflict with prior decisions of this Court, or involve a conflict among the departments of the Appellate Division. Movant shall identify the particular portions of the record where the questions sought to be reviewed are raised and preserved.

(5) A disclosure statement pursuant to section 500.1(c) of this Part, if required.

(6) Copies of the order or judgment sought to be appealed from with notice of entry, as well as copies of all relevant orders, opinions or memoranda rendered in the courts below. The papers shall state if no opinion was rendered.

(c) *Additional documents.* Movant shall file with its papers one copy of the record below, or appendix if the appendix method was used in the court below, and one copy of the briefs filed below by each of the parties.

(d) *Opposing papers.* Respondent may file an original and six copies of papers in opposition to

the motion, with proof of service of two copies on each other party. The opposing papers shall state concisely respondent's argument for dismissal or denial of the motion.

§ 500.23 *Amicus curiae* relief.

Any non party other than the Attorney General seeking to file an *amicus* brief on an appeal, certified question or motion for leave to appeal must obtain permission by motion.

(a) *Motions.*

(1) *Amicus curiae relief on normal course appeals and normal course certified questions.* Movant shall file an original and one copy of its papers, accompanied by one copy of a proposed brief, with proof of service of one copy on each other party. The motion shall be noticed for a return date no later than the Court session preceding the session in which argument or submission of the appeal or certified question is scheduled. If the motion is granted, an original and 24 copies of the brief shall be filed, with proof of service of three copies on each party, within the time set by the Court's order.

(2) *Amicus curiae relief on appeals selected for review by the alternative procedure.* Movant shall file an original and one copy of its papers, accompanied by an original and two copies of the proposed submission, with proof of service of one copy on each other party. The motion shall be noticed for a return date no later than the filing date set for respondent's submission on the appeal.

(3) *Amicus curiae relief on motions for permission to appeal in civil cases.* Movant shall file an original and one copy of its papers, accompanied by one copy of a proposed brief, with proof of service of one copy on each other party. The motion shall be noticed for a return date as soon as practicable after the return date of the motion for permission to appeal to which it relates. The granting of a motion to appear *amicus curiae* on a motion for permission to appeal does not authorize the movant to appear *amicus* on the subsequent appeal. A new motion for *amicus curiae* relief on the appeal must be brought pursuant to subsection (a) (1) or (2) above.

(4) *Criteria.* Movant shall not present issues not raised before the courts below. A motion for *amicus curiae* relief shall demonstrate that:

(i) the parties are not capable of a full and adequate presentation and that movants could remedy this deficiency;

(ii) the *amicus* could identify law or arguments that might otherwise escape the Court's consideration; or

(iii) the proposed *amicus curiae* brief otherwise would be of assistance to the Court.

(5) *Opposing papers.* Respondent may file an original and one copy of papers in opposition to

the motion, with proof of service of one copy on each other party.

(b) *Amicus curiae filings by the Attorney General.*

(1) *Amicus curiae relief on motions for permission to appeal in civil cases.* The Attorney General shall file an original and one copy of the submission with proof of service of one copy on each other party. The submission shall be filed without leave of the Court on or before the return date of the motion for permission to appeal.

(2) *Amicus curiae relief on normal course appeals and normal course certified questions.* See Rule 500.12(e).

(3) *Amicus curiae relief on appeals selected for review by the alternative procedure.* See Rule 500.11(h).

§ 500.24 Motions for reargument of appeals, motions and decisions on certified questions.

(a) *Filing and notice.* Movant shall file an original and six copies of its papers, with proof of service of two copies on each other party. An original and one copy of a motion for reargument of a motion may be served and filed if filing of an original and one copy of papers was allowed on the underlying motion pursuant to section 500.21(d)(3).

(b) *Timeliness.* Movant shall serve the notice of motion not later than 30 days after the appeal or motion sought to be reargued has been decided, unless otherwise permitted by the Court.

(c) *Content.* The motion shall state briefly the ground upon which reargument is sought and the points claimed to have been overlooked or misapprehended by the Court, with proper reference to the particular portions of the record and to the authorities relied upon.

(d) *New matters.* The motion shall not be based on the assertion for the first time of new arguments or points of law, except for extraordinary and compelling reasons.

(e) *Limitation on motions.* The Court shall entertain only one motion per party for reargument of a specific appeal, motion or certified question decision.

(f) *Opposing papers.* Except on those motions described in section 500.21(d)(3), respondent may file an original and six copies of papers in opposition to the motion, with proof of service of two copies on each other party. The opposing papers shall briefly state respondent's argument for dismissal or denial of the motion.

§ 500.25 Emergency matters; orders to show cause.

A request for emergency relief pending the determination of an appeal or a motion for permission to appeal shall be brought on by order to show cause. The applicant shall contact the clerk's office in advance of the filing. The papers shall be filed as directed by the clerk's office. The order to show cause shall include telephone and facsimile numbers for each attorney and self represented party, and a statement giving reasons for granting the request. If there is no pending appeal or motion for permission to appeal, the order to show cause shall bring on a motion for leave to appeal or be accompanied by a notice of appeal or a motion for permission to appeal complying with section 500.22 of this Part. There is no fee for filing an order to show cause. If a Judge signs an order to show cause bringing on a motion, movant shall pay the fee, if any, required by section 500.3(b) of this Part.

PRIMARY ELECTION SESSION

§ 500.26 Primary election session procedures.

(a) *Appeals as of right or by permission of the Appellate Division.*

(1) Appellant shall immediately contact the clerk's office by telephone upon receipt of the order from which the appeal is taken.

(2) Appellant shall immediately orally notify each respondent of the appeal.

(3) Within the time directed by the clerk of the Court, appellant shall file:

(i) a copy of the notice of appeal or order granting leave and a preliminary appeal statement with proof of service on each other party;

(ii) 25 copies of appellant's Appellate Division brief and, where applicable, the record or appendix;

(iii) the original file, where applicable, which appellant shall obtain;

(iv) the fee, if any, required by section 500.3(a) of this Part;

(v) an original and 24 copies of a letter setting forth appellant's arguments in this Court with proof of service of one copy on each other party; and

(vi) additional papers, if requested.

(4) Within the time directed by the clerk of the Court, respondent shall submit 25 copies of its Appellate Division brief, and may submit an original and 24 copies of a letter in opposition with proof of service of one copy on each other party.

(b) *Motions for permission to appeal.*

(1) Movant shall immediately contact the

clerk's office by telephone upon receipt of the order from which movant seeks leave to appeal.

(2) Movant shall immediately orally notify respondent of the motion.

(3) Within the time directed by the clerk of the Court, movant shall file:

(i) an original and nine copies of a letter requesting permission to appeal with proof of service of one copy on each other party;

(ii) 10 copies of the Appellate Division decision and order;

(iii) 10 copies of the Supreme Court decision and order;

(iv) 10 copies of movant's Appellate Division brief, and, where applicable, the record or appendix;

(v) the original file, where applicable, which movant shall obtain; and

(vi) the fee, if any, required by section 500.3(b) of this Part.

(4) Within the time directed by the clerk of the Court, respondent shall submit 10 copies of its Appellate Division brief, and may submit an original and nine copies of a letter in opposition with proof of service of one copy on each other party.

CERTIFIED QUESTIONS

§ 500.27 Discretionary proceedings to review certified questions from federal courts and other courts of last resort.

(a) Whenever it appears to the Supreme Court of the United States, any United States Court of Appeals, or a court of last resort of any other state that determinative questions of New York law are involved in a case pending before that court for which no controlling precedent of the Court of Appeals exists, the court may certify the dispositive questions of law to the Court of Appeals.

(b) The certifying court shall prepare a certificate which shall contain the caption of the case, a statement of facts setting forth the nature of the case and the circumstances out of which the questions of New York law arise, and the questions of New York law, not controlled by precedent, that may be determinative, together with a statement as to why the issue should be addressed in the Court of Appeals at this time.

(c) The certificate, certified by the clerk of the certifying court under its official seal, together with the original or a copy of all relevant portions of the record and other papers before the certifying court, as it may direct, shall be filed with the clerk of the Court.

(d) The Court, on its own motion, shall examine the merits presented by the certified question, to determine, first, whether to accept the certification, and second, the review procedure to be followed in determining the merits.

(e) If the certification is accepted, the clerk of the Court shall request any additional papers the Court requires for its review. The clerk of the Court shall notify the parties of the time periods for filing of briefs, if any, and calendaring of argument, if any, directed by the Court.

(f) If the constitutionality of an act of the Legislature of this state is involved in a certification to which the State of New York or an agency is not a party, the clerk of the Court shall notify the Attorney General in accordance with the provisions of Executive Law § 71.

(g) When a determination is rendered by the Court with respect to the questions certified, it shall be sent by the clerk of the Court to the certifying court.

NEW YORK STATE
COURT OF APPEALS

Preliminary Appeal Statement

Pursuant to section 500.9 of the Rules of the Court of Appeals

1. CAPTION OF CASE (as the parties should be denominated in the Court of Appeals):

STATE OF NEW YORK   COURT OF APPEALS

against

2. Name of court or tribunal where case originated, including county, if applicable:

_____

3. Civil index number, criminal indictment number or other number assigned to the matter in the court or tribunal of original instance: _____

4. Docket number assigned to the matter at the Appellate Division or other intermediate appellate court: _____

5. Jurisdictional basis for this appeal:

_____ Leave to appeal granted by the Court of Appeals or a Judge of the Court of Appeals

_____ Leave to appeal granted by the Appellate Division or a Justice of the Appellate Division

_____ CPLR 5601(a): dissents on the law at the Appellate Division

_____ CPLR 5601(b)(1): constitutional ground (Appellate Division order)

_____ CPLR 5601(b)(2): constitutional ground (judgment of court of original instance)

_____ CPLR 5601(c): Appellate Division order granting a new trial or hearing, upon stipulation for judgment absolute

_____ CPLR 5601(d): from a final judgment, order, determination or award, seeking review of a prior nonfinal Appellate Division order

_____ Other (specify) _____

6. How this appeal was taken to the Court of Appeals (choose one) (*see* CPLR 5515(1)):

NOTICE OF APPEAL
  Date filed: _____
  Clerk's office where filed: _____

ORDER GRANTING LEAVE TO APPEAL (civil case):
  Court that issued order: _____
  Date of order: _____

CERTIFICATE GRANTING LEAVE TO APPEAL (criminal case):
  Justice or Judge who issued order: _____
  Court: _____
  Date of order: _____

7. Demonstration of timeliness of appeal in civil case (CPLR 5513, 5514):

Was appellant served by its adversary with a copy of the order, judgment or determination appealed from and notice of its entry? _____ yes _____ no

If yes, date on which appellant was served (if known, or discernable from the papers served): _____

If yes, method by which appellant was served:
_____ personal delivery
_____ regular mail
_____ overnight courier
_____ other (describe _____)

Did the Appellate Division deny a motion for leave to appeal to this Court in this case? _____ yes _____ no

If yes, fill in the following information:

a. date appellant served the motion for leave to appeal made at the Appellate Division: _____

   b.   date on which appellant was served with the Appellate Division order denying such motion with notice of the order's entry: _____, and

   c.   method by which appellant was served with the Appellate Division order denying such motion:
       _____ personal service
       _____ regular mail
       _____ overnight courier
       _____ other (describe _____)

8.   Party Information:

Instructions: Fill in the name of each party to the action or proceeding, one name per line. Indicate the status of the party in the court of original instance and the party's status in this Court, if any. Examples of a party's original status include: plaintiff, defendant, petitioner, respondent, claimant, third party plaintiff, third party defendant, intervenor. Examples of a party's Court of Appeals status include: appellant, respondent, appellant respondent, respondent appellant, intervenor appellant.

No.	Party Name	Original Status	Court of Appeals Status
1			
2			
3			
4			
5			
6			
7			
8			
9			
10			

9.   Attorney information:

Instructions: For each party listed above, fill in the name of the law firm and responsible attorney, if the party is represented. Where a litigant is self represented, fill in that party's data in section 10 below.

For Party No. _____ above:
Law Firm Name: _____
Responsible Attorney: _____
Street Address: _____
City: _____ State: _____ Zip: _____
Telephone No: _____ Ext. _____ Fax: _____
If appearing *Pro Hac Vice*, has attorney satisfied requirements of section 500.4 of the Rules of the Court of Appeals? _____ yes _____ no

For Party No. _____ above:
Law Firm Name: _____
Responsible Attorney: _____
Street Address: _____
City: _____ State: _____ Zip: _____
Telephone No: _____ Ext. _____ Fax: _____
If appearing *Pro Hac Vice*, has attorney satisfied requirements of section 500.4 of the Rules of the Court of Appeals? _____ yes _____ no

For Party No. _____ above:
Law Firm Name: _____
Responsible Attorney: _____
Street Address: _____
City: _____ State: _____ Zip: _____
Telephone No: _____ Ext. _____ Fax: _____
If appearing *Pro Hac Vice*, has attorney satisfied requirements of section 500.4 of the Rules of the Court of Appeals? _____ yes _____ no

For Party No. ____ above:
Law Firm Name: _____
Responsible Attorney: _____
Street Address: _____
City: _____ State: _____ Zip: _____
Telephone No: _____ Ext. _____ Fax: _____
If appearing *Pro Hac Vice*, has attorney satisfied requirements of section 500.4 of the Rules of the Court of Appeals? ____ yes ____ no

For Party No. ____ above:
Law Firm Name: _____
Responsible Attorney: _____
Street Address: _____
City: _____ State: _____ Zip: _____
Telephone No: _____ Ext. _____ Fax: _____
If appearing *Pro Hac Vice*, has attorney satisfied requirements of section 500.4 of the Rules of the Court of Appeals? ____ yes ____ no

(Use additional sheets if necessary)

10. Self Represented Litigant information:

For Party No. ____ above:
Party's Name: _____
Street Address: _____
City: _____ State: _____ Zip: _____
Telephone No:_____ Ext. _____ Fax: _____

For Party No. ____ above:
Party's Name: _____
Street Address: _____
City: _____ State: _____ Zip: _____
Telephone No:_____ Ext. _____ Fax: _____

11. Related motions and applications:

Does any party to the appeal have any motions or applications related to this appeal pending in the Court of Appeals? ____ yes ____ no

If yes, specify:

a. the party who filed the motion or application: _____

b. the return date of the motion: _____

c. the relief sought: _____

Does any party to the appeal have any motions or applications in this case currently pending in the court from which the appeal is taken? ____ yes ____ no

If yes, specify:

a. the party who filed the motion or application: _____

b. the return date of the motion: _____

c. the relief sought: _____

Are there any other pending motions or ongoing proceedings in this case? If yes, please describe briefly the nature and the status of such motions or proceedings: _____

_____

_____

_____

12. Set forth, in point heading form, issues proposed to be raised on appeal (this is a nonbinding designation, for preliminary issue identification purposes only):

(use additional sheet, if necessary)

13. Does appellant request that this appeal be considered for resolution pursuant to section 500.11 of the Rules of the Court of Appeals (Alternative Procedure for Selected Appeals)?

_____ yes _____ no

If yes, set forth a concise statement why appellant believes that consideration pursuant to section 500.11 is appropriate (*see* section 500.11(b)): _____

_____

_____

_____

_____

14. Notice to the Attorney General.

Is any party to the appeal asserting that a statute is unconstitutional? _____ yes _____ no

If yes, has appellant met the requirement of notice to the Attorney General in section 500.9(b) of the Rules of the Court of Appeals? _____ yes _____ no

15. ITEMS REQUIRED TO BE ATTACHED TO THIS STATEMENT:

A. A copy of the filed notice of appeal, a copy of the order granting leave to appeal (civil case), or a copy of the certificate granting leave to appeal (noncapital criminal case), whichever is applicable;

B. The order, judgment or determination appealed from to this Court;

C. Any order, judgment or determination which is the subject of the order appealed from, or which is otherwise brought up for review;

D. All decisions or opinions relating to the orders set forth in subsections B and C above; and

E. If required, a copy of the notice sent to the Attorney General pursuant to section 500.9(b) of the Rules of the Court of Appeals.

Date:_____

Submitted by:

(Name of law firm)

_____

(Signature of responsible attorney)

_____

(Typed name of responsible attorney)

Attorneys for appellant_____

(Name of party)

Date:_____   or   _____

Submitted by:

_____ *pro se*

(Signature of appellant)

_____

(Typed/printed name of self represented appellant)

PART 510

CAPITAL CASES

§ 510.1 Papers.

(a) All records, briefs, appendices, motion papers and other required submissions, whether printed, typewritten, or reproduced in other form (no carbon copies), shall conform to CPLR 5529, shall be bound or securely fastened on the left edge, and shall have a fluorescent green sticker on the spine. Pages shall be consecutively numbered and each document filed shall contain an index or table of contents. Records and appendices shall be divided into volumes not to exceed two inches in thickness. Where New York authorities are cited in any paper, New York Official Law Report citations must be included.

(b) Companion filings on interactive compact disk, read-only memory (CD-ROM).

(1) (a) The submission of briefs by parties and amici curiae, and of records or appendices, on interactive compact disk, read-only memory (CD-ROM) as companions to the requisite number of printed briefs, records and appendices filed and served in accordance with the Rules of the Court of Appeals in Capital Cases is allowed and encouraged, provided that all parties have consented to the filing of the companion CD-ROM brief and record or appendix.

(b) The Court may, by order on motion of any party or sua sponte, require such filing.

(2) The companion CD-ROM brief, record or appendix must comply with the current technical specifications available from the clerk's office and must be packaged in a box or boxes with a green fluorescent sticker on the spine.

(3) The companion CD-ROM brief, record or appendix must be identical in content and format (including page numbering) to the printed version, except that each also may provide electronic links (hyperlinks) to the complete text of any authorities cited therein, and to any document or other material constituting the record on appeal.

(4) No fewer than 10 disks or sets of disks must be filed, with (a) proof of service of at least one disk or set on each other party and amicus curiae and (b) a copy of either the parties' stipulation or the Court's order permitting or requesting such filing.

(5) Appellant's filing and respondent's filing, or a joint filing by appellant and respondent, is due 10 days after the final due date for filing appellant's reply brief (see section 510.8(b) of this Part).

(6) Each amicus curiae's filing is due 10 days after the due date for filing the respective amicus brief.

§ 510.2 Duties of trial-level capital defense counsel.

(a) Where a capital trial results in a judgment including a sentence of death, capital defense counsel shall timely take an appeal. CPL 470.30(2) provides that a defendant sentenced to death may not waive review pursuant to CPL 450.70(1) of the judgment and sentence.

(b) Immediately after being served with an adverse order disposing of a capital matter appealable pursuant to CPL 450.70(2), (3), or (4) or CPL

460.40(3), capital defense counsel shall advise the defendant in writing of the right to appeal. Counsel shall ascertain whether the defendant wishes to appeal and, if so, shall timely take the appeal.

(c) In all instances, capital defense counsel shall advise the defendant in writing of the time limitations for taking an appeal, the manner of taking an appeal and of obtaining a transcript of the testimony, and the right of a defendant unable to pay the cost of an appeal to apply for permission to appeal as a poor person. Capital defense counsel shall also comply with section 510.7(a) of this Part.

§ 510.3 Notice of appeal.

(a) *CPL 450.70(1) mandatory appeal.* A timely appeal must be taken pursuant to CPL 460.10(1). In addition, counsel for defendant must file one copy of the notice of appeal, with proof of service and filing, with the clerk of the Court of Appeals.

(b) *Other capital appeals.* Any other appeal in a case involving a sentence of death shall be taken by the timely service and filing of a notice of appeal pursuant to CPL 460.10(1). In addition, counsel for appellant must file one copy of the notice of appeal, with proof of service and filing, with the clerk of the Court of Appeals.

§ 510.4 Stays of execution: automatic or determined by superior court.

(a) *Upon appeal from a judgment including a sentence of death (CPL 460.40(1)).* The taking of an appeal by a defendant directly to the Court of Appeals from a superior court judgment including a sentence of death stays the execution of such sentence until determination of the appeal.

(b) *Initial CPL article 440 proceedings (CPL 460.40(3)).* Upon motion to the superior court judge or justice who signed the warrant of execution, a defendant sentenced to death shall be granted a stay of execution of a death warrant issued pursuant to Correction Law, article 22-B to allow the defendant an opportunity to prepare and timely file an initial motion in superior court pursuant to CPL 440.10 or 440.20. The order staying execution shall provide that the stay of execution shall continue until (1) the time for taking an appeal to the Court of Appeals from the superior court's denial of such CPL article 440 motion has expired, or (2) if an appeal is taken, until the Court of Appeals determines the appeal.

(c) *Subsequent CPL article 440 proceedings (CPL 460.40(3)).* (1) In the event a defendant sentenced to death files a motion for post-conviction relief pursuant to CPL 440.10 or 440.20 subsequent to the final determination of an initial CPL article 440 motion, the superior court may grant a stay of execution of a death warrant issued pursuant to Correction Law, article 22-B only for good cause shown.

(2) The people and a defendant sentenced to death shall have an appeal as of right directly to the Court of Appeals from a superior court order granting or denying such motion for a stay of execution. On such appeal, the court may affirm, reverse, or modify such order as the court deems appropriate.

(3) By the end of business on the date a notice of appeal from a superior court order granting or denying a motion for a stay of execution has been filed, the clerk of the superior court, and appellant or appellant's counsel, shall notify the clerk of the Court of Appeals by telephone of such filing. Telephone notice to the Court of Appeals does not relieve the clerk of the superior court of the duties imposed by section 510.6 of this Part.

(4) Upon the taking of an appeal from a superior court order granting or denying such a stay, the Court of Appeals shall forthwith issue a capital appeal management order order establishing a schedule for perfecting the appeal. To the extent other provisions of this Part are inconsistent with a capital appeal management order so issued, the order shall supersede those provisions for purposes of the subject appeal only.

§ 510.5 Stays of execution: requests to the Court of Appeals.

(a) Where not otherwise provided, the Court of Appeals may grant a stay on motion brought in accordance with section 510.12 of this Part, provided that the court's jurisdiction has been invoked by the service and filing of a notice of appeal or a motion pursuant to CPL 460.30 for an extension of time to take an appeal.

(b) Emergency motions for interim stay relief shall be brought on by order to show cause filed with the clerk of the Court of Appeals. Any time a party seeks interim stay relief, that party should contact the clerk of the court at (518) 455-7700.

§ 510.6 Case history.

Within 15 days after the filing of a notice of appeal to the Court of Appeals in a case involving a sentence of death, except in those appeals taken pursuant to CPL 460.40(3) from an order of a superior court granting or denying a motion for a stay of execution, the clerk of the superior court in which the judgment or order being appealed from was rendered shall transmit to the clerk of the Court of Appeals a case history including:

(a) the duplicate notice of appeal;

(b) a chronological list of all proceedings below giving rise to this particular appeal, noting which transcripts have been, or must be, prepared; and

(c) a list of all exhibits introduced in the proceedings below giving rise to this particular appeal.

The clerk of the superior court shall transmit

to counsel for the parties copies of subdivisions (b) and (c) of this section.

§ 510.7 Poor person relief; assignment of counsel.

The following procedures shall apply in all capital appeals except those appeals taken pursuant to CPL 460.40(3) from an order of a superior court granting or denying a motion for a stay of execution.

(a) Where sought, trial counsel shall move, pursuant to section 510.12 of this Part, for assignment of appellate counsel or other items of poor person relief within 10 days after the filing of the notice of appeal. The motion papers shall include an affidavit setting forth the information required by CPLR 1101(a). On an appeal in a case in which Judiciary Law, section 35-b provides for the assignment of appellate counsel, trial counsel's affidavit shall also state whether counsel is requesting to be considered for assignment as counsel on the appeal.

(b) Where the appeal is taken from a judgment including a sentence of death pursuant to CPL 450.70(1), assigned counsel may move at any time pursuant to section 510.12 of this Part for assignment of associate counsel for good cause shown.

(c) Assignment of counsel shall proceed in compliance with any applicable Court of Appeals directives on the matter.

§ 510.8 Capital appeal management; issue identification by the parties.

The following procedures shall apply in all capital appeals except those appeals taken pursuant to CPL 460.40(3) from an order of a superior court granting or denying a motion for a stay of execution.

(a) After receipt from the superior court of the case history required by section 510.6 of this Part, the Court of Appeals shall enter and forward to counsel for the parties an initial capital appeal management order (1) determining defendant's request, if any, for items of poor person relief, (2) establishing final dates for transcription and settlement, if necessary, and (3) establishing a deadline for filing the settled record on appeal in this court.

(b) Appellant's counsel shall file, and respondent's counsel may file, a preliminary appeal statement in accordance with section 510.9 of this Part. Following either the filing of respondent's preliminary appeal statement or the expiration of respondent's time to so file, the Court of Appeals shall enter and forward to counsel for the parties a final capital appeal management order which shall:

(1) establish a briefing schedule for the appeal;

(2) state whether the appeal will proceed on the full reproduced record or on an appendix, as set forth in section 510.11 of this Part;

(3) for purposes of case management and public notice, require appellant's counsel to file periodically with the clerk of the Court of Appeals a progress report concerning the capital appeal; and

(4) establish a deadline by which all requests for *amicus curiae* relief must be noticed to be heard. Capital appeals shall receive a calendar preference. In the clerk's discretion, a capital appeal management conference may be scheduled prior to, or any time following, issuance of the initial capital appeal management order.

(c) For purposes of case management and public notice, appellant must file with the opening brief on appeal a separately bound Issue Identification Statement listing, in point-heading format, all issues raised on the appeal. The Court of Appeals may direct the parties to brief and argue specific issues on the appeal.

§ 510.9 Preliminary appeal statements.

The following procedures shall apply in all capital appeals except those appeals taken pursuant to CPL 460.40(3) from an order of a superior court granting or denying a motion for a stay of execution.

(a) For issue identification and case management purposes only, within 30 days after the filing of the record on appeal in the Court of Appeals, appellant's counsel shall file with the clerk of the Court of Appeals, with proof of service of one copy on respondent's counsel, two copies of a preliminary appeal statement, which shall include:

(1) the title of the case;

(2) the court from which the appeal is taken;

(3) a copy of the judgment or order of the superior court appealed from;

(4) a copy of any other written order brought up for review;

(5) a copy of all written decisions of the superior court; and

(6) a preliminary, nonbinding statement of issues likely to be raised on appeal.

(b) Within 10 days after service of appellant's preliminary appeal statement, respondent's counsel may file with the clerk of the Court of Appeals, with proof of service of one copy on appellant's counsel, two copies of a preliminary appeal statement which sets forth any additional matters relevant to the appeal or any disagreement with appellant's preliminary appeal statement.

(c) Where appellant's statement of issues pursuant to paragraph (a)(6) of this section includes an assertion that a statute, or a portion of a statute, is unconstitutional, notice must be given to the

Attorney General pursuant to section 510.13 of this Part prior to filing the preliminary appeal statement, and a certification of this notification shall be included in the preliminary appeal statement.

§ 510.10 Record transcription and reproduction; settlement.

(a) During the course of capital proceedings before the superior court, and at all times thereafter, the clerk of the superior court shall take all necessary steps to insure the accuracy and completeness of the record of the proceedings.

(b) The court reporter shall take minutes of all capital proceedings occurring in the superior court. Transcription shall proceed in compliance with any relevant superior court order and the Court of Appeals capital appeal management orders. Where a copy of the minutes of any proceedings in the superior court was ordered during the course of the superior court proceedings, defense counsel and the prosecutor shall preserve their respective copies of the transcript. Transcripts shall be settled pursuant to CPLR 5525(c) within such time limits and pursuant to such additional procedures as may be set by Court of Appeals order.

(c) Upon the filing of a notice of appeal, the superior court clerk shall expeditiously assemble, reproduce, and transmit to appellant the record of the proceedings. Appellant shall be responsible for the timely preparation and filing of the record on appeal in accordance with the initial capital appeal management order issued by the Court of Appeals pursuant to section 510.8(a) of this Part.

(d) The record on appeal shall comply with section 510.11(b) of this Part, and be stipulated to or settled on motion. The parties may stipulate to the correctness of the contents of the record on appeal using the process provided by CPLR 5525(c)(1). Where the parties are unable to agree and stipulate to the contents of the record on appeal, appellant shall move, on notice, to settle the record in the superior court from which the appeal is taken.

(e) Within 60 days after the superior court clerk's transmission to appellant of the reproduced record of proceedings, appellant shall file with the clerk of the Court of Appeals either the parties' stipulation to the record on appeal or a copy of appellant's notice of motion to settle the record.

(f) The parties' failure to list in the stipulation to the record on appeal any transcript, exhibit, or other document that constituted a part of the underlying prosecution shall not preclude the Court of Appeals from considering such transcript, exhibit, or other document in determining the appeal.

§ 510.11 Record on appeal; appendix; briefs.

(a) *Record on Appeal.* On an appeal in a case involving a sentence of death, appellant shall file with the clerk of the Court of Appeals 15 copies of the settled, reproduced record of the proceedings in the superior court, with proof of service on respondent of three copies of the settled, reproduced record.

(b) The settled, reproduced record shall contain the complete original file, including the transcribed stenographic minutes of all proceedings occurring in the superior court, such as proceedings on pretrial motions and hearings, opening and closing statements, jury *voir dire* examination, all trial testimony, all legal argument of counsel, including bench and chambers colloquies, the jury instructions, all communications to and from the jury after instructions, proceedings on sentencing, and post-trial motions and hearings. The record shall conform substantially with the requirements of CPLR 5526 and section 510.1 of this Part, and shall contain in the following order so many of the following items as are relevant to the case:

(1) a cover which shall contain the title of the case on the upper portion and, on the lower portion, the names, addresses, and voice and facsimile telephone numbers of counsel for the parties, and the indictment number;

(2) the statement required by CPLR 5531;

(3) a table of contents which shall list and briefly describe each paper included in the record. The part of the table relating to the transcript of testimony shall separately list each witness and the page at which direct, cross, redirect and recross examinations begin. The part of the table relating to exhibits shall concisely indicate the nature and contents of each exhibit and the page in the record where it is reproduced and where it was admitted into evidence. The table shall also contain references to pages where a motion to dismiss the indictment or to direct or set aside a verdict, or where an oral decision of the court, appears;

(4) the notice of appeal, judgment or order appealed from, judgment roll, corrected transcript, relevant exhibits and any opinions or decisions in the case;

(5) a stipulation, or order settling the transcript; and

(6) a copy of either the stipulation described in section 510.10(d) of this Part or the superior court order settling the record.

(c) The people shall file, separately from the record, one copy of all transcripts and documents concerning the nature or substance of any grand jury testimony or evidence, and any decision, result, or other matter attending a grand jury proceeding which is required by CPL 190.25(4)(a) to be kept secret. All such volumes of the record on appeal shall be identified on the cover as containing confidential grand jury material.

(d) *Appendix.* Except on appeals taken pursuant to CPL 450.70(1), the Court of Appeals *sua sponte* may order appellant, or appellant may seek permission pursuant to section 510.12 of this Part, to prosecute the appeal upon one copy of the settled, reproduced record and 15 copies of an appendix which conforms to the requirements of CPLR 5528 and 5529 and section 510.1 of this Part. The appendix shall be bound separately from the brief and shall include the following items:

(1) the notice of appeal;

(2) the statement required by CPLR 5531;

(3) the order or judgment of the superior court from which the appeal is taken;

(4) any other order sought to be reviewed;

(5) the written and oral decisions of the superior court, as relevant;

(6) findings of fact, as relevant;

(7) the indictment; and

(8) those portions of the testimony, affidavits, legal arguments, and written and photographic exhibits referenced in appellant's brief and reasonably expected to be referenced in respondent's brief, and all other portions that may be useful to the determination of the questions raised on the appeal.

The prior filing of a preliminary appeal statement pursuant to section 510.9 of this Part does not satisfy the requirements of this section. Where appellant has filed an inadequate appendix, respondent may move to strike the appendix pursuant to section 510.12 of this Part or may submit a respondent's appendix containing additional parts of the record deemed necessary for the court to consider the questions involved.

(e) *Briefs.* Briefs shall conform to the requirements of section 510.1 of this Part. The cover of the brief shall set forth the title of the case. The upper right hand section shall contain a notation stating whether the case shall be argued or submitted. If the case is to be argued, the notation shall state the name of counsel who will argue and the amount of time granted for oral argument. The lower right hand section shall contain the name, address, and voice and facsimile telephone number of counsel filing the brief, and the date the brief was filed, and shall indicate whom counsel represents. Unless authorized by the clerk of the Court of Appeals, briefs shall not contain maps, photographs, or other addenda. Boldface type shall only be used in point headings or subheadings.

(1) Appellant shall file 15 copies of the appellant's brief and the issue identification statement required by section 510.8(c) of this Part, with proof of service of three copies on respondent.

The appellant's brief shall contain in the following order:

(i) a table of contents including the titles of the points urged in the brief;

(ii) a list of all authorities cited in the brief;

(iii) a concise statement of the questions involved without names, dates, or particulars. Each question shall be numbered, set forth separately, and followed immediately by the answer, if any, of the court from which the appeal is taken;

(iv) a concise statement of the nature of the case and of the facts which should be known to determine the questions involved, with supporting references to pages in the record or the appendix, including, if such be the case, a statement that proceedings on the judgment or order appealed from have been stayed pending a determination of the appeal; and

(v) the appellant's argument, which shall be divided into points by appropriate headings distinctively printed.

(2) Respondent shall file 15 copies of the respondent's brief, with proof of service of three copies on appellant. The respondent's brief shall contain, in the following order:

(i) a table of contents including the titles of the points urged in the brief;

(ii) a list of all authorities cited in the brief;

(iii) a counter statement of the questions involved or of the nature and facts of the case, if respondent disagrees with the statement of appellant; and

(iv) the argument for respondent, which shall be divided into points by appropriate headings distinctively printed.

(3) Appellant shall file 15 copies of the appellant's reply brief, with proof of service of three copies on respondent. The appellant's reply brief shall contain, in the following order:

(i) a table of contents;

(ii) a list of all authorities cited in the brief; and

(iii) the reply for appellant, without repetition of the arguments contained in the main brief, which shall be divided into points by appropriate headings distinctively printed.

§ 510.12 Motions.

(a) Unless otherwise directed by a judge of the Court of Appeals by order to show cause, the following procedures shall apply to motions concerning capital appeals. A motion addressed to the Court of Appeals may be made on eight days' notice (personal service), nine days' notice (overnight delivery service) or 13 days' notice (service by mail) (see CPLR 2103). Motions are returnable at Court of Appeals Hall, 20 Eagle Street, Albany,

NY 12207-1095, every Monday, whether or not the court is in session. Whenever a Monday is a State holiday, motions are returnable on the next day of that week that is not a State holiday. All motions shall be submitted without oral argument. Unless otherwise permitted by the court or the clerk, the papers in support of a motion must be filed at Court of Appeals Hall no later than noon on the Friday preceding the return date. All responding papers must be served and filed at Court of Appeals Hall on or before the return date of the motion. Proof of service on each party must be filed with any papers submitted on a motion. Filings by facsimile transmission will not be accepted without prior authorization of the clerk. No adjournments are possible other than in those narrow circumstances provided by CPLR 321(c).

(b) Reply papers are not permitted by the court's motion practice. Requests for permission to file papers after the motion return date are governed by section 510.14 of this Part.

(c) *Motion for amicus curiae relief.* A brief *amicus curiae* may be filed only by leave of the Court of Appeals granted on motion, or upon the court's request. Motions for *amicus curiae* relief must be noticed to be heard no later than the deadline set forth in the final capital appeal management order. Movant must file one copy of the motion and 15 copies of the proposed brief, with proof of service of three copies on each party. Motions for *amicus curiae* relief must demonstrate to the court's satisfaction at least one of the following:

(1) that the parties are not capable of a full and adequate presentation and that movants could remedy this deficiency;

(2) that movants would invite the court's attention to law or arguments which might otherwise escape its consideration; or

(3) that *amicus curiae* briefs would otherwise be of special assistance to the court.

Proposed briefs *amicus curiae* shall conform to the requirements set forth in section 510.11(e) of this Part.

(d) *Motion for reargument.* A motion for reargument of an appeal shall be made on 10 copies of a brief or memorandum, with proof of service of three copies. A motion to reargue a motion may be made on one copy of a brief or memorandum with proof of service of one copy. A motion to reargue an appeal or motion shall state briefly the grounds upon which reargument is sought and the points claimed to have been overlooked or misapprehended by the court, with proper reference to the particular portions of the record and to the authorities relied upon. A motion to reargue may not be based on the assertion for the first time of new points except for extraordinary and compelling reasons. Unless otherwise permitted by the court, the notice of motion shall be served not

later than 30 days after the appeal or motion has been decided.

(e) *Other motions.* Motions other than those seeking *amicus curiae* relief or reargument may be made on a single set of the moving papers, with proof of service of one copy.

(f) Motion papers which do not conform to the requirements of this Part may be rejected by the clerk.

§ 510.13 Notice to the Attorney General.

Unless such notice has already been given pursuant to section 510.9(c) of this Part, where a party or an amicus asserts in its brief on appeal that a statute, or a portion of a statute, is unconstitutional, notice shall be given to the Attorney General in writing at the time the party or amicus files its brief, and a certification of the notification shall be included in the brief. The notification and a copy of the brief shall be sent to the Solicitor General, Department of Law, The Capitol, Albany, NY 12224-0341.

§ 510.14 Post-argument communications.

Post-argument and post-submission communications to the court concerning motions and appeals, in the form of letters, memoranda or briefs, are not permitted and will be returned to the sender, unless specifically requested or authorized by the Court of Appeals or authorized, in writing, by the clerk of the Court of Appeals upon submission to the clerk with a request that they be accepted.

§ 510.15 Withdrawal of appeal or motion.

With the exception of a defendant's appeal to the Court of Appeals from a judgment including a sentence of death pursuant to CPL 450.70(1), an appeal may be withdrawn and discontinued at any time prior to argument or submission by forwarding to the clerk of the Court of Appeals a duly executed stipulation of withdrawal, which must be signed by all counsel, and by the defendant personally. A motion may be withdrawn at any time prior to its return date by filing with the clerk a written request signed by counsel for the moving party. A request to withdraw a motion after submission must be supported by a stipulation of withdrawal signed by all counsel.

§ 510.16 Notice to the capital defender office.

(a) Upon a determination of the Court of Appeals affirming a judgment that includes a sentence of death, the clerk of the Court of Appeals shall notify the capital defender office of the determination by the end of business on the day such determination is handed down.

(b) Notice to the capital defender office

required pursuant to subdivision (a) of this section shall consist of telephone, facsimile, electronic mail or other prompt electronic means of communication, which shall be followed by first class mail notification within two business days after the affirmance.

(c) The clerk of the Court of Appeals shall retain a written record of the electronic and written notice given pursuant to subdivision (b) of this section.

§ 510.17 Remittitur.

The remittitur of the Court of Appeals containing the court's adjudication, together with the return papers filed with the court, shall be sent to the clerk of the court to which the case is remitted, there to be proceeded upon according to law. Any order to effect the adjudication contained in the Court of Appeals' remittitur shall be sought, entered and enforced in the superior court.

§ 510.18 Capital case data reports.

(a) In each criminal action in which the defendant has been indicted for commission of an offense defined in section 125.27 of the Penal Law, except those in which the indictment is dismissed or the defendant is acquitted, the clerk of the superior court, within 45 days after the disposition of the action in such court, shall prepare and send to the Court of Appeals a capital case data report in the form prescribed by the Court of Appeals. Data reports shall be prepared by the clerk of the superior court by reviewing the record and upon consultation with the prosecutor and counsel for the defendant. Such data

reports shall not constitute a part of the record in the underlying criminal action. The clerk of the superior court shall retain, in a confidential file kept separate from the record in the underlying criminal action, a copy of each such data report sent to the Court of Appeals, and may disclose a data report, or any part thereof, only upon order of the Court of Appeals for exceptional cause shown.

(b) All capital case data reports received by the Court of Appeals shall be compiled into a uniform capital case data report, which may consist of a computer data base containing the information in each capital case data report. Upon request, the uniform capital case data report shall be made available to the parties on appeal to the Court of Appeals in cases where a sentence of death has been imposed, and otherwise may be available upon order of the Court of Appeals to the extent and in a form and manner prescribed, and for such fee as fixed, by the Court of Appeals.

(c) If the conviction in such criminal action is subsequently reversed or modified, the capital case data report shall be notated to reflect the reversal or modification. If an intermediate appellate court reverses or modifies the conviction, that court shall forward a copy of its remittitur to the Court of Appeals within 10 days after entry. If a new disposition in the action ensues in the superior court, the superior court clerk shall prepare a new capital case data report. Upon completion, the superior court clerk shall send the new capital case data report to the clerk of the Court of Appeals with a notice that the new report should be substituted in the data base for the previous report.

PART 515

STANDARDS FOR APPELLATE AND STATE POST-CONVICTION COUNSEL IN CAPITAL CASES

515.1 Standards for appellate counsel in capital cases.

(1) Appellate qualifications and experience.

(a) *Sole appellate counsel.* To be eligible to be appointed as sole appellate counsel on direct appeal in a capital case, an attorney must demonstrate that he or she:

(1) has at least five years of criminal trial or criminal appellate or post-conviction experience, or has at least three years of concentrated criminal litigation experience;

(2) is familiar with the practice and procedure of the trial and appellate courts of New York, including the New York Court of Appeals; and

(3) also has had primary responsibility for the appeal of at least five felony convictions in any state or Federal court, at least three of which were on behalf of the defendant, and at least three of which were orally argued by the attorney.

(b) *Two appellate counsel.* To be eligible to be appointed as one of two appellate counsel on direct appeal in a capital case:

(1) one attorney must demonstrate that he or she has the qualifications set forth in subdivision (a) of this section; and

(2) the second attorney must demonstrate that he or she:

(i) has at least three years of criminal litigation or post-conviction experience;

(ii) is familiar with the practice and procedure of the trial and appellate courts of New York, including the New York Court of Appeals; and

(iii) has had primary responsibility for the appeal, in any state or Federal court, of at least three felony convictions, at least one of which was on behalf of the defendant.

(c) *Trial counsel.* If otherwise qualified under these standards, and with the consent of the client, a defendant's capital trial counsel may seek to be appointed capital appellate counsel on the same defendant's appeal.

(d) *Waiver.* If an attorney cannot meet one or more of the requirements set forth above, the screening panel, after consideration of the recommendation of the Capital Defender Office, may waive such requirement by demonstration by the attorney that he or she, by reason of extensive civil litigation and/or appellate experience or other exceptional qualifications, is capable of providing effective representation as appellate counsel in a capital case.

(2) Applications to Capital Defender Office.

(a) *Applications.* In support of an application, an attorney shall submit to the Capital Defender Office a form prescribed by the Capital Defender Office and approved by the Administrative Board of the Courts. It shall require the attorney to demonstrate that he or she has fully satisfied the requirements set forth above. The attorney shall also identify any requirements that he or she requests be waived, and shall set forth in detail his or her appellate experience or other exceptional qualifications that justify waiver.

(b) *Required submissions.* In support of an application, an attorney shall submit to the Capital Defender Office:

(1) at least two appellate briefs, written exclusively or primarily by the applicant, the opposing briefs, and the decisions;

(2) descriptions of any capital or other criminal appellate advocacy or other criminal practice program attended;

(3) the names, addresses and phone numbers of two prosecutors and two defense attorneys, current or former, including at least one appellate adversary, familiar with the applicant's work as an effective advocate;

(4) the applicant may submit the name, address and phone number of one appellate judge, if the judge is familiar with the applicant's work as an effective advocate; and

(5) any other material that may be relevant to fully evaluate the applicant's appellate qualifications and experience.

(3) Creation of Court of Appeals roster.

(a) *Delivery to screening panel.* The Capital

Defender Office shall review each application to determine that it is complete. The Capital Defender Office shall deliver all completed applications, within 30 days of their receipt, to the appropriate screening panel, together with a statement setting forth the status of the attorney's completion of the training required by section (5) below, and its recommendations to the screening panel with respect to whether the attorney is qualified for appointment as appellate counsel in a capital case. The appropriate screening panel shall be the panel in the judicial department in which the attorney has his or her principal office for the practice of law.

(1) *Designation by screening panel.* Within 30 days of receipt of the application, each screening panel shall designate those attorneys deemed qualified for appointment as appellate counsel in a capital case, and shall report those designations to the Court of Appeals.

(c) *Waiver or deferral of required submissions.* If an attorney cannot provide each of the above items, the screening panel, upon demonstration that the attorney is capable of providing effective representation as appellate counsel in a capital case, and after consideration of the recommendation of the Capital Defender Office, may:

(1) defer submission of any item(s) for a reasonable time, and in the interim designate the attorney as a qualified appellate counsel; or

(2) waive such submission.

(d) *Establishment of the roster.* The Court of Appeals shall incorporate the names of each attorney found qualified by a screening panel into a single roster of attorneys qualified for appointment as appellate counsel in a capital case.

(4) Additions to Court of Appeals roster.

(a) *Requests for reconsideration.* Any attorney whose application for designation as qualified appellate counsel is rejected by a screening panel may apply to the Court of Appeals for reconsideration of his or her application pursuant to such procedures as may be prescribed by the Court of Appeals.

(b) *Determination by the Court of Appeals.* The Court of Appeals shall review each such application pursuant to the criteria set forth in these standards, including consideration of the recommendations of the Capital Defender Office and of the screening panel, and may add that attorney to the roster of qualified appellate counsel if the court deems the attorney qualified to serve as appellate counsel in a capital case.

(5) Training.

(a) *Certification.* An attorney shall not be eligible to be appointed as appellate counsel in a capital case unless the Capital Defender Office shall certify that the attorney satisfactorily has completed a capital appellate advocacy course prescribed by the Capital Defender Office and approved by the Administrative Board of the Courts.

(b) *Interim certification.* The screening panel, or the Court of Appeals, in its discretion, may permit an attorney to be eligible for such appointment if the attorney meets all of the other requirements for qualification and experience, and the Capital Defender Office confirms that such attorney is in active pursuit of such training and certification.

(6) Retention of eligibility.

(a) *On-going training.* To remain eligible for appointment as counsel on a capital appeal, an attorney must attend and successfully complete capital training sessions as prescribed by the Capital Defender Office.

(b) *Removal from the Court of Appeals roster.* The Court of Appeals may remove from its roster of attorneys any attorney who, in the court's judgment, has not provided competent, thorough representation.

515.2 Standards for State post-conviction counsel in capital cases.

(1) State post-conviction qualifications and experience.

(a) *State post-conviction counsel.* To be eligible to be appointed as lead counsel on an initial motion pursuant to section 440.10 or 440.20 of the Criminal Procedure Law and any appeal therefrom in a capital case, an attorney must demonstrate that he or she:

(1) has at least six years criminal trial, criminal appellate or State or Federal post-conviction experience, or has at least four years of concentrated criminal or civil litigation experience;

(2) is familiar with:

(i) the practice and procedure of the trial and appellate courts of New York, including the New York Court of Appeals; and

(ii) the practice and procedure of the Federal courts with regard to Federal *habeas corpus* petitions;

(3) has conducted 12 trials before judges, arbitration panels or juries to verdict, decision, or hung jury, in serious and complex civil or criminal cases;

(4) has had primary responsibility for the appeal of at least five felony convictions in any state or Federal court, at least three of which were on behalf of the defendant, and at least three of which were orally argued by the attorney;

(5) has substantial familiarity with, and extensive experience in the use of, expert witnesses and scientific and medical evidence including, but not limited to, mental health and pathology evidence; and

(6) meets two of the following criteria:

(i) has tried five homicides to verdict or hung jury with at least three as defense counsel;

(ii) has, at the trial level, represented to disposition defendants in eight homicide cases;

(ii) has represented capital defendants in three State or Federal post-conviction proceedings;

(iv) has brought five motions, pursuant to section 440.10 or 440.20 of the Criminal Procedure Law, where hearings were held and witnesses examined.

(b) *Waiver.* If an attorney cannot meet one or more of the requirements set forth above, the screening panel, after consideration of the recommendation of the Capital Defender Office, may waive such requirement upon demonstration by the attorney that he or she, by reason of extensive criminal or civil litigation, 440 motion practice, appellate and/or post-conviction experience or other exceptional qualifications, is capable of providing effective representation as post-conviction counsel in a capital case.

(2) Applications to Capital Defender Office.

(a) *Applications.* In support of an application, an attorney shall submit to the Capital Defender Office a form prescribed by the Capital Defender Office and approved by the Administrative Board of the Courts. It shall require the attorney to demonstrate that he or she has fully satisfied the requirements set forth above. The attorney shall also identify any requirement that he or she requests be waived, and shall set forth in detail his or her criminal or civil litigation, 440 motion practice, appellate and/or post-conviction experience or other exceptional qualification that justify waiver.

(b) *Required submissions.* In support of an application, an attorney shall submit to the Capital Defender Office:

(1) a description of a trial or post-conviction strategy in a case handled by the attorney and reflective of the attorney's thorough advocacy. This strategy may have, for instance, aimed to achieve a favorable pre-trial disposition or to alter the range of sentencing options;

(2) at least two memoranda of law prepared by the attorney in connection with separate cases;

(3) at least two appellate briefs written exclusively or primarily by the applicant, the opposing briefs, and the decisions;

(4) the names, addresses, and phone numbers of two prosecutors and two defense attorneys, current or former, including at least one adversary, familiar with the applicant's work as an effective advocate;

(5) the applicant may submit the name, address, and phone number of one judge, if the judge is familiar with the applicant's work as an effective advocate;

(6) a description of specialized trial, appellate

or post-conviction capital defense training programs regularly attended; and

(7) any other material that may be relevant to fully evaluate the applicant's qualifications and experience.

(3) Creation of Court of Appeals roster.

(a) *Delivery to screening panel.* The Capital Defender Office shall review each application to determine that it is complete. The Capital Defender Office shall deliver all completed applications, within 30 days of their receipt, to the appropriate screening panel, together with a statement setting forth the status of the attorney's completion of the training required by section 5, below, and its recommendations to the screening panel with respect to whether the attorney is qualified for appointment as post-conviction counsel in a capital case. The appropriate screening panel shall be the panel in the judicial department in which the attorney has his or her principal office for the practice of law.

(b) *Designation by screening panel.* Within 30 days of receipt of the application, each screening panel shall designate those attorneys deemed qualified for appointment as post-conviction counsel in a capital case, and shall report those designations to the Court of Appeals.

(c) *Waiver or deferral of required submissions.* If an attorney cannot provide each of the above items, the screening panel, upon demonstration that the attorney is capable of providing effective representation as post-conviction counsel in a capital case, and after consideration of the recommendations of the Capital Defender Office, may:

(1) defer submission of any item(s) for a reasonable time, and in the interim designate the attorney as a qualified post-conviction counsel; or

(2) waive such submission.

(d) *Establishment of the roster.* The Court of Appeals shall incorporate the names of each attorney found qualified by a screening panel into a single roster of attorneys qualified for appointment as post-conviction counsel in a capital case.

(4) Additions to Court of Appeals roster.

(a) *Requests for reconsideration.* Any attorney whose application for designation as qualified post-conviction counsel is rejected by a screening panel may apply to the Court of Appeals for reconsideration of his or her application pursuant to such procedures as may be prescribed by the Court of Appeals.

(b) *Determination by the Court of Appeals.* The Court of Appeals shall review each such application pursuant to the criteria set forth in these standards, including consideration of the recommendations of the Capital Defender Office and of the screening panel, and may add that attorney to the roster of qualified post-conviction counsel if the court deems the attorney qualified to serve as post-conviction counsel in a capital case.

(5) Training.

(a) *Certification.* An attorney shall not be eligible to be appointed as post-conviction counsel in a capital case unless the Capital Defender Office shall certify that the attorney satisfactorily has completed a capital post-conviction course prescribed by the Capital Defender Office and approved by the Administrative Board of the Courts.

(b) *Interim certification.* The screening panel, or the Court of Appeals, in its discretion, may permit an attorney to be eligible for such appointment if the attorney meets all of the other requirements for qualification and experience, and the Capital Defender Office confirms that such attorney is in active pursuit of such training and certification.

(6) Retention of eligibility.

(a) *On-going training.* To remain eligible for appointment as counsel on an initial motion pursuant to section 440.10 or 440.20 of the Criminal Procedure Law and an appeal therefrom, an attorney must attend and successfully complete capital training sessions as prescribed by the Capital Defender Office.

(b) *Removal from the Court of Appeals roster.* The Court of Appeals may remove from its roster of attorneys any attorney who, in the court's judgment, has not provided competent, thorough representation.

PART 540

UNIFORM PROCEDURES FOR APPEALS FROM PRETRIAL FINDINGS OF MENTAL RETARDATION IN CAPITAL CASES

COURT RULES

§ 540.0 Preamble.

Acting pursuant to the rulemaking authority invested in this Court by New York Constitution, article VI, section 30 and Laws of 1995, chapter 1, section 20, the Court of Appeals establishes these Uniform Procedures for Appeals from Pretrial Findings of Mental Retardation in Capital Cases.

§ 540.1 Delegation to the Presiding Justices of the Appellate Division.

The Presiding Justices of the Appellate Division shall adopt uniform rules to ensure that appeals from pretrial findings of mental retardation in capital cases pursuant to Laws of 1995, chapter 1, section 20 are expeditiously perfected, reviewed and determined.

RULES OF THE FIRST JUDICIAL DEPARTMENT APPELLATE DIVISION

(The following rules are not a complete presentation of the First Department's Rules. Only those rules that are relevant to criminal or related matters are set forth. For a complete set of rules for civil practice, see *NY CLS Desk Edition Civil Practice Annual* **(LexisNexis).)**

PART 600

APPEALS

§ 600.1 Sessions of the court; four justices present

(a) The court will convene at 2 o'clock in the afternoon during the appointed terms of the court for the hearing of appeals except on Fridays when the court will convene at 10 o'clock in the forenoon.

(b) Special sessions of the court may be scheduled for such time or such purposes as the court may direct.

(c) When a cause is argued or submitted to the court with four justices present, it shall, whenever necessary, be deemed submitted also to any other duly qualified justice of the court, unless objection is noted at the time of argument or submission.

§ 600.2 Motions generally; special proceedings; calendars; submission.

(a) *Motions generally.*

(1) Any application, brought on by notice of motion, may be made returnable on any regular business day of the court during the period September 1 through June 30, and on Mondays during July and August, at 10 o'clock in the forenoon unless otherwise ordered by a justice of the court.

July and August, at 10 o'clock in the forenoon unless otherwise ordered by a justice of the court.

(2) Cross-motions shall be made returnable the same day as the original motion and shall be served not less than three days before the return date.

(3) The moving papers shall state the nature of the application or relief sought; the return day; and the names, addresses and telephone numbers of the attorneys for all parties in support, and who are entitled to notice, of the application. Applications made before the appeal is heard must contain a copy of the notice of appeal or other paper which first invoked the jurisdiction of the court, and the order, judgment or determination sought to be reviewed. Applications made for modification, resettlement, etc. of an order of this court shall contain a copy of the order and opinion, if any.

(4) By noon of the business day preceding the day on which a motion is returnable the moving party must file with the clerk the original moving papers with proof of service thereof within the time:

(i) prescribed by CPLR 2214(b) and 5516 or

(ii) directed by a justice of the court.

(5) Answering and replying papers, if any, must be served within the time:

(i) prescribed by CPLR 2214 (b) or

(ii) as directed by a justice of the court, and the originals thereof with proof of service must be filed by 4 o'clock in the afternoon of the business day preceding the day on which the application is returnable, unless for good cause shown they are permitted to be filed at a later time.

(6) All papers may be filed either by personal delivery or by ordinary mail. If filed by mail, they shall be considered filed only upon receipt; and the envelope must be marked "Motion Papers." If an acknowledgment of receipt of the papers is desired, there must be enclosed with the papers being filed by mail a self-addressed postage-prepaid postal card bearing the title of the cause, the nature of the motion, the date on which it is returnable and a statement of the papers filed. Such postal card, when stamped and returned by mail, shall serve as a receipt for the papers listed thereon.

(7) When an application is presented for an interim stay or other relief pending determination of a motion, the party seeking such relief must inform the clerk at the time of submission whether the opposing party has been notified of the application and whether such party opposes or consents to the granting of the relief sought. Time and manner of service of motion papers shall be directed by a justice. The relief granted to the moving party will be by brief order appended to the notice of motion. The justice's signature will

apply to the stay or provisional remedy only; there will be no direction to a party "to show cause" why an order should not be entered.

(8) All parties filing papers pertaining to a motion or special proceeding shall include therewith a stamped self-addressed envelope.

(b) *Special proceedings.* Unless a justice of the court otherwise directs, all special proceedings originating in the court, except those commenced pursuant to CPLR 506(b)(4), shall be returnable at 10 o'clock in the forenoon of any regular business day of the court during the period August 1 through June 20, and all papers shall be filed in the manner and within the time prescribed in paragraphs (a)(3) and (a)(4) of this section, except that the moving and opposing parties shall submit to the clerk seven conformed copies in addition to the original moving or opposing papers with proof of service of a copy thereof.

(c) *No calendars.* No calendar of motions and special proceedings shall be published or called.

(d) *Submission of motions and special proceedings.*

(1) All motions and special proceedings, except those commenced pursuant to CPLR 506(b)(4), unless adjourned or withdrawn, shall be deemed submitted on the return date thereof. Attendance of attorneys shall not be required and oral argument will not be heard.

(2) Applications brought on by notice of motion or order may be adjourned once by consent of the parties. Except in extraordinary circumstances, in the absence of such consent or approval of the court the application will be deemed submitted on the adjourned return date. Notices or stipulations of adjournment shall be submitted in writing.

§ 600.3 Applications for leave to appeal to Appellate Division.

(a) *When addressed to a justice.* An application to a justice of the court for leave to appeal pursuant to CPLR 5701(c) shall be made within the time prescribed by CPLR 5513(c). The papers upon which such an application is made must state whether any previous application has been made and, if so, to whom and the reason given, if any, for the denial of leave or refusal to entertain the application if that be the case.

(b) *When addressed to the court.*

(1) Where leave of this court is required for an appeal to be taken to it, the application for such leave must be made in the manner and within the time prescribed by CPLR 5513 and 5516. Applications pursuant to CPLR 5703 for leave to appeal from a determination of the Appellate Term shall be made only after denial of a motion for leave to appeal made at the Appellate Term as provided by section 640.9 of the Appellate Term rules.

(2) The papers upon which an application for leave to appeal is made must contain a copy of the order or judgment and opinion, if any, of the court below, a copy of the record in the court below, a concise statement of the grounds of alleged error and a copy of the order of the lower court denying leave to appeal, if any. If the application is to review an order of the Appellate Term granting or affirming the granting of a new trial or hearing, the papers must also contain a stipulation by the appellant consenting to the entry of judgment absolute against appellant in the event of an affirmance by the court.

(3) All applications for leave to appeal addressed to the court shall be submitted without oral argument and shall be made returnable at 10 o'clock in the forenoon of a regular business day of the court during the period September 1 through June 20.

§ 600.4 Calendars.

Appeals shall be noticed as enumerated or nonenumerated.

(a) The following appeals are to be noticed as enumerated:

(1) Appeals from final orders and judgments of the Supreme Court, other than those dismissing a cause for failure to prosecute, for failure to serve a complaint or for failure to obey an order of disclosure or to stay or compel arbitration.

(2) Appeals from decrees or orders of the Surrogate's Court finally determining a special proceeding.

(3) Appeals from orders granting or denying motions for a new trial.

(4) Appeals from orders granting or denying motions for summary judgment.

(5) Appeals from orders granting or denying motions to dismiss a complaint, a cause of action, a counter-claim or an answer in point of law.

(6) Appeals from orders to the Appellate Term.

(7) Appeals from judgments or orders in criminal proceedings.

(8) Special proceedings transferred to this court for disposition.

(9) Controversies on agreed statement of facts.

(10) Appeals from orders of the Family Court finally determining a special proceeding.

(11) Appeals from orders granting or denying custody of minors after a hearing.

(12) Special proceedings challenging determination of the New York City Tax appeals tribunal.

(13) Such other appeals as the court or a justice thereof may designate as enumerated.

(b) All other types of appeals not set forth in subdivision (a) of this section shall be noticed as nonenumerated.

§ 600.5 Alternative methods of prosecuting appeal; time to file record, appendix or agreed statement.

At appellant's option, an appeal may be prosecuted upon a record or statement authorized by CPLR 5526, 5527 or 5528.

(a) *The appendix system.*

(1) If the appeal is prosecuted by the appendix system pursuant to CPLR 5528(a)(5), appellant shall subpoena from the clerk of the court from which the appeal is taken the papers constituting the record on appeal as set forth in CPLR 5526 and cause them to be filed with the clerk of this court within 30 days after settlement of the transcript of proceedings or statement in lieu of a transcript. At the time the subpoena is served, the appellant shall deliver to the clerk two copies of the statement required by CPLR 5531.

(2) The clerk from whom the papers are subpoenaed shall prefix one copy of the statement required by CPLR 5531 to the papers and firmly fasten such papers across the top, exclusive of the transcript or statement in lieu thereof, if any, and transmit them to the clerk of this court, together with the additional copy of the statement required by CPLR 5531 and a certificate listing the papers constituting the record on appeal and stating whether all such papers are included in the papers transmitted.

(3) If a transcript of proceedings or statement in lieu of a stenographic transcript as settled is not included in the papers so subpoenaed, appellant shall file the ribbon copy of the transcript or the statement at the time of filing the appellant's brief. Where feasible, the parties shall stipulate, pursuant to CPLR 5525, subdivision (b), that only a portion of the transcript of proceedings need to be filed.

(4) Where a full or partial transcript of proceedings is made part of the record on appeal, appellant shall serve upon, or make available to, respondent a conformed copy thereof in the manner and at the time prescribed by subdivision (e), *infra.*

(b) *Agreed statement in lieu of record.*

(1) If the appeal is prosecuted pursuant to CPLR 5527, appellant shall reproduce the statement in lieu of a record on appeal as a joint appendix by printing or such other method of reproduction authorized by CPLR 5529. There shall be prefixed to these papers the statement required by CPLR 5531.

(2) Appellant shall file the original and 19 copies of the statement, with proof of service of two copies, within 30 days after approval of the statement by the court from which the appeal is taken, as required by CPLR 5527.

(c) *Optional full record.* If appellant elects to proceed on a completely reproduced record on appeal as authorized by the provisions of paragraph 5, subdivision (a), of CPLR 5528, the record shall be printed or otherwise reproduced as provided in section 600.10 of this Part, and in such case an appendix shall not be required. A copy of the record, duly certified, as provided in section 600.10(b)(1)(viii) of this Part, and 19 copies of such certified reproduced record, with proof of service of two copies, shall be filed within 30 days after settlement of the transcript of proceedings. Where feasible, the parties shall stipulate, pursuant to CPLR 5525, subdivision (b), that only a portion of the proceedings need be filed.

(d) *When record does not involve settlement or approval.* If the appeal is prosecuted upon a record which does not involve a transcript or statement requiring settlement or approval by the court from which the appeal is taken, the record on appeal must be filed or caused to be filed within 30 days after filing of the notice of appeal.

(e) *Settlement of transcript.*

(1) Within 15 days after receiving the transcript from the court reporter or any other source the appellant shall make any proposed amendments and serve them and a copy of the transcript upon the respondent. Appellant may serve on respondent, together with the copy of the transcript and the proposed amendments, a notice of settlement containing a specific reference to this subdivision, and stating that if respondent fails to propose amendments or objections within 15 days the provision of paragraph (2) of this subdivision shall apply. Within 15 days after such service the respondent shall make any proposed amendments or objections to the proposed amendments of the appellant and serve them upon the appellant. At any time thereafter and on at least four days' notice to the adverse party, the transcript and the proposed amendments and objects thereto shall be submitted for settlement to the judge or referee before whom the proceedings were had if the parties cannot agree on the amendments to the transcript. The original of the transcript shall be corrected by the appellant in accordance with the agreement of the parties or the direction of the court and its correctness shall be certified to thereon by the parties or the judge or referee before whom the proceedings were had. When he serves his brief upon the respondent the appellant shall also serve a conformed copy of the transcript or deposit it in the office of the clerk of the court of original instance who shall make it available to respondent.

(2) If the appellant has timely proposed amendments and served them and the transcript and the notice provided by paragraph (1) of this subdivision and no amendments or objections are proposed by the respondent within the time limited by this rule, the transcript, certified as correct by the court reporter, together with appellant's proposed amendments, shall be deemed correct without the necessity of a stipulation by the parties certifying to its correctness or the settlement of the transcript by the judge or referee. The appellant shall affix to such transcript an affirmation, certifying to his compliance with the time limitation and the respondent's failure to propose amendments or objections within the time prescribed.

(f) *Transcript—number to be prepared by court reporter.* Pursuant to CPLR 5525(a), in all appeals taken from judgments or orders entered in this department, the appellant may request that only the ribbon copy of the typewritten transcript be prepared by the reporter. If such request be made, only the ribbon copy shall be required to be prepared by the reporter and furnished to the appellant. If the appeal is by the appendix method, such ribbon copy shall be included in the record on appeal for use by the parties and the court.

§ 600.6 Appeals from Family Court.

An appeal from the Family Court may be prosecuted in accordance with any of the procedures specified in section 600.5 of these rules. Any party to such an appeal may elect to file eight reproduced copies of the brief and appendix, if any, with proof of service of one copy, in lieu of a printed or otherwise reproduced brief and appendix as required by section 600.10 of this Part. The appeal may also be perfected upon the original record (transcript of hearing, if any, to be ordered by appellant and filed with the clerk of the Family Court) and eight reproduced copies of the brief. There shall be prefixed to the record the statement required by CPLR 5531; an additional copy of the statement shall be filed with the clerk of this court.

§ 600.7 Action on submitted facts; transferred causes.

(a) *Submission of a controversy.* Unless the court otherwise directs, the agreed statement of facts in an action submitted to this court pursuant to CPLR 3222 shall be printed or reproduced by any other authorized method. A copy of the statement required by CPLR 5531 shall be prefixed to the papers constituting the submission. The original and 19 copies thereof with proof of service of three copies are to be filed at the time of filing plaintiff's brief and two copies of the note of issue. All such causes shall be noticed as enumerated in accordance with the provisions of section 600.11 of this Part.

(b) *Transferred causes.* Article 78 proceedings transferred to this court by an Appellate Division of another department pursuant to CPLR 5711 may be prosecuted in accordance with any of the procedures specified in section 600.5 of this Part, except that the petitioner or appellant, whichever the case may be, shall file the record or cause the same to be filed with the clerk of this court within 30 days after entry of the order of transference.

(c) *State Division of Human Rights proceedings.* State Division of Human Rights proceedings, transferred to this court pursuant to Executive Law, section 298, shall be deemed enumerated and prosecuted in accordance with sections 600.5 and 600.11 of this Part. No oral argument shall be permitted. The division, upon receipt by it of petitioner's brief, shall promptly file the original record with this court.

§ 600.8 Appeals in criminal cases.

(a) *Record and briefs.* (1) In appeals in criminal cases, other than those in which permission to proceed on the original record is granted, the appellant may elect to proceed by any of the methods specified in section 600.5 of this Part and the content and form of the record on appeal or appendix shall be as prescribed by section 600.10 of this Part.

(2) The content and form of briefs shall be as prescribed in section 600.10 of this Part and in addition thereto, there shall be included at the beginning of the main brief submitted by appellant a statement setting forth the decision and judgment appealed from; the sentence imposed, if any, and whether an application for an order of stay of judgment pending determination of the appeal was made and, if so, the date of such application, the court to which it was made, and the decision and opinion of the court.

(b) *When to be heard.* Appeals in criminal cases shall be placed on the calendar in the manner described in section 600.11 (b)-(f) of this Part, but must be brought on for argument within 120 days after the last day in which a notice of appeal was required to be filed, unless the time to perfect the appeal is enlarged by the court or a justice thereof.

(c) *Enlargements of time.* Every application for an enlargement of time within which to perfect an appeal for argument or submission, or for an extension of time to serve and file the record and brief shall be accompanied by an affidavit satisfactorily explaining the delay and stating whether there is an order of stay of judgment pending determination of the appeal outstanding and, if so, the date such order was granted and whether the appellant is free on bail or his own recognizance.

(d) *Application for certificate granting leave to appeal.* (1) Application for a certificate granting leave to appeal to this court shall be made, in writing, within 30 days after service of the order upon the applicant, shall give 15 days' notice to the district attorney, shall be filed with proof of service and shall be submitted without oral argument.

(2) The moving papers for a certificate

granting leave to appeal shall be addressed to the court for assignment to a justice, and shall state:

(i) the return day;

(ii) the name and address of the party seeking leave to appeal and the name of the district attorney;

(iii) the indictment number;

(iv) the questions of law or fact which ought to be reviewed; and

(v) that no prior application for such certificate has been made.

(3) The moving papers must include:

(i) a copy of the order sought to be reviewed; and

(ii) a copy of the memorandum or opinion of the court below or a statement that there was none.

(4) Answering papers or a statement that there is no opposition to the application shall be served and filed not later than noon of the third day before the return date stated in the application. Answering papers shall discuss the merits of the application, or shall state;

(i) that the file has been reviewed and includes a response by the district attorney covering the matters raised in the paper submitted by the applicant in the court below and an opinion or memorandum of the justice of that court; and

(ii) that the application for a certificate granting leave to appeal does not contain any new allegations.

(e) *Expedited appeal of an order reducing an indictment or dismissing an indictment and directing the filing of a prosecutor's information.* (1) This subdivision shall govern the procedure for an expedited appeal to the Appellate Division, pursuant to CPL 210.20(6)(c), 450.20(1-a) and 450.55, of an order by a superior court reducing a count or counts of an indictment or dismissing an indictment and directing the filing of a prosecutor's information.

(2) After the people file and serve a notice of appeal pursuant to CPL 460.10(1), either party may request that the court expedite the appeal. If a request is made, the court shall hear the appeal on an expedited basis as set forth in this subdivision.

(3) (i) The Appellate Division shall establish an expedited briefing schedule for the appeal. Briefs may be typewritten or reproduced. The people shall file nine copies of a brief and an appendix, which shall include a copy of the indictment and the trial court's decision and order. The respondent shall file nine copies of a brief and, if necessary, an appendix. One copy of the brief and appendix shall be served on opposing counsel.

(ii) The appeal may be taken on one original

record, which shall include copies of the indictment, the motion papers, the trial court's decision and order, and the notice of appeal.

(iii) The people shall file with the Appellate Division, separately from the record, one copy of the grand jury minutes.

(iv) The court shall give preference to the hearing of an appeal perfected pursuant to this subdivision and shall determine the appeal as expeditiously as possible.

(f) *Appeals taken by the people.* An appeal taken by the people must be perfected by serving a copy of the appellant's brief upon respondent's appellate attorney, or in the event that no appellate has appeared for respondent, upon the attorney who last appeared for him in the trial court, within nine months of the filing of the notice of appeal.

(g) *Assignment of appellate counsel.* An attorney who represents a defendant in the superior court and is a member of the Assigned Counsel Plan appellate panel, with defendant's written consent, may apply to the Appellate Division for appointment as appellate counsel.

* * *

§ 600.10 Format and content of records, appendices and briefs.

(a) *Form and size.*

(1) Generally; paper and page size. Records, appendices and briefs shall be reproduced by any method that produces a permanent, legible, black on white copy and shall be on a good grade of white, opaque, unglazed recycled paper that satisfies the requirements of paragraph (e) of this section. Paper shall measure vertically 11 inches on the bound edge and horizontally 8½ inches. The clerk may refuse to accept for filing a paper which is not legible or otherwise does not comply with the provisions of this Part.

(2) *Binding.* Every record, appendix or brief shall be securely bound on the left side; when such binding is done by means of a metal fastener or other hard material which protrudes or presents sharp edges, such binding shall be covered by linen or plastic masking tape or similar material. The use of Acco, spiral or other bulky binding edge binders is discouraged.

(3) *Typeface and type size.* Records, appendices and briefs shall be in clear serifed, proportionally-space typeface, such as times new roman, or serifed mono-spaced typeface, such as courier. Proportionally spaced typeface shall be no less than 14 point size, with the exception that footnotes shall be in type of no less than 12 point size and headings, shall be in type no greater than 15 point size. Monospaced typeface shall be no less than 12 point size, with the exception that footnotes shall be in type no less than 10 point size and headings shall be in type no greater than

14 point size. Typewritten text shall be no less than elite size.

(4) *Page format.* Records, appendices and briefs shall be double spaced, with the exception that footnotes, headlines, indented quotations, and a full size facsimile reproduction of the opinion of the trial court taken from the official state reports may be single spaced. The margin on each side of each page shall be at least one inch; the text on each page shall not exceed 9 inches by 6½ inches.

(5) *Captions.* The parties to all appeals shall be designated in the record and briefs by adding the word "Appellant," "Respondent," etc., as the case may be, following the party's name, e.g. "Plaintiff-Respondent," "Defendant-Appellant," "Petitioner-Appellant," "Respondent-Respondent," etc. Parties who have not appealed and against whom the appeal has not been taken, shall be listed separately and designated as they were in the court below, e.g. "Plaintiff," "Defendant," "Petitioner," "Respondent." In appeals from the Surrogate's Courts or from judgments on trust accountings, the captions shall contain the title used in the court below, including the name of the decedent or grantor, followed by a listing of all parties to the appeal, properly designated. In proceedings and actions originating in this court, the parties shall be designated "Petitioner" and "Respondent" or "Plaintiff" and "Defendant."

(6) *Numbering.* Page of records and briefs shall be numbered consecutively. Pages of appendices shall be separately numbered consecutively, each number preceded by the letter "A"; a respondent's appendix, if any, shall be numbered consecutively and may be preceded by the letters "RA."

(7) *Page headings.* The subject matter of each page of the record or appendix shall be stated at the top thereof, except that in the case of papers other than testimony, the subject matter of the paper may be stated at the top of the first page of each paper together with the page numbers of the first and last pages thereof. In the case of testimony, the name of the witness, by whom he was called and whether the testimony is direct, cross, redirect or re-cross examination, shall be stated at the top of each page.

(8) *Motion papers.* Each affidavit or other paper contained in a record on an appeal from an order shall be preceded by a description thereof that must specify on whose behalf it was read. The name of the affiant shall be stated at the top of each page containing an affidavit.

(9) *Questions and answers.* The answer to a question in the appendix shall not begin a new paragraph.

(10) *Quotations.* Asterisks or other appropriate means shall be used to indicate omissions in quoted excerpts. Reference shall be made to the source of the excerpts quoted. Quotations in briefs

may be single spaced, indented. Where an excerpt in the appendix is testimony of a witness quoted from the record the beginning of each page of the transcript shall be indicated by parenthetical insertion of the transcript page number.

(11) *Citation of decisions.* New York decisions shall be cited from the official reports, if any. All other decisions shall be cited from the official reports, if any, and also from the National Reporter System if they are there reported. Decisions not reported officially or in the National Reporter System shall be cited from the most available sources.

(b) *Record, what to contain.*

(1) If appellant elects to proceed on an optional full record as authorized by subdivision (c) of section 600.5 of this Part, the record shall contain, in the following order:

(i) An index of the record's contents, listing and describing each paper separately. That part of the index relating to exhibits shall concisely indicate the contents or nature and date of each exhibit and the pages in the record where it is reproduced and where it is admitted to evidence. The part of the index relating to the transcript of testimony shall separately list each witness and shall state as to each witness the page at which direct, cross, re-direct and re-cross examination begins. Such index shall also contain a reference to the pages where a motion for the dismissal of a complaint or for the direction of verdict, or an oral decision of the court, appealed from, appears.

(ii) A statement pursuant to CPLR 5531.

(iii) If the appeal be from a final judgment, the notice of appeal, the judgment roll, the corrected transcript of the proceedings or a statement pursuant to subdivision (d) of CPLR 5525 if a trial or hearing was held, any relevant exhibits, or copies of them, in the court of original instance, any other reviewable order, and any opinions in the case.

(iv) If the appeal be from an interlocutory judgment or any order, the notice of appeal, the judgment or order appealed from, the transcript, if any; the papers and other exhibits upon which the judgment or order was founded, and any opinions in the case.

(v) A stipulation or order settling the transcript pursuant to subdivision (c) of CPLR 5525.

(vi) The opinion in the case or a statement that there was none.

(vii) A stipulation, if any, dispensing with the printing or filing of exhibits.

(a) Exhibits may be omitted upon stipulation of the attorneys for the parties, approved by a justice of the court, which shall contain a list of the exhibits to be omitted and a brief description of each exhibit. Exhibits thus omitted unless of a bulk nature as defined *infra* shall be filed with the clerk of the court not later than the Wednesday preceding the first day of the term for which the appeal was noticed. Exhibits of a bulky nature (cartons, file drawers, voluminous folders, ledgers, machinery, weapons, etc.) thus omitted need not be filed with the court but shall be kept in readiness by the parties and delivered to the court on telephone notice; a letter, showing that copy has been sent to the adversary, listing such exhibits and stating that they will be available on telephone notice shall be filed with the clerk of the court not later than the Wednesday preceding the first day of the term for which the appeal was noticed.

(b) Exhibits which are not relevant to an appeal may be omitted upon stipulation of the attorneys for the parties which shall contain a list of exhibits to be omitted, a brief description of each exhibit and a statement that said exhibits will not be relied upon or cited in the briefs of the parties to the appeal.

(viii) A certificate of the proper clerk, or a stipulation waiving certification of the papers pursuant to CPLR 5532, or a certificate subscribed by the attorney certifying to the correctness of the papers pursuant to CPLR 2105.

(2) On an appeal by permission under CPLR 5701 from an order granting or denying a motion for a more definite statement of a vague or ambiguous pleading or for striking any irrelevant, redundant, scandalous or prejudicial matter unnecessarily inserted in a pleading, the portion of the pleading to which the motion is directed must be italicized if the record is printed or underscored if otherwise reproduced.

(3) On the outside front cover of the record shall appear the title of the case, the names, addresses and telephone numbers of the attorneys for the parties, and the index number in the court of original instance. (See paragraph (a)(5), *supra.*)

(c) *Appendix, what to contain.*

(1) In accordance with CPLR 5528, the appendix of appellant or the joint appendix shall contain those parts of the record necessary to consider the questions involved. A failure to comply with the requirements may result in rejection of the appendix or may effect the imposition of costs.

(2) The appendix should include at least, if in the record, the following:

(i) Notice of appeal; judgment appealed from; decree appealed from; order appealed from or sought to be enforced; notice of motion; order to show cause; opinion (or a statement that there was none); findings of fact and conclusions of law; report or referee or hearing examiner; charge to the jury; verdict; and pleadings if their sufficiency, content, or form is in issue or material.

(ii) Relevant excerpts from transcripts of testimony or papers in connection with a motion.

These must contain all the testimony or averments upon which appellant relies or upon which appellant has reason to believe respondent will rely. Such excerpts must not be misleading because of incompleteness or lack of surrounding context.

(iii) Copies of critical exhibits, including significant photographs, to the extent practicable. Critical exhibits may be omitted upon stipulation of the attorneys for the parties, approved by a justice of the court, which shall contain a list of the exhibits to be omitted and a brief description of each exhibit. A copy of this stipulation shall be included in the appendix.

(iv) Exhibits unless of a bulky nature as defined *infra* shall be filed with the clerk of the court not later than the Wednesday preceding the first day of the term for which the appeal was noticed.

(*a*) Exhibits of a bulky nature (cartons, file drawers, voluminous folders, ledgers, machinery, weapons, etc.) omitted upon stipulation pursuant to subparagraph (c)(1)(iii), *supra*, need not be filed with the court but shall be kept in readiness by the parties and delivered to the court on telephone notice; a letter, showing that copy has been sent to the adversary, listing such exhibits and stating that they will be available on telephone notice shall be filed with the clerk of the court not later than the Wednesday preceding the first day of the term for which the appeal was noticed.

(*b*) Exhibits which are not relevant to an appeal may be omitted upon stipulation of the attorneys for the parties which shall contain a list of the exhibits to be omitted, a brief description of each exhibit and a statement that said exhibit will not be relied upon or cited in the briefs of the parties to the appeal.

(3) On the outside front cover of the appendix, whether bound separately or together with the brief, shall appear the title of the case and the names, addresses and the telephone numbers of the attorneys for the parties and the index number in the court of original instance. (See paragraph (a)(5), of this section)

(4) Each appendix shall contain an index of its contents conforming to the extent feasible to the form of index prescribed by subparagraph (b)(1) (i), of this section

(d) *Briefs, what to contain.*

(1) *Generally.* (i) Except by permission of the court, principal briefs shall not exceed 70 pages or 14,000 words. The calculation of the length of a brief shall not include pages containing the table of contents, tables of citations and any authorized addendum containing statutes, rules, regulations, etc. A word count calculation shall include all printed text on each page of the body of the brief. Except by permission of the court, reply briefs shall not exceed 35 pages or 7,000 words. An application for permission to file

an oversize brief shall be by letter that demonstrates with specificity good cause for the oversize submission and asserts that the brief has been edited for conciseness and to eliminate repetition. A copy of the proposed brief shall be submitted with the letter.

(ii) The name of counsel who is to argue or submit the appeal must appear at the upper right-hand corner of the cover of all briefs regardless by whom filed. Only one counsel shall be listed except when the court shall otherwise order (see section 600.11(f)(2) of this Part).

(iii) Unless authorized by the court, briefs to which are added or appended any matter, other than specifically authorized by this rule, shall not be accepted for filing. Bold face type shall not be used except in point headings or subheadings.

(iv) The opinion and findings, if any, of a hearing officer and the determination and decision of an administrative department, board or agency shall be appended to the main brief filed by such department, board or agency in any proceeding in which a printed, reproduced or typewritten record or appendix is dispensed with by statute or court order and the proceeding is permitted to be heard on the original papers.

(v) A brief prepared on a computer shall include at the end of the brief a "Printing Specifications Statement" that specifies the processing systems, typeface, point size and word count as calculated by the processing system used to prepare the brief.

(2) *Appellant's brief.* Each respondent shall file the same number of copies of respondent's brief as appellant is required to file, with proof of service on each appellant of the same number of copies as appellant has served. The brief of the appellant shall contain, in the following order:

(i) an index or table of contents including the titles of the points urged in the brief and a table of cases (alphabetically arranged), statutes and other authorities, indicating the pages of the brief where they are cited;

(ii) a concise statement, not exceeding two pages, of the questions involved without names, dates, amounts or particulars. Each question shall be numbered, set forth separately and followed immediately by the answer, if any, of the court from which the appeal is taken;

(iii) a concise statement of the nature of the case and of the facts which should be known to determine the questions involved, with supporting references to pages in the record or the appendix, including, if such be the case, a statement that proceedings on the judgment or order appealed from have been stayed pending a determination of the appeal. Such statement shall include, if such be the case, a statement that proceedings on the judgment or order appealed from have been stayed in whole or in part, by statute or order, pending a determination of the appeal, or that an application for a stay has been denied, giving the date of any order and the court in which the order granting or denying the stay was made;

(iv) the argument for the appellant, which shall be divided into points by appropriate headings distinctively printed;

(v) the statement required by CPLR 5531, as an addendum at the end of the brief;

(vi) the opinion upon which the judgment or order appealed from was based shall also be appended to the appellant's brief in any case in which the court has dispensed with a printed, reproduced or typewritten record or appendix and has permitted the appeal to be heard on the original papers; and

(vii) if the appeal is from an order involving alimony and counsel fees, the brief shall state the date of joinder of issue, if issue was joined, and whether the case has been noticed for trial.

(3) *Respondent's brief.* The brief of the respondent shall contain, in the following order:

(i) an index or a table of contents, including the titles of the points urged in the brief and a table of cases (alphabetically arranged), statutes and other authorities, indicating the pages of the brief where they are cited;

(ii) a counterstatement of the questions involved or of the nature and facts of the case, if the respondent disagrees with the statement of the appellant; and

(iii) the argument for the respondent, which shall be divided into points by appropriate headings distinctively printed.

(4) *Appellant's reply brief.* The reply brief of the appellant shall contain, in the following order:

(i) a table of contents and a table of cases (alphabetically arranged), statutes and other authorities, indicating the pages of the brief where they are cited; and

(ii) the reply for the appellant, without repetition of the arguments contained in the main brief, which shall be divided into points by appropriate headings distinctively printed.

§ 600.11 Perfecting and hearing appeals; calendar; adjournments.

(a) *When to be noticed.*

(1) Unless otherwise ordered by the court, all appeals or causes shall be placed on the calendar within 20 days after filing the record on appeal, statement in lieu of a record, the record in a proceeding commenced pursuant to CPLR 506(b)(4), or the papers in a transferred Article 78 proceeding, except that in the case of a submission of a controversy it shall be placed on the calendar at the time of filing the agreed statement of facts.

(2) The clerk will place no appeal or cause on the calendar where the necessary papers and brief are not offered for filing within the 20-day period prescribed by this section, unless the time for filing has been enlarged by a justice of the court.

(3) The clerk will place no civil appeal or cause on the calendar where the necessary papers and briefs are not offered for filing within nine months of the date of the notice of appeal from the judgment or order appealed from, in proceedings commenced pursuant to CPLR 506(b)(4) within nine months from the date of the petition is filed, in article 78 proceedings within nine months from the date of the order transferring the proceeding to the Appellate Division and in appeals to the Appellate Division by permission within nine months from the date of the order granting leave to appeal, unless the time for filing has been enlarged by order of the court. This nine-month limitation applies to all appeals including cross-appeals and may not be extended by agreement or stipulation of the parties. This paragraph does not extend the time of any party to take any step in connection with any appeal or cause. Such times are fixed by other rules and statutes and the time periods fixed by such other rules and statutes must be complied with.

(b) *How placed on calendar.*

(1) Enumerated appeals.

(i) An appeal or cause required by section 600.4 of this Part to be noticed as enumerated shall be placed on the calendar by the appellant or moving party filing with the clerk, at least 57 days before the first day of the terms for which the matter shall have been noticed, two copies of a note of issue with proof of service stating the date the notice of appeal was served, the date the record on appeal or statement in lieu thereof was filed, the nature of the appeal or cause, the court and county in which the action was commenced, the index or indictment number, the date judgment or order was entered, the name of the justice who made the decision, the term for which noticed, and the names, addresses and telephone numbers of the attorneys for all of the parties.

(ii) Nonenumerated Appeals. All other appeals shall be noticed as nonenumerated and shall be placed on the calendar in a manner identical to that for enumerated appeals.

(2) At the time of filing the note of issue, appellant or the moving party shall also file ten copies of the brief, or brief and appendix conforming to the requirements of section 600.10 of this Part, with proof of service of two copies thereof, except that where a typewritten brief is authorized or the appeal is from the Family Court, eight reproduced copies of the brief with proof of service of one copy may be filed.

(c) *Answering and reply briefs.* At least 27 days before the first day of the term for which the appeal or cause shall have been noticed, the respondent or opposing party shall file ten copies of the answering brief, or brief and appendix conforming to the requirements of section 600.10 of this Part, with proof of service of two copies, except that where a typewritten brief is authorized or the appeal is from the Family Court eight reproduced copies of the brief with proof of service of one copy may be filed. Within nine days after such service the appellant or moving party may file a like number of copies of a reply brief as were filed of the main brief, conforming to the requirements of section 600.10 of this Part, with proof of service of the same number of copies as were served of the main brief.

(d) *Cross-appeals.* (1) The parties shall consult and thereafter file a joint record or joint appendix which shall include therein a copy of the cross-notice of appeal. The cost of the joint record or joint appendix and the transcript, if any, shall be borne equally among the parties.

(2) It shall be the duty of the first filer of a notice of appeal to perfect the appeal. Respondent-cross-appellant shall file its answering brief pursuant to the scheduled date for a respondent for that specific term and shall include therein the points and arguments on its cross-appeal. Appellant shall have nine days thereafter to file its reply brief and, thereafter, respondent-cross-appellant shall have nine days to file its reply brief.

(e) *Service by mail.* Whenever service of a record, appendix, note of issue, appellant's or respondent's briefs, is made through the post office, such service must comply with CPLR 2103(b)(2), *viz:* be made five days prior to the last day designated herein.

(f) *Time permitted for argument.* (1) Counsel for the parties shall consult and determine whether they wish to argue or submit. If they wish to argue, the clerk shall be notified by the parties in one writing of the time desired for argument by each party. The writing shall be in the possession of the clerk on or before the court's scheduled date therefor in that particular term. In the absence of such notification, the appeal shall be marked submitted with respect to all parties.

(2) On the argument of an enumerated appeal, not more than 15 minutes shall be permitted on either side and only one counsel on each side shall be heard except when the court shall otherwise order. Any party may for good cause request additional time by a writing delivered to the clerk before the day of argument.

(3) Oral argument shall not be allowed in nonenumerated appeals, except by permission of the court.

(g) *Adjournments.* Enumerated appeals or causes which have been placed on the calendar may be adjourned once upon the written stipulation of counsel, provided such stipulation is filed with the clerk not later than 26 days before the first day of the term for which the appeal has been noticed and the matter is not being adjourned to the June term. Any further adjournment by stipulation must be approved by a justice of the court. If the appeal or cause is not argued or submitted during the term to which it has been adjourned, it shall be marked off the calendar.

§ 600.12 Preference; dismissal of appeal or cause; dismissal calendar calls.

(a) *Preference.*

(1) Any party to an appeal entitled by law to a preference in the hearing of the appeal may serve and file a demand for a preference which shall set forth the provision of law relied upon for such preference. If the demand is sustained by the court, the appeal shall be preferred.

(2) A preference under CPLR 5521 may be obtained upon good cause shown in an application made to the court on notice to the other parties to the appeal.

(b) *Dismissal of appeal or cause.* In the event the appellant or moving party fails to prosecute the appeal or cause within the time prescribed by this Part, or fails to restore an appeal or cause to the calendar within 60 days after it has been marked off the calendar, any other party to the appeal may move to dismiss the appeal for lack of prosecution on eight days' notice. The moving papers on such an application must include a copy of the notice of appeal.

(c) *Dismissal calendar calls.* (1) In May of each year the clerk shall make up a calendar of all civil appeals or causes not brought on for hearing within nine months from the filing of the record or papers upon which the matter was to be heard, exclusive of such appeals or causes which are then on the calendar or were marked off the calendar less than 60 days prior to May first.

(2) In May and October of each year the clerk shall make up a calendar of all criminal appeals or causes and all appeals involving writs of *habeas corpus* in criminal causes not brought on for hearing within 18 months of the awarding of poor person relief, exclusive of such criminal appeals or causes which are then on the calendar or were marked off the calendar less than 60 days prior to the calendar call. Fifteen days' notice of the time and date of such dismissal calendar call, and of the opportunity to submit an affidavit thereupon pursuant to paragraph (4) of this subdivision, shall be given to the appellants by ordinary mail; if the appellant is a defendant such notice shall be at his last known place of residence, or if imprisoned, at the institution at which confined, and similarly to his attorney if any upon the appeal or who last appeared for him.

(3) The calendars so prepared shall be published in the *New York Law Journal* for five consecutive days and called by the clerk on the

fifth day of publication. The clerk shall cause a notice to be published in the *New York Law Journal* during the same period calling attention to the publication of the calendars and stating the date and time the calendars will be called.

(4) In the event the appellant or moving party fails to submit an affidavit with proof of service of a copy thereof prior to or on the call of any of the calendars referred to in paragraphs (1) and (2) of this subdivision satisfactorily explaining the delay and containing the following information:

(i) the nature of the order or judgment appealed from;

(ii) the date the judgment or order appealed from was entered or, if the matter was transferred to this court pursuant to CPLR 7804, the date of the order of transferral;

(iii) the date the notice of appeal was served;

(iv) whether any enlargement of time to perfect the appeal has been granted; and

(v) in the case of criminal appeals, the sentence imposed and whether the defendant is on probation or parole, or free on an order of stay of judgment pending determination of the appeal, an order will be entered dismissing the appeal or cause.

* * *

§ 600.14 Motions for reargument or leave to appeal to the Court of Appeals.

(a) *Reargument.* Motions for reargument shall be made within 30 days after the appeal has been decided and shall be submitted without oral argument. The papers in support of the motion shall include a copy of the order entered upon the decision of this court, and shall concisely state the points claimed to have been overlooked or misapprehended by the court, with proper reference to the particular portions of the record and the authorities relied upon.

(b) *Leave to appeal.* Applications for permission to appeal to the Court of Appeals shall be made in the manner and within the time prescribed by CPLR 5513(b) and 5516 and must be submitted without oral argument. The moving papers shall include a copy of the order of this court from which leave to appeal is requested, and shall set forth the questions of law to be reviewed by the Court of Appeals.

§ 600.15 Fees of the clerk of the court.

(a) On behalf of the State of New York, the clerk of the court is entitled to receive the following fees:

* * *

(3) for furnishing a copy, certified or uncertified, of an opinion, decision, order, record, or other paper in his custody, $1 for the first page and 50 cents for each additional page; and

(4) for comparing and certifying a prepared copy of an opinion, decision, order, record, or other paper in his custody, 50 cents for the first page and 25 cents for each additional page, with a minimum fee of $1; and

* * *

(b) None of the fees prescribed in paragraphs (a)(1) through (4) of this section shall be charged any department or agency of the Federal, city or State governments or any duly organized bar association. No charge shall be made for furnishing a copy of the order, opinion or decision of the court to any party to an appeal or proceeding pending in the court.

* * *

§ 600.16 Appeal from an order concerning a grand jury report; appeal from a judgment predicated upon the entry of a plea of guilty.

(a) *Appeal from an order concerning a grand jury report.* The mode, time and manner for perfecting an appeal from an order accepting a report of a grand jury pursuant to CPL 190.85(1)(a), or from an order sealing a report of a grand jury pursuant to CPL 190.85(5) shall be in accordance with the sections hereof governing appeals in criminal cases. An appeal from such an order shall be a preferred cause and may be added to the term calendar by stipulation approved by the court or upon motion made in the manner provided by section 600.2 of this Part. The record, briefs and other papers on such an appeal shall be sealed and not be available for public inspection except as permitted by CPL 190.85(3). Unless otherwise directed by the court, oral argument will be allowed.

(b) *Appeal from a judgment predicated upon the entry of a plea of guilty.* On an appeal from a judgment rendered in a criminal proceeding following entry of a guilty plea pursuant to CPL article 220, respondent may elect to file a brief that urges an affirmance of the judgment solely upon a claim that there is no reviewable issue because appellant made a valid waiver of the right to appeal. Upon the submission or argument of the appeal, the court in its discretion may direct the respondent to submit a supplemental brief addressing additional issues to which the appellant may reply.

* * *

§ 600.18 *Habeas corpus* appeals.

Appeals from judgments or orders entered in

any proceeding or action alleging that a person is illegally imprisoned or otherwise unlawfully restrained in his liberty within the state may be prosecuted in accordance with any of the methods specified in section 600.5 of this part. Such

appeals may also be brought on for hearing in such mode, time and manner and on such terms and conditions as this court or a justice thereof may direct by an order granted on the application of any party to the appeal.

* * * *

PART 603

CONDUCT OF ATTORNEYS

Section

§ 603.1 Application.

(a) This Part shall apply to all attorneys who are admitted to practice, reside in, commit acts in or who have offices in this judicial department, or who are admitted to practice by a court of another jurisdiction and who practice within this department as counsel for governmental agencies or as house counsel to corporations or other entities, or otherwise, and to all legal consultants licensed to practice pursuant to the provisions of subdivision 6 of section 53 of the Judiciary Law. In addition, any attorney from another state, territory, district or foreign country admitted *pro*

hac vice to participate in the trial or argument of a particular cause in any court in this judicial department, or who in any way participates in any action or proceeding in this judicial department shall be subject to this Part.

(b) This Part shall apply to any law firm, as that term is used in the Disciplinary Rules of the Code of Professional Responsibility, section 1200.1(b) of this Title, that has a member, employs, or otherwise retains an attorney or legal consultant described in subdivision (a) of this section.

consultant described in subdivision (a) of this section.

§ 603.2 Professional misconduct defined.

(a) Any attorney who fails to conduct himself both professionally and personally, in conformity with the standards of conduct imposed upon members of the bar as conditions for the privilege to practice law and any attorney who violates any provision of the rules of this court governing the conduct of attorneys, or with respect to conduct on or after January 1, 1970, any disciplinary rules of the Code of Professional Responsibility, as adopted by the New York State Bar Association, effective January 1, 1970, as amended, or with respect to conduct on or before December 31, 1969, any canons of the Canons of Professional Responsibility, as adopted by such bar association and effective until December 31, 1969 or with respect to conduct on or after September 1, 1990, any disciplinary rule of the Code of Professional Responsibility, as jointly adopted by the Appellate Divisions of the Supreme Court, effective September 1, 1990, or any of the special rules concerning court decorum shall be deemed to be guilty of professional misconduct within the meaning of subdivision of 2 of section 90 of the Judiciary Law.

(b) Any law firm that fails to conduct itself in conformity with the provisions of the disciplinary Rules of the Code of Professional Responsibility pertaining to law firms guilty of professional misconduct within the meaning of subdivision 2 of section 90 of the Judiciary Law.

§ 603.3 Discipline of attorneys for professional misconduct in foreign jurisdictions.

(a) Any attorney to whom this Part shall apply, pursuant to section 603.1 of this Part who has been disciplined in a foreign jurisdiction, may be disciplined by this court because of the conduct which gave rise to the discipline imposed in the foreign jurisdiction. For purposes of this Part, *foreign jurisdiction* means another state, territory or district.

(b) Upon receipt of a certified or exemplified copy of the order imposing such discipline in a foreign jurisdiction, and of the record of the proceedings upon which such order was based, this court, directly or by the Departmental Disciplinary Committee, shall give written notice to such attorney pursuant to subdivision 6 of section 90 of the Judiciary Law, according him the opportunity, within 20 days of the giving of such notice, to file a verified statement setting forth evidentiary facts for any defense to discipline enumerated under subdivision (c) of this section, and a written demand for a hearing at which consideration shall be given to any and all such defenses. Such notice shall further advise the attorney that in default of such filing such discipline or such disciplinary action as may be appropriate will be imposed or taken. When a verified statement setting forth evidentiary facts for any defense to discipline and a demand for hearing have been duly filed, no discipline shall be imposed without affording the attorney an opportunity for hearing. The court may conduct the hearing or it may appoint a referee to conduct the hearing and further refer the matter to the Departmental Disciplinary Committee. In the event the committee or the attorney desires further action by this court, a petition may be filed in this court together with the record of the proceedings before the committee.

(c) Only the following defenses may be raised:

(1) that the procedure in the foreign jurisdiction was so lacking in notice or opportunity to be heard as to constitute a deprivation of due process; or

(2) that there was such an infirmity of proof establishing the misconduct as to give rise to the clear conviction that this court could not, consistent with its duties, accept as final the finding in the foreign jurisdiction as to the attorney's misconduct; or

(3) that the misconduct for which the attorney was disciplined in the foreign jurisdiction does not constitute misconduct in this jurisdiction.

(d) Any attorney to whom these rules shall apply pursuant to section 603.1 of this Part who has been disciplined in a foreign jurisdiction shall promptly advise this court of such discipline.

(e) Whenever the Departmental Disciplinary Committee learns that an attorney to whom these rules shall apply, pursuant to section 603.1 of this Part, has been disciplined in a foreign jurisdiction, it shall ascertain whether a certified or exemplified copy of the order imposing such discipline has been filed with this court, and if it has not been filed, such committee shall cause such order to be filed.

§ 603.4 Appointment of disciplinary agencies; commencement of investigation of attorney misconduct; complaints; procedure in certain cases.

(a) (1) This court shall appoint a Departmental Disciplinary Committee for the Judicial Department, which shall be charged with the duty and empowered to investigate and prosecute matters involving alleged misconduct by attorneys who, and law firms that, are subject to this Part and to impose discipline to the extent permitted by section 603.9 of this Part. This court shall, in consultation with the Departmental Disciplinary Committee, appoint a chief counsel to such committee and such assistant counsel, special counsel and supporting staff as it deems necessary.

(2) This court shall appoint as members of the Departmental Disciplinary Committee attorneys in good standing with the bar of the State of New York and persons who are not attorneys but reside or have a principal place of business in the City of New York. Special counsel may be appointed as members of the committee. At least two-thirds of the committee shall be attorneys. Appointment to the committee shall be for a three-year term. Except for special counsel, a member who has served for two consecutive terms is not eligible for reappointment for at least one year following the expiration of the second term. (The membership of the Departmental Disciplinary Committee shall be appointed by this court for a term of three years, except members who have been appointed to complete unexpired terms, in which case such members may be reappointed for three-year or shorter terms. At least two-thirds of the members of the Departmental Disciplinary Committee shall be members of the Bar of the State of New York in good standing, each of whom shall reside or have an office in the City of New York, and up to one-third of such members shall be persons who are not members of the Bar, each of whom shall reside or have a principal place of business in the City of New York. The court may appoint special counsel who shall be full members of the committee. Appointments to the Departmental Disciplinary Committee may be made from lists of nominees submitted by the Association of the Bar of the City of New York, the New York County Lawyers' Association, and the Bronx County Bar Association, and by such other means which the court deems in the public interest with the exception of special counsel appointed by the court, a member of the bar who has served two consecutive terms shall not be eligible for reappointment until one year after the expiration of the second term. The appropriate committees of the Association of the Bar of the City of New York, the New York County Lawyers' Association, and the Bronx County Bar Association may be designated to investigate and prosecute matters involving alleged misconduct of attorneys. Upon such designation, references in sections 603.3, 603.4(a)(3), (b), and (d), 603.5, 603.6, 603.9, 603.11, 603.12(a) and (e), 603.15 and 603.16 of this Part to the Departmental Disciplinary Committee with respect to the mater or matters to which such designation applies shall mean the Committee of the Association of the Bar of the City of New York, the New York County Lawyers' Association, and the Bronx County Bar Association so designated.)

(3) The members of the Departmental Disciplinary Committee for the First Judicial Department, as volunteers, are expressly authorized to participate in a State-sponsored volunteer program within the meaning of subdivision 1 of section 17 of the Public Officers Law.

(b) The rules for the conduct of the proceedings and business of the Departmental Disciplinary Committee, set for the in Part 605 of this Title, apply to matters involving alleged misconduct by attorneys and law firms. The Departmental Disciplinary Committee may act through its chairperson, acting chairperson, subcommittees or hearing panels.

(c) Investigation of professional misconduct may be commenced upon receipt of a specific complaint by this court, or by the Departmental Disciplinary Committee or such investigation may be commenced *sua sponte* by this court or by the Departmental Disciplinary Committee. Complaints must be in writing and subscribed by the complainant but need not be verified. Whenever the Departmental Disciplinary Committee concludes that the issue involved upon the complaint is a fee dispute and, accordingly, dismisses the complaint, the Chief Counsel to the Committee or his assistant shall advise the complainant and the respondent that the dispute might be satisfactorily resolved by referring it for conciliation to the Joint Committee On Fee Disputes organized and administered by the Association of the Bar of the City of New York, the New York County Lawyers' Association and the Bronx County Bar Association and with permission of both the complainant and respondent, will forward the file to said Committee headquartered at the New York County Lawyers' Association, 14 Vesey Street, New York, NY.

(d) When the Departmental Disciplinary Committee after investigation, determines that it is appropriate to file a petition against an attorney in this court, the committee shall institute disciplinary proceedings in this court and the court may discipline an attorney on the basis of the record of hearings before such committee, or may appoint a referee, justice or judge to hold hearings.

(e) (1) An attorney who is the subject of an investigation, or of charges by the Departmental Disciplinary Committee of professional misconduct, or who is the subject of a disciplinary proceeding pending in this court against whom a petition has been filed pursuant to this section, or upon whom a notice has been served pursuant to section 603.3(b) of this Part, may be suspended from the practice of law, pending consideration of the charges against the attorney, upon a finding that the attorney is guilty of professional misconduct immediately threatening the public interest. Such a finding shall be based upon:

(i) the attorney's default in responding to the petition or notice, or the attorney's failure to submit a written answer to pending charges of professional misconduct or to comply with any lawful demand of this court or the Departmental Disciplinary Committee made in connection with any investigation, hearing or disciplinary proceeding; or

(ii) a substantial admission under oath that the attorney has committed an act or acts of professional misconduct; or

(iii) other uncontroverted evidence of professional misconduct.

(2) The suspension shall be made upon the application of the Departmental Disciplinary Committee to this court, after notice of such application has been given to the attorney pursuant to subdivision 6 of section 90 of the Judiciary Law. The court shall briefly state its reasons for its order of suspension which shall be effective immediately and until such time as the disciplinary matters before the committee have been concluded, and until further order of the court.

(f) Disciplinary proceedings shall be granted a preference by this court.

§ 603.5 Investigation of professional misconduct on the part of an attorney; subpoenas and examination of witnesses under oath.

(a) Upon application by the Departmental Disciplinary Committee, or upon application by counsel to such committee, disclosing that such committee is conducting an investigation of professional misconduct on the part of an attorney, or has commenced proceedings against an attorney, or upon application by an attorney under such investigation, or who is a party to such proceedings, the clerk of this court shall issue subpoenas in the name of the presiding justice for the attendance of any person and the production of books and papers before such committee or such counsel or any subcommittee or hearing panel thereof designated in such application at a time and place therein specified.

(b) The Departmental Disciplinary Committee, or a subcommittee or hearing panel thereof or its counsel, is empowered to take and cause to be transcribed the evidence of witnesses who may be sworn by any person authorized by law to administer oaths.

§ 603.6 Investigation of persons, firms or corporations unlawfully practicing or assuming to practice law.

(a) Upon application by the Departmental Disciplinary Committee, or of a committee of a recognized bar association authorized to inquire into possible cases of the unlawful practice of the law, disclosing that there is a reason to believe that a person, firm or corporation is unlawfully practicing or assuming to practice law, and that such committee is conducting an investigation into such matter, or upon application by any such person, firm or corporation under such investigation, the clerk of this court shall issue subpoenas

in the name of the presiding justice for the attendance of any person and production of books and papers before such committee, or any subcommittee or hearing panel thereof designated in such application, at the time and place therein specified.

(b) Each committee referred to in subdivision (a) of this section or a subcommittee or hearing panel of any of the foregoing, or its counsel, is empowered to take and cause to be transcribed the evidence of witness who may be sworn by any person authorized by law to administer oaths.

* * *

§ 603.9 Discipline by Departmental Disciplinary Committee.

The Departmental Disciplinary Committee may issue an admonition or a reprimand in those cases in which professional misconduct, not warranting proceedings before this court, is found. An admonition is discipline imposed without a hearing. A reprimand is discipline imposed after a hearing.

§ 603.10 Effect of restitution on disciplinary proceedings.

Restitution made by an attorney or on his behalf to a client for funds converted or to reimburse a person for losses suffered as a result of the attorney's wrongdoing shall not be a bar to the commencement or continuance of disciplinary proceedings.

§ 603.11 Resignation of attorneys under investigation or the subject of disciplinary proceedings.

(a) An attorney who is the subject of an investigation into allegations of misconduct or who is the subject of a disciplinary proceeding pending in the court may submit his resignation by submitting to the Departmental Disciplinary Committee an affidavit stating that he intends to resign and that:

(1) his resignation is freely and voluntarily rendered; he is not being subjected to coercion or duress; and he is fully aware of the implications of submitting his resignation;

(2) he is aware that there is pending an investigation or disciplinary proceeding into allegations that he has been guilty of misconduct, the nature of which shall be specifically set forth; and

(3) he acknowledges that if charges were predicated upon the misconduct under investigation, he could not successfully defend himself on the merits against such charges, or that he cannot successfully defend himself against the charges in the proceedings pending in the court.

(b) On receipt of the required affidavit, such committee shall file it with this court, together with either its recommendation that the resignation be accepted and the terms and conditions, if any, to be imposed upon the acceptance, or its recommendation that the resignation not be accepted.

(c) This court, in its discretion, may accept such resignation, upon such terms and conditions as it deems appropriate or it may direct that proceedings before the Departmental Disciplinary Committee or before this court go forward.

(d) This court, if it accepts such resignation shall enter an order removing the attorney on consent and may order that the affidavit referred to in subdivision (a) of this section be deemed private and confidential under subdivision 10 of section 90 of the Judiciary Law.

§ 603.12 Attorneys convicted of crimes; record of conviction; conclusive evidence.

(a) Upon receipt by the Departmental Disciplinary Committee of a certificate demonstrating that an attorney has been convicted of a crime in this State, or in any foreign jurisdiction, whether the conviction resulted from a plea of guilty or *nolo contendere* or from a verdict after trial or otherwise, the committee shall determine whether the crime is a serious crime as defined in subdivision (b) of this section. Upon a determination that a crime is a serious crime, the committee shall forthwith file the certificate of conviction with the court. This court shall thereupon enter an order directing the chairperson of the Departmental Disciplinary Committee to designate a hearing panel or appointing a referee, justice or judge, to conduct forthwith disciplinary proceedings. If the committee determines that the crime is not a serious crime as defined in subdivision (b) of this section, it may hear such evidence as is admissible under subdivision (c) of this section and take such other steps as are provided for in Part 605 of this Title.

(b) The term "serious crime" shall include any felony, not resulting in automatic disbarment under the provisions of subdivision 4 of section 90 of the Judiciary Law, and any crime, other than a felony, a necessary element of which, as determined by the statutory or common law definition of such crime, involves interference with the administration of justice, criminal contempt of court, false swearing, misrepresentation, fraud, willful failure to file income tax returns, deceit, bribery, extortion, misappropriation, theft, or an attempt or a conspiracy or solicitation of another to commit a "serious crime."

(c) A certificate of the conviction of an attorney for any crime shall be conclusive evidence of his guilt of that crime in any disciplinary proceeding instituted against him and based on the conviction, and the attorney may not offer evidence inconsistent with the essential elements of the crime for which he was convicted as determined by the statute defining the crime except such evidence as was not available at the time of the conviction or in any proceeding challenging the conviction.

(d) The clerk of any court within this judicial department in which an attorney is convicted of a crime shall within 10 days of said conviction forward a certificate thereof to the Departmental Disciplinary Committee.

(e) The pendency of an appeal shall not be grounds for delaying any action under this section unless the conviction is from a court which is not a court of record or this court or the Departmental Disciplinary Committee finds there are compelling reasons justifying a delay.

(f) Any attorney to whom these rules shall apply pursuant to section 603.1 of this Part who has been convicted of a crime shall promptly advise the Departmental Disciplinary Committee of that fact.

§ 603.13 Conduct of disbarred, suspended and resigned attorneys.

(a) *Compliance with Judiciary Law.*

Disbarred, suspended and resigned attorneys at law shall comply fully and completely with the letter and spirit of sections 478, 479, 484 and 486 of the Judiciary Law relating to practicing as attorneys at law without being admitted and registered, and soliciting of business on behalf of an attorney at law and the practice of law by an attorney who has been disbarred, suspended or convicted of a felony.

(b) *Compensation.*

A disbarred, suspended or resigned attorney may not share in any fee for legal services performed by another attorney during the period of his removal from the bar. A disbarred, suspended or resigned attorney may be compensated on a *quantum meruit* basis for legal services rendered and disbursements incurred by him prior to the effective date of the disbarment or suspension order or of his resignation. The amount and manner of payment of such compensation and recoverable disbursements shall be fixed by the court on the application of either the disbarred, suspended or resigned attorney or the new attorney, on notice to the other as well as on notice to the client. Such applications shall be made at special term in the court wherein the action is pending or at special term of the Supreme Court in the county wherein the moving attorney maintains his office if an action has not been commenced. In no event shall the combined legal fees exceed the amount the client would have been required to pay had no substitution of attorneys been required.

(c) *Notice to clients not involved in litigation.*

A disbarred, suspended or resigned attorney

shall promptly notify by registered or certified mail, return receipt requested, all clients being represented in pending matters, other than litigated or administrative matters or proceedings pending in any court or agency, of his disbarment or suspension or resignation and his consequent inability to act as an attorney after the effective date of his disbarment or suspension or resignation and shall advise said clients to seek legal advice elsewhere.

(d) *Notice to clients involved in litigation.*

(1) A disbarred or suspended or resigned attorney shall promptly notify, by registered or certified mail, return receipt requested, each of his clients whom he is representing in litigated matters or administrative proceedings, and the attorney or attorneys for every other party in such matter or proceeding, of his disbarment or suspension or resignation and consequent inability to act as an attorney after the effective date of his disbarment or suspension or resignation. The notice to be given to the client shall advise the prompt substitution of another attorney or attorneys in his place.

(2) In the event the client does not obtain substitute counsel before the effective date of the disbarment or suspension or resignation, it shall be the responsibility of the disbarred or suspended or resigned attorney to move in the court in which the action is pending, or before the body in which an administrative proceeding is pending, for leave to withdraw from the action or proceeding.

(3) The notice to be given to the attorney or attorneys for each other party shall state the place or residence of the client of the disbarred or suspended or resigned attorney. In addition, notice shall be given in like manner to the Office of Court Administration of the State of New York in each matter in which a retainer statement has been filed.

(e) *Conduct after entry of order.*

The disbarred or suspended or resigned attorney, after entry of the disbarment or suspension order, or after entry of the order accepting the resignation, shall not accept any new retainer or engage as attorney for another in any new case or legal matter of any nature. However, during the period between the entry date of the order and its effective date he may wind up and complete, on behalf of any client, all matters which were pending on the entry date.

(f) *Filing proof of compliance and attorney's address.*

Within 10 days after the effective date of the disbarment or suspension order or the order accepting the resignation, the disbarred or suspended or resigned attorney shall file with the clerk of this court, together with proof of service upon the Departmental Disciplinary Committee, an affidavit showing that he has fully complied with the provisions of the order and with these rules. Such affidavit shall also set forth the residence or other address of the disbarred or suspended or resigned attorney where communications may be directed to him.

(g) *Appointment of attorney to protect clients' interests and interests of disbarred or suspended attorney.*

Whenever it shall be brought to the court's attention that a disbarred or suspended or resigned attorney shall have failed or may fail to comply with the provisions of subdivisions (c), (d) or (f) of this section, this court, upon such notice to such attorney as this court may direct, may appoint an attorney or attorneys to inventory the files of the disbarred or suspended or resigned attorney and to take such action as seems indicated to protect the interests of his clients and for the protection of the interests of the suspended or disbarred or resigned attorney.

(h) Any attorney so appointed by this court shall not be permitted to disclose any information contained in any file so inventoried without the consent of the client to whom such file relates except as necessary to carry out the order of this court.

(i) This court may fix the compensation to be paid to any attorney appointed by this court under this section. This compensation may be directed by this court to be paid as an incident to the costs of the proceeding in which the charges are incurred and shall be charged in accordance with law.

(j) *Required records.*

A disbarred or suspended or resigned attorney shall keep and maintain records of the various steps taken by him under this Part so that, upon any subsequent proceeding instituted by or against him, proof of compliance with this Part and with the disbarment of suspension order or with the order accepting the resignation will be available.

§ 603.14 Reinstatement.

(a) (1) Unless the court directs otherwise, any attorney who has been suspended for six months or less pursuant to disciplinary proceedings shall be reinstated at the end of the period of suspension upon an order of the court. No more than 30 days prior to the expiration of the term of suspension the attorney must file with the court and serve upon the chief counsel an affidavit stating that the attorney has fully complied with the requirements of the suspension order and has paid any required fees and costs. Upon receipt of the affidavit, the chief counsel shall serve a copy of it upon each complainant in the disciplinary proceeding that led to the suspension and give notice to the complainant(s) that they may submit a response opposing or supporting the lawyer's affidavit. Such response must be filed with the chief counsel within 20 days of the date of the notice. Within 30 days of the date on which the affidavit was served upon the chief counsel, or within such longer time as the court may allow, the chief counsel may file an affidavit in opposition.

(2) Any attorney who has been disbarred after a hearing, or whose name has been stricken from the roll of attorneys pursuant to section 90(4) of the Judiciary Law or section 603.11 of this Part, may not petition for reinstatement until the expiration of seven years from the effective date of the disbarment or removal.

(3) Any attorney suspended under the provisions of this Part for more than six months shall be entitled to petition for reinstatement upon the expiration of the period of suspension.

(b) A petition for reinstatement may be granted only if the petitioner establishes by clear and convincing evidence that:

(1) the petitioner has fully complied with the provisions of the order of disbarment, removal or suspension;

(2) the petitioner possesses the requisite character and general fitness to practice law; and

(3) not more than six months prior to the filing of the petition for reinstatement, the petitioner has taken and attained a passing score on the multistate professional responsibility examination described in section 520.8(a) of this Title, the passing score being that determined by the New York State Board of Law Examiners pursuant to section 520.8(c) of this Title.

(c) In reviewing an application for reinstatement, the court may consider the misconduct for which petitioner was originally disbarred, removed or suspended and any other relevant conduct or information which may come to the attention of the court.

(d) A petition for reinstatement shall be verified and shall be accompanied by a completed questionnaire as outlined in subdivision (m) of this section.

(e) A petitioner shall serve a copy of the petition for reinstatement upon the Departmental Disciplinary Committee and upon the Lawyers' Fund for Client Protection. The court may refer the matter to the Departmental Disciplinary Committee and either direct the chairperson of the committee to designate a hearing panel, or appoint a referee, or the court may refer the matter to the Committee on Character and Fitness, to inquire into the facts submitted in support of the petition and all other relevant facts. In its discretion, the court may require the petitioner to:

(i) submit additional sworn proof;

(ii) submit to a sworn examination;

(iii) produce records and other papers in connection with the application;

(iv) provide proof of compliance with all disciplinary orders; and

(v) submit to medical or psychiatric examinations by qualified experts.

The designated committee shall report to the court in writing.

(f) The Disciplinary Committee may be heard in opposition to the petition for reinstatement.

(g) If the court determines that the petition for reinstatement satisfies the provisions of subdivision (b) of this section, the court may grant the petition, or may refer the petition to the Departmental Disciplinary Committee and direct the chairperson of the committee to designate a hearing panel or appoint a referee, or the court may refer the matter to the Committee on Character and Fitness, to conduct a hearing. At such hearing, both petitioner and counsel for the Disciplinary Committee may present evidence bearing upon all relevant issues raised by the petition.

(h) At the conclusion of the hearing, the committee that conducted it shall submit a written report and recommendation to the court; the report may include a recommendation that the court condition reinstatement upon compliance with such additional orders as are deemed appropriate, including but not limited to the payment of restitution to any person harmed by petitioner's misconduct.

(i) In the event that the court approves the application for reinstatement of an attorney who has resigned, been disbarred, or been suspended and whose petition for reinstatement is made seven or more years after the effective date of his suspension, the petition may thereupon be held in abeyance for a period of not more than two years. It may be a condition of the granting of the petition that petitioner take and attain a passing score on the New York State Bar examination described in section 520.7 of this Title within the said two-year period. Upon proof of successful completion of the said bar examination, and in the absence of further misconduct by petitioner, the petition for reinstatement shall be granted.

(j) A petition for reinstatement shall not be accepted for filing within two years following entry of this court's order denying a previous petition for reinstatement filed by or on behalf of the petitioner, unless the order denying the previous petition provides otherwise.

(k) The court may direct that notice of any reinstatement petition be published in one or more newspapers in the First Department pursuant to section 601.1 of this Title.

(l) Petitions for reinstatement under these rules shall be accompanied by payment of a fee of $315, unless waived or modified by the court upon a showing of hardship.

(m) *Petition for reinstatement.*

(Applicant's Last Name) _____

(Date) _____

TO: THE APPELLATE DIVISION OF THE SUPREME COURT

FIRST JUDICIAL DEPARTMENT

STATE OF NEW YORK

COUNTY OF

I, _____, hereby apply, pursuant to Judiciary Law, Section 90, and 22 NYCRR section 603.14, for reinstatement as an attorney and counselor-at-law licensed to practice in all the courts of the State of New York. In support of my application I submit this petition, the form of which has been prescribed by this Court. In applicable provisions have been stricken and initialed by me.

1. My full name is _____
I have also been known by the following names _____,
(If change of name was made by court order, including marriage, a certified copy of that order is attached.)

2. I was born on _____ at _____ (date).

3. I reside at _____ (city-state-country).

(If you reside in more than one place, state all places in which you reside.)

My home telephone number is _____

My office telephone number is _____

4. On _____ I was admitted as an attorney and counselor-in-law by the Appellate Division of the Supreme Court of the State of New York, _____ Judicial Department.

5. By order of this Court, dated _____, I was disciplined to the following extent: _____

A certified copy of this Court's order is attached; this Court's opinion was published in the _____ volume, page _____, of the official reports (2d series) for the Appellate Divisions. My use of the term "discipline" hereafter refers to the action of this Court by the order here referred to.

6. Since the effective date of my discipline, I have resided at the following addresses: _____

7. The discipline imposed upon me was predicated upon, or arose out of, my misappropriation or misuse of the real or personal property of others. Attached to this application is a full listing of each property, its dollar value, the name of the true owner, and the extent to which I have yet to make full restitution. Where I still owe a party under this section, I have also attached a copy of a restitution agreement, signed by that owner and myself, setting forth the terms of my repayment obligations.

8. On the date of my discipline, the following matters, which were not the basis of that order, were pending against me before the Departmental Disciplinary Committee:

9. On the effective date of my discipline, I was also admitted to practice in the following Courts/jurisdictions:

10. Based upon this Court's discipline of me, I also have been disciplined in the following way(s):

11. In addition, dating back to my original admission to the bar up until the present, I have also been disciplined for other actions or activities, in the following ways:

_____

_____

12. Prior to my discipline, my law practice involved the following areas of law:

_____

13. Since the effective date of my discipline, I have engaged in the practice of law in other jurisdiction(s), on the date(s) and in the manner specified: _____

_____

_____

14. Since the effective date of my discipline, I have been engaged in the following legal-type or law-related activities: _____

_____

_____

15. Since the effective date of my discipline I have had the following employment or been engaged in the following business (set forth names, dates, addresses): _____

_____

_____

_____

16. I am attaching copies of all Federal, State and local tax returns filed by me for the past two years.

17. At the time of my discipline, I took the following affirmative steps to notify my clients of my inability to continue representing them: _____

_____

_____

_____

18. Pursuant to 22 NYCRR section 603.13(f), I filed an affidavit of compliance on _____ (date).

-or-

I did not file an affidavit of compliance, as required by this Court's rules, because

_____

19. Since the date of my discipline, I have maintained the following bank accounts and brokerage accounts _____

_____

_____

_____

_____

20. There presently exist the following unpaid judgments against me or a partnership, corporation or other business entity of which I am an employee or in which I have an ownership interest:

_____

_____

21. Since my discipline, I, or a partnership, corporation or other business entity in which I have an ownership interest, have/has been involved in the following lawsuits, to the extent indicated _

_____

_____

22. I, or a partnership, corporation or other business entity in which I have an ownership interest, petitioned to be adjudicated a bankrupt on _____ (date).

_____ (court).

23. a) Since my discipline, I applied for the following license(s) which required proof of good character: _____

b) These applications resulted in the following action(s): _____

24. Since my admission to the bar, I have had the following licenses suspended or revoked for the stated reason(s), unrelated to this Court's order of discipline: _____

25. Since my discipline, on the date(s) specified I have been arrested, charged with, indicated, convicted, tried, and/or have pleaded guilty to the following violation(s), misdemeanor(s) and/or felony(ies): _____

26. Since my discipline, I have been the subject of the following governmental investigation(s) on the specified date(s), which resulted in the charge or complaint indicated being brought against me: _____

27. Other than the passage of time and the absence of additional misconduct, the following facts establish that I possess the requisite character and general fitness to be reinstated as an attorney in New York: _____

28. I have made the following efforts to maintain or renew my general fitness to practice law, including continuing legal education and otherwise, during the period following my disbarment, removal, or suspension: _____

29. I was treated for alcoholism and/or drug abuse on the date(s) and under the circumstances here set forth: _____

30. The following fact(s), not heretofore disclosed to this Court, are relevant to this application and might tend by some degree to induce the Court to look less favorably upon this application: .

I UNDERSTAND THAT THE DEPARTMENTAL DISCIPLINARY COMMITTEE, THE COMMITTEE ON CHARACTER AND FITNESS, OR OTHER ATTORNEY AUTHORIZED BY THE COURT, MAY TAKE ADDITIONAL INVESTIGATIVE STEPS DEEMED APPROPRIATE IN ACTING UPON THIS APPLICATION FOR REINSTATEMENT. I WILL FULLY COOPERATE WITH ANY REQUEST FOR INFORMATION AND MAKE MYSELF AVAILABLE FOR SWORN INTERVIEWS OR HEARINGS, AS REQUIRED.

_____ (SIGNATURE OF APPLICANT)

Sworn to before me this
_____ day of _____ , 19_____

STATE OF NEW YORK

COUNTY OF

I, _____ being duly sworn, say: I am the petitioner in the within action; I have read the foregoing petition and know the contents thereof; the same is true to my own knowledge, except as to the matters therein stated to be alleged on information and belief, and as to those matters I believe it to be true.

Sworn to before me this
_____ day _____ , 19_____

* * * *

§ 603.15 Random review and audit.

(a) *Availability of bookkeeping records; random review and audit.* The financial records required to be maintained pursuant to Rule DR9-102 of the Code of Professional Responsibility, as jointly adopted by the Appellate Divisions of the Supreme Court, or by any other rule of this Court, shall be made available for inspection, copying and determination of compliance with court rules, to a duly authorized representative of the court pursuant to the issuance, on a randomly selected basis, of a notice or subpoena by the Department Disciplinary Committee.

(b) *Confidentiality.* All matters, records and proceedings relating to compliance with Rule DR9-102 of the Code of Professional Responsibility and this section, including the selection of an attorney for review hereunder, shall be kept confidential in accordance with applicable law, as and to the extent required of matters relating to professional discipline.

(c) *Regulations and procedures for random review and audit.* Prior to the issuance of any notice or subpoena in connection with the random review and audit program established by this section, the Departmental Disciplinary Committee shall propose regulations and procedures for the proper administration of the program. The court shall approve such of the regulations and procedures of the Departmental Disciplinary Committee as it may deem appropriate, and only such regulations and procedures as have been approved by the court shall become effective.

(d) *Biennial affirmation of compliance.* Any attorney subject to the court's jurisdiction shall execute that portion of the biennial registration statement provided by the Office of Court Administration, affirming that the attorney had read and is in compliance with DR9-102 of the Code of Professional Responsibility, as jointly adopted by the Appellate Divisions of the Supreme Court, and with this section. The affirmation shall be available at all times to the Departmental Disciplinary Committee.

No affirmation of compliance shall be required from a full-time judge or justice of the Unified Court System of the State of New York, or of a court of any other state, or of a federal court.

§ 603.16 Proceedings where attorney is declared incompetent or alleged to be incapacitated.

(a) *Suspension upon judicial determination of incompetency or on involuntary commitment.*

Where an attorney subject to this Part pursuant to the first sentence of section 603.1 of this Part has been judicially declared incompetent or involuntarily committed to a mental hospital, this court, upon proper proof of the fact, shall enter an order suspending such attorney from the practice of the law, effective immediately and for an indefinite period and until the further order of this court. A copy of such order shall be served upon such attorney, his committee, and/or director of mental hospital in such manner as this court may direct.

(b) *Proceeding to determine alleged incapacity and suspension upon such determination.*

(1) Whenever the Departmental Disciplinary Committee shall petition this court to determine whether an attorney is incapacitated from continuing to practice law by reason of physical or mental infirmity or illness or because of addiction to drugs or intoxicants, this court may take or direct such action as it deems necessary or proper to determine whether the attorney is so incapacitated, including examination of the attorney by such qualified experts as this court shall designate. If, upon due consideration of the matter, this court is satisfied and concludes that the attorney is incapacitated from continuing to practice law, it shall enter an order suspending him on the ground of such disability for an indefinite period and until the further order of this court and any pending disciplinary proceedings against the attorney shall be held in abeyance.

(2) This court may provide for such notice to the respondent-attorney of proceedings in the matter as is deemed proper and advisable and may appoint an attorney to represent the respondent, if he is without adequate representation.

(c) *Procedure when respondent claims disability during course of proceeding.*

(1) If, during the course of a disciplinary proceeding, the respondent contends that he is suffering from a disability by reason of physical or mental infirmity or illness, or because of addiction to drugs or intoxicants, which makes it impossible for the respondent adequately to defend himself, this court thereupon shall enter an order suspending the respondent from continuing to practice law until a determination is made of the respondent's capacity to continue the practice of law is made in a proceeding instituted in accordance with the provisions of subdivision (b) of this section.

(2) If, in the course of a proceeding under this section or in a disciplinary proceeding, this court shall determine that the respondent is not incapacitated from practicing law, it shall take such action as it deems proper and advisable, including a direction for the resumption of the disciplinary proceeding against the respondent.

(d) *Appointment of attorney to protect clients' and suspended attorney's interests.*

(1) Whenever an attorney is suspended for incapacity or disability, this court, upon such notice to him as this court may direct, may appoint an attorney or attorneys to inventory the files of the suspended attorney and to take such action as seems indicated to protect the interests

of his clients and for the protection of the interests of the suspended attorney.

(2) Any attorney so appointed by this court shall not be permitted to disclose any information contained in any file so inventoried without the consent of the client to whom such file relates except as necessary to carry out the order of this court.

(e) *Reinstatement upon termination of disability.*

(1) Any attorney suspended under the provisions of this section shall be entitled to apply for reinstatement at such intervals as this court may direct in the order of suspension or any modification thereof. Such application shall be granted by this court upon showing by clear and convincing evidence that the attorney's disability has been removed and he is fit to resume the practice of law. Upon such application, this court may take or direct such action as it deems necessary or proper for a determination as to whether the attorney's disability has been removed, including a direction of an examination of the attorney by such qualified experts as this court shall designate. In its discretion, this court may direct that the expense of such an examination shall be paid by the attorney.

(2) Where an attorney has been suspended by an order in accordance with the provisions of paragraph (a) of this section and thereafter, in proceedings duly taken, he has been judicially declared to be competent, this court may dispense with further evidence that his disability has been removed and may direct his reinstatement upon such terms as are deemed proper and advisable.

(f) *Burden of proof.*

In a proceeding seeking an order of suspension under this section, the burden of proof shall rest with the petitioner. In a proceeding seeking an order terminating a suspension under this section, the burden of proof shall rest with the suspended attorney.

(g) *Waiver of doctor-patient privilege upon application for reinstatement.*

The filing of an application for reinstatement by an attorney suspended for disability shall be deemed to constitute a waiver of any doctor-patient privilege existing between the attorney and any psychiatrist, psychologist, physician or hospital who or which has examined or treated the attorney during the period of his disability. The attorney shall be required to disclose the name of every psychiatrist, psychologist, physician and hospital by whom or at which the attorney has been examined or treated since his suspension and he shall furnish to this court written consent to each to divulge such information and records as requested by court-appointed medical experts or by the clerk of this court.

(h) *Payment of expenses of proceedings.*

(1) The necessary costs and disbursements of an agency, committee or appointed attorney in conducting a proceeding under this section shall be paid in accordance with subdivision 6 of section 90 of the Judiciary Law.

(2) This court may fix the compensation to be paid to any attorney or expert appointed by this court under this section. This compensation may be directed by this court to be paid as an incident to the costs of the proceeding in which the charges are incurred and shall be charged in accordance with law.

§ 603.17 Combining or grouping of claims.

No attorney for a claimant or plaintiff shall for the purpose of settlement or payment combine or group two or more claims or causes of action or judgments therefor on behalf of separate clients, and each such demand or action shall be settled or compromised independently upon its own merits and with regard to the individual interest of the client. No attorney for a defendant shall participate in the settlement of any such claims or actions on the basis directly or indirectly of combining or grouping claims or actions belonging to different persons.

§ 603.18 Champerty and maintenance.

No attorney shall by himself, or by or in the name of another person, either before or after action brought, promise, give, or procure, or permit to be promised or given any valuable consideration to any person as an inducement to placing in his hands, or in the hands of another person, any claim for the purpose of making a claim or bringing an action or special proceeding thereon, or defending the same; nor shall any attorney, directly or indirectly, as a consideration for such retainer, pay any expenses attending the prosecution or defense of any such claim or action.

§ 603.19 Attorneys assigned by the court as counsel for a defendant in a criminal case.

No attorney assigned by a court as counsel for a defendant in any criminal case shall in any manner demand, accept, receive or agree to accept or receive any payment, compensation, emolument, gratuity or reward, or any promise of payment, compensation, emolument, gratuity or reward or any money, property or thing of value or of personal advantage from such defendant or from any other person, except as expressly authorized by statute or by written order of the court duly entered upon its minutes.

§ 603.20 Prohibition against gratuities.

No attorney shall give any gift, bequest, favor or loan to any judge or any employee of any court or any member of his family residing in his household or to any member, officer, or employee of any governmental agency or any member of his family residing in his household, where such attorney has had or is likely to have any professional or official transaction with such court or governmental agency.

§ 603.21 Practice of law by nonjudicial personnel.

(a) An attorney who is employed as a public officer or employee in any court in this judicial department shall not maintain an office for the private practice of law, alone or with others, hold himself out to be in the private practice of law, or engage in the private practice of law; such attorney shall not participate, directly or indirectly, as attorney or counsel in any action or proceeding, pending before any court or any administrative board, agency, committee or commission of any government, or in the preparation or subscription of briefs, papers, or documents pertaining thereto.

(b) By special permission secured from the Presiding Justice of this judicial department as to each professional engagement, a person referred to in subdivision (a) of this section may engage in the private practice of law as to matters not pending before a court or governmental agency, in uncontested matters in the Surrogate's Court, uncontested accountings in the Supreme Court, and other *ex parte* applications not preliminary or incidental to litigated or contested matters. Such approval, which shall continue only to the completion of the particular engagement for which permission was obtained, shall be sought by application in writing to the Presiding Justice of this judicial department (processed through the immediate supervisor and the Administrative Judge or other head of the court or agency in which applicant is employed for his comment and recommendation including restrictions, if any) which shall state the position occupied, all pertinent information as to the matter to be handled (including the name of the client engaging such attorney and the prior relationship, if any, between such client and said attorney) and that in the event of litigation the applicant will immediately withdraw as attorney and notify his Administrative Judge or other head of the court or agency thereof.

(c) A person referred to in subdivision (a) of this section shall not engage in any other practice of law which is incompatible with or would reflect adversely upon the performance of his duties.

*   *   *   *

PART 604

COURT DECORUM

Section

604.1   **Obligation of attorneys and judges.**

604.2   **Judicial exercise of contempt power.**

604.3   **Conduct of criminal trial threatened by disruptive conduct.**

§ 604.1 Obligation of attorneys and judges.

(a) *Application of rules.*

This Part shall apply to all actions and proceedings, civil and criminal, in courts subject to the jurisdiction of the Appellate Division of the Supreme Court in this Judicial Department. It is intended to supplement but not to supersede, the code of professional responsibility as adopted by the New York State Bar Association and the rules governing judicial conduct as promulgated by the Administrative Board of the Judicial Conference. In the event of any conflict between the provisions of this Part and the code of professional responsibility or the rules governing judicial conduct, the code of professional responsibility and the rules governing judicial conduct shall prevail.

(b) *Importance of decorum in court.*

The courtroom, as the place where justice is dispensed, must at all times satisfy the appearance as well as the reality of fairness and equal treatment. Dignity, order and decorum are indispensable to the proper administration of justice. Disruptive conduct by any person while the court is in session is forbidden.

(c) *Disruptive conduct defined.*

Disruptive conduct is any intentional conduct by any person in the courtroom that substantially interferes with the dignity, order and decorum of judicial proceedings.

(d) *Obligation of the attorney.*

(1) The attorney is both an officer of the court and an advocate. It is his professional obligation to conduct his case courageously, vigorously, and with all the skill and knowledge he possesses. It is also his obligation to uphold the honor and maintain the dignity of the profession. He must avoid disorder or disruption in the courtroom, and he must maintain a respectful attitude toward the court. In all respects the attorney is bound, in

court and out, by the provisions of the code of professional responsibility.

(2) The attorney shall use his best efforts to dissuade his client and witnesses from causing disorder or disruption in the courtroom.

(3) The attorney shall not engage in any examination which is intended merely to harass, annoy or humiliate the witness.

(4) (i) No attorney shall argue in support of or against an objection without permission from the court; nor shall any attorney argue with respect to a ruling of the court on an objection without such permission.

(ii) However, an attorney may make a concise statement of the particular grounds for an objection or exception, not otherwise apparent, where it is necessary to do so in order to call the court's attention thereto, or to preserve an issue for appellate review. If an attorney believes in good faith that the court has wrongly made an adverse ruling, he may respectfully request reconsideration thereof.

(5) The attorney has neither the right nor duty to execute any directive of a client which is not consistent with professional standards of conduct. Nor may he advise another to do any act or to engage in any conduct which is in any manner contrary to this Part.

(6) Once a client has employed an attorney who has entered an appearance, the attorney shall not withdraw or abandon the case without (i) justifiable cause, (ii) reasonable notice to the client, and (iii) permission of the court.

(7) The attorney is not relieved of these obligations by what he may regard as a deficiency in the conduct or ruling of a judge or in the system of justice; nor is he relieved of these obligations by what he believes to be the moral, political, social, or ideological merits of the cause of any client.

(e) *Obligations of the judge.*

(1) In the administration of justice, the judge shall safeguard the rights of the parties and the interests of the public. The judge at all times shall be dignified, courteous, and considerate of the parties, attorneys, jurors, and witnesses. In the performance of his duties and in the maintenance of proper court decorum the judge is in all respects bound by the rules governing judicial conduct.

(2) The judge shall use his judicial power to prevent disruptions of the trial.

(3) A judge before whom a case is moved for trial shall preside at such trial unless he is satisfied, upon challenge, or sua sponte, that he is unable to serve with complete impartiality, in fact or appearance, with regard to the matter, or parties in question.

(4) Where the judge deems it appropriate in order to preserve or enhance the dignity, order and decorum of the proceedings, he shall prescribe and make known the rules relating to conduct which the parties, attorneys, witnesses and others will be expected to follow in the courtroom.

(5) The judge should be the exemplar of dignity and impartiality. He shall suppress his personal predilections, control his temper and emotions, and otherwise avoid conduct on his part which tends to demean the proceedings or to undermine his authority in the courtroom. When it becomes necessary during trial for him to comment upon the conduct of witnesses, spectators, counsel, or others, or upon the testimony, he shall do so in a firm and polite manner, limiting his comments and rulings to what is reasonably required for the orderly progress of the trial, and refraining from unnecessary disparagement of persons or issues.

(6) The judge is not relieved of these obligations by what he may regard as a deficiency in the conduct of any attorney who appears before him; nor is he relieved of these obligations by what he believes to be the moral, political, social, or ideological deficiencies of the cause of any party.

§ 604.2 Judicial exercise of contempt power.

(a) *Exercise of the summary contempt power.*

(1) The power of the court to punish summarily contempt committed in its immediate view and presence shall be exercised only in exceptional and necessitous circumstances, as follows:

(i) Where the offending conduct either

(*a*) disrupts or threatens to disrupt proceedings actually in progress; or

(*b*) destroys or undermines or tends seriously to destroy or undermine the dignity and authority of the court in a manner and to the extent that it appears unlikely that the court will be able to continue to conduct its normal business in an appropriate way; and

(ii) The court reasonably believes that a prompt summary adjudication of contempt may aid in maintaining or restoring and maintaining proper order and decorum.

(2) Wherever practical punishment should be determined and imposed at the time of the adjudication of contempt. However, where the court deems it advisable the determination and imposition of punishment may be deferred following a prompt summary adjudication of contempt which satisfies the necessity for immediate judicial corrective or disciplinary action.

(3) Before summary adjudication of contempt the accused shall be given a reasonable opportunity to make a statement in his defense or in extenuation of his conduct.

(b) *Exercise of the contempt power after hearing.*

In all other cases, notwithstanding the occurrence of the contumacious conduct in the view and presence of the sitting court, the contempt shall be adjudicated at a plenary hearing with due process of law including notice, written charges, assistance of counsel, compulsory process for production of evidence and an opportunity of the accused to confront witnesses against him.

(c) *Judicial warning of possible contempts.*

Except in the case of the most flagrant and offensive misbehavior which in the court's discretion requires an immediate adjudication of contempt to preserve order and decorum, the court should warn and admonish the person engaged in alleged contumacious conduct that his conduct is deemed contumacious and give the person an opportunity to desist before adjudicating him in contempt. Where a person so warned desists from further offensive conduct, there is ordinarily no occasion for an adjudication of contempt. Where a person is summarily adjudicated in contempt and punishment deferred and such person desists from further offensive conduct, the court should consider carefully whether there is any need for punishment for the adjudicated contempt.

(d) *Disqualification of judge.*

The judge before whom the alleged contumacious conduct occurred is disqualified from presiding at the plenary hearing or trial (as distinguished from summary action) except with the defendant's consent:

(1) If the allegedly contumacious conduct consists primarily of personal disrespect to or vituperative criticism of the judge; or

(2) If the judge's recollection of, or testimony concerning the conduct allegedly constituting contempt is necessary for an adjudication; or

(3) If the judge concludes that in view of his recollection of the events he would be unable to make his decision solely on the basis of the evidence at the hearing.

(e) *Preference for appeals from criminal court contempt convictions.*

Any appeal by an attorney of his conviction for the misdemeanor of criminal contempt which is pending in any court in this judicial department, shall be granted a preference by the court.

§ 604.3 Conduct of criminal trial threatened by disruptive conduct.

(a) *Removal of disruptive defendant.*

(1) If a defendant engages in disruptive conduct by word or action in the courtroom in the course of his trial, the trial judge may order the defendant to be removed from the courtroom and placed in custody, and the trial judge may proceed with the trial in the absence of the defendant.

(2) The trial judge may not exclude the defendant except after warning that further disruptive conduct will lead to removal of the defendant from the courtroom.

(3) The defendant shall be returned to the courtroom immediately upon a determination by the court that the defendant is not likely to engage in further disruptive conduct.

(b) *Communication between defendant and courtroom.*

If the defendant is removed from the courtroom under the provisions of paragraph (1) of subdivision (a) of this section, the trial judge shall make reasonable efforts to establish methods of communication linking the defendant with the courtroom while his trial is in progress. For such defendant the judge may provide methods of communication in any way suitable to the physical facilities of the courthouse and consonant with the goal of providing adequate communication to the courtroom and to defense counsel.

(c) *Restraint of defendant.*

(1) If a defendant engages in disruptive conduct in the course of the trial, and the trial judge determines not to take action under subdivision (a) of this section, the trial judge may order the defendant to be physically restrained in the courtroom while his trial continues.

(2) The trial judge shall not apply the restraints authorized in the preceding subdivision unless he has warned the defendant, following disruptive conduct by the defendant, that further misconduct will lead to the physical restraint of the defendant in the courtroom.

(3) The physical restraint of the defendant shall be terminated immediately upon a determination by the court that the defendant is not likely to engage in further disruptive conduct.

PART 606

LEGAL AND MEDICAL SERVICES; DUTIES OF COUNSEL RESPECTING APPEALS

*   *   *   *

§ 606.1 Assignments pursuant to section 35 of the Judiciary Law.

(a) *Counsel.*

(1) Whenever in a proceeding described in section 35 of the Judiciary Law the court shall find that counsel should be assigned to represent a person who does not have legal representation and who is financially unable to obtain counsel, the court shall appoint the attorney-in-charge of the criminal courts branch or of the civil branch of the Legal Aid Society as the attorney of record to represent such person. If, however, the court deems the assignment of other counsel to be required because of either a conflict of interest or other good cause, it shall enter an order appointing the attorney designated by the administrator of the assigned counsel plan in the first judicial department from the panels of attorneys, established under that plan. Designations of counsel by the administrator shall, as nearly as practicable, be by rotation.

(2) The term "legal representation" shall include representation by a member of the bar, representation by the Director of the Mental Hygiene Legal Service, or representation by a corporation approved pursuant to the provisions of Judiciary Law § 495.

(3) A copy of each such order of appointment shall be forwarded by the court to the administrator of the assigned counsel plan. Claims for compensation by counsel or the Legal Aid Society shall be submitted to the court which made the assignment on prescribed forms, specifying the time expended (in court and out of court), the services rendered and the expenses reasonably incurred, and stating that no payment or promise of payment has been received in respect of such services and expenses.

(b) *Psychiatrists and physicians.*

(1) Whenever in a proceeding described in section 35 of the Judiciary Law the court shall find that a psychiatrist or physician should be appointed to examine and report and, if required, to testify at the hearing upon the condition of a person, the court shall request the Mental Health Information Service to designate such psychiatrist or physician for such purposes. If the court deems that because of a conflict of interest or other good cause the service should not make the designation, it shall request the Impartial Medical Panel Office

of the Supreme Court, first judicial district, to do so. Designations shall, as nearly as possible, be by rotation from panels of psychiatrists and physicians recommended by the New York Academy of Medicine in consultation with the Bronx County and New York County chapters of the American Psychiatric Association, Bronx County Medical Society, and the Medical Society of the County of New York, including the panel heretofore furnished to the Mental Health Information Service, first judicial department.

(2) A copy of each order of appointment entered by the court shall be forwarded to the director of the Mental Health Information Service. Claims for compensation by a psychiatrist or physician shall be submitted to the court which made the assignment on prescribed forms, specifying the time expended (in court and out of court), the services rendered and the expenses reasonably incurred, and stating that no payment or promise of payment has been received in respect of such services and expenses.

§ 606.2 Compensation for extraordinary services.

(a) Whenever an attorney, psychiatrist or physician, or a person providing investigative, expert or other services, seeks compensation in excess of the statutory limits prescribed by article 18-B of the County Law or section 35 of the Judiciary Law, because of extraordinary circumstances, he shall submit with his claim a detailed affidavit stating the nature of the proceeding, the manner in which the time was expended, the necessity therefor, and all other facts which tend to demonstrate extraordinary circumstances. In addition, if the claim is by an attorney he shall state the disposition of the matter.

(b) An application seeking compensation in excess of the statutory limits prescribed by article 18-b of the county law or section 35 of the judiciary law shall be reviewed, *sua sponte* or upon the request of any person or governmental body affected by the order, by the appropriate administrative judge pursuant to section 127.2 of this part.

§ 606.3 Expenses of assigned counsel, psychiatrists or physicians.

The term *expenses reasonably incurred,* whenever used herein, shall not include normal office expenses such as local telephone service, postage, secretarial and other office overhead, or mileage for use of automobile, parking fees, taxi fares, etc. in traveling to a court, hospital or place of detention located within the City of New York and readily accessible by rapid transit.

§ 606.4 Determination of financial ability.

The appointment of counsel to represent a person who does not have legal representation and who states that he is not financially able to obtain counsel, shall be made upon a finding of inability based either upon such person's affidavit or upon oral testimony in court under oath or by affirmation, or by such other proof as the court may direct.

§ 606.5 Duties of counsel with respect to representation of defendants in criminal actions.

(a) *Duties of assigned or retained counsel.* (1) It shall be the duty of counsel assigned to or retained for the defense of a defendant in a criminal action or proceeding to represent defendant in the trial court until the action or proceeding has been terminated in that court, and to comply with the provisions of paragraphs (b)(1) or (d)(2) of this section, after which the duties of assigned counsel shall be ended.

(2) It shall be the duty of counsel assigned to prosecute or defend an appeal on behalf of an indigent defendant to accept said assignment and to prosecute the appeal until entry of the order of the appellate court terminating the appeal, and to comply with the provisions of paragraphs (b)(2) or (d)(2) of this section, after which the duties of assigned counsel shall be ended.

(b) *Notification of right to appeal or to apply for a certificate granting leave to appeal.* Obligation to file profile statement with notice of appeal. (1) After conviction and sentence. Where there has been a conviction after trial or otherwise, or where there has been an adverse decision upon an application for a writ of *habeas corpus,* upon a motion to vacate a judgment made pursuant to section 440.10 of the Criminal Procedure Law, upon a motion to set aside a sentence made pursuant to section 440.20 of the Criminal Procedure Law, or where there has been a determination revoking parole, it shall be the duty of counsel, retained or assigned, immediately after the pronouncement of sentence or service of a copy of the order disposing of the application for a writ of *habeas corpus,* of a motion to vacate a judgment made pursuant to section 440.10 of the Criminal Procedure Law, of a motion to set aside a sentence made pursuant to section 440.20 of the Criminal Procedure Law, or of a notice of the determination revoking parole, to advise the defendant or parolee in writing of his right to

appeal or to apply for a certificate granting leave to appeal pursuant to subdivision 4 of section 460.10 of the Criminal Procedure Law, the time limitations involved, in the manner of instituting an appeal and of obtaining a transcript of the testimony, and of the right of a person who has an absolute right to appeal or has received a certificate granting leave to appeal and is unable to pay the cost of an appeal to apply for leave to appeal as a poor person. It shall also be the duty of such counsel to ascertain whether defendant or the parolee wishes to appeal or to apply for a certificate granting leave to appeal, and, if so, to serve and file the necessary notice of appeal from a judgment of conviction or determination revoking parole or to apply for a certificate granting leave to appeal from the denial of a motion made pursuant to section 440.10 or section 440.20 of the Criminal Procedure Law and, if granted, to file the necessary certificate and notice of appeal within the time limitations provided for in subdivision 4 of section 460.10 Criminal Procedure Law. Attached to the notices of appeal, counsel shall file two copies of a profile statement which sets forth:

(i) title of the action and indictment number;

(ii) county and court from which the appeal is taken;

(iii) full names of the defendant and any co-defendants;

(iv) name(s), address(es) and telephone number(s) of defense counsel;

(v) charges upon which defendant stands convicted and date judgment was entered;

(vi) pretrial hearings and dates held;

(vii) trial dates and/or plea dates; and

(viii) whether court ordered daily copy of hearing or trial transcripts was received and the date(s) the transcripts were returned.

(2) It shall also be the duty of such counsel to ascertain whether defendant wishes to apply for permission to appeal to the Court of Appeals, and, if so, counsel shall make a timely application therefor. If permission to appeal is granted, and poor person's relief and the assignment of counsel are necessary, counsel shall make timely application for such relief. In the case of an order affirming a judgment dismissing a writ of habeas corpus, such counsel shall advise the relator of his or her right to appeal where there is a dissent by at least two justices on a question of law, or of the right to apply for permission to appeal where the determination is unanimous or there is a dissent by fewer than two justices.

(c) *Notification to defendants who appear without counsel.* (1) After conviction or denial of a motion to vacate a judgment made pursuant to section 440.10 of the Criminal Procedure Law, or of a motion to set aside a sentence made pursuant to section 440.20 of the Criminal Procedure Law. If a defendant has appeared *pro se,* the trial court shall advise a defendant of his right to appeal from a judgment of conviction, or of his right to apply for a certificate granting leave to appeal from an order denying a motion to vacate a judgment made pursuant to section 440.10 of the Criminal Procedure Law, or of a motion to set aside a sentence made pursuant to section 440.20 of the Criminal Procedure Law. It shall also advise a defendant of the right of a person unable to pay the cost of an appeal to apply for leave to appeal as a poor person. If the defendant so requests, the clerk of the court shall prepare and file and serve forthwith a notice of appeal on behalf of the defendant from a judgment of conviction. If the defendant so requests in writing within 30 days after service upon him of a copy of an order denying a motion to vacate a judgment made pursuant to section 440.10 of the Criminal Procedure Law, or of a motion to set aside a sentence made pursuant to section 440.20 of the Criminal Procedure Law, and no previous application for a certificate granting leave to appeal has been made, the clerk of the court shall serve a copy of such request upon the district attorney and shall transmit the request and the original record of the proceedings sought to be reviewed to the appellate court. Upon determination of the application the original record of proceedings shall be returned to the trial court together with a certified copy of the order entered upon the application; a certified copy of the order shall also be sent to the defendant at his address shown in the application.

(2) After determination adverse to defendant.

(i) If on an appeal from a judgment of conviction after trial or otherwise, or on an appeal from an order or sentence appealed by the people pursuant to section 450.20 of the Criminal Procedure Law, or from an order denying a motion to vacate a judgment made pursuant to section 440.10 of the Criminal Procedure Law, or of a motion to set aside a sentence made pursuant to section 440.20 of the Criminal Procedure Law, a defendant has appeared *pro se* and the judgment, order or sentence is adverse to the defendant the copy of the order of affirmance, with notice of entry, which is served on the defendant shall have annexed or appended thereto the following notice:

NOTICE AS TO FURTHER APPEAL

Pursuant to section 460.20 of the Criminal Procedure Law, defendant has the right to apply for leave to appeal to the Court of Appeals by making application to the Chief Judge of that court by submitting such application to the clerk of that court or to a justice of the Appellate Division of the Supreme Court of this department on reasonable notice to the respondent within 30 days after service of a copy of the order or affirmance with notice of entry.

Denial of the application for permission to appeal by the judge or justice first applied to is final and no new application may thereafter be made to any other judge or justice.

(ii) Where an order determining an appeal from a judgment that determines either a writ of *habeas corpus* or a petition in an article 78 proceeding affecting a criminal case is adverse to a relator or petitioner appearing *pro se*, the following notice shall be annexed or appended to the copy of the order served, with notice of entry, upon such relator or petitioner:

NOTICE AS TO FURTHER APPEAL

If the determination by the Appellate Division is unanimous or there is a dissent by fewer than two justices, an appeal may be taken to the Court of Appeals only pursuant to section 5602 of the Civil Practice Law and Rules by permission of the Appellate Division or by permission of the Court of Appeals upon refusal of the Appellate Division to grant permission, or by direct application to the Court of Appeals.

An application for permission to appeal must be made within 30 days after service of a copy of the order of affirmance with notice of entry.

If there is a dissent in the Appellate Division or there is a modification of the judgment appealed from, relator or petitioner may take an appeal to the Court of Appeals as a matter of right pursuant to section 5601(a) of the Civil Practice Law and Rules by serving on the adverse party a notice of appeal within 30 days after service of a copy of the order appealed from, with notice of entry, and filing the notice of appeal in the office where the judgment or order of the original instance is entered.

(d) *Notification to defendants of people's appeals.* (1) It shall be the duty of trial counsel, upon service of an order appealable by the people pursuant to Criminal Procedure Law article 450 to forthwith notify defendant in writing that the people have the right to take an appeal, the consequences of the people's appeal and the defendant's rights, including the right to retain appellate counsel or, if indigent, to apply for leave to appear as a poor person.

(2) It shall be the duty of appellate counsel upon service of a notice of appeal or an order of appointment to notify the client in writing that the people have taken an appeal from an order of the trial court and the consequences of the appeal.

(3) In the event no appellate counsel has appeared on behalf of the defendant, assigned trial counsel, upon receipt of the people's brief, shall make diligent efforts to locate the defendant and notify the defendant, in writing, that the people have filed a brief, the consequences of the people's appeal and the defendant's rights, including

the right to retain appellate counsel, or if indigent, to apply for leave to appeal as a poor person.

§ 606.6 Additional duties of the court and of defendant's counsel in connection with trial court transcripts.

Where furnishing of a daily copy of a transcript is ordered by the court, the ribbon copy thereof shall be delivered to the court and a carbon copy to counsel for the defendant. Both the court and counsel for the defendant shall be duty-bound to preserve their respective copies. At the conclusion of the trial or hearing, trial counsel for the defendant shall, if an appeal is taken, deliver said carbon copy to appellant's counsel immediately on being advised of the name and address of said appellant's counsel. At the conclusion of the trial or hearing and forthwith after the decision or verdict, as the case may be, the ribbon copy shall be delivered by the court to the county clerk for filing. The ribbon copy and the carbon copy shall constitute the two transcripts of the proceedings required by section 460.70 of the Criminal Procedure Law.

* * * *

PART 611

FAMILY COURT LAW GUARDIAN PLAN

Section

§ 611.1 Introduction.

(a) (1) The Family Court panels now established in the First Judicial Department pursuant to article 18-B of the County Law and pertinent provisions of the Family Court Act, shall continue in effect and shall constitute the Family Court Panel Plan in the First Judicial Department.

(2) The law guardian roster of attorneys certified pursuant to the Rules of the Chief Administrator Part 36 and the former Rules of the Court Part 614, to accept appointment as a law guardian for an infant child or children pursuant to Family Court § 249(a), Civil Practice Law and Rules § 1202, or Uniform Rules of the Trial Court § 202.16(f)(3), shall continue in effect in this department as part of the Law Guardian Plan.

(3) The Family Court Panel Plan and the law guardian roster are merged to form the Law Guardian Plan. An attorney certified for appointment in one capacity shall be deemed certified for appointment in the other capacity and by virtue of the certification agrees to accept assignments and appointments in Supreme Court or Family Court.

(b) The Law Guardian Director, appointed by the Presiding Justice of the Appellate Division, First Department, shall administer the [Family Court] Law Guardian Plan.

§ 611.2 Assignment of counsel in Family Court.

Counsel to be assigned pursuant to the Family Court Act, section 262, shall be selected from such panels as have been established by the Assigned Counsel Plan in the First Judicial Department.

§ 611.3 Appointment of law guardians in Family Court.

Where for sufficient reason law guardians to be appointed pursuant to Family Court Act section 249, cannot otherwise be designated as provided in section 243(a) of such act, the court may draw upon such panels as have been established by the Assigned Counsel plan for the First Judicial Department as if such panels had been separately established pursuant to section 243(c) of such act.

§ 611.4 Certification of attorney.

Certification of an attorney as a member of any panel of the Law Guardian Plan shall be for a one year term subject to: (a) annual redesignation pursuant to Family Court Act § 244(b); and (b) recertification as directed by the justices of the Appellate Division, First Department.

§ 611.5 Departmental Advisory Committee.

Commencing January 1, 1980 the justices of the Appellate Division, First Department established a Departmental Advisory Committee. This Committee shall remain in operation and have the authority and responsibility to oversee the operation of the Law Guardian Plan and to consider all matters that pertain to the qualifications, performance and professional conduct of individual plan attorneys in their assignments and appointments as plan attorneys, and the representation of indigent parties in Family Court proceedings.

§ 611.6 Composition of the Departmental Advisory Committee.

(a) The Committee shall be composed of no fewer than fifteen attorneys who shall be experienced in Family Court and domestic relations proceedings, three Family Court judges, one mental health expert, one representative from each of the three bar associations designated in the Rules of the Court § 612.3, one faculty member of an accredited law school in the First Judicial Department, the Law Guardian Director and the Assigned Counsel Plan Administrator.

(b) The Justices of the Appellate Division, First Department shall nominate all Committee members, except the representatives of the three bar associations, who shall be nominated by the respective presidents of those associations. The presiding Justice may appoint such additional members to the Committee as will facilitate its operation. The term of appointment for each Committee member, except the Law Guardian Director and Assigned Counsel Plan Administrator, shall be staggered and for a period of three years subject to renomination by the justices of the Appellate Division. The term of appointment for the Law Guardian Director and the Assigned Counsel Plan Administrator shall be co-extensive with the term of their respective positions.

(c) The Presiding Justice shall designate a chair and vice-chair of the Committee.

§ 611.7 Duties of the Departmental Advisory Committee.

The Departmental Advisory Committee shall conduct its activities and carry out the duties enumerated in this Part pursuant to the Bylaws of the Assigned Counsel Plan Central Screening Committee, set forth in Part 612 Appendix A of the Rules of the Court. The Law Guardian Director shall be substituted where reference in the Bylaws is made to the Administrator.

§ 611.8 Screening process.

(a) All applicants for plan membership shall be screened by the Departmental Advisory Committee.

(b) The Committee, in accordance with standards for admission to the panels entitled *General Requirements for All Applicants to the Family Court Panels* and *General Requirements for Law Guardian to Qualify for Appointment in Domestic Relations Matters*, shall make a determination as to whether an attorney is qualified for membership on any of the panels.

§ 611.9 Continuing legal education.

(a) The Departmental Advisory Committee, in cooperation with the Assigned Counsel Plan, the Continuing Legal Education Office and the three bar associations designated in the Rules of the Court § 612.3, shall:

(1) on a continuing basis, develop and conduct training and education programs that focus on domestic relations law and practice before the Family Court;

(2) annually promulgate a list of recommended training and education programs pertaining to domestic relations and family law sponsored by independent providers of legal education; and

(3) organize and operate a co-counsel program.

(b) Members of the Law Guardian Plan biennially must complete at least eight hours of training and education programs that are either sponsored by the Departmental Advisory Committee or included on the list of recommended programs referred to in subsection (a).

§ 611.10 Annual report.

(a) No later than September 30 of each calendar year the Departmental Advisory Committee shall file with the Appellate Division a written evaluation of the panels and the panel attorneys setting forth information regarding: the performance of plan attorneys, efficiency of the panels as a means of representing indigent parties, the training and education programs sponsored and recommended by the Committee, and proposals for improving the operation of the Law Guardian

COURT RULES

Plan. In preparing the written evaluation, the Committee may consult with Family Court judges and bar associations. Plan attorneys shall cooperate with the Committee in preparing the evaluation.

(b) An annual report of the operation of the Family Court panels shall be filed by the Appellate Division with the Chief Administrator of the Unified Court System no later than January 31, of each calendar year.

§ 611.11 Continuity of powers.

Nothing contained in this Part shall be construed to limit the powers of the Appellate Division or the presiding justice thereof or the Administrator of the Assigned Counsel Plan otherwise granted pursuant to law.

§ 611.12 Members of the Departmental Advisory Committee as volunteers.

The members of the Departmental Advisory Committee, as volunteers, are expressly authorized to participate in a State-sponsored volunteer program within the meaning of Public Officers Law section 17 (a).

§ 611.13 Complaints.

The Departmental Advisory Committee may receive and investigate complaints against individual plan members appointed pursuant to this part according to the procedures set forth in Part 612 Appendix A of the Rules of the Court.

§ 611.14 Use of records.

All papers, records and documents involving a complaint relating to the discharge of a panel attorney's duties shall be sealed and deemed private and confidential. However, upon good cause being shown, the justices of the Appellate Division or the presiding justice thereof may, by written order, permit to be divulged all or any part of such papers, records and documents. In the discretion of the presiding justice, such order may be made either with notice to the persons or attorneys to be affected thereby, or upon such notice to them as the presiding justice may direct. Records of the Departmental Advisory Committee shall be made available, upon request, without the necessity for such order, to the Departmental Disciplinary Committee for the Appellate Division, First Judicial Department.

PART 612

RULES TO IMPLEMENT A CRIMINAL COURTS PANEL PLAN

(Statutory authority: County Law, art. 18-B)

Section

§ 612.0 Introduction.

The justices of the Appellate Division of the Supreme Court in and for the First Judicial Department, by virtue of the authority vested in them by law and pursuant to article 18-B of the County Law as implemented by Executive Order No. 178 of the Mayor of the City of New York effective December 1, 1965, and by the Assigned Counsel Plan, approved by the Administrative Board of the Judicial Conference of the State of New York on April 28, 1966, do hereby, effective July 1, 1980, adopt this Part to establish rules governing the Criminal Courts Panel Plan of the Assigned Counsel Plan for the Appellate Division, First Judicial Department, and to set forth rules and standards regulating the selection, designation, performance and professional conduct of individual panel plan attorneys appointed to furnish representation for indigent defendants in criminal proceedings.

§ 612.1 Previous measures continued.

The Assigned Counsel Plan and the Criminal Courts Panels previously established in the First Judicial Department pursuant to article 18-B of the County Law shall continue in effect in this department.

§ 612.2 Term of appointments.

Appointments of attorneys to any of the Indigent Defendant Legal Panels shall be for a term of not more than one year, but successive designations may be made.

§ 612.3 Authority of screening committee.

The departmental central screening committee heretofore established on January 4, 1979, upon the agreement and recommendation of the participating bar associations to the Assigned Counsel Plan (i.e., Association of the Bar of the City of New York, New York County Lawyers' Association, Bronx County Bar Association), is continued in effect in this department. The departmental screening committee shall have the authority and responsibility to oversee the operation of the panel plan and to consider all matters which pertain to the performance and professional conduct of individual panel plan attorneys in their assignments as panel attorneys and the representation of indigent parties in criminal proceedings.

§ 612.4 Membership of screening committee.

The membership of the central screening committee shall consist of 15 members, five from each of the aforesaid bar associations, such members to be nominated by the presidents of the associations. The chairman, vice-chairman and the secretary shall be designated by the presiding justice from among the nominees. The term of appointment of each member shall be for a period of three years. The term of appointment of the present committee shall be deemed to have commenced January 4, 1979.

§ 612.5 Duties of screening committee.

The central screening committee shall promulgate bylaws, subject to the approval of the Appellate Division, First Judicial Department, pursuant to which the committee may conduct its activities and carry out those duties as enumerated in this Part.

§ 612.6 Screening process.

(a) All applications for panel membership submitted to the participating bar associations shall, as agreed to by those associations, be screened by the central screening committee.

(b) The committee, in accordance with standards for admission to the panels, entitled "General Requirements for All Applicants to the Indigent Defendants Legal Panel," shall make a determination as to whether an applicant is qualified for membership on any of the panels.

(c) The committee shall inform the appropriate bar association of its determination and prepare and certify a list of qualified attorneys to the administrator of the Assigned Counsel Plan.

§ 612.7 Monitoring of criminal appeals; annual; written evaluation.

(a) As directed by the court, an employee of the Assigned Counsel Plan office shall monitor and report to the court the status of pending criminal appeals assigned to members of the appellate legal panel.

(b) No later than the last day of each calendar year, the central screening committee shall file with the Appellate Division a written evaluation of the plan and of panel attorneys, including Criminal Court, Supreme Court, homicide and appellate panels, setting forth all appropriate information with respect to the efficiency of the panel plan, problems which may exist in the operation plan, and procedures which have been or will be followed to improve the quality of legal representation in the Criminal Courts. In preparing the written evaluation, the central screening committee may seek evaluations of the plan and administrator of the Assigned Counsel Plan in the First Judicial Department, the Association of the Bar of the City of New York, the New York County Lawyers' Association, the Bronx County Bar Association and panel attorneys shall cooperate with the central screening committee in this evaluation.

§ 612.8 Training program.

Pursuant to the obligations of the participating bar associations under article 18-B of the County Law and the Assigned Counsel Plan, the bar associations shall, after consultation with the Appellate Division and the administrator of the Assigned Counsel Plan, provide a continuing program of training and education which will allow panel attorneys to improve their professional competence in criminal law. This program should provide for, but not be confined to, the establishment of a continuing co-counsel program and a professional course in criminal advocacy.

§ 612.9 Panel attorneys.

(a) The Appellate Division, pursuant to the provisions of the Assigned Counsel Plan, may at any time make additions to or deletions from the panels.

(b) The central screening committee may continue to process complaints against panel attorneys which relate to the discharge of an attorney's duties under the panel plan, and shall, in consultation with the administrator of the Assigned Counsel Plan, and subject to the approval of the Appellate Division, adopt rules for the processing of such complaints.

§ 612.10 Use of records.

All papers, records and documents involving a complaint relating to the discharge of a panel attorney's duties shall be sealed and be deemed private and confidential. However, upon good cause being shown, the justices of the Appellate Division or the presiding justice thereof may, by written order, permit to be divulged all or any part of such papers, records and documents. In the discretion of the presiding justice or the acting presiding justice, such order may be made either without notice to the persons or attorneys to be affected thereby, or upon such notice to them as he may direct. Records of the central screening committee, however, shall be made available, upon request, without the necessity for such order, to the Departmental Disciplinary Committee for the Appellate Division, First Judicial Department.

§ 612.11 Members of departmental screening committee as volunteers.

The members of the departmental central screening committee as volunteers are expressly authorized to participate in a State-sponsored volunteer program within the meaning of subdivision 1 of section 17 of the Public Officers Law.

§ 612.12 Present powers retained.

Noting contained in this Part shall be construed to limit the power of the Appellate Division, the presiding justice thereof, the participating bar associations to the Assigned Counsel Plan or the administrator of the Assigned Counsel Plan otherwise granted by the Assigned Counsel Plan.

§ 612.13 Appendix A—central screening committee indigent defendants assigned counsel plan.

The Appellate Division, First Judicial Department, in furtherance of its obligation to provide indigent criminal defendants with competent counsel, approves the bylaws contained herein. Membership on all assigned counsel panels is a privilege granted to qualified attorneys by the Appellate Division, First Judicial Department.

BYLAWS

1. **Quorum and Voting.**

1.1 A quorum of a majority of the Committee is required for the conduct of business.

1.2 Final action on proposed guidelines, applications and complaints requires a majority vote of a quorum.

2. **Application for Certification or Recertification.**

2.1 All applications for certification or recertification to the panels shall be addressed to the Administrator. The provisions of this section shall apply to applications seeking initial certification or recertification to the panels.

2.2 The Administrator shall examine each application for facial sufficiency. If it is found to be insufficient, the Administrator shall return the application to the applicant.

2.3 The Administrator shall promptly assign every application not returned pursuant to 2.2 to the Committee member for his or her review.

2.4 Within sixty days of receiving the application, the assigned committee member shall contact two-thirds of the required references, at least two in each category (judges, adversaries and colleagues) and shall recommend in writing, to the Chair, the action to be taken on the application. A copy of the recommendation shall be submitted to the Administrator. Requests for extension of the sixty day period shall be made in writing to the Administrator.

2.5 Upon receipt of the assigned committee member's recommendation, the Chair shall accept the recommendation or refer the application to the Committee for review. When the Chair refers an application to the Committee, the Chair shall invite the applicant to appear before the Committee. Upon a review of the assigned committee member's recommendation, the application and any other relevant material, the Committee shall vote on the application pursuant to § 1.2 of these bylaws. The Chair or the Committee shall take the following action on an application:

(1) Certify the applicant to the panel(s) for which he or she is qualified;

(2) Deny certification of the applicant to any of the panels for which he or she is not qualified;

(3) Set conditions that the applicant must meet to establish the necessary qualifications for certification.

2.6 Applicants shall be advised by letter of the determination. In the event the applicant is denied certification, the letter must specify the reasons therefor.

2.7 The Committee's action is appealable to the presiding justice of the Appellate Division, First Judicial Department by the submission of a letter requesting review of the Committee's determination. The presiding justice's review of the Committee's determination is final and non-appealable.

2.8 An applicant denied certification to any panel may reapply for that panel one year after the date of the letter denying certification unless a shorter time or other conditions are set by the Chair or the Committee pursuant to § 2.5.

3. Complaints and Sanctions.

3.1 The Administrator, in consultation with the Chair, shall accept and keep records of written complaints concerning the competence and conduct of panel attorneys. Complaints made to the Administrator shall be forwarded to the Chair.

3.2 The Chair, in consultation with the Administrator, may dismiss complaints. Complaints not dismissed shall be referred to a committee member designated by the Chair for further investigation within thirty days of receipt of the complaint.

3.3 Once a complaint has been referred for further investigation, a subcommittee consisting of the Chair, the Administrator, and two additional committee members shall vote as to whether the attorney should be suspended. Suspension shall be imposed upon a majority vote of the subcommittee. The suspension shall continue pending a resolution of the complaint.

3.4 A panel member who is the subject of a complaint shall receive notice of the substance of the complaint. The notice shall advise the attorney that he or she may respond in writing.

3.5 Investigation by the designated subcommittee member shall be completed within ninety days. Extension of time to investigate a complaint may be granted by the Chair. Upon the completion of an investigation, the designated committee member shall make a report, with findings and recommendations, to the Committee.

3.6 The Committee shall, upon receipt of the report, invite the attorney to appear before the Committee, and upon having duly considered the attorney's statements and other relevant submissions, shall take one or more of the following actions, as shall be appropriate:

(1) Dismiss the complaint;

(2) Adopt the recommendation;

(3) Reject the recommendation;

(4) Suspend the panel attorney from any or all panels to which the attorney is certified and impose conditions upon the attorney's restoration to the panel;

(5) Recommend the substitution of the panel attorney on some or all of the cases to which the attorney is currently assigned by notification to the trial court where the cases are pending;

(6) Remove the attorney from any or all panels to which the attorney is certified.

3.7 At any time the Committee or subcommittee may vote to transmit the information it has developed to the District Attorney or the Department Disciplinary Committee.

3.8 The Chair shall promptly notify the attorney in writing of the Committee's action. In the event the determination imposes a restriction on the attorney's panel membership, the letter shall set forth the reasons therefor.

3.9 The determination of the Committee is appealable to the presiding justice of the Appellate Division, First Judicial Department by the submission of a letter requesting review of the Committee's determination. The presiding justice's review of the Committee's determination is final and non-appealable.

3.10 Nothing contained in these bylaws limits the authority of the Appellate Division to suspend or remove an attorney from the panels.

4. Responsibilities of Committee Members.

4.1 Committee members shall act expeditiously on applications and complaints referred to them. Any Committee member who fails to take timely action twice during any twelve month period shall be removed by the Presiding Justice.

5. Responsibilities of Officers.

5.1 An executive committee shall be formed, consisting of the Chair, the Vice-chair, Administrator and three members designated by the Chair. One of the three designees shall serve as Secretary.

5.2 The executive committee may act in place of the Committee in any matter that requires action by the Committee during a period in which the Committee is not scheduled to meet for more than thirty days. Any action taken by the executive committee shall be ratified by the Committee at its next meeting.

5.3 The Chair may designate subcommittees and may designate committee members to serve as chairs therefor.

5.4 All officers and executive committee members shall serve in their respective capacities for three years and may be reappointed by the Appellate Division.

PART 613

RULES TO IMPLEMENT AN INDIGENT DEFENSE ORGANIZATION OVERSIGHT COMMITTEE

§ 613.1 Introduction.

The justices of the Appellate Division of the Supreme Court in and for the First Judicial Department, by virtue of the authority vested in them by law and pursuant to article 18-B of the County Law as implemented by Executive Order No. 178 of the Mayor of the City of New York effective December 1, 1995, the Assigned Counsel Plan approved by the Administrative Board of the Judicial Conference of the State of New York on April 28, 1966, and now upon the request of the City of New York and the participating bar associations to the Assigned Counsel Plan (i.e., Association of the Bar of the City of New York, New York County Lawyers' Association and the Bronx County Bar Association) do hereby, effective November 1, 1995, adopt this Part to establish rules governing the Indigent Defense Organization Oversight Committee for the Appellate Division, First Judicial Department, and to set forth rules and standards regulating the performance and professional conduct of indigent defense organizations and the attorneys in the employ of such organization who are appointed to furnish representation for indigent defendants in criminal proceedings.

§ 613.2 Previous measures continued.

The assigned Counsel Plan and the Criminal Courts Panels previously established in the First Judicial Department pursuant to Article 18-B of the County Law shall continue in effect in this department.

§ 613.3 Authority of oversight committee.

The indigent Defense Organization Oversight Committee hereby established, upon the agreement and recommendation of the City of New York and the participating bar associations to the Assigned Counsel Plan (i.e., Association of the Bar of the City of New York, New York County Lawyers' Association, and the Bronx County Bar Association) shall have the authority and responsibility to monitor the operation of organizations that contract with the City of New York to represent indigent defendants in criminal proceedings, and to consider all matters that pertain to the performance and professional conduct of such organizations and the individual attorneys in their employ who are assigned to represent indigent parties in criminal proceedings.

§ 613.4 Membership of oversight committee.

The membership of the Oversight Committee shall consist of lawyers to be nominated by the presidents of the bar associations and by the justices of the Appellate Division, First Department. The chair and vice-chair shall be designated by the presiding justice from among the nominees. The term of appointment for each member shall be for a period of three years subject to renomination by the justices of the Appellate Division, with the exception that four nominees will be appointed for an initial term of four years.

§ 613.5 Duties of oversight committee.

The Oversight Committee shall promulgate by laws and standards to be entitled "General Requirements for All Organized Providers of Defense Services to Indigent Defendants," subject to the approval of the Appellate Division, First Judicial Department, pursuant to which the committee may conduct its activities and carry out those duties as enumerated in this Part to ensure that indigent defendants are afforded quality legal representation.

§ 613.6 Monitoring process.

(a) All organizations awarded contracts by the City of New York for the provision of defense services shall be monitored from the time the contract is awarded by the Oversight Committee.

(b) The Committee, in accordance with the "General Requirements For All Organized Providers of Defense Services to Indigent Defendants," shall make a determination as to whether the organizations that contract with the City of New York meet those standards.

§ 613.7 Written evaluation.

The Oversight Committee shall file with the Appellate Division a written evaluation of the organizations providing indigent defense services, setting forth all appropriate information with respect to the organizations' performance, problems which may exist in their operation, and procedures which have been or will be followed to improve the quality of legal representation rendered to indigent defendants. Unless the court directs otherwise, the Oversight Committee shall file the written evaluations biennially, commencing June 1, 2002. In preparing the written evaluations, the Oversight Committee may seek evaluations of the organizations' performance and the Administrator of the Assigned Counsel Plan in the First Judicial Department, the Association of the Bar of the City of New York, the New York County Lawyers' Association and the Bronx County Bar Association shall cooperate with the Oversight Committee in this evaluation.

§ 613.8 Cooperation of indigent defense organizations.

All organizations awarded contracts by the City of New York to provide representation to indigent defendants in criminal proceedings shall cooperate with and otherwise assist the Oversight Committee in the discharge of its duties.

§ 613.9 Training program.

Pursuant to the obligations of the participating bar associations under article 18-B of the county Law and the Assigned Counsel Plan, the bar associations shall, after consultation with the Appellate Division and the Oversight Committee, provide a continuing program of training and education which will enable indigent defense organizations and the attorneys in their employ to improve their professional competence in criminal law. This program should provide for, but not be confined to, a professional course in criminal advocacy.

§ 613.10 Complaints.

The Oversight Committee may receive and investigate complaints against organizations providing representation to indigent defendants and the attorneys in their employ which relate to the discharge of an organization's or an individual attorney's duties pursuant to an order of appointment, and shall, subject to the approval of the Appellate Division, adopt rules for the processing of such complaints.

§ 613.11 Use of records.

All papers, records and documents involving a complaint against an organization providing representation to indigent defendants or an attorney in its employ shall be sealed and be deemed private and confidential. However, upon good cause being shown, the justices of the Appellate Division or the presiding justice thereof may, by written order, permit to be divulged all or any part of such papers, records and documents. In the discretion of the presiding justice such order may be made either without notice to the organization, persons or attorneys to be affected thereby, or upon such notice to them as he may direct. Records of the Oversight Committee, however, shall be made available upon request without the necessity for such order, to the Departmental Disciplinary Committee for the Appellate Division, First Judicial Department.

§ 613.12 Members of the first department indigent defense organization oversight committee as volunteers.

The members of the First Department Indigent Defense Organization Oversight Committee, as volunteers, are expressly authorized to participate in a State-sponsored volunteer program within the meaning of subdivision 1 of section 17 of the Public Officers Law.

§ 613.13 Present powers retained.

Nothing contained in this Part shall be construed to limit the power of the Appellate Division, the presiding justice thereof, or the participating bar associations to the Assigned Counsel Plan otherwise granted by the Assigned Counsel Plan.

PART 635

JOINT ADMINISTRATIVE ORDERS

Section
635.9   Joint Administrative Order No. 453: Control and supervision of city marshals.

§ 635.9 Joint Administrative Order No. 453: Control and supervision of city marshals.

The Appellate Division of the Supreme Court, First Judicial Department, and the Appellate Division of the Supreme Court, Second Judicial Department, pursuant to the authority vested in each of them, and for the purpose of providing controls and close supervision of City Marshals, do hereby jointly order as follows:

(1) The Commissioner of Investigation of the City of New York or his designee, is empowered to supervise and monitor the official acts of New York City Marshals and to take complaints, make inquiries and conduct investigations into all aspects of marshals' activities.

(2) The Commissioner of Investigation or his designee, in order to investigate and monitor the activities of city marshals, may hold hearings, compel the attendance of and examine under oath a marshal and his employees regarding the official acts of any marshal.

(3) (a) Each marshal shall keep detailed books and records and maintain bank accounts as prescribed by the Appellate Divisions or the Department of Investigation.

(b) A city marshal's official books, records and bank accounts are public records and as such are subject to unannounced inspections by the Department of Investigation or anyone designated for that purpose by the Commissioner of Investigation or the Appellate Divisions.

(c) Should the Commissioner deem it proper, the Department of Investigation may take into its custody any or all of the official records of a city marshal for the purpose of inspecting them.

(d) Each city marshal shall surrender all official books and records including, but not limited to, cash books, docket books, check books, bank statements, and cancelled checks to the Department of Investigation upon termination of office. Should it become necessary, access to such official books and records for the purpose of examination shall be accorded to the city marshal surrendering the same. Upon termination of office, each city marshal shall further prepare a final report of his official acts, as prescribed by the Department of Investigation, which shall include a final statement of monies held in trust, expenses incurred, and fees earned.

(e) A city marshal is entitled to only those fees for those services which are prescribed by law and set forth in an official schedule of fees issued by the Commissioner of Investigation. A city marshal shall perform all other services required of him by law without any other fees or charges, except as otherwise expressly prescribed by law. No fee to which a city marshal is entitled may be waived without specific written authorization of the Commissioner of Investigation.

(f) Each city marshal shall henceforth, in accordance with the procedures prescribed by the Department of Investigation, provide for a fiduciary who shall, upon the death or incapacity of said marshal, assume complete responsibility for the marshal's bank accounts and official records, and shall distribute any monies held in trust or otherwise collected by the marshal to the proper judgment creditors or to any other individual(s) to whom such monies are due and owing. Such a fiduciary shall be compensated at the marshal's own expense.

(4) (a) The Commissioner of Investigation is empowered to continue to issue directives regarding marshals' official day to day activities including, but not limited to, the official records to be kept by city marshals, the procedures for performing their duties, and the conduct of marshals and their employees. Copies of all directives shall be forwarded to the Appellate Divisions, and each directive shall remain in full force and effect unless and until nullified by joint order of both Appellate Divisions.

(b) Any handbook of regulations for city marshals which maybe promulgated by the Department of Investigation shall become effective upon approval of both Appellate Divisions. Any substantial policy changes therein shall require similar approval. However, copies of any other changes therein by directive or otherwise shall be forwarded to the Appellate Divisions and such changes shall remain in full force and effect unless and until nullified by joint order of both Appellate Divisions.

(5) The Director of the Bureau of Marshals at the Department of Investigation or any other person or persons designated by the Commissioner of Investigation may, after an investigation, present evidence of incompetency, misconduct, or other wrongdoing as set forth in Section (6) herein to the Commissioner of Investigation. The Commissioner may accordingly designate a deputy commissioner, assistant commissioner, or other qualified person to hear charges as provided herein or, in the alternative, at the option of the Commissioner, refer these charges and this

evidence to the Appellate Divisions for disciplinary action or removal proceedings.

(6) (a) The Commissioner of Investigation may, after a hearing on charges preferred against a city marshal, impose penalties upon him including, but not limited to, suspension from the performance of his official duties for a period not to exceed six months for violation of the civil laws, the rules of the Appellate Divisions of the First and Second Departments, the rules of the Civil Court of the City of New York, the directives of the Department of Investigation, or for incompetency or misconduct.

(b) A city marshal against whom such disciplinary action is proposed shall have written notice thereof and of the reasons therefor, shall be furnished a copy of the charges preferred against him, and shall be allowed at least eight days for answering the same in writing. The marshal shall be entitled to a full and complete hearing with the assistance and presence of counsel.

(c) The hearing upon which such charges shall be held by such deputy commissioner, assistant commissioner, or other person designated by the Commissioner of Investigation for that purpose. Such deputy commissioner or assistant commissioner may, pursuant to Chapter 34 of the New York City Charter, issue subpoenas, administer oaths and shall take evidence and make a record of such hearing which shall, with his recommendation, be referred to the Commissioner of Investigation for review and decision.

(d) The deputy commissioner or assistant commissioner holding such hearing shall, upon the request of the city marshal against whom charges are preferred, permit him to be represented by counsel, and shall allow him to summon witnesses in his behalf. The burden of proving incompetency, misconduct, or other wrongdoing shall be upon the Director of the Bureau of Marshals or other person designated by the Commissioner of Investigation for the purpose of preferring charges and shall be by a fair preponderance of evidence. The deputy or assistant commissioner holding such hearing shall receive evidence in the same manner as if this hearing were held pursuant to Section 75 of the Civil Service Law, in that compliance with technical rules of evidence shall not be required.

(e) If the city marshal is found guilty, a transcript of the hearing, and a written statement of the determination and the reasons therefor, shall be filed in the office of the Department of Investigation. A copy of the transcript shall, upon request of the city marshal affected, be furnished to him without charge.

(f) If desired, the city marshal may appeal any decision by the Commissioner of Investigation to the Appellate Divisions. The marshal shall file such appeal in writing within twenty days after service of written notice of the determination to be reviewed, such written notice to be delivered personally or by registered mail to the last known office address of such city marshal. When notice is given by registered mail, such city marshal shall be allowed an additional three days in which to file such an appeal.

(7) A marshal, after being furnished with a copy of the charges preferred against him, may knowingly waive a hearing as provided in Section (6) herein and agree to a penalty prescribed by the Commissioner of Investigation.

(8) Perjury by a city marshal or his failure to testify concerning his official duties at an investigative or administrative hearing held at the Department of Investigation after being granted immunity from the use of the testimony in a criminal prosecution shall be ground for removal.

(9) Failure to comply with penalties imposed by the Commissioner of Investigation shall be ground for removal. This Order is effective immediately and shall remain in full force and effect unless and until modified or nullified by Joint Order of both Appellate Divisions.

COURT RULES

RULES OF THE FIRST JUDICIAL DEPARTMENT APPELLATE TERM

PART 640

RULES OF PRACTICE

(Selected Sections)

§ 640.1 Jurisdiction.

The Appellate Term of the Supreme Court for the first judicial department shall hear and determine all appeals from the Civil Court of the City of New York and the Criminal Court of the City of New York in the Counties of New York and Bronx at such times and places as may be designated by the Appellate Division of the Supreme Court, first judicial department.

* * *

§ 640.3 Appeals from Criminal Court; papers required on appeal.

(a) Appeals from the Criminal Court shall be heard on the original papers, certified by the clerk of the Criminal Court, a stenographic transcript of the minutes of proceedings, certified by the judge before whom the action was tried, or in the case of the death or disability of such judge, in such manner as the court directs, and five copies of the briefs.

(b) For good cause shown the court may hear the appeal on an abbreviated record containing so much of the evidence or other proceedings as it may deem necessary to a consideration of the questions raised thereby, and five copies of the briefs.

(c) The appellant's brief must contain, at the

beginning, the statement required by CPLR 5531 and a statement setting forth whether defendant is presently incarcerated. If the defendant was admitted to bail, the statement should set forth the date of the order and the court which admitted defendant to bail. If a fine was paid, the statement should set forth the amount of the fine, the date of payment, the Criminal Court part or the prison in which payment was made and the receipt number.

§ 640.4 Exhibits.

Each exhibit or copies thereof shall have affixed thereto a notation as to the page of the transcript where it was admitted in evidence.

§ 640.5 Briefs—what to contain.

(a) Briefs shall be on paper of the same size and quality as is required for the record on appeal by subdivision (d) of section 640.2. The name of counsel who is to argue or submit the appeal shall appear at the upper right hand corner of the first or cover page of the brief and the calendar number of the appeal shall be stated in the upper left hand corner.

(b) In the absence of a specification that the appeal is to be argued, it shall be marked submitted and oral argument shall not be heard.

(c) Testimony referred to in a brief must be

accompanied by reference to the page of the record or transcript where such testimony appears.

(d) The main brief of any party shall not exceed 50 pages, and reply briefs shall not exceed 20 pages unless authorized by a justice of the court prior to the filing of any such brief. On appeals from the Criminal Court, appellant's brief shall contain the statement required by subdivision (c) of section 640.3.

(e) Unless authorized by the court, or these rules, briefs to which are added or appended any matter shall not be accepted for filing.

§ 640.6 Time within which to perfect appeal; calendar or pending appeal; dismissals.

* * *

(b) *Appeals from the Criminal Court.* (1) Appellant shall procure the original papers or abbreviated record to be filed within 30 days after service of the notice of appeal, and appellant shall then notice the appeal of argument or submission, within 120 days from the date of service of the notice of appeal, by filing the notice argument and briefs, with proof of service of one copy of each paper filed at least 53 days before the first day of the appointed term; proof of service of one copy of a transcript of the minutes of the proceedings shall be filed with the notice of argument, such copy to be returned to the appellant upon the argument or submission of the appeal. Unless otherwise ordered, five copies of the respondent's brief with proof of service of one copy shall be filed not later than 31 days prior to the first day of the term and five copies of a reply brief with proof of service of one copy may be filed not later than 24 days prior to the first day of the appointed term. An appellant who is incarcerated under the judgment appealed from may bring the appeal on for argument or submission on ten days' notice, after the record is filed, by filing a notice of argument and five copies of the appellant's brief, with due proof of service of one copy, in which event five copies of the respondent's brief with proof of service of one copy shall be filed not later than seven days after service of appellant's brief, and five copies of a reply brief with proof of service of one copy may be filed not later than two days after the service of respondent's brief.

(2) If appellant fails to notice the appeal within the time specified in the foregoing paragraph, the appeal will be dismissed on motion of the respondent unless an enlargement of time is granted by the court for good cause shown.

(3) Fifteen days before the first day of each term, the clerk shall cause a calendar to be published in the *New York Law Journal* of all cases in which a copy of the notice of appeal has been filed with him in accordance with the provisions of section 460.10 of the Criminal Procedure Law. If an appeal is not noticed for argument within 120 days from the date of service of the notice of appeal and no enlargement of time is obtained, such appeal may be dismissed by the court.

(4) The clerk shall prepare a special day calendar for each appointed term of the appeals subject to dismissal for failure on the part of the appellant to comply with this section. Each such special day calendar shall be published in the *New York Law Journal* at least five days prior to, as well as on the day when that calendar is to be called, and the clerk shall cause a postal card notice to be mailed to the appellant at his last known address and to his attorney five days prior to the first day of such publication.

§ 640.7 Calendar; argument of appeals.

(a) Unless otherwise ordered the calendar of appeals shall be called on the first day of the term for which they have been noticed. The calendar call shall commence at such time as the court shall direct.

(b) The clerk shall cause the calendar of appeals and the time the calendar will be called to be published in the *New York Law Journal* six days before the first day of each term.

(c) At any time prior to the call of the calendar the parties may file a stipulation submitting an appeal without oral argument provided, however, that all of the required papers have been served and filed. In the event of the filing of such stipulation, attendance at the calendar call shall not be required.

(d) Not more than 15 minutes shall be allowed to each side for argument except in such cases where additional time is granted by the court. No brief, communication or other paper shall be accepted after submission or argument of an appeal unless authorized by the court.

§ 640.8 Motions generally.

(a) Motions may be noticed for any day of the term and must be submitted without oral argument. The appropriate county clerk's index number must appear on all motion papers.

(b) If an appeal on the calendar is affected by the motion, the calendar number of the appeal must be stated on the moving papers.

(c) All moving and opposing papers, with proof of service, shall be filed with the clerk on or before the return day at 10 A.M., and submitted without oral argument.

§ 640.9 Reargument; leave to appeal to Appellate Division; stay.

(a) *Reargument.* (1) Motions for reargument shall be made within thirty days after the date of the order determining the appeal.

(2) Papers in support of a motion for reargument shall concisely state the points claimed to have been overlooked or misapprehended by the court, with proper reference to the particular portion of the record, and the authorities relied upon.

(b) Leave to appeal to the Appellate Division in civil matters. (1) Applications for permission to appeal to the Appellate Division pursuant to CPLR 5703(a) shall be made in the manner and within the time prescribed by CPLR 5513(c) and 5516.

(2) The moving papers shall set forth the questions to be reviewed by the Appellate Division. If the appeal is to review a determination granting or affirming the granting of a new trial or hearing, the moving papers must also contain a stipulation by the appellant consenting to the entry of judgment absolute against the appellant in the event of an affirmance by the Appellate Division.

(c) *Stay.* If a stay is desired pending a determination of motion for reargument or leave to appeal, application may be made for an order incorporating such stay.

§ 640.10 Leave to appeal to the court.

* * *

(c) Applications for a certificate granting leave to appeal pursuant to the provisions of sections 450.15 and 460.15 of the Criminal Procedure Law must be made in the following manner:

(1) the application must be addressed to the court for assignment to a Justice of the Appellate Term;

(2) the application must be in writing and upon reasonable notice to the people;

(3) the application must be made within 30 days after service upon the defendant of a copy of the order from which he seeks to appeal; and

(4) the application must set forth the questions of law or fact to be reviewed, and must contain a statement as to whether or not any such application has previously been made.

RULES OF THE SECOND JUDICIAL DEPARTMENT APPELLATE DIVISION

(The following rules are not a complete presentation of the Second Department's Rules. Only those rules that are relevant to criminal or related matters are set forth. For a complete set of rules, see *NY CLS Desk Edition Civil Practice Annual* (LexisNexis).)

PART 670

PROCEDURE IN THE APPELLATE DIVISION

§ 670.1 Court sessions.

(a) Unless otherwise ordered, the court will convene at 10 o'clock in the forenoon on Monday, Tuesday, Thursday, and Friday.

(b) Special sessions of the court may be held at such times and for such purposes as the court from time to time may direct.

(c) When a cause is argued or submitted with four justices present, it shall, whenever necessary, be deemed submitted also to any other duly qualified justice unless objection is noted at the time of argument or submission.

§ 670.2 General provisions and definitions.

(a) Unless the context requires otherwise, as used in this Part:

(1) The word *cause* includes an appeal, a special proceeding transferred to this court pursuant to CPLR 7804(g), a special proceeding initiated in this court, and an action submitted to this court pursuant to CPLR 3222 on a case containing the agreed statement of facts upon which the controversy depends.

(2) Any reference to the court means this court; any reference to a justice means a justice of this court; any reference to the clerk means the clerk of this court.

(3) Wherever reference is made to a judgment, order, or determination it shall also be deemed to include a sentence.

(4) The word *perfection* refers to the requirements for placing a cause on the court's calendar, *e.g.* the filing of a record and brief.

(5) The word *consolidation* refers to combining two or more causes arising out of the same action or proceeding in one record and one brief.

(6) The word *concurrent*, when used to describe appeals, is intended to refer to those appeals which have been taken separately from the same order or judgment by parties whose interests are not adverse to one another. The term *cross appeal* refers to an appeal taken by a party whose interests are adverse to a party who previously appealed from the same order or judgment.

(b) Unless the context requires otherwise, if a period of time prescribed by this Part for the performance of an act ends on a Saturday, Sunday or holiday, the act will be deemed timely if performed before 5:00 p.m. on the next business day.

(c) If a period of time prescribed by this Part is measured from the service of a record, brief, or other paper and service is by mail, five days shall be added to the prescribed period. If service is by overnight delivery, one day shall be added to the prescribed period.

(d) All records on appeal, briefs, appendices, motions, affirmations, and other papers will be deemed filed in this court only as of the time they are actually received by the clerk and they shall be accompanied by proof of service upon all necessary parties pursuant to CPLR 2103.

(e) An Appellate Division docket number will be assigned to every cause. All papers and correspondence thereafter filed shall prominently display the docket number or numbers in the upper right-hand corner of the first page opposite the title of the action or proceeding. In the event of concurrent and/or cross appeals from a judgment or order, all parties shall use the docket number first assigned to the appeal from that judgment or order.

(f) In any civil cause, and in any criminal cause where the defendant appears by retained counsel, the clerk will send to the party a copy of the decision on an appeal or a motion, if the party provides the clerk with a self-addressed, stamped envelope.

(g) If a cause or the underlying action or proceeding is wholly or partially settled or if any issues are wholly or partially rendered moot, or if any cause should not be calendared because of bankruptcy or death of a party, inability of counsel to appear, an order of rehabilitation, or for some other reason, the parties or their counsel shall immediately notify the court. Any attorney or party who, without good cause shown, fails to comply with the requirements of this subdivision shall be subject to such costs and/or sanctions as the court may direct.

(h) Any attorney or party to a civil cause who, in the prosecution or defense thereof, engages in frivolous conduct as that term is defined in section 130-1.1(c) of this Title, shall be subject to the imposition of such costs and/or sanctions authorized by subpart 130-1 of this Title as the court may direct.

(i) The original of every paper submitted for filing in the office of the clerk of this court shall be signed in ink in accordance with the provisions of section 130-1.1-a(a) of this Title. Copies of the signed original shall be served upon all opposing parties and shall be filed in the office of the clerk whenever multiple copies of a paper are required to be served and filed by this Part.

§ 670.3 Filing of notice of appeal, request for Appellate Division intervention, order of transfer.

(a) Where an appeal is taken in a civil action or proceeding, the notice of appeal, or the order of the court of original instance granting permission to appeal, shall be filed by the appellant in the office in which the judgment or order of the court of original instance is filed. Two additional copies of the notice of appeal or order granting permission to appeal shall be filed by the appellant, to each of which shall be affixed a completed

Request for Appellate Division Intervention—Civil (Form A), a copy of the order of judgment appealed from, and a copy of the opinion or decision, if any. In the event that the notice of appeal covers two or more judgments or orders, the appellant shall also complete and affix to each Form A an Additional Appeal Information form (Form B) describing the additional judgments or orders appealed from, and affix copies of the judgments or orders and the opinions or decisions upon which they were based, if any. Thereupon, the clerk of the court of original instance shall endorse the filing date upon such instruments and transmit the two additional copies to the clerk of this court.

(b) Where an appeal is taken in a criminal action, the notice of appeal shall be filed by the appellant in duplicate in the office in which the judgment or order of the court of original instance is filed. Thereupon the clerk of the court of original instance shall endorse the filing date upon such instruments, shall execute a Request for Appellate Division Intervention—Criminal (Form D) and shall transmit it together with the duplicate notice of appeal to the clerk of this court.

(c) In any case in which an order is made transferring a proceeding to this court, the petitioner shall file forthwith in the office of the clerk of this court two copies of such order, to each of which shall be affixed a copy of a Request for Appellate Division Intervention—Civil (Form A) and a copy of any opinion or decision by the transferring court.

(d) A Request for Appellate Division Intervention—Attorney Matters (Form E) shall be filed in connection with attorney disciplinary proceedings instituted in this court and applications made to this court pursuant to sections 690.17 and 690.19 of the rules of this court.

(e) In all other actions or proceedings instituted in this court, and applications pursuant to CPLR 5704, a Request for Appellate Division Intervention—Civil (Form A) shall be filed.

§ 670.4 Civil appeals management program.

(a) Active Management. (1) The court may, in the exercise of discretion, direct that the prosecution of any cause of class of causes be actively managed.

(2) The clerk shall issue a scheduling order or orders directing the parties to a cause assigned to the active management program to take specified action to expedite the prosecution thereof, including but not limited to the ordering of the transcript of the proceedings and the filing of proof of payment therefor, the making of motions, the perfection of the cause, and the filing of briefs. Notwithstanding any of the time limitations set forth in this part, a scheduling order shall set forth

the date or dates on or before which such specified action shall be taken.

(3) If any party shall establish good cause why there cannot be compliance with the provisions of a scheduling order, the clerk may amend the same consistent with the objective of insuring expedited prosecution of the cause. An application to amend a scheduling order shall be made by letter, addressed to the clerk, with a copy to the other parties to the cause. The determination of the clerk in amending or declining to amend a scheduling order shall be reviewable by motion to the court on notice pursuant to section 670.5 of this Part.

(4) No filing directed by a scheduling order shall be permitted after the time to do so has expired unless the order is amended in accordance with paragraph (3) of subdivision (a) of this section.

(5) Upon the default of any party in complying with the provisions of a scheduling order, the clerk shall issue an order to show cause, on seven days notice, why the cause should not be dismissed or such other sanction be imposed as the court may deem appropriate.

(b) Civil Appeals Management Program. (1) The court, in those cases in which it deems it appropriate, will issue a notice directing the attorneys for the parties and/or the parties themselves to attend a pre-argument conference before a designated Justice of this court or such other person as it may designate, to consider the possibility of settlement, the limitation of the issues, and any other matters which the designated Justice or other Person determines may aid in the disposition of the appeal or proceeding.

(2) Any attorney or party who, without good cause shown, fails to appear for a regularly scheduled pre-argument conference, or who fails to comply with the terms of a stipulation or order entered following a pre-argument conference, shall be subject to the imposition of such costs and/or sanctions as the court may direct.

§ 670.5 Motions and proceedings initiated in this court—generally.

(a) Unless otherwise required by statute, rule, or order of the court or any justice, every motion and every proceeding initiated in this court shall be made returnable at 9:30 a.m. on any Friday. Cross motions shall be made returnable on the same day as the original motion and shall be served and filed at least three days before the return date. Motions shall be on notice prescribed by CPLR 2214 and CPLR article 78 proceeding shall be on notice prescribed by CPLR 7804(c).

(b) All motions and proceedings initiated by notice of motion or notice of petition, shall be filed with the clerk at least one week before the return date. All papers in opposition shall be filed with the clerk before 4 p.m. of the business day preceding the return date. All papers in opposition to any motion or proceeding initiated in this court by an order to show cause shall be filed with the clerk on or before 9:30 a.m. of the return date, and shall be served by a method calculated to place the movant and other parties to the motion in receipt thereof on or before that time. The originals of all such papers shall be filed. On the return date the motion or proceeding will be deemed submitted to the court without oral argument. Counsel will not be required to attend and a note of issue need not be filed.

(c) Every notice, petition, or order to show cause instituting a motion or proceeding must state, *inter alia*:

(1) the nature of the motion or proceeding;

(2) the specific relief sought;

(3) the return date; and

(4) the names, addresses and telephone numbers of the attorneys and counsel for all parties in support of and in opposition to the motion or proceeding.

(d) The papers in support of every motion or proceeding must contain a copy of:

(1) the order, judgment or determination sought to be reviewed and the decision, if any; and

(2) the notice of appeal or other paper which first invoked the jurisdiction of this court.

(e) Except as hereinafter provided, when an order to show cause presented for signature makes provision for a temporary stay or other interim relief pending a determination of the motion, or when an application is presented pursuant to CPLR 5704, the party seeking such relief must give reasonable notice to his or her adversary of the day and time when, and the location where, the order to show cause or CPLR 5704 application will be presented and the relief being requested. If notice has been given, the order to show cause or the application will be presented and the relief being requested. If notice has been given, the order to show cause or the application pursuant to CPLR 5704 must be accompanied by an affidavit or affirmation stating the time, place, by whom given, the manner of such notification, and to the extent known, the position taken by the opposing party. If notice has not been given, the affidavit or affirmation shall state whether the applicant has made an attempt to give notice and the reasons for the lack of success. If the applicant is unwilling to give notice, the affidavit or affirmation shall state the reasons for such unwillingness. An order to show cause providing for a temporary stay or other interim relief or an application pursuant to CPLR 5704 must be personally presented for signature by the party's attorney or by the party if such party is proceeding *pro se*.

(f) The clerk may reject papers or deem a motion or proceeding to be withdrawn or abandoned for the failure to comply with any of these rules.

§ 670.6 Motions—reargue; resettle; amend; leave to appeal; admission *pro hac vice*.

(a) *Motions to reargue, resettle, or amend.* Motions to reargue a cause or motion, or to resettle or amend a decision and order, shall be made within 30 days after service of a copy of the decision and order determining the cause or motion, with notice of its entry, except that for good cause shown, the court may consider any such motion when made at a later date. The papers in support of every such motion shall concisely state the points claimed to have been overlooked or misapprehended by the court, with appropriate references to the particular portions of the record or briefs and with citation of the authorities relied upon. A copy of the order shall be attached.

(b) *Motions for leave to appeal to Appellate Division.*

(1) Motions for leave to appeal to the Appellate Division pursuant to CPLR 5701(c) and Family Court Act, § 1112 shall be addressed to the court and shall contain a copy of the order or judgment and the decision of the lower court.

(2) Motions for leave to appeal from an order of the Appellate Term shall contain a copy of the opinions, decisions, judgments and orders of the lower courts, including: a copy of the Appellate Term order denying leave to appeal; a copy of the record in the Appellate Term if such record shall have been printed or otherwise reproduced; and a concise statement of the grounds of alleged error. If the application is to review an Appellate Term order which either granted a new trial or affirmed the trial court's order granting a new trial, the papers must also contain the applicant's stipulation consenting to the entry of judgment absolute against him or her in the event that this court should affirm the order appealed from.

(c) Motions for leave to appeal to the Court of Appeals shall set forth the questions of law to be reviewed by the Court of Appeals and, where appropriate, the proposed questions of law decisive of the correctness of this court's determination or of any separable portion within it. A copy of this court's order shall be attached.

(d) Motions for leave to appeal to the Court of Appeals pursuant to CPL 460.20 shall be made to any justice who was a member of the panel which decided the matter. A copy of this court's order shall be attached.

(e) *Motions for admission pro hac vice.* An attorney and counselor-at-law or the equivalent may move for permission to appear *pro hac vice* with respect to a cause pending before this court pursuant to section 520.11(a)(1) of this Title. An affidavit in support of the motion shall state that the attorney and counselor-at-law is a member in good standing in all the jurisdictions in which he or she is admitted to practice and is associated with a member in good standing of the New York Bar, which member shall appear with him or her on the appeal or proceeding and shall be the person upon whom all papers in connection with the cause shall be served. Attached to the affidavit shall be a certificate of good standing from the bar of the state in which the attorney and counselor-at-law maintains his or her principal office for the practice of law.

§ 670.7 Calendar; Preferences; Consolidation.

(a) There shall be a general calendar for appeals. Appeals will be placed on the general calendar in the order perfected and, subject to the discretion of the court, will be heard in order.

(b) *Preferences.* (1) Any party to an appeal entitled by law to a preference in the hearing of the appeal may serve and file a demand for a preference which shall set forth the provision of law relied upon for such preference and good cause for such preference. If the demand is sustained by the court, the appeal shall be preferred.

(2) A preference under CPLR 5521 may be obtained upon good cause shown by a motion directed to the court on notice to the other parties to the appeal.

(c) *Consolidation.* (1) A party may consolidate appeals from the civil orders and/or judgments arising out of the same action or proceeding provided that each appeal is perfected timely pursuant to section 670.8(e)(1) of this Part.

(2) Appeals from orders or judgments in separate actions or proceedings cannot be consolidated but may, upon written request of a party, be scheduled by the court to be heard together on the same day.

§ 670.8 Placing civil or criminal causes on calendar; time limits for filing.

(a) *Placing cause on general calendar.* An appeal may be placed on the general calendar by filing with the clerk the record on appeal pursuant to one of the methods set forth in section 670.9 of this Part and by filing nine copies of a brief, with proof of service of two copies upon each of the other parties. Unless the court shall otherwise direct, when an appeal is prosecuted upon the original record, only one copy of the brief need be served. An extra copy of the statement required by CPLR 5531 shall be filed together with the record or appendix. If an appeal is taken on the original record, the extra copy of the statement shall be filed with the appellant's brief.

(b) *Answering and reply briefs.* Not more than 30 days after service of the appellant's brief, each respondent or opposing party shall file nine copies of the answering brief with proof of service of two copies upon each of the other parties. Not more than 10 days after service of respondent's brief, the appellant may file nine copies of a reply brief with proof of service of two copies upon each of the other parties. If one copy of the appellant's brief was served, only one copy of answering and reply briefs need be served.

(c) *Concurrent and cross appeals.*

(1) Unless otherwise ordered by the court, all parties appealing from the same order or judgment shall consult and thereafter file a joint record or joint appendix which shall include a copies of all notices of appeal. The cost of the joint record or the joint appendix, and the transcript, if any, shall be borne equally by the appealing parties.

(2) The joint record or joint appendix and the briefs of concurrent appellants shall be served and filed together. The time to do so in accordance with subdivision (e) of this section shall be measured from the latest date on the several concurrent notices of appeal.

(3) The answering brief on a cross appeal shall be served and filed not more than 30 days after service of the appellant's brief or briefs and the joint record or joint appendix, and it shall include the points of argument on the cross appeal. An appellant's reply brief may be served and filed not more than 30 days after service of the answering brief. A cross appellant's reply brief may be served and filed not more than 10 days after service of the appellant's reply brief.

(d) *Enlargements of time.* Except where a scheduling order has been issued pursuant to section 670.4(a)(2) of this Part or where the court has directed that a cause be perfected or that a brief be served and filed by a date certain, an enlargement of time to perfect or to serve and file a brief may be obtained as follows:

(1) *By Stipulation.* The parties may stipulate to enlarge the time to perfect a cause by up to 60 days, to file an answering brief by up to 30 days, and to file a reply brief by up to 10 days. Not more than one such stipulation per perfection or filing shall be permitted. Such a stipulation shall not be effective unless so ordered by the clerk.

(2) *For Cause.* Where a party shall establish a reasonable ground why there cannot or could not be compliance with the time limits prescribed by this section, or such time limits as extended by stipulation pursuant to paragraph (1) of this subdivision, the clerk or a Justice may grant reasonable enlargements of time to comply. An application pursuant to this paragraph shall be made by letter, addressed to the clerk, with a copy to the other parties to the cause. Orders made pursuant to this paragraph shall be reviewable by

motion to the court on notice pursuant to section 670.5 of this Part.

(e) Notwithstanding any of the provisions of this Part, a civil appeal or proceeding shall be deemed abandoned unless perfected:

(1) within six months after the date of the notice of appeal, order granting leave to appeal, or order transferring the proceeding to this court; or

(2) within six months of the filing of the submission with the county clerk in an action on submitted facts pursuant to CPLR 3222,

unless the time to perfect shall have been extended pursuant to subdivision (d) of this section. The clerk shall not accept any record or brief for filing after the expiration of such six-month period or such period as extended.

(f) Notwithstanding any of the provisions of this Part, an unperfected criminal appeal by a defendant shall be deemed abandoned in all cases where no application has been made by the defendant for the assignment of counsel to prosecute the appeal within nine months of the date of the notice of appeal, unless, the time to perfect shall haven been extended pursuant to subdivision (d) of this section.

(g) Notwithstanding any of the provisions of this Part, an appeal by the People pursuant to CPL 450.20(1), (1-a) or (8) shall be deemed abandoned unless perfected within three months after the date of the notice of appeal, unless the time to perfect shall have been extended pursuant to subdivision (d) of this section. All other appeals by the People shall be deemed abandoned unless perfected within six months after the date of the notice of appeal, unless the time to perfect shall have been extended pursuant to subdivision (d) of this section.

(h) Once each month the clerk shall prepare a calendar of all civil causes which have been ordered to be perfected by a date certain and which have not been perfected and a calendar of all civil causes which have been assigned an Appellate Division docket number and have not been perfected within the time limitations set forth in subdivision (e) of this section. Such calendars shall be published in the New York Law Journal for five consecutive days. Upon the failure of the appellant to make an application to enlarge time to perfect within 10 days following the last day of publication, an order shall be entered dismissing the cause.

§ 670.9 Alternate methods of prosecuting appeals.

An appellant may elect to prosecute an appeal upon a reproduced full record (CPLR 5528(a)(5)); by the appendix method (CPLR 5528(a)(5)), upon an agreed statement in lieu of record (CPLR 5527); or, where authorized by statute or this Part

or order of the court, upon a record consisting of the original papers.

(a) *Reproduced full record.* If the appellant elects to proceed on a reproduced full record on appeal as authorized by CPLR 5528(a)(5), the record shall be printed or otherwise reproduced as provided in section 670.10 of this Part. Nine copies of the record, one of which shall be marked "original", duly certified as provided in section 670.10(g), shall be filed with proof of service of two copies upon each of the other parties.

(b) *Appendix method.*

(1) If the appellant elects to proceed by the appendix method, the appellant shall subpoena from the clerk of the court from which the appeal is taken all the papers constituting the record on appeal and cause them to be filed with the clerk of this court prior to the filing of the appendix.

(2) The clerk from whom the papers are subpoenaed shall compile the original papers constituting the record on appeal and transmit them to the clerk of this court, together with a certificate listing the papers constituting the record on appeal and stating whether all such papers are included in the papers transmitted.

(3) If a settled transcript of the stenographic minutes, or an approved statement in lieu of such transcript, or any relevant exhibit is not included in the papers so filed with the clerk of this court, the appellant shall cause such transcript, statement or exhibit to be filed together with the brief.

(4) The appendix shall be printed or otherwise reproduced as provided in section 670.10 and may be bound with the brief or separately. Nine copies of the appendix, one of which shall be marked "original," duly certified as provided in section 670.10(g) shall be filed with proof of service of two copies upon each of the other parties.

(c) *Agreed statement in lieu of record method.* If the appellant elects to proceed by the agreed statement method in lieu of record (CPLR 5527), the statement shall be reproduced as provided in section 670.10 as a joint appendix. The statement required by CPLR 5531 shall be appended. Nine copies of the statement shall be filed with proof of service of two copies upon each of the other parties.

(d) *Original record.* (1) The following appeals may be prosecuted upon the original record, including a properly settled transcript of the trial or hearing, if any:

(i) appeals from the Appellate Term;

(ii) appeals from the Family Court;

(iii) appeals under the Election Law;

(iv) appeals under the Human Rights Law (Executive Law, § 298);

(v) appeals where the sole issue is compensation of a judicial appointee;

(vi) other appeals where an original record is authorized by statute;

(vii) appeals where permission to proceed upon the original record has been authorized by order of this court; and

(viii) appeals in criminal causes; and

(ix) appeals under Correction Law §§ 168-d(3) and 168-n(3).

§ 670.10 [*Repealed.*]

§ 670.10.1 Form and content of records, appendices, and briefs— generally.

(a) *Compliance with Civil Practice Law and Rules.* Briefs, appendices and to the extent practicable, reproduced full records, shall comply with the requirements of CPLR 5528 and 5529 and reproduced full records shall, in addition, comply with the requirements of CPLR 5526.

(b) *Method of reproduction.* Briefs, records, and appendices shall be reproduced by any method that produces a permanent, legible, black image on white paper. To the extent practicable, reproduction on both sides of the paper is encouraged.

(c) *Paper quality, size, and binding.* Paper shall be of a quality approved by the chief administrator of the courts and shall be opaque, unglazed, white in color, and measure 11 inches along the bound edge by 8½ inches. Records, appendices, and briefs shall be bound on the left side in a manner that shall keep all the pages securely together; however, binding by use of any metal fastener or similar hard material that protrudes or presents a bulky surface or sharp edge is prohibited. Records and appendices shall be divided into volumes not to exceed two inches in thickness.

(d) *Designation of parties.* The parties to all appeals shall be designated in the record and briefs by adding the word "Appellant," "Respondent," etc., as the case may be, following the party's name, e.g., "Plaintiff-Respondent," "Defendant-Appellant," "Petitioner-Appellant," "Respondent-Respondent," etc. Parties who have not appealed and against whom the appeal has not been taken, shall be listed separately and designated as they were in the trial court, e.g., "Plaintiff," "Defendant," "Petitioner," "Respondent."

In appeals from the Surrogate's Court or from judgments on trust accountings, the caption shall contain the title used in the trial court including the name of the decedent or grantor, followed by a listing of all parties to the appeal, properly designated. In proceedings and actions originating in this court, the parties shall be designated "Petitioner" and "Respondent" or "Plaintiff" and "Defendant."

(e) *Docket number.* The cover of all records, briefs, and appendices shall display the appellate division docket number assigned to the cause in the upper right-hand portion opposite the title.

(f) *Rejection of papers.* The clerk may refuse to accept for filing any paper that does not comply with these rules, is not legible, or is otherwise unsuitable.

§ 670.10.2 Form and content of records and appendices.

(a) *Format.* Records and appendices shall contain accurate reproductions of the papers submitted to the court of original instance, formatted in accordance with the practice in that court, except as otherwise provided in subdivision (d) of this section. Reproductions may be slightly reduced in size to fit the page and to accommodate the page headings required by CPLR 5529(c), provided, however, that such reduction does not significantly impair readability.

(b) *Reproduced full record.* The reproduced full record shall be bound separately from the brief, shall contain the items set forth in CPLR 5526, and shall contain in the following order so much of the following items as shall be applicable to the particular cause:

(1) A cover which shall contain the title of the action or proceeding on the upper portion and, on the lower portion, the names, addresses, and telephone numbers of the attorneys, the county clerk's index or file number, and the indictment number;

(2) The statement required by CPLR 5531;

(3) A table of contents which shall list and briefly describe each paper included in the record. The part of the table relating to the transcript of testimony shall separately list each witness and the page at which direct, cross, redirect and recross examinations begin. The part of the table relating to exhibits shall concisely indicate the nature or contents of each exhibit and the page in the record where it is reproduced and where it is admitted into evidence. The table shall also contain references to pages where a motion to dismiss the complaint or to direct or set aside a verdict or where an oral decision of the court appears;

(4) The notice of appeal or order of transfer, judgment or order appealed from, judgment roll, corrected transcript or statement in lieu thereof, relevant exhibits and any opinion or decision in the cause;

(5) An affirmation, stipulation or order, settling the transcript pursuant to CPLR 5525;

(6) A stipulation or order dispensing with reproducing exhibits.

(i) Exhibits which are relevant to a cause may be omitted upon a stipulation of the parties which shall contain a list of the exhibits omitted and a brief description of each exhibit or, if a party unreasonably refuses to so stipulate, upon motion directed to the court. Exhibits thus omitted, unless of a bulky or dangerous nature, shall be filed with the clerk at the same time that the appellant's brief is filed. Exhibits of a bulky or dangerous nature (cartons, file drawers, ledgers, machinery, narcotics, weapons, etc.) thus omitted need not be filed but shall be kept in readiness and delivered to the court on telephone notice. A letter, indicating that a copy has been sent to the adversary, listing such exhibits and stating that they will be available on telephone notice, shall be filed with the clerk at the same time that the appellant's brief is filed.

(ii) Exhibits which are not relevant to a cause may be omitted upon stipulation of the parties which shall contain a list of the exhibits omitted, a brief description of each exhibit, and a statement that the exhibits will not be relied upon or cited in the briefs of the parties. If a party unreasonably refuses to so stipulate, a motion to omit the exhibits may be directed to the court. Such exhibits need not be filed; and

(7) The appropriate certification or stipulation pursuant to subdivision (f) of this section.

(c) *Appendix.* (1) The appendix shall contain those portions of the record necessary to permit the court to fully consider the issues which will be raised by the appellant and the respondent including, where applicable, at least the following:

(i) notice of appeal or order of transfer;

(ii) judgment, decree, or order appealed from;

(iii) decision and opinion of the court or agency, and report of a referee, if any;

(iv) pleadings, if their sufficiency, content or form is in issue or material; in a criminal case, the indictment, or superior court information;

(v) material excerpts from transcripts of testimony or from papers in connection with a motion. Such excerpts must contain all the testimony or averments upon which the appellant relies and upon which it may be reasonably assumed the respondent will rely. Such excerpts must not be misleading or unintelligible by reason of incompleteness or lack of surrounding context;

(vi) copies of critical exhibits, including photographs, to the extent practicable; and

(vii) The appropriate certification or stipulation pursuant to subdivision (f) of this section.

(2) If bound separately from the brief, the appendix shall have a cover complying with subdivision (b)(l) of this section and shall contain the statement required by CPLR 5531 and a table of contents.

(d) *Condensed format of transcripts prohibited.* No record or appendix may contain a transcript of testimony given at a trial, hearing, or deposition that is reproduced in condensed format such that two or more pages of transcript in standard format appear on one page.

(e) *Settlement of transcript or statement.* Regardless of the method used to prosecute any civil cause, if the record contains a transcript of the stenographic minutes of the proceedings or a statement in lieu of such transcript, such transcript or statement must first be either stipulated as correct by the parties or their attorneys or settled pursuant to CPLR 5525.

(f) *Certification of record.* A reproduced full record or appendix shall be certified either by: (l) a certificate of the appellant's attorney pursuant to CPLR 2105; (2) a certificate of the proper clerk; or (3) a stipulation in lieu of certification pursuant to CPLR 5532. The reproduced copy containing the signed certification or stipulation shall be marked "Original."

§ 670.10.3 Form and content of briefs.

(a) *Computer-generated briefs.* Briefs prepared on a computer shall be printed in either a serifed, proportionally spaced typeface such as Times Roman, or a serifed, monospaced typeface such as Courier. Narrow or condensed typefaces and/or condensed font spacing may not be used. Except in headings, words may not be in bold type or type consisting of all capital letters.

(1) *Briefs set in a proportionally spaced typeface.* The body of a brief utilizing a proportionally spaced typeface shall be printed in 14-point type, but footnotes may be printed in type of no less than 12 points.

(2) *Briefs set in a monospaced typeface.* The body of a brief utilizing a monospaced typeface shall be printed in 12-point type containing no more than $10\frac{1}{2}$ characters per inch, but footnotes may be printed in type of no less than 10 points.

(3) *Length.* Computer-generated appellants' and respondents' briefs shall not exceed 14,000 words, and reply and amicus curiae briefs shall not exceed 7,000 words, inclusive of point headings and footnotes and exclusive of pages containing the table of contents, table of citations, proof of service, certificate of compliance, or any authorized addendum containing statutes, rules, regulations, etc.

(b) *Typewritten briefs.* Typewritten briefs shall be neatly prepared in clear type of no less than elite in size and in a pitch of no more than 12 characters per inch. The ribbon typescript of the brief shall be signed and filed as one of the number of copies required by section 670.8 of this Part. Typewritten appellants' and respondents' briefs shall not exceed 70 pages and reply briefs and amicus curiae briefs shall not exceed 35 pages, exclusive of pages containing the table of contents, table of citations, proof of service, certificate of compliance, or any authorized addendum containing statutes, rules, regulations, etc.

(c) *Margins, line spacing, and page numbering of computer-generated and typewritten briefs.* Computer-generated and typewritten briefs shall have margins of one inch on all sides of the page. Text shall be double-spaced, but quotations more than two lines long may be indented and single-spaced. Headings and footnotes may be single-spaced. Pages shall be numbered consecutively in the center of the bottom margin of each page.

(d) *Handwritten briefs.* Pro se litigants may serve and file handwritten briefs. Such briefs shall be neatly prepared in cursive script or hand printing in black ink. Pages shall be numbered consecutively in the center of the bottom margin of each page. The submission of handwritten briefs is not encouraged. If illegible or unreasonably long, handwritten briefs may be rejected for filing by the clerk.

(e) *Application for permission to file oversized brief.* An application for permission to file an oversized brief shall be made to the clerk by letter stating the number of words or pages by which the brief exceeds the limits set forth in this section and the reasons why submission of an oversize brief is necessary. The letter shall be accompanied by a copy of the proposed brief, including a certificate if required by subdivision (f) hereof to the effect that the brief is in all other respects compliant with this section. The determination of the clerk may be reviewed by motion to the court on notice in accordance with section 670.5 of this Part.

(f) *Certification of compliance.* Every brief, except those that are handwritten, shall have at the end thereof a certificate of compliance with this rule, stating that the brief was prepared either on a typewriter, a computer, or by some other specified means. If the brief was typewritten, the certificate shall further specify the size and pitch of the type and the line spacing used. If the brief was prepared on a computer, the certificate shall further specify the name of the typeface, point size, line spacing, and word count. A party preparing the certificate may rely on the word count of the processing system used to prepare the brief. The signing of the brief in accordance with section 130-1.1-a(a) of this Title shall also be deemed the signer's representation of the accuracy of the certificate of compliance.

(g) *Content of briefs.* (1) *Cover.* The cover shall set forth the title of the action or proceeding. The upper right hand section shall contain a notation stating: whether the cause is to be argued or submitted; if it is to be argued, the time actually required for the argument; and the name of the attorney who will argue (see § 670.20). The lower right hand section shall contain the name, address, and telephone number of the attorney filing the brief and shall indicate whom the attorney represents.

(2) *Appellant's brief.* The appellant's brief shall contain, in the following order:

(i) the statement required by CPLR 5531;

(ii) a table of contents including the titles of the points urged in the brief;

(iii) a concise statement of the questions involved without names, dates, amounts, or particulars. Each question shall be numbered, set forth separately, and followed immediately by the answer, if any, of the court from which the appeal is taken;

(iv) a concise statement of the nature of the action or proceeding and of the facts which should be known to determine the questions involved, with supporting references to pages in the record or the appendix, including, if such be the case, a statement that proceedings on the judgment or order appealed from have been stayed pending a determination of the appeal;

(v) the appellant's argument, which shall be divided into points by appropriate headings distinctively printed;

(vi) if a civil cause is perfected on the original papers, the brief shall include either a copy of the order or judgment appealed from, the decision, if any, and the notice of appeal, or a copy of any order transferring the proceeding to this court;

(vii) if the appeal is from an order involving pendente lite relief in a matrimonial action, the brief shall state whether issue has been joined and, if so, the date of joinder of issue, and whether the case has been noticed for trial;

(viii) in criminal causes, the appellant's brief at the beginning shall also set forth

(A) whether an order issued pursuant to CPL 460.50 is outstanding, the date of such order, the name of the judge who issued it and whether the defendant is free on bail or on his or her own recognizance, and

(B) whether there were co-defendants in the trial court, the disposition with respect to such co-defendants, and the status of any appeals by such co-defendants; and

(ix) a certificate of compliance, if required by subdivision (f) of this section.

(3) *Respondent's brief.* The respondent's brief shall contain, in the following order:

(i) a table of contents including the titles of points urged in the brief;

(ii) a counterstatement of the questions involved or of the nature and facts of the action or proceeding, if the respondent disagrees with the statement of the appellant;

(iii) the argument for the respondent, which

COURT RULES

shall be divided into points by appropriate headings distinctively printed; and

(iv) a certificate of compliance, if required by subdivision (f) of this section.

(4) *Appellant's reply brief.* The appellant's reply brief, unless otherwise ordered by the court, shall not contain an appendix, but shall contain, in the following order:

(i) a table of contents;

(ii) the reply for the appellant to the points raised by the respondent, without repetition of the arguments contained in the main brief, which shall be divided into points by appropriate headings distinctively printed; and

(iii) a certificate of compliance, if required by subdivision (f) of this section.

(h) *Addenda to briefs.* (1) Briefs may contain an addendum composed of decisions, statutes, ordinances, rules, regulations, local laws, or other similar matter, cited therein that were not published or that are not otherwise readily available.

(2) Unless otherwise authorized by order of the court, briefs may not contain maps, photographs, or other addenda.

(i) *Constitutionality of state statute.* Where the constitutionality of a statute of the State is involved in an appeal in which the State is not a party, the party raising the issue shall serve a copy of the brief upon the Attorney General of the State of New York who will be permitted to intervene in the appeal.

§ 670.11 *Amicus curiae* briefs.

(a) Permission to file an *amicus curiae* brief shall be obtained by persons who are not parties to the action or proceeding by motion on notice to each of the parties.

(b) An *amicus curiae* brief may not exceed 25 pages of standard typographic printing or 35 pages of printing by any other means of duplicating or copying unless otherwise ordered by the court, oral argument is not permitted.

§ 670.12 Appeals in criminal actions.

(a) Except as otherwise provided herein, an appeal in a criminal action shall be prosecuted in the same manner as a civil appeal.

(b) *Application for certificate granting leave to appeal.* (1) An application pursuant to CPL 450.15 and CPL 460.15 for leave to appeal to this court from an order shall be made in writing within 30 days after service of the order upon the applicant, on 15 days' notice to the district attorney, or other prosecutor, as the case may be.

(2) The application shall be addressed to the court for assignment to a justice and shall include:

(i) the name and address of the applicant and the name and address of the district attorney or other prosecutor, as the case may be;

(ii) the indictment, or superior court information number;

(iii) the questions of law or fact which it is claimed ought to be reviewed;

(iv) any other information, data, or matter which the applicant may deem pertinent in support of the application;

(v) a statement that no prior application for such certificate has been made; and

(vi) a copy of the order sought to be reviewed and a copy of the decision of the court of original instance or a statement that there was no decision.

(3) Within 15 days after service of a copy of the application the district attorney or other prosecutor shall file answering papers or a statement that there is no opposition to the application. Such answering papers shall include a discussion of the merits of the application or shall state, if such be the case, that the application does not contain any allegations other than those alleged in the papers submitted by the applicant in the trial court and that the prosecutor relies on the record; the answering papers in the trial court; and the decision of such court, if any.

(4) Unless the Justice designated to determine the application shall otherwise direct, the matter shall be submitted and determined upon the foregoing papers and without oral argument.

(c) *Appeal from sentence.* Where the only issue to be raised on appeal concerns the legality, propriety, or excessiveness of sentence, the appeal may be prosecuted by submitting a concise statement setting forth the reasons urged in support of the reversal or modification of sentence. Such statement shall contain the information required by CPLR 5531 and by § 670.10(d)(2)(viii) of this Part and shall contain a statement by counsel for the appellant that no other issues are asserted.

(1) Such appeals may be brought on as though they were motions made in accordance with the provisions of section 670.5 of this Part and shall be placed upon a special calendar for appeals submitted in accordance with this subdivision. The respondent shall serve and file papers in opposition within 14 days after service of the motion papers.

(2) The appellant shall submit the transcripts of sentence and the transcripts of the underlying plea or trial. The parties shall file an original and four copies of their respective papers, including the necessary transcripts.

(d) When an appeal in a criminal action is prosecuted on the original record or by the appendix method, the appellant shall serve a copy of the transcript of the proceedings upon the respondent together with the brief and appendix.

(e) Appeals by the People pursuant to CPL

450.20(1-a) shall be granted a preference upon the request of either the appellant or the respondent. The appellant's brief shall include an appendix containing a copy of the indictment, the order appealed from and the decision. The respondent's brief may also include an appendix, if necessary. The appellant shall file, separate from the record, one copy of the grand jury minutes (see Rules of the Chief Administrator of the Courts, Part 105).

(f) *Appeals to the Court of Appeals.* Service of a copy of an order on an appellant as required by CPL 460.10(5)(a) shall be made pursuant to CPLR 2103.

(g) In the event the defendant is represented by counsel the following shall be filed together with the brief filed on behalf of the defendant:

(1) Proof of mailing of a copy of the brief to the defendant at his or her last known address; and

(2) Where a brief pursuant to *Anders v. California* (386 US 738) has been filed, a copy of a letter to the defendant advising that he or she may file a *pro se* supplemental brief and if he or she wishes to file such a brief, that he or she must notify this court no later than 30 days after the date of mailing of counsel's letter of the intention to do so.

(h) A defendant represented by counsel who has not submitted a brief pursuant to *Anders v. California* (386 US 738) who wishes to file a *pro se* supplemental brief must make an application for permission to do so not later than 30 days after the date of mailing to the defendant of a copy of the brief prepared by counsel. The affidavit in support of the motion shall briefly set forth the points that the appellant intends to raise in the supplemental brief.

§ 670.13 Appeals from the Appellate Term.

(a) Appeals from the Appellate Term of the Supreme Court to this court may be prosecuted upon the record as presented to the Appellate Term; its order; its opinion or decision; and the order granting leave to appeal.

(b) When this court has made an order granting leave to appeal, the appellant shall file with the clerk of the Appellate Term a copy of the order. Within 20 days after an order granting leave to appeal shall have been filed with the clerk of the Appellate Term, such clerk or the appellant shall cause the record to be filed with the clerk of this court. Thereafter the appeal may be brought on for argument by the filing of briefs in the same manner as any other cause.

§ 670.14 Appeals from orders concerning Grand Jury reports.

The mode, time and manner for perfecting an appeal from an order accepting a report of a Grand Jury pursuant to CPL 190.85(1)(a) or from an order sealing a report of a Grand Jury pursuant to CPL 190.85(5) shall be in accordance with the provisions of this Part governing appeals in criminal cases. Appeals from such orders shall be preferred causes and may be added to the calendar by stipulation approved by the court or upon motion directed to the court. The record, briefs, and other papers on such an appeal shall be sealed and not available for public inspection except as permitted by CPL 190.85(3).

§ 670.15 Appeals where the sole issue is compensation of a judicial appointee.

If the sole issue sought to be reviewed on appeal is the amount of compensation awarded to a judicial appointee (i.e., referee, arbitrator, guardian, guardian *ad litem*, conservator, committee of the person or a committee of the property of an incompetent or patient, receiver, person designated to perform services for a receiver, such as but not limited to an agent, accountant, attorney, auctioneer, appraiser, or person designated to accept service), the appeal may be prosecuted in accordance with any of the methods specified in section 670.9 of this Part; or the appeal may be prosecuted by motion in accordance with the procedure applicable to special proceedings as set forth in section 670.5 of this Part. In such event, the review may be had on the original record and briefs may be filed at the option of any party.

§ 670.16 Transferred CPLR article 78 proceedings.

CPLR article 78 proceedings transferred to this court pursuant to CPLR 7804(g) may be prosecuted in accordance with any of the methods specified in section 670.9 of this Part. Where applicable, every such proceeding shall be governed by this Part as if it were an appeal.

§ 670.17 Transferred proceedings under the Human Rights Law (Executive Law, § 298).

(a) A proceeding under the Human Rights Law which is transferred to this court for disposition shall be prosecuted upon the original record which shall contain:

(1) copies of all papers filed in the Supreme Court;

(2) the decision of the Supreme Court, or a statement that no decision was rendered;

(3) the order of transfer; and

(4) the original record before the State Division of Human Rights, including a copy of the transcript of the public hearing.

(b) In all other respects every proceeding so

COURT RULES

transferred shall be governed by this Part as if it were an appeal.

(c) In the event that the original record which was before the State Division of Human Rights was not previously submitted to the Supreme Court, the Division shall file the original record with this court within 45 days after entry of, or service upon it of, a copy of the order of transfer.

§ 670.18 Special proceedings pursuant to Eminent Domain Procedure Law, § 207; Public Service Law, §§ 128, 170; Labor Law, § 220; Public Officers Law, § 36. or Real Property Tax Law, § 1218.

(a) Special proceedings initiated in this court pursuant to Eminent Domain Procedure Law, § 207, Public Service Law, §§ 128 or 170, Labor Law, § 220, Public Officers Law, § 36, or Real Property Tax Law, § 1218 shall be commenced by filing of a petition in the office of the clerk of this court pursuant to CPLR 304. Service of the petition with a notice of petition or order to show cause shall be made in accordance with CPLR 306-b on at least 20 days notice to the respondent. In proceedings pursuant to sections 207, 128 or 170 such notice shall be accompanied by a demand upon the respondent to file a copy of the transcript of the hearing before it and a copy of its determinations and findings.

(b) The respondent shall file an answer to the petition and, in proceedings pursuant to section 207, 128 or 170, the transcript of the hearing and the determination and findings.

(c) Within three months after service of the answer, the petitioner shall file nine copies of a brief, with proof of service of one copy upon the respondent. Not more than 30 days after service of petitioner's brief, the respondent shall file nine copies of an answering brief, with proof of service of one copy upon the petitioner. Not more than 10 days after service of the respondent's brief the petitioner may file a reply brief.

(d) The proceeding will be heard upon the original record which shall contain:

(1) the notice of petition and petition;

(2) if applicable, the demand for the transcript, determination and findings;

(3) the original record before the respondent including a copy of the transcript of the hearing, if any; and

(4) the determination and findings of the respondent.

(e) In all other respects such a proceeding shall be governed by this Part as if it were an appeal.

§ 670.19 Action on submitted facts.

(a) An action submitted to this court pursuant to CPLR 3222 shall be prosecuted on a printed submission which shall be bound separately from the brief and shall contain in the following order:

(1) a cover complying with section 670.10(b)(1) of this Part;

(2) the statement required by CPLR 5531;

(3) the case required by CPLR 3222(a), duly executed and acknowledged by all the parties in the form required to entitle a deed to be recorded, containing:

(i) the agreed statement of facts upon which the controversy depends;

(ii) a statement that the controversy is real and is made in good faith for the purpose of determining the rights of the parties;

(iii) a provision designating the particular county clerk of one of the counties within the Second Judicial Department with whom the papers are to be filed; and

(iv) a provision in conformity with CPLR 3222(b)(3) stipulating that the action be heard and determined by this court; and

(4) proof of filing of the paper comprising the submission with the designated county clerk.

(b) Where applicable, every such action shall be governed by this Part as if it were an appeal. The submission and briefs of the respective parties shall be served and filed in accordance with section 670.8 of this Part and the form of the briefs shall be governed by section 670.10(d) of this Part.

§ 670.20 Oral argument.

(a) Not more than 30 minutes shall be allowed for argument to each attorney who has filed a brief on:

(1) appeals from judgments, orders or decrees made after a trial or hearing;

(2) appeals from orders of the Appellate Term; and

(3) special proceedings transferred to or instituted in this court to review administrative determinations made after a hearing.

(b) Not more than 15 minutes shall be allowed for argument to each attorney who has filed a brief on all other causes except as set forth in subdivision (c) of this section.

(c) Argument is not permitted on issues involving maintenance; spousal support; child support; counsel fees; the legality, propriety or excessiveness of sentences; grand jury reports; and calendar and practice matters, including but not limited to preferences, bills of particulars, correction of pleadings, examinations before trial, physical examinations, discovery of records, interrogatories, change of venue, and transfers of actions to and from the Supreme Court. Applications for permission to argue such issues shall be made at the call of the calendar on the day the cause appears on the calendar. Notice of intention to make such an application shall be given to the court and the other parties at least seven days before the cause appears on the calendar.

(d) The court, in its discretion, may deny oral argument of any cause.

(e) Where the total time requested for argument by the attorneys on each side exceeds 30 minutes on appeals under subdivision (a) of this section or 15 minutes on appeals under subdivision (b) of this section, the court may, in its discretion, reduce the argument time requested. Not more than one attorney will be heard for each brief unless, upon application made before the beginning of the argument, the court shall have granted permission to allow more than one attorney to argue. A party who has not filed a brief may not argue.

(f) In the event that any party's main brief shall fail to set forth the appropriate notations indicating that the cause is to be argued and the time required for argument (see section 670.10(d)(1)(ii) of this Part), the cause will be deemed to have been submitted without oral argument by that party.

(g) If any party shall have filed the main brief late and such late brief be accepted, the court or any Justice may deem that the party has waived oral argument and has submitted the cause without argument.

(h) A party who originally elected to argue may notify the clerk of the intention to submit the cause without argument and need not appear on the calendar call.

(i) No briefs, letters or other communications in connection with a cause will be accepted after the argument or submission of a cause unless permission is granted by the court.

§ 670.21 Decisions and orders; costs.

(a) An order or judgment of this court determining a cause or an order of this court determining a motion shall be drafted by the court and shall be entered in the office of the clerk of this court. Such an order or judgment shall be deemed entered on the date upon which it was issued.

(b) Costs and disbursements upon any cause or motion shall be allowed only as directed by the court. In the absence of a contrary direction, the award by this court of costs upon any cause shall be deemed to include disbursements.

§ 670.22 Fees of the Clerk of the Court.

(a) Pursuant to CPLR 8022, the clerk is directed to charge and is entitled to receive on behalf of the State:

(1) A fee of $315, payable upon the filing of a record on a civil appeal or statement in lieu of record on a civil appeal and upon the filing of a notice of petition or order to show cause commencing a special proceeding.

(2) A fee of $45, payable upon the filing of each motion or cross motion with respect to a civil appeal or special proceeding, except that no fee shall be imposed for a motion or cross motion which seeks leave to appeal as a poor person pursuant to CPLR 1101(a).

(b) Pursuant to Judiciary Law, § 265, the clerk is directed to charge and is entitled to receive in advance the following fees on behalf of the State:

(1) For making a photocopy of an order, decision, opinion, or other filed paper of record, $1 for the first page and 50 cents for each additional page.

(2) For comparing the copy of a prepared order, decision, opinion, or other filed paper or record with the original on file, $1 for the first page and 50 cents for each additional page, with a minimum fee of $2.

(3) For certifying the copy of an order, decision, record, or other paper on file or for affixing the seal of the court, $1; and for authenticating the same, an additional $5.

(4) For certifying in any form that a search of any records in his custody has been made and giving the result of such search, $1.

(5) For an engraved parchment diploma attesting to admission as an attorney and counselor at law, $25.

(6) For a printed certificate attesting to admission or to good standing as an attorney and counselor at law, $5.

(7) [*Repealed.*]

(c) The clerk shall not, however, charge or receive any fees set forth in subdivision (b) of this section from the following parties who shall be exempt from the payment of such fees in this court:

(1) the United States or any state, city or country, or any political subdivision or agency or department of any of them;

(2) any judge, court, official character committee or board of examiners or any recognized agency serving the court or such committee or board;

(3) any duly recognized bar association;

(4) any party specifically exempt by law from the payment of fees; and

(5) any party to the cause for furnishing a copy of an opinion or order.

§ 670.23 Court's waiver of compliance.

In any civil or criminal cause, the court, either

COURT RULES

upon its own or upon any party's motion and either with or without notice to the adverse parties, may waive compliance by any party with any provision of this Part or may vary the application of any such provision.

§ 670.24 Forms [*omitted*].*

** **Editor's Note:** For forms, see NY CLS Desk Edition Civil Practice Annual (LexisNexis).*

PART 671

ADDITIONAL DUTIES OF COUNSEL, THE COURT AND THE COURT CLERK IN CRIMINAL ACTIONS, IN HABEAS CORPUS AND CPLR ARTICLE 78 PROCEEDINGS, IN PROCEEDINGS INSTITUTED BY MOTION MADE PURSUANT TO CPL 440.10 OR 440.20 AND IN FAMILY COURT ACT PROCEEDINGS

§ 671.1 Application.

(a) This Part of the rules is applicable in criminal actions or proceedings and in proceedings involving post-judgment motions made pursuant to CPL 440.10 or 440.20, and in habeas corpus and CPLR article 78 proceedings arising out of criminal actions or proceedings or accusatory instruments, indictments or informations.

(b) Unless the context requires otherwise, any reference herein to the defendant means either the defendant in a criminal action or proceeding or the defendant, the petitioner or the relator in a proceeding instituted on motion made pursuant to CPL 440.10 or 440.20 or in a proceeding under CPLR article 78 or in a habeas corpus proceeding.

(c) Unless the context requires otherwise, any reference herein to counsel for the defendant means every attorney who represents the defendant (as herein defined), regardless of whether such attorney shall have been retained or whether he shall have been assigned by the court or whether he be the public defender.

(d) Unless the context requires otherwise, any reference herein to the People's counsel means either the district attorney or other prosecutor as defined in CPL 1.20, or, as the case may be, the Attorney General or the county attorney or any other attorney who may appear for the People or for any public official joined as a party in his official capacity.

§ 671.2 Duration of representation by counsel for defendant.

In every criminal action or proceeding specified in section 671.1 hereof the duration of the representation by counsel for the defendant shall be as follows:

(a) in the trial court, until determination of the action or proceeding and until counsel shall have performed the additional duties imposed upon him by these rules; and

(b) in the appellate court, until entry of the order determining the appeal and until counsel shall have performed the additional duties imposed upon him by these rules. Thereupon such counsel's representation shall come to an end.

§ 671.3 Additional duties of defendant's counsel in the trial court.

(a) Upon conviction in the trial court or upon denial in that court of a motion made pursuant to CPL 440.10 or 440.20 or the denial or dismissal of an application in habeas corpus or CPLR article

78 proceeding, it shall be the duty of the counsel for the defendant, immediately after the pronouncement of sentence or after service upon him of a copy of the order denying the motion or of the order or judgment denying or dismissing the application, to give, either by mail or personally, written notice to his client advising him of his right to appeal or to make application for permission to appeal or for a certificate granting leave to appeal pursuant to CPL 460.10 (subdivision 4); and requesting his written instructions as to whether he desires to take an appeal or make such application. Thereafter, if the client gives to counsel timely written notice of his desire to appeal or to make such application, counsel shall promptly serve and file the necessary formal notice of appeal or application to the appropriate appellate court. If the application be granted, then within the time limitations and in the manner provided in CPL 460.10 (subdivision 4), counsel shall also file the order or certificate granting leave to appeal together with a written notice of appeal. Unless counsel shall have been retained to prosecute the appeal, the notice of appeal in every case shall contain the additional statement that it is being served and filed on appellant's behalf pursuant to this rule and that it shall not be deemed to be counsel's appearance as appellant's attorney upon the appeal.

(b) In counsel's written notice to his client advising him of the right to appeal or to make application for permission to appeal or for a certificate granting leave to appeal, counsel shall also set forth:

(1) The applicable time limitations with respect to the making of the application for permission to appeal or for a certificate granting leave to appeal and the prosecution of the appeal;

(2) the manner of instituting the appeal and, if a trial or hearing was held and stenographic minutes taken, the manner of obtaining a typewritten transcript of such minutes; and

(3) the appellant's right, upon proof of his financial inability to retain counsel and to pay the costs and expenses of the appeal, to make application to the appellate court for the following relief: for the assignment of counsel to prosecute the appeal; for leave to prosecute the appeal as a poor person and to dispense with printing; and if stenographic minutes were taken, for a direction to the clerk and the stenographer of the trial court that a typewritten transcript of such minutes be furnished without charged to the appellant's assigned counsel or, if appellant prosecutes the appeal *pro se,* to appellant.

(4) In such notice counsel shall also request the written instructions of his client, and if the client thereafter gives counsel timely written notice of his desire to make application for permission to appeal or for a certificate granting leave to appeal or to apply for the relief provided in paragraph (3) hereof, or to make any one or all of these applications, counsel shall proceed promptly to do so.

(c) Counsel shall also advise the client that in those cases where permission to appeal or where certificates granting leave to appeal are required, applications for the foregoing relief will be considered only if, as and when such permission is granted or such certificate is issued.

(d) In the event the People are the appellant and they elect to serve a copy of their notice of appeal upon the defendant, pursuant to their authority to do so under CPL 460.10, subdivision 1(c), they shall also serve a copy thereof upon the attorney who last appeared for the defendant in the court in which the order or sentence being appealed was entered.

(e) If, pursuant to CPL 460.10, subdivision 1 (c), the People as appellant elect to serve a copy of their notice of appeal in the first instance upon the attorney who last appeared for the defendant in the court in which the order or sentence being appealed was entered, or if they serve the attorney as required in subdivision (d) hereof, it shall be the duty of the attorney so served to give, either by mail or personally, written notice to his client confirming the fact that such appeal has been taken by the People. Such notice shall also advise his client of his right (1) to retain counsel to represent him as respondent on the appeal, or (2) to respond to the appeal *pro se,* or (3) upon proof of his financial inability to retain counsel and to pay the cost and expenses of responding to the appeal, to make application to the appellate court for the following relief: for the assignment of counsel to represent him as the respondent on the appeal; for leave to respond to the appeal as a poor person and to dispense with printing; and, if stenographic minutes were taken, for a direction to the clerk and the stenographer of the trial court that a typewritten transcript of such minutes be furnished without charge to the respondent's assigned counsel or, if the defendant appears as respondent *pro se,* to respondent. In such notice counsel shall also request the written instructions of his client, and, if the client thereafter gives counsel timely written notice of his desire to make such application, counsel shall proceed promptly to do so.

(f) In the event, however, the attorney was the defendant's assigned counsel in the court in which the order or sentence being appealed was entered, such assignment shall remain in effect and counsel shall continue to represent the defendant as the respondent on the appeal until entry of the order determining the appeal and until counsel shall have performed any additional applicable duties imposed upon him by these rules, or until counsel shall have been otherwise relieved of his assignment. In event the assignment remains in effect as herein provided, the written notice to the client as provided in subdivision (e) hereof may be dispensed with, except to the extent of confirming the fact that such appeal has been taken by the People.

§ 671.4 Additional duties of defendant's counsel in the Appellate Division or other intermediate appellate court.

(a) Immediately after entry of the order of the Appellate Division or other intermediate appellate court affirming the judgment of conviction or sentence or the order denying a motion made pursuant to CPL 440.10 or 440.20 or the order or judgment denying or dismissing a habeas corpus of CPLR article 78 application or proceeding, it shall be the duty of the counsel for the defendant, to give, either by mail or personally, written notice to his client advising him:

(1) of his right to make application for permission to take a further appeal or for a certificate granting leave to appeal to the Court of Appeals; and

(2) in the event such permission is granted or such certificate is issued, of his additional right, upon proof of his financial inability to retain counsel and to pay the costs and expenses of such further appeal, to make a concurrent application to the Court of Appeals for the assignment of counsel and for leave to prosecute such further appeal as a poor person and to dispense with printing. In such notice counsel shall also request the written instructions of his client. If the client thereafter gives to counsel timely written notice of his desire to make either or both of such applications, counsel shall proceed promptly to do so.

(b) In a *habeas corpus* or CPLR article 78 proceeding, however, of any two judges shall have dissented from the affirmance and if the dissent is on a stated question of law in relator's or petitioner's favor, counsel in his said written notice shall advise his client of his absolute right, without permission, to take a further appeal to the Court of Appeals. Upon receiving from the client written notice of his desire to prosecute such appeal, counsel shall file and serve promptly a formal notice of appeal accordingly. Unless counsel shall have been retained to prosecute the appeal, the notice of appeal shall contain the additional statement that it is being served and filed on appellant's behalf pursuant to this rule and that it shall not be deemed counsel's appearance as appellant's attorney upon the appeal.

(c) In the event the People are the appellant and they elect to serve a copy of their notice of appeal upon the defendant pursuant to their authority to do so under CPL 460.10, subdivision 5(c), they shall also serve a copy thereof upon the attorney who appeared for the defendant in the intermediate court.

(d) If, pursuant to said CPL 460.10 subdivision 5(c), the People as appellant elect in the first instance to serve a copy of their notice of appeal on the attorney who appeared for the defendant in the intermediate appellate court, or, if they serve the attorney as required in subdivision (c) hereof, it shall be the duty of counsel for the defendant to give, either by mail or personally, written notice to his client confirming the fact that such appeal has been taken by the People. Such notice shall also advise him of his right (1) to retain counsel to represent him as respondent on the appeal, or (2) to respond to the appeal, *pro se,* or (3) upon proof of his financial inability to retain counsel and to pay the costs and expenses of responding to such appeal, to apply to the Court of Appeals for the assignment of counsel, for leave to respond to the appeal as a poor person and to dispense with printing. In such notice counsel shall also request the written instructions of his client. If the client thereafter gives counsel timely written notice of his desire to make such application, counsel shall proceed promptly to do so.

(e) In the event the appeal by the People results in an order of an intermediate appellate court adverse or partially adverse to the defendant-respondent, it shall be the duty of counsel to comply with the written notice provisions of subdivision (a) hereof applicable to an affirmance on an appeal by the defendant except that the term "further appeal" in paragraphs (1) and (2) thereof shall be deemed to read "appeal."

§ 671.5 Additional duties of the court and the court clerk, where defendant appears pro se in the trial court.

If a defendant shall have appeared *pro se* in the trial court, then, upon imposing sentence or upon the denial of a motion made pursuant to CPL 440.10 or 440.20 or the denial or dismissal of the habeas corpus or CPLR article 78 application or proceeding, the trial court shall concurrently advise the defendant of his right to appeal or to make application for permission to appeal or for a certificate granting leave to appeal, as the case may be. The court shall also concurrently advise the defendant of his additional right, upon proof of his financial inability to retain counsel and to pay the cost and expenses of the appeal, to apply to the appellate court for the assignment of counsel and for leave to prosecute the appeal as a poor person and to dispense with printing; and that where permission to appeal or a certificate granting leave to appeal is required, such application for poor person relief will be entertained only if, as and when such permission or certificate is granted. If in open court the defendant orally so requests or if thereafter he so requests in writing and such written request be timely received by the clerk of the trial court, said clerk shall forthwith prepare and serve and file an appropriate notice of appeal on defendant's behalf, or, if a certificate granting leave to appeal is required, serve and file the application therefor in accordance with the rule herein above provided with respect to such application. As a part of every such application the clerk shall annex and transmit the original record of the proceedings to the appellate court. Upon the determination of the application, the original record of the proceedings shall be returned to the trial court together with a certified copy of the order entered upon the application. A certified copy of such order shall also be sent to the defendant at his address shown in the application.

§ 671.6 Additional duties of counsel for the People, where defendant appears pro se in appellate court on appeal in criminal action or proceeding instituted upon motion made pursuant to CPL 440.10 or 440.20.

On an appeal from a judgment of conviction or sentence or on an appeal from an order denying a motion made pursuant to CPL 440.10 or 440.20, if the defendant shall have appeared *pro se* and if the judgment, sentence or order shall have been affirmed, the copy of the order of affirmance which the People's counsel thereafter serves on the defendant shall have annexed or appended thereto or endorsed thereon the following notice:

NOTICE AS TO FURTHER APPEAL

Pursuant to CPL 460.20, within 30 days after service upon you of a copy of the order of affirmance with notice of its entry you have the right to apply for a certificate granting leave to take a further appeal to the Court of Appeals. Such application must be made either to the chief judge of the Court of Appeals by submitting it to the clerk of that court, as prescribed in CPL 460.20 (subdivisions 3b and 4), or to a justice of the Appellate Division of the Supreme Court in this department, as prescribed in section 670.7 of these rules and in CPL 460.20 (subdivisions 3a and 4).

The denial of such application by the first judge or justice to whom it is presented is final; thereafter a new application may not be made to any other judge or justice.

§ 671.7 Additional duties of counsel for the people, where defendant appears pro se in appellate court on appeal in habeas corpus or CPLR article 78 proceedings.

On an appeal from a judgment or order denying or dismissing a habeas corpus or a CPLR article 78 application or proceeding, if the defendant shall have appeared *pro se* and if the judgment or order shall have been affirmed or modified, the copy of the order which the People's counsel thereafter serves on the defendant shall have annexed or appended thereto or endorsed thereon the following notice:

NOTICE AS TO FURTHER APPEAL

If the affirmance by the Appellate Division is unanimous, then, pursuant to statute (CPLR 5602), within 30 days after service upon you of a copy of the order of affirmance with notice of its entry, you may make application for permission to take a further appeal to the Court of Appeals. Such application must be made either; to the Appellate Division, or, upon its refusal, to the Court of Appeals; or directly to the Court of Appeals without first applying to the Appellate Division. If such permission be granted by either court, the appeal to the Court of Appeals will be deemed to have been taken without the necessity of serving or filing a formal notice of appeal.

If the affirmance by the Appellate Division is not unanimous and if the dissent is in your favor with respect to a stated questions of law; or if the judgment or order appealed from be modified in a substantial respect, and if you are aggrieved by the modification and it is one which is within the power of the Court of Appeals to review, then, pursuant to statute (CPLR 5513, 5515, 5601), within 30 days after service upon you of a copy of the order with notice of its entry, you have the right (without permission) to take a further appeal to the Court of Appeals by serving your notice of appeal on the adverse party or upon his attorney and by filing such notice in the office where the judgment or order of the court of original instance was entered.

§ 671.8 [*Repealed.*]

§ 671.9 Additional duties of the court and of defendant's counsel in connection with trial court transcripts.

Where furnishing of a daily copy of a transcript is ordered by the court, the ribbon copy thereof shall be delivered to the court and a carbon copy to counsel for the defendant. Both the court and counsel for the defendant shall be duty-bound to preserve their respective copies. At the conclusion of the trial or hearing, trial counsel for the defendant shall, if an appeal is taken, deliver said carbon copy to appellant's counsel immediately on being advised of the name and address of said appellant's counsel. At the conclusion of the trial or hearing and forthwith after the decision or verdict, as the case may be, the ribbon copy shall be delivered by the court to the county clerk for filing. The ribbon copy and the carbon copy shall constitute the two transcripts of the proceedings required by section 460.70 of the Criminal Procedure Law.

§ 671.10　Duties of assigned counsel in the Family Court.

(a) Upon the entry of an order in the Family Court from which an appeal is or may be taken under section 1112 of The Family Court Act, it shall be the duty of counsel for the unsuccessful party, immediately after the entry of the order, to give, either by mail or personally, written notice to his client advising of his or her right to appeal or to make application for permission to appeal, and request written instructions as to whether he or she desires to take an appeal or to make such application. Thereafter, if the client gives to counsel timely written notice of his or her desire to appeal or to make such application, counsel shall promptly serve and file the necessary formal notice of appeal or application to this court. Unless counsel shall have been retained to prosecute the appeal, the notice of appeal shall contain the additional statement that it is being served and filed on appellant's behalf pursuant to this rule and that it shall not be deemed to be counsel's appearance as appellant's attorney on the appeal.

(b) In counsel's written notice to his client advising him of the right to appeal or to make application for permission to appeal, counsel shall also set forth:

(1) the applicable time limitations with respect to the taking of the appeal or the making of the application for permission to appeal;

(2) the manner of instituting the appeal and, if a trial hearing was held and stenographic minutes taken, the manner of obtaining a typewritten transcript of such minutes;

(3) appellant's right, upon proof of his financial inability to retain counsel and to pay the costs and expenses of the appeal, to make application to this court for the assignment of counsel to prosecute the appeal; and, if stenographic minutes were taken, for a direction to the clerk and the stenographer of the trial court that a typewritten transcript of such minutes be furnished without charge to appellant's assigned counsel or, if appellant prosecutes the appeal *pro se,* to appellant; and

(4) in such notice counsel shall also request the written instructions of his client, and if the client thereafter gives counsel timely written notice of his desire to make application for permission to appeal or to apply for the relief provided in paragraph (3) of this subdivision, or to make any one or all of these applications, counsel shall proceed promptly to do so.

(c) Counsel shall also advise the client that in those cases where permission to appeal is required, applications for the foregoing relief will be considered only if such permission is granted.

(d) In the event the unsuccessful party is the appellant, he or she must serve a copy of the notice of appeal upon the successful party and upon the attorney who last appeared for the successful party in the court in which the order being appealed was entered.

(e) If the attorney for the successful party is served with the notice of appeal, it shall be the duty of the attorney so served to give, either by mail or personally, written notice to his client of the fact that the unsuccessful party has taken an appeal. Such notice shall also advise the client of his right:

(1) to retain counsel to represent him as respondent on the appeal;

(2) to respond to the appeal *pro se;* and

(3) upon proof of his financial inability to retain counsel and to pay the costs and expenses of responding to the appeal, to make application to this court for the assignment of counsel.

In such notice counsel shall also request the written instructions of his client and, if the client thereafter gives counsel timely written notice of his desire to make such application, counsel shall proceed promptly to do so.

(f) In the event, however, that the attorney was the assigned counsel for the successful party in the court in which the order being appealed was entered, such assignment shall remain in effect and counsel shall continue to represent the successful party as the respondent on the appeal until entry of the order determining the appeal and until counsel shall have performed any additional applicable duties imposed upon him by these rules, or until counsel shall have been otherwise relieved of his assignment. In the event the assignment remains in effect as herein provided, the written notice to the client provided in subdivision (e) of this section may be dispensed with, except to the extent of confirming the fact that such appeal has been taken by the unsuccessful party.

PART 679

FAMILY COURT LAW GUARDIAN PLAN

§ 679.1 Family Court law guardian plan established.

There is hereby established in the counties of the Second Judicial Department a plan for the operation of the Family Court law guardian panels designated pursuant to Family Court Act § 243(c).

§ 679.2 Administration of law guardian plan.

The law guardian plan for the Second Judicial Department shall be administered by the director of the law guardian program who shall be appointed by the Appellate Division of the Supreme Court, Second Judicial Department, and supervised by the Presiding Justice.

§ 679.3 Law guardian director.

The director of the law guardian program shall administer the plan in accordance with the law, these rules, and with the procedures promulgated by the law guardian advisory committees.

§ 679.4 Advisory committees.

The following Family Court law guardian advisory committees shall be established:

(a) There shall be a single committee for the counties of Kings, Queens and Richmond, which shall be composed of the Deputy New York City Administrative Judge-Family Division or his or her designee, a representative of each of the county bar associations, a member of the faculty of an accredited law school, and three additional members at least one of whom shall be a non-attorney.

(b) In Nassau County, the committee shall be composed of the Deputy Administrative Judge of the Family Court, a representative of the county bar association, a member of the faculty of an accredited law school, and three additional members at least one of whom shall be a non-attorney.

(c) In Suffolk County, the committee shall be composed of the Deputy Administrative Judge of the Family Court, a representative of the county bar association, a member of the faculty of an accredited law school, and three additional members at least one of whom shall be a non-attorney.

(d) There shall be a single committee for the counties of Dutchess, Orange, Putnam, Rockland and Westchester, which shall be composed of the Deputy Administrative Judge of the Family Court, Ninth Judicial District, a representative from each county bar association, a member of the faculty of an accredited law school, and nine additional members at least three of whom shall be non-attorneys.

(e) On each advisory committee the Family Court Judge member shall serve as chairperson. All the members shall be designated by the Appellate Division, Second Judicial Department, for three-year terms, and may be reappointed for additional terms. The bar association representative members shall be appointed upon recommendation of the respective bar associations. Committee members may not serve on the law guardian panels.

(f) The director of the law guardian program shall sit as an *officio* member of each advisory committee.

(g) The members of the law guardian advisory committees as volunteers are expressly authorized to participate in a State-sponsored volunteer program within the meaning of the Public Officers Law § 17.

§ 679.5 Duties of the advisory committees.

Subject to the supervision of the Appellate Division, the advisory committees shall establish procedures for appointment and reappointment of attorneys to serve on the law guardian panels, for periodic evaluation of attorneys who serve on the law guardian panels, for training of attorneys on the law guardian panels, for investigating complaints made against members of the law guardian panels, and for removal of attorneys from the law guardian panels.

§ 679.6 Eligibility requirements.

(a) To be eligible for recommendation for appointment to a panel designated pursuant to

COURT RULES

Family Court Act § 243 or to a panel established for attorneys assigned pursuant to Family Court Act § 243, an attorney shall be admitted to the bar of the State of New York, in good standing, and shall have served as counsel or co-counsel in the Family Court in a minimum of three proceedings under Family Court Act article 3, article 6 and article 10.

(b) The advisory committees shall establish co-counsel or mentoring programs to provide experience to admitted attorneys who wish to serve on the panel but lack the qualifications required by paragraph (a).

(c) The minimum requirements may be waived if, in the opinion of the advisory committees, the applicant is otherwise qualified by reason of education, training or substantial trial experience.

(d) The advisory committees may set forth such additional requirements and procedures as they see fit, subject to approval by the Appellate Division.

§ 679.7 Designation of panels.

The Appellate Division shall designate the law guardian panel for each county from attorneys recommended by the advisory committees. Appointments to the panel shall not exceed one year, but any panel member may be reappointed.

§ 679.8 Periodic evaluation of law guardians.

The advisory committees shall establish procedures to periodically evaluate the representation provided to juveniles by each member of the law guardian panel. In conducting the periodic evaluation the advisory committees shall seek information from Family Court judges and other appropriate and knowledgeable persons. The advisory committees shall not recommend for reappointment any attorney whose representation the committees determine to be unsatisfactory.

§ 679.9 Training and education.

The advisory committees, in cooperation with the director of the law guardian program shall establish a training and education program for members of the law guardian panels. Such a program may be established in conjunction with bar associations, local law schools or other competent organizations. The advisory committees shall make attendance at training programs a requirement for continued membership on the law guardian panels.

§ 679.10 Recommendation for removal.

An advisory committee may, at any time, recommend to the Presiding Justice that an attorney be removed from the panel. Such recommendation shall be submitted in writing, together with a report of the basis for such recommendation. Such recommendation shall not be required where an attorney is not reappointed at the expiration of his or her term. The Presiding Justice shall have the power to remove members of the Family Court law guardian panels and members of panels established for attorneys assigned pursuant to Family Court Act § 262.

§ 679.11 Assignments of counsel.

Assignments of counsel by the Family Court, Supreme Court or Surrogate's Court to represent children in proceedings wherein compensation is authorized pursuant to Judiciary Law § 35 shall be made from law guardian panels designated pursuant to these rules.

§ 679.12 Annual evaluations.

On June 30th of each year, commencing with June 30, 1991, each advisory committee shall submit to the Appellate Division an evaluation of the operation of the plan and the training programs, and recommendations as to procedures, if any, which should be adopted to improve the performance of the plan and the training programs.

§ 679.13 Annual reports.

A report of the operation of the law guardian panels shall be filed by the Appellate Division with the Chief Administrator of the Courts on August 1st of each year, commencing August 1, 1991.

679.14 Construction.

Nothing contained in this Part shall be construed to limit the powers of the Appellate Division, the Presiding Justice, or the administrator of the assigned counsel plan, otherwise granted pursuant to law.

PART 691

CONDUCT OF ATTORNEYS

§ 691.1 Application.

(a) This Part shall apply to all attorneys who are admitted to practice, reside in, commit acts in or who have offices in the Second Judicial Department, or who are admitted to practice by a court of another jurisdiction and who regularly practice within this department as counsel for governmental agencies or as house counsel to corporations or other entities, or otherwise. In addition, any attorney from another state, territory, district or foreign country admitted *pro hac vice* to participate in the trial or argument of a particular cause in any court in the Second Judicial Department, or who in any way participates in an action or proceeding therein, shall be subject to this Part.

(b) The imposition of discipline pursuant to this Part shall not preclude the imposition of any further or additional sanctions prescribed or authorized by law, and nothing contained in this Part shall be construed to deny to any other court such powers as are necessary for that court to maintain control over proceedings conducted before it, such as the power of contempt, nor to prohibit bar associations from censuring, suspending or expelling their members from membership in the association or from admonishing attorneys in minor matters; provided, however, that such action by a bar association shall be reported to the appropriate committee appointed pursuant to section 691.4(a) of this Part, and provided further, that such action by a bar association shall not be a bar to the taking of other and different disciplinary action by this court or by a committee appointed pursuant to section 691.4(a) of this Part.

§ 691.2 Professional misconduct defined.

Any attorney who fails to conduct himself, either professionally or personally, in conformity with the standards of conduct imposed upon members of the bar as conditions for the privilege to practice law, and any attorney who violates any provision of the rules of this court governing the conduct of attorneys, or any disciplinary rule of the Code of Professional Responsibility, adopted jointly by the Appellate Divisions of the Supreme Court, effective September 1, 1990 or any canon of the Canons of Professional Ethics, adopted by New York State Bar Association, or any other rule or announced standard of this court governing the conduct of attorneys, shall be deemed to be guilty of professional misconduct within the meaning of subdivision 2 of section 90 of the Judiciary Law.

§ 691.3 Discipline of attorneys for professional misconduct in foreign jurisdictions.

(a) Any attorney to whom this Part shall apply pursuant to section 691.1 of this Part, who has been disciplined in another state, territory or district, may be disciplined by this court because of the conduct which gave rise to the discipline imposed in such other state, territory or district.

(b) Upon receipt from the foreign jurisdiction of a certified or exemplified copy of the order imposing such discipline and of the record of the proceedings upon which such order was based, this court, directly, or by a committee appointed pursuant to section 691.4(a) of this Part, shall give written notice to such attorney pursuant to subdivision (6) of section 90 of the Judiciary Law, according him the opportunity within 20 days of the giving of such notice, to file a verified statement setting forth any defense to discipline enumerated under subdivision (c) of this section, and a written demand for a hearing at which consideration shall be given to any and all defenses enumerated in said subdivision (c) of this section. Such notice shall further advise the attorney that in default of such filing by him, this court will impose such discipline or take such disciplinary action as it deems appropriate.

(c) This court, in default of the attorney's filing a verified statement and demand as provided for in subdivision (b) of this section, may discipline such attorney unless an examination of the entire record before this court, including the record of the foreign jurisdiction and such other evidence as this court in its discretion may receive, discloses (1) that the procedure in the foreign jurisdiction was so lacking in notice or opportunity to be heard as to constitute a deprivation of due process; or (2) that there was such an infirmity of proof establishing the misconduct as to give rise to the clear conviction that this court could not, consistent with its duties, accept as final the finding of the court in the foreign jurisdiction as to the attorney's misconduct; or (3) that the imposition of discipline by this court would be unjust.

(d) *Opportunity for hearing.* Where an attorney shall have duly filed both his verified statement setting forth any defense (as enumerated in subdivision (c) of this section) to the imposition of discipline by this court and his written demand for a hearing with respect to such defense, no discipline, by way of suspension or otherwise,

shall be imposed without affording the attorney an opportunity to have a hearing.

(e) Any attorney to whom this Part shall apply who has been disciplined in a foreign jurisdiction shall promptly advise this court of such discipline.

§ 691.4 Appointment of grievance committees; commencement of investigation of attorney misconduct; complaints; procedure.

(a) This court shall appoint three grievance committees for the Second Judicial Department. One of these grievance committees shall be charged with the duty and power to investigate and prosecute matters arising in or concerning attorneys practicing, or currently residing or having resided in the second and eleventh judicial districts at the time of their admission to practice by the Appellate Division; another shall have the duty and power to investigate and prosecute matters arising in or concerning attorneys practicing, or currently residing or having resided in the ninth judicial district at the time of their admission to practice by the Appellate Division; and the third shall have the duty and power to investigate and prosecute matters arising in or concerning attorneys practicing, or currently residing or having resided in the tenth judicial district at the time of their admission to practice by the Appellate Division. These committees shall also have the power and duty to investigate and prosecute matters concerning attorneys to whom this Part applies pursuant to section 691.1 of this Part.

(b) (1) Each grievance committee shall consist of 19 members and a chairman, all of whom shall be appointed by this court and 16 of whom shall be attorneys. The chairman shall have the power to appoint an acting chairman from among the members of the grievance committee. Appointments may be made from lists of prospective members submitted by the following county bar associations within the second judicial department; Brooklyn Bar Association, Dutchess County Bar Association, Bar Association of Nassau County, New York, Inc., Orange County Bar Association, Putnam County Bar Association, Queens County Bar Association, Richmond County Bar Association, Rockland County Bar Association, Inc., Suffolk County Bar Association and Westchester County Bar Association. This court shall, in consultation with the committees, appoint a chief counsel to each such grievance committee and such assistant counsel and supporting staff as it deems necessary.

(2) Five persons shall be appointed to each such committee for a term of one year, five persons for a term of two years, five persons for a term of three years and five persons for a term of four years. Thereafter, yearly appointments of five persons shall be made to each such committee for a term of four years. No person who has

served two consecutive terms shall be eligible for reappointment until the passage of one year from the expiration of his second such term. The person appointed chairman shall serve as chairman for a term of two years and shall be eligible for reappointment as chairman for not more than one additional term of two years.

(3) The members of the joint bar association grievance committees as volunteers are expressly authorized to participate in a State-sponsored volunteer program within the meaning of subdivision 1 of section 17 of the Public Officers Law.

(c) Investigation of professional misconduct may be commenced upon receipt of a specific complaint by this court or by any such committee, or such investigation may be commenced *sua sponte* by this court or such a committee. Complaints must be in writing and signed by the complainant but need not be verified. Complainants shall be notified by the committee of actions taken by it with respect thereto.

(d) Each grievance committee shall have the power to appoint its members to subcommittees of not less than three members, two of whom shall constitute a quorum and shall have power to act. At least two members of a subcommittee shall be attorneys. The chairman of the committee shall designate a member of the subcommittee to act as its chairman. Such subcommittees may hold hearings as hereinafter authorized.

(e) Upon receipt or initiation of a specific complaint of professional misconduct, any such committee may, after preliminary investigation and upon a majority vote of the full committee:

(1) dismiss the complaint and so advise the complainant and the attorney;

(2) conclude the matter by issuing a letter of caution to the attorney and by appropriately advising the complainant of such action;

(3) conclude the matter by privately admonishing the attorney, which admonition shall clearly indicate the improper conduct found and the disciplinary rule, canon or special rule which has been violated, and by appropriately advising the complainant of such action;

(4) serve written charges upon the attorney and hold a hearing on the matter as set forth in subdivision (f) of this section;

(5) forthwith recommend to this court the institution of a disciplinary proceeding where the public interest demands prompt action and where the available facts show probable cause for such action.

(f) Except as otherwise provided for in paragraph (5) of subdivision (e) of this section, if, after preliminary investigation, the committee shall deem a matter of sufficient importance, written charges predicated thereon, plainly stating the matter or matters charged, together with a notice of not less than 20 days, shall be served upon the person concerned, either personally, by certified mail, or in such other manner as the committee may direct. The person so served shall file a written answer at the time and place designated in the notice and the committee or a subcommittee shall proceed to hold a hearing of the case. The person concerned (hereinafter referred to as the respondent) may be represented and assisted by counsel. The committee or subcommittee shall decide all questions of evidence. Stenographic minutes of the hearing shall be kept.

(g) Whenever in the course of a hearing evidence is presented upon which another charge or charges against the respondent might be made, it shall not be necessary for the committee to prepare and serve an additional charge or charges on the respondent, but the committee or the subcommittee may, after reasonable notice to the respondent and an opportunity to answer and be heard, proceed to the consideration of such additional charge or charges as if the same had been made and served at the time of the service of the original charge or charges.

(h) If the hearing was held before a subcommittee, it shall make findings of fact and report those findings to the committee. Upon the completion of a hearing, the committee shall promptly meet and either dismiss or sustain the charges and, as to any charges sustained, shall either issue a letter of caution, admonish the respondent, or recommend that probable cause exists for the filing of disciplinary charges against the respondent in this court. A letter of caution may also be issued where the charges have been dismissed. The approval of a recommendation of the filing of disciplinary charges in this court shall be by a majority vote of the full committee.

(i) In the event that a minority of the committee disagrees with a final determination, such minority report shall be filed with this court along with any majority report and the written report of the subcommittee. Upon such filing, the committee shall await the determination of this court before otherwise disposing of the matter.

(j) Unless otherwise provided for by this court, all proceedings conducted by a grievance committee shall be sealed and be deemed private and confidential.

(k) Disciplinary proceedings shall be granted a preference by this court.

(l) (1) An attorney who is the subject of an investigation, or of charges by a grievance committee of professional misconduct, or who is the subject of a disciplinary proceeding pending in this court against whom a petition has been filed pursuant to this section, or upon whom a notice has been served pursuant to section 691.3(b) of this Part, may be suspended from the practice of law, pending consideration of the charges against the attorney, upon a finding that the attorney is guilty of professional misconduct immediately threatening the public interest. Such a finding shall be based upon:

(i) the attorney's default in responding to the petition or notice, or the attorney's failure to submit a written answer to pending charges of professional misconduct within 10 days of receipt of a demand for such an answer by the grievance committee, served either personally or by certified mail upon the attorney or the attorney's failure to comply with any lawful demand of this court or the grievance committee made in connection with any investigation, hearing, or disciplinary proceeding; or

(ii) a substantial admission under oath that the attorney has committed an act or acts of professional misconduct; or

(iii) other uncontroverted evidence of professional misconduct.

(2) The suspension shall be made upon the application of the grievance committee to this court, after notice of such application has been given to the attorney pursuant to subdivision 6 of section 90 of the Judiciary Law. The court shall briefly state its reasons for its order of suspension which shall be effective immediately and until such time as the disciplinary matters before the committee have been concluded, and until further order of this court.

(m) *Diversion Program.*

(1) If during the course of an investigation, the consideration of charges by a grievance committee, or the course of a formal disciplinary proceeding, it appears that the attorney whose conduct is the subject thereof is or may be suffering from alcoholism or other substance abuse or dependency, the court may upon application of the attorney or committee, or on its own motion, stay the investigation, charges, or proceeding and direct the attorney to complete a monitoring program sponsored by a lawyers' assistance program approved by the court. In determining whether to divert an attorney to a monitoring program, the court shall consider (i) whether the alleged misconduct occurred during a time period when the attorney suffered from alcohol or other substance abuse or dependency; (ii) whether the alleged misconduct is related to such alcohol or other substance abuse or dependency (ii) the seriousness of the alleged misconduct; and (iv) whether diversion is in the best interest of the public, the legal progression, and the attorney.

(2) Upon submission of the written proof of successful completion of the monitoring program, the court may direct the discontinuance or resumption of the investigation, charges, or proceeding, or take other appropriate action.

(3) In the event the attorney is not accepted into or fails to successfully complete the monitoring program as ordered by the court, or the attorney commits additional misconduct after diversion is directed pursuant to this subdivision,

the court may, upon notice to the attorney affording him or her the opportunity to be heard, rescind the attorney to the monitoring program and reinstate the investigation, charges, or proceeding, or take other appropriate action.

(4) Any cost associated with the attorney's participation in a monitoring program pursuant to this subdivision shall be paid by the attorney.

(n) *Medical and Psychological Evidence.* Whenever an attorney who is the subject of charges of professional misconduct and a hearing before a grievance committee or is the subject of a disciplinary proceeding pending in this court intends to offer medical or psychological evidence at a hearing in mitigation of the charges, he or she shall give written notice to counsel for the committee of the intention to do so not later than 20 days before the scheduled date of the hearing. Said notice shall be accompanied by (1) a duly executed and acknowledged written authorization permitting counsel for the committee to obtain and make copies of the records of the treating physician, psychiatrist, to obtain and make copies of the records of the treating physician, psychiatrist, psychologist, or other such health care professionals regarding the attorney's physical or mental condition at issue, and (2) a copy of the written reports, in any, of the health care professionals who the attorney proposes to call as witnesses.

(o) *Disqualification from Representation.* No former staff counsel to a grievance committee or former member of such a committee may accept a retainer or otherwise represent an attorney who is the subject of an investigation, or of charges by a grievance committee of professional misconduct, or of a disciplinary proceeding in this court, if such investigation, charges, and/or proceeding were pending before such committee during the term of service of that former staff counsel or committee member.

No former special referee appointed to hear and report on the issues raised in a formal disciplinary proceeding may accept a retainer or otherwise represent an attorney who is the subject of an investigation, or of charges by a grievance committee of professional misconduct, or of a disciplinary proceeding in this judicial department, until the expiration of two years from the date of the submission of his or her final report.

§ 691.5 Investigation of professional misconduct on the part of an attorney; subpoenas and examination of witnesses under oath.

(a) Upon application by the chairman or acting chairman of any such committee, or upon application by counsel to such committee, disclosing that such committee is conducting an investigation of professional misconduct on the part of an attorney, or upon application by an attorney under such investigation, the clerk of this court may issue subpoenas, in the name of the presiding justice, for the attendance of witnesses and the production of books and papers before such committee or such counsel, or any subcommittee thereof designated in such application, at a time and place therein specified.

(b) Any such committee thereof is empowered to take and cause to be transcribed the evidence of witnesses who may be sworn by any person authorized by law to administer oaths.

§ 691.5-a Formal disciplinary proceedings; subpoenas, depositions, and motions.

In the event that a formal disciplinary proceeding pursuant to section 90 of the Judiciary Law or other provision of this part is commenced in this court against an attorney, the following shall apply:

(a) *Subpoenas.* Upon application by the petitioner or the respondent, the clerk of this court may issue subpoenas for the attendance of the witnesses and the production of books and papers before the referee, justice, or judge designated by the court to conduct a hearing on the issues raised in the proceeding, at a time and place therein specified.

(b) *Depositions.* When there is good cause to believe that a potential witness will be unavailable at the time of a hearing, the testimony of that witness may be taken by deposition. Such a deposition shall be initiated and conducted in the manner provided by, and the use thereof at a hearing shall be in accordance with, the provisions of article 31 of the Civil Practice Law and Rules.

(c) *Motions.* Motions made during the course of a formal disciplinary proceeding shall be addressed to the court and shall be made and noticed in the manner provided in section 670.5 of this title. The court may refer the motion to a referee, justice, or judge appointed by it to either hear and determine or hear and report on the same.

§ 691.6 Reprimand; admonition; letter of caution; confidentiality.

(a) The chairman or acting chairman of any such committee may, after investigation and upon a majority vote of the full committee, issue a reprimand or an admonition or a letter of caution in those cases in which professional misconduct, not warranting proceedings before this court, is found. A reprimand is discipline imposed after a hearing. An admonition is discipline imposed without a hearing. A letter of caution may issue when it is believed that the attorney acted in a manner which, while not constituting clear professional misconduct, involved behavior requiring comment. In cases in which an admonition or a letter of caution is issued, the attorney to whom such admonition or letter of caution is directed may, within 30 days after the issuance of the admonition or letter of caution, request a hearing before the committee or a subcommittee thereof, and after such hearing, the committee shall take such steps as it deems advisable. In cases in which a reprimand is issued, the attorney to whom such reprimand is issued, may within 30 days of the issuance of the reprimand, petition this court to vacate the reprimand. Upon such petition, this court may consider the entire record and may vacate the reprimand or impose such other discipline as the record may warrant.

(b) A copy of any admonition or letter of caution given pursuant to this section shall be filed with this court.

(c) A confidential record of the proceedings resulting in such admonition or letter of caution shall be permanently maintained by such committee (except that the complainant shall be notified of any reprimand or admonition or letter of caution which has become final and is not subject to further review) and may be considered in determining the extent of discipline to be imposed in the event other charges of misconduct are brought against the attorney subsequently.

(d) The provisions for confidentiality contained in this or any other section of this Part are not intended to proscribe the free interchange of information among the committees.

§ 691.7 Attorneys convicted of serious crimes; record of conviction conclusive evidence.

(a) Upon the filing with this court of a certificate that an attorney has been convicted of a serious crime as hereinafter defined in a court of record of any state, territory or district, including this State, this court shall cause formal charges to be made and served upon the respondent and shall enter an order immediately referring the matter to a referee, justice or judge appointed by this court to conduct forthwith disciplinary proceedings, whether the conviction resulted from a plea of guilty or *nolo contendere* or from a verdict after trial or otherwise, and regardless of the pendency of an appeal.

(b) The term *serious crime* shall include any felony, not resulting in automatic disbarment under the provisions of subdivision (4) of section 90 of the Judiciary Law, and any lesser crime a necessary element of which, as determined by the statutory or common law definition of such crime, involves interference with the administration of justice, criminal contempt of court, false swearing, misrepresentation, fraud, willful failure to file income tax returns, deceit, bribery, extortion, misappropriation, theft, an attempt or a conspiracy or solicitation of another to commit a serious crime or a crime involving moral turpitude.

(c) A certificate of the conviction of an attorney for any crime shall be conclusive evidence of his guilt of that crime in any disciplinary proceeding instituted against him based on the conviction, and the attorney may not offer evidence inconsistent with the essential elements of the crime for which he was convicted as determined by the statute defining the crime.

(d) Upon the filing with the court of a certificate that an attorney has been convicted of a crime not constituting a serious crime as hereinbefore defined in a court of record in any state, territory or district, including this State, this court shall either refer the matter to a committee appointed pursuant to section 691.4(a) of this Part for whatever action may be appropriate, or cause formal charges to be made and served upon the respondent and enter an order immediately referring the matter to a referee, justice or judge appointed by this court to conduct forthwith disciplinary proceedings, whether the conviction resulted from a plea of guilty or *nolo contendere* or from a verdict after trial or otherwise, and regardless of the pendency of an appeal.

(e) The clerk of any court within the judicial department in which an attorney admitted to practice in this State is convicted of a crime shall within five days of said conviction forward a certificate thereof to the clerk of this court and to the clerk of the Appellate Division of the Supreme Court in the judicial department in which said person was admitted to practice.

(f) Any such committee, upon receiving information that an attorney to whom these rules shall apply pursuant to section 691.1 of this Part, has been convicted of a crime in a court of record of any state, territory or district, shall determine whether the clerk of the court where the conviction occurred has forwarded a certificate of the conviction to this court. If the certificate has not been forwarded by the clerk, such committee shall obtain a certificate of the conviction and forward it to this court.

§ 691.8 Effect of restitution on disciplinary proceedings.

Restitution made by an attorney or on his behalf to a client for funds converted, or to reimburse him for losses suffered as a result of the attorney's wrongdoing, shall not be a bar to the commencement or continuance of disciplinary proceedings.

§ 691.9 Resignation of attorneys under investigation.

(a) An attorney who is the subject of an investigation into allegations of misconduct may tender his resignation by submitting to the appropriate committee appointed pursuant to section 691.4(a) of this Part an affidavit stating that he intends to resign and that:

(1) his resignation is freely and voluntarily rendered; he is not being subjected to coercion or duress; and he is fully aware of the implications of submitting his resignation;

(2) he is aware that there is pending an investigation into allegations that he has been guilty of misconduct, the nature of which shall be specifically set forth; and

(3) he acknowledges that if charges were predicated upon the misconduct under investigation, he could not successfully defend himself on the merits against such charges.

(b) Upon receipt of the required affidavit, such committee shall file it with this court, which may enter an order either disbarring him or striking his name from the roll of attorneys.

§ 691.10 Conduct of disbarred, suspended or resigned attorneys; abandonment of practice by attorney.

(a) *Compliance with Judiciary Law.* Disbarred, suspended or resigned attorneys-at-law shall comply fully and completely with the letter and spirit of sections 478, 479, 484 and 486 of the Judiciary Law relating to practicing as attorneys-at-law without being admitted and registered, and soliciting of business on behalf of an attorney-at-law and the practice of law by an attorney who has been disbarred, suspended or convicted of a felony.

(b) *Compensation.* A disbarred, suspended or resigned attorney may not share in any fee for legal services performed by another attorney during the period of his removal from the bar. A disbarred, suspended or resigned attorney may be compensated on a *quantum meruit* basis for legal services rendered and disbursements incurred by him prior to the effective date of the disbarment or suspension order or of his resignation. The amount and manner of payment of such compensation and recoverable disbursements shall be fixed by the court on the application of either the disbarred, suspended or resigned attorney or the new attorney, on notice to the other as well as on notice to the client. Such applications shall be made at special term in the court wherein the action is pending or at special term in the Supreme Court in the county wherein the moving attorney maintains his office if an action has not been commenced. In no event shall the combined legal fees exceed the amount the client would have been required to pay had no substitution of attorneys been required.

(c) *Notice to clients not involved in litigation.* A disbarred, suspended or resigned attorney shall promptly notify, by registered or certified mail, return receipt requested, all clients being represented in pending matters, other than litigated or administrative matters or proceedings pending in any court or agency, of his disbarment, suspension or resignation and his consequent inability to act as an attorney after the effective date of his disbarment, suspension or resignation and shall advise said clients to seek legal advice elsewhere.

(d) *Notice to clients involved in litigation.* (1) A disbarred, suspended or resigned attorney shall promptly notify, by registered or certified mail, return receipt requested, each of his clients who is involved in litigated matters or administrative proceedings, and the attorney or attorneys for each adverse party in such matter or proceeding, of his disbarment, suspension or resignation and consequent inability to act as an attorney after the effective date of his disbarment, suspension or resignation. The notice to be given to the client shall advise of the prompt substitution of another attorney or attorneys in his place.

(2) In the event the client does not obtain substitute counsel before the effective date of the disbarment, suspension or resignation, it shall be the responsibility of the disbarred, suspended or resigned attorney to move *pro se* in the court in which the action is pending, or before the body in which an administrative proceeding is pending, for leave to withdraw from the action or proceeding.

(3) The notice given to the attorney or attorneys for an adverse party shall state the place of residence of the client of the disbarred, suspended or resigned attorney. In addition, notice shall be given in like manner to the Office of Court Administration of the State of New York in each case in which a retainer statement has been filed.

(e) *Conduct after entry of order.* The disbarred, suspended or resigned attorney, after entry of the disbarment or suspension order or after entry of the order accepting the resignation, shall not accept any new retainer or engage in any new case or legal matter of any nature as attorney for another. However, during the period between the entry date of the order and its effective date he may wind up and complete, on behalf of any client, all matters which were pending on the entry date.

(f) *Filing proof of compliance and attorney's address.* Within 10 days after the effective date of the disbarment or suspension order or accepting the resignation, the disbarred, suspended or resigned attorney shall file with the clerk of the Appellate Division for the Second Judicial Department an affidavit showing:

(1) that he has fully complied with the provisions of the order and with these rules; and

(2) that he has served a copy of such affidavit upon the petitioner or moving party. Such affidavit shall also set forth the residence or other address of the disbarred, suspended or resigned attorney where communications may be directed to him.

(g) *Appointment of attorney to protect clients' interests and interests of disbarred, suspended or resigned attorney.* Whenever it shall be brought to the court's attention that a disbarred, suspended or resigned attorney shall have failed or may fail to comply with the provisions of subdivision (c), (d) or (f) of this section, this court, upon such notice to such attorney as this court may direct, may appoint an attorney or attorneys to inventory the files of the disbarred, suspended or resigned attorney and to take such action as seems indicated to protect the interests of his clients and for the protection of the interests of the disbarred, suspended or resigned attorney.

(h) *Disclosure of information.* Any attorney so appointed by this court shall not be permitted to disclose any information contained in any file so inventoried without the consent of the client to whom such file relates except as necessary to carry out the order of this court which appointed the attorney to make such inventory.

(i) *Fixation of compensation.* This court may fix the compensation to be paid to any attorney appointed by it under this section. The compensation may be directed by this court to be paid as an incident to the costs of the proceeding in which the charges are incurred and shall be charged in accordance with law.

(j) *Required records.* A disbarred, suspended or resigned attorney shall keep and maintain records of the various steps taken by him under this Part so that, upon any subsequent proceeding instituted by or against him, proof of compliance with this Part and with the disbarment or suspension order or with the order accepting the resignation will be available.

(k) *Abandonment of practice by attorney.* When, in the opinion of this court, an attorney has abandoned his practice, this court, upon such notice to such attorney as it may direct, may appoint the chief counsel of the appropriate joint bar association grievance committee, or an individual attorney, to take custody and inventory the files of such attorney and to take such action as seems indicated to protect the interests of his clients.

§ 691.11 Reinstatement following suspension, disbarment, or striking of name from roll of attorneys.

(a) *Timing of application.* No attorney disbarred after a hearing or on consent, or whose name has been stricken from the roll of attorneys pursuant to subdivision 4 of section 90 of the Judiciary Law or section 691.9 of this Part may apply for reinstatement until expiration of at least seven years from the effective date of the disbarment or removal. An attorney suspended under the provisions of this Part shall be entitled to apply for reinstatement after such an interval as this court may direct in the order of suspension or any modification thereof.

(b) *Form and notice of application.* An application for reinstatement shall be made in the form of a motion in accordance with instructions specified by administrative order of the court. The instructions shall be available in the office of the clerk of the court and on the court's internet site. The motion for reinstatement shall be made upon notice to the appropriate grievance committee and the Lawyers' Fund for Client Protection, which may submit papers in opposition or in relation thereto.

(c) *Required showing.* An application for reinstatement may be granted by the court only upon a showing:

(1) by clear and convincing evidence, that the applicant has complied with the provisions of the order disbarring or suspending him or her, or striking his or her name from the roll of attorneys, and that he or she possesses the character and general fitness to practice law; and,

(2) if the applicant was disbarred or suspended from the practice of law for more than one year, that (i) subsequent to the entry of such order, he or she attained a passing score on the Multistate Professional Responsibility Examination described in section 520.9(a) of the rules of the Court of Appeals for the admission of attorneys and counselors-at-law, the passing score thereon being that determined by the New York State Board of Law Examiners pursuant to section 520.9(c) of such rules, and (ii) he or she has successfully completed one credit hour of continuing legal education accredited in accordance with Part 1500 of this Title for each month of disbarment or suspension up to a maximum of twenty-four credits. The continuing legal education required by clause (ii) of this paragraph shall be completed during the period of disbarment or suspension and within the two years preceding reinstatement. Compliance with clause (ii) of this paragraph may, upon request of the applicant, be deferred pending notification that the court has conditionally granted the application of reinstatement subject to the completion of required continuing legal education; or,

(3) if the applicant was suspended from the practice of law for one year, that during the period of suspension (i) he or she and successfully completed eighteen credit hours of continuing legal education accredited in accordance with Part 1500 of this Title, six credit hours of which were in the area of ethics and professionalism as defined in subdivision (c) of section 1500.2 of this Title, or (ii) he or she has successfully completed twelve credit hours of continuing legal education accredited in accordance with Part 1500 of the Title and has attained a passing score on the Multistate Professional Responsibility Examination as set forth in clause (i) of paragraph (2) of this subdivision;

(4) if the applicant was suspended from the practice of law for less than one year, that during the period of suspension he or she has successfully completed one credit hour of continuing legal education accredited in accordance with Part 1500 of this Title for each month of suspension.

(d) *Character and fitness review.* The court shall refer an application for reinstatement after a suspension of more than one year or after a disbarment to a Committee on Character and Fitness in this judicial department or to a referee, justice, or judge for a report before granting that application and, in its discretion, may similarly refer an application for reinstatement after a suspension of one year or less.

(e) *Renewed motion for reinstatement.* No renewed motion for reinstatement shall be accepted for filing within one year of the entry of an order of this court denying a prior motion for such relief, unless the order denying the prior motion provides otherwise.

(f) *Expenses.* The court may direct that the necessary expenses incurred in the investigation and processing of a motion for reinstatement be paid by the applicant.

§ 691.11-a Reinstatement after voluntary resignation.

(a) *Form and notice of application.* An application for reinstatement by a person who has voluntarily resigned from the bar of this state shall be made in the form of a motion in accordance with instructions specified by administrative order of the court. The instructions shall be available in the office of the clerk of the court and on the court's internet site. The motion for reinstatement shall be made upon notice to the grievance committee in the judicial district in which the applicant last maintained an office for the practice of law, or if none, to the grievance committee in the judicial district in which the applicant resided when admitted to practice, which may submit papers in opposition or in relation thereto.

(b) [None]

(c) *Required showing.* An application for reinstatement may be granted by the court only upon an affidavit or affirmation stating:

(1) the circumstances of the applicant's resignation from the bar and the reason for applying for reinstatement;

(2) whether the applicant has been the subject of a disciplinary complaint or proceeding in any other jurisdiction and the results thereof;

(3) that the applicant is in good standing at the bar of any other jurisdiction in which he or she is admitted to practice; and,

(4) that the applicant has successfully completed one credit hour of continuing legal education accredited in accordance with Part 1500 of this Title for each month since the date of the order of this court accepting the resignation and

removing his or her name from the roll of attorneys, up to a maximum of twenty-four credits.

Attached to the moving papers shall be a current certificate of good standing from each jurisdiction in which the applicant is admitted to practice and certificates establishing compliance with the continuing legal education requirement of paragraph (4) of this subdivision.

(d) *Character and fitness review.* The court may refer an application for reinstatement after a voluntary resignation to a Committee on character and fitness in this judicial department or to a referee, justice, or judge for a report before granting that application.

§ 691.12 Regulations and procedures for random review and audit and biennial affirmation of compliance.

(a) *Availability of bookkeeping records; random review and audit.* The financial records required by section 1200.46 of this Title shall be available at the principal New York State office of the attorneys subject hereto, for inspection, copying and determination of compliance with section 1200.46 of this Title, to a duly authorized representative of the court pursuant to the issuance, on a randomly selected basis, of a notice or subpoena by this court or the appropriate grievance committee.

(b) *Confidentiality.* All matters, records and proceedings relating to compliance with section 1200.46 of this Title, including the selection of an attorney for review hereunder, shall be kept confidential in accordance with applicable law, as and to the extent required of matters relating to professional discipline.

(c) Prior to the issuance of any notice or subpoena in connection with the random review and audit program established by this section, the appropriate grievance committee shall propose regulations and procedures for the proper administration of the program. The court shall approve such of the regulations and procedures of the grievance committee as it may deem appropriate, and only such regulations and procedures as have been approved by the court shall become effective.

(d) Any attorney subject to this court's jurisdiction shall execute that portion of the biennial registration statement provided by the Office of Court Administration affirming that the attorney has read and is in compliance with section 1200.46 of this Title. The affirmation shall be available at all times to the grievance committees. No affirmation of compliance shall be required from a full-time judge or justice of the Unified Court System of the State of New York or of a court of any other state, or of a Federal court.

§ 691.13 Proceedings where attorney is declared incompetent or alleged to be incapacitated.

(a) *Suspension upon judicial determination of incompetency or on involuntary commitment.* Where an attorney subject to the provisions of section 691.1 of this Part has been judicially declared incompetent or involuntarily committed to a mental hospital, this court, upon proper proof of the fact, shall enter an order suspending such attorney from the practice of the law, effective immediately and for an indefinite period and until the further order of this court. A copy of such order shall be served upon such attorney, his committee, and/or the director of the mental hospital in such manner as this court may direct.

(b) *Proceeding to determine alleged incapacity and suspension upon such determination.* (1) Whenever a committee appointed pursuant to section 691.4(a) of this Part shall petition this court to determine whether an attorney is incapacitated from continuing to practice law by reason of mental infirmity or illness or because of addiction to drugs or intoxicants, this court may take or direct such action as it deems necessary or proper to determine whether the attorney is so incapacitated, including examination of the attorney by such qualified medical experts as this court shall designate. If, upon due consideration of the matter, this court is satisfied and concludes that the attorney is incapacitated from continuing to practice law, it shall enter an order suspending him on the ground of such disability for an indefinite period and until the further order of this court and any pending disciplinary proceedings against the attorney shall be held in abeyance.

(2) This court may provide for such notice to the respondent-attorney of proceedings in such matter as it deems proper and advisable and may appoint an attorney to represent the respondent, if he is without adequate representation.

(3) Any report prepared by a qualified medical expert designated by the court pursuant to paragraph (1) of this subdivision and filed in the office of the clerk of this court shall be made available to counsel for the committee and the counsel for the respondent.

(c) *Procedure when respondent claims disability during course of proceeding.* (1) If, during the course of a disciplinary proceeding, the respondent contends that he is suffering from a disability by reason of mental infirmity or illness, or because of addiction to drugs or intoxicants, which makes it impossible for the respondent adequately to defend himself, this court thereupon shall enter an order suspending the respondent from continuing to practice law until a determination is made of the respondent's capacity to continue the practice of law in a proceeding instituted in accordance with the provisions of subdivision (b) of this section.

(2) If, in the course of a proceeding under this section or in a disciplinary proceeding, this court shall determine that the respondent is not incapacitated from practicing law, it shall take such action as it deems proper and advisable, including a direction for the resumption of the disciplinary proceeding against the respondent.

(d) *Appointment of attorney to protect client's and suspended attorney's interest.* (1) Whenever an attorney is suspended for incapacity or disability, this court, upon such notice to him as it may direct, may appoint an attorney or attorneys to inventory the files of the suspended attorney and to take such action as it deems proper and advisable to protect the interest of his clients and for the protection of the interest of the suspended attorney.

(2) Any attorney so appointed by this court shall not be permitted to disclose any information contained in any file so inventoried without the consent of the client to whom such file relates, except as is necessary to carry out the order of this court which appointed the attorney to make such inventory.

(e) *Reinstatement upon termination of disability.* (1) Any attorney suspended under the provisions of this section shall be entitled to apply for reinstatement at such intervals as this court may direct in the order of suspension or any modification thereof. Such application shall be granted by this court upon a showing by clear and convincing evidence that the attorney's disability has been removed and he is fit to resume the practice of law. Upon such application, this court may take or direct such action as it deems necessary or proper for a determination as to whether the attorney's disability has been removed, including the direction of an examination of the attorney by such qualified medical experts as this court shall designate. In its discretion, this court may direct that the expense of such examination shall be paid by the attorney.

(2) Where an attorney has been suspended by an order in accordance with the provisions of subdivision (a) of this section and thereafter, in proceedings duly taken, has been judicially declared to be competent, this court may dispense with further evidence that his disability has been removed and may direct his reinstatement upon such terms as it deems proper and advisable.

(f) *Burden of proof.* In a proceeding seeking an order of suspension under this section, the burden of proof shall rest with the petitioner. In a proceeding seeking an order terminating a suspension under this section, the burden of proof shall rest with the suspended attorney.

(g) *Waiver of doctor-patient privilege upon application for reinstatement.* The filing of an application for reinstatement by an attorney suspended for disability shall be deemed to constitute a waiver of any doctor-patient privilege existing between the attorney and any psychiatrist, psychologist, physician or hospital who or which has examined or treated the attorney during the period of his disability. The attorney shall be required to disclose the name of every psychiatrist, psychologist, physician and hospital by whom or at which the attorney has been examined or treated since his suspension and he shall furnish to this court written consent to each to divulge such information and records as is requested by court-appointed medical experts or by the clerk of this court.

(h) *Payment of expenses of proceedings.* (1) The necessary costs and disbursements of an agency, committee or appointed attorney in conducting a proceeding under this section shall be paid in accordance with subdivision (6) of section 90 of the Judiciary Law.

(2) The court may fix the compensation to be paid to any attorney or medical expert appointed by this court under this section. The compensation may be directed by this court to be paid as an incident to the cost of the proceeding in which the charges are incurred and shall be paid in accordance with law.

* * *

§ 691.16 Attorneys assigned by the court as counsel for a defendant in a criminal case.

(a) No attorney assigned by a court as counsel for a defendant in any criminal case shall in any manner demand, accept, receive or agree to accept or receive any payment, compensation, emolument, gratuity or reward or any promise of payment, compensation, emolument, gratuity or reward or any money, property or thing of value or of personal advantage from such defendant or from any other person, except as expressly authorized by statute.

(b) No attorney assigned by a court as counsel for an indigent defendant in any criminal case shall, during the pendency thereof, accept a private retainer to represent the defendant in that or any other case.

(c) Violation of this section shall result in the removal of the attorney's name from the panel of attorneys eligible to receive assignment pursuant to article 18 B of the County Law and shall constitute a violation of § 1200.3(5) of this Title.

* * *

§ 691.21 Preliminary investigation of any party unlawfully practicing law or assuming to practice law.

(a) Upon application by the chairman or acting chairman of the committee or subcommittee on unlawful practice of the law of any recognized bar association in any county in the second judicial department, alleging that such committee or subcommittee has reasonable cause to believe that any party (to wit: any person, firm, corporation or other organization) is unlawfully practicing law or unlawfully assuming to practice law or is engaging in any business or activity which may involve the unlawful practice of law, and further alleging that such committee or subcommittee is conducting or intends to conduct an investigation with respect to such practice, business or activity, the clerk of this court is empowered and authorized to issue, in the name of the presiding justice of the court, subpoenas directing the attendance of witnesses and the production of books, papers and records before such committee or subcommittee at the time when and at the place where it will convene. The clerk of the court is also empowered and authorized to issue such subpoenas upon the application of any such party.

(b) Every committee or subcommittee conducting such preliminary investigation is empowered to take the testimony of witnesses under oath and to transcribe such testimony. Such witnesses may be sworn by any person authorized by law to administer oaths.

*   *   *   *

PART 700

COURT DECORUM

§ 700.1 Application of rules.

These rules shall apply in all actions and proceedings, civil and criminal, in courts subject to the jurisdiction of the Appellate Division of the Supreme Court in the second judicial department. They are intended to supplement, but not to supersede, the code of professional responsibility and the canons of judicial ethics, as adopted by the New York State Bar Association. In the event of any conflict between the provisions of these rules and that code or those canons, the code and the canons shall prevail.

§ 700.2 Importance of decorum in court.

The courtroom, as the place where justice is dispensed, must at all times satisfy the appearance as well as the reality of fairness and equal treatment. Dignity, order and decorum are indispensable to the proper administration of justice. Disruptive conduct by any person while the court is in session is forbidden.

§ 700.3 Disruptive conduct defined.

Disruptive conduct is any intentional conduct by any person in the courtroom that substantially interferes with the dignity, order and decorum of judicial proceedings.

§ 700.4 Obligations of the attorney.

(a) The attorney is both an officer of the court and an advocate. It is his professional obligation to conduct his case courageously, vigorously, and with all the skill and knowledge he possesses. It is also his obligation to uphold the honor and maintain the dignity of the profession. He must avoid disorder or disruption in the courtroom and he must maintain a respectful attitude toward the court. In all respects the attorney is bound, in court and out, by the provisions of the code of professional responsibility.

(b) The attorney shall use his best efforts to dissuade his client and witnesses from causing disorder or disruption in the courtroom.

(c) The attorney shall not engage in any examination which is intended merely to harass, annoy or humiliate the witness.

(d) No attorney shall argue in support of or against an objection without permission from the court; nor shall any attorney argue with respect to a ruling of the court on any objection without such permission. However, an attorney may make a concise statement of the particular grounds for an objection or exception, not otherwise apparent, where it is necessary to do so in order to call the court's attention thereto, or to preserve an issue for appellate review. If an attorney believes in good faith that the court has wrongly made an adverse ruling, he may respectfully request reconsideration thereof.

(e) The attorney has neither the right nor duty to execute any directive of a client which is not consistent with professional standards of conduct. Nor may the attorney advise another to do any act or to engage in any conduct in any manner contrary to these rules.

COURT RULES

(f) Once a client has employed an attorney who has entered an appearance, the attorney shall not withdraw or abandon the case without:

(1) justifiable cause,

(2) reasonable notice to the client, and

(3) permission of the court.

(g) The attorney is not relieved of these obligations by what he may regard as a deficiency in the conduct or ruling of a judge or in the system of justice; nor is he relieved of these obligations by what he believes to be the moral, political, social, or ideological merits of the cause of any client.

§ 700.5 Obligations of the judge.

(a) In the administration of justice the judge shall safeguard the rights of the parties and the interests of the public. The judge at all times shall be dignified, courteous, and considerate of the parties, attorneys, jurors, and witnesses. In the performance of his duties, and in the maintenance of proper court decorum the judge is in all respects bound by the canons of judicial ethics.

(b) The judge shall use his judicial power to prevent disruptions of the trial.

(c) A judge before whom a case is moved for trial shall preside at such trial unless he is satisfied, upon challenge or *sua sponte,* that he is unable to serve with complete impartiality, in fact or appearance, with regard to the matter at issue or the parties involved.

(d) Where the judge deems it appropriate in order to preserve or enhance the dignity, order and decorum of the proceedings, he shall prescribe and make known the rules relating to conduct which the parties, attorneys, witnesses and others will be expected to follow in the courtroom.

(e) The judge should be the exemplar of dignity and impartiality. He shall suppress his personal predilections, control his temper and emotions, and otherwise avoid conduct on his part which tends to demean the proceedings or to undermine his authority in the courtroom. When it becomes necessary during trial for him to comment upon the conduct of witnesses, spectators, counsel, or others, or upon the testimony, he shall do so in a firm and polite manner, limiting his comments and rulings to what is reasonably required for the orderly progress of the trial, and refraining from unnecessary disparagement of persons or issues.

(f) The judge is not relieved of these obligations by what he may regard as a deficiency in the conduct of any attorney who appears before him; nor is he relieved of these obligations by what he believes to be the moral, political, social, or ideological deficiencies of the cause of any party.

PART 701

EXERCISE OF THE JUDICIAL CONTEMPT POWER

Section

701.1   Application of rules.

701.2   Exercise of the summary contempt power.

701.3   Exercise of the contempt power after hearing.

701.4   Judicial warning of possible contempt.

701.5   Disqualification of judge.

§ 701.1 Application of rules.

These rules shall apply in all actions and proceedings, civil and criminal, in courts subject to the jurisdiction of the Appellate Division of the Supreme Court in the second judicial department. They are intended to supplement, but not to supersede, the code of professional responsibility and the canons of judicial ethics, as adopted by the New York State Bar Association. In the event of any conflict between the provisions of these rules and that code or those canons, the code and the canons shall prevail.

§ 701.2 Exercise of the summary contempt power.

(a) The power of the court to punish summarily any contempt committed in its immediate view and presence shall be exercised only in exceptional and necessitous circumstances, as follows:

(1) Where the offending conduct disrupts or threatens to disrupt proceedings actually in progress; or

(2) where the offending conduct destroys or undermines or tends seriously to destroy or undermine the dignity and authority of the court in a manner and to the extent that it appears unlikely that the court will be able to continue to conduct its normal business in an appropriate way, provided that in either case the court reasonably believes that a prompt summary adjudication of contempt may aid in maintaining or restoring and maintaining proper order and decorum.

(b) Wherever practical, punishment should be

determined and imposed at the time of the adjudication of contempt. However, where the court deems it advisable the determination and imposition of punishment may be deferred following a prompt summary adjudication of contempt which satisfies the necessity for immediate judicial corrective or disciplinary action.

(c) Before any summary adjudication of contempt the accused shall be given a reasonable opportunity to make a statement in his defense or in extenuation of his conduct.

§ 701.3 Exercise of the contempt power after hearing.

In all other cases, notwithstanding the occurrence of the contumacious conduct in the view and presence of the sitting court, the contempt shall be adjudicated at a plenary hearing with due process of law including notice, written charges, assistance of counsel, compulsory process for production of evidence and an opportunity of the accused to confront witnesses against him.

§ 701.4 Judicial warning of possible contempt.

Except in the case of the most flagrant and offensive misbehavior which in the court's discretion requires an immediate adjudication of contempt to preserve order and decorum, the court should warn and admonish the person engaged in alleged contumacious conduct that his conduct is deemed contumacious and give him an opportunity to desist before adjudicating him in contempt. Where a person so warned desists from further offensive conduct, there is ordinarily no occasion for an adjudication of contempt. Where a person is summarily adjudicated in contempt and punishment deferred, if such person desists from further offensive conduct the court should consider carefully whether there is any need for punishment for the adjudicated contempt.

§ 701.5 Disqualification of judge.

The judge before whom the alleged contumacious conduct occurred is disqualified from presiding at the plenary hearing or trial (as distinguished from summary action) except with the defendant's consent:

(a) If the allegedly contumacious conduct consists primarily of personal disrespect to or vituperative criticism of the judge; or

(b) If the judge's recollection of, or testimony concerning the conduct allegedly constituting contempt, is necessary for an adjudication; or

(c) If the judge concludes that in view of his recollection of the events he would be unable to make his decision solely on the basis of the evidence at the hearing.

COURT RULES

RULES OF THE SECOND JUDICIAL DEPARTMENT APPELLATE TERM

PART 730

ESTABLISHMENT AND JURISDICTION OF APPELLATE TERMS

(Selected Section)

Section
730.1 Establishment and jurisdiction of Appellate Terms.

§ 730.1 Establishment and jurisdiction of Appellate Terms.

The Appellate Division of the Supreme Court, Second Judicial Department, pursuant to the authority vested in it, does hereby, effective January 2, 1968 and as amended:

(a) (1) Establish an Appellate Term of the Supreme Court in and for the second and eleventh judicial districts, which shall be held from time to time in courtroom 1902 at 111 Livingston Street, in the County of Kings, and at the courthouse located at 88-11 Sutphin Boulevard in the County of Queens and at such other places as may be designated by the Chief Administrator of the Courts.

(2) The Chief Administrator of the Courts shall, with the approval of the Presiding Justice of the Appellate Division, Second Judicial Department, designate the Supreme Court justices assigned to the Appellate Term of the Supreme Court in and for the second and eleventh judicial districts * * * [such designations shall be set forth in the orders issued from time to time].

(b) Direct that the Appellate Term of the Supreme Court in and for the second and eleventh judicial districts, hereinabove established, shall have jurisdiction to hear and determine all appeals authorized by law to be taken:

(1) from an order or judgment of the Civil Court of the City of New York entered in the counties of Kings, Queens and Richmond, and

(2) from a judgment, sentence or order of the Criminal Court of the City of New York in any of said counties.

(c) (1) Establish an Appellate Term of the Supreme Court in and for the ninth and tenth judicial districts within said department which shall be held from time to time at the courthouse located at Supreme Court Drive, in the County

of Nassau, and at the courthouse located at 111 Grove Street, in the County of Westchester, and at such other places as may be designated by the Chief Administrator of the Courts.

(2) The Chief Administrator of the Courts shall, with the approval of the Presiding Justice of the Appellate Division, Second Judicial Department, designate the Supreme Court justices assigned to the Appellate Term of the Supreme Court in and for the ninth and tenth judicial districts * * * [such designations shall be set forth in the orders issued from time to time].

(d) Direct that the Appellate Term of the Supreme Court in and for the ninth and tenth judicial districts, hereinabove established, shall have jurisdiction to hear and determine all appeals now or hereafter authorized by law to be taken to the County Court or to the Appellate Division from any court in any county within the ninth judicial district or the tenth judicial district other than appeals from the Supreme Court, the Surrogate's Court, the Family Court or criminal appeals from the County Court.

(1) Direct that an appeal authorized by CPL 450.10 and 450.20 to be taken to intermediate courts shall be taken to the Appellate Term of the Supreme Court in and for the ninth and tenth judicial districts, hereinabove established, in accordance with its rules applicable thereto but not inconsistent with the applicable provisions of the CPL, where such appeal is from a judgment, sentence or order of a local criminal court and all classifications thereof (as defined and set forth in CPL 10.10) located in this department but outside New York City.

(2) In addition to, but not in limitation of the foregoing, such Appellate Term shall have jurisdiction to hear and determine all appeals

(i) from the District Court of Nassau County, the District Court of Suffolk County and any other district court hereafter established in any county within the ninth judicial district, and

(ii) from any town, village or city court within either the ninth judicial district or the tenth judicial district, and

(iii) in civil matters, from any county court within either the ninth judicial district or the tenth judicial district.

(e) The Appellate Term of the Supreme Court in and for the second and eleventh judicial districts and the Appellate Term of the Supreme Court in and for the ninth and tenth judicial districts shall jointly employ the nonjudicial personnel heretofore appointed to and employed in the predecessor Appellate Term previously discontinued, reserving for further order the disposition to be made of the books, records, papers, documents, furniture, equipment and other property of such predecessor Appellate Term, which in the interim shall be held jointly by, and may be used in the conduct severally of the business of, the aforesaid separate Appellate Terms hereby established.

(f) Direct that all motions addressed to either of the Appellate Terms shall be made returnable in the Office of the Clerk of the Court, 111 Livingston Street, Brooklyn, New York 11201.

PART 731

RULES OF PRACTICE FOR THE SECOND AND ELEVENTH JUDICIAL DISTRICTS

(Selected Sections)

§ 731.1 Records on appeal.

* * *

(b) (1) In criminal actions or proceedings, the appeal shall be heard on the original papers, certified by the clerk of the court from which the appeal is taken, the court's return when the same is required by statute, a stenographic transcript of the proceedings settled by the judge before whom the action was tried, or in case of the death or disability of such judge, in such manner as this court directs.

(2) For good cause shown, the court may hear the appeal on an abridged record containing so much of the evidence or other proceedings as it may deem necessary to a consideration of the questions raised on the appeal.

(c) Unless otherwise ordered by the court, an appellant may, but need not, print copies of the record on appeal.

§ 731.2 Briefs.

(a) The form, style and content of all briefs shall conform to the provisions of CPLR 5528 and 5529. Briefs may, but need not, be printed and may be reproduced by any authorized method or may be typewritten.

(1) The calendar number of the appeal shall be stated at the upper left-hand corner of the *cover* page of each brief.

(2) In all cases, civil and criminal, each party's main brief, upon the upper right-hand corner of the *cover* page, shall specify whether the cause is to be *argued* or *submitted,* and shall state the *name of counsel* who is to argue or submit.

(b) In all causes, unless otherwise directed by statute, the court, or these rules, the appellant's main brief shall include at the beginning the statement required by CPLR 5531.

(c) In criminal causes, the appellant's main brief at the beginning shall also set forth:

(1) either the entire judgment or order

COURT RULES

appealed from, or its material provisions, including its date;

(2) the sentence imposed, if any; and

(3) a statement whether an order issued pursuant to CPL 460.50 is outstanding and, if so, the date of such order, the name of the judge who issued it and whether the appellant is free on bail or on his own recognizance.

§ 731.3 Court sessions.

Unless otherwise ordered, the court will convene at 9:30 o'clock in the forenoon on the first day of each appointed term. The court may be convened on any subsequent day or days during the term by order of the presiding justice or, in his absence, the associate presiding justice, which order shall specify the three justices who shall constitute the court at any such session.

§ 731.4 Calendar of appeals.

(a) The general calendar shall consist of

* * *

(2) all appeals in criminal cases in which a duplicate notice of appeal or an affidavit of errors and the court's return have been transmitted to the said clerk as provided in CPL 460.10(1)(e), 460.10(2) and 460.10(3)(d).

(b) An appeal on the general calendar in which a record has been filed may be placed on the appeal calendar to be assigned to an appointed term by the court by filing a note of issue containing the following information:

(1) the title of the appeal;

(2) the judgment or order appealed from, the date thereof and the court from which the appeal was taken;

(3) the attorneys for the respective parties, their addresses and telephone numbers, and the name, if known, of counsel who will argue the cause;

(4) the identity of the party filing the note of issue; and

(c) The note of issue, with proof of service, together with the original and three copies of appellant's brief, with proof of service of one copy, shall be filed with the court, together with blank, stamped post cards, addressed to each and every appellant and respondent on or before the first Friday of any given month; in criminal causes proof of service upon respondent of one copy of a transcript of the minutes of all proceedings shall be filed together with the note of issue, such copy to be returned by respondent to the appellant upon the argument or submission of the appeal. The original and three copies of respondent's brief, with proof of service of one copy, shall be filed on or before the third Friday of the month in which the note of issue is deemed filed.

The original and three copies of a reply brief, with proof of service of one copy, shall be filed not later than the fourth Friday of the month in which the note of issue is deemed filed.

(d) Notification of the appointed term to which an appeal has been assigned shall be published in the New York Law Journal not less than twelve days prior to the date of said term. Appellants and respondents, or their attorneys, shall be notified by postal card not less than five days prior to the date of said term.

§ 731.5 Preferences.

Any party to an appeal, for good cause shown, may move for a preference upon notice to all other parties to the appeal.

§ 731.6 Oral argument or submission.

(a) No more than 15 minutes will be allowed for argument on each side, except by express permission of the court.

(b) In the event that any party's main brief shall fail to set forth the appropriate notations with respect to the argument or submission of the cause, as required by section 731.2(a)(2) of these rules, the cause will be deemed to have been submitted without oral argument by the defaulting party.

(c) When any party shall have noted on his filed brief, or, before the cause appears on the Day Calendar, shall have filed his written consent or stipulation or otherwise notified the clerk that he intends to submit the cause without argument, such party need not appear on the calendar call.

Any provisions of the Rules requiring the filing of any papers as herein prescribed, shall mean the filing thereof, in the clerk's office of the Appellate Term, with proof of service in accordance with 2103 CPLR.

In criminal causes, proof of service of one copy of a transcript of all proceedings shall be filed together with the Note of Issue, such copy to be returned to the appellant upon the argument or submission of the appeal.

§ 731.7 Motions.

Motions may be noticed for any day of the term and must be submitted without oral argument. All papers in support of the motion (which must include a copy of the notice of appeal) or in opposition thereto shall be filed before 10 o'clock in the forenoon of the return day of the motion.

§ 731.8 Dismissals on the court's own motion.

* * *

(b) Except as otherwise provided in CPL 460.70 and subject to the applicable provisions of CPL 470.60, and unless for good cause shown an extension or enlargement of time is granted by the court, an appeal in a criminal case in which a note of issue was not filed within 90 days after the last day in which a notice of appeal was required to be filed shall be dismissed.

(c) The clerk shall prepare a special day calendar for each appointed term of the appeals subject to dismissal for failure on the part of the appellant to comply with this rule. Each such special day calendar shall be published in the *New York Law Journal* at least five days prior to, as well as on the day when that calendar is to be called, and in criminal cases, the clerk shall cause a postal card notice to be mailed to appellant or his attorney five days prior to the first day of such publication.

§ 731.9 Appeals in criminal cases; adjournments; extensions of time.

(a) Every application for an extension or enlargement of time or for and adjournment in an appeal from a judgment of conviction in a criminal case, whether on motion or stipulation, shall include, in addition to a showing of good cause, a statement subscribed by counsel setting forth:

(1) the sentence imposed and whether the defendant is free on bail or on his own recognizance by reason of the issuance of an order pursuant to CPL 460.50 and, if so, the date of such order and the name of the judge who issued the same, and

(2) whether the court has previously granted any enlargement of time.

(b) Where such application pertains to an appeal on the special day calendar referred to in subdivision (c) of section 731.8, such application shall be filed with the clerk of the court at least two days prior to the day on which the appeal is scheduled to appear on such calendar.

§ 731.10 Leave to appeal to the Appellate Term.

* * *

(c) Applications for certificates or orders granting leave to appeal under the Criminal Procedure Law (CPL 450.15, 460.15) shall be governed by the following special rules:

(1) The application shall be in writing and shall be made and filed with the clerk of this court (with proof of service upon the district attorney or any other prosecutor who appeared for the People in the criminal court in which the order sought to be reviewed was rendered) within 30 days after service upon the applicant of a copy of the order.

(2) The application shall be addressed to the court for assignment to a justice and shall include:

(i) the name and address of the applicant and the name and address of the district attorney or other prosecutor, as the case may be;

(ii) the docket or index number;

(iii) the questions of law or fact which it is claimed ought to be reviewed;

(iv) any other information, data, or matter which the applicant may deem pertinent in support of the application; and

(v) a statement that no prior application for such certificate has been made.

(3) In addition, the papers in support of the application shall include a copy of the order sought to be reviewed and a copy of the memorandum or opinion of the court below or a statement that there was none.

(4) Within 15 days after service upon him of a copy of the application and of the papers, if any, in support thereof, the district attorney or other prosecutor (as the case may be) shall file answering papers or a statement that there is no opposition to the application (with proof of service upon the applicant, if appearing *pro se,* or upon the attorney making the application on behalf of the applicant). Such answering papers shall include a discussion of the merits of the application or shall state, if such be the case, that the application does not contain any allegations other than those alleged in the papers submitted by the applicant in the court below and that the prosecutor relies on the record, his answering papers contained therein and the memorandum or opinion of such court, if there be any.

(5) Unless the justice designated to determine the application shall in his discretion otherwise direct, the matter shall be submitted and determined upon the foregoing papers and without oral argument.

§ 731.11 Motions to reargue, resettle or amend; motions for leave to appeal to Appellate Division.

(a) Motions to reargue a cause or to resettle an order or to amend a decision shall be made within 30 days after the cause shall have been decided, except that for good cause shown, the court may consider any such motion when made at a later date.

* * *

(c) The papers in support of such motion shall concisely state the points claimed to have been overlooked or misapprehended by the court, with appropriate references to the particular portions of the record or briefs and with citation of the authorities relied upon.

COURT RULES

PART 732

RULES OF PRACTICE FOR THE NINTH AND TENTH JUDICIAL DISTRICTS

(Selected Sections)

§ 732.1 Records on appeal.

*   *   *

(b) (1) In criminal actions or 200.1 proceedings, the appeal shall be heard on the original papers, certified by the clerk of the court from which the appeal is taken, the court's return when the same is required by statute, a stenographic transcript of the proceedings settled by the judge or justice before whom the action was tried, or in case of the death or disability of such judge or justice, in such manner as this court directs.

(2) For good cause shown, the court may hear the appeal on an abridged record containing so much of the evidence or other proceedings as it may deem necessary to a consideration of the questions raised on the appeal.

(c) Unless otherwise ordered by the court, an appellant may, but need not, print copies of the record on appeal.

§ 732.2 Briefs.

(a) The form, style and content of all briefs shall conform to the provisions of CPLR 5528 and 5529. Briefs may, but need not, be printed and may be reproduced by any authorized method or may be typewritten.

(1) The calendar number of the appeal shall be stated at the upper left hand corner of the *cover* page, of each brief.

(2) In all cases, civil and criminal, each party's main brief, upon the upper right-hand corner of the *cover* page, shall specify whether the cause is to be *argued or submitted*, and shall state the *name of counsel* who is to argue or submit.

(b) In all causes, unless otherwise directed by statute, the court, or these rules, the appellant's main brief shall include at the beginning the statement required by CPLR 5531.

(c) In criminal causes, the appellant's main brief at the beginning shall also set forth:

(1) either the entire judgment or order appealed from, or its material provisions, including its date;

(2) the sentence imposed, if any, and

(3) a statement whether an order issued pursuant to CPL 460.50 is outstanding and, if so, the date of such order, the name of the judge who issued it and whether the appellant is free on bail or on his own recognizance.

§ 732.3 Court sessions.

Unless otherwise ordered, the court will convene at 10 o'clock in the forenoon on the first day of each appointed term. The court may be convened on any subsequent day or days during the term by order of the presiding justice or, in his absence, the associate presiding justice, which order shall specify the three justices who shall constitute the court at any such session.

§ 732.4 Calendar of appeals.

(a) The general calendar shall consist of:

*   *   *

(2) all appeals in criminal cases in which a duplicate notice of appeal or an affidavit of errors and the court's return have been transmitted to said clerk as provided in CPL 460.10(1)(e), 460.10(2) and 460.10(3)(d).

(b) An appeal on the general calendar in which

a record has been filed may be placed on the appeal calendar to be assigned to an appointed term by the court by filing a note of issue containing the following information:

(1) the title of the appeal;

(2) the judgment or order appealed from, the date thereof and the court from which the appeal was taken;

(3) the attorneys for the respective parties, their addresses and telephone numbers and the name, if known, of counsel who will argue the cause;

(4) the identity of the party filing the note of issue.

(c) The note of issue, with proof of service, together with the original and three copies of appellant's brief, with proof of service of one copy, shall be filed with the court, together with blank, stamped post cards, addressed to each and every appellant and respondent on or before the first Friday of any given month; in criminal causes proof of service upon respondent of one copy of a transcript of the minutes of all proceedings shall be filed together with the note of issue, such copy to be returned by respondent to the appellant upon the argument or submission of the appeal. The original and three copies of respondent's brief, with proof of service of one copy, shall be filed on or before the third Friday of the month in which the note of issue is deemed filed. The original and three copies of a reply brief, with proof of service of one copy, shall be filed not later than the fourth Friday of the month in which the note of issue is deemed filed.

(d) Notification of the appointed term to which an appeal has been assigned shall be published in the New York Law Journal not less than twelve days prior to the date of said term. Appellants and respondents, or their attorneys, shall be notified by postal card not less than five days prior to the date of said term.

§ 732.5 Preferences.

Any party to an appeal, for good cause shown, may move for a preference upon notice to all other parties to the appeal.

§ 732.6 Oral argument or submission.

(a) No more than 15 minutes will be allowed for argument on each side except by express permission of the court.

(b) In the event that any party's main brief shall fail to set forth the appropriate notations with respect to the argument or submission of the cause, as required by section 732.2(a)(2) of these Rules, the cause will be deemed to have been *submitted* without oral argument by the defaulting party.

(c) When any party shall have noted on his filed brief, or, before the cause appears on the Day Calendar, shall have filed his written consent or stipulation or otherwise notified the clerk that he intends to submit the cause without argument, such party need not appear on the calendar call.

§ 732.7 Motions.

Motions may be noticed for any day of the term and must be submitted without oral argument. All papers in support of the motion (which must include a copy of the notice of appeal) or in opposition thereto shall be filed before 10 o'clock in the forenoon of the return day of the motion.

§ 732.8 Dismissals on the court's own motion.

* * *

(b) Except as otherwise provided in CPL 460.70 and subject to the applicable provisions of CPL 470.60, and unless for good cause shown an extension or enlargement of time is granted by the court, an appeal in a criminal case in which a note of issue was not filed within 90 days after the last day in which a notice of appeal was required to be filed shall be dismissed.

(c) The clerk shall prepare a special day calendar for each appointed term of the appeals subject to dismissal for failure on the part of the appellant to comply with this rule. Each such special day calendar shall be published in the *New York Law Journal* at least five days prior to, as well as on the day when that calendar is to be called, and in criminal cases, the clerk shall cause a postal card notice to be mailed to appellant or his attorney five days prior to the first day of such publication.

§ 732.9 Appeals in criminal cases; adjournments; extensions of time.

(a) Every application for an extension or enlargement of time or for an adjournment in an appeal from a judgment of conviction in a criminal case, whether on motion or stipulation, shall include, in addition to a showing of good cause, a statement subscribed by counsel setting forth:

(1) the sentence imposed and whether the defendant is free on bail or on his own recognizance by reason of the issuance of an order pursuant to CPL 460.50 and, if so, the date of such order and the name of the judge who issued the same, and

(2) whether the court has previously granted any enlargement of time.

(b) Where such application pertains to an appeal on the special day calendar referred to in subdivision (c) of section 732.8, such application shall be filed with the clerk of the court at least two days prior to the day on which the appeal is scheduled to appear on such calendar.

COURT RULES

§ 732.10 Leave to appeal to the Appellate Term.

*   *   *

(c) Applications certificates or orders granting leave to appeal under the Criminal Procedure Law (CPL 450.15, 460.15) shall be governed by the following special rules:

(1) The application shall be in writing and shall be made and filed with the clerk of this court (with proof of service upon the district attorney or any other prosecutor who appeared for the People in the criminal court in which the order sought be reviewed was rendered) within 30 days after service upon the applicant of a copy of the order.

(2) The application shall be addressed to the court for assignment to a justice and shall include:

(i) the name and address of the applicant and the name and address of the district attorney or other prosecutor, as the case may be;

(ii) the docket or index number;

(iii) the questions of law or fact which it is claimed ought to be reviewed;

(iv) any other information, data, or matter which the applicant may deem pertinent in support of the application; and

(v) a statement that no prior application for such certificate has been made.

(3) In addition, the papers in support of the application shall include a copy of the order sought to be reviewed and a copy of the memorandum or opinion of the court below or a statement that there was none.

(4) Within 15 days after service upon him of a copy of the application and of the papers, if any, in support thereof, the district attorney or other prosecutor (as the case may be) shall file answering papers or a statement that there is no opposition to the application (with proof of service upon the applicant, if appearing *pro se,* or upon the attorney making the application on behalf of the applicant). Such answering papers shall include a discussion of the merits of the application or shall state, if such be the case, that the application does not contain any allegations other than those alleged in the papers submitted by the applicant in the court below and that the prosecutor relies on the record, his answering papers contained therein and the memorandum or opinion of such court, if there be any.

(5) Unless the justice designated to determine the application shall in his discretion otherwise direct, the matter shall be submitted and determined upon the foregoing papers and without oral argument.

§ 732.11 Motions to reargue, resettle or amend; motions for leave to appeal to the Appellate Division.

(a) Motions to reargue a cause or to resettle an order or to amend a decision shall be made within 30 days after the cause shall have been decided, except that for good cause shown, the court may consider any such motion when made at a later date.

*   *   *

(c) The papers in support of such motion shall concisely state the points claimed to have been overlooked or misapprehended by the court, with appropriate references to the particular portions of the record or briefs and with citation of the authorities relied upon.

§ 732.12 Stay of judgment pending appeal to the Appellate Term.

Upon application of a defendant, pursuant to section 460.50 of the Criminal Procedure Law, for an order staying or suspending the execution of the judgment pending the determination of an appeal taken to the Appellate Term, such order may be issued by a justice of the Appellate Term or a justice of the Court of the judicial district embracing the county in which the judgment was entered.

RULES OF THE THIRD JUDICIAL DEPARTMENT APPELLATE DIVISION

(The following rules are not a complete presentation of the Third Department's rules. Only those rules that are relevant to criminal or related matters are set forth. For a complete set of rules, see *NY CLS Desk Edition Civil Practice Annual* (LexisNexis).)

PART 800

RULES OF PRACTICE

§ 800.1 Court sessions; four justices present.

Unless otherwise ordered, court sessions shall commence at 1:00 p.m., except on Friday and the last session day of a term, when they shall commence at 9:30 a.m. A term of court shall be deemed to continue until the day on which the next term convenes, and the court may reconvene at any time during recess. When a cause is argued or submitted to the court with four justices present, it shall, whenever necessary, be deemed submitted also to any other duly qualified justice of the court, unless objection is noted at the time of argument or submission.

COURT RULES

§ 800.2 Motions; special proceedings; stays.

(a) *Motions.* Unless otherwise directed by order to show cause, motions shall be made returnable on Monday (or if Monday falls on a holiday, on the next business day), whether or not court is actually in session, upon notice prescribed by CPLR 2214. Motions may not be argued except by permission of the court or a justice thereof. Counsel shall promptly notify the court clerk when such permission is granted. A notice of motion shall give notice to adverse parties that the motion will be submitted on the papers and that their personal appearance in opposition to the motion is neither required nor permitted. An order to show cause shall also give notice to adverse parties (1) whether the motion will be argued or submitted, and (2) whether their personal appearance in opposition to the motion is permitted. Papers and memoranda shall be typewritten. The original moving papers shall be filed with proof of service as soon as possible. Papers in opposition to a motion made pursuant to notice of motion shall be filed at or before 11 a.m. on Friday before the return day. Papers in opposition to an order to show cause shall be filed at or before 9 a.m. of the return date of the order. The moving papers on motions for permission to appeal to the Court of Appeals on certified questions shall state the questions proposed. A motion for permission to appeal to the Court of Appeals pursuant to CPLR 5602(a) shall be granted upon the approval of a majority of the justices comprising the panel assigned to consider the motion. On motions for reargument, a copy of the decision and any opinion of the court shall be attached to the moving papers.

(b) *Special proceedings.* Unless otherwise directed by order to show cause, original special proceedings instituted in this court (e.g., removal proceedings, mandamus and prohibition) shall be made returnable on a motion day, at 1:30 p.m., upon notice prescribed by CPLR 403 or CPLR 7804(c), unless a different time is otherwise fixed by applicable statute. The moving and opposing parties shall submit the original and six copies of their papers with proof of service of a copy on each adversary. Moving papers shall be filed within 24 hours after service upon respondent, and opposing papers shall be filed as prescribed by applicable CPLR section, unless otherwise directed by the court.

(c) *Review proceedings under Education Law, Labor Law, Public Health Law, and Tax Law.* Unless otherwise provided by order to show cause, review proceedings commenced in this court pursuant to section 6510 of the Education Law, sections 220 or 220-b of the Labor Law, section 230-c of the Public Health Law or section 2016 of the Tax Law shall be made returnable on a motion day, on not less than 20 days' notice, as provided in CPLR 7804(c). Within 60 days from the service of respondent's answer, petitioner shall file an original and nine copies of a reproduced full record on review and 10 copies of petitioner's brief, or a single copy of the record and 10 copies of petitioner's brief and appendix, with proof of service of one copy of the record and two copies of the brief, or two copies of the brief and appendix, upon respondent. Within 45 days from service of the petitioner's brief, respondent shall file 10 copies of a brief or brief and appendix, with proof of service of two copies on petitioner. Petitioner may file a reply brief within 10 days of service of respondent's brief. The record to be filed by petitioner shall be stipulated to by the parties and shall include the petition, answer, reply and affidavits, if any, the administrative determination sought to be reviewed, and the hearing transcript and exhibits. In proceedings pursuant to section 2016 of the Tax Law, the stipulated record shall also include the determination of the administrative law judge, the decision of the tax appeals tribunal, the stenographic transcript of the hearing before the administrative law judge, the transcript of any oral proceedings before the tax appeals tribunal and any exhibit or document submitted into evidence at any proceeding in the division of tax appeals upon which such decision is based.

(d) *Stays.* When an order to show cause presented for signature makes provision for a temporary stay or other interim relief, except as to the time and manner of service, the party seeking such relief must inform the justice or the clerk at the time of submission of the order that the opposing party has been notified of the application and whether such party opposes or consents to the granting of the interim relief sought.

§ 800.3 Applications to a justice for leave to appeal to Appellate Division or Court of Appeals.

An application to a justice of the appellate division for leave to appeal in a civil case (CPLR 5701(c)), or in a criminal action or proceeding (CPL 460.15; CPL 460.20), may, but need not be, addressed to a named justice, and, unless otherwise directed by order to show cause, shall be made returnable at the court's address in Albany, in the manner provided in section 800.2(a) of this Part. Such an application may not be argued unless the justice to whom it is made or referred otherwise directs.

§ 800.4 Alternative methods of prosecuting appeals and review proceedings.

An appeal or transferred review proceeding may be prosecuted upon a full record reproduced by any method approved for briefs and appendixes by CPLR 5529, by the appendix method, or upon an agreed statement in lieu of record.

(a) *Reproduced full record.* When the full record is reproduced, appellant shall file with the clerk the original and nine copies prepared in accordance with section 800.5 of this Part, with proof of service of one copy upon each adverse party.

(b) *Appendix method.* When the appendix method is used, appellant shall file with the clerk a single copy of the papers constituting the record on appeal or record on review prepared in accordance with section 800.5 of this Part, with proof of service of a copy upon each adverse party or, in lieu thereof, appellant may file with the clerk proof of service of a notice upon each adverse party that the single copy of the record has been filed in the office of the clerk of this court. In the alternative, when serving appellant's brief, appellant may serve the single copy of the record upon respondent and shall so state in an affidavit of service. A respondent upon whom the single copy of the record has been served shall file the record with the clerk of this court within 30 days from the date of its service upon him. When there are two or more adverse parties; appellant shall obtain instructions from the clerk for use of a single record by respondents and its filing with the clerk. Appellant's or petitioner's brief shall contain an appendix in compliance with section 800.8(b) of this Part.

(c) *Appeals by indigent parties.* An appeal in a criminal case, or in a civil case by a person who has been granted permission by this court to proceed as a poor person, may be prosecuted by the appendix method authorized by subdivision (b) of this section. Appellant shall file seven copies of a typewritten brief and appendix, with proof of service of one copy upon each adversary. Respondent may likewise file seven copies of a brief with proof of service of one copy upon each adversary. The clerk of the court from which the appeal is taken, after service upon him of a copy of the decision of this court, shall furnish without charge to a person granted permission to proceed as a poor person one copy of the stenographic transcript of trial or hearing minutes and one copy of any other paper or document on file in his office which is material and relevant to the appeal. In criminal and family court cases, the court may, where such is necessary for perfection of the appeal, direct the clerk of the court to send a copy of the stenographic transcript of trial or hearing minutes on file in his office to the clerk of this court, who shall attach it to the single copy record upon which the appeal shall be prosecuted.

(d) *Agreed statement in lieu of record.* If an appeal is prosecuted pursuant to CPLR 5527, appellant shall reproduce the agreed statement as a joint appendix in a manner authorized by CPLR 5529; shall prefix thereto a statement pursuant to CPLR 5531; and shall, within 30 days after approval of the statement by the court from which the appeal is taken, file the required number of copies, with proof of service of one copy upon each adverse party.

§ 800.5 Record on appeal or review.

(a) *Form and content.* A record on appeal or record on review shall be on good quality, white, unglazed paper and shall comply with CPLR 5526 as to size and form. Carbon copies will not be accepted. Bulky records shall be divided into volumes not to exceed one and one-half inches in thickness and shall be bound on the left margin with a flat clasp or similar type of fastener. The record shall contain, in the following order, so much of the following items as shall be applicable to the particular appeal or proceeding:

(1) a soft cover containing the title and names, addresses and telephone numbers of attorneys;

(2) a table of contents which shall list and briefly describe each paper included in the record, each witness' testimony and each exhibit. The part relating to a transcript of testimony shall separately state as to each witness the page at which direct, cross, redirect and recross examination begins. The part relating to exhibits shall briefly describe each exhibit and shall indicate the page where admitted in evidence and whether the exhibit has been omitted from the record;

(3) a statement pursuant to CPLR 5531;

(4) the notice of appeal or order of transfer, judgment or order appealed from, judgment roll, corrected transcript or statement in lieu thereof, any affidavits or decision relevant exhibits or copies of them, and any opinion or decision in the case;

(5) a stipulation or order settling the transcript pursuant to CPLR 5525 (c);

(6) a stipulation dispensing with reproducing any exhibits; Exhibits may be omitted from the record pursuant to stipulation of counsel or by permission of the presiding justice. Omitted exhibits which are material to the issues raised on appeal shall be filed when briefs are filed. All exhibits, whether omitted from the record or not, shall be listed and briefly described in the table of contents;

(7) the appropriate certification or stipulation as required by section 800.7 of this Part.

(b) *Exhibits.* Exhibits which are material to the issues raised by any party shall be made available to the court. Exhibits not relevant, as well as bulky, dangerous or irreplaceable exhibits, need not, however, be filed unless the clerk otherwise directs. Except in appropriation cases, appellant when filing his brief shall also file the original or a certified copy of each exhibit upon which he relies or has reason to believe a respondent will rely. Exhibits under a respondent's control or under the control of a third person shall be filed either pursuant to a five-day written demand served by appellant upon a respondent or pursuant to the subpoena duces tecum issued in accordance with CPLR, article 23. Appellant shall also file with his brief proof of service of such a demand or subpoena, together with a list of all relevant exhibits. In appropriation cases, each party shall file with his brief two copies of each appraisal report upon which he relies.

§ 800.6 Transcript.

(a) *Number required.* In civil cases, the court reporter or stenographer shall furnish petitioner or appellant with the ribbon copy of the typewritten transcript and, when the appendix method of appeal is used, the ribbon copy, or a copy of equal quality, shall be included in the single-copy record on appeal for use by the parties and the court.

(b) *Form.* Court reporters, and stenographers who report administrative agency hearings, shall furnish transcripts on 11 by 8-½-inch white, opaque paper of good quality. Pages shall contain page headings as required for appendixes by CPLR 5529(c). The transcript shall be prefaced with a table of contents showing the location of direct, cross and redirect examination of witnesses; motions for dismissal; the jury charge; the verdict and motions addressed to it; and the admission of exhibits in evidence, with a brief description of each.

(c) *Settlement of transcript.* A transcript shall be settled stipulated to by the parties or in the manner provided by CPLR 5525(c).

§ 800.7 Certification of record.

(a) *Reproduced full record.* A reproduced full record shall be certified either by: (1) a certificate of appellant's or petitioner's attorney pursuant to CPLR 2105; (2) a certificate of the proper clerk; or (3) a stipulation in lieu of certification pursuant to CPLR 5532. The reproduced copy containing the signed certification or stipulation shall be marked "Original Record." When a record contains a transcript, it shall be settled in the manner provided in section 800.6(c) of this Part.

(b) *Single copy of record.* When the appendix method is used, the single copy of the record must be stipulated to by the parties or, if the parties are unable to stipulate, settled by the judge before whom the proceedings were held. The procedure for settlement of a single copy record shall be in the manner provided by CPLR 5525 (c), except that if respondent shall fail to make any proposed amendments or objections to the record within ten days after service of it upon him, the record, certified as correct by appellant's or petitioner's attorney, shall be deemed correct and may be filed with an affirmation by appellant certifying to his compliance with the requirements of this section and respondent's noncompliance.

§ 800.8 Form and content of brief and appendix.

(a) *Briefs.* Briefs shall comply with CPLR 5528 and 5529, shall contain on the cover the name and address of counsel who will argue the appeal and the estimated time of argument, and shall be on good quality, white, unglazed paper. Carbon copies will not be accepted. Except with permission of the court, briefs shall not exceed the following limitations: petitioner's or appellant's brief, 50 printed or 70 typewritten pages; respondent's brief, 25 printed or 35 typewritten pages; reply brief, 10 printed or 15 typewritten pages; amicus curiae brief, 25 printed or 35 typewritten pages.

(b) *Appendixes.* An appendix shall comply with CPLR 5529 and may be bound in the brief or separately. Appellant's appendix shall contain such parts of the record on appeal as are necessary to consider the questions involved, including at least the following:

(1) notice of appeal;

(2) judgment, decree or order appealed from;

(3) decision and opinion of the court or agency, and report of a referee, if any;

(4) pleadings, if their sufficiency, content or form is in issue or material; in a criminal case, the indictment;

(5) relevant excerpts from transcripts of testimony or of averments in motion papers upon which appellant relies or has reason to believe respondent will rely; in addition, in a criminal case, the sentencing minutes;

(6) charge to the jury; and

(7) copies of critical exhibits, including photographs, to the extent practicable.

(c) *Inadequate appendix.* If an appendix fails to comply with this section, the adverse party, within 10 days from its receipt, may move to compel a party to file a further appendix. A respondent may also file an appendix to respondent's brief containing relevant portions of the record omitted from appellant's brief.

§ 800.9 Filing and service of papers.

(a) *Record and appellant's brief.* Except where a different time limit or a different number of copies of papers is otherwise permitted herein, appellant shall cause to be filed with the clerk of this court, within 60 days after service of the notice of appeal, either:

(1) the original and nine copies of a reproduced full record and 10 copies of appellant's brief:

(2) the single copy of the record, together with 10 copies of a brief and appendix; or

(3) ten copies of the agreed statement in lieu

of record and 10 copies of a brief; with proof of service of one copy of the record and two copies of the brief or two copies of a brief and appendix upon each respondent.

(b) *Respondent's brief.* After the record on appeal and appellant's brief, or brief and appendix, have been accepted for filing, the clerk shall mail to each respondent a scheduling memorandum which shall require respondent to serve and file respondent's brief within 45 days from the date of the memorandum or within such shorter time as the memorandum may direct. Each respondent shall file the same number of copies of respondent's brief as appellant shall have filed, with proof of service of two copies upon each appellant.

(c) *Reply brief.* Appellant may file a corresponding number of copies of a reply brief within 10 days after service of respondent's brief, with proof of service of one copy upon each respondent.

(d) *Effect of failure to comply.* Upon appellant's or petitioner's failure to comply with any provision of this Part, or for any other unreasonable delay in prosecuting an appeal or proceeding, respondent may move to dismiss for lack of prosecution. Upon respondent's failure to comply with any provision of this Part, in the discretion of the court, costs and disbursements of the appeal may be imposed against respondent or respondent's attorney, irrespective of the outcome of the appeal.

(e) *Cross-appeals.* In the case of cross-appeals, unless otherwise directed by order of the court made pursuant to a motion on notice, the plaintiff shall be appellant and shall file and serve the record and brief, or brief and appendix, first. The answering brief and appendix shall be filed and served within 30 days after service of the first brief and shall include the points of argument on the cross-appeal. A reply brief shall be filed and served within ten days after service of the answering brief. A reply brief to the cross-appeal may be served within ten days after service of appellant's reply brief.

§ 800.10 Oral argument.

(a) Unless otherwise permitted by the court, oral argument shall not be allowed in the following cases:

(1) appeals from the Workers' Compensation Board;

(2) appeals from the Unemployment Insurance Appeal Board;

(3) appeals from judgments of conviction in criminal cases challenging only the legality, propriety or excessiveness of the sentence imposed;

(4) appeals in or transfers of CPLR article 78 proceedings in which the sole issue raised is

whether there is substantial evidence to support the challenged determination; and

(5) any other case in which the court, in its discretion, determines that argument is not warranted.

(b) Any party seeking permission for oral argument in any of the cases specified in subdivision (a)(1) through (4) of this section shall submit a letter application therefor, on notice to all parties, within 10 days after the filing of applicant's brief together with proof of service upon respondent. Any party seeking permission for oral argument in a case specified in subdivision (a)(5) of this section shall submit a letter application therefor, on notice to all parties, within 10 days after being advised by the clerk that there will be no oral argument. The application shall specify the reasons why oral argument is appropriate and the amount of time requested.

(c) In cases not specified in subdivision (a) of this section, each counsel shall notify the clerk whether argument is desired and, if so, shall indicate on the cover of the brief the amount of time requested. Unless otherwise ordered, each side shall be allowed not more than 30 minutes for argument on appeals from judgments, in actions on submitted facts, and in special proceedings transferred to or instituted in this court and 15 minutes on appeals from nonfinal orders.

§ 800.11 Day calendar assignments; adjournments; additions.

The clerk shall prepare day calendars for each court term by scheduling for argument or submission cases in which the record and appellant's brief have been filed and in which the respondent's brief has been filed or the date for filing and serving respondent's brief has been fixed pursuant to section 800.9(b) of this Part. The clerk shall give counsel notice of the date on which a case will be argued. After notice of day calendar assignment has been given, a case may not be moved to a different day unless request is made at least 14 days prior to commencement of the term for which it has been scheduled. The granting of a request to reschedule a case shall not serve to extend the time to file respondent's brief. A case not argued by a party when reached shall be submitted without oral argument on the papers filed. A case may be added to a term upon written stipulation signed by counsel and approved by the court.

§ 800.12 Appeals and proceedings deemed abandoned.

A civil appeal or proceeding shall be deemed to have been abandoned where appellant or petitioner shall fail to serve and file a record and brief within nine months after the date of the notice of appeal or order of transfer, or, in the case of a proceeding instituted in this court, within nine

COURT RULES

months after the date of the order to show cause or notice of petition commencing the proceeding; and the clerk of this court shall not accept or file any record or brief attempted to be filed beyond the nine-month period unless directed to do so by order of the court. Such an order shall be granted only pursuant to a motion on notice supported by an affidavit setting forth a reasonable excuse for the delay and facts showing merit to the appeal or proceeding.

§ 800.13 Appeals from Family Court.

An appeal from Family Court shall be prosecuted by the appendix method authorized by section 800.4 (b) of this Part upon a single copy of the record prepared in accordance with section 800.5 of this Part and upon seven copies of a brief and appendix in compliance with section 800.8(b) of this Part. Application for assignment of counsel and for permission to proceed as a poor person shall be made to this court pursuant to section 1120 of the Family Court Act.

§ 800.14 Appeals in criminal cases.

An appeal authorized by the Criminal Procedure Law shall be prosecuted by the appendix method authorized by section 800.4(b) of this Part. The single copy record in a criminal case shall comply with section 800.5 of this Part, except that, in addition to the relevant items listed in section 800.5(a) of this Part, it shall also contain the indictment, hearing and trial transcripts, motion papers, if any, and sentencing minutes. When the clerk of the trial court has been directed, pursuant to section 800.4(c) of this Part, to furnish a copy of a transcript to this court, the transcript may be omitted from the single copy record.

(a) *Briefs and appendixes.* Briefs and appendixes shall comply with CPLR 5528 and section 800.8 of this Part.

(b) *When to be heard; service of briefs.* Unless appellant's time is enlarged by order, appellant's counsel shall file the single copy record and seven copies of a brief and appendix within 60 days after the last day for filing a notice of appeal, with proof of service of one copy upon the appellant and one copy upon respondent. Respondent, within 30 days after service of appellant's brief and appendix, shall file seven copies of a brief and appendix, with proof of service of two copies upon appellant's counsel, who shall forthwith furnish a copy of respondent's brief to appellant. The clerk shall schedule the appeal for argument or submission at the next term of court commencing more than 30 days after the service and filing of the record on appeal and appellant's brief and appendix, unless an extension to file respondent's brief shall have been granted pursuant to section 800.9(b) of this Part.

(c) *Enlargement of time.* Application by appellant for an enlargement of time in a criminal case shall be by motion on notice and shall be accompanied by an affidavit satisfactorily explaining the delay. The affidavit shall state (1) the date of conviction; (2) whether by trial or plea; (3) whether appellant is free on bail; (4) the date the notice of appeal was filed; (5) the date the trial transcript was ordered; (6) whether the transcript has been filed; (7) if the complete transcript has not been filed, the date it is expected to be filed; and (8) the date appellant's brief and appendix will be filed.

(d) *Oral argument.* Unless otherwise ordered by the court, appeals may be submitted without oral argument. The time allowed for oral argument shall be provided in section 800.10 of this Part.

(e) *Remittitur.* Upon entry of the order on this court's decision, the original record on appeal shall be remitted to the clerk of the criminal court with a copy of the order.

(f) *Reargument of appeal.* Motions for reargument must be made within 60 days after service upon the moving party of a copy of the court's order, with written notice of its entry, except that when a party has entered the order, the time shall be computed from the date of entry.

(g) *Where only sentence in issue.* When the sole question raised on appeal concerns the legality, propriety or excessiveness of the sentence imposed, the appeal may be heard upon a shortened record on appeal consisting of the notice of appeal, sentencing minutes, and minutes of the plea, if appellant pleaded guilty. The record which shall be clearly labeled "Record on Appeal from Sentence" shall contain a statement pursuant to CPLR 5531 and shall be stipulated to or settled in the manner provided in section 800.7(b) of this Part. The appeal shall be prosecuted, and may be scheduled for oral argument or submission, in the manner provided in subdivision (b) of this section. A copy of the presentence investigation report shall be filed with the clerk.

(h) *Expedited criminal appeal of order reducing indictment or dismissing indictment and directing filing of prosecutor's information.* (1) This subdivision shall govern the procedure for an expedited appeal, pursuant to CPL 210.20(6)(c), 450.20(1-a) and 450.55, of an order by a superior court reducing a count or counts of an indictment or dismissing an indictment and directing the filing of a prosecutor's information.

(2) After the people file and serve a notice of appeal pursuant to CPL 460.10(1), either party may request that the court expedite the appeal. If a request is made, the court shall hear the appeal on an expedited basis as set forth in this subdivision.

(3) (i) The court shall establish an expedited briefing schedule for the appeal. Briefs may be typewritten or reproduced. The people shall file nine copies of a brief and an appendix, which

shall include a copy of the indictment and the trial court's decision and order. The respondent shall file nine copies of a brief and, if necessary, an appendix. One copy of the brief and appendix shall be served on opposing counsel.

(ii) The appeal may be taken on one original record, which shall include copies of the indictment, the motion papers, the trial court's decision and order, and the notice of appeal.

(iii) The people shall file with the Appellate Division, separately from the record, one copy of the grand jury minutes.

(iv) The court shall give preference to the hearing of an appeal perfected pursuant to this subdivision and shall determine the appeal as expeditiously as possible.

(4) Unless otherwise ordered by the Appellate Division, if the defendant is represented in the superior court by court-assigned counsel, such counsel shall continue to represent the defendant in any appeal by the people of an order reducing an indictment or dismissing an indictment and directing the filing of a prosecutor's information.

(i) *Service of order.* Service of a copy of the order upon appellant in accordance with CPL 460.10(5)(a) shall be made pursuant to CPLR 2103.

§ 800.15 Appeals from orders concerning grand jury reports.

The mode, time and manner for perfecting an appeal from an order accepting a report of a grand jury pursuant to paragraph (a) of subdivision 1 of section 190.85 of the Criminal Procedure Law, or from an order sealing a report of a grand jury pursuant to subdivision 5 of section 190.85 of the Criminal Procedure Law, shall be in accordance with the section 800.14 of this Part governing appeals in criminal cases. Appeals from such orders shall be preferred causes and may be added to a term calendar either by stipulation or upon motion. The record, briefs and other papers on such an appeal shall be sealed and not be available for public inspection. Unless otherwise directed by the court, oral argument will not be allowed.

* * *

§ 800.19 Transferred proceedings.

An article 78 proceeding transferred to this court pursuant to CPLR 7804(g), and an appeal transferred from another department pursuant to CPLR 5711, may be prosecuted in any manner authorized by section 800.4 of this Part. Unless otherwise ordered by the court, the rules governing the content number and form of records briefs and appendixes shall apply, except that petitioner or appellant shall serve and file the required papers within 60 days after the entry of the order of transfer.

§ 800.20 State human rights proceedings.

(a) *Appeals.* An appeal from an order or judgment of the Supreme Court determining a proceeding pursuant to section 298 of the Executive Law shall be prosecuted upon a record consisting of the original papers and the record before the State Division of Human Rights, together with seven copies of appellant's brief and appendix, with proof of service of one copy upon each respondent. Appellant's appendix shall contain at least the notice of appeal, the order or judgment appealed from, the decision of the court below and the determination and order of the State Division of Human Rights. Each respondent shall file seven copies of a brief, with proof of service of one copy upon appellant. Briefs and appendices shall comply with and be filed within the time specified by sections 800.8 and 800.09 of this Part.

(b) *Transferred proceedings.* A proceeding transferred to this court for disposition pursuant to section 298 of the Executive Law may be prosecuted upon a single copy of the record on review, which shall consist of the notice of petition and petition, answer, reply, if any, the original record and transcript of the public hearing held before the State Division of Human Rights, and the division's determination and order. Petitioner shall file seven copies of a brief and appendix, with proof of service of one copy upon each named respondent. Each respondent shall file seven copies of a brief or brief and appendix, with proof of service of one copy, upon petitioner. Briefs and appendices shall comply with, and be filed within the time specified by, sections 800.8 and 800.19 of this Part. Unless the court directs otherwise, the division shall file the original record and transcript of public hearing within 45 days of entry of the order of transfer.

§ 800.21 Action on submitted facts.

An original agreed statement of facts in an action submitted to this court pursuant to CPLR 3222 shall be filed in the office of the county clerk, and a copy shall be appended to appellant's brief as a joint appendix. A statement required by CPLR 5531 shall be prefixed thereto. Briefs shall be served and filed in the manner and in accordance with the time requirements prescribed by sections 800.9 and 800.11 of this Part of appeals.

§ 800.22 Orders; settlement; costs.

The orders, appointments, assignments and directions of the court shall be signed by the presiding justice or the clerk of the court. Costs in workers' compensation and unemployment insurance appeals shall be taxed by the clerk in accordance with CPLR 8403.

COURT RULES

* * * *

PART 806

CONDUCT OF ATTORNEYS

§ 806.1 Application.

This part shall apply to all attorneys who reside or have an office in, or who are admitted to practice and are employed or transact business in, the Third Judicial Department.

§ 806.2 Professional misconduct defined.

Any attorney who fails to conduct himself or herself in conformity with the standards of conduct imposed upon members of the Bar as conditions for the privilege to practice law, and any attorney who violates any disciplinary rule of the Code of Professional Responsibility adopted jointly by the Appellate Divisions of the Supreme Court, effective September 1, 1990, or any other rule or announced standard of the court governing the conduct of attorneys, shall be deemed to be guilty of professional misconduct within the meaning of subdivision 2 of section 90 of the Judiciary Law.

§ 806.3 Third department grievance program.

(a) Committee on Professional Standards. This court shall appoint a committee on professional standards for the third judicial department, which shall consist of a chairperson and twenty members, three of whom shall be non-lawyers. Appointment of lawyers shall, as far as practicable, be made equally from practicing attorneys in each of the judicial districts in the third judicial department. Appointments shall be for a term of three years. A vacancy shall be filled until the following March 31 and the term of the vacancy shall be deemed to have expired on that date. No person who has served two consecutive three-year terms shall be eligible for reappointment until the passage of three years from the expiration of his or her second term. Seven members of the committee shall constitute a quorum and the concurrence of six members shall be necessary for any action taken. The chairperson and vice-chairperson shall be named by the court after considering the recommendations of the committee. The chairperson may appoint an executive committee consisting of at least on member of the committee from each judicial district.

(b) Duties of Committee on Professional Standards. The committee shall (1) consider and cause to be investigated all matters called to its attention, whether by complaint or otherwise, involving alleged misconduct by an attorney in the Third Judicial Department, (2) supervise the professional staff in the performance of its duties to the committee, (3) furnish the court quarterly statistical reports concerning the disposition of all matters before the committee and maintain such records as directed by the court, and (4) submit a proposed annual budget to the court for approval.

(c) Defense and indemnification of committee members. Members of the committee on professional standards, as volunteers, are expressly authorized to participate in a State-sponsored volunteer program within the meaning of subdivision 1 of section 17 of the Public Officers Law.

(d) Professional Staff. The court shall, in consultation with the committee, appoint a professional staff and such supporting staff as shall be necessary. The chief attorney shall be authorized to disburse funds within the amounts appropriated and allocated. The expenses of the staff and committee shall not exceed the amounts segregated and assigned by the Office of Court Administration, and shall be incurred according to rules and regulations promulgated by that office.

(e) Duties of Professional Staff. The chief attorney, under the supervision of the committee, shall (1) answer and take appropriate action respecting all inquiries concerning an attorney's conduct and (2) investigate all matters involving alleged misconduct by an attorney in the Third Judicial Department.

§ 806.4 Procedure.

(a) Investigation Generally. Investigation of professional misconduct may be commenced by the committee, through the chief attorney, upon receipt of a specific complaint, or by the committee on its own motion. Complaints must be in writing and signed by the complainant, but need not be verified. Prior to initiating an investigation on its own motion, the committee shall file as part of its record a written inquiry, signed by the chief attorney, which inquiry shall serve as the basis for such investigation.

(b) Investigation by Chief Attorney. Before initiating an investigation of a specific complaint against an attorney, the chief attorney shall determine whether the allegations, if true, are sufficient to establish a charge of professional misconduct. If deemed sufficient, the chief attorney shall forward a copy of the complaint to the attorney, together with a statement of the nature of the alleged professional misconduct and a request that the attorney furnish a written statement concerning the complaint, and shall advise the attorney that a copy of his statement may, in the discretion of the committee, be furnished to the complainant for reply. Attorneys shall be expected to cooperate with all investigations. As part of an investigation, the chief attorney may request an attorney to appear pursuant to written notice to be examined under oath by the chief attorney or a staff attorney, and may, when necessary, apply pursuant to subdivision (e) of this section for a subpoena

directing the attorney to appear for such examination. Stenographic minutes of such examination shall be made and a transcript made available to the attorney upon his request and payment of the stenographic fees. If an attorney requests that an examination be conducted before a third person, the chairman of the committee shall designate a member of the committee as the person before whom the examination shall be held. Upon the conclusion of an investigation, the chief attorney shall make a report to the committee. An attorney who fails to comply with a subpoena directing him to appear for examination may, in the court's discretion, be suspended pending his compliance or until further order of the court.

(c) *Action by committee.* (1) If, after an investigation, the committee determines that no action is warranted, the complaint shall be dismissed and the complainant and the attorney shall be so notified in writing; or, if the investigation was undertaken on the committee's own motion, the investigation shall be discontinued. If, after an investigation, the committee determines that a complaint warrants action, it may:

(i) direct that a disciplinary proceeding be commenced against the attorney; or

(ii) admonish the attorney, either orally or in writing, or both, if the acts of misconduct have been established by clear and convincing evidence and the committee determines in light of all of the circumstances that the misconduct is not serious enough to warrant commencement of a disciplinary proceeding; or

(iii) issue a letter of caution, if the acts of misconduct have been so established and the committee determines in light of all the circumstances that the misconduct is not serious enough to warrant either commencement of a disciplinary proceeding or imposition of an admonition; or

(iv) issue a letter of education, if the committee determines that the actions of the attorney warrant comment.

(2) Prior to imposition of an admonition, the committee shall give the attorney 20 days' notice by mail of the committee's proposed action. The attorney may request reconsideration of the committee's proposed admonition. Such request shall be made by letter, certified mail, return receipt requested, within 14 days from the date of mailing of the committee's notice. The request shall be considered by the executive committee. If it is determined by a majority of the executive committee that reconsideration is warranted, the matter shall be resubmitted to the committee.

(3) No prior notice to the attorney is necessary for the issuance of a letter of caution. The attorney may, however, request reconsideration of the committee's action in issuing a letter of caution. Such request shall be made by letter, certified mail, return receipt requested, within 14 days from the date of mailing of the committee's letter.

The request shall be considered by the executive committee. If it is determined by a majority of the executive committee that reconsideration is warranted, the matter shall be resubmitted to the committee.

(4) Following a request for reconsideration of a letter of admonition or caution, where the committee adheres to its action, or where consideration is not sought, the attorney may file a motion with the court for review of the letter of admonition or caution, on notice to the chief attorney, within 30 days from the mailing of the committee's determination. An attorney who receives a letter of education may similarly file a motion with the court for review thereof, upon a showing that the matter giving rise to the letter involves a fundamental constitutional right. Upon such motion, the court may consider the entire record and may confirm or vacate the letter of admonition, caution or education, or make whatever other disposition it determines to be warranted under all the circumstances.

(5) When an attorney has been admonished or cautioned, the committee shall promptly notify the complainant that appropriate action has been taken. The committee's records relating to its investigation and sanction shall be confidential. An admonition or letter of caution may be considered by the court and the committee in determining whether to impose discipline and the extent of discipline to be imposed in the event other charges of misconduct are subsequently brought against the attorney.

(d) Protective Orders. An attorney aggrieved by any investigation may apply to the court by affidavit, upon notice to the chief attorney in such manner as a justice of the court may direct, for a protective order denying, limiting, conditioning or regulating the use of any information being sought by the chief attorney.

(e) Subpoenas. If it appears that the examination of any person is necessary for a proper determination of the validity of a complaint, the chief attorney or the attorney under investigation may apply to the clerk of this court for issuance of a subpoena for the attendance of the person as a witness and for the production of relevant books and papers. Application for issuance of a subpoena shall be made by setting forth factual allegations showing the relevancy of the testimony, and of any books and papers specified, to the subject matter of the investigation. Subpoenas, which shall be entitled "In the Matter of the Investigation by the Committee on Professional Standards of the Professional Conduct of an Attorney," shall be issued by the clerk in the name of the presiding justice and may be made returnable at a time and place therein specified before the chief attorney or any member of the committee designated to conduct the examination. The committee, or a member thereof designated by the chairman, or the chief attorney or a staff attorney, is empowered to take and cause to be transcribed the testimony of a witness who may be sworn by any persons authorized by law to administer oaths. If the committee is required to obtain a subpoena in order to compel an attorney's appearance for examination, the attorney shall be required to reimburse the committee for the stenographic costs of the examination within 10 days of being advised of the amount of such costs.

(f) Suspension of attorneys pending consideration of disciplinary charges. (1) An attorney who is the subject of an investigation into allegations of misconduct and who has been examined by the committee under oath who is the subject of a disciplinary proceeding commenced in this court pursuant to a petition filed under section 806.5 of this Part, or pursuant to a notice service under section 806.19(b) of this Part, may be suspended from the practice of law pending consideration of disciplinary charges against the attorney upon a finding that the attorney is guilty of professional misconduct immediately threatening the public interest. Such a finding shall be based upon:

(i) the attorney's default in responding to the petition or notice;

(ii) a substantial admission under oath to commission of an act or acts of such professional misconduct; or

(iii) other uncontroverted evidence of the misconduct.

(2) The suspension shall be made upon application of the committee to this court, after written notice of such application has been given to the attorney, and shall commence upon service on the attorney of an order of this court granting the application. The court shall briefly state the reasons for the suspension which shall continue until such time as the disciplinary matter has been concluded and until further order of the court.

(3) An order of suspension together with any decision issued pursuant to the provisions of the subdivision shall be deemed a public record. The papers submitted in connection with the application therefor shall be deemed confidential until such time as the disciplinary matter against the attorney has been concluded and the charges are sustained by the court.

(g) Diversion program. (1) During the course of an investigation or disciplinary proceeding, when the attorney raises alcohol or other substance abuse or dependency as a mitigating factor, or upon recommendation of the committee, the Court may, upon application of the attorney or committee, stay the investigation or disciplinary proceeding and direct the attorney to complete a monitoring program sponsored by a lawyers' assistance program approved by the Court. In determining whether to divert an attorney to a monitoring program, the Court shall consider (i) whether the alleged misconduct occurred during a time period when the attorney suffered from alcohol or other substance abuse or dependency; (ii) whether the alleged misconduct is related to such alcohol or other substance abuse or dependency; (iii) the seriousness of the alleged misconduct; and (iv) whether diversion is in the best interests of the public, the legal profession, and the attorney.

(2) Upon submission of written proof of successful completion of the monitoring program, the Court may direct discontinuance of resumption of the investigation or disciplinary proceeding, or take other appropriate action.

(3) In the event the attorney is not accepted into or fails to successfully complete the monitoring program as ordered by the Court, or the attorney commits additional misconduct after the diversion is directed pursuant to this subdivision, the Court may, upon notice to the attorney affording him or her an opportunity to be heard, rescind the order diverting the attorney to the monitoring program and reinstate the investigation or disciplinary proceeding, or take other appropriate action.

(4) Any costs associated with the attorney's participation in a monitoring program pursuant to this subdivision shall be the responsibility of the attorney.

§ 806.5 Disciplinary proceedings.

Upon determining that a petition for institution of a disciplinary proceeding should be instituted, the committee shall file with the court the original petition and notice of petition with proof of service of one copy upon the attorney. Service of the petition and notice shall initially be made by certified mail to the attorney's office address; if the attorney shall fail to answer or respond on or before the return date of the notice, a copy of the petition and notice shall be served upon him personally. The court shall refer issues of fact to a judge or referee to hear and report. If no actual issue is raised, the court may, upon application of their party, fix a time at which respondent may be heard in mitigation or otherwise, or the court may refer the matter for such purpose.

§ 806.6 County bar association grievance committees and mediation programs.

(a) *County bar association grievance committees.* (1) A county bar association which receives a complaint against an attorney shall initially refer the complaint to the committee.

(2) If the chief attorney, or the committee after investigation, determines that the complaint is a matter involving undue delay in rendering legal services not constituting neglect, a fee dispute to which Part 137 of the Rules of the Chief Administrator does not apply, or inadequate representation not constituting professional misconduct, the

complaint may be referred back to the county bar association for resolution. A complaint submitted directly to the committee may also be referred by the committee or chief attorney to the county bar association in the first instance.

(3) The county bar association shall complete an investigation and attempt to resolve the complaint within 90 days after receipt of the complaint from the committee or chief attorney. If the county bar association is unable to resolve the complaint within this time period, it shall, upon request of the chief attorney, return its complete file to the committee for further consideration.

(4) The county bar association shall render a quarterly report to the committee within 15 days after the end of each calendar quarter. The report shall contain the names of all attorneys against whom complaints were received or were pending during the preceding quarter. If a county bar association resolves a complaint, it shall forward its complete original file to the committee together with its quarterly report.

(b) *County bar association mediation programs.* Upon receipt of a complaint submitted directly to the committee, or following referral of a complaint by a county bar association, the committee or chief attorney, upon determining that the matter is appropriate for mediation, may refer the complaint to a county bar association mediation program pursuant to Part 1220 of the joint rules of the Appellate Divisions.

§ 806.7 Attorneys convicted of a crime.

Upon the filing with this court of a certificate of a felony conviction of an attorney, the court shall issue an order directing the attorney to show cause why an order should not be entered striking his name from the roll of attorneys pursuant to the provisions of subdivision 4 of section 90 of the Judiciary Law. Upon the filing of the record of conviction of an attorney convicted of a serious crime, as defined in subdivision 4 of section 90 of the Judiciary Law, the court shall issue an order suspending the attorney until a further or final order is made. An attorney who has been suspended may apply for reinstatement upon expiration of the period of suspension.

§ 806.8 Resignation of attorneys.

(a) An attorney who is the subject of a disciplinary proceeding or of an investigation into allegations of misconduct may resign by tendering his resignation to the court, together with an affidavit stating that he wishes to resign and:

(1) that he is acting freely and voluntarily and is fully aware of the consequences of his resignation;

(2) that he is aware of the pending investigation or disciplinary proceeding concerning allegations of misconduct, the nature of which shall be specifically set forth; and

(3) that he does not contest the allegations of professional misconduct and recognizes that his failure to do so precludes him from asserting his innocence of the professional misconduct alleged.

(b) If the court accepts an attorney's resignation, it shall enter an order of disbarment.

§ 806.9 Conduct of disbarred, suspended or resigned attorneys.

(a) *Compliance with Judiciary Law.* Disbarred, suspended or resigned attorneys shall comply fully with sections 478, 479, 484 and 486 of the Judiciary Law.

(b) *Compensation.* A disbarred, suspended or resigned attorney may not share in any fee for legal services performed by another attorney during the period of his removal from the Bar, but he or she may be compensated on a *quantum meruit* basis for legal services rendered and disbursements incurred prior to the effective date of removal. In the absence of agreement, the amount and manner of payment of such compensation and disbursements shall be fixed by the court on application of either the disbarred, suspended or resigned attorney or the new attorney, on notice to the other, as well as on notice to the client. Such applications shall be made at special term of the court in which the action is pending, or at a special term of supreme court in the county in which the moving attorney maintains his office if an action has not been commenced. In no event shall the combined legal fees exceed the amount the client would have been required to pay had no substitution of attorneys been required.

(c) *Notice to clients not involved in litigation.* A disbarred, suspended or resigned attorney shall promptly notify by registered or certified mail, return receipt requested, all clients being represented in pending matters, other than litigated or administrative matters or proceedings pending in any court or agency, of his disbarment, suspension or resignation and shall advise said clients to seek other legal advice.

(d) *Notice to clients involved in litigation.* (1) A disbarred, suspended or resigned attorney shall promptly notify, by registered or certified mail, return receipt requested, each of his clients who is involved in litigated matters or administrative proceedings, and the attorney or attorneys for each adverse party in such matter or proceeding, of his disbarment, suspension or resignation and consequent inability to act as an attorney after the effective date of his disbarment, suspension or resignation. The notice to the client shall request the prompt substitution of another attorney. The notice to the attorney for an adverse party shall state the residence address of the client of the disbarred, suspended or resigned attorney.

(2) In the event a client does not obtain substitute counsel before the effective date of the disbarment, suspension or resignation, it shall be the responsibility of the disbarred, suspended or resigned attorney to move pro se in the court in which the action is pending, or before the body in which an administrative proceeding is pending, for leave to withdraw from the action or proceeding.

(e) *Conduct after entry of order.* A disbarred, suspended or resigned attorney, after entry of the disbarment or suspension order or after entry of the order accepting a resignation, shall not accept any new retainer or engage in any new case or legal matter of any nature as attorney for another. However, during the period between the entry date of the order and its effective date, he may wind up and complete, on behalf of any client, all matters which were pending on the entry date. After the effective date, the use of the name of a disbarred, suspended or resigned attorney, who is a member of a partnership or professional corporation, in the name of said partnership or professional corporation, shall be discontinued. The disbarred, suspended or resigned attorney shall not share in any income generated by the firm or professional corporation with which he was associated after the date of disbarment or resignation or during the period of suspension.

(f) *Filing proof of compliance and attorney's address.* Within thirty days after the effective date of the disbarment, suspension order or the order accepting a resignation, the disbarred, suspended or resigned attorney shall file with the clerk of this court an affidavit reporting that he has fully complied with the provisions of the order and with these rules and that he has served a copy of such affidavit upon the chief attorney. Such affidavit shall also set forth the residence or other address to which communications may be directed to the disbarred, suspended or resigned attorney.

(g) *Required records.* A disbarred, suspended or resigned attorney shall keep and maintain records of the steps taken by him to comply with this section so that, on any subsequent proceeding instituted by or against him, proof of compliance with this section and with the disbarment or suspension order, or with the order accepting the resignation, will be available.

§ 806.10 Mental incapacity of attorney; protection of clients of disbarred and suspended attorneys.

(a) *Proceeding to determine alleged incapacity of attorney.* Whenever, during the investigation of a complaint of professional misconduct or the prosecution of a disciplinary proceeding against an attorney, it shall appear that the attorney is incapacitated from continuing to practice law by reason of mental illness, drug addiction or alcoholism, or is otherwise mentally irresponsible, it shall be the duty of the chief attorney to petition the court to take appropriate action for determination of the attorney's mental condition, including examination by such qualified medical experts as the court shall designate. If the court is satisfied from the evidence that the attorney is so incapacitated, it shall suspend him from practice for such mental incapacity indefinitely and until further order, and any pending proceedings against him shall be held in abeyance. The court may appoint counsel to represent the attorney, if he lacks adequate representation.

(b) *Procedure when respondent claims disability during course of disciplinary proceeding.* If during the course of a disciplinary proceeding respondent contends that he is suffering from a disability by reason of mental infirmity or illness, or because of addiction to drugs or intoxicants which makes it impossible for him adequately to defend himself, the court thereupon shall enter an order suspending respondent from continuing to practice law until a determination is made of the respondent's capacity to do so.

(c) *Expenses of proceedings.* The court may fix the compensation of any attorney or medical expert appointed pursuant to this section and direct that payment be made as an incident of the expenses of a disciplinary proceeding.

§ 806.11 Appointment of attorney to protect client's interests.

Whenever an attorney is disbarred or suspended for incapacity, disability or other reason, or whenever there are reasonable grounds to believe that an attorney has abandoned or is seriously neglecting his practice to the prejudice of his clients, the court, upon such notice to him as it may direct, may appoint one or more attorneys to inventory his files and take appropriate action to protect the interests of his clients. An attorney so appointed shall not render legal services to clients of the attorney with respect to any file so inventoried, nor disclose any information contained therein without the consent of the client to whom such file relates, except as may be necessary to carry out the provisions of the order which appointed him. Whenever necessary, an attorney so appointed may apply to the court for appropriate instructions for the proper discharge of his duties.

§ 806.12 Reinstatement.

(a) An attorney who has been disbarred or whose name has been struck from the roll of attorneys pursuant to subdivision (4) of section 90 of the Judiciary Law may not apply for reinstatement until the expiration of at least seven years from the effective date of the disbarment or removal. An attorney who has been suspended may apply for reinstatement upon expiration of the period of suspension. An attorney suspended pursuant to section 806.10 of this Part who applies for reinstatement shall waive any doctor-patient privilege which would otherwise exist regarding medical or psychiatric care during his disability,

and shall submit a list of the persons by whom and the facilities at which he received treatment, together with authorizations for the release of records relating thereto. The court may direct the appointment of medical experts to examine the attorney at his own expense.

(b) An application for reinstatement may be granted by this court only upon a showing by the applicant (i) by clear and convincing evidence that he has fully complied with the provisions of the order disbarring or suspending him, or striking his name from the roll of attorneys, and that he possesses the character and general fitness to resume the practice of law, and (ii) that, subsequent to the entry of such order, he has taken and attained a passing score on the Multistate Professional Responsibility Examination described in section 520.8(a) of the Rules of the Court of Appeals for the Admission of Attorneys and Counselors at Law, the passing score thereon being that determined by the New York State Board of Law Examiners pursuant to section 520.8(c) of such rules. A copy of an application for reinstatement shall be served on the committee on professional standards. The committee shall inquire into the merits of, and may be heard in opposition to, the application. The application may be referred to the appropriate committee on character and fitness or to a judge or referee for a hearing and report to the court.

(c) The court in its discretion may direct that an applicant pay the necessary expenses incurred in connection with an application for reinstatement.

* * *

§ 806.15 Advertising by attorneys.

(a) A lawyer on behalf of himself or herself or partners or associates, shall not use or disseminate or participate in the preparation or dissemination of any public communication containing statements or claims that are false, deceptive, misleading or cast reflection on the legal profession as a whole.

(b) Advertising or other publicity by lawyers, including participation in public functions, shall not contain puffery, self-laudation, claims regarding the quality of the lawyers legal services, or claims that cannot be measured or verified.

(c) It is proper to include information, provided its dissemination does not violate the provisions of subdivisions (a) and (b) herein, as to:

(1) education, degrees and other scholastic distinctions; dates of admission to any bar; areas of the law in which the lawyer or law firm practices, as authorized by the Code of Professional Responsibility; public offices and teaching positions held; memberships in bar associations or other professional societies or organizations, including offices and committee assignments therein; foreign language fluency;

COURT RULES

(2) names of clients regularly represented, provided that the client has given prior written consent;

(3) bank references; credit arrangements accepted; prepaid group legal services programs in which the attorney or firm participates;

(4) legal fees for initial consultation; contingent fee rates in civil matters when accompanied by a statement disclosing whether percentage are computed before and after deduction of costs and disbursements; range of fees for services, provided that there be available to the public free of charge a written statement clearly describing the scope of each advertised service; hourly rates; and fixed fees for specified legal services.

(d) Advertising and publicity shall be designed to educate the public to an awareness of legal needs and to provide information relevant to the selection of the most appropriate counsel. Information other than that specifically authorized in subdivision (c) that is consistent with these purposes may be disseminated providing that it does not violate any other provisions of this rule.

(e) A lawyer or law firm advertising any fixed fee for specified legal service shall, at the time of fee publication, have available to the public a written statement clearly describing the scope of each advertised service, which statement shall be delivered to the client at the time of retainer for any such service. Such legal services shall include all those services which are recognized as reasonable and necessary under local custom in the area of practice in the community where the services are performed.

(f) If the advertisement is broadcast, it shall be prerecorded or taped and approved for broadcast by the lawyer, and recording or videotape of actual transmission shall be retained by the lawyer for a period of not less than one year following such transmission.

(g) If a lawyer or law firm advertises a range of fees or an hourly rate for services, the lawyer or law firm may not charge more than the fee advertised for such services. If a lawyer or law firm advertises a fixed fee for specified legal services, or performs services described in a fee schedule, the lawyer or law firm may not charge more than the fixed fee for such stated legal service as set forth in the advertisement or fee schedule, unless the client agrees in writing that the services performed or to be performed were not legal services referred to or implied in the advertisement or in the fee schedule and, further, that a different fee arrangement shall apply to that transaction.

(h) Unless otherwise specified in the advertisement, if a lawyer publishes any fee information authorized under this rule in a publication which is published more frequently than once per month, the lawyer shall be bound by any representation made therein for a period of not less than

30 days after such publication. If a lawyer publishes any fee information authorized under this rule in a publication which is published once per month or less frequently, the lawyer shall be bound by any representation made therein until the publication of the succeeding issue. If a lawyer publishes any fee information authorized under this rule in a publication which has no fixed date for publication of a succeeding issue, the lawyer shall be bound by any representation made therein for a reasonable period of time after publication, but in no event less than 90 days.

(i) Unless otherwise specified, if a lawyer broadcasts any fee information authorized under this rule, the lawyer shall be bound by any representation made therein for a period of not less than 30 days after such broadcast.

(j) A lawyer shall not compensate or give any thing of value to representatives of the press, radio, television or other communication medium in anticipation of or in return for professional publicity in a news item.

(k) All advertisements of legal services shall include the name, office address and telephone number of the attorney or law firm whose services are being offered.

(l) All advertisements of legal services that are mailed, or are distributed other than by radio, television, directory, newspaper, magazine or other periodical, by a lawyer or law firm with an office for the practice of law in this judicial department, shall also be subject to the following provisions:

(1) A copy of each advertisement shall at the time of its initial mailing or distribution be filed with the Committee on Professional Standards for the Third Judicial Department.

(2) Such advertisement shall contain no reference to the fact of filing.

(3) If such advertisement is directed to a predetermined addressee, a list, containing the names and addresses of all persons to whom the advertisement is being or will thereafter be mailed or distributed, shall be retained by the lawyer or law firm for a period of not less than one year following the last date of mailing or distribution.

(4) The advertisements filed pursuant to this subdivision shall be open to public inspection.

(5) The requirements of this subdivision shall not apply to such professional cards or other announcements the distribution of which is authorized by DR 2-102(A) of the Code of Professional Responsibility as adopted by the New York State Bar Association, as amended.

* * *

§ 806.18 Fiduciary responsibility to clients.

(a) *Prohibition against commingling; separate*

accounts. An attorney in possession of any asset or sum of money belonging to a client is a fiduciary and must not commingle client funds with his own funds or personal or business accounts. An attorney shall maintain in a bank or trust company within the State of New York in his own name, or in the name of a firm of attorneys of which he is a member, or in the name of the attorney or firm of attorneys by whom he is employed, a special account or accounts, separate from his personal accounts or from any accounts in which assets belonging to his firm are deposited, and separate from any accounts which may be maintained in the capacity of executor, guardian, trustee or receiver, into which special account or accounts all funds entrusted to such attorney or such firm shall be deposited.

(b) *Required Bookkeeping Records.* All such attorneys and firms of attorneys shall maintain for seven years after the events which they record:

(1) the records of all deposits in and withdrawals from the accounts specified in subdivision (a) of this section and of any other bank account which concerns or affects their practice of law;

(2) a ledger book or similar record for all special accounts, showing the source of all funds deposited in such accounts, the names of all persons for whom the funds were held, the amount of such funds, the charges or withdrawals from such accounts, and the names of all persons to whom such funds were disbursed;

(3) copies of all retainer and compensation agreements with clients;

(4) copies of all statements to clients showing the disbursement of funds to them or on their behalf;

(5) copies of all bills rendered to clients;

(6) copies of all records showing payments to attorneys, investigators or other persons, not in their regular employ, for services rendered or performed; and

(7) copies of all statements of retainer and closing statements filed with the Office of Court Administration.

All such attorneys and firms of attorneys shall make accurate entries of all financial transactions in their records of receipts and disbursements, in their special accounts, in their ledger books and similar records, and in any other books of account kept by them in the regular course of their practice, which entries shall be made at or near the time of the act, condition or event recorded.

(c) Whenever any sum of money is payable to a client and the attorney is unable to locate the client, the attorney shall apply to the court in which the action was brought, or to the Supreme Court in the county in which the attorney has his office if no action was commenced, for an order directing payment to the attorney of his fee and disbursements and to the clerk of the court of the balance due to the client.

(d) *Dissolution of a firm.* Upon the dissolution of any firm of attorneys the former partners shall make appropriate arrangements for the maintenance by one of them or by a successor firm of the records specified in subdivision (b) of this section.

(e) *Availability of records.* Any of the records required to be kept by this rule shall be produced in response to a subpoena *duces tecum* issued in connection with a complaint or investigation pending before the appropriate Departmental Disciplinary Committee or grievance committee, or shall be produced at the direction of this court before any person designated by it. When so produced, all such records shall remain confidential except for the purposes of the particular proceeding and their contents shall not be disclosed by anyone in such a way as to violate the attorney-client privilege.

(f) *Disciplinary action.* Any attorney who does not maintain and keep, or cause to be maintained and kept, the accounts and records as specified and required by this section, or who does not produce any such records pursuant to this Part, shall be subject to disciplinary proceedings.

§ 806.19 Discipline of attorneys for professional misconduct in other jurisdictions.

(a) Any attorney to whom this Part shall apply, who has been disciplined in a jurisdiction other than the State of New York, may be disciplined by the court for the conduct which gave rise to the discipline imposed in the other jurisdiction.

(b) It shall be the responsibility of the attorney to file, within 30 days of the date of the disciplinary order in the other jurisdiction, a copy of said order with the court. The failure of the attorney to do so may be deemed professional misconduct.

(c) Upon the filing by the attorney or the committee of a certified or exemplified copy of the disciplinary order, the court, either directly or upon application of the committee, shall give written notice to such attorney pursuant to subdivision 6 of section 90 of the Judiciary Law, according the attorney the opportunity within 20 days of the giving of such notice to file an affidavit or affirmation setting forth any defense to discipline enumerated in subdivision (d) of this section. The notice shall further advise the attorney that in default of such filing, the court may proceed to impose discipline or take other appropriate action. Upon the filing of such affidavit or affirmation, the court may fix a time at which the attorney can be heard in mitigation or otherwise if the attorney requests such appearance in writing.

(d) The court may impose discipline upon the attorney unless an examination of the papers before it and such other evidence as the court in its discretion may receive, discloses:

(1) that the procedure in the other jurisdiction deprived the attorney of due process; or

(2) that there was such an infirmity of proof establishing the misconduct that the court cannot accept as final the finding of misconduct made in the other jurisdiction; or

(3) that the imposition of discipline would be unjust. If the attorney raises either or both of the first two defenses enumerated in this subdivision, it shall be the attorney's responsibility to file with the court a copy of the record of the proceedings in the other jurisdiction. The court may require the attorney to file a copy of said record, or portion thereof, in any case in which such evidence is deemed necessary to determine the issues presented.

PART 821

DUTIES OF COUNSEL IN CRIMINAL ACTIONS AND HABEAS CORPUS PROCEEDINGS

Section

821.1   Duties of assigned or retained counsel.

821.2   Notification of right to appeal or to apply for certificate granting leave to appeal.

821.3   Notification to defendants who appear without counsel.

§ 821.1 Duties of assigned or retained counsel.

(a) It shall be the duty of counsel assigned to or retained for the defense of a defendant in a criminal action or proceeding to represent defendant until the action or proceeding has been terminated in the trial court, and to comply with the provisions of subdivision (a) of section 821.2 hereof, after which the duties of assigned counsel shall be ended.

(b) It shall be the duty of counsel assigned to prosecute an appeal on behalf of an indigent defendant to accept said assignment and to prosecute the appeal until entry of the order of the Appellate Court terminating the appeal, and to comply with the provisions of paragraph (b) of section 821.2 hereof, after which his duties as assigned counsel shall be ended.

§ 821.2 Notification of right to appeal or to apply for a certificate granting leave to appeal.

(a) *After conviction or denial of post-conviction or habeas corpus relief.* Where there has been a conviction after trial or otherwise, or where there has been an adverse decision upon an application for a writ of habeas corpus or upon a motion made pursuant to section 440.10 or section 440.20, Criminal Procedure Law, it shall be the duty of counsel, retained or assigned, and of the public defender, immediately after the pronouncement of sentence or the service of a copy of a judgment or order disposing of an application for a writ of habeas corpus or a motion made pursuant to section 440.10 or section 440.20, Criminal Procedure Law, to advise the defendant in writing of his right to appeal or to apply for a certificate granting leave to appeal

pursuant to subdivision 4, section 460.10, Criminal Procedure Law, the time limitations involved, the manner of instituting an appeal and of obtaining a transcript of the testimony, and of the right of a person who has an absolute right to appeal or has received a certificate granting leave to appeal and is unable to pay the cost of an appeal to apply for leave to appeal as a poor person. It shall also be the duty of such counsel to ascertain whether defendant wishes to appeal or to apply for a certificate granting leave to appeal and, if so, to serve and file the necessary notice of appeal from a judgment of conviction or to apply for a certificate granting leave to appeal from the denial of a motion made pursuant to section 440.10 or section 440.20, Criminal Procedure Law, and, if granted, to file the necessary certificate and notice of appeal within the time limitations provided for in subdivision 4, section 460.10, Criminal Procedure Law.

(b) *After affirmance of conviction or of order or judgment denying post-conviction or habeas corpus relief.* Immediately after entry of an order affirming a judgment of conviction, a judgment denying an application for a writ of habeas corpus, or an order denying a motion made pursuant to section 440.10 or section 440.20, Criminal Procedure Law, it shall be the duty of counsel retained or assigned, and of the public defender, to advise defendant of his right to apply for permission to appeal and of the additional right of a person who is unable to pay the cost of a further appeal (in the event permission shall have been granted) to apply for leave to prosecute such appeal as a poor person. It shall also be the duty of such counsel to ascertain whether defendant wishes to apply for permission to appeal and, if so, to make a timely application therefor. In the case of a non-unanimous affirmance of a judgment dismissing a writ of habeas corpus, such counsel shall also advise the relator of his absolute right to appeal without permission if the dissent is on a stated question of law in his favor.

§ 821.3 Notification to defendants who appear without counsel.

(a) *After conviction or denial of post-conviction relief.* If a defendant has appeared *pro se,* the trial court shall advise a defendant of his right to appeal from a judgment of conviction, or of his right to apply for a certificate granting leave to appeal from an order denying a motion made pursuant to section 440.10 or section 440.20, Criminal Procedure Law. It shall also advise a defendant of the right of a person unable to pay the cost of an appeal to apply for leave to appeal as a poor person. If the defendant so requests, the clerk of the court shall prepare and file and serve forthwith a notice of appeal on behalf of the defendant from a judgment of conviction. If the defendant so requests in writing, within 30 days after service upon him of a copy of an order denying a motion made pursuant to section 440.10 or section 440.20, Criminal Procedure Law, and no previous application for a certificate granting leave to appeal has been made, the clerk of the court shall serve a copy of such request upon the district attorney and shall transmit the request and the original record of the proceedings sought to be reviewed to the appellate court. Upon determination of the application the original record of proceedings shall be returned to the trial court together with a certified copy of the order entered upon the application; a certified copy of the order shall also be sent to the defendant at his address shown in the application.

(b) *After affirmance on appeal.* (1) If on an appeal from a judgment of conviction after trial or otherwise, or from an order denying a motion made pursuant to section 440.10 or section 440.20, Criminal Procedure Law, a defendant has appeared *pro se* and the judgment or order be affirmed, the copy of the order of affirmance, with notice of entry, which is served on the defendant shall have annexed or appended thereto the following notice:

NOTICE AS TO FURTHER APPEAL

Pursuant to section 460.20 of the Criminal Procedure Law, defendant has the right to apply for leave to appeal to the Court of Appeals by making application to the chief judge of that court by submitting such application to the clerk of that court, or to a justice of the Appellate Division of the Supreme Court of this department, as provided in section 800.26, Rules of Practice, Appellate Division Third Department within 30 days after service of a copy of the order of affirmance with notice of entry.

Denial of the application for permission to appeal by the judge or justice first applied to is final and no new application may thereafter be made to any other judge or justice.

(2) If on an appeal from a judgment dismissing a writ of habeas corpus or from a judgment dismissing a petition in an article 78 proceeding affecting a criminal case, the relator or petitioner has appeared pro se, the copy of the order of affirmance, with notice of entry, which is served on the relator or petitioner shall have annexed or appended thereto the following notice:

NOTICE AS TO FURTHER APPEAL

If the affirmance by the Appellate Division is by a unanimous court, an appeal may be taken to the Court of Appeals only pursuant to section 5602 of the Civil Practice Law and Rules by permission of the Appellate Division or by permission of the Court of Appeals upon refusal of the Appellate Division to grant permission, or by direct application to the Court of Appeals.

An application for permission to appeal must be made within 30 days after service of a copy of the order of affirmance with notice of entry.

If there is a dissent in the Appellate Division or there is a modification of the judgment appealed from, relator or petitioner may take an appeal to the Court of Appeals as a matter of right pursuant to section 5601(a) of the Civil Practice Law and Rules by serving on the adverse party a notice of appeal within 30 days after service of a copy of the order appealed from, with notice of entry, and filing the notice of appeal in the office where the judgment or order of the original instance is entered.

PART 835

FAMILY COURT GUARDIAN PANELS

COURT RULES

§ 835.1 Departmental advisory committee.

The presiding justice shall appoint a departmental advisory committee consisting of at least one Supreme Court Justice, one Family Court judge, one law guardian panel member, one representative of a family and child welfare agency, one law school professor, one county attorney, and such additional persons as the presiding justice deems necessary to perform the functions of the advisory committee. The clerk of the Appellate Division, Third Judicial Department, shall be a member of the committee *ex officio*. The term of appointment shall be for two years. The departmental advisory committee shall oversee the operation of the law guardian program in this department and shall annually make recommendations to the presiding justice with respect to promulgation of standards and administrative procedures for improvement of the quality of law guardian representation in the department.

§ 835.2 Law guardian panels.

(a) *Initial designation to law guardian panel.*

(1) Eligibility. An attorney is eligible for designation as a member of the law guardian panel of a county of this department when the attorney:

(A) Is a member in good standing of the Bar of the State of New York;

(B) Has attended twelve hours of introductory law guardian training conducted by the Appellate Division; and

(C) Has attained experience in law guardian representation by:

(i) Substantial participation, either as counsel of record or as co-counsel with a law guardian mentor, in:

(1) A juvenile delinquency or person in need of supervision proceeding;

(2) A child abuse, child neglect, or termination of parental rights proceeding; and

(3) A custody or visitation proceeding; and

(ii) Participation as counsel or co-counsel in, or observation of, two hearings in Family Court at which testimony is taken.

(2) Application. An attorney may, at any time, apply for membership on a law guardian panel designated for a county in this department. Such an application shall be in the form prescribed by the Appellate Division, and shall be submitted to a Family Court judge of the county.

(3) Action by the Family Court Judge. The Family Court judge shall review the application, and take one of the following actions:

(A) When the judge determines that the attorney has met the eligibility requirement of paragraph (1) above, and is otherwise qualified to provide appropriate representation for children, the judge shall approve the application and forward it to the Appellate Division with the recommendation that the attorney be added to the county law guardian panel;

(B) Except as provided in (C) below, when the judge determines that the attorney has not met the eligibility requirements of paragraph (1) above, the judge shall defer action on the application, forward a copy of the application to the Appellate Division, and refer the attorney to a law guardian mentor;

(C) When the judge determines for good cause that an attorney should not be designated as a law guardian panel member, the judge shall deny the application in writing, stating the basis for the denial, regardless of whether or not the attorney has met the eligibility requirements of paragraph (1) above. The attorney may request review of such denial by the Appellate Division.

(4) Waiver of eligibility requirements. The Appellate Division may waive the eligibility requirements set forth in paragraphs (1)(B) and (C) above when:

(A) An attorney requests such waiver in writing, endorsed by a judge of Family Court; and

(B) The attorney has sufficient relevant experience in the practice of law to demonstrate clearly his ability to represent children effectively; provided, however, that an attorney added to a law guardian panel based on a waiver granted pursuant to this paragraph must attend two days of introductory training conducted by the Appellate Division within one year of designation.

(5) Law guardian mentors. When a judge of Family Court has deferred action on the application of an attorney for membership on a law guardian panel pursuant to paragraph (3)(B) above, the judge shall designate an experience law guardian as a mentor to assist the attorney in meeting the eligibility requirements of paragraph (1)(C) above, and to familiarize the attorney with the representation of children and the operation of the Law Guardian Program. With the agreement of the mentor, the attorney may act as co-counsel in a proceeding specified in paragraph (1)(C)(i) above to which the mentor has been assigned as a law guardian, provided, however, that the mentor shall be the attorney of record in the proceeding and shall be responsible for all aspects of the representation provided. When the attorney has met the eligibility requirements, he or she shall so inform the Family Court judge, who shall then take action as provided in paragraph (3) above.

(b) *Redesignation of panels.*

(1) The Appellate Division shall, on or before January first of each year, designate an annual law guardian panel for each county in the department from lists of attorneys approved with respect to their competency by the Family Court judges of

such counties upon consideration of the following factors:

(A) Rapport with clients;

(B) Case preparation;

(C) Legal knowledge;

(D) Vigor of advocacy; and

(E) Punctuality.

(2) All current members of an annual law guardian panel for a county shall be redesignated to the annual law guardian panel, provided the law guardian has complied with the appropriate training and education requirement set forth in section 835.4(b) of this Part, and provided further that the law guardian has been found qualified for redesignation upon consideration of the factors of law guardian competency in paragraph (b)(1)(A-E) above.

(3) When a Family Court judge determines that a current law guardian should not be redesignated to the annual county law guardian panel, the judge shall submit to the Appellate Division a written recommendation to that effect, setting forth the basis of the recommendation with specific reference to the factors of law guardian competency. The Appellate Division shall provide written notice of the recommendation and a copy of the written recommendation to the law guardian concerned, who may submit to the Appellate Division a written response and such additional documentation as the law guardian believes may assist the Appellate Division in considering the judge's recommendation:

(c) *Limitations on annual law guardian panel membership.* When adequate numbers of attorneys are available in a county:

(1) Only the names of attorneys who reside or maintain an office in the county should appear on the panel list for that county; and

(2) The Family Court judge or judges of the county may decline to designate additional attorneys to the panel.

(d) *Removal from annual law guardian panel.* An attorney may, at any time, apply to a Family Court judge of the county in which he or she serves on a law guardian panel to have his or her name removed from the panel list. Upon receipt of such request, the Family Court judge may make a written recommendation to the Appellate Division that the attorney's name be removed; upon receipt of such recommendation, the Appellate Division shall remove the attorney's name from the panel list, if appropriate. If the Family Court judge denies such request, such denial shall be in writing and state the reasons for the denial. The attorney may request review of such denial by the Appellate Division.

Notwithstanding the provisions of subdivision (b) above, a Family Court judge may, at any time, recommend to the Appellate Division the removal

of an attorney's name from an annual law guardian panel for good cause, including, but not limited to, misconduct or lack of diligence in performing law guardian assignments.

The Appellate Division may, on its own motion at any time, remove an attorney's name from an annual law guardian panel.

§ 835.3 Assignment of law guardians.

(a) Any attorney designated to an annual law guardian panel in a county may also be assigned as a law guardian in any other county in the third department, provided the assigning Family Court judge has obtained the prior approval of a Family Court judge of the county in which the attorney has been designated to an annual law guardian panel and of the Appellate Division.

(b) The following factors, among others, should be considered when law guardian assignments are made:

(1) the experience and qualifications of the law guardian;

(2) the nature and difficulty of the case;

(3) continuity of representation of the minor in successive proceedings; and

(4) that assignments among law guardians on a panel are made in a fair and impartial manner.

(c) No law guardian shall be assigned to represent a minor when such assignment may involve a legal or ethical conflict of interest. Law guardians serving in the following positions or employed by any of the following offices shall not be assigned to serve as a law guardian in those types of proceedings in which, by virtue of such position or employment, they have either similar or equivalent subject matter jurisdiction or responsibilities or, in the county in which they are employed, the office by which they are employed participates as a party: judge or justice of a city, town or village court; law clerk to a judge or justice; district attorney; county attorney, or municipal corporation counsel. Whenever an attorney designated to an annual law guardian panel accepts employment in any of the above positions or offices, the attorney shall inform a Family Court judge of the county in which he or she serves on an annual law guardian panel of such employment; the attorney may complete any matter previously assigned to him, provided the Family Court judge approves of the completion of such assignment and provided completion of such assignment involves no legal or ethical conflict of interest.

§ 835.4 Training and education.

(a) Law guardians shall be expected to be thoroughly familiar with: (1) provisions of the Family Court Act and relevant provisions of the Domestic Relations Law, Social Services Law, Penal Law and Criminal Procedure Law;

(2) the basic principles of child development and behavior;

(3) the existence and availability of community-based treatment resources and residential facilities; and

(4) recent case law and legislation relating to the foregoing.

(b) To be eligible for redesignation to a law guardian panel in this department pursuant to section 835.2(b) of this Part, a law guardian shall have completed within the preceding two years at least six hours of training and education for law guardians sponsored or co-sponsored by the Appellate Division, Third Department. If prior approval is obtained from the Appellate Division, Third Department, by the law guardian or the sponsoring organization, attendance at an appropriate educational and training program sponsored or co-sponsored by one or more of the following or similar organizations may be substituted: the Appellate Divisions of the First, Second or Fourth Departments; the American Bar Association; the New York State Bar Association; a Family Court; a local or regional bar association or law guardian association; a law school; or a legal aid society. This biennial continuing education and training requirement for law guardians may also be fulfilled by (1) viewing videotapes approved for such purpose by the Appellate Division, Third Department, and filing with the Appellate Division, Third Department an affidavit attesting to such a viewing or (2) attendance at six hours of training and education for newly designated law guardians as described in section 835.2(a)(1)(ii) of this Part. For good cause shown and upon the written recommendation of a Family Court judge, the Appellate Division, Third Department, may waive or defer the training and education requirement set forth herein.

§ 835.5 Compensation.

(a) Claims by law guardians for services rendered pursuant to Family Court Act § 245 shall be submitted for approval to the Family Court Judge on forms authorized by the Chief Administrator of the Courts; after approval or modification, the Family Court shall forward the claim to the Appellate Division for approval and certification to the Comptroller for payment. If a claim is received by the Appellate Division more than 90 days after the date of completion of services, the law guardian may be requested to provide an affidavit (1) stating that counsel has not previously applied for payment or been paid for the services in question, and (2) explaining the reasons for the delay in submitting the claim for payment. The Appellate Division reserves the right to disapprove any claim for compensation by a law guardian received more than 90 days after the date of completion of services.

(b) Claims for compensation by law guardians in excess of the statutory limits set by Family Court Act § 245 and Judiciary Law § 35 shall be accompanied by a sworn statement by the law guardian describing the nature of the proceeding, specifying the time and services rendered and expenses incurred, and detailing the circumstances deemed to be extraordinary justifying a fee in excess of the statutory limits. In the absence of the attorney's affidavit in support of the excess fee, compensation in excess of statutory limits shall not be allowed.

(1) The following are among the factors which may be considered in determining whether extraordinary circumstances exist justifying a fee in excess of statutory limits:

(i) Unusually complex factual or legal issues;

(ii) Novel issues of law requiring extensive legal research;

(iii) Lengthy and necessary trial or other in-court proceedings which alone raise the compensation claim above statutory limits;

(iv) Other unique or unusual circumstances which required the law guardian to spend time on a case raising the compensation claim above statutory limits.

(2) The expenditure of time alone will not ordinarily be considered an extraordinary circumstance warranting additional compensation.

(c) When a law guardian expects the reasonable expenses, allowable pursuant to Family Court Act § 245 and Judiciary Law § 35 to exceed the sum of $1,000, for investigative, expert or other services, the law guardian, before incurring such expenses, shall obtain the approval of the judge presiding in the proceeding and of the Appellate Division.

*   *   *   *

RULES OF THE FOURTH JUDICIAL DEPARTMENT APPELLATE DIVISION

(The following rules are not a complete presentation of the Fourth Department's Rules. Only those rules that are relevant to criminal or related matters are set forth. For a complete set of rules, see *NY CLS Desk Edition Civil Practice Annual* (LexisNexis).)

PART 1000

RULES OF PRACTICE

Section

§ 1000.1 Terms and sessions of court.

The presiding justice shall designate by order the terms of court, and the clerk shall provide notice of designated terms to the bar. Unless otherwise ordered by the presiding justice, the court shall convene at 10 a.m. each day during a designated term.

§ 1000.2 Appeal defined; time limitations; perfection of appeals; responding and reply briefs.

(a) *Appeal defined.* For the purposes of these rules the word appeal shall mean appeal or cross appeal, unless otherwise indicated by text or context.

(b) *Perfecting appeals generally.* Unless otherwise provided by statute, rule or order of this court or justice of this court, all appeals shall be perfected pursuant to section 1000.3 of this Part within 60 days of service on the opposing party of the notice of appeal. An appeal not perfected within the 60-day period is subject to dismissal on motion pursuant to section 1000.12(a) of this Part. An appeal or cross appeal not perfected within nine months of service of the notice of appeal is subject to dismissal without motion pursuant to section 1000.12(b) of this Part.

(c) *Perfecting appeals in which counsel has been assigned.* (1) Appeals taken pursuant to Family Court Act. An appeal taken pursuant to the Family Court Act in which this court has assigned counsel shall be perfected within 60 days of receipt of the transcript of the proceedings upon which the order or judgment appealed from is based, as provided in Family Court Act, section 121(7).

(2) Appeals taken pursuant to Criminal Procedure Law. An appeal taken pursuant to the Criminal Procedure Law in which this court has assigned counsel shall be perfected within 120 days of receipt of the transcript of the proceedings upon which the judgment appealed from is based, as provided in section 102.1(a)(3) of this Title.

(d) *Respondent's briefs.* Unless otherwise provided by order of this court or justice of this court, a respondent or respondent-appellant shall file and serve briefs within 30 days of service of the brief of the appellant or appellant-respondent. If a respondent or respondent-appellant elects not to submit a brief, that party shall notify the court in writing prior to the expiration of the 30-day period. The failure to timely submit a brief or to timely notify the court that the party does not intend to file a brief may result in the imposition of sanctions pursuant to section 1000.16(a) of this Part.

(e) *Reply briefs.* Unless otherwise provided by order of this court or justice of this court, an appellant or appellant-respondent may file and serve reply briefs within 10 days of service of the brief of respondent or respondent-appellant.

(f) *Surreply briefs.* Unless otherwise provided by order of this court, or justice of this court, a respondent-appellant may file and serve surreply briefs within 10 days of service the reply brief of appellant-respondent. The contents of a surreply brief are to be limited to issues raised by a cross appeal. In the absence of a cross appeal, surreply briefs shall not be permitted.

(g) *Appendices.* When the filing of an appendix is authorized, it shall be filed and served by a party at the same time that the party files and serves a brief.

§ 1000.3 Necessary documents; perfection of appeals; briefs.

(a) *Complete and timely filing required.* In all appeals, a complete and timely filing is required. The clerk shall reject a partial or untimely filing.

(b) *Perfecting appeals generally.* Except in appeals in which permission to proceed as a poor person has been granted, or except as otherwise provided by rule or court order, an appellant or appellant-respondent shall make a complete filing that shall consist of: a complete record, along with the original stipulation executed by all the parties or their attorneys or the original order settling the record; 10 additional copies of the record; 10 copies of the brief; proof of service of two copies of the record and brief on each opposing party to the appeal; when necessary, a demand for

exhibits (see section 1000.49(g)(3) of this Part) with proof of service thereof; the filing fee as required by CPLR 8022; and a copy of any prior order entered by this court or the trial court affecting the appeal including, but not limited to, an order that: expedites the appeal; grants permission to proceed on appeal as a poor person or on less than the required number of records and briefs; assigns counsel; grants an extension of time to perfect the appeal; grants a stay or injunctive relief; grants relief from dismissal of the appeal; or grants permission to exceed page limitations provided for by section 1000.4(f)(3) of this Part.

(c) *Appeals in which poor person relief has been granted.* (1) Criminal appeal. Unless otherwise directed by court order, in a criminal appeal in which poor person relief has been granted by this court, the appellant shall file 10 copies of a brief with proof of service of one copy on each opposing party to the appeal; a certified transcript of the trial or hearing, if any; a copy of the presentence investigation report, if relevant to the appeal; when necessary, a demand for exhibits (see section 1000.4(g)(3)) with proof of service thereof; and one copy of an appendix with proof of service of one copy on each opposing party. The appendix shall contain the description of the action pursuant to CPLR 5531; a copy of the notice of appeal along with proof of service and filing; a copy of the certificate of conviction and the judgment of the court from which the appeal is taken; a copy of the indictment, superior court information or other accusatory instrument; a copy of any motion papers, affidavits and, to the extent practicable, written and photographic exhibits that are relevant and necessary to the determination of the appeal; and the original stipulation to the record executed by all the parties or their attorneys or the original order settling the record. The appellant shall also file a copy of any prior order entered by this court or the trial court affecting the appeal including, but not limited to, an order that: expedites the appeal; grants permission to proceed on appeal as a poor person or on less than the required number of records and briefs; assigns counsel; grants an extension of time to perfect the appeal; grants a stay or injunctive relief; grants relief from dismissal of the appeal; or grants permission to exceed page limitations provided for by section 1000.4(f)(3) of this Part.

(2) Civil appeals. In a civil appeal in which poor person relief has been granted by this court, (including appeals taken pursuant to the Family Court Act, appeals in proceedings taken pursuant to article 78 of the CPLR and appeals in habeas corpus proceedings) and, unless otherwise directed by court order, the appellant or appellant-respondent shall file 10 copies of a brief with proof of service of one copy on each opposing party to the appeal and one copy of the complete record on appeal along with the original stipulation to the record executed by all parties or their

attorneys or the original order of settlement, proof of service of one copy of the record on each other party to the appeal and, when necessary, a demand for exhibits (see section 1000.4(g)(3)), with proof of service thereof. Appellant shall also file a copy of any prior order entered by this court or the trial court affecting the appeal including, but not limited to, an order that: expedites the appeal; grants permission to proceed on appeal as a poor person or on less than the required number of records; assigns counsel; grants an extension of time to perfect the appeal; grants a stay or injunctive relief; grants relief from dismissal of the appeal; or grants permission to exceed page limitations provided for by section 1000.4(f)(3) of this Part.

(d) *Alternate methods of appeal.* (1) The appendix method. In appeals perfected on the appendix method pursuant to section 100.4(d) of this Part, the appellant or appellant-respondent shall file one complete record and, in lieu of 10 copies of the record on appeal, 10 copies of the appendix and shall serve one copy of the record on appeal and two copies of the appendix on each party. In all other respects, the appellant or appellant-respondent shall comply with the requirements of section 1000.3(b) of this Part. When a respondent's appendix, reply appendix or joint appendix is submitted, 10 copies shall be filed with proof of service of two copies on each party.

(2) Statement in lieu of a complete record. In appeals perfected pursuant to CPLR 5527 and section 1000.4(c) of this Part, the appellant or appellant-respondent shall file and serve, in lieu of the complete record and copies thereof, the joint appendix and 10 copies thereof. In all other respects, the appellant or appellant-respondent shall comply with the requirements of section 1000.3(b) of this Part.

(e) *Responding and reply briefs.* A party submitting a respondent's brief, a respondent-appellant's brief, a reply brief or, when permitted, a surreply brief, shall file 10 copies of the brief with proof of service of two copies of the brief on each party. In an appeal in which permission to proceed as a poor person has been granted, only one copy of a brief need be served on each party. When an extension of time to file and serve a brief has been granted, a copy of the order granting such permission shall be filed with the brief.

(f) *Supplemental briefs in criminal appeals.* An appellant in a criminal appeal who is represented by assigned counsel may file 10 copies of a *pro se* supplemental brief, with proof of service of one copy on assigned counsel and the people, no later than 45 days after the date on which assigned counsel mails to the appellant the brief prepared, filed and served by assigned counsel. When a *pro se* supplemental brief is filed and served, the people may file and serve 10 copies of a responding brief, with proof of service of one copy on the appellant and assigned counsel, no later than 45 days after the appellant has served the *pro se* supplemental brief.

(g) *Service of papers in criminal appeals by the people.* In an appeal taken by the people, the people shall serve the defendant in any manner authorized by CPLR 2103.

(h) (1) (i) Companion filings on interactive compact disk, read-only memory (CD-ROM). The submission of records, appendices and briefs on interactive compact disk, read-only memory (CD-ROM) as companions to the required number of printed records, appendices or briefs in accordance with this section is allowed and encouraged provided that all parties have stipulated to the filing of the companion CD-ROM.

(ii) The court may, by order on motion by any party or sua sponte, require the filing of a companion CD-ROM.

(2) Technical specifications. The companion CD-ROM record, appendix or brief shall comply with the current technical specifications available from the Office of the Clerk.

(3) Content. The companion CD-ROM record, appendix or brief shall be identical in content and format (including page numbering) to the printed record, appendix or brief, except that each may also provide electronic links (hyperlinks) to the complete text of any authorities cited therein and to any other document or other material constituting a part of the record.

(4) Number. Ten disks or sets of disks shall be filed with proof of service of one disk or set of disks on each party to the appeal, together with a copy of the stipulation of the parties to the filing of the companion CD-ROM or the order of the court directing the filing of the companion CD-ROM.

(5) Filing deadline. Unless otherwise directed by order of the court, a companion CD-ROM shall be filed no later than 10 days after the printed record, appendix or brief is filed.

§ 1000.4 Content and form of records, appendices and briefs; exhibits.

(a) *The complete record on appeal.* (1) Stipulated or settled complete record. The complete record on appeal shall be stipulated or settled.

(i) The parties or their attorneys may stipulate to the correctness of the contents of the complete record (see CPLR 5532).

(ii) When the parties or their attorneys are unable to agree and stipulate to the correctness of the contents of the complete record on appeal, the contents of the record must be settled by the court from which the appeal is taken. It shall be the obligation of the appellant to make the application to settle the record.

(iii) In a criminal matter, the failure of the

parties or their attorneys to list in the stipulation to the record on appeal any transcript, exhibit or other document that constituted a part of the underlying prosecution shall not preclude the court from considering such transcript, exhibit or other document in determining the appeal.

(2) Contents of the complete record on appeal. The complete record on appeal shall include, in the following order: the notice of appeal with proof of service and filing; the order or judgment from which the appeal is taken; the decision, if any, of the court granting the order or judgment; the judgment roll, if any; the pleadings of the action or proceeding; the corrected transcript of the action or proceeding or statement in lieu of transcript, if any; all necessary and relevant motion papers; and, to the extent practicable, all necessary and relevant exhibits (see CPLR 5526). When the appeal is from a final judgment, the complete record on appeal shall also include any other reviewable order. The complete record on appeal shall also include the description of the action required by CPLR 5531 and the stipulation to the complete record or the order settling the record.

(3) Form of the complete record.

(i) The complete record on appeal shall be bound on the left side in a manner that properly secures all the pages and keeps them firmly together; however, such binding shall not be done by using metal fastener or similar hard material that protrudes or presents a bulky surface or sharp edge.

(ii) The complete record on appeal shall be reproduced by standard typographic printing or by any other duplicating process that produces a clear black image on white paper. The record shall be reproduced on opaque, unglazed white paper, measuring 8 1/2 by 11 inches. Printing shall be of no less than 11-point size.

(iii) The cover of the complete record on appeal shall be white and shall contain the title of the matter clearly identifying the parties to the appeal and the action or proceeding; the names, addresses, and telephone numbers of counsel for the parties or, when appropriate, of the parties; in a civil matter, the index number or, in a court of claims matter, claim number or motion number assigned in the court from which the appeal is taken; in a criminal matter, the indictment or information number; and the Appellate Division docket number if one has been assigned.

(iv) The complete record on appeal shall be preceded by a table of contents listing and briefly describing the papers included in the record pursuant to paragraph (2) of this subdivision. The table of contents shall list all trial or hearing exhibits, briefly describing the nature of each exhibit, indicating the page of the record where the exhibit is admitted into evidence and indicating where in the record the exhibit is reproduced.

(v) The pages of the complete record on appeal shall be consecutively paginated. The subject matter of each page of the complete record on appeal shall be stated at the top thereof, except, for papers other than testimony the subject matter may be stated at the top of the first page of the paper, together with the first and last pages thereof. When testimony is reproduced, the name of the witness, by whom the witness was called and whether the testimony is direct, cross, redirect or recross examination shall be stated at the top of each page (see CPLR 5526).

(b) *Records in consolidated appeals.* (1) Multiple appellants. When two or more parties take an appeal from a single order or judgment, the appeals may be consolidated on motion pursuant to section 1000.13(n) of the Part or on stipulation of the parties or their attorneys. A stipulation consolidating appeals shall be signed by the parties to the appeals or their attorneys, shall designate the party bearing primary responsibility for filing the record and shall be duly filed with this court.

(2) Multiple orders or judgments. When one party appeals from two or more orders or judgments in the same action, the party may move to consolidate the appeals pursuant to section 1000.13(n) of this Part.

(3) Form and content of records. When appeals have been consolidated and are perfected on the complete record, the record shall comply with subdivision (a) of this section and the papers related to each appeal shall be clearly identified in the table of contents and shall be physically separated and conspicuously identified within the record (*i.e.*, by insertion of a tab page or colored divider).

(c) *Contents of a statement in lieu of a complete record on appeal-joint appendix.* (1) Pursuant to CPLR 5527, when the questions raised by an appeal can be determined without an examination of all the pleadings and proceedings, the parties or their attorneys may stipulate to a statement showing how the question arose and were determined by the court from which the appeal is taken and setting forth only those facts alleged and proved or sought to be proved as are necessary to the determination of the appeal. The statement may also include portions of the transcript of the proceedings and other relevant material. The statement shall include a copy of the order or judgment appealed from, the notice of appeal and a statement of the issues to be determined. The stipulated statement shall be presented for approval to the court from which the appeal is taken within 20 days after the notice of appeal has been filed and served. The court from which the appeal is taken may make corrections or additions as necessary to present fully the questions raised by the appeal. The approved statement shall constitute the record on appeal and shall be bound, along with the description required by CPLR 5531 and the order approving the statement, as a joint appendix.

(2) The joint appendix on appeal shall be bound, printed and reproduced as set forth in paragraph (a)(3) of this section.

(d) *Appendices-CPLR-article 55.* (1) Complete record on appeal. When an appeal is perfected on the appendix method pursuant to CPLR article 55, the complete record on appeal shall comply with CPLR 5525 and subdivision (a) of this section. In the case of consolidated appeals, there shall also be compliance with subdivision (b) of this section.

(2) Content of appendix.

(i) The appellant's appendix shall contain those parts of the record on appeal necessary to consider the questions involved, including those parts of the record that the appellant can reasonable expect to be relied upon by the respondent (see CPLR 5528(a)(5)).

(ii) The respondent's appendix shall contain only such additional parts of the record on appeal necessary to consider the question involved (see CPLR 5528(b)).

(iii) The appellant's reply appendix shall contain only those parts of the record necessary to consider the questions on appeal that have not been included in either the appellant's appendix or the respondent's appendix.

(iv) A joint appendix may be submitted when the parties stipulate to the contents of an appendix.

(3) Form of appendix. An appendix shall be bound, printed and reproduced as set forth in paragraph (a)(3) of this section.

(e) *Appendices-criminal appeals.* (1) Content of appendix. In a criminal appeal, when permission to proceed as a poor person has been granted (see section 1000.14 of this Part), the appendix to be filed and served by the appellant shall contain, in the following order: the description of the action required by CPLR 5531; a copy of the notice of appeal with proof of service and filing; a copy of the certificate of conviction and the judgment from which the appeal is taken; a copy of the indictment, superior court information or other accusatory instrument; all motion papers, affidavits and, to the extent practicable, written and photographic exhibits relevant and necessary to the determination of the appeal; and the stipulation of the parties or their attorneys to the complete record or the order sealing the record. The appellant shall also file a copy of any prior order entered by this court or the trial court affecting the appeal including, but not limited to, an order that: expedites the appeal; grants permission to proceed on appeal as a poor person or on less than the required number of records and briefs; assigns counsel; grants an extension of time to perfect the appeal; grants a stay or injunctive relief; grants

relief from dismissal of the appeal; or grants permission to exceed page limitations provided for by paragraph (f)(3) of this section.

(2) Form of appendix. The appendix shall be bound, printed and reproduced as set forth in subdivision (a)(3).

(f) *Briefs.* (1) Binding. A brief on appeal or a proceeding shall be bound on the left side in a manner that properly secures all the pages and keeps them firmly together; however, such binding shall not be done by any metal fastener or similar hard material that protrudes or presents a bulky surface or a sharp edge.

(2) Paper; printing. The brief shall be reproduced by standard typographical printing or other duplicating process that produces a clear black image on white paper, with margins as set forth in CPLR 5529. The brief shall be reproduced on opaque, unglazed white paper, measuring 8 1/2 by 11 inches. Printing shall be of no less than 11-point size, and shall be double-spaced. A brief shall contain no footnotes.

(3) Page limits. The brief of an appellant, petitioner, respondent or respondent-appellant shall not exceed 70 pages. The reply brief of an appellant, petitioner or respondent-appellant shall not exceed 70 pages. The reply brief of an appellant, petitioner or appellant-respondent or the surreply brief of a respondent-appellant shall not exceed 35 pages. The page shall be consecutively paginated.

(4) Cover of brief; information. The cover of a brief shall contain the title to the matter; the name, address and telephone number of the person submitting the brief; in a civil matter, the index number or, in a court of claims matter, claim number or motion number assigned in the court from which the appeal is taken; in a criminal matter, the indictment or information number; the Appellate Division docket number if one has been assigned; and, in the upper right-hand corner, the name of the person requesting oral argument and the time requested for argument, or the name of the person submitting.

(5) Cover of brief; color. Except in those appeals in which permission to proceed as a poor person has been granted, the cover of a brief of an appellant or petitioner shall be blue; the cover of a brief of a respondent shall be red; the cover of a reply brief shall be gray; the cover of a surreply brief shall be yellow; and the cover of a brief of an intervenor or an amicus curiae shall be green. The cover of a supplemental brief submitted *pro se* in a criminal appeal shall be white.

(6) Contents of brief. A brief shall contain, in the following order: a table of contents; a table of citations; a concise statement, not exceeding two pages, of the questions involved in the matter, with each question numbered and followed immediately by the answer, if any, from the court from

COURT RULES

which the appeal is taken; a concise statement of the nature of the matter and of the facts necessary and relevant to the determination of the question involved, with supporting references to pages in the record, transcript or appendix, as appropriate; and the argument of the issues, divided into points by appropriate headings distinctively printed (see CPLR 5528). A brief shall contain no footnotes.

(7) New York decisions shall be cited from the official reports, if any. All other decisions shall be cited from the official reports, if any, and also from the National Reporter System if they are there reported. Decisions not reported officially or in the National Reporter System shall be cited from the most available source (CPLR 5529(e)).

(8) When an extension of time to file and serve a brief has been granted, a copy of the order granting such permission shall be filed with the brief.

(g) *Exhibits.* (1) In general. Absent a court order or stipulation of the parties, all exhibits shall be submitted to the court. The parties or their attorneys may agree and stipulate that particular exhibits are not relevant or necessary to the determination of an appeal. In such case, the appellant shall file a stipulation of the parties or their attorneys listing the exhibits neither relevant nor necessary to the appeal.

(2) Printed exhibits. To the extents that it is practicable, all relevant and necessary exhibits shall be printed in the record on appeal.

(3) Original exhibits. Absent a stipulation of the parties pursuant to paragraph (1) or (4) of this subdivision, all original exhibits shall be submitted to the court. Upon perfecting an appeal, an appellant shall file the original exhibits or, when the exhibits are in the control of a respondent or a third party, a five-day written demand for the exhibits or a subpoena duces tecum for the exhibits issued in accordance with CPLR article 23, with proof of service thereof. The failure of a respondent to comply with a five-day demand may result in sanctions pursuant to section 10001.16(a) of this Part.

(4) Criminal appeals; physical exhibits. In a criminal appeal, in lieu of submitting original physical exhibits (weapons, contraband, *e.g.*) to the court, the appellant may file a stipulation of the parties identifying the particular exhibits, identifying the party in custody and control of each exhibit and providing that each exhibit shall be made available to the court upon the request of the clerk.

(h) *Compliance.* The clerk shall reject any record, appendix or brief that does not comply with these rules, is not legible or is otherwise unsuitable.

§ 1000.5 Appeals taken pursuant to the Election Law.

(a) *Original papers.* Appeals in proceedings brought pursuant to the Election Law shall be prosecuted upon one original record that has been stipulated to by all counsel or settled by the court from which the appeal is taken, and the original exhibits.

(b) *Briefs and oral argument.* Appeals taken pursuant to the Election Law shall be accorded a preference pursuant to Election Law, section 16-116. Upon notification by the appellant that an appeal pursuant to the Election Law is to be perfected, the clerk shall expeditiously calendar the appeal and issue a schedule for the filing and service of the record and briefs. Appellant shall file 10 copies of a brief with proof of service of one copy on each opposing party to the appeal. Each respondent shall file and serve a like number of briefs.

§ 1000.6 Actions on submitted facts.

In an action submitted to this court pursuant to CPLR 3222 and, unless otherwise ordered by this court, the agreed statement of facts shall be printed or reproduced by any method authorized by court rule. A copy of the statement required by CPLR 5531 shall be prefixed to the papers constituting the submission. Appellant shall file the original submission and 10 copies thereof along with 10 briefs and proof of service of two copies of the submission and the brief on each opposing party, and shall otherwise comply with the requirements of section 1000.3(b) of this Part.

§ 1000.7 Expedited people's appeals pursuant to CPL 450.20(1-a).

(a) *Request to expedite appeal.* When the people appeal pursuant to CPL 450.20(1-a) from an order reducing a count or counts of an indictment or dismissing an indictment and directing the filing of a prosecutor's information, either party request that the appeal be conducted on an expedited basis (see also, CPL 210.20(6)(c); 450.55; Part 105 of this Title). The request to expedite the appeal may be made after the people file and serve the notice of appeal.

(b) *Order granting expedited appeal.* When a request has been made pursuant to subdivision (a) of this section, an order shall be issued establishing an expedited briefing schedule and designating a term of court for argument of the appeal, giving a preference to the appeal. The appeal shall be expeditiously determined.

(c) Absent a contrary order of this court, if the defendant was represented in the superior court by court-assigned counsel, such counsel shall continue to represent the defendant in an appeal taken pursuant to CPL 450.20(1-a) and this section (see section 105.4 of this Title).

(d) *Brief and appendix of the people.* The people shall file nine copies of a brief and appendix. The appendix shall include a copy of the indictment and the order and decision of the court from which the appeal is taken. Briefs may be typewritten or reproduced. The form of the brief and appendix shall otherwise conform with section 1000.4 of this Part. One copy of the brief and appendix shall be served on counsel for respondent.

(e) *Brief and appendix of respondent.* Respondent shall file nine copies of a brief and shall serve one copy on counsel for the people. The brief may be typewritten or reproduced and shall otherwise conform with section 1000.4 of this Part. Respondent may, if necessary, file nine copies of an appendix and serve one copy of the appendix on counsel for the people. The appendix shall conform with section 1000.4 of this Part, in the same number as respondent's brief.

(f) *Record on appeal.* The appeal shall be heard and determined on the original papers, which shall include the notice of appeal with proof of service and filing, the indictment, the motion papers and the order and decision of the court from which the appeal is taken. The people shall file the original papers with their brief and appendix.

(g) *Grand Jury minutes.* The people shall file, separately from the record, one copy of the Grand Jury minutes with their brief and appendix.

§ 1000.8 Transferred proceedings.

(a) *Original papers.* A proceeding transferred to this court shall be prosecuted upon the original papers, which shall include the notice of petition or order to show cause and petition, answer, any other transcript or document submitted to Supreme Court, the transcript of any proceedings at Supreme Court, the order of transfer and any other order of Supreme Court. When the proceeding has been transferred prior to the filing and service of an answer, a respondent shall file and serve an answer within 25 days of filing and service of the order of transfer. When a proceeding has been transferred to this court pursuant to Executive Law, section 298, the State Division of Human Rights shall file with the clerk the record of the proceedings within 45 days of the date of entry of the order of transfer.

(b) *Briefs, transcripts and oral argument.* Upon receipt of the order of transfer and other documents from the court from which the transfer has been made, the clerk shall issue a schedule for the filing and service of briefs, if any, the production of necessary transcripts and the calendaring of the proceeding.

(1) A petitioner shall file 10 copies of a brief, with proof of service of one copy on each respondent, as set forth in the forth in the scheduling order. If the brief is not timely filed and served,

and no motion to extend the time for filing and service is made, the proceeding shall be deemed dismissed, without the necessity of an order.

(2) A respondent shall file 10 copies of a brief, with proof of service of one copy on each other party, as set forth in the scheduling order.

§ 1000.9 Original proceedings.

(a) *Return date.* Unless otherwise required by statute or by order of this court or justice of this court, original special proceeding commenced in this court shall be made returnable at 10:00 a.m. on any Monday (or, if Monday is a legal holiday, the first business day of the week), regardless of whether the court is in session. The return date shall fall not less than 25 days after service of the notice of petition and petition on each respondent.

(b) *Necessary papers.* Unless otherwise directed by statute or by order of this court or justice of this court, a petitioner shall file the original notice of petition and petition and 10 copies thereof with proof of service of two copies on each respondent, and the filing fee as required by CPLR 8022. Each respondent shall file and serve a like number of copies of an answer or other lawful response.

(1) A party commencing an original proceeding by order to show cause (see section 1000.13(b) of this Part) shall, in advance, remit the filing fee as required by CPLR 8022.

(2) Proof of service of two copies of the notice of petition and petition on each respondent shall be filed not later than 15 days after the applicable statute of limitations has expired (see CPLR 306-b).

(c) *Briefs and oral argument.* Upon the filing of a notice of petition and petition with proof of service, the clerk shall issue a schedule for the filing and service of briefs, if any, and for the calendaring of the proceeding. A party shall submit 10 copies of a brief.

§ 1000.10 Calendaring of appeals and proceedings.

(a) *Scheduling order.* After the appellant has perfected the appeal, the clerk shall issue a scheduling order. The order will specify the term of court for which the matter has been scheduled and set a deadline for the service and filing of respondent's briefs and reply briefs, if any. A proceeding shall be scheduled pursuant to section 1000.8 or 1000.9 of this Part, as appropriate.

(b) *Respondent's brief; request for extension of time.* A respondent on appeal must serve and file 10 copies of a brief on the deadline set by the clerk in the scheduling order, which shall be 30 days from service on respondent of appellant's brief. In a proceeding, a party may file 10 copies of a brief as set forth by the clerk in the scheduling order. When a respondent to an appeal or a party to a proceeding is unable to comply with a deadline, a motion for an extension of time shall be filed and served prior to the expiration of the deadline (see section 1000.13(h) of this Part). When an extension of time to file and serve a brief has been granted, a copy of the order granting such permission shall be filed with the brief.

(c) *Notice of counsel's unavailability for oral argument.* A party or his or her attorney shall notify the clerk in writing within 15 days of the date that the scheduling order was mailed of unavailability for oral argument on a specific date or dates during the term.

(d) *Expedited appeals or proceedings.* A party or his or her attorney may file and serve a motion to expedite an appeal or proceeding. The motion must be made within 15 days of the date that the scheduling order was mailed. The motion must be supported by an affidavit setting forth with particularity the compelling circumstances requiring that the appeal or proceeding be scheduled at the earliest available date (see section 1000.13(m) of this Part).

(e) *Day calendar.* The clerk shall prepare calendars for each day of a court term by designating for argument or submission appeals or proceedings that have been perfected and scheduled. A notice to appear for oral argument will be mailed by the clerk to all parties or their attorneys not less than 20 days prior to the term. Counsel must appear as directed or submit on the brief.

§ 1000.11 Oral argument.

(a) *Generally.* A party or his or her attorney who is scheduled to argue before the court shall sign in with the clerk's office prior to 10:00 a.m. on the day of the scheduled argument. When oral argument is scheduled to commence at a time other than 10:00 a.m., a party or counsel shall sign in with the clerk's office prior to the time designated for the commencement of argument. Not more than one person shall be heard on behalf of a party. When a brief has not been filed on behalf of a party, no oral argument shall be permitted except as otherwise ordered by this court.

(b) *Requests for oral argument.* Requests for oral argument shall be made by indicating on the cover of the brief the amount of time requested. The amount of time allowed shall be within the discretion of the court. When no time is indicated on the cover of the brief, the appeal or proceeding shall be deemed submitted.

(c) *No argument permitted in particular cases.* Unless otherwise provided by order of this court, oral argument shall not be permitted in the following case:

(1) an appeal from a judgment of conviction in a criminal case that challenges only the legality or length of the sentence imposed;

(2) a CPLR article 78 proceeding transferred to this court in which the sole issue is whether there is substantial evidence to support the challenged determination; and

(3) any other case in which this court, in its discretion, determines that oral argument is not warranted.

(d) *Cases deemed submitted.* An appeal or proceeding in which no argument time has been requested shall be deemed submitted. When oral argument has been requested and counsel fails to appear when the case is called by the presiding justice or justice presiding, the matter shall be deemed submitted.

(e) *Disqualification or unavailability of justice.* When a justice is absent or unavailable at the time that the appeal or proceeding is argued, the matter will be heard by the four justices present and deemed submitted to any other qualified justice unless counsel objects at the time of oral argument.

(f) *No rebuttal permitted.* Rebuttal argument is not permitted and no time may be reserved by counsel for the purpose of rebuttal.

(g) *Post-argument submissions.* Except as otherwise ordered by this court, no post-argument submissions shall be accepted unless filed, with proof of service of one copy on each other party, within five business days of the argument date.

§ 1000.12 Dismissal of appeals for failure to perfect.

(a) *On motion.* A motion to dismiss for failure to perfect an appeal may be made pursuant to section 1000.13(e) of this Part when an appellant has failed to perfect an appeal within 60 days of service of the notice of appeal.

(b) *Without motion.* A civil appeal, except an appeal taken pursuant to the Family Court Act in which this court has assigned counsel, shall be deemed abandoned and dismissed without the necessity of an order or motion, when an appellant has failed to perfect an appeal within nine months of service of the notice of appeal. A motion to vacate such an abandonment and dismissal may be made pursuant to section 1000.13(g) of this Part.

§ 1000.13 Motions.

(a) *General procedures.* (1) Return date. Unless otherwise provided by statute or by order of this court or justice of this court, a motion to this court shall be returnable at 10:00 a.m. on any Monday (or, if Monday is a legal holiday, the first business day of the week), regardless of whether the court is in session. A motion shall not be adjourned except upon the written consent or stipulation of the moving party or by order of this court.

(i) A motion for permission to appeal shall be

made returnable on a Monday (or, if Monday is a legal holiday, the first business day of the week) at least eight days but not more than 15 days after the notice of motion is served (see CPLR 5516).

(2) Notice and service of papers. A notice of motion and supporting papers shall be served with sufficient notice to all parties, as set forth in the CPLR. In computing the notice period, the date upon which service is made shall not be included (see General Construction Law, section 20).

(i) When motion papers are personally served, at least eight-days notice shall be given (CPLR 2214(b)).

(ii) When motion papers are served by regular mail, at least 13-days notice shall be given (CPLR 2103(b)(2)).

(iii) When motion papers are served by overnight delivery service, at least nine-days notice shall be given (CPLR 2103(b)(6)).

(iv) When motion papers are served by electronic means, there shall be compliance with CPLR 2103(b)(5), and at least eight days notice shall be given.

(3) Cross motions. Cross motions shall be made returnable on the same date as the original motion. A cross motion shall be served either personally or by overnight delivery service at least four days before the return date.

(4) Filings of papers. (i) All papers in support of or in opposition to a motion or cross motion shall be filed in the clerk's office no later than 5:00 p.m. on the Friday preceding the return date. When Friday is a legal holiday, papers shall be filed no later than 5:00 p.m. on the Thursday preceding the return date.

(ii) Filing is accomplished by the physical delivery of the necessary papers to the clerk's office.

(iii) A submission to the clerk's office by electronic means will be accepted, provided that it otherwise complies with these rules and the original papers and one copy thereof are sent to the clerk's office on the date of the electronic transmission.

(5) Necessary papers. (i) Except as otherwise authorized by statute or rule or by order of this court or justice of this court, the papers on a motion or cross motion shall consist of a notice of motion (CPLR 2214), supporting affidavit(s), proof of service on all parties (CPLR 306), a copy of the notice of appeal or order of transfer with proof or admission of service, a copy of the order or judgment being appealed, along with the court's decision, if any, and a copy of any prior order of this court.

(ii) When an appellate docket number has been assigned to a matter by the clerk's office, a notice of motion or cross motion and any supporting affidavits shall conspicuously bear that number.

(iii) An original and one copy of all papers shall be filed.

(iv) incomplete filings are not acceptable. A failure to comply with the rules for the submission of a motion shall result in the rejection of the motion papers.

(v) In accordance with CPLR 8022, a fee of forty-five dollars must be remitted upon the filing of each motion or cross motion with respect to a civil appeal or special proceeding, except that no fee shall be imposed for a motion or cross motion seeking poor person relief pursuant to CPLR 1101 (a) and 22 NYCRR 1000.14.

(6) Oral argument. Oral argument of motions is not permitted.

(b) Orders to show cause and applications pursuant to CPLR 5704. (1) Orders to show cause. When a moving party seeks a temporary stay or other emergency interim relief pending the return and determination of a motion, the motion may be brought by an order to show cause. The order to show cause shall be directed to a justice of this court with chambers in the judicial district from which the appeal arises. The party bringing the order to show cause must give reasonable notice to all other parties of the date and time when, and the location where, the order to show cause will be presented to a justice of this court, and all counsel may be present upon the presentation of the order to show cause. When the presence of counsel for an adverse party cannot be obtained, the papers in support of the order to show cause shall include an affidavit setting forth the manner in which reasonable notice has been given and an explanation for the failure to obtain the presence of adverse counsel. Unless otherwise ordered by a justice of this court, all papers in opposition to a motion brought by an order to show cause shall be served and filed in the clerk's office no later than noon of the return date set in the order to show cause.

(i) A party commencing an original proceeding (see section 1000.9 of this Part) by an order to show cause shall remit the filing fee in advance, as required by CPLR 8022.

(2) CPLR 5704(a). An application for relief pursuant to CPLR 5704(a) shall be made using the procedures for an order to show cause set forth in paragraph (1) of this subdivision.

(c) Stays of judgments in criminal proceedings (CPL 460.50). (1) Initial application. Unless otherwise ordered by a justice of this court, an application by a defendant or the attorney for a defendant for a stay of judgment pending appeal may be made by motion on notice, as set forth in subdivision (a) of this section, or by order to show cause, as set forth in paragraph (b)(1) of this section.

(2) Extensions. When a defendant or the attorney for a defendant seeks to extend a stay of judgment pending appeal, the application shall be

made by motion on notice, as set forth in subdivision (a) of this section. The papers in support of the motion shall include an affidavit stating either that the transcript of the proceeding to be reviewed has been filed pursuant to CPL 460.70 or that the transcript has been ordered, along with an explanation for the delay in completing and filing the transcript.

(d) *Stays in appeals pursuant to the Family Court Act (Family Court Act, section 1114).* (1) Initial application. Unless otherwise ordered by a justice of this court, an application for a stay pursuant to Family Court Act, section 1114 shall be made by order to show cause, as set forth in paragraph (b)(1) of this section (see also, Family Court Act, section 1114(d)).

(2) Extensions. An application to extend a stay granted pursuant to Family Court Act, section 1114 and paragraph (1) of this subdivision shall be made by motion on notice, as set forth in subdivision (a) of this section. The papers in support of the motion shall include an affidavit demonstrating reasonable efforts to obtain the transcript of the proceeding to be reviewed and otherwise explaining the delay.

(e) *Dismissal for failure to perfect.* A motion to dismiss for failure to perfect the appeal may be made pursuant to section 1000.12(a) of this Part. An order dismissing the appeal shall be entered, unless the appellant timely serves and files an affidavit demonstrating a reasonable excuse for the delay and intent to perfect the appeal within a reasonable time. When an appellant has made the required showing, an order shall be entered dismissing the appeal unless the appellant perfects the appeal by a date certain and further providing that the appeal shall be dismissed without further order if appellant should fail to perfect on or before the date certain.

(f) *Extension of time to perfect.* In an appeal subject to dismissal pursuant to section 1000.12(b) of this Part or order of this court, a motion for an extension of time to perfect the appeal may be made on or before the date by which the appellant must perfect the appeal. In support of the motion, the appellant shall submit an affidavit demonstrating a reasonable excuse for the delay and an intent to perfect the appeal within a reasonable time.

(g) *Vacate dismissal of appeal.* When an appeal has been dismissed pursuant to section 1000.12(b) of this Part or an order of this court, a motion to vacate the dismissal may be made within one year of the date of the dismissal. In support of the motion to vacate the dismissal may be made within one year of the dismissal. In support of the motion, the appellant shall submit an affidavit demonstrating a reasonable excuse for the delay and an intent to perfect the appeal within a reasonable time and setting forth sufficient facts to demonstrate a meritorious appeal.

(h) *Extension of time to file a brief.* A motion for an extension of time to file and serve a petitioner's brief, a respondent's brief, a reply brief or, when permitted, a surreply brief or a *pro se* supplemental brief shall be supported by an affidavit demonstrating a reasonable excuse for the delay and an intent to file and serve the brief within a reasonable time. When an extension of time to file and serve a brief has been granted, a copy of the order granting such permission shall be filed with the brief.

(i) *Extension of time to take a criminal appeal.* A motion pursuant to CPL 460.30 to extend the time to take an appeal shall be made within one year of the date on which the time to take an appeal expired. An affidavit in support of the motion shall set forth facts demonstrating that the appeal was not timely taken because of the improper conduct of a public servant, the improper conduct, death or disability of the defendant's attorney or the inability of the defendant and the defendant's attorney to communicate about whether an appeal should be taken before the time to take the appeal expired.

(j) [*Reserved.*]

(k) *Briefs amicus curiae.* A person who is not party to an appeal or proceeding may make a motion to serve and file a brief *amicus curiae.* An affidavit in support of the motion shall briefly set forth the issues to be briefed and the movant's interest in the issues. The proposed brief may not duplicate arguments made by a party to the appeal or proceeding. When permission to submit a brief *amicus curiae* is granted, the person to whom it is granted shall file 10 copies of the brief with proof of service of two copies on each party. A person granted permission to appear *amicus curiae* shall not be entitled to oral argument.

(l) *Admission pro hac vice on a particular matter.* An attorney and counselor-at-law or the equivalent may move for permission to appear pro hac vice with respect to a particular matter pending before this court (see section 520.11(a)(1) of this Title). An affidavit in support of the motion shall state that the attorney and counselor-at-law is a member in good standing in all the jurisdictions in which the attorney and counselor-at-law is admitted to practice and that the attorney is associated with a member in good standing of the New York Bar, which member shall be the attorney of record in the matter. Attached to the affidavit shall be a certificate of admission in good standing from each Bar to which the attorney and counselor-at-law is admitted.

(m) *Expedite appeal.* A motion to expedite an appeal or proceeding shall be supported by an affidavit setting forth with particularity the compelling circumstances justifying an expedited appeal or proceeding.

(n) *Consolidation.* A motion to consolidate appeals shall be supported by an affidavit setting forth the appeals to be consolidated and the reasons justifying consolidation (see section 1000.4(b)(2)).

(o) *Application for leave to appeal pursuant to CPL 460.15.* An application pursuant to CPL 460.15 for a certificate granting leave to appeal to this court shall be supported by an affidavit setting forth the questions of law or fact for which review is sought and stating that no prior application has been made. The applicant shall attach to the affidavit a copy of the order and decision, if any, sought to review and a copy of all papers submitted to the court whose order is sought to be reviewed. The motion shall be submitted to the court for determination by an individual justice thereof.

(p) *Reargument and leave to appeal to Court of Appeals.* (1) Time of motion. A motion for reargument of or leave to appeal to the Court of Appeals from an order of this court shall be made within 30 days of service of the order of this court with notice of entry. The time to make the motion shall be extended five days if the order is served by mail and by one day if the order is served by overnight delivery service.

(2) Necessary papers. Papers on a motion for reargument or leave to appeal to the Court of Appeals shall include a notice of motion (CPLR 2214), supporting affidavit, proof of service on all parties (CPLR 306) and a copy of the order and memorandum or opinion, if any, of this court.

(3) Reargument. An affidavit in support of a motion for reargument shall briefly set forth the points alleged to have been overlooked or misapprehended by this court.

(4) Leave to appeal to Court of Appeals. (i) An affidavit in support of a motion for leave to appeal to the Court of Appeals shall briefly set forth the question of law sought to be reviewed by the Court of Appeals and the reasons that the questions should be reviewed by the Court of Appeals.

(ii) In a civil matter, a motion for leave to appeal to the Court of Appeals shall be determined by the panel of justices that determined the appeal.

(iii) In a criminal matter, a motion for leave to appeal to the Court of Appeals may be submitted to and shall determined by any member of the panel of justices who determined the appeal. The affidavit in support of the motion shall state that no other application for leave to appeal to the Court of Appeals has been made.

(iv) A motion for permission to appeal shall be made returnable on a Monday (or, if Monday is a legal holiday, the first business day of the week) at least eight days but not more than 15 days after the notice of motion is served (see CPLR 5516).

(q) *Withdrawal of counsel; assigned criminal appeals.* An attorney assigned to perfect a criminal appeal on behalf of an indigent defendant pursuant to section 1022.11 of this Title may move, after conferring with the defendant and trial counsel, to be relieved of the assignment upon the submission of an affidavit accompanied by a brief in which the attorney states all points that may arguably provide a basis for appeal, with references to the record and citation of legal authorities. The brief must be supplied to the defendant at least 30 days before the return date of the motion (see *People v. Crawford*, 71 AD2d 38). Together with the motion papers and briefs, counsel shall submit the papers that would constitute the record on appeal pursuant to section 1000.3(c)(1) of this Part. If the brief is mailed to the defendant, it shall be mailed to the defendant's last known address.

(r) *Other motions.* A motion seeking relief not specifically provided for herein is not precluded. Any such motion shall be submitted to the clerk's office in conformity with subdivision (a) of this section.

§ 1000.14 Poor persons.

(a) *Motion.* A motion for permission to proceed on appeal as a poor person and for assignment of counsel may be made by any party pursuant to section 1000.13(a) of this Part.

(1) Supporting papers; all appeals. An affidavit in support of a motion for permission to proceed on appeal as a poor person and for assignment of counsel shall set forth the amount and sources of the movant's income; that the movant is unable to pay the costs, fees, and expenses necessary to prosecute or respond to the appeal; and whether any other person beneficially interested in any recovery sought and, if so, whether every such person unable to pay such costs, fees and expenses (see CPLR 110(a); Judiciary Law, section 35(1); County Law, section 722).

(2) Supporting papers; civil appeals. In a civil appeal, an affidavit in support of a motion for permission to proceed on appeal as a poor person shall also set forth sufficient facts so that the merit of the contentions can be ascertained (CPLR 1101(a)).

(i) Exceptions. This subdivision has no applications to appeals described in Family Court Act, section 1120(a), SCPA 407(1) and Judiciary Law, section 35(1).

(3) Service on county attorney. A motion for permission to appeal as a poor person and assignment of counsel shall be served with sufficient notice on the county attorney in the county from which the appeal arises (see CPLR 1101(c)).

(b) *Stenographic transcripts.* Except as provided by order of this court, the clerk of the court from which the appeal is taken shall provide a party granted permission to proceed on appeal as a poor person with a stenographic copy of the minutes of the proceeding upon which the appeal

COURT RULES

is based, along with one copy of any other paper or document on file in the clerk's office that is relevant and necessary to the appeal.

(c) *Records and briefs.* A person granted permission to proceed on appeal as a poor person shall perfect the appeal by filing 10 copies of a brief with proof of service of one copy on each respondent.

(1) In a criminal appeal, a person granted permission to proceed on appeal as a poor person shall file a properly certified transcript of the trial or hearing underlying the appeal, if any, a copy of the Pre-Sentence Investigation Report, if relevant and necessary, one copy of an appendix consisting of the documents described in section 1000.4(e) of this Part with proof of service of one copy of the appendix on each respondent, and exhibits as required by section 1000.4(g) of this Part.

(2) In a civil appeal, a person granted permission to proceed on appeal as a poor person shall file one copy of the stipulated or settled record with proof of service of one copy on each party to the appeal and shall file exhibits as required by section 1000.4(g) of this Part.

(d) *Filing fee.* A person granted permission to proceed on appeal as a poor person shall not be required to pay a filing fee (CPLR 1102(d)).

(e) *Respondent.* When an appellant has been granted permission to appeal as a poor person, a respondent shall file 10 briefs with proof of service of one copy on appellant.

§ 1000.15 Lesser number of records.

(a) *Motion.* A motion for permission to perfect an appeal on less than the required number of records and briefs may be made by any party pursuant to section 1000.13(a) of this Part.

(b) *Supporting papers.* An affidavit in support of a motion to perfect an appeal on less than the required number of records and briefs shall comply with section 1000.14(a)(1) of this Part.

(c) *Relief under motion.* When a motion to perfect an appeal on less than the required number of records and briefs has been granted, an appellant shall perfect the appeal as set forth in section 1000.14(c)(2) of this Part. A respondent shall comply with section 1000.14(e) of this Part.

§ 1000.16 Sanctions; signing of papers.

(a) *Sanctions.* An attorney or party who fails to comply with a rule or order of this court or who engages in frivolous conduct as defined in section 130-1.1(c) of this Title shall be subject to such sanction as the court may, in its discretion, impose. The imposition of sanction or costs may be made upon motion or upon the court's own initiative, after a reasonable opportunity to be heard. The court may award costs or impose sanctions upon a written decision setting forth the

conduct on which the award of costs or imposition of sanction is made and the reasons for the determination that such an award or sanction is appropriate.

(b) *Signing of papers.* In a civil appeal or proceeding, except in an appeal arising from a proceeding commenced pursuant to Family Court Act, article 3, 7, 8 or 10, the original of every paper submitted for filing with the clerk of this court shall be signed in ink by an attorney or, when a party is not represented by an attorney, a party in accordance with section 130-1.1(a) of this Title.

§ 1000.17 Orders and decisions.

(a) *Entry of orders.* An order of this court determining an appeal or motion shall be entered by the clerk in the office of the clerk of this court (see CPLR 5524(a)). Unless otherwise directed by this court or justice of this court, the clerk shall draft the order.

(b) *Service of order.* The person prevailing on an appeal or motion shall serve a copy of the order with notice of entry in the office of the clerk of this court on all parties.

(c) *Service of order; criminal appeals.* Service of a copy of an order on appellant in accordance with CPL 460.10(5)(a) shall be made pursuant to CPLR 2103.

(d) *Remittitur.* Unless otherwise ordered by this court, an order determining an appeal shall be remitted, together with the record on appeal, to the clerk of the court from which the appeal is taken (see CPLR 5524(b)).

(e) *Decisions.* Unless otherwise directed by this court, the decision-orders of this court on decided appeals and proceedings shall be published in a list at 3:00 p.m. on the day falling two weeks after the last day of a term of court. A copy of the decision-order determining the appeal or proceeding shall be mailed by the clerk's office to all parties to the appeal or proceeding.

§ 1000.18 Withdrawal of motion, appeal or proceeding; settlement of appeal or proceeding or issue therein.

(a) *Motion.* A motion may be withdrawn at any time prior to its return date upon the written request of the moving party.

(b) *Appeal or proceeding.* An appeal or proceeding may be withdrawn and discontinued at any time prior to its determination only upon the filing with this court of a written stipulation of discontinuance, which must be signed by the parties or their attorneys and, in criminal appeals and appeals in which counsel has been assigned, by the appellant personally. When an appeal or proceeding is withdrawn or discontinued, the court shall be promptly notified.

(c) *Settlement of appeal or proceeding or issue therein.* The parties or their attorneys shall promptly notify the court when there is a settlement of an appeal or proceeding or any issue therein or when an appeal or proceeding or any issue therein has been rendered moot.

§ 1000.19 Electronic recording and audio-visual coverage of court proceedings.

(a) *Generally.* Except as authorized by the presiding justice upon written application, audiotaping, photographing, filming or videotaping the proceedings of this court is prohibited.

(b) *Application for permission to conduct.* Written application for permission to photograph or conduct audio or video coverage of court proceedings must be submitted to the presiding justice at least five days prior to the scheduled proceeding. The application must specify, pursuant to section 29.2 of this Title: the type of equipment that will be utilized; the number of personnel that will be employed to conduct the coverage; and the pooling arrangements that have been made with interested members of the media.

PART 1021

INDIGENT CRIMINAL APPEALS MANAGEMENT PROGRAM

Section
　1021.1　　Establishment of program; goals.

§ 1021.1 Establishment of program; goals.

(a) An Indigent Criminal Appeals Management Program is hereby established to oversee and monitor the assigned counsel program in the Fourth Judicial Department and to improve the delivery of services of assigned appellate counsel to indigent criminal defendants.

(1) It shall be the goal of the program to implement such improvements in the operation and staffs of the legal aid and public defender offices in the Fourth Department so that existing backlogs are eliminated and appeals assigned to such offices are perfected promptly.

(2) It shall be a goal of the program to implement such improvements in the operation of the assigned counsel plans in the Fourth Department so that a disposition is made on all appeals previously assigned to private attorneys participating in such plans and so that future appeals so assigned are perfected promptly.

(3) to assure that these goals are met it shall be the duty of all assigned counsel, including the public defender and legal aid offices, to perfect appeals within a deadline of 120 days after the receipt of the transcripts unless that deadline is extended for good cause shown upon application to the associate justice assigned to chair the council in the appropriate judicial district. Notwithstanding the foregoing, the associate justice assigned to chair such council may set a different deadline for any particular appeal.

(b) In order to achieve the goals specified in subdivision (a) of this section an Indigent Criminal Appeals Council is created in each of the three judicial districts comprising the Fourth Department. The presiding justice shall designate an associate justice to chair each council which shall consist of the permanent members specified by this section, in addition to such other individuals as the presiding justice deems appropriate. The permanent members shall include:

(1) the attorneys in charge of the appeals divisions of the public defender and legal aid offices of those counties in which such offices are assigned to perfect appeals or, if no such division exists, the public defender or attorney in charge of such office;

(2) the assigned counsel administrator of those counties in which criminal appeals are assigned to private counsel participating in an assigned counsel plan pursuant to County Law, section 722(3);

(3) the assistant district attorneys in charge of the appeals divisions of the district attorney's offices or if no such division exists, the district attorney; and

(4) the administrative court reporter for each judicial district.

(c) The councils shall meet three times each year during the months of March, July and November on a date to be fixed by the chairpersons thereof. The presiding justice shall furnish to each chairperson at least five days prior to each meeting an agenda of matters to be discussed. The chairperson may add such additional matters to the agenda as are deemed appropriate. The duties of the councils shall include, but not be limited to, the following:

(1) the evaluation of the efficiency of the operation of the legal aid societies and public defender offices within the counties situate within the jurisdiction of each council with respect to:

(i) the number of assigned appeals pending, and the length of time the appeals have been pending;

(ii) the number of attorneys available to perfect assigned appeals and whether such attorneys are available on a full-time basis;

(iii) the number of appeals perfected annually;

(iv) availability of alternative representation in those cases involving conflict of interests;

(v) the length of time necessary to obtain transcripts of stenographic minutes necessary to perfect assigned appeals; and

(vi) any matter of concern raised by the presiding justice, chairperson or any member of the council relating to indigent criminal appeals;

(2) the evaluation of the operation of the assigned counsel plans in each county utilizing such a plan for the assignment of appeals with respect to:

(i) the number of attorneys in each county willing to accept assignments of appeals;

(ii) individual caseloads and the length of time such cases have been pending;

(iii) the length of time necessary to obtain transcripts of the stenographic minutes necessary for the perfection of appeals; and

(iv) any matter of concern raised by the presiding justice, chairperson or member of the council relating to indigent criminal appeals;

(3) the submission to the presiding justice of recommendations for the elimination of appeals backlogs in the public defender offices or legal aid societies and the achievement of the time and calendaring goals established by these rules.

(d) Each council shall submit to the presiding justice no later than 30 days after the date of the meeting of the council, a report of the council's deliberations and recommendations.

(e) Public defender and legal aid offices assigned to perfect criminal appeals and assigned council administrators, at least two weeks before each meeting of the council, shall file a report with the council chairperson showing the status of all assigned appeals in their counties and measures they have taken with respect to delinquent appeals.

(f) The presiding justice shall take such steps as are deemed appropriate to implement the recommendations of the councils in conjunction with this court, the Chief Administrator of the Courts, the Chief Administrative Judge of a judicial district or local authorities responsible for funding the public defender offices, legal aid offices or the assigned counsel plan.

PART 1022

ATTORNEYS

(Selected Sections)

Section

*   *   *   *

* * * *

1022.36 Application for disclosure for records pursuant to Judiciary Law, § 90(10).

* * *

§ 1022.11 Duties of criminal defense counsel.

(a) Counsel assigned to or retained for the defendant in a criminal action or proceeding shall represent the defendant until the matter has been terminated in the trial court. Where there has been a conviction or an adverse decision on an application for a writ of *habeas corpus,* or on a motion under section 440.10 or 440.20 of the Criminal Procedure Law, immediately after the pronouncement of sentence or the service of a copy of the order disposing of such application or motion, counsel shall advise the defendant in writing of his right to appeal or to apply for permission to appeal, the time limitations involved, the manner of instituting an appeal or applying for permission and of obtaining a transcript of the testimony, and of the right of the person who is unable to pay the cost of an appeal to apply for leave to appeal as a poor person. Such counsel shall also ascertain whether defendant wishes to appeal or to apply for permission to appeal, and, if so, counsel shall serve the necessary notice of appeal or application for permission with proof of service on or an admission of service by the opposing party.

(b) Counsel assigned to prosecute an appeal on behalf of an indigent defendant shall prosecute the appeal until entry of the order of the appellate court determining the appeal. Immediately upon entry of an order affirming the judgment of conviction or the order denying an application for a writ of *habeas corpus* or a motion under section 440.10 or 440.20 of the Criminal Procedure Law, counsel, assigned or retained, shall advise the defendant in writing of his right to apply for permission to appeal and of the right of a person who is unable to pay the cost of a further appeal (in the event that permission is granted) to apply for leave to appeal as a poor person. Counsel shall ascertain whether defendant wishes to apply for permission to appeal, and if so, make timely application therefor. In a *habeas corpus* proceeding, where the order of the Appellate Division is appealable to the Court of Appeals pursuant to CPLR 5601, counsel shall advise the relator of his absolute right to appeal without permission.

(c) On or before the date of filing appellant's brief, assigned counsel shall mail a copy of the brief to appellant at his last known address and advise the clerk in writing of the date of mailing.

(d) When counsel who has been assigned to perfect an appeal on behalf of an indigent defendant determines, after conferring with the defendant and trial counsel, that the appeal is frivolous, counsel may move to be relieved of the assignment pursuant to section 1000.13(q) of this Title. The motion must be accompanied by a brief in which counsel states all points that may arguably provide a basis for appeal, with references to record and citation of legal authorities. A copy of the brief must be supplied to the defendant at least 30 days before the return date of motion (see, *People v. Crawford,* 71 AD2d 38). Together with the motion papers and brief, counsel shall submit the papers that would constitute the record on appeal pursuant to section 1000.3(c)(1) of this Title. If the brief is mailed to the defendant, it shall be mailed to the defendant's last known address.

§ 1022.11a Duties of counsel in Family Court and Surrogate's Court.

(a) This rule applies in proceedings commenced pursuant to Family Court Act, articles 3, 7 and 10 and article 6 part 1, and Social Services Law, sections 358-a, 384-b and 392 (see Family Court Act, section 1121).

(b) Counsel assigned to or retained by a party and the law guardian in an applicable proceeding shall represent the client until the matter is terminated by the entry of an order. Upon the entry of an order, it shall be the duty of counsel promptly to advise the parties of the right to appeal to the Appellate Division or to make a motion for permission to appeal. In the written notice, counsel shall set forth: the time limitations applicable to taking an appeal or moving for permission to appeal; the possible reasons upon which an appeal may be based; the nature and possible consequences of the appellate process; the manner of instituting an appeal or moving for permission to appeal; the procedure for obtaining a transcript of testimony, if any; and the right to apply for permission to proceed as a poor person.

(c) When a party or the law guardian determines to appeal or to move for permission to appeal. counsel or the law guardian shall serve the notice of appeal or motion for permission and shall file the notice of appeal or motion for permission with proof of service on or an admission of service by the opposing parties, including the law guardian when a law guardian has been appointed.

(d) Except when counsel has been retained to prosecute the appeal, the notice of appeal may include the statement that it is being filed and served on behalf of appellant pursuant to subdivision (c) of this section and that it shall not be deemed an appearance by counsel as counsel for appellant on the appeal.

(e) When a party has indicated a desire to appeal, counsel shall, when appropriate, move for permission to proceed as a poor person and assignment of counsel pursuant to section 1000.14 of this Title.

§ 1022.12 Compensation of attorneys assigned as defense counsel.

(a) No attorney assigned as defense counsel in a criminal case shall demand, accept, receive or agree to accept any payment, gratuity or reward, or any promise of payment, gratuity, reward, thing of value or personal advantage from the defendant or other person, except as expressly authorized by statute or by written order of a court.

(b) All vouchers submitted by attorneys, psychiatrists or physicians pursuant to section 35 of the Judiciary Law and section 722(b) of the County Law in which the compensation sought exceeds the statutory limits shall be submitted to the judge or justice before the matter was heard for approval or modification. The attorney, psychiatrist or physician shall attach thereto an affidavit describing the unusual or extraordinary circumstances which warrant the additional fee. Time itself does not necessarily constitute an extraordinary circumstance.

(c) A judge or justice approving such fee, shall certify that the circumstances are unusual or extraordinary and that therefore a fee in excess of the statutory limit has been earned and the amount thereof. Such certification shall state circumstances, other than additional time, which justify the fee recommended. In the absence of either the attorney's affidavit of the court's certification, additional compensation shall not be allowed.

* * *

§ 1022.14 Gratuities to public employees.

No attorney shall give any gift or gratuity to any employee of any court or other governmental agency with which such attorney has had or is likely to have any professional or official transaction.

* * *

§ 1022.17 Professional misconduct defined.

A violation of any rule of the Disciplinary Rules of the Code of Professional Responsibility as set forth in Part 1200 of this Title, or any other rule or announced standard of the court governing the conduct of attorneys, shall constitute professional misconduct within the meaning of Judiciary Law, section 90(2).

§ 1022.18 Effect of restitution on disciplinary proceedings.

The restitution by an attorney of client funds converted or misapplied by the attorney shall not bar the commencement or continuation of grievance or disciplinary proceedings.

§ 1022.19 Fourth Judicial Department grievance plan.

(a) *Attorney grievance committee structure.* (1) There shall be an attorney grievance committee for each judicial district in the Fourth Judicial Department. the [sic] committees shall be composed of members recommended by the presidents of the local bar associations in each district, and there shall be at least one member from each county in a judicial district.

(2) The Appellate Division shall appoint the members of the committees, including a chairperson. An appointment shall be for a term of three years. A member who has completed two consecutive three-year terms shall not be eligible for reappointment until three years after the expiration of the second term and vacancies on the committee shall be filled for the remainder of the unexpired term. Each committee shall be composed of 21 members, including three non-lawyers. All members of a committee shall reside in the respective judicial district. Twelve members of a committee constitute a quorum. Members of the committees are volunteers and are expressly authorized to participate in a State-sponsored volunteer program, pursuant to Public Officers Law, section 17(1).

(3) A member of a current or former committee member's law firm shall not be prohibited from representing a respondent in a disciplinary proceeding, or during an investigation conducted pursuant to these rules, provided that such representation is in accordance with section 1200.45 of this Title.

(b) *Duties of Attorney Grievance Committee.* The attorney grievance committee shall: (1) consider and investigate all matters presented or referred to it by complaint or otherwise, which involve allegations of misconduct by an attorney practicing in the respective district;

(2) supervise staff attorneys in the performance of their duties before the committee;

(3) appoint sub-committees to assist in investigations when necessary and appropriate;

(4) refer cases directly to the Appellate Division when the public interest requires prompt action or when the matter requires [sic] involves an attorney who has been convicted of a felony or a crime involving conduct that adversely reflects upon the attorney's honesty, trustworthiness or fitness as an attorney; and

(5) maintain and provide to the Appellate

Division statistical reports summarizing the processing and disposition of all matters before the committee.

(c) *Staff structure.* (1) There shall be a legal staff, which shall include a chief attorney and such staff attorney positions as may be provided for in the State budget. Staff attorneys shall be recommended by the committee chairpersons and appointed by the Appellate Division. Staff attorneys shall reside within the Fourth Department. The chief attorney may hire investigative and clerical staff as provided for in the State budget.

(d) *Duties and authority of legal staff.* (1) Investigation of complaints. Investigation of all complaints shall be initiated by the chief attorney and conducted by the staff attorneys. Staff attorneys are authorized to:

(i) request from the subject of a complaint that a written response be filed within 14 days; a copy of the response may be provided to the complainant;

(ii) interview witnesses and obtain any records and reports necessary to determine the validity of a complaint;

(iii) direct the subject of the complaint to appear before the chief attorney or a staff attorney for a formal interview or examination under oath;

(iv) when it appears necessary that the examination of any person is necessary for a proper determination of the validity of a complaint or that the production of relevant books and papers is necessary, the chief attorney may apply to the clerk of the Appellate Division for a judicial subpoena to compel the attendance of the person as a witness or the production of relevant books and papers; the application for the subpoena shall be supported by sufficient facts to demonstrate the relevancy of the testimony and of any books and papers specified; subpoenas shall be issued by the clerk in the name of the presiding justice and may be made returnable before the chief attorney or staff attorney at a time and place specified therein; and

(v) when it appears that a complaint involves a minor matter, such as a personality conflict between attorney and client, a fee dispute or a delay that resulted in no harm to the client, the staff attorney may refer the complaint, upon notice to the attorney and the complainant, to an appropriate committee of the local bar association.

(2) Authorized dispositions of matters not warranting institution of formal disciplinary proceedings. After an investigation of a complaint and consultation with the appropriate committee chairperson, the chief attorney or designated staff attorney may:

(i) dismiss a complaint as unfounded by letter to the complainant and subject attorney; or

(ii) refer a complaint to a mediation or monitoring program, pursuant to 22 NYCRR 1220.2; or

(iii) when it appears that the factors set forth in 22 NYCRR 1022.20(d)(3)(a) are present, make a written recommendation to the Appellate Division, on notice to the attorney who is the subject of the complaint or investigation, that the matter under investigation be stayed and that the attorney be diverted to a monitoring program approved by the Appellate Division; or

(iv) when it appears that the subject attorney has engaged in inappropriate behavior that does not constitute professional misconduct, issue a Letter of Caution to the attorney, with written notification to the complainant that such action has been taken; or

(v) recommend to the appropriate committee that a Letter of Admonition be issued to the subject attorney. A report summarizing the matter along with the recommendation shall be provided to the attorney. The attorney shall be afforded the right to appear before the committee and be heard. A Letter of Admonition shall be issued upon the approval of a majority of the committee members present. The Letter of Admonition shall state the nature of the inappropriate conduct and the basis for the determination. The issuance of a Letter of Admonition shall constitute the imposition of formal discipline. The complainant shall receive written notification that such action has been taken.

In the event that a majority of the committee members decline to approve the issuance of a Letter of Admonition, the matter may be disposed of in any manner set forth in 22 NYCRR 1022.19(d)(2)(i), (ii) or (iv).

(3) Appeals.

(i) Appeal from letter of caution. An attorney may appeal to the committee from a letter of caution by filing a letter stating objections to the letter of caution. The letter appeal shall be directed to the chairperson of the appropriate district committee, and shall be served on the chief attorney. The letter appeal shall be filed within 30 days of the date on the letter of caution. The chief attorney may file a reply within 10 days of service of the letter appeal. Oral argument of the appeal is not permitted.

(ii) Appeal from letter of admonition. An attorney may appeal to the three district committee chairpersons from a letter of admonition by filing a letter stating objections to the letter of admonition. The letter appeal shall be filed within 30 days of the date on the letter of admonition, and shall be served on the chief attorney. The chief attorney may file a reply within 10 days of service of the letter appeal. Appearances on such appeals shall be within the discretion of the committee chairpersons.

(iii) Appeal by chief attorney. The chief attorney may appeal to the three committee

COURT RULES

chairpersons from a committee determination declining to approve the issuance of a letter of admonition by filing a letter stating objections to the determination. The letter appeal shall be filed within 30 days of the date of the adverse determination, and shall be served on the subject attorney. The attorney may file a reply within 10 days of service of the letter appeal. Appearances on such appeals shall be within the discretion of the committee chairpersons.

(e) *Duties of county and local bar associations.* A county or local bar association may review, investigate and determine complaints against attorneys involving allegations of minor delay that resulted in no harm to the client, fee disputes, personality conflicts between attorney and client, and other minor matters.

(1) The bar association shall provide to the chief attorney, within 20 days of receipt of a complaint, a report, in a form prescribed by the chief attorney, a copy of the complaint and any other relevant correspondence.

(2) When a bar association retains jurisdiction over a complaint after notifying the chief attorney as required by section 1022.19(e)(i) of this Title, the association shall complete its investigation and forward the file along with a status report in a form prescribed by the chief attorney, to the chief attorney within 60 days of the date of receipt of the complaint. When the bar association has not reached a determination resolving the complaint within the 60-day period, the district committee shall assume jurisdiction of the matter. The association may make a written request to the chief attorney for an extension of the 60-day period.

(3) A complaint received by a bar association that involves a matter other than a minor delay, fee dispute or personality conflict shall be forwarded to the chief attorney as soon as possible and in no event more than 20 days after receipt.

(4) Each bar association shall file quarterly reports on attorney grievance matters in a form prescribed by the chief attorney. The report shall be filed within 15 days of the end of each quarter.

§ 1022.20 Formal disciplinary proceedings.

(a) *Authorization for commencement of proceedings.* The chief attorney may recommend to the committee that disciplinary proceedings be commenced when there is probable cause to believe that an attorney has committed professional misconduct or when an attorney has been convicted of a crime involving conduct that adversely reflects upon the attorney's honesty, trustworthiness or fitness as an attorney. The chief attorney shall present the matter to the committee along with a written recommendation, which shall be provided to the attorney who is the subject of the proceeding. The attorney shall have the right

to appear before the committee and to be heard in response to the charges. When a majority of the committee members present vote to approve the filing of charges, the chief attorney shall institute formal proceedings against the attorney.

(b) *Procedure for filing charges.* (1) To commence a proceeding in the Appellate Division, the chief attorney shall file the original notice of petition and petition and 12 copies thereof with proof of service of one copy on the respondent attorney. Unless otherwise proof of service of one copy on the respondent attorney. [*sic*] Unless otherwise directed by the Appellate Division, the proceeding shall be made returnable at 3 p.m. on the second Tuesday of the next scheduled court term. The notice of petition and petition shall be served with sufficient notice to all parties, as set forth in the CPLR, and shall be filed at least 20 days prior to the commencement of the court term when it is returnable.

(2) An attorney subject to formal disciplinary charges shall personally appear before the Appellate Division on the return date of the matter and thereafter on any adjourned date, except as provided in paragraph (c)(1) of this section.

(3) Answer. An attorney subject to formal disciplinary charges shall file in the Appellate Division the original answer and 12 copies thereof with proof of service of one copy on the chief attorney or staff counsel within 20 days from the date of service of the petition.

(c) *Procedure for filing charges.* (1) To commence a proceeding in the Appellate Division, the chief attorney shall file the original notice of petition and petition and five copies thereof with proof of service of one copy on the respondent attorney. Unless otherwise directed by the Appellate Division, the proceeding shall be made returnable at 2 p.m. on the second Tuesday of the next scheduled Court term. The notice of petition and petition shall be served in the manner set forth in Judiciary Law § 90(6), and with sufficient notice to all parties, as set forth in the CPLR, and shall be filed at least 20 days prior to the commencement of the Court term when it is returnable.

(d) (3) (a) *Disposition by Appellate Division.* When an attorney who is the subject of a disciplinary investigation or proceeding raises in defense of the charges or as a mitigating factor alcohol or substance abuse, or, upon the recommendation of chief counsel or a designated staff attorney pursuant to 22 NYCRR 1022.19 (d) (2) (iii), the Appellate Division may stay the matter under investigation or the determination of the charges and direct that the attorney complete a monitoring program sponsored by a lawyers' assistance program approved by the Appellate Division upon a finding that:

(i) the alleged misconduct occurred during a time period when the attorney suffered from alcohol or other substance abuse or dependency;

(ii) the alleged misconduct is not such that disbarment from the practice of law would be an appropriate sanction; and

(iii) diverting the attorney to a monitoring program is in the public interest.

(b) Upon submission of written proof of successful completion of the monitoring program, the Appellate Division may dismiss the disciplinary charges. In the event of an attorney's failure to successfully complete a Court ordered monitoring program, or, the commission of additional misconduct by the attorney during the pendency of the proceeding, the Appellate Division may, upon notice to the attorney and after affording the attorney an opportunity to be heard, rescind the order diverting the attorney to the monitoring program and reinstate the disciplinary charges or investigation.

(c) Any costs associated with the attorney's participation in a monitoring program pursuant to this section shall be the responsibility of the attorney.

§ 1022.21 Attorneys convicted of a crime.

(a) *Attorneys convicted of a felony.* The Appellate Division shall, upon receipt of proof that an attorney has been convicted of a felony, as that term is defined in Judiciary Law, section 90(4)(e), enter an order striking the attorney's name from the roll of attorneys.

(b) *Attorneys convicted of a serious crime.* (1) The Appellate Division shall, upon receipt of proof that an attorney has been convicted of a serious crime, as that term is defined in Judiciary Law, section 90(4)(d), enter an order suspending the attorney pending the entry of a final order of disposition. The Appellate Division may, upon the application of the attorney and for good cause shown, as provided in Judiciary Law, section 90(4)(f), vacate the suspension.

(2) The Appellate Division shall, upon entry of the judgment of conviction, direct the attorney to show cause why a final order of discipline should not be entered. When an attorney requests a hearing, the Appellate Division shall refer the matter to a referee for a hearing, report and recommendation.

(c) *Referral to a grievance committee.* When it is determined by Appellate Division that the crime of which the attorney has been convicted is not a serious crime, pursuant to Judiciary Law, section 90(4)(d), the Appellate Division may refer the matter to a district grievance committee for investigation and appropriate disciplinary action.

(d) *Effect of reversal of conviction or pardon.* When an attorney has been suspended or disbarred based upon a conviction of a serious crime or felony and the conviction is subsequently reversed on appeal, or, the attorney is pardoned by the President of the United States or a governor

of any state, the Appellate Division may vacate or modify the order of suspension or disbarment, as provided in Judiciary Law, section 90(5).

§ 1022.22 Imposition of discipline for misconduct committed in other jurisdiction.

When the Appellate Division receives notice that an attorney admitted to practice by the Fourth Department has been disciplined by another state, territory or district, it shall direct the attorney to appear and show cause why similar discipline should not be imposed for the underlying misconduct. The attorney may file, within 20 days of service of the order to show cause, an affidavit stating any defense to the imposition of discipline and raising any mitigating factors. After the attorney has been heard, or, after the appearance has been waived, and upon review of the attorney's affidavit, the order entered by the foreign jurisdiction and the record of the proceeding in that jurisdiction, the Appellate Division may discipline the attorney for the misconduct committed in the foreign jurisdiction unless it finds that the procedure in the foreign jurisdiction deprived the attorney of due process of law, that there was insufficient proof that the attorney committed the misconduct, or, that the imposition of discipline would be unjust.

§ 1022.23 Incompetency or incapacity of attorney.

(a) When the Appellate Division is presented with proof that an attorney has been judicially declared incompetent or has been committed to a mental facility, it shall enter an order immediately suspending the attorney from the practice of law. The chief attorney shall serve a copy of the order upon the attorney, a committee appointed on behalf of the attorney or upon the director of the appropriate facility, as directed by the Appellate Division.

(b) At any time during the pendency of a disciplinary proceeding or an investigation conducted pursuant to these rules, the chief attorney, or the attorney who is the subject of the proceeding or investigation, may apply to the Appellate Division for a determination that the attorney is incapacitated from practicing law by reason of mental illness or infirmity, addition [sic] to alcohol or illegal substances or any other condition that renders the attorney incapacitated from practicing law. The application shall be by notice of motion and shall be served with sufficient notice to all parties, as set forth in the CPLR. An affidavit shall be filed in support of the application, setting forth facts demonstrating that the attorney is incapacitated. The Appellate Division may appoint a medical expert to examine the attorney and render a report and may assign counsel to represent the attorney. When the Appellate Division finds that an attorney is incapacitated from practicing law, the Appellate Division shall enter an order immediately suspending the attorney from the practice of law and may stay the pending proceeding or investigation.

§ 1022.24 Appointment of attorney to protect clients of suspended, disbarred, incapacitated, or deceased attorney.

(a) *Suspension, disbarment, incapacitation or death.* When an attorney is suspended, disbarred, incapacitated from practicing law pursuant to section 1022.23 of this Part, has abandoned the practice of law, or is deceased or is otherwise unable to adequately protect the interests of clients, the Appellate Division may appoint one or more attorneys to take possession of the attorney's files, examine the files, advise the clients to secure another attorney or take any other action necessary to protect the client's interests.

(b) *Report to court.* An attorney appointed pursuant to this section shall file, within 30 days of the order of appointment or any other time period set by the Appellate Division, a status report, which shall include the name and address of each client and the disposition of each client's file.

(c) *Compensation.* The Appellate Division may fix the compensation of any attorney appointed pursuant to subdivision (a) of this section, and may direct that compensation shall be a cost of the underlying disciplinary or incapacitation proceeding.

§ 1022.25 Responsibilities of retired attorneys.

(a) An attorney shall, at least 60 days prior to retirement from the practice of law, notify by certified mail, return receipt requested, each client and the attorney for each adverse party in any pending matter involving the client, that the attorney is retiring and shall advise each client to secure another attorney. The attorney shall also, with respect to each matter in which a retainer statement has been filed pursuant to section 1022.2 of this Part notify the Office of Court Administration that the attorney is retiring.

(b) In the event that a retired attorney fails to comply with subdivision (a) of this section, the Appellate Division may appoint an attorney to take possession of the retired attorney's files, examine the files, advise the clients to secure another attorney or take any other action necessary to protect the clients' interest.

§ 1022.26 Resignation from practice of law.

(a) *Resignation of attorney during pendency of disciplinary proceeding or investigation.* The

Appellate Division shall enter an order striking from the roll of attorneys the name of an attorney who is the subject of a disciplinary proceeding or an investigation conducted pursuant to these rules upon receipt of an affidavit or affirmation in the form included in Appendix A (see section 1022.28 of this Part), with proof of service on the chief attorney, which sets forth the nature of the charges or the allegations under investigation and shows that:

(1) the resignation is voluntarily rendered without duress and with full awareness of the consequences;

(2) the resignor admits the charges or allegations of misconduct;

(3) the resignor has no defense to the charges or allegations of misconduct; and

(4) when the charges or allegations include the wilful misappropriation or misapplication of clients' funds or property, the resignor consents to the entry of an order of restitution.

(b) *Resignation of attorney for non-disciplinary reasons.* An attorney may resign from the practice of law for non-disciplinary reasons by submitting to the Appellate Division an affidavit or affirmation in the form included in Appendix A (see section 1022.28 of this Part), showing:

(1) the jurisdiction or jurisdictions where the attorney is admitted, along with the respective dates of admission;

(2) the attorney's current address and, when applicable, date that the attorney left the State of New York;

(3) that the attorney is in good standing in each jurisdiction where admitted and that the attorney is not currently the subject of a disciplinary proceeding or complaint;

(4) the specific reason for the resignation; and

(5) when the resignation is submitted by an attorney residing out-of-state who does not want to submit attorney registration fees, that the attorney does not intend to return to the State of New York to resume the practice of law.

When the Appellate Division determines that an attorney is eligible to resign for non-disciplinary reasons, it shall enter an order removing from the roll of attorneys the attorney's name and stating the non-disciplinary nature of the resignation.

§ 1022.27 Conduct of disbarred, suspended or resigned attorneys.

(a) *Prohibition against practicing law.* Attorneys disbarred, suspended or resigned from practice shall comply with Judiciary Law, sections 478, 479, 484 and 486.

(b) *Notification of clients.* When an attorney

is disbarred, suspended from the practice of law or removed from the roll of attorneys after resignation, the attorney shall promptly notify, by registered or certified mail, each client, the attorney for each party in a pending matter and, for each action where a retainer statement has been filed pursuant to former 22 NYCRR 1022.2, the Office of Court Administration. The notice shall state that the attorney is unable to act as counsel due to disbarment, suspension or removal from the roll of attorneys. A notice to a client shall advise the client to obtain new counsel. A notice to counsel for a party in a pending action or to the Office of Court Administration in connection with an action where a retainer statement has been filed pursuant to former 22 NYCRR 1022.2 shall include the name and address of the disbarred, suspended or resigned attorney's client.

(c) *Duty to withdraw from pending action or proceeding.* When a client in a pending action or proceeding fails to obtain new counsel, the disbarred, suspended or resigned attorney shall move, in the court where the action or proceeding is pending, for permission to withdraw as counsel.

(d) *Affidavit of compliance.* A disbarred, suspended or resigned attorney shall file with the Appellate Division, no later than 30 days after the date of the order of disbarment, suspension or removal from the roll of attorneys, an affidavit showing a current mailing address for the attorney and that the attorney has complied with the order and these rules. The affidavit shall be served on the chief attorney and proof of service shall be filed with the Appellate Division.

(e) *Compensation.* A disbarred, suspended or resigned attorney may not share in any fee for legal services rendered by another attorney during the period of disbarment, suspension or removal from the roll of attorneys but may be compensated on a *quantum meruit* basis for services rendered prior to the effective date of the disbarment, suspension or removal from the roll of attorneys. The amount and manner of compensation shall be determined, on motion of the disbarred, suspended or resigned attorney, by the court or agency where the action is pending, or, if the action has not been commenced, at a special term of the Supreme Court in the county where the moving attorney maintained an office. The total amount of the legal fee shall not exceed the amount that the client would have owed if no substitution of counsel had been required.

(f) *Required records.* A disbarred, suspended or resigned attorney shall keep and maintain records of the attorney's compliance with this section and with the order of disbarment, suspension or removal from the roll of attorneys.

§ 1022.28 Reinstatement.

The Appellate Division may enter an order reinstating an attorney who has been disbarred, suspended or removed from the roll of attorneys for non-disciplinary reasons, when it appears to the satisfaction of the Appellate Division that: the attorney has complied with the order of disbarment, suspension or the order removing the attorney from the roll; the attorney has complied with the rules of the court; the attorney has the requisite character and fitness to practice law; and it would be in the public interest to reinstate the attorney to the practice of law.

(a) *Disbarred attorneys.* (1) Time of application. An attorney disbarred by order of the Appellate Division for misconduct, or stricken from the roll of attorneys pursuant to Judiciary Law, section 90(4) or section 1022.26(a) of this Part, may apply for reinstatement to practice after the expiration of seven years from the entry of the order of disbarment or the order striking the attorney from the roll of attorneys. The Appellate Division may deny the application with leave to renew upon submission of proof of successful completion of the New York State Bar Examination described in section 520.8 of this Title.

(2) Procedure. An application for reinstatement shall be made by motion, which shall be served with sufficient notice to all parties as set forth in the CPLR. The motion shall be returnable at 2 p.m. on the date scheduled by the Appellate Division for disciplinary matters, or as otherwise directed by the Appellate Division. The disbarred attorney shall personally appear before the Appellate Division on the return date of the application, unless otherwise directed by the Appellate Division. The motion and all supporting papers, as set forth in 22 NYCRR 1022.28 (3), shall be filed in the Appellate Division no later than the Friday preceding the return date.

(3) Necessary papers. An applicant for reinstatement shall file an original and 12 copies of the application. Papers on an application for reinstatement following disbarment shall include: a notice of motion; a copy of the order of disbarment or the order striking the attorney from the roll of attorneys; a copy of the Per Curiam Opinion of the Appellate Division, if any; a completed questionnaire in the form included in Appendix A of this section; proof of successful completion of the Multistate Professional Responsibility Examination described in section 520.9 of this Title; and proof of service of one copy of the application on the chief attorney.

(4) Responding papers. Papers in response to an application for reinstatement must be in the form of an affidavit or affirmation and shall be filed, along with 12 copies thereof and proof of service of one copy of the disbarred attorney, no later than the Friday preceding the return date of the application.

(b) *Attorneys suspended for misconduct.* (1) Time of application. A suspended attorney may apply for reinstatement after the expiration of the period of suspension and as provided in the order of suspension. When an attorney has been suspended for a period of more than one year, the Appellate Division may deny the application with leave to renew upon submission of proof of successful completion of the New York State Bar Examination described in section 520.8 of this Title.

(2) Procedure. An attorney suspended for misconduct by order of the Appellate Division may apply for reinstatement by making a motion, as provided in paragraph (a)(2) of this section. When an attorney has been suspended for a period of more than six months, the attorney shall personally appear before the Appellate Division on the return date of the application, unless otherwise directed by the Appellate Division. An attorney suspended for a period of six months or less shall not be required to appear before the Appellate Division, unless otherwise directed by the Appellate Division.

(3) Necessary papers. An applicant for reinstatement shall file an original and 12 copies of the application. When an attorney has been suspended for a period of more than six months, papers on an application for reinstatement following suspension shall include: a notice of motion; a copy of the order of suspension; a copy of the per curiam opinion of the Appellate Division, if any; a completed questionnaire in the form included in Appendix A of this section; proof of successful completion of the Multistate Professional Responsibility Examination described in section 520.9 of this Title; and proof of service of one copy of the application on the chief attorney. When an attorney has been suspended for a period of six months or less, papers on an application for reinstatement following suspension shall include: an affidavit of the suspended attorney demonstrating compliance with the order of suspension and with section 1022.27 of this Part; a copy of the order of suspension; a copy of the per curiam opinion of the Appellate Division, if any; and proof of service of one copy of the application on the chief attorney. The Appellate Division may direct an attorney to file a completed questionnaire in the form included in Appendix A of this section.

(4) Responding papers. Responding papers may be filed as provided in paragraph (a)(4) of this section.

(c) *Attorneys suspended pursuant to section 1022.23 of this Part.* (1) Time of application. An attorney suspended pursuant to section 1022.23(a) of this Part may apply for reinstatement at such time as the attorney is declared competent. An attorney suspended pursuant to section 1022.2(b) of this Part may apply for reinstatement as provided in the order of suspension or at such time as the attorney is no longer incapacitated from practicing law.

(2) Procedure. An attorney suspended pursuant to section 1022.23(a) or (b) of this Part may apply for reinstatement by making a motion as provided in paragraph (a)(2) of this section. The attorney shall personally appear before the Appellate Division on the return date of the application, unless otherwise directed by the Appellate Division. The Appellate Division may appoint a medical expert to examine the suspended attorney or may require the suspended attorney to be examined at the attorney's expense. The Appellate Division may require the suspended attorney to submit records of medical or psychiatric care made during the period of disability.

(3) Necessary papers. An applicant for reinstatement shall file an original and 12 copies of the application. Papers on an application for reinstatement following suspension pursuant to section 1022.23 of this Part shall include a notice of motion; a copy of the order of suspension; a copy of the per curiam opinion of the Appellate Division, if any; proof, in evidentiary form, of a declaration of competency or of the attorney's capacity to practice law; proof of service of one copy of the application on the chief attorney; and, when the suspension was for a period of one year or more, a completed questionnaire in the form included in Appendix A of this section; proof of successful completion of the Multistate Professional Responsibility Examination described in section 520.9 of this Title; and proof of service of one copy of the application on the chief attorney.

(4) Responding papers. Responding papers may be filed, as provided in paragraph (a)(4) of this section.

(d) *Attorneys removed from roll of attorneys after voluntary resignation.* (1) Time of application. Attorneys removed from the roll of attorneys after voluntarily resigning from practice pursuant to section 1022.26(b) of this Part may apply for reinstatement to practice at any time upon a showing of changed circumstances. When the attorney has been removed from the roll of attorneys for a period of one year or more, the Appellate Division may require that the attorney submit proof of successful completion of the Multistate Professional Responsibility Examination described in section 520.9 of this Title or may direct that the application be denied with leave to renew upon submission of proof of successful completion of the New York State Bar Examination described in section 520.8 of this Title.

(2) Procedure. An attorney removed from the roll of attorneys pursuant to 22 NYCRR 1022.26 (b) may apply for reinstatement to practice by submitting to the Appellate Division an affidavit along with supporting documentation showing:

(i) the jurisdiction or jurisdictions where the attorney is admitted and that the attorney is in good standing in each jurisdiction where admitted and is not the subject of a pending disciplinary proceeding or complaint;

(ii) the attorney's current address and, when

applicable, date that the attorney left the State of New York;

(iii) facts demonstrating a change of circumstances subsequent to entry of the order accepting the attorney's voluntary resignation; and

(iv) payment of attorney registration fees outstanding at the time of the voluntary resignation and that accrued during the period between the entry of the order removing the attorney from the roll of attorneys and the filing of the application for reinstatement.

When the attorney has been removed from the roll of attorneys for a period of one year or more, the attorney shall personally appear before the Appellate Division at 2 p.m. on the next date scheduled for disciplinary proceedings following the filing of the application, unless otherwise directed by the Appellate Division. Attorneys removed from the roll of attorneys for a period of less than one year prior to the application for reinstatement shall not be required to appear before the Appellate Division, unless otherwise directed by the Appellate Division.

Twelve copies of the application shall be filed, along with proof of service of one copy of the application on the chief attorney, in the Appellate Division no later than the Friday preceding the next scheduled disciplinary date.

(3) Necessary papers. Unless otherwise directed by the Appellate Division pursuant to paragraph (2) of this subdivision, papers on an application for reinstatement following the entry of an order of voluntary resignation shall include the affidavit described in paragraph (2) of this subdivision; a copy of the order removing the attorney from the roll of attorneys; the per curiam opinion of the Appellate Division, if any; and proof of service of one copy of the application on the chief attorney. The Appellate Division may direct an attorney to file a completed questionnaire in the form included in Appendix A of this section.

(4) Responding papers. Responding papers may be filed as provided in paragraph (a)(4) of this section.

[Appendix omitted.]

* * * *

§ 1022.36 Application for disclosure of records pursuant to Judiciary Law, § 90(10).

(a) An application made pursuant to Judiciary Law, section 90(10), shall consist of a notice of petition and petition returnable on the opening day of a term of this court or on the first business day of any week during the term. If the requested disclosure relates to a complaint, inquiry, investigation or proceeding involving the Office of Grievance Committees for the Fourth Judicial Department, the application shall be on notice to such office as provided by CPLR 2214(b). It shall also be served upon the subject attorney, unless the application requests, and the Presiding Justice approves, dispensing with such service.

(b) The petition shall specify:

(1) the nature and scope of the inquiry or investigation for which disclosure is sought;

(2) the papers, records or documents sought to be disclosed; and

(3) other methods, if any, of obtaining the information sought, and the reasons such methods are unavailable or impractical.

(c) Upon written request of a representative of The Lawyers' Fund for Client Protection certifying that a person or persons has filed a claim or claims seeking reimbursement from The Lawyers' Fund for Client Protection for the wrongful taking of client money or property by an attorney who has been disciplined by this court, the offices of the Grievance Committees for the Fourth Judicial Department are authorized to disclose to The Lawyers' Fund for Client Protection such information as they may have on file relating thereto.

PART 1039

MISCELLANEOUS RULES

Section

1039.3 Notification of right to appeal to defendants appearing *pro se*.

§ 1039.3 Notification of right to appeal to defendants appearing *pro se*.

(a) Upon conviction or denial of a motion under section 440.10 or 440.20 of the Criminal Procedure Law, the trial court shall advise a defendant appearing *pro se* of his right to appeal or to apply for permission to appeal and of the right of a person unable to pay the cost to apply for leave to appeal as a poor person. If the defendant requests, the clerk shall forthwith prepare, file and serve a notice of appeal on behalf of the defendant.

(b) Upon affirmance of a judgment of conviction or an order denying a motion under section 440.10 or 440.20 of the Criminal Procedure Law, a defendant appearing *pro se* shall be served with a copy of the order of affirmance, with notice of entry, which has annexed or appended thereto the following notice:

NOTICE AS TO FURTHER APPEAL

Pursuant to section 460.20 of the Criminal Procedure Law, defendant has the right to apply for leave to appeal to the Court of Appeals by making application to the chief judge of that court by submitting such application to the clerk of that court, or to a justice of the Appellate Division of the Supreme Court of this department within 30 days after service of a copy of the order of affirmance with notice of entry.

Denial of the application for permission to appeal by the judge or justice first applied to is final and no new application may thereafter be made to any other judge or justice.

(c) Upon affirmance of a judgment dismissing a writ of habeas corpus or an article 78 proceeding affecting a criminal case, a relator or petitioner appearing *pro se* shall be served with a copy of the order of affirmance, with notice of entry, which has annexed or appended thereto the following notice:

NOTICE AS TO FURTHER APPEAL

If the affirmance by the Appellate Division is by an unanimous court, an appeal may be taken to the Court of Appeals only pursuant to section 5602 of the Civil Practice Law and Rules by permission of the Appellate Division or by permission of the Court of Appeals upon refusal of the Appellate Division to grant permission, or by direct application to the Court of Appeals.

An application for permission to appeal must be made within 30 days after service of a copy of the order of affirmance with notice of entry.

If there is a dissent in the Appellate Division or there is a modification of the judgment appealed from, relator or petitioner may take an appeal to the Court of Appeals as a matter of right pursuant to section 5601(a) of the Civil Practice Law and Rules by serving on the adverse party a notice of appeal within 30 days after service of a copy of the order appealed from, with notice of entry, and filing the notice of appeal in the office where the judgment or order of the original instance is entered.

* * * * *

RULES FOR ALL DEPARTMENTS

PART 1100

UNIFORM PROCEDURES FOR APPEALS FROM PRETRIAL FINDINGS OF MENTAL RETARDATION IN CAPITAL CASES

Section
- 1100.1   General.
- 1100.2   Procedure.
- 1100.3   Representation by court-assigned counsel in the Appellate Division.

§ 1100.1 General.

This Part shall govern the procedure for an expedited appeal by the People to the Appellate Division, pursuant to Criminal Procedure Law 400.27(12)(f) and 450.20(10), of an order by a superior court finding a defendant charged with Murder in the First Degree to be mentally retarded.

§ 1100.2 Procedure.

(a) Upon filing the notice of appeal, the People shall give notice to the Appellate Division that an appeal is pending pursuant to Criminal Procedure Law 400.27(12)(f) and request that an expedited briefing schedule be set.

(b) The Appellate Division shall establish an expedited briefing schedule for the appeal. Briefs may be typewritten or reproduced. Both the People and the defendant shall file nine copies of a brief, and one copy of the brief shall be served on opposing counsel.

(c) The appeal may be taken on one original record, which shall include copies of the indictment, the motion papers, the minutes of, and all exhibits in, the hearing on mental retardation held in the superior court, the court's decision and order, and the notice of appeal.

(d) The Appellate Division shall give preference to the hearing of an appeal perfected pursuant to this Part and shall determine the appeal as expeditiously as possible.

§ 1100.3 Representation by Court-Assigned Counsel in the Appellate Division.

In any appeal by the People from an order pursuant to this Part, the Appellate Division shall assign counsel to represent a defendant who is represented in the superior court by court-assigned counsel, and may direct that the court-assigned counsel in the superior court represent the defendant on appeal.

PART 1210

STATEMENT OF CLIENT'S RIGHTS

Section
- 1210.1   Posting.

§ 1210.1 Posting.

Every attorney with an office located in the State of New York shall insure that there is posted in that office, in a manner visible to clients of the attorney, a statement of client's rights in the form set forth below. Attorneys in offices that provide legal service without a fee may delete from the statement those provisions dealing with fees. The statement shall contain the following:

STATEMENT OF CLIENT'S RIGHTS

1. You are entitled to be treated with courtesy and consideration at all times by your lawyer and the other lawyers and personnel in your lawyer's office.

2. You are entitled to an attorney capable of handling your legal matter competently and diligently, in accordance with the highest standards of the profession. If you are not satisfied with how your matter is being handled, you have the right to withdraw from the attorney-client relationship at any time (court approval may be required in some matters and your attorney may have a claim against you for the value of services rendered to you up to the point of discharge).

3. You are entitled to your lawyer's independent professional judgment and undivided loyalty uncompromised by conflicts of interest.

4. You are entitled to be charged a reasonable fee and to have your lawyer explain at the outset how the fee will be computed and the manner and frequency of billing. You are entitled to request and receive a written itemized bill from your attorney at reasonable intervals. You may refuse to enter into any fee arrangement that you find unsatisfactory. In the event of a fee dispute, you may have the right to seek arbitration; your attorney will provide you with the necessary information regarding arbitration in the event of a fee dispute, or upon your request.

5. You are entitled to have your questions and concerns addressed in a prompt manner and to have your telephone calls returned promptly.

6. You are entitled to be kept informed as to the status of your matter and to request and receive copies of papers. You are entitled to sufficient information to allow you to participate meaningfully in the development of your matter.

7. You are entitled to have your legitimate objectives respected by your attorney, including whether or not to settle your matter (court approval of a settlement is required in some matters).

8. You have the right to privacy in your dealings with your lawyer and to have your secrets and confidences preserved to the extent permitted by law.

9. You are entitled to have your attorney conduct himself or herself ethically in accordance with the Code of Professional Responsibility.

10. You may not be refused representation on the basis of race, creed, color, religion, sex, sexual orientation, age, national origin or disability.

PART 4

SENTENCING GUIDES

SENTENCING GUIDES
by Barry Kamins, Esq. *

TABLE OF CONTENTS

---

* Barry Kamins, a partner in Flamhaft, Levy, Kamins, Hirsch & Rendeiro, is the author of *New York Search and Seizure* (LexisNexis Matthew Bender).

I. INTRODUCTION TO USE OF THE SENTENCING GUIDES

The following guides are designed to assist the practitioner in understanding the sentencing statutes contained in the Penal Law and Criminal Procedure Law. These guides include classifications of felonies, misdemeanors, and violations as designated under the New York Penal Law. The terms of imprisonment for these crimes are enumerated, as are specified crimes for youthful and juvenile offenders. *

To use the Sentencing Guides, certain terminology should be defined:

(1) Indeterminate Sentence of Imprisonment (§ 70.00(1)). An indeterminate sentence is imposed by the court for a felony. A minimum and a maximum period are fixed in the sentence, the maximum being the completion of the term. The minimum period may not be less than one year and the maximum period may not be less than three years.

(2) Definite Sentence of Imprisonment (§ 70.15). A definite sentence is a term of imprisonment for a specific time not to exceed one year. Typically, such a sentence is imposed for misdemeanors and lesser crimes.

(3) Sentence of Intermittent Imprisonment (§ 85.00). A sentence of intermittent imprisonment is a revocable sentence of imprisonment to be served on days or during certain periods of days, or both, specified by the court as part of the sentence. The duration of the sentence of intermittent imprisonment may be for any term that could be imposed as a definite sentence of imprisonment. The sentence of intermittent imprisonment may be used when: (1) the court is imposing sentence on a person other than a second or persistent felony offender, for a Class D or E felony or for any offense that is not a felony; (2) the court is not imposing any other sentence of imprisonment on the defendant at the same time; and (3) the defendant is not under any other sentence of imprisonment with a term in excess of 15 days imposed by any other court.

(4) Determinate Sentence (§ 70.06(6)). A determinate sentence is a fixed period of years and fractions thereof, which must be imposed on: (1) first time violent felony offenders; (2) second violent felony offenders and (3) those individuals who are convicted of a violent felony and who also have a previous non-violent felony conviction.

---

* For a chart outlining the New York court structure, see Part 5 *infra*.

II. SENTENCING GUIDE FOR FELONIES

Classification of Crime	Section	Term of Imprisonment

NOTE: *Class A-I, A-II, B and C (violent) felonies carry mandatory determinate sentences (no definite or intermittent permitted). Certain Class C nonviolent felonies (§ 60.05(4)) carry mandatory imprisonment which must be indeterminate sentences (no definite or intermittent) but Class C drug felonies also permit definite sentences (§ 70.00(4)). All Class D felonies have permissible definite or intermittent terms of up to 1 year (see § 70.02-2b). All Class E felonies have permissible definite or intermittent terms of up to 1 year (§§ 70.00-4, 85.00-2(a), 3). Where a definite sentence is permitted, a sentence from one day to six months incarceration plus probation (a "split" sentence) is permitted. (Penal Law §§ 60.01-2(d), 60.05(4), 70.00.) Where an intermittent sentence is permitted, a period of up to four months incarceration plus probation (a "split" sentence) is permitted. (Penal Law § 60.01-2(d).) Where imprisonment is not mandatory, a period of probation not to exceed five years may be imposed as well as the following sentences: probation plus a fine; an unconditional discharge; a conditional discharge of three years; a conditional discharge plus a fine. (Penal Law §§ 60.01-2(c); 65.00-1(a), 3(a); 65.20-1.)*

NOTE: *Effective February 1, 2001, probation periods for a felony sexual assault (Penal Law Article 130, § 263 offense or incest) will be 10 years. The period for a misdemeanor sexual assault will be 6 years. (Penal Law § 65.00(3); see Sexual Assault Reform Act, Chap. 1, Laws 2000.)*

NOTE: *Effective November 1, 2000, a court may enhance a sentence by 3 to 5 years when a defendant is convicted of a "specified offense" against a driver of a "for-hire" vehicle (§ 60.07, Penal Law).*

NOTE: *Effective January 13, 2005, sentences for drug offenses have changed pursuant to Penal Law §§ 70.70 and 70.71 (see chart).*

CLASS A	Section	Minimum	Maximum
I (Murder-1)	§ 70.00(3)(a)(i) § 125.27	A defendant can receive a death sentence, life imprisonment without parole or a minimum of 20 to 25 years and a maximum of life imprisonment.	
I (Excluding Murder-1)	§ 70.00-1	Not Less than 15 yrs. Not More than 25 yrs. § 70.00-3(a)(i)	LIFE § 70.00-2(a)
Arson- 1	§ 150.20		
Kidnapping- 1	§ 135.25		
Conspiracy- 1	§ 105.17		
Sale Drugs-1	§ 220.43		

NOTE: *When a defendant is convicted of Murder in the Second Degree and the victim is killed during the course of certain enumerated sex crimes, the victim is less than fourteen years of age and the defendant is over eighteen, the defendant must be sentenced to life imprisonment without the possibility of parole. PL §§ 125.25(5); 60.06; 70.00(5)(3); 70.00(3)(a)(i).*

NOTE: *For A-II drug felonies lifetime probation is permitted where defendant gives material assistance. §§ 60.05(3); 65.00.*

Classification of Crime	Section	Term of Imprisonment
CLASS B	§ 70.00	
Violent Felony	§ 70.02-1(a)	Determinate Sentence between 5–25 years (for crimes committed after 9/1/98; prior crimes require an indeterminate sentence) § 70.02(3)

(1)	Attempt to Commit A-I Felony, Murder-2	§ 125.25

NOTE: *In domestic violence cases, can be an indeterminate sentence. Maximum sentence must be 6–25 years and minimum must be ½ maximum. § 60.12.*

(2)	Kidnapping-2	§ 135.20	Determinate Sentence
(3)	Manslaughter-1	§ 125.20	between 5–25 years
(4)	Rape-1	§ 130.35	§ 70.02(3)
(5)	Criminal Sexual Act-1 (formerly Sodomy-1)	§ 130.50	
(6)	Aggravated Sexual Abuse-1	§ 130.70	
(7)	Kidnapping-2	§ 135.20	
(8)	Burglary-1	§ 140.30	
(9)	Arson-2	§ 150.15	
(10)	Possession of Weapon- 1	§ 265.04	
(11)	Robbery-1	§ 160.15	
(12)	Firearm Use-1	§ 265.09	
(13)	Aggravated Assault on Peace Officer	§ 120.11	
(14)	Intimidating a Victim or Witness-1	§ 215.17	
(15)	Course of sexual conduct against a child in the first degree	§ 130.75	
(16)	Gang assault in the first degree	§ 120.07	
(17)	Assault in the first degree	§ 120.10	

Nonviolent Felony	§ 55.05-1	Minimum	Maximum
All other Class B felonies not enumerated above.		Not Less than 1 year (Minimum time cannot exceed ⅓ of the maximum term.) See § 70.00-2, 3(b)	Not Less than 3 yrs. Not More than 25 yrs. § 70.00-2, 2(b)

NOTE: *When a Class B second felony drug offender gives material assistance, lifetime probation is permitted. When a Class B felony drug offender gives material assistance, probation for 25 years is permitted.*

An individual who is convicted of Criminal Use of a Firearm in the First Degree, for using a weapon during the commission of a Class B violent felony for which the defendant is also convicted, must be sentenced to an additional consecutive sentence of 5 years which is added to the minimum term of the indeterminate sentence imposed on the underlying Class B violent felony, unless the court finds it would be "unduly harsh" to do so.

NOTE: *An enhanced sentence is required for a "hate crime". PL § 485.05.*

Classification of Crime	Section	Term of Imprisonment	
CLASS C			
Violent Felony	§ 70.02-1(b)	Determinate Sentence between 3½–15 years (for crimes committed after 9/1/98; prior crimes require an indeterminate sentence) § 70.02(3)	
(1) Any attempt to commit Class B Violent Felony	§ 70.02-1(b)		
(2) Burglary-2	§ 140.25		
(3) Robbery-2	§ 160.10		
(4) Weapon Possession-2	§ 265.03		
(5) Firearm Use-2	§ 265.08		
(6) Aggravated Sexual Abuse-2	§ 130.67		
(7) Crim. Firearm Sale-1	§ 265.13		
(8) Gang assault in the second degree	§ 120.06		
(9) Assault on a peace officer, police officer, fireman or emergency medical service professional	§ 120.08		

Nonviolent Felony § 55.05-1			
Nonviolent Felony *(NOTE: See § 60.05 for various classifications)*	§ 55.05-1	**Minimum**	**Maximum**
		Must impose minimum at ½ the maximum sentence See § 70.02(a), 4	Not less than 4½ yrs. Not more than 15 yrs. § 70.02-2(a), 3(b)
		Not Less than 1 year Not More than 5 yrs. (Minimum time cannot exceed ⅓ of the maximum term.) See § 70.00-2, 3(b), 4	Not Less than 3 yrs. Not Less than 15 yrs. § 70.00-1, 2(c)

NOTE: *In domestic violence cases, can be an indeterminate sentence. Maximum must be 4½–15 years and minimum must be ½ maximum. § 60.12.*

NOTE: *Definite sentence is permitted in Class C drug conviction; thus split sentence is also permitted. §§ 60.01-2(d); 60.05-4; 70.00.*

NOTE: *Enhanced sentence if victim is operator of a "for hire" vehicle. PL § 60.07.*

Classification of Crime	Section	Term of Imprisonment
CLASS D		
Violent Felony	§ 70.02-1(c)	Determinate Sentence between 2–7
(1) Assault-2	§ 120.05	years (for crimes committed after 9/1/98;
(2) Sexual Abuse- 1	§ 130.65	prior crimes require an indeterminate
(3) Crim. Weapon Possession-3	§ 265.02-4, 5	sentence § 70.02(3)
(4) Crim. Firearm Sale-2	§ 265.12	
(5) Crim. Firearm Sale—Aid of Minor	§ 265.14	Determinate Sentence between 2–7 years (for crimes committed after 9/1/98; prior crimes require an indeterminate sentence) § 70.02(3)
(6) Crim. Firearm Sale to Minor	§ 265.16	
(7) Attempt to Commit Any Class C Violent Felony	§ 70.02-1(c)	
(8) Intimidating Witness/Victim-2	§ 215.16	
(9) Course of sexual conduct against a child in the second degree	§ 130.80	
(10) Aggravated sexual abuse in the third degree	§ 130.66	

NOTE: *In domestic violence cases, can be an indeterminate sentence. Maximum must be 3–7 years and minimum must be ½ maximum. § 60.12.*

NOTE: *The following D violent felonies carry mandatory jail sentences but can be satisfied in several ways:*

Assault-2 and Att. Assault-1: definite sentence available as well as an intermittent sentence of up to four months plus probation or a definite jail sentence of up to 6 months plus probation. §§ 70.00-4; 70.02(2)(b), (c); 85.00-2(a), 3.

Criminal Sale Weapon-2 and Criminal Possession Weapon-3: either an indeterminate sentence or a one year definite sentence unless the following situations in which probation is permissible:

(1) defendant has no previous conviction for a felony or Class A misdemeanor within preceding 5 years and jail sentence would be "unduly harsh";

(2) defendant has prior conviction within preceding five years, but court finds "mitigating circumstances."

Nonviolent Felony	§ 55.05-1	**Minimum**	**Maximum**
		Not Less than 1 year	Not less than 3 yrs.
		Not More than 2⅓ yrs.	Not More than 7 yrs.
		(Minimum time cannot exceed ⅓ maximum term) § 70.00-3	§ 70.00-2

NOTE: *(See § 60.05-5). Class D nonviolent felonies carry the same range of sentences as Class D violent felonies, i.e., definite and intermittent sentences are permitted.*

Classification of Crime	Section	Term of Imprisonment

CLASS E

Violent Felony	§ 70.02-1(d)	Determinate Sentence between 1½ to 4 years (for crimes committed after 9/1/98; prior crimes require an indeterminate sentence) § 70.02(3)

NOTE: *A lesser term may be imposed for a definite period. (See §§ 70.00-4, 85.00-2(a), 3).*
NOTE: *In domestic violence cases, can be an indeterminate sentence. Maximum must be 3–4 years and minimum must be ½ maximum, § 60.12.*

		Minimum	Maximum
Nonviolent Felony	§ 55.05-1	Not Less than	Not Less than
		1 year	3 yrs.
		(Minimum time may	Not More than
		not exceed ⅓ maximum	4 yrs.
		term)	§ 70.00-2(e)
		See § 70.00-3(b), 4	

NOTE: *Class E violent and nonviolent offenses carry definite and intermittent sentences.*

A. JAIL SENTENCES FOR FELONY DRUG OFFENSES (P.L. 70.70) (P.L. 70.71)

Effective January 13, 2005, for crimes committed on or after that date.

The following are determinate sentences:

Class A-I Felony

First Offender:	8–20 years
Prior Non-violent Felony:	12–24 years
Prior Violent Felony:	15–30 years

Class A-II Felony

First Offender:	3–10 years
Prior Non-violent Felony:	6–14 years
Prior Violent Felony:	8–17 years

Class B Felony

First Offender:	1–9 years (2–9 years if near a school)
Prior Non-violent Felony:	3½–12 years
Prior Violent Felony:	6–15 years

Class C Felony

First Offender:	1–5½ years
Prior Non-violent Felony:	2–8 years
Prior Violent Felony:	3½–9 years

Class D Felony

First Offender:	1–2½ years
Prior Non-violent Felony:	1½–4 years
Prior Violent Felony:	2½–4½ years

Class E Felony

First Offender:	1–1½ years
Prior Non-violent Felony:	1½–2 years
Prior Violent Felony:	2–2½ years

Post-Release Supervision Periods

Class A-I and Class A-II Offender:	5 years
Class B or C First Offender:	1–2 years
Class D or E First Offender:	1 year
Class B or C Second Offender:	1½–3 years
Class D or E Second Offender:	1–2 years
Class B or C Violent Felony Offender:	2½–5 years
Class D or E Violent Felony Offender:	1½–3 years

NOTE: *1) The weight thresholds for Class A-I and A-II possession crimes have been doubled from 4 ounces to 8 ounces for class A-I felonies and from 2 ounces to 4 ounces for class A-II felonies.*
2) Class A-I felony offenders serving sentences of 15–25 years to life can apply for a resentencing consistent with the new sentencing structure for A-I felonies. An inmate can appeal either a denial of a resentencing application or a grant of resentencing with which the inmate does not agree.
*3) Class A-II felony offenders can also apply for a resentencing consistent with the new sentencing structure of A-II felonies. The resentencing provision applies to those inmates who are more than three years from a parole eligibility date (and 12 months from work release eligibility) and who are **eligible** for merit time.*

Classification of Crime	Section	Term of Imprisonment

B. SECOND FELONY OFFENDER (Where second felony is not a violent felony offense and first felony is either a non-violent or violent felony)

		Minimum	Maximum
Class B			
(Nonviolent)	§ 70.06	Minimum time may not exceed ½ maximum § 70.06-4(b)	Not Less than 9 yrs. Not More than 25 yrs. § 70.06-3(b)
Class C			
(Nonviolent)	§ 70.06	Minimum time may not exceed ½ the maximum § 70.06-4(b)	Not Less than 6 yrs. Not More than 15 yrs. § 70.06-3(c)
Class D			
(Nonviolent)	§ 70.06	Minimum time may not exceed ½ the maximum § 70.06-4(b)	Not Less than 4 yrs. Not More than 7 yrs. § 70.06-3(d)
Class E			
(Nonviolent)	§ 70.06	Minimum time may not exceed ½ the maximum § 70.06-4(b)	Not Less than 3 yrs. Not More than 4 yrs. § 70.06-3(e)

NOTE: *Certain Second Felony Offenders are eligible for a sentence of "parole supervision." See PL § 410.91 (eff. 10/1/95.)*

NOTE: *For a Class B "hate" crime, the maximum term of the indeterminate sentence must be at least 10 years. In addition, for the Class C felony of Manslaughter in the Second Degree where the victim was operating a "for hire" vehicle, the sentence is enhanced. § 60.07(1), (2)*

NOTE: *See chart for drug offense sentences.*

Classification of Crime	Section	Term of Imprisonment

SECOND FELONY OFFENDER (Where second felony is a violent offense but first felony is not a violent offense)

		Determinate Sentence Between
Class B VFO	§ 70.06(6)	8–25 yrs.
Class C VFO	§ 70.06(6)	5–15 yrs.
Class D VFO	§ 70.06(6)	3–7 yrs.
Class E VFO	§ 70.06(6)	2–4 yrs.

NOTE: *Sentence can be in fractions of years.*

NOTE: *See chart for drug offense sentences.*

C. SECOND VIOLENT FELONY OFFENDER

		Determinate Sentence Between
Class B (Violent) *(Listed § 70.02-1(a))*	§ 70.04(3)	10–25 yrs.
Class C (Violent) *(Listed § 70.02-1(b))*	§ 70.04(3)	7–15 yrs.
Class D (Violent) *(Listed § 70.02-1(c))*	§ 70.04(3)	5–7 yrs.
Class E (Violent)	§ 70.04(3)	3–4 yrs.

NOTE: *Sentence must be in whole or half years. PL § 70.04(2)*

NOTE: *There are enhanced sentences for Class B violent "hate crimes" and Class B or C violent felonies where the victim was operating a "for hire" vehicle. § 60.07(1)*

NOTE: *See chart for drug offense sentences.*

D. PERSISTENT FELONY OFFENDER (3 or more felony convictions).

NOTE: *Where defendant's conviction is a third felony conviction, the court <u>may</u> impose an indeterminate sentence authorized for a Class A-I felony (15–25 years to life). If the court does not impose an A-I sentence, then the court must sentence the defendant as a second felony offender.*

NOTE: *For a Class C felony of manslaughter in the second degree, there are enhanced sentences when the victim of the crime was operating a "for hire" vehicle. § 60.07(1)*

Classification of Crime	Section	Term of Imprisonment

E. PERSISTENT VIOLENT FELONY OFFENDER

NOTE: *Where defendant's conviction is a third <u>violent</u> felony offense (as defined in PL § 70.02), the court <u>must</u> sentence the defendant as follows*

		Minimum	Maximum
Class B			
(Violent)	§ 70.08	Not Less than	LIFE
(Listed § 70.02-1(a))		20 yrs.	§ 70.08-2
		Not More than	
		25 yrs.	
		§ 70.08-3(a)	
Class C			
(Violent)	§ 70.08	Not Less than	LIFE
(Listed § 70.02-1(b))		16 yrs.	§ 70.08-2
		Not More than	
		25 yrs.	
		§ 70.08-3(b)	
Class D			
(Violent)	§ 70.08	Not Less than	LIFE
(Listed § 70.02-1(c))		12 yrs.	§ 70.08-2
		Not More than	
		25 yrs.	
		§ 70.08-3(c)	
Class E			
(Violent)	§ 70.08	No Classification	LIFE
			§ 70.08-2

NOTE: *For a Class B or C violent felony there are enhanced sentences when the victim of the crime was operating a "for hire" vehicle. § 60.07(1)*

F. SECOND CHILD SEXUAL ASSAULT FELONY OFFENDER (eff. 2/1/00) (Where a person stands convicted of a felony sex offense (Penal Law—Articles 130, § 263, or § 255.25) involving a victim under the age of 15 and within the preceding 15 years (exclusive of time in jail) was previously convicted of a felony sex offense involving a victim under the age of 15 (P.L. § 70.07).)

Present Conviction	Predicate Conviction	New Sentence Range
Class B	Class B or C felony	15–25 years to Life (indeterminate)
Class B	Class D or E felony	12–30 years (determinate)
Class C	Class B or C felony	12–30 years (determinate) or 15–25 years to Life (indeterminate)
Class C	Class D or E felony	10–25 years (determinate)
Class D	Any degree felony	5–15 years (determinate)
Class E	Any degree felony	4–12 years (determinate)

G. INCREASED SENTENCES FOR HATE CRIMES (eff. 10/8/00) (When an individual is convicted of a specified offense that is found to be a hate crime (P.L. § 485.05, § 485.10).)

Specified Offense	Minimum Sentence
A-1 Felony	20 years to Life
Class B Violent (first felony)	8 years (determinate)
Class B Violent (second felony)	12 years (determinate)
Class B Non-violent (first felony)	6 years (indeterminate) i.e., 2 to 6 years
Class B Non-violent (second felony)	10 years (determinate)
Class B (juvenile offender)	4 years (indeterminate) i.e., 1⅓ to 4 years

H. PROBATION AND CONDITIONAL DISCHARGE

1. Periods of Probation (PL § 65.00(3))

Class A-II or Class B felony (PL § 220)	Life
Felony Defined in PL § 130, 263 or 255.25	10 years
Any Other Felony	5 years
Class A Misdemeanor in PL § 130, 263 or 225.25	6 years
Any Other Class A Misdemeanor	3 years
Class B Misdemeanor in PL § 245.00	3 years
Any Other Class B Misdemeanor	1 year

2. Periods of Conditional Discharge (PL § 65.05(3))

Felony	3 years
Misdemeanor	1 year

III. SENTENCING GUIDE FOR MISDEMEANORS AND VIOLATIONS

Classification of Offense	Section	Jail Sentence	Non-Jail Sentence
CLASS A MISDEMEANOR	§ 55.10-2(a) §§ 70.15-1; 85.00-2(a), 3	Up to 1 year	Probation (up to 3 years) (but see chart on previous page for exceptions); probation plus fine; probation plus up to 60 days in jail; probation plus up to 4 months intermittent sentence; conditional discharge (one year) with or without a fine up to $1000. PL §§ 60.01-2(c); 60.01-2(d); 60.01-3(d); 65.00-1; 65.00-3(b); 65.03-3(b); 65.05-1; 65.20-1
CLASS B MISDEMEANOR	§ 55.10-2(a) §§ 70.15-2; 85.00-2(a)	Up to 3 months	Probation (up to one year) (but see chart on previous page for exceptions); all sentences for A misdemeanor except an intermittent sentence cannot exceed 3 months
UNCLASSIFIED MISDEMEANOR (Outside Penal Law where a sentence is provided)	§ 55.10-2(c)	Shall be in accordance with sentence specified in law that defines crime	Shall be in accordance with sentence specified in law that defines crime
UNCLASSIFIED MISDEMEANOR (Outside Penal Law where no sentence/is provided)	§ 55.10-2(b)	Up to 1 year	Same as sentences for Class A misdemeanor
VIOLATION	§§ 55.10-3 70.15-4 85.00-2(a), 3	Up to 15 days	Conditional discharge (up to 1 year); unconditional discharge; fine up to $250.
MARIHUANA VIOLATIONS			
First Offense (no previous drug or marihuana conviction in 3 yrs.)	§ 221.05	NONE	Up to $100 fine
Second Offense (within 3 years)	§ 221.05	NONE	Up to $200 fine
Third Offense (within 3 years)	§ 221.05	Up to 15 days	Up to $250 fine

IV. SENTENCING GUIDE FOR JUVENILE OFFENDERS

PART I—CLASSIFICATIONS

Age	Type of Juvenile Offender Felony	Felony
13	Class A-I Felony	**Murder-2** (Excluding Felony Murder)
14, 15	Class A Felony	**Murder-2** (Felony Murder if Underlying Felony Is a Juvenile Offender Felony) **Arson-1** **Kidnapping-1**
14, 15	Class B Felony	**Aggravated Sexual Abuse** (§ 130.70) **Arson-2** **Attempted Kidnapping-1** **Attempted Murder-2** **Burglary-1** **Manslaughter-1** **Rape-1** (§ 130.35) **Robbery-1** **Criminal Sexual Act-1** (formerly Sodomy-1) (§ 130.50-1, 2)
14, 15	Class C Felony	**Assault-1** (Intentional § 120.10-1, 2) **Burglary-2** (§ 140.25-1) **Robbery-2** (§ 160.10-2(a), (b)) **Crim. Poss. Weapon-2** (§ 265.03) (On School Grounds)
14, 15	Class D Felony	**Crim. Poss. Weapon-3** (§ 265.02(4)) (On School Grounds)

TERMS OF IMPRISONMENT—JUVENILE OFFENDERS

Classification of Crime By Juvenile Offenders	Mandatory Term of Imprisonment	
	Minimum	Maximum

NOTE: *Under § 70.05 there shall be an indeterminate sentence for the following felonies committed by a juvenile offender. Imprisonment is mandatory unless Youthful Offender Treatment is granted.*

(a) Class A Felony
  (i) Murder-2

Intentional Murder	Not less than 7½ yrs. Not more than 15 yrs.		Life
Depraved Indifference Murder	Not less than 7½ yrs. Not more than 15 yrs.		Life
Felony Murder	Not less than 5 yrs. Not more than 9 yrs. § 70.05-3(a)		Life

(ii) Arson-1
      Kidnapping-1

Not less than 4 yrs.
Not more than 6 yrs.
§ 70.05-3(b)

Not less than 12 yrs.
Not more than 15 yrs.
§ 70.05-2(c)

(b) Class B Felony

No more than ⅓
the Maximum
Sentence
§ 70.05-3(c)

Not less than 3 yrs.
Not more than 10 yrs.
§ 70.05-2(c)

(c) Class C Felony

No more than ⅓
the Maximum
Sentence
§ 70.05-3(c)

Not less than 3 yrs.
Not more than 7 yrs.
§ 70.05-2(d)

(d) Class D Felony

No more than ⅓
the Maximum
Sentence
§ 70.05-3(c)

Not less than 3 yrs.
Not more than 4 yrs.
§ 70.05(2-e)

V. SENTENCING GUIDE FOR YOUTHFUL OFFENDERS

WHO QUALIFIES AS A YOUTHFUL OFFENDER

Eligibility   (Article 720)

A person is eligible for youthful offender treatment if he or she is between the ages of 14 and 19 at the time a crime is committed and stands convicted of any crime *except* an A-I or A-II felony. If a person stands convicted of an armed felony, Rape in the First Degree, Criminal Sexual Act in the First Degree (Sodomy) or Aggravated Sexual Abuse, a person is eligible if he or she can establish mitigating factors. A person is not eligible for youthful offender treatment if he or she has been sentenced on a prior felony conviction, was adjudicated as a youthful offender for a felony, or has a previous juvenile delinquent adjudication based on a Family Court Act Designated Felony.

TERMS OF IMPRISONMENT FOR YOUTHFUL OFFENDERS

Crimes by Youthful Offenders

Classification of Crime	Definite or Intermittent Term
(a) Misdemeanors *(Note: There are no indeterminate terms allowed in the statute for misdemeanors by youthful offenders (see PL § 60.02-1). Alternative, non-jail sentences, which are available to adult offenders, are available to youthful offenders.*	
(i) Class A	Up to 1 year for Discretionary Youthful Offenders (PL §§ 60.01-3(a), 70.15-1) Up to 6 months for Mandatory Youthful Offenders (CPL § 720.20-1(b); PL § 60.02-2)
(ii) Class B	Up to 3 months for all Youthful Offenders (PL §§ 60.01-3(a), 70.15-2)
(iii) Unclassified	A sentence of imprisonment for an unclassified misdemeanor shall be a definite sentence. When such a sentence is imposed, the term shall be fixed by the court and shall be in accordance with the sentence specified in the law or ordinance that defines the crime (PL §§ 60.01-3(a), 70.15-3)

TERMS OF IMPRISONMENT FOR YOUTHFUL OFFENDERS
(Continued)

(b) Felonies	Section	Definite or Intermittent Term	Indeterminate Term	
			Minimum	Maximum
(i) Class B	§ 60.02	Up to 1 year	Not less than	Not less
	§ 70.00	§ 85.00	1 year	than 3 yrs.
			Not more than	Not more
			1½ yrs.	than 4 yrs.
(ii) Class C	§ 60.02	Up to 1 year	Not less than	Not less
	§ 70.00	§ 85.00	1 year	than 3 yrs.
			Not more than	Not more
			1½ yrs	than 4 yrs.
(iii) Class D	§ 60.02	Up to 1 year	Not less than	Not less than
	§ 70.00	§ 85.00	1 year	3 yrs.
			Not more than	Not more than
			1½ yrs.	4 yrs.
(iv) Class E	§ 60.02	Up to 1 year	Not less than	Not less than
	§ 70.00	§ 85.00	1 year	3 yrs.
			Not more than	Not more than
			1½ yrs.	4 yrs.

NOTE: *Alternative non-jail sentences, which are available to adult offenders for felony convictions, are available to youthful offenders.*

VI. PLEA BARGAINING RESTRICTIONS
(Reduction of Charge)

A. Limitations on reducing a Felony complaint to a Misdemeanor.

When a local criminal court determines that there is reasonable cause to believe a defendant has committed either a Class A felony other than those defined in Article 220 [*] of the Penal Law **or** any armed felony as defined in § 1.20(41) of the C.P.L., the court **may not reduce** such felony to a misdemeanor. **See C.P.L. §§ 180.50, 180.70.**

B. Post-indictment limitations on pleas of Guilty to a Felony charge under C.P.L. Article 220.

Crime Charged	Lowest Possible Plea
Class A-I Felony (controlled substances as defined in Art. 220, Penal Law)	A-II Felony (**exception:** eligible youths (C.P.L. § 720.10) may plead B Felony under youthful offender procedure) (See C.P.L. § 220.10(5)(a)(i))
Other Class A-I Felonies (except Murder-I)	Class C Violent Felony (See C.P.L. § 220.10(5)(d)(i))
Class A-I Felony (Murder-I)	Class A-I (with consent of court and People; sentence of life without parole or 20–25 years to life)
Class A-II Felony (controlled substances as defined in Art. 220, Penal Law)	Class B Felony (See C.P.L. § 220.10(5)(a)(ii))
Class B Violent and Armed Felony	Class C violent felony offense (See C.P.L. § 220.10(5)(d)(i))
Class B Violent Felony	Class D violent felony offense (See C.P.L. § 220.10(5)(d)(ii))
Class B Felony (controlled substances as defined in Art. 220, Penal Law)	Class D Felony (See C.P.L. § 220.10(5)(a)(iii))
Any other Class B Felony	Class E Felony (See C.P.L. § 220.10(5)(b))

[*] For definitions and schedules of controlled substances, see Public Health Law §§ 3302 and 3306, reproduced in Part 2 *supra.*

Crime Charged	Lowest Possible Plea *(continued)*
Class C Violent Felony	Class D Violent Felony (See C.P.L. § 220.10(5)(d)(ii))
Any other Class C Felony	No limitations (**exception:** if defendant has predicate felony conviction, then Class E) (See C.P.L. § 220.10(5)(c) and Penal Law § 70.06)
Class D Violent Felony (Criminal Sale of Firearm-2nd degree, § 265.12 Penal Law) or (Criminal Possession of Weapon-3rd degree under § 265.02(4) Penal Law) (Where there is a previous Class A misdemeanor conviction in 5 years.)	Class E Violent Felony (See C.P.L. § 220.10(5)(d)(iv))
Class D Violent Felony (Criminal Possession of Weapon-3rd degree under § 265.02(4) Penal Law) (Where there is no previous Class A misdemeanor conviction in 5 years.)	Class E Violent Felony or Class A Misdemeanor of Criminal Possession of Weapon-4th degree under § 265.01(1) Penal Law (See C.P.L. § 220.10(5)(d)(iii))
Class D Violent Felony (Criminal Sale of Firearm-2nd degree, § 265.12 Penal Law)	Class E Violent Felony (See C.P.L. § 220.10(5)(d)(iv))
Any other Class D Felony	No limitations (**exception:** if defendant has predicate felony conviction, then Class E Felony (See C.P.L. § 220.10(5)(c) and Penal Law § 70.06)
Class E Felony of Aggravated Harassment of an Employee by an Inmate	Class E Felony (See C.P.L. § 220.10(5)(h))
Any other Class E felony	No limitations (**exception:** if defendant has predicate felony conviction, then Class E Felony (See C.P.L. § 220.10(5)(c) and Penal Law § 70.06)

NOTE: *(1) A defendant may always plead guilty (as a matter of right) to the crime charged except for Murder-1. (See C.P.L. §§ 220.10(2), (5)(e), 220.30(3)(b)(vii).)*

(2) A defendant may plead to a "lesser included offense" or any one of multiple counts in satisfaction of an entire indictment or in satisfaction of one or more other indictments. (See C.P.L. §§ 220.10(3), (4), 220.30(3)(a)(i).)

(3) Consent of the District Attorney and the Court is required for all pleas except a plea of guilty to an entire indictment. (See C.P.L. §§ 180.50, 180.70, 220.10(2), 220.30.)

VII. ADJOURNMENT IN CONTEMPLATION OF DISMISSAL IN FELONY CASES

(Article 215—Criminal Procedure Law)

NOTE: *Effective 11/1/02, a superior court can grant an adjournment in contemplation of dismissal, when the sole remaining count or counts of an indictment charge only a Misdemeanor offense and both parties consent. (CPL § 210.47)*

(A) The court, with the consent of both sides, and with reasonable notice to the victim of the crime and an opportunity for the victim to be heard, and after arraignment of an action in a local criminal court or superior court, and before final disposition, may adjourn in contemplation of dismissal for the purpose of referring certain selected felonies (see below for exceptions) to a community dispute center, as established pursuant to Article 21-A of the Judiciary Law. However, when the court makes a determination that an Adjournment in Contemplation of Dismissal is not proper for the reason outlined, *infra,* the court may restore the action in the time limits specified.

(B) Who is not eligible—defendant who is charged with:

    (a) a class A felony;
    (b) a violent felony offense as defined under § 70.02 of Penal Law;
    (c) any drug offense as defined under Article 220 of Penal Law;
    (d) a felony upon the conviction of which a defendant must be sentenced as a second felony offender or persistent felony offender as defined by §§ 70.04, 70.06, 70.08, or 70.10 of the Penal Law.

(C) Restoration of Action to Calendar

Situation	Time Limit
(a) Resolution Center must inform district attorney as to whether changes against defendant have been resolved.	Not more than 45 days
(b) Application to restore action to calendar upon determination that dismissal of accusatory instrument would not be in furtherance of justice.	Not more than 6 months
(c) Application to restore action where defendant has agreed to pay a fine, restitution or reparation and has failed to.	Not more than 1 year

(D) Action Not Restored To Calendar

Situation	Effect
(a) No application made within 6 months to restore action to calendar; **or** — (b) Defendant agreed to pay fine, restitution or reparation but has not paid such within one year of the issuance of an order adjourning an action in contemplation of dismissal.	Accusatory instrument deemed to have been dismissed by court in furtherance of justice at expiration of 6 months or one year period. The arrest and prosecution is deemed a nullity, and defendant is restored to status he or she was at before arrest and prosecution.

VIII. MANDATORY SURCHARGE AND FEES

	Mandatory Surcharge	
Felony	Misdemeanor	Violation
$250	$140	$75
	Crime Victim Assistance Fee	
Felony	Misdemeanor	Violation
$20	$20	$20

Sex Offender Registration Fee:	$50
DNA Databank Fee:	$50
Supplemental Sex Offender Victim Fee:	$1000 (imposed upon each person convicted of a felony or misdemeanor under Penal Law Article 130)

SENT. GUIDES

IX. DRIVER'S LICENSE REVOCATION AND SUSPENSION

Based on certain convictions, a defendant's driver's license may be revoked or suspended. The following convictions will result in revocation or suspension for the period indicated:

Conviction	Action Taken
Homicide or Assault Arising out of Operating a Motor Vehicle	Revocation (VTL § 510(2)(a)(i))
Drug Conviction for any Felony or Misdemeanor under Penal Law § 220 or 221	6 mo. Suspension (VTL § 510(2)(b)(v)) (absent compelling circumstances)

PART 5

NEW YORK COURT STRUCTURE CHART AND DIRECTORY

NEW YORK COURT STRUCTURE

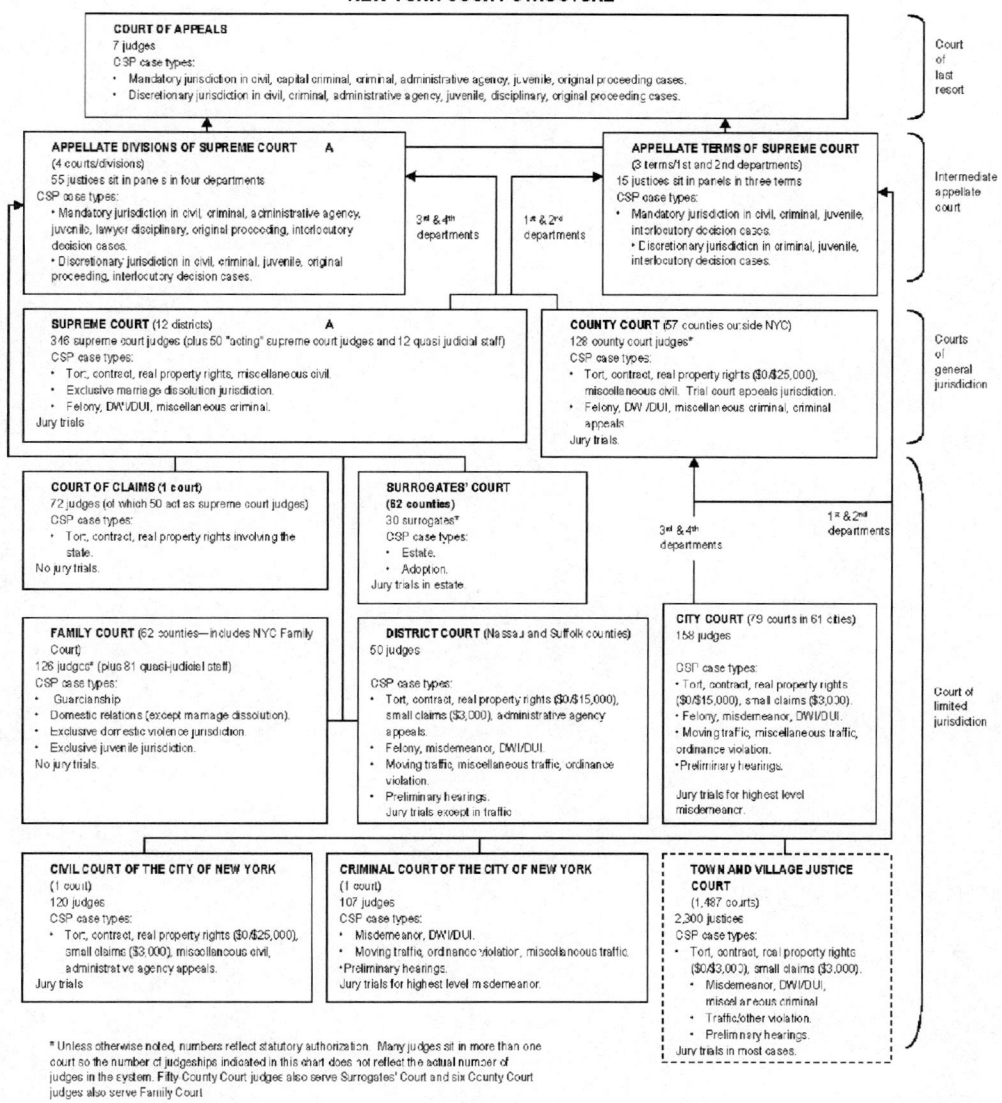

Source: Court Statistics Project, *State Court Caseload Statistics, 2003* **(National Center for State Courts 2004).**

CHART–1

COURT DIRECTORY

STATE-WIDE COURT ADMINISTRATIVE OFFICES

Office of Court Administration

25 Beaver Street–11th Floor
New York, New York 10004
Honorable Jonathan Lippman, Chief Administrative Judge
(212) 428-2150 (New York City Office)
Fax: (212) 428-2188
Internet: http://www.courts.state.ny.us

Commission on Judicial Conduct

61 Broadway, 12th Floor
New York, New York 10006
(212) 809-0566
Fax: (212) 809-3664
www.scjc.state.ny.us (for all offices)

38-40 State Street
Albany, New York 12207
(518) 474-5617
Fax: (518) 486-1750
www.scjc.state.ny.us

400 Andrews Street, Suite 700
Rochester, New York 14604
(585) 232-5756
Fax: (585) 232-7834
www.scjc.state.ny.us

Lawyers' Fund for Client Protection

119 Washington Avenue
Albany, New York 12210
(518) 434-1935
(800) 442-3863
Fax: (518) 434-5641
E-mail: raywood@nylawfund.org
Internet: http://www.nylawfund.org

Department of State

41 State Street
Albany, New York 12231-1001
(518) 474-4750; (518) 474-6740
Fax: (518) 474-4765; (518) 473-9211
E-mail: info@dos.state.ny.us; counsel @dos.state.ny.us
Internet: http://www.dos.state.ny.us

New York City Regional Office

123 William Street
19th Floor
New York, New York 10038
(212) 417-5800
Fax: (212) 417-5805
www.dos.state.ny.us

Division of Corporations and State Records

41 State Street
Albany, New York 12231
(518) 473-2492
Fax: (518) 474-5173 or (518) 474-1418
Record Searches: 1-900-TEL-CORP; 1-900-835-2677
State Records: (518) 478-4770
Uniform Commercial Codes: (518) 474-4763
Fax: (518) 474-4478
Email: corporations@dos.state.ny.us
Internet: http://www.dos.state.ny.us

NEW YORK STATE COURTS
www.nycourts.gov (Information for all NYS courts)

Court of Appeals

Court of Appeals Hall
20 Eagle Street
Albany, New York 12207-1095
(518) 455-7700
Internet: http://www.courts.state.ny.us/ctapps

Appellate Division

First Department

27 Madison Avenue at 25th Street
New York, New York 10010
(212) 340-0400
Fax: (212) 889-4412

Second Department

45 Monroe Place
Brooklyn, New York 11201
(718) 875-1300
Clerk: (718) 858-2446
www.nycourts.gov/court/ad2/

Third Department

Justice Building
Empire State Plaza, Fifth Floor, Room 505
Albany, New York 12203
(518) 471-4708
Fax: (518) 471-4750
www.courts.state.ny.us

mailing address:
Capitol Station
P.O. Box 7288
Albany, New York 12224

Fourth Department

50 East Avenue
Suite 200
Rochester, New York 14604
(585) 530-3100
Clerk: (585) 530-3247
www.courts.state.ny.us

Court of Claims

Justice Building
P.O. Box 7344
Capitol Station
Albany, New York 12224-0902
(518) 465-8881
Clerk: David B. Klingaman
(518) 432-3437, 3480
Fax for filing: (866) 413-1069
www.nyscourtofclaims.state.ny.us

26 Broadway, 10th Floor
New York, New York 10014
Clerk: (212) 361-8100
Receptionist: (212) 361-8150
Fax: (212) 361-8163

COUNTY DIRECTORY

Albany County

(Third Department, Third Judicial District)
www.nycourts.gov

Supreme Court

32 North Russell Road
Albany, New York 12206
(518) 487-5100; (518) 487-5012
Fax: (518) 487-5099; (518) 487-5020

Surrogate's Court

16 Eagle Street
Courthouse, Rm 125
Albany, New York 12207
(518) 487-5393
Chief Clerk: (518) 487-5391
Fax: (518) 487-5087; (518) 487-5020

County Court

16 Eagle Street
Courthouse, Rm 102

Albany, New York 12207
(518) 487-5011; (518) 487-5012
Chief Clerk: (518) 487-5018
Fax: (518) 487-5020

Family Court

30 Clinton Avenue
Albany, New York 12207
(518) 285-8600

City Court

Civil Court

Rm 209 City Hall
Eagle & Corning Pl.
Albany, New York 12207
(518) 434-5115
Fax: (518) 434-5034
www.nycourts.gov

97 Mohawk Street
P.O. Box 678
Cohoes, New York 12047-0678
(518) 233-2133
Fax: (518) 233-8202

City Hall
15th Street & Broadway
Watervliet, New York 12189
(518) 270-3815; (518) 270-3803
Fax: (518) 270-3812

Sheriff

16 Eagle Street
Albany, New York 12207
(518) 487-5400
Civil Unit Fax: (518) 487-5352

Allegany County

(Fourth Department, Eighth Judicial District)

Supreme Court

Courthouse
7 Court Street
Belmont, New York 14813
(585) 268-5813; (585) 268-5800
Fax: (585) 268-7090

Surrogate's Court

Courthouse
7 Court Street
Belmont, New York 14813
(585) 268-5815; (585) 268-5816
Fax: (585) 268-7090

County Court

Courthouse
7 Court Street
Belmont, New York 14813
(585) 268-5813; (585) 268-5800
Fax: (585) 268-7090

Family Court

Courthouse
7 Court Street
Belmont, New York 14813
(585) 268-5816
Fax: (585) 268-7090

Sheriff

7 Court Street
Belmont, New York 14813
(716) 268-9200, 08
Fax: (716) 268-9475

Bronx County

(First Department, Twelfth Judicial District)

Supreme Court

851 Grand Concourse, Rm 217
Bronx, New York 10451
General Information: (718) 590-3803
Civil Division: (718) 590-3722, 3
Chief Clerk: (718) 590-3985
Fax: (718) 590-8914
Internet: www.nycourts.gov

Surrogate's Court

851 Grand Concourse, Rm 326
Bronx, New York 10451
General Information: (718) 590-3318
Records: (718) 590-3618
Chief Clerk: (718) 590-4515
Fax: (718) 537-5158

Family Court

900 Sheridan Avenue
Bronx, New York 10451
Judge's Chambers: (718) 590-3377
Clerk of Court: (718) 590-3318, 21
Fax: (718) 590-2681

Civil Court

851 Grand Concourse, Basement/Ground Floor
Bronx, New York 10451
(718) 590-3600
Clerk: (718) 590-3603

Broome County

(Third Department, Sixth Judicial District)

Supreme Court

92 Court Street
Courthouse, Rm 204
P.O. Box 1766
Binghamton, New York 13902-1766
(607) 778-2448
Fax: (607) 778-6426

Surrogate's Court

Courthouse, Rm 109
P.O. Box 1766
Binghamton, New York 13902-1766
(607) 778-2111
Fax: (607) 778-2308

County Court

George Harvey Justice Building
65 Hawley Street
P.O. Box 1766
Binghamton, New York 13902-1766
(607) 778-2448
Fax: (607) 778-6426

Family Court

65 Hawley Street
P.O. Box 1766
Binghamton, New York 13902-1766
(607) 778-2156
Fax: (607) 778-2439
District Office: (607) 721-8541

City Court

Governmental Plaza
38 Hawley Street
Binghamton, New York 13901
(607) 772-7006
Fax: (607) 772-7041
District Office: (607) 721-8541

Sheriff

155 Lt. Van Winkle Drive
Binghamton, New York 13905
(607) 778-2492
Fax: (607) 778-2100

Cattaraugus County

(Fourth Department, Eighth Judicial District)

Supreme Court

County Center
303 Court Street
Little Valley, New York 14755
(716) 938-9111, Ext. 388, Ext. 384
Fax: (716) 938-6413

Surrogate's Court

County Center
303 Court Street
Little Valley, New York 14755-1096
(716) 938-9111, Ext. 2327
Fax: (716) 938-6983

County Court

County Center
303 Court Street
Little Valley, New York 14755
(716) 938-9111, Ext. 387, Ext. 388
Fax: (716) 938-6413

Family Court

1 Leomoff Drive
Olean, New York 14760
(716) 373-8035
Fax: (716) 373-0449

City Court

Municipal Building
101 East State Street
P.O. Box 631
Olean, New York 14760-0631
(716) 376-5620
Fax: (716) 376-5623

Municipal Center
225 Wildwood Avenue
Salamanca, New York 14779
(716) 945-4153
Fax: (716) 945-2362

Sheriff

County Center
301 Court Street
Little Valley, New York 14755
(716) 938-9111

Cayuga County

(Fourth Department, Seventh Judicial District)

Supreme Court

Courthouse
154 Genesee Street

Auburn, New York 13021-3474
(315) 255-4320
Fax: (315) 255-4322
Internet: www.courts.state.ny.us

Surrogate's Court

Courthouse
154 Genesee Street
Auburn, New York 13021-3471
(315) 255-4316
Fax: (315) 255-4322

County Court

Courthouse
154 Genesee Street
Auburn, New York 13021-3474
(315) 255-4320
Fax: (315) 255-4322

Family Court

Courthouse
Historic Post Office Building
157 Genesee Street
Auburn, New York 13021-3476
(315) 255-4306
Fax: (315) 255-4312

City Court

Historic Post Office
157 Genesee Street
Auburn, New York 13021-3434
(315) 253-1570
Fax: (315) 253-1085

Sheriff

Public Safety Building
7445 County House Road
Auburn, New York 13021
(315) 253-1222
Fax: (315) 253-1192

Chautauqua County

(Fourth Department, Eighth Judicial District)

Supreme Court

Courthouse
1 North Erie Street
P.O. Box 292
Mayville, New York 14757-0292
(716) 753-4266
Fax: (716) 753-4585; (716) 753-4993

Surrogate's Court

Gerace Office Building
Erie Street
P.O. Box C
Mayville, New York 14757-0299
(716) 753-4339
Fax: (716) 753-4600

County Court

Courthouse
1 North Erie Street
P.O. Box 292
Mayville, New York 14757-0292
(716) 753-4266
Fax: (716) 753-4162; (716) 753-4993

Family Court

Gerace Office Building
3 North Erie Street
P.O. Box 149
Mayville, New York 14757-0149
(716) 753-4351
Fax: (716) 753-4350
Chief Clerk: (716) 753-4351

City Court

Dunkirk City Court—City Hall
342 Central Avenue
Dunkirk, New York 14048-2122
(716) 366-2055
Fax: (716) 366-3622

City Hall
Municipal Building
200 East 3rd Street
Jamestown, New York 14701-5433
(716) 483-7561, 2
Fax: (716) 483-7519

Sheriff

Sheriff's Office
15 East Chautauqua Street
P.O. Box 128
Mayville, New York 14757
(716) 753-2131
(716) 753-4276

Chemung County

(Third Department, Sixth Judicial District)

Supreme Court

Hazlett Building
203 Lake Street, 6th Floor
P.O. Box 588

Elmira, New York 14902-0588
(607) 737-2847
Chief Clerk: (607) 737-2084
Fax: (607) 732-8879

Surrogate's Court

Courthouse
224 Lake Street
P.O. Box 588
Elmira, New York 14902-0588
General Number: (607) 737-2946
(607) 737-2873
Fax: (607) 737-2874
Chief Clerk: (607) 737-2873

County Court

Courthouse
224 Lake Street
P.O. Box 588
Elmira, New York 14902-0588
Chief Clerk: (607) 737-2084

Family Court

Justice Building
203-209 William Street
Elmira, New York 14902-0588
(607) 737-2902, 3
Fax: (607) 737-2898

City Court

City Hall
317 East Church Street
Elmira, New York 14901-2790
(607) 737-5681
Fax: (607) 737-5820

Sheriff

Justice Building
203 William Street
Elmira, New York 14902-0588
(607) 737-2987
Fax: (607) 737-2931

Chenango County

(Third Department, Sixth Judicial District)

Supreme Court

Courthouse
West Park Place
Norwich, New York 13815-1676
(607) 337-1740
Court Clerk: (607) 337-1457

Clerk Fax: (607) 337-1835
Chambers Fax: (607) 336-3648

Surrogate's Court

County Office Building
5 Court Street
Norwich, New York 13815-1676
(607) 337-1827, 22
Fax: (607) 337-1834

County Court

County Office Building
5 Court Street
Norwich, New York 13815-1676
Judge Chambers: (607) 337-1825
Court Clerk: (607) 337-1457

Family Court

County Office Building
5 Court Street
Norwich, New York 13815-1676
(607) 337-1824; (607) 337-1820
Fax: (607) 337-1835

City Court

1 Court Plaza
Norwich, New York 13815
(607) 334-1224
Fax: (607) 334-8494

Sheriff

14 West Park Place
Norwich, New York 13815
(607) 334-2000
Fax: (607) 336-1568

Clinton County

(Third Department, Fourth Judicial District)

Supreme Court
Clerk's Office

County Government Center
137 Margaret Street
Plattsburgh, New York 12901-2933
(518) 565-4715
Fax: (607) 565-4708

Surrogate's Court

County Government Center
137 Margaret Street, Suite 315
Plattsburgh, New York 12901-2933

(518) 565-4630
Fax: (518) 565-4769; (518) 565-4688

County Court

County Government Center
137 Margaret Street
Plattsburgh, New York 12901-2933
Chief Clerk: (518) 565-4715
Fax: (518) 565-4708

Family Court

County Government Center
137 Margaret Street
Plattsburgh, New York 12901-2933
(518) 565-4658
Fax: (518) 565-4688

City Court

City Hall
24 U.S. Oval
Plattsburgh, New York 12903
(518) 563-7870
Fax: (518) 563-3124

Sheriff

25 McCarthy Drive
Plattsburgh, New York 12901
(518) 561-4338
Fax: (518) 565-4333

Columbia County

(Third Department, Third Judicial District)

Supreme Court

Courthouse
401 Union Street
Hudson, New York 12534
(518) 828-7858
Fax: (518) 828-1603

Surrogate's Court

Courthouse
401 Union Street
Hudson, New York 12534
(518) 828-0414
Fax: (518) 828-1603

County Court

Courthouse
401 Union Street
Hudson, New York 12534

(518) 828-7909
Chief Clerk: (518) 828-7858
Fax: (518) 828-1603

Family Court

Courthouse
401 Union Street
Hudson, New York 12534
(518) 828-0315
Fax: (518) 828-1603

City Court

429 Warren Street
Hudson, New York 12534
(518) 828-3100
Fax: (518) 828-3628

Sheriff

85 Industrial Tract
Hudson, New York 12534
Emergency: (518) 828-3344
Business: (518) 828-0601
Fax: (518) 828-9088

Cortland County

(Third Department, Sixth Judicial District)

Supreme Court

Courthouse
46 Greenbush Street, Suite 301
Cortland, New York 13045-2725
Chief Clerk: (607) 753-5013
Fax: (607) 756-3409

Surrogate's Court

Courthouse
46 Greenbush Street, Suite 301
Cortland, New York 13045-2725
(607) 753-5355
Fax: (607) 756-3409

County Court

Courthouse
46 Greenbush Street, Suite 301
Cortland, New York 13045-2772
(607) 753-5010
Fax: (607) 756-3409

Family Court

Courthouse
46 Greenbush Street, Suite 301

Cortland, New York 13045-2725
(607) 753-5353
Fax: (607) 756-3409

City Court

City Hall
25 Court Street
Cortland, New York 13045
(607) 753-1811
Fax: (607) 753-9932

Sheriff

Courthouse
54 Greenbush Street
Cortland, New York 13045-5590
(607) 753-3311
Fax: (607) 753-7815

Delaware County

(Third Department, Sixth Judicial District)

Supreme Court

Courthouse
3 Court Street
Delhi, New York 13753
(607) 746-2131
Fax: (607) 746-3253

Surrogate's Court

Courthouse
3 Court Street
Delhi, New York 13753
(607) 746-2126
Fax: (607) 746-3253

County Court

Courthouse
3 Court Street
Delhi, New York 13753
Clerk: (607) 746-2131
Fax: (607) 746-3253

Family Court

Courthouse
3 Court Street
Delhi, New York 13753
(607) 746-2298
Fax: (607) 746-3253

Sheriff

280 Phoebe Lane
Suite 1

Delhi, New York 13753
(607) 746-2336
(607) 746-2632

Dutchess County

(Second Department, Ninth Judicial District)

Supreme Court

Courthouse
10 Market Street
Poughkeepsie, New York 12601
(845) 486-2260
Fax: (845) 473-5403

Surrogate's Court

Courthouse
10 Market Street
Poughkeepsie, New York 12601-3203
(845) 486-2235
Chief Clerk: (845) 486-2235
Fax: (845) 486-2234

County Court

Courthouse
10 Market Street
Poughkeepsie, New York 12601-3203
Chief Clerk: (845) 486-2260
Fax: (845) 473-5403

Family Court

50 Market Street
Poughkeepsie, New York 12601-3204
(845) 486-2500
Fax: (845) 486-2510; (845) 486-2505

City Court

1 Municipal Plaza
Suite 2
Beacon, New York 12508
(845) 838-5030
Fax: (845) 838-5041

Civic Center Plaza
P.O. Box 300
Poughkeepsie, New York 12602
Street Address:
62 Civic Center Plaza
Poughkeepsie, New York 12601
(845) 451-4091
Fax: (845) 485-6795; (845) 451-4094

Sheriff

150 North Hamilton Street
Poughkeepsie, New York 12601
(845) 486-3800
Fax: (845) 452-2987

Erie County

(Fourth Department, Eighth Judicial District)

Supreme Court

Erie County Hall
92 Franklin Street
Buffalo, New York 14202
(716) 851-3291; (716) 845-9300
Fax: (716) 851-3293

Surrogate's Court

Erie County Hall
92 Franklin Street
Buffalo, New York 14202
(716) 845-2560
Fax: (716) 853-3741

County Court

Erie County Hall
92 Franklin Street
Buffalo, New York 14202
Fax: (716) 851-3293; (716) 845-9300
Chief Clerk: (716) 858-8452

Family Court

1 Niagara Plaza
Buffalo, New York 14202
(716) 845-7400
Fax: (716) 858-8175
Clerk: (716) 858-8111

City Court

50 Delaware Avenue
Buffalo, New York 14202
(716) 847-8200
Fax: (716) 847-8257

City Hall
714 Ridge Road
Lackawanna, New York 14218
(716) 827-6486
Fax: (716) 825-1874
Chief Clerk: (716) 827-6672

City Hall
200 Niagara Street
Tonawanda, New York 14150
(716) 845-2160
Fax: (716) 693-1612

Sheriff

10 Delaware Avenue
Buffalo, New York 14202
(716) 858-7608
Fax: (716) 858-7680

Essex County

(Third Department, Fourth Judicial District)

Supreme Court

Courthouse
7559 Court Street
P.O. Box 217
Elizabethtown, New York 12932
(518) 873-3370, 1
Law Library: (518) 873-3789
Fax: (518) 873-3376

Surrogate's Court

Courthouse
7559 Court Street
P.O. Box 217
Elizabethtown, New York 12932
(518) 873-3384

County Court

Courthouse
7559 Court Street
P.O. Box 217
Elizabethtown, New York 12932
(518) 873-3370, 1
Chief Clerk III: (518) 873-3375

Family Court

Courthouse
7559 Court Street
P.O. Box 217
Elizabethtown, New York 12932
(518) 873-3320
Fax: (518) 873-3626

Sheriff

7551 Court Street
P.O. Box 278
Elizabethtown, New York 12932
(518) 873-6321
Fax: (518) 873-3340

Franklin County

(Third Department, Fourth Judicial District)

Supreme Court

Courthouse
355 West Main Street
Malone, New York 12953-1817
(518) 481-1749
Fax: (518) 481-5456

Surrogate's Court

Courthouse
355 West Main Street
Malone, New York 12953
(518) 481-1737
Chief Clerk: (518) 481-1736
Fax: (518) 483-7583

County Court

Courthouse
355 West Main Street
Malone, New York 12953
(518) 481-1748
Clerk: (518) 481-1748; (518) 481-1749
Fax: (518) 483-5456

Family Court

Courthouse
355 West Main Street
Malone, New York 12953-1893
(518) 481-1742
Fax: (518) 481-5453

Commissioner of Jurors

Courthouse
355 West Main Street
Malone, New York 12953
(518) 481-1756
Fax: (518) 481-6204

Sheriff

Courthouse
45 Bare Hill Road
Malone, New York 12953
(518) 483-3304
Fax: (518) 483-3139

Fulton County

(Third Department, Fourth Judicial District)

Supreme Court

County Building
223 West Main Street
Johnstown, New York 12095
Chief Clerk: (518) 736-5539
Fax: (518) 762-5078

Surrogate's Court

County Building
223 West Main Street
Johnstown, New York 12095
Chief Clerk: (518) 736-5697; (518) 736-5685
Fax: (518) 762-6372

County Court

County Building
223 West Main Street
Johnstown, New York 12095
Chief Clerk: (518) 736-5539
Fax: (518) 762-5078

Family Court

11 North William Street
Johnstown, New York 12095
(518) 762-3840
Fax: (518) 762-9540

City Court

City Hall
3 Frontage Road
Gloversville, New York 12078
(518) 773-4527
Fax: (518) 773-4599

City Hall
33-41 East Main Street
Johnstown, New York 12095
(518) 762-0007
(518) 762-2720

Sheriff

2712 State Highway 29
P.O. Box 20
Johnstown, New York 12095
(518) 736-2100
Fax: (518) 736-2126

Genesee County

(Fourth Department, Eighth Judicial District)

Supreme Court

Courts Facility
1 West Main Street
Batavia, New York 14020-0462
(585) 344-2550, Ext. 2239
Chief Clerk Nelson Green: (585) 344-2550, Ext. 2238
Fax: (585) 344-8517

Surrogate's Court

Courts Facility
1 West Main Street
Batavia, New York 14020-0462
Chief Clerk Colleen Kelly: (585) 344-2550, Ext. 2237
Fax: (585) 344-8517

County Court

Courts Facility
1 West Main Street
P.O. Box 462
Batavia, New York 14020-2019
(585) 344-2550, Ext. 2239
Fax: (585) 344-8517

Family Court

Courts Facility
1 West Main Street
Batavia, New York 14020
(585) 344-2550, Ext. 2228
Fax: (585) 344-8520

City Court

Courts Facility
1 West Main Street
Batavia, New York 14020
(585) 344-2550, Ext. 2418
Fax: (585) 344--8556

Sheriff

14 West Main Street
P.O. Box 151
Batavia, New York 14020-0151
(585) 343-0911
Fax: (585) 343-9129

Greene County

(Third Department, Third Judicial District)

Supreme Court

Courthouse
320 Main Street
Catskill, New York 12414
Fax: (518) 943-7763
Chief Clerk: (518) 943-2230

Surrogate's Court

Courthouse
320 Main Street
Catskill, New York 12414
(518) 943-2484
Fax: (518) 943-1864

County Court

Courthouse
320 Main Street
Catskill, New York 12414
(518) 943-2230, 2171
Fax: (518) 943-7763
Chief Clerk: (518) 943-2230

Family Court

Courthouse
320 Main Street
Catskill, New York 12414
(518) 943-5711
Fax: (518) 943-1864

Sheriff

80 Bridge Street
P.O. Box 231
Catskill, New York 12414
(518) 943-3300
Fax: (518) 943-6832

Hamilton County

(Third Department, Fourth Judicial District)

Supreme Court

No sessions held (*See Fulton County for information*)

Surrogate's Court

mailing address:
P.O. Box 780
Indian Lake, New York 12842-0780

Court sessions held at:
Lake Pleasant, New York 12108
(518) 648-5411
Fax: (518) 648-6286

County Court

mailing address:
P.O. Box 780
Indian Lake, New York 12842-0780

Court sessions held at:
Courthouse
Route 8
Lake Pleasant, New York 12108
(518) 548-3211

Chambers
White Birch Lane
Indian Lake, New York 12842-0780
(518) 648-5411
Fax: (518) 648-6286

Family Court

mailing address:
White Birch Lane
P.O. Box 780
Indian Lake, New York 12842-0780

Court sessions held at:
Courthouse
Route 8
Lake Pleasant, New York 12108
(518) 648-5411
Fax: (518) 648-6286

Sheriff

P.O. Box 210
South Shore Road
Lake Pleasant, New York 12108
(518) 548-3113
(518)548-3113 (call to fax)

Herkimer County

(Fourth Department, Fifth Judicial District)

Supreme Court

Courthouse
301 North Washington Street
Herkimer, New York 13350-0749
Chief Clerk: (315) 867-1367; (315) 867-1282
Fax: (315) 866-1802

Surrogate's Court

Courthouse
301 North Washington Street
Herkimer, New York 13350-0749
(315) 867-1170
Fax: (315) 866-1722

County Court

Courthouse
301 North Washington Street
Herkimer, New York 13350-0749
Deputy Chief Clerk: (315) 867-1346
Fax: (315) 866-1802

Family Court

County Office Building
109 Mary Street
P.O. Box 749
Herkimer, New York 13350-0749
(315) 867-1139
Fax: (315) 867-1369

City Court

City Hall
659 East Main Street
Little Falls, New York 13365
(315) 823-1690
Fax: (315) 823-1623

Sheriff

320 North Main Street, Suite 2900
Herkimer, New York 13350-1949
(315) 867-1167
Fax: (315) 867-1354

Jefferson County

(Fourth Department, Fifth Judicial District)

Supreme Court

Dulles State Office Building
317 Washington Street, 10th Floor
Watertown, New York 13601
Chief Clerk: (315) 785-7906
Fax: (315) 785-7909

Surrogate's Court

County Office Building, 3rd Floor
163 Arsenal Street
Watertown, New York 13601
(315) 785-3019
Fax: (315) 785-5194

County Court

Courthouse
163 Arsenal Street
Watertown, New York 13601
(315) 785-3044
Chief Clerk: (315) 785-7906
Fax: (315) 785-3226

Family Court

County Office Building
163 Arsenal Street
Watertown, New York 13601
(315) 785-3001
Fax: (315) 785-3198

City Court

Municipal Building
245 Washington Street
Watertown, New York 13601
(315) 785-7785
Fax: (315) 785-7817

Sheriff

753 Waterman Drive
Watertown, New York 13601
(315) 786-2600, 2700
Fax: (315) 786-2684

Kings County

(Second Department, Second Judicial District)

Supreme Court

360 Adams Street, Room 189
Brooklyn, New York 11201
(718) 643-8076
Chief Clerk: (718) 643-5268
Fax: (718) 643-4221

Surrogate's Court

2 Johnson Street
Brooklyn, New York 11201
(718) 643-5262
Chief Clerk: (718) 643-7098
Fax: (718) 643-6237

Family Court

330 Jay Street
Brooklyn, New York 11201
Main Telephone: (347) 401-9600
Clerk of Court: (347) 401-9610

Civil Court

141 Livingston Street
Brooklyn, New York 11201
(718) 643-5069
Fax: (718) 643-3733
Clerk: (718) 643-8126

Under Sheriff

Municipal Building
210 Joralemon Street
Brooklyn, New York 11201
(718) 802-3543
Fax: (718) 802-3517

Lewis County

(Fourth Department, Fifth Judicial District)

Supreme Court

Courthouse
7660 North State Street
Lowville, New York 13367-1396
(315) 376-5380
Fax: (315) 376-5398

Clerk of Courts: (315) 376-5380
County Clerk: (315) 376-5333

Surrogate's Court

Courthouse
7660 North State Street
Lowville, New York 13367-1396
(315) 376-5344
Fax: (315) 376-4145

County Court

Courthouse
7660 North State Street
Lowville, New York 13367-1396
(315) 376-5366
Clerk of Courts: (315) 376-5380
Fax: (315) 376-4145; (315) 376-5398

Family Court

Courthouse
7660 North State Street
Lowville, New York 13367-1396
(315) 376-5345
Fax: (315) 376-5189

Sheriff

Public Safety Building
P.O. Box 233
Outer Stowe Street
Lowville, New York 13367
(315) 376-3511
Fax: (315) 376-5232

Livingston County

(Fourth Department, Seventh Judicial District)

Supreme Court

Courthouse
2 Court Street
Geneseo, New York 14454-1030
Fax: (585) 243-7067
Chief Clerk: (585) 243-7060

Surrogate's Court

Courthouse
2 Court Street
Geneseo, New York 14454-1030
(585) 243-7095
Fax: (585) 243-7583

County Court

Courthouse
2 Court Street
Geneseo, New York 14454-1030
Fax: (585) 243-7067
Chief Clerk: (585) 243-7060

Family Court

Courthouse
2 Court Street
Geneseo, New York 14454-1030
(585) 243-7070
Fax: (585) 243-7076

Sheriff

4 Court Street
Geneseo, New York 14454
(585) 243-7120
(585) 243-7926

Madison County

(Third Department, Sixth Judicial District)

Supreme Court

Courthouse
North Court Street
P.O. Box 545
Wampsville, New York 13163
Fax: (315) 366-2539
Chief Clerk: (315) 366-2267

Surrogate's Court

Courthouse
North Court Street
P.O. Box 607
Wampsville, New York 13163
Chief Clerk: (315) 366-2392
Fax: (315) 366-2539

County Court

Courthouse
North Court Street
P.O. Box 545
Wampsville, New York 13163
(315) 366-2266
Chief Clerk: (315) 366-2267
Fax: (315) 366-2539

Family Court

Courthouse
North Court Street
P.O. Box 607
Wampsville, New York 13163

(315) 366-2291
Fax: (315) 366-2828

City Court

109 North Main Street
Oneida, New York 13421
(315) 363-1310
Fax: (315) 363-3230

Sheriff

County Correctional Facility
North Court Street
Wampsville, New York 13163
(315) 366-2289
Fax: (315) 366-2286

Monroe County

(Fourth Department, Seventh Judicial District)

Supreme Court

Room 545 Hall of Justice
99 Exchange Boulevard
Rochester, New York 14614-2185
(585) 428-2020
Fax: (585) 428-2190 or (585) 428-2684
Chief Clerk: (585) 428-5001
Internet: http://www.courts.state.ny.us

Surrogate's Court

Room 541 Hall of Justice
99 Exchange Boulevard
Rochester, New York 14614-2186
(585) 428-5200
Fax: (585) 428-2650
Chief Court Clerk: (585) 428-1779

County Court

545 Hall of Justice
99 Exchange Boulevard
Rochester, New York 14614-2185
(585) 428-2331
Fax: (585) 428-2190
Chief Court Clerk: (585) 428-5001

Family Court

Hall of Justice
99 Exchange Boulevard Room 360
Rochester, New York 14614-2187
(585) 428-5429
Chief Clerk: (585) 428-2002
Fax: (585) 428-2597

City Court

Civil Branch
Room 6 Hall of Justice
99 Exchange Boulevard
Rochester, New York 14614
(585) 428-2444
Fax: (585) 428-2588

Sheriff

130 South Plymouth Avenue
Rochester, New York 14614
(585) 428-5780, 1
Fax: (585) 428-5851

Montgomery County

(Third Department, Fourth Judicial District)

Supreme Court

Courthouse
58 Broadway
P.O. Box 1500
Fonda, New York 12068-1500
(518) 853-4432
Fax: (518) 853-8378

Surrogate's Court

Courthouse
58 Broadway
P.O. Box 1500
Fonda, New York 12068-1500
(518) 853-8108
Fax: (518) 853-8230

County Court

Courthouse
58 Broadway
P.O. Box 1500
Fonda, New York 12068-1500
(518) 853-3431, 3834
Fax: (518) 853-8396
Chief Clerk: (518) 853-4516

Family Court

Courthouse
58 Broadway
P.O. Box 1500
Fonda, New York 12068-1500
(518) 853-8133, 5
Chief Clerk: (518) 853-8134
Fax: (518) 853-8148

City Court

Public Safety Building, Room 208
1 Guy Park Avenue Extension

Amsterdam, New York 12010
(518) 842-9510
Fax: (518) 843-8474

Sheriff

Sheriff's Office
200 Clark Drive
Fultonville, New York 12072
Civil: (518) 853-5515
Sheriff Fax: (518) 853-4969

Nassau County

(Second Department, Tenth Judicial District)

Supreme Court

Supreme Court Building
100 Supreme Court Drive
Mineola, New York 11501
Deputy Chief Clerk Fax: (516) 571-1427
Chief Clerk: (516) 571-2904
Fax: (516) 571-1575

Surrogate's Court

262 Old Country Road
Mineola, New York 11501
(516) 571-2082
Chief Clerk-Referee: (516) 571-2082
Fax: (516) 571-3864, 3803

County Court

262 Old Country Road
Mineola, New York 11501
(516) 571-2800, 01
Chief Clerk: (516) 571-2720
Fax: (516) 571-2160

Family Court

1200 Old Country Road
Westbury, New York 11590
(516) 571-9033
Fax: (516) 571-9335

District Court

First District Court

99 Main Street
Hempstead, New York 11550
Civil Court: (516) 572-2264 or (516) 572-2256
Fax: (516) 572-2291, 2507

Second District Court

Town Hall
99 Main Street

Hempstead, New York 11550
(516) 572-2264
Fax: (516) 572-2507

Third District Court

435 Middleneck Road
Great Neck, New York 11023
(516) 571-8400
Fax: (516) 571-8403, 02

Fourth District Court

99 Main Street
Hempstead, New York 11550
(516) 572-2261

City Court

13 Glen Street
Glen Cove, New York 11542-2776
(516) 676-0109
Fax: (516) 676-1570

1 West Chester Street
Long Beach, New York 11561
(516) 431-1000
Fax: (516) 889-3511

Sheriff

Civil Bureau
Nassau County Office Building
240 Old Country Road
Mineola, New York 11501
(516) 571-2113
Fax: (516) 571-5086

New York County

(First Department, First Judicial District)

Supreme Court

60 Centre Street
New York, New York 10007-1474
(646) 386-3685
Chief Clerk and Executive Officer, Civil Branch: (646) 386-3685
Fax: (646) 386-3001

Surrogate's Court

31 Chambers Street
New York, New York 10007
Chief Clerk & Clerk of Court: (212) 374-8557

Family Court

60 Lafayette Street, Suite 11B
New York, New York 10013

(646) 386-5170
Clerk of Court: (646) 386-5206

Civil Court

111 Centre Street
New York, New York 10013
Civil Court Information Line (*all 5 boroughs*): (212) 791-6000

Sheriff

31 Chambers Street Room 608
New York, New York 10007
(212) 788-8731
Fax: (212) 766-9666

Niagara County

(Fourth Department, Eighth Judicial District)

Supreme Court

775 3rd Street
Niagara Falls, New York 14302-1710
(716) 278-1800
Fax: (716) 278-1809

Surrogate's Court

Courthouse
175 Hawley Street
Lockport, New York 14094-2758
(716) 439-7319
Fax: (716) 439-7157
Chief Clerk: (716) 439-7130

County Court

Courthouse
175 Hawley Street
Lockport, New York 14094-2758
(716) 439-7148
Fax: (716) 439-7157
Chief Clerk: (716) 439-7145

Family Court

Niagara County Civil Building
775 Third Street at Cedar
Niagara Falls, New York 14302-1710
(716) 278-1880
Fax: (716) 278-1877

City Court

Niagara County Courthouse
175 Hawley Street 2nd Floor
Lockport, New York 14094
General Information: (716) 439-7172
Fax: (716) 278-1877

Public Safety Building
520 Hyde Park Boulevard
Niagara Falls, New York 14302-2725
Civil: (716) 278-9860
Fax: (716) 278-9869

City Hall
216 Payne Avenue
North Tonawanda, New York 14120-5446
(716) 693-1010
Fax: (716) 743-1754

Sheriff

P.O. Box 496
5526 Niagara Street
Lockport, New York 14094-1898
(716) 438-3393
Fax: (716) 438-3302

Oneida County

(Fourth Department, Fifth Judicial District)

Supreme Court

Courthouse
200 Elizabeth Street
Utica, New York 13501
(315) 798-5889, 90
Deputy Chief Clerk: (315) 798-5889
Chief Clerk: (315) 798-5890
Fax: (315) 798-6436

Surrogate's Court

Oneida County Office Building
800 Park Avenue
Eighth Floor
Utica, New York 13501
(315) 797-9230
Fax: (315) 797-9237

County Court

Courthouse
200 Elizabeth Street
Utica, New York 13501
(315) 798-5716
Chief Clerk: (315) 798-5890
Fax: (315) 793-6047, 6436

Family Court

Courthouse
200 Elizabeth Street
Utica, New York 13501
Fax: (315) 798-6404
Chief Clerk: (315) 798-5925

Oneida County Office Building
301 West Dominick Street
Rome, New York 13440-5196
(315) 337-7492
Fax: (315) 336-3828

City Court

100 West Court Street
Rome, New York 13440
(315) 337-6440
Fax: (315) 338-0343

373 Sherrill Road
Sherrill, New York 13461
(315) 363-0996
Fax: (315) 363-1176

411 Oriskany Street West
Utica, New York 13502
(315) 724-8157
Chief Clerk: (315) 724-8150
Fax: (315) 792-8038

Sheriff

Law Enforcement Building
6065 Judd Road
Oriskany, New York 13424
(315) 765-2222
Fax: (315) 765-2205

Onondaga County

(Fourth Department, Fifth Judicial District)

Supreme Court

Courthouse
401 Montgomery Street
Syracuse, New York 13202
Chief Clerk: (315) 671-1020
Fax: (315) 671-1176

Surrogate's Court

Courthouse
401 Montgomery Street
Syracuse, New York 13202-2173
(315) 671-2100
Fax: (315) 671-1162

County Court

Courthouse
401 Montgomery Street
Syracuse, New York 13202
(315) 671-1030
Fax: (315) 671-1191

Family Court

Courthouse
401 Montgomery Street
Syracuse, New York 13202
Chief Clerk: (315) 671-2060
Fax: (315) 671-1163

City Court

Public Safety Building
505 South State Street
Syracuse, New York 13202-2179
(315) 671-2785
Chief Clerk: (315) 671-2776
Fax: (315) 671-2740

Sheriff

407 South State Street
Syracuse, New York 13202
(315) 435-3044
Fax: (315) 435-2942

Ontario County

(Fourth Department, Seventh Judicial District)

Supreme Court

Courthouse
27 North Main Street, Rm 130
Canandaigua, New York 14424-1447
(585) 396-4239
Fax: (585) 396-4576

Surrogate's Court

Courthouse
27 North Main Street, Rm 130
Canandaigua, New York 14424-1447
(585) 396-4055
Fax: (585) 396-4576

County Court

Courthouse
27 North Main Street, Rm 130
Canandaigua, New York 14424-1447
(585) 396-4239
Fax: (585) 396-4576

Family Court

Courthouse
27 North Main Street, Rm 130
Canandaigua, New York 14424-1447
(585) 396-4272
Fax: (585) 396-4576

City Court

City Hall
2 North Main Street
Canandaigua, New York 14424-1448
(585) 396-5011
Fax: (585) 396-5012

Public Safety Building
255 Exchange Street
Geneva, New York 14456
(315) 789-6560
Fax: (315) 781-2802

Sheriff

Sheriff's Office
74 Ontario Street
Canandaigua, New York 14424
(585) 394-4560
Fax: (585) 394-3245

Orange County

(Second Department, Ninth Judicial District)

Supreme Court

Orange County Government Center
30 Park Place
Goshen, New York 10924
(845) 291-3111, 3114
Fax: (845) 291-2595

Surrogate's Court

Surrogate's Courthouse
30 Park Place
Goshen, New York 10924
(845) 291-2193, 94
Fax: (845) 291-2196

County Court

Orange County Government Center
255-275 Main Street
Goshen, New York 10924
(845) 291-3100
Chief Court Clerk: (845) 291-3111
Fax: (845) 291-2525

Family Court

Orange County Courthouse
285 Main Street
Goshen, New York 10924
(845) 291-3030
Chief Clerk V: (845) 291-3031
Fax: (845) 291-3054

City Court

2 James Street
Middletown, New York 10940
(845) 346-4050
Fax: (845) 343-5737

Public Safety Building
57 Broadway
Newburgh, New York 12550
(845) 565-3208
Fax: (845) 565-1244

20 Hammond Street
Port Jervis, New York 12771
(845) 858-4034
Fax: (845) 856-2767

Sheriff

110 Wells Farm Road
Goshen, New York 10924
(845) 294-4033
Fax: (845) 294-1590; (845) 291-7603 (Civil Unit)

Orleans County

(Fourth Department, Eighth Judicial District)

Supreme Court

Courthouse
Courthouse Square
3 South Main Street
Albion, New York 14411-1497
(585) 589-5458
Fax: (585) 589-0632

Surrogate's Court

Surrogate's Office
Courthouse Square
3 South Main Street
Albion, New York 14411-1497
(585) 589-4457
Fax: (585) 589-0632

County Court

Courthouse
Courthouse Square
3 South Main Street
Albion, New York 14411-1497
(585) 589-5458
Fax: (585) 589-0632

Family Court

Courthouse
Courthouse Square

3 South Main Street
Albion, New York 14411-1497
(585) 589-4457
Fax: (585) 589-0632

Sheriff

13925 Route 31
Albion, New York 14411
(585) 589-5528
Fax: (585) 589-6761

Oswego County

(Fourth Department, Fifth Judicial District)

Supreme Court

Courthouse
25 East Oneida Street
Oswego, New York 13126-2693
(315) 349-3277
Fax: (315) 349-8513

Surrogate's Court

Courthouse
25 East Oneida Street
Oswego, New York 13126-2693
(315) 349-3295
Fax: (315) 349-8514

County Court

Courthouse
25 East Oneida Street
Oswego, New York 13126
(315) 349-3280, 3288
Fax: (315) 349-8513
Court Clerk: (315) 349-3280

Family Court

Public Safety Center
39 Churchill Road
Oswego, New York 13126
(315) 349-3350
Fax: (315) 349-3457

City Court

Municipal Building
141 South First Street
Fulton, New York 13069
(315) 593-8400
Fax: (315) 592-3415

Conway Municipal Building
20 West Oneida Street

Oswego, New York 13126
(315) 343-0415
Fax: (315) 343-0531

Sheriff

39 Churchill Road
Oswego, New York 13126-6613
(315) 349-3309
Civil Division Fax: (315) 349-3303
Sheriff Direct Fax: (315) 349-3483
Corrections Fax: (315) 349-3349

Otsego County

(Third Department, Sixth Judicial District)

Supreme Court

County Office Building
197 Main Street
P.O. Box 710
Cooperstown, New York 13326
(607) 547-4364
Fax: (607) 547-7567

Surrogate's Court

Surrogate's Office
County Office Building
197 Main Street
Cooperstown, New York 13326
(607) 547-4213
Fax: (607) 547-7566

County Court

County Office Building
197 Main Street
P.O. Box 710
Cooperstown, New York 13326
(607) 547-4388
Chief Clerk: (607) 547-7567

Family Court

County Office Building
197 Main Street
Cooperstown, New York 13326
(607) 547-4288
Fax: (607) 547-6412

City Court

Public Safety Building
81 Main Street
Oneonta, New York 13820
(607) 432-4480
Fax: (607) 432-2328

Sheriff

Sheriff's Office

172 County Highway 33 West
Cooperstown, New York 13326
(607) 547-4271
Fax: (607) 547-6413

Putnam County

(Second Department, Ninth Judicial District)

Supreme Court
County Office Building
40 Gleneida Avenue
Carmel, New York 10512
(845) 225-3641, Ext. 227
Fax: (845) 228-0656

Judge John W. Sweeny, Jr.
44 Gleneida Avenue
Carmel, New York 10512
(845) 225-3641, Ext. 222
Fax: (845) 228-0837

Surrogate's Court

Historic Courthouse
44 Gleneida Avenue
Carmel, New York 10512
(845) 225-3641, Ext. 295, 296, 332
Fax: (845) 228-5761

County Court

County Office Building
40 Gleneida Avenue
Carmel, New York 10512
(845) 225-3641, Ext. 338

Family Court

County Office Building
40 Gleneida Avenue
Carmel, New York 10512
(845) 225-3641, Ext. 286
Fax: (845) 225-4395

Sheriff

3 County Center
Carmel, New York 10512
(845) 225-4300
Fax: (845) 228-5227

Queens County

(Second Department, Eleventh Judicial District)

Supreme Court

Civil Term:

88-11 Sutphin Boulevard
Jamaica, New York 11435
(718) 520-3713
Chief Clerk (Civil & Matrimonial): (718) 298-1160
Fax: (718) 520-2204

Surrogate's Court

88-11 Sutphin Boulevard
Jamaica, New York 11435
(718) 520-0500

Family Court

151-20 Jamaica Avenue
Jamaica, New York 11432
(718) 298-0197
Fax: (718) 297-2826

Civil Court

89-17 Sutphin Boulevard
Jamaica, New York 11435
(718) 262-7100
Fax: (718) 262-7107

Sheriff

144-06 94th Avenue
Jamaica, New York 11435
Family Court Warrants: (718) 298-7500
Private Sector: (718) 298-7550

Rensselaer County

(Third Department, Third Judicial District)

Supreme Court

Courthouse
72 Congress Street (Congress and 2nd Street
Troy, New York 12180
(518) 270-3711
Fax: (518) 270-3714, 11

Surrogate's Court

Courthouse
80 Second Street (Congress and 2nd Street)
Troy, New York 12180
(518) 270-3724
Fax: (518) 272-5452

County Court

Courthouse
Congress and 2nd Street

Troy, New York 12180
(518) 270-3734
Chief Clerk: (518) 270-3711

Family Court

Rensselaer Family Court Center
1504 Fifth Avenue
Troy, New York 12180
(518) 270-3761
Fax: (518) 272-6573

City Court

City Hall
505 Broadway
Rensselaer, New York 12144
(518) 462-6751
Fax: (518) 462-3307

51 State Street
Third Floor
Troy, New York 12180
(518) 273-2434
Fax: (518) 271-2360

Sheriff

4000 Main Street
P.O. Box 389
Troy, New York 12181-0389
(518) 270-5448
Fax: (518) 270-5447

Richmond County

(Second Department, Second Judicial District)

Supreme Court

Courthouse
18 Richmond Terrace
Staten Island, New York 10301
(718) 390-5201
Chief Clerk: (718) 390-5290
Fax: (718) 380-5435
Mail Delivery for Jail:
355 Front Street
Staten Island, New York 10304

Surrogate's Court

Courthouse
18 Richmond Terrace
Staten Island, New York 10301
(718) 390-5400
Fax: (718) 390-8741

Family Court

100 Richmond Terrace
Staten Island, New York 10301
(718) 390-5460,1
Clerk of Court: (718) 390-5466
Fax: (718) 390-5247

Civil Court

927 Castleton Avenue
Staten Island, New York 10310
(718) 390-5417
Fax: (718) 390-8108

Under Sheriff

350 Saint Marks Place
Staten Island, New York 10301
(718) 815-8407
Fax: (718) 815-8416

Rockland County

(Second Department, Ninth Judicial District)

Supreme Court

Courthouse
1 South Main Street
New City, New York 10956
Civil: (845) 638-5393
Chief Clerk: (845) 638-5393
Fax: (845) 638-5312

Surrogate's Court

1 South Main Street
Suite 270
New City, New York 10956
(845) 638-5330
Fax: (845) 638-5632
Chief Clerk: (845) 638-5335

County Court

Courthouse
1 South Main Street
New City, New York 10956
Civil: (845) 638-5393
Chief Clerk: (845) 638-5393
Fax: (845) 638-5312

Family Court

Rockland County Courthouse
1 South Main Street, Suite 300
New City, New York 10956
(845) 638-5300
Fax: (845) 638-5319

Sheriff

55 New Hempstead Road
New City, New York 10956
(845) 638-5456
Fax: (845) 638-5460

St. Lawrence County

(Third Department, Fourth Judicial District)

Supreme Court

Courthouse
48 Court Street
Canton, New York 13617-1169
(315) 379-0326
Chief Clerk: (315) 379-2219
Chief Clerk Fax: (315) 379-2423
Chambers Fax: (315) 379-2311

Surrogate's Court

Courthouse
48 Court Street
Canton, New York 13617-1199
(315) 379-2217, 9427
Fax: (315) 379-2372

County Court

Courthouse
48 Court Street
Canton, New York 13617
(315) 379-2219
Fax: (315) 379-2423
Chief Clerk: (315) 379-2219

Family Court

Courthouse
48 Court Street
Canton, New York 13617-1199
(315) 379-2410
Fax: (315) 386-3197

City Court

330 Ford Street
Ogdensburg, New York 13669
(315) 393-3941
Fax: (315) 393-6839

Sheriff

Courthouse
48 Court Street
Canton, New York 13617
(315) 379-2222
Fax: (315) 379-0335

Saratoga County

(Third Department, Fourth Judicial District)

Supreme Court

30 McMaster Street, Building 3
Ballston Spa, New York 12020-0600
(518) 885-2224
Fax: (518) 884-4758

Surrogate's Court

30 McMaster Street, Building 3
Ballston Spa, New York 12020-0600
(518) 884-4722
Fax: (518) 884-4774

County Court

30 McMaster Street, Building 3
Ballston Spa, New York 12020-0600
(518) 885-2214
Chief Clerk: (518) 885-2224
Fax: (518) 884-4758

Family Court

Saratoga County Municipal Center
35 West High Street
Ballston Spa, New York 12020-0600
(518) 884-9207
Fax: (518) 884-8735

City Court

City Hall
36 North Main Street
Mechanicville, New York 12118
(518) 664-9876
Fax: (518) 664-8606

City Hall
474 Broadway, Suite 3
Saratoga Springs, New York 12866
(518) 581-1797
Fax: (518) 584-3097

Sheriff

6010 County Farm Road
Ballston Spa, New York 12020-0600
(518) 885-6761
Civil Division: (518) 885-2469
Fax: (518) 885-2453

Schenectady County

(Third Department, Fourth Judicial District)

Supreme Court

612 State Street
Schenectady, New York 12305
(518) 388-4322
Chief Clerk: (518) 388-4322
Fax: (518) 388-4520

Surrogate's Court

Courthouse
612 State Street
Schenectady, New York 12305-2113
(518) 388-4293
Fax: (518) 377-6378

County Court

Courthouse
612 State Street
Schenectady, New York 12305
(518) 388-4215
Chief Clerk IV: (518) 388-4322
Fax: (518) 388-4520

Family Court

620 State Street
Schenectady, New York 12305-2114
Chief Clerk Melissa Mills: (518) 388-4305
Fax: (518) 388-4496

City Court

Civil Division:
City Hall
105 Jay Street
Schenectady, New York 12305
(518) 382-5077, 8
Fax: (518) 382-5080

Sheriff

Schenectady County Correctional Facility
320 Veeder Avenue
Schenectady, New York 12307
(518) 388-4596
Civil: (518) 388-4304
Fax: (518) 393-5111

Schoharie County

(Third Department, Third Judicial District)

Supreme Court

Courthouse
300 Main Street
P.O. Box 669

Schoharie, New York 12157-0669
(518) 295-8342
Fax: (518) 295-7226

Surrogate's Court

Courthouse
300 Main Street
P.O. Box 669
Schoharie, New York 12157-0669
(518) 295-8383
Chief Clerk: (518) 295-8387
Fax: (518) 295-8451

County Court

Courthouse
290 Main Street
P.O. Box 669
Schoharie, New York 12157-0669
(518) 295-8342
Fax: (518) 295-7226

Family Court

Courthouse
300 Main Street
P.O. Box 669
Schoharie, New York 12157-0669
(518) 295-8383
Fax: (518) 295-8451

Sheriff

157 Depot Lane
P.O. Box 689
Schoharie, New York 12157-0089
Administration: (518) 295-7066
Civil: (518) 296-8888, (518) 295-7080
Fax: (518)295-7094

Schuyler County

(Third Department, Sixth Judicial District)

Supreme Court

Courthouse
Unit 35
105 9th Street
Watkins Glen, New York 14891
(607) 535-7760
Fax: (607) 535-4918

Surrogate's Court

Courthouse
105 9th Street
Watkins Glen, New York 14891

(607) 535-7144
Fax: (607) 535-4918

County Court

Courthouse
105 9th Street
Watkins Glen, New York 14891
(607) 535-7015
Fax: (607) 535-4918
Chief Clerk: (607) 535-7760

Family Court

Courthouse
105 9th Street
Watkins Glen, New York 14891
(607) 535-7143; (607) 535-7760
Fax: (607) 535-4918

Sheriff

106 10th Street
Watkins Glen, New York 14891
(607) 535-8222
Fax: (607) 535-8216

Seneca County

(Fourth Department, Seventh Judicial District)

Supreme Court

Courthouse
48 W. Williams Street
Waterloo, New York 13165
(315) 539-7021
Fax: (315) 539-7929

Surrogate's Court

Courthouse
48 W. Williams Street
Waterloo, New York 13165
(315) 539-7531
Fax: (315) 539-3267

County Court

Courthouse
48 W. Williams Street
Waterloo, New York 13165
(315) 539-7021
Fax: (315) 539-7929

Family Court

Courthouse
48 W. Williams Street

Waterloo, New York 13165
(315) 539-4917
Fax: (315) 539-4225

Sheriff

44 W. Williams Street
Waterloo, New York 13165
(315) 539-9241
Fax: (315) 539-0121

Steuben County

(Fourth Department, Seventh Judicial District)

Supreme Court

3 East Pulteney Square
Bath, New York 14810-1575
(607) 776-7879
Fax: (607) 776-5226

Surrogate's Court

13 East Pulteney Square
Bath, New York 14810-1598
(607) 776-7126
Fax: (607) 776-4987
Chief Clerk: (607) 776-7126

County Court

Courthouse
3 East Pulteney Square
Bath, New York 14810-1575
(607) 776-7879
Fax: (607) 776-5226
Court Clerk: (607) 776-7879

Family Court

Courthouse
3 East Pulteney Square
Bath, New York 14810-1621
(607) 776-9631, Ext. 3450
Fax: (607) 776-7857

City Court

City Hall
12 Civic Center Plaza
Corning, New York 14830-2884
(607) 936-4111
Fax: (607) 936-0519

82 Main Street
P.O. Box 627
Hornell, New York 14843-0627
(607) 324-7531
Fax: (607) 324-6325

Sheriff

Steuben County Jail
7007 Rumsey Street Extension
Bath, New York 14810
(607) 776-7009
Fax: (607) 776-7100

Suffolk County

(Second Department, Tenth Judicial District)

Supreme Court

235 Griffing Avenue
Riverhead, New York 11901
(631) 852-2333
Fax: (631) 852-2340
Email: www.courts.states.ny.us

Surrogate's Court

320 Center Drive
Riverhead, New York 11901
(631) 852-1745
Fax: (631) 852-1777

County Court

210 Center Drive
Riverhead, New York 11901
Civil Dept.: (631) 852-2120
Fax: (631) 852-2568
Chief Clerk: (631) 852-2120, 21

District Court

First District Court

Civil:
3105 Veterans' Memorial Highway
Ronkonkoma, New York 11779-7614
(631) 854-9678, 76
Fax: (631) 854-9681

Second District Court

375 Commack Road
Deer Park, New York 11729
(631) 854-1950
General Information (Central Islip Main District Court): (631) 853-7500
Fax: (631) 854-1956

Third District Court

1850 New York Avenue
Huntington Station, New York 11746
(631) 854-4545
Fax: (631) 854-4549

Fourth District Court

North County Complex Building 158
P.O. Box 6100
Veterans' Memorial Highway
Hauppauge, New York 11788
(631) 853-5400
Fax: (631) 853-5951

Fifth District Court

3105 Veterans' Memorial Highway
Ronkonkoma, New York 11779
(631) 854-9673
(631) 854-9696, 81, 83

Sixth District Court

150 West Main Street
Patchogue, New York 11772
(631) 854-1440
Fax: (631) 854-1444

Family Court

400 Carleton Avenue
Central Islip, New York 11722
(631) 853-4647, 48
Fax: (631) 853-5851; (631) 853-4283

Sheriff

100 Center Drive
Riverhead, New York 11901-3389
(631) 852-2200

Sullivan County

(Third Department, Third Judicial District)

Supreme Court

Courthouse
414 Broadway
Monticello, New York 12701
(845) 794-8811 (Appeal Division)
Chief Clerk: (845) 794-4066
Fax: (845) 7891-6170

Surrogate's Court

Government Center
100 North Street
P.O. Box 5012
Monticello, New York 12701
(845) 794-3000, Ext. 3450
Fax: (845) 794-0310

County Court

Courthouse
414 Broadway
Monticello, New York 12701
Chief Clerk: (845) 794-4066
Fax: (845) 791-6170

Family Court

Government Center
100 North Street
Monticello, New York 12701
(845) 794-3000, Ext. 3460
Fax: (845) 794-0199

Sheriff

County Jail
4 Bushnell Avenue
Monticello, New York 12701
(845) 794-7102
Fax: (845) 794-4060

Tioga County

(Third Department, Sixth Judicial District)

Supreme Court

16 Court Street
P.O. Box 307
Owego, New York 13827
(607) 687-0544
Fax: (607) 687-3240

Surrogate's Court

Court Annex
20 Court Street
P.O. Box 10
Owego, New York 13827
(607) 687-1303
Fax: (607) 687-3240

County Court

16 Court Street
P.O. Box 307
Owego, New York 13827
Chief Clerk: (607) 687-0544
Fax: (607) 687-3240

Family Court

Court Annex
20 Court Street
P.O. Box 10
Owego, New York 13827
(607) 687-1730
Fax: (607) 687-3240

Sheriff

103 Corporate Drive
Owego, New York 13827
(607) 687-1010
Fax: (607) 687-6755

Tompkins County

(Third Department, Sixth Judicial District)

Supreme Court

Courthouse
320 N. Tioga Street
P.O. Box 70
Ithaca, New York 14851-0070
(607) 272-0466
Fax: (607) 256-0301

Surrogate's Court

Courthouse
320 N. Tioga Street
P.O. Box 70
Ithaca, New York 14851-0070
(607) 277-0622
Fax: (607) 256-2572

County Court

Courthouse
320 N. Tioga Street
P.O. Box 70
Ithaca, New York 14851-0070
(607) 272-0466
Fax: (607) 256-0301

Family Court

Courthouse
320 N. Tioga Street
P.O. Box 70
Ithaca, New York 14851-0070
(607) 277-1517
Fax: (607) 277-5027

City Court

118 E. Clinton St.
Ithaca, New York 14850
(607) 273-2263
Fax: (607) 277-3702

Sheriff

779 Warren Road
Ithaca, New York 14850
(607) 257-1345
Fax: (607) 266-5436

Ulster County

(Third Department, Third Judicial District)

Supreme Court

Courthouse
285 Wall Street
Kingston, New York 12401
Clerks: (845) 340-3377
Filings: (845) 340-3288
Fax: (845) 340-3387
Chief Clerk: (845) 340-3370

Surrogate's Court

240 Fair Street
P.O. Box 1800
Kingston, New York 12402-1800
(845) 340-3348
Fax: (845) 340-3352
Chief Clerk: (845) 340-3347
Fax: (845) 256-0301

County Court

Courthouse
285 Wall Street
Kingston, New York 12401-0906
(845) 340-3377
Chief Clerk: (845) 340-3770
Fax: (845) 340-3729

Family Court

16 Lucas Avenue
Kingston, New York 12401-0906
(845) 340-3600
Fax: (845) 340-3626
Chief Clerk: (845) 340-3608

City Court

1 Garraghan Drive
Kingston, New York 12401
(845) 338-2974
Fax: (845) 338-1443

Sheriff

129 Schwenk Drive
Kingston, New York 12401-2941
(845) 340-3802
Fax: (845) 334-8125

Warren County

(Third Department, Fourth Judicial District)

Supreme Court

Warren County Municipal Center
1340 State Route 9
Lake George, New York 12845
(518) 761-6547
Fax: (518) 761-6465; (518) 761-6253
Court Clerk: (518) 761-6431

Surrogate's Court

Warren County Municipal Center
1340 State Route 9
Lake George, New York 12845
(518) 761-6514
Fax: (518) 761-6511; (518) 761-6465

County Court

Warren County Municipal Center
1340 State Route 9
Lake George, New York 12845-9803
Judge Hall Chambers: (518) 761-7695
Fax: (518) 761-7698

Family Court

Warren County Municipal Center
1340 State Route 9
Lake George, New York 12845
(518) 761-6500
Fax: (518) 761-6230

City Court

42 Ridge Street
Glens Falls, New York 12801
(518) 798-4714
Fax: (518) 798-0137

Sheriff

Warren County Municipal Center
1340 State Route 9
Lake George, New York 12845-9803
(518) 761-6477
Fax: (518) 761-6234

Washington County

(Third Department, Fourth Judicial District)

Supreme Court

Courthouse
383 Broadway
Fort Edward, New York 12828
(518) 746-2521
Fax: (518) 746-2519

Surrogate's Court

Courthouse
383 Broadway
Fort Edward, New York 12828
(518) 746-2545
Fax: (518) 746-2547

County Court

Courthouse
383 Broadway
Fort Edward, New York 12828
Clerk: (518) 746-2521
Fax: (518) 746-2519

Family Court

Courthouse
383 Broadway
Fort Edward, New York 12828
(518) 746-2501
Fax: (518) 746-2503

Sheriff

383 Broadway
Fort Edward, New York 12828
(518) 854-9245
Main Fax: (518) 746-2483
Substation Fax: (518) 854-9720

Wayne County

(Fourth Department, Seventh Judicial District)

Supreme Court

Room 106 Hall of Justice
54 Broad Street
Lyons, New York 14489-1199
(315) 946-5457
Fax: (315) 946-5456

Surrogate's Court

Room 106 Hall of Justice
54 Broad Street
Lyons, New York 14489-1199
(315) 946-5430
Fax: (315) 946-5433

County Court

Room 106 Hall of Justice
54 Broad Street
Lyons, New York 14489-1199
(315) 946-5459
Chief Clerk: (315) 946-5457
Fax: (315) 946-5456

Family Court

Room 106 Hall of Justice
54 Broad Street
Lyons, New York 14489-1199
(315) 946-5420
Chief Clerk: (315) 946-5421
Fax: (315) 946-5456

Sheriff

County Jail
7368 Route 31
Lyons, New York 14489-9107
(315) 946-9711
Fax: (315) 946-5811

Westchester County

(Second Department, Ninth Judicial District)

Supreme Court

111 Dr. Martin Luther King Jr. Blvd., Rm. 803
White Plains, New York 10601
Administrative Office: (914) 995-4100
(914) 995-3838
Chief Clerk: (914) 995-4336
Fax: (914) 995-3427

Surrogate's Court

140 Grand Street
White Plains, New York 10601
(914) 995-3712
Chief Clerk: (914) 824-5653
Fax: (914) 995-3728

County Court

111 Dr. Martin Luther King Jr. Blvd.
White Plains, New York 10601
(914) 824-5316
Chief Clerk: (914) 995-4336
Fax: (914) 995-3427

Family Court

111 Dr. Martin Luther King Jr. Blvd.
White Plains, New York 10601
(914) 995-3600
Fax (Clerk): (914) 995-4468

420 North Avenue
New Rochelle, New York 10801
(914) 813-5650
Fax (Clerk): (914) 813-5580; (914) 633-4680

53 South Broadway
Yonkers, New York 10701
(914) 231-2950

Support Matters: (914) 231-2978
Fax: (914) 966-6861

City Court

Two North Roosevelt Square
Mount Vernon, New York 10550-2019
(914) 665-2400
Fax: (914) 699-1230

475 North Avenue
New Rochelle, New York 10801
(914) 654-2291
Fax: (914) 654-0344

2 Nelson Avenue
Peekskill, New York 10566
(914) 737-3405
Fax: (914) 736-1889

21 McCullough Place (formerly Third Street)
Rye, New York 10580
(914) 967-1599
Fax: (914) 967-3308

77 South Lexington Avenue
White Plains, New York 10601
(914) 824-5675, 76
Fax: (914) 422-6058

Robert W. Cacace Justice Center
100 South Broadway
Yonkers, New York 10701
(914) 377-6377
Fax: (914) 377-6395

Sheriff

Westchester County Police
Saw Mill River Parkway
Hawthorne, New York 10532
(914) 864-7700
Fax: (914) 741-4444

Wyoming County

(Fourth Department, Eighth Judicial District)

Supreme Court

Courthouse
147 North Main Street
Warsaw, New York 14569-1193
(716) 786-3148, Ext. 4
Fax: (716) 786-2818

Surrogate's Court

Courthouse
147 North Main Street

Warsaw, New York 14569-1193
(716) 786-3148, Ext. 5
Fax: (716) 786-3800

County Court

Courthouse
147 North Main Street
Warsaw, New York 14569-1193
(716) 786-3148, Ext. 4
Fax: (716) 786-2818

Family Court

Courthouse
147 North Main Street
Warsaw, New York 14569-1193
(716) 786-3148 Ext. 5
Fax: (716) 786-3800

Sheriff

151 North Main Street
Warsaw, New York 14569
(716) 786-8989
Fax: 786-8961

Yates County

(Fourth Department, Seventh Judicial District)

Supreme Court

Courthouse
415 Liberty Street
Penn Yan, New York 14527-1191
(315) 536-5126
Fax: (315) 536-5190

Surrogate's Court

415 Liberty Street
Penn Yan, New York 14527-1176
(315) 536-5130
Fax: (315) 536-5190

County Court

Courthouse
415 Liberty Street
Penn Yan, New York 14527-1191
(315) 536-5126
Fax: (315) 536-5190

Family Court

415 Liberty Street
Penn Yan, New York 14527-1182
(315) 536-5127

Fax: (315) 536-5190
Chief Clerk: (315) 536-5127

Sheriff

Public Safety Building
227 Main Street
Penn Yan, New York 14527
(315) 536-5182
Fax: (315) 572-4365

PART 6

INDEX

Index

INDEX

References in the Index to the Laws are abbreviated as follows:

COR	Correction Law
CPL	Criminal Procedure Law
CPLR	Civil Practice Law and Rules
EXEC	Executive Law
FCA	Family Court Act
JUD	Judiciary Law
MISC	Miscellaneous Death Penalty Provisions
PHL	Public Health Law
PL	Penal Law
VTL	Vehicle and Traffic Law

INDEX

INDEX

[References are to sections of Laws as abbreviated on Page iii. The abbreviation MISC before the section refers to the Miscellaneous Death Penalty Provision following Judiciary Law.]

A

ABANDONMENT OF CHILD
Generally . . . PL 260.00
Child protective proceedings . . . FCA 1059
Defense to . . . PL 260.03

ABORTION
Articles, issuing abortional . . . PL 125.60
Definition . . . PL 125.05
First degree . . . PL 125.45
Issuing abortional articles . . . PL 125.60
Second degree . . . PL 125.40
Self-abortion
 First degree . . . PL 125.55
 Second degree . . . PL 125.50

ABSCONDING FROM CUSTODY (See CUSTODY)

ABSENCE OF INMATES (See INMATES)

ABSTRACT COMPANIES
Search by . . . CPLR 4523

ABUSE
Child protective proceedings (See CHILD PROTECTIVE PROCEEDINGS)
Sexual abuse (See SEXUAL ABUSE)

ACCESSORIAL CONDUCT
Generally . . . PL 20.00
Convictions . . . PL 20.15
Corporations, liability of
 Generally . . . PL 20.20
 Individual's liability for corporate conduct . . . PL 20.25
Defense, lack of . . . PL 20.05
Exemptions . . . PL 20.10

ACCIDENTS AND ACCIDENT REPORTS
Animals, leaving scene of accident without reporting injury to certain . . . VTL 601
Arrest for leaving scene of accident without reporting . . . VTL 602
Leaving scene of accident without reporting
 Generally . . . VTL 600
 Animals, injury to certain . . . VTL 601
 Arrest for violations . . . VTL 602

ACCOMPLICES
Corroboration of accomplice testimony, evidentiary rules on . . . CPL 60.22

ACCOMPLICES—Cont.
Juvenile delinquency; accomplice testimony at fact-finding hearings . . . FCA 343.2
Prostitution, promotion of . . . PL 230.35

ACCUSATORY INSTRUMENTS
Appearance ticket, local criminal court accusatory instrument requirements after issuance of . . . CPL 150.50
Arrest without warrant, dismissal of insufficient accusatory instrument in case involving . . . CPL 140.45
District attorney on local criminal court accusatory instrument, notice to . . . CPL 110.20
Local criminal court accusatory instrument
 Appearance ticket, requirements after issuance of . . . CPL 150.50
 Arrest without warrant, dismissal of insufficient accusatory instrument in case involving . . . CPL 140.45
 Definition . . . CPL 100.10
 Dismissal of insufficient instrument . . . CPL 150.50
 District attorney, notice to . . . CPL 110.20
 Filing procedures . . . CPL 100.55
 Sufficiency on face . . . CPL 100.40
 Youthful offender, sealing of accusatory instrument filed against . . . CPL 720.15
New trial, accusatory instrument status upon order of . . . CPL 470.55
Pre-pleading status, accusatory instrument status upon restoration of action to . . . CPL 470.55
Warrant of arrest, attachment of accusatory instrument to . . . CPL 120.40
Youthful offender, sealing of accusatory instrument filed against . . . CPL 720.15

ACQUITTAL
Discharge of defendant after verdict of . . . . . CPL 330.10

ADJOURNMENT IN CONTEMPLATION OF DISMISSAL
Generally . . . CPL 170.55
Child protective proceedings . . . . FCA 1039; FCA 1039-a
Dispute resolution, for purposes of referral to . . . . CPL 215.30
Fact-finding hearings . . . FCA 748; FCA 749
Family offenses proceeding hearings . . . FCA 836
Juvenile delinquency
 Initial appearance . . . FCA 320.2

[References are to sections of Laws as abbreviated on Page iii. The abbreviation MISC before the section refers to the Miscellaneous Death Penalty Provision following Judiciary Law.]

[References are to sections of Laws as abbreviated on Page iii. The abbreviation MISC before the section refers to the Miscellaneous Death Penalty Provision following Judiciary Law.]

Index

[References are to sections of Laws as abbreviated on Page iii. The abbreviation MISC before the section refers to the Miscellaneous Death Penalty Provision following Judiciary Law.]

ARRAIGNMENT—Cont.

Local criminal courts for arraignment, methods of requiring defendant's appearance in . . . . . CPL 110.10

Material witness order . . . CPL 620.40

Misdemeanor complaint . . . CPL 170.10

Pre-arraignment bail, issuance and service of appearance ticket upon posting of . . . CPL 150.30

Prosecutor's information on misdemeanor complaint . . . CPL 170.10

Simplified traffic information . . . CPL 170.10

Traffic violations . . . VTL 1807

ARREST

Conveyance of prisoner after arrest . . . COR 613

Extradition, arrest for (See EXTRADITION)

Physical force, use of

Escape, prevention of . . . PL 35.30

Making of arrest, prohibitions against use of physical force in . . . PL 35.30

Resisting arrest, prohibitions against use of physical force in . . . PL 35.27

Resisting arrest

Generally . . . PL 205.30

Physical force, prohibitions against use of . . . PL 35.27

Vehicle and Traffic Law (See VEHICLE AND TRAFFIC LAW)

Warrant of (See WARRANT OF ARREST)

Without warrant (See ARREST WITHOUT WARRANT)

ARREST WITHOUT WARRANT

Generally . . . CPL 140.05

Extradition, arrest for . . . CPL 570.34

Local criminal court accusatory instrument, dismissal of insufficient . . . CPL 140.45

Peace officers, arrest by

Generally . . . CPL 140.25

Close pursuit, by officers of other states in . . . CPL 140.55

Post-arrest procedure . . . CPL 140.27

Procedure for . . . CPL 140.27

When authorized . . . CPL 140.30

Where authorized . . . CPL 140.30

Police officers, arrest by

Post-arrest procedure . . . CPL 140.20

Procedure for . . . CPL 140.15

When authorized . . . CPL 140.10

Where authorized . . . CPL 140.10

Private persons, arrest by

Post-arrest procedure . . . CPL 140.40

Procedure for . . . CPL 140.35

When authorized . . . CPL 140.30

Where authorized . . . CPL 140.30

Public places, temporary questioning of persons in . . . CPL 140.50

ARREST WITHOUT WARRANT—Cont.

Search for weapons . . . CPL 140.50

Temporary questioning of persons in public places . . . CPL 140.50

Uniform Close Pursuit Act . . . CPL 140.55

ARSON

Definitions . . . PL 150.00

Fifth degree . . . PL 150.01

Firefighter applicants, search for arson conviction records of volunteer . . . EXEC 837-o

First degree . . . PL 150.20

Fourth degree . . . PL 150.05

Reparation . . . PL 60.27

Restitution . . . PL 60.27

Second degree . . . PL 150.15

Third degree . . . PL 150.10

ARTICLE 78 PROCEEDINGS

Judgments . . . CPLR 7806

Nature of proceeding . . . CPLR 7801

Parties . . . CPLR 7802

Procedure . . . CPLR 7804

Questions raised . . . CPLR 7803

Stays . . . CPLR 7805

ASSAULT

Aggravated assault

Eleven years of age, upon person less than . . . PL 120.12

Peace officers, upon . . . PL 120.11

Police officers, upon . . . PL 120.11

Child day care provider, reckless assault upon person less than eleven years of age by . . . PL 120.01

Child sexual assault (See CHILD SEXUAL ASSAULT)

Emergency medical services professional, on . . . PL 120.08

Firefighter, on . . . PL 120.08

First degree . . . PL 120.10

Gang assault

First degree . . . PL 120.07

Second degree . . . PL 120.06

Paramedic, on . . . PL 120.08

Peace officer, on . . . PL 120.08

Police officer, on . . . PL 120.08

Second degree . . . PL 120.05

Third degree . . . PL 120.00

Vehicular assault

First degree . . . PL 120.04

Second degree . . . PL 120.03

ATTACHMENT

Forfeiture actions (See FORFEITURE—PROCEEDS OF CRIME)

ATTEMPT TO COMMIT CRIME

Generally . . . PL 110.00

Defense, lack of . . . PL 110.10

[References are to sections of Laws as abbreviated on Page iii. The abbreviation MISC before the section refers to the Miscellaneous Death Penalty Provision following Judiciary Law.]

ATTEMPT TO COMMIT CRIME—Cont.
Punishment . . . PL 110.05

ATTENDANCE (See APPEARANCE)

ATTORNEY GENERAL
Undertaking, prosecution of . . . JUD 779

ATTORNEYS
Child protective proceedings
    Appointment of attorney . . . FCA 1022-a
    Duties, attorney's . . . FCA 1052-b
Death penalty (See DEATH PENALTY, subhead: Counsel)
Dispositional hearings, duties at juvenile delinquency . . . FCA 354.2
District attorney (See DISTRICT ATTORNEY)
Evidentiary issues concerning . . . CPLR 4503
Grand jury proceedings, witness' right to attorney in . . . CPL 190.52
Juvenile delinquency
    Dispositional hearings, attorney's duties at . . . FCA 354.2
    Initial appearance, appointment of attorney for . . . FCA 320.2
Supervision, attorney's duties to persons in need of . . . FCA 760

AUTHENTICATION
Newspapers, self-authentication of periodicals of general circulation and . . . CPLR 4532
Official records . . . CPLR 4540
Periodicals of general circulation, self-authentication of . . . CPLR 4532
Self-authentication of newspapers and periodicals of general circulation . . . CPLR 4532

AUTHORIZED DISPOSITIONS OF OFFENDERS
Generally . . . PL 60.01
Applicability of provisions . . . PL 60.00
Cemetery desecration . . . PL 60.29
Civil penalties . . . PL 60.30
Class A, B, certain C and D felonies . . . PL 60.05
Controlled substance offenders, resentencing of . . . PL 60.08; PL 60.09
Corporations . . . PL 60.25
Domestic violence cases . . . PL 60.12
Graffiti, making of; possession of graffiti instruments . . . PL 60.28
Juvenile offenders . . . PL 60.10
Multiple felony offenders . . . PL 60.05
Murder in first degree . . . PL 60.06
Operators of for-hire vehicles, criminal attack on . . . PL 60.07
Penalties (See FINES AND PENALTIES)
Possession of weapon in fourth degree . . . PL 60.11
Reparation . . . PL 60.27
Restitution . . . PL 60.27

AUTHORIZED DISPOSITIONS OF OFFENDERS—Cont.
Traffic infractions . . . PL 60.20
Weapon, possession in fourth degree of . . PL 60.11
Youthful offenders . . . PL 60.02

AUTOMOBILES
Assault, vehicular
    First degree . . . PL 120.04
    Second degree . . . PL 120.03
Auto stripping
    First degree . . . PL 165.10
    Second degree . . . PL 165.11
    Third degree . . . PL 165.09
Identification numbers
    Forgery . . . PL 170.65
    Illegal possession of
        Generally . . . PL 170.70
        Presumptions . . . PL 170.71
    Presumptions as to illegal possession of . . PL 170.71
Livery vehicle safety training program
    Eligibility . . . EXEC 837-h
    Establishment of . . . EXEC 837-g
    Standards . . . EXEC 837-h
Manslaughter, vehicular
    First degree . . . PL 125.13
    Second degree . . . PL 125.12
Operators of for-hire vehicles
    Authorized disposition of offenders for attack on . . . PL 60.07
    Livery vehicle safety training program (See subhead: Livery vehicle safety training program)
    Special information . . . CPL 200.61
Parking violations
    Enforcement and disposition program . . . . . EXEC 837-j
    Uniform parking tickets . . . EXEC 837-i
Presumptions as to illegal possession of identification numbers . . . PL 170.71
Seizure and forfeiture of vehicles used to transport gambling records . . . PL 415.00
Stripping, auto (See subhead: Auto stripping)
Taximeter accelerating device, criminal possession of . . . PL 145.70
Unauthorized use of
    First degree . . . PL 165.08
    Second degree . . . PL 165.06
    Third degree . . . PL 165.05
Vehicle and Traffic Law (See VEHICLE AND TRAFFIC LAW)

AUTOPSY
Prisoners, state liability for expense of autopsy on . . . COR 16

[References are to sections of Laws as abbreviated on Page iii. The abbreviation MISC before the section refers to the Miscellaneous Death Penalty Provision following Judiciary Law.]

Index

[References are to sections of Laws as abbreviated on Page iii. The abbreviation MISC before the section refers to the Miscellaneous Death Penalty Provision following Judiciary Law.]

BRIBERY
Commercial bribery
    First degree
        Generally . . . PL 180.03
        Receiving in . . . PL 180.08
    Second degree
        Generally . . . PL 180.00
        Receiving in . . . PL 180.05
Jurors
    Generally . . . PL 215.19
    Receiving bribe . . . PL 215.20
Labor officials, bribery of
    Generally . . . PL 180.15
    Defenses . . . PL 180.20; PL 180.30
    Definition . . . PL 180.10
    Lack of defense . . . PL 180.30
    Receiving bribe . . . PL 180.25
Public servants, bribery involving (See PUBLIC SERVANTS)
Rent gouging (See RENT GOUGING)
Sports bribery (See SPORTS)
Witnesses (See WITNESSES)

BURDEN OF PROOF
Defenses . . . PL 25.00

BURGLARY
Definition . . . PL 140.00
First degree . . . PL 140.30
Physical force; justification for use in defense of person in course burglary . . . PL 35.20
Possession of burglar's tools . . . PL 140.35
Second degree . . . PL 140.25
Third degree . . . PL 140.20
Tools, possession of burglar's . . . PL 140.35

BURN INJURIES
Failure to report . . . PL 265.26

BUSINESS RECORDS
Evidence, as . . . CPLR 4518
Falsifying (See WRITTEN FALSE STATEMENTS)

C

CANADA
Driver's license, suspension and revocation of; reciprocal agreements . . . VTL 516-a

CAPITAL PUNISHMENT (See DEATH PENALTY)

CAREGIVER
Criminal history information . . . EXEC 837-n
Endangering welfare of vulnerable elderly person
    First degree . . . PL 260.34
    Second degree . . . PL 260.32

CEMETERY DESECRATION
Authorized disposition of offenders . . . PL 60.29

CEMETERY DESECRATION—Cont.
Conditional discharge . . . PL 65.10
First degree . . . PL 145.23
Second degree . . . PL 145.22

CERTIFICATES AND CERTIFICATION
Appeal, certificate granting leave to
    Court of appeals, to . . . CPL 460.20
    Intermediate appellate court, to . . CPL 460.15
Controlled substances, revocation and suspension of certificate of approval for . . . PHL 3390-3396
Conviction, certificate concerning judgment of . . . CPL 60.60
Disabilities, certificate of relief from (See DISABILITIES)
Evidence, certificates as (See EVIDENCE)
Execution, certificate as to . . . COR 661
False certificates, issuing . . . PL 175.40
Fingerprints . . . CPL 60.60
Good conduct . . . COR 703-a; COR 703-b
Inspection certificate issued by Agriculture Department . . . CPLR 4529
Jail time records and certificates . . . COR 600-a
Post-mortem certificate; death penalty cases . . COR 661
Public officers . . . CPLR 4520
Retarded persons, delivery and filing of copy of certificate of conviction to institution for . . . COR 443
Social services, delivery of certificate of conviction to commissioner of . . . COR 71; CPL 380.80
Vehicle and Traffic Law (See VEHICLE AND TRAFFIC LAW)

CHALLENGES (See JURY AND JURORS)

CHARGE TO JURY (See JURY AND JURORS)

CHECKS
Bad checks, issuance of (See FRAUD, subhead: Bad checks, issuance of)
Definition . . . PL 190.00

CHEMICAL TESTS
Age of 21, persons under . . VTL 1192-a; VTL 1194; VTL 1194-a
Alcohol, for . . . VTL 1195
Analysis . . . VTL 1192-a; VTL 1194; VTL 1194-a
Drugs, for . . . VTL 1195
Evidence . . . CPL 60.75; VTL 1195
Hearings . . . VTL 1194-a
Reports . . . VTL 1194-a

CHEMICAL WEAPONS (See TERRORISM, CRIMES OF)

CHILD DAY CARE PROVIDER
Assault by provider upon person less than eleven years old . . . PL 120.01
Misrepresentation by . . . PL 260.30

[References are to sections of Laws as abbreviated on Page iii. The abbreviation MISC before the section refers to the Miscellaneous Death Penalty Provision following Judiciary Law.]

[References are to sections of Laws as abbreviated on Page iii. The abbreviation MISC before the section refers to the Miscellaneous Death Penalty Provision following Judiciary Law.]

COMMISSION OF CORRECTION—Cont.
Chairman . . . COR 44
Citizen's policy . . . COR 42
Complaint review council . . . COR 42
Definitions . . . COR 40
Duties
    Generally . . . COR 45; COR 46
    Medical review board . . . COR 47
Functions
    Generally . . . COR 45; COR 46
    Medical review board . . . COR 47
Medical review board
    Functions, powers and duties . . . COR 47
    Organization of . . . COR 43
Organization
    Generally . . . COR 41
    Medical review board . . . COR 43
Powers
    Generally . . . COR 45; COR 46
    Medical review board . . . COR 47
Preference of action commenced by . . . COR 48

COMMISSION ON FORENSIC SCIENCE (See FORENSIC SCIENCE COMMISSION)

COMMITMENT
Definition . . . CPL 500.10
Sixteen years of age, principal under . . CPL 510.15

COMMUNICATIONS
Eavesdropping (See EAVESDROPPING)
Privacy, right to (See PRIVACY, RIGHT TO)
Privileged (See PRIVILEGED COMMUNICATIONS)

COMMUNITY DISPUTE RESOLUTION CENTER PROGRAM
Administration of centers . . . JUD 849-b
Application procedures . . . JUD 849-c
Definitions . . . JUD 849-a
Establishment . . . JUD 849-b
Funding . . . JUD 849-e
Payment procedures . . . JUD 849-d
Regulations . . . JUD 849-f
Reports . . . JUD 849-g
Rules and regulations . . . JUD 849-f

COMMUNITY TREATMENT FACILITIES
Absconding from . . . PL 205.19
Transfer of eligible inmates to . . . COR 72-a

COMMUTATION OF SENTENCE (See EXECUTIVE CLEMENCY)

COMPLAINT REVIEW COUNCIL
Role of . . . COR 42

COMPOUNDING A CRIME
Generally . . . PL 215.45

COMPUTER CRIMES
Defenses . . . PL 156.50
Definitions . . . PL 156.00
Duplication of computer related material, unlawful . . . PL 156.30
Notice of defenses involving . . . CPL 250.30
Related material, computer
    Duplication, unlawful . . . PL 156.30
    Possession, criminal . . . PL 156.35
Tampering
    First degree . . . PL 156.27
    Fourth degree . . . PL 156.20
    Second degree . . . PL 156.26
    Third degree . . . PL 156.25
Trespass . . . PL 156.10
Unauthorized use of computer . . . PL 156.05

CONDITIONAL DISCHARGE (See PROBATION AND CONDITIONAL DISCHARGE)

CONDITIONAL SALE CONTRACTS
Fraudulent dispositions of property subject to . . PL 185.05

CONFIDENTIALITY
Controlled substances, records or reports relating to . . . PHL 3371; PHL 3373
DNA testing . . . EXEC 995-d
Pre-sentence reports
    Generally . . . CPL 390.50
    HIV-related testing requirement . . CPL 390.15
Privileged communications (See PRIVILEGED COMMUNICATIONS)

CONSPIRACY
Defense, lack of . . . PL 105.30
Enterprise corruption . . . PL 105.35
Evidence . . . PL 105.20
Fifth degree . . . PL 105.05
First degree . . . PL 105.17
Fourth degree . . . PL 105.10
Jurisdiction and venue . . . PL 105.25
Overt act, necessity of . . . PL 105.20
Pleading and proof . . . PL 105.20
Second degree . . . PL 105.15
Sixth degree . . . PL 105.00
Third degree . . . PL 105.13
Venue . . . PL 105.25

CONSTITUTIONALITY
Extradition . . . CPL 570.66

CONSUMER PRODUCTS
Definition . . . PL 145.35
Tampering with
    Consumer product defined . . . PL 145.35
    First degree . . . PL 145.45
    Second degree . . . PL 145.40

Index

[References are to sections of Laws as abbreviated on Page iii. The abbreviation MISC before the section refers to the Miscellaneous Death Penalty Provision following Judiciary Law.]

CONTAGIOUS DISEASES
Outbreak in correctional facility . . . COR 141

CONTEMPT
Aggravated criminal contempt . . . PL 215.52
Appearance, offender's failure to put in . . JUD 777
Application to punish for . . . JUD 756
Civil contempt
    Fines, amount of . . . JUD 773
    Imprisonment, length of . . . JUD 774
    Labor disputes, contempt in cases involving or growing out of . . . JUD 753-a
    Notice to accused . . . JUD 761
    Periodic review of proceedings . . . JUD 774
    Powers of courts to punish . . . JUD 753
    Release of offender . . . JUD 775
    Special proceeding to punish for . . . JUD 754; JUD 760
Court, contempt of . . . JUD 757
Criminal contempt
    Final order directing punishment . . . JUD 770
    Fines, amount of . . . JUD 773
    Habeas corpus
        Generally . . . JUD 767
        Punishment upon return of . . . JUD 771
    Labor disputes, contempt in cases involving or growing out of . . . JUD 753-a
    Power of courts to punish . . . JUD 750
    Punishment for . . . JUD 751
    Requisites of; review of mandates . . JUD 752
    Return of application, punishment upon . . . . JUD 772
First degree . . . PL 215.51
Habeas corpus; criminal contempt
    Generally . . . JUD 767
    Punishment upon return of . . . JUD 771
Indictment, offender liable to . . . JUD 776
Judicial conduct, criminal contempt of state commission of . . . PL 215.66
Labor disputes, contempt in cases involving or growing out of . . . JUD 753-a
Legislature, of . . . PL 215.60
Misconduct at trial term, punishment of . . JUD 781
Notice
    Civil contempt . . . JUD 761
    Show cause, notice to delinquent officer to . . JUD 758
Prosecution and punishment . . . PL 215.54
Punishment . . . PL 215.54
Second degree . . . PL 215.50
State commission on judicial conduct, of . . . . PL 215.66
Summary punishment . . . JUD 755
Sureties, sheriff liable for . . . JUD 780
Temporary state commission, of . . . PL 215.65
Undertaking, prosecution of
    Aggrieved person, by . . . JUD 778

CONTEMPT—Cont.
Undertaking, prosecution of—Cont.
    Attorney-general, by . . . JUD 779
    District attorney, by . . . JUD 779

CONTRACTS
Conditional sale contract, fraudulent disposition of property subject to . . . PL 185.05
Employees' interest in contracts for institution, penalty for . . . COR 22
Evidence, contracts in small print as . . CPLR 4544
Interstate Corrections Compact . . . COR 103
Labor time of inmates in correctional facilities, prohibitions against contracts for . . . COR 103
Officers and employees' interest in contracts for institution, penalty for . . . COR 22

CONTROLLED SUBSTANCES
Addicts and habitual users, dispensing to
    Medical use, dispensing for . . . PHL 3351
    Prohibitions . . . PHL 3350
    Records . . . PHL 3352
    Reports and records . . . PHL 3352
Alcohol and drug rehabilitation program (See ALCOHOL AND DRUG REHABILITATION PROGRAM)
Analysis of dangerous drugs . . . CPL 715.50
Appearance in public under the influence of drugs . . . PL 240.40
Applicability of article to actions and matters occurring or arising before and after effective date . . PHL 3301
Authorized dispositions of offenders . . PL 60.08; PL 60.09
Cannabis grown by unlicensed persons . . PHL 3382
Certificate of approval, revocation and suspension of . . . PHL 3390-3396
Child day care facility, criminal sale in or near . . . PL 220.44
Commissioner, powers and duties of . . . PHL 3308
Criminal possession of (See subhead: Possession of, criminal)
Criminal sale of (See subhead: Sale of, criminal)
Definitions . . . PHL 3302; PL 220.00
Distribution of (See subhead: Manufacture and distribution of)
Drug paraphernalia, criminally using
    First degree . . . PL 220.55
    Hypodermic instruments (See HYPODERMIC INSTRUMENTS)
    Second degree . . . PL 220.50
Enforcement . . . PHL 3385
Exception from schedules of controlled substances . . . PHL 3307
Exemptions . . . PHL 3305
Forfeiture
    Generally . . . PHL 3387

[References are to sections of Laws as abbreviated on Page iii. The abbreviation MISC before the section refers to the Miscellaneous Death Penalty Provision following Judiciary Law.]

Index

[References are to sections of Laws as abbreviated on Page iii. The abbreviation MISC before the section refers to the Miscellaneous Death Penalty Provision following Judiciary Law.]

CORRECTIONAL FACILITIES—Cont.

Information on inmate transfers to foreign nations, availability of . . . COR 71

Inmates (See INMATES)

Interstate Corrections Compact (See INTERSTATE CORRECTIONS COMPACT)

Labor in (See LABOR IN CORRECTIONAL FACILITIES)

Library, availability of information on international offender transfer in . . . COR 71

Local facilities (See LOCAL CORRECTIONAL FACILITIES)

Management of (See MANAGEMENT OF CORRECTIONAL FACILITIES)

Mentally ill inmates, establishment of programs inside facilities for . . . COR 401

New York City (See NEW YORK CITY)

Officers and employees (See CORRECTION OFFICERS AND EMPLOYEES)

Prisoners (See PRISONS AND PRISONERS)

Reformatories, duties of . . . COR 618

Residential treatment facilities

    Coordinated use of state and local facilities . . COR 94

    Transfer of inmates to . . . COR 73

Riot in the first degree . . . PL 240.06

Sex offender, notification requirements upon discharge of (See SEX OFFENDER REGISTRATION ACT)

Social Services Department, cooperation of institution with . . . COR 619

Superintendents of (See SUPERINTENDENTS OF CORRECTIONAL FACILITIES)

Use and designation of . . . COR 70

Work release program (See WORK RELEASE PROGRAM)

CORRECTIONAL SERVICES DEPARTMENT

Confinement of persons by . . . COR 72

Custody of, persons received into . . . COR 71

Employees (See CORRECTION OFFICERS AND EMPLOYEES)

Library of . . . COR 20

Mentally ill inmates, Department's duty to director of hospital concerning . . . COR 405

Officers and employees (See CORRECTION OFFICERS AND EMPLOYEES)

Organization of . . . COR 7

Real property, acquisition of . . . COR 21

Social services, notification of conviction to commissioner of . . . COR 71; CPL 380.80

Statistical analysis . . . COR 29

Testing of certain applicants for employment . . . . COR 8

CORRECTION LAW (GENERALLY)

Alternate correctional facilities; New York City (See ALTERNATE CORRECTIONAL FACILITIES: NEW YORK CITY)

CORRECTION LAW (GENERALLY)—Cont.

Clemency (See EXECUTIVE CLEMENCY)

Commission of correction (See COMMISSION OF CORRECTION)

Commutation of sentence (See EXECUTIVE CLEMENCY)

Correctional services department (See CORRECTIONAL SERVICES DEPARTMENT)

Death penalty (See DEATH PENALTY)

Definitions . . . COR 2

Department of correctional services (See CORRECTIONAL SERVICES DEPARTMENT)

Disabilities, certificate of relief from (See DISABILITIES)

Executive clemency (See EXECUTIVE CLEMENCY)

Facilities, correctional (See CORRECTIONAL FACILITIES)

Furloughs (See FURLOUGHS)

Good behavior (See GOOD BEHAVIOR)

Interstate corrections compact (See INTERSTATE CORRECTIONS COMPACT)

Local conditional release commission (See LOCAL CONDITIONAL RELEASE COMMISSION)

Local correctional facilities (See LOCAL CORRECTIONAL FACILITIES)

Pardons (See EXECUTIVE CLEMENCY)

Shock incarceration program (See SHOCK INCARCERATION PROGRAM)

Short title . . . COR 1

Temporary release program (See TEMPORARY RELEASE PROGRAM)

Work release program (See WORK RELEASE PROGRAM)

CORRECTION OFFICERS AND EMPLOYEES

Appointment by commissioner . . . COR 7

Civil action against . . . COR 24

Closure of facility, notice to employees regarding . . . COR 79-a

Commissioner, appointment by . . . COR 7

Contracts for institution, penalty for interest in . . . COR 22

Death benefits . . . COR 472

Disability benefits . . . COR 472

Oaths by certain officers, administration of . . COR 600

Qualification for employment as correction officer . . . COR 22-a

Retarded persons, institutions for . . . COR 435

Retirement

    Generally . . . COR 470; COR 473

    Compulsory separation from members of department . . . COR 472-a

    Death benefits . . . COR 472

    Disability benefits . . . COR 472

    Guards . . . COR 470

[References are to sections of Laws as abbreviated on Page iii. The abbreviation MISC before the section refers to the Miscellaneous Death Penalty Provision following Judiciary Law.]

CORRECTION OFFICERS AND EMPLOYEES—
Cont.
Retirement—Cont.
    Options . . . COR 470-b
    Revocation by governor, retirement subject to
    . . . COR 471
    Salary basis for computing benefits . . . COR
    470-a
Salary basis for computing benefits . . . COR 470-a
Testing of certain applicants for employment . . . .
  COR 8

CORROBORATION
Accomplice testimony . . . CPL 60.22
Adultery . . . PL 255.30
Child, endangering welfare of . . . PL 260.11
Defendant's statements . . . CPL 60.50
Facilitation, criminal . . . PL 115.15
Incest . . . PL 255.30
Juvenile delinquency; fact-finding hearings
    Accomplice testimony . . . FCA 343.2
    Respondent, statements of . . . FCA 344.2
Perjury . . . PL 210.50
Sex offenses . . . PL 130.16
Stolen property, criminal possession of . . PL 165.65

CORRUPTION
Bribery (See BRIBERY)
Enterprise corruption (See ENTERPRISE CORRUP-
  TION)

COSTS AND FEES
Alternate correctional facilities for New York City;
  costs for establishment, operation and maintenance
  . . . COR 89-g
Crime victim assistance fee . . . CPL 420.35
Discovery . . . CPL 240.70
Extradition, expense of . . . CPL 570.56
Felony prisoners, reimbursement of costs for . . . .
  COR 601-c
Health care in local correction facilities, costs for
  . . . COR 500-h
Inmates, costs for
    Generally (See INMATES)
    Transportation of inmates (See TRANSPORTA-
    TION OF INMATES)
Local correction facilities, health care costs for . . .
  COR 500-h
Mandatory surcharge
    Generally . . . CPL 420.35
    Deferral of . . . CPL 420.40
Sex offender registration, fee charged upon change of
  address for . . . COR 168-b
Transportation of inmates (See TRANSPORTATION
  OF INMATES)
Witnesses
    Material witness . . . CPL 620.80

COSTS AND FEES—Cont.
Witnesses—Cont.
    Subpoenaed witness . . . CPL 610.50

COUNTERFEITING (See TRADEMARK COUN-
  TERFEITING)

COUNTIES
Correctional facilities (See LOCAL CORRECTIONAL
  FACILITIES)
Geographical jurisdiction of offenses . . . CPL 20.40
Jails
    Generally (See LOCAL CORRECTIONAL
    FACILITIES)
    Work release program for (See WORK RELEASE
    PROGRAM, subhead: County jails)
Leasing of state institutions to cities or counties for
  confinement of prisoners . . . COR 79
Work release program for (See WORK RELEASE
  PROGRAM, subhead: County jails)

COUNTY COURTS
Removal action to and from Supreme Court . . CPL
  230.10; CPL 230.20

COURT OF APPEALS
Death sentence, motion for setting aside
    Generally . . . CPL 450.70; CPL 450.80
    Judicial review, basis of . . . CPL 470.30
    Racial bias . . . CPL 470.30
    Stay of judgment . . . CPL 460.40
Defendant, appeal by . . . CPL 450.70
Determination of appeals taken directly upon judgments
  and orders of criminal courts . . . CPL 470.30
Intermediate appellate court, appeals from
    Corrective action . . . CPL 470.40
    Order of appellate court, appeals from . . CPL
    450.90; CPL 470.35
People, direct appeal by . . . CPL 450.80
Stay of judgment
    Death sentence, motion for setting aside . . . .
    CPL 460.40
    Intermediate appellate court to court of appeals,
    pending appeal from . . . CPL 460.60

CREDIT CARDS
Unlawful use of . . . PL 165.17

CREDITORS
Fraud (See FRAUD)

CREDIT TERMS
False statement of, making . . . PL 190.55

CRIME VICTIMS (See VICTIMS)

CRIMINAL CONTEMPT (See CONTEMPT)

[References are to sections of Laws as abbreviated on Page iii. The abbreviation MISC before the section refers to the Miscellaneous Death Penalty Provision following Judiciary Law.]

CRIMINAL COURTS
Appeals
    Court of appeals, judgments and orders of criminal court for direct appeal to . . . CPL 470.30
    Remission of case by appellate court to criminal court upon reversal or modification of judgment . . . CPL 470.45
Chief administrator's power to prescribe forms . . . CPL 10.40
Court of appeals, judgments and orders of criminal court for direct appeal to . . . CPL 470.30
Definitions . . . CPL 10.10
Enumeration . . . CPL 10.10
Family offenses proceedings to, transfer of . . FCA 813
Jurisdiction
    Local criminal courts
        Generally . . . CPL 10.30
        Divestiture of jurisdiction by indictment . . . CPL 170.20; CPL 170.25
    Superior courts . . . CPL 10.20
Local criminal courts (See LOCAL CRIMINAL COURTS)
Superior courts, jurisdiction of . . . CPL 10.20

CRIMINAL FACILITATION (See FACILITATION, CRIMINAL)

CRIMINAL JUSTICE SERVICES DIVISION
Accreditation council, law enforcement agency . . . EXEC 846-h
Ballistic armor vests for police officers . . . EXEC 837-d
Capital prosecution extraordinary assistance program, creation of . . . EXEC 837-l
Children (See MINORS)
Commissioner of
    Municipal police training council, powers and duties with respect to . . . EXEC 841
    Role of . . . EXEC 836
    Security guard advisory council, powers and duties with respect to . . . EXEC 841-c
Courts, duties of . . . EXEC 837-b
Definitions . . . EXEC 835
Duties . . . EXEC 837; EXEC 837-a
Elderly persons
    Committee for coordination of police services to; effective April 1, 1994 . . . EXEC 844-b
    Programs for . . . EXEC 846
Employees . . . EXEC 836
Fingerprinting
    Duties of Division . . . CPL 160.30
    Transmission of report received by police to Division . . . CPL 160.40
Functions . . . EXEC 837; EXEC 837-a
Internet homepage . . . EXEC 843

CRIMINAL JUSTICE SERVICES DIVISION— Cont.
Law enforcement agency accreditation council . . . . EXEC 846-h
Minors (See MINORS)
Missing persons (See MISSING PERSONS)
Municipal police training council (See MUNICIPAL POLICE TRAINING COUNCIL)
Organization . . . EXEC 836
Parking violations
    Enforcement and disposition program . . . . . EXEC 837-j
    Uniform parking tickets . . . EXEC 837-i
Peace officers (See PEACE OFFICERS)
Police department requests, processing . . . . EXEC 837-c
Police officers (See POLICE OFFICERS)
Powers . . . EXEC 837; EXEC 837-a
Security guard advisory council (See SECURITY GUARD ADVISORY COUNCIL)
Soft ballistic armor vests for police officers . . . . . EXEC 837-d
Telecommunications committee, statewide law enforcement . . . EXEC 844-a
Unknown dead persons, identification of . . . EXEC 838
Westchester County for policing special parkways, payments to . . . EXEC 837-q

CRIMINAL NEGLIGENCE
Definition . . . PL 15.05

CRIMINAL PROCEDURE LAW (GENERALLY)
Accusatory instruments (See ACCUSATORY INSTRUMENTS)
Appeals (See APPEALS)
Appearance (See APPEARANCE)
Application of law . . . CPL 1.10
Arraignment (See ARRAIGNMENT)
Arrest
    Warrant of (See WARRANT OF ARREST)
    Without warrant (See ARREST WITHOUT WARRANT)
Bail (See BAIL)
Conditional discharge (See PROBATION AND CONDITIONAL DISCHARGE)
Criminal courts
    Generally (See CRIMINAL COURTS)
    Local criminal courts (See LOCAL CRIMINAL COURTS)
Definitions . . . CPL 1.20
Discovery (See DISCOVERY)
Evidence (See EVIDENCE)
Extradition (See EXTRADITION)
Fingerprinting (See FINGERPRINTING)
Geographical jurisdiction of offenses (See GEOGRAPHICAL JURISDICTION OF OFFENSES)

Index

[References are to sections of Laws as abbreviated on Page iii. The abbreviation MISC before the section refers to the Miscellaneous Death Penalty Provision following Judiciary Law.]

[References are to sections of Laws as abbreviated on Page iii. The abbreviation MISC before the section refers to the Miscellaneous Death Penalty Provision following Judiciary Law.]

[References are to sections of Laws as abbreviated on Page iii. The abbreviation MISC before the section refers to the Miscellaneous Death Penalty Provision following Judiciary Law.]

DEFENSES—Cont.

Child—Cont.

Endangering welfare of, to . . . PL 260.15

Coercion . . . PL 135.70; PL 135.75

Computer crimes . . . PL 156.50

Conspiracy . . . PL 105.30

Culpability, defenses involving lack of (See CULPABILITY)

Entrapment . . . PL 40.05

Forged instrument, criminal possession of . . . . PL 170.35

Gambling offenses (See GAMBLING OFFENSES)

Imprisonment, unlawful . . . PL 135.15

Infancy, defense of . . . PL 30.00

Justification (See JUSTIFICATION)

Juvenile delinquency . . . FCA 303.3

Kidnapping . . . PL 135.30

Labor officials, bribery of . . . PL 180.20; PL 180.30

Lack of

Attempt to commit crime . . . PL 110.10

Coercion . . . PL 135.70

Conspiracy . . . PL 105.30

Facilitation, lack of . . . PL 115.10

Forged instrument, criminal possession of . . . . PL 170.35

Labor officials, bribery of . . . PL 180.30

Larceny . . . PL 155.10

Lottery offenses . . . PL 225.40

Perjury . . . PL 210.30

Prostitute, patronizing . . . PL 230.10

Public servants, receipt of bribery by . . . PL 200.15

Solicitation, criminal . . . PL 100.15

Stolen property, criminal possession of . . PL 165.60

Larceny . . . PL 155.10; PL 155.15

Lottery offenses . . . PL 225.40

Marriage license, unlawfully procuring . . PL 255.20

Minors, dissemination of indecent material to . . PL 235.23

Obscenity . . . PL 235.15

Perjury . . . PL 210.25; PL 210.30

Prostitute, patronizing . . . PL 230.07; PL 230.10

Public servants, bribery involving . . . PL 200.05

Sex offenses . . . PL 130.10

Sexual performance by child; affirmative defenses . . . PL 263.20

Solicitation, criminal . . . PL 100.15

Stolen property, criminal possession of . . PL 165.60

Unlawful imprisonment . . . PL 135.15

DEFINITE SENTENCE

Alternate correctional facilities, good behavior time allowances against definite sentences served in; New York City . . . COR 89-b

Custody of definite sentence inmates, agreements for . . . COR 91; COR 92

DEFINITE SENTENCE—Cont.

Good behavior allowances against; revised Penal Law provisions . . . COR 804

DELIBERATIONS (See JURY AND JURORS)

DENTISTS

Dispositional hearings on dental services for respondent placed in division for youth . . . FCA 355.4

Evidentiary issues concerning . . . CPLR 4504

Malpractice, loss of earnings and impairment of earning ability in actions for . . . CPLR 4546

DEPARTMENT OF AGRICULTURE (See AGRICULTURE DEPARTMENT)

DEPARTMENT OF CORRECTIONAL SERVICES (See CORRECTIONAL SERVICES DEPARTMENT)

DEPOSITION

Supporting (See SUPPORTING DEPOSITION)

DESTRUCTION

Counterfeit goods . . . PL 165.74

Drugs, dangerous (See DRUGS)

Fireworks . . . PL 405.05

Recording of sound, unauthorized . . . PL 420.00

DETAINERS

Agreement on . . . CPL 580.20

DETENTION

Escape from detention facility (See CUSTODY, subhead: Escape from)

Juvenile delinquency

Generally . . . FCA 304.1

Hearing following . . . FCA 307.4

Initial appearance . . . FCA 320.5

Redetention after discharge . . . CPLR 7012

Supervision, persons in need of

Generally . . . FCA 720

Duration of detention . . . FCA 729

Hearing, detention by judge after . . . FCA 728

Preliminary procedures . . . FCA 739

DIAGNOSTIC CLINICS

Establishment and conduct of . . . COR 148

DISABILITIES

Certificate of relief from

Generally . . . COR 701

Courts, issued by . . . COR 702

Definitions . . . COR 700

Filing . . . COR 705

Forms . . . COR 705

Pardon, no status as . . . COR 706

Parole board, issued by . . . COR 703

Revocation of . . . COR 704

Employee disability benefits . . . COR 472

[References are to sections of Laws as abbreviated on Page iii. The abbreviation MISC before the section refers to the Miscellaneous Death Penalty Provision following Judiciary Law.]

DISABILITIES—Cont.

Relief from, certificate of (See subhead: Certificate of relief from)

DISABLED PERSONS

Animal trained to aid, harming
    First degree . . . PL 195.12
    Restitution to person with disability . . . . PL 60.21
    Second degree . . . PL 195.11
Endangering welfare of physically disabled persons . . . PL 260.25

DISCLOSURE

Discovery (See DISCOVERY)
DNA testing
    Generally . . . EXEC 995-d
    Penalties for disclosure . . . EXEC 995-f
Eavesdropping, information obtained through . . . . CPL 700.65
Enterprise corruption; court ordered disclosure . . . . PL 460.80
Forfeiture actions . . . CPLR 1326
Grand jury disclosure, unlawful . . . PL 215.70
HIV-related testing
    Requirement . . . CPL 390.15
    Sexual offense case, testing of defendant in . . . FCA 347.1
Indictment, unlawful disclosure of . . . PL 215.75
Library circulation records . . . CPLR 4509
Privileged communications (See PRIVILEGED COMMUNICATIONS)
Video surveillance, information obtained through . . . CPL 700.65

DISCOVERY

Child protective proceedings . . . . FCA 1038; FCA 1038-a
Continuing duty to disclose . . . CPL 240.60
Court order . . . CPL 240.40
Criminal acts, disclosure of prior uncharged . . CPL 240.43
Criminal history of witnesses, discovery upon trial of . . . CPL 240.45
Defendant's demand . . . CPL 240.20
Definitions . . . CPL 240.10
Demand for
    Defendant's demand . . . CPL 240.20
    Procedure . . . CPL 240.80
    Prosecutor's demand . . . CPL 240.30
    Refusal of . . . CPL 240.35; CPL 240.80
Duty to disclose, continuing . . . CPL 240.60
Fees . . . CPL 240.70
Immoral acts, disclosure of prior uncharged . . CPL 240.43
Interrogatories of witnesses on commission . . CPL 680.50

DISCOVERY—Cont.

Juvenile delinquency (See DISCOVERY: JUVENILE DELINQUENCY)
Motion procedure . . . CPL 240.90
Pre-trial discovery, prosecution of information and . . . CPL 340.30
Pre-trial hearing, upon . . . CPL 240.44
Prior statements of witnesses, discovery upon trial of . . . CPL 240.45
Prior uncharged acts, disclosure of . . . CPL 240.43
Prosecutor's demand . . . CPL 240.30
Protective orders . . . CPL 240.50
Refusal of demand . . . CPL 240.35
Sanctions . . . CPL 240.70
Supporting deposition (See SUPPORTING DEPOSITION)
Vicious or immoral acts, disclosure of prior uncharged . . . CPL 240.43
Violations . . . CPL 240.75
Witnesses, discovery upon trial of prior statements and criminal history of . . . CPL 240.45

DISCOVERY: JUVENILE DELINQUENCY

Continuing duty to disclose . . . FCA 331.5
Court order, discovery upon . . . FCA 331.3
Demand
    Motion procedure and . . . FCA 331.7
    Party, discovery upon demand of . . FCA 331.2
Discovery defined . . . FCA 331.1
History of witnesses . . . FCA 331.4
Motion procedures . . . FCA 331.7
Pre-trial motions
    Definition . . . FCA 332.1
    Procedure . . . FCA 332.2
Prior statements . . . FCA 331.4
Protective orders . . . FCA 331.5
Sanctions . . . FCA 331.6

DISCRETIONARY REDUCTION OF SENTENCE

Work release program for county jails, eligibility of person participating in . . . COR 876

DISCRIMINATION

Death penalty case, racial bias issues in
    Court of Appeals, review by . . . CPL 470.30
    Prospective jurors, of . . . CPL 270.16
Prior convictions, application for license or employment by persons with; prohibitions against unfair discrimination . . . COR 752

DISMISSAL OF CHARGES

Adjournment in contemplation of dismissal (See ADJOURNMENT IN CONTEMPLATION OF DISMISSAL)
Effect of . . . CPL 215.40
Grand jury . . . CPL 190.75

[References are to sections of Laws as abbreviated on Page iii. The abbreviation MISC before the section refers to the Miscellaneous Death Penalty Provision following Judiciary Law.]

[References are to sections of Laws as abbreviated on Page iii. The abbreviation MISC before the section refers to the Miscellaneous Death Penalty Provision following Judiciary Law.]

DRIVER'S LICENSE: SUSPENSION AND REVO-CATION—Cont.

Forfeitures

    Certification to commissioner . . . VTL 514

    Unlicensed operation of vehicle under certain circumstances, seizure and forfeitures for . . . VTL 511-c

Fraudulent license, sale or purchase of . . VTL 392-a

Nonappearance, certification of . . . VTL 514

Notification of . . . VTL 514-a

Probationary periods, for violations committed during . . . VTL 510-b

Reciprocal agreements

    Canada, agreements with provinces of . . VTL 516-a

    Traffic offenses, reporting of . . . VTL 516-b

Redemption of unlawfully operated vehicles, seizure and . . . VTL 511-b

Reissuance . . . VTL 510

Seizures

    Unlawfully operated vehicles, seizure and redemption of . . . VTL 511-b

    Unlicensed operation of vehicle under certain circumstances . . . VTL 511-c

Stolen or fraudulent license, sale or purchase of . . . VTL 392-a

DRIVING WHILE INTOXICATED

Vehicle and Traffic Law (See VEHICLE AND TRAFFIC LAW, subhead: Alcohol and drug-related offenses)

DRUGS

Analysis of dangerous drugs . . . CPL 715.50

Appearance in public under the influence of . . . PL 240.40

Controlled substances (See CONTROLLED SUBSTANCES)

Destruction of dangerous drugs

    Affidavit of destruction . . . CPL 715.40

    Court order, pursuant to . . . . CPL 60.70; CPL 715.30

    Definition . . . CPL 715.05

    Notice, proceedings on motion upon . . . CPL 715.20

    Pre-trial motion . . . CPL 715.10

Injection of narcotics, criminal . . . PL 220.46

Marijuana (See MARIJUANA)

Methamphetamine (See CONTROLLED SUBSTANCES)

Prescriptions (See PRESCRIPTIONS)

Special narcotics parts of supreme court in cities with population of one million or more (See JUDICIARY LAW, subhead: Special narcotics parts of supreme court in cities with population of one million or more)

DURESS

Defense of . . . PL 40.00

E

EAVESDROPPING

Generally . . . PL 250.05

Admissibility . . . CPLR 4506

Definitions . . . PL 250.00

Devices, possession of . . . PL 250.10

Electronic access device; defined . . . PL 170.00

Failure to report wiretapping . . . PL 250.15

Suppression of evidence . . . CPLR 4506

Unlawful surveillance (See UNLAWFUL SURVEILLANCE)

Warrant (See EAVESDROPPING OR VIDEO SURVEILLANCE WARRANTS)

EAVESDROPPING OR VIDEO SURVEILLANCE WARRANTS

Generally . . . CPL 700.10

Administrative office of United States courts, reports to . . . CPL 700.60

Amendment, order of . . . CPL 700.65

Application

    Generally . . . CPL 700.20

    Content . . . CPL 700.20

    Custody of . . . CPL 700.55

    Determination of . . . CPL 700.25

Content . . . CPL 700.30

Custody of warrants, applications and recordings . . . CPL 700.55

Definitions . . . CPL 700.05

Determination of application . . . CPL 700.25

Disclosure and use of information . . . CPL 700.65

Divulging warrant . . . PL 250.20

Emergency situations, temporary authorization for . . . CPL 700.21

Execution, manner and time of . . . CPL 700.35

Extension, order of . . . CPL 700.40

Form and content . . . CPL 700.30

Intention to use, notice of . . . CPL 700.70

Issuance of . . . CPL 700.15

Manner of execution . . . CPL 700.35

Notice . . . CPL 700.50; CPL 700.70

Order of extension . . . CPL 700.40

Progress reports . . . CPL 700.50

Recordings, custody of . . . CPL 700.55

Reports

    Administrative office of United States courts, reports to . . . CPL 700.60

    Progress reports . . . CPL 700.50

Temporary authorization for emergency situations . . . CPL 700.21

Time of execution . . . CPL 700.35

Use of information, disclosure and . . . CPL 700.65

EDUCATION

Correctional education . . . COR 136

[References are to sections of Laws as abbreviated on Page iii. The abbreviation MISC before the section refers to the Miscellaneous Death Penalty Provision following Judiciary Law.]

EDUCATION—Cont.

Death penalty cases, continuing legal education classes for attorneys assigned to . . . EXEC 837-a

Director of, appointment of . . . COR 15-b

EDUCATION DEPARTMENT

Licensed professional convicted of felony, notice to department where . . . CPL 440.55

ELDERLY PERSONS

Criminal justice services

    Police services, committee for coordination of; effective April 1, 1994 . . . EXEC 844-b

    Programs for aging . . . EXEC 846

Endangering welfare of vulnerable elderly person

    First degree . . . PL 260.34

    Second degree . . . PL 260.32

Vulnerable elderly person

    Definition . . . PL 260.30

    Endangering welfare of

        First degree . . . PL 260.34

        Second degree . . . PL 260.32

ELECTRONIC APPEARANCE (See APPEARANCE)

ELECTRONIC SURVEILLANCE (See EAVESDROPPING)

EMERGENCY MEDICAL SERVICES PROFESSIONAL

Assault on . . . PL 120.08

Obstruction of . . . PL 195.16

EMINENT DOMAIN

Correctional Services Department, acquisition of real property by . . . COR 21

EMPLOYERS AND EMPLOYEES

Aggravated harassment of employee of local correctional facility by inmate . . . PL 240.32

Bribery (See BRIBERY)

Caregivers, criminal history information of . . . . . EXEC 837-n

Correction officers and employees (See CORRECTION OFFICERS AND EMPLOYEES)

Criminal Justice Services Division . . . EXEC 836

Government employees (See PUBLIC SERVANTS)

Prior convictions, employment applications by persons with (See PRIOR CONVICTIONS, subhead: License or employment application by persons with)

Public servants (See PUBLIC SERVANTS)

Witness, employer unlawfully penalizing . . . . . PL 215.14

EMPLOYMENT

Correctional facilities, of inmates in . . . COR 171

Prior convictions, license or employment application by persons with (See PRIOR CONVICTIONS, subhead: License or employment application by persons with)

EMPLOYMENT—Cont.

Temporary release program

    Prohibitions against employment . . . COR 859

    Work release program (See WORK RELEASE PROGRAM)

Work release program (See WORK RELEASE PROGRAM)

ENTERPRISE CORRUPTION

Generally . . . PL 460.20

Civil actions notice . . . CPLR 1355

Civil remedies . . . CPLR 1353

Consent to prosecute . . . PL 460.60

Court ordered disclosure . . . PL 460.80

Definitions . . . PL 460.10

Disclosure, court ordered . . . PL 460.80

Forfeiture . . . PL 460.30

Indictment . . . CPL 200.65

Joinder of party . . . CPLR 1354

Jurisdiction . . . PL 460.40

Legislative findings . . . PL 460.00

Limitations . . . PL 460.25

Previous prosecution, exemption from prosecution by reason of . . . CPL 40.50

Prosecution

    Generally . . . PL 460.50

    Consent to prosecute . . . PL 460.60

    Previous prosecution, exemption from prosecution by reason of . . . CPL 40.50

Provisional remedies . . . PL 460.70

Remedies, provisional . . . PL 460.70

ENTRAPMENT

Defense of . . . PL 40.05

ESCAPE

Custody, from (See CUSTODY)

Inmates (See INMATES)

EVIDENCE

Generally . . . CPL 60.10

Admissibility of (See ADMISSIBILITY OF EVIDENCE)

Age of child, proof of . . . CPLR 4516

Alcohol and drugs, chemical test evidence for . . . . VTL 1195

Anatomically correct dolls, use of . . . CPL 60.44

Attorneys, issues concerning . . . CPLR 4503

Authentication (See AUTHENTICATION)

Burden of proof; defenses . . . PL 25.00

Business records . . . CPLR 4518

Certificates

    Inspection certificates issued by U.S. Department of Agriculture . . . CPLR 4529

    Judgments of conviction and fingerprints, concerning . . . CPL 60.60

    Marriage certificate . . . CPLR 4526

    Population, certificate of . . . CPLR 4530

[References are to sections of Laws as abbreviated on Page iii. The abbreviation MISC before the section refers to the Miscellaneous Death Penalty Provision following Judiciary Law.]

EVIDENCE—Cont.

Chemical test evidence . . . CPL 60.75; VTL 1195

Child protective proceedings . . . FCA 1046

Chiropractors, issues concerning . . . CPLR 4504

Compulsion of evidence

    Grand jury proceedings . . . CPL 190.40

    Immunity, by offer of (See IMMUNITY, subhead: Compulsion of evidence by offer of)

Confidential communications (See PRIVILEGED COMMUNICATIONS)

Conspiracy . . . PL 105.20

Contracts in small print . . . CPLR 4544

Convictions (See CONVICTIONS)

Copies of statements under Uniform Commercial Code, Article 9 . . . CPLR 4525

Corroboration

    Accomplice testimony . . . CPL 60.22

    Defendant's statements . . . CPL 60.50

Damages, prima facie proof of . . . CPLR 4533-a

Dangerous drugs destroyed pursuant to court order . . . CPL 60.70

Dentists, issues concerning . . . CPLR 4504

Disclosure (See DISCLOSURE)

Discovery (See DISCOVERY)

DNA testing, records and reports of . . . CPLR 4518

Drugs, chemical test evidence for alcohol and . . . . VTL 1195

Eavesdropping evidence . . . CPLR 4506

Fact-finding hearings, juvenile delinquency (See FACT-FINDING HEARINGS: JUVENILE DELINQUENCY)

Family offenses proceedings

    Hearings . . . FCA 834

    Rules of evidence for proceedings in family court . . . CPL 60.46

Fingerprints, certificates concerning . . . CPL 60.60

Grand jury (See GRAND JURY)

Grand larceny . . . PL 155.45

Handwriting comparison . . . CPLR 4536

Immunity, compulsion of evidence by offer of (See IMMUNITY, subhead: Compulsion of evidence by offer of)

Imprisonment evidence in pre-sentence proceedings . . . CPL 400.22

Inconsistent statements, proof as to . . . PL 210.20

Inspection certificates issued by U.S. Department of Agriculture . . . CPLR 4529

Joint tort-feasor, proof of payment by . . . . CPLR 4533-b

Judicial notice of law . . . CPLR 4511

Justice of the peace, proof of proceedings before . . . CPLR 4541

Juvenile delinquency (See JUVENILE DELIN-QUENCY)

Market reports . . . CPLR 4533

Marriage certificate . . . CPLR 4526

EVIDENCE—Cont.

Measurement used by surveyor, standard of . . . . . CPLR 4534

Medical malpractice, loss of earnings and impairment of earning ability in actions for . . . CPLR 4546

Methods other than those authorized by article . . . CPLR 4543

Missing persons, death or other status of . . . CPLR 4527

Murder in first degree, pre-sentence proceeding for defendant convicted of . . . CPL 400.27

Nurses, issues concerning . . . CPLR 4504

Physicians, issues concerning . . . CPLR 4504

Podiatrists, issues concerning . . . CPLR 4504

Pre-sentence proceeding for defendant convicted of murder in first degree . . . CPL 400.27

Prior convictions, proof of . . . CPL 60.40

Privileged communications (See PRIVILEGED COMMUNICATIONS)

Psychiatric evidence, notice of intent to proffer . . . CPL 250.10

Public officers, certificate or affidavit of . . . CPLR 4520

Rape crisis counselor evidence . . CPL 60.76; CPLR 4510

Real property (See REAL PROPERTY)

Records (See RECORDS AND REPORTS)

Reproduction of original . . . CPLR 4539

Self-incrimination, privilege against; witnesses . . . . CPLR 4501

Sex offenses (See SEX OFFENSES)

Social workers, issues concerning . . . CPLR 4508

Spouse, issues concerning . . . CPLR 4502

Standards of proof

    Conviction . . . CPL 70.20

    Definitions . . . CPL 70.10

Subpoenaed evidence, possession of . . CPL 610.25

Support payments as, records of . . . CPLR 4518

Suppression of (See SUPPRESSION OF EVIDENCE)

Tampering with physical evidence

    Generally . . . PL 215.40

    Definitions . . . PL 215.35

Testimony (See WITNESSES)

Unavailability of person at trial, affidavit of service or posting notice for . . . CPLR 4531

Uniform Commercial Code, copies of statements under Article 9 of . . . CPLR 4525

Weather conditions . . . CPLR 4528

Witnesses (See WITNESSES)

Writings (See WRITINGS)

EXECUTIVE CLEMENCY

Application for clemency . . . COR 261

Appointment of person to hear application . . COR 262

Certificate of relief from disability; no status as pardon . . . COR 706

[References are to sections of Laws as abbreviated on Page iii. The abbreviation MISC before the section refers to the Miscellaneous Death Penalty Provision following Judiciary Law.]

[References are to sections of Laws as abbreviated on Page iii. The abbreviation MISC before the section refers to the Miscellaneous Death Penalty Provision following Judiciary Law.]

[References are to sections of Laws as abbreviated on Page iii. The abbreviation MISC before the section refers to the Miscellaneous Death Penalty Provision following Judiciary Law.]

[References are to sections of Laws as abbreviated on Page iii. The abbreviation MISC before the section refers to the Miscellaneous Death Penalty Provision following Judiciary Law.]

FELONY COMPLAINT—Cont.

Reduction of charges . . . CPL 180.50

Release of defendant from custody upon failure of timely disposition . . . CPL 180.80

Removal of action from one local criminal court to another . . . CPL 180.20

Termination of prosecution . . . CPL 180.85

Verification . . . CPL 100.30

FEMALE INMATES (See WOMEN)

FIFTH DEGREE OFFENSES (See specific headings)

FINANCIAL STATEMENTS

False statements, issuing . . . PL 175.45

FINES AND PENALTIES

Attempt to commit crime . . . PL 110.05

Civil penalties . . . PL 60.30

Collection of

     Generally . . . CPL 420.10

     Corporation, fines imposed on . . . CPL 420.20

Contempt . . . JUD 773

Corporations . . . CPL 420.20; PL 80.10

Credit card, payment by . . . CPL 420.05

Crime victim assistance fee . . CPL 420.35; PL 60.35

Defendant's gain from offense, based of . . . . CPL 400.30

DNA databank fee . . . PL 60.35

DNA tests or analysis, disclosure of . . . EXEC 995-f

Extradition proceedings, penalties for violation of rights of accused in . . . CPL 570.26

Felonies . . . PL 80.00

Leaving scene of accident without reporting injury to certain animals . . . VTL 601

Littering on railroad tracks and rights-of-ways . . . . PL 145.50

Mandatory surcharge

     Generally . . . CPL 420.35; PL 60.35

     Deferral of . . . CPL 420.40

Misdemeanors . . . PL 80.05

Money laundering . . . PL 470.20

Multiple offenses . . . PL 80.15

Railroad tracks, littering on . . . PL 145.50

Remission of . . . CPL 420.30

Rights-of-ways, littering on . . . PL 145.50

Sex offenders

     Failure to register or verify as, penalty upon . . . COR 168-t

     Registration fee . . . PL 60.35

     Supplemental sex offender victim fee . . . PL 60.35

Vehicle and Traffic Law (See VEHICLE AND TRAFFIC LAW)

Violations . . . PL 80.05

FINGERPRINTING

Appearance ticket, fingerprinting in conjunction with . . . CPL 150.70

FINGERPRINTING—Cont.

Certificates concerning, evidentiary rules on . . CPL 60.60

Criminal history records search for certain employment, appointments, licenses, registrations or permits

     Caregivers . . . EXEC 837-n

     New York City . . . EXEC 837-m

     Westchester County . . . EXEC 837-p

Criminal justice services division

     Duties of . . . CPL 160.30

     Transmission of report received by police . . . CPL 160.40

Forwarding of . . . CPL 160.20

Juvenile delinquents (See JUVENILE DELINQUENCY)

Pre-sentence report . . . CPL 390.10

Procedure . . . CPL 160.20

Requirements . . . CPL 160.10

Summons procedure, fingerprinting . . . CPL 130.60

Termination of criminal action, return of fingerprints upon . . . CPL 160.50; CPL 160.55

FIRE

Arson (See ARSON)

Burn injuries, failure to report . . . PL 265.26

Correctional facility, fire in . . . COR 25; COR 507

Mutual assistance by institutional and local fire fighting facilities . . . COR 25

Removal of inmates in case of . . . COR 507

FIREARMS

Criminal sale of (See subhead: Sale of, criminal)

Criminal use of (See subhead: Use of, criminal)

Definitions . . . PL 265.00

Family Court Act

     Surrender, order to . . . FCA 842-a

     Suspension and revocation of license . . FCA 842-a

Licenses to carry, possess, repair and dispose of

     Certification . . . PL 400.00

     Expiration . . . PL 400.00

     Ineligibility for license . . . FCA 842-a

     Renewal . . . PL 400.00

     Requirements . . . PL 400.00

     Retired sworn members of state police, granting to . . . PL 400.01

     Suspension and revocation . . CPL 530.14; FCA 842-a

Loss of, report of . . . PL 400.10

Minors

     Aid of minor, sale with . . . PL 265.14

     Possession by . . . PL 265.20

     Sale to . . . PL 265.16

Purchase of

     Contiguous states, rifles and/or shotguns in . . PL 265.40

     Criminal purchase . . . PL 265.17

Report of theft or loss of . . . PL 400.10

[References are to sections of Laws as abbreviated on Page iii. The abbreviation MISC before the section refers to the Miscellaneous Death Penalty Provision following Judiciary Law.]

FIREARMS—Cont.

Sale of, criminal

First degree . . . PL 265.13

Minors

Aid of minor, sale with . . . PL 265.14

Sale to . . . PL 265.16

Second degree . . . PL 265.12

Third degree . . . PL 265.11

Surrender firearms, order to . . . FCA 342-a

Suspension and revocation of licenses to carry, possess, repair and dispose of . . . CPL 530.14; FCA 842-a

Theft, report of . . . PL 400.10

Use of, criminal

First degree . . . PL 265.09

Second degree . . . PL 265.08

FIREFIGHTERS AND FIREFIGHTING

Arson conviction records of volunteer firefighter applicants, search for . . . EXEC 837-o

Assault on firefighter . . . PL 120.08

Obstruction of firefighting operations . . . PL 195.15

Volunteer firefighter applicants, search for arson conviction records of . . . EXEC 837-o

FIREWORKS

Dangerous fireworks, unlawfully dealing with . . PL 270.00

Destruction of, seizure and . . . PL 405.05

Seizure and destruction of . . . PL 405.05

Unlawfully dealing with . . . PL 270.00

FIRST DEGREE OFFENSES (See specific headings)

FITNESS TO PROCEED (See MENTAL DISEASE OR DEFECT)

FOREIGN COUNTRIES

Extradition of defendants in . . . CPL 590.10

Transfer of inmates to . . . COR 71

FOREIGN RECORDS

Evidence, as . . . CPLR 4542

FORENSIC SCIENCE COMMISSION

Generally . . . EXEC 995-a

Definitions . . . EXEC 995

DNA testing (See DNA TESTING)

Duties . . . EXEC 995-b

Powers . . . EXEC 995-b

FORFEITURE

Aircraft used to transport or conceal gambling records . . . PL 415.00

Bail (See BAIL)

Controlled substances (See CONTROLLED SUBSTANCES)

Crime, proceeds of (See FORFEITURE—PROCEEDS OF CRIME)

FORFEITURE—Cont.

Dispositions of assets subject to, unlawful . . . . PL 215.80

Driver's license, suspension and revocation of

Certification of forfeitures to commissioner . . . VTL 514

Unlicensed operation of vehicle under certain circumstances . . . VTL 511-c

Enterprise corruption . . . PL 460.30

Gambling records; seizure of any vehicles, vessels or aircraft used to transport or conceal . . PL 415.00

Pornography, equipment used to promote . . . . PL 410.00

Proceeds of crime (See FORFEITURE—PROCEEDS OF CRIME)

Recording of sound, equipment used in unauthorized . . . PL 420.05

Unlicensed operation of vehicle under certain circumstances . . . VTL 511-c

Vehicle and Traffic Law

Dispositions . . . VTL 1803

Driver's license, suspension and revocation of

Certification of forfeitures to commissioner . . . VTL 514

Unlicensed operation of vehicle under certain circumstances . . . VTL 511-c

Vehicles, vessels or aircraft used to transport gambling records . . . PL 415.00

Vessels

Controlled substances, any vehicles or vessels used for transportation or conveyance . . . . PHL 3388

Gambling records, vessels used to transport . . . PL 415.00

FORFEITURE—PROCEEDS OF CRIME

Actions . . . CPLR 1311

Adverse claims, proceedings to determine . . CPLR 1327

Application of article . . . CPLR 1351

Attachment

Annulment of . . . CPLR 1330

Creditor's rights in personal property . . CPLR 1314

Debt or property subject to, proper garnishee for . . . CPLR 1313

Discharge of . . . CPLR 1328

Disposition of attachment property after execution issued . . . CPLR 1332

Garnishee (See subhead: Garnishee)

Levy (See subhead: Levy)

Modification of . . . CPLR 1329

Notice

Order of attachment on . . . CPLR 1316

Order of attachment without . . . CPLR 1317

[References are to sections of Laws as abbreviated on Page iii. The abbreviation MISC before the section refers to the Miscellaneous Death Penalty Provision following Judiciary Law.]

[References are to sections of Laws as abbreviated on Page iii. The abbreviation MISC before the section refers to the Miscellaneous Death Penalty Provision following Judiciary Law.]

FOR-HIRE VEHICLES (See AUTOMOBILES, subhead: Operators of for-hire vehicles)

FORTUNE TELLING
Definition . . . PL 165.35

FOSTER CARE
Permanency hearing
    Generally . . . FCA 355.5
    Notice of . . . FCA 741-a; FCA 1040
    Opportunity to be heard . . . . FCA 741-a; FCA 1040

FOURTH DEGREE OFFENSES (See specific headings)

FRAUD
Accosting, fraudulent . . . PL 165.30
Anti-security items, criminal possession of . . . PL 170.47
Bad checks, issuance of
    Generally . . . PL 190.05
    Defenses . . . PL 190.15
    Definitions . . . PL 190.00
    Presumptions . . . PL 190.10
Bribery (See BRIBERY)
Collection practices, unlawful . . . PL 190.50
Conditional sale contract, fraudulent disposition of property subject to . . . PL 185.15
Controlled substances, obtaining . . . PHL 3397
Corporate official, misconduct by . . . PL 190.35
Creditors
    Conditional sale contract, fraudulent disposition of property subject to . . . PL 185.15
    Insolvency, fraud in . . . PL 185.00
    Mortgaged property, fraudulent disposition of . . . PL 185.10
    Security interests . . . PL 185.05
False advertising . . . PL 190.20
False personation . . . PL 190.23
False written statements (See WRITTEN FALSE STATEMENTS)
Forgery (See FORGERY)
Government, defrauding . . . PL 195.20
Impersonation, criminal
    First degree . . . PL 190.26
    Second degree . . . PL 190.25
Insolvency, fraud in . . . PL 185.00
Insurance fraud (See INSURANCE FRAUD)
Misconduct by corporate official . . . PL 190.35
Mortgaged property, fraudulent disposition of . . PL 185.10
Police uniforms, criminal sale of . . . PL 190.27
Prescriptions, unlawful sale of . . . PL 190.70
Scheme to defraud
    First degree . . . PL 190.65
    Prescriptions, unlawful sale of . . . PL 190.70
    Second degree . . . PL 190.60

FRAUD—Cont.
Security interests . . . PL 185.05
Signatures, fraudulently obtaining . . . PL 165.20
Simulation, criminal . . . PL 170.45
Slugs, unlawfully using (See SLUGS)
Usury, criminal
    First degree . . . PL 190.42
    Second degree . . . PL 190.40
Welfare fraud (See WELFARE FRAUD)
Wills, unlawful concealment of . . . PL 190.30
Written false statements (See WRITTEN FALSE STATEMENTS)

FUNERAL SERVICE
Absence of inmate for . . . COR 113; COR 509

FURLOUGHS
Generally . . . COR 630
Absconding from furlough program . . . PL 205.18
Conduct of inmates participating in program . . . . . COR 634
Definitions . . . COR 631
Eligible inmates, procedure for furlough release of . . . COR 633
Establishment of furlough program . . . COR 632

G

GAMBLING OFFENSES
Defenses
    Devices, possession of gambling . . PL 225.32
    Lottery offenses . . . PL 225.40
    Records, possession of gambling . . PL 225.25
Definitions . . . PL 225.00
Devices, possession of gambling
    Generally . . . PL 225.30
    Defenses . . . PL 225.32
Lottery offenses . . . PL 225.40
Presumptions . . . PL 225.35
Promotion of gambling
    First degree . . . PL 225.10
    Second degree . . . PL 225.05
Records, possession of gambling
    Defenses . . . PL 225.25
    First degree . . . PL 225.20
    Second degree . . . PL 225.15

GANG ASSAULT
First degree . . . PL 120.07
Second degree . . . PL 120.06

GEOGRAPHICAL JURISDICTION OF OFFENSES
Cities . . . CPL 20.50
Communications between jurisdictions . . CPL 20.60
Counties . . . CPL 20.40
Definitions . . . CPL 20.10
Partly committed within state, offense . . CPL 20.30

[References are to sections of Laws as abbreviated on Page iii. The abbreviation MISC before the section refers to the Miscellaneous Death Penalty Provision following Judiciary Law.]

GEOGRAPHICAL JURISDICTION OF OF-FENSES—Cont.

State jurisdiction . . . CPL 20.20

Towns . . . CPL 20.50

Transportation of property between jurisdictions . . . CPL 20.60

Villages . . . CPL 20.50

GIFTS

Commissioner of correction, acceptance by . . COR 15-c

GOOD BEHAVIOR

Alternate correctional facilities, good behavior time allowances against definite sentences served in; New York City . . . COR 89-b

Certificate of good conduct . . . . COR 703-a; COR 703-b

Civil commitments, provisions for certain . . . COR 804-a

Definite sentence, good behavior allowances against . . . COR 804

Determinate sentence, good behavior allowances against . . . COR 803

Indeterminate sentence, good behavior allowances against . . . COR 803

Penal Law, provisions under revised

Civil commitments, provisions for certain . . . COR 804-a

Definite sentence, good behavior allowances against . . . COR 804

Indeterminate sentence, good behavior allowances against . . . COR 803

GOVERNMENT

Custody of persons convicted of crimes against . . . COR 143

Defrauding . . . PL 195.20

Employees (See PUBLIC SERVANTS)

GOVERNOR

Death penalty cases, role in (See DEATH PENALTY)

Extradition of fugitive (See EXTRADITION)

GRAFFITI

Authorized disposition of offenders . . . PL 60.28

Conditional discharge . . . PL 60.28; PL 65.10

Making graffiti . . . PL 145.60

Possession of graffiti instruments . . . PL 145.65

GRAND JURY

Generally . . . CPL 190.05

Actions to be taken by . . . CPL 190.60

Appeal from order concerning grand jury reports . . CPL 190.90

Attorney, witnesses' right to . . . CPL 190.52

Courts drawn from . . . CPL 190.10

Definition . . . CPL 190.05; CPL 190.35

GRAND JURY—Cont.

Direction to file

Family court, request for removal to . . . CPL 190.71

Prosecutor's information and related matters . . . CPL 190.70

Discharge . . . CPL 190.15

Disclosure, unlawful . . . PL 215.70

Dismissal of charges . . . CPL 190.75

District attorney, duties and authority of . . . . CPL 190.55

Duration of term . . . CPL 190.15

Duties of . . . CPL 190.20

Evidence

Compulsion of . . . CPL 190.40

Definitions . . . CPL 50.10

District attorney, duties and authority of . . . . CPL 190.55

Examination of . . . CPL 190.55

Insufficiency of, motion to dismiss or reduce indictment on ground of . . . CPL 210.30

Rules of . . . CPL 190.30

Witnesses (See subhead: Witnesses)

Family court, direction to file request for removal to . . . CPL 190.71

Formation . . . CPL 190.20

Function of . . . CPL 190.05

Hearing of evidence in . . . CPL 190.55

Immunity

Generally . . . CPL 190.40

Waiver of immunity . . . CPL 190.45

Indictment (See INDICTMENT)

Minutes, motion to inspect . . . CPL 210.30

Operation and proceedings . . . CPL 190.25

Organization . . . CPL 190.20

Proceedings and operation . . . CPL 190.25

Prosecutor's information, direction to file . . . CPL 190.70

Release of defendant upon failure of timely grand jury action . . . CPL 190.80

Reports

Generally . . . CPL 190.85

Appeal from order concerning . . . CPL 190.90

Timely grand jury action, release of defendant upon failure of . . . CPL 190.80

Videotaped examination . . . CPL 190.32

Waiver

Immunity, waiver by witness . . . CPL 190.45

Indictment (See INDICTMENT)

Witnesses

Generally . . . CPL 190.40

Attorney, right to . . . CPL 190.52

Defendant as witness . . . CPL 190.50

Immunity

Generally . . . CPL 190.40

Waiver of . . . CPL 190.45

GRAND JURY—Cont.

Witnesses—Cont.

    Videotaped examination . . . CPL 190.32

    Who may call . . . CPL 190.50

GRAND LARCENY

Evidence . . . PL 155.45

First degree . . . PL 155.42

Fourth degree . . . PL 155.30

Pleading and proof . . . PL 155.45

Second degree . . . PL 155.40

Third degree . . . PL 155.35

GRANTS

Commissioner of correction, acceptance by . . COR 15-c

GRATUITIES

Public servants, unlawful gratuities to

    Giving . . . PL 200.30

    Receiving . . . PL 200.35

GUARDIANS

Law guardians (See LAW GUARDIANS)

GUARDS

Retirement, requirements for . . . COR 470

GUNS (See FIREARMS)

H

HABEAS CORPUS

Appeal . . . CPLR 7011

Application of article . . . CPLR 7001

Contempt, criminal

    Generally . . . JUD 767

    Punishment upon return of habeas corpus . . . JUD 771

Content of writ . . . CPLR 7004

Determination of proceeding . . . CPLR 7010

Discharge of detained person, redetention after . . . CPLR 7012

Extradition proceedings . . . CPL 570.24

Hearing . . . CPLR 7009

Issuance of writ . . . CPLR 7003

Mentally ill inmates . . . COR 446

Obedience to writ . . . CPLR 7006

Petitions . . . CPLR 7002

Redetention after discharge . . . CPLR 7012

Return . . . CPLR 7008

Service of writ . . . CPLR 7005

Special proceeding . . . CPLR 7001

Warrants preceding or accompanying writ . . CPLR 7007

HANDWRITING

Proof of writing by comparison of . . . CPLR 4536

HARASSMENT

Aggravated harassment

    First degree . . . PL 240.31

    Inmate, harassment of employee by . . . . PL 240.32

    Second degree . . . PL 240.30

Employee by inmate, aggravated harassment of . . . PL 240.32

First degree . . . PL 240.25

Inmate, aggravated harassment of employee by . . . PL 240.32

Rent regulated tenant, of

    Generally . . . PL 241.05

    Definition . . . PL 241.00

Second degree . . . PL 240.26

HATE CRIMES

Definitions . . . PL 485.05

Legislative findings . . . PL 485.00

Sentencing . . . PL 485.10

HAZARDOUS SUBSTANCES

False, placement of

    Generally . . . PL 240.63

    First degree . . . PL 240.62

    Second degree . . . PL 240.61

HAZING

First degree . . . PL 120.16

Second degree . . . PL 120.17

HEALTH CARE

Criminal interference with health care service

    First degree . . . PL 240.71

    Second degree . . . PL 240.70

Interference with, criminal (See subhead: Criminal interference with health care service)

Local correctional facilities, costs for medical and dental services for inmates in . . . COR 500-h

Medical review board (See MEDICAL REVIEW BOARD)

Minors, right to consent of incarcerated . . . . COR 140; PL 70.20

Outside hospitals, requirements for permitting inmates treatment in . . . COR 23

Persons rendering services at request of Department, action against . . . COR 24-a

HEARING OFFICERS

Parole division . . . EXEC 259-d

HEARINGS

Chemical test report and hearing for persons operating vehicle after consumption of alcohol . . . . VTL 1194-a

Child protective proceedings (See CHILD PROTECTIVE PROCEEDINGS)

Clemency, appointment of persons to hear application for . . . COR 262

[References are to sections of Laws as abbreviated on Page iii. The abbreviation MISC before the section refers to the Miscellaneous Death Penalty Provision following Judiciary Law.]

HEARINGS—Cont.

Conditional discharge sentence, violation of . . CPL 410.70

Detention of persons in need of supervision after hearing . . . FCA 728

Discovery upon pre-trial . . . CPL 240.44

Dispositional hearings
    Generally (See DISPOSITIONAL HEARINGS)
    Juvenile delinquency (See DISPOSITIONAL HEARINGS: JUVENILE DELINQUENCY)

Fact-finding hearings (See FACT-FINDING HEARINGS)

Family offenses proceedings (See FAMILY OFFENSES PROCEEDINGS)

Felony complaint (See FELONY COMPLAINT)

Financial hardship; mandatory surcharge, deferral of . . . CPL 420.40

Grand jury proceeding, hearing of evidence in . . . . CPL 190.55

Habeas corpus . . . CPLR 7009

Juvenile delinquency (See JUVENILE DELINQUENCY)

Mandatory surcharge, deferral of; financial hardship . . . CPL 420.40

Material witness, adjudgment of . . . CPL 620.50

Parole violations, interstate hearings for . . . EXEC 259-o

Permanency hearing (See FOSTER CARE)

Predicate felony conviction . . . CPL 220.35

Probation sentence, violation of . . . CPL 410.70

Supervision, persons in need of (See PERSONS IN NEED OF SUPERVISION)

HINDERING PROSECUTION

Definition . . . PL 205.50

First degree . . . PL 205.65

Second degree . . . PL 205.60

Third degree . . . PL 205.55

HIV-RELATED TESTING

Pre-sentence reports . . . CPL 390.15

Victim of sexual assault upon defendant, request by . . . FCA 347.1

HOMICIDE

Criminally negligent . . . PL 125.10

Definition . . . PL 125.00; PL 125.05

Manslaughter (See MANSLAUGHTER)

Murder (See MURDER)

Victim of; defined . . . PL 125.05

HORSE RACING

Pari-mutuel betting system, impairing integrity of
    First degree . . . PL 180.53
    Second degree . . . PL 180.52

HOSPITALS

Mental disease or defect, commitment of inmates with (See MENTAL DISEASE OR DEFECT)

HOSPITALS—Cont.

Outside hospitals, requirements for permitting inmates treatment in . . . COR 23

Pre-sentence report to accompany defendant to mental health facility . . . CPL 390.60

HUSBAND AND WIFE (See SPOUSE)

HYPODERMIC INSTRUMENTS

Criminal possession of . . . PL 220.45

Destruction of . . . PHL 3381-a

Distribution of single-use syringes . . . PHL 3381

Narcotic drugs, criminal injection of . . . PL 220.46

Possession of
    Criminal . . . PL 220.45
    Sale and . . . PHL 3381

Sale and possession of . . . PHL 3381

I

IDENTITY THEFT

Defenses . . . PL 190.84

Definitions . . . PL 190.77

First degree offense . . . PL 190.80

Geographical jurisdiction of . . . CPL 20.40

Personal identification information, unlawful possession of
    Defenses . . . PL 190.84
    First degree offense . . . PL 190.83
    Second degree offense . . . PL 190.82
    Third degree offense . . . PL 190.81

Restitution and reparations for . . . PL 60.27

Second degree offense . . . PL 190.79

Terrorism, defined as specified offense for . . . PL 490.05

Third degree offense . . . PL 190.78

Warrants for eavesdropping and video surveillance, designated offense for . . . CPL 700.05

IGNITION INTERLOCK DEVICE PROGRAM

Generally . . . VTL 1198

IMMUNITY

Compulsion of evidence by offer of
    Generally . . . CPL 50.20
    Court as competent authority to confer immunity . . . CPL 50.30
    Definitions . . . CPL 50.10

Extradition
    Other criminal prosecutions while in this state . . . CPL 570.60
    Service of process in civil actions in connection with . . . CPL 570.58

Grand jury proceedings
    Generally . . . CPL 190.40
    Waiver of immunity . . . CPL 190.45

Sex Offender Registration Act, officials' immunity from liability for disclosure under . . . COR 168-r

[References are to sections of Laws as abbreviated on Page iii. The abbreviation MISC before the section refers to the Miscellaneous Death Penalty Provision following Judiciary Law.]

IMPEACHMENT

Contradictory statement, impeachment of own witness by proof of prior . . . CPL 60.35

Witness, of (See WITNESSES)

IMPERSONATION

Criminal impersonation

    First degree . . . PL 190.26

    Physician, as; first degree . . . PL 190.26

    Police officer, as; first degree . . . PL 190.26

    Second degree . . . PL 190.25

IMPRISONMENT

Civil contempt . . . JUD 774

Inmates (See INMATES)

Sentence (See IMPRISONMENT SENTENCE)

Unlawful imprisonment (See UNLAWFUL IMPRIS-ONMENT)

IMPRISONMENT SENTENCE

Calculation of terms of . . . PL 70.30

Change after commencement . . . CPL 430.10

Child sexual assault felony, for second . . PL 70.07

Commitment of defendant . . . CPL 430.20

Concurrent terms . . . PL 70.25

Conditional release . . . PL 70.40

Consecutive terms . . . PL 70.25

Definite and indeterminate sentence, merger of . . . PL 70.35

Duty to deliver defendant . . . CPL 430.30

Felonies

    Generally . . . PL 70.00

    Second felony offenders (See subhead: Second felony offenders)

    Violent felony offense (See subhead: Violent felony offense)

Indeterminate sentence, merger of definite and . . . PL 70.35

Intermittent imprisonment

    Generally . . . PL 85.00

    Commitment . . . PL 85.10

    Modifications . . . PL 85.05

    Notification . . . PL 85.10

    Revocation . . . PL 85.05

    Subsequent sentence . . . PL 85.15

    Warrants . . . PL 85.10

Juvenile offenders . . . PL 70.05

Merger of definite and indeterminate sentence . . PL 70.35

Misdemeanors . . . PL 70.15

Murder in first degree, conviction for . . . PL 70.00

Parole . . . CPL 410.91; PL 70.40

Persistent offenders

    Generally . . . PL 70.10

    Violent felony offenders . . . PL 70.08

Place of imprisonment . . . PL 70.20

IMPRISONMENT SENTENCE—Cont.

Pre-sentence proceedings, evidence of imprisonment in . . . CPL 400.22

Presumptive release . . . PL 70.40

Second felony offenders

    Generally . . . PL 70.06

    Child sexual assault offender . . . PL 70.07

    Violent felony offense . . . PL 70.04

Social services, notification of sentence to commissioner of . . . COR 71; CPL 380.80

Violations . . . PL 70.15

Violent felony offense

    Generally . . . PL 70.02

    Persistent violent felony offenders . . PL 70.08

    Second violent felony offender . . . PL 70.04

    Victim notification of release of violent felony offender . . . CPL 380.50

INCAPACITATED PERSONS

Juvenile delinquency

    Examination reports . . . FCA 322.1

    Proceedings to determine capacity . . . . FCA 322.2

INCEST

Generally . . . PL 255.25

Corroboration . . . PL 255.30

INCOMPETENT PERSONS (See MENTAL DISEASE OR DEFECT)

INDEMNIFICATIONS

Alternate correctional facilities in New York City . . . COR 89-l

INDETERMINATE SENTENCE

Commissioner of Correction, conversion by . . . . . COR 5

Domestic violence cases . . . PL 60.12

Good behavior allowances against . . . COR 803

Parole supervision . . . CPL 410.91

INDICTMENT

Amendment of . . . CPL 200.70

Appeal by people from order reducing count of . . . CPL 450.55

Arraignment

    Appearance of defendant, securing . . . . CPL 210.10

    Procedure . . . CPL 210.15

Authorization . . . CPL 190.65

Bill of particulars . . . CPL 200.95

Biological weapon, possession or use of . . . . CPL 200.65

Chargeable offenses . . . CPL 200.20

Charge to jury (See JURY AND JURORS, subhead: Charge to jury)

Chemical weapon, possession or use of . . . . CPL 200.65

[References are to sections of Laws as abbreviated on Page iii. The abbreviation MISC before the section refers to the Miscellaneous Death Penalty Provision following Judiciary Law.]

INDICTMENT—Cont.

Child sexual assault offender, special information for . . . CPL 200.62

Consolidation of indictments
     Generally . . . CPL 200.20
     Different defendants, against . . . CPL 200.40

Contempt, offender liable to indictment for . . JUD 776

Content . . . CPL 200.50

Definition . . . CPL 200.10

Disclosure of, unlawful . . . PL 215.75

Dismissal, motion for (See subhead: Motion for dismissal)

Duplicitous counts, prohibitions against . . . . CPL 200.30

Enterprise corruption . . . CPL 200.65

Form and content . . . CPL 200.50

Joinder
     Defendants . . . CPL 200.40
     Offenses . . . CPL 200.20

Juvenile offenders, motion for removal to family court of . . . CPL 210.43

Local criminal court, divestiture of . . . CPL 170.20; CPL 170.25

Marijuana cases; adjournment in contemplation of dismissal in superior court . . . CPL 210.46

Mental examination, fitness to proceed after . . CPL 730.50

Minutes, inspection of . . . CPL 210.30

Mistrial, indictment status upon new trial resulting from declaration of . . . CPL 280.20

Motion for dismissal
     Generally . . . CPL 210.20
     Defective grand jury proceeding . . CPL 210.35
     Defective indictment . . . CPL 210.25
     Inspection of minutes . . . CPL 210.30
     Insufficiency of grand jury evidence . . . CPL 210.30
     Justice, in interest of . . . CPL 210.40
     Procedure . . . CPL 210.45

Operators of for-hire vehicles, special information for . . . CPL 200.61

Plea (See PLEA)

Prior convictions, prohibitions against allegations of . . . CPL 200.60

Reduction of, motion for . . . CPL 210.20

Superior court information
     Content . . . CPL 200.15
     Definition . . . CPL 200.15
     Prosecution, exclusive methods of . . . . CPL 210.05
     Waiver of indictment, filing information upon . . . CPL 200.15

Superseding indictments . . . CPL 200.80

Waiver
     Generally . . . CPL 195.10

INDICTMENT—Cont.

Waiver—Cont.
     Approval of waiver by court . . . CPL 195.30
     Superior court information, filing of . . . CPL 195.40
     Written instrument . . . CPL 195.20

INFANTS (See MINORS)

INFORMATION

Amendment . . . CPL 100.45

Arraignment upon . . . CPL 170.10

Bill of particulars . . . CPL 100.45

Child sexual assault offender, special information for . . . CPL 200.62

Consolidation . . . CPL 100.45

Content . . . CPL 100.15

Dismissal of, motion for
     Generally . . . CPL 170.30
     Adjournment in contemplation of dismissal
         Generally . . . CPL 170.55
         Marijuana cases . . . CPL 170.56
     Defective information . . . CPL 170.35
     Justice, in interest of . . . CPL 170.40
     Procedure . . . CPL 170.45

Form and content . . . CPL 100.15

Misdemeanor complaint, replacement of (See MISDEMEANOR COMPLAINT)

Non-jury trials
     Judicial hearing officer, trial by . . CPL 350.20
     Single judge trial, conduct of . . . CPL 350.10

Operators of for-hire vehicles, special information for . . . CPL 200.61

Plea
     Prosecution of information . . . CPL 340.20
     Requirements . . . CPL 170.60

Prosecution of information
     Definitions . . . CPL 340.10
     Deliberations . . . CPL 360.55
     Jury and jurors (See JURY AND JURORS)
     Modes of trial . . . CPL 340.40
     Non-jury trials
         Judicial hearing officer, trial by . . . CPL 350.20
         Single judge trial, conduct of . . . . CPL 350.10
     Notice of defenses . . . CPL 340.30
     Plea . . . CPL 340.20
     Presence of defendant at trial . . . CPL 340.50
     Pre-trial discovery . . . CPL 340.30
     Sentence, proceedings from verdict to . . CPL 370.10
     Verdict
         Generally . . . CPL 360.55
         Sentence, proceedings from verdict to . . CPL 370.10

Index

[References are to sections of Laws as abbreviated on Page iii. The abbreviation MISC before the section refers to the Miscellaneous Death Penalty Provision following Judiciary Law.]

[References are to sections of Laws as abbreviated on Page iii. The abbreviation MISC before the section refers to the Miscellaneous Death Penalty Provision following Judiciary Law.]

[References are to sections of Laws as abbreviated on Page iii. The abbreviation MISC before the section refers to the Miscellaneous Death Penalty Provision following Judiciary Law.]

INTERMEDIATE APPELLATE COURT—Cont.

Determination of appeals—Cont.

Modification or reversal, corrective action upon . . . CPL 470.20; CPL 470.40

Reversal or modification, corrective action upon . . . CPL 470.20; CPL 470.40

People, appeal by . . . CPL 450.20

Stay of judgment pending appeal to or from . . CPL 460.50; CPL 460.60

Taking appeal to . . . CPL 450.60

INTERMITTENT IMPRISONMENT (See IMPRIS-ONMENT SENTENCE)

INTERROGATORIES

Commission, examination of witnesses on . . . CPL 680.50

INTERSTATE COOPERATION

Law enforcement officers and agencies of other states and federal government . . . COR 621

INTERSTATE CORRECTIONS COMPACT

Acts not reviewable in receiving state . . . COR 105

Adoption of . . . COR 100

Construction of . . . COR 109

Contracts . . . COR 103

Definitions . . . COR 102

Entry into force . . . COR 107

Extradition provisions . . . COR 105

Federal aid . . . COR 106

Force, entry into . . . COR 107

Procedures . . . COR 104

Purpose of . . . COR 101

Rights of inmates . . . COR 104

Severability of provisions . . . COR 109

Short title . . . COR 101

Termination of . . . COR 108

Withdrawal of . . . COR 108

INTOXICATION

Criminal liability, effect on . . . PL 15.25

INVESTIGATIONS

Child protective proceedings . . . FCA 1034

Extradition, investigation by governor of . . . . CPL 570.10

Pre-sentence reports, scope of . . . CPL 390.30

Probation; juvenile delinquency . . FCA 351.1; FCA 750

J

JAILS (See CORRECTIONAL FACILITIES)

JOINDER OF PARTIES

Enterprise corruption . . . CPLR 1354

JOINT TORT-FEASORS

Proof of payment by . . . CPLR 4533-b

JOSTLING

Definition . . . PL 165.25

JUDGMENT

Appeals (See APPEALS)

Article 78 proceeding . . . CPLR 7806

Certificates concerning judgments of conviction and fingerprints . . . CPL 60.60

Suspended judgments; supervision, persons in need of . . . FCA 755; FCA 776

Vacation of, motion for

Generally . . . CPL 440.10

Procedure . . . CPL 440.30

Vehicle and Traffic Law provisions for fines and penalties

Default judgment . . . VTL 1806-a

Stay order on appeal from judgment of conviction of offense, effect of . . . VTL 1808

JUDICIARY LAW

Community dispute resolution center program (See COMMUNITY DISPUTE RESOLUTION CENTER PROGRAM)

Contempt proceedings (See CONTEMPT)

Death penalty provisions, miscellaneous (See DEATH PENALTY)

Special narcotics parts of supreme court in cities with population of one million or more

Declaration . . . JUD 177-a

Establishment . . . JUD 177-b

Intent . . . JUD 177-a

Legislative findings . . . JUD 177-a

Probation services . . . JUD 177-e

Procedure . . . JUD 177-d

Prosecutional organization . . . JUD 177-c

JURISDICTION

Child protective proceedings (See CHILD PROTEC-TIVE PROCEEDINGS)

Conspiracy . . . PL 105.25

Criminal courts (See CRIMINAL COURTS)

Enterprise corruption . . . PL 460.40

Extradition (See EXTRADITION)

Family offenses proceedings (See FAMILY OF-FENSES PROCEEDINGS)

Geographical jurisdiction of offenses (See GEO-GRAPHICAL JURISDICTION OF OFFENSES)

Juvenile delinquency (See JUVENILE DELIN-QUENCY)

Local criminal courts

Generally . . . CPL 10.30

Divestiture of jurisdiction by indictment . . . . CPL 170.20; CPL 170.25

Superior courts . . . CPL 10.20

[References are to sections of Laws as abbreviated on Page iii. The abbreviation MISC before the section refers to the Miscellaneous Death Penalty Provision following Judiciary Law.]

[References are to sections of Laws as abbreviated on Page iii. The abbreviation MISC before the section refers to the Miscellaneous Death Penalty Provision following Judiciary Law.]

[References are to sections of Laws as abbreviated on Page iii. The abbreviation MISC before the section refers to the Miscellaneous Death Penalty Provision following Judiciary Law.]

[References are to sections of Laws as abbreviated on Page iii. The abbreviation MISC before the section refers to the Miscellaneous Death Penalty Provision following Judiciary Law.]

LABOR IN CORRECTIONAL FACILITIES— Cont.

Receipts and expenditure statement for industries, monthly . . . COR 190

Report concerning industries . . . COR 183

State and local facilities . . . COR 177

Violation of institutional labor regulations . . . COR 196

Work release program, participation in . . COR 178

LABOR OFFICIALS

Bribery of (See BRIBERY)

LARCENY

Defenses . . . PL 155.10; PL 155.15

Definitions . . . PL 155.00; PL 155.05

Grand larceny (See GRAND LARCENY)

Petit larceny . . . PL 155.25

Physical force; justification for use to prevent or terminate larceny . . . PL 35.25

Value of stolen property . . . PL 155.20

LASER DETECTORS

Prohibitions . . . VTL 397-a

LAW ENFORCEMENT AGENCY ACCREDITATION COUNCIL

Membership . . . EXEC 846-h

Organization . . . EXEC 846-h

Procedure . . . EXEC 846-h

LAW GUARDIANS

Child protective proceedings . . . FCA 1016

Juvenile delinquency; dispositional hearings . . FCA 354.2

Supervision, persons in need of . . . FCA 760

LEVY

Forfeiture actions, levy upon personal property in (See FORFEITURE—PROCEEDS OF CRIME)

LIBRARIES

Circulation records, disclosure of . . . CPLR 4509

Correctional facility library, availability of information on international offender transfers . . . COR 71

Correctional Services Department, of . . . COR 20

LICENSES

Controlled substances

    Cannabis grown by unlicensed persons . . PHL 3382

    Chemical analysis (See subhead: Research, instructional activities and chemical analysis relating to controlled substances)

    Distribution of (See subhead: Controlled substances, manufacture and distribution of)

    Instructional activities (See subhead: Research, instructional activities and chemical analysis relating to controlled substances)

LICENSES—Cont.

Controlled substances—Cont.

    Manufacture and distribution of (See subhead: Controlled substances, manufacture and distribution of)

    Research activities (See subhead: Research, instructional activities and chemical analysis relating to controlled substances)

    Revocation of licenses

        Generally . . . PHL 3390; PHL 3391

        Hearing procedure . . . PHL 3393

        Judicial review . . . PHL 3394

    Suspension of licenses . . . PHL 3391 -PHL 3394

Controlled substances, manufacture and distribution of

    Generally . . . PHL 3310

    Amended licenses . . . PHL 3311

    Initial licenses

        Application for . . . PHL 3312

        Authority to issues . . . PHL 3311

        Granting of . . . PHL 3313

    Renewal of licenses

        Applications for . . . PHL 3315

        Authority to issue . . . PHL 3311

        Granting of . . . PHL 3316

Driver's license, suspension and revocation (See DRIVER'S LICENSE: SUSPENSION AND REVOCATION)

Firearms, license to carry, possess, repair and dispose of (See FIREARMS)

Fireworks, permits for public display of . . . . . PL 405.00

Marriage license, unlawfully procuring

    Generally . . . PL 255.10

    Defense . . . PL 255.20

Permits for public display of fireworks . . PL 405.00

Prior convictions, application for license by persons with (See PRIOR CONVICTIONS, subhead: License or employment application by persons with)

Public display of fireworks, permits for . . . . . PL 405.00

Research, instructional activities and chemical analysis relating to controlled substances

    Generally . . . PHL 3324

    Applications . . . PHL 3325

    Authority to issue licenses . . . PHL 3325

    Exemptions from title . . . PHL 3328

    Institutional research licenses . . . PHL 3326

    Procedure . . . PHL 3327

    Records . . . PHL 3329

    Reports and records . . . PHL 3329

Suspension and revocation

    Driver's license (See DRIVER'S LICENSE: SUSPENSION AND REVOCATION)

    Firearms; licenses to carry, possess, repair or dispose . . . CPL 530.14; FCA 842-a

[References are to sections of Laws as abbreviated on Page iii. The abbreviation MISC before the section refers to the Miscellaneous Death Penalty Provision following Judiciary Law.]

LIQUOR (See ALCOHOL)

LITTERING

Railroad tracks, penalties for littering on . . . . . PL 145.50

Rights-of-way, penalties for littering on . . . . . PL 145.50

LOCAL CONDITIONAL RELEASE COMMISSION

Application procedures . . . COR 273

Definitions . . . COR 270

Delinquency, declaration of . . . COR 274

Determinations, procedures for . . . COR 273

Duties . . . COR 272

Functions . . . COR 272

Organization . . . COR 271

Powers . . . COR 272

Revocation procedures . . . COR 274

Supervision of conditional release . . . COR 275

Transfer of custody and supervision of conditional release . . . COR 275

Violation, procedures for . . . COR 274

Warrants, procedures for . . . COR 274

LOCAL CORRECTIONAL FACILITIES

Generally . . . COR 5; COR 611-a

Absence of inmate for funeral or deathbed visits . . COR 509

Aggravated harassment of employee by inmate . . . PL 240.32

Alcoholic beverages, use of . . . COR 502; COR 503

Application of article . . . COR 500

Civil prisoners . . . COR 500-n; COR 514

Custody and control of inmates . . . COR 500-c

Deathbed visits, absence of inmate for . . . COR 509

Dental services, payment of costs for . . COR 500-h

Designation of jail

    Revocation of . . . COR 523; COR 524

    Substitute jail . . . COR 504

Duties of . . . COR 618

Fire, removal of inmates in case of . . . COR 507

Food provisions . . . COR 500-d

Funeral service, absence of inmate for . . . COR 509

Health care costs . . . COR 500-h

Holidays, release on . . . COR 500-l

Housing of inmates and other persons . . COR 500-b

Labor . . . COR 500-d

Liquor in jails, use of . . . COR 502; COR 503

Medical services, payment of costs for . . . . COR 500-h

New York City, special provision relating to . . . . COR 500-m

Physicians, appointment of . . . COR 501

Reading matter . . . COR 500-e

Recaptured prisoner, term of imprisonment of . . . . COR 529

LOCAL CORRECTIONAL FACILITIES—Cont.

Record of commitments and discharges . . . . COR 500-f

Release on holidays, Saturdays and Sundays . . . . . COR 500-l

Religious services . . . COR 500-e

Revocation of designation of jail . . COR 523; COR 524

Saturdays, release on . . . COR 500-l

Segregation of inmates, rooms for . . . COR 500-b

Sex offender, notification requirements upon release of (See SEX OFFENDER REGISTRATION ACT)

Sick persons, removal of . . . COR 508

Substitute jail, designation of . . . COR 504

Sundays, release on . . . COR 500-l

Treatment of inmates . . . COR 500-k

United States courts, commitment by . . . COR 500-g

Unlawful fees, prohibitions against charging to inmates . . . COR 500-n

Use of jails . . . COR 500-a

Visitations . . . COR 500-j

Westchester County correctional facilities, provision relating to . . . COR 118

Workhouses

    Generally . . . COR 500-i

    Visitations . . . COR 500-j

Work release program (See WORK RELEASE PROGRAM, subhead: County jails)

LOCAL CRIMINAL COURTS

Accusatory instruments (See ACCUSATORY INSTRUMENTS)

Arraignment, methods of requiring defendant's appearance in local court for . . . CPL 110.10

Bail

    Forfeiture of . . . CPL 540.20

    Recognizance or, order when action pending . . . CPL 530.20

Cash bail transfer to superior court from . . . . CPL 520.40

Commencement of action

    Generally . . . CPL 100.05

    Family court proceeding, effect of . . . . CPL 100.07

Deposition, supporting (See SUPPORTING DEPOSITION)

Felony complaint (See FELONY COMPLAINT)

Information (See INFORMATION)

Jurisdiction of

    Generally . . . CPL 10.30

    Divestiture of jurisdiction by indictment . . . . CPL 170.20; CPL 170.25

Misdemeanor complaint (See MISDEMEANOR COMPLAINT)

Prosecutor's information (See PROSECUTOR'S INFORMATION)

LOCAL CRIMINAL COURTS—Cont.

Recognizance or bail, order when action pending . . . CPL 530.20

Removal of action to or from (See REMOVAL OF ACTION)

Simplified information (See SIMPLIFIED INFORMATION)

Supporting deposition (See SUPPORTING DEPOSITION)

Warrant of arrest, issuance of . . . CPL 120.30

LOITERING

Generally . . . PL 240.35

First degree . . . PL 240.36

Prostitution offense, for purposes of engaging in . . . PL 240.37

LOTTERY OFFENSES

Defense, lack of . . . PL 225.40

M

MALPRACTICE

Medical malpractice, loss of earnings and impairment of earning ability in actions for . . . CPLR 4546

MANAGEMENT OF CORRECTIONAL FACILITIES

Alien inmates . . . COR 147

Alternate facilities . . . COR 89-a

Commissioner of correction, powers and duties of . . . COR 112

Contagious disease in facility . . . COR 141

Daily report on inmates . . . COR 119

Deathbed visits, absence of inmate for . . . COR 113

Death sentence commuted by governor, custody of inmate where . . . COR 130

Debts, recovery of . . . COR 122

Diagnostic clinics . . . COR 148

Discipline program for inmates . . . COR 137

Education, correctional . . . COR 136

Estimates of expenses . . . COR 117

Fire in facility . . . COR 142

Fiscal accounts and records . . . COR 115

Fiscal transactions, control of . . . COR 122

Funeral service, allowing inmates to attend . . COR 113

Government, custody of persons convicted of crimes against . . . COR 143

Grievance procedures . . . COR 139

Inmates

    Alien inmates . . . COR 147

    Daily report on . . . COR 119

    Deathbed visits, absence of inmate for . . COR 113

    Death sentence commuted by governor, custody of inmate where . . . COR 130

MANAGEMENT OF CORRECTIONAL FACILITIES—Cont.

Inmates—Cont.

    Discipline program for inmates . . . COR 137

    Funds . . . COR 116

    Funeral service, allowing inmates to attend . . COR 113

    Grievance procedures . . . COR 139

    Mentally ill when crime committed, superintendent to report concerning inmate believed to be . . . COR 133

    Minors to routine medical, dental and mental health services, right to consent of incarcerated . . . COR 140

    Released inmates (See RELEASED INMATES)

    Retaking of escaped inmate . . . COR 132

    Rules and regulations at all facilities for . . . . COR 138

    Treatment, control and disciple program for inmates . . . COR 137

Minors to routine medical, dental and mental health services, right to consent of incarcerated . . COR 140

Psychiatric and diagnostic clinics . . . COR 148

Records, fiscal accounts and . . . COR 115

Recovery of debts . . . COR 122

Released inmates (See RELEASED INMATES)

Retaking of escaped inmate . . . COR 132

Retarded persons, institutions for . . . COR 431

Superintendents

    Mentally ill when crime committed, superintendent to report concerning inmate believed to be . . . COR 133

    Punishment for neglect of duty . . . COR 126

Treatment, control and disciple program for inmates . . . COR 137

United States, custody of persons convicted of crimes against . . . COR 143

Visitation of facility, persons authorized for . . COR 146

MANSLAUGHTER

First degree . . . PL 125.20

Second degree . . . PL 125.15

Vehicular manslaughter

    First degree . . . PL 125.13

    Second degree . . . PL 125.12

MAPS

Real property . . . CPLR 4522

MARIJUANA

Adjournment in contemplation of dismissal of charges . . . CPL 170.56; CPL 210.46

Definitions . . . PL 221.00

Possession of

    First degree . . . PL 221.30

[References are to sections of Laws as abbreviated on Page iii. The abbreviation MISC before the section refers to the Miscellaneous Death Penalty Provision following Judiciary Law.]

MARIJUANA—Cont.
Possession of—Cont.
   Second degree . . . PL 221.25
   Third degree . . . PL 221.20
   Fourth degree . . . PL 221.15
   Fifth degree . . . PL 221.10
Sale of
   First degree . . . PL 221.55
   Second degree . . . PL 221.50
   Third degree . . . PL 221.45
   Fourth degree . . . PL 221.40
   Fifth degree . . . PL 221.35
Sentencing for felony offense
   Authorized disposition . . . PL 60.04
   Class A felonies . . . PL 70.71
   Other than Class A felonies . . . PL 70.70
Unlawful possession of . . . PL 221.05

MARKET REPORTS
Evidence, as . . . CPLR 4533

MARRIAGE
Adultery (See ADULTERY)
Bigamy
   Generally . . . PL 255.15
   Defense . . . PL 255.20
Certificate as evidence . . . CPLR 4526
Dissolution decree, unlawfully issuing . . PL 255.05
Incest
   Generally . . . PL 255.25
   Corroboration . . . PL 255.30
License, unlawfully procuring
   Generally . . . PL 255.10
   Defense . . . PL 255.20
Solemnizing marriage unlawfully . . . PL 255.00

MATERIAL WITNESS ORDER
Amendment . . . CPL 620.60
Appearance of prospective witness . . . CPL 620.30
Arraignment . . . CPL 620.40
Authorization . . . CPL 620.20
Commencement of proceedings . . . CPL 620.30
Courts authorized to issue . . . CPL 620.20
Definition . . . CPL 620.10
Determination and execution of . . . CPL 620.50
Duration of . . . CPL 620.20
Execution of . . . CPL 620.50
Failure to appear on, compelling appearance of witness
   for . . . CPL 620.70
Fees of material witness . . . CPL 620.80
Hearing . . . CPL 620.50
Modification . . . CPL 620.60
Procurement of appearance of prospective witness
   . . . CPL 620.30
Vacation . . . CPL 620.60

MEDICAL ASSISTANCE CARDS
Unlawful use of . . . PL 165.17

MEDICAL CARE (See HEALTH CARE)

MEDICAL REVIEW BOARD
Duties . . . COR 47
Functions . . . COR 47
Organization . . . COR 43
Powers . . . COR 47

MEDICAL TREATMENT (See HEALTH CARE)

MEGAN'S LAW (See SEX OFFENDER REGISTRA-
TION ACT)

MENACING
First degree . . . PL 120.13
Second degree . . . PL 120.14
Third degree . . . PL 120.15

MENTAL DISEASE OR DEFECT
Conditional release of mentally ill inmate . . . COR
   404
Correctional Services Department duty to director of
   hospital concerning inmates . . . COR 405
Custody of defendant by commissioner, procedure
   following
      Generally . . . CPL 730.60
      Termination of . . . CPL 730.70
Death sentence, incompetent persons under . . COR
   656
Defense . . . PL 40.15
Definitions . . . COR 400
Endangering welfare of incompetent persons . . PL
   260.25
Establishment of programs inside correctional facilities
   . . . COR 401
Evidentiary rules for giving testimony . . CPL 60.20
Examination (See subhead: Fitness to proceed)
Expiration of sentence, disposition of inmate upon
   . . . COR 404; COR 441
Fitness to proceed
   Generally . . . CPL 730.20
   Custody of defendant by commissioner, procedure
     following
      Generally . . . CPL 730.60
      Termination of . . . CPL 730.70
   Definitions . . . CPL 730.10
   Indictment . . . CPL 730.50
   Local criminal court accusatory instrument . . .
     CPL 730.40
   Order of examination . . . CPL 730.30
Habeas corpus . . . COR 446
Institutions for retarded persons (See INSTITUTIONS
   FOR RETARDED PERSONS)
Murder in first degree, pre-sentence proceeding for
   defendant convicted of . . . CPL 400.27
Notice of defense of . . . FCA 335.1
Notice of intent to proffer psychiatric evidence . . .
   CPL 250.10

Index

[References are to sections of Laws as abbreviated on Page iii. The abbreviation MISC before the section refers to the Miscellaneous Death Penalty Provision following Judiciary Law.]

[References are to sections of Laws as abbreviated on Page iii. The abbreviation MISC before the section refers to the Miscellaneous Death Penalty Provision following Judiciary Law.]

MINORS—Cont.
Testimony by
    Closed-circuit television for (See subhead: Closed-circuit television for child witnesses)
    Definitions . . . CPL 65.00
    Evidentiary rules on testimony by . . . . CPL 60.20
Weapons (See WEAPONS)
Welfare of, endangering (See subhead: Endangering welfare of child)
Witnesses
    Fair treatment standards for child victims as . . . EXEC 642-a
    Testimony (See subhead: Testimony by)

MINUTES
Grand jury minutes, motion to inspect . . . . . CPL 210.30
Sentence . . . CPL 380.70

MISCHIEF
First degree . . . PL 145.12
Fourth degree . . . PL 145.00
Physical force; justification for use to prevent or terminate criminal mischief . . . PL 35.25
Second degree . . . PL 145.10
Third degree . . . PL 145.05

MISCONDUCT
Corporate official . . . PL 190.35
Jurors, by
    First degree . . . PL 215.30
    Second degree . . . PL 215.28
Official misconduct (See PUBLIC SERVANTS, subhead: Official misconduct)

MISDEMEANOR
(See also specific crimes)
Classification of . . . PL 55.05
Complaint (See MISDEMEANOR COMPLAINT)
Fines . . . PL 80.05
Imprisonment sentence . . . PL 70.15
Sentences . . . PL 55.05

MISDEMEANOR COMPLAINT
Amendment . . . CPL 100.45
Arraignment upon . . . CPL 170.10
Bill of particulars . . . CPL 100.45
Consolidation . . . CPL 100.45
Content . . . CPL 100.15
Dismissal of, motion for
    Generally . . . CPL 170.30
    Adjournment in contemplation of dismissal
        Generally . . . CPL 170.55
        Marijuana, cases involving . . CPL 170.56
    Defective complaint . . . CPL 170.35
    Justice, in interest of . . . CPL 170.40
    Procedure . . . CPL 170.45

MISDEMEANOR COMPLAINT—Cont.
Form and content . . . CPL 100.15
Information, replacement by
    Generally . . . CPL 170.65
    Release of defendant upon failure to replace . . . CPL 170.70
    Waiver of . . . CPL 170.65
Removal of action (See REMOVAL OF ACTION)
Severance . . . CPL 100.45
Verification . . . CPL 100.30

MISSING PERSONS
Children
    Clearinghouse . . . EXEC 837-f
    Reporting duties of law enforcement departments . . . EXEC 837-m
    Statewide central register for . . . EXEC 837-e
Death or other status of . . . CPLR 4527
Identification of . . . EXEC 838
Toll-free telephone number to obtain information regarding resources available in assisting recovery of . . . EXEC 837

MISTRIAL
Generally . . . CPL 280.10
Indictment status upon new trial . . . CPL 280.20

MONEY LAUNDERING
Definitions . . . PL 470.00
Fines . . . PL 470.20
First degree . . . PL 470.15
Second degree . . . PL 470.10
Terrorism, in support of (See TERRORISM, CRIMES OF)
Third degree . . . PL 470.05

MORTGAGED PROPERTY
Fraudulent disposition of . . . PL 185.10

MOTION PICTURE THEATERS
Recording device in, unauthorized operation of . . . PL 275.32

MOTIONS (See specific subject headings, e.g., PRETRIAL MOTIONS)

MOTOR VEHICLES (See AUTOMOBILES; VEHICLE AND TRAFFIC LAW)

MULTIPLE OFFENSES
Fines . . . PL 80.15

MUNICIPAL POLICE TRAINING COUNCIL
Generally . . . EXEC 839
Commissioner, duties and powers of . . . EXEC 841
Duties
    Generally . . . EXEC 840
    Commissioner . . . EXEC 841
Functions . . . EXEC 840

Index

[References are to sections of Laws as abbreviated on Page iii. The abbreviation MISC before the section refers to the Miscellaneous Death Penalty Provision following Judiciary Law.]

[References are to sections of Laws as abbreviated on Page iii. The abbreviation MISC before the section refers to the Miscellaneous Death Penalty Provision following Judiciary Law.]

[References are to sections of Laws as abbreviated on Page iii. The abbreviation MISC before the section refers to the Miscellaneous Death Penalty Provision following Judiciary Law.]

[References are to sections of Laws as abbreviated on Page iii. The abbreviation MISC before the section refers to the Miscellaneous Death Penalty Provision following Judiciary Law.]

[References are to sections of Laws as abbreviated on Page iii. The abbreviation MISC before the section refers to the Miscellaneous Death Penalty Provision following Judiciary Law.]

[References are to sections of Laws as abbreviated on Page iii. The abbreviation MISC before the section refers to the Miscellaneous Death Penalty Provision following Judiciary Law.]

PERSONS IN NEED OF SUPERVISION—Cont.
Summons—Cont.
    Issuance of . . . FCA 736
    Service of . . . FCA 737
Suspended judgment . . . FCA 755
Temporary order of protection . . . FCA 740
Transfer of records and information to institutions and agencies . . . FCA 782-a
Vacation of order . . . FCA 762
Warrants
    Failure to produce minor pursuant to . . . FCA 725
    Preliminary procedures for issuance of . . FCA 738

PETITIONS
Child protective proceedings (See CHILD PROTECTIVE PROCEEDINGS)
Family offenses proceedings, petition alleging violation of court order in . . . FCA 846; FCA 847
Habeas corpus . . . CPLR 7002
Juvenile delinquency (See JUVENILE DELINQUENCY)
Supervision, persons in need of (See PERSONS IN NEED OF SUPERVISION)

PETIT LARCENY
Generally . . . PL 155.25

PHOTOGRAPHS
Termination of criminal action
    Fingerprints upon, return of . . . CPL 160.55
    Return upon . . . CPL 160.50

PHYSICAL FORCE
Arrest, use of force during (See ARREST)
Justification for use of (See JUSTIFICATION)

PHYSICAL INJURY (See ASSAULT)

PHYSICIANS
Evidentiary issues concerning . . . CPLR 4504
Impersonation as; first degree . . . PL 190.26
Local correctional facilities, appointment at . . COR 501

PLEA
Change of . . . CPL 220.60
Deportation of non-citizen defendant; guilty plea . . CPL 220.50
Entry of . . . CPL 220.50
Guilty plea; deportation of non-citizen defendant . . CPL 220.50
Information
    Prosecution of . . . CPL 340.20
    Requirements for . . . CPL 170.60
Lesser included offense for purposes of . . . . CPL 220.20

PLEA—Cont.
Mental disease or defect, plea of not responsible by reason of
    Generally . . . CPL 220.15
    Procedure following . . . CPL 330.20
Non-citizen defendant, deportation of; guilty plea . . . CPL 220.50
Not guilty plea . . . CPL 220.40
Part of indictment, guilty plea to . . . CPL 220.30
Predicate felony conviction, hearing on . . . . CPL 220.35
Prosecutor's information, requirements for . . . CPL 170.60
Requirement . . . CPL 210.50
Simplified information, requirements for . . . . CPL 170.60
Types of . . . CPL 220.10

PLEADING
Conspiracy . . . PL 105.20
Grand larceny . . . PL 155.45
Inconsistent statements, pleading as to . . PL 210.20

PODIATRISTS
Evidentiary issues concerning . . . CPLR 4504
Malpractice, loss of earnings and impairment of earning ability in actions for . . . CPLR 4546

POLICE DEPARTMENT
Criminal justice services division, department requests processed by . . . EXEC 837-c

POLICE OFFICERS
Aggravate assault upon . . . PL 120.11
Arrest without warrant (See ARREST WITHOUT WARRANT)
Assault on . . . PL 120.08
Ballistic armor vests for . . . EXEC 837-d
Central state register of . . . EXEC 845
Impersonation as; first degree . . . PL 190.26
Minor, custody by police officer without warrant of . . . FCA 305.2
Municipal police training council (See MUNICIPAL POLICE TRAINING COUNCIL)
Records and reports (See POLICE RECORDS AND REPORTS)
Refusal to aid . . . PL 195.10
Retired sworn members of state police licenses to carry and possess firearms, granting . . . PL 400.01
Supervision, custody of persons in need of . . FCA 724
Warrant of arrest (See WARRANT OF ARREST, subhead: State university appointed police and peace officers)

POLICE RECORDS AND REPORTS
Fair treatment standards . . . EXEC 646
Juvenile delinquents . . . FCA 381.3

[References are to sections of Laws as abbreviated on Page iii. The abbreviation MISC before the section refers to the Miscellaneous Death Penalty Provision following Judiciary Law.]

POLICE RECORDS AND REPORTS—Cont.
Missing children, with respect to . . . EXEC 837-m
Supervision, persons in need of . . . FCA 784

POLICE UNIFORMS
Criminal sale of . . . PL 190.27

POLYGRAPH TESTS
Prohibitions against use . . . CPL 160.45

PORNOGRAPHY
Seizure and forfeiture of equipment used to promote . . . PL 410.00

POST-RELEASE SUPERVISION
Generally . . . PL 70.45
Determinate sentence . . . PL 70.45
Victim notification upon release of violent felony offender to . . . CPL 380.50

PRELIMINARY INJUNCTIONS
Forfeiture actions (See FORFEITURE—PROCEEDS OF CRIME)

PREMISES
Physical force; justification for use in defense of premises . . . PL 35.20

PRESCRIPTIONS
Criminal sale prescription for controlled substances . . . PL 220.65
Diversion, criminal
    Definitions . . . PL 178.00
    First degree . . . PL 178.25
    Fourth degree . . . PL 178.10
    Limitations . . . PL 178.05
    Second degree . . . PL 178.20
    Third degree . . . PL 178.15
Emergency oral prescriptions for schedule II drugs . . . PHL 3334
Official New York state prescriptions for scheduled substances
    Dispensing upon . . . PHL 3333
    Forms . . . PHL 3338
    Making of . . . PHL 3332
Oral prescriptions
    Emergency oral prescriptions for schedule II drugs . . . PHL 3334
    Schedule III, IV and V substances . . . PHL 3337
Refilling prescriptions . . . PHL 3339
Scheme to defraud state by unlawful sale of . . . PL 190.70
Written prescriptions
    Dispensing upon . . . PHL 3336
    Making of . . . PHL 3335

PRE-SENTENCE PROCEEDINGS
Conference . . . CPL 400.10

PRE-SENTENCE PROCEEDINGS—Cont.
Death penalty cases . . . CPL 400.27
Fine based upon defendant's gain from offense . . . CPL 400.30
Imprisonment, evidence of . . . CPL 400.22
Murder in first degree . . . CPL 400.27
Persistent violent felony offender . . . . CPL 400.16; CPL 400.20
Prior convictions, determination of . . . CPL 400.40
Reports (See PRE-SENTENCE REPORTS)
Second violent felony offender . . CPL 400.15; CPL 400.21

PRE-SENTENCE REPORTS
Accompanying defendant sentenced to imprisonment or to mental health facility, copy of report . . . CPL 390.60
Confidentiality
    Generally . . . CPL 390.50
    HIV-related testing requirement . . CPL 390.15
Copy of report to accompany defendant sentenced to imprisonment or to mental health facility . . CPL 390.60
Fingerprint report requirement . . . CPL 390.10
HIV-related testing requirement . . . CPL 390.15
Investigation and report, scope of . . . CPL 390.30
Memorandum, defendant's pre-sentence . . . . CPL 390.40
Mental health facility, copy of report to accompany defendant to . . . CPL 390.60
Requirement of . . . CPL 390.20

PRESUMPTIONS
Bad checks, issuance of . . . PL 190.10
Controlled substances
    Criminal possession of . . . PL 220.25
    Proceeds from; rebuttable presumption . . . PL 480.35
Forged instrument, criminal possession of; second degree . . . PL 170.27
Gambling offenses . . . PL 225.35
Minors, dissemination of indecent material to . . PL 235.23
Obscenity . . . PL 235.10
Stolen property, criminal possession of . . PL 165.55
Vehicle identification numbers, illegal possession of . . . PL 170.71
Weapons; presumptions of possession, unlawful intent and defacement . . . PL 265.15

PRE-TRIAL MOTIONS
Dangerous drugs, destruction of . . . CPL 715.10
Definitions . . . CPL 255.10
Juvenile delinquency; discovery
    Pre-trial motion defined . . . FCA 332.1
    Procedure . . . FCA 332.2
Pre-trial motion defined . . . FCA 332.1

[References are to sections of Laws as abbreviated on Page iii. The abbreviation MISC before the section refers to the Miscellaneous Death Penalty Provision following Judiciary Law.]

[References are to sections of Laws as abbreviated on Page iii. The abbreviation MISC before the section refers to the Miscellaneous Death Penalty Provision following Judiciary Law.]

[References are to sections of Laws as abbreviated on Page iii. The abbreviation MISC before the section refers to the Miscellaneous Death Penalty Provision following Judiciary Law.]

[References are to sections of Laws as abbreviated on Page iii. The abbreviation MISC before the section refers to the Miscellaneous Death Penalty Provision following Judiciary Law.]

PUBLIC BENEFIT CARDS
Unlawful use of . . . PL 165.17
Welfare fraud (See WELFARE FRAUD)

PUBLIC HEALTH LAW
Controlled substances (See CONTROLLED SUB-STANCES)
Purpose of article . . . PHL 3300-a

PUBLIC OFFICERS
Affidavits of . . . CPLR 4520
Certificates of . . . CPLR 4520

PUBLIC ORDER, OFFENSES AGAINST
Anarchy, criminal . . . PL 240.15
Appearance in public under the influence of narcotics or drugs other than alcohol . . . PL 240.40
Assembly, unlawful . . . PL 240.10
Bomb, placement of false
    First degree . . . PL 240.62
    Second degree . . . PL 240.61
Definitions . . . PL 240.00
Disorderly conduct . . . PL 240.20
Drugs, appearance in public under the influence of . . . PL 240.40
Falsely reporting incident
    First degree . . . PL 240.60
    Second degree . . . PL 240.55
    Third degree . . . PL 240.50
Harassment (See HARASSMENT)
Loitering (See LOITERING)
Narcotics, appearance in public under the influence of . . . PL 240.40
Nuisance
    First degree . . . PL 240.46
    Second degree . . . PL 240.45
Records, unlawful prevention public access to . . PL 240.65
Religious services, disruption or disturbance of . . . PL 240.21

PUBLIC SAFETY, OFFENSES AGAINST
Body vest, unlawful wearing of . . . PL 270.20
Dangerous fireworks, unlawfully dealing with . . PL 270.00
Fireworks, unlawfully dealing with . . . PL 270.00
Hazard, creation of . . . PL 270.10
Noxious material, possession of . . . PL 270.05
Party line, refusal to yield to . . . PL 270.15
Weapons
    Generally (See WEAPONS)
    Firearms (See FIREARMS)

PUBLIC SENSIBILITIES, OFFENSES AGAINST
Exposure of person . . . PL 245.01; PL 245.02
Lewdness . . . PL 245.00
Obscenity (See OBSCENITY)
Offensive exhibition . . . PL 245.05

PUBLIC SENSIBILITIES, OFFENSES AGAINST—
Cont.
Sexual material, public display of offensive . . . PL 245.10; PL 245.11

PUBLIC SERVANTS
Bribery
    Defenses . . . PL 200.05; PL 200.15
    First degree . . . PL 200.04; PL 200.12
    Gratuities, unlawful
        Giving . . . PL 200.30
        Receiving . . . PL 200.35
    Official misconduct, reward for (See subhead: Official misconduct)
    Public office
        Giving for . . . PL 200.40; PL 200.45
        Receiving for . . . PL 200.40; PL 200.50
    Receiving bribe
        Defense, lack of . . . PL 200.15
        First degree . . . PL 200.12
        Public office, for . . PL 200.40; PL 200.50
        Second degree . . . PL 200.11
        Third degree . . . PL 200.10
    Second degree . . . PL 200.03; PL 200.11
    Third degree . . . PL 200.00; PL 200.10
Defrauding government . . . PL 195.20
Gratuities, unlawful
    Giving . . . PL 200.30
    Receiving . . . PL 200.35
Misconduct, official (See subhead: Official misconduct)
Obstruction of (See OBSTRUCTION OF PUBLIC SERVANTS)
Official misconduct
    Generally . . . PL 195.00
    Receiving reward for
        First degree . . . PL 200.27
        Second degree . . . PL 200.25
    Rewarding
        First degree . . . PL 200.22
        Second degree . . . PL 200.20
Peace officers (See PEACE OFFICERS)
Police officers (See POLICE OFFICERS)

PUBLIC TRANSPORTATION
Unauthorized sale of unlimited or doctored farecard . . . PL 165.16

R

RADAR DETECTORS
Prohibitions . . . VTL 397-a

RADIO DEVICES
Unlawful possession of . . . PL 140.40

RADIO RECEIVING SETS
Equipping motor vehicles with sets capable of receiving signals on frequencies allocated for police use . . VTL 397

[References are to sections of Laws as abbreviated on Page iii. The abbreviation MISC before the section refers to the Miscellaneous Death Penalty Provision following Judiciary Law.]

RAILROAD TRACKS
Littering on, penalties for . . . PL 145.50

RAPE
First degree . . . PL 130.35
Rape crisis counselors, evidentiary issues concerning . . . CPL 60.76; CPLR 4510
Second degree . . . PL 130.30
Third degree . . . PL 130.25

REAL PROPERTY
Abstract companies, search by . . . CPLR 4523
Commissioner of correction, acquisition by . . COR 21
Conveyance of property without state evidence . . . CPLR 4524; CPLR 4538
Evidence
    Abstract companies, search by . . . CPLR 4523
    Conveyance of property without state . . . . . CPLR 4524; CPLR 4538
    Maps . . . CPLR 4522
    Records . . . CPLR 4522
    Search by title insurance or abstract companies . . . CPLR 4523
    Surveys . . . CPLR 4522
    Title insurance companies, search by . . CPLR 4523
Forfeiture actions, levy upon real property in . . . . CPLR 1322
Maps . . . CPLR 4522
Records . . . CPLR 4522
Rent gouging (See RENT GOUGING)
Search by title insurance or abstract companies . . . CPLR 4523
Surveys . . . CPLR 4522
Title insurance companies, search by . . CPLR 4523

RECKLESS ENDANGERMENT
First degree . . . PL 120.25
Property, of . . . PL 145.25
Second degree . . . PL 120.20

RECKLESSNESS
Definition . . . PL 15.05

RECOGNIZANCE, RELEASE ON OWN (See BAIL)

RECORDINGS
Advertisement or sale of unauthorized recording of sound
    First degree . . . PL 275.30
    Second degree . . . PL 275.25
Definitions . . . PL 275.00
Destruction of equipment used in unauthorized recording of sound . . . PL 420.00
Forfeiture of equipment used in production of recordings, seizure and . . . PL 420.05

RECORDINGS—Cont.
Manufacturer of unauthorized recording of sound
    First degree . . . PL 275.10
    Second degree . . . PL 275.05
Motion picture theater, unauthorized operation of recording device in . . . PL 275.32
Performances, unauthorized recording of
    First degree . . . PL 275.20
    Second degree . . . PL 275.15
Sale of unauthorized recording of sound
    First degree . . . PL 275.30
    Second degree . . . PL 275.25
Seizures of unauthorized recordings
    Destruction and . . . PL 420.00
    Equipment used in production of recordings . . . PL 420.05
Unauthorized recording of sound
    Advertisement or sale of
        First degree . . . PL 275.30
        Second degree . . . PL 275.25
    Definitions . . . PL 275.00
    Destruction of equipment used in . . PL 420.00
    Equipment used in, seizure and forfeiture of . . . PL 420.05
    Forfeiture of equipment used in production of recordings, seizure and . . . PL 420.05
    Limitations of application of statute . . . . PL 275.45
    Manufacturer of
        First degree . . . PL 275.10
        Second degree . . . PL 275.05
    Origin of recording, failure to disclose
        First degree . . . PL 275.40
        Second degree . . . PL 275.35
    Performances
        First degree . . . PL 275.20
        Second degree . . . PL 275.15
    Sale of
        First degree . . . PL 275.30
        Second degree . . . PL 275.25
    Seizures
        Destruction and . . . PL 420.00
        Equipment used in production of recordings . . . PL 420.05

RECORDS AND REPORTS
Accident reports (See ACCIDENTS AND ACCIDENT REPORTS)
Alcohol and drug rehabilitation program . . VTL 523
Authentication of official records . . . CPLR 4540
Business records
    Evidence, as . . . CPLR 4518
    Falsifying statements (See WRITTEN FALSE STATEMENTS)
Chemical test report of persons operating vehicle after consumption of alcohol . . . VTL 1194-a

[References are to sections of Laws as abbreviated on Page iii. The abbreviation MISC before the section refers to the Miscellaneous Death Penalty Provision following Judiciary Law.]

RECORDS AND REPORTS—Cont.

Child protective proceedings . . . FCA 1038

Community dispute resolution center program . . . . JUD 849-g

Controlled substances (See CONTROLLED SUBSTANCES)

Criminal history records search for certain employment, appointments, licenses, registrations or permits

    Caregivers . . . EXEC 837-n

    New York City . . . EXEC 837-m

    Westchester County . . . EXEC 837-p

Death penalty cases, required reports in . . . EXEC 837-a

Eavesdropping or video surveillance warrants

    Administrative office of United States courts, reports to . . . CPL 700.60

    Progress reports . . . CPL 700.50

False statements (See WRITTEN FALSE STATEMENTS)

Firearms, theft or loss of . . . PL 400.10

Foreign records . . . CPLR 4542

Gambling records, possession of (See GAMBLING OFFENSES)

Grand jury

    Generally . . . CPL 190.85

    Appeal from order concerning grand jury reports . . . CPL 190.90

Incapacitated persons, examination reports on . . . . FCA 322.1

Jail time records and certificates . . . COR 600-a

Juvenile delinquency (See JUVENILE DELINQUENCY)

Lack of . . . CPLR 4521

Library circulation records, disclosure of . . . CPLR 4509

Loan records, possession of usurious . . . PL 190.45

Local correctional facilities . . . COR 500-f

Management of correctional facilities; fiscal accounts and records . . . COR 115

Mentally ill inmates . . . COR 403

Official records, authentication of . . . CPLR 4540

Parole division, access by . . . EXEC 259-k

Police records and reports (See POLICE RECORDS AND REPORTS)

Pre-sentence reports (See PRE-SENTENCE REPORTS)

Public access to, unlawful prevention of . . . . . PL 240.65

Real property . . . CPLR 4522

Rehabilitation program . . . VTL 523

Sentences of students, notification to school officials of convictions and . . . CPL 380.90

Supervision, persons in need of (See PERSONS IN NEED OF SUPERVISION)

Support payments as evidence, of . . . CPLR 4518

RECORDS AND REPORTS—Cont.

Tampering with public records

    First degree . . . PL 175.25

    Second degree . . . PL 175.20

Temporary release programs . . . COR 853

Waiver, termination of criminal action by entry of; sealed records . . . CPL 160.55

Youthful offender adjudication . . . CPL 720.35

REFORMATORIES

Duties of . . . COR 618

RELEASED INMATES

Clothing furnished upon . . . COR 125

Money furnished upon . . . COR 125

Notification of

    District attorney . . . COR 149

    Sheriff and police . . . COR 149

    Victim notification of release of violent felony offender . . . CPL 380.50

Sex offender, notification requirements upon release of (See SEX OFFENDER REGISTRATION ACT)

RELEASE ON OWN RECOGNIZANCE (See BAIL)

RELIGION AND RELIGIOUS SERVICES

Criminal interference with service

    First degree . . . PL 240.71

    Second degree . . . PL 240.70

Disruption or disturbance of services . . . PL 240.21

Freedom of worship . . . COR 610

Local correctional facilities . . . COR 500-e

REMOVAL OF ACTION

County court to supreme court . . . CPL 230.10; CPL 230.20

Determinations and rulings before and after . . CPL 230.40

Grand jury's direction to file request for removal to family court . . . CPL 190.71

Juvenile offenders, removal to family court (See JUVENILE DELINQUENCY)

Local criminal court to another, removal from

    Generally . . . CPL 170.15

    Felony complaint, proceedings upon . . . CPL 180.20

Rulings and determinations before and after . . CPL 230.40

Stay of trial pending motion . . . CPL 230.30

Superior court, removal from local criminal court to

    Defendant's request . . . CPL 170.25

    District attorney's request . . . CPL 170.20

Supreme court to county court . . . CPL 230.10

Venue, change of . . . CPL 230.20

Verdict, after . . . CPL 330.25

RENT GOUGING

Definition . . . PL 180.54

[References are to sections of Laws as abbreviated on Page iii. The abbreviation MISC before the section refers to the Miscellaneous Death Penalty Provision following Judiciary Law.]

Index

[References are to sections of Laws as abbreviated on Page iii. The abbreviation MISC before the section refers to the Miscellaneous Death Penalty Provision following Judiciary Law.]

SECOND FELONY OFFENDERS
Child sexual assault felony offender, determination if defendant is second . . . CPL 400.19

Imprisonment sentence (See IMPRISONMENT SENTENCE, subhead: Second felony offenders)

Procedure for determining if defendant is . . . CPL 400.21

Violent felony offender, procedure for determining if defendant is second . . . CPL 400.15

SECURING APPEARANCE OF DEFENDANT (See APPEARANCE)

SECURITY
Anti-security items, criminal possession of . . . PL 170.47

SECURITY GUARD ADVISORY COUNCIL
Generally . . . EXEC 841-a

Commissioner, duties and powers of . . EXEC 841-c

Duties
> Generally . . . EXEC 841-b
> Commissioner . . . EXEC 841-c

Functions . . . EXEC 841-b

Governor, rules and regulations promulgated by . . . EXEC 842

Powers
> Generally . . . EXEC 841-b
> Commissioner . . . EXEC 841-b

Saving clause . . . EXEC 841-d

SECURITY INTERESTS
Fraud involving . . . PL 185.05

SEIZURES
Aircraft used to transport or conceal gambling records . . . PL 415.00

Automobiles used to transport or conceal gambling records, of . . . PL 415.00

Controlled substances
> Generally . . . PHL 3387
> Transportation or conveyance of controlled substances, any vehicles or vessels used for . . . PHL 3388

Counterfeit goods, seizure and destruction of . . PL 165.74

Driver's license
> Unlawfully operated vehicles, seizure and redemption of . . . VTL 511-b
> Unlicensed operation of vehicle under certain circumstances . . . VTL 511-c

Fireworks . . . PL 405.05

Forfeiture actions, levy upon personal property by seizure in . . . CPLR 1321

Gambling records; seizure of any vehicles, vessels or aircraft used to transport or conceal . . PL 415.00

Pornography, equipment used to promote . . . . PL 410.00

SEIZURES—Cont.
Recording of sound, unauthorized
> Destruction of recordings . . . PL 420.00
> Equipment used in unauthorized . . PL 420.05

Search warrants, seizure of property under
> Generally . . . CPL 690.10
> Disposition of seized property . . . CPL 690.55

Vehicles, vessels or aircraft used to transport gambling records . . . PL 415.00

Vessels
> Controlled substances, any vehicles or vessels used for transportation or conveyance of . . PHL 3388
> Gambling records, seizure of any vehicles, vessels or aircraft used to transport or conceal . . . . PL 415.00

SELF-AUTHENTICATION
Newspapers . . . CPLR 4532

Periodicals of general circulation . . . CPLR 4532

SELF-DEFENSE SPRAY DEVICE
Obstruction of governmental administration by use of . . . PL 195.08

Police or peace officer, used to obstruct . . . . . PL 195.08

Possession of . . . PL 265.20; PL 270.05

Unlawful possession or sale of . . . PL 270.05

SELF-INCRIMINATION
Witnesses . . . CPLR 4501

SENIOR CITIZENS (See ELDERLY PERSONS)

SENTENCE
Appeals (See APPEALS)

Applicability of article . . . CPL 380.10; PL 55.00

Attempt to commit crime . . . PL 110.05

Authority for execution of . . . CPL 380.60

Authorized dispositions of offenders (See AUTHORIZED DISPOSITIONS OF OFFENDERS)

Bail or recognizance, order before sentence of . . . . CPL 530.45

Capital punishment (See DEATH PENALTY)

Classification of felonies and misdemeanors . . . PL 55.05

Clemency (See EXECUTIVE CLEMENCY)

Commutation of sentence (See EXECUTIVE CLEMENCY)

Conditional discharge (See PROBATION AND CONDITIONAL DISCHARGE)

Controlled substances (See CONTROLLED SUBSTANCES)

Death penalty (See DEATH PENALTY)

Definite sentence (See DEFINITE SENTENCE)

Designation of offenses . . . PL 55.10

Determinate sentence
> Good behavior allowances against . . COR 803

[References are to sections of Laws as abbreviated on Page iii. The abbreviation MISC before the section refers to the Miscellaneous Death Penalty Provision following Judiciary Law.]

Index

[References are to sections of Laws as abbreviated on Page iii. The abbreviation MISC before the section refers to the Miscellaneous Death Penalty Provision following Judiciary Law.]

[References are to sections of Laws as abbreviated on Page iii. The abbreviation MISC before the section refers to the Miscellaneous Death Penalty Provision following Judiciary Law.]

SEX OFFENSES—Cont.
Fines and penalties (See FINES AND PENALTIES)
Forcible touching . . . PL 130.52
HIV-related testing requirement . . . CPL 390.15
Lack of consent . . . PL 130.05
Minors, course of sexual conduct against
    Female genital mutilation . . . PL 130.85
    First degree . . . PL 130.75
    Imprisonment sentence running concurrently for offenses against . . . PL 70.25
    Second degree . . . PL 130.80
    Sexual assault (See CHILD SEXUAL ASSAULT)
    Sexual performance by child (See SEXUAL PERFORMANCE BY CHILD)
    Statute of limitations for prosecution of sex offenses against child . . . CPL 30.10
Misconduct, sexual . . . PL 130.20
Rape (See RAPE)
Sex Offender Registration Act (See SEX OFFENDER REGISTRATION ACT)
Sexual abuse (See SEXUAL ABUSE)
Sexual assault, child (See CHILD SEXUAL ASSAULT)

SEXUAL ABUSE
Aggravated sexual abuse
    First degree . . . PL 130.70
    Second degree . . . PL 130.67
    Third degree . . . PL 130.66
    Fourth degree . . . PL 130.65-a
First degree . . . PL 130.65
Persistent sexual abuse . . . PL 130.53
Second degree . . . PL 130.60
Statute of limitations for prosecution of course sexual conduct against child . . . CPL 30.10
Third degree . . . PL 130.55

SEXUAL PERFORMANCE BY CHILD
Generally . . . PL 263.05
Affirmative defenses . . . PL 263.20
Age of child, proof of . . . PL 263.25
Control of performance . . . PL 263.16
Definitions . . . PL 263.00
Obscene sexual performance by child
    Control of performance . . . PL 263.11
    Defined . . . PL 263.00
    Possession of performance . . . PL 263.11
    Promotion of . . . PL 263.10
Possession of performance . . . PL 263.16
Promotion of . . . PL 263.10; PL 263.15

SHOCK INCARCERATION PROGRAM
Definitions . . . COR 865
Establishment of . . . COR 866
Selection of participants, procedure for . . COR 867

SIGNATURES
Fraudulently obtaining . . . PL 165.20

SIMPLIFIED INFORMATION
Appearance ticket, issuance of . . . CPL 100.25
Dismissal of, motion for
    Generally . . . CPL 170.30
    Adjournment in contemplation of dismissal
        Generally . . . CPL 170.55
        Marijuana cases involving . . CPL 170.56
    Defective information . . . CPL 170.35
    Traffic information
        Justice, dismissal in interest of . . . CPL 170.40
        Procedure . . . CPL 170.45
Form and content . . . CPL 100.25
Notice requirement . . . CPL 100.25
Plea requirements . . . CPL 170.60
Removal of action (See REMOVAL OF ACTION)
Supporting deposition of defendant arraigned upon . . . CPL 100.25
Traffic information
    Arraignment upon . . . CPL 170.10
    Dismissal of, motion for
        Justice, dismissal in interest of . . . CPL 170.40
        Procedure . . . CPL 170.45

SIMULATION
Criminal . . . PL 170.45

SLUGS
Definitions . . . PL 170.50
Unlawfully using
    Definitions . . . PL 170.50
    First degree . . . PL 170.60
    Second degree . . . PL 170.55

SOCIAL SERVICES DEPARTMENT
Cooperation of correctional institutions with . . . . . . COR 619
Imprisonment sentence of social services recipient to commissioner, notification of . . . CPL 380.80
Sex offenders, notice to local departments upon release of . . . COR 72-c

SOCIAL WORKERS
Evidentiary issues concerning . . . CPLR 4508

SOLICITATION, CRIMINAL
Defense, lack of . . . PL 100.15
Exemptions . . . PL 100.20
Fifth degree . . . PL 100.00
First degree . . . PL 100.13
Fourth degree . . . PL 100.05
Second degree . . . PL 100.10
Third degree . . . PL 100.08

SOUND RECORDINGS (See RECORDINGS)

SPEED RESTRICTIONS (See VEHICLE AND TRAFFIC LAW)

Index

[References are to sections of Laws as abbreviated on Page iii. The abbreviation MISC before the section refers to the Miscellaneous Death Penalty Provision following Judiciary Law.]

[References are to sections of Laws as abbreviated on Page iii. The abbreviation MISC before the section refers to the Miscellaneous Death Penalty Provision following Judiciary Law.]

[References are to sections of Laws as abbreviated on Page iii. The abbreviation MISC before the section refers to the Miscellaneous Death Penalty Provision following Judiciary Law.]

TAMPERING—Cont.

First degree . . . PL 145.20

Jurors, with

First degree . . . PL 215.25

Second degree . . . PL 215.23

Private communications . . . PL 250.25

Public records

First degree . . . PL 175.25

Second degree . . . PL 175.20

Second degree . . . PL 145.15

Sports (See SPORTS)

Third degree . . . PL 145.14

Witnesses, with (See WITNESSES)

TELECOMMUNICATIONS

Access device, criminal use of

First degree . . . PL 190.76

Second degree . . . PL 190.75

Electronic access device

Defined . . . PL 170.00

Fraudulent making of; second degree . . . PL 170.75

TELECOMMUNICATIONS COMMITTEE

Statewide law enforcement . . . EXEC 844-a

TEMPORARY RELEASE PROGRAM

Absconding from

First degree . . . PL 205.17

Second degree . . . PL 205.16

Absence of inmates (See INMATES, subhead: Absence of)

Abuses, review of complaint of . . . COR 857

Agent of state, status of inmate as . . . COR 861

Complaint and abuse review . . . COR 857

Conduct of inmates participating in . . . COR 856

Definitions . . . COR 851

Employment, prohibitions against . . . COR 859

Establishment of . . . COR 852

Evaluation and recommendation . . . COR 854

Furloughs (See FURLOUGHS)

Information on, maintenance of . . . COR 853

Procedure . . . COR 855

Recommendation for . . . COR 854

Records . . . COR 853

Reports, maintenance of . . . COR 853

Work release programs (See WORK RELEASE PROGRAM)

TEMPORARY RESTRAINING ORDERS

Forfeiture actions (See FORFEITURE—PROCEEDS OF CRIME)

TERMINATION OF CRIMINAL ACTION

Administrative findings . . . CPL 160.55

Favor of accused

Effect of termination in . . . CPL 160.60

Order upon termination in . . . CPL 160.50

TERMINATION OF CRIMINAL ACTION—Cont.

Orders

Favor of accused, order upon termination in . . . CPL 160.55

Noncriminal offenses, order upon termination by conviction for . . . CPL 160.55

Waiver, termination upon entry of . . . CPL 160.55

TERRORISM, CRIMES OF

Generally . . . PL 490.25

Biological and chemical weapons

Defined . . . PL 490.05

Eavesdropping and video surveillance warrants, defined as designated offense for . . . CPL 700.05

Indictment for use or possession of . . . . CPL 200.65

Possession

Exclusions . . . PL 490.70

First degree . . . PL 490.45

Second degree . . . PL 490.40

Third degree . . . PL 490.37

Use of

Exclusions . . . PL 490.70

First degree . . . PL 490.55

Second degree . . . PL 490.50

Third degree . . . PL 490.47

Chemical weapons (See subhead: Biological and chemical weapons)

Definitions related to . . . PL 490.05

Eavesdropping and video surveillance warrants, defined as designated offense for . . . CPL 700.05

First degree murder, death as a result of terrorist act defined as . . . PL 125.27

Hindering prosecution of

First degree . . . PL 490.35

Second degree . . . PL 490.30

Legislative findings . . . PL 490.00

Money laundering in support of

First degree . . . PL 470.24

Fourth degree . . . PL 470.21

Second degree . . . PL 470.23

Third degree . . . PL 470.22

Sentence of life imprisonment without parole . . PL 70.00

Solicitation or providing support for

First degree . . . PL 490.15

Second degree . . . PL 490.10

Threats, making of terroristic . . . PL 490.20

Violent felony, acts aiding or abetting terrorism defined as . . . PL 70.02

TESTIMONY (See WITNESSES)

THEFT

Accosting, fraudulent . . . PL 165.30

[References are to sections of Laws as abbreviated on Page iii. The abbreviation MISC before the section refers to the Miscellaneous Death Penalty Provision following Judiciary Law.]

THEFT—Cont.
Automobiles, unauthorized use of (See AUTOMO-BILES, subhead: Unauthorized use of)
Burglary (See BURGLARY)
Credit cards, unlawful use of . . . PL 165.17
Criminal possession of stolen property; fifth degree . . . PL 165.40
Debit cards, unlawful use of . . . PL 165.17
Fraud
    Accosting, fraudulent . . . PL 165.30
    Signatures, fraudulently obtaining . . PL 165.20
Jostling . . . PL 165.25
Larceny (See LARCENY)
Medical assistance cards, unlawful use of . . . . PL 165.17
Misapplication of property . . . PL 165.00
Possession of stolen property, criminal . . PL 165.40
Public transportation, unauthorized sale of unlimited or doctored farecard for use on . . . PL 165.16
Robbery (See ROBBERY)
Scientific material, unlawful use of secret . . . . PL 165.07
Services, of . . . PL 165.15
Signatures, fraudulently obtaining . . . PL 165.20
Stolen property (See STOLEN PROPERTY)
Vehicles, unauthorized use of (See AUTOMOBILES, subhead: Unauthorized use of)

THIRD DEGREE OFFENSES (See specific headings)

TIMBER
Restitution and reparation for stolen . . . PL 60.27

TITLE INSURANCE COMPANIES
Search by . . . CPLR 4523

TOWN COURTS
Geographical jurisdiction of offenses . . . CPL 20.50
Warrant of arrest, attachment of accusatory instrument to . . . CPL 120.40

TRACE DEVICES (See TRAP AND TRACE DEVICES)

TRADEMARK COUNTERFEITING
Definition . . . PL 165.70
Destruction of goods, seizure and . . . PL 165.74
First degree . . . PL 165.73
Second degree . . . PL 165.72
Seizure and destruction of goods . . . PL 165.74
Third degree . . . PL 165.71

TRAFFIC INFRACTIONS
Generally . . . PL 60.20
Authorized dispositions of offenders . . . PL 60.20
Definition . . . VTL155
Penalties for . . . VTL 1800

TRAFFIC INFRACTIONS—Cont.
Simplified information (See SIMPLIFIED INFORMATION)

TRANSCRIPTS
Examination of witnesses on commission, use of transcript of . . . CPL 680.80

TRANSPORTATION OF INMATES
Alternate correction facilities . . . COR 89-d
Arrest, conveyance after . . . COR 613
Coram nobis prisoners, reimbursement of costs for . . . COR 601-b
Costs for
    Coram nobis prisoners, reimbursement of costs for . . . COR 601-b
    Institution for retarded persons, state liability for expenses for transportation to . . . COR 449
    Sheriff's expenses . . . COR 602
Female inmates . . . COR 605-a
Institution for retarded persons, state liability for expenses for transportation to . . . COR 449
Rendering accounts for . . . COR 603
Same time, prisoners sentenced at one session of court to be transported at . . . COR 605
Sheriff's expenses . . . COR 602

TRAP AND TRACE DEVICES
Generally . . . CPL 705.05
Assistance in installation of . . . CPL 705.35
Definitions . . . CPL 705.00
Installation of, assistance in . . . CPL 705.35
Nondisclosure of existence of . . . CPL 705.30
Order authorizing use of
    Application for
        Generally . . . CPL 705.15
        Content . . . CPL 705.15
        Determination of . . . CPL 705.20
    Extensions . . . CPL 705.25
    Issuance of . . . CPL 705.10
    Time period . . . CPL 705.25

TRESPASS
Generally . . . PL 140.05
Computer trespass . . . PL 156.10
Criminal
    Definition . . . PL 140.00
    First degree . . . PL 140.17
    Second degree . . . PL 140.15
    Third degree . . . PL 140.10

TRIAL
Discovery upon trial of prior statements and criminal history of witnesses . . . CPL 240.45
Information, prosecution of (See INFORMATION)
Jury trial (See JURY TRIAL)
Non-jury trial (See NON-JURY TRIAL)

Index

[References are to sections of Laws as abbreviated on Page iii. The abbreviation MISC before the section refers to the Miscellaneous Death Penalty Provision following Judiciary Law.]

TRIAL—Cont.

Removal of action, stay of trial pending motion for . . . CPL 230.30

Speedy trial (See SPEEDY TRIAL)

Transcript of examination of witness on commission, use of . . . CPL 680.80

U

UNCONDITIONAL DISCHARGE

Sentence of . . . PL 65.20

UNDERTAKINGS

Contempt (See CONTEMPT)

Forfeiture actions (See FORFEITURE—PROCEEDS OF CRIME)

UNIFORM CLOSE PURSUIT ACT

Provisions . . . CPL 140.55

UNIFORM COMMERCIAL CODE

Copies of statements under Article 9 . . CPLR 4525

UNIFORM CRIMINAL EXTRADITION ACT (See EXTRADITION)

UNIFORMS

Police uniforms, criminal sale of . . . PL 190.27

UNLAWFUL IMPRISONMENT

Defense . . . PL 135.15

Definition . . . PL 135.00

First degree . . . PL 135.10

Second degree . . . PL 135.05

UNLAWFUL SURVEILLANCE

Additional provisions . . . PL 250.65

Definitions . . . PL 250.40

First degree

    Generally . . . PL 250.50

    Dissemination of an image . . . PL 250.60

Second degree

    Generally . . . PL 250.45

    Dissemination of an image . . . PL 250.55

USURY

Criminal usury

    First degree . . . PL 190.42

    Second degree . . . PL 190.40

Loan records, possession of usurious . . . PL 190.45

V

VEHICLE AND TRAFFIC LAW

Accidents and accident reports (See ACCIDENTS AND ACCIDENT REPORTS)

Age of 21, consumption of alcohol by persons under (See subhead: Alcohol and drug-related offenses)

VEHICLE AND TRAFFIC LAW—Cont.

Alcohol and drug-related offenses

    Age of 21, persons under

        Chemical tests . . VTL 1192-a; VTL 1194; VTL 1194-a

        Procedure . . . VTL 1194-a

        Rehabilitation program . . . VTL 1196

        Restrictions . . . VTL 1192-a

        Sanctions . . . VTL 1194

    Arrests . . . VTL 1194

    Chemical tests (See CHEMICAL TESTS)

    Ignition interlock device program . . VTL 1198

    Operation of vehicle under influence of . . . . VTL 1192

    Rehabilitation program (See ALCOHOL AND DRUG REHABILITATION PROGRAM)

    Sanctions . . . VTL 1193

    School bus driver . . . VTL 1193

    Special traffic options for driving while intoxicated . . . VTL 1197

Alteration of records in connection with examination . . . VTL 392

Arrests

    Alcohol and drug-related offenses . . VTL 1194

    Compensation of officers not dependent upon apprehension or arrests . . . VTL 1810

    Drug-related offenses . . . VTL 1194

    Scene of accident, leaving without reporting . . . VTL 602

Certificate of magistrate . . . VTL 513

Certificate of registration

    Fraudulent, sale or purchase of . . . VTL 392-a

    Reissuance of . . . VTL 510

    Revoked, operation while registration or privilege . . . VTL 512

    Stolen or fraudulent, sale or purchase of . . . . VTL 392-a

    Suspended or revoked, operation while registration or privilege . . . VTL 512

Chemical tests (See CHEMICAL TESTS)

Compensation of officers not dependent upon apprehension or arrests . . . VTL 1810

Construction or maintenance areas, mandatory surcharges for violation of maximum speed limits in highway . . . VTL 1809-d

Convictions

    Alteration of convictions endorsed on licenses . . . VTL 515

    Certification of . . . VTL 514; VTL 514-b

    Notification of . . . VTL 514-a

    Recording . . . VTL 514

Crime victim assistance fee . . . VTL 1809

Disposition of fines and forfeitures . . . VTL 1803

Driver's license, suspension and revocation of (See DRIVER'S LICENSE: SUSPENSION AND REVOCATION)

[References are to sections of Laws as abbreviated on Page iii. The abbreviation MISC before the section refers to the Miscellaneous Death Penalty Provision following Judiciary Law.]

VEHICLE AND TRAFFIC LAW—Cont.

Drug-related offenses (See subhead: Alcohol and drug-related offenses)

Examination, false statements or alteration of records in connection with . . . VTL 392

False statements in connection with examination . . VTL 392

Fines and penalties

Arraignments for traffic violations . . . . VTL 1807

Compensation of officers not dependent upon apprehension or arrests . . . VTL 1810

Crime victim assistance fee . . . VTL 1809

Default judgment in cases of failure to answer . . . VTL 1806-a

Disposition of fines and forfeitures . . . . VTL 1803

Driver's license, suspension and revocation for failure to pay fines . . . VTL 511-d

Driving while intoxicated or impaired, additional surcharge for . . . VTL 1809-c

Guilty plea . . . VTL 1805

Local surcharges . . . VTL 1809-d

Mandatory surcharges (See subhead: Mandatory surcharges)

Misdemeanors . . . VTL 1801

Not guilty plea . . . VTL 1806

Receipts for fines or bail . . . VTL 1802

Stay order on appeal from judgment of conviction of offense, effect of . . . VTL 1808

Traffic infractions . . . VTL 1800

Forfeiture issues (See FORFEITURE)

Handicapped parking spaces violations, mandatory surcharge for . . . VTL 1809-b

Identification card, stolen or fraudulent; sale or purchase . . . VTL 392-a

Ignition interlock device program . . . VTL 1198

Judgments on fines and penalties

Default judgment in cases of failure to answer . . . VTL 1806-a

Stay order on appeal from judgment of conviction of offense, effect of . . . VTL 1808

Laser detectors, prohibitions against . . . VTL 397-a

Licenses, stolen or fraudulent; sale or purchase . . . VTL 392-a

Magistrate, certificate . . . VTL 513

Mandatory surcharges

Generally . . . VTL 1809

Parking stopping . . . VTL 1809-a

Speed limits in highway construction or maintenance areas, violation of maximum . . VTL 1809-d

Standing violations . . . VTL 1809-a

Number plate, stolen or fraudulent; sale or purchase . . . VTL 392-a

VEHICLE AND TRAFFIC LAW—Cont.

Parking stopping, mandatory surcharges for . . VTL 1809-a

Penalties (See subhead: Fines and penalties)

Prior conviction . . . VTL 1192

Radar detectors, prohibitions against . . . VTL 397-a

Radio receiving sets capable of receiving signals on frequencies allocated for police use, equipping motor vehicles with . . . VTL 397

Rehabilitation program, alcohol and drug (See ALCO-HOL AND DRUG REHABILITATION PROGRAM)

Revocation (See subhead: Suspension and revocation)

School bus driver, alcohol or drug-related offenses by . . . VTL 1193

Speed restrictions

Basic rule . . . VTL 1180

Construction or maintenance areas, mandatory surcharges in highway . . . VTL 1809-d

Contests . . . VTL 1182

Maximum limits . . . VTL 1180

Races . . . VTL 1182

Standing violations, mandatory surcharges for . . . . VTL 1809-a

Suspension and revocation

Certificate of magistrate . . . VTL 513

Certificate of registration . . . VTL 512

Driver's license (See DRIVER'S LICENSE: SUSPENSION AND REVOCATION)

Traffic infractions (See TRAFFIC INFRACTIONS)

VEHICULAR ASSAULT

First degree . . . PL 120.04

Second degree . . . PL 120.03

VEHICULAR MANSLAUGHTER

First degree . . . PL 125.13

Second degree . . . PL 125.12

VENUE

Child protective proceedings . . . FCA 1015

Conspiracy . . . PL 105.25

Family offenses proceeding . . . FCA 818

Juvenile delinquency proceeding . . . FCA 302.3

Removal of action . . . CPL 230.20

Supervision, persons in need of . . . FCA 717

VERDICT

Acquittal, discharge of defendant after verdict of . . CPL 330.10

Checking of . . . CPL 310.80

Defective verdict, reconsideration of . . CPL 310.50

Discharge of defendant after verdict of acquittal . . . CPL 330.10

Discharge of jury before rendition of verdict, effect of . . . CPL 310.60

Form . . . CPL 310.50

[References are to sections of Laws as abbreviated on Page iii. The abbreviation MISC before the section refers to the Miscellaneous Death Penalty Provision following Judiciary Law.]

VERDICT—Cont.

Guilty verdict where defendant not criminally responsible . . . CPL 310.85

Information, prosecution of

Generally . . . CPL 360.55

Sentence, proceedings from verdict to . . CPL 370.10

Mental disease or defect, procedure following verdict or plea of not responsible by reason of . . . . . CPL 330.20

Partial verdict, effect of . . . CPL 310.70

Polling of jury . . . CPL 310.80

Procedure for rendition of . . . CPL 310.40

Recording and checking of . . . CPL 310.80

Removal of action after . . . CPL 330.25

Setting aside

Grounds for . . . CPL 330.30

Motion for

Order granting motion . . . CPL 330.50

Procedure . . . CPL 330.40

VESSELS

Seizures and forfeitures

Controlled substances, any vehicles or vessels used for transportation or conveyance of . . PHL 3388

Gambling records, vessels used to transport . . . PL 415.00

VICTIMS

Audiotaped, videotaped or written victim impact statement, notice to crime victim of right to submit . . . CPL 440.50

Bail or recognizance for protection of, order of . . . CPL 530.13

Crime victim assistance fee . . CPL 420.35; PL 60.35; VTL 1809

Disposition of case, notice to crime victims of . . . CPL 440.50

Dispute resolution, defined for purposes of . . CPL 215.20

Fair treatment standards for crime victims (See FAIR TREATMENT STANDARDS FOR CRIME VICTIMS)

HIV-related testing of defendant, request by victim of sexual assault for . . . FCA 347.1

Homicide victim defined . . . PL 125.05

Intimidation of

First degree . . . PL 215.17

Second degree . . . PL 215.16

Third degree . . . PL 215.15

Notification upon release of violent felony offender . . . CPL 380.50

Protection orders

Family offenses . . . CPL 530.12

Other crimes . . . CPL 530.13

VICTIMS—Cont.

Release of violent felony offender, notification upon . . . CPL 380.50

Sex offenses (See SEX OFFENSES)

Videotaped, audiotaped or written victim impact statement, notice to crime victim of right to submit . . . CPL 440.50

VIDEO SURVEILLANCE (See EAVESDROPPING OR VIDEO SURVEILLANCE WARRANTS)

VIDEOTAPES

Grand jury proceedings, examination of witnesses in . . . CPL 190.32

Victim impact statement, notice to crime victim of right to submit videotaped . . . CPL 440.50

VILLAGE COURTS

Geographical jurisdiction of offenses . . . CPL 20.50

Warrant of arrest, attachment of accusatory instrument to . . . CPL 120.40

VIOLENT FELONY OFFENSE (See IMPRISONMENT SENTENCE)

VISITATION

Correctional facilities, persons authorized for visitation of . . . COR 146

Local correctional facilities . . . COR 500-j

Workhouses . . . COR 500-j

W

WAIVERS

Extradition

Non-waiver . . . CPL 570.62

Written waiver . . . CPL 570.50

Felony complaint, procedure upon waiver of hearing on

Generally . . . CPL 180.30

Superior court, application in . . . CPL 180.40

Grand jury proceedings

Immunity, waiver of . . . CPL 190.45

Indictment (See INDICTMENT)

Indictment (See INDICTMENT)

Information, waiver of replacement of misdemeanor complaint by . . . CPL 170.65

Jury trial, consent to non-jury trial upon waiver of . . . CPL 320.10

Mandatory surcharge . . . CPL 420.35

Termination of criminal action by entry of . . . CPL 160.55

WARRANT OF ARREST

Accusatory instrument to warrant of town, village or city court, attachment of . . . CPL 120.40

Addressing warrant to police and peace officers appointed by state university . . . CPL 120.50

[References are to sections of Laws as abbreviated on Page iii. The abbreviation MISC before the section refers to the Miscellaneous Death Penalty Provision following Judiciary Law.]

[References are to sections of Laws as abbreviated on Page iii. The abbreviation MISC before the section refers to the Miscellaneous Death Penalty Provision following Judiciary Law.]

[References are to sections of Laws as abbreviated on Page iii. The abbreviation MISC before the section refers to the Miscellaneous Death Penalty Provision following Judiciary Law.]

[References are to sections of Laws as abbreviated on Page iii. The abbreviation MISC before the section refers to the Miscellaneous Death Penalty Provision following Judiciary Law.]

X

Y

QUICK FIND INDEX

◄ **Criminal Procedure Law**

◄ **Court Directory**

◄ **Penal Law**

◄ **Index**

◄ **Correction Law**

◄ **Related Miscellaneous Criminal Provisions**

◄ **Vehicle and Traffic Law**

◄ **Miscellaneous Court Rules**

◄ **Sentencing Guides**